The Pro Football

Encyclopedia

The Complete and Definitive Record of Professional Football

THE

PRO FOOTBALL

ENCYCLOPEDIA

THE COMPLETE AND DEFINITIVE RECORD OF PROFESSIONAL FOOTBALL

EDITED BY TOD MAHER AND BOB GILL

Macmillan · USA

MACMILLAN

A Simon & Schuster Macmillan Company
1633 Broadway
New York, NY 10019

Macmillan is a registered trademark of Macmillan, Inc.

A catalogue record is available from the Library of Congress

ISBN 0-02-861989-7

Macmillan books are available at special discounts for bulk purchases for sales promotions, premiums, fund-raising, or educational use. For details, contact:

Special Sales Director
Macmillan Books
1633 Broadway
New York, NY 10019

Electronic book design and composition by Stephen Ogata

First Edition
10 9 8 7 6 5 4 3 2 1

Printed in the United States of America

CONTENTS

ACKNOWLEDGMENTS

A book of this size and scope could not have been possible without the help of the following people:

Ken Samelson, our editor at Macmillan. Many of you know him from his excellent work as editor of *The Macmillan® Baseball Encyclopedia*.

The production staff of Macmillan, including Seiji Ogata, Chris Dreyer, Bob Kerler, Helen Chin, and Sheri Hyman.

Richard Topp introduced us to Ken and helped us put together the biographical database. Joe Cronin, who not only entrusted us with his near-bottomless collection of media guides and record manuals, but always answered our nearly endless list of questions about pro football.

Others who made valuable contributions to this work are Mel Bashore, Rich Bozzone, Steve Brainerd, Bob Carroll, William Himmelman, John Hogrogian, David Neft, Mark Speck, and Chris Willis.

As usual, the staff at the Pro Football Hall of Fame Library—Joe Horrigan, Pete Fierle, Melissa Meadows, and Tricia Trilli—went out of their way to help.

Howard Siner, sports editor with the Newspaper Enterprise Association, supplied several of NEA's all-pro teams from the 1950s and '60s.

Another valuable "resource" we've drawn upon is the Pro Football Researchers Association, an organization founded in 1979 to bring together people like us with an interest in pro football history. In particular, our participation in PFRA projects to assemble biographical information for players and a compilation of annual all-pro teams has added a lot to those sections of this book. Many of the all-pro teams we've listed from before 1950 are the result of the PFRA project—in particular, the work of John Hogrogian, who discovered the important early teams chosen by the *Green Bay Press-Gazette*.

And finally, a special thanks to Marilyn Graham for her support, patience, and understanding.

TEAM ABBREVIATIONS

AKR	1920–1921	APFA	Akron Pros		1970–1996	NFL	Cincinnati Bengals
	1922–1925	NFL	Akron Pros	**CLE**	1920–1921	APFA	Cleveland Tigers
	1926	NFL	Akron Indians		1923	NFL	Cleveland Indians
ARI	1994–1996	NFL	Arizona Cardinals		1924–1925	NFL	Cleveland Bulldogs
ATL	1966–1996	NFL	Atlanta Falcons		1926	AFL	Cleveland Panthers
BAL	1947–1949	AAFC	Baltimore Colts		1927	NFL	Cleveland Bulldogs
	1950	NFL	Baltimore Colts		1931	NFL	Cleveland Indians
	1953–1983	NFL	Baltimore Colts		1937–1942	NFL	Cleveland Rams
	1996	NFL	Baltimore Ravens		1944–1945	NFL	Cleveland Rams
BKN	1926	AFL	Brooklyn Horsemen		1946–1949	AAFC	Cleveland Browns
	1926	NFL	Brooklyn Lions		1950–1995	NFL	Cleveland Browns
	1930–1943	NFL	Brooklyn Dodgers	**COL**	1920–1921	APFA	Columbus Panhandles
	1944	NFL	Brooklyn Tigers		1922	NFL	Columbus Panhandles
	1946–1948	AAFC	Brooklyn Dodgers		1923–1926	NFL	Columbus Tigers
B-NY	1949	AAFC	Brooklyn-New York Yankees	**DAL**	1952	NFL	Dallas Texans
BOS	1926	AFL	Boston Bulldogs		1960–1996	NFL	Dallas Cowboys
	1929	NFL	Boston Bulldogs		1960–1962	AFL	Dallas Texans
	1932	NFL	Boston Braves	**DAY**	1920–1921	APFA	Dayton Triangles
	1933–1936	NFL	Boston Redskins		1922–1929	NFL	Dayton Triangles
	1944–1948	NFL	Boston Yanks	**DEC**	1920–1921	APFA	Decatur Staleys
	1960–1969	AFL	Boston Patriots	**DEN**	1960–1969	AFL	Denver Broncos
	1970	NFL	Boston Patriots		1970–1996	NFL	Denver Broncos
BUF	1920–1921	APFA	Buffalo All-Americans	**DET**	1920	APFA	Detroit Heralds
	1922–1923	NFL	Buffalo All-Americans		1921	APFA	Detroit Tigers
	1924–1925	NFL	Buffalo Bisons		1925–1926	NFL	Detroit Panthers
	1926	NFL	Buffalo Rangers		1928	NFL	Detroit Wolverines
	1927	NFL	Buffalo Bisons		1934–1996	NFL	Detroit Lions
	1929	NFL	Buffalo Bisons	**DUL**	1923–1925	NFL	Duluth Kelleys
	1946–1949	AAFC	Buffalo Bills		1926–1927	NFL	Duluth Eskimos
	1960–1969	AFL	Buffalo Bills	**EVA**	1921	APFA	Evansville Crimson Giants
	1970–1996	NFL	Buffalo Bills		1922	NFL	Evansville Crimson Giants
C-P	1944	NFL	Chicago Cardinals-Pittsburgh Steelers	**FRA**	1924–1931	NFL	Frankford Yellow Jackets
C-S	1934	NFL	Cincinnati Reds-St. Louis Gunners	**GB**	1921	APFA	Green Bay Packers
					1922–1996	NFL	Green Bay Packers
CAN	1920–1921	APFA	Canton Bulldogs	**HAM**	1920–1921	APFA	Hammond Pros
	1922–1923	NFL	Canton Bulldogs		1922–1926	NFL	Hammond Pros
	1925–1926	NFL	Canton Bulldogs	**HAR**	1926	NFL	Hartford Blues
CAR	1995–1996	NFL	Carolina Panthers	**HOU**	1960–1969	AFL	Houston Oilers
CHI	1921	APFA	Chicago Cardinals		1970–1996	NFL	Houston Oilers
	1926	AFL	Chicago Bulls	**IND**	1984–1996	NFL	Indianapolis Colts
	1946–1948	AAFC	Chicago Rockets	**JAC**	1995–1996	NFL	Jacksonville Jaguars
	1949	AAFC	Chicago Hornets	**KC**	1924	NFL	Kansas City Blues
	1960–1996	NFL	Chicago Bears		1925–1926	NFL	Kansas City Cowboys
CHIB	1922–1959	NFL	Chicago Bears		1963–1969	AFL	Kansas City Chiefs
CHIC	1920	APFA	Chicago Cardinals		1970–1996	NFL	Kansas City Chiefs
	1922–1943	NFL	Chicago Cardinals	**KEN**	1924	NFL	Kenosha Maroons
	1945–1959	NFL	Chicago Cardinals	**LA**	1926	AFL	Los Angeles Wildcats
CHIT	1920	APFA	Chicago Tigers		1926	NFL	Los Angeles Buccaneers
CIN	1921	APFA	Cincinnati Celts		1946–1949	AAFC	Los Angeles Dons
	1933	NFL	Cincinnati Reds		1960	AFL	Los Angeles Chargers
	1968–1969	AFL	Cincinnati Bengals		1946–1981	NFL	Los Angeles Rams
				LARI	1982–1994	NFL	Los Angeles Raiders

LARM	1982–1994	NFL	Los Angeles Rams
LOU	1921	APFA	Louisville Brecks
	1922–1923	NFL	Louisville Brecks
	1926	NFL	Louisville Colonels
MIA	1946	AAFC	Miami Seahawks
	1966–1996	NFL	Miami Dolphins
MIL	1922–1926	NFL	Milwaukee Badgers
MIN	1921	APFA	Minneapolis Marines
	1922–1924	NFL	Minneapolis Marines
	1929–1930	NFL	Minneapolis Redjackets
	1961–1996	NFL	Minnesota Vikings
MUN	1920–1921	APFA	Muncie Flyers
NE	1971–1996	NFL	New England Patriots
NEW	1926	AFL	Newark Demons
	1930	NFL	Newark Tornadoes
NO	1967–1996	NFL	New Orleans Saints
NY	1921	APFA	New York Giants
	1926	AFL	New York Yankees
	1946–1948	AAFC	New York Yankees
	1960–1962	AFL	New York Titans
	1963–1969	AFL	New York Jets
NYB	1949	NFL	New York Bulldogs
NYG	1925–1996	NFL	New York Giants
NYJ	1970–1996	NFL	New York Jets
NYY	1927–1929	NFL	New York Yankees
	1950–1951	NFL	New York Yanks
OAK	1960–1969	AFL	Oakland Raiders
	1970–1981	NFL	Oakland Raiders
	1995–1996	NFL	Oakland Raiders
OOR	1922–1923	NFL	Oorang Indians
ORA	1929	NFL	Orange Tornadoes
P-P	1943	NFL	Philadelphia Eagles-Pittsburgh Steelers
PHI	1926	AFL	Philadelphia Quakers
	1933–1942	NFL	Philadelphia Eagles
	1944–1996	NFL	Philadelphia Eagles
PHX	1988–1993	NFL	Phoenix Cardinals
PIT	1933–1939	NFL	Pittsburgh Pirates
	1940–1942	NFL	Pittsburgh Steelers
	1945–1996	NFL	Pittsburgh Steelers
POR	1930–1933	NFL	Portsmouth Spartans
POT	1925–1928	NFL	Pottsville Maroons
PRO	1925–1931	NFL	Providence Steam Roller
RAC	1922–1924	NFL	Racine Legion
	1926	NFL	Racine Tornadoes
RI	1920–1921	APFA	Rock Island Independents
	1922–1925	NFL	Rock Island Independents
	1926	AFL	Rock Island Independents
ROC	1920–1921	APFA	Rochester Jeffersons
	1922–1925	NFL	Rochester Jeffersons
SD	1961–1969	AFL	San Diego Chargers
	1970–1996	NFL	San Diego Chargers
SEA	1976–1996	NFL	Seattle Seahawks
SF	1946–1949	AAFC	San Francisco 49ers
	1950–1996	NFL	San Francisco 49ers
SI	1929–1932	NFL	Staten Island Stapletons
STL	1923	NFL	St. Louis All-Stars
	1934	NFL	St. Louis Gunners
	1960–1987	NFL	St. Louis Cardinals
	1995–1996	NFL	St. Louis Rams
SYR	1921	APFA	Syracuse Pros
TB	1976–1996	NFL	Tampa Bay Buccaneers
TOL	1922–1923	NFL	Toledo Maroons
TON	1921	APFA	Tonawanda Kardex
WAS	1921	APFA	Washington Pros
	1937–1996	NFL	Washington Redskins

The Pro Football

Encyclopedia

The Complete and Definitive Record of Professional Football

PART ONE

Introduction
A Short History of Pro Football

Introduction

The Pro Football Encyclopedia presents in one publication the most complete and accurate statistical account of the game of professional football, as *The Macmillan Baseball Encyclopedia*® does for major league baseball.

Most of the information presented here has never been seen before by the general public. Much of it has been hidden, buried in long-forgotten newspapers and team and league media guides. Much of the information did not exist prior to the publication of this book. The authors have painstakingly reconstructed statistics and records as completely as possible in an effort to fill in the gaps in the official records of professional football.

Part Two lists every coach of the year, player of the year, rookie of the year, and all-pro team ever selected by a panel of players, coaches, sportswriters, or other expert observers—many of which were uncovered by our research team. Also included are all of the first round draft picks, a list of Hall of Famers, and results of every All-Star/Pro Bowl game ever played.

The All-Time Leaders section lists the top performers in each of nine major statistical categories.

The Game Scores chapter lists the result of every game ever played, with dates, sites, and attendance figures.

The Playoffs section contains summaries for every playoff game.

The Yearly Record gives the year-by-year standings, home and road records, and individual leaders.

The Player Register lists every player who played in a major professional football league game. Also, for the first time, complete biographical data is given for each player. Another first is the listing of each player's games played from year to year.

The Statistical Registers (again for the first time ever) list each player's complete season-by-season statistics in each of the six major individual statistical categories.

The Coaches Register lists every coach who coached a major professional football league game. For the first time, complete biographical information is given for each coach. Another first is the inclusion of each coach's playoff record.

And finally, we have even included standings and other statistical information for the World League and the USFL.

A Short History of Pro Football

As near as anyone can say for certain, professional football was born on November 12, 1892, when the Allegheny Athletic Association in Pittsburgh paid guard Pudge Heffelfinger, a three-time All-American at Yale, $500 to play in a game against the Pittsburgh A.C. Though others may well have been paid before that, Heffelfinger is the first documented pro football player; the ledger sheet showing his payment is on display today at the Pro Football Hall of Fame.

At the time, no one was bragging about hiring the Yale star, though, because the Alleghenies, like everyone else in those days, were playing under Amateur Athletic Association rules—which forbade any sort of payment to athletes. Teams tried to get around this ban by giving players "gifts," by setting them up in cushy jobs, or simply by paying them under the table and keeping quiet, as in Heffelfinger's case.

Heffelfinger proved to be worth the outlay, forcing a fumble, then recovering it and rumbling for the game's only score. The result was a 4–0 win for the A.A.A. (In those days a touchdown was worth only four points, a field goal five.)

A week later an ex-Princeton end named Sport Donnelly picked up $250 to play for the A.A.A. against Washington & Jefferson. And the following season the Alleghenies signed three players to season-long contracts for $50 a game.

Other teams in western Pennsylvania picked up the professional banner: the Duquesne Country and Athletic Club in Pittsburgh, and two small towns to the southeast, Greensburg and Latrobe. John Brallier, an 18-year-old quarterback who got $10 to play for Latrobe in an 1895 game, was believed for years to have been the first professional player, until the facts about Heffelfinger and others came to light.

The first attempt at a professional league came in 1902, when three baseball teams—the Pittsburgh Pirates, the Philadelphia Athletics, and the Philadelphia Phillies—sponsored gridiron squads. The teams featured a number of well-known football players, including a fullback from Bucknell named Christy Mathewson, who played for Pittsburgh. By the end of the season the only thing for sure was that the Phillies had finished third. Pittsburgh's management said their team had won the league title; the Athletics' backers said their guys had won. Few people knew who to believe, or cared.

Another interesting innovation came that same season: a football "World Series" played indoors at Madison Square Garden in late December. It was less like a World Series than a Christmas tournament of the sort held in high school and college basketball, but it did well enough that a second—and final—tournament was held in 1903.

Meanwhile, pro football was spreading into Ohio, where the undefeated Massillon Tigers were head and shoulders above the state's other pro teams by 1904. The Canton Bulldogs mounted a serious challenge in 1905, signing halfback Willie Heston, a Michigan All-American, before the season's climactic game with the Tigers. But Heston went nowhere and Massillon came away with a 14–4 win and another state title.

Canton broke through in 1906, handing Massillon its first defeat in years, but the Tigers took the rematch and claimed another championship. The latter game attracted extraordinary interest from gamblers, and almost immediately afterward there were charges of a fix. That certainly didn't endear pro football to the sporting public, and the fact that Canton and Massillon had lost money by paying exorbitant salaries to imported college stars certainly didn't endear the game to the team's backers. As a result, for the next few seasons Ohio cities fielded teams made up almost entirely of local players without college pedigrees.

That started to change around 1914, however, as rivalries grew more heated and team managers again found themselves tempted to add high-priced "ringers" for important games. Then in 1915 Massillon finally returned to the football wars and revived the old Bulldog–Tiger rivalry. And before the season's climactic home-and-home series with Massillon, Canton manager Jack Cusack took the plunge and signed Jim Thorpe to a contract calling for $250 a game. (As a sign of how things had changed, that was still only half as much as Pudge Heffelfinger got more than 20 years earlier.)

The signing of the legendary Carlisle All-American and Olympic decathlon winner didn't work out exactly as planned for Canton, as the Bulldogs split two games with Massillon and left the 1915 championship forever up in the air. But it did mark the end of the low-budget era in Ohio pro football. Starting in 1916, teams all over the state threw fiscal caution to the wind in bidding for the nation's top football talent.

But no one could find a match for Thorpe. The best running back in the game, the best punter, and an intimidating defensive back (actually, more of a linebacker in the run-oriented game of that period), he was something like a combination of Walter Payton, Ray Guy and Lawrence Taylor. Thorpe led Canton to championships in the unofficial "Ohio League" in 1916, 1917 and 1919, missing in 1918 only because most teams in the region—including the Bulldogs—suspended operations for World War I.

At this point in football's history, the game would have been recognizable to any modern fan. A touchdown's value had been increased to six points, a field goal's decreased to three from the original five (it had previously been reduced to four points); the team with the ball had four downs to gain ten yards; and the forward pass had been introduced in 1906. However, few teams made the pass a part of their offensive scheme. And the T formation that had dominated pro football's first decade or so had been superseded by the single wing, which was something like a tight shotgun formation, to use a modern analogy.

The lack of passing meant that defenses could focus on the run, of course, and combined with the lack of wide receivers, this would have made almost every play look like third-and-

one. As a result, it was very difficult to gain through the line, but long runs were about as common as they are today. Just picture John Riggins's famous fourth-down touchdown run in Super Bowl XVII—but with Jim Thorpe carrying the ball.

Though Ohio teams got most of the publicity, there were other strong teams in Indiana and Detroit. In 1917, for instance, the Detroit Heralds may have been second only to Canton, and in 1919 the Hammond All-Stars, featuring an end named George Halas and a halfback named Paddy Driscoll, mounted a serious though unsuccessful challenge to the Bulldogs' reign.

Once again, though, teams found themselves falling into the red as they offered increasingly high salaries to college stars. Players jumped from team to team, even during the season, whenever a better offer came along. Besides driving salaries up, that made things tough for fans, who often found the local team's lineup full of unfamiliar players. Some managers began to think seriously about forming a league as a means of restricting this revolving-door system. (In light of the labor squabbles of the 1980s and '90s, it's worth noting that the NFL was born in part so the owners could hold down salaries and keep players from leaving one team for another.)

Birth of the NFL

In August 1920 the managers of ten teams gathered in Canton in Ralph Hay's auto dealership to inaugurate a new era in pro football. Hay had taken over the Bulldogs' management from Jack Cusack; other teams represented at the meeting were the Akron Pros, the Dayton Triangles, the Cleveland Tigers, the Chicago Cardinals, the Muncie Flyers, the Rock Island Independents, and the Rochester Jeffersons. And a new team called the Decatur Staleys sent their manager and coach, George Halas.

The result of their work that night was called the American Professional Football Association. Jim Thorpe, still a player-coach with the Bulldogs, was named president, but he was just a figurehead; Ralph Hay wielded the real power that first year.

Actually, there wasn't much power to be wielded in the loosely organized league; in fact, for the first two years of its existence, it wasn't always clear just who was in and who was out, partly because the championship was awarded by a vote of the owners and standings were scarce or non-existent. As near as we can tell, though, four other teams joined the new league before the 1920 season was over, and Akron, Decatur, and the Buffalo All-Americans staged a spirited three-way race for the first official championship. In the end, the Akron Pros, led by halfback Fritz Pollard, one of the game's early black stars, took the title with a 6–0–3 record.

A couple of important firsts occurred in 1921: The league installed Joe Carr as president, and George Halas won his first championship as the Staleys, now calling Chicago their home, edged Buffalo for the title. Carr's appointment was probably more important in the long run. He gave the fledgling league sound leadership until his death in 1939.

In 1922 the APFA became the National Football League and the Chicago Staleys became the Chicago Bears, but a name from the past made the season's biggest news. The Canton Bulldogs launched the league's first dynasty, winning the first of three straight championships, the last of which came in Cleveland after a complicated franchise shift.

The Bulldogs' streak came to an end in 1925, when the race for the title culminated in a confusing chain of events that were still capable of fueling controversy six decades after the fact.

The season's two top contenders were the Chicago Cardinals and the Pottsville Maroons, a new franchise from the coal mining region of Pennsylvania. When the Maroons came to Chicago on the first Sunday in December and whipped the Cardinals 21–7, it appeared that the newcomers had clinched the title with a 10–2 record to the Cardinals' 9–2–1. However, Chicago owner Chris O'Brien quickly scheduled two games in the next six days with Hammond and Milwaukee, teams that had already disbanded for the season. The resulting easy victories lifted the Cardinals back into first place with a record of 11–2–1.

The Maroons, though, had begun celebrating immediately after the victory over the Cardinals. Apparently no one in Pottsville was aware that the season didn't end until December 20. In the euphoria after their return from Chicago, the Maroons booked an exhibition game December 12 against a team of former Notre Dame stars. Trouble was, they were scheduled to play in Philadelphia's Shibe Park—and the Frankford Yellow Jackets, based in a Philadelphia suburb, were playing at home on the same day.

The Yellow Jackets protested that the Pottsville–Notre Dame game violated their territorial rights, and Joe Carr ordered Pottsville to cancel the game. The Maroons ignored the warning and played anyway, posting a 9–6 win over the ex-collegians. That forced Carr's hand, and he suspended Pottsville from the league, leaving the Cardinals securely in first place. Even today, though, there are those in Pottsville who still believe their team was robbed of a championship it had won fair and square on the field.

Adding to the confusion was the fact that one of the Cardinals' final two games, against Milwaukee, was a farcical affair at which the few spectators didn't even have to pay their way in. And when it came out that the hastily assembled Milwaukee team had included four local high school players to fill out its lineup for the 58–0 fiasco, Carr fined the Milwaukee owner $500 and forced him to sell the team. He also banned halfback Art Folz of the Cardinals for life for helping to recruit the ineligible players.

It was an ugly end to the season, but what could have been a major scandal received comparatively little notice in the nation's newspapers. For the only time in NFL history, the battle for the championship had taken a back seat to the exploits of a single player—a rookie, at that.

Red Grange, college football's biggest star, made coast-to-coast headlines when he signed with the Bears in late November, right after his last game at the University of Illinois.

The Bears rushed to cash in on their new star's notoriety, playing ten games (including three non-league contests) in seven cities from November 26 to December 13. The rigorous schedule wore the team down, and losses in the last three games cost the Bears a shot at another championship, but winning wasn't the issue. Money was the name of this game, and in that regard the Bears cleaned up, as did Grange and his manager, C. C. (Cash and Carry) Pyle.

Incidentally, the success of the Grange tour helps to explain Chris O'Brien's strategy in scheduling that ill-fated Milwaukee game. Apparently he hoped to arrange another lucrative date with Grange & Co., and thought he would have a better bargaining position if his team were in first place. But an injury Grange suffered on the latter part of the tour scuttled his plan for an all-Chicago finale.

Though the Bears' last few games weren't anything to write home about, the team turned in a good performance in the most important stop on the tour, in New York. Joe Carr, realizing that the NFL needed to establish itself in bigger cities than Canton, Hammond, and Rock Island, had finally succeeded in placing a team in the Big Apple for 1925. But New York Giants owner Tim Mara was losing money until 70,000 fans—the most for a pro game to that time—turned out to see Grange hit Manhattan. Grange played one of his best games as the Bears won 19–7, but Mara was the biggest winner, as the huge crowd saw pro football at its best. From that day on, the Giants were a fixture in New York.

The huge throng that came to see Grange at the Polo Grounds also made quite an impression on C. C. Pyle, and in the offseason he came to the league meeting and demanded a New York franchise for himself and his big star. Mara, of course, refused to relinquish his territorial rights, Carr backed him up, and Pyle left the meeting vowing to get even.

By the fall of 1926, Pyle's revenge had taken shape as the first American Football League. To prove it meant business, the AFL lured several established stars and one whole team, the Rock Island Independents, away from the established league. The NFL, worried that the strong Pottsville team would follow Rock Island into the new league, swallowed its pride and welcomed the Maroons back into the fold—thus obscuring the fact that the team had been ineligible for the 1925 championship and adding credence to latter-day conspiracy theories originating in Pottsville.

Besides tweaking the NFL's nose by arranging Rock Island's defection, the AFL also managed to sign a number of major college stars. Among them were Colgate's Eddie Tryon, who joined Grange's New York Yankees; Washington's George "Wildcat" Wilson, star of a traveling team nominally representing Los Angeles; and Harry Stuhldreher, one of the Four Horsemen of Notre Dame, who played for Brooklyn. (Still, the league's most important rookies may have been Mike Michalske and Ray Flaherty, who went on to Hall of Fame careers in the NFL.) To advertise the presence of Wilson and Stuhldreher, their teams were nicknamed the Wildcats and the Horsemen, respectively.

Such star power posed a real threat to the NFL, which wasn't exactly turning fans away at the gates. But during the course of the season AFL teams began falling by the wayside, and by the end of November only four of the original nine teams were still in business. One of them, the Philadelphia Quakers, surprised most observers by edging the Yankees for the championship. It was to be the only one in the AFL's short history, because the league folded soon thereafter.

(Trivia experts should note that the Frankford Yellow Jackets won the NFL title, giving the City of Brotherly Love two championship teams in the same season—the only time that's ever happened.)

The rival leagues made peace in the offseason. The NFL agreed to take in Grange's New York team, but in deference to Mara the Yankees agreed to play almost no home games, serving instead as a traveling attraction, much like Ernie Nevers and the Duluth Eskimos, another team that showcased a great college star.

Perhaps more important was the NFL's decision to cut back from 22 teams to only 12 for 1927. Including nine in the AFL, there had been 31 major league teams in 1926, and this consolidation—a 60 percent reduction—caused a major improvement in the quality of play. Financially, the purging of smaller cities like Canton, Hammond, Akron, and Racine was a further indication of Joe Carr's desire to establish his league in larger cities that could provide a better fan base. It also helped that the New York Giants, from the biggest city of them all, picked that year to win their first NFL title.

One team that refused to cooperate with Carr's grand strategy was the Green Bay Packers, who represented the smallest city in the NFL but captured three straight championships starting in 1929. Other successes followed, and today the Packers are still hanging in there, the last remnant of the early small-town NFL.

The Turning Point

Green Bay came up short in its bid for a fourth title in 1932, but that failure brought about one of the key moments in pro football history. When the season ended, the Chicago Bears (6-1-6) and the Portsmouth Spartans (6-1-4) stood in a flat-footed tie atop the standings. (In those days, tie games were thrown out when figuring a team's record.) A playoff game was scheduled for December 18 in Chicago, but a snowstorm made the field unplayable, and the game was shifted indoors to Chicago Stadium (which later hosted NBA championship games as the home of the Chicago Bulls).

The indoor site was far from ideal, with a truncated 60-yard field and a fence right at the sidelines, but a couple of rule changes made it acceptable. First, kickoffs were made from the kicking team's 10-yard line; second, and more important, the ball was brought in 10 yards from the sideline after out-of-bounds plays. The latter was a big change from the normal practice, which was to start the next play with the ball only a yard from the sideline, severely limiting the offense's play selection.

Under these unusual conditions, the two teams battled through three scoreless quarters. But in the game's waning minutes an interception gave the Bears a chance deep in Spartan territory. On fourth-and-goal, Bronko Nagurski faked a plunge into the line, then straightened up and flipped a short pass to Red Grange for the winning score. The Spartans complained that Nagurski wasn't five yards behind the line of scrimmage, as the rules required on passing plays, but the play stood, and the Bears went on to a 9–0 win.

Even more important than the result of the game was the effect it had on the NFL rule book. At the league meetings in 1933, George Halas and George Preston Marshall, owner of a new team in Boston that was about to change its name from Braves to Redskins, pushed through a number of rule changes that really opened up pro football. Three of them resulted from that indoor game:

1. From now on, officials would bring the ball in 10 yards from the sideline after any play that ended within five yards of the line.
2. Passing became legal from anywhere behind the line of scrimmage, thus allowing more deception in the aerial game and making offenses more creative.
3. The league was divided into two five-team divisions, with the winners to play a championship game at the end of each season like the one between the Bears and the Spartans (but preferably outside).

The other major change involved the placement of the goal posts. In 1927 the league had moved them to the back of the end zone, where the colleges had them, but that had reduced the number of field goals drastically. Restoring the posts to their old position more than quadrupled the number of successful three-pointers in 1933.

All of these changes immediately made the NFL much more attractive to fans. Three of them provided a needed boost to the offense, resulting in more scoring and more wide-open play. And the institution of an annual championship game gave the NFL season a climactic event to parallel baseball's World Series. And it didn't hurt that the very first matchup was one of the best games ever.

Played in Chicago on December 17, 1933, the title game between the Bears and the New York Giants provided a spectacular demonstration of the new-look NFL. Pulling off several trick plays made possible by the new rules, the teams passed for well over 300 yards and four touchdowns (very high totals for that era), including a TD pass by Nagurski with less than three minutes left that pulled out a 23–21 win for the Bears.

Though football was still a run-oriented game, the move toward the NFL's modern offensive fireworks had begun.

The decade's other major innovation originated with Bert Bell, owner of the Philadelphia Eagles: In 1936 the NFL held its first draft of college players. Designed to help weaker teams and cut down on bidding for college stars, the draft survives today in virtually its original form, and has become an annual spectacle on cable television.

The draft made its debut as the NFL was facing its second challenge from a rival league—this one also called the AFL. Opening play in 1936, this upstart league operated on a slightly smaller scale than its 1926 predecessor, with fewer teams and fewer name players. Its two biggest stars came from the Giants' backfield: future Hall-of-Famer Ken Strong and passing standout Harry Newman. But the league's best player may have been Hank Soar, who led the Boston Shamrocks to the championship, then began a long NFL career with the Giants in 1937.

The AFL also included two ends who were bound for the Hall of Fame: Red Badgro, who jumped ship after only three games as player-coach with the Syracuse Braves; and future coaching great Sid Gillman, who starred for the Cleveland Rams in his only active season of pro football.

The NFL, which had fielded an awkward nine teams two seasons in a row, took in Cleveland (sans Gillman) as its tenth member in 1937, thus allowing the establishment of uniform scheduling. With several of its top players also defecting to the established league, the AFL staggered through its second season before admitting defeat. Despite that failure, yet another AFL appeared in 1940 to do battle with the established NFL. The new league scored a coup in 1941 when its New York franchise signed Tom Harmon and John Kimbrough, two of college football's biggest stars at Michigan and Texas A&M, respectively. But that was its high water mark, and this AFL folded when the United States entered in World War II.

The increased emphasis on the passing game picked up steam in the late 1930s, when a group of outstanding college passers came into the NFL. Chief among them was Sammy Baugh, who joined Marshall's transplanted Washington Redskins in 1937 and led them to their first NFL title that same year. Great receivers were a little slower in appearing, but in 1935 the Green Bay Packers signed rookie end Don Hutson, who soon proved to be head and shoulders above everyone who had gone before him.

The stage was set for a real offensive explosion, and in 1940 the Chicago Bears provided the spark. George Halas had assembled possibly the greatest array of talent any team ever had, including Sid Luckman, one of the new breed of star passers, who joined the team in 1939. Throughout the 1920s and '30s, while other teams used variations of the single wing, the Bears had stuck to the outmoded T formation. And in 1940, with help from offensive mastermind Clark Shaughnessy, Halas revamped the T, turning it into a high-powered attack based on speed and deception. It took a while for the new offense to click, but by the end of the season the Bears were unbeatable. Their 73–0 demolition of the Redskins in the championship game left no doubt about the future of football, and it wasn't long before every team was using the T formation.

Football Goes to War

No other team could match the Bears' personnel, though. With a line featuring the likes of Danny Fortmann, Bulldog Turner,

and Joe Stydahar, plus George McAfee, Bill Osmanski, Norm Standlee, and a whole host of others in the backfield, the Monsters of the Midway added two more championships in 1941 and '43, and only an upset loss to the Redskins in the 1942 title game kept them from winning an unprecedented four in a row.

World War II finally put an end to the Chicago dynasty, and threatened to do the same to the league as a whole. By 1943 a serious shortage of players prompted talk of closing down the NFL for the duration; instead, the owners circled the wagons and cut back to eight teams. The Cleveland Rams suspended operations, and the Eagles and Steelers combined to form a new "Phil-Pitt" franchise. The Steagles, as they were soon known, posted a winning record, but the Eagles withdrew from the partnership after a year and the Steelers merged with the Chicago Cardinals for 1944. The resulting Card-Pitt club failed to win a game, but the return of Cleveland and the addition of a new franchise called the Boston Yanks brought league membership back up to ten teams.

It wasn't always pretty, but the NFL survived the war years intact—and emerged only to find itself in the middle of a football war, against its most serious competition yet.

The All-America Football Conference was the brainchild of Arch Ward, sports editor of the Chicago *Tribune*. It placed teams in major cities from New York to Los Angeles and signed dozens of NFL players; moreover, the AAFC managed to lure one whole team, Dan Topping's Brooklyn Tigers, from the established league. Rechristened the New York Yankees, Topping's troops played in AAFC title games in 1946 and '47.

They weren't the class of the new league, however. That title belonged to the Cleveland Browns, named for their brilliant coach, Paul Brown, whose revolutionary ideas about strategy and organization revolutionized pro football. With an array of stars including Otto Graham, Lou Groza, Dante Lavelli, and Mac Speedie, the Browns captured the championship in all four years of the AAFC's existence. They also made history in 1946 by hiring two black players—Marion Motley and Bill Willis, both of whom wound up in the Hall of Fame.

A number of blacks had played in the NFL in the 1920s; Duke Slater, an all-pro tackle with Rock Island and the Chicago Cardinals, may have been the best. But after 1933 the league's owners instituted an unspoken ban on black players. It lasted until 1946, when the Cleveland Rams went west to Los Angeles, where they battled for West Coast supremacy with the L.A. Dons and the San Francisco 49ers of the AAFC. In an effort to appeal to fans in their new locale, the Rams signed Kenny Washington and Woody Strode, two UCLA stars who had played several seasons in the Pacific Coast Football League.

There was a change of command in the league office as Bert Bell took over as commissioner, succeeding Elmer Layden, one of the fabled Four Horsemen of Notre Dame, who had been tapped in 1941 to succeed Joe Carr. Besides the challenge from the AAFC, at the end of his first season Bell was faced with the NFL's first gambling crisis. It began when a high roller named Alvin Paris tried to bribe fullback Merle Hapes and quarterback

Frank Filchock of the Giants to throw the championship game against the Bears. Both men turned him down, but neither reported the offer.

The attempted fix came to light on the night before the game, and Hapes and Filchock were called in for questioning. Hapes admitted that Paris had approached him, and Bell immediately ruled him ineligible for the title game. Filchock denied everything and was allowed to play; he threw for two touchdowns, but also suffered six interceptions and a broken nose as the Bears prevailed, 24-14. After the game he admitted that he too had been offered a bribe.

Bell suspended Hapes and Filchock indefinitely, and both wound up playing in Canada. Filchock, though, kept pushing for reinstatement to the NFL, and in 1950 Bell finally relented. By then Filchock was an established star north of the border, but he signed with the Baltimore Colts at the tail end of the NFL season and got into one game, completing a single pass for one yard. Then, having made his point, he returned to Canada.

By then the struggle between the NFL and the AAFC had run its course. After a costly four-year struggle, the warring leagues signed a peace treaty for the 1950 season. The NFL took in the AAFC's two best teams, the Browns and the 49ers, plus the Baltimore Colts. The latter choice is hard to figure, since the Colts had won but a single game in 1949. They matched that performance in the NFL, posting another 1–11 record and folding after one season.

The biggest question surrounding the merger was whether Cleveland could dominate the NFL as it had the "inferior" AAFC. The Browns silenced the skeptics by advancing to the championship game in 1950, where they defeated the Rams 30-28 in what may have been the greatest game in NFL history. And it didn't stop there: Paul Brown's charges won division championships every year through 1955 and captured two more NFL titles.

The offensive explosion of the late 1940s, fueled by the T-formation, was finally brought under control in the '50s, thanks to a 1950 rule change allowing free substitution. Though some players still played both ways, as necessitated by the 33-man roster limit, most soon became offensive or defensive specialists. Defensive standouts like Detroit's Jack Christiansen and Les Bingaman were soon as well-known as their offensive counterparts. And in the latter part of the decade—in response to their fans' chants of "Dee-fense!"—the Giants began introducing the defensive team instead of the offense before every home game.

On the other side of the ball, the NFL of the 1950s featured stars like quarterbacks Y.A. Tittle, Norm Van Brocklin, Bobby Layne, and Johnny Unitas, running backs Joe Perry, Lenny Moore, and Jim Brown, and receivers like Elroy "Crazy Legs" Hirsch, Pete Pihos, and Raymond Berry. The result was the most exciting game pro football fans had seen.

And thanks to television, more fans than ever were watching the sport. A national TV deal brought NFL games into homes across the country and fueled a big rise in attendance as well.

The decade's climactic moment occurred on December 28, 1958, when the Baltimore Colts and the Giants squared off in the championship game at Yankee Stadium. The matchup of the famed Giants' defense against the Colts' explosive offense resulted in one of the best games ever played. At the end of regulation time it was 17–17, and millions of fans around the U.S. were glued to their TV screens for the first overtime period in the league's history. Eight minutes later Alan Ameche went over from a yard out to give the Colts a 23–17 "sudden-death" victory.

It was a great game, and it did more than any other single event to establish pro football as a legitimate contender for the title of America's national pastime.

Birth of the AFL

The game's new status didn't go unnoticed in the world of high finance, and in August 1959 Dallas multimillionaire Lamar Hunt announced his plans to launch yet another American Football League to rival the NFL. Only two months later, on October 11, NFL Commissioner Bert Bell died while watching a game between the Eagles and the Steelers. He had been a strong leader since assuming the post in 1946, but someone else would have to take the helm for the ensuing battle with Hunt's upstart league.

At the league meeting after the season, the search for a new commissioner deteriorated into a stalemate when no candidate could win the required two-thirds majority of the twelve owners. Finally the magnates settled on a compromise choice: Pete Rozelle, a one-time publicist and more recently general manager of the Rams. To that point Rozelle was best-known as the man who had traded nine players to the Cardinals for halfback Ollie Matson, but he proved to be the ideal choice to lead the league into its era of greatest prosperity.

The NFL took a hard line against the new AFL when it awarded franchises to two expansion teams within days of Rozelle's election. One, the Dallas Cowboys, would go head-to-head with Hunt's Dallas Texans; the other, the Minnesota Vikings, was owned by a group that had been expected to operate a Minneapolis team in the new league. The AFL was forced to replace Minneapolis with a franchise in Oakland, which because of its late organization would be the league's weak sister for the first few years.

On a more positive note, the AFL chose former South Dakota governor and war hero Joe Foss as its first commissioner, and scored a major coup by signing a national TV contract with ABC. This gave the league's owners a guaranteed income to offset the expected losses in the circuit's formative years. And it gave the unproven AFL unprecedented exposure to viewers across the country.

What those viewers saw was a more wide-open game than the NFL played. For one thing, after a touchdown teams had the option of running or passing for a two-point conversion, thus increasing strategy as well as second-guessing by armchair quarterbacks. For another, the AFL emphasized passing—in part because it would appeal to casual fans, but also because a passing attack requires less practice time than a running attack, and time was in short supply at the league's training camps in that first chaotic summer.

To direct this aerial circus, most AFL teams in the early years relied on quarterbacks with experience in the NFL, the Canadian Football League, or both. As a group, grizzled signal-callers like George Blanda, Babe Parilli, and Frank Tripucka were by far the league's oldest players, but they offered a degree of credibility from the start. But perhaps the more important pickups from the NFL were those who had sat on the bench for a couple of years without getting a real chance. The latter group included quarterbacks Jack Kemp and Len Dawson and wide receivers Don Maynard and Art Powell; they and others like them starred throughout the AFL's first decade.

Of course, the new league also offered a great opportunity for rookies, some of whom turned out to be real gems. Heisman Trophy winner Billy Cannon, a running back from Louisiana State University who signed with the Houston Oilers, was the biggest name, but he was outgained by two other members of the Class of 1960—the Dallas Texans' Abner Haynes and the Los Angeles (later San Diego) Chargers' Paul Lowe. The AFL's rookie stars in 1960 also included kicker Gino Cappelletti, who became a perennial scoring leader after the Boston Patriots moved him from defensive back to offensive end; Ron Mix, a future Hall of Fame tackle; and center Jim Otto, who began a string of 13 straight seasons as an all-pro center with the Oakland Raiders.

Meanwhile, in the NFL, coach Vince Lombardi was building one of the league's greatest dynasties in Green Bay. The Packers' defense, featuring the likes of Willie Davis, Henry Jordan, Ray Nitschke, Herb Adderley, and Willie Wood, held opponents at bay while Jim Taylor and Paul Hornung piled up yardage running behind an offensive line led by Forrest Gregg, Jim Ringo, and Jerry Kramer. And when opposing defenses loaded up to stop the run, Bart Starr picked them apart with passes to Boyd Dowler and Max McGee.

It was as uncomplicated as water running downhill—and nearly as hard to stop.

The Green Bay juggernaut won its first Western Division title in 1960, Lombardi's second year at the helm, but dropped a 17–13 nail-biter to the Philadelphia Eagles for the championship. The Packers rebounded to win back-to-back titles in 1961 and '62, dropped to second place in each of the next two seasons, then came back with a vengeance to win it all in 1965, '66 and '67—making them the first to win three in a row since Green Bay's first great team turned the trick from 1929 to '31.

While the Packers were dominating the NFL, the young AFL was making steady progress on the road toward parity. The league's stature was enhanced by the exciting 1962 championship game between the Houston Oilers and the Dallas Texans. At the end of the fourth quarter the score was 17-17, necessitating pro football's second sudden-death overtime. The first fifteen minutes were scoreless, and the teams changed ends

for an unprecedented sixth period. Shortly thereafter the Texans moved deep into Houston territory, and Tommy Brooker kicked a 25-yard field goal for a 20–17 victory.

For anyone who thought that game had put the AFL on the map, however, the offseason brought a rude awakening when Lamar Hunt moved his title-winning Texans to Kansas City, where they were renamed the Chiefs. His championship team had barely won the battle of the turnstiles against the NFL Cowboys, who had yet to post a winning season, and Hunt saw a bleak future in Dallas if the Cowboys ever turned the corner.

The NFL had its own problems during that offseason, when the league was rocked by the first gambling scandal since the 1946 championship game. Though it was established that none of the players involved had bet against their own teams, commissioner Rozelle suspended two stars—the Packers' Hornung and Detroit defensive tackle Alex Karras—for one season and fined five other members of the Lions, including perennial all-pro linebacker Joe Schmidt.

The $400,000 Quarterback

Probably the most important event of 1963 in the battle for supremacy between the two leagues took place on March 28, when a group led by David "Sonny" Werblin bought the AFL's New York Titans from Harry Wismer. Constant financial troubles had made the Titans a laughingstock, but the new ownership brought professionalism to the AFL's most important franchise. And in 1964, when the new Shea Stadium opened, the renamed Jets shattered all league attendance marks.

They did even better in 1965, after Werblin shocked the sports world by shelling out an unheard-of $427,000 to sign Alabama quarterback Joe Namath. Before long Namath was a household name, and the presence of the league's biggest drawing card in the nation's largest city spelled instant success at the gate: In Namath's rookie season the Jets became the first AFL team to draw more than 50,000 fans per game.

The large crowds that turned out to see Namath put the whole AFL on a much firmer financial footing. The Jets' success also brought a costly escalation in the bidding for top draft choices; and for perhaps the first time, NFL leaders saw no chance for a quick end to their war with the upstart league. So in early 1966, Lamar Hunt and Tex Schramm of the Dallas Cowboys began holding secret talks to arrange a merger between the two leagues.

Before the peace talks could bear fruit, however, the war broke out again in earnest. The New York Giants launched the first strike when they signed Pete Gogolak, the game's first soccer-style kicker, away from the AFL's Buffalo Bills. Looking for a more militant leader, AFL owners forced the resignation of commissioner Joe Foss and replaced him with Al Davis, coach and general manager of the Oakland Raiders. Under Davis's direction, the AFL declared all-out war with the NFL, raiding the established league and signing stars like the 49ers' John Brodie, the Rams' Roman Gabriel, and the Bears' Mike Ditka.

These developments infused the merger negotiations with a new sense of urgency, and on June 8 Pete Rozelle announced an agreement by which the two leagues would become a single entity. Besides voiding the AFL's post-Gogolak signings, the pact provided for a common draft and interleague preseason games to begin in 1967, followed by realignment into a single league with two conferences, the AFC and NFC, in 1970. Rozelle was chosen to head pro football's new monolith, relegating the AFL commissioner to essentially the role of a figurehead; firebrand Al Davis, upset that the peace treaty had foiled his aggressive strategy, resigned the latter post and returned to the Raiders with the new title of managing general partner.

For most fans, however, the most notable detail of the peace treaty was the provision for a championship game between the two league's champions—a game that would soon be dubbed the Super Bowl.

The first meeting between the best of both leagues took place on January 15, 1967, in Los Angeles. The Kansas City Chiefs represented the AFL in the historic game, but proved to be no match for Lombardi's Green Bay Packers, who validated the pregame analysis with a workmanlike 35-10 victory. The Packers turned the trick again a year later in Miami, this time trouncing the Raiders 33-14.

Despite posting the third-best record in the NFL's Western Conference, the 9–4–1 Packers had returned to the Super Bowl as a result of the league's new four-division alignment. The addition of Atlanta and New Orleans had given the NFL sixteen teams, eight in each conference and four in each division. The winners of the Capitol and Century divisions played for the eastern title, while the champs of the Central and Coastal divisions faced each other in the western playoff. Then the two winners played for the NFL championship.

The Los Angeles Rams and the Baltimore Colts compiled matching 11–1–2 records, tied for the best in the NFL; but they were both in the Coastal Division. The Rams were awarded the division title on the basis of their record in head-to-head competition with the Colts—the first use of a "tie-breaker" to determine a division champion, but far from the last.

Meanwhile, the Packers had easily won the Central Division despite two more losses than the Rams and the Colts combined. But Green Bay trounced the Rams in the western playoff, then beat the Dallas Cowboys 21–17 in the famous "Ice Bowl" game, scoring the winning touchdown on Bart Starr's quarterback sneak with 13 seconds left.

Lombardi's retirement from the coaching ranks in 1968 brought a quick end to the Packers' dynasty, and Don Shula's Colts stepped into the breach, winning the NFL title with a 13–1 record despite an injury that sidelined quarterback Johnny Unitas for almost the whole season. Like the Packers before them, the Colts were overwhelming favorites in the third Super Bowl against the Jets, who had upset the Raiders to win their first AFL crown.

At a banquet a few days before the game, Namath shocked the audience and made national headlines when he guaranteed that his

Jets would beat the Colts. The Jets provided a bigger shock on the day of the game, stifling the Baltimore attack and playing mistake-free football en route to a stunning 16-7 victory.

More than any other moment in the football war of the 1960s, this was the one that put the AFL over the top.

To underline the new status of the former upstart league, Lamar Hunt's Kansas City Chiefs repeated the Jets' accomplishment a year later, drubbing the heavily favored Minnesota Vikings in the last Super Bowl between champions of the AFL and the NFL. That gave the AFL a split in the four games played to date, and gave the realignment of 1970 much more credibility as a true partnership of equals.

One Plus One Equals . . . One

With sixteen teams in the NFL and ten in the AFL, the realignment plan called for two thirteen-team conferences. This required shifting three established NFL teams to the new AFC. After considerable debate, it was decided to move Baltimore and Cleveland, two franchises that had combined for seven NFL titles in the past twenty years, plus a third team that had been playing since 1933 without ever coming close to a championship: the 1–13 Pittsburgh Steelers.

The new NFL had three divisions apiece in the NFC and the AFC, with a playoff format that included all six division champs plus one "wild card" team from each conference—the second-place team with the best record. The wild card concept may have been devised to prevent a repeat of 1967, when the Colts had been left out of the playoffs despite tying for the NFL's best record. Otherwise, the new system essentially continued the playoff format the NFL had been using for the past three years.

The 1972 season brought two significant rule changes: The hash marks were moved in to match the position of the goal posts; and tie games, which had previously been discounted in figuring a team's percentage, were now counted as a half-game won and a half-game lost.

On the field, 1972 marked the high-water mark of a great team in Miami, and the first flowering of an even greater dynasty in Pittsburgh. The Dolphins, an AFL expansion team in only their seventh season, finished the regular season with a 14–0 record, won two playoff games to capture the AFC title, then capped a landmark season with a 14–7 Super Bowl win over the Washington Redskins. Winning 17 straight games, coach Don Shula's team became the first and only one to go undefeated through the regular season and the playoffs.

Meanwhile, in Pittsburgh, the once-woeful Steelers had rebounded from back-to-back 1–13 seasons to win their first division title under a young coach named Chuck Noll. They followed that with the franchise's first playoff victory when running back Franco Harris picked Terry Bradshaw's deflected pass off his shoetops and sprinted 40 yards for a touchdown with only seconds remaining. The play, soon to be known as "the immaculate reception," gave the Steelers a 13–7 decision over the Raiders; but a week later they came up short against Miami's team of destiny.

By 1974, though, the Steelers were ready to fulfill their own destiny. Noll and his staff had built one of the NFL's great teams. The offense featured Bradshaw at quarterback, plus running backs Harris and Rocky Bleier, receivers Lynn Swann and John Stallworth, and center Mike Webster; but the heart of the team was its defense. With L.C. Greenwood, Dwight White, and Mean Joe Greene on the line, Jack Ham, Jack Lambert, and Andy Russell at linebacker, and Mel Blount, Donnie Shell, and Mike Wagner in the secondary, the "Steel Curtain" may have been the best defense ever assembled. The Pittsburgh juggernaut won four Super Bowls over the next six seasons.

The first year of the Steelers' dynasty was also the first year of yet another competitor for the NFL, this one called the World Football League. Playing an ambitious 20-week July-to-November schedule made up mostly of weeknight games, the WFL hoped to appeal to fans with a number of rules that were new to pro football. The most unusual of these changed the value of a touchdown to seven points and replaced the traditional conversion with an "action point" that could be accomplished only by running or passing.

The new league boosted its credibility by signing several NFL stars for delivery in 1975, after they had played out their options with their current teams. The most publicized jumpers were Paul Warfield, Larry Csonka, and Jim Kiick of the Miami Dolphins, who signed with the Memphis Southmen; but the WFL also signed other big names like the Cowboys' Calvin Hill, the Vikings' John Gilliam, and the 49ers' Ted Kwalick. The opening of the season provided further evidence of the WFL's clout, as 258,000 fans turned out for six games in the league's first week.

After two more weeks of good attendance, though, it was revealed that most of the figures had been drastically inflated—some by 500 percent or more. That admission damaged the league's credibility almost as much as the signing of Warfield, Csonka, and Kiick had helped it.

Without the benefit of inflated crowds, it soon became clear that several teams were in financial trouble. By early October, two of the WFL's twelve teams had folded and two others had been forced to move. And when the Birmingham Americans hosted the Florida Blazers in the WFL championship game (dubbed the "World Bowl") on December 5, neither team's players had been paid for a month or more. Despite talk of a strike, both teams elected to go on with the game, and the Americans' 22–21 victory earned them what turned out to be the only WFL title.

Despite the arrival of those previously signed NFL stars in 1975, the WFL's monetary problems were too much to overcome, and the league went belly-up in midseason.

Though it failed on the field and at the box office, the WFL left its mark in the rule book, as several of the league's innovative rule changes were adopted by the NFL over the next few years.

The most obvious changes were made in 1974—not coincidentally, the year of the WFL's debut. The NFL moved the goal posts from the goal line, where they had been for 40 years, back to the end line. As a further deterrent to the kicking game, missed field goals from outside the 20-yard line, which had

been touchbacks in the past, would be brought back to the line of scrimmage. Meanwhile, the passing game received a boost when the penalty for offensive holding was reduced from fifteen to ten yards and the new "illegal contact" rule limited defensive backs' use of "bump-and-run" coverage.

At the same time, the NFL adopted a sudden-death overtime period for regular-season games that were tied after 60 minutes, plus other less visible rule changes that opened things up for punt and kickoff returners. All these new rules had one thing in common: They were very similar, if not identical, to rules adopted by the WFL a few weeks earlier.

Despite the offense-oriented changes instituted in 1974, defense continued to dominate in the NFL. So in 1978 the league tried again, further restricting bump-and-run coverage while liberalizing the pass-blocking rules to allow extended arms and open hands. This time the results were immediately apparent, as interception rates plummeted and passing yardage totals soared—a trend that continued for the next decade and beyond.

Also in 1978, the NFL increased its regular season to 16 games and added a second wild card team in each conference. The four wild cards were to play each other in a preliminary playoff round, giving the division winners a week to rest up before starting postseason play.

Off the Field, Into the Courts

The 1970s had brought unprecedented prosperity to the NFL, but as the decade drew to a close there were a few storm clouds on the horizon.

The first squalls appeared in Los Angeles, where the Rams left the L.A. Coliseum, their home since 1946, and moved to Anaheim Stadium for the 1980 season. Suddenly without a tenant, the coliseum's management made an offer to Al Davis, the Oakland Raiders' maverick principal owner. The prospect of playing in a 100,000-seat stadium in the nation's second-largest city proved irresistible, and Davis announced that the Raiders would move to Los Angeles in 1981. The league's owners vetoed the move, but Davis and the L.A. Coliseum Commission filed an antitrust suit against the NFL. The case was finally decided in 1982. On May 7 a federal court ruled in favor of the Raiders, and in September the NFL season opened for the first time with two teams in the City of Angels.

Just four days after losing its case against the Raiders, the NFL got more bad news when a group of wealthy backers announced plans for a new rival league, this one called the United States Football League. Though the USFL planned to avoid a direct confrontation with the established league by playing in the spring and summer, it still raised the specter of bidding wars and skyrocketing salaries.

But before the USFL launched its first season in March 1983, the NFL had to face an even more dangerous threat—this one from within.

The league had suffered periodic labor problems since 1968, when a threatened strike by the NFL Players Association had been settled just days before training camps opened. Six years later, in 1974, failed negotiations for a new collective bar-

gaining agreement brought a training camp walkout that wasn't settled until August 28, when the players opted to play without a collective agreement. A year later, five teams voted to strike after the NFLPA rejected the latest offer from the NFL Management Council. Once again, the players finally agreed to play without a labor contract, and the season was saved. At last, in early 1977, the NFLPA reached a five-year agreement with the league after three seasons without one.

In 1982, though, it was time to negotiate a new deal, and this time the talks were more antagonistic than ever. No agreement had been reached when the season opened, and after two weeks of the regular season the players turned in their shoulder pads and hit the picket lines. The strike lasted 57 days while negotiations dragged on. Finally, in mid-November, the owners and players agreed on a new contract, which was ratified on December 11. To salvage the season, the NFL added an extra week to the schedule, giving each team nine games. Then the playoffs were expanded to include the top eight teams from each conference.

Unfortunately, the strike-ending agreement lasted only five years, and in 1987 the same scenario was repeated, with the players walking out two weeks into the season. This time, after a week with no games, the owners elected to continue the schedule with "replacement" players. The replacement games lasted three weeks, as attendance and the number of union players crossing the picket lines increased each time out. Finally the NFLPA was forced to admit defeat, and the players returned to work despite the absence of a new collective bargaining agreement.

One thing that limited the players' options was the absence of the USFL, which had played its last game in the summer of 1985. The league's owners had signed their death warrant when they approved New Jersey Generals owner Donald Trump's proposal to begin playing a fall schedule in 1986, going head-to-head against the NFL.

Trump's plan also included an antitrust suit against the NFL, and in July 1986 a federal court found in favor of the USFL—sort of. Though the jury agreed that the NFL had conspired to block the new league, it also decided that the USFL's own management had been primarily responsible for its financial woes, and awarded damages of $1. Awards in antitrust cases are routinely trebled, but the increase to $3 still fell far short of the windfall USFL owners had been counting on to enable them to pay off their debts.

That ignominious end condemned the USFL to be remembered as "the $3 league." But even the league's critics had to admit that the USFL had managed to attract a fine crop of talented young players. The league made headlines by signing the Heisman Trophy winner in each year of its existence: Herschel Walker in 1983, Mike Rozier in 1984, and Doug Flutie in 1985. Walker and Rozier made their mark in the NFL after the USFL's demise, though Flutie was a disappointment until he found a home in the Canadian Football League. These three were only the tip of the iceberg, however.

For instance, what do Gary Clark, Kent Hull, Jim Kelly, Sean Landeta, Sam Mills, Frank Minnifield, Reggie White, Steve Young, and Gary Zimmerman have in common? All of

13

them broke in with the USFL and were later named to all-pro teams in the NFL—but they're far from the only ones who fit that description.

Then there's Jim Mora, Coach of the Year in 1987 with the New Orleans Saints. He got his start as a head coach with the USFL's Philadelphia (later Baltimore) Stars and led them to championships in 1984 and '85, after a two-point loss in the 1983 title game. He was the outstanding coach in a league that included George Allen and Jack Pardee, two former Coach of the Year choices in the NFL.

Taken altogether, the talent in the USFL—on the field and on the sidelines—was at least comparable to what the AFL produced in its first three seasons, 1960 to '62. That's not a bad showing for a "$3 league."

The USFL was gone for good, but the NFL still had to cope with after-effects from the two other major stumbling blocks of the early 1980s. The court ruling that allowed the Raiders to move to Los Angeles in 1982 made it inevitable that other teams would follow suit, and they did—the Baltimore Colts escaping to Indianapolis in 1984, the St. Louis Cardinals fleeing to Phoenix in 1988. Both moves were handled in the worst possible fashion, but the commissioner could do nothing more to stop them than the bitter fans in the abandoned cities.

Even the NFL's apparently decisive triumph over the players' union in 1987 proved to be only temporary, and by 1989 that dispute too had found its way into the courts, where the players sought the free agency that would give them the bargaining power enjoyed by their counterparts in baseball and basketball. In an effort to head off legal action, the NFL came up with a system of limited free agency called Plan B. Though it allowed a team to reserve most of its players, this system did result in far more free agent signings than ever before.

The league's first season under Plan B was also its first since 1960 without the leadership of Pete Rozelle, who had served the league well in his 29 years as commissioner, guiding pro football through an extraordinary era of unprecedented growth. After several months of debate, the owners chose the relatively obscure Paul Tagliabue as their new commissioner.

Tagliabue's first years were fairly calm, but the league's labor troubles were never far from the surface. No collective bargaining agreement had been signed since 1982, and the players continued to seek free agency in the courts. Finally, early in the 1992 season, a federal court ruled that Plan B was illegal and declared four players free agents. The most sought-after was all-pro tight end Keith Jackson, who signed with the Miami Dolphins shortly thereafter.

Finally, at the end of the season, the owners and the players signed a new seven-year collective contract that included a free-agent system similar to those in other sports, plus a salary cap to limit teams' expenses. Free agency brought unprecedented turnover on rosters all over the league, but the salary cap proved unpopular with the players when highly paid veterans started losing their jobs. That didn't stop the stars and near-stars from continuing to look elsewhere for sweeter deals, or general managers from dangling mega-contracts to lure players who they hoped would be their ticket to the Super Bowl.

Meanwhile, team owners took a tip from the players and started selling the teams themselves to the highest bidder, playing one city off another in a high-stakes game of "franchise free agency." This was perhaps the natural outgrowth of the court ruling on the Raiders' move to Los Angeles in 1982, which left the league virtually powerless to stop the practice, but it didn't set well with the public or the media, and the NFL's image suffered.

The most blatant case occurred in 1995, when Cleveland Browns owner Art Modell, claiming financial distress, despite consistent home crowds of 70,000 and more, accepted a sweetheart deal worth more than $200 million to take his team to Baltimore, where fans had been clamoring for another team ever since the Colts' departure more than a decade earlier. The fact that the deal was announced in midseason made it even worse, as did the fact that the team was renamed the Baltimore Ravens for the 1996 season and had all Cleveland records removed from its publications. The fact that the Browns, considered Super Bowl contenders when the 1995 season started, collapsed after the move was announced didn't seem to matter when stacked up against the financial windfall.

Before long, the Houston Oilers had arranged to move to Nashville, but logistical problems delayed the move until at least 1998. After one season as a lame-duck team in their home of 35 years, the Oilers opted for an interim move to Memphis for 1997. And the most ironic franchise shift occurred when Al Davis and the Raiders pulled out of Los Angeles for the greener pastures of . . . Oakland. Combined with the Los Angeles Rams' move to St. Louis a year earlier, this left the NFL without a team in the nation's second-largest city.

The NFL reacted to the latest round of moves by promising to place expansion teams in Cleveland and Los Angeles, but that proved to be small consolation to fans in the jilted cities. And for every team that did move, another was rumored to be in the market, and the guessing game continued: Would Tampa Bay be able to keep the Buccaneers? Would the Bengals stay in Cincinnati? Could the Seahawks be happy in Seattle?

But all was not gloom and doom in the NFL. On the positive side, the league's two newest members, the Carolina Panthers and the Jacksonville Jaguars, played the new game of salary caps and free agency so well that they reached their respective conference championship games in 1996, only their second season of existence—in the process giving new hope to fans of also-rans all around the league. And the Green Bay Packers, a community-owned small-town team that seemed an anachronism in the megabucks world of pro football in the '90s, captured their twelfth championship (the first since the Lombardi era three decades earlier) by winning Super Bowl XXXI in January 1997.

Besides thrilling the fans in Green Bay, the Packers' victory reaffirmed the NFL's connection with its own colorful history.

PART TWO

The Draft
All-Pro
All-Star Games
The Hall of Fame

NO. 1 DRAFT CHOICES

1936 Jay Berwanger, HB, Chicago by Philadelphia

1937 Sam Francis, FB, Nebraska by Philadelphia

1938 Corby Davis, FB, Indiana by Cleveland Rams

1939 Charles (Ki) Aldrich, C, TCU by Chicago Cardinals

1940 George Cafego, HB, Tennessee by Chicago Cardinals

1941 Tom Harmon, HB, Michigan by Chicago Bears

1942 Bill Dudley, HB, Virginia by Pittsburgh

1943 Frank Sinkwich, HB, Georgia by Detroit

1944 Angelo Bertelli, QB, Notre Dame by Boston Yanks

1945 Charley Trippi, HB, Georgia by Chicago Cardinals

1946 Boley Dancewicz, QB, Notre Dame by Boston Yanks

1947 Bob Fenimore, HB, Oklahoma A&M by Chicago Bears

1948 Harry Gilmer, QB, Alabama by Washington

Tony Minisi, B, Pennsylvania by Chicago (AAFC)

1949 Chuck Bednarik, C, Pennsylvania by Philadelphia

Stan Heath, QB, Nevada-Reno by Chicago (AAFC)

1950 Leon Hart, E, Notre Dame by Detroit

1951 Kyle Rote, HB, SMU by New York Giants

1952 Bill Wade, QB, Vanderbilt by Los Angeles

1953 Harry Babcock, E, Georgia by San Francisco

1954 Bobby Garrett, QB, Stanford by Cleveland

1955 George Shaw, QB, Oregon by Baltimore

1956 Gary Glick, DB, Colorado A&M by Pittsburgh

1957 Paul Hornung, HB, Notre Dame by Green Bay

1958 King Hill, QB, Rice by Chicago Cardinals

1959 Randy Duncan, QB, Iowa by Green Bay

1960 Billy Cannon, RB, LSU by Los Angeles

1961 Tommy Mason, RB, Tulane by Minnesota

Ken Rice, G, Auburn by Buffalo (AFL)

1962 Ernie Davis, RB, Syracuse by Washington

Roman Gabriel, QB, N.C. State by Oakland (AFL)

1963 Terry Baker, QB, Oregon State by Los Angeles

Buck Buchanan, DT, Grambling by Kansas City (AFL)

1964 Dave Parks, E, Texas Tech by San Francisco

Jack Concannon, QB, Boston College by Boston (AFL)

1965 Tucker Frederickson, RB, Auburn by New York Giants

Larry Elkins, E, Baylor by Houston (AFL)

1966 Tommy Nobis, LB, Texas by Atlanta

Jim Grabowski, RB, Illinois by Miami (AFL)

1967 Bubba Smith, DT, Michigan State by Baltimore

1968 Ron Yary, T, USC by Minnesota

1969 O.J. Simpson, RB, USC by Buffalo

1970 Terry Bradshaw, QB, Louisiana Tech by Pittsburgh

1971 Jim Plunkett, QB, Stanford by New England

1972 Walt Patulski, DE, Notre Dame by Buffalo

1973 John Matuszak, DE, Tampa by Houston

1974 Ed Jones, DE, Tennessee State by Dallas

1975 Steve Bartkowski, QB, California by Atlanta

1976 Lee Roy Selmon, DE, Oklahoma by Tampa Bay

1977 Ricky Bell, RB, USC by Tampa Bay

1978 Earl Campbell, RB, Texas by Houston

1979 Tom Cousineau, LB, Ohio State by Buffalo

1980 Billy Sims, RB, Oklahoma by Detroit

1981 George Rogers, RB, South Carolina by New Orleans

1982 Kenneth Sims, DT, Texas by New England

1983 John Elway, QB, Stanford by Baltimore

1984 Irving Fryar, WR, Nebraska by New England

1985 Bruce Smith, DE, Virginia Tech by Buffalo

1986 Bo Jackson, RB, Auburn by Tampa Bay

1987 Vinny Testaverde, QB, Miami by Tampa Bay

1988 Aundray Bruce, LB, Auburn by Atlanta

1989 Troy Aikman, QB, UCLA by Dallas

1990 Jeff George, QB, Illinois by Indianapolis

1991 Russell Maryland, DT, Miami by Dallas

1992 Steve Emtman, DT, Washington by Indianapolis

1993 Drew Bledsoe, QB, Washington State by New England

1994 Dan Wilkinson, DT, Ohio State by Cincinnati

1995 Ki-Jana Carter, RB, Penn State by Cincinnati

1996 Keyshawn Johnson, WR, USC by New York Jets

1997 Orlando Pace, T, Ohio State by St. Louis Rams

FIRST-ROUND DRAFT CHOICES

ARIZONA CARDINALS
Chicago Cardinals
1936 Jim Lawrence, B, TCU
1937 Ray Buivid, B, Marquette
1938 Jack Robbins, B, Arkansas
1939 Ki Aldrich, C, TCU
1940 George Cafego, HB, Tennessee
1941 John Kimbrough, FB, Texas A&M
1942 Steve Lach, B, Duke
1943 Glenn Dobbs, B, Tulsa
1944 Pat Harder, FB, Wisconsin
1945 Charley Trippi, HB, Georgia
1946 Dub Jones, B, LSU
1947 DeWitt (Tex) Coulter, T, Army
1948 Jim Spavital, B, Oklahoma A&M
1949 Bill Fischer, G, Notre Dame
1950 none
1951 Jerry Groom, C, Notre Dame
1952 Ollie Matson, HB, USF
1953 Johnny Olszewski, B, California
1954 Lamar McHan, QB, Arkansas
1955 Max Boydston, E, Oklahoma
1956 Joe Childress, B, Auburn
1957 Jerry Tubbs, C, Oklahoma
1958 King Hill, QB, Rice
      John David Crow, B, Texas A&M
1959 Bill Stacy, B, Mississippi State

St. Louis Cardinals
1960 George Izo, QB, Notre Dame
1961 Ken Rice, T, Auburn
1962 Fate Echols, DT, Northwestern
      Irv Goode, C, Kentucky
1963 Jerry Stovall, DB, LSU
      Don Brumm, DE, Purdue
1964 Ken Kortas, DT, Louisville
1965 Joe Namath, QB, Alabama
1966 Carl McAdams, LB, Oklahoma
1967 Dave Williams, WR, Washington
1968 MacArthur Lane, RB, Utah State
1969 Roger Wehrli, DB, Missouri
1970 Larry Stegent, RB, Texas A&M
1971 Norm Thompson, CB, Utah
1972 Bobby Moore, RB/WR, Oregon
1973 Dave Butz, DT, Purdue
1974 J.V. Cain, TE, Colorado
1975 Tim Gray, DB, Texas A&M
1976 Mike Dawson, DT, Arizona
1977 Steve Pisarkiewicz, QB, Missouri
1978 Steve Little, K, Arkansas
      Ken Greene, DB, Washington State
1979 Ottis Anderson, RB, Miami
1980 Curtis Greer, DE, Michigan

1981 E.J. Junior, LB, Alabama
1982 Luis Sharpe, T, UCLA
1983 Leonard Smith, DB, McNeese State
1984 Clyde Duncan, WR, Tennessee
1985 Freddie Joe Nunn, LB, Mississippi
1986 Anthony Bell, LB, Michigan State
1987 Kelly Stouffer, QB, Colorado State

Phoenix Cardinals
1988 Ken Harvey, LB, California
1989 Eric Hill, LB, LSU
      Joe Wolf, G, Boston College
1990 none
1991 Eric Swann, DE (no college)
1992 none
1993 Garrison Hearst, RB, Georgia
      Ernest Dye, T, South Carolina

Arizona Cardinals
1994 Jamir Miller, LB, UCLA
1995 none
1996 Simeon Rice, DE, Illinois
1997 Tom Knight, DB, Iowa

ATLANTA FALCONS
1966 Tommy Nobis, LB, Texas
      Randy Johnson, QB, Texas A&I
1967 none
1968 Claude Humphrey, DE, Tennessee State
1969 George Kunz, T, Notre Dame
1970 John Small, LB, Citadel
1971 Joe Profit, RB, Northeast Louisiana
1972 Clarence Ellis, DB, Notre Dame
1973 none
1974 none
1975 Steve Bartkowski, QB, California
1976 Bubba Bean, RB, Texas A&M
1977 Warren Bryant, T, Kentucky
      Wilson Faumuina, DT, San Jose State
1978 Mike Kenn, T, Michigan
1979 Don Smith, DE, Miami
1980 Junior Miller, TE, Nebraska
1981 Bobby Butler, DB, Florida State
1982 Gerald Riggs, RB, Arizona State
1983 Mike Pitts, DE, Alabama
1984 Rick Bryan, DT, Oklahoma
1985 Bill Fralic, T, Pittsburgh
1986 Tony Casillas, DT, Oklahoma
      Tim Green, LB, Syracuse
1987 Chris Miller, QB, Oregon
1988 Aundray Bruce, LB, Auburn
1989 Deion Sanders, DB, Florida State
      Shawn Collins, WR, Northern Arizona
1990 Steve Broussard, RB, Washington State

1991 Bruce Pickens, DB, Nebraska
      Mike Pritchard, WR, Colorado
1992 Bob Whitfield, T, Stanford
      Tony Smith, RB, Southern Mississippi
1993 Lincoln Kennedy, T, Washington
1994 none
1995 Devin Bush, DB, Florida State
1996 none
1997 Michael Booker, DB, Nebraska

BALTIMORE COLTS (AAFC)
1947 Arnold Tucker, QB, Army
      Ernie Case, B, UCLA
1948 Bobby Layne, QB, Texas
1949 George Sims, B, Baylor

Baltimore Colts (NFL)
1950 Adrian Burk, QB, Baylor

CAROLINA PANTHERS
1995 Kerry Collins, QB, Penn State
      Tyrone Poole, DB, Fort Valley State
      Blake Brockermeyer, T, Texas
1996 Tim Biakabutuka, RB, Michigan
1997 Rae Carruth, WR, Colorado

CHICAGO ROCKETS
1947 Johnny Lujack, QB, Notre Dame
      Bernie Gallagher, T, Pennsylvania
1948 Tony Minisi, B, Pennsylvania
1949 Stan Heath, QB, Nevada-Reno

BALTIMORE RAVENS
Cleveland Browns (AAFC)
1947 Dick Hoerner, B, Iowa
      Robert Rice, C, Tulane

Cleveland Browns (NFL)
1948 Jeff Durkota, B, Penn State
1949 Jack Mitchell, QB, Oklahoma
1950 Ken Carpenter, B, Oregon State
1951 Ken Konz, B, LSU
1952 Bert Rechichar, DB, Tennessee
      Harry Agganis, QB, Boston University
1953 Doug Atkins, DE, Tennessee
1954 Bobby Garrett, QB, Stanford
      John Bauer, G, Illinois
1955 Kurt Burris, C, Oklahoma
1956 Preston Carpenter, B, Arkansas
1957 Jim Brown, FB, Syracuse
1958 Jim Shofner, DB, TCU
1959 Rich Kreitling, DE, Illinois
1960 Jim Houston, DE, Ohio State
1961 Bobby Crespino, TE, Mississippi

1962 Gary Collins, WR, Maryland
     Leroy Jackson, RB, Western Illinois
1963 Tom Hutchinson, WR, Kentucky
1964 Paul Warfield, WR, Ohio State
1965 none
1966 Milt Morin, TE, Massachusetts
1967 Bob Matheson, LB, Duke
1968 Marvin Upshaw, DT/DE, Trinity
     (Texas)
1969 Ron Johnson, RB, Michigan
1970 Mike Phipps, QB, Purdue
     Bob McKay, T, Texas
1971 Clarence Scott, DB, Kansas State
1972 Thom Darden, DB, Michigan
1973 Steve Holden, WR, Arizona State
     Pete Adams, T, USC
1974 none
1975 Mack Mitchell, DE, Houston
1976 Mike Pruitt, RB, Purdue
1977 Robert Jackson, LB, Texas A&M
1978 Clay Matthews, LB, USC
     Ozzie Newsome, TE, Alabama
1979 Willis Adams, WR, Houston
1980 Charles White, RB, USC
1981 Hanford Dixon, DB, Southern
     Mississippi
1982 Chip Banks, LB, USC
1983 none
1984 Don Rogers, DB, UCLA
1985 none
1986 none
1987 Mike Junkin, LB, Duke
1988 Clifford Charlton, LB, Florida
1989 Eric Metcalf, RB, Texas
1990 none
1991 Eric Turner, DB, UCLA
1992 Tommy Vardell, RB, Stanford
1993 Steve Everitt, C, Michigan
1994 Antonio Langham, DB, Alabama
     Derrick Alexander, WR, Michigan
1995 Craig Powell, LB, Ohio State

Baltimore Ravens

1996 Jonathan Ogden, T, UCLA
     Ray Lewis, LB, Miami
1997 Peter Boulware, DE, Florida State

BOSTON YANKS

1944 Angelo Bertelli, QB, Notre Dame
1945 Eddie Prokop, B, Georgia Tech
1946 Frank (Boley) Dancewicz, QB, Notre
     Dame
1947 Fritz Barzilauskas, G, Yale
1948 Vaughn Mancha, C, Alabama

New York Bulldogs

1949 Doak Walker, HB, SMU

New York Yanks

1950 none
1951 none

BROOKLYN DODGERS

1936 Dick Crayne, B, Iowa
1937 Ed Goddard, B, Washington State
1938 Boyd Brumbaugh, B, Duquesne
     Joe Kilgrow, B, Alabama
1939 Bob MacLeod, B, Dartmouth
1940 Banks McFadden, B, Clemson
1941 Dean McAdams, B, Washington
1942 Bobby Robertson, B, USC
1943 Paul Governali, B, Columbia

Brooklyn Tigers

1944 Creighton Miller, B, Notre Dame
1945 Joe Renfroe, B, Tulane

BROOKLYN DODGERS (AAFC)

1947 Felix (Doc) Blanchard, FB, Army
     Gene (Choo-Choo) Roberts, B,
     Tennessee-Chattanooga
1948 Harry Gilmer, QB, Alabama
1949 Joe Sullivan, B, Dartmouth

BUFFALO BILLS (AAFC)

1947 Bob Fenimore, B, Oklahoma A&M
     Frank Aschenbrenner, B, Northwestern
     Cal Richardson, E, Tulsa
     John (Red) Cochran, B, Wake Forest
1948 Clyde Scott, B, Arkansas
1949 Bill Kay, T, Iowa

BUFFALO BILLS

1960 Richie Lucas, QB, Penn State
1961 Ken Rice, T, Auburn
1962 Ernie Davis, RB, Syracuse
1963 Dave Behrman, C, Michigan State
1964 Carl Eller, DE, Minnesota
1965 Jim Davidson, T, Ohio State
1966 Mike Dennis, RB, Mississippi
1967 John Pitts, DB, Arizona State
1968 Haven Moses, WR, San Diego State
1969 O.J. Simpson, RB, USC
1970 Al Cowlings, DE, USC
1971 J.D. Hill, WR, Arizona State
1972 Walt Patulski, DE, Notre Dame
1973 Paul Seymour, TE, Michigan
     Joe DeLamielleure, G, Michigan State
1974 Reuben Gant, TE, Oklahoma State
1975 Tom Rudd, LB, Nebraska
1976 Mario Clark, DB, Oregon
1977 Phil Dokes, DT, Oklahoma State
1978 Terry Miller, RB, Oklahoma State

1979 Tom Cousineau, LB, Ohio State
     Jerry Butler, WR, Clemson
1980 Jim Ritcher, C, North Carolina State
1981 Booker Moore, RB, Penn State
1982 Perry Tuttle, WR, Clemson
1983 Tony Hunter, TE, Notre Dame
     Jim Kelly, QB, Miami
1984 Greg Bell, RB, Notre Dame
1985 Bruce Smith, DE, Virginia Tech
     Derrick Burroughs, DB, Memphis State
1986 Ronnie Harmon, RB, Iowa
     Will Wolford, T, Vanderbilt
1987 Shane Conlan, LB, Penn State
1988 none
1989 none
1990 James Williams, DB, Fresno State
1991 Henry Jones, DB, Illinois
1992 John Fina, T, Arizona
1993 Thomas Smith, DB, North Carolina
1994 Jeff Burris, DB, Notre Dame
1995 Ruben Brown, G, Pittsburgh
1996 Eric Moulds, WR, Mississippi State
1997 Antowain Smith, RB, Houston

CHICAGO BEARS

1936 Joe Stydahar, T, West Virginia
1937 Les McDonald, E, Nebraska
1938 Joe Gray, B, Oregon State
1939 Sid Luckman, QB, Columbia
     Bill Osmanski, FB, Holy Cross
1940 Clyde (Bulldog) Turner, C, Hardin-
     Simmons
1941 Tom Harmon, HB, Michigan
     Norm Standlee, FB, Stanford
     Don Scott, B, Ohio State
1942 Frankie Albert, QB, Stanford
1943 Bob Steuber, HB, Missouri
1944 Ray Evans, B, Kansas
1945 Don Lund, B, Michigan
1946 Johnny Lujack, QB, Notre Dame
1947 Bob Fenimore, B, Oklahoma State
     Don Kindt, B, Wisconsin
1948 Bobby Layne, QB, Texas
     Max Bumgardner, E, Texas
1949 Dick Harris, C, Texas
1950 Chuck Hunsinger, B, Florida
     Fred Morrison, B, Ohio State
1951 Bob Williams, B, Notre Dame
     Billy Stone, B, Bradley
     Gene Schroeder, E, Virginia
1952 Jim Dooley, B, Miami
1953 Billy Anderson, B, Compton J.C.
1954 Stan Wallace, B, Illinois
1955 Ron Drzewiecki, B, Marquette
1956 Menan (Tex) Schriewer, E, Texas

1957 Earl Leggett, T, LSU
1958 Chuck Howley, G, West Virginia
1959 Don Clark, B, Ohio State
1960 Roger Davis, G, Syracuse
1961 Mike Ditka, TE, Pittsburgh
1962 Ronnie Bull, RB, Baylor
1963 Dave Behrman, C, Michigan State
1964 Dick Evey, DT, Tennessee
1965 Dick Butkus, LB, Illinois
      Gale Sayers, RB, Kansas
      Steve DeLong, T, Tennessee
1966 George Rice, DT, LSU
1967 Loyd Phillips, DE, Arkansas
1968 Mike Hull, RB, USC
1969 Rufus Mayes, T, Ohio State
1970 none
1971 Joe Moore, RB, Missouri
1972 Lionel Antoine, T, Southern Illinois
      Craig Clemons, DB, Iowa
1973 Wally Chambers, DT, Eastern
        Kentucky
1974 Waymond Bryant, LB, Tennessee State
      Dave Gallagher, DT, Michigan
1975 Walter Payton, RB, Jackson State
1976 Dennis Lick, T, Wisconsin
1977 Ted Albrecht, T, California
1978 none
1979 Dan Hampton, DT, Arkansas
      Al Harris, DE, Arizona State
1980 Otis Wilson, LB, Louisville
1981 Keith Van Horne, T, USC
1982 Jim McMahon, QB, BYU
1983 Jim Covert, T, Pittsburgh
      Willie Gault, WR, Tennessee
1984 Wilber Marshall, LB, Florida
1985 William Perry, DT, Clemson
1986 Neal Anderson, RB, Florida
1987 Jim Harbaugh, QB, Michigan
1988 Brad Muster, RB, Stanford
      Wendell Davis, WR, LSU
1989 Donnell Woolford, DB, Clemson
      Trace Armstrong, DE, Florida
1990 Mark Carrier, DB, USC
1991 Stan Thomas, T, Texas
1992 Alonzo Spellman, DE, Ohio State
1993 Curtis Conway, WR, USC
1994 John Thierry, DE, Alcorn State
1995 Rashaan Salaam, RB, Colorado
1996 Walt Harris, DB, Mississippi State
1997 none

CINCINNATI BENGALS

1968 Bob Johnson, C, Tennessee
1969 Greg Cook, QB, Cincinnati
1970 Mike Reid, DT, Penn State

1971 Vernon Holland, T, Tennessee State
1972 Sherman White, DE, California
1973 Isaac Curtis, WR, San Diego State
1974 Bill Kollar, DT, Montana State
1975 Glenn Cameron, LB, Florida
1976 Billy Brooks, WR, Oklahoma
      Archie Griffin, RB, Ohio State
1977 Eddie Edwards, DT, Miami
      Wilson Whitley, DT, Houston
      Mike Cobb, TE, Michigan State
1978 Ross Browner, DT, Notre Dame
      Blair Bush, C, Washington
1979 Jack Thompson, QB, Washington State
      Charles Alexander, RB, LSU
1980 Anthony Munoz, T, USC
1981 David Verser, WR, Kansas
1982 Glen Collins, DE, Mississippi State
1983 Dave Rimington, C, Nebraska
1984 Ricky Hunley, LB, Arizona
      Pete Koch, DE, Maryland
      Brian Blados, T, North Carolina
1985 Eddie Brown, WR, Miami
      Emanuel King, LB, Alabama
1986 Joe Kelly, LB, Washington
      Tim McGee, WR, Tennessee
1987 Jason Buck, DE, BYU
1988 Rickey Dixon, DB, Oklahoma
1989 none
1990 James Francis, LB, Baylor
1991 Alfred Williams, LB, Colorado
1992 David Klingler, QB, Houston
      Darryl Williams, DB, Miami
1993 John Copeland, DE, Alabama
1994 Dan Wilkinson, DT, Ohio State
1995 Ki-Jana Carter, RB, Penn State
1996 Willie Anderson, T, Auburn
1997 Reinard Wilson, LB, Florida State

DALLAS COWBOYS

1960 none
1961 Bob Lilly, DT, TCU
1962 none
1963 Lee Roy Jordan, LB, Alabama
1964 Scott Appleton, DT, Texas
1965 Craig Morton, QB, California
1966 John Niland, G, Iowa
1967 none
1968 Dennis Homan, WR, Alabama
1969 Calvin Hill, RB, Yale
1970 Duane Thomas, RB, West Texas State
1971 Tody Smith, DE, USC
1972 Bill Thomas, RB, Boston College
1973 Billy Joe DuPree, TE, Michigan State
1974 Ed Jones, DE, Tennessee State
      Charley Young, RB, N.C. State

1975 Randy White, LB, Maryland
      Thomas Henderson, LB, Langston
1976 Aaron Kyle, DB, Wyoming
1977 Tony Dorsett, RB, Pittsburgh
1978 Larry Bethea, DE, Michigan State
1979 Robert Shaw, C, Tennessee
1980 none
1981 Howard Richards, T, Missouri
1982 Rod Hill, DB, Kentucky State
1983 Jim Jeffcoat, DE, Arizona State
1984 Billy Cannon Jr., LB, Texas A&M
1985 Kevin Brooks, DE, Michigan
1986 Mike Sherrard, WR, UCLA
1987 Danny Noonan, DT, Nebraska
1988 Michael Irvin, WR, Miami
1989 Troy Aikman, QB, UCLA
1990 Emmitt Smith, RB, Florida
1991 Russell Maryland, DT, Miami
      Alvin Harper, WR, Tennessee
      Kelvin Pritchett, DT, Mississippi
1992 Kevin Smith, DB, Texas A&M
      Robert Jones, LB, East Carolina
1993 none
1994 Shante Carver, DE, Arizona State
1995 none
1996 none
1997 David LaFleur, TE, LSU

DALLAS TEXANS (NFL)

1952 Les Richter, G, California

DENVER BRONCOS

1960 Roger LeClerc, C, Trinity (Conn.)
1961 Bob Gaiters, RB, New Mexico State
1962 Merlin Olsen, DT, Utah State
1963 Kermit Alexander, DB, UCLA
1964 Bob Brown, T, Nebraska
1965 none
1966 Jerry Shay, DT, Purdue
1967 Floyd Little, RB, Syracuse
1968 none
1969 none
1970 Bob Anderson, RB, Colorado
1971 Marv Montgomery, T, USC
1972 Riley Odoms, TE, Houston
1973 Otis Armstrong, RB, Purdue
1974 Randy Gradishar, LB, Ohio State
1975 Louis Wright, DB, San Jose State
1976 Tom Glassic, G, Virginia
1977 Steve Schindler, G, Boston College
1978 Don Latimer, DT, Miami
1979 Kelvin Clark, T, Nebraska
1980 none
1981 Dennis Smith, DB, USC
1982 Gerald Willhite, RB, San Jose State

1983 Chris Hinton, G, Northwestern
1984 none
1985 Steve Sewell, RB, Oklahoma
1986 none
1987 Ricky Nattiel, WR, Florida
1988 Ted Gregory, DT, Syracuse
1989 Steve Atwater, DB, Arkansas
1990 none
1991 Mike Croel, LB, Nebraska
1992 Tommy Maddox, QB, UCLA
1993 Dan Williams, DE, Toledo
1994 none
1995 none
1996 John Mobley, LB, Kutztown
1997 Trevor Pryce, DT, Clemson

DETROIT LIONS

1936 Sid Wagner, G, Michigan State
1937 Lloyd Cardwell, HB, Nebraska
1938 Alex Wojciechowicz, C, Fordham
1939 John Pingel, B, Michigan State
1940 Doyle Nave, B, USC
1941 Jim Thomason, B, Texas A&M
1942 Bob Westfall, B, Michigan
1943 Frank Sinkwich, HB, Georgia
1944 Otto Graham, B, Northwestern
1945 Frank Szymanski, C, Notre Dame
1946 Bill Dellastatious, B, Missouri
1947 Glenn Davis, HB, Army
1948 Y.A. Tittle, QB, LSU
1949 John Rauch, B, Georgia
1950 Leon Hart, E, Notre Dame
     Joe Watson, C, Rice
1951 none
1952 none
1953 Harley Sewell, G, Texas
1954 Dick Chapman, T, Rice
1955 Dave Middleton, B, Auburn
1956 Hopalong Cassady, B, Ohio State
1957 Bill Glass, G, Baylor
1958 Alex Karras, DT, Iowa
1959 Nick Pietrosante, B, Notre Dame
1960 John Robinson, DB, LSU
1961 none
1962 John Hadl, QB, Kansas
1963 Daryl Sanders, T, Ohio State
1964 Pete Beathard, QB, USC
1965 Tom Nowatzke, RB, Indiana
1966 none
1967 Mel Farr, RB, UCLA
1968 Greg Landry, QB, Massachusetts
     Earl McCullouch, WR, USC
1969 none
1970 Steve Owens, RB, Oklahoma
1971 Bob Bell, DT, Cincinnati

1972 Herb Orvis, DE, Colorado
1973 Ernie Price, DE, Texas A&I
1974 Ed O'Neil, LB, Penn State
1975 Lynn Boden, G, South Dakota State
1976 James Hunter, DB, Grambling
     Lawrence Gaines, RB, Wyoming
1977 none
1978 Luther Bradley, DB, Notre Dame
1979 Keith Dorney, T, Penn State
1980 Billy Sims, RB, Oklahoma
1981 Mark Nichols, WR, San Jose State
1982 Jimmy Williams, LB, Nebraska
1983 James Jones, RB, Florida
1984 David Lewis, TE, California
1985 Lomas Brown, T, Florida
1986 Chuck Long, QB, Iowa
1987 Reggie Rogers, DE, Washington
1988 Bennie Blades, DB, Miami
1989 Barry Sanders, RB, Oklahoma State
1990 Andre Ware, QB, Houston
1991 Herman Moore, WR, Virginia
1992 Robert Porcher, DE, South Carolina
     State
1993 none
1994 Johnnie Morton, WR, USC
1995 Luther Elliss, DT, Utah
1996 Reggie Brown, LB, Texas A&M
     Jeff Hartings, G, Penn State
1997 Bryant Westbrook, DB, Texas

GREEN BAY PACKERS

1936 Russ Letlow, G, USF
1937 Ed Jankowski, B, Wisconsin
1938 Cecil Isbell, B, Purdue
1939 Larry Buhler, B, Minnesota
1940 Harold Van Every, B, Minnesota
1941 George Paskvan, B, Wisconsin
1942 Urban Odson, T, Minnesota
1943 Dick Wildung, T, Minnesota
1944 Merv Pregulman, G, Michigan
1945 Walt Schlinkman, B, Texas Tech
1946 Johnny Strzykalski, B, Marquette
1947 Ernie Case, B, UCLA
1948 Earl (Jug) Girard, B, Wisconsin
1949 Stan Heath, QB, Nevada-Reno
1950 Clayton Tonnemaker, C, Minnesota
1951 Bob Gain, T, Kentucky
1952 Babe Parilli, QB, Kentucky
1953 Al Carmichael, B, USC
1954 Art Hunter, T, Notre Dame
     Veryl Switzer, B, Kansas State
1955 Tom Bettis, G, Purdue
1956 Jack Losch, B, Miami
1957 Paul Hornung, B, Notre Dame
     Ron Kramer, E, Michigan

1958 Dan Currie, C, Michigan State
1959 Randy Duncan, B, Iowa
1960 Tom Moore, RB, Vanderbilt
1961 Herb Adderley, DB, Michigan State
1962 Earl Gros, RB, LSU
1963 Dave Robinson, LB, Penn State
1964 Lloyd Voss, DT, Nebraska
1965 Donny Anderson, RB, Texas Tech
     Lawrence Elkins, E, Baylor
1966 Jim Grabowski, RB, Illinois
     Gale Gillingham, T, Minnesota
1967 Bob Hyland, C, Boston College
     Don Horn, QB, San Diego State
1968 Fred Carr, LB, Texas-El Paso
     Bill Lueck, G, Arizona
1969 Rich Moore, DT, Villanova
1970 Mike McCoy, DT, Notre Dame
     Rich McGeorge, TE, Elon
1971 John Brockington, RB, Ohio State
1972 Willie Buchanon, DB, San Diego State
     Jerry Tagge, QB, Nebraska
1973 Barry Smith, WR, Florida State
1974 Barty Smith, RB, Richmond
1975 none
1976 Mark Koncar, T, Colorado
1977 Mike Butler, DE, Kansas
     Ezra Johnson, DE, Morris Brown
1978 James Lofton, WR, Stanford
     John Anderson, LB, Michigan
1979 Eddie Lee Ivery, RB, Georgia Tech
1980 Bruce Clark, DE, Penn State
     George Cumby, LB, Oklahoma
1981 Rich Campbell, QB, California
1982 Ron Hallstrom, G, Iowa
1983 Tim Lewis, DB, Pittsburgh
1984 Alphonso Carreker, DE, Florida State
1985 Ken Ruettgers, T, USC
1986 none
1987 Brent Fullwood, RB, Auburn
1988 Sterling Sharpe, WR, South Carolina
1989 Tony Mandarich, T, Michigan State
1990 Tony Bennett, LB, Mississippi
     Darrell Thompson, RB, Minnesota
1991 Vinnie Clark, DB, Ohio State
1992 Terrell Buckley, DB, Florida State
1993 Wayne Simmons, LB, Clemson
     George Teague, DB, Alabama
1994 Aaron Taylor, T, Notre Dame
1995 Craig Newsome, DB, Arizona State
1996 John Michels, T, USC
1997 Ross Verba, T, Iowa

HOUSTON OILERS

1960 Billy Cannon, RB, LSU
1961 Mike Ditka, TE, Pittsburgh

21

1962 Ray Jacobs, DT, Howard Payne
1963 Danny Brabham, LB, Arkansas
1964 Scott Appleton, DT, Texas
1965 Larry Elkins, WR, Baylor
1966 Tommy Nobis, LB, Texas
1967 George Webster, LB, Michigan State
    Tom Regner, G, Notre Dame
1968 none
1969 Ron Pritchard, LB, Arizona State
1970 Doug Wilkerson, G, North Carolina
    Central
1971 Dan Pastorini, QB, Santa Clara
1972 Greg Sampson, DE, Stanford
1973 John Matuszak, DE, Tampa
    George Amundson, RB, Iowa State
1974 none
1975 Robert Brazile, LB, Jackson State
    Don Hardeman, RB, Texas A&I
1976 none
1977 Morris Towns, T, Missouri
1978 Earl Campbell, RB, Texas
1979 none
1980 none
1981 none
1982 Mike Munchak, G, Penn State
1983 Bruce Matthews, T, USC
1984 Dean Steinkuhler, T, Nebraska
1985 Ray Childress, DE, Texas A&M
    Richard Johnson, DB, Wisconsin
1986 Jim Everett, QB, Purdue
1987 Alonzo Highsmith, RB, Miami
    Haywood Jeffires, WR, N.C. State
1988 Lorenzo White, RB, Michigan State
1989 David Williams, T, Florida
1990 Lamar Lathon, LB, Houston
1991 none
1992 none
1993 Brad Hopkins, T, Illinois
1994 Henry Ford, DE, Arkansas
1995 Steve McNair, QB, Alcorn State
1996 Eddie George, RB, Ohio State
1997 Kenny Holmes, DE, Miami

INDIANAPOLIS COLTS
Baltimore Colts
1953 Billy Vessels, HB, Oklahoma
1954 Cotton Davidson, QB, Baylor
1955 George Shaw, QB, Oregon
    Alan Ameche, FB, Wisconsin
1956 Lenny Moore, HB, Penn State
1957 Jim Parker, G, Ohio State
1958 Lenny Lyles, B, Louisville
1959 Jackie Burkett, C, Auburn
1960 Ron Mix, T, USC
1961 Tom Matte, RB, Ohio State

1962 Wendell Harris, DB, LSU
1963 Bob Vogel, T, Ohio State
1964 Marv Woodson, DB, Indiana
1965 Mike Curtis, LB, Duke
1966 Sam Ball, T, Kentucky
1967 Bubba Smith, DT, Michigan State
    Jim Detwiler, RB, Michigan
1968 John Williams, G, Minnesota
1969 Eddie Hinton, WR, Oklahoma
1970 Norm Bulaich, RB, TCU
1971 Don McCauley, RB, North Carolina
    Leonard Dunlap, DB, North Texas
    State
1972 Tom Drougas, T, Oregon
1973 Bert Jones, QB, LSU
    Joe Ehrmann, DT, Syracuse
1974 John Dutton, DE, Nebraska
    Roger Carr, WR, Louisiana Tech
1975 Ken Huff, G, North Carolina
1976 Ken Novak, DT, Purdue
1977 Randy Burke, WR, Kentucky
1978 Reese McCall, TE, Auburn
1979 Barry Krauss, LB, Alabama
1980 Curtis Dickey, RB, Texas A&M
    Derrick Hatchett, DB, Texas
1981 Randy McMillan, RB, Pittsburgh
    Donnell Thompson, DT, North
    Carolina
1982 Johnie Cooks, LB, Mississippi State
    Art Schlichter, QB, Ohio State
1983 John Elway, QB, Stanford

Indianapolis Colts
1984 Leonard Coleman, DB, Vanderbilt
    Ron Solt, G, Maryland
1985 Duane Bickett, LB, USC
1986 Jon Hand, DE, Alabama
1987 Cornelius Bennett, LB, Alabama
1988 none
1989 Andre Rison, WR, Michigan State
1990 Jeff George, QB, Illinois
1991 none
1992 Steve Emtman, DT, Washington
    Quentin Coryatt, LB, Texas A&M
1993 Sean Dawkins, WR, California
1994 Marshall Faulk, RB, San Diego State
    Trev Alberts, LB, Nebraska
1995 Ellis Johnson, DT, Florida
1996 Marvin Harrison, WR, Syracuse
1997 Tarik Glenn, T, California

JACKSONVILLE JAGUARS
1995 Tony Boselli, T, USC
    James Stewart, RB, Tennessee
1996 Kevin Hardy, LB, Illinois
1997 Renaldo Wynn, DT, Notre Dame

KANSAS CITY CHIEFS
Dallas Texans (AFL)
1960 Don Meredith, QB, SMU
1961 E.J. Holub, C, Texas Tech
1962 Ronnie Bull, RB, Baylor

Kansas City Chiefs
1963 Buck Buchanan, DT, Grambling
    Ed Budde, G, Michigan State
1964 Pete Beathard, QB, USC
1965 Gale Sayers, RB, Kansas
1966 Aaron Brown, DE, Minnesota
1967 Gene Trosch, DE/DT, Miami
1968 Mo Moorman, G, Texas A&M
    George Daney, G, Texas-El Paso
1969 Jim Marsalis, DB, Tennessee State
1970 Sid Smith, T, USC
1971 Elmo Wright, WR, Houston
1972 Jeff Kinney, RB, Nebraska
1973 none
1974 Woody Green, RB, Arizona State
1975 none
1976 Rod Walters, G, Iowa
1977 Gary Green, DB, Baylor
1978 Art Still, DE, Kentucky
1979 Mike Bell, DE, Colorado State
    Steve Fuller, QB, Clemson
1980 Brad Budde, G, USC
1981 Willie Scott, TE, South Carolina
1982 Anthony Hancock, WR, Tennessee
1983 Todd Blackledge, QB, Penn State
1984 Bill Maas, DT, Pittsburgh
    John Alt, T, Iowa
1985 Ethan Horton, RB, North Carolina
1986 Brian Jozwiak, T, West Virginia
1987 Paul Palmer, RB, Temple
1988 Neil Smith, DE, Nebraska
1989 Derrick Thomas, LB, Alabama
1990 Percy Snow, LB, Michigan State
1991 Harvey Williams, RB, LSU
1992 Dale Carter, DB, Tennessee
1993 none
1994 Greg Hill, RB, Texas A&M
1995 Trezelle Jenkins, T, Michigan
1996 Jerome Woods, DB, Memphis
1997 Tony Gonzalez, TE, California

LOS ANGELES DONS (AAFC)
1947 Herman Wedemeyer, B, St. Mary's
    (Calif.)
1948 Vaughn Mancha, C, Alabama
1949 George Taliaferro, B, Indiana

MIAMI DOLPHINS
1966 Jim Grabowski, RB, Illinois

Rick Norton, QB, Kentucky
1967 Bob Griese, QB, Purdue
1968 Larry Csonka, RB, Syracuse
Doug Crusan, T, Indiana
1969 Bill Stanfill, DE, Georgia
1970 none
1971 none
1972 Mike Kadish, DT, Notre Dame
1973 none
1974 Donald Reese, DE, Jackson State
1975 Darryl Carlton, T, Tampa
1976 Larry Gordon, LB, Arizona State
Kim Bokamper, LB, San Jose State
1977 A.J. Duhe, DT, LSU
1978 none
1979 Jon Giesler, T, Michigan
1980 Don McNeal, DB, Alabama
1981 David Overstreet, RB, Oklahoma
1982 Roy Foster, G, USC
1983 Dan Marino, QB, Pittsburgh
1984 Jackie Shipp, LB, Oklahoma
1985 Lorenzo Hampton, RB, Florida
1986 none
1987 John Bosa, DE, Boston College
1988 Eric Kumerow, DE, Ohio State
1989 Sammie Smith, RB, Florida State
Louis Oliver, DB, Florida
1990 Richmond Webb, T, Texas A&M
1991 Randal Hill, WR, Miami
1992 Troy Vincent, DB, Wisconsin
Marco Coleman, LB, Georgia Tech
1993 O.J. McDuffie, WR, Penn State
1994 Tim Bowens, DT, Mississippi
1995 Billy Milner, T, Houston
1996 Daryl Gardener, DT, Baylor
1997 Yatil Green, WR, Miami

MINNESOTA VIKINGS

1961 Tommy Mason, RB, Tulane
1962 none
1963 Jim Dunaway, T, Mississippi
1964 Carl Eller, DE, Minnesota
1965 Jack Snow, WR, Notre Dame
1966 Jerry Shay, DT, Purdue
1967 Clint Jones, RB, Michigan State
Gene Washington, WR, Michigan State
Alan Page, DT, Notre Dame
1968 Ron Yary, T, USC
1969 none
1970 John Ward, DT, Oklahoma State
1971 Leo Hayden, RB, Ohio State
1972 Jeff Siemon, LB, Stanford
1973 Chuck Foreman, RB, Miami
1974 Fred McNeill, LB, UCLA
Steve Riley, T, USC

1975 Mark Mullaney, DE, Colorado State
1976 James White, DT, Oklahoma State
1977 Tommy Kramer, QB, Rice
1978 Randy Holloway, DE, Pittsburgh
1979 Ted Brown, RB, North Carolina State
1980 Doug Martin, DT, Washington
1981 none
1982 Darrin Nelson, RB, Stanford
1983 Joey Browner, DB, USC
1984 Keith Millard, DE, Washington State
1985 Chris Doleman, LB, Pittsburgh
1986 Gerald Robinson, DE, Auburn
1987 D.J. Dozier, RB, Penn State
1988 Randall McDaniel, G, Arizona State
1989 none
1990 none
1991 none
1992 none
1993 Robert Smith, RB, Ohio State
1994 DeWayne Washington, DB, North
Carolina State
Todd Steussie, T, California
1995 Derrick Alexander, DE, Florida State
Korey Stringer, T, Ohio State
1996 Duane Clemons, DE, California
1997 Dwayne Rudd, LB, Alabama

NEW ENGLAND PATRIOTS
Boston Patriots
1960 Ron Burton, RB, Northwestern
1961 Tommy Mason, RB, Tulane
1962 Gary Collins, WR, Maryland
1963 Art Graham, WR, Boston College
1964 Jack Concannon, QB, Boston College
1965 Jerry Rush, DE, Michigan State
1966 Karl Singer, T, Purdue
1967 John Charles, DB, Purdue
1968 Dennis Byrd, DE, North Carolina State
1969 Ron Sellers, WR, Florida State
1970 Phil Olsen, DE, Utah State

New England Patriots
1971 Jim Plunkett, QB, Stanford
1972 none
1973 John Hannah, G, Alabama
Sam Cunningham, RB, USC
Darryl Stingley, WR, Purdue
1974 none
1975 Russ Francis, TE, Oregon
1976 Mike Haynes, DB, Arizona State
Pete Brock, C, Colorado
Tim Fox, DB, Ohio State
1977 Raymond Clayborn, DB, Texas
Stanley Morgan, WR, Tennessee
1978 Bob Cryder, G, Alabama
1979 Rick Sanford, DB, South Carolina

1980 Roland James, DB, Tennessee
Vagas Ferguson, RB, Notre Dame
1981 Brian Holloway, T, Stanford
1982 Kenneth Sims, DT, Texas
Lester Williams, DT, Miami
1983 Tony Eason, QB, Illinois
1984 Irving Fryar, WR, Nebraska
1985 Trevor Matich, C, BYU
1986 Reggie Dupard, RB, SMU
1987 Bruce Armstrong, T, Louisville
1988 John Stephens, RB, Northwestern State
(La.)
1989 Hart Lee Dykes, WR, Oklahoma State
1990 Chris Singleton, LB, Arizona
Ray Agnew, DE, North Carolina State
1991 Pat Harlow, T, USC
Leonard Russell, RB, Arizona State
1992 Eugene Chung, T, Virginia Tech
1993 Drew Bledsoe, QB, Washington State
1994 Willie McGinest, DE, USC
1995 Ty Law, DB, Michigan
1996 Terry Glenn, WR, Ohio State
1997 Chris Canty, DB, Kansas State

NEW ORLEANS SAINTS

1967 Les Kelley, RB, Alabama
1968 Kevin Hardy, DE, Notre Dame
1969 John Shinners, G, Xavier
1970 Ken Burrough, WR, Texas Southern
1971 Archie Manning, QB, Mississippi
1972 Royce Smith, G, Georgia
1973 none
1974 Rick Middleton, LB, Ohio State
1975 Larry Burton, WR, Purdue
Kurt Schumacher, T, Ohio State
1976 Chuck Muncie, RB, California
1977 Joe Campbell, DE, Maryland
1978 Wes Chandler, WR, Florida
1979 Russell Erxleben, P/K, Texas
1980 Stan Brock, T, Colorado
1981 George Rogers, RB, South Carolina
1982 Lindsay Scott, WR, Georgia
1983 none
1984 James Geathers, DE, Wichita State
1985 Alvin Toles, LB, Tennessee
1986 Jim Dombrowski, T, Virginia
1987 Shawn Knight, DT, BYU
1988 Craig Heyward, RB, Pittsburgh
1989 Wayne Martin, DE, Arkansas
1990 Renaldo Turnbull, DE, West Virginia
1991 none
1992 Vaughn Dunbar, RB, Indiana
1993 William Roaf, T, Louisiana Tech
Irv Smith, TE, Notre Dame
1994 Joe Johnson, DE, Louisville

1995 Mark Fields, LB, Washington State
1996 Alex Molden, DB, Oregon
1997 Chris Naeole, G, Colorado

NEW YORK GIANTS

1936 Art Lewis, T, Ohio University
1937 Ed Widseth, T, Minnesota
1938 George Karamatic, B, Gonzaga
1939 Walt Nielsen, B, Arizona
1940 Grenville Lansdell, B, USC
1941 George Franck, B, Minnesota
1942 Merle Hapes, B, Mississippi
1943 Steve Filipowicz, B, Fordham
1944 Billy Hillenbrand, B, Indiana
1945 Elmer Barbour, B, Wake Forest
1946 George Connor, T, Notre Dame
1947 Vic Schwall, B, Northwestern
1948 Tony Minisi, B, Pennsylvania
1949 Paul Page, B, SMU
1950 Travis Tidwell, B, Auburn
1951 Kyle Rote, B, SMU
     Jim Spavital, B, Oklahoma A&M
1952 Frank Gifford, B, USC
1953 Bobby Marlow, B, Alabama
1954 none
1955 Joe Heap, B, Notre Dame
1956 none
1957 none
1958 Phil King, B, Vanderbilt
1959 Lee Grosscup, QB, Utah
1960 Lou Cordileone, G, Clemson
1961 none
1962 Jerry Hillebrand, LB, Colorado
1963 none
1964 Joe Don Looney, RB, Oklahoma
1965 Tucker Frederickson, RB, Auburn
1966 Francis Peay, T, Missouri
1967 none
1968 none
1969 Fred Dryer, DE, San Diego State
1970 Jim Files, LB, Oklahoma
1971 Rocky Thompson, WR, West Texas
     State
1972 Eldridge Small, DB, Texas A&I
     Larry Jacobson, DE, Nebraska
1973 none
1974 John Hicks, G, Ohio State
1975 none
1976 Troy Archer, DE, Colorado
1977 Gary Jeter, DT, USC
1978 Gordon King, T, Stanford
1979 Phil Simms, QB, Morehead State
1980 Mark Haynes, DB, Colorado
1981 Lawrence Taylor, LB, North Carolina
1982 Butch Woolfolk, RB, Michigan

1983 Terry Kinard, DB, Clemson
1984 Carl Banks, LB, Michigan State
     William Roberts, T, Ohio State
1985 George Adams, RB, Kentucky
1986 Eric Dorsey, DE, Notre Dame
1987 Mark Ingram, WR, Michigan State
1988 Eric Moore, T, Indiana
1989 Brian Williams, C/G, Minnesota
1990 Rodney Hampton, RB, Georgia
1991 Jarrod Bunch, RB, Michigan
1992 Derek Brown, TE, Notre Dame
1993 none
1994 Thomas Lewis, WR, Indiana
1995 Tyrone Wheatley, RB, Michigan
1996 Cedric Jones, DE, Oklahoma
1997 Ike Hilliard, WR, Florida

NEW YORK JETS

New York Titans

1960 George Izo, QB, Notre Dame
1961 Tom Brown, G, Minnesota
1962 Sandy Stephens, QB, Minnesota

New York Jets

1963 Jerry Stovall, DB, LSU
1964 Matt Snell, FB, Ohio State
1965 Joe Namath, QB, Alabama
     Tom Nowatzke, RB, Indiana
1966 Bill Yearby, DT, Michigan
1967 Paul Seiler, T, Notre Dame
1968 Lee White, RB, Weber State
1969 Dave Foley, T, Ohio State
1970 Steve Tannen, DB, Florida
1971 John Riggins, RB, Kansas
1972 Jerome Barkum, WR, Jackson State
     Mike Taylor, LB, Michigan
1973 Burgess Owens, DB, Miami
1974 Carl Barzilauskas, DT, Indiana
1975 none
1976 Richard Todd, QB, Alabama
1977 Marvin Powell, T, USC
1978 Chris Ward, T, Ohio State
1979 Marty Lyons, DE, Alabama
1980 Johnny (Lam) Jones, WR, Texas
1981 Freeman McNeil, RB, UCLA
1982 Bob Crable, LB, Notre Dame
1983 Ken O'Brien, QB, Cal-Davis
1984 Russell Carter, DB, SMU
     Ron Faurot, DE, Arkansas
1985 Al Toon, WR, Wisconsin
1986 Mike Haight, T, Iowa
1987 Roger Vick, RB, Texas A&M
1988 Dave Cadigan, T, USC
1989 Jeff Lageman, LB, Virginia
1990 Blair Thomas, RB, Penn State
1991 none

1992 Johnny Mitchell, TE, Nebraska
1993 Marvin Jones, LB, Florida State
1994 Aaron Glenn, DB, Texas A&M
1995 Kyle Brady, TE, Penn State
     Hugh Douglas, DE, Central State
     (Ohio)
1996 Keyshawn Johnson, WR, USC
1997 James Farrior, LB, Virginia

NEW YORK YANKEES (AAFC)

1947 Buddy Young, HB, Illinois
     Charley Trippi, HB, Georgia
1948 Lowell Tew, B, Alabama
1949 Bobby Thomason, QB, VMI

OAKLAND RAIDERS

Oakland Raiders

1960 Dale Hackbart, DB, Wisconsin
1961 Joe Rutgens, DT, Illinois
1962 Roman Gabriel, QB, N.C. State
1963 none
1964 Tony Lorick, RB, Arizona State
1965 Harry Schuh, T, Memphis State
1966 Rodger Bird, DB, Kentucky
1967 Gene Upshaw, G, Texas A&I
1968 Eldridge Dickey, QB, Tennessee State
1969 Art Thoms, DT, Syracuse
1970 Raymond Chester, TE, Morgan State
1971 Jack Tatum, DB, Ohio State
1972 Mike Siani, WR, Villanova
1973 Ray Guy, P, Southern Mississippi
1974 Henry Lawrence, T, Florida A&M
1975 Neal Colzie, DB, Ohio State
1976 none
1977 none
1978 none
1979 none
1980 Marc Wilson, QB, BYU
1981 Ted Watts, DB, Texas Tech
     Curt Marsh, T, Washington

Los Angeles Raiders

1982 Marcus Allen, RB, USC
1983 Don Mosebar, T, USC
1984 none
1985 Jessie Hester, WR, Florida State
1986 Bob Buczkowski, DE, Pittsburgh
1987 John Clay, T, Missouri
1988 Tim Brown, WR, Notre Dame
     Terry McDaniel, DB, Tennessee
     Scott Davis, DE, Illinois
1989 none
1990 Anthony Smith, DE, Arizona
1991 Todd Marinovich, QB, USC
1992 Chester McGlockton, DE, Clemson

1993 Patrick Bates, DB, Texas A&M
1994 Rob Fredrickson, LB, Michigan State

Oakland Raiders

1995 Napoleon Kaufman, RB, Washington
1996 Rickey Dudley, TE, Ohio State
1997 Darrell Russell, DT, USC

PHILADELPHIA EAGLES

1936 Jay Berwanger, B, Chicago
1937 Sam Francis, B, Nebraska
1938 Jim McDonald, B, Ohio State
1939 Davey O'Brien, QB, TCU
1940 George McAfee, HB, Duke
1941 none
1942 Pete Kmetovic, B, Stanford
1943 Joe Muha, B, VMI
1944 Steve Van Buren, B, LSU
1945 John Yonaker, E, Notre Dame
1946 Leo Riggs, B, USC
1947 Neill Armstrong, E, Oklahoma A&M
1948 Clyde Scott, B, Arkansas
1949 Chuck Bednarik, C, Pennsylvania
     Frank Tripucka, QB, Notre Dame
1950 Harry (Bud) Grant, E, Minnesota
1951 Ebert Van Buren, B, LSU
1952 Johnny Bright, B, Drake
1953 none
1954 Neil Worden, B, Notre Dame
1955 Dick Bielski, B, Maryland
1956 Bob Pellegrini, C, Maryland
1957 Clarence Peaks, B, Michigan State
1958 Walt Kowalczyk, B, Michigan State
1959 none
1960 Ron Burton, RB, Northwestern
1961 Art Baker, RB, Syracuse
1962 none
1963 Ed Budde, G, Michigan State
1964 Bob Brown, T, Nebraska
1965 none
1966 Randy Beisler, DE, Indiana
1967 Harry Jones, RB, Arkansas
1968 Tim Rossovich, DE, USC
1969 Leroy Keyes, RB, Purdue
1970 Steve Zabel, TE, Oklahoma
1971 Richard Harris, DE, Grambling
1972 John Reaves, QB, Florida
1973 Jerry Sisemore, T, Texas
     Charlie Young, TE, USC
1974 none
1975 none
1976 none
1977 none
1978 none
1979 Jerry Robinson, LB, UCLA
1980 Roynell Young, DB, Alcorn State

1981 Leonard Mitchell, DE, Houston
1982 Mike Quick, WR, North Carolina State
1983 Michael Haddix, RB, Mississippi State
1984 Kenny Jackson, WR, Penn State
1985 Kevin Allen, T, Indiana
1986 Keith Byars, RB, Ohio State
1987 Jerome Brown, DT, Miami
1988 Keith Jackson, TE, Oklahoma
1989 none
1990 Ben Smith, DB, Georgia
1991 Antone Davis, T, Tennessee
1992 none
1993 Lester Holmes, T, Jackson State
     Leonard Renfro, DT, Colorado
1994 Bernard Williams, T, Georgia
1995 Mike Mamula, DE, Boston College
1996 Jermane Mayberry, T, Texas A&M-
     Kingsville
1997 Jon Harris, DE, Virginia

PITTSBURGH STEELERS

Pittsburgh Pirates

1936 Bill Shakespeare, B, Notre Dame
1937 Mike Basrak, C, Duquesne
1938 Byron (Whizzer) White, HB, Colorado
1939 none

Pittsburgh Steelers

1940 Kay Eakin, B, Arkansas
1941 none
1942 Bill Dudley, HB, Virginia
1943 Bill Daley, B, Minnesota
1944 Johnny Podesto, B, St. Mary's (Calif.)
1945 Paul Duhart, B, Florida
1946 Felix (Doc) Blanchard, FB, Army
1947 Hub Bechtol, E, Texas
1948 Dan Edwards, E, Georgia
1949 Bobby Gage, B, Clemson
1950 Lynn Chandnois, B, Michigan State
1951 Butch Avinger, B, Alabama
1952 Ed Modzelewski, B, Maryland
1953 Ted Marchibroda, QB, St. Bonaventure
1954 Johnny Lattner, B, Notre Dame
1955 Frank Varrichione, T, Notre Dame
1956 Gary Glick, B, Colorado A&M
     Art Davis, B, Mississippi State
1957 Len Dawson, QB, Purdue
1958 none
1959 none
1960 Jack Spikes, RB, TCU
1961 none
1962 Bob Ferguson, RB, Ohio State
1963 none
1964 Paul Martha, DB, Pittsburgh
1965 none
1966 Dick Leftridge, RB, West Virginia

1967 none
1968 Mike Taylor, T, USC
1969 Joe Greene, DT, North Texas State
1970 Terry Bradshaw, QB, Louisiana Tech
1971 Frank Lewis, WR, Grambling
1972 Franco Harris, RB, Penn State
1973 J.T. Thomas, DB, Florida State
1974 Lynn Swann, WR, USC
1975 Dave Brown, DB, Michigan
1976 Bennie Cunningham, TE, Clemson
1977 Robin Cole, LB, New Mexico
1978 Ron Johnson, DB, Eastern Michigan
1979 Greg Hawthorne, RB, Baylor
1980 Mark Malone, QB, Arizona State
1981 Keith Gary, DE, Oklahoma
1982 Walter Abercrombie, RB, Baylor
1983 Gabriel Rivera, DT, Texas Tech
1984 Louis Lipps, WR, Southern Mississippi
1985 Darryl Sims, DE, Wisconsin
1986 John Rienstra, G, Temple
1987 Rod Woodson, DB, Purdue
1988 Aaron Jones, DE, Eastern Kentucky
1989 Tim Worley, RB, Georgia
     Tom Ricketts, T, Pittsburgh
1990 Eric Green, TE, Liberty
1991 Huey Richardson, DE, Florida
1992 Leon Searcy, T, Miami
1993 Deon Figures, DB, Colorado
1994 Charles Johnson, WR, Colorado
1995 Mark Bruener, TE, Washington
1996 Jamain Stephens, T, North Carolina
     A&T
1997 Chad Scott, DB, Maryland

ST. LOUIS RAMS

Cleveland Rams

1937 Johnny Drake, FB, Purdue
1938 Corby Davis, B, Indiana
1939 Parker Hall, B, Mississippi
1940 Ollie Cordill, B, Rice
1941 Rudy Mucha, C, Washington
1942 Jack Wilson, B, Baylor
1943 Mike Holovak, B, Boston College
1944 Tony Butkovich, B, Illinois
1945 Elroy Hirsch, HB, Wisconsin

Los Angeles Rams

1946 Emil Sitko, B, Notre Dame
1947 Herman Wedemeyer, B, St. Mary's
     (Calif.)
1948 none
1949 Bobby Thomason, QB, VMI
1950 Ralph Pasquariello, B, Villanova
     Stan West, G, Oklahoma
1951 Bud McFadin, G, Texas
1952 Bill Wade, QB, Vanderbilt

Bob Carey, E, Michigan State
1953 Donn Moomaw, C, UCLA
Ed Barker, E, Washington State
1954 Ed Beatty, C, Cincinnati
1955 Larry Morris, C, Georgia Tech
1956 Joe Marconi, B, West Virginia
Charles Horton, B, Vanderbilt
1957 Jon Arnett, HB, USC
Del Shofner, E, Baylor
1958 Lou Michaels, T, Kentucky
Jim Phillips, E, Auburn
1959 Dick Bass, B, Pacific
Paul Dickson, T, Baylor
1960 Billy Cannon, RB, LSU
1961 Marlin McKeever, E/LB, USC
1962 Roman Gabriel, QB, N.C. State
Merlin Olsen, DT, Utah State
1963 Terry Baker, QB, Oregon State
Rufus Guthrie, G, Georgia Tech
1964 Bill Munson, QB, Utah State
1965 Clancy Williams, DB, Washington State
1966 Tom Mack, G, Michigan
1967 none
1968 none
1969 Larry Smith, RB, Florida
Jim Seymour, WR, Notre Dame
Bob Klein, TE, USC
1970 Jack Reynolds, LB, Tennessee
1971 Isiah Robertson, LB, Southern
Jack Youngblood, DE, Florida
1972 none
1973 none
1974 John Cappelletti, RB, Penn State
1975 Mike Fanning, DT, Notre Dame
Dennis Harrah, T, Miami
Doug France, T, Ohio State
1976 Kevin McLain, LB, Colorado State
1977 Bob Brudzinski, LB, Ohio State
1978 Elvis Peacock, RB, Oklahoma
1979 George Andrews, LB, Nebraska
Kent Hill, T, Georgia Tech
1980 Johnnie Johnson, DB, Texas
1981 Mel Owens, LB, Michigan
1982 Barry Redden, RB, Richmond
1983 Eric Dickerson, RB, SMU
1984 none
1985 Jerry Gray, DB, Texas
1986 Mike Schad, T, Queen's University (Can.)
1987 none
1988 Gaston Green, RB, UCLA
Aaron Cox, WR, Arizona State
1989 Bill Hawkins, DE, Miami
Cleveland Gary, RB, Miami
1990 Bern Brostek, C, Washington

1991 Todd Lyght, DB, Notre Dame
1992 Sean Gilbert, DE, Pittsburgh
1993 Jerome Bettis, RB, Notre Dame
1994 Wayne Gandy, T, Auburn

St. Louis Rams
1995 Kevin Carter, DE, Florida
1996 Lawrence Phillips, RB, Nebraska
Eddie Kennison, WR, LSU
1997 Orlando Pace, T, Ohio State

SAN DIEGO CHARGERS
Los Angeles Chargers
1960 Monty Stickles, E, Notre Dame

San Diego Chargers
1961 Earl Faison, DE, Indiana
1962 Bob Ferguson, RB, Ohio State
1963 Walt Sweeney, G, Syracuse
1964 Ted Davis, LB, Georgia Tech
1965 Steve DeLong, DE, Tennessee
1966 Don Davis, DT, Cal State-Los Angeles
1967 Ron Billingsley, DE, Wyoming
1968 Russ Washington, DT, Missouri
Jimmy Hill, DB, Texas A&I
1969 Marty Domres, QB, Columbia
Bob Babich, LB, Miami (Ohio)
1970 Walker Gillette, WR, Richmond
1971 Leon Burns, RB, Long Beach State
1972 none
1973 Johnny Rodgers, WR, Nebraska
1974 Bo Matthews, RB, Colorado
Don Goode, LB, Kansas
1975 Gary Johnson, DT, Grambling
Mike Williams, DB, LSU
1976 Joe Washington, RB, Oklahoma
1977 Bob Rush, C, Memphis State
1978 John Jefferson, WR, Arizona State
1979 Kellen Winslow, TE, Missouri
1980 none
1981 James Brooks, RB, Auburn
1982 none
1983 Billy Ray Smith, LB, Arkansas
Gary Anderson, WR, Arkansas
Gill Byrd, DB, San Jose State
1984 Mossy Cade, DB, Texas
1985 Jim Lachey, T, Ohio State
1986 Leslie O'Neal, DE, Oklahoma State
James FitzPatrick, T, USC
1987 Rod Bernstine, TE, Texas A&M
1988 Anthony Miller, WR, Tennessee
1989 Burt Grossman, DE, Pittsburgh
1990 Junior Seau, LB, USC
1991 Stanley Richard, DB, Texas
1992 Chris Mims, DE, Tennessee
1993 Darrien Gordon, DB, Stanford

1994 none
1995 none
1996 none
1997 none

SAN FRANCISCO 49ERS
San Francisco 49ers (AAFC)
1947 Glenn Davis, HB, Army
1948 Joe Scott, B, USF
1949 Chester Fritz, T, Missouri

San Francisco 49ers (NFL)
1950 Leo Nomellini, T, Minnesota
1951 none
1952 Hugh McElhenny, HB, Washington
1953 Harry Babcock, E, Georgia
Tom Stolhandske, E, Texas
1954 Bernie Faloney, B, Maryland
1955 Dickie Moegle, B, Rice
1956 Earl Morrall, QB, Michigan State
1957 John Brodie, QB, Stanford
1958 Jim Pace, B, Michigan
Charlie Krueger, T, Texas A&M
1959 Dave Baker, B, Oklahoma
Dan James, C, Ohio State
1960 Monty Stickles, E, Notre Dame
1961 Jimmy Johnson, DB, UCLA
Bernie Casey, WR, Bowling Green
Bill Kilmer, QB, UCLA
1962 Lance Alworth, WR, Arkansas
1963 Kermit Alexander, DB, UCLA
1964 Dave Parks, WR, Texas Tech
1965 Ken Willard, RB, North Carolina
George Donnelly, DB, Illinois
1966 Stan Hindman, DE, Mississippi
1967 Steve Spurrier, QB, Florida
Cas Banaszek, T, Northwestern
1968 Forrest Blue, C, Auburn
1969 Ted Kwalick, TE, Penn State
Gene Washington, WR, Stanford
1970 Cedrick Hardman, DE, North Texas State
Bruce Taylor, DB, Boston University
1971 Tim Anderson, DB, Ohio State
1972 Terry Beasley, WR, Auburn
1973 Mike Holmes, DB, Texas Southern
1974 Wilbur Jackson, RB, Alabama
Bill Sandifer, DT, UCLA
1975 Jimmy Webb, DT, Mississippi State
1976 none
1977 none
1978 Ken MacAfee, TE, Notre Dame
Dan Bunz, LB, Cal State-Long Beach
1979 none
1980 Earl Cooper, RB, Rice
Jim Stuckey, DT, Clemson

1981 Ronnie Lott, DB, USC
1982 none
1983 none
1984 Todd Shell, LB, Brigham Young
1985 Jerry Rice, WR, Mississippi Valley State
1986 none
1987 Harris Barton, T, North Carolina
     Terrence Flagler, RB, Clemson
1988 none
1989 Keith DeLong, LB, Tennessee
1990 Dexter Carter, RB, Florida State
1991 Ted Washington, DT, Louisville
1992 Dana Hall, DB, Washington
1993 Dana Stubblefield, DT, Kansas
     Todd Kelly, DE, Tennessee
1994 Bryant Young, DT, Notre Dame
     William Floyd, RB, Florida State
1995 J.J. Stokes, WR, UCLA
1996 none
1997 Jim Druckenmiller, QB, Virginia Tech

SEATTLE SEAHAWKS

1976 Steve Niehaus, DT, Notre Dame
1977 Steve August, G, Tulsa
1978 Keith Simpson, DB, Memphis State
1979 Manu Tuiasosopo, DT, UCLA
1980 Jacob Green, DE, Texas A&M
1981 Kenny Easley, DB, UCLA
1982 Jeff Bryant, DE, Clemson
1983 Curt Warner, RB, Penn State
1984 Terry Taylor, DB, Southern Illinois
1985 none
1986 John L. Williams, RB, Florida
1987 Tony Woods, LB, Pittsburgh
1988 none
1989 Andy Heck, T, Notre Dame
1990 Cortez Kennedy, DT, Miami
1991 Dan McGwire, QB, San Diego State
1992 Ray Roberts, T, Virginia
1993 Rick Mirer, QB, Notre Dame
1994 Sam Adams, DT, Texas A&M
1995 Joey Galloway, WR, Ohio State
1996 Pete Kendall, T, Boston College
1997 Shawn Springs, CB, Ohio State
     Walter Jones, T, Florida State

TAMPA BAY BUCCANEERS

1976 Lee Roy Selmon, DT, Oklahoma
1977 Ricky Bell, RB, USC
1978 Doug Williams, QB, Grambling
1979 none
1980 Ray Snell, G, Wisconsin
1981 Hugh Green, LB, Pittsburgh
1982 Sean Farrell, G, Penn State
1983 none

1984 none
1985 Ron Holmes, DE, Washington
1986 Bo Jackson, RB, Auburn
     Roderick Jones, DB, SMU
1987 Vinny Testaverde, QB, Miami
1988 Paul Gruber, T, Wisconsin
1989 Broderick Thomas, LB, Nebraska
1990 Keith McCants, LB, Alabama
1991 Charles McRae, T, Tennessee
1992 none
1993 Eric Curry, DE, Alabama
1994 Trent Dilfer, QB, Fresno State
1995 Warren Sapp, DT, Miami
     Derrick Brooks, LB, Florida State
1996 Regan Upshaw, DE, California
     Marcus Jones, DT, North Carolina
1997 Warrick Dunn, RB, Florida State
     Reidel Anthony, WR, Florida

WASHINGTON REDSKINS
Boston Redskins
1936 Riley Smith, B, Alabama

Washington Redskins
1937 Sammy Baugh, B, TCU
1938 Andy Farkas, B, Detroit
1939 I.B. Hale, T, TCU
1940 Ed Boell, B, NYU
1941 Forest Evashevski, B, Michigan
1942 Orban (Spec) Sanders, B, Texas
1943 Jack Jenkins, B, Missouri
1944 Mike Micka, B, Colgate
1945 Jim Hardy, B, USC
1946 Cal Rossi, B, UCLA
1947 Cal Rossi, B, UCLA
1948 Harry Gilmer, QB, Alabama
     Lowell Tew, B, Alabama
1949 Rob Goode, B, Texas A&M
1950 George Thomas, B, Oklahoma
1951 Leon Heath, B, Oklahoma
1952 Larry Isbell, B, Baylor
1953 Jack Scarbath, QB, Maryland
1954 Steve Meilinger, E, Kentucky
1955 Ralph Guglielmi, QB, Notre Dame
1956 Ed Vereb, B, Maryland
1957 Don Bosseler, B, Miami
1958 none
1959 Don Allard, B, Boston College
1960 Richie Lucas, QB, Penn State
1961 Norm Snead, QB, Wake Forest
     Joe Rutgens, DT, Illinois
1962 Ernie Davis, RB, Syracuse
1963 Pat Richter, TE, Wisconsin
1964 Charley Taylor, RB, Arizona State
1965 none
1966 Charlie Gogolak, K, Princeton

1967 Ray McDonald, RB, Idaho
1968 Jim (Yazoo) Smith, DB, Oregon
1969 none
1970 none
1971 none
1972 none
1973 none
1974 none
1975 none
1976 none
1977 none
1978 none
1979 none
1980 Art Monk, WR, Syracuse
1981 Mark May, T, Pittsburgh
1982 none
1983 Darrell Green, DB, Texas A&I
1984 none
1985 none
1986 none
1987 none
1988 none
1989 none
1990 none
1991 Bobby Wilson, DT, Michigan State
1992 Desmond Howard, WR, Michigan
1993 Tom Carter, DB, Notre Dame
1994 Heath Shuler, QB, Tennessee
1995 Michael Westbrook, WR, Colorado
1996 Andre Johnson, T, Penn State
1997 Kenard Lang, DE, Miami

Introduction to the All-Pro Teams

One of the favorite topics for football fans and experts alike is comparing players: Who was the best quarterback of the 1960s, or the best running back ever?

Such discussions are often handicapped by fading memories—not to mention changing statistical standards that can make yesterday's stars seem no better than today's role players. And of course, for offensive linemen and many defensive standouts, there are no statistical standards at all, because these players have virtually no stats.

All-pro teams are the best tools we have for getting around those problems because these selections don't rely on distant memories—they're chosen by contemporary observers; and they avoid the pitfalls of statistical comparisons because they're already adjusted for context. Bill Osmanski's league-leading total of 699 yards rushing in 1939 wouldn't even crack the top ten today, but the fact that he was a unanimous all-pro selection means exactly what it's always meant: that qualified observers at the time thought he was the best player in the league at his position.

For offensive linemen and other "non-stat" positions, all-pro selections take the place of statistics. We don't know how many times Ron Mix led the AFL in blocking because there's no such record; but we do know how many times he was chosen to the all-AFL team, and in that way we can compare him to other top players from his and other eras.

This section of the book includes every all-pro team ever chosen by a poll of players, coaches, sportswriters, etc. Teams selected by the staff of a single publication or by a single expert, no matter how influential, aren't included, on the theory that a consensus of opinion eliminates local biases or personal quirks.

For each season (and each league, or conference) we've listed every player who was named to a first team by any of these polls. A short abbreviation for each selector shows which teams a player was chosen for. In 1960, for example, tackle Roosevelt Brown of the New York Giants was a first-team all-NFL choice of United Press International and the *New York Daily News*; his listing for that season shows his name and his position, followed by UPI and NYN. Another tackle, Jim Parker of the Baltimore Colts, was named to all four all-NFL teams included for that year: AP (Associated Press), UPI, NYN, and NEA (Newspaper Enterprise Association).

If two players are tied for one position on an all-pro team, the tie is indicated by a "plus" sign (+). For example, Ed Flanagan and Len Hauss tied in balloting for *The Sporting News'* 1971 all-NFC team, so the listing for each of them is SN+.

From 1946 to '49, when the NFL and the AAFC coexisted, some selectors chose all-league teams and others chose genuine all-pro teams covering both leagues. The first teams listed in those years cover just the NFL or the AAFC; the ones to the right are combined teams. The same arrangement applies in 1968 and '69, to distinguish all-AFL and all-NFL teams from true all-pro teams.

From 1970 on, the same sort of distinction has been made between all-AFC or all-NFC teams and all-NFL teams that cover both conferences.

Sometimes a selector picks all-star teams for two different leagues (NFL and AAFC, NFL and AFL) or different conferences and also names a combined team for the same season. Such choices are listed as all-conference teams, but the overall selections are followed by an asterisk (i.e., AP* or PFW*).

Names printed all in capital letters are "consensus" all-pros. These are the players with the most first-team selections at their positions. Sometimes, though, determining the consensus requires more information than is listed here. To take another example from 1960: Sonny Randle of St. Louis and Tommy McDonald were both first-team choices of two all-NFL selectors. Randle gets the nod as the consensus choice, however, because he was a second-team choice of Newspaper Enterprise Association and the *New York Daily News*; McDonald was a second-team selection of only UPI. Thus, though second-team choices aren't included in this listing, they're still a part of it in some cases.

Two other annual selections that aren't included here are also used as tie-breakers. From 1956 to '69 *The Sporting News* picked all-conference teams for the NFL—that is, one quarterback from the West and one from the East, etc. These teams just don't equate with standard all-pro teams (it's not clear which QB would have been the first choice), and so they've been omitted here. Pro Bowl selections from 1950 to '69 are missing for exactly the same reason. But *The Sporting News* and Pro Bowl teams have been used as tie-breakers, along with second-team choices from the other selectors.

(In case you're wondering about Randle and McDonald, both of them were chosen as Pro Bowl starters and members of *The Sporting News'* all-conference team in 1960.)

Sometimes, though, even the tie-breakers fail to eliminate a deadlock—for instance, between Gale Gillingham and Tom Mack for the second guard spot on the 1971 all-NFC team. In such cases, both players are shown as consensus choices, with a plus sign after their position.

Consensus choices are indicated by league through 1969, and by conference from 1970 to '76. From 1977 on, however, consensus choices cover the whole NFL—one quarterback, two running backs, one center, etc.—because there were as many all-NFL teams chosen as all-AFC or all-NFC teams, and sometimes more, starting in 1977.

Following is a description of the various all-pro selectors. The abbreviation given after each selector's name is the one used in the all-pro listings.

Green Bay Press-Gazette (PG): Individual sportswriters were picking all-pro teams before the NFL was formed, but the first all-pro poll was conducted by the *Green Bay Press-Gazette* in 1923. The team was picked annually through 1931; it disappeared for a year, then returned from 1933 to '35. It was selected

by coaches, sportswriters and game officials, in varying combinations. The *Green Bay Press-Gazette* teams were discovered by John Hogrogian in 1982.

Official teams (OFF): In 1931 the NFL adopted the annual *Green Bay Press-Gazette* team as the first "official" all-pro team. Starting in 1932, the league polled its own head coaches for the official team. The coaches poll lasted through 1939; from 1940 to '42 the official team was chosen by the Pro Football Writers Association (see below.) The AAFC picked its own all-star team for its entire history, 1946–49. The AFL released an official team in 1960, chosen by sportswriters and coaching staffs; in 1961, chosen by coaches; and from 1962 to '66, chosen by the players in a poll conducted by *The Sporting News* (see below). The Hall of Fame selection committee picked a combined NFL-AFL all-pro team in 1969 that was given the "official" label. And in 1970 and '71 the new Pro Football Writers Association chose the official all-NFL team. The only teams denoted by OFF in the all-pro listing are those for the 1932–39 NFL, the 1946–49 AAFC, the 1960–61 AFL, and the 1969 NFL-AFL. The others are credited to the organizations that did the selecting—i.e., PG or FWA.

United Press (UP): The United Press all-pro team, started in 1931, is the oldest annual team that's still being chosen. With some slight variations, it's generally been done by a poll of the organization's sportswriters or editors. In 1958 UP combined with I.N.S. to form **United Press International (UPI)**. From 1946 to '49 UP picked separate teams for the NFL and the AAFC. Since 1970 UPI has chosen separate teams for the AFC and the NFC. No UP all-pro teams have been found for the NFL in 1942 and the AAFC in 1947.

New York Daily News (NYN): From 1937 to '69 the *New York Daily News* selected an annual all-pro team by polling sportswriters from each league city. The voters were listed each year, and they included many nationally known writers. The *New York Daily News* didn't pick an all-star team for the AFL in 1960, the league's inaugural season, but did so from 1961 on. In 1962, however, the paper printed no all-pro teams at all, because a strike shut down the paper from December 1962 until April 1963. The annual poll was discontinued after 1969; though the *New York Daily News* revived its all-pro teams in the mid-1970s, those selections were made by the newspaper's staff alone, and thus are outside the scope of this compilation.

Associated Press (AP): After distributing the official coaches poll from 1932 to '39, AP began polling its sportswriters for an all-pro team in 1940. From 1946 to '49 AP picked a true all-pro team, covering the NFL *and* the AAFC, but each year the 22 players on the first and second teams included exactly eleven from each league. In essence, AP was picking an NFL team, an AAFC team, and a combined team—and that's how they're listed here. AP has chosen an all-NFL team since 1970; from 1970 to '76 it also selected separate teams for the NFC and AFC.

Pro Football Writers Association (FWA): This organization chose its first all-pro team in 1938—allegedly with 205 voters, though that seems very unlikely. When the coaches poll stopped after the 1939 season, the NFL adopted the PFWA

selections as its "official" team. That arrangement continued through 1942, but the PFWA seems to have stopped conducting annual polls after that. In those years the balloting was done by nine voters, one from each NFL city. The PFWA returned to the all-pro scene in 1968, picking a combined NFL-AFL team, and continued without interruption until 1992, when its selections were combined with those of *Pro Football Weekly*. The Pro Football Writers Association all-pro team was considered the NFL's "official" team in 1970 and '71.

The Sporting News (SN): No selector has changed its all-pro format as often as *The Sporting News*. *The Sporting News's* first effort was a combined NFL-AAFC team in 1948. The paper made no choices in 1949, then printed the *New York Daily News* teams from 1950 to '53, adopting them as its own. *The Sporting News* picked its own squad in 1954—a single platoon of only 11 players; by that time everyone else was naming an offensive and defensive team. In 1955 TSN chose a 33-man squad, which was the size of an NFL roster at the time. From 1956 to '69 TSN picked all-conference teams by polling its correspondents. *The Sporting News* selected its first all-AFL team in 1961; a year later it began polling AFL players for what was recognized as the official all-AFL team through 1966. *The Sporting News* continued polling the players from 1967 to '69, though without the "official" designation. From 1970 to '79 the paper picked all-AFC and all-NFC teams; since 1980 it's named a single all-NFL team. *The Sporting News* chose no team in 1982, because of the first NFL strike, but did select one in 1987, the year of the replacement games. For the past few years the teams have been chosen by players, coaches, correspondents, and broadcasters in various combinations.

Newspaper Enterprise Association (NEA): The NEA began polling NFL players in 1955 to determine its all-pro team. It chose an all-AFL team from 1963 to '69 by polling the league's coaches. Coaches in both leagues were polled for a combined AFL-NFL team in 1969. Starting in 1970 the NEA picked a single all-NFL team, and the players poll was replaced by several different methods of selection. Team captains were polled in 1970; later, captains and player representatives did the balloting. Later still, the NEA team was chosen by a group of sportswriters, and finally an unspecified "panel of experts." As a result of some changes in ownership of NEA, the teams were published in the *World Almanac* starting in 1986, and the last few were listed as *World Almanac* selections. The NEA teams stopped after the 1992 selections. NEA sports editor Howard Siner supplied a few of the early teams and helped in explaining the selection and publishing process of the latter years.

Pro Football Weekly (PFW): Today's most influential pro football publication was founded in 1967 and chose its first all-pro team in 1968. Selections have always been made by PFW's correspondents. For most seasons, *Pro Football Weekly* has picked all-AFC and all-NFC teams, plus a combined all-NFL team. No all-conference teams were chosen in 1972 (no explanation) and 1982 (because of the first NFL strike). There were no picks at all for 1985, because *Pro Football Weekly* had ceased publication for a time. Starting in 1992, *Pro Football Weekly's* choices were combined with those of the Pro Football Writers

Association. Since the selections are announced in the magazine, they're listed as *Pro Football Weekly* teams.

Pro Bowl (PB): Starting in 1970, Pro Bowl teams for the AFC and the NFC have been chosen by players and coaches. Players selected as starters are considered first-team choices, even if they actually missed the game because of an injury.

International News Service (INS): This Hearst organization began picking all-pro teams in 1937 and continued sporadically through 1949. No teams have been found for 1941, 1943, and 1946-48, and none at all after 1949. The teams were presumably chosen by a poll of INS sportswriters or sports editors. The 1949 INS all-pro team covered the NFL and the AAFC, and was the first poll to pick separate offensive and defensive platoons.

Pro Football Illustrated (PFI): This annual fall publication of the 1940s selected all-pro teams from 1943 to '48; the teams appeared in the editions for the following season—that is, the 1944-49 editions. The 1949 edition was PFI's last, so the all-pro teams stopped with 1948. At least in its early years, PFI was an official publication of the NFL, and it's possible that the magazine's all-pro teams were considered "official." If not, it appears that the editors intended them to be.

Twelve years after the original PFI ceased publication, a new *Pro Football Illustrated* appeared, a weekly paper based in Chicago, in many ways a predecessor of *Pro Football Weekly*. *Pro Football Illustrated* polled its correspondents to select all-NFL teams in 1961 and '62, plus an all-AFL team in 1962. Since this *Pro Football Illustrated* survived until sometime in 1964, it presumably chose all-pro teams for 1963 as well, but so far they haven't surfaced.

Sportswriters Inc. (SP): This panel was organized by Christy Walsh, a nationally known writer and broadcaster whose All-America Board chose one of the most respected college All-America teams. His foray into professional football lasted only two seasons, 1946 and '47. A group of nine sportswriters from around the country chose the 1946 team, and a group of eight, with some repeaters, did the honors in 1947.

Coaches & Officials (C&O): The method of selection for this team is self-explanatory. It was a one-shot poll conducted in 1947, picking separate teams for the NFL and the AAFC.

Sports Illustrated (SI): In 1969 *Sports Illustrated* conducted a one-shot poll of assistant coaches to select all-AFL and all-NFL teams. Later *Sports Illustrated* selections made solely by football writer Paul Zimmerman don't qualify for inclusion here.

MVP and Other Awards

There are a lot of annual awards, from comeback player of the year to assistant coach of the year, and they're presented by any number of groups and individual experts. Once again, though, we're concerned with only the awards selected by a poll of players, coaches, sportswriters, or similar groups. And we'll list only the major award categories: Rookie of the Year, Coach of the Year, and Most Valuable Player or its alter ego, player of the year. Some organizations choose an offensive and defensive rookie of the year, or an offensive and defensive player of the year,

which are indicated with a suffix of -o or -d (for example, **AP-o**).

First a description of who chose what, and when.

Official (OFF): The NFL named its own MVP from 1938 to '46. The AAFC did the same from 1946 to '48, but not in its final season. The AFL named an official MVP in 1960 and '61, and Rookie of the Year in 1961.

United Press International (UPI): UP, as it was known then, chose an MVP in 1938, again in 1948 (one for each leagues), then started for good in 1953. It added an MVP for the AFL from 1960 to '69, and continued with separate choices for the NFC and AFC from 1970. Since 1975, with three exceptions, UPI has named Offensive and Defensive MVPs for each conference. Its Coach of the Year selections began in 1954 for the NFL and 1960 for the AFL, with separate choices for the NFC and AFC since 1970. UPI picked its first Rookie of the Year in 1948, then started for good in 1954, adding the AFL in 1960 and continuing with separate selections for the NFC and AFC since 1970.

New York Daily News (NYN): The *New York Daily News* was the first to name a Coach of the Year; it did so 1945 to '69. There was no choice in 1947 and 1959 (no explanation), nor for the AFL in 1960 and both leagues in 1962, because of the newspaper strike. The New York Daily News named an AAFC Coach of the Year in 1946, '48, and '49.

The Sporting News (SN): *The Sporting News* has chosen an MVP from 1954, but the awards 1957 and '58 awards aren't included here because for those years the award was based simply on rushing yardage, not any kind of selection process. MVPs were chosen for each season of the AFL, followed by separate choices for the NFC and the AFC from 1970 to '79; since 1980, TSN has chosen one MVP for the NFL as a whole. Rookie of the Year choices cover the same seasons as the MVP award, and 1957 and '58 have been omitted for the same reason. TSN's Coach of the Year choices began in 1955, and were hit and miss for a while, but have appeared annually for the NFL since 1963. AFL coaches were honored in 1961, 1963-66, and '69; Since 1970, TSN has named one coach for the whole NFL. This award deserves special mention because it's chosen by the coaches themselves.

Newspaper Enterprise Association (NEA): The Newspaper Enterprise Association began polling the NFL players for an MVP award in 1955, with the Jim Thorpe trophy going to the winner. The George Halas trophy for Defensive Player of the Year appeared in 1966; the Rookie of the Year award started in 1964 for the NFL only. NEA made a single choice for the whole NFL in 1970 and '74 (indicated by an asterisk), but otherwise made separate selections for the NFC and the AFC through 1976. In 1977 NEA finally settled on a single league-wide choice, which continued through 1992.

Associated Press (AP): The Associated Press began naming a player of the year, a coach of the year, and a rookie of the year in 1957 for the NFL, and 1961 for the AFL. Since 1970 AP has chosen a single Coach of the Year for the whole NFL. In 1970 an offensive and '71 AP made a single choice for player of the year, but in 1972 it added an offensive and a defensive player of the year. Generally, the offensive player is also the

MVP, and in that case the offensive selection is indicated by **AP**, the defensive choice by **AP-d**. If the defensive player is also the MVP, as in 1986, the offensive player gets the suffix: **AP-o**. But occasionally the MVP is neither the offensive nor defensive player, as in 1996; in that case, **AP** denotes the MVP, **AP-o** the offensive player, and **AP-d** the defensive player. In Rookie of the Year balloting, AP began choosing offensive and defensive rookies for each league in 1967, then cut back to a single offensive and defensive choice for the whole NFL in 1970. AP's awards receive wider circulation than any others, and when a TV announcer refers to someone as the MVP, that almost always means he was chosen by AP.

Maxwell Club (MAX): Based in Philadelphia, this group distributes more than 1,000 ballots to sportswriters and other experts across the country to select its MVP. The selections began in 1959, with a single player chosen each year for the whole NFL (none for the AFL in the 1960s).

Pro Football Illustrated (PFI): The annual magazine from the 1940s chose an MVP for the NFL in 1947, apparently intending this as a continuation of the league's official award from 1938 to '46. It also chose a coach of the year (a single selection covering each league) for 1947 and '48. The later *Pro Football Illustrated*, the short-lived publication from the early 1960s, chose an offensive and defensive player of the year for the NFL in 1961 and '62, and for the AFL in 1962. It was the first to pick a defensive player of the year (though defensive standout Gino Marchetti had been AP's choice for MVP in 1958). PFI also named an NFL Coach of the Year and Rookie of the Year in 1961.

Pro Football Weekly (PFW): *Pro Football Weekly* selected MVPs for the NFL and the AFL in 1968 and '69. In 1970, it began selecting offensive and defensive players of the year, cov-ering the whole NFL. PFW chose a Coach of the Year for the NFL and the AFL in 1968 and '69, then one for the whole NFL since 1970. *Pro Football Weekly* named an offensive and defensive Rookie of the Year for each league in 1969, then for the whole NFL starting in 1970.

Pro Football Writers Association (FWA): The writers started selecting an MVP for the whole NFL in 1975, and a Rookie of the Year in 1976. They chose a Coach of the Year for the NFC and the AFC from 1970 to '89, then made a single choice for the whole NFL in 1990 and '91. The writers' selections were combined with those of *Pro Football Weekly* in 1992, and they're listed as PFW's choices from then.

Key

AP	Associated Press
C&O	Coaches & Officials
FWA	Pro Football Writers Association
INS	International News Service
NEA	Newspaper Enterprise Association
NYN	New York Daily News
OFF	Official teams
PB	Pro Bowl
PFI	*Pro Football Illustrated*
PFW	*Pro Football Weekly*
PG	*Green Bay Press-Gazette*
SI	*Sports Illustrated*
SN	*The Sporting News*
SP	Sportswriters Inc.
UP	United Press
UPI	United Press International

ALL-PRO SELECTIONS

1923 ALL-NFL

E	GUS TEBELL, Cle	PG
E	INKY WILLIAMS, Ham	PG
T	WILBUR HENRY, Can	PG
T	ED HEALEY, ChiB	PG
G	SWEDE YOUNGSTROM, Buf	PG
G	BUB WELLER, StL	PG
C	HARRY MEHRE, Min	PG
QB	PADDY DRISCOLL, ChiC	PG
HB	AL MICHAELS, Akr	PG
HB	JIM THORPE, Oor	PG
FB	DOC ELLIOTT, Can	PG

1924 ALL-NFL

E	JOE LITTLE TWIG, RI	PG
E	TILLIE VOSS, GB	PG
T	ED HEALEY, ChiB	PG
T	BONI PETCOFF, Col	PG
G	STAN MUIRHEAD, Day	PG
G	SWEDE YOUNGSTROM, Buf	PG
C	GEORGE TRAFTON, ChiB	PG
QB	JOE STERNAMAN, ChiB	PG
HB	BEN BOYNTON, Buf	PG
HB	PIE WAY, Fra	PG
FB	DOC ELLIOTT, Can	PG

1925 ALL-NFL

E	CHARLIE BERRY, Pot	PG
E	ED LYNCH, Roc	PG
T	GUS SONNENBERG, Det	PG
T	ED HEALEY, ChiB	PG
G	JIM MCMILLEN, ChiB	PG
G	ART CARNEY, NY	PG
C	RALPH CLAYPOOL, ChiC	PG
QB	JOE STERNAMAN, ChiB	PG
HB	PADDY DRISCOLL, ChiC	PG
HB	DAVE NOBLE, Cle	PG
FB	JACK MCBRIDE, NY	PG

1926 ALL-NFL

E	BRICK MULLER, LA	PG
E	CHARLIE BERRY, Pot	PG
T	ED HEALEY, ChiB	PG
T	WALT ELLIS, ChiC	PG
G	JOHNNY BUDD, Fra	PG
G	GUS SONNENBERG, Det	PG
C	CLYDE SMITH, KC	PG
QB	TUT IMLAY, LA	PG
HB	PADDY DRISCOLL, ChiB	PG
HB	VERNE LEWELLEN, GB	PG
FB	ERNIE NEVERS, Dul	PG

1927 ALL-NFL

E	LAVERN DILWEG, GB	PG
E	CAL HUBBARD, NYG	PG
T	GUS SONNENBERG, Pro	PG
T	ED WEIR, Fra	PG
G	MIKE MICHALSKE, NYY	PG
G	STEVE OWEN, NYG	PG
C	CLYDE SMITH, Cle	PG
QB	BENNY FRIEDMAN, Cle	PG
HB	PADDY DRISCOLL, ChiB	PG
HB	VERNE LEWELLEN, GB	PG
FB	ERNIE NEVERS, Dul	PG

1928 ALL-NFL

E	LAVERN DILWEG, GB	PG
E	RAY FLAHERTY, NYY	PG
T	BILL OWEN, Det	PG
T	BULL BEHMAN, Fra	PG
G	JIM MCMILLEN, ChiB	PG
G	MIKE MICHALSKE, NYY	PG
C	CLYDE SMITH, Pro	PG
QB	BENNY FRIEDMAN, Det	PG
HB	WILDCAT WILSON, Pro	PG
HB	VERNE LEWELLEN, GB	PG
FB	WALLY DIEHL, Fra	PG

1929 ALL-NFL

E	LAVERN DILWEG, GB	PG
E	RAY FLAHERTY, NY	PG
T	BULL BEHMAN, Fra	PG
T	BOB BEATTIE, Ora	PG
G	MIKE MICHALSKE, GB	PG
G	MILT REHNQUIST, Pro	PG
C	JOE WESTOUPAL, NY	PG
QB	BENNY FRIEDMAN, NY	PG
HB	VERNE LEWELLEN, GB	PG
HB	TONY PLANSKY, NY	PG
FB	ERNIE NEVERS, ChiC	PG

1930 ALL-NFL

E	LAVERN DILWEG, GB	PG
E	LUKE JOHNSOS, ChiB	PG
T	JAP DOUDS, Pro-Por	PG
T	LINK LYMAN, ChiB	PG
G	WALT KIESLING, ChiC	PG
G	MIKE MICHALSKE, GB	PG
C	SWEDE HAGBERG, Bkn	PG
QB	BENNY FRIEDMAN, NY	PG
HB	RED GRANGE, ChiB	PG
HB	KEN STRONG, SI	PG
FB	ERNIE NEVERS, ChiC	PG

1931 ALL-NFL

E	LAVERN DILWEG, GB	PG*	UP
E	LUKE JOHNSOS, ChiB		UP
E	Red Badgro, NY	PG*	
T	CAL HUBBARD, GB	PG*	UP
T+	GEORGE CHRISTENSEN, Por	PG*	
T+	LEN GRANT, NY		UP
G	BUTCH GIBSON, NY	PG*	UP
G	MIKE MICHALSKE, GB	PG*	UP
C	FRANK MCNALLY, ChiC	PG*	UP
QB	DUTCH CLARK, Por	PG*	UP
HB	RED GRANGE, ChiB	PG*	UP
HB+	JOHNNY BLOOD, GB	PG*	
HB+	KEN STRONG, SI		UP
FB	ERNIE NEVERS, ChiC	PG*	UP

1932 ALL-NFL

E	RAY FLAHERTY, NY	OFF	UP
E+	LUKE JOHNSOS, ChiB	OFF	
E+	TOM NASH, GB		UP
T	CAL HUBBARD, GB	OFF	UP
T+	TURK EDWARDS, BOS	OFF	
T+	LEN GRANT, NY		UP
G	ZUCK CARLSON, ChiB	OFF	UP
G+	OX EMERSON, Por		UP
G+	WALT KIESLING, ChiC	OFF	
C	NATE BARRAGER, GB	OFF	
C	Tim Moynihan, ChiC		UP
QB	DUTCH CLARK, Por	OFF	UP
HB	ARNIE HERBER, GB	OFF	UP
HB	FATHER LUMPKIN, Por	OFF	UP
FB	BRONKO NAGURSKI, ChiB	OFF	UP

1933 ALL-NFL

E	BILL HEWITT, ChiB	OFF	UP	PG
E	RED BADGRO, NY	OFF		PG
E	Harry Ebding, Por		UP	
T	CAL HUBBARD, GB	OFF	UP	PG-g
T	TURK EDWARDS, Bos	OFF		PG
T	George Christensen, Por		UP	PG
G	HERMAN HICKMAN, Bkn	OFF		PG
G	JOE KOPCHA, ChiB	OFF	UP	
G	Ox Emerson, Por		UP	
C	OOKIE MILLER, ChiB		UP	PG
C	Mel Hein, NY	OFF		
QB	GLENN PRESNELL, Por	OF-h	UP	PG
QB	Harry Newman, NY	OFF		
HB	CLIFF BATTLES, Bos	OFF	UP	PG
HB	KEN STRONG, NY		UP	PG
FB	BRONKO NAGURSKI, ChiB	OFF	UP	PG

1934 ALL-NFL

E	BILL HEWITT, ChiB	OFF	UP	PG
E	BILL MCKALIP, Det			PG
E	Red Badgro, NY	OFF		
E	Buster Mitchell, Det		UP	
T	LINK LYMAN, ChiB		UP	PG
T	BILL MORGAN, NY	OFF		PG
T	Turk Edwards, Bos		UP	
T	George Christensen, Det	OFF		
G	JOE KOPCHA, ChiB	OFF	UP	PG
G+	OX EMERSON, Det		UP	
G+	MIKE MICHALSKE, GB			PG
G	Butch Gibson, NY	OFF		
C	MEL HEIN, NY	OFF	UP	PG
QB	DUTCH CLARK, Det	OFF	UP	PG
HB	BEATTIE FEATHERS, ChiB	OFF	UP	PG
HB	KEN STRONG, NY	OFF		PG
HB	Cliff Battles, Bos		UP	
FB	BRONKO NAGURSKI, ChiB	OFF	UP	PG
UT	Jack Manders, ChiB		UP	

1935 All-NFL

Pos	Player	OFF	UP	PG
E	BILL KARR, ChiB	OFF	UP	PG
E	BILL SMITH, ChiC	OFF	UP	PG
T	BILL MORGAN, NY	OFF	UP	PG
T	GEORGE MUSSO, ChiB	OFF		
T	Turk Edwards, Bos			PG
T	Ad Schwammel, GB		UP	
G+	OX EMERSON, Det		UP	PG
G+	MIKE MICHALSKE, GB	OFF		PG
G+	JOE KOPCHA, ChiB	OFF	UP	
C	MEL HEIN, NY	OFF	UP	
QB	DUTCH CLARK, Det	OFF	UP	PG
HB	ED DANOWSKI, NY	OFF	UP	PG
HB	GENE RONZANI, ChiB		UP	
HB	Ernie Caddel, Det	OFF		
HB	George Sauer, GB			PG
FB	MIKE MIKULAK, ChiC	OFF		PG
FB	Clarke Hinkle, GB		UP	

1936 All-NFL

E	BILL HEWITT, ChiB	OFF	UP
E+	MILT GANTENBEIN, GB		UP
E+	DON HUTSON, GB	OFF	
T	TURK EDWARDS, Bos	OFF	UP
T	ERNIE SMITH, GB	OFF	UP
G	LON EVANS, GB	OFF	UP
G	OX EMERSON, Det	OFF	UP
C+	MEL HEIN, NY	OFF	
C+	FRANK BAUSCH, Bos		UP
QB	DUTCH CLARK, Det	OFF	UP
HB	CLIFF BATTLES, Bos	OFF	UP
HB+	TUFFY LEEMANS, NY	OFF	
FB	CLARKE HINKLE, GB	OFF	UP-H
FB+	BRONKO NAGURSKI, ChiB		UP

1937 All-NFL

Pos	Player	OFF	UP	NYN	INS
E	GAYNELL TINSLEY, ChiC	OFF	UP	NYN	
E+	BILL HEWITT, PHI	OFF			INS
E+	DON HUTSON, GB			NYN	INS
E	Ed Klewicki, Det		UP		
T	TURK EDWARDS, Bos	OFF	UP	NYN	INS
T	JOE STYDAHAR, ChiB	OFF	UP	NYN	
T	Ed Widseth, NY				INS
G	GEORGE MUSSO, ChiB	OFF	UP	NYN	INS
G	LON EVANS, GB	OFF	UP		
G	Ox Emerson, Det				INS
G	Dan Fortmann, ChiB			NYN	
C	MEL HEIN, NY	OFF		NYN	INS
C	Mike Basrak, Pit		UP		
QB	DUTCH CLARK, Det	OFF	UP	NYN	INS
HB	SAMMY BAUGH, Was	OFF	UP	NYN	INS
HB	CLIFF BATTLES, Was	OFF		NYN	INS
HB	Jack Manders, ChiB		UP		
FB	CLARKE HINKLE, GB	OFF	UP	NYN	INS

1938 All-NFL

Pos	Player	OFF	UP	NYN	INS	FWA
E	DON HUTSON, GB	OFF	UP	NYN	INS	FWA
E	GAYNELL TINSLEY, ChiC	OFF			INS	FWA
E	Bill Hewitt, Phi		UP	NYN		
T	ED WIDSETH, NY	OFF	UP	NYN	INS	
T	JOE STYDAHAR, ChiB	OFF	UP	NYN	INS	
T	Bruiser Kinard, Bkn					FWA
G	DAN FORTMANN, ChiB	OFF	UP	NYN	INS	FWA
G	RUSS LETLOW, GB	OFF			INS	FWA
G	Byron Gentry, Pit		UP			
G	Les Olssen, Was			NYN		
C	MEL HEIN, NY	OFF	UP	NYN	INS	
C	Frank Bausch, ChiC					FWA
QB	ACE PARKER, Bkn	OFF	UP	NYN	INS	FWA
HB	ED DANOWSKI, NY	OFF	UP	NYN	INS	FWA
HB	WHIZZER WHITE, Pit		UP		INS	FWA
HB	Lloyd Cardwell, Det	OFF				
HB	Bill Shepherd, Det			NYN		
FB	CLARKE HINKLE, GB	OFF	UP	NYN	INS	FWA

1939 All-NFL

Pos	Player	OFF	UP	NYN	INS	FWA
E	DON HUTSON, GB	OFF	UP	NYN	INS	FWA
E	JIM POOLE, NY	OFF	UP		INS	FWA
E	Perry Schwartz, Bkn			NYN		
T	JOE STYDAHAR, ChiB	OFF	UP	NYN	INS	FWA
T	JIM BARBER, Was	OFF	UP			FWA
T	Turk Edwards, Was			NYN	INS	
G	DAN FORTMANN, ChiB	OFF	UP	NYN	INS	FWA
G	JOHN DELL ISOLA, NY	OFF		NYN		FWA
G	Byron Gentry, Pit				INS	
G	John Wiethe, Det		UP			
C	MEL HEIN, NY	OFF	UP	NYN	INS	FWA
QB	PARKER HALL, Cle		UP	NYN	INS	FWA-h
QB	Davey O'Brien, Phi	OFF				
QB	Ace Parker, Bkn					FWA
HB	ANDY FARKAS, Was	OFF	UP	NYN		FWA
HB	TUFFY LEEMANS, NY	OFF	UP	NYN	INS	
HB	Frank Filchock, Was				INS	
FB	BILL OSMANSKI, ChiB	OFF	UP	NYN	INS	FWA

1940 All-NFL

Pos	Player	AP	UP	NYN	INS	FWA
E	DON HUTSON, GB	AP	UP	NYN	INS	FWA*
E	PERRY SCHWARTZ, Bkn	AP	UP	NYN	INS	FWA*
E	Jim Poole, NY		UP		INS	
T	BRUISER KINARD, Bkn	AP	UP	NYN	INS	FWA*
T	JOE STYDAHAR, ChiB	AP	UP	NYN	INS	FWA*
T	Jim Barber, Was		UP			
G	DAN FORTMANN, ChiB	AP		NYN	INS	FWA*
G	JOHN WIETHE, Det	AP		NYN	INS	FWA*
G	Steve Slivinski, Was		UP		INS	
C	MEL HEIN, NY	AP	UP	NYN	INS	FWA*
QB	ACE PARKER, Bkn	AP	UP	NYN	INS	FWA*
HB	WHIZZER WHITE, Det	AP	UP	NYN		FWA*
HB	SAMMY BAUGH, Was	AP	UP	NYN		FWA*
HB	Dick Todd, Was				INS	
FB	JOHNNY DRAKE, Cle	AP	UP	NYN		FWA*
FB	Clarke Hinkle, GB				INS	

1941 All-NFL

Pos	Player	AP	UP	NYN	FWA
E	DON HUTSON, GB	AP	UP	NYN	FWA*
E	PERRY SCHWARTZ, Bkn	AP		NYN	FWA*
E	Dick Plasman, ChiB		UP		
T	BRUISER KINARD, Bkn		UP	NYN	FWA*
T	WILLIE WILKIN, Was	AP		NYN	FWA*
T	John Mellus, NY	AP			
T	Baby Ray, GB		UP		
G	DAN FORTMANN, ChiB	AP	UP	NYN	FWA*
G	JOE KUHARICH, ChiC	AP			FWA*
G	Riley Matheson, Cle		UP		
G	Bob Suffridge, Phi			NYN	
C	BULLDOG TURNER, ChiB	AP	UP	NYN	FWA*
QB	SID LUCKMAN, ChiB	AP	UP	NYN	FWA*
QB	Ward Cuff, NY		UP		
HB	CECIL ISBELL, GB	AP	UP	NYN	FWA*
HB	GEORGE MCAFEE, ChiB	AP	UP	NYN	FWA*
FB	PUG MANDERS, Bkn	AP	UP	NYN	
FB	Clarke Hinkle, GB				FWA*

1942 All-NFL

Pos	Player	AP	NYN	INS	FWA
E	DON HUTSON, GB	AP	NYN	INS	FWA*
E	GEORGE WILSON, ChiB	AP	NYN		
E	Ed Cifers, Was			INS	
E	Bob Masterson, Was				FWA*
T	LEE ARTOE, ChiB	AP	NYN		FWA*
T	WILLIE WILKIN, Was	AP	NYN		FWA*
T	Bruiser Kinard, Bkn			INS	
T	Ed Kolman, ChiB			INS	
G	DAN FORTMANN, ChiB	AP	NYN	INS	FWA*
G	BILL EDWARDS, NY			INS	FWA*
G	Riley Matheson, Cle	AP			
G	Milt Simington, Pit		NYN		
C	BULLDOG TURNER, ChiB	AP	NYN	INS	FWA*
QB	SID LUCKMAN, ChiB	AP	NYN	INS	FWA*
HB	BILL DUDLEY, Pit	AP	NYN	INS	FWA*
HB	SAMMY BAUGH, Was	AP	NYN	INS	
HB+	CECIL ISBELL, GB		NYN		FWA*
FB+	GARY FAMIGLIETTI, ChiB			INS	FWA*
FB	Andy Farkas, Was	AP			

1943 All-NFL

Pos	Player	AP	UP	NYN	PFI
E	DON HUTSON, GB	AP	UP	NYN	PFI
E	ED RUCINSKI, ChiC	AP	UP		
E	Joe Aguirre, Was			NYN	
E	George Wilson, ChiB				PFI
T	AL BLOZIS, NY	AP	UP	NYN	PFI
T	BABY RAY, GB			NYN	PFI
T	Bruiser Kinard, Bkn	AP			
T	Vic Sears, Ph/P		UP		
G	DAN FORTMANN, ChiB	AP	UP	NYN	
G	DICK FARMAN, Was	AP	UP	NYN	
G	Eberle Schultz, Ph/P				PFI
C	BULLDOG TURNER, ChiB	AP	UP	NYN	PFI
QB	SID LUCKMAN, ChiB	AP	UP	NYN	PFI
HB	SAMMY BAUGH, Was	AP	UP	NYN	PFI
HB+	HARRY CLARK, ChiB	AP	UP		
HB	Bill Paschal, NY				PFI
HB	Frank Sinkwich, Det			NYN	
FB+	TONY CANADEO, GB	AP		NYN	
FB+	WARD CUFF, NY		UP		PFI

1944 All-NFL

Pos	Player	AP	UP	NYN	INS	PFI
E	JOE AGUIRRE, Was	AP	UP	NYN	INS	PFI
E	DON HUTSON, GB	AP	UP	NYN	INS	PFI
T	AL WISTERT, Phi	AP	UP	NYN	INS	

		AP	UP	NYN	INS	PFI
T	FRANK COPE, NY		UP		INS	PFI
T	Bruiser Kinard, Bkn	AP		NYN		
T	Baby Ray, GB					PFI
G	LEN YOUNCE, NY	AP	UP	NYN		PFI
G	RILEY MATHESON, Cle	AP	UP	NYN		PFI
G	Augie Lio, Bos				INS	
C	BULLDOG TURNER, ChiB	AP	UP	NYN	INS	
C	Alex Wojciechowicz, Det					PFI
QB	SID LUCKMAN, ChiB	AP		NYN	INS	PFI
QB	Roy Zimmerman, Phi		UP			
HB	FRANK SINKWICH, Det	AP	UP	NYN	INS	
HB+	WARD CUFF, NY		UP			PFI
HB	Steve Van Buren, Phi	AP				
FB	BILL PASCHAL, NY	AP	UP	NYN	INS	PFI
FB+	JOHN GRIGAS, Ch/P			NYN	INS	

1945 ALL-NFL

		AP	UP	NYN	INS	PFI
E	DON HUTSON, GB	AP	UP			PFI
E	JIM BENTON, Cle	AP		NYN		PFI
E	Steve Pritko, Cle		UP		INS	
E	Joe Aguirre, Was				INS	
T	AL WISTERT, Phi	AP	UP	NYN	INS	PFI
T	EMIL UREMOVICH, Det		UP	NYN		
T	John Adams, Was					PFI
T	Frank Cope, NY	AP				
T	Eberle Schultz, Phi				INS	
G	RILEY MATHESON, Cle	AP	UP	NYN		PFI
G	BILL RADOVICH, Det	AP	UP		INS	
G	Augie Lio, Bos			NYN	INS	
G	Stan Batinski, Det					PFI
C	CHARLEY BROCK, GB	AP	UP	NYN	INS	PFI
QB	BOB WATERFIELD, Cle	AP	UP-h	NYN		PFI
QB	SAMMY BAUGH, Was	AP	UP	NYN	INS	
HB	STEVE VAN BUREN, Phi	AP	UP	NYN	INS	PFI
HB	Steve Bagarus, Was	AP				
HB	Fred Gehrke, Cle					PFI
HB	Jim Gillette, Cle				INS	
HB	Bob Margarita, ChiB			NYN		
FB	FRANK AKINS, Was				INS	PFI
FB	Ted Fritsch, GB		UP			
FB	Bob Westfall, Det	AP				

1946 ALL-NFL

E	JIM BENTON, LA	AP*	UP	NYN	PFI	SP
E	JIM POOLE, NY	AP*			PFI	
E	Bill Dewell, ChiC			NYN		
E	Ken Kavanaugh, ChiB		UP			
T	AL WISTERT, Phi	AP*	UP	NYN	PFI	
T	JIM WHITE, NY	AP	UP	NYN		SP
T	John Adams, Was				PFI	
G	RILEY MATHESON, LA	AP*	UP	NYN	PFI	
G	LEN YOUNCE, NY	AP		NYN		
G	Ray Bray, ChiB				PFI	
G	Augie Lio, Phi		UP			
C	BULLDOG TURNER, ChiB	AP*	UP	NYN		SP
C	Charley Brock, GB				PFI	
QB	SID LUCKMAN, ChiB	AP		NYN	PFI	SP
QB	BOB WATERFIELD, LA	AP*	UP			
HB	BILL DUDLEY, Pit	AP	UP	NYN	PFI	SP
HB	Frank Filchock, NY		UP			
HB	Hugh Gallarneau, ChiB				PFI	
HB	Steve Van Buren, Phi			NYN		
FB	TED FRITSCH, GB	AP*	UP	NYN	PFI	SP

1946 ALL-AAFC

		AP	UP	NYN	OFF	SP
E	DANTE LAVELLI, Cle	AP			OFF	
E+	ALYN BEALS, SF		UP		OFF	
E+	JACK RUSSELL, NY	AP				SP
E+	MAC SPEEDIE, Cle		UP	NYN		
E	Joe Aguirre, LA			NYN		
T	BRUISER KINARD, NY	AP*	UP	NYN	OFF	
T	MARTIN RUBY, Bkn	AP	UP	NYN	OFF	
T	Lou Rymkus, Cle					SP
G	BRUNO BANDUCCI, SF	AP	UP	NYN	OFF	
G	BILL RADOVICH, LA	AP*	UP	NYN		
G	Bill Willis, Cle				OFF	SP
C	BOB NELSON, LA	AP			OFF	
C	Mike Scarry, Cle			NYN		
QB	FRANKIE ALBERT, SF	AP				
QB	Otto Graham, Cle		UP		OFF	
HB	GLENN DOBBS, Bkn	AP*	UP	NYN	OFF	SP
HB	SPEC SANDERS, NY	AP*	UP	NYN	OFF	
FB	MARION MOTLEY, Cle	AP	UP	NYN	OFF	

1947 ALL-NFL

		AP	UP	NYN	PFI	C&O	SP
E	KEN KAVANAUGH, ChiB	AP	UP	NYN			SP
E	MAL KUTNER, ChiB	AP	UP		PFI		
E	Larry Craig, GB				PFI	C&O	
E	Bill Dewell, ChiC					C&O	
E	Val Jansante, Pit			NYN			
T	AL WISTERT, Phi	AP*	UP	NYN			SP
T	FRED DAVIS, ChiB		UP	NYN	PFI		
T	Stan Mauldin, ChiC				PFI	C&O	
T	Dick Huffman, LA	AP*					
T	Jim White, NY					C&O	
G	RILEY MATHESON, LA	AP*		NYN		C&O	SP
G	BUSTER RAMSEY, ChiC	AP		NYN	PFI		
G	Len Younce, NY		UP			C&O	
G	Bill Moore, Pit		UP				
G	Dick Wildung, GB				PFI		
C	BULLDOG TURNER, ChiB	AP*		NYN	PFI		SP
C	Vince Banonis, ChiC		UP				
QB	SID LUCKMAN, ChiB	AP*		NYN	PFI	C&O	
HB	STEVE VAN BUREN, Phi	AP*		NYN	PFI	C&O	SP
HB	SAMMY BAUGH, Was	AP	UP	NYN			
HB	Bill Dudley, Det			NYN	PFI		
HB	Tony Canadeo, GB					C&O	
HB	John Clement, Pit	AP					
FB	PAT HARDER, ChiC		UP	NYN	PFI	C&O	SP

1947 ALL-AAFC

E	MAC SPEEDIE, Cle	AP*	NYN	OFF	C&O	
E	BRUCE ALFORD, NY	AP*	NYN		C&O	
E	Dante Lavelli, Cle			OFF		
E	Jack Russell, NY		NYN			
T	LOU RYMKUS, Cle		NYN	OFF	C&O	SP
T	NATE JOHNSON, NY		NYN	OFF	C&O	
T	Martin Ruby, Bkn	AP				
T	John Woudenberg, SF	AP				
G	BRUNO BANDUCCI, SF	AP*	NYN	OFF	C&O	
G	DICK BARWEGAN, NY	AP	NYN		C&O	SP
G	Bill Willis, Cle			OFF		
C	BOB NELSON, LA	AP	NYN	OFF		
C	Mike Scarry, Cle				C&O	
QB	OTTO GRAHAM, Cle	AP*	NYN		C&O	SP
QB	Frankie Albert, SF	AP				
HB	SPEC SANDERS, NY	AP*	NYN	OFF	C&O	SP
HB	CHET MUTRYN, Buf		NYN	OFF	C&O	
FB	MARION MOTLEY, Cle	AP	NYN	OFF	C&O	

1948 ALL-NFL

		AP	UP	NYN	PFI	SN
E	MAL KUTNER, ChiC	AP*	UP	NYN	PFI	SN
E	PETE PIHOS, Phi	AP*	UP	NYN	PFI	
T	DICK HUFFMAN, LA	AP*	UP	NYN	PFI	SN
T	AL WISTERT, Phi		UP	NYN	PFI	SN
T	Fred Davis, ChiB	AP				
G	BUSTER RAMSEY, ChiC	AP*	UP	NYN	PFI	SN
G	RAY BRAY, ChiB		UP	NYN	PFI	
G	Chuck Drulis, ChiB	AP				
C	BULLDOG TURNER, ChiB	AP*	UP		PFI	SN
C	Vince Banonis, ChiC			NYN		
QB	SAMMY BAUGH, Was	AP	UP	NYN	PFI	
QB	Tommy Thompson, Phi	AP				
HB	CHARLIE TRIPPI, ChiC	AP*	UP	NYN	PFI	SN
HB	STEVE VAN BUREN, Phi	AP*	UP	NYN	PFI	SN
FB	PAT HARDER, ChiC		UP	NYN	PFI	

1948 ALL-AAFC

		AP	UP	NYN	OFF	SN
E	MAC SPEEDIE, Cle	AP	UP	NYN	OFF	SN
E	ALYN BEALS, SF	AP	UP	NYN	OFF	
T	BOB REINHARD, LA	AP*	UP	NYN	OFF	
T	LOU RYMKUS, Cle	AP	UP		OFF	
T	John Woudenberg, SF			NYN		
G	DICK BARWEGAN, Bal	AP*	UP	NYN	OFF	SN
G	BILL WILLIS, Cle		UP	NYN		
C	LOU SABAN, Cle		UP	NYN		
C	Bob Nelson, LA				OFF	
C	George Strohmeyer, Bkn	AP				
QB	OTTO GRAHAM, Cle	AP*			OFF	
QB	Frankie Albert, SF			NYN		SN
HB	CHET MUTRYN, Buf	AP	UP	NYN	OFF	
HB	JOHN STRZYKALSKI, SF	AP	UP	NYN	OFF	
FB	MARION MOTLEY, Cle	AP*	UP	NYN	OFF	SN

1949 ALL-NFL

		AP	UP	NYN	INS
E	PETE PIHOS, Phi	AP*	UP	NYN	
E	TOM FEARS, LA	AP*	UP	NYN	
E	Ed Sprinkle, ChiB				INS-d
T	DICK HUFFMAN, LA	AP*	UP	NYN	INS-d
T	GEORGE CONNOR, ChiB	AP			
T	Vic Sears, Phi		UP		
T	Dick Wildung, GB			NYN	
T	Al Wistert, Phi				INS-o
G	RAY BRAY, ChiB	AP	UP	NYN	
G	BUSTER RAMSEY, ChiC	AP*	UP		
G	Bucko Kilroy, Phi			NYN	
G	Darrell Hogan, Pit				INS-d
G	Milan Lazetich, LA				INS-d
G	Wash Serini, ChiB				INS-d
C	FRED NAUMETZ, LA	AP*	UP	NYN	
C	Vince Banonis, ChiC				INS-o
QB	BOB WATERFIELD, LA	AP*	UP		

QB	Johnny Lujack, ChiB			NYN		
HB	STEVE VAN BUREN, Phi	AP*	UP	NYN	INS-o	
HB	TONY CANADEO, GB	AP	UP		INS-o	
HB	Elmer Angsman, ChiC	AP				
HB	Gene Roberts, NYG			NYN		
HB	Don Doll, Det				INS-d	
HB	Emlen Tunnell, NY				INS-d	
FB	PAT HARDER, ChiC					

1949 All-AAFC

E	MAC SPEEDIE, Cle	AP*	UP	NYN	OFF	INS-o
E	ALYN BEALS, SF	AP	UP	NYN	OFF	
T	ARNIE WEINMEISTER, NY	AP*	UP	NYN	OFF	
T+	JOHN KISSELL, Buf			NYN		INS-d
T+	BOB REINHARD, LA	AP			OFF	
T+	LOU RYMKUS, Cle		UP			INS-o
G	DICK BARWEGAN, Bal	AP*	UP	NYN	OFF	
G	VISCO GRGICH, SF	AP	UP	NYN	OFF	
G	Joe Signaigo, NY					INS-o
C	LOU SABAN, Cle	AP	UP	NYN	OFF	INS-d
QB	OTTO GRAHAM, Cle	AP*	UP	NYN	OFF	INS-o
QB	FRANKIE ALBERT, SF	AP			OFF	
HB	CHET MUTRYN, Buf	AP*			OFF	INS-o
HB	Buddy Young, NY		UP	NYN		
HB	Jim Cason, SF					INS-d
HB	Herman Wedemeyer, Bal					INS-d
FB	JOE PERRY, SF	AP	UP	NYN	OFF	
FB	Marion Motley, Cle			NYN		

1950 All-NFL

Offense

E	TOM FEARS, LA	AP	UP	NYN
E	MAC SPEEDIE, Cle		UP	NYN
E	Dan Edwards, NYY	AP		
T	GEORGE CONNOR, ChiB	AP	UP	NYN
T	ARNIE WEINMEISTER, NYG*	AP	UP	*
T	Dick Huffman, LA			NYN
G	DICK BARWEGAN, ChiB	AP	UP	NYN
G	BILL WILLIS, Cle*		UP	*
G	Bucko Kilroy, Phi			NYN
G	Joe Signaigo, NYY	AP		
C	CLAYTON TONNEMAKER, GB*	UP	*	
C	Chuck Bednarik, Phi	AP		
C	John Rapacz, NYG			NYN
QB	JOHN LUJACK, ChiB	AP	UP	NYN
HB	JOE GERI, Pit	AP	UP	NYN
HB	DOAK WALKER, Det	AP	UP	
HB	Billy Joe Grimes, GB			NYN
FB	MARION MOTLEY, Cle	AP	UP	NYN

Defense

E	Ray Poole, NYG	-	-	NYN
E	Ed Sprinkle, ChiB	-	-	NYN
T	Arnie Weinmeister, NYG*	*	*	NYN
T	Bob Reinhard, LA	-	-	NYN
G	Ray Bray, ChiB	-	-	NYN
G	Bill Willis, Cle*	-	*	NYN
LB	Joe Muha, Phi	-	-	NYN
LB	Clayton Tonnemaker, GB*	-	*	NYN
HB	Don Doll, Det	-	-	NYN
HB	Otto Schnellbacher, NYG	-	-	NYN
S	Spec Sanders, NYY	-	-	NYN

1951 All-NFL

Offense

E	CRAZY LEGS HIRSCH, LA	AP	UP	NYN
E	DANTE LAVELLI, Cle		UP	NYN
E	Leon Hart, Det*	AP	*	
T	TEX COULTER, NYG		UP	NYN
T	LOU GROZA, Cle		UP	NYN
T	George Connor, ChiB*	AP	*	*
T	Leo Nomellini, SF	AP		
G	DICK BARWEGAN, ChiB	AP	UP	NYN
G	LOU CREEKMUR, Det	AP	UP	NYN
C	FRANK GATSKI, Cle	AP	UP	NYN
C	Vic Lindskog, Phi	AP		
QB	OTTO GRAHAM, Cle	AP	UP	NYN
HB	DUB JONES, Cle	AP	UP	NYN
HB	DOAK WALKER, Det	AP	UP	NYN
FB	DAN TOWLER, LA	AP	UP	NYN
FB	Eddie Price, NYG	AP		

Defense

E	LEN FORD, Cle	AP	UP	NYN
E	LARRY BRINK, LA	AP		NYN
E	Leon Hart, Det*	*	UP	
T	ARNIE WEINMEISTER, NYG	AP	UP	NYN
T	GEORGE CONNOR, ChiB*	*	UP	NYN

T	Al DeRogatis, NYG	AP		
G	BILL WILLIS, Cle	AP	UP	NYN
G+	LES BINGAMAN, Det	AP		
G+	STAN WEST, LA			NYN
G	Jon Baker, NYG		UP	
LB	CHUCK BEDNARIK, Phi	AP	UP	NYN
LB	TONY ADAMLE, Cle	AP	UP	NYN
LB	Tank Younger, LA	AP		
HB	OTTO SCHNELLBACHER, NYG	AP	UP	NYN
HB	WARREN LAHR, Cle		UP	NYN
HB	Jerry Shipkey, Pit	AP		
S	EMLEN TUNNELL, NYG	AP	UP	NYN

1952 All-NFL

Offense

E	GORDIE SOLTAU, SF	AP	UP	NYN
E	BILLY HOWTON, GB			NYN
E	Cloyce Box, Det	AP		
E	Mac Speedie, Cle		UP	
T	LEO NOMELLINI, SF	AP	UP	NYN
T	LOU GROZA, Cle	AP-g	UP	NYN
T	George Connor, ChiB*	AP	*	*
G	LOU CREEKMUR, Det	AP	UP	NYN
G	BILL FISCHER, ChiC		UP	
G	Bruno Banducci, SF			NYN
C	FRANK GATSKI, Cle	AP		NYN
C	Bill Walsh, Pit		UP	
QB	OTTO GRAHAM, Cle		UP	NYN
QB	Bobby Layne, Det	AP		
HB	HUGH MCELHENNY, SF	AP	UP	NYN
HB	DAN TOWLER, LA	AP	UP	
HB	Bob Hoernschemeyer, Det			NYN
FB	EDDIE PRICE, NY	AP	UP	NYN

Defense

E	LEN FORD, Cle	AP	UP	NYN
E	PETE PIHOS, Phi	AP		NYN
E	Larry Brink, LA		UP	
T	THURMAN MCGRAW, Det	AP	UP	NYN
T	ARNIE WEINMEISTER, NY	AP	UP	NYN
G	STAN WEST, LA	AP	UP	NYN
G	BILL WILLIS, Cle	AP		NYN
G	Les Bingaman, Det		UP	
LB	GEORGE CONNOR, ChiB*	*	UP	NYN
LB	JERRY SHIPKEY, Pit	AP		NYN
LB	Chuck Bednarik, Phi	AP	UP	
HB	HERB RICH, LA		UP	NYN
HB	JIM SMITH, Det		UP	NYN
HB	Jack Christiansen, Det	AP		
HB	Ollie Matson, ChiC	AP		
S	EMLEN TUNNELL, NY	AP	UP	
S	John Williams, Was			NYN

1953 All-NFL

Offense

E	PETE PIHOS, Phi	AP	UP	NYN
E	DANTE LAVELLI, Cle		UP	NYN
E	Crazy Legs Hirsch, LA	AP		
T	LOU CREEKMUR, Det	AP-g	UP	NYN
T	LOU GROZA, Cle	AP	UP	NYN
T	George Connor, ChiB*	AP	*	*
G	DICK STANFEL, Det	AP	UP	NYN
G	ABE GIBRON, Cle			NYN
G	Bruno Banducci, SF		UP	
C	FRANK GATSKI, Cle	AP	UP	NYN
QB	OTTO GRAHAM, Cle	AP	UP	NYN
HB	HUGH MCELHENNY, SF	AP	UP	NYN
HB	DOAK WALKER, Det	AP		
HB	Bob Hoernschemeyer, Det			NYN
HB	Dan Towler, LA		UP	
FB	JOE PERRY, SF	AP	UP	NYN

Defense

E	LEN FORD, Cle	AP	UP	NYN
E	NORM WILLEY, Phi		UP	NYN
E	Andy Robustelli, LA	AP		
T	ARNIE WEINMEISTER, NY	AP	UP	NYN
T	LEO NOMELLINI, SF	AP	UP	NYN-g
T	Thurman McGraw, Det			NYN
G	LES BINGAMAN, Det	AP	UP	NYN
G	BILL WILLIS, Cle	AP		
G	Dale Dodrill, Pit		UP	
LB	GEORGE CONNOR, ChiB*	*	UP	NYN
LB	CHUCK BEDNARIK, Phi	AP		NYN
LB	Tommy Thompson, Cle	AP-b	UP	
LB	Don Paul, LA	AP		
HB	JACK CHRISTIANSEN, Det	AP	UP	NYN
HB	TOM KEANE, Bal	AP	UP	NYN
S	KEN GORGAL, Cle		UP	NYN

1954 ALL-NFL

Offense

		AP	UP	NYN	SN
E	HARLON HILL, ChiB		UP	NYN	SN
E	PETE PIHOS, Phi	AP	UP		SN
E	Bob Boyd, LA	AP		NYN	
T	LOU CREEKMUR, Det	AP	UP	NYN	SN
T	LOU GROZA, Cle	AP	UP	NYN	SN
G	BRUNO BANDUCCI, SF	AP	UP	NYN	SN
G	DICK STANFEL, Det	AP	UP	NYN	
G	Les Bingaman, Det*	*	*	*	SN
C	BILL WALSH, Pit	AP	UP		
C	Chuck Bednarik, Phi*	*	*	*	SN
C	Bill Johnson, SF			NYN	
QB	OTTO GRAHAM, Cle	AP	UP	NYN	SN
HB	DOAK WALKER, Det	AP	UP	NYN	SN
HB	OLLIE MATSON, ChiC*	AP	UP	*	SN
HB	Hugh McElhenny, SF			NYN	
FB	JOE PERRY, SF	AP	UP	NYN	SN

Defense

		AP	UP	NYN	
E	LEN FORD, Cle	AP	UP	NYN	
E	NORM WILLEY, Phi	AP	UP	NYN	
T	LEO NOMELLINI, SF	AP	UP	NYN	
T	ART DONOVAN, Bal	AP	UP		
T	Ray Krouse, NY			NYN	
G	LES BINGAMAN, Det*	AP	UP	NYN	
G	Dale Dodrill, Pit	AP			
G	Bucko Kilroy, Phi		UP		
LB	CHUCK BEDNARIK, Phi*	AP	UP	NYN	
LB	JOE SCHMIDT, Det	AP			
LB	Clayton Tonnemaker, GB			NYN	
LB	Roger Zatkoff, GB		UP		
HB	JIM DAVID, Det		UP	NYN	
HB	TOM LANDRY, NY	AP	UP		
HB	Ollie Matson, ChiC*	*	*	NYN	
HB	Bobby Dillon, GB	AP			
S	JACK CHRISTIANSEN, Det	AP	UP	NYN	
S	EMLEN TUNNELL, NY			NYN	

1955 ALL-NFL

Offense

		AP	UP	NYN	NEA
E	HARLON HILL, ChiB	AP	UP	NYN	NEA
E	BILLY WILSON, SF		UP	NYN	NEA
E	Pete Pihos, Phi	AP			
T	LOU GROZA, Cle	AP	UP	NYN	NEA
T	BOB ST. CLAIR, SF		UP		NEA
T	Mike McCormack, Cle			NYN	
T	Bill Wightkin, ChiB	AP			
G	ABE GIBRON, Cle		UP	NYN	NEA
G	DUANE PUTNAM, LA	AP		NYN	NEA
G	Bill Austin, NY		UP		
G	Stan Jones, ChiB	AP			
C	FRANK GATSKI, Cle	AP	UP	NYN	NEA
QB	OTTO GRAHAM, Cle	AP	UP	NYN	NEA
QB	Tobin Rote, GB				NEA
HB	OLLIE MATSON, ChiC	AP	UP	NYN	NEA
HB	FRANK GIFFORD, NY	AP			NEA
HB	Rick Casares, ChiB			NYN	
HB	Ron Waller, LA		UP		
FB	ALAN AMECHE, Bal	AP	UP	NYN	
FB	Howie Ferguson, GB				NEA

Defense

		AP	UP	NYN	NEA
E	GENE BRITO, Was	AP	UP		NEA
E	LEN FORD, Cle		UP	NYN	NEA
E	Andy Robustelli, LA	AP		NYN	
T	ART DONOVAN, Bal	AP	UP	NYN	NEA
T	BOB TONEFF, SF	AP		NYN	
T	Don Colo, Cle		UP		NEA
MG	DALE DODRILL, Pit		UP	NYN	NEA
MG	Bill George, ChiB	AP			
LB	GEORGE CONNOR, ChiB		UP	NYN	NEA
LB	JOE SCHMIDT, Det	AP			NEA
LB	Chuck Bednarik, Phi		UP		
LB	Les Richter, LA			NYN	
LB	Roger Zatkoff, GB	AP			
DB	JACK CHRISTIANSEN, Det	AP	UP	NYN	NEA
DB	BOBBY DILLON, GB	AP	UP	NYN	NEA
DB	WILL SHERMAN, LA	AP	UP	NYN	NEA
DB	BERT RECHICHAR, Bal			NYN	NEA
DB	Don Paul, Cle		UP		
DB	Emlen Tunnell, NY	AP			

1956 ALL-NFL

Offense

		AP	UP	NYN	NEA
E	HARLON HILL, ChiB	AP	UP	NYN	NEA
E	BILLY HOWTON, GB	AP	UP	NYN	NEA
T	ROOSEVELT BROWN, NY	AP	UP	NYN	NEA
T	LOU CREEKMUR, Det	AP	UP		
T	Bob St. Clair, SF				NEA
T	Bill Wightkin, ChiB			NYN	
G	STAN JONES, ChiB	AP	UP	NYN	
G	DICK STANFEL, Was	AP	UP		NEA
G	Duane Putnam, LA			NYN	NEA
C	LARRY STRICKLAND, ChiB	AP		NYN	
C	Charlie Ane, Det		UP		NEA
QB	BOBBY LAYNE, Det	AP	UP	NYN	NEA
HB	FRANK GIFFORD, NY	AP	UP	NYN	NEA
HB	OLLIE MATSON, ChiC	AP	UP	NYN	NEA
FB	RICK CASARES, ChiB	AP	UP	NYN	NEA

Defense

		AP	UP	NYN	NEA
E	GENE BRITO, Was	AP	UP	NYN	
E	ANDY ROBUSTELLI, NY	AP	UP	NYN	
E	Gino Marchetti, Bal				NEA
T	ROSEY GRIER, NY	AP	UP	NYN	
T	ART DONOVAN, Bal	AP			NEA
T	Ernie Stautner, Pit		UP		NEA
T	Ray Krouse, Det			NYN	
MG	BILL GEORGE, ChiB	AP	UP	NYN	NEA
LB	JOE SCHMIDT, Det	AP	UP	NYN	NEA
LB	CHUCK BEDNARIK, Phi		UP	NYN	NEA
LB	Les Richter, LA	AP		NYN	
HB	NIGHT TRAIN LANE, ChiC		UP	NYN	NEA
HB	EMLEN TUNNELL, NY	AP	UP		NEA
HB	J.C. Caroline, ChiB			NYN	
S	JACK CHRISTIANSEN, Det	AP	UP	NYN	NEA
S	BOBBY DILLON, GB		UP	NYN	NEA
S	Yale Lary, Det	AP			

1957 ALL-NFL

Offense

		AP	UP	NYN	NEA
E	BILLY HOWTON, GB	AP	UP	NYN	NEA
E	BILLY WILSON, SF	AP	UP	NYN	NEA
T	ROOSEVELT BROWN, NY	AP	UP	NYN	NEA
T	LOU GROZA, Cle		UP	NYN	
T	Lou Creekmur, Det	AP			
T	Mike McCormack, Cle				NEA
G	DUANE PUTNAM, LA	AP	UP	NYN	NEA
G	DICK STANFEL, Was	AP	UP	NYN	NEA
C	JIM RINGO, GB	AP			NEA
C	Larry Strickland, ChiB		UP	NYN	
QB	Y.A. TITTLE, SF	AP	UP		
QB	Johnny Unitas, Bal			NYN	NEA
HB	FRANK GIFFORD, NY	AP	UP	NYN	NEA
HB	OLLIE MATSON, ChiC	AP	UP	NYN	NEA
FB	JIM BROWN, Cle	AP	UP	NYN	NEA

Defense

		AP	UP	NYN	NEA
E	GINO MARCHETTI, Bal	AP	UP	NYN	NEA
E+	GENE BRITO, Was	AP			NEA
E+	ANDY ROBUSTELLI, NY		UP	NYN	
T	ART DONOVAN, Bal	AP	UP	NYN	NEA
T	LEO NOMELLINI, SF	AP	UP		
T	Don Colo, Cle			NYN	NEA
LB	BILL GEORGE, ChiB	AP	UP	NYN	NEA
LB	JOE SCHMIDT, Det	AP	UP	NYN	NEA
LB	MARV MATUSZAK, SF	AP	UP		NEA
LB	Chuck Bednarik, Phi			NYN	
DB	JACK BUTLER, Pit	AP	UP	NYN	NEA
DB	JACK CHRISTIANSEN, Det	AP	UP	NYN	NEA
DB	BOBBY DILLON, GB	AP	UP	NYN	NEA
DB	YALE LARY, Det		UP		NEA
DB	Milt Davis, Bal	AP			
DB	Dick Moegle, SF			NYN	

1958 ALL-NFL

Offense

		AP	UPI	NYN	NEA
E	RAYMOND BERRY, Bal	AP	UPI	NYN	NEA
E	DEL SHOFNER, LA	AP	UPI	NYN	NEA
T	ROOSEVELT BROWN, NY	AP	UPI	NYN	NEA
T	JIM PARKER, Bal	AP	UPI	NYN	NEA
G	DUANE PUTNAM, LA	AP	UPI	NYN	NEA
G	DICK STANFEL, Was	AP	UPI	NYN	NEA
C	RAY WIETECHA, NY	AP	UPI		NEA
C	Jim Ringo, GB			NYN	
QB	JOHNNY UNITAS, Bal	AP	UPI	NYN	NEA
HB	JON ARNETT, LA	AP	UPI	NYN	NEA
HB	LENNY MOORE, Bal	AP	UPI	NYN	NEA
FB	JIM BROWN, Cle	AP	UPI	NYN	NEA

Defense

		AP	UPI	NYN	NEA
E	GINO MARCHETTI, Bal	AP	UPI	NYN	NEA
E	GENE BRITO, Was		UPI		NEA
E	Doug Atkins, ChiB			NYN	
E	Andy Robustelli, NY	AP			

Pos	Player	AP	UPI	NYN	NEA
T	BIG DADDY LIPSCOMB, Bal	AP	UPI	NYN	NEA
T	ERNIE STAUTNER, Pit	AP	UPI		
T	Art Donovan, Bal			NYN	
T	Bob Gain, Cle				NEA
LB	BILL GEORGE, ChiB	AP	UPI	NYN	NEA
LB	SAM HUFF, NY	AP	UPI	NYN	NEA
LB	JOE SCHMIDT, Det	AP	UPI	NYN	NEA
HB	JACK BUTLER, Pit	AP	UPI	NYN	NEA
HB	YALE LARY, Det	AP	UPI	NYN	NEA
HB	Andy Nelson, Bal			NYN	
S	BOBBY DILLON, GB	AP	UPI	NYN	NEA
S	JIM PATTON, NY	AP	UPI		NEA

1959 ALL-NFL

Offense

Pos	Player	AP	UPI	NYN	NEA
E	RAYMOND BERRY, Bal	AP	UPI	NYN	NEA
E	DEL SHOFNER, LA	AP	UPI	NYN	NEA
T	ROOSEVELT BROWN, NY	AP	UPI	NYN	NEA
T	JIM PARKER, Bal	AP	UPI	NYN	NEA
G	JIM RAY SMITH, Cle	AP	UPI	NYN	NEA
G	ART SPINNEY, Bal		UPI	NYN	
G	Stan Jones, ChiB	AP			
G	Duane Putnam, LA				NEA
C	JIM RINGO, GB	AP	UPI	NYN	NEA
QB	JOHNNY UNITAS, Bal	AP	UPI	NYN	NEA
HB	FRANK GIFFORD, NY	AP	UPI	NYN	NEA
HB	LENNY MOORE, Bal	AP		NYN	NEA
HB	J.D. Smith, SF		UPI		
FB	JIM BROWN, Cle	AP	UPI	NYN	NEA

Defense

Pos	Player	AP	UPI	NYN	NEA
E	GINO MARCHETTI, Bal	AP	UPI	NYN	NEA
E	ANDY ROBUSTELLI, NY	AP	UPI	NYN	NEA
T	LEO NOMELLINI, SF	AP	UPI	NYN	NEA
T	BIG DADDY LIPSCOMB, Bal	AP	UPI	NYN	
T	Ernie Stautner, Pit				NEA
LB	SAM HUFF, NY	AP	UPI	NYN	NEA
LB	JOE SCHMIDT, Det	AP	UPI	NYN	NEA
LB	BILL GEORGE, ChiB	AP	UPI		NEA
LB	Walt Michaels, Cle			NYN	
HB	JACK BUTLER, Pit	AP	UPI	NYN	NEA
HB	ABE WOODSON, SF	AP	UPI		
HB	Tom Brookshier, Phi				NEA
HB	Yale Lary, Det				NEA
S	JIM PATTON, NY		UPI	NYN	NEA
S	DEAN DERBY, Pit		UPI	NYN	
S	Andy Nelson, Bal	AP		NYN	

1960 ALL-NFL

Offense

Pos	Player	AP	UPI	NYN	NEA
E	RAYMOND BERRY, Bal	AP	UPI	NYN	NEA
E	SONNY RANDLE, StL	AP	UPI		
E	Tommy McDonald, Phi			NYN	NEA
T	JIM PARKER, Bal	AP	UPI	NYN	NEA
T	ROOSEVELT BROWN, NY		UPI	NYN	
T	Forrest Gregg, GB	AP			
T	Bob St. Clair, SF				NEA
G	JIM RAY SMITH, Cle	AP	UPI	NYN	NEA
G	STAN JONES, Chi		UPI	NYN	
G	Jerry Kramer, GB	AP			
G	Jack Stroud, NY				NEA
C	JIM RINGO, GB	AP	UPI	NYN	NEA
QB	NORM VAN BROCKLIN, Phi	AP	UPI	NYN	NEA
HB	PAUL HORNUNG, GB	AP	UPI	NYN	NEA+
HB	LENNY MOORE, Bal	AP	UPI	NYN	NEA
HB	John David Crow, StL				NEA+
FB	JIM BROWN, Cle	AP	UPI	NYN	NEA

Defense

Pos	Player	AP	UPI	NYN	NEA
E	GINO MARCHETTI, Bal	AP	UPI	NYN	NEA
E	DOUG ATKINS, Chi		UPI	NYN	NEA
E	Andy Robustelli, NY	AP			
T	HENRY JORDAN, GB	AP	UPI	NYN	
T	ALEX KARRAS, Det	AP	UPI		
T	Big Daddy Lipscomb, Bal			NYN	NEA
T	Bob Toneff, Was				NEA
LB	BILL GEORGE, Chi	AP	UPI	NYN	NEA
LB	CHUCK BEDNARIK, Phi	AP	UPI	NYN	
LB+	BILL FORESTER, GB	AP	UPI		
LB+	SAM HUFF, NY			NYN	NEA
LB	Joe Schmidt, Det				NEA
HB	TOM BROOKSHIER, Phi	AP	UPI	NYN	NEA
HB	ABE WOODSON, SF	AP		NYN	
HB	Night Train Lane, Det		UPI		NEA
S	JERRY NORTON, StL	AP	UPI	NYN	NEA
S	JIM PATTON, NY	AP	UPI	NYN	NEA

1960 ALL-AFL

Offense

E	LIONEL TAYLOR, Den	OFF	AP	UPI

E	BILL GROMAN, Hou	OFF		UPI
E	Art Powell, Oak		AP	
T	RON MIX, LA	OFF	AP	UPI
T	RICH MICHAEL, Hou	OFF		UPI
T	Al Jamison, Hou		AP	
G	BOB MISCHAK, NY	OFF	AP	UPI
G	BILL KRISHER, Dal	OFF	AP	
G	Jack Davis, Bos			UPI
C	JIM OTTO, Oak	OFF	AP	
C	Walt Cudzik, Bos			UPI
QB	JACK KEMP, LA	OFF	AP	UPI
HB	ABNER HAYNES, Dal	OFF	AP	UPI
HB	PAUL LOWE, LA	OFF	AP	UPI
FB	DAVE SMITH, Hou	OFF	AP	UPI

Defense

E	MEL BRANCH, Dal	OFF	AP	UPI
E	LAVERNE TORCZON, Buf	OFF	AP	UPI
T	BUD McFADIN, Den	OFF	AP	UPI
T	SID YOUNGELMAN, NY			UPI
T	Chuck McMurtry, Buf		AP	
T	Volney Peters, LA	OFF		
LB	ARCHIE MATSOS, Buf	OFF	AP	UPI
LB	SHERRILL HEADRICK, Dal	OFF	AP	
LB+	LARRY GRANTHAM, NY		AP	
LB+	PAUL MAGUIRE, LA			UPI
LB	Tom Addison, Bos	OFF		
LB	Mike Dukes, Hou			UPI
DB	GOOSE GONSOULIN, Den	OFF	AP	
DB	DICK HARRIS, LA	OFF	AP	
DB	RICHIE McCABE, Buf	OFF	AP	
DB+	MARK JOHNSTON, Hou		AP	
DB+	EDDIE MACON, Oak			UPI
DB	Johnny Bookman, Dal			UPI
DB	Fred Bruney, Bos			UPI
DB	Ross O'Hanley, Bos	OFF		
DB	Julian Spence, Hou			UPI

1961 ALL-NFL

Offense

Pos	Player	AP	UPI	NYN	NEA	PFI
E	DEL SHOFNER, NY	AP	UPI	NYN	NEA	PFI
E	JIM PHILLIPS, LA	AP	UPI	NYN		
E	Mike Ditka, Chi				NEA	
E	Ron Kramer, GB					PFI
T	ROOSEVELT BROWN, NY	AP	UPI	NYN	NEA	PFI
T	JIM PARKER, Bal	AP		NYN	NEA	
T	Forrest Gregg, GB		UPI			PFI
G	JIM RAY SMITH, Cle	AP	UPI	NYN	NEA	PFI
G	FUZZY THURSTON, GB	AP	UPI	NYN	NEA	PFI
C	JIM RINGO, GB	AP	UPI	NYN	NEA	PFI
QB	SONNY JURGENSEN, Phi	AP	UPI			PFI
QB	Y.A. Tittle, NY			NYN	NEA	
HB	LENNY MOORE, Bal	AP	UPI	NYN	NEA	
HB	PAUL HORNUNG, GB	AP	UPI	NYN		PFI
FB	JIM BROWN, Cle	AP	UPI	NYN	NEA	
RB	Jim Taylor, GB				NEA	PFI

Defense

Pos	Player	AP	UPI	NYN	NEA	PFI
E	GINO MARCHETTI, Bal	AP	UPI	NYN	NEA	PFI
E	JIM KATCAVAGE, NY	AP	UPI	NYN		PFI
E	Doug Atkins, Chi				NEA	
T	HENRY JORDAN, GB	AP	UPI	NYN	NEA	PFI
T	ALEX KARRAS, Det	AP	UPI			PFI
T	Big Daddy Lipscomb, Pit				NEA	
T	Dick Modzelewski, NY			NYN		
LB	BILL FORESTER, GB	AP	UPI	NYN		PFI
LB	JOE SCHMIDT, Det	AP	UPI	NYN	NEA	
LB	BILL GEORGE, Chi	AP			NEA	PFI
LB	Dan Currie, GB		UPI		NEA	PFI
LB	Maxie Baughan, Phi			NYN		
HB	ERICH BARNES, NY	AP	UPI	NYN		
HB	JESSE WHITTENTON, GB	AP	UPI			PFI
HB	Jimmy Hill, StL				NEA	
HB	Jerry Norton, StL				NEA	
HB	Abe Woodson, SF			NYN		
S	JIM PATTON, NY	AP	UPI	NYN	NEA	PFI
S	NIGHT TRAIN LANE, Det	AP			NEA	PFI
S	Johnny Sample, Pit		UPI	NYN		PFI

1961 ALL-AFL

Offense

Pos	Player	OFF	SN	AP	UPI	NYN
E	CHARLEY HENNIGAN, Hou	OFF	SN	AP	UPI	NYN
E	LIONEL TAYLOR, Den	OFF		AP	UPI	NYN
E	Bill Groman, Hou		SN	AP		
T	AL JAMISON, Hou	OFF	SN		UPI	NYN
T	RON MIX, SD	OFF		AP	UPI	NYN
T	Jerry Cornelison, Dal		SN			
G	BOB MISCHAK, NY	OFF	SN	AP	UPI	NYN
G	TONY SARDISCO, Bos				UPI	NYN
G	Ken Adamson, Den			AP		
G	Wayne Hawkins, Oak		SN			
G	Chuck Leo, Bos	OFF				

Pos	Player	OFF	SN	AP	UPI	NYN
C	JIM OTTO, Oak	OFF	SN	AP	UPI	NYN
QB	GEORGE BLANDA, Hou	OFF	SN	AP	UPI	NYN
HB	BILLY CANNON, Hou	OFF	SN	AP	UPI	NYN
HB	ABNER HAYNES, Dal	OFF		AP	UPI	NYN
FB	BILL MATHIS, NY	OFF	SN	AP	UPI	NYN

Defense

Pos	Player	OFF	SN	AP	UPI	NYN
E	EARL FAISON, SD	OFF	SN	AP	UPI	NYN
E	RON NERY, SD		SN	AP		
E	Laverne Torczon, Buf				UPI	NYN
E	Don Floyd, Hou	OFF				
T	BUD MCFADIN, Den	OFF	SN	AP	UPI	NYN
T	ERNIE LADD, SD		SN	AP	UPI	NYN
T	Chuck McMurtry, Buf	OFF				
LB	SHERRILL HEADRICK, Dal	OFF	SN	AP	UPI	NYN
LB	LARRY GRANTHAM, NY		SN	AP	UPI	NYN
LB	TOM ADDISON, Bos		SN	AP	UPI	
LB	Archie Matsos, Buf	OFF				NYN
LB	Chuck Allen, SD	OFF				
CB	DICK HARRIS, SD	OFF	SN	AP	UPI	NYN
CB	TONY BANFIELD, Hou	OFF	SN	AP	UPI	
CB	Mark Johnston, Hou					NYN
S	CHARLIE MCNEIL, SD	OFF	SN	AP	UPI	NYN
S	BILLY ATKINS, Buf		SN	AP	UPI	NYN
S	Dave Webster, Dal	OFF				

1962 ALL-NFL

Offense

Pos	Player	AP	UPI	NEA	PFI
SE	DEL SHOFNER, NY	AP	UPI	NEA	PFI
TE	MIKE DITKA, Chi		UPI	NEA	PFI
TE	Ron Kramer, GB	AP			
FL	BOBBY MITCHELL, Was	AP	UPI	NEA	PFI
T	FORREST GREGG, GB	AP	UPI	NEA	PFI
T	JIM PARKER, Bal	AP-g		NEA	PFI
T	Roosevelt Brown, NY	AP	UPI		
G	JERRY KRAMER, GB	AP	UPI	NEA	
G	FUZZY THURSTON, GB		UPI		PFI
G	Jim Ray Smith, Cle			NEA	
C	JIM RINGO, GB	AP	UPI	NEA	PFI
QB	Y.A. TITTLE, NY	AP	UPI	NEA	PFI
HB	DICK BASS, LA		UPI		PFI
HB	Don Perkins, Dal	AP		NEA	
FB	JIM TAYLOR, GB	AP	UPI	NEA	PFI

Defense

Pos	Player	AP	UPI	NEA	PFI
E	GINO MARCHETTI, Bal	AP	UPI	NEA	PFI
E	JIM KATCAVAGE, NY	AP	UPI	NEA	
E	Willie Davis, GB	AP			PFI
T	ROGER BROWN, Det	AP	UPI	NEA	PFI
T	ALEX KARRAS, Det		UPI	NEA	PFI
T	Henry Jordan, GB	AP			
LB	DAN CURRIE, GB	AP	UPI	NEA	PFI
LB	BILL FORESTER, GB	AP	UPI	NEA	PFI
LB	JOE SCHMIDT, Det	AP	UPI	NEA	PFI
CB	NIGHT TRAIN LANE, Det	AP	UPI	NEA	PFI
CB	HERB ADDERLEY, GB	AP	UPI		
CB	Jesse Whittenton, GB				PFI
CB	Abe Woodson, SF			NEA	
S	JIM PATTON, NY	AP	UPI	NEA	
S	YALE LARY, Det	AP	UPI	NEA	
S	Willie Wood, GB				PFI

1962 ALL-AFL

Offense

Pos	Player	SN	AP	UPI	PFI
WR	CHRIS BURFORD, Dal	SN*	AP	UPI	PFI
WR	CHARLEY HENNIGAN, Hou	SN*	AP	UPI	PFI
TE	DAVE KOCOUREK, SD	SN*	AP	UPI	
TE	Fred Arbanas, Dal				PFI
E	Lionel Taylor		AP		
T	AL JAMISON, Hou		AP	UPI	PFI
T	ELDON DANENHAUER, Den	SN*			PFI
T	Charley Long, Bos			UPI	
T	Harold Olson, Buf		AP		
T	Jim Tyrer, Dal	SN*			
G	RON MIX, SD	SN*	AP	UPI	PFI
G	BOB TALAMINI, Hou	SN*		UPI	PFI
G	Billy Shaw, Buf		AP		
C	JIM OTTO, Oak	SN*	AP	UPI	PFI
QB	LEN DAWSON, Dal	SN*	AP	UPI	PFI
HB	ABNER HAYNES, Dal	SN*	AP	UPI	PFI
FB	COOKIE GILCHRIST, Buf	SN*	AP	UPI	PFI

Defense

Pos	Player	SN	AP	UPI	PFI
E	DON FLOYD, Hou	SN*	AP	UPI	
E	MEL BRANCH, Dal	SN*			PFI
E	Larry Eisenhauer, Bos		AP	UPI	
E	Bob Dee, Bos				PFI
T	BUD MCFADIN, Den	SN*	AP	UPI	PFI
T	ED HUSMANN, Hou		AP	UPI	PFI
T	Jerry Mays, Dal	SN*			
LB	LARRY GRANTHAM, NY	SN*	AP	UPI	PFI
LB	SHERRILL HEADRICK, Dal	SN*	AP	UPI	PFI
LB	E.J. HOLUB, Dal	SN*	AP	UPI	PFI
CB	TONY BANFIELD, Hou	SN*	AP	UPI	PFI
CB	FRED WILLIAMSON, Oak	SN*	AP	UPI	PFI
S	BOBBY HUNT, Dal		AP	UPI	PFI
S	BOB ZEMAN, Den	SN*			PFI
S	Goose Gonsoulin, Den	SN*	AP		
S	Jim Norton, Hou			UPI	

1963 ALL-NFL

Offense

Pos	Player	AP	UPI	NYN	NEA
SE	DEL SHOFNER, NY	AP	UPI	NYN	NEA
TE	MIKE DITKA, Chi	AP	UPI	NYN	NEA
FL	BOBBY JOE CONRAD, StL	AP	UPI	NYN	
FL	Bobby Mitchell, Was				NEA
T	FORREST GREGG, GB	AP	UPI	NYN	NEA
T	ROOSEVELT BROWN, NY		UPI	NYN	NEA
T	Dick Schafrath, Cle	AP			
G	JERRY KRAMER, GB	AP	UPI	NYN	NEA
G	KEN GRAY, StL		UPI	NYN	
G	Jim Parker, Bal	AP			NEA
C	JIM RINGO, GB	AP	UPI	NYN	NEA
QB	Y.A. TITTLE, NY	AP	UPI	NYN	NEA
HB	TOMMY MASON, Min	AP	UPI	NYN	NEA
FB	JIM BROWN, Cle	AP	UPI	NYN	NEA

Defense

Pos	Player	AP	UPI	NYN	NEA
E	DOUG ATKINS, Chi	AP	UPI	NYN	NEA
E	JIM KATCAVAGE, NY	AP	UPI	NYN	
E	Gino Marchetti, Bal				NEA
T	ROGER BROWN, Det	AP	UPI	NYN	NEA
T	HENRY JORDAN, GB	AP	UPI	NYN	
LB	JOE FORTUNATO, Chi	AP	UPI	NYN	NEA
LB	BILL GEORGE, Chi	AP	UPI	NYN	
LB+	JACK PARDEE, LA		UPI		
LB+	MYRON POTTIOS, Pit				NEA
LB	Dan Currie, GB			NYN	
LB	Bill Forester, GB	AP			
LB	Joe Schmidt, Det				NEA
CB	DICK LYNCH, NY	AP	UPI	NYN	NEA
CB	NIGHT TRAIN LANE, Det		UPI	NYN	
CB	Herb Adderley, GB	AP			
CB	Abe Woodson, SF				NEA
S	RICHIE PETITBON, Chi	AP	UPI	NYN	
S	ROSEY TAYLOR, Chi	AP		NYN	NEA
S	Larry Wilson, StL		UPI		
S	Willie Wood, GB				NEA

1963 ALL-AFL

Offense

Pos	Player	SN	AP	UPI	NYN	NEA
SE	ART POWELL, Oak	SN*	AP	UPI	NYN	NEA
TE	FRED ARBANAS, KC	SN*	AP	UPI		
TE	Dave Kocourek, SD				NYN	NEA
FL	LANCE ALWORTH, SD	SN*	AP	UPI	NYN	NEA
T	RON MIX, SD	SN*	AP	UPI	NYN	NEA
T	STEW BARBER, Buf		AP	UPI	NYN	
T	Jim Tyrer, KC	SN*				NEA
G	BILLY SHAW, Buf	SN*	AP	UPI	NYN	
G	BOB TALAMINI, Hou	SN*	AP			NEA
G	Billy Neighbors, Bos			UPI		
C	JIM OTTO, Oak	SN*	AP	UPI	NYN	NEA
QB	TOBIN ROTE, SD	SN*	AP	UPI	NYN	NEA
HB	CLEM DANIELS, Oak	SN*	AP	UPI	NYN	NEA
FB	KEITH LINCOLN, SD	SN*	AP	UPI		NEA
FB	Cookie Gilchrist, Buf				NYN	

Defense

Pos	Player	SN	AP	UPI	NYN	NEA
E	LARRY EISENHAUER, Bos	SN*	AP	UPI	NYN	NEA
E	EARL FAISON, SD	SN*	AP	UPI	NYN	
E	Dalva Allen, Oak					NEA
T	HOUSTON ANTWINE, Bos	SN*	AP	UPI	NYN	NEA
T	TOM SESTAK, Buf	SN*	AP	UPI	NYN	NEA
LB	E.J. HOLUB, KC	SN*	AP	UPI	NYN	NEA
LB	LARRY GRANTHAM, NY		AP	UPI	NYN	NEA
LB	ARCHIE MATSOS, Oak	SN*	AP	UPI	NYN	
LB	Tom Addison, Bos	SN*				
LB	Nick Buoniconti, Bos					NEA
CB	FRED WILLIAMSON, Oak	SN*	AP	UPI	NYN	NEA
CB	TONY BANFIELD, Hou		AP	UPI	NYN	
CB	Dave Grayson, KC	SN*				
CB	Dick Westmoreland, SD					NEA
S	FRED GLICK, Hou	SN*	AP	UPI	NYN	NEA
S	TOM MORROW, Oak		AP	UPI	NYN	NEA
S	Goose Gonsoulin, Den	SN*				

1964 ALL-NFL

Offense

Pos	Player	AP	UPI	NYN	NEA
SE	FRANK CLARKE, Dal	AP		NYN	
SE	Bobby Mitchell, Was		UPI		
SE	Paul Warfield, Cle				NEA
TE	MIKE DITKA, Chi	AP	UPI	NYN	NEA

Pos	Player	AP	UPI	NYN	NEA
FL	JOHNNY MORRIS, Chi	AP	UPI	NYN	NEA
T	FORREST GREGG, GB	AP	UPI	NYN	NEA
T	DICK SCHAFRATH, Cle	AP	UPI	NYN	
T	Bob Vogel, Bal				NEA
G	JIM PARKER, Bal	AP	UPI	NYN	NEA
G	KEN GRAY, StL	AP	UPI	NYN	
G	John Gordy, Det				NEA
C+	BOB DEMARCO, StL			NYN	NEA
C+	MICK TINGLEHOFF, Min	AP	UPI		
QB	JOHNNY UNITAS, Bal	AP	UPI	NYN	NEA
HB	LENNY MOORE, Bal	AP	UPI	NYN	NEA
FB	JIM BROWN, Cle	AP	UPI	NYN	NEA

Defense

Pos	Player	AP	UPI	NYN	NEA
E	WILLIE DAVIS, GB	AP	UPI	NYN	NEA
E	GINO MARCHETTI, Bal	AP	UPI	NYN	NEA
T	BOB LILLY, Dal	AP	UPI	NYN	NEA
T	HENRY JORDAN, GB	AP	UPI	NYN	
T	Merlin Olsen, LA				NEA
LB	JOE FORTUNATO, Chi	AP	UPI		NEA
LB	RAY NITSCHKE, GB	AP	UPI	NYN	
LB	MAXIE BAUGHAN, Phi	AP		NYN	
LB	Jim Houston, Cle				NEA
LB	Dale Meinert, StL				NEA
LB	Wayne Walker, Det		UPI		
CB	PAT FISCHER, StL	AP	UPI	NYN	NEA
CB	BOBBY BOYD, Bal	AP	UPI	NYN	
CB	Erich Barnes, NY				NEA
S	PAUL KRAUSE, Was	AP	UPI	NYN	NEA
S	WILLIE WOOD, GB	AP	UPI		NEA
S	Mel Renfro, Dal			NYN	

1964 ALL-AFL

Offense

Pos	Player	SN	AP	UPI	NYN	NEA
SE	CHARLEY HENNIGAN, Hou	+SN*	AP	UPI	NYN	NEA
SE	Art Powell, Oak	+SN*				
TE	FRED ARBANAS, KC	SN*	AP	UPI	NYN	NEA
FL	LANCE ALWORTH, SD	SN*	AP	UPI	NYN	NEA
T	RON MIX, SD	SN*	AP	UPI	NYN	NEA
T	STEW BARBER, Buf		AP	UPI	NYN	NEA
T	Jim Tyrer, KC	SN*				
G	BILLY SHAW, Buf	SN*	AP	UPI	NYN	
G	BILLY NEIGHBORS, Bos		AP	UPI	NYN	
G	Bob Talamini, Hou	SN*				NEA
C	JIM OTTO, Oak	SN*	AP	UPI	NYN	
QB	BABE PARILLI, Bos	SN*	AP	UPI	NYN	NEA
HB	KEITH LINCOLN, SD	SN*	AP	UPI	NYN	NEA
FB	COOKIE GILCHRIST, Buf	SN*	AP	UPI	NYN	NEA

Defense

Pos	Player	SN	AP	UPI	NYN	NEA
E	EARL FAISON, SD	SN*	AP	UPI	NYN	NEA
E	LARRY EISENHAUER, Bos	SN*	AP		NYN	NEA
E	Bobby Bell, KC			UPI		
T	TOM SESTAK, Buf	SN*	AP	UPI	NYN	NEA
T	ERNIE LADD, SD		AP	UPI	NYN	NEA
T	Jerry Mays, KC	SN*				
LB	NICK BUONICONTI, Bos	SN*	AP		NYN	NEA
LB	LARRY GRANTHAM, NY	SN*	AP	UPI	NYN	NEA
LB	MIKE STRATTON, Buf	SN*	AP		NYN	
LB	Tom Addison, Bos	SN*				
CB	WILLIE BROWN, Den	SN*	AP	UPI	NYN	NEA
CB	DAVE GRAYSON, KC	SN*	AP		NYN	
CB	Dick Westmoreland, SD					NEA
CB	Fred Williamson, KC			UPI		
S	RON HALL, Bos		AP	UPI	NYN	NEA
S	DAINARD PAULSON, NY	SN*		UPI		NEA
S	George Saimes, Buf		AP		NYN	
S	Fred Glick, Hou	SN*				

1965 ALL-NFL

Offense

Pos	Player	AP	UPI	NYN	NEA
SE	DAVE PARKS, SF	AP	UPI	NYN	NEA
TE	PETE RETZLAFF, Phi	AP	UPI	NYN	NEA
FL	JIMMY ORR, Bal	AP			NEA
FL	Gary Collins, Cle		UPI	NYN	
T	DICK SCHAFRATH, Cle	AP	UPI	NYN	
T	BOB VOGEL, Bal			NYN	NEA
T	Bob Brown, Phi	AP			NEA
T	Forrest Gregg, GB	AP-g	UPI		
G	JIM PARKER, Bal	AP	UPI	NYN	NEA
G	KEN GRAY, StL		UPI	NYN	
G	John Gordy, Det				NEA
C	MICK TINGLEHOFF, Min	AP	UPI	NYN	NEA
QB	JOHNNY UNITAS, Bal	AP	UPI	NYN	NEA
HB	GALE SAYERS, Chi	AP	UPI	NYN	NEA
FB	JIM BROWN, Cle	AP	UPI	NYN	NEA

Defense

Pos	Player	AP	UPI	NYN	NEA
E	WILLIE DAVIS, GB	AP	UPI	NYN	NEA
E	DEACON JONES, LA	AP	UPI	NYN	NEA
T	ALEX KARRAS, Det	AP	UPI	NYN	NEA
T	BOB LILLY, Dal	AP	UPI	NYN	NEA
LB	WAYNE WALKER, Det	AP	UPI	NYN	NEA
LB	DICK BUTKUS, Chi	AP		NYN	NEA
LB	JOE FORTUNATO, Chi	AP			NEA
LB	Jim Houston, Cle		UPI		
LB	Ray Nitschke, GB		UPI		
LB	Steve Stonebreaker, Bal			NYN	
CB	HERB ADDERLEY, GB	AP	UPI	NYN	NEA
CB	BOBBY BOYD, Bal	AP	UPI	NYN	NEA
S	WILLIE WOOD, GB	AP	UPI	NYN	NEA
S	PAUL KRAUSE, Was	AP	UPI	NYN	
S	Mel Renfro, Dal				NEA

1965 ALL-AFL

Offense

Pos	Player	SN	AP	UPI	NYN	NEA
SE	LIONEL TAYLOR, Den	+SN*	AP	UPI	NYN	NEA
SE	Art Powell, Oak	+SN*				
TE	WILLIE FRAZIER, Hou	SN*	AP	UPI	NYN	NEA
FL	LANCE ALWORTH, SD	SN*	AP	UPI	NYN	NEA
T	JIM TYRER, KC	SN*	AP	UPI	NYN	NEA
T	RON MIX, SD		AP	UPI	NYN	NEA
T	Eldon Danenhauer, Den	SN*				
G	BILLY SHAW, Buf	SN*	AP	UPI	NYN	NEA
G	BOB TALAMINI, Hou	SN*	AP	UPI	NYN	
G	Wayne Hawkins, Oak					NEA
C	JIM OTTO, Oak	SN*	AP	UPI	NYN	NEA
QB	JACK KEMP, Buf	SN*	AP	UPI	NYN	NEA
HB	PAUL LOWE, SD	SN*	AP	UPI	NYN	NEA
FB	COOKIE GILCHRIST, Den	SN*	AP	UPI	NYN	NEA
K	Pete Gogolak, Buf	SN*	-	-	-	-

Defense

Pos	Player	SN	AP	UPI	NYN	NEA
E	EARL FAISON, SD	SN*	AP	UPI	NYN	NEA
E	JERRY MAYS, KC	SN*	AP		NYN	NEA
E	Ron McDole, Buf			UPI		
T	TOM SESTAK, Buf	SN*	AP	UPI	NYN	NEA
T	ERNIE LADD, SD	SN*	AP	UPI	NYN	NEA
LB	BOBBY BELL, KC	SN*	AP	UPI	NYN	NEA
LB	NICK BUONICONTI, Bos	SN*	AP	UPI	NYN	NEA
LB	MIKE STRATTON, Buf	SN*	AP	UPI	NYN	NEA
CB	DAVE GRAYSON, Oak	SN*	AP	UPI	NYN	NEA
CB	BUTCH BYRD, Buf	SN*	AP		NYN	
CB	Speedy Duncan, SD					NEA
CB	Fred Williamson, KC			UPI		
S	GEORGE SAIMES, Buf	SN*	AP	UPI	NYN	NEA
S	DAINARD PAULSON, NY			UPI	NYN	NEA
S	Johnny Robinson, KC	SN*	AP			
P	Curley Johnson, NY	SN*	-	-	-	-

1966 ALL-NFL

Offense

Pos	Player	AP	UPI	NYN	NEA
WR	BOB HAYES, Dal	AP	UPI	NYN	NEA
WR	PAT STUDSTILL, Det	AP	UPI	NYN	
WR	Dave Parks, SF				NEA
TE	JOHN MACKEY, Bal	AP	UPI	NYN	NEA
T	BOB BROWN, Phi	AP	UPI	NYN	NEA
T	FORREST GREGG, GB	AP	UPI	NYN	NEA
G	JERRY KRAMER, GB	AP	UPI	NYN	
G	JOHN THOMAS, SF	AP			NEA
G	John Gordy, Det		UPI		
G	Gene Hickerson, Cle				NEA
G	John Wooten, Cle			NYN	
C	MICK TINGLEHOFF, Min	AP	UPI	NYN	NEA
QB	BART STARR, GB	AP	UPI	NYN	NEA
RB	LEROY KELLY, Cle	AP	UPI	NYN	NEA
RB	GALE SAYERS, Chi	AP	UPI	NYN	NEA

Defense

Pos	Player	AP	UPI	NYN	NEA
E	WILLIE DAVIS, GB	AP	UPI	NYN	NEA
E	DEACON JONES, LA	AP	UPI	NYN	NEA
T	BOB LILLY, Dal	AP	UPI	NYN	NEA
T	MERLIN OLSEN, LA	AP	UPI	NYN	NEA
LB	RAY NITSCHKE, GB	AP	UPI	NYN	NEA
LB	LEE ROY CAFFEY, GB	AP	UPI	NYN	
LB	CHUCK HOWLEY, Dal	AP	UPI		NEA
LB	Maxie Baughan, LA				NEA
LB	Wayne Walker, Det			NYN	
CB	HERB ADDERLEY, GB	AP	UPI	NYN	NEA
CB	CORNELL GREEN, Dal	AP		NYN	NEA
CB	Bobby Boyd, Bal		UPI		
S	LARRY WILSON, StL	AP	UPI	NYN	NEA
S	WILLIE WOOD, GB	AP	UPI	NYN	NEA

1966 ALL-AFL

Offense

Pos	Player	SN	AP	UPI	NYN	NEA
SE	OTIS TAYLOR, KC		AP	UPI		NEA
SE	Art Powell, Oak	SN*			NYN	

TE	FRED ARBANAS, KC	SN*	AP	UPI	NYN	NEA
FL	LANCE ALWORTH, SD	SN*	AP	UPI	NYN	NEA
T	JIM TYRER, KC	SN*	AP	UPI	NYN	NEA
T	RON MIX, SD	SN*	AP	UPI	NYN	NEA
T	Sherman Plunkett, NY	SN*				
G	BILLY SHAW, Buf	SN*	AP	UPI	NYN	NEA
G	WAYNE HAWKINS, Oak			UPI	NYN	NEA
G	Ed Budde, KC		AP			
G	Bob Talamini, Hou	SN*				
C	JIM OTTO, Oak	SN*	AP	UPI	NYN	NEA
C	Jon Morris, Bos		AP			
QB	LEN DAWSON, KC	SN*	AP	UPI	NYN	NEA
HB	CLEM DANIELS, Oak	SN*	AP	UPI		
HB	Bobby Burnett, Buf				NYN	
FB	JIM NANCE, Bos	SN*	AP	UPI	NYN	NEA
K	Gino Cappelletti, Bos	SN*	-	-	-	-

Defense

E	JERRY MAYS, KC	SN*	AP	UPI	NYN	NEA
E	VERLON BIGGS, NY			UPI		NEA
E	Ron McDole, Buf		AP		NYN	
E	Larry Eisenhauer, Bos	SN*				
T	HOUSTON ANTWINE, Bos	SN*		UPI	NYN	NEA+
T	BUCK BUCHANAN, KC	SN*	AP	UPI		
T	Tom Sestak, Buf				NYN	NEA+
T	Jim Dunaway, Buf		AP			
T	Tom Keating, Oak					NEA
LB	BOBBY BELL, KC	SN*	AP	UPI	NYN	NEA
LB	NICK BUONICONTI, Bos	SN*	AP	UPI	NYN	NEA
LB	MIKE STRATTON, Buf	SN*	AP	UPI	NYN	NEA
CB	BUTCH BYRD, Buf	SN*	AP	UPI	NYN	NEA
CB	DAVE GRAYSON, Oak	SN*			NYN	NEA
CB	Kent McCloughan, Oak		AP	UPI		
S	JOHNNY ROBINSON, KC	SN*	AP	UPI	NYN	NEA
S	KENNY GRAHAM, SD		AP	UPI		NEA
S	George Saimes, Buf	SN*			NYN	
P	Bob Scarpitto, Den	SN*	-	-	-	-

1967 ALL-NFL
Offense

WR	HOMER JONES, NY		UPI	NYN	NEA
WR	CHARLEY TAYLOR, Was	AP	UPI		NEA
WR	Bob Hayes, Dal			NYN	
WR	Willie Richardson, Bal	AP			
TE	JOHN MACKEY, Bal	AP		NYN	NEA
TE	Jackie Smith, StL		UPI		
T	FORREST GREGG, GB	AP	UPI	NYN	
T	RALPH NEELY, Dal	AP	UPI	NYN	
T	Ernie McMillan, StL				NEA
T	Bob Vogel, Bal				NEA
G	GENE HICKERSON, Cle	AP	UPI	NYN	NEA
G	JERRY KRAMER, GB	AP	UPI	NYN	
G	Howard Mudd, SF				NEA
C	MICK TINGLEHOFF, Min		UPI	NYN	NEA
C	Bob DeMarco, StL	AP			
QB	JOHNNY UNITAS, Bal	AP	UPI	NYN	NEA
RB	LEROY KELLY, Cle	AP	UPI	NYN	NEA
RB	GALE SAYERS, Chi	AP	UPI	NYN	NEA

Defense

E	WILLIE DAVIS, GB	AP	UPI	NYN	NEA
E	DEACON JONES, LA	AP	UPI	NYN	NEA
T	BOB LILLY, Dal	AP	UPI	NYN	NEA
T	MERLIN OLSEN, LA	AP	UPI	NYN	NEA
LB	DAVE ROBINSON, GB	AP	UPI	NYN	NEA
LB	MAXIE BAUGHAN, LA		UPI	NYN	
LB	TOMMY NOBIS, Atl	AP		NYN	
LB	Dick Butkus, Chi		UPI		NEA
LB	Chuck Howley, Dal	AP			
LB	Dave Wilcox, SF				NEA
CB	CORNELL GREEN, Dal	AP	UPI	NYN	NEA
CB	BOB JETER, GB	AP	UPI	NYN	NEA
S	LARRY WILSON, StL	AP		NYN	NEA
S	WILLIE WOOD, GB	AP	UPI	NYN	
S	Eddie Meador, LA		UPI		NEA

1967 ALL-AFL
Offense

SE	GEORGE SAUER, NY	SN	AP	UPI	NYN	
SE	Al Denson, Den					NEA
TE	FRED ARBANAS, KC				NYN	NEA
TE	Billy Cannon, Oak		AP	UPI		
TE	Willie Frazier, SD	SN				
FL	LANCE ALWORTH, SD	SN	AP	UPI	NYN	NEA
T	RON MIX, SD		AP	UPI	NYN	NEA
T	JIM TYRER, KC	SN	AP		NYN	
T	Harry Schuh, Oak			UPI		NEA
T	Walt Suggs, Hou	SN				
G	WALT SWEENEY, SD		AP	UPI	NYN	NEA
G	BOB TALAMINI, Hou	SN	AP	UPI		NEA

G	Dave Herman, NY				NYN	
G	Gene Upshaw, Oak	SN				
C	JIM OTTO, Oak	SN	AP	UPI	NYN	NEA
QB	DARYLE LAMONICA, Oak	SN	AP	UPI		
QB	Joe Namath, NY				NYN	NEA
RB	MIKE GARRETT, KC	SN	AP	UPI	NYN	NEA
RB	JIM NANCE, Bos		AP	UPI	NYN	NEA
RB	Hewritt Dixon, Oak	SN				
K	George Blanda, Oak	SN	-	-	-	-

Defense

E	BEN DAVIDSON, Oak	SN	AP	UPI	NYN	
E	PAT HOLMES, Hou		AP	UPI		NEA
E	Jerry Mays, KC	SN				
E	Ron McDole, Buf					NEA
E	Gerry Philbin, NY				NYN	
T	BUCK BUCHANAN, KC	SN	AP	UPI	NYN	NEA
T	TOM KEATING, Oak	SN	AP	UPI		NEA
T	Houston Antwine, Bos				NYN	
LB	GEORGE WEBSTER, Hou	SN	AP	UPI	NYN	NEA
LB	BOBBY BELL, KC	SN	AP	UPI	NYN	
LB	NICK BUONICONTI, Bos	SN	AP	UPI	NYN	
LB	Dan Conners, Oak					NEA
LB	Mike Stratton, Buf					NEA
CB	MILLER FARR, Hou	SN	AP	UPI	NYN	NEA
CB	KENT MCCLOUGHAN, Oak	SN	AP	UPI	NYN	NEA
S	GEORGE SAIMES, Buf	SN	AP	UPI	NYN	NEA
S	JOHNNY ROBINSON, KC		AP	UPI	NYN	NEA
S	Kenny Graham, SD	SN				
P	Bob Scarpitto, Den	SN	-	-	-	-

1968 ALL-NFL
Offense

WR	CLIFTON MCNEIL, SF	AP	UPI	NYN	NEA	PFW	FWA
WR	PAUL WARFIELD, Cle		UPI		NEA	PFW	
WR	Bob Hayes, Dal	AP		NYN			
TE	JOHN MACKEY, Bal	AP	UPI	NYN	NEA	PFW*	FWA
T	RALPH NEELY, Dal	AP	UPI	NYN	NEA	PFW*	FWA
T	BOB BROWN, Phi	AP			NEA	PFW	
T	Bob Vogel, Bal		UPI	NYN			FWA
G	GENE HICKERSON, Cle	AP	UPI	NYN	NEA	PFW	FWA
G	HOWARD MUDD, SF	AP	UPI	NYN	NEA	PFW	FWA
C	MICK TINGLEHOFF, Min	AP	UPI	NYN	NEA	PFW	FWA
QB	EARL MORRALL, Bal	AP	UPI	NYN	NEA	PFW	
RB	LEROY KELLY, Cle	AP	UPI	NYN	NEA	PFW*	FWA
RB	GALE SAYERS, Chi	AP	UPI	NYN	NEA	PFW*	FWA
K	Mac Percival, Chi	-	-	-	-	PFW	

Defense

E	DEACON JONES, LA	AP	UPI	NYN	NEA	PFW*	FWA
E	CARL ELLER, Min	AP	UPI	NYN	NEA	PFW	FWA
T	BOB LILLY, Dal	AP	UPI	NYN	NEA	PFW	FWA
T	MERLIN OLSEN, LA	AP	UPI	NYN	NEA	PFW	FWA
LB	DICK BUTKUS, Chi	AP	UPI		NEA	PFW	FWA
LB	MIKE CURTIS, Bal	AP	UPI	NYN		PFW*	FWA
LB	CHUCK HOWLEY, Dal	AP			NEA	PFW	
LB	Dave Robinson, GB		UPI	NYN	NEA		
LB	Tommy Nobis, Atl			NYN			
CB	LEM BARNEY, Det	AP	UPI	NYN	NEA	PFW*	FWA
CB	BOBBY BOYD, Bal	AP	UPI	NYN		PFW	FWA
CB	Cornell Green, Dal				NEA		
S	LARRY WILSON, StL	AP	UPI	NYN	NEA	PFW*	FWA
S	WILLIE WOOD, GB		UPI	NYN		PFW	
S	Rick Volk, Bal				NEA		FWA
S	Eddie Meador, LA	AP					
P	Billy Lothridge, Atl	-	-	-	-	PFW	FWA

1968 ALL-AFL
Offense

WR	LANCE ALWORTH, SD	SN	AP	UPI	NYN	NEA	PFW*	FWA
WR	GEORGE SAUER, NY	SN	AP	UPI		NEA	PFW*	
WR	Don Maynard, NY				NYN			
TE	JIM WHALEN, Bos		AP	UPI		NEA	PFW	
TE	Alvin Reed, Hou	SN			NYN			
T	RON MIX, SD	SN	AP	UPI	NYN	NEA	PFW*	
T	JIM TYRER, KC		AP	UPI		NEA	PFW	
T	Harry Schuh, Oak				NYN			
T	Walt Suggs, Hou	SN						
G	WALT SWEENEY, SD	SN	AP	UPI	NYN	NEA	PFW*	
G	GENE UPSHAW, Oak	SN	AP	UPI			PFW	
G	Ed Budde, KC				NYN			
G	Dave Herman, NY					NEA		
C	JIM OTTO, Oak	SN	AP	UPI		NEA		
C	John Schmitt, NY				NYN			
QB	JOE NAMATH, NY	SN	AP	UPI	NYN	NEA	PFW	FWA
RB	HEWRITT DIXON, Oak	SN	AP	UPI	NYN	NEA	PFW	
RB	PAUL ROBINSON, Cin	SN	AP	UPI	NYN	NEA	PFW	
K	Jim Turner, NY		-	-	-	-	PFW	FWA
K	Jan Stenerud, KC	SN	-	-	-	-		

Defense

Pos	Player	SN	AP	UPI	NYN	NEA	PFW	FWA
E	GERRY PHILBIN, NY	SN	AP	UPI	NYN	NEA	PFW*	
E	RICH JACKSON, Den		AP	UPI			PFW	
E	Ike Lassiter, Oak				NYN			
E	Jerry Mays, KC	SN						
E	Ron McDole, Buf					NEA		
T	BUCK BUCHANAN, KC		AP	UPI	NYN	NEA	PFW	
T	DAN BIRDWELL, Oak	SN	AP	UPI			PFW	
T	Houston Antwine, Bos	SN				NEA		
T	John Elliott, NY				NYN			
LB	GEORGE WEBSTER, Hou	SN	AP	UPI	NYN	NEA	PFW	FWA
LB	BOBBY BELL, KC	SN	AP	UPI	NYN	NEA	PFW	
LB	DAN CONNERS, Oak			UPI	NYN		PFW	
LB	Willie Lanier, KC		AP			NEA		
LB	Nick Buoniconti, Bos	SN						
CB	MILLER FARR, Hou	SN	AP	UPI	NYN	NEA	PFW	
CB	WILLIE BROWN, Oak	SN	AP	UPI		NEA	PFW	
CB	Butch Byrd, Buf				NYN			
S	JOHNNY ROBINSON, KC	SN	AP	UPI	NYN	NEA	PFW	
S	DAVE GRAYSON, Oak		AP	UPI		NEA	PFW	
S	Kenny Graham, SD	SN						
S	Jim Hudson, NY				NYN			
S	George Saimes, Buf				NYN			
P	Jerrel Wilson, KC	SN	-	-	-	-	PFW	

1969 ALL-NFL

Offense

Pos	Player	AP	UPI	NYN	NEA	PFW	SI	FWA	OFF
WR	ROY JEFFERSON, Pit	AP+	UPI	NYN	NEA				
WR	PAUL WARFIELD, Cle				NEA*	PFW	SI		OFF
WR	Gene Washington, Min			NYN		PFW	SI		
WR	Gary Collins, Cle	AP							
WR	Dan Abramowicz, NO	AP+							
TE	JERRY SMITH, Was	AP	UPI	NYN	NEA*	PFW		FWA	
TE	Jackie Smith, StL						SI		
T	BOB BROWN, LA	AP	UPI	NYN	NEA*	PFW*	SI		OFF
T	RALPH NEELY, Dal	AP	UPI	NYN	NEA	PFW*	SI		OFF
T	Charley Cowan, LA						SI		
G	GENE HICKERSON, Cle	AP	UPI	NYN	NEA*	PFW*	SI	FWA	OFF
G	TOM MACK, LA		UPI		NEA				OFF
G	John Niland, Dal	AP				PFW			
G	Gale Gillingham, GB				NEA				
C	MICK TINGLEHOFF, Min	AP	UPI	NYN	NEA*	PFW*	SI	FWA	OFF
QB	ROMAN GABRIEL, LA	AP	UPI	NYN	NEA*	PFW*	SI	FWA	OFF
QB	Sonny Jurgensen, Was				NEA				
RB	GALE SAYERS, Chi	AP	UPI	NYN	NEA*	PFW*	SI	FWA	OFF
RB	CALVIN HILL, Dal	AP	UPI	NYN	NEA	PFW*	SI	FWA	OFF
RB	Leroy Kelly, Cle				NEA*				
K	Fred Cox, Min		-	-	-	PFW*	-		

Defense

Pos	Player	AP	UPI	NYN	NEA	PFW	SI	FWA	OFF
E	CARL ELLER, Min	AP	UPI	NYN	NEA*	PFW*		FWA	OFF
E	DEACON JONES, LA	AP	UPI	NYN	NEA*	PFW*	SI	FWA	OFF
T	MERLIN OLSEN, LA	AP	UPI	NYN	NEA*	PFW*	SI	FWA	OFF
T	BOB LILLY, Dal	AP		NYN	NEA*	PFW	SI	FWA	OFF
T	Alan Page, Min		UPI						
LB	DICK BUTKUS, Chi	AP	UPI	NYN	NEA*	PFW*	SI		OFF
LB	CHUCK HOWLEY, Dal	AP	UPI	NYN	NEA*	PFW*	SI		OFF
LB	DAVE ROBINSON, GB	AP	UPI	NYN	NEA	PFW	SI		
CB	LEM BARNEY, Det	AP	UPI	NYN	NEA*	PFW*	SI	FWA	OFF
CB	HERB ADDERLEY, GB	AP				PFW	SI+		
CB	Bobby Bryant, Min			NYN					
CB	Cornell Green, Dal		UPI				SI+		
CB	Jimmy Johnson, SF				NEA				
S	LARRY WILSON, StL	AP	UPI	NYN	NEA	PFW	SI	FWA	OFF
S	EDDIE MEADOR, LA	AP	UPI	NYN		PFW			
S	Mel Renfro, Dal				NEA*	PFW*			
S	Willie Wood, GB						SI		
P	DAVID LEE, Bal	-	-		NEA*	PFW*	-	FWA	OFF

1969 ALL-AFL

Offense

Pos	Player	SN	AP	UPI	NYN	NEA	PFW	SI	FWA	OFF
WR	FRED BILETNIKOFF, Oak	SN	AP		NYN	NEA	PFW*	SI	FWA	
WR	LANCE ALWORTH, SD	SN		UPI		NEA*	PFW*		FWA	OFF
WR	Don Maynard, NY		AP	UPI						
WR	Warren Wells, Oak			UPI						
TE	BOB TRUMPY, Cin		AP	UPI	NYN	NEA	PFW*	SI		OFF
TE	Alvin Reed, Hou	SN								
T	JIM TYRER, KC	SN	AP	UPI	NYN	NEA	PFW*	SI		OFF
T	WINSTON HILL, NY	SN			NYN	NEA*		SI		
T	Harry Schuh, Oak		AP				PFW			
G	ED BUDDE, KC	SN	AP		NYN	NEA*	PFW			
G	GENE UPSHAW, Oak	SN	AP	UPI	NYN			SI	FWA	
G	Walt Sweeney, SD			UPI		NEA*	PFW*	SI		
C	JIM OTTO, Oak	SN	AP	UPI	NYN	NEA	PFW*	SI	FWA	
QB	DARYLE LAMONICA, Oak	SN	AP	UPI			PFW*		FWA	
QB	Joe Namath, NY				NYN	NEA*	PFW*	SI		
RB	FLOYD LITTLE, Den	SN	AP	UPI	NYN	NEA	PFW*	SI		
RB	MATT SNELL, NY	SN	AP	UPI	NYN	NEA	PFW*	SI		
K	JAN STENERUD, KC	SN	-	-	-	NEA*	PFW	-		OFF
K	Jim Turner, NY		-	-	-				FWA	

Defense

Pos	Player	SN	AP	UPI	NYN	NEA	PFW	SI	FWA	OFF
E	RICH JACKSON, Den	SN	AP	UPI	NYN	NEA	PFW	SI		
E	GERRY PHILBIN, NY	SN	AP	UPI	NYN		PFW	SI		
E	Ron McDole, Buf					NEA				
T	BUCK BUCHANAN, KC	SN	AP	UPI	NYN		PFW*	SI		
T	JOHN ELLIOTT, NY		AP	UPI	NYN	NEA	PFW	SI		
T	Houston Antwine, Hou	SN								
T	Tom Keating, Oak					NEA				
LB	BOBBY BELL, KC	SN	AP	UPI	NYN	NEA*	PFW*	SI	FWA	OFF
LB	GEORGE WEBSTER, Hou	SN	AP	UPI	NYN	NEA	PFW		FWA	
LB	NICK BUONICONTI, Mia		AP	UPI		NEA		SI		
LB	Willie Lanier, KC				NYN		PFW			
LB	Dan Conners, Oak	SN								
CB	WILLIE BROWN, Oak	SN	AP	UPI	NYN	NEA*	PFW*	SI	FWA	OFF
CB	BUTCH BYRD, Buf		AP	UPI	NYN	NEA	PFW	SI		
CB	Miller Farr, Hou	SN								
S	DAVE GRAYSON, Oak	SN	AP	UPI		NEA*	PFW*	SI	FWA	
S	JERRY ROBINSON, KC	SN	AP	UPI	NYN	NEA	PFW			OFF
S	Ken Houston, Hou				NYN			SI		
P	Dennis Partee, SD	SN	-	-	-					
P	Paul Maguire, Buf						PFW			

1970 ALL-NFC

Offense

Pos	Player	AP	UPI	SN	PB	PFW	FWA	NEA
WR	DICK GORDON, Chi	AP*	UPI	SN	PB	PFW*	FWA	NEA
WR	GENE WASHINGTON, SF	AP*	UPI	SN	PB	PFW*	FWA	NEA
TE	CHARLIE SANDERS, Det	AP*	UPI	SN	PB	PFW	FWA	NEA
T	BOB BROWN, LA	AP*		SN	PB	PFW*	FWA	NEA
T	ERNIE MCMILLAN, StL		UPI	SN	PB			
T	Cas Banaszek, SF	AP						
T	Rocky Freitas, Det					PFW		
T	Ron Yary, Min			SN				
G	GALE GILLINGHAM, GB	AP*	UPI	SN	PB	PFW		NEA
G	TOM MACK, LA	AP	UPI	SN	PB	PFW*		
G	John Niland, Dal		UPI					
C	MICK TINGLEHOFF, Min					PFW*	FWA	
C	Ed Flanagan, Det		UPI	SN	PB			
QB	JOHN BRODIE, SF	AP*	UPI	SN	PB	PFW	FWA	NEA
RB	LARRY BROWN, Was	AP*	UPI	SN	PB	PFW*	FWA	NEA
RB	MACARTHUR LANE, StL							NEA
RB	Ron Johnson, NY	AP*				PFW*	FWA	
K	Fred Cox, Min		-	SN	PB	-	-	
KR	Cecil Turner, Chi		-		PB	-		

Defense

Pos	Player	AP	UPI	SN	PB	PFW	FWA	NEA
E	CARL ELLER, Min	AP*	UPI	SN	PB	PFW*	FWA	NEA
E	DEACON JONES, LA		UPI	SN	PB	PFW*		
E	Claude Humphrey, Atl	AP				PFW		
T	MERLIN OLSEN, LA	AP*	UPI	SN	PB	PFW*	FWA	NEA
T	ALAN PAGE, Min	AP*	UPI	SN	PB	PFW*	FWA	NEA
LB	DICK BUTKUS, Chi	AP*	UPI	SN	PB	PFW*	FWA	NEA
LB	CHUCK HOWLEY, Dal	AP*	UPI	SN	PB			
LB+	PAUL NAUMOFF, Det	AP				PFW		
LB+	DAVE WILCOX, SF				PB			NEA
LB	Larry Stallings, StL				PB			
LB	Chris Hanburger, Was			SN				
CB	JIMMY JOHNSON, SF	AP*	UPI	SN	PB	PFW	FWA	NEA
CB	ROGER WEHRLI, StL	AP*	UPI	SN	PB	PFW		
CB	Mel Renfro, Dal	AP						
S	LARRY WILSON, StL	AP*	UPI	SN	PB	PFW*	FWA	NEA
S+	SPIDER LOCKHART, NY	AP						
S+	WILLIE WOOD, GB			SN	PB			
S	Paul Krause, Min		UPI					
P	Julian Fagan, NO		-	-		-	-	
P	Bobby Joe Green, Chi		-		PB	-	-	

1970 ALL-AFC

Offense

Pos	Player	AP	UPI	SN	PB	PFW	FWA	NEA
WR	MARLIN BRISCOE, Buf	AP	UPI	SN+	PB	PFW		
WR	WARREN WELLS, Oak		UPI	SN+	PB	PFW		
WR	Fred Biletnikoff, Oak	AP						
WR	Paul Warfield, Mia			SN				
TE	BOB TRUMPY, Cin	AP		SN				
TE	Alvin Reed, Hou		UPI			PFW		
TE	Raymond Chester, Oak				PB			
T	JIM TYRER, KC	AP*	UPI	SN	PB	PFW*	FWA	NEA
T	WINSTON HILL, NY	AP	UPI	SN	PB			
T	Harry Schuh, Oak				PB	PFW		
G	GENE UPSHAW, Oak	AP*		SN		PFW*	FWA	
G	WALT SWEENEY, SD	AP	UPI	SN	PB			NEA
G	Ed Budde, KC		UPI					
G	Gene Hickerson, Cle		UPI				FWA	
G	Randy Rasmussen, NY				PB			
C	JIM OTTO, Oak	AP*	UPI	SN	PB			NEA
QB	DARYLE LAMONICA, Oak	AP	UPI		PB	PFW		
QB	Bob Griese, Mia			SN				
RB	FLOYD LITTLE, Den	AP	UPI	SN	PB			
RB	HEWRITT DIXON, Oak	AP	UPI		PB			
RB	Larry Csonka, Mia					PFW		
RB	Leroy Kelly, Cle				PB			

Pos	Player	AP	UPI	SN	PB	PFW	FWA	NEA
RB	Jess Phillips, Cin			SN				
K	JAN STENERUD, KC	AP*		SN	PB	-	FWA	-
KR	Lemar Parrish, Cin				PB	-	-	-

Defense

Pos	Player	AP	UPI	SN	PB	PFW	FWA	NEA
E	RICH JACKSON, Den	AP*	UPI	SN	PB	PFW	FWA	NEA
E	BUBBA SMITH, Bal		UPI	SN	PB	PFW		
E	Aaron Brown, KC	AP						
T	JOHN ELLIOTT, NY	AP	UPI			PFW		
T	JOE GREENE, Pit		UPI	SN	PB			
T	Buck Buchanan, KC	AP			PB			
T	Tom Keating, Oak			SN		PFW		
LB	BOBBY BELL, KC	AP*	UPI	SN	PB	PFW*	FWA	NEA
LB	WILLIE LANIER, KC	AP	UPI	SN	PB	PFW		
LB	ANDY RUSSELL, Pit	AP	UPI	SN	PB	PFW		
CB	WILLIE BROWN, Oak	AP	UPI	SN	PB	PFW*	FWA	
CB	JIM MARSALIS, KC	AP*	UPI	SN	PB	PFW*		
S	JOHNNY ROBINSON, KC	AP*	UPI	SN	PB	PFW*	FWA	NEA
S	KEN HOUSTON, Hou				PB	PFW		
S	Jerry Logan, Bal	AP	UPI					
S	Rick Volk, Bal			SN				
P	Dave Lewis, Cin	AP*	-				FWA	-
P	David Lee, Bal	-	-	SN				
P	Jerrel Wilson, KC	-	-		PB	-	-	-

1971 ALL-NFC

Offense

Pos	Player	AP	UPI	SN	PB	PFW	FWA	NEA
WR	GENE WASHINGTON, SF	AP	UPI	SN	PB	PFW		
WR	ROY JEFFERSON, Was	AP				PFW		
WR	Bob Grim, Min		UPI	SN				
WR	Dick Gordon, Chi				PB			
TE	CHARLIE SANDERS, Det	AP*	UPI	SN	PB	PFW	FWA	NEA
T	RON YARY, Min	AP*	UPI	SN	PB	PFW*	FWA	NEA
T	RAYFIELD WRIGHT, Dal	AP*					FWA	
T	Cas Banaszek, SF					PFW		
T	Charley Cowan, LA			SN				
T	George Kunz, Atl				PB			
T	Ernie McMillan, StL		UPI					
G	JOHN NILAND, Dal	AP*		SN	PB	PFW		
G+	GALE GILLINGHAM, GB		UPI	SN	PB	PFW		NEA
G+	TOM MACK, LA	AP	UPI	SN	PB			NEA
C	FORREST BLUE, SF	AP*	UPI		PB	PFW	FWA	
C	Ed Flanagan, Det			SN+				
C	Len Hauss, Was			SN+				
QB	ROGER STAUBACH, Dal	AP		SN	PB	PFW		
QB	Greg Landry, Det		UPI					
RB	JOHN BROCKINGTON, GB	AP*	UPI	SN	PB	PFW	FWA	NEA
RB	LARRY BROWN, Was		UPI	SN	PB	PFW		
RB	Steve Owens, Det	AP						
K	CURT KNIGHT, Was	-	-	SN				NEA
K	Fred Cox, Min	-	-			PFW		-
KR	Speedy Duncan, Was	-	-		PB			-

Defense

Pos	Player	AP	UPI	SN	PB	PFW	FWA	NEA
E	CARL ELLER, Min	AP*	UPI	SN		PFW*	FWA	NEA
E	CLAUDE HUMPHREY, Atl	AP	UPI	SN	PB	PFW		NEA
E	Cedrick Hardman, SF				PB			
T	BOB LILLY, Dal	AP*	UPI	SN	PB	PFW	FWA	NEA
T	ALAN PAGE, Min	AP*	UPI	SN	PB	PFW*	FWA	NEA
LB	DAVE WILCOX, SF	AP*	UPI	SN	PB	PFW	FWA	NEA
LB	DICK BUTKUS, Chi	AP	UPI	SN	PB	PFW		
LB	JACK PARDEE, Was	AP	UPI	SN		PFW		
LB	Chuck Howley, Dal				PB			
LB	Mike Lucci, Det			SN				
LB	Isiah Robertson, LA			SN				
CB	JIMMY JOHNSON, SF	AP*	UPI		PB	PFW*	FWA	
CB	MEL RENFRO, AP	AP						NEA
CB	Roger Wehrli, StL		UPI	SN				
S	BILL BRADLEY, Phi	AP*	UPI	SN+	PB	PFW*	FWA	
S	PAUL KRAUSE, Min		UPI			PFW		NEA
S	Cornell Green, Dal	AP			PB			
S	Willie Wood, GB			SN+				
P	Ron Widby, Dal	-	-	SN	PB			-
P	Tom McNeill, Phi					PFW		

1971 ALL-AFC

Offense

Pos	Player	AP	UPI	SN	PB	PFW	FWA	NEA
WR	PAUL WARFIELD, Mia	AP*	UPI	SN	PB	PFW*	FWA	
WR	OTIS TAYLOR, KC	AP*	UPI	SN		PFW*	FWA	NEA
WR	Fred Biletnikoff, Oak				PB			
TE	RAYMOND CHESTER, Oak			SN		PFW		
TE	Milt Morin, Cle	AP	UPI					
T	JIM TYRER, KC	AP	UPI			PFW		
T	BOB BROWN, Oak	AP		SN				NEA
T	Winston Hill, NY		UPI					
T	Bob Vogel, Bal					PFW		
G	LARRY LITTLE, Mia	AP*	UPI	SN	PB	PFW*	FWA	
G	WALT SWEENEY, SD	AP	UPI		PB			
G	Gene Upshaw, Oak			SN		PFW		
C	BILL CURRY, Bal	AP	UPI		PB			
C	Jim Otto, Oak			SN				NEA

Pos	Player	AP	UPI	SN	PB	PFW	FWA	NEA
QB	BOB GRIESE, Mia	AP*	UPI	SN	PB	PFW	FWA	NEA
RB	LARRY CSONKA, Mia	AP*	UPI	SN	PB	PFW	FWA	
RB	FLOYD LITTLE, Den	AP	UPI	SN	PB	PFW*		
RB	Leroy Kelly, Cle							NEA
K	GARO YEPREMIAN, Mia	AP*	-	SN		PFW*	FWA+	
K	Jan Stenerud, KC		-	-			FWA+	-
KR	Mercury Morris, Mia		-	-			-	-

Defense

Pos	Player	AP	UPI	SN	PB	PFW	FWA	NEA
E	BUBBA SMITH, Bal	AP*	UPI	SN	PB	PFW	FWA	
E	ELVIN BETHEA, Hou				PB	PFW		
E	Aaron Brown, KC	AP						
E	Rich Jackson, Den			SN				
E	Bill Stanfill, Mia		UPI					
T	JOE GREENE, Pit	AP	UPI	SN	PB	PFW		
T	MIKE REID, Cin	AP	UPI	SN+				
T	Buck Buchanan, KC				PB	PFW		
T	Manny Fernandez, Mia			SN+				
LB	TED HENDRICKS, Bal	AP*	UPI	SN	PB	PFW	FWA	NEA
LB	WILLIE LANIER, KC	AP*	UPI	SN		PFW	FWA	NEA
LB	BOBBY BELL, KC	AP	UPI	SN	PB	PFW*		
LB	Mike Curtis, Bal				PB			
CB	WILLIE BROWN, Oak	AP*	UPI	SN	PB	PFW*	FWA	
CB	EMMITT THOMAS, KC	AP			PB	PFW		
CB	Jim Marsalis, KC		UPI	SN				
S	KEN HOUSTON, Hou		UPI	SN	PB	PFW*		
S	RICK VOLK, Bal	AP*			PB	PFW	FWA	NEA
S	Jake Scott, Mia	AP	UPI					
S	Jerry Logan, Bal			SN+				
S	Johnny Robinson, KC			SN+				
P	JERREL WILSON, KC	-	-	SN		PFW*	FWA	-

1972 ALL-NFC

Offense

Pos	Player	AP	UPI	SN	PB	PFW	FWA	NEA
WR	GENE WASHINGTON, SF	AP*	UPI	SN	PB	PFW	FWA	
WR	HAROLD JACKSON, Phi	AP	UPI	SN				
WR	John Gilliam, Min				PB			
TE	TED KWALICK, SF	AP*	UPI			PFW*		NEA
TE	Bob Tucker, NY			SN			FWA	
T	RAYFIELD WRIGHT, Dal	AP*	UPI	SN	PB	PFW*	FWA	NEA
T	RON YARY, Min	AP*	UPI	SN	PB	PFW		
T	George Kunz, Atl							NEA
G	JOHN NILAND, Dal	AP*	UPI	SN	PB	PFW*		
G	TOM MACK, LA	AP	UPI	SN	PB			
G	Blaine Nye, Dal							NEA
C	FORREST BLUE, SF	AP*	UPI	SN	PB	PFW*	FWA	
C	Len Hauss, Was							NEA
QB	BILLY KILMER, Was	AP			PB			
QB	Fran Tarkenton, Min		UPI	SN				
RB	LARRY BROWN, Was	AP*	UPI	SN	PB	PFW*	FWA	NEA
RB	JOHN BROCKINGTON, GB	AP	UPI	SN	PB			
K	CHESTER MARCOL, GB	AP*	-	SN	PB	PFW*	FWA	NEA
KR	Ron Smith, Chi		-	-		PB	-	-	-

Defense

Pos	Player	AP	UPI	SN	PB	PFW	FWA	NEA
E	CLAUDE HUMPHREY, Atl	AP*	UPI	SN	PB	PFW	FWA	NEA
E	JACK GREGORY, NY	AP	UPI			PFW*	FWA	NEA
E	Coy Bacon, LA				PB			
E	Carl Eller, Min			SN				
T	BOB LILLY, Dal	AP	UPI	SN	PB	PFW*		
T	ALAN PAGE, Min	AP	UPI	SN	PB			
T	Merlin Olsen, LA				PB			
LB	CHRIS HANBURGER, Was	AP*	UPI	SN	PB	PFW*	FWA	NEA
LB	DAVE WILCOX, SF	AP*	UPI	SN	PB	PFW*	FWA	NEA
LB	DICK BUTKUS, Chi	AP	UPI	SN			FWA	
LB	Tommy Nobis, Atl				PB			
CB	JIMMY JOHNSON, SF	AP*		SN	PB	PFW*	FWA	NEA
CB	LEM BARNEY, Det		UPI	SN	PB			
CB	Ken Ellis, GB	AP*	UPI					
S	BILL BRADLEY, Phi	AP*	UPI	SN	PB	PFW*	FWA	
S	PAUL KRAUSE, Min	AP	UPI	SN				
S	Cornell Green, Dal				PB			
P	Dave Chapple, LA	-	-	SN	PB			

1972 ALL-AFC

Offense

Pos	Player	AP	UPI	SN	PB	PFW	FWA	NEA
WR	FRED BILETNIKOFF, Oak	AP*	UPI	SN	PB	PFW*		NEA
WR	PAUL WARFIELD, Mia	AP	UPI	SN	PB			NEA
WR	Otis Taylor, KC		UPI				FWA	
TE	RAYMOND CHESTER, Oak	AP	UPI	SN	PB			
T	BOB BROWN, Oak	AP	UPI	SN	PB	PFW*		
T	WINSTON HILL, NY	AP	UPI	SN	PB			
T	Art Shell, Oak				PB			
G	LARRY LITTLE, Mia	AP*	UPI	SN	PB	PFW*	FWA	
G	GENE UPSHAW, Oak	AP	UPI		PB		FWA	
G	Bruce Van Dyke, Pit			SN				
C	JIM OTTO, Oak	AP		SN	PB			
C	Bob Johnson, Cin		UPI					
QB	JOE NAMATH, NY		UPI	SN	PB	PFW*	FWA	NEA
QB	Earl Morrall, Mia	AP*						
RB	O.J. SIMPSON, Buf	AP*	UPI	SN+	PB		FWA	NEA

Pos	Player	AP	UPI	SN	PB	PFW	FWA	NEA
RB	LARRY CSONKA, Mia	AP	UPI	SN+	PB	PFW*		
RB	Franco Harris, Pit			SN				
K	Roy Gerela, Pit		-	SN	PB			
KR	Mercury Morris, Mia				PB	-	-	-

Defense

Pos	Player	AP	UPI	SN	PB	PFW	FWA	NEA
E	BILL STANFILL, Mia	AP*	UPI	SN	PB			
E+	ELVIN BETHEA, Hou			SN				
E+	DEACON JONES, SD				PB			
E	Vern Den Herder, Mia	AP						
E	Dwight White, Pit		UPI					
T	JOE GREENE, Pit	AP*	UPI	SN		PFW*	FWA	NEA
T	MIKE REID, Cin	AP*	UPI	SN			FWA	
LB	ANDY RUSSELL, Pit	AP	UPI	SN	PB			
LB	TED HENDRICKS, Bal	AP	UPI		PB			
LB	WILLIE LANIER, KC		UPI	SN		PFW*		
LB	Nick Buoniconti, Mia	AP			PB			
LB	Bobby Bell, KC			SN				
CB	WILLIE BROWN, Oak	AP	UPI		PB			
CB	ROBERT JAMES, Buf	AP	UPI					
CB	Lemar Parrish, Cin			SN				
S	DICK ANDERSON, Mia	AP*	UPI	SN			FWA	NEA
S	JAKE SCOTT, Mia	AP	UPI	SN	PB	PFW*		
S	Ken Houston, Hou				PB			
P	JERREL WILSON, KC	-	-	SN	PB	PFW*	FWA	
P	Don Cockroft, Cle	-	-					NEA

1973 ALL-NFC
Offense

Pos	Player	AP	UPI	SN	PB	PFW	FWA	NEA
WR	HAROLD JACKSON, LA	AP*	UPI	SN	PB	PFW*	FWA	NEA
WR	HAROLD CARMICHAEL, Phi	AP				PFW*	FWA	
WR	John Gilliam, Min		UPI	SN				NEA
WR	Charley Taylor, Was				PB			
TE	CHARLE YOUNG, Phi	AP*				PFW*	FWA	
TE	Ted Kwalick, SF		UPI	SN	PB			
T	RON YARY, Min	AP*	UPI	SN	PB	PFW*	FWA	
T	RAYFIELD WRIGHT, Dal	AP*	UPI	SN	PB		FWA	
T	George Kunz, Atl					PFW*		NEA
G	TOM MACK, LA	AP	UPI	SN	PB	PFW*		
G	JOHN NILAND, Dal	AP	UPI	SN	PB			
G	Gale Gillingham, GB				PB	PFW		
G	Joe Scibelli, LA							NEA
C	FORREST BLUE, SF	AP*	UPI	SN	PB	PFW*	FWA	
QB	JOHN HADL, LA	AP*	UPI	SN		PFW*	FWA	
QB	Fran Tarkenton, Min							NEA
RB	JOHN BROCKINGTON, GB	AP	UPI	SN	PB	PFW		NEA
RB	CALVIN HILL, Dal	AP	UPI	SN	PB	PFW	FWA	
K	NICK MIKE-MAYER, Atl	AP	-	SN+	PB			
K	Bruce Gossett, SF		-	SN+		PFW		
KR	Herb Mulkey, Was		-	-	PB	-	-	

Defense

Pos	Player	AP	UPI	SN	PB	PFW	FWA	NEA
E	CLAUDE HUMPHREY, Atl	AP	UPI	SN	PB	PFW*	FWA	
E	CARL ELLER, Min	AP*	UPI	SN	PB	PFW*		
T	ALAN PAGE, Min	AP*	UPI	SN	PB	PFW*	FWA	NEA-e
T	MERLIN OLSEN, LA	AP	UPI	SN	PB	PFW		
LB	LEE ROY JORDAN, Dal	AP	UPI	SN		PFW*	FWA	NEA
LB	CHRIS HANBURGER, Was	AP*	UPI	SN	PB	PFW*		NEA
LB	DAVE WILCOX, SF		UPI	SN	PB	PFW*	FWA	NEA
LB	Isiah Robertson, LA	AP*					FWA	
CB	MEL RENFRO, Dal	AP	UPI	SN	PB	PFW*	FWA	NEA
CB	KEN ELLIS, GB	AP	UPI	SN	PB	PFW		
CB	Lem Barney, Det				PB			
CB	Bobby Bryant, Min					PFW		
S	KEN HOUSTON, Was	AP	UPI	SN	PB	PFW		
S	PAUL KRAUSE, Min	AP	UPI	SN	PB	PFW		
S	Bill Bradley, Phi							NEA
P	TOM WITTUM, SF	-	UPI	SN	PB			

1973 ALL-AFC
Offense

Pos	Player	AP	UPI	SN	PB	PFW	FWA	NEA
WR	PAUL WARFIELD, Mia	AP*	UPI	SN		PFW		
WR	FRED BILETNIKOFF, Oak	AP		SN		PFW		
WR	Ron Shanklin, Pit		UPI		PB			
WR	Isaac Curtis, Cin				PB			
TE	RILEY ODOMS, Den	AP	UPI	SN	PB	PFW		NEA
T	ART SHELL, Oak	AP	UPI		PB	PFW		NEA
T	WINSTON HILL, NY		UPI	SN	PB	PFW		
T	Norm Evans, Mia	AP						
T	Russ Washington, SD			SN				
G	LARRY LITTLE, Mia	AP*	UPI	SN	PB	PFW		NEA
G	REGGIE MCKENZIE, Buf	AP*	UPI	SN			FWA	
G	Gene Upshaw, Oak				PB	PFW		
C	JIM LANGER, Mia		UPI	SN	PB	PFW		
C	Bob Johnson, Cin							NEA
C	Jack Rudnay, KC	AP						
QB+	CHARLEY JOHNSON, Den		UPI					
QB+	KEN STABLER, Oak	AP						
QB	Bob Griese, Mia			SN				
RB	O.J. SIMPSON, Buf	AP*	UPI	SN	PB	PFW*		
RB	LARRY CSONKA, Mia	AP*	UPI	SN	PB	PFW*		

Pos	Player	AP	UPI	SN	PB	PFW	FWA	NEA
K	GARO YEPREMIAN, Mia	AP*	-	SN+	PB	PFW*	FWA	NEA
K	George Blanda, Oak		-	SN+				
KR	Greg Pruitt, Cle		-	-	PB	-	-	-

Defense

Pos	Player	AP	UPI	SN	PB	PFW	FWA	NEA
E	BILL STANFILL, Mia	AP	UPI	SN	PB	PFW	FWA	NEA
E	DWIGHT WHITE, Pit	AP	UPI	SN				
E	L.C. Greenwood, Pit				PB	PFW		
T	JOE GREENE, Pit	AP*	UPI	SN	PB	PFW*	FWA	NEA
T	MIKE REID, Cin	AP	UPI	SN	PB			NEA
T	Paul Smith, Den					PFW		
LB	WILLIE LANIER, KC	AP*	UPI	SN	PB	PFW		
LB	JACK HAM, Pit	AP	UPI	SN	PB	PFW		
LB	ANDY RUSSELL, Pit		UPI	SN	PB	PFW		
LB	Ted Hendricks, Bal	AP						
CB	WILLIE BROWN, Oak	AP*		SN	PB	PFW*	FWA	NEA
CB	ROBERT JAMES, Buf	AP*	UPI	SN		PFW		
CB	Clarence Scott, Cle		UPI		PB			
S	DICK ANDERSON, Mia	AP*	UPI	SN	PB	PFW	FWA	
S	JAKE SCOTT, Mia	AP*	UPI	SN			FWA	
S	Mike Wagner, Pit					PFW*		
S	Jack Tatum, Oak					PFW		
P	RAY GUY, Oak	-	-	SN	PB	PFW*	FWA	NEA

1974 ALL-NFC
Offense

Pos	Player	AP	UPI	SN	PB	PFW	FWA	NEA
WR	DREW PEARSON, Dal	AP*	UPI	SN	PB	PFW*	FWA	
WR	CHARLEY TAYLOR, Was	AP	UPI	SN	PB			
WR	Mel Gray, StL					PFW		NEA
TE	CHARLE YOUNG, Phi	AP	UPI	SN	PB	PFW		
T	RON YARY, Min	AP*	UPI	SN	PB	PFW*	FWA	
T	RAYFIELD WRIGHT, Dal	AP	UPI	SN	PB	PFW		
G	TOM MACK, LA	AP	UPI	SN	PB	PFW*	FWA	
G	GALE GILLINGHAM, GB	AP	UPI	SN	PB	PFW		
G	John Niland, Dal					PFW		
G	Ed White, Min							NEA
C	FORREST BLUE, SF		UPI	SN+		PFW		
C	Len Hauss, Was	AP		SN+				
C	Jeff Van Note, Atl				PB			
QB	JIM HART, StL	AP	UPI	SN	PB	PFW		
RB	LAWRENCE MCCUTCHEON, LA	AP	UPI	SN	PB	PFW		NEA
RB	CHUCK FOREMAN, Min	AP	UPI	SN	PB	PFW		
K	CHESTER MARCOL, GB	AP*	UPI	SN	PB	PFW*	FWA	
KR	Dick Jauron, Det	-	-		PB	-	-	-

Defense

Pos	Player	AP	UPI	SN	PB	PFW	FWA	NEA
E	CLAUDE HUMPHREY, Atl	AP	UPI	SN	PB	PFW*		
E	JACK YOUNGBLOOD, LA	AP*	UPI	SN		PFW	FWA	
E	Fred Dryer, LA							NEA
E	Carl Eller, Min				PB			
T	ALAN PAGE, Min	AP*	UPI	SN	PB	PFW*	FWA	NEA
T	WALLY CHAMBERS, Chi	AP		SN				
T	Larry Brooks, LA					PFW		
T	John Mendenhall, NY		UPI					
T	Merlin Olsen, LA				PB			
LB	BILL BERGEY, Phi	AP*	UPI	SN	PB	PFW	FWA	
LB	TED HENDRICKS, GB	AP	UPI	SN	PB	PFW		
LB	CHRIS HANBURGER, Was	AP	UPI	SN	PB	PFW		
CB	ROGER WEHRLI, StL	AP	UPI	SN	PB	PFW*		NEA
CB	MIKE BASS, Was	AP	UPI	SN				
CB	Willie Buchanon, GB				PB			
CB	Nate Wright, Min					PFW		
S	KEN HOUSTON, Was	AP	UPI	SN	PB	PFW	FWA	
S	CLIFF HARRIS, Dal		UPI	SN	PB	PFW		
S	Dave Elmendorf, LA	AP						
S	Paul Krause, Min				PB			
P	TOM WITTUM, SF	-	UPI	SN	PB	PFW		

1974 ALL-AFC
Offense

Pos	Player	AP	UPI	SN	PB	PFW	FWA	NEA
WR	CLIFF BRANCH, Oak	AP*	UPI	SN	PB	PFW*	FWA	NEA
WR	ISAAC CURTIS, Cin	AP	UPI	SN	PB			
WR	Paul Warfield, Mia					PFW		
TE	RILEY ODOMS, Den	AP*	UPI	SN	PB	PFW*	FWA	NEA
T	ART SHELL, Oak	AP*	UPI	SN	PB	PFW*	FWA	NEA
T	RUSS WASHINGTON, SD	AP		SN+	PB			
T	Winston Hill, NY		UPI			PFW		
T	Norm Evans, Mia			SN+				
G	LARRY LITTLE, Mia	AP*	UPI	SN+	PB		FWA	
G	GENE UPSHAW, Oak	AP*			PB	PFW*		
G	Reggie McKenzie, Buf		UPI	SN				
G	John Hannah, NE			SN+				
G	Bob Kuechenberg, Mia					PFW		
C	JIM LANGER, Mia	AP	UPI	SN	PB	PFW	FWA	NEA
QB	KEN STABLER, Oak	AP*	UPI	SN	PB	PFW*	FWA	NEA
RB	O.J. SIMPSON, Buf	AP*	UPI	SN	PB	PFW*	FWA	NEA
RB	OTIS ARMSTRONG, Den	AP*	UPI	SN	PB	PFW*	FWA	
K	ROY GERELA, Pit	AP	UPI	SN	PB			
K	John Leypoldt, Buf					PFW		
K	Jan Stenerud, KC							NEA
KR	Greg Pruitt, Cle	-	-	-	PB	-	-	

Defense

		AP	UPI	SN	PB	PFW	FWA	NEA
E	L.C. GREENWOOD, Pit	AP*	UPI	SN	PB	PFW*	FWA	
E	BILL STANFILL, Mia	AP*	UPI	SN	PB			
E	Elvin Bethea, Hou					PFW		
T	JOE GREENE, Pit	AP*	UPI	SN	PB	PFW*	FWA	NEA
T	OTIS SISTRUNK, Oak	AP	UPI					
T	Mike Reid, Cin					PFW		
T	Jerry Sherk, Cle				PB			
T	Art Thoms, Oak			SN				
LB	JACK HAM, Pit	AP*	UPI	SN	PB	PFW*	FWA	NEA
LB	WILLIE LANIER, KC	AP	UPI	SN		PFW		NEA
LB	PHIL VILLAPIANO, Oak	AP	UPI	SN				
LB	Andy Russell, Pit				PB	PFW		
LB	Mike Curtis, Bal				PB			
CB	ROBERT JAMES, Buf	AP*	UPI	SN	PB	PFW*	FWA	
CB	EMMITT THOMAS, KC	AP*	UPI	SN	PB	PFW	FWA	
S	TONY GREENE, Buf	AP*	UPI	SN	PB	PFW*	FWA	NEA
S	DICK ANDERSON, Mia			SN	PB			NEA
S	Jake Scott, Mia	AP*				PFW*		
S	Jack Tatum, Oak		UPI		PB			
P	RAY GUY, Oak	-	UPI	SN	PB	PFW*	FWA	NEA

		AP	UPI	SN	PB	PFW	FWA	NEA
E	JOHN DUTTON, Bal	AP		SN	PB			
E	Dwight White, Pit		UPI			PFW		
E	Elvin Bethea, Hou		UPI					
T	CURLEY CULP, Hou	AP*	UPI	SN		PFW*	FWA	NEA
T	JOE GREENE, Pit	AP*	UPI		PB	PFW+		
T	Jerry Sherk, Cle			SN	PB			
T	Otis Sistrunk, Oak					PFW+		
LB	JACK HAM, Pit	AP*	UPI	SN	PB	PFW*	FWA	NEA
LB	JACK LAMBERT, Pit	AP	UPI	SN		PFW*	FWA	
LB	ANDY RUSSELL, Pit						FWA	
LB	Willie Lanier, KC				PB			NEA
LB	Phil Villapiano, Oak	AP				PFW*		
LB	Tom MacLeod, Bal		UPI					
CB	MEL BLOUNT, Pit	AP*	UPI	SN	PB	PFW*	FWA	NEA
CB	EMMITT THOMAS, KC		UPI			PFW		NEA
CB	Ken Riley, Cin	AP		SN				
CB	Lemar Parrish, Cin				PB			
S	JAKE SCOTT, Mia	AP	UPI	SN	PB			
S	JACK TATUM, Oak		UPI	SN	PB			
S	Mike Wagner, Pit				PB	PFW		
S	Tommy Casanova, Cin	AP						
P	RAY GUY, Oak	-	UPI	SN	PB	PFW*	FWA	NEA

1975 All-NFC

Offense

		AP	UPI	SN	PB	PFW	FWA	NEA
WR	MEL GRAY, StL	AP*	UPI	SN	PB	PFW*	FWA	
WR	JOHN GILLIAM, Min			SN	PB	PFW+		
WR	Charley Taylor, Was	AP	UPI					
WR	Drew Pearson, Dal					PFW+		
TE	CHARLE YOUNG, Phi	AP	UPI	SN	PB	PFW*	FWA	NEA
T	RON YARY, Min	AP*	UPI	SN	PB	PFW*	FWA	NEA
T	DAN DIERDORF, StL	AP	UPI		PB	PFW	FWA	
T	Rayfield Wright, Dal			SN				NEA
G	ED WHITE, Min	AP	UPI	SN				NEA
G	TOM MACK, LA	AP	UPI	SN		PFW+		
G	Conrad Dobler, StL				PB	PFW		
C	LEN HAUSS, Was	AP	UPI	SN				
C	Tom Banks, StL				PB	PFW		
QB	FRAN TARKENTON, Min	AP*	UPI	SN	PB	PFW*	FWA	NEA
RB	CHUCK FOREMAN, Min	AP*	UPI	SN	PB	PFW*	FWA	NEA
RB	TERRY METCALF, StL	AP	UPI	SN	PB	PFW		
K	JIM BAKKEN, StL	AP*	UPI	SN	PB	PFW*	FWA	NEA
KR	Steve Odom, GB	-	-	-	PB			
KR	Terry Metcalf, StL	-	-	-		PFW	-	-

Defense

		AP	UPI	SN	PB	PFW	FWA	NEA
E	JACK YOUNGBLOOD, LA	AP*	UPI	SN	PB	PFW*	FWA	NEA
E	CEDRICK HARDMAN, SF			SN	PB			
E	Carl Eller, Min	AP	UPI					
E	Fred Dryer, LA					PFW		
T	ALAN PAGE, Min	AP	UPI	SN		PFW		
T	WALLY CHAMBERS, Chi	AP	UPI	SN		PFW		NEA
T	Merlin Olsen, LA				PB			
LB	CHRIS HANBURGER, Was	AP*	UPI	SN	PB	PFW		
LB	ISIAH ROBERTSON, LA	AP	UPI		PB	PFW*		
LB	BILL BERGEY, Phi	AP*	UPI					
LB	Lee Roy Jordan, Dal			SN		PFW		
LB	Fred Carr, GB			SN				
LB	Jeff Siemon, Min				PB			
CB	ROGER WEHRLI, StL	AP*	UPI	SN	PB	PFW*	FWA	
CB	LEM BARNEY, Det				PB	PFW		
CB	Rolland Lawrence, Atl		UPI	SN				
CB	Pat Fischer, Was	AP						
S	KEN HOUSTON, Was	AP*	UPI	SN	PB	PFW*	FWA	NEA
S	PAUL KRAUSE, Min	AP*	UPI			PFW*	FWA	
S	Cliff Harris, Dal			SN				NEA
P	JOHN JAMES, Atl	-	UPI	SN	PB	PFW		

1975 All-AFC

Offense

		AP	UPI	SN	PB	PFW	FWA	NEA
WR	LYNN SWANN, Pit	AP	UPI	SN	PB	PFW	FWA	
WR	ISAAC CURTIS, Cin			SN	PB	PFW*		NEA
WR	Cliff Branch, Oak	AP*	UPI					NEA
TE	RILEY ODOMS, Den	AP*	UPI	SN	PB			
TE	Rich Caster, NY		UPI			PFW		
T	GEORGE KUNZ, Bal	AP*	UPI	SN	PB	PFW*		
T	ART SHELL, Oak	AP	UPI	SN	PB			
T	Jon Kolb, Pit					PFW		
G	JOE DELAMIELLEURE, Buf	AP*	UPI	SN	PB	PFW*	FWA	
G	LARRY LITTLE, Mia	AP*	UPI			PFW*	FWA	
G	Bob Kuechenberg, Mia			SN	PB			NEA
G	Gene Upshaw, Oak				PB			
C	JIM LANGER, Mia	AP*	UPI	SN	PB	PFW*	FWA	NEA
QB	KEN ANDERSON, Cin	AP	UPI	SN	PB	PFW		
QB	Terry Bradshaw, Pit				PB			
RB	O.J. SIMPSON, Buf	AP*	UPI	SN	PB	PFW*	FWA	NEA
RB	FRANCO HARRIS, Pit	AP	UPI	SN	PB	PFW		
K	JAN STENERUD, KC	AP	UPI	SN	PB	PFW		
KR	Billy Johnson, Hou	-	-	-	PB	PFW*	-	-

Defense

		AP	UPI	SN	PB	PFW	FWA	NEA
E	L.C. GREENWOOD, Pit	AP*		SN	PB	PFW*	FWA	NEA

1976 All-NFC

Offense

		AP	UPI	SN	PB	PFW	FWA	NEA
WR	DREW PEARSON, Dal	AP*	UPI	SN	PB	PFW*	FWA	
WR	MEL GRAY, StL	AP		SN	PB			
WR	Sammie White, Min		UPI			PFW		
TE	BILLY JOE DUPREE, Dal	AP	UPI	SN	PB			
T	DAN DIERDORF, StL	AP*	UPI	SN	PB	PFW*	FWA	NEA
T	RON YARY, Min	AP	UPI	SN	PB	PFW	FWA	NEA
G	CONRAD DOBLER, StL	AP	UPI	SN	PB	PFW		
G	ED WHITE, Min		UPI	SN	PB			
G	Blaine Nye, Dal	AP				PFW		
C	TOM BANKS, StL	AP*	UPI	SN	PB	PFW		
QB	FRAN TARKENTON, Min		UPI		PB	PFW		
QB	Roger Staubach, Dal	AP		SN				
RB	CHUCK FOREMAN, Min	AP	UPI	SN	PB	PFW		NEA
RB	WALTER PAYTON, Chi	AP*	UPI	SN	PB	PFW*	FWA	
K	JIM BAKKEN, StL	AP*	UPI	SN	PB	PFW*	FWA	NEA
KR	Eddie Brown, Was	-	-	-	PB	PFW	-	
KR	Cullen Bryant, LA	-	-	-		PFW	-	

Defense

		AP	UPI	SN	PB	PFW	FWA	NEA
E	JACK YOUNGBLOOD, LA	AP*	UPI	SN	PB	PFW*	FWA	NEA
E	TOMMY HART, SF	AP	UPI	SN	PB	PFW*	FWA	NEA
T	WALLY CHAMBERS, Chi	AP*	UPI	SN	PB	PFW	FWA	NEA
T	ALAN PAGE, Min	AP	UPI	SN	PB	PFW		
LB	BILL BERGEY, Phi	AP	UPI	SN	PB	PFW		
LB	ISIAH ROBERTSON, LA	AP*	UPI	SN	PB	PFW		
LB	CHRIS HANBURGER, Was		UPI	SN	PB	PFW		NEA
LB	Brad Van Pelt, NY	AP						
CB	MONTE JACKSON, LA	AP	UPI	SN	PB	PFW*	FWA	NEA
CB	ROGER WEHRLI, StL	AP	UPI	SN	PB	PFW	FWA	
S	CLIFF HARRIS, Dal	AP*	UPI	SN	PB	PFW*	FWA	
S	KEN HOUSTON, Was	AP	UPI	SN	PB	PFW*	FWA	NEA
P	JOHN JAMES, Atl	AP	UPI	SN	PB	PFW		

1976 All-AFC

Offense

		AP	UPI	SN	PB	PFW	FWA	NEA
WR	CLIFF BRANCH, Oak	AP*	UPI	SN	PB	PFW*	FWA	NEA
WR	ROGER CARR, Bal	AP	UPI			PFW		
WR	Isaac Curtis, Cin			SN	PB			NEA
TE	DAVE CASPER, Oak	AP*	UPI	SN	PB	PFW*	FWA	NEA
T	ART SHELL, Oak	AP	UPI	SN	PB	PFW*		
T	GEORGE KUNZ, Bal	AP	UPI	SN	PB	PFW		
G	JOE DELAMIELLEURE, Buf	AP*	UPI	SN	PB	PFW*	FWA	
G	JOHN HANNAH, NE	AP*	UPI	SN	PB	PFW*	FWA	
C	JIM LANGER, Mia	AP*	UPI	SN	PB	PFW*	FWA	NEA
QB	BERT JONES, Bal	AP*	UPI				FWA	NEA
QB	Ken Stabler, Oak			SN	PB	PFW*		
RB	O.J. SIMPSON, Buf	AP*	UPI	SN	PB	PFW*	FWA	NEA
RB	LYDELL MITCHELL, Bal	AP	UPI	SN				
RB	Franco Harris, Pit				PB	PFW		
K	TONI LINHART, Bal		UPI	SN	PB	PFW		
K	Jan Stenerud, KC	AP						
KR	Rick Upchurch, Den	AP*	-	-	PB	PFW*	-	-
KR	Duriel Harris, Mia					PFW*	-	-

Defense

		AP	UPI	SN	PB	PFW	FWA	NEA
E	COY BACON, Cin	AP	UPI	SN	PB	PFW		
E	JOHN DUTTON, Bal	AP	UPI	SN	PB	PFW		
T	JERRY SHERK, Cle	AP*	UPI	SN	PB	PFW*	FWA	NEA
T	CURLEY CULP, Hou			SN	PB	PFW*		
T	Joe Greene, Pit	AP				PFW+		
T	Joe Ehrmann, Bal		UPI					
LB	JACK HAM, Pit	AP*	UPI	SN	PB	PFW*	FWA	NEA
LB	JACK LAMBERT, Pit	AP*	UPI	SN	PB	PFW*	FWA	NEA
LB	ROBERT BRAZILE, Hou		UPI	SN	PB	PFW*	FWA	
LB	Ted Hendricks, Oak	AP						
CB	MEL BLOUNT, Pit		UPI	SN	PB	PFW*		

CB	MIKE HAYNES, NE	AP	UPI	SN		PFW		
CB	Lemar Parrish, Cin				PB			NEA
CB	Ken Riley, Cin	AP						
S	TOMMY CASANOVA, Cin	AP*	UPI		PB	PFW		
S	MIKE WAGNER, Pit		UPI	SN		PFW		
S	Glen Edwards, Pit	AP			PB			
S	Jack Tatum, Oak			SN				
P	RAY GUY, Oak	AP*	UPI	SN	PB	PFW*	FWA	NEA

CB	Mel Blount, Pit			SN				NEA
CB	Lemar Parrish, Cin				PB			
S	BILL THOMPSON, Den	UPI	SN	PB	PFW	AP		
S	Jack Tatum, Oak	UPI	SN					
S	Tommy Casanova, Cin			PB	PFW			
P	RAY GUY, Oak	UPI	SN	PB	PFW*	AP	FWA	NEA

1977 ALL-NFC

Offense

WR	DREW PEARSON, Dal	UPI	SN	PB	PFW*	AP	FWA	NEA
WR	Harold Jackson, LA	UPI	SN					
WR	Sammie White, Min			PB	PFW			
TE	Jean Fugett, Was	UPI	SN		PFW			
TE	Billy Joe DuPree, Dal			PB				
T	DAN DIERDORF, StL	UPI	SN	PB	PFW*	AP	FWA	NEA
T	Ron Yary, Min	UPI	SN	PB	PFW			
G	Tom Mack, LA	UPI	SN		PFW			
G	Revie Sorey, Chi	UPI			PFW			
G	Conrad Dobler, StL			PB				
G	Ed White, Min			PB				
G	Bob Young, StL		SN					
C	Tom Banks, StL	UPI	SN	PB	PFW			
QB	Roger Staubach, Dal	UPI	SN	PB	PFW			
RB	WALTER PAYTON, Chi	UPI	SN	PB	PFW*	AP	FWA	NEA
RB	Chuck Foreman, Min		SN		PFW			
RB	Lawrence McCutcheon, LA	UPI		PB				
K	EFREN HERRERA, Dal	UPI	SN	PB	PFW*	AP	FWA	NEA
KR	Eddie Brown, Was	-	-	PB	PFW		-	
KR	Bob Hammond, NY	-	-		PFW			-

Defense

E	HARVEY MARTIN, Dal	UPI	SN	PB	PFW*	AP	FWA	NEA
E	Jack Youngblood, LA	UPI	SN	PB	PFW			
E	Claude Humphrey, Atl				PFW			
T	CLEVELAND ELAM, SF	UPI	SN	PB	PFW*	AP	FWA	NEA
T	Larry Brooks, LA		SN	PB	PFW			
T	Randy White, Dal				PFW*			
T	Alan Page, Min	UPI						
LB	BILL BERGEY, Phi	UPI	SN	PB	PFW		FWA	NEA
LB	Isiah Robertson, LA	UPI	SN	PB	PFW			
LB	Brad Van Pelt, NY	UPI		PB	PFW			
LB	Matt Blair, Min		SN					
CB	MONTE JACKSON, LA	UPI	SN	PB	PFW		FWA	
CB	ROLLAND LAWRENCE, Atl	UPI	SN		PFW*	AP	FWA	
CB	Roger Wehrli, StL			PB		AP		NEA
S	CLIFF HARRIS, Dal	UPI	SN	PB	PFW	AP	FWA	NEA
S	Ken Houston, Was	UPI			PFW*			NEA
S	Charlie Waters, Dal			PB			FWA	
S	Bill Simpson, LA		SN					
P	John James, Atl	UPI	SN	PB	PFW			

1977 ALL-AFC

Offense

WR	NAT MOORE, Mia	UPI	SN	PB	PFW	AP	FWA	
WR	Lynn Swann, Pit	UPI	SN	PB	PFW*			
WR	Cliff Branch, Oak							NEA
TE	DAVE CASPER, Oak	UPI	SN	PB	PFW*	AP	FWA	NEA
T	ART SHELL, Oak	UPI	SN	PB	PFW*	AP	FWA	NEA
T	George Kunz, Bal	UPI	SN	PB	PFW			
G	JOE DELAMIELLEURE, Buf		SN	PB	PFW	AP	FWA+	NEA
G	GENE UPSHAW, Oak	UPI	SN	PB	PFW*	AP	FWA	
G	John Hannah, NE	UPI						NEA
G	Larry Little, Mia						FWA+	
C	JIM LANGER, Mia	UPI	SN	PB	PFW*	AP	FWA	NEA
QB	BOB GRIESE, Mia	UPI		PB	PFW*	FWA	NEA	
QB	Craig Morton, Den		SN	RB				
RB	FRANCO HARRIS, Pit	UPI	SN	PB	PFW*	AP	FWA	NEA
RB	Lydell Mitchell, Bal	UPI	SN	PB	PFW			
K	Errol Mann, Oak	UPI			PFW			
K	Chris Bahr, Cin		SN					
K	Toni Linhart, Bal			PB				
KR	BILLY JOHNSON, Hou	-	-	PB	PFW*	AP	FWA	-
KR	Ray Clayborn, NE	-	-		PFW*			-

Defense

E	LYLE ALZADO, Den	UPI	SN	PB	PFW*	AP	FWA	
E	John Dutton, Bal	UPI		PB	PFW			
E	Fred Cook, Bal		SN					
T	Louie Kelcher, SD	UPI	SN		PFW			NEA
T	Mike Barnes, Bal		SN	PB				
T	Curley Culp, Hou			PB	PFW			
T	Joe Greene, Pit	UPI				AP		
LB	JACK HAM, Pit	UPI	SN	PB	PFW*	AP	FWA	NEA
LB	RANDY GRADISHAR, Den	UPI	SN	PB	PFW	AP		
LB	TOM JACKSON, Den	UPI	SN	PB	PFW*	AP		
LB	Robert Brazile, Hou			PB	PFW			NEA
CB	Mike Haynes, NE	UPI		PB	PFW*			
CB	Louis Wright, Den	UPI	SN		PFW			

1978 ALL-NFC

Offense

WR	Harold Carmichael, Phi	UPI	SN	PB	PFW			
WR	Ahmad Rashad, Min		SN	PB				
WR	Tony Hill, Dal				PFW			
WR	Sammy White, Min	UPI						
TE	Billy Joe DuPree, Dal	UPI	SN	PB	PFW			
T	DAN DIERDORF, StL	UPI	SN	PB	PFW*	AP	FWA	NEA
T	Doug France, LA		SN	PB	PFW			
T	Stan Walters, Phi	UPI						
G	Dennis Harrah, LA	UPI		PB	PFW			
G	Bob Young, StL		SN	PB	PFW			
G	Tom Mack, LA		SN					
G	Herb Scott, Dal	UPI						
C	Tom Banks, StL	UPI	SN	PB	PFW			
QB	Archie Manning, NO							
QB	Roger Staubach, Dal			PB	PFW			
RB	WALTER PAYTON, Chi	UPI	SN	PB	PFW*		FWA	NEA
RB	Tony Dorsett, Dal	UPI		PB				
RB	Terdell Middleton, GB		SN					
RB	Wilbert Montgomery, Phi				PFW			
K	FRANK CORRAL, LA	UPI	SN	PB	PFW*		FWA	NEA
KR	Tony Green, Was	-	-	PB	PFW*			-
KR	Jackie Wallace, LA	-	-		PFW			-

Defense

E	JACK YOUNGBLOOD, LA	UPI	SN	PB	PFW*	AP	FWA	NEA
E	AL (BUBBA) BAKER, Det			PB	PFW*	AP	FWA	NEA
E	Lee Roy Selmon, TB	UPI	SN					
T	RANDY WHITE, Dal	UPI	SN	PB	PFW*	AP	FWA	NEA
T	Larry Brooks, LA	UPI	SN	PB	PFW			
LB	Bill Bergey, Phi	UPI	SN	PB	PFW*			
LB	Matt Blair, Min	UPI	SN	PB	PFW			
LB	Brad Van Pelt, NY		SN	PB	PFW			
LB	Harry Carson, NY				PFW			
LB	Fulton Kuykendall, Atl				PFW			
LB	Jim Youngblood, LA	UPI						
CB	WILLIE BUCHANON, GB	UPI	SN	PB	PFW*	AP	FWA+	
CB	Pat Thomas, LA	UPI	SN	PB	PFW			
CB	Rod Perry, LA		SN					
S	CLIFF HARRIS, Dal	UPI	SN	PB	PFW*	AP	FWA+	
S	Charlie Waters, Dal	UPI	SN	PB			FWA	NEA
S	Ken Houston, Was					AP		
S	Bill Simpson, LA				PFW			
P	Tom Skladany, Det	UPI	SN		PFW			
P	Dave Jennings, NY			PB				

1978 ALL-AFC

Offense

WR	LYNN SWANN, Pit	UPI	SN	PB	PFW*	AP	FWA	NEA
WR	WESLEY WALKER, NY	UPI		PB	PFW*	AP	FWA	NEA
WR	Steve Largent, Sea		SN					
TE	DAVE CASPER, Oak	UPI	SN	PB	PFW*	AP	FWA	NEA
T	LEON GRAY, NE	UPI	SN	PB	PFW*	AP	FWA	
T	Russ Washington, SD			PB				NEA
T	Jon Kolb, Pit				PFW			
T	Art Shell, Oak	UPI						
G	JOHN HANNAH, NE	UPI	SN	PB	PFW*	AP	FWA	NEA
G	JOE DELAMIELLEURE, Buf	UPI	SN	PB	PFW++		FWA	NEA
G	Bob Kuechenberg, Mia		SN-t		PFW++	AP		
C	MIKE WEBSTER, Pit	UPI	SN	PB	PFW*	AP	FWA	
QB	TERRY BRADSHAW, Pit	UPI	SN	PB	PFW*	AP	FWA	
QB	Jim Zorn, Sea							NEA
RB	EARL CAMPBELL, Hou	UPI	SN	PB	PFW*	AP	FWA	NEA
RB	Delvin Williams, Mia	UPI	SN	PB	PFW	AP		
K	Pat Leahy, NY	UPI	SN		PFW			
K	Garo Yepremian, Mia			PB				
KR	RICK UPCHURCH, Den	-	-	PB	PFW*	AP	FWA	-
KR	Keith Wright, Cle	-	-		PFW			-

Defense

E	Lyle Alzado, Den	UPI	SN	PB	PFW			
E	Elvin Bethea, Hou	UPI		PB	PFW			
E	L.C. Greenwood, Pit		SN					
T	LOUIE KELCHER, SD	UPI	SN	PB	PFW*	AP	FWA	NEA
T	Joe Greene, Pit			PB	PFW			
LB	ROBERT BRAZILE, Hou	UPI	SN	PB	PFW*	AP	FWA	NEA
LB	RANDY GRADISHAR, Den	UPI	SN	PB	PFW*	AP	FWA	NEA
LB	JACK HAM, Pit	UPI	SN	PB	PFW*	AP	FWA	NEA
LB	Jack Lambert, Pit	UPI	SN	PB	PFW			
CB	LOUIS WRIGHT, Den	UPI	SN	PB	PFW*	AP	FWA	NEA
CB	Mike Haynes, NE	UPI					FWA+	NEA
S	THOM DARDEN, Cle	UPI	SN	PB	PFW*		FWA+	NEA

		UPI	SN	PB	PFW	AP	FWA	NEA
S	Bill Thompson, Den	UPI	SN	PB	PFW			
P	RAY GUY, Oak	UPI	SN	PB	PFW*	AP	FWA	NEA

1979 All-NFC

Offense

		UPI	SN	PB	PFW	AP	FWA	NEA
WR	Harold Carmichael, Phi	UPI	SN	PB	PFW			
WR	Ahmad Rashad, Min	UPI	SN	PB	PFW			
TE	Henry Childs, NO			PB	PFW			
TE	Keith Krepfle, Phi	UPI	SN					
T	Pat Donovan, Dal	UPI	SN	PB	PFW			
T	Stan Walters, Phi	UPI	SN	PB	PFW			
G	Bob Young, StL	UPI	SN	PB	PFW*	AP		
G	Herb Scott, Dal	UPI	SN					
G	Dennis Harrah, LA			PB	PFW			
C	Tom Banks, StL	UPI	SN					
C	Rich Saul, LA			PB	PFW			
QB	Roger Staubach, Dal	UPI	SN	PB	PFW			
RB	OTTIS ANDERSON, StL	UPI	SN	PB	PFW	AP	FWA	
RB	Walter Payton, Chi	UPI	SN	PB	PFW*			NEA
K	Mark Moseley, Was	UPI	SN	PB	PFW*			
KR+	WALLY HENRY, Phi	-	SN	PB	PFW+			-
KR	Roy Green, StL	-	SN		PFW			-

Defense

		UPI	SN	PB	PFW	AP	FWA	NEA
E	LEE ROY SELMON, TB	UPI	SN	PB	PFW*	AP	FWA	NEA
E	JACK YOUNGBLOOD, LA	UPI	SN	PB	PFW*	AP	FWA	NEA
T	RANDY WHITE, Dal	UPI	SN	PB	PFW*	AP	FWA	NEA
T+	CHARLIE JOHNSON, Phi	UPI	SN	PB	PFW			NEA
T	Larry Brooks, LA					AP		
LB	Harry Carson, NY	UPI	SN	PB	PFW			
LB	Brad Van Pelt, NY	UPI	SN	PB	PFW			
LB	Jim Youngblood, LA		SN	PB				
LB	Matt Blair, Min				PFW			
LB	Bob Breunig, Dal				PFW			
LB	David Lewis, TB	UPI						
LB	Jack Reynolds, LA		SN					
CB	LEMAR PARRISH, Was	UPI	SN	PB	PFW*	AP	FWA	NEA
CB	Roger Wehrli, StL	UPI	SN	PB	PFW			
S	Gary Fencik, Chi		SN		PFW		FWA	
S	Tom Myers, NO	UPI		PB				
S	Ken Houston, Was	UPI		PB				
S	Cliff Harris, Dal		SN					
P	Dave Jennings, NY	UPI	SN	PB	PFW	AP		

1979 All-AFC

		UPI	SN	PB	PFW	AP	FWA	NEA
WR	JOHN JEFFERSON, SD	UPI	SN	PB	PFW*	AP	FWA	NEA
WR	JOHN STALLWORTH, Pit	UPI	SN	PB	PFW*	AP	FWA	NEA
TE+	DAVE CASPER, Oak	UPI	SN	PB	PFW*	AP	FWA	NEA
TE+	OZZIE NEWSOME, Cle	UPI	SN				FWA	
TE	Raymond Chester, Oak							NEA
T	LEON GRAY, Hou	UPI	SN	PB	PFW*	AP	FWA	
T	MARVIN POWELL, NY	UPI	SN	PB	PFW*	AP	FWA	
T	Jon Kolb, Pit							NEA
T	Russ Washington, SD			PB				
G	JOHN HANNAH, NE	UPI	SN	PB	PFW*	AP	FWA	NEA
G	JOE DELAMIELLEURE, Buf	UPI	SN	PB	PFW		FWA	NEA
C	MIKE WEBSTER, Pit	UPI	SN	PB	PFW*	AP	FWA	NEA
QB	DAN FOUTS, SD	UPI	SN	PB	PFW*	AP	FWA	NEA
RB	EARL CAMPBELL, Hou	UPI	SN	PB	PFW*	AP	FWA	NEA
RB	Mike Pruitt, Cle	UPI	SN	PB	PFW			
RB	Franco Harris, Pit			PB				
K	TONI FRITSCH, Hou	UPI	SN	PB	PFW*	AP	FWA	NEA
KR+	RICK UPCHURCH, Den	-		PB	PFW*			-
KR	Ira Matthews, Oak	-	SN		PFW*			-
KR	Tony Nathan, Mia	-	SN			AP		
KR	J.T. Smith, KC						FWA	-

Defense

		UPI	SN	PB	PFW	AP	FWA	NEA
E	Fred Dean, SD	UPI	SN	PB	PFW			
E	L.C. Greenwood, Pit	UPI	SN	PB				
E	Lyle Alzado, Cle				PFW			
T+	JOE GREENE, Pit	UPI	SN	PB	PFW*			
T	Bob Baumhower, Mia		SN	PB	PFW			
T	Wilbur Young, SD	UPI						
LB	ROBERT BRAZILE, Hou	UPI	SN	PB	PFW	AP	FWA	NEA
LB	JACK HAM, Pit	UPI	SN	PB	PFW*	AP	FWA	NEA
LB	JACK LAMBERT, Pit	UPI	SN	PB	PFW*			NEA
LB	Randy Gradishar, Den		SN		PFW*			
CB	LOUIS WRIGHT, Den	UPI	SN	PB	PFW*	AP	FWA	
CB	Mike Haynes, NE	UPI	SN	PB	PFW			
S	MIKE REINFELDT, Hou	UPI	SN	PB	PFW*	AP	FWA	NEA
S	DONNIE SHELL, Pit		SN	PB	PFW		FWA	NEA
S	Thom Darden, Cle				PFW			
S	Bill Thompson, Den	UPI						
P	BOB GRUPP, KC	UPI	SN	PB	PFW*		FWA	NEA

1980 All-NFC

Offense

		UPI	PB	PFW	AP	SN	FWA	NEA
WR	JAMES LOFTON, GB	UPI	PB	PFW*		SN	FWA	NEA
WR	Ahmad Rashad, Min	UPI		PFW				
WR	Harold Carmichael, Phi		PB					
TE	Junior Miller, Atl	UPI		PFW				
TE	Jimmie Giles, TB		PB					
T	MIKE KENN, Atl	UPI	PB	PFW*	AP	SN	FWA	NEA
T	Dan Dierdorf, StL		PB					NEA
T	Pat Donovan, Dal	UPI						
T	Doug France, LA			PFW				
G	Herb Scott, Dal	UPI	PB	PFW	AP			NEA
G	Kent Hill, LA	UPI	PB	PFW*				
G	Randy Cross, SF			PFW				
C	Rich Saul, LA		PB					
C	Jeff Van Note, Atl	UPI		PFW				
QB	Ron Jaworski, Phi	UPI		PFW				
QB	Steve Bartkowski, Atl		PB					
RB	WALTER PAYTON, Chi	UPI	PB	PFW*	AP	SN	FWA	NEA
RB	Billy Sims, Det	UPI		PFW				
RB	Ottis Anderson, StL		PB					
K	EDDIE MURRAY, Det	UPI	PB	PFW*	AP		FWA	NEA
KR	Mike Nelms, Was	-	PB					-
KR	Rich Mauti, NO	-		PFW				-
KR	Freddy Solomon, SF	-		PFW				-

Defense

		UPI	PB	PFW	AP	SN	FWA	NEA
E	LEE ROY SELMON, TB	UPI	PB			SN	FWA	NEA
E	Al (Bubba) Baker, Det		PB					
E	Carl Hairston, Phi			PFW				
E	Dan Hampton, Chi			PFW				
E	Jack Youngblood, LA	UPI						
T	RANDY WHITE, Dal	UPI	PB	PFW*	AP			
T	Charlie Johnson, Phi	UPI	PB	PFW	AP			
T	Alan Page, Chi			PFW				
LB	Matt Blair, Min	UPI	PB	PFW	AP			
LB	Bob Bruenig, Dal	UPI	PB					
LB	Jerry Robinson, Phi	UPI		PFW*+				
LB	Bill Bergey, Phi			PFW				
LB	Buddy Curry, Atl			PFW				
LB	Brad Van Pelt, NY		PB					
CB	LEMAR PARRISH, Was	UPI	PB	PFW*		SN	FWA	NEA
CB	Pat Thomas, LA	UPI	PB	PFW	AP			
S	NOLAN CROMWELL, LA	UPI	PB	PFW*	AP	SN	FWA	NEA
S	Gary Fencik, Chi	UPI	PB	PFW*				
S	Randy Logan, Phi		PB					
P	DAVE JENNINGS, NY	UPI	PB	PFW*	AP	SN	FWA	NEA

1980 All-AFC

Offense

		UPI	PB	PFW	AP	SN	FWA	NEA
WR	JOHN JEFFERSON, SD	UPI	PB	PFW*	AP	SN	FWA	NEA
WR	Stanley Morgan, NE	UPI	PB	PFW				
WR	Charlie Joiner, SD				AP			
TE	KELLEN WINSLOW, SD	UPI	PB	PFW*	AP	SN	FWA	NEA
T	LEON GRAY, Hou	UPI	PB	PFW*	AP		FWA	
T	Marvin Powell, NY	UPI	PB	PFW				
G	JOHN HANNAH, NE	UPI	PB	PFW*	AP	SN	FWA	NEA
G	JOE DELAMIELLEURE, Cle	UPI	PB	PFW*	AP	SN	FWA	NEA
C	MIKE WEBSTER, Pit	UPI	PB	PFW*	AP	SN	FWA	NEA
QB	BRIAN SIPE, Cle	UPI	PB	PFW*	AP	SN	FWA	NEA
RB	EARL CAMPBELL, Hou	UPI	PB	PFW*	AP	SN	FWA	NEA
RB	Joe Cribbs, Buf	UPI	PB	PFW				
K	Fred Steinfort, Den	UPI		PFW++		SN		
K	John Smith, NE		PB	PFW++				
KR	J.T. SMITH, KC	-	PB	PFW*	AP		FWA	
KR	Horace Ivory, NE	-		PFW*		SN	FWA	-

Defense

		UPI	PB	PFW	AP	SN	FWA	NEA
E	ART STILL, KC	UPI	PB	PFW*		SN	FWA	NEA
E	Fred Dean, SD	UPI	PB	PFW*	AP			
E	Lyle Alzado, Cle	UPI			AP			
T	GARY JOHNSON, SD	UPI	PB	PFW*	AP	SN	FWA	NEA
T	Louie Kelcher, SD		PB	PFW				
T	Fred Smerlas, Buf	UPI		PFW*				
LB	TED HENDRICKS, Oak	UPI	PB	PFW*	AP	SN	FWA	NEA
LB	ROBERT BRAZILE, Hou	UPI	PB	PFW*		SN	FWA	NEA
LB	JACK LAMBERT, Pit		PB	PFW*	AP		FWA	NEA
LB	Steve Nelson, NE			PFW*+		SN		
LB	Randy Gradishar, Den					SN		
LB	Jim Haslett, Buff	UPI						
CB	LESTER HAYES, Oak	UPI	PB	PFW*	AP	SN	FWA	NEA
CB	Mike Haynes, NE	UPI	PB	PFW				
S	DONNIE SHELL, Pit	UPI	PB	PFW+	AP		FWA	NEA
S	Gary Barbaro, KC	UPI	PB	PFW				
S	Bruce Laird, Bal			PFW+				
P	Ray Guy, Oak	UPI	PB	PFW				

1981 All-NFC

Offense

		UPI	PB	PFW	AP	SN	FWA	NEA
WR	JAMES LOFTON, GB	UPI	PB	PFW*	AP	SN	FWA	NEA
WR	ALFRED JENKINS, Atl	UPI	PB	PFW*+	AP	SN	FWA	NEA
TE	Joe Senser, Min	UPI		PFW				
TE	Jimmie Giles, TB		PB					

		UPI	PB	PFW	AP	SN	FWA	NEA
T	Mike Kenn, Atl	UPI	PB	PFW				
T	Pat Donovan, Dal		PB	PFW				
T	Keith Dorney, Det	UPI						
G+	RANDY CROSS, SF	UPI	PB	PFW*			FWA	NEA
G	Herb Scott, Dal	UPI	PB	PFW	AP	SN		
C	Larry McCarren, GB			PFW				
C	Guy Morriss, Phi	UPI						
C	Rich Saul, LA		PB					
QB	Joe Montana, SF	UPI	PB	PFW				
RB	TONY DORSETT, Dal	UPI	PB	PFW*	AP	SN	FWA	NEA
RB	BILLY SIMS, Det		PB	PFW*			FWA	NEA
RB	George Rogers, NO	UPI			AP	SN		
K	RAFAEL SEPTIEN, Dal	UPI	PB	PFW*	AP	SN	FWA	
KR+	LEROY IRVIN, LA	-		PFW*		SN	FWA	-
KR+	MIKE NELMS, Was	-	PB	PFW*		SN	FWA	-

Defense

		UPI	PB	PFW	AP	SN	FWA	NEA
E	FRED DEAN, SF	UPI	PB	PFW*	AP	SN	FWA	
E	Ed Jones, Dal	UPI	PB	PFW				
E	Lee Roy Selmon, TB		PB					
T	RANDY WHITE, Dal	UPI	PB	PFW*	AP	SN	FWA	NEA
T	Doug English, Det		PB	PFW*				NEA
T	Charlie Johnson, Phi	UPI			AP			
LB	LAWRENCE TAYLOR, NY	UPI	PB	PFW*	AP	SN	FWA	NEA
LB	Harry Carson, NY	UPI	PB	PFW*				
LB	Jerry Robinson, Phi	UPI		PFW			FWA	
LB	Matt Blair, Min		PB					
CB	RONNIE LOTT, SF	UPI	PB	PFW*	AP	SN	FWA	NEA
CB	Mark Haynes, NY			PFW*				NEA
CB	Roynell Young, Phi		PB					
S	NOLAN CROMWELL, LA		PB	PFW*	AP	SN	FWA	
S+	GARY FENCIK, Chi	UPI	PB		AP	SN		
S	Dwight Hicks, SF	UPI		PFW*				
P	Tom Skladany, Det	UPI	PB	PFW*				

1981 ALL-AFC
Offense

		UPI	PB	PFW	AP	SN	FWA	NEA
WR	Steve Watson, Den	UPI	PB	PFW*				
WR	Frank Lewis, Buf	UPI	PB	PFW				
TE	KELLEN WINSLOW, SD	UPI	PB	PFW*	AP	SN	FWA	NEA
T	ANTHONY MUNOZ, Cin	UPI	PB	PFW*	AP	SN	FWA	NEA
T	MARVIN POWELL, NY	UPI	PB	PFW*	AP	SN	FWA	NEA
G	JOHN HANNAH, NE	UPI	PB	PFW*	AP	SN	FWA	NEA
G	Doug Wilkerson, SD	UPI	PB	PFW				
C	MIKE WEBSTER, Pit	UPI	PB	PFW*	AP	SN	FWA	NEA
QB	KEN ANDERSON, Cin	UPI	PB	PFW*	AP	SN	FWA	NEA
RB	Joe Delaney, KC	UPI	PB	PFW				
RB	Chuck Muncie, SD	UPI		PFW				
RB	Earl Campbell, Hou		PB					
K	Nick Lowery, KC	UPI	PB	PFW				NEA
KR	Carl Roaches, Hou	-	PB	PFW				-
KR	J.T. Smith, KC			PFW				-

Defense

		UPI	PB	PFW	AP	SN	FWA	NEA
E	JOE KLECKO, NY	UPI	PB	PFW*	AP	SN	FWA	NEA
E	Mark Gastineau, NY	UPI	PB	PFW				
T+	BOB BAUMHOWER, Mia	UPI	PB	PFW		SN		
T+	GARY JOHNSON, SD		PB	PFW	AP		FWA	
T	Fred Smerlas, Buf	UPI		PFW*				
LB	JACK LAMBERT, Pit		PB	PFW*	AP	SN	FWA	NEA
LB	BOB SWENSON, Den			PFW*		SN		
LB	Randy Gradishar, Den	UPI		PFW*		SN		
LB	Ted Hendricks, Oak	UPI	PB	PFW				
LB	Bob Brazile, Hou		PB					
LB	A.J. Duhe, Mia	UPI						
CB	MEL BLOUNT, Pit	UPI	PB	PFW	AP		FWA	
CB	Gary Green, KC	UPI		PFW				
CB	Lester Hayes, Oak		PB			SN		
S+	GARY BARBARO, KC		PB				FWA	NEA
S	Darrol Ray, NY	UPI		PFW				
S	Donnie Shell, Pit		PB					
S	Bill Thompson, Den	UPI						
P	PAT MCINALLY, Cin	UPI	PB	PFW*	AP	SN	FWA	NEA

1982 ALL-NFC
Offense

		UPI	PB	PFW	AP	SN	FWA	NEA
WR	DWIGHT CLARK, SF	UPI	PB	PFW*	AP		FWA	NEA
WR	James Lofton, GB	UPI	PB					
TE	Jimmie Giles, TB	UPI	PB					
T	Pat Donovan, Dal	UPI	PB					
T	Mike Kenn, Atl	UPI	PB					
G	R.C. Thielemann, Atl	UPI	PB		AP			
G	Randy Cross, SF		PB					
G	Kent Hill, LA	UPI						
C	Larry McCarren, GB	UPI						
C	Jeff Van Note, Atl		PB					
QB	Joe Theismann, Was	UPI	PB					
RB	William Andrews, Atl	UPI	PB					
RB	Tony Dorsett, Dal	UPI	PB					
K	MARK MOSELEY, Was	UPI	PB	PFW*	AP		FWA	NEA
KR	MIKE NELMS, Was	-	PB	PFW*			FWA	-
KR	LeRoy Irvin, LA	-					FWA	-

Defense

		UPI	PB	PFW	AP	SN	FWA	NEA
E	LEE ROY SELMON, TB	UPI	PB				FWA	NEA
E	Ed Jones, Dal		PB		AP			
E	Doug Martin, Min	UPI		PFW*				
T	RANDY WHITE, Dal	UPI	PB	PFW*			FWA	NEA
T	DAN HAMPTON, Chi			PFW*				
T	Doug English, Det		PB		AP			
LB	LAWRENCE TAYLOR, NY	UPI	PB	PFW*	AP		FWA	NEA
LB	HUGH GREEN, TB	UPI	PB	PFW*			FWA	
LB	Harry Carson, NY	UPI	PB					
LB	Mike Douglass, GB			PFW*				
LB	Bob Bruenig, Dal	UPI						
CB	MARK HAYNES, NY	UPI	PB	PFW*	AP		FWA	
CB	EVERSON WALLS, Dal	UPI	PB	PFW*			FWA	
S	NOLAN CROMWELL, LA	UPI	PB		AP		FWA	
S	Tony Peters, Was	UPI	PB					
S	Gary Fencik, Chi			PFW*				
P	DAVE JENNINGS, NY	UPI	PB	PFW*			FWA	

1982 ALL-AFC
Offense

		UPI	PB	PFW	AP	SN	FWA	NEA
WR	WES CHANDLER, SD	UPI	PB	PFW*	AP		FWA	NEA
WR	Cris Collinsworth, Cin		PB					
WR	Wesley Walker, NY	UPI						
TE	KELLEN WINSLOW, SD	UPI	PB	PFW*	AP		FWA	NEA
T	ANTHONY MUNOZ, CIN	UPI	PB	PFW*	AP		FWA	NEA
T	MARVIN POWELL, NY	UPI	PB	PFW*	AP		FWA	NEA
G	DOUG WILKERSON, SD	UPI	PB	PFW*	AP		FWA	NEA
G	JOHN HANNAH, NE		PB	PFW*			FWA	
G	Ed Newman, Mia	UPI						NEA
C	MIKE WEBSTER, Pit	UPI	PB	PFW*			FWA	
C	Joe Fields, NY				AP			NEA
QB	DAN FOUTS, SD	UPI	PB	PFW*	AP		FWA	NEA
RB	MARCUS ALLEN, LA	UPI	PB	PFW*	AP		FWA	NEA
RB	FREEMAN MCNEIL, NY	UPI	PB	PFW*	AP		FWA	NEA
K	Rolf Benirschke, SD	UPI	PB					
KR	Rick Upchurch, Den	-	PB	PFW*				-

Defense

		UPI	PB	PFW	AP	SN	FWA	NEA
E	MARK GASTINEAU, NY	UPI	PB	PFW*	AP		FWA	NEA
E	Lyle Alzado, LA	UPI						
E	Art Still, KC		PB					
T	Fred Smerlas, Buf		PB		AP			
T	Bob Baumhower, Mia	UPI						
T	Gary Johnson, SD		PB					
LB	JACK LAMBERT, Pit	UPI	PB	PFW*	AP		FWA	NEA
LB	Ted Hendricks, LA	UPI	PB		AP			
LB	Robert Brazile, Hou	UPI	PB					
LB	Randy Gradishar, Den	UPI						
LB	Rod Martin, LA							NEA
CB	Mike Haynes, NE	UPI	PB					NEA
CB	Louis Breeden, Cin				AP			NEA
CB	Lester Hayes, LA	UPI	PB					
S	Gary Barbaro, KC	UPI	PB					NEA
S+	KENNY EASLEY, Sea	UPI		PFW*				
S+	DONNIE SHELL, Pit		PB		AP		FWA	
P	Luke Prestridge, Den	UPI	PB		AP			

1983 ALL-NFC
Offense

		UPI	PB	PFW	AP	SN	FWA	NEA
WR	ROY GREEN, StL	UPI		PFW*	AP	SN	FWA	NEA
WR	MIKE QUICK, Phi	UPI	PB	PFW*	AP			NEA
WR	James Lofton, GB		PB				FWA	
TE	Paul Coffman, GB	UPI	PB	PFW				
T	JOE JACOBY, Was	UPI	PB	PFW*	AP	SN	FWA	NEA
T	Mike Kenn, Atl		PB	PFW*				
T	Keith Fahnhorst, SF							NEA
T	Jackie Slater, LA	UPI						
G	RUSS GRIMM, Was	UPI	PB	PFW*	AP		FWA	NEA
G	Kent Hill, LA	UPI	PB	PFW*		SN		
C	Jeff Bostic, Was	UPI	PB	PFW				
QB	JOE THEISMANN, Was	UPI	PB	PFW*	AP	SN	FWA	NEA
RB	ERIC DICKERSON, LA	UPI	PB	PFW*	AP	SN	FWA	NEA
RB	JOHN RIGGINS, Was	UPI	PB	PFW*		SN	FWA	
RB	William Andrews, Atl		PB			SN		NEA
K	ALI HAJI-SHEIKH, NY	UPI	PB	PFW*	AP	SN	FWA	NEA
KR	BILLY JOHNSON, Atl		PB	PFW*		SN	FWA	-
KR	Mike Nelms, Was	-		PFW	AP			-

Defense

		UPI	PB	PFW	AP	SN	FWA	NEA
E	Ed Jones, Dal	UPI	PB	PFW				
E	Fred Dean, SF			PFW				
E	William Gay, Det	UPI						
E	Lee Roy Selmon, TB		PB					
T	RANDY WHITE, Dal	UPI	PB	PFW*	AP	SN	FWA	
T	Dave Butz, Was			PFW*	AP	SN		NEA

		UPI	PB	PFW	AP	SN	FWA	NEA
T	Doug English, Det		PB				FWA	
T	David Logan, TB			PFW				
LB	LAWRENCE TAYLOR, NY	UPI	PB	PFW*	AP	SN	FWA	NEA
LB	Mike Singletary, Chi	UPI	PB	PFW*				NEA
LB	Hugh Green, TB	UPI	PB			SN		
LB	Bob Bruenig, Dal	UPI						
LB	Rickey Jackson, NO			PFW				
CB	Ronnie Lott, SF		PB	PFW			FWA	
CB	Everson Walls, Dal		PB	PFW	AP			
CB	Johnnie Poe, NO	UPI						
CB	Eric Wright, SF	UPI						
S	MARK MURPHY, Was	UPI	PB	PFW*	AP	SN	FWA	
S	Nolan Cromwell, LA		PB	PFW				
S	Russell Gary, NO	UPI						
S	Johnnie Johnson, LA							NEA
P	Carl Birdsong, StL	UPI	PB	PFW				

		UPI	PB	PFW	AP	SN	FWA	NEA
T	DAN HAMPTON, Chi		PB	PFW*	AP	SN		NEA
T	RANDY WHITE, Dal	UPI		PFW*	AP		FWA	NEA
T	David Logan, TB			PFW		SN		
LB	MIKE SINGLETARY, Chi	UPI	PB	PFW*	AP	SN	FWA	NEA
LB	LAWRENCE TAYLOR, NY	UPI	PB	PFW		SN	FWA	NEA
LB	E.J. JUNIOR, StL	UPI	PB		AP		FWA	NEA
LB	Rickey Jackson, NO	UPI	PB	PFW				
LB	Harry Carson, NY					SN		
LB	Jim Collins, LA			PFW*				
CB	MARK HAYNES, NY	UPI	PB	PFW	AP			NEA
CB	Darrell Green, Was		PB					
CB	Everson Walls, Dal	UPI						
CB	Eric Wright, SF			PFW				
S	TODD BELL, Chi		PB	PFW		SN		
S	Michael Downs, Dal	UPI					FWA	
S	Dwight Hicks, SF	UPI	PB					
S	Wes Hopkins, Phi			PFW				NEA
P	Brian Hansen, NO		PB					
P	Mike Horan, Phi			PFW				
P	Bucky Scribner, GB	UPI						
ST	Bill Bates, Dal	-	PB	PFW	-		-	-

1983 ALL-AFC

Offense

		UPI	PB	PFW	AP	SN	FWA	NEA
WR	Cris Collinsworth, Cin	UPI	PB	PFW				
WR	Carlos Carson, KC	UPI	PB					
WR	Steve Largent, Sea					SN		
WR	Tim Smith, Hou			PFW				
TE	TODD CHRISTENSEN, LA	UPI	PB	PFW*	AP	SN	FWA	NEA
T	ANTHONY MUNOZ, Cin	UPI	PB		AP		FWA	
T	Marvin Powell, NY		PB	PFW				
T	Brian Holloway, NE			PFW				
T	Eric Laakso, Mia					SN		
T	Cody Risien, Cle	UPI						
G	JOHN HANNAH, NE	UPI	PB	PFW*	AP	SN	FWA	NEA
G	Chris Hinton, Bal		PB	PFW				
G	Ed Newman, Mia			PFW				
C	DWIGHT STEPHENSON, Mia	UPI	PB	PFW*				
C	Mike Webster, Pit				AP	SN		
QB	Dan Marino, Mia	UPI	PB	PFW				
RB	Curt Warner, Sea	UPI	PB	PFW				
RB	Joe Cribbs, Buf	UPI		PFW				
RB	Earl Campbell, Hou		PB					
K	Gary Anderson, Pit	UPI	PB	PFW				
KR	Fulton Walker, Mia	-		PFW*		SN	FWA	-
KR	Greg Pruitt, LA	-	PB					-

Defense

		UPI	PB	PFW	AP	SN	FWA	NEA
E	DOUG BETTERS, Mia	UPI	PB	PFW*	AP	SN	FWA	NEA
E	HOWIE LONG, LA		PB	PFW*			FWA	NEA
E	Mark Gastineau, NY	UPI			AP	SN		
T	Bob Baumhower, Mia	UPI	PB	PFW*				
T	Fred Smerlas, Buf		PB	PFW				NEA
T	Joe Klecko, NY			PFW				
LB	JACK LAMBERT, Pit	UPI	PB	PFW*	AP	SN	FWA	
LB	CHIP BANKS, Cle	UPI	PB	PFW*	AP		FWA	
LB	ROD MARTIN, LA	UPI	PB	PFW		SN		NEA
LB	Tom Cousineau, Cle	UPI						
LB	Lance Mehl, NY			PFW				
CB	GARY GREEN, KC	UPI	PB				FWA	NEA
CB	LESTER HAYES, LA	UPI	PB					
CB	Ken Riley, Cin			PFW*	AP	SN		
CB	Ray Clayborn, NE					SN		
CB	Louis Wright, Den							NEA
S	KENNY EASLEY, Sea	UPI	PB	PFW*	AP	SN	FWA	NEA
S	Deron Cherry, KC	UPI	PB	PFW				
S	Steve Freeman, Buf					SN		
P	RICH CAMARILLO, NE	UPI	PB	PFW*		SN	FWA	NEA
P	Rohn Stark, Bal				AP			

1984 ALL-NFC

Offense

		UPI	PB	PFW	AP	SN	FWA	NEA
WR	ROY GREEN, StL	UPI	PB	PFW*	AP	SN	FWA	NEA
WR	ART MONK, Was	UPI		PFW*	AP	SN	FWA	
WR	James Lofton, GB		PB					NEA
TE	Paul Coffman, GB	UPI	PB	PFW				
T	KEITH FAHNHORST, SF	UPI		PFW*	AP	SN	FWA	
T+	JOE JACOBY, Was	UPI	PB		AP	SN	FWA	
T	Mike Kenn, Atl		PB					
T	Bill Bain, LA			PFW*				
G	RUSS GRIMM, Was	UPI	PB		AP	SN	FWA	NEA
G	Randy Cross, SF	UPI	PB	PFW*				
G	John Ayers, SF			PFW				
G	Sean Farrell, TB					SN		
C	Fred Quillan, SF	UPI	PB	PFW				
QB	Joe Montana, SF	UPI	PB	PFW				
RB	ERIC DICKERSON, LA	UPI	PB	PFW*	AP	SN	FWA	NEA
RB	WALTER PAYTON, Chi	UPI	PB	PFW*	AP	SN	FWA	NEA
K	Jan Stenerud, Min	UPI	PB	PFW				NEA
KR	HENRY ELLARD, LA	-	PB	PFW	AP	SN		-
KR	Stump Mitchell, StL	-		PFW				-

Defense

		UPI	PB	PFW	AP	SN	FWA	NEA
E	Richard Dent, Chi	UPI	PB	PFW*				
E	Lee Roy Selmon, TB	UPI	PB	PFW				

1984 ALL-AFC

Offense

		UPI	PB	PFW	AP	SN	FWA	NEA
WR	John Stallworth, Pit	UPI	PB	PFW				
WR	Mark Duper, Mia	UPI	PB					
WR	Mark Clayton, Mia			PFW				
TE	OZZIE NEWSOME, Cle	UPI	PB	PFW*	AP	SN	FWA	NEA
T+	ANTHONY MUNOZ, Cin	UPI	PB	PFW		SN		NEA
T	Brian Holloway, NE		PB	PFW				
T	Henry Lawrence, LA	UPI						
G	JOHN HANNAH, NE	UPI	PB			SN	FWA	NEA
G	Ed Newman, Mia	UPI	PB	PFW*	AP			
G	Mike Munchak, Hou			PFW				
C	DWIGHT STEPHENSON, Mia	UPI	PB	PFW*	AP	SN	FWA	NEA
QB	DAN MARINO, Mia	UPI	PB	PFW*	AP	SN	FWA	NEA
RB	Marcus Allen, LA	UPI	PB	PFW				
RB	Freeman McNeil, NY			PFW				
RB	Earnest Jackson, SD			PFW				
K	NORM JOHNSON, Sea	UPI	PB	PFW*	AP	SN	FWA	
KR	Bobby Humphrey, NY	-		PFW*		SN	FWA	-
KR	Louis Lipps, Pit	-	PB	PFW*			FWA	-

Defense

		UPI	PB	PFW	AP	SN	FWA	NEA
E	MARK GASTINEAU, NY	UPI	PB	PFW*	AP	SN	FWA	NEA
E	HOWIE LONG, LA	UPI	PB	PFW	AP		FWA	NEA
E	Jacob Green, Sea					SN		
T	Joe Nash, Sea	UPI	PB	PFW*	AP			
LB	Rod Martin, LA	UPI	PB		AP		FWA	
LB	Mike Merriweather, Pit	UPI	PB	PFW				
LB	Clay Matthews, Cle			PFW				
LB	Steve Nelson, NE	UPI	PB					
LB	Robin Cole, Pit		PB					
LB	Tom Cousineau, Cle	UPI						
LB	Tom Jackson, Den			PFW				
LB	Andre Tippett, NE			PFW				
CB	MIKE HAYNES, LA	UPI	PB	PFW*	AP	SN	FWA	NEA
CB	Lester Hayes, LA	UPI	PB				FWA	
CB	Louis Wright, Den			PFW*		SN		
S	KENNY EASLEY, Sea	UPI	PB	PFW*	AP	SN	FWA	NEA
S	Deron Cherry, KC	UPI			AP			
S	Vann McElroy, LA		PB					
S	Dennis Smith, Den			PFW*				
P	REGGIE ROBY, Mia	UPI	PB	PFW*	AP	SN	FWA	NEA
ST	Fredd Young, Sea	-	PB	PFW*	-		-	-

1985 ALL-NFC

Offense

		UPI	PB	PFW	AP	SN	FWA	NEA
WR	MIKE QUICK, Phi	UPI	PB		AP	SN		NEA
WR	Art Monk, Was	UPI	PB			SN		
TE	Doug Cosbie, Dal	UPI	PB					
T	JIM COVERT, Chi	UPI	PB		AP	SN	FWA	NEA
T	Keith Dorney, Det	UPI						
T	Jackie Slater, LA		PB					
G	RUSS GRIMM, Was	UPI	PB		AP	SN	FWA	NEA
G	Dennis Harrah, LA	UPI						
G	Kent Hill, LA		PB					
G	Randy Cross, SF							NEA
C	Jay Hilgenberg, Chi	UPI	PB					
QB	Joe Montana, SF	UPI	PB					
RB	WALTER PAYTON, Chi	UPI	PB		AP	SN	FWA	NEA
RB	Gerald Riggs, Atl	UPI						
RB	Roger Craig, SF		PB					
K	MORTEN ANDERSEN, NO	UPI	PB			SN		
KR	RON BROWN, LA	-	PB		AP	SN	FWA	-
KR	Henry Ellard, LA	-				SN		-

Defense

		UPI	PB	PFW	AP	SN	FWA	NEA
E	RICHARD DENT, Chi	UPI	PB		AP		FWA	
E	Leonard Marshall, NY	UPI	PB					

Pos	Player	UPI	PB	AP	SN	FWA	NEA
T	RANDY WHITE, Dal	UPI	PB	AP	SN		NEA
T	Steve McMichael, Chi			AP			
LB	LAWRENCE TAYLOR, NY	UPI	PB	AP	SN	FWA	NEA
LB	MIKE SINGLETARY, Chi	UPI	PB	AP	SN	FWA	NEA
LB	E.J. Junior, StL	UPI					
LB	Otis Wilson, Chi	UPI					
LB	Harry Carson, NY		PB				
LB	Rickey Jackson, NO		PB				
LB	Jim Collins, LA				SN		
CB	ERIC WRIGHT, SF	UPI	PB	AP	SN		NEA
CB	Everson Walls, Dal	UPI	PB			FWA	
S	WES HOPKINS, Phi	UPI	PB	AP	SN	FWA	NEA
S	Michael Downs, Dal	UPI					
S	Carlton Williamson, SF		PB				
P	DALE HATCHER, LA	UPI	PB	AP	SN	FWA	
ST	Joey Browner, Min	-	PB	-	-	-	-

1985 ALL-AFC
Offense

Pos	Player	UPI	PB	AP	SN	FWA	NEA
WR+	STEVE LARGENT, Sea	UPI	PB	AP		FWA	
WR+	LOUIS LIPPS, Pit	UPI	PB			FWA	NEA
TE	TODD CHRISTENSEN, LA	UPI		AP	SN	FWA	NEA
TE	Ozzie Newsome, Cle		PB				
T	ANTHONY MUNOZ, Cin	UPI	PB	AP	SN	FWA	NEA
T	Chris Hinton, Ind	UPI					
T	Brian Holloway, NE		PB				
G	JOHN HANNAH, NE	UPI	PB	AP			
G	Roy Foster, Mia	UPI					
G	Mike Munchak, Hou		PB				
C	DWIGHT STEPHENSON, Mia	UPI	PB	AP	SN		
QB	DAN MARINO, Mia	UPI	PB	AP	SN	FWA	
QB	Dan Fouts, SD						NEA
RB	MARCUS ALLEN, LA	UPI	PB	AP	SN	FWA	NEA
RB	Freeman McNeil, NY	UPI	PB				
K	Gary Anderson, Pit	UPI	PB			FWA	
K	Nick Lowery, KC			AP			NEA
KR	Irving Fryar, NE	-	PB				-

Defense

Pos	Player	UPI	PB	AP	SN	FWA	NEA
E	HOWIE LONG, LA	UPI	PB	AP		FWA	NEA
E	Mark Gastineau, NY				SN		NEA
E	Rulon Jones, Den	UPI			SN		
T	Joe Klecko, NY	UPI	PB	AP		FWA	
T	Bob Golic, Cle				SN		
LB	ANDRE TIPPETT, NE	UPI	PB	AP		FWA	NEA
LB	KARL MECKLENBURG, Den	UPI	PB	AP		FWA	NEA
LB	Chip Banks, Cle	UPI	PB				
LB	Lance Mehl, NY	UPI					
LB	Steve Nelson, NE		PB				
CB	MIKE HAYNES, LA	UPI	PB	AP	SN	FWA	NEA
CB	Louis Wright, Den	UPI	PB				
S	KENNY EASLEY, Sea	UPI	PB	AP	SN	FWA	NEA
S	Deron Cherry, Sea	UPI	PB				
P	Rohn Stark, Ind	UPI	PB				NEA
ST	Fredd Young, Sea	-	PB	-		-	-

1986 ALL-NFC
Offense

Pos	Player	UPI	PB	PFW	AP	SN	FWA	NEA
WR	JERRY RICE, SF	UPI	PB	PFW*	AP	SN	FWA	NEA
WR	Gary Clark, Was	UPI	PB	PFW				
TE	MARK BAVARO, NY	UPI	PB	PFW*	AP	SN	FWA	
T	JIM COVERT, Chi	UPI	PB	PFW*	AP	SN	FWA	
T	Jackie Slater, LA	UPI	PB	PFW				
G	DENNIS HARRAH, LA	UPI	PB	PFW*	AP	SN		
G	BILL FRALIC, Atl		PB	PFW*	AP	SN		NEA
G	Russ Grimm, Was	UPI					FWA	NEA
C	Jay Hilgenberg, Chi	UPI	PB	PFW				
QB	Tommy Kramer, Min	UPI	PB	PFW				
QB	Phil Simms, NY							NEA
RB	ERIC DICKERSON, LA	UPI	PB	PFW*	AP	SN	FWA	NEA
RB	JOE MORRIS, NY	UPI		PFW*	AP	SN	FWA	NEA
RB	Walter Payton, Chi		PB					
K	MORTEN ANDERSEN, NO	UPI	PB	PFW*	AP	SN	FWA	NEA
KR	Dennis Gentry, Chi	-		PFW*			FWA	-
KR	Vai Sikahema, StL	-	PB	PFW				-
KR	Mel Gray, NO	-				SN		

Defense

Pos	Player	UPI	PB	PFW	AP	SN	FWA	NEA
E	DEXTER MANLEY, Was	UPI	PB	PFW*	AP	SN	FWA	NEA
E	Dan Hampton, Chi	UPI						NEA
T	REGGIE WHITE, Phi	UPI	PB-e	PFW-e	AP		FWA	NEA
T	Steve McMichael, Chi		PB	PFW*		SN	FWA	
T	Jim Burt, NY			PFW				
T	Michael Carter, SF							NEA
LB	LAWRENCE TAYLOR, NY	UPI	PB	PFW*	AP	SN	FWA	NEA
LB	MIKE SINGLETARY, Chi	UPI	PB	PFW*	AP	SN	FWA	NEA
LB	WILBER MARSHALL, Chi	UPI	PB	PFW*	AP	SN	FWA	
LB	Harry Carson, NY	UPI	PB	PFW				
LB	Rickey Jackson, NO							NEA
CB	LEROY IRVIN, LA	UPI	PB		AP	SN	FWA	
CB	Darrell Green, Was		PB	PFW				NEA
CB	Jerry Gray, LA	UPI		PFW				
S	RONNIE LOTT, SF	UPI	PB	PFW*	AP		FWA	NEA
S	DAVE DUERSON, Chi	UPI	PB	PFW*		SN	FWA	
P	SEAN LANDETA, NY	UPI	PB	PFW*	AP	SN	FWA	
ST	Ron Wolfley, StL	-	PB		-	-	-	
ST	Neal Anderson, Chi	-		PFW				

1986 ALL-AFC
Offense

Pos	Player	UPI	PB	PFW	AP	SN	FWA	NEA
WR	AL TOON, NY	UPI	PB	PFW*	AP		FWA	NEA
WR	Stanley Morgan, NE	UPI		PFW		SN		
WR	Steve Largent, Sea		PB					
TE	Todd Christensen, LA	UPI	PB	PFW				NEA
T	ANTHONY MUNOZ, Cin	UPI	PB	PFW*	AP	SN	FWA	NEA
T	Cody Risien, Cle		PB	PFW				
T	Chris Hinton, Ind	UPI						
T	Brian Holloway, NE							NEA
G	Max Montoya, Cin	UPI	PB	PFW				
G	Roy Foster, Mia	UPI		PFW				
G	Keith Bishop, Den		PB					
C	DWIGHT STEPHENSON, Mia	UPI	PB	PFW*	AP	SN	FWA	NEA
QB	DAN MARINO, Mia	UPI	PB	PFW*	AP	SN	FWA	
RB	James Brooks, Cin	UPI	PB	PFW				
RB	Curt Warner, Sea	UPI	PB	PFW				
K	Tony Franklin, NE	UPI	PB	PFW				
KR	BOBBY JOE EDMONDS, Sea	-	PB	PFW*	AP	SN	FWA	-
KR	Tim McGee, Cin	-		PFW				

Defense

Pos	Player	UPI	PB	PFW	AP	SN	FWA	NEA
E	RULON JONES, Den	UPI	PB	PFW*	AP	SN	FWA	NEA
E	Howie Long, LA		PB	PFW				
E	Art Still, KC	UPI						
T	Bill Pickel, LA	UPI			AP			
T	Bill Maas, KC		PB	PFW*				
LB	KARL MECKLENBURG, Den	UPI	PB	PFW*	AP	SN	FWA	NEA
LB	Chip Banks, Cle	UPI	PB	PFW				
LB	John Offerdahl, Mia	UPI	PB	PFW				
LB	Andre Tippett, NE	UPI	PB	PFW				
CB	HANFORD DIXON, Cle	UPI	PB	PFW*	AP	SN	FWA	NEA
CB	Ray Clayborn, NE			PFW*				
CB	Mike Haynes, LA		PB					
CB	Ronnie Lippett, NE	UPI						
S	Deron Cherry, KC	UPI	PB	PFW	AP			NEA
S	Dennis Smith, Den		PB	PFW				NEA
S	Lloyd Burruss, KC	UPI						
P	Rohn Stark, Ind	UPI	PB	PFW				NEA
ST	Mosi Tatupu, NE	-	PB	PFW*	-	-	-	-

1987 ALL-NFC
Offense

Pos	Player	UPI	PB	PFW	AP	SN	FWA	NEA
WR	JERRY RICE, SF	UPI	PB	PFW*	AP	SN	FWA	NEA
WR	J.T. Smith, StL	UPI		PFW*		SN		
WR	Mike Quick, Phi		PB					NEA
WR	Gary Clark, Was				AP			
TE	MARK BAVARO, NY	UPI	PB	PFW*	AP	SN	FWA	NEA
T	GARY ZIMMERMAN, Min		PB	PFW*	AP	SN	FWA	
T	Jackie Slater, LA	UPI	PB	PFW				NEA
T	Jim Covert, Chi	UPI						
T	Joe Jacoby, Was							NEA
G	BILL FRALIC, Atl	UPI	PB	PFW*	AP	SN	FWA	
G	Tom Newberry, LA	UPI	PB	PFW				
G	Dennis Harrah, LA		PB					
C	Jay Hilgenberg, Chi	UPI	PB	PFW		SN		
QB	JOE MONTANA, SF	UPI	PB	PFW*	AP	SN	FWA	
RB	CHARLES WHITE, LA	UPI	PB	PFW*	AP	SN	FWA	
RB	Rueben Mayes, NO	UPI	PB					
RB	Herschel Walker, Dal			PFW				
K	MORTEN ANDERSEN, NO	UPI	PB	PFW*	AP	SN	FWA	NEA
KR	MEL GRAY, NO	-		PFW*		SN	FWA	-
KR	Vai Sikahema, StL	-	PB		AP			-
KR	Sylvester Stamps, Atl	-		PFW*				-
KR	Dennis Gentry, Chi	-					FWA	-

Defense

Pos	Player	UPI	PB	PFW	AP	SN	FWA	NEA
E	REGGIE WHITE, Phi	UPI	PB	PFW*	AP	SN	FWA	NEA
E	Chris Doleman, Min	UPI	PB	PFW				NEA
T	MICHAEL CARTER, SF	UPI	PB	PFW	AP	SN	FWA	NEA
T	Steve McMichael, Chi			PFW*	AP	SN	FWA	
LB	CARL BANKS, NY				AP	SN	FWA	NEA
LB	MIKE SINGLETARY, Chi	UPI	PB	PFW*	AP	SN	FWA	
LB	Rickey Jackson, NO					SN		NEA
LB	Vaughan Johnson, NO	UPI		PFW				
LB	Wilber Marshall, Chi		PB	PFW				
LB	Harry Carson, NY		PB					
LB	Pat Swilling, NO	UPI						
LB	Lawrence Taylor, NY			PFW*				
CB	Barry Wilburn, Was	UPI		PFW	AP			
CB	Jerry Gray, LA		PB	PFW				

		UPI	PB	PFW	AP	SN	FWA	NEA
CB	Darrell Green, Was		PB					NEA
CB	Dave Waymer, NO	UPI						
S	JOEY BROWNER, Min	UPI	PB	PFW*	AP	SN	FWA	NEA
S	RONNIE LOTT, SF	UPI	PB	PFW*	AP	SN	FWA	
P	JIM ARNOLD, Det	UPI	PB	PFW*	-	-	FWA	NEA
ST	Ron Wolfley, StL	-	PB	PFW*	-	-	-	-

1987 All-AFC

Offense

		UPI	PB	PFW	AP	SN	FWA	NEA
WR	STEVE LARGENT, Sea	UPI	PB	PFW			FWA	
WR	Al Toon, NY	UPI	PB	PFW*				
TE	Kellen Winslow, SD	UPI	PB					
TE	Todd Christensen, LA			PFW				
T	ANTHONY MUNOZ, Cin	UPI	PB	PFW*	AP		FWA	
T	Chris Hinton, Ind		PB	PFW		SN		
T	Jim Lachey, SD	UPI						
G	MIKE MUNCHAK, Hou	UPI	PB	PFW*	AP	SN	FWA	NEA
G	Ron Solt, Ind	UPI		PFW				NEA
G	Keith Bishop, Den		PB					
C	DWIGHT STEPHENSON, Mia	UPI		PFW*	AP		FWA	
C	Ray Donaldson, Ind		PB					
C	Mike Webster, Pit							NEA
QB	John Elway, Den	UPI	PB	PFW		SN		NEA
RB	ERIC DICKERSON, Ind	UPI	PB	PFW*	AP	SN	FWA	NEA
RB	Curt Warner, Sea	UPI	PB	PFW				NEA
K	Dean Biasucci, Ind	UPI	PB	PFW				
KR	Lionel James, SD	-		PFW				-
KR	Gerald McNeil, Cle	-	PB					-
KR	Paul Palmer, KC	-		PFW				-

Defense

		UPI	PB	PFW	AP	SN	FWA	NEA
E	BRUCE SMITH, Buf	UPI	PB	PFW*	AP	SN	FWA	
E	Jacob Green, Sea	UPI	PB	PFW				
T	Bill Maas, KC	UPI	PB	PFW*				
LB	FREDD YOUNG, Sea	UPI	PB	PFW*	AP	SN	FWA	NEA
LB	ANDRE TIPPETT, NE	UPI	PB	PFW*	AP		FWA	
LB	Karl Mecklenburg, Den	UPI	PB	PFW				NEA
LB	Duane Bickett, Ind	UPI	PB	PFW				
CB	HANFORD DIXON, Cle	UPI	PB	PFW*	AP		FWA	NEA
CB	FRANK MINNIFIELD, Cle	UPI	PB	PFW*		SN	FWA	
S	Keith Bostic, Hou	UPI		PFW				
S	Kenny Easley, Sea		PB	PFW				
S	Vann McElroy, LA	UPI						
S	Deron Cherry, KC		PB					
P	Ralf Mojsiejenko, SD	UPI	PB					
P	Reggie Roby, Mia			PFW				
ST	Steve Tasker, Buf	-	PB	PFW	-	-	-	-

1988 All-NFC

Offense

		UPI	PB	PFW	AP	SN	FWA	NEA
WR	JERRY RICE, SF	UPI	PB	PFW*	AP	SN	FWA	
WR	HENRY ELLARD, LA	UPI		PFW	AP	SN	FWA	NEA
WR	Anthony Carter, Min		PB					
TE	KEITH JACKSON, Phi	UPI	PB	PFW*	AP	SN	FWA	
T	GARY ZIMMERMAN, Min	UPI	PB		AP		FWA	
T	Luis Sharpe, Pho	UPI		PFW				
T	Jackie Slater, LA		PB	PFW*				
T	Irv Pankey, LA							NEA
G	TOM NEWBERRY, LA	UPI	PB	PFW*	AP	SN	FWA	
G	Bill Fralic, Atl	UPI	PB					NEA
G	Mark May, Was			PFW				
C	JAY HILGENBERG, Chi	UPI	PB	PFW*	AP	SN	FWA	
QB	Randall Cunningham, Phi	UPI	PB	PFW				
RB	ROGER CRAIG, SF	UPI	PB	PFW*	AP	SN	FWA	NEA
RB	Herschel Walker, Dal	UPI	PB	PFW				
K	Morten Anderson, NO	UPI	PB					
K	Eddie Murray, Det			PFW				
KR+	JOHN TAYLOR, SF	-	PB	PFW*	-	SN	FWA	-
KR	Dennis Gentry, Chi	-		PFW	-			-

Defense

		UPI	PB	PFW	AP	SN	FWA	NEA
E	REGGIE WHITE, Phi	UPI	PB	PFW*	AP	SN	FWA	NEA
E	Richard Dent, Chi	UPI		PFW				
E	Chris Doleman, Min		PB					
T	Keith Millard, Min		PB		AP	SN	FWA	
T	Dan Hampton, Chi	UPI		PFW*				NEA
T	Michael Carter, SF			PFW				NEA
LB	MIKE SINGLETARY, Chi	UPI	PB	PFW*	AP	SN	FWA	NEA
LB	LAWRENCE TAYLOR, NY	UPI	PB	PFW*	AP	SN	FWA	
LB	Vaughan Johnson, NO	UPI						NEA
LB	Tim Harris, GB			PFW				NEA
LB	Mike Cofer, Det		PB					
LB	Charles Haley, SF	UPI						
LB	Sam Mills, NO		PB					
CB	CARL LEE, Min	UPI	PB	PFW*	AP	SN	FWA	
CB	Jerry Gray, LA		PB	PFW				
CB	Scott Case, Atl	UPI						
S	JOEY BROWNER, Min	UPI	PB	PFW*	AP	SN	FWA	NEA
S	Ronnie Lott, SF	UPI	PB					NEA
S	Dave Duerson, Chi			PFW				

		UPI	PB	PFW	AP	SN	FWA	NEA
P	Jim Arnold, Det	UPI	PB	PFW*			FWA+	NEA
ST	Ron Wolfley, Pho	-	PB	PFW*	-	-	-	
ST	Robert Delpino, LA	-		PFW	-	-	-	

1988 All-AFC

Offense

		UPI	PB	PFW	AP	SN	FWA	NEA
WR	Eddie Brown, Cin	UPI	PB	PFW				NEA
WR	Al Toon, NY	UPI	PB	PFW*				
TE	Mickey Shuler, NY	UPI	PB	PFW				NEA
T	ANTHONY MUNOZ, Cin	UPI	PB	PFW*	AP	SN	FWA	NEA
T	Bruce Armstrong, NE	UPI				SN		
T	Chris Hinton, Ind		PB					
T	Tunch Ilkin, Pit			PFW				
G	BRUCE MATTHEWS, Hou	UPI	PB	PFW*	AP	SN	FWA	
G	Max Montoya, Cin	UPI	PB					
G	Mike Munchak, Hou			PFW				NEA
C	Ray Donaldson, Ind		PB	PFW				
C	Kent Hull, Buf	UPI						
QB	BOOMER ESIASON, Cin	UPI	PB	PFW*	AP	SN	FWA	NEA
RB	ERIC DICKERSON, Ind	UPI	PB	PFW*	AP	SN	FWA	NEA
RB	John Stephens, NE	UPI	PB	PFW*	AP			
K	SCOTT NORWOOD, Buf	UPI	PB	PFW*	AP		FWA	
K	Dean Biasucci, Ind					SN		
K	Nick Lowery, KC							NEA
KR+	TIM BROWN, LA	-	PB	PFW*	-	SN	FWA	-
KR	JoJo Townsell, NY	-		PFW	-	-	-	

Defense

		UPI	PB	PFW	AP	SN	FWA	NEA
E	BRUCE SMITH, Buf	UPI	PB	PFW*	AP	SN	FWA	NEA
E	Ray Childress, Hou	UPI	PB	PFW				
E	Lee Williams, SD		PB					
T	TIM KRUMRIE, Cin		PB	PFW*	AP	SN	FWA	
T	Fred Smerlas, Buf	UPI						
LB	CORNELIUS BENNETT, Buf	UPI	PB	PFW*		SN	FWA	NEA
LB	SHANE CONLAN, Buf	UPI	PB	PFW*		SN	FWA	
LB	John Offerdahl, Mia	UPI	PB	PFW				
LB	Andre Tippett, NE	UPI	PB	PFW				
CB	FRANK MINNIFIELD, Cle	UPI	PB	PFW*	AP	SN	FWA	
CB	Albert Lewis, KC	UPI	PB	PFW				
CB	Ronnie Lippett, NE							NEA
S	DERON CHERRY, KC	UPI	PB	PFW*	AP	SN	FWA	
S	David Fulcher, Cin	UPI	PB	PFW				
P	MIKE HORAN, Den	UPI	PB	PFW	AP	SN	FWA+	
ST	Rufus Porter, Sea	-	PB		-	-	-	
ST	Eugene Seale, Hou	-		PFW*	-	-	-	

1989 All-NFC

Offense

		UPI	PB	PFW	AP	SN	FWA	NEA
WR	JERRY RICE, SF	UPI	PB	PFW*	AP	SN	FWA	NEA
WR	STERLING SHARPE, GB	UPI	PB	PFW*	AP	SN	FWA	NEA
TE	KEITH JACKSON, Phi	UPI	PB	PFW	AP	SN	FWA	
T	JIM LACHEY, Was	UPI		PFW*	AP	SN		
T	Jackie Slater, LA		PB	PFW				NEA
T	Gary Zimmerman, Min		PB				FWA	
T	Paul Gruber, TB	UPI						
G	TOM NEWBERRY, LA	UPI	PB	PFW*	AP	SN	FWA	
G	Randall McDaniel, Min		PB	PFW				
G	Bill Fralic, Atl	UPI						
G	Rich Moran, GB							NEA
C	JAY HILGENBERG, Chi	UPI	PB	PFW*	AP		FWA	NEA
QB	JOE MONTANA, SF	UPI	PB	PFW*	AP	SN	FWA	NEA
RB	BARRY SANDERS, Det	UPI	PB	PFW*	AP	SN	FWA	
RB	Neal Anderson, Chi	UPI	PB	PFW				
K	EDDIE MURRAY, Det		PB	PFW*			FWA	
K	Mike Cofer, SF	UPI			AP			NEA
K	Mike Lansford, LA					SN		
KR	Dave Meggett, NY	-	PB		-		FWA	-
KR	Walter Stanley, Det	-		PFW*	-	SN		
KR	Mel Gray, Det	-		PFW	-			

Defense

		UPI	PB	PFW	AP	SN	FWA	NEA
E	CHRIS DOLEMAN, Min	UPI	PB	PFW*	AP	SN	FWA	NEA
E	REGGIE WHITE, Phi	UPI	PB	PFW*	AP		FWA	NEA
T	KEITH MILLARD, Min	UPI	PB	PFW*	AP	SN	FWA	NEA
T	Jerry Ball, Det			PFW*				
T	Michael Carter, SF							NEA

Pos	Player	UPI	PB	PFW	AP	SN	FWA	NEA
LB	TIM HARRIS, GB	UPI	PB	PFW*	AP	SN	FWA	NEA
LB	MIKE SINGLETARY, Chi	UPI	PB	PFW*	AP	SN	FWA	
LB	LAWRENCE TAYLOR, NY	UPI	PB	PFW*	AP		FWA	
LB	Vaughan Johnson, NO	UPI		PFW				NEA
LB	Kevin Greene, LA					SN		NEA
LB	Eugene Lockhart, Dal					SN		
LB	Chris Spielman, Det		PB					
CB	ERIC ALLEN, Phi	UPI	PB	PFW*	AP			
CB	Jerry Gray, LA		PB	PFW			FWA	
CB	Mark Collins, NY							NEA
CB	Don Griffin, SF	UPI						
CB	Carl Lee, Min		PB					
S	RONNIE LOTT, SF	UPI	PB	PFW*	AP		FWA	
S	Tim McDonald, Pho	UPI		PFW+				NEA
S	Joey Browner, Min		PB	PFW+				NEA
S	Harry Hamilton, TB					SN		
P	SEAN LANDETA, NY	UPI		PFW*	AP	SN	FWA	
P	Rich Camarillo, Pho		PB					
ST	Ron Wolfley, Pho	-	PB	PFW	-	-	-	-

1989 ALL-AFC

Offense

Pos	Player	UPI	PB	PFW	AP	SN	FWA	NEA
WR	Andre Reed, Buf	UPI	PB	PFW				
WR	Webster Slaughter, Cle	UPI	PB					
WR	Anthony Miller, SD			PFW				
TE	Rodney Holman, Cin	UPI	PB	PFW*				NEA
T	ANTHONY MUNOZ, Cin	UPI	PB	PFW*	AP	SN	FWA	NEA
T	Chris Hinton, Ind	UPI	PB	PFW				
G+	BRUCE MATTHEWS, Hou	UPI	PB	PFW*	AP	SN		
G+	MIKE MUNCHAK, Hou	UPI	PB	PFW*			FWA	NEA
C	Kent Hull, Buf	UPI		PFW		SN		
C	Ray Donaldson, Ind		PB					
QB	Warren Moon, Hou	UPI	PB					
QB	Boomer Esiason, Cin			PFW				
RB	CHRISTIAN OKOYE, KC	UPI	PB	PFW*	AP	SN	FWA	NEA
RB	Thurman Thomas, Buf	UPI		PFW				NEA
RB	James Brooks, Cin		PB					
K	David Treadwell, Den	UPI	PB	PFW				
KR	ROD WOODSON, Pit*	-		PFW*	-	SN	FWA	-
KR	Clarence Verdin, Ind	-		PFW				

Defense

Pos	Player	UPI	PB	PFW	AP	SN	FWA	NEA
E	Lee Williams, SD	UPI	PB	PFW		SN		
E	Bruce Smith, Buf	UPI	PB	PFW				
T	MICHAEL DEAN PERRY, Cle	UPI	PB	PFW	AP	SN	FWA	
T	Greg Kragen, Den			PFW				
LB	Karl Mecklenburg, Den	UPI	PB	PFW*				NEA
LB	Derrick Thomas, KC	UPI	PB	PFW				
LB	Mike Johnson, Cle	UPI		PFW				
LB	Leslie O'Neal, SD	UPI		PFW				
LB	Clay Matthews, Cle		PB					
LB	John Offerdahl, Mia		PB					
CB	ALBERT LEWIS, KC	UPI	PB	PFW*	AP	SN	FWA	NEA
CB	Frank Minnifield, Cle	UPI	PB					
CB	Gill Byrd, SD					SN		
CB	Rod Woodson, Pit*			PFW				
S	DAVID FULCHER, Cin	UPI	PB	PFW*	AP	SN	FWA	
S	Erik McMillan, NY	UPI	PB					
S	Dennis Smith, Den			PFW				
P	Greg Montgomery, Hou	UPI		PFW				NEA
P	Reggie Roby, Mia		PB					
ST	Rufus Porter, Sea	-	PB	PFW*	-	-	-	-

1990 ALL-NFC

Offense

Pos	Player	UPI	PB	PFW	AP	SN	FWA	NEA
WR	JERRY RICE, SF	UPI	PB	PFW*	AP	SN	FWA	NEA
WR	ANDRE RISON, Atl	UPI	PB	PFW*	AP	SN	FWA	NEA
TE	KEITH JACKSON, Phi	UPI	PB	PFW*	AP	SN	FWA	NEA
T	JIM LACHEY, Was	UPI	PB	PFW*	AP	SN	FWA	NEA
T	Jackie Slater, LA		PB	PFW				
T	Lomas Brown, Det	UPI						
G	Randall McDaniel, Min	UPI	PB	PFW	AP			
G	Mark Bortz, Chi		PB	PFW				NEA
G	Guy McIntyre, SF	UPI						
C	Jay Hilgenberg, Chi	UPI	PB	PFW				
QB	Randall Cunningham, Phi	UPI		PFW*			FWA	
QB	Joe Montana, SF		PB		AP			NEA
RB	BARRY SANDERS, Det	UPI	PB	PFW*	AP	SN	FWA	NEA
RB	Neal Anderson, Chi	UPI	PB	PFW				
K	Steve Christie, TB	UPI		PFW				
K	Morten Andersen, NO		PB					
KR	MEL GRAY, Det	UPI	PB	PFW*	AP	SN	FWA	-
KR	DAVE MEGGETT, NY	UPI	PB	PFW		SN	FWA	-

Defense

Pos	Player	UPI	PB	PFW	AP	SN	FWA	NEA
E	REGGIE WHITE, Phi	UPI	PB	PFW*	AP		FWA	NEA-t
E	Richard Dent, Chi	UPI		PFW				
E	Chris Doleman, Min		PB					
T	Jerome Brown, Phi	UPI	PB	PFW	AP			
T	Jerry Ball, Det			PFW				

Pos	Player	UPI	PB	PFW	AP	SN	FWA	NEA
LB	CHARLES HALEY, SF	UPI	PB	PFW*	AP		FWA	NEA
LB	PEPPER JOHNSON, NY	UPI	PB	PFW*	AP	SN	FWA	NEA
LB	Mike Singletary, Chi	UPI	PB	PFW				
LB	Lawrence Taylor, NY	UPI	PB	PFW				
CB	Darrell Green, Was	UPI	PB	PFW*				
CB	Mark Collins, NY	UPI						
CB	Wayne Haddix, TB			PFW				
CB	Carl Lee, Min		PB					
S	JOEY BROWNER, Min	UPI	PB	PFW*	AP	SN	FWA	NEA
S	RONNIE LOTT, SF		PB		AP	SN	FWA	NEA
S	Mark Carrier, Chi	UPI		PFW*				
P	SEAN LANDETA, NY	UPI	PB	PFW*	AP	SN	FWA	NEA
ST	Reyna Thompson, NY	-	PB	PFW*	-	-	-	-

1990 ALL-AFC

Offense

Pos	Player	UPI	PB	PFW	AP	SN	FWA	NEA
WR	Andre Reed, Buf	UPI	PB	PFW				
WR	Anthony Miller, SD		PB	PFW				
WR	Ernest Givins, Hou	UPI						
TE	Rodney Holman, Cin	UPI	PB	PFW				
T	ANTHONY MUNOZ, Cin	UPI	PB	PFW*	AP		FWA	NEA
T	John Alt, KC	UPI				SN		
T	Bruce Armstrong, NE		PB	PFW				
G	BRUCE MATTHEWS, Hou	UPI	PB	PFW*	AP		FWA	NEA
G	STEVE WISNIEWSKI, LA	UPI		PFW*		SN	FWA	
G	Mike Munchak, Hou		PB					
C	KENT HULL, Buf	UPI	PB	PFW*	AP		FWA	NEA
QB	WARREN MOON, Hou	UPI	PB	PFW		SN		
RB	THURMAN THOMAS, Buf	UPI	PB	PFW*	AP		FWA	NEA
RB	Marion Butts, SD	UPI	PB	PFW				
K	NICK LOWERY, KC	UPI	PB	PFW*	AP	SN	FWA	NEA
KR	Clarence Verdin, Ind	UPI	PB	PFW*				-
KR	Rod Woodson, Pit	UPI		PFW				

Defense

Pos	Player	UPI	PB	PFW	AP	SN	FWA	NEA
E	BRUCE SMITH, Buf	UPI	PB	PFW*	AP	SN	FWA	NEA
E	Greg Townsend, LA	UPI	PB	PFW		SN		NEA
T	MICHAEL DEAN PERRY, Cle	UPI	PB	PFW*	AP	SN	FWA	NEA
T	Ray Childress, Hou					SN	FWA	
T	Dan Saleaumua, KC			PFW*				
LB	JOHN OFFERDAHL, Mia	UPI	PB	PFW*	AP	SN	FWA	NEA
LB	DERRICK THOMAS, KC	UPI	PB	PFW*	AP	SN	FWA	NEA
LB	David Little, Pit	UPI		PFW				
LB	Darryl Talley, Buf			PFW		SN		
LB	Cornelius Bennett, Buf	UPI						
LB	Shane Conlan, Buf		PB					
LB	Leslie O'Neal, SD		PB					
CB	ROD WOODSON, Pit	UPI	PB	PFW*	AP	SN	FWA	NEA
CB	ALBERT LEWIS, KC	UPI	PB	PFW	AP	SN	FWA	NEA
S	David Fulcher, Cin	UPI	PB	PFW				
S	Steve Atwater, Den	UPI	PB	PFW				
P	Rohn Stark, Ind	UPI	PB	PFW				
ST	Steve Tasker, Buf	-	PB	PFW	-	-	-	-

1991 ALL-NFC

Offense

Pos	Player	UPI	PB	PFW	AP	SN	FWA	NEA
WR	MICHAEL IRVIN, Dal	UPI	PB	PFW*	AP		FWA	NEA
WR	Jerry Rice, SF		PB	PFW*		SN		
WR	Gary Clark, Was	UPI						NEA
WR	Andre Rison, Atl							NEA
TE	Jay Novacek, Dal	UPI	PB	PFW				
T	JIM LACHEY, Was	UPI	PB	PFW*	AP	SN	FWA	NEA
T	MIKE KENN, Atl	UPI	PB	PFW*	AP		FWA	
T	Lomas Brown, Det		PB					NEA
G	Randall McDaniel, Min		PB	PFW		SN		NEA
G	Guy McIntyre, SF	UPI	PB	PFW				
G	Raleigh McKenzie, Was	UPI						
C	Jay Hilgenberg, Chi	UPI	PB	PFW				
QB	Mark Rypien, Was	UPI	PB	PFW				
RB	BARRY SANDERS, Det	UPI	PB	PFW*	AP		FWA	NEA
RB	Emmitt Smith, Dal	UPI	PB	PFW				
K	Chip Lohmiller, Was					SN		
KR	MEL GRAY, Det	-	PB	PFW*	AP	SN	FWA	-

Defense

Pos	Player	UPI	PB	PFW	AP	SN	FWA	NEA
E	CLYDE SIMMONS, Phi	UPI	PB	PFW*	AP	SN	FWA	NEA
E	REGGIE WHITE, Phi	UPI	PB	PFW*	AP	SN	FWA	NEA
T	JERRY BALL, Det	UPI		PFW*	AP	SN	FWA	NEA
T	JEROME BROWN, Phi		PB	PFW*	AP	SN	FWA	NEA
LB	PAT SWILLING, NO	UPI	PB	PFW*	AP	SN	FWA	NEA
LB	SAM MILLS, NO		PB	PFW		SN	FWA	
LB	Seth Joyner, Phi		PB	PFW			FWA	NEA
LB	Mike Singletary, Chi	UPI			AP	SN		
LB	Vaughan Johnson, NO	UPI		PFW				
LB	Wilber Marshall, Was	UPI						
LB	Chris Spielman, Det				AP			
LB	Jessie Tuggle, Atl	UPI						
CB	DARRELL GREEN, Was	UPI	PB	PFW*	AP	SN	FWA	NEA
CB	DEION SANDERS, Atl	UPI	PB	PFW		SN	FWA	NEA
S	Mark Carrier, Chi		PB			SN		NEA
S	Bennie Blades, Det	UPI		PFW				

Pos	Player	UPI	PB	PFW	AP	SN	FWA	NEA
S	Tim McDonald, Pho		PB	PFW				
S	Andre Waters, Phi	UPI						
P	Rich Camarillo, Pho	UPI	PB	PFW				
ST	Bennie Thompson, NO	-	PB	PFW	-	-	-	

Pos	Player	UPI	PB	PFW	AP	SN	FWA	NEA
CB	Ricky Reynolds, TB			PFW				
S	Tim McDonald, Pho		PB	PFW				NEA
S	Chuck Cecil, GB		PB	PFW				
S	Brad Edwards, Was	UPI						
S	Todd Scott, Min	UPI						
P	RICH CAMARILLO, Pho	UPI	PB	PFW*	AP			
ST	Elbert Shelley, Atl	-	PB	PFW	-	-	-	

1991 All-AFC

Offense

Pos	Player	UPI	PB	PFW	AP	SN	FWA	NEA
WR	HAYWOOD JEFFIRES, Hou	UPI	PB	PFW	AP		FWA	
WR	Andre Reed, Buf	UPI	PB	PFW				
TE	MARV COOK, NE	UPI	PB	PFW*	AP	SN	FWA	NEA
T	Bruce Armstrong, NE	UPI	PB	PFW				
T	Anthony Munoz, Cin		PB			SN		
T	John Alt, KC	UPI						
T	Howard Ballard, Buf			PFW				
G	STEVE WISNIEWSKI, LA	UPI	PB	PFW*	AP	SN	FWA	NEA
G	MIKE MUNCHAK, Hou	UPI	PB	PFW*	AP		FWA	
C	BRUCE MATTHEWS, Hou		PB	PFW*				NEA
C	Kent Hull, Buf	UPI			AP		FWA	
C	Don Mosebar, LA					SN		
QB	JIM KELLY, Buf	UPI	PB	PFW*	AP		FWA	NEA
RB	THURMAN THOMAS, Buf	UPI	PB	PFW*	AP	SN	FWA	NEA
RB	Christian Okoye, KC		PB	PFW				
RB	Gaston Green, Den	UPI						
K	JEFF JAEGER, LA	UPI	PB	PFW*	AP		FWA	
K	Pete Stoyanovich, Mia							NEA
KR	Tim Brown, LA	-	PB	PFW			-	
KR	Nate Lewis, SD			PFW				

Defense

Pos	Player	UPI	PB	PFW	AP	SN	FWA	NEA
E	William Fuller, Hou	UPI	PB	PFW				
E	Greg Townsend, LA	UPI	PB	PFW				
T	Ray Childress, Hou	UPI		PFW				NEA
T	Michael Dean Perry, Cle		PB	PFW		SN		
T	Greg Kragen, Den	UPI						
LB	DERRICK THOMAS, KC	UPI	PB	PFW*	AP	SN		
LB	Al Smith, Hou	UPI	PB	PFW*			FWA	
LB	Cornelius Bennett, Buf	UPI	PB	PFW				NEA
LB	Junior Seau, SD		PB					NEA
LB	Vincent Brown, NE			PFW				
LB	Karl Mecklenburg, Den	UPI						
CB	Cris Dishman, Hou	UPI	PB	PFW*	AP			
CB	Gill Byrd, SD		PB	PFW				
CB	Nate Odomes, Buf	UPI						
S	RONNIE LOTT, LA	UPI	PB	PFW*	AP	SN	FWA	
S	STEVE ATWATER, Den	UPI	PB	PFW*	AP		FWA	NEA
P	JEFF GOSSETT, LA		PB	PFW*	AP	SN	FWA	NEA
P	Reggie Roby, Mia	UPI						
ST	Steve Tasker, Buf	-	PB	PFW*	-	-	-	

1992 All-AFC

Offense

Pos	Player	UPI	PB	PFW	AP	SN	NEA
WR	Haywood Jeffires, Hou	UPI	PB	PFW			
WR	Anthony Miller, SD	UPI	PB	PFW			
TE	Keith Jackson, Mia	UPI	PB	PFW		SN	
T	RICHMOND WEBB, Mia	UPI	PB	PFW	AP	SN	
T+	HOWARD BALLARD, Buf	UPI	PB	PFW			
G	STEVE WISNIEWSKI, LA		PB	PFW*	AP	SN	
G	Mike Munchak, Hou	UPI	PB	PFW			
G	Carlton Haselrig, Pit	UPI					
C	BRUCE MATTHEWS, Hou	UPI	PB	PFW*		SN	NEA-g
QB	Dan Marino, Mia	UPI	PB	PFW			
RB	BARRY FOSTER, Pit	UPI	PB	PFW*	AP	SN	NEA
RB	Thurman Thomas, Buf	UPI	PB	PFW			
K	Pete Stoyanovich, Mia	UPI	PB	PFW	AP	SN	
K	Nick Lowery, KC		PB				
KR	Clarence Verdin, Ind	UPI	PB	PFW			
KR	Jon Vaughn, NE			PFW			

Defense

Pos	Player	UPI	PB	PFW	AP	SN	NEA
E	Bruce Smith, Buf	UPI	PB	PFW		SN	
E	Leslie O'Neal, SD	UPI	PB	PFW			
T	CORTEZ KENNEDY, Sea	UPI	PB	PFW*	AP	SN	NEA
T	Ray Childress, Hou			PFW*	AP		NEA
T	Michael Dean Perry, Cle					SN	
LB	JUNIOR SEAU, SD	UPI	PB	PFW*	AP	SN	NEA
LB	DERRICK THOMAS, KC	UPI	PB	PFW		SN	NEA
LB	Bryan Cox, Mia	UPI	PB	PFW			
LB	Al Smith, Hou		PB	PFW	AP		
LB	Cornelius Bennet, Buf						NEA
LB	Vincent Brown, NE	UPI					
CB	ROD WOODSON, Pit	UPI	PB	PFW*	AP	SN	NEA
CB+	GILL BYRD, SD	UPI	PB	PFW			
S	HENRY JONES, Buf	UPI	PB	PFW*	AP	SN	
S	STEVE ATWATER, Den		PB	PFW*	AP	SN	NEA
S	Louis Oliver, Mia	UPI					
P	Rohn Stark, Ind		PB	PFW		SN	NEA
P	Greg Montgomery, Hou	UPI					
ST	Steve Tasker, Buf	-	PB	PFW*		-	-

1992 All-NFC

Offense

Pos	Player	UPI	PB	PFW	AP	SN	NEA
WR	JERRY RICE, SF	UPI	PB	PFW*	AP	SN	NEA
WR	STERLING SHARPE, GB	UPI	PB	PFW*	AP	SN	NEA
TE	JAY NOVACEK, Dal	UPI	PB	PFW*			
TE	Brent Jones, SF						NEA
T+	GARY ZIMMERMAN, Min	UPI	PB				NEA
T	Harris Barton, SF			PFW*			NEA
T	Steve Wallace, SF	UPI		PFW*			
T	Lomas Brown, Det		PB			SN	
T	Paul Gruber, TB						NEA
G	RANDALL MCDANIEL, Min		PB	PFW*	AP	SN	NEA
G	Guy McIntyre, SF	UPI	PB				
G	Nate Newton, Dal	UPI					
C	Mark Stepnoski, Dal	UPI		PFW			NEA
C	Joel Hilgenberg, NO		PB				
QB	STEVE YOUNG, SF	UPI	PB	PFW*	AP	SN	NEA
RB	EMMITT SMITH, Dal	UPI	PB	PFW*	AP	SN	NEA
RB	Barry Sanders, Det	UPI	PB	PFW			
K	MORTEN ANDERSEN, NO	UPI	PB	PFW*			NEA
KR	DEION SANDERS, Atl*			PFW*	AP	SN	
KR	Johnny Bailey, Pho	UPI	PB				
KR	Kelvin Martin, Dal			PFW*			
KR	Mel Gray, Det					SN	NEA

Defense

Pos	Player	UPI	PB	PFW	AP	SN	NEA
E	CHRIS DOLEMAN, Min	UPI	PB	PFW*	AP	SN	NEA
E	REGGIE WHITE, Phi	UPI	PB	PFW*			NEA
E	Clyde Simmons, Phi				AP		
T	Pierce Holt, SF	UPI	PB	PFW			
T	Henry Thomas, Min			PFW			
LB	WILBER MARSHALL, Was	UPI		PFW*	AP	SN	NEA
LB	SAM MILLS, NO	UPI	PB	PFW*		SN	
LB	Rickey Jackson, NY	UPI	PB	PFW			
LB	Pat Swilling, NO		PB		AP	SN	
LB	Byron Evans, Phi			PFW			
LB	Vaughan Johnson, NO	UPI					
LB	Jessie Tuggle, Atl		PB				
CB	DEION SANDERS, Atl*		PB			SN	NEA
CB	Audray McMillian, Min	UPI		PFW*	AP		
CB	Eric Allen, Phi	UPI					
CB	Robert Massey, Pho		PB				

1993 All-NFC

Offense

Pos	Player	UPI	PB	PFW	AP	SN
WR	JERRY RICE, SF	UPI	PB	PFW*	AP	SN
WR	STERLING SHARPE, GB	UPI		PFW*	AP	SN
WR	Michael Irvin, Dal		PB			
TE	Brent Jones, SF	UPI		PFW		
TE	Jay Novacek, Dal		PB			
T	HARRIS BARTON, SF	UPI	PB	PFW*	AP	SN
T	ERIK WILLIAMS, Dal	UPI	PB	PFW*	AP	SN
G	RANDALL MCDANIEL, Min	UPI	PB	PFW*	AP	SN
G	Chris Hinton, Atl	UPI			AP	
G	Nate Newton, Dal		PB	PFW		
C	Mark Stepnoski, Dal	UPI	PB	PFW		
QB	STEVE YOUNG, SF	UPI	PB	PFW*	AP	
QB	Troy Aikman, Dal		PB			SN
RB	EMMITT SMITH, Dal	UPI	PB	PFW*	AP	SN
RB	JEROME BETTIS, LA	UPI		PFW*		SN
RB	Barry Sanders, Det		PB			SN
K	NORM JOHNSON, Atl	UPI	PB	PFW*		
K	Jason Hanson, Det					SN
K	Chris Jacke, GB				AP	
KR	Tyrone Hughes, NO	UPI	PB	PFW*		
KR	Mel Gray, Det					SN

Defense

Pos	Player	UPI	PB	PFW	AP	SN
E	Reggie White, GB	UPI	PB	PFW		SN
E	Richard Dent, Chi		PB	PFW		
E	Chris Doleman, Min	UPI				
T	JOHN RANDLE, Min	UPI	PB	PFW*	AP	SN
T	Sean Gilbert, LA	UPI	PB	PFW		SN
LB	HARDY NICKERSON, TB		PB	PFW*	AP	SN
LB	Rickey Jackson, NO	UPI	PB	PFW		SN
LB	Renaldo Turnbull, NO	UPI	PB		AP	
LB	Michael Brooks, NY	UPI				
LB	Seth Joyner, Phi			PFW*		
CB	DEION SANDERS, Atl	UPI	PB	PFW*	AP	SN
CB	Eric Allen, Phi	UPI	PB	PFW		
S	LEROY BUTLER, GB	UPI	PB	PFW*	AP	SN
S	Tim McDonald, SF	UPI	PB	PFW		
S	Mark Carrier, Chi		PB			
P	Rich Camarillo, Pho	UPI	PB	PFW		
ST	Elbert Shelley, Atl	-	PB	PFW	-	-

1993 All-AFC

Offense

WR	Tim Brown, LA	UPI	PB	PFW		
WR	Anthony Miller, SD	UPI		PFW		
WR	Webster Slaughter, Hou		PB			
TE	SHANNON SHARPE, Den	UPI	PB	PFW*	AP	SN
T	Howard Ballard, Buf	UPI	PB			
T	Richmond Webb, Mia	UPI	PB			
T	John Jackson, Pit			PFW		
T	Gary Zimmerman, Den			PFW		
G	STEVE WISNIEWSKI, LA	UPI	PB	PFW*		SN
G	Mike Munchak, Hou	UPI	PB	PFW		
C	BRUCE MATTHEWS, Hou	UPI	PB	PFW*		SN
C	Dermontti Dawson, Pit				AP	
QB	John Elway, Den	UPI	PB	PFW		
RB	Marcus Allen, KC	UPI	PB	PFW		
RB	Thurman Thomas, Buf	UPI	PB	PFW		
K	Gary Anderson, Pit	UPI	PB	PFW		
KR	ERIC METCALF, Cle	UPI	PB	PFW*	AP	SN
KR	O.J. McDuffie, Mia			PFW		

Defense

E	BRUCE SMITH, Buf	UPI	PB	PFW*	AP	SN
E	NEIL SMITH, KC	UPI	PB	PFW*	AP	
T	CORTEZ KENNEDY, Sea	UPI	PB	PFW*	AP	SN
T	Ray Childress, Hou	UPI	PB	PFW		
T	Michael Dean Perry, Cle					SN
LB	JUNIOR SEAU, SD	UPI	PB	PFW*	AP	SN
LB	GREG LLOYD, Pit	UPI	PB	PFW*	AP	
LB	Darryl Talley, Buf			PFW		SN
LB	Derrick Thomas, KC	UPI	PB			
LB	Vincent Brown, NE			PFW		
CB	ROD WOODSON, Pit	UPI	PB	PFW*	AP	SN
CB	Nate Odomes, Buf	UPI	PB			
CB	Terry McDaniel, LA			PFW		
S	MARCUS ROBERTSON, Hou	UPI		PFW	AP	SN
S	Steve Atwater, Den	UPI	PB			
S	Eugene Robinson, Sea			PFW*		
S	Dennis Smith, Den		PB			
P	GREG MONTGOMERY, Hou	UPI	PB	PFW*	AP	SN
ST	Steve Tasker, Buf	-	PB	PFW*	-	-

1994 All-NFC

Offense

WR	JERRY RICE, SF	UPI	PB	PFW*	AP	SN
WR	CRIS CARTER, Min	UPI	PB	PFW*	AP	SN
TE	Brent Jones, SF	UPI	PB	PFW		
T	WILLIAM ROAF, NO	UPI	PB	PFW*	AP	SN
T	Lomas Brown, Det	UPI	PB	PFW		
G	RANDALL MCDANIEL, Min	UPI	PB	PFW*	AP	SN
G	NATE NEWTON, Dal	UPI	PB	PFW*	AP	
C	Mark Stepnoski, Dal	UPI	PB			
C	Kevin Glover, Det			PFW		
QB	STEVE YOUNG, SF	UPI	PB	PFW*	AP	SN
RB	BARRY SANDERS, Det	UPI	PB	PFW*	AP	SN
RB	EMMITT SMITH, Dal	UPI	PB	PFW*	AP	SN
K	Fuad Reveiz, Min	UPI	PB	PFW*		
KR	MEL GRAY, Det	-	PB	PFW*	AP	SN
KR	Brian Mitchell, Was	-		PFW*		

Defense

E	CHARLES HALEY, Dal	UPI	PB	PFW*	AP	SN
E	Reggie White, GB	UPI	PB	PFW		
T	JOHN RANDLE, Min	UPI	PB	PFW*	AP	SN
T	Leon Lett, Dal	UPI	PB			
T	Dana Stubblefield, SF			PFW		
LB	CHRIS SPIELMAN, Det	UPI	PB	PFW*		SN
LB	Ken Harvey, Was	UPI	PB	PFW		
LB	Bryce Paup, GB	UPI	PB	PFW		
LB	Jack Del Rio, Min			PFW		
CB	DEION SANDERS, SF	UPI	PB	PFW*	AP	SN
CB	Aeneas Williams, Ari	UPI	PB			
CB	Donnell Woolford, Chi			PFW		
S	DARREN WOODSON, Dal	UPI	PB	PFW*	AP	SN
S	Merton Hanks, SF	UPI	PB	PFW		SN
P	REGGIE ROBY, Was	UPI	PB	PFW*	AP	SN
ST	Elbert Shelley, Atl	-	PB		-	-
ST	Maurice Douglass, Chi	-		PFW	-	-

1994 All-AFC

Offense

WR	Andre Reed, Buf	UPI	PB	PFW		
WR	Tim Brown, LA		PB	PFW		
WR	Irving Fryar, Mia	UPI				
TE	BEN COATES, NE	UPI	PB	PFW*	AP	SN
T	RICHMOND WEBB, Mia	UPI	PB	PFW*	AP	SN
T	Bruce Armstrong, NE	UPI	PB			
T	Tony Jones, Cle			PFW		
G	Steve Wisniewski, LA	UPI	PB	PFW		SN
G	Keith Sims, Mia	UPI	PB	PFW		
C	DERMONTTI DAWSON, Pit	UPI	PB	PFW*	AP	SN
QB	Dan Marino, Mia	UPI	PB	PFW		
RB	Marshall Faulk, Ind	UPI	PB	PFW		
RB	Chris Warren, Sea	UPI		PFW		
RB	Natrone Means, SD		PB			
K	JOHN CARNEY, SD	UPI	PB	PFW	AP	SN
KR	Eric Metcalf, Cle	-	PB			SN
KR	Andre Coleman, SD			PFW		
KR	Darien Gordon, SD	-		PFW		

Defense

E	BRUCE SMITH, Buf	UPI	PB	PFW*	AP	SN
E	Leslie O'Neal, SD	UPI	PB	PFW		
T	CORTEZ KENNEDY, Sea	UPI	PB	PFW	AP	
T	Chester McGlockton, LA			PFW*		SN
T	Michael Dean Perry, Cle	UPI	PB			
LB	GREG LLOYD, Pit	UPI	PB	PFW*	AP	SN
LB	JUNIOR SEAU, SD	UPI	PB	PFW*	AP	SN
LB	Kevin Greene, Pit			PFW*	AP	SN
LB	Derrick Thomas, KC	UPI	PB			
LB	Bryan Cox, Mia			PFW		
CB	ROD WOODSON, Pit	UPI	PB	PFW*	AP	SN
CB	Terry McDaniel, LA	UPI	PB	PFW		
S	ERIC TURNER, Cle	UPI	PB	PFW*	AP	
S	Carnell Lake, Pit	UPI	PB	PFW		
P	Rick Tuten, Sea	UPI	PB	PFW		
ST	Steve Tasker, Buf	-	PB	PFW*	-	-

1995 All-NFC

Offense

WR	JERRY RICE, SF	UPI	PB	PFW*	AP	SN
WR	HERMAN MOORE, Det	UPI	PB	PFW*	AP	SN
TE	Jay Novacek, Dal	UPI	PB			
TE	Mark Chmura, GB			PFW		
T	WILLIAM ROAF, NO	UPI	PB	PFW*	AP	SN
T	LOMAS BROWN, Det	UPI	PB	PFW*	AP	
T	Erik Williams, Dal					SN
G	RANDALL MCDANIEL, Min	UPI	PB	PFW*	AP	
G	NATE NEWTON, Dal	UPI	PB		AP	SN
G	Larry Allen, Dal			PFW*		SN
C	Kevin Glover, Det	UPI	PB	PFW		
QB	BRETT FAVRE, GB	UPI	PB	PFW*	AP	SN
RB	BARRY SANDERS, Det	UPI	PB	PFW*	AP	SN
RB	EMMITT SMITH, Dal	UPI	PB	PFW*	AP	SN
K	MORTEN ANDERSEN, Atl	UPI	PB	PFW*	AP	SN
KR	BRIAN MITCHELL, Was	-	PB	PFW*	AP	SN

Defense

E	REGGIE WHITE, GB	UPI	PB	PFW*	AP	SN
E	William Fuller, Phi	UPI		PFW		
E	Charles Haley, Dal		PB			
T	JOHN RANDLE, Min	UPI	PB	PFW*	AP	SN
T	Dana Stubblefield, SF	UPI		PFW		
T	Eric Swann, Ari		PB			SN
LB	Ken Harvey, Was	UPI	PB	PFW		
LB	Ken Norton, SF	UPI		PFW	AP	
LB	Lee Woodall, SF	UPI	PB			
LB	William Thomas, Phi			PFW		
LB	Jessie Tuggle, Atl		PB			
CB	AENEAS WILLIAMS, Ari	UPI	PB	PFW*	AP	SN
CB	ERIC DAVIS, SF	UPI	PB	PFW*	AP	
CB	Deion Sanders, Dal					SN
S	MERTON HANKS, SF	UPI	PB	PFW*	AP	SN
S	DARREN WOODSON, Dal	UPI	PB	PFW*	AP	SN
P	Jeff Feagles, Ari	UPI	PB	PFW		
ST	Elbert Shelley, Atl	-	PB	PFW	-	-

1995 All-AFC

Offense

WR	Tim Brown, Oak	UPI	PB	PFW		
WR	Carl Pickens, Cin	UPI	PB	PFW		
TE	BEN COATES, NE	UPI	PB	PFW*	AP	SN
T	Richmond Webb, Mia	UPI	PB	PFW		
T	Bruce Armstrong, NE		PB	PFW		
T	Gary Zimmerman, Den	UPI				
G	Bruce Matthews, Hou	UPI	PB	PFW		
G	Steve Wisniewski, Oak	UPI		PFW		
G	Keith Sims, Mia		PB			
C	DERMONTTI DAWSON, Pit	UPI	PB	PFW*	AP	SN
QB	Jim Harbaugh, Ind	UPI		PFW		
QB	Dan Marino, Mia		PB			
RB	Chris Warren, Sea	UPI	PB	PFW		
RB	Curtis Martin, NE	UPI		PFW		
RB	Marshall Faulk, Sea		PB			
K	Jason Elam, Den	UPI	PB	PFW		
KR	Glyn Milburn, Den	-	PB	PFW		SN

KR	Andre Coleman, SD	-		PFW		

Defense

E	BRUCE SMITH, Buf	UPI	PB	PFW*	AP	SN
E	Neil Smith, KC	UPI	PB	PFW		
T	CHESTER MCGLOCKTON, Oak	UPI	PB	PFW*	AP	
T	Dan Saleaumua, KC	UPI	PB	PFW		
LB	GREG LLOYD, Pit	UPI	PB	PFW*	AP	SN
LB	BRYCE PAUP, Buf	UPI	PB	PFW*	AP	SN
LB	JUNIOR SEAU, SD	UPI	PB	PFW*		SN
CB	Dale Carter, KC	UPI	PB	PFW		
CB	Terry McDaniel, Oak	UPI	PB	PFW		
S	Carnell Lake, Pit	UP-c	PB	PFW		
S	Steve Atwater, Den	UPI	PB			
S	Blaine Bishop, Hou	UPI		PFW		
P	DARREN BENNETT, SD	UPI	PB	PFW*	AP	SN
ST	Steve Tasker, Buf	-	PB	PFW*	-	-

1996 ALL-NFC

Offense

WR	JERRY RICE, SF	UPI	PB	PFW*	AP	TSN
WR	HERMAN MOORE, Det	UPI	PB	PFW	AP	TSN
TE	Wesley Walls, Car	UPI	PB	PFW		
T	WILLIAM ROAF, NO	UPI	PB	PFW*		TSN
T	Lomas Brown, Ari	UPI		PFW		
T	Erik Williams, Dal		PB		AP	
G	LARRY ALLEN, Dal	UPI	PB	PFW*	AP	TSN
G	RANDALL MCDANIEL, Min	UPI	PB	PFW*	AP	TSN
C	Kevin Glover, Det	UPI	PB	PFW		
QB	BRETT FAVRE, GB	UPI	PB	PFW*	AP	TSN
RB	BARRY SANDERS, Det	UPI	PB	PFW*		TSN
RB	Terry Allen, Was	UPI	PB	PFW		
FB	Larry Centers, Ari				AP	
K	John Kasay, Car	UPI	PB	PFW		
KR	MICHAEL BATES, Car		PB	PFW*	AP	TSN
KR	Desmond Howard, GB	UPI		PFW*		TSN

Defense

E	Reggie White, GB	UPI	PB	PFW		
E	Tony Tolbert, Dal	UPI	PB	PFW		
T	JOHN RANDLE, Min	UPI	PB	PFW*	AP	TSN
T	BRYANT YOUNG, SF	UPI	PB	PFW*	AP	TSN
LB	KEVIN GREENE, Car	UPI	PB	PFW*	AP	
LB	SAM MILLS, Car	UPI	PB	PFW*	AP	
LB	Lamar Lathon, Car	UPI	PB	PFW		TSN
CB	DEION SANDERS, Dal	UPI	PB	PFW*	AP	TSN
CB	Aeneas Williams, Ari	UPI	PB	PFW*		
S	LEROY BUTLER, GB	UPI	PB	PFW*	AP	TSN
S	DARREN WOODSON, Dal	UPI		PFW*	AP	TSN
S	Merton Hanks, SF		PB			
P	Matt Turk, Was	UPI	PB	PFW	AP+	
ST	Jim Schwantz, Dal	-	PB	PFW*	-	-

1996 ALL-AFC

Offense

WR	Carl Pickens, Cin	UPI	PB	PFW*		
WR	Tony Martin, SD		PB	PFW		
WR	Terry Glenn, NE	UPI				
TE	SHANNON SHARPE, Den	UPI	PB	PFW*	AP	TSN
T	GARY ZIMMERMAN, Den	UPI	PB	PFW*	AP	TSN
T	Bruce Armstrong, NE	UPI	PB	PFW		
G	Bruce Matthews, Hou	UPI	PB	PFW		
G	Will Shields, KC		PB	PFW		
G	Steve Wisniewski, Oak	UPI				
C	DERMONTTI DAWSON, Pit	UPI	PB	PFW*	AP	TSN
QB	John Elway, Den	UPI	PB	PFW		
RB	TERRELL DAVIS, Den	UPI	PB	PFW*	AP	TSN
RB	Jerome Bettis, Pit	UPI	PB	PFW	AP	
FB	Kimble Anders, KC		PB			
K	CARY BLANCHARD, Ind	UPI	PB	PFW*	AP	TSN
KR	Dave Meggett, NE	UPI	PB			
KR	Tamarick Vanover, KC			PFW		
KR	Darrien Gordon, SD			PFW		

Defense

E	BRUCE SMITH, Buf	UPI	PB	PFW*	AP	TSN
E	ALFRED WILLIAMS, Den	UPI	PB	PFW*	AP	TSN
T	Chester McGlockton, Oak	UPI	PB	PFW		
T	Cortez Kennedy, Sea	UPI	PB	PFW		
LB	CHAD BROWN, Pit	UPI	PB	PFW*	AP	TSN
LB	Junior Seau, SD	UPI	PB		AP	TSN
LB	Derrick Thomas, KC	UPI	PB	PFW		
LB	Levon Kirkland, Pit			PFW		
CB+	ASHLEY AMBROSE, Cin	UPI	PB	PFW	AP	
CB+	DALE CARTER, KC	UPI	PB	PFW		TSN
S	Steve Atwater, Den	UPI	PB	PFW		
S	Carnell Lake, Pit	UPI	PB	PFW		
P	CHRIS GARDOCKI, Ind	UPI	PB	PFW*	AP+	TSN
ST	John Henry Mills, Hou	-	PB	PFW	-	-

PLAYER OF THE YEAR

1938 NFL

Mel Hein, C, NY	OFF	
Ace Parker, QB, Bkn		UP

1939 NFL

Parker Hall, QB, Cle	OFF

1940 NFL

Ace Parker, QB, Bkn	OFF

1941 NFL

Don Hutson, E, GB	OFF

1942 NFL

Don Hutson, E, GB	OFF

1943 NFL

Sid Luckman, QB, ChiB	OFF

1944 NFL

Frankie Sinkwich, HB, Det	OFF

1945 NFL

Bob Waterfield, QB, Cle	OFF

1946 NFL

Bill Dudley, HB, Pit	OFF

1946 AAFC

Glenn Dobbs, HB, Bkn	OFF

1947 NFL

Mal Kutner, E, ChiC	PFI

1947 AAFC

Otto Graham, QB, Cle	OFF

1948 NFL

Pat Harder, FB, ChiC	UP

1948 AAFC

Otto Graham, QB, Cle	OFF*	UP
Frankie Albert, QB, SF	OFF*	

1949 AAFC

Otto Graham, QB, Cle	OFF

1953 NFL

Otto Graham, QB, Cle	UP

1954 NFL

Joe Perry, FB, SF	UP	
Lou Groza, TK, Cle		TSN

1955 NFL

Otto Graham, QB, Cle	UP	TSN	
Harlon Hill, E, ChiB			NEA

1956 NFL

Frank Gifford, HB, NY	UP	TSN	NEA

1957 NFL

Y.A. Tittle, QB, SF	UP	-	
Johnny Unitas, QB, Bal	-		NEA
Jim Brown, FB, Cle	-	AP	

1958 NFL

Jim Brown, FB, Cle	UPI	-	NEA
Gino Marchetti, DT, Bal	-	AP	

1959 NFL

Player	Awards
Johnny Unitas, QB, Bal	UPI TSN MAX
Charley Conerly, QB, NY	AP NEA

1960 NFL

Player	Awards
Norm Van Brocklin, QB, Phi	UPI TSN AP* NEA MAX
Joe Schmidt, LB, Det	AP*

1960 AFL

Player	Awards
Abner Haynes, HB, Dal	UPI TSN OFF

1961 NFL

Player	Awards
Paul Hornung, HB, GB	UPI TSN AP MAX PFI-o
Y.A. Tittle, QB, NY	NEA
Henry Jordan, DT, GB	PFI-d

1961 AFL

Player	Awards
George Blanda, QB, Hou	UPI TSN AP OFF

1962 NFL

Player	Awards
Jim Taylor, FB, GB	AP NEA PFI-o
Y.A. Tittle, QB, NY	UPI TSN
Andy Robustelli, DE, NY	MAX
Joe Schmidt, LB, Det	PFI-d

1962 AFL

Player	Awards
Cookie Gilchrist, FB, Buf	UPI AP
Len Dawson, QB, Dal	TSN PFI-o
E.J. Holub, LB, Dal	PFI-d

1963 NFL

Player	Awards
Jim Brown, FB, Cle	UPI NEA* MAX
Y.A. Tittle, QB, NY	TSN AP NEA*

1963 AFL

Player	Awards
Lance Alworth, FL, SD	UPI
Clem Daniels, HB, Oak	TSN
Tobin Rote, QB, SD	AP

1964 NFL

Player	Awards
Johnny Unitas, QB, Bal	UPI TSN AP MAX
Lenny Moore, HB, Bal	NEA

1964 AFL

Player	Awards
Gino Cappelletti, EK, Bos	UPI TSN AP

1965 NFL

Player	Awards
Jim Brown, FB, Cle	UPI TSN AP NEA
Pete Retzlaff, TE, Phi	MAX

1965 AFL

Player	Awards
Paul Lowe, HB, SD	UPI TSN
Jack Kemp, QB, Buf	AP

1966 NFL

Player	Awards
Bart Starr, QB, GB	UPI TSN AP NEA
Don Meredith, QB, Dal	MAX
Larry Wilson, S, StL	NEA-d

1966 AFL

Player	Awards
Jim Nance, FB, Bos	UPI TSN AP

1967 NFL

Player	Awards
Johnny Unitas, QB, Bal	UPI TSN AP NEA MAX
Deacon Jones, DE, LA	NEA-d

1967 AFL

Player	Awards
Daryle Lamonica, QB, Oak	UPI TSN AP

1968 NFL

Player	Awards
Earl Morrall, QB, Bal	UPI TSN AP PFW NEA
Leroy Kelly, RB, Cle	MAX
Deacon Jones, DE, LA	NEA-d

1968 AFL

Player	Awards
Joe Namath, QB, NY	UPI TSN AP PFW

1969 NFL

Player	Awards
Roman Gabriel, QB, LA	UPI TSN AP PFW NEA MAX
Dick Butkus, LB, Chi	NEA-d

1969 AFL

Player	Awards
Daryle Lamonica, QB, Oak	UPI TSN AP PFW

1970 NFC

Player	Awards
John Brodie, QB, SF	UPI TSN AP NEA PFW-o
Dick Butkus, LB, Chi	NEA-d PFW-d

1970 AFC

Player	Awards
George Blanda, QBK, Oak	UPI TSN MAX

1971 NFC

Player	Awards
Alan Page, DT, Min	UPI NEA-d PFW-d
Roger Staubach, QB, Dal	TSN MAX

1971 AFC

Player	Awards
Bob Griese, QB, Mia	TSN NEA
Otis Taylor, WR, KC	UPI PFW-o

1972 NFC

Player	Awards
Larry Brown, RB, Was	UPI TSN AP NEA MAX PFW-o

1972 AFC

Player	Awards
Joe Greene, DT, Pit	AP-d NEA-d PFW-d
O.J. Simpson, RB, Buf	UPI
Earl Morrall, QB, Mia	TSN

1973 NFC

Player	Awards
John Hadl, QB, LA	UPI TSN
Alan Page, DT, Min	NEA-d PFW-d*

1973 AFC

Player	Awards
O.J. Simpson, RB, Buf	UPI TSN AP NEA MAX PFW-o
Dick Anderson, S, Mia	AP-d
Paul Smith, DT, Den	PFW-d*

1974 NFC

Player	Awards
Jim Hart, QB, StL	UPI PFW-o
Chuck Foreman, RB, Min	TSN
Merlin Olsen, DT, LA	MAX

1974 AFC

Player	Awards
Ken Stabler, QB, Oak	UPI TSN AP NEA
Joe Greene, DT, Pit	AP-d NEA-d PFW-d

1975 NFC

Player	Awards
Fran Tarkenton, QB, Min	UP-o TSN AP NEA MAX FWA PFW-o
Jack Youngblood, DE, LA	UP-d

1975 AFC

Player	Awards
O.J. Simpson, RB, Buf	UP-o TSN
Mel Blount, CB, Pit	UP-d AP-d
Curley Culp, DT, Hou	NEA-d
Jack Ham, LB, Pit	PFW-d

1976 NFC

Player	Awards
Walter Payton, RB, Chi	TSN
Chuck Foreman, RB, Min	UP-o
Wally Chambers, DT, Chi	UP-d

1976 AFC

Player	Awards
Bert Jones, QB, Bal	UP-o AP NEA FWA
Ken Stabler, QB, Oak	TSN MAX PFW-o
Jack Lambert, LB, Pit	UP-d AP-d PFW-d
Jerry Sherk, DT, Cle	NEA-d

1977 NFC

Player	Awards
Walter Payton, RB, Chi	UP-o TSN AP NEA FWA PFW-o
Harvey Martin, DE, Dal	UP-d AP-d NEA-d PFW-d

1977 AFC

Player	Awards
Craig Morton, QB, Den	UP-o TSN
Bob Griese, QB, Mia	MAX
Lyle Alzado, DE, Den	UP-d

1978 NFC

Player	UPI	TSN	AP	NEA	MAX	FWA	PFW
Archie Manning, QB, NO	UP-o	TSN					
Randy White, DT, Dal	UP-d						

1978 AFC

Player	UPI	TSN	AP	NEA	MAX	FWA	PFW
Earl Campbell, RB, Hou	UP-o	TSN	AP-o	NEA		FWA	PFW-o
Randy Gradishar, LB, Den	UP-d		AP-d	NEA-d			PFW-d
Terry Bradshaw, QB, Pit			AP		MAX		

1979 NFC

Player	UPI	TSN	AP	NEA	MAX	FWA	PFW
Lee Roy Selmon, DE, TB			AP-d	NEA-d			PFW-d
Ottis Anderson, RB, StL	UPI	TSN					

1979 AFC

Player	UPI	TSN	AP	NEA	MAX	FWA	PFW
Earl Campbell, RB, Hou			AP	NEA	MAX	FWA	PFW-o
Dan Fouts, QB, SD	UPI	TSN					

1980 NFC

Player	UPI	TSN	AP	NEA	MAX	FWA	PFW
Ron Jaworski, QB, Phi	UPI				MAX		

1980 AFC

Player	UPI	TSN	AP	NEA	MAX	FWA	PFW
Brian Sipe, QB, Cle	UPI	TSN	AP			FWA	PFW-o
Lester Hayes, CB, Oak			AP-d	NEA-d			PFW-d
Earl Campbell, RB, Hou			AP-o	NEA			

1981 NFC

Player	UPI	TSN	AP	NEA	MAX	FWA	PFW
Tony Dorsett, RB, Dal	UPI-o						
Fred Dean, DE, SF	UPI-d						
Lawrence Taylor, LB, NY			AP-d				

1981 AFC

Player	UPI	TSN	AP	NEA	MAX	FWA	PFW
Ken Anderson, QB, Cin	UPI-o	TSN	AP	NEA	MAX	FWA	PFW-o
Joe Klecko, DE, NY	UPI-d			NEA-d			PFW-d

1982 NFC

Player	UPI	TSN	AP	NEA	MAX	FWA	PFW
Mark Moseley, K, Was	UPI	TSN	AP				
Joe Theismann, QB, Was					MAX		
Lawrence Taylor, LB, NY			AP-d				
Dan Hampton, DT, Chi							PFW-d

1982 AFC

Player	UPI	TSN	AP	NEA	MAX	FWA	PFW
Dan Fouts, QB, SD	UPI		AP-o	NEA		FWA	PFW-o
Mark Gastineau, DE, NY				NEA-d			

1983 NFC

Player	UPI	TSN	AP	NEA	MAX	FWA	PFW
Joe Theismann, QB, Was			AP	NEA		FWA	PFW-o
Eric Dickerson, RB, LA	UPI-o	TSN					
John Riggins, RB, Was					MAX		
Lawrence Taylor, LB, NY	UPI-d						

1983 AFC

Player	UPI	TSN	AP	NEA	MAX	FWA	PFW
Curt Warner, RB, Sea	UPI-o						
Rod Martin, LB, LA	UPI-d						
Bob Baumhower, DT, Mia							PFW-d
Doug Betters, DE, Mia			AP-d				
Jack Lambert, LB, Pit				NEA-d			

1984 NFC

Player	UPI	TSN	AP	NEA	MAX	FWA	PFW
Eric Dickerson, RB, LA	UPI-o						
Mike Singletary, LB, Chi	UPI-d						

1984 AFC

Player	UPI	TSN	AP	NEA	MAX	FWA	PFW
Dan Marino, QB, Mia	UPI-o	TSN	AP	NEA	MAX	FWA	PFW-o
Kenny Easley, S, Sea			AP-d				PFW-d
Mark Gastineau, DE, NY	UPI-d						
Mike Haynes, CB, Oak				NEA-d			

1985 NFC

Player	UPI	TSN	AP	NEA	MAX	FWA	PFW
Walter Payton, RB, Chi	UPI-o			NEA	MAX		
Mike Singletary, LB, Chi	UPI-d		AP-d				

1985 AFC

Player	UPI	TSN	AP	NEA	MAX	FWA	PFW
Marcus Allen, RB, LA	UPI-o	TSN	AP			FWA	
Andre Tippett, LB, NE	UPI-d			NEA-d*			
Howie Long, DE, LA				NEA-d*			

1986 NFC

Player	UPI	TSN	AP	NEA	MAX	FWA	PFW
Lawrence Taylor, LB, NY	UPI-d	TSN	AP	NE-d	MAX	FWA	PFW-d
Phil Simms, QB, NY				NEA			
Eric Dickerson, RB, LA	UPI-o		AP-o				
Jerry Rice, WR, SF							PFW-o

1986 AFC

Player	UPI	TSN	AP	NEA	MAX	FWA	PFW
Curt Warner, RB, Sea	UPI-o						
Rulon Jones, DE, Den	UPI-d						

1987 NFC

Player	UPI	TSN	AP	NEA	MAX	FWA	PFW
Jerry Rice, WR, SF	UPI-o	TSN	AP-o	NEA	MAX	FWA	PFW-o
Reggie White, DE, Phi	UPI-d		AP-d	NEA-d			PFW-d

1987 AFC

Player	UPI	TSN	AP	NEA	MAX	FWA	PFW
John Elway, QB, Den	UPI-o		AP				
Bruce Smith, DE, Buf	UPI-d						

1988 NFC

Player	UPI	TSN	AP	NEA	MAX	FWA	PFW
Mike Singletary, LB, Chi	UPI-d		AP-d	NEA-d			PFW-d
Roger Craig, RB, SF	UPI-o		AP-o	NEA			
Randall Cunningham, QB, Phi					MAX		

1988 AFC

Player	UPI	TSN	AP	NEA	MAX	FWA	PFW
Boomer Esiason, QB, Cin	UPI-o	TSN	AP			FWA	PFW-o
Cornelius Bennett, LB, Buf	UPI-d*						
Bruce Smith, DE, Buf	UPI-d*						

1989 NFC

Player	UPI	TSN	AP	NEA	MAX	FWA	PFW
Joe Montana, QB, SF	UPI-o	TSN	AP	NEA	MAX	FWA	PFW-o
Keith Millard, DT, Min	UPI-d		AP-d				PFW-d
Tim Harris, LB, GB				NEA-d			

1989 AFC

Player	UPI	TSN	AP	NEA	MAX	FWA	PFW
Christian Okoye, RB, KC	UPI-o						
Michael Dean Perry, DT, Cle	UPI-d						

1990 NFC

Player	UPI	TSN	AP	NEA	MAX	FWA	PFW
Randall Cunningham, QB, Phi	UPI-o				MAX	FWA	PFW-o
Charles Haley, LB, SF	UPI-d						
Jerry Rice, WR, SF		TSN					
Joe Montana, QB, SF			AP				

1990 AFC

Player	UPI	TSN	AP	NEA	MAX	FWA	PFW
Bruce Smith, DE, Buf	UPI-d		AP-d	NEA-d			PFW-d
Warren Moon, QB, Hou	UPI-o		AP-o	NEA			

1991 NFC

Player	UPI	TSN	AP	NEA	MAX	FWA	PFW
Reggie White, DE, Phi							PFW-d
Pat Swilling, LB, NO			AP-d	NEA-d			
Barry Sanders, RB, Det					MAX		
Mark Rypien, QB, Was	UPI-o						

1991 AFC

Player	UPI	TSN	AP	NEA	MAX	FWA	PFW
Thurman Thomas, RB, Buf	UPI-o	TSN	AP	NEA		FWA	PFW-o
Cornelius Bennett, LB, Buf	UPI-d						

1992 NFC

Player	UPI	TSN	AP	NEA	MAX	FWA	PFW
Steve Young, QB, SF	UPI-o	TSN	AP	NEA	MAX		PFW-o
Chris Doleman, DE, Min	UPI-d						

1992 AFC

Player	UPI	TSN	AP	NEA	MAX	FWA	PFW
Cortez Kennedy, DT, Sea			AP-d				PFW-d
Junior Seau, LB, SD				NEA-d			
Barry Foster, RB, Pit	UPI-o						

1993 NFC

Player	UPI	TSN	AP	NEA	MAX	FWA	PFW
Emmitt Smith, RB, Dal	UPI-o	TSN	AP	NEA	MAX		PFW-o
Eric Allen, CB, Phi	UPI-d						
Jerry Rice, WR, SF			AP-o				

1993 AFC

Player	UPI	TSN	AP	NEA	MAX	FWA	PFW
Bruce Smith, DE, Buf				NEA-d			PFW-d
Rod Woodson, CB, Pit	UPI-d		AP-d				
John Elway, QB, Den	UPI-o						

1994 NFC

Player	UPI	TSN	AP	NEA	MAX	FWA	PFW
Steve Young, QB, SF	UPI-o	TSN	AP		MAX		PFW-o
Deion Sanders, CB, SF			AP-d				PFW-d
Charles Haley, DE, Dal	UPI-d						
Barry Sanders, RB, Det			AP-o				

1994 AFC

Greg Lloyd, LB, Pit	UPI-d				
Dan Marino, QB, Mia	UPI-o				

1995 NFC

Brett Favre, QB, GB	UPI-o	TSN	AP		MAX	PFW-o
Reggie White, DE, GB	UPI-d					

1995 AFC

Jim Harbaugh, QB, Ind	UPI-o			
Bryce Paup, LB, Buf	UPI-d		AP-d	PFW-d

1996 NFC

Brett Favre, QB, GB	UPI-o	TSN	AP	NEA	MAX	PFW-o
Kevin Greene, LB, Car	UPI-d			NEA-d		

1996 AFC

Terrell Davis, RB, Den	UPI-o	AP-o		
Bruce Smith, DE, Buf	UPI-d	AP-d		PFW-d

COACH OF THE YEAR

1945 NFL

Adam Walsh, Cleveland	NYN

1946 NFL

Steve Owen, New York	NYN

1946 AAFC

Ray Flaherty, New York	NYN

1947 NFL

Jimmy Conzelman, Chi. Cards	TSN

1947 AAFC

Paul Brown, Cleveland	PFI

1948 NFL

George Halas, Chicago Bears	NYN		
Greasy Neale, Philadelphia		TSN	PFI

1948 AAFC

Paul Brown, Cleveland	NYN

1949 NFL

Greasy Neale, Philadelphia	NYN

1949 AAFC

Paul Brown, Cleveland	NYN TSN

1950 NFL

Steve Owen, N.Y. Giants	NYN

1951 NFL

Paul Brown, Cleveland	NYN

1952 NFL

Hampton Pool, Los Angeles	NYN

1953 NFL

Paul Brown, Cleveland	NYN

1954 NFL

Buddy Parker, Detroit	NYN
Paul Brown, Cleveland	UP

1955 NFL

Joe Kuharich, Washington	UP	TSN
George Halas, Chicago Bears	NYN	

1956 NFL

Buddy Parker, Detroit	NYN UP	
Jim Lee Howell, New York		TSN

1957 NFL

Paul Brown, Cleveland	NYN UP		
George Wilson, Detroit			AP

1958 NFL

Weeb Ewbank, Baltimore	NYN UPI		AP

1959 NFL

Vince Lombardi, Green Bay	UPI	AP

1960 NFL

Buck Shaw, Philadelphia	NYN UPI	AP

1960 AFL

Lou Rymkus, Houston	UPI

1961 NFL

Allie Sherman, New York	NYN UPI			
Vince Lombardi, Green Bay		TSN		PFI

1961 AFL

Wally Lemm, Houston	NYN UPI	TSN	AP

1962 NFL

Allie Sherman, New York	-	UPI	-	AP

1962 AFL

Jack Faulkner, Denver	-	UPI	-	AP

1963 NFL

George Halas, Chicago	NYN UPI	TSN	AP

1963 AFL

Al Davis, Oakland	NYN UPI	TSN	AP

1964 NFL

Don Shula, Baltimore	NYN UPI	TSN	AP

1964 AFL

Lou Saban, Buffalo	UPI	TSN	
Mike Holovak, Boston	NYN		AP

1965 NFL

George Halas, Chicago	NYN UPI	TSN	AP

1965 AFL

Lou Saban, Buffalo	NYN UPI	TSN	AP

1966 NFL

Tom Landry, Dallas	NYN UPI	TSN	AP

1966 AFL

Mike Holovak, Boston	UPI	TSN	
Hank Stram, Kansas City	NYN		AP

1967 NFL

George Allen, Los Angeles	UPI	TSN	AP*
Don Shula, Baltimore	NYN		AP*

1967 AFL

Johnny Rauch, Oakland	UPI	-	AP
Wally Lemm, Houston	NYN	-	

1968 NFL

Don Shula, Baltimore	NYN UPI	TSN	AP	PFW

1968 AFL

Hank Stram, Kansas City	UPI	-	AP	PFW
Weeb Ewbank, New York	NYN	-		

1969 NFL

Bud Grant, Minnesota	NYN UPI	TSN	AP	PFW

1969 AFL

Paul Brown, Cincinnati — NYN UPI AP
John Madden, Oakland — TSN PFW

1970 NFC

Alex Webster, New York — UPI
Dick Nolan, San Francisco — FWA

1970 AFC

Don Shula, Miami — TSN PFW
Paul Brown, Cincinnati — UPI FWA AP

1971 NFC

George Allen, Washington — UPI FWA TSN AP PFW

1971 AFC

Don Shula, Miami — UPI FWA

1972 NFC

Dan Devine, Green Bay — UPI FWA

1972 AFC

Don Shula, Miami — FWA TSN AP PFW
Chuck Noll, Pittsburgh — UPI

1973 NFC

Chuck Knox, Los Angeles — UPI FWA TSN AP PFW

1973 AFC

John Ralston, Denver — UPI FWA

1974 NFC

Don Coryell, St. Louis — UPI FWA TSN AP PFW

1974 AFC

Sid Gillman, Houston — UPI FWA

1975 NFC

Tom Landry, Dallas — UPI FWA

1975 AFC

Ted Marchibroda, Baltimore — UPI FWA TSN AP PFW

1976 NFC

Jack Pardee, Chicago — UPI FWA

1976 AFC

Chuck Fairbanks, New England — UPI FWA TSN PFW
Forrest Gregg, Cleveland — AP

1977 NFC

Leeman Bennett, Atlanta — UPI

1977 AFC

Red Miller, Denver — UPI FWA* TSN AP PFW

1978 NFC

Dick Vermeil, Philadelphia — UPI FWA

1978 AFC

Walt Michaels, New York — UPI FWA PFW
Jack Patera, Seattle — TSN AP

1979 NFC

Dick Vermeil, Philadelphia — FWA TSN PFW
Jack Pardee, Washington — UPI AP

1979 AFC

Sam Rutigliano, Cleveland — UPI
Don Coryell, San Diego — FWA

1980 NFC

Leeman Bennett, Atlanta — UPI FWA

1980 AFC

Chuck Knox, Buffalo — FWA TSN AP PFW
Sam Rutigliano, Cleveland — UPI

1981 NFC

Bill Walsh, San Francisco — UPI FWA TSN AP PFW

1981 AFC

Forrest Gregg, Cincinnati — UPI FWA

1982 NFC

Joe Gibbs, Washington — UPI FWA TSN AP PFW

1982 AFC

Tom Flores, Los Angeles — UPI FWA

1983 NFC

Joe Gibbs, Washington — FWA TSN AP PFW
John Robinson, Los Angeles — UPI

1983 AFC

Chuck Knox, Seattle — UPI
Chuck Noll, Pittsburgh — FWA

1984 NFC

Bill Walsh, San Francisco — UPI FWA

1984 AFC

Chuck Knox, Seattle — UPI FWA TSN AP
Dan Reeves, Denver — PFW

1985 NFC

Mike Ditka, Chicago — UPI FWA TSN AP

1985 AFC

Raymond Berry, New England — UPI FWA

1986 NFC

Bill Parcells, Giants — UPI FWA TSN AP PFW

1986 AFC

Marty Schottenheimer, Cleve. — UPI FWA

1987 NFC

Jim Mora, New Orleans — UPI FWA TSN AP PFW

1987 AFC

Ron Meyer, Indianapolis — UPI FWA

1988 NFC

Mike Ditka, Chicago — UPI FWA AP PFW

1988 AFC

Marv Levy, Buffalo — UPI TSN
Sam Wyche, Cincinnati — FWA

1989 NFC

Lindy Infante, Green Bay — UPI FWA TSN AP
George Seifert, San Fran. — PFW

1989 AFC

Dan Reeves, Denver — UPI
Chuck Noll, Pittsburgh — FWA

1990 NFC

Jimmy Johnson, Dallas — UPI AP
George Seifert, San Fran. — TSN

1990 AFC

Art Shell, Oakland — UPI FWA PFW

1991 NFC

Wayne Fontes, Detroit — UPI AP FWA PFW
Joe Gibbs, Washington — TSN

1991 AFC

Dan Reeves, Denver	UPI			

1992 NFC

Dennis Green, Minnesota	UPI			

1992 AFC

Bobby Ross, San Diego	UPI			PFW
Bill Cowher, Pittsburgh		TSN	AP	

1993 NFC

Dan Reeves, New York	UPI	TSN	AP	PFW	MAX

1993 AFC

Marv Levy, Buffalo	UPI	

1994 NFC

George Seifert, San Fran.		TSN
Dave Wannstedt, Chicago	UPI	

1994 AFC

Bill Parcells, New England	UPI	AP	PFW	MAX

1995 NFC

Ray Rhodes, Philadelpia	UPI	TSN	AP		MAX
Dom Capers, Carolina				PFW	

1995 AFC

Marv Levy, Buffalo	UPI	

1996 NFC

Dom Capers, Carolina	UPI	TSN	AP	PFW	MAX

1996 AFC

Tom Coughlin, Jacksonville	UPI	

ROOKIE OF THE YEAR

1948 NFL

Charlie Conerly, QB, NY	UP

1955 NFL

Alan Ameche, FB, Bal	UP	TSN

1956 NFL

Lenny Moore, HB, Bal	UP	
J.C. Caroline, HB-DB, Chi		TSN

1957 NFL

Jim Brown, FB, Cle	UP	-	AP

1958 NFL

Jimmy Orr, FL, Bal	UPI	-	AP

1959 NFL

Nick Pietrosante, FB, Det		TSN	AP
Boyd Dowler, FL, GB	UPI	

1960 NFL

Gail Cogdill, SE, Det	UPI	TSN	AP

1960 AFL

Abner Haynes, HB, Dal	UPI	TSN

1961 NFL

Mike Ditka, TE, Chi	UPI	TSN	AP	PFI

1961 AFL

Earl Faison, DE, SD	UPI	TSN	AP	OFF

1962 NFL

Ronnie Bull, FB, Chi	UPI	TSN	AP

1962 AFL

Curtis McClinton, FB, Dal	UPI	TSN	AP

1963 NFL

Paul Flatley, FL, Min	UPI	TSN	AP

1963 AFL

Billy Joe, FB, Den	UPI	TSN	AP

1964 NFL

Charley Taylor, HB, Was	UPI	TSN	AP	NEA

1964 AFL

Matt Snell, FB, NY	UPI	TSN	AP

1965 NFL

Gale Sayers, HB, Chi	UPI	TSN	AP	NEA

1965 AFL

Joe Namath, QB, NY	UPI	TSN	AP

1966 NFL

Johnny Roland, HB, StL	UPI		AP	
Tommy Nobis, LB, Atl		TSN		NEA

1966 AFL

Bobby Burnett, HB, Buf	UPI	TSN	AP

1967 NFL

Mel Farr, RB, Det	UPI	TSN	AP-o	NEA
Lem Barney, CB, Det			AP-d	

1967 AFL

George Webster, LB, Hou	UPI	TSN	AP-d
Dickie Post, RB, SD			AP-o

1968 NFL

Earl McCullouch, FL, Det	UPI	TSN	AP-o	NEA
Claude Humphrey, DE, Atl			AP-d	

1968 AFL

Paul Robinson, RB, Cin	UPI	TSN	AP-o
Dick Anderson, S, Mia			AP-d*
George Atkinson, S, Oak			AP-d*

1969 NFL

Calvin Hill, RB, Dal	UPI	TSN	AP-o	NEA	PFW-o
Joe Greene, DT, Pit			AP-d		PFW-d

1969 AFL

Greg Cook, QB, Cin	UPI		AP-o		PFW-o
Carl Garrett, RB, Bos		TSN			
Bill Bergey, LB, Cin			AP-d		
Jim Marsalis, CB, KC					PFW-d

1970 NFC

Bruce Taylor, CB, SF	UPI	TSN	AP-d	PFW-d

1970 AFC

Dennis Shaw, QB, Buf	UPI	TSN	AP-o	PFW-o
Raymond Chester, TE, Oak			NEA*	

1971 NFC

John Brockington, RB, GB	UPI	TSN	NEA	AP-o	
Isiah Robertson, LB, LA				AP-d	PFW-d

1971 AFC

Jim Plunkett, QB, NE	UPI	TSN	NEA	PFW-o

1972 NFC

Chester Marcol, K, GB	UPI	TSN		
Willie Buchanon, CB, GB			NEA	AP-d

1972 AFC

Franco Harris, RB, Pit	UPI	TSN	NEA	AP-o	PFW-o
Sherman White, DE, Cin					PFW-d

1973 NFC
Chuck Foreman, RB, Min — TSN NEA AP-o PFW-o
Wally Chambers, DT, Chi — AP-d PFW-d
Charlie Young, TE, Phi — UPI

1973 AFC
Boobie Clark, RB, Cin — UPI TSN NEA

1974 NFC
John Hicks, G, NY — UPI
Wilbur Jackson, RB, SF — TSN

1974 AFC
Don Woods, RB, SD — UPI TSN NEA* AP-o PFW-o
Jack Lambert, LB, Pit — AP-d PFW-d

1975 NFC
Steve Bartkowski, QB, Atl — TSN NEA PFW-o*
Mike Thomas, RB, Was — UPI AP-o PFW-o*

1975 AFC
Robert Brazile, LB, Hou — UPI TSN NEA AP-d PFW-d

1976 NFC
Sammy White, WR, Min — UPI TSN NEA AP-o FWA PFW-o

1976 AFC
Mike Haynes, CB, NE — UPI TSN NEA AP-d PFW-d

1977 NFC
Tony Dorsett, RB, Dal — UPI TSN AP-o NEA FWA PFW-o

1977 AFC
A.J. Duhe, DE, Mia — UPI TSN AP-d PFW-d

1978 NFC
Al (Bubba) Baker, DE, Det — UPI TSN AP-d PFW-d

1978 AFC
Earl Campbell, RB, Hou — UPI TSN AP-o NEA FWA PFW-d

1979 NFC
Ottis Anderson, RB, StL — UPI TSN AP-o NEA FWA PFW-o

1979 AFC
Jerry Butler, WR, Buf — UPI TSN
Jim Haslett, LB, Buf — AP-d
Jesse Baker, DE, Hou — PFW-d

1980 NFC
Billy Sims, RB, Det — UPI TSN AP-o NEA FWA PFW-o
Buddy Curry, LB, Atl — AP-d* PFW-d
Al Richardson, LB, Atl — AP-d*

1980 AFC
Joe Cribbs, RB, Buf — UPI

1981 NFC
George Rogers, RB, NO — UPI TSN AP-o FWA PFW-o
Lawrence Taylor, LB, NY — AP-d NEA PFW-d

1981 AFC
Joe Delaney, RB, KC — UPI

1982 NFC
Jim McMahon, QB, Chi — UPI

1982 AFC
Marcus Allen, RB, LA — UPI TSN AP-o NEA FWA PFW-d
Chip Banks, LB, Cle — AP-d PFW-d

1983 NFC
Eric Dickerson, RB, LA — UPI AP-o NEA FWA PFW-o

1983 AFC
Vernon Maxwell, LB, Bal — AP-d PFW-d
Curt Warner, RB, Sea — UPI
Dan Marino, QB, Mia — TSN

1984 NFC
Paul McFadden, K, Phi — UPI
Tom Flynn, S, GB — PFW-d

1984 AFC
Louis Lipps, WR, Pit — UPI TSN AP-o NEA FWA PFW-o
Bill Maas, DT, KC — AP-d

1985 NFC
Jerry Rice, WR, SF — UPI

1985 AFC
Eddie Brown, WR, Cin — TSN AP-o NEA FWA
Kevin Mack, RB, Cle — UPI
Duane Bickett, LB, Ind — AP-d

1986 NFC
Rueben Mayes, RB, NO — UPI TSN AP-o NEA FWA PFW-o

1986 AFC
Leslie O'Neal, DE, SD — UPI AP-d PFW-d*
John Offerdahl, LB, Mia — PFW-d*

1987 NFC
Rob Awalt, TE, StL — UPI TSN

1987 AFC
Shane Conlan, LB, Buf — UPI AP-d FWA PFW-d
Troy Stradford, HB, Mia — AP-o PFW-o
Bo Jackson, LA — NEA

1988 NFC
Keith Jackson, TE, Phi — UPI TSN PFW-o

1988 AFC
John Stephens, RB, NE — UPI AP-o NEA FWA
Erik McMillan, S, NY — AP-d PFW-d

1989 NFC
Barry Sanders, RB, Det — UPI TSN AP-o NEA FWA PFW-o

1989 AFC
Derrick Thomas, LB, KC — UPI AP-d PFW-d

1990 NFC
Mark Carrier, S, Chi — UPI AP-d FWA PFW-d
Emmitt Smith, RB, Dal — AP-o PFW-o

1990 AFC
Richmond Webb, T, Mia — UPI TSN
Eric Green, TE, Pit — NEA

1991 NFC
Lawrence Dawsey, WR, TB — UPI

1991 AFC
Mike Croel, LB, Den — UPI TSN AP-d NEA FWA PFW-d
Leonard Russell, RB, NE — AP-o PFW-o

1992 NFC
Robert Jones, LB, Dal — UPI
Santana Dotson, DE, TB — TSN
Jason Hanson, K, Det — PFW-o

1992 AFC
Dale Carter, CB, KC — UPI AP-d NEA PFW-d
Carl Pickens, WR, Cin — AP-o

1993 NFC
Jerome Bettis, RB, LA — UPI TSN AP-o PFW-o
Dana Stubblefield, SF — AP-d PFW-d

1993 AFC

| Rick Mirer, QB, Sea | UPI | | | |

1994 NFC

| Bryant Young, DT, SF | UPI | | | |

1994 AFC

| Marshall Faulk, RB, Ind | UPI | TSN | AP-o | PFW-o |
| Tim Bowens, DT, Mia | | | AP-d | PFW-d |

1995 NFC

| Rashaan Salaam, RB, Chi | UPI | | | |

1995 AFC

| Hugh Douglas, DE, NYJ | | | AP-d | PFW-d |
| Curtis Martin, RB, NE | UPI | TSN | AP-o | PFW-o |

1996 NFC

| Simeon Rice, DE, Ari | UPI | | AP-d | PFW-d |

1996 AFC

| Eddie George, RB, Hou | | TSN | AP-o NEA | PFW-o |
| Terry Glenn, WR, NE | UPI | | | |

ALL-PRO REGISTER
1923–1996

Dan Abramowicz, WR: 1969
Tony Adamle, LB: **1951**
John Adams, T: 1945, 1946
Ken Adamson, G: 1961
Herb Adderley, CB: **1962**, 1963, **1965**, **1966**, **1969**
Tom Addison, LB: 1960, **1961**, 1963, 1964
Joe Aguirre, E: 1943, **1944**, 1945, 1946
Troy Aikman, QB: 1993
Frank Akins, FB: 1945
Frankie Albert, QB: **1946**, 1947, 1948, **1949**
Bruce Alford, E: **1947**
Chuck Allen, LB: 1961
Dalva Allen, DE: 1963
Eric Allen, CB: **1989**, 1992, 1993
Larry Allen, G: 1995, **1996**
Marcus Allen, RB: **1982**, 1984, **1985**, 1993
Terry Allen, RB: 1996
John Alt, T: 1990, 1991
Lance Alworth, FL: **1963**, **1964**, **1965**, **1966**, **1967**, **1968**, **1969**
Lyle Alzado, DE: **1977**, 1978, 1979, 1980, 1982
Ashley Ambrose, CB: **1996**
Alan Ameche, FB: **1955**
Kimble Anders, FB: 1995, 1996
Morten Andersen, K: **1985**, **1986**, **1987**, 1988, 1990, **1992**, **1995**
Dick Anderson, S: **1972**, **1973**, **1974**
Gary Anderson, K: 1983, 1985, 1993
Ken Anderson, QB: **1975**, **1981**
Neal Anderson, RB-ST: 1986, 1989, 1990
Ottis Anderson, RB: **1979**, 1980
William Andrews, RB: 1982, 1983
Charlie Ane, C: 1956
Elmer Angsman, HB: 1949
Houston Antwine, DT: **1963**, **1966**, 1967, 1968, 1969
Fred Arbanas, TE: 1962, **1963**, **1964**, **1966**, **1967**
Bruce Armstrong, T: 1988, 1990, 1991, 1994, 1995, 1996
Otis Armstrong, RB: **1974**
Jon Arnett, HB: **1958**
Jim Arnold, P: **1987**, 1988
Lee Artoe, T: **1942**
Billy Atkins, S: **1961**
Doug Atkins, DE: 1958, **1960**, 1961, **1963**
Steve Atwater, S: 1990, **1991**, **1992**, 1993, 1995, 1996
Bill Austin, G: 1955
John Ayers, G: 1984
Coy Bacon, DE: 1972, **1976**
Red Badgro, E: 1931, **1933**, 1934
Steve Bagarus, HB: 1945
Chris Bahr, K: 1977
Johnny Bailey, KR: 1992
Bill Bain, T: 1984
Al (Bubba) Baker, DE: **1978**, 1980
Jon Baker, DG: 1951
Jim Bakken, K: **1975**, **1976**
Jerry Ball, DT: 1989, 1990, **1991**
Howard Ballard, T: 1991, **1992**, 1993
Cas Banaszek, T: 1970, 1971
Bruno Banducci, G: **1946**, **1947**, 1952, **1953**, **1954**
Tony Banfield, CB: **1961**, **1962**, **1963**
Carl Banks, LB: **1987**
Chip Banks, LB: **1983**, 1985, 1986
Tom Banks, C: 1975, **1976**, 1977, 1978, 1979
Vince Banonis, C: 1947, 1948, 1949
Gary Barbaro, S: 1980, **1981**, 1982
Jim Barber, T: **1939**, 1940
Stew Barber, T: **1963**, **1964**

Erich Barnes, CB: **1961**, 1964
Mike Barnes, T: 1977
Lem Barney, CB: **1968**, **1969**, **1972**, 1973, **1975**
Nate Barrager, C: **1932**
Steve Bartkowski, QB: 1980
Harris Barton, T: 1992, **1993**
Dick Barwegan, G: **1947**, **1948**, **1949**, **1950**, **1951**
Mike Barzak, C: 1937
Dick Bass, HB: **1962**
Mike Bass, CB: **1974**
Bill Bates, ST: 1984
Michael Bates, KR: **1996**
Stan Batinski, G: 1945
Cliff Battles, HB: **1933**, 1934, **1936**, **1937**
Sammy Baugh, HB-QB: **1937**, **1940**, **1942**, **1943**, **1945**, **1947**, **1948**
Maxie Baughan, LB: 1961, **1964**, 1966, **1967**
Bob Baumhower, DT: 1979, **1981**, 1982, 1983
Frank Bausch, C: **1936**, 1938
Mark Bavaro, TE: **1986**, **1987**
Alyn Beals, E: **1946**, **1948**, **1949**
Bob Beattie, T: **1929**
Chuck Bednarik, C-LB: 1950, **1951**, 1952, **1953**, **1954**, 1955, **1956**, 1957, **1960**
Bull Behman, T: **1928**, **1929**
Bobby Bell, LB-DE: 1964, **1965**, **1966**, **1967**, **1968**, **1969**, **1970**, **1971**, 1972
Todd Bell, S: **1984**
Rolf Benirschke, K: 1982
Cornelius Bennett, LB: **1988**, 1990, 1991, 1992
Darren Bennett, P: **1995**
Jim Benton, E: **1945**, **1946**
Bill Bergey, LB: **1974**, **1975**, **1976**, **1977**, 1978, 1980
Charlie Berry, E: **1925**, **1926**
Raymond Berry, E: **1958**, **1959**, **1960**
Elvin Bethea, DE: **1971**, **1972**, 1974, 1975, 1978
Doug Betters, DE: **1983**
Jerome Bettis, RB: **1993**, 1996
Dean Biasucci, K: 1987, 1988
Duane Bickett, LB: 1987
Verlon Biggs, DE: **1966**
Fred Biletnikoff, WR: **1969**, 1970, 1971, **1972**, **1973**
Les Bingaman, DG: **1951**, 1952, **1953**, **1954**
Carl Birdsong, P: 1983
Dan Birdwell, DT: **1968**
Blaine Bishop, S: 1995
Keith Bishop, G: 1986, 1987
Bennie Blades, S: 1991
Matt Blair, LB: 1977, 1978, 1979, 1980, 1981
Cary Blanchard, K: **1996**
George Blanda, K-QB: **1961**, 1967, 1973
Johnny Blood, HB: **1931**
Mel Blount, CB: **1975**, **1976**, 1977, **1981**
Al Blozis, T: **1943**
Forrest Blue, C: **1971**, **1972**, **1973**, **1974**
Johnny Bookman, DB: 1960
Mark Bortz, G: 1990
Jeff Bostic, C: 1983
Keith Bostic, S: 1987
Cloyce Box, E: 1952
Bob Boyd, E: 1954
Bobby Boyd, CB: **1964**, **1965**, 1966, **1968**
Ben Boynton, HB: **1924**
Bill Bradley, S: **1971**, **1972**, 1973
Terry Bradshaw, QB: 1975, **1978**
Cliff Branch, WR: **1974**, 1975, **1976**, 1977
Mel Branch, DE: **1960**, **1962**
Ray Bray, G-DG: 1946, **1948**, **1949**
Robert Brazile, LB: **1976**, 1977, **1978**, **1979**, **1980**, 1981, 1982
Louis Breeden, CB: 1982
Larry Brink, DE: **1951**, 1952

Marlin Briscoe, WR: **1970**
Gene Brito, DE: **1955**, **1956**, **1957**, **1958**
Charley Brock, C: **1945**, 1946
John Brockington, RB: **1971**, **1972**, **1973**
John Brodie, QB: **1970**
James Brooks, RB: 1986, 1989
Larry Brooks, DT: 1974, 1977, 1978, 1979
Michael Brooks, LB: 1993
Tom Brookshier, HB: 1959, **1960**
Aaron Brown, DE: 1970, 1971
Bob Brown, T: 1965, **1966**, **1968**, **1969**, **1970**, **1971**, 1972
Chad Brown, LB: **1996**
Eddie Brown, KR: 1976, 1977
Eddie Brown, WR: 1988
Jerome Brown, DT: 1990, **1991**
Jim Brown, FB: **1957**, **1958**, **1959**, **1960**, **1961**, **1963**, **1964**, **1965**
Larry Brown, RB: **1970**, **1971**, **1972**
Lomas Brown, T: 1990, 1991, 1992, 1994, **1995**, 1996
Roger Brown, DT: **1962**, **1963**
Ron Brown, KR: **1985**
Roosevelt Brown, T: **1956**, **1957**, **1958**, **1959**, **1960**, 1961, **1962**, **1963**
Tim Brown, WR-KR: **1988**, 1991, 1993, 1994, 1995
Vincent Brown, LB: 1991, 1992, 1993
Willie Brown, CB: **1964**, **1968**, **1969**, **1970**, **1971**, **1972**, **1973**
Joey Browner, S-ST: 1985, **1987**, **1988**, 1989, **1990**
Bob Bruenig, LB: 1979, 1980, 1982, 1983
Fred Bruney, DB: 1960
Bobby Bryant, CB: 1969, 1973
Cullen Bryant, KR: 1976
Buck Buchanan, DT: **1966**, **1967**, **1968**, **1969**, 1970, 1971
Willie Buchanon, CB: 1974, **1978**
Johnny Budd, G: **1926**
Ed Budde, G: 1966, 1968, **1969**, 1970
Nick Buoniconti, LB: 1963, **1964**, **1965**, **1966**, **1967**, 1968, **1969**, 1972
Chris Burford, FL: **1962**
Bobby Burnett, HB: 1966
Lloyd Burruss, S: 1986
Jim Burt, DT: 1986
Dick Butkus, LB: **1965**, 1967, **1968**, **1969**, **1970**, **1971**, **1972**
Jack Butler, DB: **1957**, **1958**, **1959**
LeRoy Butler, S: **1993**, **1996**
Marion Butts, RB: 1990
Dave Butz, DT: 1983
Keith Byars, FB: 1993
Butch Byrd, CB: **1965**, **1966**, 1968, **1969**
Gill Byrd, CB: 1989, 1991, **1992**
Ernie Caddel, HB: 1935
Lee Roy Caffey, LB: **1966**
Rich Camarillo, P: **1983**, 1989, 1991, **1992**, 1993
Earl Campbell, RB: **1978**, **1979**, **1980**, 1981, 1983
Tony Canadeo, HB-FB: **1943**, 1947, **1949**
Billy Cannon, HB-TE: **1961**, 1967
Gino Cappelletti, K: 1966
Lloyd Cardwell, HB: 1938
Zuck Carlson, G: **1932**
J.C. Caroline, DB: 1956
Harold Carmichael, WR: **1973**, 1978, 1979, 1980
Art Carney, G: **1925**
John Carney, K: **1994**
Fred Carr, LB: 1975
Roger Carr, WR: **1976**
Mark Carrier, S: 1990, 1991, 1993
Carlos Carson, WR: 1983
Harry Carson, LB: 1978, 1979, 1981, 1982, 1984, 1985, 1986, 1987

Anthony Carter, WR: 1988
Cris Carter, WR: **1994**
Dale Carter, CB: 1995, **1996**
Michael Carter, DT: 1986, **1987**, 1988, 1989
Tommy Casanova, S: 1975, **1976**, 1977
Rick Casares, FB-HB: 1955, **1956**
Scott Case, CB: 1988
Jim Cason, DB: 1949
Dave Casper, TE: **1976, 1977, 1978, 1979**
Rich Caster, TE: 1975
Chuck Cecil, S: 1992
Larry Centers, FB: 1995, 1996
Wally Chambers, DT: **1974, 1975, 1976**
Wes Chandler, WR: **1982**
Dave Chapple, P: 1972
Deron Cherry, S: 1983, 1984, 1985, 1986, 1987, **1988**
Raymond Chester, TE: 1970, **1971, 1972**, 1979
Ray Childress, DT-DE: 1988, 1990, 1991, 1992, 1993
Henry Childs, TE: 1979
Mark Chmura, TE: 1995
George Christensen, T: **1931**, 1933, 1934
Todd Christensen, TE: **1983, 1985**, 1986, 1987
Jack Christiansen, DB: 1952, **1953, 1954, 1955, 1956, 1957**
Steve Christie, K: 1990
Ed Cifers, E: 1942
Dutch Clark, QB: **1931, 1932, 1934, 1935, 1936, 1937**
Dwight Clark, WR: **1982**
Gary Clark, WR: 1986, 1987, 1991
Harry Clark, HB: **1943**
Frank Clarke, SE: **1964**
Ray Clayborn, CB-KR: 1977, 1983, 1986
Ralph Claypool, C: **1925**
Mark Clayton, WR: 1984
John Clement, HB: 1947
Ben Coates, TE: **1994, 1995**
Don Cockroft, P: 1972
Mike Cofer, LB: 1988
Mike Cofer, K: 1989
Paul Coffman, TE: 1983, 1984
Robin Cole, LB: 1984
Andre Coleman, KR: 1994, 1995
Gary Collins, WR: 1965, 1969
Jim Collins, LB: 1984, 1985
Mark Collins, CB: 1989, 1990
Cris Collinsworth, WR: 1982, 1983
Don Colo, DT: 1955, 1957
Shane Conlan, LB: **1988**, 1990
Dan Conners, LB: 1967, **1968**, 1969
George Connor, T-DT-LB: **1949, 1950, 1951, 1952, 1953, 1955**
Bobby Joe Conrad, FL: **1963**
Fred Cook, DE: 1977
Marv Cook, TE: **1991**
Frank Cope, T: **1944**, 1945
Jerry Cornelison, T: 1961
Frank Corral, K: **1978**
Doug Cosbie, TE: 1985
Tom Cousineau, LB: 1983, 1984
Tex Coulter, T: **1951**
Jim Covert, T: **1985, 1986**, 1987
Charley Cowan, T: 1969, 1971
Bryan Cox, LB: 1992, 1994
Fred Cox, K: 1969, 1970
Larry Craig, E: 1947
Roger Craig, RB: 1985, **1988**
Lou Creekmur, G-T: **1951, 1952, 1953, 1954, 1956, 1957**
Joe Cribbs, RB: 1980, 1983
Nolan Cromwell, S: **1980, 1981, 1982**, 1983

Randy Cross, G: 1980, **1981**, 1982, 1984, 1985
John David Crow, HB: 1960
Larry Csonka, RB: 1970, **1971, 1972, 1973**
Walt Cudzik, C: 1960
Ward Cuff, QB-HB-FB: 1941, **1943, 1944**
Curley Culp, DT: **1975, 1976**, 1977
Randall Cunningham, QB: 1988, 1990
Dan Currie, LB: 1961, **1962**, 1963
Bill Curry, C: **1971**
Buddy Curry, LB: 1980
Isaac Curtis, WR: 1973, **1974, 1975**, 1976
Mike Curtis, LB: **1968**, 1971, 1974
Eldon Danenhauer, T: **1962**, 1965
Clem Daniels, HB: **1963, 1966**
Ed Danowski, HB: **1935, 1938**
Thom Darden, S: **1978**, 1979
Jim David, DB: **1954**
Ben Davidson, DE: **1967**
Eric Davis, CB: **1995**
Fred Davis, T: **1947**, 1948
Jack Davis, G: 1960
Milt Davis, DB: 1957
Terrell Davis, RB: **1996**
Willie Davis, DE: 1962, **1964, 1965, 1966, 1967**
Dermontti Dawson, C: 1993, **1994, 1995, 1996**
Len Dawson, QB: **1962, 1966**
Fred Dean, DE: 1979, 1980, **1981**, 1983
Bob Dee, DE: 1962
Joe DeLamielleure, G: **1975, 1976, 1977, 1978, 1979, 1980**
Joe Delaney, RB: 1981
John Dell Isola, G: **1939**
Robert Delpino, ST: 1988
Jack Del Rio, LB: 1994
Bob DeMarco, C: **1964**, 1967
Vern Den Herder, DE: 1972
Al Denson, SE: 1967
Richard Dent, DE: 1984, **1985**, 1988, 1990, 1993
Dean Derby, S: **1959**
Al DeRogatis, DT: 1951
Bill Dewell, E: 1946, 1947
Eric Dickerson, RB: **1983, 1984, 1986, 1987, 1988**
Wally Diehl, FB: **1928**
Dan Dierdorf, T: **1975, 1976, 1977, 1978**, 1980
Bobby Dillon, DB: 1954, **1955, 1956, 1957, 1958**
Lavern Dilweg, E: **1927, 1928, 1929, 1930, 1931**
Cris Dishman, CB: 1991
Mike Ditka, TE: 1961, **1962, 1963, 1964**
Hanford Dixon, CB: **1986, 1987**
Hewritt Dixon, RB: 1967, **1968, 1970**
Glenn Dobbs, HB: **1946**
Conrad Dobler, G: 1975, **1976**, 1977
Dale Dodrill, DG-LB: 1953, 1954, **1955**
Chris Doleman, DE: 1987, 1988, **1989**, 1990, **1992**, 1993
Don Doll, DB: 1949, 1950
Ray Donaldson, C: 1987, 1988, 1989
Art Donovan, DT: **1954, 1955, 1956, 1957**, 1958
Pat Donovan, T: 1979, 1980, 1981, 1982
Keith Dorney, T: 1981, 1985
Tony Dorsett, RB: 1978, **1981**, 1982
Jap Douds, T: **1930**
Maurice Douglass, ST: 1994
Mike Douglass, LB: 1982
Michael Downs, S: 1984, 1985
Johnny Drake, FB: **1940**
Paddy Driscoll, QB-HB: **1923, 1925, 1926, 1927**
Fred Dryer, DE: 1974, 1975
Bill Dudley, HB: **1942, 1946**, 1947
Dave Duerson, S: **1986**, 1988
A.J. Duhe, LB: 1981
Mike Dukes, LB: 1960
Jim Dunaway, DT: 1966

Speedy Duncan, CB-KR: 1965, 1971
Mark Duper, WR: 1984
Billy Joe DuPree, TE: **1976**, 1977, 1978
John Dutton, DE: **1975, 1976**, 1977
Kenny Easley, S: **1982, 1983, 1984, 1985**, 1987
Harry Ebding, E: 1933
Bobby Joe Edmonds, KR: **1986**
Bill Edwards, G: **1942**
Brad Edwards, S: 1992
Dan Edwards, E: 1950
Glen Edwards, S: 1976
Turk Edwards, T: **1932, 1933**, 1934, 1935, **1936, 1937**, 1939
Joe Ehrmann, DT: 1976
Larry Eisenhauer, DE: 1962, **1963, 1964**, 1966
Cleveland Elam, DT: **1977**
Jason Elam, K: 1995
Henry Ellard, KR-WR: **1984**, 1985, **1988**
Carl Eller, DE: **1968, 1969, 1970, 1971**, 1972, **1973**, 1974, 1975
Doc Elliott, FB: **1923, 1924**
John Elliott, DT: 1968, **1969, 1970**
Ken Ellis, CB: 1972, **1973**
Walt Ellis, T: **1926**
Dave Elmendorf, S: 1974
John Elway, QB: 1987, 1993, 1996
Ox Emerson, G: **1932**, 1933, **1934, 1935, 1936**, 1937
Doug English, DT: 1981, 1982, 1983
Boomer Esiason, QB: **1988**, 1989
Byron Evans, LB: 1992
Lon Evans, G: **1936, 1937**
Norm Evans, T: 1973, 1974
Julian Fagan, P: 1970
Keith Fahnhorst, T: 1983, **1984**
Earl Faison, DE: **1961, 1963, 1964, 1965**
Gary Famiglietti, FB: **1942**
Andy Farkas, HB: **1939**, 1942
Dick Farman, G: **1943**
Miller Farr, CB: **1967, 1968**, 1969
Sean Farrell, G: 1984
Marshall Faulk, RB: **1994**, 1995
Brett Favre, QB: **1995, 1996**
Jeff Feagles, P: 1995
Tom Fears, E: 1949, **1950**
Beattie Feathers, HB: **1934**
Gary Fencik, S: 1979, 1980, **1981**, 1982
Howie Ferguson, FB: 1955
Manny Fernandez, DT: 1971
Joe Fields, C: 1982
Frank Filchock, HB: 1939, 1946
Bill Fischer, G: **1952**
Pat Fischer, CB: **1964**, 1975
Ray Flaherty, E: **1928, 1929, 1932**
Ed Flanagan, C: 1970, 1971
Don Floyd, DE: 1961, **1962**
Len Ford, DE: **1951, 1952, 1953, 1954, 1955**
Chuck Foreman, RB: **1974, 1975, 1976**, 1977
Bill Forester, LB: **1960, 1961, 1962**, 1963
Dan Fortmann, G: 1937, **1938, 1939, 1940, 1941, 1942, 1943**
Joe Fortunato, LB: **1963, 1964, 1965**
Barry Foster, RB: **1992**
Roy Foster, G: 1985, 1986
Dan Fouts, QB: **1979, 1982**, 1985
Bill Fralic, G: **1986, 1987**, 1988, 1989
Doug France, T: 1978, 1980
Tony Franklin, K: 1986
Willie Frazier, TE: **1965**, 1967
Steve Freeman, S: 1983
Rocky Freitas, T: 1970
Benny Friedman, QB: **1927, 1928, 1929, 1930**
Ted Fritsch, FB: 1945, **1946**

Toni Fritsch, K: **1979**
Irving Fryar, KR-WR: 1985, 1994
Jean Fugett, TE: 1977
David Fulcher, S: 1988, **1989**, 1990
William Fuller, DE: 1991, 1995
Roman Gabriel, QB: **1969**
Bob Gain, DT: 1958
Hugh Gallarneau, HB: 1946
Milt Gantenbein, E: **1936**
Chris Gardocki, P: **1996**
Mike Garrett, RB: **1967**
Russell Gary, S: 1983
Mark Gastineau, DE: 1981, **1982**, 1983, **1984**, 1985
Frank Gatski, C: **1951**, **1952**, **1953**, **1955**
William Gay, DE: 1983
Fred Gehrke, HB: 1945
Byron Gentry, G: 1938, 1939
Dennis Gentry, KR: 1986, 1987, 1988
Bill George, LB: 1955, **1956**, **1957**, **1958**, **1959**, **1960**, **1961**, **1963**
Roy Gerela, K: 1972, **1974**
Joe Geri, HB: **1950**
Abe Gibron, G: **1953**, **1955**
Butch Gibson, G: **1931**, 1934
Frank Gifford, HB: **1955**, **1956**, **1957**, **1959**
Sean Gilbert, DT: 1993
Cookie Gilchrist, FB: **1962**, 1963, **1964**, **1965**
Jimmie Giles, TE: 1980, 1981, 1982
Jim Gillette, HB: 1945
John Gilliam, WR: 1972, 1973, **1975**
Gale Gillingham, G: 1969, **1970**, **1971**, 1973, **1974**
Ernest Givins, WR: 1990
Terry Glenn, WR: 1996
Fred Glick, S: **1963**, 1964
Kevin Glover, C: 1994, 1995, 1996
Pete Gogolak, K: 1965
Bob Golic, DT: 1985
Goose Gonsoulin, DB: **1960**, 1962, 1963
Darrien Gordon, KR: 1994, 1996
Dick Gordon, WR: **1970**, 1971
John Gordy, G: 1964, 1965, 1966
Ken Gorgal, S: **1953**
Bruce Gossett, K: 1973
Jeff Gossett, P: **1991**
Randy Gradishar, LB: **1977**, **1978**, 1979, 1980, 1981, 1982
Kenny Graham, S: **1966**, 1967, 1968
Otto Graham, QB: 1946, **1947**, **1948**, **1949**, **1951**, **1952**, **1953**, **1954**, **1955**
Red Grange, HB: **1930**, **1931**
Len Grant, T: **1931**, **1932**
Larry Grantham, LB: **1960**, **1961**, **1962**, **1963**, **1964**
Jerry Gray, CB: 1986, 1987, 1988, 1989
Ken Gray, G: **1963**, **1964**, **1965**
Leon Gray, T: **1978**, **1979**, **1980**
Mel Gray, WR: 1974, **1975**, **1976**
Mel Gray, KR: 1986, **1987**, 1989, **1990**, **1991**, 1992, 1993, **1994**
Dave Grayson, CB-S: 1963, **1964**, **1965**, **1966**, **1968**, **1969**
Cornell Green, CB-S: **1966**, **1967**, 1968, 1969, 1971, 1972
Darrell Green, CB: 1984, 1986, 1987, 1990, **1991**
Gary Green, CB: 1981, **1983**
Gaston Green, RB: 1991
Hugh Green, LB: **1982**, 1983
Jacob Green, DE: 1984, 1987
Roy Green, WR-KR: 1979, **1983**, **1984**
Tony Green, KR: 1978
Joe Greene, DT: **1970**, **1971**, **1972**, **1973**, **1974**, **1975**, 1976, 1977, 1978, **1979**
Kevin Greene, LB: 1989, 1994, **1996**

Tony Greene, S: **1974**
L.C. Greenwood, DE: 1973, **1974**, **1975**, 1978, 1979
Forrest Gregg, T: 1960, 1961, **1962**, **1963**, **1964**, 1965, **1966**, **1967**
Jack Gregory, DE: **1972**
Visco Grgich, G: **1949**
Rosey Grier, DT: **1956**
Bob Griese, QB: 1970, **1971**, 1973, **1977**
Don Griffin, CB: 1989
John Grigas, FB: **1944**
Bob Grim, WR: 1971
Billy Joe Grimes, HB: 1950
Russ Grimm, G: **1983**, **1984**, **1985**, 1986
Bill Groman, E: **1960**, 1961
Lou Groza, T: **1951**, **1952**, **1953**, **1954**, **1955**, **1957**
Paul Gruber, T: 1989, 1992
Bob Grupp, P: **1979**
Ray Guy, P: **1973**, **1974**, **1975**, **1976**, **1977**, **1978**, 1980
Wayne Haddix, CB: 1990
John Hadl, QB: **1973**
Swede Hagberg, C: **1930**
Carl Hairston, DE: 1980
Ali Haji-Sheikh, K: **1983**
Charles Haley, LB-DE: 1988, **1990**, **1994**, 1995
Parker Hall, QB: **1939**
Ron Hall, S: **1964**
Jack Ham, LB: **1973**, **1974**, **1975**, **1976**, **1977**, **1978**, **1979**
Harry Hamilton, S: 1989
Bob Hammond, KR: 1977
Dan Hampton, DT-DE: 1980, **1982**, **1984**, 1986, 1988
Chris Hanburger, LB: 1970, **1972**, **1973**, **1974**, **1975**, **1976**
Merton Hanks, S: 1994, 1995, 1996
John Hannah, G: 1974, **1976**, 1977, **1978**, **1979**, **1980**, **1981**, **1982**, **1983**, **1984**, **1985**
Brian Hansen, P: 1984
Jason Hanson, K: 1993
Jim Harbaugh, QB: 1995
Pat Harder, FB: **1947**, **1948**, **1949**
Cedrick Hardman, DE: 1971, **1975**
Dennis Harrah, G: 1978, 1979, 1985, **1986**, 1987
Cliff Harris, S: **1974**, 1975, **1976**, **1977**, **1978**, 1979
Dick Harris, CB: **1960**, **1961**
Duriel Harris, KR: 1976
Franco Harris, RB: 1972, **1975**, 1976, **1977**, 1979
Tim Harris, LB: 1988, **1989**
Jim Hart, QB: **1974**
Leon Hart, E-DE: 1951
Tommy Hart, DE: **1976**
Ken Harvey, LB: 1994, 1995
Carlton Haselrig, G: 1992
Jim Haslett, LB: 1980
Dale Hatcher, P: **1985**
Len Hauss, C: 1971, 1972, 1974, **1975**
Wayne Hawkins, G: 1961, 1965, **1966**
Bob Hayes, WR: **1966**, 1967, 1968
Lester Hayes, CB: **1980**, 1981, 1982, **1983**, 1984
Abner Haynes, HB: **1960**, **1961**, **1962**
Mark Haynes, CB: 1981, **1982**, **1984**
Mike Haynes, CB: **1976**, 1977, 1978, 1979, 1980, 1982, **1984**, **1985**, 1986
Sherrill Headrick, LB: **1960**, **1961**, **1962**
Ed Healey, T: **1923**, **1924**, **1925**, **1926**
Mel Hein, C: 1933, **1934**, **1935**, **1936**, **1937**, **1938**, **1939**, **1940**
Ted Hendricks, LB: **1971**, **1972**, 1973, **1974**, 1976, **1980**, 1981, 1982
Charley Hennigan, SE: **1961**, **1962**, **1964**
Wally Henry, KR: **1979**
Wilbur Henry, T: **1923**

Arnie Herber, HB: **1932**
Dave Herman, G: 1967, 1968
Efren Herrera, K: **1977**
Bill Hewitt, E: **1933**, **1934**, **1936**, **1937**, 1938
Gene Hickerson, G: 1966, **1967**, **1968**, **1969**, 1970
Herman Hickman, G: **1933**
Dwight Hicks, S: 1981, 1984
Jay Hilgenberg, C: 1985, 1986, 1987, **1988**, **1989**, 1990, 1991
Joel Hilgenberg, C: 1992
Calvin Hill, RB: **1969**, **1973**
Harlon Hill, E: **1954**, **1955**, **1956**
Jimmy Hill, DB: 1961
Kent Hill, G: 1980, 1982, 1983, 1985
Tony Hill, WR: 1978
Winston Hill, T: **1969**, **1970**, 1971, **1972**, **1973**, 1974
Clarke Hinkle, FB: 1935, **1936**, **1937**, **1938**, 1940, 1941
Chris Hinton, T-G: 1983, 1985, 1986, 1987, 1988, 1989, 1993
Crazy Legs Hirsch, E: **1951**, 1953
Leroy Hoard, FB: 1994
Bob Hoernschemeyer, HB: 1952, 1953
Darrell Hogan, DG: 1949
Brian Holloway, T: 1983, 1984, 1985, 1986
Rodney Holman, TE: 1989, 1990
Pat Holmes, DE: **1967**
Pierce Holt, DT: 1992
E.J. Holub, LB: **1962**, **1963**
Wes Hopkins, S: 1984, **1985**
Mike Horan, P: 1984, **1988**
Paul Hornung, HB: **1960**, **1961**
Jim Houston, LB: 1964, 1965
Ken Houston, S: 1969, **1970**, **1971**, 1972, **1973**, **1974**, **1975**, **1976**, 1977, 1978, 1979
Desmond Howard, KR: 1996
Chuck Howley, LB: **1966**, 1967, **1968**, **1969**, **1970**, 1971
Billy Howton, E: **1952**, **1956**, **1957**
Cal Hubbard, T-E: **1927**, **1931**, **1932**, **1933**
Jim Hudson, S: 1968
Sam Huff, LB: **1958**, **1959**, **1960**
Dick Huffman, T-DT: 1947, **1948**, **1949**, 1950
Tyrone Hughes, KR: 1993
Kent Hull, C: 1988, 1989, **1990**, 1991
Bobby Humphrey, KR: 1984
Claude Humphrey, DE: 1970, **1971**, **1972**, **1973**, **1974**, 1977
Bobby Hunt, S: **1962**
Ed Husmann, DT: **1962**
Don Hutson, E: **1936**, **1937**, **1938**, **1939**, **1940**, **1941**, **1942**, **1943**, **1944**, **1945**
Tunch Ilkin, T: 1988
Tut Imlay, QB: **1926**
LeRoy Irvin, KR: **1981**, 1982, **1986**
Michael Irvin, WR: **1991**, 1993
Cecil Isbell, HB: **1941**, **1942**
Horace Ivory, KR: 1980
Chris Jacke, K: 1993
Earnest Jackson, RB: 1984
Harold Jackson, WR: **1972**, **1973**, 1977
John Jackson, T: 1993
Keith Jackson, TE: **1988**, **1989**, **1990**, 1992
Monte Jackson, CB: **1976**, **1977**
Rich Jackson, DE: **1968**, **1969**, **1970**, 1971
Rickey Jackson, LB: 1983, 1984, 1985, 1986, 1987, 1992, 1993
Tom Jackson, LB: **1977**, 1984
Joe Jacoby, T: **1983**, **1984**, 1987
Jeff Jaeger, K: **1991**
John James, P: 1975, **1976**, 1977
Lionel James, KR: 1987

65

Robert James, CB: **1972**, **1973**, **1974**
Al Jamison, T: 1960, **1961**, **1962**
Val Jansante, E: 1947
Dick Jauron, KR: 1974
Ron Jaworski, QB: 1980
John Jefferson, WR: **1979**, **1980**
Roy Jefferson, WR: **1969**, **1971**
Haywood Jeffires, WR: **1991**, 1992
Alfred Jenkins, WR: **1981**
Dave Jennings, P: 1978, 1979, **1980**, **1982**
Bob Jeter, CB: **1967**
Bill Johnson, C: 1954
Billy Johnson, KR: 1975, **1977**, **1983**
Bob Johnson, C: 1972, 1973
Charley Johnson, QB: **1973**
Charlie Johnson, DT: **1979**, 1980, 1981
Curley Johnson, P: 1965
Gary Johnson, DT: **1980**, **1981**, 1982
Jimmy Johnson, CB: 1969, **1970**, **1971**, **1972**
Johnnie Johnson, S: 1983
Mike Johnson, LB: 1989
Nate Johnson, T: **1947**
Norm Johnson, K: **1984**, **1993**
Pepper Johnson, LB: **1990**
Ron Johnson, RB: 1970
Vaughan Johnson, LB: 1987, 1988, 1989, 1991, 1992
Luke Johnsos, E: **1930**, **1931**, **1932**
Daryl Johnston, FB: 1993, 1994
Mark Johnston, CB: **1960**, 1961
Charlie Joiner, WR: 1980
Bert Jones, QB: **1976**
Brent Jones, TE: 1992, 1993, 1994
Deacon Jones, DE: **1965**, **1966**, **1967**, **1968**, **1969**, **1970**, **1972**
Dub Jones, HB: **1951**
Ed Jones, DE: 1981, 1982, 1983
Henry Jones, S: **1992**
Homer Jones, WR: **1967**
Rulon Jones, DE: 1985, **1986**
Stan Jones, G: 1955, **1956**, 1959, **1960**
Tony Jones, T: 1994
Henry Jordan, DT: **1960**, **1961**, 1962, **1963**, **1964**
Lee Roy Jordan, LB: **1973**, 1975
Seth Joyner, LB: 1991, 1993
E.J. Junior, LB: **1984**, 1985
Sonny Jurgensen, QB: **1961**, 1969
Bill Karr, E: **1935**
Alex Karras, DT: **1960**, **1961**, **1962**, **1965**
John Kasay, K: 1996
Jim Katcavage, DE: **1961**, **1962**, **1963**
Ken Kavanaugh, E: 1946, **1947**
Tom Keane, DB: **1953**
Tom Keating, DT: 1966, **1967**, 1969, 1970
Louie Kelcher, DT: 1977, **1978**, 1980
Leroy Kelly, RB: **1966**, **1967**, **1968**, 1969, 1970, 1971
Jim Kelly, QB: **1991**
Jack Kemp, QB: **1960**, 1965
Mike Kenn, T: **1980**, 1981, 1982, 1983, 1984, **1991**
Cortez Kennedy, DT: **1992**, **1993**, **1994**, 1996
Walt Kiesling, G: **1930**, **1932**
Bucko Kilroy, G-DG: 1949, 1950, 1954
Billy Kilmer, QB: **1972**
Bruiser Kinard, T: 1938, **1940**, **1941**, 1942, 1943, 1944, **1946**
Levon Kirkland, LB: 1996
John Kissell, T-DT: **1949**
Joe Klecko, DT-DE: **1981**, 1983, 1985
Ed Klewicki, E: 1937
Curt Knight, K: **1971**
Dave Kocourek, TE: **1962**, 1963
Jon Kolb, T: 1975, 1978, 1979
Ed Kolman, T: 1942

Joe Kopcha, G: **1933**, **1934**, **1935**
Greg Kragen, DT: 1989, 1991
Jerry Kramer, G: 1960, **1962**, **1963**, **1966**, **1967**
Ron Kramer, TE: 1961, 1962
Tommy Kramer, QB: 1986
Paul Krause, S: **1964**, **1965**, 1970, **1971**, **1972**, **1973**, 1974, **1975**
Keith Krepfle, TE: 1979
Bill Krisher, G: **1960**
Ray Krouse, DT: 1954, 1956
Tim Krumrie, DT: **1988**
Bob Kuechenberg, G: 1974, 1975, 1978
Joe Kuharich, G: **1941**
George Kunz, T: 1971, 1972, 1973, **1975**, **1976**, 1977
Mal Kutner, E: **1947**, **1948**
Fulton Kuykendall, LB: 1978
Ted Kwalick, TE: **1972**, 1973
Eric Laakso, T: 1983
Jim Lachey, T: 1987, **1989**, **1990**, **1991**
Ernie Ladd, DT: **1961**, **1964**, **1965**
Warren Lahr, DB: **1951**
Bruce Laird, S: 1980
Carnell Lake, S: 1994, 1995, 1996
Jack Lambert, LB: **1975**, **1976**, 1978, **1979**, **1980**, **1981**, **1982**, **1983**
Daryle Lamonica, QB: **1967**, 1969, **1970**
Sean Landeta, P: **1986**, **1989**, **1990**
Greg Landry, QB: 1971
Tom Landry, DB: **1954**
MacArthur Lane, RB: **1970**
Night Train Lane, CB-S: **1956**, 1960, **1961**, **1962**, **1963**
Jim Langer, C: **1973**, **1974**, **1975**, **1976**, **1977**
Willie Lanier, LB: 1968, 1969, **1970**, **1971**, **1972**, **1973**, **1974**, 1975
Mike Lansford, K: 1989
Steve Largent, WR: 1978, 1983, **1985**, 1986, **1987**
Yale Lary, S: 1956, **1957**, **1958**, 1959, **1962**
Ike Lassiter, DE: 1968
Lamar Lathon, LB: 1996
Dante Lavelli, E: **1946**, 1947, **1951**, **1953**
Henry Lawrence, T: 1984
Rolland Lawrence, CB: 1975, **1977**
Bobby Layne, QB: 1952, **1956**
Milan Lazetich, DG: 1949
Pat Leahy, K: 1978
Carl Lee, CB: **1988**, 1989, 1990
David Lee, P: **1969**, 1970
Tuffy Leemans, HB: **1936**, **1939**
Chuck Leo, G: 1961
Russ Letlow, G: **1938**
Leon Lett, DT: 1994
Verne Lewellen, HB: **1926**, **1927**, **1928**, **1929**
Albert Lewis, CB: 1988, **1989**, **1990**
Dave Lewis, P: 1970
David Lewis, LB: 1979
Frank Lewis, WR: 1981
Nate Lewis, KR: 1991
John Leypoldt, K: 1974
Bob Lilly, DT: **1964**, **1965**, **1966**, **1967**, **1968**, **1969**, **1971**, **1972**
Keith Lincoln, FB-HB: **1963**, **1964**
Vic Lindskog, C: 1951
Toni Linhart, K: **1976**, 1977
Augie Lio, G: 1944, 1945, 1946
Ronnie Lippett, CB: 1986, 1988
Louis Lipps, KR-WR: 1984, **1985**
Big Daddy Lipscomb, DT: **1958**, **1959**, 1960, 1961
David Little, LB: 1990
Floyd Little, RB: **1969**, **1970**, **1971**
Larry Little, G: **1971**, **1972**, **1973**, **1974**, **1975**, 1977

Joe Little Twig, E: **1924**
Greg Lloyd, LB: **1993**, **1994**, **1995**
Eugene Lockhart, LB: 1989
Spider Lockhart, S: **1970**
James Lofton, WR: **1980**, **1981**, 1982, 1983, 1984
David Logan, DT: 1983, 1984
Jerry Logan, S: 1970, 1971
Randy Logan, S: 1980
Chip Lohmiller, K: 1991
Charley Long, T: 1962
Howie Long, DE: **1983**, **1984**, **1985**, 1986
Billy Lothridge, P: 1968
Ronnie Lott, S-CB: **1981**, 1983, **1986**, **1987**, 1988, **1989**, **1990**, **1991**
Paul Lowe, HB: **1960**, **1965**
Nick Lowery, K: 1981, 1985, 1988, **1990**, 1992
Mike Lucci, LB: 1971
Sid Luckman, QB: **1941**, **1942**, **1943**, **1944**, **1946**, **1947**
Johnny Lujack, QB: 1949, **1950**
Father Lumpkin, HB: **1932**
Link Lyman, T: **1930**, **1934**
Dick Lynch, CB: **1963**
Ed Lynch, E: **1925**
Bill Maas, DT: 1986, 1987
Tom Mack, G: **1969**, **1970**, **1971**, **1972**, **1973**, **1974**, **1975**, 1977, 1978
John Mackey, TE: **1966**, **1967**, **1968**
Tom MacLeod, LB: 1975
Eddie Macon, DB: **1960**
Paul Maguire, LB-P: **1960**, 1969
Jack Manders, HB: 1934, 1937
Pug Manders, FB: **1941**
Dexter Manley, DE: **1986**
Errol Mann, K: 1977
Archie Manning, QB: 1978
Gino Marchetti, DE: 1956, **1957**, **1958**, **1959**, **1960**, **1961**, **1962**, 1963, **1964**
Chester Marcol, K: **1972**, **1974**
Bob Margarita, HB: 1945
Dan Marino, QB: 1983, **1984**, **1985**, **1986**, 1992, 1994, 1995
Jim Marsalis, CB: **1970**, 1971
Leonard Marshall, DE: 1985
Wilber Marshall, LB: **1986**, 1987, 1991, **1992**
Curtis Martin, RB: 1995
Doug Martin, DE: 1982
Harvey Martin, DE: **1977**
Kelvin Martin, KR: 1992
Rod Martin, LB: 1982, **1983**, 1984
Tony Martin, WR: 1996
Tommy Mason, HB: **1963**
Robert Massey, CB: 1992
Bob Masterson, E: 1942
Riley Matheson, G: 1941, 1942, **1944**, **1945**, **1946**, **1947**
Bill Mathis, FB: **1961**
Ollie Matson, HB-DB: 1952, **1954**, **1955**, **1956**, **1957**
Archie Matsos, LB: **1960**, 1961, **1963**
Bruce Matthews, G-C: **1988**, **1989**, **1990**, **1991**, **1992**, **1993**, 1995, 1996
Clay Matthews, LB: 1984, 1989
Ira Matthews, KR: 1979
Marv Matuszak, LB: **1957**
Stan Mauldin, T: 1947
Rich Mauti, KR: 1980
Mark May, G: 1988
Rueben Mayes, RB: 1987
Don Maynard, WR: 1968, 1969
Jerry Mays, DE-DT: 1962, 1964, **1965**, **1966**, 1967, 1968
George McAfee, HB: **1941**

Jack McBride, FB: **1925**
Richie McCabe, S: **1960**
Larry McCarren, C: 1980, 1982
Kent McCloughan, CB: 1966, **1967**
Mike McCormack, T: 1954, 1957
Lawrence McCutcheon, RB: **1974**, 1977
Randall McDaniel, G: 1989, 1990, 1991, **1992, 1993, 1994, 1995, 1996**
Terry McDaniel, CB: 1993, 1994, 1995
Ron McDole, DE: 1965, 1966, 1967, 1968, 1969
Tim McDonald, S: 1989, 1991, 1992, 1993
Tommy McDonald, E: 1960
O.J. McDuffie, KR: 1993
Hugh McElhenny, HB: **1952, 1953**, 1954
Vann McElroy, S: 1984, 1987
Bud McFadin, DT: **1960, 1961, 1962**
Tim McGee, KR: 1986
Chester McGlockton, DT: 1994, **1995**, 1996
Thurman McGraw, DT: **1952**, 1953
Pat McInally, P: **1981**
Guy McIntyre, G: 1990, 1991, 1992
Bill McKalip, E: **1934**
Raleigh McKenzie, G: 1991
Reggie McKenzie, G: **1973**, 1974
Steve McMichael, DT: 1985, 1986, 1987
Erik McMillan, S: 1989
Ernie McMillan, T: 1967, **1970**, 1971
Jim McMillen, G: **1925, 1928**
Audray McMillian, CB: 1992
Chuck McMurtry, DT: 1960, 1961
Frank McNally, C: **1931**
Charlie McNeil, S: **1961**
Clifton McNeil, WR: **1968**
Freeman McNeil, RB: **1982**, 1984, 1985
Gerald McNeil, KR: 1987
Eddie Meador, S: 1967, 1968, **1969**
Natrone Means, RB: 1994
Karl Mecklenburg, LB: **1985, 1986**, 1987, 1989, 1991
Dave Meggett, KR: 1989, **1990**, 1996
Lance Mehl, LB: 1983, 1985
Harry Mehre, C: **1923**
Dale Meinert, LB: 1964
John Mellus, T: 1941
John Mendenhall, DT: 1974
Mike Merriweather, LB: 1984
Eric Metcalf, KR: **1993**, 1994
Terry Metcalf, RB/KR: **1975**
Rich Michael, T: **1960**
Al Michaels, HB: **1923**
Walt Michaels, LB: 1959
Mike Michalske, G: **1927, 1928, 1929, 1930, 1931, 1934, 1935**
Terdell Middleton, RB: 1978
Nick Mike-Mayer, K: **1973**
Mike Mikulak, FB: **1935**
Glyn Milburn, KR: 1995
Keith Millard, DT: 1988, **1989**
Anthony Miller, WR: 1989, 1990, 1992, 1993
Junior Miller, TE: 1980
Ookie Miller, C: **1933**
John Henry Mills, ST: 1996
Sam Mills, LB: 1988, **1991, 1992, 1996**
Frank Minnifield, CB: **1987, 1988**, 1989
Bob Mischak, G: **1960, 1961**
Bobby Mitchell, WR: **1962**, 1963, 1964
Brian Mitchell, KR: 1994, **1995**
Buster Mitchell, E: 1934
Lydell Mitchell, RB: **1976**, 1977
Stump Mitchell, KR: 1984
Ron Mix, T-G: **1960, 1961, 1962, 1963, 1964, 1965, 1966, 1967, 1968**
Dick Modzelewski, DT: 1961

Dick Moegle, S: 1957
Ralf Mojsiejenko, P: 1987
Art Monk, WR: **1984**, 1985
Joe Montana, QB: 1981, 1984, 1985, **1987, 1989**, 1990
Greg Montgomery, P: 1989, 1992, **1993**
Wilbert Montgomery, RB: 1978
Max Montoya, G: 1986, 1988
Warren Moon, QB: 1989, **1990**
Bill Moore, G: 1947
Herman Moore, WR: **1995, 1996**
Lenny Moore, HB: **1958, 1959, 1960, 1961, 1964**
Nat Moore, WR: **1977**
Rich Moran, G: 1989
Bill Morgan, T: **1934, 1935**
Stanley Morgan, WR: 1980, 1986
Milt Morin, TE: 1971
Earl Morrall, QB: **1968**, 1972
Joe Morris, RB: **1986**
Johnny Morris, FL: **1964**
Jon Morris, C: 1966
Mercury Morris, KR: 1971, 1972
Guy Morriss, C: 1981
Tom Morrow, S: **1963**
Craig Morton, QB: 1977
Don Mosebar, C: 1991
Mark Moseley, K: 1979, **1982**
Marion Motley, FB: **1946, 1947, 1948**, 1949, **1950**
Tim Moynihan, C: 1932
Howard Mudd, G: 1967, **1968**
Joe Muha, LB: 1950
Stan Muirhead, G: **1924**
Herb Mul-Key, KR: 1973
Brick Muller, E: **1926**
Mike Munchak, G: 1984, 1985, **1987**, 1988, **1989**, 1990, **1991**, 1992, 1993
Chuck Muncie, RB: 1981
Anthony Munoz, T: **1981, 1982, 1983, 1984, 1985, 1986, 1987, 1988, 1989, 1990**, 1991
Mark Murphy, S: **1983**
Eddie Murray, K: **1980**, 1988, **1989**
George Musso, T: **1935, 1937**
Chet Mutryn, HB: **1947, 1948, 1949**
Tom Myers, S: 1979
Bronko Nagurski, FB: **1932, 1933, 1934, 1936**
Joe Namath, QB: 1967, **1968**, 1969, **1972**
Jim Nance, FB: **1966, 1967**
Joe Nash, DT: 1984
Tom Nash, E: 1932
Tony Nathan, KR: 1979
Fred Naumetz, C: **1949**
Paul Naumoff, LB: **1970**
Ralph Neely, T: **1967, 1968, 1969**
Billy Neighbors, G: 1963, **1964**
Mike Nelms, KR: 1980, **1981, 1982**, 1983
Andy Nelson, S: 1958, 1959
Bob Nelson, C: **1946, 1947**, 1948
Steve Nelson, LB: 1980, 1984, 1985
Ron Nery, DE: **1961**
Ernie Nevers, FB: **1926, 1927, 1929, 1930, 1931**
Tom Newberry, G: 1987, **1988, 1989**
Ed Newman, G: 1982, 1983, 1984
Harry Newman, QB: 1933
Ozzie Newsome, TE: **1979, 1984**, 1985
Nate Newton, G: 1992, 1993, **1994, 1995**
Hardy Nickerson, LB: **1993**
John Niland, G: 1969, 1970, **1971, 1972, 1973**, 1974
Ray Nitschke, LB: **1964**, 1965, **1966**
Tommy Nobis, LB: **1967**, 1968, 1972
Dave Noble, HB: **1925**
Leo Nomellini, T-DT: 1951, **1952, 1953, 1954, 1957, 1959**

Jerry Norton, DB: **1960**, 1961
Jim Norton, S: 1962
Ken Norton, LB: 1995
Scott Norwood, K: **1988**
Jay Novacek, TE: 1991, **1992**, 1993, 1995
Blaine Nye, G: 1972, 1976
Davey O'Brien, QB: 1939
Steve Odom, KR: 1975
Nate Odomes, CB: 1991, 1993
Riley Odoms, TE: **1973, 1974, 1975**
John Offerdahl, LB: 1986, 1988, 1989, **1990**
Ross O'Hanley, S: 1960
Christian Okoye, RB: **1989**, 1991
Louis Oliver, S: 1992
Merlin Olsen, T: 1964, **1966, 1967, 1968, 1969, 1970**, 1972, **1973**, 1974, 1975
Harold Olson, T: 1962
Les Olssen, G: 1938
Leslie O'Neal, LB-DE: 1989, 1990, 1992, 1994
Jimmy Orr, FL: **1965**
Bill Osmanski, FB: **1939**
Jim Otto, C: **1960, 1961, 1962, 1963, 1964, 1965, 1966, 1967, 1968, 1969, 1970**, 1971, **1972**
Bill Owen, T: **1928**
Steve Owen, G: **1927**
Steve Owens, RB: 1971
Alan Page, DT: 1969, **1970, 1971, 1972, 1973, 1974, 1975, 1976**, 1977, 1980
Paul Palmer, KR: 1987
Irv Pankey, T: 1988
Jack Pardee, LB: **1963, 1971**
Babe Parilli, QB: **1964**
Ace Parker, QB: **1938**, 1939, **1940**
Jim Parker, T-G: **1958, 1959, 1960, 1961, 1962**, 1963, **1964, 1965**
Dave Parks, SE: **1965**, 1966
Lemar Parrish, CB-KR: 1970, 1972, 1975, 1976, 1977, **1979, 1980**
Dennis Partee, P: 1969
Bill Paschal, HB-FB: 1943, **1944**
Jim Patton, S: **1958, 1959, 1960, 1961, 1962**
Don Paul, LB-DB: 1953, 1955
Dainard Paulson, S: **1964, 1965**
Bryce Paup, LB: 1994, **1995**
Walter Payton, RB: **1976, 1977, 1978**, 1979, **1980, 1984, 1985**, 1986
Drew Pearson, WR: **1974**, 1975, **1976, 1977**
Mac Percival, K: 1968
Don Perkins, HB: 1962
Joe Perry, FB: **1949, 1953, 1954**
Michael Dean Perry, DT: **1989, 1990**, 1991, 1992, 1993, 1994
Rod Perry, CB: 1978
Boni Petcoff, T: **1924**
Tony Peters, S: 1982
Volney Peters, DT: 1960
Richie Petitbon, S: **1963**
Gerry Philbin, DE: 1967, **1968, 1969**
Jess Phillips, RB: 1970
Jim Phillips, E: **1961**
Bill Pickel, DT: 1986
Carl Pickens, WR: 1995, 1996
Pete Pihos, E-DE: **1948, 1949, 1952, 1953, 1954**, 1955
Tony Plansky, HB: **1929**
Dick Plasman, E: 1941
Sherman Plunkett, T: 1966
Johnnie Poe, CB: 1983
Jim Poole, E: **1939**, 1940, **1946**
Ray Poole, DE: 1950
Rufus Porter, ST: 1988, 1989
Myron Pottios, LB: **1963**
Art Powell, SE: 1960, **1963**, 1964, 1965, 1966

Marvin Powell, T: **1979**, 1980, **1981**, **1982**, 1983
Glenn Presnell, QB: **1933**
Luke Prestridge, P: 1982
Eddie Price, FB: 1951, **1952**
Steve Pritko, E: 1945
Greg Pruitt, KR: 1973, 1974, 1983
Mike Pruitt, RB: 1979
Duane Putnam, G: **1955**, 1956, **1957**, **1958**, 1959
Mike Quick, WR: **1983**, **1985**, 1987
Fred Quillan, C: 1984
Bill Radovich, G: **1945**, **1946**
Buster Ramsey, G: **1947**, **1948**, **1949**
John Randle, DT: **1993**, **1994**, **1995**, **1996**
Sonny Randle, E: **1960**
John Rapacz, C: 1950
Ahmad Rashad, WR: 1978, 1979, 1980
Randy Rasmussen, G: 1970
Baby Ray, T: 1941, **1943**, 1944
Darrol Ray, S: 1981
Bert Rechichar, DB: **1955**
Alvin Reed, TE: 1968, 1969, 1970
Andre Reed, WR: 1989, 1990, 1991, 1994
Milt Rehnquist, G: **1929**
Mike Reid, DT: **1971**, **1972**, **1973**, 1974
Mike Reinfeldt, S: **1979**
Bob Reinhard, T-DT: **1948**, **1949**, 1950
Mel Renfro, S-CB: 1964, 1965, 1969, 1970, **1971**, **1973**
Pete Retzlaff, TE: **1965**
Fuad Reveiz, K: 1994
Jack Reynolds, LB: 1979
Ricky Reynolds, CB: 1992
Jerry Rice, WR: **1986**, **1987**, **1988**, **1989**, **1990**, 1991, **1992**, **1993**, **1994**, **1995**, **1996**
Herb Rich, DB: **1952**
Willie Richardson, WR: 1967
Les Richter, LB: 1955, 1956
John Riggins, RB: **1983**
Gerald Riggs, RB: 1985
Ken Riley, CB: 1975, 1976, 1983
Jim Ringo, C: **1957**, 1958, **1959**, **1960**, **1961**, **1962**, **1963**
Cody Risien, T: 1983, 1986
Andre Rison, WR: **1990**, 1991
Carl Roaches, KR: 1981
William Roaf, T: **1994**, **1995**, **1996**
Gene Roberts, HB: 1949
Isiah Robertson, LB: 1971, 1973, **1975**, **1976**, 1977
Marcus Robertson, S: **1993**
Dave Robinson, LB: **1967**, 1968, **1969**
Eugene Robinson, S: 1993
Jerry Robinson, LB: 1980, 1981
Johnny Robinson, S: 1965, **1966**, **1967**, **1968**, **1969**, **1970**, 1971
Paul Robinson, RB: **1968**
Andy Robustelli, DE: 1953, 1955, **1956**, **1957**, 1958, **1959**, 1960
Reggie Roby, P: **1984**, 1987, 1989, 1991, **1994**
George Rogers, RB: 1981
Gene Ronzani, HB: **1935**
Tobin Rote, QB: 1955, **1963**
Martin Ruby, T: **1946**, 1947
Ed Rucinski, E: **1943**
Jack Rudnay, C: 1973
Andy Russell, LB: **1970**, **1972**, **1973**, 1974, **1975**
Jack Russell, E: **1946**, 1947
Lou Rymkus, T: 1946, **1947**, **1948**, **1949**
Mark Rypien, QB: 1991
Lou Saban, C-LB: **1948**, **1949**
George Saimes, S: 1964, **1965**, 1966, **1967**, 1968
Bob St. Clair, T: **1955**, 1956, 1960
Dan Saleaumua, DT: 1990, 1995
Johnny Sample, S: 1961

Barry Sanders, RB: **1989**, **1990**, **1991**, 1992, 1993, **1994**, **1995**, **1996**
Charlie Sanders, TE: **1970**, **1971**
Deion Sanders, CB-KR: **1991**, **1992**, **1993**, **1994**, 1995, **1996**
Spec Sanders, HB-S: **1946**, **1947**, 1950
Tony Sardisco, G: **1961**
George Sauer, HB: 1935
George Sauer, SE: **1967**, **1968**
Rich Saul, C: 1979, 1980, 1981
Gale Sayers, HB: **1965**, **1966**, **1967**, **1968**, **1969**
Bob Scarpitto, P: 1966, 1967
Mike Scarry, C: 1946, 1947
Dick Schafrath, T: 1963, **1964**, **1965**
Joe Schmidt, LB: **1954**, **1955**, **1956**, **1957**, **1958**, **1959**, 1960, **1961**, **1962**, 1963
John Schmitt, C: 1968
Otto Schnellbacher, DB: 1950, **1951**
Harry Schuh, T: 1967, 1968, 1969, 1970
Eberle Schultz, G-T: 1943, 1945
Ad Schwammel, T: 1935
Jim Schwantz, ST: 1996
Perry Schwartz, E: 1939, **1940**, **1941**
Joe Scibelli, G: 1973
Clarence Scott, CB: 1973
Herb Scott, G: 1978, 1979, 1980, 1981
Jake Scott, S: 1971, **1972**, **1973**, 1974, **1975**
Todd Scott, S: 1992
Bucky Scribner, P: 1984
Eugene Seale, ST: 1988
Vic Sears, T: 1943, 1949
Junior Seau, LB: 1991, **1992**, **1993**, **1994**, **1995**, 1996
Lee Roy Selmon, DE: 1978, **1979**, **1980**, 1981, **1982**, 1983, 1984
Joe Senser, TE: 1981
Rafael Septien, K: **1981**
Wash Serini, G: 1949
Tom Sestak, DT: **1963**, **1964**, **1965**, 1966
Ron Shanklin, WR: 1973
Luis Sharpe, T: 1988
Shannon Sharpe, TE: **1993**, **1996**
Sterling Sharpe, WR: **1989**, **1992**, **1993**
Billy Shaw, G: 1962, **1963**, **1964**, **1965**, **1966**
Art Shell, T: 1972, **1973**, **1974**, **1975**, **1976**, **1977**, 1978
Donnie Shell, S: **1979**, **1980**, 1981, **1982**
Elbert Shelley, ST: 1992, 1993, 1994, 1995
Bill Shepherd, HB: 1938
Jerry Sherk, DT: 1974, 1975, **1976**
Will Sherman, DB: **1955**
Will Shields, G: 1996
Jerry Shipkey, DB-LB: 1951, **1952**
Del Shofner, SE: **1958**, **1959**, **1961**, **1962**, **1963**
Mickey Shuler, TE: 1988
Jeff Siemon, LB: 1975
Joe Signaigo, G: 1949, 1950
Vai Sikahema, KR: 1986, 1987
Milt Simington, G: 1942
Clyde Simmons, DE: **1991**, 1992
Phil Simms, QB: 1986
Bill Simpson, S: 1977, 1978
O.J. Simpson, RB: **1972**, **1973**, **1974**, **1975**, **1976**
Billy Sims, RB: 1980, **1981**
Keith Sims, G: 1994, 1995
Mike Singletary, LB: 1983, **1984**, **1985**, **1986**, **1987**, **1988**, **1989**, 1990, 1991
Frank Sinkwich, HB: 1943, **1944**
Brian Sipe, QB: **1980**
Otis Sistrunk, DT: **1974**, 1975
Tom Skladany, P: 1978, 1981
Jackie Slater, T: 1983, 1985, 1986, 1987, 1988, 1989, 1990

Webster Slaughter, WR: 1989, 1993
Steve Slivinski, G: 1940
Fred Smerlas, DT: 1980, 1981, 1982, 1983, 1988
Al Smith, LB: 1991, 1992
Bill Smith, E: **1935**
Bruce Smith, DE: **1987**, **1988**, 1989, **1990**, 1992, **1993**, **1994**, **1995**, **1996**
Bubba Smith, DE: **1970**, **1971**
Clyde Smith, C: **1926**, **1927**, **1928**
Dave Smith, FB: **1960**
Dennis Smith, S: 1984, 1986, 1989, 1993
Emmitt Smith, RB: 1991, **1992**, **1993**, **1994**, **1995**
Ernie Smith, T: **1936**
J.D. Smith, HB: 1959
J.T. Smith, KR-WR: 1979, **1980**, 1981, 1987
Jackie Smith, TE: 1967, 1969
Jerry Smith, TE: **1969**
Jim Smith, DB: **1952**
Jim Ray Smith, G: **1959**, **1960**, **1961**, 1962
John Smith, K: 1980
Neil Smith, DE: **1993**, 1995
Paul Smith, DT: 1973
Ron Smith, KR: 1972
Tim Smith, WR: 1983
Matt Snell, RB: **1969**
Freddy Solomon, KR: 1980
Ron Solt, G: 1987
Gordie Soltau, E: **1952**
Gus Sonnenberg, T-G: **1925**, **1926**, **1927**
Revie Sorey, G: 1977
Mac Speedie, E: **1946**, **1947**, **1948**, **1949**, **1950**, 1952
Julian Spence, DB: 1960
Chris Spielman, LB: 1989, 1991, **1994**
Art Spinney, G: **1959**
Ed Sprinkle, DE: 1949, 1950
Ken Stabler, QB: **1973**, **1974**, 1976
Larry Stallings, LB: 1970
John Stallworth, WR: **1979**, 1984
Sylvester Stamps, KR: 1987
Dick Stanfel, G: **1953**, **1954**, **1956**, **1957**, **1958**
Bill Stanfill, DE: 1971, **1972**, **1973**, **1974**
Walter Stanley, KR: 1989
Rohn Stark, P: 1983, 1985, 1986, 1990, 1992
Bart Starr, QB: **1966**
Roger Staubach, QB: **1971**, 1976, 1977, 1978, 1979
Ernie Stautner, DT: 1956, **1958**, 1959
Fred Steinfort, K: 1980
Jan Stenerud, K: 1968, **1969**, **1970**, 1971, 1974, **1975**, 1976, 1984
John Stephens, RB: 1988
Dwight Stephenson, C: **1983**, **1984**, **1985**, **1986**, **1987**
Mark Stepnoski, C: 1992, 1993, 1994
Joe Sternaman, QB: **1924**, **1925**
Art Still, DE: **1980**, 1982, 1986
Steve Stonebreaker, LB: 1965
Pete Stoyanovich, K: 1991, 1992
Mike Stratton, LB: **1964**, **1965**, **1966**, 1967
Larry Strickland, C: **1956**, 1957
Ken Strong, HB: **1930**, **1931**, **1933**, **1934**
Jack Stroud, G: 1960
John Strzykalski, HB: **1948**
Dana Stubblefield, DT: 1994, 1995
Pat Studstill, WR: **1966**
Joe Stydahar, T: **1937**, **1938**, **1939**, **1940**
Bob Suffridge, G: 1941
Walt Suggs, T: 1967, 1968
Eric Swann, DT: 1995
Lynn Swann, WR: **1975**, 1977, **1978**
Walt Sweeney, G: **1967**, **1968**, 1969, **1970**, **1971**
Bob Swenson, LB: **1981**
Pat Swilling, LB: 1987, **1991**, 1992

Bob Talamini, G: 1962, **1963**, 1964, **1965**, 1966, **1967**
Darryl Talley, LB: 1990, 1993
Fran Tarkenton, QB: 1972, 1973, **1975**, **1976**
Steve Tasker, ST: 1987, 1990, 1991, 1992, 1993, 1994, 1995
Jack Tatum, S: 1973, 1974, **1975**, 1976, 1977
Mosi Tatupu, ST: 1986
Charley Taylor, WR: **1967**, 1973, **1974**, 1975
Jim Taylor, FB: 1961, **1962**
John Taylor, KR: **1988**
Lawrence Taylor, LB: **1981**, **1982**, **1983**, **1984**, **1985**, **1986**, 1987, **1988**, **1989**, 1990
Lionel Taylor, SE: **1960**, **1961**, 1962, **1965**
Otis Taylor, WR: **1966**, **1971**, 1972
Rosey Taylor, S: **1963**
Gus Tebell, E: **1923**
Joe Theismann, QB: 1982, **1983**
R.C. Thielemann, G: 1982
Derrick Thomas, LB: 1989, **1990**, **1991**, **1992**, 1993, 1994, 1996
Emmitt Thomas, CB: **1971**, **1974**, **1975**
Henry Thomas, DT: 1992
John Thomas, G: **1966**
Pat Thomas, CB: 1978, 1980
Thurman Thomas, RB: 1989, **1990**, **1991**, 1992, 1993
William Thomas, LB: 1995
Benny Thompson, ST: 1991
Bill Thompson, S: **1977**, 1978, 1979, 1981
Reyna Thompson, ST: 1990
Tommy Thompson, QB: 1948
Tommy Thompson, LB: 1953
Art Thoms, DT: 1974
Jim Thorpe, HB: **1923**
Fuzzy Thurston, G: **1961**, **1962**
Mick Tinglehoff, C: **1964**, **1965**, **1966**, **1967**, **1968**, **1969**, **1970**
Gaynell Tinsley, E: **1937**, **1938**
Andre Tippett, LB: 1984, **1985**, 1986, **1987**, 1988
Y.A. Tittle, QB: **1957**, 1961, **1962**, **1963**
Dick Todd, HB: 1940
Tony Tolbert, DE: 1996
Bob Toneff, DT: **1955**, 1960
Clayton Tonemaker, C-LB: **1950**, 1954
Al Toon, WR: **1986**, 1987, 1988
Laverne Torczon, DE: **1960**, 1961
Dan Towler, FB-HB: **1951**, **1952**, 1953
JoJo Townsell, KR: 1988
Greg Townsend, DE: 1990, 1991
George Trafton, C: **1924**
David Treadwell, K: 1989
Charlie Trippi, HB; **1948**
Bob Trumpy, TE: **1969**, **1970**
Bob Tucker, TE: 1972
Jessie Tuggle, LB: 1991, 1992, 1995
Emlen Tunnell, S: 1949, **1951**, **1952**, **1954**, 1955, **1956**
Matt Turk, P: 1996
Renaldo Turnbull, LB: 1993
Bulldog Turner, C: **1941**, **1942**, **1943**, **1944**, 1946, **1947**, **1948**
Cecil Turner, KR: 1970
Eric Turner, S: **1994**
Jim Turner, K: 1968, 1969
Rick Tuten, P: 1994
Jim Tyrer, T: 1962, 1963, 1964, **1965**, **1966**, **1967**, **1968**, **1969**, **1970**, **1971**
Johnny Unitas, QB: 1957, **1958**, **1959**, 1964, **1965**, **1967**
Rick Upchurch, KR: 1976, **1978**, **1979**, 1982
Gene Upshaw, G: 1967, **1968**, **1969**, **1970**, 1971, **1972**, 1973, **1974**, 1975, **1977**

Emil Uremovich, T: **1945**
Norm Van Brocklin, QB: **1960**
Steve Van Buren, HB: 1944, **1945**, 1946, **1947**, **1948**, **1949**
Bruce Van Dyke, G: 1972
Jeff Van Note, C: 1974, 1980, 1982
Tamarick Vanover, KR: 1996
Brad Van Pelt, LB: 1976, 1977, 1978, 1979, 1980
Jon Vaughn, KR: 1992
Clarence Verdin, KR: 1989, 1990, 1992
Phil Villapiano, LB: **1974**, 1975
Bob Vogel, T: 1964, **1965**, 1967, 1968, 1971
Rick Volk, S: 1968, 1970, **1971**
Tillie Voss, E: **1924**
Mike Wagner, S: 1973, 1975, **1976**
Doak Walker, HB: **1950**, **1951**, **1953**, **1954**
Fulton Walker, KR: 1983
Herschel Walker, RB: 1987, 1988
Wayne Walker, LB: 1964, **1965**, 1966
Wesley Walker, WR: **1978**, 1982
Jackie Wallace, KR: 1978
Steve Wallace, T: 1992
Ron Waller, HB: 1955
Everson Walls, CB: **1982**, 1983, 1984, 1985
Wesley Walls, TE: 1996
Bill Walsh, C: 1952, **1954**
Stan Walters, T: 1978, 1979
Paul Warfield, WR: 1964, **1968**, **1969**, 1970, **1971**, **1972**, **1973**, 1974
Curt Warner, RB: 1983, 1986, 1987
Chris Warren, RB: 1994, 1995
Gene Washington (Vikings), WR: 1969
Gene Washington (49ers), WR: **1970**, **1971**, **1972**
Russ Washington, T: 1973, **1974**, 1978, 1979
Bob Waterfield, QB: **1945**, **1946**, **1949**
Andre Waters: 1991
Charlie Waters, S: 1977, 1978
Steve Watson, WR: 1981
Pie Way, HB: **1924**
Dave Waymer, CB: 1987
Richmond Webb, T: **1992**, 1993, **1994**, 1995
Dave Webster, S: 1961
George Webster, LB: **1967**, **1968**, **1969**
Mike Webster, C: **1978**, **1979**, **1980**, **1981**, **1982**, 1983, 1987
Herman Wedemeyer, DB: 1949
Roger Wehrli, CB: **1970**, 1971, **1974**, **1975**, **1976**, 1977, 1979
Arnie Weinmeister, T-DT: **1949**, **1950**, **1951**, **1952**, **1953**
Ed Weir, T: **1927**
Bub Weller, G: **1923**
Warren Wells, WR: 1969, **1970**
Stan West, DG: **1951**, **1952**
Bob Westfall, FB: 1945
Dick Westmoreland, CB: 1963, 1964
Joe Westoupal, C: **1929**
Jim Whalen, TE: **1968**
Charles White, RB: **1987**
Dwight White, DE: 1972, **1973**, 1975
Ed White, G: 1974, **1975**, **1976**, 1977
Jim White, T: **1946**, 1947
Randy White, DT: 1977, **1978**, **1979**, **1980**, **1981**, **1982**, **1983**, **1984**, **1985**
Reggie White, DE-DT: **1986**, **1987**, **1988**, **1989**, **1990**, **1991**, **1992**, 1993, 1994, **1995**, 1996
Sammie White, WR: 1976, 1977, 1978
Whizzer White, HB: **1938**, **1940**
Jesse Whittenton, DB: **1961**, 1962
Ron Widby, P: 1971
Ed Widseth, T: 1937, **1938**
Ray Wietecha, C: **1958**
John Wiethe, G: 1939, **1940**

Bill Wightkin, T: 1955, 1956
Barry Wilburn, CB: 1987
Dave Wilcox, LB: 1967, **1970**, **1971**, **1972**, **1973**
Dick Wildung, G-T: 1947, 1949
Doug Wilkerson, G: 1981, **1982**
Willie Wilkin, T: **1941**, **1942**
Norm Willey, DE: **1953**, **1954**
Aeneas Williams, CB: 1994, **1995**, 1996
Alfred Williams, DE: **1996**
Delvin Williams, RB: 1978
Erik Williams, T: **1993**, 1995, 1996
Inky Williams, E: **1923**
John Williams, S: 1952
Lee Williams, DE: 1988, 1989
Carlton Williamson, S: 1985
Fred Williamson, CB: **1962**, **1963**, 1964, 1965
Bill Willis, G-DG: 1946, 1947, **1948**, **1950**, **1951**, **1952**, **1953**
Billy Wilson, E: **1955**, **1957**
George Wilson, E: **1942**, 1943
Jerrel Wilson, P: 1968, **1971**, **1972**
Larry Wilson, S: 1963, **1966**, **1967**, **1968**, **1969**, **1970**
Otis Wilson, LB: 1985
Wildcat Wilson, HB: **1928**
Kellen Winslow, TE: **1980**, **1981**, **1982**, 1987
Steve Wisniewski, G: **1990**, **1991**, **1992**, **1993**, 1994, 1995, 1996
Al Wistert, T: **1944**, **1945**, **1946**, **1947**, **1948**, 1949
Tom Wittum, P: **1973**, **1974**
Alex Wojciechowicz, C: 1944
Ron Wolfley, ST: 1986, 1987, 1988, 1989
Willie Wood, S: 1962, 1963, **1964**, **1965**, **1966**, **1967**, **1968**, 1969, **1970**, 1971
Lee Woodall, LB: 1995
Abe Woodson, CB: **1959**, **1960**, 1961, 1962, 1963
Darren Woodson, S: **1994**, **1995**, **1996**
Rod Woodson, CB-KR: 1989, **1990**, **1992**, **1993**, **1994**
Donnell Woolford, CB: 1994
John Wooten, G: 1966
John Woudenberg, T: 1947, 1948
Eric Wright, CB: 1983, 1984, **1985**
Keith Wright, KR: 1978
Louis Wright, CB: 1977, **1978**, **1979**, 1983, 1984, 1985
Nate Wright, CB: 1974
Rayfield Wright, T: **1971**, **1972**, **1973**, **1974**, 1975
Ron Yary, T: 1970, **1971**, **1972**, **1973**, **1974**, **1975**, **1976**, 1977
Garo Yepremian, K: **1971**, **1973**, 1978
Len Younce, G: **1944**, **1946**, 1947
Bob Young, G: 1977, 1978, 1979
Bryant Young, DE: **1996**
Buddy Young, HB: 1949
Charle Young, TE: **1973**, **1974**, **1975**
Fredd Young, ST-LB: 1984, 1985, **1987**
Roynell Young, CB: 1981
Steve Young, QB: **1992**, **1993**, **1994**
Wilbur Young, DT: 1979
Jack Youngblood, DE: **1974**, **1975**, **1976**, 1977, **1978**, **1979**, 1980
Jim Youngblood, LB: 1978, 1979
Sid Youngelman, DT: **1960**
Tank Younger, LB: 1951
Swede Youngstrom, G: **1923**, **1924**
Roger Zatkoff, LB: 1954, 1955
Bob Zeman, S: **1962**
Gary Zimmerman, T: **1987**, **1988**, 1989, **1992**, 1993, 1995, **1996**
Roy Zimmerman, QB: 1944
Jim Zorn, QB: 1978

ALL-STAR GAMES

The first attempt at what's now known as the Pro Bowl occurred at the end of the 1938 season, when a team of all-stars played the New York Giants, who had just won the NFL championship. The game was played in Los Angeles, and fans were allowed to vote for the all-stars; as a result, the squad included three players from the Los Angeles Bulldogs and the Hollywood Stars, the two best professional teams on the West Coast that season. One of them, Ernie Smith, kicked a field goal for the all-stars' first score.

The game was played in Los Angeles for three years, then moved to the East Coast as a safety measure after the bombing of Pearl Harbor. After the December 1942 game in Philadelphia, though, it was discontinued because of the war. When the game reappeared in 1950, it was in its modern form, matching two teams of all-stars from different conferences.

Jan. 15, 1939
Wrigley Field, Los Angeles (20,000)

New York Giants	0	3	0	10	- 13
All-Stars	0	3	7	0	- 10

NY - Barnum 18 FG
AS - E. Smith 25 FG
AS - Cardwell 71 pass from Baugh (Stydahar)
NY - Gelatka 22 pass from Danowski (Cuff)
NY - Cuff 18 FG

Jan. 14, 1940
Gilmore Stadium, Los Angeles (18,000)

Green Bay Packers	3	10	0	3	- 16
All-Stars	0	0	7	0	- 7

GB - Hinkle 45 FG
GB - Smith 15 FG
GB - Hutson 92 pass from Isbell (Smith)
AS - Carter 4 pass from O'Brien (Cuff)
GB - Smith 14 FG

Dec. 29, 1940
Gilmore Stadium, Los Angeles (21,624)

Chicago Bears	7	7	7	7	- 28
All-Stars	0	14	0	0	- 14

Chi - Pool 35 lateral from Plasman 23 pass from Luckman (Martinovich)
AS - Livingston 7 interception return (Hinkle)
Chi - Clark 59 pass from Luckman (Snyder)
AS - Looney 4 pass from Baugh (Hutson)
Chi - Luckman 1 run (Snyder)
Chi - Maniaci 2 run (Maniaci)

Jan. 4, 1942
Polo Grounds, New York (17,725)

Chicago Bears	0	21	7	7	- 35
All-Stars	3	0	14	7	- 24

AS - Cuff 19 FG
Chi - McAfee 3 run (Snyder)
Chi - McAfee 68 punt return (Artoe)
Chi - Swisher 4 run (Stydahar)
AS - Schwartz 15 pass from Baugh (Cuff)
AS - Dewell 24 pass from Baugh (Cuff)
Chi - McLean 43 pass from Luckman (Snyder)
Chi - Kavanaugh 7 pass from Bussey (Stydahar)
AS - Schwartz 26 pass from Baugh (Cuff)

Dec. 27, 1942
Shibe Park, Philadelphia (18,671)

Wash. Redskins	7	0	7	0	- 14
All-Stars	0	0	14	3	- 17

Was - Aldrich 30 punt return (Masterson)

AS - Dudley 97 interception return (Maznicki)
AS - Petty 1 run (Maznicki)
Was - Seymour 14 pass from Zimmerman (Masterson)
AS - Artoe 43 FG

AAFC ALL-STAR GAME
Dec. 17, 1949
Rice Stadium, Houston (10,000)

Cleveland Browns	0	7	0	0	- 7
AAFC All-Stars	6	6	0	0	- 12

AS - Mutryn 2 run (Albert miss)
Cle - D. Jones 40 pass from Graham (Groza)
AS - Baldwin 12 pass from Albert (Albert miss)

PRO BOWL
Jan. 14, 1951
Memorial Coliseum, Los Angeles (53,676)

American Conf.	7	7	14	0	- 28
National Conf.	7	13	7	0	- 27

Nat - Fears 22 pass from Waterfield (Waterfield)
Amer- Dudley 47 punt return (Groza)
Nat - Waterfield 30 FG
Amer- Shaw 49 pass from Graham (Groza)
Nat - Waterfield 27 FG
Nat - Fears 5 pass from Van Brocklin (Waterfield)
Nat - Edwards 65 pass from Waterfield (Waterfield)
Amer- Graham 6 run (Harder)
Amer- Graham 10 run (Harder)
MVP: Otto Graham, Cleveland

Jan. 12, 1952
Memorial Coliseum, Los Angeles (19,400)

American Conf.	7	6	0	0	- 13
National Conf.	3	7	0	20	- 30

Amer- Jones 44 pass from Graham (Groza)
Nat - Waterfield 30 FG
Amer- Groza 45 FG
Amer- Groza 11 FG
Nat - Soltau 1 pass from Van Brocklin (Waterfield)
Nat - Dottley 2 run (Waterfield miss)
Nat - Nomellini 20 fumble return (Waterfield)
Nat - Hirsch 7 pass from Walker (Lujack)
MVP: Dan Towler, Los Angeles

Jan. 10, 1953
Memorial Coliseum, Los Angeles (34,208)

American Conf.	0	0	0	7	- 7
National Conf.	14	0	3	10	- 27

Nat - McElhenny 13 pass from Towler (Harder)
Nat - Howton 74 pass from Van Brocklin (Harder)
Nat - Harder 23 FG
Amer- Graham 1 run (Groza)
Nat - Harder 13 FG
Nat - McElhenny 7 pass from Van Brocklin (Harder)
MVP: Don Doll, Detroit

Jan. 17, 1954
Memorial Coliseum, Los Angeles (44,214)

Eastern Conf.	3	0	10	7	- 20
Western Conf.	0	2	0	7	- 9

East - Groza 11 FG
West - Safety, Kindt tackled Graham in end zone
East - Groza 25 FG
East - Bednarik 24 interception return (Groza)
West - Perry 16 run (Walker)
East - Renfro 25 run (Groza)
MVP: Chuck Bednarik, Philadelphia

Jan. 16, 1955
Memorial Coliseum, Los Angeles (43,972)

Eastern Conf.	13	6	0	0	- 19
Western Conf.	3	6	7	10	- 26

East - Matson 6 pass from Graham (Groza)
East - Willey 5 fumble return (Groza miss)
West - Walker 35 FG
East - Taylor 33 pass from Burk (Groza miss)
West - Wilson 14 pass from Tittle (Walker miss)
West - Hill 42 pass from Tittle (Walker)
West - Walker 30 FG
West - Perry 1 run (Walker)
MVP: Billy Wilson, San Francisco

Jan. 15, 1956
Memorial Coliseum, Los Angeles (37,867)

Eastern Conf.	7	0	14	10	- 31
Western Conf.	7	7	9	7	- 30

West - Christiansen 103 kickoff return (Richter)
East - Pihos 12 pass from LeBaron (Groza)
West - Howton 73 pass from Brown (Richter)
East - Matson 91 kickoff return (Groza)
West - Ferguson 1 run (Richter miss)
East - Matson 15 run (Groza)
West - Rechichar 46 FG
East - Groza 50 FG
East - Mathews 20 pass from LeBaron (Groza)
West - Waller 3 run (Richter)
MVP: Ollie Matson, Chicago Cards

Jan. 13, 1957
Memorial Coliseum, Los Angeles (44,177)

Eastern Conf.	0	7	3	0	- 10
Western Conf.	7	3	3	6	- 19

West - Brown 1 run (Layne)
East - Rote fumble recovery in end zone (Baker)
West - Rechichar 41 FG
East - Baker 52 FG
West - Rechichar 44 FG
West - Rechichar 44 FG
West - Rechichar 52 FG
   Outstanding back: Bert Rechichar, Baltimore
   Outstanding lineman: Ernie Stautner, Pittsburgh

Jan. 12, 1958
Memorial Coliseum, Los Angeles (66,634)

Eastern Conf.	0	7	0	0	- 7
Western Conf.	6	3	10	7	- 26

West - Dillon 39 interception return (Rechichar miss)
East - Renfro 39 pass from Morrall (Groza)
West - Rechichar 9 FG
West - Rechichar 23 FG
West - T. Wilson 10 run (Rechichar)
West - Ameche 8 pass from Unitas (Rechichar)
   Outstanding back: Hugh McElhenny,
     San Francisco
   Outstanding lineman: Gene Brito, Washington

Jan. 11, 1959
Memorial Coliseum, Los Angeles (72,250)

Eastern Conf.	9	7	0	12	- 28
Western Conf.	7	7	7	0	- 21

West - Ameche 1 run (Richter)
East - Groza 25 FG
East - Webster 40 pass from Gifford (Groza miss)
West - McElhenny 20 pass from Wade (Richter)
East - Nagler 7 pass from LeBaron (Groza)
West - Wade 10 run (Richter)
East - Groza 25 FG
East - Retzlaff 15 pass from Van Brocklin (Groza)
East - Safety, Scott tackled McElhenny in end zone
   Outstanding back: Frank Gifford, New York
   Outstanding lineman: Doug Atkins,
     Chicago Bears

Jan. 17, 1960
Memorial Coliseum, Los Angeles (56,876)

Eastern Conf.	7	7	0	7	- 21
Western Conf.	10	21	0	7	- 38

East - Patton 22 interception return (Groza)
West - Berry 22 pass from Unitas (Hornung)
West - Hornung 16 FG
East - McDonald 63 pass from Layne (Groza)
West - Moore 13 pass from Tittle (Hornung)
West - Moore 65 pass from Unitas (Hornung)
West - Smith 6 pass from Unitas (Hornung)
East - J. Brown 2 pass from Layne (Groza)

West - Hornung 2 run (Hornung)
   Outstanding back: Johnny Unitas, Baltimore
   Outstanding lineman: Big Daddy Lipscomb,
     Baltimore

Jan. 15, 1961
Memorial Coliseum, Los Angeles (62,971)

Eastern Conf.	3	14	7	7	- 31
Western Conf.	7	14	7	7	- 35

West - Taylor 2 run (Hornung)
West - Walston 22 FG
West - Taylor 1 run (Hornung)
East - Randle 51 pass from Plum (Walston)
East - McDonald 46 pass from Van Brocklin (Walston)
West - Moore 44 pass from Unitas (Hornung)
West - Taylor 1 run (Hornung)
East - Retzlaff 43 pass from Van Brocklin (Walston)
West - Arnett 20 run (Hornung)
East - Randle 36 pass from Van Brocklin (Walston)
   Outstanding back: Johnny Unitas, Baltimore
   Outstanding lineman: Sam Huff, New York

Jan. 14, 1962
Memorial Coliseum, Los Angeles (57,409)

Eastern Conf.	3	7	6	14	- 30
Western Conf.	14	3	7	7	- 31

East - Walston 33 FG
West - Berry 16 pass from Unitas (Martin)
West - Lane 42 interception return (Martin)
East - Bielski 10 pass from Tittle (Walston)
West - Martin 27 FG
West - McElhenny 10 pass from Starr (Martin)
East - Walston 12 pass from Plum (Walston miss)
East - Webster 2 pass from Tittle (Walston)
East - Brown 70 run (Walston)
West - Arnett 12 pass from Unitas (Martin)
   Outstanding back: Jim Brown, Cleveland
   Outstanding lineman: Henry Jordan, Green Bay

Jan. 13, 1963
Memorial Coliseum, Los Angeles (61,374)

Eastern Conf.	13	0	0	17	- 30
Western Conf.	0	3	17	0	- 20

East - J. Brown 1 run (Michaels)
East - J. Brown 50 run (Michaels miss)
West - Davis 49 FG
West - Bass 1 run (Davis)
West - Davis 32 FG
West - Ditka 6 pass from Unitas (Davis)
East - Carpenter 19 pass from Tittle (Gain)
East - Michaels 27 FG
East - Bishop 20 fumble return (Michaels)
   Outstanding back: Jim Brown, Cleveland
   Outstanding lineman: Big Daddy Lipscomb,
     Pittsburgh

Jan. 12, 1964
Memorial Coliseum, Los Angeles (67,242)

Eastern Conf.	3	0	0	14	- 17
Western Conf.	7	7	14	3	- 31

East - Baker 30 FG
West - Taylor 37 run (T. Davis)
West - Berry 4 pass from Unitas (T. Davis)
West - Whittenton 26 interception return (T. Davis)
West - Cogdill 5 pass from Unitas (T. Davis)
East - J. Brown 8 run (Baker)
West - T. Davis 38 FG
East - J. Brown 3 run (Baker)
   Outstanding back: Johnny Unitas, Baltimore
   Outstanding lineman: Gino Marchetti, Baltimore

Jan. 10, 1965
Memorial Coliseum, Los Angeles (60,598)

Eastern Conf.	0	7	0	7	- 14
Western Conf.	3	14	10	7	- 34

West - Walker 15 FG
West - B. Brown 2 run (Walker)
East - Renfro 47 interception return (Baker)
West - B. Brown 2 pass from Tarkenton (Walker)
West - Nitschke 42 interception return (Walker)
West - Walker 28 FG
West - Moore 2 run (Walker)
East - J. Brown 27 pass from Jurgensen (Baker)
   Outstanding back: Fran Tarkenton, Minnesota
   Outstanding lineman: Terry Barr, Detroit

Jan. 16, 1966
Memorial Coliseum, Los Angeles (60,124)

Eastern Conf.	10	13	3	10	- 36
Western Conf.	0	0	0	7	- 7

East - Bakken 41 FG
East - J. Brown 2 run (Bakken)
East - J. Brown 2 run (Bakken)
East - J. Brown 1 run (Bakken miss)
East - Bakken 36 FG
East - Bakken 42 FG
East - Renfro 20 interception return (Bakken)
West - McDonald 31 pass from Brodie (Walker)
   Outstanding back: Jim Brown, Cleveland
   Outstanding lineman: Dale Meinert, St. Louis

Jan. 22, 1967
Memorial Coliseum, Los Angeles (15,062)

Eastern Conf.	6	14	0	0	- 20
Western Conf.	0	0	3	7	- 10

East - Clark 18 FG
East - Clark 17 FG
East - Roland 1 run (Clark)
East - Collins 18 pass from Ryan (Clark)
West - Gossett 27 FG
West - Willard 51 pass from Starr (Gossett)
   Outstanding back: Gale Sayers, Chicago
   Outstanding lineman: Floyd Peters, Philadelphia

Jan. 21, 1968
Memorial Coliseum, Los Angeles (53,289)

Eastern Conf.	0	13	7	0	- 20
Western Conf.	10	7	0	21	- 38

West - Chandler 26 FG
West - Josephson 4 run (Chandler)
East - Bakken 45 FG
East - Bakken 25 FG
West - Farr 39 pass from Gabriel (Chandler)
East - Kelly 1 run (Bakken)
East - Taylor 9 pass from Meredith (Bakken)
West - Sayers 3 run (Chandler)
West - Petitbon 70 interception return (Chandler)
West - B. Brown 19 run (Chandler)
Outstanding back: Gale Sayers, Chicago
Outstanding lineman: Dave Robinson, Green Bay

Jan. 19, 1969
Memorial Coliseum, Los Angeles (32,050)

Eastern Conf.	0	0	7	0	- 7
Western Conf.	0	3	0	7	- 10

West - Gossett 20 FG
East - Warfield 3 pass from Meredith (Baker)
West - Brown 1 run (Gossett)
Outstanding back: Roman Gabriel, Los Angeles
Outstanding lineman: Merlin Olsen, Los Angeles

Jan. 18, 1970
Memorial Coliseum, Los Angeles (57,786)

Eastern Conf.	7	6	0	0	- 13
Western Conf.	0	7	0	9	- 16

East - Kelly 10 run (Dempsey)
East - Dempsey 46 FG
West - Gabriel 1 run (Etter)
East - Dempsey 27 FG
West - Safety, Brezina tackled Walden in end zone
West - Dale 28 pass from Gabriel (Etter)
Outstanding back: Gale Sayers, Chicago
Outstanding lineman: George Andrie, Dallas

Jan. 24, 1971
Memorial Coliseum, Los Angeles (48,222)

AFC	0	3	3	0	- 6
NFC	0	3	10	14	- 27

AFC - Stenerud 37 FG
NFC - Cox 13 FG
NFC - Osborn 23 pass from Brodie (Cox)
NFC - Cox 35 FG
AFC - Stenerud 16 FG
NFC - Renfro 82 punt return (Cox)
NFC - Renfro 56 punt return (Cox)
Outstanding back: Mel Renfro, Dallas
Outstanding lineman: Fred Carr, Green Bay

Jan. 23, 1972
Memorial Coliseum, Los Angeles (53,647)

AFC	0	3	13	10	- 26
NFC	0	6	0	7	- 13

NFC - Grim 50 pass from Landry (Knight miss)

AFC - Stenerud 25 FG
AFC - Stenerud 23 FG
AFC - Stenerud 48 FG
AFC - Morin 5 pass from Dawson (Stenerud)
AFC - Stenerud 42 FG
NFC - V. Washington 2 run (Knight)
AFC - F. Little 6 run (Stenerud)
Offensive MVP: Jan Stenerud, Kansas City
Defensive MVP: Willie Lanier, Kansas City

Jan. 21, 1973
Texas Stadium, Irving (37,091)

AFC	0	10	10	13	- 33
NFC	14	0	0	14	- 28

NFC - Brockington 1 run (Marcol)
NFC - Brockington 3 pass from Kilmer (Marcol)
AFC - Simpson 7 run (Gerela)
AFC - Gerela 18 FG
AFC - Gerela 22 FG
AFC - Hubbard 11 run (Gerela)
AFC - Taylor 5 pass from Lamonica (bad snap)
AFC - Bell 12 interception return (Gerela)
NFC - Brockington 1 run (Marcol)
NFC - Kwalick 12 pass from Snead (Marcol)
MVP: O.J. Simpson, Buffalo

Jan. 20, 1974
Arrowhead Stadium, Kansas City (66,918)

NFC	0	10	0	3	- 13
AFC	3	3	3	6	- 15

AFC - Yepremian 16 FG
NFC - Mike - Mayer 27 FG
NFC - McCutcheon 14 pass from Gabriel (Mike - Mayer)
AFC - Yepremian 37 FG
AFC - Yepremian 27 FG
AFC - Yepremian 41 FG
NFC - Mike - Mayer 21 FG
AFC - Yepremian 42 FG
MVP: Garo Yepremian, Miami

Jan. 20, 1975
Orange Bowl, Miami (26,484)

NFC	0	3	0	14	- 17
AFC	0	0	10	0	- 10

NFC - Marcol 33 FG
AFC - Warfield 32 pass from Griese (Gerela)
AFC - Gerela 33 FG
NFC - Gray 8 pass from J. Harris (Marcol)
NFC - Taylor 8 pass from J. Harris (Marcol)
MVP: James Harris, Los Angeles

Jan. 26, 1976
Superdome, New Orleans (30,546)

AFC	0	13	0	7	- 20
NFC	0	0	9	14	- 23

AFC - Stenerud 20 FG
AFC - Stenerud 35 FG
AFC - Burrough 64 pass from Pastorini (Stenerud)
NFC - Bakken 42 FG

NFC - Foreman 4 pass from Hart (Bakken miss)
AFC - Johnson 90 punt return (Stenerud)
NFC - Metcalf 14 pass from Boryla (Bakken)
NFC - Gray 8 pass from Boryla (Bakken)
MVP: Billy Johnson, Houston

Jan. 17, 1977
Kingdome, Seattle (64,752)

AFC	10	7	0	7	- 24
NFC	0	14	0	0	- 14

AFC - Simpson 3 run (Linhart)
AFC - Linhart 31 FG
NFC - Thomas 15 run (Bakken)
AFC - Joiner 12 pass from Anderson (Linhart)
NFC - McCutcheon 1 run (Bakken)
AFC - Branch 27 pass from Anderson (Linhart)
MVP: Mel Blount, Pittsburgh

Jan. 23, 1978
Tampa Stadium (51,337)

AFC	3	10	0	0	- 13
NFC	0	0	7	7	- 14

AFC - Linhart 21 FG
AFC - Branch 10 pass from Stabler (Linhart)
AFC - Linhart 39 FG
NFC - Metcalf 4 pass from Haden (Herrera)
NFC - Payton 1 run (Herrera)
MVP: Walter Payton, Chicago

Jan. 29, 1979
Memorial Coliseum, Los Angeles (46,281)

AFC	0	7	0	0	- 7
NFC	0	6	7	0	- 13

NFC - Montgomery 2 run (Corral miss)
AFC - Largent 8 pass from Griese (Yepremian)
NFC - T. Hill 19 pass from Staubach (Corral)
MVP: Ahmad Rashad, Minnesota

Jan. 27, 1980
Aloha Stadium, Honolulu (49,800)

AFC	3	7	10	7	- 27
NFC	3	20	7	7	- 37

NFC - Moseley 37 FG
AFC - Fritsch 19 FG
NFC - Muncie 1 run (Moseley)
AFC - Pruitt 1 pass from Bradshaw (Fritsch)
NFC - D. Hill 13 pass from Manning (Moseley miss)
NFC - T. Hill 25 pass from Muncie (Moseley)
NFC - Henry 86 punt return (Moseley)
AFC - Campbell 2 run (Fritsch)
AFC - Fritsch 29 FG
NFC - Muncie 11 run (Moseley)
AFC - Campbell 1 run (Fritsch)
MVP: Chuck Muncie, New Orleans

Feb. 1, 1981
Aloha Stadium, Honolulu (50,360)

AFC	0	7	0	0	- 7
NFC	3	6	0	12	- 12

NFC - Murray 31 FG
AFC - Morgan 9 pass from Sipe (J. Smith)
NFC - Murray 31 FG
NFC - Murray 34 FG
NFC - Jenkins 55 pass from Bartkowski (Murray)
NFC - Murray 36 FG
NFC - Safety, Shell called for holding in end zone
MVP: Eddie Murray, Detroit

Jan. 31, 1982
Aloha Stadium, Honolulu (50,402)

AFC	0	0	13	3	- 16
NFC	0	6	0	7	- 13

NFC - Giles 4 pass from Montana (Septien miss)
AFC - Muncie 2 run (Lowery miss)
AFC - Campbell 1 run (Lowery)
NFC - Dorsett 4 run (Septien)
AFC - Lowery 23 FG
MVP: Kellen Winslow, San Diego and Lee Roy Selmon, Tampa Bay

Feb. 6, 1983
Aloha Stadium, Honolulu (49,883)

AFC	9	3	7	0	- 19
NFC	0	10	0	10	- 20

AFC - Walker 34 pass from Fouts (Benirschke)
AFC - Safety, Still tackled Theismann in end zone
NFC - Andrews 3 run (Moseley)
NFC - Moseley 35 FG
AFC - Benirschke 29 FG
AFC - Allen 1 run (Benirschke)
NFC - Moseley 41 FG
NFC - Jefferson 11 pass from D. White (Moseley)
MVP: Dan Fouts, San Diego and John Jefferson, Green Bay

Jan. 29, 1984
Aloha Stadium, Honolulu (50,445)

AFC	0	3	0	0	- 3
NFC	3	14	14	14	- 45

NFC - Haji-Sheikh 23 FG
NFC - Andrews 16 pass from Theismann (Haji-Sheikh)
NFC - Andrews 2 pass from Montana (Haji-Sheikh)
AFC - Anderson 43 FG
NFC - Cromwell 44 interception return (Haji-Sheikh)
NFC - Lofton 8 pass from Theismann (Haji-Sheikh)
NFC - Coffman 6 pass from Theismann (Haji-Sheikh)
NFC - Dickerson 14 run (Haji-Sheikh)
MVP: Joe Theismann, Washington

Jan. 27, 1985
Aloha Stadium, Honolulu (50,385)

AFC	0	9	0	13	- 22
NFC	0	0	7	7	- 14

AFC - Safety, Gastineau tackled Dickerson in end zone
AFC - Allen 6 pass from Marino (Johnson)
NFC - Lofton 13 pass from Montana (Stenerud)
NFC - Payton 1 run (Stenerud)
AFC - Johnson 33 FG
AFC - Still 83 fumble return (Johnson)
AFC - Johnson 22 FG
MVP: Mark Gastineau, New York Jets

Feb. 2, 1986
Aloha Stadium, Honolulu (50,101)

AFC	7	17	0	0	- 24
NFC	0	7	7	14	- 28

AFC - Allen 2 run (Anderson)
NFC - Browner 48 interception return (Andersen)
AFC - Chandler 51 pass from Allen (Anderson)
AFC - Anderson 34 FG
AFC - Lipps 11 pass from O'Brien (Anderson)
NFC - Monk 15 pass from Simms (Andersen)
NFC - Cosbie 2 pass from Simms (Andersen)
NFC - Giles 15 pass from Simms (Andersen)
MVP: Phil Simms, New York Giants

Feb. 1, 1987
Aloha Stadium, Honolulu (50,101)

AFC	7	3	0	0	- 10
NFC	0	0	3	3	- 6

AFC - Christensen 10 pass from Elway (Franklin)
AFC - Franklin 26 FG
NFC - Andersen 38 FG
NFC - Andersen 19 FG
MVP: Reggie White, Philadelphia

Feb. 7, 1988
Aloha Stadium, Honolulu (50,113)

AFC	0	7	6	2	- 15
NFC	0	6	0	0	- 6

NFC - Andersen 25 FG
AFC - Kelly 1 run (Biasucci)
NFC - Andersen 36 FG
AFC - Biasucci 37 FG
AFC - Biasucci 30 FG
AFC - Safety, Montana forced out of end zone
MVP: Bruce Smith, Buffalo

Jan. 29, 1989
Aloha Stadium, Honolulu (50,113)

AFC	3	0	0	0	- 3
NFC	7	7	10	10	- 34

AFC - Norwood 38 FG
NFC - Walker 4 run (Andersen)
NFC - Settle 1 run (Andersen)
NFC - Andersen 27 FG
NFC - Walker 7 run (Andersen)
NFC - Andersen 51 FG
NFC - Ellard 8 pass from Wilson (Andersen)
MVP: Randall Cunningham, Philadelphia

Feb. 4, 1990
Aloha Stadium, Honolulu (50,445)

AFC	0	7	0	14	- 21
NFC	3	3	21	0	- 27

NFC - Murray 23 FG
NFC - Murray 41 FG
AFC - Okoye 1 run (Treadwell)
NFC - Meggett 11 pass from Cunningham (Murray)
NFC - Gray 51 interception return (Murray)
NFC - Millard 8 fumble return (Murray)
AFC - Edmunds 5 pass from Krieg (Treadwell)
AFC - M. Johnson 22 interception return (Treadwell)
MVP: Jerry Gray, Los Angeles Rams

Feb. 3, 1991
Aloha Stadium, Honolulu (50,345)

AFC	3	0	3	17	- 23
NFC	0	7	7	7	- 21

AFC - Lowery 26 FG
NFC - J. Johnson 1 run (Andersen)
AFC - Lowery 43 FG
NFC - J. Johnson 9 run (Andersen)
AFC - Reed 20 pass from Kelly (Lowery)
NFC - Sanders 22 run (Andersen)
AFC - Lowery 34 FG
AFC - Givins 13 pass from Kelly (Lowery)
MVP: Jim Kelly, Buffalo

Feb. 2, 1992
Aloha Stadium, Honolulu (50,209)

AFC	7	5	0	3	- 15
NFC	7	7	0	7	- 21

AFC - Clayton 4 pass from Kelly (Jaeger)
NFC - Irvin 13 pass from Rypien (Lohmiller)
AFC - Safety, Townsend tackled Byner in end zone
AFC - Jaeger 48 FG
NFC - Clark 35 pass from Rypien (Lohmiller)
AFC - Jaeger 27 FG
NFC - Rice 11 pass from Miller (Lohmiller)
MVP: Michael Irvin, Dallas

Feb. 7, 1993
Aloha Stadium, Honolulu (50,007)

AFC	0	10	3	7	3	- 23
NFC	3	10	0	7	0	- 20

NFC - Andersen 27 FG
AFC - Seau 31 interception return (Lowery)
NFC - Andersen 37 FG
NFC - Irvin 9 pass from Aikman (Andersen)
AFC - Lowery 42 FG
AFC - Lowery 29 FG
AFC - McDaniel 28 blocked field goal return (Lowery)
NFC - Hampton 23 pass from Young (Andersen)
AFC - Lowery 33 FG
MVP: Steve Tasker, Buffalo

Feb. 6, 1994
Aloha Stadium, Honolulu (50,026)

AFC	0	3	0	0	- 3
NFC	3	0	7	7	- 17

NFC - Johnson 35 FG
AFC - Anderson 25 FG
NFC - Bettis 4 run (Johnson)
NFC - Carter 15 pass from Hebert (Johnson)
MVP: Andre Rison, Atlanta

Feb. 5, 1995
Aloha Stadium, Honolulu (49,121)

AFC	0	17	3	21	- 41
NFC	10	0	3	0	- 13

NFC - Reveiz 28 FG
NFC - Carter 51 pass from Young (Reveiz kick)
AFC - Green 22 pass from Elway (Carney kick)
AFC - Carney 22 FG
AFC - Hoard 4 run (Carney kick)
NFC - Reveiz 49 FG
AFC - Carney 23 FG
AFC - Warren 11 run (Carney kick)
AFC - Green 16 pass from Hostetler (Carney kick)
AFC - Faulk 49 run (Carney kick)
MVP: Marshall Faulk, Indianapolis

Feb. 4, 1996
Aloha Stadium, Honolulu (50,034)

AFC	7	0	6	0	- 13
NFC	3	17	0	0	- 20

AFC - Thigpen 93 pass from Blake (Elam kick)
NFC - Andersen 36 FG
NFC - Rice 1 pass from Favre (Andersen kick)
NFC - Harvey 36 interception return (Andersen kick)
NFC - Andersen 24 FG
AFC - Martin 17 pass from Harbaugh (Elam miss)
MVP: Jerry Rice, San Francisco

Feb. 2, 1997
Aloha Stadium, Honolulu (50,031)

AFC	0	3	7	13	3	- 26
NFC	9	0	6	8	0	- 23

NFC - Kasay 20 FG
NFC - McDaniel 5 pass from Favre (Kasay miss)
AFC - Blanchard 28 FG
NFC - Sanders 6 run (pass failed)
AFC - C. Martin 3 run (Blanchard kick)
AFC - Ambrose 54 interception return (pass failed)
NFC - C. Carter 53 pass from Frerotte (Walls pass from Frerotte)
AFC - T. Brown 80 pass from Brunell (Blanchard kick)
AFC - Blanchard 37 FG
MVP: Mark Brunell, Jacksonville

AFL ALL-STAR GAME
Jan. 7, 1962
Balboa Stadium, San Diego (20,973)

Eastern Division	5	7	7	8	- 27
Western Division	0	21	14	12	- 47

East - Blanda 32 FG
East - Safety, Haynes tackled in end zone
West - Stone 45 pass from Davidson (Blair)

East - Cannon 34 pass from Blanda (Blanda)
West - Haynes 12 run (Blair)
West - Kocourek 24 pass from Davidson (Blair)
West - Haynes 66 punt return (Blair)
West - Norton 10 pass from Davidson (Blair)
East - Cappelletti 5 pass from Blanda (Blanda)
West - Williamson 53 interception return (Blanda miss)
East - Hennigan 3 pass from Dorow (Dorow run)
West - Stone 15 run (pass failed)
MVP: Cotton Davidson, Dallas

Jan. 13, 1963
Balboa Stadium, San Diego (27,641)

Eastern Division	0	0	14	0	- 14
Western Division	7	7	0	7	- 21

West - McClinton 64 run (Mingo)
West - Kocourek 11 pass from Dawson (Mingo)
East - Hennigan 8 pass from Blanda (Blanda)
East - Grantham 29 interception return (Blanda)
West - Taylor 20 pass from Tripucka (Mingo)
Offensive MVP: Curtis McClinton, Dallas
Defensive MVP: Earl Faison, San Diego

Jan. 19, 1964
Balboa Stadium, San Diego (20,016)

Eastern Division	10	14	0	0	- 24
Western Division	0	3	14	10	- 27

East - Gilchrist 1 run (Cappelletti)
East - Cappelletti 35 FG
West - Fraser 19 FG
East - Garron 12 pass from Parilli (Cappelletti)
East - Mathis 3 pass from Parilli (Cappelletti)
West - Lincoln 64 run (Fraser)
West - Lowe 5 run (Fraser)
West - Fraser 7 FG
West - Powell 25 pass from Davidson (Fraser)
Offensive MVP: Keith Lincoln, San Diego
Defensive MVP: Archie Matsos, Oakland

Jan. 16, 1965
Jeppesen Stadium, Houston (15,446)

Western Division	7	10	14	7	- 38
Eastern Division	0	14	0	0	- 14

West - Lincoln 73 pass from Dawson (Brooker)
West - Daniels 5 pass from Hadl (Brooker)
East - Blanks 5 run (Cappelletti)
West - Brooker 46 FG
East - Buoniconti 17 fumble return (Cappelletti)
West - Lincoln 80 run (Brooker)
West - Alworth 7 pass from Hadl (Brooker)
West - Powell 17 pass from Hadl (Brooker)
Offensive MVP: Keith Lincoln, San Diego
Defensive MVP: Willie Brown, Denver

Jan. 15, 1966
Rice Stadium, Houston (35,572)

Buffalo Bills	10	3	0	6	- 19
All-Stars	0	6	17	7	- 30

Buf - Gogolak 20 FG
Buf - Saimes 61 fumble return (Gogolak)
AS - Cappelletti 46 FG

Buf - Gogolak 11 FG
AS - Cappelletti 14 FG
AS - Cappelletti 32 FG
AS - Lowe 1 run (Cappelletti)
AS - Alworth 43 pass from Namath (Cappelletti)
AS - Alworth 10 pass from Namath (Cappelletti)
Buf - Carlton 34 pass from Lamonica (run failed)
Offensive MVP: Joe Namath, New York
Defensive MVP: Frank Buncom, San Diego

Jan. 21, 1967
Oakland-Alameda County Coliseum (18,876)

Eastern Division	0	0	16	14	- 30
Western Division	9	7	7	0	- 23

West - McClinton 31 pass from Dawson (Van Raaphorst)
West - Safety, bad snap through end zone
West - Dixon 17 pass from Flores (Van Raaphorst)
East - Safety, Dawson tackled in end zone
West - Buchanan 39 fumble return (Van Raaphorst)
East - Biggs 50 interception return (Cappelletti)
East - Carlton 3 pass from Parilli (Cappelletti)
East - Burnett 12 run (Cappelletti)
East - Frazier 17 pass from Parilli (Cappelletti)
Offensive MVP: Babe Parilli, Boston
Defensive MVP: Verlon Biggs, New York

Jan. 21, 1968
Gator Bowl, Jacksonville, Fla. (40,103)

Western Division	7	14	0	3	- 24
Eastern Division	3	10	0	12	- 25

East - Mercer 10 FG
West - Duncan 90 kickoff return (Blanda)
West - Frazier 3 pass from Lamonica (Blanda)
East - Lammons 35 pass from Namath (Mercer)
West - Alworth 9 pass from Lamonica (Blanda)
East - Mercer 33 FG
West - Blanda 28 FG
East - Maynard 24 pass from Namath (pass failed)
East - Namath 1 run (run failed)
Offensive MVPs: Joe Namath, New York and Don Maynard, New York
Defensive MVP: Speedy Duncan, San Diego

Jan. 19, 1969
Gator Bowl, Jacksonville, Fla. (41,058)

Western Division	3	0	10	25	- 38
Eastern Division	3	16	3	3	- 25

East - Turner 27 FG
West - Stenerud 51 FG
East - Kiick 2 run (Turner)
East - Turner 16 FG
East - Turner 19 FG
East - Turner 13 FG
West - Trumpy 6 pass from Dawson (Stenerud)
East - Turner 18 FG
West - Stenerud 30 FG

East - Turner 21 FG
West - Dixon 1 run (Stenerud)
West - Robinson 1 run (Robinson run)
West - Robinson 1 run (Stenerud)
West - Stenerud 32 FG
    Offensive MVP: Len Dawson, Kansas City
    Defensive MVP: George Webster, Houston

Jan. 17, 1970
Astrodome, Houston (30,170)

Western Division	13	0	3	10	- 26
Eastern Division	0	0	3	0	- 3

West - Post 1 run (pass failed)
West - Alworth 21 pass from Hadl (Stenerud)

West - Stenerud 38 FG
East - Turner 44 FG
West - Stenerud 30 FG
West - Livingston 11 run (Stenerud)
    MVP: John Hadl, San Diego

PLAYOFF BOWL

The Playoff Bowl was an unusual game that matched the second-place finishers in the East and the West. It made its debut after the 1960 season, and the Detroit Lions won the first three games. After the NFL instituted a playoff system in 1967, the Playoff Bowl took on the look of a consolation game, since it involved the losers in the conference championship games. Teams began taking it less seriously, and it lasted only through the 1969 season, after which it was abolished.

Jan. 7, 1961
Orange Bowl, Miami (34,981)

Cleveland	0	7	0	9	- 16
Detroit	0	0	10	7	- 17

Cle - Kreitling 9 pass from Plum (Baker)
Det - Pietrosante 5 run (Martin)
Det - Martin 12 FG
Cle - Baker 27 FG
Det - Webb 1 run (Martin)
Cle - Mitchell 89 pass from Plum (Baker miss)

Jan. 6, 1962
Orange Bowl, Miami (25,612)

Detroit	10	14	7	7	- 38
Philadelphia	0	0	10	0	- 10

Det - Martin 38 FG
Det - Barr 69 pass from Ninowski (Martin)
Det - Morrall 5 run (Martin)
Det - Studstill 18 pass from Morrall (Martin)
Phi - Retzlaff 9 pass from Hill (Walston)
Phi - Walston 22 FG
Det - Barr 14 pass from Ninowski (Martin)
Det - Williams 19 pass from Morrall (Martin)

Jan. 6, 1963
Orange Bowl, Miami (36,284)

Detroit	0	10	7	0	- 17
Pittsburgh	0	7	3	0	- 10

Det - Walker 27 FG
Pit - Hoak 5 run (Michaels)
Det - Webb 20 pass from Plum (Walker)
Pit - Michaels 40 FG
Det - Webb 2 run (Walker)

Jan. 5, 1964
Orange Bowl, Miami (54,921)

Cleveland	0	10	0	13	- 23
Green Bay	14	14	7	5	- 40

GB - R. Kramer 18 pass from Starr (J. Kramer)

GB - Moore 99 pass from Starr (J. Kramer)
Cle - Groza 36 FG
GB - McGee 15 pass from Starr (J. Kramer)
Cle - Green 5 run (Groza)
GB - Taylor 2 run (J. Kramer)
GB - Moore 2 run (J. Kramer)
GB - J. Kramer 8 FG
Cle - Kreitling 20 pass from Ryan (Groza)
Cle - Crespino 25 pass from Ryan (Groza miss)
GB - Safety, Aldridge tackled Ryan in end zone

Jan. 3, 1965
Orange Bowl, Miami (56,218)

Green Bay	3	0	0	14	- 17
St. Louis	0	7	10	7	- 24

GB - Hornung 40 FG
StL - Gambrell 80 pass from Johnson (Bakken)
StL - Bakken 7 FG
StL - Gambrell 10 pass from Johnson (Bakken)
GB - Taylor 7 run (Hornung)
StL - Stovall 30 interception return (Bakken)
GB - Taylor 1 run (Hornung)

Jan. 9, 1966
Orange Bowl, Miami (65,569)

Baltimore	0	14	14	7	- 35
Dallas	0	3	0	0	- 3

Bal - Moore 6 run (Michaels)
Dal - Villanueva 12 FG
Bal - Hill 3 run (Michaels)
Bal - Hill 1 run (Michaels)
Bal - Orr 15 pass from Matte (Michaels)
Bal - Orr 20 pass from Matte (Michaels)

Jan. 8, 1967
Orange Bowl, Miami (58,088)

Baltimore	3	7	3	7	- 20
Philadelphia	0	14	0	0	- 14

Bal - Michaels 23 FG
Phi - K. Hill 1 run (Baker)
Bal - Berry 14 pass from Unitas (Michaels)
Phi - Lang 2 run (Baker)
Bal - Michaels 14 FG
Bal - Matte 1 run (Michaels)

Jan. 7, 1968
Orange Bowl, Miami (37,102)

Cleveland	0	0	0	6	- 6
Los Angeles	10	7	3	10	- 30

LA - Casey 21 pass from Gabriel (Gossett)
LA - Gossett 41 FG
LA - Truax 2 pass from Gabriel (Gossett)
LA - Gossett 46 FG
Cle - Kelly 2 run (Groza miss)
LA - Ellison 9 run (Gossett)
LA - Gossett 19 FG

Jan. 5, 1969
Orange Bowl, Miami (22,961)

Dallas	0	10	7	0	- 17
Minnesota	13	0	0	0	- 13

Min - Bryant 81 punt return (Cox)
Min - Cox 37 FG
Min - Cox 23 FG
Dal - Hayes 51 pass from Meredith (Clark)
Dal - Clark 11 FG
Dal - Baynham 20 pass from Morton (Clark)

Jan. 3, 1970
Orange Bowl, Miami (30,824)

Dallas	0	0	0	0	- 0
Los Angeles	14	0	7	10	- 31

LA - Josephson 35 pass from Gabriel (Gossett)
LA - Snow 67 pass from Gabriel (Gossett)
LA - Klein 16 pass from Gabriel (Gossett)
LA - Snow 49 pass from Gabriel (Gossett)
LA - Gossett 42 FG

PRO FOOTBALL HALL OF FAME
Canton, Ohio

Herb Adderley	1980	Player		Joe Gibbs	1996	Coach
Lance Alworth	1978	Player		Frank Gifford	1977	Player
Doug Atkins	1982	Player		Sid Gillman	1983	Coach
Red Badgro	1981	Player		Otto Graham	1965	Player
Lem Barney	1992	Player		Red Grange	1963	Player
Cliff Battles	1968	Player		Bud Grant	1994	Coach
Sammy Baugh	1963	Player		Joe Greene	1987	Player
Chuck Bednarik	1967	Player		Forrest Gregg	1977	Player
Bert Bell	1963	Owner/Commissioner		Bob Griese	1990	Player
Bobby Bell	1983	Player		Lou Groza	1974	Player
Raymond Berry	1973	Player		Joe Guyon	1966	Player
Charles Bidwill	1967	Owner		George Halas	1963	Coach/Owner
Fred Biletnikoff	1988	Player		Jack Ham	1988	Player
George Blanda	1981	Player		John Hannah	1991	Player
Mel Blount	1989	Player		Franco Harris	1990	Player
Terry Bradshaw	1989	Player		Mike Haynes	1997	Player
Jim Brown	1971	Player		Ed Healey	1964	Player
Paul Brown	1967	Coach		Mel Hein	1963	Player
Roosevelt Brown	1975	Player		Ted Hendricks	1990	Player
Willie Brown	1984	Player		Pete Henry	1963	Player
Buck Buchanan	1990	Player		Arnie Herber	1966	Player
Dick Butkus	1979	Player		Bill Hewitt	1971	Player
Earl Campbell	1991	Player		Clarke Hinkle	1964	Player
Tony Canadeo	1974	Player		Elroy Hirsch	1968	Player
Joe Carr	1963	Administrator		Paul Hornung	1986	Player
Guy Chamberlain	1965	Player/Coach		Ken Houston	1986	Player
Jack Christiansen	1970	Player		Cal Hubbard	1963	Player
Dutch Clark	1963	Player		Sam Huff	1982	Player
George Connor	1975	Player		Lamar Hunt	1972	Owner
Jimmy Conzelman	1964	Player/Coach		Don Hutson	1963	Player
Lou Creekmur	1996	Player		Jimmy Johnson	1994	Player
Larry Csonka	1987	Player		John Henry Johnson	1987	Player
Al Davis	1992	Owner/Administrator		Charlie Joiner	1996	Player
Willie Davis	1981	Player		Deacon Jones	1980	Player
Len Dawson	1987	Player		Stan Jones	1991	Player
Dan Dierdorf	1996	Player		Henry Jordan	1995	Player
Mike Ditka	1988	Player		Sonny Jurgensen	1983	Player
Art Donovan	1968	Player		Leroy Kelly	1994	Player
Tony Dorsett	1994	Player		Walt Kiesling	1966	Player/Coach
Paddy Driscoll	1965	Player		Bruiser Kinard	1971	Player
Bill Dudley	1966	Player		Curly Lambeau	1963	Coach
Turk Edwards	1969	Player		Jack Lambert	1990	Player
Weeb Ewbank	1978	Coach		Tom Landry	1990	Coach
Tom Fears	1970	Player		Night Train Lane	1974	Player
Jim Finks	1995	Administrator		Jim Langer	1987	Player
Ray Flaherty	1976	Coach		Willie Lanier	1986	Player
Len Ford	1976	Player		Steve Largent	1995	Player
Dan Fortmann	1965	Player		Yale Lary	1979	Player
Dan Fouts	1993	Player		Dante Lavelli	1975	Player
Frank Gatski	1985	Player		Bobby Layne	1967	Player
Bill George	1974	Player		Tuffy Leemans	1978	Player

Bob Lilly	1980	Player		Andy Robustelli	1971	Player
Larry Little	1993	Player		Art Rooney	1964	Owner
Vince Lombardi	1971	Coach		Pete Rozelle	1985	Commissioner
Sid Luckman	1965	Player		Bob St. Clair	1990	Player
Link Lyman	1964	Player		Gale Sayers	1977	Player
John Mackey	1992	Player		Joe Schmidt	1973	Player
Tim Mara	1963	Owner		Tex Schramm	1991	Administrator
Wellington Mara	1997	Owner		Lee Roy Selmon	1995	Player
Gino Marchetti	1972	Player		Art Shell	1989	Player
George Preston Marshall	1963	Owner		Don Shula	1997	Coach
Ollie Matson	1972	Player		O.J. Simpson	1985	Player
Don Maynard	1987	Player		Jackie Smith	1994	Player
George McAfee	1966	Player		Bart Starr	1977	Player
Mike McCormack	1984	Player		Roger Staubach	1985	Player
Hugh McElhenny	1970	Player		Ernie Stautner	1969	Player
Johnny (Blood) McNally	1963	Player		Jan Stenerud	1991	Player
Mike Michalske	1964	Player		Ken Strong	1967	Player
Wayne Millner	1968	Player		Joe Stydahar	1967	Player
Bobby Mitchell	1983	Player		Fran Tarkenton	1986	Player
Ron Mix	1979	Player		Charley Taylor	1984	Player
Lenny Moore	1975	Player		Jim Taylor	1976	Player
Marion Motley	1968	Player		Jim Thorpe	1963	Player
George Musso	1982	Player		Y.A. Tittle	1971	Player
Bronko Nagurski	1963	Player		George Trafton	1964	Player
Joe Namath	1985	Player		Charley Trippi	1968	Player
Greasy Neale	1969	Coach		Emlen Tunnell	1967	Player
Ernie Nevers	1963	Player		Bulldog Turner	1966	Player
Ray Nitschke	1978	Player		Johnny Unitas	1979	Player
Chuck Noll	1993	Coach		Gene Upshaw	1987	Player
Leo Nomellini	1969	Player		Norm Van Brocklin	1971	Player
Merlin Olsen	1982	Player		Steve Van Buren	1965	Player
Jim Otto	1980	Player		Doak Walker	1986	Player
Steve Owen	1966	Player/Coach		Bill Walsh	1993	Coach
Alan Page	1988	Player		Paul Warfield	1983	Player
Ace Parker	1972	Player		Bob Waterfield	1965	Player
Jim Parker	1973	Player		Mike Webster	1997	Player
Walter Payton	1993	Player		Arnie Weinmeister	1984	Player
Joe Perry	1969	Player		Randy White	1994	Player
Pete Pihos	1970	Player		Bob Willis	1977	Player
Shorty Ray	1966	Administrator		Larry Wilson	1978	Player
Dan Reeves	1967	Owner		Kellen Winslow	1995	Player
Mel Renfro	1996	Player		Alex Wojciechowicz	1968	Player
John Riggins	1992	Player		Willie Wood	1989	Player
Jim Ringo	1981	Player				

PART THREE

All-Time Leaders

The All-Time Leaders

The All-Time Leaders section lists for the first time the career regular season, career playoff, and single season leaders for all the major statistical categories.

Regular Season Career Leaders

The top 25 players are listed for Games played, Scoring (points scored), Rushing (net yards gained), Passing (NFL passer rating points), Pass Receiving (receptions), Interceptions, Punting (average), Sacks, Kickoff Returns (average return), and Punt Returns (average return).

To qualify for inclusion in the Passing, Punting, Punt Return, and Kickoff Return categories, the following minimums were used:

> Passing, 1500 attempts.
> Punting, 250 net punts.
> Punt Returns, 75 returns.
> Kickoff Returns, 75 returns.

Playoff Career Leaders

The top ten players are listed for Scoring (points scored), Rushing (net yards gained), Passing (NFL passer rating points), Pass Receiving (pass receptions), Interceptions, Punting (average), Sacks, Kickoff Returns (average return), and Punt Returns (average return).

To qualify for inclusion in the Passing, Punting, Punt Return, and Kickoff Return categories, the following minimums were used:

> Passing, 150 attempts.
> Punting, 25 net punts.
> Punt Returns, 10 returns.
> Kickoff Returns, 10 returns.

Single Season Leaders

The top 25 players are listed for Scoring (points scored), Rushing (net yards gained), Passing (NFL passer rating points), Pass Receiving (pass receptions), Interceptions, Punting (average), Sacks, Kickoff Returns (average return), and Punt Returns (average return).

To qualify for inclusion in the Passing, Punting, Punt Return, and Kickoff Return categories, the following per game minimums were established:

> Passing, 14 attempts per game.
> Punting, 2.5 net punts per game.
> Punt Returns, 1 return per game.
> Kickoff Returns, 1 return per game.

These per game qualifications are the current standards used by the NFL. The minimums in these categories have changed over the years (in all cases increasing from the initial minimums established in the 1940s). However, for many years in the late 1930s and the 1940s the NFL (and the AAFC for Passing and Punting) did not publish the minimums necessary to qualify for these categories; thus we've decided to use the current standards for the purposes of providing top 25 lists for these four categories.

Key

Scoring

TD	Touchdowns
1XP	Points after touchdown
2XP	2 point conversions
FG	Field Goals
SAF	Safeties
PTS	Total number of points scored

Rushing

ATT	Attempts
YDS	Yards
AVG	Average gain per attempt
TD	Touchdowns

Passing

ATT	Attempts
COM	Completions
PCT	Completion percentage
YDS	Yards
AVG	Average gain per attempt
TD	Touchdowns
TD%	Touchdown percentage
INT	Interceptions
INT%	Interception percentage
RTG	Passer rating

Receiving

NO	Number of receptions
YDS	Yards
AVG	Average gain per reception
TD	Touchdowns

Interceptions

NO	Number of interceptions
YDS	Yards
AVG	Average gain per interception
TD	Touchdowns

Punting

NO	Number of punts
YDS	Yards
AVG	Average length of punt

Sacks

NO	Number of sacks

Kickoff/Punt Returns

NO	Number of kick/punt returns
YDS	Yards
AVG	Average gain per return
TD	Touchdowns

Games Played

	Player	NO
1.	George Blanda	339
2.	Jim Marshall	282
3.	Clay Matthews	278
4.	Lou Groza	268
5.	Jan Stenerud	263
6.	Nick Lowery	260
7.	Jackie Slater	259
8.	Earl Morrall	255
9.	Mike Kenn	252
10.	Pat Leahy	250
11.	Blair Bush	246
	Fran Tarkenton	246
13.	Jeff Van Note	245
	Mike Webster	245
15.	Ray Donaldson	244
16.	Ed White	241
17.	Ron McDole	240
	Mick Tinglehoff	240
19.	Paul Krause	239
20.	Charlie Joiner	235
	Matt Bahr	235
22.	Jim Bakken	234
	Stan Brock	234
24.	James Lofton	233
25.	Gary Anderson	229
	Rohn Stark	229

Scoring

	Player	Year	TD	1XP	2XP	FG	SAF	PTS
Career								
1.	George Blanda		9	943	0	335	0	2002
2.	Nick Lowery		0	562	0	383	0	1711
3.	Jan Stenerud		0	580	0	373	0	1699
4.	Lou Groza		1	810		264	0	1608
5.	Gary Anderson		0	488	0	356	0	1556
6.	Morten Andersen		0	472	0	355	0	1537
7.	Eddie Murray		0	498	0	325	0	1473
8.	Pat Leahy		0	558		304	0	1470
9.	Norm Johnson		0	552	0	300	0	1452
10.	Jim Turner		1	521	0	304	0	1439
11.	Matt Bahr		0	522	0	300	0	1422
12.	Mark Moseley		0	482		300	0	1382
13.	Jim Bakken		0	534		282	0	1380
14.	Fred Cox		0	519		282	0	1365
15.	Jim Breech		0	517		243	0	1246
16.	Chris Bahr		0	490		241	0	1213
17.	Kevin Butler		0	404	0	257	0	1175
18.	Gino Cappelletti		42	342	4	176	0	1130
19.	Ray Wersching		0	458		222	0	1124
20.	Al Del Greco		0	403	0	236	0	1111
21.	Don Cockroft		0	432		216	0	1080

	Player	Year	TD	1XP	2XP	FG	SAF	PTS
22.	Garo Yepremian		0	444		210	0	1074
23.	Bruce Gossett		0	374		219	0	1031
24.	Jerry Rice		165	0	2	0	0	994
25.	Sam Baker		2	428		179	0	977

Playoffs

	Player	Year	TD	1XP	2XP	FG	SAF	PTS
1.	Emmitt Smith		20	0	0	0	0	120
	Thurman Thomas		20	0	0	0	0	120
3.	George Blanda		0	49	0	22	0	115
4.	Franco Harris		18	0	0	0	0	108
	Jerry Rice		18	0	0	0	0	108
6.	Matt Bahr		0	40	0	21	0	103
7.	Rafael Septien		0	41	0	18	0	95
8.	Norm Johnson		0	28	0	22	0	94
9.	Steve Christie		0	28	0	20	0	88
10.	Gary Anderson		0	30	0	19	0	87

Single Season

	Player	Year	TD	1XP	2XP	FG	SAF	PTS
1.	Paul Hornung	1960	15	41		15	0	176
2.	Mark Moseley	1983	0	62		33	0	161
3.	Gino Cappelletti	1964	7	36	1	25	0	155
4.	Emmitt Smith	1995	25	0	0	0	0	150
5.	Chip Lohmiller	1991	0	56		31	0	149
6.	Gino Cappelletti	1961	8	48	0	17	0	147
7.	Paul Hornung	1961	10	41		15	0	146
	Jim Turner	1968	0	43	0	34	0	145
	John Kasay	1996	0	34	0	37	0	145
10.	John Riggins	1983	24	0		0	0	144
	Kevin Butler	1985	0	51		31	0	144
12.	Norm Johnson	1995	0	39	0	34	0	141
13.	Tony Franklin	1986	0	44		32	0	140
14.	Gary Anderson	1985	0	40		33	0	139
	Nick Lowery	1990	0	37		34	0	139
16.	Don Hutson	1942	17	33		1	0	138
	O.J. Simpson	1975	23	0		0	0	138
	Jerry Rice	1987	23	0		0	0	138
19.	Gene Mingo	1962	4	32	0	27	0	137
20.	Mike Cofer	1989	0	49		29	0	136
21.	John Carney	1994	0	33	0	34	0	135
	Cary Blanchard	1996	0	27	0	36	0	135

Rushing

	Player	Year	ATT	YDS	AVG	TD
Career						
1.	Walter Payton		3838	16726	4.4	110
2.	Eric Dickerson		2996	13259	4.4	90
3.	Tony Dorsett		2936	12739	4.3	77
4.	Jim Brown		2359	12312	5.2	106
5.	Franco Harris		2949	12120	4.1	91
6.	Marcus Allen		2898	11738	4.1	112
7.	Barry Sanders		2384	11725	4.9	84
8.	John Riggins		2916	11352	3.9	104
9.	O.J. Simpson		2404	11236	4.7	61

	Player	Year	ATT	YDS	AVG	TD
10.	Thurman Thomas		2566	10762	4.2	62
11.	O.J. Anderson		2562	10273	4.0	81
12.	Emmitt Smith		2334	10160	4.4	108
13.	Joe Perry		1929	9723	5.0	71
14.	Earl Campbell		2187	9407	4.3	74
15.	Jim Taylor		1941	8597	4.4	83
16.	Herschel Walker		1948	8205	4.2	61
17.	Roger Craig		1991	8189	4.1	56
18.	Gerald Riggs		1989	8188	4.1	69
19.	Larry Csonka		1891	8081	4.3	64
20.	Freeman McNeil		1798	8074	4.5	38
21.	James Brooks		1685	7962	4.7	49
22.	Earnest Byner		2011	7948	4.0	56
23.	Mike Pruitt		1844	7378	4.0	51
24.	Leroy Kelly		1727	7274	4.2	74
25.	George Rogers		1692	7176	4.2	54

Playoffs

	Player	Year	ATT	YDS	AVG	TD
1.	Franco Harris		400	1556	3.9	16
2.	Emmitt Smith		318	1413	4.4	18
3.	Thurman Thomas		327	1399	4.3	15
4.	Tony Dorsett		302	1383	4.6	9
5.	Marcus Allen		255	1310	5.1	11
6.	John Riggins		251	996	4.0	12
7.	Larry Csonka		225	891	4.0	9
8.	Chuck Foreman		229	860	3.8	7
9.	Roger Craig		207	840	4.1	7
10.	Earnest Byner		186	839	4.5	5

Single Season

	Player	Year	ATT	YDS	AVG	TD
1.	Eric Dickerson	1984	379	2105	5.6	14
2.	O.J. Simpson	1973	332	2003	6.0	12
3.	Earl Campbell	1980	373	1934	5.2	13
4.	Barry Sanders	1994	331	1883	5.7	7
5.	Jim Brown	1963	291	1863	6.4	12
6.	Walter Payton	1977	339	1852	5.5	14
7.	Eric Dickerson	1986	404	1821	4.5	11
8.	O.J. Simpson	1975	329	1817	5.5	16
9.	Eric Dickerson	1983	390	1808	4.6	18
10.	Emmitt Smith	1995	377	1773	4.7	25
11.	Marcus Allen	1985	380	1759	4.6	11
12.	Gerald Riggs	1985	397	1719	4.3	10
13.	Emmitt Smith	1992	373	1713	4.6	18
14.	Earl Campbell	1979	368	1697	4.6	19
15.	Barry Foster	1992	390	1690	4.3	11
16.	Walter Payton	1984	381	1684	4.4	11
17.	George Rogers	1981	378	1674	4.4	13
18.	Eric Dickerson	1988	388	1659	4.3	14
19.	Tony Dorsett	1981	342	1646	4.8	4
20.	Walter Payton	1979	369	1610	4.4	14
21.	O.J. Anderson	1979	331	1605	4.8	8
22.	William Andrews	1983	331	1567	4.7	7
23.	Emmitt Smith	1991	365	1563	4.3	12
24.	Barry Sanders	1996	307	1553	5.1	11
25.	Walter Payton	1985	324	1551	4.8	9

Passing

Player	Year	ATT	COM	PCT	YDS	AVG	TD	TD%	INT	INT%	RTG
Career											
1. Steve Young		3192	2059	64.5	25479	8.0	174	5.5	85	2.7	96.17
2. Joe Montana		5391	3409	63.2	40551	7.5	273	5.1	139	2.6	92.26
3. Brett Favre		2693	1667	61.9	18724	7.0	147	5.5	79	2.9	88.61
4. Dan Marino		6904	4134	59.9	51636	7.5	369	5.3	209	3.0	88.35
5. Otto Graham		2626	1464	55.8	23584	9.0	174	6.6	135	5.1	86.63
6. Jim Kelly		4779	2874	60.1	35467	7.4	237	5.0	175	3.7	84.39
7. Roger Staubach		2958	1685	57.0	22700	7.7	153	5.2	109	3.7	83.42
8. Troy Aikman		3178	2000	62.9	22733	7.2	110	3.5	98	3.1	83.02
9. Neil Lomax		3153	1817	57.6	22771	7.2	136	4.3	90	2.9	82.68
10. Sonny Jurgensen		4262	2433	57.1	32224	7.6	255	6.0	189	4.4	82.62
11. Len Dawson		3741	2136	57.1	28711	7.7	239	6.4	183	4.9	82.56
12. Jeff Hostetler		2194	1278	58.2	15531	7.1	89	4.1	61	2.8	82.06
13. Ken Anderson		4475	2654	59.3	32838	7.3	197	4.4	160	3.6	81.86
14. Bernie Kosar		3365	1994	59.3	23301	6.9	124	3.7	87	2.6	81.83
15. Danny White		2950	1761	59.7	21959	7.4	155	5.3	132	4.5	81.71
16. Dave Krieg		5288	3092	58.5	37946	7.2	261	4.9	199	3.8	81.48
17. Warren Moon		6000	3514	58.6	43787	7.3	254	4.2	208	3.5	80.96
18. Neil O'Donnell		2059	1179	57.3	14014	6.8	72	3.5	46	2.2	80.51
19. Scott Mitchell		1507	853	56.6	10516	7.0	71	4.7	49	3.3	80.48
20. Bart Starr		3149	1808	57.4	24718	7.8	152	4.8	138	4.4	80.47
21. Ken O'Brien		3602	2110	58.6	25094	7.0	128	3.6	98	2.7	80.44
22. Fran Tarkenton		6467	3686	57.0	47003	7.3	342	5.3	266	4.1	80.35
23. Dan Fouts		5604	3297	58.8	43040	7.7	254	4.5	242	4.3	80.23
24. Boomer Esiason		5019	2851	56.8	36442	7.3	234	4.7	182	3.6	80.11
25. Tony Eason		1564	911	58.2	11142	7.1	61	3.9	51	3.3	79.72
Playoffs											
1. Bart Starr		213	130	61.0	1753	8.2	15	7.0	4	1.9	102.89
2. Troy Aikman		415	276	66.5	3372	8.1	22	5.3	13	3.1	95.98
3. Joe Montana		734	460	62.7	5772	7.9	45	6.1	21	2.9	95.59
4. Brett Favre		317	194	61.2	2430	7.7	18	5.7	7	2.2	94.75
5. Ken Anderson		166	110	66.3	1321	8.0	9	5.4	6	3.6	93.47
6. Joe Theismann		211	128	60.7	1782	8.4	11	5.2	7	3.3	91.38
7. Steve Young		334	207	62.0	2381	7.1	15	4.5	7	2.1	89.67
8. Warren Moon		403	259	64.3	2870	7.1	17	4.2	14	3.5	84.90
9. Ken Stabler		351	203	57.8	2641	7.5	19	5.4	13	3.7	84.24
10. Bernie Kosar		270	152	56.3	1953	7.2	16	5.9	10	3.7	83.46
Single Season											
1. Steve Young	1994	461	324	70.3	3969	8.6	35	7.6	10	2.2	112.79
2. Joe Montana	1989	386	271	70.2	3521	9.1	26	6.7	8	2.1	112.41
3. Milt Plum	1960	250	151	60.4	2297	9.2	21	8.4	5	2.0	110.37
4. Sammy Baugh	1945	182	128	70.3	1669	9.2	11	6.0	4	2.2	109.89
5. Otto Graham	1947	269	163	60.6	2753	10.2	25	9.3	11	4.1	109.16
6. Dan Marino	1984	564	362	64.2	5084	9.0	48	8.5	17	3.0	108.94
7. Sid Luckman	1943	202	110	54.5	2194	10.9	28	13.9	12	5.9	107.55
8. Steve Young	1992	402	268	66.7	3465	8.6	25	6.2	7	1.7	107.03
9. Bart Starr	1966	251	156	62.2	2257	9.0	14	5.6	3	1.2	104.96
10. Roger Staubach	1971	211	126	59.7	1882	8.9	15	7.1	4	1.9	104.81
11. Y.A. Tittle	1963	367	221	60.2	3145	8.6	36	9.8	14	3.8	104.77
12. Ken Stabler	1976	291	194	66.7	2737	9.4	27	9.3	17	5.8	103.41

	Player	Year	ATT	COM	PCT	YDS	AVG	TD	TD%	INT	INT%	RTG
13.	Frankie Albert	1948	264	154	58.3	1990	7.5	29	11.0	10	3.8	102.94
14.	Joe Montana	1984	432	279	64.6	3630	8.4	28	6.5	10	2.3	102.87
15.	Charlie Conerly	1959	194	113	58.2	1706	8.8	14	7.2	4	2.1	102.73
16.	Bert Jones	1976	343	207	60.3	3104	9.0	24	7.0	9	2.6	102.47
17.	Joe Montana	1987	398	266	66.8	3054	7.7	31	7.8	13	3.3	102.10
18.	Steve Young	1991	279	180	64.5	2517	9.0	17	6.1	8	2.9	101.80
19.	Len Dawson	1966	284	159	56.0	2527	8.9	26	9.2	10	3.5	101.66
20.	Steve Young	1993	462	314	68.0	4023	8.7	29	6.3	16	3.5	101.50
21.	Jim Kelly	1990	346	219	63.3	2829	8.2	24	6.9	9	2.6	101.18
22.	Jim Harbaugh	1995	314	200	63.7	2575	8.2	17	5.4	5	1.6	100.74
23.	Otto Graham	1953	258	167	64.7	2722	10.6	11	4.3	9	3.5	99.66
24.	Brett Favre	1995	570	359	63.0	4413	7.7	38	6.7	13	2.3	99.55
25.	Troy Aikman	1993	392	271	69.1	3100	7.9	15	3.8	6	1.5	99.02

Receiving

	Player	Year	NO	YDS	AVG	TD

Career

	Player	NO	YDS	AVG	TD
1.	Jerry Rice	1050	16377	15.6	154
2.	Art Monk	940	12721	13.5	68
3.	Steve Largent	819	13089	16.0	100
4.	Henry Ellard	775	13177	17.0	61
5.	Andre Reed	766	10884	14.2	75
6.	James Lofton	764	14004	18.3	75
7.	Charlie Joiner	750	12146	16.2	65
8.	Gary Clark	699	10856	15.5	65
9.	Cris Carter	667	8367	12.5	76
10.	Ozzie Newsome	662	7980	12.1	47
11.	Irving Fryar	650	10111	15.6	69
12.	Charley Taylor	649	9110	14.0	79
13.	Drew Hill	634	9831	15.5	60
14.	Don Maynard	633	11834	18.7	88
15.	Raymond Berry	631	9275	14.7	68
16.	Sterling Sharpe	595	8134	13.7	65
17.	Michael Irvin	591	9500	16.1	52
18.	Harold Carmichael	590	8985	15.2	79
19.	Fred Biletnikoff	589	8974	15.2	76
20.	Bill Brooks	583	8001	13.7	46
21.	Mark Clayton	582	8974	15.4	84
22.	Harold Jackson	579	10372	17.9	76
23.	Marcus Allen	576	5325	9.2	21
24.	Ernest Givins	571	8215	14.4	49
25.	Andre Rison	569	7747	13.6	66

Playoffs

	Player	NO	YDS	AVG	TD
1.	Jerry Rice	120	1742	14.5	18
2.	Michael Irvin	83	1283	15.5	8
3.	Andre Reed	80	1169	14.6	9
4.	Thurman Thomas	75	669	8.9	5
5.	Cliff Branch	73	1289	17.7	5
6.	Fred Biletnikoff	70	1167	16.7	10
7.	Drew Pearson	69	1131	16.4	8
	Art Monk	69	1062	15.4	7

	Player	Year	NO	YDS	AVG	TD
9.	Tony Nathan		65	649	10.0	2
10.	Roger Craig		63	606	9.6	2

Single Season

	Player	Year	NO	YDS	AVG	TD
1.	Herman Moore	1995	123	1686	13.7	14
2.	Jerry Rice	1995	122	1848	15.1	15
	Cris Carter	1995	122	1371	11.2	17
	Cris Carter	1994	122	1256	10.3	7
5.	Isaac Bruce	1995	119	1781	15.0	13
6.	Jerry Rice	1994	112	1499	13.4	13
	Sterling Sharpe	1993	112	1274	11.4	11
8.	Michael Irvin	1995	111	1603	14.4	10
	Terance Mathis	1994	111	1342	12.1	11
10.	Brett Perriman	1995	108	1488	13.8	9
	Sterling Sharpe	1992	108	1461	13.5	13
	Jerry Rice	1996	108	1254	11.6	8
13.	Art Monk	1984	106	1372	12.9	7
	Herman Moore	1996	106	1296	12.2	9
15.	Eric Metcalf	1995	104	1189	11.4	8
16.	Robert Brooks	1995	102	1497	14.7	13
17.	Charley Hennigan	1964	101	1546	15.3	8
	Larry Centers	1995	101	962	9.5	2
19.	Jerry Rice	1990	100	1502	15.0	13
	Haywood Jeffires	1991	100	1181	11.8	7
	Carl Pickens	1996	100	1180	11.8	12
	Lionel Taylor	1961	100	1176	11.8	4
23.	Carl Pickens	1995	99	1234	12.5	17
	Larry Centers	1996	99	766	7.7	7
25.	Jerry Rice	1993	98	1503	15.3	15

Interceptions

	Player	Year	NO	YDS	AVG	TD

Career

	Player	Year	NO	YDS	AVG	TD
1.	Paul Krause		81	1185	14.6	3
2.	Emlen Tunnell		79	1282	16.2	4
3.	Night Train Lane		68	1207	17.8	5
4.	Ken Riley		65	596	9.2	5
5.	Ronnie Lott		63	730	11.6	5
6.	Dick LeBeau		62	762	12.3	3
	Dave Brown		62	698	11.3	5
8.	Emmitt Thomas		58	937	16.2	5
9.	Bobby Boyd		57	994	17.4	4
	Johnny Robinson		57	741	13.0	1
	Mel Blount		57	736	12.9	2
	Everson Walls		57	504	8.8	1
13.	Lem Barney		56	1077	19.2	7
	Pat Fischer		56	941	16.8	4
15.	Willie Brown		54	472	8.7	2
16.	Bobby Dillon		52	976	18.8	5
	Jack Butler		52	827	15.9	3
	Larry Wilson		52	800	15.4	5
	Jimmy Patton		52	712	13.7	2
	Mel Renfro		52	626	12.0	3

	Player	Year	NO	YDS	AVG	TD
21.	Bobby Bryant		51	749	14.7	3
	Donnie Shell		51	490	9.6	2
23.	Yale Lary		50	787	15.7	2
	Deron Cherry		50	688	13.8	1
	Don Burroughs		50	564	11.3	0
	John Harris		50	560	11.2	2

Playoffs

	Player	Year	NO	YDS	AVG	TD
1.	Ronnie Lott		9	187	20.8	2
	Bill Simpson		9	149	16.6	1
	Charlie Waters		9	124	13.8	0
4.	Lester Hayes		8	107	13.4	2
5.	Willie Brown		7	196	28.0	3
	Dennis Thurman		7	126	18.0	1
7.	Glen Edwards		6	151	25.2	0
	Cliff Harris		6	103	17.2	0
	Bobby Bryant		6	80	13.3	1
	Vernon Perry		6	75	12.5	1
	Eric Davis		6	50	8.3	1

Single Season

	Player	Year	NO	YDS	AVG	TD
1.	Night Train Lane	1952	14	298	21.3	2
2.	Lester Hayes	1980	13	273	21.0	1
	Dan Sandifer	1948	13	258	19.8	2
	Spec Sanders	1950	13	199	15.3	0
5.	Woodley Lewis	1950	12	275	22.9	0
	Jack Christiansen	1953	12	238	19.8	1
	Emmitt Thomas	1974	12	214	17.8	2
	Mike Reinfeldt	1979	12	205	17.1	0
	Freddy Glick	1963	12	180	15.0	1
	Don Doll	1950	12	163	13.6	1
	Bob Nussbaumer	1949	12	157	13.1	0
	Dainard Paulson	1964	12	157	13.1	1
	Paul Krause	1964	12	140	11.7	1
14.	Don Doll	1949	11	301	27.4	1
	Bill Bradley	1971	11	248	22.5	0
	Otto Schnellbacher	1948	11	239	21.7	1
	Otto Schnellbacher	1951	11	194	17.6	2
	Jimmy Patton	1958	11	183	16.6	0
	Lindon Crow	1956	11	170	15.5	0
	Ron Hall	1964	11	148	13.5	0
	Everson Walls	1981	11	133	12.1	0
	Lee Riley	1962	11	122	11.1	0
	Mel Blount	1975	11	121	11.0	0
	Tom Keane	1953	11	118	10.7	0
	Sammy Baugh	1943	11	112	10.2	0
	Will Sherman	1955	11	101	9.2	0
	Goose Gonsoulin	1960	11	98	8.9	0

Punting

	Player	Year	NO	YDS	AVG
Career					
1.	Sammy Baugh		329	15180	46.14
2.	Tommy Davis		509	22833	44.86

	Player	Year	NO	YDS	AVG
3.	Bob Scarpitto		279	12408	44.47
4.	Jerry Norton		356	15671	44.02
5.	Greg Montgomery		441	19291	43.744
6.	Sean Landeta		807	35295	43.736
7.	Don Chandler		656	28679	43.72
8.	Dave Lewis		285	12447	43.67
9.	Horace Gillom		486	21207	43.64
10.	Reggie Roby		859	37391	43.53
11.	Rick Tuten		566	24622	43.50
12.	Jerrel Wilson		1062	46139	43.45
13.	Rohn Stark		1121	48658	43.41
14.	Jim Fraser		271	11736	43.31
15.	Bob Waterfield		310	13380	43.16
16.	Norm Van Brocklin		520	22433	43.14
17.	Tom Rouen		260	11181	43.00
18.	Danny Villanueva		486	20862	42.93
19.	Curley Johnson		552	23650	42.84
20.	Sam Baker		701	29974	42.80
21.	Rich Camarillo		1027	43895	42.74
22.	Bobby Joe Green		967	41317	42.73
23.	Tommy Barnhardt		619	26403	42.65
24.	Jim Norton		515	21961	42.64
25.	Yale Lary		499	22279	42.52

Playoffs

	Player	Year	NO	YDS	AVG
1.	Rich Camarillo		35	1559	44.54
2.	Lee Johnson		28	1244	44.43
3.	John Kidd		37	1612	43.57
4.	Don Chandler		50	2168	43.36
5.	John Jett		33	1415	42.88
6.	Marv Bateman		29	1235	42.59
7.	Bob Waterfield		35	1490	42.57
8.	Bryan Barker		51	2167	42.49
9.	Ray Guy		111	4705	42.39
10.	Craig Colquitt		26	1094	42.08

Single Season

	Player	Year	NO	YDS	AVG
1.	Sammy Baugh	1940	34	1799	52.91
2.	Glenn Dobbs	1948	65	3336	51.32
3.	Frank Reagan	1950	54	2770	51.30
4.	Glenn Dobbs	1946	78	3824	49.00
5.	Yale Lary	1963	35	1713	48.94
6.	Sammy Baugh	1943	47	2295	48.83
7.	Sammy Baugh	1941	30	1462	48.73
8.	Yale Lary	1961	52	2519	48.44
9.	Frankie Albert	1949	31	1495	48.23
10.	Bob Reinhard	1947	27	1279	47.37
11.	Joe Muha	1948	57	2962	47.20
	George Gulyanics	1949	29	1369	47.20
13.	Yale Lary	1959	45	2121	47.13
14.	Yale Lary	1962	51	2402	47.10
15.	Bobby Joe Green	1961	73	3431	47.00
16.	Greg Montgomery	1992	53	2487	46.92
17.	Pat Brady	1953	80	3752	46.90
18.	Gary Collins	1965	65	3035	46.69

	Player	Year	NO	YDS	AVG
19.	Don Chandler	1959	55	2565	46.64
20.	Tommy Davis	1963	71	3311	46.63
21.	Sammy Baugh	1942	37	1725	46.62
22.	Bobby Joe Green	1963	64	2974	46.47
23.	Horace Gillom	1952	60	2787	46.45
24.	Bobby Walden	1964	72	3341	46.403
25.	Bob Reinhard	1946	43	1996	46.400
	Sammy Baugh	1947	33	1530	46.400

Sacks (since 1982)

	Player	Year	NO

Career

1.	Reggie White	166
2.	Bruce Smith	140
3.	Richard Dent	133
	Lawrence Taylor	133
5.	Rickey Jackson	128
6.	Kevin Greene	123
7.	Chris Doleman	116
8.	Sean Jones	113
	Leslie O'Neal	113
10.	Greg Townsend	110
11.	Pat Swilling	106
12.	Jim Jeffcoat	102
13.	Clyde Simmons	101
14.	Andre Tippett	100
15.	Derrick Thomas	98
16.	Charles Haley	97.5
	Dexter Manley	97.5
	Jacob Green	97.5
	Simon Fletcher	97.5
20.	Steve McMichael	95
21.	William Fuller	94.5
22.	Neil Smith	86.5
23.	Howie Long	84
24.	Leonard Marshall	83.5
25.	Charles Mann	83

Playoffs

1.	Bruce Smith	12
2.	Richard Dent	11
	Charles Haley	11
	Reggie White	11
5.	Tony Tolbert	9.5
6.	Charles Mann	9
	Jeff Wright	9
8.	Sean Jones	8
9.	Kevin Greene	7.5
	Jim Jeffcoat	7.5

Single Season

1.	Mark Gastineau	1984	22
2.	Reggie White	1987	21
	Chris Doleman	1989	21

	Player	Year	NO			
4.	Lawrence Taylor	1986	20.5			
5.	Derrick Thomas	1990	20			
6.	Tim Harris	1989	19.5			
7.	Mark Gastineau	1983	19			
	Bruce Smith	1990	19			
	Clyde Simmons	1992	19			
10.	Andre Tippett	1984	18.5			
	Dexter Manley	1986	18.5			
12.	Reggie White	1986	18			
	Reggie White	1988	18			
	Keith Millard	1989	18			
15.	Fred Dean	1983	17.5			
	Richard Dent	1984	17.5			
	Bryce Paup	1995	17.5			
18.	Richard Dent	1985	17			
	Pat Swilling	1991	17			
	Tim Harris	1992	17			
	Leslie O'Neal	1992	17			
22.	Andre Tippett	1985	16.5			
	Kevin Greene	1988	16.5			
	Kevin Greene	1989	16.5			
	Pat Swilling	1989	16.5			

Kickoff Returns

	Player	Year	NO	YDS	AVG	TD
Career						
1.	Gale Sayers		91	2781	30.6	6
2.	Lynn Chandnois		92	2720	29.6	3
3.	Abe Woodson		193	5538	28.7	5
4.	Buddy Young		125	3465	27.7	4
5.	Travis Williams		102	2801	27.5	6
6.	Joe Arenas		139	3798	27.3	1
7.	Clarence Davis		79	2140	27.1	0
8.	Steve Van Buren		76	2030	26.71	3
9.	Lenny Lyles		81	2161	26.67	3
10.	Mercury Morris		111	2947	26.55	3
11.	Bobby Jancik		158	4185	26.48	0
12.	Mel Renfro		85	2246	26.42	2
13.	Bobby Mitchell		102	2690	26.37	5
14.	Ollie Matson		143	3746	26.2	6
15.	Alvin Haymond		170	4438	26.11	2
16.	Noland Smith		82	2137	26.06	1
17.	Al Nelson		101	2625	25.99	0
18.	Timmy Brown		184	4781	25.98	5
19.	Vic Washington		129	3341	25.90	1
20.	Dave Hampton		113	2923	25.87	3
21.	Larry Garron		89	2299	25.83	2
22.	Clarence Childs		134	3454	25.78	2
23.	Herb Adderley		120	3080	25.7	2
24.	Tamarick Vanover		76	1949	25.6	3
25.	Terry Metcalf		121	3087	25.5	2
Playoffs						
1.	Carl Garrett		16	481	30.1	0
2.	George Atkinson		12	335	27.9	0

	Player	Year	NO	YDS	AVG	TD
3.	Dennis Gentry		17	435	25.6	0
4.	Andre Coleman		19	481	25.3	1
5.	O.J. McDuffie		10	249	24.9	0
6.	Mel Gray		16	388	24.3	0
7.	Larry Anderson		16	387	24.2	0
8.	Mike Nelms		13	308	23.7	0
9.	Fulton Walker		29	677	23.3	1
10.	Antonio Freeman		11	255	23.2	0

Single Season

	Player	Year	NO	YDS	AVG	TD
1.	Travis Williams	1967	18	739	41.1	4
2.	Gale Sayers	1967	16	603	37.7	3
3.	Ollie Matson	1958	14	497	35.5	2
4.	Jim Duncan	1970	20	707	35.4	1
5.	Lynn Chandnois	1952	17	599	35.2	2
6.	Preston Pearson	1968	15	527	35.1	2
7.	Joe Arenas	1953	16	551	34.43	0
8.	Tommy Watkins	1965	17	584	34.35	0
9.	Vitamin Smith	1950	22	742	33.7	3
10.	Bobby Ray Williams	1969	17	563	33.12	1
11.	Tom Moore	1960	12	397	33.08	0
12.	Chet Mutryn	1947	21	691	32.90	1
13.	Duriel Harris	1976	17	559	32.88	0
14.	Ron Brown	1985	28	918	32.8	3
15.	Cecil Turner	1970	23	752	32.7	4
16.	Lynn Chandnois	1951	12	390	32.5	0
17.	Abe Woodson	1963	29	935	32.2	3
18.	Tommy Wilson	1956	15	477	31.8	1
19.	Gary Ballman	1963	22	698	31.73	1
20.	Walter Payton	1975	14	444	31.71	0
21.	Jack Salschneider	1949	15	474	31.6	1
22.	Gale Sayers	1965	21	660	31.43	1
23.	Frank Seno	1946	13	408	31.38	1
24.	Abe Woodson	1962	37	1157	31.27	0
25.	Ken Hall	1960	19	594	31.26	1

Punt Returns

	Player	Year	NO	YDS	AVG	TD

Career

	Player	Year	NO	YDS	AVG	TD
1.	Darrien Gordon		103	1407	13.66	3
2.	Desmond Howard		92	1230	13.37	4
3.	George McAfee		112	1431	12.78	2
4.	Jack Christiansen		85	1084	12.75	8
5.	Claude Gibson		110	1381	12.55	3
6.	Bill Dudley		124	1515	12.22	3
7.	Rick Upchurch		248	3008	12.13	8
8.	Billy Johnson		282	3317	11.76	6
9.	Mack Herron		84	982	11.69	0
10.	Billy Thompson		157	1814	11.55	0
11.	Henry Ellard		135	1527	11.311	4
12.	Rodger Bird		94	1063	11.309	0
13.	Bosh Pritchard		95	1072	11.28	2
14.	Brian Mitchell		195	2196	11.26	6
15.	Terry Metcalf		84	936	11.14	1
16.	Bob Hayes		104	1158	11.13	3

	Player	Year	NO	YDS	AVG	TD
17.	Mel Gray		233	2592	11.12	3
18.	Floyd Little		81	893	11.025	2
19.	Louis Lipps		112	1234	11.018	3
20.	Bobby Joe Edmonds		134	1471	10.98	1
21.	Speedy Duncan		202	2201	10.90	4
22.	Vai Sikahema		292	3169	10.85	4
23.	Jeff Burris		79	847	10.72	0
24.	Jo Jo Townsell		127	1360	10.709	2
25.	Dave Meggett		299	3201	10.706	7

Playoffs

	Player	Year	NO	YDS	AVG	TD
1.	Anthony Carter		17	259	15.24	1
2.	Antonio Freeman		10	143	14.30	1
3.	Brian Mitchell		11	142	12.91	0
4.	Bob Hayes		12	151	12.58	0
5.	Mike Fuller		13	161	12.38	0
6.	Neal Colzie		18	221	12.28	0
7.	Jahine Arnold		10	111	11.10	0
8.	Butch Johnson		19	208	10.95	0
9.	Mike Nelms		15	164	10.93	0
10.	John Taylor		18	189	10.50	0

Single Season

	Player	Year	NO	YDS	AVG	TD
1.	Herb Rich	1950	12	276	23.00	1
2.	Jack Christiansen	1952	15	322	21.47	2
3.	Dick Christy	1961	18	383	21.28	2
4.	Rex Bamgardner	1948	16	336	21.00	2
5.	Red Cochran	1949	15	314	20.93	2
6.	Jerry Davis	1948	16	334	20.88	2
7.	Bob Hayes	1968	15	312	20.80	2
8.	Frankie Sinkwich	1943	11	228	20.73	0
9.	Buddy Young	1951	12	231	19.25	1
10.	Billy Joe Grimes	1950	29	555	19.14	2
11.	Jack Christiansen	1951	18	343	19.06	4
12.	Ollie Matson	1955	13	245	18.85	2
13.	Lemar Parrish	1974	18	338	18.78	2
14.	Chuck Fenenbock	1946	16	299	18.69	0
15.	Woodley Lewis	1952	19	351	18.47	2
16.	Frank Seno	1947	12	213	17.75	1
17.	Billy Reinhard	1948	16	276	17.25	1
18.	Bob Livingstone	1949	17	292	17.18	1
19.	Sam Catchcart	1949	18	306	17.00	0
	Dick Todd	1941	14	238	17.00	1
21.	Floyd Little	1967	16	270	16.88	1
22.	Dick Jauron	1974	17	286	16.82	0
23.	Jim Cason	1949	21	351	16.71	0
24.	Dick Christy	1962	15	250	16.67	2
25.	Andy Tomasic	1942	12	199	16.58	1

Part Four

Game Scores

Key

THE GAME SCORES

SAN FRANCISCO 49ERS

Day	Date		Opp	Score/R		Attend
Sun	9/4	A	NO	34-33	W	66,357
Sun	9/11	A	NYG	20-17	W	75,943
Sun	9/18	H	ATL	17-34	L	60,168
Sun	9/25	A	SEA	38-7	W	62,382
Sun	10/2	H	DET	20-13	W	58,285
Sun	10/9	H	DEN	*13-16	L	61,711
Sun	10/16	A	LARM	24-21	W	65,450
Mon	10/24	A	CHI	9-10	L	65,293
Sun	10/30	H	MIN	24-21	W	60,738
Sun	11/6	A	PHX	23-24	L	64,544
Sun	11/13	H	LARI	3-9	L	54,448
Mon	11/21	H	WAS	37-21	W	59,268
Sun	11/27	A	SD	48-10	W	51,484
Sun	12/4	A	ATL	13-3	W	44,048
Sun	12/11	H	NO	30-17	W	62,977
Sun	12/18	H	LARM	16-38	L	62,444
			NFC DIVISIONAL PLAYOFF			
Sun	1/1	H	MIN	34-9	W	61,848
			NFC CHAMPIONSHIP			
Sun	1/8	A	CHI	28-3	W	66,946
			SUPER BOWL XXIII			
Sun	1/22	N	CIN	20-16	W	75,129

A—Away game
H—Home game
N—Neutral site game

* Overtime game
** Double overtime game

OPP   Opponent, using the standard abbreviation for each team, according to the list on page ix.
SCORE/R   The score and result (**W**in, **L**oss or **T**ie) of each game.
ATTEND   The attendance for each game.

1920 APFA

AKRON PROS

Sun	10/10	H	COL	37-0	W	1,500
Sun	10/24	H	CLE	7-0	W	5,000
Sun	10/31	A	CAN	10-0	W	6,000
Sun	11/14	A	CLE	7-7	T	8,000
Sun	11/21	H	DAY	13-0	W	3,700
Thu	11/25	H	CAN	7-0	W	6,500
Sun	11/28	A	DAY	14-0	W	5,000
Sun	12/5	A	BUF	0-0	T	3,000
Sun	12/12	N	DEC	0-0	T	12,000

BUFFALO ALL-AMERICANS

Sun	10/31	H	ROC	17-6	W	7,500
Sun	11/14	H	COL	43-7	W	
Sun	11/21	H	CAN	0-3	L	9,000
Sun	11/28	H	CLE	7-0	W	5,000
Sat	12/4	N	CAN	7-3	W	12,000
Sun	12/5	H	AKR	0-0	T	3,000

CANTON BULLDOGS

Sun	10/17	H	CLE	7-0	W	7,000
Sun	10/24	A	DAY	20-20	T	5,000
Sun	10/31	H	AKR	0-10	L	6,000
Sun	11/7	A	CLE	18-0	W	8,000
Sun	11/14	H	CHIT	21-0	W	8,000
Sun	11/21	A	BUF	3-0	W	9,000
Thu	11/25	A	AKR	0-7	L	6,500
Sat	12/4	N	BUF	3-7	L	12,000

CHICAGO CARDINALS

Sun	10/10	A	CHIT	0-0	T	8,000
Sun	10/24	A	RI	0-7	L	4,000
Sun	10/31	H	DET	21-0	W	3,000
Sun	11/7	A	CHIT	6-3	W	7,000
Sun	11/28	H	DEC	7-6	W	5,300
Sun	12/5	H	DEC	0-10	L	8,500

CHICAGO TIGERS

Sun	10/10	H	CHIC	0-0	T	8,000
Sun	10/17	H	DET	12-0	W	5,000
Sun	10/24	H	DEC	0-10	L	4,000
Sun	10/31	A	RI	7-20	L	
Sun	11/7	H	CHIC	3-6	L	7,000
Sun	11/14	A	CAN	0-21	L	8,000
Thu	11/25	H	DEC	0-6	L	8,000

CLEVELAND TIGERS

Sun	10/10	A	DAY	0-0	T	
Sun	10/17	A	CAN	0-7	L	7,000
Sun	10/24	A	AKR	0-7	L	5,000
Sun	10/31	H	COL	7-0	W	3,000
Sun	11/7	H	CAN	0-18	L	8,000
Sun	11/14	H	AKR	7-7	T	8,000
Sun	11/28	A	BUF	0-7	L	5,000

COLUMBUS PANHANDLES

Sun	10/3	A	DAY	0-14	L	
Sun	10/10	A	AKR	0-37	L	1,500
Sun	10/24	A	DET	0-6	L	
Sun	10/31	A	CLE	0-7	L	3,000
Sun	11/14	A	BUF	7-43	L	

DAYTON TRIANGLES

Sun	10/3	H	COL	14-0	W	
Sun	10/10	H	CLE	0-0	T	
Sun	10/17	H	HAM	44-0	W	2,000
Sun	10/24	H	CAN	20-20	T	5,000
Sun	11/14	A	RI	21-0	W	
Sun	11/21	A	AKR	0-13	L	3,700
Thu	11/25	H	DET	28-0	W	
Sun	11/28	H	AKR	0-14	L	5,000

DECATUR STALEYS

Sun	10/17	A	RI	7-0	W	7,000
Sun	10/24	A	CHIT	10-0	W	4,000
Sun	11/7	A	RI	0-0	T	4,991
Sun	11/21	H	HAM	28-7	W	2,000
Thu	11/25	A	CHIT	6-0	W	8,000
Sun	11/28	A	CHIC	6-7	L	5,300
Sun	12/5	A	CHIC	10-0	W	8,500
Sun	12/12	N	AKR	0-0	T	12,000

DETROIT HERALDS

Sun	10/17	A	CHIT	0-12	L	5,000
Sun	10/24	H	COL	6-0	W	
Sun	10/31	A	CHIC	0-21	L	3,000
Thu	11/25	A	DAY	0-28	L	

HAMMOND PROS

Sun	10/10	A	RI	0-26	L	2,554
Sun	10/17	A	DAY	0-44	L	2,000
Sun	11/21	A	DEC	7-28	L	2,000

MUNCIE FLYERS

Sun	10/3	A	RI	0-45	L	3,100

ROCHESTER JEFFERSONS

Sun	10/31	A	BUF	6-17	L	7,500

ROCK ISLAND INDEPENDENTS

Sun	10/3	H	MUN	45-0	W	3,100
Sun	10/10	H	HAM	26-0	W	2,554
Sun	10/17	H	DEC	0-7	L	7,000
Sun	10/24	H	CHIC	7-0	W	4,000
Sun	10/31	H	CHIT	20-7	W	
Sun	11/7	H	DEC	0-0	T	4,991
Sun	11/14	H	DAY	0-21	L	

1921 APFA

AKRON PROS

Sun	9/25	H	COL	14-0	W	1,700
Sun	10/2	H	CIN	41-0	W	2,500
Sun	10/9	A	CHIC	23-0	W	6,000
Sun	10/16	A	DET	20-0	W	6,000
Sun	10/23	A	CAN	3-0	W	7,000
Sun	10/30	H	ROC	19-0	W	4,000
Sun	11/6	A	COL	21-0	W	4,100
Sun	11/13	A	BUF	0-0	T	4,600
Sun	11/20	A	DAY	0-3	L	
Thu	11/24	H	CAN	0-14	L	4,000
Sat	12/3	A	BUF	0-14	L	
Sun	12/4	A	CHIC	7-0	W	3,500

BUFFALO ALL-AMERICANS

Sun	10/2	H	HAM	17-0	W	3,500
Sun	10/9	H	COL	38-0	W	
Sun	10/16	H	NY	55-0	W	7,500
Sun	10/23	H	ROC	28-0	W	10,000
Sun	10/30	H	DET	21-0	W	7,000
Sun	11/6	H	CLE	10-6	W	3,000
Sun	11/13	H	AKR	0-0	T	4,600
Sun	11/20	H	CAN	7-7	T	3,500
Thu	11/24	A	DEC	7-6	W	
Sun	11/27	H	DAY	7-0	W	
Sat	12/3	H	AKR	14-0	W	
Sun	12/4	A	DEC	7-10	L	12,000

CANTON BULLDOGS

Sun	10/9	H	HAM	7-7	T	
Sun	10/16	A	DAY	14-14	T	
Sun	10/23	H	AKR	0-3	L	7,000
Sun	11/6	H	DAY	14-0	W	
Sun	11/13	A	CLE	7-0	W	3,500
Sun	11/20	A	BUF	7-7	T	3,500
Thu	11/24	A	AKR	14-0	W	4,000
Sun	11/27	A	WAS	15-0	W	4,000
Sun	12/11	A	DEC	0-10	L	1,900
Sun	12/18	A	WAS	28-14	W	3,500

CHICAGO CARDINALS

Sun	10/2	H	MIN	20-0	W	4,000
Sun	10/9	H	AKR	0-23	L	6,000
Sun	10/16	H	RI	7-14	L	4,000
Sun	10/23	H	COL	17-6	W	6,000
Sun	11/6	H	HAM	7-0	W	
Sun	11/20	H	GB	3-3	T	2,000
Sun	12/4	H	AKR	0-7	L	3,500
Sun	12/18	A	DEC	0-0	T	2,700

CINCINNATI CELTS

Sun	10/2	A	AKR	0-41	L	2,500
Sun	10/16	A	MUN	14-0	W	
Sun	10/23	A	CLE	0-28	L	
Sun	11/27	A	EVA	0-48	L	

CLEVELAND TIGERS

Sun	10/16	H	COL	35-9	W	3,000
Sun	10/23	H	CIN	28-0	W	
Sun	10/30	A	DAY	2-3	L	4,000
Sun	11/6	A	BUF	6-10	L	3,000
Sun	11/13	H	CAN	0-7	L	3,500
Sun	11/20	A	DEC	7-22	L	8,500
Sat	12/3	A	NY	17-0	W	3,000
Sun	12/11	A	WAS	0-7	L	5,000

COLUMBUS PANHANDLES

Sun	9/25	A	AKR	0-14	L	1,700
Sun	10/2	A	DAY	13-42	L	
Sun	10/9	A	BUF	0-38	L	
Sun	10/16	A	CLE	9-35	L	3,000
Sun	10/23	A	CHIC	6-17	L	6,000
Sun	10/30	A	MIN	0-28	L	
Sun	11/6	H	AKR	0-21	L	4,100
Sun	11/20	A	ROC	13-27	L	2,500
Sun	12/4	A	LOU	6-0	W	

DAYTON TRIANGLES

Sun	10/2	H	COL	42-13	W	
Sun	10/9	A	DET	7-10	L	
Sun	10/16	H	CAN	14-14	T	
Sun	10/23	A	DEC	0-7	L	8,000
Sun	10/30	H	CLE	3-2	W	4,000
Sun	11/6	A	CAN	0-14	L	
Sun	11/13	H	DET	27-0	W	
Sun	11/20	H	AKR	3-0	W	
Sun	11/27	A	BUF	0-7	L	

DECATUR STALEYS

Mon	10/10	H	RI	14-10	W	4,000
Sun	10/16	H	ROC	16-13	W	7,500
Sun	10/23	H	DAY	7-0	W	8,000
Sun	11/6	H	DET	20-9	W	6,500
Sun	11/13	H	RI	3-0	W	2,500
Sun	11/20	H	CLE	22-7	W	8,500
Thu	11/24	H	BUF	6-7	L	
Sun	11/27	H	GB	20-0	W	7,000
Sun	12/4	H	BUF	10-7	W	12,000
Sun	12/11	H	CAN	10-0	W	1,900
Sun	12/18	H	CHIC	0-0	T	2,700

DETROIT HERALDS

Sun	10/2	A	RI	0-0	T	3,304
Sun	10/9	H	DAY	10-7	W	
Sun	10/16	H	AKR	0-20	L	6,000
Sun	10/23	H	RI	0-14	L	3,000
Sun	10/30	A	BUF	0-21	L	7,000
Sun	11/6	A	DEC	9-20	L	6,500
Sun	11/13	A	DAY	0-27	L	

EVANSVILLE CRIMSON GIANTS

Sun	10/2	H	LOU	21-0	W	1,500
Sun	10/9	H	MUN	14-0	W	
Sun	10/16	H	HAM	0-3	L	
Sun	11/6	A	GB	6-43	L	
Sun	11/27	H	CIN	48-0	W	

GREEN BAY PACKERS

Sun	10/23	H	MIN	7-6	W	6,000
Sun	10/30	H	RI	3-13	L	6,000
Sun	11/6	H	EVA	43-6	W	
Sun	11/13	H	HAM	14-7	W	4,000
Sun	11/20	A	CHIC	3-3	T	2,000
Sun	11/27	A	DEC	0-20	L	7,000

HAMMOND PROS

Sun	10/2	A	BUF	0-17	L	3,500
Sun	10/9	A	CAN	7-7	T	
Sun	10/16	A	EVA	3-0	W	
Sun	11/6	A	CHIC	0-7	L	
Sun	11/13	A	GB	7-14	L	4,000

LOUISVILLE BRECKS

Sun	10/2	A	EVA	0-21	L	1,500
Sun	12/4	H	COL	0-6	L	

MINNEAPOLIS MARINES

Sun	10/2	A	CHIC	0-20	L	4,000
Sun	10/23	A	GB	6-7	L	6,000
Sun	10/30	H	COL	28-0	W	
Sun	11/6	A	RI	3-14	L	1,700

MUNCIE FLYERS

Sun	10/9	A	EVA	0-14	L	
Sun	10/16	H	CIN	0-14	L	

NEW YORK GIANTS

Sun	10/16	A	BUF	0-55	L	7,500
Sat	12/3	H	CLE	0-17	L	3,000

ROCHESTER JEFFERSONS

Sun	10/16	A	DEC	13-16	L	7,500
Sun	10/23	A	BUF	0-28	L	10,000
Sun	10/30	A	AKR	0-19	L	4,000
Sun	11/6	H	TON	45-0	W	2,700
Sun	11/20	H	COL	27-13	W	2,500
Sun	11/27	H	SYR	12-0	W	1,500
Sun	12/4	A	WAS	Forfeit Loss		400

ROCK ISLAND INDEPENDENTS

Sun	10/2	H	DET	0-0	T	3,304
Mon	10/10	A	DEC	10-14	L	4,000
Sun	10/16	A	CHIC	14-7	W	4,000
Sun	10/23	A	DET	14-0	W	3,000
Sun	10/30	A	GB	13-3	W	6,000
Sun	11/6	H	MIN	14-3	W	1,700
Sun	11/13	A	DEC	0-3	L	2,500

SYRACUSE PROS

Sun	10/9	H	TON	0-0	T	800
Sun	11/13	A	WAS	7-20	L	
Sun	11/27	A	ROC	0-12	L	1,500

TONAWANDA KARDEX

Sun	10/9	A	SYR	0-0	T	800
Sun	11/6	A	ROC	0-45	L	2,700

WASHINGTON PROS

Sun	11/13	H	SYR	20-7	W	
Sun	11/27	H	CAN	0-15	L	4,000
Sun	12/4	H	ROC	Forfeit Win		400
Sun	12/11	H	CLE	7-0	W	5,000
Sun	12/18	H	CAN	14-28	L	3,500

1922 NFL

AKRON PROS

Sun	10/1	H	COL	36-0	W	3,000
Thu	10/12	H	ROC	13-13	T	2,000
Sun	10/22	H	CAN	0-22	L	7,000
Sun	10/29	H	OOR	62-0	W	3,000
Sun	11/5	H	HAM	22-0	W	
Sun	11/12	A	CHIC	0-7	L	2,000
Sun	11/19	A	BUF	3-3	T	4,000
Sun	11/26	A	CHIB	10-20	L	6,000
Thu	11/30	A	CAN	0-14	L	3,500
Sun	12/3	A	BUF	0-16	L	

BUFFALO ALL-AMERICANS

Sun	10/1	H	HAM	7-0	W	3,500

Sun 10/15 H COL 19-0 W
Sun 10/22 A CHIB 0-7 L
Sun 10/29 A DAY 7-0 W 5,000
Sun 11/5 A CHIC 7-9 L 4,000
Sun 11/12 A CAN 0-3 L
Sun 11/19 H AKR 3-3 T 4,000
Sun 11/26 A OOR 7-19 L
Thu 11/30 A ROC 21-0 W 2,200
Sun 12/3 H AKR 16-0 W

CANTON BULLDOGS
Sun 10/1 H LOU 38-0 W 3,000
Sun 10/8 A DAY 0-0 T 3,000
Sun 10/15 H OOR 14-0 W 7,000
Sun 10/22 A AKR 22-0 W 7,000
Sun 10/29 A CHIB 7-6 W 10,000
Sun 11/5 H TOL 0-0 T
Sun 11/12 H BUF 3-0 W
Sun 11/19 A CHIC 7-0 W 7,500
Sun 11/26 H CHIC 20-3 W 2,500
Thu 11/30 A AKR 14-0 W 3,500
Sun 12/3 H MIL 40-6 W 3,000
Sun 12/10 A TOL 19-0 W 4,200

CHICAGO BEARS
Sun 10/1 A RAC 6-0 W 4,000
Sun 10/8 A RI 10-6 W 4,749
Sun 10/15 H ROC 7-0 W 7,000
Sun 10/22 H BUF 7-0 W
Sun 10/29 H CAN 6-7 L 10,000
Sun 11/5 H DAY 9-0 W
Sun 11/12 H OOR 33-6 W
Sun 11/19 H RI 3-0 W 5,600
Sun 11/26 H AKR 20-10 W 6,000
Thu 11/30 A CHIC 0-6 L 12,000
Sun 12/3 H TOL 22-0 W 6,000
Sun 12/10 A CHIC 0-9 L 12,000

CHICAGO CARDINALS
Sun 10/1 H MIL 3-0 W 3,500
Sun 10/15 H GB 16-3 W 3,500
Sun 10/22 H MIN 3-0 W 4,000
Sun 10/29 H COL 37-6 W 5,000
Sun 11/5 H BUF 9-7 W 4,000
Sun 11/12 H AKR 7-0 W 2,000
Sun 11/19 H CAN 0-7 L 7,500
Sun 11/26 A CAN 3-20 L 2,500
Thu 11/30 H CHIB 6-0 W 12,000
Sun 12/3 H DAY 3-7 L 8,000
Sun 12/10 H CHIB 9-0 W 12,000

COLUMBUS PANHANDLES
Sun 10/1 A AKR 0-36 L 3,000
Sun 10/8 A OOR 6-20 L 1,200
Sun 10/15 A BUF 0-19 L
Sun 10/29 A CHIC 6-37 L 5,000
Sun 11/5 A GB 0-3 L 2,000
Sat 11/11 A RAC 0-34 L 4,000
Sun 11/26 A TOL 6-7 L 1,700
Thu 11/30 H OOR 6-18 L 3,000

DAYTON TRIANGLES
Sun 10/1 H OOR 36-0 W
Sun 10/8 H CAN 0-0 T 3,000
Sun 10/15 H MIN 17-0 W
Sun 10/22 H HAM 20-0 W
Sun 10/29 H BUF 0-7 L 5,000
Sun 11/5 A CHIB 0-9 L
Sun 11/12 A RI 0-43 L
Sun 12/3 A CHIC 7-3 W 8,000

EVANSVILLE CRIMSON GIANTS
Sun 10/1 A TOL 0-15 L 2,000
Sun 10/15 A RI 0-60 L 1,200
Sun 11/12 A LOU 6-13 L

GREEN BAY PACKERS
Sun 10/1 A RI 14-19 L 3,500
Sun 10/8 H RAC 6-10 L 3,603
Sun 10/15 A CHIC 3-16 L 3,500
Sun 10/22 A MIL 0-0 T 6,500
Sun 10/29 H RI 0-0 T 3,100
Sun 11/5 H COL 3-0 W 2,000
Sun 11/12 H MIN 14-6 W 4,000
Sun 11/19 A RAC 3-3 T 3,000
Sun 11/26 H MIL 13-0 W
Sun 12/3 N RAC 14-0 W 4,500

HAMMOND PROS
Sun 10/1 A BUF 0-7 L 3,500
Sun 10/15 A TOL 0-14 L 2,500
Sun 10/22 A DAY 0-20 L
Sun 10/29 A MIL 0-0 T 4,000
Sun 11/5 A AKR 0-22 L
Sun 11/26 A RAC 0-6 L 1,084

LOUISVILLE BRECKS
Sun 10/1 A CAN 0-38 L 3,000
Sun 10/29 A TOL 0-39 L 2,500
Sun 11/5 A RAC 0-57 L 1,000
Sun 11/12 H EVA 13-6 W

MILWAUKEE BADGERS
Sun 10/1 A CHIC 0-3 L 3,500
Sun 10/8 A TOL 12-12 T 1,200
Sun 10/15 H RAC 20-0 W 5,003
Sun 10/22 H GB 0-0 T 6,500
Sun 10/29 H HAM 0-0 T 4,000
Sun 11/19 A OOR 13-0 W 6,500
Sun 11/26 A GB 0-13 L
Thu 11/30 A RAC 0-3 L 3,500
Sun 12/3 A CAN 6-40 L 3,000

MINNEAPOLIS MARINES
Sun 10/15 A DAY 0-17 L
Sun 10/22 A CHIC 0-3 L 4,000
Sun 11/5 H OOR 13-6 W 4,000
Sun 11/12 A GB 6-14 L 2,000

OORANG INDIANS
Sun 10/1 A DAY 0-36 L
Sun 10/8 H COL 20-6 W 1,200
Sun 10/15 A CAN 0-14 L 7,000
Sun 10/29 A AKR 0-62 L 3,000
Sun 11/5 A MIN 6-13 L 4,000
Sun 11/12 A CHIB 6-33 L
Sun 11/19 A MIL 0-13 L 6,500
Sun 11/26 A BUF 19-7 W
Thu 11/30 A COL 18-6 W 3,000

RACINE LEGION
Sun 10/1 H CHIB 0-6 L 4,000
Sun 10/8 A GB 10-6 W 3,603
Sun 10/15 A MIL 0-20 L 5,003
Sun 10/22 H TOL 0-7 L 3,000
Sun 10/29 H ROC 9-0 W 3,000
Sun 11/5 H LOU 57-0 W 1,000
Sat 11/11 H COL 34-0 W 4,000
Sun 11/19 H GB 3-3 T 3,000
Sun 11/26 H HAM 6-0 W 1,084
Thu 11/30 H MIL 3-0 W 3,500
Sun 12/3 N GB 0-14 L 4,500

ROCHESTER JEFFERSONS
Thu 10/12 A AKR 13-13 T 2,000
Sun 10/15 A CHIB 0-7 L 7,000
Sun 10/22 A RI 0-26 L 1,500
Sun 10/29 A RAC 0-9 L 3,000
Thu 11/30 H BUF 0-21 L 2,200

ROCK ISLAND INDEPENDENTS
Sun 10/1 H GB 19-14 W 3,500
Sun 10/8 H CHIB 6-10 L 4,749
Sun 10/15 H EVA 60-0 W 1,200
Sun 10/22 H ROC 26-0 W 1,500
Sun 10/29 A GB 0-0 T 3,100
Sun 11/12 H DAY 43-0 W
Sun 11/19 H CHIB 0-3 L 5,600

TOLEDO MAROONS
Sun 10/1 H EVA 15-0 W 2,000
Sun 10/8 H MIL 12-12 T 1,200
Sun 10/15 H HAM 14-0 W 2,500
Sun 10/22 A RAC 7-0 W 3,500
Sun 10/29 H LOU 39-0 W 2,500
Sun 11/5 A CAN 0-0 T
Sun 11/26 H COL 7-6 W 1,700
Sun 12/3 A CHIB 0-22 L 6,000
Sun 12/10 H CAN 0-19 L 4,200

1923 NFL

AKRON PROS
Sun 9/30 A DUL 7-10 L 3,000
Sun 10/7 A BUF 0-9 L
Sun 10/14 A CHIC 0-19 L
Sun 10/21 A RAC 7-9 L
Sun 10/28 A CAN 3-7 L 2,500
Sun 11/11 A CHIB 6-20 L 4,000
Thu 11/29 H BUF 2-0 W 1,700

BUFFALO ALL-AMERICANS
Sun 9/30 A CHIC 0-3 L
Sun 10/7 H AKR 9-0 W
Sun 10/14 A COL 3-0 W 3,500
Sun 10/21 H OOR 57-0 W
Sun 10/28 A CHIB 3-18 L
Sun 11/4 H CLE 0-0 T 3,000
Sun 11/11 H CAN 3-3 T 10,000
Sun 11/18 H DAY 3-0 W 3,500
Sun 11/25 H TOL 3-3 T
Thu 11/29 A AKR 0-2 L 1,700
Sat 12/1 A ROC 13-0 W
Sun 12/2 A CAN 0-14 L 3,000

CANTON BULLDOGS
Sun 9/30 H HAM 17-0 W 5,000
Sun 10/7 H LOU 37-0 W
Sun 10/14 H DAY 30-0 W
Sun 10/21 A CHIB 6-0 W
Sun 10/28 H AKR 7-3 W 2,500
Sun 11/4 A CHIC 7-3 W 5,500
Sun 11/11 A BUF 3-3 T 10,000
Sun 11/18 A OOR 41-0 W 5,000
Sun 11/25 A CLE 46-10 W 17,000
Thu 11/29 H TOL 28-0 W 3,000
Sun 12/2 H BUF 14-0 W 3,000
Sun 12/9 A COL 10-0 W 1,700

CHICAGO BEARS
Sun 9/30 A RI 0-3 L 3,500
Sun 10/7 A RAC 3-0 W 4,000
Sun 10/14 A GB 3-0 W 4,451
Sun 10/21 H CAN 0-6 L
Sun 10/28 H BUF 18-3 W
Sun 11/4 H OOR 26-0 W 1,000
Sun 11/11 H AKR 20-6 W 4,000
Sun 11/18 H RI 7-3 W 6,500
Sun 11/25 H HAM 14-7 W 3,500
Thu 11/29 H CHIC 3-0 W 13,500
Sun 12/2 H MIL 0-0 T
Sun 12/9 H RI 29-7 W 6,000
Sun 12/16 H MIL 7-7 T 7,500

CHICAGO CARDINALS
Sun 9/30 H BUF 3-0 W
Sun 10/7 H ROC 60-0 W 5,000
Sun 10/14 H AKR 19-0 W
Sun 10/21 H MIN 9-0 W 4,000
Sun 10/28 H DAY 13-3 W 5,000
Sun 11/4 H CAN 3-7 L 5,500
Sun 11/11 H HAM 6-0 W 3,500
Sun 11/18 H DUL 10-0 W 5,500
Sun 11/25 H RAC 4-10 L 6,500
Thu 11/29 A CHIB 0-3 L 13,500
Sun 12/2 H OOR 22-19 W 1,200
Sun 12/9 H MIL 12-14 L 5,500

CLEVELAND INDIANS
Sun 10/7 A RI 0-0 T 3,500
Sun 10/21 H STL 6-0 W 7,000
Sun 10/28 H OOR 27-0 W
Sun 11/4 A BUF 0-0 T 3,000
Sun 11/11 H DAY 0-0 T 11,000
Sun 11/18 H COL 9-3 W 6,000
Sun 11/25 H CAN 10-46 L 17,000

COLUMBUS TIGERS
Sun 9/30 A DAY 6-7 L 6,000
Sun 10/7 A MIL 0-0 T 2,000
Sun 10/14 H BUF 0-3 L 3,500
Sun 10/21 H LOU 34-0 W 2,500
Sun 10/28 H TOL 3-0 W 4,000
Sun 11/11 H TOL 16-0 W 3,500
Sun 11/18 A CLE 3-9 L 6,000
Sun 11/25 H OOR 27-3 W
Sun 12/2 H DAY 30-3 W 3,000
Sun 12/9 H CAN 0-10 L 1,700

DAYTON TRIANGLES
Sun 9/30 H COL 7-6 W 6,000
Sun 10/7 H HAM 0-7 L
Sun 10/14 H CAN 0-30 L
Sun 10/21 H TOL 3-6 L 3,000
Sun 10/28 A CHIC 3-13 L 5,000
Sun 11/11 A CLE 0-0 T 11,000
Sun 11/18 A BUF 0-3 L 3,500
Sun 12/2 A COL 3-30 L 3,000

DULUTH KELLEYS
Sun 9/30 H AKR 10-7 W 3,000
Sun 10/7 A MIN 10-0 W 2,500
Sun 10/21 H HAM 3-0 W
Sun 10/28 H MIN 9-0 W 3,000
Sun 11/11 A MIL 3-6 L 5,000
Sun 11/18 A CHIC 0-10 L 5,500
Sun 11/25 A GB 0-10 L 3,000

GREEN BAY PACKERS
Sun 9/30 H MIN 12-0 W 3,008
Sun 10/7 H STL 0-0 T 2,831
Sun 10/14 H CHIB 0-3 L 4,451
Sun 10/21 H MIL 12-0 W 5,000
Sun 10/28 H RAC 3-24 L 2,800
Sun 11/4 A STL 3-0 W 750
Sun 11/11 A RAC 16-0 W 5,000
Sun 11/18 A MIL 10-7 W 5,400
Sun 11/25 H DUL 10-0 W 3,000
Thu 11/29 H HAM 19-0 W

HAMMOND PROS
Sun 9/30 A CAN 0-17 L 5,000
Sun 10/7 H DAY 7-0 W
Sun 10/14 A STL 0-0 T 600
Sun 10/21 A DUL 0-3 L
Sun 11/11 A CHIC 0-6 L 3,500
Sun 11/25 A CHIB 7-14 L 3,500
Thu 11/29 A GB 0-19 L

LOUISVILLE BRECKS
Sun 10/7 A CAN 0-37 L
Sun 10/21 A COL 0-34 L 2,500
Sun 12/9 H OOR 0-12 L

MILWAUKEE BADGERS

Sun	9/30	H	OOR	13-2	W	4,000
Sun	10/7	H	COL	0-0	T	2,000
Sun	10/14	H	RAC	7-7	T	4,000
Sun	10/21	A	GB	0-12	L	5,000
Sun	10/28	H	STL	6-0	W	1,700
Sun	11/4	A	RI	14-3	W	2,500
Sun	11/11	H	DUL	6-3	W	5,000
Sun	11/18	H	GB	7-10	L	5,400
Sat	11/24	A	STL	17-0	W	2,395
Thu	11/29	A	RAC	16-0	W	
Sun	12/2	A	CHIB	0-0	T	
Sun	12/9	A	CHIC	14-12	W	5,500
Sun	12/16	A	CHIB	7-7	T	7,500

MINNEAPOLIS MARINES

Sun	9/30	A	GB	0-12	L	3,008
Sun	10/7	H	DUL	0-10	L	2,500
Sun	10/14	H	OOR	23-0	W	4,000
Sun	10/21	A	CHIC	0-9	L	4,000
Sun	10/28	A	DUL	0-9	L	3,000
Sun	11/4	H	RAC	13-6	W	1,200
Sun	11/11	H	RI	6-6	T	
Sun	11/25	A	RI	6-6	T	
Sun	12/2	A	RAC	0-23	L	

OORANG INDIANS

Sun	9/30	A	MIL	2-13	L	4,000
Sun	10/7	A	TOL	0-7	L	5,500
Sun	10/14	A	MIN	0-23	L	4,000
Sun	10/21	A	BUF	0-57	L	
Sun	10/28	A	CLE	0-27	L	
Sun	11/4	A	CHIB	0-26	L	1,000
Sun	11/11	A	STL	7-14	L	5,000
Sun	11/18	A	CAN	0-41	L	5,000
Sun	11/25	A	COL	3-27	L	
Sun	12/2	A	CHIC	19-22	L	1,200
Sun	12/9	A	LOU	12-0	W	

RACINE LEGION

Sun	9/30	H	TOL	7-7	T	3,500
Sun	10/7	H	CHIB	0-3	L	4,000
Sun	10/14	A	MIL	7-7	T	4,000
Sun	10/21	H	AKR	9-7	W	
Sun	10/28	A	GB	24-3	W	2,800
Sun	11/4	A	MIN	6-13	L	1,200
Sun	11/11	H	GB	0-16	L	3,500
Sun	11/25	A	CHIC	10-4	W	6,500
Thu	11/29	H	MIL	0-16	L	
Sun	12/2	H	MIN	23-0	W	

ROCHESTER JEFFERSONS

Sun	10/7	A	CHIC	0-60	L	5,000
Sun	10/14	A	RI	0-56	L	2,500
Sat	11/24	H	TOL	6-12	L	
Sat	12/1	H	BUF	0-13	L	

ROCK ISLAND INDEPENDENTS

Sun	9/30	H	CHIB	3-0	W	3,500
Sun	10/7	H	CLE	0-0	T	3,500
Sun	10/14	H	ROC	56-0	W	2,500
Sun	11/4	H	MIL	3-14	L	2,500
Sun	11/11	A	MIN	6-6	T	
Sun	11/18	A	CHIB	3-7	L	6,500
Sun	11/25	H	MIN	6-6	T	
Sun	12/9	A	CHIB	7-29	L	6,000

ST. LOUIS ALL-STARS

Sun	10/7	A	GB	0-0	T	2,831
Sun	10/14	H	HAM	0-0	T	600
Sun	10/21	A	CLE	0-6	L	7,000
Sun	10/28	A	MIL	0-6	L	1,700
Sun	11/4	H	GB	0-3	L	750
Sun	11/11	H	OOR	14-7	W	5,000
Sat	11/24	H	MIL	0-17	L	2,395

TOLEDO MAROONS

Sun	9/30	A	RAC	7-7	T	3,500
Sun	10/7	H	OOR	7-0	W	5,500
Sun	10/21	H	DAY	6-3	W	3,000
Sun	10/28	A	COL	0-3	L	4,000
Sun	11/11	A	COL	0-16	L	3,500
Sat	11/24	A	ROC	12-6	W	
Sun	11/25	A	BUF	3-3	T	
Thu	11/29	A	CAN	0-28	L	3,000

1924 NFL

AKRON PROS

Sun	10/5	A	ROC	3-0	W	1,200
Sun	10/12	A	CLE	14-29	L	
Sun	10/26	A	BUF	13-17	L	8,000
Sat	11/1	A	FRA	0-23	L	8,000
Sun	11/2	A	COL	0-30	L	3,000
Sun	11/9	H	CLE	7-20	L	5,000
Sun	11/16	A	CHIC	0-13	L	2,500
Thu	11/27	H	BUF	22-0	W	1,000

BUFFALO BISONS

Sun	10/5	H	COL	13-0	W	5,000
Sun	10/12	H	DAY	0-7	L	6,000
Sun	10/19	H	ROC	26-0	W	5,000
Sun	10/26	H	AKR	17-13	W	8,000
Sun	11/2	H	FRA	0-24	L	6,000
Sun	11/9	H	KEN	27-0	W	3,500
Sun	11/16	H	DAY	14-6	W	2,700
Sat	11/22	A	ROC	16-0	W	
Sun	11/23	H	MIL	0-23	L	
Thu	11/27	A	AKR	0-22	L	1,000
Sat	11/29	A	FRA	7-45	L	7,000

CHICAGO BEARS

Sun	9/28	A	RI	0-0	T	4,500
Sun	10/5	A	CLE	14-16	L	
Sun	10/12	H	RAC	10-10	T	10,000
Sun	10/19	H	CHIC	6-0	W	12,000
Sun	10/26	H	FRA	33-3	W	6,000
Sun	11/2	H	RI	3-3	T	6,000
Sun	11/9	H	COL	12-6	W	6,000
Sun	11/16	H	RAC	3-3	T	6,500
Sun	11/23	H	GB	3-0	W	6,000
Thu	11/27	A	CHIC	21-0	W	6,000
Sun	11/30	H	MIL	31-14	W	1,000

CHICAGO CARDINALS

Sun	9/28	H	MIL	17-7	W	4,000
Sun	10/5	H	GB	3-0	W	2,852
Sun	10/12	H	MIN	13-0	W	8,000
Sun	10/19	A	CHIB	0-6	L	12,000
Sun	10/26	H	HAM	3-6	L	2,500
Sun	11/2	H	MIL	8-17	L	3,000
Sun	11/9	H	DAY	23-0	W	2,500
Sun	11/16	H	AKR	13-0	W	2,500
Sun	11/23	H	RAC	10-10	T	4,000
Thu	11/27	H	CHIB	0-21	L	6,000

CLEVELAND BULLDOGS

Sun	10/5	H	CHIB	16-14	W	
Sat	10/11	A	FRA	3-3	T	
Sun	10/12	H	AKR	29-14	W	
Sun	10/26	H	ROC	59-0	W	5,000
Sun	11/2	H	DAY	35-0	W	
Sun	11/9	A	AKR	20-7	W	5,000
Sun	11/16	H	FRA	7-12	L	
Sun	11/23	H	COL	7-0	W	
Thu	11/27	N	MIL	53-10	W	4,000

COLUMBUS TIGERS

Sun	10/5	A	BUF	0-13	L	5,000
Sun	10/12	A	ROC	15-7	W	2,000
Sat	10/18	A	FRA	7-23	L	10,000
Sun	10/26	A	DAY	17-6	W	3,000
Sun	11/2	H	AKR	30-0	W	3,000
Sun	11/9	A	CHIB	6-12	L	6,000
Sun	11/16	H	ROC	16-0	W	2,500
Sun	11/23	A	CLE	0-7	L	

DAYTON TRIANGLES

Sun	10/5	H	FRA	19-7	W	4,000
Sun	10/12	A	BUF	7-0	W	6,000
Sun	10/19	A	RI	0-20	L	4,500
Sun	10/26	H	COL	6-17	L	3,000
Sun	11/2	A	CLE	0-35	L	
Sun	11/9	A	CHIC	0-23	L	2,500
Sun	11/16	A	BUF	6-14	L	2,700
Thu	11/27	A	FRA	7-32	L	18,000

DULUTH KELLEYS

Sun	9/28	H	GB	6-3	W	2,200
Sun	10/5	H	MIN	3-0	W	3,000
Sun	10/26	H	KEN	32-0	W	
Sun	11/2	A	MIN	6-0	W	
Sun	11/9	A	GB	0-13	L	2,700
Sun	11/23	A	RI	9-0	W	2,500

FRANKFORD YELLOW JACKETS

Sat	9/27	H	ROC	21-0	W	7,000
Sat	10/4	H	KEN	31-6	W	7,000
Sun	10/5	A	DAY	7-19	L	4,000
Sat	10/11	H	CLE	3-3	T	
Sat	10/18	H	COL	23-7	W	10,000
Sun	10/26	A	CHIB	3-33	L	6,000
Sat	11/1	H	AKR	23-0	W	8,000
Sun	11/2	A	BUF	24-0	W	6,000
Sat	11/8	H	KC	42-7	W	10,000
Sat	11/15	H	MIN	39-7	W	8,000
Sun	11/16	A	CLE	12-7	W	
Sat	11/22	H	MIL	21-6	W	5,000
Thu	11/27	H	DAY	32-7	W	18,000
Sat	11/29	H	BUF	45-7	W	7,000

GREEN BAY PACKERS

Sun	9/28	A	DUL	3-6	L	2,200
Sun	10/5	A	CHIC	0-3	L	2,852
Sun	10/12	H	KC	16-0	W	2,800
Sun	10/19	H	MIL	17-0	W	4,150
Sun	10/26	H	MIN	19-0	W	2,500
Sun	11/2	H	RAC	6-3	W	4,000
Sun	11/9	H	DUL	13-0	W	2,700
Sun	11/16	A	MIL	17-10	W	3,800
Sun	11/23	A	CHIB	0-3	L	6,000
Thu	11/27	A	KC	17-6	W	1,543
Sun	11/30	A	RAC	0-7	L	2,200

HAMMOND PROS

Sun	9/28	A	RAC	0-10	L	3,000
Sun	10/12	A	RI	0-26	L	3,000
Sun	10/19	A	KEN	6-6	T	600
Sun	10/26	A	CHIC	6-3	W	2,500
Sun	11/2	A	KC	6-0	W	

KANSAS CITY BLUES

Sun	10/5	A	MIL	0-3	L	
Sun	10/12	A	GB	0-16	L	2,800
Sun	10/19	A	RAC	3-13	L	
Sun	10/26	H	RI	23-7	W	
Sun	11/2	H	HAM	0-6	L	
Sat	11/8	A	FRA	7-42	L	10,000
Tue	11/11	H	MIL	7-3	W	3,000
Sun	11/16	A	RI	0-17	L	3,000
Thu	11/27	H	GB	6-17	L	1,543

KENOSHA MAROONS

Sat	10/4	A	FRA	6-31	L	7,000
Sun	10/12	A	MIL	0-21	L	1,000
Sun	10/19	H	HAM	6-6	T	600
Sun	10/26	A	DUL	0-32	L	
Sun	11/9	A	BUF	0-27	L	3,500

MILWAUKEE BADGERS

Sun	9/28	A	CHIC	7-17	L	4,000
Sun	10/5	H	KC	3-0	W	
Sun	10/12	H	KEN	21-0	W	1,000
Sun	10/19	A	GB	0-17	L	4,150
Sun	10/26	H	RAC	0-10	L	4,000
Sun	11/2	A	CHIC	17-8	W	3,000
Sun	11/9	H	MIN	28-7	W	
Tue	11/11	A	KC	3-7	L	3,000
Sun	11/16	H	GB	10-17	L	3,800
Sat	11/22	A	FRA	6-21	L	5,000
Sun	11/23	A	BUF	23-0	W	
Thu	11/27	N	CLE	10-53	L	4,000
Sun	11/30	A	CHIB	14-31	L	1,000

MINNEAPOLIS MARINES

Sun	10/5	A	DUL	0-3	L	3,000
Sun	10/12	A	CHIC	0-13	L	8,000
Sun	10/26	A	GB	0-19	L	2,500
Sun	11/2	H	DUL	0-6	L	
Sun	11/9	A	MIL	7-28	L	
Sat	11/15	A	FRA	7-39	L	8,000

RACINE LEGION

Sun	9/28	H	HAM	10-0	W	3,000
Sun	10/5	A	RI	0-9	L	3,500
Sun	10/12	A	CHIB	10-10	T	10,000
Sun	10/19	H	KC	13-3	W	
Sun	10/26	A	MIL	10-0	W	4,000
Sun	11/2	A	GB	3-6	L	4,000
Sun	11/9	H	RI	3-6	L	3,500
Sun	11/16	A	CHIB	3-3	T	6,500
Sun	11/23	A	CHIC	10-10	T	4,000
Sun	11/30	H	GB	7-0	W	2,200

ROCHESTER JEFFERSONS

Sat	9/27	A	FRA	0-21	L	7,000
Sun	10/5	H	AKR	0-3	L	1,200
Sun	10/12	H	COL	7-15	L	2,000
Sun	10/19	A	BUF	0-26	L	5,000
Sun	10/26	A	CLE	0-59	L	5,000
Sun	11/16	A	COL	0-16	L	2,500
Sat	11/22	H	BUF	0-16	L	

ROCK ISLAND INDEPENDENTS

Sun	9/28	H	CHIB	0-0	T	4,500
Sun	10/5	H	RAC	9-0	W	3,500
Sun	10/12	H	HAM	26-0	W	3,000
Sun	10/19	H	DAY	20-0	W	4,500
Sun	10/26	A	KC	7-23	L	
Sun	11/2	A	CHIB	3-3	T	6,000
Sun	11/9	A	RAC	6-3	W	3,500
Sun	11/16	H	KC	17-0	W	3,000
Sun	11/23	H	DUL	0-9	L	2,500

1925 NFL

AKRON PROS

Sun	9/27	H	CLE	7-0	W	1,500
Sun	10/4	H	KC	14-7	W	
Sun	10/11	A	BUF	0-0	T	
Sun	10/18	A	CAN	20-3	W	4,500
Sun	10/25	A	DET	0-0	T	5,400
Sun	11/1	H	DAY	17-3	W	2,500
Sat	11/7	A	FRA	7-17	L	12,000
Sun	11/8	A	POT	0-21	L	

BUFFALO BISONS

Sat	9/26	A	FRA	7-27	L	15,000
Sun	9/27	A	POT	0-28	L	3,500
Sun	10/4	H	ROC	0-0	T	5,000
Sun	10/11	H	AKR	0-0	T	
Sun	10/18	H	COL	17-6	W	4,500
Sun	11/1	H	FRA	3-12	L	8,000
Tue	11/3	A	NYG	0-7	L	16,000

Sun	11/8	A	PRO	0-10	L	
Sun	11/15	A	CHIC	6-23	L	4,000

CANTON BULLDOGS

Sun	9/27	H	ROC	14-7	W	
Sun	10/4	H	DAY	14-0	W	5,000
Sat	10/10	A	FRA	7-12	L	16,000
Sun	10/11	A	POT	0-28	L	
Sun	10/18	H	AKR	3-20	L	4,500
Sun	11/8	H	CLE	6-0	W	2,000
Sun	11/22	H	COL	6-0	W	
Sun	12/6	A	CLE	0-6	L	1,500

CHICAGO BEARS

Sun	9/20	A	RI	0-0	T	2,000
Sun	9/27	A	GB	10-14	L	5,889
Sun	10/4	A	DET	0-0	T	3,700
Sun	10/11	H	HAM	28-7	W	
Sun	10/18	H	CLE	7-0	W	
Sun	10/25	A	CHIC	0-9	L	13,000
Sun	11/1	H	RI	6-0	W	8,000
Sun	11/8	H	FRA	19-0	W	6,500
Sun	11/15	H	DET	14-0	W	6,200
Sun	11/22	H	GB	21-0	W	6,898
Thu	11/26	H	CHIC	0-0	T	39,000
Sun	11/29	H	COL	14-13	W	28,000
Sat	12/5	A	FRA	14-7	W	23,000
Sun	12/6	A	NYG	19-7	W	68,000
Wed	12/9	N	PRO	6-9	L	15,000
Sat	12/12	A	DET	0-21	L	5,000
Sun	12/13	H	NYG	0-9	L	18,000

CHICAGO CARDINALS

Sun	9/27	H	HAM	6-10	L	
Sun	10/4	H	MIL	34-0	W	2,500
Sun	10/11	H	COL	19-9	W	
Sun	10/18	H	KC	20-7	W	
Sun	10/25	H	CHIB	9-0	W	13,000
Sun	11/1	H	DUL	10-6	W	20,000
Sun	11/8	H	GB	9-6	W	4,000
Sun	11/15	H	BUF	23-6	W	4,000
Sun	11/22	H	DAY	14-0	W	3,000
Thu	11/26	A	CHIB	0-0	T	39,000
Sun	11/29	H	RI	7-0	W	3,000
Sun	12/6	H	POT	7-21	L	5,000
Thu	12/10	H	MIL	59-0	W	250
Sat	12/12	H	HAM	13-0	W	1,000

CLEVELAND BULLDOGS

Sun	9/27	A	AKR	0-7	L	1,500
Sun	10/4	H	COL	3-0	W	4,000
Sun	10/11	H	KC	16-13	W	2,000
Sun	10/18	A	CHIB	0-7	L	
Sun	11/1	A	NYG	0-19	L	18,000
Sun	11/8	A	CAN	0-6	L	2,000
Wed	11/11	A	DET	13-22	L	5,000
Sat	11/21	A	FRA	14-0	W	7,000
Sun	11/22	A	POT	6-24	L	
Thu	11/26	N	KC	0-17	L	1,000
Sun	11/29	A	PRO	7-7	T	7,000
Sun	12/6	H	CAN	6-0	W	1,500
Sat	12/12	A	FRA	3-0	W	7,000
Sun	12/20	H	FRA	7-13	L	1,000

COLUMBUS TIGERS

Sun	9/27	A	DET	0-7	L	3,500
Sun	10/4	A	CLE	0-3	L	4,000
Sun	10/11	A	CHIC	9-19	L	
Sun	10/18	A	BUF	6-17	L	4,500
Sat	10/31	A	FRA	0-19	L	8,000
Sun	11/1	A	POT	0-20	L	3,000
Sun	11/8	A	NYG	0-19	L	4,000
Sun	11/22	A	CAN	0-6	L	
Sun	11/29	A	CHIB	13-14	L	28,000

DAYTON TRIANGLES

Sun	9/27	A	RI	0-0	T	
Sun	10/4	A	CAN	0-14	L	5,000
Sun	10/18	A	DET	0-6	L	4,132
Sat	10/24	A	FRA	0-3	L	2,000
Sun	11/1	A	AKR	3-17	L	2,500
Sun	11/15	A	GB	0-7	L	3,000
Sun	11/22	A	CHIC	0-14	L	3,000
Sun	11/29	A	NYG	0-23	L	18,000

DETROIT PANTHERS

Sun	9/27	H	COL	7-0	W	3,500
Sun	10/4	H	CHIB	0-0	T	3,700
Sun	10/11	H	FRA	6-0	W	4,132
Sun	10/18	H	DAY	6-0	W	4,132
Sun	10/25	H	AKR	0-0	T	5,400
Sun	11/1	H	HAM	26-6	W	
Sun	11/8	H	MIL	21-0	W	
Wed	11/11	H	CLE	22-13	W	5,000
Sun	11/15	A	CHIB	0-14	L	6,200
Sun	11/22	H	ROC	20-0	W	
Thu	11/26	H	RI	3-6	L	
Sat	12/12	H	CHIB	21-0	W	5,000

DULUTH KELLEYS

Sun	9/27	H	KC	0-3	L	
Sun	10/11	H	RI	0-12	L	4,000
Sun	11/1	A	CHIC	6-10	L	20,000

FRANKFORD YELLOW JACKETS

Sat	9/26	H	BUF	27-7	W	15,000
Sat	10/3	H	PRO	7-0	W	8,000
Sat	10/10	H	CAN	12-7	W	16,000
Sun	10/11	A	DET	0-3	L	3,400
Sat	10/17	H	NYG	5-3	W	13,000
Sun	10/18	A	NYG	14-0	W	27,000
Sat	10/24	H	DAY	3-0	W	2,000
Sat	10/31	H	COL	19-0	W	8,000
Sun	11/1	A	BUF	12-3	W	8,000
Sat	11/7	H	AKR	17-7	W	12,000
Sun	11/8	A	CHIB	0-19	L	6,500
Sat	11/14	H	POT	20-0	W	20,000
Sat	11/21	H	CLE	0-14	L	7,000
Sun	11/22	A	PRO	7-20	L	14,000
Sat	11/28	H	GB	13-7	W	12,000
Sun	11/29	A	POT	0-49	L	9,000
Sat	12/5	H	CHIB	7-14	L	23,000
Sat	12/12	H	CLE	0-3	L	7,000
Sun	12/13	A	PRO	14-6	W	
Sun	12/20	A	CLE	13-7	W	1,000

GREEN BAY PACKERS

Sun	9/20	H	HAM	14-0	W	3,000
Sun	9/27	H	CHIB	14-10	W	5,889
Sun	10/4	A	RI	0-3	L	3,000
Sun	10/11	H	MIL	31-0	W	2,300
Sun	10/18	H	RI	20-0	W	7,000
Sun	10/25	H	ROC	33-13	W	2,700
Sun	11/1	A	MIL	6-0	W	2,300
Sun	11/8	A	CHIC	6-9	L	4,000
Sun	11/15	H	DAY	7-0	W	3,000
Sun	11/22	A	CHIB	0-21	L	6,898
Thu	11/26	A	POT	0-31	L	3,500
Sat	11/28	A	FRA	7-13	L	12,000
Sun	12/6	A	PRO	13-10	W	7,000

HAMMOND PROS

Sun	9/20	A	GB	0-14	L	3,000
Sun	9/27	A	CHIC	10-6	W	
Sun	10/11	A	CHIB	7-28	L	
Sun	11/1	A	DET	6-26	L	
Sat	12/12	A	CHIC	0-13	L	1,000

KANSAS CITY COWBOYS

Sun	9/27	A	DUL	3-0	W	
Sun	10/4	A	AKR	7-14	L	
Sun	10/11	A	CLE	13-16	L	2,000
Sun	10/18	A	CHIC	7-20	L	
Sun	10/25	A	RI	3-3	T	1,500
Sun	11/15	A	RI	12-35	L	1,500
Sun	11/22	A	NYG	3-9	L	28,000
Thu	11/26	N	CLE	17-0	W	1,000

MILWAUKEE BADGERS

Sun	10/4	A	CHIC	0-34	L	2,500
Sun	10/11	A	GB	0-31	L	2,300
Sun	11/1	H	GB	0-6	L	2,300
Sun	11/8	A	DET	0-21	L	
Sun	11/22	A	RI	7-40	L	1,200
Thu	12/10	A	CHIC	0-59	L	250

NEW YORK GIANTS

Sun	10/11	A	PRO	0-14	L	8,000
Sat	10/17	A	FRA	3-5	L	13,000
Sun	10/18	H	FRA	0-14	L	27,000
Sun	11/1	H	CLE	19-0	W	18,000
Tue	11/3	H	BUF	7-0	W	16,000
Sun	11/8	H	COL	19-0	W	4,000
Wed	11/11	H	ROC	13-0	W	8,000
Sun	11/15	H	PRO	13-12	W	15,000
Sun	11/22	H	KC	9-3	W	28,000
Sun	11/29	H	DAY	23-0	W	18,000
Sun	12/6	H	CHIB	7-19	L	68,000
Sun	12/13	A	CHIB	9-0	W	18,000

POTTSVILLE MAROONS

Sun	9/27	H	BUF	28-0	W	3,500
Sun	10/4	H	PRO	0-6	L	2,000
Sun	10/11	H	CAN	28-0	W	
Sun	10/18	A	PRO	34-0	W	7,500
Sun	11/1	H	COL	20-0	W	3,000
Sun	11/8	H	AKR	21-0	W	
Sat	11/14	A	FRA	0-20	L	20,000
Sun	11/15	H	ROC	14-6	W	
Sun	11/22	H	CLE	24-6	W	
Thu	11/26	H	GB	31-0	W	3,500
Sun	11/29	H	FRA	49-0	W	9,000
Sun	12/6	A	CHIC	21-7	W	5,000

PROVIDENCE STEAM ROLLER

Sat	10/3	A	FRA	0-7	L	8,000
Sun	10/4	A	POT	6-0	W	2,000
Sun	10/11	H	NYG	14-0	W	8,000
Sun	10/18	H	POT	0-34	L	7,500
Sun	11/1	H	ROC	17-0	W	
Sun	11/8	H	BUF	10-0	W	
Sun	11/15	A	NYG	12-13	L	15,000
Sun	11/22	H	FRA	20-7	W	14,000
Sun	11/29	H	CLE	7-7	T	7,000
Sun	12/6	H	GB	10-13	L	7,000
Wed	12/9	N	CHIB	9-6	W	15,000
Sun	12/13	H	FRA	6-14	L	

ROCHESTER JEFFERSONS

Sun	9/27	A	CAN	7-14	L	
Sun	10/4	A	BUF	0-0	T	5,000
Sun	10/25	A	GB	13-33	L	2,700
Sun	11/1	A	PRO	0-17	L	
Wed	11/11	A	NYG	0-13	L	8,000
Sun	11/15	A	POT	6-14	L	
Sun	11/22	A	DET	0-20	L	

ROCK ISLAND INDEPENDENTS

Sun	9/20	H	CHIB	0-0	T	2,000
Sun	9/27	H	DAY	0-0	T	
Sun	10/4	H	GB	3-0	W	3,000
Sun	10/11	A	DUL	12-0	W	4,000
Sun	10/18	A	GB	0-20	L	7,000
Sun	10/25	H	KC	3-3	T	1,500
Sun	11/1	A	CHIB	0-6	L	8,000
Sun	11/15	H	KC	35-12	W	1,500
Sun	11/22	H	MIL	40-7	W	1,200
Thu	11/26	A	DET	6-3	W	
Sun	11/29	A	CHIC	0-7	L	3,000

1926 AFL

BOSTON BULLDOGS

Sun	10/3	A	NEW	3-0	W	1,000
Sat	10/9	H	NY	0-13	L	12,000
Sat	10/16	H	LA	0-21	L	2,000
Sun	10/17	A	BKN	17-0	W	4,000
Sun	10/31	A	CHI	0-23	L	4,000
Sun	11/14	A	NY	0-24	L	20,000

BROOKLYN HORSEMEN

Sun	10/3	H	CHI	12-7	W	10,000
Sun	10/10	H	LA	0-23	L	6,000
Sun	10/17	H	BOS	0-17	L	4,000
Sun	11/7	A	NY	13-21	L	28,000

Merged with Brooklyn Lions [NFL], playing remainder of season in the NFL.

CHICAGO BULLS

Sun	9/26	A	NEW	7-7	T	2,000
Sat	10/2	A	PHI	3-9	L	8,000
Sun	10/3	A	BKN	7-12	L	10,000
Sun	10/10	A	RI	3-7	L	1,700
Sun	10/17	H	NY	14-0	W	16,000
Sun	10/24	H	CLE	19-12	W	3,000
Sun	10/31	H	BOS	23-0	W	4,000
Sun	11/7	H	LA	3-3	T	7,500
Sun	11/14	H	PHI	3-0	W	2,500
Sun	11/21	H	RI	3-0	W	1,800
Thu	11/25	H	LA	0-0	T	3,500
Sun	11/28	A	NY	0-7	L	15,000
Sun	12/5	H	LA	0-5	L	3,000
Sun	12/12	H	NY	3-7	L	8,000

CLEVELAND PANTHERS

Sun	9/26	H	NY	10-0	W	22,000
Sun	10/3	H	LA	17-14	W	
Sun	10/17	H	RI	23-7	W	6,000
Sun	10/24	A	CHI	12-19	L	3,000
Sun	10/31	H	LA	0-6	L	1,000

LOS ANGELES WILDCATS

Sun	9/26	A	RI	3-7	L	2,500
Sun	10/3	A	CLE	14-17	L	
Sat	10/9	A	PHI	0-3	L	35,000
Sun	10/10	A	BKN	23-0	W	6,000
Sat	10/16	A	BOS	21-0	W	2,000
Sun	10/17	A	NEW	7-0	W	2,000
Sun	10/24	A	NY	0-6	L	11,560
Sun	10/31	A	CLE	6-0	W	1,000
Sun	11/7	A	CHI	3-3	T	7,500
Mon	11/8	N	NY	0-28	L	10,000
Sat	11/20	A	PHI	7-13	L	4,000
Sun	11/21	A	NY	16-6	W	18,827
Thu	11/25	A	CHI	0-0	T	3,500
Sun	12/5	A	CHI	5-0	W	3,000

NEWARK BEARS

Sun	9/26	H	CHI	7-7	T	2,000
Sun	10/3	H	BOS	0-3	L	1,000
Sat	10/16	A	PHI	0-9	L	40,000
Sun	10/17	H	LA	0-7	L	2,000
Sun	10/24	H	RI	0-0	T	400

NEW YORK YANKEES

Sun	9/26	A	CLE	0-10	L	22,000
Sun	10/3	A	RI	26-0	W	5,000
Sat	10/9	A	BOS	13-0	W	12,000
Sun	10/17	A	CHI	0-14	L	16,000
Sun	10/24	H	LA	6-0	W	11,560
Sat	10/30	A	PHI	23-0	W	30,000
Tue	11/2	H	RI	35-0	W	30,000
Sun	11/7	H	BKN	21-13	W	28,000
Mon	11/8	N	LA	28-0	W	10,000
Sun	11/14	H	BOS	24-0	W	20,000
Sun	11/21	H	LA	6-16	L	18,827
Thu	11/25	H	PHI	10-13	L	22,000
Sat	11/27	A	PHI	6-13	L	15,000

Sun	11/28	H	CHI	7-0	W	15,000
Sun	12/12	A	CHI	7-3	W	8,000

PHILADELPHIA QUAKERS

Sat	10/2	H	CHI	9-3	W	8,000
Sat	10/9	H	LA	3-0	W	35,000
Sat	10/16	H	NEW	9-0	W	40,000
Sat	10/23	H	RI	9-0	W	15,000
Sat	10/30	H	NY	0-23	L	30,000
Sat	11/6	H	RI	24-0	W	5,000
Sun	11/14	A	CHI	0-3	L	2,500
Sat	11/20	H	LA	13-7	W	4,000
Thu	11/25	A	NY	13-10	W	22,000
Sat	11/27	H	NY	13-6	W	15,000

ROCK ISLAND INDEPENDENTS

Sun	9/26	H	LA	7-3	W	2,500
Sun	10/3	H	NY	0-26	L	5,000
Sun	10/10	H	CHI	7-3	W	1,700
Sun	10/17	A	CLE	7-23	L	6,000
Sat	10/23	A	PHI	0-9	L	15,000
Sun	10/24	A	NEW	0-0	T	400
Tue	11/2	A	NY	0-35	L	30,000
Sat	11/6	A	PHI	0-24	L	5,000
Sun	11/21	A	CHI	0-3	L	1,800

1926 NFL

AKRON INDIANS

Sat	9/25	A	FRA	6-6	T	6,000
Sun	9/26	A	BUF	0-7	L	2,500
Sun	10/3	H	HAM	17-0	W	
Sun	10/10	H	CAN	0-0	T	2,500
Sun	10/24	A	DET	0-25	L	
Sun	10/31	A	CHIB	0-17	L	6,500
Sun	11/7	A	POT	0-34	L	
Thu	11/25	A	CAN	0-0	T	

BROOKLYN LIONS

Sun	9/26	A	PRO	0-13	L	7,000
Sun	10/10	H	HAR	6-0	W	1,000
Sat	10/16	H	POT	0-21	L	8,000
Sun	10/17	A	POT	0-14	L	
Sat	10/23	H	COL	20-12	W	
Sun	10/24	A	HAR	6-16	L	1,000
Sun	11/7	H	KC	9-10	L	4,000
Sun	11/14	H	CAN	19-0	W	7,000
Sun	11/21	H	LA	0-20	L	10,000
Thu	11/25	H	NY	0-17	L	10,000
Sun	11/28	A	NY	0-27	L	7,000

BUFFALO RANGERS

Sun	9/26	H	AKR	7-0	W	2,500
Sun	10/3	H	DAY	0-3	L	5,000
Sat	10/9	A	FRA	0-30	L	6,000
Sun	10/17	A	DAY	7-6	W	1,500
Sun	10/24	H	LA	0-0	T	2,500
Sun	10/31	A	POT	0-14	L	
Sun	11/7	H	COL	26-0	W	3,500
Sun	11/14	A	HAR	13-7	W	
Sun	11/21	H	KC	0-2	L	
Sun	11/28	H	POT	0-0	T	

CANTON BULLDOGS

Sun	9/26	H	COL	2-14	L	
Sun	10/3	H	LOU	13-0	W	3,000
Sun	10/10	A	AKR	0-0	T	2,500
Sun	10/17	H	LA	13-16	L	5,000
Sat	10/23	A	FRA	0-17	L	4,000
Sun	10/31	A	DET	0-6	L	
Tue	11/2	A	NYG	7-7	T	40,000
Sun	11/7	A	HAR	7-16	L	4,000
Thu	11/11	A	PRO	2-21	L	4,000
Sun	11/14	A	BKN	0-19	L	7,000
Sun	11/21	H	DUL	2-10	L	
Thu	11/25	H	AKR	0-0	T	
Sun	11/28	A	CHIB	0-35	L	5,000

CHICAGO BEARS

Sun	9/19	A	MIL	10-7	W	
Sun	9/26	A	GB	6-6	T	7,000
Sun	10/3	A	DET	10-7	W	10,000
Sun	10/10	H	NYG	7-0	W	8,000
Sun	10/17	H	CHIC	16-0	W	12,000
Sun	10/24	H	DUL	24-6	W	12,000
Sun	10/31	H	AKR	17-0	W	6,500
Sun	11/7	H	LOU	34-0	W	7,000
Thu	11/11	A	CHIC	10-0	W	10,000
Sun	11/14	H	MIL	10-7	W	3,500
Sun	11/21	H	GB	19-13	W	7,500
Thu	11/25	H	CHIC	0-0	T	8,000
Sun	11/28	H	CAN	35-0	W	5,000
Sat	12/4	A	FRA	6-7	L	11,000
Sun	12/12	H	POT	9-7	W	5,500
Sun	12/19	H	GB	3-3	T	

CHICAGO CARDINALS

Sun	9/19	H	COL	14-0	W	2,500
Sun	9/26	H	LA	15-0	W	7,500
Sun	10/3	H	RAC	20-0	W	3,000
Sun	10/10	A	GB	13-7	W	5,000
Sun	10/17	H	CHIB	0-16	L	12,000
Sun	10/24	A	MIL	3-2	W	
Sun	10/31	H	GB	0-3	L	2,500
Sat	11/6	A	FRA	7-33	L	8,000
Sun	11/7	A	NYG	0-20	L	5,000
Thu	11/11	A	CHIB	0-10	L	10,000
Thu	11/25	A	CHIB	0-0	T	8,000
Sun	11/28	H	KC	2-7	L	12,000

COLUMBUS TIGERS

Sun	9/19	A	CHIC	0-14	L	2,500
Sun	9/26	A	CAN	14-2	W	
Sun	10/3	A	POT	0-3	L	
Sun	10/10	A	PRO	0-19	L	
Sat	10/16	H	KC	0-9	L	5,000
Sat	10/23	A	BKN	12-20	L	
Sun	11/7	A	BUF	0-26	L	3,500

DAYTON TRIANGLES

Sun	10/3	A	BUF	3-0	W	5,000
Sun	10/10	A	POT	6-24	L	
Sun	10/17	H	BUF	6-7	L	1,500
Sun	11/14	A	DET	0-0	T	
Sat	11/20	A	FRA	0-35	L	6,000
Sun	11/21	A	HAR	0-16	L	

DETROIT PANTHERS

Sun	9/19	A	GB	0-21	L	4,500
Sun	9/26	A	MIL	0-6	L	2,500
Sun	10/3	H	CHIB	7-10	L	10,000
Sun	10/10	H	KC	10-0	W	
Sun	10/17	H	LOU	47-0	W	
Sun	10/24	H	AKR	25-0	W	
Sun	10/31	H	CAN	6-0	W	
Sun	11/7	H	DUL	0-0	T	21,000
Sun	11/14	H	DAY	0-0	T	
Thu	11/25	H	LA	6-9	L	
Sat	11/27	A	FRA	6-7	L	3,000
Sun	11/28	H	GB	0-7	L	1,000

DULUTH ESKIMOS

Sun	9/19	H	KC	7-0	W	6,000
Sun	10/3	A	GB	0-0	T	2,500
Sun	10/10	A	HAM	26-0	W	2,000
Sun	10/17	A	RAC	21-0	W	2,600
Sun	10/24	A	CHIB	6-24	L	12,000
Sun	10/31	A	MIL	7-6	W	
Sun	11/7	A	DET	0-0	T	21,000
Thu	11/11	A	NYG	13-14	L	4,000
Sat	11/13	A	FRA	0-10	L	9,000
Sun	11/14	A	POT	0-13	L	
Sun	11/21	A	CAN	10-2	W	
Sat	11/27	A	HAR	16-0	W	
Sun	11/28	A	PRO	0-0	T	11,560
Sun	12/12	A	KC	7-12	L	

FRANKFORD YELLOW JACKETS

Sat	9/25	H	AKR	6-6	T	6,000
Sat	10/2	H	HAR	13-0	W	
Sun	10/3	A	HAR	10-0	W	
Sat	10/9	H	BUF	30-0	W	6,000
Sat	10/16	H	NYG	6-0	W	7,000
Sun	10/17	A	NYG	6-0	W	15,000
Sat	10/23	H	CAN	17-0	W	4,000
Sat	10/30	H	PRO	6-7	L	8,000
Sun	10/31	A	PRO	6-3	W	
Sat	11/6	H	CHIC	33-7	W	8,000
Sat	11/13	H	DUL	10-0	W	9,000
Sat	11/20	H	DAY	35-0	W	6,000
Thu	11/25	H	GB	20-14	W	11,000
Sat	11/27	H	DET	7-6	W	3,000
Sat	12/4	H	CHIB	7-6	W	11,000
Sat	12/11	H	PRO	24-0	W	4,500
Sat	12/18	H	POT	0-0	T	8,000

GREEN BAY PACKERS

Sun	9/19	H	DET	21-0	W	4,500
Sun	9/26	H	CHIB	6-6	T	7,000
Sun	10/3	H	DUL	0-0	T	2,500
Sun	10/10	H	CHIC	7-13	L	5,000
Sun	10/17	H	MIL	7-0	W	3,000
Sun	10/24	H	RAC	35-0	W	
Sun	10/31	A	CHIC	3-0	W	2,500
Sun	11/7	A	MIL	21-0	W	4,300
Sun	11/14	H	LOU	14-0	W	1,300
Sun	11/21	A	CHIB	13-19	L	7,500
Thu	11/25	A	FRA	14-20	L	11,000
Sun	11/28	A	DET	7-0	W	1,000
Sun	12/19	A	CHIB	3-3	T	

HAMMOND PROS

Sun	9/26	A	RAC	3-6	L	2,500
Sun	10/3	A	AKR	0-17	L	
Sun	10/10	H	DUL	0-26	L	2,000
Sun	11/21	A	POT	0-7	L	

HARTFORD BLUES

Sun	9/26	H	NYG	0-21	L	17,000
Sat	10/2	A	FRA	0-13	L	
Sun	10/3	H	FRA	0-10	L	
Sun	10/10	A	BKN	0-6	L	1,000
Sun	10/24	H	BKN	16-6	W	1,000
Sun	10/31	H	KC	2-7	L	500
Sun	11/7	H	CAN	16-7	W	4,000
Sun	11/14	H	BUF	7-13	L	
Sun	11/21	H	DAY	16-0	W	
Sat	11/27	H	DUL	0-16	L	

KANSAS CITY COWBOYS

Sun	9/19	A	DUL	0-7	L	6,000
Sun	10/10	A	DET	0-10	L	
Sat	10/16	A	COL	9-0	W	5,000
Sun	10/24	A	NYG	0-13	L	5,000
Sun	10/31	A	HAR	7-2	W	500
Sun	11/7	A	BKN	10-9	W	4,000
Sun	11/14	A	PRO	22-0	W	
Sun	11/21	A	BUF	2-0	W	
Sun	11/28	A	CHIC	7-2	W	12,000
Sun	12/5	H	LA	7-3	W	3,000
Sun	12/12	H	DUL	12-7	W	

LOS ANGELES BUCCANEERS

Sun	9/26	A	CHIC	0-15	L	7,500
Sun	10/3	A	MIL	6-0	W	
Sun	10/17	A	CAN	16-13	W	5,000
Sun	10/24	A	BUF	0-0	T	2,500
Sun	11/7	A	PRO	7-6	W	11,000
Thu	11/11	A	POT	0-10	L	3,000
Sun	11/14	A	NYG	6-0	W	20,000
Sun	11/21	A	BKN	20-0	W	10,000
Thu	11/25	A	DET	9-6	W	
Sun	12/5	A	KC	3-7	L	3,000

LOUISVILLE COLONELS

Sun	10/3	A	CAN	0-13	L	3,000
Sun	10/17	A	DET	0-47	L	
Sun	11/7	A	CHIB	0-34	L	7,000
Sun	11/14	A	GB	0-14	L	1,300

MILWAUKEE BADGERS

Sun	9/19	H	CHIB	7-10	L	
Sun	9/26	H	DET	6-0	W	2,500
Sun	10/3	H	LA	0-6	L	
Sun	10/10	A	RAC	13-2	W	1,500
Sun	10/17	A	GB	0-7	L	3,000
Sun	10/24	H	CHIC	2-3	L	
Sun	10/31	H	DUL	6-7	L	
Sun	11/7	H	GB	0-21	L	4,300
Sun	11/14	A	CHIB	7-10	L	3,500

NEW YORK GIANTS

Sun	9/26	A	HAR	21-0	W	17,000
Sun	10/3	A	PRO	7-6	W	8,000
Sun	10/10	A	CHIB	0-7	L	8,000
Sat	10/16	A	FRA	0-6	L	7,000
Sun	10/17	H	FRA	0-6	L	15,000
Sun	10/24	H	KC	13-0	W	5,000
Tue	11/2	H	CAN	7-7	T	40,000
Sun	11/7	H	CHIC	20-0	W	5,000
Thu	11/11	H	DUL	14-13	W	4,000
Sun	11/14	H	LA	0-6	L	20,000
Sun	11/21	H	PRO	21-0	W	10,000
Thu	11/25	A	BKN	17-0	W	10,000
Sun	11/28	H	BKN	27-0	W	7,000

POTTSVILLE MAROONS

Sun	10/3	H	COL	3-0	W	
Sun	10/10	H	DAY	24-6	W	
Sat	10/16	A	BKN	21-0	W	8,000
Sun	10/17	H	BKN	14-0	W	
Sun	10/24	A	PRO	0-14	L	4,500
Sun	10/31	H	BUF	14-0	W	
Sun	11/7	H	AKR	34-0	W	
Thu	11/11	H	LA	10-0	W	3,000
Sun	11/14	H	DUL	13-0	W	
Sun	11/21	H	HAM	7-0	W	
Thu	11/25	H	PRO	8-0	W	
Sun	11/28	A	BUF	0-0	T	
Sun	12/12	A	CHIB	7-9	L	5,500
Sat	12/18	A	FRA	0-0	T	8,000

PROVIDENCE STEAM ROLLER

Sun	9/26	H	BKN	13-0	W	7,000
Sun	10/3	H	NYG	6-7	L	8,000
Sun	10/10	H	COL	19-0	W	
Sun	10/24	H	POT	14-0	W	4,500
Sat	10/30	A	FRA	7-0	W	8,000
Sun	10/31	H	FRA	3-6	L	
Sun	11/7	H	LA	6-7	L	11,000
Thu	11/11	H	CAN	21-2	W	4,000
Sun	11/14	H	KC	0-22	L	
Sun	11/21	A	NYG	0-21	L	10,000
Thu	11/25	A	POT	0-8	L	
Sun	11/28	H	DUL	0-0	T	
Sat	12/11	A	FRA	0-24	L	4,500

RACINE TORNADOES

Sun	9/26	H	HAM	6-3	W	2,500
Sun	10/3	A	CHIC	0-20	L	3,000
Sun	10/10	H	MIL	2-13	L	1,500
Sun	10/17	H	DUL	0-21	L	2,600
Sun	10/24	A	GB	0-35	L	

1927 NFL

BUFFALO BISONS

Sun	9/25	A	POT	0-22	L	
Sun	10/2	A	PRO	0-5	L	3,500

Wed	10/12	H	NYY	8-19	L	3,000
Sat	10/15	A	FRA	0-54	L	7,000
Sun	10/16	H	FRA	0-23	L	

CHICAGO BEARS

Sun	9/25	A	CHIC	9-0	W	4,000
Sun	10/2	A	GB	7-6	W	5,500
Sun	10/16	H	NYY	12-0	W	25,000
Sun	10/23	H	CLE	14-12	W	20,000
Sun	10/30	H	DAY	14-6	W	8,000
Sun	11/6	H	PRO	0-0	T	8,000
Tue	11/8	A	NYY	6-26	L	6,000
Sun	11/13	H	POT	30-12	W	8,000
Sun	11/20	H	GB	14-6	W	14,000
Thu	11/24	H	CHIC	0-3	L	6,000
Sun	11/27	A	NYG	7-13	L	10,000
Sat	12/3	A	FRA	0-0	T	4,000
Sun	12/4	H	FRA	9-0	W	2,500
Sun	12/11	H	DUL	27-14	W	2,500

CHICAGO CARDINALS

Sun	9/25	H	CHIB	0-9	L	4,000
Sun	10/2	H	POT	19-7	W	2,000
Sun	10/9	H	DAY	7-0	W	2,500
Sun	10/16	A	GB	0-13	L	4,500
Sun	10/30	H	NYY	6-7	L	15,000
Sun	11/6	H	GB	6-6	T	3,500
Sun	11/13	A	NYY	6-20	L	10,000
Sat	11/19	A	FRA	8-12	L	7,000
Sun	11/20	A	NYG	7-28	L	10,000
Thu	11/24	A	CHIB	3-0	W	6,000
Sun	11/27	H	CLE	7-32	L	5,000

CLEVELAND BULLDOGS

Sun	9/25	A	GB	7-12	L	4,400
Sun	10/2	H	NYG	0-0	T	3,000
Sun	10/9	N	NYY	7-13	L	16,000
Sun	10/16	A	NYG	6-0	W	15,000
Sun	10/23	A	CHIB	12-14	L	20,000
Sun	10/30	H	DUL	21-20	W	12,000
Sun	11/6	H	NYY	15-0	W	2,500
Sat	11/12	A	FRA	0-22	L	6,000
Sun	11/13	H	FRA	37-0	W	5,000
Sun	11/20	A	PRO	22-0	W	12,000
Thu	11/24	A	NYY	30-19	W	15,000
Sun	11/27	A	CHIC	32-7	W	5,000
Sat	12/3	H	DUL	20-0	W	11,000

DAYTON TRIANGLES

Sun	9/18	A	GB	0-14	L	3,600
Sat	9/24	A	FRA	6-3	W	7,000
Sun	10/2	H	NYY	3-6	L	6,000
Sat	10/8	A	FRA	0-0	T	3,000
Sun	10/9	A	CHIC	0-7	L	2,500
Sun	10/23	A	PRO	0-7	L	
Sun	10/30	A	CHIB	6-14	L	8,000
Sun	11/13	A	GB	0-6	L	2,500

DULUTH ESKIMOS

Sun	10/9	A	GB	0-20	L	4,000
Sun	10/23	A	POT	27-0	W	
Sun	10/30	A	CLE	20-21	L	12,000
Sun	11/6	A	NYG	0-21	L	15,000
Sun	11/13	A	PRO	7-13	L	
Sun	11/20	A	POT	0-6	L	
Sat	11/26	A	FRA	0-6	L	4,500
Sat	12/3	A	CLE	0-20	L	11,000
Sun	12/11	A	CHIB	14-27	L	2,500

FRANKFORD YELLOW JACKETS

Sat	9/24	H	DAY	3-6	L	7,000
Sat	10/8	H	DAY	0-0	T	3,000
Sat	10/15	H	BUF	54-0	W	7,000
Sun	10/16	A	BUF	23-0	W	
Sat	10/22	H	NYG	0-13	L	8,000
Sun	10/23	A	NYG	0-27	L	15,000
Sat	10/29	H	PRO	7-20	L	5,000
Sun	10/30	A	PRO	0-14	L	9,000
Sat	11/5	H	POT	10-0	W	6,000
Sun	11/6	A	POT	0-9	L	
Sat	11/12	H	CLE	22-0	W	6,000
Sun	11/13	A	CLE	0-37	L	5,000
Sat	11/19	H	CHIC	12-8	W	7,000
Thu	11/24	H	GB	9-17	L	9,000
Sat	11/26	H	DUL	6-0	W	4,500
Sat	12/3	H	CHIB	0-0	T	4,000
Sun	12/4	A	CHIB	0-9	L	2,500
Sat	12/10	H	NYY	6-6	T	4,500

GREEN BAY PACKERS

Sun	9/18	H	DAY	14-0	W	3,600
Sun	9/25	H	CLE	12-7	W	4,400
Sun	10/2	H	CHIB	6-7	L	5,500
Sun	10/9	H	DUL	20-0	W	4,000
Sun	10/16	H	CHIC	13-0	W	4,500
Sun	10/23	H	NYY	13-0	W	11,000
Sun	11/6	A	CHIC	6-6	T	3,500
Sun	11/13	H	DAY	6-0	W	2,500
Sun	11/20	A	CHIB	6-14	L	14,000
Thu	11/24	A	FRA	17-9	W	9,000

NEW YORK GIANTS

Sun	9/25	A	PRO	8-0	W	7,500
Sun	10/2	A	CLE	0-0	T	3,000
Sun	10/9	A	POT	19-0	W	5,000
Sun	10/16	H	CLE	0-6	L	15,000
Sat	10/22	A	FRA	13-0	W	8,000
Sun	10/23	H	FRA	27-0	W	15,000
Sun	10/30	H	POT	16-0	W	15,000
Sun	11/6	H	DUL	21-0	W	15,000
Tue	11/8	H	PRO	25-0	W	38,000
Sun	11/20	H	CHIC	28-7	W	10,000
Sun	11/27	H	CHIB	13-7	W	10,000
Sun	12/4	H	NYY	14-0	W	5,000
Sun	12/11	A	NYY	13-0	W	8,000

NEW YORK YANKEES

Sun	10/2	A	DAY	6-3	W	6,000
Sun	10/9	N	CLE	13-7	W	16,000
Wed	10/12	A	BUF	19-8	W	3,000
Sun	10/16	A	CHIB	0-12	L	25,000
Sun	10/23	A	GB	0-13	L	11,000
Sun	10/30	A	CHIC	7-6	W	15,000
Sun	11/6	A	CLE	0-15	L	2,500
Tue	11/8	H	CHIB	26-6	W	6,000
Fri	11/11	A	POT	19-12	W	
Sun	11/13	H	CHIC	20-6	W	10,000
Thu	11/24	H	CLE	19-30	L	15,000
Sun	11/27	A	PRO	7-14	L	10,000
Sat	12/3	N	PRO	0-9	L	5,000
Sun	12/4	A	NYG	0-14	L	5,000
Sat	12/10	A	FRA	6-6	T	4,500
Sun	12/11	H	NYG	0-13	L	8,000

POTTSVILLE MAROONS

Sun	9/25	H	BUF	22-0	W	
Sun	10/2	A	CHIC	7-19	L	2,000
Sun	10/9	H	NYG	0-19	L	5,000
Sun	10/16	A	PRO	6-3	W	6,000
Sun	10/23	H	DUL	0-27	L	
Sun	10/30	A	NYG	0-16	L	15,000
Sat	11/5	A	FRA	0-10	L	6,000
Sun	11/6	H	FRA	9-0	W	
Fri	11/11	H	NYY	12-19	L	
Sun	11/13	A	CHIB	12-30	L	8,000
Sun	11/20	H	DUL	6-0	W	
Thu	11/24	H	PRO	6-0	W	4,000
Sun	12/4	A	PRO	0-20	L	1,500

PROVIDENCE STEAM ROLLER

Sun	9/25	H	NYG	0-8	L	7,500
Sun	10/2	H	BUF	5-0	W	3,500
Sun	10/16	H	POT	3-6	L	6,000
Sun	10/23	H	DAY	7-0	W	
Sat	10/29	A	FRA	20-7	W	5,000
Sun	10/30	H	FRA	14-0	W	9,000
Sun	11/6	A	CHIB	0-0	T	8,000
Tue	11/8	A	NYG	0-25	L	38,000
Sun	11/13	H	DUL	13-7	W	
Sun	11/20	H	CLE	0-22	L	12,000
Thu	11/24	A	POT	0-6	L	4,000
Sun	11/27	H	NYY	14-7	W	10,000
Sat	12/3	N	NYY	9-0	W	5,000
Sun	12/4	H	POT	20-0	W	1,500

1928 NFL

CHICAGO BEARS

Sun	9/23	A	CHIC	15-0	W	4,000
Sun	9/30	A	GB	12-12	T	8,500
Sun	10/14	H	NYG	13-0	W	14,000
Sun	10/21	H	GB	6-16	L	15,000
Sun	10/28	H	DET	0-6	L	20,000
Sun	11/4	H	NYY	27-0	W	10,000
Sun	11/11	H	DAY	27-0	W	5,000
Sun	11/18	H	POT	13-6	W	5,000
Sun	11/25	H	DET	7-14	L	15,000
Thu	11/29	H	CHIC	34-0	W	10,000
Sun	12/2	H	FRA	28-6	W	12,000
Sun	12/9	H	GB	0-6	L	14,000
Sat	12/15	A	FRA	0-19	L	7,000

CHICAGO CARDINALS

Sun	9/23	H	CHIB	0-15	L	4,000
Sun	10/7	H	DAY	7-0	W	
Sun	10/14	A	GB	0-20	L	4,200
Sat	11/24	A	FRA	0-19	L	8,000
Sun	11/25	A	NYY	0-19	L	7,000
Thu	11/29	A	CHIB	0-34	L	10,000

DAYTON TRIANGLES

Sat	9/29	A	FRA	0-6	L	4,000
Sun	10/7	A	CHIC	0-7	L	
Sun	10/14	A	PRO	0-28	L	7,000
Sat	10/20	A	FRA	9-13	L	7,000
Sun	10/28	A	GB	0-17	L	3,100
Sun	11/11	A	CHIB	0-27	L	5,000
Thu	11/29	A	DET	0-33	L	

DETROIT WOLVERINES

Sun	10/14	A	NYY	35-12	W	10,000
Sun	10/21	H	NYG	28-0	W	12,000
Sun	10/28	A	CHIB	6-0	W	20,000
Sat	11/3	A	FRA	7-25	L	8,000
Sun	11/4	A	PRO	0-7	L	8,000
Sun	11/11	A	NYG	19-19	T	25,000
Sun	11/18	H	NYY	13-0	W	8,000
Sun	11/25	A	CHIB	14-7	W	15,000
Thu	11/29	H	DAY	33-0	W	
Sun	12/9	A	NYY	34-6	W	3,500

FRANKFORD YELLOW JACKETS

Sun	9/23	A	GB	19-9	W	6,500
Sat	9/29	H	DAY	6-0	W	4,000
Sun	10/7	A	PRO	10-6	W	8,000
Sat	10/13	H	NYY	0-13	L	
Sat	10/20	H	DAY	13-9	W	7,000
Sat	11/3	H	DET	25-7	W	8,000
Sun	11/4	A	NYG	0-0	T	8,000
Sat	11/10	H	POT	19-0	W	
Sun	11/11	A	POT	24-0	W	
Sat	11/17	H	PRO	6-6	T	8,000
Sun	11/18	A	PRO	0-6	L	9,727
Sat	11/24	H	CHIC	19-0	W	8,000
Thu	11/29	H	GB	2-0	W	8,000
Sun	12/2	A	CHIB	6-28	L	11,000
Sat	12/8	H	NYG	7-0	W	3,500
Sat	12/15	H	CHIB	19-0	W	7,000

GREEN BAY PACKERS

Sun	9/23	H	FRA	9-19	L	6,500
Sun	9/30	H	CHIB	12-12	T	8,500
Sun	10/7	H	NYG	0-6	L	7,000
Sun	10/14	H	CHIC	20-0	W	4,200
Sun	10/21	A	CHIB	16-6	W	15,000
Sun	10/28	H	DAY	17-0	W	3,100
Sun	11/4	H	POT	26-14	W	5,000
Sun	11/11	H	NYY	0-0	T	6,000
Sun	11/18	A	NYG	7-0	W	12,000
Sun	11/25	A	POT	0-26	L	1,600
Thu	11/29	A	FRA	0-2	L	8,000
Sun	12/2	A	PRO	7-7	T	9,000
Sun	12/9	A	CHIB	6-0	W	14,000

NEW YORK GIANTS

Sun	9/30	A	POT	12-6	W	7,000
Sun	10/7	A	GB	6-0	W	7,000
Sun	10/14	A	CHIB	0-13	L	14,000
Sun	10/21	A	DET	0-28	L	12,000
Sun	10/28	A	NYY	10-7	W	25,000
Sun	11/4	H	FRA	0-0	T	8,000
Tue	11/6	H	POT	13-7	W	15,000
Sun	11/11	H	DET	19-19	T	25,000
Sun	11/18	H	GB	0-7	L	12,000
Sun	11/25	A	PRO	0-16	L	11,987
Sun	12/2	H	NYY	13-19	L	15,000
Sat	12/8	A	FRA	0-7	L	3,500
Sun	12/16	A	NYY	6-7	L	15,000

NEW YORK YANKEES

Sun	9/30	A	PRO	7-20	L	4,000
Sun	10/7	A	POT	7-9	L	5,000
Sat	10/13	A	FRA	13-0	W	
Sun	10/14	H	DET	12-35	L	10,000
Sun	10/21	H	PRO	6-12	L	7,000
Sun	10/28	H	NYG	7-10	L	25,000
Sun	11/4	A	CHIB	0-27	L	10,000
Sun	11/11	A	GB	0-0	T	6,000
Sun	11/18	A	DET	0-13	L	8,000
Sun	11/25	H	CHIC	19-0	W	7,000
Sun	12/2	A	NYG	19-13	W	15,000
Sun	12/9	H	DET	6-34	L	3,500
Sun	12/16	H	NYG	7-6	W	15,000

POTTSVILLE MAROONS

Sun	9/30	H	NYG	6-12	L	7,000
Sun	10/7	H	NYY	9-7	W	5,000
Sun	10/28	A	PRO	6-13	L	8,000
Sun	11/4	A	GB	14-26	L	5,000
Tue	11/6	A	NYG	7-13	L	15,000
Sat	11/10	A	FRA	0-19	L	
Sun	11/11	H	FRA	0-24	L	
Sun	11/18	A	CHIB	6-13	L	5,000
Sun	11/25	H	GB	26-0	W	1,600
Thu	11/29	H	PRO	0-7	L	10,000

PROVIDENCE STEAM ROLLER

Sun	9/30	H	NYY	20-7	W	4,000
Sun	10/7	H	FRA	6-10	L	8,000
Sun	10/14	H	DAY	28-0	W	7,000
Sun	10/21	A	NYY	12-6	W	7,000
Sun	10/28	H	POT	13-6	W	8,000
Sun	11/4	H	DET	7-0	W	8,500
Sat	11/17	A	FRA	6-6	T	8,000
Sun	11/18	H	FRA	6-0	W	9,727
Sun	11/25	H	NYG	16-0	W	11,987
Thu	11/29	A	POT	7-0	W	10,000
Sun	12/2	H	GB	7-7	T	9,000

1929 NFL

BOSTON BULLDOGS

Sun	10/6	A	ORA	0-7	L	7,000
Sun	10/13	H	DAY	41-0	W	800
Sun	10/20	H	ORA	13-19	L	6,000

Sun	10/27	N	BUF	14-6	W	700
Tue	10/29	N	ORA	6-0	W	2,000
Sun	11/10	A	SI	6-14	L	7,500
Sun	11/17	H	BUF	12-7	W	
Sun	11/24	A	PRO	6-20	L	

BUFFALO BISONS

Sun	9/29	H	CHIC	3-9	L	4,000
Sat	10/5	A	FRA	0-19	L	6,000
Sun	10/6	H	FRA	0-13	L	
Sun	10/13	H	CHIB	0-16	L	5,200
Sun	10/20	A	PRO	7-7	T	8,500
Sun	10/27	N	BOS	6-14	L	700
Tue	11/5	H	NYG	6-45	L	
Sun	11/17	A	BOS	7-12	L	
Sun	11/24	A	CHIB	19-7	W	3,500

CHICAGO BEARS

Sun	9/22	N	MIN	19-6	W	6,000
Sun	9/29	A	GB	0-23	L	13,000
Sun	10/6	A	MIN	7-6	W	6,000
Sun	10/13	A	BUF	16-0	W	5,200
Sun	10/20	H	CHIC	0-0	T	18,000
Sun	10/27	H	MIN	27-0	W	9,400
Sun	11/3	H	NYG	14-26	L	26,000
Sun	11/10	H	GB	0-14	L	13,000
Sat	11/16	A	FRA	14-20	L	9,000
Sun	11/17	A	NYG	0-34	L	12,000
Sun	11/24	H	BUF	7-19	L	3,500
Thu	11/28	A	CHIC	6-40	L	7,000
Sun	12/1	H	FRA	0-0	T	1,500
Sun	12/8	H	GB	0-25	L	6,000
Sun	12/15	H	NYG	9-14	L	5,000

CHICAGO CARDINALS

Sun	9/29	A	BUF	9-3	W	4,000
Sun	10/6	A	GB	2-9	L	6,000
Sun	10/13	A	MIN	7-14	L	
Sun	10/20	A	CHIB	0-0	T	18,000
Sun	10/27	H	GB	6-7	L	8,000
Sat	11/2	A	FRA	0-8	L	5,000
Wed	11/6	A	PRO	16-0	W	6,000
Sun	11/10	H	MIN	8-0	W	6,000
Sun	11/17	H	GB	0-12	L	10,000
Sun	11/24	H	DAY	19-0	W	300
Thu	11/28	H	CHIB	40-6	W	7,000
Sun	12/1	A	NYG	21-24	L	15,000
Sun	12/8	A	ORA	26-0	W	

DAYTON TRIANGLES

Sun	9/22	A	GB	0-9	L	5,000
Sat	9/28	A	FRA	7-14	L	6,500
Sun	9/29	A	PRO	0-41	L	8,500
Sun	10/6	A	SI	0-12	L	6,000
Sun	10/13	A	BOS	0-41	L	800
Sun	11/24	A	CHIC	0-19	L	300

FRANKFORD YELLOW JACKETS

Sat	9/28	H	DAY	14-7	W	6,500
Sat	10/5	H	BUF	19-0	W	6,000
Sun	10/6	A	BUF	13-0	W	
Sun	10/13	A	GB	2-14	L	9,000
Sat	10/19	H	ORA	6-6	T	6,000
Sun	10/20	A	NYG	0-32	L	30,000
Sat	10/26	H	SI	6-6	T	6,000
Sun	10/27	A	SI	3-0	W	10,000
Sat	11/2	H	CHIC	8-0	W	5,000
Sat	11/9	H	PRO	7-0	W	6,000
Sun	11/10	A	PRO	7-6	W	
Sat	11/16	H	CHIB	20-14	W	9,000
Sun	11/17	A	ORA	0-0	T	1,500
Sat	11/23	H	MIN	24-0	W	4,000
Thu	11/28	H	GB	0-0	T	15,000
Sun	12/1	A	CHIB	0-0	T	1,500
Sat	12/7	H	NYG	0-12	L	7,000
Sun	12/8	A	NYG	0-31	L	10,000
Sat	12/14	H	ORA	10-0	W	3,000

GREEN BAY PACKERS

Sun	9/22	H	DAY	9-0	W	5,000
Sun	9/29	H	CHIB	23-0	W	13,000
Sun	10/6	H	CHIC	9-2	W	6,000
Sun	10/13	H	FRA	14-2	W	9,000
Sun	10/20	H	MIN	24-0	W	6,000
Sun	10/27	A	CHIC	7-6	W	8,000
Sun	11/3	A	MIN	16-6	W	3,000
Sun	11/10	A	CHIB	14-0	W	13,000
Sun	11/17	A	CHIC	12-0	W	10,000
Sun	11/24	A	NYG	20-6	W	25,000
Thu	11/28	A	FRA	0-0	T	15,000
Sun	12/1	A	PRO	25-0	W	6,500
Sun	12/8	A	CHIB	25-0	W	6,000

MINNEAPOLIS REDJACKETS

Sun	9/22	N	CHIB	6-19	L	6,000
Sun	10/6	H	CHIB	6-7	L	6,000
Sun	10/13	H	CHIC	14-7	W	
Sun	10/20	A	GB	0-24	L	6,000
Sun	10/27	A	CHIB	0-27	L	9,400
Sun	11/3	H	GB	6-16	L	3,000
Sun	11/10	A	CHIC	0-8	L	6,000
Sun	11/17	A	PRO	16-19	L	8,500
Sat	11/23	A	FRA	0-24	L	4,000
Sun	11/24	A	SI	0-34	L	2,000

NEW YORK GIANTS

Sun	9/29	A	ORA	0-0	T	9,000
Sun	10/6	A	PRO	7-0	W	14,000
Sun	10/13	H	SI	19-9	W	30,000
Sun	10/20	H	FRA	32-0	W	30,000
Sun	10/27	H	PRO	19-0	W	25,000
Sun	11/3	A	CHIB	26-14	W	26,000
Tue	11/5	A	BUF	45-6	W	
Sun	11/10	H	ORA	22-0	W	15,000
Sun	11/17	H	CHIB	34-0	W	12,000
Sun	11/24	H	GB	6-20	L	25,000
Thu	11/28	A	SI	21-7	W	12,000
Sun	12/1	H	CHIC	24-21	W	15,000
Sat	12/7	A	FRA	12-0	W	7,000
Sun	12/8	H	FRA	31-0	W	10,000
Sun	12/15	A	CHIB	14-9	W	5,000

ORANGE TORNADOES

Sun	9/29	H	NYG	0-0	T	9,000
Sun	10/6	H	BOS	7-0	W	7,000
Sun	10/13	A	PRO	0-7	L	9,000
Sat	10/19	A	FRA	6-6	T	6,000
Sun	10/20	A	BOS	19-13	W	6,000
Tue	10/29	N	BOS	0-6	L	2,000
Sun	11/3	A	SI	0-0	T	
Sun	11/10	A	NYG	0-22	L	15,000
Sun	11/17	H	FRA	0-0	T	1,500
Sun	12/1	H	SI	3-0	W	8,000
Sun	12/8	H	CHIC	0-26	L	
Sat	12/14	A	FRA	0-10	L	3,000

PROVIDENCE STEAM ROLLER

Sun	9/29	H	DAY	41-0	W	8,500
Sun	10/6	H	NYG	0-7	L	14,000
Sun	10/13	H	ORA	7-0	W	9,000
Sun	10/20	H	BUF	7-7	T	8,500
Sun	10/27	A	NYG	0-19	L	25,000
Tue	11/5	A	SI	7-7	T	10,000
Wed	11/6	H	CHIC	0-16	L	6,000
Sat	11/9	A	FRA	0-7	L	6,000
Sun	11/10	H	FRA	6-7	L	
Sun	11/17	H	MIN	19-16	W	8,500
Sun	11/24	H	BOS	20-6	W	
Sun	12/1	H	GB	0-25	L	6,500

STATEN ISLAND STAPLETONS

Sun	10/6	H	DAY	12-0	W	6,000
Sun	10/13	A	NYG	9-19	L	30,000
Sat	10/26	A	FRA	6-6	T	6,000
Sun	10/27	H	FRA	0-3	L	10,000
Sun	11/3	H	ORA	0-0	T	
Tue	11/5	H	PRO	7-7	T	10,000
Sun	11/10	H	BOS	14-6	W	7,500
Sun	11/24	H	MIN	34-0	W	2,000
Thu	11/28	H	NYG	7-21	L	12,000
Sun	12/1	A	ORA	0-3	L	8,000

1930 NFL

BROOKLYN DODGERS

Sun	9/21	A	CHIB	0-0	T	10,000
Wed	9/24	A	POR	0-12	L	6,000
Sun	10/5	A	SI	20-0	W	3,500
Sun	10/12	H	NEW	32-0	W	7,000
Sat	10/18	A	FRA	14-7	W	3,000
Sun	10/19	A	NEW	14-0	W	
Sun	11/2	A	PRO	0-3	L	
Sun	11/9	H	MIN	34-0	W	12,000
Sun	11/23	H	SI	0-6	L	18,000
Thu	11/27	H	PRO	33-12	W	7,000
Sun	11/30	A	NYG	7-6	W	25,000
Sun	12/7	H	NYG	0-13	L	20,000

CHICAGO BEARS

Sun	9/21	H	BKN	0-0	T	10,000
Sun	9/28	A	GB	0-7	L	10,000
Sun	10/5	A	MIN	20-0	W	7,000
Sun	10/12	H	NYG	0-12	L	12,000
Sun	10/19	A	CHIC	32-6	W	7,000
Wed	10/22	A	POR	6-7	L	7,500
Sun	10/26	H	FRA	13-7	W	5,000
Sun	11/2	H	MIN	20-7	W	4,000
Sun	11/9	H	GB	12-13	L	22,000
Sun	11/16	A	NYG	12-0	W	5,000
Sat	11/22	A	FRA	13-6	W	6,500
Thu	11/27	H	CHIC	6-0	W	8,175
Sun	11/30	H	POR	14-6	W	6,000
Sun	12/7	H	GB	21-0	W	22,000

CHICAGO CARDINALS

Sun	9/21	A	GB	0-14	L	8,000
Sun	9/28	A	MIN	7-7	T	
Sun	10/5	A	POR	0-0	T	6,500
Wed	10/8	A	NEW	13-0	W	5,000
Sun	10/12	A	PRO	7-9	L	6,500
Thu	10/16	A	NYG	12-25	L	15,000
Sun	10/19	H	CHIB	6-32	L	7,000
Sat	10/25	A	FRA	34-7	W	
Sun	10/26	H	POR	23-13	W	8,000
Sun	11/2	H	FRA	6-0	W	3,000
Sun	11/9	H	NYG	7-13	L	4,000
Sun	11/16	H	GB	13-6	W	12,000
Thu	11/27	A	CHIB	0-6	L	8,175

FRANKFORD YELLOW JACKETS

Tue	9/24	A	NEW	13-6	W	2,000
Sat	9/27	H	SI	7-3	W	6,000
Sun	9/28	A	SI	0-21	L	6,000
Wed	10/1	A	PRO	0-14	L	3,500
Sat	10/4	H	NEW	0-19	L	5,000
Wed	10/8	A	POR	7-39	L	
Sun	10/12	A	GB	12-27	L	8,000
Sat	10/18	H	BKN	7-14	L	3,000
Sun	10/19	A	NYG	0-53	L	12,000
Sat	10/25	H	CHIC	7-34	L	
Sun	10/26	A	CHIB	7-13	L	5,000
Sun	11/2	A	CHIC	0-6	L	3,000
Sat	11/8	H	PRO	20-7	W	4,000
Sun	11/9	A	PRO	7-7	T	
Sat	11/15	H	POR	7-6	W	3,500
Sat	11/22	H	CHIB	6-13	L	6,500
Thu	11/27	H	GB	7-25	L	8,000
Sat	12/6	H	NYG	6-14	L	4,000

GREEN BAY PACKERS

Sun	9/21	H	CHIC	14-0	W	8,000
Sun	9/28	H	CHIB	7-0	W	10,000
Sun	10/5	H	NYG	14-7	W	11,000
Sun	10/12	H	FRA	27-12	W	8,000
Sun	10/19	A	MIN	13-0	W	
Sun	10/26	H	MIN	19-0	W	6,000
Sun	11/2	H	POR	47-13	W	7,500
Sun	11/9	A	CHIB	13-12	W	22,000
Sun	11/16	A	CHIC	6-13	L	12,000
Sun	11/23	A	NYG	6-13	L	37,000
Thu	11/27	A	FRA	25-7	W	8,000
Sun	11/30	A	SI	37-7	W	9,500
Sun	12/7	A	CHIB	0-21	L	22,000
Sun	12/14	A	POR	6-6	T	4,500

MINNEAPOLIS REDJACKETS

Sun	9/28	H	CHIC	7-7	T	
Sun	10/5	H	CHIB	0-20	L	7,000
Sun	10/12	H	POR	13-0	W	2,000
Sun	10/19	H	GB	0-13	L	
Sun	10/26	A	GB	0-19	L	6,000
Sun	11/2	A	CHIB	7-20	L	4,000
Sun	11/9	A	BKN	0-34	L	12,000
Sun	11/23	A	PRO	0-10	L	
Sun	12/7	A	POR	0-42	L	3,500

NEWARK TORNADOES

Sun	9/14	A	POR	6-13	L	4,000
Wed	9/17	H	NYG	0-32	L	6,000
Sun	9/21	A	SI	6-12	L	7,500
Wed	9/24	H	FRA	6-13	L	2,000
Wed	10/1	H	SI	7-7	T	8,000
Sat	10/4	A	FRA	19-0	W	5,000
Sun	10/5	A	PRO	0-14	L	4,500
Wed	10/8	H	CHIC	0-13	L	5,000
Sun	10/12	A	BKN	0-32	L	7,000
Sun	10/19	H	BKN	0-14	L	
Sun	10/26	H	SI	0-6	L	
Thu	10/30	A	NYG	7-34	L	5,000

NEW YORK GIANTS

Wed	9/17	A	NEW	32-0	W	6,000
Sun	9/28	A	PRO	27-7	W	12,000
Sun	10/5	A	GB	7-14	L	11,000
Sun	10/12	A	CHIB	12-0	W	12,000
Thu	10/16	H	CHIC	25-12	W	15,000
Sun	10/19	H	FRA	53-0	W	12,000
Sun	10/26	H	PRO	25-0	W	10,000
Thu	10/30	H	NEW	34-7	W	5,000
Sun	11/2	H	SI	9-7	W	18,000
Wed	11/5	A	POR	19-6	W	7,000
Sun	11/9	A	CHIC	13-7	W	4,000
Sun	11/16	H	CHIB	0-12	L	5,000
Sun	11/23	H	GB	13-6	W	37,000
Thu	11/27	A	SI	6-7	L	12,000
Sun	11/30	H	BKN	6-7	L	25,000
Sat	12/6	A	FRA	14-6	W	4,000
Sun	12/7	A	BKN	13-0	W	20,000

PORTSMOUTH SPARTANS

Sun	9/14	H	NEW	13-6	W	4,000
Wed	9/24	H	BKN	12-0	W	6,000
Sun	10/5	H	CHIC	0-0	T	6,500
Wed	10/8	H	FRA	39-7	W	
Sun	10/12	A	MIN	0-13	L	2,000
Wed	10/22	H	CHIB	7-6	W	7,500
Sun	10/26	A	CHIC	13-23	L	8,000
Sun	11/2	A	GB	13-47	L	7,500
Wed	11/5	H	NYG	6-19	L	7,000
Sun	11/9	A	SI	13-13	T	8,000
Sat	11/15	A	FRA	6-7	L	3,500
Sun	11/30	A	CHIB	6-14	L	6,000

Sun	12/7	H	MIN	42-0	W	3,500
Sun	12/14	H	GB	6-6	T	4,500

PROVIDENCE STEAM ROLLER

Sun	9/28	H	NYG	7-27	L	12,000
Wed	10/1	H	FRA	14-0	W	3,500
Sun	10/5	H	NEW	14-0	W	4,500
Sun	10/12	H	CHIC	9-7	W	6,500
Sun	10/19	H	SI	7-6	W	5,000
Sun	10/26	A	NYG	0-25	L	10,000
Sun	11/2	H	BKN	3-0	W	
Sat	11/8	A	FRA	7-20	L	4,000
Sun	11/9	H	FRA	7-7	T	
Sun	11/23	H	MIN	10-0	W	
Thu	11/27	A	BKN	12-33	L	7,000

STATEN ISLAND STAPLETONS

Sun	9/21	H	NEW	12-6	W	7,500
Sat	9/27	A	FRA	3-7	L	6,000
Sun	9/28	H	FRA	21-0	W	6,000
Wed	10/1	A	NEW	7-7	T	8,000
Sun	10/5	H	BKN	0-20	L	3,500
Sun	10/19	A	PRO	6-7	L	5,000
Sun	10/26	A	NEW	6-0	W	
Sun	11/2	A	NYG	7-9	L	18,000
Sun	11/9	H	POR	13-13	T	8,000
Sun	11/23	A	BKN	6-0	W	18,000
Thu	11/27	H	NYG	7-6	W	12,000
Sun	11/30	H	GB	7-37	L	9,500

1931 NFL

BROOKLYN DODGERS

Sun	9/13	A	POR	0-14	L	7,000
Sun	9/20	A	GB	0-6	L	8,000
Sat	9/26	A	CLE	0-6	L	8,000
Fri	10/2	A	FRA	20-0	W	2,000
Sun	10/4	A	SI	7-9	L	12,000
Sun	10/11	H	SI	18-6	W	15,000
Sun	10/18	H	POR	0-19	L	10,000
Sun	10/25	A	NYG	0-27	L	22,000
Sun	11/1	H	CHIC	7-14	L	15,000
Wed	11/4	A	SI	0-13	L	6,000
Sun	11/8	A	PRO	0-7	L	4,000
Sun	11/22	H	CHIB	0-26	L	25,000
Sun	11/29	H	GB	0-7	L	15,000
Sun	12/6	H	NYG	6-19	L	25,000

CHICAGO BEARS

Fri	9/18	H	CLE	21-0	W	6,000
Sun	9/27	A	GB	0-7	L	13,500
Sun	10/11	H	NYG	6-0	W	8,000
Sun	10/18	H	CHIC	26-13	W	8,000
Sun	10/25	H	FRA	12-13	L	26,000
Sun	11/1	H	GB	2-6	L	29,000
Sun	11/8	H	POR	9-6	W	25,000
Sun	11/15	A	NYG	12-6	W	20,000
Sun	11/22	A	BKN	26-0	W	25,000
Thu	11/26	H	CHIC	18-7	W	14,000
Sun	11/29	A	POR	0-3	L	9,000
Sun	12/6	H	GB	7-6	W	18,000
Sun	12/13	H	NYG	6-25	L	8,000

CHICAGO CARDINALS

Wed	9/23	A	POR	3-13	L	8,000
Sun	10/11	A	GB	7-26	L	8,000
Sun	10/18	A	CHIB	13-26	L	8,000
Sun	11/1	A	BKN	14-7	W	15,000
Sun	11/8	A	CLE	14-6	W	10,000
Sun	11/15	H	GB	21-13	W	9,000
Sun	11/22	H	POR	20-19	W	5,000
Thu	11/26	A	CHIB	7-18	L	14,000
Sat	11/28	H	CLE	21-0	W	1,500

CLEVELAND INDIANS

Sun	9/13	A	GB	0-26	L	6,000
Fri	9/18	A	CHIB	0-21	L	6,000
Sat	9/26	H	BKN	6-0	W	8,000
Wed	10/7	A	POR	0-6	L	
Sun	10/18	A	PRO	13-6	W	6,000
Sun	11/8	H	CHIC	6-14	L	10,000
Sun	11/15	N	POR	6-14	L	4,742
Sat	11/21	A	PRO	7-13	L	
Sun	11/22	A	SI	7-16	L	
Sat	11/28	A	CHIC	0-21	L	1,500

FRANKFORD YELLOW JACKETS

Fri	10/2	H	BKN	0-20	L	2,000
Sun	10/4	A	PRO	0-0	T	
Sat	10/10	H	PRO	0-6	L	3,000
Thu	10/15	A	POR	0-19	L	5,000
Sun	10/18	A	GB	0-15	L	6,000
Sun	10/25	A	CHIB	13-12	W	26,000
Sat	10/31	H	POR	0-14	L	5,000
Sun	11/8	A	NYG	0-13	L	25,000

GREEN BAY PACKERS

Sun	9/13	H	CLE	26-0	W	6,000
Sun	9/20	H	BKN	32-6	W	7,000
Sun	9/27	H	CHIB	7-0	W	13,500
Sun	10/4	H	NYG	27-7	W	15,550
Sun	10/11	H	CHIC	26-7	W	8,000
Sun	10/18	H	FRA	15-0	W	6,000
Sun	10/25	H	PRO	48-20	W	6,000
Sun	11/1	A	CHIB	6-2	W	29,000
Sun	11/8	H	SI	26-0	W	7,000
Sun	11/15	A	CHIC	13-21	L	9,000
Sun	11/22	A	NYG	14-10	W	35,000
Thu	11/26	A	PRO	38-7	W	5,000
Sun	11/29	A	BKN	7-0	W	15,000
Sun	12/6	A	CHIB	6-7	L	18,000

NEW YORK GIANTS

Sun	9/27	A	PRO	14-6	W	8,000
Wed	9/30	A	POR	6-14	L	9,000
Sun	10/4	A	GB	7-27	L	15,550
Sun	10/11	A	CHIB	0-6	L	8,000
Sun	10/18	H	SI	7-0	W	25,000
Sun	10/25	H	BKN	27-0	W	22,000
Sun	11/1	H	POR	14-0	W	32,500
Sun	11/8	H	FRA	13-0	W	25,000
Sun	11/15	H	CHIB	6-12	L	20,000
Sun	11/22	H	GB	10-14	L	35,000
Thu	11/26	A	SI	6-9	L	10,000
Sun	11/29	H	PRO	0-0	T	10,000
Sun	12/6	A	BKN	19-6	W	25,000
Sun	12/13	A	CHIB	25-6	W	8,000

PORTSMOUTH SPARTANS

Sun	9/13	H	BKN	14-0	W	7,000
Wed	9/23	H	CHIC	13-3	W	8,000
Wed	9/30	H	NYG	14-6	W	9,000
Wed	10/7	H	CLE	6-0	W	
Thu	10/15	H	FRA	19-0	W	5,000
Sun	10/18	A	BKN	19-0	W	10,000
Sun	10/25	A	SI	20-7	W	12,000
Sat	10/31	A	FRA	14-0	W	5,000
Sun	11/1	A	NYG	0-14	L	32,500
Sun	11/8	A	CHIB	6-9	L	25,000
Wed	11/11	H	SI	14-12	W	
Sun	11/15	N	CLE	14-6	W	4,742
Sun	11/22	A	CHIC	19-20	L	5,000
Sun	11/29	H	CHIB	3-0	W	9,000

PROVIDENCE STEAM ROLLER

Sun	9/27	H	NYG	6-14	L	8,000
Sun	10/4	H	FRA	0-0	T	
Sat	10/10	A	FRA	6-0	W	3,000
Sun	10/18	H	CLE	6-13	L	6,000
Sun	10/25	A	GB	20-48	L	6,000
Sun	11/1	A	SI	7-7	T	
Sun	11/8	H	BKN	7-0	W	4,000
Sun	11/15	H	SI	6-0	W	2,000
Sat	11/21	H	CLE	13-7	W	
Thu	11/26	H	GB	7-38	L	5,000
Sun	11/29	A	NYG	0-0	T	10,000

STATEN ISLAND STAPLETONS

Sun	10/4	H	BKN	9-7	W	12,000
Sun	10/11	A	BKN	6-18	L	15,000
Sun	10/18	A	NYG	0-7	L	25,000
Sun	10/25	H	POR	7-20	L	12,000
Sun	11/1	H	PRO	7-7	T	
Wed	11/4	H	BKN	13-0	W	6,000
Sun	11/8	A	GB	0-26	L	7,000
Wed	11/11	A	POR	12-14	L	
Sun	11/15	A	PRO	0-6	L	2,000
Sun	11/22	H	CLE	16-7	W	
Thu	11/26	H	NYG	9-6	W	10,000

1932 NFL

BOSTON BRAVES

Sun	10/2	H	BKN	0-14	L	6,000
Sun	10/9	H	NYG	14-6	W	8,000
Sun	10/16	H	CHIC	0-9	L	15,000
Sun	10/23	A	NYG	0-0	T	15,000
Sun	10/30	H	CHIB	7-7	T	18,000
Sun	11/6	H	SI	19-6	W	
Sun	11/13	H	GB	0-21	L	16,500
Sun	11/20	A	POR	0-10	L	5,000
Sun	11/27	A	CHIC	8-6	W	6,200
Sun	12/4	A	BKN	7-0	W	20,000

BROOKLYN DODGERS

Sun	9/25	A	SI	7-0	W	9,000
Sun	10/2	A	BOS	14-0	W	6,000
Sun	10/9	H	SI	6-7	L	15,000
Sun	10/16	A	NYG	12-20	L	26,000
Sun	10/23	A	GB	0-13	L	7,000
Sun	10/30	A	CHIC	7-27	L	7,159
Sun	11/6	H	POR	7-17	L	25,000
Sun	11/13	H	CHIC	3-0	W	17,000
Sun	11/20	A	CHIB	0-20	L	6,500
Thu	11/24	H	GB	0-7	L	17,000
Sun	11/27	H	NYG	7-13	L	10,000
Sun	12/4	H	BOS	0-7	L	20,000

CHICAGO BEARS

Sun	9/25	A	GB	0-0	T	13,000
Sun	10/2	A	SI	0-0	T	8,000
Sun	10/9	A	CHIC	0-0	T	7,234
Sun	10/16	H	GB	0-2	L	18,000
Sun	10/23	H	SI	27-7	W	27,540
Sun	10/30	A	BOS	7-7	T	18,000
Sun	11/6	A	NYG	28-8	W	12,000
Sun	11/13	H	POR	13-13	T	5,500
Sun	11/20	H	BKN	20-0	W	6,500
Thu	11/24	H	CHIC	34-0	W	6,800
Sun	11/27	A	POR	7-7	T	7,500
Sun	12/4	H	NYG	6-0	W	
Sun	12/11	H	GB	9-0	W	5,000
	PLAYOFF					
Sun	12/18	H	POR	9-0	W	11,198

CHICAGO CARDINALS

Sun	9/18	A	GB	7-15	L	3,500
Sun	10/2	A	POR	7-7	T	3,725
Sun	10/9	H	CHIB	0-0	T	7,234
Sun	10/16	A	BOS	9-0	W	15,000
Sun	10/30	H	BKN	27-7	W	7,159
Sun	11/6	H	GB	9-19	L	11,000
Sun	11/13	A	BKN	0-3	L	17,000
Sun	11/20	A	SI	7-21	L	5,000
Thu	11/24	A	CHIB	0-34	L	6,800
Sun	11/27	H	BOS	6-8	L	6,200

GREEN BAY PACKERS

Sun	9/18	H	CHIC	15-7	W	3,500
Sun	9/25	H	CHIB	0-0	T	13,000
Sun	10/2	H	NYG	13-0	W	5,500
Sun	10/9	H	POR	15-10	W	5,500
Sun	10/16	A	CHIB	2-0	W	18,000
Sun	10/23	H	BKN	13-0	W	7,000
Sun	10/30	H	SI	26-0	W	
Sun	11/6	A	CHIC	19-9	W	11,000
Sun	11/13	A	BOS	21-0	W	16,500
Sun	11/20	A	NYG	0-6	L	17,000
Thu	11/24	A	BKN	7-0	W	17,000
Sun	11/27	A	SI	21-3	W	3,500
Sun	12/4	A	POR	0-19	L	12,000
Sun	12/11	A	CHIB	0-9	L	5,000

NEW YORK GIANTS

Sun	9/25	A	POR	0-7	L	4,606
Sun	10/2	A	GB	0-13	L	5,500
Sun	10/9	A	BOS	20-12	W	26,000
Sun	10/16	H	BKN	20-12	W	26,000
Sun	10/23	H	BOS	0-0	T	15,000
Sun	10/30	H	POR	0-6	L	20,000
Sun	11/6	H	CHIB	8-28	L	12,000
Sun	11/13	H	SI	27-7	W	15,000
Sun	11/20	H	GB	6-0	W	17,000
Thu	11/24	A	SI	13-13	T	8,000
Sun	11/27	A	BKN	13-7	W	10,000
Sun	12/4	A	CHIB	0-6	L	

PORTSMOUTH SPARTANS

Sun	9/25	H	NYG	7-0	W	4,606
Sun	10/2	H	CHIC	7-7	T	3,725
Sun	10/9	A	GB	10-15	L	5,500
Sun	10/16	A	SI	7-7	T	7,500
Thu	10/20	A	SI	13-6	W	5,000
Sun	10/30	A	NYG	6-0	W	20,000
Sun	11/6	A	BKN	17-7	W	25,000
Sun	11/13	A	CHIB	13-13	T	5,500
Sun	11/20	H	BOS	10-0	W	5,000
Sun	11/27	H	CHIB	7-7	T	7,500
Sun	12/4	H	GB	19-0	W	12,000
	PLAYOFF					
Sun	12/18	A	CHIB	0-9	L	11,198

STATEN ISLAND STAPLETONS

Sun	9/25	H	BKN	0-7	L	9,000
Sun	10/2	H	CHIB	0-0	T	8,000
Sun	10/9	A	BKN	7-6	W	15,000
Sun	10/16	H	POR	7-7	T	7,500
Thu	10/20	H	POR	6-13	L	5,000
Sun	10/23	A	CHIB	7-27	L	27,540
Sun	10/30	A	GB	0-26	L	
Sun	11/6	A	BOS	6-19	L	
Sun	11/13	A	NYG	7-27	L	15,000
Sun	11/20	H	CHIC	21-7	W	5,000
Thu	11/24	H	NYG	13-13	T	8,000
Sun	11/27	H	GB	3-21	L	3,500

1933 NFL

BOSTON REDSKINS

Sun	9/17	A	GB	7-7	T	5,000
Sun	10/1	A	CHIB	0-7	L	8,000
Wed	10/4	A	PIT	21-6	W	15,000
Sun	10/8	H	NYG	21-20	W	17,000
Sun	10/15	H	POR	0-13	L	21,000
Sun	10/22	H	CHIC	10-0	W	18,000
Sun	10/29	H	PIT	14-16	L	7,500
Sun	11/5	H	CHIB	10-0	W	22,820
Sun	11/12	A	NYG	0-7	L	17,601
Sun	11/19	H	GB	20-7	W	16,399
Sun	11/26	A	BKN	0-14	L	15,000
Sun	12/3	A	CHIC	0-0	T	7,000

BROOKLYN DODGERS

Sun	10/8	H	CHIB	0-10	L	20,000
Sun	10/15	H	CIN	27-0	W	12,000
Sun	10/22	A	NYG	7-21	L	35,000

Sun 10/29 H CHIC 7-0 W 18,000
Sun 11/5 H PIT 3-3 T 15,000
Sun 11/12 A PIT 32-0 W 12,000
Sun 11/19 A CHIC 3-0 W 4,000
Sun 11/26 H BOS 14-0 W 15,000
Thu 11/30 H NYG 0-10 L 28,000
Sun 12/3 A CIN 0-10 L 3,500

CHICAGO BEARS

Sun 9/24 A GB 14-7 W 12,000
Sun 10/1 H BOS 7-0 W 8,000
Sun 10/8 A BKN 10-0 W 20,000
Sun 10/15 A CHIC 12-9 W 12,000
Sun 10/22 H GB 10-7 W 19,000
Sun 10/29 H NYG 14-10 W 28,000
Sun 11/5 A BOS 0-10 L 22,820
Sun 11/12 H PHI 3-3 T 17,850
Sun 11/19 A NYG 0-3 L 22,000
Sun 11/26 H POR 17-14 W 9,000
Thu 11/30 H CHIC 22-6 W 8,000
Sun 12/3 A POR 17-7 W 7,000
Sun 12/10 H GB 7-6 W 7,000

LEAGUE CHAMPIONSHIP

Sun 12/17 H NYG 23-21 W 26,000

CHICAGO CARDINALS

Wed 9/27 A PIT 13-14 L 6,000
Sun 10/1 A POR 6-7 L
Sun 10/8 A CIN 3-0 W 1,500
Sun 10/15 H CHIB 9-12 L 12,000
Sun 10/22 A BOS 0-10 L 18,000
Sun 10/29 A BKN 0-7 L 18,000
Sun 11/5 H GB 6-14 L 5,000
Sun 11/12 H CIN 9-12 L 6,000
Sun 11/19 H BKN 0-3 L 4,000
Thu 11/30 A CHIB 6-22 L 8,000
Sun 12/3 H BOS 0-0 T 7,000

CINCINNATI REDS

Sun 9/17 A POR 0-21 L 4,500
Sun 10/8 H CHIC 0-3 L 1,500
Wed 10/11 A PIT 3-17 L 5,000
Sun 10/15 H BKN 0-27 L 12,000
Sun 10/22 H PIT 0-0 T 900
Sun 11/5 H PHI 0-6 L 500
Sun 11/12 A CHIC 12-9 W 6,000
Sun 11/19 H POR 10-7 W 7,500
Sun 11/26 A PHI 3-20 L 10,000
Sun 12/3 H BKN 10-0 W 3,500

GREEN BAY PACKERS

Sun 9/17 H BOS 7-7 T 5,000
Sun 9/24 H CHIB 7-14 L 12,000
Sun 10/1 N NYG 7-10 L 12,467
Sun 10/8 H POR 47-0 W 5,200
Sun 10/15 H PIT 47-0 W 4,000
Sun 10/22 A CHIB 7-10 L 19,000
Sun 10/29 H PHI 35-9 W 3,007
Sun 11/5 A CHIC 14-6 L 5,000
Sun 11/12 A POR 0-7 L 7,500
Sun 11/19 A BOS 7-20 L 16,399
Sun 11/26 A NYG 6-17 L 17,000
Sun 12/3 A PHI 10-0 W 9,500
Sun 12/10 A CHIB 6-7 L 7,000

NEW YORK GIANTS

Wed 9/20 A PIT 23-2 W 20,000
Sun 9/24 A POR 7-17 L 7,000
Sun 10/1 N GB 10-7 W 12,467
Sun 10/8 A BOS 20-21 L 17,000
Sun 10/15 H PHI 56-0 W 18,000
Sun 10/22 H BKN 21-7 W 35,000
Sun 10/29 A CHIB 10-14 L 28,000
Sun 11/5 H POR 3-10 W 15,000
Sun 11/12 H BOS 7-0 W 17,601
Sun 11/19 H CHIB 3-0 W 22,000
Sun 11/26 H GB 17-6 W 17,000
Thu 11/30 A BKN 10-0 W 28,000
Sun 12/3 H PIT 27-3 W 12,000
Sun 12/10 A PHI 20-14 W 8,000

LEAGUE CHAMPIONSHIP

Sun 12/17 A CHIB 21-23 L 26,000

PHILADELPHIA EAGLES

Sun 10/15 A NYG 0-56 L 18,000
Wed 10/18 H POR 0-25 L 3,500
Sun 10/29 A GB 9-35 L 3,007
Sun 11/5 A CIN 6-0 W 500
Sun 11/12 H CHIB 3-3 T 17,850
Sun 11/19 H PIT 25-6 W 7,500
Sun 11/26 H CIN 20-3 W 10,000
Sun 12/3 H GB 0-10 L 9,500
Sun 12/10 H NYG 14-20 L 8,000

PITTSBURGH PIRATES

Wed 9/20 H NYG 2-23 L 20,000
Wed 9/27 H CHIC 14-13 W 6,000
Wed 10/4 H BOS 6-21 L 15,000
Wed 10/11 H CIN 17-3 W 5,000
Sun 10/15 A GB 0-47 L 4,000
Sun 10/22 A CIN 0-0 T 900
Sun 10/29 A BOS 16-14 W 7,500
Sun 11/5 A BKN 3-3 T 15,000
Sun 11/12 H BKN 0-32 L 12,000
Sun 11/19 A PHI 6-25 L 7,500
Sun 12/3 A NYG 3-27 L 12,000

PORTSMOUTH SPARTANS

Sun 9/17 H CIN 21-0 W 4,500
Sun 9/24 H NYG 17-7 W 7,000
Sun 10/1 H CHIC 7-6 W
Sun 10/8 A GB 0-17 L 5,200
Sun 10/15 A BOS 13-0 W 21,000
Wed 10/18 A PHI 25-0 W 3,500
Sun 11/5 A NYG 10-13 L 15,000
Sun 11/12 H GB 7-0 W 7,500
Sun 11/19 A CIN 7-10 L 7,500
Sun 11/26 A CHIB 14-17 L 9,000
Sun 12/3 H CHIB 7-17 L 7,000

1934 NFL

BOSTON REDSKINS

Sun 9/16 A PIT 7-0 W 17,171
Sun 9/30 A BKN 6-10 L 12,500
Sun 10/7 H NYG 13-16 L 17,033
Sun 10/14 H PIT 39-0 W 15,500
Wed 10/17 A DET 0-24 L 12,000
Sun 10/21 H PHI 6-0 W 10,344
Sun 10/28 H CHIC 9-0 W 15,000
Sun 11/4 H GB 0-10 L 23,722
Sun 11/11 H CHIB 0-21 L 26,000
Sun 11/18 A PHI 14-7 W 8,500
Sun 11/25 A NYG 0-3 L 20,000
Sun 12/2 H BKN 13-3 W 13,000

BROOKLYN DODGERS

Sun 9/30 H BOS 10-6 W 12,500
Sun 10/7 H CHIB 7-21 L 20,000
Sun 10/14 H NYG 0-14 L 30,000
Mon 10/22 A DET 0-28 L 11,000
Sun 10/28 H PIT 21-3 W 8,000
Tue 11/6 H CHIC 0-21 L 7,000
Sun 11/11 A PHI 10-7 W 8,000
Sun 11/18 A PIT 10-0 W 9,000
Sun 11/25 H PHI 0-13 L 8,000
Thu 11/29 H NYG 0-27 L 15,000
Sun 12/2 A BOS 3-13 L 13,000

CHICAGO BEARS

Sun 9/23 A GB 24-10 W 13,500
Sun 9/30 A CIN 21-3 W 5,500
Sun 10/7 A BKN 21-7 W 20,000
Wed 10/10 A PIT 28-0 W 19,386
Sun 10/14 A CHIC 20-0 W 15,000
Sun 10/21 H CIN 41-7 W 10,000
Sun 10/28 H GB 27-14 W 11,000
Sun 11/4 H NYG 27-7 W 23,200
Sun 11/11 A BOS 21-0 W 26,000
Sun 11/18 A NYG 10-9 W 45,600
Sun 11/25 H CHIC 17-6 W 13,800
Thu 11/29 A DET 19-16 W 26,000
Sun 12/2 H DET 10-7 W 34,412

LEAGUE CHAMPIONSHIP

Sun 12/9 A NYG 13-30 L 35,059

CHICAGO CARDINALS

Sun 9/23 N CIN 9-0 W 6,000
Sun 9/30 A DET 0-6 L 18,000
Sun 10/7 A CIN 16-0 W 2,500
Sun 10/14 H CHIB 0-20 L 15,000
Sun 10/21 A GB 0-15 L 4,000
Sun 10/28 A BOS 0-9 L 10,000
Tue 11/6 A BKN 21-0 W 7,000
Sun 11/11 H DET 13-17 L 7,500
Sun 11/18 A GB 9-0 W 3,000
Sun 11/25 A CHIB 6-17 L 13,800
Thu 11/29 H GB 6-0 W 1,738

CINCINNATI REDS-
ST. LOUIS GUNNERS

Cincinnati

Sun 9/9 A PIT 0-13 L 14,164
Sun 9/23 N CHIC 0-9 L 6,000
Sun 9/30 H CHIB 3-21 L 5,500
Sun 10/7 H CHIC 0-16 L 2,500
Sun 10/14 A GB 0-41 L 3,000
Sun 10/21 A CHIB 7-41 L 10,000
Sun 10/28 N DET 0-38 L 4,800
Tue 11/6 A PHI 0-64 L 2,000

St. Louis

Sun 11/11 A PIT 6-0 W 13,678
Sun 11/18 A DET 7-40 L 13,000
Sun 12/2 H GB 14-21 L 10,088

DETROIT LIONS

Sun 9/23 A NYG 0-9 L 12,000
Sun 9/30 H CHIC 6-0 W 18,000
Sun 10/7 A GB 3-0 W 7,500
Sun 10/14 A PHI 10-0 W 9,860
Wed 10/17 H BOS 24-0 W 12,000
Mon 10/22 H BKN 28-0 W 11,000
Sun 10/28 N CIN 38-0 W 4,800
Sun 11/4 A PIT 40-7 W 6,000
Sun 11/11 A CHIC 17-13 W 7,500
Sun 11/18 H STL 40-7 W 13,000
Sun 11/25 H GB 0-3 L 12,000
Thu 11/29 H CHIB 16-19 L 26,000
Sun 12/2 A CHIB 7-10 L 34,412

GREEN BAY PACKERS

Sun 9/16 H PHI 19-6 W 5,500
Sun 9/23 H CHIB 10-24 L 13,500
Sun 9/30 H NYG 20-6 W 11,000
Sun 10/7 H DET 0-3 L 7,500
Sun 10/14 H CIN 41-0 W 3,000
Sun 10/21 H CHIC 15-0 W 4,000
Sun 10/28 A CHIB 14-27 L 11,000
Sun 11/4 A BOS 10-0 W 23,722
Sun 11/11 A NYG 3-17 L 27,000
Sun 11/18 H CHIC 0-9 L 3,000
Sun 11/25 A DET 3-0 W 12,000
Thu 11/29 A CHIC 0-6 L 1,738
Sun 12/2 A STL 21-14 W 10,088

NEW YORK GIANTS

Sun 9/23 A DET 0-9 L 12,000
Sun 9/30 A GB 6-20 L 11,000
Wed 10/3 A PIT 14-12 W 13,020
Sun 10/7 A BOS 16-13 W 17,033
Sun 10/14 H BKN 14-0 W 30,000
Sun 10/21 H PIT 17-7 W 11,000
Sun 10/28 H PHI 17-0 W 8,500
Sun 11/4 A CHIB 7-27 L 23,200
Sun 11/11 H GB 17-3 W 27,000
Sun 11/18 H CHIB 9-10 L 45,600
Sun 11/25 H BOS 3-0 W 20,000
Thu 11/29 A BKN 27-0 W 15,000
Sun 12/2 A PHI 0-6 L 12,471

LEAGUE CHAMPIONSHIP

Sun 12/9 H CHIB 30-13 W 35,059

PHILADELPHIA EAGLES

Sun 9/16 A GB 6-19 L 5,500
Wed 9/26 A PIT 17-0 W 11,559
Sun 10/7 H PIT 7-9 L 9,000
Sun 10/14 H DET 0-10 L 9,860
Sun 10/21 A BOS 0-6 L 10,344
Sun 10/28 A NYG 0-17 L 8,500
Tue 11/6 H CIN 64-0 W 2,000
Sun 11/11 H BKN 7-10 L 8,000
Sun 11/18 H BOS 7-14 L 8,500
Sun 11/25 A BKN 13-0 W 8,000
Sun 12/2 H NYG 6-0 W 12,471

PITTSBURGH PIRATES

Sun 9/9 H CIN 13-0 W 14,164
Sun 9/16 H BOS 0-7 L 17,171
Wed 9/26 H PHI 0-17 L 11,559
Wed 10/3 H NYG 12-14 L 13,020
Sun 10/7 A PHI 9-7 W 9,000
Wed 10/10 A CHIB 0-28 L 19,386
Sun 10/14 A BOS 0-39 L 15,500
Sun 10/21 A NYG 7-17 L 11,000
Sun 10/28 A BKN 3-21 L 8,000
Sun 11/4 A DET 7-40 L 6,000
Sun 11/11 A STL 0-6 L 13,678
Sun 11/18 H BKN 0-10 L 9,000

1935 NFL

BOSTON REDSKINS

Sun 9/29 H BKN 7-3 W 17,930
Sun 10/6 H NYG 12-20 L 8,000
Sun 10/13 H DET 7-17 L 18,737
Sun 10/20 A NYG 6-17 L 20,000
Sun 10/27 A PIT 0-6 L 11,379
Wed 10/30 A DET 0-14 L 14,000
Sun 11/3 H PHI 6-7 L 10,000
Sun 11/10 H CHIB 14-30 L 16,423
Sun 11/24 H CHIC 0-6 L 4,152
Sun 12/1 H PIT 13-3 W 5,000
Sun 12/8 A BKN 0-0 T 7,500

BROOKLYN DODGERS

Sun 9/29 A BOS 3-7 L 17,930
Sun 10/6 H DET 12-10 W 10,000
Sun 10/13 A NYG 7-10 L 30,000
Sun 10/20 A CHIB 14-24 L 13,620
Sun 10/27 H PHI 17-6 W 20,000
Sun 11/3 A PIT 13-7 W 13,390
Tue 11/5 A PHI 3-0 W 10,000
Sun 11/10 H PIT 7-16 L 18,000
Tue 11/19 H CHIC 14-12 W 18,000
Thu 11/28 H NYG 0-21 L 25,000
Sun 12/1 A DET 0-28 L 12,000
Sun 12/8 H BOS 0-0 T 7,500

CHICAGO BEARS

Sun 9/22 A GB 0-7 L 13,600
Sun 9/29 A PIT 23-7 W 11,858
Sun 10/13 H PHI 39-0 W 22,000
Sun 10/20 H BKN 24-14 W 13,620
Sun 10/27 H GB 14-17 L 29,386

Sun	11/3	A	NYG	20-3	W	40,000
Sun	11/10	A	BOS	30-14	W	16,423
Sun	11/17	H	NYG	0-3	L	18,651
Sun	11/24	H	DET	20-20	T	14,624
Thu	11/28	A	DET	2-14	L	18,000
Sun	12/1	H	CHIC	7-7	T	12,167
Sun	12/8	A	CHIC	13-0	W	17,373

CHICAGO CARDINALS

Sun	9/15	A	GB	7-6	W	10,000
Sun	9/29	A	DET	10-10	T	8,200
Sun	10/13	A	GB	3-0	W	13,000
Sun	10/20	A	PIT	13-17	L	6,991
Sun	10/27	A	NYG	14-13	W	32,000
Sun	11/3	H	DET	6-7	L	5,000
Sun	11/10	H	PHI	12-3	W	6,000
Tue	11/19	A	BKN	12-14	L	18,000
Sun	11/24	A	BOS	6-0	W	4,152
Thu	11/28	H	GB	9-7	W	7,500
Sun	12/1	A	CHIB	7-7	T	12,167
Sun	12/8	H	CHIB	0-13	L	17,373

DETROIT LIONS

Fri	9/20	H	PHI	35-0	W	12,000
Sun	9/29	H	CHIC	10-10	T	8,200
Sun	10/6	A	BKN	10-12	L	10,000
Sun	10/13	A	BOS	17-7	W	18,737
Sun	10/20	A	GB	9-13	L	9,500
Wed	10/30	H	BOS	14-0	W	14,000
Sun	11/3	A	CHIC	7-6	W	5,000
Sun	11/10	A	GB	7-31	L	12,200
Sun	11/17	H	GB	20-10	W	12,500
Sun	11/24	A	CHIB	20-20	T	14,624
Thu	11/28	H	CHIB	14-2	W	18,000
Sun	12/1	H	BKN	28-0	W	12,000

League Championship

Sun	12/15	H	NYG	26-7	W	15,000

GREEN BAY PACKERS

Sun	9/15	H	CHIC	6-7	L	10,000
Sun	9/22	H	CHIB	7-0	W	13,600
Sun	9/29	H	NYG	16-7	W	10,000
Sun	10/6	H	PIT	27-0	W	5,000
Sun	10/13	H	CHIC	0-3	L	13,000
Sun	10/20	H	DET	13-9	W	9,500
Sun	10/27	A	CHIB	17-14	W	29,386
Sun	11/10	H	DET	31-7	W	12,200
Sun	11/17	A	DET	10-20	L	12,500
Sun	11/24	A	PIT	34-14	W	12,902
Thu	11/28	A	CHIC	7-9	L	7,500
Sun	12/8	A	PHI	13-6	W	4,000

NEW YORK GIANTS

Sun	9/22	A	PIT	42-7	W	23,298
Sun	9/29	A	GB	7-16	L	10,000
Sun	10/6	A	BOS	20-12	W	8,000
Sun	10/13	H	BKN	10-7	W	30,000
Sun	10/20	H	BOS	17-6	W	20,000
Sun	10/27	H	CHIC	13-14	L	32,000
Sun	11/3	H	CHIB	3-20	L	40,000
Sun	11/17	A	CHIB	3-0	W	18,651
Sun	11/24	H	PHI	10-0	W	15,000
Thu	11/28	A	BKN	21-0	W	25,000
Sun	12/1	A	PHI	21-14	W	6,500
Sun	12/8	H	PIT	13-0	W	8,500

League Championship

Sun	12/15	A	DET	7-26	L	15,000

PHILADELPHIA EAGLES

Fri	9/13	H	PIT	7-17	L	20,000
Fri	9/20	A	DET	0-35	L	12,000
Wed	10/9	A	PIT	17-6	W	6,271
Sun	10/13	H	CHIB	0-39	L	22,000
Sun	10/27	A	BKN	6-17	L	20,000
Sun	11/3	A	BOS	7-6	W	10,000
Tue	11/5	H	BKN	0-3	L	10,000
Sun	11/10	A	CHIC	3-12	L	6,000
Sun	11/24	A	NYG	0-10	L	15,000
Sun	12/1	H	NYG	14-21	L	6,500
Sun	12/8	H	GB	6-13	L	4,000

PITTSBURGH PIRATES

Fri	9/13	A	PHI	17-7	W	20,000
Sun	9/22	H	NYG	7-42	L	23,298
Sun	9/29	H	CHIB	7-23	L	11,858
Sun	10/6	A	GB	0-27	L	5,000
Wed	10/9	H	PHI	6-17	L	6,271
Sun	10/20	H	CHIC	17-13	W	6,991
Sun	10/27	H	BOS	6-0	W	11,379
Sun	11/3	H	BKN	7-13	L	13,390
Sun	11/10	A	BKN	16-7	W	18,000
Sun	11/24	H	GB	14-34	L	12,902
Sun	12/1	A	BOS	3-13	L	5,000
Sun	12/8	A	NYG	0-13	L	8,500

1936 NFL

BOSTON REDSKINS

Sun	9/13	A	PIT	0-10	L	15,622
Sun	9/20	A	PHI	26-3	W	20,000
Sun	9/27	A	BKN	14-3	W	15,000
Sun	10/4	H	NYG	0-7	L	14,133
Sun	10/11	A	GB	2-31	L	6,100
Sun	10/18	H	PHI	17-7	W	4,000
Sun	11/1	H	CHIC	13-10	W	7,000
Sun	11/8	H	GB	3-7	L	11,220
Sun	11/15	H	CHIB	0-26	L	12,000
Sun	11/22	H	BKN	30-6	W	4,197
Sun	11/29	H	PIT	30-0	W	4,813
Sun	12/6	A	NYG	14-0	W	18,000

League Championship

Sun	12/13	N	GB	6-21	L	29,545

BROOKLYN DODGERS

Wed	9/23	H	PIT	6-10	L	10,000
Sun	9/27	H	BOS	3-14	L	15,000
Sun	10/4	H	PHI	18-0	W	10,000
Sun	10/11	A	NYG	10-10	T	25,000
Wed	10/14	H	DET	7-14	L	8,000
Sun	10/25	H	CHIC	9-0	W	20,000
Sun	11/1	A	PIT	7-10	L	9,573
Sun	11/15	H	GB	7-38	L	25,325
Sun	11/22	A	BOS	6-30	L	4,197
Thu	11/26	H	NYG	0-14	L	18,000
Sun	11/29	A	PHI	13-7	W	5,000
Sun	12/6	A	DET	6-14	L	11,000

CHICAGO BEARS

Sun	9/20	A	GB	30-3	W	14,312
Sun	9/27	A	PHI	17-0	W	25,000
Sun	10/4	A	PIT	27-9	W	28,777
Sun	10/11	H	CHIC	7-3	W	16,288
Sun	10/18	H	PIT	26-7	W	20,000
Sun	10/25	H	DET	12-10	W	27,424
Sun	11/1	H	GB	10-21	L	31,264
Sun	11/8	A	NYG	25-7	W	34,789
Sun	11/15	A	BOS	26-0	W	12,000
Sun	11/22	A	PHI	28-7	W	10,000
Thu	11/26	A	DET	7-13	L	22,000
Sun	11/29	A	CHIC	7-14	L	13,704

CHICAGO CARDINALS

Sun	9/13	A	GB	7-10	L	8,900
Mon	9/28	A	DET	0-39	L	15,000
Sun	10/4	A	GB	0-24	L	11,000
Sun	10/11	A	CHIB	3-7	L	16,288
Sun	10/18	A	NYG	6-14	L	17,000
Sun	10/25	A	BKN	0-9	L	20,000
Sun	11/1	A	BOS	10-13	L	7,000
Sun	11/8	H	PHI	13-0	W	1,500
Sun	11/15	H	PIT	14-6	W	3,856
Sun	11/22	H	DET	7-14	L	7,579
Sun	11/29	H	CHIB	14-7	W	13,704
Sun	12/6	H	GB	0-0	T	4,793

DETROIT LIONS

Mon	9/28	H	CHIC	39-0	W	15,000
Sun	10/11	A	PHI	23-0	W	17,000
Wed	10/14	A	BKN	14-7	W	8,000
Sun	10/18	A	GB	18-20	L	13,500
Sun	10/25	A	CHIB	10-12	L	27,424
Sun	11/1	A	NYG	7-14	L	26,243
Sun	11/8	H	PIT	28-3	W	18,000
Sun	11/15	H	NYG	38-0	W	20,000
Sun	11/22	A	CHIC	14-7	W	7,579
Thu	11/26	H	CHIB	13-7	W	22,000
Sun	11/29	H	GB	17-26	L	22,000
Sun	12/6	H	BKN	14-6	W	11,000

GREEN BAY PACKERS

Sun	9/13	H	CHIC	10-7	W	8,900
Sun	9/20	H	CHIB	3-30	L	14,312
Sun	10/4	H	CHIC	24-0	W	11,000
Sun	10/11	H	BOS	31-2	W	6,100
Sun	10/18	H	DET	20-18	W	13,500
Sun	10/25	H	PIT	42-10	W	10,000
Sun	11/1	A	CHIB	21-10	W	31,264
Sun	11/8	A	BOS	7-3	W	11,220
Sun	11/15	A	BKN	38-7	W	25,325
Sun	11/22	A	NYG	26-14	W	26,000
Sun	11/29	A	DET	26-17	W	22,000
Sun	12/6	A	CHIC	0-0	T	4,793

League Championship

Sun	12/13	N	BOS	21-6	W	29,545

NEW YORK GIANTS

Sun	9/13	A	PHI	7-10	L	20,000
Sun	9/27	A	PIT	7-10	L	25,800
Sun	10/4	A	BOS	7-0	W	14,133
Sun	10/11	H	BKN	10-10	T	25,000
Sun	10/18	H	CHIC	14-6	W	17,000
Sun	10/25	H	PHI	21-17	W	15,000
Sun	11/1	H	DET	14-7	W	26,243
Sun	11/8	H	CHIB	7-25	L	34,789
Sun	11/15	A	DET	0-38	L	20,000
Sun	11/22	H	GB	14-26	L	26,000
Thu	11/26	A	BKN	14-0	W	18,000
Sun	12/6	H	BOS	0-14	L	18,000

PHILADELPHIA EAGLES

Sun	9/13	H	NYG	10-7	W	20,000
Sun	9/20	H	BOS	3-26	L	20,000
Sun	9/27	H	CHIB	0-17	L	25,000
Sun	10/4	A	BKN	0-18	L	10,000
Sun	10/11	H	DET	0-23	L	17,000
Wed	10/14	A	PIT	0-17	L	10,042
Sun	10/18	A	BOS	7-17	L	4,000
Sun	10/25	A	NYG	17-21	L	15,000
Thu	11/5	N	PIT	0-6	L	7,891
Sun	11/8	A	CHIC	0-13	L	1,500
Sun	11/22	H	CHIB	7-28	L	10,000
Sun	11/29	H	BKN	7-13	L	5,000

PITTSBURGH PIRATES

Sun	9/13	H	BOS	10-0	W	15,622
Wed	9/23	A	BKN	10-6	W	10,000
Sun	9/27	H	NYG	10-7	W	25,800
Sun	10/4	H	CHIB	9-27	L	28,777
Wed	10/14	H	PHI	17-0	W	10,042
Sun	10/18	A	CHIB	7-26	L	20,000
Sun	10/25	A	GB	10-42	L	10,000
Sun	11/1	H	BKN	10-7	W	9,573
Thu	11/5	N	PHI	6-0	W	7,891
Sun	11/8	A	DET	3-28	L	18,000
Sun	11/15	A	CHIC	6-14	L	3,856
Sun	11/29	A	BOS	0-30	L	4,813

1937 NFL

BROOKLYN DODGERS

Fri	9/10	A	PHI	13-7	W	5,221
Sun	9/19	H	PIT	0-21	L	18,000
Sun	9/26	H	CLE	9-7	W	12,000
Sun	10/3	A	WAS	7-11	L	16,000
Sun	10/17	A	DET	0-30	L	18,000
Sun	10/24	A	NYG	0-21	L	25,000
Sun	10/31	H	WAS	0-21	L	22,500
Sun	11/7	H	PHI	10-14	L	8,373
Sun	11/14	A	CHIB	7-29	L	7,065
Sun	11/21	A	PIT	23-0	W	3,706
Thu	11/25	H	NYG	13-13	T	27,000

CHICAGO BEARS

Sun	9/19	A	GB	14-2	W	16,658
Mon	10/4	A	PIT	7-0	W	22,511
Sun	10/10	A	CLE	20-2	W	5,000
Sun	10/17	H	CHIC	16-7	W	22,978
Sun	10/24	H	DET	28-20	W	34,530
Sun	10/31	A	NYG	3-3	T	50,449
Sun	11/7	H	GB	14-24	L	44,977
Sun	11/14	H	BKN	29-7	W	7,065
Thu	11/25	A	DET	13-0	W	24,173
Sun	11/28	H	CLE	15-7	W	4,188
Sun	12/5	A	CHIC	42-28	W	7,313

League Championship

Sun	12/12	H	WAS	21-28	L	15,870

CHICAGO CARDINALS

Sun	9/12	A	GB	14-7	W	10,000
Sun	9/19	A	DET	7-16	L	17,000
Fri	9/24	A	WAS	21-14	W	22,367
Sun	9/26	A	PHI	6-6	T	3,912
Sun	10/3	A	CLE	6-0	W	10,400
Sun	10/10	A	GB	13-34	L	16,181
Sun	10/17	A	CHIB	7-16	L	22,978
Sun	10/24	A	PIT	13-7	W	8,963
Sun	10/31	H	CLE	13-7	W	9,923
Sun	11/21	H	DET	7-16	L	8,576
Sun	12/5	H	CHIB	28-42	L	7,313

CLEVELAND RAMS

Fri	9/10	H	DET	0-28	L	15,500
Tue	9/21	A	PHI	21-3	W	11,376
Sun	9/26	A	BKN	7-9	L	12,000
Sun	10/3	H	CHIC	0-6	L	10,400
Sun	10/10	H	CHIB	2-20	L	5,000
Sun	10/17	H	GB	10-35	L	12,100
Sun	10/24	A	GB	7-35	L	8,600
Sun	10/31	A	CHIC	7-13	L	9,923
Sun	11/7	A	DET	7-27	L	24,800
Sun	11/21	H	WAS	7-16	L	3,500
Sun	11/28	A	CHIB	7-15	L	4,188

DETROIT LIONS

Fri	9/10	A	CLE	28-0	W	15,500
Sun	9/19	H	CHIC	16-7	W	17,000
Sun	10/3	A	GB	6-26	L	17,553
Sun	10/10	H	PIT	7-3	W	16,000
Sun	10/17	H	BKN	30-0	W	18,000
Sun	10/24	A	CHIB	20-28	L	34,530
Sun	10/31	H	GB	13-14	L	23,000
Sun	11/7	H	CLE	27-7	W	24,800
Sun	11/14	A	NYG	17-0	W	35,790
Sun	11/21	A	CHIC	16-7	W	8,576
Thu	11/25	H	CHIB	0-13	L	24,173

GREEN BAY PACKERS

Sun	9/12	H	CHIC	7-14	L	10,000
Sun	9/19	H	CHIB	2-14	L	16,658
Sun	10/3	H	DET	26-6	W	17,553
Sun	10/10	H	CHIC	34-13	W	16,181
Sun	10/17	A	CLE	35-10	W	12,100
Sun	10/24	H	CLE	35-7	W	8,600

Sun	10/31	A	DET	14-13	W	23,000
Sun	11/7	A	CHIB	24-14	W	44,977
Sun	11/14	H	PHI	37-7	W	13,340
Sun	11/21	A	NYG	0-10	L	38,965
Sun	11/28	A	WAS	6-14	L	30,000

NEW YORK GIANTS

Thu	9/16	A	WAS	3-13	L	25,000
Sun	9/26	A	PIT	10-7	W	33,095
Sun	10/3	A	PHI	16-7	W	12,127
Sun	10/17	H	PHI	21-0	W	20,089
Sun	10/24	H	BKN	21-0	W	25,000
Sun	10/31	H	CHIB	3-3	T	50,449
Sun	11/7	H	PIT	17-0	W	21,447
Sun	11/14	H	DET	0-17	L	35,790
Sun	11/21	H	GB	10-0	W	38,965
Thu	11/25	A	BKN	13-13	T	27,000
Sun	12/5	H	WAS	14-49	L	58,285

PHILADELPHIA EAGLES

Sun	9/5	A	PIT	14-27	L	8,588
Fri	9/10	H	BKN	7-13	L	5,221
Tue	9/21	H	CLE	3-21	L	11,376
Sun	9/26	H	CHIC	6-6	T	3,912
Sun	10/3	H	NYG	7-16	L	12,127
Sun	10/10	A	WAS	14-0	W	7,370
Sun	10/17	A	NYG	0-21	L	20,089
Sun	10/24	H	WAS	7-10	L	13,167
Sun	10/31	A	PIT	7-16	L	2,772
Sun	11/7	A	BKN	14-10	W	8,373
Sun	11/14	A	GB	7-37	L	13,340

PITTSBURGH PIRATES

Sun	9/5	H	PHI	27-14	W	8,588
Sun	9/19	A	BKN	21-0	W	18,000
Sun	9/26	H	NYG	7-10	L	33,095
Mon	10/4	H	CHIB	0-7	L	22,511
Sun	10/10	A	DET	3-7	L	16,000
Sun	10/17	A	WAS	20-34	L	12,835
Sun	10/24	H	CHIC	7-13	L	8,963
Sun	10/31	H	PHI	16-7	W	2,772
Sun	11/7	A	NYG	0-17	L	21,447
Sun	11/14	H	WAS	21-13	W	12,242
Sun	11/21	H	BKN	0-23	L	3,706

WASHINGTON REDSKINS

Thu	9/16	H	NYG	13-3	W	25,000
Fri	9/24	H	CHIC	14-21	L	22,367
Sun	10/3	H	BKN	11-7	W	16,000
Sun	10/10	H	PHI	0-14	L	7,370
Sun	10/17	H	PIT	34-20	W	12,835
Sun	10/24	A	PHI	10-7	W	13,167
Sun	10/31	A	BKN	21-0	W	22,500
Sun	11/14	A	PIT	13-21	L	12,242
Sun	11/21	A	CLE	16-7	W	3,500
Sun	11/28	H	GB	14-6	W	30,000
Sun	12/5	A	NYG	49-14	W	58,285

League Championship

Sun	12/12	A	CHIB	28-21	W	15,870

1938 NFL

BROOKLYN DODGERS

Sun	9/18	A	WAS	16-16	T	23,000
Fri	9/23	H	PIT	3-17	L	21,494
Sun	10/2	H	CHIC	13-0	W	17,129
Sun	10/9	A	PIT	17-7	W	8,372
Sun	10/16	A	GB	7-35	L	11,892
Sun	10/23	A	NYG	14-28	L	36,228
Sun	10/30	H	WAS	6-6	T	29,913
Sun	11/6	A	PHI	10-7	W	11,477
Sun	11/13	H	PHI	32-14	W	13,052
Sun	11/20	H	CHIB	6-24	L	26,416
Thu	11/24	H	NYG	7-7	T	17,400

CHICAGO BEARS

Sun	9/11	H	CHIC	16-13	W	20,000
Sun	9/18	A	GB	2-0	W	15,172
Sun	10/2	A	PHI	28-6	W	22,245
Sun	10/9	A	CLE	7-14	L	8,024
Sun	10/16	A	CHIC	34-28	W	21,614
Sun	10/23	H	CLE	21-23	L	18,705
Sun	10/30	H	DET	7-13	L	24,356
Sun	11/6	H	GB	17-24	L	40,208
Sun	11/13	H	WAS	31-7	W	21,817
Sun	11/20	A	BKN	24-6	W	26,416
Thu	11/24	A	DET	7-14	L	26,278

CHICAGO CARDINALS

Sun	9/11	A	CHIB	13-16	L	20,000
Sat	9/17	A	CLE	7-6	W	7,448
Sun	9/25	A	GB	7-28	L	18,000
Wed	9/28	N	GB	22-24	L	10,678
Sun	10/2	A	BKN	0-13	L	17,129
Sun	10/16	H	CHIB	28-34	L	21,614
Sun	10/23	A	DET	0-10	L	17,917
Wed	10/26	N	PHI	0-7	L	15,000
Sun	11/6	A	NYG	0-6	L	19,648
Sun	11/20	H	DET	3-7	L	8,279
Sun	11/27	H	CLE	31-17	W	2,200

CLEVELAND RAMS

Sun	9/11	A	GB	17-26	L	8,247
Sat	9/17	H	CHIC	6-7	L	7,448
Sun	9/25	A	WAS	13-37	L	27,000
Sun	10/2	H	DET	21-17	W	8,012
Sun	10/9	H	CHIB	14-7	W	8,024
Sun	10/23	A	CHIB	23-21	W	18,705
Sun	10/30	H	GB	7-28	L	18,843
Sun	11/6	A	DET	0-6	L	31,140
Sun	11/13	A	NYG	0-28	L	25,000
Sun	11/27	A	CHIC	17-31	L	2,200
Sun	12/4	N	PIT	13-7	W	7,500

DETROIT LIONS

Fri	9/9	H	PIT	16-7	W	17,000
Sun	10/2	A	CLE	17-21	L	8,012
Sun	10/9	A	GB	17-7	W	21,968
Sun	10/16	H	WAS	5-7	L	42,855
Sun	10/23	H	CHIC	10-0	W	17,917
Sun	10/30	A	CHIB	13-7	W	24,356
Sun	11/6	H	CLE	6-0	W	31,140
Sun	11/13	H	GB	7-28	L	45,139
Sun	11/20	A	CHIC	7-3	W	8,279
Thu	11/24	H	CHIB	14-7	W	26,278
Sun	12/4	H	PHI	7-21	L	18,985

GREEN BAY PACKERS

Sun	9/11	H	CLE	26-17	W	8,247
Sun	9/18	H	CHIB	0-2	L	15,172
Sun	9/25	H	CHIC	28-7	W	18,000
Wed	9/28	N	CHIC	24-22	W	10,678
Sun	10/9	H	DET	7-17	L	21,968
Sun	10/16	H	BKN	35-7	W	11,892
Sun	10/23	H	PIT	20-0	W	12,142
Sun	10/30	A	CLE	28-7	W	18,843
Sun	11/6	A	CHIB	24-17	W	40,208
Sun	11/13	A	DET	28-7	W	45,139
Sun	11/20	A	NYG	3-15	L	48,279

League Championship

Sun	12/11	A	NYG	17-23	L	48,120

NEW YORK GIANTS

Sun	9/11	A	PIT	27-14	W	17,340
Sun	9/25	A	PHI	10-14	L	23,877
Mon	10/3	H	PIT	10-13	L	18,805
Sun	10/9	A	WAS	10-7	W	37,500
Sun	10/16	H	PHI	17-7	W	33,187
Sun	10/23	H	BKN	28-14	W	36,228
Sun	11/6	H	CHIC	6-0	W	19,648
Sun	11/13	H	CLE	28-0	W	25,000
Sun	11/20	H	GB	15-3	W	48,279
Thu	11/24	A	BKN	7-7	T	17,400
Sun	12/4	H	WAS	36-0	W	57,461

League Championship

Sun	12/11	H	GB	23-17	W	48,120

PHILADELPHIA EAGLES

Sun	9/11	H	WAS	23-26	L	20,000
Fri	9/16	N	PIT	27-7	W	19,749
Sun	9/25	H	NYG	14-10	W	23,877
Sun	10/2	H	CHIB	7-17	L	33,187
Sun	10/16	A	NYG	7-17	L	33,187
Sun	10/23	A	WAS	14-20	L	3,000
Wed	10/26	N	CHIC	7-0	W	15,000
Sun	11/6	H	BKN	7-10	L	11,477
Sun	11/13	A	BKN	14-32	L	13,052
Sun	11/20	N	PIT	14-7	W	6,500
Sun	12/4	A	DET	21-7	W	18,985

PITTSBURGH PIRATES

Fri	9/9	A	DET	7-16	L	17,000
Sun	9/11	H	NYG	14-27	L	17,340
Fri	9/16	N	PHI	7-27	L	19,749
Fri	9/23	A	BKN	17-3	W	21,494
Mon	10/3	A	NYG	13-10	W	18,805
Sun	10/9	H	BKN	7-17	L	8,372
Sun	10/23	A	GB	0-20	L	12,142
Sun	11/6	H	WAS	0-7	L	12,910
Sun	11/20	N	PHI	7-14	L	6,500
Sun	11/27	A	WAS	0-15	L	22,000
Sun	12/4	N	CLE	7-13	L	7,500

WASHINGTON REDSKINS

Sun	9/11	A	PHI	26-23	W	20,000
Sun	9/18	H	BKN	16-16	T	23,000
Sun	9/25	H	CLE	37-13	W	27,000
Sun	10/9	H	NYG	7-10	L	37,500
Sun	10/16	A	DET	7-5	W	42,855
Sun	10/23	H	PHI	20-14	W	3,000
Sun	10/30	A	BKN	6-6	T	29,913
Sun	11/6	A	PIT	7-0	W	12,910
Sun	11/13	A	CHIB	7-31	L	21,817
Sun	11/27	H	PIT	15-0	W	22,000
Sun	12/4	A	NYG	0-36	L	57,461

1939 NFL

BROOKLYN DODGERS

Thu	9/14	H	PIT	12-7	W	19,444
Wed	9/20	H	CLE	23-12	W	12,423
Sun	9/24	A	DET	7-27	L	15,515
Sun	10/1	A	PHI	0-0	T	1,880
Sun	10/8	A	WAS	13-41	L	27,092
Sun	10/22	H	PHI	23-14	W	13,051
Sun	10/29	H	NYG	6-7	L	34,032
Mon	11/6	H	PIT	17-13	W	8,951
Sun	11/12	H	WAS	0-42	L	28,541
Sun	11/19	H	GB	0-28	L	19,843
Sun	11/26	A	NYG	7-28	L	30,144

CHICAGO BEARS

Fri	9/15	H	CLE	30-21	W	10,000
Sun	9/24	A	GB	16-21	L	19,192
Mon	10/2	A	PIT	32-0	W	10,325
Sun	10/8	A	CLE	35-21	W	18,209
Sun	10/15	H	CHIC	44-7	W	29,592
Sun	10/22	A	NYG	13-16	L	58,693
Sun	10/29	H	DET	0-10	L	30,903
Sun	11/5	H	GB	30-27	W	40,537
Sun	11/12	A	DET	23-13	W	42,684
Sun	11/19	H	PHI	27-14	W	21,398
Sun	11/26	A	CHIC	48-7	W	16,055

CHICAGO CARDINALS

Sun	9/10	A	DET	13-21	L	15,075
Sun	9/17	A	GB	10-14	L	11,792
Sun	9/24	A	PIT	10-0	W	19,008
Sun	10/1	H	DET	3-17	L	9,000
Sun	10/8	A	GB	20-27	L	18,965
Sun	10/15	A	CHIB	7-44	L	29,592
Sun	10/22	H	CLE	0-24	L	10,043
Sun	11/5	A	CLE	0-14	L	8,378
Sun	11/12	A	NYG	7-17	L	28,217
Sun	11/19	A	WAS	7-28	L	26,667
Sun	11/26	H	CHIB	7-48	L	16,055

CLEVELAND RAMS

Fri	9/15	A	CHIB	21-30	L	10,000
Wed	9/20	A	BKN	12-23	L	12,423
Sun	10/1	A	GB	27-24	W	9,888
Sun	10/8	H	CHIB	21-35	L	18,209
Sun	10/15	A	DET	7-15	L	30,096
Sun	10/22	A	CHIC	24-0	W	10,043
Sun	10/29	H	PIT	14-14	T	11,579
Sun	11/5	H	CHIC	14-0	W	8,378
Sun	11/19	H	DET	14-3	W	28,142
Sun	11/26	H	GB	6-7	L	30,691
Sun	12/3	N	PHI	35-13	W	9,189

DETROIT LIONS

Sun	9/10	H	CHIC	21-13	W	15,075
Sun	9/24	H	BKN	27-7	W	15,515
Sun	10/1	A	CHIC	17-3	W	9,000
Sun	10/15	H	CLE	15-7	W	30,096
Sun	10/22	A	GB	7-26	L	22,558
Sun	10/29	A	CHIB	10-0	W	30,903
Sun	11/5	H	NYG	18-14	W	48,492
Sun	11/12	H	CHIB	13-23	L	42,684
Sun	11/19	A	CLE	3-14	L	28,142
Sun	11/26	A	WAS	7-31	L	36,183
Sun	12/3	H	GB	7-12	L	30,699

GREEN BAY PACKERS

Sun	9/17	H	CHIC	14-10	W	11,792
Sun	9/24	H	CHIB	21-16	W	19,192
Sun	10/1	H	CLE	24-27	L	9,888
Sun	10/8	H	CHIC	27-20	W	18,965
Sun	10/22	H	DET	26-7	W	22,558
Sun	10/29	H	WAS	24-14	W	24,308
Sun	11/5	A	CHIB	27-30	L	40,537
Sun	11/12	A	PHI	23-16	W	23,862
Sun	11/19	A	BKN	28-0	W	19,843
Sun	11/26	A	CLE	7-6	W	30,691
Sun	12/3	A	DET	12-7	W	30,699

League Championship

Sun	12/10	H	NYG	27-0	W	32,279

NEW YORK GIANTS

Sun	9/24	A	PHI	13-3	W	30,864
Sun	10/1	A	WAS	0-0	T	26,341
Sun	10/8	A	PIT	14-7	W	9,663
Sun	10/15	H	PHI	27-10	W	34,471
Sun	10/22	H	CHIB	16-13	W	58,693
Sun	10/29	A	BKN	7-6	W	34,032
Sun	11/5	A	DET	14-18	L	48,492
Sun	11/12	H	CHIC	17-7	W	28,217
Sun	11/19	H	PIT	23-7	W	19,372
Sun	11/26	H	BKN	28-7	W	30,144
Sun	12/3	H	WAS	9-7	W	62,404

League Championship

Sun	12/10	A	GB	0-27	L	32,279

PHILADELPHIA EAGLES

Sun	9/17	H	WAS	0-7	L	33,528
Sun	9/24	H	NYG	3-13	L	30,864
Sun	10/1	H	BKN	0-0	T	1,880
Sun	10/15	A	NYG	10-27	L	34,471
Sun	10/22	A	BKN	14-23	L	13,051
Sun	11/5	A	WAS	6-7	L	20,444
Sun	11/12	H	GB	16-23	L	23,862
Sun	11/19	A	CHIB	14-27	L	21,398
Thu	11/23	H	PIT	17-14	W	20,000

Sun	11/26	A	PIT	12-24	L	8,788
Sun	12/3	N	CLE	13-35	L	9,189

PITTSBURGH PIRATES

Thu	9/14	A	BKN	7-12	L	19,444
Sun	9/24	H	CHIC	0-10	L	19,008
Mon	10/2	H	CHIB	0-32	L	10,325
Sun	10/8	H	NYG	7-14	L	9,663
Sun	10/15	A	WAS	14-44	L	25,982
Sun	10/22	H	WAS	14-21	L	8,602
Sun	10/29	A	CLE	14-14	T	11,579
Mon	11/6	A	BKN	13-17	L	8,951
Sun	11/19	A	NYG	7-23	L	19,372
Thu	11/23	A	PHI	14-17	L	20,000
Sun	11/26	H	PHI	24-12	W	8,788

WASHINGTON REDSKINS

Sun	9/17	A	PHI	7-0	W	33,528
Sun	10/1	H	NYG	0-0	T	26,341
Sun	10/8	H	BKN	41-13	W	27,092
Sun	10/15	H	PIT	44-14	W	25,982
Sun	10/22	A	PIT	21-14	W	8,602
Sun	10/29	A	GB	14-24	L	24,308
Sun	11/5	H	PHI	7-6	W	20,444
Sun	11/12	A	BKN	42-0	W	28,541
Sun	11/19	H	CHIC	28-7	W	26,667
Sun	11/26	H	DET	31-7	W	36,183
Sun	12/3	A	NYG	7-9	L	62,404

1940 NFL

BROOKLYN DODGERS

Sun	9/15	A	WAS	17-24	L	32,763
Sun	9/29	A	PIT	10-3	W	26,618
Fri	10/4	H	PHI	30-17	W	24,008
Sun	10/13	H	PIT	21-0	W	19,468
Sun	10/20	A	CHIB	7-16	L	31,101
Sat	10/26	A	PHI	21-7	W	6,500
Sun	11/3	H	NYG	7-10	L	32,958
Sun	11/10	H	WAS	16-14	W	33,846
Sun	11/17	H	CLE	29-14	W	19,212
Sun	11/24	H	CHIC	14-9	W	16,619
Sun	12/1	A	NYG	14-6	W	54,993

CHICAGO BEARS

Sun	9/22	A	GB	41-10	W	22,557
Wed	9/25	A	CHIC	7-21	L	23,181
Sun	10/6	A	CLE	21-14	W	18,998
Sun	10/13	H	DET	7-0	W	34,217
Sun	10/20	H	BKN	16-7	W	31,101
Sun	10/27	A	NYG	37-21	W	44,219
Sun	11/3	H	GB	14-7	W	45,434
Sun	11/10	A	DET	14-17	L	21,735
Sun	11/17	A	WAS	3-7	L	35,231
Sun	11/24	H	CLE	47-25	W	20,717
Sun	12/1	H	CHIC	31-23	W	13,902

League Championship

Sun	12/8	A	WAS	73-0	W	36,034

CHICAGO CARDINALS

Sun	9/8	A	PIT	7-7	T	22,000
Sun	9/15	N	DET	0-0	T	18,048
Wed	9/25	H	CHIB	21-7	W	23,181
Sun	9/29	A	GB	6-31	L	20,234
Sat	10/5	A	DET	14-43	L	20,619
Sun	10/13	A	WAS	21-28	L	33,691
Sun	10/20	A	CLE	14-26	L	13,683
Sun	10/27	H	CLE	17-7	W	10,313
Sun	11/10	H	GB	7-28	L	11,364
Sun	11/24	A	BKN	9-14	L	16,619
Sun	12/1	A	CHIB	23-31	L	13,902

CLEVELAND RAMS

Sun	9/22	H	PHI	21-13	W	15,941
Sun	9/29	A	DET	0-6	L	15,347
Sun	10/6	H	CHIB	14-21	L	18,998
Sun	10/13	A	GB	14-31	L	16,299
Sun	10/20	H	CHIC	26-14	W	13,683
Sun	10/27	A	CHIC	7-17	L	10,313
Sun	11/3	H	DET	24-0	W	18,881
Sun	11/10	A	NYG	13-0	W	23,614
Sun	11/17	A	BKN	14-29	L	19,212
Sun	11/24	A	CHIB	25-47	L	20,717
Sun	12/1	H	GB	13-13	T	16,249

DETROIT LIONS

Sun	9/15	N	CHIC	0-0	T	18,048
Sun	9/22	H	PIT	7-10	L	15,310
Sun	9/29	H	CLE	6-0	W	15,347
Sat	10/5	H	CHIC	43-14	W	20,619
Sun	10/13	A	CHIB	0-7	L	34,217
Sun	10/20	A	GB	23-14	W	21,001
Sun	10/27	H	WAS	14-20	L	28,909
Sun	11/3	A	CLE	0-24	L	18,881
Sun	11/10	H	CHIB	17-14	W	21,735
Sun	11/17	A	PHI	21-0	W	6,327
Sun	11/24	H	GB	7-50	L	26,019

GREEN BAY PACKERS

Sun	9/15	H	PHI	27-20	W	11,657
Sun	9/22	H	CHIB	10-41	L	22,557
Sun	9/29	H	CHIC	31-6	W	20,234
Sun	10/13	H	CLE	31-14	W	16,299
Sun	10/20	H	DET	14-23	L	21,001
Sun	10/27	H	PIT	24-3	W	13,703
Sun	11/3	A	CHIB	7-14	L	45,434
Sun	11/10	A	CHIC	28-7	W	11,364
Sun	11/17	A	NYG	3-7	L	28,262
Sun	11/24	A	DET	50-7	W	26,019
Sun	12/1	A	CLE	13-13	T	16,249

NEW YORK GIANTS

Sun	9/15	A	PIT	10-10	T	18,601
Sun	9/22	A	WAS	7-21	L	34,712
Sat	9/28	A	PHI	20-14	W	26,431
Sun	10/13	H	PHI	17-7	W	30,317
Sun	10/20	H	PIT	12-0	W	19,798
Sun	10/27	H	CHIB	21-37	L	44,219
Sun	11/3	A	BKN	10-7	W	32,958
Sun	11/10	H	CLE	0-13	L	23,614
Sun	11/17	H	GB	7-3	W	28,262
Sun	11/24	H	WAS	21-7	W	46,439
Sun	12/1	H	BKN	6-14	L	54,993

PHILADELPHIA EAGLES

Sun	9/15	A	GB	20-27	L	11,657
Sun	9/22	A	CLE	13-21	L	15,941
Sat	9/28	H	NYG	14-20	L	26,431
Fri	10/4	A	BKN	17-30	L	24,008
Sun	10/13	A	NYG	7-17	L	30,317
Sun	10/20	H	WAS	17-34	L	26,083
Sat	10/26	H	BKN	7-21	L	6,500
Sun	11/10	A	PIT	3-7	L	9,556
Sun	11/17	H	DET	0-21	L	6,327
Thu	11/28	H	PIT	7-0	W	4,200
Sun	12/1	A	WAS	6-13	L	25,838

PITTSBURGH STEELERS

Sun	9/8	H	CHIC	7-7	T	22,000
Sun	9/15	H	NYG	10-10	T	18,601
Sun	9/22	A	DET	10-7	W	15,310
Sun	9/29	H	BKN	3-10	L	26,618
Sun	10/6	H	WAS	10-40	L	25,213
Sun	10/13	A	BKN	0-21	L	19,468
Sun	10/20	A	NYG	0-12	L	19,798
Sun	10/27	A	GB	3-24	L	13,703
Sun	11/3	A	WAS	10-37	L	31,204
Sun	11/10	H	PHI	7-3	W	9,556
Thu	11/28	A	PHI	0-7	L	4,200

WASHINGTON REDSKINS

Sun	9/15	H	BKN	24-17	W	32,763
Sun	9/22	H	NYG	21-7	W	34,712
Sun	10/6	A	PIT	40-10	W	25,213
Sun	10/13	H	CHIC	28-21	W	33,691
Sun	10/20	A	PHI	34-17	W	26,083
Sun	10/27	A	DET	20-14	W	28,909
Sun	11/3	H	PIT	37-10	W	31,204
Sun	11/10	A	BKN	14-16	L	33,846
Sun	11/17	H	CHIB	7-3	W	35,231
Sun	11/24	A	NYG	7-21	L	46,439
Sun	12/1	H	PHI	13-6	W	25,838

League Championship

Sun	12/8	H	CHIB	0-73	L	36,034

1941 NFL

BROOKLYN DODGERS

Sun	9/21	H	DET	14-7	W	19,269
Sat	9/27	A	PHI	24-13	W	16,341
Sun	10/5	A	WAS	0-3	L	32,642
Sun	10/12	A	GB	7-30	L	15,621
Sun	10/19	H	CHIC	6-20	L	12,054
Sun	10/26	H	NYG	16-13	W	28,675
Sun	11/2	H	PHI	15-6	W	15,899
Sun	11/9	H	WAS	13-7	W	31,713
Sun	11/16	A	PIT	7-14	L	20,843
Sun	11/30	H	PIT	35-7	W	12,336
Sun	12/7	A	NYG	21-7	W	55,051

CHICAGO BEARS

Sun	9/28	A	GB	25-17	W	24,876
Sun	10/5	A	CLE	48-21	W	23,850
Sun	10/12	H	CHIC	53-7	W	34,668
Sun	10/19	H	DET	49-0	W	29,980
Sun	10/26	H	PIT	34-7	W	17,217
Sun	11/2	H	GB	14-16	L	46,484
Sun	11/9	H	CLE	31-13	W	18,102
Sun	11/16	H	WAS	35-21	W	30,095
Sun	11/23	A	DET	24-7	W	28,657
Sun	11/30	A	PHI	49-14	W	32,608
Sun	12/7	A	CHIC	34-24	W	18,879

Western Division Playoff

Sun	12/14	H	GB	33-14	W	43,425

League Championship

Sun	12/21	H	NYG	37-9	W	13,341

CHICAGO CARDINALS

Tue	9/16	H	CLE	6-10	L	15,000
Sat	9/27	H	DET	14-14	T	17,458
Sun	10/5	A	GB	13-14	L	10,000
Sun	10/12	A	CHIB	7-53	L	34,668
Sun	10/19	A	BKN	20-6	W	12,054
Sun	10/26	A	PHI	14-21	L	12,683
Sun	11/2	A	NYG	10-7	W	29,289
Sun	11/16	A	GB	9-17	L	15,495
Sun	11/23	A	CLE	7-0	W	5,000
Sun	11/30	A	DET	3-21	L	17,051
Sun	12/7	H	CHIB	24-34	L	18,879

CLEVELAND RAMS

Sun	9/7	N	PIT	17-14	W	23,720
Tue	9/16	A	CHIC	10-6	W	15,000
Sun	9/21	A	GB	7-24	L	18,463
Sun	10/5	H	CHIB	21-48	L	23,850
Sun	10/12	A	DET	7-17	L	26,481
Sun	10/19	H	GB	14-17	L	13,086
Sun	10/26	A	WAS	13-17	L	32,820
Sun	11/2	H	DET	0-14	L	10,554
Sun	11/9	A	CHIB	13-31	L	18,102
Sun	11/16	A	NYG	14-49	L	32,740
Sun	11/23	H	CHIC	0-7	L	5,000

DETROIT LIONS

Sun	9/14	A	GB	0-23	L	16,734
Sun	9/21	A	BKN	7-14	L	19,269
Sat	9/27	A	CHIC	14-14	T	17,458
Sun	10/12	H	CLE	17-7	W	26,481
Sun	10/19	A	CHIB	0-49	L	29,980
Sun	10/26	H	GB	7-24	L	30,269
Sun	11/2	A	CLE	14-0	W	10,554
Sun	11/9	A	NYG	13-20	L	27,875
Sun	11/16	H	PHI	21-17	W	16,306
Sun	11/23	H	CHIB	7-24	L	28,657
Sun	11/30	H	CHIC	21-3	W	17,051

GREEN BAY PACKERS

Sun	9/14	H	DET	23-0	W	16,734
Sun	9/21	H	CLE	24-7	W	18,463
Sun	9/28	H	CHIB	17-25	L	24,876
Sun	10/5	H	CHIC	14-13	W	10,000
Sun	10/12	H	BKN	30-7	W	15,621
Sun	10/19	A	CLE	17-14	W	13,086
Sun	10/26	A	DET	24-7	W	30,269
Sun	11/2	A	CHIB	16-14	W	46,484
Sun	11/16	H	CHIC	17-9	W	15,495
Sun	11/23	A	PIT	54-7	W	15,202
Sun	11/30	A	WAS	22-17	W	35,594

Western Division Playoff

Sun	12/14	A	CHIB	14-33	L	43,425

NEW YORK GIANTS

Sat	9/13	A	PHI	24-0	W	38,747
Sun	9/28	A	WAS	17-10	W	35,677
Sun	10/5	A	PIT	37-10	W	13,458
Sun	10/12	H	PHI	16-0	W	35,842
Sun	10/19	H	PIT	28-7	W	24,604
Sun	10/26	A	BKN	13-16	L	28,675
Sun	11/2	H	CHIC	7-10	L	29,289
Sun	11/9	H	DET	20-13	W	27,875
Sun	11/16	H	CLE	49-14	W	32,740
Sun	11/23	H	WAS	20-13	W	49,317
Sun	12/7	H	BKN	7-21	L	55,051

League Championship

Sun	12/21	A	CHIB	9-37	L	13,341

PHILADELPHIA EAGLES

Sat	9/13	H	NYG	0-24	L	38,747
Sun	9/21	A	PIT	10-7	W	12,893
Sat	9/27	H	BKN	13-24	L	16,341
Sun	10/12	A	NYG	0-16	L	35,842
Sun	10/19	H	WAS	17-21	L	19,071
Sun	10/26	H	CHIC	21-14	W	12,683
Sun	11/2	A	BKN	6-15	L	15,899
Sun	11/9	H	PIT	7-7	T	15,601
Sun	11/16	A	DET	17-21	L	16,306
Sun	11/30	H	CHIB	14-49	L	32,608
Sun	12/7	A	WAS	14-20	L	27,102

PITTSBURGH STEELERS

Sun	9/7	N	CLE	14-17	L	23,720
Sun	9/21	H	PHI	7-10	L	12,893
Sun	10/5	H	NYG	10-37	L	13,458
Sun	10/12	H	WAS	20-24	L	18,733
Sun	10/19	A	NYG	7-28	L	24,604
Sun	10/26	A	CHIB	7-34	L	17,217
Sun	11/2	A	WAS	3-23	L	30,755
Sun	11/9	A	PHI	7-7	T	15,601
Sun	11/16	H	BKN	14-7	W	20,843
Sun	11/23	H	GB	7-54	L	15,202
Sun	11/30	A	BKN	7-35	L	12,336

WASHINGTON REDSKINS

Sun	9/28	H	NYG	10-17	L	35,677
Sun	10/5	H	BKN	3-0	W	32,642
Sun	10/12	A	PIT	24-20	W	18,733
Sun	10/19	A	PHI	21-17	W	19,071
Sun	10/26	H	CLE	17-13	W	32,820
Sun	11/2	H	PIT	23-3	W	30,755
Sun	11/9	A	BKN	7-13	L	31,713
Sun	11/16	A	CHIB	21-35	L	30,095
Sun	11/23	A	NYG	13-20	L	49,317
Sun	11/30	H	GB	17-22	L	35,594
Sun	12/7	H	PHI	20-14	W	27,102

1942 NFL
BROOKLYN DODGERS
Sun 9/27 N PHI 35-14 W 5,682
Sun 10/4 A DET 28-7 W 12,598
Sun 10/11 H PIT 0-7 L 17,689
Sun 10/18 H WAS 10-21 L 25,635
Sun 10/25 H NYG 17-7 W 23,244
Sun 11/1 A CLE 0-17 L 6,329
Sun 11/8 A CHIB 0-35 L 31,643
Sun 11/15 H PHI 7-14 L 3,858
Sun 11/22 A WAS 3-23 L 34,450
Sun 11/29 A PIT 0-13 L 5,340
Sun 12/6 A NYG 0-10 L 27,449

CHICAGO BEARS
Sun 9/27 A GB 44-28 W 20,007
Sun 10/4 A CLE 21-7 W 17,161
Sun 10/11 H CHIC 41-14 W 38,500
Sun 10/18 H NYG 26-7 W 32,000
Sun 10/25 H PHI 45-14 W 15,372
Sun 11/1 H DET 16-0 W 12,205
Sun 11/8 A BKN 35-0 W 31,643
Sun 11/15 H GB 38-7 W 42,787
Sun 11/22 A DET 42-0 W 17,348
Sun 11/29 H CLE 47-0 W 13,195
Sun 12/6 A CHIC 21-7 W 8,251
LEAGUE CHAMPIONSHIP
Sun 12/13 A WAS 6-14 L 36,006

CHICAGO CARDINALS
Sun 9/13 N CLE 7-0 W 18,698
Sun 9/20 H DET 13-0 W 14,742
Sun 10/4 H GB 13-17 L 24,897
Sun 10/11 A CHIB 14-41 L 38,500
Sun 10/18 A DET 7-0 W 14,100
Sun 10/25 A CLE 3-7 L 7,896
Sun 11/1 A GB 24-55 L 14,782
Sun 11/8 A WAS 0-28 L 35,425
Sun 11/22 A PIT 3-19 L 20,711
Sun 11/29 A NYG 7-21 L 20,354
Sun 12/6 H CHIB 7-21 L 8,251

CLEVELAND RAMS
Sun 9/13 N CHIC 0-7 L 18,698
Sun 9/20 N PHI 24-14 W 6,434
Sun 9/27 A DET 14-0 W 14,646
Sun 10/4 H CHIB 7-21 L 17,161
Sun 10/11 A WAS 14-33 L 33,250
Sun 10/18 A GB 28-45 L 12,847
Sun 10/25 H CHIC 7-3 W 7,896
Sun 11/1 A BKN 17-0 W 6,329
Sun 11/8 H GB 12-30 L 16,473
Sun 11/15 H DET 27-7 W 4,029
Sun 11/29 A CHIB 0-47 L 13,195

DETROIT LIONS
Sun 9/20 A CHIC 0-13 L 14,742
Sun 9/27 H CLE 0-14 L 14,646
Sun 10/4 H BKN 7-28 L 12,598
Sun 10/11 A GB 7-38 L 19,500
Sun 10/18 H CHIC 0-7 L 14,100
Sun 10/25 H GB 7-28 L 19,097
Sun 11/1 A CHIB 0-16 L 12,205
Sun 11/8 H PIT 7-35 L 16,679
Sun 11/15 A CLE 7-27 L 4,029
Sun 11/22 H CHIB 0-42 L 17,348
Sun 11/29 H WAS 3-15 L 6,044

GREEN BAY PACKERS
Sun 9/27 H CHIB 28-44 L 20,007
Sun 10/4 A CHIC 17-13 W 24,897
Sun 10/11 H DET 38-7 W 19,500
Sun 10/18 H CLE 45-28 W 12,847
Sun 10/25 A DET 28-7 W 19,097
Sun 11/1 H CHIC 55-24 W 14,782

Sun 11/8 A CLE 30-12 W 16,473
Sun 11/15 A CHIB 7-38 L 42,787
Sun 11/22 A NYG 21-21 T 30,246
Sun 11/29 A PHI 7-0 W 13,700
Sun 12/6 H PIT 24-21 W 5,138

NEW YORK GIANTS
Sun 9/27 A WAS 14-7 W 34,700
Sun 10/4 A PIT 10-13 L 9,600
Sun 10/11 H PHI 35-17 W 28,264
Sun 10/18 A CHIB 7-26 L 32,000
Sun 10/25 A BKN 7-17 L 23,244
Sun 11/1 H PIT 9-17 L 19,346
Sun 11/8 A PHI 14-0 W 13,548
Sun 11/15 H WAS 7-14 L 30,879
Sun 11/22 H GB 21-21 T 30,246
Sun 11/29 H CHIC 21-7 W 20,354
Sun 12/6 H BKN 10-0 W 27,449

PHILADELPHIA EAGLES
Sun 9/13 A PIT 24-14 W 13,349
Sun 9/20 N CLE 14-24 L 6,434
Sun 9/27 N BKN 14-35 L 5,682
Sun 10/4 H WAS 10-14 L 15,500
Sun 10/11 A NYG 17-35 L 28,264
Sun 10/18 A PIT 0-14 L 12,500
Sun 10/25 A CHIB 14-45 L 15,372
Sun 11/1 A WAS 27-30 L 32,658
Sun 11/8 H NYG 0-14 L 13,548
Sun 11/15 A BKN 14-7 W 3,858
Sun 11/29 H GB 0-7 L 13,700

PITTSBURGH STEELERS
Sun 9/13 H PHI 14-24 L 13,349
Sun 9/20 A WAS 14-28 L 25,000
Sun 10/4 H NYG 13-10 W 9,600
Sun 10/11 A BKN 7-0 W 17,689
Sun 10/18 A PHI 14-0 W 12,500
Sun 10/25 H BKN 0-14 L 37,764
Sun 11/1 A NYG 17-9 W 19,346
Sun 11/8 A DET 35-7 W 16,679
Sun 11/22 H CHIC 19-3 W 20,711
Sun 11/29 H BKN 13-0 W 5,340
Sun 12/6 A GB 21-24 L 5,138

WASHINGTON REDSKINS
Sun 9/20 H PIT 28-14 W 25,000
Sun 9/27 H NYG 7-14 W 34,700
Sun 10/4 A PHI 14-10 W 15,500
Sun 10/11 H CLE 33-14 W 33,250
Sun 10/18 A BKN 21-10 W 25,635
Sun 10/25 A PIT 14-0 W 37,764
Sun 11/1 H PHI 30-27 W 32,658
Sun 11/8 H CHIC 28-0 W 35,425
Sun 11/15 A NYG 14-7 W 30,879
Sun 11/22 H BKN 23-3 W 34,450
Sun 11/29 A DET 15-3 W 6,044
LEAGUE CHAMPIONSHIP
Sun 12/13 H CHIB 14-6 W 36,006

1943 NFL
BROOKLYN DODGERS
Sun 9/26 A DET 0-27 L 23,768
Sat 10/2 P-P 0-17 L 11,131
Sun 10/10 A WAS 0-27 L 35,540
Sun 10/17 H NYG 0-20 L 18,361
Sun 10/24 A CHIB 21-33 L 9,600
Sun 10/31 H WAS 10-48 L 11,471
Sun 11/7 H CHIC 7-0 W 13,340
Sun 11/14 H P-P 13-7 W 7,614
Sun 11/21 H GB 7-31 L 18,992
Sun 11/28 A NYG 7-24 L 28,706

CHICAGO BEARS
Sun 9/26 A GB 21-21 T 23,675
Sun 10/3 A DET 27-21 W 48,118

Sun 10/10 H CHIC 20-0 W 24,658
Sun 10/17 P-P 48-21 W 21,744
Sun 10/24 H BKN 33-21 W 9,600
Sun 10/31 H DET 35-14 W 25,187
Sun 11/7 H GB 21-7 W 43,425
Sun 11/14 A NYG 56-7 W 56,681
Sun 11/21 A WAS 7-21 L 35,672
Sun 11/28 A CHIC 35-24 W 17,219
LEAGUE CHAMPIONSHIP
Sun 12/26 H WAS 41-21 W 34,320

CHICAGO CARDINALS
Sun 9/19 A DET 17-35 L 23,408
Sun 10/3 H GB 7-28 L 15,563
Sun 10/10 A CHIB 0-20 L 24,658
Sun 10/17 N DET 0-7 L 15,072
Sun 10/24 A WAS 7-13 L 35,540
Sun 10/31 P-P 13-34 L 16,351
Sun 11/7 A BKN 0-7 L 13,340
Sun 11/14 A GB 14-35 L 10,831
Sun 11/21 A NYG 13-24 L 19,804
Sun 11/28 H CHIB 24-35 L 17,219

DETROIT LIONS
Sun 9/19 H CHIC 35-17 W 23,408
Sun 9/26 H BKN 27-0 W 23,768
Sun 10/3 H CHIB 21-27 L 48,118
Sun 10/10 A GB 14-35 L 21,396
Sun 10/17 N CHIC 7-0 W 15,072
Sun 10/24 A GB 6-27 L 41,463
Sun 10/31 A CHIB 14-35 L 25,187
Sun 11/7 H NYG 0-0 T 16,992
Sun 11/14 A WAS 20-42 L 35,540
Sun 11/21 A P-P 34-35 L 23,338

GREEN BAY PACKERS
Sun 9/26 H CHIB 21-21 T 23,675
Sun 10/3 A CHIC 28-7 W 15,563
Sun 10/10 H DET 35-14 W 21,396
Sun 10/17 H WAS 7-33 L 23,058
Sun 10/24 A DET 27-6 W 41,463
Sun 10/31 A NYG 35-21 W 46,208
Sun 11/7 A CHIB 7-21 L 43,425
Sun 11/14 H CHIC 35-14 W 10,831
Sun 11/21 A BKN 31-7 W 18,992
Sun 12/5 A P-P 38-28 W 34,294

NEW YORK GIANTS
Sun 10/9 A P-P 14-28 L 15,340
Sun 10/17 A BKN 20-0 W 18,361
Sun 10/24 P-P 42-14 W 42,681
Sun 10/31 H GB 21-35 L 46,208
Sun 11/7 A DET 0-0 T 16,992
Sun 11/14 H CHIB 7-56 L 56,681
Sun 11/21 H CHIC 24-13 W 19,804
Sun 11/28 H BKN 24-7 W 28,706
Sun 12/5 H WAS 14-10 W 51,308
Sun 12/12 A WAS 31-7 W 35,540
EASTERN DIVISION PLAYOFF
Sun 12/19 H WAS 0-28 L 42,800

PHILADELPHIA EAGLES-PITTSBURGH STEELERS
Sat 10/2 H BKN 17-0 W 11,131
Sat 10/9 H NYG 28-14 W 15,340
Sun 10/17 A CHIB 21-48 L 21,744
Sun 10/24 A NYG 14-42 L 42,681
Sun 10/31 H CHIC 34-13 W 16,351
Sun 11/7 H WAS 14-14 T 28,893
Sun 11/14 A BKN 7-13 L 7,614
Sun 11/21 H DET 35-34 W 23,338
Sun 11/28 A WAS 27-14 W 35,826
Sun 12/5 H GB 28-38 L 34,294

WASHINGTON REDSKINS
Sun 10/10 H BKN 27-0 W 35,540

Sun 10/17 A GB 33-7 W 23,058
Sun 10/24 H CHIC 13-7 W 35,540
Sun 10/31 A BKN 48-10 W 11,471
Sun 11/7 A P-P 14-14 T 28,893
Sun 11/14 H DET 42-20 W 35,540
Sun 11/21 H CHIB 21-7 W 35,672
Sun 11/28 P-P 14-27 L 35,826
Sun 12/5 A NYG 10-14 L 51,308
Sun 12/12 H NYG 7-31 L 35,540
EASTERN DIVISION PLAYOFF
Sun 12/19 A NYG 28-0 W 42,800
LEAGUE CHAMPIONSHIP
Sun 12/26 A CHIB 21-41 L 34,320

1944 NFL
BOSTON YANKS
Tue 9/26 H PHI 7-28 L 25,061
Sun 10/8 H NYG 10-22 L 17,404
Sun 10/15 H WAS 14-21 L 17,758
Sun 10/22 H PHI 0-38 L 24,638
Sun 10/29 H BKN 17-14 W 13,237
Sun 11/5 A NYG 0-31 L 28,364
Sun 11/12 A CHIB 7-21 L 19,374
Sun 11/19 H BKN 13-6 W 16,487
Sun 11/26 A WAS 7-14 L 35,540
Sun 12/3 A DET 7-38 L 15,027

BROOKLYN TIGERS
Sun 9/17 A GB 7-14 L 12,994
Sun 10/8 A DET 14-19 L 15,702
Sun 10/15 H NYG 7-14 L 24,854
Sun 10/22 A WAS 14-17 L 35,000
Sun 10/29 H BOS 14-17 L 13,237
Sun 11/5 H PHI 7-21 L 15,289
Sun 11/12 H WAS 0-10 L 20,404
Sun 11/19 A BOS 6-13 L 16,487
Sun 11/26 A NYG 0-7 L 29,387
Sun 12/3 A PHI 0-34 L 13,467

CHICAGO BEARS
Sun 9/24 A GB 28-42 L 24,362
Sun 10/8 A CLE 7-19 L 15,750
Sun 10/15 H C-P 34-7 W 20,940
Sun 10/22 H DET 21-21 L 23,835
Sun 10/29 H CLE 28-21 W 23,644
Sun 11/5 H GB 21-0 W 45,553
Sun 11/12 H BOS 21-7 W 19,374
Sun 11/19 A DET 21-41 L 21,960
Sun 11/26 A PHI 28-7 W 34,035
Sun 12/3 A C-P 49-7 W 9,069

CHICAGO CARDINALS-PITTSBURGH STEELERS
Sun 9/24 A CLE 28-30 L 20,968
Sun 10/8 A GB 7-34 L 16,535
Sun 10/15 A CHIB 0-23 L 40,734
Sun 10/22 A NYG 0-23 L 40,734
Sun 10/29 A WAS 20-42 L 35,540
Sun 11/5 H DET 6-27 L 17,743
Sun 11/12 A DET 7-21 L 13,239
Sun 11/19 H CLE 20-35 L 7,158
Sun 11/26 H GB 20-35 L 7,158
Sun 12/3 H CHIB 7-49 L 9,069

CLEVELAND RAMS
Sun 9/24 A C-P 30-28 W 20,968
Sun 10/8 H CHIB 19-7 W 15,750
Sun 10/15 A DET 20-17 W 21,115
Sun 10/22 A GB 21-30 L 18,780
Sun 10/29 A CHIB 21-28 L 23,644
Sun 11/5 A WAS 10-14 L 35,540
Sun 11/12 H DET 7-42 L 17,166
Sun 11/19 A C-P 33-6 W 14,632
Sun 11/26 H DET 14-26 L 7,462
Sun 12/10 A PHI 13-26 L 24,123

DETROIT LIONS

Sun	10/1	A	GB	6-27	L	18,556
Sun	10/8	H	BKN	19-14	W	15,702
Sun	10/15	H	CLE	17-20	L	21,115
Sun	10/22	A	CHIB	21-21	T	23,835
Sun	10/29	H	GB	0-14	L	30,844
Sun	11/5	A	C-P	27-6	W	17,743
Sun	11/12	H	C-P	21-7	W	13,239
Sun	11/19	H	CHIB	41-21	W	21,960
Sun	11/26	A	CLE	26-14	W	7,462
Sun	12/3	H	BOS	38-7	W	15,027

GREEN BAY PACKERS

Sun	9/17	H	BKN	14-7	W	12,994
Sun	9/24	H	CHIB	42-28	W	24,362
Sun	10/1	H	DET	27-6	W	18,556
Sun	10/8	H	C-P	34-7	W	16,535
Sun	10/22	H	CLE	30-21	W	18,780
Sun	10/29	A	DET	14-0	W	30,844
Sun	11/5	A	CHIB	0-21	L	45,553
Sun	11/12	A	CLE	42-7	W	17,166
Sun	11/19	A	NYG	0-24	L	56,481
Sun	11/26	A	C-P	35-20	W	7,158

League Championship

Sun	12/17	A	NYG	14-7	W	46,016

NEW YORK GIANTS

Sun	10/8	A	BOS	22-10	W	17,404
Sun	10/15	A	BKN	14-7	W	24,854
Sun	10/22	H	C-P	23-0	W	40,734
Sun	10/29	H	PHI	17-24	L	42,639
Sun	11/5	H	BOS	31-0	W	28,364
Sun	11/12	A	PHI	21-21	T	33,248
Sun	11/19	H	GB	24-0	W	56,481
Sun	11/26	H	BKN	7-0	W	29,387
Sun	12/3	H	WAS	16-13	W	47,457
Sun	12/10	A	WAS	31-0	W	35,540

League Championship

Sun	12/17	H	GB	7-14	L	46,016

PHILADELPHIA EAGLES

Tue	9/26	A	BOS	28-7	W	25,061
Sun	10/8	H	WAS	31-31	T	32,548
Sun	10/22	H	BOS	38-0	W	24,638
Sun	10/29	A	NYG	24-17	W	42,639
Sun	11/5	A	BKN	21-7	W	15,289
Sun	11/12	H	NYG	21-21	T	33,248
Sun	11/19	A	WAS	37-7	W	35,540
Sun	11/26	H	CHIB	7-28	L	34,035
Sun	12/3	H	BKN	34-0	W	13,467
Sun	12/10	H	CLE	26-13	W	24,123

WASHINGTON REDSKINS

Sun	10/8	A	PHI	31-31	T	32,549
Sun	10/15	A	BOS	21-14	W	17,758
Sun	10/22	H	BKN	17-14	W	35,000
Sun	10/29	H	C-P	42-20	W	35,540
Sun	11/5	H	CLE	14-10	W	35,540
Sun	11/12	A	BKN	10-0	W	20,404
Sun	11/19	H	PHI	7-37	L	35,540
Sun	11/26	H	BOS	14-7	W	35,540
Sun	12/3	A	NYG	13-16	L	47,457
Sun	12/10	H	NYG	0-31	L	35,540

1945 NFL

BOSTON YANKS

Tue	9/25	H	PIT	28-7	W	27,502
Sun	10/7	H	WAS	28-20	W	22,685
Sun	10/14	A	NYG	13-13	T	33,113
Sun	10/21	A	GB	14-38	L	20,846
Sun	10/28	A	PIT	10-6	W	25,447
Sun	11/4	H	DET	9-10	L	17,631
Sun	11/11	A	WAS	7-34	L	34,788
Sun	11/18	H	GB	0-28	L	33,748
Sun	12/2	A	CLE	7-20	L	18,470
Sun	12/9	A	PHI	7-35	L	27,905

CHICAGO BEARS

Sun	9/30	A	GB	21-31	L	24,525
Sun	10/7	A	CLE	0-17	L	19,580
Sun	10/14	H	CHIC	7-16	L	20,784
Sun	10/21	H	CLE	21-41	L	28,273
Sun	10/28	A	DET	10-16	L	37,260
Sun	11/4	H	GB	28-24	W	45,527
Sun	11/11	H	DET	28-35	L	24,798
Sun	11/18	A	WAS	21-28	L	34,788
Sun	11/25	H	PIT	28-7	W	20,689
Sun	12/2	A	CHIC	28-20	W	13,925

CHICAGO CARDINALS

Sun	9/23	N	DET	0-10	L	5,461
Sun	9/30	A	CLE	0-21	L	10,872
Sun	10/7	A	PHI	6-21	L	25,581
Sun	10/14	A	CHIB	16-7	W	20,784
Sun	10/21	A	DET	0-26	L	32,644
Sun	10/28	A	GB	14-33	L	19,221
Sun	11/4	A	WAS	21-24	L	35,000
Sun	11/11	A	PIT	0-23	L	13,153
Sun	11/18	H	CLE	21-35	L	18,000
Sun	12/2	H	CHIB	20-28	L	13,925

CLEVELAND RAMS

Sun	9/30	H	CHIC	21-0	W	10,872
Sun	10/7	H	CHIB	17-0	W	19,580
Sun	10/14	A	GB	27-14	W	24,607
Sun	10/21	A	CHIB	41-21	W	28,273
Sun	10/28	A	PHI	14-28	L	38,149
Sun	11/4	A	NYG	21-17	W	46,219
Sun	11/11	H	GB	20-7	W	28,688
Sun	11/18	A	CHIC	35-21	W	18,000
Thu	11/22	A	DET	28-21	W	40,017
Sun	12/2	H	BOS	20-7	W	18,470

League Championship

Sun	12/16	H	WAS	15-14	W	32,178

DETROIT LIONS

Sun	9/23	N	CHIC	10-0	W	5,461
Sun	10/7	A	GB	21-57	L	20,463
Sun	10/14	H	PHI	28-24	W	22,580
Sun	10/21	H	CHIC	26-0	W	32,644
Sun	10/28	H	CHIB	16-10	W	37,260
Sun	11/4	A	BOS	10-9	W	17,631
Sun	11/11	A	CHIB	35-28	W	24,798
Sun	11/18	A	NYG	14-35	L	38,215
Thu	11/22	H	CLE	21-28	L	40,017
Sun	12/2	H	GB	14-3	W	23,468

GREEN BAY PACKERS

Sun	9/30	H	CHIB	31-21	W	24,525
Sun	10/7	H	DET	57-21	W	20,463
Sun	10/14	H	CLE	14-27	L	24,607
Sun	10/21	H	BOS	38-14	W	20,846
Sun	10/28	H	CHIC	33-14	W	19,221
Sun	11/4	A	CHIB	24-28	L	45,527
Sun	11/11	A	CLE	7-20	L	28,686
Sun	11/18	A	BOS	28-0	W	33,748
Sun	11/25	A	NYG	23-14	W	52,681
Sun	12/2	A	DET	3-14	L	23,468

NEW YORK GIANTS

Sun	10/7	A	PIT	34-6	W	20,097
Sun	10/14	H	BOS	13-13	T	33,113
Sun	10/21	H	PIT	7-21	L	43,070
Sun	10/28	H	WAS	14-24	L	55,641
Sun	11/4	H	CLE	17-21	L	46,219
Sun	11/11	A	PHI	17-38	L	30,047
Sun	11/18	H	DET	35-14	W	38,215
Sun	11/25	H	GB	14-23	L	52,681
Sun	12/2	H	PHI	28-21	W	45,372
Sun	12/9	A	WAS	0-17	L	34,788

PHILADELPHIA EAGLES

Sun	10/7	H	CHIC	21-6	W	25,581
Sun	10/14	A	DET	24-28	L	22,580
Sun	10/21	A	WAS	14-24	L	34,788
Sun	10/28	H	CLE	28-14	W	38,149
Sun	11/4	A	PIT	45-3	W	23,018
Sun	11/11	H	NYG	38-17	W	30,047
Sun	11/18	H	PIT	30-6	W	23,838
Sun	11/25	H	WAS	16-0	W	37,306
Sun	12/2	A	NYG	21-28	L	45,372
Sun	12/9	H	BOS	35-7	W	27,905

PITTSBURGH STEELERS

Tue	9/25	A	BOS	7-28	L	27,502
Sun	10/7	H	NYG	6-34	L	20,097
Sun	10/14	H	WAS	0-14	L	14,050
Sun	10/21	A	NYG	21-7	W	43,070
Sun	10/28	H	BOS	6-10	L	25,447
Sun	11/4	H	PHI	3-45	L	23,018
Sun	11/11	H	CHIC	23-0	W	13,153
Sun	11/18	A	PHI	6-30	L	23,838
Sun	11/25	A	CHIB	7-28	L	20,689
Sun	12/2	A	WAS	0-24	L	34,788

WASHINGTON REDSKINS

Sun	10/7	A	BOS	20-28	L	22,685
Sun	10/14	A	PIT	14-0	W	14,050
Sun	10/21	H	PHI	24-14	W	34,788
Sun	10/28	A	NYG	24-14	W	55,641
Sun	11/4	H	CHIC	24-21	W	35,000
Sun	11/11	H	BOS	34-7	W	34,788
Sun	11/18	H	CHIB	28-21	W	34,788
Sun	11/25	A	PHI	0-16	L	37,306
Sun	12/2	H	PIT	24-0	W	34,788
Sun	12/9	H	NYG	17-0	W	34,788

League Championship

Sun	12/16	A	CLE	14-15	L	32,178

1946 AAFC

BROOKLYN DODGERS

Sun	9/8	A	BUF	27-14	W	25,489
Fri	9/13	A	LA	14-20	L	19,153
Sun	9/22	A	SF	13-32	L	35,000
Sun	10/6	A	CLE	7-26	L	43,713
Fri	10/11	H	CHI	21-21	T	16,211
Sat	10/19	A	NY	10-21	L	30,212
Fri	10/25	H	MIA	30-7	W	15,200
Sat	11/2	A	CHI	21-14	W	17,924
Sun	11/10	H	BUF	14-17	L	12,820
Sun	11/17	H	LA	14-19	L	7,500
Sun	11/24	H	SF	14-30	L	15,100
Thu	11/28	H	NY	7-21	L	16,240
Sun	12/8	H	CLE	14-66	L	14,600
Fri	12/13	A	MIA	20-31	L	2,340

BUFFALO BILLS

Sun	9/8	H	BKN	14-27	L	25,489
Sat	9/14	A	NY	10-21	L	40,606
Sun	9/22	H	CLE	0-28	L	30,302
Wed	9/25	A	CHI	35-38	L	20,678
Sun	9/29	H	LA	21-21	T	18,163
Fri	10/4	H	NY	13-21	L	17,101
Fri	10/11	H	MIA	14-17	L	5,040
Sat	10/19	H	SF	17-14	W	6,101
Sun	10/27	H	CHI	49-17	W	15,738
Sat	11/2	A	SF	14-27	L	12,500
Sun	11/10	A	BKN	17-14	W	12,820
Mon	11/18	A	MIA	14-21	L	5,592
Sun	11/24	A	CLE	17-42	L	37,054
Sun	12/1	A	LA	14-62	L	27,000

CHICAGO ROCKETS

Fri	9/13	H	CLE	6-20	L	51,962
Fri	9/20	H	NY	17-17	T	25,000
Wed	9/25	H	BUF	38-35	W	20,678
Sun	9/29	H	SF	21-7	W	28,675
Sat	10/5	H	LA	9-21	L	31,076
Fri	10/11	A	BKN	21-21	T	16,211
Fri	10/18	H	MIA	28-7	W	20,172
Sun	10/27	A	BUF	17-49	L	15,738
Sat	11/2	H	BKN	14-21	L	17,924
Mon	11/11	A	MIA	20-7	W	7,438
Sun	11/17	A	CLE	14-51	L	60,457
Sun	11/24	A	NY	38-28	W	21,270
Sat	11/30	A	SF	0-14	L	12,000
Sun	12/15	A	LA	17-17	T	22,515

CLEVELAND BROWNS

Fri	9/6	H	MIA	44-0	W	60,135
Fri	9/13	A	CHI	20-6	W	51,962
Sun	9/22	A	BUF	28-0	W	30,302
Sun	9/29	H	NY	24-7	W	57,084
Sun	10/6	H	BKN	26-7	W	43,713
Sun	10/12	A	NY	7-0	W	34,252
Sun	10/20	H	LA	31-14	W	71,134
Sun	10/27	H	SF	20-34	L	70,386
Sun	11/3	A	LA	16-17	L	24,800
Sun	11/10	A	SF	14-7	W	41,061
Sun	11/17	H	CHI	51-14	W	60,457
Sun	11/24	H	BUF	42-17	W	37,054
Tue	12/3	A	MIA	34-0	W	9,083
Sun	12/8	A	BKN	66-14	W	14,600

League Championship

Sun	12/22	H	NY	14-9	W	41,181

LOS ANGELES DONS

Fri	9/13	H	BKN	20-14	W	19,153
Fri	9/20	H	MIA	30-14	W	19,585
Sun	9/29	A	BUF	21-21	T	18,163
Sat	10/5	A	CHI	21-9	W	31,076
Sat	10/12	H	SF	14-23	L	12,500
Sat	10/20	A	CLE	14-31	L	71,134
Sun	10/27	H	NY	17-31	L	15,000
Sun	11/3	H	CLE	17-16	W	24,800
Sun	11/10	A	NY	12-17	L	30,765
Sun	11/17	A	BKN	19-14	W	7,500
Mon	11/25	A	MIA	34-21	W	9,987
Sun	12/1	H	BUF	62-14	W	27,000
Sun	12/8	A	SF	7-48	L	25,000
Sun	12/15	H	CHI	17-17	T	22,515

MIAMI SEAHAWKS

Fri	9/6	A	CLE	0-44	L	60,135
Sun	9/15	A	SF	14-21	L	25,000
Fri	9/20	A	LA	14-30	L	19,585
Tue	10/8	H	SF	7-34	L	7,621
Fri	10/11	A	BUF	17-14	W	5,040
Fri	10/18	A	CHI	7-28	L	20,172
Fri	10/25	A	BKN	7-30	L	15,200
Sun	11/3	A	NY	21-24	L	18,800
Mon	11/11	H	CHI	7-20	L	7,438
Mon	11/18	H	BUF	21-14	W	5,592
Mon	11/25	H	LA	21-34	L	9,987
Tue	12/3	H	CLE	0-34	L	9,083
Mon	12/9	H	NY	0-31	L	7,090
Fri	12/13	H	BKN	31-20	W	2,340

NEW YORK YANKEES

Sun	9/8	A	SF	21-7	W	35,000
Sat	9/14	H	BUF	21-10	W	40,606
Fri	9/20	A	CHI	17-17	T	25,000
Sun	9/29	A	CLE	7-24	L	57,084
Fri	10/4	A	BUF	21-13	W	17,101
Sat	10/12	H	CLE	0-7	L	34,252
Sat	10/19	H	BKN	21-10	W	30,212
Sun	10/27	A	LA	31-17	W	15,000
Sun	11/3	H	MIA	24-21	W	18,800
Sun	11/10	H	LA	17-12	W	30,765
Sun	11/17	H	SF	10-9	W	18,695
Sun	11/24	H	CHI	28-38	L	21,270
Thu	11/28	A	BKN	21-7	W	16,240
Mon	12/9	A	MIA	31-0	W	7,090

League Championship

Sun	12/22	A	CLE	9-14	L	41,181

San Francisco 49ers

Sun	9/8	H	NY	7-21	L	35,000
Sun	9/15	H	MIA	21-14	T	25,000
Sun	9/22	H	BKN	32-13	W	35,000
Sun	9/29	A	CHI	7-21	L	28,675
Tue	10/8	A	MIA	34-7	W	7,621
Sat	10/12	A	LA	23-14	W	12,500
Sat	10/19	A	BUF	14-17	L	6,101
Sun	10/27	A	CLE	34-20	W	70,386
Sat	11/2	H	BUF	27-14	W	12,500
Sun	11/10	H	CLE	7-14	L	41,061
Sun	11/17	A	NY	9-10	L	18,695
Sun	11/24	A	BKN	30-14	W	15,100
Sat	11/30	H	CHI	14-0	W	12,000
Sun	12/8	H	LA	48-7	W	25,000

1946 NFL

Boston Yanks

Tue	10/1	H	NYG	0-17	L	16,500
Sun	10/6	A	PHI	25-49	L	33,986
Sun	10/13	A	PIT	7-16	L	34,297
Sun	10/20	H	WAS	6-14	L	24,357
Sun	10/27	H	PIT	7-33	L	13,797
Sun	11/3	H	CHIC	14-28	L	10,556
Sun	11/10	A	WAS	14-17	L	33,691
Sun	11/17	A	NYG	28-28	T	35,583
Sun	11/24	H	LA	40-21	W	23,689
Thu	11/28	A	DET	34-10	W	13,010
Sun	12/8	H	PHI	14-40	L	29,555

Chicago Bears

Sun	9/29	A	GB	30-7	W	25,049
Sun	10/6	A	CHIC	34-17	W	39,263
Sun	10/13	H	LA	28-28	T	44,211
Sun	10/20	H	PHI	21-14	W	41,221
Sun	10/27	A	NYG	0-14	L	62,359
Sun	11/3	H	GB	10-7	W	46,321
Sun	11/10	A	LA	27-21	W	68,381
Sun	11/17	H	WAS	24-20	W	43,315
Sun	11/24	H	DET	42-6	W	24,270
Sun	12/1	H	CHIC	28-35	L	47,511
Sun	12/8	A	DET	45-24	W	19,579

League Championship

Sun	12/15	A	NYG	24-14	W	58,346

Chicago Cardinals

Fri	9/20	A	PIT	7-14	L	32,851
Mon	9/30	H	DET	34-14	W	14,667
Sun	10/6	H	CHIB	17-34	L	39,263
Sun	10/13	A	DET	36-14	W	21,939
Sun	10/20	A	NYG	24-28	L	50,681
Sun	10/27	H	LA	34-10	W	38,180
Sun	11/3	A	BOS	28-14	W	10,556
Sun	11/10	H	GB	7-19	L	30,681
Sun	11/17	A	LA	14-17	L	38,271
Sun	11/24	A	GB	24-6	W	16,150
Sun	12/1	A	CHIB	35-28	W	47,511

Detroit Lions

Mon	9/30	A	CHIC	14-34	L	14,667
Sun	10/6	A	WAS	16-17	L	33,569
Sun	10/13	H	CHIC	14-36	L	21,939
Sun	10/20	A	LA	14-35	L	27,928
Sun	10/27	A	GB	7-10	L	17,073
Sun	11/3	H	LA	20-41	L	34,447
Sun	11/10	H	PIT	17-7	W	13,621
Sun	11/17	H	GB	0-9	L	21,055
Sun	11/24	A	CHIB	6-42	L	24,270
Thu	11/28	H	BOS	10-34	L	13,010
Sun	12/8	H	CHIB	24-45	L	19,579

Green Bay Packers

Sun	9/29	H	CHIB	7-30	L	25,049
Sun	10/6	H	LA	17-21	L	27,094
Sun	10/13	A	PHI	19-7	W	36,127
Sun	10/20	H	PIT	17-7	W	22,588
Sun	10/27	H	DET	10-7	W	17,073
Sun	11/3	A	CHIB	7-10	L	46,321
Sun	11/10	A	CHIC	19-7	W	30,681
Sun	11/17	A	DET	9-0	W	21,055
Sun	11/24	H	CHIC	6-24	L	16,150
Sun	12/1	A	WAS	20-7	W	33,691
Sun	12/8	A	LA	17-38	L	46,838

Los Angeles Rams

Sun	9/29	H	PHI	14-25	L	30,500
Sun	10/6	A	GB	21-17	W	27,094
Sun	10/13	A	CHIB	28-28	T	44,211
Sun	10/20	H	DET	35-14	W	27,928
Sun	10/27	A	CHIC	10-34	L	38,180
Sun	11/3	A	DET	41-20	W	34,447
Sun	11/10	H	CHIB	21-27	L	68,381
Sun	11/17	H	CHIC	17-14	W	38,271
Sun	11/24	A	BOS	21-40	L	23,689
Sun	12/1	A	NYG	31-21	W	47,366
Sun	12/8	H	GB	38-17	W	46,838

New York Giants

Tue	10/1	A	BOS	17-0	W	16,500
Sun	10/6	A	PIT	17-14	W	33,702
Sun	10/13	A	WAS	14-24	L	33,651
Sun	10/20	H	CHIC	28-24	W	50,681
Sun	10/27	H	CHIB	14-0	W	62,359
Sun	11/3	A	PHI	14-24	L	40,059
Sun	11/10	H	PHI	45-17	W	60,784
Sun	11/17	H	BOS	28-28	T	35,583
Sun	11/24	H	PIT	7-0	W	45,347
Sun	12/1	H	LA	21-31	L	47,366
Sun	12/8	H	WAS	31-0	W	60,337

League Championship

Sun	12/15	H	CHIB	14-24	L	58,346

Philadelphia Eagles

Sun	9/29	A	LA	25-14	W	30,500
Sun	10/6	H	BOS	49-25	W	33,986
Sun	10/13	H	GB	7-19	L	36,127
Sun	10/20	A	CHIB	14-21	L	41,221
Sun	10/27	A	WAS	28-24	W	33,691
Sun	11/3	H	NYG	24-14	W	40,059
Sun	11/10	A	NYG	17-45	L	60,784
Sun	11/17	A	PIT	7-10	L	38,882
Sun	11/24	H	WAS	10-27	L	36,633
Sun	12/1	H	PIT	10-7	W	29,943
Sun	12/8	A	BOS	40-14	W	29,555

Pittsburgh Steelers

Fri	9/20	H	CHIC	14-7	W	32,851
Sun	9/29	A	WAS	14-14	T	33,620
Sun	10/6	H	NYG	14-17	L	33,702
Sun	10/13	H	BOS	16-7	W	34,297
Sun	10/20	A	GB	7-17	L	22,588
Sun	10/27	A	BOS	33-7	W	13,797
Sun	11/3	H	WAS	14-7	W	39,060
Sun	11/10	A	DET	7-17	L	13,621
Sun	11/17	H	PHI	10-7	W	38,883
Sun	11/24	A	NYG	0-7	L	45,347
Sun	12/1	A	PHI	7-10	L	29,943

Washington Redskins

Sun	9/29	H	PIT	14-14	T	33,620
Sun	10/6	H	DET	17-16	W	33,569
Sun	10/13	H	NYG	24-14	W	33,651
Sun	10/20	A	BOS	14-6	W	24,357
Sun	10/27	H	PHI	24-28	L	33,691
Sun	11/3	A	PIT	7-14	L	39,060
Sun	11/10	H	BOS	17-14	W	33,691
Sun	11/17	A	CHIB	20-24	L	43,315
Sun	11/24	A	PHI	27-10	W	36,633
Sun	12/1	H	GB	7-20	L	33,691
Sun	12/8	A	NYG	0-31	L	60,337

1947 AAFC

Baltimore Colts

Sun	9/7	H	BKN	16-7	W	27,418
Sun	9/14	A	SF	7-14	L	25,787
Sun	9/21	A	CLE	0-28	L	44,251
Sun	9/28	H	NY	7-21	L	51,583
Sun	10/5	H	SF	28-28	T	29,556
Sun	10/12	A	BUF	15-20	L	27,345
Sun	10/19	H	LA	10-38	L	36,852
Sun	10/26	A	LA	0-56	L	27,000
Sun	11/2	A	NY	21-35	L	21,714
Fri	11/7	A	CHI	21-27	L	5,395
Sun	11/16	A	BKN	14-21	L	9,604
Sun	11/23	H	BUF	14-33	L	19,593
Sun	11/30	H	CHI	14-7	W	14,085
Sun	12/7	H	CLE	0-42	L	20,574

Brooklyn Dodgers

Sun	8/31	A	SF	7-23	L	31,874
Sun	9/7	A	BAL	7-16	L	27,418
Fri	9/12	H	CLE	7-55	L	18,872
Fri	9/19	A	LA	21-48	L	38,817
Fri	10/3	A	CHI	35-31	W	16,844
Sun	10/12	A	NY	7-31	L	21,882
Fri	10/17	H	BUF	14-14	T	9,972
Sun	10/26	A	BUF	7-35	L	23,762
Fri	10/31	H	CHI	7-3	W	2,960
Sun	11/9	A	CLE	12-13	L	30,279
Sun	11/16	H	BAL	21-14	W	9,604
Sun	11/23	H	LA	12-16	L	11,866
Thu	11/27	H	SF	7-21	L	9,837
Sun	12/7	H	NY	17-20	L	14,166

Buffalo Bills

Sun	8/31	H	NY	28-24	W	32,385
Fri	9/5	A	CLE	14-30	L	61,442
Sun	9/14	H	CHI	28-20	W	33,648
Fri	9/19	A	CHI	31-14	W	22,685
Sun	9/28	H	SF	24-41	L	36,099
Sun	10/5	A	LA	27-25	W	36,087
Sun	10/12	H	BAL	20-15	W	27,345
Fri	10/17	A	BKN	14-14	T	9,972
Sun	10/26	H	BKN	35-7	W	23,762
Sun	11/2	H	CLE	7-28	L	43,167
Sun	11/9	H	LA	25-0	W	21,293
Sun	11/23	A	BAL	33-14	W	19,593
Sun	11/30	A	NY	13-35	L	39,012
Sun	12/7	A	SF	21-21	T	22,943

Chicago Rockets

Fri	8/29	H	LA	21-24	L	41,182
Fri	9/5	A	NY	26-48	L	36,777
Sun	9/14	A	BUF	20-28	L	33,648
Fri	9/19	H	BUF	14-31	L	22,685
Fri	9/26	H	CLE	21-41	L	18,450
Fri	10/3	H	BKN	31-35	L	16,844
Sun	10/12	A	SF	28-42	L	23,300
Sun	10/19	A	CLE	28-31	L	35,266
Fri	10/24	H	NY	7-28	L	20,310
Fri	10/31	A	BKN	3-7	L	2,960
Fri	11/7	H	BAL	27-21	W	5,395
Sun	11/21	H	SF	16-41	L	5,791
Sun	11/30	A	BAL	7-14	L	14,085
Sun	12/7	A	LA	14-34	L	20,856

Cleveland Browns

Fri	9/5	H	BUF	30-14	W	61,442
Fri	9/12	A	BKN	55-7	W	18,872
Sun	9/21	H	BAL	28-0	W	44,251
Fri	9/26	A	CHI	41-21	W	18,450
Sun	10/5	H	NY	26-17	W	80,067
Sun	10/12	H	LA	10-13	L	63,124
Sun	10/19	H	CHI	31-28	W	35,266
Sun	10/26	A	SF	14-7	W	54,325
Sun	11/2	A	BUF	28-7	W	43,167
Sun	11/9	H	BKN	13-12	W	30,279
Sun	11/16	H	SF	37-14	W	76,504
Sun	11/23	A	NY	28-28	T	70,060
Thu	11/27	A	LA	27-17	W	45,009
Sun	12/7	A	BAL	42-0	W	20,574

League Championship

Sun	12/14	A	NY	14-3	W	60,103

Los Angeles Dons

Fri	8/29	A	CHI	24-21	W	41,182
Sun	9/7	A	SF	14-17	L	31,298
Fri	9/12	H	NY	14-30	L	82,675
Fri	9/19	H	BKN	48-21	W	38,817
Sun	10/5	H	BUF	25-27	L	36,087
Sun	10/12	A	CLE	13-10	W	63,124
Sun	10/19	A	BAL	38-10	W	36,852
Sun	10/26	H	BAL	56-0	W	27,000
Sun	11/2	H	SF	16-26	L	53,726
Sun	11/9	A	BUF	0-25	L	21,293
Sun	11/16	A	NY	13-16	L	37,625
Sun	11/23	A	BKN	16-12	W	11,866
Thu	11/27	H	CLE	17-27	L	45,009
Sun	12/7	H	CHI	34-14	W	20,856

New York Yankees

Sun	8/31	A	BUF	24-28	L	32,385
Fri	9/5	H	CHI	48-26	W	36,777
Fri	9/12	A	LA	30-14	W	82,675
Sun	9/21	A	SF	21-16	W	52,819
Sun	9/28	A	BAL	21-7	W	51,583
Sun	10/5	A	CLE	17-26	L	80,067
Sun	10/12	H	BKN	31-7	W	21,882
Fri	10/24	A	CHI	28-7	W	20,310
Sun	11/2	H	BAL	35-21	W	21,714
Sun	11/9	H	SF	24-16	W	37,342
Sun	11/16	H	LA	16-13	W	37,625
Sun	11/23	H	CLE	28-28	T	70,060
Sun	11/30	H	BUF	35-13	W	39,012
Sun	12/7	A	BKN	20-17	W	14,166

League Championship

Sun	12/14	H	CLE	3-14	L	60,103

San Francisco 49ers

Sun	8/31	H	BKN	23-7	W	31,874
Sun	9/7	H	LA	17-14	W	31,298
Sun	9/14	H	BAL	14-7	W	25,787
Sun	9/21	H	NY	16-21	L	52,819
Sun	9/28	A	BUF	41-24	W	36,099
Sun	10/5	A	BAL	28-28	T	29,556
Sun	10/12	H	CHI	42-28	W	23,300
Sun	10/26	H	CLE	7-14	L	54,325
Sun	11/2	A	LA	26-16	W	53,726
Sun	11/9	A	NY	16-24	L	37,342
Sun	11/16	A	CLE	14-37	L	76,504
Fri	11/21	A	CHI	41-16	W	5,791
Thu	11/27	A	BKN	21-7	W	9,837
Sun	12/7	H	BUF	21-21	T	22,943

1947 NFL

Boston Yanks

Mon	9/29	H	NYG	7-7	T	21,905
Sun	10/5	H	DET	7-21	L	16,097
Sun	10/12	H	PIT	14-30	L	18,894
Sun	10/19	A	NY	14-0	W	37,144
Sun	10/26	A	CHIC	7-27	L	22,286
Sun	11/2	H	CHIB	24-28	L	24,894
Sun	11/9	A	LA	27-16	W	19,415
Sun	11/16	A	PHI	0-32	L	26,498
Sun	11/23	H	PHI	21-14	W	15,368
Sun	11/30	H	WAS	27-24	W	24,800
Sun	12/7	A	PIT	7-17	L	31,398
Sun	12/14	A	WAS	13-40	L	33,226

Chicago Bears

Sun	9/28	A	GB	20-29	L	25,461

Sun	10/5	A	CHIC	7-31	L	51,123
Sun	10/12	H	PHI	40-7	W	34,338
Sun	10/19	H	DET	33-24	W	31,960
Sun	10/26	A	WAS	56-20	W	36,591
Sun	11/2	A	BOS	28-24	W	24,894
Sun	11/9	H	GB	20-17	W	46,112
Sun	11/16	A	LA	41-21	W	37,934
Sun	11/23	H	PIT	49-7	W	34,142
Thu	11/27	A	DET	34-14	W	27,214
Sun	12/7	H	LA	14-17	L	34,215
Sun	12/14	H	CHIC	21-30	L	48,632

CHICAGO CARDINALS

Sun	9/28	H	DET	45-21	W	22,245
Sun	10/5	H	CHIB	31-7	W	51,123
Sun	10/12	A	GB	14-10	W	25,502
Sun	10/19	A	LA	7-27	L	69,631
Sun	10/26	H	BOS	27-7	W	22,286
Sun	11/2	H	LA	17-10	W	40,075
Sun	11/9	A	DET	17-7	W	25,296
Sun	11/16	H	GB	21-20	W	40,086
Sun	11/23	A	WAS	21-45	L	35,362
Sun	11/30	A	NYG	31-35	L	28,744
Sun	12/7	A	PHI	45-21	W	32,322
Sun	12/14	A	CHIB	30-21	W	48,632

League Championship

Sun	12/28	H	PHI	28-21	W	30,759

DETROIT LIONS

Sun	9/21	A	PIT	10-17	L	34,681
Sun	9/28	A	CHIC	21-45	L	22,245
Sun	10/5	A	BOS	21-7	W	16,097
Sun	10/12	H	LA	13-27	L	42,955
Sun	10/19	A	CHIB	24-33	L	31,960
Sun	10/26	A	GB	17-34	L	23,100
Sun	11/2	H	NYG	35-7	W	28,812
Sun	11/9	H	CHIC	7-17	L	25,296
Sun	11/16	H	WAS	38-21	W	17,003
Sun	11/23	A	LA	17-28	L	17,693
Thu	11/27	H	CHIB	14-34	L	27,214
Sun	12/7	H	GB	14-35	L	14,055

GREEN BAY PACKERS

Sun	9/28	H	CHIB	29-20	W	25,461
Sun	10/5	H	LA	17-14	W	31,613
Sun	10/12	H	CHIC	10-14	L	25,502
Sun	10/19	H	WAS	27-10	W	28,572
Sun	10/26	H	DET	34-17	W	23,100
Sun	11/2	H	PIT	17-18	L	30,073
Sun	11/9	A	CHIB	17-20	L	46,112
Sun	11/16	A	CHIC	20-21	L	40,086
Sun	11/23	A	NYG	24-24	T	27,939
Sun	11/30	A	LA	30-10	W	31,040
Sun	12/7	A	DET	35-14	W	14,055
Sun	12/14	A	PHI	14-28	L	24,216

LOS ANGELES RAMS

Mon	9/29	A	PIT	48-7	W	35,658
Sun	10/5	A	GB	14-17	L	31,613
Sun	10/12	A	DET	27-13	W	42,955
Sun	10/19	H	CHIC	27-7	W	69,631
Sun	10/26	A	PHI	7-14	L	36,364
Sun	11/2	A	CHIC	10-17	L	40,075
Sun	11/9	H	BOS	16-27	L	19,415
Sun	11/16	H	CHIB	21-41	L	37,934
Sun	11/23	H	DET	28-17	W	17,693
Sun	11/30	H	GB	10-30	L	31,040
Sun	12/7	A	CHIB	17-14	W	34,215
Sun	12/14	H	NYG	34-10	W	24,000

NEW YORK GIANTS

Mon	9/29	A	BOS	7-7	T	21,905
Sun	10/5	A	PHI	0-23	L	29,823
Sun	10/12	A	WAS	20-28	L	36,533
Sun	10/19	H	BOS	0-14	L	37,144
Sun	10/26	H	PIT	21-38	L	41,736
Sun	11/2	A	DET	7-35	L	28,812
Sun	11/9	H	PHI	24-41	L	29,016
Sun	11/16	A	PIT	7-24	L	35,000
Sun	11/23	H	GB	24-24	T	27,939
Sun	11/30	H	CHIC	35-31	W	28,744
Sun	12/7	H	WAS	35-10	W	25,594
Sun	12/14	A	LA	10-34	L	24,000

PHILADELPHIA EAGLES

Sun	9/28	H	WAS	45-42	W	35,406
Sun	10/5	H	NYG	23-0	W	29,823
Sun	10/12	A	CHIB	7-40	L	34,338
Sun	10/19	A	PIT	24-35	L	33,538
Sun	10/26	H	LA	14-7	W	36,364
Sun	11/2	A	WAS	38-14	W	36,591
Sun	11/9	A	NYG	41-24	W	29,016
Sun	11/16	H	BOS	32-0	W	26,498
Sun	11/23	A	BOS	14-21	L	15,368
Sun	11/30	H	PIT	21-0	W	37,218
Sun	12/7	H	CHIC	21-45	L	32,322
Sun	12/14	H	GB	28-14	W	24,216

Eastern Division Playoff

Sun	12/21	A	PIT	21-0	W	35,729

League Championship

Sun	12/28	A	CHIC	21-28	L	30,759

PITTSBURGH STEELERS

Sun	9/21	H	DET	17-10	W	34,681
Mon	9/29	H	LA	7-48	L	35,658
Sun	10/5	A	WAS	26-27	L	36,585
Sun	10/12	A	BOS	30-14	W	18,894
Sun	10/19	H	PHI	35-24	W	33,538
Sun	10/26	A	NYG	38-21	W	41,736
Sun	11/2	A	GB	18-17	W	30,073
Sun	11/9	H	WAS	21-14	W	36,257
Sun	11/16	H	NYG	24-7	W	35,000
Sun	11/23	A	CHIB	7-49	L	34,142
Sun	11/30	A	PHI	0-21	L	37,218
Sun	12/7	H	BOS	17-7	W	31,398

Eastern Division Playoff

Sun	12/21	H	PHI	0-21	L	35,729

WASHINGTON REDSKINS

Sun	9/28	A	PHI	42-45	W	35,406
Sun	10/5	H	PIT	27-26	W	36,585
Sun	10/12	H	NYG	28-20	W	36,533
Sun	10/19	A	GB	10-27	L	28,572
Sun	10/26	H	CHIB	20-56	L	36,591
Sun	11/2	H	PHI	14-38	L	36,591
Sun	11/9	A	PIT	14-21	L	36,257
Sun	11/16	A	DET	21-38	L	17,003
Sun	11/23	H	CHIC	45-21	W	35,362
Sun	11/30	A	BOS	24-27	L	24,800
Sun	12/7	A	NYG	10-35	L	25,594
Sun	12/14	H	BOS	40-13	W	33,226

1948 AAFC

BALTIMORE COLTS

Sun	9/5	H	NY	45-28	W	31,800
Fri	9/10	A	CHI	14-21	L	15,642
Thu	9/16	A	NY	27-14	W	18,959
Sun	9/26	H	BKN	35-20	W	34,554
Tue	10/5	H	CLE	10-14	L	22,329
Sun	10/10	H	SF	14-56	L	37,209
Fri	10/15	A	LA	29-14	W	40,019
Sun	10/24	A	SF	10-21	L	27,978
Sun	10/31	A	BUF	17-35	L	23,964
Sun	11/7	A	CLE	7-28	L	32,314
Sun	11/14	H	CHI	38-24	W	21,899
Sun	11/21	H	LA	14-17	L	25,228
Sun	11/28	A	BKN	38-20	W	7,629
Sun	12/5	H	BUF	35-15	W	33,090

Eastern Division Playoff

Sun	12/12	H	BUF	17-28	L	27,327

BROOKLYN DODGERS

Thu	8/27	H	NY	3-21	L	16,411
Sun	9/5	A	SF	20-36	L	32,606
Fri	9/10	A	LA	7-17	L	35,246
Sun	9/26	A	BAL	20-35	L	34,554
Sun	10/3	A	BUF	21-31	L	17,694
Sun	10/10	A	CLE	17-30	L	31,187
Fri	10/15	H	CHI	21-7	W	8,671
Sun	10/24	A	CHI	35-14	W	5,964
Sun	10/31	H	LA	0-17	L	12,825
Sun	11/7	H	BUF	21-26	L	7,805
Sun	11/14	A	NY	7-21	L	17,642
Sun	11/21	H	SF	40-63	L	9,336
Sun	11/28	H	BAL	20-38	L	7,629
Sun	12/5	H	CLE	21-31	L	9,821

BUFFALO BILLS

Sun	8/29	A	SF	14-35	L	33,946
Mon	9/6	H	CHI	42-7	W	25,816
Sun	9/12	H	CLE	13-42	L	35,340
Sun	9/26	H	SF	28-38	L	31,103
Sun	10/3	H	BKN	31-21	W	17,694
Sun	10/10	H	NY	13-14	L	18,825
Sun	10/17	A	CLE	14-31	L	28,054
Sun	10/24	A	LA	35-21	W	26,818
Sun	10/31	H	BAL	35-17	W	23,694
Sun	11/7	A	BKN	26-21	W	7,805
Sun	11/14	H	LA	20-27	L	23,725
Thu	11/25	A	CHI	39-35	W	6,305
Sun	11/28	A	NY	35-14	W	18,376
Sun	12/5	A	BAL	15-35	L	33,090

Eastern Division Playoff

Sun	12/12	A	BAL	28-17	W	27,327

League Championship

Sun	12/19	A	CLE	7-49	L	22,981

CHICAGO ROCKETS

Fri	8/27	H	LA	0-7	L	26,479
Mon	9/6	A	BUF	7-42	L	25,816
Fri	9/10	H	BAL	21-14	W	15,642
Fri	9/17	H	CLE	7-28	L	30,608
Sun	9/26	A	CLE	10-21	L	37,190
Fri	10/1	H	SF	14-31	L	14,553
Fri	10/8	A	LA	28-49	L	31,119
Fri	10/15	A	BKN	7-21	L	8,671
Sun	10/24	H	BKN	14-35	L	5,964
Sun	10/31	A	NY	7-42	L	13,239
Sun	11/7	A	SF	21-44	L	25,306
Sun	11/14	A	BAL	24-38	L	21,899
Thu	11/25	H	BUF	35-39	L	6,305
Sat	12/4	H	NY	7-28	L	4,930

CLEVELAND BROWNS

Fri	9/3	H	LA	19-14	W	60,193
Sun	9/12	A	BUF	42-13	W	35,340
Fri	9/17	A	CHI	28-7	W	30,608
Sun	9/26	H	CHI	21-10	W	37,190
Tue	10/5	A	BAL	14-10	W	22,329
Sun	10/10	H	BKN	30-17	W	31,187
Sun	10/17	H	BUF	31-14	W	28,054
Sun	10/24	H	NY	35-7	W	46,912
Sun	11/7	H	BAL	28-7	W	32,314
Sun	11/14	H	SF	14-7	W	82,769
Sun	11/21	A	NY	34-21	W	49,981
Thu	11/25	A	LA	31-14	W	60,031
Sun	11/28	A	SF	31-28	W	59,785
Sun	12/5	A	BKN	31-21	W	9,821

League Championship

Sun	12/19	H	BUF	49-7	W	22,981

LOS ANGELES DONS

Fri	8/27	A	CHI	7-0	W	26,479
Fri	9/3	A	CLE	14-19	L	60,193
Fri	9/10	H	BKN	17-7	W	35,246
Sun	9/19	A	SF	14-36	L	45,420
Wed	9/29	H	NY	20-10	W	35,655
Fri	10/8	H	CHI	49-28	W	31,119
Fri	10/15	H	BAL	14-29	L	40,019
Sun	10/24	H	BUF	21-35	L	26,818
Sun	10/31	A	BKN	17-0	W	12,825
Sun	11/7	A	NY	6-38	L	17,386
Sun	11/14	A	BUF	27-20	W	23,725
Sun	11/21	A	BAL	17-14	W	25,228
Thu	11/25	H	CLE	14-31	L	60,031
Sun	12/5	H	SF	21-38	L	51,460

NEW YORK YANKEES

Fri	8/27	A	BKN	21-3	W	16,411
Sun	9/5	A	BAL	28-45	L	31,800
Sun	9/12	A	SF	0-41	L	60,927
Thu	9/16	H	BAL	14-27	L	18,959
Wed	9/29	A	LA	10-20	L	35,655
Sun	10/10	A	BUF	14-13	W	18,825
Sun	10/17	H	SF	7-21	L	29,743
Sun	10/24	A	CLE	7-35	L	46,912
Sun	10/31	H	CHI	42-7	W	13,239
Sun	11/7	H	LA	38-6	W	17,386
Sun	11/14	H	BKN	21-7	W	17,642
Sun	11/21	H	CLE	21-34	L	49,981
Sun	11/28	H	BUF	14-35	L	18,376
Sat	12/4	A	CHI	28-7	W	4,930

SAN FRANCISCO 49ERS

Sun	8/29	H	BUF	35-14	W	33,946
Sun	9/5	H	BKN	36-20	W	32,606
Sun	9/12	H	NY	41-0	W	60,927
Sun	9/19	H	LA	36-14	W	45,420
Sun	9/26	A	BUF	38-28	W	31,103
Fri	10/1	A	CHI	31-14	W	14,553
Sun	10/10	A	BAL	56-14	W	37,209
Sun	10/17	A	NY	21-7	W	29,743
Sun	10/24	H	BAL	21-10	W	27,978
Sun	11/7	H	CHI	44-21	W	25,306
Sun	11/14	A	CLE	7-14	L	82,769
Sun	11/21	A	BKN	63-40	W	9,336
Sun	11/28	H	CLE	28-31	L	59,785
Sun	12/5	A	LA	38-21	W	51,460

1948 NFL

BOSTON YANKS

Fri	9/17	H	GB	0-31	L	15,443
Thu	9/23	H	NYG	7-27	L	7,428
Sun	10/3	A	PIT	14-24	L	26,216
Sat	10/9	A	DET	17-14	W	18,747
Sun	10/17	H	PIT	13-7	W	7,208
Sun	10/24	A	CHIC	27-49	L	23,423
Sun	10/31	A	WAS	21-59	L	29,758
Sun	11/7	H	WAS	7-23	L	13,659
Sun	11/14	A	PHI	0-45	L	22,958
Sun	11/21	H	CHIB	17-51	L	18,048
Sun	11/28	A	NYG	14-28	L	19,636
Sun	12/5	H	PHI	37-14	W	9,652

CHICAGO BEARS

Sun	9/26	A	GB	45-7	W	25,546
Mon	10/4	A	CHIC	28-17	W	52,765
Sun	10/10	H	LA	42-21	W	43,707
Sun	10/17	H	DET	28-0	W	35,425
Sun	10/24	A	PHI	7-12	L	36,227
Sun	10/31	H	NYG	35-14	W	41,608
Sun	11/7	A	LA	21-6	W	56,263
Sun	11/14	H	GB	7-6	W	48,113
Sun	11/21	A	BOS	51-17	W	18,048
Sun	11/28	H	WAS	48-13	W	42,299
Sun	12/5	A	DET	42-14	W	25,781
Sun	12/12	H	CHIC	21-24	L	51,283

CHICAGO CARDINALS

Fri	9/24	H	PHI	21-14	W	25,875
Mon	10/4	H	CHIB	17-28	L	52,765

```
Sun  10/10  A  GB    17-7    W  34,369
Sun  10/17  A  NYG   63-35   W  35,342
Sun  10/24  H  BOS   49-27   W  23,423
Sun  10/31  A  LA    27-22   W  32,149
Sun  11/7   H  DET   56-20   W  22,311
Sun  11/14  A  PIT   24-7    W  33,364
Sun  11/21  H  DET   27-24   W  29,031
Thu  11/25  A  DET   28-14   W  22,099
Sun  12/5   H  GB    42-7    W  26,072
Sun  12/12  A  CHIB  24-21   W  51,283
```

LEAGUE CHAMPIONSHIP
```
Sun  12/19  A  PHI   0-7     L  38,909
```

DETROIT LIONS
```
Wed  9/22   A  LA    7-44    L  12,941
Sun  10/3   A  GB    21-33   L  21,403
Sat  10/9   H  BOS   14-17   L  18,747
Sun  10/17  A  CHIB  0-28    L  35,425
Sun  10/24  H  LA    27-34   L  17,444
Sun  10/31  A  GB    24-20   W  15,045
Sun  11/7   A  CHIC  20-56   L  22,311
Sun  11/14  A  WAS   21-46   L  32,528
Sun  11/21  H  PIT   17-14   W  13,646
Thu  11/25  H  CHIC  14-28   L  22,099
Sun  12/5   H  CHIB  14-42   L  25,781
Sun  12/12  A  PHI   21-45   L  15,327
```

GREEN BAY PACKERS
```
Fri  9/17   A  BOS   31-0    W  15,443
Sun  9/26   H  CHIB  7-45    L  25,546
Sun  10/3   H  DET   33-21   W  21,403
Sun  10/10  A  CHIC  7-17    L  34,369
Sun  10/17  H  LA    16-0    W  25,119
Sun  10/24  H  WAS   7-23    L  13,433
Sun  10/31  A  DET   20-24   L  15,045
Sun  11/7   A  PIT   7-38    L  26,058
Sun  11/14  A  CHIB  6-7     L  48,113
Sun  11/21  H  NYG   3-49    L  12,639
Sun  11/28  A  LA    10-24   L  23,874
Sun  12/5   A  CHIC  7-42    L  26,072
```

LOS ANGELES RAMS
```
Wed  9/22   H  DET   44-7    W  12,941
Sun  10/3   H  PHI   28-28   T  36,884
Sun  10/10  A  CHIB  21-42   L  43,707
Sun  10/17  A  GB    0-16    L  25,119
Sun  10/24  H  DET   34-27   W  17,444
Sun  10/31  H  CHIC  22-27   L  32,149
Sun  11/7   A  CHIB  6-21    L  56,263
Sun  11/14  H  NYG   52-37   W  22,766
Sun  11/21  A  CHIC  24-27   L  29,031
Sun  11/28  H  GB    24-10   W  23,874
Sun  12/5   A  WAS   41-13   W  32,970
Sun  12/12  H  PIT   31-14   W  27,967
```

NEW YORK GIANTS
```
Thu  9/23   A  BOS   27-7    W  7,428
Sun  10/3   A  WAS   10-41   L  32,593
Sun  10/10  H  PHI   0-45    L  22,804
Sun  10/17  H  CHIC  35-63   L  35,342
Sun  10/24  A  PIT   34-27   W  13,443
Sun  10/31  A  CHIB  14-35   L  41,608
Sun  11/7   H  PHI   14-35   L  24,983
Sun  11/14  H  LA    37-52   L  22,766
Sun  11/21  A  GB    49-3    W  12,639
Sun  11/28  H  BOS   28-14   W  19,636
Sun  12/5   A  PIT   28-38   L  27,645
Sun  12/12  H  WAS   21-28   L  23,156
```

PHILADELPHIA EAGLES
```
Fri  9/24   A  CHIC  14-21   L  25,875
Sun  10/3   A  LA    28-28   T  36,884
Sun  10/10  H  NYG   45-0    W  22,804
Sun  10/17  A  WAS   45-0    W  35,584
Sun  10/24  H  CHIB  12-7    W  36,227
Sun  10/31  A  PIT   34-7    W  32,474
Sun  11/7   A  NYG   35-14   W  24,983
Sun  11/14  H  BOS   45-0    W  22,958
Sun  11/21  H  WAS   42-21   W  36,254
Sun  11/28  H  PIT   17-0    W  22,001
Sun  12/5   A  BOS   14-37   L  9,652
Sun  12/12  H  DET   45-21   W  15,327
```

LEAGUE CHAMPIONSHIP
```
Sun  12/19  H  CHIC  7-0     W  36,909
```

PITTSBURGH STEELERS
```
Sun  9/26   A  WAS   14-17   L  32,084
Sun  10/3   H  BOS   24-14   W  26,216
Sun  10/10  H  WAS   10-7    W  28,969
Sun  10/17  A  BOS   7-13    L  7,208
Sun  10/24  A  NYG   27-34   L  13,443
Sun  10/31  H  PHI   7-34    L  32,474
Sun  11/7   H  GB    38-7    W  26,058
Sun  11/14  H  CHIC  7-24    L  33,364
Sun  11/21  A  DET   14-17   L  13,646
Sun  11/28  A  PHI   0-17    L  22,001
Sun  12/5   H  NYG   38-28   W  27,645
Sun  12/12  A  LA    14-31   L  27,967
```

WASHINGTON REDSKINS
```
Sun  9/26   H  PIT   17-14   W  32,084
Sun  10/3   H  NYG   41-10   W  32,593
Sun  10/10  A  PIT   7-10    L  28,969
Sun  10/17  H  PHI   0-45    L  35,584
Sun  10/24  A  GB    23-7    W  13,433
Sun  10/31  H  BOS   59-21   W  29,758
Sun  11/7   A  BOS   23-7    W  13,659
Sun  11/14  H  DET   46-21   W  32,528
Sun  11/21  A  PHI   21-42   L  36,254
Sun  11/28  A  CHIB  13-48   L  42,299
Sun  12/5   H  LA    13-41   L  32,970
Sun  12/12  A  NYG   28-21   W  23,156
```

1949 AAFC
BALTIMORE COLTS
```
Sun  8/28   A  SF    17-31   L  29,095
Fri  9/2    A  LA    17-49   L  20,211
Sun  9/11   A  CLE   0-21    L  21,621
Fri  9/16   A  CHI   7-35    L  18,483
Sun  9/25   H  CLE   20-28   L  34,879
Sun  10/2   A  BUF   35-28   W  25,692
Sun  10/16  H  B-NY  21-24   L  32,645
Sun  10/23  H  CHI   7-17    L  32,107
Sun  10/30  A  B-NY  14-21   L  10,692
Sun  11/6   H  SF    10-28   L  23,704
Sun  11/20  H  LA    10-21   L  19,503
Sun  11/27  H  BUF   14-38   L  16,323
```

BROOKLYN-NEW YORK YANKEES
```
Sun  9/11   A  BUF   17-14   W  30,410
Sun  9/18   A  CLE   3-14    L  26,312
Thu  9/22   H  LA    10-7    W  14,437
Fri  10/7   A  CHI   38-24   W  17,098
Sun  10/16  A  BAL   24-21   W  32,645
Sun  10/23  H  SF    24-3    W  36,197
Sun  10/30  H  BAL   21-14   W  10,692
Sun  11/6   H  BUF   14-17   L  16,758
Sun  11/13  H  CHI   14-10   W  9,091
Sun  11/20  H  CLE   0-31    L  48,069
Thu  11/24  A  LA    17-16   W  20,096
Sun  11/27  A  SF    14-35   L  44,828
```

PLAYOFF
```
Sun  12/4   A  SF    7-17    L  41,393
```

BUFFALO BILLS
```
Fri  8/26   A  CHI   14-17   L  23,800
Mon  9/5    H  CLE   28-28   T  31,839
Sun  9/11   H  B-NY  14-17   L  30,410
Sun  9/25   A  SF    28-17   W  32,097
Sun  10/2   H  BAL   28-35   L  25,692
Sun  10/9   A  LA    28-42   L  16,575
Sun  10/16  A  SF    7-51    L  35,476
Sun  10/23  H  LA    17-14   W  21,310
Sun  11/6   A  B-NY  17-14   W  16,758
Sun  11/13  A  CLE   7-7     T  22,511
Sun  11/20  H  CHI   10-0    W  18,494
Sun  11/27  A  BAL   38-14   W  16,323
```

PLAYOFF
```
Sun  12/4   A  CLE   21-31   L  17,270
```

CHICAGO HORNETS
```
Fri  8/26   H  BUF   17-14   W  23,800
Sun  9/4    A  SF    7-42    L  28,311
Fri  9/9    A  LA    23-21   W  30,193
Fri  9/16   H  BAL   35-7    W  18,483
Fri  9/30   H  SF    24-42   L  31,561
Fri  10/7   H  B-NY  24-38   L  17,098
Sun  10/23  A  BAL   17-7    W  23,107
Fri  10/28  A  LA    14-11   L  11,249
Sun  11/6   A  CLE   2-35    L  16,506
Sun  11/13  A  B-NY  10-14   L  9,091
Sun  11/20  A  BUF   0-10    L  18,494
Thu  11/24  H  CLE   6-14    L  5,031
```

CLEVELAND BROWNS
```
Mon  9/5    A  BUF   28-28   T  31,839
Sun  9/11   H  BAL   21-0    W  21,621
Sun  9/18   H  B-NY  14-3    W  26,312
Sun  9/25   A  BAL   28-20   W  34,879
Sun  10/2   H  LA    42-7    W  30,466
Sun  10/9   A  SF    28-56   L  59,770
Fri  10/14  A  LA    61-14   W  27,437
Sun  10/30  H  SF    30-28   W  72,189
Sun  11/6   H  CHI   35-2    W  16,506
Sun  11/13  H  BUF   7-7     T  22,511
Sun  11/20  A  B-NY  31-0    W  48,069
Thu  11/24  A  CHI   14-6    W  5,031
```

PLAYOFF
```
Sun  12/4   H  BUF   31-21   W  17,270
```

LEAGUE CHAMPIONSHIP
```
Sun  12/11  H  SF    21-7    W  22,550
```

LOS ANGELES DONS
```
Fri  9/2    H  BAL   49-17   W  20,211
Fri  9/9    H  CHI   21-23   L  30,193
Sun  9/18   A  SF    14-42   L  31,960
Thu  9/22   A  B-NY  7-10    L  14,437
Sun  10/2   A  CLE   7-42    L  30,466
Sun  10/9   H  BUF   42-28   W  16,575
Fri  10/14  H  CLE   14-61   L  27,437
Sun  10/23  A  BUF   14-17   L  21,310
Fri  10/28  H  CHI   24-14   W  11,249
Sun  11/13  H  SF    24-41   L  17,880
Sun  11/20  A  BAL   21-10   W  19,503
Thu  11/24  H  B-NY  16-17   L  20,096
```

SAN FRANCISCO 49ERS
```
Sun  8/28   H  BAL   31-17   W  29,095
Sun  9/4    H  CHI   42-7    W  28,311
Sun  9/18   H  LA    42-14   W  31,960
Sun  9/25   A  BUF   17-28   L  32,097
Fri  9/30   A  CHI   42-24   W  31,561
Sun  10/9   H  CLE   56-28   W  59,770
Sun  10/16  H  BUF   51-7    W  35,746
Sun  10/23  A  B-NY  3-24    L  36,197
Sun  10/30  A  CLE   28-30   L  72,189
Sun  11/6   A  BAL   28-10   W  23,704
Sun  11/13  A  LA    41-24   W  17,880
Sun  11/27  H  B-NY  35-14   W  44,828
```

PLAYOFF
```
Sun  12/4   H  B-NY  17-7    W  41,393
```

LEAGUE CHAMPIONSHIP
```
Sun  12/11  A  CLE   7-21    L  22,550
```

1949 NFL
CHICAGO BEARS
```
Sun  9/25   A  GB    17-0    W  25,571
Sun  10/2   A  CHIC  17-7    W  52,867
Sun  10/9   H  LA    16-31   L  42,124
Sun  10/16  H  PHI   38-21   W  50,129
Sun  10/23  A  NYG   28-35   L  30,587
Sun  10/30  A  LA    24-27   L  86,080
Sun  11/6   H  GB    24-3    W  47,218
Sun  11/13  H  DET   27-24   W  32,716
Sun  11/20  A  WAS   31-21   W  30,418
Thu  11/24  A  DET   28-7    W  22,912
Sun  12/4   H  PIT   30-21   W  36,071
Sun  12/11  H  CHIC  52-21   W  50,101
```

CHICAGO CARDINALS
```
Mon  9/26   H  WAS   38-7    W  24,136
Sun  10/2   H  CHIB  7-17    L  52,867
Sat  10/8   A  PHI   3-28    L  34,596
Sun  10/16  A  GB    39-17   W  18,464
Sun  10/23  H  DET   7-24    L  19,490
Sun  10/30  A  NYG   38-41   L  21,339
Sun  11/6   A  DET   42-19   W  19,465
Sun  11/13  A  NYB   65-20   W  9,072
Sun  11/20  H  LA    28-28   T  34,100
Sun  11/27  H  GB    41-21   W  16,787
Sun  12/4   A  LA    31-27   W  74,673
Sun  12/11  A  CHIB  21-52   L  50,101
```

DETROIT LIONS
```
Fri  9/23   A  LA    24-27   L  17,878
Mon  10/3   H  PHI   14-22   L  20,163
Sat  10/8   A  PIT   7-14    L  21,355
Sun  10/16  H  LA    10-21   L  19,839
Sun  10/23  A  CHIC  24-7    W  19,490
Sun  10/30  A  GB    14-16   L  6,177
Sun  11/6   H  CHIC  19-42   L  19,465
Sun  11/13  A  CHIB  24-27   L  32,716
Sun  11/20  A  NYG   45-21   W  14,661
Thu  11/24  H  CHIB  7-28    L  22,912
Sun  12/4   H  NYB   28-27   W  11,956
Sun  12/11  H  GB    21-7    W  9,722
```

GREEN BAY PACKERS
```
Sun  9/25   H  CHIB  0-17    L  25,571
Sun  10/2   H  LA    7-48    L  24,308
Fri  10/7   A  NYB   19-0    W  5,099
Sun  10/16  H  CHIC  17-39   L  18,464
Sun  10/23  A  LA    7-35    L  37,546
Sun  10/30  H  DET   16-14   W  6,177
Sun  11/6   A  CHIB  3-24    L  47,218
Sun  11/13  H  NYG   10-30   L  20,151
Sun  11/20  H  PIT   7-30    L  5,483
Sun  11/27  A  CHIC  21-41   L  16,787
Sun  12/4   A  WAS   0-30    L  23,200
Sun  12/11  A  DET   7-21    L  9,722
```

LOS ANGELES RAMS
```
Fri  9/23   H  DET   27-24   W  17,878
Sun  10/2   A  GB    48-7    W  24,308
Sun  10/9   A  CHIB  31-16   W  42,124
Sun  10/16  A  DET   21-10   W  19,839
Sun  10/23  H  GB    35-7    W  37,546
Sun  10/30  H  CHIB  27-24   W  86,080
Sun  11/6   A  PHI   14-38   L  38,320
Sun  11/13  A  PIT   7-7     T  20,510
Sun  11/20  A  CHIC  28-28   T  34,100
Sun  11/27  H  NYB   42-20   W  38,052
Sun  12/4   H  CHIC  27-31   L  74,673
Sun  12/11  H  WAS   53-27   W  44,899
```

LEAGUE CHAMPIONSHIP
```
Sun  12/18  H  PHI   0-14    L  22,245
```

NEW YORK BULLDOGS
```
Thu  9/22   H  PHI   0-7     L  8,426
```

Fri   9/30 H NYG   14-38 L 17,704
Fri 10/7   H GB   0-19 L   5,099
Sun 10/16 A WAS   14-38 L 26,278
Sun 10/23 A PIT   13-24 L 22,042
Sun 10/30 H WAS   14-14 T   3,678
Sun 11/6   A NYG   31-24 W 23,222
Sun 11/13 H CHIC 20-65 L   9,072
Sun 11/20 A PHI   0-42 L 22,165
Sun 11/27 A LA   20-42 L 38,052
Sun 12/4   A DET   27-28 L 11,956
Sun 12/11 H PIT   0-27 L   4,028

NEW YORK GIANTS
Sun   9/25 A PIT   7-28 L 20,957
Fri   9/30 A NYB   38-14 W 17,704
Sun 10/9   A WAS   45-35 W 30,073
Sun 10/16 H PIT   17-21 L 29,911
Sun 10/23 A CHIB 35-28 W 30,587
Sun 10/30 A CHIC 41-38 W 21,339
Sun 11/6   H NYB   24-31 L 23,222
Sun 11/13 A GB   30-10 W 20,151
Sun 11/20 H DET   21-45 L 14,661
Sun 11/27 H WAS   23-7   W 12,985
Sun 12/4   H PHI   3-24 L 25,446
Sun 12/11 H PHI   3-17 L 21,022

PHILADELPHIA EAGLES
Thu   9/22 A NYB   7-0   W   8,426
Mon 10/3   A DET   22-14 W 20,163
Sat 10/8   H CHIC 28-3   W 34,596
Sun 10/16 A CHIB 21-38 L 50,129
Sun 10/23 H WAS   49-14 W 28,855
Sun 10/30 A PIT   38-7   W 37,803
Sun 11/6   H LA   38-14 W 38,230
Sun 11/13 A WAS   44-21 W 31,107
Sun 11/20 H NYB   42-0   W 22,165
Sun 11/27 A PIT   34-17 W 22,191
Sun 12/4   A NYG   24-3   W 25,446
Sun 12/11 H NYG   17-3   W 21,022

LEAGUE CHAMPIONSHIP
Sun 12/18 A LA   14-0   W 22,245

PITTSBURGH STEELERS
Sun   9/25 H NYG   28-7   W 20,957
Mon 10/3   H WAS   14-27 L 30,000
Sat 10/8   H DET   14-7   W 21,355
Sun 10/16 A NYG   21-17 W 29,911
Sun 10/23 H NYB   24-13 W 22,042
Sun 10/30 H PHI   7-38 L 37,803
Sun 11/6   A WAS   14-27 L 26,038
Sun 11/13 H LA   7-7   T 20,510
Sun 11/20 A GB   30-7   W   5,483
Sun 11/27 H PHI   17-34 L 22,191
Sun 12/4   A CHIB 21-30 L 36,071
Sun 12/11 A NYB   27-0   W   4,028

WASHINGTON REDSKINS
Mon   9/26 A CHIC   7-38 L 24,136
Mon 10/3   A PIT   27-14 W 30,000
Sun 10/9   H NYG   35-45 L 30,073
Sun 10/16 H NYB   38-14 W 26,278
Sun 10/23 A PHI   14-49 L 28,855
Sun 10/30 A NYB   14-14 T   3,678
Sun 11/6   H PIT   27-14 W 26,038
Sun 11/13 H PHI   21-44 L 31,107
Sun 11/20 H CHIB 21-31 L 30,418
Sun 11/27 A NYG   7-23 L 12,985
Sun 12/4   H GB   30-0   W 23,200
Sun 12/11 A LA   27-53 L 44,899

1950 NFL
BALTIMORE COLTS
Sun   9/17 H WAS   14-38 L 29,000
Sun   9/24 H CLE   0-31 L 15,201
Mon 10/2   A CHIC 13-55 L 14,439
Sun 10/15 H PHI   14-24 L 14,413
Sun 10/22 A LA   27-70 L 16,026
Sun 10/29 A SF   14-17 L 15,091
Sun 11/5   H GB   41-21 W 12,971
Sun 11/12 A PIT   7-17 L 24,141
Sun 11/19 H NYG   20-55 L 14,573
Sun 11/26 A WAS   38-28 L 21,275
Sun 12/3   H DET   21-45 L 12,059
Sun 12/10 A NYY   14-51 L   6,836

CHICAGO BEARS
Sun   9/17 A LA   24-20 W 18,219
Sun   9/24 A SF   32-20 W 35,558
Sun 10/1   A GB   21-31 L 24,893
Sun 10/8   H CHIC 27-6   W 48,025
Sun 10/15 H GB   28-14 W 51,065
Sun 10/29 A NYY   27-38 L 48,642
Sun 11/5   A DET   35-21 W 32,000
Sun 11/12 H NYY   28-20 W 50,102
Sun 11/19 H SF   17-0   W 38,105
Sun 11/26 H LA   24-14 W 43,478
Sun 12/3   A CHIC 10-20 L 31,919
Sun 12/10 H DET   6-3   W 34,604

NATIONAL CONFERENCE PLAYOFF
Sun 12/17 H LA   14-24 L 83,501

CHICAGO CARDINALS
Sun   9/17 H PHI   7-45 L 24,914
Mon 10/2   H BAL   55-13 W 14,439
Sun 10/8   A CHIB   6-27 L 48,025
Sun 10/15 A CLE   24-34 L 33,774
Sun 10/22 A WAS   38-28 W 27,856
Sun 10/29 H NYG   17-3   W 23,964
Sun 11/5   H CLE   7-10 L 38,456
Sun 11/12 A NYG   21-51 L 22,380
Sun 11/19 A PHI   14-10 W 28,368
Thu 11/23 H PIT   17-28 L 11,622
Sun 12/3   H CHIB 20-10 W 31,919
Sun 12/10 A PIT   7-28 L 18,301

CLEVELAND BROWNS
Sat   9/16 A PHI   35-10 W 71,237
Sun   9/24 A BAL   31-0   W 15,201
Sun 10/1   H NYG   0-6   L 37,647
Sat 10/7   A PIT   17-30 L 35,399
Sun 10/15 H CHIC 34-24 W 33,774
Sun 10/22 A NYG   13-17 L 41,734
Sun 10/29 H PIT   45-7   W 40,714
Sun 11/5   A CHIC 10-7   W 38,456
Sun 11/12 H SF   34-14 W 28,786
Sun 11/19 H WAS   20-14 W 21,908
Sun 12/3   H PHI   13-7   W 37,490
Sun 12/10 A WAS   45-21 W 30,143

AMERICAN CONFERENCE PLAYOFF
Sun 12/17 H NYG   8-3   W 33,054

LEAGUE CHAMPIONSHIP
Sun 12/24 H LA   30-28 W 29,751

DETROIT LIONS
Sun   9/17 A GB   45-7   W 20,285
Sun   9/24 H PIT   10-7   W 18,707
Fri   9/29 A NYY   21-44 L 11,096
Sun 10/8   H SF   24-7   W 17,337
Sun 10/15 H LA   28-30 L 32,589
Sun 10/22 A SF   27-28 L 26,252
Sun 10/29 A LA   24-65 L 27,475
Sun 11/5   H CHIB 21-35 L 32,000
Sun 11/19 H GB   24-21 W 17,752
Thu 11/23 H NYY   49-14 W 30,206
Sun 12/3   A BAL   45-21 W 12,059
Sun 12/10 A CHIB   3-6   L 34,604

GREEN BAY PACKERS
Sun   9/17 H DET   7-45 L 20,285
Sun   9/24 H WAS   35-21 W 14,109
Sun 10/1   H CHIB 31-21 W 24,893
Sun 10/8   H NYY   31-44 L 23,871
Sun 10/15 A CHIB 14-28 L 51,065
Thu 10/19 A NYY   17-35 L 13,661
Sun 11/5   A BAL   21-41 L 12,971
Sun 11/12 H LA   14-45 L 20,456
Sun 11/19 A DET   21-24 L 17,752
Sun 11/26 H SF   25-21 W 13,196
Sun 12/3   A LA   14-51 L 39,323
Sun 12/10 A SF   14-30 L 19,204

LOS ANGELES RAMS
Sun   9/17 H CHIB 20-24 L 18,219
Fri   9/22 H NYY   45-28 W 23,768
Sun 10/1   A SF   35-14 W 27,262
Sat 10/7   A PHI   20-56 L 24,134
Sun 10/15 A DET   30-28 W 32,589
Sun 10/22 H BAL   70-27 W 16,026
Sun 10/29 H DET   65-24 W 27,475
Sun 11/5   H SF   28-21 W 15,952
Sun 11/12 A GB   45-14 W 20,456
Sun 11/19 A NYY   43-35 W 42,673
Sun 11/26 A CHIB 14-24 L 43,478
Sun 12/3   H GB   51-14 W 39,323

NATIONAL CONFERENCE PLAYOFF
Sun 12/17 A CHIB 24-14 W 83,501

LEAGUE CHAMPIONSHIP
Sun 12/24 A CLE   28-30 L 29,751

NEW YORK GIANTS
Sun   9/17 A PIT   18-7   W 24,699
Sun 10/1   A CLE   6-0   W 37,647
Sun 10/8   A WAS   21-17 W 19,288
Sun 10/15 H PIT   6-17 L 21,725
Sun 10/22 H CLE   17-13 W 41,734
Sun 10/29 A CHIC   3-17 L 23,964
Sun 11/5   H WAS   24-21 W 23,909
Sun 11/12 H CHIC 51-21 W 22,380
Sun 11/19 A BAL   55-20 W 14,573
Sun 11/26 H PHI   7-3   W 24,903
Sun 12/3   H NYY   51-7   W 41,630
Sun 12/10 A PHI   9-7   W 26,440

AMERICAN CONFERENCE PLAYOFF
Sun 12/17 A CLE   3-8   L 33,054

NEW YORK YANKS
Sun   9/17 A SF   21-17 W 29,992
Fri   9/22 A LA   28-45 L 23,768
Fri   9/29 H DET   44-21 W 11,096
Sun 10/8   A GB   44-31 W 23,871
Thu 10/12 H SF   29-24 W   5,740
Thu 10/19 H GB   35-17 W 13,661
Sun 10/29 H CHIB 38-27 W 48,462
Sun 11/12 H CHIB 20-28 L 50,102
Sun 11/19 H LA   35-43 L 42,673
Thu 11/23 A DET   14-49 L 30,206
Sun 12/3   A NYG   7-51 L 41,630
Sun 12/10 H BAL   51-14 W   6,836

PHILADELPHIA EAGLES
Sat   9/16 H CLE   10-35 L 71,237
Sun   9/24 A CHIC 45-7   W 24,914
Sat 10/7   H LA   56-20 W 24,134
Sun 10/15 A BAL   24-14 W 14,413
Sun 10/22 A PIT   17-10 W 35,662
Sun 10/29 H WAS   35-3   W 33,707
Sun 11/5   H PIT   7-9   L 24,629
Sun 11/12 A WAS   33-0   W 29,407
Sun 11/19 H CHIC 10-14 L 28,368
Sun 11/26 A NYG   3-7   L 24,903
Sun 12/3   A CLE   7-13 L 37,490
Sun 12/10 H NYG   7-9   L 26,440

PITTSBURGH STEELERS
Sun   9/17 H NYG   7-18 L 24,699
Sun   9/24 A DET   7-10 L 18,707
Sun 10/1   A WAS   26-7   W 25,008
Sat 10/7   H CLE   17-30 L 35,399
Sun 10/15 A NYG   17-6   W 21,725
Sun 10/22 H PHI   10-17 L 35,662
Sun 10/29 A CLE   7-45 L 40,714
Sun 11/5   A PHI   9-7   W 24,629
Sun 11/12 H BAL   17-7   W 24,141
Thu 11/23 A CHIC 28-17 W 11,622
Sun 12/3   H WAS   7-24 L 19,741
Sun 12/10 H CHIC 28-7   W 18,301

SAN FRANCISCO 49ERS
Sun   9/17 H NYY   17-21 L 29,992
Sun   9/24 H CHIB 20-32 L 35,558
Sun 10/1   H LA   14-35 L 27,262
Sun 10/8   A DET   7-24 L 17,337
Thu 10/12 A NYY   24-29 L   5,740
Sun 10/22 H DET   28-27 W 26,252
Sun 10/29 H BAL   17-14 W 15,091
Sun 11/5   A LA   21-28 L 15,952
Sun 11/12 A CLE   14-34 L 28,786
Sun 11/19 A CHIB   0-17 L 38,105
Sun 11/26 A GB   21-25 L 13,196
Sun 12/10 H GB   30-14 W 19,204

WASHINGTON REDSKINS
Sun   9/17 A BAL   38-14 W 29,000
Sun   9/24 A GB   21-35 L 14,109
Sun 10/1   H PIT   7-26 L 25,008
Sun 10/8   H NYG   17-21 L 19,288
Sun 10/22 H CHIC 28-38 L 27,856
Sun 10/29 A PHI   3-35 L 33,707
Sun 11/5   A NYG   21-24 L 23,909
Sun 11/12 H PHI   0-33 L 29,407
Sun 11/19 A CLE   14-20 L 21,908
Sun 11/26 H BAL   38-28 W 21,275
Sun 12/3   A PIT   24-7   W 19,741
Sun 12/10 H CLE   21-45 L 30,143

1951 NFL
CHICAGO BEARS
Sun   9/30 A GB   31-20 W 24,666
Sun 10/7   A CHIC 14-28 L 33,781
Sun 10/14 H NYY   24-21 W 37,697
Sun 10/21 H SF   13-7   W 43,727
Sun 10/28 A DET   28-23 W 34,778
Sun 11/4   A WAS   27-0   W 31,737
Sun 11/11 H DET   28-41 L 43,709
Sun 11/18 H GB   24-13 W 36,771
Sun 11/25 A CLE   21-42 L 40,969
Sun 12/2   H LA   17-42 L 50,286
Sun 12/9   A NYY   45-21 W 13,075
Sun 12/16 H CHIC 14-24 L 15,085

CHICAGO CARDINALS
Sun   9/30 H PHI   14-17 L 16,129
Sun 10/7   H CHIB 28-14 W 33,781
Sun 10/14 A NYG   17-28 L 28,095
Sun 10/21 A WAS   3-7   L 22,960
Sun 10/28 H PIT   14-28 L 14,773
Sun 11/4   H CLE   17-34 L 19,742
Sun 11/11 A LA   21-45 L 29,995
Sun 11/18 A SF   27-21 W 19,658
Sun 11/25 H NYG   0-10 L 11,892
Sun 12/2   A CLE   28-49 L 30,550
Sun 12/9   H WAS   17-20 L   9,459
Sun 12/16 A CHIB 24-14 W 15,085

CLEVELAND BROWNS
Sun   9/30 A SF   10-24 L 48,263
Sun 10/7   A LA   38-23 W 67,186
Sun 10/14 H WAS   45-0   W 33,968
Sun 10/21 A PIT   17-0   W 32,409
Sun 10/28 H NYG   14-13 W 56,942
Sun 11/4   A CHIC 34-17 W 19,742
Sun 11/11 H PHI   20-17 W 36,571

Sun	11/18	A	NYG	10-0	W	52,215
Sun	11/25	H	CHIB	42-21	W	40,969
Sun	12/2	H	CHIC	49-28	W	30,550
Sun	12/9	A	PIT	28-0	W	24,229
Sun	12/16	A	PHI	24-9	W	16,623

League Championship

Sun	12/23	A	LA	17-24	L	57,540

DETROIT LIONS

Sun	9/30	H	WAS	35-17	W	28,900
Mon	10/8	A	NYY	37-10	W	24,194
Sun	10/14	H	LA	21-27	L	50,567
Sun	10/21	H	NYY	24-24	T	21,807
Sun	10/28	H	CHIB	23-28	L	34,778
Sun	11/4	A	GB	24-17	W	18,165
Sun	11/11	A	CHIB	41-28	W	43,709
Sun	11/18	A	PHI	28-10	W	25,350
Thu	11/22	H	GB	52-35	W	32,247
Sun	12/2	H	SF	10-20	L	45,757
Sun	12/9	A	LA	24-22	W	52,937
Sun	12/16	A	SF	17-21	L	26,465

GREEN BAY PACKERS

Sun	9/30	H	CHIB	20-31	L	24,666
Sun	10/7	H	PIT	35-33	W	8,324
Sun	10/14	H	PHI	37-24	W	18,489
Sun	10/21	H	LA	0-28	L	21,393
Sun	10/28	A	NYY	29-27	W	7,351
Sun	11/4	H	DET	17-24	L	18,165
Sun	11/11	A	PIT	7-28	L	20,080
Sun	11/18	A	CHIB	13-24	L	36,771
Thu	11/22	A	DET	35-52	L	32,247
Sun	12/2	H	NYY	28-31	L	14,297
Sun	12/9	A	SF	19-31	L	15,121
Sun	12/16	A	LA	14-42	L	23,698

LOS ANGELES RAMS

Fri	9/28	H	NYY	54-14	W	30,315
Sun	10/7	H	CLE	23-38	L	67,186
Sun	10/14	A	DET	27-21	W	50,567
Sun	10/21	A	GB	28-0	W	21,393
Sun	10/28	A	SF	17-44	L	51,987
Sun	11/4	H	SF	23-16	W	54,346
Sun	11/11	H	CHIC	45-21	W	29,995
Sun	11/18	H	NYY	48-21	W	34,717
Sun	11/25	A	WAS	21-31	L	26,307
Sun	12/2	A	CHIB	42-17	W	50,286
Sun	12/9	H	DET	22-24	L	52,937
Sun	12/16	H	GB	42-14	W	23,698

League Championship

Sun	12/23	H	CLE	24-17	W	57,540

NEW YORK GIANTS

Mon	10/1	A	PIT	13-13	T	27,984
Sun	10/7	A	WAS	35-14	W	23,800
Sun	10/14	H	CHIC	28-17	W	28,095
Sun	10/21	H	PHI	26-24	W	28,656
Sun	10/28	A	CLE	13-14	L	56,942
Sun	11/4	H	NYY	37-31	W	25,682
Sun	11/11	H	WAS	28-14	W	21,242
Sun	11/18	H	CLE	0-10	L	52,515
Sun	11/25	A	CHIC	10-0	W	11,892
Sun	12/2	H	PIT	14-0	W	18,186
Sun	12/9	A	PHI	23-7	W	19,342
Sun	12/16	A	NYY	27-17	W	16,658

NEW YORK YANKS

Fri	9/28	A	LA	14-54	L	30,315
Mon	10/8	A	DET	10-37	L	24,194
Sun	10/14	A	CHIB	21-24	L	37,697
Sun	10/21	A	DET	24-24	T	21,807
Sun	10/28	H	GB	27-29	L	7,351
Sun	11/4	A	NYG	31-37	L	25,682
Sun	11/11	A	SF	14-19	L	25,538
Sun	11/18	A	LA	21-48	L	34,717
Sun	11/25	H	SF	10-10	T	10,184
Sun	12/2	A	GB	31-28	W	14,297
Sun	12/9	H	CHIB	21-45	L	13,075
Sun	12/16	H	NYG	17-27	L	16,658

PHILADELPHIA EAGLES

Sun	9/30	A	CHIC	17-14	W	16,129
Sat	10/6	H	SF	21-14	W	23,432
Sun	10/14	A	GB	24-37	L	18,489
Sun	10/21	A	NYG	24-26	L	28,656
Sun	10/28	H	WAS	23-27	L	20,437
Sun	11/4	A	PIT	34-13	W	19,649
Sun	11/11	A	CLE	17-20	L	36,571
Sun	11/18	H	DET	10-28	L	25,350
Sun	11/25	H	PIT	13-17	L	15,537
Sun	12/2	A	WAS	35-21	W	23,738
Sun	12/9	H	NYG	7-23	L	19,342
Sun	12/16	H	CLE	9-24	L	16,263

PITTSBURGH STEELERS

Mon	10/1	H	NYG	13-13	T	27,984
Sun	10/7	A	GB	33-35	L	8,324
Sun	10/14	H	SF	24-28	L	27,124
Sun	10/21	A	CLE	0-17	L	32,409
Sun	10/28	A	CHIC	28-14	W	14,773
Sun	11/4	H	PHI	13-34	L	19,649
Sun	11/11	H	GB	28-7	W	20,080
Sun	11/18	H	WAS	7-22	L	15,060
Sun	11/25	A	PHI	17-13	W	15,537
Sun	12/2	A	NYG	0-14	L	18,186
Sun	12/9	H	CLE	0-28	L	24,229
Sun	12/16	A	WAS	20-10	W	18,096

SAN FRANCISCO 49ERS

Sun	9/30	H	CLE	24-10	W	48,263
Sat	10/6	A	PHI	14-21	L	23,432
Sun	10/14	A	PIT	28-24	W	27,124
Sun	10/21	A	CHIB	7-13	L	43,427
Sun	10/28	H	LA	44-17	W	51,987
Sun	11/4	A	LA	16-23	L	54,346
Sun	11/11	H	NYY	19-14	W	25,538
Sun	11/18	H	CHIC	21-27	L	19,658
Sun	11/25	A	NYY	10-10	T	10,184
Sun	12/2	A	DET	20-10	W	45,757
Sun	12/9	H	GB	31-19	W	15,121
Sun	12/16	H	DET	21-17	W	26,465

WASHINGTON REDSKINS

Sun	9/30	A	DET	17-35	L	28,900
Sun	10/7	H	NYG	14-35	L	23,800
Sun	10/14	A	CLE	0-45	L	33,968
Sun	10/21	H	CHIC	7-3	W	22,960
Sun	10/28	A	PHI	27-23	W	20,437
Sun	11/4	H	CHIB	0-27	L	31,737
Sun	11/11	A	NYG	14-28	L	21,242
Sun	11/18	A	PIT	22-7	W	15,060
Sun	11/25	H	LA	31-21	W	26,307
Sun	12/2	H	PHI	21-35	L	23,738
Sun	12/9	A	CHIC	20-17	W	9,459
Sun	12/16	H	PIT	10-20	L	18,096

1952 NFL

CHICAGO BEARS

Sun	9/28	A	GB	24-14	W	24,656
Sun	10/5	A	CHIC	10-21	L	34,697
Sun	10/12	H	DAL	38-20	W	35,429
Sun	10/19	H	SF	16-40	L	48,338
Sun	10/26	A	LA	7-31	L	43,574
Sun	11/2	A	SF	20-17	W	58,255
Sun	11/9	H	GB	28-41	L	41,751
Sun	11/16	H	LA	24-40	L	40,737
Sun	11/23	H	DET	24-23	W	37,508
Thu	11/27	N	DAL	23-27	L	2,500
Sun	12/7	A	DET	21-45	L	50,410
Sun	12/14	H	CHIC	10-7	W	32,578

CHICAGO CARDINALS

Mon	9/29	H	WAS	7-23	L	17,837
Sun	10/5	H	CHIB	21-10	W	34,697
Sun	10/12	A	WAS	17-6	W	24,600
Sun	10/19	A	NYG	24-23	W	41,182
Sun	10/26	H	PIT	28-34	L	20,395
Sun	11/2	H	NYG	6-28	L	27,195
Sun	11/9	A	CLE	13-28	L	34,097
Sun	11/16	A	PHI	7-10	L	18,908
Sun	11/23	A	PIT	14-17	L	18,330
Sun	11/30	H	PHI	28-22	W	13,577
Sun	12/7	H	CLE	0-10	L	24,541
Sun	12/14	A	CHIB	7-10	L	32,578

CLEVELAND BROWNS

Sun	9/28	H	LA	37-7	W	57,832
Sat	10/4	A	PIT	21-20	W	27,923
Sun	10/12	H	NYG	9-17	L	51,858
Sun	10/19	A	PHI	49-7	W	27,874
Sun	10/26	H	WAS	19-15	W	32,496
Sun	11/2	A	DET	6-17	L	56,029
Sun	11/9	H	CHIC	28-13	W	34,097
Sun	11/16	H	PIT	29-28	W	34,973
Sun	11/23	H	PHI	20-28	L	28,948
Sun	11/30	A	WAS	48-24	W	22,679
Sun	12/7	A	CHIC	10-0	W	24,541
Sun	12/14	A	NYG	34-37	L	41,610

League Championship

Sun	12/28	H	DET	7-17	L	50,934

DALLAS TEXANS

Sun	9/28	H	NYG	6-24	L	17,500
Sun	10/5	H	SF	14-37	L	12,566
Sun	10/12	A	CHIB	20-38	L	35,429
Sat	10/18	H	GB	14-24	L	14,000
Sun	10/26	A	SF	21-48	L	26,887
Sun	11/2	A	LA	20-42	L	30,702
Sun	11/9	H	LA	6-27	L	10,000
Sun	11/16	A	DET	13-43	L	33,304
Sun	11/23	A	GB	14-42	L	16,340
Thu	11/27	N	CHIB	27-23	W	2,500
Sun	12/7	A	PHI	21-38	L	18,376
Sat	12/13	A	DET	6-41	L	12,452

DETROIT LIONS

Sun	9/28	A	SF	3-17	L	54,761
Fri	10/3	A	LA	17-14	W	42,743
Sun	10/12	H	SF	0-28	L	48,842
Sun	10/19	H	LA	24-16	W	40,152
Sun	10/26	A	GB	52-17	W	24,656
Sun	11/2	H	CLE	17-6	W	56,029
Sun	11/9	A	PIT	31-6	W	26,170
Sun	11/16	H	DAL	43-13	W	33,304
Sun	11/23	A	CHIB	23-24	L	37,508
Thu	11/27	H	GB	48-24	W	39,101
Sun	12/7	H	CHIB	45-21	W	50,410
Sat	12/13	H	DAL	41-6	W	12,452

National Conference Playoff

Sun	12/21	H	LA	31-21	W	47,645

League Championship

Sun	12/28	A	CLE	17-7	W	50,934

GREEN BAY PACKERS

Sun	9/28	H	CHIB	14-24	L	24,656
Sat	10/4	H	WAS	35-20	W	9,657
Sun	10/12	H	LA	28-30	L	21,693
Sat	10/18	A	DAL	24-14	W	14,000
Sun	10/26	H	DET	17-52	L	24,656
Sun	11/2	H	PHI	12-10	W	10,149
Sun	11/9	A	CHIB	41-28	W	41,751
Sun	11/16	A	NYG	17-3	W	26,723
Sun	11/23	H	DAL	42-14	W	16,340
Thu	11/27	A	DET	24-48	L	39,101
Sun	12/7	A	LA	27-45	L	49,822
Sun	12/14	A	SF	14-24	L	17,579

LOS ANGELES RAMS

Sun	9/28	A	CLE	7-37	L	57,832
Fri	10/3	H	DET	14-17	L	42,743
Sun	10/12	A	GB	30-28	W	21,693
Sun	10/19	A	DET	16-24	L	40,152
Sun	10/26	H	CHIB	31-7	W	43,574
Sun	11/2	H	DAL	42-20	W	30,702
Sun	11/9	A	DAL	27-6	W	10,000
Sun	11/16	A	CHIB	40-24	W	40,737
Sun	11/23	H	SF	35-9	W	64,450
Sun	11/30	A	SF	34-21	W	48,731
Sun	12/7	H	GB	45-27	W	49,822
Sun	12/14	H	PIT	28-14	W	71,130

National Conference Playoff

Sun	12/21	A	DET	21-31	L	47,645

NEW YORK GIANTS

Sun	9/28	A	DAL	24-6	W	17,500
Sat	10/4	A	PHI	31-7	W	22,512
Sun	10/12	A	CLE	17-9	W	51,858
Sun	10/19	H	CHIC	23-24	L	41,182
Sun	10/26	H	PHI	10-14	L	21,458
Sun	11/2	A	CHIC	28-6	W	27,195
Sun	11/9	H	SF	23-14	W	50,880
Sun	11/16	H	GB	3-17	L	26,723
Sun	11/23	A	WAS	14-10	W	21,125
Sun	11/30	A	PIT	7-63	L	15,140
Sun	12/7	H	WAS	17-27	L	21,237
Sun	12/14	H	CLE	37-34	W	41,610

PHILADELPHIA EAGLES

Sun	9/28	A	PIT	31-25	W	22,501
Sat	10/4	H	NYG	7-31	L	22,512
Sun	10/12	H	PIT	26-21	W	18,648
Sun	10/19	H	CLE	7-49	L	27,874
Sun	10/26	A	NYG	14-10	W	21,458
Sun	11/2	A	GB	10-12	L	10,149
Sun	11/9	H	WAS	38-20	W	16,932
Sun	11/16	H	CHIC	10-7	W	18,906
Sun	11/23	A	CLE	28-20	W	28,948
Sun	11/30	A	CHIC	22-28	L	13,577
Sun	12/7	H	DAL	38-21	W	18,376
Sun	12/14	A	WAS	21-27	L	22,468

PITTSBURGH STEELERS

Sun	9/28	H	PHI	25-31	L	22,501
Sun	10/4	H	CLE	20-21	L	27,923
Sun	10/12	A	PHI	21-26	L	18,648
Sun	10/19	H	WAS	24-28	L	22,605
Sun	10/26	A	CHIC	34-28	W	20,395
Sun	11/2	A	WAS	24-23	W	25,866
Sun	11/9	H	DET	6-31	L	26,170
Sun	11/16	A	CLE	28-29	L	34,973
Sun	11/23	H	CHIC	17-14	W	18,330
Sun	11/30	H	NYG	63-7	W	15,140
Sun	12/7	A	SF	24-7	W	13,866
Sun	12/14	A	LA	14-28	L	71,130

SAN FRANCISCO 49ERS

Sun	9/28	H	DET	17-3	W	54,761
Sun	10/5	A	DAL	37-14	W	12,566
Sun	10/12	A	DET	28-0	W	48,842
Sun	10/19	A	CHIB	40-16	W	48,338
Sun	10/26	H	DAL	48-21	W	26,887
Sun	11/2	H	CHIB	17-20	L	58,255
Sun	11/9	A	NYG	14-23	L	50,880
Sun	11/16	A	WAS	23-17	W	28,997
Sun	11/23	A	LA	9-35	L	64,450
Sun	11/30	H	LA	21-34	L	48,731
Sun	12/7	H	PIT	7-24	L	13,886
Sun	12/14	H	GB	24-14	W	17,579

WASHINGTON REDSKINS

Mon	9/29	A	CHIC	23-7	W	17,837
Sat	10/4	A	GB	20-35	L	9,657

Sun	10/12	H	CHIC	6-17	L	24,600
Sun	10/19	A	PIT	28-24	W	22,605
Sun	10/26	A	CLE	15-19	L	32,496
Sun	11/2	H	PIT	23-24	L	25,866
Sun	11/9	A	PHI	20-38	L	16,932
Sun	11/16	H	SF	17-23	L	28,997
Sun	11/23	H	NYG	10-14	L	21,125
Sun	11/30	H	CLE	24-48	L	22,679
Sun	12/7	A	NYG	27-17	W	21,237
Sun	12/14	H	PHI	27-21	W	22,468

1953 NFL

BALTIMORE COLTS

Sun	9/27	H	CHIB	13-9	W	23,715
Sat	10/3	H	DET	17-27	L	25,159
Sun	10/11	A	CHIB	16-14	W	35,316
Sun	10/18	A	GB	14-37	L	18,713
Sun	10/25	H	WAS	27-17	W	34,031
Sat	10/31	H	GB	24-35	L	33,797
Sat	11/7	A	DET	7-17	L	46,508
Sun	11/15	A	PHI	14-45	L	27,813
Sun	11/22	H	LA	13-21	L	27,268
Sun	11/29	H	SF	21-38	L	26,005
Sat	12/5	A	LA	2-45	L	26,696
Sun	12/13	A	SF	14-45	L	23,932

CHICAGO BEARS

Sun	9/27	A	BAL	9-13	L	23,715
Sun	10/4	A	GB	17-13	W	24,835
Sun	10/11	H	BAL	14-16	L	35,316
Sun	10/18	H	SF	28-35	L	36,909
Sun	10/25	A	LA	24-38	L	49,546
Sun	11/1	A	SF	14-24	L	26,308
Sun	11/8	H	GB	21-21	T	39,899
Sun	11/15	A	WAS	27-24	W	21,392
Sun	11/22	H	DET	16-20	L	36,165
Sun	11/29	H	LA	24-21	W	31,626
Sun	12/6	A	DET	7-13	L	58,056
Sun	12/13	H	CHIC	17-24	L	38,059

CHICAGO CARDINALS

Sun	9/27	H	WAS	13-24	L	16,055
Sun	10/4	H	CLE	7-27	L	24,374
Sun	10/11	A	PIT	28-31	L	25,935
Sun	10/18	A	NYG	7-21	L	30,301
Sun	10/25	H	PHI	17-56	L	22,064
Sun	11/1	H	NYG	20-23	L	17,499
Sun	11/8	A	WAS	17-28	L	19,654
Sun	11/15	H	LA	24-24	T	26,674
Sat	11/21	A	PHI	0-38	L	19,402
Sun	11/29	A	CLE	16-27	L	24,499
Sun	12/6	H	PIT	17-21	L	14,138
Sun	12/13	A	CHIB	24-17	W	38,059

CLEVELAND BROWNS

Sun	9/27	A	GB	27-0	W	22,604
Sun	10/4	A	CHIC	27-7	W	24,374
Sat	10/10	H	PHI	37-13	W	45,802
Sun	10/18	A	WAS	30-14	W	33,963
Sun	10/25	A	NYG	7-0	W	30,773
Sun	11/1	H	WAS	27-3	W	47,845
Sun	11/8	H	PIT	34-16	W	35,592
Sun	11/15	H	SF	23-21	W	80,698
Sun	11/22	A	PIT	20-16	W	32,904
Sun	11/29	H	CHIC	27-16	W	24,499
Sun	12/6	H	NYG	62-14	W	40,235
Sun	12/13	A	PHI	27-42	L	38,654

League Championship

Sun	12/27	A	DET	16-17	L	54,577

DETROIT LIONS

Sun	9/27	H	PIT	38-21	W	44,587
Sat	10/3	A	BAL	27-17	W	25,159
Sun	10/11	H	SF	24-21	W	58,079
Sun	10/18	H	LA	19-31	L	55,772
Sun	10/25	A	SF	14-10	W	54,862
Sun	11/1	A	LA	24-37	L	93,751
Sat	11/7	H	BAL	17-7	W	46,508
Sun	11/15	A	GB	14-7	W	20,834
Sun	11/22	A	CHIB	20-16	W	36,165
Thu	11/26	H	GB	34-15	W	52,547
Sun	12/6	H	CHIB	13-7	W	58,056
Sun	12/13	A	NYG	27-16	W	28,390

League Championship

Sun	12/27	H	CLE	17-16	W	54,577

GREEN BAY PACKERS

Sun	9/27	H	CLE	0-27	L	22,604
Sun	10/4	H	CHIB	13-17	L	24,835
Sun	10/11	H	LA	20-38	L	23,352
Sun	10/18	H	BAL	37-14	W	18,713
Sat	10/24	A	PIT	14-31	L	22,918
Sat	10/31	A	BAL	35-24	W	33,797
Sun	11/8	A	CHIB	21-21	T	39,899
Sun	11/15	H	DET	7-14	L	20,834
Sun	11/22	H	SF	7-37	L	16,378
Thu	11/26	A	DET	15-34	L	52,547
Sun	12/6	A	SF	14-48	L	31,337
Sat	12/12	A	LA	17-33	L	23,069

LOS ANGELES RAMS

Sun	9/27	H	NYG	21-7	W	49,579
Sun	10/4	A	SF	30-31	L	43,922
Sun	10/11	A	GB	38-20	W	23,352
Sun	10/18	A	DET	31-19	W	55,772
Sun	10/25	H	CHIB	38-24	W	49,546
Sun	11/1	H	DET	37-24	W	93,751
Sun	11/8	H	SF	27-31	L	85,505
Sun	11/15	A	CHIC	24-24	T	26,674
Sun	11/22	A	BAL	21-13	W	27,268
Sun	11/29	A	CHIB	21-24	L	31,626
Sat	12/5	H	BAL	45-2	W	26,696
Sat	12/12	H	GB	33-17	W	23,069

NEW YORK GIANTS

Sun	9/27	A	LA	7-21	L	49,579
Sat	10/3	A	PIT	14-24	L	31,500
Sun	10/11	A	WAS	9-13	L	26,241
Sun	10/18	H	CHIC	21-7	W	30,301
Sun	10/25	H	CLE	0-7	L	30,773
Sun	11/1	A	CHIC	23-20	W	17,499
Sun	11/8	A	PHI	7-30	L	24,331
Sun	11/15	H	PIT	10-14	L	20,411
Sun	11/22	H	WAS	21-24	L	16,887
Sun	11/29	H	PHI	37-28	W	20,294
Sun	12/6	A	CLE	14-62	L	40,235
Sun	12/13	H	DET	16-27	L	28,390

PHILADELPHIA EAGLES

Sun	9/27	A	SF	21-31	L	27,819
Fri	10/2	H	WAS	21-21	T	19,099
Sat	10/10	A	CLE	13-37	L	45,802
Sat	10/17	H	PIT	23-7	W	18,681
Sun	10/25	A	CHIC	56-17	W	22,064
Sun	11/1	A	PIT	35-7	W	27,547
Sun	11/8	H	NYG	30-7	W	24,331
Sun	11/15	H	BAL	45-14	W	27,813
Sat	11/21	H	CHIC	38-0	W	19,402
Sun	11/29	A	NYG	28-37	L	20,294
Sun	12/6	A	WAS	0-10	L	21,579
Sun	12/13	H	CLE	42-27	W	38,654

PITTSBURGH STEELERS

Sun	9/27	A	DET	21-38	L	44,587
Sat	10/3	H	NYG	24-14	W	31,500
Sun	10/11	H	CHIC	31-28	W	25,935
Sat	10/17	A	PHI	7-23	L	18,681
Sat	10/24	H	GB	31-14	W	22,918
Sun	11/1	H	PHI	7-35	L	27,547
Sun	11/8	A	CLE	16-34	L	35,592
Sun	11/15	A	NYG	14-10	W	20,411
Sun	11/22	H	CLE	16-20	L	32,904
Sun	11/29	H	WAS	9-17	L	17,026
Sun	12/6	A	CHIC	21-17	W	14,138
Sun	12/13	A	WAS	14-13	W	22,057

SAN FRANCISCO 49ERS

Sun	9/27	H	PHI	31-21	W	27,819
Sun	10/4	H	LA	31-30	W	43,922
Sun	10/11	A	DET	21-24	L	58,079
Sun	10/18	A	CHIB	35-28	W	36,909
Sun	10/25	H	DET	10-14	L	54,862
Sun	11/1	H	CHIB	24-14	W	26,308
Sun	11/8	A	LA	31-27	W	85,505
Sun	11/15	A	CLE	21-23	L	80,698
Sun	11/22	A	GB	37-7	W	16,378
Sun	11/29	A	BAL	38-21	W	26,005
Sun	12/6	H	GB	48-14	W	31,337
Sun	12/13	H	BAL	45-14	W	23,932

WASHINGTON REDSKINS

Sun	9/27	A	CHIC	24-13	W	16,055
Fri	10/2	A	PHI	21-21	T	19,099
Sun	10/11	H	NYG	13-9	W	26,241
Sun	10/18	H	CLE	14-30	L	33,963
Sun	10/25	A	BAL	17-27	L	34,031
Sun	11/1	A	CLE	3-27	L	47,845
Sun	11/8	H	CHIC	28-17	W	19,654
Sun	11/15	H	CHIB	24-27	L	21,392
Sun	11/22	A	NYG	24-21	W	16,887
Sun	11/29	A	PIT	17-9	W	17,026
Sun	12/6	H	PHI	10-0	W	21,579
Sun	12/13	H	PIT	13-14	L	22,057

1954 NFL

BALTIMORE COLTS

Sun	9/26	H	LA	0-48	L	36,215
Sat	10/2	H	NYG	20-14	W	27,088
Sun	10/10	A	CHIB	9-28	L	27,845
Sat	10/16	A	DET	0-35	L	48,272
Sun	10/24	H	GB	6-7	L	28,680
Sun	10/31	A	WAS	21-24	L	23,567
Sat	11/6	H	DET	3-27	L	25,287
Sat	11/13	A	GB	13-24	L	19,786
Sun	11/21	H	CHIB	13-28	L	23,093
Sun	11/28	H	SF	17-13	W	23,875
Sat	12/4	A	LA	22-21	W	30,744
Sat	12/11	A	SF	7-10	L	25,456

CHICAGO BEARS

Sun	9/26	A	DET	23-48	L	52,343
Sun	10/3	A	GB	10-3	W	24,414
Sun	10/10	H	BAL	28-9	W	27,845
Sun	10/17	H	SF	24-31	L	42,935
Sun	10/24	A	LA	38-42	L	48,174
Sun	10/31	A	SF	31-27	W	49,833
Sun	11/7	H	GB	28-23	W	47,038
Sun	11/14	H	CLE	10-39	L	48,722
Sun	11/21	A	BAL	28-13	W	23,093
Sun	11/28	H	LA	24-13	W	32,338
Sun	12/5	A	CHIC	29-7	W	33,594
Sun	12/12	H	DET	28-24	W	37,240

CHICAGO CARDINALS

Sun	9/26	H	NYG	10-41	L	16,780
Sun	10/3	H	PHI	16-35	L	17,084
Sun	10/10	A	CLE	7-31	L	24,101
Sun	10/17	A	NYG	17-31	L	31,256
Sun	10/24	H	CLE	3-35	L	23,823
Sun	10/31	H	PIT	17-14	W	18,765
Sun	11/7	A	PHI	14-30	L	21,963
Sun	11/14	A	LA	17-28	L	40,739
Sun	11/21	H	WAS	38-16	W	15,619
Sun	11/28	A	PIT	17-20	L	14,460
Sun	12/5	H	CHIB	7-29	L	33,594
Sun	12/12	A	WAS	20-37	L	18,107

CLEVELAND BROWNS

Sun	9/26	A	PHI	10-28	L	26,546
Sun	10/10	H	CHIC	31-7	W	24,101
Sun	10/17	A	PIT	27-55	L	33,262
Sun	10/24	A	CHIC	35-3	W	23,823
Sun	10/31	H	NYG	24-14	W	30,448
Sun	11/7	H	WAS	62-3	W	25,158
Sun	11/14	A	CHIB	39-10	W	48,722
Sun	11/21	H	PHI	6-0	W	41,537
Sun	11/28	A	NYG	16-7	W	45,936
Sun	12/5	A	WAS	34-14	W	21,761
Sun	12/12	H	PIT	42-7	W	28,064
Sun	12/19	H	DET	10-14	L	34,168

League Championship

Sun	12/26	H	DET	56-10	W	43,827

DETROIT LIONS

Sun	9/26	H	CHIB	48-23	W	52,343
Sun	10/10	H	LA	21-3	W	55,008
Sat	10/16	H	BAL	35-0	W	48,272
Sun	10/24	A	SF	31-37	L	58,891
Sun	10/31	A	LA	27-24	W	74,315
Sat	11/6	A	BAL	27-3	W	25,287
Sun	11/14	H	SF	48-7	W	58,431
Sun	11/21	A	GB	21-17	W	20,767
Thu	11/25	H	GB	28-24	W	55,532
Sun	12/5	H	PHI	13-13	T	54,939
Sun	12/12	A	CHIB	24-28	L	37,240
Sun	12/19	A	CLE	14-10	W	34,168

League Championship

Sun	12/26	A	CLE	10-56	L	43,827

GREEN BAY PACKERS

Sun	9/26	H	PIT	20-21	L	20,675
Sun	10/3	H	CHIB	3-10	L	24,414
Sun	10/10	H	SF	17-23	L	15,571
Sun	10/17	H	LA	35-17	W	17,455
Sun	10/24	A	BAL	7-6	W	28,680
Sat	10/30	A	PHI	37-14	W	25,378
Sun	11/7	A	CHIB	23-28	L	47,038
Sat	11/13	H	BAL	24-13	W	19,786
Sun	11/21	H	DET	17-21	L	20,767
Thu	11/25	A	DET	24-28	L	55,532
Sun	12/5	A	SF	0-35	L	32,012
Sun	12/12	A	LA	27-35	L	38,839

LOS ANGELES RAMS

Sun	9/26	A	BAL	48-0	W	36,215
Sun	10/3	H	SF	24-24	T	79,208
Sun	10/10	A	DET	3-21	L	55,008
Sun	10/17	A	GB	17-35	L	17,455
Sun	10/24	H	CHIB	42-38	W	48,174
Sun	10/31	H	DET	24-27	L	74,315
Sun	11/7	A	SF	42-34	W	58,758
Sun	11/14	H	CHIC	28-17	W	40,739
Sun	11/21	A	NYG	17-16	W	27,077
Sun	11/28	A	CHIB	13-24	L	32,338
Sat	12/4	H	BAL	21-22	L	30,744
Sun	12/12	H	GB	35-27	W	38,839

NEW YORK GIANTS

Sun	9/26	A	CHIC	41-10	W	16,780
Sat	10/2	A	BAL	14-20	L	27,088
Sun	10/10	A	WAS	51-21	W	21,217
Sun	10/17	H	CHIC	31-17	W	31,256
Sun	10/24	H	WAS	24-7	W	22,597
Sun	10/31	A	CLE	14-24	L	30,448
Sun	11/7	A	PIT	30-6	W	36,358
Sun	11/14	H	PHI	27-14	W	46,565
Sun	11/21	H	LA	16-17	L	27,077
Sun	11/28	H	CLE	7-16	L	45,936
Sun	12/5	H	PIT	24-3	W	16,856
Sun	12/12	A	PHI	14-29	L	28,449

PHILADELPHIA EAGLES

Sun	9/26	H	CLE	28-10	W	26,546

Sun	10/3	A	CHIC	35-16	W	17,084
Sat	10/9	H	PIT	24-22	W	37,322
Sun	10/17	A	WAS	49-21	W	22,051
Sat	10/23	A	PIT	7-17	L	39,075
Sat	10/30	H	GB	14-37	L	25,378
Sun	11/7	H	CHIC	30-14	W	21,963
Sun	11/14	A	NYG	14-27	L	46,565
Sun	11/21	A	CLE	0-6	L	41,537
Sun	11/28	H	WAS	41-33	W	18,517
Sun	12/5	A	DET	13-13	T	54,939
Sun	12/12	H	NYG	29-14	W	28,449

PITTSBURGH STEELERS

Sun	9/26	A	GB	21-20	W	20,675
Sat	10/2	H	WAS	37-7	W	22,492
Sat	10/9	A	PHI	22-24	L	37,322
Sun	10/17	H	CLE	55-27	W	33,262
Sat	10/23	H	PHI	17-7	W	39,075
Sun	10/31	A	CHIC	14-17	L	18,765
Sun	11/7	H	NYG	7-30	L	36,358
Sun	11/14	A	WAS	14-17	L	19,388
Sat	11/20	H	SF	3-31	L	35,520
Sun	11/28	H	CHIC	20-17	W	14,460
Sun	12/5	A	NYG	3-24	L	16,856
Sun	12/12	A	CLE	7-42	L	28,064

SAN FRANCISCO 49ERS

Sun	9/26	H	WAS	41-7	W	32,085
Sun	10/3	A	LA	24-24	T	79,208
Sun	10/10	A	GB	23-17	W	15,571
Sun	10/17	A	CHIB	31-24	W	42,935
Sun	10/24	H	DET	37-31	W	58,891
Sun	10/31	H	CHIB	27-31	L	49,833
Sun	11/7	H	LA	34-42	L	58,758
Sun	11/14	A	DET	7-48	L	58,431
Sat	11/20	A	PIT	31-3	W	35,520
Sun	11/28	A	BAL	13-17	L	23,875
Sun	12/5	H	GB	35-0	W	32,012
Sat	12/11	H	BAL	10-7	W	25,456

WASHINGTON REDSKINS

Sun	9/26	A	SF	7-41	L	32,085
Sat	10/2	A	PIT	7-37	L	22,492
Sun	10/10	H	NYG	21-51	L	21,217
Sun	10/17	H	PHI	21-49	L	22,051
Sun	10/24	A	NYG	7-24	L	22,597
Sun	10/31	H	BAL	24-21	W	23,567
Sun	11/7	A	CLE	3-62	L	25,158
Sun	11/14	H	PIT	17-14	W	19,388
Sun	11/21	A	CHIC	16-38	L	15,619
Sun	11/28	A	PHI	33-41	L	18,517
Sun	12/5	H	CLE	14-34	L	21,761
Sun	12/12	H	CHIC	37-20	W	18,107

1955 NFL

BALTIMORE COLTS

Sun	9/25	H	CHIB	23-17	W	36,167
Sat	10/1	H	DET	28-13	W	40,030
Sat	10/8	A	GB	24-20	W	40,199
Sun	10/16	A	CHIB	10-38	L	40,184
Sun	10/23	H	WAS	13-14	L	51,387
Sat	10/29	H	GB	14-10	W	34,411
Sat	11/5	A	DET	14-24	L	53,874
Sun	11/13	A	NYG	7-17	L	33,982
Sun	11/20	H	LA	17-17	T	41,146
Sun	11/27	H	SF	26-14	W	33,485
Sun	12/4	A	LA	14-20	L	37,024
Sun	12/11	A	SF	24-35	L	33,471

CHICAGO BEARS

Sun	9/25	A	BAL	17-23	L	36,167
Sun	10/2	A	GB	3-24	L	24,662
Sun	10/9	H	SF	19-20	L	41,651
Sun	10/16	H	BAL	38-10	W	40,184
Sun	10/23	A	SF	34-23	W	56,350
Sun	10/30	A	LA	31-20	W	69,587
Sun	11/6	H	GB	52-31	W	48,890
Sun	11/13	H	LA	24-3	W	50,187
Sun	11/20	A	DET	24-14	W	53,610
Sun	11/27	A	CHIC	14-53	L	47,314
Sun	12/4	H	DET	21-20	W	39,388
Sun	12/11	H	PHI	17-10	W	34,783

CHICAGO CARDINALS

Mon	9/26	A	PIT	7-14	L	26,359
Sun	10/2	H	NYG	28-17	W	9,555
Sun	10/9	A	WAS	24-10	W	26,337
Sun	10/16	A	NYG	0-10	L	7,000
Sun	10/23	H	PHI	24-24	T	24,620
Sun	10/30	H	CLE	20-26	L	29,471
Sat	11/5	H	PIT	27-13	W	23,310
Sun	11/13	A	GB	14-31	L	20,104
Sun	11/20	H	WAS	0-31	L	16,901
Sun	11/27	H	CHIB	53-14	W	47,314
Sun	12/4	A	PHI	3-27	L	19,478
Sun	12/11	A	CLE	24-35	L	25,914

CLEVELAND BROWNS

Sun	9/25	H	WAS	17-27	L	30,041
Sun	10/2	A	SF	38-3	W	43,595
Sun	10/9	H	PHI	21-17	W	43,974
Sun	10/16	A	WAS	24-14	W	29,168
Sun	10/23	H	GB	41-10	W	51,482
Sun	10/30	A	CHIC	26-20	W	29,471
Sun	11/6	H	NYG	24-14	W	46,524
Sun	11/13	A	PHI	17-33	L	39,303
Sun	11/20	H	PIT	41-14	W	54,509
Sun	11/27	A	NYG	35-35	T	45,699
Sun	12/4	A	PIT	30-7	W	31,101
Sun	12/11	H	CHIC	35-24	W	25,914

League Championship

Mon	12/26	A	LA	38-14	W	87,695

DETROIT LIONS

Sun	9/25	A	GB	17-20	L	22,217
Sat	10/1	A	BAL	13-28	L	40,030
Sun	10/9	H	LA	10-17	L	54,836
Sun	10/16	H	SF	24-27	L	50,179
Sun	10/23	A	LA	13-24	L	68,690
Sun	10/30	A	SF	21-38	L	44,831
Sat	11/5	H	BAL	24-14	W	53,874
Sun	11/13	A	PIT	31-28	W	34,441
Sun	11/20	H	CHIB	14-24	L	53,610
Thu	11/24	H	GB	24-10	W	51,685
Sun	12/4	A	CHIB	20-21	L	39,388
Sun	12/11	H	NYG	19-24	L	45,929

GREEN BAY PACKERS

Sun	9/25	H	DET	20-17	W	22,217
Sun	10/2	H	CHIB	24-3	W	24,662
Sat	10/8	H	BAL	20-24	L	40,199
Sun	10/16	H	LA	30-28	W	26,960
Sun	10/23	A	CLE	10-41	L	51,482
Sat	10/29	A	BAL	10-14	L	34,411
Sun	11/6	A	CHIB	31-52	L	48,890
Sun	11/13	H	CHIC	31-14	W	20,104
Sun	11/20	H	SF	27-21	W	19,099
Thu	11/24	A	DET	10-24	L	51,685
Sun	12/4	A	SF	28-7	W	32,897
Sun	12/11	A	LA	17-31	L	90,535

LOS ANGELES RAMS

Sun	9/25	A	SF	23-14	W	58,772
Sun	10/2	H	PIT	27-26	W	45,816
Sun	10/9	A	DET	17-10	W	54,836
Sun	10/16	A	GB	28-30	L	26,960
Sun	10/23	H	DET	24-13	W	68,690
Sun	10/30	H	CHIB	20-31	L	69,587
Sun	11/6	H	SF	27-14	W	71,832
Sun	11/13	A	CHIB	3-24	L	50,187
Sun	11/20	A	BAL	17-17	T	41,146
Sun	11/27	A	PHI	23-21	W	31,648
Sun	12/4	H	BAL	20-14	W	37,024
Sun	12/11	H	GB	31-17	W	90,535

League Championship

Mon	12/26	H	CLE	14-38	L	87,695

NEW YORK GIANTS

Sat	9/24	A	PHI	17-27	L	29,597
Sun	10/2	A	CHIC	17-28	L	9,555
Sun	10/9	A	PIT	23-30	L	29,422
Sun	10/16	H	CHIC	10-0	W	7,000
Sun	10/23	H	PIT	17-19	L	27,365
Sun	10/30	H	WAS	35-7	W	17,402
Sun	11/6	A	CLE	14-24	L	46,524
Sun	11/13	H	BAL	17-7	W	33,982
Sun	11/20	H	PHI	31-7	W	22,075
Sun	11/27	H	CLE	35-35	T	45,699
Sun	12/4	A	WAS	27-20	W	28,556
Sun	12/11	A	DET	24-19	W	45,929

PHILADELPHIA EAGLES

Sat	9/24	H	NYG	27-17	W	29,597
Sat	10/1	H	WAS	30-31	L	31,891
Sun	10/9	A	CLE	17-21	L	43,974
Sat	10/15	A	PIT	7-13	L	33,413
Sun	10/23	A	CHIC	24-24	T	24,620
Sun	10/30	H	PIT	24-0	W	31,164
Sun	11/6	A	WAS	21-34	L	25,741
Sun	11/13	H	CLE	33-17	W	39,303
Sun	11/20	A	NYG	7-31	L	22,075
Sun	11/27	H	LA	21-23	L	31,648
Sun	12/4	H	CHIC	27-3	W	19,478
Sun	12/11	A	CHIB	10-17	L	34,783

PITTSBURGH STEELERS

Mon	9/26	H	CHIC	14-7	W	26,359
Sun	10/2	A	LA	26-27	L	45,816
Sun	10/9	H	NYG	30-23	W	29,422
Sat	10/15	H	PHI	13-7	W	33,413
Sun	10/23	A	NYG	19-17	W	27,365
Sun	10/30	A	PHI	0-24	L	31,164
Sat	11/5	A	CHIC	13-27	L	23,310
Sun	11/13	H	DET	28-31	L	34,441
Sun	11/20	A	CLE	14-41	L	54,509
Sun	11/27	H	WAS	14-23	L	21,760
Sun	12/4	H	CLE	7-30	L	31,101
Sun	12/11	A	WAS	17-28	L	20,547

SAN FRANCISCO 49ERS

Sun	9/25	H	LA	14-23	L	58,772
Sun	10/2	H	CLE	3-38	L	43,595
Sun	10/9	A	CHIB	20-19	W	41,651
Sun	10/16	A	DET	27-24	W	50,179
Sun	10/23	H	CHIB	23-34	L	56,350
Sun	10/30	H	DET	38-21	W	44,831
Sun	11/6	A	LA	14-27	L	71,832
Sun	11/13	A	WAS	0-7	L	25,112
Sun	11/20	A	GB	21-27	L	19,099
Sun	11/27	A	BAL	14-26	L	33,485
Sun	12/4	H	GB	7-28	L	32,897
Sun	12/11	H	BAL	35-24	W	33,471

WASHINGTON REDSKINS

Sun	9/25	A	CLE	27-17	W	30,041
Sat	10/1	A	PHI	31-30	W	31,891
Sun	10/9	H	CHIC	10-24	L	26,337
Sun	10/16	H	CLE	14-24	L	29,168
Sun	10/23	A	BAL	14-13	W	51,387
Sun	10/30	A	NYG	7-35	L	17,402
Sun	11/6	H	PHI	34-21	W	25,741
Sun	11/13	H	SF	7-0	W	25,112
Sun	11/20	A	CHIC	31-0	W	16,901
Sun	11/27	A	PIT	23-14	W	21,760
Sun	12/4	H	NYG	20-27	L	28,556
Sun	12/11	H	PIT	28-17	W	20,547

1956 NFL

BALTIMORE COLTS

Sun	9/30	H	CHIB	28-21	W	45,221
Sat	10/6	H	DET	14-31	L	42,622
Sun	10/14	A	GB	33-38	L	24,214
Sun	10/21	A	CHIB	27-58	L	48,364
Sun	10/28	H	GB	28-21	W	40,086
Sun	11/11	A	CLE	21-7	W	42,404
Sun	11/18	A	DET	3-27	L	55,788
Sun	11/25	H	LA	56-21	W	40,321
Sun	12/2	H	SF	17-20	L	37,227
Sun	12/9	A	LA	7-31	L	51,037
Sun	12/16	A	SF	17-30	L	43,791
Sun	12/23	H	WAS	19-17	W	32,994

CHICAGO BEARS

Sun	9/30	A	BAL	21-28	L	45,221
Sun	10/7	A	GB	37-21	W	24,668
Sun	10/14	H	SF	31-7	W	47,526
Sun	10/21	H	BAL	58-27	W	48,364
Sun	10/28	A	SF	38-21	W	53,612
Sun	11/4	A	LA	35-24	W	69,894
Sun	11/11	H	GB	38-14	W	49,172
Sun	11/18	H	LA	30-21	W	48,102
Sun	11/25	A	NYG	17-17	T	55,191
Sun	12/2	A	DET	10-42	L	57,024
Sun	12/9	H	CHIC	10-3	W	48,606
Sun	12/16	H	DET	38-21	W	49,086

League Championship

Sun	12/30	A	NYG	7-47	L	56,836

CHICAGO CARDINALS

Sun	9/30	H	CLE	9-7	W	20,966
Sun	10/7	H	NYG	35-27	W	21,799
Sun	10/14	A	WAS	31-3	W	25,794
Sun	10/21	A	PHI	20-6	W	36,545
Sun	10/28	H	WAS	14-17	L	30,553
Sun	11/4	H	PHI	28-17	W	22,609
Sun	11/11	A	NYG	10-23	L	62,410
Sun	11/18	A	PIT	7-14	L	24,086
Sun	11/25	H	PIT	38-27	W	17,724
Sun	12/2	H	GB	21-24	L	22,620
Sun	12/9	A	CHIB	3-10	L	48,606
Sun	12/16	A	CLE	24-7	W	25,312

CLEVELAND BROWNS

Sun	9/30	A	CHIC	7-9	L	20,966
Sat	10/6	A	PIT	14-10	W	35,398
Sun	10/14	H	NYG	9-21	L	60,042
Sun	10/21	A	WAS	9-20	L	23,332
Sun	10/28	H	PIT	16-24	L	50,358
Sun	11/4	A	GB	24-7	W	28,590
Sun	11/11	H	BAL	7-21	L	42,404
Sun	11/18	A	PHI	16-0	W	25,894
Sun	11/25	H	WAS	17-20	L	22,878
Sun	12/2	H	PHI	17-14	W	20,654
Sun	12/9	A	NYG	24-7	W	27,707
Sun	12/16	H	CHIC	7-24	L	25,312

DETROIT LIONS

Sun	9/30	A	GB	20-16	W	24,668
Sat	10/6	A	BAL	31-14	W	42,622
Sun	10/14	H	LA	24-21	W	56,281
Sun	10/21	H	SF	20-17	W	55,662
Sun	10/28	A	LA	16-7	W	76,758
Sun	11/4	A	SF	17-13	W	46,708
Sun	11/11	A	WAS	17-18	L	28,003
Sun	11/18	H	BAL	27-3	W	55,788
Thu	11/22	H	GB	20-24	L	54,087
Sun	12/2	H	CHIB	42-10	W	57,024
Sun	12/9	H	PIT	45-7	W	52,124
Sun	12/16	A	CHIB	21-38	L	49,086

GREEN BAY PACKERS

Sun	9/30	H	DET	16-20	L	24,668

Sun 10/7   H   CHIB   21-37   L   24,668
Sun 10/14   H   BAL   38-33   W   24,214
Sun 10/21   H   LA   42-17   W   24,200
Sun 10/28   A   BAL   21-28   L   40,086
Sun 11/4   H   CLE   7-24   L   28,590
Sun 11/11   A   CHIB   14-38   L   49,172
Sun 11/18   H   SF   16-17   L   17,986
Thu 11/22   A   DET   24-20   W   54,087
Sun 12/2   A   CHIC   24-21   W   22,620
Sat 12/8   A   SF   20-38   L   32,436
Sun 12/16   A   LA   21-49   L   45,209

LOS ANGELES RAMS
Sun 9/30   H   PHI   27-7   W   54,412
Sun 10/7   A   SF   30-33   L   56,489
Sun 10/14   A   DET   21-24   L   56,281
Sun 10/21   A   GB   17-42   L   24,200
Sun 10/28   H   DET   7-16   L   76,758
Sun 11/4   A   CHIB   24-35   L   69,894
Sun 11/11   H   SF   30-6   W   69,828
Sun 11/18   A   CHIB   21-30   L   48,102
Sun 11/25   A   BAL   21-56   L   40,321
Sun 12/2   A   PIT   13-30   L   20,540
Sun 12/9   H   BAL   31-7   W   51,037
Sun 12/16   H   GB   49-21   W   45,209

NEW YORK GIANTS
Sun 9/30   A   SF   38-21   W   41,751
Sun 10/7   A   CHIC   27-35   L   21,799
Sun 10/14   A   CLE   21-9   W   60,042
Sun 10/21   H   PIT   38-10   W   48,108
Sun 10/28   H   PHI   20-3   W   40,960
Sun 11/4   A   PIT   17-14   W   31,240
Sun 11/11   H   CHIC   23-10   W   62,410
Sun 11/18   A   WAS   7-33   L   26,261
Sun 11/25   H   CHIB   17-17   T   55,191
Sun 12/2   H   WAS   28-14   W   46,351
Sun 12/9   H   CLE   7-24   L   27,707
Sat 12/15   A   PHI   21-7   W   16,562

LEAGUE CHAMPIONSHIP
Sun 12/30   H   CHIB   47-7   W   56,836

PHILADELPHIA EAGLES
Sun 9/30   A   LA   7-27   L   54,412
Sat 10/6   A   WAS   13-9   W   26,607
Sun 10/14   A   PIT   35-21   W   31,375
Sun 10/21   H   CHIC   6-20   L   36,545
Sun 10/28   A   NYG   3-20   L   40,960
Sun 11/4   A   CHIC   17-28   L   22,609
Sun 11/11   H   PIT   14-7   W   22,652
Sun 11/18   H   CLE   0-16   L   25,894
Sun 11/25   H   SF   10-10   T   19,326
Sun 12/2   A   CLE   14-17   L   20,654
Sun 12/9   A   WAS   17-19   L   22,333
Sat 12/15   H   NYG   7-21   L   16,562

PITTSBURGH STEELERS
Sun 9/30   H   WAS   30-13   W   27,718
Sat 10/6   H   CLE   10-14   L   35,398
Sun 10/14   H   PHI   21-35   L   31,375
Sun 10/21   A   NYG   10-38   L   48,108
Sun 10/28   A   CLE   24-16   W   50,358
Sun 11/4   H   NYG   14-17   L   31,240
Sun 11/11   A   PHI   7-14   L   22,652
Sun 11/18   H   CHIC   14-7   W   24,086
Sun 11/25   A   CHIC   27-38   L   17,724
Sun 12/2   H   LA   30-13   W   20,540
Sun 12/9   A   DET   7-45   L   52,124
Sun 12/16   A   WAS   23-0   W   21,097

SAN FRANCISCO 49ERS
Sun 9/30   H   NYG   21-38   L   41,751
Sun 10/7   H   LA   33-30   W   56,489
Sun 10/14   A   CHIB   7-31   L   47,526
Sun 10/21   A   DET   17-20   L   55,662

Sun 10/28   H   CHIB   21-38   L   53,612
Sun 11/4   H   DET   13-17   L   46,708
Sun 11/11   A   LA   6-30   L   69,828
Sun 11/18   A   GB   17-16   W   17,986
Sun 11/25   A   PHI   10-10   T   19,326
Sun 12/2   A   BAL   20-17   W   37,227
Sat 12/8   H   GB   38-20   W   32,436
Sun 12/16   H   BAL   30-17   W   43,791

WASHINGTON REDSKINS
Sun 9/30   A   PIT   13-30   L   27,718
Sat 10/6   A   PHI   9-13   L   26,607
Sun 10/14   H   CHIC   3-31   L   25,794
Sun 10/21   H   CLE   20-9   W   23,332
Sun 10/28   A   CHIC   17-14   W   30,553
Sun 11/11   H   DET   18-17   W   28,003
Sun 11/18   H   NYG   33-7   W   26,261
Sun 11/25   A   CLE   20-17   W   22,878
Sun 12/2   A   NYG   14-28   L   46,351
Sun 12/9   H   PHI   19-17   W   22,333
Sun 12/16   H   PIT   0-23   L   21,097
Sun 12/23   A   BAL   17-19   L   32,994

1957 NFL
BALTIMORE COLTS
Sun 9/29   H   DET   34-14   W   40,112
Sat 10/5   H   CHIB   21-10   W   46,558
Sun 10/13   A   GB   45-17   W   26,322
Sun 10/20   A   DET   27-31   L   55,764
Sun 10/27   H   GB   21-24   L   48,510
Sun 11/3   H   PIT   13-19   L   42,575
Sun 11/10   A   WAS   21-17   W   33,149
Sun 11/17   A   CHIB   29-14   W   47,168
Sun 11/24   H   SF   27-21   W   50,073
Sun 12/1   H   LA   31-14   W   52,060
Sun 12/8   A   SF   13-17   L   59,686
Sun 12/15   A   LA   21-37   L   52,560

CHICAGO BEARS
Sun 9/29   A   GB   17-21   L   32,132
Sat 10/5   A   BAL   10-21   L   46,558
Sun 10/13   H   SF   17-21   L   45,310
Sun 10/20   H   LA   34-26   W   47,337
Sun 10/27   A   SF   17-21   L   59,593
Sun 11/3   H   LA   16-10   W   80,456
Sun 11/10   H   GB   21-14   W   47,183
Sun 11/17   H   BAL   14-29   L   47,168
Sun 11/24   A   DET   27-7   W   55,749
Sun 12/1   H   WAS   3-14   L   39,148
Sun 12/8   A   CHIC   14-6   W   43,735
Sun 12/15   A   DET   13-21   L   41,088

CHICAGO CARDINALS
Sun 9/29   A   SF   20-10   W   35,743
Sun 10/6   H   WAS   14-37   L   18,278
Sun 10/13   A   PIT   20-29   L   29,446
Sun 10/20   A   WAS   44-14   W   23,159
Sun 10/27   H   CLE   7-17   L   26,341
Sun 11/3   H   PHI   21-38   L   18,718
Sun 11/10   A   NYG   14-27   L   46,402
Sun 11/24   H   NYG   21-28   L   19,200
Sun 12/1   A   CLE   0-31   L   40,525
Sun 12/8   H   CHIB   6-14   L   43,735
Sat 12/14   A   PHI   31-27   W   12,555
Sun 12/22   H   PIT   2-27   L   10,084

CLEVELAND BROWNS
Sun 9/29   H   NYG   6-3   W   58,095
Sat 10/5   A   PIT   23-12   W   35,750
Sun 10/13   H   PHI   24-7   W   53,493
Sun 10/20   A   PHI   7-17   L   22,443
Sun 10/27   A   CHIC   17-7   W   26,341
Sun 11/3   H   WAS   21-17   W   52,936
Sun 11/10   H   PIT   24-0   W   53,709
Sun 11/17   A   WAS   30-30   T   27,722

Sun 11/24   H   LA   45-31   W   65,407
Sun 12/1   H   CHIC   31-0   W   40,525
Sun 12/8   A   DET   7-20   L   55,814
Sun 12/15   A   NYG   34-28   W   54,294

LEAGUE CHAMPIONSHIP
Sun 12/29   A   DET   14-59   L   55,263

DETROIT LIONS
Sun 9/29   A   BAL   14-34   L   40,112
Sun 10/6   A   GB   24-14   W   32,120
Sun 10/13   H   LA   10-7   W   55,914
Sun 10/20   H   BAL   31-27   W   55,764
Sun 10/27   A   LA   17-35   L   77,314
Sun 11/3   A   SF   31-35   L   59,702
Sun 11/10   A   PHI   27-16   W   29,302
Sun 11/17   H   SF   31-10   W   56,915
Sun 11/24   H   CHIB   7-27   L   55,749
Thu 11/28   H   GB   18-6   W   54,301
Sun 12/8   H   CLE   20-7   W   55,814
Sun 12/15   H   CHIB   21-13   W   41,088

WESTERN CONFERENCE PLAYOFF
Sun 12/22   A   SF   31-27   W   60,118

LEAGUE CHAMPIONSHIP
Sun 12/29   H   CLE   59-14   W   55,263

GREEN BAY PACKERS
Sun 9/29   H   CHIB   21-17   W   32,132
Sun 10/6   H   DET   14-24   L   32,120
Sun 10/13   H   BAL   17-45   L   26,322
Sun 10/20   H   SF   14-24   L   18,919
Sun 10/27   A   BAL   24-21   W   48,510
Sun 11/3   H   NYG   17-31   L   32,070
Sun 11/10   A   CHIB   14-21   L   47,183
Sun 11/17   H   LA   27-31   L   19,540
Sun 11/24   A   PIT   27-10   W   29,701
Thu 11/28   A   DET   6-18   L   54,301
Sun 12/8   A   LA   17-42   L   70,572
Sun 12/15   A   SF   20-27   L   59,522

LOS ANGELES RAMS
Sun 9/29   H   PHI   17-13   W   62,506
Sun 10/6   A   SF   20-23   L   59,637
Sun 10/13   A   DET   7-10   L   55,914
Sun 10/20   A   CHIB   26-34   L   47,337
Sun 10/27   H   DET   35-17   W   77,314
Sun 11/3   H   CHIB   10-16   L   80,456
Sun 11/10   H   SF   37-24   W   102,368
Sun 11/17   A   GB   31-27   W   19,540
Sun 11/24   A   CLE   31-45   L   65,407
Sun 12/1   A   BAL   14-31   L   52,060
Sun 12/8   H   GB   42-17   W   70,572
Sun 12/15   H   BAL   37-21   L   52,560

NEW YORK GIANTS
Sun 9/29   A   CLE   3-6   L   58,095
Sat 10/5   A   PHI   24-20   W   28,342
Sun 10/13   A   WAS   24-20   W   30,086
Sun 10/20   H   PIT   35-0   W   52,589
Sun 10/27   A   WAS   14-31   L   40,416
Sun 11/3   A   GB   31-17   W   32,070
Sun 11/10   H   CHIC   27-14   W   46,402
Sun 11/17   A   PHI   13-0   W   42,845
Sun 11/24   A   CHIC   28-21   W   19,200
Sun 12/1   H   SF   17-27   L   54,121
Sat 12/7   A   PIT   10-21   L   19,772
Sun 12/15   H   CLE   28-34   L   54,294

PHILADELPHIA EAGLES
Sun 9/29   A   LA   13-17   L   62,506
Sat 10/5   H   NYG   20-24   L   28,342
Sun 10/13   A   CLE   7-24   L   53,493
Sun 10/20   H   CLE   17-7   W   22,443
Sun 10/27   A   PIT   0-6   L   27,016
Sun 11/3   A   CHIC   38-21   W   18,718
Sun 11/10   H   DET   16-27   L   29,302

Sun 11/17   A   NYG   0-13   L   42,845
Sun 11/24   H   WAS   21-12   W   20,730
Sun 12/1   H   PIT   7-6   W   16,364
Sun 12/8   A   WAS   7-42   L   21,304
Sat 12/14   H   CHIC   27-31   L   12,555

PITTSBURGH STEELERS
Sun 9/29   H   WAS   28-7   W   27,452
Sat 10/5   H   CLE   12-23   L   35,750
Sun 10/13   H   CHIC   29-20   W   29,446
Sun 10/20   A   NYG   0-35   L   52,589
Sun 10/27   H   PHI   6-0   W   27,016
Sun 11/3   A   BAL   19-13   W   42,575
Sun 11/10   A   CLE   0-24   L   53,709
Sun 11/24   H   GB   10-27   L   29,701
Sun 12/1   A   PHI   6-7   L   16,364
Sat 12/7   H   NYG   21-10   W   19,772
Sun 12/15   A   WAS   3-10   L   22,577
Sun 12/22   A   CHIC   27-2   W   10,084

SAN FRANCISCO 49ERS
Sun 9/29   H   CHIC   10-20   L   35,743
Sun 10/6   H   LA   23-20   W   59,637
Sun 10/13   A   CHIB   21-17   W   45,310
Sun 10/20   A   GB   24-14   W   18,919
Sun 10/27   H   CHIB   21-17   W   59,593
Sun 11/3   H   DET   35-31   W   59,702
Sun 11/10   A   LA   24-37   L   102,368
Sun 11/17   A   DET   10-31   L   56,915
Sun 11/24   A   BAL   21-27   L   50,073
Sun 12/1   A   NYG   27-17   W   54,121
Sun 12/8   H   BAL   17-13   W   59,686
Sun 12/15   H   GB   27-20   W   59,522

WESTERN CONFERENCE PLAYOFF
Sun 12/22   H   DET   27-31   L   60,118

WASHINGTON REDSKINS
Sun 9/29   A   PIT   7-28   L   27,452
Sun 10/6   A   CHIC   37-14   W   18,278
Sun 10/13   H   NYG   20-24   L   30,086
Sun 10/20   H   CHIC   14-44   L   23,159
Sun 10/27   H   NYG   31-14   W   40,416
Sun 11/3   A   CLE   17-21   L   52,936
Sun 11/10   H   BAL   17-21   L   33,149
Sun 11/17   H   CLE   30-30   T   27,722
Sun 11/24   A   PHI   12-21   L   20,730
Sun 12/1   A   CHIB   14-3   W   39,148
Sun 12/8   H   PHI   42-7   W   21,304
Sun 12/15   H   PIT   10-3   W   22,577

1958 NFL
BALTIMORE COLTS
Sun 9/28   H   DET   28-15   W   48,377
Sat 10/4   H   CHIB   51-38   W   52,622
Sun 10/12   A   GB   24-17   W   24,553
Sun 10/19   A   DET   40-14   W   55,190
Sun 10/26   H   WAS   35-10   W   54,403
Sun 11/2   H   GB   56-0   W   51,333
Sun 11/9   A   NYG   21-24   L   71,163
Sun 11/16   A   CHIB   17-0   W   48,664
Sun 11/23   H   LA   34-7   W   57,577
Sun 11/30   H   SF   35-27   W   57,557
Sat 12/6   A   LA   28-30   L   100,202
Sun 12/14   A   SF   12-21   L   53,334

LEAGUE CHAMPIONSHIP
Sun 12/28   A   NYG   *23-17   W   64,185

CHICAGO BEARS
Sun 9/28   A   GB   34-20   W   32,150
Sat 10/4   A   BAL   38-51   L   52,622
Sun 10/12   H   SF   28-6   W   48,286
Sun 10/19   H   LA   31-10   W   48,326
Sun 10/26   A   SF   27-14   W   59,441
Sun 11/2   A   LA   35-41   L   100,470
Sun 11/9   H   GB   24-10   W   48,424

Sun 11/16 H BAL 0-17 L 48,664
Sun 11/23 A DET 20-7 W 55,280
Sun 11/30 A PIT 10-24 L 20,094
Sun 12/7 H CHIC 30-14 W 41,617
Sun 12/14 H DET 21-16 W 38,346

CHICAGO CARDINALS

Sun 9/28 N NYG 7-37 L 21,923
Sat 10/4 H WAS 37-10 W 21,824
Sun 10/12 A CLE 28-35 L 65,403
Sun 10/19 A NYG 23-6 W 52,684
Sun 10/26 H CLE 24-38 L 30,933
Sun 11/2 A PHI 21-21 T 17,486
Sun 11/9 A WAS 31-45 L 26,196
Sun 11/16 A PHI 21-49 L 18,315
Sun 11/23 H PIT 20-27 L 15,946
Sun 11/30 H LA 14-20 L 13,014
Sun 12/7 A CHIB 14-30 L 41,617
Sat 12/13 A PIT 21-38 L 16,660

CLEVELAND BROWNS

Sun 9/28 A LA 30-27 W 69,993
Sun 10/5 A PIT 45-12 W 31,130
Sun 10/12 H CHIC 35-28 W 65,403
Sun 10/19 H PIT 27-10 W 66,852
Sun 10/26 A CHIC 38-24 W 30,933
Sun 11/2 H NYG 17-21 L 78,404
Sun 11/9 H DET 10-30 L 75,563
Sun 11/16 A WAS 20-10 W 32,372
Sun 11/23 H PHI 28-14 W 51,319
Sun 11/30 H WAS 21-14 W 33,240
Sun 12/7 A PHI 21-14 W 36,773
Sun 12/14 A NYG 10-13 L 63,192

EASTERN CONFERENCE PLAYOFF
Sun 12/21 A NYG 0-10 L 61,174

DETROIT LIONS

Sun 9/28 A BAL 15-28 L 48,377
Sun 10/5 A GB 13-13 T 32,053
Sun 10/12 H LA 28-42 L 55,648
Sun 10/19 H BAL 14-40 L 55,190
Sun 10/26 A LA 41-24 W 81,703
Sun 11/2 A SF 21-24 L 59,213
Sun 11/9 A CLE 30-10 W 75,563
Sun 11/16 H SF 35-21 W 54,253
Sun 11/23 A CHIB 7-20 L 55,280
Thu 11/27 H GB 24-14 W 50,971
Sun 12/7 H NYG 17-19 L 50,115
Sun 12/14 A CHIB 16-21 L 38,346

GREEN BAY PACKERS

Sun 9/28 H CHIB 20-34 L 32,150
Sun 10/5 H DET 13-13 T 32,053
Sun 10/12 H BAL 17-24 L 24,553
Sun 10/19 A WAS 21-37 L 25,228
Sun 10/26 H PHI 38-35 W 31,043
Sun 11/2 A BAL 0-56 L 51,333
Sun 11/9 A CHIB 12-48 L 48,424
Sun 11/16 H LA 7-20 L 28,051
Sun 11/23 H SF 12-33 L 19,786
Thu 11/27 A DET 14-24 L 50,971
Sun 12/7 A SF 21-48 L 50,792
Sun 12/14 A LA 20-34 L 54,634

LOS ANGELES RAMS

Sun 9/28 H CLE 27-30 L 69,993
Sun 10/5 A SF 33-3 W 59,826
Sun 10/12 A DET 42-28 W 55,648
Sun 10/19 A CHIB 10-31 L 48,326
Sun 10/26 H DET 24-41 L 81,703
Sun 11/2 H CHIB 41-35 W 100,470
Sun 11/9 H SF 56-7 W 95,082
Sun 11/16 A GB 20-7 W 28,051
Sun 11/23 A BAL 7-34 L 57,577
Sun 11/30 A CHIC 20-14 W 13,014
Sat 12/6 H BAL 30-28 W 100,202
Sun 12/14 H GB 34-20 W 54,634

NEW YORK GIANTS

Sun 9/28 N CHIC 37-7 W 21,923
Sun 10/5 A PHI 24-27 L 23,178
Sun 10/12 A WAS 21-14 W 30,348
Sun 10/19 H CHIC 6-23 L 52,684
Sun 10/26 H PIT 17-6 W 25,007
Sun 11/2 A CLE 21-17 W 78,404
Sun 11/9 H BAL 24-21 W 71,163
Sun 11/16 A PIT 10-31 L 30,030
Sun 11/23 H WAS 30-0 W 46,752
Sun 11/30 A PHI 24-10 W 35,438
Sun 12/7 A DET 19-17 W 50,115
Sun 12/14 A CLE 13-10 W 63,192

EASTERN CONFERENCE PLAYOFF
Sun 12/21 H CLE 10-0 W 61,174

LEAGUE CHAMPIONSHIP
Sun 12/28 H BAL *17-23 L 64,185

PHILADELPHIA EAGLES

Sun 9/28 H WAS 14-24 L 36,853
Sun 10/5 H NYG 27-24 W 23,178
Sun 10/12 A PIT 3-24 L 23,153
Sun 10/19 H SF 24-30 L 33,110
Sun 10/26 A GB 35-38 L 31,043
Sun 11/2 A CHIC 21-21 T 17,486
Sun 11/9 H PIT 24-31 L 26,306
Sun 11/16 H CHIC 49-21 W 18,315
Sun 11/23 A CLE 14-28 L 51,319
Sun 11/30 H NYG 10-24 L 35,438
Sun 12/7 H CLE 14-21 L 36,773
Sun 12/14 A WAS 0-20 L 22,621

PITTSBURGH STEELERS

Sun 9/28 A SF 20-23 L 51,856
Sun 10/5 H CLE 12-45 L 31,130
Sun 10/12 H PHI 24-3 W 23,153
Sun 10/19 A CLE 10-27 L 66,852
Sun 10/26 A NYG 6-17 L 25,007
Sun 11/2 H WAS 24-16 W 19,525
Sun 11/9 A PHI 31-24 W 26,306
Sun 11/16 H NYG 31-10 W 30,030
Sun 11/23 A CHIC 27-20 W 15,946
Sun 11/30 H CHIB 24-10 W 20,094
Sun 12/7 A WAS 14-14 T 23,370
Sat 12/13 H CHIC 38-21 W 16,660

SAN FRANCISCO 49ERS

Sun 9/28 H PIT 23-20 W 51,856
Sun 10/5 H LA 3-33 L 59,826
Sun 10/12 A CHIB 6-28 L 48,286
Sun 10/19 A PHI 30-24 W 33,110
Sun 10/26 H CHIB 14-27 L 59,441
Sun 11/2 H DET 24-21 W 59,213
Sun 11/9 A LA 7-56 L 95,082
Sun 11/16 A DET 21-35 L 54,253
Sun 11/23 A GB 33-12 W 19,786
Sun 11/30 A BAL 27-35 L 57,557
Sun 12/7 H GB 48-21 W 50,792
Sun 12/14 H BAL 21-12 W 53,334

WASHINGTON REDSKINS

Sun 9/28 A PHI 24-14 W 36,853
Sat 10/4 A CHIC 10-37 L 21,824
Sun 10/12 H NYG 14-21 L 30,348
Sun 10/19 H GB 37-21 W 25,228
Sun 10/26 A BAL 10-35 L 54,403
Sun 11/2 A PIT 16-24 L 19,525
Sun 11/9 H CHIC 45-31 W 26,196
Sun 11/16 H CLE 10-20 L 32,372
Sun 11/23 A NYG 0-30 L 46,752
Sun 11/30 A CLE 14-21 L 33,240
Sun 12/7 H PIT 14-14 T 23,370
Sun 12/14 H PHI 20-0 W 22,621

1959 NFL

BALTIMORE COLTS

Sun 9/27 H DET 21-9 W 55,588
Sat 10/3 H CHIB 21-26 L 57,557
Sun 10/11 A DET 31-24 W 54,197
Sun 10/18 A CHIB 21-7 W 48,430
Sun 10/25 H GB 38-21 W 57,557
Sun 11/1 H CLE 31-38 L 57,557
Sun 11/8 A WAS 24-27 L 32,773
Sun 11/15 A GB 28-24 W 25,521
Sun 11/22 H SF 45-14 W 57,557
Sun 11/29 H LA 35-21 W 57,557
Sat 12/5 A SF 34-14 W 59,075
Sat 12/12 A LA 45-26 W 65,528

LEAGUE CHAMPIONSHIP
Sun 12/27 H NYG 31-16 W 57,545

CHICAGO BEARS

Sun 9/27 A GB 6-9 L 32,150
Sat 10/3 A BAL 26-21 W 57,557
Sun 10/11 H LA 21-28 L 47,036
Sun 10/18 H BAL 7-21 L 48,430
Sun 10/25 A SF 17-20 L 59,045
Sun 11/1 A LA 26-21 W 77,943
Sun 11/8 H GB 28-17 W 46,205
Sun 11/15 H SF 14-3 W 44,406
Sun 11/22 A DET 24-14 W 54,059
Sun 11/29 A CHIC 31-7 W 48,687
Sun 12/6 H PIT 27-21 W 41,476
Sun 12/13 H DET 25-14 W 40,890

CHICAGO CARDINALS

Sun 9/27 H WAS 49-21 W 21,892
Sun 10/4 H CLE 7-34 L 19,935
Sun 10/11 A WAS 14-23 L 25,937
Sun 10/18 A CLE 7-17 L 46,422
Sun 10/25 N PHI 24-28 L 20,112
Sun 11/1 H PIT 45-24 W 23,187
Sun 11/8 A NYG 3-9 L 56,779
Sun 11/15 A PHI 17-27 L 28,887
Sun 11/22 N NYG 20-30 L 26,625
Sun 11/29 H CHIB 7-31 L 48,687
Sun 12/6 A DET 21-45 L 45,811
Sun 12/13 A PIT 20-35 L 19,011

CLEVELAND BROWNS

Sat 9/26 A PIT 7-17 L 33,844
Sun 10/4 A CHIC 34-7 W 19,935
Sun 10/11 H NYG 6-10 L 65,534
Sun 10/18 A CHIB 17-7 W 46,422
Sun 10/25 H WAS 34-7 W 42,732
Sun 11/1 A BAL 38-31 W 57,557
Sun 11/8 H PHI 28-7 W 58,275
Sun 11/15 A WAS 31-17 W 32,266
Sun 11/22 H PIT 20-21 L 68,563
Sun 11/29 H SF 20-21 L 56,854
Sun 12/6 A NYG 7-48 L 68,436
Sun 12/13 A PHI 28-21 W 45,952

DETROIT LIONS

Sun 9/27 A BAL 9-21 L 55,588
Sun 10/4 A GB 10-28 L 32,150
Sun 10/11 H BAL 24-31 L 54,197
Sun 10/18 H SF 13-34 L 52,585
Sun 10/25 A LA 17-7 W 74,288
Sun 11/1 A SF 7-33 L 59,064
Sun 11/8 A PIT 10-10 T 24,619
Sun 11/15 H LA 10-10 T 24,619
Sun 11/22 H CHIB 14-24 L 54,059
Thu 11/26 H GB 17-24 L 49,221
Sun 12/6 H CHIC 45-21 W 45,811
Sun 12/13 A CHIB 14-25 L 40,890

GREEN BAY PACKERS

Sun 9/27 H CHIB 9-6 W 32,150
Sun 10/4 H DET 28-10 W 32,150
Sun 10/11 H SF 21-20 W 32,150
Sun 10/18 A LA 6-45 L 36,174
Sun 10/25 A BAL 21-38 L 57,557
Sun 11/1 A NYG 3-20 L 67,837
Sun 11/8 A CHIB 17-28 L 46,205
Sun 11/15 H BAL 24-28 L 25,521
Sun 11/22 H WAS 21-0 W 31,853
Thu 11/26 A DET 24-17 W 49,221
Sun 12/6 A LA 38-20 W 61,044
Sun 12/13 A SF 36-14 W 55,997

LOS ANGELES RAMS

Sat 9/26 H NYG 21-23 L 71,297
Sun 10/4 A SF 0-34 L 56,028
Sun 10/11 A CHIB 28-21 W 47,036
Sun 10/18 A GB 45-6 W 36,174
Sun 10/25 H DET 7-17 L 74,288
Sun 11/1 H CHIB 21-26 L 77,943
Sun 11/8 H SF 16-24 L 94,376
Sun 11/15 A DET 17-23 L 52,271
Sun 11/22 A PHI 20-23 L 47,425
Sun 11/29 A BAL 21-35 L 57,557
Sun 12/6 H GB 20-38 L 61,044
Sat 12/12 H BAL 26-45 L 65,528

NEW YORK GIANTS

Sat 9/26 A LA 23-21 W 71,297
Sun 10/4 A PHI 21-49 L 27,023
Sun 10/11 A CLE 10-6 W 65,534
Sun 10/18 H PHI 24-7 W 68,783
Sun 10/25 A PIT 21-16 W 33,596
Sun 11/1 H GB 20-3 W 67,837
Sun 11/8 H CHIC 9-3 W 56,779
Sun 11/15 H PIT 9-14 L 66,786
Sun 11/22 N CHIC 30-20 W 26,625
Sun 11/29 H WAS 45-14 W 60,982
Sun 12/6 H CLE 48-7 W 68,436
Sun 12/13 A WAS 24-10 W 26,198

LEAGUE CHAMPIONSHIP
Sun 12/27 A BAL 16-31 L 57,545

PHILADELPHIA EAGLES

Sun 9/27 A SF 14-24 L 41,697
Sun 10/4 H NYG 49-21 W 27,023
Sun 10/11 H PIT 28-24 W 27,343
Sun 10/18 A NYG 7-24 L 68,783
Sun 10/25 N CHIC 28-24 W 20,112
Sun 11/1 H WAS 30-23 W 39,854
Sun 11/8 A CLE 7-28 L 58,275
Sun 11/15 H CHIC 27-17 W 28,887
Sun 11/22 H LA 23-20 W 47,425
Sun 11/29 A PIT 0-31 L 22,191
Sun 12/6 A WAS 34-14 W 24,325
Sun 12/13 H CLE 21-28 L 45,952

PITTSBURGH STEELERS

Sat 9/26 H CLE 17-7 W 33,844
Sun 10/4 H WAS 17-23 L 26,570
Sun 10/11 A PHI 24-28 L 27,343
Sun 10/18 A WAS 27-6 W 28,218
Sun 10/25 H NYG 16-21 L 33,596
Sun 11/1 A CHIC 24-45 L 23,187
Sun 11/8 H DET 10-10 T 24,619
Sun 11/15 A NYG 14-9 W 66,786
Sun 11/22 A CLE 21-20 W 68,563
Sun 11/29 H PHI 31-0 W 22,191
Sun 12/6 A CHIB 21-27 L 41,476
Sun 12/13 H CHIC 35-20 W 19,011

SAN FRANCISCO 49ERS

Sun 9/27 H PHI 24-14 W 41,697
Sun 10/4 H LA 34-0 W 56,028
Sun 10/11 A GB 20-21 L 32,150
Sun 10/18 A DET 34-13 W 52,585
Sun 10/25 H CHIB 20-17 W 59,045

Sun	11/1	H	DET	33-7	W	59,064
Sun	11/8	A	LA	24-16	W	94,376
Sun	11/15	A	CHIB	3-14	L	44,406
Sun	11/22	A	BAL	14-45	L	57,557
Sun	11/29	A	CLE	21-20	W	56,854
Sat	12/5	H	BAL	14-34	L	59,075
Sun	12/13	H	GB	14-36	L	55,997

WASHINGTON REDSKINS

Sun	9/27	A	CHIC	21-49	L	21,892
Sun	10/4	A	PIT	23-17	W	26,570
Sun	10/11	H	CHIC	23-14	W	25,937
Sun	10/18	H	PIT	6-27	L	28,218
Sun	10/25	A	CLE	7-34	L	42,732
Sun	11/1	A	PHI	23-30	L	39,854
Sun	11/8	H	BAL	27-24	W	32,773
Sun	11/15	H	CLE	17-31	L	32,266
Sun	11/22	A	GB	0-21	L	31,853
Sun	11/29	A	NYG	14-45	L	60,982
Sun	12/6	H	PHI	14-34	L	24,325
Sun	12/13	H	NYG	10-24	L	26,198

1960 AFL

BOSTON PATRIOTS

Fri	9/9	H	DEN	10-13	L	21,597
Sat	9/17	A	NY	28-24	W	19,200
Fri	9/23	H	BUF	0-13	L	20,732
Sat	10/8	A	LA	35-0	W	18,226
Sun	10/16	A	OAK	14-27	L	11,500
Sun	10/23	A	DEN	24-31	L	12,683
Fri	10/28	H	LA	16-45	L	13,988
Fri	11/4	H	OAK	34-28	W	8,446
Fri	11/11	H	NY	38-21	W	11,653
Fri	11/18	H	DAL	42-14	W	14,721
Fri	11/25	H	HOU	10-24	L	27,123
Sun	12/4	A	BUF	14-38	L	14,335
Sun	12/11	A	DAL	0-34	L	12,000
Sun	12/18	A	HOU	21-37	L	22,352

BUFFALO BILLS

Sun	9/11	A	NY	3-27	L	9,607
Sun	9/18	H	DEN	21-27	L	15,229
Fri	9/23	A	BOS	13-0	W	20,732
Sun	10/2	H	LA	10-24	L	15,821
Sun	10/16	H	NY	13-17	L	14,998
Sun	10/23	H	OAK	38-9	W	8,876
Sun	10/30	H	HOU	25-24	W	23,001
Sun	11/6	H	DAL	28-45	L	19,610
Sun	11/13	A	OAK	7-20	L	8,800
Sun	11/20	A	LA	32-3	W	16,161
Sun	11/27	A	DEN	38-38	T	7,785
Sun	12/4	H	BOS	38-14	W	14,335
Sun	12/11	A	HOU	23-31	L	25,243
Sun	12/18	A	DAL	7-24	L	18,000

DALLAS TEXANS

Sat	9/10	A	LA	20-21	L	17,724
Fri	9/16	A	OAK	34-16	W	8,021
Sun	9/25	H	LA	17-0	W	42,000
Sun	10/2	H	NY	35-37	L	37,500
Sun	10/9	H	OAK	19-20	L	21,000
Sun	10/16	A	HOU	10-20	L	19,026
Sun	10/30	A	DEN	17-14	W	13,102
Sun	11/6	A	BUF	45-28	W	19,610
Sun	11/13	H	DEN	34-7	W	21,000
Fri	11/18	A	BOS	14-42	L	14,721
Thu	11/24	A	NY	35-41	L	14,344
Sun	12/4	H	HOU	24-0	W	20,000
Sun	12/11	H	BOS	34-0	W	12,000
Sun	12/18	H	BUF	24-7	W	18,000

DENVER BRONCOS

Fri	9/9	A	BOS	13-10	W	21,597
Sun	9/18	A	BUF	27-21	W	15,229
Fri	9/23	A	NY	24-28	L	20,462
Sun	10/2	H	OAK	31-14	W	18,372
Sun	10/16	H	LA	19-23	L	19,141
Sun	10/23	H	BOS	31-24	W	12,683
Sun	10/30	H	DAL	14-17	L	13,102
Sun	11/6	H	HOU	25-45	L	14,489
Sun	11/13	A	DAL	7-34	L	21,000
Sun	11/20	A	HOU	10-20	L	20,788
Sun	11/27	H	BUF	38-38	T	7,785
Sun	12/4	H	NY	27-30	L	5,861
Sat	12/10	A	LA	33-41	L	9,928
Sat	12/17	A	OAK	10-48	L	7,000

HOUSTON OILERS

Sun	9/11	A	OAK	37-22	W	12,703
Sun	9/18	H	LA	38-28	W	20,156
Sun	9/25	H	OAK	13-14	L	16,421
Sun	10/9	H	NY	27-21	W	16,151
Sun	10/16	H	DAL	20-10	W	19,026
Sun	10/23	A	NY	42-28	W	20,000
Sun	10/30	A	BUF	24-25	L	23,001
Sun	11/6	A	DEN	45-25	W	14,489
Sun	11/13	A	LA	21-24	L	21,805
Sun	11/20	H	DEN	20-10	W	20,788
Fri	11/25	A	BOS	24-10	W	27,123
Sun	12/4	A	DAL	0-24	L	20,000
Sun	12/11	H	BUF	31-23	W	25,243
Sun	12/18	H	BOS	37-21	W	22,352

LEAGUE CHAMPIONSHIP

Sun	1/1	H	LA	24-16	W	32,183

LOS ANGELES CHARGERS

Sat	9/10	H	DAL	21-20	W	17,724
Sun	9/18	A	HOU	28-38	L	20,156
Sun	9/25	A	DAL	0-17	L	42,000
Sun	10/2	A	BUF	24-10	W	15,821
Sat	10/8	H	BOS	0-35	L	18,226
Sun	10/16	A	DEN	23-19	W	19,141
Fri	10/28	A	BOS	45-16	W	13,988
Fri	11/4	A	NY	21-7	W	19,402
Sun	11/13	H	HOU	24-21	W	21,805
Sun	11/20	H	BUF	3-32	L	16,161
Sun	11/27	H	OAK	52-28	W	15,075
Sun	12/4	A	OAK	41-17	W	12,061
Sat	12/10	H	DEN	41-33	W	9,928
Sun	12/18	H	NY	50-43	W	11,457

LEAGUE CHAMPIONSHIP

Sun	1/1	A	HOU	16-24	L	32,183

NEW YORK TITANS

Sun	9/11	H	BUF	27-3	W	9,607
Sat	9/17	H	BOS	24-28	L	19,200
Fri	9/23	H	DEN	28-24	W	20,462
Sun	10/2	A	DAL	37-35	W	37,500
Sun	10/9	A	HOU	21-27	L	16,151
Sun	10/16	A	BUF	17-13	W	14,998
Sun	10/23	H	HOU	28-42	L	20,000
Fri	10/28	H	OAK	27-28	L	10,000
Fri	11/4	H	LA	7-21	L	19,402
Fri	11/11	A	BOS	21-38	L	11,653
Thu	11/24	H	DAL	41-35	W	14,344
Sun	12/4	A	DEN	30-27	W	5,861
Sun	12/11	A	OAK	31-28	W	9,037
Sun	12/18	A	LA	43-50	L	11,457

OAKLAND RAIDERS

Sun	9/11	H	HOU	22-37	L	12,703
Fri	9/16	H	DAL	16-34	L	8,021
Sun	9/25	A	HOU	14-13	W	16,241
Sun	10/2	A	DEN	14-31	L	18,372
Sun	10/9	A	DAL	20-19	W	21,000
Sun	10/16	H	BOS	27-14	W	11,500
Sun	10/23	A	BUF	9-38	L	8,876
Fri	10/28	A	NY	28-27	W	10,000
Fri	11/4	A	BOS	28-34	L	8,446
Sun	11/13	H	BUF	20-7	W	8,800
Sun	11/27	A	LA	28-52	L	15,075
Sun	12/4	H	LA	17-41	L	12,061
Sun	12/11	H	NY	28-31	L	9,037
Sat	12/17	H	DEN	48-10	W	7,000

1960 NFL

BALTIMORE COLTS

Sun	9/25	H	WAS	20-0	W	53,818
Sun	10/2	H	CHIB	42-7	W	57,808
Sun	10/9	A	GB	21-35	L	32,150
Sun	10/16	H	LA	31-17	W	57,808
Sun	10/23	A	DET	17-30	L	53,854
Sun	10/30	A	DAL	45-7	W	25,500
Sun	11/6	H	GB	38-24	W	57,808
Sun	11/13	A	CHIB	24-20	W	48,713
Sun	11/27	H	SF	22-30	L	57,808
Sun	12/4	H	DET	15-20	L	57,808
Sun	12/11	A	LA	3-10	L	75,461
Sun	12/18	A	SF	10-34	L	57,269

CHICAGO BEARS

Sun	9/25	A	GB	17-14	W	32,150
Sun	10/2	A	BAL	7-42	L	57,808
Sun	10/9	H	LA	34-27	W	47,776
Sun	10/16	H	SF	27-10	W	48,226
Sun	10/23	A	LA	24-24	T	63,438
Sun	10/30	A	SF	7-25	L	55,071
Sun	11/13	H	BAL	20-24	L	48,713
Sun	11/20	H	DET	28-7	W	42,267
Sun	11/27	H	DAL	17-7	W	39,951
Sun	12/4	H	GB	13-41	L	46,406
Sun	12/11	A	CLE	0-42	L	38,155
Sun	12/18	A	DET	0-36	L	51,017

CLEVELAND BROWNS

Sun	9/25	A	PHI	41-24	W	56,303
Sun	10/2	H	PIT	28-20	W	67,692
Sun	10/16	A	DAL	48-7	W	28,500
Sun	10/23	H	PHI	29-31	L	64,850
Sun	10/30	A	WAS	31-10	W	32,086
Sun	11/6	H	NYG	13-17	L	82,872
Sun	11/13	H	STL	28-27	W	49,192
Sun	11/20	A	PIT	10-14	L	35,215
Sun	11/27	A	STL	17-17	T	26,146
Sun	12/4	H	WAS	27-16	W	35,211
Sun	12/11	H	CHIB	42-0	W	38,155
Sun	12/18	A	NYG	48-34	W	56,517

DALLAS COWBOYS

Sat	9/24	H	PIT	28-35	L	30,000
Fri	9/30	H	PHI	25-27	L	18,500
Sun	10/9	A	WAS	14-26	L	21,142
Sun	10/16	H	CLE	7-48	L	28,500
Sun	10/23	A	STL	10-12	L	23,128
Sun	10/30	H	BAL	7-45	L	25,500
Sun	11/6	H	LA	13-38	L	16,000
Sun	11/13	A	GB	7-41	L	32,294
Sun	11/20	H	SF	14-26	L	10,000
Sun	11/27	A	CHIB	7-17	L	39,951
Sun	12/4	A	NYG	31-31	T	55,033
Sun	12/11	A	DET	14-23	L	43,272

DETROIT LIONS

Sun	10/2	A	GB	9-28	L	32,150
Sun	10/9	H	SF	10-14	L	49,825
Sun	10/16	A	PHI	10-28	L	38,065
Sun	10/23	H	BAL	30-17	W	53,854
Sun	10/30	A	LA	35-48	L	53,295
Sun	11/6	A	SF	24-0	W	48,447
Sun	11/13	H	LA	12-10	W	54,019
Sun	11/20	A	CHIB	7-28	L	42,267
Thu	11/24	H	GB	23-10	W	54,123
Sun	12/4	A	BAL	20-15	W	57,808
Sun	12/11	H	DAL	23-14	W	43,272
Sun	12/18	H	CHIB	36-0	W	51,017

GREEN BAY PACKERS

Sun	9/25	H	CHIB	14-17	L	32,150
Sun	10/2	H	DET	28-9	W	32,150
Sun	10/9	H	BAL	35-21	W	32,150
Sun	10/23	H	SF	41-14	W	39,914
Sun	10/30	A	PIT	19-13	W	30,155
Sun	11/6	A	BAL	24-38	L	57,808
Sun	11/13	H	DAL	41-7	W	32,294
Sun	11/20	H	LA	31-33	L	35,763
Thu	11/24	A	DET	10-23	L	54,123
Sun	12/4	A	CHIB	41-13	W	46,406
Sat	12/10	A	SF	13-0	W	53,612
Sat	12/17	A	LA	35-21	W	53,445

LEAGUE CHAMPIONSHIP

Mon	12/26	A	PHI	13-17	L	67,325

LOS ANGELES RAMS

Fri	9/23	H	STL	21-43	L	47,448
Sun	10/2	A	SF	9-13	L	53,633
Sun	10/9	A	CHIB	27-34	L	47,776
Sun	10/16	A	BAL	17-31	L	57,808
Sun	10/23	H	CHIB	24-24	T	63,438
Sun	10/30	H	DET	48-35	W	53,295
Sun	11/6	A	DAL	38-13	W	16,000
Sun	11/13	A	DET	10-12	L	54,019
Sun	11/20	A	GB	33-31	W	35,763
Sun	12/4	H	SF	7-23	L	77,254
Sun	12/11	H	BAL	10-3	W	75,461
Sat	12/17	H	GB	21-35	L	53,445

NEW YORK GIANTS

Sun	9/25	A	SF	21-19	W	44,598
Sun	10/2	A	STL	35-14	W	26,089
Sun	10/9	A	PIT	19-17	W	40,323
Sun	10/16	H	WAS	24-24	T	60,625
Sun	10/30	H	STL	13-20	L	58,516
Sun	11/6	A	CLE	17-13	W	82,872
Sun	11/13	H	PIT	27-24	W	63,321
Sun	11/20	H	PHI	10-17	L	63,571
Sun	11/27	A	PHI	23-31	L	60,547
Sun	12/4	H	DAL	31-31	T	55,033
Sun	12/11	A	WAS	17-3	W	14,077
Sun	12/18	H	CLE	34-48	L	56,517

PHILADELPHIA EAGLES

Sun	9/25	H	CLE	24-41	L	56,303
Fri	9/30	A	DAL	27-25	W	18,500
Sun	10/9	H	STL	31-27	W	33,701
Sun	10/16	H	DET	28-10	W	38,065
Sun	10/23	A	CLE	31-29	W	64,850
Sun	11/6	H	PIT	34-7	W	58,324
Sun	11/13	H	WAS	19-13	W	39,361
Sun	11/20	A	NYG	17-10	W	63,571
Sun	11/27	H	NYG	31-23	W	60,547
Sun	12/4	A	STL	20-6	W	21,358
Sun	12/11	A	PIT	21-27	L	22,101
Sun	12/18	A	WAS	38-28	W	20,558

LEAGUE CHAMPIONSHIP

Mon	12/26	H	GB	17-13	W	67,325

PITTSBURGH STEELERS

Sat	9/24	A	DAL	35-28	W	30,000
Sun	10/2	A	CLE	20-28	L	67,692
Sun	10/9	H	NYG	17-19	L	40,323
Sun	10/16	H	STL	27-14	W	22,971
Sun	10/23	A	WAS	27-27	T	25,292
Sun	10/30	H	GB	13-19	L	30,155
Sun	11/6	A	PHI	7-34	L	58,324
Sun	11/13	A	NYG	24-27	L	63,321
Sun	11/20	H	CLE	14-10	W	35,215
Sun	11/27	H	WAS	22-10	W	22,334
Sun	12/11	H	PHI	27-21	W	22,101
Sun	12/18	A	STL	7-38	L	20,840

ST. LOUIS CARDINALS

Fri	9/23	A	LA	43-21	W	47,448
Sun	10/2	H	NYG	14-35	L	26,089
Sun	10/9	A	PHI	27-31	L	33,701
Sun	10/16	A	PIT	14-27	L	22,971
Sun	10/23	H	DAL	12-10	W	23,128

Sun 10/30 A NYG 20-13 W 58,516
Sun 11/6 H WAS 44-7 W 22,458
Sun 11/13 A CLE 27-28 L 49,192
Sun 11/20 A WAS 26-14 W 23,848
Sun 11/27 H CLE 17-17 T 26,146
Sun 12/4 A PHI 6-20 L 21,358
Sun 12/18 H PIT 38-7 W 20,840

SAN FRANCISCO 49ERS
Sun 9/25 H NYG 19-21 L 44,598
Sun 10/2 H LA 13-9 W 53,633
Sun 10/9 A DET 14-10 W 49,825
Sun 10/16 A CHIB 10-27 L 48,226
Sun 10/23 A GB 14-41 L 39,914
Sun 10/30 H CHIB 25-7 W 55,071
Sun 11/6 H DET 0-24 L 48,447
Sun 11/20 A DAL 26-14 W 10,000
Sun 11/27 A BAL 30-22 W 57,808
Sun 12/4 A LA 23-7 W 77,254
Sat 12/10 A GB 0-13 L 53,612
Sun 12/18 H BAL 34-10 W 57,269

WASHINGTON REDSKINS
Sun 9/25 A BAL 0-20 L 53,818
Sun 10/9 H DAL 26-14 W 21,142
Sun 10/16 A NYG 24-24 T 60,625
Sun 10/23 H PIT 27-27 T 25,292
Sun 10/30 H CLE 10-31 L 32,086
Sun 11/6 A STL 7-44 L 22,458
Sun 11/13 A PHI 13-19 L 39,361
Sun 11/20 A STL 14-26 L 23,848
Sun 11/27 A PIT 10-22 L 22,334
Sun 12/4 A CLE 16-27 L 35,211
Sun 12/11 H NYG 3-17 L 14,077
Sun 12/18 H PHI 28-38 L 20,558

1961 AFL
BOSTON PATRIOTS
Sat 9/9 A NY 20-21 L 16,531
Sat 9/16 H DEN 45-17 W 14,479
Sat 9/23 A BUF 23-21 W 21,504
Sun 10/1 A NY 30-37 L 15,189
Sat 10/7 H SD 27-38 L 17,748
Fri 10/13 H HOU 31-31 T 15,070
Sun 10/22 H BUF 52-21 W 9,398
Sun 10/29 A DAL 18-17 W 20,500
Fri 11/3 A DAL 28-21 W 25,036
Sun 11/12 A HOU 15-27 L 35,649
Fri 11/17 A OAK 20-17 W 18,169
Sun 12/3 H DEN 28-24 W 9,303
Sat 12/9 A OAK 35-21 W 6,500
Sun 12/17 A SD 41-0 W 21,339

BUFFALO BILLS
Sun 9/10 H DEN 10-22 L 16,636
Sun 9/17 H NY 41-31 W 15,584
Sat 9/23 H BOS 21-23 L 21,504
Sat 9/30 H SD 11-19 L 20,742
Sun 10/8 A HOU 22-12 W 22,761
Sun 10/15 H DAL 27-24 W 20,678
Sun 10/22 A BOS 21-52 L 9,398
Sun 10/29 H HOU 16-28 L 21,237
Sun 11/5 A OAK 22-31 L 17,027
Sun 11/12 A DAL 30-20 W 15,000
Sun 11/19 A DEN 23-10 W 7,642
Thu 11/23 A NY 14-21 L 12,023
Sun 12/3 A OAK 26-21 W 8,011
Sun 12/10 A SD 10-28 L 24,486

DALLAS TEXANS
Sun 9/10 H SD 10-26 L 24,500
Sun 9/24 A OAK 42-35 W 6,737
Sun 10/1 H HOU 26-21 W 28,000
Sun 10/8 A DEN 19-12 W 14,500
Sun 10/15 H BUF 24-27 L 20,678
Sun 10/22 A HOU 7-38 L 23,228
Sun 10/29 H BOS 17-18 L 20,500
Fri 11/3 A BOS 21-28 L 25,036
Sun 11/12 H BUF 20-30 L 15,000
Sun 11/19 A SD 14-24 L 33,788
Sun 11/26 H OAK 43-11 W 14,500
Sun 12/3 A NY 7-28 L 14,117
Sun 12/10 H DEN 49-21 W 8,000
Sun 12/17 H NY 35-24 W 12,500

DENVER BRONCOS
Sun 9/10 A BUF 22-10 W 16,636
Sat 9/16 A BOS 17-45 L 14,479
Sun 9/24 A NY 28-35 L 14,381
Sun 10/1 A OAK 19-33 L 8,361
Sun 10/8 H DAL 12-19 L 14,500
Sun 10/15 H OAK 27-24 W 11,129
Sun 10/22 H NY 27-10 W 12,508
Sun 10/29 A SD 0-37 L 32,584
Sun 11/5 H HOU 14-55 L 11,564
Sun 11/12 H SD 16-19 L 7,859
Sun 11/19 H BUF 10-23 L 7,642
Sun 11/26 A HOU 14-45 L 27,874
Sun 12/3 H BOS 24-28 L 9,303
Sun 12/10 A DAL 21-49 L 8,000

HOUSTON OILERS
Sat 9/9 H OAK 55-0 W 16,231
Sun 9/24 A SD 24-34 L 29,210
Sun 10/1 A DAL 21-26 L 28,000
Sun 10/8 H BUF 12-22 L 22,761
Fri 10/13 A BOS 31-31 T 15,070
Sun 10/22 H DAL 38-7 W 23,228
Sun 10/29 H BUF 28-16 W 21,237
Sun 11/5 A DEN 55-14 W 11,564
Sun 11/12 H BOS 27-15 W 35,649
Sun 11/19 H NY 49-13 W 33,428
Sun 11/26 H DEN 45-14 W 27,874
Sun 12/3 H SD 33-13 W 37,845
Sun 12/10 A NY 48-21 W 9,462
Sun 12/17 A OAK 47-16 W 4,821

LEAGUE CHAMPIONSHIP
Sun 12/24 A SD 10-3 W 29,556

NEW YORK TITANS
Sat 9/9 A BOS 21-20 W 16,531
Sun 9/17 A BUF 31-41 L 15,584
Sun 9/24 H DEN 35-28 W 14,381
Sun 10/1 H BOS 37-30 W 15,189
Sun 10/15 H SD 10-25 L 25,136
Sun 10/22 A DEN 10-27 L 12,508
Sun 10/29 A OAK 14-6 W 7,138
Sun 11/5 A SD 13-48 L 33,391
Sat 11/11 H OAK 23-12 W 16,811
Sun 11/19 A HOU 13-49 L 33,428
Thu 11/23 H BUF 21-14 W 12,023
Sun 12/3 H DAL 28-7 W 14,117
Sun 12/10 H HOU 21-48 L 9,462
Sun 12/17 A DAL 24-35 L 12,500

OAKLAND RAIDERS
Sat 9/9 A HOU 0-55 L 16,231
Sun 9/17 A SD 0-44 L 20,216
Sun 9/24 H DAL 35-42 L 6,737
Sun 10/1 H DEN 33-19 W 8,361
Sun 10/15 A DEN 24-27 L 11,129
Sun 10/22 A SD 10-41 L 12,014
Sun 10/29 H NY 6-14 L 7,138
Sun 11/5 H BUF 31-22 W 17,027
Sat 11/11 A NY 12-23 L 16,811
Fri 11/17 H BOS 17-20 L 18,169
Sun 11/26 A DAL 11-43 L 14,500
Sun 12/3 H BUF 21-26 L 8,011
Sat 12/9 H BOS 21-35 L 6,500
Sun 12/17 H HOU 16-47 L 4,821

SAN DIEGO CHARGERS
Sun 9/10 A DAL 26-10 W 24,500
Sun 9/17 H OAK 44-0 W 20,216
Sun 9/24 H HOU 34-24 W 29,210
Sat 9/30 A BUF 19-11 W 20,742
Sat 10/7 A BOS 38-27 W 17,748
Sun 10/15 A NY 25-10 W 25,136
Sun 10/22 A OAK 41-10 W 12,014
Sun 10/29 H DEN 37-0 W 32,584
Sun 11/5 H NY 48-13 W 33,391
Sun 11/12 A DEN 19-16 W 7,859
Sun 11/19 H DAL 24-14 W 33,788
Sun 12/3 A HOU 13-33 L 37,845
Sun 12/10 H BUF 28-10 W 24,486
Sun 12/17 H BOS 0-41 L 21,339

LEAGUE CHAMPIONSHIP
Sun 12/24 H HOU 3-10 L 29,556

1961 NFL
BALTIMORE COLTS
Sun 9/17 H LA 27-24 W 54,259
Sun 9/24 H DET 15-16 L 54,259
Sun 10/1 H MIN 34-33 W 54,259
Sun 10/8 A GB 7-45 L 38,669
Sun 10/15 A CHI 10-24 L 48,719
Sun 10/22 A DET 17-14 W 53,016
Sun 10/29 H CHI 20-21 L 57,641
Sun 11/5 H GB 45-21 W 57,641
Sun 11/12 A MIN 20-28 L 38,010
Sun 11/19 H STL 16-0 L 56,112
Sun 11/26 A WAS 27-6 W 41,062
Sun 12/3 H SF 20-17 W 57,641
Sat 12/9 A LA 17-34 L 41,268
Sat 12/16 A SF 27-24 W 45,517

CHICAGO BEARS
Sun 9/17 A MIN 13-37 L 32,326
Sat 9/23 A LA 21-17 W 53,315
Sun 10/1 A GB 0-24 L 38,669
Sun 10/8 A DET 31-17 W 50,521
Sun 10/15 H BAL 24-10 W 48,719
Sun 10/22 H SF 31-0 W 49,070
Sun 10/29 A BAL 21-20 W 57,641
Sun 11/5 A PHI 14-16 L 60,671
Sun 11/12 H GB 28-31 L 49,711
Sun 11/19 H SF 31-41 L 52,972
Sun 11/26 H LA 28-24 W 45,965
Sun 12/3 H DET 15-16 L 47,394
Sun 12/10 H CLE 17-14 W 38,717
Sun 12/17 H MIN 52-35 W 34,539

CLEVELAND BROWNS
Sun 9/17 A PHI 20-27 L 60,671
Sun 9/24 H STL 20-17 W 50,443
Sun 10/1 H DAL 25-7 W 43,638
Sun 10/8 H WAS 31-7 W 46,186
Sun 10/15 H GB 17-49 L 75,042
Sun 10/22 H PIT 30-28 W 29,266
Sun 10/29 A STL 21-10 W 26,696
Sun 11/5 H PIT 13-17 L 62,723
Sun 11/12 A WAS 17-6 W 28,975
Sun 11/19 H PHI 45-24 W 68,399
Sun 11/26 H NYG 21-37 L 80,455
Sun 12/3 A DAL 38-17 W 23,500
Sun 12/10 A CHI 14-17 L 38,717
Sun 12/17 A NY 7-7 T 61,084

DALLAS COWBOYS
Sun 9/17 H PIT 27-24 W 23,500
Sun 9/24 H MIN 21-7 W 12,992
Sun 10/1 A CLE 7-25 L 43,638
Sun 10/8 A MIN 28-0 W 33,070
Sun 10/15 H NYG 10-31 L 41,500
Sun 10/22 H PHI 7-43 L 25,000
Sun 10/29 A NYG 17-16 W 60,284
Sun 11/5 H STL 17-31 L 20,500
Sun 11/12 A PIT 7-37 L 17,519
Sun 11/19 H WAS 28-28 T 17,500

Sun 11/26 A PHI 13-35 L 60,127
Sun 12/3 H CLE 17-38 L 23,500
Sun 12/10 A STL 13-31 L 15,384
Sun 12/17 A WAS 24-34 L 21,451

DETROIT LIONS
Sun 9/17 A GB 17-13 W 44,307
Sun 9/24 A BAL 16-15 W 54,259
Sun 10/1 H SF 0-49 L 53,155
Sun 10/8 H CHI 17-31 L 50,521
Sun 10/15 H LA 14-13 W 45,873
Sun 10/22 H BAL 14-17 L 53,016
Sun 10/29 A LA 28-10 W 49,123
Sun 11/5 A SF 20-20 T 56,878
Sun 11/12 A STL 45-14 W 20,320
Sun 11/19 A MIN 37-10 W 32,296
Thu 11/23 H GB 9-17 L 55,662
Sun 12/3 H CHI 16-15 W 47,394
Sun 12/10 H MIN 13-7 W 42,655
Sun 12/17 H PHI 24-27 L 44,231

GREEN BAY PACKERS
Sun 9/17 H DET 13-17 L 44,307
Sun 9/24 H SF 30-10 W 38,624
Sun 10/1 H CHI 24-0 W 38,669
Sun 10/8 H BAL 45-7 W 38,669
Sun 10/15 A CLE 49-17 W 75,042
Sun 10/22 A MIN 33-7 W 42,007
Sun 10/29 H MIN 28-10 W 44,112
Sun 11/5 A BAL 21-45 L 57,641
Sun 11/12 A CHI 31-28 W 49,711
Sun 11/19 H LA 35-17 W 38,669
Thu 11/23 A DET 17-9 W 55,662
Sun 12/3 H NYG 20-17 W 47,012
Sun 12/10 A SF 21-22 L 55,722
Sun 12/17 A LA 24-17 W 49,169

LEAGUE CHAMPIONSHIP
Sun 12/31 H NYG 37-0 W 39,029

LOS ANGELES RAMS
Sun 9/17 A BAL 24-27 L 54,259
Sat 9/23 H CHI 17-21 L 53,315
Sun 10/1 H PIT 24-14 W 40,707
Sun 10/8 A SF 0-35 L 59,004
Sun 10/15 A DET 13-14 L 45,873
Sun 10/22 A NYG 14-24 L 63,053
Sun 10/29 H DET 10-28 L 49,123
Sun 11/5 H MIN 31-17 W 38,594
Sun 11/12 H SF 17-7 W 63,766
Sun 11/19 A GB 17-35 L 38,669
Sun 11/26 A CHI 24-28 L 45,965
Sun 12/3 A MIN 21-42 L 30,068
Sat 12/9 H BAL 34-17 W 41,268
Sun 12/17 H GB 17-24 L 49,169

MINNESOTA VIKINGS
Sun 9/17 H CHI 37-13 W 32,326
Sun 9/24 A DAL 7-21 L 12,992
Sun 10/1 A BAL 33-34 L 54,259
Sun 10/8 H DAL 0-28 L 33,070
Sun 10/15 H SF 24-38 L 34,415
Sun 10/22 A GB 7-33 L 42,007
Sun 10/29 A GB 10-28 L 44,112
Sun 11/5 A LA 17-31 L 38,594
Sun 11/12 H BAL 28-20 W 38,010
Sun 11/19 A DET 10-37 L 32,296
Sun 11/26 A SF 28-38 L 43,905
Sun 12/3 H LA 42-21 W 30,068
Sun 12/10 A DET 7-13 L 42,655
Sun 12/17 A CHI 35-52 L 34,539

NEW YORK GIANTS
Sun 9/17 H STL 10-21 L 58,059
Sun 9/24 A PIT 17-14 W 35,587
Sun 10/1 A WAS 24-21 W 36,767
Sun 10/8 H DAL 24-9 W 23,713
Sun 10/15 A DAL 31-10 W 41,500

Sun 10/22 H LA 24-14 W 63,053
Sun 10/29 A DAL 16-17 L 60,284
Sun 11/5 H WAS 53-0 W 56,077
Sun 11/12 H PHI 38-21 W 62,800
Sun 11/19 H PIT 42-21 W 62,592
Sun 11/26 A CLE 37-21 W 80,455
Sun 12/3 A GB 17-20 L 47,012
Sun 12/10 H PHI 28-24 W 60,671
Sun 12/17 H CLE 7-7 T 61,084

League Championship
Sun 12/31 A GB 0-37 L 39,029

PHILADELPHIA EAGLES
Sun 9/17 H CLE 27-20 W 60,671
Sun 9/24 H WAS 14-7 W 50,108
Sun 10/1 H STL 27-30 L 59,399
Sun 10/8 H PIT 21-16 W 60,671
Sun 10/15 A STL 20-7 W 20,262
Sun 10/22 A DAL 43-7 W 25,000
Sun 10/29 A WAS 27-24 W 31,066
Sun 11/5 H CHI 16-14 W 60,671
Sun 11/12 A NYG 21-38 L 62,800
Sun 11/19 A CLE 24-45 L 68,399
Sun 11/26 H DAL 35-13 W 60,127
Sun 12/3 H PIT 35-24 W 21,653
Sun 12/10 H NYG 24-28 L 60,671
Sun 12/17 A DET 27-24 W 44,231

PITTSBURGH STEELERS
Sun 9/17 A DAL 24-27 L 23,500
Sun 9/24 H NYG 14-17 L 35,587
Sun 10/1 A LA 14-24 L 40,707
Sun 10/8 A PHI 16-21 L 60,671
Sun 10/15 H WAS 20-0 W 15,072
Sun 10/22 H CLE 28-30 L 29,266
Sun 10/29 A SF 20-10 W 21,686
Sun 11/5 A CLE 17-13 W 62,723
Sun 11/12 H DAL 37-7 W 17,519
Sun 11/19 A NYG 21-42 L 62,592
Sun 11/26 H STL 30-27 W 17,090
Sun 12/3 A PHI 24-35 L 21,653
Sun 12/10 A WAS 30-14 W 21,134
Sun 12/17 A STL 0-20 L 16,298

ST. LOUIS CARDINALS
Sun 9/17 A NYG 21-10 W 58,059
Sun 9/24 A CLE 17-20 L 50,443
Sun 10/1 A PHI 30-27 W 59,399
Sun 10/8 H NYG 9-24 L 23,713
Sun 10/15 H PHI 7-20 L 20,262
Sun 10/22 A WAS 24-0 W 28,037
Sun 10/29 H CLE 10-21 L 26,696
Sun 11/5 A DAL 31-17 W 20,500
Sun 11/12 H DET 14-45 L 20,320
Sun 11/19 A BAL 0-16 L 56,112
Sun 11/26 A PIT 27-30 L 17,090
Sun 12/3 H WAS 38-24 W 16,204
Sun 12/10 H DAL 31-13 W 15,384
Sun 12/17 H PIT 20-0 W 16,298

SAN FRANCISCO 49ERS
Sun 9/17 H WAS 35-3 W 43,142
Sun 9/24 A GB 10-30 L 38,624
Sun 10/1 A DET 49-0 W 53,155
Sun 10/8 H LA 35-0 W 59,004
Sun 10/15 A MIN 38-24 W 34,415
Sun 10/22 A CHI 0-31 L 49,070
Sun 10/29 A PIT 10-20 L 21,686
Sun 11/5 H DET 20-20 T 56,878
Sun 11/12 A LA 7-17 L 63,766
Sun 11/19 A CHI 41-31 W 52,972
Sun 11/26 A MIN 38-28 W 43,905
Sun 12/3 A BAL 17-20 L 57,641
Sun 12/10 H GB 22-21 W 55,722
Sat 12/16 H BAL 24-27 L 45,517

WASHINGTON REDSKINS
Sun 9/17 A SF 3-35 L 43,142
Sun 9/24 A PHI 7-14 L 50,108
Sun 10/1 H NYG 21-24 L 36,767
Sun 10/8 A CLE 7-31 L 46,186
Sun 10/15 A PIT 0-20 L 15,072
Sun 10/22 H STL 0-24 L 28,037
Sun 10/29 H PHI 24-27 L 31,066
Sun 11/5 A NYG 0-53 L 56,077
Sun 11/12 H CLE 6-17 L 28,975
Sun 11/19 A DAL 28-28 T 17,500
Sun 11/26 H BAL 6-27 L 41,062
Sun 12/3 A STL 24-38 L 16,204
Sun 12/10 H PIT 14-30 L 21,134
Sun 12/17 H DAL 34-24 W 21,451

1962 AFL
BOSTON PATRIOTS
Sat 9/8 A DAL 28-42 L 32,000
Sun 9/16 H HOU 34-21 W 32,276
Fri 9/21 H DEN 41-16 W 21,038
Sat 10/6 A NY 43-14 W 14,412
Fri 10/12 H DAL 7-27 L 23,874
Fri 10/19 H SD 24-20 W 20,888
Fri 10/26 H OAK 26-16 W 12,514
Sat 11/3 A BUF 28-28 T 33,247
Sun 11/11 A DEN 33-29 W 28,187
Sun 11/18 H HOU 17-21 L 35,250
Fri 11/23 H BUF 21-10 W 20,021
Fri 11/30 H NY 24-17 W 20,015
Sun 12/9 A SD 20-14 W 19,887
Sun 12/16 A OAK 0-20 L 8,000

BUFFALO BILLS
Sun 9/9 H HOU 23-28 L 31,236
Sat 9/15 H DEN 20-23 L 30,557
Sat 9/22 H NY 6-17 L 24,024
Sun 9/30 A DAL 21-41 L 25,500
Sun 10/7 A HOU 14-17 L 26,350
Sat 10/13 H SD 35-10 W 20,074
Sat 10/20 H OAK 14-6 W 21,037
Sun 10/28 A DEN 45-38 W 26,051
Sat 11/3 H BOS 28-28 T 33,247
Sun 11/11 A SD 40-20 W 22,204
Sun 11/18 A OAK 10-6 W 11,700
Fri 11/23 A BOS 10-21 L 20,021
Sun 12/2 H DAL 23-14 W 35,261
Sat 12/8 A NY 20-3 L 16,453

DALLAS TEXANS
Sat 9/8 H BOS 42-28 W 32,000
Sun 9/23 A OAK 26-16 W 12,500
Sun 9/30 H BUF 41-21 W 25,500
Sun 10/7 A SD 28-32 L 23,092
Fri 10/12 A BOS 27-7 W 23,874
Sun 10/21 H NY 20-17 W 17,814
Sun 10/28 A HOU 31-7 W 31,750
Sun 11/4 H HOU 6-14 L 29,017
Sun 11/11 A NY 52-31 W 13,725
Sun 11/18 H DEN 24-3 W 23,523
Sun 11/25 H OAK 35-7 W 13,557
Sun 12/2 A BUF 14-23 L 35,261
Sun 12/9 H DEN 17-10 W 19,137
Sun 12/16 H SD 26-17 W 18,384

League Championship
Sun 12/23 A HOU**20-17 W 37,981

DENVER BRONCOS
Fri 9/7 H SD 30-21 W 28,000
Sat 9/15 A BUF 23-20 W 30,557
Fri 9/21 A BOS 16-41 L 21,038
Sun 9/30 A NY 32-10 W 17,213
Fri 10/5 H OAK 44-7 W 22,452
Sun 10/14 A OAK 23-6 W 7,000
Sun 10/21 H HOU 20-10 W 34,496
Sun 10/28 H BUF 38-45 L 26,051
Sun 11/4 A SD 23-20 W 20,827
Sun 11/11 H BOS 29-33 L 28,187
Sun 11/18 H DAL 3-24 L 23,523
Thu 11/22 H NY 45-46 L 15,776
Sun 12/2 A HOU 17-34 L 30,650
Sun 12/9 A DAL 10-17 L 19,137

HOUSTON OILERS
Sun 9/9 A BUF 28-23 W 31,236
Sun 9/16 A BOS 21-34 L 32,276
Sun 9/23 A SD 42-17 W 28,061
Sun 10/7 H BUF 17-14 W 26,350
Sun 10/14 H NY 56-17 W 20,650
Sun 10/21 A DEN 10-20 L 34,496
Sun 10/28 H DAL 7-31 L 31,750
Sun 11/4 A DAL 14-6 W 29,017
Sun 11/11 A OAK 28-20 W 11,500
Sun 11/18 A BOS 21-17 W 35,250
Sun 11/25 H SD 33-27 W 28,235
Sun 12/2 H DEN 34-17 W 30,650
Sun 12/9 H OAK 32-17 W 27,400
Sat 12/15 A NY 44-10 W 8,167

League Championship
Sun 12/23 H DAL **17-20 L 37,981

NEW YORK TITANS
Sun 9/9 A OAK 28-17 W 12,893
Sun 9/16 A SD 14-40 L 22,003
Sat 9/22 A BUF 17-6 W 24,024
Sun 9/30 H DEN 10-32 L 17,213
Sat 10/6 H BOS 14-43 L 14,412
Sun 10/14 A HOU 17-56 L 20,650
Sun 10/21 A DAL 17-20 L 17,814
Sun 10/28 H SD 23-3 W 21,467
Sun 11/4 H OAK 31-21 W 13,247
Sun 11/11 H DAL 31-52 L 13,725
Thu 11/22 A DEN 46-45 W 15,776
Fri 11/30 A BOS 17-24 L 20,105
Sat 12/8 H BUF 3-20 L 16,453
Sat 12/15 H HOU 10-44 L 8,167

OAKLAND RAIDERS
Sun 9/9 H NY 17-28 L 12,893
Sun 9/23 H DAL 16-26 L 12,500
Sun 9/30 H SD 33-42 L 13,000
Fri 10/5 A DEN 7-44 L 22,452
Sun 10/14 H DEN 6-23 L 7,000
Sat 10/20 A BUF 6-14 L 21,037
Fri 10/26 A BOS 16-26 L 12,514
Sun 11/4 A NY 21-31 L 13,247
Sun 11/11 H HOU 20-28 L 11,500
Sun 11/18 H BUF 6-10 L 11,700
Sun 11/25 A DAL 7-35 L 13,557
Sun 12/2 A SD 21-31 L 17,874
Sun 12/9 A HOU 17-32 L 27,400
Sun 12/16 H BOS 20-0 W 8,000

SAN DIEGO CHARGERS
Fri 9/7 A DEN 21-30 L 28,000
Sun 9/16 H NY 40-14 W 22,003
Sun 9/23 H HOU 17-42 L 28,061
Sun 9/30 A OAK 42-33 W 13,000
Sun 10/7 H DAL 32-28 W 23,092
Sat 10/13 A BUF 10-35 L 20,074
Fri 10/19 A BOS 20-24 L 20,888
Sun 10/28 A NY 3-23 L 21,467
Sun 11/4 H DEN 20-23 L 20,827
Sun 11/11 H BUF 20-40 L 22,204
Sun 11/25 A HOU 27-33 L 28,235
Sun 12/2 H OAK 31-21 W 17,874
Sun 12/9 H BOS 14-20 L 19,887
Sun 12/16 A DAL 17-26 L 18,384

1962 NFL
BALTIMORE COLTS
Sun 9/16 H LA 30-27 W 54,796
Sun 9/23 A MIN 34-7 W 30,787
Sun 9/30 H DET 20-29 L 57,966
Sun 10/7 H SF 13-21 L 54,158
Sun 10/14 A CLE 36-14 W 80,132
Sun 10/21 A CHI 15-35 L 49,066
Sun 10/28 H GB 6-17 L 57,966
Sun 11/4 H SF 22-3 W 44,875
Sun 11/11 A LA 14-2 W 39,502
Sun 11/18 A GB 13-17 L 38,669
Sun 11/25 H CHI 0-57 L 56,164
Sun 12/2 A DET 14-21 L 52,012
Sat 12/8 H WAS 34-21 W 56,964
Sun 12/16 H MIN 42-17 W 53,645

CHICAGO BEARS
Sun 9/16 H SF 30-14 W 46,052
Sun 9/23 A LA 27-23 W 44,376
Sun 9/30 A GB 0-49 L 38,669
Sun 10/7 A MIN 13-0 W 33,141
Sun 10/14 H SF 27-34 L 48,902
Sun 10/21 H BAL 35-15 W 49,066
Sun 10/28 A DET 3-11 L 53,432
Sun 11/4 A GB 7-38 L 48,753
Sun 11/11 H MIN 31-30 W 46,984
Sun 11/18 A DAL 34-33 W 12,692
Sun 11/25 A BAL 57-0 W 56,164
Sun 12/2 H NYG 24-26 L 49,043
Sun 12/9 H LA 30-14 W 38,685
Sun 12/16 H DET 3-0 W 44,948

CLEVELAND BROWNS
Sun 9/16 H NYG 17-7 W 81,115
Sun 9/23 H WAS 16-17 L 57,491
Sun 9/30 H PHI 7-35 L 60,671
Sun 10/7 H DAL 19-10 W 44,040
Sun 10/14 H BAL 14-36 L 80,132
Sun 10/21 A STL 34-7 W 23,256
Sun 10/28 A PIT 41-14 W 35,417
Sun 11/4 H PHI 14-14 T 63,848
Sun 11/11 A WAS 9-17 L 48,169
Sun 11/18 A STL 38-14 W 41,815
Sun 11/25 H PIT 35-14 W 53,601
Sun 12/2 H DAL 21-45 L 24,226
Sun 12/9 A NYG 13-17 L 62,794
Sat 12/15 A SF 13-10 W 35,274

DALLAS COWBOYS
Sun 9/16 H WAS 35-35 T 15,730
Sun 9/23 H PIT 28-30 L 19,478
Sun 9/30 A LA 27-17 W 26,907
Sun 10/7 A CLE 10-19 L 44,040
Sun 10/14 H PHI 41-19 W 18,645
Sun 10/21 H PIT 42-27 W 23,106
Sun 10/28 H STL 24-28 L 16,027
Sun 11/4 A WAS 38-10 W 49,888
Sun 11/11 H NYG 10-41 L 45,668
Sun 11/18 H CHI 33-34 L 12,692
Sun 11/25 A PHI 14-28 L 58,070
Sun 12/2 H CLE 45-21 W 24,226
Sun 12/9 A STL 20-52 L 14,102
Sun 12/16 A NYG 31-41 L 62,694

DETROIT LIONS
Sun 9/16 H PIT 45-7 W 46,641
Sun 9/23 H SF 45-24 W 51,032
Sun 9/30 A BAL 29-20 W 57,966
Sun 10/7 A GB 7-9 L 38,669
Sun 10/14 H LA 13-10 W 53,714
Sun 10/21 A NYG 14-17 L 62,856
Sun 10/28 H CHI 11-3 W 53,432
Sun 11/4 A LA 12-3 W 44,241
Sun 11/11 A SF 38-24 W 43,449

Sun	11/18	A	MIN	17-6	W	31,257
Thu	11/22	H	GB	26-14	W	57,598
Sun	12/2	H	BAL	21-14	W	52,012
Sun	12/9	H	MIN	37-23	W	42,256
Sun	12/16	A	CHI	0-3	L	44,948

GREEN BAY PACKERS

Sun	9/16	H	MIN	34-7	W	38,669
Sun	9/23	H	STL	17-0	W	44,885
Sun	9/30	H	CHI	49-0	W	38,669
Sun	10/7	H	DET	9-7	W	38,669
Sun	10/14	A	MIN	48-21	W	41,475
Sun	10/21	H	SF	31-13	W	46,012
Sun	10/28	A	BAL	17-6	W	57,966
Sun	11/4	A	CHI	38-7	W	48,753
Sun	11/11	A	PHI	49-0	W	60,671
Sun	11/18	H	BAL	17-13	W	38,669
Thu	11/22	A	DET	14-26	L	57,598
Sun	12/2	H	LA	41-10	W	46,833
Sun	12/9	A	SF	31-21	W	53,769
Sun	12/16	A	LA	20-17	W	60,353

League Championship

Sun	12/30	A	NYG	16-7	W	64,892

LOS ANGELES RAMS

Sun	9/16	A	BAL	27-30	L	54,796
Sun	9/23	H	CHI	23-27	L	44,376
Sun	9/30	H	DAL	17-27	L	26,907
Sun	10/7	A	WAS	14-20	L	38,264
Sun	10/14	A	DET	10-13	L	53,714
Sun	10/21	H	MIN	14-38	L	33,071
Sun	10/28	A	SF	28-14	W	51,033
Sun	11/4	H	DET	3-12	L	44,241
Sun	11/11	H	BAL	2-14	L	39,502
Sun	11/18	H	SF	17-24	L	42,554
Sun	11/25	A	MIN	24-24	T	26,728
Sun	12/2	A	GB	10-41	L	46,833
Sun	12/9	A	CHI	14-30	L	38,685
Sun	12/16	H	GB	17-20	L	60,353

MINNESOTA VIKINGS

Sun	9/16	A	GB	7-34	L	38,669
Sun	9/23	H	BAL	7-34	L	30,787
Sun	9/30	A	SF	7-21	L	38,407
Sun	10/7	H	CHI	0-13	L	33,141
Sun	10/14	H	GB	21-48	L	41,475
Sun	10/21	A	LA	38-14	W	33,071
Sun	10/28	H	PHI	31-21	W	30,071
Sun	11/4	A	PIT	31-39	L	14,642
Sun	11/11	A	CHI	30-31	L	46,984
Sun	11/18	H	DET	6-17	L	31,257
Sun	11/25	H	LA	24-24	T	26,728
Sun	12/2	H	SF	12-35	L	33,076
Sun	12/9	A	DET	23-37	L	42,256
Sun	12/16	A	BAL	14-42	L	53,645

NEW YORK GIANTS

Sun	9/16	A	CLE	7-17	L	81,115
Sun	9/23	A	PHI	29-13	W	60,671
Sun	9/30	A	PIT	31-27	W	40,916
Sun	10/7	A	STL	31-14	W	20,627
Sun	10/14	H	PIT	17-20	L	62,808
Sun	10/21	H	DET	17-14	W	62,856
Sun	10/28	H	WAS	49-34	W	62,844
Sun	11/4	H	STL	31-28	W	62,755
Sun	11/11	A	DAL	41-10	W	45,668
Sun	11/18	H	PHI	19-14	W	62,705
Sun	11/25	A	WAS	42-24	W	49,219
Sun	12/2	A	CHI	26-24	W	49,043
Sun	12/9	H	CLE	17-13	W	62,974
Sun	12/16	H	DAL	41-31	W	62,694

League Championship

Sun	12/30	H	GB	7-16	L	64,892

PHILADELPHIA EAGLES

Sun	9/16	H	STL	21-27	L	58,910
Sun	9/23	H	NYG	13-29	L	60,671
Sun	9/30	H	CLE	35-7	W	60,671
Sat	10/6	A	PIT	7-13	L	23,164
Sun	10/14	A	DAL	19-41	L	18,645
Sun	10/21	H	WAS	21-27	L	60,671
Sun	10/28	A	MIN	21-31	L	30,071
Sun	11/4	A	CLE	14-14	T	63,848
Sun	11/11	H	GB	0-49	L	60,671
Sun	11/18	A	NYG	14-19	L	62,705
Sun	11/25	H	DAL	28-14	W	58,070
Sun	12/2	A	WAS	37-14	W	32,229
Sun	12/9	H	PIT	17-26	L	60,671
Sun	12/16	A	STL	35-45	L	14,989

PITTSBURGH STEELERS

Sun	9/16	A	DET	7-45	L	46,461
Sun	9/23	A	DAL	30-28	W	19,478
Sun	9/30	H	NYG	27-31	L	40,916
Sat	10/6	H	PHI	13-7	W	23,164
Sun	10/14	A	NYG	20-17	W	62,808
Sun	10/21	H	DAL	27-42	L	23,106
Sun	10/28	H	CLE	14-41	L	35,417
Sun	11/4	H	MIN	39-31	W	14,642
Sun	11/11	A	STL	26-17	W	20,264
Sun	11/18	H	WAS	23-21	W	21,231
Sun	11/25	A	CLE	14-35	L	53,601
Sun	12/2	H	STL	19-7	W	17,265
Sun	12/9	A	PHI	26-17	W	60,671
Sun	12/16	A	WAS	27-24	W	34,508

ST. LOUIS CARDINALS

Sun	9/16	A	PHI	27-21	W	58,910
Sun	9/23	A	GB	0-17	L	44,885
Sun	9/30	A	WAS	14-24	L	37,419
Sun	10/7	H	NYG	14-31	L	20,627
Sun	10/14	H	WAS	17-17	T	18,104
Sun	10/21	H	CLE	7-34	L	23,256
Sun	10/28	A	DAL	28-24	W	16,027
Sun	11/4	A	NYG	28-31	L	62,755
Sun	11/11	H	PIT	17-26	L	20,264
Sun	11/18	A	CLE	14-38	L	41,815
Sun	11/25	H	SF	17-24	L	17,532
Sun	12/2	A	PIT	7-19	L	17,265
Sun	12/9	H	DAL	52-20	W	14,102
Sun	12/16	H	PHI	45-35	W	14,989

SAN FRANCISCO 49ERS

Sun	9/16	H	CHI	14-30	L	46,052
Sun	9/23	A	DET	24-45	L	51,032
Sun	9/30	H	MIN	21-7	W	38,407
Sun	10/7	A	BAL	21-13	W	54,158
Sun	10/14	A	CHI	34-27	W	48,902
Sun	10/21	A	GB	13-31	L	46,012
Sun	10/28	H	LA	14-28	L	51,033
Sun	11/4	H	BAL	3-22	L	44,875
Sun	11/11	H	DET	24-38	L	43,449
Sun	11/18	A	LA	24-17	W	42,554
Sun	11/25	A	STL	24-17	W	17,532
Sun	12/2	A	MIN	35-12	W	33,076
Sun	12/9	H	GB	21-31	L	53,769
Sat	12/15	H	CLE	10-13	L	35,274

WASHINGTON REDSKINS

Sun	9/16	A	DAL	35-35	T	15,730
Sun	9/23	A	CLE	17-16	W	57,491
Sun	9/30	H	STL	24-14	W	37,419
Sun	10/7	H	LA	20-14	W	38,264
Sun	10/14	A	STL	17-17	T	18,104
Sun	10/21	A	PHI	27-21	W	60,671
Sun	10/28	A	NYG	34-49	L	62,844
Sun	11/4	H	DAL	10-38	L	49,888
Sun	11/11	H	CLE	17-9	W	48,169
Sun	11/18	A	PIT	21-23	L	21,231
Sun	11/25	H	NYG	24-42	L	49,219
Sun	12/2	H	PHI	14-37	L	32,229
Sat	12/8	A	BAL	21-34	L	56,964
Sun	12/16	H	PIT	24-27	L	34,508

1963 AFL

BOSTON PATRIOTS

Sun	9/8	H	NY	38-14	W	24,120
Sat	9/14	A	SD	13-17	L	26,097
Sun	9/22	A	OAK	20-14	W	17,131
Sun	9/29	A	DEN	10-14	L	18,636
Sat	10/5	A	NY	24-31	L	16,769
Fri	10/11	H	OAK	20-14	W	26,494
Fri	10/18	H	DEN	40-21	W	25,418
Sat	10/26	A	BUF	21-28	L	29,243
Fri	11/1	H	HOU	45-3	W	31,185
Sun	11/10	H	SD	6-7	L	28,402
Sun	11/17	H	KC	24-24	T	17,270
Sun	12/1	H	BUF	17-7	W	16,981
Sun	12/8	A	HOU	46-28	W	23,462
Sat	12/14	A	KC	3-35	L	12,598

Eastern Division Playoff

Sat	12/28	A	BUF	26-8	W	33,044

League Championship

Sun	1/5	A	SD	10-51	L	30,127

BUFFALO BILLS

Sun	9/8	A	SD	10-14	L	22,344
Sun	9/15	A	OAK	17-35	L	17,568
Sun	9/22	H	KC	27-27	T	33,487
Sat	9/28	H	HOU	20-31	L	32,340
Sat	10/5	H	OAK	12-0	W	24,846
Sun	10/13	A	KC	35-26	W	25,519
Sun	10/20	A	HOU	14-28	L	23,948
Sat	10/26	H	BOS	28-21	W	29,243
Sun	11/3	A	DEN	30-28	W	19,424
Sat	11/9	H	DEN	27-17	W	30,989
Sun	11/17	H	SD	13-23	L	38,592
Sun	12/1	A	BOS	7-17	L	16,981
Sun	12/8	H	NY	45-14	W	20,222
Sat	12/14	A	NY	19-10	W	5,826

Eastern Division Playoff

Sat	12/28	H	BOS	8-26	L	33,044

DENVER BRONCOS

Sat	9/7	H	KC	7-59	L	21,115
Sat	9/14	A	HOU	14-20	L	22,855
Sun	9/29	H	BOS	14-10	W	18,636
Sun	10/6	H	SD	50-34	W	18,428
Sun	10/13	H	HOU	24-33	L	24,087
Fri	10/18	A	BOS	21-40	L	25,418
Sat	10/26	A	NY	35-35	T	20,377
Sun	11/3	H	BUF	28-30	L	19,424
Sat	11/9	A	BUF	17-27	L	30,989
Sun	11/17	H	NY	9-14	L	14,247
Thu	11/28	H	OAK	10-26	L	14,763
Sun	12/8	A	KC	21-52	L	17,443
Sun	12/15	A	OAK	31-35	L	15,223
Sun	12/22	A	SD	20-58	L	31,312

HOUSTON OILERS

Sat	9/7	H	OAK	13-24	L	24,749
Sat	9/14	H	DEN	20-14	W	22,855
Sun	9/22	A	NY	17-24	L	9,336
Sat	9/28	A	BUF	31-20	W	32,340
Sun	10/6	A	KC	7-28	L	27,801
Sun	10/13	A	DEN	33-24	W	24,087
Sun	10/20	H	BUF	28-14	W	23,948
Sun	10/27	H	KC	28-7	W	26,331
Fri	11/1	A	BOS	3-45	L	31,185
Sun	11/10	H	NY	31-27	W	23,619
Sun	12/1	A	SD	0-27	L	31,713
Sun	12/8	H	BOS	28-46	L	23,462
Sun	12/15	H	SD	14-20	L	18,540
Sun	12/22	A	OAK	49-52	L	17,401

KANSAS CITY CHIEFS

Sat	9/7	A	DEN	59-7	W	21,115
Sun	9/22	A	BUF	27-27	T	33,487
Sun	9/29	A	SD	10-24	L	22,654
Sun	10/6	H	HOU	28-7	W	27,801
Sun	10/13	H	BUF	26-35	L	25,519
Sun	10/20	H	SD	17-38	L	30,107
Sun	10/27	A	HOU	7-28	L	26,331
Sun	11/3	A	OAK	7-10	L	18,919
Fri	11/8	H	OAK	7-22	L	24,897
Sun	11/17	A	BOS	24-24	T	17,270
Sun	12/1	A	NY	0-17	L	11,615
Sun	12/8	H	DEN	52-21	W	17,443
Sat	12/14	H	BOS	35-3	W	12,598
Sun	12/22	H	NY	48-0	W	12,202

NEW YORK JETS

Sun	9/8	A	BOS	14-38	L	24,120
Sun	9/22	H	HOU	24-17	W	9,336
Sat	9/28	H	OAK	10-7	W	18,925
Sat	10/5	H	BOS	31-24	W	16,769
Sun	10/13	A	SD	20-24	L	27,189
Sun	10/20	A	OAK	26-49	L	15,557
Sat	10/26	H	DEN	35-35	T	20,377
Sat	11/2	H	SD	7-53	L	20,798
Sun	11/10	A	HOU	27-31	L	23,619
Sun	11/17	A	DEN	14-9	W	14,247
Sun	12/1	H	KC	17-0	W	11,615
Sun	12/8	A	BUF	14-45	L	20,222
Sat	12/14	H	BUF	10-19	L	5,826
Sun	12/22	A	KC	0-48	L	12,202

OAKLAND RAIDERS

Sat	9/7	A	HOU	24-13	W	24,749
Sun	9/15	H	BUF	35-17	W	17,568
Sun	9/22	H	BOS	14-20	L	17,131
Sat	9/28	A	NY	7-10	L	18,925
Sat	10/5	A	BUF	0-12	L	24,846
Fri	10/11	A	BOS	14-20	L	26,494
Sun	10/20	H	NY	49-26	W	15,557
Sun	10/27	A	SD	34-33	W	30,182
Sun	11/3	H	KC	10-7	W	18,919
Fri	11/8	A	KC	22-7	W	24,897
Thu	11/28	A	DEN	26-10	W	14,763
Sun	12/8	H	SD	41-27	W	20,249
Sun	12/15	H	DEN	35-31	W	15,223
Sun	12/22	H	HOU	52-49	W	17,401

SAN DIEGO CHARGERS

Sun	9/8	H	BUF	14-10	W	22,344
Sat	9/14	H	BOS	17-13	W	26,097
Sun	9/29	H	KC	24-10	W	22,654
Sun	10/6	A	DEN	34-50	L	18,428
Sun	10/13	H	NY	24-20	W	27,189
Sun	10/20	A	KC	38-17	W	30,107
Sun	10/27	H	OAK	33-34	L	30,182
Sat	11/2	A	NY	53-7	W	20,798
Sun	11/10	A	BOS	7-6	W	28,402
Sun	11/17	A	BUF	23-13	W	38,592
Sun	12/1	H	HOU	27-0	W	31,713
Sun	12/8	A	OAK	27-41	L	20,249
Sun	12/15	A	HOU	20-14	W	18,540
Sun	12/22	H	DEN	58-20	W	31,312

League Championship

Sun	1/5	H	BOS	51-10	W	30,127

1963 NFL

BALTIMORE COLTS

Sun	9/15	H	NYG	28-37	L	60,029
Sun	9/22	A	SF	20-14	W	31,006
Sun	9/29	A	GB	20-31	L	42,327
Sun	10/6	A	CHI	3-10	L	48,998
Sun	10/13	H	SF	20-3	W	56,962
Sun	10/20	A	DET	25-21	W	51,901

Sun 10/27 H GB 20-34 L 60,065
Sun 11/3 H CHI 7-17 L 60,065
Sun 11/10 H DET 24-21 W 59,758
Sun 11/17 A MIN 37-34 W 33,136
Sun 11/24 A LA 16-17 L 48,555
Sun 12/1 A WAS 36-20 W 44,006
Sun 12/8 H MIN 41-10 W 54,122
Sun 12/15 H LA 19-16 W 52,834

CHICAGO BEARS

Sun 9/15 A GB 10-3 W 42,327
Sun 9/22 A MIN 28-7 W 33,923
Sun 9/29 A DET 37-21 W 55,400
Sun 10/6 H BAL 10-3 W 48,998
Sun 10/13 H LA 52-14 W 40,476
Sun 10/20 A SF 14-20 L 35,837
Sun 10/27 H PHI 16-7 W 48,514
Sun 11/3 A BAL 17-7 W 60,065
Sun 11/10 H LA 6-0 W 48,312
Sun 11/17 H GB 26-7 W 49,166
Sun 11/24 H PIT 17-17 T 36,465
Sun 12/1 H MIN 17-17 T 47,249
Sun 12/8 H SF 27-7 W 46,994
Sun 12/15 H DET 24-14 W 45,317

LEAGUE CHAMPIONSHIP
Sun 12/29 H NYG 14-10 W 45,801

CLEVELAND BROWNS

Sun 9/15 H WAS 37-14 W 57,618
Sun 9/22 A DAL 41-24 W 28,710
Sun 9/29 H LA 20-6 W 54,713
Sat 10/5 H PIT 35-23 W 84,684
Sun 10/13 A NYG 35-24 W 62,986
Sun 10/20 H PHI 37-7 W 75,174
Sun 10/27 H NYG 6-33 L 84,213
Sun 11/3 A PHI 23-17 W 60,671
Sun 11/10 A PIT 7-9 L 54,497
Sun 11/17 H STL 14-20 L 75,932
Sun 11/24 H DET 27-17 W 55,096
Sun 12/1 A STL 24-10 W 32,531
Sun 12/8 A DET 10-38 L 51,382
Sun 12/15 A WAS 27-20 W 40,865

DALLAS COWBOYS

Sat 9/14 H STL 7-34 L 36,432
Sun 9/22 H CLE 24-41 L 28,710
Sun 9/29 A WAS 17-21 L 40,101
Sun 10/6 A PHI 21-24 L 60,671
Sun 10/13 H DET 17-14 W 27,264
Sun 10/20 A NYG 21-37 L 62,889
Sun 10/27 A PIT 21-27 L 19,047
Sun 11/3 H WAS 35-20 W 18,838
Sun 11/10 A SF 24-31 L 29,563
Sun 11/17 H PHI 27-20 W 23,694
Sun 11/24 A CLE 17-27 L 55,096
Sun 12/1 H NYG 27-34 L 29,653
Sun 12/8 H PIT 19-24 L 24,136
Sun 12/15 A STL 28-24 W 12,695

DETROIT LIONS

Sat 9/14 A LA 23-2 W 49,342
Sun 9/22 A GB 10-31 L 45,912
Sun 9/29 H CHI 21-37 L 55,400
Sun 10/6 H SF 26-3 W 44,088
Sun 10/13 A DAL 14-17 L 27,264
Sun 10/20 H BAL 21-25 L 51,901
Sun 10/27 H MIN 28-10 W 44,509
Sun 11/3 A SF 45-7 W 33,511
Sun 11/10 A BAL 21-24 L 59,758
Sun 11/17 H LA 21-28 L 44,951
Sun 11/24 A MIN 31-34 L 28,763
Thu 11/28 A GB 13-13 T 54,016
Sun 12/8 H CLE 38-10 W 51,382
Sun 12/15 A CHI 14-24 L 45,317

GREEN BAY PACKERS

Sun 9/15 H CHI 3-10 L 42,327
Sun 9/22 H DET 31-10 W 45,912
Sun 9/29 H BAL 31-20 W 42,327
Sun 10/6 H LA 42-10 W 42,327
Sun 10/13 A MIN 37-28 W 42,567
Sun 10/20 A STL 30-7 W 32,224
Sun 10/27 A BAL 34-20 W 60,065
Sun 11/3 H PIT 33-14 W 46,293
Sun 11/10 H MIN 28-7 W 42,327
Sun 11/17 A CHI 7-26 L 49,166
Sun 11/24 H SF 28-10 W 45,905
Thu 11/28 A DET 13-13 T 54,016
Sat 12/7 A LA 31-14 W 52,357
Sat 12/14 A SF 21-17 W 31,031

LOS ANGELES RAMS

Sat 9/14 H DET 2-23 L 49,342
Sat 9/21 H WAS 14-37 L 29,295
Sun 9/29 A CLE 6-20 L 54,713
Sun 10/6 A GB 10-42 L 42,327
Sun 10/13 A CHI 14-52 L 40,476
Sun 10/20 H MIN 27-24 W 30,555
Sun 10/27 H SF 28-21 W 45,532
Sun 11/3 A MIN 13-21 L 33,567
Sun 11/10 A CHI 0-6 L 48,312
Sun 11/17 A DET 28-21 W 44,951
Sun 11/24 H BAL 17-16 W 48,555
Sun 12/1 A SF 21-17 W 33,321
Sat 12/7 H GB 14-31 L 52,357
Sun 12/15 A BAL 16-19 L 52,834

MINNESOTA VIKINGS

Sun 9/15 A SF 24-20 W 30,781
Sun 9/22 H CHI 7-28 L 33,923
Sun 9/29 H SF 45-14 W 28,567
Sun 10/6 H STL 14-56 L 30,220
Sun 10/13 H GB 28-37 L 42,567
Sun 10/20 A LA 24-27 L 30,555
Sun 10/27 A DET 10-28 L 44,509
Sun 11/3 H LA 21-13 W 33,567
Sun 11/10 A GB 7-28 L 42,327
Sun 11/17 H BAL 34-37 L 33,136
Sun 11/24 H DET 34-31 W 28,763
Sun 12/1 A CHI 17-17 T 47,249
Sun 12/8 H BAL 10-41 L 54,122
Sun 12/15 A PHI 34-13 W 54,403

NEW YORK GIANTS

Sun 9/15 H BAL 37-28 W 60,029
Sun 9/22 A PIT 0-31 L 46,068
Sun 9/29 H PHI 37-14 W 60,671
Sun 10/6 A WAS 24-14 W 49,219
Sun 10/13 H CLE 24-35 L 62,986
Sun 10/20 H DAL 37-21 W 62,889
Sun 10/27 A CLE 33-6 W 84,213
Sun 11/3 A STL 38-21 W 29,482
Sun 11/10 H PHI 42-14 W 62,936
Sun 11/17 H SF 48-14 W 62,982
Sun 11/24 H STL 17-24 L 62,992
Sun 12/1 A DAL 34-27 W 29,653
Thu 12/8 H WAS 44-14 W 62,992
Sun 12/15 H PIT 33-17 W 63,240

LEAGUE CHAMPIONSHIP
Sun 12/29 A CHI 10-14 L 45,801

PHILADELPHIA EAGLES

Sun 9/15 H PIT 21-21 T 58,205
Sun 9/22 H STL 24-28 L 60,671
Sun 9/29 H NYG 14-37 L 60,671
Sun 10/6 H DAL 24-21 W 60,671
Sun 10/13 A WAS 37-24 W 49,219
Sun 10/20 A CLE 7-37 L 75,174
Sun 10/27 A CHI 7-16 L 48,514
Sun 11/3 H CLE 17-23 L 60,671
Sun 11/10 A NYG 14-42 L 62,936
Sun 11/17 A DAL 20-27 L 23,694
Sun 11/24 H WAS 10-13 L 60,671
Sun 12/1 A PIT 20-20 T 15,721
Sun 12/8 A STL 14-38 L 15,979
Sun 12/15 H MIN 13-34 L 54,403

PITTSBURGH STEELERS

Sun 9/15 A PHI 21-21 T 58,205
Sun 9/22 H NYG 31-0 W 46,068
Sun 9/29 H STL 23-10 W 28,225
Sat 10/5 A CLE 23-35 L 84,684
Sun 10/13 A STL 23-24 L 23,715
Sun 10/20 H WAS 38-27 W 41,987
Sun 10/27 H DAL 27-21 W 19,047
Sun 11/3 A GB 14-33 L 42,693
Sun 11/10 H CLE 9-7 W 54,497
Sun 11/17 A WAS 34-28 W 49,219
Sun 11/24 H CHI 17-17 T 36,465
Sun 12/1 H PHI 20-20 T 15,721
Sun 12/8 A DAL 24-19 W 24,136
Sun 12/15 A NYG 17-33 L 63,240

ST. LOUIS CARDINALS

Sat 9/14 A DAL 34-7 W 36,432
Sun 9/22 A PHI 28-24 W 60,671
Sun 9/29 A PIT 10-23 L 28,225
Sun 10/6 A MIN 56-14 W 30,220
Sun 10/13 H PIT 24-23 W 23,715
Sun 10/20 H GB 7-30 L 32,224
Sun 10/27 A WAS 21-7 W 46,921
Sun 11/3 H NYG 21-38 L 29,482
Sun 11/10 H WAS 24-20 W 18,197
Sun 11/17 A CLE 20-14 W 75,932
Sun 11/24 A NYG 24-17 W 62,992
Sun 12/1 H CLE 10-24 L 32,531
Sun 12/8 H PHI 38-14 W 15,979
Sun 12/15 H DAL 24-28 L 12,695

SAN FRANCISCO 49ERS

Sun 9/15 H MIN 20-24 L 30,781
Sun 9/22 H BAL 14-20 L 31,006
Sun 9/29 A MIN 14-45 L 28,567
Sun 10/6 A DET 3-26 L 44,088
Sun 10/13 A BAL 3-20 L 56,962
Sun 10/20 H CHI 20-14 W 35,837
Sun 10/27 A LA 21-28 L 45,532
Sun 11/3 H DET 7-45 L 33,511
Sun 11/10 H DAL 31-24 W 29,563
Sun 11/17 A NYG 14-48 L 62,982
Sun 11/24 A GB 10-28 L 45,905
Sun 12/1 H LA 17-21 L 33,321
Sun 12/8 H CHI 7-27 L 46,994
Sat 12/14 A GB 17-21 L 31,031

WASHINGTON REDSKINS

Sun 9/15 A CLE 14-37 L 57,618
Sat 9/21 A LA 37-14 W 29,295
Sun 9/29 H DAL 21-17 W 40,101
Sun 10/6 H NYG 14-24 L 49,219
Sun 10/13 H PHI 24-37 L 49,219
Sun 10/20 A PIT 27-38 L 41,987
Sun 10/27 H STL 7-21 L 46,921
Sun 11/3 A DAL 20-35 L 18,838
Sun 11/10 A STL 20-24 L 18,197
Sun 11/17 H PIT 28-34 L 49,219
Sun 11/24 A PHI 13-10 W 60,671
Sun 12/1 H BAL 20-36 L 44,006
Sun 12/8 A NYG 14-44 L 62,992
Sun 12/15 H CLE 20-27 L 40,865

1964 AFL

BOSTON PATRIOTS

Sun 9/13 A OAK 17-14 W 21,126
Sun 9/20 A SD 33-28 W 20,568
Sun 9/27 H NY 26-10 W 22,716
Sun 10/4 A DEN 39-10 W 15,485
Fri 10/9 H SD 17-26 L 35,096
Fri 10/16 H OAK 43-43 T 23,279
Fri 10/23 H KC 24-7 W 27,456
Sat 10/31 A NY 14-35 L 41,910
Fri 11/6 H HOU 25-24 W 28,161
Fri 11/15 A BUF 36-28 W 42,308
Fri 11/20 H DEN 12-7 W 24,979
Sun 11/29 A HOU 34-17 W 17,560
Sun 12/6 A KC 31-24 W 13,166
Sun 12/20 H BUF 14-24 L 38,021

BUFFALO BILLS

Sun 9/13 H KC 34-17 W 30,157
Sun 9/20 H DEN 30-13 W 28,501
Sat 9/26 H SD 30-3 W 40,167
Sat 10/3 H OAK 23-20 W 36,461
Sun 10/11 H HOU 48-17 W 26,218
Sun 10/18 A KC 35-22 W 20,904
Sat 10/24 H NY 34-24 W 39,621
Sun 11/1 H HOU 24-10 W 40,119
Sun 11/8 A NY 20-7 W 60,300
Sun 11/15 H BOS 28-36 L 42,308
Thu 11/26 A SD 27-24 W 34,865
Sun 12/6 A OAK 13-16 L 18,134
Sun 12/13 H DEN 30-19 W 14,431
Sun 12/20 A BOS 24-14 W 38,021

LEAGUE CHAMPIONSHIP
Sat 12/26 H SD 20-7 W 40,242

DENVER BRONCOS

Sat 9/12 A NY 6-30 L 45,665
Sun 9/20 A BUF 13-30 L 28,501
Sun 9/27 H HOU 17-38 L 22,651
Sun 10/4 H BOS 10-39 L 15,485
Sun 10/11 H KC 33-27 W 16,285
Sun 10/18 A SD 14-42 L 23,332
Sun 10/25 A OAK 7-40 L 17,858
Sun 11/1 A KC 39-49 L 15,053
Sun 11/8 H SD 20-31 L 19,670
Sun 11/15 H NY 20-16 W 11,309
Fri 11/20 A BOS 7-12 L 24,979
Sun 11/29 H OAK 20-20 T 15,958
Sun 12/13 A BUF 19-30 L 14,431
Sun 12/20 A HOU 15-34 L 15,839

HOUSTON OILERS

Sat 9/12 A SD 21-27 L 22,632
Sat 9/19 H OAK 42-28 W 26,482
Sun 9/27 A DEN 38-17 W 22,651
Sun 10/4 A KC 7-28 L 22,727
Sun 10/11 A BUF 17-48 L 26,218
Sat 10/17 A NY 21-24 L 32,840
Sun 10/25 H SD 17-20 L 21,671
Sun 11/1 A BUF 10-24 L 40,119
Fri 11/6 A BOS 24-25 L 28,161
Sun 11/15 A OAK 10-20 L 16,375
Sun 11/22 H KC 19-28 L 17,782
Sun 11/29 H BOS 17-34 L 17,560
Sun 12/13 H NY 33-17 W 16,225
Sun 12/20 H DEN 34-15 W 15,839

KANSAS CITY CHIEFS

Sun 9/13 A BUF 17-34 L 30,157
Sun 9/20 A OAK 21-9 W 18,925
Sun 10/4 H HOU 28-7 W 22,727
Sun 10/11 A DEN 27-33 L 16,285
Sun 10/18 H BUF 22-35 L 20,904
Fri 10/23 A BOS 7-24 L 27,456
Sun 11/1 H DEN 49-39 W 15,053
Sun 11/8 H OAK 42-7 W 21,023
Sun 11/15 H SD 14-28 L 19,782
Sun 11/22 A HOU 28-19 W 17,782
Sun 11/29 A NY 14-27 L 38,135

Sun 12/6 H BOS 24-31 L 13,166
Sun 12/13 A SD 49-6 W 26,562
Sun 12/20 H NY 24-7 W 14,216

NEW YORK JETS
Sat 9/12 H DEN 30-6 W 45,665
Sun 9/27 A BOS 10-26 L 22,716
Sat 10/3 H SD 17-17 T 46,828
Sat 10/10 H OAK 35-13 W 32,376
Sat 10/17 H HOU 24-21 W 32,840
Sat 10/24 A BUF 24-34 L 39,621
Sat 10/31 H BOS 35-14 W 41,910
Sun 11/8 H BUF 7-20 L 60,300
Sun 11/15 A DEN 16-20 L 11,309
Sun 11/22 A OAK 26-35 L 15,589
Sun 11/29 H KC 27-14 W 38,135
Sun 12/6 A SD 3-38 L 25,753
Sun 12/13 A HOU 17-33 L 16,225
Sun 12/20 A KC 7-24 L 14,216

OAKLAND RAIDERS
Sun 9/13 H BOS 14-17 L 21,126
Sat 9/19 A HOU 28-42 L 26,482
Sun 9/27 H KC 9-21 L 18,925
Sat 10/3 A BUF 20-23 L 36,461
Sat 10/10 A NY 13-35 L 32,376
Fri 10/16 A BOS 43-43 T 23,279
Sun 10/25 H DEN 40-7 W 17,858
Sun 11/1 A SD 17-31 L 25,557
Sun 11/8 A KC 7-42 L 21,023
Sun 11/15 A HOU 20-10 W 16,375
Sun 11/22 H NY 35-26 W 15,589
Sun 11/29 A DEN 20-20 T 15,958
Sun 12/6 H BUF 21-20 W 20,124

SAN DIEGO CHARGERS
Sat 9/12 H HOU 27-21 W 22,632
Sun 9/20 H BOS 28-33 L 20,568
Sat 9/26 A BUF 3-30 L 40,167
Sat 10/3 A NY 17-17 T 46,828
Fri 10/9 A BOS 26-17 W 35,096
Sun 10/18 H DEN 42-14 W 23,332
Sun 10/25 A HOU 20-17 W 21,671
Sun 11/1 H OAK 31-17 W 25,557
Sun 11/8 A DEN 31-20 W 19,670
Sun 11/15 A KC 28-14 W 19,782
Thu 11/26 H BUF 24-27 L 34,865
Sun 12/6 H NY 38-3 W 25,753
Sun 12/13 A KC 6-49 L 26,562
Sun 12/20 A OAK 16-13 W 18,134
Sun 12/20 H SD 20-21 L 20,124

LEAGUE CHAMPIONSHIP
Sun 12/27 A BUF 7-20 L 40,242

1964 NFL
BALTIMORE COLTS
Sun 9/13 A MIN 24-34 L 35,563
Sun 9/20 A GB 21-20 W 42,327
Sun 9/27 H CHI 52-0 W 56,537
Sun 10/4 H LA 35-20 W 56,537
Mon 10/12 H STL 47-27 W 60,213
Sun 10/18 H GB 24-21 W 60,213
Sun 10/25 A DET 34-0 W 57,814
Sun 11/1 H SF 37-7 W 60,213
Sun 11/8 A CHI 40-24 W 47,891
Sun 11/15 H MIN 17-14 W 60,213
Sun 11/22 A LA 24-7 W 72,137
Sun 11/29 A SF 14-3 W 33,642
Sun 12/6 H DET 14-31 L 60,213
Sun 12/13 H WAS 45-17 W 60,213

LEAGUE CHAMPIONSHIP
Sun 12/27 A CLE 0-27 L 79,544

CHICAGO BEARS
Sun 9/13 A GB 12-23 L 42,327
Sun 9/20 A MIN 34-28 W 41,387
Sun 9/27 A BAL 0-52 L 56,537
Sun 10/4 A SF 21-31 L 33,132
Sun 10/11 H LA 38-17 W 47,358
Sun 10/18 H DET 0-10 L 47,547
Sun 10/25 A WAS 20-27 L 49,219
Sun 11/1 H DAL 10-24 L 47,527
Sun 11/8 A BAL 24-40 L 47,891
Sun 11/15 A LA 34-24 W 61,115
Sun 11/22 H SF 23-21 W 46,722
Thu 11/26 A DET 27-24 W 52,231
Sat 12/5 H GB 3-17 L 43,636
Sun 12/13 H MIN 14-41 L 46,486

CLEVELAND BROWNS
Sun 9/13 A WAS 27-13 W 47,577
Sun 9/20 H STL 33-33 T 76,954
Sun 9/27 A PHI 28-20 W 60,671
Sun 10/4 H DAL 27-6 W 72,062
Sat 10/10 A PIT 7-23 L 80,530
Sun 10/18 A DAL 20-16 W 37,456
Sun 10/25 H NYG 42-20 W 81,050
Sun 11/1 A PIT 30-17 W 49,568
Sun 11/8 H WAS 34-24 W 76,385
Sun 11/15 H DET 37-21 W 83,064
Sun 11/22 A GB 21-28 L 48,065
Sun 11/29 H PHI 38-24 W 79,289
Sun 12/6 A STL 19-28 L 31,585
Sat 12/12 A NYG 52-20 W 63,007

LEAGUE CHAMPIONSHIP
Sun 12/27 H BAL 27-0 W 79,544

DALLAS COWBOYS
Sat 9/12 H STL 6-16 L 36,605
Sun 9/20 H WAS 24-18 W 25,158
Sun 9/27 A PIT 17-23 L 35,594
Sun 10/4 A CLE 6-27 L 72,062
Sun 10/11 H NYG 13-13 T 33,224
Sun 10/18 H CLE 16-20 L 37,456
Sun 10/25 A STL 31-13 W 28,253
Sun 11/1 A CHI 24-10 W 47,527
Sun 11/8 A NYG 31-21 W 63,031
Sun 11/15 H PHI 14-17 L 55,972
Sun 11/22 A WAS 16-28 L 49,219
Sun 11/29 H GB 21-45 L 44,975
Sun 12/6 A PHI 14-24 L 60,671
Sun 12/13 H PIT 17-14 W 35,271

DETROIT LIONS
Sun 9/13 A SF 26-17 W 33,204
Sat 9/19 A LA 17-17 T 52,001
Mon 9/28 H GB 10-14 L 59,203
Sun 10/4 H NYG 26-3 W 54,836
Sun 10/11 A MIN 24-20 W 40,840
Sun 10/18 A CHI 10-0 W 47,547
Sun 10/25 H BAL 0-34 L 57,814
Sun 11/1 H LA 37-17 W 52,064
Sun 11/8 A GB 7-30 L 42,327
Sun 11/15 A CLE 21-37 L 83,064
Thu 11/22 H MIN 23-23 T 48,291
Thu 11/26 H CHI 24-27 L 52,231
Sun 12/6 A BAL 31-14 W 60,213
Sun 12/13 H SF 24-7 W 41,854

GREEN BAY PACKERS
Sun 9/13 H CHI 23-12 W 42,327
Sun 9/20 H BAL 20-21 L 42,327
Mon 9/28 A DET 14-10 W 59,203
Sun 10/4 H MIN 23-24 L 42,327
Sun 10/11 H SF 24-14 W 47,380
Sun 10/18 H BAL 21-24 L 60,213
Sun 10/25 H LA 17-27 L 46,617
Sun 11/1 A MIN 42-13 W 44,278
Sun 11/8 H DET 30-7 W 42,327
Sun 11/15 A SF 14-24 L 38,483
Sun 11/22 H CLE 28-21 W 48,065
Sun 11/29 A DAL 45-21 W 44,975
Sat 12/5 A CHI 17-3 W 43,636
Sun 12/13 A LA 24-24 T 40,735

LOS ANGELES RAMS
Sun 9/13 A PIT 26-14 W 33,988
Sat 9/19 H DET 17-17 T 52,001
Sun 9/27 H MIN 22-13 W 50,009
Sun 10/4 A BAL 20-35 L 56,537
Sun 10/11 A CHI 17-38 L 47,358
Sun 10/18 H SF 42-14 W 54,355
Sun 10/25 A GB 27-17 W 46,617
Sun 11/1 A DET 17-37 L 52,064
Sun 11/8 H PHI 20-10 W 53,994
Sun 11/15 A CHI 24-34 L 61,115
Sun 11/22 H BAL 7-24 L 72,137
Sun 11/29 A MIN 13-34 L 31,677
Sun 12/6 A SF 7-28 L 31,791
Sun 12/13 H GB 24-24 T 40,735

MINNESOTA VIKINGS
Sun 9/13 H BAL 34-24 W 35,563
Sun 9/20 H CHI 28-34 L 41,387
Sun 9/27 A LA 13-22 L 50,009
Sun 10/4 A GB 24-23 W 42,327
Sun 10/11 H DET 20-24 L 40,840
Sun 10/18 H PIT 30-10 W 39,873
Sun 10/25 A SF 27-22 W 31,845
Sun 11/1 H GB 13-42 L 44,278
Sun 11/8 H SF 27-40 L 40,408
Sun 11/15 A BAL 14-17 L 60,213
Sun 11/22 A DET 23-23 T 48,291
Sun 11/29 H LA 34-13 W 31,677
Sun 12/6 A NYG 30-21 W 62,802
Sun 12/13 A CHI 41-14 W 46,486

NEW YORK GIANTS
Sun 9/13 A PHI 7-38 L 60,671
Sun 9/20 A PIT 24-27 L 33,053
Fri 9/25 H WAS 13-10 W 62,996
Sun 10/4 A DET 3-26 L 54,836
Sun 10/11 A DAL 13-13 T 33,224
Sun 10/18 H PHI 17-23 L 62,978
Sun 10/25 A CLE 20-42 L 81,050
Sun 11/1 H STL 34-17 W 63,012
Sun 11/8 H DAL 21-31 L 63,031
Sun 11/15 A STL 10-10 T 29,608
Sun 11/22 H PIT 17-44 L 62,691
Sun 11/29 A WAS 21-36 L 49,219
Sun 12/6 H MIN 21-30 L 62,802
Sat 12/12 H CLE 20-52 L 63,007

PHILADELPHIA EAGLES
Sun 9/13 H NYG 38-7 W 60,671
Sun 9/20 H SF 24-28 L 57,353
Sun 9/27 H CLE 20-28 L 60,671
Sun 10/4 H PIT 21-7 W 59,394
Sun 10/11 A WAS 20-35 L 49,219
Sun 10/18 A NYG 23-17 W 62,978
Sun 10/25 A PIT 34-10 W 38,393
Sun 11/1 H WAS 10-21 L 60,671
Sun 11/8 A LA 10-20 L 53,994
Sun 11/15 A DAL 17-14 W 55,972
Sun 11/22 H STL 13-38 L 60,671
Sun 11/29 A CLE 24-38 L 79,289
Sun 12/6 H DAL 24-14 W 60,671
Sun 12/13 A STL 34-36 L 24,636

PITTSBURGH STEELERS
Sun 9/13 H LA 14-26 L 33,988
Sun 9/20 H NYG 27-24 W 33,053
Sun 9/27 H DAL 23-17 W 35,594
Sun 10/4 A PHI 7-21 L 59,394
Sat 10/10 A CLE 23-7 W 80,530
Sun 10/18 A MIN 10-30 L 39,873
Sun 10/25 H PHI 10-34 L 38,393
Sun 11/1 H CLE 17-30 L 49,568
Sun 11/8 A STL 30-34 L 28,245
Sun 11/15 H WAS 0-30 L 31,587
Sun 11/22 A NYG 44-17 W 62,691
Sun 11/29 A STL 20-21 L 27,807
Sun 12/6 A WAS 14-7 W 49,219
Sun 12/13 A DAL 14-17 L 35,271

ST. LOUIS CARDINALS
Sat 9/12 A DAL 16-6 W 36,605
Sun 9/20 A CLE 33-33 T 76,954
Sun 9/27 A SF 23-13 W 30,969
Sun 10/4 A WAS 23-17 W 49,219
Mon 10/12 A BAL 27-47 L 60,213
Sun 10/18 H WAS 38-24 W 23,748
Sun 10/25 H DAL 13-31 L 28,253
Sun 11/1 H NYG 17-34 L 63,012
Sun 11/8 H PIT 34-30 W 28,245
Sun 11/15 H NYG 10-10 T 29,608
Sun 11/22 A PHI 38-13 W 60,671
Sun 11/29 H PIT 21-20 W 27,807
Sun 12/6 H CLE 28-19 W 31,585
Sun 12/13 H PHI 36-34 W 24,636

SAN FRANCISCO 49ERS
Sun 9/13 H DET 17-26 L 33,204
Sun 9/20 A PHI 28-24 W 57,353
Sun 9/27 H STL 13-23 L 30,969
Sun 10/4 A CHI 31-21 W 33,132
Sun 10/11 A GB 14-24 L 47,380
Sun 10/18 A LA 14-42 L 54,355
Sun 10/25 H MIN 22-27 L 31,845
Sun 11/1 A BAL 7-37 L 60,213
Sun 11/8 A MIN 7-24 L 40,408
Sun 11/15 H GB 24-14 W 38,483
Sun 11/22 A CHI 21-23 L 46,722
Sun 11/29 H BAL 3-14 L 33,642
Sun 12/6 H LA 28-7 W 31,791
Sun 12/13 A DET 7-24 L 41,854

WASHINGTON REDSKINS
Sun 9/13 H CLE 13-27 L 47,577
Sun 9/20 A DAL 18-24 L 25,158
Fri 9/25 A NYG 10-13 L 62,996
Sun 10/4 H STL 17-23 L 49,219
Sun 10/11 H PHI 35-20 W 49,219
Sun 10/18 A STL 34-38 L 23,748
Sun 10/25 H CHI 27-20 W 49,219
Sun 11/1 A PHI 21-10 W 60,671
Sun 11/8 H CLE 24-34 L 76,385
Sun 11/15 A PIT 30-0 W 31,587
Sun 11/22 H DAL 28-16 W 49,219
Sun 11/29 H NYG 36-21 W 49,219
Sun 12/6 H PIT 7-14 L 49,219
Sun 12/13 A BAL 17-45 L 60,213

1965 AFL
BOSTON PATRIOTS
Sat 9/11 A BUF 7-24 L 45,502
Sun 9/19 A HOU 10-31 L 32,445
Fri 9/24 H DEN 10-27 L 26,782
Sun 10/3 A KC 17-27 L 26,773
Fri 10/8 A OAK 10-24 L 24,824
Sun 10/17 H SD 13-13 T 20,924
Sun 10/24 A OAK 21-30 L 20,858
Sun 10/31 A SD 22-6 W 33,366
Sun 11/7 H BUF 7-23 L 24,415
Sun 11/14 H NY 20-30 L 18,589
Sun 11/21 H KC 10-10 T 13,056
Sun 11/28 A NY 27-23 W 56,511
Sun 12/12 A DEN 28-20 W 27,207
Sat 12/18 H HOU 42-14 W 14,508

BUFFALO BILLS
Sat 9/11 H BOS 24-7 W 45,502
Sun 9/19 A DEN 30-15 W 30,682
Sun 9/26 H NY 33-21 W 45,056
Sun 10/3 H OAK 17-12 W 41,246
Sun 10/10 H SD 3-34 L 45,260
Sun 10/17 A KC 23-7 W 26,941
Sun 10/24 H DEN 31-13 W 45,046
Sun 10/31 H HOU 17-19 L 44,267
Sun 11/7 A BOS 23-7 W 24,415
Sun 11/14 A OAK 17-14 W 19,352
Thu 11/25 A SD 20-20 T 27,473
Sun 12/5 A HOU 29-18 W 23,087
Sun 12/12 H KC 34-25 W 40,298
Sun 12/19 A NY 12-14 L 55,427

LEAGUE CHAMPIONSHIP
Sun 12/26 A SD 23-0 W 30,361

DENVER BRONCOS
Sat 9/11 A SD 31-34 L 27,022
Sun 9/19 H BUF 15-30 L 30,682
Fri 9/24 A BOS 27-10 W 26,782
Sun 10/3 H NY 16-13 W 34,988
Sun 10/10 H KC 23-31 L 31,001
Sun 10/17 H HOU 28-17 W 32,492
Sun 10/24 A BUF 13-31 L 45,046
Sun 10/31 A NY 10-45 L 53,717
Sun 11/7 H SD 21-35 L 33,073
Sun 11/14 A HOU 31-21 W 28,126
Sun 11/21 H OAK 20-28 L 30,369
Sun 12/5 A OAK 13-24 L 19,023
Sun 12/12 H BOS 20-28 L 27,207
Sun 12/19 A KC 35-45 L 14,421

HOUSTON OILERS
Sun 9/12 H NY 27-21 W 52,680
Sun 9/19 H BOS 31-10 W 32,445
Sun 9/26 A OAK 17-21 L 18,116
Sun 10/3 A SD 14-31 L 28,190
Sun 10/17 A DEN 17-28 L 32,492
Sun 10/24 H KC 38-36 W 34,670
Sun 10/31 A BUF 19-17 W 44,267
Sun 11/7 H OAK 21-33 L 35,729
Sun 11/14 H DEN 21-31 L 28,126
Sun 11/21 A NY 14-41 L 52,888
Sun 11/28 A KC 21-52 L 16,459
Sun 12/5 H BUF 18-29 L 23,087
Sun 12/12 H SD 26-37 L 24,120
Sat 12/18 A BOS 14-42 L 14,508

KANSAS CITY CHIEFS
Sun 9/12 A OAK 10-37 L 18,659
Sat 9/18 A NY 14-10 W 53,658
Sun 9/26 A SD 10-10 T 28,126
Sun 10/3 H BOS 27-17 W 26,773
Sun 10/10 A DEN 31-23 W 31,001
Sun 10/17 H BUF 7-23 L 26,941
Sun 10/24 A HOU 36-38 L 34,670
Sun 10/31 H OAK 14-7 W 18,354
Sun 11/7 H NY 10-13 L 25,523
Sun 11/14 H SD 31-7 W 21,968
Sun 11/21 A BOS 10-10 T 13,056
Sun 11/28 H HOU 52-21 W 16,459
Sun 12/12 A BUF 25-34 L 40,298
Sun 12/19 H DEN 45-35 W 14,421

NEW YORK JETS
Sun 9/12 A HOU 21-27 L 52,680
Sat 9/18 H KC 10-14 L 53,658
Sun 9/26 A BUF 21-33 L 45,056
Sun 10/3 A DEN 13-16 L 34,988
Sat 10/16 H OAK 24-24 T 53,122
Sun 10/23 H SD 9-34 L 59,001
Sun 10/31 H DEN 45-10 W 53,717
Sun 11/7 A KC 13-10 W 25,523
Sun 11/14 A BOS 30-20 W 18,589
Sun 11/21 H HOU 41-14 W 52,888
Sun 11/28 H BOS 23-27 L 56,511
Sat 12/4 A SD 7-38 L 32,169
Sun 12/12 A OAK 14-24 L 19,013
Sun 12/19 H BUF 14-12 W 55,427

OAKLAND RAIDERS
Sun 9/12 H KC 37-10 W 18,659
Sun 9/19 H SD 6-17 L 21,406
Sun 9/26 H HOU 21-17 W 18,116
Sun 10/3 A BUF 12-17 L 41,246
Fri 10/8 A BOS 24-10 W 24,824
Sat 10/16 A NY 24-24 T 53,122
Sun 10/24 H BOS 30-21 W 20,858
Sun 10/31 A KC 7-14 L 18,354
Sun 11/7 A HOU 33-21 W 35,729
Sun 11/14 H BUF 14-17 L 19,352
Sun 11/21 A DEN 28-20 W 30,369
Sun 12/5 H DEN 24-13 W 19,023
Sun 12/12 H NY 24-14 W 19,013
Sun 12/19 A SD 14-24 L 26,056

SAN DIEGO CHARGERS
Sat 9/11 H DEN 34-31 W 27,022
Sun 9/19 A OAK 17-6 W 21,406
Sun 9/26 H KC 10-10 T 28,126
Sun 10/3 H HOU 31-14 W 28,190
Sun 10/10 A BUF 34-3 W 45,260
Sun 10/17 A BOS 13-13 T 20,924
Sat 10/23 A NY 34-9 W 59,001
Sun 10/31 H BOS 6-22 L 33,366
Sun 11/7 A DEN 35-21 W 33,073
Sun 11/14 A KC 7-31 L 21,968
Thu 11/25 H BUF 20-20 T 27,473
Sat 12/4 H NY 38-7 W 32,169
Sun 12/12 A HOU 37-26 W 24,120
Sun 12/19 H OAK 24-14 W 26,056

LEAGUE CHAMPIONSHIP
Sun 12/26 H BUF 0-23 L 30,361

1965 NFL
BALTIMORE COLTS
Sun 9/19 H MIN 35-16 W 56,562
Sun 9/26 A GB 17-20 L 48,130
Sun 10/3 H SF 27-24 W 58,609
Sun 10/10 H DET 31-7 W 60,238
Sun 10/17 A WAS 38-7 W 50,405
Sun 10/24 H LA 35-20 W 60,238
Sun 10/31 A SF 34-28 W 45,827
Sun 11/7 A CHI 26-21 W 45,656
Sun 11/14 A MIN 41-21 W 47,426
Sun 11/21 H PHI 34-24 W 60,238
Thu 11/25 A DET 24-24 T 55,036
Sun 12/5 H CHI 0-13 L 60,238
Sun 12/12 H GB 27-42 L 60,238
Sat 12/18 A LA 20-17 W 46,636

WESTERN CONFERENCE PLAYOFF
Sun 12/26 A GB *10-13 L 50,484

CHICAGO BEARS
Sun 9/19 A SF 24-52 L 33,211
Sat 9/25 A LA 28-30 L 36,359
Sun 10/3 A GB 14-23 L 50,852
Sun 10/10 H LA 31-6 W 45,760
Sun 10/17 A MIN 45-37 W 47,426
Sun 10/24 H DET 38-10 W 45,658
Sun 10/31 H GB 31-10 W 45,664
Sun 11/7 H BAL 21-26 L 45,656
Sun 11/14 H STL 34-13 W 45,663
Sun 11/21 A DET 17-10 W 51,499
Sun 11/28 A NYG 35-14 W 62,933
Sun 12/5 A BAL 13-0 W 60,238
Sun 12/12 H SF 61-20 W 46,278

Sun 12/19 H MIN 17-24 L 46,604

CLEVELAND BROWNS
Sun 9/19 A WAS 17-7 W 48,208
Sun 9/26 H STL 13-49 L 80,161
Sun 10/3 H PHI 35-17 W 60,759
Sat 10/9 H PIT 24-19 W 80,187
Sun 10/17 H DAL 23-17 W 80,432
Sun 10/24 A NYG 38-14 W 62,864
Sun 10/31 H MIN 17-27 L 83,505
Sun 11/7 H PHI 38-34 W 72,807
Sun 11/14 A NYG 34-21 W 82,426
Sun 11/21 A DAL 24-17 W 76,251
Sun 11/28 A PIT 42-21 W 42,757
Sun 12/5 H WAS 24-16 W 77,765
Sun 12/12 A LA 7-42 L 49,048
Sun 12/19 A STL 27-24 W 29,348

LEAGUE CHAMPIONSHIP
Sun 1/2 A GB 12-23 L 50,777

DALLAS COWBOYS
Sun 9/19 H NYG 31-2 W 59,366
Sun 9/26 H WAS 27-7 W 61,577
Mon 10/4 A STL 13-20 L 32,034
Sun 10/10 H PHI 24-35 L 56,249
Sun 10/17 A CLE 17-23 L 80,432
Sun 10/24 A GB 3-13 L 48,311
Sun 10/31 A PIT 13-22 L 37,804
Sun 11/7 H SF 39-31 W 39,677
Sun 11/14 H PIT 24-17 W 57,293
Sun 11/21 H CLE 17-24 L 76,251
Sun 11/28 A WAS 31-34 L 50,205
Sun 12/5 H PHI 21-19 W 54,714
Sat 12/11 H STL 27-13 W 38,499
Sun 12/19 A NYG 38-20 W 62,871

DETROIT LIONS
Sun 9/19 H LA 20-0 W 46,941
Sun 9/26 A MIN 31-29 W 46,826
Sun 10/3 H WAS 14-10 W 52,627
Sun 10/10 A BAL 7-31 L 60,238
Sun 10/17 A GB 21-31 L 56,712
Sun 10/24 A CHI 10-38 L 45,658
Sun 10/31 A LA 31-7 W 35,187
Sun 11/7 A GB 12-7 W 50,852
Sun 11/14 H SF 21-27 L 54,534
Sun 11/21 H CHI 10-17 L 51,499
Thu 11/25 H BAL 24-24 T 55,036
Sun 12/5 A SF 14-17 L 38,463
Sun 12/12 H MIN 7-29 L 45,420
Sun 12/19 A PHI 35-28 W 56,718

GREEN BAY PACKERS
Sun 9/19 A PIT 41-9 W 38,383
Sun 9/26 H BAL 20-17 W 48,130
Sun 10/3 H CHI 23-14 W 50,852
Sun 10/10 H SF 27-10 W 50,852
Sun 10/17 A DET 31-21 W 56,712
Sun 10/24 H DAL 13-3 W 48,311
Sun 10/31 A CHI 10-31 L 45,664
Sun 11/7 H DET 7-12 L 50,852
Sun 11/14 H LA 6-3 W 48,485
Sun 11/21 A MIN 38-13 W 47,426
Sun 11/28 A LA 10-21 L 39,733
Sun 12/5 H MIN 24-19 W 50,852
Sun 12/12 A BAL 42-27 W 60,238
Sun 12/19 A SF 24-24 T 45,710

WESTERN CONFERENCE PLAYOFF
Sun 12/26 H BAL *13-10 W 50,484

LEAGUE CHAMPIONSHIP
Sun 1/2 H CLE 23-12 W 50,777

LOS ANGELES RAMS
Sun 9/19 A DET 0-20 L 46,941
Sat 9/25 H CHI 30-28 W 36,359
Sun 10/3 H MIN 35-38 L 36,755
Sun 10/10 A CHI 6-31 L 45,760
Sun 10/17 H SF 21-45 L 38,615
Sun 10/24 A BAL 20-35 L 60,238
Sun 10/31 H DET 7-31 L 35,187
Sun 11/7 A MIN 13-24 L 47,426
Sun 11/14 H GB 3-6 L 48,485
Sun 11/21 H SF 27-30 L 39,253
Sun 11/28 H GB 21-10 W 39,733
Sun 12/5 A STL 27-3 W 27,943
Sun 12/12 H CLE 42-7 W 49,048
Sat 12/18 H BAL 17-20 L 46,636

MINNESOTA VIKINGS
Sun 9/19 A BAL 16-35 L 56,562
Sun 9/26 H DET 29-31 L 46,826
Sun 10/3 A LA 38-35 W 36,755
Sat 10/9 H NYG 40-14 W 44,283
Sun 10/17 H CHI 37-45 L 47,426
Sun 10/24 A SF 42-41 W 42,680
Sun 10/31 A CLE 27-17 W 83,505
Sun 11/7 H LA 24-13 W 47,426
Sun 11/14 H BAL 21-41 L 47,426
Sun 11/21 H GB 13-38 L 47,426
Sun 11/28 A SF 24-45 L 40,306
Sun 12/5 A GB 19-24 L 50,852
Sun 12/12 A DET 29-7 W 45,420
Sun 12/19 A CHI 24-17 W 46,604

NEW YORK GIANTS
Sun 9/19 A DAL 2-31 L 59,366
Sun 9/26 A PHI 16-14 W 57,154
Sun 10/3 A PIT 23-13 W 31,871
Sat 10/9 A MIN 14-40 L 44,283
Sun 10/17 H PHI 35-27 W 62,815
Sun 10/24 H CLE 14-38 L 62,864
Sun 10/31 H STL 14-10 W 62,807
Sun 11/7 H WAS 7-23 L 62,788
Sun 11/14 A CLE 21-34 L 82,426
Sun 11/21 A STL 28-15 W 31,704
Sun 11/28 H CHI 14-35 L 62,933
Sun 12/5 H PIT 35-10 W 62,735
Sun 12/12 A WAS 27-10 W 50,373
Sun 12/19 H DAL 20-38 L 62,871

PHILADELPHIA EAGLES
Sun 9/19 H STL 34-27 W 54,260
Sun 9/26 A NYG 14-16 L 57,154
Sun 10/3 H CLE 17-35 L 60,759
Sun 10/10 A DAL 35-24 W 56,249
Sun 10/17 A NYG 27-35 L 62,815
Sun 10/24 H PIT 14-20 L 56,515
Sun 10/31 A WAS 21-23 L 50,301
Sun 11/7 A CLE 34-38 L 72,807
Sun 11/14 H WAS 21-14 W 60,444
Sun 11/21 A BAL 24-34 L 60,238
Sun 11/28 A STL 28-24 W 28,706
Sun 12/5 H DAL 19-21 L 54,714
Sun 12/12 H PIT 47-13 W 22,002
Sun 12/19 H DET 28-35 L 56,718

PITTSBURGH STEELERS
Sun 9/19 H GB 9-41 L 38,383
Sun 9/26 A SF 17-27 L 30,140
Sun 10/3 H NYG 13-23 L 31,871
Sat 10/9 A CLE 19-24 L 80,187
Sun 10/17 H STL 7-20 L 31,085
Sun 10/24 A PHI 20-14 W 56,515
Sun 10/31 H DAL 22-13 W 37,804
Sun 11/7 A STL 17-21 L 31,899
Sun 11/14 A DAL 17-24 L 57,293
Sun 11/21 H WAS 3-31 L 25,052
Sun 11/28 H CLE 21-42 L 42,757
Sun 12/5 A NYG 10-35 L 62,735
Sun 12/12 H PHI 13-47 L 22,002

Sun 12/19 A WAS 14-35 L 49,806

ST. LOUIS CARDINALS
Sun 9/19 A PHI 27-34 L 54,260
Sun 9/26 A CLE 49-13 W 80,161
Mon 10/4 H DAL 20-13 W 32,034
Sun 10/10 A WAS 37-16 W 50,205
Sun 10/17 A PIT 20-7 W 31,085
Sun 10/24 H WAS 20-24 L 32,228
Sun 10/31 A NYG 10-14 L 62,807
Sun 11/7 H PIT 21-17 W 31,899
Sun 11/14 A CHI 13-34 L 45,663
Sun 11/21 H NYG 15-28 L 31,704
Sun 11/28 H PHI 24-28 L 28,706
Sun 12/5 H LA 3-27 L 27,943
Sat 12/11 A DAL 13-27 L 38,499
Sun 12/19 H CLE 24-27 L 29,348

SAN FRANCISCO 49ERS
Sun 9/19 H CHI 52-24 W 33,211
Sun 9/26 H PIT 27-17 W 30,140
Sun 10/3 A BAL 24-27 L 58,609
Sun 10/10 A GB 10-27 L 50,852
Sun 10/17 A LA 45-21 W 38,615
Sun 10/24 H MIN 41-42 L 42,680
Sun 10/31 H BAL 28-34 L 45,827
Sun 11/7 A DAL 31-39 L 39,677
Sun 11/14 A DET 27-21 W 54,534
Sun 11/21 H LA 30-27 W 39,253
Sun 11/28 A MIN 45-24 W 40,306
Sun 12/5 H DET 17-14 W 38,463
Sun 12/12 A CHI 20-61 L 46,278
Sun 12/19 H GB 24-24 T 45,710

WASHINGTON REDSKINS
Sun 9/19 H CLE 7-17 L 48,208
Sun 9/26 A DAL 7-27 L 61,577
Sun 10/3 A DET 10-14 L 52,627
Sun 10/10 H STL 16-37 L 50,205
Sun 10/17 H BAL 7-38 L 50,405
Sun 10/24 A STL 24-20 W 32,228
Sun 10/31 H PHI 23-21 W 50,301
Sun 11/7 A NYG 23-7 W 62,788
Sun 11/14 A PHI 14-21 L 60,444
Sun 11/21 A PIT 31-3 W 25,052
Sun 11/28 H DAL 34-31 W 50,205
Sun 12/5 A CLE 16-24 L 77,765
Sun 12/12 H NYG 10-27 L 50,373
Sun 12/19 H PIT 35-14 W 49,806

1966 AFL
BOSTON PATRIOTS
Sat 9/10 A SD 0-24 L 29,539
Sun 9/18 A DEN 24-10 W 25,337
Sun 9/25 H KC 24-43 L 22,641
Sun 10/2 A NY 24-24 T 27,255
Sat 10/8 A BUF 20-10 W 45,542
Sun 10/23 H SD 35-17 W 32,371
Sun 10/30 H OAK 24-21 W 26,941
Sun 11/6 H DEN 10-17 L 18,154
Sun 11/13 A HOU 27-21 W 23,426
Sun 11/20 A KC 27-27 T 41,475
Sun 11/27 A MIA 20-14 W 22,754
Sun 12/4 H BUF 14-3 W 39,350
Sun 12/11 A HOU 38-14 W 17,100
Sat 12/17 A NY 28-38 L 58,921

BUFFALO BILLS
Sun 9/4 A SD 7-27 L 27,572
Sun 9/11 H KC 20-42 L 42,023
Sun 9/18 H MIA 58-24 W 37,546
Sun 9/25 H HOU 27-20 W 42,526
Sun 10/2 A KC 29-14 W 43,885
Sat 10/8 H BOS 10-20 L 45,542
Sun 10/16 H SD 17-17 T 45,169

Sun 10/30 A NY 33-23 W 61,552
Sun 11/6 A MIA 29-0 W 37,177
Sun 11/13 H NY 14-3 W 45,738
Sun 11/20 A HOU 42-20 W 27,312
Thu 11/24 A OAK 31-10 W 36,781
Sun 12/4 A BOS 3-14 L 39,530
Sun 12/18 H DEN 38-21 W 40,583

LEAGUE CHAMPIONSHIP
Sun 1/1 H KC 7-31 L 42,080

DENVER BRONCOS
Sat 9/3 A HOU 7-45 L 30,156
Sun 9/18 H BOS 10-24 L 25,337
Sun 9/25 H NY 7-16 L 29,878
Sun 10/2 H HOU 40-38 W 27,203
Sat 10/8 A KC 10-37 L 33,929
Sun 10/16 A MIA 7-24 L 23,393
Sun 10/23 H KC 10-56 L 23,196
Sun 10/30 A SD 17-24 L 25,819
Sun 11/6 A BOS 17-10 W 18,154
Sun 11/20 H OAK 3-17 L 26,703
Sun 11/27 H SD 20-17 W 24,860
Sun 12/4 H MIA 17-7 W 33,306
Sun 12/11 A OAK 10-28 L 31,765
Sun 12/18 A BUF 21-38 L 40,583

HOUSTON OILERS
Sat 9/3 H DEN 45-7 W 30,156
Sat 9/10 H OAK 31-0 W 31,763
Sun 9/18 A NY 13-52 L 54,681
Sun 9/25 A BUF 20-27 L 42,526
Sun 10/2 A DEN 38-40 L 27,203
Sun 10/16 H NY 24-0 W 30,823
Sun 10/23 H MIA 13-20 L 23,173
Sun 10/30 A KC 23-48 L 31,676
Sun 11/6 A OAK 23-38 L 34,102
Sun 11/13 H BOS 21-27 L 23,426
Sun 11/20 H BUF 20-42 L 27,312
Sun 12/4 H SD 22-28 L 17,569
Sun 12/11 H BOS 14-38 L 17,100
Sun 12/18 A MIA 28-29 L 20,045

KANSAS CITY CHIEFS
Sun 9/11 A BUF 42-20 W 42,023
Sun 9/18 A OAK 32-10 W 50,746
Sun 9/25 A BOS 43-24 W 22,641
Sun 10/2 H BUF 14-29 L 43,885
Sat 10/8 H DEN 37-10 W 33,929
Sun 10/16 H OAK 13-34 L 33,057
Sun 10/23 A DEN 56-10 W 23,196
Sun 10/30 H HOU 48-23 W 31,676
Sun 11/6 H SD 24-14 W 40,986
Sun 11/13 H MIA 34-16 W 34,063
Sun 11/20 H BOS 27-27 T 41,475
Sun 11/27 A NY 32-24 W 60,318
Sun 12/11 A MIA 19-18 W 17,881
Sun 12/18 A SD 27-17 W 28,348

LEAGUE CHAMPIONSHIP
Sun 1/1 A BUF 31-7 W 42,080

AFL-NFL WORLD CHAMPIONSHIP (SUPER BOWL I)
Sun 1/15 N GB 10-35 L 61,946

MIAMI DOLPHINS
Fri 9/2 H OAK 14-23 L 26,767
Fri 9/9 H NY 14-19 L 35,402
Sun 9/18 A BUF 24-58 L 37,546
Sun 10/2 A SD 10-44 L 26,444
Sun 10/9 A OAK 10-21 L 30,787
Sun 10/16 H DEN 24-7 W 23,393
Sun 10/23 A HOU 20-13 W 23,173
Sun 11/6 H BUF 0-29 L 37,177
Sun 11/13 A KC 16-34 L 34,063
Sun 11/20 A NY 13-30 L 58,664
Sun 11/27 H BOS 14-20 L 22,754
Sun 12/4 A DEN 7-17 L 33,306

Sun 12/11 H KC 18-19 L 17,881
Sun 12/18 H HOU 29-28 W 20,045

NEW YORK JETS
Fri 9/9 A MIA 19-14 W 35,402
Sun 9/18 H HOU 52-13 W 54,681
Sun 9/25 A DEN 16-7 W 29,878
Sun 10/2 A BOS 24-24 T 27,255
Sat 10/8 H SD 17-16 W 63,497
Sun 10/16 A HOU 0-24 L 30,823
Sun 10/23 H OAK 21-24 L 58,135
Sun 10/30 H BUF 23-33 L 61,552
Sun 11/13 A BUF 3-14 L 45,738
Sun 11/20 H MIA 30-13 W 58,664
Sun 11/27 H KC 24-32 L 60,318
Sat 12/3 A OAK 28-28 T 31,144
Sun 12/11 A SD 27-42 L 25,712
Sat 12/17 H BOS 38-28 W 58,921

OAKLAND RAIDERS
Fri 9/2 A MIA 23-14 W 26,767
Sat 9/10 A HOU 0-31 L 31,763
Sun 9/18 H KC 10-32 L 50,746
Sun 9/25 H SD 20-29 L 37,183
Sun 10/9 H MIA 21-20 W 30,787
Sun 10/16 A KC 34-13 W 33,057
Sun 10/23 A NY 24-21 W 58,135
Sun 10/30 A BOS 21-24 L 26,941
Sun 11/6 H HOU 38-23 W 34,102
Sun 11/13 A SD 41-19 W 26,230
Sun 11/20 A DEN 17-3 W 26,703
Thu 11/24 H BUF 10-31 L 36,781
Sat 12/3 H NY 28-28 T 31,144
Sun 12/11 H DEN 28-10 W 31,765

SAN DIEGO CHARGERS
Sun 9/4 H BUF 27-7 W 27,572
Sat 9/10 H BOS 24-0 W 29,539
Sun 9/25 A OAK 29-20 W 37,183
Sun 10/2 H MIA 44-10 W 26,444
Sat 10/8 A NY 16-17 L 63,497
Sun 10/16 A BUF 17-17 T 45,169
Sun 10/23 A BOS 17-35 L 32,371
Sun 10/30 H DEN 24-17 W 25,819
Sun 11/6 A KC 14-24 L 40,986
Sun 11/13 H OAK 19-41 L 26,230
Sun 11/27 A DEN 17-20 L 24,860
Sun 12/4 H HOU 28-22 W 17,569
Sun 12/11 H NY 42-27 W 25,712
Sun 12/18 H KC 17-27 L 28,348

1966 NFL
ATLANTA FALCONS
Sun 9/11 H LA 14-19 L 54,418
Sun 9/18 A PHI 10-23 L 54,049
Sun 9/25 A DET 10-28 L 47,615
Sun 10/2 H DAL 14-47 L 56,990
Sun 10/9 A WAS 20-33 L 50,116
Sun 10/16 H SF 7-44 L 54,788
Sun 10/23 A GB 3-56 L 48,623
Sun 10/30 H CLE 17-49 L 57,235
Sun 11/13 A BAL 7-19 L 58,850
Sun 11/20 A NYG 27-16 W 62,746
Sun 11/27 A CHI 6-23 L 44,777
Sun 12/4 A MIN 20-13 W 37,117
Sun 12/11 A STL 16-10 W 57,169
Sun 12/18 H PIT 33-57 L 56,229

BALTIMORE COLTS
Sat 9/10 A GB 3-24 L 48,650
Sun 9/18 A MIN 38-23 W 47,426
Sun 9/25 A SF 36-14 W 56,715
Sun 10/9 A CHI 17-27 L 47,452
Sun 10/16 H DET 45-14 W 60,238
Sun 10/23 A MIN 20-17 W 60,238

Sun 10/30 A LA 17-3 W 57,898
Sun 11/6 A WAS 37-10 W 60,238
Sun 11/13 A ATL 19-7 W 58,850
Sun 11/20 A DET 14-20 L 52,383
Sun 11/27 H LA 7-23 W 60,238
Sun 12/4 H CHI 21-16 W 60,238
Sat 12/10 H GB 10-14 L 60,238
Sun 12/18 A SF 30-14 W 40,005

CHICAGO BEARS
Sun 9/11 A DET 3-14 L 52,225
Fri 9/16 A LA 17-31 L 58,916
Sun 10/2 A MIN 13-10 W 47,426
Sun 10/9 H BAL 27-17 W 47,452
Sun 10/16 H GB 0-17 L 48,573
Sun 10/23 H LA 17-10 W 47,475
Mon 10/31 A STL 17-24 L 49,516
Sun 11/6 H DET 10-10 T 47,041
Sun 11/13 H SF 30-30 T 47,078
Sun 11/20 A GB 6-13 L 50,861
Sun 11/27 H ATL 23-6 W 44,777
Sun 12/4 H BAL 16-21 L 60,238
Sun 12/11 A SF 14-41 L 37,170
Sun 12/18 H MIN 41-28 W 45,191

CLEVELAND BROWNS
Sun 9/11 A WAS 38-14 W 48,643
Sun 9/18 A GB 20-21 L 83,943
Sun 9/25 H STL 28-34 L 74,814
Sun 10/2 A NYG 28-7 W 62,916
Sat 10/8 H PIT 41-10 W 82,687
Sun 10/23 H DAL 30-21 W 84,721
Sun 10/30 A ATL 49-17 W 57,235
Sun 11/6 A PIT 6-16 L 39,690
Sun 11/13 H PHI 27-7 W 77,968
Sun 11/20 H WAS 14-3 W 78,466
Thu 11/24 A DAL 14-26 L 80,259
Sun 12/4 H NYG 49-40 W 61,651
Sun 12/11 A PHI 21-33 L 58,074
Sat 12/17 A STL 38-10 W 47,721

DALLAS COWBOYS
Sun 9/18 H NYG 52-7 W 60,010
Sun 9/25 H MIN 28-17 W 64,116
Sun 10/2 A ATL 47-14 W 56,990
Sun 10/9 H PHI 56-7 W 69,372
Sun 10/16 A STL 10-10 T 50,673
Sun 10/23 A CLE 21-30 L 84,721
Sun 10/30 H PIT 52-21 W 58,453
Sun 11/6 A PHI 23-24 L 60,658
Sun 11/13 A WAS 31-30 W 50,927
Sun 11/20 A PIT 20-7 W 42,185
Thu 11/24 H CLE 26-14 W 80,259
Sun 12/4 H STL 31-17 W 76,965
Sun 12/11 H WAS 31-34 L 64,198
Sun 12/18 A NYG 17-7 W 62,735

LEAGUE CHAMPIONSHIP
Sun 1/1 H GB 27-34 L 74,152

DETROIT LIONS
Sun 9/11 H CHI 14-3 W 52,225
Sun 9/18 A PIT 3-17 L 35,473
Sun 9/25 H ATL 28-10 W 47,615
Sun 10/2 A GB 14-23 L 50,861
Sun 10/9 H LA 7-14 L 52,793
Sun 10/16 A BAL 14-45 L 60,238
Sun 10/23 A SF 24-27 L 36,745
Sun 10/30 H GB 7-31 L 56,954
Sun 11/6 A CHI 10-10 T 47,041
Sun 11/13 A MIN 32-31 W 43,939
Sun 11/20 H BAL 20-14 W 52,383
Thu 11/24 H SF 14-41 L 53,189
Sun 12/4 A LA 3-23 L 40,039
Sun 12/11 H MIN 16-28 L 43,023

GREEN BAY PACKERS

Sat	9/10	H	BAL	24-3	W	48,650
Sun	9/18	A	CLE	21-20	W	83,943
Sun	9/25	H	LA	24-13	W	50,861
Sun	10/2	H	DET	23-14	W	50,861
Sun	10/9	A	SF	20-21	L	39,290
Sun	10/16	A	CHI	17-0	W	48,573
Sun	10/23	H	ATL	56-3	W	48,623
Sun	10/30	A	DET	31-7	W	56,954
Sun	11/6	H	MIN	17-20	L	50,861
Sun	11/20	H	CHI	13-6	W	50,861
Sun	11/27	A	MIN	28-16	W	47,426
Sun	12/4	H	SF	20-7	W	48,725
Sat	12/10	A	BAL	14-10	W	60,238
Sun	12/18	A	LA	27-23	W	72,416

League Championship

Sun	1/1	A	DAL	34-27	W	74,152

AFL-NFL World Championship (Super Bowl I)

Sun	1/15	N	KC	35-10	W	61,946

LOS ANGELES RAMS

Sun	9/11	A	ATL	19-14	W	54,418
Fri	9/16	H	CHI	31-17	W	58,916
Sun	9/25	A	GB	13-24	L	50,861
Fri	9/30	H	SF	34-3	W	45,642
Sun	10/9	A	DET	14-7	W	52,793
Sun	10/16	A	MIN	7-35	L	47,426
Sun	10/23	A	CHI	10-17	L	47,475
Sun	10/30	H	BAL	3-17	L	57,898
Sun	11/6	A	SF	13-21	L	35,372
Sun	11/13	H	NYG	55-14	W	34,746
Sun	11/20	H	MIN	21-6	W	38,775
Sun	11/27	A	BAL	23-7	W	60,238
Sun	12/4	H	DET	23-3	W	40,039
Sun	12/18	H	GB	23-27	L	72,416

MINNESOTA VIKINGS

Sun	9/11	A	SF	20-20	T	29,312
Sun	9/18	H	BAL	23-38	L	47,426
Sun	9/25	A	DAL	17-28	L	64,116
Sun	10/2	H	CHI	10-13	L	47,426
Sun	10/16	H	LA	35-7	W	47,426
Sun	10/23	A	BAL	17-20	L	60,238
Sun	10/30	H	SF	28-3	W	45,077
Sun	11/6	A	GB	20-17	W	50,861
Sun	11/13	H	DET	31-32	L	43,939
Sun	11/20	A	LA	6-21	L	38,775
Sun	11/27	H	GB	16-28	L	47,426
Sun	12/4	H	ATL	13-20	L	37,117
Sun	12/11	A	DET	28-16	W	43,023
Sun	12/18	A	CHI	28-41	L	45,191

NEW YORK GIANTS

Sun	9/11	A	PIT	34-34	T	37,693
Sun	9/18	A	DAL	7-52	L	60,010
Sun	9/25	A	PHI	17-35	L	60,177
Sun	10/2	H	CLE	7-28	L	62,916
Sun	10/9	A	STL	19-24	L	43,893
Sun	10/16	H	WAS	13-10	W	62,865
Sun	10/23	H	PHI	3-31	L	63,018
Sun	11/6	H	STL	17-20	L	62,967
Sun	11/13	A	LA	14-55	L	34,746
Sun	11/20	H	ATL	16-27	L	62,746
Sun	11/27	A	WAS	41-72	L	50,439
Sun	12/4	A	CLE	40-49	L	61,651
Sun	12/11	H	PIT	28-47	L	62,658
Sun	12/18	H	DAL	7-17	L	62,735

PHILADELPHIA EAGLES

Sun	9/11	A	STL	13-16	L	39,066
Sun	9/18	H	ATL	23-10	W	54,049
Sun	9/25	H	NYG	35-17	W	60,177
Sun	10/2	H	STL	10-41	L	59,305
Sun	10/9	A	DAL	7-56	L	69,372
Sun	10/16	A	PIT	31-14	W	28,233
Sun	10/23	A	NYG	31-3	W	63,018
Sun	10/30	H	WAS	13-27	L	60,658
Sun	11/6	H	DAL	24-23	W	60,658
Sun	11/13	A	CLE	7-27	L	77,968
Sun	11/20	A	SF	35-34	W	31,993
Sun	12/4	H	PIT	27-23	W	54,275
Sun	12/11	H	CLE	33-21	W	58,074
Sun	12/18	A	WAS	37-28	W	50,405

PITTSBURGH STEELERS

Sun	9/11	H	NYG	34-34	T	37,693
Sun	9/18	H	DET	17-3	W	35,473
Sun	9/25	H	WAS	27-33	L	37,505
Sun	10/2	A	WAS	10-24	L	47,360
Sat	10/8	A	CLE	10-41	L	82,687
Sun	10/16	H	PHI	14-31	L	28,233
Sun	10/30	A	DAL	21-52	L	58,453
Sun	11/6	H	CLE	16-6	W	39,690
Sun	11/13	H	STL	30-9	W	28,552
Sun	11/20	H	DAL	7-20	L	42,185
Sun	11/27	A	STL	3-6	L	46,099
Sun	12/4	A	PHI	23-27	L	54,275
Sun	12/11	A	NYG	47-28	W	62,658
Sun	12/18	A	ATL	57-33	W	56,229

ST. LOUIS CARDINALS

Sun	9/11	H	PHI	16-13	W	39,066
Sun	9/18	H	WAS	23-7	W	40,198
Sun	9/25	A	CLE	34-28	W	74,814
Sun	10/2	A	PHI	41-10	W	59,305
Sun	10/9	H	NYG	24-19	W	43,893
Sun	10/16	H	DAL	10-10	T	50,673
Sun	10/23	A	WAS	20-26	L	50,154
Mon	10/31	H	CHI	24-17	W	49,516
Sun	11/6	A	NYG	20-17	W	62,967
Sun	11/13	A	PIT	9-30	L	28,552
Sun	11/27	H	PIT	6-3	W	46,099
Sun	12/4	A	DAL	17-31	L	76,965
Sun	12/11	A	ATL	10-16	L	57,169
Sat	12/17	H	CLE	10-38	L	47,721

SAN FRANCISCO 49ERS

Sun	9/11	H	MIN	20-20	T	29,312
Sun	9/25	A	BAL	14-36	L	56,715
Fri	9/30	A	LA	3-34	L	45,642
Sun	10/9	H	GB	21-20	W	39,290
Sun	10/16	A	ATL	44-7	W	54,788
Sun	10/23	H	DET	27-24	W	36,745
Sun	10/30	A	MIN	3-28	L	45,077
Sun	11/6	H	LA	21-13	W	35,372
Sun	11/13	A	CHI	30-30	T	47,078
Sun	11/20	H	PHI	34-35	L	31,993
Thu	11/24	A	DET	41-14	W	53,189
Sun	12/4	A	GB	7-20	L	48,725
Sun	12/11	H	CHI	41-14	W	37,170
Sun	12/18	H	BAL	14-30	L	40,005

WASHINGTON REDSKINS

Sun	9/11	H	CLE	14-38	L	48,643
Sun	9/18	A	STL	7-23	L	40,198
Sun	9/25	A	PIT	33-27	W	37,505
Sun	10/2	H	PIT	24-10	W	47,360
Sun	10/9	H	ATL	33-20	W	50,116
Sun	10/16	A	NYG	10-13	L	62,865
Sun	10/23	H	STL	26-20	W	50,154
Sun	10/30	A	PHI	27-13	W	60,658
Sun	11/6	A	BAL	10-37	L	60,238
Sun	11/13	H	DAL	30-31	L	50,927
Sun	11/20	A	CLE	3-14	L	78,466
Sun	11/27	H	NYG	72-41	W	50,439
Sun	12/11	A	DAL	34-31	W	64,198
Sun	12/18	H	PHI	28-37	L	50,405

1967 AFL

BOSTON PATRIOTS

Sun	9/3	A	DEN	21-26	L	35,488
Sat	9/9	A	SD	14-28	L	39,337
Sun	9/17	A	OAK	7-35	L	26,289
Sun	9/24	A	BUF	23-0	W	45,748
Sat	10/7	A	SD	31-31	T	23,620
Sun	10/15	H	MIA	41-10	W	23,955
Sun	10/22	H	OAK	14-48	L	25,057
Sun	10/29	A	NY	23-30	L	62,784
Sun	11/5	H	HOU	18-7	W	19,422
Sun	11/12	H	KC	10-33	L	23,010
Sun	11/19	H	NY	24-29	L	26,790
Sun	11/26	A	HOU	6-27	L	28,044
Sat	12/9	H	BUF	16-44	L	20,627
Sun	12/17	A	MIA	32-41	L	25,967

BUFFALO BILLS

Sun	9/10	H	NY	20-17	W	45,748
Sun	9/17	H	HOU	3-20	L	41,384
Sun	9/24	H	BOS	0-23	L	45,748
Sun	10/1	H	SD	17-37	L	39,310
Sun	10/8	A	DEN	17-16	W	35,188
Sun	10/15	H	OAK	20-24	L	45,758
Sun	10/29	A	HOU	3-10	L	30,060
Sun	11/5	H	MIA	35-13	W	31,622
Sun	11/12	A	NY	10-20	L	62,671
Sun	11/19	H	DEN	20-21	L	30,891
Sun	11/26	A	MIA	14-17	L	27,050
Sun	12/3	A	KC	13-23	L	41,948
Sat	12/9	A	BOS	44-16	W	20,627
Sun	12/24	A	OAK	21-28	L	30,738

DENVER BRONCOS

Sun	9/3	H	BOS	26-21	W	35,488
Sun	9/10	A	OAK	0-51	L	25,423
Sun	9/17	A	MIA	21-35	L	29,381
Sun	9/24	H	NY	24-38	L	35,565
Sun	10/1	A	HOU	6-10	L	21,798
Sun	10/8	H	BUF	16-17	L	35,188
Sun	10/22	H	SD	21-38	L	34,464
Sun	10/29	A	KC	9-52	L	44,002
Sun	11/5	H	OAK	17-21	L	29,043
Sun	11/12	H	HOU	18-20	L	30,392
Sun	11/19	A	BUF	21-20	W	30,891
Thu	11/23	A	SD	20-24	L	34,586
Sun	12/3	A	NY	33-24	W	61,615
Sun	12/17	H	KC	24-38	L	31,660

HOUSTON OILERS

Sat	9/9	H	KC	20-25	L	28,003
Sun	9/17	A	BUF	20-3	W	41,384
Sun	9/24	A	SD	3-13	L	36,032
Sun	10/1	H	DEN	10-6	W	21,798
Sun	10/15	A	NY	28-28	T	62,729
Sun	10/22	A	KC	24-19	W	46,365
Sun	10/29	H	BUF	10-3	W	30,060
Sun	11/5	A	BOS	7-18	L	19,422
Sun	11/12	A	DEN	20-18	W	30,392
Sun	11/26	H	BOS	27-6	W	28,044
Sun	12/3	H	MIA	17-14	W	20,979
Sun	12/10	H	OAK	7-19	L	36,375
Sat	12/16	H	SD	24-17	W	19,870
Sat	12/23	A	MIA	41-10	W	25,982

League Championship

Sun	12/31	A	OAK	7-40	L	53,330

KANSAS CITY CHIEFS

Sat	9/9	A	HOU	25-20	W	28,003
Sun	9/24	A	MIA	24-0	W	36,272
Sun	10/1	A	OAK	21-23	L	50,268
Sun	10/8	H	MIA	41-0	W	45,291
Sun	10/15	A	SD	31-45	L	45,355
Sun	10/22	H	HOU	19-24	L	46,365
Sun	10/29	H	DEN	52-9	W	44,002
Sun	11/5	H	NY	42-18	W	46,642
Sun	11/12	A	BOS	33-10	W	23,010
Sun	11/19	H	SD	16-17	L	46,738
Thu	11/23	H	OAK	22-44	L	44,020
Sun	12/3	H	BUF	23-13	W	41,948
Sun	12/10	A	NY	21-7	W	62,891
Sun	12/17	A	DEN	38-24	W	31,660

MIAMI DOLPHINS

Sun	9/17	H	DEN	35-21	W	29,381
Sun	9/24	H	KC	0-24	L	36,272
Sun	10/1	A	NY	7-29	L	61,240
Sun	10/8	A	KC	0-41	L	45,291
Sun	10/15	A	BOS	10-41	L	23,955
Sun	10/22	H	NY	14-33	L	30,049
Sun	11/5	A	BUF	13-35	L	31,622
Sun	11/12	A	SD	0-24	L	34,751
Sun	11/19	A	OAK	17-31	L	37,295
Sun	11/26	H	BUF	17-14	W	27,050
Sun	12/3	A	HOU	14-17	L	20,979
Sun	12/10	H	SD	41-24	W	23,007
Sun	12/17	H	BOS	41-32	W	25,967
Sat	12/23	H	HOU	10-41	L	25,982

NEW YORK JETS

Sun	9/10	A	BUF	17-20	L	45,748
Sun	9/24	A	DEN	38-24	W	35,565
Sun	10/1	H	MIA	29-7	W	61,240
Sat	10/7	H	OAK	27-14	W	63,106
Sun	10/15	H	HOU	28-28	T	62,729
Sun	10/22	A	MIA	33-14	W	30,049
Sun	10/29	H	BOS	30-23	W	62,784
Sun	11/5	A	KC	18-42	L	46,642
Sun	11/12	H	BUF	20-10	W	62,671
Sun	11/19	A	BOS	29-24	W	26,790
Sun	12/3	H	DEN	24-33	L	61,615
Sun	12/10	H	KC	7-21	L	62,891
Sun	12/17	A	OAK	29-38	L	53,011
Sun	12/24	A	SD	42-31	W	34,580

OAKLAND RAIDERS

Sun	9/10	H	DEN	51-0	W	25,423
Sun	9/17	H	BOS	35-7	W	26,289
Sun	10/1	H	KC	23-21	W	50,268
Sat	10/7	A	NY	14-27	L	63,106
Sun	10/15	A	BUF	24-20	W	45,758
Sun	10/22	A	BOS	48-14	W	25,057
Sun	10/29	H	SD	51-10	W	53,474
Sun	11/5	A	DEN	21-17	W	29,043
Sun	11/19	H	MIA	31-17	W	37,295
Thu	11/23	A	KC	44-22	W	44,020
Sun	12/3	A	SD	41-21	W	52,661
Sun	12/10	A	HOU	19-7	W	36,375
Sun	12/17	H	NY	38-29	W	53,011
Sun	12/24	H	BUF	28-21	W	30,738

League Championship

Sun	12/31	H	HOU	40-7	W	53,330

Super Bowl II

Sun	1/14	N	GB	14-33	L	75,546

SAN DIEGO CHARGERS

Sat	9/9	H	BOS	28-14	W	39,337
Sun	9/24	H	HOU	13-3	W	36,032
Sun	10/1	A	BUF	37-17	W	39,310
Sat	10/7	H	BOS	31-31	T	23,620
Sun	10/15	H	KC	45-31	W	45,355
Sun	10/22	A	DEN	38-21	W	34,464
Sun	10/29	A	OAK	10-51	L	53,474
Sun	11/12	H	MIA	24-0	W	34,751
Sun	11/19	A	KC	17-16	W	46,738
Thu	11/23	H	DEN	24-20	W	34,586
Sun	12/3	H	OAK	21-41	L	52,661
Sun	12/10	A	MIA	24-41	L	23,007
Sat	12/16	A	HOU	17-24	L	19,870
Sun	12/24	H	NY	31-42	L	34,580

1967 NFL

ATLANTA FALCONS

Sun	9/17	A	BAL	31-38	L	56,715
Sun	9/24	A	SF	7-38	L	30,207
Sun	10/1	A	GB	0-23	L	49,467

Sun	10/8	H	PHI	7-38	L	53,868
Sun	10/15	H	WAS	20-20	T	56,538
Sun	10/22	A	DET	3-24	L	50,601
Sun	10/29	H	MIN	21-20	W	52,859
Sun	11/5	A	DAL	7-37	L	54,751
Sun	11/12	H	BAL	7-49	L	58,850
Sun	11/19	H	LA	3-31	L	56,871
Sun	11/26	A	NO	24-27	L	83,437
Sun	12/3	A	LA	3-20	L	40,395
Sun	12/10	H	SF	28-34	L	51,798
Sun	12/17	H	CHI	14-23	L	54,107

BALTIMORE COLTS

Sun	9/17	H	ATL	38-31	W	56,715
Sun	9/24	A	PHI	38-6	W	60,755
Sun	10/1	H	SF	41-7	W	60,238
Sun	10/8	A	CHI	24-3	W	47,190
Sun	10/15	H	LA	24-24	T	60,238
Sun	10/22	A	MIN	20-20	T	47,693
Sun	10/29	A	WAS	17-13	W	50,574
Sun	11/5	H	GB	13-10	W	60,238
Sun	11/12	A	ATL	49-7	W	58,850
Sun	11/19	H	DET	41-7	W	60,238
Sun	11/26	A	SF	26-9	W	44,815
Sun	12/3	H	DAL	23-17	W	60,238
Sun	12/10	H	NO	30-10	W	60,238
Sun	12/17	A	LA	10-34	L	77,277

CHICAGO BEARS

Sun	9/17	A	PIT	13-41	L	53,365
Sun	9/24	A	GB	10-13	L	50,861
Sun	10/1	A	MIN	17-7	W	44,868
Sun	10/8	H	BAL	3-24	L	47,190
Sun	10/15	H	DET	14-3	W	46,024
Sun	10/22	A	CLE	0-24	L	83,183
Sun	10/29	H	LA	17-28	L	46,073
Sun	11/5	A	DET	27-13	W	55,606
Sun	11/12	H	NYG	34-7	W	46,223
Sun	11/19	H	STL	30-3	W	47,147
Sun	11/26	H	GB	13-17	L	47,513
Sun	12/3	A	SF	28-14	W	25,613
Sun	12/10	H	MIN	10-10	T	40,110
Sun	12/17	A	ATL	23-14	W	54,107

CLEVELAND BROWNS

Sun	9/17	H	DAL	14-21	L	81,039
Sun	9/24	A	DET	14-31	L	57,383
Sun	10/1	A	NO	42-7	W	77,045
Sat	10/7	H	PIT	21-10	W	82,949
Sun	10/15	H	STL	20-16	W	77,813
Sun	10/22	H	CHI	24-0	W	83,183
Sun	10/29	A	NYG	34-38	L	62,903
Sun	11/5	A	PIT	34-14	W	47,131
Sun	11/12	A	GB	7-55	L	50,074
Sun	11/19	H	MIN	14-10	W	68,431
Sun	11/26	H	WAS	42-37	W	72,798
Sun	12/3	H	NYG	24-14	W	78,594
Sun	12/10	A	STL	20-16	W	47,782
Sun	12/17	A	PHI	24-28	L	60,658

Eastern Conference Championship

Sun	12/24	A	DAL	14-52	L	70,786

DALLAS COWBOYS

Sun	9/17	A	CLE	21-14	W	81,039
Sun	9/24	H	NYG	38-24	W	66,209
Sun	10/1	H	LA	13-35	L	75,229
Sun	10/8	A	WAS	17-14	W	50,566
Sun	10/15	H	NO	14-10	W	64,128
Sun	10/22	A	PIT	24-21	W	39,641
Sun	10/29	A	PHI	14-21	L	60,740
Sun	11/5	H	ATL	37-7	W	54,751
Sun	11/12	A	NO	27-10	W	83,437
Sun	11/19	H	WAS	20-27	L	75,538
Thu	11/23	H	STL	46-21	W	68,787
Sun	12/3	A	BAL	17-23	L	60,238
Sun	12/10	H	PHI	38-17	W	55,834
Sat	12/16	A	SF	16-24	L	27,182

Eastern Conference Championship

Sun	12/24	H	CLE	52-14	W	70,786

League Championship

Sun	12/31	A	GB	17-21	L	50,861

DETROIT LIONS

Sun	9/17	A	GB	17-17	T	50,861
Sun	9/24	H	CLE	31-14	W	57,383
Sun	10/1	A	STL	28-38	L	43,821
Sun	10/8	H	GB	17-27	L	57,877
Sun	10/15	A	CHI	3-14	L	46,024
Sun	10/22	H	ATL	24-3	W	50,601
Sun	10/29	A	SF	45-3	W	37,990
Sun	11/5	H	CHI	13-27	L	55,606
Sun	11/12	A	MIN	10-10	T	40,032
Sun	11/19	A	BAL	7-41	L	60,238
Thu	11/23	H	LA	7-31	L	54,389
Sun	12/3	H	PIT	14-24	L	47,713
Sun	12/10	A	NYG	30-7	W	63,011
Sun	12/17	H	MIN	14-3	W	44,874

GREEN BAY PACKERS

Sun	9/17	H	DET	17-17	T	50,861
Sun	9/24	H	CHI	13-10	W	50,861
Sun	10/1	H	ATL	23-0	W	49,467
Sun	10/8	A	DET	27-17	W	57,877
Sun	10/15	H	MIN	7-10	L	49,601
Sun	10/22	A	NYG	48-21	W	62,585
Mon	10/30	A	STL	31-23	W	49,792
Sun	11/5	A	BAL	10-13	L	60,238
Sun	11/12	H	CLE	55-7	W	50,074
Sun	11/19	H	SF	13-0	W	50,861
Sun	11/26	A	CHI	17-13	W	47,513
Sun	12/3	A	MIN	30-27	W	47,693
Sat	12/9	A	LA	24-27	L	76,637
Sun	12/17	H	PIT	17-24	L	50,861

Western Conference Championship

Sat	12/23	H	LA	28-7	W	49,861

League Championship

Sun	12/31	H	DAL	21-17	W	50,861

Super Bowl II

Sun	1/14	N	OAK	33-14	W	75,546

LOS ANGELES RAMS

Sun	9/17	A	NO	27-13	W	80,879
Fri	9/22	H	MIN	39-3	W	52,255
Sun	10/1	A	DAL	35-13	W	75,229
Sun	10/8	H	SF	24-27	L	60,424
Sun	10/15	A	BAL	24-24	T	60,238
Sun	10/22	H	WAS	28-28	T	55,381
Sun	10/29	A	CHI	28-17	W	46,073
Sun	11/5	A	SF	17-7	W	53,794
Sun	11/12	H	PHI	33-17	W	57,628
Sun	11/19	A	ATL	31-3	W	56,871
Thu	11/23	A	DET	31-7	W	54,389
Sun	12/3	H	ATL	20-3	W	40,395
Sat	12/9	H	GB	27-24	W	76,637
Sun	12/17	H	BAL	34-10	W	77,277

Western Conference Championship

Sat	12/23	A	GB	7-28	L	49,861

MINNESOTA VIKINGS

Sun	9/17	H	SF	21-27	L	39,638
Fri	9/22	A	LA	3-39	L	52,255
Sun	10/1	H	CHI	7-17	L	44,868
Sun	10/8	H	STL	24-34	L	40,017
Sun	10/15	A	GB	10-7	W	49,601
Sun	10/22	H	BAL	20-20	T	47,693
Sun	10/29	A	ATL	20-21	L	52,859
Sun	11/5	H	NYG	27-24	W	44,960
Sun	11/12	H	DET	10-10	T	40,032
Sun	11/19	A	CLE	10-14	L	68,431
Sun	11/26	A	PIT	41-27	W	23,773
Sun	12/3	H	GB	27-30	L	47,693
Sun	12/10	A	CHI	10-10	T	40,110
Sun	12/17	A	DET	3-14	L	44,874

NEW ORLEANS SAINTS

Sun	9/17	H	LA	13-27	L	80,879
Sun	9/24	H	WAS	10-30	L	74,937
Sun	10/1	H	CLE	7-42	L	77,045
Sun	10/8	A	NYG	21-27	L	62,670
Sun	10/15	A	DAL	10-14	L	64,128
Sun	10/22	A	SF	13-27	L	34,285
Sun	10/29	H	PIT	10-14	L	68,911
Sun	11/5	H	PHI	31-24	W	59,596
Sun	11/12	H	DAL	10-27	L	83,437
Sun	11/19	A	PHI	21-48	L	60,751
Sun	11/26	H	ATL	27-24	W	83,437
Sun	12/3	A	STL	20-31	L	41,171
Sun	12/10	A	BAL	10-30	L	60,238
Sun	12/17	A	WAS	30-14	W	50,486

NEW YORK GIANTS

Sun	9/17	A	STL	37-20	W	40,801
Sun	9/24	A	DAL	24-38	L	66,209
Sun	10/1	A	WAS	34-38	L	50,266
Sun	10/8	H	NO	27-21	W	62,670
Sun	10/15	A	PIT	27-24	W	39,782
Sun	10/22	H	GB	21-48	L	62,585
Sun	10/29	H	CLE	38-34	W	62,903
Sun	11/5	A	MIN	24-27	L	44,960
Sun	11/12	A	CHI	7-34	L	46,223
Sun	11/19	H	PIT	28-20	W	62,892
Sun	11/26	H	PHI	44-7	W	63,027
Sun	12/3	A	CLE	14-24	L	78,594
Sun	12/10	H	DET	7-30	L	63,011
Sun	12/17	H	STL	37-14	W	62,955

PHILADELPHIA EAGLES

Sun	9/17	H	WAS	35-24	W	60,709
Sun	9/24	H	BAL	6-38	L	60,755
Sun	10/1	H	PIT	34-24	W	60,335
Sun	10/8	A	ATL	38-7	W	53,868
Sun	10/15	H	SF	27-28	L	60,825
Sun	10/22	A	STL	14-48	L	46,562
Sun	10/29	H	DAL	21-14	W	60,740
Sun	11/5	A	NO	24-31	L	59,596
Sun	11/12	A	LA	17-33	L	57,628
Sun	11/19	H	NO	48-21	W	60,751
Sun	11/26	A	NYG	7-44	L	63,027
Sun	12/3	A	WAS	35-35	T	50,451
Sun	12/10	A	DAL	17-38	L	55,834
Sun	12/17	H	CLE	28-24	W	60,658

PITTSBURGH STEELERS

Sun	9/17	H	CHI	41-13	W	53,365
Sun	9/24	H	STL	14-28	L	45,579
Sun	10/1	A	PHI	24-34	L	60,335
Sat	10/7	A	CLE	10-21	L	82,949
Sun	10/15	H	NYG	24-27	L	39,782
Sun	10/22	H	DAL	21-24	L	39,641
Sun	10/29	A	NO	14-10	W	68,911
Sun	11/5	H	CLE	14-34	L	47,131
Sun	11/12	A	STL	14-14	T	46,994
Sun	11/19	A	NYG	20-28	L	62,892
Sun	11/26	H	MIN	27-41	L	23,773
Sun	12/3	A	DET	24-14	W	47,713
Sun	12/10	H	WAS	10-15	L	22,251
Sun	12/17	A	GB	24-17	W	50,861

ST. LOUIS CARDINALS

Sun	9/17	H	NYG	20-37	L	40,801
Sun	9/24	A	PIT	28-14	W	45,579
Sun	10/1	H	DET	38-28	W	43,821
Sun	10/8	A	MIN	34-24	W	40,017
Sun	10/15	A	CLE	16-20	L	77,813
Sun	10/22	H	PHI	48-14	W	46,562
Mon	10/30	H	GB	23-31	L	49,792
Sun	11/5	A	WAS	27-21	W	50,480
Sun	11/12	H	PIT	14-14	T	46,994
Sun	11/19	A	CHI	3-30	L	47,147
Thu	11/23	A	DAL	21-46	L	68,787
Sun	12/3	H	NO	31-20	W	41,171
Sun	12/10	H	CLE	16-20	L	47,782
Sun	12/17	A	NYG	14-37	L	62,955

SAN FRANCISCO 49ERS

Sun	9/17	A	MIN	27-21	W	39,638
Sun	9/24	H	ATL	38-7	W	30,207
Sun	10/1	A	BAL	7-41	L	60,238
Sun	10/8	A	LA	27-24	W	60,424
Sun	10/15	A	PHI	28-27	W	60,825
Sun	10/22	H	NO	27-13	W	34,285
Sun	10/29	H	DET	3-45	L	37,990
Sun	11/5	H	LA	7-17	L	53,794
Sun	11/12	A	WAS	28-31	L	50,326
Sun	11/19	A	GB	0-13	L	50,861
Sun	11/26	H	BAL	9-26	L	44,815
Sun	12/3	H	CHI	14-28	L	25,613
Sun	12/10	A	ATL	34-28	W	51,798
Sat	12/16	H	DAL	24-16	W	27,182

WASHINGTON REDSKINS

Sun	9/17	A	PHI	24-35	L	60,709
Sun	9/24	A	NO	30-10	W	74,937
Sun	10/1	H	NYG	38-34	W	50,266
Sun	10/8	H	DAL	14-17	L	50,566
Sun	10/15	A	ATL	20-20	T	56,538
Sun	10/22	A	LA	28-28	T	55,381
Sun	10/29	H	BAL	13-17	L	50,574
Sun	11/5	H	STL	21-27	L	50,480
Sun	11/12	H	SF	31-28	W	50,326
Sun	11/19	A	DAL	27-20	W	75,538
Sun	11/26	A	CLE	37-42	L	72,798
Sun	12/3	H	PHI	35-35	T	50,451
Sun	12/10	A	PIT	15-10	W	22,251
Sun	12/17	H	NO	14-30	L	50,486

1968 AFL

BOSTON PATRIOTS

Sun	9/8	A	BUF	16-7	W	38,865
Sun	9/22	N	NY	31-47	L	29,192
Sun	9/29	A	DEN	20-17	W	37,024
Sun	10/6	A	OAK	10-41	L	44,253
Sun	10/13	H	HOU	0-16	L	32,502
Sun	10/20	H	BUF	23-6	W	21,082
Sun	10/27	A	NY	14-48	L	62,351
Sun	11/3	H	DEN	14-35	L	18,304
Sun	11/10	H	SD	17-27	L	19,278
Sun	11/17	A	KC	17-31	L	48,271
Sun	11/24	H	MIA	10-34	L	18,305
Sun	12/1	H	CIN	33-14	W	17,796
Sat	12/7	A	MIA	7-38	L	24,242
Sun	12/15	A	HOU	17-45	L	34,198

BUFFALO BILLS

Sun	9/8	H	BOS	7-16	L	38,865
Sun	9/15	H	OAK	6-48	L	43,056
Sun	9/22	A	CIN	23-34	L	24,405
Sun	9/29	H	NY	37-35	W	38,044
Sat	10/5	H	KC	7-18	L	40,748
Sat	10/12	A	MIA	14-14	T	28,559
Sun	10/20	A	BOS	6-23	L	21,082
Sun	10/27	H	HOU	7-30	L	34,339
Sun	11/3	A	NY	21-25	L	61,452
Sun	11/10	H	MIA	17-21	L	28,759
Sun	11/17	H	SD	6-21	L	27,993
Sun	11/24	A	DEN	32-34	L	35,142
Thu	11/28	A	OAK	10-13	L	39,883
Sat	12/7	A	HOU	6-35	L	34,110

CINCINNATI BENGALS

Fri	9/6	A	SD	13-29	L	33,686
Sun	9/15	H	DEN	24-10	W	25,049
Sun	9/22	H	BUF	34-23	W	24,045
Sun	9/29	H	SD	10-31	L	28,642

Sun	10/6	A	DEN	7-10	L	41,257
Sun	10/13	A	KC	3-13	L	47,096
Sun	10/20	H	MIA	22-24	L	25,936
Sun	10/27	A	OAK	10-31	L	37,083
Sun	11/3	H	HOU	17-27	L	24,012
Sun	11/10	H	KC	9-16	L	25,537
Sun	11/17	A	MIA	38-21	W	31,747
Sun	11/24	H	OAK	0-34	L	27,116
Sun	12/1	A	BOS	14-33	L	17,796
Sun	12/8	A	NY	14-27	L	61,111

DENVER BRONCOS

Sun	9/15	A	CIN	10-24	L	25,049
Sun	9/22	A	KC	2-34	L	45,821
Sun	9/29	H	BOS	17-20	L	37,024
Sun	10/6	H	CIN	10-7	W	41,257
Sun	10/13	A	NY	21-13	W	62,052
Sun	10/20	A	SD	24-55	L	42,953
Sun	10/27	H	MIA	21-14	W	44,115
Sun	11/3	A	BOS	35-14	W	18,304
Sun	11/10	H	OAK	7-43	L	50,002
Sun	11/17	A	HOU	17-38	L	36,075
Sun	11/24	H	BUF	34-32	W	35,142
Sun	12/1	H	SD	23-47	L	35,312
Sun	12/8	A	OAK	27-33	L	47,754
Sat	12/14	H	KC	7-30	L	38,463

HOUSTON OILERS

Mon	9/9	H	KC	21-26	L	45,083
Sat	9/14	A	MIA	24-10	W	40,067
Sat	9/21	A	SD	14-30	L	46,217
Sun	9/29	H	OAK	15-24	L	46,098
Sun	10/6	H	MIA	7-24	L	36,109
Sun	10/13	A	BOS	16-0	W	32,502
Sun	10/20	H	NY	14-20	L	51,710
Sun	10/27	A	BUF	30-7	W	34,339
Sun	11/3	A	CIN	27-17	W	24,012
Sun	11/10	A	NY	7-26	L	60,242
Sun	11/17	H	DEN	38-17	W	36,075
Thu	11/28	A	KC	10-24	L	48,493
Sat	12/7	H	BUF	35-6	W	34,110
Sun	12/15	H	BOS	45-17	W	34,198

KANSAS CITY CHIEFS

Mon	9/9	A	HOU	26-21	W	45,083
Sun	9/15	H	NY	19-20	L	48,871
Sun	9/22	H	DEN	34-2	W	45,821
Sat	9/28	A	MIA	48-3	W	28,501
Sat	10/5	A	BUF	18-7	W	40,748
Sun	10/13	H	CIN	13-3	W	47,096
Sun	10/20	H	OAK	24-10	W	50,015
Sun	10/27	H	SD	27-20	W	50,344
Sun	11/3	A	OAK	21-38	L	53,357
Sun	11/10	A	CIN	16-9	W	25,537
Sun	11/17	H	BOS	31-17	W	48,271
Thu	11/28	H	HOU	24-10	W	48,493
Sun	12/8	A	SD	40-3	W	51,174
Sat	12/14	A	DEN	30-7	W	38,463

Western Division Playoff

Sun	12/22	A	OAK	6-41	L	53,605

MIAMI DOLPHINS

Sat	9/14	H	HOU	10-24	L	40,067
Sat	9/21	H	OAK	21-47	L	30,021
Sat	9/28	H	KC	3-48	L	28,501
Sun	10/6	A	HOU	24-7	W	36,109
Sat	10/12	H	BUF	14-14	T	28,559
Sun	10/20	A	CIN	24-22	W	25,936
Sun	10/27	A	DEN	14-21	L	44,115
Sun	11/3	A	SD	28-34	L	37,284
Sun	11/10	A	BUF	21-17	W	28,759
Sun	11/17	H	CIN	21-38	L	31,747
Sun	11/24	A	BOS	34-10	W	18,305
Sun	12/1	A	NY	17-35	L	61,766
Sat	12/7	H	BOS	38-7	W	24,242
Sun	12/15	H	NY	7-31	L	32,843

NEW YORK JETS

Sun	9/15	A	KC	20-19	W	48,871
Sun	9/22	N	BOS	47-31	W	29,192
Sun	9/29	A	BUF	35-37	L	38,044
Sat	10/5	H	SD	23-20	W	63,786
Sun	10/13	H	DEN	13-21	L	62,052
Sun	10/20	A	HOU	20-14	W	51,710
Sun	10/27	H	BOS	48-14	W	62,351
Sun	11/3	H	BUF	25-21	W	61,452
Sun	11/10	H	HOU	26-7	W	60,242
Sun	11/17	A	OAK	32-43	L	53,318
Sun	11/24	A	SD	37-15	W	51,175
Sun	12/1	H	MIA	35-17	W	61,766
Sun	12/8	H	CIN	27-14	W	61,111
Sun	12/15	A	MIA	31-7	W	32,843

League Championship

Sun	12/29	H	OAK	27-23	W	62,627

Super Bowl III

Sun	1/12	N	BAL	16-7	W	75,377

OAKLAND RAIDERS

Sun	9/15	A	BUF	48-6	W	43,056
Sat	9/21	A	MIA	47-21	W	30,021
Sun	9/29	A	HOU	24-15	W	46,098
Sun	10/6	H	BOS	41-10	W	44,253
Sun	10/13	H	SD	14-23	L	53,257
Sun	10/20	A	KC	10-24	L	50,015
Sun	10/27	H	CIN	31-10	W	37,083
Sun	11/3	H	KC	38-21	W	53,357
Sun	11/10	A	DEN	43-7	W	50,002
Sun	11/17	H	NY	43-32	W	53,318
Sun	11/24	A	CIN	34-0	W	27,116
Thu	11/28	H	BUF	13-10	W	39,883
Sun	12/8	H	DEN	33-27	W	47,754
Sun	12/15	A	SD	34-27	W	40,698

Western Division Playoff

Sun	12/22	H	KC	41-6	W	53,605

League Championship

Sun	12/29	A	NY	23-27	L	62,627

SAN DIEGO CHARGERS

Fri	9/6	H	CIN	29-13	W	33,686
Sat	9/21	H	HOU	30-14	W	46,217
Sun	9/29	A	CIN	31-10	W	28,642
Sat	10/5	A	NY	20-23	L	63,786
Sun	10/13	A	OAK	23-14	W	53,257
Sun	10/20	H	DEN	55-24	W	42,953
Sun	10/27	A	KC	20-27	L	50,344
Sun	11/3	H	MIA	34-28	W	37,284
Sun	11/10	A	BOS	27-17	W	19,278
Sun	11/17	A	BUF	21-6	W	27,993
Sun	11/24	H	NY	15-37	L	51,175
Sun	12/1	A	DEN	47-23	W	35,312
Sun	12/8	H	KC	3-40	L	51,174
Sun	12/15	H	OAK	27-34	L	40,698

1968 NFL

ATLANTA FALCONS

Sat	9/14	A	MIN	7-47	L	45,563
Sun	9/22	H	BAL	20-28	L	50,428
Sun	9/29	A	SF	13-28	L	27,741
Sun	10/6	H	GB	7-38	L	58,850
Sun	10/13	H	NYG	24-21	W	49,962
Sun	10/20	A	LA	14-27	L	54,443
Sun	10/27	A	CLE	7-30	L	67,723
Sun	11/3	H	PIT	21-41	L	47,727
Sun	11/10	H	LA	10-17	L	53,979
Sun	11/17	A	CHI	16-13	W	44,214
Sun	11/24	A	STL	12-17	L	43,246
Sun	12/1	A	BAL	0-44	L	60,238
Sun	12/8	H	DET	7-24	L	49,437
Sun	12/15	H	SF	12-14	L	44,977

BALTIMORE COLTS

Sun	9/15	H	SF	27-10	W	56,864
Sun	9/22	A	ATL	28-20	W	50,428
Sun	9/29	A	PIT	41-7	W	44,480
Sun	10/6	H	CHI	28-7	W	60,228
Sun	10/13	A	SF	42-14	W	32,822
Sun	10/20	H	CLE	20-30	L	60,238
Sun	10/27	H	LA	27-10	W	60,238
Sun	11/3	A	NYG	26-0	W	62,973
Sun	11/10	A	DET	27-10	W	55,170
Sun	11/17	H	STL	27-0	W	60,238
Sun	11/24	H	MIN	21-9	W	60,238
Sun	12/1	H	ATL	44-0	W	60,238
Sat	12/7	A	GB	16-3	W	50,861
Sun	12/15	A	LA	28-24	W	69,397

Western Conference Championship

Sun	12/22	H	MIN	24-14	W	60,238

League Championship

Sun	12/29	A	CLE	34-0	W	80,628

Super Bowl III

Sun	1/12	N	NYJ	7-16	L	75,377

CHICAGO BEARS

Sun	9/15	H	WAS	28-38	L	41,321
Sun	9/22	A	DET	0-42	L	50,688
Sun	9/29	A	MIN	27-17	W	47,644
Sun	10/6	A	BAL	7-28	L	60,228
Sun	10/13	H	DET	10-28	L	46,996
Sun	10/20	A	PHI	29-16	W	60,858
Sun	10/27	H	MIN	26-24	W	46,562
Sun	11/3	A	GB	13-10	W	50,861
Sun	11/10	H	SF	27-19	W	46,978
Sun	11/17	H	ATL	13-16	L	44,214
Sun	11/24	H	DAL	3-34	L	46,667
Sun	12/1	A	NO	23-17	W	78,285
Sun	12/8	A	LA	17-16	W	66,368
Sun	12/15	H	GB	27-28	L	46,435

CLEVELAND BROWNS

Sun	9/15	A	NO	24-10	W	74,215
Sun	9/22	A	DAL	7-28	L	68,733
Sun	9/29	H	LA	6-24	L	82,514
Sat	10/5	H	PIT	31-24	W	81,865
Sun	10/13	H	STL	21-27	L	79,349
Sun	10/20	A	BAL	30-20	W	60,238
Sun	10/27	H	ATL	30-7	W	67,723
Sun	11/3	A	SF	33-21	W	31,359
Sun	11/10	H	NO	35-17	W	71,025
Sun	11/17	A	PIT	45-24	W	41,572
Sun	11/24	H	PHI	47-13	W	62,338
Sun	12/1	H	NYG	45-10	W	83,193
Sun	12/8	A	WAS	24-21	W	50,661
Sat	12/14	A	STL	16-27	L	48,174

Eastern Conference Championship

Sat	12/21	H	DAL	31-20	W	81,497

League Championship

Sun	12/29	H	BAL	0-34	L	80,628

DALLAS COWBOYS

Sun	9/15	H	DET	59-13	W	61,382
Sun	9/22	H	CLE	28-7	W	68,733
Sun	9/29	A	PHI	45-13	W	60,858
Sun	10/6	A	STL	27-10	W	48,296
Sun	10/13	H	PHI	34-14	W	72,083
Sun	10/20	A	MIN	20-7	W	47,644
Mon	10/28	H	GB	17-28	L	74,604
Sun	11/3	A	NO	17-3	W	84,728
Sun	11/10	H	NYG	21-27	L	72,163
Sun	11/17	A	WAS	44-24	W	50,816
Sun	11/24	A	CHI	34-3	W	46,667
Thu	11/28	H	WAS	29-20	W	66,076
Sun	12/8	H	PIT	28-7	W	55,069
Sun	12/15	A	NY	28-10	W	62,617

Eastern Conference Championship

Sat	12/21	A	CLE	20-31	L	81,497

DETROIT LIONS

Sun	9/15	A	DAL	13-59	L	61,382
Sun	9/22	H	CHI	42-0	W	50,688
Sun	9/29	A	GB	23-17	W	50,861
Sun	10/6	A	MIN	10-24	L	44,289
Sun	10/13	A	CHI	28-10	W	46,996
Sun	10/20	H	GB	14-14	T	57,302
Sun	10/27	H	SF	7-14	L	53,555
Sun	11/3	A	LA	7-10	L	77,982
Sun	11/10	H	BAL	10-27	L	55,170
Sun	11/17	H	MIN	6-13	L	48,654
Sun	11/24	H	NO	20-20	T	46,152
Thu	11/28	H	PHI	0-12	L	47,909
Sun	12/8	A	ATL	24-7	W	49,437
Sun	12/15	A	WAS	3-14	L	50,123

GREEN BAY PACKERS

Sun	9/15	H	PHI	30-13	W	50,861
Sun	9/22	H	MIN	13-26	L	49,346
Sun	9/29	H	DET	17-23	L	50,861
Sun	10/6	A	ATL	38-7	W	58,850
Sun	10/13	H	LA	14-16	L	49,646
Sun	10/20	A	DET	14-14	T	57,302
Mon	10/28	A	DAL	28-17	W	74,604
Sun	11/3	H	CHI	10-13	L	50,861
Sun	11/10	A	MIN	10-14	L	47,644
Sun	11/17	H	NO	29-7	W	49,644
Sun	11/24	A	WAS	27-7	W	50,621
Sun	12/1	A	SF	20-27	L	47,218
Sat	12/7	H	BAL	3-16	L	50,861
Sun	12/15	A	CHI	28-27	W	46,435

LOS ANGELES RAMS

Mon	9/16	A	STL	24-13	W	49,757
Sun	9/22	H	PIT	45-10	W	49,647
Sun	9/29	A	CLE	24-6	W	82,514
Sun	10/6	H	SF	24-10	W	69,520
Sun	10/13	A	GB	16-14	W	49,646
Sun	10/20	H	ATL	27-14	W	54,443
Sun	10/27	A	BAL	10-27	L	60,238
Sun	11/3	H	DET	10-7	W	77,982
Sun	11/10	A	ATL	17-10	W	53,979
Sun	11/17	A	SF	20-20	T	41,815
Sun	11/24	H	NYG	24-21	W	68,534
Sun	12/1	A	MIN	31-3	W	47,644
Sun	12/8	H	CHI	16-17	L	66,368
Sun	12/15	H	BAL	24-28	L	69,397

MINNESOTA VIKINGS

Sat	9/14	H	ATL	47-7	W	45,563
Sun	9/22	A	GB	26-13	W	49,346
Sun	9/29	H	CHI	17-27	L	47,644
Sun	10/6	H	DET	24-10	W	44,289
Sun	10/13	A	NO	17-20	L	71,105
Sun	10/20	H	DAL	7-20	L	47,644
Sun	10/27	A	CHI	24-26	L	46,562
Sun	11/3	H	WAS	27-14	W	47,644
Sun	11/10	H	GB	14-10	W	47,644
Sun	11/17	A	DET	13-6	W	48,654
Sun	11/24	A	BAL	9-21	L	60,238
Sun	12/1	H	LA	3-31	L	47,644
Sun	12/8	A	SF	30-20	W	29,049
Sun	12/15	A	PHI	24-17	W	54,530

Western Conference Championship

Sun	12/22	A	BAL	14-24	L	60,238

NEW ORLEANS SAINTS

Sun	9/15	H	CLE	10-24	L	74,215
Sun	9/22	H	WAS	37-17	W	65,941
Sun	9/29	H	STL	20-21	L	79,021
Sun	10/6	A	NYG	21-38	L	62,967
Sun	10/13	H	MIN	20-17	W	71,105
Sun	10/20	A	PIT	16-12	W	32,303
Sun	10/27	A	STL	17-31	L	45,476
Sun	11/3	H	DAL	3-17	L	84,728
Sun	11/10	A	CLE	17-35	L	71,025
Sun	11/17	A	GB	7-29	L	49,644
Sun	11/24	A	DET	20-20	T	46,152

Sun 12/1 H CHI 17-23 L 78,285
Sun 12/8 A PHI 17-29 L 57,128
Sun 12/15 H PIT 24-14 W 66,131

NEW YORK GIANTS
Sun 9/15 A PIT 34-20 W 45,698
Sun 9/22 A PHI 34-25 W 60,858
Sun 9/29 H WAS 48-21 W 62,797
Sun 10/6 H NO 38-21 W 62,967
Sun 10/13 A ATL 21-24 L 49,962
Sun 10/20 H SF 10-26 L 62,958
Sun 10/27 A WAS 13-10 W 50,839
Sun 11/3 A BAL 0-26 L 62,973
Sun 11/10 A DAL 27-21 W 72,163
Sun 11/17 H PHI 7-6 W 62,896
Sun 11/24 A LA 21-24 L 68,534
Sun 12/1 A CLE 10-45 L 83,193
Sun 12/8 H STL 21-28 L 62,709
Sun 12/15 H DAL 10-28 L 62,617

PHILADELPHIA EAGLES
Sun 9/15 A GB 13-30 L 50,861
Sun 9/22 H NYG 25-34 L 60,858
Sun 9/29 A DAL 13-45 L 60,858
Sun 10/6 A WAS 14-17 L 50,816
Sun 10/13 A DAL 14-34 L 72,083
Sun 10/20 H CHI 16-29 L 60,858
Sun 10/27 H PIT 3-6 L 26,908
Sun 11/3 A STL 17-45 L 59,208
Sun 11/10 H WAS 10-16 L 59,133
Sun 11/17 A NYG 6-7 L 62,896
Sun 11/24 A CLE 13-47 L 62,338
Thu 11/28 A DET 12-0 W 47,909
Sun 12/8 H NO 29-17 W 57,128
Sun 12/15 H MIN 17-24 L 54,530

PITTSBURGH STEELERS
Sun 9/15 H NYG 20-34 L 45,698
Sun 9/22 A LA 10-45 L 49,647
Sun 9/29 H BAL 7-41 L 44,480
Sat 10/5 A CLE 24-31 L 81,865
Sun 10/13 A WAS 13-16 L 50,659
Sun 10/20 H NO 12-16 L 32,303
Sun 10/27 H PHI 6-3 W 26,908
Sun 11/3 A ATL 41-21 W 47,727
Sun 11/10 H STL 28-28 T 45,432
Sun 11/17 H CLE 24-45 L 41,572
Sun 11/24 H SF 28-45 L 21,408
Sun 12/1 H STL 10-20 L 22,682
Sun 12/8 A DAL 7-28 L 55,069
Sun 12/15 A NO 14-24 L 66,131

ST. LOUIS CARDINALS
Mon 9/16 H LA 13-24 L 49,757
Sun 9/22 A SF 17-35 L 27,557
Sun 9/29 A NO 21-20 W 79,021
Sun 10/6 H DAL 10-27 L 48,296
Sun 10/13 A CLE 27-21 W 79,349
Sun 10/20 H WAS 41-14 W 46,456
Sun 10/27 A NO 31-17 W 45,476
Sun 11/3 A PHI 45-17 W 59,208
Sun 11/10 H PIT 28-28 T 45,432
Sun 11/17 A BAL 0-27 L 60,238
Sun 11/24 H ATL 17-12 W 43,246
Sun 12/1 A PIT 20-10 W 22,682
Sun 12/8 A NYG 28-21 W 62,709
Sat 12/14 H CLE 27-16 W 48,174

SAN FRANCISCO 49ERS
Sun 9/15 A BAL 10-27 L 56,864
Sun 9/22 H STL 35-17 W 27,557
Sun 9/29 H ATL 28-13 W 27,741
Sun 10/6 A LA 10-24 L 69,520
Sun 10/13 H BAL 14-42 L 32,822
Sun 10/20 A NYG 26-10 W 62,958
Sun 10/27 A DET 14-7 W 53,555
Sun 11/3 H CLE 21-33 L 31,359
Sun 11/10 A CHI 19-27 L 46,978
Sun 11/17 H LA 20-20 T 41,815
Sun 11/24 A PIT 45-28 W 21,408
Sun 12/1 H GB 27-20 W 47,218
Sun 12/8 H MIN 20-30 L 29,049
Sun 12/15 A ATL 14-12 W 44,977

WASHINGTON REDSKINS
Sun 9/15 A CHI 38-28 W 41,321
Sun 9/22 A NO 17-37 L 65,941
Sun 9/29 A NYG 21-48 L 62,797
Sun 10/6 H PHI 17-14 W 50,816
Sun 10/13 H PIT 16-13 W 50,659
Sun 10/20 A STL 14-41 L 46,456
Sun 10/27 H NYG 10-13 L 50,839
Sun 11/3 A MIN 14-27 L 47,644
Sun 11/10 A PHI 16-10 W 59,133
Sun 11/17 H DAL 24-44 L 50,816
Sun 11/24 H GB 7-27 L 50,621
Thu 11/28 A DAL 20-29 L 66,076
Sun 12/8 H CLE 21-24 L 50,661
Sun 12/15 H DET 14-3 W 50,123

1969 AFL
BOSTON PATRIOTS
Sun 9/14 A DEN 7-35 L 43,679
Sun 9/21 H KC 0-31 L 22,002
Sun 9/28 H OAK 23-38 L 19,069
Sun 10/5 H NY 14-23 L 25,584
Sat 10/11 A BUF 16-23 L 46,201
Sun 10/19 H SD 10-13 L 18,346
Sun 10/26 A NY 17-23 L 62,298
Sun 11/2 H HOU 24-0 W 19,006
Sun 11/9 H MIA 16-17 L 19,821
Sun 11/16 H CIN 25-14 W 27,927
Sun 11/23 H BUF 35-21 W 25,584
Sun 11/30 N MIA 38-23 W 32,121
Sun 12/7 A SD 18-28 L 33,146
Sun 12/14 A HOU 23-27 L 39,215

BUFFALO BILLS
Sun 9/14 H NY 19-33 L 46,165
Sun 9/21 H HOU 3-17 L 40,146
Sun 9/28 H DEN 41-28 W 40,302
Sun 10/5 A HOU 14-28 L 46,485
Sat 10/11 H BOS 23-16 W 46,201
Sun 10/19 A OAK 21-50 L 54,418
Sun 10/26 A MIA 6-24 L 39,837
Sun 11/2 H KC 7-29 L 45,844
Sun 11/9 A NY 6-16 L 62,680
Sun 11/16 H MIA 28-3 W 32,868
Sun 11/23 A BOS 21-35 L 25,584
Sun 11/30 H CIN 16-13 W 35,122
Sun 12/7 A KC 19-22 L 47,112
Sun 12/14 A SD 6-45 L 47,582

CINCINNATI BENGALS
Sun 9/14 H MIA 27-21 W 25,335
Sun 9/21 H SD 34-20 W 26,243
Sun 9/28 H KC 24-19 W 27,812
Sat 10/4 A SD 14-21 L 52,748
Sat 10/11 H NY 7-21 L 27,927
Sun 10/19 H DEN 23-30 L 27,920
Sun 10/26 A KC 22-42 L 50,934
Sun 11/2 H OAK 31-17 W 27,927
Sun 11/9 A HOU 31-31 T 45,298
Sun 11/16 H BOS 14-25 L 27,927
Sun 11/23 A NY 7-40 L 62,128
Sun 11/30 A BUF 13-16 L 35,122
Sun 12/7 A OAK 17-37 L 54,427
Sun 12/14 A DEN 16-27 L 42,198

DENVER BRONCOS
Sun 9/14 H BOS 35-7 W 43,679
Sun 9/21 H NY 21-19 W 50,583
Sun 9/28 A BUF 28-41 L 40,302
Sun 10/5 H KC 13-26 L 50,564
Sun 10/12 A OAK 14-24 L 49,511
Sun 10/19 A CIN 30-23 W 27,920
Sun 10/26 A HOU 21-24 L 45,348
Sun 11/2 H SD 13-0 W 45,511
Sun 11/9 A OAK 10-41 L 54,416
Sun 11/16 H HOU 20-20 T 45,002
Sun 11/23 A SD 24-45 L 34,664
Thu 11/27 A KC 17-31 L 48,773
Sun 12/7 A MIA 24-27 L 25,332
Sun 12/14 H CIN 27-16 W 42,198

HOUSTON OILERS
Sun 9/14 A OAK 17-21 L 49,361
Sun 9/21 A BUF 17-3 W 40,146
Sun 9/28 H MIA 22-10 W 41,086
Sun 10/5 H BUF 28-14 W 46,485
Sun 10/12 A KC 0-24 L 45,805
Mon 10/20 A NY 17-26 L 63,841
Sun 10/26 H DEN 24-21 W 45,348
Sun 11/2 H BOS 0-24 L 19,006
Sun 11/9 H CIN 31-31 T 45,298
Sun 11/16 A DEN 20-20 T 45,002
Sun 11/23 A MIA 32-7 W 27,218
Thu 11/27 H SD 17-21 L 40,065
Sat 12/6 H NY 26-34 L 51,923
Sun 12/14 H BOS 27-23 W 39,215

INTER-DIVISIONAL PLAYOFF
Sun 12/21 A OAK 7-56 L 53,539

KANSAS CITY CHIEFS
Sun 9/14 A SD 27-9 W 47,988
Sun 9/21 A BOS 31-0 W 22,002
Sun 9/28 A CIN 19-24 L 27,812
Sun 10/5 A DEN 26-13 W 50,564
Sun 10/12 H HOU 24-0 W 45,805
Sun 10/19 H MIA 17-10 W 49,809
Sun 10/26 A CIN 42-22 W 50,934
Sun 11/2 A BUF 29-7 W 45,844
Sun 11/9 H SD 27-3 W 51,014
Sun 11/16 A NY 34-16 W 63,849
Sun 11/23 H OAK 24-27 L 51,982
Thu 11/27 H DEN 31-17 W 48,773
Sun 12/7 H BUF 22-19 W 47,112
Sat 12/13 A OAK 6-10 L 54,443

INTER-DIVISIONAL PLAYOFF
Sat 12/20 A NY 13-6 W 62,977
LEAGUE CHAMPIONSHIP
Sun 1/4 A OAK 17-7 W 53,564
SUPER BOWL IV
Sun 1/11 N MIN 23-7 W 80,562

MIAMI DOLPHINS
Sun 9/14 A CIN 21-27 L 25,335
Sat 9/20 A OAK 17-20 L 50,277
Sun 9/28 A HOU 10-22 L 41,086
Sat 10/4 H OAK 20-20 T 35,614
Sat 10/11 H SD 14-21 L 34,585
Sun 10/19 A KC 10-17 L 49,809
Sun 10/26 H BUF 24-6 W 39,837
Sun 11/2 H NY 31-34 L 61,761
Sun 11/9 H BOS 17-16 W 19,821
Sun 11/16 A BUF 3-28 L 32,868
Sun 11/23 H HOU 7-32 L 27,218
Sun 11/30 N BOS 23-38 L 32,121
Sun 12/7 H DEN 27-24 W 25,332
Sun 12/14 H NY 9-27 L 48,108

NEW YORK JETS
Sun 9/14 A BUF 33-19 W 46,165
Sun 9/21 A DEN 19-21 L 50,583
Sun 9/28 A SD 27-34 L 54,042
Sun 10/5 A BOS 23-14 W 25,584
Sat 10/11 A CIN 21-7 W 27,927
Mon 10/20 H HOU 26-17 W 63,841
Sun 10/26 H BOS 23-17 W 62,298
Sun 11/2 H MIA 34-31 W 61,761
Sun 11/9 H BUF 16-6 W 62,680
Sun 11/16 H KC 16-34 L 63,849
Sun 11/23 H CIN 40-7 W 62,128
Sun 11/30 H OAK 14-27 L 63,865
Sat 12/6 A HOU 34-26 W 51,923
Sun 12/14 A MIA 27-9 W 48,108

INTER-DIVISIONAL PLAYOFF
Sat 12/20 H KC 6-13 L 62,977

OAKLAND RAIDERS
Sun 9/14 H HOU 21-17 W 49,361
Sat 9/20 H MIA 20-17 W 50,277
Sun 9/28 H BOS 38-23 W 19,069
Sat 10/4 A MIA 20-20 T 35,614
Sun 10/12 H DEN 24-14 W 49,511
Sun 10/19 H BUF 50-21 W 54,418
Sun 10/26 A SD 24-12 W 54,008
Sun 11/2 A CIN 17-31 L 27,927
Sun 11/9 H DEN 41-10 W 54,416
Sun 11/16 H SD 21-16 W 54,372
Sun 11/23 A KC 27-24 W 51,982
Sun 11/30 A NY 27-14 W 63,865
Sun 12/7 H CIN 37-17 W 54,427
Sat 12/13 H KC 10-6 W 54,443

INTER-DIVISIONAL PLAYOFF
Sun 12/21 H HOU 56-7 W 53,539
LEAGUE CHAMPIONSHIP
Sun 1/4 H KC 7-17 L 53,564

SAN DIEGO CHARGERS
Sun 9/14 H KC 9-27 L 47,988
Sun 9/21 A CIN 20-34 L 26,243
Sun 9/28 H NY 34-27 W 54,042
Sat 10/4 H CIN 21-14 W 52,748
Sat 10/11 A MIA 21-14 W 34,585
Sun 10/19 A BOS 13-10 W 18,346
Sun 10/26 H OAK 12-24 L 54,008
Sun 11/2 A DEN 0-13 L 45,511
Sun 11/9 A KC 3-27 L 51,104
Sun 11/16 A OAK 16-21 L 54,372
Sun 11/23 H DEN 45-24 W 34,664
Thu 11/27 A HOU 21-17 W 40,065
Sun 12/7 H BOS 26-18 W 33,146
Sun 12/14 H BUF 45-6 W 47,582

1969 NFL
ATLANTA FALCONS
Sun 9/21 H SF 24-12 W 45,940
Sun 9/28 A LA 7-17 L 58,031
Sun 10/5 H BAL 14-21 L 57,806
Sun 10/12 H DAL 17-24 L 54,833
Sun 10/19 A SF 21-7 W 28,684
Sun 10/26 A GB 10-28 L 50,861
Sun 11/2 H LA 6-38 L 54,357
Sun 11/9 A DET 21-27 L 53,242
Sun 11/16 H CHI 48-31 W 53,722
Sun 11/23 A WAS 20-27 L 50,345
Sun 11/30 A BAL 6-13 L 60,238
Sun 12/7 H NO 45-17 W 51,021
Sun 12/14 H PHI 27-3 W 60,658
Sun 12/21 H MIN 10-3 L 52,872

BALTIMORE COLTS
Sun 9/21 H LA 20-27 L 56,864
Sun 9/28 A MIN 14-52 L 47,900
Sun 10/5 A ATL 21-14 W 57,806
Mon 10/13 H PHI 24-20 W 56,864
Sun 10/19 A NO 30-10 W 80,636
Sun 10/26 H SF 21-24 L 60,238
Sun 11/2 H WAS 41-17 W 60,238
Sun 11/9 H GB 14-6 W 60,238
Sun 11/16 A SF 17-20 L 38,472
Sun 11/23 A CHI 24-21 W 45,455
Sun 11/30 H ATL 13-6 W 60,238

Sun 12/7 H DET 17-17 T 60,238
Sat 12/13 A DAL 10-27 L 63,191
Sun 12/21 A LA 13-7 W 73,326

CHICAGO BEARS
Sun 9/21 A GB 0-17 L 50,861
Sun 9/28 A STL 17-20 L 50,039
Sun 10/5 A NYG 24-28 L 62,583
Sun 10/12 H MIN 0-31 L 45,757
Sun 10/19 A DET 7-13 L 54,732
Sun 10/26 H LA 7-9 L 45,985
Sun 11/2 A MIN 14-31 L 47,900
Sun 11/9 H PIT 38-7 W 45,856
Sun 11/16 H ATL 31-48 L 53,722
Sun 11/23 H BAL 21-24 L 45,455
Sun 11/30 H CLE 24-28 L 45,050
Sat 12/6 A SF 21-42 L 32,826
Sun 12/14 H GB 3-21 L 45,216
Sun 12/21 H DET 3-20 L 41,879

CLEVELAND BROWNS
Sun 9/21 A PHI 27-20 W 60,658
Sun 9/28 H WAS 27-23 W 82,581
Sun 10/5 H DET 21-28 L 82,933
Sun 10/12 A NO 27-17 W 71,274
Sat 10/18 H PIT 42-31 W 84,078
Sun 10/26 H STL 21-21 T 81,186
Sun 11/2 H DAL 42-10 W 84,850
Sun 11/9 A MIN 3-51 L 47,900
Sun 11/16 H PIT 24-3 W 47,670
Sun 11/23 H NYG 28-17 W 80,595
Sun 11/30 A CHI 28-24 W 45,050
Sun 12/7 H GB 20-7 W 82,137
Sun 12/14 A STL 27-21 W 44,924
Sun 12/21 A NYG 14-27 L 62,966

EASTERN CONFERENCE CHAMPIONSHIP
Sun 12/28 A DAL 38-14 W 69,321

LEAGUE CHAMPIONSHIP
Sun 1/4 A MIN 7-27 L 47,900

DALLAS COWBOYS
Sun 9/21 H STL 24-3 W 62,134
Sun 9/28 A NO 21-17 W 79,567
Sun 10/5 H PHI 38-7 W 60,658
Sun 10/12 A ATL 24-17 W 54,833
Sun 10/19 H PHI 49-14 W 71,509
Mon 10/27 H NYG 25-3 W 58,964
Sun 11/2 A CLE 10-42 L 84,850
Sun 11/9 H NO 33-17 W 68,282
Sun 11/16 A WAS 41-28 W 50,474
Sun 11/23 A LA 23-24 L 79,105
Thu 11/27 H SF 24-24 T 62,348
Sun 12/7 A PIT 10-7 W 24,990
Sat 12/13 A BAL 27-10 W 63,191
Sun 12/21 H WAS 20-10 W 56,924

EASTERN CONFERENCE CHAMPIONSHIP
Sun 12/28 H CLE 14-38 L 69,321

DETROIT LIONS
Sun 9/21 A PIT 13-16 L 51,360
Sun 9/28 H NYG 24-0 W 54,358
Sun 10/5 A CLE 28-21 W 82,933
Sun 10/12 H GB 17-28 L 58,384
Sun 10/19 H CHI 13-7 W 54,732
Sun 10/26 A MIN 10-24 L 47,900
Sun 11/2 A SF 26-14 W 35,100
Sun 11/9 H ATL 27-21 W 53,242
Sun 11/16 H STL 20-0 W 51,749
Sun 11/23 A GB 16-10 W 50,861
Thu 11/27 H MIN 0-27 L 57,906
Sun 12/7 A BAL 17-17 T 60,238
Sun 12/14 H LA 28-0 W 53,256
Sun 12/21 A CHI 20-3 W 41,879

GREEN BAY PACKERS
Sun 9/21 H CHI 17-0 W 50,861

Sun 9/28 H SF 14-7 W 48,184
Sun 10/5 A MIN 7-19 L 60,740
Sun 10/12 A DET 28-17 W 58,384
Sun 10/19 A LA 21-34 L 78,947
Sun 10/26 H ATL 28-10 W 50,861
Sun 11/2 H PIT 38-34 W 46,403
Sun 11/9 H BAL 6-14 L 60,238
Sun 11/16 H MIN 7-9 L 48,321
Sun 11/23 H DET 10-16 L 50,861
Sun 11/30 H NYG 20-10 W 48,156
Sun 12/7 A CLE 7-20 L 82,137
Sun 12/14 H CHI 21-3 W 45,216
Sun 12/21 H STL 45-28 L 50,861

LOS ANGELES RAMS
Sun 9/21 A BAL 27-20 W 56,864
Sun 9/28 H ATL 17-7 W 58,031
Sun 10/5 H NO 36-17 W 54,879
Sun 10/12 A SF 27-21 W 45,995
Sun 10/19 H GB 34-21 W 78,947
Sun 10/26 A CHI 9-7 W 45,985
Sun 11/2 A ATL 38-6 W 54,357
Sun 11/9 H SF 41-30 W 73,975
Sun 11/16 H PHI 23-17 W 60,658
Sun 11/23 H DAL 24-23 W 79,105
Sun 11/30 A WAS 24-13 W 50,352
Sun 12/7 H MIN 13-20 L 80,430
Sun 12/14 H DET 0-28 L 53,256
Sun 12/21 H BAL 7-13 L 73,326

WESTERN CONFERENCE CHAMPIONSHIP
Sat 12/27 A MIN 20-23 L 47,900

MINNESOTA VIKINGS
Sun 9/21 A NYG 23-24 L 62,920
Sun 9/28 H BAL 52-14 W 47,900
Sun 10/5 H GB 19-7 W 60,740
Sun 10/12 A CHI 31-0 W 45,757
Sun 10/19 A STL 27-10 W 49,430
Sun 10/26 H DET 24-10 W 47,900
Sun 11/2 H CHI 31-14 W 47,900
Sun 11/9 H CLE 51-3 W 47,900
Sun 11/16 H GB 9-7 W 48,321
Sun 11/23 H PIT 52-14 W 47,202
Thu 11/27 A DET 27-0 W 57,906
Sun 12/7 H LA 20-13 W 80,430
Sun 12/14 H SF 10-7 W 43,028
Sun 12/21 A ATL 3-10 L 52,872

WESTERN CONFERENCE CHAMPIONSHIP
Sat 12/27 H LA 23-20 W 47,900

LEAGUE CHAMPIONSHIP
Sun 1/4 H CLE 27-7 W 47,900

SUPER BOWL IV
Sun 1/11 N KC 7-23 L 80,562

NEW ORLEANS SAINTS
Sun 9/21 H WAS 20-26 L 73,147
Sun 9/28 H DAL 17-21 L 79,567
Sun 10/5 A LA 17-36 L 54,879
Sun 10/12 H CLE 17-27 L 71,274
Sun 10/19 H BAL 10-30 L 80,636
Sun 10/26 A PHI 10-13 L 60,658
Sun 11/2 A STL 51-42 W 46,718
Sun 11/9 A DAL 17-33 L 68,282
Sun 11/16 A NYG 25-24 W 62,927
Sun 11/23 H SF 43-38 W 71,448
Sun 11/30 H PHI 26-17 W 72,805
Sun 12/7 A ATL 17-45 L 57,021
Sun 12/14 A WAS 14-17 L 50,354
Sun 12/21 H PIT 27-24 W 72,256

NEW YORK GIANTS
Sun 9/21 H MIN 24-23 W 62,920
Sun 9/28 A DET 0-24 L 54,358
Sun 10/5 H CHI 28-24 W 62,583
Sun 10/12 H PIT 10-7 W 62,987

Sun 10/19 A WAS 14-20 L 50,352
Mon 10/27 A DAL 3-25 L 58,954
Sun 11/2 H PHI 20-23 L 62,962
Sun 11/9 A STL 17-42 L 49,194
Sun 11/16 H NO 24-25 L 62,927
Sun 11/23 A CLE 17-28 L 80,595
Sun 11/30 A GB 10-20 L 48,156
Sun 12/7 H STL 49-6 W 62,973
Sun 12/14 A PIT 21-17 W 21,067
Sun 12/21 H CLE 27-14 W 62,966

PHILADELPHIA EAGLES
Sun 9/21 H CLE 20-27 L 60,658
Sun 9/28 H PIT 41-27 W 60,658
Sun 10/5 H DAL 7-38 L 60,658
Mon 10/13 A BAL 20-24 L 56,864
Sun 10/19 A DAL 14-49 L 71,509
Sun 10/26 H NO 13-10 W 60,658
Sun 11/2 A NYG 23-20 W 62,962
Sun 11/9 A WAS 28-28 T 50,502
Sun 11/16 H LA 17-23 L 60,658
Sun 11/23 A STL 34-30 W 45,512
Sun 11/30 A NO 17-26 L 72,805
Sun 12/7 H WAS 29-34 L 60,658
Sun 12/14 A ATL 3-27 L 60,658
Sun 12/21 A SF 13-14 L 25,391

PITTSBURGH STEELERS
Sun 9/21 H DET 16-13 W 51,360
Sun 9/28 A PHI 27-41 L 60,658
Sun 10/5 H STL 14-27 L 45,011
Sun 10/12 A NYG 7-10 L 62,987
Sat 10/18 A CLE 31-42 L 84,078
Sun 10/26 H WAS 7-14 L 47,557
Sun 11/2 H GB 34-38 L 46,403
Sun 11/9 A CHI 7-38 L 45,856
Sun 11/16 H CLE 3-24 L 47,670
Sun 11/23 A MIN 14-52 L 47,202
Sun 11/30 A STL 10-47 L 43,721
Sun 12/7 H DAL 7-10 L 24,990
Sun 12/14 H NYG 17-21 L 21,067
Sun 12/21 A NO 24-27 L 72,256

ST. LOUIS CARDINALS
Sun 9/21 A DAL 3-24 L 62,134
Sun 9/28 H CHI 20-17 W 50,039
Sun 10/5 H PIT 27-14 W 45,011
Sun 10/12 A WAS 17-33 L 50,481
Sun 10/19 H MIN 10-27 L 49,430
Sun 10/26 A CLE 21-21 T 81,186
Sun 11/2 H NO 42-51 L 46,718
Sun 11/9 H NYG 42-17 W 49,194
Sun 11/16 H DET 0-20 L 51,749
Sun 11/23 H PHI 30-34 L 45,512
Sun 11/30 H PIT 47-10 W 43,721
Sun 12/7 A NYG 6-49 L 62,973
Sun 12/14 H CLE 21-27 L 44,924
Sun 12/21 A GB 28-45 L 50,861

SAN FRANCISCO 49ERS
Sun 9/21 A ATL 12-24 L 45,940
Sun 9/28 A GB 7-14 L 48,184
Sun 10/5 H WAS 17-17 T 35,642
Sun 10/12 H LA 21-27 L 45,995
Sun 10/19 H ATL 7-21 L 28,684
Sun 10/26 A BAL 24-21 W 60,238
Sun 11/2 H DET 14-26 L 35,100
Sun 11/9 A LA 30-41 L 73,975
Sun 11/16 H BAL 20-17 W 38,472
Sun 11/23 A NO 38-43 L 71,448
Thu 11/27 A DAL 24-24 T 62,348
Sat 12/6 H CHI 42-21 W 32,826
Sun 12/14 A MIN 7-10 L 43,028
Sun 12/21 H PHI 14-13 W 25,391

WASHINGTON REDSKINS
Sun 9/21 A NO 26-20 W 73,147

Sun 9/28 A CLE 23-27 L 82,581
Sun 10/5 A SF 17-17 T 35,642
Sun 10/12 H STL 33-17 W 50,481
Sun 10/19 H NYG 20-14 W 50,352
Sun 10/26 A PIT 14-7 W 46,557
Sun 11/2 A BAL 17-41 L 60,238
Sun 11/9 H PHI 28-28 T 50,502
Sun 11/16 H DAL 28-41 L 50,474
Sun 11/23 H ATL 27-20 W 50,345
Sun 11/30 A LA 13-24 L 50,352
Sun 12/7 A PHI 34-29 W 60,658
Sun 12/14 H NO 17-14 W 50,354
Sun 12/21 A DAL 10-20 L 56,924

1970 NFL
ATLANTA FALCONS
Sun 9/20 A NO 14-3 W 77,042
Sun 9/27 A GB 24-27 L 56,263
Sun 10/4 H SF 21-20 W 58,850
Sun 10/11 A DAL 0-13 L 53,611
Sun 10/18 A DEN 10-24 L 50,705
Sun 10/25 H NO 32-14 W 58,850
Sun 11/1 H CHI 13-16 L 58,850
Sun 11/8 A LA 10-10 T 67,232
Sun 11/15 H PHI 13-13 T 55,425
Sun 11/22 H LA 7-17 L 58,850
Mon 11/30 H MIA 7-20 L 54,036
Sun 12/6 A SF 20-24 L 41,387
Sun 12/13 H PIT 27-16 W 54,162
Sun 12/20 H MIN 7-37 L 57,992

BALTIMORE COLTS
Sun 9/20 A SD 16-14 W 47,782
Mon 9/28 A KC 24-44 L 53,911
Sun 10/4 A BOS 14-6 W 38,235
Sun 10/11 A HOU 24-20 W 48,050
Sun 10/18 H NYJ 29-22 W 63,301
Sun 10/25 H BOS 27-3 W 60,240
Sun 11/1 H MIA 35-0 W 60,240
Mon 11/9 A GB 13-10 W 48,063
Sun 11/15 H BUF 17-17 T 60,240
Sun 11/22 H MIA 17-34 L 67,699
Sun 11/29 H CHI 21-20 W 60,240
Sun 12/6 H PHI 29-10 W 60,240
Sun 12/13 A BUF 20-14 W 34,346
Sat 12/19 H NYJ 35-20 W 60,240

AFC DIVISIONAL PLAYOFF
Sat 12/26 H CIN 17-0 W 51,127

AFC CHAMPIONSHIP
Sun 1/3 H OAK 27-17 W 56,368

SUPER BOWL V
Sun 1/17 N DAL 16-13 W 79,204

BOSTON PATRIOTS
Sun 9/20 H MIA 27-14 W 32,607
Sun 9/27 H NYJ 21-31 L 36,040
Sun 10/4 H BAL 6-14 L 38,235
Sun 10/11 A KC 10-23 L 50,698
Sun 10/18 A NYG 0-16 L 39,091
Sun 10/25 A BAL 3-27 L 60,240
Sun 11/1 H BUF 10-45 L 31,148
Sun 11/8 A STL 0-31 L 46,466
Sun 11/15 H SD 14-16 L 30,597
Sun 11/22 H NYJ 3-17 L 61,822
Sun 11/29 A BUF 14-10 W 31,427
Sun 12/6 A MIA 20-37 L 51,032
Sun 12/13 H MIN 14-35 L 37,819
Sun 12/20 A CIN 7-45 L 60,157

BUFFALO BILLS
Sun 9/20 H DEN 10-25 L 34,882
Sun 9/27 H LA 0-19 L 46,206
Sun 10/4 H NYJ 34-31 W 46,206
Sun 10/11 A PIT 10-23 L 42,140
Sun 10/18 H MIA 14-33 L 41,312

Sun 10/25 A NYJ 10-6 W 62,712
Sun 11/1 A BOS 45-10 W 31,148
Sun 11/8 H CIN 14-43 L 43,587
Sun 11/15 A BAL 17-17 T 60,240
Sun 11/22 A CHI 13-31 L 41,015
Sun 11/29 H BOS 10-14 L 31,427
Sun 12/6 A NYG 6-20 L 62,870
Sun 12/13 H BAL 14-20 L 34,346
Sun 12/20 A MIA 7-45 L 70,990

CHICAGO BEARS
Sat 9/19 A NYG 24-16 W 62,936
Sun 9/27 H PHI 20-16 W 53,643
Mon 10/5 A DET 14-28 L 58,210
Sun 10/11 H MIN 0-24 L 45,485
Sun 10/18 H SD 7-20 L 45,278
Sun 10/25 H DET 10-16 L 45,632
Sun 11/1 A ATL 23-14 W 58,850
Sun 11/8 H SF 16-37 L 45,607
Sun 11/15 A GB 19-20 L 56,263
Sun 11/22 A BUF 31-13 W 41,015
Sun 11/29 A BAL 20-21 L 60,240
Sat 12/5 A MIN 13-16 L 47,900
Sun 12/13 H GB 35-17 W 44,957
Sun 12/20 A NO 24-3 W 63,518

CINCINNATI BENGALS
Sun 9/20 H OAK 31-21 W 56,616
Sun 9/27 A DET 3-38 L 58,202
Sun 10/4 H HOU 13-20 L 55,094
Sun 10/11 A CLE 27-30 L 83,520
Sun 10/18 A KC 19-27 L 57,265
Sun 10/25 A WAS 0-20 L 50,415
Mon 11/2 A PIT 10-21 L 38,968
Sun 11/8 A BUF 43-14 W 43,587
Sun 11/15 H CLE 14-10 W 60,007
Sun 11/22 H PIT 34-7 W 59,276
Sun 11/29 H NO 26-6 W 59,342
Sun 12/6 A SD 17-14 W 41,461
Sun 12/13 A HOU 30-20 W 34,435
Sun 12/20 H BOS 45-7 W 60,157

AFC Divisional Playoff
Sat 12/26 A BAL 0-17 L 51,127

CLEVELAND BROWNS
Mon 9/21 H NYJ 31-21 W 85,703
Sun 9/27 A SF 31-34 L 37,502
Sat 10/3 H PIT 15-7 W 84,349
Sun 10/11 H CIN 30-27 W 83,520
Sun 10/18 H DET 24-41 L 83,577
Sun 10/25 H MIA 28-0 W 75,313
Sun 11/1 H SD 10-27 L 80,047
Sun 11/8 A OAK 20-23 L 54,463
Sun 11/15 A CIN 10-14 L 60,007
Sun 11/22 H HOU 28-14 W 74,723
Sun 11/29 A PIT 9-28 L 50,214
Mon 12/7 A HOU 21-10 W 50,582
Sat 12/12 A DAL 2-6 L 75,458
Sun 12/20 A DEN 27-13 W 51,001

DALLAS COWBOYS
Sun 9/20 A PHI 17-7 W 59,728
Sun 9/27 H NYG 28-10 W 57,239
Sun 10/4 A STL 7-20 L 50,780
Sun 10/11 H ATL 13-0 W 53,611
Sun 10/18 A MIN 13-54 L 47,900
Sun 10/25 A KC 27-16 W 51,158
Sun 11/1 H PHI 21-17 W 55,736
Sun 11/8 A NYG 20-23 L 62,938
Mon 11/16 A STL 0-38 L 69,323
Sun 11/22 H WAS 45-21 W 50,415
Thu 11/26 H GB 16-3 W 67,182
Sun 12/6 H WAS 34-0 W 57,936
Sat 12/12 A CLE 6-2 W 75,458
Sun 12/20 H HOU 52-10 W 50,504

NFC Divisional Playoff
Sat 12/26 H DET 5-0 W 73,167
NFC Championship
Sun 1/3 A SF 17-10 W 59,625
Super Bowl V
Sun 1/17 N BAL 13-16 L 79,204

DENVER BRONCOS
Sun 9/20 A BUF 25-10 W 34,882
Sun 9/27 H PIT 16-13 W 50,705
Sun 10/4 H KC 26-13 W 50,705
Sun 10/11 A OAK 23-35 L 54,436
Sun 10/18 A ATL 24-10 W 50,705
Sun 10/25 A SF 14-19 L 39,515
Sun 11/1 H WAS 3-19 L 50,705
Sun 11/8 A SD 21-24 L 48,327
Sun 11/15 H OAK 19-24 L 50,959
Sun 11/22 A NO 31-6 W 66,837
Sun 11/29 H HOU 21-31 L 35,733
Sun 12/6 A KC 0-16 L 50,454
Sun 12/13 H SD 17-17 T 50,959
Sun 12/20 H CLE 13-27 L 51,001

DETROIT LIONS
Sun 9/20 A GB 40-0 W 56,263
Sun 9/27 H CIN 38-3 W 58,202
Mon 10/5 H CHI 28-14 W 58,210
Sun 10/11 A WAS 10-31 L 50,415
Sun 10/18 A CLE 41-24 W 83,577
Sun 10/25 A CHI 16-10 W 45,632
Sun 11/1 H MIN 17-30 L 58,210
Sun 11/8 A NO 17-19 L 66,910
Sun 11/15 A MIN 20-24 L 47,900
Sun 11/22 H SF 28-7 W 56,232
Thu 11/26 H OAK 28-14 W 56,597
Sun 12/6 H STL 16-3 W 56,362
Mon 12/14 A LA 28-23 W 79,441
Sun 12/20 H GB 20-0 W 57,387

NFC Divisional Playoff
Sat 12/26 A DAL 0-5 L 73,167

GREEN BAY PACKERS
Sun 9/20 H DET 0-40 L 56,263
Sun 9/27 H ATL 27-24 W 56,263
Sun 10/4 H MIN 13-10 W 47,967
Mon 10/12 A SD 22-20 W 53,064
Sun 10/18 H LA 21-31 L 56,263
Sun 10/25 H PHI 30-17 W 48,022
Sun 11/1 A SF 10-26 L 59,335
Mon 11/9 H BAL 10-13 L 48,063
Sun 11/15 H CHI 20-19 W 56,263
Sun 11/22 A MIN 3-10 L 47,900
Thu 11/26 A DAL 3-16 L 67,182
Sun 12/6 A PIT 20-12 W 46,418
Sun 12/13 A CHI 17-35 L 44,957
Sun 12/20 A DET 0-20 L 57,387

HOUSTON OILERS
Sun 9/20 A PIT 19-7 W 45,538
Sun 9/27 A MIA 10-20 L 39,840
Sun 10/4 A CIN 20-13 W 55,094
Sun 10/11 H BAL 20-24 L 48,050
Sun 10/18 H PIT 3-7 L 42,799
Sun 10/25 A SD 31-31 T 41,427
Sun 11/1 A STL 0-44 L 47,911
Sun 11/8 A KC 9-24 L 49,810
Sun 11/15 H SF 20-30 L 43,040
Sun 11/22 A CLE 14-28 L 74,723
Sun 11/29 H DEN 31-21 W 35,733
Mon 12/7 H CLE 10-21 L 50,582
Sun 12/13 H CIN 20-30 L 34,435
Sun 12/20 A DAL 10-52 L 50,504

KANSAS CITY CHIEFS
Sun 9/20 A MIN 10-27 L 47,900
Mon 9/28 A BAL 44-24 W 53,911
Sun 10/4 A DEN 13-26 L 50,705
Sun 10/11 H BOS 23-10 W 50,698
Sun 10/18 A CIN 27-19 W 57,265
Sun 10/25 H DAL 16-27 L 51,158
Sun 11/1 H OAK 17-17 T 51,334
Sun 11/8 H HOU 24-9 W 49,810
Sun 11/15 A PIT 31-14 W 50,081
Sun 11/22 H STL 6-6 T 50,711
Sun 11/29 H SD 26-14 W 50,315
Sun 12/6 H DEN 16-0 W 50,454
Sat 12/12 A OAK 6-20 L 54,496
Sun 12/20 A SD 13-31 L 41,379

LOS ANGELES RAMS
Fri 9/18 H STL 34-13 W 63,130
Sun 9/27 A BUF 19-0 W 46,206
Sun 10/4 H SD 37-10 W 69,564
Sun 10/11 H SF 6-20 L 77,272
Sun 10/18 A GB 31-21 W 56,263
Mon 10/26 A MIN 3-13 L 47,900
Sun 11/1 A NO 30-17 W 77,861
Sun 11/8 H ATL 10-10 T 67,232
Sun 11/15 H NYJ 20-31 L 76,378
Sun 11/22 A ATL 17-7 W 58,850
Sun 11/29 A SF 30-13 W 59,602
Sun 12/6 H NO 34-16 W 66,410
Mon 12/14 H DET 23-28 L 79,441
Sun 12/20 A NYG 31-3 W 62,870

MIAMI DOLPHINS
Sun 9/20 A BOS 14-27 L 32,607
Sun 9/27 A HOU 20-10 W 39,840
Sat 10/3 H OAK 20-13 W 57,140
Sat 10/10 A NYJ 20-6 W 62,712
Sun 10/18 A BUF 33-14 W 41,312
Sun 10/25 H CLE 0-28 L 75,313
Sun 11/1 A BAL 0-35 L 60,240
Sun 11/8 H PHI 17-24 L 58,171
Sun 11/15 H NO 21-10 W 42,866
Sun 11/22 H BAL 34-17 W 67,699
Mon 11/30 A ATL 20-7 W 54,036
Sun 12/6 H BOS 37-20 W 51,032
Sun 12/13 H NYJ 16-10 W 75,099
Sun 12/20 H BUF 45-7 W 70,990

AFC Divisional Playoff
Sun 12/27 A OAK 14-21 L 54,401

MINNESOTA VIKINGS
Sun 9/20 H KC 27-10 W 47,900
Sun 9/27 H NO 26-0 W 47,900
Sun 10/4 H GB 10-13 L 47,967
Sun 10/11 A CHI 24-0 W 45,485
Sun 10/18 H DAL 54-13 W 47,900
Mon 10/26 H LA 13-3 W 47,900
Sun 11/1 A DET 30-17 W 58,210
Sun 11/8 A WAS 19-10 W 50,415
Sun 11/15 H DET 24-20 W 47,900
Sun 11/22 H GB 10-3 W 47,900
Sun 11/29 A NYJ 10-20 L 62,333
Sat 12/5 H CHI 16-13 W 47,900
Sun 12/13 A BOS 35-14 W 37,819
Sun 12/20 A ATL 37-7 W 57,992

NFC Divisional Playoff
Sun 12/27 H SF 14-17 L 47,900

NEW ORLEANS SAINTS
Sun 9/20 H ATL 3-14 L 77,042
Sun 9/27 A MIN 0-26 L 47,900
Sun 10/4 H NYG 14-10 W 69,126
Sun 10/11 A STL 17-24 L 45,294
Sun 10/18 A SF 20-20 T 39,446
Sun 10/25 A ATL 14-32 L 58,850
Sun 11/1 H LA 17-30 L 77,861
Sun 11/8 H DET 19-17 W 66,910
Sun 11/15 A MIA 10-21 L 42,866
Sun 11/22 H DEN 6-31 L 66,837
Sun 11/29 A CIN 6-26 L 59,342
Sun 12/6 A LA 16-34 L 66,410
Sun 12/13 H SF 27-38 L 61,940
Sun 12/20 H CHI 3-24 L 63,518

NEW YORK GIANTS
Sat 9/19 H CHI 16-24 L 62,936
Sun 9/27 A DAL 10-28 L 57,239
Sun 10/4 A NO 10-14 L 69,126
Sun 10/11 H PHI 30-23 W 62,820
Sun 10/18 A BOS 16-0 W 39,091
Sun 10/25 A STL 35-17 W 62,984
Sun 11/1 A NYJ 22-10 W 63,903
Sun 11/8 H DAL 23-20 L 62,938
Sun 11/15 H WAS 35-33 W 62,915
Mon 11/23 A PHI 20-23 L 59,117
Sun 11/29 A WAS 27-24 W 50,415
Sun 12/6 H BUF 20-6 W 62,870
Sun 12/13 A STL 34-17 W 50,845
Sun 12/20 H LA 3-31 L 62,870

NEW YORK JETS
Mon 9/21 A CLE 21-31 L 85,703
Sun 9/27 A BOS 31-21 W 36,040
Sun 10/4 A BUF 31-34 L 46,206
Sat 10/10 H MIA 6-20 L 62,712
Sun 10/18 H BAL 22-29 L 63,301
Sun 10/25 H BUF 6-10 L 62,712
Sun 11/1 H NYG 10-22 L 63,903
Sun 11/8 A PIT 17-21 L 50,028
Sun 11/15 A LA 31-20 L 76,378
Sun 11/22 H BOS 17-3 L 61,822
Sun 11/29 H MIN 20-10 W 62,333
Sun 12/6 H OAK 13-14 L 62,905
Sun 12/13 A MIA 10-16 L 75,099
Sat 12/19 A BAL 20-35 L 60,240

OAKLAND RAIDERS
Sun 9/20 A CIN 21-31 L 56,616
Sun 9/27 A SD 27-27 T 42,109
Sat 10/3 A MIA 13-20 L 57,140
Sun 10/11 H DEN 35-23 W 54,436
Mon 10/19 H WAS 34-20 W 54,471
Sun 10/25 H PIT 31-14 W 54,423
Sun 11/1 A KC 17-17 T 51,334
Sun 11/8 H CLE 23-20 W 54,463
Sun 11/15 A DEN 24-19 W 50,959
Sun 11/22 H SD 20-17 W 54,594
Thu 11/26 A DET 14-28 L 56,597
Sun 12/6 A NYJ 14-13 W 62,905
Sat 12/12 H KC 20-6 W 54,496
Sun 12/20 H SF 7-38 L 54,535

AFC Divisional Playoff
Sun 12/27 H MIA 21-14 W 54,401
AFC Championship
Sun 1/3 A BAL 17-27 L 56,368

PHILADELPHIA EAGLES
Sun 9/20 H DAL 7-17 L 59,728
Sun 9/27 A CHI 16-20 L 53,643
Sun 10/4 H WAS 21-33 L 60,658
Sun 10/11 A NYG 23-30 L 62,820
Sun 10/18 H STL 20-35 L 59,002
Sun 10/25 A GB 17-30 L 48,022
Sun 11/1 A DAL 17-21 L 55,736
Sun 11/8 H MIA 24-17 W 58,171
Sun 11/15 H ATL 13-13 T 55,425
Mon 11/23 H NYG 23-20 W 59,117
Sun 11/29 A STL 14-23 L 46,581
Sun 12/6 A BAL 10-29 L 60,240
Sun 12/13 A WAS 6-24 L 50,415
Sun 12/20 H PIT 30-20 W 55,252

PITTSBURGH STEELERS
Sun 9/20 H HOU 7-19 L 45,538

Sun 9/27 A DEN 13-16 L 50,705
Sat 10/3 A CLE 7-15 L 84,349
Sun 10/11 H BUF 23-10 W 42,140
Sun 10/18 A HOU 7-3 W 42,799
Sun 10/25 A OAK 14-31 L 54,423
Mon 11/2 H CIN 21-10 W 38,968
Sun 11/8 H NYJ 21-17 W 50,028
Sun 11/15 H KC 14-31 L 50,081
Sun 11/22 A CIN 7-34 L 59,276
Sun 11/29 A CLE 28-9 W 50,214
Sun 12/6 H GB 12-20 L 46,418
Sun 12/13 A ATL 16-27 L 54,162
Sun 12/20 A PHI 20-30 L 55,252

ST. LOUIS CARDINALS
Fri 9/18 A LA 13-34 L 63,130
Sun 9/27 H WAS 27-17 W 44,246
Sun 10/4 H DAL 20-7 W 50,780
Sun 10/11 H NO 24-17 W 45,294
Sun 10/18 A PHI 35-20 W 59,002
Sun 10/25 A NYG 17-35 L 62,984
Sun 11/1 H HOU 44-0 W 47,911
Sun 11/8 H BOS 31-0 W 46,466
Mon 11/16 A DAL 38-0 W 69,323
Sun 11/22 A KC 6-6 T 50,711
Sun 11/29 H PHI 23-14 W 46,581
Sun 12/6 A DET 3-16 L 56,362
Sun 12/13 H NYG 17-34 L 50,845
Sun 12/20 A WAS 27-28 L 50,415

SAN DIEGO CHARGERS
Sun 9/20 H BAL 14-16 L 47,782
Sun 9/27 H OAK 27-27 T 42,109
Sun 10/4 A LA 10-37 L 69,564
Mon 10/12 H GB 20-22 L 53,064
Sun 10/18 A CHI 20-7 W 45,278
Sun 10/25 H HOU 31-31 T 41,427
Sun 11/1 A CLE 27-10 W 80,047
Sun 11/8 H DEN 24-21 W 48,327
Sun 11/15 A BOS 16-14 W 30,597
Sun 11/22 A OAK 17-20 L 54,594
Sun 11/29 A KC 14-26 L 50,315
Sun 12/6 H CIN 14-17 L 41,461
Sun 12/13 A DEN 17-17 T 50,959
Sun 12/20 A KC 31-13 W 41,379

SAN FRANCISCO 49ERS
Sun 9/20 H WAS 26-17 W 34,984
Sun 9/27 H CLE 34-31 W 37,502
Sun 10/4 A ATL 20-21 L 58,850
Sun 10/11 A LA 20-6 W 77,272
Sun 10/18 H NO 20-20 T 39,446
Sun 10/25 H DEN 19-14 W 39,515
Sun 11/1 H GB 26-10 W 59,335
Sun 11/8 A CHI 37-16 W 45,607
Sun 11/15 H HOU 30-20 W 43,040
Sun 11/22 A DET 7-28 L 56,232
Sun 11/29 A LA 13-30 L 56,902
Sun 12/6 H ATL 24-20 W 41,387
Sun 12/13 A NO 38-27 W 61,940
Sun 12/20 A OAK 38-7 W 54,535

NFC DIVISIONAL PLAYOFF
Sun 12/27 A MIN 17-14 W 47,900

NFC CHAMPIONSHIP
Sun 1/3 H DAL 10-17 L 59,625

WASHINGTON REDSKINS
Sun 9/20 A SF 17-26 L 34,984
Sun 9/27 A STL 17-27 L 44,246
Sun 10/4 A PHI 33-21 W 60,658
Sun 10/11 H DET 31-10 W 50,415
Mon 10/19 A OAK 20-34 L 54,471
Sun 10/25 H CIN 20-0 W 50,415
Sun 11/1 A DEN 19-3 W 50,705
Sun 11/8 H MIN 10-19 L 50,415
Sun 11/15 A NYG 33-35 L 62,915
Sun 11/22 H DAL 21-45 L 50,415
Sun 11/29 H NYG 24-27 L 50,415
Sun 12/6 A DAL 0-34 L 57,936
Sun 12/13 H PHI 24-6 W 50,415
Sun 12/20 H STL 28-27 W 50,415

1971 NFL

ATLANTA FALCONS
Sun 9/19 H SF 20-17 W 56,990
Sun 9/26 A LA 20-20 T 57,895
Sun 10/3 A DET 38-41 L 54,418
Sun 10/10 H STL 9-26 L 58,850
Sun 10/17 H LA 16-24 L 58,850
Sun 10/24 H NO 28-6 W 58,850
Sun 10/31 A CLE 31-14 W 76,825
Sun 11/7 A CIN 9-6 W 59,604
Sun 11/14 H NYG 17-21 L 58,850
Mon 11/22 H GB 28-21 W 58,850
Sun 11/28 A MIN 7-24 L 49,784
Sun 12/5 H OAK 24-13 W 58,850
Sun 12/12 A SF 3-24 L 44,582
Sun 12/19 A NO 24-20 W 75,954

BALTIMORE COLTS
Sun 9/19 H NYJ 22-0 W 56,458
Sun 9/26 A CLE 13-14 L 56,837
Sun 10/3 A NE 23-3 W 61,232
Sun 10/10 A BUF 43-0 W 46,206
Sun 10/17 A NYG 31-7 W 62,860
Mon 10/25 A MIN 3-10 L 49,784
Sun 10/31 H PIT 34-21 W 60,238
Mon 11/8 H LA 24-17 W 57,722
Sun 11/14 A NYJ 14-13 W 63,947
Sun 11/21 A MIA 14-17 L 75,312
Sun 11/28 A OAK 37-14 W 54,689
Sun 12/5 H BUF 24-0 W 58,476
Sat 12/11 H MIA 14-3 W 60,238
Sun 12/19 A NE 17-21 L 57,942

AFC DIVISIONAL PLAYOFF
Sun 12/26 A CLE 20-3 W 70,734

AFC CHAMPIONSHIP
Sun 1/2 A MIA 0-21 L 76,622

BUFFALO BILLS
Sun 9/19 H DAL 37-49 L 46,206
Sun 9/26 H MIA 14-29 L 45,139
Sun 10/3 A MIN 0-19 L 47,900
Sun 10/10 H BAL 0-43 L 46,206
Sun 10/17 A NYJ 17-28 L 61,498
Sat 10/23 A SD 3-20 L 49,261
Sun 10/31 H STL 23-28 L 40,040
Sun 11/7 A MIA 0-34 L 61,016
Sun 11/14 A NE 33-38 L 57,446
Sun 11/21 H NYJ 7-20 L 41,577
Sun 11/28 H NE 27-20 W 27,166
Sun 12/5 A BAL 0-24 L 58,476
Sun 12/12 H HOU 14-20 L 28,107
Sun 12/19 A KC 9-22 L 48,121

CHICAGO BEARS
Sun 9/19 H PIT 17-15 W 55,049
Sun 9/26 A MIN 20-17 W 47,900
Sun 10/3 A LA 3-17 L 66,957
Sun 10/10 H NO 35-14 W 55,049
Sun 10/17 A SF 0-13 L 44,000
Sun 10/24 A DET 28-23 W 54,418
Sun 10/31 H DAL 23-19 W 55,049
Sun 11/7 H GB 14-17 L 55,049
Sun 11/14 H WAS 16-15 W 55,049
Sun 11/21 H DET 3-28 L 55,049
Mon 11/29 A MIA 3-34 L 75,312
Sun 12/5 A DEN 3-6 L 51,200
Sun 12/12 A GB 10-31 L 56,263
Sun 12/19 H MIN 10-27 L 55,049

CINCINNATI BENGALS
Sun 9/19 H PHI 37-14 W 55,880
Sun 9/26 A PIT 10-21 L 48,448
Sun 10/3 A GB 17-20 L 56,263
Sun 10/10 H MIA 13-23 L 60,099
Sun 10/17 H CLE 24-27 L 60,284
Sun 10/24 A OAK 27-31 L 54,699
Sun 10/31 A HOU 6-10 L 37,947
Sun 11/7 H ATL 6-9 L 59,604
Sun 11/14 A DEN 24-10 W 51,200
Sun 11/21 H HOU 28-13 W 59,390
Sun 11/28 H SD 31-0 W 59,580
Sun 12/5 A CLE 27-31 L 82,705
Sun 12/12 H PIT 13-21 L 60,022
Sun 12/19 A NYJ 21-35 L 63,151

CLEVELAND BROWNS
Sun 9/19 H HOU 31-0 W 73,387
Sun 9/26 A BAL 14-13 W 56,837
Mon 10/4 A OAK 34-20 L 84,285
Sun 10/10 H PIT 27-17 W 83,391
Sun 10/17 A CIN 27-24 W 60,284
Sun 10/24 H DEN 0-27 L 75,674
Sun 10/31 H ATL 14-31 L 76,825
Sun 11/7 A PIT 9-26 L 50,202
Sun 11/14 A KC 7-13 L 50,388
Sun 11/21 H NE 27-7 W 65,238
Sun 11/28 H HOU 37-24 W 37,921
Sun 12/5 H CIN 31-27 W 82,705
Sun 12/12 A NO 21-17 W 72,794
Sun 12/19 A WAS 20-13 W 53,041

AFC DIVISIONAL PLAYOFF
Sun 12/26 H BAL 3-20 L 70,734

DALLAS COWBOYS
Sun 9/19 A BUF 49-37 W 46,206
Sun 9/26 A PHI 42-7 W 65,358
Sun 10/3 H WAS 16-20 L 61,554
Mon 10/11 H NYG 20-13 W 68,378
Sun 10/17 A NO 14-24 L 83,088
Sun 10/24 H NE 44-21 W 65,708
Sun 10/31 A CHI 19-23 L 55,049
Sun 11/7 A STL 16-13 W 50,486
Sun 11/14 H PHI 20-7 W 60,178
Sun 11/21 A WAS 13-0 W 53,041
Thu 11/25 H LA 28-21 W 66,595
Sat 12/4 H NYJ 52-10 W 66,689
Sun 12/12 A NYG 42-14 W 62,815
Sat 12/18 H STL 31-12 W 66,672

NFC DIVISIONAL PLAYOFF
Sat 12/25 A MIN 20-12 W 47,307

NFC CHAMPIONSHIP
Sun 1/2 H SF 14-3 W 63,409

SUPER BOWL VI
Sun 1/16 N MIA 24-3 W 81,023

DENVER BRONCOS
Sun 9/19 H MIA 10-10 T 51,228
Sun 9/26 A GB 13-34 L 47,957
Sun 10/3 H KC 3-16 L 51,200
Sun 10/10 H OAK 16-27 L 51,200
Sun 10/17 H SD 20-16 W 51,200
Sun 10/24 A CLE 0-27 L 75,674
Sun 10/31 A PHI 16-17 L 65,358
Sun 11/7 H DET 20-24 L 51,200
Sun 11/14 H CIN 10-24 L 51,200
Sun 11/21 A KC 10-28 L 49,945
Sun 11/28 A PIT 22-10 W 39,710
Sun 12/5 H CHI 6-3 W 51,200
Sun 12/12 A SD 17-45 L 44,347
Sun 12/19 A OAK 13-21 L 54,651

DETROIT LIONS
Mon 9/20 H MIN 13-16 L 54,418
Sun 9/26 A NE 34-7 W 61,057
Sun 10/3 H ATL 41-38 W 54,418
Sun 10/10 H GB 31-28 W 54,418
Sun 10/17 A HOU 31-7 W 45,885
Sun 10/24 H CHI 23-28 L 54,418
Mon 11/1 A GB 14-14 T 47,961
Sun 11/7 A DEN 24-20 W 51,200
Sun 11/14 H LA 13-21 L 54,418
Thu 11/21 A CHI 28-3 W 55,049
Thu 11/25 H KC 32-21 W 54,418
Sun 12/5 H PHI 20-23 L 54,418
Sat 12/11 A MIN 10-29 L 49,784
Sun 12/19 A SF 27-31 L 45,850

GREEN BAY PACKERS
Sun 9/19 H NYG 40-42 L 56,263
Sun 9/26 H DEN 34-13 W 47,957
Sun 10/3 H CIN 20-17 W 56,263
Sun 10/10 A DET 28-31 L 54,418
Sun 10/17 H MIN 13-24 L 56,263
Sun 10/24 A LA 13-30 L 75,351
Mon 11/1 H DET 14-14 T 47,961
Sun 11/7 A CHI 17-14 W 55,049
Sun 11/14 H MIN 0-3 L 49,784
Mon 11/22 A ATL 21-28 L 58,850
Sun 11/28 H NO 21-29 L 48,035
Sun 12/5 A STL 16-16 T 50,443
Sun 12/12 H CHI 31-10 W 56,263
Sun 12/19 A MIA 6-27 L 76,812

HOUSTON OILERS
Sun 9/19 A CLE 0-31 L 73,387
Sun 9/26 H KC 16-20 L 46,498
Sun 10/3 H NO 13-13 T 47,966
Sun 10/10 A WAS 13-22 L 53,041
Sun 10/17 H DET 7-31 L 45,885
Sun 10/24 A PIT 16-23 L 45,872
Sun 10/31 H CIN 10-6 W 37,947
Sun 11/7 A NE 20-28 L 53,155
Sun 11/14 A OAK 21-41 L 54,705
Sun 11/21 A CIN 13-28 L 59,390
Sun 11/28 A CLE 24-37 L 37,921
Sun 12/5 H PIT 29-3 W 37,778
Sun 12/12 A BUF 20-14 W 28,107
Sun 12/19 H SD 49-33 W 35,959

KANSAS CITY CHIEFS
Sun 9/19 A SD 14-21 L 54,061
Sun 9/26 A HOU 20-16 W 46,498
Sun 10/3 A DEN 16-3 W 51,200
Sun 10/10 H SD 31-10 W 50,514
Mon 10/18 H PIT 38-16 W 49,533
Sun 10/24 H WAS 27-20 W 51,989
Sun 10/31 A OAK 20-20 T 54,715
Sun 11/7 A NYJ 10-13 L 62,812
Sun 11/14 H CLE 13-7 W 50,388
Sun 11/21 H DEN 28-10 W 49,945
Thu 11/25 A DET 21-32 L 54,418
Mon 12/6 H SF 26-17 W 45,306
Sun 12/12 H OAK 16-14 W 51,215
Sun 12/19 H BUF 22-9 W 48,121

AFC DIVISIONAL PLAYOFF
Sat 12/25 H MIA **24-27 L 45,822

LOS ANGELES RAMS
Sun 9/19 A NO 20-24 L 70,915
Sun 9/26 H ATL 20-20 T 57,895
Sun 10/3 H CHI 17-3 W 66,957
Sun 10/10 H SF 20-13 W 44,000
Sun 10/17 A ATL 24-16 W 58,850
Sun 10/24 H GB 30-13 W 75,351
Sun 10/31 H MIA 14-20 L 72,903
Mon 11/8 A BAL 17-24 L 57,722
Sun 11/14 A DET 21-13 W 54,418
Sun 11/21 H SF 17-6 W 80,050
Thu 11/25 A DAL 21-28 L 66,595

Sun	12/5	H	NO	45-28	W	73,610
Mon	12/13	H	WAS	24-38	L	80,402
Sun	12/19	A	PIT	23-14	W	45,233

MIAMI DOLPHINS

Sun	9/19	A	DEN	10-10	T	51,228
Sun	9/26	A	BUF	29-14	W	45,139
Sun	10/3	H	NYJ	10-14	L	70,670
Sun	10/10	A	CIN	23-13	W	60,099
Sun	10/17	H	NE	41-3	W	58,822
Sun	10/24	A	NYJ	30-14	W	62,130
Sun	10/31	A	LA	20-14	W	72,903
Sun	11/7	H	BUF	34-0	W	61,016
Sun	11/14	H	PIT	24-21	W	66,435
Sun	11/21	H	BAL	17-14	W	75,312
Mon	11/29	H	CHI	34-3	W	75,312
Sun	12/5	A	NE	13-34	L	61,457
Sat	12/11	A	BAL	3-14	L	60,238
Sun	12/19	H	GB	27-6	W	76,812

AFC Divisional Playoff

Sat	12/25	A	KC	**27-24	W	45,822

AFC Championship

Sun	1/2	H	BAL	21-0	W	76,622

Super Bowl VI

Sun	1/16	N	DAL	3-24	L	81,023

MINNESOTA VIKINGS

Mon	9/20	A	DET	16-13	W	54,418
Sun	9/26	H	CHI	17-20	L	47,900
Sun	10/3	H	BUF	19-0	W	47,900
Sun	10/10	A	PHI	13-0	W	65,358
Sun	10/17	A	GB	24-13	W	56,263
Mon	10/25	H	BAL	10-3	W	49,784
Sun	10/31	A	NYG	17-10	W	62,829
Sun	11/7	H	SF	9-13	L	49,784
Sun	11/14	H	GB	3-0	W	49,784
Sun	11/21	A	NO	23-10	W	83,130
Sun	11/28	H	ATL	24-7	W	49,784
Sun	12/5	A	SD	14-30	L	54,505
Sat	12/11	H	DET	29-10	W	49,784
Sun	12/19	A	CHI	27-10	W	55,049

NFC Divisional Playoff

Sat	12/25	H	DAL	12-20	L	47,307

NEW ENGLAND PATRIOTS

Sun	9/19	H	OAK	20-6	W	55,405
Sun	9/26	H	DET	7-34	L	61,057
Sun	10/3	H	BAL	3-23	L	61,232
Sun	10/10	H	NYJ	20-0	W	61,357
Sun	10/17	A	MIA	3-41	L	58,822
Sun	10/24	A	DAL	21-44	L	65,708
Sun	10/31	A	SF	10-27	L	45,092
Sun	11/7	H	HOU	28-20	W	53,155
Sun	11/14	H	BUF	38-33	W	57,446
Sun	11/21	A	CLE	7-27	L	65,238
Sun	11/28	A	BUF	20-27	L	27,166
Sun	12/5	H	MIA	34-13	W	61,457
Sun	12/12	A	NYJ	6-13	L	63,175
Sun	12/19	A	BAL	21-17	W	57,942

NEW ORLEANS SAINTS

Sun	9/19	H	LA	24-20	W	70,915
Sun	9/26	H	SF	20-38	L	81,595
Sun	10/3	A	HOU	13-13	T	47,966
Sun	10/10	A	CHI	14-35	L	55,049
Sun	10/17	H	DAL	24-14	W	83,088
Sun	10/24	A	ATL	6-28	L	58,850
Sun	10/31	A	WAS	14-24	L	53,041
Sun	11/7	H	OAK	21-21	T	83,102
Sun	11/14	A	SF	26-20	W	45,138
Sun	11/21	H	MIN	10-23	L	83,130
Sun	11/28	A	GB	29-21	W	48,035
Sun	12/5	A	LA	28-45	L	73,610
Sun	12/12	H	CLE	17-21	L	72,794
Sun	12/19	H	ATL	20-24	L	75,954

NEW YORK GIANTS

Sun	9/19	A	GB	42-40	W	56,263
Sun	9/26	H	WAS	3-30	L	62,795
Sun	10/3	A	STL	21-20	W	49,571
Mon	10/11	A	DAL	13-20	L	68,378
Sun	10/17	H	BAL	7-31	L	62,860
Sun	10/24	A	PHI	7-23	L	65,358
Sun	10/31	H	MIN	10-17	L	62,829
Sun	11/7	H	SD	35-17	W	62,905
Sun	11/14	A	ATL	21-17	W	58,850
Sun	11/21	A	PIT	13-17	L	50,008
Sun	11/28	H	STL	7-24	L	62,878
Sun	12/5	A	WAS	7-23	L	53,041
Sun	12/12	H	DAL	14-42	L	62,815
Sun	12/19	H	PHI	28-41	L	62,774

NEW YORK JETS

Sun	9/19	A	BAL	0-22	L	56,458
Mon	9/27	A	STL	10-17	L	50,358
Sun	10/3	A	MIA	14-10	W	70,670
Sun	10/10	A	NE	0-20	L	61,357
Sun	10/17	H	BUF	28-17	W	61,948
Sun	10/24	H	MIA	14-30	L	62,130
Sun	10/31	A	SD	21-49	L	44,786
Sun	11/7	H	KC	13-10	W	62,812
Sun	11/14	H	BAL	13-14	L	63,947
Sun	11/21	A	BUF	20-7	W	41,577
Sun	11/28	H	SF	21-24	L	63,936
Sat	12/4	A	DAL	10-52	L	66,689
Sun	12/12	H	NE	13-6	W	63,175
Sun	12/19	H	CIN	35-21	W	63,151

OAKLAND RAIDERS

Sun	9/19	A	NE	6-20	L	55,405
Sun	9/26	A	SD	34-0	W	54,084
Mon	10/4	A	CLE	34-20	W	84,285
Sun	10/10	A	DEN	27-16	W	51,200
Sun	10/17	H	PHI	34-10	W	54,615
Sun	10/24	H	CIN	31-27	W	54,699
Sun	10/31	H	KC	20-20	T	54,715
Sun	11/7	A	NO	21-21	T	83,102
Sun	11/14	H	HOU	41-21	W	54,705
Sun	11/21	H	SD	34-33	W	54,681
Sun	11/28	H	BAL	14-37	L	54,689
Sun	12/5	A	ATL	13-24	L	58,850
Sun	12/12	A	KC	14-16	L	51,215
Sun	12/19	H	DEN	21-13	W	54,651

PHILADELPHIA EAGLES

Sun	9/19	A	CIN	14-37	L	55,880
Sun	9/26	H	DAL	7-42	L	65,358
Sun	10/3	H	SF	3-31	L	65,358
Sun	10/10	H	MIN	0-13	L	65,358
Sun	10/17	A	OAK	10-34	L	54,615
Sun	10/24	H	NYG	23-7	W	65,358
Sun	10/31	H	DEN	17-16	W	65,358
Sun	11/7	A	WAS	7-7	T	53,041
Sun	11/14	A	DAL	7-20	L	60,178
Sun	11/21	A	STL	37-20	W	48,658
Sun	11/28	H	WAS	13-20	L	65,358
Sun	12/5	A	DET	23-20	W	54,418
Sun	12/12	H	STL	19-7	W	65,358
Sun	12/19	A	NYG	41-28	W	62,774

PITTSBURGH STEELERS

Sun	9/19	A	CHI	15-17	L	55,049
Sun	9/26	H	CIN	21-10	W	48,448
Sun	10/3	H	SD	21-17	W	44,339
Sun	10/10	A	CLE	17-27	L	83,391
Mon	10/18	A	KC	16-38	L	49,533
Sun	10/24	H	HOU	23-16	W	45,872
Sun	10/31	A	BAL	21-34	L	60,238
Sun	11/7	H	CLE	26-9	W	50,202
Sun	11/14	A	MIA	21-24	L	66,435
Sun	11/21	H	NYG	17-13	W	50,008
Sun	11/28	H	DEN	10-22	L	39,710
Sun	12/5	A	HOU	3-29	L	37,778
Sun	12/12	A	CIN	21-13	W	60,022
Sun	12/19	H	LA	14-23	L	45,233

ST. LOUIS CARDINALS

Sun	9/19	H	WAS	17-24	L	46,805
Mon	9/27	H	NYJ	17-10	W	50,358
Sun	10/3	H	NYG	20-21	L	49,571
Sun	10/10	A	ATL	26-9	W	58,850
Sun	10/17	A	WAS	0-20	L	53,041
Sun	10/24	H	SF	14-26	L	50,419
Sun	10/31	A	BUF	28-23	W	40,040
Sun	11/7	H	DAL	13-16	L	50,486
Mon	11/15	A	SD	17-20	L	46,486
Sun	11/21	H	PHI	20-37	L	48,658
Sun	11/28	A	NYG	24-7	W	62,878
Sun	12/5	H	GB	16-16	T	50,443
Sun	12/12	A	PHI	7-19	L	65,358
Sat	12/18	A	DAL	12-31	L	66,672

SAN DIEGO CHARGERS

Sun	9/19	H	KC	21-14	W	54,061
Sun	9/26	H	OAK	0-34	L	54,084
Sun	10/3	A	PIT	17-21	L	44,339
Sun	10/10	A	KC	10-31	L	50,514
Sun	10/17	A	DEN	16-20	L	51,200
Sat	10/23	H	BUF	20-3	W	49,261
Sun	10/31	H	NYJ	49-21	W	44,786
Sun	11/7	A	NYG	17-35	L	62,905
Mon	11/15	H	STL	20-17	W	46,486
Sun	11/21	A	OAK	33-34	L	54,681
Sun	11/28	A	CIN	0-31	L	59,580
Sun	12/5	H	MIN	30-14	W	54,505
Sun	12/12	H	DEN	45-17	W	44,347
Sun	12/19	A	HOU	33-49	L	35,959

SAN FRANCISCO 49ERS

Sun	9/19	A	ATL	17-20	L	56,990
Sun	9/26	A	NO	38-20	W	81,595
Sun	10/3	A	PHI	31-3	W	65,358
Sun	10/10	H	LA	13-20	L	44,000
Sun	10/17	H	CHI	13-0	W	44,000
Sun	10/24	A	STL	26-14	W	50,419
Sun	10/31	H	NE	27-10	W	45,092
Sun	11/7	A	MIN	13-9	W	49,784
Sun	11/14	H	NO	20-26	L	45,138
Sun	11/21	A	LA	6-17	L	80,050
Sun	11/28	A	NYJ	24-21	W	63,936
Mon	12/6	H	KC	17-26	L	45,306
Sun	12/12	H	ATL	24-3	W	44,582
Sun	12/19	H	DET	31-27	W	45,580

NFC Divisional Playoff

Sun	12/26	H	WAS	24-20	W	45,327

NFC Championship

Sun	1/2	A	DAL	3-14	L	63,409

WASHINGTON REDSKINS

Sun	9/19	A	STL	24-17	W	46,805
Sun	9/26	A	NYG	30-3	W	62,795
Sun	10/3	A	DAL	20-16	W	61,554
Sun	10/10	H	HOU	22-13	W	53,041
Sun	10/17	H	STL	20-0	W	53,041
Sun	10/24	A	KC	20-27	L	51,989
Sun	10/31	H	NO	24-14	W	53,041
Sun	11/7	H	PHI	7-7	T	53,041
Sun	11/14	A	CHI	15-16	L	55,049
Sun	11/21	H	DAL	0-13	L	53,041
Sun	11/28	A	PHI	20-13	W	65,358
Sun	12/5	H	NYG	23-7	W	53,041
Mon	12/13	A	LA	38-24	W	80,402
Sun	12/19	H	CLE	13-20	L	53,041

NFC Divisional Playoff

Sun	12/26	A	SF	20-24	L	45,327

1972 NFL

ATLANTA FALCONS

Sun	9/17	A	CHI	37-21	W	55,701
Sun	9/24	A	NE	20-21	L	60,999
Sun	10/1	H	LA	31-3	W	57,122
Sun	10/8	H	DET	23-26	L	58,850
Sun	10/15	A	NO	21-14	W	66,294
Sun	10/22	A	GB	10-9	W	47,967
Sun	10/29	H	SF	14-49	L	58,850
Sun	11/5	A	LA	7-20	L	75,018
Sun	11/12	H	NO	36-20	W	58,850
Mon	11/20	A	WAS	13-24	L	53,039
Sun	11/26	H	DEN	23-20	W	58,850
Sun	12/3	H	HOU	20-10	W	58,850
Sun	12/10	A	SF	0-20	L	61,214
Sun	12/17	H	KC	14-17	L	58,860

BALTIMORE COLTS

Sun	9/17	H	STL	3-10	L	53,632
Sun	9/24	H	NYJ	34-44	L	56,626
Sun	10/1	A	BUF	17-0	W	46,206
Sun	10/8	H	SD	20-23	L	55,459
Sun	10/15	H	DAL	0-21	L	58,992
Sun	10/22	A	NYJ	20-24	L	62,948
Sun	10/29	H	MIA	0-23	L	60,000
Mon	11/6	A	NE	24-17	W	60,999
Sun	11/12	A	SF	21-24	L	61,214
Sun	11/19	A	CIN	20-19	W	49,512
Sun	11/26	H	NE	31-0	W	54,907
Sun	12/3	H	BUF	35-7	W	55,390
Sun	12/10	A	KC	10-24	L	44,175
Sat	12/16	A	MIA	0-16	L	80,010

BUFFALO BILLS

Sun	9/17	H	NYJ	24-41	L	46,206
Sun	9/24	H	SF	27-20	W	45,845
Sun	10/1	H	BAL	0-17	L	46,206
Sun	10/8	H	NE	38-14	W	41,749
Sun	10/15	A	OAK	16-28	L	53,501
Sun	10/22	A	MIA	23-24	L	80,010
Sun	10/29	H	PIT	21-38	L	45,882
Sun	11/5	H	MIA	16-30	L	46,206
Sun	11/12	A	NYJ	3-41	L	62,853
Sun	11/19	A	NE	27-24	W	60,999
Sun	11/26	A	CLE	10-27	L	70,104
Sun	12/3	A	BAL	7-35	L	55,390
Sun	12/10	H	DET	21-21	T	41,583
Sun	12/17	A	WAS	24-17	W	53,039

CHICAGO BEARS

Sun	9/17	H	ATL	21-37	L	55,701
Sun	9/24	H	LA	13-13	T	55,701
Sun	10/1	H	DET	24-38	L	55,701
Sun	10/8	A	GB	17-20	L	56,263
Sun	10/15	A	CLE	17-0	W	72,339
Mon	10/23	H	MIN	13-10	W	55,701
Sun	10/29	A	STL	27-10	W	50,464
Sun	11/5	A	DET	0-14	L	54,418
Sun	11/12	H	GB	17-23	L	55,701
Sun	11/19	H	SF	21-34	L	55,701
Sun	11/26	H	CIN	3-13	L	55,701
Sun	12/3	A	MIN	10-23	L	49,784
Sun	12/10	A	PHI	21-12	W	65,720
Sun	12/17	A	OAK	21-28	L	54,711

CINCINNATI BENGALS

Sun	9/17	A	NE	31-7	W	60,999
Sun	9/24	H	PIT	15-10	W	54,292
Sun	10/1	A	CLE	6-27	L	81,564
Sun	10/8	H	DEN	21-10	W	55,812
Sun	10/15	A	KC	23-16	W	79,068
Sun	10/22	A	LA	12-15	L	73,385
Sun	10/29	H	HOU	30-7	W	59,409
Sun	11/5	A	PIT	17-40	L	50,350
Sun	11/12	H	OAK	14-20	L	59,485

Sun	11/19	H	BAL	19-20	L	49,512
Sun	11/26	A	CHI	13-3	W	55,701
Sun	12/3	H	NYG	13-10	W	59,523
Sat	12/9	H	CLE	24-27	L	59,524
Sun	12/17	A	HOU	61-17	W	32,482

CLEVELAND BROWNS

Sun	9/17	H	GB	10-26	L	75,771
Sun	9/24	A	PHI	27-17	W	65,720
Sun	10/1	H	CIN	27-6	W	81,564
Sun	10/8	H	KC	7-31	L	83,819
Sun	10/15	H	CHI	0-17	L	72,339
Sun	10/22	A	HOU	23-17	W	38,113
Sun	10/29	A	DEN	27-20	W	51,656
Sun	11/5	H	HOU	20-0	W	61,985
Mon	11/13	A	SD	21-17	W	54,205
Sun	11/19	H	PIT	26-24	W	83,009
Sun	11/26	H	BUF	27-10	W	70,104
Sun	12/3	A	PIT	0-30	L	50,350
Sat	12/9	A	CIN	27-24	W	59,524
Sun	12/17	A	NYJ	26-10	W	45,084

AFC Divisional Playoff

Sun	12/24	A	MIA	14-20	L	80,010

DALLAS COWBOYS

Sun	9/17	H	PHI	28-6	W	55,850
Sun	9/24	A	NYG	23-14	W	62,725
Sun	10/1	A	GB	13-16	L	47,103
Sun	10/8	H	PIT	17-13	W	65,682
Sun	10/15	A	BAL	21-0	W	58,992
Sun	10/22	A	WAS	20-24	L	53,039
Mon	10/30	H	DET	28-24	W	65,378
Sun	11/5	A	SD	34-28	W	54,476
Sun	11/12	H	STL	33-24	W	65,218
Sun	11/19	A	PHI	28-7	W	65,720
Thu	11/23	H	SF	10-31	L	65,124
Sun	12/3	A	STL	27-6	W	49,797
Sat	12/9	H	WAS	34-24	W	65,136
Sun	12/17	H	NYG	3-23	L	64,602

NFC Divisional Playoff

Sat	12/23	A	SF	30-28	W	61,214

NFC Championship

Sun	12/31	A	WAS	3-26	L	53,129

DENVER BRONCOS

Sun	9/17	H	HOU	30-17	W	51,656
Sun	9/24	A	SD	14-37	L	49,048
Sun	10/1	H	KC	24-45	L	51,656
Sun	10/8	A	CIN	10-21	L	55,812
Sun	10/15	H	MIN	20-23	L	51,656
Sun	10/22	A	OAK	30-23	W	53,551
Sun	10/29	H	CLE	20-27	L	51,656
Sun	11/5	A	NYG	17-29	L	62,689
Sun	11/12	A	LA	16-10	W	65,398
Sun	11/19	H	OAK	20-37	L	51,656
Sun	11/26	A	ATL	20-23	L	58,850
Sun	12/3	A	KC	21-24	L	66,725
Sun	12/10	H	SD	38-13	W	51,478
Sun	12/17	H	NE	45-21	W	51,656

DETROIT LIONS

Sun	9/17	H	NYG	30-16	W	54,418
Sun	9/24	H	MIN	10-34	L	54,418
Sun	10/1	A	CHI	38-24	W	55,701
Sun	10/8	A	ATL	26-23	W	58,850
Mon	10/16	H	GB	23-24	L	54,418
Sun	10/22	H	SD	34-20	W	54,371
Mon	10/30	A	DAL	24-28	L	65,378
Sun	11/5	H	CHI	14-0	W	54,418
Sun	11/12	A	MIN	14-16	L	49,784
Sun	11/19	H	NO	27-14	W	53,752
Thu	11/23	H	NYJ	37-20	W	54,418
Sun	12/3	A	GB	7-33	L	56,263
Sun	12/10	A	BUF	21-21	T	41,583
Sun	12/17	A	LA	34-17	W	71,761

GREEN BAY PACKERS

Sun	9/17	A	CLE	26-10	W	75,771
Sun	9/24	H	OAK	14-20	L	56,263
Sun	10/1	H	DAL	16-13	W	47,103
Sun	10/8	H	CHI	20-17	W	56,263
Mon	10/16	A	DET	24-23	W	54,418
Sun	10/22	H	ATL	9-10	L	47,967
Sun	10/29	H	MIN	13-27	L	56,263
Sun	11/5	H	SF	34-24	W	47,897
Sun	11/12	A	CHI	23-17	W	55,701
Sun	11/19	A	HOU	23-10	W	41,752
Sun	11/26	A	WAS	16-21	L	53,039
Sun	12/3	H	DET	33-7	W	56,263
Sun	12/10	A	MIN	23-7	W	49,784
Sun	12/17	A	NO	30-20	W	65,881

NFC Divisional Playoff

Sun	12/24	A	WAS	3-16	L	53,140

HOUSTON OILERS

Sun	9/17	A	DEN	17-30	L	51,656
Sun	9/24	A	MIA	13-34	L	77,821
Sun	10/1	H	NYJ	26-20	W	51,423
Mon	10/9	H	OAK	0-34	L	51,378
Sun	10/15	A	PIT	7-24	L	42,923
Sun	10/22	H	CLE	17-23	L	38,113
Sun	10/29	A	CIN	7-30	L	59,409
Sun	11/5	A	CLE	0-20	L	61,985
Sun	11/12	H	PHI	17-18	L	34,175
Sun	11/19	H	GB	10-23	L	41,752
Sun	11/26	A	SD	20-34	L	46,289
Sun	12/3	A	ATL	10-20	L	58,850
Sun	12/10	H	PIT	3-9	L	36,528
Sun	12/17	H	CIN	17-61	L	32,482

KANSAS CITY CHIEFS

Sun	9/17	H	MIA	10-20	L	78,829
Mon	9/25	A	NO	20-17	W	70,793
Sun	10/1	A	DEN	45-24	W	51,656
Sun	10/8	A	CLE	31-7	W	83,819
Sun	10/15	H	CIN	16-23	L	79,068
Sun	10/22	H	PHI	20-21	L	78,389
Sun	10/29	A	SD	26-14	W	54,533
Sun	11/5	H	OAK	27-14	W	82,094
Sun	11/12	A	PIT	7-16	L	50,350
Sun	11/19	H	SD	17-27	L	79,011
Sun	11/26	A	OAK	3-26	L	54,801
Sun	12/3	H	DEN	24-21	W	66,725
Sun	12/10	H	BAL	24-10	W	44,175
Sun	12/17	A	ATL	17-14	W	58,860

LOS ANGELES RAMS

Sun	9/17	H	NO	34-14	W	66,303
Sun	9/24	A	CHI	13-13	T	55,701
Sun	10/1	A	ATL	3-31	L	57,122
Sun	10/8	H	SF	31-7	W	77,382
Sun	10/15	A	PHI	34-3	W	65,720
Sun	10/22	H	CIN	15-12	W	73,385
Sun	10/29	A	OAK	17-45	L	54,660
Sun	11/5	H	ATL	20-7	W	75,018
Sun	11/12	H	DEN	10-16	L	65,398
Sun	11/19	H	MIN	41-45	L	77,982
Sun	11/26	A	NO	16-19	L	64,325
Mon	12/4	A	SF	26-16	W	61,214
Sun	12/10	A	STL	14-24	L	36,873
Sun	12/17	H	DET	17-34	L	71,761

MIAMI DOLPHINS

Sun	9/17	A	KC	20-10	W	79,829
Sun	9/24	H	HOU	34-13	W	77,821
Sun	10/1	A	MIN	16-14	W	47,900
Sun	10/8	A	NYJ	27-17	W	63,841
Sun	10/15	H	SD	24-10	W	80,010
Sun	10/22	H	BUF	24-23	W	80,010
Sun	10/29	A	BAL	23-0	W	60,000
Sun	11/5	A	BUF	30-16	W	46,206
Sun	11/12	H	NE	52-0	W	80,010
Sun	11/19	H	NYJ	28-24	W	80,010
Mon	11/27	H	STL	31-10	W	80,010
Sun	12/3	A	NE	37-21	W	60,999
Sun	12/10	A	NYG	23-13	W	62,728
Sat	12/16	H	BAL	16-0	W	80,010

AFC Divisional Playoff

Sun	12/24	H	CLE	20-14	W	80,010

AFC Championship

Sun	12/31	A	PIT	21-17	W	50,350

Super Bowl VII

Sun	1/14	N	WAS	14-7	W	90,182

MINNESOTA VIKINGS

Mon	9/18	H	WAS	21-24	L	47,900
Sun	9/24	A	DET	34-10	W	54,418
Sun	10/1	H	MIA	14-16	L	47,900
Sun	10/8	H	STL	17-19	L	49,687
Sun	10/15	A	DEN	23-20	W	51,656
Mon	10/23	A	CHI	10-13	L	55,701
Sun	10/29	A	GB	27-13	W	56,263
Sun	11/5	H	NO	37-6	W	49,784
Sun	11/12	H	DET	16-14	W	49,784
Sun	11/19	A	LA	45-41	W	77,982
Sun	11/26	A	PIT	10-23	L	50,348
Sun	12/3	H	CHI	23-10	W	49,784
Sun	12/10	H	GB	7-23	L	49,784
Sat	12/16	A	SF	17-20	L	61,214

NEW ENGLAND PATRIOTS

Sun	9/17	H	CIN	7-31	L	60,999
Sun	9/24	H	ATL	21-20	W	60,999
Sun	10/1	H	WAS	24-23	W	60,999
Sun	10/8	A	BUF	14-38	L	41,749
Sun	10/15	H	NYJ	13-41	L	60,999
Sun	10/22	A	PIT	3-33	L	46,081
Sun	10/29	A	NYJ	10-34	L	62,867
Mon	11/6	H	BAL	17-24	L	60,999
Sun	11/12	A	MIA	0-52	L	80,010
Sun	11/19	H	BUF	24-27	L	60,999
Sun	11/26	A	BAL	0-31	L	54,907
Sun	12/3	H	MIA	21-37	L	60,999
Sun	12/10	A	NO	17-10	W	64,889
Sun	12/17	A	DEN	21-45	L	51,656

NEW ORLEANS SAINTS

Sun	9/17	A	LA	14-34	L	66,303
Mon	9/25	H	KC	17-20	L	70,793
Sun	10/1	H	SF	2-37	L	69,840
Sun	10/8	A	NYG	21-45	L	62,507
Sun	10/15	H	ATL	14-21	L	66,294
Sun	10/22	A	SF	20-20	T	59,167
Sun	10/29	H	PHI	21-3	W	65,664
Sun	11/5	A	MIN	6-37	L	49,784
Sun	11/12	A	ATL	20-36	L	58,850
Sun	11/19	A	DET	14-27	L	53,752
Sun	11/26	H	LA	19-16	W	64,325
Sun	12/3	A	NYJ	17-18	L	62,496
Sun	12/10	H	NE	10-17	L	64,889
Sun	12/17	H	GB	20-30	L	65,881

NEW YORK GIANTS

Sun	9/17	A	DET	16-30	L	54,418
Sun	9/24	H	DAL	14-23	L	62,725
Mon	10/2	A	PHI	27-12	W	65,720
Sun	10/8	H	NO	45-21	W	62,507
Sun	10/15	A	SF	23-17	W	58,606
Sun	10/22	H	STL	27-21	W	62,756
Sun	10/29	H	WAS	16-23	L	62,878
Sun	11/5	H	DEN	29-17	W	62,689
Sun	11/12	A	WAS	13-27	L	53,039
Sun	11/19	A	STL	13-7	W	48,014
Sun	11/26	H	PHI	62-10	W	62,586
Sun	12/3	A	CIN	10-13	L	59,523
Sun	12/10	H	MIA	13-23	L	62,728
Sun	12/17	A	DAL	23-3	W	64,602

NEW YORK JETS

Sun	9/17	A	BUF	41-24	W	46,206
Sun	9/24	A	BAL	44-34	W	56,626
Sun	10/1	A	HOU	20-26	L	51,423
Sun	10/8	H	MIA	17-27	L	63,841
Sun	10/15	A	NE	41-13	W	60,999
Sun	10/22	H	BAL	24-20	W	62,948
Sun	10/29	H	NE	34-10	W	62,867
Sun	11/5	H	WAS	17-35	L	63,962
Sun	11/12	H	BUF	41-3	W	62,853
Sun	11/19	A	MIA	24-28	L	80,010
Thu	11/23	A	DET	20-37	L	54,418
Sun	12/3	H	NO	18-17	W	62,496
Mon	12/11	A	OAK	16-24	L	54,843
Sun	12/17	H	CLE	10-26	L	45,084

OAKLAND RAIDERS

Sun	9/17	A	PIT	28-34	L	50,141
Sun	9/24	A	GB	20-14	W	56,263
Sun	10/1	H	SD	17-17	T	53,455
Mon	10/9	A	HOU	34-0	W	51,378
Sun	10/15	H	BUF	28-16	W	53,501
Sun	10/22	H	DEN	23-30	L	53,551
Sun	10/29	H	LA	45-17	W	54,660
Sun	11/5	A	KC	14-27	L	82,094
Sun	11/12	A	CIN	20-14	W	59,485
Sun	11/19	A	DEN	37-20	W	51,656
Sun	11/26	H	KC	26-3	W	54,801
Sun	12/3	A	SD	21-19	W	54,611
Mon	12/11	H	NYJ	24-16	W	54,843
Sun	12/17	H	CHI	28-21	W	54,711

AFC Divisional Playoff

Sat	12/23	A	PIT	7-13	L	50,350

PHILADELPHIA EAGLES

Sun	9/17	A	DAL	6-28	L	58,850
Sun	9/24	H	CLE	17-27	L	65,720
Mon	10/2	H	NYG	12-27	L	65,720
Sun	10/8	A	WAS	0-14	L	53,039
Sun	10/15	H	LA	3-34	L	65,720
Sun	10/22	A	KC	21-20	W	78,389
Sun	10/29	A	NO	3-21	L	65,664
Sun	11/5	H	STL	6-6	T	65,720
Sun	11/12	A	HOU	18-17	W	34,175
Sun	11/19	H	DAL	7-28	L	65,720
Sun	11/26	A	NYG	10-62	L	62,586
Sun	12/3	H	WAS	7-23	L	65,720
Sun	12/10	H	CHI	12-21	L	65,720
Sun	12/17	A	STL	23-24	L	34,872

PITTSBURGH STEELERS

Sun	9/17	H	OAK	34-28	W	50,141
Sun	9/24	A	CIN	10-15	L	54,292
Sun	10/1	A	STL	25-19	W	49,140
Sun	10/8	A	DAL	13-17	L	65,682
Sun	10/15	H	HOU	24-7	W	42,923
Sun	10/22	H	NE	33-3	W	46,081
Sun	10/29	A	BUF	38-21	W	45,882
Sun	11/5	H	CIN	40-17	W	50,350
Sun	11/12	H	KC	16-7	W	50,350
Sun	11/19	A	CLE	24-26	L	83,009
Sun	11/26	H	MIN	23-10	W	50,348
Sun	12/3	H	CLE	30-0	W	50,350
Sun	12/10	A	HOU	9-3	W	36,528
Sun	12/17	A	SD	24-2	W	52,873

AFC Divisional Playoff

Sat	12/23	H	OAK	13-7	W	50,350

AFC Championship

Sun	12/31	H	MIA	17-21	L	50,350

ST. LOUIS CARDINALS

Sun	9/17	A	BAL	10-3	W	53,632
Sun	9/24	A	WAS	10-24	L	53,039

Sun	10/1	H	PIT	19-25	L	49,140
Sun	10/8	A	MIN	19-17	W	49,687
Sun	10/15	H	WAS	3-33	L	50,454
Sun	10/22	A	NYG	21-27	L	62,756
Sun	10/29	H	CHI	10-27	L	50,464
Sun	11/5	A	PHI	6-6	T	65,720
Sun	11/12	A	DAL	24-33	L	65,218
Sun	11/19	H	NYG	7-13	L	48,014
Mon	11/27	A	MIA	10-31	L	80,010
Sun	12/3	H	DAL	6-27	L	49,797
Sun	12/10	H	LA	24-14	W	36,873
Sun	12/17	H	PHI	24-23	W	34,872

SAN DIEGO CHARGERS

Sun	9/17	A	SF	3-34	L	59,438
Sun	9/24	H	DEN	37-14	W	49,048
Sun	10/1	A	OAK	17-17	T	53,455
Sun	10/8	A	BAL	23-20	W	55,459
Sun	10/15	A	MIA	10-24	L	80,010
Sun	10/22	A	DET	20-34	L	54,371
Sun	10/29	H	KC	14-26	L	54,533
Sun	11/5	H	DAL	28-34	L	54,476
Mon	11/13	H	CLE	17-21	L	54,205
Sun	11/19	A	KC	27-17	W	79,011
Sun	11/26	H	HOU	34-20	W	46,289
Sun	12/3	H	OAK	19-21	L	54,611
Sun	12/10	A	DEN	13-38	L	51,478
Sun	12/17	H	PIT	2-24	L	52,873

SAN FRANCISCO 49ERS

Sun	9/17	H	SD	34-3	W	59,438
Sun	9/24	A	BUF	20-27	L	45,845
Sun	10/1	A	NO	37-2	W	69,840
Sun	10/8	A	LA	7-31	L	77,382
Sun	10/15	H	NYG	17-23	L	58,606
Sun	10/22	H	NO	20-20	T	59,167
Sun	10/29	A	ATL	49-14	W	58,850
Sun	11/5	A	GB	24-34	L	47,897
Sun	11/12	H	BAL	24-21	W	61,214
Sun	11/19	A	CHI	34-21	W	55,701
Thu	11/23	A	DAL	31-10	W	65,124
Mon	12/4	H	LA	16-26	L	61,214
Sun	12/10	H	ATL	20-0	W	61,214
Sat	12/16	H	MIN	20-17	W	61,214

NFC Divisional Playoff

Sat	12/23	H	DAL	28-30	L	61,214

WASHINGTON REDSKINS

Mon	9/18	A	MIN	24-21	W	47,900
Sun	9/24	H	STL	24-10	W	53,039
Sun	10/1	A	NE	23-24	L	60,999
Sun	10/8	H	PHI	14-0	W	53,039
Sun	10/15	A	STL	33-3	W	50,454
Sun	10/22	H	DAL	24-20	W	53,039
Sun	10/29	A	NYG	23-16	W	62,878
Sun	11/5	A	NYJ	35-17	W	63,962
Sun	11/12	H	NYG	27-13	W	53,039
Mon	11/20	H	ATL	24-13	W	53,039
Sun	11/26	H	GB	21-16	W	53,039
Sun	12/3	A	PHI	23-7	W	65,720
Sat	12/9	A	DAL	24-34	L	65,136
Sun	12/17	H	PHI	17-24	L	53,039

NFC Divisional Playoff

Sun	12/24	H	GB	16-3	W	53,140

NFC Championship

Sun	12/31	H	DAL	26-3	W	53,129

Super Bowl VII

Sun	1/14	A	MIA	7-14	L	90,182

1973 NFL

ATLANTA FALCONS

Sun	9/16	A	NO	62-7	W	66,428
Sun	9/23	A	LA	0-31	L	61,197
Mon	10/1	A	DET	6-31	L	45,599
Sun	10/7	H	SF	9-13	L	51,107
Sun	10/14	H	CHI	46-6	W	47,342
Sun	10/21	A	SD	41-0	W	41,527
Sun	10/28	A	SF	17-3	W	56,825
Sun	11/4	H	LA	15-13	W	55,837
Sun	11/11	A	PHI	44-27	W	63,114
Mon	11/19	H	MIN	20-14	W	56,519
Sun	11/25	A	NYJ	28-20	W	47,283
Sun	12/2	H	BUF	6-17	L	54,607
Sun	12/9	H	STL	10-32	L	48,030
Sun	12/16	H	NO	14-10	W	34,147

BALTIMORE COLTS

Sun	9/16	A	CLE	14-24	L	74,303
Sun	9/23	H	NYJ	10-34	L	55,942
Sun	9/30	H	NO	14-10	W	52,393
Sun	10/7	A	NE	16-24	L	57,044
Sun	10/14	A	BUF	13-31	L	78,875
Sun	10/21	A	DET	29-27	W	48,058
Sun	10/28	H	OAK	21-34	L	54,147
Sun	11/4	H	HOU	27-31	L	46,207
Sun	11/11	A	MIA	0-44	L	60,332
Sun	11/18	A	WAS	14-22	L	52,675
Sun	11/25	H	BUF	17-24	L	52,250
Sun	12/2	A	NYJ	17-20	L	51,167
Sun	12/9	H	MIA	16-3	W	41,005
Sun	12/16	H	NE	18-13	W	52,065

BUFFALO BILLS

Sun	9/16	A	NE	31-13	W	56,119
Sun	9/23	A	SD	7-34	L	47,588
Sun	9/30	H	NYJ	9-7	W	77,425
Sun	10/7	H	PHI	27-26	W	72,364
Sun	10/14	H	BAL	31-13	W	78,875
Sun	10/21	A	MIA	6-27	L	65,241
Mon	10/29	H	KC	23-14	W	76,071
Sun	11/4	A	NO	0-13	L	74,770
Sun	11/11	H	CIN	13-16	L	76,927
Sun	11/18	H	MIA	0-17	L	77,138
Sun	11/25	A	BAL	24-17	W	52,250
Sun	12/2	A	ATL	17-6	W	54,607
Sun	12/9	H	NE	37-13	W	72,470
Sun	12/16	A	NYJ	34-14	W	47,790

CHICAGO BEARS

Sun	9/16	H	DAL	17-20	L	49,790
Sun	9/23	H	MIN	13-22	L	52,035
Sun	9/30	A	DEN	33-14	W	51,159
Sun	10/7	A	NO	16-21	L	56,561
Sun	10/14	A	ATL	6-46	L	47,342
Sun	10/21	H	NE	10-13	L	47,643
Sun	10/28	H	HOU	35-14	W	43,755
Sun	11/4	A	GB	31-17	W	53,231
Mon	11/12	A	KC	7-19	L	70,664
Sun	11/18	H	DET	7-30	L	48,625
Sun	11/25	A	MIN	13-31	L	46,430
Sun	12/2	H	LA	0-26	L	47,620
Sun	12/9	A	DET	7-40	L	41,729
Sun	12/16	H	GB	0-21	L	29,157

CINCINNATI BENGALS

Sun	9/16	A	DEN	10-28	L	49,059
Sun	9/23	H	HOU	24-10	W	51,823
Sun	9/30	A	SD	20-13	W	46,733
Sun	10/7	A	CLE	10-17	L	70,805
Sun	10/14	H	PIT	19-7	W	55,819
Sun	10/21	H	KC	14-6	W	56,397
Sun	10/28	A	PIT	13-20	L	45,761
Sun	11/4	A	DAL	10-38	L	54,944
Sun	11/11	A	BUF	16-13	W	76,927
Sun	11/18	H	NYJ	20-14	W	55,745
Sun	11/25	H	STL	42-24	W	50,918
Sun	12/2	H	MIN	27-0	W	57,859
Sun	12/9	H	CLE	34-17	W	58,266
Sun	12/16	A	HOU	27-24	W	21,955

AFC Divisional Playoff

Sun	12/23	A	MIA	16-34	L	74,651

CLEVELAND BROWNS

Sun	9/16	H	BAL	24-14	W	74,303
Sun	9/23	A	PIT	6-33	L	49,396
Sun	9/30	H	NYG	12-10	W	76,065
Sun	10/7	H	CIN	17-10	W	70,805
Mon	10/15	H	MIA	9-17	L	72,070
Sun	10/21	H	HOU	42-13	W	61,146
Sun	10/28	H	SD	16-16	T	68,244
Sun	11/4	A	MIN	3-26	L	46,722
Sun	11/11	A	HOU	23-13	W	37,230
Sun	11/18	A	OAK	7-3	W	47,398
Sun	11/25	H	PIT	21-16	W	67,773
Sun	12/2	A	KC	20-20	T	70,296
Sun	12/9	A	CIN	17-34	L	58,266
Sun	12/16	A	LA	17-30	L	73,948

DALLAS COWBOYS

Sun	9/16	A	CHI	20-17	W	49,790
Mon	9/24	H	NO	40-3	W	52,715
Sun	9/30	H	STL	45-10	W	64,729
Mon	10/8	A	WAS	7-14	L	54,314
Sun	10/14	A	LA	31-37	L	81,428
Sun	10/21	H	NYG	45-28	W	58,741
Sun	10/28	A	PHI	16-30	L	63,300
Sun	11/4	H	CIN	38-10	W	54,944
Sun	11/11	A	NYG	23-10	W	70,128
Sun	11/18	H	PHI	31-10	W	59,375
Thu	11/22	H	MIA	7-14	L	58,089
Sun	12/2	A	DEN	22-10	W	51,508
Sun	12/9	H	WAS	27-7	W	62,195
Sun	12/16	A	STL	30-3	W	43,946

NFC Divisional Playoff

Sun	12/23	H	LA	27-16	W	62,081

NFC Championship

Sun	12/30	H	MIN	10-27	L	59,688

DENVER BRONCOS

Sun	9/16	H	CIN	28-10	W	49,059
Sun	9/23	H	SF	34-36	L	51,706
Sun	9/30	H	CHI	14-33	L	51,159
Sun	10/7	A	KC	14-16	L	71,414
Sun	10/14	A	HOU	48-20	W	32,801
Mon	10/22	H	OAK	23-23	T	51,270
Sun	10/28	A	NYJ	40-28	W	55,108
Sun	11/4	A	STL	17-17	T	46,565
Sun	11/11	H	SD	30-19	W	51,034
Sun	11/18	A	PIT	23-13	W	48,580
Sun	11/25	H	KC	14-10	W	51,331
Sun	12/2	H	DAL	10-22	L	51,508
Sun	12/9	A	SD	42-28	W	44,954
Sun	12/16	A	OAK	17-21	L	51,910

DETROIT LIONS

Sun	9/16	A	PIT	10-24	L	48,913
Sun	9/23	A	GB	13-13	T	55,495
Mon	10/1	H	ATL	31-6	W	45,599
Sun	10/7	H	MIN	9-23	L	49,544
Sun	10/14	A	NO	13-20	L	57,810
Sun	10/21	H	BAL	27-29	L	48,058
Sun	10/28	H	GB	34-0	W	43,616
Sun	11/4	H	SF	30-20	W	49,310
Sun	11/11	A	MIN	7-28	L	47,911
Sun	11/18	A	CHI	30-7	W	48,625
Thu	11/22	H	WAS	0-20	L	46,807
Sun	12/2	A	STL	20-16	W	44,982
Sun	12/9	H	CHI	40-7	W	41,729
Sat	12/15	A	MIA	7-34	L	53,375

GREEN BAY PACKERS

Mon	9/17	H	NYJ	23-7	W	47,124
Sun	9/23	H	DET	13-13	T	55,495
Sun	9/30	A	MIN	3-11	L	48,176
Sun	10/7	A	NYG	16-14	W	70,050
Sun	10/14	H	KC	10-10	T	46,583
Sun	10/21	A	LA	7-24	L	80,558
Sun	10/28	A	DET	0-34	L	43,616
Sun	11/4	H	CHI	17-31	L	53,231
Sun	11/11	H	STL	25-21	W	52,922
Sun	11/18	A	NE	24-33	L	60,525
Mon	11/26	A	SF	6-20	L	49,244
Sun	12/2	H	NO	30-10	W	46,092
Sat	12/8	H	MIN	7-31	L	53,830
Sun	12/16	A	CHI	21-0	W	29,157

HOUSTON OILERS

Sun	9/16	A	NYG	14-34	L	57,979
Sun	9/23	A	CIN	10-24	L	51,823
Sun	9/30	H	PIT	7-36	L	39,331
Sun	10/7	H	LA	26-31	L	34,875
Sun	10/14	H	DEN	20-48	L	32,801
Sun	10/21	A	CLE	13-42	L	61,146
Sun	10/28	A	CHI	14-35	L	43,755
Sun	11/4	A	BAL	31-27	W	46,207
Sun	11/11	H	CLE	13-23	L	37,230
Sun	11/18	A	KC	14-38	L	68,444
Sun	11/25	H	NE	0-32	L	27,344
Sun	12/2	H	OAK	6-17	L	25,801
Sun	12/9	A	PIT	7-33	L	38,004
Sun	12/16	H	CIN	24-27	L	21,955

KANSAS CITY CHIEFS

Sun	9/16	H	LA	13-23	L	62,315
Sun	9/23	A	NE	10-7	W	57,918
Sun	9/30	H	OAK	16-3	W	72,631
Sun	10/7	H	DEN	16-14	W	71,414
Sun	10/14	A	GB	10-10	T	46,583
Sun	10/21	A	CIN	6-14	L	56,397
Mon	10/29	A	BUF	14-23	L	76,071
Sun	11/4	A	SD	19-0	W	50,234
Mon	11/12	H	CHI	19-7	W	70,664
Sun	11/18	H	HOU	38-14	W	68,444
Sun	11/25	A	DEN	10-14	L	51,331
Sun	12/2	H	CLE	20-20	T	70,296
Sat	12/8	A	OAK	7-37	L	53,061
Sun	12/16	H	SD	33-6	W	43,755

LOS ANGELES RAMS

Sun	9/16	A	KC	23-13	W	62,315
Sun	9/23	H	ATL	31-0	W	61,197
Sun	9/30	A	SF	40-20	W	57,487
Sun	10/7	A	HOU	31-26	W	34,875
Sun	10/14	H	DAL	37-31	W	81,428
Sun	10/21	H	GB	24-7	W	80,558
Sun	10/28	A	MIN	9-10	L	47,787
Sun	11/4	A	ATL	13-15	L	55,837
Sun	11/11	H	NO	29-7	W	70,358
Sun	11/18	H	SF	31-13	W	78,358
Sun	11/25	A	NO	24-13	W	67,192
Sun	12/2	A	CHI	26-0	W	47,620
Mon	12/10	H	NYG	40-6	W	73,328
Sun	12/16	H	CLE	30-17	W	73,948

NFC Divisional Playoff

Sun	12/23	A	DAL	16-27	L	62,081

MIAMI DOLPHINS

Sun	9/16	H	SF	21-13	W	68,275
Sun	9/23	A	OAK	7-12	L	74,121
Sun	9/30	H	NE	44-23	W	62,508
Sun	10/7	H	NYJ	31-3	W	63,850
Mon	10/15	A	CLE	17-9	W	72,070
Sun	10/21	H	BUF	27-6	W	65,241
Sun	10/28	A	NE	30-14	W	57,919
Sun	11/4	A	NYJ	24-14	W	57,491
Sun	11/11	H	BAL	44-0	W	60,332
Sun	11/18	A	BUF	17-0	W	77,138
Thu	11/22	A	DAL	14-7	W	58,089
Mon	12/3	H	PIT	30-26	W	68,901

Sun	12/9	A	BAL	3-16	L	41,005
Sat	12/15	H	DET	34-7	W	53,375

AFC Divisional Playoff

Sun	12/23	H	CIN	34-16	W	74,651

AFC Championship

Sun	12/30	H	OAK	27-10	W	74,384

Super Bowl VIII

Sun	1/13	N	MIN	24-7	W	68,142

MINNESOTA VIKINGS

Sun	9/16	H	OAK	24-16	W	44,818
Sun	9/23	A	CHI	22-13	W	52,035
Sun	9/30	H	GB	11-3	W	48,176
Sun	10/7	A	DET	23-9	W	49,544
Sun	10/14	A	SF	17-13	W	56,438
Sun	10/21	H	PHI	28-21	W	47,478
Sun	10/28	H	LA	10-9	W	47,787
Sun	11/4	H	CLE	26-3	W	46,722
Sun	11/11	H	DET	28-7	W	47,911
Mon	11/19	A	ATL	14-20	L	56,519
Sun	11/25	H	CHI	31-13	W	46,430
Sun	12/2	A	CIN	0-27	L	57,859
Sat	12/8	A	GB	31-7	W	53,830
Sun	12/16	A	NYG	31-7	W	70,041

NFC Divisional Playoff

Sat	12/22	H	WAS	27-20	W	46,065

NFC Championship

Sun	12/30	A	DAL	27-10	W	59,688

Super Bowl VIII

Sun	1/13	N	MIA	7-24	L	68,142

NEW ENGLAND PATRIOTS

Sun	9/16	H	BUF	13-31	L	56,119
Sun	9/23	H	KC	7-10	L	57,918
Sun	9/30	A	MIA	23-44	L	62,508
Sun	10/7	H	BAL	24-16	W	57,044
Sun	10/14	H	NYJ	7-9	L	57,781
Sun	10/21	A	CHI	13-10	W	47,643
Sun	10/28	H	MIA	14-30	L	57,919
Sun	11/4	A	PHI	23-24	L	65,070
Sun	11/11	A	NYJ	13-33	L	51,034
Sun	11/18	H	GB	33-24	W	60,525
Sun	11/25	A	HOU	32-0	W	27,344
Sun	12/2	H	SD	30-14	W	58,150
Sun	12/9	A	BUF	13-37	L	72,470
Sun	12/16	A	BAL	13-18	L	52,065

NEW ORLEANS SAINTS

Sun	9/16	H	ATL	7-62	L	66,428
Mon	9/24	A	DAL	3-40	L	52,715
Sun	9/30	A	BAL	10-14	L	52,393
Sun	10/7	H	CHI	21-16	W	56,561
Sun	10/14	H	DET	20-13	W	57,810
Sun	10/21	A	SF	0-40	L	52,881
Sun	10/28	H	WAS	19-3	W	66,315
Sun	11/4	H	BUF	13-0	W	74,770
Sun	11/11	A	LA	7-29	L	70,358
Sun	11/18	A	SD	14-17	L	34,848
Sun	11/25	H	LA	13-24	L	67,192
Sun	12/2	A	GB	10-30	L	46,092
Sun	12/9	H	SF	16-10	W	62,490
Sun	12/16	A	ATL	10-14	L	34,147

NEW YORK GIANTS

Sun	9/16	H	HOU	34-14	W	57,979
Sun	9/23	H	PHI	23-23	T	57,138
Sun	9/30	A	CLE	10-12	L	76,065
Sun	10/7	H	GB	14-16	L	70,050
Sun	10/14	H	WAS	3-21	L	70,168
Sun	10/21	A	DAL	28-45	L	58,741
Sun	10/28	A	STL	27-35	L	47,589
Sun	11/4	A	OAK	0-42	L	51,200
Sun	11/11	H	DAL	10-23	L	70,128
Sun	11/18	H	STL	24-13	W	65,795
Sun	11/25	A	PHI	16-20	L	63,086
Sun	12/2	A	WAS	24-27	L	52,036
Mon	12/10	A	LA	6-40	L	73,328
Sun	12/16	H	MIN	7-31	L	70,041

NEW YORK JETS

Mon	9/17	A	GB	7-23	L	47,124
Sun	9/23	A	BAL	34-10	W	55,942
Sun	9/30	A	BUF	7-9	L	77,425
Sun	10/7	A	MIA	3-31	L	63,850
Sun	10/14	A	NE	9-7	W	57,781
Sun	10/21	A	PIT	14-26	L	48,682
Sun	10/28	H	DEN	28-40	L	55,108
Sun	11/4	H	MIA	14-24	L	57,491
Sun	11/11	H	NE	33-13	W	51,034
Sun	11/18	A	CIN	14-20	L	55,745
Sun	11/25	H	ATL	20-28	L	47,283
Sun	12/2	H	BAL	20-17	W	51,167
Sun	12/9	A	PHI	23-24	L	34,621
Sun	12/16	H	BUF	14-34	L	47,790

OAKLAND RAIDERS

Sun	9/16	A	MIN	16-24	L	44,818
Sun	9/23	H	MIA	12-7	W	74,121
Sun	9/30	A	KC	3-16	L	72,631
Sun	10/7	A	STL	17-10	W	49,051
Sun	10/14	H	SD	27-17	W	50,672
Mon	10/22	A	DEN	23-23	T	51,270
Sun	10/28	A	BAL	34-21	W	54,147
Sun	11/4	H	NYG	42-0	W	51,200
Sun	11/11	H	PIT	9-17	L	47,535
Sun	11/18	H	CLE	3-7	L	47,398
Sun	11/25	A	SD	31-3	W	40,195
Sun	12/2	A	HOU	17-6	W	25,801
Sat	12/8	H	KC	37-7	W	53,061
Sun	12/16	H	DEN	21-17	W	51,910

AFC Divisional Playoff

Sat	12/22	H	PIT	33-14	W	50,094

AFC Championship

Sun	12/30	A	MIA	10-27	L	74,384

PHILADELPHIA EAGLES

Sun	9/16	H	STL	23-34	L	61,103
Sun	9/23	A	NYG	23-23	T	57,138
Sun	9/30	H	WAS	7-28	L	64,147
Sun	10/7	A	BUF	26-27	L	72,364
Sun	10/14	A	STL	27-24	W	44,400
Sun	10/21	A	MIN	21-28	L	47,478
Sun	10/28	H	DAL	30-16	W	63,300
Sun	11/4	H	NE	24-23	W	65,070
Sun	11/11	H	ATL	27-44	L	63,114
Sun	11/18	A	DAL	10-31	L	59,375
Sun	11/25	H	NYG	20-16	W	63,086
Sun	12/2	A	SF	28-38	L	51,155
Sun	12/9	H	NYJ	24-23	W	34,621
Sun	12/16	A	WAS	20-38	L	49,484

PITTSBURGH STEELERS

Sun	9/16	H	DET	24-10	W	48,913
Sun	9/23	H	CLE	33-6	W	49,396
Sun	9/30	A	HOU	36-7	W	39,331
Sun	10/7	H	SD	38-21	W	48,795
Sun	10/14	A	CIN	7-19	L	55,819
Sun	10/21	H	NYJ	26-14	W	48,682
Sun	10/28	H	CIN	20-13	W	45,761
Mon	11/5	H	WAS	21-16	W	49,220
Sun	11/11	A	OAK	17-9	W	47,535
Sun	11/18	H	DEN	13-23	L	48,580
Sun	11/25	A	CLE	16-21	L	67,773
Mon	12/3	A	MIA	26-30	L	68,901
Sun	12/9	H	HOU	33-7	W	38,004
Sat	12/15	A	SF	37-14	W	52,252

AFC Divisional Playoff

Sat	12/22	A	OAK	14-33	L	50,094

ST. LOUIS CARDINALS

Sun	9/16	A	PHI	34-23	W	61,103
Sun	9/23	H	WAS	34-27	W	50,316
Sun	9/30	A	DAL	10-45	L	64,729
Sun	10/7	H	OAK	10-17	L	49,051
Sun	10/14	H	PHI	24-27	L	44,400
Sun	10/21	A	WAS	13-31	L	54,381
Sun	10/28	H	NYG	35-27	W	47,589
Sun	11/4	H	DEN	17-17	T	46,565
Sun	11/11	A	GB	21-25	L	52,922
Sun	11/18	A	NYG	13-24	L	65,795
Sun	11/25	A	CIN	24-42	L	50,918
Sun	12/2	H	DET	16-20	L	44,982
Sun	12/9	A	ATL	32-10	W	48,030
Sun	12/16	H	DAL	3-30	L	43,946

SAN DIEGO CHARGERS

Sun	9/16	A	WAS	0-38	L	52,718
Sun	9/23	H	BUF	34-7	W	47,588
Sun	9/30	H	CIN	13-20	L	46,733
Sun	10/7	A	PIT	21-38	L	48,795
Sun	10/14	A	OAK	17-27	L	50,672
Sun	10/21	H	ATL	0-41	L	41,527
Sun	10/28	A	CLE	16-16	T	68,244
Sun	11/4	H	KC	0-19	L	50,234
Sun	11/11	A	DEN	19-30	L	51,034
Sun	11/18	H	NO	17-14	W	34,848
Sun	11/25	H	OAK	3-31	L	40,195
Sun	12/2	A	NE	14-30	L	58,150
Sun	12/9	H	DEN	28-42	L	44,954
Sun	12/16	A	KC	6-33	L	43,755

SAN FRANCISCO 49ERS

Sun	9/16	A	MIA	13-21	L	68,275
Sun	9/23	A	DEN	36-34	W	51,706
Sun	9/30	H	LA	20-40	L	57,487
Sun	10/7	A	ATL	13-9	W	51,107
Sun	10/14	H	MIN	13-17	L	56,438
Sun	10/21	H	NO	40-0	W	52,881
Sun	10/28	H	ATL	3-17	L	56,825
Sun	11/4	A	DET	20-30	L	49,310
Sun	11/11	A	WAS	9-33	L	54,267
Sun	11/18	A	LA	13-31	L	78,358
Mon	11/26	H	GB	20-6	W	49,244
Sun	12/2	H	PHI	38-28	W	51,155
Sun	12/9	A	NO	10-16	L	62,490
Sat	12/15	H	PIT	14-37	L	52,252

WASHINGTON REDSKINS

Sun	9/16	H	SD	38-0	W	52,718
Sun	9/23	A	STL	27-34	L	50,316
Sun	9/30	A	PHI	28-7	W	64,147
Mon	10/8	H	DAL	14-7	W	54,314
Sun	10/14	A	NYG	21-3	W	70,168
Sun	10/21	H	STL	31-13	W	54,381
Sun	10/28	A	NO	3-19	L	66,315
Mon	11/5	A	PIT	16-21	L	49,220
Sun	11/11	H	SF	33-9	W	54,267
Sun	11/18	H	BAL	22-14	W	52,675
Thu	11/22	A	DET	20-0	W	46,807
Sun	12/2	H	NYG	27-24	W	52,036
Sun	12/9	A	DAL	7-27	L	62,195
Sun	12/16	H	PHI	38-20	W	49,484

NFC Divisional Playoff

Sat	12/22	A	MIN	20-27	L	46,065

1974 NFL

ATLANTA FALCONS

Sun	9/15	H	DAL	0-24	L	52,322
Sun	9/22	H	SF	10-16	L	47,686
Sun	9/29	A	NO	13-14	L	55,025
Sun	10/6	A	NYG	14-7	W	42,379
Sun	10/13	H	CHI	13-10	W	47,835
Sun	10/20	H	NO	3-13	L	47,127
Mon	10/28	A	PIT	17-24	L	48,094
Sun	11/3	A	MIA	7-42	L	64,399
Sun	11/10	A	LA	0-21	L	62,133
Sun	11/17	H	BAL	7-17	L	41,278
Sun	11/24	A	SF	0-27	L	45,435
Sun	12/1	H	LA	7-30	L	18,648
Sat	12/7	A	MIN	10-23	L	47,105
Sun	12/15	H	GB	10-3	W	10,020

BALTIMORE COLTS

Sun	9/15	A	PIT	0-30	L	48,890
Sun	9/22	H	GB	13-20	L	35,873
Sun	9/29	A	PHI	10-30	L	64,205
Sun	10/6	A	NE	3-42	L	55,820
Sun	10/13	H	BUF	14-27	L	36,314
Sun	10/20	A	NYJ	35-20	W	51,745
Sun	10/27	A	MIA	7-17	L	65,868
Sun	11/3	H	CIN	14-24	L	35,110
Sun	11/10	H	DEN	6-17	L	32,244
Sun	11/17	A	ATL	17-7	W	41,278
Sun	11/24	H	NE	17-27	L	33,782
Sun	12/1	A	BUF	0-6	L	75,325
Sun	12/8	H	MIA	16-17	L	33,320
Sun	12/15	H	NYJ	38-45	L	31,651

BUFFALO BILLS

Mon	9/16	H	OAK	21-20	W	79,791
Sun	9/22	H	MIA	16-24	L	78,990
Sun	9/29	H	NYJ	16-12	W	76,866
Sun	10/6	A	GB	27-7	W	51,919
Sun	10/13	A	BAL	27-14	W	36,314
Sun	10/20	H	NE	30-28	W	78,935
Sun	10/27	H	CHI	16-6	W	78,084
Sun	11/3	A	NE	29-28	W	58,932
Sun	11/10	H	HOU	9-21	L	79,144
Sun	11/17	A	MIA	28-35	L	69,313
Sun	11/24	A	CLE	15-10	W	66,504
Sun	12/1	H	BAL	6-0	W	75,325
Sun	12/8	A	NYJ	10-20	L	31,982
Sun	12/15	A	LA	14-19	L	78,967

AFC Divisional Playoff

Sun	12/22	A	PIT	14-32	L	48,321

CHICAGO BEARS

Sun	9/15	H	DET	17-9	W	48,134
Sun	9/22	H	NYJ	21-23	L	50,213
Sun	9/29	A	MIN	7-11	L	46,217
Sun	10/6	H	NO	24-10	W	45,818
Sun	10/13	A	ATL	10-13	L	47,835
Mon	10/21	H	GB	10-9	W	50,623
Sun	10/27	A	BUF	6-16	L	78,084
Sun	11/3	H	MIN	0-17	L	33,343
Sun	11/10	A	GB	3-20	L	46,567
Sun	11/17	H	SF	0-34	L	42,686
Sun	11/24	A	DET	17-34	L	40,930
Sun	12/1	H	NYG	16-13	W	18,802
Sun	12/8	A	SD	21-28	L	33,662
Sun	12/15	A	WAS	0-42	L	52,085

CINCINNATI BENGALS

Sun	9/15	H	CLE	33-7	W	53,113
Sun	9/22	H	SD	17-20	L	51,178
Sun	9/29	A	SF	21-3	W	49,895
Sun	10/6	H	WAS	28-17	W	56,175
Sun	10/13	A	CLE	34-24	W	70,897
Sun	10/20	A	OAK	27-30	L	51,821
Sun	10/27	H	HOU	21-34	L	55,434
Sun	11/3	A	BAL	24-14	W	35,110
Sun	11/10	H	PIT	17-10	W	57,532
Sun	11/17	A	HOU	3-20	L	44,054
Sun	11/24	H	KC	33-6	W	49,777
Mon	12/2	A	MIA	3-24	L	71,962
Sun	12/8	H	DET	19-23	L	45,159
Sat	12/14	A	PIT	3-27	L	42,878

CLEVELAND BROWNS

Sun	9/15	A	CIN	7-33	L	53,113
Sun	9/22	H	HOU	20-7	W	55,242
Sun	9/29	A	STL	7-29	L	43,472

Sun	10/6	H	OAK	24-40	L	65,247
Sun	10/13	H	CIN	24-34	L	70,897
Sun	10/20	A	PIT	16-20	L	48,100
Sun	10/27	H	DEN	23-21	W	60,478
Sun	11/3	A	SD	35-36	L	34,087
Sun	11/10	A	NE	21-14	W	57,263
Sun	11/17	H	PIT	16-26	L	77,195
Sun	11/24	H	BUF	10-15	L	66,504
Sun	12/1	H	SF	7-0	W	24,559
Sat	12/7	A	DAL	17-41	L	48,754
Sun	12/15	A	HOU	24-28	L	33,299

DALLAS COWBOYS

Sun	9/15	A	ATL	24-0	W	52,322
Mon	9/23	A	PHI	10-13	L	64,089
Sun	9/29	H	NYG	6-14	L	45,841
Sun	10/6	H	MIN	21-23	L	57,847
Sun	10/13	A	STL	28-31	L	49,885
Sun	10/20	H	PHI	31-24	W	43,586
Sun	10/27	A	NYG	21-7	W	57,381
Sun	11/3	H	STL	17-14	W	64,146
Sun	11/10	H	SF	20-14	W	50,018
Sun	11/17	A	WAS	21-28	L	54,395
Sun	11/24	A	HOU	10-0	W	49,775
Thu	11/28	H	WAS	24-23	W	63,243
Sat	12/7	H	CLE	41-17	W	48,754
Sat	12/14	A	OAK	23-27	L	45,840

DENVER BRONCOS

Sun	9/15	H	LA	10-17	L	56,981
Sun	9/22	H	PIT	*35-35	T	50,858
Mon	9/30	A	WAS	3-30	L	54,395
Sun	10/6	A	KC	17-14	W	67,298
Sun	10/13	H	NO	33-17	W	50,751
Sun	10/20	H	SD	27-7	W	50,748
Sun	10/27	A	CLE	21-23	L	60,478
Sun	11/3	H	OAK	17-28	L	45,766
Sun	11/10	A	BAL	17-6	W	33,244
Mon	11/18	H	KC	34-42	L	50,236
Sun	11/24	A	OAK	20-17	W	51,224
Thu	11/28	A	DET	31-27	W	51,157
Sun	12/8	H	HOU	37-14	W	46,942
Sun	12/15	A	SD	0-17	L	35,756

DETROIT LIONS

Sun	9/15	A	CHI	9-17	L	48,134
Sun	9/22	H	MIN	6-7	L	44,546
Sun	9/29	A	GB	19-21	L	45,970
Sun	10/6	A	LA	13-16	L	56,599
Mon	10/14	H	SF	17-13	W	45,199
Sun	10/20	A	MIN	20-16	W	47,807
Sun	10/27	H	GB	19-17	W	51,775
Sun	11/3	H	NO	19-14	W	43,256
Sun	11/10	A	OAK	13-35	L	51,973
Sun	11/17	H	NYG	20-19	W	40,431
Sun	11/24	H	CHI	34-17	W	40,930
Thu	11/28	H	DEN	27-31	L	51,157
Sun	12/8	A	CIN	23-19	W	45,159
Sun	12/15	A	PHI	17-28	L	57,157

GREEN BAY PACKERS

Sun	9/15	H	MIN	17-32	L	55,131
Sun	9/22	A	BAL	20-13	W	35,873
Sun	9/29	H	DET	21-19	W	45,970
Sun	10/6	H	BUF	7-27	L	51,919
Sun	10/13	H	LA	17-6	W	45,938
Mon	10/21	A	CHI	9-10	L	50,623
Sun	10/27	A	DET	17-19	L	51,775
Sun	11/3	H	WAS	6-17	L	55,288
Sun	11/10	H	CHI	20-3	W	46,567
Sun	11/17	A	MIN	19-7	W	47,924
Sun	11/24	H	SD	34-0	W	50,321
Sun	12/1	A	PHI	14-36	L	42,030
Sun	12/8	A	SF	6-7	L	45,475
Sun	12/15	A	ATL	3-10	L	10,020

HOUSTON OILERS

Sun	9/15	H	SD	21-14	W	25,317
Sun	9/22	A	CLE	7-20	L	55,242
Sun	9/29	H	KC	7-17	L	28,538
Sun	10/6	H	PIT	7-13	L	30,049
Sun	10/13	A	MIN	10-51	L	48,006
Sun	10/20	H	STL	27-31	L	26,371
Sun	10/27	A	CIN	34-21	W	55,434
Sun	11/3	A	NYJ	27-22	W	47,218
Sun	11/10	A	BUF	21-9	W	79,144
Sun	11/17	H	CIN	20-3	W	44,054
Sun	11/24	H	DAL	0-10	L	49,775
Sun	12/1	A	PIT	13-10	W	41,195
Sun	12/8	A	DEN	14-37	L	46,942
Sun	12/15	H	CLE	28-24	W	33,299

KANSAS CITY CHIEFS

Sun	9/15	H	NYJ	24-16	W	73,959
Sun	9/22	A	OAK	7-27	L	48,108
Sun	9/29	A	HOU	17-7	W	28,538
Sun	10/6	H	DEN	14-17	L	67,298
Sun	10/13	H	PIT	24-34	L	65,517
Sun	10/20	A	MIA	3-9	L	67,779
Sun	10/27	A	SD	24-14	W	33,898
Sun	11/3	H	NYG	27-33	L	61,437
Sun	11/10	H	SD	7-14	L	48,551
Mon	11/18	A	DEN	42-34	W	50,236
Sun	11/24	A	CIN	6-33	L	49,777
Sun	12/1	A	STL	17-13	W	41,863
Sun	12/8	H	OAK	6-7	L	60,577
Sat	12/14	H	MIN	15-35	L	35,480

LOS ANGELES RAMS

Sun	9/15	A	DEN	17-10	W	56,981
Sun	9/22	H	NO	24-0	W	57,314
Sun	9/29	A	NE	14-20	L	59,712
Sun	10/6	H	DET	16-13	W	56,599
Sun	10/13	A	GB	6-17	L	45,938
Sun	10/20	H	SF	37-14	W	67,319
Sun	10/27	A	NYJ	20-13	W	56,110
Mon	11/4	A	SF	15-13	W	57,526
Sun	11/10	H	ATL	21-0	W	62,133
Sun	11/17	A	NO	7-20	L	35,727
Sun	11/24	H	MIN	20-17	W	87,138
Sun	12/1	A	ATL	30-7	W	18,648
Mon	12/9	H	WAS	17-23	L	84,327
Sun	12/15	H	BUF	19-14	W	78,967

NFC Divisional Playoff

Sun	12/22	H	WAS	19-10	W	80,118

NFC Championship

Sun	12/29	A	MIN	10-14	L	47,404

MIAMI DOLPHINS

Sun	9/15	A	NE	24-34	L	51,508
Sun	9/22	A	BUF	24-16	W	78,990
Sun	9/29	A	SD	28-21	W	44,706
Mon	10/7	H	NYJ	21-17	W	61,527
Sun	10/13	A	WAS	17-20	L	54,395
Sun	10/20	H	KC	9-3	W	67,779
Sun	10/27	H	BAL	17-7	W	65,868
Sun	11/3	H	ATL	42-7	W	64,399
Sun	11/10	A	NO	21-0	W	68,339
Sun	11/17	H	BUF	35-28	W	69,313
Sun	11/24	A	NYJ	14-17	L	57,162
Mon	12/2	H	CIN	24-3	W	71,962
Sun	12/8	A	BAL	17-16	W	33,320
Sun	12/15	H	NE	34-27	W	56,920

AFC Divisional Playoff

Sat	12/21	A	OAK	26-28	L	52,817

MINNESOTA VIKINGS

Sun	9/15	A	GB	32-17	W	55,131
Sun	9/22	A	DET	7-6	W	44,546
Sun	9/29	H	CHI	11-7	W	46,217
Sun	10/6	A	DAL	23-21	W	57,847
Sun	10/13	H	HOU	51-10	W	48,006
Sun	10/20	H	DET	16-20	L	47,807
Sun	10/27	H	NE	14-17	L	48,177
Sun	11/3	A	CHI	17-0	W	33,343
Mon	11/11	A	STL	28-24	W	50,183
Sun	11/17	H	GB	7-19	L	47,924
Sun	11/24	A	LA	17-20	L	87,138
Sun	12/1	H	NO	29-9	W	44,202
Sat	12/7	H	ATL	23-10	W	47,105
Sat	12/14	A	KC	35-15	W	35,480

NFC Divisional Playoff

Sat	12/21	H	STL	30-14	W	44,626

NFC Championship

Sun	12/29	H	LA	14-10	W	47,404

Super Bowl IX

Sun	1/12	N	PIT	6-16	L	80,997

NEW ENGLAND PATRIOTS

Sun	9/15	H	MIA	34-24	W	51,508
Sun	9/22	A	NYG	28-20	W	44,082
Sun	9/29	H	LA	20-14	W	59,712
Sun	10/6	H	BAL	42-3	W	55,820
Sun	10/13	A	NYJ	24-0	W	57,828
Sun	10/20	A	BUF	28-30	L	78,935
Sun	10/27	A	MIN	17-14	W	48,177
Sun	11/3	H	BUF	28-29	L	58,932
Sun	11/10	H	CLE	14-21	L	57,263
Sun	11/17	H	NYJ	16-21	L	57,165
Sun	11/24	A	BAL	27-17	W	33,782
Sun	12/1	A	OAK	26-41	L	50,120
Sun	12/8	H	PIT	17-21	L	52,107
Sun	12/15	A	MIA	27-34	L	56,920

NEW ORLEANS SAINTS

Sun	9/15	H	SF	13-17	L	59,945
Sun	9/22	A	LA	0-24	L	57,314
Sun	9/29	H	ATL	14-13	W	55,025
Sun	10/6	A	CHI	10-24	L	45,818
Sun	10/13	A	DEN	17-33	L	50,751
Sun	10/20	A	ATL	13-3	W	47,127
Sun	10/27	H	PHI	14-10	W	57,136
Sun	11/3	A	DET	14-19	L	43,256
Sun	11/10	H	MIA	0-21	L	68,339
Sun	11/17	H	LA	20-7	W	35,727
Mon	11/25	H	PIT	7-28	L	69,010
Sun	12/1	A	MIN	9-29	L	44,202
Sun	12/8	H	STL	14-0	W	47,172
Sun	12/15	A	SF	21-35	L	40,418

NEW YORK GIANTS

Sun	9/15	H	WAS	10-13	L	49,849
Sun	9/22	H	NE	20-28	L	44,082
Sun	9/29	A	DAL	14-6	W	45,841
Sun	10/6	H	ATL	7-14	L	42,379
Sun	10/13	A	PHI	7-35	L	64,801
Sun	10/20	A	WAS	3-24	L	53,879
Sun	10/27	H	DAL	7-21	L	57,381
Sun	11/3	A	KC	33-27	W	61,437
Sun	11/10	H	NYJ	*20-26	L	64,327
Sun	11/17	A	DET	19-20	L	40,431
Sun	11/24	H	STL	21-23	L	40,615
Sun	12/1	A	CHI	13-16	L	18,802
Sun	12/8	H	PHI	7-20	L	21,170
Sun	12/15	A	STL	14-26	L	47,414

NEW YORK JETS

Sun	9/15	A	KC	16-24	L	73,959
Sun	9/22	A	CHI	23-21	W	50,213
Sun	9/29	A	BUF	12-16	L	76,866
Mon	10/7	A	MIA	17-21	L	61,527
Sun	10/13	H	NE	0-24	L	57,828
Sun	10/20	H	BAL	20-35	L	51,745
Sun	10/27	H	LA	13-20	L	56,110
Sun	11/3	H	HOU	22-27	L	47,218
Sun	11/10	A	NYG	*26-20	W	64,327
Sun	11/17	A	NE	21-16	W	57,165
Sun	11/24	H	MIA	17-14	W	57,162
Sun	12/1	H	SD	27-14	W	44,888
Sun	12/8	H	BUF	20-10	W	31,982
Sun	12/15	A	BAL	45-38	W	31,651

OAKLAND RAIDERS

Mon	9/16	A	BUF	20-21	L	79,791
Sun	9/22	H	KC	27-7	W	48,108
Sun	9/29	A	PIT	17-0	W	48,304
Sun	10/6	A	CLE	40-24	W	65,247
Sun	10/13	A	SD	14-10	W	40,013
Sun	10/20	H	CIN	30-27	W	51,821
Sun	10/27	A	SF	35-24	W	58,524
Sun	11/3	A	DEN	28-17	W	45,766
Sun	11/10	H	DET	35-13	W	51,973
Sun	11/17	H	SD	17-10	W	50,178
Sun	11/24	H	DEN	17-20	L	51,224
Sun	12/1	H	NE	41-26	W	50,120
Sun	12/8	A	KC	7-6	W	60,577
Sat	12/14	H	DAL	27-23	W	45,840

AFC Divisional Playoff

Sat	12/21	H	MIA	28-26	W	52,817

AFC Championship

Sun	12/29	H	PIT	13-24	L	53,515

PHILADELPHIA EAGLES

Sun	9/15	A	STL	3-7	L	40,322
Mon	9/23	H	DAL	13-10	W	64,089
Sun	9/29	H	BAL	30-10	W	64,205
Sun	10/6	A	SD	13-7	W	36,013
Sun	10/13	H	NYG	35-7	W	64,801
Sun	10/20	A	DAL	24-31	L	43,586
Sun	10/27	A	NO	10-14	L	57,136
Sun	11/3	A	PIT	0-27	L	47,996
Sun	11/10	H	WAS	20-27	L	65,947
Sun	11/17	H	STL	3-13	L	61,982
Sun	11/24	A	WAS	7-26	L	54,395
Sun	12/1	H	GB	36-14	W	42,030
Sun	12/8	A	NYG	20-7	W	21,170
Sun	12/15	H	DET	28-17	W	57,157

PITTSBURGH STEELERS

Sun	9/15	H	BAL	30-0	W	48,890
Sun	9/22	A	DEN	*35-35	T	50,858
Sun	9/29	H	OAK	0-17	L	48,304
Sun	10/6	A	HOU	13-7	W	30,049
Sun	10/13	A	KC	34-24	W	65,517
Sun	10/20	H	CLE	20-16	W	48,100
Mon	10/28	H	ATL	24-17	W	48,094
Sun	11/3	H	PHI	27-0	W	47,996
Sun	11/10	A	CIN	10-17	L	57,532
Sun	11/17	A	CLE	26-16	W	77,195
Mon	11/25	A	NO	28-7	W	69,010
Sun	12/1	H	HOU	10-13	L	41,195
Sun	12/8	A	NE	21-17	W	52,107
Sat	12/14	H	CIN	27-3	W	42,878

AFC Divisional Playoff

Sun	12/22	H	BUF	32-14	W	48,321

AFC Championship

Sun	12/29	A	OAK	24-13	W	53,515

Super Bowl IX

Sun	1/12	N	MIN	16-6	W	80,997

ST. LOUIS CARDINALS

Sun	9/15	H	PHI	7-3	W	40,322
Sun	9/22	A	WAS	17-10	W	53,888
Sun	9/29	H	CLE	29-7	W	43,472
Sun	10/6	A	SF	34-9	W	47,675
Sun	10/13	H	DAL	31-28	W	49,885
Sun	10/20	A	HOU	31-27	W	26,371
Sun	10/27	H	WAS	23-20	W	49,410
Sun	11/3	A	DAL	14-17	L	64,146
Mon	11/11	H	MIN	24-28	L	50,183
Sun	11/17	A	PHI	13-3	W	61,982

Sun 11/24 A NYG 23-21 W 40,615
Sun 12/1 H KC 13-17 L 41,863
Sun 12/8 A NO 0-14 L 47,172
Sun 12/15 H NYG 26-14 W 47,414

NFC DIVISIONAL PLAYOFF
Sat 12/21 A MIN 14-30 L 44,626

SAN DIEGO CHARGERS
Sun 9/15 A HOU 14-21 L 25,317
Sun 9/22 A CIN 20-17 W 51,178
Sun 9/29 H MIA 21-28 L 44,706
Sun 10/6 H PHI 7-13 L 36,013
Sun 10/13 H OAK 10-14 L 40,013
Sun 10/20 A DEN 7-27 L 50,748
Sun 10/27 H KC 14-24 L 33,898
Sun 11/3 H CLE 36-35 W 34,087
Sun 11/10 A KC 14-7 W 48,551
Sun 11/17 A OAK 10-17 L 50,178
Sun 11/24 A GB 0-34 L 50,321
Sun 12/1 A NYJ 14-27 L 44,888
Sun 12/8 H CHI 28-21 W 33,662
Sun 12/15 H DEN 17-0 W 35,756

SAN FRANCISCO 49ERS
Sun 9/15 A NO 17-13 W 59,945
Sun 9/22 A ATL 16-10 W 47,686
Sun 9/29 H CIN 3-21 L 49,895
Sun 10/6 H STL 9-34 L 47,675
Mon 10/14 A DET 13-17 L 45,199
Sun 10/20 A LA 14-37 L 67,391
Sun 10/27 H OAK 24-35 L 58,524
Mon 11/4 H LA 13-15 L 57,526
Sun 11/10 A DAL 14-20 L 50,018
Sun 11/17 H CHI 34-0 W 42,686
Sun 11/24 H ATL 27-0 W 45,435
Sun 12/1 A CLE 0-7 L 24,559
Sun 12/8 H GB 7-6 W 45,475
Sun 12/15 H NO 35-21 W 40,418

WASHINGTON REDSKINS
Sun 9/15 A NYG 13-10 W 49,849
Sun 9/22 H STL 10-17 L 53,888
Mon 9/30 H DEN 30-3 W 54,395
Sun 10/6 A CIN 17-28 L 56,175
Sun 10/13 H MIA 20-17 W 54,395
Sun 10/20 H NYG 24-3 W 53,879
Sun 10/27 A STL 20-23 L 49,410
Sun 11/3 A GB 17-6 W 55,288
Sun 11/10 A PHI 27-20 W 65,947
Sun 11/17 H DAL 28-21 W 54,395
Sun 11/24 H PHI 26-7 W 54,395
Thu 11/28 A DAL 23-24 L 63,243
Mon 12/9 A LA 23-17 W 84,327
Sun 12/15 H CHI 42-0 W 52,085

NFC DIVISIONAL PLAYOFF
Sun 12/22 A LA 10-19 L 80,118

1975 NFL
ATLANTA FALCONS
Sun 9/21 A STL 20-23 L 42,172
Sun 9/28 H DET 14-17 L 45,218
Sun 10/5 H NO 14-7 W 29,444
Sun 10/12 A SF 17-3 W 44,043
Sun 10/19 A LA 7-22 L 60,581
Sun 10/26 H CIN 14-21 L 45,811
Sun 11/2 A NO 7-23 L 49,342
Sun 11/9 A MIN 0-38 L 43,751
Sun 11/16 H LA 7-16 L 44,595
Sun 11/23 H DEN 35-21 W 28,686
Sun 11/30 A OAK *34-37 L 50,860
Sun 12/7 H WAS 27-30 L 52,809
Sun 12/14 H SF 31-9 W 38,501
Sun 12/21 A GB 13-22 L 38,565

BALTIMORE COLTS
Sun 9/21 A CHI 35-7 W 51,678
Sun 9/28 H OAK 20-31 L 39,084
Sun 10/5 A LA 13-24 L 60,011
Sun 10/12 H BUF 31-38 L 43,907
Sun 10/19 A NE 10-21 L 51,417
Sun 10/26 A NYJ 45-28 W 55,137
Sun 11/2 H CLE 21-7 W 35,235
Sun 11/9 A BUF 42-35 W 77,320
Sun 11/16 H NYJ 52-19 W 52,097
Sun 11/23 H MIA 33-17 W 61,968
Sun 11/30 H KC 28-14 W 42,122
Sun 12/7 A NYG 21-0 W 49,863
Sun 12/14 H MIA *10-7 W 59,398
Sun 12/21 H NE 34-21 W 51,926

AFC DIVISIONAL PLAYOFF
Sat 12/27 A PIT 10-28 L 49,557

BUFFALO BILLS
Sun 9/21 H NYJ 42-14 W 77,837
Sun 9/28 A PIT 31-21 W 49,438
Sun 10/5 H DEN 38-14 W 79,798
Sun 10/12 A BAL 38-31 W 43,907
Mon 10/20 A NYG 14-17 L 79,428
Sun 10/26 H MIA 30-35 L 79,080
Sun 11/2 A NYJ 24-23 W 58,343
Sun 11/9 H BAL 35-42 L 77,320
Mon 11/17 A CIN 24-33 L 56,666
Sun 11/23 H NE 45-31 W 65,655
Thu 11/27 A STL 32-14 W 41,899
Sun 12/7 H MIA 21-31 L 74,573
Sun 12/14 A NE 34-14 W 58,393
Sat 12/20 H MIN 13-35 L 54,993

CHICAGO BEARS
Sun 9/21 H BAL 7-35 L 51,678
Sun 9/28 H PHI 15-13 W 48,071
Sun 10/5 A MIN 3-28 L 47,578
Sun 10/12 A DET 7-27 L 73,477
Sun 10/19 A PIT 3-34 L 47,579
Mon 10/27 H MIN 9-13 L 51,259
Sun 11/2 H MIA 13-46 L 51,298
Sun 11/9 H GB 27-14 W 48,738
Sun 11/16 A SF 3-31 L 41,726
Sun 11/23 A LA 10-38 L 58,690
Sun 11/30 A GB 7-28 L 46,821
Sun 12/7 H DET 25-21 W 37,772
Sun 12/14 H STL 20-34 L 35,052
Sun 12/21 A NO 42-17 W 33,371

CINCINNATI BENGALS
Sun 9/21 H CLE 24-17 W 52,874
Sun 9/28 A NO 21-0 W 52,637
Sun 10/5 A HOU 21-19 W 42,412
Sun 10/12 H NE 27-10 W 51,220
Sun 10/19 H OAK 14-10 W 48,122
Sun 10/26 A ATL 21-14 W 45,811
Sun 11/2 H PIT 24-30 L 58,418
Sun 11/9 A DEN 17-16 W 49,702
Mon 11/17 H BUF 33-24 W 56,666
Sun 11/23 A CLE 23-35 L 56,427
Sun 11/30 H HOU 23-19 W 46,128
Sun 12/7 A PHI 31-0 W 56,984
Sat 12/13 A PIT 14-35 L 48,889
Sun 12/21 H SD 47-17 W 46,474

AFC DIVISIONAL PLAYOFF
Sun 12/28 A OAK 28-31 L 53,030

CLEVELAND BROWNS
Sun 9/21 A CIN 17-24 L 52,874
Sun 9/28 H MIN 10-42 L 63,163
Sun 10/5 H PIT 6-42 L 73,217
Sun 10/12 H HOU 10-40 L 46,531
Sun 10/19 A DEN 15-16 L 52,540
Sun 10/26 H WAS 7-23 L 56,702
Sun 11/2 A BAL 7-21 L 35,235
Sun 11/9 A DET 10-21 L 74,653
Sun 11/16 A OAK 17-38 L 50,461
Sun 11/23 H CIN 35-23 W 56,427
Sun 11/30 H NO 17-16 W 44,753
Sun 12/7 A PIT 17-31 L 47,962
Sun 12/14 H KC 40-14 W 44,368
Sun 12/21 A HOU 10-21 L 43,770

DALLAS COWBOYS
Sun 9/21 H LA 18-7 W 49,091
Sun 9/28 H STL *37-31 W 52,417
Mon 10/6 A DET 36-10 W 79,384
Sun 10/12 A NYG 13-7 W 56,511
Sun 10/19 H GB 17-19 L 64,189
Sun 10/26 A PHI 20-17 W 64,889
Sun 11/2 A WAS *24-30 L 55,004
Mon 11/10 H KC 31-34 L 63,539
Sun 11/16 A NE 34-31 W 60,905
Sun 11/23 H PHI 27-17 W 57,893
Sun 11/30 H NYG 14-3 W 53,329
Sun 12/7 A STL 17-31 L 49,701
Sat 12/13 H WAS 31-10 W 61,091
Sun 12/21 A NYJ 31-21 W 37,279

NFC DIVISIONAL PLAYOFF
Sun 12/28 A MIN 17-14 W 48,050

NFC CHAMPIONSHIP
Sun 1/4 A LA 37-7 W 88,919

SUPER BOWL X
Sun 1/18 N PIT 17-21 L 80,187

DENVER BRONCOS
Sun 9/21 H KC 37-33 W 51,858
Mon 9/29 H GB 23-13 W 52,491
Sun 10/5 A BUF 14-38 L 79,798
Sun 10/12 A PIT 9-20 L 49,164
Sun 10/19 H CLE 16-15 W 52,540
Sun 10/26 A KC 13-26 L 70,043
Sun 11/2 A OAK 17-42 L 52,330
Sun 11/9 H CIN 16-17 L 49,702
Sun 11/16 A SD 27-17 W 26,048
Sun 11/23 A ATL 21-35 L 28,686
Sun 11/30 H SD *13-10 W 44,982
Mon 12/8 A OAK 10-17 L 51,075
Sun 12/14 H PHI 25-10 W 36,860
Sat 12/20 A MIA 13-14 L 43,064

DETROIT LIONS
Sun 9/21 A GB 30-16 W 50,781
Sun 9/28 A ATL 17-14 W 45,218
Mon 10/6 H DAL 10-36 L 79,384
Sun 10/12 H CHI 27-7 W 73,477
Sun 10/19 A MIN 19-25 L 47,872
Sun 10/26 A HOU 8-24 L 46,904
Sun 11/2 A SF 28-17 W 43,209
Sun 11/9 H CLE 21-10 W 74,653
Sun 11/16 H GB 13-10 W 76,356
Sun 11/23 A KC *21-24 L 55,161
Thu 11/27 H LA 0-20 L 69,152
Sun 12/7 A CHI 21-25 L 37,772
Sun 12/14 H MIN 17-10 W 72,742
Sun 12/21 A STL 13-24 L 64,272

GREEN BAY PACKERS
Sun 9/21 H DET 16-30 L 50,781
Mon 9/29 A DEN 13-23 L 52,491
Sun 10/5 H MIA 7-31 L 55,396
Sun 10/12 A NO 19-20 L 51,371
Sun 10/19 A DAL 19-17 W 64,189
Sun 10/26 H PIT 13-16 L 52,258
Sun 11/2 H MIN 17-28 L 55,378
Sun 11/9 A CHI 14-27 L 48,738
Sun 11/16 H NYG 40-14 W 50,150
Sun 11/23 H CHI 28-7 W 46,821
Sun 11/30 A MIN 3-24 L 46,147
Sun 12/7 A MIN 3-24 L 46,147
Sun 12/14 A LA 5-22 L 59,312
Sun 12/21 H ATL 22-13 W 38,565

HOUSTON OILERS
Sun 9/21 A NE 7-0 W 51,934
Sun 9/28 H SD 33-17 W 33,765
Sun 10/5 H CIN 19-21 L 42,412
Sun 10/12 A CLE 40-10 W 46,531
Sun 10/19 H WAS 13-10 W 49,566
Sun 10/26 H DET 24-8 W 46,904
Sun 11/2 A KC 17-13 W 62,989
Sun 11/9 A PIT 17-24 L 49,460
Sun 11/16 H MIA 20-19 W 48,892
Mon 11/24 H PIT 9-32 L 49,947
Sun 11/30 A CIN 19-23 L 46,128
Sun 12/7 A SF 27-13 W 44,015
Sun 12/14 A OAK 27-26 W 50,719
Sun 12/21 H CLE 21-10 W 43,770

KANSAS CITY CHIEFS
Sun 9/21 A DEN 33-37 L 51,858
Sun 9/28 H NYJ 24-30 L 73,939
Sun 10/5 H SF 3-20 L 54,490
Sun 10/12 H OAK 42-10 W 60,045
Sun 10/19 A SD 12-10 W 26,469
Sun 10/26 H DEN 26-13 W 70,043
Sun 11/2 H HOU 13-17 L 62,989
Mon 11/10 A DAL 34-31 W 63,539
Sun 11/16 A PIT 3-28 L 48,803
Sun 11/23 H DET *24-21 W 55,161
Sun 11/30 A BAL 14-28 L 42,122
Sun 12/7 H SD 20-28 L 46,888
Sun 12/14 A CLE 14-40 L 44,368
Sun 12/21 A OAK 20-28 L 48,604

LOS ANGELES RAMS
Sun 9/21 A DAL 7-18 L 49,091
Sun 9/28 A SF 23-14 W 55,072
Sun 10/5 H BAL 24-13 W 60,011
Sun 10/12 A SD *13-10 W 37,382
Sun 10/19 H ATL 22-7 W 60,581
Sun 10/26 H NO 38-14 W 54,723
Mon 11/3 A PHI 42-3 W 64,601
Sun 11/9 H SF 23-24 L 74,064
Sun 11/16 A ATL 16-7 W 44,595
Sun 11/23 H CHI 38-10 W 58,690
Thu 11/27 A DET 20-0 W 69,152
Sun 12/7 A NO 14-7 W 39,958
Sun 12/14 H GB 22-5 W 59,312
Sat 12/20 H PIT 10-3 W 69,389

NFC DIVISIONAL PLAYOFF
Sat 12/27 H STL 35-23 W 73,459

NFC CHAMPIONSHIP
Sun 1/4 H DAL 7-37 L 88,919

MIAMI DOLPHINS
Mon 9/22 H OAK 21-31 L 78,744
Sun 9/28 A NE 22-14 W 59,967
Sun 10/5 A GB 31-7 W 55,396
Sun 10/12 H PHI 24-16 W 60,127
Sun 10/19 A NYJ 43-0 W 47,191
Sun 10/26 A BUF 35-30 W 79,080
Sun 11/2 A CHI 46-13 W 51,298
Sun 11/9 H NYJ 27-7 W 72,896
Sun 11/16 A HOU 19-20 L 48,892
Sun 11/23 H BAL 17-33 L 61,968
Mon 12/1 H NE 20-7 W 61,963
Sun 12/7 H BUF 31-21 W 74,573
Sun 12/14 A BAL *7-10 L 59,398
Sat 12/20 H DEN 14-13 W 43,064

MINNESOTA VIKINGS
Sun 9/21 H SF 27-17 W 46,479
Sun 9/28 A CLE 42-10 W 63,163
Sun 10/5 H CHI 28-3 W 47,578
Sun 10/12 H NYJ 29-21 W 47,739
Sun 10/19 A DET 25-19 W 47,872
Mon 10/27 A CHI 13-9 W 51,259
Sun 11/2 A GB 28-17 W 55,378

Sun	11/9	H	ATL	38-0	W	43,751
Sun	11/16	A	NO	20-7	W	52,765
Sun	11/23	H	SD	28-13	W	43,737
Sun	11/30	A	WAS	30-31	L	54,498
Sun	12/7	H	GB	24-3	W	46,147
Sun	12/14	A	DET	10-17	L	72,742
Sat	12/20	A	BUF	35-13	W	54,993

NFC DIVISIONAL PLAYOFF

Sun	12/28	H	DAL	14-17	L	48,050

NEW ENGLAND PATRIOTS

Sun	9/21	H	HOU	0-7	L	51,934
Sun	9/28	H	MIA	14-22	L	59,967
Sun	10/5	A	NYJ	7-36	L	57,365
Sun	10/12	A	CIN	10-27	L	51,220
Sun	10/19	H	BAL	21-10	W	51,417
Sun	10/26	H	SF	24-16	W	60,358
Sun	11/2	A	STL	17-24	L	45,907
Sun	11/9	A	SD	33-19	W	24,161
Sun	11/16	H	DAL	31-34	L	60,905
Sun	11/23	A	BUF	31-45	L	65,655
Mon	12/1	A	MIA	7-20	L	61,963
Sun	12/7	H	NYJ	28-30	L	53,989
Sun	12/14	H	BUF	14-34	L	58,393
Sun	12/21	A	BAL	21-34	L	51,926

NEW ORLEANS SAINTS

Sun	9/21	A	WAS	3-41	L	54,414
Sun	9/28	H	CIN	0-21	L	52,637
Sun	10/5	A	ATL	7-14	L	29,444
Sun	10/12	H	GB	20-19	W	51,371
Sun	10/19	A	SF	21-35	L	39,990
Sun	10/26	A	LA	14-38	L	54,723
Sun	11/2	H	ATL	23-7	W	49,342
Sun	11/9	A	OAK	10-48	L	51,267
Sun	11/16	H	MIN	7-20	L	52,765
Sun	11/23	H	SF	6-16	L	40,328
Sun	11/30	A	CLE	16-17	L	44,753
Sun	12/7	H	LA	7-14	L	39,958
Sun	12/14	A	NYG	14-28	L	40,150
Sun	12/21	H	CHI	17-42	L	33,371

NEW YORK GIANTS

Sun	9/21	A	PHI	23-14	W	60,798
Sun	9/28	A	WAS	13-49	L	54,953
Sun	10/5	A	STL	14-26	L	44,919
Sun	10/12	H	DAL	7-13	L	56,511
Mon	10/20	A	BUF	17-14	W	79,428
Sat	10/25	H	STL	13-20	L	49,598
Sat	11/1	H	SD	35-24	W	52,032
Sun	11/9	H	WAS	13-21	L	57,242
Sun	11/16	H	PHI	10-13	L	53,434
Sun	11/23	A	GB	14-40	L	50,150
Sun	11/30	A	DAL	3-14	L	53,329
Sun	12/7	H	BAL	0-21	L	49,863
Sun	12/14	H	NO	28-14	W	40,150
Sun	12/21	A	SF	26-23	W	34,354

NEW YORK JETS

Sun	9/21	A	BUF	14-42	L	77,837
Sun	9/28	A	KC	30-24	W	73,939
Sun	10/5	H	NE	36-7	W	57,365
Sun	10/12	A	MIN	21-29	L	47,739
Sun	10/19	H	MIA	0-43	L	47,191
Sun	10/26	H	BAL	28-45	L	55,137
Sun	11/2	H	BUF	23-24	L	58,343
Sun	11/9	A	MIA	7-27	L	72,896
Sun	11/16	A	BAL	19-52	L	52,097
Sun	11/23	H	STL	6-37	L	53,169
Sun	11/30	H	PIT	7-20	L	52,618
Sun	12/7	A	NE	30-28	W	53,989
Mon	12/15	A	SD	16-24	L	49,706
Sun	12/21	H	DAL	21-31	L	37,279

OAKLAND RAIDERS

Mon	9/22	A	MIA	31-21	W	78,744
Sun	9/28	A	BAL	31-20	W	39,084
Sun	10/5	A	SD	6-0	W	31,095
Sun	10/12	A	KC	10-42	L	60,425
Sun	10/19	A	CIN	10-14	L	48,122
Sun	10/26	H	SD	25-0	W	42,796
Sun	11/2	A	DEN	42-17	W	52,330
Sun	11/9	H	NO	48-10	W	51,267
Sun	11/16	H	CLE	38-17	W	50,461
Sun	11/23	A	WAS	*26-23	W	53,582
Sun	11/30	H	ATL	*37-34	W	50,860
Mon	12/8	H	DEN	17-10	W	51,075
Sun	12/14	H	HOU	26-27	L	50,719
Sun	12/21	H	KC	28-20	W	48,604

AFC DIVISIONAL PLAYOFF

Sun	12/28	H	CIN	31-28	W	53,030

AFC CHAMPIONSHIP

Sun	1/4	A	PIT	10-16	L	50,609

PHILADELPHIA EAGLES

Sun	9/21	H	NYG	14-23	L	60,798
Sun	9/28	A	CHI	13-15	L	48,071
Sun	10/5	H	WAS	26-10	W	64,397
Sun	10/12	A	MIA	16-24	L	60,127
Sun	10/19	A	STL	20-31	L	45,242
Sun	10/26	H	DAL	17-20	L	64,889
Mon	11/3	H	LA	3-42	L	64,601
Sun	11/9	H	STL	23-24	L	60,277
Sun	11/16	A	NYG	13-10	W	53,434
Sun	11/23	A	DAL	17-27	L	57,893
Sun	11/30	H	SF	27-17	W	56,694
Sun	12/7	H	CIN	0-31	L	56,984
Sun	12/14	A	DEN	10-25	L	36,860
Sun	12/21	A	WAS	26-3	W	49,385

PITTSBURGH STEELERS

Sun	9/21	A	SD	37-0	W	35,853
Sun	9/28	H	BUF	21-30	L	49,438
Sun	10/5	A	CLE	42-6	W	73,217
Sun	10/12	H	DEN	20-9	W	49,164
Sun	10/19	H	CHI	34-3	W	47,579
Sun	10/26	A	GB	16-13	W	52,258
Sun	11/2	A	CIN	30-24	W	58,418
Sun	11/9	H	HOU	24-17	W	49,460
Sun	11/16	H	KC	28-3	W	48,803
Mon	11/24	A	HOU	32-9	W	49,947
Sun	11/30	A	NYJ	20-7	W	52,618
Sun	12/7	H	CLE	31-17	W	47,962
Sat	12/13	H	CIN	35-14	W	48,889
Sat	12/20	A	LA	3-10	L	69,389

AFC DIVISIONAL PLAYOFF

Sat	12/27	H	BAL	28-10	W	49,557

AFC CHAMPIONSHIP

Sun	1/4	H	OAK	16-10	W	50,609

SUPER BOWL X

Sun	1/18	N	DAL	21-17	W	80,187

ST. LOUIS CARDINALS

Sun	9/21	H	ATL	23-20	W	42,172
Sun	9/28	A	DAL	*31-37	L	52,417
Sun	10/5	H	NYG	26-14	W	44,919
Mon	10/13	A	WAS	17-27	L	54,693
Sun	10/19	H	PHI	31-20	W	45,242
Sat	10/25	A	NYG	20-13	W	49,598
Sun	11/2	H	NE	24-17	W	45,907
Sun	11/9	A	PHI	24-23	W	60,277
Sun	11/16	H	WAS	*20-17	W	49,919
Sun	11/23	A	NYJ	37-6	W	53,169
Thu	11/27	H	BUF	14-32	L	41,899
Sun	12/7	H	DAL	31-17	W	49,701
Sun	12/14	A	CHI	34-20	W	35,052
Sun	12/21	A	DET	24-13	W	64,272

NFC DIVISIONAL PLAYOFF

Sat	12/27	A	LA	23-35	L	73,459

SAN DIEGO CHARGERS

Sun	9/21	H	PIT	0-37	L	35,853
Sun	9/28	A	HOU	17-33	L	33,765
Sun	10/5	H	OAK	0-6	L	31,095
Sun	10/12	H	LA	*10-13	L	37,382
Sun	10/19	H	KC	10-12	L	26,469
Sun	10/26	A	OAK	0-25	L	42,796
Sat	11/1	A	NYG	24-35	L	52,032
Sun	11/9	H	NE	19-33	L	24,161
Sun	11/16	H	DEN	17-27	L	26,048
Sun	11/23	A	MIN	13-28	L	43,737
Sun	11/30	A	DEN	*10-13	L	44,982
Sun	12/7	A	KC	28-20	W	46,888
Mon	12/15	H	NYJ	24-16	W	49,706
Sun	12/21	A	CIN	17-47	L	46,474

SAN FRANCISCO 49ERS

Sun	9/21	A	MIN	17-27	L	46,479
Sun	9/28	H	LA	14-23	L	55,072
Sun	10/5	A	KC	20-3	W	54,490
Sun	10/12	H	ATL	3-17	L	44,043
Sun	10/19	H	NO	35-21	W	39,990
Sun	10/26	A	NE	16-24	L	60,358
Sun	11/2	H	DET	17-28	L	43,209
Sun	11/9	A	LA	24-23	W	74,064
Sun	11/16	H	CHI	31-3	W	41,726
Sun	11/23	A	NO	16-6	W	40,328
Sun	11/30	A	PHI	17-27	L	56,694
Sun	12/7	H	HOU	13-27	L	44,015
Sun	12/14	A	ATL	9-31	L	38,501
Sun	12/21	H	NYG	23-26	L	34,354

WASHINGTON REDSKINS

Sun	9/21	H	NO	41-3	W	54,414
Sun	9/28	H	NYG	49-13	W	54,953
Sun	10/5	A	PHI	10-26	L	64,397
Mon	10/13	H	STL	27-17	W	54,963
Sun	10/19	A	HOU	10-13	L	49,566
Sun	10/26	A	CLE	23-7	W	56,702
Sun	11/2	H	DAL	*30-24	W	55,004
Sun	11/9	A	NYG	21-13	W	57,242
Sun	11/16	A	STL	*17-20	L	49,919
Sun	11/23	H	OAK	*23-26	L	53,582
Sun	11/30	H	MIN	31-30	W	54,498
Sun	12/7	A	ATL	30-27	W	52,809
Sat	12/13	A	DAL	10-31	L	61,091
Sun	12/21	H	PHI	3-26	L	49,385

1976 NFL

ATLANTA FALCONS

Sun	9/12	H	LA	14-30	L	53,607
Sun	9/19	A	DET	10-24	L	50,115
Sun	9/26	A	CHI	10-0	W	41,029
Sun	10/3	H	PHI	13-14	L	45,535
Sun	10/10	A	NO	0-30	L	51,521
Sun	10/17	H	CLE	17-20	L	32,837
Sat	10/23	A	SF	0-15	L	50,240
Sun	10/31	H	NO	23-20	W	33,702
Sun	11/7	A	SEA	13-30	L	57,985
Sun	11/14	H	SF	21-16	W	19,733
Sun	11/21	H	DAL	17-10	W	54,992
Sun	11/28	A	HOU	14-20	L	25,838
Sat	12/4	A	LA	0-59	L	57,366
Sun	12/12	H	GB	20-24	L	23,116

BALTIMORE COLTS

Sun	9/12	A	NE	27-13	W	39,512
Sun	9/19	H	CIN	28-27	W	50,621
Sun	9/26	A	DAL	27-30	L	63,725
Sun	10/3	H	TB	42-17	W	40,053
Sun	10/10	H	MIA	28-14	W	58,832
Sun	10/17	A	BUF	31-13	W	71,009
Sun	10/24	A	NYJ	20-0	W	49,768
Mon	11/1	H	HOU	38-14	W	59,732
Sun	11/7	A	SD	37-21	W	42,827
Sun	11/14	H	NE	14-21	L	58,226
Mon	11/22	A	MIA	17-16	W	62,104
Sun	11/28	H	NYJ	33-16	W	43,823
Sat	12/4	A	STL	17-24	L	48,282
Sun	12/12	H	BUF	58-20	W	50,451

AFC DIVISIONAL PLAYOFF

Sun	12/19	H	PIT	14-40	L	60,020

BUFFALO BILLS

Mon	9/13	H	MIA	21-30	L	77,683
Sun	9/19	H	HOU	3-13	L	61,364
Sun	9/26	A	TB	14-9	W	42,805
Sun	10/3	H	KC	50-17	W	51,909
Sun	10/10	A	NYJ	14-17	L	52,416
Sun	10/17	H	BAL	13-31	L	71,009
Sun	10/24	H	NE	22-26	L	45,144
Sun	10/31	H	NYJ	14-19	L	41,285
Sun	11/7	A	NE	10-20	L	61,157
Mon	11/15	A	DAL	10-17	L	51,779
Sun	11/21	H	SD	13-34	L	36,539
Thu	11/25	A	DET	14-27	L	66,569
Sun	12/5	A	MIA	27-45	L	43,475
Sun	12/12	A	BAL	20-58	L	50,451

CHICAGO BEARS

Sun	9/12	H	DET	10-3	W	54,125
Sun	9/19	A	SF	19-12	W	44,158
Sun	9/26	H	ATL	0-10	L	41,029
Sun	10/3	H	WAS	33-7	W	52,105
Sun	10/10	A	MIN	19-20	L	47,498
Sun	10/17	A	LA	12-20	L	71,751
Sun	10/24	A	DAL	21-31	L	60,790
Sun	10/31	H	MIN	14-13	W	53,602
Sun	11/7	H	OAK	27-28	L	57,359
Sun	11/14	H	GB	24-13	W	52,907
Sun	11/21	A	DET	10-14	L	77,731
Sun	11/28	A	GB	16-10	W	56,267
Sun	12/5	A	SEA	34-7	W	60,510
Sun	12/12	H	DEN	14-28	L	44,459

CINCINNATI BENGALS

Sun	9/12	H	DEN	17-7	W	53,464
Sun	9/19	A	BAL	27-28	L	50,621
Sun	9/26	H	GB	28-7	W	44,103
Sun	10/3	A	CLE	45-24	W	75,817
Sun	10/10	H	TB	21-0	W	49,700
Sun	10/17	A	PIT	6-23	L	48,311
Sun	10/24	A	HOU	27-7	W	45,499
Sun	10/31	H	CLE	21-6	W	54,776
Mon	11/8	H	LA	20-12	W	52,480
Sun	11/14	H	HOU	31-27	W	53,243
Sun	11/21	A	KC	27-24	W	46,259
Sun	11/28	H	PIT	3-7	L	55,142
Mon	12/6	A	OAK	20-35	L	52,430
Sun	12/12	A	NYJ	42-3	W	31,067

CLEVELAND BROWNS

Sun	9/12	H	NYJ	38-17	W	67,496
Sun	9/19	A	PIT	14-31	L	49,169
Sun	9/26	A	DEN	13-44	L	62,758
Sun	10/3	H	CIN	24-45	L	75,817
Sun	10/10	H	PIT	18-16	W	75,769
Sun	10/17	A	ATL	20-17	W	32,837
Sun	10/24	H	SD	21-17	W	60,018
Sun	10/31	A	CIN	6-21	L	54,776
Sun	11/7	A	HOU	21-7	W	39,828
Sun	11/14	H	PHI	24-3	W	62,120
Sun	11/21	A	TB	24-7	W	39,948
Sun	11/28	H	MIA	17-13	W	74,715
Sun	12/5	H	HOU	13-10	W	56,025
Sun	12/12	A	KC	14-39	L	34,340

DALLAS COWBOYS

Sun	9/12	H	PHI	27-7	W	53,540
Sun	9/19	A	NO	24-6	W	61,413
Sun	9/26	H	BAL	30-27	W	63,725
Sun	10/3	A	SEA	28-13	W	62,027
Sun	10/10	A	NYG	24-14	W	76,042

Sun 10/17 A STL 17-21 L 50,317
Sun 10/24 H CHI 31-21 W 60,790
Sun 10/31 A WAS 20-7 W 55,004
Sun 11/7 H NYG 9-3 W 58,230
Mon 11/15 H BUF 17-10 W 51,779
Sun 11/21 A ATL 10-17 L 54,992
Thu 11/25 H STL 19-14 W 62,498
Sun 12/5 A PHI 26-7 W 55,072
Sun 12/12 H WAS 14-27 L 59,916

NFC Divisional Playoff
Sun 12/19 H LA 12-14 L 62,436

DENVER BRONCOS
Sun 9/12 A CIN 7-17 L 53,464
Sun 9/19 H NYJ 46-3 W 62,519
Sun 9/26 H CLE 44-13 W 62,758
Sun 10/3 H SD 26-0 W 62,486
Sun 10/10 A HOU 3-17 L 47,928
Sun 10/17 H OAK 10-17 L 63,241
Sun 10/24 A KC 35-26 W 57,961
Sun 10/31 A OAK 6-19 L 52,169
Sun 11/7 H TB 48-13 W 62,503
Sun 11/14 A SD 17-0 W 32,017
Sun 11/21 H NYG 14-13 W 62,961
Sun 11/28 A NE 14-38 L 61,128
Sun 12/5 H KC 17-16 W 57,995
Sun 12/12 A CHI 28-14 W 44,459

DETROIT LIONS
Sun 9/12 A CHI 3-10 L 54,125
Sun 9/19 H ATL 24-10 W 50,115
Sun 9/26 H MIN 9-10 L 76,914
Sun 10/3 A GB 14-24 L 54,758
Sun 10/10 H NE 30-10 W 59,730
Sun 10/17 A WAS 7-20 L 45,908
Sun 10/24 A SEA 41-14 W 61,280
Sun 10/31 H GB 27-6 W 74,582
Sun 11/7 A MIN 23-31 L 46,735
Sun 11/14 A NO 16-17 L 42,048
Sun 11/21 H CHI 14-10 W 77,731
Thu 11/25 H BUF 27-14 W 66,569
Sun 12/5 A NYG 10-24 L 66,069
Sat 12/11 H LA 17-20 L 73,155

GREEN BAY PACKERS
Sun 9/12 H SF 14-26 L 54,628
Sun 9/19 A STL 0-29 L 48,842
Sun 9/26 A CIN 7-28 L 44,103
Sun 10/3 H DET 24-14 W 54,758
Sun 10/10 H SEA 27-20 W 54,983
Sun 10/17 H PHI 28-13 W 55,115
Sun 10/24 A OAK 14-18 L 52,232
Sun 10/31 A DET 6-27 L 74,582
Sun 11/7 H NO 32-27 W 52,936
Sun 11/14 A CHI 13-24 L 52,907
Sun 11/21 H MIN 10-17 L 53,104
Sun 11/28 H CHI 10-16 L 56,267
Sun 12/5 A MIN 9-20 L 43,700
Sun 12/12 A ATL 24-20 W 23,116

HOUSTON OILERS
Sun 9/12 H TB 20-0 W 42,228
Sun 9/19 A BUF 13-3 W 61,364
Sun 9/26 H OAK 13-14 L 42,338
Sun 10/3 A NO 31-26 W 51,973
Sun 10/10 H DEN 17-3 W 47,928
Sun 10/17 A SD 27-30 L 31,950
Sun 10/24 H CIN 7-27 L 45,499
Mon 11/1 A BAL 14-38 L 59,732
Sun 11/7 H CLE 7-21 L 39,828
Sun 11/14 A CIN 27-31 L 53,243
Sun 11/21 A PIT 16-32 L 47,947
Sun 11/28 H ATL 20-14 W 25,838
Sun 12/5 A CLE 10-13 L 56,025
Sat 12/11 H PIT 0-21 L 44,743

KANSAS CITY CHIEFS
Sun 9/12 H SD 16-30 L 53,133
Mon 9/20 H OAK 21-24 L 60,884
Sun 9/26 H NO 17-27 L 53,918
Sun 10/3 A BUF 17-50 L 51,909
Sun 10/10 A WAS 33-30 W 53,060
Sun 10/17 A MIA *20-17 W 43,325
Sun 10/24 H DEN 26-35 L 57,961
Sun 10/31 A TB 28-19 W 40,079
Sun 11/7 H PIT 0-45 L 71,516
Sun 11/14 A OAK 10-21 L 48,859
Sun 11/21 H CIN 24-27 L 46,259
Sun 11/28 A SD 23-20 W 29,272
Sun 12/5 A DEN 16-17 L 57,995
Sun 12/12 H CLE 39-14 W 34,340

LOS ANGELES RAMS
Sun 9/12 A ATL 30-14 W 53,607
Sun 9/19 A MIN *10-10 T 47,310
Sun 9/26 H NYG 24-10 W 60,698
Sun 10/3 A MIA 31-28 W 60,753
Mon 10/11 A SF 0-16 W 80,532
Sun 10/17 H CHI 20-12 W 71,751
Sun 10/24 A NO 16-10 W 51,984
Sun 10/31 H SEA 45-6 W 52,035
Mon 11/8 A CIN 12-20 L 52,480
Sun 11/14 H STL 28-30 L 64,698
Sun 11/21 A SF 23-3 W 58,573
Sun 11/28 H NO 33-14 W 54,906
Sat 12/4 H ATL 59-0 W 57,366
Sat 12/11 A DET 20-17 W 73,155

NFC Divisional Playoff
Sun 12/19 A DAL 14-12 W 62,436

NFC Championship
Sun 12/26 A MIN 13-24 L 47,191

MIAMI DOLPHINS
Mon 9/13 A BUF 30-21 W 77,683
Sun 9/19 A NE 14-30 L 41,879
Sun 9/26 H NYJ 16-0 W 49,754
Sun 10/3 H LA 28-31 L 60,753
Sun 10/10 A BAL 14-28 L 58,832
Sun 10/17 H KC *17-20 L 43,325
Sun 10/24 A TB 23-20 W 59,115
Sun 10/31 H NE 10-3 W 52,863
Sun 11/7 A NYJ 27-7 W 53,344
Sun 11/14 A PIT 3-14 L 48,945
Mon 11/22 H BAL 16-17 L 62,104
Sun 11/28 A CLE 13-17 L 74,715
Sun 12/5 H BUF 45-27 W 43,475
Sat 12/11 H MIN 7-29 L 45,853

MINNESOTA VIKINGS
Sun 9/12 A NO 40-9 W 58,156
Sun 9/19 H LA *10-10 T 47,310
Sun 9/26 A DET 10-9 W 76,914
Mon 10/4 A PIT 17-6 W 47,809
Sun 10/10 H CHI 20-19 W 47,948
Sun 10/17 H NYG 24-7 W 47,156
Sun 10/24 A PHI 31-12 W 56,233
Sun 10/31 A CHI 13-14 L 53,602
Sun 11/7 H DET 31-23 W 46,735
Sun 11/14 H SEA 27-21 W 45,087
Sun 11/21 A GB 17-10 W 53,104
Mon 11/29 A SF 16-20 L 56,775
Sun 12/5 H GB 20-9 W 43,700
Sat 12/11 A MIA 29-7 W 45,853

NFC Divisional Playoff
Sat 12/18 H WAS 35-20 W 47,221

NFC Championship
Sun 12/26 H LA 24-13 W 47,191

Super Bowl XI
Sun 1/9 N OAK 14-32 L 100,421

NEW ENGLAND PATRIOTS
Sun 9/12 H BAL 13-27 L 39,512
Sun 9/19 H MIA 30-14 W 47,379
Sun 9/26 A PIT 30-27 W 41,379
Sun 10/3 H OAK 48-17 W 61,068
Sun 10/10 A DET 10-30 L 59,730
Mon 10/18 H NYJ 41-7 W 50,883
Sun 10/24 A BUF 26-22 W 45,144
Sun 10/31 A MIA 3-10 L 52,863
Sun 11/7 H BUF 20-10 W 61,157
Sun 11/14 A BAL 21-14 W 58,226
Sun 11/21 A NYJ 38-24 W 49,983
Sun 11/28 H DEN 38-14 W 61,128
Sun 12/5 H NO 27-6 W 53,592
Sun 12/12 A TB 31-14 W 39,606

AFC Divisional Playoff
Sat 12/18 A OAK 21-24 L 53,045

NEW ORLEANS SAINTS
Sun 9/12 H MIN 9-40 L 58,156
Sun 9/19 H DAL 6-24 L 61,413
Sun 9/26 A KC 27-17 W 53,918
10/3 H HOU 26-31 L 51,973
Sun 10/10 H ATL 30-0 W 51,521
Sun 10/17 A SF 3-33 L 43,160
Sun 10/24 H LA 10-16 L 51,984
Sun 10/31 A ATL 20-23 L 33,702
Sun 11/7 A GB 27-32 L 52,936
Sun 11/14 H DET 17-16 W 42,048
Sun 11/21 A SEA 51-27 W 61,855
Sun 11/28 A LA 14-33 L 54,906
Sun 12/5 A NE 6-27 L 53,592
Sun 12/12 H SF 7-27 L 42,536

NEW YORK GIANTS
Sun 9/12 A WAS 17-19 L 54,245
Sun 9/19 A PHI 7-20 L 60,643
Sun 9/26 A LA 10-24 L 60,698
Sun 10/3 A STL 21-27 L 48,039
Sun 10/10 H DAL 14-24 L 76,042
Sun 10/17 A MIN 7-24 L 47,156
Sun 10/24 H PIT 0-27 L 69,783
Sun 10/31 H PHI 0-10 L 68,690
Sun 11/7 A DAL 3-9 L 58,230
Sun 11/14 H WAS 12-9 W 72,975
Sun 11/21 A DEN 13-14 L 62,961
Sun 11/28 H SEA 28-16 W 65,111
Sun 12/5 H DET 24-10 W 66,069
Sun 12/12 H STL 14-17 L 60,553

NEW YORK JETS
Sun 9/12 A CLE 17-38 L 67,496
Sun 9/19 A DEN 3-46 L 62,519
Sun 9/26 A MIA 0-16 L 49,754
Sun 10/3 A SF 6-17 L 42,961
Sun 10/10 H BUF 17-14 W 52,416
Mon 10/18 A NE 7-41 L 50,883
Sun 10/24 H BAL 0-20 L 49,768
Sun 10/31 A BUF 19-14 W 41,285
Sun 11/7 H MIA 7-27 L 53,344
Sun 11/14 H TB 34-0 W 46,427
Sun 11/21 H NE 24-38 L 49,983
Sun 11/28 A BAL 16-33 L 43,823
Sun 12/5 H WAS 16-37 L 46,638
Sun 12/12 H CIN 3-42 L 31,067

OAKLAND RAIDERS
Sun 9/12 H PIT 31-28 W 51,371
Mon 9/20 A KC 24-21 W 60,884
Sun 9/26 A HOU 14-13 W 42,338
Sun 10/3 A NE 17-48 L 61,068
Sun 10/10 A SD 27-17 W 50,223
Sun 10/17 A DEN 17-10 W 63,241
Sun 10/24 H GB 18-14 W 52,232
Sun 10/31 H DEN 19-6 W 52,169
Sun 11/7 A CHI 28-27 W 57,359
Sun 11/14 H KC 21-10 W 48,859
Sun 11/21 A PHI 26-7 W 62,133
Sun 11/28 H TB 49-16 W 49,990
Mon 12/6 H CIN 35-20 W 52,430
Sun 12/12 H SD 24-0 W 50,102

AFC Divisional Playoff
Sat 12/18 H NE 24-21 W 53,045

AFC Championship
Sun 12/26 H PIT 24-7 W 53,739

Super Bowl XI
Sun 1/9 N MIN 32-14 W 100,421

PHILADELPHIA EAGLES
Sun 9/12 A DAL 7-27 L 53,540
Sun 9/19 H NYG 20-7 W 60,643
Mon 9/27 H WAS *17-20 L 60,131
Sun 10/3 A ATL 14-13 W 45,535
Sun 10/10 A STL 14-33 L 44,933
Sun 10/17 A GB 13-28 L 55,115
Sun 10/24 H MIN 12-31 L 56,233
Sun 10/31 A NYG 10-0 W 68,690
Sun 11/7 A STL 14-17 L 60,760
Sun 11/14 A CLE 3-24 L 62,120
Sun 11/21 H OAK 7-26 L 62,133
Sun 11/28 A WAS 0-24 L 54,292
Sun 12/5 H DAL 7-26 L 55,072
Sun 12/12 H SEA 27-10 W 37,949

PITTSBURGH STEELERS
Sun 9/12 A OAK 28-31 L 51,371
Sun 9/19 H CLE 31-14 W 49,169
Sun 9/26 H NE 27-30 L 47,379
Mon 10/4 A MIN 6-17 L 47,809
Sun 10/10 A CLE 16-18 L 75,769
Sun 10/17 H CIN 23-6 W 48,311
Sun 10/24 A NYG 27-0 W 69,783
Sun 10/31 H SD 23-0 W 45,484
Sun 11/7 A KC 45-0 W 71,516
Sun 11/14 H MIA 14-3 W 48,945
Sun 11/21 H HOU 32-16 W 47,947
Sun 11/28 A CIN 7-3 W 55,142
Sun 12/5 H TB 42-0 W 43,385
Sat 12/11 A HOU 21-0 W 44,743

AFC Divisional Playoff
Sun 12/19 A BAL 40-14 W 60,020

AFC Championship
Sun 12/26 A OAK 7-24 L 53,739

ST. LOUIS CARDINALS
Sun 9/12 A SEA 30-24 W 58,441
Sun 9/19 H GB 29-0 W 48,842
Sun 9/26 A SD 24-43 L 39,911
Sun 10/3 H NYG 27-21 W 48,039
Sun 10/10 H PHI 33-14 W 44,933
Sun 10/17 H DAL 21-17 W 50,317
Mon 10/25 A WAS 10-20 L 48,325
Sun 10/31 H SF *23-20 W 50,365
Sun 11/7 H PHI 17-14 W 60,760
Sun 11/14 A LA 30-28 W 64,698
Sun 11/21 H WAS 10-16 L 49,833
Thu 11/25 A DAL 14-19 L 62,498
Sat 12/4 H BAL 24-17 W 48,282
Sun 12/12 A NYG 17-14 W 60,553

SAN DIEGO CHARGERS
Sun 9/12 A KC 30-16 W 53,133
Sun 9/19 A TB 23-0 W 38,276
Sun 9/26 H STL 43-24 W 39,911
Sun 10/3 A DEN 0-26 L 62,486
Sun 10/10 H OAK 17-27 L 50,223
Sun 10/17 H HOU 30-27 W 31,950
Sun 10/24 A CLE 17-21 L 60,018
Sun 10/31 A PIT 0-23 L 45,484
Sun 11/7 H BAL 21-37 L 42,827

Sun	11/14	H	DEN	0-17	L	32,017
Sun	11/21	A	BUF	34-13	W	36,539
Sun	11/28	H	KC	20-23	L	29,272
Sun	12/5	H	SF	*13-7	W	33,539
Sun	12/12	A	OAK	0-24	L	50,102

SAN FRANCISCO 49ERS

Sun	9/12	A	GB	26-14	W	54,628
Sun	9/19	H	CHI	12-19	L	44,158
Sun	9/26	A	SEA	37-21	W	59,108
Sun	10/3	H	NYJ	17-6	W	42,961
Mon	10/11	A	LA	16-0	W	80,532
Sun	10/17	H	NO	33-3	W	43,160
Sat	10/23	H	ATL	15-0	W	50,240
Sat	10/31	A	STL	*20-23	L	50,365
Sun	11/7	H	WAS	21-24	L	56,134
Sun	11/14	A	ATL	16-21	L	19,733
Sun	11/21	H	LA	3-23	L	58,573
Mon	11/29	H	MIN	20-16	W	56,775
Sun	12/5	A	SD	*7-13	L	33,539
Sun	12/12	A	NO	27-7	W	42,536

SEATTLE SEAHAWKS

Sun	9/12	H	STL	24-30	L	58,441
Sun	9/19	A	WAS	7-31	L	53,174
Sun	9/26	H	SF	21-37	L	59,108
Sun	10/3	H	DAL	13-28	L	62,027
Sun	10/10	A	GB	20-27	L	54,983
Sun	10/17	A	TB	13-10	W	41,112
Sun	10/24	H	DET	14-41	L	61,280
Sun	10/31	A	LA	6-45	L	52,035
Sun	11/7	H	ATL	30-13	W	57,985
Sun	11/14	A	MIN	21-27	L	45,087
Sun	11/21	H	NO	27-51	L	61,855
Sun	11/28	A	NYG	16-28	L	65,111
Sun	12/5	H	CHI	7-34	L	60,510
Sun	12/12	A	PHI	10-27	L	37,949

TAMPA BAY BUCCANEERS

Sun	9/12	A	HOU	0-20	L	42,228
Sun	9/19	H	SD	0-23	L	38,276
Sun	9/26	H	BUF	9-14	L	42,805
Sun	10/3	A	BAL	17-42	L	40,053
Sun	10/10	A	CIN	0-21	L	49,700
Sun	10/17	H	SEA	10-13	L	41,112
Sun	10/24	H	MIA	20-23	L	59,115
Sun	10/31	H	KC	19-28	L	40,079
Sun	11/7	A	DEN	13-48	L	62,503
Sun	11/14	A	NYJ	0-34	L	46,427
Sun	11/21	H	CLE	7-24	L	39,948
Sun	11/28	A	OAK	16-49	L	49,990
Sun	12/5	A	PIT	0-42	L	43,385
Sun	12/12	H	NE	14-31	L	39,606

WASHINGTON REDSKINS

Sun	9/12	H	NYG	19-17	W	54,245
Sun	9/19	H	SEA	31-7	W	53,174
Mon	9/27	A	PHI	*20-17	W	60,131
Sun	10/3	A	CHI	7-33	L	52,105
Sun	10/10	H	KC	30-33	L	53,060
Sun	10/17	H	DET	20-7	W	45,908
Mon	10/25	H	STL	20-10	W	48,325
Sun	10/31	H	DAL	7-20	L	55,004
Sun	11/7	A	SF	24-21	W	56,134
Sun	11/14	A	NYG	9-12	L	72,975
Sun	11/21	A	STL	16-10	W	49,833
Sun	11/28	H	PHI	24-0	W	54,292
Sun	12/5	A	NYJ	37-16	W	46,638
Sun	12/12	A	DAL	27-14	W	59,916

NFC Divisional Playoff

Sat	12/18	A	MIN	20-35	L	47,221

1977 NFL

ATLANTA FALCONS

Sun	9/18	H	LA	17-6	W	55,649
Sun	9/25	A	WAS	6-10	L	55,031
Sun	10/2	H	NYG	17-3	W	46,174
Sun	10/9	A	SF	7-0	W	38,009
Sun	10/16	A	BUF	0-3	L	27,348
Sun	10/23	A	CHI	16-10	W	49,407
Sun	10/30	H	MIN	7-14	L	59,257
Sun	11/6	H	SF	3-10	L	46,577
Sun	11/13	H	DET	17-6	W	47,141
Sun	11/20	A	NO	20-21	L	43,135
Sun	11/27	A	TB	17-0	W	43,592
Sun	12/4	H	NE	10-16	L	57,911
Sun	12/11	A	LA	7-23	L	52,574
Sun	12/18	H	NO	35-7	W	36,575

BALTIMORE COLTS

Sun	9/18	A	SEA	29-14	W	58,991
Sun	9/25	A	NYJ	20-12	W	43,439
Sun	10/2	H	BUF	17-14	W	47,717
Sun	10/9	H	MIA	45-28	W	57,005
Sun	10/16	A	KC	17-6	W	63,076
Sun	10/23	A	NE	3-17	L	60,976
Sun	10/30	H	PIT	31-21	W	60,225
Mon	11/7	H	WAS	10-3	W	57,740
Sun	11/13	A	BUF	31-13	W	39,444
Sun	11/20	H	NYJ	33-12	W	49,957
Sun	11/27	A	DEN	13-27	L	74,717
Mon	12/5	A	MIA	6-17	L	68,977
Sun	12/11	H	DET	10-13	L	39,401
Sun	12/18	H	NE	30-24	W	42,250

AFC Divisional Playoff

Sat	12/24	H	OAK	**31-37	L	60,763

BUFFALO BILLS

Sun	9/18	H	MIA	0-13	L	76,097
Sun	9/25	A	DEN	6-26	L	74,737
Sun	10/2	A	BAL	14-17	L	47,717
Sun	10/9	H	NYJ	19-24	L	32,046
Sun	10/16	H	ATL	3-0	W	27,348
Sun	10/23	H	CLE	16-27	L	60,905
Sun	10/30	A	SEA	17-56	L	61,180
Sun	11/6	A	NE	24-14	W	60,263
Sun	11/13	H	BAL	13-31	L	39,444
Sun	11/20	H	NE	7-20	L	27,598
Mon	11/28	A	OAK	13-34	L	51,558
Sun	12/4	H	WAS	0-10	L	22,975
Sun	12/11	A	NYJ	14-10	W	31,929
Sat	12/17	A	MIA	14-31	L	39,626

CHICAGO BEARS

Sun	9/18	H	DET	30-20	W	51,530
Sun	9/25	A	STL	13-16	L	49,878
Sun	10/2	H	NO	24-42	L	51,488
Mon	10/10	H	LA	24-23	W	51,412
Sun	10/16	A	MIN	*16-22	L	47,708
Sun	10/23	H	ATL	10-16	L	49,407
Sun	10/30	A	GB	26-0	W	56,002
Sun	11/6	A	HOU	0-47	L	46,237
Sun	11/13	H	KC	28-27	W	49,583
Sun	11/20	H	MIN	10-7	W	49,563
Thu	11/24	A	DET	31-14	W	71,172
Sun	12/4	A	TB	10-0	W	48,948
Sun	12/11	H	GB	*21-10	W	33,557
Sun	12/18	A	NYG	*12-9	W	50,152

NFC Divisional Playoff

Mon	12/26	A	DAL	7-37	L	62,920

CINCINNATI BENGALS

Sun	9/18	H	CLE	3-13	L	52,847
Sun	9/25	H	SEA	42-20	W	45,579
Sun	10/2	A	SD	3-24	L	40,352
Sun	10/9	A	GB	17-7	W	53,653
Mon	10/17	A	PIT	14-20	L	47,950
Sun	10/23	H	DEN	13-24	L	54,395
Sun	10/30	H	HOU	*13-10	W	53,194
Sun	11/6	A	CLE	10-7	W	81,932
Sun	11/13	A	MIN	10-42	L	45,371
Sun	11/20	H	MIA	23-17	W	46,733
Sun	11/27	H	NYG	30-13	W	32,705
Sun	12/4	A	KC	27-7	W	48,488
Sat	12/10	H	PIT	17-10	W	36,133
Sun	12/18	A	HOU	16-21	L	45,263

CLEVELAND BROWNS

Sun	9/18	A	CIN	13-3	W	52,847
Mon	9/26	H	NE	*30-27	W	76,418
Sun	10/2	H	PIT	14-28	L	79,021
Sun	10/9	H	OAK	10-26	L	79,178
Sun	10/16	A	HOU	24-23	W	46,877
Sun	10/23	A	BUF	27-16	W	60,905
Sun	10/30	H	KC	44-7	W	60,381
Sun	11/6	H	CIN	7-10	L	81,932
Sun	11/13	A	PIT	31-35	L	47,055
Sun	11/20	A	NYG	21-7	W	72,576
Sun	11/27	H	LA	0-9	L	70,352
Sun	12/4	A	SD	14-37	L	37,312
Sun	12/11	H	HOU	15-19	L	30,898
Sun	12/18	A	SEA	19-20	L	61,583

DALLAS COWBOYS

Sun	9/18	A	MIN	*16-10	W	47,678
Sun	9/25	H	NYG	41-21	W	64,215
Sun	10/2	H	TB	23-7	W	55,316
Sun	10/9	A	STL	30-24	W	50,129
Sun	10/16	H	WAS	34-16	W	62,115
Sun	10/23	A	PHI	16-10	W	65,507
Sun	10/30	H	DET	37-0	W	63,160
Sun	11/6	A	NYG	24-10	W	74,532
Mon	11/14	H	STL	17-24	L	64,038
Sun	11/20	A	PIT	13-28	L	49,761
Sun	11/27	A	WAS	14-7	W	55,031
Sun	12/4	H	PHI	24-14	W	60,289
Mon	12/12	A	SF	42-35	W	55,848
Sun	12/18	H	DEN	14-6	W	63,752

NFC Divisional Playoff

Mon	12/26	H	CHI	37-7	W	62,920

NFC Championship

Sun	1/1	H	MIN	23-6	W	61,968

Super Bowl XII

Sun	1/15	N	DEN	27-10	W	75,583

DENVER BRONCOS

Sun	9/18	H	STL	7-0	W	74,812
Sun	9/25	H	BUF	26-6	W	74,737
Sun	10/2	A	SEA	24-13	W	53,108
Sun	10/9	H	KC	23-7	W	74,718
Sun	10/16	A	OAK	30-7	W	53,616
Sun	10/23	A	CIN	24-13	W	54,395
Sun	10/30	H	OAK	14-24	L	74,787
Sun	11/6	H	PIT	21-7	W	74,787
Sun	11/13	A	SD	17-14	W	45,211
Sun	11/20	A	KC	14-7	W	54,050
Sun	11/27	H	BAL	27-13	W	74,717
Sun	12/4	A	HOU	24-14	W	45,514
Sun	12/11	H	SD	17-9	W	74,685
Sun	12/18	A	DAL	6-14	L	63,752

AFC Divisional Playoff

Sat	12/24	H	PIT	34-21	W	75,011

AFC Championship

Sun	1/1	H	OAK	20-17	W	74,982

Super Bowl XII

Sun	1/15	N	DAL	10-27	L	75,583

DETROIT LIONS

Sun	9/18	A	CHI	20-30	L	51,530
Sun	9/25	H	NO	23-19	W	51,458
Sun	10/2	H	PHI	17-13	W	56,877
Sun	10/9	A	MIN	7-14	L	45,860
Sun	10/16	H	GB	10-6	W	78,087
Sun	10/23	A	SF	7-28	L	39,392
Sun	10/30	A	DAL	0-37	L	63,160
Sun	11/6	H	SD	20-0	W	72,248
Sun	11/13	A	ATL	6-17	L	47,141
Sun	11/20	H	TB	16-7	W	49,354
Thu	11/24	H	CHI	14-31	L	71,172
Sun	12/4	A	GB	9-10	L	50,000
Sun	12/11	A	BAL	13-10	W	39,401
Sat	12/17	H	MIN	21-30	L	78,298

GREEN BAY PACKERS

Sun	9/18	A	NO	24-20	W	56,250
Sun	9/25	H	HOU	10-16	L	55,071
Sun	10/2	A	MIN	7-19	L	47,143
Sun	10/9	H	CIN	7-17	L	53,653
Sun	10/16	A	DET	6-10	L	78,087
Sun	10/23	A	TB	13-0	W	47,635
Sun	10/30	H	CHI	0-26	L	56,002
Sun	11/6	A	KC	10-20	L	62,687
Sun	11/13	H	LA	6-24	L	52,948
Mon	11/21	A	WAS	9-10	L	51,498
Sun	11/27	H	MIN	6-13	L	50,000
Sun	12/4	H	DET	10-9	W	50,000
Sun	12/11	A	CHI	10-21	L	33,557
Sun	12/18	H	SF	16-14	W	44,902

HOUSTON OILERS

Sun	9/18	H	NYJ	20-0	W	39,488
Sun	9/25	A	GB	16-10	W	55,071
Sun	10/2	A	MIA	7-27	L	49,619
Sun	10/9	H	PIT	27-10	W	47,777
Sun	10/16	H	CLE	23-24	L	46,877
Sun	10/23	A	PIT	10-27	L	48,517
Sun	10/30	A	CIN	*10-13	L	53,194
Sun	11/6	H	CHI	47-0	W	46,237
Sun	11/13	A	OAK	29-34	L	53,667
Sun	11/20	H	SEA	22-10	W	61,519
Sun	11/27	H	KC	34-20	W	42,934
Sun	12/4	H	DEN	14-24	L	45,514
Sun	12/11	A	CLE	19-15	W	30,898
Sun	12/18	H	CIN	21-16	W	45,263

KANSAS CITY CHIEFS

Sun	9/18	A	NE	17-21	L	58,185
Sun	9/25	H	SD	7-23	L	56,146
Mon	10/3	H	OAK	28-37	L	60,684
Sun	10/9	A	DEN	7-23	L	74,718
Sun	10/16	H	BAL	6-17	L	63,076
Sun	10/23	A	SD	21-16	W	33,010
Sun	10/30	A	CLE	7-44	L	60,381
Sun	11/6	H	GB	20-10	W	62,687
Sun	11/13	A	CHI	27-28	L	49,583
Sun	11/20	H	DEN	7-14	L	54,050
Sun	11/27	A	HOU	20-34	L	42,394
Sun	12/4	H	CIN	7-27	L	48,488
Sun	12/11	H	SEA	31-34	L	22,262
Sun	12/18	A	OAK	20-21	L	50,304

LOS ANGELES RAMS

Sun	9/18	A	ATL	6-17	L	55,649
Sun	9/25	H	PHI	20-0	W	46,031
Sun	10/2	H	SF	34-14	W	55,466
Mon	10/10	A	CHI	23-24	L	51,412
Sun	10/16	H	NO	14-7	W	46,045
Mon	10/24	H	MIN	35-3	W	62,414
Sun	10/30	A	NO	26-27	L	59,023
Sun	11/6	H	TB	31-0	W	45,493
Sun	11/13	A	GB	24-6	W	52,948
Sun	11/20	A	SF	23-10	W	56,779
Sun	11/27	A	CLE	9-0	W	70,352
Sun	12/4	H	OAK	20-14	W	67,075
Sun	12/11	H	ATL	23-7	W	52,574
Sat	12/17	A	WAS	14-17	L	54,208

NFC Divisional Playoff

Mon	12/26	H	MIN	7-14	L	62,538

MIAMI DOLPHINS

Sun	9/18	A	BUF	13-0	W	76,097

Sun	9/25	A	SF	19-15	W	40,503
Sun	10/2	H	HOU	27-7	W	49,619
Sun	10/9	A	BAL	28-45	L	57,005
Sun	10/16	H	NYJ	21-17	W	43,446
Sun	10/23	H	SEA	31-13	W	29,858
Sun	10/30	H	SD	13-14	L	40,670
Sun	11/6	A	NYJ	14-10	W	52,325
Sun	11/13	H	NE	17-5	W	67,502
Sun	11/20	A	CIN	17-23	L	46,733
Thu	11/24	A	STL	55-14	W	50,269
Mon	12/5	H	BAL	17-6	W	68,977
Sun	12/11	A	NE	10-14	L	61,064
Sat	12/17	H	BUF	31-14	W	39,626

MINNESOTA VIKINGS

Sun	9/18	H	DAL	*10-16	L	47,678
Sat	9/24	A	TB	9-3	W	66,272
Sun	10/2	H	GB	19-7	W	47,143
Sun	10/9	H	DET	14-7	W	45,860
Sun	10/16	H	CHI	*22-16	W	47,708
Mon	10/24	A	LA	3-35	L	62,414
Sun	10/30	A	ATL	14-7	W	59,257
Sun	11/6	H	STL	7-27	L	47,066
Sun	11/13	H	CIN	42-10	W	45,371
Sun	11/20	A	CHI	7-10	L	49,563
Sun	11/27	A	GB	13-6	W	50,000
Sun	12/4	H	SF	28-27	W	40,745
Sun	12/11	A	OAK	13-35	L	52,771
Sat	12/17	A	DET	30-21	W	78,298

NFC Divisional Playoff

Mon	12/26	A	LA	14-7	W	62,538

NFC Championship

Sun	1/1	A	DAL	6-23	L	61,968

NEW ENGLAND PATRIOTS

Sun	9/18	H	KC	21-17	W	58,185
Mon	9/26	A	CLE	*27-30	L	76,418
Sun	10/2	A	NYJ	27-30	L	38,277
Sun	10/9	H	SEA	31-0	W	45,297
Sun	10/16	A	SD	24-20	W	50,327
Sun	10/23	H	BAL	17-3	W	60,976
Sun	10/30	H	NYJ	24-13	W	61,042
Sun	11/6	H	BUF	14-24	L	60,263
Sun	11/13	A	MIA	5-17	L	67,502
Sun	11/20	A	BUF	20-7	W	27,598
Sun	11/27	H	PHI	14-6	W	57,893
Sun	12/4	A	ATL	16-10	W	57,911
Sun	12/11	H	MIA	14-10	W	61,064
Sun	12/18	A	BAL	24-30	L	42,250

NEW ORLEANS SAINTS

Sun	9/18	H	GB	20-24	L	56,250
Sun	9/25	A	DET	19-23	L	51,458
Sun	10/2	A	CHI	42-24	W	51,488
Sun	10/9	H	SD	0-14	L	53,942
Sun	10/16	A	LA	7-14	L	46,045
Sun	10/23	A	STL	31-49	L	48,417
Sun	10/30	H	LA	27-26	W	59,023
Sun	11/6	A	PHI	7-28	L	53,482
Sun	11/13	H	SF	*7-10	L	41,564
Sun	11/20	H	ATL	21-20	W	43,135
Sun	11/27	A	SF	17-20	L	33,702
Sun	12/4	H	NYJ	13-16	L	40,464
Sun	12/11	H	TB	14-33	L	40,124
Sun	12/18	A	ATL	7-35	L	36,575

NEW YORK GIANTS

Sun	9/18	H	WAS	20-17	W	76,086
Sun	9/25	A	DAL	21-41	L	64,215
Sun	10/2	A	ATL	3-17	L	46,174
Sun	10/9	H	PHI	10-28	L	48,824
Sun	10/16	H	SF	20-17	W	70,366
Sun	10/23	A	WAS	17-6	W	53,903
Mon	10/31	A	STL	0-28	L	50,323
Sun	11/6	H	DAL	10-24	L	74,532
Sun	11/13	A	TB	10-0	W	46,518
Sun	11/20	H	CLE	7-21	L	72,526
Sun	11/27	A	CIN	13-30	L	32,705
Sun	12/4	H	STL	27-7	W	71,826
Sun	12/11	A	PHI	14-17	L	47,731
Sun	12/18	H	CHI	*9-12	L	50,152

NEW YORK JETS

Sun	9/18	A	HOU	0-20	L	39,488
Sun	9/25	H	BAL	12-20	L	43,439
Sun	10/2	H	NE	30-27	W	38,277
Sun	10/9	A	BUF	24-19	W	32,046
Sun	10/16	A	MIA	17-21	L	43,446
Sun	10/23	H	OAK	27-28	L	56,734
Sun	10/30	A	NE	13-24	L	61,042
Sun	11/6	H	MIA	10-14	L	52,325
Sun	11/13	H	SEA	0-17	L	43,973
Sun	11/20	A	BAL	12-33	L	49,957
Sun	11/27	H	PIT	20-23	L	47,385
Sun	12/4	A	NO	16-13	W	40,464
Sun	12/11	H	BUF	10-14	L	31,929
Sun	12/18	A	PHI	0-27	L	19,241

OAKLAND RAIDERS

Sun	9/18	H	SD	24-0	W	51,022
Sun	9/25	A	PIT	16-7	W	50,398
Mon	10/3	A	KC	37-28	W	60,684
Sun	10/9	A	CLE	26-10	W	79,178
Sun	10/16	H	DEN	7-30	L	53,616
Sun	10/23	A	NYJ	28-27	W	56,734
Sun	10/30	A	DEN	24-14	W	74,787
Sun	11/6	H	SEA	44-7	W	50,929
Sun	11/13	H	HOU	34-29	W	53,667
Sun	11/20	A	SD	7-12	L	50,887
Mon	11/28	H	BUF	34-13	W	51,558
Sun	12/4	A	LA	14-20	L	67,075
Sun	12/11	H	MIN	35-13	W	52,771
Sun	12/18	H	KC	21-20	W	50,304

AFC Divisional Playoff

Sat	12/24	A	BAL	**37-31	W	60,763

AFC Championship

Sun	1/1	A	DEN	17-20	L	74,982

PHILADELPHIA EAGLES

Sun	9/18	H	TB	13-3	W	61,549
Sun	9/25	A	LA	0-20	L	46,031
Sun	10/2	A	DET	13-17	L	56,877
Sun	10/9	A	NYG	28-10	W	48,824
Sun	10/16	H	STL	17-21	L	60,535
Sun	10/23	H	DAL	10-16	L	65,507
Sun	10/30	A	WAS	17-23	L	55,031
Sun	11/6	H	NO	28-7	W	53,482
Sun	11/13	H	WAS	14-17	L	60,702
Sun	11/20	A	STL	16-21	L	48,768
Sun	11/27	A	NE	6-14	L	57,893
Sun	12/4	A	DAL	14-24	L	60,289
Sun	12/11	H	NYG	17-14	W	47,731
Sun	12/18	H	NYJ	27-0	W	19,241

PITTSBURGH STEELERS

Mon	9/19	H	SF	27-0	W	48,046
Sun	9/25	H	OAK	7-16	L	50,398
Sun	10/2	A	CLE	28-14	W	79,021
Sun	10/9	A	HOU	10-27	L	47,777
Mon	10/17	H	CIN	20-14	W	47,950
Sun	10/23	H	HOU	27-10	W	48,517
Sun	10/30	A	BAL	21-31	L	60,225
Sun	11/6	A	DEN	7-21	L	74,787
Sun	11/13	H	CLE	35-31	W	47,055
Sun	11/20	H	DAL	28-13	W	49,761
Sun	11/27	A	NYJ	23-20	W	47,385
Sun	12/4	H	SEA	30-20	W	45,429
Sat	12/10	A	CIN	10-17	L	36,133
Sun	12/18	A	SD	10-9	W	50,727

AFC Divisional Playoff

Sat	12/24	A	DEN	21-34	L	75,011

ST. LOUIS CARDINALS

Sun	9/18	A	DEN	0-7	L	74,182
Sun	9/25	H	CHI	16-13	W	49,878
Sun	10/2	A	WAS	14-24	L	55,031
Sun	10/9	H	DAL	24-30	L	50,129
Sun	10/16	A	PHI	21-17	W	60,535
Sun	10/23	H	NO	49-31	W	48,417
Mon	10/31	H	NYG	28-0	W	50,323
Sun	11/6	A	MIN	27-7	W	47,066
Mon	11/14	A	DAL	24-17	W	64,038
Sun	11/20	H	PHI	21-16	W	48,768
Thu	11/24	H	MIA	14-55	L	50,269
Sun	12/4	A	NYG	7-27	L	71,826
Sat	12/10	H	WAS	20-26	L	36,067
Sun	12/18	A	TB	7-17	L	56,922

SAN DIEGO CHARGERS

Sun	9/18	A	OAK	0-24	L	51,022
Sun	9/25	A	KC	23-7	W	56,146
Sun	10/2	H	CIN	24-3	W	40,352
Sun	10/9	A	NO	14-0	W	53,942
Sun	10/16	H	NE	20-24	L	50,327
Sun	10/23	H	KC	16-21	L	33,010
Sun	10/30	A	MIA	14-13	W	40,670
Sun	11/6	A	DET	0-20	L	72,248
Sun	11/13	H	DEN	14-17	L	45,211
Sun	11/20	H	OAK	12-7	W	50,887
Sun	11/27	A	SEA	30-28	W	55,338
Sun	12/4	H	CLE	37-14	W	37,312
Sun	12/11	A	DEN	9-17	L	74,685
Sun	12/18	H	PIT	9-10	L	50,727

SAN FRANCISCO 49ERS

Mon	9/19	A	PIT	0-27	L	48,046
Sun	9/25	H	MIA	15-19	L	40,503
Sun	10/2	A	LA	14-34	L	55,466
Sun	10/9	H	ATL	0-7	L	38,009
Sun	10/16	A	NYG	17-20	L	70,366
Sun	10/23	H	DET	28-7	W	39,392
Sun	10/30	H	TB	20-10	W	34,750
Sun	11/6	A	ATL	10-3	W	46,577
Sun	11/13	A	NO	*10-7	W	41,564
Sun	11/20	H	LA	10-23	L	56,779
Sun	11/27	H	NO	20-17	W	33,702
Sun	12/4	A	MIN	27-28	L	40,745
Mon	12/12	H	DAL	35-42	L	55,848
Sun	12/18	A	GB	14-16	L	44,902

SEATTLE SEAHAWKS

Sun	9/18	H	BAL	14-29	L	58,991
Sun	9/25	A	CIN	20-42	L	45,579
Sun	10/2	H	DEN	13-24	L	53,108
Sun	10/9	A	NE	0-31	L	45,927
Sun	10/16	H	TB	30-23	W	54,783
Sun	10/23	A	MIA	13-31	L	29,858
Sun	10/30	H	BUF	56-17	W	61,180
Sun	11/6	A	OAK	7-44	L	50,929
Sun	11/13	A	NYJ	17-0	W	43,973
Sun	11/20	H	HOU	10-22	L	61,519
Sun	11/27	H	SD	28-30	L	55,338
Sun	12/4	A	PIT	20-30	L	45,429
Sun	12/11	A	KC	34-31	W	22,262
Sun	12/18	H	CLE	20-19	W	61,583

TAMPA BAY BUCCANEERS

Sun	9/18	A	PHI	3-13	L	61,549
Sat	9/24	H	MIN	3-9	L	66,272
Sun	10/2	A	DAL	7-23	L	55,316
Sun	10/9	H	WAS	0-10	L	58,571
Sun	10/16	A	SEA	23-30	L	54,783
Sun	10/23	H	GB	0-13	L	47,635
Sun	10/30	A	SF	10-20	L	34,750
Sun	11/6	A	LA	0-31	L	45,493
Sun	11/13	H	NYG	0-10	L	46,518
Sun	11/20	A	DET	7-16	L	49,354
Sun	11/27	H	ATL	0-17	L	43,592
Sun	12/4	H	CHI	0-10	L	48,948
Sun	12/11	A	NO	33-14	W	40,124
Sun	12/18	H	STL	17-7	W	56,922

WASHINGTON REDSKINS

Sun	9/18	A	NYG	17-20	L	76,086
Sun	9/25	H	ATL	10-6	W	55,031
Sun	10/2	H	STL	24-14	W	55,031
Sun	10/9	A	TB	10-0	W	58,571
Sun	10/16	A	DAL	16-34	L	62,115
Sun	10/23	H	NYG	6-17	L	53,903
Sun	10/30	H	PHI	23-17	W	55,031
Mon	11/7	A	BAL	3-10	L	57,740
Sun	11/13	A	PHI	17-14	W	60,702
Mon	11/21	H	GB	10-9	W	51,498
Sun	11/27	H	DAL	7-14	L	55,031
Sun	12/4	A	BUF	10-0	W	22,975
Sat	12/10	A	STL	26-20	W	36,067
Sat	12/17	H	LA	17-14	W	54,208

1978 NFL

ATLANTA FALCONS

Sun	9/3	H	HOU	20-14	W	57,326
Sun	9/10	A	LA	0-10	L	46,201
Sun	9/17	H	CLE	16-24	L	56,648
Sun	9/24	A	TB	9-14	L	58,073
Sun	10/1	H	NYG	23-20	W	47,765
Sun	10/8	A	PIT	7-31	L	48,202
Sun	10/15	H	DET	14-0	W	50,804
Sun	10/22	A	SF	20-17	W	34,133
Mon	10/30	H	LA	15-7	W	57,250
Sun	11/5	H	SF	21-10	W	55,468
Sun	11/12	A	NO	20-17	W	70,323
Sun	11/19	A	CHI	7-13	L	46,022
Sun	11/26	H	NO	20-17	W	54,895
Sun	12/3	A	CIN	7-37	L	25,336
Sun	12/10	H	WAS	20-17	W	54,178
Sun	12/17	A	STL	21-42	L	40,022

NFC Wild-Card Playoff

Sun	12/24	H	PHI	14-13	W	49,447

NFC Divisional Playoff

Sat	12/30	A	DAL	20-27	L	60,338

BALTIMORE COLTS

Mon	9/4	A	DAL	0-38	L	64,224
Sun	9/10	H	MIA	0-42	L	46,426
Mon	9/18	A	NE	34-27	W	57,284
Sun	9/24	A	BUF	17-24	L	55,270
Sun	10/1	H	PHI	14-17	L	47,639
Sun	10/8	A	STL	30-17	W	47,479
Sun	10/15	H	NYJ	10-33	L	45,563
Sun	10/22	H	DEN	7-6	W	54,057
Sun	10/29	A	MIA	8-26	L	53,524
Mon	11/6	H	WAS	21-17	W	57,631
Sun	11/12	A	SEA	17-14	W	61,905
Sun	11/19	H	CLE	24-45	L	44,341
Sun	11/26	H	NE	14-35	L	42,828
Sun	12/3	A	NYJ	16-24	L	50,248
Sat	12/9	A	PIT	13-35	L	41,957
Sun	12/17	H	BUF	14-21	L	25,415

BUFFALO BILLS

Sun	9/3	H	PIT	17-28	L	64,147
Sun	9/10	H	NYJ	20-21	L	40,985
Sun	9/17	A	MIA	24-31	L	48,373
Sun	9/24	H	BAL	24-17	W	55,270
Sun	10/1	H	KC	28-13	W	47,310

Sun 10/8 A NYJ 14-45 L 44,545
Sun 10/15 A HOU 10-17 L 47,727
Sun 10/22 H CIN 5-0 W 47,754
Sun 10/29 A CLE 20-41 L 51,409
Sun 11/5 H NE 10-14 L 44,897
Sun 11/12 H MIA 24-25 L 48,623
Sun 11/19 A TB 10-31 L 61,383
Sun 11/26 H NYG 41-17 W 28,496
Sun 12/3 A KC 10-14 L 25,781
Sun 12/10 A NE 24-26 L 59,598
Sun 12/17 A BAL 21-14 W 25,415

CHICAGO BEARS

Sun 9/3 H STL 17-10 W 52,791
Sun 9/10 A SF 16-13 W 49,502
Sun 9/17 A DET 19-0 W 65,982
Mon 9/25 H MIN 20-24 L 53,561
Sun 10/1 H OAK *19-25 L 52,848
Sun 10/8 A GB 14-24 L 55,352
Mon 10/16 A DEN 7-16 L 74,878
Sun 10/22 A TB 19-33 L 68,146
Sun 10/29 H DET 17-21 L 53,378
Sun 11/5 H SEA 29-31 L 50,697
Sun 11/12 A MIN 14-17 L 43,286
Sun 11/19 H ATL 13-7 W 46,022
Sun 11/26 H TB 14-3 W 42,373
Mon 12/4 A SD 7-40 L 48,492
Sun 12/10 H GB 14-0 W 34,306
Sat 12/16 A WAS 14-10 W 49,774

CINCINNATI BENGALS

Sun 9/3 H KC 23-24 L 41,810
Sun 9/10 A CLE *10-13 L 72,691
Sun 9/17 H PIT 3-28 L 50,260
Sun 9/24 H NO 18-20 L 40,455
Sun 10/1 A SF 12-28 L 41,107
Mon 10/9 A MIA 0-21 L 54,729
Sun 10/15 H NE 3-10 L 48,699
Sun 10/22 A BUF 0-5 L 47,754
Sun 10/29 H HOU 28-13 W 50,532
Sun 11/5 A SD 13-22 L 43,639
Mon 11/13 H OAK 21-34 L 51,374
Sun 11/19 A PIT 6-7 L 47,578
Sun 11/26 A HOU 10-17 L 43,245
Sun 12/3 H ATL 37-7 W 25,336
Mon 12/11 A LA 20-19 W 47,471
Sun 12/17 H CLE 48-16 W 46,985

CLEVELAND BROWNS

Sun 9/3 H SF 24-7 W 68,973
Sun 9/10 H CIN *13-10 W 72,691
Sun 9/17 A ATL 24-16 W 56,648
Sun 9/24 A PIT *9-15 L 49,573
Sun 10/1 H HOU 13-16 L 72,776
Sun 10/8 A NO 24-16 W 50,158
Sun 10/15 H PIT 14-34 L 81,302
Sun 10/22 A KC 3-17 L 41,157
Sun 10/29 H BUF 41-20 W 51,409
Sun 11/5 A HOU 10-14 L 45,827
Sun 11/12 H DEN 7-19 L 70,856
Sun 11/19 A BAL 45-24 W 44,341
Sun 11/26 H LA 30-19 W 55,158
Sun 12/3 A SEA 24-47 L 62,262
Sun 12/10 H NYJ *37-34 W 36,881
Sun 12/17 A CIN 16-48 L 46,985

DALLAS COWBOYS

Mon 9/4 H BAL 38-0 W 64,224
Sun 9/10 A NYG 34-24 W 73,265
Sun 9/17 A LA 14-27 L 65,749
Sun 9/24 H STL 21-12 W 62,760
Mon 10/2 A WAS 5-9 L 55,031
Sun 10/8 H NYG 24-3 W 63,420
Sun 10/15 A STL *24-21 W 48,991
Sun 10/22 H PHI 14-7 W 60,525
Thu 10/26 H MIN 10-21 L 61,848
Sun 11/5 A MIA 16-23 L 70,414
Sun 11/12 A GB 42-14 W 55,256
Sun 11/19 H NO 27-7 W 57,920
Thu 11/23 H WAS 37-10 W 64,905
Sun 12/3 H NE 17-10 W 63,263
Sun 12/10 A PHI 31-13 W 64,667
Sun 12/17 A NYJ 30-7 W 52,532

NFC Divisional Playoff

Sat 12/30 H ATL 27-20 W 60,338

NFC Championship

Sun 1/7 A LA 28-0 W 67,470

Super Bowl XIII

Sun 1/21 N PIT 31-35 L 79,484

DENVER BRONCOS

Sun 9/3 H OAK 14-6 W 74,754
Mon 9/11 A MIN *9-12 L 46,508
Sun 9/17 H SD 27-14 W 74,827
Sun 9/24 A KC *23-17 W 60,593
Sun 10/1 H SEA 28-7 W 74,989
Sun 10/8 A SD 0-23 L 50,077
Mon 10/16 H CHI 16-7 W 74,878
Sun 10/22 A BAL 6-7 L 54,057
Sun 10/29 A SEA *20-17 W 62,948
Sun 11/5 H NYJ 28-31 L 74,803
Sun 11/12 A CLE 19-7 W 70,856
Sun 11/19 H GB 16-3 W 74,743
Thu 11/23 A DET 14-17 L 71,785
Sun 12/3 A OAK 21-6 W 53,932
Sun 12/10 H KC 24-3 W 74,019
Sat 12/16 H PIT 17-21 L 73,924

AFC Divisional Playoff

Sat 12/30 A PIT 10-33 L 48,921

DETROIT LIONS

Sun 9/3 H GB 7-13 L 51,187
Sat 9/9 A TB 15-7 W 63,808
Sun 9/17 H CHI 0-19 L 65,982
Sun 9/24 A SEA 16-28 L 56,781
Sun 10/1 A GB 14-35 L 54,606
Sun 10/8 H WAS 19-21 L 60,555
Sun 10/15 A ATL 0-14 L 50,804
Sun 10/22 H SD 31-14 W 54,031
Sun 10/29 A CHI 21-17 W 53,378
Sun 11/5 A MIN 7-17 L 46,008
Sun 11/12 H TB 34-23 W 60,320
Sun 11/19 A OAK 17-29 L 44,517
Thu 11/23 H DEN 17-14 W 71,785
Sun 12/3 A STL 14-21 L 39,200
Sat 12/9 H MIN 45-14 W 78,328
Sun 12/17 H SF 33-14 W 56,674

GREEN BAY PACKERS

Sun 9/3 A DET 13-7 W 51,187
Sun 9/10 H NO 28-17 W 52,646
Sun 9/17 H OAK 3-28 L 55,903
Sun 9/24 A SD 24-3 W 42,755
Sun 10/1 H DET 35-14 W 54,606
Sun 10/8 H CHI 24-14 W 55,352
Sun 10/15 H SEA 45-28 W 52,712
Sun 10/22 A MIN 7-21 L 47,411
Sun 10/29 H TB 9-7 W 55,108
Sun 11/5 A PHI 3-10 L 64,214
Sun 11/12 H DAL 14-42 L 55,256
Sun 11/19 A DEN 3-16 L 74,743
Sun 11/26 H MIN *10-10 T 51,354
Sun 12/3 A TB 17-7 W 67,754
Sun 12/10 A CHI 0-14 L 34,306
Sun 12/17 A LA 14-31 L 42,500

HOUSTON OILERS

Sun 9/3 A ATL 14-20 L 57,326
Sun 9/10 A KC 20-17 W 40,213
Sun 9/17 H SF 20-19 W 46,161
Sun 9/24 H LA 6-10 L 45,749
Sun 10/1 A CLE 16-13 W 72,776
Sun 10/8 A OAK 17-21 L 52,550
Sun 10/15 H BUF 17-10 W 47,727
Mon 10/23 A PIT 24-17 W 48,021
Sun 10/29 A CIN 13-28 L 50,532
Sun 11/5 H CLE 14-10 W 45,827
Sun 11/12 A NE 26-23 W 60,356
Mon 11/20 H MIA 35-30 W 50,290
Sun 11/26 H CIN 17-10 W 43,245
Sun 12/3 H PIT 3-13 L 54,261
Sun 12/10 A NO 17-12 W 63,169
Sun 12/17 H SD 24-45 L 49,554

AFC Wild-Card Playoff

Sun 12/24 A MIA 17-9 W 70,036

AFC Divisional Playoff

Sun 12/31 A NE 31-14 W 60,881

AFC Championship

Sun 1/7 A PIT 5-34 L 49,417

KANSAS CITY CHIEFS

Sun 9/3 A CIN 24-23 W 41,810
Sun 9/10 H HOU 17-20 L 40,213
Sun 9/17 A NYG 10-26 L 70,546
Sun 9/24 H DEN *17-23 L 60,593
Sun 10/1 A BUF 13-28 L 47,310
Sun 10/8 H TB 13-30 L 38,201
Sun 10/15 A OAK 6-28 L 50,759
Sun 10/22 H CLE 17-3 W 41,157
Sun 10/29 A PIT 24-27 L 48,185
Sun 11/5 H OAK 10-20 L 75,418
Sun 11/12 A SD *23-29 L 41,395
Sun 11/19 H SEA 10-13 L 35,252
Sun 11/26 H SD 23-0 W 26,248
Sun 12/3 H BUF 14-10 W 25,781
Sun 12/10 A DEN 3-24 L 74,019
Sun 12/17 A SEA 19-23 L 58,490

LOS ANGELES RAMS

Sun 9/3 A PHI 16-14 W 64,721
Sun 9/10 H ATL 10-0 W 46,201
Sun 9/17 H DAL 27-14 W 65,749
Sun 9/24 A HOU 10-6 W 45,749
Sun 10/1 A NO 26-20 W 61,654
Sun 10/8 H SF 27-10 W 59,337
Sun 10/15 A MIN 34-17 W 46,551
Sun 10/22 H NO 3-10 L 47,574
Mon 10/30 A ATL 7-15 L 57,250
Sun 11/5 H TB 26-23 W 55,182
Sun 11/12 H PIT 10-7 W 63,089
Sun 11/19 A SF 31-28 W 45,022
Sun 11/26 A CLE 19-30 L 55,158
Sun 12/3 A NYG 20-17 W 62,629
Mon 12/11 H CIN 19-20 L 47,471
Sun 12/17 H GB 31-14 W 42,500

NFC Divisional Playoff

Sun 12/31 H MIN 34-10 W 69,631

NFC Championship

Sun 1/7 H DAL 0-28 L 67,470

MIAMI DOLPHINS

Sun 9/3 A NYJ 20-33 L 49,598
Sun 9/10 A BAL 42-0 W 46,426
Sun 9/17 H BUF 31-24 W 48,373
Sun 9/24 A PHI 3-17 L 62,998
Sun 10/1 H STL 24-10 W 43,882
Mon 10/9 H CIN 21-0 W 54,729
Sun 10/15 A SD 28-21 W 50,637
Sun 10/22 A NE 24-33 L 60,424
Sun 10/29 H BAL 26-8 W 53,524
Sun 11/5 H DAL 23-16 W 70,414
Sun 11/12 A BUF 25-24 W 48,623
Mon 11/20 A HOU 30-35 L 50,290
Sun 11/26 H NYJ 13-24 L 49,255
Sun 12/3 A WAS 16-0 W 52,860
Sun 12/10 H OAK 23-6 W 73,003
Mon 12/18 H NE 23-3 W 72,071

AFC Wild-Card Playoff

Sun 12/24 H HOU 9-17 L 70,036

MINNESOTA VIKINGS

Sun 9/3 A NO 24-31 L 54,187
Mon 9/11 H DEN *12-9 W 46,508
Sun 9/17 H TB 10-16 L 46,152
Mon 9/25 A CHI 24-20 W 53,561
Sun 10/1 A TB 24-7 W 65,972
Sun 10/8 A SEA 28-29 L 62,031
Sun 10/15 H LA 17-34 L 46,551
Sun 10/22 H GB 21-7 W 47,411
Thu 10/26 A DAL 21-10 W 61,848
Sun 11/5 H DET 17-7 W 46,008
Sun 11/12 H CHI 17-14 W 43,286
Sun 11/19 H SD 7-13 L 40,086
Sun 11/26 A GB *10-10 T 51,354
Sun 12/3 H PHI 28-27 W 38,722
Sat 12/9 A DET 14-45 L 78,328
Sun 12/17 A OAK 20-27 L 44,643

NFC Divisional Playoff

Sun 12/31 A LA 10-34 L 69,631

NEW ENGLAND PATRIOTS

Sun 9/3 H WAS 14-16 L 55,037
Sun 9/10 A STL 16-6 W 48,233
Mon 9/18 H BAL 27-34 L 57,284
Sun 9/24 A OAK 21-14 W 52,904
Sun 10/1 H SD 28-23 W 60,781
Sun 10/8 H PHI 24-14 W 61,016
Sun 10/15 A CIN 10-3 W 48,699
Sun 10/22 H MIA 33-24 W 60,424
Sun 10/29 H NYJ 55-21 W 60,585
Sun 11/5 A BUF 14-10 W 44,897
Sun 11/12 H HOU 23-26 L 60,356
Sun 11/19 A NYJ 19-17 W 55,568
Sun 11/26 A BAL 35-14 W 42,828
Sun 12/3 A DAL 10-17 L 63,263
Sun 12/10 H BUF 26-24 W 59,598
Mon 12/18 A MIA 3-23 L 72,071

AFC Divisional Playoff

Sun 12/31 H HOU 14-31 L 60,881

NEW ORLEANS SAINTS

Sun 9/3 H MIN 31-24 W 54,187
Sun 9/10 A GB 17-28 L 52,646
Sun 9/17 H PHI 17-24 L 49,242
Sun 9/24 A CIN 20-18 W 40,455
Sun 10/1 H LA 20-26 L 61,654
Sun 10/8 H CLE 16-24 L 50,158
Sun 10/15 A SF 14-7 W 37,671
Sun 10/22 A LA 10-3 W 47,574
Sun 10/29 H NYG 28-17 W 58,806
Sun 11/5 A PIT 14-20 L 48,526
Sun 11/12 H ATL 17-20 L 70,323
Sun 11/19 A DAL 7-27 L 57,920
Sun 11/26 A ATL 17-20 L 54,895
Sun 12/3 H SF 24-13 W 50,068
Sun 12/10 H HOU 12-17 L 63,169
Sun 12/17 A TB 17-10 W 51,207

NEW YORK GIANTS

Sat 9/2 A TB 19-13 W 67,456
Sun 9/10 H DAL 24-34 L 73,265
Sun 9/17 H KC 26-10 W 70,546
Sun 9/24 H SF 27-10 W 71,536
Sun 10/1 A ATL 20-23 L 47,765
Sun 10/8 A DAL 3-24 L 63,420

Sun 10/15 H TB 17-14 W 68,025
Sun 10/22 H WAS 17-6 W 76,192
Sun 10/29 A NO 17-28 L 58,806
Sun 11/5 A STL 10-20 L 48,820
Sun 11/12 A WAS *13-16 L 53,271
Sun 11/19 H PHI 17-19 L 70,318
Sun 11/26 A BUF 17-41 L 28,496
Sun 12/3 H LA 17-20 L 62,629
Sun 12/10 H STL 17-0 W 52,226
Sun 12/17 A PHI 3-20 L 56,396

NEW YORK JETS
Sun 9/3 H MIA 33-20 W 49,598
Sun 9/10 A BUF 21-20 W 40,985
Sun 9/17 H SEA 17-24 L 46,911
Sun 9/24 A WAS 3-23 L 54,729
Sun 10/1 H PIT 17-28 L 52,058
Sun 10/8 H BUF 45-14 W 44,545
Sun 10/15 A BAL 33-10 W 45,563
Sun 10/22 H STL 23-10 W 49,244
Sun 10/29 A NE 21-55 L 60,585
Sun 11/5 A DEN 31-28 W 74,803
Sun 11/12 A PHI 9-17 L 60,249
Sun 11/19 H NE 17-19 L 55,568
Sun 11/26 H MIA 24-13 W 49,255
Sun 12/3 H BAL 24-16 W 50,248
Sun 12/10 A CLE *34-37 L 36,881
Sun 12/17 H DAL 7-30 L 52,532

OAKLAND RAIDERS
Sun 9/3 A DEN 6-14 L 74,754
Sun 9/10 A SD 21-20 W 51,653
Sun 9/17 A GB 28-3 W 55,903
Sun 9/24 H NE 14-21 L 52,904
Sun 10/1 A CHI *25-19 W 52,848
Sun 10/8 H HOU 21-17 W 52,550
Sun 10/15 H KC 28-6 W 50,759
Sun 10/22 A SEA 7-27 L 62,559
Sun 10/29 H SD 23-27 L 52,612
Sun 11/5 A KC 20-10 W 75,418
Mon 11/13 A CIN 34-21 W 51,374
Sun 11/19 H DET 29-17 W 44,517
Sun 11/26 H SEA 16-17 L 52,978
Sun 12/3 H DEN 6-21 L 53,932
Sun 12/10 A MIA 6-23 L 73,003
Sun 12/17 H MIN 27-20 W 44,643

PHILADELPHIA EAGLES
Sun 9/3 H LA 14-16 L 64,721
Sun 9/10 A WAS 30-35 L 54,380
Sun 9/17 A NO 24-17 W 49,242
Sun 9/24 H MIA 17-3 W 62,998
Sun 10/1 H BAL 17-14 W 64,721
Sun 10/8 H NE 14-24 L 61,016
Sun 10/15 H WAS 17-10 W 65,722
Sun 10/22 A DAL 7-14 L 60,525
Sun 10/29 H STL 10-16 L 62,989
Sun 11/5 H GB 10-3 W 64,214
Sun 11/12 H NYJ 17-9 W 60,249
Sun 11/19 A NYG 19-17 W 70,318
Sun 11/26 A STL 14-10 W 39,693
Sun 12/3 A MIN 27-28 L 38,722
Sun 12/10 H DAL 13-31 L 64,667
Sun 12/17 H NYG 20-3 W 56,396

NFC WILD-CARD PLAYOFF
Sun 12/24 A ATL 13-14 L 49,447

PITTSBURGH STEELERS
Sun 9/3 A BUF 28-17 W 64,147
Sun 9/10 H SEA 21-10 W 48,277
Sun 9/17 A CIN 28-3 W 50,260
Sun 9/24 H CLE *15-9 W 49,573
Sun 10/1 A NYJ 28-17 W 52,058
Sun 10/8 H ATL 31-7 W 48,202
Sun 10/15 A CLE 34-14 W 81,302

Mon 10/23 H HOU 17-24 L 48,021
Sun 10/29 H KC 27-24 W 48,185
Sun 11/5 H NO 20-14 W 48,526
Sun 11/12 A LA 7-10 L 63,089
Sun 11/19 H CIN 7-6 W 47,578
Mon 11/27 A SF 24-7 W 51,657
Sun 12/3 A HOU 13-3 L 54,261
Sat 12/9 H BAL 35-13 W 41,957
Sat 12/16 A DEN 21-17 W 73,924

AFC DIVISIONAL PLAYOFF
Sat 12/30 H DEN 33-10 W 48,921

AFC CHAMPIONSHIP
Sun 1/7 H HOU 34-5 W 49,417

SUPER BOWL XIII
Sun 1/21 N DAL 35-31 W 79,484

ST. LOUIS CARDINALS
Sun 9/3 A CHI 10-17 L 52,791
Sun 9/10 H NE 6-16 L 48,233
Sun 9/17 H WAS 10-28 L 49,282
Sun 9/24 A DAL 12-21 L 62,760
Sun 10/1 A MIA 10-24 L 43,882
Sun 10/8 H BAL 17-30 L 47,479
Sun 10/15 H DAL *21-24 L 48,991
Sun 10/22 A NYJ 10-23 L 49,244
Sun 10/29 H PHI 16-10 W 62,989
Sun 11/5 H NYG 20-10 W 48,820
Sun 11/12 A SF 16-10 W 33,155
Sun 11/19 A WAS 27-17 W 52,460
Sun 11/26 H PHI 10-14 L 39,693
Sun 12/3 H DET 21-14 W 39,200
Sun 12/10 A NYG 0-17 L 52,226
Sun 12/17 H ATL 42-21 W 40,022

SAN DIEGO CHARGERS
Sun 9/3 H SEA 24-20 W 56,778
Sun 9/10 H OAK 20-21 L 51,653
Sun 9/17 A DEN 14-27 L 74,827
Sun 9/24 H GB 3-24 L 42,755
Sun 10/1 A NE 23-28 L 60,781
Sun 10/8 H DEN 23-0 W 50,077
Sun 10/15 A MIA 21-28 L 60,781
Sun 10/22 A DET 14-31 L 54,031
Sun 10/29 A OAK 27-23 W 52,612
Sun 11/5 H CIN 22-13 L 43,639
Sun 11/12 H KC *29-23 W 41,395
Sun 11/19 A MIN 13-7 W 40,086
Sun 11/26 A KC 0-23 L 26,248
Mon 12/4 H CHI 40-7 W 48,492
Sun 12/10 H SEA 37-10 W 49,975
Sun 12/17 A HOU 45-24 W 49,554

SAN FRANCISCO 49ERS
Sun 9/3 A CLE 7-24 L 68,973
Sun 9/10 H CHI 13-16 L 49,502
Sun 9/17 A HOU 19-20 L 46,161
Sun 9/24 A NYG 10-27 L 71,536
Sun 10/1 H CIN 28-12 W 41,107
Sun 10/8 A LA 10-27 L 59,337
Sun 10/15 H NO 7-14 L 37,671
Sun 10/22 H ATL 17-20 L 34,133
Sun 10/29 A WAS 20-38 L 53,706
Sun 11/5 A ATL 10-21 L 55,468
Sun 11/12 H STL 10-16 L 33,155
Sun 11/19 H LA 28-31 L 45,022
Mon 11/27 H PIT 7-24 L 51,657
Sun 12/3 A NO 13-24 L 50,068
Sun 12/10 H TB 6-3 W 30,931
Sun 12/17 A DET 14-33 L 56,674

SEATTLE SEAHAWKS
Sun 9/3 H SD 20-24 L 56,778
Sun 9/10 A PIT 10-21 L 48,277
Sun 9/17 A NYJ 24-17 W 46,911
Sun 9/24 H DET 28-16 W 56,781

Sun 10/1 A DEN 7-28 L 74,989
Sun 10/8 H MIN 29-28 W 62,031
Sun 10/15 A GB 28-45 L 52,712
Sun 10/22 H OAK 27-7 W 62,559
Sun 10/29 H DEN *17-20 L 62,948
Sun 11/5 A CHI 31-29 W 50,697
Sun 11/12 H BAL 14-17 L 61,905
Sun 11/19 A KC 13-10 W 35,252
Sun 11/26 A OAK 17-16 W 52,978
Sun 12/3 H CLE 47-24 W 62,262
Sun 12/10 A SD 10-37 L 49,975
Sun 12/17 H KC 23-19 W 58,490

TAMPA BAY BUCCANEERS
Sat 9/2 H NYG 13-19 L 67,456
Sat 9/9 H DET 7-15 L 63,808
Sun 9/17 A MIN 16-10 W 46,152
Sun 9/24 H ATL 14-9 W 58,073
Sun 10/1 H MIN 7-24 L 65,972
Sun 10/8 A KC 30-13 W 38,201
Sun 10/15 H NYG 14-17 L 68,025
Sun 10/22 H CHI 33-19 W 68,146
Sun 10/29 A GB 7-9 L 55,108
Sun 11/5 A LA 23-26 L 55,182
Sun 11/12 H DET 23-34 L 60,230
Sun 11/19 H BUF 31-10 W 61,383
Sun 11/26 A CHI 3-14 L 42,373
Sun 12/3 H GB 7-17 L 67,754
Sun 12/10 A SF 3-6 L 30,931
Sun 12/17 H NO 10-17 L 51,207

WASHINGTON REDSKINS
Sun 9/3 A NE 16-14 W 55,037
Sun 9/10 H PHI 35-30 W 54,380
Sun 9/17 A STL 28-10 W 49,282
Sun 9/24 H NYJ 23-3 W 54,729
Mon 10/2 H DAL 9-5 W 55,031
Sun 10/8 A DET 21-19 W 60,555
Sun 10/15 A PHI 10-17 L 65,722
Sun 10/22 A NYG 6-17 L 76,192
Sun 10/29 H SF 38-20 W 53,706
Mon 11/6 A BAL 17-21 L 57,631
Sun 11/12 H NYG *16-13 W 53,271
Sun 11/19 A STL 17-27 L 52,460
Thu 11/23 A DAL 10-37 L 64,905
Sun 12/3 H MIA 0-16 L 52,860
Sun 12/10 A ATL 17-20 L 54,178
Sat 12/16 H CHI 10-14 L 49,774

1979 NFL
ATLANTA FALCONS
Sun 9/2 A NO *40-34 W 70,940
Mon 9/10 A PHI 14-10 W 66,935
Sun 9/16 H DEN *17-20 L 57,677
Sun 9/23 A DET 23-24 L 56,249
Sun 9/30 H WAS 7-16 L 56,819
Sun 10/7 H GB 25-7 W 56,184
Sun 10/14 A OAK 19-50 L 52,900
Sun 10/21 A SF 15-20 L 33,952
Mon 10/29 H SEA 28-31 L 52,566
Sun 11/4 H TB 17-14 W 55,150
Sun 11/11 A NYG 3-24 L 60,860
Mon 11/19 A LA 14-20 L 54,097
Sun 11/25 H NO 6-37 L 42,815
Sun 12/2 A SD 20-35 L 50,198
Sun 12/9 H LA 13-34 L 49,236
Sun 12/16 A SF 31-21 W 37,211

BALTIMORE COLTS
Sun 9/2 A KC 0-14 L 50,442
Sun 9/9 H TB *26-29 L 36,374
Sun 9/16 A CLE 10-13 L 72,070
Sun 9/23 A PIT 13-17 L 49,483
Sun 9/30 H BUF 13-31 L 31,904

Sun 10/7 H NYJ 10-8 W 32,142
Sun 10/14 H HOU 16-28 L 45,021
Sun 10/21 A BUF 14-13 W 50,581
Sun 10/28 H NE 31-26 W 41,029
Sun 11/4 H CIN 38-28 W 37,740
Sun 11/11 A MIA 0-19 L 50,193
Sun 11/18 H NE 21-50 L 60,879
Sun 11/25 H MIA 24-28 L 38,016
Sun 12/2 A NYJ 17-30 L 47,744
Sun 12/9 H KC 7-10 L 37,226
Sun 12/16 A NYG 31-7 W 58,711

BUFFALO BILLS
Sun 9/2 H MIA 7-9 L 69,441
Sun 9/9 H CIN 51-24 W 43,504
Sun 9/16 A SD 19-27 L 50,709
Sun 9/23 H NYJ 46-31 W 68,731
Sun 9/30 A BAL 31-13 W 31,904
Sun 10/7 H CHI 0-7 L 73,383
Sun 10/14 A MIA 7-17 L 45,597
Sun 10/21 H BAL 13-14 L 50,581
Sun 10/28 A DET 20-17 W 61,911
Sun 11/4 H NE 6-26 L 67,935
Sun 11/11 A NYJ 14-12 W 50,647
Sun 11/18 H GB 19-12 W 39,679
Sun 11/25 A NE *16-13 L 60,991
Sun 12/2 H DEN 16-19 L 37,886
Sun 12/9 A MIN 3-10 L 42,239
Sun 12/16 A PIT 0-28 L 48,002

CHICAGO BEARS
Sun 9/2 H GB 6-3 W 56,515
Sun 9/9 H MIN 26-7 W 53,231
Sun 9/16 A DAL 20-24 L 64,056
Sun 9/23 A MIA 16-31 L 66,011
Sun 9/30 H TB 13-17 L 55,258
Sun 10/7 A BUF 7-0 W 73,383
Sun 10/14 H NE 7-27 L 54,128
Sun 10/21 A MIN 27-30 L 41,164
Sun 10/28 A SF 28-27 W 42,773
Sun 11/4 H DET 35-7 W 50,018
Sun 11/11 H LA 27-23 W 51,483
Sun 11/18 H NYJ 23-13 W 53,635
Thu 11/22 A DET 0-20 L 66,219
Sun 12/2 A TB 14-0 W 69,508
Sun 12/9 A GB 15-14 W 54,207
Sun 12/16 H STL 42-6 W 42,810

NFC WILD-CARD PLAYOFF
Sun 12/23 A PHI 17-27 L 69,397

CINCINNATI BENGALS
Sun 9/2 A DEN 0-10 L 74,788
Sun 9/9 A BUF 24-51 L 43,504
Sun 9/16 H MIA 14-20 L 41,805
Sun 9/23 H HOU *27-30 L 45,615
Sun 9/30 A DAL 13-38 L 63,179
Sun 10/7 H KC 7-10 L 40,041
Sun 10/14 H PIT 34-10 W 52,381
Sun 10/21 A CLE 27-28 L 75,119
Sun 10/28 H PHI 37-13 W 42,036
Sun 11/4 A BAL 28-38 L 37,740
Sun 11/11 H SD 24-26 L 40,782
Sun 11/18 A HOU 21-42 L 49,829
Sun 11/25 H STL 34-28 W 25,103
Sun 12/2 A PIT 17-37 L 46,521
Sun 12/9 A WAS 14-28 L 52,882
Sun 12/16 H CLE 16-12 W 42,183

CLEVELAND BROWNS
Sun 9/2 A NYJ *25-22 W 48,472
Sun 9/9 A KC 27-24 W 42,181
Sun 9/16 H BAL 13-10 W 72,070
Mon 9/24 H DAL 26-7 W 80,123
Sun 9/30 A HOU 10-31 L 48,915
Sun 10/7 H PIT 35-51 L 81,260

Sun	10/14	H	WAS	9-13	L	63,323
Sun	10/21	H	CIN	28-27	W	75,119
Sun	10/28	A	STL	38-20	W	47,845
Sun	11/4	A	PHI	24-19	W	69,019
Sun	11/11	H	SEA	24-29	L	72,440
Sun	11/18	H	MIA	*30-24	W	80,374
Sun	11/25	A	PIT	*30-33	L	48,773
Sun	12/2	H	HOU	14-7	W	69,112
Sun	12/9	A	OAK	14-19	L	52,641
Sun	12/16	A	CIN	12-16	L	42,183

DALLAS COWBOYS

Sun	9/2	A	STL	22-21	W	50,855
Sun	9/9	A	SF	21-13	W	56,728
Sun	9/16	H	CHI	24-20	W	64,056
Mon	9/24	A	CLE	7-26	L	80,123
Sun	9/30	H	CIN	38-13	W	63,179
Sun	10/7	A	MIN	36-20	W	47,572
Sun	10/14	H	LA	30-6	W	64,462
Sun	10/21	H	STL	22-13	W	64,300
Sun	10/28	A	PIT	3-14	L	50,199
Sun	11/4	A	NYG	16-14	W	76,490
Mon	11/12	H	PHI	21-31	L	62,417
Sun	11/18	A	WAS	20-34	L	55,031
Thu	11/22	H	HOU	24-30	L	63,897
Sun	12/2	H	NYG	28-7	W	63,787
Sat	12/8	A	PHI	24-17	W	71,434
Sun	12/16	H	WAS	35-34	W	62,867

NFC Divisional Playoff

Sun	12/30	H	LA	19-21	L	64,792

DENVER BRONCOS

Sun	9/2	H	CIN	10-0	W	74,788
Thu	9/6	H	LA	9-13	L	74,884
Sun	9/16	A	ATL	*20-17	W	57,677
Sun	9/23	H	SEA	37-34	W	74,879
Sun	9/30	A	OAK	3-27	L	52,632
Sun	10/7	H	SD	7-0	W	74,997
Sun	10/14	A	KC	24-10	W	74,292
Mon	10/22	A	PIT	7-42	L	49,699
Sun	10/28	H	KC	20-3	W	74,908
Sun	11/4	H	NO	10-3	W	74,482
Sun	11/11	H	NE	45-10	W	74,379
Sun	11/18	A	SF	38-28	W	42,910
Sun	11/25	H	OAK	10-14	L	74,186
Sun	12/2	A	BUF	19-16	W	37,886
Sat	12/8	A	SEA	23-28	L	60,038
Mon	12/17	A	SD	7-17	L	51,906

AFC Wild-Card Playoff

Sun	12/23	A	HOU	7-13	L	48,776

DETROIT LIONS

Sat	9/1	A	TB	16-31	L	68,225
Sun	9/9	H	WAS	24-27	L	54,991
Sun	9/16	A	NYJ	10-31	L	49,612
Sun	9/23	H	ATL	24-23	W	56,249
Sun	9/30	H	MIN	10-13	L	75,295
Sun	10/7	A	NE	17-24	L	60,629
Sun	10/14	A	GB	16-24	L	53,950
Sun	10/21	A	NO	7-17	L	57,428
Sun	10/28	H	BUF	17-20	L	61,911
Sun	11/4	A	CHI	7-35	L	50,018
Sun	11/11	H	TB	14-16	L	70,461
Sun	11/18	A	MIN	7-14	L	43,650
Thu	11/22	H	CHI	20-0	W	66,219
Sun	12/2	A	PHI	7-44	L	66,128
Sun	12/9	H	MIA	10-28	L	78,075
Sat	12/15	H	GB	13-18	L	57,376

GREEN BAY PACKERS

Sun	9/2	A	CHI	3-6	L	56,515
Sun	9/9	H	NO	28-19	W	53,184
Sun	9/16	H	TB	10-21	L	55,498
Sun	9/23	A	MIN	*21-27	L	46,524
Mon	10/1	H	NE	27-14	W	52,842
Sun	10/7	A	ATL	7-25	L	56,184
Sun	10/14	H	DET	24-16	W	53,950
Sun	10/21	A	TB	3-21	L	67,186
Sun	10/28	A	MIA	7-27	L	47,741
Sun	11/4	H	NYJ	22-27	L	54,201
Sun	11/11	H	MIN	19-7	W	52,706
Sun	11/18	A	BUF	12-19	L	39,679
Sun	11/25	H	PHI	10-21	L	50,023
Sun	12/2	A	WAS	21-38	L	51,682
Sun	12/9	H	CHI	14-15	L	54,207
Sat	12/15	A	DET	18-13	W	57,376

HOUSTON OILERS

Sun	9/2	A	WAS	29-27	W	54,582
Sun	9/9	A	PIT	7-38	L	49,792
Sun	9/16	H	KC	20-6	W	45,684
Sun	9/23	A	CIN	*30-27	W	45,615
Sun	9/30	H	CLE	31-10	W	48,915
Sun	10/7	H	STL	17-24	L	53,043
Sun	10/14	A	BAL	28-16	W	45,021
Sun	10/21	A	SEA	14-34	L	60,705
Sun	10/28	H	NYJ	*27-24	W	45,825
Mon	11/5	A	MIA	9-6	W	72,073
Sun	11/11	H	OAK	31-17	W	48,000
Sun	11/18	H	CIN	42-21	W	49,829
Thu	11/22	A	DAL	30-24	W	63,897
Sun	12/2	A	CLE	7-14	L	69,112
Mon	12/10	H	PIT	20-17	W	55,293
Sun	12/16	H	PHI	20-26	L	53,897

AFC Wild-Card Playoff

Sun	12/23	H	DEN	13-7	W	48,776

AFC Divisional Playoff

Sat	12/29	A	SD	17-14	W	51,192

AFC Championship

Sun	1/6	A	PIT	13-27	L	50,475

KANSAS CITY CHIEFS

Sun	9/2	H	BAL	14-0	W	50,442
Sun	9/9	H	CLE	24-27	L	42,181
Sun	9/16	A	HOU	6-20	L	45,684
Sun	9/23	H	OAK	35-7	W	67,821
Sun	9/30	A	SEA	24-6	W	61,169
Sun	10/7	A	CIN	10-7	W	40,041
Sun	10/14	H	DEN	10-24	L	74,292
Sun	10/21	H	NYG	17-21	L	44,362
Sun	10/28	A	DEN	3-20	L	74,908
Sun	11/4	H	SD	14-20	L	59,353
Sun	11/11	H	PIT	3-30	L	70,132
Sun	11/18	A	OAK	24-21	W	53,596
Sun	11/25	A	SD	7-28	L	50,078
Sun	12/2	H	SEA	37-21	W	42,160
Sun	12/9	A	BAL	10-7	W	37,226
Sun	12/16	A	TB	0-3	L	63,624

LOS ANGELES RAMS

Sun	9/2	H	OAK	17-24	L	59,000
Thu	9/6	A	DEN	13-9	W	74,884
Sun	9/16	H	SF	27-24	W	44,303
Sun	9/23	A	TB	6-21	L	69,497
Sun	9/30	H	STL	21-0	W	48,160
Sun	10/7	A	NO	35-17	W	68,986
Sun	10/14	A	DAL	6-30	L	64,462
Sun	10/21	H	SD	16-40	L	64,245
Sun	10/28	H	NYG	14-20	L	43,376
Sun	11/4	A	SEA	24-0	W	62,048
Sun	11/11	A	CHI	23-27	L	51,483
Mon	11/19	H	ATL	20-14	W	54,097
Sun	11/25	A	SF	26-20	W	49,282
Sun	12/2	H	MIN	*27-21	W	56,700
Sun	12/9	A	ATL	34-13	W	49,236
Sun	12/16	H	NO	14-29	L	53,879

NFC Divisional Playoff

Sun	12/30	A	DAL	21-19	W	64,792

NFC Championship

Sun	1/6	A	TB	9-0	W	72,033

Super Bowl XIV

Sun	1/20	N	PIT	19-31	L	103,985

MIAMI DOLPHINS

Sun	9/2	A	BUF	9-7	W	69,441
Sun	9/9	H	SEA	19-10	W	56,233
Sun	9/16	A	MIN	27-12	W	46,187
Sun	9/23	H	CHI	31-16	W	66,011
Sun	9/30	A	NYJ	27-33	L	51,496
Mon	10/8	A	OAK	3-13	L	52,419
Sun	10/14	H	BUF	17-7	W	45,597
Sun	10/21	A	NE	13-28	L	61,096
Sun	10/28	H	GB	27-7	W	47,471
Mon	11/5	H	HOU	6-9	L	72,073
Sun	11/11	H	BAL	19-0	W	50,193
Sun	11/18	A	CLE	*24-30	L	80,374
Sun	11/25	A	BAL	28-24	W	38,016
Thu	11/29	H	NE	39-24	W	69,174
Sun	12/9	A	DET	28-10	W	78,075
Sat	12/15	H	NYJ	24-27	L	49,915

AFC Divisional Playoff

Sun	12/30	A	PIT	14-34	L	50,214

MINNESOTA VIKINGS

Sun	9/2	H	SF	28-22	W	46,539
Sun	9/9	A	CHI	7-26	L	53,231
Sun	9/16	H	MIA	12-27	L	46,187
Sun	9/23	H	GB	*27-21	W	46,524
Sun	9/30	A	DET	13-10	W	75,295
Sun	10/7	H	DAL	20-36	L	47,572
Mon	10/15	A	NYJ	7-14	L	54,479
Sun	10/21	H	CHI	30-27	W	41,164
Sun	10/28	H	TB	10-12	L	46,906
Sun	11/4	A	STL	7-37	L	47,213
Sun	11/11	A	GB	7-19	L	52,706
Sun	11/18	H	DET	14-7	W	43,650
Sun	11/25	A	TB	23-22	W	70,039
Sun	12/2	A	LA	*21-27	L	56,700
Sun	12/9	H	BUF	10-3	W	42,239
Sun	12/16	A	NE	23-27	L	54,719

NEW ENGLAND PATRIOTS

Mon	9/3	H	PIT	*13-16	L	60,978
Sun	9/9	H	NYJ	56-3	W	53,113
Sun	9/16	A	CIN	20-14	W	41,805
Sun	9/23	H	SD	27-21	W	60,916
Mon	10/1	A	GB	14-27	L	52,842
Sun	10/7	H	DET	24-17	W	60,629
Sun	10/14	A	CHI	27-7	W	54,128
Sun	10/21	H	MIA	28-13	W	61,096
Sun	10/28	A	BAL	26-31	L	41,029
Sun	11/4	A	BUF	26-6	W	67,935
Sun	11/11	A	DEN	10-45	L	74,379
Sun	11/18	H	BAL	50-21	W	60,879
Sun	11/25	H	BUF	*13-16	L	60,991
Thu	11/29	A	MIA	24-39	L	69,174
Sun	12/9	A	NYJ	26-27	L	45,131
Sun	12/16	H	MIN	27-23	W	54,719

NEW ORLEANS SAINTS

Sun	9/2	H	ATL	*34-40	L	70,940
Sun	9/9	A	GB	19-28	L	53,184
Sun	9/16	H	PHI	14-26	L	54,212
Sun	9/23	A	SF	30-21	W	39,727
Sun	9/30	H	NYG	24-14	W	51,543
Sun	10/7	H	LA	17-35	L	68,986
Sun	10/14	A	TB	42-14	W	67,640
Sun	10/21	H	DET	17-7	W	57,428
Sun	10/28	A	WAS	14-10	W	53,133
Sun	11/4	A	DEN	3-10	L	74,482
Sun	11/11	H	SF	31-20	W	65,551
Sun	11/18	A	SEA	24-38	L	60,055
Sun	11/25	A	ATL	37-6	W	42,815
Mon	12/3	H	OAK	35-42	L	65,541
Sun	12/9	H	SD	0-35	L	61,059
Sun	12/16	A	LA	29-14	W	53,879

NEW YORK GIANTS

Sun	9/2	A	PHI	17-23	L	67,366
Sun	9/9	H	STL	14-27	L	71,370
Mon	9/17	A	WAS	0-27	L	55,031
Sun	9/23	H	PHI	13-17	L	74,370
Sun	9/30	A	NO	14-24	L	51,543
Sun	10/7	H	TB	17-14	W	72,841
Sun	10/14	H	SF	32-16	W	70,352
Sun	10/21	A	KC	21-17	W	44,362
Sun	10/28	A	LA	20-14	W	43,376
Sun	11/4	H	DAL	14-16	L	76,490
Sun	11/11	H	ATL	24-3	W	60,860
Sun	11/18	A	TB	3-31	L	70,261
Sun	11/25	H	WAS	14-6	W	72,641
Sun	12/2	A	DAL	7-28	L	63,787
Sun	12/9	A	STL	20-29	L	39,802
Sun	12/16	H	BAL	7-31	L	58,711

NEW YORK JETS

Sun	9/2	H	CLE	*22-25	L	48,472
Sun	9/9	A	NE	3-56	L	53,113
Sun	9/16	H	DET	31-10	W	49,612
Sun	9/23	A	BUF	31-46	L	68,731
Sun	9/30	H	MIA	33-27	W	51,496
Sun	10/7	A	BAL	8-10	L	32,142
Mon	10/15	H	MIN	14-7	W	54,479
Sun	10/21	H	OAK	28-19	W	55,802
Sun	10/28	A	HOU	*24-27	L	45,825
Sun	11/4	A	GB	27-22	W	54,201
Sun	11/11	H	BUF	12-14	L	50,647
Sun	11/18	A	CHI	13-23	L	53,635
Mon	11/26	A	SEA	7-30	L	59,977
Sun	12/2	H	BAL	30-17	W	47,744
Sun	12/9	H	NE	27-26	W	45,131
Sat	12/15	A	MIA	27-24	W	49,915

OAKLAND RAIDERS

Sun	9/2	A	LA	24-17	W	59,000
Sun	9/9	A	SD	10-30	L	50,255
Sun	9/16	A	SEA	10-27	L	61,602
Sun	9/23	A	KC	7-35	L	67,821
Sun	9/30	H	DEN	27-3	W	52,632
Mon	10/8	H	MIA	13-3	W	52,419
Sun	10/14	H	ATL	50-19	W	52,900
Sun	10/21	A	NYJ	19-28	L	55,802
Thu	10/25	H	SD	45-22	W	53,709
Sun	11/4	H	SF	23-10	W	52,764
Sun	11/11	A	HOU	17-31	L	48,000
Sun	11/18	H	KC	21-24	L	53,596
Sun	11/25	A	DEN	14-10	W	74,186
Mon	12/3	A	NO	42-35	W	65,541
Sun	12/9	H	CLE	19-14	W	52,641
Sun	12/16	H	SEA	24-29	L	53,177

PHILADELPHIA EAGLES

Sun	9/2	H	NYG	23-17	W	67,366
Mon	9/10	H	ATL	10-14	L	66,935
Sun	9/16	A	NO	26-14	W	54,212
Sun	9/23	A	NYG	17-13	W	74,370
Sun	9/30	H	PIT	17-14	W	70,352
Sun	10/7	A	WAS	28-17	W	69,142
Sun	10/14	A	STL	24-20	W	48,367
Sun	10/21	H	WAS	7-17	L	54,442
Sun	10/28	A	CIN	13-37	L	42,036
Sun	11/4	H	CLE	19-24	L	69,019
Mon	11/12	A	DAL	31-21	W	62,417
Sun	11/18	H	STL	16-13	W	70,235
Sun	11/25	A	GB	21-10	W	50,023
Sun	12/2	H	DET	44-7	W	66,128
Sat	12/8	H	DAL	17-24	L	71,434
Sun	12/16	A	HOU	26-20	W	53,879

NFC Wild-Card Playoff

Sun	12/23	H	CHI	27-17	W	69,397

NFC DIVISIONAL PLAYOFF
Sat 12/29 A TB 17-24 L 71,402

PITTSBURGH STEELERS
Mon 9/3 A NE *16-13 W 60,978
Sun 9/9 H HOU 38-7 W 49,792
Sun 9/16 A STL 24-21 W 50,416
Sun 9/23 H BAL 17-13 W 49,483
Sun 9/30 A PHI 14-17 L 70,352
Sun 10/7 A CLE 51-35 W 81,260
Sun 10/14 A CIN 10-34 L 52,381
Mon 10/22 H DEN 42-7 W 49,699
Sun 10/28 H DAL 14-3 W 50,199
Sun 11/4 H WAS 38-7 W 49,462
Sun 11/11 A KC 30-3 W 70,132
Sun 11/18 A SD 7-35 L 51,910
Sun 11/25 H CLE *33-30 W 48,773
Sun 12/2 H CIN 37-17 W 46,521
Mon 12/10 A HOU 17-20 L 55,293
Sun 12/16 H BUF 28-0 W 48,002

AFC DIVISIONAL PLAYOFF
Sun 12/30 H MIA 34-14 W 50,214

AFC CHAMPIONSHIP
Sun 1/6 H HOU 27-13 W 50,475

SUPER BOWL XIV
Sun 1/20 N LA 31-19 W 103,985

ST. LOUIS CARDINALS
Sun 9/2 H DAL 21-22 L 50,855
Sun 9/9 A NYG 27-14 W 71,370
Sun 9/16 H PIT 21-24 L 50,416
Sun 9/23 H WAS 7-17 L 50,680
Sun 9/30 A LA 0-21 L 48,160
Sun 10/7 A HOU 24-17 W 53,043
Sun 10/14 H PHI 20-24 L 48,367
Sun 10/21 A DAL 13-22 L 64,300
Sun 10/28 H CLE 20-38 L 47,845
Sun 11/4 H MIN 37-7 W 47,213
Sun 11/11 A WAS 28-30 L 50,868
Sun 11/18 A PHI 13-16 L 70,235
Sun 11/25 H CIN 28-34 L 25,103
Sun 12/2 H SF 13-10 W 41,593
Sun 12/9 H NYG 29-20 W 39,802
Sun 12/16 A CHI 6-42 L 42,810

SAN DIEGO CHARGERS
Sun 9/2 A SEA 33-16 W 62,287
Sun 9/9 H OAK 30-10 W 50,255
Sun 9/16 H BUF 27-19 W 50,709
Sun 9/23 A NE 21-27 L 60,916
Sun 9/30 H SF 31-9 W 50,893
Sun 10/7 A DEN 0-7 L 74,997
Sun 10/14 H SEA 20-10 W 50,007
Sun 10/21 A LA 40-16 W 64,245
Thu 10/25 A OAK 22-45 L 53,709
Sun 11/4 A KC 20-14 W 59,353
Sun 11/11 A CIN 26-24 W 40,782
Sun 11/18 H PIT 35-7 W 51,910
Sun 11/25 H KC 28-7 W 50,078
Sun 12/2 H ATL 26-28 L 50,198
Sun 12/9 A NO 35-0 W 61,059
Mon 12/17 H DEN 17-7 W 51,906

AFC DIVISIONAL PLAYOFF
Sat 12/29 H HOU 14-17 L 51,192

SAN FRANCISCO 49ERS
Sun 9/2 A MIN 22-28 L 46,539
Sun 9/9 H DAL 13-21 L 56,728
Sun 9/16 A LA 24-27 L 44,303
Sun 9/23 H NO 21-30 L 39,727
Sun 9/30 A SD 9-31 L 50,893
Sun 10/7 A SEA 24-35 L 44,592
Sun 10/14 A NYG 16-32 L 70,352
Sun 10/21 H ATL 20-15 W 33,952

Sun 10/28 H CHI 27-28 L 42,773
Sun 11/4 A OAK 10-23 L 52,764
Sun 11/11 A NO 20-31 L 65,551
Sun 11/18 H DEN 28-38 L 42,910
Sun 11/25 H LA 20-26 L 49,282
Sun 12/2 A STL 10-13 L 41,593
Sun 12/9 H TB 23-7 W 44,506
Sun 12/16 A ATL 21-31 L 37,211

SEATTLE SEAHAWKS
Sun 9/2 H SD 16-33 L 62,287
Sun 9/9 A MIA 10-19 L 56,233
Sun 9/16 H OAK 27-10 W 61,602
Sun 9/23 A DEN 34-37 L 74,879
Sun 9/30 H KC 6-24 L 61,169
Sun 10/7 A SF 35-24 W 44,592
Sun 10/14 A SD 10-20 L 50,007
Sun 10/21 H HOU 34-14 W 60,705
Mon 10/29 A ATL 31-28 W 52,266
Sun 11/4 H LA 0-24 L 62,048
Sun 11/11 A CLE 29-24 W 72,440
Sun 11/18 H NO 38-24 W 60,055
Mon 11/26 H NYJ 30-7 W 59,977
Sun 12/2 A KC 21-37 L 42,160
Sat 12/8 H DEN 28-23 W 60,038
Sun 12/16 A OAK 29-24 W 53,177

TAMPA BAY BUCCANEERS
Sat 9/1 H DET 31-16 W 68,225
Sun 9/9 A BAL *29-26 W 36,374
Sun 9/16 H GB 21-10 W 55,498
Sun 9/23 H LA 21-6 W 69,497
Sun 9/30 A CHI 17-13 W 55,258
Sun 10/7 A NYG 14-17 L 72,841
Sun 10/14 H NO 14-42 L 67,640
Sun 10/21 H GB 21-3 W 67,186
Sun 10/28 A MIN 12-10 W 46,906
Sun 11/4 A ATL 14-17 L 55,150
Sun 11/11 A DET 16-14 W 70,461
Sun 11/18 A NYG 31-3 W 70,261
Sun 11/25 H MIN 22-23 L 70,039
Sun 12/2 H CHI 0-14 L 69,508
Sun 12/9 A SF 7-23 L 44,506
Sun 12/16 H KC 3-0 W 63,624

NFC DIVISIONAL PLAYOFF
Sat 12/29 H PHI 24-17 W 71,402

NFC CHAMPIONSHIP
Sun 1/6 H LA 0-9 L 72,033

WASHINGTON REDSKINS
Sun 9/2 H HOU 27-29 L 54,582
Sun 9/9 A DET 27-24 W 54,991
Mon 9/17 H NYG 27-0 W 55,031
Sun 9/23 A STL 17-7 W 50,680
Sun 9/30 A ATL 16-7 W 56,819
Sun 10/7 H PHI 17-28 L 69,142
Sun 10/14 A CLE 13-9 W 63,323
Sun 10/21 A PHI 17-7 W 54,442
Sun 10/28 H NO 10-14 L 53,133
Sun 11/4 A PIT 7-38 L 49,462
Sun 11/11 H STL 30-28 W 50,868
Sun 11/18 H DAL 34-20 W 55,031
Sun 11/25 A NYG 6-14 L 72,641
Sun 12/2 H GB 38-21 W 51,682
Sun 12/9 H CIN 28-14 W 52,882
Sun 12/16 A DAL 34-35 L 62,867

1980 NFL
ATLANTA FALCONS
Sun 9/7 A MIN 23-24 L 44,773
Sun 9/14 A NE 37-21 W 48,321
Sun 9/21 H MIA 17-20 L 55,479
Sun 9/28 A SF 20-17 W 56,518
Sun 10/5 H DET 43-28 W 57,652

Sun 10/12 H NYJ 7-14 L 57,458
Sun 10/19 A NO 41-14 W 62,651
Sun 10/26 H LA 13-10 W 57,401
Sun 11/2 A BUF 30-14 W 57,959
Sun 11/9 A STL *33-27 W 48,662
Sun 11/16 H NO 31-13 W 53,871
Sun 11/23 H CHI 28-17 W 49,164
Sun 11/30 H WAS 10-6 W 55,665
Sun 12/7 A PHI 20-17 W 70,205
Sun 12/14 H SF 35-10 W 55,767
Sun 12/21 A LA *17-20 L 62,469

NFC DIVISIONAL PLAYOFF
Sun 1/4 H DAL 27-30 L 60,022

BALTIMORE COLTS
Sun 9/7 A NYJ 17-14 W 50,777
Sun 9/14 H PIT 17-20 L 54,914
Sun 9/21 A HOU 16-21 L 47,878
Sun 9/28 H NYJ 35-21 W 33,373
Sun 10/5 A MIA 30-17 W 50,631
Sun 10/12 A BUF 17-12 W 73,634
Sun 10/19 H NE 21-37 L 53,924
Sun 10/26 H STL 10-17 L 33,506
Sun 11/2 A KC 31-24 W 52,383
Sun 11/9 H CLE 27-28 L 45,369
Sun 11/16 A DET 10-9 W 77,307
Sun 11/23 H NE 21-47 L 60,994
Sun 11/30 H BUF 28-24 W 36,184
Sun 12/7 A CIN 33-34 L 35,651
Sun 12/14 H MIA 14-24 L 30,564
Sun 12/21 H KC 28-38 L 16,941

BUFFALO BILLS
Sun 9/7 H MIA 17-7 W 79,598
Sun 9/14 H NYJ 20-10 W 65,315
Sun 9/21 A NO 35-26 W 51,154
Sun 9/28 H OAK 24-7 W 77,259
Sun 10/5 A SD 26-24 W 51,982
Sun 10/12 H BAL 12-17 L 73,634
Sun 10/19 A MIA 14-17 L 41,636
Sun 10/26 H NE 31-13 W 75,092
Sun 11/2 H ATL 14-30 L 57,959
Sun 11/9 A NYJ 31-24 W 45,677
Sun 11/16 A CIN 14-0 W 40,836
Sun 11/23 H PIT 28-13 W 79,659
Sun 11/30 A BAL 24-28 L 36,184
Sun 12/7 H LA *10-7 W 77,133
Sun 12/14 A NE 2-24 L 58,324
Sun 12/21 A SF 18-13 W 37,476

AFC DIVISIONAL PLAYOFF
Sat 1/3 A SD 14-20 L 52,028

CHICAGO BEARS
Sun 9/7 A GB *6-12 L 54,381
Sun 9/14 H NO 22-3 W 62,523
Sun 9/21 H MIN 14-34 L 59,983
Sun 9/28 A PIT 3-38 L 53,987
Mon 10/6 H TB 23-0 W 61,350
Sun 10/12 A MIN 7-13 L 46,751
Sun 10/19 H DET 24-7 W 58,508
Sun 10/26 A PHI 14-17 L 68,752
Mon 11/3 A CLE 21-27 L 83,224
Sun 11/9 H WAS 35-21 W 57,159
Sun 11/16 H HOU 6-10 L 59,390
Sun 11/23 A ATL 17-28 L 49,164
Thu 11/27 A DET *23-17 W 75,397
Sun 12/7 H GB 61-7 W 57,176
Sun 12/14 H CIN *14-17 L 48,808
Sat 12/20 H TB 14-13 W 55,298

CINCINNATI BENGALS
Sun 9/7 H TB 12-17 L 38,280
Sun 9/14 A MIA 16-17 L 38,322
Sun 9/21 H PIT 30-28 W 52,490
Sun 9/28 H HOU 10-13 L 50,413

Sun 10/5 A GB 9-14 L 55,006
Sun 10/12 A PIT 17-16 W 53,668
Sun 10/19 H MIN 14-0 W 44,487
Sun 10/26 A HOU 3-23 L 49,189
Sun 11/2 H SD 14-31 L 46,406
Sun 11/9 A OAK 17-28 L 44,132
Sun 11/16 H BUF 0-14 L 40,836
Sun 11/23 A CLE 7-31 L 79,523
Sun 11/30 A KC 20-6 W 41,594
Sun 12/7 H BAL 34-33 W 35,651
Sun 12/14 A CHI *17-14 W 48,808
Sun 12/21 H CLE 24-27 L 50,058

CLEVELAND BROWNS
Sun 9/7 A NE 17-34 L 49,222
Mon 9/15 H HOU 7-16 L 79,438
Sun 9/21 H KC 20-13 W 63,614
Sun 9/28 A TB 34-27 W 65,540
Sun 10/5 H DEN 16-19 L 81,065
Sun 10/12 A SEA 27-3 W 61,366
Sun 10/19 H GB 26-21 W 75,540
Sun 10/26 H PIT 27-26 W 79,095
Mon 11/3 H CHI 27-21 W 83,224
Sun 11/9 A BAL 28-27 W 45,369
Sun 11/16 H PIT 13-16 L 54,563
Sun 11/23 H CIN 31-7 W 79,523
Sun 11/30 A HOU 17-14 W 51,514
Sun 12/7 H NYJ 17-14 W 78,454
Sun 12/14 A MIN 23-28 L 42,202
Sun 12/21 A CIN 27-24 W 50,058

AFC DIVISIONAL PLAYOFF
Sun 1/4 H OAK 12-14 L 77,655

DALLAS COWBOYS
Mon 9/8 A WAS 17-3 W 55,045
Sun 9/14 A DEN 20-41 L 74,919
Sun 9/21 H TB 28-17 W 62,750
Sun 9/28 A GB 28-7 W 54,776
Sun 10/5 H NYG 24-3 W 59,126
Sun 10/12 H SF 59-14 W 63,399
Sun 10/19 A PHI 10-17 L 70,696
Sun 10/26 H SD 42-31 W 60,639
Sun 11/2 A STL 27-24 W 50,701
Sun 11/9 A NYG 35-38 L 68,343
Sun 11/16 H STL 31-21 W 52,567
Sun 11/23 H WAS 14-10 W 58,809
Thu 11/27 H SEA 51-7 W 57,540
Sun 12/7 A OAK 19-13 W 53,194
Mon 12/15 A LA 14-38 L 65,154
Sun 12/21 H PHI 35-27 W 62,548

NFC WILD-CARD PLAYOFF
Sun 12/28 H LA 34-13 W 64,533

NFC DIVISIONAL PLAYOFF
Sun 1/4 A ATL 30-27 W 60,022

NFC CHAMPIONSHIP
Sun 1/11 A PHI 7-20 L 70,696

DENVER BRONCOS
Sun 9/7 A PHI 6-27 L 70,307
Sun 9/14 H DAL 41-20 W 74,919
Sun 9/21 H SD 13-30 L 74,970
Mon 9/29 A NE 14-23 L 59,602
Sun 10/5 A CLE 19-16 W 81,065
Mon 10/13 H WAS 20-17 W 74,657
Sun 10/19 H KC 17-23 L 74,459
Sun 10/26 A NYG 14-9 W 67,598
Sun 11/2 H HOU 16-20 L 74,717
Sun 11/9 A SD 20-13 W 51,435
Sun 11/16 H NYJ 31-24 W 72,114
Sun 11/23 H SEA 36-20 W 73,274
Mon 12/1 A OAK 3-9 L 51,583
Sun 12/7 A KC 14-31 L 40,237
Sun 12/14 A OAK 21-24 L 73,274
Sun 12/21 H SEA 25-17 W 51,853

DETROIT LIONS

Sun	9/7	A	LA	41-20	W	64,892
Sun	9/14	A	GB	29-7	W	53,099
Sun	9/21	H	STL	20-7	W	79,587
Sun	9/28	H	MIN	27-7	W	80,291
Sun	10/5	A	ATL	28-43	L	57,652
Sun	10/12	H	NO	24-13	W	78,147
Sun	10/19	A	CHI	7-24	L	58,508
Sun	10/26	A	KC	17-20	L	59,391
Sun	11/2	H	SF	17-13	W	78,845
Sun	11/9	A	MIN	0-34	L	46,264
Sun	11/16	H	BAL	9-10	L	77,307
Sun	11/23	A	TB	24-10	W	64,976
Thu	11/27	H	CHI	*17-23	L	75,397
Sun	12/7	A	STL	23-24	L	46,966
Sun	12/14	H	TB	27-14	W	76,893
Sun	12/21	H	GB	24-3	W	75,111

GREEN BAY PACKERS

Sun	9/7	H	CHI	*12-6	W	54,381
Sun	9/14	H	DET	7-29	L	53,099
Sun	9/21	A	LA	21-51	L	63,850
Sun	9/28	H	DAL	7-28	L	54,776
Sun	10/5	H	CIN	14-9	W	55,006
Sun	10/12	A	TB	*14-14	T	64,854
Sun	10/19	A	CLE	21-26	L	75,540
Sun	10/26	H	MIN	16-3	W	56,191
Sun	11/2	A	PIT	20-22	L	52,165
Sun	11/9	H	SF	23-16	W	54,675
Sun	11/16	A	NYG	21-27	L	72,368
Sun	11/23	A	MIN	25-13	W	47,234
Sun	11/30	H	TB	17-20	L	54,225
Sun	12/7	A	CHI	7-61	L	57,176
Sun	12/14	H	HOU	3-22	L	53,168
Sun	12/21	A	DET	3-24	L	75,111

HOUSTON OILERS

Sun	9/7	A	PIT	17-31	L	54,386
Mon	9/15	A	CLE	16-7	W	79,438
Sun	9/21	H	BAL	21-16	W	47,878
Sun	9/28	A	CIN	13-10	W	50,413
Sun	10/5	H	SEA	7-26	L	46,860
Sun	10/12	A	KC	20-21	L	75,048
Sun	10/19	H	TB	20-14	W	48,167
Sun	10/26	H	CIN	23-3	W	49,189
Sun	11/2	A	DEN	20-16	W	74,717
Mon	11/10	H	NE	38-34	W	51,524
Sun	11/16	A	CHI	10-6	W	59,390
Sun	11/23	A	NYJ	*28-31	L	52,358
Sun	11/30	H	CLE	14-17	L	51,514
Thu	12/4	H	PIT	6-0	W	53,960
Sun	12/14	A	GB	22-3	W	53,168
Sun	12/21	H	MIN	20-16	W	51,064

AFC Wild-Card Playoff

Sun	12/28	A	OAK	7-27	L	52,762

KANSAS CITY CHIEFS

Sun	9/7	H	OAK	14-27	L	54,269
Sun	9/14	H	SEA	16-17	L	42,403
Sun	9/21	A	CLE	13-20	L	63,614
Sun	9/28	H	SD	7-24	L	45,161
Sun	10/5	A	OAK	31-17	W	40,153
Sun	10/12	H	HOU	21-20	W	75,048
Sun	10/19	A	DEN	23-17	W	74,459
Sun	10/26	H	DET	20-17	W	59,391
Sun	11/2	H	BAL	24-31	L	52,383
Sun	11/9	A	SEA	31-30	W	58,976
Sun	11/16	A	SD	7-20	L	50,248
Sun	11/23	A	STL	21-13	W	42,871
Sun	11/30	H	CIN	6-20	L	41,594
Sun	12/7	H	DEN	31-14	W	40,237
Sun	12/14	A	PIT	16-21	L	50,013
Sun	12/21	A	BAL	38-28	W	16,941

LOS ANGELES RAMS

Sun	9/7	H	DET	20-41	L	64,892
Thu	9/11	A	TB	9-10	L	66,576
Sun	9/21	H	GB	51-21	W	63,850
Sun	9/28	A	NYG	28-7	W	73,414
Sun	10/5	H	SF	48-26	W	62,188
Sun	10/12	A	STL	21-13	W	50,230
Sun	10/19	A	SF	31-17	W	55,360
Sun	10/26	A	ATL	10-13	L	57,401
Sun	11/2	H	NO	45-31	W	59,909
Sun	11/9	H	MIA	14-35	L	62,198
Sun	11/16	A	NE	17-14	W	60,609
Mon	11/24	A	NO	27-7	W	53,448
Sun	11/30	H	NYJ	38-13	W	59,743
Sun	12/7	A	BUF	*7-10	L	77,133
Mon	12/15	H	DAL	38-14	W	65,154
Sun	12/21	H	ATL	*20-17	W	62,469

NFC Wild-Card Playoff

Sun	12/28	A	DAL	13-34	L	64,533

MIAMI DOLPHINS

Sun	9/7	A	BUF	7-17	L	79,598
Sun	9/14	H	CIN	17-16	W	38,322
Sun	9/21	A	ATL	20-17	W	55,479
Sun	9/28	H	NO	21-16	W	40,946
Sun	10/5	H	BAL	17-30	L	50,631
Sun	10/12	A	NE	0-34	L	60,377
Sun	10/19	H	BUF	17-14	W	41,636
Mon	10/27	A	NYJ	14-17	L	53,046
Sun	11/2	A	OAK	10-16	L	46,378
Sun	11/9	A	LA	35-14	W	62,198
Sun	11/16	H	SF	17-13	W	45,135
Thu	11/20	H	SD	*24-27	L	63,013
Sun	11/30	A	PIT	10-23	L	51,384
Mon	12/8	H	NE	*16-13	W	63,292
Sun	12/14	A	BAL	24-14	W	30,564
Sat	12/20	H	NYJ	17-24	L	41,854

MINNESOTA VIKINGS

Sun	9/7	H	ATL	24-23	W	44,773
Sun	9/14	H	PHI	7-42	L	46,460
Sun	9/21	A	CHI	34-14	W	59,983
Sun	9/28	A	DET	7-27	L	80,291
Sun	10/5	H	PIT	17-23	L	47,583
Sun	10/12	H	CHI	13-7	W	46,751
Sun	10/19	A	CIN	0-14	L	44,487
Sun	10/26	A	GB	3-16	L	56,191
Sun	11/2	A	WAS	39-14	W	52,060
Sun	11/9	H	DET	34-0	W	46,264
Sun	11/16	H	TB	38-30	W	46,032
Sun	11/23	H	GB	13-25	L	47,234
Sun	11/30	A	NO	23-20	W	30,936
Sun	12/7	A	TB	21-10	W	65,649
Sun	12/14	H	CLE	28-23	W	42,202
Sun	12/21	A	HOU	16-20	L	51,064

NFC Divisional Playoff

Sat	1/3	A	PHI	16-31	L	68,434

NEW ENGLAND PATRIOTS

Sun	9/7	H	CLE	34-17	W	49,222
Sun	9/14	H	ATL	21-37	L	48,321
Sun	9/21	A	SEA	37-31	W	61,035
Mon	9/29	H	DEN	23-14	W	59,602
Sun	10/5	A	NYJ	21-11	W	53,603
Sun	10/12	H	MIA	34-0	W	60,377
Sun	10/19	A	BAL	37-21	W	53,924
Sun	10/26	A	BUF	13-31	L	75,092
Sun	11/2	H	NYJ	34-21	W	60,834
Mon	11/10	A	HOU	34-38	L	51,524
Sun	11/16	H	LA	14-17	L	60,609
Sun	11/23	H	BAL	47-21	W	60,994
Sun	11/30	A	SF	17-21	L	45,254
Mon	12/8	A	MIA	*13-16	L	63,292
Sun	12/14	H	BUF	24-2	W	58,324
Sun	12/21	A	NO	38-27	W	38,277

NEW ORLEANS SAINTS

Sun	9/7	H	SF	23-26	L	58,621
Sun	9/14	A	CHI	3-22	L	62,523
Sun	9/21	H	BUF	26-35	L	51,154
Sun	9/28	A	MIA	16-21	L	40,946
Sun	10/5	H	STL	7-40	L	45,388
Sun	10/12	A	DET	13-24	L	78,147
Sun	10/19	H	ATL	14-41	L	62,651
Sun	10/26	A	WAS	14-22	L	51,375
Sun	11/2	A	LA	31-45	L	59,909
Sun	11/9	H	PHI	21-34	L	44,340
Sun	11/16	A	ATL	13-31	L	53,871
Mon	11/24	H	LA	7-27	L	53,448
Sun	11/30	H	MIN	20-23	L	30,936
Sun	12/7	A	SF	*35-38	L	37,949
Sun	12/14	A	NYJ	21-20	W	38,077
Sun	12/21	H	NE	27-38	L	38,277

NEW YORK GIANTS

Sun	9/7	A	STL	41-35	W	49,122
Sun	9/14	H	WAS	21-23	L	73,343
Mon	9/22	A	PHI	3-35	L	70,767
Sun	9/28	H	LA	7-28	L	73,414
Sun	10/5	A	DAL	3-24	L	59,126
Sun	10/12	H	PHI	16-31	L	71,051
Sun	10/19	A	SD	7-44	L	50,397
Sun	10/26	H	DEN	9-14	L	67,598
Sun	11/2	A	TB	13-30	L	68,256
Sun	11/9	H	DAL	38-35	W	68,343
Sun	11/16	H	GB	27-21	W	72,368
Sun	11/23	A	SF	0-12	L	38,574
Sun	11/30	H	STL	7-23	L	65,852
Sun	12/7	A	SEA	27-21	W	51,617
Sat	12/13	A	WAS	13-16	L	44,443
Sun	12/21	H	OAK	17-33	L	61,287

NEW YORK JETS

Sun	9/7	H	BAL	14-17	L	50,777
Sun	9/14	A	BUF	10-20	L	65,315
Sun	9/21	H	SF	27-37	L	50,608
Sun	9/28	A	BAL	21-35	L	33,373
Sun	10/5	H	NE	11-21	L	53,603
Sun	10/12	A	ATL	14-7	W	57,458
Sun	10/19	H	SEA	17-27	L	52,496
Mon	10/27	H	MIA	17-14	W	53,046
Sun	11/2	A	NE	21-34	L	60,834
Sun	11/9	H	BUF	24-31	L	45,677
Sun	11/16	A	DEN	24-31	L	72,114
Sun	11/23	H	HOU	*31-28	W	52,358
Sun	11/30	A	LA	13-38	L	59,743
Sun	12/7	A	CLE	14-17	L	78,454
Sun	12/14	H	NO	20-21	L	38,077
Sat	12/20	A	MIA	24-17	W	41,854

OAKLAND RAIDERS

Sun	9/7	A	KC	27-14	W	54,269
Sun	9/14	A	SD	*24-30	L	51,943
Sun	9/21	H	WAS	24-21	W	45,163
Sun	9/28	A	BUF	7-24	L	77,259
Sun	10/5	H	KC	17-31	L	40,153
Sun	10/12	H	SD	38-24	W	44,826
Mon	10/20	A	PIT	45-34	W	53,940
Sun	10/26	H	SEA	33-14	W	50,185
Sun	11/2	H	MIA	16-10	W	46,378
Sun	11/9	H	CIN	28-17	W	44,132
Mon	11/17	A	SEA	19-17	W	60,480
Sun	11/23	A	PHI	7-10	L	68,585
Mon	12/1	H	DEN	9-3	W	51,583
Sun	12/7	H	DAL	13-19	L	53,194
Sun	12/14	A	DEN	24-21	W	73,274
Sun	12/21	A	NYG	33-17	W	61,287

AFC Wild-Card Playoff

Sun	12/28	H	HOU	27-7	W	52,762

AFC Divisional Playoff

Sun	1/4	A	CLE	14-12	W	77,655

AFC Championship

Sun	1/11	A	SD	34-27	W	52,438

Super Bowl XV

Sun	1/25	N	PHI	27-10	W	75,500

PHILADELPHIA EAGLES

Sun	9/7	H	DEN	27-6	W	70,307
Sun	9/14	A	MIN	42-7	W	46,460
Mon	9/22	H	NYG	35-3	W	70,767
Sun	9/28	A	STL	14-24	L	49,079
Sun	10/5	H	WAS	24-14	W	69,044
Sun	10/12	A	NYG	31-16	W	71,051
Sun	10/19	H	DAL	17-10	W	70,696
Sun	10/26	H	CHI	17-14	W	68,752
Sun	11/2	A	SEA	27-20	W	61,047
Sun	11/9	A	NO	34-21	W	44,340
Sun	11/16	A	WAS	24-0	W	51,897
Sun	11/23	H	OAK	10-7	W	68,585
Sun	11/30	A	SD	21-22	L	51,760
Sun	12/7	H	ATL	17-20	L	70,205
Sun	12/14	H	STL	17-3	W	68,969
Sun	12/21	A	DAL	27-35	L	62,548

NFC Divisional Playoff

Sat	1/3	H	MIN	31-16	W	68,434

NFC Championship

Sun	1/11	H	DAL	20-7	W	70,696

Super Bowl XV

Sun	1/25	N	OAK	10-27	L	75,500

PITTSBURGH STEELERS

Sun	9/7	H	HOU	31-17	W	54,386
Sun	9/14	A	BAL	20-17	W	54,914
Sun	9/21	A	CIN	28-30	L	52,490
Sun	9/28	H	CHI	38-3	W	53,987
Sun	10/5	A	MIN	23-17	W	47,583
Sun	10/12	H	CIN	16-17	L	53,668
Mon	10/20	H	OAK	34-45	L	53,940
Sun	10/26	A	CLE	26-27	L	79,095
Sun	11/2	H	GB	22-20	W	52,165
Sun	11/9	A	TB	24-21	W	71,636
Sun	11/16	H	CLE	16-13	W	54,563
Sun	11/23	A	BUF	13-28	L	79,659
Sun	11/30	H	MIA	23-10	W	51,384
Thu	12/4	A	HOU	0-6	L	53,960
Sun	12/14	H	KC	21-16	W	50,013
Mon	12/22	A	SD	17-26	L	51,785

ST. LOUIS CARDINALS

Sun	9/7	H	NYG	35-41	L	49,122
Sun	9/14	A	SF	*21-24	L	49,999
Sun	9/21	A	DET	7-20	L	79,587
Sun	9/28	H	PHI	24-14	W	49,079
Sun	10/5	A	NO	40-7	W	45,388
Sun	10/12	H	LA	13-21	L	50,230
Sun	10/19	A	WAS	0-23	L	51,060
Sun	10/26	A	BAL	17-10	W	33,506
Sun	11/2	H	DAL	24-27	L	50,701
Sun	11/9	H	ATL	*27-33	L	48,662
Sun	11/16	A	DAL	21-31	L	52,567
Sun	11/23	H	KC	13-21	L	42,871
Sun	11/30	A	NYG	23-7	W	65,852
Sun	12/7	H	DET	24-23	W	46,966
Sun	12/14	A	PHI	3-17	L	68,969
Sun	12/21	H	WAS	7-31	L	35,942

SAN DIEGO CHARGERS

Sun	9/7	A	SEA	34-13	W	62,042
Sun	9/14	H	OAK	*30-24	W	51,943
Sun	9/21	A	DEN	30-13	W	74,970
Sun	9/28	A	KC	24-7	W	45,161
Sun	10/5	H	BUF	24-26	L	51,982
Sun	10/12	A	OAK	24-38	L	44,826
Sun	10/19	H	NYG	44-7	W	50,397

Sun	10/26	A	DAL	31-42	L	60,639
Sun	11/2	A	CIN	31-14	W	46,406
Sun	11/9	H	DEN	13-20	L	51,435
Sun	11/16	H	KC	20-7	W	50,248
Thu	11/20	A	MIA	*27-24	W	63,013
Sun	11/30	H	PHI	22-21	W	51,760
Sun	12/7	A	WAS	17-40	L	48,556
Sat	12/13	H	SEA	21-14	W	49,980
Mon	12/22	H	PIT	26-17	W	51,785

AFC Divsional Playoff

Sat	1/3	H	BUF	20-14	W	52,028

AFC Championship

Sun	1/11	H	OAK	27-34	L	52,438

SAN FRANCISCO 49ERS

Sun	9/7	A	NO	26-23	W	58,621
Sun	9/14	H	STL	*24-21	W	49,999
Sun	9/21	A	NYJ	37-27	W	50,608
Sun	9/28	H	ATL	17-20	L	56,518
Sun	10/5	A	LA	26-48	L	62,188
Sun	10/12	A	DAL	14-59	L	63,399
Sun	10/19	H	LA	17-31	L	55,360
Sun	10/26	H	TB	23-24	L	51,925
Sun	11/2	A	DET	13-17	L	78,845
Sun	11/9	A	GB	16-23	L	54,675
Sun	11/16	A	MIA	13-17	L	45,135
Sun	11/23	H	NYG	12-0	W	38,574
Sun	11/30	H	NE	21-17	W	45,254
Sun	12/7	H	NO	*38-35	W	37,949
Sun	12/14	A	ATL	10-35	L	55,767
Sun	12/21	H	BUF	13-18	L	37,476

SEATTLE SEAHAWKS

Sun	9/7	H	SD	13-34	L	62,042
Sun	9/14	A	KC	17-16	W	42,403
Sun	9/21	H	NE	31-37	L	61,035
Sun	9/28	A	WAS	14-0	W	53,263
Sun	10/5	A	HOU	26-7	W	46,860
Sun	10/12	H	CLE	3-27	L	61,366
Sun	10/19	A	NYJ	27-17	W	52,496
Sun	10/26	A	OAK	14-33	L	50,185
Sun	11/2	H	PHI	20-27	L	61,047
Sun	11/9	H	KC	30-31	L	58,976
Mon	11/17	H	OAK	17-19	L	60,480
Sun	11/23	A	DEN	20-36	L	73,274
Thu	11/27	A	DAL	7-51	L	57,540
Sun	12/7	H	NYG	21-27	L	51,617
Sat	12/13	A	SD	14-21	L	49,980
Sun	12/21	H	DEN	17-25	L	51,853

TAMPA BAY BUCCANEERS

Sun	9/7	A	CIN	17-12	W	38,280
Thu	9/11	H	LA	10-9	W	66,576
Sun	9/21	A	DAL	17-28	L	62,750
Sun	9/28	H	CLE	27-34	L	65,540
Mon	10/6	A	CHI	0-23	L	61,350
Sun	10/12	H	GB	*14-14	T	64,854
Sun	10/19	A	HOU	14-20	L	48,167
Sun	10/26	A	SF	24-23	W	51,925
Sun	11/2	H	NYG	30-13	W	68,256
Sun	11/9	H	PIT	21-24	L	71,636
Sun	11/16	A	MIN	30-38	L	46,032
Sun	11/23	H	DET	10-24	L	64,976
Sun	11/30	A	GB	20-17	W	54,225
Sun	12/7	H	MIN	10-21	L	65,649
Sun	12/14	A	DET	14-27	L	76,893
Sat	12/20	H	CHI	13-14	L	55,298

WASHINGTON REDSKINS

Mon	9/8	H	DAL	3-17	L	55,045
Sun	9/14	A	NYG	23-21	W	73,343
Sun	9/21	A	OAK	21-24	L	45,163
Sun	9/28	H	SEA	0-14	L	53,263
Sun	10/5	A	PHI	14-24	L	69,044
Mon	10/13	A	DEN	17-20	L	74,657
Sun	10/19	H	STL	23-0	W	51,060
Sun	10/26	H	NO	22-14	W	51,375
Sun	11/2	H	MIN	14-39	L	52,060
Sun	11/9	A	CHI	21-35	L	57,159
Sun	11/16	H	PHI	0-24	L	51,897
Sun	11/23	A	DAL	10-14	L	58,809
Sun	11/30	A	ATL	6-10	L	55,665
Sun	12/7	H	SD	40-17	W	48,556
Sat	12/13	H	NYG	16-13	W	44,443
Sun	12/21	A	STL	31-7	W	35,942

1981 NFL

ATLANTA FALCONS

Sun	9/6	H	NO	27-0	W	57,406
Sun	9/13	A	GB	31-17	W	54,574
Sun	9/20	H	SF	34-17	W	56,653
Sun	9/27	A	CLE	17-28	L	78,283
Mon	10/5	A	PHI	13-16	L	71,488
Sun	10/11	H	LA	35-37	L	57,841
Sun	10/18	H	STL	41-20	W	51,428
Sun	10/25	H	NYG	*24-27	L	48,410
Sun	11/1	A	NO	41-10	W	63,637
Sun	11/8	A	SF	14-17	L	59,127
Sun	11/15	H	PIT	20-34	L	57,485
Mon	11/23	H	MIN	31-30	W	54,086
Sun	11/29	A	HOU	31-27	W	40,201
Sun	12/6	A	TB	23-24	L	69,221
Mon	12/14	A	LA	16-21	L	57,054
Sun	12/20	H	CIN	28-30	L	35,972

BALTIMORE COLTS

Sun	9/6	A	NE	29-28	W	49,572
Sun	9/13	H	BUF	3-35	L	43,953
Sun	9/20	A	DEN	10-28	L	74,804
Sun	9/27	H	MIA	28-31	L	39,273
Sun	10/4	A	BUF	17-23	L	77,720
Sun	10/11	H	CIN	19-41	L	33,060
Sun	10/18	H	SD	14-43	L	41,921
Sun	10/25	A	CLE	28-42	L	78,986
Sun	11/1	A	MIA	10-27	L	46,061
Sun	11/8	H	NYJ	14-41	L	31,521
Sun	11/15	A	PHI	13-38	L	68,618
Sun	11/22	H	STL	24-35	L	24,784
Sun	11/29	A	NYJ	0-25	L	53,593
Sun	12/6	H	DAL	13-37	L	54,871
Sun	12/13	A	WAS	14-38	L	46,706
Sun	12/20	H	NE	23-21	W	17,073

BUFFALO BILLS

Sun	9/6	H	NYJ	31-0	W	79,665
Sun	9/13	A	BAL	35-3	W	43,953
Thu	9/17	H	PHI	14-20	L	78,236
Sun	9/27	A	CIN	*24-27	L	46,418
Sun	10/4	H	BAL	23-17	W	77,720
Mon	10/12	H	MIA	31-21	W	78,485
Sun	10/18	A	NYJ	14-33	L	54,607
Sun	10/25	H	DEN	9-7	W	77,631
Sun	11/1	H	CLE	22-13	W	78,184
Mon	11/9	A	DAL	14-27	L	62,583
Sun	11/15	A	STL	0-24	L	46,214
Sun	11/22	H	NE	20-17	W	71,593
Sun	11/29	H	WAS	21-14	W	59,664
Sun	12/6	A	SD	28-27	W	51,488
Sun	12/13	A	NE	19-10	W	42,529
Sat	12/19	A	MIA	6-16	L	72,956

AFC Wild-Card Playoff

Sun	12/27	A	NYJ	31-27	W	57,050

AFC Divisional Playoff

Sun	1/3	A	CIN	21-28	L	55,420

CHICAGO BEARS

Sun	9/6	H	GB	9-16	L	62,411
Sun	9/13	A	SF	17-28	L	49,520
Sun	9/20	H	TB	28-17	W	60,130
Mon	9/28	H	LA	7-24	L	62,461
Sun	10/4	A	MIN	21-24	L	43,827
Sun	10/11	H	WAS	7-24	L	57,683
Mon	10/19	A	DET	17-48	L	71,273
Sun	10/25	H	SD	*20-17	W	52,906
Sun	11/1	A	TB	10-20	L	63,688
Sun	11/8	A	KC	*16-13	W	60,605
Sun	11/15	A	GB	17-21	L	55,338
Sun	11/22	H	DET	7-23	L	50,082
Thu	11/26	A	DAL	9-10	L	63,499
Sun	12/6	H	MIN	10-9	W	50,766
Sun	12/13	A	OAK	23-6	W	40,384
Sun	12/20	H	DEN	35-24	W	40,125

CINCINNATI BENGALS

Sun	9/6	H	SEA	27-21	W	41,177
Sun	9/13	A	NYJ	31-30	W	49,454
Sun	9/20	H	CLE	17-20	L	52,170
Sun	9/27	H	BUF	*27-24	W	46,418
Sun	10/4	A	HOU	10-17	L	44,350
Sun	10/11	A	BAL	41-19	W	33,060
Sun	10/18	H	PIT	34-7	W	57,090
Sun	10/25	A	NO	7-17	L	46,336
Sun	11/1	H	HOU	34-21	W	54,736
Sun	11/8	A	SD	40-17	W	51,259
Sun	11/15	H	LA	24-10	W	58,836
Sun	11/22	H	DEN	38-21	W	57,207
Sun	11/29	A	CLE	41-21	W	75,186
Sun	12/6	H	SF	3-21	L	56,796
Sun	12/13	A	PIT	17-10	W	50,923
Sun	12/20	A	ATL	30-28	W	35,972

AFC Divisional Playoff

Sun	1/3	H	BUF	28-21	W	55,420

AFC Championship

Sun	1/10	H	SD	27-7	W	46,302

Super Bowl XVI

Sun	1/24	N	SF	21-26	L	81,270

CLEVELAND BROWNS

Mon	9/7	H	SD	14-44	L	78,904
Sun	9/13	H	HOU	3-9	L	79,843
Sun	9/20	A	CIN	20-17	W	52,170
Sun	9/27	H	ATL	28-17	W	78,283
Sun	10/4	A	LA	16-27	L	63,294
Sun	10/11	A	PIT	7-13	L	53,225
Sun	10/18	H	NO	20-17	W	76,059
Sun	10/25	H	BAL	42-28	W	78,986
Sun	11/1	A	BUF	13-22	L	78,184
Sun	11/8	A	DEN	*20-23	L	74,859
Sun	11/15	A	SF	15-12	W	52,445
Sun	11/22	H	PIT	10-32	L	77,958
Sun	11/29	H	CIN	21-41	L	75,186
Thu	12/3	A	HOU	13-17	L	44,502
Sat	12/12	H	NYJ	13-14	L	56,866
Sun	12/20	A	SEA	21-42	L	51,435

DALLAS COWBOYS

Sun	9/6	A	WAS	26-10	W	55,045
Sun	9/13	H	STL	30-17	W	63,602
Mon	9/21	A	NE	35-21	W	60,311
Sun	9/27	H	NYG	18-10	W	63,449
Sun	10/4	A	STL	17-20	L	49,477
Sun	10/11	A	SF	14-45	L	57,574
Sun	10/18	H	LA	29-17	W	64,649
Sun	10/25	H	MIA	28-27	W	64,221
Sun	11/1	A	PHI	17-14	W	72,111
Mon	11/9	H	BUF	27-14	W	62,583
Sun	11/15	A	DET	24-27	L	79,694
Sun	11/22	H	WAS	24-10	W	64,583
Thu	11/26	H	CHI	10-9	W	63,499
Sun	12/6	A	BAL	37-13	W	54,871
Sun	12/13	H	PHI	21-10	W	64,955
Sat	12/19	A	NYG	*10-13	L	73,009

NFC Divisional Playoff

Sat	1/2	H	TB	38-0	W	64,848

NFC Championship

Sun	1/10	A	SF	27-28	L	60,525

DENVER BRONCOS

Sun	9/6	H	OAK	9-7	W	74,796
Sun	9/13	A	SEA	10-13	L	58,513
Sun	9/20	H	BAL	28-10	W	74,804
Sun	9/27	H	SD	42-24	W	74,844
Sun	10/4	A	OAK	17-0	W	51,035
Sun	10/11	H	DET	27-21	W	74,816
Sun	10/18	A	KC	14-28	L	74,672
Sun	10/25	A	BUF	7-9	L	77,631
Mon	11/2	H	MIN	19-17	W	74,834
Sun	11/8	H	CLE	*23-20	W	74,859
Sun	11/15	A	TB	24-7	W	64,518
Sun	11/22	A	CIN	21-38	L	57,207
Sun	11/29	A	SD	17-34	L	51,533
Sun	12/6	H	KC	16-13	W	74,744
Sun	12/13	H	SEA	23-13	W	74,705
Sun	12/20	A	CHI	24-35	L	40,125

DETROIT LIONS

Sun	9/6	H	SF	24-17	W	62,123
Sun	9/13	A	SD	23-28	L	51,624
Sun	9/20	A	MIN	24-26	L	45,350
Sun	9/27	H	OAK	16-0	W	77,919
Sun	10/4	A	TB	10-28	L	71,733
Sun	10/11	A	DEN	21-27	L	74,816
Mon	10/19	H	CHI	48-17	W	71,273
Sun	10/25	H	GB	31-27	W	76,063
Sun	11/1	A	LA	13-20	L	61,814
Sun	11/8	A	WAS	31-33	L	52,096
Sun	11/15	H	DAL	27-24	W	79,694
Sun	11/22	A	CHI	23-7	W	50,082
Thu	11/26	H	KC	27-10	W	76,735
Sun	12/6	A	GB	17-31	L	54,481
Sat	12/12	H	MIN	45-7	W	79,428
Sun	12/20	H	TB	17-20	L	80,444

GREEN BAY PACKERS

Sun	9/6	A	CHI	16-9	W	62,411
Sun	9/13	H	ATL	17-31	L	54,574
Sun	9/20	A	LA	23-35	L	61,286
Sun	9/27	H	MIN	13-30	L	55,012
Sun	10/4	A	NYG	27-14	W	73,684
Sun	10/11	H	TB	10-21	L	55,264
Sun	10/18	H	SF	3-13	L	50,171
Sun	10/25	A	DET	27-31	L	76,063
Sun	11/1	H	SEA	34-24	W	54,099
Sun	11/8	H	NYG	26-24	W	54,138
Sun	11/15	H	CHI	21-17	W	55,338
Sun	11/22	A	TB	3-37	L	63,251
Sun	11/29	A	MIN	35-23	W	46,025
Sun	12/6	H	DET	31-17	W	54,481
Sun	12/13	A	NO	35-7	W	45,518
Sun	12/20	A	NYJ	3-28	L	56,340

HOUSTON OILERS

Sun	9/6	A	LA	27-20	W	63,198
Sun	9/13	A	CLE	9-3	W	79,483
Sun	9/20	H	MIA	10-16	L	47,379
Sun	9/27	A	NYJ	17-33	L	50,309
Sun	10/4	H	CIN	17-10	W	44,350
Sun	10/11	H	SEA	35-17	W	42,671
Sun	10/18	A	NE	10-38	L	60,474
Mon	10/26	A	PIT	13-26	L	52,732
Sun	11/1	A	CIN	21-34	L	54,736
Sun	11/8	H	OAK	17-16	W	45,519
Sun	11/15	A	KC	10-23	L	73,984
Sun	11/22	H	NO	24-27	L	49,581
Sun	11/29	H	ATL	27-31	L	40,201
Thu	12/3	H	CLE	17-13	W	44,502
Sun	12/13	A	SF	6-28	L	55,707
Sun	12/20	H	PIT	21-20	W	41,056

KANSAS CITY CHIEFS

Sun	9/6	A	PIT	37-33	W	53,305
Sun	9/13	H	TB	19-10	W	50,555
Sun	9/20	H	SD	31-42	L	63,866

Sun 9/27 A SEA 20-14 W 59,255
Sun 10/4 A NE 17-33 L 55,931
Sun 10/11 H OAK 27-0 W 76,543
Sun 10/18 H DEN 28-14 W 74,672
Sun 10/25 A OAK 28-17 W 42,914
Sun 11/1 A SD 20-22 L 51,307
Sun 11/8 H CHI *13-16 L 60,605
Sun 11/15 H HOU 23-10 W 73,984
Sun 11/22 H SEA 40-13 W 49,002
Thu 11/26 A DET 10-27 L 76,735
Sun 12/6 A DEN 13-16 L 74,744
Sun 12/13 H MIA 7-17 L 57,407
Sun 12/20 A MIN 10-6 W 41,110

LOS ANGELES RAMS
Sun 9/6 H HOU 20-27 L 63,198
Sun 9/13 A NO 17-23 L 62,023
Sun 9/20 H GB 35-23 W 61,286
Mon 9/28 A CHI 24-7 W 62,461
Sun 10/4 H CLE 27-16 W 63,294
Sun 10/11 A ATL 37-35 W 57,841
Sun 10/18 A DAL 17-29 L 64,649
Sun 10/25 A SF 20-17 L 59,190
Sun 11/1 H DET 20-13 W 61,814
Sun 11/8 H NO 13-21 L 61,008
Sun 11/15 H CIN 10-24 L 56,836
Sun 11/22 H SF 31-33 L 63,456
Sun 11/29 A PIT 0-24 L 51,854
Sun 12/6 A NYG 7-10 L 59,659
Mon 12/14 H ATL 21-16 W 57,054
Sun 12/20 H WAS 7-30 L 52,224

MIAMI DOLPHINS
Sun 9/6 A STL 20-7 W 50,351
Thu 9/10 H PIT 30-10 W 74,190
Sun 9/20 A HOU 16-10 W 47,379
Sun 9/27 A BAL 31-28 W 39,273
Sun 10/4 H NYJ *28-28 L 68,723
Mon 10/12 A BUF 21-31 L 78,485
Sun 10/18 H WAS 13-10 W 47,367
Sun 10/25 A DAL 27-28 L 64,221
Sun 11/1 H BAL 27-10 W 46,061
Sun 11/8 A NE *30-27 L 60,436
Sun 11/15 H OAK 17-33 L 61,777
Sun 11/22 H NYJ 15-16 L 59,962
Mon 11/30 H PHI 13-10 W 67,797
Sun 12/6 H NE 24-14 W 50,421
Sun 12/13 H KC 17-7 W 57,407
Sat 12/19 H BUF 16-6 W 72,956

AFC DIVISIONAL PLAYOFF
Sat 1/2 H SD *38-41 L 73,735

MINNESOTA VIKINGS
Sat 9/5 A TB 13-21 L 66,287
Mon 9/14 H OAK 10-36 L 47,186
Sun 9/20 H DET 26-24 W 45,350
Sun 9/27 A GB 30-13 W 55,012
Sun 10/4 H CHI 24-21 W 43,287
Sun 10/11 A SD 33-31 W 50,708
Sun 10/18 H PHI 35-23 W 45,459
Sun 10/25 A STL 17-30 L 48,039
Mon 11/2 A DEN 17-19 L 74,834
Sun 11/8 H TB 25-10 W 47,038
Sun 11/15 H NO 20-10 W 45,215
Mon 11/23 A ATL 30-31 L 54,086
Sun 11/29 H GB 23-35 L 46,025
Sun 12/6 H CHI 9-10 L 50,766
Sat 12/12 A DET 7-45 L 79,428
Sun 12/20 H KC 6-10 L 41,110

NEW ENGLAND PATRIOTS
Sun 9/6 H BAL 28-29 L 49,572
Sun 9/13 A PHI 3-13 L 71,089
Mon 9/21 H DAL 21-35 L 60,311
Sun 9/27 A PIT *21-27 L 53,344
Sun 10/4 H KC 33-17 W 55,931
Sun 10/11 A NYJ 24-28 L 50,093
Sun 10/18 H HOU 38-10 W 60,474
Sun 10/25 A WAS 22-24 L 50,394
Sun 11/1 A OAK 17-27 L 44,246
Sun 11/8 H MIA *27-30 L 60,436
Sun 11/15 H NYJ 6-17 L 45,342
Sun 11/22 A BUF 17-20 L 71,593
Sun 11/29 H STL 20-27 L 39,946
Sun 12/6 A MIA 14-24 L 50,421
Sun 12/13 H BUF 10-19 L 42,529
Sun 12/20 A BAL 21-23 L 17,073

NEW ORLEANS SAINTS
Sun 9/6 A ATL 0-27 L 57,406
Sun 9/13 H LA 23-17 W 62,023
Sun 9/20 A NYG 7-20 L 69,814
Sun 9/27 A SF 14-21 L 44,433
Sun 10/4 H PIT 6-20 L 64,578
Sun 10/11 H PHI 14-31 L 52,728
Sun 10/18 A CLE 17-20 L 76,059
Sun 10/25 A CIN 17-7 W 46,336
Sun 11/1 H ATL 10-41 L 63,637
Sun 11/8 A LA 21-13 W 61,008
Sun 11/15 A MIN 10-20 L 45,215
Sun 11/22 A HOU 27-24 W 49,581
Sun 11/29 H TB 14-31 L 62,209
Sun 12/6 A STL 3-30 L 46,923
Sun 12/13 H GB 7-35 L 45,518
Sun 12/20 H SF 17-21 L 43,639

NEW YORK GIANTS
Sun 9/6 H PHI 10-24 L 71,459
Sun 9/13 A WAS 17-7 W 53,343
Sun 9/20 H NO 20-7 W 69,814
Sun 9/27 A DAL 10-18 L 63,449
Sun 10/4 H GB 14-27 L 73,684
Sun 10/11 H STL 34-14 W 67,128
Sun 10/18 A SEA 32-0 W 56,134
Sun 10/25 A ATL *27-24 W 48,410
Sun 11/1 H NYJ 7-26 L 74,740
Sun 11/8 A BAL 24-26 L 34,138
Sun 11/15 A WAS *27-30 L 63,133
Sun 11/22 A PHI 20-10 W 66,827
Sun 11/29 A SF 10-17 L 57,186
Sun 12/6 H LA 10-7 W 59,659
Sun 12/13 A STL 20-10 W 47,358
Sat 12/19 H DAL *13-10 W 73,009

NFC WILD-CARD PLAYOFF
Sun 12/27 H PHI 27-21 W 71,611

NFC DIVISIONAL PLAYOFF
Sun 1/3 A SF 24-38 L 58,360

NEW YORK JETS
Sun 9/6 A BUF 0-31 L 79,665
Sun 9/13 H CIN 30-31 L 49,454
Sun 9/20 A PIT 10-38 L 52,973
Sun 9/27 H HOU 33-17 W 50,309
Sun 10/4 A MIA *28-28 T 68,723
Sun 10/11 H NE 28-24 W 50,093
Sun 10/18 A BUF 33-14 W 54,607
Sun 10/25 H SEA 3-19 L 49,678
Sun 11/1 A NYG 26-7 W 74,740
Sun 11/8 A BAL 41-14 W 31,521
Sun 11/15 A NE 17-6 W 45,342
Sun 11/22 H MIA 16-15 W 59,962
Sun 11/29 H BAL 25-0 W 53,593
Sun 12/6 A SEA 23-27 L 53,105
Sat 12/12 A CLE 14-13 W 56,866
Sun 12/20 H GB 28-3 W 56,340

AFC WILD-CARD PLAYOFF
Sun 12/27 H BUF 27-31 L 57,050

OAKLAND RAIDERS
Sun 9/6 A DEN 7-9 L 74,796
Mon 9/14 A MIN 36-10 W 47,186
Sun 9/20 H SEA 20-10 W 45,725
Sun 9/27 A DET 0-16 L 77,919
Sun 10/4 H DEN 0-17 L 51,035
Sun 10/11 A KC 0-27 L 76,543
Sun 10/18 H TB 18-16 W 42,288
Sun 10/25 H KC 17-28 L 42,914
Sun 11/1 H NE 27-17 W 44,246
Sun 11/8 A HOU 16-17 L 45,519
Sun 11/15 A MIA 33-17 L 61,777
Sun 11/22 H SD 21-55 L 50,199
Sun 11/29 A SEA 32-31 W 57,147
Mon 12/7 H PIT 30-27 W 51,769
Sun 12/13 H CHI 6-23 L 40,384
Mon 12/21 A SD 10-23 L 52,279

PHILADELPHIA EAGLES
Sun 9/6 A NYG 24-10 W 71,459
Sun 9/13 H NE 13-3 W 71,089
Thu 9/17 A BUF 20-14 W 78,236
Sun 9/27 H WAS 36-13 W 70,664
Mon 10/5 H ATL 16-13 W 71,488
Sun 10/11 A NO 31-14 W 52,728
Sun 10/18 A MIN 23-35 L 45,459
Sun 10/25 H TB 20-10 W 70,718
Sun 11/1 H DAL 14-17 L 72,111
Sun 11/8 A STL 52-10 W 48,421
Sun 11/15 H BAL 38-13 W 68,618
Sun 11/22 H NYG 10-20 L 66,827
Mon 11/30 A MIA 10-13 L 67,797
Sun 12/6 A WAS 13-15 L 52,206
Sun 12/13 A DAL 10-21 L 64,955
Sun 12/20 H STL 38-0 W 56,656

NFC WILD-CARD PLAYOFF
Sun 12/27 H NYG 21-27 L 71,611

PITTSBURGH STEELERS
Sun 9/6 H KC 33-37 L 53,305
Thu 9/10 A MIA 10-30 L 74,190
Sun 9/20 H NYJ 38-10 W 52,973
Sun 9/27 H NE *27-21 W 53,344
Sun 10/4 A NO 20-6 W 64,578
Sun 10/11 A CLE 13-7 W 53,225
Sun 10/18 A CIN 7-34 L 57,090
Mon 10/26 H HOU 26-13 W 52,732
Sun 11/1 H SF 14-17 L 52,878
Sun 11/8 A SEA 21-24 L 59,058
Sun 11/15 A ATL 34-20 W 57,485
Sun 11/22 A CLE 32-10 W 77,958
Sun 11/29 H LA 24-0 W 51,854
Mon 12/7 A OAK 27-30 L 51,769
Sun 12/13 H CIN 10-17 L 50,923
Sun 12/20 A HOU 20-21 L 41,056

ST. LOUIS CARDINALS
Sun 9/6 H MIA 7-20 L 50,351
Sun 9/13 A DAL 17-30 L 63,602
Sun 9/20 H WAS 40-30 W 47,592
Sun 9/27 A TB 10-20 L 65,850
Sun 10/4 H DAL 20-17 L 49,477
Sun 10/11 A NYG 14-34 L 67,128
Sun 10/18 A ATL 20-41 L 51,428
Sun 10/25 H MIN 30-17 W 48,039
Sun 11/1 A WAS 21-42 L 50,643
Sun 11/8 H PHI 10-52 L 48,421
Sun 11/15 H BUF 24-0 W 46,214
Sun 11/22 A BAL 35-24 W 24,784
Sun 11/29 H NE 27-20 W 39,946
Sun 12/6 H NO 30-3 W 46,923
Sun 12/13 H NYG 10-20 L 47,358
Sun 12/20 A PHI 0-38 L 56,656

SAN DIEGO CHARGERS
Mon 9/7 A CLE 44-14 W 78,904
Sun 9/13 H DET 28-23 W 51,624
Sun 9/20 A KC 42-31 W 63,866
Sun 9/27 A DEN 24-42 L 74,844
Sun 10/4 H SEA 24-10 W 51,463
Sun 10/11 H MIN 31-33 L 50,708
Sun 10/18 A BAL 43-14 W 41,921
Sun 10/25 A CHI *17-20 L 52,906
Sun 11/1 H KC 22-20 W 51,307
Sun 11/8 A CIN 17-40 L 51,259
Mon 11/16 A SEA 23-44 L 58,628
Sun 11/22 A OAK 55-21 W 50,199
Sun 11/29 H DEN 34-17 W 51,533
Sun 12/6 H BUF 27-28 L 51,488
Sun 12/13 A TB 24-23 W 67,388
Mon 12/21 H OAK 23-10 W 52,279

AFC DIVISIONAL PLAYOFF
Sat 1/2 A MIA *41-38 W 73,735

AFC CHAMPIONSHIP
Sun 1/10 A CIN 7-27 L 46,302

SAN FRANCISCO 49ERS
Sun 9/6 A DET 17-24 L 62,123
Sun 9/13 H CHI 28-17 W 49,520
Sun 9/20 A ATL 17-34 L 56,653
Sun 9/27 H NO 21-14 W 44,433
Sun 10/4 A WAS 30-17 W 51,843
Sun 10/11 H DAL 45-14 W 57,574
Sun 10/18 A GB 13-3 W 50,171
Sun 10/25 H LA 20-17 W 59,190
Sun 11/1 A PIT 17-14 W 52,878
Sun 11/8 H ATL 17-14 W 59,127
Sun 11/15 H CLE 12-15 L 52,445
Sun 11/22 A LA 33-31 W 63,456
Sun 11/29 H NYG 17-10 W 57,186
Sun 12/6 A CIN 21-3 W 56,796
Sun 12/13 H HOU 28-6 W 55,707
Sun 12/20 A NO 21-17 W 43,639

NFC DIVISIONAL PLAYOFF
Sun 1/3 H NYG 38-24 W 58,360

NFC CHAMPIONSHIP
Sun 1/10 H DAL 28-27 W 60,525

SUPER BOWL XVI
Sun 1/24 N CIN 26-21 W 81,270

SEATTLE SEAHAWKS
Sun 9/6 A CIN 21-27 L 41,177
Sun 9/13 H DEN 13-10 W 58,513
Sun 9/20 A OAK 10-20 L 45,725
Sun 9/27 H KC 14-20 L 59,255
Sun 10/4 A SD 10-24 L 51,463
Sun 10/11 A HOU 17-35 L 42,671
Sun 10/18 H NYG 0-32 L 56,134
Sun 10/25 A NYJ 19-3 W 49,678
Sun 11/1 H GB 24-34 L 54,099
Sun 11/8 H PIT 24-21 W 59,058
Mon 11/16 H SD 44-23 W 58,628
Sun 11/22 A KC 13-40 L 49,002
Sun 11/29 H OAK 31-32 L 57,147
Sun 12/6 H NYJ 27-23 W 53,105
Sun 12/13 A DEN 13-23 L 74,705
Sun 12/20 H CLE 42-21 W 51,435

TAMPA BAY BUCCANEERS
Sat 9/5 H MIN 21-13 W 66,287
Sun 9/13 A KC 10-19 L 50,555
Sun 9/20 A CHI 17-28 L 60,130
Sun 9/27 H STL 20-10 W 65,850
Sun 10/4 H DET 28-10 W 71,733
Sun 10/11 A GB 21-10 W 55,264
Sun 10/18 A OAK 16-18 L 42,288
Sun 10/25 A PHI 10-20 L 70,718
Sun 11/1 H CHI 20-10 W 63,688
Sun 11/8 A MIN 10-25 L 47,038
Sun 11/15 H DEN 7-24 L 64,518
Sun 11/22 H GB 37-3 W 63,251
Sun 11/29 A NO 31-14 W 62,209
Sun 12/6 H ATL 24-23 W 69,221
Sun 12/13 H SD 23-24 L 67,388
Sun 12/20 A DET 20-17 W 80,444

NFC DIVISIONAL PLAYOFF
| Sat | 1/2 | A | DAL | 0-38 | L | 64,848 |

WASHINGTON REDSKINS
Sun	9/6	H	DAL	10-26	L	55,045
Sun	9/13	H	NYG	7-17	L	53,343
Sun	9/20	A	STL	30-40	L	47,592
Sun	9/27	A	PHI	13-36	L	70,664
Sun	10/4	H	SF	17-30	L	51,843
Sun	10/11	H	CHI	24-7	W	57,683
Sun	10/18	A	MIA	10-13	L	47,367
Sun	10/25	H	NE	24-22	W	50,394
Sun	11/1	H	STL	42-21	W	50,643
Sun	11/8	H	DET	33-31	W	52,096
Sun	11/15	A	NYG	*30-27	W	63,133
Sun	11/22	A	DAL	10-24	L	64,583
Sun	11/29	A	BUF	14-21	L	59,624
Sun	12/6	H	PHI	15-13	W	52,206
Sun	12/13	H	BAL	38-14	W	46,706
Sun	12/20	A	LA	30-7	W	52,224

1982 NFL

ATLANTA FALCONS
Sun	9/12	A	NYG	16-14	W	74,286
Sun	9/19	H	LARI	14-38	L	54,774
Sun	11/21	H	LARM	34-17	W	39,686
Sun	11/28	A	STL	20-23	L	33,411
Sun	12/5	A	DEN	34-27	W	73,984
Sun	12/12	H	NO	35-0	W	39,535
Sun	12/19	A	SF	17-7	W	53,234
Sun	12/26	H	GB	7-38	L	50,245
Sun	1/2	A	NO	6-35	L	47,336

NFC FIRST-ROUND PLAYOFF
| Sun | 1/9 | A | MIN | 24-30 | L | 60,560 |

BALTIMORE COLTS
Sun	9/12	H	NE	13-24	L	39,055
Sun	9/19	A	MIA	20-24	L	51,999
Sun	11/21	A	NYJ	0-37	L	46,970
Sun	11/28	A	BUF	0-20	L	33,985
Sun	12/5	H	CIN	17-20	L	23,598
Sun	12/12	A	MIN	10-13	L	53,981
Sun	12/19	H	GB	*20-20	T	25,920
Sun	12/26	A	SD	26-44	L	49,711
Sun	1/2	H	MIA	7-34	L	19,073

BUFFALO BILLS
Sun	9/12	H	KC	14-9	W	79,306
Thu	9/16	H	MIN	23-22	W	77,733
Sun	11/21	H	MIA	7-9	L	52,945
Sun	11/28	H	BAL	20-0	W	33,985
Sun	12/5	A	GB	21-33	L	46,655
Sun	12/12	H	PIT	13-0	W	58,391
Sun	12/19	A	TB	23-24	L	62,510
Mon	12/27	A	MIA	10-27	L	73,924
Sun	1/2	A	NE	19-30	L	36,218

CHICAGO BEARS
Sun	9/12	A	DET	10-17	L	71,337
Sun	9/19	H	NO	0-10	L	56,600
Sun	11/21	A	DET	20-17	W	46,783
Sun	11/28	A	MIN	7-35	L	54,724
Sun	12/5	H	NE	26-13	W	36,973
Sun	12/12	A	SEA	14-20	L	53,826
Sun	12/19	H	STL	7-10	L	43,270
Sun	12/26	A	LARM	34-26	W	46,502
Sun	1/2	A	TB	*23-26	L	68,112

CINCINNATI BENGALS
Sun	9/12	H	HOU	27-6	W	53,268
Sun	9/19	A	PIT	*20-26	L	53,973
Sun	11/21	A	PHI	18-14	W	65,172
Sun	11/28	H	LARI	31-17	W	53,330
Sun	12/5	A	BAL	20-17	W	23,598
Sun	12/12	H	CLE	23-10	W	54,305
Mon	12/20	A	SD	34-50	L	51,296
Sun	12/26	H	SEA	24-10	W	55,330
Sun	1/2	A	HOU	35-27	W	26,522

AFC FIRST-ROUND PLAYOFF
| Sun | 1/9 | H | NYJ | 17-44 | L | 57,560 |

CLEVELAND BROWNS
Sun	9/12	A	SEA	21-7	W	55,907
Sun	9/19	H	PHI	21-24	L	78,830
Sun	11/21	H	NE	10-7	W	47,281
Thu	11/25	A	DAL	14-31	L	46,267
Sun	12/5	H	SD	13-30	L	54,064
Sun	12/12	A	CIN	10-23	L	54,305
Sun	12/19	H	PIT	10-9	W	67,139
Sun	12/26	A	HOU	20-14	W	36,559
Sun	1/2	A	PIT	21-37	L	52,312

AFC FIRST-ROUND PLAYOFF
| Sat | 1/8 | A | LARI | 10-27 | L | 56,555 |

DALLAS COWBOYS
Mon	9/13	H	PIT	28-36	L	63,431
Sun	9/19	A	STL	24-7	W	50,705
Sun	11/21	H	TB	14-9	W	49,578
Thu	11/25	H	CLE	31-14	W	46,267
Sun	12/5	A	WAS	24-10	W	54,633
Mon	12/13	A	HOU	37-7	W	51,808
Sun	12/19	H	NO	21-7	W	64,506
Sun	12/26	H	PHI	20-24	L	46,199
Mon	1/3	A	MIN	27-31	L	60,007

NFC FIRST-ROUND PLAYOFF
| Sun | 1/9 | H | TB | 30-17 | W | 65,042 |

NFC SECOND-ROUND PLAYOFF
| Sun | 1/16 | H | GB | 37-26 | W | 63,972 |

NFC CHAMPIONSHIP
| Sat | 1/22 | A | WAS | 17-31 | L | 55,045 |

DENVER BRONCOS
Sun	9/12	H	SD	3-23	L	73,564
Sun	9/19	H	SF	24-21	W	73,899
Sun	11/21	H	SEA	10-17	L	73,916
Sun	11/28	A	SD	20-30	L	47,629
Sun	12/5	H	ATL	27-34	L	73,984
Sun	12/12	A	LARM	27-24	W	48,112
Sun	12/19	H	KC	16-37	L	74,192
Sun	12/26	A	LARI	10-27	L	44,160
Sun	1/2	A	SEA	11-13	L	43,145

DETROIT LIONS
Sun	9/12	H	CHI	17-10	W	71,337
Sun	9/19	A	LARM	19-14	W	59,470
Sun	11/21	A	CHI	17-20	L	46,783
Thu	11/25	H	NYG	6-13	L	64,348
Mon	12/6	H	NYJ	13-28	L	79,361
Sun	12/12	A	GB	30-10	W	51,875
Sun	12/19	H	MIN	31-34	L	73,058
Sun	12/26	A	TB	21-23	L	65,997
Sun	1/2	H	GB	27-24	W	64,377

NFC FIRST-ROUND PLAYOFF
| Sat | 1/8 | A | WAS | 7-31 | L | 55,045 |

GREEN BAY PACKERS
Sun	9/12	H	LARM	35-23	W	53,964
Mon	9/20	A	NYG	27-19	W	68,405
Sun	11/21	H	MIN	26-7	W	44,681
Sun	11/28	A	NYJ	13-15	L	53,872
Sun	12/5	H	BUF	33-21	W	46,655
Sun	12/12	H	DET	10-30	L	51,875
Sun	12/19	A	BAL	*20-20	T	25,920
Sun	12/26	A	ATL	38-7	W	50,245
Sun	1/2	A	DET	24-27	L	64,377

NFC FIRST-ROUND PLAYOFF
| Sat | 1/8 | H | STL | 41-16 | W | 54,282 |

NFC SECOND-ROUND PLAYOFF
| Sun | 1/16 | A | DAL | 26-37 | L | 63,972 |

HOUSTON OILERS
Sun	9/12	A	CIN	6-27	L	53,268
Sun	9/19	H	SEA	23-21	W	43,117
Sun	11/21	H	PIT	10-24	L	42,338
Sun	11/28	A	NE	21-29	L	33,602
Sun	12/5	A	NYG	14-17	L	71,184
Mon	12/13	H	DAL	7-37	L	51,808
Sun	12/19	A	PHI	14-35	L	44,119
Sun	12/26	H	CLE	14-20	L	36,559
Sun	1/2	H	CIN	27-35	L	26,522

KANSAS CITY CHIEFS
Sun	9/12	A	BUF	9-14	L	79,306
Sun	9/19	H	SD	19-12	W	60,514
Sun	11/21	H	NO	17-27	L	39,341
Sun	11/28	A	LARM	14-20	L	45,793
Sun	12/5	A	PIT	14-35	L	52,090
Sun	12/12	H	LARI	16-21	L	26,307
Sun	12/19	A	DEN	37-16	W	74,192
Sun	12/26	H	SF	13-26	L	24,319
Sun	1/2	H	NYJ	37-13	W	11,902

LOS ANGELES RAIDERS
Sun	9/12	A	SF	23-17	W	59,748
Sun	9/19	A	ATL	38-14	W	54,774
Mon	11/22	H	SD	28-24	W	42,162
Sun	11/28	A	CIN	17-31	L	53,330
Sun	12/5	H	SEA	28-23	W	42,170
Sun	12/12	A	KC	21-16	W	26,307
Sat	12/18	A	LARM	37-31	W	56,646
Sun	12/26	H	DEN	27-10	W	44,160
Sun	1/2	A	SD	41-34	W	51,612

AFC FIRST-ROUND PLAYOFF
| Sat | 1/8 | H | CLE | 27-10 | W | 56,555 |

AFC SECOND-ROUND PLAYOFF
| Sat | 1/15 | H | NYJ | 14-17 | L | 90,037 |

LOS ANGELES RAMS
Sun	9/12	A	GB	23-35	L	53,964
Sun	9/19	H	DET	14-19	L	59,470
Sun	11/21	A	ATL	17-34	L	39,686
Sun	11/28	H	KC	20-14	W	45,793
Thu	12/2	H	SF	24-30	L	58,574
Sun	12/12	H	DEN	24-27	L	48,112
Sat	12/18	H	LARI	31-37	L	56,646
Sun	12/26	H	CHI	26-34	L	46,502
Sun	1/2	A	SF	21-20	W	54,256

MIAMI DOLPHINS
Sun	9/12	A	NYJ	45-28	W	53,360
Sun	9/19	H	BAL	24-20	W	51,999
Sun	11/21	H	BUF	9-7	W	52,945
Mon	11/29	A	TB	17-23	L	65,854
Sun	12/5	H	MIN	22-14	W	45,721
Sun	12/12	A	NE	0-3	L	25,716
Sat	12/18	H	NYJ	20-19	W	67,307
Mon	12/27	H	BUF	27-10	W	73,924
Sun	1/2	A	BAL	34-7	W	19,073

AFC FIRST-ROUND PLAYOFF
| Sat | 1/8 | H | NE | 28-13 | W | 68,842 |

AFC SECOND-ROUND PLAYOFF
| Sun | 1/16 | H | SD | 34-13 | W | 71,383 |

AFC CHAMPIONSHIP
| Sun | 1/23 | H | NYJ | 14-0 | W | 67,396 |

SUPER BOWL XVII
| Sun | 1/30 | N | WAS | 17-27 | L | 103,667 |

MINNESOTA VIKINGS
Sun	9/12	H	TB	17-10	W	58,440
Thu	9/16	A	BUF	22-23	L	77,733
Sun	11/21	A	GB	7-26	L	44,681
Sun	11/28	H	CHI	35-7	W	54,724
Sun	12/5	A	MIA	14-22	L	45,721
Sun	12/12	H	BAL	13-10	W	53,981
Sun	12/19	A	DET	34-31	W	73,058
Sun	12/26	H	NYJ	14-42	L	58,672
Mon	1/3	H	DAL	31-27	W	60,007

NFC FIRST-ROUND PLAYOFF
| Sun | 1/9 | H | ATL | 30-24 | W | 60,560 |

NFC SECOND-ROUND PLAYOFF
| Sat | 1/15 | A | WAS | 7-21 | L | 54,593 |

NEW ENGLAND PATRIOTS
Sun	9/12	A	BAL	24-13	W	39,055
Sun	9/19	H	NYJ	7-31	L	53,515
Sun	11/21	A	CLE	7-10	L	47,281
Sun	11/28	H	HOU	29-21	W	33,602
Sun	12/5	A	CHI	13-26	L	36,973
Sun	12/12	H	MIA	3-0	W	25,716
Sun	12/19	A	SEA	16-0	W	53,457
Sun	12/26	A	PIT	14-37	L	51,515
Sun	1/2	H	BUF	30-19	W	36,218

AFC FIRST-ROUND PLAYOFF
| Sat | 1/8 | A | MIA | 13-28 | L | 68,842 |

NEW ORLEANS SAINTS
Sun	9/12	H	STL	7-21	L	58,673
Sun	9/19	A	CHI	10-0	W	56,600
Sun	11/21	H	KC	27-17	W	39,341
Sun	11/28	A	SF	23-20	W	51,611
Sun	12/5	H	TB	10-13	L	61,709
Sun	12/12	A	ATL	0-35	L	39,535
Sun	12/19	A	DAL	7-21	L	64,506
Sun	12/26	H	WAS	10-27	L	48,667
Sun	1/2	H	ATL	35-6	W	47,336

NEW YORK GIANTS
Sun	9/12	H	ATL	14-16	L	74,286
Mon	9/20	H	GB	19-27	L	68,405
Sun	11/21	H	WAS	17-27	L	70,766
Thu	11/25	A	DET	13-6	W	64,348
Sun	12/5	H	HOU	17-14	W	71,184
Sat	12/11	H	PHI	23-7	W	66,053
Sun	12/19	A	WAS	14-15	L	50,030
Sun	12/26	A	STL	21-24	L	39,824
Sun	1/2	A	PHI	26-24	W	55,797

NEW YORK JETS
Sun	9/12	H	MIA	28-45	L	53,360
Sun	9/19	A	NE	31-7	W	53,515
Sun	11/21	H	BAL	37-0	W	46,970
Sun	11/28	H	GB	15-13	W	53,872
Mon	12/6	A	DET	28-13	W	79,361
Sun	12/12	H	TB	32-17	W	28,147
Sat	12/18	A	MIA	19-20	L	67,307
Sun	12/26	A	MIN	42-14	W	58,672
Sun	1/2	A	KC	13-37	L	11,902

AFC FIRST-ROUND PLAYOFF
| Sun | 1/9 | A | CIN | 44-17 | W | 57,560 |

AFC SECOND-ROUND PLAYOFF
| Sat | 1/15 | A | LARI | 17-14 | W | 90,037 |

AFC CHAMPIONSHIP
| Sun | 1/23 | A | MIA | 0-14 | L | 67,396 |

PHILADELPHIA EAGLES
Sun	9/12	H	WAS	*34-37	L	68,885
Sun	9/19	A	CLE	24-21	W	78,830
Sun	11/21	H	CIN	14-18	L	65,172
Sun	11/28	A	WAS	9-13	L	48,313
Sun	12/5	H	STL	20-23	L	63,622
Sat	12/11	A	NYG	7-23	L	66,053
Sun	12/19	H	HOU	35-14	W	44,119
Sun	12/26	A	DAL	24-20	W	46,199
Sun	1/2	H	NYG	24-26	L	55,797

PITTSBURGH STEELERS
Mon	9/13	A	DAL	36-28	W	63,431
Sun	9/19	H	CIN	*26-20	W	53,973
Sun	11/21	A	HOU	24-10	W	42,338
Sun	11/28	A	SEA	0-16	L	55,553
Sun	12/5	H	KC	35-14	W	52,090
Sun	12/12	A	BUF	0-13	L	58,391
Sun	12/19	A	CLE	9-10	L	67,139
Sun	12/26	H	NE	37-14	W	51,515
Sun	1/2	H	CLE	37-21	W	52,312

<table>
<tbody>
<tr><td colspan="6">AFC First-Round Playoff</td></tr>
</tbody>
</table>

AFC First-Round Playoff
Sun 1/9 H SD 28-31 L 53,546

ST. LOUIS CARDINALS
Sun 9/12 A NO 21-7 W 58,673
Sun 9/19 H DAL 7-24 L 50,705
Sun 11/21 H SF 20-31 L 38,064
Sun 11/28 A ATL 23-20 W 33,411
Sun 12/5 A PHI 23-20 W 63,622
Sun 12/12 H WAS 7-12 L 35,308
Sun 12/19 A CHI 10-7 W 43,270
Sun 12/26 H NYG 24-21 W 39,824
Sun 1/2 A WAS 0-28 L 52,554

NFC First-Round Playoff
Sat 1/8 A GB 16-41 L 54,282

SAN DIEGO CHARGERS
Sun 9/12 A DEN 23-3 W 73,564
Sun 9/19 A KC 12-19 L 60,514
Mon 11/22 A LARI 24-28 L 42,162
Sun 11/28 H DEN 30-20 W 47,629
Sun 12/5 A CLE 30-13 W 54,064
Sat 12/11 H SF 41-37 W 55,988
Mon 12/20 H CIN 50-34 W 51,296
Sun 12/26 H BAL 44-26 W 49,711
Sun 1/2 H LARI 34-41 L 51,612

AFC First-Round Playoff
Sun 1/9 A PIT 31-28 W 53,546

AFC Second-Round Playoff
Sun 1/16 A MIA 13-34 L 71,383

SAN FRANCISCO 49ERS
Sun 9/12 H LARI 17-23 L 59,748
Sun 9/19 A DEN 21-24 L 73,899
Sun 11/21 A STL 31-20 W 38,064
Sun 11/28 H NO 20-23 L 51,611
Thu 12/2 A LARM 30-24 W 58,574
Sat 12/11 H SD 37-41 L 55,988
Sun 12/19 H ATL 7-17 L 53,234
Sun 12/26 A KC 26-13 W 24,319
Sun 1/2 H LARM 20-21 L 54,256

SEATTLE SEAHAWKS
Sun 9/12 H CLE 7-21 L 55,907
Sun 9/19 A HOU 21-23 L 43,117
Sun 11/21 A DEN 17-10 W 73,916
Sun 11/28 H PIT 16-0 W 55,553
Sun 12/5 A LARI 23-28 L 42,170
Sun 12/12 H CHI 20-14 W 53,826
Sun 12/19 H NE 0-16 L 53,457
Sun 12/26 A CIN 10-24 L 55,330
Sun 1/2 H DEN 13-11 W 43,145

TAMPA BAY BUCCANEERS
Sun 9/12 A MIN 10-17 L 58,440
Sun 9/19 H WAS 13-21 L 66,824
Sun 11/21 A DAL 9-14 L 49,578
Mon 11/29 H MIA 23-17 W 65,854
Sun 12/5 A NO 13-10 W 61,709
Sun 12/12 A NYJ 17-32 L 28,147
Sun 12/19 H BUF 24-23 W 62,510
Sun 12/26 H DET 23-21 W 65,997
Sun 1/2 H CHI *26-23 W 68,112

NFC First-Round Playoff
Sun 1/9 A DAL 17-30 L 65,042

WASHINGTON REDSKINS
Sun 9/12 A PHI *37-34 W 68,885
Sun 9/19 A TB 21-13 W 66,824
Sun 11/21 A NYG 27-17 W 70,766
Sun 11/28 H PHI 13-9 W 48,313
Sun 12/5 H DAL 10-24 L 54,633
Sun 12/12 A STL 12-7 W 35,308
Sun 12/19 H NYG 15-14 W 50,030
Sun 12/26 A NO 27-10 W 48,667
Sun 1/2 H STL 28-0 W 52,544

NFC First-Round Playoff
Sat 1/8 H DET 31-7 W 55,045

NFC Second-Round Playoff
Sat 1/15 H MIN 21-7 W 54,593

NFC Championship
Sat 1/22 H DAL 31-17 W 55,045

Super Bowl XVII
Sun 1/30 N MIA 27-17 W 103,667

1983 NFL

ATLANTA FALCONS
Sun 9/4 A CHI 20-17 W 60,165
Sun 9/11 H NYG *13-16 L 52,850
Sun 9/18 A DET *30-14 W 54,622
Sun 9/25 A SF 20-24 L 57,814
Sun 10/2 H PHI 24-28 L 50,621
Sun 10/9 H NO 17-19 L 51,654
Sun 10/16 A LARM 21-27 L 50,404
Sun 10/23 A NYJ 27-21 W 46,878
Sun 10/30 H NE 24-13 W 47,546
Sun 11/6 A NO 24-17 W 67,062
Mon 11/14 H LARM 13-36 L 31,203
Sun 11/20 H SF 28-24 W 32,782
Sun 11/27 H GB *47-41 W 35,688
Sun 12/4 A WAS 21-37 L 52,074
Sat 12/10 A MIA 24-31 L 56,725
Sun 12/18 H BUF 31-14 W 31,015

BALTIMORE COLTS
Sun 9/4 A NE *29-23 W 45,526
Sun 9/11 H DEN 10-17 L 51,482
Sun 9/18 A BUF 23-28 L 40,937
Sun 9/25 A CHI *22-19 W 34,350
Sun 10/2 A CIN 34-31 W 48,104
Sun 10/9 A NE 12-7 W 35,618
Sun 10/16 H BUF 7-30 L 38,565
Sun 10/23 H MIA 7-21 L 32,343
Sun 10/30 A PHI 22-21 W 59,150
Sun 11/6 A NYJ 17-14 W 53,323
Sun 11/13 H PIT 13-24 L 57,319
Sun 11/20 A MIA 0-37 L 54,482
Sun 11/27 A CLE 23-41 L 65,812
Sun 12/4 H NYJ 6-10 L 29,431
Sun 12/11 A DEN 19-21 L 74,854
Sun 12/18 H HOU 20-10 W 20,418

BUFFALO BILLS
Sun 9/4 H MIA 0-12 L 78,683
Sun 9/11 A CIN 10-6 W 46,841
Sun 9/18 H BAL 28-23 W 40,937
Sun 9/25 H HOU 30-13 W 60,070
Mon 10/3 H NYJ 10-34 L 79,833
Sun 10/9 A MIA *38-35 W 59,948
Sun 10/16 A BAL 30-7 W 38,565
Sun 10/23 H NE 0-31 L 60,424
Sun 10/30 H NO 27-21 W 49,413
Sun 11/6 H NE 7-21 L 42,604
Sun 11/13 A NYJ 24-17 W 48,513
Sun 11/20 H LARI 24-27 L 72,393
Sun 11/27 A LARM 17-41 L 48,246
Sun 12/4 A KC 14-9 W 27,104
Sun 12/11 H SF 10-23 L 38,039
Sun 12/18 A ATL 14-31 L 31,015

CHICAGO BEARS
Sun 9/4 H ATL 17-20 L 60,165
Sun 9/11 H TB 17-10 W 58,186
Sun 9/18 A NO *31-34 L 64,692
Sun 9/25 H BAL *19-22 L 34,350
Sun 10/2 H DEN 31-14 W 58,210
Sun 10/9 H MIN 14-23 L 59,632
Sun 10/16 A DET 17-31 L 66,709
Sun 10/23 A PHI 7-6 W 45,263
Sun 10/30 H DET 17-38 L 58,764
Sun 11/6 A LARM 14-21 L 53,010
Sun 11/13 H PHI 17-14 W 47,524
Sun 11/20 A TB 27-0 W 36,816
Sun 11/27 H SF 13-3 W 40,483
Sun 12/4 A GB 28-31 L 51,244
Sun 12/11 A MIN 19-13 W 57,880
Sun 12/18 H GB 23-21 W 35,807

CINCINNATI BENGALS
Sun 9/4 H LARI 10-20 L 50,956
Sun 9/11 H BUF 6-10 L 46,841
Thu 9/15 A CLE 7-17 L 79,574
Sun 9/25 A TB 23-17 W 56,023
Sun 10/2 H BAL 31-34 L 48,104
Mon 10/10 H PIT 14-24 L 56,086
Sun 10/16 A DEN 17-24 L 74,305
Sun 10/23 A CLE 28-21 W 50,047
Sun 10/30 H GB 34-14 W 53,349
Sun 11/6 A HOU 55-14 W 39,706
Sun 11/13 A KC 15-20 L 41,711
Sun 11/20 H HOU 38-10 W 46,375
Mon 11/28 A MIA 14-38 L 74,506
Sun 12/4 A PIT 23-10 W 55,832
Sun 12/11 H DET 17-9 W 45,728
Sat 12/17 A MIN 14-20 L 51,565

CLEVELAND BROWNS
Sun 9/4 H MIN 21-27 L 70,087
Sun 9/11 A DET 31-26 W 60,095
Thu 9/15 H CIN 17-7 W 79,574
Sun 9/25 A SD *30-24 W 49,482
Sun 10/2 H SEA 9-24 L 75,446
Sun 10/9 H NYJ 10-7 W 78,235
Sun 10/16 A PIT 17-44 L 59,263
Sun 10/23 A CIN 21-28 L 50,047
Sun 10/30 H HOU *25-19 W 66,955
Sun 11/6 H GB 21-35 L 54,089
Sun 11/13 H TB 20-0 W 56,091
Sun 11/20 A NE 30-0 W 40,987
Sun 11/27 H BAL 41-23 W 65,812
Sun 12/4 A DEN 6-27 L 70,912
Sun 12/11 H HOU 27-34 L 29,746
Sun 12/18 H PIT 30-17 W 72,313

DALLAS COWBOYS
Mon 9/5 A WAS 31-30 W 55,045
Sun 9/11 A STL 34-17 W 48,532
Sun 9/18 H NYG 28-13 W 62,347
Sun 9/25 H NO 21-20 W 62,136
Sun 10/2 A MIN 37-24 W 60,774
Sun 10/9 H TB *27-24 W 63,808
Sun 10/16 A PHI 37-7 W 63,070
Sun 10/23 H LARI 38-40 L 64,991
Sun 10/30 A NYG 38-20 W 76,142
Sun 11/6 H PHI 27-20 W 71,236
Sun 11/13 H SD 23-24 L 46,192
Sun 11/20 H KC 41-21 W 64,103
Thu 11/24 H STL 35-17 W 60,764
Sun 12/4 A SEA 35-10 W 63,352
Sun 12/11 H WAS 10-31 L 65,074
Mon 12/19 A SF 17-42 L 59,957

NFC Wild-Card Playoff
Mon 12/26 H LARM 17-24 L 62,118

DENVER BRONCOS
Sun 9/4 A PIT 14-10 W 58,233
Sun 9/11 A BAL 17-10 W 51,482
Sun 9/18 H PHI 10-13 L 74,202
Sun 9/25 H LARI 7-22 L 74,289
Sun 10/2 A CHI 14-31 L 58,210
Sun 10/9 A HOU 26-14 W 44,209
Sun 10/16 H CIN 24-17 W 74,305
Sun 10/23 H SD 14-6 W 74,581
Sun 10/30 H KC 27-24 W 74,640
Sun 11/6 A SEA 19-27 L 61,189
Sun 11/13 A LARI 20-22 L 51,945
Sun 11/20 H SEA 38-27 W 74,710
Sun 11/27 A SD 7-31 L 44,050
Sun 12/4 H CLE 27-6 W 70,912
Sun 12/11 H BAL 21-19 W 74,854
Sun 12/18 A KC 17-48 L 11,377

AFC Wild-Card Playoff
Sat 12/24 A SEA 7-31 L 64,275

DETROIT LIONS
Sun 9/4 A TB 11-0 W 62,154
Sun 9/11 H CLE 26-31 L 60,095
Sun 9/18 H ATL 14-30 L 54,622
Sun 9/25 A MIN 17-20 L 58,254
Sun 10/2 A LARM 10-21 L 49,403
Sun 10/9 H GB 38-14 W 67,738
Sun 10/16 H CHI 31-17 W 66,709
Sun 10/23 A WAS 17-38 L 43,189
Sun 10/30 A CHI 38-17 W 58,764
Mon 11/7 H NYG 15-9 W 68,985
Sun 11/13 A HOU 17-27 L 40,660
Sun 11/20 A GB *23-20 W 50,050
Thu 11/24 H PIT 45-3 W 77,724
Mon 12/5 H MIN 13-2 W 79,169
Sun 12/11 A CIN 9-17 L 45,375
Sun 12/18 H TB 23-20 W 78,553

NFC Divisional Playoff
Sat 12/31 A SF 23-24 L 59,979

GREEN BAY PACKERS
Sun 9/4 A HOU *41-38 W 44,073
Sun 9/11 H PIT 21-25 L 55,204
Sun 9/18 H LARM 27-24 W 54,037
Mon 9/26 A NYG 3-27 L 75,308
Sun 10/2 H TB 55-14 W 54,272
Sun 10/9 A DET 14-38 L 67,738
Mon 10/17 H WAS 48-47 W 55,255
Sun 10/23 H MIN *17-20 L 55,236
Sun 10/30 A CIN 14-34 L 53,349
Sun 11/6 H CLE 35-21 W 54,089
Sun 11/13 A MIN 29-21 W 60,113
Sun 11/20 H DET *20-23 L 50,050
Sun 11/27 A ATL *41-47 L 35,688
Sun 12/4 H CHI 31-28 W 51,244
Mon 12/12 A TB *12-9 W 50,763
Sun 12/18 A CHI 21-23 L 35,807

HOUSTON OILERS
Sun 9/4 H GB *38-41 L 44,073
Sun 9/11 A LARI 6-20 L 37,526
Sun 9/18 H PIT 28-40 L 44,150
Sun 9/25 A BUF 13-30 L 60,070
Sun 10/2 A PIT 10-17 L 56,901
Sun 10/9 H DEN 14-26 L 44,209
Sun 10/16 A MIN 14-34 L 58,910
Sun 10/23 H KC *10-13 L 39,462
Sun 10/30 A CLE *19-25 L 66,955
Sun 11/6 H CIN 14-55 L 39,706
Sun 11/13 H DET 27-17 W 40,660
Sun 11/20 A CIN 10-38 L 46,375
Sun 11/27 A TB 24-33 L 38,625
Sun 12/4 H MIA 17-24 L 39,434
Sun 12/11 A CLE 34-27 W 29,746
Sun 12/18 H BAL 10-20 L 20,418

KANSAS CITY CHIEFS
Sun 9/4 H SEA 17-13 W 42,531
Mon 9/12 H SD 14-17 L 62,150
Sun 9/18 A WAS 12-27 L 52,610
Sun 9/25 A MIA 6-14 L 50,785
Sun 10/2 H STL 38-14 W 59,875
Sun 10/9 A LARI 20-21 L 40,492
Sun 10/16 H NYG 38-17 W 55,449
Sun 10/23 A HOU *13-10 W 39,462
Sun 10/30 A DEN 24-27 L 74,640
Sun 11/6 H LARI 20-28 L 73,497
Sun 11/13 H CIN 20-15 W 41,711
Sun 11/20 A DAL 21-41 L 64,103

Sun	11/27	A	SEA	*48-51	L	56,793
Sun	12/4	H	BUF	9-14	L	27,104
Sun	12/11	A	SD	38-41	L	35,910
Sun	12/18	H	DEN	48-17	W	11,377

LOS ANGELES RAIDERS

Sun	9/4	A	CIN	20-10	W	50,956
Sun	9/11	H	HOU	20-6	W	37,526
Mon	9/19	H	MIA	27-14	W	57,796
Sun	9/25	A	DEN	22-7	W	74,289
Sun	10/2	A	WAS	35-37	L	54,016
Sun	10/9	H	KC	21-20	W	40,492
Sun	10/16	A	SEA	36-38	L	60,967
Sun	10/23	A	DAL	40-38	W	64,991
Sun	10/30	H	SEA	21-34	L	49,708
Sun	11/6	A	KC	28-20	W	73,497
Sun	11/13	H	DEN	22-20	W	51,945
Sun	11/20	A	BUF	27-24	W	72,393
Sun	11/27	H	NYG	27-12	W	41,473
Thu	12/1	A	SD	42-10	W	47,760
Sun	12/11	H	STL	24-34	L	32,111
Sun	12/18	H	SD	30-14	W	57,325

AFC Divisional Playoff

Sun	1/1	H	PIT	38-10	W	90,380

AFC Championship

Sun	1/8	H	SEA	30-14	W	88,734

Super Bowl XVII

Sun	1/22	N	WAS	38-9	W	72,920

LOS ANGELES RAMS

Sun	9/4	A	NYG	16-6	W	75,281
Sun	9/11	H	NO	30-27	W	45,662
Sun	9/18	A	GB	24-27	L	54,037
Sun	9/25	A	NYJ	*24-27	L	52,070
Sun	10/2	H	DET	21-10	W	49,403
Sun	10/9	A	SF	10-7	W	59,119
Sun	10/16	H	ATL	27-21	W	50,404
Sun	10/23	H	SF	35-45	L	66,070
Sun	10/30	A	MIA	14-30	L	72,175
Sun	11/6	H	CHI	21-14	W	53,010
Mon	11/14	A	ATL	36-13	W	31,203
Sun	11/20	H	WAS	20-42	L	63,031
Sun	11/27	H	BUF	41-17	W	48,246
Sun	12/4	A	PHI	9-13	L	32,867
Sun	12/11	H	NE	7-21	L	46,503
Sun	12/18	A	NO	26-24	W	70,148

NFC Wild-Card Playoff

Mon	12/26	A	DAL	24-17	W	62,118

NFC Divisional Playoff

Sun	1/1	A	WAS	7-51	L	54,440

MIAMI DOLPHINS

Sun	9/4	A	BUF	12-0	W	78,683
Sun	9/11	H	NE	34-24	W	59,343
Mon	9/19	A	LARI	14-27	L	57,796
Sun	9/25	H	KC	14-6	W	50,785
Sun	10/2	A	NO	7-17	L	66,489
Sun	10/9	H	BUF	*35-38	L	59,948
Sun	10/16	A	NYJ	32-14	W	58,615
Sun	10/23	A	BAL	21-7	W	32,343
Sun	10/30	H	LARM	30-14	W	72,175
Sun	11/6	A	SF	20-17	W	57,832
Sun	11/13	A	NE	6-17	L	60,771
Sun	11/20	H	BAL	37-0	W	54,482
Mon	11/28	H	CIN	38-14	W	74,506
Sun	12/4	A	HOU	24-17	W	39,434
Sat	12/10	H	ATL	31-24	W	56,725
Fri	12/16	H	NYJ	34-14	W	59,975

AFC Divisional Playoff

Sat	12/31	H	SEA	20-27	L	74,136

MINNESOTA VIKINGS

Sun	9/4	A	CLE	27-21	W	70,087
Thu	9/8	H	SF	17-48	L	58,167
Sun	9/18	A	TB	*19-16	W	57,657
Sun	9/25	H	DET	20-17	W	58,254
Sun	10/2	H	DAL	24-37	L	60,774
Sun	10/9	A	CHI	23-14	W	59,632
Sun	10/16	H	HOU	34-14	W	58,910
Sun	10/23	A	GB	*20-17	W	55,236
Sun	10/30	A	STL	31-41	L	38,796
Sun	11/6	H	TB	12-17	L	59,239
Sun	11/13	H	GB	21-29	L	60,113
Sun	11/20	A	PIT	17-14	W	58,417
Sun	11/27	A	NO	16-17	L	59,502
Mon	12/5	A	DET	2-13	L	79,169
Sun	12/11	H	CHI	13-19	L	57,880
Sat	12/17	H	CIN	20-14	W	51,565

NEW ENGLAND PATRIOTS

Sun	9/4	H	BAL	*23-29	L	45,526
Sun	9/11	A	MIA	24-34	L	59,343
Sun	9/18	H	NYJ	23-13	W	43,182
Sun	9/25	A	PIT	28-23	W	58,282
Sun	10/2	H	SF	13-33	L	54,293
Sun	10/9	A	BAL	7-12	L	35,618
Sun	10/16	H	SD	37-21	W	59,016
Sun	10/23	A	BUF	31-0	W	60,424
Sun	10/30	A	ATL	13-24	L	47,546
Sun	11/6	H	BUF	21-7	W	42,604
Sun	11/13	H	MIA	17-6	W	60,771
Sun	11/20	H	CLE	0-30	L	40,987
Sun	11/27	A	NYJ	3-26	L	48,620
Sun	12/4	H	NO	7-0	W	24,579
Sun	12/11	A	LARM	21-7	W	46,503
Sun	12/18	A	SEA	6-24	L	59,688

NEW ORLEANS SAINTS

Sun	9/4	H	STL	28-17	W	65,225
Sun	9/11	A	LARM	27-30	L	45,662
Sun	9/18	H	CHI	*34-31	W	64,692
Sun	9/25	A	DAL	20-21	L	62,136
Sun	10/2	H	MIA	17-7	W	66,489
Sun	10/9	A	ATL	19-17	W	51,654
Sun	10/16	H	SF	13-32	L	68,154
Sun	10/23	A	TB	24-21	W	48,242
Sun	10/30	A	BUF	21-27	L	49,413
Sun	11/6	H	ATL	27-10	W	67,062
Sun	11/13	A	SF	0-27	L	40,022
Mon	11/21	H	NYJ	28-31	L	68,606
Sun	11/27	H	MIN	17-16	W	59,502
Sun	12/4	A	NE	0-7	L	24,579
Sun	12/11	A	PHI	*20-17	W	45,182
Sun	12/18	H	LARM	24-26	L	70,148

NEW YORK GIANTS

Sun	9/4	H	LARM	6-16	L	75,281
Sun	9/11	A	ATL	*16-13	W	52,850
Sun	9/18	A	DAL	13-28	L	62,347
Mon	9/26	H	GB	27-3	W	75,308
Sun	10/2	H	SD	34-41	L	73,892
Sun	10/9	H	PHI	13-17	L	73,291
Sun	10/16	A	KC	17-38	L	55,449
Mon	10/24	A	STL	*20-20	T	45,630
Sun	10/30	H	DAL	20-38	L	76,142
Mon	11/7	A	DET	9-15	L	68,985
Sun	11/13	H	WAS	17-33	L	71,482
Sun	11/20	A	PHI	23-0	W	57,977
Sun	11/27	A	LARI	12-27	L	41,473
Sun	12/4	H	STL	6-10	L	25,156
Sun	12/11	H	SEA	12-17	L	48,942
Sat	12/17	A	WAS	22-31	L	53,874

NEW YORK JETS

Sun	9/4	A	SD	41-29	W	51,004
Sun	9/11	H	SEA	10-17	L	50,066
Sun	9/18	A	NE	13-23	L	43,182
Sun	9/25	H	LARM	*27-24	W	52,070
Mon	10/3	A	BUF	34-10	W	79,833
Sun	10/9	A	CLE	7-10	L	78,235
Sun	10/16	H	MIA	14-32	L	58,615
Sun	10/23	H	ATL	21-27	L	46,878
Sun	10/30	A	SF	27-13	W	54,796
Sun	11/6	H	BAL	14-17	L	53,323
Sun	11/13	H	BUF	17-24	L	48,513
Mon	11/21	A	NO	31-28	W	68,606
Sun	11/27	H	NE	26-3	W	48,620
Sun	12/4	A	BAL	10-6	W	29,431
Sat	12/10	H	PIT	7-34	L	53,996
Fri	12/16	A	MIA	14-34	L	59,975

PHILADELPHIA EAGLES

Sat	9/3	A	SF	22-17	W	55,775
Sun	9/11	H	WAS	13-23	L	69,544
Sun	9/18	A	DEN	13-10	W	74,202
Sun	9/25	H	STL	11-14	L	64,465
Sun	10/2	A	ATL	28-24	W	50,621
Sun	10/9	A	NYG	17-13	W	73,291
Sun	10/16	H	DAL	7-37	L	63,070
Sun	10/23	H	CHI	6-7	L	45,263
Sun	10/30	H	BAL	21-22	L	59,150
Sun	11/6	A	DAL	20-27	L	71,236
Sun	11/13	A	CHI	14-17	L	47,524
Sun	11/20	H	NYG	0-23	L	57,977
Sun	11/27	A	WAS	24-28	L	54,324
Sun	12/4	H	LARM	13-9	W	32,867
Sun	12/11	H	NO	*17-20	L	45,182
Sun	12/18	A	STL	7-31	L	21,902

PITTSBURGH STEELERS

Sun	9/4	H	DEN	10-14	L	58,233
Sun	9/11	A	GB	25-21	W	55,204
Sun	9/18	A	HOU	40-28	W	44,150
Sun	9/25	H	NE	23-28	L	58,282
Sun	10/2	H	HOU	17-10	W	56,901
Mon	10/10	A	CIN	24-14	W	56,086
Sun	10/16	H	CLE	44-17	W	59,263
Sun	10/23	A	SEA	27-21	W	61,615
Sun	10/30	H	TB	17-12	W	57,648
Sun	11/6	H	SD	26-3	W	58,191
Sun	11/13	A	BAL	24-13	W	57,319
Sun	11/20	H	MIN	14-17	L	58,417
Thu	11/24	A	DET	3-45	L	77,724
Sun	12/4	H	CIN	10-23	L	55,832
Sat	12/10	A	NYJ	34-7	W	53,996
Sun	12/18	A	CLE	17-30	L	72,313

AFC Divisional Playoff

Sun	1/1	A	LARI	10-38	L	90,380

ST. LOUIS CARDINALS

Sun	9/4	A	NO	17-28	L	65,225
Sun	9/11	H	DAL	17-34	L	48,532
Sun	9/18	H	SF	27-42	L	38,130
Sun	9/25	A	PHI	14-11	W	64,465
Sun	10/2	A	KC	14-38	L	59,875
Sun	10/9	H	WAS	14-38	L	42,698
Sun	10/16	A	TB	34-27	W	48,244
Mon	10/24	H	NYG	*20-20	T	45,630
Sun	10/30	H	MIN	41-31	W	38,796
Sun	11/6	A	WAS	7-45	L	51,380
Sun	11/13	H	SEA	33-28	W	33,280
Sun	11/20	H	SD	44-14	W	40,644
Thu	11/24	A	DAL	17-35	L	60,764
Sun	12/4	A	NYG	10-6	W	25,156
Sun	12/11	A	LARI	34-24	W	32,111
Sun	12/18	H	PHI	31-7	W	21,902

SAN DIEGO CHARGERS

Sun	9/4	H	NYJ	29-41	L	51,004
Mon	9/12	A	KC	17-14	W	62,150
Sun	9/18	A	SEA	31-34	L	61,714
Sun	9/25	H	CLE	*24-30	L	49,482
Sun	10/2	A	NYG	41-34	W	73,892
Sun	10/9	H	SEA	28-21	W	49,132
Sun	10/16	A	NE	21-37	L	59,016
Sun	10/23	A	DEN	6-14	L	74,581
Mon	10/31	H	WAS	24-27	L	46,414
Sun	11/6	A	PIT	3-26	L	58,191
Sun	11/13	H	DAL	24-23	W	46,192
Sun	11/20	A	STL	14-44	L	40,644
Sun	11/27	H	DEN	31-7	W	44,050
Thu	12/1	H	LARI	10-42	L	47,760
Sun	12/11	H	KC	41-38	W	35,910
Sun	12/18	A	LARI	14-30	L	57,325

SAN FRANCISCO 49ERS

Sat	9/3	H	PHI	17-22	L	55,775
Thu	9/8	A	MIN	48-17	W	58,167
Sun	9/18	A	STL	42-27	W	38,130
Sun	9/25	H	ATL	24-20	W	57,814
Sun	10/2	A	NE	33-13	W	54,293
Sun	10/9	H	LARM	7-10	L	59,119
Sun	10/16	A	NO	32-13	W	68,154
Sun	10/23	A	LARM	45-35	W	66,070
Sun	10/30	H	NYJ	13-27	L	54,796
Sun	11/6	H	MIA	17-20	L	57,832
Sun	11/13	H	NO	27-0	W	40,022
Sun	11/20	A	ATL	24-28	L	32,782
Sun	11/27	A	CHI	3-13	L	40,483
Sun	12/4	H	TB	35-21	W	49,773
Sun	12/11	A	BUF	23-10	W	38,039
Mon	12/19	H	DAL	42-17	W	59,957

NFC Divisional Playoff

Sat	12/31	H	DET	24-23	W	59,979

NFC Championship

Sun	1/8	A	WAS	21-24	L	55,363

SEATTLE SEAHAWKS

Sun	9/4	A	KC	13-17	L	42,531
Sun	9/11	A	NYJ	17-10	W	50,066
Sun	9/18	H	SD	34-31	W	61,714
Sun	9/25	H	WAS	17-27	L	60,718
Sun	10/2	A	CLE	24-9	W	75,446
Sun	10/9	A	SD	21-28	L	49,132
Sun	10/16	H	LARI	38-36	W	60,967
Sun	10/23	H	PIT	21-27	L	61,615
Sun	10/30	A	LARI	34-21	W	49,708
Sun	11/6	H	DEN	27-19	W	61,189
Sun	11/13	A	STL	28-33	L	33,280
Sun	11/20	A	DEN	27-38	L	74,710
Sun	11/27	H	KC	*51-48	W	56,793
Sun	12/4	H	DAL	10-35	L	63,352
Sun	12/11	A	NYG	17-12	W	48,942
Sun	12/18	H	NE	24-6	W	59,688

AFC Wild-Card Playoff

Sat	12/24	H	DEN	31-7	W	64,275

AFC Divisional Playoff

Sat	12/31	A	MIA	27-20	W	74,136

AFC Championship

Sun	1/8	A	LARI	14-30	L	88,734

TAMPA BAY BUCCANEERS

Sun	9/4	H	DET	0-11	L	62,154
Sun	9/11	A	CHI	10-17	L	58,186
Sun	9/18	H	MIN	*16-19	L	57,657
Sun	9/25	H	CIN	17-23	L	56,023
Sun	10/2	A	GB	14-55	L	54,272
Sun	10/9	A	DAL	*24-27	L	63,808
Sun	10/16	H	STL	27-34	L	48,224
Sun	10/23	H	NO	21-24	L	48,242
Sun	10/30	A	PIT	12-17	L	57,648
Sun	11/6	A	MIN	17-12	W	59,239
Sun	11/13	A	CLE	0-20	L	56,091
Sun	11/20	H	CHI	0-27	L	36,816
Sun	11/27	H	HOU	33-24	W	38,625
Sun	12/4	A	SF	21-35	L	49,773
Mon	12/12	H	GB	*9-12	L	50,763
Sun	12/18	A	DET	20-23	L	78,553

WASHINGTON REDSKINS

Mon	9/5	H	DAL	30-31	L	55,045
Sun	9/11	A	PHI	23-13	W	69,544
Sun	9/18	H	KC	27-12	W	52,610
Sun	9/25	A	SEA	27-17	W	60,718

Sun	10/2	H	LARI	37-35	W	54,016
Sun	10/9	A	STL	38-14	W	42,698
Mon	10/17	A	GB	47-48	L	55,255
Sun	10/23	H	DET	38-17	W	43,189
Mon	10/31	A	SD	27-24	W	46,414
Sun	11/6	H	STL	45-7	W	51,380
Sun	11/13	A	NYG	33-17	W	71,482
Sun	11/20	A	LARM	42-20	W	63,031
Sun	11/27	H	PHI	28-24	W	54,324
Sun	12/4	H	ATL	37-21	W	52,074
Sun	12/11	A	DAL	31-10	W	65,074
Sat	12/17	H	NYG	31-22	W	53,874

NFC Divisional Playoff

Sun	1/1	H	LARM	51-7	W	54,440

NFC Championship

Sun	1/8	H	SF	24-21	W	55,363

Super Bowl XVIII

Sun	1/22	N	LARI	9-38	L	72,920

1984 NFL

ATLANTA FALCONS

Sun	9/2	A	NO	36-28	W	66,652
Sun	9/9	H	DET	*24-27	L	49,878
Sun	9/16	A	MIN	20-27	L	53,955
Sun	9/23	H	HOU	42-10	W	45,248
Sun	9/30	A	SF	5-14	L	57,990
Sun	10/7	A	LARM	30-28	W	47,832
Sun	10/14	H	NYG	7-19	L	50,268
Mon	10/22	H	LARM	10-24	L	52,861
Sun	10/28	A	PIT	10-35	L	55,971
Mon	11/5	A	WAS	14-27	L	51,301
Sun	11/11	H	NO	13-17	L	40,590
Sun	11/18	H	CLE	7-23	L	28,280
Sun	11/25	A	CIN	14-35	L	44,678
Sun	12/2	H	SF	17-35	L	29,644
Sun	12/9	A	TB	6-23	L	33,808
Sun	12/16	H	PHI	26-10	W	15,582

BUFFALO BILLS

Sun	9/2	H	NE	17-21	L	48,528
Sun	9/9	A	STL	7-37	L	35,785
Mon	9/17	H	MIA	17-21	L	65,455
Sun	9/23	H	NYJ	26-28	L	48,330
Sun	9/30	A	IND	17-31	L	60,032
Sun	10/7	H	PHI	17-27	L	37,555
Sun	10/14	A	SEA	28-31	L	59,034
Sun	10/21	H	DEN	7-37	L	31,204
Sun	10/28	A	MIA	7-38	L	58,824
Sun	11/4	H	CLE	10-13	L	33,343
Sun	11/11	A	NE	10-38	L	43,313
Sun	11/18	H	DAL	14-3	W	74,391
Sun	11/25	A	WAS	14-41	L	51,513
Sun	12/2	H	IND	21-15	W	20,693
Sat	12/8	A	NYJ	17-21	L	45,378
Sun	12/16	A	CIN	21-52	L	55,771

CHICAGO BEARS

Sun	9/2	H	TB	34-14	W	58,802
Sun	9/9	H	DEN	27-0	W	54,335
Sun	9/16	A	GB	9-7	W	55,942
Sun	9/23	A	SEA	9-38	L	61,520
Sun	9/30	H	DAL	14-23	L	63,623
Sun	10/7	H	NO	20-7	W	53,752
Sun	10/14	A	STL	21-38	L	49,554
Sun	10/21	A	TB	44-9	W	60,003
Sun	10/28	H	MIN	16-7	W	57,517
Sun	11/4	H	LARI	17-6	W	59,858
Sun	11/11	A	LARM	13-29	L	62,021
Sun	11/18	H	DET	16-14	W	54,911
Sun	11/25	A	MIN	34-3	W	56,881
Mon	12/3	A	SD	7-20	L	45,470
Sun	12/9	H	GB	14-20	L	59,374
Sun	12/16	A	DET	30-13	W	53,252

NFC Divisional Playoff

Sun	12/30	A	WAS	23-19	W	55,431

NFC Championship

Sun	1/6	A	SF	0-23	L	61,040

CINCINNATI BENGALS

Sun	9/2	A	DEN	17-20	L	74,178
Sun	9/9	H	KC	22-27	L	47,111
Sun	9/16	A	NYJ	23-43	L	64,193
Sun	9/23	H	LARM	14-24	L	45,406
Mon	10/1	A	PIT	17-38	L	57,098
Sun	10/7	H	HOU	13-3	W	43,637
Sun	10/14	A	NE	14-20	L	48,154
Sun	10/21	H	CLE	12-9	W	50,667
Sun	10/28	A	HOU	31-13	W	34,010
Sun	11/4	A	SF	17-23	L	58,324
Sun	11/11	H	PIT	22-20	W	52,497
Sun	11/18	H	SEA	6-26	L	50,280
Sun	11/25	H	ATL	35-14	W	44,678
Sun	12/2	A	CLE	*20-17	W	51,774
Sun	12/9	A	NO	24-21	W	40,855
Sun	12/16	H	BUF	52-21	W	55,771

CLEVELAND BROWNS

Mon	9/3	A	SEA	0-33	L	59,540
Sun	9/9	A	LARM	17-20	L	43,043
Sun	9/16	H	DEN	14-24	L	61,980
Sun	9/23	H	PIT	20-10	W	77,312
Sun	9/30	A	KC	6-10	L	39,225
Sun	10/7	H	NE	16-17	L	53,036
Sun	10/14	H	NYJ	20-24	L	55,673
Sun	10/21	A	CIN	9-12	L	50,667
Sun	10/28	H	NO	14-16	L	52,489
Sun	11/4	A	BUF	13-10	W	33,343
Sun	11/11	H	SF	7-41	L	60,092
Sun	11/18	A	ATL	23-7	W	28,280
Sun	11/25	H	HOU	27-10	W	46,077
Sun	12/2	H	CIN	*17-20	L	51,774
Sun	12/9	A	PIT	20-23	L	55,825
Sun	12/16	A	HOU	27-20	W	33,676

DALLAS COWBOYS

Mon	9/3	A	LARM	20-13	W	65,403
Sun	9/9	A	NYG	7-28	L	75,921
Sun	9/16	H	PHI	23-17	W	64,695
Sun	9/23	H	GB	20-6	W	64,425
Sun	9/30	A	CHI	23-14	W	63,623
Sun	10/7	H	STL	20-31	L	61,678
Sun	10/14	A	WAS	14-34	L	55,431
Sun	10/21	H	NO	*30-27	W	51,161
Sun	10/28	H	IND	22-3	W	58,724
Sun	11/4	H	NYG	7-19	L	60,235
Sun	11/11	A	STL	24-17	W	48,721
Sun	11/18	A	BUF	3-14	L	74,391
Thu	11/22	H	NE	20-17	W	55,341
Sun	12/2	A	PHI	26-10	W	66,322
Sun	12/9	H	WAS	28-30	L	64,286
Mon	12/17	A	MIA	21-28	L	74,139

DENVER BRONCOS

Sun	9/2	H	CIN	20-17	W	74,178
Sun	9/9	A	CHI	0-27	L	54,335
Sun	9/16	A	CLE	24-14	W	61,980
Sun	9/23	H	KC	21-0	W	74,263
Sun	9/30	H	LARI	16-13	W	74,833
Sun	10/7	A	DET	28-7	W	55,836
Mon	10/15	H	GB	17-14	W	62,546
Sun	10/21	A	BUF	37-7	W	31,204
Sun	10/28	A	LARI	*22-19	W	91,020
Sun	11/4	H	NE	26-19	W	74,908
Sun	11/11	A	SD	16-13	W	53,181
Sun	11/18	H	MIN	42-21	W	74,716
Sun	11/25	H	SEA	24-27	L	74,922
Sun	12/2	A	KC	13-16	L	35,537
Sun	12/9	H	SD	16-13	W	74,867
Sat	12/15	A	SEA	31-14	W	64,411

AFC Divisional Playoff

Sun	12/30	H	PIT	17-24	L	74,981

DETROIT LIONS

Sun	9/2	H	SF	27-30	L	56,782
Sun	9/9	A	ATL	*27-24	W	49,878
Sun	9/16	A	TB	17-21	L	44,560
Sun	9/23	H	MIN	28-29	L	57,511
Sun	9/30	A	SD	24-27	L	53,887
Sun	10/7	H	DEN	7-28	L	55,836
Sun	10/14	H	TB	*13-7	W	44,308
Sun	10/21	A	MIN	16-14	W	57,953
Sun	10/28	A	GB	9-41	L	54,289
Sun	11/4	H	PHI	*23-23	T	59,141
Sun	11/11	A	WAS	14-28	L	50,212
Sun	11/18	A	CHI	14-16	L	54,911
Thu	11/22	H	GB	31-28	W	63,698
Sun	12/2	A	SEA	17-38	L	62,441
Mon	12/10	H	LARI	3-24	L	66,710
Sun	12/16	H	CHI	13-30	L	53,252

GREEN BAY PACKERS

Sun	9/2	H	STL	24-23	W	53,738
Sun	9/9	A	LARI	7-28	L	46,269
Sun	9/16	H	CHI	7-9	L	55,942
Sun	9/23	A	DAL	6-20	L	64,425
Sun	9/30	A	TB	*27-30	L	47,487
Sun	10/7	H	SD	28-34	L	54,045
Mon	10/15	A	DEN	14-17	L	62,546
Sun	10/21	H	SEA	24-30	L	52,286
Sun	10/28	H	DET	41-9	W	54,289
Sun	11/4	A	NO	23-13	W	57,426
Sun	11/11	H	MIN	45-17	W	52,931
Sun	11/18	H	LARM	31-6	W	52,031
Thu	11/22	A	DET	28-31	L	63,698
Sun	12/2	H	TB	27-14	W	46,800
Sun	12/9	A	CHI	20-14	W	59,374
Sun	12/16	A	MIN	38-14	W	51,197

HOUSTON OILERS

Sun	9/2	H	LARI	14-24	L	49,092
Sun	9/9	H	IND	21-35	L	43,820
Sun	9/16	A	SD	14-31	L	52,726
Sun	9/23	A	ATL	10-42	L	45,248
Sun	9/30	H	NO	10-27	L	43,108
Sun	10/7	A	CIN	3-13	L	43,637
Sun	10/14	A	MIA	10-28	L	54,080
Sun	10/21	H	SF	21-34	L	39,900
Sun	10/28	H	CIN	13-31	L	34,010
Sun	11/4	A	PIT	7-35	L	48,892
Sun	11/11	A	KC	17-16	W	39,472
Sun	11/18	H	NYJ	31-20	W	40,141
Sun	11/25	A	CLE	10-27	L	46,077
Sun	12/2	H	PIT	*23-20	W	39,782
Sun	12/9	A	LARM	16-27	L	49,092
Sun	12/16	H	CLE	20-27	L	33,676

INDIANAPOLIS COLTS

Sun	9/2	H	NYJ	14-23	L	60,398
Sun	9/9	A	HOU	35-21	W	43,820
Sun	9/16	H	STL	33-34	L	60,274
Sun	9/23	A	MIA	7-44	L	55,415
Sun	9/30	H	BUF	31-17	W	60,032
Sun	10/7	H	WAS	7-35	L	60,012
Sun	10/14	A	PHI	7-16	L	50,277
Sun	10/21	H	PIT	17-16	W	60,026
Sun	10/28	A	DAL	3-22	L	58,724
Sun	11/4	H	SD	10-38	L	60,143
Sun	11/11	A	NYJ	9-5	W	51,066
Sun	11/18	H	NE	17-50	L	60,009
Sun	11/25	A	LARI	7-21	L	40,289
Sun	12/2	A	BUF	15-21	L	20,693
Sun	12/9	H	MIA	17-35	L	60,411
Sun	12/16	A	NE	10-16	L	22,383

KANSAS CITY CHIEFS

Sun	9/2	A	PIT	37-27	W	56,709
Sun	9/9	A	CIN	27-22	W	47,111
Sun	9/16	H	LARI	20-22	L	75,111
Sun	9/23	A	DEN	0-21	L	74,263
Sun	9/30	H	CLE	10-6	W	39,225
Sun	10/7	H	NYJ	16-17	L	48,895
Sun	10/14	H	SD	31-13	W	62,233
Sun	10/21	A	NYJ	7-28	L	66,782
Sun	10/28	H	TB	24-20	W	38,984
Sun	11/4	A	SEA	0-45	L	61,396
Sun	11/11	H	HOU	16-17	L	39,472
Sun	11/18	A	LARI	7-17	L	48,575
Sun	11/25	A	NYG	27-28	L	74,383
Sun	12/2	H	DEN	16-13	W	35,537
Sun	12/9	H	SEA	34-7	W	31,860
Sun	12/16	A	SD	42-21	W	40,221

LOS ANGELES RAIDERS

Sun	9/2	A	HOU	24-14	W	49,092
Sun	9/9	H	GB	28-7	W	46,269
Sun	9/16	A	KC	22-20	W	75,111
Mon	9/24	H	SD	33-30	W	76,131
Sun	9/30	A	DEN	13-16	L	74,833
Sun	10/7	H	SEA	28-14	W	77,904
Sun	10/14	H	MIN	23-20	W	49,276
Sun	10/21	A	SD	44-37	W	57,442
Sun	10/28	H	DEN	*19-22	L	91,020
Sun	11/4	A	CHI	6-17	L	59,858
Mon	11/12	A	SEA	14-17	L	64,001
Sun	11/18	H	KC	17-7	W	48,575
Sun	11/25	H	IND	21-7	W	40,289
Sun	12/2	A	MIA	45-34	W	71,222
Mon	12/10	A	DET	24-3	W	66,710
Sun	12/16	H	PIT	7-13	L	83,056

AFC Wild-Card Playoff

Sat	12/22	A	SEA	7-13	L	62,049

LOS ANGELES RAMS

Mon	9/3	H	DAL	13-20	L	65,403
Sun	9/9	H	CLE	20-17	W	43,043
Sun	9/16	A	PIT	14-24	L	58,104
Sun	9/23	A	CIN	24-14	W	45,406
Sun	9/30	H	NYG	33-12	W	53,417
Sun	10/7	H	ATL	28-30	L	47,832
Sun	10/14	A	NO	28-10	W	63,161
Mon	10/22	A	ATL	24-10	W	52,861
Sun	10/28	H	SF	0-33	L	65,481
Sun	11/4	A	STL	16-13	W	51,010
Sun	11/11	H	CHI	29-13	W	62,021
Sun	11/18	A	GB	6-31	L	52,031
Sun	11/25	A	TB	34-33	W	42,242
Sun	12/2	H	NO	34-21	W	49,348
Sun	12/9	H	HOU	27-16	W	49,092
Fri	12/14	A	SF	16-19	L	59,743

NFC Wild-Card Playoff

Sun	12/23	H	NYG	13-16	L	67,037

MIAMI DOLPHINS

Sun	9/2	A	WAS	35-17	W	52,683
Sun	9/9	H	NE	28-7	W	66,083
Mon	9/17	A	BUF	21-17	W	65,455
Sun	9/23	H	IND	44-7	W	55,415
Sun	9/30	A	STL	36-28	W	46,991
Sun	10/7	A	PIT	31-7	W	59,103
Sun	10/14	H	HOU	28-10	W	54,080
Sun	10/21	A	NE	44-24	W	60,711
Sun	10/28	H	BUF	38-7	W	58,824
Sun	11/4	A	NYJ	31-17	W	72,655
Sun	11/11	H	PHI	24-23	W	70,227
Sun	11/18	A	SD	*28-34	L	53,041
Mon	11/26	H	NYJ	28-17	W	74,884
Sun	12/2	H	LARI	34-45	L	71,222
Sun	12/9	A	IND	35-17	W	60,411
Mon	12/17	H	DAL	28-21	W	74,139

AFC Divisional Playoff

Sat	12/29	H	SEA	31-10	W	73,469

AFC Championship

Sun	1/6	H	PIT	45-28	W	76,029

SUPER BOWL XIX
Sun 1/20 N SF 16-38 L 84,059

MINNESOTA VIKINGS
Sun 9/2 H SD 13-42 L 57,276
Sun 9/9 A PHI 17-19 L 55,942
Sun 9/16 H ATL 27-20 W 53,955
Sun 9/23 A DET 29-28 W 57,511
Sun 9/30 H SEA 12-20 L 57,171
Sun 10/7 A TB 31-35 L 47,405
Sun 10/14 A LARI 20-23 L 49,276
Sun 10/21 H DET 14-16 L 57,953
Sun 10/28 A CHI 7-16 L 57,517
Sun 11/4 H TB 27-24 W 54,949
Sun 11/11 A GB 17-45 L 52,931
Sun 11/18 H DEN 21-42 L 74,716
Sun 11/25 A CHI 3-34 L 56,881
Thu 11/29 H WAS 17-31 L 55,017
Sat 12/8 A SF 7-51 L 56,670
Sun 12/16 H GB 14-38 L 51,197

NEW ENGLAND PATRIOTS
Sun 9/2 A BUF 21-17 W 48,528
Sun 9/9 A MIA 7-28 L 66,083
Sun 9/16 H SEA 38-23 W 43,140
Sun 9/23 H WAS 10-26 L 60,503
Sun 9/30 A NYJ 28-21 W 68,978
Sun 10/7 A CLE 17-16 W 53,036
Sun 10/14 H CIN 20-14 W 48,154
Sun 10/21 H MIA 24-44 L 60,711
Sun 10/28 H NYJ 30-20 W 60,513
Sun 11/4 A DEN 19-26 L 74,908
Sun 11/11 H BUF 38-10 W 43,313
Sun 11/18 A IND 50-17 W 60,009
Thu 11/22 A DAL 17-20 L 55,341
Sun 12/2 H STL 10-33 L 53,540
Sun 12/9 A PHI 17-27 L 41,581
Sun 12/16 H IND 16-10 W 22,383

NEW ORLEANS SAINTS
Sun 9/2 H ATL 28-36 L 66,652
Sun 9/9 H TB 17-13 W 54,686
Sun 9/16 A SF 20-30 L 57,611
Sun 9/23 H STL 34-24 W 58,723
Sun 9/30 A HOU 27-10 W 43,108
Sun 10/7 A CHI 7-20 L 53,752
Sun 10/14 H LARM 10-28 L 63,161
Sun 10/21 A DAL *27-30 L 51,161
Sun 10/28 A CLE 16-14 W 52,489
Sun 11/4 H GB 13-23 L 57,426
Sun 11/11 A ATL 17-13 W 40,590
Mon 11/19 H PIT 27-24 W 66,005
Sun 11/25 H SF 3-35 L 65,177
Sun 12/2 A LARM 21-34 L 49,348
Sun 12/9 H CIN 21-24 L 40,855
Sat 12/15 A NYG 10-3 W 63,739

NEW YORK GIANTS
Sun 9/2 H PHI 28-27 W 71,520
Sun 9/9 H DAL 28-7 W 75,921
Sun 9/16 A WAS 14-30 L 52,997
Sun 9/23 H TB 17-14 W 72,650
Sun 9/30 A LARM 12-33 L 53,417
Mon 10/8 H SF 10-31 L 76,112
Sun 10/14 A ATL 19-7 W 50,268
Sun 10/21 H PHI 10-24 L 64,677
Sun 10/28 H WAS 37-13 W 76,192
Sun 11/4 A DAL 19-7 W 60,235
Sun 11/11 A TB 17-20 L 46,534
Sun 11/18 H STL 19-16 L 73,428
Sun 11/25 H KC 28-27 W 74,383
Sun 12/2 A NYJ 20-10 W 74,975
Sun 12/9 A STL 21-31 L 49,973
Sat 12/15 H NO 3-10 L 63,739

NFC WILD-CARD PLAYOFF
Sun 12/23 A LARM 16-13 W 67,037

NFC DIVISIONAL PLAYOFF
Sat 12/29 A SF 10-21 L 60,303

NEW YORK JETS
Sun 9/2 A IND 23-14 W 60,398
Thu 9/6 H PIT 17-23 L 70,564
Sun 9/16 H CIN 43-23 W 64,193
Sun 9/23 A BUF 28-26 W 48,330
Sun 9/30 H NE 21-28 L 68,978
Sun 10/7 A KC 17-16 W 48,895
Sun 10/14 A CLE 24-20 W 55,673
Sun 10/21 H KC 28-7 W 66,782
Sun 10/28 A NE 20-30 L 60,513
Sun 11/4 H MIA 17-31 L 72,655
Sun 11/11 H IND 5-9 L 51,066
Sun 11/18 H HOU 20-31 L 40,141
Mon 11/26 A MIA 17-28 L 74,884
Sun 12/2 H NYG 10-20 L 74,975
Sat 12/8 H BUF 21-17 W 45,378
Sun 12/16 A TB 21-41 L 43,817

PHILADELPHIA EAGLES
Sun 9/2 A NYG 27-28 L 71,520
Sun 9/9 H MIN 19-17 W 55,942
Sun 9/16 A DAL 17-23 L 64,695
Sun 9/23 H SF 9-21 L 62,771
Sun 9/30 A WAS 0-20 L 53,064
Sun 10/7 H BUF 27-17 W 37,555
Sun 10/14 H IND 16-7 W 50,277
Sun 10/21 H NYG 24-10 W 64,677
Sun 10/28 H STL 14-34 L 54,310
Sun 11/4 A DET *23-23 T 59,141
Sun 11/11 A MIA 23-24 L 70,227
Sun 11/18 H WAS 16-10 W 63,117
Sun 11/25 A STL 16-17 L 39,858
Sun 12/2 H DAL 10-26 L 66,322
Sun 12/9 H NE 27-17 W 41,581
Sun 12/16 A ATL 10-26 L 15,582

PITTSBURGH STEELERS
Sun 9/2 H KC 27-37 L 56,709
Thu 9/6 A NYJ 23-17 W 70,564
Sun 9/16 H LARM 24-14 W 58,104
Sun 9/23 A CLE 10-20 L 77,312
Mon 10/1 H CIN 38-17 W 57,098
Sun 10/7 H MIA 7-31 L 59,103
Sun 10/14 A SF 20-17 W 59,110
Sun 10/21 A IND 16-17 L 60,026
Sun 10/28 A ATL 35-10 W 55,971
Sun 11/4 H HOU 35-7 W 48,892
Sun 11/11 A CIN 20-22 L 52,497
Mon 11/19 A NO 24-27 L 66,005
Sun 11/25 H SD 52-24 W 55,856
Sun 12/2 A HOU *20-23 L 39,782
Sun 12/9 H CLE 23-20 W 55,825
Sun 12/16 A LARM 13-7 W 83,056

AFC DIVISIONAL PLAYOFF
Sun 12/30 A DEN 24-17 W 74,981

AFC CHAMPIONSHIP
Sun 1/6 A MIA 28-45 L 76,029

ST. LOUIS CARDINALS
Sun 9/2 A GB 23-24 L 53,738
Sun 9/9 H BUF 37-7 W 35,785
Sun 9/16 A IND 34-33 W 60,274
Sun 9/23 H NO 24-34 L 58,723
Sun 9/30 H MIA 28-36 L 46,991
Sun 10/7 A DAL 31-20 W 61,678
Sun 10/14 A CHI 38-21 W 49,554
Sun 10/21 H WAS 26-24 W 50,262
Sun 10/28 A PHI 34-14 W 54,310
Sun 11/4 H LARM 13-16 L 51,010
Sun 11/11 H DAL 17-24 L 48,721
Sun 11/18 A NYG 16-19 L 73,428
Sun 11/25 H PHI 17-16 W 39,858
Sun 12/2 A NE 33-10 W 53,540
Sun 12/9 H NYG 31-21 W 49,973
Sun 12/16 A WAS 27-29 L 54,299

SAN DIEGO CHARGERS
Sun 9/2 A MIN 42-13 W 57,276
Sun 9/9 A SEA 17-31 L 61,314
Sun 9/16 H HOU 31-14 W 52,726
Mon 9/24 A LARI 30-33 L 76,131
Sun 9/30 H DET 27-24 W 53,887
Sun 10/7 H GB 34-28 W 54,045
Sun 10/14 A KC 13-31 L 62,233
Sun 10/21 H LARI 37-44 L 57,442
Mon 10/29 H SEA 0-24 L 53,974
Sun 11/4 A IND 38-10 W 60,143
Sun 11/11 H DEN 13-16 L 53,181
Sun 11/18 H MIA *34-28 W 53,041
Sun 11/25 A PIT 24-52 L 55,856
Mon 12/3 H CHI 20-7 W 45,470
Sun 12/9 H DEN 13-16 L 74,867
Sun 12/16 A KC 21-42 L 40,221

SAN FRANCISCO 49ERS
Sun 9/2 A DET 30-27 W 56,782
Mon 9/10 H WAS 37-31 W 59,707
Sun 9/16 H NO 30-20 W 57,611
Sun 9/23 A PHI 21-9 W 62,771
Sun 9/30 H ATL 14-5 W 57,990
Mon 10/8 A NYG 31-10 W 76,112
Sun 10/14 H PIT 17-20 L 59,110
Sun 10/21 A HOU 34-21 W 39,900
Sun 10/28 A LARM 33-0 W 65,481
Sun 11/4 H CIN 23-17 W 58,324
Sun 11/11 A CLE 41-7 W 60,092
Sun 11/18 H TB 24-17 W 57,704
Sun 11/25 A NO 35-3 W 65,177
Sun 12/2 A ATL 35-17 W 29,644
Sat 12/8 H MIN 51-7 W 56,670
Fri 12/14 H LARM 19-16 W 59,743

NFC DIVISIONAL PLAYOFF
Sat 12/29 H NYG 21-10 W 60,303

NFC CHAMPIONSHIP
Sun 1/6 H CHI 23-0 W 61,040

SUPER BOWL XIX
Sun 1/20 N MIA 38-16 W 84,059

SEATTLE SEAHAWKS
Mon 9/3 H CLE 33-0 W 59,540
Sun 9/9 H SD 31-17 W 61,314
Sun 9/16 A NE 23-38 L 43,140
Sun 9/23 H CHI 38-9 W 61,520
Sun 9/30 A MIN 20-12 W 57,171
Sun 10/7 A LARI 14-28 L 77,904
Sun 10/14 H BUF 31-28 W 59,034
Sun 10/21 A GB 30-24 W 52,286
Mon 10/29 A SD 24-0 W 53,974
Sun 11/4 H KC 45-0 W 61,396
Mon 11/12 H LARI 17-14 W 64,001
Sun 11/18 A CIN 26-6 W 50,280
Sun 11/25 A DEN 27-24 W 74,922
Sun 12/2 H DET 38-17 W 62,441
Sun 12/9 A KC 7-34 L 31,860
Sat 12/15 H DEN 14-31 L 64,411

AFC WILD-CARD PLAYOFF
Sat 12/22 H LARI 13-7 W 62,049

AFC DIVISIONAL PLAYOFF
Sat 12/29 A MIA 10-31 L 73,469

TAMPA BAY BUCCANEERS
Sun 9/2 A CHI 14-34 L 58,802
Sun 9/9 A NO 13-17 L 54,686
Sun 9/16 H DET 21-17 W 44,560
Sun 9/23 A NYG 14-17 L 72,650
Sun 9/30 H GB *30-27 W 47,487
Sun 10/7 H MIN 35-31 W 47,405
Sun 10/14 A DET *7-13 L 44,308
Sun 10/21 H CHI 9-44 L 60,003
Sun 10/28 A KC 20-24 L 38,984
Sun 11/4 A MIN 24-27 L 54,949
Sun 11/11 H NYG 20-17 W 46,534
Sun 11/18 A SF 17-24 L 57,704
Sun 11/25 A LARM 33-34 L 42,242
Sun 12/2 H GB 14-27 L 46,800
Sun 12/9 H ATL 23-6 W 33,808
Sun 12/16 H NYJ 41-21 W 43,817

WASHINGTON REDSKINS
Sun 9/2 H MIA 17-35 L 52,683
Mon 9/10 A SF 31-37 L 59,707
Sun 9/16 H NYG 30-14 W 52,997
Sun 9/23 A NE 26-10 W 60,503
Sun 9/30 H PHI 20-0 W 53,064
Sun 10/7 A IND 35-7 W 60,012
Sun 10/14 H DAL 34-14 W 55,431
Sun 10/21 A STL 24-26 L 50,262
Sun 10/28 A NYG 13-37 L 76,192
Mon 11/5 H ATL 27-14 W 51,301
Sun 11/11 H DET 28-14 W 50,212
Sun 11/18 A PHI 10-16 L 63,117
Sun 11/25 H BUF 41-14 W 51,513
Thu 11/29 A MIN 31-17 W 55,017
Sun 12/9 A DAL 30-28 W 64,286
Sun 12/16 H STL 29-27 W 54,299

NFC DIVISIONAL PLAYOFF
Sun 12/30 H CHI 19-23 L 55,431

1985 NFL
ATLANTA FALCONS
Sun 9/8 H DET 27-28 L 37,785
Sun 9/15 A SF 16-35 L 58,923
Sun 9/22 H DEN 28-44 L 37,903
Sun 9/29 A LARM 6-17 L 49,870
Sun 10/6 A SF 17-38 L 44,740
Sun 10/13 H SEA 26-30 L 60,430
Sun 10/20 H NO 31-24 W 44,784
Sun 10/27 A DAL 10-24 L 57,941
Sun 11/3 H WAS 10-44 L 42,209
Sun 11/10 A PHI *17-23 L 63,694
Sun 11/17 A LARM 30-14 W 29,960
Sun 11/24 A CHI 0-36 L 61,769
Sun 12/1 H LARI 24-34 L 20,585
Sun 12/8 A KC 10-38 L 18,199
Sun 12/15 H MIN 14-13 W 14,167
Sun 12/22 A NO 16-10 W 37,717

BUFFALO BILLS
Sun 9/8 H SD 9-14 L 67,597
Sun 9/15 A NYJ 3-42 L 63,449
Sun 9/22 H NE 14-17 L 40,334
Sun 9/29 H MIN 20-27 L 45,667
Sun 10/6 A IND 17-49 L 28,430
Sun 10/13 A NE 3-14 L 40,462
Sun 10/20 H IND 21-9 W 28,430
Sun 10/27 A PHI 17-21 L 60,987
Sun 11/3 H CIN 17-23 L 25,640
Sun 11/10 H HOU 20-0 W 21,881
Sun 11/17 A CLE 7-17 L 44,915
Sun 11/24 H MIA 14-23 L 50,474
Sun 12/1 A SD 7-40 L 45,487
Sun 12/8 H NYJ 7-27 L 23,122
Sun 12/15 A PIT 24-30 L 35,953
Sun 12/22 A MIA 0-28 L 64,811

CHICAGO BEARS
Sun 9/8 H TB 38-28 W 57,828
Sun 9/15 H NE 20-7 W 60,533
Thu 9/19 A MIN 33-24 W 61,242
Sun 9/29 H WAS 45-10 W 63,708
Sun 10/6 A TB 27-19 W 51,795
Sun 10/13 A SF 26-10 W 60,523
Mon 10/21 H GB 23-7 W 65,095
Sun 10/27 H MIN 27-9 W 63,815
Sun 11/3 A GB 16-10 W 56,895

Sun	11/10	H	DET	24-3	W	53,467
Sun	11/17	A	DAL	44-0	W	63,750
Sun	11/24	H	ATL	36-0	W	61,769
Mon	12/2	A	MIA	24-38	L	75,594
Sun	12/8	H	IND	17-10	W	59,997
Sat	12/14	A	NYJ	19-6	W	74,752
Sun	12/22	A	DET	37-17	W	74,042

NFC Divisional Playoff

Sun	1/5	H	NYG	21-0	W	65,670

NFC Championship

Sun	1/12	H	LARM	24-0	W	66,030

Super Bowl XX

Sun	1/26	N	NE	46-10	W	73,818

CINCINNATI BENGALS

Sun	9/8	H	SEA	24-28	L	51,625
Sun	9/15	A	STL	27-41	L	46,321
Sun	9/22	H	SD	41-44	L	52,270
Mon	9/30	A	PIT	37-24	W	59,541
Sun	10/6	H	NYJ	20-29	L	51,785
Sun	10/13	H	NYG	35-30	W	53,112
Sun	10/20	A	HOU	27-44	L	35,590
Sun	10/27	H	PIT	26-21	W	55,421
Sun	11/3	A	BUF	23-17	W	25,640
Sun	11/10	H	CLE	27-10	W	57,293
Sun	11/17	A	LARI	6-13	L	52,501
Sun	11/24	A	CLE	6-24	L	69,439
Sun	12/1	H	HOU	45-27	W	46,140
Sun	12/8	H	DAL	50-24	W	56,936
Sun	12/15	A	WAS	24-27	L	50,544
Sun	12/22	A	NE	23-34	L	57,953

CLEVELAND BROWNS

Sun	9/8	H	STL	*24-27	L	62,107
Mon	9/16	H	PIT	17-7	W	76,042
Sun	9/22	A	DAL	7-20	L	61,456
Sun	9/29	A	SD	21-7	W	52,107
Sun	10/6	H	NE	24-20	W	60,639
Sun	10/13	A	HOU	21-6	W	38,386
Sun	10/20	H	LARI	20-21	L	77,928
Sun	10/27	H	WAS	7-14	L	75,540
Sun	11/3	A	PIT	9-10	L	51,976
Sun	11/10	A	CIN	10-27	L	57,293
Sun	11/17	H	BUF	17-7	W	44,915
Sun	11/24	H	CIN	24-6	W	69,439
Sun	12/1	A	NYG	35-33	W	66,482
Sun	12/8	A	SEA	13-31	L	58,477
Sun	12/15	H	HOU	28-21	W	40,793
Sun	12/22	A	NYJ	10-37	L	59,073

AFC Divisional Playoff

Sat	1/4	A	MIA	21-24	L	74,667

DALLAS COWBOYS

Mon	9/9	H	WAS	44-14	W	61,543
Sun	9/15	A	DET	21-26	L	72,985
Sun	9/22	H	CLE	20-7	W	61,456
Sun	9/29	A	HOU	17-10	W	49,686
Sun	10/6	A	NYG	30-29	W	74,981
Sun	10/13	H	PIT	27-13	W	62,932
Sun	10/20	A	PHI	14-16	L	70,114
Sun	10/27	H	ATL	24-10	W	57,941
Mon	11/4	A	STL	10-21	L	49,347
Sun	11/10	A	WAS	13-7	W	55,750
Sun	11/17	H	CHI	0-44	L	63,750
Sun	11/24	H	PHI	34-17	W	54,047
Thu	11/28	H	STL	35-17	W	54,125
Sun	12/8	A	CIN	24-50	L	56,936
Sun	12/15	H	NYG	28-21	W	62,310
Sun	12/22	A	SF	16-31	L	60,114

NFC Divisional Playoff

Sat	1/4	A	LARM	0-20	L	66,581

DENVER BRONCOS

Sun	9/8	A	LARM	16-20	L	52,522
Sun	9/15	H	NO	34-23	W	74,488
Sun	9/22	A	ATL	44-28	W	37,903
Sun	9/29	H	MIA	26-30	L	73,614
Sun	10/6	H	HOU	31-20	W	74,699
Sun	10/13	A	IND	15-10	W	60,128
Sun	10/20	H	SEA	*13-10	W	74,899
Sun	10/27	A	KC	30-10	W	68,248
Sun	11/3	A	SD	10-30	L	57,312
Mon	11/11	H	SF	17-16	W	73,173
Sun	11/17	H	SD	*30-24	W	74,376
Sun	11/24	A	LARI	*28-31	L	63,161
Sun	12/1	A	PIT	31-23	W	56,797
Sun	12/8	H	LARI	*14-17	L	75,042
Sat	12/14	H	KC	14-13	W	69,209
Fri	12/20	A	SEA	27-24	W	56,283

DETROIT LIONS

Sun	9/8	A	ATL	28-27	W	37,785
Sun	9/15	H	DAL	26-21	W	72,985
Sun	9/22	A	IND	6-14	L	60,042
Sun	9/29	H	TB	30-9	W	45,023
Sun	10/6	A	GB	10-43	L	55,914
Sun	10/13	A	WAS	3-24	L	52,845
Sun	10/20	H	SF	23-21	W	67,715
Sun	10/27	H	MIA	31-21	W	75,291
Sun	11/3	A	MIN	13-16	L	58,012
Sun	11/10	A	CHI	3-24	L	53,467
Sun	11/17	H	MIN	41-21	W	54,647
Sun	11/24	A	TB	*16-19	L	43,471
Thu	11/28	H	NYJ	31-20	W	65,531
Sun	12/8	A	NE	6-23	L	59,078
Sun	12/15	H	GB	23-26	L	49,379
Sun	12/22	H	CHI	17-37	L	74,042

GREEN BAY PACKERS

Sun	9/8	A	NE	20-26	L	49,488
Sun	9/15	H	NYG	23-20	W	56,149
Sun	9/22	H	NYJ	3-24	L	53,667
Sun	9/29	A	STL	28-43	L	48,598
Sun	10/6	H	DET	43-10	W	55,914
Sun	10/13	H	MIN	20-17	W	54,674
Mon	10/21	A	CHI	7-23	L	65,095
Sun	10/27	A	IND	10-37	L	59,708
Sun	11/3	H	CHI	10-16	L	56,895
Sun	11/10	A	MIN	27-17	W	59,970
Sun	11/17	H	NO	38-14	W	52,104
Sun	11/24	A	LARM	17-34	L	52,710
Sun	12/1	H	TB	21-0	W	19,856
Sun	12/8	H	MIA	24-34	L	52,671
Sun	12/15	A	DET	26-23	W	49,379
Sun	12/22	A	TB	20-17	W	33,992

HOUSTON OILERS

Sun	9/8	H	MIA	26-23	W	47,656
Sun	9/15	A	WAS	13-16	L	53,553
Sun	9/22	A	PIT	0-20	L	58,752
Sun	9/29	H	DAL	10-17	L	49,686
Sun	10/6	A	DEN	20-31	L	74,699
Sun	10/13	H	CLE	6-21	L	38,386
Sun	10/20	H	CIN	44-27	W	35,590
Sun	10/27	A	STL	20-10	W	43,190
Sun	11/3	H	KC	23-20	W	41,238
Sun	11/10	A	BUF	0-20	L	21,881
Sun	11/17	H	PIT	7-30	L	45,977
Sun	11/24	H	SD	37-35	W	34,336
Sun	12/1	A	CIN	27-45	L	46,140
Sun	12/8	H	NYG	14-35	L	36,576
Sun	12/15	A	CLE	21-28	L	40,793
Sun	12/22	A	IND	16-34	L	55,818

INDIANAPOLIS COLTS

Sun	9/8	A	PIT	3-45	L	57,279
Sun	9/15	A	MIA	13-30	L	53,693
Sun	9/22	H	DET	14-6	W	60,042
Sun	9/29	A	NYJ	20-25	L	61,987
Sun	10/6	H	BUF	49-17	W	60,003
Sun	10/13	H	DEN	10-15	L	60,128
Sun	10/20	A	BUF	9-21	L	28,430
Sun	10/27	H	GB	37-10	W	59,708
Sun	11/3	H	NYJ	17-35	L	59,683
Sun	11/10	A	NE	15-34	L	53,824
Sun	11/17	H	MIA	20-34	L	59,666
Sun	11/24	A	KC	7-20	L	19,762
Sun	12/1	H	NE	31-38	L	56,740
Sun	12/8	A	CHI	10-17	L	59,997
Sun	12/15	A	TB	31-23	W	25,577
Sun	12/22	H	HOU	34-16	W	55,818

KANSAS CITY CHIEFS

Sun	9/8	A	NO	47-27	W	57,760
Thu	9/12	H	LARI	36-20	W	72,686
Sun	9/22	A	MIA	0-31	L	70,244
Sun	9/29	H	SEA	28-7	W	50,485
Sun	10/6	A	LARI	10-19	L	55,133
Sun	10/13	A	SD	20-31	L	50,067
Sun	10/20	H	LARM	0-16	L	64,474
Sun	10/27	H	DEN	10-30	L	68,248
Sun	11/3	A	HOU	20-23	L	41,238
Sun	11/10	H	PIT	28-36	L	46,126
Sun	11/17	A	SF	3-31	L	56,447
Sun	11/24	H	IND	20-7	W	19,762
Sun	12/1	A	SEA	6-24	L	52,655
Sun	12/8	H	ATL	38-10	W	18,199
Sat	12/14	A	DEN	13-14	L	69,209
Sun	12/22	H	SD	38-24	W	18,178

LOS ANGELES RAIDERS

Sun	9/8	H	NYJ	31-0	W	57,123
Thu	9/12	A	KC	20-36	L	72,686
Sun	9/22	H	SF	10-34	L	87,006
Sun	9/29	A	NE	35-20	W	60,893
Sun	10/6	H	KC	19-10	W	55,133
Sun	10/13	H	NO	23-13	W	48,152
Sun	10/20	A	CLE	21-20	W	77,928
Mon	10/28	H	SD	34-21	W	69,297
Sun	11/3	A	SEA	3-33	L	64,060
Sun	11/10	A	SD	*34-40	L	58,566
Sun	11/17	H	CIN	13-6	W	52,501
Sun	11/24	H	DEN	*31-28	W	63,161
Sun	12/1	A	ATL	34-24	W	20,585
Sun	12/8	A	DEN	*17-14	W	75,042
Sun	12/15	H	SEA	13-3	W	77,425
Mon	12/23	A	LARM	16-6	W	66,676

AFC Divisional Playoff

Sun	1/5	H	NE	20-27	L	87,163

LOS ANGELES RAMS

Sun	9/8	H	DEN	20-16	W	52,522
Sun	9/15	A	PHI	17-6	W	60,920
Mon	9/23	A	SEA	35-24	W	63,292
Sun	9/29	H	ATL	17-6	W	49,870
Sun	10/6	H	MIN	13-10	W	61,139
Sun	10/13	A	TB	31-27	W	39,607
Sun	10/20	A	KC	16-0	W	64,474
Sun	10/27	H	SF	14-28	L	65,939
Sun	11/3	H	NO	28-10	W	49,030
Sun	11/10	A	NYG	19-24	L	74,603
Sun	11/17	A	ATL	14-30	L	29,960
Sun	11/24	H	GB	34-17	W	52,710
Sun	12/1	A	NO	3-29	L	44,122
Mon	12/9	A	SF	27-20	W	60,581
Sun	12/15	H	STL	46-14	W	52,052
Mon	12/23	H	LARI	6-16	L	66,676

NFC Divisional Playoff

Sat	1/4	H	DAL	20-0	W	66,581

NFC Championship

Sun	1/12	A	CHI	0-24	L	66,030

MIAMI DOLPHINS

Sun	9/8	A	HOU	23-26	L	47,656
Sun	9/15	H	IND	30-13	W	53,693
Sun	9/22	H	KC	31-0	W	70,244
Sun	9/29	A	DEN	30-26	W	73,614
Sun	10/6	H	PIT	24-20	W	72,820
Mon	10/14	A	NYJ	7-23	L	73,807
Sun	10/20	H	TB	41-38	W	62,335
Sun	10/27	A	DET	21-31	L	75,291
Sun	11/3	A	NE	13-17	L	58,811
Sun	11/10	H	NYJ	21-17	W	73,965
Sun	11/17	A	IND	34-20	W	59,666
Sun	11/24	A	BUF	23-14	W	50,474
Mon	12/2	H	CHI	38-24	W	75,594
Sun	12/8	A	GB	34-24	W	52,671
Mon	12/16	H	NE	30-27	W	69,489
Sun	12/22	H	BUF	28-0	W	64,811

AFC Divisional Playoff

Sat	1/4	H	CLE	24-21	W	74,667

AFC Championship

Sun	1/12	H	NE	14-31	L	75,662

MINNESOTA VIKINGS

Sun	9/8	H	SF	28-21	W	57,375
Sun	9/15	A	TB	31-16	W	46,188
Thu	9/19	H	CHI	24-33	L	61,242
Sun	9/29	A	BUF	27-20	W	45,667
Sun	10/6	A	LARM	10-13	L	61,139
Sun	10/13	A	GB	17-20	L	54,674
Sun	10/20	H	SD	21-17	W	61,670
Sun	10/27	A	CHI	9-27	L	63,815
Sun	11/3	H	DET	16-13	W	58,012
Sun	11/10	H	GB	17-27	L	59,970
Sun	11/17	A	DET	21-41	L	54,647
Sun	11/24	H	NO	23-30	L	54,117
Sun	12/1	A	PHI	28-23	W	54,688
Sun	12/8	H	TB	26-7	W	51,593
Sun	12/15	A	ATL	13-14	L	14,167
Sun	12/22	H	PHI	35-37	L	49,722

NEW ENGLAND PATRIOTS

Sun	9/8	H	GB	26-20	W	49,488
Sun	9/15	A	CHI	7-20	L	60,533
Sun	9/22	A	BUF	17-14	W	40,334
Sun	9/29	H	LARI	20-35	L	60,893
Sun	10/6	A	CLE	20-24	L	60,639
Sun	10/13	H	BUF	14-3	W	40,462
Sun	10/20	H	NYJ	20-13	W	58,163
Sun	10/27	A	TB	32-14	W	34,661
Sun	11/3	H	MIA	17-13	W	58,811
Sun	11/10	H	IND	34-15	W	53,824
Sun	11/17	A	SEA	20-13	W	60,345
Sun	11/24	A	NYJ	*13-16	L	74,100
Sun	12/1	A	IND	38-31	W	56,740
Sun	12/8	H	DET	23-6	W	59,078
Mon	12/16	A	MIA	27-30	L	69,489
Sun	12/22	H	CIN	34-23	W	57,953

AFC Wild-Card Playoff

Sat	12/28	A	NYJ	26-14	W	75,945

AFC Divisional Playoff

Sun	1/5	A	LARI	27-20	W	87,163

AFC Championship

Sun	1/12	A	MIA	31-14	W	75,662

Super Bowl XX

Sun	1/26	N	CHI	10-46	L	73,818

NEW ORLEANS SAINTS

Sun	9/8	H	KC	27-47	L	57,760
Sun	9/15	A	DEN	23-34	L	74,488
Sun	9/22	H	TB	20-13	W	45,320
Sun	9/29	A	SF	20-17	W	58,053
Sun	10/6	H	PHI	23-21	W	56,364
Sun	10/13	A	LARI	13-23	L	48,152
Sun	10/20	A	ATL	24-31	L	44,784
Sun	10/27	H	NYG	13-21	L	54,082
Sun	11/3	A	LARM	10-28	L	49,030
Sun	11/10	H	SEA	3-27	L	47,365
Sun	11/17	A	GB	14-38	L	52,104
Sun	11/24	A	MIN	30-23	W	54,117
Sun	12/1	H	LARM	29-3	W	44,122
Sun	12/8	A	STL	16-28	L	29,527

Sun 12/15 H SF 19-31 L 46,065
Sun 12/22 H ATL 10-16 L 37,717

NEW YORK GIANTS
Sun 9/8 H PHI 21-0 W 76,141
Sun 9/15 A GB 20-23 L 56,149
Sun 9/22 H STL 27-17 W 74,987
Sun 9/29 A PHI *16-10 W 66,696
Sun 10/6 H DAL 29-30 L 74,981
Sun 10/13 A CIN 30-35 L 53,112
Sun 10/20 H WAS 17-3 W 74,389
Sun 10/27 A NO 21-13 W 54,082
Sun 11/3 H TB 22-20 W 72,031
Sun 11/10 H LARM 24-19 W 74,603
Mon 11/18 A WAS 21-23 L 53,571
Sun 11/24 H STL 34-3 W 41,428
Sun 12/1 H CLE 33-35 L 66,482
Sun 12/8 A HOU 35-14 W 36,576
Sun 12/15 A DAL 21-28 L 62,310
Sat 12/21 H PIT 28-10 W 66,785

NFC Wild-Card Playoff
Sat 12/29 H SF 17-3 W 75,131

NFC Divisional Playoff
Sun 1/5 A CHI 0-21 L 65,670

NEW YORK JETS
Sun 9/8 A LARI 0-31 L 57,123
Sun 9/15 H BUF 42-3 W 63,449
Sun 9/22 A GB 24-3 W 53,667
Sun 9/29 H IND 25-20 W 61,987
Sun 10/6 A CIN 29-20 W 51,785
Mon 10/14 H MIA 23-7 W 73,807
Sun 10/20 A NE 13-20 L 58,163
Sun 10/27 H SEA 17-14 W 69,320
Sun 11/3 A IND 35-17 W 59,683
Sun 11/10 A MIA 17-21 L 73,965
Sun 11/17 H TB 62-28 W 65,344
Sun 11/24 H NE *16-13 W 74,100
Thu 11/28 A DET 20-31 L 65,531
Sun 12/8 A BUF 27-7 W 23,122
Sat 12/14 H CHI 6-19 L 74,752
Sun 12/22 H CLE 37-10 W 59,073

AFC Wild-Card Playoff
Sat 12/28 H NE 14-26 L 75,945

PHILADELPHIA EAGLES
Sun 9/8 A NYG 0-21 L 76,141
Sun 9/15 H LARM 6-17 L 60,920
Sun 9/22 A WAS 19-6 W 53,748
Sun 9/29 H NYG *10-16 L 66,696
Sun 10/6 A NO 21-23 L 56,364
Sun 10/13 A STL 30-7 W 48,186
Sun 10/20 H DAL 16-14 W 70,014
Sun 10/27 H BUF 21-17 W 60,987
Sun 11/3 A SF 13-24 L 58,383
Sun 11/10 H ATL *23-17 W 63,694
Sun 11/17 H STL 24-14 W 39,032
Sun 11/24 A DAL 17-34 L 54,047
Sun 12/1 H MIN 23-28 L 54,688
Sun 12/8 H WAS 12-17 L 60,737
Sun 12/15 A SD 14-20 L 45,569
Sun 12/22 A MIN 37-35 W 49,722

PITTSBURGH STEELERS
Sun 9/8 H IND 45-3 W 57,279
Mon 9/16 A CLE 7-17 L 76,042
Sun 9/22 H HOU 20-0 W 58,752
Mon 9/30 H CIN 24-37 L 59,541
Sun 10/6 A MIA 20-24 L 72,820
Sun 10/13 A DAL 13-27 L 62,932
Sun 10/20 H STL 23-10 W 56,478
Sun 10/27 A CIN 21-26 L 55,421
Sun 11/3 H CLE 10-9 W 51,976
Sun 11/10 A KC 36-28 W 46,126
Sun 11/17 A HOU 30-7 W 45,977

Sun 11/24 H WAS 23-30 L 59,293
Sun 12/1 H DEN 23-31 L 56,797
Sun 12/8 A SD 44-54 L 52,098
Sun 12/15 H BUF 30-24 L 35,953
Sat 12/21 A NYG 10-28 L 66,785

ST. LOUIS CARDINALS
Sun 9/8 A CLE *27-24 W 62,107
Sun 9/15 H CIN 41-27 W 46,321
Sun 9/22 A NYG 17-27 L 74,987
Sun 9/29 H GB 43-28 W 48,598
Mon 10/7 A WAS 10-27 L 53,134
Sun 10/13 H PHI 7-30 L 48,186
Sun 10/20 A PIT 10-23 L 56,478
Sun 10/27 H HOU 10-20 L 43,190
Mon 11/4 H DAL 21-10 W 49,347
Sun 11/10 A TB 0-16 L 34,736
Sun 11/17 A PHI 14-24 L 39,032
Sun 11/24 H NYG 3-34 L 41,248
Thu 11/28 A DAL 17-35 L 54,125
Sun 12/8 H NO 28-16 W 29,527
Sun 12/15 A LARM 14-46 L 52,052
Sat 12/21 H WAS 16-27 L 28,090

SAN DIEGO CHARGERS
Sun 9/8 A BUF 14-9 W 67,597
Sun 9/15 H SEA 35-49 L 54,420
Sun 9/22 A CIN 44-41 W 52,270
Sun 9/29 H CLE *7-21 L 52,107
Sun 10/6 A SEA 21-26 L 61,300
Sun 10/13 H KC 31-20 W 50,067
Sun 10/20 A MIN 17-21 L 61,670
Mon 10/28 A LARI 21-34 L 69,297
Sun 11/3 H DEN 30-10 W 57,312
Sun 11/10 H LARI *40-34 W 58,566
Sun 11/17 H DEN *24-30 L 74,376
Sun 11/24 A HOU 35-37 L 34,336
Sun 12/1 H BUF 40-7 W 45,487
Sun 12/8 H PIT 54-44 W 52,098
Sun 12/15 H PHI 20-14 W 45,569
Sun 12/22 A KC 34-38 L 18,178

SAN FRANCISCO 49ERS
Sun 9/8 A MIN 21-28 L 57,375
Sun 9/15 H ATL 35-16 W 58,923
Sun 9/22 A LARI 34-10 W 87,006
Sun 9/29 H NO 17-20 L 58,053
Sun 10/6 A ATL 38-17 W 44,740
Sun 10/13 H CHI 10-26 L 60,523
Sun 10/20 A DET 21-23 L 67,715
Sun 10/27 A LARM 28-14 W 65,939
Sun 11/3 H PHI 24-13 W 58,383
Mon 11/11 A DEN 16-17 L 73,173
Sun 11/17 A KC 31-3 W 56,447
Mon 11/25 H SEA 19-6 W 57,482
Sun 12/1 A WAS 35-8 W 51,321
Mon 12/9 H LARM 20-27 L 60,581
Sun 12/15 A NO 31-19 W 46,065
Sun 12/22 H DAL 31-16 W 60,114

NFC Wild-Card Playoff
Sat 12/29 A NYG 3-17 L 75,131

SEATTLE SEAHAWKS
Sun 9/8 A CIN 28-24 W 51,625
Sun 9/15 A SD 49-35 W 54,420
Mon 9/23 H LARM 24-35 L 63,292
Sun 9/29 A KC 7-28 L 50,485
Sun 10/6 H SD 26-21 W 61,300
Sun 10/13 H ATL 30-26 W 60,430
Sun 10/20 A DEN *10-13 L 74,899
Sun 10/27 A NYJ 14-17 L 69,320
Sun 11/3 H LARI 33-3 W 64,060
Sun 11/10 A NO 27-3 W 47,365
Sun 11/17 H NE 13-20 L 60,345
Mon 11/25 A SF 6-19 L 57,482

Sun 12/1 H KC 24-6 W 52,655
Sun 12/8 H CLE 31-13 W 58,477
Sun 12/15 A LARI 3-13 L 77,425
Fri 12/20 H DEN 24-27 L 56,283

TAMPA BAY BUCCANEERS
Sun 9/8 A CHI 28-38 L 57,828
Sun 9/15 H MIN 16-31 L 46,188
Sun 9/22 A NO 13-20 L 45,320
Sun 9/29 A DET 9-30 L 45,023
Sun 10/6 H CHI 19-27 L 51,795
Sun 10/13 A LARM 27-31 L 39,607
Sun 10/20 H MIA 38-41 L 62,335
Sun 10/27 H NE 14-32 L 34,661
Sun 11/3 A NYG 20-22 L 72,031
Sun 11/10 H STL 16-0 W 34,736
Sun 11/17 A NYJ 28-62 L 65,344
Sun 11/24 H DET *19-16 W 43,471
Sun 12/1 A GB 0-21 L 19,856
Sun 12/8 A MIN 7-26 L 51,593
Sun 12/15 H IND 23-31 L 25,577
Sun 12/22 H GB 17-20 L 33,992

WASHINGTON REDSKINS
Mon 9/9 A DAL 14-44 L 61,543
Sun 9/15 H HOU 16-13 W 53,553
Sun 9/22 H PHI 6-19 L 53,748
Sun 9/29 A CHI 10-45 L 63,708
Mon 10/7 H STL 27-10 W 53,134
Sun 10/13 H DET 24-3 W 52,845
Sun 10/20 A NYG 3-17 L 74,389
Sun 10/27 A CLE 14-7 W 75,540
Sun 11/3 H ATL 44-10 W 42,209
Sun 11/10 H DAL 7-13 L 55,750
Mon 11/18 H NYG 23-21 W 53,571
Sun 11/24 A PIT 30-23 W 59,293
Sun 12/1 H SF 8-35 L 51,321
Sun 12/8 A PHI 17-12 W 60,737
Sun 12/15 H CIN 27-24 W 50,544
Sat 12/21 A STL 27-16 W 28,090

1986 NFL
ATLANTA FALCONS
Sun 9/7 A NO 31-10 W 67,950
Sun 9/14 H STL 33-13 W 46,463
Sun 9/21 H DAL 37-35 W 62,880
Sun 9/28 A TB *23-20 W 38,950
Sun 10/5 H PHI 0-16 L 57,104
Sun 10/12 H LARM 26-14 W 51,662
Sun 10/19 H SF *10-10 T 55,306
Sun 10/26 A LARM 7-14 L 56,993
Sun 11/2 A NE 17-25 L 60,597
Sun 11/9 H NYJ 14-28 L 53,476
Sun 11/16 H CHI 10-13 L 55,520
Sun 11/23 A SF 0-20 L 58,747
Sun 11/30 A MIA 20-14 W 53,762
Sun 12/7 H IND 23-28 L 30,397
Sun 12/14 H NO 9-14 L 39,994
Sun 12/21 A DET 20-6 W 35,255

BUFFALO BILLS
Sun 9/7 H NYJ 24-28 L 79,951
Sun 9/14 A CIN *33-36 L 52,714
Sun 9/21 H STL 17-10 W 65,762
Sun 9/28 H KC 17-20 L 67,555
Sun 10/5 A NYJ 13-14 L 69,504
Sun 10/12 A MIA 14-27 L 49,467
Sun 10/19 H IND 24-13 W 50,050
Sun 10/26 H NE 3-23 L 77,808
Sun 11/2 H TB 28-34 L 32,806
Sun 11/9 H PIT 16-12 W 72,000
Sun 11/16 H MIA 24-34 L 76,474
Sun 11/23 A NE 19-22 L 60,455
Sun 11/30 A KC 17-14 W 31,492

Sun 12/7 H CLE 17-21 L 42,213
Sun 12/14 A IND 14-24 L 52,783
Sun 12/21 A HOU 7-16 L 31,409

CHICAGO BEARS
Sun 9/7 H CLE 41-31 W 66,030
Sun 9/14 H PHI *13-10 W 65,130
Mon 9/22 A GB 25-12 W 55,527
Sun 9/28 A CIN 44-7 W 55,146
Sun 10/5 H MIN 23-0 W 63,921
Sun 10/12 A HOU 20-7 W 46,026
Sun 10/19 A MIN 7-23 L 62,851
Sun 10/26 H DET 13-7 W 62,064
Mon 11/3 H LARM 17-20 L 64,877
Sun 11/9 H TB 23-3 W 70,097
Sun 11/16 A ATL 13-10 W 55,520
Sun 11/23 H GB 12-10 W 59,291
Sun 11/30 A PIT *13-10 W 61,425
Sun 12/7 H TB 48-14 W 52,746
Mon 12/15 A DET 16-13 W 75,602
Sun 12/21 A DAL 24-10 W 57,256

NFC Divisional Playoff
Sat 1/3 H WAS 13-27 L 65,524

CINCINNATI BENGALS
Sun 9/7 A KC 14-24 L 43,430
Sun 9/14 H BUF *36-33 W 52,714
Thu 9/18 A CLE 30-13 W 78,779
Sun 9/28 H CHI 7-44 L 55,146
Sun 10/5 A GB 34-28 W 51,230
Mon 10/13 H PIT 24-22 W 54,283
Sun 10/19 H HOU 31-28 W 53,844
Sun 10/26 A PIT 9-30 L 50,815
Sun 11/2 A DET 24-17 W 52,423
Sun 11/9 A HOU 28-32 L 32,130
Sun 11/16 H SEA 34-7 W 54,410
Sun 11/23 H MIN 24-20 W 53,003
Sun 11/30 A DEN 28-34 L 58,705
Sun 12/7 A NE 31-7 W 60,633
Sun 12/14 H CLE 3-34 L 58,062
Sun 12/21 H NYJ 52-21 W 51,619

CLEVELAND BROWNS
Sun 9/7 A CHI 31-41 L 66,030
Sun 9/14 A HOU 23-20 W 46,049
Thu 9/18 H CIN 13-30 L 78,779
Sun 9/28 H DET 24-21 W 72,029
Sun 10/5 A PIT 27-24 W 57,327
Sun 10/12 H KC 20-7 W 71,278
Sun 10/19 H GB 14-17 L 76,438
Sun 10/26 A MIN 23-20 W 59,133
Sun 11/2 A IND 24-9 W 57,962
Mon 11/10 H MIA 26-16 W 77,949
Sun 11/16 A LARI 14-27 L 65,461
Sun 11/23 H PIT *37-31 W 76,452
Sun 11/30 H HOU *13-10 W 62,309
Sun 12/7 A BUF 21-17 W 42,213
Sun 12/14 A CIN 34-3 W 58,062
Sun 12/21 H SD 47-17 W 68,505

AFC Divisional Playoff
Sat 1/3 H NYJ **23-20 W 79,720

AFC Championship
Sun 1/11 H DEN *20-23 L 79,973

DALLAS COWBOYS
Mon 9/8 H NYG 31-28 W 59,804
Sun 9/14 A DET 31-7 W 73,812
Sun 9/21 H ATL 35-37 L 62,880
Mon 9/29 A STL 31-7 W 49,077
Sun 10/5 A DEN 14-29 L 76,082
Sun 10/12 H WAS 30-6 W 63,264
Sun 10/19 H PHI 17-14 W 68,572
Sun 10/26 A STL 37-6 W 60,756
Sun 11/2 A NYG 14-17 L 74,871
Sun 11/9 H LARI 13-17 L 61,706

Sun	11/16	A	SD	24-21	W	55,622
Sun	11/23	A	WAS	14-41	L	55,642
Thu	11/27	H	SEA	14-31	L	58,023
Sun	12/7	A	LARM	10-29	L	64,949
Sun	12/14	H	PHI	21-23	L	46,117
Sun	12/21	H	CHI	10-24	L	57,256

DENVER BRONCOS

Sun	9/7	H	LARI	38-36	W	75,695
Mon	9/15	A	PIT	21-10	W	57,305
Sun	9/21	A	PHI	33-7	W	63,839
Sun	9/28	H	NE	27-20	W	75,804
Sun	10/5	H	DAL	29-14	W	76,082
Sun	10/12	A	SD	31-14	W	55,662
Mon	10/20	A	NYJ	10-22	L	73,759
Sun	10/26	H	SEA	20-13	W	76,089
Sun	11/2	A	LARI	21-10	W	90,153
Sun	11/9	H	SD	3-9	L	75,012
Sun	11/16	H	KC	38-17	W	75,745
Sun	11/23	A	NYG	16-19	L	75,116
Sun	11/30	H	CIN	34-28	W	58,705
Sun	12/7	A	KC	10-37	L	47,019
Sat	12/13	H	WAS	31-30	W	75,905
Sat	12/20	A	SEA	16-41	L	63,697
AFC Divisional Playoff						
Sun	1/4	H	NE	22-17	W	76,105
AFC Championship						
Sun	1/11	A	CLE	*23-20	W	79,973
Super Bowl XXI						
Sun	1/25	N	NYG	20-39	L	101,063

DETROIT LIONS

Sun	9/7	A	MIN	13-10	W	54,851
Sun	9/14	H	DAL	7-31	L	73,812
Sun	9/21	H	TB	20-24	L	38,453
Sun	9/28	A	CLE	21-24	L	72,029
Sun	10/5	H	HOU	24-13	W	41,960
Sun	10/12	A	GB	21-14	W	52,290
Sun	10/19	A	LARM	10-14	L	50,992
Sun	10/26	A	CHI	7-13	L	62,064
Sun	11/2	H	CIN	17-24	L	52,423
Sun	11/9	H	MIN	10-24	L	53,725
Sun	11/16	A	PHI	13-11	W	54,568
Sun	11/23	A	TB	38-17	W	30,029
Thu	11/27	H	GB	40-44	L	61,199
Sun	12/7	A	PIT	17-27	L	45,042
Mon	12/15	H	CHI	13-16	L	75,602
Sun	12/21	H	ATL	6-20	L	35,255

GREEN BAY PACKERS

Sun	9/7	H	HOU	3-31	L	54,065
Sun	9/14	A	NO	10-24	L	46,383
Mon	9/22	H	CHI	12-25	L	55,527
Sun	9/28	A	MIN	7-42	L	60,478
Sun	10/5	H	CIN	28-34	L	51,230
Sun	10/12	H	DET	14-21	L	52,290
Sun	10/19	A	CLE	17-14	W	76,438
Sun	10/26	H	SF	17-31	L	50,557
Sun	11/2	A	PIT	3-27	L	52,831
Sun	11/9	H	WAS	7-16	L	47,728
Sun	11/16	H	TB	31-7	W	48,271
Sun	11/23	A	CHI	10-12	L	59,291
Thu	11/27	A	DET	44-40	W	61,199
Sun	12/7	H	MIN	6-32	L	47,637
Sun	12/14	A	TB	21-7	W	30,099
Sat	12/20	A	NYG	24-55	L	71,351

HOUSTON OILERS

Sun	9/7	A	GB	31-3	W	54,065
Sun	9/14	H	CLE	20-23	L	46,049
Sun	9/21	A	KC	13-27	L	43,699
Sun	9/28	H	PIT	*16-22	L	42,001
Sun	10/5	A	DET	13-24	L	41,960
Sun	10/12	H	CHI	7-20	L	46,026
Sun	10/19	A	CIN	28-31	L	53,844
Sun	10/26	H	LARI	17-28	L	41,641
Sun	11/2	A	MIA	7-28	L	43,804
Sun	11/9	H	CIN	32-28	W	32,130
Sun	11/16	A	PIT	10-21	L	49,724
Sun	11/23	H	IND	31-17	W	31,792
Sun	11/30	A	CLE	*10-13	L	62,309
Sun	12/7	A	SD	0-27	L	40,103
Sun	12/14	H	MIN	23-10	W	32,738
Sun	12/21	H	BUF	16-7	W	31,409

INDIANAPOLIS COLTS

Sun	9/7	A	NE	3-33	L	55,208
Sun	9/14	A	MIA	10-30	L	51,848
Sun	9/21	H	LARM	7-24	L	59,012
Sun	9/28	H	NYJ	7-26	L	56,075
Sun	10/5	A	SF	14-35	L	57,252
Sun	10/12	H	NO	14-17	L	53,512
Sun	10/19	A	BUF	13-24	L	50,050
Sun	10/26	H	MIA	13-17	L	58,350
Sun	11/2	H	CLE	9-24	L	57,962
Sun	11/9	H	NE	21-30	L	56,890
Sun	11/16	A	NYJ	16-31	L	65,149
Sun	11/23	A	HOU	17-31	L	31,792
Sun	11/30	H	SD	3-17	L	47,950
Sun	12/7	A	ATL	28-23	W	30,397
Sun	12/14	H	BUF	24-14	W	52,783
Sun	12/21	A	LARI	30-24	W	41,349

KANSAS CITY CHIEFS

Sun	9/7	H	CIN	24-14	W	43,430
Sun	9/14	A	SEA	17-23	L	61,068
Sun	9/21	H	HOU	27-13	W	43,699
Sun	9/28	A	BUF	20-17	W	67,555
Sun	10/5	H	LARI	17-24	L	74,430
Sun	10/12	A	CLE	7-20	L	71,278
Sun	10/19	H	SD	42-41	W	55,767
Sun	10/26	H	TB	27-20	W	36,230
Sun	11/2	A	SD	24-23	W	44,518
Sun	11/9	H	SEA	27-7	W	53,628
Sun	11/16	A	DEN	17-38	L	75,745
Sun	11/23	A	STL	14-23	L	29,680
Sun	11/30	H	BUF	14-17	L	31,492
Sun	12/7	H	DEN	37-10	W	47,019
Sun	12/14	A	LARI	20-17	W	60,952
Sun	12/21	A	PIT	24-19	W	47,150
AFC Wild-Card Playoff						
Sun	12/28	A	NYJ	15-35	L	75,210

LOS ANGELES RAIDERS

Sun	9/7	A	DEN	36-38	L	75,695
Sun	9/14	A	WAS	6-10	L	55,235
Sun	9/21	H	NYG	9-14	L	71,164
Sun	9/28	H	SD	17-13	W	63,153
Sun	10/5	A	KC	24-17	W	74,430
Sun	10/12	H	SEA	14-10	W	70,635
Sun	10/19	A	MIA	30-28	W	53,421
Sun	10/26	A	HOU	28-17	W	41,641
Sun	11/2	H	DEN	10-21	L	90,153
Sun	11/9	A	DAL	17-13	W	61,706
Sun	11/16	H	CLE	27-14	W	65,461
Thu	11/20	A	SD	*37-31	W	56,031
Sun	11/30	H	PHI	*27-33	L	53,338
Mon	12/8	A	SEA	0-37	L	62,923
Sun	12/14	H	KC	17-20	L	60,952
Sun	12/21	H	IND	24-30	L	41,349

LOS ANGELES RAMS

Sun	9/7	A	STL	16-10	W	40,347
Sun	9/14	H	SF	16-13	W	65,195
Sun	9/21	A	IND	24-7	W	59,012
Sun	9/28	A	PHI	20-34	L	65,646
Sun	10/5	H	TB	*26-20	W	50,585
Sun	10/12	A	ATL	14-26	L	51,662
Sun	10/19	H	DET	14-10	W	50,992
Sun	10/26	H	ATL	14-7	W	56,993
Mon	11/3	A	CHI	20-17	W	64,877
Sun	11/9	A	NO	0-6	L	62,352
Sun	11/16	H	NE	28-30	L	64,339
Sun	11/23	H	NO	26-13	W	58,600
Sun	11/30	A	NYJ	17-3	W	70,539
Sun	12/7	H	DAL	29-10	W	64,949
Sun	12/14	H	MIA	*31-37	L	62,629
Fri	12/19	A	SF	14-24	L	60,366
NFC Wild-Card Playoff						
Sun	12/28	A	WAS	7-19	L	54,567

MIAMI DOLPHINS

Sun	9/7	A	SD	28-50	L	57,726
Sun	9/14	H	IND	30-10	W	51,848
Sun	9/21	A	NYJ	*45-51	L	71,025
Sun	9/28	H	SF	16-31	L	70,264
Sun	10/5	A	NE	7-34	L	60,689
Sun	10/12	H	BUF	27-14	W	49,467
Sun	10/19	H	LARI	28-30	L	53,421
Sun	10/26	A	IND	17-13	W	58,350
Sun	11/2	H	HOU	28-7	W	43,804
Mon	11/10	A	CLE	16-26	L	77,949
Sun	11/16	A	BUF	34-24	W	76,474
Mon	11/24	H	NYJ	45-3	W	70,206
Sun	11/30	H	ATL	14-20	L	53,762
Sun	12/7	A	NO	31-27	W	64,761
Sun	12/14	A	LARM	*37-31	W	62,629
Mon	12/22	H	NE	27-34	L	74,516

MINNESOTA VIKINGS

Sun	9/7	H	DET	10-13	L	54,851
Sun	9/14	A	TB	23-10	W	34,579
Sun	9/21	H	PIT	31-7	W	56,795
Sun	9/28	H	GB	42-7	W	60,478
Sun	10/5	A	CHI	0-23	L	63,921
Sun	10/12	A	SF	*27-24	W	58,637
Sun	10/19	H	CHI	23-7	W	62,851
Sun	10/26	H	CLE	20-23	L	59,133
Sun	11/2	A	WAS	*38-44	L	51,928
Sun	11/9	A	DET	24-10	W	53,725
Sun	11/16	H	NYG	20-22	L	62,003
Sun	11/23	A	CIN	20-24	L	53,003
Sun	11/30	H	TB	45-13	W	56,235
Sun	12/7	A	GB	32-6	W	47,637
Sun	12/14	A	HOU	10-23	L	32,738
Sun	12/21	H	NO	33-17	W	51,209

NEW ENGLAND PATRIOTS

Sun	9/7	H	IND	33-3	W	55,208
Thu	9/11	A	NYJ	20-6	W	72,422
Sun	9/21	H	SEA	31-38	L	58,977
Sun	9/28	A	DEN	20-27	L	75,804
Sun	10/5	H	MIA	34-7	W	60,689
Sun	10/12	H	NYJ	24-31	L	60,342
Sun	10/19	A	PIT	34-0	W	54,743
Sun	10/26	A	BUF	23-3	W	77,808
Sun	11/2	H	ATL	25-17	W	60,597
Sun	11/9	A	IND	30-21	W	56,890
Sun	11/16	A	LARM	30-28	W	64,339
Sun	11/23	H	BUF	22-19	W	60,455
Sun	11/30	A	NO	21-20	W	58,259
Sun	12/7	H	CIN	7-31	L	60,633
Sun	12/14	H	SF	24-29	L	60,787
Mon	12/22	A	MIA	34-27	W	74,516
AFC Divisional Playoff						
Sun	1/4	A	DEN	17-22	L	76,105

NEW ORLEANS SAINTS

Sun	9/7	H	ATL	10-31	L	67,950
Sun	9/14	H	GB	24-10	W	46,383
Sun	9/21	A	SF	17-26	L	58,297
Sun	9/28	A	NYG	17-20	L	72,769
Sun	10/5	H	WAS	6-14	L	57,378
Sun	10/12	A	IND	17-14	W	53,512
Sun	10/19	H	TB	38-7	W	43,355
Sun	10/26	A	NYJ	23-28	L	44,246
Sun	11/2	H	SF	23-10	W	53,234
Sun	11/9	H	LARM	6-0	W	62,352
Sun	11/16	A	STL	16-7	W	32,069
Sun	11/23	A	LARM	13-26	L	58,600
Sun	11/30	H	NE	20-21	L	58,259
Sun	12/7	H	MIA	27-31	L	64,761
Sun	12/14	A	ATL	14-9	W	39,994
Sun	12/21	A	MIN	17-33	L	51,209

NEW YORK GIANTS

Mon	9/8	A	DAL	28-31	L	59,804
Sun	9/14	H	SD	20-7	W	74,921
Sun	9/21	A	LARI	14-9	W	71,164
Sun	9/28	H	NO	20-17	W	72,769
Sun	10/5	A	STL	13-6	W	40,562
Sun	10/12	H	PHI	35-3	W	74,221
Sun	10/19	A	SEA	12-17	L	62,282
Mon	10/27	H	WAS	27-20	W	75,923
Sun	11/2	H	DAL	17-14	W	74,871
Sun	11/9	A	PHI	17-14	W	60,601
Sun	11/16	A	MIN	22-20	W	62,003
Sun	11/23	H	DEN	19-16	W	75,116
Mon	12/1	A	SF	21-17	W	59,777
Sun	12/7	A	WAS	24-14	W	55,642
Sun	12/14	H	STL	27-7	W	75,261
Sat	12/20	H	GB	55-24	W	71,351
NFC Divisional Playoff						
Sun	1/4	H	SF	49-3	W	75,691
NFC Championship						
Sun	1/11	H	WAS	17-0	W	76,891
Super Bowl XXI						
Sun	1/25	N	DEN	39-20	W	101,063

NEW YORK JETS

Sun	9/7	A	BUF	28-24	W	79,951
Thu	9/11	H	NE	6-20	L	72,422
Sun	9/21	H	MIA	*51-45	W	71,025
Sun	9/28	A	IND	26-7	W	56,075
Sun	10/5	H	BUF	14-13	W	69,504
Sun	10/12	A	NE	31-24	W	60,342
Mon	10/20	H	DEN	22-10	W	73,759
Sun	10/26	H	NO	28-23	W	44,246
Sun	11/2	A	SEA	38-7	W	62,497
Sun	11/9	A	ATL	28-14	W	53,476
Sun	11/16	H	IND	31-16	W	65,149
Mon	11/24	A	MIA	3-45	L	70,206
Sun	11/30	H	LARM	3-17	L	70,539
Sun	12/7	A	SF	10-24	L	58,091
Sat	12/13	H	PIT	24-45	L	58,044
Sun	12/21	A	CIN	21-52	L	51,619
AFC Wild-Card Playoff						
Sun	12/28	H	KC	35-15	W	75,210
AFC Divisional Playoff						
Sat	1/3	A	CLE	**20-23	L	79,720

PHILADELPHIA EAGLES

Sun	9/7	A	WAS	14-41	L	53,982
Sun	9/14	A	CHI	*10-13	L	65,130
Sun	9/21	H	DEN	7-33	L	63,839
Sun	9/28	H	LARM	34-20	W	65,646
Sun	10/5	A	ATL	16-0	W	57,104
Sun	10/12	A	NYG	3-35	L	74,221
Sun	10/19	H	DAL	14-17	L	68,572
Sun	10/26	H	SD	23-7	W	41,469
Sun	11/2	A	STL	10-13	L	33,051
Sun	11/9	H	NYG	14-17	L	60,601
Sun	11/16	H	DET	11-13	L	54,568
Sun	11/23	A	SEA	20-24	L	55,786
Sun	11/30	A	LARI	*33-27	W	53,338
Sun	12/7	H	STL	*10-10	T	50,148
Sun	12/14	A	DAL	23-21	W	46,117
Sun	12/21	H	WAS	14-21	L	61,816

PITTSBURGH STEELERS

Sun	9/7	A	SEA	0-30	L	61,461
Mon	9/15	H	DEN	10-21	L	57,305
Sun	9/21	A	MIN	7-31	L	56,795
Sun	9/28	A	HOU	*22-16	W	42,001
Sun	10/5	H	CLE	24-27	L	57,327
Mon	10/13	A	CIN	22-24	L	54,283
Sun	10/19	H	NE	0-34	L	54,743
Sun	10/26	H	CIN	30-9	W	50,815
Sun	11/2	H	GB	27-3	W	52,831
Sun	11/9	A	BUF	12-16	L	72,000
Sun	11/16	H	HOU	21-10	W	49,724
Sun	11/23	A	CLE	*31-37	L	76,452
Sun	11/30	A	CHI	*10-13	L	61,425
Sun	12/7	H	DET	27-17	W	45,042
Sat	12/13	A	NYJ	45-24	W	58,044
Sun	12/21	H	KC	19-24	L	47,150

ST. LOUIS CARDINALS

Sun	9/7	H	LARM	10-16	L	40,347
Sun	9/14	A	ATL	13-33	L	46,463
Sun	9/21	A	BUF	10-17	L	65,762
Mon	9/29	H	DAL	7-31	L	49,077
Sun	10/5	H	NYG	6-13	L	40,562
Sun	10/12	A	TB	30-19	W	33,307
Sun	10/19	A	WAS	21-28	L	53,494
Sun	10/26	A	DAL	6-37	L	60,756
Sun	11/2	H	PHI	13-10	W	33,051
Sun	11/9	A	SF	17-43	L	59,172
Sun	11/16	H	NO	7-16	L	32,069
Sun	11/23	H	KC	23-14	W	29,680
Sun	11/30	H	WAS	17-20	L	35,637
Sun	12/7	A	PHI	*10-10	T	50,148
Sun	12/14	A	NYG	7-27	L	75,261
Sun	12/21	H	TB	21-17	W	23,957

SAN DIEGO CHARGERS

Sun	9/7	H	MIA	50-28	W	57,726
Sun	9/14	A	NYG	7-20	L	74,921
Sun	9/21	H	WAS	27-30	L	57,853
Sun	9/28	A	LARI	13-17	L	63,153
Mon	10/6	A	SEA	7-33	L	63,207
Sun	10/12	H	DEN	14-31	L	55,662
Sun	10/19	A	KC	41-42	L	55,767
Sun	10/26	A	PHI	7-23	L	41,469
Sun	11/2	H	KC	23-24	L	44,518
Sun	11/9	A	DEN	9-3	W	75,012
Sun	11/16	H	DAL	21-24	L	55,622
Thu	11/20	H	LARI	*31-37	L	56,031
Sun	11/30	A	IND	17-3	W	47,950
Sun	12/7	H	HOU	27-0	W	40,103
Sun	12/14	H	SEA	24-34	L	47,096
Sun	12/21	A	CLE	17-47	L	68,505

SAN FRANCISCO 49ERS

Sun	9/7	A	TB	31-7	W	50,780
Sun	9/14	A	LARM	13-16	L	65,195
Sun	9/21	H	NO	26-17	W	58,297
Sun	9/28	A	MIA	31-16	W	70,264
Sun	10/5	H	IND	35-14	W	57,252
Sun	10/12	H	MIN	*24-27	L	58,637
Sun	10/19	A	ATL	*10-10	T	55,306
Sun	10/26	A	GB	31-17	W	50,557
Sun	11/2	A	NO	10-23	L	53,234
Sun	11/9	H	STL	43-17	W	59,172
Mon	11/17	A	WAS	6-14	L	54,774
Sun	11/23	H	ATL	20-0	W	58,747
Mon	12/1	H	NYG	17-21	L	59,777
Sun	12/7	H	NYJ	24-10	W	58,091
Sun	12/14	A	NE	29-24	W	60,787
Fri	12/19	H	LARM	24-14	W	60,366

NFC DIVISIONAL PLAYOFF

Sun	1/4	A	NYG	3-49	L	75,691

SEATTLE SEAHAWKS

Sun	9/7	H	PIT	30-0	W	61,461
Sun	9/14	H	KC	23-17	W	61,068
Sun	9/21	A	NE	38-31	W	58,977
Sun	9/28	A	WAS	14-19	L	54,157
Mon	10/6	H	SD	33-7	W	63,207
Sun	10/12	A	LARI	10-14	L	70,635
Sun	10/19	H	NYG	17-12	W	62,282
Sun	10/26	A	DEN	13-20	L	76,089
Sun	11/2	H	NYJ	7-38	L	62,497
Sun	11/9	A	KC	7-27	L	53,628
Sun	11/16	A	CIN	7-34	L	54,410
Sun	11/23	H	PHI	24-20	W	55,786
Thu	11/27	A	DAL	31-14	W	58,023
Mon	12/8	H	LARI	37-0	W	62,923
Sun	12/14	A	SD	34-24	W	47,096
Sat	12/20	H	DEN	41-16	W	63,697

TAMPA BAY BUCCANEERS

Sun	9/7	H	SF	7-31	L	50,780
Sun	9/14	H	MIN	10-23	L	34,579
Sun	9/21	A	DET	24-20	W	38,453
Sun	9/28	H	ATL	*20-23	L	38,950
Sun	10/5	A	LARM	*20-26	L	50,585
Sun	10/12	H	STL	19-30	L	33,307
Sun	10/19	A	NO	7-38	L	43,355
Sun	10/26	A	KC	20-27	L	36,230
Sun	11/2	H	BUF	34-28	W	32,806
Sun	11/9	H	CHI	3-23	L	70,097
Sun	11/16	A	GB	7-31	L	48,271
Sun	11/23	H	DET	17-38	L	30,029
Sun	11/30	A	MIN	13-45	L	56,235
Sun	12/7	A	CHI	14-48	L	52,746
Sun	12/14	H	GB	7-21	L	30,099
Sun	12/21	A	STL	17-21	L	23,957

WASHINGTON REDSKINS

Sun	9/7	H	PHI	41-14	W	53,982
Sun	9/14	H	LARI	10-6	W	55,235
Sun	9/21	A	SD	30-27	W	57,853
Sun	9/28	H	SEA	19-14	W	54,157
Sun	10/5	A	NO	14-6	W	57,378
Sun	10/12	A	DAL	6-30	L	63,264
Sun	10/19	H	STL	28-21	W	53,494
Mon	10/27	A	NYG	20-27	L	57,378
Sun	11/2	H	MIN	*44-38	W	51,928
Sun	11/9	A	GB	16-7	W	47,728
Mon	11/17	H	SF	14-6	W	54,774
Sun	11/23	H	DAL	41-14	W	55,662
Sun	11/30	A	STL	20-17	W	35,637
Sun	12/7	H	NYG	14-24	L	55,642
Sat	12/13	A	DEN	30-31	L	75,905
Sun	12/21	A	PHI	21-14	W	61,816

NFC WILD-CARD PLAYOFF

Sun	12/28	H	LARM	19-7	W	54,567

NFC DIVISIONAL PLAYOFF

Sat	1/3	A	CHI	27-13	W	65,524

NFC CHAMPIONSHIP

Sun	1/11	A	NYG	0-17	L	76,891

1987 NFL

ATLANTA FALCONS

Sun	9/13	A	TB	10-48	L	51,250
Sun	9/20	H	WAS	21-20	W	50,882
Sun	10/4	H	PIT	12-28	L	16,667
Sun	10/11	H	SF	17-25	L	8,684
Sun	10/18	H	LARM	24-20	W	15,813
Sun	10/25	A	HOU	33-37	L	29,062
Sun	11/1	H	NO	0-38	L	42,196
Sun	11/8	A	CLE	3-38	L	71,135
Sun	11/15	H	CIN	10-16	L	25,758
Sun	11/22	A	MIN	13-24	L	53,866
Sun	11/29	H	STL	21-34	L	15,909
Sun	12/6	A	DAL	21-10	W	40,103
Sun	12/13	A	LARM	0-33	L	43,310
Sun	12/20	A	SF	7-35	L	54,698
Sun	12/27	H	DET	13-30	L	13,906

BUFFALO BILLS

Sun	9/13	H	NYJ	28-31	L	76,718
Sun	9/20	H	HOU	34-30	W	58,534
Sun	10/4	H	IND	6-47	L	9,860
Sun	10/11	A	NE	7-14	L	11,878
Sun	10/18	H	NYG	*6-3	W	15,737
Sun	10/25	A	MIA	*34-31	W	61,295
Sun	11/1	H	WAS	7-27	L	71,640
Sun	11/8	H	DEN	21-14	W	63,698
Sun	11/15	A	CLE	21-27	L	78,409
Sun	11/22	A	NYJ	17-14	W	58,407
Sun	11/29	H	MIA	27-0	W	68,055
Sun	12/6	A	LARI	21-34	L	43,143
Sun	12/13	A	IND	27-3	W	60,253
Sun	12/20	H	NE	7-13	L	74,945
Sun	12/27	A	PHI	7-17	L	57,547

CHICAGO BEARS

Mon	9/14	H	NYG	34-19	W	65,704
Sun	9/20	H	TB	20-3	W	63,551
Sun	10/4	A	PHI	35-3	W	4,074
Sun	10/11	H	MIN	27-7	W	32,113
Sun	10/18	H	NO	17-19	L	46,813
Sun	10/25	A	TB	27-26	W	70,747
Sun	11/1	H	KC	31-28	W	63,498
Sun	11/8	A	GB	26-24	W	53,320
Mon	11/16	A	DEN	29-31	L	75,783
Sun	11/22	H	DET	30-10	W	63,357
Sun	11/29	H	GB	23-10	W	61,638
Sun	12/6	A	MIN	30-24	W	62,331
Mon	12/14	A	SF	0-41	L	63,509
Sun	12/20	H	SEA	21-34	L	62,518
Sun	12/27	A	LARI	6-3	W	78,019

NFC DIVISIONAL PLAYOFF

Sun	1/10	H	WAS	17-21	L	66,030

CINCINNATI BENGALS

Sun	9/13	A	IND	23-21	W	59,387
Sun	9/20	H	SF	26-27	L	53,498
Sun	10/4	H	SD	9-10	L	26,209
Sun	10/11	A	SEA	17-10	W	31,739
Sun	10/18	H	CLE	0-34	L	40,179
Sun	10/25	A	PIT	20-23	L	53,692
Sun	11/1	H	HOU	29-31	L	52,700
Sun	11/8	H	MIA	14-20	L	53,840
Sun	11/15	A	ATL	16-10	W	25,758
Sun	11/22	H	PIT	16-30	L	52,795
Sun	11/29	A	NYJ	20-27	L	41,135
Sun	12/6	H	KC	*30-27	W	46,489
Sun	12/13	A	CLE	24-38	L	77,331
Sun	12/20	H	NO	24-41	L	43,424
Sun	12/27	A	HOU	17-21	L	49,775

CLEVELAND BROWNS

Sun	9/13	A	NO	21-28	L	59,900
Sun	9/20	H	PIT	34-10	W	79,543
Sun	10/4	A	NE	20-10	W	14,830
Sun	10/11	H	HOU	10-15	L	38,927
Sun	10/18	A	CIN	34-0	W	40,179
Mon	10/26	H	LARM	30-17	W	76,933
Sun	11/1	A	SD	*24-27	L	55,381
Sun	11/8	H	ATL	38-3	W	71,135
Sun	11/15	H	BUF	27-21	W	78,409
Sun	11/22	A	HOU	40-7	W	51,161
Sun	11/29	A	SF	24-38	L	60,248
Sun	12/6	H	IND	7-9	L	70,661
Sun	12/13	H	CIN	38-24	W	77,331
Sun	12/20	A	LARI	24-17	W	40,275
Sat	12/26	A	PIT	19-13	W	56,394

AFC DIVISIONAL PLAYOFF

Sat	1/9	H	IND	38-21	W	78,586

AFC CHAMPIONSHIP

Sun	1/17	A	DEN	33-38	L	75,993

DALLAS COWBOYS

Sun	9/13	A	STL	13-24	L	47,241
Sun	9/20	A	NYG	16-14	W	73,426
Sun	10/4	A	NYJ	38-24	W	12,370
Sun	10/11	H	PHI	41-22	W	40,622
Mon	10/19	H	WAS	7-13	L	60,415
Sun	10/25	A	PHI	20-37	L	61,630
Mon	11/2	H	NYG	33-24	W	55,730
Sun	11/8	A	DET	17-27	L	45,325
Sun	11/15	A	NE	*23-17	W	60,567
Sun	11/22	H	MIA	14-20	L	56,519
Thu	11/26	H	MIN	*38-44	L	54,229
Sun	12/6	H	ATL	10-21	L	40,103
Sun	12/13	A	WAS	20-24	L	54,882
Mon	12/21	A	LARM	29-21	W	60,700
Sun	12/27	H	STL	21-16	W	36,788

DENVER BRONCOS

Sun	9/13	H	SEA	40-17	W	75,999
Sun	9/20	A	GB	*17-17	T	50,624
Sun	10/4	H	HOU	10-40	L	38,494
Mon	10/12	H	LARI	30-14	W	61,230
Sun	10/18	A	KC	26-17	W	20,296
Mon	10/26	A	MIN	27-34	L	51,011
Sun	11/1	H	DET	34-0	W	75,172
Sun	11/8	A	BUF	14-21	L	63,698
Mon	11/16	H	CHI	31-29	W	75,783
Sun	11/22	A	LARI	23-17	W	61,318
Sun	11/29	A	SD	31-17	W	61,880
Sun	12/6	H	NE	31-20	W	75,795
Sun	12/13	A	SEA	21-28	L	61,759
Sat	12/19	H	KC	20-17	W	75,053
Sun	12/27	H	SD	24-0	W	21,189

AFC DIVISIONAL PLAYOFF

Sun	1/10	H	HOU	34-10	W	75,968

AFC CHAMPIONSHIP

Sun	1/17	H	CLE	38-33	W	75,993

SUPER BOWL XXII

Sun	1/31	N	WAS	10-42	L	73,302

DETROIT LIONS

Sun	9/13	A	MIN	19-34	L	57,061
Sun	9/20	A	LARI	7-27	L	50,300
Sun	10/4	H	TB	27-31	L	4,919
Sun	10/11	A	GB	*19-16	W	35,779
Sun	10/18	H	SEA	14-37	L	8,310
Sun	10/25	H	GB	33-34	L	27,278
Sun	11/1	A	DEN	0-34	L	75,172
Sun	11/8	H	DAL	27-17	W	45,325
Sun	11/15	A	WAS	13-20	L	53,593
Sun	11/22	A	CHI	10-30	L	63,357
Thu	11/26	H	KC	20-27	L	43,820
Sun	12/6	H	LARM	16-37	L	33,413
Sun	12/13	A	TB	20-10	W	41,699
Sun	12/20	H	MIN	14-17	L	27,693
Sun	12/27	A	ATL	30-13	W	13,906

GREEN BAY PACKERS

Sun	9/13	H	LARI	0-20	L	54,983
Sun	9/20	H	DEN	*17-17	T	50,624
Sun	10/4	A	MIN	23-16	W	13,911
Sun	10/11	H	DET	*16-19	L	35,779
Sun	10/18	H	PHI	*16-10	W	35,842
Sun	10/25	A	DET	34-33	W	27,278
Sun	11/1	H	TB	17-23	L	50,308
Sun	11/8	H	CHI	24-26	L	53,320
Sun	11/15	A	SEA	13-24	L	60,963
Sun	11/22	A	KC	23-3	W	34,611
Sun	11/29	A	CHI	10-23	L	61,638
Sun	12/6	H	SF	12-23	L	51,118
Sun	12/13	H	MIN	16-10	W	47,059
Sat	12/19	A	NYG	10-20	L	51,013
Sun	12/27	A	NO	24-33	L	68,364

HOUSTON OILERS

Sun	9/13	H	LARM	20-16	W	33,186
Sun	9/20	A	BUF	30-34	L	56,534
Sun	10/4	A	DEN	40-10	W	38,494

Sun	10/11	A	CLE	15-10	W	38,927
Sun	10/18	H	NE	7-21	L	26,294
Sun	10/25	H	ATL	37-33	W	29,062
Sun	11/1	A	CIN	31-29	W	52,700
Sun	11/8	A	SF	20-27	L	59,740
Sun	11/15	A	PIT	23-3	W	56,177
Sun	11/22	H	CLE	7-40	L	51,161
Sun	11/29	A	IND	27-51	L	54,999
Sun	12/6	H	SD	33-18	W	31,714
Sun	12/13	A	NO	10-24	L	68,257
Sun	12/20	H	PIT	24-16	W	38,683
Sun	12/27	H	CIN	21-17	W	49,775

AFC Wild-Card Playoff

Sun	1/3	H	SEA	*23-20	W	49,622

AFC Divisional Playoff

Sun	1/10	A	DEN	10-34	L	75,968

INDIANAPOLIS COLTS

Sun	9/13	H	CIN	21-23	L	59,387
Sun	9/20	H	MIA	10-23	L	57,524
Sun	10/4	A	BUF	47-6	W	9,860
Sun	10/11	H	NYJ	6-0	W	34,927
Sun	10/18	A	PIT	7-21	L	34,627
Sun	10/25	H	NE	30-16	W	48,850
Sun	11/1	A	NYJ	19-14	W	60,863
Sun	11/8	H	SD	13-16	L	60,459
Sun	11/15	A	MIA	40-21	W	65,433
Sun	11/22	A	NE	0-24	L	56,906
Sun	11/29	H	HOU	51-27	W	54,999
Sun	12/6	A	CLE	9-7	W	70,661
Sun	12/13	H	BUF	3-27	L	60,253
Sun	12/20	A	SD	20-7	W	46,211
Sun	12/27	H	TB	24-6	W	60,468

AFC Divisional Playoff

Sat	1/9	A	CLE	21-38	L	78,586

KANSAS CITY CHIEFS

Sun	9/13	H	SD	20-13	W	56,940
Sun	9/20	A	SEA	14-43	L	61,667
Sun	10/4	A	LARI	17-35	L	10,708
Sun	10/11	A	MIA	0-42	L	25,867
Sun	10/18	H	DEN	17-26	L	20,296
Sun	10/25	A	SD	21-42	L	47,972
Sun	11/1	A	CHI	28-31	L	63,498
Sun	11/8	H	PIT	16-17	L	45,249
Sun	11/15	H	NYJ	9-16	L	40,718
Sun	11/22	H	GB	3-23	L	34,611
Thu	11/26	A	DET	27-20	W	43,820
Sun	12/6	A	CIN	*27-30	L	46,489
Sun	12/13	H	LARI	16-10	W	63,834
Sat	12/19	A	DEN	17-20	L	75,053
Sun	12/27	H	SEA	41-20	W	20,370

LOS ANGELES RAIDERS

Sun	9/13	A	GB	20-0	W	54,983
Sun	9/20	H	DET	27-7	W	50,300
Sun	10/4	H	KC	35-17	W	10,708
Mon	10/12	A	DEN	14-30	L	61,230
Sun	10/18	H	SD	17-23	L	23,541
Sun	10/25	H	SEA	13-35	L	52,735
Sun	11/1	A	NE	23-26	L	60,664
Sun	11/8	A	MIN	20-31	L	57,150
Sun	11/15	A	SD	14-16	L	60,639
Sun	11/22	H	DEN	17-23	L	61,318
Mon	11/30	A	SEA	37-14	W	62,802
Sun	12/6	H	BUF	34-21	W	43,143
Sun	12/13	A	KC	10-16	L	63,834
Sun	12/20	H	CLE	17-24	L	40,275
Sun	12/27	H	CHI	3-6	L	78,019

LOS ANGELES RAMS

Sun	9/13	A	HOU	16-20	L	33,186
Sun	9/20	H	MIN	16-21	L	63,367
Sun	10/4	A	NO	10-37	L	29,745
Sun	10/11	H	PIT	31-21	W	20,219
Sun	10/18	A	ATL	20-24	L	15,813
Mon	10/26	A	CLE	17-30	L	76,933
Sun	11/1	H	SF	10-31	L	55,328
Sun	11/8	H	NO	14-31	L	43,379
Sun	11/15	A	STL	27-24	W	27,730
Mon	11/23	A	WAS	30-26	W	53,614
Sun	11/29	H	TB	35-3	W	45,188
Sun	12/6	A	DET	37-16	W	33,413
Sun	12/13	H	ATL	33-0	W	43,310
Mon	12/21	H	DAL	21-29	L	60,700
Sun	12/27	A	SF	0-48	L	57,950

MIAMI DOLPHINS

Sun	9/13	A	NE	21-28	L	54,642
Sun	9/20	A	IND	23-10	W	57,524
Sun	10/4	A	SEA	20-24	L	19,448
Sun	10/11	H	KC	42-0	W	25,867
Sun	10/18	A	NYJ	*31-37	L	18,249
Sun	10/25	H	BUF	*31-34	L	61,295
Sun	11/1	H	PIT	35-24	W	52,578
Sun	11/8	A	CIN	20-14	W	53,840
Sun	11/15	H	IND	21-40	L	65,433
Sun	11/22	A	DAL	20-14	W	56,519
Sun	11/29	A	BUF	0-27	L	68,055
Mon	12/7	H	NYJ	37-28	W	62,592
Sun	12/13	A	PHI	28-10	W	63,841
Sun	12/20	H	WAS	23-21	W	65,715
Mon	12/28	H	NE	10-24	L	61,192

MINNESOTA VIKINGS

Sun	9/13	H	DET	34-19	W	57,061
Sun	9/20	A	LARM	21-16	W	63,367
Sun	10/4	H	GB	16-23	L	13,911
Sun	10/11	A	CHI	7-27	L	32,113
Sun	10/18	A	TB	10-20	L	20,850
Mon	10/26	H	DEN	34-27	W	51,011
Sun	11/1	A	SEA	17-28	L	61,134
Sun	11/8	H	LARI	31-20	W	57,150
Sun	11/15	H	TB	23-17	W	48,605
Sun	11/22	H	ATL	24-13	W	53,866
Thu	11/26	A	DAL	*44-38	W	54,229
Sun	12/6	H	CHI	24-30	L	62,331
Sun	12/13	A	GB	10-16	L	47,059
Sun	12/20	A	DET	17-14	W	27,693
Sat	12/26	H	WAS	*24-27	L	59,160

NFC Wild-Card Playoff

Sun	1/3	A	NO	44-10	W	68,127

NFC Divisional Playoff

Sat	1/9	A	SF	36-24	W	62,547

NFC Championship

Sun	1/17	A	WAS	10-17	L	55,212

NEW ENGLAND PATRIOTS

Sun	9/13	H	MIA	28-21	W	54,642
Mon	9/21	A	NYJ	24-43	L	70,847
Sun	10/4	H	CLE	10-20	L	14,830
Sun	10/11	H	BUF	14-7	W	11,878
Sun	10/18	A	HOU	21-7	W	26,294
Sun	10/25	A	IND	16-30	L	48,550
Sun	11/1	H	LARI	26-23	W	60,664
Sun	11/8	A	NYG	10-17	L	73,817
Sun	11/15	H	DAL	*17-23	L	60,567
Sun	11/22	H	IND	24-0	W	56,906
Sun	11/29	H	PHI	*31-34	L	54,198
Sun	12/6	A	DEN	20-31	L	75,795
Sun	12/13	H	NYJ	42-20	W	60,617
Sun	12/20	A	BUF	13-7	W	74,945
Mon	12/28	A	MIA	24-10	W	61,192

NEW ORLEANS SAINTS

Sun	9/13	H	CLE	28-21	W	59,900
Sun	9/20	A	PHI	17-27	L	57,485
Sun	10/4	H	LARM	37-10	W	29,745
Sun	10/11	A	STL	19-24	L	11,795
Sun	10/18	A	CHI	19-17	W	46,813
Sun	10/25	H	SF	22-24	L	60,497
Sun	11/1	A	ATL	38-0	W	42,196
Sun	11/8	A	LARM	31-14	W	43,379
Sun	11/15	A	SF	26-24	W	60,436
Sun	11/22	H	NYG	23-14	W	67,639
Sun	11/29	A	PIT	20-16	W	47,896
Sun	12/6	H	TB	44-34	W	66,471
Sun	12/13	H	HOU	24-10	W	68,257
Sun	12/20	A	CIN	41-24	W	43,424
Sun	12/27	H	GB	33-24	W	68,364

NFC Wild-Card Playoff

Sun	1/3	H	MIN	10-44	L	68,127

NEW YORK GIANTS

Mon	9/14	A	CHI	19-34	L	65,704
Sun	9/20	H	DAL	14-16	L	73,426
Mon	10/5	H	SF	21-41	L	16,471
Sun	10/11	H	WAS	12-38	L	9,123
Sun	10/18	A	BUF	*3-6	L	15,737
Sun	10/25	H	STL	30-7	W	74,391
Mon	11/2	A	DAL	24-33	L	55,730
Sun	11/8	H	NE	17-10	W	73,817
Sun	11/15	A	PHI	20-17	W	66,172
Sun	11/22	A	NO	14-23	L	67,639
Sun	11/29	A	WAS	19-23	L	45,815
Sun	12/6	H	PHI	*23-20	W	65,874
Sun	12/13	A	STL	24-27	L	29,623
Sat	12/19	H	GB	20-10	W	51,013
Sun	12/27	H	NYJ	20-7	W	68,318

NEW YORK JETS

Sun	9/13	A	BUF	31-28	W	76,718
Mon	9/21	H	NE	43-24	W	70,847
Sun	10/4	H	DAL	24-38	L	12,370
Sun	10/11	A	IND	0-6	L	34,927
Sun	10/18	H	MIA	*37-31	W	18,249
Sun	10/25	A	WAS	16-17	L	53,497
Sun	11/1	H	IND	14-19	L	60,863
Mon	11/9	H	SEA	30-14	W	60,452
Sun	11/15	A	KC	16-9	W	40,718
Sun	11/22	H	BUF	14-17	L	58,407
Sun	11/29	H	CIN	27-20	W	41,135
Mon	12/7	A	MIA	28-37	L	62,592
Sun	12/13	A	NE	20-42	L	60,617
Sun	12/20	H	PHI	27-38	L	30,572
Sun	12/27	A	NYG	7-20	L	68,318

PHILADELPHIA EAGLES

Sun	9/13	A	WAS	24-34	L	52,188
Sun	9/20	H	NO	27-17	W	57,485
Sun	10/4	H	CHI	3-35	L	4,074
Sun	10/11	A	DAL	22-41	L	40,622
Sun	10/18	A	GB	*10-16	L	35,842
Sun	10/25	H	DAL	37-20	W	61,630
Sun	11/1	A	STL	28-23	W	24,586
Sun	11/8	H	WAS	31-27	W	63,609
Sun	11/15	H	NYG	17-20	L	66,172
Sun	11/22	H	STL	19-31	L	55,592
Sun	11/29	A	NE	*34-31	W	54,198
Sun	12/6	A	NYG	*20-23	L	65,874
Sun	12/13	H	MIA	10-28	L	63,841
Sun	12/20	A	NYJ	38-27	W	30,572
Sun	12/27	H	BUF	17-7	W	57,547

PITTSBURGH STEELERS

Sun	9/13	H	SF	30-17	W	55,735
Sun	9/20	A	CLE	10-34	L	79,543
Sun	10/4	A	ATL	28-12	W	16,667
Sun	10/11	A	LARM	21-31	L	20,219
Sun	10/18	H	IND	21-7	W	34,627
Sun	10/25	H	CIN	23-20	W	53,692
Sun	11/1	A	MIA	24-35	L	52,578
Sun	11/8	A	KC	17-16	W	45,249
Sun	11/15	H	HOU	3-23	L	56,177
Sun	11/22	A	CIN	30-16	W	52,795
Sun	11/29	H	NO	16-20	L	47,896
Sun	12/6	H	SEA	13-9	W	48,881
Sun	12/13	A	SD	20-16	W	51,605
Sun	12/20	A	HOU	16-24	L	38,683
Sat	12/26	H	CLE	13-19	L	56,394

ST. LOUIS CARDINALS

Sun	9/13	H	DAL	24-13	W	47,241
Sun	9/20	A	SD	24-28	L	47,988
Sun	10/4	A	WAS	21-28	L	27,728
Sun	10/11	H	NO	24-19	W	11,795
Sun	10/18	A	SF	28-34	L	38,094
Sun	10/25	A	NYG	7-30	L	74,391
Sun	11/1	H	PHI	23-28	L	24,586
Sun	11/8	H	TB	31-28	W	22,449
Sun	11/15	H	LARM	24-27	L	27,730
Sun	11/22	A	PHI	31-19	W	55,592
Sun	11/29	A	ATL	34-21	W	15,909
Sun	12/6	H	WAS	17-34	L	31,324
Sun	12/13	H	NYG	27-24	W	29,623
Sun	12/20	A	TB	31-14	W	32,046
Sun	12/27	A	DAL	16-21	L	36,788

SAN DIEGO CHARGERS

Sun	9/13	A	KC	13-20	L	56,940
Sun	9/20	H	STL	28-24	W	47,988
Sun	10/4	A	CIN	10-9	W	26,209
Sun	10/11	A	TB	17-13	W	23,873
Sun	10/18	A	LARI	23-17	W	23,541
Sun	10/25	H	KC	42-21	W	47,972
Sun	11/1	H	CLE	*27-24	W	55,381
Sun	11/8	A	IND	16-13	W	60,459
Sun	11/15	H	LARI	16-14	W	60,639
Sun	11/22	A	SEA	3-34	L	62,444
Sun	11/29	H	DEN	17-31	L	61,880
Sun	12/6	A	HOU	18-33	L	31,714
Sun	12/13	H	PIT	16-20	L	51,605
Sun	12/20	H	IND	7-20	L	46,211
Sun	12/27	A	DEN	0-24	L	21,189

SAN FRANCISCO 49ERS

Sun	9/13	A	PIT	17-30	L	55,735
Sun	9/20	A	CIN	27-26	W	53,498
Mon	10/5	A	NYG	41-21	W	16,471
Sun	10/11	A	ATL	25-17	W	8,684
Sun	10/18	H	STL	34-28	W	38,094
Sun	10/25	A	NO	24-22	W	60,497
Sun	11/1	A	LARM	31-10	W	55,328
Sun	11/8	H	HOU	27-20	W	59,740
Sun	11/15	H	NO	24-26	L	60,436
Sun	11/22	A	TB	24-10	W	63,211
Sun	11/29	H	CLE	38-24	W	60,248
Sun	12/6	A	GB	23-12	W	51,118
Mon	12/14	H	CHI	41-0	W	63,509
Sun	12/20	H	ATL	35-7	W	54,698
Sun	12/27	H	LARM	48-0	W	57,950

NFC Divisional Playoff

Sat	1/9	H	MIN	24-36	L	62,547

SEATTLE SEAHAWKS

Sun	9/13	A	DEN	17-40	L	75,999
Sun	9/20	H	KC	43-14	W	61,667
Sun	10/4	H	MIA	24-20	W	19,448
Sun	10/11	H	CIN	10-17	L	31,739
Sun	10/18	A	DET	37-14	W	8,310
Sun	10/25	A	LARI	35-13	W	52,735
Sun	11/1	H	MIN	28-17	W	61,134
Mon	11/9	A	NYJ	14-30	L	60,452
Sun	11/15	H	GB	24-13	W	60,963
Sun	11/22	H	SD	34-3	W	62,444
Mon	11/30	H	LARI	14-37	L	62,802
Sun	12/6	A	PIT	9-13	L	48,881
Sun	12/13	H	DEN	28-21	W	61,759
Sun	12/20	A	CHI	34-21	W	62,518
Sun	12/27	A	KC	20-41	L	20,370

AFC Wild-Card Playoff

Sun	1/3	A	HOU	*20-23	L	49,622

TAMPA BAY BUCCANEERS

Sun	9/13	H	ATL	48-10	W	51,250

Sun 9/20 A CHI 3-20 L 63,551
Sun 10/4 A DET 31-27 W 4,919
Sun 10/11 H SD 13-17 L 23,873
Sun 10/18 H MIN 20-10 W 20,850
Sun 10/25 H CHI 26-27 L 70,747
Sun 11/1 A GB 23-17 W 50,308
Sun 11/8 A STL 28-31 L 22,449
Sun 11/15 A MIN 17-23 L 48,605
Sun 11/22 H SF 10-24 L 63,211
Sun 11/29 A LARM 3-35 L 45,188
Sun 12/6 A NO 34-44 L 66,471
Sun 12/13 H DET 10-20 L 41,699
Sun 12/20 H STL 14-31 L 32,046
Sun 12/27 A IND 6-24 L 60,468

WASHINGTON REDSKINS

Sun 9/13 A PHI 34-24 W 52,188
Sun 9/20 A ATL 20-21 L 50,882
Sun 10/4 H STL 28-21 W 27,728
Sun 10/11 A NYG 38-12 W 9,123
Mon 10/19 A DAL 13-7 W 60,415
Sun 10/25 H NYJ 17-16 W 53,497
Sun 11/1 A BUF 27-7 W 71,640
Sun 11/8 A PHI 27-31 L 63,609
Sun 11/15 H DET 20-13 W 53,593
Mon 11/23 H LARM 26-30 L 53,614
Sun 11/29 H NYG 23-19 W 45,815
Sun 12/6 A STL 34-17 W 31,324
Sun 12/13 H DAL 24-20 W 54,882
Sun 12/20 A MIA 21-23 L 65,715
Sat 12/26 H MIN *27-24 W 59,160

NFC DIVISIONAL PLAYOFF
Sun 1/10 A CHI 21-17 W 66,030

NFC CHAMPIONSHIP
Sun 1/17 H MIN 17-10 W 55,212

SUPER BOWL XXII
Sun 1/31 N DEN 42-10 W 73,302

1988 NFL

ATLANTA FALCONS

Sun 9/4 A DET 17-31 L 31,075
Sun 9/11 H NO 21-29 L 48,901
Sun 9/18 A SF 34-17 W 60,168
Sun 9/25 A DAL 20-26 L 39,702
Sun 10/2 H SEA 20-31 L 28,619
Sun 10/9 H LARM 0-33 L 30,852
Sun 10/16 A DEN 14-30 L 75,287
Sun 10/23 H NYG 16-23 L 45,092
Sun 10/30 A PHI 27-24 W 60,091
Sun 11/6 H GB 20-0 W 29,952
Sun 11/13 A SD 7-10 L 26,329
Sun 11/20 A LARI 12-6 W 40,967
Sun 11/27 H TB 17-10 W 14,020
Sun 12/4 H SF 3-13 L 44,048
Sun 12/11 A LARM 7-22 L 42,828
Sun 12/18 A NO 9-10 L 60,566

BUFFALO BILLS

Sun 9/4 H MIN 13-10 W 76,783
Sun 9/11 H MIA 9-6 W 79,520
Sun 9/18 A NE 16-14 W 55,945
Sun 9/25 H PIT 36-28 W 78,735
Sun 10/2 A CHI 3-24 L 62,793
Sun 10/9 H IND 34-23 W 76,018
Mon 10/17 A NYJ 37-14 W 70,218
Sun 10/23 H NE 23-20 W 76,824
Sun 10/30 H GB 28-0 W 79,176
Sun 11/6 A SEA 13-3 W 61,074
Mon 11/14 A MIA 31-6 W 67,091
Sun 11/20 H NYJ *9-6 L 78,389
Sun 11/27 A CIN 21-35 L 58,672
Sun 12/4 A TB 5-10 L 49,498
Sun 12/11 H LARI 37-21 W 77,348
Sun 12/18 A IND 14-17 L 59,908

AFC DIVISIONAL PLAYOFF
Sun 1/1 H HOU 17-10 W 79,532

AFC CHAMPIONSHIP
Sun 1/8 A CIN 10-21 L 59,747

CHICAGO BEARS

Sun 9/4 H MIA 34-7 W 63,330
Sun 9/11 A IND 17-13 W 60,503
Sun 9/18 H MIN 7-31 L 63,990
Sun 9/25 A GB 24-6 W 56,492
Sun 10/2 H BUF 24-3 W 62,793
Sun 10/9 A DET 24-7 W 64,526
Sun 10/16 H DAL 17-7 W 64,759
Mon 10/24 H SF 10-9 W 65,293
Sun 10/30 A NE 7-30 L 60,821
Sun 11/6 H TB 28-10 W 56,892
Sun 11/13 A WAS 34-14 W 52,418
Sun 11/20 A TB 27-15 W 67,070
Sun 11/27 H GB 16-0 W 62,026
Mon 12/5 A LARM 3-23 L 65,579
Sun 12/11 H DET 13-12 W 55,010
Mon 12/19 A MIN 27-28 L 62,067

NFC DIVISIONAL PLAYOFF
Sat 12/31 H PHI 20-12 W 65,534

NFC CHAMPIONSHIP
Sun 1/8 H SF 3-28 L 66,946

CINCINNATI BENGALS

Sun 9/4 H PHX 21-14 W 50,404
Sun 9/11 A PHI 28-24 W 66,459
Sun 9/18 A PIT 17-12 W 56,647
Sun 9/25 H CLE 24-17 W 54,943
Sun 10/2 A LARI 45-21 W 42,594
Sun 10/9 H NYJ 36-19 W 57,482
Sun 10/16 A NE 21-27 L 59,969
Sun 10/23 H HOU 44-21 W 54,659
Sun 10/30 A CLE 16-23 L 79,147
Sun 11/6 H PIT 42-7 W 56,403
Sun 11/13 A KC 28-31 L 34,614
Sun 11/20 A DAL 38-24 W 37,865
Sun 11/27 H BUF 35-21 W 58,672
Sun 12/4 H SD 27-10 W 58,866
Sun 12/11 A HOU 6-41 L 50,269
Sat 12/17 H WAS *20-17 W 52,157

AFC DIVISIONAL PLAYOFF
Sat 12/31 H SEA 21-13 W 58,560

AFC CHAMPIONSHIP
Sun 1/8 H BUF 21-10 W 59,747

SUPER BOWL XXIII
Sun 1/22 N SF 16-20 L 75,129

CLEVELAND BROWNS

Sun 9/4 A KC 6-3 W 55,654
Sun 9/11 H NYJ 3-23 L 74,434
Mon 9/19 H IND 23-17 W 75,148
Sun 9/25 A CIN 17-24 L 54,943
Sun 10/2 A PIT 23-9 W 56,410
Sun 10/9 H SEA 10-16 L 78,605
Sun 10/16 H PHI 19-3 W 78,787
Sun 10/23 H PHX 29-21 W 61,261
Sun 10/30 H CIN 23-16 W 79,147
Mon 11/7 A HOU 17-24 L 51,467
Sun 11/13 A DEN 7-30 L 75,806
Sun 11/20 H PIT 27-7 W 77,131
Sun 11/27 A WAS 17-13 L 51,604
Sun 12/4 A DAL 24-21 W 77,683
Mon 12/12 A MIA 31-38 L 61,884
Sun 12/18 H HOU 28-23 W 74,610

AFC WILD-CARD PLAYOFF
Sat 12/24 H HOU 23-24 L 74,977

DALLAS COWBOYS

Sun 9/4 A PIT 21-24 L 56,813
Mon 9/12 A PHX 17-14 W 67,139
Sun 9/18 H NYG 10-12 L 55,325
Sun 9/25 H ATL 26-20 W 39,702
Mon 10/3 A NO 17-20 L 68,474
Sun 10/9 H WAS 17-35 L 63,325
Sun 10/16 A CHI 7-17 L 64,759
Sun 10/23 A PHI 23-24 L 66,309
Sun 10/30 H PHX 10-16 L 42,196
Sun 11/6 H NYG 21-29 L 75,826
Sun 11/13 H MIN 3-43 L 57,830
Sun 11/20 H CIN 24-38 L 37,865
Thu 11/24 H HOU 17-25 L 50,845
Sun 12/4 A CLE 21-24 L 77,683
Sun 12/11 A WAS 24-17 L 51,526
Sun 12/18 H PHI 7-23 L 46,131

DENVER BRONCOS

Sun 9/4 H SEA 14-21 L 75,986
Sun 9/11 A SD 34-3 W 75,359
Sun 9/18 A KC 13-20 L 63,268
Mon 9/26 H LARI *27-30 L 75,964
Sun 10/2 A SD 12-0 W 55,763
Sun 10/9 A SF *16-13 W 61,711
Sun 10/16 H ATL 30-14 W 75,287
Sun 10/23 A PIT 21-39 L 49,811
Mon 10/31 A IND 23-55 L 60,544
Sun 11/6 H KC 17-11 W 74,227
Sun 11/13 H CLE 30-7 W 75,806
Sun 11/20 A NO 0-42 L 68,075
Sun 11/27 H LARM 35-24 W 74,141
Sun 12/4 A LARI 20-21 L 65,561
Sun 12/11 H SEA 14-42 L 62,838
Sat 12/17 H NE 21-10 W 70,910

DETROIT LIONS

Sun 9/4 H ATL 31-17 W 31,075
Sun 9/11 A LARM 10-17 L 46,262
Sun 9/18 A NO 14-22 L 32,943
Sun 9/25 H NYJ 10-17 L 29,250
Sun 10/2 A SF 13-20 L 58,285
Sun 10/9 H CHI 7-24 L 64,526
Sun 10/16 A NYG 10-30 L 74,813
Sun 10/23 A KC 7-6 W 66,926
Sun 10/30 H NYG *10-13 L 38,354
Sun 11/6 A MIN 17-44 L 55,573
Sun 11/13 H TB 20-23 L 25,956
Sun 11/20 A GB 19-9 W 44,327
Thu 11/24 H MIN 0-23 L 46,379
Sun 12/4 H GB 30-14 W 28,124
Sun 12/11 A CHI 12-13 L 55,010
Sun 12/18 A TB 10-21 L 37,778

GREEN BAY PACKERS

Sun 9/4 H LARM 7-34 L 53,769
Sun 9/11 H TB 10-13 L 52,584
Sun 9/18 A MIA 17-24 L 54,409
Sun 9/25 H CHI 6-24 L 56,492
Sun 10/2 A TB 24-27 L 40,003
Sun 10/9 H NE 45-3 W 51,932
Sun 10/16 A MIN 34-14 W 59,053
Sun 10/23 H WAS 17-20 L 51,767
Sun 10/30 A BUF 0-28 L 79,176
Sun 11/6 H ATL 0-20 L 29,952
Sun 11/13 H IND 13-20 L 53,492
Sun 11/20 H DET 9-19 L 44,327
Sun 11/27 A CHI 0-16 L 62,026
Sun 12/4 A DET 14-30 L 28,124
Sun 12/11 H MIN 18-6 W 48,892
Sun 12/18 A PHX 26-17 W 44,586

HOUSTON OILERS

Sun 9/4 A IND *17-14 W 57,251
Sun 9/11 A LARI 38-35 W 46,050
Sun 9/18 A NYJ 3-45 L 64,683
Sun 9/25 H NE 31-6 W 38,646
Sun 10/2 A PHI 23-32 L 64,692
Sun 10/9 H KC 7-6 W 39,134
Sun 10/16 A PIT 34-14 W 52,229
Sun 10/23 A CIN 21-44 L 54,659
Sun 10/30 H WAS 41-17 W 48,781
Mon 11/7 H CLE 24-17 W 51,467
Sun 11/13 A SEA 24-27 L 60,446
Sun 11/20 H PHX 38-20 W 43,843
Thu 11/24 A DAL 25-17 W 50,845
Sun 12/4 H PIT 34-37 L 47,791
Sun 12/11 H CIN 41-6 W 50,269
Sun 12/18 A CLE 23-28 L 74,610

AFC WILD-CARD PLAYOFF
Sat 12/24 A CLE 24-23 W 74,977

AFC DIVISIONAL PLAYOFF
Sun 1/1 A BUF 10-17 L 79,532

INDIANAPOLIS COLTS

Sun 9/4 H HOU *14-17 L 57,251
Sun 9/11 A CHI 13-17 L 60,503
Mon 9/19 A CLE 17-23 L 75,148
Sun 9/25 H MIA 15-13 W 59,638
Sun 10/2 A NE 17-21 L 58,050
Sun 10/9 A BUF 23-34 L 76,018
Sun 10/16 H TB 35-31 W 53,135
Sun 10/23 A SD 16-0 W 37,722
Mon 10/31 H DEN 55-23 W 60,544
Sun 11/6 H NYJ 38-14 W 59,233
Sun 11/13 A GB 20-13 W 53,492
Sun 11/20 A MIN 3-12 L 58,342
Sun 11/27 H NE 24-21 W 58,157
Sun 12/4 A MIA 31-28 W 45,236
Sat 12/10 A NYJ 16-34 L 46,284
Sun 12/18 A BUF 17-14 W 59,908

KANSAS CITY CHIEFS

Sun 9/4 H CLE 3-6 L 55,654
Sun 9/11 A SEA 10-31 L 61,512
Sun 9/18 H DEN 20-13 W 63,268
Sun 9/25 H SD 23-24 L 45,498
Sun 10/2 A NYJ *17-17 T 66,110
Sun 10/9 A HOU 6-7 L 39,134
Sun 10/16 H LARI 17-27 L 77,078
Sun 10/23 H DET 6-7 L 66,926
Sun 10/30 A LARI 10-17 L 36,103
Sun 11/6 A DEN 11-17 L 74,227
Sun 11/13 H CIN 31-28 W 34,614
Sun 11/20 H SEA 27-24 W 33,152
Sun 11/27 A PIT 10-16 L 42,057
Sun 12/4 H NYJ 38-34 W 30,059
Sun 12/11 A NYG 12-28 L 69,807
Sun 12/18 A SD 13-24 L 26,339

LOS ANGELES RAIDERS

Sun 9/4 H SD 24-13 W 39,029
Sun 9/11 H HOU 35-38 L 46,050
Sun 9/18 H LARM 17-22 L 84,870
Mon 9/26 A DEN *30-27 W 75,964
Sun 10/2 H CIN 21-45 L 42,594
Sun 10/9 H MIA 14-24 L 50,751
Sun 10/16 A KC 27-17 W 77,078
Sun 10/23 A NO 6-20 L 66,249
Sun 10/30 H KC 17-10 W 36,103
Sun 11/6 A SD 13-3 W 55,134
Sun 11/13 A SF 9-3 W 54,448
Sun 11/20 H ATL 6-12 L 40,967
Mon 11/28 A SEA 27-35 L 62,641
Sun 12/4 H DEN 21-20 W 65,561
Sun 12/11 A BUF 21-37 L 77,348
Sun 12/18 H SEA 37-43 L 61,127

LOS ANGELES RAMS

Sun 9/4 A GB 34-7 W 53,769
Sun 9/11 A DET 17-10 W 46,262
Sun 9/18 A LARI 22-17 W 84,870
Sun 9/25 A NYG 45-31 W 75,617
Sun 10/2 H PHX 27-41 L 49,830

Sun	10/9	A	ATL	33-0	W	30,852
Sun	10/16	H	SF	21-24	L	65,450
Sun	10/23	H	SEA	31-10	W	57,033
Sun	10/30	A	NO	12-10	W	68,238
Sun	11/6	A	PHI	24-30	L	65,624
Sun	11/13	H	NO	10-14	L	63,305
Sun	11/20	H	SD	24-38	L	45,462
Sun	11/27	A	DEN	24-35	L	74,141
Mon	12/5	H	CHI	23-3	W	65,579
Sun	12/11	H	ATL	22-7	W	42,828
Sun	12/18	A	SF	38-16	W	62,444

NFC Wild-Card Playoff

Mon	12/26	A	MIN	17-28	L	57,666

MIAMI DOLPHINS

Sun	9/4	A	CHI	7-34	L	63,330
Sun	9/11	A	BUF	6-9	L	79,520
Sun	9/18	H	GB	24-17	W	54,409
Sun	9/25	A	IND	13-15	L	59,638
Sun	10/2	H	MIN	24-7	W	59,867
Sun	10/9	A	LARI	24-14	W	50,751
Sun	10/16	H	SD	31-28	W	58,972
Sun	10/23	H	NYJ	30-44	L	68,292
Sun	10/30	A	TB	17-14	W	67,352
Sun	11/6	A	NE	10-21	L	60,840
Mon	11/14	H	BUF	6-31	L	67,091
Sun	11/20	H	NE	3-6	L	53,526
Sun	11/27	A	NYJ	34-38	L	52,752
Sun	12/4	H	IND	28-31	L	45,236
Mon	12/12	H	CLE	38-31	W	61,884
Sun	12/18	A	PIT	24-40	L	36,051

MINNESOTA VIKINGS

Sun	9/4	A	BUF	10-13	L	76,783
Sun	9/11	H	NE	36-6	W	55,545
Sun	9/18	A	CHI	31-7	W	63,990
Sun	9/25	H	PHI	23-21	W	56,012
Sun	10/2	A	MIA	7-24	L	59,867
Sun	10/9	H	TB	14-13	W	55,274
Sun	10/16	H	GB	14-34	L	59,053
Sun	10/23	A	TB	49-20	W	48,020
Sun	10/30	A	SF	21-24	L	60,738
Sun	11/6	H	DET	44-17	W	55,573
Sun	11/13	A	DAL	43-3	W	57,830
Sun	11/20	H	IND	12-3	W	58,342
Thu	11/24	A	DET	23-0	W	46,379
Sun	12/4	H	NO	45-3	W	61,215
Sun	12/11	A	GB	6-18	L	48,892
Mon	12/19	H	CHI	28-27	W	62,067

NFC Wild-Card Playoff

Mon	12/26	H	LARM	28-17	W	57,666

NFC Divisional Playoff

Sun	1/1	A	SF	9-34	L	61,848

NEW ENGLAND PATRIOTS

Sun	9/4	H	NYJ	28-3	W	44,027
Sun	9/11	A	MIN	6-36	L	55,545
Sun	9/18	H	BUF	14-16	L	55,945
Sun	9/25	A	HOU	6-31	L	38,646
Sun	10/2	H	IND	21-17	W	58,050
Sun	10/9	A	GB	3-45	L	51,932
Sun	10/16	H	CIN	27-21	W	59,969
Sun	10/23	A	BUF	20-23	L	76,824
Sun	10/30	H	CHI	30-7	W	60,821
Sun	11/6	H	MIA	21-10	W	60,840
Sun	11/13	A	NYJ	14-13	W	48,358
Sun	11/20	A	MIA	6-3	W	53,526
Sun	11/27	A	IND	21-24	L	58,157
Sun	12/4	H	SEA	13-7	W	59,086
Sun	12/11	H	TB	*10-7	W	39,889
Sat	12/17	A	DEN	10-21	L	70,910

NEW ORLEANS SAINTS

Sun	9/4	H	SF	33-34	L	66,357
Sun	9/11	A	ATL	29-21	W	48,901
Sun	9/18	A	DET	22-14	W	32,943
Sun	9/25	H	TB	13-9	W	66,671
Mon	10/3	H	DAL	20-17	W	68,474
Sun	10/9	A	SD	23-17	W	42,693
Sun	10/16	A	SEA	20-19	W	63,569
Sun	10/23	H	LARI	20-6	W	66,249
Sun	10/30	H	LARM	10-12	L	68,238
Sun	11/6	A	WAS	24-27	L	54,183
Sun	11/13	A	LARM	14-10	W	63,305
Sun	11/20	H	DEN	42-0	W	68,075
Sun	11/27	H	NYG	12-13	L	66,526
Sun	12/4	A	MIN	3-45	L	61,215
Sun	12/11	A	SF	17-30	L	62,977
Sun	12/18	H	ATL	10-9	W	60,566

NEW YORK GIANTS

Mon	9/5	H	WAS	27-20	W	76,417
Sun	9/11	H	SF	17-20	L	75,943
Sun	9/18	A	DAL	12-10	W	55,325
Sun	9/25	H	LARM	31-45	L	75,617
Sun	10/2	A	WAS	24-23	W	54,601
Mon	10/10	A	PHI	13-24	L	63,736
Sun	10/16	H	DET	30-10	W	74,813
Sun	10/23	A	ATL	23-16	W	45,092
Sun	10/30	A	DET	*13-10	W	38,354
Sun	11/6	H	DAL	29-21	W	75,826
Sun	11/13	A	PHX	17-24	L	65,324
Sun	11/20	H	PHI	*17-23	L	43,621
Sun	11/27	A	NO	13-12	W	66,526
Sun	12/4	H	PHX	44-7	W	73,438
Sun	12/11	H	KC	28-12	W	69,807
Sun	12/18	A	NYJ	21-27	L	69,770

NEW YORK JETS

Sun	9/4	A	NE	3-28	L	44,027
Sun	9/11	A	CLE	23-3	W	74,434
Sun	9/18	H	HOU	45-3	W	64,683
Sun	9/25	A	DET	17-10	W	29,250
Sun	10/2	H	KC	*17-17	T	66,110
Sun	10/9	A	CIN	19-36	L	57,482
Mon	10/17	H	BUF	14-37	L	70,218
Sun	10/23	A	MIA	44-30	W	68,292
Sun	10/30	H	PIT	24-20	W	64,862
Sun	11/6	A	IND	14-38	L	59,233
Sun	11/13	H	NE	13-14	L	48,358
Sun	11/20	A	BUF	*6-9	L	78,389
Sun	11/27	H	MIA	38-34	W	52,752
Sun	12/4	A	KC	34-38	L	30,059
Sat	12/10	H	IND	34-16	W	46,284
Sun	12/18	H	NYG	27-21	W	69,770

PHILADELPHIA EAGLES

Sun	9/4	A	TB	41-14	W	43,502
Sun	9/11	H	CIN	24-28	L	66,459
Sun	9/18	A	WAS	10-17	L	53,920
Sun	9/25	A	MIN	21-23	L	56,012
Sun	10/2	H	HOU	32-23	W	64,692
Mon	10/10	H	NYG	24-13	W	63,736
Sun	10/16	A	CLE	3-19	L	78,787
Sun	10/23	H	DAL	24-23	W	66,309
Sun	10/30	H	ATL	24-27	L	60,091
Sun	11/6	H	LARM	30-24	W	65,624
Sun	11/13	A	PIT	27-26	W	46,026
Sun	11/20	A	NYG	*23-17	W	43,621
Sun	11/27	H	PHX	31-21	W	57,918
Sun	12/4	H	WAS	19-20	L	65,947
Sat	12/10	A	PHX	23-17	W	54,832
Sun	12/18	A	DAL	23-7	W	46,131

NFC Divisional Playoff

Sat	12/31	A	CHI	12-20	L	65,534

PHOENIX CARDINALS

Sun	9/4	A	CIN	14-21	L	50,404
Mon	9/12	H	DAL	14-17	L	67,139
Sun	9/18	A	TB	30-24	W	35,034
Sun	9/25	H	WAS	30-21	W	61,973
Sun	10/2	A	LARM	41-27	W	49,830
Sun	10/9	H	PIT	31-14	W	53,278
Sun	10/16	A	WAS	17-33	L	54,402
Sun	10/23	H	CLE	21-29	L	61,261
Sun	10/30	A	DAL	16-10	W	42,196
Sun	11/6	H	SF	24-23	W	64,544
Sun	11/13	H	NYG	24-17	W	65,324
Sun	11/20	A	HOU	20-38	L	43,843
Sun	11/27	A	PHI	21-31	L	57,918
Sun	12/4	A	NYG	7-44	L	73,438
Sat	12/10	H	PHI	17-23	L	54,832
Sun	12/18	H	GB	17-26	L	44,586

PITTSBURGH STEELERS

Sun	9/4	H	DAL	24-21	W	56,813
Sun	9/11	A	WAS	29-30	L	54,083
Sun	9/18	H	CIN	12-17	L	56,647
Sun	9/25	A	BUF	28-36	L	78,735
Sun	10/2	H	CLE	9-23	L	56,410
Sun	10/9	A	PHX	14-31	L	53,278
Sun	10/16	H	HOU	14-34	L	52,229
Sun	10/23	H	DEN	39-21	W	49,811
Sun	10/30	A	NYJ	20-24	L	64,862
Sun	11/6	A	CIN	7-42	L	56,403
Sun	11/13	H	PHI	26-27	L	46,026
Sun	11/20	A	CLE	7-27	L	77,131
Sun	11/27	H	KC	16-10	W	42,057
Sun	12/4	A	HOU	37-34	W	47,791
Sun	12/11	A	SD	14-20	L	33,816
Sun	12/18	H	MIA	40-24	W	36,051

SAN DIEGO CHARGERS

Sun	9/4	A	LARI	13-24	L	39,029
Sun	9/11	A	DEN	3-34	L	75,359
Sun	9/18	H	SEA	17-6	W	44,449
Sun	9/25	A	KC	24-23	W	45,498
Sun	10/2	H	DEN	0-12	L	55,763
Sun	10/9	H	NO	17-23	L	42,693
Sun	10/16	A	MIA	28-31	L	58,972
Sun	10/23	H	IND	0-16	L	37,722
Sun	10/30	A	SEA	14-17	L	59,641
Sun	11/6	H	LARI	3-13	L	55,134
Sun	11/13	A	ATL	10-7	W	26,329
Sun	11/20	A	LARM	38-24	W	45,462
Sun	11/27	H	SF	10-48	L	51,484
Sun	12/4	A	CIN	10-27	L	56,866
Sun	12/11	H	PIT	20-14	W	33,816
Sun	12/18	H	KC	24-13	W	26,339

SAN FRANCISCO 49ERS

Sun	9/4	A	NO	34-33	W	66,357
Sun	9/11	A	NYG	20-17	W	75,943
Sun	9/18	H	ATL	17-34	L	60,168
Sun	9/25	A	SEA	38-7	W	62,382
Sun	10/2	H	DET	20-13	W	58,285
Sun	10/9	H	DEN	*13-16	L	61,711
Sun	10/16	A	LARM	24-21	W	65,450
Mon	10/24	A	CHI	9-10	L	65,293
Sun	10/30	H	MIN	24-21	W	60,738
Sun	11/6	A	PHX	23-24	L	64,544
Sun	11/13	H	LARI	3-9	L	54,448
Mon	11/21	H	WAS	37-21	W	59,268
Sun	11/27	A	SD	48-10	W	51,484
Sun	12/4	A	ATL	13-3	W	44,048
Sun	12/11	H	NO	30-17	W	62,977
Sun	12/18	H	LARM	16-38	L	62,444

NFC Divisional Playoff

Sun	1/1	H	MIN	34-9	W	61,848

NFC Championship

Sun	1/8	A	CHI	28-3	W	66,946

Super Bowl XXIII

Sun	1/22	N	CIN	20-16	W	75,129

SEATTLE SEAHAWKS

Sun	9/4	A	DEN	21-14	W	75,986
Sun	9/11	H	KC	31-10	W	61,512
Sun	9/18	A	SD	6-17	L	44,449
Sun	9/25	H	SF	7-38	L	62,382
Sun	10/2	A	ATL	31-20	W	28,619
Sun	10/9	A	CLE	16-10	W	78,605
Sun	10/16	H	NO	19-20	L	63,569
Sun	10/23	A	LARM	10-31	L	57,033
Sun	10/30	H	SD	17-14	W	59,641
Sun	11/6	H	BUF	3-13	L	61,074
Sun	11/13	H	HOU	27-24	W	60,446
Sun	11/20	A	KC	24-27	L	33,152
Mon	11/28	H	LARI	35-27	W	62,641
Sun	12/4	A	NE	7-13	L	59,086
Sun	12/11	H	DEN	42-14	W	62,838
Sun	12/18	A	LARI	43-37	W	61,127

AFC Divisional Playoff

Sat	12/31	A	CIN	13-21	L	58,560

TAMPA BAY BUCCANEERS

Sun	9/4	H	PHI	14-41	L	43,502
Sun	9/11	A	GB	13-10	W	52,584
Sun	9/18	H	PHX	24-30	L	35,034
Sun	9/25	A	NO	9-13	L	66,671
Sun	10/2	H	GB	27-24	W	40,003
Sun	10/9	A	MIN	13-14	L	55,274
Sun	10/16	A	IND	31-35	L	53,135
Sun	10/23	H	MIN	20-49	L	48,020
Sun	10/30	H	MIA	14-17	L	67,352
Sun	11/6	A	CHI	10-28	L	56,892
Sun	11/13	A	DET	23-20	W	25,956
Sun	11/20	H	CHI	15-27	L	67,070
Sun	11/27	A	ATL	10-17	L	14,020
Sun	12/4	H	BUF	10-5	W	49,498
Sun	12/11	A	NE	*7-10	L	39,889
Sun	12/18	H	DET	21-10	W	37,778

WASHINGTON REDSKINS

Mon	9/5	A	NYG	20-27	L	76,417
Sun	9/11	H	PIT	30-29	W	54,083
Sun	9/18	H	PHI	17-10	W	53,920
Sun	9/25	A	PHX	21-30	L	61,973
Sun	10/2	H	NYG	23-24	L	54,601
Sun	10/9	A	DAL	35-17	W	63,325
Sun	10/16	H	PHX	33-17	W	54,402
Sun	10/23	A	GB	20-17	W	51,767
Sun	10/30	A	HOU	17-41	L	48,781
Sun	11/6	H	NO	27-24	W	54,183
Sun	11/13	H	CHI	14-34	L	52,418
Mon	11/21	A	SF	21-37	L	59,268
Sun	11/27	H	CLE	13-17	L	51,604
Sun	12/4	A	PHI	20-19	W	65,947
Sun	12/11	H	DAL	17-24	L	51,526
Sat	12/17	A	CIN	*17-20	L	52,157

1989 NFL

ATLANTA FALCONS

Sun	9/10	H	LARM	21-31	L	38,708
Sun	9/17	H	DAL	27-21	W	55,285
Sun	9/24	A	IND	9-13	L	57,816
Sun	10/1	A	GB	21-23	L	54,647
Sun	10/8	A	LARM	14-26	L	52,182
Sun	10/15	H	NE	16-15	W	39,697
Sun	10/22	A	PHX	20-34	L	33,894
Sun	10/29	A	NO	13-20	L	65,153
Sun	11/5	H	BUF	30-28	W	45,267
Sun	11/12	A	SF	3-45	L	59,914
Sun	11/19	H	NO	17-26	L	53,173
Sun	11/26	A	NYJ	7-27	L	40,429
Sun	12/3	H	SF	10-23	L	43,128
Sun	12/10	A	MIN	17-43	L	58,116
Sun	12/17	H	WAS	30-31	L	37,501
Sun	12/24	H	DET	24-31	L	7,792

The Game Scores

BUFFALO BILLS

Sun	9/10	A	MIA	27-24	W	54,541
Mon	9/18	H	DEN	14-28	L	78,176
Sun	9/24	A	HOU	*47-41	W	57,278
Sun	10/1	H	NE	31-10	W	78,921
Sun	10/8	A	IND	14-37	L	58,890
Mon	10/16	H	LARM	23-20	W	76,231
Sun	10/22	H	NYJ	34-3	W	76,811
Sun	10/29	H	MIA	31-17	W	80,208
Sun	11/5	A	ATL	28-30	L	45,267
Sun	11/12	H	IND	30-7	W	79,256
Sun	11/19	A	NE	24-33	L	49,663
Sun	11/26	H	CIN	24-7	W	80,074
Mon	12/4	A	SEA	16-17	L	57,682
Sun	12/10	H	NO	19-22	L	70,037
Sun	12/17	A	SF	10-21	L	60,927
Sat	12/23	A	NYJ	37-0	W	21,148

AFC Divisional Playoff

Sat	1/6	A	CLE	30-34	L	78,921

CHICAGO BEARS

Sun	9/10	H	CIN	17-14	W	64,730
Sun	9/17	H	MIN	38-7	W	66,475
Sun	9/24	A	DET	47-27	W	71,418
Mon	10/2	H	PHI	27-13	W	66,625
Sun	10/8	A	TB	35-42	L	72,077
Sun	10/15	H	HOU	28-33	L	64,383
Mon	10/23	A	CLE	7-27	L	78,722
Sun	10/29	H	LARM	20-10	W	65,506
Sun	11/5	A	GB	13-14	L	56,556
Sun	11/12	A	PIT	20-0	W	56,505
Sun	11/19	H	TB	31-32	L	63,826
Sun	11/26	A	WAS	14-38	L	50,044
Sun	12/3	A	MIN	16-27	L	60,664
Sun	12/10	H	DET	17-27	L	52,650
Sun	12/17	H	GB	28-40	L	44,781
Sun	12/24	A	SF	0-26	L	60,207

CINCINNATI BENGALS

Sun	9/10	A	CHI	14-17	L	64,730
Sun	9/17	H	PIT	41-10	W	53,885
Mon	9/25	H	CLE	21-14	W	55,996
Sun	10/1	A	KC	21-17	W	61,165
Sun	10/8	A	PIT	26-16	W	52,785
Sun	10/15	H	MIA	13-20	L	58,184
Sun	10/22	H	IND	12-23	L	57,642
Sun	10/29	H	TB	56-23	W	57,225
Sun	11/5	A	LARI	7-28	L	51,080
Mon	11/13	A	HOU	24-26	L	60,694
Sun	11/19	H	DET	42-7	W	55,720
Sun	11/26	A	BUF	7-24	L	80,074
Sun	12/3	A	CLE	21-0	W	76,236
Sun	12/10	H	SEA	17-24	L	54,744
Sun	12/17	H	HOU	61-7	W	47,510
Mon	12/25	A	MIN	21-29	L	58,829

CLEVELAND BROWNS

Sun	9/10	A	PIT	51-0	W	57,928
Sun	9/17	H	NYJ	38-24	W	73,516
Mon	9/25	A	CIN	14-21	L	55,996
Sun	10/1	H	DEN	16-13	W	78,637
Sun	10/8	A	MIA	*10-13	L	58,444
Sun	10/15	H	PIT	7-17	L	78,840
Mon	10/23	H	CHI	27-7	W	78,722
Sun	10/29	H	HOU	28-17	W	78,765
Sun	11/5	A	TB	42-31	W	69,162
Sun	11/12	A	SEA	17-7	W	58,978
Sun	11/19	H	KC	*10-10	T	77,922
Thu	11/23	A	DET	10-13	L	65,624
Sun	12/3	H	CIN	0-21	L	76,236
Sun	12/10	A	IND	*17-23	L	58,550
Sun	12/17	H	MIN	*23-17	W	70,777
Sat	12/23	A	HOU	24-20	W	58,852

AFC Divisional Playoff

Sat	1/6	H	BUF	34-30	W	78,921

AFC Championship

Sun	1/14	A	DEN	21-37	L	76,046

DALLAS COWBOYS

Sun	9/10	A	NO	0-28	L	66,977
Sun	9/17	A	ATL	21-27	L	55,285
Sun	9/24	H	WAS	7-30	L	63,200
Sun	10/1	H	NYG	13-30	L	51,785
Sun	10/8	A	GB	13-31	L	56,656
Sun	10/15	H	SF	14-31	L	61,077
Sun	10/22	A	KC	28-36	L	76,841
Sun	10/29	H	PHX	10-19	L	44,431
Sun	11/5	A	WAS	13-3	W	53,187
Sun	11/12	A	PHX	20-24	L	49,657
Sun	11/19	H	MIA	14-17	L	56,044
Thu	11/23	H	PHI	0-27	L	54,444
Sun	12/3	H	LARM	31-35	L	46,100
Sun	12/10	A	PHI	10-20	L	59,842
Sat	12/16	A	NYG	0-15	L	72,141
Sun	12/24	H	GB	10-20	L	41,265

DENVER BRONCOS

Sun	9/10	H	KC	34-20	W	74,284
Mon	9/18	A	BUF	28-14	W	78,176
Sun	9/24	H	LARI	31-21	W	75,754
Sun	10/1	A	CLE	13-16	L	78,637
Sun	10/8	H	SD	16-10	W	75,222
Sun	10/15	H	IND	14-3	W	74,680
Sun	10/22	A	SEA	*24-21	W	62,353
Sun	10/29	H	PHI	24-28	L	75,065
Sun	11/5	H	PIT	34-7	W	74,739
Sun	11/12	A	KC	16-13	W	76,245
Mon	11/20	A	WAS	14-10	W	52,975
Sun	11/26	H	SEA	41-14	W	75,117
Sun	12/3	A	LARI	*13-16	L	87,560
Sun	12/10	H	NYG	7-14	L	63,283
Sat	12/16	A	PHX	37-0	W	56,071
Sun	12/24	A	SD	16-19	L	50,524

AFC Divisional Playoff

Sun	1/7	H	PIT	24-23	W	75,477

AFC Championship

Sun	1/14	H	CLE	37-21	W	76,046

Super Bowl XXIV

Sun	1/28	N	SF	10-55	L	72,919

DETROIT LIONS

Sun	9/10	H	PHX	13-16	L	36,735
Sun	9/17	A	NYG	14-24	L	76,021
Sun	9/24	H	CHI	27-47	L	71,418
Sun	10/1	H	PIT	3-23	L	43,804
Sun	10/8	A	MIN	17-24	L	55,380
Sun	10/15	A	TB	17-16	W	46,225
Sun	10/22	H	MIN	7-20	L	51,579
Sun	10/29	A	GB	*20-23	L	53,731
Sun	11/5	A	HOU	31-35	L	48,056
Sun	11/12	H	GB	31-22	W	44,324
Sun	11/19	A	CIN	7-42	L	55,720
Thu	11/23	H	CLE	13-10	W	65,624
Sun	12/3	H	NO	21-14	W	38,550
Sun	12/10	A	CHI	27-17	W	52,650
Sun	12/17	H	TB	33-7	W	40,362
Sun	12/24	A	ATL	31-24	W	7,792

GREEN BAY PACKERS

Sun	9/10	H	TB	21-23	L	55,650
Sun	9/17	H	NO	35-34	W	55,809
Sun	9/24	A	LARM	38-41	L	57,701
Sun	10/1	H	ATL	23-21	W	54,647
Sun	10/8	H	DAL	31-13	W	56,656
Sun	10/15	A	MIN	14-26	L	62,075
Sun	10/22	A	MIA	20-23	L	56,624
Sun	10/29	H	DET	*23-20	W	53,731
Sun	11/5	H	CHI	14-13	W	56,556
Sun	11/12	A	DET	22-31	L	44,324
Sun	11/19	A	SF	21-17	W	62,219
Sun	11/26	H	MIN	20-19	W	55,592
Sun	12/3	A	TB	17-16	W	58,120
Sun	12/10	H	KC	3-21	L	56,694
Sun	12/17	A	CHI	40-28	W	44,781
Sun	12/24	A	DAL	20-10	W	41,265

HOUSTON OILERS

Sun	9/10	A	MIN	7-38	L	54,015
Sun	9/17	A	SD	34-27	W	42,013
Sun	9/24	H	BUF	*41-47	L	57,278
Sun	10/1	H	MIA	39-7	W	53,326
Sun	10/8	A	NE	13-23	L	59,828
Sun	10/15	A	CHI	33-28	W	64,383
Sun	10/22	H	PIT	27-0	W	59,091
Sun	10/29	A	CLE	17-28	L	78,765
Sun	11/5	H	DET	35-31	W	48,056
Mon	11/13	H	CIN	26-24	W	60,694
Sun	11/19	H	LARI	23-7	W	59,198
Sun	11/26	A	KC	0-34	L	51,342
Sun	12/3	A	PIT	23-16	W	40,541
Sun	12/10	H	TB	20-17	W	54,532
Sun	12/17	A	CIN	7-61	L	47,510
Sat	12/23	H	CLE	20-24	L	58,852

AFC Wild-Card Playoff

Sun	12/31	H	PIT	*23-26	L	59,406

INDIANAPOLIS COLTS

Sun	9/10	H	SF	24-30	L	60,111
Sun	9/17	A	LARM	17-31	L	63,995
Sun	9/24	H	ATL	13-9	W	57,816
Sun	10/1	A	NYJ	17-10	W	65,542
Sun	10/8	H	BUF	37-14	W	58,890
Sun	10/15	A	DEN	3-14	L	74,680
Sun	10/22	A	CIN	23-12	W	57,642
Sun	10/29	H	NE	*20-23	L	59,356
Sun	11/5	A	MIA	13-19	L	52,680
Sun	11/12	A	BUF	7-30	L	79,256
Sun	11/19	H	NYJ	27-10	W	58,236
Sun	11/26	H	SD	10-6	W	58,822
Sun	12/3	A	NE	16-22	L	32,234
Sun	12/10	H	CLE	*23-17	W	58,550
Sun	12/17	H	MIA	42-13	W	55,665
Sun	12/24	A	NO	6-41	L	49,009

KANSAS CITY CHIEFS

Sun	9/10	A	DEN	20-34	L	74,284
Sun	9/17	H	LARI	24-19	W	71,741
Sun	9/24	A	SD	6-21	L	40,128
Sun	10/1	H	CIN	17-21	L	61,165
Sun	10/8	A	SEA	20-16	W	60,715
Sun	10/15	A	LARI	14-20	L	40,453
Sun	10/22	H	DAL	36-28	W	76,841
Sun	10/29	A	PIT	17-23	L	54,194
Sun	11/5	H	SEA	20-10	W	54,489
Sun	11/12	H	DEN	13-16	L	76,245
Sun	11/19	A	CLE	*10-10	T	77,922
Sun	11/26	H	HOU	34-0	W	51,342
Sun	12/3	H	MIA	26-21	W	54,610
Sun	12/10	A	GB	21-3	W	56,694
Sun	12/17	H	SD	13-20	L	40,623
Sun	12/24	A	MIA	27-24	W	43,612

LOS ANGELES RAIDERS

Sun	9/10	H	SD	40-14	W	40,237
Sun	9/17	A	KC	19-24	L	71,741
Sun	9/24	A	DEN	21-31	L	75,754
Sun	10/1	H	SEA	20-24	L	44,319
Mon	10/9	A	NYJ	14-7	W	68,040
Sun	10/15	H	KC	20-14	W	40,453
Sun	10/22	A	PHI	7-10	L	64,019
Sun	10/29	H	WAS	37-24	W	52,781
Sun	11/5	H	CIN	28-7	W	51,080
Sun	11/12	A	SD	12-14	L	59,151
Sun	11/19	A	HOU	7-23	L	59,198
Sun	11/26	H	NE	24-21	W	38,747
Sun	12/3	H	DEN	*16-13	W	87,560
Sun	12/10	H	PHX	16-14	W	41,785
Sun	12/17	A	SEA	17-23	L	61,076
Sun	12/24	A	NYG	17-34	L	70,306

LOS ANGELES RAMS

Sun	9/10	A	ATL	31-21	W	38,708
Sun	9/17	H	IND	31-17	W	63,995
Sun	9/24	H	GB	41-38	W	57,701
Sun	10/1	A	SF	13-12	W	64,250
Sun	10/8	H	ATL	26-14	W	52,182
Mon	10/16	A	BUF	20-23	L	76,231
Sun	10/22	H	NO	21-40	L	57,567
Sun	10/29	A	CHI	10-20	L	65,506
Sun	11/5	A	MIN	*21-23	L	59,600
Sun	11/12	H	NYG	31-10	W	65,127
Sun	11/19	H	PHX	37-14	W	53,176
Sun	11/26	A	NO	*20-17	W	64,274
Sun	12/3	A	DAL	35-31	W	46,100
Mon	12/11	H	SF	27-30	L	67,959
Sun	12/17	H	NYJ	38-14	W	53,063
Sun	12/24	A	NE	24-20	W	27,940

NFC Wild-Card Playoff

Sun	12/31	A	PHI	21-7	W	65,479

NFC Divisional Playoff

Sun	1/7	A	NYG	*19-13	W	76,526

NFC Championship

Sun	1/14	A	SF	3-30	L	65,634

MIAMI DOLPHINS

Sun	9/10	H	BUF	24-27	L	54,541
Sun	9/17	A	NE	24-10	W	57,043
Sun	9/24	H	NYJ	33-40	L	65,908
Sun	10/1	A	HOU	7-39	L	53,326
Sun	10/8	H	CLE	*13-10	W	58,444
Sun	10/15	A	CIN	20-13	W	58,184
Sun	10/22	H	GB	23-20	W	56,624
Sun	10/29	A	BUF	17-31	L	80,208
Sun	11/5	H	IND	19-13	W	52,680
Sun	11/12	A	NYJ	31-23	W	65,923
Sun	11/19	A	DAL	17-14	W	56,044
Sun	11/26	H	PIT	14-34	L	59,936
Sun	12/3	A	KC	21-26	L	54,610
Sun	12/10	H	NE	31-10	W	55,918
Sun	12/17	A	IND	13-42	L	55,665
Sun	12/24	H	KC	24-27	L	43,612

MINNESOTA VIKINGS

Sun	9/10	H	HOU	38-7	W	54,015
Sun	9/17	A	CHI	7-38	L	66,475
Sun	9/24	A	PIT	14-27	L	50,744
Sun	10/1	H	TB	17-3	W	54,817
Sun	10/8	H	DET	24-17	W	55,380
Sun	10/15	H	GB	26-14	W	62,075
Sun	10/22	A	DET	20-7	W	51,579
Mon	10/30	A	NYG	14-24	L	76,041
Sun	11/5	H	LARM	*23-21	W	59,600
Sun	11/12	A	TB	24-10	W	56,271
Sun	11/19	A	PHI	9-10	L	65,944
Sun	11/26	A	GB	19-20	L	55,592
Sun	12/3	H	CHI	27-16	W	60,664
Sun	12/10	H	ATL	43-17	W	58,116
Sun	12/17	A	CLE	*17-23	L	70,777
Mon	12/25	H	CIN	29-21	W	58,829

NFC Divisional Playoff

Sat	1/6	A	SF	13-41	L	64,918

NEW ENGLAND PATRIOTS

Sun	9/10	A	NYJ	27-24	W	64,541
Sun	9/17	H	MIA	10-24	L	57,043
Sun	9/24	H	SEA	3-24	L	48,025
Sun	10/1	A	BUF	10-31	L	78,921
Sun	10/8	H	HOU	23-13	W	59,828
Sun	10/15	A	ATL	15-16	L	39,697
Sun	10/22	A	SF	20-37	L	51,781
Sun	10/29	A	IND	*23-20	W	59,356
Sun	11/5	H	NYJ	26-27	L	53,366
Sun	11/12	H	NO	24-28	L	47,680

Sun	11/19	H	BUF	33-24	W	49,663
Sun	11/26	A	LARI	21-24	L	38,747
Sun	12/3	H	IND	22-16	W	32,234
Sun	12/10	A	MIA	10-31	L	55,918
Sun	12/17	A	PIT	10-28	L	26,594
Sun	12/24	H	LARM	20-24	L	27,940

New Orleans Saints

Sun	9/10	H	DAL	28-0	W	66,977
Sun	9/17	A	GB	34-35	L	55,809
Sun	9/24	A	TB	10-20	L	44,053
Sun	10/1	H	WAS	14-16	L	64,358
Sun	10/8	A	SF	20-24	L	60,488
Sun	10/15	H	NYJ	29-14	W	59,521
Sun	10/22	A	LARM	40-21	W	57,567
Sun	10/29	H	ATL	20-13	W	65,153
Mon	11/6	H	SF	13-31	L	60,667
Sun	11/12	A	NE	28-24	W	47,680
Sun	11/19	A	ATL	26-17	W	53,173
Sun	11/26	H	LARM	*17-20	L	64,274
Sun	12/3	A	DET	14-21	L	38,550
Sun	12/10	A	BUF	22-19	W	70,037
Mon	12/18	H	PHI	30-20	W	59,218
Sun	12/24	H	IND	41-6	W	49,009

New York Giants

Mon	9/11	A	WAS	27-24	W	54,160
Sun	9/17	H	DET	24-14	W	76,021
Sun	9/24	H	PHX	35-7	W	75,742
Sun	10/1	A	DAL	30-13	W	51,785
Sun	10/8	A	PHI	19-21	L	65,688
Sun	10/15	H	WAS	20-17	W	76,245
Sun	10/22	A	SD	20-13	W	48,556
Mon	10/30	H	MIN	24-14	W	76,041
Sun	11/5	A	PHX	20-13	W	46,588
Sun	11/12	A	LARM	10-31	L	65,127
Sun	11/19	H	SEA	15-3	W	75,014
Mon	11/27	A	SF	24-34	L	63,461
Sun	12/3	H	PHI	17-24	L	74,809
Sun	12/10	A	DEN	14-7	W	63,283
Sat	12/16	H	DAL	15-0	W	72,141
Sun	12/24	H	LARI	34-17	W	70,306

NFC Divisional Playoff

Sun	1/7	H	LARM	*13-19	L	76,526

New York Jets

Sun	9/10	H	NE	24-27	L	64,541
Sun	9/17	A	CLE	24-38	L	73,516
Sun	9/24	A	MIA	40-33	W	65,908
Sun	10/1	H	IND	10-17	L	65,542
Mon	10/9	H	LARI	7-14	L	68,040
Sun	10/15	A	NO	14-29	L	59,521
Sun	10/22	A	BUF	3-34	L	76,811
Sun	10/29	H	SF	10-23	L	62,805
Sun	11/5	A	NE	27-26	W	53,366
Sun	11/12	H	MIA	23-31	L	65,923
Sun	11/19	A	IND	10-27	L	58,236
Sun	11/26	H	ATL	27-7	W	40,429
Sun	12/3	A	SD	20-17	W	38,954
Sun	12/10	H	PIT	0-13	L	41,037
Sun	12/17	A	LARM	14-38	L	53,063
Sat	12/23	H	BUF	0-37	L	21,148

Philadelphia Eagles

Sun	9/10	H	SEA	31-7	W	64,287
Sun	9/17	A	WAS	42-37	W	53,493
Sun	9/24	H	SF	28-38	L	66,042
Mon	10/2	A	CHI	13-27	L	66,625
Sun	10/8	H	NYG	21-19	W	65,688
Sun	10/15	A	PHX	17-5	W	42,620
Sun	10/22	H	LARI	10-7	W	64,019
Sun	10/29	A	DEN	28-24	W	75,065
Sun	11/5	A	SD	17-20	L	47,019
Sun	11/12	H	WAS	3-10	L	65,443
Sun	11/19	H	MIN	10-9	W	65,944
Thu	11/23	A	DAL	27-0	W	54,444
Sun	12/3	A	NYG	24-17	W	74,809
Sun	12/10	H	DAL	20-10	W	59,842
Mon	12/18	A	NO	20-30	L	59,218
Sun	12/24	H	PHX	31-14	W	43,287

NFC Wild-Card Playoff

Sun	12/31	H	LARM	7-21	L	65,479

Phoenix Cardinals

Sun	9/10	A	DET	16-13	W	36,735
Sun	9/17	A	SEA	34-24	W	60,444
Sun	9/24	A	NYG	7-35	L	75,742
Sun	10/1	H	SD	13-24	L	44,201
Sun	10/8	A	WAS	28-30	L	53,335
Sun	10/15	H	PHI	5-17	L	42,620
Sun	10/22	H	ATL	34-20	W	33,894
Sun	10/29	A	DAL	19-10	W	44,431
Sun	11/5	H	NYG	13-20	L	46,588
Sun	11/12	H	DAL	24-20	W	49,657
Sun	11/19	A	LARM	14-37	L	53,176
Sun	11/26	H	TB	13-14	L	33,297
Sun	12/3	H	WAS	10-29	L	38,870
Sun	12/10	A	LARI	14-16	L	41,785
Sat	12/16	H	DEN	0-37	L	56,071
Sun	12/24	A	PHI	14-31	L	43,287

Pittsburgh Steelers

Sun	9/10	H	CLE	0-51	L	57,928
Sun	9/17	A	CIN	10-41	L	53,885
Sun	9/24	H	MIN	27-14	W	50,744
Sun	10/1	A	DET	23-3	W	43,804
Sun	10/8	H	CIN	16-26	L	52,785
Sun	10/15	A	CLE	17-7	W	78,840
Sun	10/22	A	HOU	0-27	L	59,091
Sun	10/29	H	KC	23-17	W	54,194
Sun	11/5	A	DEN	7-34	L	74,739
Sun	11/12	H	CHI	0-20	L	56,505
Sun	11/19	H	SD	20-17	W	44,203
Sun	11/26	A	MIA	34-14	W	59,936
Sun	12/3	H	HOU	16-23	L	40,541
Sun	12/10	A	NYJ	13-0	W	41,037
Sun	12/17	H	NE	28-10	W	26,594
Sun	12/24	A	TB	31-22	W	29,690

AFC Wild-Card Playoff

Sun	12/31	A	HOU	*26-23	W	59,406

AFC Divisional Playoff

Sun	1/7	A	DEN	23-24	L	75,477

San Diego Chargers

Sun	9/10	A	LARI	14-40	L	40,237
Sun	9/17	H	HOU	27-34	L	42,013
Sun	9/24	H	KC	21-6	W	40,128
Sun	10/1	A	PHX	24-13	W	44,201
Sun	10/8	A	DEN	10-16	L	75,222
Sun	10/15	H	SEA	16-17	L	50,079
Sun	10/22	H	NYG	13-20	L	48,566
Sun	10/29	A	SEA	7-10	L	59,691
Sun	11/5	H	PHI	20-17	W	47,019
Sun	11/12	H	LARI	14-12	W	59,151
Sun	11/19	A	PIT	17-20	L	44,203
Sun	11/26	A	IND	6-10	L	58,822
Sun	12/3	H	NYJ	17-20	L	38,954
Sun	12/10	A	WAS	21-26	L	47,693
Sun	12/17	A	KC	20-13	W	40,623
Sun	12/24	H	DEN	19-16	W	50,524

San Francisco 49ers

Sun	9/10	A	IND	30-24	W	60,111
Sun	9/17	A	TB	20-16	W	64,087
Sun	9/24	A	PHI	38-28	W	66,042
Sun	10/1	H	LARM	12-13	L	64,250
Sun	10/8	H	NO	24-20	W	60,488
Sun	10/15	A	DAL	31-14	W	61,077
Sun	10/22	H	NE	37-20	W	51,781
Sun	10/29	A	NYJ	23-10	W	62,805
Mon	11/6	A	NO	31-13	W	60,667
Sun	11/12	H	ATL	45-3	W	59,914
Sun	11/19	H	GB	17-21	L	62,219
Mon	11/27	H	NYG	34-24	W	63,461
Sun	12/3	A	ATL	23-10	W	43,128
Mon	12/11	A	LARM	30-27	W	67,959
Sun	12/17	H	BUF	21-10	W	60,927
Sun	12/24	H	CHI	26-0	W	60,207

NFC Divisional Playoff

Sat	1/6	H	MIN	41-13	W	64,918

NFC Championship

Sun	1/14	H	LARM	30-3	W	65,634

Super Bowl XXIV

Sun	1/28	N	DEN	55-10	W	72,919

Seattle Seahawks

Sun	9/10	A	PHI	7-31	L	64,287
Sun	9/17	H	PHX	24-34	L	60,444
Sun	9/24	A	NE	24-3	W	48,025
Sun	10/1	A	LARI	24-20	W	44,319
Sun	10/8	H	KC	16-20	L	60,715
Sun	10/15	A	SD	17-16	W	50,079
Sun	10/22	H	DEN	*21-24	L	62,353
Sun	10/29	H	SD	10-7	W	59,691
Sun	11/5	A	KC	10-20	L	54,489
Sun	11/12	H	CLE	7-17	L	58,978
Sun	11/19	A	NYG	3-15	L	75,014
Sun	11/26	A	DEN	14-41	L	75,117
Mon	12/4	H	BUF	17-16	W	57,682
Sun	12/10	A	CIN	24-17	W	54,744
Sun	12/17	H	LARI	23-17	W	61,076
Sat	12/23	H	WAS	0-29	L	60,294

Tampa Bay Buccaneers

Sun	9/10	A	GB	23-21	W	55,650
Sun	9/17	H	SF	16-20	L	64,087
Sun	9/24	H	NO	20-10	W	44,053
Sun	10/1	A	MIN	3-17	L	54,817
Sun	10/8	H	CHI	42-35	W	72,077
Sun	10/15	H	DET	16-17	L	46,225
Sun	10/22	A	WAS	28-32	L	53,862
Sun	10/29	A	CIN	23-56	L	57,225
Sun	11/5	H	CLE	31-42	L	69,162
Sun	11/12	H	MIN	10-24	L	56,271
Sun	11/19	A	CHI	32-31	W	63,826
Sun	11/26	A	PHX	14-13	W	33,297
Sun	12/3	H	GB	16-17	L	58,120
Sun	12/10	A	HOU	17-20	L	54,532
Sun	12/17	A	DET	7-33	L	40,362
Sun	12/24	H	PIT	22-31	L	29,690

Washington Redskins

Mon	9/11	H	NYG	24-27	L	54,160
Sun	9/17	H	PHI	37-42	L	53,493
Sun	9/24	A	DAL	30-7	W	63,200
Sun	10/1	A	NO	16-14	W	64,358
Sun	10/8	H	PHX	30-28	W	53,335
Sun	10/15	A	NYG	17-20	L	76,245
Sun	10/22	H	TB	32-28	W	53,862
Sun	10/29	A	LARI	24-37	L	52,781
Sun	11/5	H	DAL	3-13	L	53,187
Sun	11/12	A	PHI	10-3	W	65,443
Mon	11/20	H	DEN	10-14	L	52,975
Sun	11/26	H	CHI	38-14	W	50,044
Sun	12/3	A	PHX	29-10	W	38,870
Sun	12/10	H	SD	26-21	W	47,693
Sun	12/17	A	ATL	31-30	W	37,501
Sat	12/23	A	SEA	29-0	W	60,294

1990 NFL

Atlanta Falcons

Sun	9/9	H	HOU	47-27	W	56,222
Sun	9/16	A	DET	14-21	L	48,961
Sun	9/23	A	SF	13-19	L	62,858
Sun	10/7	H	NO	28-27	W	57,401
Sun	10/14	H	SF	35-45	L	57,921
Sun	10/21	A	LARM	24-44	L	54,761
Sun	10/28	H	CIN	38-17	W	53,214
Sun	11/4	A	PIT	9-21	L	57,093
Sun	11/11	A	CHI	24-30	L	62,855
Sun	11/18	H	PHI	23-24	L	53,755
Sun	11/25	A	NO	7-10	L	68,629
Sun	12/2	A	TB	17-23	L	42,839
Sun	12/9	H	PHX	13-24	L	36,222
Sun	12/16	A	CLE	10-13	L	46,536
Sun	12/23	H	LARM	20-13	W	30,021
Sun	12/30	H	DAL	26-7	W	50,097

Buffalo Bills

Sun	9/9	H	IND	26-10	W	78,899
Sun	9/16	A	MIA	7-30	L	68,142
Mon	9/24	A	NYJ	30-7	W	69,927
Sun	9/30	H	DEN	29-28	W	74,393
Sun	10/7	H	LARI	38-24	W	80,076
Sun	10/21	H	NYJ	30-27	W	79,002
Sun	10/28	A	NE	27-10	W	51,959
Sun	11/4	A	CLE	42-0	W	78,331
Sun	11/11	H	PHX	45-14	W	74,904
Sun	11/18	H	NE	14-0	W	74,720
Mon	11/26	A	HOU	24-27	L	60,130
Sun	12/2	H	PHI	30-23	W	79,320
Sun	12/9	A	IND	31-7	W	53,268
Sat	12/15	A	NYG	17-13	W	66,893
Sun	12/23	H	MIA	24-14	W	80,235
Sun	12/30	A	WAS	14-29	L	52,397

AFC Divisional Playoff

Sat	1/12	H	MIA	44-34	W	77,087

AFC Championship

Sun	1/20	H	LARI	51-3	W	80,324

Super Bowl XXV

Sun	1/27	N	NYG	19-20	L	73,813

Chicago Bears

Sun	9/9	H	SEA	17-0	W	64,400
Sun	9/16	A	GB	31-13	W	58,938
Sun	9/23	H	MIN	19-16	W	65,420
Sun	9/30	A	LARI	10-24	L	80,156
Sun	10/7	H	GB	27-13	W	59,929
Sun	10/14	H	LARM	38-9	W	59,383
Sun	10/28	A	PHX	31-21	W	71,233
Sun	11/4	A	TB	26-6	W	68,555
Sun	11/11	H	ATL	30-24	W	62,855
Sun	11/18	A	DEN	*16-13	W	75,013
Sun	11/25	A	MIN	13-41	L	58,866
Sun	12/2	H	DET	*23-17	W	62,313
Sun	12/9	A	WAS	9-10	L	53,920
Sun	12/16	A	DET	21-38	L	67,759
Sun	12/23	H	TB	27-14	W	46,456
Sat	12/29	H	KC	10-21	L	60,262

NFC Wild-Card Playoff

Sun	1/6	H	NO	16-6	W	60,767

NFC Divisional Playoff

Sun	1/13	A	NYG	3-31	L	77,025

Cincinnati Bengals

Sun	9/9	H	NYJ	25-20	W	56,467
Sun	9/16	A	SD	21-16	W	48,098
Sun	9/23	H	NE	41-7	W	56,470
Mon	10/1	A	SEA	16-31	L	60,135
Sun	10/7	A	LARM	*34-31	W	62,619
Sun	10/14	A	HOU	17-48	L	53,501
Mon	10/22	A	CLE	34-13	W	78,567
Sun	10/28	A	ATL	17-38	L	53,214
Sun	11/4	H	NO	7-21	L	60,067
Sun	11/18	H	PIT	27-3	W	60,064
Sun	11/25	H	IND	20-34	L	60,051
Sun	12/2	A	PIT	16-12	W	58,200
Sun	12/9	H	SF	*17-20	L	60,084
Sun	12/16	A	LARI	7-24	L	54,132
Sun	12/23	H	HOU	40-20	W	60,044
Sun	12/30	H	CLE	21-14	W	60,041

AFC Wild-Card Playoff

Sun	1/6	H	HOU	41-14	W	60,012

AFC Divisional Playoff
Sun 1/13 A LARI 10-20 L 92,045

CLEVELAND BROWNS
Sun 9/9 H PIT 13-3 W 78,298
Sun 9/16 A NYJ 21-24 L 67,354
Sun 9/23 H SD 14-24 L 77,429
Sun 9/30 A KC 0-34 L 75,462
Mon 10/8 A DEN 30-29 W 74,814
Sun 10/14 A NO 20-25 L 68,608
Mon 10/22 H CIN 13-34 L 78,567
Sun 10/28 A SF 17-20 L 63,672
Sun 11/4 H BUF 0-42 L 78,331
Sun 11/18 A HOU 23-35 L 76,726
Sun 11/25 H MIA 13-30 L 70,225
Sun 12/2 H LARM 23-38 L 61,981
Sun 12/9 A HOU 14-58 L 54,469
Sun 12/16 H ATL 13-10 W 46,536
Sun 12/23 A PIT 0-35 L 51,665
Sun 12/30 A CIN 14-21 L 60,041

DALLAS COWBOYS
Sun 9/9 H SD 17-14 W 48,063
Sun 9/16 H NYG 7-28 L 61,090
Sun 9/23 A WAS 15-19 L 53,804
Sun 9/30 A NYG 17-31 L 75,923
Sun 10/7 H TB 14-10 W 60,076
Sun 10/14 A PHX 3-20 L 45,235
Sun 10/21 A TB 17-13 W 68,315
Sun 10/28 H PHI 20-21 L 62,605
Sun 11/4 A NYJ 9-24 L 68,086
Sun 11/11 H SF 6-24 L 62,966
Sun 11/18 A LARM 24-21 W 58,589
Thu 11/22 H WAS 27-17 W 60,355
Sun 12/2 H NO 17-13 W 60,087
Sun 12/16 H PHX 41-10 W 60,190
Sun 12/23 A PHI 3-17 L 63,895
Sun 12/30 A ATL 7-26 L 50,097

DENVER BRONCOS
Sun 9/9 A LARI 9-14 L 54,206
Mon 9/17 H KC 24-23 W 75,277
Sun 9/23 H SEA *34-31 W 75,290
Sun 9/30 A BUF 28-29 L 74,393
Mon 10/8 A CLE 29-30 L 74,814
Sun 10/14 H PIT 17-34 L 74,285
Sun 10/21 A IND 27-17 W 59,850
Sun 11/4 A MIN 22-27 L 57,331
Sun 11/11 H SD 7-19 L 59,557
Sun 11/18 H CHI *13-16 L 75,013
Thu 11/22 A DET 27-40 L 73,896
Sun 12/2 H LARI 20-23 L 74,162
Sun 12/9 A KC 20-31 L 74,347
Sun 12/16 H SD 20-10 W 64,919
Sun 12/23 A SEA 12-17 L 55,845
Sun 12/30 H GB 22-13 W 46,943

DETROIT LIONS
Sun 9/9 H TB 21-38 L 56,692
Sun 9/16 H ATL 21-14 W 48,961
Sun 9/23 A TB 20-23 L 55,075
Sun 9/30 H GB 21-24 L 64,509
Sun 10/7 A MIN 34-27 W 57,586
Sun 10/14 A KC 24-43 L 74,312
Sun 10/28 A NO 27-10 W 64,368
Sun 11/4 H WAS *38-41 L 69,326
Sun 11/11 H MIN 7-17 L 68,264
Sun 11/18 A NYG 0-20 L 76,109
Thu 11/22 H DEN 40-27 W 73,896
Mon 12/2 A CHI *17-23 L 62,313
Mon 12/10 H LARI 31-38 L 72,190
Sun 12/16 A CHI 38-21 W 67,759
Sat 12/22 A GB 24-17 W 46,700
Sun 12/30 A SEA 10-30 L 50,681

GREEN BAY PACKERS
Sun 9/9 H LARM 36-24 W 57,685

Sun 9/16 H CHI 13-31 L 58,938
Sun 9/23 H KC 3-17 L 58,817
Sun 9/30 A DET 24-21 W 64,509
Sun 10/7 A CHI 13-27 L 59,929
Sun 10/14 A TB 14-26 L 67,472
Sun 10/28 H MIN 24-10 W 55,125
Sun 11/4 H SF 20-24 L 58,835
Sun 11/11 A LARI 29-16 W 50,855
Sun 11/18 A PHX 24-21 W 46,878
Sun 11/25 H TB 20-10 W 53,677
Sun 12/2 A MIN 7-23 L 62,058
Sun 12/9 H SEA 14-20 L 52,015
Sun 12/16 A PHI 0-31 L 65,627
Sat 12/22 H DET 17-24 L 46,700
Sun 12/30 A DEN 13-22 L 46,943

HOUSTON OILERS
Sun 9/9 A ATL 27-47 L 56,222
Sun 9/16 A PIT 9-20 L 54,814
Sun 9/23 H IND 24-10 W 50,093
Sun 9/30 A SD 17-7 W 48,762
Sun 10/7 H SF 21-24 L 59,931
Sun 10/14 H CIN 48-17 W 53,501
Sun 10/21 H NO 23-10 W 57,908
Sun 10/28 H NYJ 12-17 L 56,337
Sun 11/4 A LARM 13-17 L 52,628
Sun 11/18 A CLE 35-23 W 76,726
Mon 11/26 H BUF 27-24 W 60,130
Sun 12/2 A SEA *10-13 L 57,592
Sun 12/9 H CLE 58-14 W 54,469
Sun 12/16 A KC 27-10 W 61,756
Sun 12/23 A CIN 20-40 L 60,044
Sun 12/30 H PIT 34-14 W 56,906

AFC Wild-Card Playoff
Sun 1/6 A CIN 14-41 L 60,012

INDIANAPOLIS COLTS
Sun 9/9 A BUF 10-26 L 78,899
Sun 9/16 H NE 14-16 L 49,256
Sun 9/23 A HOU 10-24 L 50,093
Sun 9/30 A PHI 24-23 W 62,067
Sun 10/7 H KC 23-19 W 54,950
Sun 10/21 H DEN 17-27 L 59,850
Sun 10/28 H MIA 7-27 L 59,213
Mon 11/5 H NYG 7-24 L 58,688
Sun 11/11 A NE 13-10 W 28,924
Sun 11/18 A NYJ 17-14 W 47,283
Sun 11/25 A CIN 34-20 W 60,051
Sun 12/2 H PHX 17-20 L 31,885
Sun 12/9 H BUF 7-31 L 53,268
Sun 12/16 H NYJ 29-21 W 41,423
Sat 12/22 H WAS 35-28 W 58,173
Sun 12/30 A MIA 17-23 L 59,547

KANSAS CITY CHIEFS
Sun 9/9 H MIN 24-21 W 68,363
Mon 9/17 A DEN 23-24 L 75,277
Sun 9/23 A GB 17-3 W 58,817
Sun 9/30 H CLE 34-0 W 75,462
Sun 10/7 A IND 19-23 L 54,950
Sun 10/14 H DET 43-24 W 74,312
Sun 10/21 A SEA 7-19 L 60,358
Sun 11/4 H LARI 9-7 W 70,951
Sun 11/11 H SEA 16-17 L 71,285
Sun 11/18 H SD 27-10 W 63,717
Sun 11/25 A LARI 27-24 W 65,710
Sun 12/2 A NE 37-7 W 26,280
Sun 12/9 H DEN 31-20 W 74,347
Sun 12/16 H HOU 10-27 L 61,756
Sun 12/23 A SD 24-21 W 45,135
Sat 12/29 A CHI 21-10 W 60,262

AFC Wild-Card Playoff
Sat 1/5 A MIA 16-17 L 67,276

LOS ANGELES RAIDERS
Sun 9/9 H DEN 14-9 W 54,206

Sun 9/16 A SEA 17-13 W 61,889
Sun 9/23 H PIT 20-3 W 50,657
Sun 9/30 H CHI 24-10 W 80,156
Sun 10/7 A BUF 24-38 L 80,076
Sun 10/14 H SEA 24-17 W 50,624
Sun 10/21 A SD 24-9 W 60,569
Sun 11/4 A KC 7-9 L 70,951
Sun 11/11 H GB 16-29 L 50,855
Mon 11/19 A MIA 13-10 W 70,553
Sun 11/25 H KC 24-27 L 65,710
Sun 12/2 A DEN 23-20 W 74,162
Mon 12/10 A DET 38-31 W 72,190
Sun 12/16 H CIN 24-7 W 54,132
Sat 12/22 H MIN 28-24 W 53,899
Sun 12/30 H SD 17-12 W 62,593

AFC Divisional Playoff
Sun 1/13 H CIN 20-10 W 92,045

AFC Championship
Sun 1/20 A BUF 3-51 L 80,324

LOS ANGELES RAMS
Sun 9/9 A GB 24-36 L 57,685
Sun 9/16 A TB 35-14 W 59,705
Sun 9/23 H PHI 21-27 L 63,644
Sun 10/7 H CIN *31-34 L 62,619
Sun 10/14 A CHI 9-38 L 59,383
Sun 10/21 H ATL 44-24 W 54,761
Mon 10/29 A PIT 10-41 L 56,466
Sun 11/4 H HOU 17-13 W 52,628
Sun 11/11 H NYG 7-31 L 64,632
Sun 11/18 H DAL 21-24 L 58,589
Sun 11/25 A SF 18-17 W 62,633
Sun 12/2 A CLE 38-23 W 61,981
Sun 12/9 H NO 20-24 L 56,864
Mon 12/17 H SF 10-26 L 65,619
Sun 12/23 A ATL 13-20 L 30,021
Mon 12/31 A NO 17-20 L 68,647

MIAMI DOLPHINS
Sun 9/9 A NE 27-24 W 45,305
Sun 9/16 H BUF 30-7 W 68,142
Sun 9/23 A NYG 3-20 L 76,483
Sun 9/30 A PIT 28-6 W 54,691
Sun 10/7 H NYJ 20-16 W 69,678
Thu 10/18 A NE 17-10 W 62,630
Sun 10/28 A IND 27-7 W 59,213
Sun 11/4 H PHX 23-3 W 54,924
Sun 11/11 A NYJ 17-3 L 68,362
Mon 11/19 H LARI 10-13 L 70,553
Sun 11/25 A CLE 30-13 W 70,225
Sun 12/2 A WAS 20-42 L 53,599
Sun 12/9 H PHI *23-20 W 67,034
Sun 12/16 H SEA 24-17 W 57,851
Sun 12/23 A BUF 14-24 L 80,235
Sun 12/30 H IND 23-17 W 59,547

AFC Wild-Card Playoff
Sat 1/5 H KC 17-16 W 67,276

AFC Divisional Playoff
Sat 1/12 A BUF 34-44 L 77,087

MINNESOTA VIKINGS
Sun 9/9 A KC 21-24 L 68,363
Sun 9/16 H NO 32-3 W 56,272
Sun 9/23 A CHI 16-19 L 65,420
Sun 9/30 H TB *20-23 L 54,462
Sun 10/7 H DET 27-34 L 57,586
Mon 10/15 A PHI 24-32 L 66,296
Sun 10/28 A GB 10-24 L 55,125
Sun 11/4 H DEN 27-22 W 57,331
Sun 11/11 A DET 17-7 W 68,264
Sun 11/18 A SEA 24-21 W 59,735
Sun 11/25 H CHI 41-13 W 58,866
Sun 12/2 H GB 23-7 W 62,058
Sun 12/9 A NYG 15-23 L 76,121
Sun 12/16 H TB 13-26 L 47,272
Sat 12/22 A LARI 24-28 L 53,899

Sun 12/30 H SF 17-20 L 51,590

NEW ENGLAND PATRIOTS
Sun 9/9 H MIA 24-27 L 45,305
Sun 9/16 A IND 16-14 W 49,256
Sun 9/23 H CIN 7-41 L 56,470
Sun 9/30 H NYJ 13-37 L 36,724
Sun 10/7 H SEA 20-33 L 39,735
Thu 10/18 A MIA 10-17 L 62,630
Sun 10/28 H BUF 10-27 L 51,959
Sun 11/4 H PHI 20-48 L 65,514
Sun 11/11 H IND 10-13 L 28,924
Sun 11/18 H BUF 0-14 L 74,720
Sun 11/25 H PHX 14-34 L 30,110
Sun 12/2 H KC 7-37 L 26,280
Sun 12/9 A PIT 3-24 L 48,354
Sat 12/15 H WAS 10-25 L 22,286
Sun 12/23 A NYJ 7-42 L 30,250
Sun 12/30 H NYG 10-13 L 60,410

NEW ORLEANS SAINTS
Mon 9/10 H SF 12-13 L 68,629
Sun 9/16 A MIN 3-32 L 56,672
Sun 9/23 H PHX 28-7 W 61,110
Sun 10/7 A ATL 27-28 L 57,401
Sun 10/14 H CLE 25-20 W 68,608
Sun 10/21 A HOU 10-23 L 57,908
Sun 10/28 H DET 10-27 L 64,368
Sun 11/4 A CIN 21-7 W 60,067
Sun 11/11 H TB 35-7 W 67,855
Sun 11/18 A WAS 17-31 L 52,573
Sun 11/25 H ATL 10-7 W 68,629
Sun 12/2 A DAL 13-17 L 60,087
Sun 12/9 A LARM 24-20 W 56,864
Sun 12/16 H PIT 6-9 L 68,582
Sun 12/23 A SF 13-10 W 60,112
Mon 12/31 H LARM 20-17 W 68,647

NFC Wild-Card Playoff
Sun 1/6 A CHI 6-16 L 60,767

NEW YORK GIANTS
Sun 9/9 H PHI 27-20 W 76,202
Sun 9/16 A DAL 28-7 W 61,090
Sun 9/23 H MIA 20-3 W 76,483
Sun 9/30 H DAL 31-17 W 75,923
Sun 10/14 A WAS 24-20 W 54,737
Sun 10/21 H PHX 20-19 W 76,518
Sun 10/28 A WAS 21-10 W 75,321
Mon 11/5 A IND 24-7 W 58,688
Sun 11/11 A LARM 31-7 W 64,632
Sun 11/18 H DET 20-0 W 76,109
Sun 11/25 A PHI 13-31 L 66,706
Mon 12/3 A SF 3-7 L 66,092
Sun 12/9 H MIN 23-15 W 76,121
Sat 12/15 H BUF 13-17 L 66,893
Sun 12/23 A PHX 24-21 W 41,212
Sun 12/30 A NE 13-10 W 60,410

NFC Divisional Playoff
Sun 1/13 H CHI 31-3 W 77,025

NFC Championship
Sun 1/20 A SF 15-13 W 66,334

Super Bowl XXV
Sun 1/27 N BUF 20-19 W 73,813

NEW YORK JETS
Sun 9/9 A CIN 20-25 L 56,467
Sun 9/16 H CLE 24-21 W 67,354
Mon 9/24 H BUF 7-30 L 69,927
Sun 9/30 A NE 37-13 W 36,724
Sun 10/7 A MIA 16-20 L 69,678
Sun 10/14 H SD 3-39 L 63,311
Sun 10/21 A BUF 27-30 L 79,002
Sun 10/28 A HOU 17-12 W 56,337
Sun 11/4 H DAL 24-9 W 68,086
Sun 11/11 H MIA 3-17 L 68,362
Sun 11/18 A IND 14-17 L 47,283

Sun 11/25 H PIT 7-24 L 57,806
Sun 12/2 A SD 17-38 L 40,877
Sun 12/16 H IND 21-29 L 41,423
Sun 12/23 H NE 42-7 W 30,250
Sun 12/30 A TB 16-14 W 46,543

PHILADELPHIA EAGLES
Sun 9/9 A NYG 20-27 L 76,202
Sun 9/16 H PHX 21-23 L 64,396
Sun 9/23 A LARM 27-21 W 63,644
Sun 9/30 H IND 23-24 L 62,067
Mon 10/15 H MIN 32-24 W 66,296
Sun 10/21 A WAS 7-13 L 53,567
Sun 10/28 A DAL 21-20 W 62,605
Sun 11/4 H NE 48-20 W 65,514
Mon 11/12 H WAS 28-14 W 65,857
Sun 11/18 A ATL 24-23 W 53,755
Sun 11/25 A NYG 31-13 W 66,706
Sun 12/2 A BUF 23-30 L 79,320
Sun 12/9 H MIA *20-23 L 67,034
Sun 12/16 H GB 31-0 W 65,627
Sun 12/23 H DAL 17-3 W 63,895
Sat 12/29 A PHX 23-21 W 31,796

NFC WILD-CARD PLAYOFF
Sat 1/5 H WAS 6-20 L 65,287

PHOENIX CARDINALS
Sun 9/9 A WAS 0-31 L 52,649
Sun 9/16 A PHI 23-21 W 64,396
Sun 9/23 A NO 7-28 L 61,110
Sun 9/30 H WAS 10-38 L 49,303
Sun 10/14 H DAL 20-3 W 45,235
Sun 10/21 A NYG 19-20 L 76,518
Sun 10/28 H CHI 21-31 L 71,233
Sun 11/4 A MIA 3-23 L 54,924
Sun 11/11 A BUF 14-45 L 74,904
Sun 11/18 A GB 21-24 L 46,878
Sun 11/25 H NE 34-14 W 30,110
Sun 12/2 H IND 20-17 W 31,885
Sun 12/9 A ATL 24-13 W 36,222
Sun 12/16 A DAL 10-41 L 60,190
Sun 12/23 H NYG 21-24 L 41,212
Sat 12/29 H PHI 21-23 L 31,796

PITTSBURGH STEELERS
Sun 9/9 A CLE 3-13 L 78,298
Sun 9/16 H HOU 20-9 W 54,814
Sun 9/23 A LARI 3-20 L 50,657
Sun 9/30 H MIA 6-28 L 54,691
Sun 10/7 H SD 36-14 W 53,486
Sun 10/14 A DEN 34-17 W 74,285
Sun 10/21 A SF 7-27 L 64,301
Mon 10/29 H LARM 41-10 W 56,466
Sun 11/4 H ATL 21-9 W 57,093
Sun 11/18 A CIN 3-27 L 60,064
Sun 11/25 A NYJ 24-7 W 57,806
Sun 12/2 H CIN 12-16 L 58,200
Sun 12/9 H NE 24-3 W 48,354
Sun 12/16 A NO 9-6 W 68,582
Sun 12/23 H CLE 35-0 W 51,665
Sun 12/30 A HOU 14-34 L 56,906

SAN DIEGO CHARGERS
Sun 9/9 A DAL 14-17 L 48,063
Sun 9/16 A CIN 16-21 L 48,098
Sun 9/23 A CLE 24-14 W 77,429
Sun 9/30 H HOU 7-17 L 48,762
Sun 10/7 A PIT 14-36 L 53,486
Sun 10/14 A NYJ 39-3 W 63,311
Sun 10/21 H LARI 9-24 L 60,569
Sun 10/28 H TB 41-10 W 40,653
Sun 11/4 A SEA 31-14 W 59,646
Sun 11/11 H DEN 19-7 W 59,557
Sun 11/18 A KC 10-27 L 63,717
Sun 11/25 H SEA *10-13 L 50,097
Sun 12/2 H NYJ 38-17 W 40,877
Sun 12/16 A DEN 10-20 L 64,919
Sun 12/23 H KC 21-24 L 45,135
Sun 12/30 A LARI 12-17 L 62,593

SAN FRANCISCO 49ERS
Mon 9/10 A NO 13-12 W 68,629
Sun 9/16 H WAS 26-13 W 64,287
Sun 9/23 H ATL 19-13 W 62,858
Sun 10/7 A HOU 24-21 W 59,931
Sun 10/14 A ATL 45-35 W 57,921
Sun 10/21 H PIT 27-7 W 64,301
Sun 10/28 H CLE 20-17 W 63,672
Sun 11/4 A GB 24-20 W 58,835
Sun 11/11 A DAL 24-6 W 62,966
Sun 11/18 H TB 31-7 W 62,221
Sun 11/25 H LARM 17-28 L 62,633
Mon 12/3 H NYG 7-3 W 66,092
Sun 12/9 A CIN *20-17 W 60,084
Mon 12/17 A LARM 26-10 W 65,619
Sun 12/23 H NO 10-13 L 60,112
Sun 12/30 A MIN 20-17 W 51,590

NFC DIVISIONAL PLAYOFF
Sat 1/12 H WAS 28-10 W 65,292

NFC CHAMPIONSHIP
Sun 1/20 H NYG 13-15 L 66,334

SEATTLE SEAHAWKS
Sun 9/9 A CHI 0-17 L 64,400
Sun 9/16 H LARI 13-17 L 61,889
Sun 9/23 A DEN *31-14 W 75,290
Mon 10/1 A CIN 31-16 W 60,135
Sun 10/7 A NE 33-20 W 39,735
Sun 10/14 A LARI 17-24 L 50,624
Sun 10/21 H KC 19-7 W 60,358
Sun 11/4 H SD 14-31 L 59,646
Sun 11/11 A KC 17-16 W 71,285
Sun 11/18 H MIN 21-24 L 59,735
Sun 11/25 A SD *13-10 W 50,097
Sun 12/2 H HOU *13-10 W 57,592
Sun 12/9 A GB 20-14 W 52,015
Sun 12/16 A MIA 17-24 L 57,851
Sun 12/23 H DEN 17-12 W 55,845
Sun 12/30 H DET 30-10 W 50,681

TAMPA BAY BUCCANEERS
Sun 9/9 A DET 38-21 W 56,692
Sun 9/16 H LARM 14-35 L 59,705
Sun 9/23 H DET 23-20 W 55,075
Sun 9/30 A MIN *23-20 W 54,462
Sun 10/7 A DAL 10-14 L 60,076
Sun 10/14 H GB 26-14 W 67,472
Sun 10/21 H DAL 13-17 L 68,315
Sun 10/28 A SD 10-41 L 40,653
Sun 11/4 H CHI 6-26 L 68,555
Sun 11/11 A NO 7-35 L 67,855
Sun 11/18 A SF 7-31 L 62,221
Sun 11/25 A GB 10-20 L 53,677
Sun 12/2 H ATL 23-17 L 42,839
Sun 12/16 H MIN 26-13 W 47,272
Sun 12/23 A CHI 14-27 L 46,456
Sun 12/30 H NYJ 14-16 L 46,543

WASHINGTON REDSKINS
Sun 9/9 H PHX 31-0 W 52,649
Sun 9/16 A SF 13-26 L 64,287
Sun 9/23 H DAL 19-15 W 53,804
Sun 9/30 A PHX 38-10 W 49,303
Sun 10/14 H NYG 20-24 L 54,737
Sun 10/21 H PHI 13-7 W 53,567
Sun 10/28 A NYG 10-21 L 75,321
Sun 11/4 A DET *41-38 W 69,326
Mon 11/12 A PHI 14-28 L 65,857
Sun 11/18 H NO 31-17 W 52,573
Thu 11/22 A DAL 17-27 L 60,355
Sun 12/2 H MIA 42-20 W 53,599
Sun 12/9 A CHI 10-9 W 53,920
Sat 12/15 A NE 25-10 W 22,286
Sat 12/22 A IND 28-35 L 58,173

Sun 12/30 H BUF 29-14 W 52,397

NFC WILD-CARD PLAYOFF
Sat 1/5 A PHI 20-6 W 65,287

NFC DIVISIONAL PLAYOFF
Sat 1/12 A SF 10-28 L 65,292

1991 NFL
ATLANTA FALCONS
Sun 9/1 A KC 3-14 L 74,246
Sun 9/8 H MIN 19-20 L 50,936
Sun 9/15 A SD 13-10 W 44,804
Sun 9/22 H LARI 21-17 W 53,615
Sun 9/29 H NO 6-27 L 56,556
Sun 10/13 H SF 39-34 W 66,210
Sun 10/20 A PHX 10-16 L 24,124
Sun 10/27 H LARM 31-14 W 50,187
Sun 11/3 A SF 17-14 W 51,259
Sun 11/10 A WAS 17-56 L 52,461
Sun 11/17 H TB 43-7 W 41,274
Sun 11/24 A NO *23-20 W 68,591
Sun 12/1 H GB 35-31 W 43,270
Sun 12/8 A LARM 31-14 W 35,315
Sun 12/15 H SEA 26-13 W 53,834
Sun 12/22 A DAL 27-31 L 60,962

NFC WILD-CARD PLAYOFF
Sat 12/28 A NO 27-20 W 68,299

NFC DIVISIONAL PLAYOFF
Sat 1/4 A WAS 7-24 L 55,181

BUFFALO BILLS
Sun 9/1 H MIA 35-31 W 80,252
Sun 9/8 H PIT 52-34 W 79,545
Sun 9/15 A NYG 23-20 W 65,309
Sun 9/22 H TB 17-10 W 57,323
Sun 9/29 H CHI 35-20 W 80,366
Mon 10/7 A KC 6-33 L 76,120
Sun 10/13 H IND 42-6 W 79,015
Mon 10/21 H CIN 35-16 W 80,131
Sun 11/3 H NE 22-17 W 78,278
Sun 11/10 A GB 34-24 W 52,175
Mon 11/18 A MIA 41-27 W 71,062
Sun 11/24 A NE 13-16 L 47,053
Sun 12/1 H NYJ 24-13 W 80,243
Sun 12/8 A LARI *30-27 W 85,081
Sun 12/15 A IND 35-7 W 48,286
Sun 12/22 A DET *14-17 L 78,059

AFC DIVISIONAL PLAYOFF
Sun 1/5 H KC 37-14 W 80,182

AFC CHAMPIONSHIP
Sun 1/12 H DEN 10-7 W 80,272

SUPER BOWL XXVI
Sun 1/26 N WAS 24-37 L 63,130

CHICAGO BEARS
Sun 9/1 H MIN 10-6 W 64,112
Sun 9/8 A TB 21-20 W 62,409
Sun 9/15 H NYG 20-17 W 64,829
Mon 9/23 H NYJ *19-13 W 65,255
Sun 9/29 A BUF 20-35 L 80,366
Sun 10/6 H WAS 7-20 L 64,941
Thu 10/17 A GB 10-0 W 58,435
Sun 10/27 A NO 20-17 W 68,591
Sun 11/3 H DET 20-10 W 57,281
Mon 11/11 A MIN 34-17 W 59,001
Sun 11/17 A IND 31-17 W 60,519
Sun 11/24 A MIA *13-16 L 58,288
Thu 11/28 A DET 6-16 L 78,879
Sun 12/8 H GB 27-13 W 62,353
Sat 12/14 H TB 27-0 W 54,719
Mon 12/23 A SF 14-52 L 60,419

NFC WILD-CARD PLAYOFF
Sun 12/29 H DAL 13-17 L 66,213

CINCINNATI BENGALS
Sun 9/1 A DEN 14-45 L 72,855
Sun 9/8 H HOU 7-30 L 56,463
Sun 9/15 A CLE 13-14 L 78,269
Sun 9/22 H WAS 27-34 L 52,038
Sun 10/6 H SEA 7-13 L 60,010
Sun 10/13 A DAL 23-35 L 63,275
Mon 10/21 A BUF 16-35 L 80,131
Sun 10/27 A HOU 3-35 L 58,634
Sun 11/3 H CLE 23-21 W 55,077
Sun 11/10 H PIT *27-33 L 55,503
Sun 11/17 A PHI 10-17 L 63,189
Sun 11/24 H LARI 14-38 L 52,044
Sun 12/1 H NYG 27-24 W 45,063
Mon 12/9 A MIA 13-37 L 60,616
Sun 12/15 A PIT 10-17 L 35,420
Sun 12/22 H NE 29-7 W 46,394

CLEVELAND BROWNS
Sun 9/1 H DAL 14-26 L 78,860
Sun 9/8 A NE 20-0 W 35,377
Sun 9/15 H CIN 14-13 W 78,269
Sun 9/22 A NYG 10-13 L 75,891
Sun 10/6 H NYJ 14-17 L 71,042
Sun 10/13 A WAS 17-42 L 54,715
Sun 10/20 A SD *30-24 W 48,440
Sun 10/27 H PIT 17-14 W 78,285
Sun 11/3 A CIN 21-23 L 55,077
Sun 11/10 H PHI 30-32 L 72,086
Sun 11/17 A HOU 24-28 L 58,155
Sun 11/24 H KC 20-15 W 63,991
Sun 12/1 A IND 31-0 W 57,539
Sun 12/8 H DEN 7-17 L 73,539
Sun 12/15 H HOU 14-17 L 55,680
Sun 12/22 A PIT 10-17 L 47,070

DALLAS COWBOYS
Sun 9/1 A CLE 26-14 W 78,860
Mon 9/9 H WAS 31-33 L 63,025
Sun 9/15 A PHI 0-24 L 62,656
Sun 9/22 A PHX 17-9 W 68,814
Sun 9/29 H NYG 21-16 W 64,010
Sun 10/6 A GB 20-17 W 53,695
Sun 10/13 H CIN 35-23 W 63,275
Sun 10/27 A DET 10-34 L 74,906
Sun 11/3 H PHX 27-7 W 61,190
Sun 11/10 A HOU *23-26 L 63,001
Sun 11/17 A NYG 9-22 L 76,410
Sun 11/24 A WAS 24-21 W 55,561
Thu 11/28 H PIT 20-10 W 62,253
Sun 12/8 H NO 23-14 W 64,530
Sun 12/15 A PHI 25-13 W 65,854
Sun 12/22 A ATL 31-27 W 60,962

NFC WILD-CARD PLAYOFF
Sun 12/29 A CHI 17-13 W 66,213

NFC DIVISIONAL PLAYOFF
Sun 1/5 A DET 6-38 L 79,166

DENVER BRONCOS
Sun 9/1 H CIN 45-14 W 72,855
Sun 9/8 A LARI 13-16 L 50,812
Sun 9/15 H SEA 16-10 W 74,152
Sun 9/22 H SD 27-19 W 73,258
Sun 9/29 A MIN 13-6 W 55,031
Sun 10/6 A HOU 14-42 L 59,145
Sun 10/20 H KC 19-16 W 75,866
Sun 10/27 A NE 9-6 W 43,994
Sun 11/3 H PIT 20-13 W 70,973
Sun 11/10 A LARI 16-17 L 75,896
Sun 11/17 A KC 24-20 W 74,661
Sun 11/24 A SEA 10-13 L 60,430
Sun 12/1 H NE 20-3 W 67,116
Sun 12/8 A CLE 17-7 W 73,539
Sun 12/15 H PHX 24-19 W 74,098
Sun 12/22 A SD 17-14 W 51,449

AFC DIVISIONAL PLAYOFF
Sat 1/4 H HOU 26-24 W 75,301

AFC CHAMPIONSHIP
Sun 1/12 A BUF 7-10 L 80,272

DETROIT LIONS

Sun	9/1	A	WAS	0-45	L	52,958
Sun	9/8	H	GB	23-14	W	43,132
Sun	9/15	H	MIA	17-13	W	56,896
Sun	9/22	A	IND	33-24	W	53,396
Sun	9/29	H	TB	31-3	W	48,784
Sun	10/6	H	MIN	24-20	W	63,423
Sun	10/20	A	SF	3-35	L	61,240
Sun	10/27	H	DAL	34-10	W	74,906
Sun	11/3	A	CHI	10-20	L	57,281
Sun	11/10	A	TB	21-30	L	37,742
Sun	11/17	H	LARM	21-10	W	60,873
Sun	11/24	A	MIN	34-14	W	51,644
Thu	11/28	H	CHI	16-6	W	78,879
Sun	12/8	H	NYJ	34-20	W	69,304
Sun	12/15	A	GB	21-17	W	43,881
Sun	12/22	A	BUF	*17-14	W	78,059

NFC Divisional Playoff

Sun	1/5	H	DAL	38-6	W	79,166

NFC Championship

Sun	1/12	A	WAS	10-41	L	55,585

GREEN BAY PACKERS

Sun	9/1	H	PHI	3-20	L	58,991
Sun	9/8	A	DET	14-23	L	43,132
Sun	9/15	H	TB	15-13	W	58,114
Sun	9/22	A	MIA	13-16	L	56,583
Sun	9/29	A	LARM	21-23	L	54,736
Sun	10/6	H	DAL	17-20	L	53,695
Thu	10/17	H	CHI	0-10	L	58,435
Sun	10/27	A	TB	27-0	W	40,275
Sun	11/3	A	NYJ	*16-19	L	67,435
Sun	11/10	H	BUF	24-34	L	52,175
Sun	11/17	H	MIN	21-35	L	57,614
Sun	11/24	H	IND	14-10	W	42,132
Sun	12/1	A	ATL	31-35	L	43,270
Sun	12/8	A	CHI	13-27	L	62,353
Sun	12/15	H	DET	17-21	L	43,881
Sat	12/21	A	MIN	27-7	W	52,860

HOUSTON OILERS

Sun	9/1	H	LARI	47-17	W	61,367
Sun	9/8	A	CIN	30-7	W	56,463
Mon	9/16	H	KC	17-7	W	61,058
Sun	9/22	A	NE	20-24	L	30,702
Sun	10/6	H	DEN	42-14	W	59,145
Sun	10/13	A	NYJ	23-20	W	70,758
Sun	10/20	A	MIA	17-13	W	60,705
Sun	10/27	H	CIN	35-3	W	58,634
Sun	11/3	A	WAS	*13-16	L	55,096
Sun	11/10	H	DAL	26-23	W	63,001
Sun	11/17	H	CLE	28-24	W	58,155
Sun	11/24	A	PIT	14-26	L	45,795
Mon	12/2	H	PHI	6-13	L	62,141
Sun	12/8	H	PIT	31-6	W	59,225
Sun	12/15	A	CLE	17-14	W	55,680
Sat	12/21	A	NYG	20-24	L	63,421

AFC Wild-Card Playoff

Sun	12/29	H	NYJ	17-10	W	61,485

AFC Divisional Playoff

Sat	1/4	A	DEN	24-26	L	75,301

INDIANAPOLIS COLTS

Sun	9/1	H	NE	7-16	L	49,961
Sun	9/8	A	MIA	6-17	L	51,155
Sun	9/15	A	LARI	0-16	L	40,287
Sun	9/22	H	DET	24-33	L	53,396
Sun	9/29	A	SEA	3-31	L	56,656
Sun	10/6	H	PIT	3-21	L	55,383
Sun	10/13	A	BUF	6-42	L	79,015
Sun	10/20	H	NYJ	6-17	L	53,025
Sun	11/3	H	MIA	6-10	L	55,899
Sun	11/10	A	NYJ	28-27	W	44,792
Sun	11/17	H	CHI	17-31	L	60,519
Sun	11/24	A	GB	10-14	L	42,132
Sun	12/1	H	CLE	0-31	L	57,539
Sun	12/8	A	NE	*17-23	L	20,131
Sun	12/15	H	BUF	7-35	L	42,286
Sun	12/22	A	TB	3-17	L	28,043

KANSAS CITY CHIEFS

Sun	9/1	H	ATL	14-3	W	74,246
Sun	9/8	H	NO	10-17	L	74,816
Mon	9/16	A	HOU	7-17	L	61,058
Sun	9/22	H	SEA	20-13	W	71,789
Sun	9/29	A	SD	14-13	W	44,907
Mon	10/7	H	BUF	33-6	W	76,120
Sun	10/13	H	MIA	42-7	W	76,021
Sun	10/20	A	DEN	16-19	L	75,866
Mon	10/28	H	LARI	24-21	W	77,111
Sun	11/10	A	LARM	27-20	W	52,511
Sun	11/17	H	DEN	20-24	L	74,661
Sun	11/24	A	CLE	15-20	L	63,991
Sun	12/1	A	SEA	19-6	W	57,248
Sun	12/8	H	SD	*20-17	W	73,330
Sat	12/14	A	SF	14-28	L	62,672
Sun	12/22	A	LARI	27-21	W	65,144

AFC Wild-Card Playoff

Sat	12/28	H	LARI	10-6	W	75,827

AFC Divisional Playoff

Sun	1/5	A	BUF	14-37	L	80,182

LOS ANGELES RAIDERS

Sun	9/1	A	HOU	17-47	L	61,367
Sun	9/8	H	DEN	16-13	W	50,812
Sun	9/15	H	IND	16-0	W	40,287
Sun	9/22	A	ATL	17-21	L	53,615
Sun	9/29	H	SF	12-6	W	91,494
Sun	10/6	H	SD	13-21	L	42,787
Sun	10/13	A	SEA	*23-20	W	61,974
Sun	10/20	H	LARM	20-17	W	85,102
Mon	10/28	A	KC	21-24	L	77,111
Sun	11/10	A	DEN	17-16	W	75,896
Sun	11/17	H	SEA	31-7	W	49,317
Sun	11/24	A	CIN	38-14	W	52,044
Sun	12/1	A	SD	9-7	W	56,780
Sun	12/8	H	BUF	*27-30	L	85,081
Mon	12/16	A	NO	0-27	L	68,625
Sun	12/22	H	KC	21-27	L	65,144

AFC Wild-Card Playoff

Sat	12/28	A	KC	6-10	L	75,827

LOS ANGELES RAMS

Sun	9/1	H	PHX	14-24	L	47,069
Sun	9/8	A	NYG	19-13	W	76,541
Sun	9/15	A	NO	7-24	L	68,583
Sun	9/22	A	SF	10-27	L	63,871
Sun	9/29	H	GB	23-21	W	54,736
Sun	10/13	H	SD	30-24	W	47,433
Sun	10/20	A	LARI	17-20	L	85,102
Sun	10/27	A	ATL	14-31	L	50,187
Sun	11/3	H	NO	17-24	L	58,713
Sun	11/10	H	KC	20-27	L	52,511
Sun	11/17	A	DET	10-21	L	60,873
Mon	11/25	H	SF	10-33	L	61,881
Sun	12/1	H	WAS	6-27	L	55,027
Sun	12/8	H	ATL	14-31	L	35,315
Sun	12/15	A	MIN	14-20	L	61,518
Sun	12/22	A	SEA	9-23	L	51,100

MIAMI DOLPHINS

Sun	9/1	A	BUF	31-35	L	80,252
Sun	9/8	H	IND	17-6	W	51,155
Sun	9/15	A	DET	13-17	L	56,896
Sun	9/22	H	GB	16-13	W	56,583
Sun	9/29	A	NYJ	23-41	L	71,170
Sun	10/6	A	NE	20-10	W	49,749
Sun	10/13	A	KC	7-42	L	76,021
Sun	10/20	H	HOU	13-17	L	60,705
Sun	11/3	A	IND	10-6	W	55,899
Sun	11/10	H	NE	30-20	W	56,065
Mon	11/18	H	BUF	27-41	L	71,062
Sun	11/24	A	CHI	*16-13	W	58,288
Sun	12/1	H	TB	33-14	W	51,036
Mon	12/9	H	CIN	37-13	W	60,616
Sun	12/15	A	SD	30-38	L	47,731
Sun	12/22	H	NYJ	*20-23	L	69,636

MINNESOTA VIKINGS

Sun	9/1	A	CHI	6-10	L	64,112
Sun	9/8	A	ATL	20-19	W	50,936
Sun	9/15	H	SF	17-14	W	59,148
Sun	9/22	A	NO	0-26	L	68,591
Sun	9/29	H	DEN	6-13	L	55,031
Sun	10/6	A	DET	20-24	L	63,423
Sun	10/13	H	PHX	34-7	W	51,209
Sun	10/20	A	NE	*23-26	L	45,367
Sun	10/27	A	PHX	28-0	W	45,447
Sun	11/3	H	TB	28-13	W	35,737
Mon	11/11	H	CHI	17-34	L	59,001
Sun	11/17	A	GB	35-21	W	57,614
Sun	11/24	H	DET	14-34	L	51,644
Sun	12/8	A	TB	26-24	W	41,091
Sun	12/15	H	LARM	20-14	W	61,518
Sat	12/21	H	GB	7-27	L	52,860

NEW ENGLAND PATRIOTS

Sun	9/1	A	IND	16-7	W	49,961
Sun	9/8	H	CLE	0-20	L	35,377
Sun	9/15	A	PIT	6-20	L	53,703
Sun	9/22	H	HOU	24-20	W	30,702
Sun	9/29	A	PHX	10-24	L	26,043
Sun	10/6	H	MIA	10-20	L	49,749
Sun	10/20	H	MIN	*26-23	W	45,367
Sun	10/27	H	DEN	6-9	L	43,394
Sun	11/3	A	BUF	17-22	L	78,278
Sun	11/10	A	MIA	20-30	L	56,065
Sun	11/17	H	NYJ	21-28	L	30,743
Sun	11/24	H	BUF	16-13	W	47,053
Sun	12/1	A	DEN	3-20	L	67,116
Sun	12/8	H	IND	*23-17	W	20,131
Sun	12/15	A	NYJ	6-3	W	55,689
Sun	12/22	A	CIN	7-29	L	46,394

NEW ORLEANS SAINTS

Sun	9/1	H	SEA	27-24	W	68,492
Sun	9/8	A	KC	17-10	W	74,816
Sun	9/15	H	LARM	24-7	W	68,583
Sun	9/22	H	MIN	26-0	W	68,591
Sun	9/29	A	ATL	27-6	W	56,556
Sun	10/13	A	PHI	13-6	W	64,224
Sun	10/20	H	TB	23-7	W	68,591
Sun	10/27	H	CHI	17-20	L	68,591
Sun	11/3	A	LARM	24-17	W	58,713
Sun	11/10	H	SF	10-3	W	68,591
Sun	11/17	A	SD	21-24	L	48,420
Sun	11/24	H	ATL	*20-23	L	68,591
Sun	12/1	A	SF	24-38	L	62,092
Sun	12/8	A	DAL	14-23	L	64,530
Mon	12/16	H	LARI	27-0	W	68,625
Sun	12/22	A	PHX	27-3	W	30,928

NFC Wild-Card Playoff

Sat	12/28	H	ATL	20-27	L	68,299

NEW YORK GIANTS

Mon	9/2	H	SF	16-14	W	76,319
Sun	9/8	H	LARM	13-19	L	76,541
Sun	9/15	A	CHI	17-20	L	64,829
Sun	9/22	H	CLE	13-10	W	75,891
Sun	9/29	A	DAL	16-21	L	64,010
Sun	10/6	H	PHX	20-9	W	75,891
Mon	10/14	A	PIT	23-20	W	57,608
Sun	10/27	H	WAS	13-17	L	76,627
Mon	11/4	A	PHI	7-30	L	65,816
Sun	11/10	A	PHX	21-14	W	50,048
Sun	11/17	H	DAL	22-9	W	76,410
Sun	11/24	A	TB	21-14	W	63,698
Sun	12/1	A	CIN	24-27	L	45,063
Sun	12/8	H	PHI	14-19	L	76,099
Sun	12/15	A	WAS	17-34	L	54,722
Sat	12/21	H	HOU	24-20	W	63,421

NEW YORK JETS

Sun	9/1	H	TB	16-13	W	61,204
Sun	9/8	A	SEA	13-20	L	56,770
Sun	9/15	H	BUF	20-23	L	65,309
Mon	9/23	A	CHI	*13-19	L	65,255
Sun	9/29	H	MIA	41-23	W	71,170
Sun	10/6	A	CLE	17-14	W	71,042
Sun	10/13	H	HOU	20-23	L	70,758
Sun	10/20	A	IND	17-6	W	53,025
Sun	11/3	H	GB	*19-16	W	67,435
Sun	11/10	H	IND	27-28	L	44,792
Sun	11/17	A	NE	28-21	W	30,743
Sun	11/24	H	SD	24-3	W	59,025
Sun	12/1	A	BUF	13-24	L	80,243
Sun	12/8	A	DET	20-34	L	69,304
Sun	12/15	H	NE	3-6	L	55,689
Sun	12/22	A	MIA	*23-20	W	69,636

AFC Wild-Card Playoff

Sun	12/29	A	HOU	10-17	L	61,485

PHILADELPHIA EAGLES

Sun	9/1	A	GB	20-3	W	58,991
Sun	9/8	H	PHX	10-26	L	63,818
Sun	9/15	A	DAL	24-0	W	62,656
Sun	9/22	H	PIT	23-14	W	65,511
Mon	9/30	A	WAS	0-23	L	55,198
Sun	10/6	A	TB	13-14	L	41,219
Sun	10/13	H	NO	6-13	L	64,224
Sun	10/27	H	SF	7-23	L	65,796
Mon	11/4	H	NYG	30-7	W	65,816
Sun	11/10	A	CLE	32-30	W	72,086
Sun	11/17	H	CIN	17-10	W	63,189
Sun	11/24	A	PHX	34-14	W	37,307
Mon	12/2	A	HOU	13-6	W	62,141
Sun	12/8	A	NYG	19-14	W	76,099
Sun	12/15	H	DAL	13-25	L	65,854
Sun	12/22	H	WAS	24-22	W	58,988

PHOENIX CARDINALS

Sun	9/1	A	LARM	24-14	W	47,069
Sun	9/8	A	PHI	26-10	W	63,818
Sun	9/15	A	WAS	0-34	L	54,662
Sun	9/22	H	DAL	9-17	L	68,814
Sun	9/29	H	NE	24-10	W	26,043
Sun	10/6	A	NYG	9-20	L	75,891
Sun	10/13	A	MIN	7-34	L	51,209
Sun	10/20	H	ATL	16-10	W	24,124
Sun	10/27	H	MIN	0-28	L	45,447
Sun	11/3	A	DAL	7-27	L	61,190
Sun	11/10	H	NYG	14-21	L	50,048
Sun	11/17	A	SF	10-14	L	50,180
Sun	11/24	H	PHI	14-34	L	37,307
Sun	12/8	H	WAS	14-20	L	48,373
Sun	12/15	A	DEN	19-24	L	74,098
Sun	12/22	H	NO	3-27	L	30,928

PITTSBURGH STEELERS

Sun	9/1	H	SD	26-20	W	55,848
Sun	9/8	A	BUF	34-52	L	79,545
Sun	9/15	H	NE	20-6	W	53,703
Sun	9/22	A	PHI	14-23	L	65,511
Sun	10/6	A	IND	21-3	W	55,383
Mon	10/14	H	NYG	20-23	L	57,608
Sun	10/20	H	SEA	7-27	L	54,678
Sun	10/27	A	CLE	14-17	L	78,285
Sun	11/3	A	DEN	13-20	L	70,973
Sun	11/10	A	CIN	*33-27	W	55,503
Sun	11/17	H	WAS	14-41	L	56,813
Sun	11/24	H	HOU	26-14	W	45,795
Thu	11/28	A	DAL	10-20	L	62,253
Sun	12/8	A	HOU	6-31	L	59,225

Sun	12/15	H	CIN	17-10	W	35,420
Sun	12/22	H	CLE	17-10	W	47,070

SAN DIEGO CHARGERS

Sun	9/1	A	PIT	20-26	L	55,848
Sun	9/8	A	SF	14-34	L	60,753
Sun	9/15	H	ATL	10-13	L	44,804
Sun	9/22	A	DEN	19-27	L	73,258
Sun	9/29	H	KC	13-14	L	44,907
Sun	10/6	A	LARI	21-13	W	42,787
Sun	10/13	A	LARM	24-30	L	47,433
Sun	10/20	H	CLE	*24-30	L	48,440
Sun	10/27	A	SEA	9-20	L	58,025
Sun	11/10	H	SEA	17-14	W	43,597
Sun	11/17	H	NO	24-21	W	48,420
Sun	11/24	A	NYJ	3-24	L	59,025
Sun	12/1	H	LARI	7-9	L	56,780
Sun	12/8	A	KC	*17-20	L	73,330
Sun	12/15	H	MIA	38-30	W	47,731
Sun	12/22	H	DEN	14-17	L	51,449

SAN FRANCISCO 49ERS

Mon	9/2	A	NYG	14-16	L	76,319
Sun	9/8	H	SD	34-14	W	60,753
Sun	9/15	A	MIN	14-17	L	59,148
Sun	9/22	H	LARM	27-10	W	63,871
Sun	9/29	A	LARI	6-12	L	91,494
Sun	10/13	A	ATL	34-39	L	66,210
Sun	10/20	H	DET	35-3	W	61,240
Sun	10/27	A	PHI	23-7	W	65,796
Sun	11/3	H	ATL	14-17	L	51,259
Sun	11/10	A	NO	3-10	L	68,591
Sun	11/17	H	PHX	14-10	W	50,180
Mon	11/25	A	LARM	33-10	W	61,881
Sun	12/1	H	NO	38-24	W	62,092
Sun	12/8	A	SEA	24-22	W	56,711
Sat	12/14	H	KC	28-14	W	62,672
Mon	12/23	H	CHI	52-14	W	60,419

SEATTLE SEAHAWKS

Sun	9/1	A	NO	24-27	L	68,492
Sun	9/8	H	NYJ	20-13	W	56,770
Sun	9/15	A	DEN	10-16	L	74,152
Sun	9/22	A	KC	13-20	L	71,789
Sun	9/29	H	IND	31-3	W	56,656
Sun	10/6	A	CIN	13-7	W	60,010
Sun	10/13	H	LARI	*20-23	L	61,974
Sun	10/20	A	PIT	27-7	W	54,678
Sun	10/27	H	SD	20-9	W	58,025
Sun	11/10	A	SD	14-17	L	43,597
Sun	11/17	A	LARI	7-31	L	49,317
Sun	11/24	H	DEN	13-10	W	60,430
Sun	12/1	H	KC	6-19	L	57,248
Sun	12/8	H	SF	22-24	L	56,711
Sun	12/15	A	ATL	13-26	L	53,834
Sun	12/22	H	LARM	23-9	W	51,100

TAMPA BAY BUCCANEERS

Sun	9/1	A	NYJ	13-16	L	61,204
Sun	9/8	H	CHI	20-21	L	62,409
Sun	9/15	A	GB	13-15	L	58,114
Sun	9/22	H	BUF	10-17	L	57,323
Sun	9/29	A	DET	3-31	L	48,784
Sun	10/6	H	PHI	14-13	W	41,219
Sun	10/20	A	NO	7-23	L	68,591
Sun	10/27	H	GB	0-27	L	40,275
Sun	11/3	A	MIN	13-28	L	35,737
Sun	11/10	H	DET	30-21	W	37,742
Sun	11/17	A	ATL	7-43	L	41,274
Sun	11/24	H	NYG	14-21	L	63,698
Sun	12/1	A	MIA	14-33	L	51,036
Sun	12/8	H	MIN	24-26	L	41,091
Sat	12/14	A	CHI	0-27	L	54,719
Sun	12/22	H	IND	17-3	W	28,043

WASHINGTON REDSKINS

Sun	9/1	H	DET	45-0	W	52,958
Mon	9/9	A	DAL	33-31	W	63,025
Sun	9/15	H	PHX	34-0	W	54,662
Sun	9/22	A	CIN	34-27	W	52,038
Mon	9/30	H	PHI	23-0	W	55,198
Sun	10/6	A	CHI	20-7	W	64,941
Sun	10/13	H	CLE	42-17	W	54,715
Sun	10/27	A	NYG	17-13	W	76,627
Sun	11/3	H	HOU	*16-13	W	55,096
Sun	11/10	H	ATL	56-17	W	52,461
Sun	11/17	A	PIT	41-14	W	56,813
Sun	11/24	H	DAL	21-24	L	55,561
Sun	12/1	A	LARM	27-6	W	55,027
Sun	12/8	A	PHX	20-14	W	48,373
Sun	12/15	H	NYG	34-17	W	54,722
Sun	12/22	A	PHI	22-24	L	58,988

NFC Divisional Playoff

Sat	1/4	H	ATL	24-7	W	55,181

NFC Championship

Sun	1/12	H	DET	41-10	W	55,585

Super Bowl XXVI

Sun	1/26	N	BUF	37-24	W	63,130

1992 NFL

ATLANTA FALCONS

Sun	9/6	H	NYJ	20-17	W	69,045
Sun	9/13	A	WAS	17-24	L	55,456
Sun	9/20	H	NO	7-10	L	69,820
Sun	9/27	A	CHI	31-41	L	66,094
Sun	10/4	H	GB	24-10	W	69,120
Sun	10/11	A	MIA	17-21	L	70,765
Sun	10/18	A	SF	17-56	L	65,446
Sun	11/1	H	LARM	30-28	W	69,503
Mon	11/9	H	SF	3-41	L	69,898
Sun	11/15	H	PHX	20-17	W	68,377
Sun	11/22	A	BUF	14-41	L	78,983
Sun	11/29	H	NE	34-0	W	68,416
Thu	12/3	A	NO	14-22	L	67,604
Sun	12/13	A	TB	35-7	W	42,783
Mon	12/21	H	DAL	17-41	L	69,800
Sun	12/27	A	LARM	27-38	L	44,627

BUFFALO BILLS

Sun	9/6	H	LARM	40-7	W	78,851
Sun	9/13	A	SF	34-31	W	65,401
Sun	9/20	H	IND	38-0	W	78,997
Sun	9/27	A	NE	41-7	W	58,925
Sun	10/4	H	MIA	10-37	L	78,998
Sun	10/11	A	LARI	3-20	L	50,548
Mon	10/26	A	NYJ	24-20	W	75,925
Sun	11/1	H	NE	16-7	W	78,840
Sun	11/8	H	PIT	28-20	W	78,870
Mon	11/16	A	MIA	26-20	W	71,274
Sun	11/22	H	ATL	41-14	W	78,983
Sun	11/29	A	IND	*13-16	L	47,483
Sun	12/6	H	NYJ	17-24	L	78,752
Sat	12/12	H	DEN	27-17	W	78,687
Sun	12/20	A	NO	20-16	W	67,636
Sun	12/27	A	HOU	3-27	L	62,803

AFC Wild-Card Playoff

Sun	1/3	H	HOU	*41-38	W	75,141

AFC Divisional Playoff

Sat	1/9	A	PIT	24-3	W	60,407

AFC Championship

Sun	1/17	A	MIA	29-10	W	72,703

Super Bowl XXVII

Sun	1/31	N	DAL	17-52	L	98,374

CHICAGO BEARS

Sun	9/6	H	DET	27-24	W	66,101
Sun	9/13	A	NO	6-28	L	67,633
Mon	9/21	H	NYG	14-27	L	66,091
Sun	9/27	H	ATL	41-31	W	66,094
Sun	10/4	A	MIN	20-21	L	62,510
Sun	10/18	H	TB	31-14	W	65,973
Sun	10/25	A	GB	30-10	W	58,672
Mon	11/2	H	MIN	10-38	L	66,091
Sun	11/8	H	CIN	*28-31	L	66,006
Sun	11/15	A	TB	17-20	L	72,607
Sun	11/22	H	GB	3-17	L	66,075
Sun	11/29	A	CLE	14-27	L	73,727
Mon	12/7	A	HOU	7-24	L	62,408
Sun	12/13	H	PIT	30-6	W	66,034
Sun	12/20	A	DET	3-16	L	75,804
Sun	12/27	A	DAL	14-27	L	63,208

CINCINNATI BENGALS

Sun	9/6	A	SEA	21-3	W	64,601
Sun	9/13	H	LARI	*24-21	W	55,551
Sun	9/20	A	GB	23-24	L	58,500
Sun	9/27	H	MIN	7-42	L	55,526
Sun	10/11	H	HOU	24-38	L	59,029
Mon	10/19	A	PIT	0-20	L	59,307
Sun	10/25	A	HOU	10-26	L	61,303
Sun	11/1	H	CLE	30-10	W	59,140
Sun	11/8	A	CHI	*31-28	W	66,006
Sun	11/15	A	NYJ	14-17	L	75,442
Sun	11/22	H	DET	13-19	L	58,921
Sun	11/29	H	PIT	9-21	L	59,123
Sun	12/6	A	CLE	21-37	L	69,609
Sun	12/13	A	SD	10-27	L	48,843
Sun	12/20	H	NE	20-10	W	58,125
Sun	12/27	H	IND	17-21	L	58,519

CLEVELAND BROWNS

Sun	9/6	A	IND	3-14	L	51,315
Mon	9/14	H	MIA	23-27	L	75,912
Sun	9/20	A	LARI	28-16	W	46,198
Sun	9/27	H	DEN	0-12	L	78,069
Sun	10/11	H	PIT	17-9	W	78,256
Sun	10/18	H	GB	17-6	W	69,682
Sun	10/25	A	NE	19-17	W	38,442
Sun	11/1	A	CIN	10-30	L	59,140
Sun	11/8	A	HOU	24-14	W	61,282
Sun	11/15	H	SD	13-14	L	59,610
Sun	11/22	A	MIN	13-17	L	60,798
Sun	11/29	H	CHI	27-14	W	73,727
Sun	12/6	H	CIN	37-21	W	69,609
Sun	12/13	A	DET	14-24	L	70,746
Sun	12/20	H	HOU	14-17	L	60,060
Sun	12/27	A	PIT	13-23	L	59,431

DALLAS COWBOYS

Mon	9/7	H	WAS	23-10	W	62,652
Sun	9/13	A	NYG	34-28	W	76,034
Sun	9/20	H	PHX	31-20	W	62,200
Mon	10/5	A	PHI	7-31	L	65,740
Sun	10/11	H	SEA	27-0	W	62,569
Sun	10/18	H	KC	17-10	W	62,775
Sun	10/25	A	LARI	28-13	W	91,505
Sun	11/1	H	PHI	20-10	W	63,290
Sun	11/8	A	DET	37-3	W	78,815
Sun	11/15	H	LARM	23-27	L	62,993
Sun	11/22	A	PHX	16-10	W	71,628
Thu	11/26	H	NYG	30-3	W	62,974
Sun	12/6	A	DEN	31-27	W	74,929
Sun	12/13	A	WAS	17-20	L	55,455
Mon	12/21	A	ATL	41-17	W	69,800
Sun	12/27	H	CHI	27-14	W	63,208

NFC Divisional Playoff

Sun	1/10	H	PHI	34-10	W	63,721

NFC Championship

Sun	1/17	A	SF	30-20	W	64,920

Super Bowl XXVII

Sun	1/31	N	BUF	52-17	W	98,374

DENVER BRONCOS

Sun	9/6	H	LARI	17-13	W	74,824
Sun	9/13	H	SD	21-13	W	72,180
Sun	9/20	A	PHI	0-30	L	65,507
Sun	9/27	A	CLE	12-0	W	78,069
Sun	10/4	H	KC	20-19	W	74,372
Mon	10/12	A	WAS	3-34	L	55,455
Sun	10/18	H	HOU	27-21	W	73,825
Sun	10/25	A	SD	21-24	L	52,149
Sun	11/8	H	NYJ	27-16	W	73,036
Sun	11/15	H	NYG	27-13	W	74,161
Sun	11/22	A	LARI	0-24	L	47,786
Mon	11/30	A	SEA	*13-16	L	64,482
Sun	12/6	H	DAL	27-31	L	74,929
Sat	12/12	A	BUF	17-27	L	78,687
Sun	12/20	H	SEA	10-6	W	72,763
Sun	12/27	A	KC	20-42	L	76,608

DETROIT LIONS

Sun	9/6	A	CHI	24-27	L	66,101
Sun	9/13	H	MIN	31-17	W	57,353
Sun	9/20	A	WAS	10-13	L	55,482
Sun	9/27	H	TB	23-27	L	52,779
Sun	10/4	H	NO	7-13	L	68,428
Thu	10/15	A	MIN	14-31	L	61,010
Sun	10/25	A	TB	38-7	W	58,649
Sun	11/1	H	GB	13-27	L	62,372
Sun	11/8	H	DAL	3-37	L	78,815
Sun	11/15	A	PIT	14-17	L	58,993
Sun	11/22	A	CIN	19-13	W	58,921
Thu	11/26	H	HOU	21-24	L	76,105
Sun	12/6	A	GB	10-38	L	54,681
Sun	12/13	H	CLE	24-14	W	70,746
Sun	12/20	H	CHI	16-3	W	75,804
Mon	12/28	A	SF	6-24	L	65,432

GREEN BAY PACKERS

Sun	9/6	H	MIN	*20-23	L	58,704
Sun	9/13	A	TB	3-31	L	50,725
Sun	9/20	H	CIN	24-23	W	58,500
Sun	9/27	H	PIT	17-3	W	58,700
Sun	10/4	A	ATL	10-24	L	69,120
Sun	10/18	A	CLE	6-17	L	69,682
Sun	10/25	H	CHI	10-30	L	58,672
Sun	11/1	A	DET	27-13	W	62,372
Sun	11/8	A	NYG	7-27	L	76,069
Sun	11/15	H	PHI	27-24	W	54,867
Sun	11/22	A	CHI	17-3	W	66,075
Sun	11/29	H	TB	19-14	W	54,172
Sun	12/6	H	DET	38-10	W	54,681
Sun	12/13	A	HOU	16-14	W	61,115
Sun	12/20	H	LARM	28-13	W	58,648
Sun	12/27	A	MIN	7-27	L	62,597

HOUSTON OILERS

Sun	9/6	H	PIT	24-29	L	63,705
Sun	9/13	A	IND	20-10	W	45,274
Sun	9/20	H	KC	*23-20	W	62,672
Sun	9/27	H	SD	27-0	W	59,159
Sun	10/11	A	CIN	38-24	W	59,029
Sun	10/18	A	DEN	21-27	L	73,825
Sun	10/25	H	CIN	26-10	W	61,303
Sun	11/1	A	PIT	20-21	L	59,504
Sun	11/8	H	CLE	14-24	L	61,282
Sun	11/15	A	MIN	17-13	W	61,073
Sun	11/22	A	MIA	16-19	L	70,439
Thu	11/26	A	DET	24-21	W	76,105
Mon	12/7	H	CHI	24-7	W	62,408
Sun	12/13	H	GB	14-16	L	61,115
Sun	12/20	A	CLE	17-14	W	60,060
Sun	12/27	H	BUF	27-3	W	62,803

AFC Wild-Card Playoff

Sun	1/3	A	BUF	*38-41	L	75,141

INDIANAPOLIS COLTS

Sun	9/6	H	CLE	14-3	W	51,315
Sun	9/13	H	HOU	10-20	L	45,274
Sun	9/20	A	BUF	0-38	L	78,997
Sun	10/4	A	TB	24-14	W	56,229
Sun	10/11	H	NYJ	*6-3	W	45,188
Sun	10/18	H	SD	14-34	L	43,805
Sun	10/25	A	MIA	31-20	W	61,245

Sun	11/1	A	SD	0-26	L	38,832
Sun	11/8	H	MIA	0-28	L	58,599
Sun	11/15	H	NE	*34-37	L	41,426
Sun	11/22	A	PIT	14-30	L	58,611
Sun	11/29	H	BUF	*16-13	W	47,483
Sun	12/6	A	NE	6-0	W	26,196
Sun	12/13	A	NYJ	10-6	W	74,636
Sun	12/20	H	PHX	16-13	W	43,135
Sun	12/27	A	CIN	21-17	W	58,519

KANSAS CITY CHIEFS

Sun	9/6	A	SD	24-10	W	43,403
Sun	9/13	H	SEA	26-7	W	76,591
Sun	9/20	A	HOU	*20-23	L	62,672
Mon	9/28	H	LARI	27-7	W	76,607
Sun	10/4	A	DEN	19-20	L	74,372
Sun	10/11	H	PHI	24-17	W	76,570
Sun	10/18	A	DAL	10-17	L	62,775
Sun	10/25	H	PIT	3-27	L	76,610
Sun	11/8	H	SD	16-14	W	76,590
Sun	11/15	H	WAS	35-16	W	76,617
Sun	11/22	A	SEA	24-14	W	64,017
Sun	11/29	A	NYJ	23-7	W	75,473
Sun	12/6	A	LARI	7-28	L	44,029
Sun	12/13	H	NE	27-20	W	76,580
Sat	12/19	A	NYG	21-35	L	75,981
Sun	12/27	H	DEN	42-20	W	76,608

AFC Wild-Card Playoff

Sat	1/2	A	SD	0-17	L	58,278

LOS ANGELES RAIDERS

Sun	9/6	A	DEN	13-17	L	74,824
Sun	9/13	A	CIN	*21-24	L	55,551
Sun	9/20	H	CLE	16-28	L	46,198
Mon	9/28	A	KC	7-27	L	76,607
Sun	10/4	H	NYG	13-10	W	40,919
Sun	10/11	H	BUF	20-3	W	50,548
Sun	10/18	A	SEA	19-0	W	64,646
Sun	10/25	H	DAL	13-28	L	91,505
Sun	11/8	A	PHI	10-31	L	65,736
Sun	11/15	H	SEA	20-3	W	31,805
Sun	11/22	H	DEN	24-0	W	47,786
Sun	11/29	A	SD	3-27	L	59,224
Sun	12/6	H	KC	28-7	W	44,029
Mon	12/14	A	MIA	7-20	L	71,005
Sun	12/20	H	SD	14-36	L	37,163
Sat	12/26	A	WAS	21-20	W	55,460

LOS ANGELES RAMS

Sun	9/6	A	BUF	7-40	L	78,851
Sun	9/13	H	NE	14-0	W	44,000
Sun	9/20	A	MIA	10-26	L	57,701
Sun	9/27	H	NYJ	18-10	W	45,735
Sun	10/4	A	SF	24-27	L	65,340
Sun	10/11	A	NO	10-13	L	67,591
Sun	10/18	H	NYG	38-17	W	56,549
Sun	11/1	A	ATL	28-30	L	69,503
Sun	11/8	H	PHX	14-20	L	44,241
Sun	11/15	A	DAL	27-23	W	62,993
Sun	11/22	H	SF	10-27	L	67,461
Sun	11/29	H	MIN	17-31	L	58,882
Sun	12/6	A	TB	31-27	W	39,056
Sun	12/13	H	NO	14-37	L	53,007
Sun	12/20	A	GB	13-28	L	58,648
Sun	12/27	H	ATL	38-27	W	44,627

MIAMI DOLPHINS

Mon	9/14	A	CLE	27-23	W	75,912
Sun	9/20	H	LARI	26-10	W	57,701
Sun	9/27	A	SEA	19-17	W	64,629
Sun	10/4	A	BUF	37-10	W	78,998
Sun	10/11	H	ATL	21-17	W	70,765
Sun	10/18	H	NE	38-17	W	59,981
Sun	10/25	H	IND	20-31	L	61,245
Sun	11/1	A	NYJ	14-26	L	75,903
Sun	11/8	A	IND	28-0	W	58,599
Mon	11/16	H	BUF	20-26	L	71,274
Sun	11/22	H	HOU	19-16	W	70,439
Sun	11/29	A	NO	13-24	L	67,664
Sun	12/6	A	SF	3-27	L	65,461
Mon	12/14	H	LARI	20-7	W	71,005
Sun	12/20	H	NYJ	19-17	W	70,907
Sun	12/27	A	NE	*16-13	W	41,451

AFC Divisional Playoff

Sun	1/10	H	SD	31-0	W	71,224

AFC Championship

Sun	1/17	H	BUF	10-29	L	72,703

MINNESOTA VIKINGS

Sun	9/6	A	GB	*23-20	W	58,704
Sun	9/13	A	DET	17-31	L	57,353
Sun	9/20	H	TB	26-20	W	53,371
Sun	9/27	A	CIN	42-7	W	55,526
Sun	10/4	H	CHI	21-20	W	62,510
Thu	10/15	H	DET	31-14	W	61,010
Sun	10/25	H	WAS	13-15	L	61,801
Mon	11/2	A	CHI	38-10	W	66,091
Sun	11/8	A	TB	35-7	W	51,658
Sun	11/15	H	HOU	13-17	L	61,073
Sun	11/22	H	CLE	17-13	W	60,798
Sun	11/29	A	LARM	31-17	W	58,882
Sun	12/6	A	PHI	17-28	L	65,698
Sun	12/13	H	SF	17-20	L	62,456
Sun	12/20	A	PIT	6-3	W	59,005
Sun	12/27	H	GB	27-7	W	62,597

NFC Wild-Card Playoff

Sat	1/2	H	WAS	7-24	L	57,353

NEW ENGLAND PATRIOTS

Sun	9/13	A	LARM	0-14	L	44,000
Sun	9/20	H	SEA	6-10	L	45,785
Sun	9/27	H	BUF	7-41	L	58,925
Sun	10/4	A	NYJ	21-30	L	75,004
Sun	10/11	H	SF	12-24	L	59,437
Sun	10/18	A	MIA	17-38	L	59,981
Sun	10/25	H	CLE	17-19	L	38,442
Sun	11/1	A	BUF	7-16	L	78,840
Sun	11/8	H	NO	14-31	L	51,878
Sun	11/15	A	IND	*37-34	W	41,426
Sun	11/22	H	NYJ	24-3	W	34,301
Sun	11/29	A	ATL	0-34	L	68,416
Sun	12/6	H	IND	0-6	L	26,196
Sun	12/13	A	KC	20-27	L	76,580
Sun	12/20	A	CIN	10-20	L	58,125
Sun	12/27	H	MIA	*13-16	L	41,451

NEW ORLEANS SAINTS

Sun	9/6	A	PHI	13-15	L	65,418
Sun	9/13	H	CHI	28-6	W	67,633
Sun	9/20	A	ATL	10-7	W	69,820
Sun	9/27	H	SF	10-16	L	67,627
Sun	10/4	A	DET	13-7	W	68,428
Sun	10/11	H	LARM	13-10	W	67,591
Sun	10/18	A	PHX	30-21	W	28,117
Sun	11/1	H	TB	23-21	W	67,601
Sun	11/8	A	NE	31-14	W	51,878
Sun	11/15	A	SF	20-21	L	65,484
Mon	11/23	H	WAS	20-3	W	67,723
Sun	11/29	H	MIA	24-13	W	67,664
Thu	12/3	H	ATL	22-14	W	67,604
Sun	12/13	A	LARM	37-14	W	53,007
Sun	12/20	H	BUF	16-20	L	67,636
Sat	12/26	A	NYJ	20-0	W	45,614

NFC Wild-Card Playoff

Sun	1/3	H	PHI	20-36	L	68,993

NEW YORK GIANTS

Sun	9/6	H	SF	14-31	L	76,241
Sun	9/13	H	DAL	28-34	L	76,034
Mon	9/21	A	CHI	27-14	W	66,091
Sun	10/4	A	LARI	10-13	L	40,919
Sun	10/11	H	PHX	31-21	W	76,007
Sun	10/18	A	LARM	17-38	L	56,549
Sun	10/25	H	SEA	23-10	W	76,021
Sun	11/1	A	WAS	24-7	W	55,458
Sun	11/8	H	GB	27-7	W	76,069
Sun	11/15	A	DEN	13-27	L	74,161
Sun	11/22	H	PHI	34-47	L	76,191
Thu	11/26	A	DAL	3-30	L	62,974
Sun	12/6	H	WAS	10-28	L	76,162
Sat	12/12	A	PHX	0-19	L	31,905
Sat	12/19	H	KC	35-21	W	75,981
Sun	12/27	A	PHI	10-20	L	65,655

NEW YORK JETS

Sun	9/6	A	ATL	17-20	L	69,045
Sun	9/13	A	PIT	10-27	L	58,327
Sun	9/20	H	SF	14-31	L	75,945
Sun	9/27	A	LARM	10-18	L	45,735
Sun	10/4	H	NE	30-21	W	75,004
Sun	10/11	A	IND	*3-6	L	45,188
Mon	10/26	H	BUF	20-24	L	75,925
Sun	11/1	H	MIA	26-14	W	75,903
Sun	11/8	A	DEN	16-27	L	73,036
Sun	11/15	H	CIN	17-14	W	75,442
Sun	11/22	A	NE	3-24	L	34,301
Sun	11/29	H	KC	7-23	L	75,473
Sun	12/6	A	BUF	24-17	W	78,752
Sun	12/13	H	IND	6-10	L	74,636
Sun	12/20	A	MIA	17-19	L	70,907
Sat	12/26	H	NO	0-20	L	45,614

PHILADELPHIA EAGLES

Sun	9/6	H	NO	15-13	W	65,418
Sun	9/13	A	PHX	31-14	W	44,120
Sun	9/20	H	DEN	31-0	W	65,507
Mon	10/5	H	DAL	31-7	W	65,740
Sun	10/11	A	KC	17-24	L	76,570
Sun	10/18	A	WAS	12-16	L	55,454
Sun	10/25	H	PHX	7-3	W	65,438
Sun	11/1	A	DAL	10-20	L	63,290
Sun	11/8	H	LARI	31-10	W	65,736
Sun	11/15	A	GB	24-27	L	54,867
Sun	11/22	A	NYG	47-34	W	76,191
Sun	11/29	A	SF	14-20	L	65,486
Sun	12/6	H	MIN	28-17	W	65,698
Sun	12/13	A	SEA	*20-17	W	64,102
Sun	12/20	H	WAS	17-13	W	65,809
Sun	12/27	H	NYG	20-10	W	65,655

NFC Wild-Card Playoff

Sun	1/3	A	NO	36-20	W	68,893

NFC Divisional Playoff

Sun	1/10	A	DAL	10-34	L	63,721

PHOENIX CARDINALS

Sun	9/6	A	TB	7-23	L	44,779
Sun	9/13	H	PHI	14-31	L	44,120
Sun	9/20	A	DAL	20-31	L	62,200
Sun	10/4	H	WAS	27-24	W	37,657
Sun	10/11	A	NYG	21-31	L	76,007
Sun	10/18	H	NO	21-30	L	28,117
Sun	10/25	A	PHI	3-7	L	65,438
Sun	11/1	H	SF	24-14	W	50,482
Sun	11/8	A	LARM	20-14	W	44,241
Sun	11/15	A	ATL	17-20	L	68,377
Sun	11/22	H	DAL	10-16	L	71,628
Sun	11/29	A	WAS	3-41	L	55,455
Sun	12/6	H	SD	21-27	L	26,663
Sat	12/12	H	NYG	19-0	W	31,905
Sun	12/20	A	IND	13-16	L	43,135
Sun	12/27	H	TB	3-7	L	28,790

PITTSBURGH STEELERS

Sun	9/6	A	HOU	29-24	W	63,705
Sun	9/13	H	NYJ	27-10	W	58,327
Sun	9/20	A	SD	23-6	W	44,764
Sun	9/27	A	GB	3-17	L	58,700
Sun	10/11	A	CLE	9-17	L	78,256
Mon	10/19	H	CIN	20-0	W	59,307
Sun	10/25	A	KC	27-3	W	76,610
Sun	11/1	H	HOU	21-20	W	59,504
Sun	11/8	A	BUF	20-28	L	78,870
Sun	11/15	H	DET	17-14	W	58,993
Sun	11/22	H	IND	30-14	W	58,611
Sun	11/29	A	CIN	21-9	W	59,123
Sun	12/6	H	SEA	20-14	W	58,128
Sun	12/13	A	CHI	6-30	L	66,034
Sun	12/20	H	MIN	3-6	L	59,005
Sun	12/27	H	CLE	23-13	W	59,431

AFC Divisional Playoff

Sat	1/9	H	BUF	3-24	L	60,407

SAN DIEGO CHARGERS

Sun	9/6	H	KC	10-24	L	43,403
Sun	9/13	A	DEN	13-21	L	72,180
Sun	9/20	H	PIT	6-23	L	44,764
Sun	9/27	A	HOU	0-27	L	59,159
Sun	10/4	H	SEA	17-6	W	37,344
Sun	10/18	A	IND	34-14	W	43,805
Sun	10/25	H	DEN	24-21	W	52,149
Sun	11/1	H	IND	26-0	W	38,832
Sun	11/8	A	KC	14-16	L	76,590
Sun	11/15	A	CLE	14-13	W	59,610
Sun	11/22	H	TB	29-14	W	40,646
Sun	11/29	H	LARI	27-3	W	59,224
Sun	12/6	A	PHX	27-21	W	26,663
Sun	12/13	H	CIN	27-10	W	48,843
Sun	12/20	A	LARI	36-14	W	37,163
Sun	12/27	A	SEA	31-14	W	63,834

AFC Wild-Card Playoff

Sat	1/2	H	KC	17-0	W	58,278

AFC Divisional Playoff

Sun	1/10	A	MIA	0-31	L	71,224

SAN FRANCISCO 49ERS

Sun	9/6	A	NYG	31-14	W	76,241
Sun	9/13	H	BUF	31-34	L	65,401
Sun	9/20	A	NYJ	31-14	W	75,945
Sun	9/27	A	NO	16-10	W	67,627
Sun	10/4	H	LARM	27-24	W	65,340
Sun	10/11	A	NE	24-12	W	59,437
Sun	10/18	H	ATL	56-17	W	65,446
Sun	11/1	A	PHX	14-24	L	50,482
Mon	11/9	A	ATL	41-3	W	69,898
Sun	11/15	H	NO	21-20	W	65,484
Sun	11/22	A	LARM	27-10	W	67,461
Sun	11/29	H	PHI	20-14	W	65,486
Sun	12/6	H	MIA	27-3	W	65,461
Sun	12/13	A	MIN	20-17	W	52,456
Sat	12/19	H	TB	21-14	W	65,305
Mon	12/28	H	DET	24-6	W	65,432

NFC Divisional Playoff

Sat	1/9	H	WAS	20-13	W	64,991

NFC Championship

Sun	1/17	H	DAL	20-30	L	64,920

SEATTLE SEAHAWKS

Sun	9/6	H	CIN	3-21	L	64,601
Sun	9/13	A	KC	7-26	L	76,591
Sun	9/20	A	NE	10-6	W	45,785
Sun	9/27	H	MIA	17-19	L	64,629
Sun	10/4	A	SD	6-17	L	37,344
Sun	10/11	A	DAL	0-27	L	62,569
Sun	10/18	H	LARI	0-19	L	64,646
Sun	10/25	A	NYG	10-23	L	76,021
Sun	11/8	H	WAS	3-16	L	64,673
Sun	11/15	A	LARI	3-20	L	31,805
Sun	11/22	H	KC	14-24	L	64,017
Mon	11/30	H	DEN	*16-13	W	64,482

Sun	12/6	A	PIT	14-20	L	58,128
Sun	12/13	H	PHI	*17-20	L	64,102
Sun	12/20	A	DEN	6-10	L	72,763
Sun	12/27	H	SD	14-31	L	63,834

TAMPA BAY BUCCANEERS

Sun	9/6	H	PHX	23-7	W	44,779
Sun	9/13	H	GB	31-3	W	50,725
Sun	9/20	A	MIN	20-26	L	53,371
Sun	9/27	A	DET	27-23	W	52,779
Sun	10/4	H	IND	14-24	L	56,229
Sun	10/18	A	CHI	14-31	L	65,973
Sun	10/25	H	DET	7-38	L	58,649
Sun	11/1	A	NO	21-23	L	67,601
Sun	11/8	H	MIN	7-35	L	51,658
Sun	11/15	H	CHI	20-17	W	72,607
Sun	11/22	A	SD	14-29	L	40,646
Sun	11/29	A	GB	14-19	L	54,172
Sun	12/6	H	LARM	27-31	L	39,056
Sun	12/13	H	ATL	7-35	L	42,783
Sat	12/19	A	SF	14-21	L	65,305
Sun	12/27	A	PHX	7-3	W	28,790

WASHINGTON REDSKINS

Mon	9/7	A	DAL	10-23	L	62,652
Sun	9/13	H	ATL	24-17	W	55,456
Sun	9/20	H	DET	13-10	W	55,482
Sun	10/4	A	PHX	24-27	L	37,657
Mon	10/12	H	DEN	34-3	W	55,455
Sun	10/18	H	PHI	16-12	W	55,454
Sun	10/25	A	MIN	15-13	W	61,801
Sun	11/1	H	NYG	7-24	L	55,458
Sun	11/8	A	SEA	16-3	W	64,673
Sun	11/15	A	KC	16-35	L	76,617
Mon	11/23	A	NO	3-20	L	67,723
Sun	11/29	H	PHX	41-3	W	55,455
Sun	12/6	A	NYG	28-10	W	76,162
Sun	12/13	H	DAL	20-17	W	55,455
Sun	12/20	A	PHI	13-17	L	65,809
Sat	12/26	H	LARI	20-21	L	55,460

NFC WILD-CARD PLAYOFF

Sat	1/2	A	MIN	24-7	W	57,353

NFC DIVISIONAL PLAYOFF

Sat	1/9	A	SF	13-20	L	64,991

1993 NFL

ATLANTA FALCONS

Sun	9/5	A	DET	13-30	L	56,216
Sun	9/12	H	NO	31-34	L	64,287
Sun	9/19	A	SF	30-37	L	63,032
Mon	9/27	H	PIT	17-45	L	65,477
Sun	10/3	A	CHI	0-6	L	57,441
Thu	10/14	H	LARM	30-24	W	45,231
Sun	10/24	A	NO	26-15	W	69,043
Sun	10/31	H	TB	24-31	L	50,647
Sun	11/14	A	LARM	13-0	W	37,073
Sun	11/21	H	DAL	27-14	W	67,337
Sun	11/28	H	CLE	17-14	W	54,510
Sun	12/5	A	HOU	17-33	L	58,186
Sat	12/11	H	SF	27-24	W	64,688
Sun	12/19	A	WAS	17-30	L	50,192
Sun	12/26	A	CIN	17-21	L	27,014
Sun	1/2	H	PHX	10-27	L	44,360

BUFFALO BILLS

Sun	9/5	H	NE	38-14	W	79,751
Sun	9/12	A	DAL	13-10	W	63,226
Sun	9/26	H	MIA	13-22	L	79,635
Sun	10/3	H	NYG	17-14	W	79,283
Mon	10/11	H	HOU	35-7	W	79,613
Sun	10/24	A	NYJ	19-10	W	71,541
Mon	11/1	H	WAS	24-10	W	79,106
Sun	11/7	A	NE	*13-10	W	54,326
Mon	11/15	A	PIT	0-23	L	60,265
Sun	11/21	H	IND	23-9	W	79,101
Sun	11/28	A	KC	7-23	L	74,452
Sun	12/5	H	LARI	24-25	L	79,478
Sun	12/12	A	PHI	10-7	W	60,769
Sun	12/19	A	MIA	47-34	W	71,597
Sun	12/26	H	NYJ	16-14	W	70,817
Sun	1/2	A	IND	30-10	W	43,028

AFC DIVISIONAL PLAYOFF

Sat	1/15	H	LARI	29-23	W	61,923

AFC CHAMPIONSHIP

Sun	1/23	H	KC	30-13	W	76,642

SUPER BOWL XXVIII

Sun	1/30	N	DAL	13-30	L	72,817

CHICAGO BEARS

Sun	9/5	H	NYG	20-26	L	66,900
Sun	9/12	A	MIN	7-10	L	57,921
Sun	9/26	H	TB	47-17	W	58,329
Sun	10/3	H	ATL	6-0	W	57,441
Sun	10/10	A	PHI	17-6	W	63,601
Sun	10/25	H	MIN	12-19	L	64,677
Sun	10/31	A	GB	3-17	L	58,945
Sun	11/7	H	LARI	14-16	L	59,750
Sun	11/14	A	SD	16-13	W	58,459
Sun	11/21	A	KC	19-17	W	76,872
Thu	11/25	A	DET	10-6	W	76,699
Sun	12/5	H	GB	30-17	W	62,236
Sun	12/12	A	TB	10-13	L	56,667
Sat	12/18	H	DEN	3-13	L	53,056
Sun	12/26	H	DET	14-20	L	43,443
Sun	1/2	A	LARM	6-20	L	39,147

CINCINNATI BENGALS

Sun	9/5	A	CLE	14-27	L	75,508
Sun	9/12	H	IND	6-9	L	50,299
Sun	9/19	A	PIT	7-34	L	53,682
Sun	9/26	H	SEA	10-19	L	46,880
Sun	10/10	A	KC	15-17	L	75,394
Sun	10/17	H	CLE	17-28	L	55,647
Sun	10/24	A	HOU	12-28	L	50,039
Sun	11/7	H	PIT	16-24	L	51,202
Sun	11/14	H	HOU	3-38	L	42,347
Sun	11/21	A	NYJ	12-17	L	64,264
Sun	11/28	H	LARI	16-10	W	43,272
Sun	12/5	A	SF	8-21	L	60,039
Sun	12/12	A	NE	2-7	L	29,794
Sun	12/19	H	LARM	15-3	W	36,612
Sun	12/26	H	ATL	21-17	W	27,014
Sun	1/2	A	NO	13-20	L	58,036

CLEVELAND BROWNS

Sun	9/5	H	CIN	27-14	W	75,508
Mon	9/13	H	SF	23-13	W	78,218
Sun	9/19	A	LARI	19-16	W	48,617
Sun	9/26	A	IND	10-23	L	59,654
Sun	10/10	H	MIA	14-24	L	78,138
Sun	10/17	A	CIN	28-17	W	55,647
Sun	10/24	H	PIT	28-23	W	78,118
Sun	11/7	H	DEN	14-29	L	77,818
Sun	11/14	A	SEA	5-22	L	54,622
Sun	11/21	H	HOU	20-27	L	71,668
Sun	11/28	A	ATL	14-17	L	54,510
Sun	12/5	H	NO	17-13	W	60,388
Sun	12/12	A	HOU	17-19	L	58,720
Sun	12/19	H	NE	17-20	L	48,618
Sun	12/26	A	LARM	42-14	W	34,155
Sun	1/2	A	PIT	9-16	L	49,208

DALLAS COWBOYS

Mon	9/6	A	WAS	16-35	L	56,345
Sun	9/12	H	BUF	10-13	L	63,226
Sun	9/19	A	PHX	17-10	W	73,025
Sun	10/3	H	GB	36-14	W	63,568
Sun	10/10	A	IND	27-3	W	60,453
Sun	10/17	H	SF	26-17	W	65,099
Sun	10/31	A	PHI	23-10	W	61,912
Sun	11/7	H	NYG	31-9	W	64,735
Sun	11/14	H	PHX	20-15	W	64,224
Sun	11/21	A	ATL	14-27	L	67,337
Thu	11/25	H	MIA	14-16	L	60,198
Mon	12/6	H	PHI	23-17	W	64,521
Sun	12/12	A	MIN	37-20	W	63,321
Sat	12/18	A	NYJ	28-7	W	73,233
Sun	12/26	H	WAS	38-3	W	64,497
Sun	1/2	A	NYG	*16-13	W	77,356

NFC DIVISIONAL PLAYOFF

Sun	1/16	H	GB	27-17	W	64,790

NFC CHAMPIONSHIP

Sun	1/23	H	SF	38-21	W	64,902

SUPER BOWL XXVIII

Sun	1/30	N	BUF	30-13	W	72,817

DENVER BRONCOS

Sun	9/5	A	NYJ	26-20	W	68,130
Sun	9/12	H	SD	34-17	W	75,074
Mon	9/20	A	KC	7-15	L	78,453
Sun	10/3	H	IND	35-13	W	74,953
Sun	10/10	A	GB	27-30	L	58,943
Mon	10/18	H	LARI	20-23	L	75,712
Sun	10/31	H	SEA	28-17	W	73,644
Sun	11/7	A	CLE	29-14	W	77,818
Sun	11/14	H	MIN	23-26	L	67,329
Sun	11/21	H	PIT	37-13	W	74,840
Sun	11/28	A	SEA	17-9	W	57,812
Sun	12/5	A	SD	10-13	L	60,233
Sun	12/12	H	KC	27-21	W	75,822
Sat	12/18	A	CHI	13-3	W	53,056
Sun	12/26	H	TB	10-17	L	73,434
Sun	1/2	A	LARI	*30-33	L	66,904

AFC WILD-CARD PLAYOFF

Sun	1/9	A	LARI	24-42	L	65,314

DETROIT LIONS

Sun	9/5	H	ATL	30-13	W	56,216
Sun	9/12	A	NE	*19-16	W	54,151
Sun	9/19	A	NO	3-14	L	69,039
Sun	9/26	H	PHX	26-20	W	57,180
Sun	10/3	A	TB	10-27	L	40,794
Sun	10/17	H	SEA	30-10	W	60,801
Sun	10/24	A	LARM	16-13	W	43,850
Sun	10/31	A	MIN	30-27	W	53,428
Sun	11/7	H	TB	23-0	W	65,295
Sun	11/21	A	GB	17-26	L	55,119
Thu	11/25	H	CHI	6-10	L	76,699
Sun	12/5	H	MIN	0-13	L	63,216
Sun	12/12	A	PHX	21-14	W	39,993
Sun	12/19	H	SF	17-55	L	77,052
Sun	12/26	A	CHI	20-14	W	43,443
Sun	1/2	H	GB	30-20	W	77,510

NFC WILD-CARD PLAYOFF

Sat	1/8	H	GB	24-28	L	68,479

GREEN BAY PACKERS

Sun	9/5	H	LARM	36-6	W	54,648
Sun	9/12	H	PHI	17-20	L	59,061
Sun	9/26	A	MIN	13-15	L	61,746
Sun	10/3	A	DAL	14-36	L	63,568
Sun	10/10	H	DEN	30-27	W	58,943
Sun	10/24	A	TB	37-14	W	47,354
Sun	10/31	H	CHI	17-3	W	58,945
Mon	11/8	A	KC	16-23	L	76,742
Sun	11/14	A	NO	19-17	W	69,043
Sun	11/21	H	DET	26-17	W	55,119
Sun	11/28	H	TB	13-10	W	56,995
Sun	12/5	A	CHI	17-30	L	62,236
Sun	12/12	A	SD	20-13	W	57,930
Sun	12/19	H	MIN	17-21	L	54,773
Sun	12/26	H	LARI	28-0	W	54,482
Sun	1/2	A	DET	20-30	L	77,510

NFC WILD-CARD PLAYOFF

Sat	1/8	A	DET	28-24	W	68,479

NFC DIVISIONAL PLAYOFF

Sun	1/16	A	DAL	17-27	L	64,790

HOUSTON OILERS

Sun	9/5	A	NO	21-33	L	69,029
Sun	9/12	H	KC	30-0	W	59,780
Sun	9/19	A	SD	17-18	L	58,519
Sun	9/26	H	LARM	13-28	L	53,072
Mon	10/11	A	BUF	7-35	L	79,613
Sun	10/17	A	NE	28-14	W	51,037
Sun	10/24	H	CIN	28-12	W	50,039
Sun	11/7	H	SEA	24-14	W	50,447
Sun	11/14	A	CIN	38-3	W	42,347
Sun	11/21	A	CLE	27-20	W	71,668
Sun	11/28	H	PIT	23-3	W	61,238
Sun	12/5	H	ATL	33-17	W	58,186
Sun	12/12	H	CLE	19-17	W	58,720
Sun	12/19	A	PIT	26-17	W	57,592
Sat	12/25	A	SF	10-7	W	61,744
Sun	1/2	H	NYJ	24-0	W	61,040

AFC DIVISIONAL PLAYOFF

Sun	1/16	H	KC	20-28	L	64,011

INDIANAPOLIS COLTS

Sun	9/5	H	MIA	20-24	L	51,858
Sun	9/12	A	CIN	9-6	W	50,299
Sun	9/26	H	CLE	23-10	W	59,654
Sun	10/3	A	DEN	13-35	L	74,953
Sun	10/10	H	DAL	3-27	L	60,453
Sun	10/24	A	MIA	27-41	L	57,301
Sun	10/31	H	NE	9-6	W	46,522
Sun	11/7	A	WAS	24-30	L	50,523
Sun	11/14	H	NYJ	17-31	L	47,351
Sun	11/21	A	BUF	9-23	L	79,101
Mon	11/29	H	SD	0-31	L	54,110
Sun	12/5	A	NYJ	9-6	W	45,799
Sun	12/12	A	NYG	6-20	L	70,411
Sun	12/19	H	PHI	10-20	L	44,952
Sun	12/26	A	NE	0-38	L	26,571
Sun	1/2	H	BUF	10-30	L	43,028

KANSAS CITY CHIEFS

Sun	9/5	A	TB	27-3	W	63,378
Sun	9/12	A	HOU	0-30	L	59,780
Mon	9/20	H	DEN	15-7	W	78,453
Sun	10/3	H	LARI	24-9	W	77,395
Sun	10/10	H	CIN	17-15	W	75,394
Sun	10/17	A	SD	17-14	W	60,729
Sun	10/31	A	MIA	10-30	L	67,765
Mon	11/8	H	GB	23-16	W	76,742
Sun	11/14	A	LARI	31-20	W	66,553
Sun	11/21	H	CHI	17-19	L	76,872
Sun	11/28	H	BUF	23-7	W	74,452
Sun	12/5	A	SEA	31-16	W	58,551
Sun	12/12	A	DEN	21-27	L	75,822
Sun	12/19	H	SD	28-24	W	74,778
Sun	12/26	A	MIN	10-30	L	59,236
Sun	1/2	H	SEA	34-24	W	72,136

AFC WILD-CARD PLAYOFF

Sat	1/8	H	PIT	*27-24	W	74,515

AFC DIVISIONAL PLAYOFF

Sun	1/16	A	HOU	28-20	W	64,011

AFC CHAMPIONSHIP

Sun	1/23	A	BUF	13-30	L	76,642

LOS ANGELES RAIDERS

Sun	9/5	H	MIN	24-7	W	44,120
Sun	9/12	A	SEA	17-13	W	58,836
Sun	9/19	H	CLE	16-19	L	48,617
Sun	10/3	A	KC	9-24	L	77,395
Sun	10/10	H	NYJ	24-20	W	41,627
Mon	10/18	A	DEN	23-20	W	75,712
Sun	10/31	H	SD	23-30	L	45,122

Sun	11/7	A	CHI	16-14	W	59,750
Sun	11/14	H	KC	20-31	L	66,553
Sun	11/21	A	SD	12-7	W	60,615
Sun	11/28	A	CIN	10-16	L	43,272
Sun	12/5	A	BUF	25-24	W	79,478
Sun	12/12	H	SEA	27-23	W	38,161
Sun	12/19	H	TB	27-20	W	40,532
Sun	12/26	A	GB	0-28	L	54,482
Sun	1/2	H	DEN	*33-30	W	66,904

AFC Wild-Card Playoff

Sun	1/9	H	DEN	42-24	W	65,314

AFC Divisional Playoff

Sat	1/15	A	BUF	23-29	L	61,923

LOS ANGELES RAMS

Sun	9/5	A	GB	6-36	L	54,648
Sun	9/12	H	PIT	27-0	W	50,588
Sun	9/19	A	NYG	10-20	L	76,213
Sun	9/26	A	HOU	28-13	W	53,072
Sun	10/3	H	NO	6-37	L	50,709
Thu	10/14	A	ATL	24-30	L	45,231
Sun	10/24	H	DET	13-16	L	43,850
Sun	10/31	A	SF	17-40	L	63,417
Sun	11/14	H	ATL	0-13	L	37,073
Sun	11/21	H	WAS	10-6	W	45,546
Sun	11/28	H	SF	10-35	L	62,143
Sun	12/5	A	PHX	10-38	L	33,964
Sun	12/12	A	NO	23-20	W	69,033
Sun	12/19	A	CIN	3-15	L	36,612
Sun	12/26	H	CLE	14-42	L	34,155
Sun	1/2	H	CHI	20-6	W	39,147

MIAMI DOLPHINS

Sun	9/5	A	IND	24-20	W	51,858
Sun	9/12	H	NYJ	14-24	L	70,314
Sun	9/26	A	BUF	22-13	W	79,635
Mon	10/4	H	WAS	17-10	W	68,568
Sun	10/10	A	CLE	24-14	W	78,138
Sun	10/24	H	IND	41-27	W	57,301
Sun	10/31	H	KC	30-10	W	67,765
Sun	11/7	A	NYJ	10-27	L	71,306
Sun	11/14	A	PHI	19-14	W	64,213
Sun	11/21	H	NE	17-13	W	59,982
Thu	11/25	A	DAL	16-14	W	60,198
Sun	12/5	H	NYG	14-19	L	72,161
Mon	12/13	H	PIT	20-21	L	70,232
Sun	12/19	H	BUF	34-47	L	71,597
Mon	12/27	A	SD	20-45	L	60,311
Sun	1/2	A	NE	*27-33	L	53,883

MINNESOTA VIKINGS

Sun	9/5	A	LARI	7-24	L	44,120
Sun	9/12	H	CHI	10-7	W	57,921
Sun	9/26	H	GB	15-13	W	61,746
Sun	10/3	A	SF	19-38	L	63,071
Sun	10/10	H	TB	15-0	W	54,215
Mon	10/25	A	CHI	19-12	W	64,677
Sun	10/31	H	DET	27-30	L	53,428
Sun	11/7	H	SD	17-30	L	55,527
Sun	11/14	A	DEN	26-23	W	67,329
Sun	11/21	A	TB	10-23	L	40,848
Sun	11/28	H	NO	14-17	L	53,030
Sun	12/5	A	DET	13-0	W	63,216
Sun	12/12	H	DAL	20-37	L	63,321
Sun	12/19	A	GB	21-17	W	54,773
Sun	12/26	H	KC	30-10	W	59,236
Fri	12/31	A	WAS	14-9	W	42,836

NFC Wild-Card Playoff

Sat	1/9	A	NYG	10-17	L	75,089

NEW ENGLAND PATRIOTS

Sun	9/5	A	BUF	14-38	L	79,751
Sun	9/12	H	DET	*16-19	L	54,151
Sun	9/19	H	SEA	14-17	L	50,392
Sun	9/26	A	NYJ	7-45	L	64,836
Sun	10/10	A	PHX	23-21	W	36,115
Sun	10/17	H	HOU	14-28	L	51,037
Sun	10/24	A	SEA	9-10	L	56,526
Sun	10/31	A	IND	6-9	L	46,522
Sun	11/7	H	BUF	*10-13	L	54,326
Sun	11/21	A	MIA	13-17	L	59,982
Sun	11/28	H	NYJ	0-6	L	42,810
Sun	12/5	A	PIT	14-17	L	51,358
Sun	12/12	H	CIN	7-2	W	29,794
Sun	12/19	A	CLE	20-17	W	48,618
Sun	12/26	H	IND	38-0	W	26,571
Sun	1/2	H	MIA	*33-27	W	53,883

NEW ORLEANS SAINTS

Sun	9/5	H	HOU	33-21	W	69,029
Sun	9/12	A	ATL	34-31	W	64,287
Sun	9/19	H	DET	14-3	W	69,039
Sun	9/26	H	SF	16-13	W	69,041
Sun	10/3	A	LARM	37-6	W	50,709
Sun	10/17	A	PIT	14-37	L	56,056
Sun	10/24	H	ATL	15-26	L	69,043
Sun	10/31	A	PHX	20-17	W	36,778
Sun	11/14	H	GB	17-19	L	69,043
Mon	11/22	A	SF	7-42	L	66,500
Sun	11/28	A	MIN	17-14	W	53,030
Sun	12/5	A	CLE	13-17	L	60,388
Sun	12/12	H	LARM	20-23	L	69,033
Mon	12/20	H	NYG	14-24	L	69,036
Sun	12/26	A	PHI	26-37	L	50,085
Sun	1/2	H	CIN	20-13	W	58,036

NEW YORK GIANTS

Sun	9/5	A	CHI	26-20	W	66,900
Sun	9/12	H	TB	23-7	W	75,891
Sun	9/19	H	LARM	20-10	W	76,213
Sun	10/3	A	BUF	14-17	L	79,283
Sun	10/10	A	WAS	41-7	W	53,715
Sun	10/17	H	PHI	21-10	W	76,050
Sun	10/31	H	NYJ	6-10	L	71,659
Sun	11/7	A	DAL	9-31	L	64,735
Sun	11/14	H	WAS	20-6	W	76,606
Sun	11/21	A	PHI	7-3	W	62,928
Sun	11/28	H	PHX	19-17	W	59,979
Sun	12/5	A	MIA	19-14	W	72,161
Sun	12/12	H	IND	20-6	W	70,411
Mon	12/20	A	NO	24-14	W	69,036
Sun	12/26	A	PHX	6-17	L	53,414
Sun	1/2	H	DAL	*13-16	L	77,356

NFC Wild-Card Playoff

Sun	1/9	H	MIN	17-10	W	75,089

NFC Divisional Playoff

Sat	1/15	A	SF	3-44	L	67,143

NEW YORK JETS

Sun	9/5	H	DEN	20-26	L	68,130
Sun	9/12	A	MIA	24-14	W	70,314
Sun	9/26	H	NE	45-7	W	64,836
Sun	10/3	H	PHI	30-35	L	72,593
Sun	10/10	A	LARI	20-24	L	41,627
Sun	10/24	H	BUF	10-19	L	71,541
Sun	10/31	A	NYG	10-6	W	71,659
Sun	11/7	H	MIA	27-10	W	71,306
Sun	11/14	A	IND	31-17	W	47,351
Sun	11/21	H	CIN	17-12	W	64,264
Sun	11/28	A	NE	6-0	W	42,810
Sun	12/5	H	IND	6-9	L	45,799
Sat	12/11	A	WAS	3-0	W	47,970
Sat	12/18	H	DAL	7-28	L	73,233
Sun	12/26	A	BUF	14-16	L	70,817
Sun	1/2	A	HOU	0-24	L	61,040

PHILADELPHIA EAGLES

Sun	9/5	H	PHX	23-17	W	59,831
Sun	9/12	A	GB	20-17	W	59,061
Sun	9/19	H	WAS	34-31	W	65,435
Sun	10/3	A	NYJ	35-30	W	72,593
Sun	10/10	H	CHI	6-17	L	63,601
Sun	10/17	A	NYG	10-21	L	76,050
Sun	10/31	H	DAL	10-23	L	61,912
Sun	11/7	A	PHX	3-16	L	41,634
Sun	11/14	H	MIA	14-19	L	64,213
Sun	11/21	H	NYG	3-7	L	62,928
Sun	11/28	A	WAS	17-14	W	46,663
Mon	12/6	A	DAL	17-23	L	64,521
Sun	12/12	H	BUF	7-10	L	60,769
Sun	12/19	A	IND	20-10	W	44,952
Sun	12/26	H	NO	37-26	W	50,085
Mon	1/3	A	SF	*37-34	W	61,653

PHOENIX CARDINALS

Sun	9/5	A	PHI	17-23	L	59,831
Sun	9/12	A	WAS	17-10	W	53,525
Sun	9/19	H	DAL	10-17	L	73,025
Sun	9/26	A	DET	20-26	L	57,180
Sun	10/10	H	NE	21-23	L	36,115
Sun	10/17	H	WAS	36-6	W	48,143
Sun	10/24	A	SF	14-28	L	62,020
Sun	10/31	H	NO	17-20	L	36,778
Sun	11/7	H	PHI	16-3	W	41,634
Sun	11/14	A	DAL	15-20	L	64,224
Sun	11/28	A	NYG	17-19	L	59,979
Sun	12/5	H	LARM	38-10	W	33,964
Sun	12/12	H	DET	14-21	L	39,393
Sun	12/19	A	SEA	*30-27	W	45,737
Sun	12/26	H	NYG	17-6	W	53,414
Sun	1/2	A	ATL	27-10	W	44,360

PITTSBURGH STEELERS

Sun	9/5	H	SF	13-24	L	57,502
Sun	9/12	A	LARM	0-27	L	50,588
Sun	9/19	H	CIN	34-7	W	53,682
Mon	9/27	A	ATL	45-17	W	65,477
Sun	10/10	H	SD	16-3	W	55,264
Sun	10/17	H	NO	37-14	W	56,056
Sun	10/24	A	CLE	23-28	L	78,118
Sun	11/7	A	CIN	24-16	W	51,202
Mon	11/15	H	BUF	23-0	W	60,265
Sun	11/21	A	DEN	13-37	L	74,840
Sun	11/28	A	HOU	3-23	L	61,238
Sun	12/5	H	NE	17-14	W	51,358
Mon	12/13	A	MIA	21-20	W	70,232
Sun	12/19	H	HOU	17-26	L	57,592
Sun	12/26	A	SEA	6-16	L	51,814
Sun	1/2	H	CLE	16-9	W	49,208

AFC Wild-Card Playoff

Sat	1/8	A	KC	*24-27	L	74,515

SAN DIEGO CHARGERS

Sun	9/5	H	SEA	18-12	W	58,039
Sun	9/12	A	DEN	17-34	L	75,074
Sun	9/19	H	HOU	18-17	W	58,519
Sun	10/3	A	SEA	14-31	L	54,778
Sun	10/10	A	PIT	3-16	L	55,264
Sun	10/17	H	KC	14-17	L	60,729
Sun	10/31	A	LARI	30-23	W	45,122
Sun	11/7	A	MIN	30-17	W	55,527
Sun	11/14	H	CHI	13-16	L	58,459
Sun	11/21	H	LARI	7-12	L	60,615
Mon	11/29	A	IND	31-0	W	54,110
Sun	12/5	H	DEN	13-10	W	60,233
Sun	12/12	H	GB	13-20	L	57,930
Sun	12/19	A	KC	24-28	L	74,778
Mon	12/27	H	MIA	45-20	W	60,311
Sun	1/2	A	TB	32-17	W	35,857

SAN FRANCISCO 49ERS

Sun	9/5	A	PIT	24-13	W	57,502
Mon	9/13	A	CLE	13-23	L	78,218
Sun	9/19	H	ATL	37-30	W	63,032
Sun	9/26	A	NO	13-16	L	69,041
Sun	10/3	H	MIN	38-19	W	63,071
Sun	10/17	A	DAL	17-26	L	65,099
Sun	10/24	H	PHX	28-14	W	62,020
Sun	10/31	H	LARM	40-17	W	63,417
Sun	11/14	A	TB	45-21	W	43,835
Mon	11/22	H	NO	42-7	W	66,500
Sun	11/28	A	LARM	35-10	W	62,143
Sun	12/5	H	CIN	21-8	W	60,039
Sat	12/11	A	ATL	24-27	L	64,688
Sun	12/19	A	DET	55-17	W	77,052
Sat	12/25	H	HOU	7-10	L	61,744
Mon	1/3	H	PHI	*34-37	L	61,653

NFC Divisional Playoff

Sat	1/15	H	NYG	44-3	W	67,143

NFC Championship

Sun	1/23	A	DAL	21-38	L	64,902

SEATTLE SEAHAWKS

Sun	9/5	A	SD	12-18	L	58,039
Sun	9/12	H	LARI	13-17	L	58,836
Sun	9/19	A	NE	17-14	W	50,392
Sun	9/26	A	CIN	19-10	W	46,880
Sun	10/3	H	SD	31-14	W	54,778
Sun	10/17	A	DET	10-30	L	60,801
Sun	10/24	H	NE	10-9	W	56,526
Sun	10/31	A	DEN	17-28	L	73,644
Sun	11/7	A	HOU	14-24	L	50,447
Sun	11/14	H	CLE	22-5	W	54,622
Sun	11/28	H	DEN	9-17	L	57,812
Sun	12/5	H	KC	16-31	L	58,551
Sun	12/12	A	LARI	23-27	L	38,161
Sun	12/19	H	PHX	*27-30	L	45,737
Sun	12/26	H	PIT	16-6	W	51,814
Sun	1/2	A	KC	24-34	L	72,136

TAMPA BAY BUCCANEERS

Sun	9/5	H	KC	3-27	L	63,378
Sun	9/12	A	NYG	7-23	L	75,891
Sun	9/26	A	CHI	17-47	L	58,329
Sun	10/3	H	DET	27-10	W	40,794
Sun	10/10	A	MIN	0-15	L	54,215
Sun	10/24	H	GB	14-37	L	47,354
Sun	10/31	A	ATL	31-24	W	50,647
Sun	11/7	A	DET	0-23	L	65,295
Sun	11/14	H	SF	21-45	L	43,835
Sun	11/21	H	MIN	23-10	W	40,848
Sun	11/28	A	GB	10-13	L	56,995
Sun	12/5	H	WAS	17-23	L	49,035
Sun	12/12	H	CHI	13-10	W	56,667
Sun	12/19	A	LARI	20-27	L	40,532
Sun	12/26	A	DEN	17-10	W	73,434
Sun	1/2	H	SD	17-32	L	35,587

WASHINGTON REDSKINS

Mon	9/6	H	DAL	35-16	W	56,345
Sun	9/12	H	PHX	10-17	L	53,525
Sun	9/19	A	PHI	31-34	L	65,435
Mon	10/4	A	MIA	10-17	L	68,568
Sun	10/10	H	NYG	7-41	L	53,715
Sun	10/17	A	PHX	6-36	L	48,143
Mon	11/1	A	BUF	10-24	L	79,106
Sun	11/7	H	IND	30-24	W	50,523
Sun	11/14	A	NYG	6-20	L	76,606
Sun	11/21	A	LARM	6-10	L	45,546
Sun	11/28	H	PHI	14-17	L	46,663
Sun	12/5	A	TB	23-17	W	49,035
Sat	12/11	H	NYJ	0-3	L	47,970
Sun	12/19	H	ATL	30-17	W	50,192
Sun	12/26	A	DAL	3-38	L	64,497
Fri	12/31	H	MIN	9-14	L	42,836

1994 NFL

ARIZONA CARDINALS

Sun	9/4	A	LARM	12-14	L	32,969
Sun	9/11	H	NYG	17-20	L	60,066
Sun	9/18	A	CLE	0-32	L	62,818
Sun	10/2	H	MIN	17-7	W	67,950
Sun	10/9	A	DAL	3-38	L	64,518

Sun	10/16	A	WAS	*19-16	W	50,019
Sun	10/23	H	DAL	21-28	L	71,023
Sun	10/30	H	PIT	*20-17	W	73,400
Sun	11/6	A	PHI	7-17	L	64,952
Sun	11/13	A	NYG	10-9	W	71,719
Sun	11/20	H	PHI	12-6	W	62,779
Sun	11/27	H	CHI	*16-19	L	72,199
Sun	12/4	A	HOU	30-12	W	39,821
Sun	12/11	H	WAS	17-15	W	53,790
Sun	12/18	H	CIN	28-7	W	50,110
Sat	12/24	A	ATL	6-10	L	35,311

ATLANTA FALCONS

Sun	9/4	A	DET	*28-31	L	60,740
Sun	9/11	H	LARM	31-13	W	55,378
Sun	9/18	H	KC	10-30	L	67,357
Sun	9/25	A	WAS	27-20	W	53,238
Sun	10/2	A	LARM	8-5	W	34,599
Sun	10/9	H	TB	34-13	W	52,633
Sun	10/16	H	SF	3-42	L	67,298
Sun	10/23	A	LARI	17-30	L	42,192
Sun	11/6	H	SD	10-9	W	59,217
Sun	11/13	A	NO	32-33	L	60,313
Sun	11/20	A	DEN	28-32	L	70,594
Sun	11/27	H	PHI	28-21	W	60,008
Sun	12/4	A	SF	14-50	L	60,549
Sun	12/11	H	NO	20-29	L	61,307
Sun	12/18	A	GB	17-21	L	54,885
Sat	12/24	H	ARI	10-6	W	35,311

BUFFALO BILLS

Sun	9/4	H	NYJ	3-23	L	79,460
Sun	9/11	A	NE	38-35	W	60,274
Sun	9/18	A	HOU	15-7	W	55,424
Mon	9/26	H	DEN	27-20	W	75,373
Sun	10/2	A	CHI	13-20	L	62,406
Sun	10/9	H	MIA	21-11	W	79,491
Sun	10/16	H	IND	17-27	L	79,404
Sun	10/30	H	KC	44-10	W	79,501
Sun	11/6	A	NYJ	17-22	L	67,030
Mon	11/14	A	PIT	10-23	L	59,019
Sun	11/20	H	GB	29-20	W	79,029
Thu	11/24	A	DET	21-35	L	75,672
Sun	12/4	A	MIA	42-31	W	69,358
Sun	12/11	H	MIN	17-21	L	66,501
Sun	12/18	H	NE	17-41	L	56,784
Sat	12/24	A	IND	9-10	L	38,458

CHICAGO BEARS

Sun	9/4	H	TB	21-9	W	61,844
Mon	9/12	A	PHI	22-30	L	64,890
Sun	9/18	H	MIN	14-42	L	61,073
Sun	9/25	A	NYJ	19-7	W	70,806
Sun	10/2	H	BUF	20-13	W	62,406
Sun	10/9	H	NO	17-7	W	63,822
Sun	10/23	A	DET	16-21	L	73,574
Mon	10/31	H	GB	6-33	L	47,381
Sun	11/6	A	TB	20-6	W	60,821
Sun	11/13	A	MIA	17-14	W	65,006
Sun	11/20	H	DET	20-10	W	55,035
Sun	11/27	A	ARI	*19-16	W	72,199
Thu	12/1	A	MIN	*27-33	L	61,483
Sun	12/11	A	GB	3-40	L	57,927
Sun	12/18	H	LARM	27-13	W	56,276
Sat	12/24	H	NE	3-13	L	60,178

NFC Wild-Card Playoff

Sun	1/1	A	MIN	35-18	W	60,347

NFC Divisional Playoff

Sat	1/7	A	SF	15-44	L	64,644

CINCINNATI BENGALS

Sun	9/4	H	CLE	20-28	L	52,778
Sun	9/11	A	SD	10-27	L	53,217
Sun	9/18	H	NE	28-31	L	46,640
Sun	9/25	A	HOU	13-20	L	44,253
Sun	10/2	H	MIA	7-23	L	55,056
Sun	10/16	A	PIT	10-14	L	55,353
Sun	10/23	A	CLE	13-37	L	77,588
Sun	10/30	H	DAL	20-23	L	57,096
Sun	11/6	A	SEA	*20-17	W	46,630
Sun	11/13	H	HOU	34-31	W	54,908
Sun	11/20	H	IND	13-17	L	55,566
Sun	11/27	A	DEN	13-15	L	69,714
Sun	12/4	H	PIT	15-38	L	59,997
Sun	12/11	A	NYG	20-27	L	67,530
Sun	12/18	A	ARI	7-28	L	50,110
Sat	12/24	H	PHI	33-30	W	39,923

CLEVELAND BROWNS

Sun	9/4	A	CIN	28-20	W	52,778
Sun	9/11	H	PIT	10-17	L	77,774
Sun	9/18	H	ARI	32-0	W	62,818
Sun	9/25	A	IND	21-14	W	55,821
Sun	10/2	H	NYJ	27-7	W	76,188
Thu	10/13	A	HOU	11-8	W	50,364
Sun	10/23	H	CIN	37-13	W	77,588
Sun	10/30	A	DEN	14-26	L	73,190
Sun	11/6	H	NE	13-6	W	73,878
Sun	11/13	A	PHI	26-7	W	65,233
Sun	11/20	A	KC	13-20	L	66,129
Sun	11/27	H	HOU	34-10	W	65,088
Sun	12/4	H	NYG	13-16	L	72,068
Sat	12/10	A	DAL	19-14	W	64,286
Sun	12/18	A	PIT	7-17	L	60,808
Sat	12/24	H	SEA	35-9	W	54,180

AFC Wild-Card Playoff

Sun	1/1	H	NE	20-13	W	77,452

AFC Divisional Playoff

Sat	1/7	A	PIT	9-29	L	58,185

DALLAS COWBOYS

Sun	9/4	A	PIT	26-9	W	60,156
Sun	9/11	H	HOU	20-17	W	64,402
Mon	9/19	H	DET	*17-20	L	64,102
Sun	10/2	A	WAS	34-7	W	55,394
Sun	10/9	H	ARI	38-3	W	64,518
Sun	10/16	H	PHI	24-13	W	64,703
Sun	10/23	A	ARI	28-21	W	71,023
Sun	10/30	A	CIN	23-20	W	57,096
Mon	11/7	H	NYG	38-10	W	64,836
Sun	11/13	A	SF	14-21	L	69,014
Sun	11/20	H	WAS	31-7	W	64,644
Thu	11/24	H	GB	42-31	W	64,597
Sun	12/4	A	PHI	31-19	W	65,974
Sat	12/10	H	CLE	14-19	L	64,286
Mon	12/19	A	NO	24-16	W	67,323
Sat	12/24	A	NYG	10-15	L	66,943

NFC Divisional Playoff

Sun	1/8	H	GB	35-9	W	64,745

NFC Championship

Sun	1/15	A	SF	28-39	L	69,125

DENVER BRONCOS

Sun	9/4	H	SD	34-37	L	74,032
Sun	9/11	A	NYJ	*22-25	L	73,436
Sun	9/18	H	LARI	16-48	L	75,764
Mon	9/26	A	BUF	20-27	L	75,373
Sun	10/9	A	SEA	16-9	W	63,872
Mon	10/17	H	KC	28-31	L	75,151
Sun	10/23	A	SD	20-15	W	61,626
Sun	10/30	H	CLE	26-14	W	73,190
Sun	11/6	A	LARM	21-27	L	48,103
Sun	11/13	H	SEA	17-10	W	71,290
Sun	11/20	H	ATL	32-28	W	70,594
Sun	11/27	H	CIN	15-13	W	69,714
Sun	12/4	A	KC	*20-17	W	77,631
Sun	12/11	A	LARI	13-23	L	60,016
Sat	12/17	A	SF	19-42	L	64,884
Sat	12/24	H	NO	28-30	L	64,445

DETROIT LIONS

Sun	9/4	H	ATL	*31-28	W	60,740
Sun	9/11	A	MIN	3-10	L	57,349
Mon	9/19	A	DAL	*20-17	W	64,102
Sun	9/25	H	NE	17-23	L	59,618
Sun	10/2	A	TB	14-24	L	38,012
Sun	10/9	H	SF	21-27	L	77,340
Sun	10/23	H	CHI	21-16	W	73,574
Sun	10/30	A	NYG	*28-25	W	75,124
Sun	11/6	A	GB	30-38	L	54,995
Sun	11/13	H	TB	14-9	W	50,814
Sun	11/20	A	CHI	10-20	L	55,035
Thu	11/24	H	BUF	35-21	W	75,672
Sun	12/4	H	GB	34-31	W	76,338
Sat	12/10	A	NYJ	18-7	W	56,080
Sat	12/17	H	MIN	41-19	W	73,881
Sun	12/25	A	MIA	20-27	L	70,980

NFC Wild-Card Playoff

Sat	12/31	A	GB	12-16	L	58,125

GREEN BAY PACKERS

Sun	9/4	H	MIN	16-10	W	59,487
Sun	9/11	H	MIA	14-24	L	55,011
Sun	9/18	A	PHI	7-13	L	63,922
Sun	9/25	H	TB	30-3	W	58,551
Sun	10/2	A	NE	16-17	L	57,522
Sun	10/9	H	LARM	24-17	W	58,911
Thu	10/20	A	MIN	*10-13	L	63,041
Mon	10/31	A	CHI	33-6	W	47,381
Sun	11/6	H	DET	38-30	W	54,995
Sun	11/13	H	NYJ	17-10	W	58,307
Sun	11/20	A	BUF	20-29	L	79,029
Thu	11/24	A	DAL	31-42	L	64,597
Sun	12/4	A	DET	31-34	L	76,338
Sun	12/11	H	CHI	40-3	W	57,927
Sun	12/18	H	ATL	21-17	W	54,885
Sat	12/24	A	TB	34-19	W	65,076

NFC Wild-Card Playoff

Sat	12/31	H	DET	16-12	W	58,125

NFC Divisional Playoff

Sun	1/8	A	DAL	9-35	L	64,745

HOUSTON OILERS

Sun	9/4	A	IND	21-45	L	47,372
Sun	9/11	A	DAL	17-20	L	64,402
Sun	9/18	H	BUF	7-15	L	55,424
Sun	9/25	H	CIN	20-13	W	44,253
Mon	10/3	A	PIT	14-30	L	57,274
Thu	10/13	H	CLE	8-11	L	50,364
Mon	10/24	A	PHI	6-21	L	65,233
Sun	10/30	A	LARI	14-17	L	40,473
Sun	11/6	H	PIT	*9-12	L	47,822
Sun	11/13	A	CIN	31-34	L	54,908
Mon	11/21	H	NYG	10-13	L	53,201
Sun	11/27	A	CLE	10-34	L	65,088
Sun	12/4	H	ARI	12-30	L	39,821
Sun	12/11	H	SEA	14-16	L	31,453
Sun	12/18	A	KC	9-31	L	74,474
Sat	12/24	H	NYJ	24-10	W	31,176

INDIANAPOLIS COLTS

Sun	9/4	H	HOU	45-21	W	47,372
Sun	9/11	A	TB	10-24	L	36,631
Sun	9/18	A	PIT	21-31	L	54,040
Sun	9/25	H	CLE	14-21	L	55,821
Sun	10/2	H	SEA	17-15	W	49,876
Sun	10/9	A	NYJ	6-16	L	66,244
Sun	10/16	A	BUF	27-17	W	79,404
Sun	10/23	H	WAS	27-41	L	57,879
Sun	10/30	H	NYJ	28-25	W	44,350
Sun	11/6	A	MIA	21-22	L	67,863
Sun	11/20	A	CIN	17-13	W	55,566
Sun	11/27	H	NE	10-12	L	43,839
Sun	12/4	A	SEA	31-19	W	39,574
Sun	12/11	A	NE	13-28	L	57,656
Sun	12/18	H	MIA	10-6	W	58,867
Sat	12/24	H	BUF	10-9	W	38,458

KANSAS CITY CHIEFS

Sun	9/4	A	NO	30-17	W	69,362
Sun	9/11	H	SF	24-17	W	79,907
Sun	9/18	A	ATL	30-10	W	67,357
Sun	9/25	H	LARM	0-16	L	78,184
Sun	10/9	A	SD	6-20	L	62,923
Mon	10/17	A	DEN	31-28	W	75,151
Sun	10/23	H	SEA	38-23	W	78,847
Sun	10/30	A	BUF	10-44	L	79,501
Sun	11/6	H	LARI	13-3	W	78,709
Sun	11/13	H	SD	13-14	L	76,997
Sun	11/20	H	CLE	20-13	W	66,129
Sun	11/27	A	SEA	9-10	L	54,120
Sun	12/4	H	DEN	*17-20	L	77,631
Mon	12/12	A	MIA	28-45	L	71,578
Sun	12/18	H	HOU	31-9	W	74,474
Sat	12/24	A	LARI	19-9	W	64,130

AFC Wild-Card Playoff

Sat	12/31	A	MIA	17-27	L	67,487

LOS ANGELES RAIDERS

Mon	9/5	A	SF	14-44	L	68,032
Sun	9/11	H	SEA	9-38	L	47,319
Sun	9/18	A	DEN	48-16	W	75,764
Sun	9/25	H	SD	24-26	L	55,385
Sun	10/9	A	NE	21-17	W	59,889
Sun	10/16	A	MIA	*17-20	L	69,380
Sun	10/23	H	ATL	30-17	W	42,192
Sun	10/30	H	HOU	17-14	W	40,473
Sun	11/6	A	KC	3-13	L	78,709
Sun	11/13	A	LARM	20-17	W	65,208
Sun	11/20	H	NO	24-19	W	41,722
Sun	11/27	H	PIT	3-21	L	58,327
Mon	12/5	A	SD	24-17	W	63,012
Sun	12/11	H	DEN	23-13	W	60,016
Sun	12/18	A	SEA	17-16	W	53,301
Sat	12/24	H	KC	9-19	L	64,130

LOS ANGELES RAMS

Sun	9/4	H	ARI	14-12	W	32,969
Sun	9/11	A	ATL	13-31	L	55,378
Sun	9/18	H	SF	19-34	L	56,479
Sun	9/25	A	KC	16-0	W	78,184
Sun	10/2	H	ATL	5-8	L	34,599
Sun	10/9	A	GB	17-24	L	58,911
Sun	10/16	H	NYG	17-10	W	40,474
Sun	10/23	A	NO	34-37	L	47,908
Sun	11/6	H	DEN	27-21	W	48,103
Sun	11/13	H	LARI	17-20	L	65,208
Sun	11/20	A	SF	27-31	L	62,774
Sun	11/27	A	SD	17-31	L	59,579
Sun	12/4	H	NO	15-31	L	34,960
Sun	12/11	A	TB	14-24	L	34,150
Sun	12/18	A	CHI	13-27	L	56,276
Sat	12/24	H	WAS	21-24	L	25,705

MIAMI DOLPHINS

Sun	9/4	H	NE	39-35	W	69,613
Sun	9/11	A	GB	24-14	W	55,011
Sun	9/18	H	NYJ	28-14	W	68,192
Sun	9/25	A	MIN	35-38	L	64,035
Sun	10/2	A	CIN	23-7	W	55,056
Sun	10/9	A	BUF	11-21	L	79,491
Sun	10/16	H	LARI	*20-17	W	69,380
Sun	10/30	A	NE	23-3	W	59,167
Sun	11/6	H	IND	22-21	W	67,863
Sun	11/13	H	CHI	14-17	L	65,006
Sun	11/20	A	PIT	*13-16	L	59,148
Sun	11/27	A	NYJ	28-24	W	75,606
Sun	12/4	H	BUF	31-42	L	69,358
Mon	12/12	H	KC	45-28	W	71,578
Sun	12/18	A	IND	6-10	L	58,867
Sun	12/25	H	DET	27-20	W	70,980

AFC Wild-Card Playoff

Sat	12/31	H	KC	27-17	W	67,487

MINNESOTA VIKINGS

Sun 9/4   A GB   10-16   L 59,487
Sun 9/11   H DET 10-3   W 57,349
Sun 9/18   A CHI 42-14   W 61,073
Sun 9/25   H MIA 38-35   W 64,035
Sun 10/2   A ARI 7-17   L 67,950
Mon 10/10 A NYG 27-10   W 77,294
Thu 10/20 H GB   *13-10 W 63,041
Sun 10/30 H TB   36-13   W 42,110
Sun 11/6   H NO   21-20   W 57,564
Sun 11/13 A NE   *20-26 L 58,382
Sun 11/20 H NYJ 21-31   L 60,687
Sun 11/27 H TB   *17-20 L 47,259
Thu 12/1   H CHI *33-27 W 61,483
Sun 12/11 A BUF 21-17   W 66,501
Sat 12/17 A DET 19-41   L 73,881
Mon 12/26 H SF   21-14   W 63,326

NFC WILD-CARD PLAYOFF
Sun 1/1   H CHI 18-35   L 60,347

NEW ENGLAND PATRIOTS

Sun 9/4   A MIA 35-39   L 69,613
Sun 9/11   H BUF 35-38   L 60,274
Sun 9/18   A CIN 31-28   W 46,640
Sun 9/25   A DET 23-17   W 59,618
Sun 10/2   H GB   17-16   W 57,522
Sun 10/9   H LARI 17-21   L 59,889
Sun 10/16 A NYJ 17-24   L 71,123
Sun 10/30 H MIA 3-23   L 59,167
Sun 11/6   A CLE 6-13   L 73,878
Sun 11/13 H MIN *26-20 W 58,382
Sun 11/20 H SD   23-17   W 59,690
Sun 11/27 A IND 12-10   W 43,839
Sun 12/4   H NYJ 24-13   W 60,138
Sun 12/11 H IND 28-13   W 57,656
Sun 12/18 A BUF 41-17   W 56,784
Sat 12/24 A CHI 13-3   W 60,178

AFC WILD-CARD PLAYOFF
Sun 1/1   A CLE 13-20   L 77,452

NEW ORLEANS SAINTS

Sun 9/4   H KC   17-30   L 69,362
Sun 9/11   H WAS 24-38   L 58,049
Sun 9/18   A TB   9-7   W 45,522
Sun 9/25   A SF   13-24   L 63,971
Sun 10/2   H NYG 27-22   W 55,076
Sun 10/9   A CHI 7-17   L 63,822
Sun 10/16 H SD   22-36   L 50,565
Sun 10/23 H LARM 37-34   W 47,908
Sun 11/6   A MIN 20-21   L 57,564
Sun 11/13 H ATL 33-32   W 60,313
Sun 11/20 A LARI 19-24   L 41,722
Mon 11/28 H SF   14-35   L 61,304
Sun 12/4   A LARM 31-15   W 34,960
Sun 12/11 H ATL 29-20   W 61,307
Mon 12/19 H DAL 16-24   L 67,323
Sat 12/24 A DEN 30-28   W 64,445

NEW YORK GIANTS

Sun 9/4   H PHI 28-23   W 76,130
Sun 9/11   A ARI 20-17   W 60,066
Sun 9/18   H WAS 31-23   W 77,298
Sun 10/2   A NO   22-27   L 55,076
Mon 10/10 H MIN 10-27   L 77,294
Sun 10/16 H LARM 10-17   L 40,474
Sun 10/23 H PIT 6-10   L 71,819
Sun 10/30 H DET *25-28 L 75,124
Mon 11/7   A DAL 10-38   L 64,836
Sun 11/13 A ARI 9-10   L 71,719
Mon 11/21 A HOU 13-10   W 53,201
Sun 11/27 A WAS 21-19   W 43,384
Sun 12/4   A CLE 16-13   W 72,068

Sun 12/11 H CIN 27-20   W 67,530
Sun 12/18 A PHI 16-13   W 64,540
Sat 12/24 H DAL 15-10   W 66,943

NEW YORK JETS

Sun 9/4   A BUF 23-3   L 79,460
Sun 9/11   H DEN *25-22 W 73,436
Sun 9/18   A MIA 14-28   L 68,192
Sun 9/25   H CHI 7-19   L 70,806
Sun 10/2   A CLE 7-27   L 76,188
Sun 10/9   H IND 16-6   W 66,244
Sun 10/16 H NE   24-17   W 71,123
Sun 10/30 A IND 25-28   L 44,350
Sun 11/6   H BUF 22-17   W 67,030
Sun 11/13 A GB   10-17   L 58,307
Sun 11/20 A MIN 31-21   W 60,687
Sun 11/27 H MIA 24-28   L 75,606
Sun 12/4   A NE   13-24   L 60,138
Sat 12/10 H DET 7-18   L 56,080
Sun 12/18 H SD   6-21   L 48,213
Sat 12/24 A HOU 10-24   L 31,176

PHILADELPHIA EAGLES

Sun 9/4   A NYG 23-28   L 76,130
Mon 9/12   H CHI 30-22   W 64,890
Sun 9/18   H GB   13-7   W 63,922
Sun 10/2   A SF   40-8   W 64,771
Sun 10/9   H WAS 21-17   W 63,947
Sun 10/16 A DAL 13-24   L 64,703
Mon 10/24 H HOU 21-6   W 65,233
Sun 10/30 A WAS 31-29   W 53,530
Sun 11/6   H ARI 17-7   W 64,952
Sun 11/13 H CLE 7-26   L 65,233
Sun 11/20 A ARI 6-12   L 62,779
Sun 11/27 A ATL 21-28   L 60,008
Sun 12/4   H DAL 19-31   L 65,974
Sun 12/11 A PIT 3-14   L 55,474
Sun 12/18 H NYG 13-16   L 64,540
Sat 12/24 A CIN 30-33   L 39,923

PITTSBURGH STEELERS

Sun 9/4   H DAL 9-26   L 60,156
Sun 9/11   A CLE 17-10   W 77,774
Sun 9/18   H IND 31-21   W 54,040
Sun 9/25   A SEA 13-30   L 59,637
Mon 10/3   H HOU 30-14   W 57,274
Sun 10/16 H CIN 14-10   W 55,353
Sun 10/23 A NYG 10-6   L 71,819
Sun 10/30 A ARI *17-20 L 73,400
Sun 11/6   A HOU *12-9   L 47,822
Mon 11/14 H BUF 23-10   W 59,019
Sun 11/20 H MIA *16-13 W 59,148
Sun 11/27 A LARI 21-3   W 58,327
Sun 12/4   A CIN 38-15   W 59,997
Sun 12/11 H PHI 14-3   W 55,474
Sun 12/18 H CLE 17-7   W 60,808
Sat 12/24 A SD   34-37   L 58,379

AFC DIVISIONAL PLAYOFF
Sat 1/7   H CLE 29-9   W 58,185

AFC CHAMPIONSHIP
Sun 1/15   H SD   13-17   L 61,545

SAN DIEGO CHARGERS

Sun 9/4   A DEN 37-34   W 74,032
Sun 9/11   H CIN 27-10   W 53,217
Sun 9/18   A SEA 24-10   W 65,356
Sun 9/25   A LARI 26-24   W 55,385
Sun 10/9   H KC   20-6   W 62,923
Sun 10/16 A NO   36-22   W 50,565
Sun 10/23 H DEN 15-20   L 61,626
Sun 10/30 H SEA 35-15   W 59,001
Sun 11/6   A ATL 9-10   L 59,217
Sun 11/13 A KC   14-13   W 76,997
Sun 11/20 A NE   17-23   L 59,690
Sun 11/27 H LARI 31-17   W 59,579

Mon 12/5   H LARI 17-24   L 63,012
Sun 12/11 H SF   15-38   L 62,105
Sun 12/18 A NYJ 21-6   W 48,213
Sat 12/24 H PIT 37-34   W 58,379

AFC DIVISIONAL PLAYOFF
Sun 1/8   H MIA 22-21   W 63,381

AFC CHAMPIONSHIP
Sun 1/15   A PIT 17-13   W 61,545

SUPER BOWL XXIX
Sun 1/29   N SF   26-49   L 74,107

SAN FRANCISCO 49ERS

Mon 9/5   H LARI 44-14   W 68,032
Sun 9/11   A KC   17-24   L 79,907
Sun 9/18   A LARM 34-19   W 56,479
Sun 9/25   H NO   24-13   W 63,971
Sun 10/2   H PHI 8-40   L 64,771
Sun 10/9   A DET 27-21   W 77,340
Sun 10/16 A ATL 42-3   W 67,298
Sun 10/23 H TB   41-16   W 62,741
Sun 11/6   A WAS 37-22   W 54,335
Sun 11/13 H DAL 21-14   W 69,014
Sun 11/20 H LARM 31-27   W 62,774
Mon 11/28 H NO   35-14   W 61,304
Sun 12/4   H ATL 50-14   W 60,549
Sun 12/11 A SD   38-15   W 62,105
Sat 12/17 H DEN 42-19   W 64,884
Mon 12/26 A MIN 14-21   L 63,326

NFC DIVISIONAL PLAYOFF
Sat 1/7   H CHI 44-15   W 64,644

NFC CHAMPIONSHIP
Sun 1/15   H DAL 38-28   W 69,125

SUPER BOWL XXIX
Sun 1/29   N SD   49-26   W 74,107

SEATTLE SEAHAWKS

Sun 9/4   A WAS 28-7   W 56,454
Sun 9/11   A LARI 38-9   W 47,319
Sun 9/18   H SD   10-24   L 65,536
Sun 9/25   H PIT 30-13   W 59,637
Sun 10/2   H IND 15-17   L 49,876
Sun 10/9   H DEN 9-16   L 63,872
Sun 10/23 A KC   23-38   L 78,847
Sun 10/30 A SD   15-35   L 59,001
Sun 11/6   A CIN *17-20 L 46,630
Sun 11/13 A DEN 10-17   L 71,290
Sun 11/20 H TB   22-21   W 37,466
Sun 11/27 H KC   10-9   W 54,120
Sun 12/4   H IND 19-31   L 39,574
Sun 12/11 A HOU 16-14   W 31,453
Sun 12/18 A LARI 16-17   L 53,301
Sat 12/24 A CLE 9-35   L 54,180

TAMPA BAY BUCCANEERS

Sun 9/4   A CHI 9-21   L 61,844
Sun 9/11   H IND 24-10   W 36,631
Sun 9/18   H NO   7-9   L 45,522
Sun 9/25   A GB   3-30   L 58,551
Sun 10/2   H DET 24-14   W 38,012
Sun 10/9   H ATL 13-34   L 52,633
Sun 10/23 A SF   16-41   L 62,741
Sun 10/30 A MIN 13-36   L 42,110
Sun 11/6   H CHI 6-20   L 60,821
Sun 11/13 A DET 9-14   L 50,814
Sun 11/20 A SEA 21-22   L 37,466
Sun 11/27 A MIN *20-17 L 47,259
Sun 12/4   H WAS 26-21   W 45,121
Sun 12/11 H LARM 24-14   W 34,150
Sun 12/18 A WAS 17-14   W 47,315
Sat 12/24 A GB   19-34   L 65,076

WASHINGTON REDSKINS

Sun 9/4   H SEA 7-28   L 56,454
Sun 9/11   A NO   38-24   W 58,049
Sun 9/18   A NYG 23-31   L 77,298

Sun 9/25   H ATL 20-27   L 53,238
Sun 10/2   H DAL 7-34   L 55,394
Sun 10/9   A PHI 17-21   L 63,947
Sun 10/16 H ARI *16-19 L 50,019
Sun 10/23 A IND 41-27   W 57,879
Sun 10/30 H PHI 29-31   L 53,530
Sun 11/6   H SF   22-37   L 54,335
Sun 11/20 A DAL 7-31   L 64,644
Sun 11/27 H NYG 19-21   L 43,384
Sun 12/4   A TB   21-26   L 45,121
Sun 12/11 A ARI 15-17   L 53,790
Sun 12/18 H TB   14-17   L 47,315
Sat 12/24 A LARM 24-21   W 25,705

1995 NFL

ARIZONA CARDINALS

Sun 9/3   A WAS 7-27   L 52,731
Sun 9/10   H PHI 19-31   L 45,004
Sun 9/17   A DET 20-17   W 58,727
Sun 9/24   A DAL 20-34   L 64,560
Sun 10/1   H KC   3-24   L 50,211
Sun 10/8   A NYG *21-27 L 68,463
Sun 10/15 H WAS 24-20   W 42,370
Sun 10/29 H SEA *20-14 W 39,600
Sun 11/5   A DEN 6-38   L 71,488
Sun 11/12 H MIN *24-30 L 51,342
Sun 11/19 A CAR 7-27   L 49,582
Sun 11/26 H ATL *40-37 W 35,147
Thu 11/30 H NYG 6-10   L 44,246
Sat 12/9   A SD   25-28   L 55,258
Sun 12/17 A PHI 20-21   L 62,076
Mon 12/25 H DAL 13-37   L 72,394

ATLANTA FALCONS

Sun 9/3   H CAR *23-20 W 58,808
Sun 9/10   A SF   10-41   L 63,627
Sun 9/17   A NO   *27-24 W 57,442
Sun 9/24   H NYJ 13-3   W 40,778
Sun 10/1   H NE   30-17   W 47,114
Thu 10/12 A STL 19-21   L 59,700
Sun 10/22 A TB   24-21   W 66,135
Sun 10/29 H DAL 13-28   L 70,089
Sun 11/5   H DET 34-22   W 49,619
Sun 11/12 H BUF 17-23   L 62,690
Sun 11/19 H STL 31-6   W 46,309
Sun 11/26 A ARI *37-40 L 35,147
Sun 12/3   A MIA 20-21   L 63,395
Sun 12/10 H NO   19-14   W 54,603
Sun 12/17 A CAR 17-21   L 53,833
Sun 12/24 H SF   28-27   W 51,785

NFC WILD-CARD PLAYOFF
Sun 12/31 A GB   20-37   L 60,453

BUFFALO BILLS

Sun 9/3   A DEN 7-22   L 75,743
Sun 9/10   H CAR 31-9   W 79,190
Sun 9/17   H IND 20-14   W 62,499
Mon 9/25   A CLE *22-19 W 76,211
Sun 10/8   H NYJ 29-10   W 79,485
Sun 10/15 H SEA 27-21   W 74,362
Mon 10/23 A NE   14-27   L 60,203
Sun 10/29 A MIA 6-23   L 71,060
Sun 11/5   A IND 16-10   W 59,612
Sun 11/12 A ATL 23-17   W 62,690
Sun 11/19 A NYJ 28-26   W 54,436
Sun 11/26 H NE   25-35   L 69,384
Sun 12/3   A SF   17-27   L 65,568
Sun 12/10 A STL 45-27   W 64,623
Sun 12/17 H MIA 23-20   W 79,531
Sun 12/24 H HOU 17-28   L 45,253

AFC WILD-CARD PLAYOFF
Sat 12/30 H MIA 37-22   W 73,103

AFC DIVISIONAL PLAYOFF
Sat 1/6   A PIT 21-40   L 59,072

CAROLINA PANTHERS

Sun	9/3	A	ATL	*20-23	L	58,808
Sun	9/10	A	BUF	9-31	L	79,190
Sun	9/17	H	STL	10-31	L	54,060
Sun	10/1	H	TB	13-20	L	50,076
Sun	10/8	A	CHI	27-31	L	59,668
Sun	10/15	H	NYJ	26-15	W	52,613
Sun	10/22	H	NO	20-3	W	55,484
Sun	10/29	A	NE	*20-17	W	60,064
Sun	11/5	A	SF	13-7	W	61,722
Sun	11/12	A	STL	17-28	L	65,598
Sun	11/19	H	ARI	27-7	W	49,582
Sun	11/26	A	NO	26-34	L	39,580
Sun	12/3	H	IND	13-10	W	49,841
Sun	12/10	H	SF	10-31	L	76,136
Sun	12/17	H	ATL	21-17	W	53,833
Sun	12/24	A	WAS	17-20	L	42,903

CHICAGO BEARS

Sun	9/3	H	MIN	31-14	W	63,036
Mon	9/11	H	GB	24-27	L	64,855
Sun	9/17	A	TB	25-6	W	71,507
Sun	9/24	A	STL	28-34	L	59,679
Sun	10/8	H	CAR	31-27	W	59,668
Sun	10/15	A	JAC	30-27	W	72,020
Sun	10/22	H	HOU	35-32	W	63,545
Mon	10/30	A	MIN	14-6	W	58,217
Sun	11/5	H	PIT	*34-37	L	61,838
Sun	11/12	A	GB	28-35	L	59,996
Sun	11/19	H	DET	17-24	L	61,779
Sun	11/26	A	NYG	27-24	W	70,015
Mon	12/4	A	DET	7-27	L	77,230
Sun	12/10	A	CIN	10-16	L	38,642
Sun	12/17	H	TB	31-10	W	49,475
Sun	12/24	H	PHI	20-14	W	52,391

CINCINNATI BENGALS

Sun	9/3	A	IND	*24-21	W	42,445
Sun	9/10	H	JAC	24-17	W	48,318
Sun	9/17	A	SEA	21-24	L	39,492
Sun	9/24	H	HOU	28-38	L	46,332
Sun	10/1	H	MIA	23-26	L	52,671
Sun	10/8	A	TB	16-19	L	41,732
Thu	10/19	A	PIT	27-9	W	56,684
Sun	10/29	H	CLE	*26-29	L	58,632
Sun	11/5	H	OAK	17-20	L	51,265
Sun	11/12	A	HOU	32-25	W	32,998
Sun	11/19	H	PIT	31-49	L	54,636
Sun	11/26	A	JAC	17-13	W	68,249
Sun	12/3	A	GB	10-24	L	60,318
Sun	12/10	H	CHI	16-10	W	38,642
Sun	12/17	A	CLE	10-26	L	55,875
Sun	12/24	H	MIN	27-24	W	34,568

CLEVELAND BROWNS

Sun	9/3	A	NE	14-17	L	60,126
Sun	9/10	H	TB	22-6	W	61,083
Sun	9/17	A	HOU	14-7	W	36,077
Sun	9/24	H	KC	35-17	W	74,280
Mon	10/2	H	BUF	19-22	L	76,211
Sun	10/8	A	DET	20-38	L	74,171
Sun	10/22	H	JAC	15-23	L	64,405
Sun	10/29	A	CIN	*29-26	W	58,632
Sun	11/5	H	HOU	10-37	L	57,881
Mon	11/13	A	PIT	3-20	L	58,675
Sun	11/19	H	GB	20-31	L	55,388
Sun	11/26	H	PIT	17-20	L	67,269
Sun	12/3	A	SD	13-31	L	56,358
Sat	12/9	A	MIN	11-27	L	47,984
Sun	12/17	H	CIN	26-10	W	55,875
Sun	12/24	A	JAC	21-24	L	66,007

DALLAS COWBOYS

Mon	9/4	A	NYG	35-0	W	77,454
Sun	9/10	H	DEN	31-21	W	64,576
Sun	9/17	A	MIN	*23-17	W	60,088
Sun	9/24	H	ARI	34-20	W	64,560
Sun	10/1	A	WAS	23-27	L	55,489
Sun	10/8	H	GB	34-24	W	64,806
Sun	10/15	A	SD	23-9	W	62,664
Sun	10/29	A	ATL	28-13	W	70,089
Mon	11/6	H	PHI	34-12	W	64,876
Sun	11/12	H	SF	20-38	L	65,180
Sun	11/19	A	OAK	34-21	W	54,444
Thu	11/23	H	KC	24-12	W	64,901
Sun	12/3	H	WAS	17-24	L	64,866
Sun	12/10	A	PHI	17-20	L	66,198
Sun	12/17	H	NYG	21-20	W	64,400
Mon	12/25	A	ARI	37-13	W	72,394

NFC Divisional Playoff

Sun	1/7	H	PHI	30-11	W	64,371

NFC Championship

Sun	1/14	H	GB	38-27	W	65,135

Super Bowl XXX

Sun	1/28	N	PIT	27-17	W	76,347

DENVER BRONCOS

Sun	9/3	H	BUF	22-7	W	75,743
Sun	9/10	A	DAL	21-31	L	64,576
Sun	9/17	H	WAS	38-31	W	71,930
Sun	9/24	A	SD	6-17	L	58,978
Sun	10/1	A	SEA	10-27	L	56,483
Sun	10/8	A	NE	37-3	W	60,074
Mon	10/16	H	OAK	27-0	W	75,491
Sun	10/22	H	KC	7-21	L	71,044
Sun	11/5	H	ARI	38-6	W	71,488
Sun	11/12	A	PHI	13-31	L	60,842
Sun	11/19	H	SD	30-27	W	74,681
Sun	11/26	A	HOU	33-42	L	36,113
Sun	12/3	H	JAC	31-23	W	72,231
Sun	12/10	H	SEA	27-31	L	71,488
Sun	12/17	A	KC	17-20	L	75,061
Sun	12/24	A	OAK	31-28	W	50,074

DETROIT LIONS

Sun	9/3	A	PIT	20-23	L	58,002
Sun	9/10	A	MIN	10-20	L	52,234
Sun	9/17	H	ARI	17-20	L	58,727
Mon	9/25	H	SF	27-24	W	76,236
Sun	10/8	H	CLE	38-20	W	74,171
Sun	10/15	A	GB	21-30	L	60,302
Sun	10/22	A	WAS	*30-36	L	52,332
Sun	10/29	H	GB	24-16	W	73,462
Sun	11/5	A	ATL	22-34	L	49,619
Sun	11/12	H	TB	27-24	W	60,644
Sun	11/19	A	CHI	24-17	W	61,779
Thu	11/23	H	MIN	44-38	W	74,559
Mon	12/4	H	CHI	27-7	W	77,230
Sun	12/10	A	HOU	24-17	W	35,842
Sun	12/17	H	JAC	44-0	W	70,204
Sat	12/23	A	TB	37-10	W	50,049

NFC Wild-Card Playoff

Sat	12/30	A	PHI	37-58	L	66,099

GREEN BAY PACKERS

Sun	9/3	H	STL	14-17	L	60,104
Mon	9/11	A	CHI	27-24	W	64,855
Sun	9/17	H	NYG	14-6	W	60,117
Sun	9/24	A	JAC	24-14	W	66,744
Sun	10/8	A	DAL	24-34	L	64,806
Sun	10/15	H	DET	30-21	W	60,302
Sun	10/22	H	MIN	38-21	W	60,332
Sun	10/29	A	DET	16-24	L	73,462
Sun	11/5	A	MIN	24-27	L	62,839
Sun	11/12	H	CHI	35-28	W	59,996
Sun	11/19	A	CLE	31-20	W	55,388
Sun	11/26	H	TB	35-13	W	59,218
Sun	12/3	H	CIN	24-10	W	60,318
Sun	12/10	A	TB	*10-13	L	67,557
Sat	12/16	A	NO	34-23	W	50,132
Sun	12/24	H	PIT	24-19	W	60,649

NFC Wild-Card Playoff

Sun	12/31	H	ATL	37-20	W	60,453

NFC Divisional Playoff

Sat	1/6	A	SF	27-17	W	69,311

NFC Championship

Sun	1/14	A	DAL	27-38	L	65,135

HOUSTON OILERS

Sun	9/3	A	JAC	10-3	W	72,363
Sun	9/10	H	PIT	17-34	L	44,122
Sun	9/17	H	CLE	7-14	L	36,077
Sun	9/24	A	CIN	38-28	W	46,332
Sun	10/1	H	JAC	16-17	L	36,346
Sun	10/8	A	MIN	*17-23	L	56,430
Sun	10/22	A	CHI	32-35	L	63,545
Sun	10/29	H	TB	19-7	W	31,489
Sun	11/5	A	CLE	37-10	W	57,881
Sun	11/12	H	CIN	25-32	L	32,998
Sun	11/19	A	KC	13-20	L	77,576
Sun	11/26	H	DEN	42-33	W	36,113
Sun	12/3	A	PIT	7-21	L	56,013
Sun	12/10	H	DET	17-24	L	35,842
Sun	12/17	H	NYJ	23-6	W	35,873
Sun	12/24	A	BUF	28-17	W	45,253

INDIANAPOLIS COLTS

Sun	9/3	H	CIN	*21-24	L	42,445
Sun	9/10	A	NYJ	*27-24	W	65,134
Sun	9/17	A	BUF	14-20	L	62,499
Sun	10/1	H	STL	21-18	W	58,616
Sun	10/8	A	MIA	*27-24	W	68,471
Sun	10/15	H	SF	18-17	W	60,273
Sun	10/22	A	OAK	17-30	L	53,543
Sun	10/29	H	NYJ	17-10	W	49,250
Sun	11/5	H	BUF	10-16	L	59,612
Sun	11/12	A	NO	14-17	L	44,122
Sun	11/19	A	NE	24-10	W	59,544
Sun	11/26	H	MIA	36-28	W	60,414
Sun	12/3	A	CAR	10-13	L	49,841
Sun	12/10	A	JAC	41-31	W	66,099
Sun	12/17	H	SD	24-27	L	55,318
Sat	12/23	H	NE	10-7	W	54,685

AFC Wild-Card Playoff

Sun	12/31	A	SD	35-20	W	61,182

AFC Divisional Playoff

Sun	1/7	A	KC	10-7	W	77,594

AFC Championship

Sun	1/14	A	PIT	16-20	L	61,062

JACKSONVILLE JAGUARS

Sun	9/3	H	HOU	3-10	L	72,363
Sun	9/10	A	CIN	17-24	L	48,318
Sun	9/17	A	NYJ	10-27	L	49,970
Sun	9/24	H	GB	14-24	L	66,744
Sun	10/1	A	HOU	17-16	W	36,346
Sun	10/8	H	PIT	20-16	W	72,042
Sun	10/15	H	CHI	27-30	L	72,020
Sun	10/22	A	CLE	23-15	W	64,405
Sun	10/29	A	PIT	7-24	L	54,516
Sun	11/12	H	SEA	30-47	L	71,290
Sun	11/19	A	TB	16-17	L	71,629
Sun	11/26	H	CIN	13-17	L	68,249
Sun	12/3	A	DEN	23-31	L	72,231
Sun	12/10	H	IND	31-41	L	66,099
Sun	12/17	A	DET	0-44	L	70,204
Sun	12/24	H	CLE	24-21	W	66,007

KANSAS CITY CHIEFS

Sun	9/3	A	SEA	34-10	W	54,062
Sun	9/10	H	NYG	*20-17	W	77,962
Sun	9/17	H	OAK	*23-17	W	78,696
Sun	9/24	A	CLE	17-35	L	74,280
Sun	10/1	A	ARI	24-3	W	50,211
Mon	10/9	H	SD	*29-23	W	79,288
Sun	10/15	H	NE	31-26	W	77,992
Sun	10/22	A	DEN	21-7	W	71,044
Sun	11/5	H	WAS	24-3	W	77,821
Sun	11/12	A	SD	22-7	W	59,285
Sun	11/19	H	HOU	20-13	W	77,576
Thu	11/23	A	DAL	12-24	L	64,901
Sun	12/3	A	OAK	29-23	W	53,930
Mon	12/11	A	MIA	6-13	L	70,321
Sun	12/17	H	DEN	20-17	W	75,061
Sun	12/24	H	SEA	26-3	W	75,784

AFC Divisional Playoff

Sun	1/7	H	IND	7-10	L	77,594

MIAMI DOLPHINS

Sun	9/3	H	NYJ	52-14	W	71,317
Sun	9/10	A	NE	20-3	W	60,239
Mon	9/18	H	PIT	23-10	W	72,874
Sun	10/1	A	CIN	26-23	W	52,671
Sun	10/8	H	IND	*24-27	L	68,471
Sun	10/15	A	NO	30-33	L	55,628
Sun	10/22	A	NYJ	16-17	L	67,228
Sun	10/29	H	BUF	23-6	W	71,060
Sun	11/5	A	SD	24-14	W	61,966
Sun	11/12	H	NE	17-34	L	70,399
Mon	11/20	H	SF	20-44	L	73,080
Sun	11/26	A	IND	28-36	L	60,414
Sun	12/3	H	ATL	21-20	W	63,395
Mon	12/11	H	KC	13-6	W	70,321
Sun	12/17	A	BUF	20-23	L	79,531
Sun	12/24	A	STL	41-22	W	63,876

AFC Wild-Card Playoff

Sat	12/30	A	BUF	22-37	L	73,103

MINNESOTA VIKINGS

Sun	9/3	A	CHI	14-31	L	63,036
Sun	9/10	H	DET	20-10	W	52,234
Sun	9/17	H	DAL	*17-23	L	60,088
Sun	9/24	A	PIT	44-24	W	57,853
Sun	10/8	H	HOU	*23-17	W	56,430
Sun	10/15	A	TB	*17-20	L	55,703
Sun	10/22	A	GB	21-38	L	60,332
Mon	10/30	H	CHI	6-14	L	58,217
Sun	11/5	H	GB	27-24	W	62,839
Sun	11/12	A	ARI	*30-24	W	51,342
Sun	11/19	H	NO	43-24	W	58,108
Thu	11/23	A	DET	38-44	L	74,559
Sun	12/3	H	TB	31-17	W	52,879
Sat	12/9	H	CLE	27-11	W	47,984
Mon	12/18	A	SF	30-37	L	64,975
Sun	12/24	A	CIN	24-27	L	34,568

NEW ENGLAND PATRIOTS

Sun	9/3	H	CLE	17-14	W	60,126
Sun	9/10	H	MIA	3-20	L	60,239
Sun	9/17	A	SF	3-28	L	66,179
Sun	10/1	H	ATL	17-30	L	47,114
Sun	10/8	H	DEN	3-37	L	60,074
Sun	10/15	A	KC	26-31	L	77,992
Mon	10/23	H	BUF	27-14	W	60,203
Sun	10/29	H	CAR	*17-20	L	60,064
Sun	11/5	A	NYJ	20-7	W	61,462
Sun	11/12	A	MIA	34-17	W	70,399
Sun	11/19	H	IND	10-24	L	59,544
Sun	11/26	A	BUF	35-25	W	69,384
Sun	12/3	H	NO	17-31	L	59,876
Sun	12/10	H	NYJ	31-28	W	46,617
Sat	12/16	A	PIT	27-41	L	57,158
Sat	12/23	A	IND	7-10	L	54,685

NEW ORLEANS SAINTS

Sun	9/3	H	SF	22-24	L	66,627
Sun	9/10	A	STL	13-17	L	58,186
Sun	9/17	H	ATL	*24-27	L	57,442
Sun	9/24	A	NYG	29-45	L	72,619

Sun 10/1   H   PHI   10-15   L   43,938
Sun 10/15   H   MIA   33-30   W   55,628
Sun 10/22   A   CAR   3-20   L   55,484
Sun 10/29   A   SF   11-7   W   65,272
Sun 11/5   H   STL   19-10   W   43,120
Sun 11/12   H   IND   17-14   W   44,122
Sun 11/19   A   MIN   24-43   L   58,108
Sun 11/26   H   CAR   34-26   W   39,580
Sun 12/3   A   NE   31-17   W   59,876
Sun 12/10   A   ATL   14-19   L   54,603
Sat 12/16   H   GB   23-34   L   50,132
Sun 12/24   A   NYJ   12-0   W   28,885

NEW YORK GIANTS

Mon 9/4   H   DAL   0-35   L   77,454
Sun 9/10   A   KC   *17-20   L   77,962
Sun 9/17   A   GB   6-14   L   60,117
Sun 9/24   H   NO   45-29   W   72,619
Sun 10/1   A   SF   6-20   L   65,536
Sun 10/8   H   ARI   *27-21   W   68,463
Sun 10/15   H   PHI   17-14   L   74,252
Sun 10/29   A   WAS   24-15   W   53,310
Sun 11/5   A   SEA   28-30   L   42,100
Sun 11/12   A   OAK   13-17   L   71,160
Sun 11/19   A   PHI   19-28   L   63,562
Sun 11/26   H   CHI   24-27   L   70,015
Thu 11/30   A   ARI   10-6   W   44,246
Sun 12/10   H   WAS   20-13   W   48,247
Sun 12/17   A   DAL   20-21   L   64,400
Sat 12/23   H   SD   17-27   L   50,243

NEW YORK JETS

Sun 9/3   A   MIA   14-52   L   71,317
Sun 9/10   H   IND   *24-27   L   65,134
Sun 9/17   H   JAC   27-10   W   49,970
Sun 9/24   A   ATL   3-13   L   40,778
Sun 10/1   H   OAK   10-47   L   68,941
Sun 10/8   A   BUF   10-29   L   79,485
Sun 10/15   A   CAR   15-26   L   52,613
Sun 10/22   H   MIA   17-16   W   67,228
Sun 10/29   A   IND   10-17   L   49,250
Sun 11/5   H   NE   7-20   L   61,462
Sun 11/19   H   BUF   26-28   L   54,436
Sun 11/26   A   SEA   16-10   W   41,160
Sun 12/3   H   STL   20-23   L   52,023
Sun 12/10   A   NE   28-31   L   46,617
Sun 12/17   H   HOU   6-23   L   35,873
Sun 12/24   H   NO   0-12   L   28,885

OAKLAND RAIDERS

Sun 9/3   H   SD   17-7   W   50,323
Sun 9/10   A   WAS   20-8   W   54,548
Sun 9/17   A   KC   *17-23   L   78,696
Sun 9/24   H   PHI   48-17   W   48,875
Sun 10/1   A   NYJ   47-10   W   68,941
Sun 10/8   H   SEA   34-14   W   50,213
Mon 10/16   A   DEN   0-27   L   75,491
Sun 10/22   H   IND   30-17   W   53,543
Sun 11/5   A   CIN   20-17   W   51,265
Sun 11/12   A   NYG   17-13   W   71,160
Sun 11/19   H   DAL   21-34   L   54,444
Mon 11/27   A   SD   6-12   L   60,607
Sun 12/3   H   KC   23-29   L   53,930
Sun 12/10   H   PIT   10-29   L   53,516
Sun 12/17   A   SEA   10-44   L   58,428
Sun 12/24   H   DEN   28-31   L   50,074

PHILADELPHIA EAGLES

Sun 9/3   H   TB   6-21   L   66,266
Sun 9/10   A   ARI   31-19   W   45,004
Sun 9/17   H   SD   21-27   L   63,081
Sun 9/24   A   OAK   17-48   L   48,875
Sun 10/1   A   NO   15-10   W   43,938
Sun 10/8   H   WAS   *37-34   W   65,498

Sun 10/15   A   NYG   17-14   W   74,252
Sun 10/29   A   STL   20-9   W   62,172
Mon 11/6   H   DAL   12-34   L   64,876
Sun 11/12   H   DEN   31-13   W   60,842
Sun 11/19   H   NYG   28-19   W   63,562
Sun 11/26   A   WAS   14-7   W   50,539
Sun 12/3   A   SEA   14-26   L   39,893
Sun 12/10   H   DAL   20-17   W   66,198
Sun 12/17   H   ARI   21-20   W   62,076
Sun 12/24   A   CHI   14-20   L   52,391

NFC WILD-CARD PLAYOFF

Sat 12/30   H   DET   58-37   W   66,099

NFC DIVISIONAL PLAYOFF

Sun 1/7   A   DAL   11-30   L   64,371

PITTSBURGH STEELERS

Sun 9/3   H   DET   23-20   W   58,002
Sun 9/10   A   HOU   34-17   W   44,122
Mon 9/18   A   MIA   10-23   L   72,874
Sun 9/24   H   MIN   24-44   L   57,853
Sun 10/1   A   SD   31-16   W   57,012
Sun 10/8   A   JAC   16-20   L   72,042
Thu 10/19   H   CIN   9-27   L   56,684
Sun 10/29   H   JAC   24-7   W   54,516
Sun 11/5   A   CHI   *37-34   W   61,838
Mon 11/13   H   CLE   20-3   W   58,675
Sat 11/19   A   CIN   49-31   W   54,636
Sun 11/26   A   CLE   20-17   W   67,269
Sun 12/3   H   HOU   21-7   W   56,013
Sun 12/10   A   OAK   29-10   W   53,516
Sat 12/16   H   NE   41-27   W   57,158
Sun 12/24   A   GB   19-24   L   60,649

AFC DIVISIONAL PLAYOFF

Sat 1/6   H   BUF   40-21   W   59,072

AFC CHAMPIONSHIP

Sun 1/14   H   IND   20-16   W   61,062

SUPER BOWL XXX

Sun 1/28   N   DAL   17-27   L   76,347

ST. LOUIS RAMS

Sun 9/3   A   GB   17-14   W   60,104
Sun 9/10   H   NO   17-13   W   58,186
Sun 9/17   A   CAR   31-10   W   54,060
Sun 9/24   A   CHI   34-28   W   59,679
Sun 10/1   H   IND   18-21   L   58,616
Thu 10/12   H   ATL   21-19   W   59,700
Sun 10/22   H   SF   10-44   L   59,915
Sun 10/29   A   PHI   9-20   L   62,172
Sun 11/5   A   NO   10-19   L   43,120
Sun 11/12   H   CAR   28-17   W   65,598
Sun 11/19   A   ATL   6-31   L   46,309
Sun 11/26   A   SF   13-41   L   66,049
Sun 12/3   A   NYJ   23-20   W   52,023
Sun 12/10   H   BUF   27-45   L   64,623
Sun 12/17   A   WAS   23-35   L   63,760
Sun 12/24   H   MIA   22-41   L   63,876

SAN DIEGO CHARGERS

Sun 9/3   A   OAK   7-17   L   50,323
Sun 9/10   H   SEA   14-10   W   54,420
Sun 9/17   A   PHI   27-21   W   63,081
Sun 9/24   H   DEN   17-6   W   58,978
Sun 10/1   A   PIT   16-31   L   57,012
Mon 10/9   A   KC   *23-29   L   79,288
Sun 10/15   H   DAL   9-23   L   62,664
Sun 10/22   A   SEA   35-25   W   45,821
Sun 11/5   H   MIA   14-24   L   61,966
Sun 11/12   H   KC   7-22   L   59,285
Sun 11/19   A   DEN   27-30   L   74,681
Mon 11/27   H   OAK   12-6   W   60,607
Sun 12/3   H   CLE   31-13   W   56,358
Sat 12/9   H   ARI   28-25   W   55,258
Sun 12/17   A   IND   27-24   W   55,318
Sat 12/23   A   NYG   27-17   W   50,243

AFC WILD-CARD PLAYOFF

Sun 12/31   H   IND   20-35   L   61,182

SAN FRANCISCO 49ERS

Sun 9/3   A   NO   24-22   W   66,627
Sun 9/10   H   ATL   41-10   W   63,627
Sun 9/17   H   NE   28-3   W   66,179
Mon 9/25   A   DET   24-27   L   76,236
Sun 10/1   H   NYG   20-6   W   65,536
Sun 10/15   A   IND   17-18   L   60,273
Sun 10/22   A   STL   44-10   W   59,915
Sun 10/29   H   NO   7-11   L   65,272
Sun 11/5   H   CAR   7-13   L   61,722
Sun 11/12   A   DAL   38-20   W   65,180
Mon 11/20   A   MIA   44-20   W   73,080
Sun 11/26   H   STL   41-13   W   66,049
Sun 12/3   H   BUF   27-17   W   65,568
Sun 12/10   A   CAR   31-10   W   76,136
Mon 12/18   H   MIN   37-30   W   64,975
Sun 12/24   A   ATL   27-28   L   51,785

NFC DIVISIONAL PLAYOFF

Sat 1/6   H   GB   17-27   L   69,311

SEATTLE SEAHAWKS

Sun 9/3   H   KC   10-34   L   54,062
Sun 9/10   A   SD   10-14   L   54,420
Sun 9/17   H   CIN   24-21   W   39,492
Sun 10/1   H   DEN   27-10   W   56,483
Sun 10/8   A   OAK   14-34   L   50,213
Sun 10/15   A   BUF   21-27   L   74,362
Sun 10/22   H   SD   25-35   L   45,821
Sun 10/29   A   ARI   *14-20   L   39,600
Sun 11/5   H   NYG   30-28   W   42,100
Sun 11/12   A   JAC   47-30   W   71,290
Sun 11/19   A   WAS   27-20   W   51,298
Sun 11/26   H   NYJ   10-16   L   41,160
Sun 12/3   H   PHI   26-14   W   39,893
Sun 12/10   A   DEN   31-27   W   71,488
Sun 12/17   H   OAK   44-10   W   58,428
Sun 12/24   H   KC   3-26   L   75,784

TAMPA BAY BUCCANEERS

Sun 9/3   A   PHI   21-6   W   66,266
Sun 9/10   A   CLE   6-22   L   61,083
Sun 9/17   H   CHI   6-25   L   71,507
Sun 9/24   H   WAS   14-6   W   49,234
Sun 10/1   A   CAR   20-13   W   50,076
Sun 10/8   H   CIN   19-16   W   41,732
Sun 10/15   H   MIN   *20-17   W   55,703
Sun 10/22   A   ATL   21-24   L   66,135
Sun 10/29   A   HOU   7-19   L   31,489
Sun 11/12   A   DET   24-27   L   60,644
Sun 11/19   H   JAC   17-16   W   71,629
Sun 11/26   A   GB   13-35   L   59,218
Sun 12/3   A   MIN   17-31   L   52,879
Sun 12/10   H   GB   *13-10   W   67,557
Sun 12/17   A   CHI   10-31   L   49,475
Sat 12/23   H   DET   10-37   L   50,049

WASHINGTON REDSKINS

Sun 9/3   H   ARI   27-7   W   52,731
Sun 9/10   H   OAK   8-20   L   54,548
Sun 9/17   A   DEN   31-38   L   71,930
Sun 9/24   A   TB   6-14   L   49,234
Sun 10/1   H   DAL   27-23   W   55,489
Sun 10/8   A   PHI   *34-37   L   65,498
Sun 10/15   A   ARI   20-24   L   42,370
Sun 10/22   H   DET   *36-30   W   52,332
Sun 10/29   H   NYG   15-24   L   53,310
Sun 11/5   A   KC   3-24   L   77,821
Sun 11/19   H   SEA   20-27   L   51,298
Sun 11/26   H   PHI   7-14   L   50,539
Sun 12/3   A   DAL   24-17   W   64,866
Sun 12/10   A   NYG   13-20   L   48,247

Sun 12/17   A   STL   35-23   W   63,760
Sun 12/24   H   CAR   20-17   W   42,903

1996 NFL

ARIZONA CARDINALS

Sun 9/1   A   IND   13-20   L   48,133
Sun 9/8   H   MIA   10-38   L   55,444
Sun 9/15   A   NE   0-31   L   59,118
Sun 9/22   A   NO   34-16   W   34,316
Sun 9/29   H   STL   *31-28   W   33,116
Sun 10/13   A   DAL   3-17   L   64,096
Sun 10/20   H   TB   13-9   W   27,738
Sun 10/27   H   NYJ   21-31   L   28,088
Sun 11/3   A   NYG   8-16   L   68,262
Sun 11/10   A   WAS   *37-34   W   51,929
Sun 11/17   H   NYG   31-23   W   34,924
Sun 11/24   H   PHI   36-30   W   36,175
Sun 12/1   A   MIN   17-41   L   45,767
Sun 12/8   H   DAL   6-10   L   70,763
Sun 12/15   H   WAS   27-26   W   34,260
Sun 12/22   A   PHI   19-29   L   63,658

ATLANTA FALCONS

Sun 9/1   A   CAR   6-29   L   69,522
Sun 9/8   H   MIN   17-23   L   42,688
Sun 9/22   H   PHI   18-33   L   40,107
Sun 9/29   A   SF   17-39   L   62,995
Sun 10/6   A   DET   24-28   L   58,666
Sun 10/13   H   HOU   13-23   L   35,401
Sun 10/20   A   DAL   28-32   L   64,091
Sun 10/27   H   PIT   17-20   L   58,760
Sun 11/3   H   CAR   20-17   W   42,726
Sun 11/10   A   STL   16-59   L   58,776
Sun 11/17   H   NO   17-15   W   43,119
Sun 11/24   A   CIN   31-41   L   44,868
Mon 12/2   H   SF   10-34   L   46,318
Sun 12/8   A   NO   31-15   W   32,923
Sun 12/15   H   STL   27-34   L   26,519
Sun 12/22   A   JAC   17-19   L   71,449

BALTIMORE RAVENS

Sun 9/1   H   OAK   19-14   W   64,124
Sun 9/8   A   PIT   17-31   L   57,241
Sun 9/15   A   HOU   13-29   L   20,082
Sun 9/29   H   NE   17-10   W   61,063
Sun 10/6   H   NE   38-46   L   63,569
Sun 10/13   A   IND   21-26   L   56,978
Sun 10/20   A   DEN   34-45   L   70,453
Sun 10/27   H   STL   *37-31   W   60,256
Sun 11/3   H   CIN   21-24   L   60,743
Sun 11/10   A   JAC   24-28   L   64,628
Sun 11/17   A   SF   20-38   L   51,596
Sun 11/24   A   JAC   *25-28   L   57,384
Sun 12/1   H   PIT   31-17   W   51,882
Sun 12/8   A   CIN   14-21   L   43,022
Sun 12/15   A   CAR   16-27   L   70,075
Sun 12/22   H   HOU   21-24   L   52,704

BUFFALO BILLS

Sun 9/1   A   NYG   *23-20   W   74,218
Sun 9/8   H   NE   17-10   W   78,104
Mon 9/16   A   PIT   6-24   L   59,002
Sun 9/22   H   DAL   10-7   W   78,098
Sun 10/6   H   IND   *16-13   W   79,401
Sun 10/13   H   MIA   7-21   L   79,642
Sun 10/20   A   NYJ   25-22   W   49,775
Sun 10/27   A   NE   25-28   L   58,858
Sun 11/3   H   WAS   38-13   W   78,002
Sun 11/10   A   PHI   24-17   W   66,613
Sun 11/17   H   CIN   31-17   W   75,549
Sun 11/24   H   NYJ   35-10   W   60,854
Sun 12/1   A   IND   *10-13   L   53,804
Sun 12/8   H   SEA   18-26   L   41,373
Mon 12/16   A   MIA   14-16   L   67,016

Sun 12/22 H KC 20-9 W 68,671

AFC Wild-Card Playoff
Sat 12/28 H JAC 27-30 L 70,213

CAROLINA PANTHERS
Sun 9/1 H ATL 29-6 W 69,522
Sun 9/8 A NO 22-20 W 43,288
Sun 9/22 H SF 23-7 W 72,224
Sun 9/29 A JAC 14-24 L 71,537
Sun 10/6 A MIN 12-14 L 60,894
Sun 10/13 H STL 45-13 W 70,535
Sun 10/20 H NO 19-7 W 70,888
Sun 10/27 A PHI 9-20 L 65,982
Sun 11/3 A ATL 17-20 L 42,726
Sun 11/10 H NYG 27-17 W 70,298
Sun 11/17 A STL 20-10 W 60,652
Sun 11/24 A HOU 31-6 W 20,107
Sun 12/1 H TB 24-0 W 57,623
Sun 12/8 A SF 30-24 W 66,291
Sun 12/15 H BAL 27-16 W 70,075
Sun 12/22 H PIT 18-14 W 72,217

NFC Divisional Playoff
Sun 1/5 H DAL 26-17 W 72,808

NFC Championship
Sun 1/12 A GB 13-30 L 60,216

CHICAGO BEARS
Mon 9/2 H DAL 22-6 W 63,076
Sun 9/8 A WAS 3-10 L 52,711
Sun 9/15 H MIN 14-20 L 61,301
Sun 9/22 A DET 16-35 L 70,022
Sun 9/29 A OAK 19-17 W 57,062
Sun 10/6 A GB 6-37 L 65,480
Sun 10/13 A NO 24-27 L 43,512
Mon 10/28 A MIN 15-13 W 58,143
Sun 11/3 H TB 13-10 W 58,727
Sun 11/10 A DEN 12-17 L 75,555
Sun 11/17 A KC 10-14 L 76,762
Sun 11/24 H DET 31-14 W 55,864
Sun 12/1 A GB 17-28 L 59,682
Sun 12/8 H STL 35-9 W 45,075
Sat 12/14 H SD 27-14 W 49,763
Sun 12/22 A TB 19-34 L 51,572

CINCINNATI BENGALS
Sun 9/1 A STL 16-26 L 62,659
Sun 9/8 A SD 14-27 L 55,880
Sun 9/15 H NO 30-15 W 45,412
Sun 9/29 H DEN 10-14 L 51,798
Sun 10/6 H HOU *27-30 L 44,680
Sun 10/13 A PIT 10-20 L 58,875
Sun 10/20 A SF 21-28 L 63,218
Sun 10/27 H JAC 28-21 W 45,890
Sun 11/3 A BAL 24-21 W 60,743
Sun 11/10 H PIT 34-24 W 57,265
Sun 11/17 A BUF 17-31 L 75,549
Sun 11/24 A ATL 41-31 W 44,868
Sun 12/1 A JAC 23-30 L 57,408
Sun 12/8 H BAL 21-14 W 43,022
Sun 12/15 A HOU 21-13 W 15,131
Sun 12/22 H IND 31-24 W 49,389

DALLAS COWBOYS
Mon 9/2 A CHI 6-22 L 63,076
Sun 9/8 H NYG 27-0 W 63,069
Sun 9/15 H IND 24-25 L 63,021
Sun 9/22 A BUF 7-10 L 78,098
Mon 9/30 A PHI 23-19 W 67,201
Sun 10/13 H ARI 7-4 W 64,096
Sun 10/20 H ATL 32-28 W 64,091
Sun 10/27 A MIA 29-10 W 75,283
Sun 11/3 H PHI 21-31 L 64,952
Sun 11/10 A SF *20-17 W 68,919
Mon 11/18 H GB 21-6 W 65,032

Sun 11/24 A NYG 6-20 L 77,081
Thu 11/28 H WAS 21-10 W 64,955
Sun 12/8 A ARI 10-6 W 70,763
Sun 12/15 H NE 12-6 W 64,578
Sun 12/22 A WAS 10-37 L 56,454

NFC Wild-Card Playoff
Sat 12/28 H MIN 40-15 W 64,682

NFC Divisional Playoff
Sun 1/5 A CAR 17-26 L 72,808

DENVER BRONCOS
Sun 9/1 H NYJ 31-6 W 70,595
Sun 9/8 A SEA 30-20 W 43,671
Sun 9/15 H TB 27-23 W 71,535
Sun 9/22 A KC 14-17 L 79,439
Sun 9/29 A CIN 14-10 W 51,798
Sun 10/6 H SD 28-17 W 75,058
Sun 10/20 H BAL 45-34 W 70,453
Sun 10/27 H KC 34-7 W 75,652
Mon 11/4 A OAK 22-21 W 61,179
Sun 11/10 H CHI 17-12 W 75,555
Sun 11/17 A NE 34-8 W 59,452
Sun 11/24 A MIN 21-17 W 59,142
Sun 12/1 H SEA 34-7 W 74,982
Sun 12/8 A GB 6-41 L 60,712
Sun 12/15 H OAK 24-19 W 75,466
Sun 12/22 A SD 10-16 L 46,801

AFC Divisional Playoff
Sat 1/4 H JAC 27-30 L 75,678

DETROIT LIONS
Sun 9/1 A MIN 13-17 L 52,972
Sun 9/8 H TB 21-6 W 54,229
Sun 9/15 A PHI 17-24 L 66,007
Sun 9/22 H CHI 35-16 W 70,022
Sun 9/29 A TB 27-0 W 34,961
Sun 10/6 H ATL 28-24 W 58,666
Sun 10/13 A OAK 21-37 L 50,037
Sun 10/27 H NYG 7-35 L 63,501
Sun 11/3 A GB 18-28 L 60,695
Mon 11/11 A SD 21-27 L 60,425
Sun 11/17 H SEA 17-16 W 51,194
Sun 11/24 A CHI 14-31 L 55,864
Thu 11/28 H KC 24-28 L 75,079
Sun 12/8 H MIN 22-24 L 46,043
Sun 12/15 H GB 3-31 L 73,214
Mon 12/23 A SF 14-24 L 61,291

GREEN BAY PACKERS
Sun 9/1 A TB 34-3 W 54,102
Mon 9/9 H PHI 39-13 W 60,666
Sun 9/15 H SD 42-10 W 60,584
Sun 9/22 A MIN 21-30 L 64,168
Sun 9/29 A SEA 31-10 W 59,973
Sun 10/6 A CHI 37-6 W 65,480
Mon 10/14 H SF *23-20 W 60,716
Sun 10/27 H TB 13-7 W 60,627
Sun 11/3 H DET 28-18 W 60,695
Sun 11/10 A KC 20-27 L 79,281
Mon 11/18 A DAL 6-21 L 65,032
Sun 11/24 A STL 24-9 W 61,499
Sun 12/1 H CHI 28-17 W 59,682
Sun 12/8 H DEN 41-6 W 60,712
Sun 12/15 A DET 31-3 W 73,214
Sun 12/22 H MIN 38-10 W 59,306

NFC Divisional Playoff
Sat 1/4 H SF 35-14 W 60,787

NFC Championship
Sun 1/12 H CAR 30-13 W 60,216

Super Bowl XXXI
Sun 1/26 N NE 35-21 W 72,301

HOUSTON OILERS
Sun 9/1 H KC 19-20 L 27,725

Sun 9/8 A JAC 34-27 W 66,468
Sun 9/15 H BAL 29-13 W 20,082
Sun 9/29 A PIT 16-30 L 58,608
Sun 10/6 A CIN *30-27 W 44,680
Sun 10/13 A ATL 23-13 W 35,401
Sun 10/20 H PIT 23-13 W 50,337
Sun 10/27 H SF 9-10 L 53,664
Sun 11/3 A SEA 16-23 L 36,320
Sun 11/10 A NO 31-14 W 34,121
Sun 11/17 H MIA 20-23 L 47,358
Sun 11/24 H CAR 6-31 L 20,107
Sun 12/1 A NYJ 35-10 W 21,731
Sun 12/8 H JAC 17-23 L 20,196
Sun 12/15 H CIN 13-21 L 15,131
Sun 12/22 A BAL 24-21 W 52,704

INDIANAPOLIS COLTS
Sun 9/1 H ARI 20-13 W 48,133
Sun 9/8 A NYJ 21-7 W 63,534
Sun 9/15 A DAL 25-24 W 63,021
Mon 9/23 H MIA 6-10 L 60,891
Sun 10/6 A BUF 13-16 L 79,401
Sun 10/13 H BAL 26-21 W 56,978
Sun 10/20 H NE 9-27 L 58,725
Sun 10/27 A WAS 16-31 L 54,254
Sun 11/3 H SD 19-26 L 58,484
Sun 11/10 A MIA 13-37 L 66,623
Sun 11/17 H NYJ 34-29 W 48,322
Sun 11/24 A NE 13-27 L 58,226
Sun 12/1 H BUF *13-10 W 53,804
Thu 12/5 H PHI 37-10 W 52,689
Sun 12/15 A KC 24-19 W 71,136
Sun 12/22 A CIN 24-31 L 49,389

AFC Wild-Card Playoff
Sun 12/29 A PIT 14-42 L 58,078

JACKSONVILLE JAGUARS
Sun 9/1 H PIT 24-9 W 70,210
Sun 9/8 H HOU 27-34 L 66,468
Sun 9/15 A OAK 3-17 L 46,291
Sun 9/22 A NE *25-28 L 59,446
Sun 9/29 H CAR 24-14 W 71,537
Sun 10/6 A NO 13-17 L 34,231
Sun 10/13 H NYJ 21-17 W 65,699
Sun 10/20 A STL 14-17 L 60,066
Sun 10/27 A CIN 21-28 L 45,890
Sun 11/10 H BAL 30-27 W 64,628
Sun 11/17 A PIT 3-28 L 58,879
Sun 11/24 H BAL 828-25 W 57,384
Sun 12/1 H CIN 30-27 W 57,408
Sun 12/8 A HOU 23-17 W 20,196
Sun 12/15 H SEA 20-13 W 66,134
Sun 12/22 A ATL 19-17 W 71,449

AFC Wild-Card Playoff
Sat 12/28 A BUF 30-27 W 70,213

AFC Divisional Playoff
Sat 1/4 A DEN 30-27 W 75,678

AFC Championship
Sun 1/12 A NE 6-20 L 60,190

KANSAS CITY CHIEFS
Sun 9/1 A HOU 20-19 W 27,725
Sun 9/8 H OAK 19-3 W 79,281
Sun 9/15 A SEA 35-17 W 39,790
Sun 9/22 H DEN 17-14 W 79,439
Sun 9/29 A SD 19-22 L 59,384
Mon 10/7 H PIT 7-17 L 79,189
Thu 10/17 H SEA 34-16 W 76,057
Sun 10/27 H DEN 7-34 L 75,652
Sun 11/3 A MIN 21-6 W 59,552
Sun 11/10 H GB 27-20 W 79,281
Sun 11/17 H CHI 14-10 W 76,762
Sun 11/24 H SD 14-28 L 69,472
Thu 11/28 A DET 28-24 W 75,079

Mon 12/9 A OAK 7-26 L 57,082
Sun 12/15 H IND 19-24 L 71,136
Sun 12/22 A BUF 9-20 L 68,671

MIAMI DOLPHINS
Sun 9/1 H NE 24-10 W 71,542
Sun 9/8 A ARI 38-10 W 55,444
Sun 9/15 H NYJ 36-27 W 68,137
Mon 9/23 A IND 6-10 L 60,891
Sun 10/6 H SEA 15-22 L 59,539
Sun 10/13 A BUF 21-7 W 79,642
Sun 10/20 A PHI 28-35 L 66,240
Sun 10/27 H DAL 10-29 L 75,283
Sun 11/3 A NE 23-42 L 58,942
Sun 11/10 H IND 37-13 W 66,623
Sun 11/17 A HOU 23-20 L 47,358
Mon 11/25 H PIT 17-24 L 73,489
Sun 12/1 A OAK 7-17 L 60,591
Sun 12/8 H NYG 7-17 L 63,889
Mon 12/16 H BUF 16-14 W 67,016
Sun 12/22 A NYJ 31-28 W 47,271

MINNESOTA VIKINGS
Sun 9/1 H DET 17-13 W 52,972
Sun 9/8 A ATL 23-17 W 42,688
Sun 9/15 A CHI 20-14 W 61,301
Sun 9/22 H GB 30-21 W 64,168
Sun 9/29 A NYG 10-15 L 70,970
Sun 10/6 H CAR 14-12 W 60,894
Sun 10/13 A TB 13-24 L 32,175
Mon 10/28 H CHI 13-15 L 58,143
Sun 11/3 H KC 6-21 L 59,552
Sun 11/10 A SEA 23-42 L 50,794
Sun 11/17 A OAK *16-13 W 41,183
Sun 11/24 H DEN 17-21 L 59,142
Sun 12/1 H ARI 41-17 W 45,767
Sun 12/8 A DET 24-22 W 46,043
Sun 12/15 H TB 21-10 W 49,202
Sun 12/22 A GB 10-38 L 59,306

NFC Wild-Card Playoff
Sat 12/28 A DAL 15-40 L 64,682

NEW ENGLAND PATRIOTS
Sun 9/1 A MIA 10-24 L 71,542
Sun 9/8 A BUF 10-17 L 78,104
Sun 9/15 H ARI 31-0 W 59,118
Sun 9/22 H JAC *28-25 W 59,446
Sun 10/6 A BAL 46-38 W 63,569
Sun 10/13 H WAS 22-27 L 59,638
Sun 10/20 A IND 27-9 W 58,725
Sun 10/27 H BUF 28-25 W 58,858
Sun 11/3 H MIA 42-23 W 58,942
Sun 11/10 A NYJ 31-27 W 61,843
Sun 11/17 H DEN 8-34 L 59,452
Sun 11/24 H IND 27-13 W 58,226
Sun 12/1 A SD 45-7 W 59,209
Sun 12/8 H NYJ 34-10 W 55,621
Sun 12/15 H DAL 6-12 L 64,578
Sat 12/21 A NYG 23-22 W 65,387

AFC Divisional Playoff
Sun 1/5 H PIT 28-3 W 60,188

AFC Championship
Sun 1/12 H JAC 20-6 W 60,190

Super Bowl XXXI
Sun 1/26 N GB 21-35 L 72,301

NEW ORLEANS SAINTS
Sun 9/1 A SF 11-27 L 63,970
Sun 9/8 H CAR 20-22 L 43,288
Sun 9/15 A CIN 15-30 L 45,412
Sun 9/22 H ARI 14-28 L 34,316
Sun 9/29 A BAL 10-17 L 61,063
Sun 10/6 H JAC 17-13 W 34,231
Sun 10/13 H CHI 27-24 W 43,512

Sun	10/20	A	CAR	7-19	L	70,888
Sun	11/3	H	SF	17-24	L	53,297
Sun	11/10	H	HOU	14-31	L	34,121
Sun	11/17	A	ATL	15-17	L	43,119
Sun	11/24	A	TB	7-13	L	40,203
Sun	12/1	H	STL	10-26	L	26,310
Sun	12/8	H	ATL	15-31	L	32,923
Sun	12/15	A	NYG	17-3	W	52,530
Sat	12/21	A	STL	13-14	L	57,681

NEW YORK GIANTS

Sun	9/1	H	BUF	*20-23	L	74,218
Sun	9/8	A	DAL	0-27	L	63,069
Sun	9/15	H	WAS	10-31	L	71,693
Sun	9/22	A	NYJ	13-6	W	58,339
Sun	9/29	H	MIN	15-10	W	70,970
Sun	10/13	H	PHI	10-19	L	72,729
Sun	10/20	A	WAS	21-31	L	52,684
Sun	10/27	A	DET	35-7	W	63,501
Sun	11/3	H	ARI	16-8	W	68,262
Sun	11/10	A	CAR	17-27	L	70,298
Sun	11/17	A	ARI	23-31	L	34,924
Sun	11/24	H	DAL	20-6	W	77,081
Sun	12/1	A	PHI	0-24	L	51,468
Sun	12/8	A	MIA	17-7	W	63,889
Sun	12/15	H	NO	3-17	L	52,530
Sat	12/21	H	NE	22-23	L	65,387

NEW YORK JETS

Sun	9/1	A	DEN	6-31	L	70,595
Sun	9/8	H	IND	7-21	L	63,534
Sun	9/15	A	MIA	27-36	L	68,137
Sun	9/22	H	NYG	6-13	L	58,339
Sun	9/29	A	WAS	16-31	L	52,068
Sun	10/6	H	OAK	13-34	L	63,611
Sun	10/13	A	JAC	17-21	L	65,699
Sun	10/20	H	BUF	22-25	L	49,775
Sun	10/27	A	ARI	31-21	W	28,088
Sun	11/10	H	NE	27-31	L	61,843
Sun	11/17	A	IND	29-34	L	48,322
Sun	11/24	A	BUF	10-35	L	60,854
Sun	12/1	H	HOU	10-35	L	21,731
Sun	12/8	A	NE	10-34	L	55,621
Sat	12/14	H	PHI	20-21	L	29,178
Sun	12/22	H	MIA	28-31	L	47,271

OAKLAND RAIDERS

Sun	9/1	A	BAL	14-19	L	64,124
Sun	9/8	A	KC	3-19	L	79,281
Sun	9/15	H	JAC	17-3	W	46,291
Sun	9/22	H	SD	34-40	L	49,097
Sun	9/29	A	CHI	17-19	L	57,062
Sun	10/6	A	NYJ	34-13	W	63,611
Sun	10/13	H	DET	37-21	W	50,037
Mon	10/21	A	SD	23-14	W	62,350
Mon	11/4	H	DEN	21-22	L	61,179
Sun	11/10	A	TB	*17-20	L	45,392
Sun	11/17	H	MIN	*13-16	L	41,183
Sun	11/24	A	SEA	27-21	W	47,506
Sun	12/1	H	MIA	17-7	W	60,591
Mon	12/9	H	KC	26-7	W	57,082
Sun	12/15	A	DEN	19-24	L	75,466
Sun	12/22	H	SEA	21-28	L	33,456

PHILADELPHIA EAGLES

Sun	9/1	A	WAS	17-14	W	53,415
Mon	9/9	A	GB	13-39	L	60,666
Sun	9/15	H	DET	24-17	W	66,007
Sun	9/22	A	ATL	33-18	W	40,107
Mon	9/30	H	DAL	19-23	L	67,201
Sun	10/13	A	NYG	19-10	W	72,729
Sun	10/20	H	MIA	35-28	W	66,240
Sun	10/27	H	CAR	20-9	W	65,982
Sun	11/3	A	DAL	31-21	W	64,952
Sun	11/10	H	BUF	17-24	L	66,613
Sun	11/17	H	WAS	21-26	L	66,834
Sun	11/24	A	ARI	30-36	L	36,175
Sun	12/1	H	NYG	24-0	W	51,468
Thu	12/5	A	IND	10-37	L	52,689
Sat	12/14	A	NYJ	21-20	W	29,178
Sun	12/22	H	ARI	29-19	W	63,658

NFC WILD-CARD PLAYOFF

Sun	12/29	A	SF	0-14	L	56,460

PITTSBURGH STEELERS

Sun	9/1	A	JAC	9-24	L	70,210
Sun	9/8	H	BAL	31-17	W	57,241
Mon	9/16	H	BUF	24-6	W	59,002
Sun	9/29	H	HOU	30-16	W	58,608
Mon	10/7	A	KC	17-7	W	79,189
Sun	10/13	H	CIN	20-10	W	58,875
Sun	10/20	A	HOU	13-23	L	50,337
Sun	10/27	A	ATL	20-17	W	58,760
Sun	11/3	H	STL	42-6	W	58,148
Sun	11/10	A	CIN	24-34	L	57,265
Sun	11/17	H	JAC	28-3	W	58,879
Mon	11/25	A	MIA	24-17	W	73,489
Sun	12/1	A	BAL	17-31	L	51,882
Sun	12/8	H	SD	16-3	W	56,368
Sun	12/15	H	SF	15-25	L	59,823
Sun	12/22	A	CAR	14-18	L	72,217

AFC WILD-CARD PLAYOFF

Sun	12/29	H	IND	42-14	W	58,078

AFC DIVISIONAL PLAYOFF

Sun	1/5	A	NE	3-28	L	60,188

ST. LOUIS RAMS

Sun	9/1	H	CIN	26-16	W	62,659
Sun	9/8	A	SF	0-34	L	63,624
Sun	9/22	H	WAS	10-17	L	62,303
Sun	9/29	A	ARI	*28-31	L	33,116
Sun	10/6	H	SF	11-28	L	61,260
Sun	10/13	A	CAR	13-45	L	70,535
Sun	10/20	H	JAC	17-14	W	60,066
Sun	10/27	A	BAL	*31-37	L	60,256
Sun	11/3	A	PIT	6-42	L	58,148
Sun	11/10	H	ATL	59-16	W	58,776
Sun	11/17	H	CAR	10-20	L	60,652
Sun	11/24	A	GB	9-24	L	61,499
Sun	12/1	A	NO	26-10	W	26,310
Sun	12/8	H	CHI	9-35	L	45,075
Sun	12/15	A	ATL	34-27	W	26,519
Sat	12/21	H	NO	14-13	W	57,681

SAN DIEGO CHARGERS

Sun	9/1	H	SEA	29-7	W	58,780
Sun	9/8	H	CIN	27-14	W	55,880
Sun	9/15	A	GB	10-42	L	60,584
Sun	9/22	A	OAK	40-34	W	49,097
Sun	9/29	H	KC	22-19	W	59,384
Sun	10/6	A	DEN	17-28	L	75,058
Mon	10/21	H	OAK	14-23	L	62,350
Sun	10/27	A	SEA	13-32	L	38,143
Sun	11/3	A	IND	26-19	W	58,484
Mon	11/11	H	DET	27-21	W	60,425
Sun	11/17	A	TB	17-25	L	57,526
Sun	11/24	A	KC	28-14	W	69,472
Sun	12/1	H	NE	7-45	L	59,209
Sun	12/8	H	PIT	3-16	L	56,368
Sat	12/14	A	CHI	14-27	L	49,763
Sun	12/22	H	DEN	16-10	W	46,801

SAN FRANCISCO 49ERS

Sun	9/1	H	NO	27-11	W	63,970
Sun	9/8	H	STL	34-0	W	63,624
Sun	9/22	A	CAR	7-23	L	72,224
Sun	9/29	H	ATL	39-17	W	62,995
Sun	10/6	A	STL	28-11	W	61,260
Mon	10/14	A	GB	*20-23	L	60,716
Sun	10/20	H	CIN	28-21	W	63,218
Sun	10/27	A	HOU	10-9	W	53,664
Sun	11/3	A	NO	24-17	W	53,297
Sun	11/10	H	DAL	*17-20	L	68,919
Sun	11/17	H	BAL	38-20	W	51,596
Sun	11/24	A	WAS	*19-16	W	54,235
Mon	12/2	A	ATL	34-10	W	46,318
Sun	12/8	H	CAR	24-30	L	66,291
Sun	12/15	H	PIT	25-15	W	59,823
Mon	12/23	H	DET	24-14	W	61,291

NFC WILD-CARD PLAYOFF

Sun	12/29	H	PHI	14-0	W	56,460

NFC DIVISIONAL PLAYOFF

Sat	1/4	A	GB	14-35	L	60,787

SEATTLE SEAHAWKS

Sun	9/1	A	SD	7-29	L	58,780
Sun	9/8	H	DEN	20-30	L	43,671
Sun	9/15	H	KC	17-35	L	39,790
Sun	9/22	A	TB	17-13	W	30,212
Sun	9/29	H	GB	10-31	L	59,973
Sun	10/6	A	MIA	22-15	W	59,539
Thu	10/17	A	KC	16-34	L	76,057
Sun	10/27	H	SD	32-13	W	38,143
Sun	11/3	H	HOU	23-16	W	36,320
Sun	11/10	H	MIN	42-23	W	50,794
Sun	11/17	A	DET	16-17	L	51,194
Sun	11/24	H	OAK	21-27	L	47,506
Sun	12/1	A	DEN	7-34	L	74,982
Sun	12/8	H	BUF	26-18	W	41,373
Sun	12/15	A	JAC	13-20	L	66,134
Sun	12/22	A	OAK	28-21	W	33,456

TAMPA BAY BUCCANEERS

Sun	9/1	H	GB	3-34	L	54,102
Sun	9/8	A	DET	6-21	L	54,229
Sun	9/15	A	DEN	23-27	L	71,535
Sun	9/22	H	SEA	13-17	L	30,212
Sun	9/29	H	DET	0-27	L	34,961
Sun	10/13	H	MIN	24-13	W	32,175
Sun	10/20	A	ARI	9-13	L	27,738
Sun	10/27	A	GB	7-13	L	60,627
Sun	11/3	A	CHI	10-13	L	58,727
Sun	11/10	H	OAK	*20-17	W	45,392
Sun	11/17	A	SD	25-17	W	57,526
Sun	11/24	H	NO	13-7	W	40,203
Sun	12/1	A	CAR	0-24	L	57,681
Sun	12/8	H	WAS	24-10	W	44,733
Sun	12/15	A	MIN	10-21	L	49,202
Sun	12/22	H	CHI	34-19	W	51,572

WASHINGTON REDSKINS

Sun	9/1	H	PHI	14-17	L	53,415
Sun	9/8	H	DEN	10-3	W	52,711
Sun	9/15	A	NYG	31-10	W	71,693
Sun	9/22	A	STL	17-10	W	62,303
Sun	9/29	H	NYJ	31-16	W	52,068
Sun	10/13	A	NE	27-22	W	56,938
Sun	10/20	H	NYG	31-21	W	52,684
Sun	10/27	H	IND	31-16	W	54,254
Sun	11/3	H	BUF	13-38	L	78,002
Sun	11/10	A	ARI	*34-37	L	51,929
Sun	11/17	A	PHI	26-21	W	66,834
Sun	11/24	H	SF	*16-19	L	54,235
Thu	11/28	A	DAL	10-21	L	64,955
Sun	12/8	A	TB	10-24	L	44,733
Sun	12/15	A	ARI	26-27	L	34,260
Sun	12/22	H	DAL	37-10	W	56,454

PART FIVE

The Playoffs

NFL Championship Game
Dec. 17, 1933
Wrigley Field, Chicago–26,000

New York	0	7	7	–	21	
Chicago Bears	3	3	10	7	–	23

Chi - Manders 16 FG
Chi - Manders 40 FG
NY - Badgro 29 pass from Newman (Strong)
Chi - Manders 28 FG
NY - Krause 1 run (Strong)
Chi - Karr 8 pass from Nagurski (Manders)
NY - Strong 8 pass from Newman (Strong)
Chi - Karr 33 lateral from Hewitt 3 on pass from Nagurski (Manders)

TEAM STATISTICS	NY	Chi
First Downs	13	12
Offensive plays - yards	45 - 307	66 - 312
Rushes - yards	25 - 99	50 - 162
Passes	20 - 14 - 1	16 - 7 - 1
Passing yards	208	150
Interceptions - yards	1 - 13	1 - 11
Punts - average	13 - 29.4	10 - 39.8
Punt returns - yards	5 - 59	5 - 58
Kickoff returns - yards		
Fumbles - lost	0 - 0	0 - 0
Penalties - yards	3 - 15	8 - 40

NFL Championship Game
Dec. 9, 1934
Polo Grounds, New York–35,059

Chicago Bears	0	10	3	0	–	13
New York	3	0	0	27	–	30

NY - Strong 38 FG
Chi - Nagurski 1 run (Manders)
Chi - Manders 17 FG
Chi - Manders 24 FG
NY - Frankian 28 pass from Danowski (Strong)
NY - Strong 42 run (Strong)
NY - Strong 11 run (Molenda miss)
NY - Danowski 9 run (Molenda)

TEAM STATISTICS	Chi	NY
First Downs	10	12
Offensive plays - yards	61 - 165	49 - 276
Rushes - yards	46 - 89	37 - 173
Passes	15 - 6 - 3	12 - 7 - 2
Passing yards	76	103
Interceptions - yards	2 - 16	3 - 10
Punts - average	9 - 40.7	6 - 45.7
Punt returns - yards	46	12
Kickoff returns - yards		
Fumbles - lost	5 - 0	5 - 2
Penalties - yards	4 - 30	0 - 0

NFL Championship Game
Dec. 15, 1935
Detroit University Stadium–15,000

New York	0	0	7	0	–	7
Detroit	13	0	0	13	–	26

Det - Gutowsky 5 run (Presnell)
Det - Clark 42 run (Clark miss)
NY - Strong 42 pass from Danowski (Strong)
Det - Caddel 1 run (Clark)
Det - Parker 4 run (Parker miss)

TEAM STATISTICS	NY	Det
First Downs	8	13
Offensive plays - yards	194	286
Rushes - yards	106	235
Passes	13 - 4 - 2	5 - 2 - 0
Passing yards	88	51
Interceptions - yards	0 - 0	2 - 51
Punts - average	- 43	- 39
Had blocked	2	0
Punt returns - yards		
Kickoff returns - yards		
Fumbles - lost	3 - 0	4 - 2
Penalties - yards	- 15	- 25

NFL Championship Game
Dec. 13, 1936
Polo Grounds, New York–29,545

Green Bay	7	0	7	7	–	21
Boston	0	6	0	0	–	6

GB - Hutson 48 pass from Herber (E. Smith)
Bos - Rentner 2 run (R. Smith miss)
GB - Gantenbein 8 pass from Herber (E. Smith)
GB - Monnett 3 run (Engebretsen)

TEAM STATISTICS	GB	Bos
First Downs	7	8
Rushing	2	4
Passing	4	3
Penalty	1	1
Offensive plays - yards	67 - 232	57 - 147
Rushes - yards	44 - 71	34 - 66
Passes	23 - 9 - 2	23 - 6 - 1
Passing yards	161	81
Sacked - yards lost	0 - 0	2 - 12
Interceptions - yards	1 - 0	2 - 22
Punts - average	8 - 37.6	11 - 29.9
Had blocked	0	2
Punt returns - yards	3 - 27	5 - 58
Kickoff returns - yards	3 - 57	3 - 30
Fumbles - lost	2 - 1	5 - 2
Penalties - yards	3 - 15	3 - 25

NFL Championship Game
Dec. 12, 1937
Wrigley Field, Chicago–15,878

Washington	7	0	7	14	–	28
Chicago Bears	7	7	7	0	–	21

Was - Battles 7 run (R. Smith)
Chi - Manders 10 run (Manders)
Chi - Manders 37 pass from Masterson (Manders)
Was - Millner 55 pass from Baugh (R. Smith)
Chi - Manske 3 pass from Masterson (Manders)
Was - Millner 77 pass from Baugh (R. Smith)
Was - Justice 35 pass from Baugh (R. Smith)

TEAM STATISTICS	Was	Chi
First Downs	18	11
Rushing	8	7
Passing	10	4
Offensive plays - yards	75 - 482	64 - 332
Rushes - yards	35 - 90	34 - 125
Passes	40 - 22 - 3	30 - 8 - 3
Passing yards	392	207

NFL Championship Game
Dec. 11, 1938
Polo Grounds, New York–48,120

Green Bay	0	14	3	0	–	17
New York	9	7	7	0	–	23

NY - Cuff 14 FG
NY - Leemans 6 run (Gildea miss)
GB - C. Mulleneaux 40 pass from Herber (Engebretsen)
NY - Barnard 20 pass from Danowski (Cuff)
GB - Hinkle 1 run (Engebretsen)
GB - Engebretsen 15 FG
NY - Soar 23 pass from Danowski (Cuff)

TEAM STATISTICS	GB	NY
First Downs	14	10
Rushing	9	6
Passing	4	2
Penalty	1	2
Offensive plays - yards	65 - 378	58 - 212
Rushes - yards	46 - 164	43 - 115
Passes	19 - 8 - 1	15 - 8 - 1
Passing yards	214	97
Sacked - yards lost	0 - 0	0 - 0
Interceptions - yards	1 - 4	1 - 0
Punts - average	6 - 26.8	8 - 40.6
Had blocked	2	0
Punt returns - yards	4 - 10	2 - 34
Kickoff returns - yards	3 - 66	4 - 56
Fumbles - lost	4 - 2	2 - 0
Penalties - yards	2 - 20	2 - 10

NFL Championship Game
Dec. 10, 1939
State Fair Park, Milwaukee–32,279

New York	0	0	0	0	–	0
Green Bay	7	0	10	10	–	27

GB - Gantenbein 7 pass from Herber (Engebretsen)
GB - Engebretsen 29 FG
GB - Laws 31 pass from Isbell (Engebretsen)
GB - Smith 42 FG
GB - Jankowski 1 run (Smith)

TEAM STATISTICS	NY	GB
First Downs	9	10
Rushing	5	6
Passing	3	2
Penalty	1	2
Offensive plays - yards	59 - 164	62 - 232
Rushes - yards	34 - 70	52 - 136
Passes	25 - 8 - 6	10 - 7 - 3
Passing yards	94	96
Sacked - yards lost	1 - 9	1 - 6
Interceptions - yards	3 - 27	6 - 39
Punts - average	6 - 40.3	7 - 23.7
Had blocked	0	2

Punt returns - yards	2 - 25	2 - 25
Kickoff returns - yards	4 - 54	0 - 0
Fumbles - lost	1 - 0	2 - 0
Penalties - yards	- 20	- 45

NFL Championship Game
Dec. 8, 1940
Griffith Stadium, Washington–36,034

Chicago Bears	21	7	26	19	–	73
Washington	0	0	0	0	–	0

Chi - Osmanski 68 run (Manders)
Chi - Luckman 1 run (Snyder)
Chi - Maniaci 42 run (Martinovich)
Chi - Kavanaugh 30 pass from Luckman (Snyder)
Chi - Pool 15 interception return (Plasman)
Chi - Nolting 23 run (Plasman miss)
Chi - McAfee 34 interception return (Stydahar)
Chi - Turner 21 interception return (Maniaci miss)
Chi - Clark 44 run (Famiglietti miss)
Chi - Famiglietti 2 run (Maniaci pass from Sherman)
Chi - Clark 1 run (Snyder pass failed)

TEAM STATISTICS	Chi	Was
First Downs	17	17
Rushing	13	4
Passing	3	10
Penalty	1	3
Offensive plays - yards	63 - 519	66 - 231
Rushes - yards	53 - 381	15 - 5
Passes	10 - 7 - 0	51 - 20 - 8
Passing yards	138	226
Sacked - yards lost	2 - 18	1 - 17
Interceptions - yards	8 - 106	0 - 0
Punts - average	2 - 48.0	3 - 42.3
Punt returns - yads	3 - 29	1 - 6
Kickoff returns - yards	1 - 22	8 - 203
Fumbles - lost	2 - 1	4 - 1
Penalties - yards	3 - 25	8 - 70

NFL Western Division Playoff
Dec. 14, 1941
Wrigley Field, Chicago–43,425

Green Bay	7	0	7	0	–	14
Chicago Bears	6	24	0	3	–	33

GB - Hinkle 1 run (Hutson)
Chi - Gallarneau 81 punt return (Snyder miss)
Chi - Snyder 24 FG
Chi - Standlee 3 run (Stydahar)
Chi - Standlee 2 run (Stydahar)
Chi - Swisher 9 run (Stydahar)
GB - Van Every 10 pass from Isbell (Hutson)
Chi - Snyder 26 FG

TEAM STATISTICS	GB	Chi
First Downs	12	14
Rushing	4	10
Passing	7	3
Penalty	1	1
Offensive plays - yards	63 - 255	60 - 325
Rushes - yards	36 - 33	48 - 277
Passes	27 - 11 - 2	12 - 5 - 0
Passing yards	222	48

Sacked - yards lost	- 54	- 15
Interceptions - yards	0 - 0	2 - 9
Punts - average	4 - 28.5	6 - 38.7
Punt returns - yards	60	87
Kickoff returns - yards	5 - 95	3 - 43
Fumbles - lost	3 - 3	5 - 3
Penalties - yards	3 - 46	12 - 128

NFL Championship Game
Dec. 21, 1941
Wrigley Field, Chicago–13,341

New York	6	0	3	0	–	9
Chicago Bears	3	6	14	14	–	37

Chi - Snyder 14 FG
NY - Franck 31 pass from Leemans (Cuff miss)
Chi - Snyder 39 FG
Chi - Snyder 37 FG
NY - Cuff 16 FG
Chi - Standlee 3 run (Snyder)
Chi - Standlee 7 run (Maniaci)
Chi - McAfee 3 run (Artoe)
Chi - Kavanaugh 42 fumble return (McLean)

TEAM STATISTICS	NY	Chi
First Downs	8	20
Rushing	4	14
Passing	2	5
Penalty	2	1
Offensive plays - yards	40 - 157	75 - 389
Rushes - yards	25 - 84	56 - 207
Passes	15 - 3 - 3	19 - 11 - 0
Passing yards	73	182
Sacked - yards lost	- 5	- 12
Interceptions - yards	0 - 0	3 - 19
Punts - average	4 - 37.8	2 - 43.5
Punt returns - yards	0	0
Kickoff returns - yards	5 - 124	2 - 36
Fumbles - lost	3 - 1	2 - 2
Penalties - yards	9 - 65	3 - 31

NFL Championship Game
Dec. 13, 1942
Griffith Stadium, Washington–36,006

Chicago Bears	0	6	0	0	–	6
Washington	0	7	7	0	–	14

Chi - Artoe 50 fumble return (Artoe miss)
Was - Moore 39 pass from Baugh (Masterson)
Was - Farkas 1 run (Masterson)

TEAM STATISTICS	Chi	Was
First Downs	10	9
Rushing	4	5
Passing	5	2
Penalty	1	2
Offensive plays - yards	59 - 188	49 - 170
Rushes - yards	41 - 69	36 - 104
Passes	18 - 9 - 3	13 - 5 - 2
Passing yards	119	66
Sacked - yards lost	3 - 33	0 - 0
Interceptions - yards	2 - 0	3 - 14
Punts - average	6 - 41.0	6 - 52.2
Punt returns - yards	2 - 20	2 - 10
Kickoff returns - yards	3 - 63	2 - 52
Fumbles - lost	2 - 1	1 - 0
Penalties - yards	7 - 47	4 - 26

NFL Eastern Division Playoff
Dec. 19, 1943
Polo Grounds, New York–42,800

Washington	0	14	0	14	–	28
New York	0	0	0	0	–	0

Was - Farkas 2 run (Masterson)
Was - Farkas 2 run (Masterson)
Was - Farkas 1 run (Masterson)
Was - Lapka 11 pass from Baugh (Masterson)

TEAM STATISTICS	Was	NY
First Downs	13	8
Rushing	2	5
Passing	10	1
Penalty	1	2
Offensive plays - yards	61 - 296	53 - 112
Rushes - yards	39 - 83	33 - 55
Passes	22 - 17 - 2	20 - 4 - 3
Passing yards	213	57
Interceptions - yards	3 - 66	2 - 5
Punts - average	7 - 44.	10 - 36.
Had blocked	1	1
Punt returns - yards	7 - 58	3 - 41
Kickoff returns - yards	2 - 42	4 - 80
Fumbles - lost	2 - 1	0 - 0
Penalties - yards	9 - 83	5 - 35

NFL Championship Game
Dec. 26, 1943
Wrigley Field, Chicago–34,320

Washington	0	7	7	7	–	21
Chicago Bears	0	14	13	14	–	41

Was - Farkas 1 run (Masterson)
Chi - Clark 31 pass from Luckman (Snyder)
Chi - Nagurski 3 run (Snyder)
Chi - Magnani 36 pass from Luckman (Snyder)
Chi - Magnani 66 pass from Luckman (Snyder miss)
Was - Farkas 17 pass from Baugh (Masterson)
Chi - Benton 29 pass from Luckman (Snyder)
Chi - Clark 16 pass from Luckman (Snyder)
Was - Aguirre 25 pass from Baugh (Aguirre)

TEAM STATISTICS	Was	Chi
First Downs	11	14
Rushing	4	8
Passing	6	6
Penalty	1	0
Offensive plays - yards	51 - 249	71 - 455
Rushes - yards	27 - 50	44 - 169
Passes	24 - 11 - 4	27 - 15 - 0
Passing yards	199	286
Interceptions - yards	0 - 0	4 - 68
Punts - average	5 - 40.8	5 - 32.0
Punt returns - yards	2 - 37	5 - 66
Kickoff returns - yards	7 - 167	2 - 21
Fumbles - lost	2 - 2	0 - 0
Penalties - yards	3 - 35	8 - 81

NFL Championship Game
Dec. 17, 1944
Polo Grounds, New York–46,016

Green Bay	0	14	0	0	–	14
New York	0	0	0	7	–	7

GB - Fritsch 2 run (Hutson)
GB - Fritsch 26 pass from Comp (Hutson)
NY - Cuff 1 run (Strong)

TEAM STATISTICS	GB	NY
First Downs	11	10
Rushing	9	5
Passing	2	4
Penalty	0	1
Offensive plays - yards	60 - 237	52 - 199
Rushes - yards	49 - 163	30 - 85
Passes	11 - 3 - 3	22 - 8 - 4
Passing yards	74	114
Interceptions - yards	4 - 28	3 - 2
Punts - average	10 - 39.5	10 - 39.7
Punt returns - yards	8 - 92	4 - 31
Kickoff returns - yards	1 - 9	4 - 79
Kick returns - yards	101	107
Fumbles - lost	2 - 0	1 - 0
Penalties - yards	4 - 48	11 - 90

NFL Championship Game
Dec. 16, 1945
Municipal Stadium, Cleveland–32,178

Washington	0	7	7	0	–	14
Cleveland	2	7	6	0	–	15

Cle - Safety, Baugh's pass hit goal post
Was - Bagarus 38 pass from Filchock (Aguirre)
Cle - Benton 37 pass from Waterfield (Waterfield)
Cle - Gillette 44 pass from Waterfield (Waterfield miss)
Was - Seymour 8 pass from Filchock (Aguirre)

TEAM STATISTICS	Was	Cle
First Downs	8	14
Rushing	3	9
Passing	4	4
Penalty	1	1
Offensive plays - yards	54 - 214	71 - 372
Rushes - yards	34 - 35	44 - 180
Passes	20 - 9 - 2	27 - 14 - 2
Passing yards	179	192
Interceptions - yards	2 - 11	2 - 35
Punts - average	7 - 38.9	8 - 37.9
Punt returns - yards	5 - 67	5 - 34
Kickoff returns - yards	3 - 77	3 - 50
Fumbles - lost	1 - 0	1 - 1
Penalties - yards	4 - 29	6 - 60

AAFC Championship Game
Dec. 22, 1946
Municipal Stadium, Cleveland–41,181

New York	3	0	6	0	–	9
Cleveland	0	7	0	7	–	14

NY - H. Johnson 12 FG
Cle - Motley 1 run (Groza)
NY - Sanders 2 run (H. Johnson miss)
Cle - Lavelli 16 pass from Graham (Groza)

TEAM STATISTICS	NY	Cle
First Downs	10	18
Rushing	6	8
Passing	4	10
Offensive plays - yards	49 - 146	64 - 325

Rushes - yards	29 - 65	37 - 112
Passes	20 - 8 - 1	27 - 16 - 1
Passing yards	81	213
Interceptions - yards	1 - 16	1 - 4
Punts - average	5 - 32.2	2 - 38.5
Punt returns - yards	1 - 5	5 - 20
Kickoff returns - yards	3 - 77	3 - 37
Fumbles - lost	2 - 1	3 - 0
Penalties - yards	4 - 20	5 - 25

NFL Championship Game
Dec. 15, 1946
Polo Grounds, New York–58,346

Chicago Bears	14	0	0	10	–	24
New York	7	0	7	0	–	14

Chi - Kavanaugh 21 pass from Luckman (Maznicki)
Chi - Magnani 19 interception return (Maznicki)
NY - Liebel 38 pass from Filchock (Strong)
NY - Filipowicz 5 pass from Filchock (Strong)
Chi - Luckman 19 run (Maznicki)
Chi - Maznicki 26 FG

TEAM STATISTICS	Chi	NY
First Downs	10	13
Rushing	5	6
Passing	4	4
Penalty	1	3
Offensive plays - yards	62 - 245	59 - 248
Rushes - yards	40 - 101	33 - 120
Passes	22 - 9 - 2	26 - 9 - 6
Passing yards	144	128
Interceptions - yards	6 - 84	2 - 10
Punts - average	7 - 41.4	4 - 31.7
Punt returns - yards	2 - 13	3 - 9
Kickoff returns - yards	4 - 91	4 - 51
Fumbles - lost	2 - 1	3 - 2
Penalties - yards	9 - 112	6 - 70

AAFC Championship Game
Dec. 14, 1947
Yankee Stadium, New York–60,103

Cleveland	7	0	7	0	–	14
New York	0	3	0	0	–	3

Cle - Graham 1 run (Groza)
NY - H. Johnson 12 FG
Cle - Jones 4 run (Saban)

TEAM STATISTICS	Cle	NY
First Downs	15	13
Rushing	10	8
Passing	4	5
Penalty	1	0
Offensive plays - yards	54 - 284	51 - 212
Rushes - yards	33 - 172	33 - 123
Passes	21 - 14 - 0	18 - 7 - 1
Passing yards	112	89
Interceptions - yards	1 - 13	0 - 0
Punts - average	5 - 45.0	6 - 36.0
Punt returns - yards	4 - 27	3 - 14
Kickoff returns - yards	2 - 26	3 - 83
Fumbles - lost	2 - 1	3 - 2
Penalties - yards	7 - 45	3 - 21

NFL Eastern Division Playoff
Dec. 21, 1947
Forbes Field, Pittsburgh–35,729

Philadelphia	7	7	7	0	–	21
Pittsburgh	0	0	0	0	–	0

Phi - Van Buren 15 pass from Thompson (Patton)
Phi - Ferrante 28 pass from Thompson (Patton)
Phi - Pritchard 79 punt return (Patton)

TEAM STATISTICS	Phi	Pit
First Downs	17	7
Rushing	6	5
Passing	8	2
Penalty	3	0
Offensive plays - yards	70 - 255	145
Rushes - yards	52 - 124	29 - 102
Passes	18 - 11 - 0	18 - 4 - 0
Gross passing yards	131	52
Sacked - yards lost	0 - 0	- 9
Net yards passing	131	43
Interceptions - yards	0 - 0	0 - 0
Punts - average	6 - 36.3	9 - 40.0
Had blocked	0	1
Punt returns - yards	5 - 112	4 - 34
Kickoff returns - yards	1 - 15	2 - 31
Fumbles - lost	3 - 2	3 - 2
Penalties - yards	7 - 49	5 - 65

NFL Championship Game
Dec. 28, 1947
Comiskey Park, Chicago–30,759

Philadelphia	0	7	7	7	–	21
Chicago Cards	7	7	7	7	–	28

Chi - Trippi 44 run (Harder)
Chi - Angsman 70 run (Harder)
Phi - McHugh 70 pass from Thompson (Patton)
Chi - Trippi 75 punt return (Harder)
Phi - Van Buren 1 run (Patton)
Chi - Angsman 70 run (Harder)
Phi - Craft 1 run (Patton)

TEAM STATISTICS	Phi	Chi
First Downs	22	10
Rushing	10	7
Passing	11	2
Penalty	1	1
Offensive plays - yards	329	311
Rushes - yards	37 - 60	39 - 282
Passes	44 - 27 - 3	14 - 3 - 2
Gross passing yards	297	54
Sacked - yards lost	- 28	- 25
Net passing yards	269	29
Interceptions - yards	2 - 11	3 - 45
Punts - average	8 - 34.5	8 - 32.0
Punt returns - yards	4 - 10	4 - 150
Kickoff returns - yards	5 - 63	3 - 90
Fumbles - lost	2 - 0	2 - 1
Penalties - yards	7 - 55	10 - 97

AAFC Eastern Division Playoff
Dec. 12, 1948
Municipal Stadium, Baltimore–27,327

Buffalo	0	7	0	21	–	28
Baltimore	3	0	14	0	–	17

Bal - Grossman 16 FG
Buf - O'Connor 6 pass from Ratterman (Armstrong)
Bal - Mertes 9 run (Grossman)
Bal - Mertes 1 run (Grossman)
Buf - Gompers 66 pass from Ratterman (Armstrong)
Buf - Baldwin 26 pass from Ratterman (Armstrong)
Buf - Hirsch 20 interception return (Armstrong)

TEAM STATISTICS	Buf	Bal
First Downs	11	24
Rushing		
Passing		
Penalty		
Offensive plays - yards	297	367
Rushes - yards	162	177
Passes	18 - 10 - 1	36 - 17 - 1
Gross passing yards	135	217
Sacked - yards lost	0 - 0	- 27
Net passing yards	135	190
Interceptions - yards	1 - 20	1 - 0
Punts - average	3 - 40	5 - 42.4
Kick return yards	75	68
Punt returns - yards	5 - 42	2 - 14
Kickoff returns - yards	2 - 14	4 - 54
Fumbles - lost	4 - 33	7 - 2
Penalties - yards	5 - 25	8 - 80

AAFC Championship Game
Dec. 19, 1948
Municipal Stadium, Cleveland–22,981

Buffalo	0	0	7	0	–	7
Cleveland	7	7	14	21	–	49

Cle - E. Jones 3 run (Groza)
Cle - Young 18 fumble return (Groza)
Cle - E. Jones 9 pass from Graham (Groza)
Cle - Motley 29 run (Groza)
Buf - A. Baldwin 10 pass from Still (Armstrong)
Cle - Motley 31 run (Groza)
Cle - Motley 5 run (Groza)
Cle - Saban 39 interception return (Groza)

TEAM STATISTICS	Buf	Cle
First Downs	12	15
Rushing	4	6
Passing	6	7
Penalty	2	2
Offensive plays - yards	69 - 167	66 - 333
Rushes - yards	33 - 63	40 - 215
Passes	36 - 11 - 5	26 - 11 - 1
Passing yards	104	118
Interceptions - yards	1 - 2	5 - 80
Punts - average	6 - 42.5	3 - 32.7
Punt returns - yards	0 - 0	4 - 41
Kickoff returns - yards	3 - 51	2 - 66
Fumbles - lost	3 - 3	6 - 3
Penalties - yards	7 - 27	9 - 90

NFL Championship Game
Dec. 19, 1948
Shibe Park, Philadelphia–28,864

Chicago Cards	0	0	0	0	–	0
Philadelphia	0	0	0	7	–	7

Phi - Van Buren 5 run (Patton)

TEAM STATISTICS	Chi	Phi
First Downs	6	16
Rushing	3	15
Passing	3	0
Penalty	0	1
Offensive plays - yards	47 - 107	69 - 232
Rushes - yards	34 - 96	57 - 225
Passes	11 - 3 - 1	12 - 2 - 2
Gross passing yards	35	7
Sacked - yards lost	2 - 24	0 - 0
Net passing yards	11	7
Interceptions - yards	2 - 20	1 - 0
Punts - average	8 - 37.4	5 - 36.6
Punt returns - yards	2 - 11	2 - 22
Kickoff returns - yards	2 - 35	1 - 18
Fumbles - lost	3 - 2	1 - 1
Penalties - yards	4 - 33	3 - 17

AAFC First-Round Playoff
Dec. 4, 1949
Municipal Stadium, Cleveland–17,270

Buffalo	0	14	7	0	–	21
Cleveland	10	0	14	7	–	31

Cle - Lavelli 48 pass from Graham (Groza)
Cle - Groza 31 FG
Buf - Tomasetti 4 pass from Ratterman (Adams)
Buf - Mutryn 8 pass from Ratterman (Adams)
Cle - E. Jones 2 run (Groza)
Buf - Mutryn 30 pass from Ratterman (Adams)
Cle - D. Jones 49 pass from Graham (Groza)
Cle - Lahr 52 interception return (Groza)

TEAM STATISTICS	Buf	Cle
First Downs	19	15
Rushing	3	4
Passing	13	10
Penalty	3	1
Offensive plays - yards	373	398
Rushes - yards	25 - 80	20 - 72
Passes	42 - 21 - 2	43 - 22 - 2
Passing yards	293	326
Interceptions - yards	2 - 14	2 - 88
Punts - average	5 - 40	4 - 41
Kick return yards	111	95
Fumbles - lost	3 - 2	0 - 0
Penalties - yards	2 - 20	5 - 58

AAFC First-Round Playoff
Dec. 4, 1949
Kezar Stadium, San Francisco–41,393

Brooklyn-NY	0	7	0	0	–	7
San Francisco	7	3	7	0	–	17

SF - Lillywhite 40 run (Vetrano)
B-NY - Howard 7 run (H. Johnson)
SF - Vetrano 37 FG
SF - Garlin 6 pass from Albert (Vetrano)

TEAM STATISTICS	B-NY	SF
First Downs	9	10
Rushing	3	8
Passing	5	2
Penalty	1	0
Offensive plays - yards	190	260
Rushes - yards	33 - 74	33 - 164
Passes	25 - 7 - 3	17 - 8 - 2
Passing yards	116	96

Interceptions - yards	2 - 16	3 - 31
Punts - average	10 - 55.0	9 - 46.6
Punt returns - yards	5 - 56	10 - 137
Kickoff returns - yards	3 - 45	2 - 42
Fumbles - lost	1 - 0	4 - 1
Penalties - yards	3 - 35	2 - 10

AAFC Championship Game
Dec. 11, 1949
Municipal Stadium, Cleveland–22,550

San Francisco	0	0	7	0	–	7
Cleveland	7	0	7	7	–	21

Cle - E. Jones 2 run (Groza)
Cle - Motley 63 run (Groza)
SF - Salata 23 pass from Albert (Vetrano)
Cle - D. Jones 4 run (Groza)

TEAM STATISTICS	SF	Cle
First Downs	14	16
Rushing	7	11
Passing	7	5
Offensive plays - yards	58 - 230	58 - 345
Rushes - yards	33 - 122	41 - 217
Passes	25 - 9 - 0	17 - 7 - 0
Passing yards	108	128
Interceptions - yards	0 - 0	0 - 0
Punts - average	6 - 44.0	4 - 43.0
Punt returns - yards	2 - 23	5 - 61
Kickoff returns - yards	1 - 22	2 - 41
Fumbles - lost	2 - 0	0 - 0
Penalties - yards	0 - 0	1 - 5

NFL Championship Game
Dec. 18, 1949
Memorial Coliseum, Los Angeles–22,245

Philadelphia	0	7	7	0	–	14
Los Angeles	0	0	0	0	–	0

Phi - Pihos 31 pass from Thompson (Patton)
Phi - Skladany 2 blocked punt return (Patton)

TEAM STATISTICS	Phi	LA
First Downs	17	7
Rushing	12	0
Passing	4	6
Penalty	1	1
Offensive plays - yards	70 - 342	109
Rushes - yards	61 - 274	24 - 21
Passes	9 - 5 - 2	27 - 10 - 1
Gross passing yards	68	98
Sacked - yards lost	0 - 0	- 10
Net passing yards	68	88
Interceptions - yards	1 - 0	2 - 0
Punts - average	6 - 36.3	9 - 38.1
Had blocked	0	1
Punt returns - yards	4 - 14	2 - 17
Kickoff returns - yards	1 - 35	1 - 20
Fumbles - lost	4 - 1	1 - 0
Penalties - yards	6 - 40	4 - 25

NFL American Conference Playoff
Dec. 17, 1950
Municipal Stadium, Cleveland–33,054

New York	0	0	0	3	–	3
Cleveland	3	0	0	5	–	8

Cle - Groza 11 FG

NY - Clay 20 FG
Cle - Groza 29 FG
Cle - Safety, Willis tackled Conerly in end zone

TEAM STATISTICS	NY	Cle
First Downs	11	9
Rushing	8	7
Passing	2	2
Penalty	1	0
Offensive plays - yards	189	196
Rushes - yards	37 - 141	40 - 153
Passes	15 - 3 - 2	9 - 3 - 1
Gross passing yards	48	43
Sacked - yards lost		
Net passing yards		
Interceptions - yards	1 - 0	2 - 9
Punts - average	9 - 40.0	9 - 40.3
Punt returns - yards	5 - 22	3 - 11
Kickoff returns - yards	3 - 53	3 - 65
Fumbles - lost	2 - 0	0 - 0
Penalties - yards	5 - 45	9 - 54

NFL National Conference Playoff
Dec. 17, 1950
Memorial Coliseum, Los Angeles–83,501

Chicago Bears	0	7	0	7	–	14
Los Angeles	3	14	7	0	–	24

LA - Waterfield 43 FG
Chi - Campana 22 run (Lujack)
LA - Fears 43 pass from Waterfield (Waterfield)
LA - Fears 68 pass from Waterfield (Waterfield)
LA - Fears 27 pass from Waterfield (Waterfield)
Chi - Morrison 4 run (Lujack)

TEAM STATISTICS	Chi	LA
First Downs	23	11
Rushing	12	4
Passing	10	6
Penalty	1	1
Offensive plays - yards	83 - 370	63 - 371
Rushes - yards	48 - 229	32 - 74
Passes	29 - 15 - 3	31 - 16 - 1
Gross passing yards	193	297
Sacked - yards lost	6 - 52	0 - 0
Net passing yards	141	297
Interceptions - yards	1 - 20	3 - 56
Punts - average	7 - 44.0	10 - 42.4
Punt returns - yards	7 - 82	3 - 22
Kickoff returns - yards	2 - 31	0 - 0
Fumbles - lost	3 - 2	1 - 1
Penalties - yards	5 - 45	8 - 74

NFL Championship Game
Dec. 24, 1950
Municipal Stadium, Cleveland–29,751

Los Angeles	14	0	14	0	–	28
Cleveland	7	6	7	10	–	30

LA - Davis 82 pass from Waterfield (Waterfield)
Cle - Jones 27 pass from Graham (Groza)
LA - Hoerner 3 run (Waterfield)
Cle - Lavelli 37 pass from Graham (James pass failed)
Cle - Lavelli 39 pass from Graham (Groza)
LA - Hoerner 1 run (Waterfield)
LA - Brink 6 fumble return (Waterfield)
Cle - Bumgardner 14 pass from Graham (Groza)
Cle - Groza 16 FG

TEAM STATISTICS	LA	Cle
First Downs	22	22
Rushing	9	8
Passing	12	13
Penalty	1	1
Offensive plays - yards	69 - 407	373
Rushes - yards	36 - 106	25 - 116
Passes	32 - 18 - 5	33 - 22 - 1
Gross passing yards	312	298
Sacked - yards lost	1 - 11	- 41
Net passing yards	301	257
Interceptions - yards	1 - 11	5 - 54
Punts - average	4 - 50.8	5 - 38.4
Punt returns - yards	2 - 14	2 - 22
Kickoff returns - yards	5 - 126	3 - 58
Fumbles - lost	0 - 0	3 - 3
Penalties - yards	4 - 48	3 - 25

NFL Championship Game
Dec. 23, 1951
Memorial Coliseum, Los Angeles–57,522

Cleveland	0	10	0	7	–	17
Los Angeles	0	7	7	10	–	24

LA - Hoerner 1 run (Waterfield)
Cle - Groza 52 FG
Cle - Jones 17 pass from Graham (Groza)
LA - Towler 1 run (Waterfield)
LA - Waterfield 17 FG
Cle - Carpenter 2 run (Groza)
LA - Fears 73 pass from Van Brocklin (Waterfield)

TEAM STATISTICS	Cle	LA
First Downs	22	20
Rushing	6	9
Passing	16	9
Penalty	0	2
Offensive plays - yards	69 - 325	73 - 334
Rushes - yards	23 - 92	43 - 81
Passes	41 - 19 - 3	30 - 13 - 2
Gross passing yards	280	253
Sacked - yards lost	5 - 47	0 - 0
Net passing yards	233	253
Interceptions - yards	2 - 0	3 - 76
Punts - average	4 - 37.3	5 - 43.4
Punt returns - yards	1 - 13	0 - 0
Kickoff returns - yards	5 - 132	0 - 0
Fumbles - lost	4 - 1	2 - 1
Penalties - yards	6 - 41	5 - 25

NFL National Conference Playoff
Dec. 21, 1952
Briggs Stadium, Detroit–47,645

Los Angeles	0	7	0	14	–	21
Detroit	7	7	10	7	–	31

Det - Harder 12 run (Harder)
Det - Harder 4 run (Harder)
LA - Fears 14 pass from Van Brocklin (Waterfield)
Det - Hart 24 pass from Walker (Harder)
Det - Harder 43 FG
LA - Towler 5 run (Waterfield)
LA - Smith 57 punt return (Waterfield)
Det - Hoernschemeyer 9 run (Harder)

TEAM STATISTICS	LA	Det
First Downs	15	18
Rushing	5	11
Passing	8	7
Penalty	2	0
Offensive plays - yards	276	360
Rushes - yards	29 - 128	39 - 173
Passes	28 - 18 - 1	23 - 11 - 4
Gross passing yards	179	192
Sacked - yards lost	- 31	- 5
Net passing yards	148	187
Interceptions - yards	4 - 32	1 - 0
Punts - average	6 - 30.7	5 - 43.8
Punt returns - yards	4 - 76	2 - 7
Kickoff returns - yards	6 - 129	4 - 96
Fumbles - lost	2 - 2	0 - 0
Penalties - yards	2 - 14	5 - 35

NFL Championship Game
Dec. 28, 1952
Municipal Stadium, Cleveland–50,934

Detroit	0	7	7	3	–	17
Cleveland	0	0	7	0	–	7

Det - Layne 2 run (Harder)
Det - Walker 67 run (Harder)
Cle - Jagade 7 run (Groza)
Det - Harder 36 FG

TEAM STATISTICS	Det	Cle
First Downs	10	22
Rushing	8	15
Passing	2	7
Offensive plays - yards	258	384
Rushes - yards	34 - 199	34 - 227
Passes	10 - 7 - 0	36 - 20 - 1
Gross passing yards	68	191
Sacked - yards lost	- 9	- 34
Net passing yards	59	157
Interceptions - yards	1 - 7	0 - 0
Punts - average	6 - 40.8	3 - 43.3
Punt returns - yards	1 - 18	6 - 18
Kickoff returns - yards	2 - 39	4 - 84
Fumbles - lost	0 - 0	1 - 1
Penalties - yards	3 - 25	7 - 65

NFL Championship Game
Dec. 27, 1953
Briggs Stadium, Detroit–54,577

Cleveland	0	3	7	6	–	16
Detroit	7	3	0	7	–	17

Det - Walker 1 run (Walker)
Cle - Groza 13 FG
Det - Walker 23 FG
Cle - Jagade 9 run (Groza)
Cle - Groza 15 FG
Cle - Groza 43 FG
Det - Doran 33 pass from Layne (Walker)

TEAM STATISTICS	Cle	Det
First Downs	11	18
Rushing	9	10
Passing	1	7
Penalty	1	1
Offensive plays - yards	55 - 191	67 - 293
Rushes - yards	36 - 182	39 - 129
Passes	16 - 3 - 2	26 - 12 - 2
Gross passing yards	38	179
Sacked - yards lost	3 - 29	2 - 15
Net passing yards	9	164
Interceptions - yards	2 - 9	2 - 48
Punts - average	5 - 42.6	4 - 49.3
Punt returns - yards	3 - 35	0 - 0
Kickoff returns - yards	4 - 70	3 - 46
Fumbles - lost	2 - 2	3 - 2
Penalties - yards	4 - 30	4 - 50

NFL Championship Game
Dec. 26, 1954
Municipal Stadium, Cleveland–43,827

Detroit	3	7	0	0	– 10
Cleveland	14	21	14	7	– 56

Det - Walker 36 FG
Cle - Renfro 35 pass from Graham (Groza)
Cle - Brewster 8 pass from Graham (Groza)
Cle - Graham 1 run (Groza)
Det - Bowman 5 run (Walker)
Cle - Graham 5 run (Groza)
Cle - Renfro 31 pass from Graham (Groza)
Cle - Graham 1 run (Groza)
Cle - Morrison 12 run (Groza)
Cle - Hanulak 10 run (Groza)

TEAM STATISTICS	Det	Cle
First Downs	16	17
Rushing	5	8
Passing	9	6
Penalty	2	3
Offensive plays - yards	73 - 331	57 - 303
Rushes - yards	28 - 152	45 - 140
Passes	44 - 19 - 6	12 - 9 - 2
Gross passing yards	195	163
Sacked - yards lost	1 - 16	0 - 0
Net passing yards	179	163
Interceptions - yards	2 - 14	6 - 122
Punts - average	6 - 41.3	4 - 43.0
Punt returns - yards	1 - 0	2 - 42
Kickoff returns - yards	6 - 108	3 - 85
Fumbles - lost	3 - 3	2 - 2
Penalties - yards	5 - 63	4 - 40

NFL Championship Game
Dec. 26, 1955
Memorial Coliseum, Los Angeles–85,693

Cleveland	3	14	14	7	– 38
Los Angeles	0	7	0	7	– 14

Cle - Groza 26 FG
Cle - Paul 65 interception return (Groza)
LA - Quinlan 67 pass from Van Brocklin (Richter)
Cle - Lavelli 50 pass from Graham (Groza)
Cle - Graham 15 run (Groza)
Cle - Graham 2 run (Groza)
Cle - Renfro 35 pass from Graham (Groza)

LA - Waller 4 run (Richter)

TEAM STATISTICS	Cle	LA
First Downs	17	17
Rushing	7	8
Passing	10	8
Penalty	0	1
Offensive plays - yards	74 - 371	56 - 259
Rushes - yards	47 - 175	26 - 116
Passes	25 - 14 - 3	28 - 11 - 7
Gross passing yards	209	166
Sacked - yards lost	2 - 13	2 - 23
Net passing yards	196	143
Interceptions - yards	7 - 103	3 - 46
Punts - average	3 - 42.7	4 - 45.0
Punt returns - yards	3 - 27	1 - 9
Kickoff returns - yards	3 - 41	7 - 215
Fumbles - lost	0 - 0	1 - 0
Penalties - yards	5 - 74	2 - 10

NFL Championship Game
Dec. 30, 1956
Yankee Stadium, New York–56,836

Chicago Bears	0	7	0	0	– 7
New York	13	21	6	7	– 47

NY - Triplett 17 run (Agajanian)
NY - Agajanian 17 FG
NY - Agajanian 43 FG
NY - Webster 3 run (Agajanian)
Chi - Casares 9 run (Blanda)
NY - Webster 1 run (Agajanian)
NY - H. Moore blocked punt recovery (Agajanian)
NY - Rote 9 pass from Conerly (Agajanian miss)
NY - Gifford 14 pass from Conerly (Agajanian)

TEAM STATISTICS	Chi	NY
First Downs	19	16
Rushing	8	8
Passing	10	8
Penalty	1	0
Offensive plays - yards	280	348
Rushes - yards	32 - 67	34 - 126
Passes	47 - 20 - 2	20 - 11 - 0
Gross passing yards	237	228
Sacked - yards lost	- 24	- 6
Net passing yards	213	222
Interceptions - yards	0 - 0	2 - 48
Punts - average	8 - 34.0	3 - 37.0
Had blocked	1	0
Punt returns - yards	1 - 1	5 - 46
Kickoff returns - yards	9 - 143	2 - 83
Fumbles - lost	2 - 1	3 - 2
Penalties - yards	4 - 50	6 - 40

NFL Western Conference Playoff
Dec. 22, 1957
Kezar Stadium, San Francisco–60,118

Detroit	0	7	14	10	– 31
San Francisco	14	10	3	0	– 27

SF - Owens 34 pass from Tittle (Soltau)
SF - McElhenny 47 pass from Tittle (Soltau)
Det - Junker 4 pass from Rote (Martin)

SF - Wilson 12 pass from Tittle (Soltau)
SF - Soltau 25 FG
SF - Soltau 10 FG
Det - Tracy 2 run (Martin)
Det - Tracy 58 run (Martin)
Det - Gedman 3 run (Martin)
Det - Martin 14 FG

TEAM STATISTICS	Det	SF
First Downs	22	20
Rushing	6	4
Passing	13	14
Penalty	3	2
Offensive plays - yards	62 - 324	66 - 351
Rushes - yards	29 - 129	33 - 127
Passes	30 - 16 - 1	31 - 18 - 3
Gross passing yards	214	248
Sacked - yards lost	3 - 19	2 - 24
Net passing yards	195	224
Interceptions - yards	3 - 26	1 - 17
Punts - average	4 - 43.3	3 - 34.3
Punt returns - yards	2 - 0	2 - 16
Kickoff returns - yards	4 - 89	2 - 34
Fumbles - lost	3 - 3	6 - 2
Penalties - yards	7 - 61	6 - 70

NFL Championship Game
Dec. 29, 1957
Briggs Stadium, Detroit–55,263

Cleveland	0	7	7	0	– 14
Detroit	17	14	14	14	– 59

Det - Martin 31 FG
Det - Rote 1 run (Martin)
Det - Gedman 1 run (Martin)
Cle - Brown 29 run (Groza)
Det - Junker 26 pass from Rote (Martin)
Det - Barr 19 interception return (Martin)
Cle - L. Carpenter 5 run (Groza)
Det - Doran 78 pass from Rote (Martin)
Det - Junker 23 pass from Rote (Martin)
Det - Middleton 32 pass from Rote (Martin)
Det - Cassady 16 pass from Reichow (Martin)

TEAM STATISTICS	Cle	Det
First Downs	17	22
Rushing	11	9
Passing	5	10
Penalty	1	3
Offensive plays - yards	62 - 313	58 - 438
Rushes - yards	38 - 218	36 - 142
Passes	22 - 9 - 5	22 - 13 - 0
Gross passing yards	112	296
Sacked - yards lost	2 - 17	0 - 0
Net passing yards	95	296
Interceptions - yards	0 - 0	5 - 38
Punts - average	4 - 35.5	4 - 36.3
Punt returns - yards	2 - 1	2 - 10
Kickoff returns - yards	7 - 163	3 - 75
Fumbles - lost	2 - 2	3 - 1
Penalties - yards	4 - 60	7 - 52

NFL Eastern Conference Playoff
Dec. 21, 1958
Yankee Stadium, New York–61,274

Cleveland	0	0	0	0	– 0
New York	7	3	0	0	– 10

NY - Conerly 10 lateral from Gifford 8 run (Summerall)
NY - Summerall 26 FG

TEAM STATISTICS	Cle	NY
First Downs	7	17
Rushing	2	12
Passing	5	5
Offensive plays - yards	46 - 86	71 - 317
Rushes - yards	13 - 24	53 - 211
Passes	27 - 10 - 3	18 - 8 - 2
Gross passing yards	114	106
Sacked - yards lost	6 - 52	0 - 0
Net passing yards	62	106
Interceptions - yards	2 - 24	3 - 23
Punts - average	8 - 38.0	7 - 47.0
Punt returns - yards	4 - 11	5 - 6
Kickoff returns - yards	3 - 72	1 - 21
Fumbles - lost	1 - 1	6 - 2
Penalties - yards	2 - 20	4 - 35

NFL Championship Game
Dec. 28, 1958
Yankee Stadium, New York—64,185

Baltimore	0	14	0	3	6	— 23
New York	3	0	7	7	0	— 17

NY - Summerall 36 FG
Bal - Ameche 2 run (Myhra)
Bal - Berry 15 pass from Unitas (Myhra)
NY - Triplett 1 run (Summerall)
NY - Gifford 15 pass from Conerly (Summerall)
Bal - Myhra 20 FG
Bal - Ameche 1 run (no attempt)

TEAM STATISTICS	Bal	NY
First Downs	27	10
Rushing	9	3
Passing	17	7
Penalty	1	0
Offensive plays - yards	83 - 460	53 - 259
Rushes - yards	38 - 139	31 - 88
Passes	40 - 26 - 1	18 - 12 - 0
Gross passing yards	361	200
Sacked - yards lost	5 - 39	4 - 29
Net passing yards	322	171
Interceptions - yards	0 - 0	1 - 5
Punts - average	4 - 47.8	6 - 45.5
Punt returns - yards	3 - 8	4 - 17
Kickoff returns - yards	3 - 61	3 - 49
Fumbles - lost	2 - 2	6 - 4
Penalties - yards	3 - 15	2 - 22

NFL Championship Game
Dec. 27, 1959
Memorial Stadium, Baltimore—57,545

New York	3	3	3	7	— 16
Baltimore	7	0	0	24	— 31

Bal - Moore 59 pass from Unitas (Myhra)
NY - Summerall 23 FG
NY - Summerall 37 FG
NY - Summerall 23 FG
Bal - Unitas 4 run (Myhra)
Bal - Richardson 12 pass from Unitas (Myhra)
Bal - Sample 42 interception return (Myhra)
Bal - Myhra 25 FG

NY - Schnelker 32 pass from Conerly (Summerall)

TEAM STATISTICS	NY	Bal
First Downs	16	13
Rushing	4	3
Passing	11	10
Penalty	1	0
Offensive plays - yards	67 - 332	61 - 280
Rushes - yards	25 - 118	25 - 73
Passes	38 - 17 - 3	29 - 18 - 0
Gross passing yards	253	264
Sacked - yards lost	4 - 39	7 - 57
Net passing yards	214	207
Interceptions - yards	0 - 0	3 - 93
Punts - average	6 - 47.8	6 - 36.3
Punt returns - yards	1 - 5	3 - 33
Kickoff returns - yards	5 - 136	4 - 64
Fumbles - lost	1 - 0	1 - 0
Penalties - yards	3 - 23	4 - 20

AFL Championship Game
Jan. 1, 1961
Jeppesen Stadium, Houston—32,183

Los Angeles	6	3	7	0	— 16
Houston	0	10	7	7	— 24

LA - Agajanian 38 FG
LA - Agajanian 22 FG
Hou - Smith 17 pass from Blanda (Blanda)
Hou - Blanda 18 FG
LA - Agajanian 27 FG
Hou - Groman 7 pass from Blanda (Blanda)
LA - Lowe 2 run (Agajanian)
Hou - Cannon 88 pass from Blanda (Blanda)

TEAM STATISTICS	LA	Hou
First Downs	21	17
Rushing	11	4
Passing	9	13
Penalty	1	0
Offensive plays - yards	74 - 333	72 - 401
Rushes - yards	33 - 162	40 - 100
Passes	41 - 21 - 2	32 - 16 - 0
Passing yards	171	301
Interceptions - yards	0 - 0	2 - 35
Punts - average	4 - 41.0	5 - 34.0
Punt returns - yards	2 - 42	0 - 0
Kickoff returns - yards	5 - 123	5 - 128
Fumbles - lost	2 - 0	0 - 0
Penalties - yards	3 - 15	4 - 54

NFL Championship Game
Dec. 26, 1960
Franklin Field, Philadelphia—67,325

Green Bay	3	3	0	7	— 13
Philadelphia	0	10	0	7	— 17

GB - Hornung 20 FG
GB - Hornung 23 FG
Phi - McDonald 35 pass from Van Brocklin (Walston)
Phi - Walston 15 FG
GB - McGee 7 pass from Starr (Hornung)
Phi - Dean 5 run (Walston)

TEAM STATISTICS	GB	Phi
First Downs	22	13
Rushing	14	5
Passing	8	6
Penalty	0	2
Offensive plays - yards	77 - 401	49 - 296
Rushes - yards	42 - 223	28 - 99
Passes	35 - 21 - 1	20 - 9 - 1
Gross passing yards	178	204
Sacked - yards lost	0 - 0	1 - 7
Net passing yards	178	197
Interceptions - yards	1 - 0	0 - 0
Punts - average	5 - 45.2	6 - 39.5
Punt returns - yards	5 - 18	1 - 10
Kickoff returns - yards	2 - 49	4 - 91
Fumbles - lost	1 - 1	3 - 2
Penalties - yards	4 - 27	0 - 0

AFL Championship Game
Dec. 24, 1961
Balboa Stadium, San Diego—29,556

Houston	0	3	7	0	— 10
San Diego	0	0	0	3	— 3

Hou - Blanda 46 FG
Hou - Cannon 35 pass from Blanda (Blanda)
SD - Blair 12 FG

TEAM STATISTICS	Hou	SD
First Downs	18	15
Rushing	6	6
Passing	8	8
Penalty	4	1
Offensive plays - yards	74 - 256	58 - 256
Rushes - yards	33 - 96	20 - 79
Passes	41 - 18 - 6	32 - 17 - 4
Gross passing yards	160	226
Sacked - yards lost	0 - 0	6 - 49
Net passing yards	160	177
Interceptions - yards	4 - 7	6 - 60
Punts - average	4 - 41.5	6 - 33.3
Punt returns - yards	0 - 0	1 - 16
Kickoff returns - yards	0 - 0	2 - 50
Fumbles - lost	5 - 1	2 - 2
Penalties - yards	5 - 68	10 - 106

NFL Championship Game
Dec. 31, 1961
City Stadium, Green Bay—39,029

New York	0	0	0	0	— 0
Green Bay	0	24	10	3	— 37

GB - Hornung 6 run (Hornung)
GB - Dowler 13 pass from Starr (Hornung)
GB - R. Kramer 14 pass from Starr (Hornung)
GB - Hornung 17 FG
GB - Hornung 22 FG
GB - R. Kramer 13 pass from Starr (Hornung)
GB - Hornung 19 FG

TEAM STATISTICS	NY	GB
First Downs	6	19
Rushing	1	10
Passing	4	8
Penalty	1	1
Offensive plays - yards	46 - 130	63 - 345
Rushes - yards	14 - 31	44 - 185
Passes	29 - 10 - 4	19 - 10 - 0
Gross passing yards	119	164

Sacked - yards lost	3 - 20	0 - 0
Net passing yards	99	164
Interceptions - yards	0 - 0	4 - 36
Punts - average	5 - 39.2	5 - 41.6
Punt returns - yards	3 - 10	1 - 4
Kickoff returns - yards	6 - 119	1 - 18
Fumbles - lost	5 - 1	1 - 0
Penalties - yards	4 - 38	4 - 16

AFL Championship Game
Dec. 23, 1962
Jeppesen Stadium, Houston–37,981

Dallas	3	14	0	0	0	3	- 20
Houston	0	0	7	10	0	0	- 17

Dal - Brooker 16 FG
Dal - Haynes 28 pass from Dawson (Brooker)
Dal - Haynes 2 run (Brooker)
Hou - Dewveall 15 pass from Blanda (Blanda)
Hou - Blanda 31 FG
Hou - Tolar 1 run (Blanda)
Dal - Brooker 25 FG

TEAM STATISTICS	Dal	Hou
First Downs	19	21
Rushing	10	6
Passing	5	15
Penalty	4	0
Offensive plays - yards	68 - 237	76 - 359
Rushes - yards	54 - 199	30 - 98
Passes	14 - 9 - 0	46 - 23 - 5
Gross passing yards	88	261
Sacked - yards lost	6 - 50	0 - 0
Net passing yards	38	261
Interceptions - yards	5 - 136	0 - 0
Punts - average	8 - 31.2	3 - 39.3
Punt returns - yards	1 - 0	1 - 0
Kickoff returns - yards	4 - 86	5 - 139
Fumbles - lost	2 - 1	0 - 0
Penalties - yards	6 - 42	6 - 50

NFL Championship Game
Dec. 30, 1962
Yankee Stadium, New York–64,892

Green Bay	3	7	3	3	- 16
New York	0	0	7	0	- 7

GB - J. Kramer 26 FG
GB - Taylor 7 run (J. Kramer)
NY - Collier blocked punt recovery (Chandler)
GB - J. Kramer 29 FG
GB - J. Kramer 30 FG

TEAM STATISTICS	GB	NY
First Downs	18	18
Rushing	11	5
Passing	6	11
Penalty	1	2
Offensive plays - yards	69 - 244	67 - 291
Rushes - yards	46 - 148	26 - 94
Passes	22 - 10 - 0	41 - 18 - 1
Gross passing yards	106	197
Sacked - yards lost	1 - 10	0 - 0
Net passing yards	96	197
Interceptions - yards	1 - 30	0 - 0
Punts - average	6 - 26.7	7 - 41.7
Had blocked	1	0
Punt returns - yards	2 - 36	1 - 0

Kickoff returns - yards	2 - 62	4 - 88
Fumbles - lost	2 - 0	3 - 2
Penalties - yards	5 - 44	4 - 62

AFL Eastern Division Playoff
Dec. 28, 1963
War Memorial Stadium, Buffalo–33,044

Boston	10	6	0	10	- 26
Buffalo	0	0	8	0	- 8

Bos - Cappelletti 28 FG
Bos - Garron 59 pass from Parilli (Cappelletti)
Bos - Cappelletti 12 FG
Bos - Cappelletti 33 FG
Buf - Dubenion 93 pass from Lamonica (Tracey pass from Lamonica)
Bos - Garron 17 pass from Parilli (Cappelletti)
Bos - Cappelletti 36 FG

TEAM STATISTICS	Bos	Buf
First Downs	16	13
Rushing	5	0
Passing	9	11
Penalty	2	2
Offensive plays - yards	72 - 375	59 - 286
Rushes - yards	36 - 83	12 - 7
Passes	35 - 14 - 1	45 - 19 - 4
Gross passing yards	300	301
Sacked - yards lost	1 - 8	2 - 22
Net passing yards	292	279
Interceptions - yards	4 - 13	1 - 9
Punts - average	7 - 32.3	8 - 35.1
Punt returns - yards	2 - 34	3 - 8
Kickoff returns - yards	2 - 38	7 - 157
Fumbles - lost	0 - 0	3 - 2
Penalties - yards	7 - 65	9 - 100

AFL Championship Game
Jan. 5, 1964
Balboa Stadium, San Diego–30,127

Boston	7	3	0	0	- 10
San Diego	21	10	7	13	- 51

SD - Rote 2 run (Blair)
SD - Lincoln 67 run (Blair)
Bos - Garron 7 run (Cappelletti)
SD - Lowe 58 run (Blair)
SD - Blair 11 FG
Bos - Cappelletti 15 FG
SD - Norton 14 pass from Rote (Blair)
SD - Alworth 48 pass from Rote (Blair)
SD - Lincoln 25 pass from Hadl (pass failed)
SD - Hadl 1 run (Blair)

TEAM STATISTICS	Bos	SD
First Downs	14	21
Rushing	6	11
Passing	8	9
Penalty	0	1
Offensive plays - yards	59 - 261	60 - 610
Rushes - yards	16 - 75	32 - 318
Passes	37 - 17 - 2	26 - 17 - 0
Gross passing yards	228	305
Sacked - yards lost	6 - 42	2 - 13
Net passing yards	186	292
Interceptions - yards	0 - 0	2 - 15
Punts - average	7 - 46.9	2 - 43.5
Punt returns - yards	0 - 0	0 - 0

Kickoff returns - yards	9 - 122	3 - 70
Fumbles - lost	1 - 0	1 - 1
Penalties - yards	1 - 18	6 - 30

NFL Championship Game
Dec. 29, 1963
Wrigley Field, Chicago–45,801

New York	7	3	0	0	- 10
Chicago	7	0	7	0	- 14

NY - Gifford 14 pass from Tittle (Chandler)
Chi - Wade 2 run (Jencks)
NY - Chandler 13 FG
Chi - Wade 1 run (Jencks)

TEAM STATISTICS	NY	Chi
First Downs	17	14
Rushing	8	6
Passing	9	7
Penalty	0	1
Offensive plays - yards	69 - 268	60 - 222
Rushes - yards	38 - 128	31 - 93
Passes	30 - 11 - 5	28 - 10 - 0
Gross passing yards	147	138
Sacked - yards lost	1 - 7	1 - 9
Net passing yards	140	129
Interceptions - yards	0 - 0	5 - 71
Punts - average	4 - 43.3	7 - 41.9
Punt returns - yards	3 - 21	3 - 5
Kickoff returns - yards	3 - 97	3 - 35
Fumbles - lost	2 - 1	2 - 2
Penalties - yards	3 - 25	5 - 35

AFL Championship Game
Dec. 26, 1964
War Memorial Stadium, Buffalo–40,242

San Diego	7	0	0	0	- 7
Buffalo	3	10	0	7	- 20

SD - Kocourek 26 pass from Rote (Lincoln)
Buf - Gogolak 12 FG
Buf - Carlton 4 run (Gogolak)
Buf - Gogolak 17 FG
Buf - Kemp 1 run (Gogolak)

TEAM STATISTICS	SD	Buf
First Downs	15	21
Rushing	7	12
Passing	7	8
Penalty	1	1
Offensive plays - yards	259	387
Rushes - yards	18 - 124	41 - 219
Passes	36 - 13 - 3	20 - 10 - 0
Gross passing yards	149	188
Sacked - yards lost	- 14	- 20
Net passing yards	135	168
Interceptions - yards	0 - 0	3 - 8
Punts - average	5 - 36.4	5 - 46.8
Punt returns - yards	2 - 58	1 - 6
Kickoff returns - yards	4 - 175	2 - 44
Fumbles - lost	1 - 0	0 - 0
Penalties - yards	3 - 20	3 - 45

NFL Championship Game
Dec. 27, 1964
Municipal Stadium, Cleveland–79,544

Baltimore	0	0	0	0	- 0
Cleveland	0	0	17	10	- 27

Cle - Groza 43 FG
Cle - Collins 18 pass from Ryan (Groza)
Cle - Collins 42 pass from Ryan (Groza)
Cle - Groza 9 FG
Cle - Collins 51 pass from Ryan (Groza)

TEAM STATISTICS	Bal	Cle
First Downs	11	20
Rushing	5	8
Passing	4	9
Penalty	2	3
Offensive plays - yards	47 - 181	60 - 339
Rushes - yards	25 - 92	41 - 142
Passes	20 - 12 - 2	18 - 11 - 1
Gross passing yards	95	206
Sacked - yards lost	2 - 6	1 - 9
Net passing yards	89	197
Interceptions - yards	1 - 14	2 - 10
Punts - average	4 - 33.8	3 - 44.0
Punt returns - yards	2 - 18	1 - 13
Kickoff returns - yards	3 - 29	1 - 21
Fumbles - lost	2 - 2	0 - 0
Penalties - yards	5 - 48	7 - 59

AFL Championship Game
Dec. 26, 1965
Balboa Stadium, San Diego–30,361

Buffalo	0	14	6	3	– 23
San Diego	0	0	0	0	– 0

Buf - Warlick 18 pass from Kemp (Gogolak)
Buf - Byrd 74 punt return (Gogolak)
Buf - Gogolak 11 FG
Buf - Gogolak 39 FG
Buf - Gogolak 32 FG

TEAM STATISTICS	Buf	SD
First Downs	23	12
Rushing	13	5
Passing	9	7
Penalty	1	0
Offensive plays - yards	58 - 260	57 - 223
Rushes - yards	36 - 108	27 - 104
Passes	20 - 9 - 1	25 - 12 - 2
Gross passing yards	167	164
Sacked - yards lost	2 - 15	5 - 45
Net passing yards	152	119
Interceptions - yards	2 - 36	1 - 0
Punts - average	4 - 46.3	7 - 40.7
Punt returns - yards	3 - 87	1 - 12
Kickoff returns - yards	1 - 17	3 - 97
Fumbles - lost	0 - 0	4 - 2
Penalties - yards	2 - 21	3 - 41

NFL Western Conference Playoff
Dec. 26, 1965
Lambeau Field, Green Bay–50,484

Baltimore	7	3	0	0	0	– 10
Green Bay	0	0	7	3	3	– 13

Bal - Shinnick 25 fumble return (Michaels)
Bal - Michaels 15 FG
GB - Hornung 1 run (Chandler)
GB - Chandler 22 FG
GB - Chandler 25 FG

TEAM STATISTICS	Bal	GB
First Downs	9	23
Rushing	6	9

Passing	2	11
Penalty	1	3
Offensive plays - yards	60 - 175	81 - 362
Rushes - yards	47 - 143	39 - 112
Passes	12 - 5 - 0	41 - 23 - 2
Gross passing yards	40	258
Sacked - yards lost	1 - 8	1 - 8
Net passing yards	32	250
Interceptions - yards	2 - 18	0 - 0
Punts - average	8 - 41.3	5 - 42.6
Punt returns - yards	5 - 21	6 - 20
Kickoff returns - yards	2 - 44	4 - 73
Fumbles - lost	1 - 1	3 - 2
Penalties - yards	- 59	- 40

NFL Championship Game
Jan. 2, 1966
Lambeau Field, Green Bay–50,777

Cleveland	9	3	0	0	– 12
Green Bay	7	6	7	3	– 23

GB - Dale 47 pass from Starr (Chandler)
Cle - Collins 17 pass from Ryan (fumbled snap)
Cle - Groza 24 FG
GB - Chandler 15 FG
GB - Chandler 23 FG
Cle - Groza 28 FG
GB - Hornung 13 run (Chandler)
GB - Chandler 29 FG

TEAM STATISTICS	Cle	GB
First Downs	8	21
Rushing	2	10
Passing	5	9
Penalty	1	2
Offensive plays - yards	39 - 161	69 - 332
Rushes - yards	18 - 64	47 - 204
Passes	18 - 8 - 2	19 - 10 - 1
Gross passing yards	115	147
Sacked - yards lost	3 - 18	3 - 19
Net passing yards	97	128
Interceptions - yards	1 - 0	2 - 15
Punts - average	4 - 46.0	3 - 38.3
Punt returns - yards	1 - 11	2 - (-10
Kickoff returns - yards	5 - 155	3 - 66
Fumbles - lost	0 - 0	0 - 0
Penalties - yards	3 - 35	2 - 20

AFL Championship Game
Jan. 1, 1967
War Memorial Stadium, Buffalo–42,080

Kansas City	7	10	0	14	– 31
Buffalo	7	0	0	0	– 7

KC - Arbanas 29 pass from Dawson (Mercer)
Buf - Dubenion 69 pass from Kemp (Lusteg)
KC - Taylor 29 pass from Dawson (Mercer)
KC - Mercer 32 FG
KC - Garrett 1 run (Mercer)
KC - Garrett 18 run (Mercer)

TEAM STATISTICS	KC	Buf
First Downs	14	9
Rushing	6	2
Passing	8	7
Offensive plays - yards	65 - 277	44 - 255
Rushes - yards	33 - 113	13 - 40
Passes	24 - 16 - 0	27 - 12 - 2

Gross passing yards	227	253
Sacked - yards lost	8 - 63	4 - 38
Net passing yards	164	215
Interceptions - yards	2 - 98	0 - 0
Punts - average	6 - 42.3	8 - 39.3
Punt returns - yards	3 - 37	5 - 16
Kickoff returns - yards	2 - 38	6 - 99
Fumbles - lost	1 - 0	3 - 2
Penalties - yards	4 - 40	3 - 23

NFL Championship Game
Jan. 1, 1967
Cotton Bowl, Dallas–74,152

Green Bay	14	7	7	6	– 34
Dallas	14	3	3	7	– 27

GB - Pitts 17 pass from Starr (Chandler)
GB - Grabowski 18 fumble return (Chandler)
Dal - Reeves 3 run (Villanueva)
Dal - Perkins 23 run (Villanueva)
GB - Dale 51 pass from Starr (Chandler)
Dal - Villanueva 11 FG
Dal - Villanueva 32 FG
GB - Dowler 16 pass from Starr (Chandler)
GB - McGee 28 pass from Starr (Chandler miss)
Dal - Clarke 68 pass from Meredith (Villanueva)

TEAM STATISTICS	GB	Dal
First Downs	19	23
Rushing	3	12
Passing	14	10
Penalty	2	1
Offensive plays - yards	57 - 367	73 - 418
Rushes - yards	24 - 102	40 - 187
Passes	28 - 19 - 0	31 - 15 - 1
Gross passing yards	304	238
Sacked - yards lost	5 - 39	2 - 7
Net passing yards	265	231
Interceptions - yards	1 - 0	0 - 0
Punts - average	4 - 40.0	4 - 32.3
Punt returns - yards	0 - 0	3 - (-9
Kickoff returns - yards	6 - 110	6 - 153
Fumbles - lost	1 - 1	3 - 1
Penalties - yards	2 - 23	6 - 29

Super Bowl I
Jan. 15, 1967
Memorial Coliseum, Los Angeles–61,946

Kansas City	0	10	0	0	– 10
Green Bay	7	7	14	7	– 35

GB - McGee 37 pass from Starr (Chandler)
KC - McClinton 7 pass from Dawson (Mercer)
GB - Taylor 14 run (Chandler)
KC - Mercer 31 FG
GB - Pitts 5 run (Chandler)
GB - McGee 13 pass from Starr (Chandler)
GB - Pitts 1 run (Chandler)
MVP: Bart Starr, QB, Green Bay

TEAM STATISTICS	KC	GB
First Downs	17	21
Rushing	4	10
Passing	12	11
Penalty	1	0
Offensive plays - yards	64 - 239	64 - 358

	Hou	Oak
Rushes - yards	19 - 72	33 - 130
Passes	32 - 17 - 1	24 - 16 - 1
Gross passing yards	228	250
Sacked - yards lost	6 - 61	3 - 22
Net passing yards	167	228
Interceptions - yards	1 - 0	1 - 50
Punts - average	7 - 45.3	4 - 43.3
Punt returns - yards	3 - 19	4 - 23
Kickoff returns - yards	6 - 130	3 - 65
Fumbles - lost	1 - 0	1 - 0
Penalties - yards	4 - 26	4 - 40

AFL Championship Game
Dec. 31, 1967
Oakland - Alameda County Coliseum—53,330

Houston	0 0 0 7	– 7
Oakland	3 14 10 13	– 40

Oak - Blanda 37 FG
Oak - Dixon 69 run (Blanda)
Oak - Kocourek 17 pass from Lamonica (Blanda)
Oak - Lamonica 1 run (Blanda)
Oak - Blanda 40 FG
Oak - Blanda 42 FG
Hou - Frazier 5 pass from Beathard (Wittenborn)
Oak - Blanda 36 FG
Oak - Miller 12 pass from Lamonica (Blanda)

TEAM STATISTICS	Hou	Oak
First Downs	11	18
Rushing	4	11
Passing	6	6
Penalty	1	1
Offensive plays - yards	60 - 146	75 - 364
Rushes - yards	22 - 38	48 - 263
Passes	35 - 15 - 1	26 - 10 - 0
Gross passing yards	142	111
Sacked - yards lost	3 - 34	1 - 10
Net passing yards	108	101
Interceptions - yards	0 - 0	1 - 2
Punts - average	11 - 38.5	4 - 44.3
Punt returns - yards	0 - 0	6 - 47
Kickoff returns - yards	9 - 215	2 - 79
Fumbles - lost	4 - 2	0 - 0
Penalties - yards	7 - 45	4 - 69

NFL Western Conference Playoff
Dec. 23, 1967
County Stadium, Milwaukee—49,861

Los Angeles	7 0 0 0	– 7
Green Bay	0 14 7 7	– 28

LA - Casey 29 pass from Gabriel (Gossett)
GB - Williams 46 run (Chandler)
GB - Dale 17 pass from Starr (Chandler)
GB - Mercein 6 run (Chandler)
GB - Williams 2 run (Chandler)

TEAM STATISTICS	LA	GB
First Downs	12	20
Rushing	2	11
Passing	9	8
Penalty	1	1
Offensive plays - yards	64 - 217	69 - 374

	Cle	Dal
Rushes - yards	28 - 75	45 - 163
Passes	31 - 11 - 1	23 - 17 - 1
Gross passing yards	186	222
Sacked - yards lost	5 - 44	1 - 11
Net passing yards	142	211
Interceptions - yards	1 - 24	1 - 20
Punts - average	6 - 39.3	5 - 32.6
Punt returns - yards	1 - 0	3 - 44
Kickoff returns - yards	4 - 80	2 - 19
Fumbles - lost	0 - 0	3 - 3
Penalties - yards	3 - 25	7 - 44

NFL Eastern Conference Playoff
Dec. 24, 1967
Cotton Bowl, Dallas—70,786

Cleveland	0 7 0 7	– 14
Dallas	14 10 21 7	– 52

Dal - Baynham 3 pass from Meredith (Villanueva)
Dal - Perkins 4 run (Villanueva)
Dal - Hayes 86 pass from Meredith (Villanueva)
Dal - Villanueva 10 FG
Cle - Morin 13 pass from Ryan (Groza)
Dal - Baynham 1 run (Villanueva)
Dal - Perkins 1 run (Villanueva)
Dal - Green 60 interception return (Villanueva)
Dal - Baynham 1 run (Villanueva)
Cle - Warfield 75 pass from Ryan (Groza)

TEAM STATISTICS	Cle	Dal
First Downs	15	22
Rushing	4	13
Passing	10	7
Penalty	1	2
Offensive plays - yards	62 - 322	62 - 401
Rushes - yards	27 - 159	46 - 178
Passes	30 - 14 - 1	15 - 11 - 1
Gross passing yards	194	225
Sacked - yards lost	5 - 31	1 - 2
Net passing yards	163	223
Interceptions - yards	1 - 0	1 - 60
Punts - average	7 - 39.9	2 - 44.5
Punt returns - yards	2 - 11	4 - 155
Kickoff returns - yards	7 - 112	1 - 4
Fumbles - lost	0 - 0	2 - 1
Penalties - yards	2 - 18	2 - 10

NFL Championship Game
Dec. 31, 1967
Lambeau Field, Green Bay—50,861

Dallas	0 10 0 7	– 17
Green Bay	7 7 0 7	– 21

GB - Dowler 8 pass from Starr (Chandler)
GB - Dowler 43 pass from Starr (Chandler)
Dal - Andrie 7 fumble return (Villanueva)
Dal - Villanueva 21 FG
Dal - Rentzel 50 pass from Reeves (Villanueva)
GB - Starr 1 run (Chandler)

TEAM STATISTICS	Dal	GB
First Downs	11	18
Rushing	4	5
Passing	6	10
Penalty	1	3

	GB	Oak
Offensive plays - yards	60 - 192	64 - 195
Rushes - yards	33 - 92	32 - 80
Passes	26 - 11 - 1	24 - 14 - 0
Gross passing yards	109	191
Sacked - yards lost	1 - 9	8 - 76
Net passing yards	100	115
Interceptions - yards	0 - 0	1 - 15
Punts - average	8 - 39.1	8 - 28.8
Punt returns - yards	0 - 0	5 - 19
Kickoff returns - yards	3 - 43	3 - 10
Fumbles - lost	3 - 1	3 - 2
Penalties - yards	7 - 58	2 - 10

Super Bowl II
Jan. 14, 1968
Orange Bowl, Miami—75,546

Green Bay	3 13 10 7	– 33
Oakland	0 7 0 7	– 14

GB - Chandler 39 FG
GB - Chandler 20 FG
GB - Dowler 62 pass from Starr (Chandler)
Oak - Miller 23 pass from Lamonica (Blanda)
GB - Chandler 43 FG
GB - Anderson 2 run (Chandler)
GB - Chandler 31 FG
GB - Adderley 60 interception return (Chandler)
Oak - Miller 23 pass from Lamonica (Blanda)
MVP: Bart Starr, QB, Green Bay

TEAM STATISTICS	GB	Oak
First Downs	19	16
Rushing	11	5
Passing	7	10
Penalty	1	1
Offensive plays - yards	69 - 322	57 - 293
Rushes - yards	41 - 160	20 - 107
Passes	24 - 13 - 0	34 - 15 - 1
Gross passing yards	202	208
Sacked - yards lost	4 - 40	3 - 22
Net passing yards	162	186
Interceptions - yards	1 - 60	0 - 0
Punts - average	6 - 39.0	6 - 44.0
Punt returns - yards	5 - 35	3 - 12
Kickoff returns - yards	3 - 49	7 - 127
Fumbles - lost	0 - 0	3 - 2
Penalties - yards	1 - 12	4 - 31

AFL Western Division Playoff
Dec. 22, 1968
Oakland - Alameda County Coliseum—53,605

Kansas City	0 6 0 0	– 6
Oakland	21 7 0 13	– 41

Oak - Biletnikoff 24 pass from Lamonica (Blanda)
Oak - Wells 23 pass from Lamonica (Blanda)
Oak - Biletnikoff 44 pass from Lamonica (Blanda)
KC - Stenerud 10 FG
KC - Stenerud 8 FG
Oak - Biletnikoff 54 pass from Lamonica (Blanda)
Oak - Wells 35 pass from Lamonica (Blanda)

Oak - Blanda 41 FG
Oak - Blanda 40 FG

TEAM STATISTICS	KC	Oak
First Downs	13	22
Rushing	3	7
Passing	9	14
Penalty	1	1
Offensive plays - yards	61 - 312	70 - 454
Rushes - yards	24 - 70	30 - 118
Passes	36 - 17 - 4	39 - 19 - 0
Gross passing yards	253	347
Sacked - yards lost	1 - 11	1 - 11
Net passing yards	242	336
Interceptions - yards	0 - 0	4 - 26
Punts - average	6 - 50.3	5 - 45.4
Punt returns - yards	2 - 9	3 - 29
Kickoff returns - yards	8 - 117	1 - 34
Fumbles - lost	2 - 0	1 - 0
Penalties - yards	6 - 49	1 - 5

AFL Championship Game
Dec. 29, 1968
Shea Stadium, New York–62,627

Oakland	0	10	3	10	–	23
New York	10	3	7	7	–	27

NY - Maynard 14 pass from Namath (J. Turner)
NY - J. Turner 33 FG
Oak - Biletnikoff 29 pass from Lamonica (Blanda)
NY - J. Turner 36 FG
Oak - Blanda 26 FG
Oak - Blanda 9 FG
NY - Lammons 20 pass from Namath (J. Turner)
Oak - Blanda 20 FG
Oak - Banaszak 4 run (Blanda)
NY - Maynard 6 pass from Namath (J. Turner)

TEAM STATISTICS	Oak	NY
First Downs	18	25
Rushing	3	9
Passing	14	15
Penalty	1	1
Offensive plays - yards	68 - 443	85 - 400
Rushes - yards	19 - 50	34 - 144
Passes	47 - 20 - 0	49 - 19 - 1
Gross passing yards	401	266
Sacked - yards lost	2 - 8	2 - 10
Net passing yards	393	256
Interceptions - yards	1 - 32	0 - 0
Punts - average	7 - 42.7	10 - 41.5
Punt returns - yards	4 - 17	3 - 8
Kickoff returns - yards	5 - 129	4 - 110
Fumbles - lost	2 - 0	1 - 1
Penalties - yards	2 - 23	4 - 26

NFL Eastern Conference Playoff
Dec. 21, 1968
Municipal Stadium, Cleveland–81,497

Dallas	7	3	3	7	–	20
Cleveland	3	7	14	7	–	31

Cle - Cockroft 38 FG
Dal - Howley 44 fumble return (Clark)

Dal - Clark 16 FG
Cle - Kelly 45 pass from Nelsen (Cockroft)
Cle - Lindsey 27 interception return (Cockroft)
Cle - Kelly 35 run (Cockroft)
Dal - Clark 47 FG
Cle - Green 2 run (Cockroft)
Dal - Garrison 2 pass from Morton (Clark)

TEAM STATISTICS	Dal	Cle
First Downs	13	12
Rushing	5	4
Passing	8	8
Offensive plays - yards	63 - 286	57 - 280
Rushes - yards	30 - 86	30 - 102
Passes	32 - 12 - 4	25 - 13 - 1
Gross passing yards	205	203
Sacked - yards lost	1 - 5	2 - 25
Net passing yards	200	178
Interceptions - yards	1 - 6	4 - 52
Punts - average	5 - 41.0	7 - 36.1
Punt returns - yards	0 - 0	3 - 6
Kickoff returns - yards	5 - 72	4 - 67
Fumbles - lost	1 - 0	1 - 1
Penalties - yards	4 - 20	6 - 40

NFL Western Conference Playoff
Dec. 22, 1968
Memorial Stadium, Baltimore–60,238

Minnesota	0	0	0	14	–	14
Baltimore	0	7	14	3	–	24

Bal - Mitchell 3 pass from Morrall (Michaels)
Bal - Mackey 49 pass from Morrall (Michaels)
Bal - Curtis 60 fumble return (Michaels)
Min - Martin 1 pass from Kapp (Cox)
Bal - Michaels 33 FG
Min - Brown 7 pass from Kapp (Cox)

TEAM STATISTICS	Min	Bal
First Downs	22	15
Rushing	4	2
Passing	17	12
Penalty	1	1
Offensive plays - yards	75 - 351	53 - 295
Rushes - yards	28 - 85	27 - 50
Passes	44 - 26 - 2	22 - 13 - 1
Gross passing yards	287	280
Sacked - yards lost	3 - 21	4 - 35
Net passing yards	266	245
Interceptions - yards	1 - 21	2 - 44
Punts - average	6 - 39.7	5 - 40.4
Punt returns - yards	1 - (-3)	2 - 11
Kickoff returns - yards	5 - 113	3 - 54
Fumbles - lost	2 - 1	1 - 1
Penalties - yards	4 - 30	2 - 38

NFL Championship Game
Dec. 29, 1968
Municipal Stadium, Cleveland–78,410

Baltimore	0	17	7	10	–	34
Cleveland	0	0	0	0	–	0

Bal - Michaels 28 FG
Bal - Matte 1 run (Michaels)
Bal - Matte 12 run (Michaels)
Bal - Matte 2 run (Michaels)
Bal - Michaels 10 FG

Bal - Brown 4 run (Michaels)

TEAM STATISTICS	Bal	Cle
First Downs	22	12
Rushing	13	2
Passing	8	8
Penalty	1	2
Offensive plays - yards	64 - 353	58 - 173
Rushes - yards	39 - 184	22 - 56
Passes	25 - 11 - 1	32 - 13 - 2
Gross passing yards	169	151
Sacked - yards lost	0 - 0	4 - 34
Net passing yards	169	117
Interceptions - yards	2 - 26	1 - 0
Punts - average	2 - 37.0	5 - 33.4
Punt returns - yards	1 - 0	1 - 4
Kickoff returns - yards	1 - 21	6 - 91
Fumbles - lost	2 - 1	2 - 1
Penalties - yards	3 - 15	7 - 54

Super Bowl III
Jan. 12, 1969
Orange Bowl, Miami–75,377

New York Jets	0	7	6	3	–	16
Baltimore	0	0	0	7	–	7

NY - Snell 4 run (Turner)
NY - Turner 32 FG
NY - Turner 30 FG
NY - Turner 9 FG
Bal - Hill 1 run (Michaels)
MVP: Joe Namath, QB, New York

TEAM STATISTICS	NY	Bal
First Downs	21	18
Rushing	10	7
Passing	10	9
Penalty	1	2
Offensive plays - yards	74 - 337	64 - 324
Rushes - yards	43 - 142	23 - 143
Passes	29 - 17 - 0	41 - 17 - 4
Gross passing yards	206	181
Sacked - yards lost	2 - 11	0 - 0
Net passing yards	195	181
Interceptions - yards	4 - 9	0 - 0
Punts - average	4 - 38.8	3 - 44.3
Punt returns - yards	1 - 0	4 - 34
Kickoff returns - yards	1 - 25	4 - 105
Fumbles - lost	1 - 1	1 - 1
Penalties - yards	5 - 28	3 - 23

AFL Inter-Divisional Playoff
Dec. 20, 1969
Shea Stadium, New York–62,977

Kansas City	0	3	3	7	–	13
New York	3	0	0	3	–	6

NY - J. Turner 27 FG
KC - Stenerud 23 FG
KC - Stenerud 25 FG
NY - J. Turner 7 FG
KC - Richardson 19 pass from Dawson (Stenerud)

TEAM STATISTICS	KC	NY
First Downs	14	19
Rushing	3	5

Passing	9	11
Penalty	2	3
Offensive plays - yards	59 - 276	64 - 235
Rushes - yards	30 - 99	22 - 87
Passes	27 - 12 - 0	40 - 14 - 3
Gross passing yards	201	164
Sacked - yards lost	2 - 24	2 - 16
Net passing yards	177	148
Interceptions - yards	3 - 42	0 - 0
Punts - average	6 - 33.5	5 - 37.2
Punt returns - yards	2 - 14	2 - 10
Kickoff returns - yards	3 - 64	4 - 97
Fumbles - lost	0 - 0	1 - 1
Penalties - yards	5 - 63	3 - 15

AFL Inter-Divisional Playoff
Dec. 21, 1969
Oakland - Alameda County Coliseum–53,539

Houston	0	0	0	7	–	7
Oakland	28	7	14	7	–	56

Oak - Biletnikoff 13 pass from Lamonica (Blanda)
Oak - Atkinson 57 interception return (Blanda)
Oak - Sherman 24 pass from Lamonica (Blanda)
Oak - Biletnikoff 31 pass from Lamonica (Blanda)
Oak - Smith 60 pass from Lamonica (Blanda)
Oak - Sherman 23 pass from Lamonica (Blanda)
Oak - Cannon 3 pass from Lamonica (Blanda)
Hou - Reed 8 pass from Beathard (Gerela)
Oak - Hubbard 4 run (Blanda)

TEAM STATISTICS	Hou	Oak
First Downs	14	17
Rushing	1	5
Passing	10	11
Penalty	3	1
Offensive plays - yards	71 - 197	60 - 412
Rushes - yards	19 - 28	37 - 110
Passes	46 - 18 - 3	22 - 14 - 3
Gross passing yards	209	309
Sacked - yards lost	6 - 40	1 - 7
Net passing yards	169	302
Interceptions - yards	3 - 0	3 - 72
Punts - average	11 - 41.4	5 - 42.0
Punt returns - yards	2 - 4	3 - 27
Kickoff returns - yards	7 - 130	2 - 64
Fumbles - lost	3 - 2	3 - 1
Penalties - yards	3 - 48	7 - 63

AFL Championship Game
Jan. 4, 1970
Oakland - Alameda County Coliseum–53,564

Kansas City	0	7	7	3	–	17
Oakland	7	0	0	0	–	7

Oak - Smith 3 run (Blanda)
KC - Hayes 1 run (Stenerud)
KC - Holmes 5 run (Stenerud)
KC - Stenerud 22 FG

TEAM STATISTICS	KC	Oak
First Downs	13	18

Rushing	5	6
Passing	6	10
Penalty	2	2
Offensive plays - yards	57 - 207	77 - 233
Rushes - yards	39 - 86	28 - 79
Passes	17 - 7 - 0	45 - 17 - 4
Gross passing yards	129	191
Sacked - yards lost	1 - 8	4 - 37
Net passing yards	121	154
Interceptions - yards	4 - 109	0 - 0
Punts - average	8 - 42.9	6 - 48.5
Punt returns - yards	4 - 9	2 - (-1
Kickoff returns - yards	2 - 43	4 - 112
Fumbles - lost	5 - 4	1 - 0
Penalties - yards	5 - 43	5 - 45

NFL Western Conference Playoff
Dec. 27, 1969
Metropolitan Stadium, Bloomington–47,900

Los Angeles	7	10	0	3	–	20
Minnesota	7	0	7	9	–	23

LA - Klein 3 pass from Gabriel (Gossett)
Min - Osborn 1 run (Cox)
LA - Gossett 20 FG
LA - Truax 2 pass from Gabriel (Gossett)
Min - Osborn 1 run (Cox)
LA - Gossett 27 FG
Min - Kapp 2 run (Cox)
Min - Safety, Eller tackled Gabriel in end zone

TEAM STATISTICS	LA	Min
First Downs	19	18
Rushing	10	7
Passing	9	10
Penalty	0	1
Offensive plays - yards	65 - 255	50 - 275
Rushes - yards	30 - 126	29 - 97
Passes	32 - 22 - 1	19 - 12 - 2
Gross passing yards	150	196
Sacked - yards lost	3 - 21	2 - 18
Net passing yards	129	178
Interceptions - yards	2 - 19	1 - 29
Punts - average	3 - 36.3	3 - 39.3
Punt returns - yards	2 - 8	1 - 6
Kickoff returns - yards	4 - 69	6 - 111
Fumbles - lost	1 - 0	3 - 1
Penalties - yards	4 - 37	4 - 36

NFL Eastern Conference Playoff
Dec. 28, 1969
Cotton Bowl, Dallas–69,321

Cleveland	7	10	7	14	–	38
Dallas	0	0	7	7	–	14

Cle - Scott 2 run (Cockroft)
Cle - Morin 6 pass from Nelsen (Cockroft)
Cle - Cockroft 29 FG
Cle - Scott 2 run (Cockroft)
Dal - Morton 2 run (M. Clark)
Cle - Kelly 1 run (Cockroft)
Cle - Sumner 88 interception return (Cockroft)
Dal - Rentzel 5 pass from Staubach (M. Clark)

TEAM STATISTICS	Cle	Dal
First Downs	22	17
Rushing	4	9
Passing	17	6

Penalty	1	2
Offensive plays - yards	65 - 344	57 - 217
Rushes - yards	35 - 97	25 - 100
Passes	29 - 20 - 0	29 - 12 - 2
Gross passing yards	254	136
Sacked - yards lost	1 - 7	3 - 19
Net passing yards	247	117
Interceptions - yards	2 - 123	0 - 0
Punts - average	1 - 34.0	5 - 36.2
Punt returns - yards	2 - 11	1 - 0
Kickoff returns - yards	3 - 56	5 - 106
Fumbles - lost	1 - 0	2 - 1
Penalties - yards	6 - 50	6 - 51

NFL Championship Game
Jan. 4, 1970
Metropolitan Stadium, Bloomington–46,503

Cleveland	0	0	0	7	–	7
Minnesota	14	10	3	0	–	27

Min - Kapp 7 run (Cox)
Min - Washington 75 pass from Kapp (Cox)
Min - Cox 30 FG
Min - Osborn 20 run (Cox)
Min - Cox 32 FG
Cle - Collins 3 pass from Nelsen (Cockroft)

TEAM STATISTICS	Cle	Min
First Downs	14	18
Rushing	4	13
Passing	10	5
Offensive plays - yards	56 - 268	59 - 383
Rushes - yards	21 - 97	45 - 222
Passes	33 - 17 - 2	13 - 7 - 0
Gross passing yards	181	169
Sacked - yards lost	2 - 10	1 - 8
Net passing yards	171	161
Interceptions - yards	0 - 0	2 - 0
Punts - average	3 - 33.0	3 - 41.0
Punt returns - yards	3 - 21	1 - 1
Kickoff returns - yards	5 - 83	2 - 42
Fumbles - lost	2 - 1	0 - 0
Penalties - yards	1 - 5	3 - 33

Super Bowl IV
Jan. 11, 1970
Tulane Stadium, New Orleans–80,562

Minnesota	0	0	7	0	–	7
Kansas City	3	13	7	0	–	23

KC - Stenerud 48 FG
KC - Stenerud 32 FG
KC - Stenerud 25 FG
KC - Garrett 5 run (Stenerud)
Min - Osborn 4 run (Cox)
KC - Taylor 46 pass from Dawson (Stenerud)
MVP: Len Dawson, QB, Kansas City

TEAM STATISTICS	Min	KC
First Downs	13	18
Rushing	2	8
Passing	10	7
Penalty	1	3
Offensive plays - yards	50 - 239	62 - 273
Rushes - yards	19 - 67	42 - 151
Passes	28 - 17 - 3	17 - 12 - 1
Gross passing yards	199	142
Sacked - yards lost	3 - 27	3 - 20

Net passing yards	172	122
Interceptions - yards	1 - 0	3 - 24
Punts - average	3 - 37.0	4 - 48.5
Punt returns - yards	2 - 18	1 - 0
Kickoff returns - yards	4 - 79	2 - 36
Fumbles - lost	3 - 2	0 - 0
Penalties - yards	6 - 67	4 - 47

AFC Divisional Playoff
Dec. 26, 1970
Memorial Stadium, Baltimore—51,127

Cincinnati	0	0	0	0	–	0
Baltimore	7	3	0	7	–	17

Bal - Jefferson 45 pass from Unitas (O'Brien)
Bal - O'Brien 44 FG
Bal - Hinton 53 pass from Unitas (O'Brien)

TEAM STATISTICS	Cin	Bal
First Downs	7	15
Rushing	2	12
Passing	5	3
Offensive plays - yards	46 - 139	66 - 299
Rushes - yards	22 - 63	47 - 170
Passes	21 - 8 - 1	17 - 6 - 0
Gross passing yards	93	145
Sacked - yards lost	3 - 17	2 - 16
Net passing yards	76	129
Interceptions - yards	0 - 0	1 - 0
Punts - average	8 - 39.1	6 - 38.3
Punt returns - yards	2 - 6	7 - 28
Kickoff returns - yards	3 - 46	1 - 0
Fumbles - lost	1 - 0	0 - 0
Penalties - yards	1 - 5	6 - 63

NFC Divisional Playoff
Dec. 26, 1970
Cotton Bowl, Dallas—73,167

Detroit	0	0	0	0	–	0
Dallas	3	0	0	2	–	5

Dal - Clark 26 FG
Dal - Safety, Andrie and Pugh tackled Landry in end zone

TEAM STATISTICS	Det	Dal
First Downs	7	14
Rushing	2	11
Passing	5	3
Offensive plays - yards	50 - 156	69 - 231
Rushes - yards	27 - 76	50 - 209
Passes	20 - 7 - 1	18 - 4 - 1
Gross passing yards	92	38
Sacked - yards lost	3 - 12	1 - 16
Net passing yards	80	22
Interceptions - yards	1 - 31	1 - 13
Punts - average	8 - 48.9	8 - 44.8
Punt returns - yards	6 - 21	4 - 23
Kickoff returns - yards	2 - 37	2 - 25
Fumbles - lost	3 - 2	0 - 0
Penalties - yards	0 - 0	6 - 47

AFC Divisional Playoff
Dec. 27, 1970
Oakland - Alameda County Coliseum—54,401

Miami	0	7	0	7	–	14
Oakland	0	7	7	7	–	21

Mia - Warfield 16 pass from Griese (Yepremian)
Oak - Biletnikoff 22 pass from Lamonica (Blanda)
Oak - Brown 50 interception return (Blanda)
Oak - Sherman 82 pass from Lamonica (Blanda)
Mia - W. Richardson 7 pass from Griese (Yepremian)

TEAM STATISTICS	Mia	Oak
First Downs	16	12
Rushing	5	5
Passing	9	7
Penalty	2	0
Offensive plays - yards	63 - 242	52 - 307
Rushes - yards	33 - 118	36 - 120
Passes	27 - 13 - 1	16 - 8 - 0
Gross passing yards	155	187
Sacked - yards lost	3 - 31	0 - 0
Net passing yards	124	187
Interceptions - yards	0 - 0	1 - 50
Punts - average	5 - 39.2	4 - 32.3
Punt returns - yards	2 - (-5)	1 - (-1
Kickoff returns - yards	4 - 56	3 - 41
Fumbles - lost	2 - 0	4 - 2
Penalties - yards	0 - 0	4 - 30

NFC Divisional Playoff
Dec. 27, 1970
Metropolitan Stadium, Bloomington—41,050

San Francisco	7	3	0	7	–	17
Minnesota	7	0	0	7	–	14

Min - Krause 22 fumble return (Cox)
SF - Witcher 24 pass from Brodie (Gossett)
SF - Gossett 40 FG
SF - Brodie 1 run (Gossett)
Min - Washington 24 pass from Cuozzo (Cox)

TEAM STATISTICS	SF	Min
First Downs	14	14
Rushing	5	7
Passing	8	6
Penalty	1	1
Offensive plays - yards	71 - 289	60 - 241
Rushes - yards	38 - 96	30 - 117
Passes	32 - 16 - 0	27 - 9 - 2
Gross passing yards	201	146
Sacked - yards lost	1 - 8	3 - 22
Net passing yards	193	124
Interceptions - yards	2 - 5	0 - 0
Punts - average	8 - 33.8	7 - 39.4
Punt returns - yards	5 - 69	0 - 0
Kickoff returns - yards	3 - 30	4 - 72
Fumbles - lost	5 - 3	3 - 2
Penalties - yards	3 - 37	1 - 5

AFC Championship Game
Jan. 3, 1971
Memorial Stadium, Baltimore—56,368

Oakland	0	3	7	7	–	17
Baltimore	3	7	10	7	–	27

Bal - O'Brien 16 FG
Bal - Bulaich 2 run (O'Brien)
Oak - Blanda 48 FG
Oak - Biletnikoff 38 pass from Blanda (Blanda)

Bal - O'Brien 23 FG
Bal - Bulaich 11 run (O'Brien)
Oak - Wells 15 pass from Blanda (Blanda)
Bal - Perkins 68 pass from Unitas (O'Brien)

TEAM STATISTICS	Oak	Bal
First Downs	16	18
Rushing	5	7
Passing	10	11
Penalty	1	0
Offensive plays - yards	63 - 336	71 - 363
Rushes - yards	22 - 107	38 - 126
Passes	36 - 18 - 3	30 - 11 - 0
Gross passing yards	277	245
Sacked - yards lost	5 - 48	3 - 8
Net passing yards	229	237
Interceptions - yards	0 - 0	3 - 16
Punts - average	5 - 40.0	6 - 45.3
Punt returns - yards	2 - 10	2 - 1
Kickoff returns - yards	3 - 60	4 - 105
Fumbles - lost	1 - 1	0 - 0
Penalties - yards	2 - 20	2 - 10

NFC Championship Game
Jan. 3, 1971
Kezar Stadium, San Francisco—59,625

Dallas	0	3	14	0	–	17
San Francisco	3	0	7	0	–	10

SF - Gossett 16 FG
Dal - Clark 21 FG
Dal - Thomas 13 run (Clark)
Dal - Garrison 5 pass from Morton (Clark)
SF - Witcher 26 pass from Brodie (Gossett)

TEAM STATISTICS	Dal	SF
First Downs	22	15
Rushing	16	2
Passing	5	12
Penalty	1	1
Offensive plays - yards	75 - 319	61 - 307
Rushes - yards	51 - 229	19 - 61
Passes	22 - 7 - 0	40 - 19 - 2
Gross passing yards	101	262
Sacked - yards lost	2 - 11	2 - 16
Net passing yards	90	246
Interceptions - yards	2 - 23	0 - 0
Punts - average	6 - 40.2	5 - 41.0
Punt returns - yards	2 - 8	2 - 5
Kickoff returns - yards	3 - 46	4 - 89
Fumbles - lost	4 - 1	1 - 0
Penalties - yards	7 - 75	5 - 51

Super Bowl V
Jan. 17, 1971
Orange Bowl, Miami—79,204

Baltimore	0	6	0	10	–	16
Dallas	3	10	0	0	–	13

Dal - Clark 14 FG
Dal - Clark 30 FG
Bal - Mackey 75 pass from Unitas (O'Brien miss)
Dal - Thomas 7 pass from Morton (Clark)
Bal - Nowatzke 3 run (O'Brien)
Bal - O'Brien 32 FG

MVP: Chuck Howley, LB, Dallas

TEAM STATISTICS	Bal	Dal
First Downs	14	10
Rushing	4	4
Passing	6	5
Penalty	4	1
Offensive plays - yards	56 - 329	59 - 215
Rushes - yards	31 - 69	31 - 102
Passes	25 - 11 - 3	26 - 12 - 3
Gross passing yards	260	127
Sacked - yards lost	0 - 0	2 - 14
Net passing yards	260	113
Interceptions - yards	3 - 57	3 - 22
Punts - average	4 - 41.5	9 - 41.9
Punt returns - yards	5 - 12	3 - 9
Kickoff returns - yards	4 - 90	3 - 34
Fumbles - lost	5 - 4	1 - 1
Penalties - yards	4 - 31	10 - 133

AFC Divisional Playoff
Dec. 25, 1971
Municipal Stadium, Kansas City–45,822

Miami	0	10	7	7	0	3	– 27
Kansas City	10	0	7	7	0	0	– 24

KC - Stenerud 24 FG
KC - Podolak 7 pass from Dawson (Stenerud)
Mia - Csonka 1 run (Yepremian)
Mia - Yepremian 14 FG
KC - Otis 1 run (Stenerud)
Mia - Kiick 1 run (Yepremian)
KC - Podolak 3 run (Stenerud)
Mia - Fleming 5 pass from Griese (Yepremian)
Mia - Yepremian 37 FG

TEAM STATISTICS	Mia	KC
First Downs	22	23
Rushing	6	13
Passing	14	10
Penalty	2	0
Offensive plays - yards	78 - 407	71 - 451
Rushes - yards	43 - 144	44 - 213
Passes	35 - 20 - 2	26 - 18 - 2
Gross passing yards	263	246
Sacked - yards lost	0 - 0	1 - 8
Net passing yards	263	238
Interceptions - yards	2 - 13	2 - 17
Punts - average	6 - 40.0	2 - 51.0
Punt returns - yards	1 - 18	2 - 1
Kickoff returns - yards	2 - 61	4 - 154
Fumbles - lost	1 - 0	3 - 2
Penalties - yards	5 - 26	6 - 44

NFC Divisional Playoff
Dec. 25, 1971
Metropolitan Stadium, Bloomington–47,307

Dallas	3	3	14	0	– 20
Minnesota	0	3	0	9	– 12

Dal - Clark 26 FG
Min - Cox 27 FG
Dal - Clark 44 FG
Dal - D. Thomas 13 run (Clark)
Dal - Hayes 9 pass from Staubach (Clark)
Min - Safety, Page tackled Staubach in end zone

Min - Voigt 6 pass from Cuozzo (Cox)

TEAM STATISTICS	Dal	Min
First Downs	10	17
Rushing	5	5
Passing	5	12
Offensive plays - yards	55 - 183	64 - 311
Rushes - yards	39 - 98	26 - 101
Passes	14 - 10 - 0	38 - 19 - 4
Gross passing yards	99	210
Sacked - yards lost	2 - 14	0 - 0
Net passing yards	85	210
Interceptions - yards	4 - 69	0 - 0
Punts - average	7 - 37.0	4 - 43.5
Punt returns - yards	2 - 37	2 - 6
Kickoff returns - yards	3 - 52	6 - 188
Fumbles - lost	0 - 0	1 - 1
Penalties - yards	2 - 10	2 - 18

AFC Divisional Playoff
Dec. 26, 1971
Municipal Stadium, Cleveland–70,734

Baltimore	0	14	3	3	– 20
Cleveland	0	0	3	0	– 3

Bal - Nottingham 1 run (O'Brien)
Bal - Nottingham 7 run (O'Brien)
Cle - Cockroft 14 FG
Bal - O'Brien 42 FG
Bal - O'Brien 15 FG

TEAM STATISTICS	Bal	Cle
First Downs	16	11
Rushing	7	5
Passing	8	5
Penalty	1	1
Offensive plays - yards	64 - 271	56 - 165
Rushes - yards	43 - 128	24 - 69
Passes	21 - 13 - 1	27 - 12 - 3
Gross passing yards	143	131
Sacked - yards lost	0 - 0	5 - 35
Net passing yards	143	96
Interceptions - yards	3 - 79	1 - 23
Punts - average	6 - 37.2	5 - 40.8
Punt returns - yards	4 - 27	4 - 74
Kickoff returns - yards	1 - 25	5 - 98
Fumbles - lost	2 - 2	6 - 2
Penalties - yards	5 - 43	3 - 16

NFC Divisional Playoff
Dec. 26, 1971
Candlestick Park, San Francisco–45,327

Washington	7	3	3	7	– 20
San Francisco	0	3	14	7	– 24

Was - Smith 5 pass from Kilmer (Knight)
SF - Gossett 23 FG
Was - Knight 40 FG
SF - G. Washington 78 pass from Brodie (Gossett)
SF - Windsor 2 pass from Brodie (Gossett)
Was - Knight 36 FG
SF - Hoskins fumble recovery (Gossett)
Was - Brown 16 pass from Kilmer (Knight)

TEAM STATISTICS	Was	SF
First Downs	13	11
Rushing	6	2
Passing	5	9
Penalty	2	0
Offensive plays - yards	67 - 192	59 - 285
Rushes - yards	39 - 99	39 - 112
Passes	27 - 11 - 1	19 - 10 - 0
Gross passing yards	106	176
Sacked - yards lost	1 - 13	1 - 3
Net passing yards	93	173
Interceptions - yards	0 - 0	1 - 17
Punts - average	5 - 46.2	10 - 33.7
Had blocked	0	1
Punt returns - yards	4 - 58	3 - 13
Kickoff returns - yards	4 - 189	5 - 79
Fumbles - lost	3 - 2	0 - 0
Penalties - yards	4 - 55	3 - 41

AFC Championship Game
Jan. 2, 1972
Orange Bowl, Miami–76,622

Baltimore	0	0	0	0	– 0
Miami	7	0	7	7	– 21

Mia - Warfield 75 pass from Griese (Yepremian)
Mia - Anderson 62 interception return (Yepremian)
Mia - Csonka 5 run (Yepremian)

TEAM STATISTICS	Bal	Mia
First Downs	16	13
Rushing	6	8
Passing	10	4
Penalty	0	1
Offensive plays - yards	68 - 302	45 - 286
Rushes - yards	29 - 93	35 - 144
Passes	36 - 20 - 3	8 - 4 - 1
Gross passing yards	224	158
Sacked - yards lost	3 - 15	2 - 16
Net passing yards	209	142
Interceptions - yards	1 - 0	3 - 73
Punts - average	3 - 45.3	6 - 42.7
Punt returns - yards	5 - 20	2 - 20
Kickoff returns - yards	2 - 58	1 - 22
Fumbles - lost	1 - 0	0 - 0
Penalties - yards	1 - 5	2 - 27

NFC Championship Game
Jan. 2, 1972
Texas Stadium, Irving–63,409

San Francisco	0	0	3	0	– 3
Dallas	0	7	0	7	– 14

Dal - Hill 1 run (Clark)
SF - Gossett 28 FG
Dal - D. Thomas 2 run (Clark)

TEAM STATISTICS	SF	Dal
First Downs	9	16
Rushing	2	9
Passing	7	7
Offensive plays - yards	47 - 239	70 - 244
Rushes - yards	16 - 61	46 - 172
Passes	30 - 14 - 3	18 - 9 - 0
Gross passing yards	184	103
Sacked - yards lost	1 - 6	6 - 31

Net passing yards	178	72
Interceptions - yards	0 - 0	3 - 32
Punts - average	6 - 38.2	6 - 45.0
Punt returns - yards	3 - 10	2 - 4
Kickoff returns - yards	3 - 56	1 - 19
Fumbles - lost	0 - 0	2 - 1
Penalties - yards	1 - 12	2 - 30

Super Bowl VI
Jan. 16, 1972
Tulane Stadium, New Orleans–80,591

Dallas	3	7	7	–	24
Miami	0	3	0	–	3

Dal - Clark 9 FG
Dal - Alworth 7 pass from Staubach (Clark)
Mia - Yepremian 31 FG
Dal - D. Thomas 3 run (Clark)
Dal - Ditka 7 pass from Staubach (Clark)
MVP: Roger Staubach, QB, Dallas

TEAM STATISTICS	Dal	Mia
First Downs	23	10
Rushing	15	3
Passing	8	7
Offensive plays - yards	69 - 352	44 - 185
Rushes - yards	48 - 252	20 - 80
Passes	19 - 12 - 0	23 - 12 - 1
Gross passing yards	119	134
Sacked - yards lost	2 - 19	1 - 29
Net passing yards	100	105
Interceptions - yards	1 - 41	0 - 0
Punts - average	5 - 37.2	5 - 40.0
Punt returns - yards	1 - (-1)	1 - 21
Kickoff returns - yards	2 - 34	5 - 122
Fumbles - lost	1 - 1	2 - 2
Penalties - yards	3 - 15	0 - 0

AFC Divisional Playoff
Dec. 23, 1972
Three Rivers Stadium, Pittsburgh–50,350

Oakland	0	0	0	7	–	7
Pittsburgh	0	0	3	10	–	13

Pit - Gerela 18 FG
Pit - Gerela 29 FG
Oak - Stabler 30 run (Blanda)
Pit - Harris 60 pass from Bradshaw (Gerela)

TEAM STATISTICS	Oak	Pit
First Downs	13	13
Rushing	9	7
Passing	4	6
Offensive plays - yards	65 - 216	64 - 252
Rushes - yards	31 - 138	36 - 108
Passes	30 - 12 - 2	25 - 11 - 1
Gross passing yards	102	175
Sacked - yards lost	4 - 24	3 - 31
Net passing yards	78	144
Interceptions - yards	1 - 7	2 - 0
Punts - average	7 - 45.1	6 - 48.3
Punt returns - yards	1 - 37	3 - 39
Kickoff returns - yards	1 - 26	1 - 21
Fumbles - lost	3 - 2	0 - 0
Penalties - yards	2 - 15	1 - 5

NFC Divisional Playoff
Dec. 23, 1972
Candlestick Park, San Francisco–61,214

Dallas	3	10	0	17	–	30
San Francisco	7	14	7	0	–	28

SF - V. Washington 97 kickoff return (Gossett)
Dal - Fritsch 37 FG
SF - Schreiber 1 run (Gossett)
SF - Schreiber 1 run (Gossett)
Dal - Fritsch 45 FG
Dal - Alworth 28 pass from Morton (Fritsch)
SF - Schreiber 1 run (Gossett)
Dal - Fritsch 27 FG
Dal - Parks 20 pass from Staubach (Fritsch)
Dal - Sellers 10 pass from Staubach (Fritsch)

TEAM STATISTICS	Dal	SF
First Downs	22	13
Rushing	5	7
Passing	15	6
Penalty	2	0
Offensive plays - yards	77 - 402	59 - 255
Rushes - yards	31 - 165	37 - 105
Passes	41 - 20 - 2	22 - 12 - 2
Gross passing yards	270	150
Sacked - yards lost	5 - 33	0 - 0
Net passing yards	237	150
Interceptions - yards	2 - 12	2 - 4
Punts - average	6 - 41.8	6 - 37.3
Punt returns - yards	1 - 2	1 - (-5)
Kickoff returns - yards	3 - 83	5 - 146
Fumbles - lost	4 - 3	5 - 1
Penalties - yards	3 - 35	7 - 56

AFC Divisional Playoff
Dec. 24, 1972
Orange Bowl, Miami–80,010

Cleveland	0	0	7	7	–	14
Miami	10	0	0	10	–	20

Mia - Babb 5 blocked punt return (Yepremian)
Mia - Yepremian 40 FG
Cle - Phipps 5 run (Cockroft)
Mia - Yepremian 46 FG
Cle - Hooker 27 pass from Phipps (Cockroft)
Mia - Kiick 8 run (Yepremian)

TEAM STATISTICS	Cle	Mia
First Downs	15	17
Rushing	9	11
Passing	6	4
Penalty	0	2
Offensive plays - yards	57 - 283	64 - 272
Rushes - yards	32 - 165	47 - 198
Passes	23 - 9 - 5	13 - 6 - 0
Gross passing yards	131	88
Sacked - yards lost	2 - 13	4 - 14
Net passing yards	118	74
Interceptions - yards	0 - 0	5 - 64
Punts - average	6 - 34.7	5 - 42.0
Had blocked	1	0
Punt returns - yards	2 - 46	1 - (-1)
Kickoff returns - yards	3 - 56	0 - 0
Fumbles - lost	2 - 0	2 - 2
Penalties - yards	3 - 25	3 - 25

NFC Divisional Playoff
Dec. 24, 1972
RFK Stadium, Washington–53,140

Green Bay	0	3	0	0	–	3
Washington	0	10	0	6	–	16

GB - Marcol 17 FG
Was - Jefferson 32 pass from Kilmer (Knight)
Was - Knight 42 FG
Was - Knight 35 FG
Was - Knight 46 FG

TEAM STATISTICS	GB	Was
First Downs	10	13
Rushing	2	6
Passing	8	4
Penalty	0	3
Offensive plays - yards	55 - 211	51 - 232
Rushes - yards	29 - 78	36 - 138
Passes	24 - 12 - 1	14 - 7 - 0
Gross passing yards	150	100
Sacked - yards lost	2 - 17	1 - 6
Net passing yards	133	94
Interceptions - yards	0 - 0	1 - 15
Punts - average	8 - 36.6	6 - 46.5
Punt returns - yards	4 - 33	3 - 19
Kickoff returns - yards	4 - 62	2 - 60
Fumbles - lost	0 - 0	1 - 1
Penalties - yards	6 - 54	4 - 39

AFC Championship Game
Dec. 31, 1972
Three Rivers Stadium, Pittsburgh–50,350

Miami	0	7	7	7	–	21
Pittsburgh	7	0	3	7	–	17

Pit - Mullins offensive fumble recovery (Gerela)
Mia - Csonka 9 pass from Morrall (Yepremian)
Pit - Gerela 14 FG
Mia - Kiick 2 run (Yepremian)
Mia - Kiick 3 run (Yepremian)
Pit - Young 12 pass from Bradshaw (Gerela)

TEAM STATISTICS	Mia	Pit
First Downs	19	13
Rushing	11	6
Passing	6	6
Penalty	2	1
Offensive plays - yards	65 - 314	48 - 250
Rushes - yards	49 - 193	26 - 128
Passes	16 - 10 - 1	20 - 10 - 2
Gross passing yards	121	137
Sacked - yards lost	0 - 0	2 - 15
Net passing yards	121	122
Interceptions - yards	2 - 11	1 - 28
Punts - average	4 - 35.5	4 - 51.3
Punt returns - yards	0 - 0	1 - 5
Kickoff returns - yards	1 - 23	3 - 85
Fumbles - lost	0 - 0	2 - 0
Penalties - yards	2 - 19	4 - 30

NFC Championship Game
Dec. 31, 1972
RFK Stadium, Washington–53,129

Dallas	0	3	0	0	–	3
Washington	0	10	0	16	–	26

Was - Knight 18 FG
Was - C. Taylor 15 pass from Kilmer (Knight)
Dal - Fritsch 35 FG
Was - C. Taylor 45 pass from Kilmer (Knight)
Was - Knight 39 FG
Was - Knight 46 FG
Was - Knight 45 FG

TEAM STATISTICS	Dal	Was
First Downs	8	16
Rushing	3	4
Passing	3	11
Penalty	2	1
Offensive plays - yards	45 - 169	62 - 316
Rushes - yards	21 - 96	44 - 122
Passes	21 - 9 - 0	18 - 14 - 0
Gross passing yards	98	194
Sacked - yards lost	3 - 25	0 - 0
Net passing yards	73	194
Interceptions - yards	0 - 0	0 - 0
Punts - average	7 - 43.1	4 - 36.0
Punt returns - yards	3 - (-5)	4 - 10
Kickoff returns - yards	3 - 54	0 - 0
Fumbles - lost	1 - 1	2 - 1
Penalties - yards	4 - 30	4 - 38

Super Bowl VII
Jan. 14, 1973
Memorial Coliseum, Los Angeles—90,192

Miami	7	7	0	0	–	14
Washington	0	0	0	7	–	7

Mia - Twilley 28 pass from Griese (Yepremian)
Mia - Kiick 1 run (Yepremian)
Was - Bass 49 fumble return (Knight)
MVP: Jake Scott, S, Miami

TEAM STATISTICS	Mia	Was
First Downs	12	16
Rushing	7	9
Passing	5	7
Offensive plays - yards	50 - 253	66 - 228
Rushes - yards	37 - 184	36 - 141
Passes	11 - 8 - 1	28 - 14 - 3
Gross passing yards	88	104
Sacked - yards lost	2 - 19	2 - 17
Net passing yards	69	87
Interceptions - yards	3 - 95	1 - 0
Punts - average	7 - 43.0	5 - 31.2
Punt returns - yards	2 - 4	4 - 9
Kickoff returns - yards	2 - 33	3 - 45
Fumbles - lost	2 - 1	1 - 0
Penalties - yards	3 - 35	3 - 25

AFC Divisional Playoff
Dec. 22, 1973
Oakland - Alameda County Coliseum—50,094

Pittsburgh	0	7	0	7	–	14
Oakland	7	3	13	10	–	33

Oak - Hubbard 1 run (Blanda)
Oak - Blanda 25 FG
Pit - B. Pearson 4 pass from Bradshaw (Gerela)
Oak - Blanda 31 FG
Oak - Blanda 22 FG

Oak - W. Brown 54 interception return (Blanda)
Oak - Blanda 10 FG
Pit - Lewis 26 pass from Bradshaw (Gerela)
Oak - Hubbard 1 run (Blanda)

TEAM STATISTICS	Pit	Oak
First Downs	15	24
Rushing	2	14
Passing	10	8
Penalty	3	2
Offensive plays - yards	46 - 223	74 - 361
Rushes - yards	20 - 65	55 - 232
Passes	25 - 12 - 3	17 - 14 - 0
Gross passing yards	167	142
Sacked - yards lost	1 - 9	2 - 13
Net passing yards	158	129
Interceptions - yards	0 - 0	3 - 62
Punts - average	5 - 41.6	2 - 39.0
Punt returns - yards	1 - 20	2 - 11
Kickoff returns - yards	7 - 156	3 - 58
Fumbles - lost	1 - 0	0 - 0
Penalties - yards	4 - 60	9 - 75

NFC Divisional Playoff
Dec. 22, 1973
Metropolitan Stadium, Bloomington—45,475

Washington	0	7	3	10	–	20
Minnesota	0	3	7	17	–	27

Min - Cox 19 FG
Was - L. Brown 3 run (Knight)
Min - B. Brown 2 run (Cox)
Was - Knight 52 FG
Was - Knight 42 FG
Min - Gilliam 28 pass from Tarkenton (Cox)
Min - Gilliam 8 pass from Tarkenton (Cox)
Was - Jefferson 28 pass from Kilmer (Knight)
Min - Cox 30 FG

TEAM STATISTICS	Was	Min
First Downs	18	17
Rushing	10	6
Passing	7	11
Penalty	1	0
Offensive plays - yards	66 - 314	63 - 359
Rushes - yards	42 - 155	34 - 141
Passes	24 - 13 - 1	28 - 16 - 1
Gross passing yards	159	222
Sacked - yards lost	0 - 0	1 - 4
Net passing yards	159	218
Interceptions - yards	1 - 28	1 - 26
Punts - average	4 - 37.3	6 - 31.9
Had blocked	0	1
Punt returns - yards	4 - 18	2 - 3
Kickoff returns - yards	5 - 104	5 - 127
Fumbles - lost	2 - 1	2 - 1
Penalties - yards	0 - 0	2 - 9

AFC Divisional Playoff
Dec. 23, 1973
Orange Bowl, Miami—74,651

Cincinnati	3	13	0	0	–	16
Miami	14	7	10	3	–	34

Mia - Warfield 13 pass from Griese (Yepremian)
Cin - Muhlmann 24 FG

Mia - Csonka 1 run (Yepremian)
Mia - Morris 4 run (Yepremian)
Cin - Craig 45 interception return (Muhlmann)
Cin - Muhlmann 46 FG
Cin - Muhlmann 12 FG
Mia - Mandich 7 pass from Griese (Yepremian)
Mia - Yepremian 50 FG
Mia - Yepremian 46 FG

TEAM STATISTICS	Cin	Mia
First Downs	11	27
Rushing	5	18
Passing	6	9
Offensive plays - yards	50 - 194	71 - 400
Rushes - yards	20 - 97	52 - 241
Passes	27 - 14 - 1	19 - 11 - 2
Gross passing yards	113	159
Sacked - yards lost	3 - 16	0 - 0
Net passing yards	97	159
Interceptions - yards	2 - 45	1 - 19
Punts - average	7 - 36.3	2 - 49.0
Punt returns - yards	2 - 26	2 - 6
Kickoff returns - yards	2 - 42	2 - 14
Fumbles - lost	0 - 0	2 - 1
Penalties - yards	2 - 19	1 - 5

NFC Divisional Playoff
Dec. 23, 1973
Texas Stadium, Irving—62,081

Los Angeles	0	6	0	10	–	16
Dallas	14	3	0	10	–	27

Dal - Hill 3 run (Fritsch)
Dal - Pearson 4 pass from Staubach (Fritsch)
Dal - Fritsch 39 FG
LA - Ray 33 FG
LA - Ray 37 FG
LA - Ray 40 FG
LA - Baker 5 run (Ray)
Dal - Pearson 83 pass from Staubach (Fritsch)
Dal - Fritsch 12 FG

TEAM STATISTICS	LA	Dal
First Downs	11	15
Rushing	5	11
Passing	5	4
Penalty	1	0
Offensive plays - yards	59 - 192	68 - 298
Rushes - yards	30 - 93	45 - 162
Passes	24 - 7 - 1	16 - 8 - 2
Gross passing yards	133	180
Sacked - yards lost	5 - 34	7 - 44
Net passing yards	99	136
Interceptions - yards	2 - 4	1 - 2
Punts - average	5 - 43.6	7 - 46.7
Punt returns - yards	5 - 53	2 - 3
Kickoff returns - yards	6 - 155	2 - 42
Fumbles - lost	2 - 2	2 - 2
Penalties - yards	2 - 20	5 - 44

AFC Championship Game
Dec. 30, 1973
Orange Bowl, Miami—74,384

Oakland	0	0	10	0	–	10
Miami	7	7	3	10	–	27

Mia - Csonka 11 run (Yepremian)

Mia - Csonka 2 run (Yepremian)
Oak - Blanda 21 FG
Mia - Yepremian 42 FG
Oak - Siani 25 pass from Stabler (Blanda)
Mia - Yepremian 27 FG
Mia - Csonka 2 run (Yepremian)

TEAM STATISTICS	Oak	Mia
First Downs	15	21
Rushing	4	18
Passing	9	2
Penalty	2	1
Offensive plays - yards	49 - 236	60 - 292
Rushes - yards	26 - 107	53 - 266
Passes	23 - 15 - 1	6 - 3 - 1
Gross passing yards	129	34
Sacked - yards lost	0 - 0	1 - 8
Net passing yards	129	26
Interceptions - yards	1 - 0	1 - 29
Punts - average	2 - 51.0	1 - 39.0
Punt returns - yards	1 - 0	2 - 10
Kickoff returns - yards	4 - 89	3 - 90
Fumbles - lost	1 - 0	1 - 0
Penalties - yards	3 - 35	3 - 26

NFC Championship Game
Dec. 30, 1973
Texas Stadium, Irving–59,688

Minnesota	3	7	7	10	–	27
Dallas	0	0	10	0	–	10

Min - Cox 44 FG
Min - Foreman 5 run (Cox)
Dal - Richards 63 punt return (Fritsch)
Min - Gilliam 54 pass from Tarkenton (Cox)
Dal - Fritsch 17 FG
Min - Bryant 63 interception return (Cox)
Min - Cox 34 FG

TEAM STATISTICS	Min	Dal
First Downs	20	9
Rushing	14	3
Passing	6	5
Penalty	0	1
Offensive plays - yards	72 - 306	49 - 153
Rushes - yards	47 - 203	25 - 90
Passes	21 - 10 - 1	21 - 10 - 4
Gross passing yards	133	89
Sacked - yards lost	4 - 30	3 - 26
Net passing yards	103	63
Interceptions - yards	4 - 76	1 - 1
Punts - average	3 - 43.3	4 - 39.5
Punt returns - yards	1 - 0	1 - 63
Kickoff returns - yards	3 - 66	3 - 72
Fumbles - lost	4 - 3	2 - 2
Penalties - yards	3 - 33	2 - 20

Super Bowl VIII
Jan. 13, 1974
Rice Stadium, Houston–68,142

Minnesota	0	0	0	7	–	7
Miami	14	3	7	0	–	24

Mia - Csonka 5 run (Yepremian)
Mia - Kiick 1 run (Yepremian)
Mia - Yepremian 28 FG
Mia - Csonka 2 run (Yepremian)

Min - Tarkenton 4 run (Cox)
MVP: Larry Csonka, RB, Miami

TEAM STATISTICS	Min	Mia
First Downs	14	21
Rushing	5	13
Passing	8	4
Penalty	1	4
Offensive plays - yards	54 - 238	61 - 259
Rushes - yards	24 - 72	53 - 196
Passes	28 - 18 - 1	7 - 6 - 0
Gross passing yards	182	73
Sacked - yards lost	2 - 16	1 - 10
Net passing yards	166	63
Interceptions - yards	0 - 0	1 - 10
Punts - average	5 - 42.2	3 - 39.7
Punt returns - yards	0 - 0	3 - 20
Kickoff returns - yards	4 - 69	2 - 47
Fumbles - lost	2 - 1	1 - 0
Penalties - yards	7 - 65	1 - 4

AFC Divisional Playoff
Dec. 21, 1974
Oakland - Alameda County
Coliseum–52,817

Miami	7	3	6	10	–	26
Oakland	0	7	7	14	–	28

Mia - N. Moore 89 kickoff return (Yepremian)
Oak - C. Smith 31 pass from Stabler (Blanda)
Mia - Yepremian 33 FG
Oak - Biletnikoff 13 pass from Stabler (Blanda)
Mia - Warfield 16 pass from Griese (Yepremian miss)
Mia - Yepremian 46 FG
Oak - Branch 72 pass from Stabler (Blanda)
Mia - Malone 23 run (Yepremian)
Oak - Davis 8 pass from Stabler (Blanda)

TEAM STATISTICS	Mia	Oak
First Downs	18	19
Rushing	10	8
Passing	6	11
Penalty	2	0
Offensive plays - yards	57 - 294	64 - 411
Rushes - yards	41 - 213	32 - 135
Passes	14 - 7 - 1	30 - 20 - 1
Gross passing yards	101	293
Sacked - yards lost	2 - 20	2 - 17
Net passing yards	81	276
Interceptions - yards	1 - 14	1 - 5
Punts - average	6 - 33.2	7 - 42.7
Punt returns - yards	2 - 5	3 - 16
Kickoff returns - yards	5 - 183	6 - 135
Fumbles - lost	0 - 0	0 - 0
Penalties - yards	3 - 15	3 - 59

NFC Divisional Playoff
Dec. 21, 1974
Metropolitan Stadium, Bloomington–44,626

St. Louis	0	7	0	7	–	14
Minnesota	0	7	16	7	–	30

Stl - Thomas 13 pass from Hart (Bakken)
Min - Gilliam 16 pass from Tarkenton (Cox)
Min - Cox 37 FG
Min - N. Wright 20 fumble return (Cox)

Min - Gilliam 38 pass from Tarkenton (Cox miss)
Min - Foreman 4 run (Cox)
StL - Metcalf 11 run (Bakken)

TEAM STATISTICS	StL	Min
First Downs	17	19
Rushing	6	12
Passing	10	7
Penalty	1	0
Offensive plays - yards	67 - 284	66 - 363
Rushes - yards	25 - 100	42 - 197
Passes	40 - 18 - 1	23 - 13 - 2
Gross passing yards	200	169
Sacked - yards lost	2 - 16	1 - 3
Net passing yards	184	166
Interceptions - yards	2 - 17	1 - 18
Punts - average	7 - 36.4	5 - 38.2
Punt returns - yards	3 - 18	1 - 3
Kickoff returns - yards	6 - 99	3 - 49
Fumbles - lost	2 - 1	0 - 0
Penalties - yards	1 - 15	4 - 39

AFC Divisional Playoff
Dec. 22, 1974
Three Rivers Stadium, Pittsburgh–48,321

Buffalo	7	0	7	0	–	14
Pittsburgh	3	26	0	3	–	32

Pit - Gerela 21 FG
Buf - Seymour 22 pass from Ferguson (Leypoldt)
Pit - Bleier 27 pass from Bradshaw (Gerela miss)
Pit - Harris 1 run (Gerela)
Pit - Harris 4 run (Gerela miss)
Pit - Harris 1 run (Gerela)
Buf - Simpson 3 pass from Ferguson (Leypoldt)
Pit - Gerela 22 FG

TEAM STATISTICS	Buf	Pit
First Downs	15	29
Rushing	5	18
Passing	10	9
Penalty	0	2
Offensive plays - yards	47 - 264	72 - 438
Rushes - yards	21 - 100	51 - 235
Passes	26 - 11 - 0	21 - 12 - 0
Gross passing yards	164	203
Sacked - yards lost	0 - 0	0 - 0
Net passing yards	164	203
Interceptions - yards	0 - 0	0 - 0
Punts - average	5 - 39.4	3 - 38.7
Punt returns - yards	2 - 11	4 - 25
Kickoff returns - yards	6 - 118	3 - 86
Fumbles - lost	2 - 1	2 - 0
Penalties - yards	3 - 15	2 - 10

NFC Divisional Playoff
Dec. 22, 1974
Memorial Coliseum, Los Angeles–80,118

Washington	3	7	0	0	–	10
Los Angeles	7	0	3	9	–	19

LA - Klein 10 pass from Harris (Ray)
Was - Bragg 35 FG
Was - Denson 1 run (Bragg)

LA - Ray 37 FG
LA - Ray 26 FG
LA - Robertson 59 interception return (bad snap)

TEAM STATISTICS	Was	LA
First Downs	13	14
Rushing	4	8
Passing	7	6
Penalty	2	0
Offensive plays - yards	58 - 218	66 - 226
Rushes - yards	27 - 49	42 - 131
Passes	30 - 13 - 3	24 - 8 - 2
Gross passing yards	177	95
Sacked - yards lost	1 - 8	0 - 0
Net passing yards	169	95
Interceptions - yards	2 - 24	3 - 71
Punts - average	5 - 45.2	5 - 43.0
Punt returns - yards	5 - 31	2 - 16
Kickoff returns - yards	5 - 95	3 - 82
Fumbles - lost	3 - 3	2 - 0
Penalties - yards	1 - 5	5 - 49

AFC Championship Game
Dec. 29, 1974
Oakland - Alameda County Coliseum–53,515

Pittsburgh	0	3	0	21	– 24
Oakland	3	0	7	3	– 13

Oak - Blanda 40 FG
Pit - Gerela 23 FG
Oak - Branch 38 pass from Stabler (Blanda)
Pit - Harris 8 run (Gerela)
Pit - Swann 6 pass from Bradshaw (Gerela)
Oak - Blanda 24 FG
Pit - Harris 21 run (Gerela)

TEAM STATISTICS	Pit	Oak
First Downs	20	15
Rushing	11	0
Passing	7	13
Penalty	2	2
Offensive plays - yards	68 - 305	59 - 278
Rushes - yards	50 - 224	21 - 29
Passes	17 - 8 - 1	36 - 19 - 3
Gross passing yards	95	271
Sacked - yards lost	1 - 14	2 - 22
Net passing yards	95	249
Interceptions - yards	3 - 56	1 - 37
Punts - average	4 - 41.0	5 - 43.4
Punt returns - yards	4 - 45	0 - 0
Kickoff returns - yards	4 - 104	5 - 105
Fumbles - lost	3 - 2	0 - 0
Penalties - yards	4 - 30	5 - 60

NFC Championship Game
Dec. 29, 1974
Metropolitan Stadium, Bloomington–47,404

Los Angeles	0	3	0	7	– 10
Minnesota	0	7	0	7	– 14

Min - Lash 29 pass from Tarkenton (Cox)
LA - Ray 27 FG
Min - Osborn 1 run (Cox)
LA - Jackson 44 pass from Harris (Ray)

TEAM STATISTICS	LA	Min
First Downs	15	18
Rushing	5	9
Passing	10	7
Penalty	0	2
Offensive plays - yards	58 - 340	69 - 269
Rushes - yards	33 - 121	47 - 164
Passes	23 - 13 - 2	20 - 10 - 1
Gross passing yards	248	123
Sacked - yards lost	2 - 29	2 - 18
Net passing yards	219	105
Interceptions - yards	1 - 0	2 - 16
Punts - average	5 - 43.8	6 - 39.2
Punt returns - yards	5 - 19	4 - 23
Kickoff returns - yards	3 - 57	3 - 78
Fumbles - lost	3 - 3	5 - 2
Penalties - yards	7 - 70	2 - 20

Super Bowl IX
Jan. 12, 1975
Tulane Stadium, New Orleans–80,997

Pittsburgh	0	2	7	7	– 16
Minnesota	0	0	0	6	– 6

Pit - Safety, White tackled Tarkenton in end zone
Pit - Harris 9 run (Gerela)
Min - T. Brown blocked punt recovery (Cox miss)
Pit - Brown 4 pass from Bradshaw (Gerela)
MVP: Franco Harris, RB, Pittsburgh

TEAM STATISTICS	Pit	Min
First Downs	17	9
Rushing	11	2
Passing	5	5
Penalty	1	2
Offensive plays - yards	73 - 333	47 - 119
Rushes - yards	57 - 249	21 - 17
Passes	14 - 9 - 0	26 - 11 - 3
Gross passing yards	96	102
Sacked - yards lost	2 - 12	0 - 0
Net passing yards	84	102
Interceptions - yards	3 - 46	0 - 0
Punts - average	7 - 34.7	6 - 37.2
Had blocked	1	0
Punt returns - yards	5 - 36	4 - 12
Kickoff returns - yards	3 - 32	3 - 50
Fumbles - lost	4 - 2	3 - 2
Penalties - yards	8 - 122	4 - 18

AFC Divisional Playoff
Dec. 27, 1975
Three Rivers Stadium, Pittsburgh–49,053

Baltimore	0	7	3	0	– 10
Pittsburgh	7	0	7	14	– 28

Pit - Harris 8 run (Gerela)
Bal - Doughty 5 pass from Domres (Linhart)
Bal - Linhart 21 FG
Pit - Bleier 7 run (Gerela)
Pit - Bradshaw 2 run (Gerela)
Pit - Russell 93 fumble return (Gerela)

TEAM STATISTICS	Bal	Pit
First Downs	10	16
Rushing	4	13

Passing	4	3
Penalty	2	0
Offensive plays - yards	68 - 154	59 - 287
Rushes - yards	41 - 82	43 - 211
Passes	22 - 8 - 2	13 - 8 - 2
Gross passing yards	100	103
Sacked - yards lost	5 - 28	3 - 27
Net passing yards	72	76
Interceptions - yards	2 - 67	2 - 26
Punts - average	9 - 40.1	4 - 39.8
Punt returns - yards	4 - 30	4 - 46
Kickoff returns - yards	5 - 103	3 - 74
Fumbles - lost	2 - 1	3 - 3
Penalties - yards	6 - 53	5 - 45

NFC Divisional Playoff
Dec. 27, 1975
Memorial Coliseum, Los Angeles–72,650

St. Louis	0	9	7	7	– 23
Los Angeles	14	14	0	7	– 35

LA - Jaworski 5 run (Dempsey)
LA - Jack Youngblood 47 interception return (Dempsey)
LA - Simpson 65 interception return (Dempsey)
StL - Otis 2 run (Bakken miss)
LA - H. Jackson 66 pass from Jaworski (Dempsey)
StL - Bakken 29 FG
StL - M. Gray 11 pass from Hart (Bakken)
LA - Jessie 2 fumble recovery (Dempsey)
StL - Jones 3 run (Bakken)

TEAM STATISTICS	StL	LA
First Downs	22	26
Rushing	5	14
Passing	16	10
Penalty	1	2
Offensive plays - yards	70 - 363	73 - 440
Rushes - yards	27 - 95	50 - 237
Passes	41 - 22 - 3	23 - 12 - 0
Gross passing yards	291	203
Sacked - yards lost	2 - 23	0 - 0
Net passing yards	268	203
Interceptions - yards	0 - 0	3 - 130
Punts - average	6 - 42.7	5 - 31.6
Punt returns - yards	2 - 6	3 - 19
Kickoff returns - yards	7 - 191	5 - 90
Fumbles - lost	3 - 2	5 - 3
Penalties - yards	6 - 70	5 - 38

AFC Divisional Playoff
Dec. 28, 1975
Oakland - Alameda County Coliseum–53,039

Cincinnati	0	7	7	14	– 28
Oakland	3	14	7	7	– 31

Oak - Blanda 27 FG
Oak - Siani 9 pass from Stabler (Blanda)
Cin - Fritts 1 run (Green)
Oak - Moore 8 pass from Stabler (Blanda)
Oak - Banaszak 6 run (Blanda)
Cin - Elliott 6 run (Green)
Oak - Casper 2 pass from Stabler (Blanda)
Cin - Joiner 25 pass from Anderson (Green)

Cin - Curtis 14 pass from Anderson (Green)

TEAM STATISTICS	Cin	Oak
First Downs	17	27
Rushing	8	9
Passing	6	15
Penalty	3	3
Offensive plays - yards	57 - 258	75 - 358
Rushes - yards	25 - 97	51 - 173
Passes	27 - 17 - 0	23 - 17 - 1
Gross passing yards	201	199
Sacked - yards lost	5 - 40	1 - 14
Net passing yards	161	185
Interceptions - yards	1 - 34	0 - 0
Punts - average	6 - 35.8	1 - 38.0
Punt returns - yards	1 - 7	4 - 64
Kickoff returns - yards	4 - 71	5 - 121
Fumbles - lost	1 - 0	1 - 1
Penalties - yards	5 - 37	7 - 64

NFC Divisional Playoff
Dec. 28, 1975
Metropolitan Stadium, Bloomington–46,425

Dallas	0	0	7	10	– 17
Minnesota	0	7	0	7	– 14

Min - Foreman 1 run (Cox)
Dal - Dennison 4 run (Fritsch)
Dal - Fritsch 24 FG
Min - McClanahan 1 run (Cox)
Dal - D. Pearson 50 pass from Staubach (Fritsch)

TEAM STATISTICS	Dal	Min
First Downs	19	12
Rushing	7	6
Passing	11	6
Penalty	1	0
Offensive plays - yards	76 - 356	57 - 215
Rushes - yards	42 - 131	27 - 115
Passes	29 - 17 - 0	26 - 12 - 1
Gross passing yards	246	135
Sacked - yards lost	5 - 21	4 - 35
Net passing yards	225	100
Interceptions - yards	1 - 0	0 - 0
Punts - average	6 - 38.5	7 - 39.6
Punt returns - yards	4 - 18	4 - 5
Kickoff returns - yards	3 - 39	4 - 41
Fumbles - lost	4 - 1	2 - 0
Penalties - yards	4 - 30	7 - 60

AFC Championship Game
Jan. 4, 1976
Three Rivers Stadium, Pittsburgh–49,103

Oakland	0	0	0	10	– 10
Pittsburgh	0	3	0	13	– 16

Pit - Gerela 36 FG
Pit - Harris 25 run (Gerela)
Oak - Siani 14 pass from Stabler (Blanda)
Pit - Stallworth 20 pass from Bradshaw (bad snap)
Oak - Blanda 41 FG

TEAM STATISTICS	Oak	Pit
First Downs	18	16
Rushing	3	5
Passing	13	10
Penalty	2	1
Offensive plays - yards	76 - 321	64 - 332
Rushes - yards	32 - 93	39 - 117
Passes	42 - 18 - 2	25 - 15 - 3
Gross passing yards	246	215
Sacked - yards lost	2 - 18	0 - 0
Net passing yards	228	215
Interceptions - yards	3 - 19	2 - 34
Punts - average	8 - 37.8	4 - 38.5
Punt returns - yards	1 - 0	3 - 28
Kickoff returns - yards	4 - 71	3 - 59
Fumbles - lost	4 - 3	5 - 5
Penalties - yards	4 - 40	3 - 32

NFC Championship Game
Jan. 4, 1976
Memorial Coliseum, Los Angeles–84,483

Dallas	7	14	13	3	– 37
Los Angeles	0	0	0	7	– 7

Dal - P. Pearson 18 pass from Staubach (Fritsch)
Dal - Richards 4 pass from Staubach (Fritsch)
Dal - P. Pearson 15 pass from Staubach (Fritsch)
Dal - P. Pearson 19 pass from Staubach (Fritsch)
Dal - Fritsch 40 FG
Dal - Fritsch 26 FG
LA - Cappelletti 1 run (Dempsey)
Dal - Fritsch 26 FG

TEAM STATISTICS	Dal	LA
First Downs	24	9
Rushing	8	1
Passing	15	7
Penalty	1	1
Offensive plays - yards	78 - 441	45 - 118
Rushes - yards	50 - 195	16 - 22
Passes	28 - 18 - 1	24 - 11 - 3
Gross passing yards	246	147
Sacked - yards lost	0 - 0	5 - 51
Net passing yards	246	96
Interceptions - yards	3 - 42	1 - 37
Punts - average	4 - 34.8	7 - 35.4
Punt returns - yards	4 - 26	2 - 3
Kickoff returns - yards	2 - 47	8 - 167
Fumbles - lost	1 - 0	1 - 0
Penalties - yards	5 - 59	4 - 25

Super Bowl X
Jan. 18, 1976
Orange Bowl, Miami–80,187

Dallas	7	3	0	7	– 17
Pittsburgh	7	0	0	14	– 21

Dal - D. Pearson 29 pass from Staubach (Fritsch)
Pit - Grossman 7 pass from Bradshaw (Gerela)
Dal - Fritsch 36 FG
Pit - Safety, Harrison blocked Hoopes' punt
Pit - Gerela 36 FG
Pit - Gerela 18 FG
Pit - Swann 64 pass from Bradshaw (Gerela miss)
Dal - P. Howard 34 pass from Staubach (Fritsch)
MVP: Lynn Swann, WR, Pittsburgh

TEAM STATISTICS	Dal	Pit
First Downs	14	13
Rushing	6	7
Passing	8	6
Offensive plays - yards	62 - 270	67 - 339
Rushes - yards	31 - 108	46 - 149
Passes	24 - 15 - 3	19 - 9 - 0
Gross passing yards	204	209
Sacked - yards lost	7 - 42	2 - 19
Net passing yards	162	190
Interceptions - yards	0 - 0	3 - 89
Punts - average	7 - 35.0	4 - 39.8
Had blocked	1	0
Punt returns - yards	1 - 5	4 - 31
Kickoff returns - yards	4 - 96	4 - 89
Fumbles - lost	4 - 0	4 - 0
Penalties - yards	2 - 20	0 - 0

AFC Divisional Playoff
Dec. 18, 1976
Oakland - Alameda County Coliseum–53,045

New England	7	0	14	0	– 21
Oakland	3	7	0	14	– 24

NE - Johnson 1 run (Smith)
Oak - Mann 40 FG
Oak - Biletnikoff 31 pass from Stabler (Mann)
NE - Francis 26 pass from Grogan (Smith)
NE - Phillips 3 run (Smith)
Oak - van Eeghen 1 run (Mann)
Oak - Stabler 1 run (Mann)

TEAM STATISTICS	NE	Oak
First Downs	23	20
Rushing	10	5
Passing	6	13
Penalty	7	2
Offensive plays - yards	73 - 331	60 - 282
Rushes - yards	49 - 164	24 - 81
Passes	24 - 12 - 2	32 - 19 - 0
Gross passing yards	167	233
Sacked - yards lost	0 - 0	4 - 32
Net passing yards	167	201
Interceptions - yards	0 - 0	2 - 18
Punts - average	3 - 44.0	5 - 37.8
Punt returns - yards	1 - 13	3 - 53
Kickoff returns - yards	5 - 67	4 - 119
Fumbles - lost	1 - 1	1 - 1
Penalties - yards	10 - 83	11 - 93

NFC Divisional Playoff
Dec. 18, 1976
Metropolitan Stadium, Bloomington–47,221

Washington	3	0	3	14	– 20
Minnesota	14	7	14	0	– 35

Min - Voigt 18 pass from Tarkenton (Cox)
Was - Moseley 47 FG
Min - S. White 27 pass from Tarkenton (Cox)
Min - Foreman 2 run (Cox)
Min - Foreman 30 run (Cox)

Was - Moseley 35 FG
Min - S. White 9 pass from Tarkenton (Cox)
Was - Grant 12 pass from Kilmer (Moseley)
Was - Jefferson 3 pass from Kilmer (Moseley)

TEAM STATISTICS	Was	Min
First Downs	19	21
Rushing	3	11
Passing	15	9
Penalty	1	1
Offensive plays - yards	68 - 365	69 - 384
Rushes - yards	18 - 75	46 - 221
Passes	49 - 26 - 2	22 - 12 - 2
Gross passing yards	298	170
Sacked - yards lost	1 - 8	1 - 7
Net passing yards	290	163
Interceptions - yards	2 - 25	2 - 0
Punts - average	6 - 32.8	6 - 46.0
Punt returns - yards	6 - 55	2 - 12
Kickoff returns - yards	6 - 136	3 - 41
Fumbles - lost	0 - 0	2 - 0
Penalties - yards	7 - 57	5 - 30

AFC Divisional Playoff
Dec. 19, 1976
Memorial Stadium, Baltimore–60,020

Pittsburgh	9	17	0	14	– 40
Baltimore	7	0	0	7	– 14

Pit - Lewis 76 pass from Bradshaw (Gerela miss)
Pit - Gerela 45 FG
Bal - Carr 17 pass from Jones (Linhart)
Pit - Harrison 1 run (Gerela)
Pit - Swann 29 pass from Bradshaw (Gerela)
Pit - Gerela 25 FG
Pit - Swann 11 pass from Bradshaw (Gerela)
Bal - Leaks 1 run (Linhart)
Pit - Harrison 10 run (Mansfield)

TEAM STATISTICS	Pit	Bal
First Downs	29	16
Rushing	12	4
Passing	15	8
Penalty	2	4
Offensive plays - yards	65 - 526	53 - 170
Rushes - yards	40 - 225	23 - 71
Passes	24 - 19 - 0	25 - 11 - 2
Gross passing yards	308	144
Sacked - yards lost	1 - 7	5 - 45
Net passing yards	301	99
Interceptions - yards	2 - 38	0 - 0
Punts - average	1 - 33.0	4 - 40.5
Punt returns - yards	3 - 12	1 - 11
Kickoff returns - yards	2 - 79	7 - 110
Fumbles - lost	2 - 1	0 - 0
Penalties - yards	12 - 88	7 - 59

NFC Divisional Playoff
Dec. 19, 1976
Texas Stadium, Irving–62,436

Los Angeles	0	7	0	7	– 14
Dallas	3	7	0	2	– 12

Dal - Herrera 44 FG
LA - Haden 4 run (Dempsey)
Dal - Laidlaw 1 run (Herrera)

LA - McCutcheon 1 run (Dempsey)
Dal - Safety, Jensen tackled R. Jackson in end zone

TEAM STATISTICS	LA	Dal
First Downs	17	14
Rushing	6	4
Passing	8	9
Penalty	3	1
Offensive plays - yards	73 - 250	69 - 211
Rushes - yards	49 - 120	28 - 85
Passes	21 - 10 - 3	37 - 15 - 3
Gross passing yards	152	150
Sacked - yards lost	3 - 22	4 - 24
Net passing yards	130	126
Interceptions - yards	3 - 20	3 - 9
Punts - average	9 - 28.1	6 - 38.7
Had blocked	2	0
Punt returns - yards	2 - 23	4 - 64
Kickoff returns - yards	3 - 71	2 - 49
Fumbles - lost	0 - 0	3 - 1
Penalties - yards	8 - 94	6 - 34

AFC Championship Game
Dec. 26, 1976
Oakland - Alameda County Coliseum–53,739

Pittsburgh	0	7	0	0	– 7
Oakland	3	14	7	0	– 24

Oak - Mann 39 FG
Oak - Davis 1 run (Mann)
Pit - Harrison 3 run (Mansfield)
Oak - Bankston 4 pass from Stabler (Mann)
Oak - Banaszak 5 pass from Stabler (Mann)

TEAM STATISTICS	Pit	Oak
First Downs	13	15
Rushing	3	7
Passing	8	7
Penalty	2	1
Offensive plays - yards	59 - 237	68 - 228
Rushes - yards	21 - 72	51 - 157
Passes	35 - 14 - 1	16 - 10 - 0
Gross passing yards	176	88
Sacked - yards lost	3 - 11	1 - 17
Net passing yards	165	71
Interceptions - yards	0 - 0	1 - 25
Punts - average	7 - 37.3	7 - 44.0
Punt returns - yards	3 - 18	2 - 19
Kickoff returns - yards	5 - 97	2 - 35
Fumbles - lost	1 - 0	2 - 0
Penalties - yards	5 - 29	7 - 34

NFC Championship Game
Dec. 26, 1976
Metropolitan Stadium, Bloomington–47,191

Los Angeles	0	0	13	0	– 13
Minnesota	7	3	7	7	– 24

Min - Bryant 90 blocked FG return (Cox)
Min - Cox 25 FG
Min - Foreman 1 run (Cox)
LA - McCutcheon 10 run (Dempsey miss)
LA - H. Jackson 5 pass from Haden (Dempsey)
Min - Johnson 12 run (Cox)

TEAM STATISTICS	LA	Min
First Downs	21	13
Rushing	14	6
Passing	7	7
Offensive plays - yards	71 - 336	60 - 267
Rushes - yards	46 - 193	29 - 158
Passes	22 - 9 - 2	27 - 12 - 1
Gross passing yards	161	143
Sacked - yards lost	3 - 18	4 - 34
Net passing yards	143	109
Interceptions - yards	1 - 0	2 - 17
Punts - average	7 - 29.4	8 - 35.1
Had blocked	1	0
Punt returns - yards	7 - 50	3 - 20
Kickoff returns - yards	5 - 79	3 - 69
Fumbles - lost	4 - 2	1 - 1
Penalties - yards	3 - 33	4 - 32

Super Bowl XI
Jan. 9, 1977
Rose Bowl, Pasadena–103,438

Oakland	0	16	3	13	– 32
Minnesota	0	0	7	7	– 14

Oak - Mann 24 FG
Oak - Casper 1 pass from Stabler (Mann)
Oak - Banaszak 1 run (Mann miss)
Oak - Mann 40 FG
Min - S. White 8 pass from Tarkenton (Cox)
Oak - Banaszak 2 run (Mann)
Oak - Brown 75 interception return (Mann miss)
Min - Voigt 13 pass from Lee (Cox)
MVP: Fred Biletnikoff, WR, Oakland

TEAM STATISTICS	Oak	Min
First Downs	21	20
Rushing	13	2
Passing	8	15
Penalty	0	3
Offensive plays - yards	73 - 429	71 - 353
Rushes - yards	52 - 266	26 - 71
Passes	19 - 12 - 0	44 - 24 - 2
Gross passing yards	180	286
Sacked - yards lost	2 - 17	1 - 4
Net passing yards	163	282
Interceptions - yards	2 - 91	0 - 0
Punts - average	5 - 32.4	7 - 37.9
Had blocked	1	0
Punt returns - yards	4 - 43	3 - 14
Kickoff returns - yards	2 - 47	7 - 136
Fumbles - lost	0 - 0	1 - 1
Penalties - yards	4 - 30	2 - 25

AFC Divisional Playoff
Dec. 24, 1977
Mile High Stadium, Denver–75,011

Pittsburgh	0	14	0	7	– 21
Denver	7	7	7	13	– 34

Den - Lytle 7 run (Turner)
Pit - Bradshaw 1 run (Gerela)
Den - Armstrong 10 run (Turner)
Pit - Harris 1 run (Gerela)
Den - Odoms 30 pass from Morton (Turner)
Pit - Brown 1 pass from Bradshaw (Gerela)
Den - Turner 44 FG

Den - Turner 25 FG
Den - Dolbin 34 pass from Morton (Turner)

TEAM STATISTICS	Pit	Den
First Downs	18	15
Rushing	10	5
Passing	8	9
Penalty	0	1
Offensive plays - yards	76 - 304	61 - 258
Rushes - yards	39 - 127	37 - 103
Passes	37 - 19 - 3	23 - 11 - 0
Gross passing yards	177	164
Sacked - yards lost	0 - 0	1 - 9
Net passing yards	177	155
Interceptions - yards	0 - 0	3 - 64
Punts - average	6 - 34.0	5 - 37.6
Had blocked	1	0
Punt returns - yards	4 - 31	4 - 12
Kickoff returns - yards	5 - 104	4 - 85
Fumbles - lost	2 - 1	3 - 1
Penalties - yards	10 - 67	3 - 20

AFC Divisional Playoff
Dec. 24, 1977
Memorial Stadium, Baltimore—59,925

Oakland	7	0	14	10	0	6	– 37
Baltimore	0	10	7	14	0	0	– 31

Oak - Davis 30 run (Mann)
Bal - Laird 61 interception return (Linhart)
Bal - Linhart 36 FG
Oak - Casper 8 pass from Stabler (Mann)
Bal - Johnson 87 kickoff return (Linhart)
Oak - Casper 10 pass from Stabler (Mann)
Bal - R. Lee 1 run (Linhart)
Oak - Banaszak 1 run (Mann)
Bal - R. Lee 13 run (Linhart)
Oak - Mann 22 FG
Oak - Casper 10 pass from Stabler (no attempt)

TEAM STATISTICS	Oak	Bal
First Downs	28	22
Rushing	8	10
Passing	17	8
Penalty	3	4
Offensive plays - yards	89 - 491	82 - 301
Rushes - yards	47 - 167	50 - 187
Passes	40 - 21 - 2	26 - 12 - 0
Gross passing yards	345	164
Sacked - yards lost	2 - 21	6 - 50
Net passing yards	324	114
Interceptions - yards	0 - 0	2 - 61
Punts - average	8 - 46.8	13 - 33.7
Had blocked	0	1
Punt returns - yards	6 - 42	3 - 22
Kickoff returns - yards	6 - 186	6 - 193
Fumbles - lost	4 - 2	1 - 0
Penalties - yards	7 - 65	8 - 82

NFC Divisional Playoff
Dec. 26, 1977
Texas Stadium, Irving—62,920

Chicago	0	0	0	7	– 7
Dallas	7	10	17	3	– 37

Dal - Dennison 2 run (Herrera)
Dal - DuPree 28 pass from Staubach (Herrera)
Dal - Herrera 21 FG
Dal - Dorsett 23 run (Herrera)
Dal - Herrera 31 FG
Dal - Dorsett 7 run (Herrera)
Dal - Herrera 27 FG
Chi - Schubert 34 pass from Avellini (Thomas)

TEAM STATISTICS	Chi	Dal
First Downs	15	20
Rushing	4	13
Passing	9	7
Penalty	2	0
Offensive plays - yards	55 - 224	64 - 365
Rushes - yards	27 - 81	48 - 233
Passes	25 - 15 - 4	14 - 8 - 1
Gross passing yards	177	134
Sacked - yards lost	3 - 34	2 - 2
Net passing yards	143	132
Interceptions - yards	1 - 8	4 - 76
Punts - average	6 - 42.5	3 - 37.0
Punt returns - yards	1 - 7	4 - 38
Kickoff returns - yards	8 - 162	2 - 44
Fumbles - lost	3 - 3	2 - 2
Penalties - yards	4 - 43	3 - 35

NFC Divisional Playoff
Dec. 26, 1977
Memorial Coliseum, Los Angeles—62,538

Minnesota	7	0	0	7	– 14
Los Angeles	0	0	0	7	– 7

Min - Foreman 5 run (Cox)
Min - Johnson 1 run (Cox)
LA - H. Jackson 1 pass from Haden (Septien)

TEAM STATISTICS	Min	LA
First Downs	14	14
Rushing	9	7
Passing	4	6
Penalty	1	1
Offensive plays - yards	60 - 189	62 - 267
Rushes - yards	49 - 144	29 - 149
Passes	10 - 5 - 0	32 - 14 - 3
Gross passing yards	57	130
Sacked - yards lost	1 - 12	1 - 12
Net passing yards	45	118
Interceptions - yards	3 - 17	0 - 0
Punts - average	8 - 40.8	5 - 37.6
Punt returns - yards	2 - 30	5 - 34
Kickoff returns - yards	1 - 25	2 - 43
Fumbles - lost	1 - 0	1 - 0
Penalties - yards	7 - 50	2 - 15

AFC Championship Game
Jan. 1, 1978
Mile High Stadium, Denver—74,982

Oakland	3	0	0	14	– 17
Denver	7	0	7	6	– 20

Oak - Mann 20 FG
Den - Moses 74 pass from Morton (Turner)
Den - Keyworth 1 run (Turner)
Oak - Casper 7 pass from Stabler (Mann)
Den - Moses 12 pass from Morton (fumbled snap)
Oak - Casper 17 pass from Stabler (Mann)

TEAM STATISTICS	Oak	Den
First Downs	20	16
Rushing	6	6
Passing	11	8
Penalty	3	2
Offensive plays - yards	72 - 298	58 - 308
Rushes - yards	36 - 94	37 - 91
Passes	35 - 17 - 1	20 - 10 - 1
Gross passing yards	215	224
Sacked - yards lost	1 - 11	1 - 7
Net passing yards	204	217
Interceptions - yards	1 - 11	1 - 14
Punts - average	5 - 36.0	4 - 40.8
Punt returns - yards	2 - 5	2 - 12
Kickoff returns - yards	4 - 136	4 - 67
Fumbles - lost	2 - 2	0 - 0
Penalties - yards	2 - 6	2 - 12

NFC Championship Game
Jan. 1, 1978
Texas Stadium, Irving—61,968

Minnesota	0	6	0	0	– 6
Dallas	6	10	0	7	– 23

Dal - Richards 32 pass from Staubach (Herrera miss)
Dal - Newhouse 5 run (Herrera)
Min - Cox 32 FG
Min - Cox 37 FG
Dal - Herrera 21 FG
Dal - Dorsett 11 run (Herrera)

TEAM STATISTICS	Min	Dal
First Downs	12	16
Rushing	4	7
Passing	6	7
Penalty	2	2
Offensive plays - yards	63 - 214	64 - 328
Rushes - yards	30 - 66	39 - 170
Passes	31 - 14 - 1	23 - 12 - 1
Gross passing yards	158	165
Sacked - yards lost	2 - 10	2 - 7
Net passing yards	148	158
Interceptions - yards	1 - 0	1 - 1
Punts - average	8 - 34.8	8 - 36.6
Punt returns - yards	3 - 2	5 - 57
Kickoff returns - yards	5 - 122	3 - 36
Fumbles - lost	5 - 3	1 - 1
Penalties - yards	5 - 32	5 - 84

Super Bowl XII
Jan. 15, 1978
Louisiana Superdome, New Orleans—75,583

Dallas	10	3	7	7	– 27
Denver	0	0	10	0	– 10

Dal - Dorsett 3 run (Herrera)
Dal - Herrera 35 FG
Dal - Herrera 43 FG
Den - Turner 47 FG
Dal - Johnson 45 pass from Staubach (Herrera)
Den - Lytle 1 run (Turner)
Dal - Richards 29 pass from Newhouse (Herrera)
MVP: Randy White, DT, Dallas and Harvey Martin, DE, Dallas

TEAM STATISTICS	Dal	Den
First Downs	17	11
Rushing	8	8
Passing	8	1
Penalty	1	2
Offensive plays - yards	71 - 325	58 - 156
Rushes - yards	38 - 143	29 - 121
Passes	28 - 19 - 0	25 - 8 - 4
Gross passing yards	217	61
Sacked - yards lost	5 - 35	4 - 26
Net passing yards	182	35
Interceptions - yards	4 - 46	0 - 0
Punts - average	5 - 41.6	4 - 38.3
Punt returns - yards	1 - 0	4 - 22
Kickoff returns - yards	3 - 51	6 - 173
Fumbles - lost	6 - 2	4 - 4
Penalties - yards	12 - 94	8 - 60

AFC Wild Card Game
Dec. 24, 1978
Orange Bowl, Miami–70,036

Houston	7	0	0	10	–	17
Miami	7	0	0	2	–	9

Mia - Tillman 13 pass from Griese (Yepremian)
Hou - T. Wilson 13 pass from Pastorini (Fritsch)
Hou - Fritsch 35 FG
Hou - Campbell 1 run (Fritsch)
Mia - Safety, Pastorini stepped out of end zone

TEAM STATISTICS	Hou	Mia
First Downs	23	14
Rushing	9	6
Passing	14	7
Penalty	0	1
Offensive plays - yards	77 - 455	57 - 209
Rushes - yards	45 - 165	25 - 91
Passes	30 - 20 - 0	30 - 12 - 3
Gross passing yards	306	137
Sacked - yards lost	2 - 16	2 - 19
Net passing yards	290	118
Interceptions - yards	3 - 4	0 - 0
Punts - average	5 - 44.0	5 - 48.6
Punt returns - yards	3 - 11	1 - 24
Kickoff returns - yards	2 - 55	5 - 109
Fumbles - lost	3 - 1	2 - 2
Penalties - yards	5 - 37	1 - 5

NFC Wild Card Game
Dec. 24, 1978
Atlanta-Fulton County Stadium–49,447

Philadelphia	6	0	7	0	–	13
Atlanta	0	0	0	14	–	14

Phi - Carmichael 13 pass from Jaworski (Michel miss)
Phi - Montgomery 1 run (Michel)
Atl - Mitchell 20 pass from Bartkowski (Mazzetti)
Atl - Francis 37 pass from Bartkowski (Mazzetti)

TEAM STATISTICS	Phi	Atl
First Downs	15	14
Rushing	4	4
Passing	10	9
Penalty	1	1
Offensive plays - yards	70 - 217	61 - 298
Rushes - yards	32 - 53	27 - 75
Passes	35 - 19 - 0	32 - 18 - 2
Gross passing yards	190	243
Sacked - yards lost	3 - 26	2 - 20
Net passing yards	164	223
Interceptions - yards	2 - 48	0 - 0
Punts - average	9 - 33.7	7 - 33.1
Punt returns - yards	3 - 27	5 - 14
Kickoff returns - yards	3 - 72	3 - 69
Fumbles - lost	3 - 2	3 - 3
Penalties - yards	5 - 60	6 - 63

AFC Divisional Playoff
Dec. 30, 1978
Three Rivers Stadium, Pittsburgh–48,921

Denver	3	7	0	0	–	10
Pittsburgh	6	13	0	14	–	33

Den - Turner 37 FG
Pit - Harris 1 run (Gerela miss)
Pit - Harris 18 run (Gerela)
Pit - Gerela 24 FG
Den - Preston 3 run (Turner)
Pit - Gerela 27 FG
Pit - Stallworth 45 pass from Bradshaw (Gerela)
Pit - Swann 38 pass from Bradshaw (Gerela)

TEAM STATISTICS	Den	Pit
First Downs	15	24
Rushing	5	9
Passing	8	11
Penalty	2	4
Offensive plays - yards	55 - 218	69 - 425
Rushes - yards	27 - 87	40 - 153
Passes	22 - 12 - 0	29 - 16 - 1
Gross passing yards	168	272
Sacked - yards lost	6 - 37	0 - 0
Net passing yards	131	272
Interceptions - yards	1 - 10	0 - 0
Punts - average	6 - 34.0	2 - 36.0
Punt returns - yards	2 - 30	4 - 28
Kickoff returns - yards	6 - 70	3 - 65
Fumbles - lost	2 - 2	4 - 1
Penalties - yards	8 - 104	11 - 88

NFC Divisional Playoff
Dec. 30, 1978
Texas Stadium, Irving–60,338

Atlanta	7	13	0	0	–	20
Dallas	10	3	7	7	–	27

Dal - Septien 34 FG
Atl - Bean 14 run (Mazzetti)
Dal - Laidlaw 13 run (Septien)
Atl - Mazzetti 42 FG
Dal - Septien 48 FG
Atl - Francis 17 pass from Bartkowski (Mazzetti)
Atl - Mazzetti 22 FG
Dal - Smith 2 pass from D. White (Septien)
Dal - Laidlaw 1 run (Septien)

TEAM STATISTICS	Atl	Dal
First Downs	16	26
Rushing	10	9
Passing	5	15
Penalty	1	2
Offensive plays - yards	64 - 216	75 - 369
Rushes - yards	36 - 164	37 - 148
Passes	23 - 8 - 3	37 - 17 - 1
Gross passing yards	95	232
Sacked - yards lost	5 - 43	1 - 11
Net passing yards	52	221
Interceptions - yards	1 - 0	3 - 37
Punts - average	6 - 37.5	3 - 36.0
Punt returns - yards	0 - 0	4 - 32
Kickoff returns - yards	5 - 124	5 - 85
Fumbles - lost	0 - 0	6 - 3
Penalties - yards	7 - 69	7 - 65

AFC Divisional Playoff
Dec. 31, 1978
Schaefer Stadium, Foxboro–60,881

Houston	0	21	3	7	–	31
New England	0	0	7	7	–	14

Hou - Burrough 71 pass from Pastorini (Fritsch)
Hou - Barber 19 pass from Pastorini (Fritsch)
Hou - Barber 13 pass from Pastorini (Fritsch)
Hou - Fritsch 30 FG
NE - Jackson 24 pass from Johnson (Posey)
NE - Francis 24 pass from Owen (Posey)
Hou - Campbell 2 run (Fritsch)

TEAM STATISTICS	Hou	NE
First Downs	21	15
Rushing	11	6
Passing	8	8
Penalty	2	1
Offensive plays - yards	72 - 344	59 - 263
Rushes - yards	54 - 174	20 - 83
Passes	15 - 12 - 1	35 - 16 - 3
Gross passing yards	200	206
Sacked - yards lost	3 - 30	4 - 26
Net passing yards	170	180
Interceptions - yards	3 - 46	1 - 0
Punts - average	5 - 34.8	4 - 43.3
Punt returns - yards	3 - 6	3 - 6
Kickoff returns - yards	3 - 53	5 - 136
Fumbles - lost	1 - 0	2 - 0
Penalties - yards	2 - 25	8 - 92

NFC Divisional Playoff
Dec. 31, 1978
Memorial Coliseum, Los Angeles–69,631

Minnesota	3	7	0	0	–	10
Los Angeles	0	10	14	10	–	34

Min - Danmeier 42 FG
LA - Miller 9 pass from Haden (Corral)
LA - Corral 43 FG
Min - Rashad 1 pass from Tarkenton (Danmeier)
LA - Bryant 3 run (Corral)
LA - Jessie 27 pass from Haden (Corral)
LA - Corral 28 FG
LA - Jodat 3 run (Corral)

TEAM STATISTICS	Min	LA
First Downs	12	25
Rushing	2	13
Passing	10	12
Offensive plays - yards	55 - 244	77 - 409

Rushes - yards	16 - 36	48 - 200
Passes	38 - 18 - 2	29 - 15 - 1
Gross passing yards	219	209
Sacked - yards lost	1 - 11	0 - 0
Net passing yards	208	209
Interceptions - yards	1 - 11	2 - 17
Punts - average	6 - 41.3	4 - 31.0
Had blocked	0	1
Punt returns - yards	2 - (-1)	6 - 82
Kickoff returns - yards	6 - 126	3 - 58
Fumbles - lost	2 - 0	1 - 0
Penalties - yards	2 - 12	4 - 35

AFC Championship Game
Jan. 7, 1979
Three Rivers Stadium, Pittsburgh–49,417

Houston	0	3	2	0	– 5
Pittsburgh	14	17	3	0	– 34

Pit - Harris 7 run (Gerela)
Pit - Bleier 15 run (Gerela)
Hou - Fritsch 19 FG
Pit - Swann 29 pass from Bradshaw (Gerela)
Pit - Stallworth 17 pass from Bradshaw (Gerela)
Pit - Gerela 37 FG
Pit - Gerela 22 FG
Hou - Safety, Washington tackled Bleier in end zone

TEAM STATISTICS	Hou	Pit
First Downs	10	21
Rushing	5	8
Passing	3	11
Penalty	2	2
Offensive plays - yards	56 - 142	66 - 379
Rushes - yards	26 - 72	47 - 179
Passes	12 - 26 - 5	11 - 19 - 2
Gross passing yards	96	200
Sacked - yards lost	4 - 26	0 - 0
Net passing yards	70	200
Interceptions - yards	2 - 0	5 - 90
Punts - average	6 - 39.5	1 - 53.0
Punt returns - yards	0 - 0	6 - 91
Kickoff returns - yards	8 - 179	2 - 36
Fumbles - lost	6 - 4	6 - 3
Penalties - yards	5 - 48	4 - 32

NFC Championship Game
Jan. 7, 1979
Memorial Coliseum, Los Angeles–67,470

Dallas	0	0	7	21	– 28
Los Angeles	0	0	0	0	– 0

Dal - Dorsett 5 run (Septien)
Dal - Laidlaw 4 pass from Staubach (Septien)
Dal - DuPree 11 pass from Staubach (Septien)
Dal - Henderson 68 interception return (Septien)

TEAM STATISTICS	Dal	LA
First Downs	16	15
Rushing	7	3
Passing	7	11
Penalty	2	1
Offensive plays - yards	61 - 235	69 - 277
Rushes - yards	33 - 126	31 - 81

Passes	13 - 25 - 2	14 - 35 - 5
Gross passing yards	126	206
Sacked - yards lost	3 - 17	3 - 10
Net passing yards	109	196
Interceptions - yards	5 - 123	2 - 0
Punts - average	8 - 35.0	5 - 39.0
Punt returns - yards	4 - 40	2 - 22
Kickoff returns - yards	0 - 0	5 - 106
Fumbles - lost	2 - 1	3 - 2
Penalties - yards	10 - 85	5 - 40

Super Bowl XIII
Jan. 21, 1979
Orange Bowl, Miami–79,484

Pittsburgh	7	14	0	14	– 35
Dallas	7	7	3	14	– 31

Pit - Stallworth 28 pass from Bradshaw (Gerela)
Dal - Hill 39 pass from Staubach (Septien)
Dal - Hegman 37 fumble return (Septien)
Pit - Stallworth 75 pass from Bradshaw (Gerela)
Pit - Bleier 7 pass from Bradshaw (Gerela)
Dal - Septien 27 FG
Pit - Harris 22 run (Gerela)
Pit - Swann 18 pass from Bradshaw (Gerela)
Dal - DuPree 7 pass from Staubach (Septien)
Dal - Johnson 4 pass from Staubach (Septien)
MVP: Terry Bradshaw, QB, Pittsburgh

TEAM STATISTICS	Pit	Dal
First Downs	19	20
Rushing	2	6
Passing	15	13
Penalty	2	1
Offensive plays - yards	58 - 357	67 - 330
Rushes - yards	24 - 66	32 - 154
Passes	17 - 30 - 1	17 - 30 - 1
Gross passing yards	318	228
Sacked - yards lost	4 - 27	5 - 52
Net passing yards	291	176
Interceptions - yards	1 - 13	1 - 21
Punts - average	3 - 43.0	5 - 39.6
Punt returns - yards	4 - 27	2 - 33
Kickoff returns - yards	3 - 45	6 - 104
Fumbles - lost	2 - 2	3 - 2
Penalties - yards	5 - 35	9 - 89

AFC Wild Card Game
Dec. 23, 1979
Astrodome, Houston–48,776

Denver	7	0	0	0	– 7
Houston	3	7	0	3	– 13

Hou - Fritsch 31 FG
Den - Preston 7 pass from Morton (Turner)
Hou - Campbell 3 run (Fritsch)
Hou - Fritsch 20 FG

TEAM STATISTICS	Den	Hou
First Downs	17	15
Rushing	7	8
Passing	9	6
Penalty	1	1
Offensive plays - yards	65 - 216	65 - 282
Rushes - yards	32 - 112	42 - 135

Passes	27 - 14 - 1	22 - 10 - 2
Gross passing yards	144	158
Sacked - yards lost	6 - 40	1 - 11
Net passing yards	104	147
Interceptions - yards	2 - 12	1 - 15
Punts - average	6 - 46.0	5 - 43.2
Punt returns - yards	2 - 25	5 - 42
Kickoff returns - yards	4 - 83	1 - 26
Fumbles - lost	1 - 0	0 - 0
Penalties - yards	7 - 70	2 - 19

NFC Wild Card Game
Dec. 23, 1979
Veterans Stadium, Philadelphia–69,397

Chicago	7	10	0	0	– 17
Philadelphia	7	3	7	10	– 27

Phi - Carmichael 17 pass from Jaworski (Franklin)
Chi - Payton 2 run (Thomas)
Phi - Franklin 29 FG
Chi - Payton 1 run (Thomas)
Chi - Thomas 30 FG
Phi - Carmichael 29 pass from Jaworski (Franklin)
Phi - Campfield 63 pass from Jaworski (Franklin)
Phi - Franklin 34 FG

TEAM STATISTICS	Chi	Phi
First Downs	15	18
Rushing	7	8
Passing	7	8
Penalty	1	2
Offensive plays - yards	60 - 241	63 - 315
Rushes - yards	29 - 99	37 - 139
Passes	30 - 13 - 2	23 - 12 - 1
Gross passing yards	142	204
Sacked - yards lost	1 - 0	3 - 28
Net passing yards	142	176
Interceptions - yards	1 - 25	2 - 5
Punts - average	6 - 39.0	4 - 40.5
Punt returns - yards	0 - 0	4 - 51
Kickoff returns - yards	6 - 124	3 - 76
Fumbles - lost	1 - 1	4 - 2
Penalties - yards	4 - 35	4 - 46

AFC Divisional Playoff
Dec. 29, 1979
San Diego Stadium–51,192

Houston	0	10	7	0	– 17
San Diego	7	0	7	0	– 14

SD - C. Williams 1 run (Wood)
Hou - Fritsch 26 FG
Hou - Clark 1 run (Fritsch)
SD - Mitchell 8 run (Wood)
Hou - Renfro 47 pass from Nielsen (Fritsch)

TEAM STATISTICS	Hou	SD
First Downs	15	25
Rushing	9	6
Passing	5	17
Penalty	1	2
Offensive plays - yards	59 - 259	68 - 380
Rushes - yards	40 - 148	19 - 63
Passes	19 - 10 - 1	47 - 25 - 5

Gross passing yards	111	333
Sacked - yards lost	0 - 0	2 - 16
Net passing yards	111	317
Interceptions - yards	5 - 11	1 - 0
Punts - average	6 - 40.7	2 - 32.0
Punt returns - yards	1 - 25	3 - 29
Kickoff returns - yards	3 - 53	4 - 84
Fumbles - lost	0 - 0	0 - 0
Penalties - yards	5 - 45	6 - 30

NFC Divisional Playoff
Dec. 29, 1979
Tampa Stadium–71,402

Philadelphia	0	7	3	7	– 17
Tampa Bay	7	10	0	7	– 24

TB - Bell 4 run (O'Donoghue)
TB - O'Donoghue 40 FG
TB - Bell 1 run (O'Donoghue)
Phi - Smith 11 pass from Jaworski (Franklin)
Phi - Franklin 42 FG
TB - Giles 9 pass from Williams (O'Donoghue)
Phi - Carmichael 37 pass from Jaworski (Franklin)

TEAM STATISTICS	Phi	TB
First Downs	15	17
Rushing	4	10
Passing	10	6
Penalty	1	1
Offensive plays - yards	58 - 227	70 - 318
Rushes - yards	18 - 48	55 - 186
Passes	38 - 15 - 0	15 - 7 - 1
Gross passing yards	199	132
Sacked - yards lost	2 - 20	0 - 0
Net passing yards	179	132
Interceptions - yards	1 - 37	0 - 0
Punts - average	5 - 44.2	5 - 42.6
Punt returns - yards	4 - 48	3 - 33
Kickoff returns - yards	4 - 87	4 - 59
Fumbles - lost	2 - 1	0 - 0
Penalties - yards	8 - 62	9 - 105

AFC Divisional Playoff
Dec. 30, 1979
Three Rivers Stadium, Pittsburgh–50,214

Miami	0	0	7	7	– 14
Pittsburgh	20	0	7	7	– 34

Pit - Thornton 1 run (Bahr)
Pit - Stallworth 17 pass from Bradshaw (Bahr miss)
Pit - Swann 20 pass from Bradshaw (Bahr)
Mia - Harris 7 pass from Griese (von Schamann)
Pit - Bleier 1 run (Bahr)
Pit - Harris 5 run (Bahr)
Mia - Csonka 1 run (von Schamann)

TEAM STATISTICS	Mia	Pit
First Downs	16	27
Rushing	2	14
Passing	11	12
Penalty	3	1
Offensive plays - yards	65 - 249	72 - 379
Rushes - yards	22 - 25	40 - 159

Passes	40 - 22 - 2	31 - 21 - 0
Gross passing yards	243	230
Sacked - yards lost	3 - 19	1 - 10
Net passing yards	224	220
Interceptions - yards	0 - 0	2 - 3
Punts - average	4 - 36.3	2 - 29.5
Punt returns - yards	0 - 0	4 - 31
Kickoff returns - yards	6 - 87	2 - 46
Fumbles - lost	0 - 0	3 - 3
Penalties - yards	4 - 35	8 - 41

NFC Divisional Playoff
Dec. 30, 1979
Texas Stadium, Irving–64,792

Los Angeles	0	14	0	7	– 21
Dallas	2	3	7	7	– 19

Dal - Safety, R. White tackled Ferragamo in end zone
LA - Tyler 32 pass from Ferragamo (Corral)
Dal - Septien 33 FG
LA - R. Smith 43 pass from Ferragamo (Corral)
Dal - Springs 1 run (Septien)
Dal - Saldi 2 pass from Staubach (Septien)
LA - Waddy 50 pass from Ferragamo (Corral)

TEAM STATISTICS	LA	Dal
First Downs	16	17
Rushing	8	8
Passing	7	8
Penalty	1	1
Offensive plays - yards	61 - 361	64 - 306
Rushes - yards	39 - 159	34 - 156
Passes	21 - 9 - 2	29 - 13 - 1
Gross passing yards	210	150
Sacked - yards lost	1 - 8	1 - 0
Net passing yards	202	150
Interceptions - yards	1 - 21	2 - 40
Punts - average	5 - 41.4	8 - 36.8
Punt returns - yards	3 - 17	2 - 10
Kickoff returns - yards	4 - 76	4 - 79
Fumbles - lost	0 - 0	0 - 0
Penalties - yards	6 - 44	6 - 55

AFC Championship Game
Jan. 6, 1980
Three Rivers Stadium, Pittsburgh–50,475

Houston	7	3	0	3	– 13
Pittsburgh	3	14	0	10	– 27

Hou - Perry 75 interception return (Fritsch)
Pit - Bahr 21 FG
Hou - Fritsch 21 FG
Pit - Cunningham 16 pass from Bradshaw (Bahr)
Pit - Stallworth 20 pass from Bradshaw (Bahr)
Hou - Fritsch 23 FG
Pit - Bahr 39 FG
Pit - Bleier 4 run (Bahr)

TEAM STATISTICS	Hou	Pit
First Downs	11	22
Rushing	2	9
Passing	7	13
Penalty	2	0
Offensive plays - yards	52 - 227	69 - 358

Rushes - yards	22 - 24	36 - 161
Passes	20 - 29 - 1	18 - 30 - 1
Gross passing yards	212	219
Sacked - yards lost	1 - 9	3 - 22
Net passing yards	203	197
Interceptions - yards	1 - 75	1 - 0
Punts - average	4 - 30.0	3 - 51.0
Punt returns - yards	3 - 8	3 - 8
Kickoff returns - yards	6 - 64	4 - 82
Fumbles - lost	4 - 2	1 - 1
Penalties - yards	2 - 10	5 - 34

NFC Championship Game
Jan. 6, 1980
Tampa Stadium–72,033

Los Angeles	0	6	0	3	– 9
Tampa Bay	0	0	0	0	– 0

LA - Corral 19 FG
LA - Corral 21 FG
LA - Corral 23 FG

TEAM STATISTICS	LA	TB
First Downs	23	7
Rushing	13	3
Passing	8	4
Penalty	2	0
Offensive plays - yards	77 - 369	54 - 177
Rushes - yards	53 - 216	26 - 92
Passes	12 - 23 - 0	5 - 27 - 1
Gross passing yards	163	96
Sacked - yards lost	1 - 10	1 - 11
Net passing yards	153	85
Interceptions - yards	1 - 10	0 - 0
Punts - average	5 - 37.2	8 - 37.1
Punt returns - yards	6 - 67	3 - 14
Kickoff returns - yards	1 - 27	4 - 106
Fumbles - lost	1 - 1	1 - 0
Penalties - yards	3 - 20	4 - 45

Super Bowl XIV
Jan. 20, 1980
Rose Bowl, Pasadena–103,985

Pittsburgh	3	7	7	14	– 31
Los Angeles	7	6	6	0	– 19

Pit - Bahr 41 FG
LA - Bryant 1 run (Corral)
Pit - Harris 1 run (Bahr)
LA - Corral 31 FG
LA - Corral 45 FG
Pit - Swann 47 pass from Bradshaw (Bahr)
LA - Smith 24 pass from McCutcheon (Corral miss)
Pit - Stallworth 73 pass from Bradshaw (Bahr)
Pit - Harris 1 run (Bahr)
MVP: Terry Bradshaw, QB, Pittsburgh

TEAM STATISTICS	LA	Pit
First Downs	16	19
Rushing	6	8
Passing	9	10
Penalty	1	1
Offensive plays - yards	59 - 301	58 - 393
Rushes - yards	29 - 107	37 - 84
Passes	16 - 26 - 1	14 - 21 - 3
Gross passing yards	236	309

Sacked - yards lost	4 - 42	0 - 0
Net passing yards	194	309
Interceptions - yards	3 - 21	1 - 16
Punts - average	5 - 44.0	2 - 42.5
Punt returns - yards	1 - 4	4 - 31
Kickoff returns - yards	6 - 79	5 - 162
Fumbles - lost	0 - 0	0 - 0
Penalties - yards	2 - 26	6 - 65

AFC Wild Card Game
Dec. 28, 1980
Oakland - Alameda County
Coliseum–52,762

Houston	7	0	0	0	– 7
Oakland	3	7	0	17	– 27

Oak - Bahr 47 FG
Hou - Campbell 1 run (Fritsch)
Oak - Christensen 1 pass from Plunkett (Bahr)
Oak - Whittington 44 pass from Plunkett (Bahr)
Oak - Bahr 37 FG
Oak - Hayes 20 interception return (Bahr)

TEAM STATISTICS	Hou	Oak
First Downs	18	12
Rushing	5	4
Passing	11	7
Penalty	2	1
Offensive plays - yards	67 - 275	61 - 250
Rushes - yards	33 - 97	35 - 111
Passes	27 - 15 - 2	23 - 8 - 1
Gross passing yards	243	168
Sacked - yards lost	7 - 65	3 - 29
Net passing yards	178	139
Interceptions - yards	1 - 0	2 - 26
Punts - average	9 - 44.0	9 - 51.1
Punt returns - yards	7 - 84	6 - 29
Kickoff returns - yards	6 - 118	2 - 47
Fumbles - lost	1 - 1	2 - 0
Penalties - yards	8 - 64	14 - 91

NFC Wild Card Game
Dec. 28, 1980
Texas Stadium, Irving–64,533

Los Angeles	6	7	0	0	– 13
Dallas	3	10	14	7	– 34

Dal - Septien 28 FG
LA - J. Thomas 1 run (Corral miss)
Dal - Septien 29 FG
LA - Dennard 21 pass from Ferragamo (Corral)
Dal - Dorsett 12 run (Septien)
Dal - Dorsett 10 pass from D. White (Septien)
Dal - Johnson 35 pass from D. White (Septien)
Dal - D. Pearson 11 pass from D. White (Septien)

TEAM STATISTICS	LA	Dal
First Downs	15	29
Rushing	6	19
Passing	7	9
Penalty	2	1
Offensive plays - yards	55 - 260	71 - 528
Rushes - yards	24 - 92	46 - 338
Passes	30 - 14 - 3	25 - 12 - 3
Gross passing yards	176	190

Sacked - yards lost	1 - 8	0 - 0
Net passing yards	168	190
Interceptions - yards	3 - 51	3 - 22
Punts - average	6 - 39.3	2 - 44.5
Punt returns - yards	1 - 2	5 - 81
Kickoff returns - yards	6 - 120	3 - 72
Fumbles - lost	1 - 0	2 - 0
Penalties - yards	5 - 50	11 - 79

AFC Divisional Playoff
Jan. 3, 1981
Jack Murphy Stadium, San Diego–52,028

Buffalo	0	14	0	0	– 14
San Diego	3	0	7	10	– 20

SD - Benirschke 22 FG
Buf - Leaks 1 run (Mike - Mayer)
Buf - Lewis 9 pass from Ferguson (Mike - Mayer)
SD - Joiner 9 pass from Fouts (Benirschke)
SD - Benirschke 22 FG
SD - Smith 50 pass from Fouts (Benirschke)

TEAM STATISTICS	Buf	SD
First Downs	17	21
Rushing	6	6
Passing	9	14
Penalty	2	1
Offensive plays - yards	66 - 244	64 - 397
Rushes - yards	33 - 97	25 - 96
Passes	30 - 15 - 3	37 - 22 - 1
Gross passing yards	180	314
Sacked - yards lost	3 - 33	2 - 13
Net passing yards	147	301
Interceptions - yards	1 - 0	3 - 47
Punts - average	6 - 44.5	4 - 27.8
Had blocked	0	1
Punt returns - yards	2 - 13	3 - 29
Kickoff returns - yards	5 - 84	3 - 50
Fumbles - lost	0 - 0	3 - 2
Penalties - yards	5 - 40	6 - 66

NFC Divisional Playoff
Jan. 3, 1981
Veterans Stadium, Philadelphia–68,434

Minnesota	7	7	2	0	– 16
Philadelphia	0	7	14	10	– 31

Min - S. White 30 pass from Kramer (Danmeier)
Min - Brown 1 run (Danmeier)
Phi - Carmichael 9 pass from Jaworski (Franklin)
Phi - Montgomery 8 run (Franklin)
Min - Safety, Martin and Blair tackled Jaworski in end zone
Phi - Montgomery 5 run (Franklin)
Phi - Franklin 33 FG
Phi - Harrington 2 run (Franklin)

TEAM STATISTICS	Min	Phi
First Downs	14	24
Rushing	3	12
Passing	10	12
Penalty	1	0
Offensive plays - yards	55 - 215	82 - 305
Rushes - yards	13 - 36	42 - 126

Passes	39 - 19 - 5	38 - 17 - 2
Gross passing yards	209	190
Sacked - yards lost	3 - 30	2 - 11
Net passing yards	179	179
Interceptions - yards	2 - 0	5 - 22
Punts - average	5 - 40.0	4 - 33.8
Punt returns - yards	2 - 18	3 - 21
Kickoff returns - yards	7 - 117	3 - 55
Fumbles - lost	3 - 3	1 - 1
Penalties - yards	5 - 27	4 - 30

AFC Divisional Playoff
Jan. 4, 1981
Municipal Stadium, Cleveland–77,655

Oakland	0	7	0	7	– 14
Cleveland	0	6	6	0	– 12

Cle - Bolton 42 interception return (Cockroft miss)
Oak - van Eeghen 1 run (Bahr)
Cle - Cockroft 30 FG
Cle - Cockroft 30 FG
Oak - van Eeghen 1 run (Bahr)

TEAM STATISTICS	Oak	Cle
First Downs	12	17
Rushing	4	6
Passing	8	8
Penalty	0	3
Offensive plays - yards	70 - 208	69 - 254
Rushes - yards	38 - 76	27 - 85
Passes	30 - 14 - 2	40 - 13 - 3
Gross passing yards	149	183
Sacked - yards lost	2 - 17	2 - 14
Net passing yards	132	169
Interceptions - yards	3 - 3	2 - 42
Punts - average	9 - 38.3	6 - 39.5
Punt returns - yards	1 - 1	7 - 81
Kickoff returns - yards	4 - 65	3 - 75
Fumbles - lost	2 - 1	6 - 1
Penalties - yards	5 - 39	2 - 10

NFC Divisional Playoff
Jan. 4, 1981
Atlanta-Fulton County Stadium–60,022

Dallas	3	7	0	20	– 30
Atlanta	10	7	7	3	– 27

Atl - Mazzetti 38 FG
Atl - Jenkins 60 pass from Bartkowski (Mazzetti)
Dal - Septien 38 FG
Dal - DuPree 5 pass from D. White (Septien)
Atl - Cain 1 run (Mazzetti)
Atl - Andrews 12 pass from Bartkowski (Mazzetti)
Dal - Newhouse 1 run (Septien)
Atl - Mazzetti 34 FG
Dal - D. Pearson 14 pass from D. White (Septien)
Dal - D. Pearson 23 pass from D. White (bad snap)

TEAM STATISTICS	Dal	Atl
First Downs	22	18
Rushing	5	6
Passing	16	11

Penalty	1	1
Offensive plays - yards	65 - 422	64 - 371
Rushes - yards	24 - 112	27 - 86
Passes	40 - 25 - 1	33 - 18 - 1
Gross passing yards	322	320
Sacked - yards lost	1 - 12	4 - 35
Net passing yards	310	285
Interceptions - yards	1 - 0	1 - 22
Punts - average	4 - 38.8	4 - 36.0
Punt returns - yards	2 - (-4)	3 - 8
Kickoff returns - yards	6 - 104	5 - 108
Fumbles - lost	4 - 1	1 - 1
Penalties - yards	6 - 72	4 - 48

AFC Championship Game
Jan. 11, 1981
Jack Murphy Stadium, San Diego–52,428

Oakland	21	7	3	3	– 34
San Diego	7	7	10	3	– 27

Oak - Chester 65 pass from Plunkett (Bahr)
SD - Joiner 48 pass from Fouts (Benirschke)
Oak - Plunkett 5 run (Bahr)
Oak - King 21 pass from Plunkett (Bahr)
Oak - van Eeghen 3 run (Bahr)
SD - Joiner 8 pass from Fouts (Benirschke)
SD - Benirschke 26 FG
SD - Muncie 6 run (Benirschke)
Oak - Bahr 27 FG
Oak - Bahr 33 FG
SD - Benirschke 27 FG

TEAM STATISTICS	Oak	SD
First Downs	21	26
Rushing	8	6
Passing	12	17
Penalty	1	3
Offensive plays - yards	66 - 362	71 - 434
Rushes - yards	42 - 138	23 - 83
Passes	18 - 14 - 0	46 - 23 - 2
Gross passing yards	261	364
Sacked - yards lost	6 - 37	2 - 13
Net passing yards	224	351
Interceptions - yards	2 - 41	0 - 0
Punts - average	4 - 56.0	2 - 40.5
Punt returns - yards	2 - 20	2 - 41
Kickoff returns - yards	6 - 103	6 - 99
Fumbles - lost	0 - 0	5 - 1
Penalties - yards	7 - 54	6 - 45

NFC Championship Game
Jan. 11, 1981
Veterans Stadium, Philadelphia–70,696

Dallas	0	7	0	0	– 7
Philadelphia	7	0	10	3	– 20

Phi - Montgomery 42 run (Franklin)
Dal - Dorsett 3 run (Septien)
Phi - Franklin 26 FG
Phi - Harris 9 run (Franklin)
Phi - Franklin 20 FG

TEAM STATISTICS	Dal	Phi
First Downs	11	19
Rushing	5	13
Passing	6	5
Penalty	0	1

Offensive plays - yards	55 - 206	71 - 340
Rushes - yards	22 - 90	40 - 263
Passes	32 - 12 - 1	29 - 9 - 2
Gross passing yards	127	91
Sacked - yards lost	1 - 11	2 - 14
Net passing yards	116	77
Interceptions - yards	2 - 0	1 - 5
Punts - average	7 - 33.7	4 - 34.3
Punt returns - yards	3 - 4	6 - 69
Kickoff returns - yards	5 - 104	2 - 40
Fumbles - lost	5 - 3	4 - 0
Penalties - yards	5 - 40	5 - 45

Super Bowl XV
Jan. 25, 1981
Louisiana Superdome, New Orleans–76,135

Oakland	14	0	10	3	– 27
Philadelphia	0	3	0	7	– 10

Oak - Branch 2 pass from Plunkett (Bahr)
Oak - King 80 pass from Plunkett (Bahr)
Phi - Franklin 30 FG
Oak - Branch 29 pass from Plunkett (Bahr)
Oak - Bahr 46 FG
Phi - Krepfle 8 pass from Jaworski (Franklin)
Oak - Bahr 35 FG

MVP: Jim Plunkett, QB, Oakland

TEAM STATISTICS	Oak	Phi
First Downs	17	19
Rushing	6	3
Passing	10	14
Penalty	1	2
Offensive plays - yards	56 - 377	64 - 360
Rushes - yards	34 - 117	26 - 69
Passes	21 - 13 - 0	38 - 18 - 3
Gross passing yards	261	291
Sacked - yards lost	1 - 1	0 - 0
Net passing yards	260	291
Interceptions - yards	3 - 44	0 - 0
Punts - average	3 - 42.0	3 - 36.7
Punt returns - yards	2 - 1	3 - 20
Kickoff returns - yards	3 - 48	6 - 87
Fumbles - lost	0 - 0	1 - 1
Penalties - yards	5 - 37	6 - 57

AFC Wild Card Game
Dec. 27, 1981
Shea Stadium, New York–57,050

Buffalo	17	7	0	7	– 31
New York	0	10	3	14	– 27

Buf - Romes 26 fumble return (Mike - Mayer)
Buf - Lewis 50 pass from Ferguson (Mike - Mayer)
Buf - Mike - Mayer 29 FG
Buf - Lewis 26 pass from Ferguson (Mike - Mayer)
NY - Shuler 30 pass from Todd (Leahy)
NY - Leahy 26 FG
NY - Leahy 19 FG
Buf - Cribbs 45 run (Mike - Mayer)
NY - B. Jones 30 pass from Todd (Leahy)
NY - Long 1 run (Leahy)

TEAM STATISTICS	Buf	NY
First Downs	15	23

Rushing	4	3
Passing	11	17
Penalty	0	3
Offensive plays - yards	58 - 321	77 - 419
Rushes - yards	22 - 91	22 - 71
Passes	34 - 17 - 4	50 - 28 - 4
Gross passing yards	268	377
Sacked - yards lost	2 - 38	5 - 29
Net passing yards	230	348
Interceptions - yards	4 - 79	4 - 62
Punts - average	4 - 43.8	4 - 33.0
Punt returns - yards	2 - 11	3 - 31
Kickoff returns - yards	6 - 101	5 - 110
Fumbles - lost	1 - 0	3 - 1
Penalties - yards	8 - 62	6 - 55

NFC Wild Card Game
Dec. 27, 1981
Veterans Stadium, Philadelphia–71,611

New York	20	7	0	0	– 27
Philadelphia	0	7	7	7	– 21

NY - Bright 9 pass from Brunner (Danelo miss)
NY - Mistler 10 pass from Brunner (Danelo)
NY - Haynes fumble recovery (Danelo)
Phi - Carmichael 15 pass from Jaworski (Franklin)
NY - Mullady 22 pass from Brunner (Danelo)
Phi - Montgomery 6 run (Franklin)
Phi - Montgomery 1 run (Franklin)

TEAM STATISTICS	NY	Phi
First Downs	16	19
Rushing	10	8
Passing	6	8
Penalty	0	3
Offensive plays - yards	57 - 275	56 - 226
Rushes - yards	42 - 183	29 - 93
Passes	14 - 9 - 1	24 - 13 - 0
Gross passing yards	96	154
Sacked - yards lost	1 - 4	3 - 21
Net passing yards	92	133
Interceptions - yards	0 - 0	1 - 1
Punts - average	4 - 44.8	7 - 42.4
Punt returns - yards	5 - 41	3 - 16
Kickoff returns - yards	4 - 87	5 - 59
Fumbles - lost	1 - 0	5 - 2
Penalties - yards	5 - 54	4 - 23

AFC Divisional Playoff
Jan. 2, 1982
Orange Bowl, Miami–73,735

San Diego	24	0	7	3	– 41	
Miami	0	17	14	7	0	– 38

SD - Benirschke 32 FG
SD - Chandler 56 punt return (Benirschke)
SD - Muncie 1 run (Benirschke)
SD - Brooks 8 pass from Fouts (Benirschke)
Mia - von Schamann 34 FG
Mia - Rose 1 pass from Strock (von Schamann)
Mia - Nathan 25 lateral from Harris 15 pass from Strock (von Schamann)
Mia - Rose 15 pass from Strock (von Schamann)

SD - Winslow 25 pass from Fouts (Benirschke)
Mia - Hardy 50 pass from Strock (von Schamann)
Mia - Nathan 12 run (von Schamann)
SD - Brooks 9 pass from Fouts (Benirschke)
SD - Benirschke 29 FG

TEAM STATISTICS	SD	Mia
First Downs	34	25
Rushing	10	3
Passing	21	21
Penalty	3	1
Offensive plays - yards	85 - 564	79 - 472
Rushes - yards	29 - 149	28 - 78
Passes	54 - 33 - 1	48 - 31 - 2
Gross passing yards	433	423
Sacked - yards lost	2 - 18	3 - 29
Net passing yards	415	394
Interceptions - yards	2 - 35	1 - 30
Punts - average	4 - 40.3	5 - 42.0
Punt returns - yards	2 - 64	1 - 12
Kickoff returns - yards	6 - 100	6 - 98
Fumbles - lost	3 - 3	2 - 1
Penalties - yards	9 - 55	7 - 50

NFC Divisional Playoff
Jan. 2, 1982
Texas Stadium, Irving–64,848

Tampa Bay	0	0	0	0	– 0
Dallas	0	10	21	7	– 38

Dal - Hill 9 pass from D. White (Septien)
Dal - Septien 32 FG
Dal - Springs 1 run (Septien)
Dal - Dorsett 5 run (Septien)
Dal - J. Jones 5 run (Septien)
Dal - Newsome 1 run (Septien)

TEAM STATISTICS	TB	Dal
First Downs	12	26
Rushing	3	15
Passing	7	10
Penalty	2	1
Offensive plays - yards	55 - 222	73 - 345
Rushes - yards	22 - 74	46 - 212
Passes	29 - 10 - 4	26 - 15 - 0
Gross passing yards	187	143
Sacked - yards lost	4 - 39	1 - 10
Net passing yards	148	133
Interceptions - yards	0 - 0	4 - 71
Punts - average	5 - 38.4	4 - 30.0
Punt returns - yards	1 - 1	3 - 53
Kickoff returns - yards	5 - 147	0 - 0
Fumbles - lost	2 - 0	0 - 0
Penalties - yards	10 - 105	8 - 40

AFC Divisional Playoff
Jan. 3, 1982
Riverfront Stadium, Cincinnati–55,240

Buffalo	0	7	7	7	– 21
Cincinnati	14	0	7	7	– 28

Cin - Alexander 4 run (Breech)
Cin - Johnson 1 run (Breech)
Buf - Cribbs 1 run (Mike - Mayer)
Buf - Cribbs 44 run (Mike - Mayer)
Cin - Alexander 20 run (Breech)

Buf - Butler 21 pass from Ferguson (Mike - Mayer)
Cin - Collinsworth 16 pass from Anderson (Breech)

TEAM STATISTICS	Buf	Cin
First Downs	21	22
Rushing	11	11
Passing	8	9
Penalty	2	2
Offensive plays - yards	59 - 336	58 - 305
Rushes - yards	28 - 134	33 - 136
Passes	31 - 15 - 2	21 - 14 - 0
Gross passing yards	202	192
Sacked - yards lost	0 - 0	4 - 23
Net passing yards	202	169
Interceptions - yards	0 - 0	2 - 16
Punts - average	3 - 42.0	4 - 44.5
Punt returns - yards	2 - 8	1 - 27
Kickoff returns - yards	5 - 82	4 - 94
Fumbles - lost	0 - 0	0 - 0
Penalties - yards	6 - 56	5 - 44

NFC Divisional Playoff
Jan. 3, 1982
Candlestick Park, San Francisco–58,360

New York	7	3	7	7	– 24
San Francisco	7	17	0	14	– 38

SF - Young 8 pass from Montana (Wersching)
NY - Gray 72 pass from Brunner (Danelo)
SF - Wersching 22 FG
SF - Solomon 58 pass from Montana (Wersching)
SF - Patton 25 run (Wersching)
NY - Danelo 48 FG
NY - Perkins 59 pass from Brunner (Danelo)
SF - Ring 3 run (Wersching)
SF - Lott 20 interception return (Wersching)
NY - Perkins 17 pass from Brunner (Danelo)

TEAM STATISTICS	NY	SF
First Downs	13	24
Rushing	3	8
Passing	9	13
Penalty	1	3
Offensive plays - yards	61 - 346	68 - 423
Rushes - yards	22 - 65	34 - 135
Passes	37 - 16 - 2	31 - 20 - 1
Gross passing yards	290	304
Sacked - yards lost	2 - 9	3 - 16
Net passing yards	281	288
Interceptions - yards	1 - 2	2 - 32
Punts - average	4 - 43.8	5 - 41.2
Punt returns - yards	3 - 18	1 - 22
Kickoff returns - yards	7 - 142	5 - 93
Fumbles - lost	4 - 2	2 - 0
Penalties - yards	9 - 61	14 - 145

AFC Championship Game
Jan. 10, 1982
Riverfront Stadium, Cincinnati–46,302

San Diego	0	7	0	0	– 7
Cincinnati	10	7	3	7	– 27

Cin - Breech 31 FG
Cin - M. Harris 8 pass from Anderson (Breech)

Cin - Johnson 1 run (Breech)
SD - Winslow 33 pass from Fouts (Benirschke)
Cin - Breech 38 FG
Cin - Bass 3 pass from Anderson (Breech)

TEAM STATISTICS	SD	Cin
First Downs	18	19
Rushing	11	8
Passing	7	11
Offensive plays - yards	61 - 301	59 - 318
Rushes - yards	31 - 128	36 - 143
Passes	28 - 15 - 2	23 - 15 - 0
Gross passing yards	185	175
Sacked - yards lost	2 - 12	0 - 0
Net passing yards	173	175
Interceptions - yards	0 - 0	2 - 24
Punts - average	2 - 29.5	3 - 30.7
Punt returns - yards	1 - 7	0 - 0
Kickoff returns - yards	7 - 132	1 - 40
Fumbles - lost	4 - 2	3 - 1
Penalties - yards	2 - 15	3 - 25

NFC Championship Game
Jan. 10, 1982
Candlestick Park, San Francisco–60,525

Dallas	10	7	0	10	– 27
San Francisco	7	7	7	7	– 28

SF - Solomon 8 pass from Montana (Wersching)
Dal - Septien 44 FG
Dal - Hill 26 pass from D. White (Septien)
SF - Clark 20 pass from Montana (Wersching)
Dal - Dorsett 5 run (Septien)
SF - Davis 2 run (Wersching)
Dal - Septien 22 FG
Dal - Cosbie 21 pass from D. White (Septien)
SF - Clark 6 pass from Montana (Wersching)

TEAM STATISTICS	Dal	SF
First Downs	16	26
Rushing	5	6
Passing	9	17
Penalty	2	3
Offensive plays - yards	60 - 250	69 - 393
Rushes - yards	32 - 115	31 - 127
Passes	24 - 16 - 1	35 - 22 - 3
Gross passing yards	173	286
Sacked - yards lost	4 - 38	3 - 20
Net passing yards	135	266
Interceptions - yards	3 - 0	1 - 5
Punts - average	6 - 39.3	3 - 35.7
Punt returns - yards	3 - 13	3 - 24
Kickoff returns - yards	5 - 89	6 - 107
Fumbles - lost	4 - 2	3 - 3
Penalties - yards	5 - 39	7 - 106

Super Bowl XVI
Jan. 24, 1982
Pontiac Silverdome–81,270

San Francisco	7	13	0	6	– 26
Cincinnati	0	0	7	14	– 21

SF - Montana 1 run (Wersching)
SF - Cooper 11 pass from Montana (Wersching)
SF - Wersching 22 FG

SF - Wersching 26 FG
Cin - Anderson 5 run (Breech)
Cin - Ross 4 pass from Anderson (Breech)
SF - Wersching 40 FG
SF - Wersching 23 FG
Cin - Ross 3 pass from Anderson (Breech)
MVP: Joe Montana, QB, San Francisco

TEAM STATISTICS	SF	Cin
First Downs	20	24
Rushing	9	7
Passing	9	13
Penalty	2	4
Offensive plays - yards	63 - 275	63 - 356
Rushes - yards	40 - 127	24 - 72
Passes	22 - 14 - 0	34 - 25 - 2
Gross passing yards	157	300
Sacked - yards lost	1 - 9	5 - 16
Net passing yards	148	284
Interceptions - yards	2 - 52	0 - 0
Punts - average	4 - 46.3	3 - 43.7
Punt returns - yards	1 - 6	4 - 35
Kickoff returns - yards	2 - 40	7 - 52
Fumbles - lost	2 - 1	2 - 2
Penalties - yards	8 - 65	8 - 57

AFC First-Round Playoff
Jan. 8, 1983
Orange Bowl, Miami–68,842

New England	0	3	3	7	– 13
Miami	0	14	7	7	– 28

NE - J. Smith 23 FG
Mia - Hardy 2 pass from Woodley (von Schamann)
Mia - Franklin 1 run (von Schamann)
NE - J. Smith 42 FG
Mia - Bennett 2 run (von Schamann)
Mia - Hardy 2 pass from Woodley (von Schamann)
NE - Hasselbeck 22 pass from Grogan (J. Smith)

TEAM STATISTICS	NE	Mia
First Downs	14	27
Rushing	6	12
Passing	8	14
Penalty	0	1
Offensive plays - yards	52 - 237	66 - 448
Rushes - yards	18 - 77	45 - 214
Passes	30 - 16 - 2	19 - 16 - 0
Gross passing yards	189	246
Sacked - yards lost	4 - 29	2 - 12
Net passing yards	160	234
Interceptions - yards	0 - 0	2 - 25
Punts - average	5 - 43.6	1 - 51.0
Punt returns - yards	0 - 0	4 - 40
Kickoff returns - yards	3 - 54	3 - 73
Fumbles - lost	1 - 1	3 - 3
Penalties - yards	4 - 27	2 - 15

AFC First-Round Playoff
Jan. 8, 1983
Memorial Coliseum, Los Angeles–56,555

Cleveland	0	10	0	0	– 10
Los Angeles	3	10	7	7	– 27

LA - C. Bahr 27 FG
Cle - M. Bahr 52 FG
LA - Allen 2 run (C. Bahr)
Cle - Feacher 43 pass from McDonald (M. Bahr)
LA - C. Bahr 37 FG
LA - Allen 3 run (C. Bahr)
LA - Hawkins 1 run (C. Bahr)

TEAM STATISTICS	Cle	LA
First Downs	17	25
Rushing	1	11
Passing	11	14
Penalty	5	0
Offensive plays - yards	61 - 284	75 - 510
Rushes - yards	18 - 56	36 - 140
Passes	37 - 18 - 0	37 - 24 - 2
Gross passing yards	281	386
Sacked - yards lost	6 - 53	2 - 16
Net passing yards	228	370
Interceptions - yards	2 - 3	0 - 0
Punts - average	6 - 48.5	3 - 39.0
Punt returns - yards	1 - 10	5 - 45
Kickoff returns - yards	4 - 86	3 - 83
Fumbles - lost	2 - 1	2 - 0
Penalties - yards	4 - 35	6 - 65

NFC First-Round Playoff
Jan. 8, 1983
RFK Stadium, Washington–55,045

Detroit	0	0	7	0	– 7
Washington	10	14	7	0	– 31

Was - White 77 interception return (Moseley)
Was - Moseley 26 FG
Was - Garrett 21 pass from Theismann (Moseley)
Was - Garrett 21 pass from Theismann (Moseley)
Was - Garrett 27 pass from Theismann (Moseley)
Det - Hill 15 pass from Hipple (Murray)

TEAM STATISTICS	Det	Was
First Downs	20	18
Rushing	6	10
Passing	12	8
Penalty	2	0
Offensive plays - yards	63 - 364	59 - 366
Rushes - yards	21 - 95	38 - 175
Passes	38 - 22 - 2	19 - 14 - 0
Gross passing yards	298	210
Sacked - yards lost	4 - 29	2 - 19
Net passing yards	269	191
Interceptions - yards	0 - 0	2 - 77
Punts - average	3 - 38.3	4 - 31.3
Punt returns - yards	2 - 13	3 - 60
Kickoff returns - yards	6 - 123	2 - 37
Fumbles - lost	3 - 3	0 - 0
Penalties - yards	5 - 29	4 - 20

NFC First-Round Playoff
Jan. 8, 1983
Lambeau Field, Green Bay–54,282

St. Louis	3	6	0	7	– 16
Green Bay	7	21	10	3	– 41

StL - O'Donoghue 18 FG
GB - Jefferson 60 pass from Dickey (Stenerud)
GB - Lofton 20 pass from Dickey (Stenerud)
GB - Ivery 2 run (Stenerud)
GB - Ivery 4 pass from Dickey (Stenerud)
StL - Tilley 5 pass from Lomax (O'Donoghue miss)
GB - Stenerud 46 FG
GB - Jefferson 7 pass from Dickey (Stenerud)
GB - Stenerud 34 FG
StL - Shumann 18 pass from Lomax (O'Donoghue)

TEAM STATISTICS	StL	GB
First Downs	28	22
Rushing	8	7
Passing	19	13
Penalty	1	2
Offensive plays - yards	79 - 453	57 - 394
Rushes - yards	23 - 106	31 - 108
Passes	51 - 32 - 2	26 - 19 - 0
Gross passing yards	385	286
Sacked - yards lost	5 - 38	0 - 0
Net passing yards	347	286
Interceptions - yards	0 - 0	2 - 22
Punts - average	0 - 0	1 - 28.0
Punt returns - yards	0 - 0	0 - 0
Kickoff returns - yards	7 - 178	3 - 59
Fumbles - lost	3 - 2	1 - 1
Penalties - yards	6 - 78	5 - 35

AFC First-Round Playoff
Jan. 9, 1983
Riverfront Stadium, Cincinnati–57,560

New York	3	17	3	21	– 44
Cincinnati	14	0	3	0	– 17

Cin - Curtis 32 pass from Anderson (Breech)
NY - Leahy 33 FG
Cin - Ross 2 pass from Anderson (Breech)
NY - Gaffney 14 pass from McNeil (Leahy)
NY - Walker 4 pass from Todd (Leahy)
NY - Leahy 24 FG
NY - Leahy 47 FG
Cin - Breech 20 FG
NY - McNeil 20 run (Leahy)
NY - Ray 98 interception return (Leahy)
NY - Crutchfield 1 run (Leahy)

TEAM STATISTICS	NY	Cin
First Downs	27	23
Rushing	12	2
Passing	13	18
Penalty	2	3
Offensive plays - yards	63 - 517	61 - 395
Rushes - yards	34 - 234	21 - 62
Passes	29 - 21 - 1	36 - 26 - 3
Gross passing yards	283	354
Sacked - yards lost	0 - 0	4 - 21
Net passing yards	283	333
Interceptions - yards	3 - 138	1 - 0
Punts - average	0 - 0	2 - 43.0
Punt returns - yards	1 - 2	0 - 0
Kickoff returns - yards	4 - 69	8 - 138
Fumbles - lost	2 - 1	2 - 1
Penalties - yards	12 - 95	7 - 60

AFC First-Round Playoff
Jan. 9, 1983
Three Rivers Stadium, Pittsburgh–53,546

San Diego	3	14	0	14	– 31
Pittsburgh	14	0	7	7	– 28

Pit	-	Ruff fumble recovery (Anderson)
SD	-	Benirschke 25 FG
Pit	-	Bradshaw 1 run (Anderson)
SD	-	Brooks 18 run (Benirschke)
SD	-	Sievers 10 pass from Fouts (Benirschke)
Pit	-	Cunningham 2 pass from Bradshaw (Anderson)
Pit	-	Stallworth 14 pass from Bradshaw (Anderson)
SD	-	Winslow 8 pass from Fouts (Benirschke)
SD	-	Winslow 12 pass from Fouts (Benirschke)

TEAM STATISTICS	SD	Pit
First Downs	29	26
Rushing	6	6
Passing	19	19
Penalty	4	1
Offensive plays - yards	71 - 479	62 - 422
Rushes - yards	29 - 146	23 - 97
Passes	42 - 27 - 0	39 - 28 - 2
Gross passing yards	333	325
Sacked - yards lost	0 - 0	0 - 0
Net passing yards	333	325
Interceptions - yards	2 - 43	0 - 0
Punts - average	1 - 48.0	2 - 32.5
Punt returns - yards	0 - 0	1 - 12
Kickoff returns - yards	3 - 33	5 - 90
Fumbles - lost	3 - 2	1 - 0
Penalties - yards	6 - 51	6 - 54

NFC First-Round Playoff
Jan. 9, 1983
Texas Stadium, Irving–65,042

Tampa Bay	0	10	7	0	– 17
Dallas	6	7	3	14	– 30

Dal	-	Septien 33 FG
Dal	-	Septien 33 FG
TB	-	Green 60 fumble return (Capece)
TB	-	Capece 32 FG
Dal	-	Springs 6 pass from D. White (Septien)
Dal	-	Septien 19 FG
TB	-	Jones 49 pass from Williams (Capece)
Dal	-	Hunter 19 interception return (Septien)
Dal	-	Newsome 10 pass from D. White (Septien)

TEAM STATISTICS	TB	Dal
First Downs	8	29
Rushing	3	9
Passing	4	19
Penalty	1	1
Offensive plays - yards	49 - 218	92 - 456
Rushes - yards	21 - 105	42 - 179
Passes	28 - 8 - 3	45 - 27 - 2
Gross passing yards	113	312
Sacked - yards lost	0 - 0	5 - 35
Net passing yards	113	277
Interceptions - yards	2 - 50	3 - 30
Punts - average	6 - 43.5	3 - 37.3

Punt returns - yards	1 - 8	5 - 57
Kickoff returns - yards	5 - 110	4 - 71
Fumbles - lost	0 - 0	1 - 1
Penalties - yards	4 - 41	6 - 45

NFC First-Round Playoff
Jan. 9, 1983
Metrodome, Minneapolis–60,560

Atlanta	7	0	14	3	– 24
Minnesota	3	10	3	14	– 30

Atl	-	Rogers blocked punt recovery (Luckhurst)
Min	-	Danmeier 33 FG
Min	-	S. White 36 pass from Kramer (Danmeier)
Min	-	Danmeier 30 FG
Atl	-	Luckhurst 17 run (Luckhurst)
Atl	-	Glazebrook 35 interception return (Luckhurst)
Min	-	Danmeier 39 FG
Min	-	McCullum 11 pass from Kramer (Danmeier)
Atl	-	Luckhurst 41 FG
Min	-	Brown 5 run (Danmeier)

TEAM STATISTICS	Atl	Min
First Downs	14	24
Rushing	5	8
Passing	5	12
Penalty	4	4
Offensive plays - yards	50 - 235	76 - 378
Rushes - yards	24 - 120	42 - 125
Passes	23 - 9 - 2	34 - 20 - 1
Gross passing yards	134	253
Sacked - yards lost	3 - 19	0 - 0
Net passing yards	115	253
Interceptions - yards	1 - 35	2 - 25
Punts - average	5 - 42.6	5 - 32.0
Had blocked	0	1
Punt returns - yards	1 - 0	5 - 65
Kickoff returns - yards	7 - 120	4 - 88
Fumbles - lost	1 - 0	4 - 0
Penalties - yards	7 - 98	10 - 84

AFC Second-Round Playoff
Jan. 15, 1983
Memorial Coliseum, Los Angeles–90,037

New York	7	3	0	7	– 17
Los Angeles	0	0	14	0	– 14

NY	-	Walker 20 pass from Todd (Leahy)
NY	-	Leahy 30 FG
LA	-	Allen 3 run (Bahr)
LA	-	Barnwell 57 pass from Plunkett (Bahr)
NY	-	Dierking 1 run (Leahy)

TEAM STATISTICS	NY	LA
First Downs	21	19
Rushing	8	7
Passing	11	11
Penalty	2	1
Offensive plays - yards	62 - 391	65 - 339
Rushes - yards	34 - 139	30 - 93
Passes	24 - 15 - 2	33 - 21 - 3
Gross passing yards	277	266
Sacked - yards lost	4 - 25	2 - 20

Net passing yards	252	246
Interceptions - yards	3 - 30	2 - 0
Punts - average	2 - 31.5	4 - 41.3
Punt returns - yards	1 - 4	2 - 0
Kickoff returns - yards	0 - 0	2 - 49
Fumbles - lost	4 - 3	2 - 2
Penalties - yards	7 - 64	5 - 55

NFC Second-Round Playoff
Jan. 15, 1983
RFK Stadium, Washington–54,593

Minnesota	0	7	0	0	– 7
Washington	14	7	0	0	– 21

Was	-	Warren 3 pass from Theismann (Moseley)
Was	-	Riggins 2 run (Moseley)
Min	-	Brown 18 run (Danmeier)
Was	-	Garrett 18 pass from Theismann (Moseley)

TEAM STATISTICS	Min	Was
First Downs	15	23
Rushing	3	12
Passing	11	11
Penalty	1	0
Offensive plays - yards	59 - 317	67 - 415
Rushes - yards	18 - 79	42 - 204
Passes	39 - 18 - 0	23 - 17 - 1
Gross passing yards	252	213
Sacked - yards lost	2 - 14	2 - 2
Net passing yards	238	211
Interceptions - yards	1 - 0	0 - 0
Punts - average	4 - 39.3	2 - 30.0
Punt returns - yards	0 - 0	1 - 9
Kickoff returns - yards	3 - 45	2 - 40
Fumbles - lost	1 - 0	0 - 0
Penalties - yards	5 - 39	3 - 25

AFC Second-Round Playoff
Jan. 16, 1983
Orange Bowl, Miami–71,383

San Diego	0	13	0	0	– 13
Miami	7	20	0	7	– 34

Mia	-	Moore 3 pass from Woodley (von Schamann)
Mia	-	Franklin 3 run (von Schamann)
Mia	-	Lee 6 pass from Woodley (von Schamann)
Mia	-	von Schamann 24 FG
SD	-	Joiner 28 pass from Fouts (Benirschke miss)
Mia	-	von Schamann 23 FG
SD	-	Muncie 1 run (Benirschke)
Mia	-	Woodley 7 run (von Schamann)

TEAM STATISTICS	SD	Mia
First Downs	17	29
Rushing	5	15
Passing	9	11
Penalty	3	3
Offensive plays - yards	54 - 247	80 - 413
Rushes - yards	17 - 79	56 - 214
Passes	34 - 15 - 5	23 - 18 - 1
Gross passing yards	191	215
Sacked - yards lost	3 - 23	1 - 16

Net passing yards	168	199
Interceptions - yards	1 - 18	5 - 54
Punts - average	4 - 41.3	3 - 40.3
Punt returns - yards	3 - 16	2 - 4
Kickoff returns - yards	7 - 93	3 - 40
Fumbles - lost	3 - 2	2 - 1
Penalties - yards	7 - 62	6 - 70

NFC Second-Round Playoff
Jan. 16, 1983
Texas Stadium, Irving–63,972

Green Bay	0	7	6	13	– 26
Dallas	6	14	3	14	– 37

Dal - Septien 50 FG
Dal - Septien 34 FG
GB - Lofton 6 pass from Dickey (Stenerud)
Dal - Newsome 2 run (Septien)
Dal - Thurman 39 interception return (Septien)
GB - Stenerud 30 FG
GB - Stenerud 33 FG
Dal - Septien 24 FG
GB - Lofton 71 run (Stenerud miss)
Dal - Cosbie 7 pass from D. White (Septien)
GB - Lee 22 interception return (Stenerud)
Dal - Newhouse 1 run (Septien)

TEAM STATISTICS	GB	Dal
First Downs	21	24
Rushing	5	10
Passing	16	13
Penalty	0	1
Offensive plays - yards	57 - 466	77 - 375
Rushes - yards	17 - 158	39 - 109
Passes	36 - 19 - 3	37 - 24 - 1
Gross passing yards	332	274
Sacked - yards lost	4 - 24	1 - 8
Net passing yards	308	266
Interceptions - yards	1 - 22	3 - 58
Punts - average	4 - 42.0	4 - 34.8
Punt returns - yards	1 - 8	3 - 23
Kickoff returns - yards	7 - 148	6 - 173
Fumbles - lost	4 - 2	1 - 1
Penalties - yards	3 - 35	5 - 30

NFC Championship Game
Jan. 22, 1983
RFK Stadium, Washington–55,045

Dallas	3	0	14	0	– 17
Washington	7	7	7	10	– 31

Dal - Septien 27 FG
Was - Brown 19 pass from Theismann (Moseley)
Was - Riggins 1 run (Moseley)
Dal - Pearson 6 pass from Hogeboom (Septien)
Was - Riggins 4 run (Moseley)
Dal - Johnson 23 pass from Hogeboom (Septien)
Was - Moseley 29 FG
Was - Grant 10 interception return (Moseley)

TEAM STATISTICS	Dal	Was
First Downs	21	18
Rushing	2	11
Passing	19	5
Penalty	0	2

Offensive plays - yards	65 - 340	63 - 260
Rushes - yards	21 - 65	40 - 137
Passes	44 - 23 - 2	20 - 12 - 0
Gross passing yards	275	150
Sacked - yards lost	0 - 0	3 - 27
Net passing yards	275	123
Interceptions - yards	0 - 0	2 - 12
Punts - average	3 - 31.0	5 - 40.2
Punt returns - yards	3 - 10	2 - 14
Kickoff returns - yards	5 - 94	4 - 128
Fumbles - lost	2 - 1	1 - 0
Penalties - yards	3 - 15	3 - 25

AFC Championship Game
Jan. 23, 1983
Orange Bowl, Miami–67,396

New York	0	0	0	0	– 0
Miami	0	0	7	7	– 14

Mia - Bennett 7 run (von Schamann)
Mia - Duhe 35 interception return (von Schamann)

TEAM STATISTICS	NY	Mia
First Downs	10	13
Rushing	2	7
Passing	6	5
Penalty	2	1
Offensive plays - yards	65 - 139	66 - 198
Rushes - yards	24 - 62	41 - 138
Passes	37 - 15 - 5	21 - 9 - 3
Gross passing yards	103	87
Sacked - yards lost	4 - 26	4 - 27
Net passing yards	77	60
Interceptions - yards	3 - 1	5 - 48
Punts - average	10 - 35.7	10 - 33.3
Had blocked	1	0
Punt returns - yards	6 - 65	3 - 20
Kickoff returns - yards	1 - 31	1 - 20
Fumbles - lost	1 - 0	3 - 1
Penalties - yards	6 - 42	3 - 15

Super Bowl XVII
Jan. 30, 1983
Rose Bowl, Pasadena–103,667

Miami	7	10	0	0	– 17
Washington	0	10	3	14	– 27

Mia - Cefalo 76 pass from Woodley (von Schamann)
Was - Moseley 31 FG
Mia - von Schamann 20 FG
Was - Garrett 4 pass from Theismann (Moseley)
Mia - Walker 98 kickoff return (von Schamann)
Was - Moseley 20 FG
Was - Riggins 43 run (Moseley)
Was - Brown 6 pass from Theismann (Moseley)
MVP: John Riggins, RB, Washington

TEAM STATISTICS	Mia	Was
First Downs	9	24
Rushing	7	14
Passing	2	9
Penalty	0	1
Offensive plays - yards	47 - 176	78 - 400
Rushes - yards	29 - 96	52 - 276
Passes	17 - 4 - 1	23 - 15 - 2

Gross passing yards	97	143
Sacked - yards lost	1 - 17	3 - 19
Net passing yards	80	124
Interceptions - yards	2 - 0	1 - 0
Punts - average	6 - 37.8	4 - 42.0
Punt returns - yards	2 - 22	6 - 52
Kickoff returns - yards	6 - 222	3 - 57
Fumbles - lost	2 - 1	0 - 0
Penalties - yards	4 - 55	5 - 36

AFC Wild Card Game
Dec. 24, 1983
Kingdome, Seattle–60,752

Denver	7	0	0	0	– 7
Seattle	7	3	7	14	– 31

Sea - Largent 17 pass from Krieg (N. Johnson)
Den - Myles 13 pass from DeBerg (Karlis)
Sea - N. Johnson 37 FG
Sea - Metzelaars 5 pass from Krieg (N. Johnson)
Sea - Johns 18 pass from Krieg (N. Johnson)
Sea - Hughes 2 run (N. Johnson)

TEAM STATISTICS	Den	Sea
First Downs	21	17
Rushing	5	8
Passing	14	9
Penalty	2	0
Offensive plays - yards	69 - 360	53 - 324
Rushes - yards	33 - 125	38 - 145
Passes	34 - 24 - 2	13 - 12 - 0
Gross passing yards	254	200
Sacked - yards lost	2 - 19	2 - 21
Net passing yards	235	179
Interceptions - yards	0 - 0	2 - 45
Punts - average	4 - 47.8	3 - 41.7
Punt returns - yards	3 - 10	4 - 58
Kickoff returns - yards	6 - 118	2 - 43
Fumbles - lost	1 - 1	1 - 0
Penalties - yards	5 - 35	3 - 34

NFC Wild Card Game
Dec. 26, 1983
Texas Stadium, Irving–43,521

Los Angeles	7	0	10	7	– 24
Dallas	0	7	3	7	– 17

LA - D. Hill 18 pass from Ferragamo (Lansford)
Dal - T. Hill 14 pass from D. White (Septien)
Dal - Septien 41 FG
LA - Dennard 16 pass from Ferragamo (Lansford)
LA - Farmer 8 pass from Ferragamo (Lansford)
LA - Lansford 20 FG
Dal - Cosbie 2 pass from D. White (Septien)

TEAM STATISTICS	LA	Dal
First Downs	19	24
Rushing	5	4
Passing	11	20
Penalty	3	0
Offensive plays - yards	63 - 243	76 - 363
Rushes - yards	30 - 94	20 - 63
Passes	31 - 16 - 0	53 - 32 - 3
Gross passing yards	163	330

Sacked - yards lost	2 - 14	3 - 30
Net passing yards	149	300
Interceptions - yards	3 - 111	0 - 0
Punts - average	6 - 37.3	5 - 31.4
Punt returns - yards	2 - 10	4 - 16
Kickoff returns - yards	3 - 46	5 - 80
Fumbles - lost	0 - 0	2 - 1
Penalties - yards	4 - 18	6 - 40

AFC Divisional Playoff
Dec. 31, 1983
Orange Bowl, Miami–71,032

Seattle	0	7	7	13	–	27
Miami	0	13	0	7	–	20

Mia - Johnson 19 pass from Marino (von Schamann miss)
Sea - C. Bryant 6 pass from Krieg (N. Johnson)
Mia - Duper 32 pass from Marino (von Schamann)
Sea - Warner 1 run (N. Johnson)
Sea - N. Johnson 27 FG
Mia - Bennett 3 run (von Schamann)
Sea - Warner 2 run (N. Johnson)
Sea - N. Johnson 37 FG

TEAM STATISTICS	Sea	Mia
First Downs	21	21
Rushing	12	9
Passing	9	11
Penalty	0	1
Offensive plays - yards	72 - 334	56 - 321
Rushes - yards	42 - 151	30 - 128
Passes	29 - 15 - 1	26 - 15 - 2
Gross passing yards	192	193
Sacked - yards lost	1 - 9	0 - 0
Net passing yards	183	193
Interceptions - yards	2 - 0	1 - 18
Punts - average	4 - 38.0	4 - 35.5
Punt returns - yards	0 - 0	2 - 32
Kickoff returns - yards	4 - 130	6 - 104
Fumbles - lost	0 - 0	3 - 3
Penalties - yards	2 - 15	5 - 30

NFC Divisional Playoff
Dec. 31, 1983
Candlestick Park, San Francisco–58,286

Detroit	3	6	0	14	–	23
San Francisco	7	7	3	7	–	24

Det - Murray 37 FG
SF - Craig 1 run (Wersching)
SF - Tyler 2 run (Wersching)
Det - Murray 21 FG
Det - Murray 54 FG
SF - Wersching 19 FG
Det - Sims 11 run (Murray)
Det - Sims 3 run (Murray)
SF - Solomon 14 pass from Montana (Wersching)

TEAM STATISTICS	Det	SF
First Downs	22	20
Rushing	9	9
Passing	11	10
Penalty	2	1
Offensive plays - yards	75 - 412	60 - 291

Rushes - yards	35 - 188	27 - 103
Passes	38 - 24 - 5	31 - 18 - 1
Gross passing yards	236	201
Sacked - yards lost	2 - 12	2 - 13
Net passing yards	224	188
Interceptions - yards	1 - 24	5 - 41
Punts - average	2 - 36.5	5 - 34.8
Punt returns - yards	4 - 30	0 - 0
Kickoff returns - yards	4 - 88	5 - 92
Fumbles - lost	2 - 0	2 - 1
Penalties - yards	7 - 63	5 - 25

AFC Divisional Playoff
Jan. 1, 1984
Memorial Coliseum, Los Angeles–90,334

Pittsburgh	3	0	7	0	–	10
Los Angeles	7	10	21	0	–	38

Pit - Anderson 17 FG
LA - Hayes 18 interception return (Bahr)
LA - Allen 4 run (Bahr)
LA - Bahr 45 FG
LA - King 9 run (Bahr)
LA - Allen 49 run (Bahr)
Pit - Stallworth 58 pass from Stoudt (Anderson)
LA - Hawkins 2 run (Bahr)

TEAM STATISTICS	Pit	LA
First Downs	17	24
Rushing	9	13
Passing	8	9
Penalty	0	2
Offensive plays - yards	64 - 331	68 - 413
Rushes - yards	32 - 162	33 - 188
Passes	27 - 13 - 1	34 - 21 - 0
Gross passing yards	209	232
Sacked - yards lost	5 - 40	1 - 7
Net passing yards	169	225
Interceptions - yards	0 - 0	1 - 18
Punts - average	8 - 40.9	6 - 41.3
Punt returns - yards	3 - 21	6 - 52
Kickoff returns - yards	5 - 103	3 - 87
Fumbles - lost	2 - 1	2 - 0
Penalties - yards	4 - 30	2 - 15

NFC Divisional Playoff
Jan. 1, 1984
RFK Stadium, Washington–55,363

Los Angeles	0	7	0	0	–	7
Washington	17	21	6	7	–	51

Was - Riggins 3 run (Moseley)
Was - Monk 40 pass from Theismann (Moseley)
Was - Moseley 42 FG
Was - Riggins 1 run (Moseley)
LA - Dennard 32 pass from Ferragamo (Lansford)
Was - Monk 21 pass from Theismann (Moseley)
Was - Riggins 1 run (Moseley)
Was - Moseley 36 FG
Was - Moseley 41 FG
Was - Green 72 interception return (Moseley)

TEAM STATISTICS	LA	Was
First Downs	12	23
Rushing	2	10

Passing	9	12
Penalty	1	1
Offensive plays - yards	62 - 204	65 - 445
Rushes - yards	16 - 51	40 - 130
Passes	43 - 20 - 3	25 - 20 - 0
Gross passing yards	175	315
Sacked - yards lost	3 - 22	0 - 0
Net passing yards	153	315
Interceptions - yards	0 - 0	3 - 72
Punts - average	7 - 33.9	3 - 28.0
Punt returns - yards	1 - 4	3 - 56
Kickoff returns - yards	10 - 151	2 - 47
Fumbles - lost	2 - 1	2 - 1
Penalties - yards	7 - 41	6 - 55

AFC Championship Game
Jan. 8, 1984
Memorial Coliseum, Los Angeles–88,734

Seattle	0	0	7	7	–	14
Los Angeles	3	17	7	3	–	30

LA - Bahr 20 FG
LA - Hawkins 1 run (Bahr)
LA - Hawkins 5 run (Bahr)
LA - Bahr 45 FG
LA - Allen 3 pass from Plunkett (Bahr)
Sea - Doornink 11 pass from Zorn (N. Johnson)
LA - Bahr 35 FG
Sea - Young 9 pass from Zorn (N. Johnson)

TEAM STATISTICS	Sea	LA
First Downs	16	21
Rushing	4	10
Passing	10	11
Penalty	2	0
Offensive plays - yards	58 - 167	72 - 401
Rushes - yards	18 - 65	46 - 205
Passes	36 - 17 - 5	24 - 17 - 2
Gross passing yards	146	214
Sacked - yards lost	4 - 44	2 - 18
Net passing yards	102	196
Interceptions - yards	2 - 8	5 - 53
Punts - average	5 - 32.0	2 - 34.0
Punt returns - yards	0 - 0	1 - 1
Kickoff returns - yards	7 - 136	2 - 46
Fumbles - lost	1 - 0	3 - 2
Penalties - yards	2 - 20	7 - 53

NFC Championship Game
Jan. 8, 1984
RFK Stadium, Washington–55,363

San Francisco	0	0	0	21	–	21
Washington	0	7	14	3	–	24

Was - Riggins 4 run (Moseley)
Was - Riggins 1 run (Moseley)
Was - Brown 70 pass from Theismann (Moseley)
SF - Wilson 5 pass from Montana (Wersching)
SF - Solomon 76 pass from Montana (Wersching)
SF - Wilson 12 pass from Montana (Wersching)
Was - Moseley 25 FG

TEAM STATISTICS	SF	Was
First Downs	19	24

Rushing	3	11
Passing	16	10
Penalty	0	3
Offensive plays - yards	64 - 434	75 - 410
Rushes - yards	16 - 87	45 - 172
Passes	48 - 27 - 1	27 - 15 - 1
Gross passing yards	347	265
Sacked - yards lost	0 - 0	3 - 27
Net passing yards	347	238
Interceptions - yards	1 - 0	1 - 5
Punts - average	7 - 33.6	5 - 40.2
Punt returns - yards	2 - 7	4 - 31
Kickoff returns - yards	5 - 98	4 - 48
Fumbles - lost	4 - 2	2 - 1
Penalties - yards	6 - 72	4 - 35

Super Bowl XVIII
Jan. 22, 1984
Tampa Stadium–72,920

Washington	0	3	6	0	– 9
L.A. Raiders	7	14	14	3	– 38

LA	- Jensen blocked punt recovery (Bahr)
LA	- Branch 12 pass from Plunkett (Bahr)
Was	- Moseley 24 FG
LA	- Squirek 5 interception return (Bahr)
Was	- Riggins 1 run (Moseley miss)
LA	- Allen 5 run (Bahr)
LA	- Allen 74 run (Bahr)
LA	- Bahr 21 FG

MVP: Marcus Allen, RB, Los Angeles

TEAM STATISTICS	Was	LA
First Downs	19	18
Rushing	7	8
Passing	10	9
Penalty	2	1
Offensive plays - yards	73 - 283	60 - 385
Rushes - yards	32 - 90	33 - 231
Passes	35 - 16 - 2	25 - 16 - 0
Gross passing yards	243	172
Sacked - yards lost	6 - 50	2 - 18
Net passing yards	193	154
Interceptions - yards	0 - 0	2 - 5
Punts - average	8 - 32.4	7 - 42.7
Had blocked	1	0
Punt returns - yards	2 - 35	2 - 8
Kickoff returns - yards	7 - 132	1 - 17
Fumbles - lost	1 - 1	3 - 2
Penalties - yards	4 - 62	7 - 56

AFC Wild Card Game
Dec. 22, 1984
Kingdome, Seattle–62,049

Los Angeles	0	0	0	7	– 7
Seattle	0	7	3	3	– 13

Sea	- Turner 26 pass from Krieg (Johnson)
Sea	- Johnson 35 FG
Sea	- Johnson 44 FG
LA	- Allen 46 pass from Plunkett (Bahr)

TEAM STATISTICS	LA	Sea
First Downs	14	17
Rushing	5	12
Passing	8	4
Penalty	1	1

Offensive plays - yards	58 - 240	63 - 251
Rushes - yards	25 - 105	51 - 205
Passes	27 - 14 - 2	10 - 4 - 0
Gross passing yards	184	70
Sacked - yards lost	6 - 49	2 - 24
Net passing yards	135	46
Interceptions - yards	0 - 0	2 - 21
Punts - average	8 - 41.9	8 - 37.8
Punt returns - yards	3 - 5	5 - 52
Kickoff returns - yards	2 - 28	2 - 38
Fumbles - lost	2 - 1	0 - 0
Penalties - yards	8 - 68	7 - 55

NFC Wild Card Game
Dec. 23, 1984
Anaheim Stadium–67,037

New York	10	0	6	0	– 16
Los Angeles	0	3	7	3	– 13

NY	- Haji - Sheikh 37 FG
NY	- Carpenter 1 run (Haji - Sheikh)
LA	- Lansford 38 FG
NY	- Haji - Sheikh 39 FG
LA	- Dickerson 14 run (Lansford)
NY	- Haji - Sheikh 36 FG
LA	- Lansford 22 FG

TEAM STATISTICS	NY	LA
First Downs	16	12
Rushing	5	5
Passing	8	5
Penalty	3	2
Offensive plays - yards	62 - 192	43 - 214
Rushes - yards	27 - 40	26 - 107
Passes	31 - 22 - 0	15 - 11 - 0
Gross passing yards	179	109
Sacked - yards lost	4 - 27	2 - 2
Net passing yards	152	107
Interceptions - yards	0 - 0	0 - 0
Punts - average	4 - 38.8	4 - 37.8
Punt returns - yards	3 - 25	2 - 17
Kickoff returns - yards	4 - 69	5 - 92
Fumbles - lost	3 - 0	2 - 2
Penalties - yards	5 - 81	10 - 75

AFC Divisional Playoff
Dec. 29, 1984
Orange Bowl, Miami–73,469

Seattle	0	10	0	0	– 10
Miami	7	7	14	3	– 31

Mia	- Nathan 14 run (von Schamann)
Sea	- Johnson 27 FG
Mia	- Cefalo 34 pass from Marino (von Schamann)
Sea	- Largent 56 pass from Krieg (Johnson)
Mia	- Hardy 3 pass from Marino (von Schamann)
Mia	- Clayton 33 pass from Marino (von Schamann)
Mia	- von Schamann 37 FG

TEAM STATISTICS	Sea	Mia
First Downs	8	22
Rushing	2	8
Passing	6	12

Penalty	0	2
Offensive plays - yards	55 - 267	70 - 405
Rushes - yards	18 - 51	36 - 143
Passes	35 - 20 - 0	34 - 21 - 2
Gross passing yards	234	262
Sacked - yards lost	2 - 18	0 - 0
Net passing yards	216	262
Interceptions - yards	2 - 45	0 - 0
Punts - average	7 - 37.0	3 - 37.0
Punt returns - yards	1 - 5	3 - 30
Kickoff returns - yards	4 - 77	3 - 51
Fumbles - lost	1 - 1	0 - 0
Penalties - yards	4 - 20	1 - 5

NFC Divisional Playoff
Dec. 29, 1984
Candlestick Park, San Francisco–60,303

New York	0	10	0	0	– 10
San Francisco	14	7	0	0	– 21

SF	- D. Clark 21 pass from Montana (Wersching)
SF	- Francis 9 pass from Montana (Wersching)
NY	- Haji - Sheikh 46 FG
NY	- Carson 14 interception return (Haji - Sheikh)
SF	- Solomon 29 pass from Montana (Wersching)

TEAM STATISTICS	NY	SF
First Downs	18	22
Rushing	7	5
Passing	10	16
Penalty	1	1
Offensive plays - yards	75 - 260	71 - 412
Rushes - yards	25 - 87	28 - 131
Passes	44 - 25 - 2	39 - 25 - 3
Gross passing yards	218	309
Sacked - yards lost	6 - 45	4 - 28
Net passing yards	173	281
Interceptions - yards	3 - 47	2 - 50
Punts - average	6 - 37.7	5 - 42.0
Punt returns - yards	3 - 22	2 - 7
Kickoff returns - yards	4 - 109	3 - 40
Fumbles - lost	2 - 1	0 - 0
Penalties - yards	2 - 25	5 - 29

AFC Divisional Playoff
Dec. 30, 1984
Mile High Stadium, Denver–74,981

Pittsburgh	0	10	7	7	– 24
Denver	7	0	10	0	– 17

Den	- J. Wright 9 pass from Elway (Karlis)
Pit	- Anderson 28 FG
Pit	- Pollard 1 run (Anderson)
Den	- Karlis 21 FG
Den	- Watson 20 pass from Elway (Karlis)
Pit	- Lipps 10 pass from Malone (Anderson)
Pit	- Pollard 2 run (Anderson)

TEAM STATISTICS	Pit	Den
First Downs	25	15
Rushing	12	4
Passing	13	11
Offensive plays - yards	70 - 381	64 - 250

Rushes - yards	40 - 169	22 - 51
Passes	28 - 17 - 0	38 - 20 - 2
Gross passing yards	224	236
Sacked - yards lost	2 - 12	4 - 37
Net passing yards	212	199
Interceptions - yards	2 - 34	0 - 0
Punts - average	3 - 28.3	4 - 42.3
Had blocked	1	0
Punt returns - yards	3 - 9	2 - 17
Kickoff returns - yards	4 - 102	2 - 56
Fumbles - lost	3 - 2	2 - 0
Penalties - yards	4 - 30	1 - 5

NFC Divisional Playoff
Dec. 30, 1984
RFK Stadium, Washington–55,431

Chicago	0 10 13 0	– 23
Washington	3 0 14 2	– 19

Was - Moseley 25 FG
Chi - B. Thomas 34 FG
Chi - Dunsmore 19 pass from Payton (B. Thomas)
Chi - Gault 75 pass from Fuller (B. Thomas miss)
Was - Riggins 1 run (Moseley)
Chi - McKinnon 16 pass from Fuller (B. Thomas)
Was - Riggins 1 run (Moseley)
Was - Safety, Finzer stepped out of end zone

TEAM STATISTICS	Chi	Was
First Downs	13	22
Rushing	5	6
Passing	7	14
Penalty	1	2
Offensive plays - yards	57 - 310	76 - 336
Rushes - yards	35 - 114	27 - 93
Passes	17 - 10 - 0	42 - 22 - 1
Gross passing yards	230	292
Sacked - yards lost	5 - 34	7 - 49
Net passing yards	196	243
Interceptions - yards	1 - 0	0 - 0
Punts - average	5 - 39.4	5 - 36.8
Punt returns - yards	2 - 17	3 - 29
Kickoff returns - yards	3 - 74	6 - 112
Fumbles - lost	2 - 1	3 - 2
Penalties - yards	6 - 34	7 - 55

AFC Championship Game
Jan. 6, 1985
Orange Bowl, Miami–76,029

Pittsburgh	7 7 7 7	– 28
Miami	7 17 14 7	– 45

Mia - Clayton 40 pass from Marino (von Schamann)
Pit - Erenberg 7 run (Anderson)
Mia - von Schamann 26 FG
Pit - Stallworth 65 pass from Malone (Anderson)
Mia - Duper 41 pass from Marino (von Schamann)
Mia - Nathan 2 run (von Schamann)
Mia - Duper 36 pass from Marino (von Schamann)

Pit - Stallworth 19 pass from Malone (Anderson)
Mia - Bennett 1 run (von Schamann)
Mia - Moore 6 pass from Marino (von Schamann)
Pit - Capers 29 pass from Malone (Anderson)

TEAM STATISTICS	Pit	Mia
First Downs	22	28
Rushing	8	10
Passing	14	18
Offensive plays - yards	68 - 455	71 - 569
Rushes - yards	32 - 143	38 - 134
Passes	36 - 20 - 3	33 - 22 - 1
Gross passing yards	312	435
Sacked - yards lost	0 - 0	0 - 0
Net passing yards	312	435
Interceptions - yards	1 - 18	3 - 42
Punts - average	3 - 43.7	2 - 42.5
Punt returns - yards	1 - 7	3 - 12
Kickoff returns - yards	5 - 106	3 - 62
Fumbles - lost	2 - 1	1 - 1
Penalties - yards	3 - 30	3 - 25

NFC Championship Game
Jan. 6, 1985
Candlestick Park, San Francisco–61,336

Chicago	0 0 0 0	– 0
San Francisco	3 3 7 10	– 23

SF - Wersching 21 FG
SF - Wersching 22 FG
SF - Tyler 9 run (Wersching)
SF - Solomon 10 pass from Montana (Wersching)
SF - Wersching 34 FG

TEAM STATISTICS	Chi	SF
First Downs	13	25
Rushing	9	9
Passing	3	14
Penalty	1	2
Offensive plays - yards	63 - 186	67 - 387
Rushes - yards	32 - 149	29 - 159
Passes	22 - 13 - 1	35 - 19 - 2
Gross passing yards	87	236
Sacked - yards lost	9 - 50	3 - 8
Net passing yards	37	228
Interceptions - yards	2 - 5	1 - 0
Punts - average	7 - 43.1	3 - 39.0
Punt returns - yards	2 - 12	4 - 69
Kickoff returns - yards	4 - 67	1 - 15
Fumbles - lost	1 - 0	1 - 0
Penalties - yards	7 - 50	3 - 20

Super Bowl XIX
Jan. 20, 1985
Stanford Stadium, Palo Alto–84,059

Miami	10 6 0 0	– 16
San Francisco	7 21 10 0	– 38

Mia - von Schamann 37 FG
SF - Monroe 33 pass from Montana (Wersching)
Mia - D. Johnson 2 pass from Marino (von Schamann)
SF - Craig 8 pass from Montana (Wersching)

SF - Montana 6 run (Wersching)
SF - Craig 2 run (Wersching)
Mia - von Schamann 31 FG
Mia - von Schamann 30 FG
SF - Wersching 27 FG
SF - Craig 16 pass from Montana (Wersching)

MVP: Joe Montana, QB, San Francisco

TEAM STATISTICS	Mia	SF
First Downs	19	31
Rushing	2	16
Passing	17	15
Offensive plays - yards	63 - 314	76 - 537
Rushes - yards	9 - 25	40 - 211
Passes	50 - 29 - 2	35 - 24 - 0
Gross passing yards	318	331
Sacked - yards lost	4 - 29	1 - 5
Net passing yards	289	326
Interceptions - yards	0 - 0	2 - 0
Punts - average	6 - 39.3	3 - 32.7
Punt returns - yards	2 - 15	5 - 51
Kickoff returns - yards	7 - 140	4 - 40
Fumbles - lost	1 - 0	2 - 2
Penalties - yards	1 - 10	2 - 10

AFC Wild Card Game
Dec. 28, 1985
Giants Stadium, East Rutherford, N.J.–70,958

New England	3 10 10 3	– 26
New York Jets	0 7 7 0	– 14

NE - Franklin 33 FG
NY - Hector 11 pass from O'Brien (Leahy)
NE - Franklin 41 FG
NE - Morgan 36 pass from Eason (Franklin)
NE - Franklin 20 FG
NE - Rembert 15 fumble return (Franklin)
NY - Shuler 12 pass from Ryan (Leahy)
NE - Franklin 26 FG

TEAM STATISTICS	NE	NY
First Downs	12	15
Rushing	5	3
Passing	6	12
Penalty	1	0
Offensive plays - yards	58 - 258	60 - 240
Rushes - yards	39 - 99	21 - 58
Passes	16 - 12 - 0	34 - 23 - 2
Gross passing yards	179	233
Sacked - yards lost	3 - 20	5 - 51
Net passing yards	159	182
Interceptions - yards	2 - 46	0 - 0
Punts - average	5 - 40.0	5 - 38.4
Punt returns - yards	4 - 12	1 - 3
Kickoff returns - yards	2 - 30	7 - 165
Fumbles - lost	2 - 0	3 - 2
Penalties - yards	1 - 10	6 - 48

NFC Wild Card Game
Dec. 29, 1985
Giants Stadium, East Rutherford, N.J.–75,842

San Francisco	0 3 0 0	– 3
New York Giants	3 7 7 0	– 17

NY - Schubert 47 FG

NY - Bavaro 18 pass from Simms (Schubert)
SF - Wersching 21 FG
NY - Hasselbeck 3 pass from Simms (Schubert)

TEAM STATISTICS	SF	NY
First Downs	19	21
Rushing	6	9
Passing	10	11
Penalty	3	1
Offensive plays - yards	74 - 362	72 - 355
Rushes - yards	22 - 94	41 - 174
Passes	48 - 26 - 1	31 - 15 - 1
Gross passing yards	296	181
Sacked - yards lost	4 - 28	0 - 0
Net passing yards	268	181
Interceptions - yards	1 - 2	1 - 15
Punts - average	6 - 38.0	5 - 36.6
Punt returns - yards	1 - 5	4 - 29
Kickoff returns - yards	3 - 42	2 - 35
Fumbles - lost	2 - 1	0 - 0
Penalties - yards	6 - 41	5 - 45

AFC Divisional Playoff
Jan. 4, 1986
Orange Bowl, Miami–75,128

Cleveland	7	7	7	0	–	21
Miami	3	0	14	7	–	24

Mia - Reveiz 51 FG
Cle - Newsome 16 pass from Kosar (Bahr)
Cle - Byner 21 run (Bahr)
Cle - Byner 66 run (Bahr)
Mia - N. Moore 6 pass from Marino (Reveiz)
Mia - Davenport 31 run (Reveiz)
Mia - Davenport 1 run (Reveiz)

TEAM STATISTICS	Cle	Mia
First Downs	17	20
Rushing	11	6
Passing	5	13
Penalty	1	1
Offensive plays - yards	57 - 313	64 - 330
Rushes - yards	37 - 251	19 - 92
Passes	19 - 10 - 1	45 - 25 - 1
Gross passing yards	66	238
Sacked - yards lost	1 - 4	0 - 0
Net passing yards	62	238
Interceptions - yards	1 - 45	1 - 2
Punts - average	6 - 37.2	5 - 41.6
Punt returns - yards	1 - 1	4 - 23
Kickoff returns - yards	3 - 75	4 - 89
Fumbles - lost	1 - 0	1 - 0
Penalties - yards	6 - 49	2 - 20

NFC Divisional Playoff
Jan. 4, 1986
Anaheim Stadium–66,351

Dallas	0	0	0	0	–	0
Los Angeles	3	0	10	7	–	20

LA - Lansford 33 FG
LA - Dickerson 55 run (Lansford)
LA - Lansford 34 FG
LA - Dickerson 40 run (Lansford)

TEAM STATISTICS	Dal	LA
First Downs	15	15

Rushing	3	11
Passing	12	3
Penalty	0	1
Offensive plays - yards	66 - 243	64 - 316
Rushes - yards	18 - 61	41 - 269
Passes	43 - 24 - 3	22 - 6 - 1
Gross passing yards	217	50
Sacked - yards lost	5 - 35	1 - 3
Net passing yards	182	47
Interceptions - yards	1 - 20	3 - 66
Punts - average	7 - 46.9	7 - 40.7
Punt returns - yards	4 - 30	4 - 37
Kickoff returns - yards	5 - 110	1 - 14
Fumbles - lost	3 - 3	3 - 1
Penalties - yards	5 - 30	4 - 29

AFC Divisional Playoff
Jan. 5, 1986
Memorial Coliseum, Los Angeles–88,936

New England	7	10	10	0	–	27
Los Angeles	3	17	0	0	–	20

NE - Dawson 13 pass from Eason (Franklin)
LA - Bahr 29 FG
LA - Hester 16 pass from Wilson (Bahr)
LA - Allen 11 run (Bahr)
NE - C. James 2 run (Franklin)
NE - Franklin 45 FG
LA - Bahr 32 FG
NE - Franklin 32 FG
NE - Bowman fumble recovery in end zone (Franklin)

TEAM STATISTICS	NE	LA
First Downs	15	17
Rushing	9	11
Passing	5	6
Penalty	1	0
Offensive plays - yards	67 - 254	56 - 287
Rushes - yards	49 - 156	27 - 163
Passes	15 - 8 - 0	27 - 11 - 3
Gross passing yards	125	135
Sacked - yards lost	3 - 27	2 - 11
Net passing yards	98	124
Interceptions - yards	3 - 23	0 - 0
Punts - average	6 - 37.5	2 - 34.0
Punt returns - yards	0 - 0	4 - 36
Kickoff returns - yards	4 - 54	5 - 66
Fumbles - lost	3 - 2	5 - 3
Penalties - yards	6 - 45	6 - 53

NFC Divisional Playoff
Jan. 5, 1986
Soldier Field, Chicago–62,076

New York	0	0	0	0	–	0
Chicago	7	0	14	0	–	21

Chi - Gayle 5 punt return (Butler)
Chi - McKinnon 23 pass from McMahon (Butler)
Chi - McKinnon 20 pass from McMahon (Butler)

TEAM STATISTICS	NY	Chi
First Downs	10	17
Rushing	1	9
Passing	8	8
Penalty	1	0

Offensive plays - yards	55 - 181	65 - 363
Rushes - yards	14 - 32	44 - 147
Passes	35 - 14 - 0	21 - 11 - 0
Gross passing yards	209	216
Sacked - yards lost	6 - 60	0 - 0
Net passing yards	149	216
Interceptions - yards	0 - 0	0 - 0
Punts - average	9 - 38.1	6 - 37.3
Punt returns - yards	2 - 9	6 - 27
Kickoff returns - yards	4 - 95	1 - 21
Fumbles - lost	3 - 1	0 - 0
Penalties - yards	4 - 25	2 - 20

AFC Championship Game
Jan. 12, 1986
Orange Bowl, Miami–74,978

New England	3	14	7	7	–	31
Miami	0	7	0	7	–	14

NE - Franklin 23 FG
Mia - Johnson 10 pass from Marino (Reveiz)
NE - Collins 4 pass from Eason (Franklin)
NE - D. Ramsey 1 pass from Eason (Franklin)
NE - Weathers 2 pass from Eason (Franklin)
Mia - Nathan 10 pass from Marino (Reveiz)
NE - Tatupu 1 run (Franklin)

TEAM STATISTICS	NE	Mia
First Downs	21	18
Rushing	15	3
Passing	6	15
Offensive plays - yards	71 - 326	62 - 302
Rushes - yards	59 - 255	13 - 68
Passes	12 - 10 - 0	48 - 20 - 2
Gross passing yards	71	248
Sacked - yards lost	0 - 0	1 - 14
Net passing yards	71	234
Interceptions - yards	2 - 21	0 - 0
Punts - average	5 - 40.2	4 - 41.3
Punt returns - yards	2 - 2	1 - 8
Kickoff returns - yards	3 - 67	6 - 91
Fumbles - lost	2 - 2	5 - 4
Penalties - yards	2 - 15	4 - 35

NFC Championship Game
Jan. 12, 1986
Soldier Field, Chicago–66,030

Los Angeles	0	0	0	0	–	0
Chicago	10	0	7	7	–	24

Chi - McMahon 16 run (Butler)
Chi - Butler 34 FG
Chi - Gault 22 pass from McMahon (Butler)
Chi - Marshall 52 fumble return (Butler)

TEAM STATISTICS	LA	Chi
First Downs	9	13
Rushing	5	5
Passing	3	8
Penalty	1	0
Offensive plays - yards	60 - 130	61 - 232
Rushes - yards	26 - 86	33 - 91
Passes	31 - 10 - 1	25 - 16 - 0
Gross passing yards	66	164
Sacked - yards lost	3 - 22	3 - 23
Net passing yards	44	141
Interceptions - yards	0 - 0	1 - (- 3

Punts - average	11 - 39.2	10 - 36.3
Punt returns - yards	4 - 16	5 - 21
Kickoff returns - yards	4 - 76	1 - 22
Fumbles - lost	4 - 2	3 - 1
Penalties - yards	4 - 25	6 - 48

Super Bowl XX

Jan. 26, 1986
Louisiana Superdome, New Orleans–73,818

Chicago	13	10	21	2	– 46
New England	3	0	0	7	– 10

NE - Franklin 36 FG
Chi - Butler 28 FG
Chi - Butler 24 FG
Chi - Suhey 11 run (Butler)
Chi - McMahon 2 run (Butler)
Chi - Butler 24 FG
Chi - McMahon 1 run (Butler)
Chi - Phillips 28 interception return (Butler)
Chi - Perry 1 run (Butler)
NE - Fryar 8 pass from Grogan (Franklin)
Chi - Safety, Waechter tackled Grogan in end zone

MVP: Richard Dent, DE, Chicago

TEAM STATISTICS	Chi	NE
First Downs	23	12
Rushing	13	1
Passing	9	10
Penalty	1	1
Offensive plays - yards	76 - 408	54 - 123
Rushes - yards	49 - 167	11 - 7
Passes	24 - 12 - 0	36 - 17 - 2
Gross passing yards	256	177
Sacked - yards lost	3 - 15	7 - 61
Net passing yards	241	116
Interceptions - yards	2 - 75	0 - 0
Punts - average	4 - 43.3	6 - 43.8
Punt returns - yards	2 - 20	2 - 22
Kickoff returns - yards	4 - 49	7 - 153
Fumbles - lost	3 - 2	4 - 4
Penalties - yards	7 - 40	5 - 35

AFC Wild Card Game

Dec. 28, 1986
Giants Stadium, East Rutherford, N.J.–69,307

Kansas City	6	0	0	9	– 15
New York Jets	7	14	7	7	– 35

KC - Smith 1 run (Lowery miss)
NY - McNeil 4 run (Leahy)
NY - McNeil 1 pass from Ryan (Leahy)
NY - Toon 11 pass from Ryan (Leahy)
NY - McArthur 21 interception return (Leahy)
KC - Lewis blocked punt recovery (Lowery)
NY - Griggs 6 pass from Ryan (Leahy)
KC - Safety, Jennings stepped out of end zone

TEAM STATISTICS	KC	NY
First Downs	15	19
Rushing	4	9
Passing	8	10
Penalty	3	0
Offensive plays - yards	59 - 241	61 - 306
Rushes - yards	20 - 67	36 - 165
Passes	37 - 20 - 2	23 - 16 - 0
Gross passing yards	177	153
Sacked - yards lost	2 - 3	2 - 12
Net passing yards	174	141
Interceptions - yards	0 - 0	2 - 33
Punts - average	3 - 41.3	4 - 29.0
Had blocked	0	1
Punt returns - yards	3 - 5	1 - 4
Kickoff returns - yards	6 - 85	3 - 27
Fumbles - lost	2 - 1	1 - 0
Penalties - yards	1 - 5	8 - 54

NFC Wild Card Game

Dec. 28, 1986
RFK Stadium, Washington–54,180

Los Angeles	0	0	0	7	– 7
Washington	10	3	3	3	– 19

Was - Atkinson 25 FG
Was - Bryant 14 pass from Schroeder (Atkinson)
Was - Atkinson 20 FG
Was - Atkinson 38 FG
LA - House 12 pass from Everett (Lansford)
Was - Atkinson 19 FG

TEAM STATISTICS	LA	Was
First Downs	16	15
Rushing	9	9
Passing	6	5
Penalty	1	1
Offensive plays - yards	53 - 324	64 - 228
Rushes - yards	34 - 198	41 - 138
Passes	18 - 9 - 2	23 - 13 - 0
Gross passing yards	136	90
Sacked - yards lost	1 - 10	0 - 0
Net passing yards	126	90
Interceptions - yards	0 - 0	2 - 18
Punts - average	3 - 38.3	5 - 42.2
Punt returns - yards	2 - 23	2 - 8
Kickoff returns - yards	6 - 86	2 - 27
Fumbles - lost	4 - 4	1 - 0
Penalties - yards	8 - 78	6 - 45

AFC Divisional Playoff

Jan. 3, 1987
Municipal Stadium, Cleveland–79,650

New York	7	3	3	7	0	0	– 20
Cleveland	7	3	0	10	0	3	– 23

NY - Walker 42 pass from Ryan (Leahy)
Cle - Fontenot 37 pass from Kosar (Moseley)
Cle - Moseley 38 FG
NY - Leahy 46 FG
NY - Leahy 37 FG
NY - McNeil 25 run (Leahy)
Cle - Mack 1 run (Moseley)
Cle - Moseley 22 FG
Cle - Moseley 27 FG

TEAM STATISTICS	NY	Cle
First Downs	14	33
Rushing	6	6
Passing	8	21
Penalty	0	6
Offensive plays - yards	71 - 287	96 - 558
Rushes - yards	31 - 104	27 - 75
Passes	30 - 17 - 0	65 - 34 - 2
Gross passing yards	237	494
Sacked - yards lost	9 - 54	4 - 11
Net passing yards	183	483
Interceptions - yards	2 - 0	0 - 0
Punts - average	14 - 37.9	8 - 38.8
Punt returns - yards	3 - 23	7 - 65
Kickoff returns - yards	5 - 91	5 - 46
Fumbles - lost	0 - 0	2 - 0
Penalties - yards	10 - 94	4 - 40

NFC Divisional Playoff

Jan. 3, 1987
Soldier Field, Chicago–65,141

Washington	7	0	7	13	– 27
Chicago	0	13	0	0	– 13

Was - Monk 28 pass from Schroeder (Atkinson)
Chi - Gault 50 pass from Flutie (Butler)
Chi - Butler 23 FG
Chi - Butler 41 FG
Was - Monk 23 pass from Schroeder (Atkinson)
Was - Rogers 1 run (Atkinson)
Was - Atkinson 35 FG
Was - Atkinson 25 FG

TEAM STATISTICS	Was	Chi
First Downs	19	14
Rushing	8	8
Passing	8	5
Penalty	3	1
Offensive plays - yards	73 - 302	56 - 220
Rushes - yards	39 - 134	24 - 93
Passes	32 - 15 - 1	31 - 11 - 2
Gross passing yards	184	134
Sacked - yards lost	2 - 16	1 - 7
Net passing yards	168	127
Interceptions - yards	2 - 33	1 - 43
Punts - average	7 - 39.3	5 - 40.6
Punt returns - yards	3 - 22	5 - 27
Kickoff returns - yards	3 - 71	6 - 159
Fumbles - lost	2 - 0	3 - 2
Penalties - yards	8 - 65	4 - 42

AFC Divisional Playoff

Jan. 4, 1987
Mile High Stadium, Denver–76,105

New England	0	10	7	0	– 17
Denver	3	7	10	2	– 22

Den - Karlis 27 FG
NE - Morgan 19 pass from Eason (Franklin)
Den - Elway 22 run (Karlis)
NE - Franklin 38 FG
Den - Karlis 22 FG
NE - Morgan 45 pass from Eason (Franklin)
Den - Johnson 48 pass from Elway (Karlis)
Den - Safety, Jones tackled Eason in end zone

TEAM STATISTICS	NE	Den
First Downs	12	23
Rushing	6	12
Passing	6	9
Penalty	0	2
Offensive plays - yards	54 - 271	75 - 444
Rushes - yards	24 - 121	42 - 188

Passes	24 - 13 - 0	32 - 13 - 2
Gross passing yards	194	257
Sacked - yards lost	6 - 44	1 - 4
Net passing yards	150	253
Interceptions - yards	2 - 2	0 - 0
Punts - average	9 - 50.2	6 - 46.0
Punt returns - yards	2 - 13	4 - 35
Kickoff returns - yards	2 - 31	4 - 84
Fumbles - lost	1 - 0	0 - 0
Penalties - yards	5 - 45	3 - 20

NFC Divisional Playoff
Jan. 4, 1987
Giants Stadium, East Rutherford,
N.J.–76,034

San Francisco	3	0	0	0	– 3
New York	7	21	21	0	– 49

NY - Bavaro 24 pass from Simms (Allegre)
SF - Wersching 26 FG
NY - Morris 45 run (Allegre)
NY - B. Johnson 15 pass from Simms (Allegre)
NY - Taylor 34 interception return (Allegre)
NY - McConkey 28 pass from Simms (Allegre)
NY - Mowatt 29 pass from Simms (Allegre)
NY - Morris 2 run (Allegre)

TEAM STATISTICS	SF	NY
First Downs	9	21
Rushing	2	12
Passing	6	6
Penalty	1	3
Offensive plays - yards	58 - 184	65 - 366
Rushes - yards	20 - 29	44 - 216
Passes	37 - 15 - 3	20 - 10 - 0
Gross passing yards	162	159
Sacked - yards lost	1 - 7	1 - 9
Net passing yards	155	150
Interceptions - yards	0 - 0	3 - 77
Punts - average	10 - 40.0	7 - 43.9
Punt returns - yards	2 - 11	7 - 57
Kickoff returns - yards	7 - 119	2 - 32
Fumbles - lost	2 - 1	0 - 0
Penalties - yards	11 - 62	3 - 23

AFC Championship Game
Jan. 11, 1987
Municipal Stadium, Cleveland–79,915

Denver	0	10	3	7	3	– 23
Cleveland	7	3	0	10	0	– 20

Cle - Fontenot 6 pass from Kosar (Moseley)
Den - Karlis 19 FG
Den - Willhite 1 run (Karlis)
Cle - Moseley 29 FG
Den - Karlis 26 FG
Cle - Moseley 24 FG
Cle - Brennan 48 pass from Kosar (Moseley)
Den - M. Jackson 5 pass from Elway (Karlis)
Den - Karlis 33 FG

TEAM STATISTICS	Den	Cle
First Downs	22	17
Rushing	6	4
Passing	13	12
Penalty	3	1
Offensive plays - yards	77 - 374	66 - 356

Rushes - yards	37 - 149	33 - 100
Passes	38 - 22 - 1	32 - 18 - 2
Gross passing yards	244	259
Sacked - yards lost	2 - 19	1 - 3
Net passing yards	225	256
Interceptions - yards	2 - 40	1 - 0
Punts - average	7 - 37.6	6 - 43.2
Punt returns - yards	3 - 10	3 - 37
Kickoff returns - yards	5 - 33	6 - 105
Fumbles - lost	1 - 0	3 - 2
Penalties - yards	6 - 39	9 - 76

NFC Championship Game
Jan. 11, 1987
Giants Stadium, East Rutherford,
N.J.–76,633

Washington	0	0	0	0	– 0
New York	10	7	0	0	– 17

NY - Allegre 47 FG
NY - Manuel 11 pass from Simms (Allegre)
NY - Morris 1 run (Allegre)

TEAM STATISTICS	Was	NY
First Downs	12	12
Rushing	2	8
Passing	7	3
Penalty	3	1
Offensive plays - yards	70 - 190	61 - 199
Rushes - yards	16 - 40	46 - 117
Passes	50 - 20 - 1	14 - 7 - 0
Gross passing yards	195	90
Sacked - yards lost	4 - 45	1 - 8
Net passing yards	150	82
Interceptions - yards	0 - 0	1 - 15
Punts - average	9 - 35.6	6 - 42.3
Punt returns - yards	3 - 19	5 - 27
Kickoff returns - yards	2 - 15	0 - 0
Fumbles - lost	3 - 1	4 - 3
Penalties - yards	3 - 15	6 - 48

Super Bowl XXI
Jan. 25, 1987
Rose Bowl, Pasadena–101,063

Denver	10	0	0	10	– 20
New York Giants	7	2	17	13	– 39

Den - Karlis 48 FG
NY - Mowatt 6 pass from Simms (Allegre)
Den - Elway 4 run (Karlis)
NY - Safety, Martin tackled Elway in end zone
NY - Bavaro 13 pass from Simms (Allegre)
NY - Allegre 21 FG
NY - Morris 1 run (Allegre)
NY - McConkey 6 pass from Simms (Allegre)
Den - Karlis 28 FG
NY - Anderson 2 run (Allegre miss)
Den - Johnson 47 pass from Elway (Karlis)
MVP: Phil Simms, QB, New York

TEAM STATISTICS	Den	NY
First Downs	23	24
Rushing	5	10
Passing	16	13
Penalty	2	1
Offensive plays - yards	64 - 372	64 - 399
Rushes - yards	19 - 52	38 - 136

Passes	41 - 26 - 1	25 - 22 - 0
Gross passing yards	352	268
Sacked - yards lost	4 - 32	1 - 5
Net passing yards	320	263
Interceptions - yards	0 - 0	1 - (-7
Punts - average	2 - 41.0	3 - 46.0
Punt returns - yards	1 - 9	1 - 25
Kickoff returns - yards	5 - 84	4 - 53
Fumbles - lost	2 - 0	0 - 0
Penalties - yards	4 - 28	6 - 48

NFC Wild Card Game
Jan. 3, 1988
Louisiana Superdome, New Orleans–68,127

Minnesota	10	21	3	10	– 44
New Orleans	7	3	0	0	– 10

NO - Martin 10 pass from Hebert (Andersen)
Min - C. Nelson 42 FG
Min - Carter 84 punt return (C. Nelson)
Min - Jordan 5 pass from Wilson (C. Nelson)
Min - Carter 10 pass from Rice (C. Nelson)
NO - Andersen 40 FG
Min - Jones 44 pass from Wilson (C. Nelson)
Min - C. Nelson 32 FG
Min - C. Nelson 19 FG
Min - Dozier 8 run (C. Nelson)

TEAM STATISTICS	Min	NO
First Downs	28	9
Rushing	14	0
Passing	14	7
Penalty	0	2
Offensive plays - yards	86 - 417	47 - 149
Rushes - yards	50 - 210	14 - 53
Passes	30 - 17 - 0	31 - 11 - 4
Gross passing yards	249	104
Sacked - yards lost	6 - 42	2 - 8
Net passing yards	207	96
Interceptions - yards	4 - 45	0 - 0
Punts - average	3 - 32.0	6 - 44.2
Punt returns - yards	6 - 143	1 - 0
Kickoff returns - yards	0 - 0	7 - 101
Fumbles - lost	4 - 2	3 - 2
Penalties - yards	5 - 42	4 - 26

AFC Wild Card Game
Jan. 3, 1988
Astrodome, Houston–49,622

Seattle	7	3	3	7	0	– 20
Houston	3	10	7	0	3	– 23

Sea - Largent 20 pass from Krieg (N. Johnson)
Hou - Zendejas 47 FG
Hou - Rozier 1 run (Zendejas)
Hou - Zendejas 49 FG
Sea - N. Johnson 33 FG
Sea - N. Johnson 41 FG
Hou - Drewrey 29 pass from Moon (Zendejas)
Sea - Largent 12 pass from Krieg (N. Johnson)
Hou - Zendejas 42 FG

TEAM STATISTICS	Sea	Hou
First Downs	11	27
Rushing	1	9
Passing	10	18
Offensive plays - yards	52 - 250	84 - 437

Rushes - yards	11 - 29	50 - 178
Passes	39 - 16 - 0	32 - 21 - 1
Gross passing yards	237	273
Sacked - yards lost	2 - 16	2 - 14
Net passing yards	221	259
Interceptions - yards	1 - 28	0 - 0
Punts - average	7 - 44.3	3 - 35.0
Punt returns - yards	2 - 66	4 - 27
Kickoff returns - yards	6 - 132	4 - 65
Fumbles - lost	1 - 1	2 - 1
Penalties - yards	3 - 20	4 - 25

NFC Divisional Playoff
Jan. 9, 1988
Candlestick Park, San Francisco—62,547

Minnesota	3	17	10	6	–	36
San Francisco	3	0	14	7	–	24

Min - C. Nelson 21 FG
SF - Wersching 43 FG
Min - Hilton 7 pass from Wilson (C. Nelson)
Min - C. Nelson 23 FG
Min - Rutland 45 interception return (C. Nelson)
SF - Fuller 48 interception return (Wersching)
Min - Jones 5 pass from Wilson (C. Nelson)
SF - Young 5 run (Wersching)
Min - C. Nelson 40 FG
Min - C. Nelson 46 FG
SF - Frank 16 pass from Young (Wersching)
Min - C. Nelson 23 FG

TEAM STATISTICS	Min	SF
First Downs	22	17
Rushing	5	6
Passing	15	10
Penalty	2	1
Offensive plays - yards	70 - 397	66 - 358
Rushes - yards	34 - 117	18 - 115
Passes	34 - 20 - 1	44 - 24 - 2
Gross passing yards	298	267
Sacked - yards lost	2 - 18	4 - 24
Net passing yards	280	243
Interceptions - yards	2 - 40	1 - 48
Punts - average	5 - 36.4	6 - 40.8
Punt returns - yards	3 - 29	3 - 17
Kickoff returns - yards	3 - 76	8 - 130
Fumbles - lost	0 - 0	1 - 0
Penalties - yards	2 - 20	8 - 75

AFC Divisional Playoff
Jan. 9, 1988
Municipal Stadium, Cleveland—78,546

Indianapolis	7	7	0	7	–	21
Cleveland	7	7	7	17	–	38

Cle - Byner 10 pass from Kosar (Bahr)
Ind - Beach 2 pass from Trudeau (Biasucci)
Cle - Langhorne 39 pass from Kosar (Bahr)
Ind - Dickerson 19 pass from Trudeau (Biasucci)
Cle - Byner 2 run (Bahr)
Cle - Bahr 22 FG
Cle - Brennan 2 pass from Kosar (Bahr)
Ind - Bentley 1 run (Biasucci)
Cle - Minnifield 48 interception return (Bahr)

TEAM STATISTICS	Ind	Cle
First Downs	23	25

Rushing	4	10
Passing	16	13
Penalty	3	2
Offensive plays - yards	62 - 315	65 - 404
Rushes - yards	21 - 63	34 - 175
Passes	39 - 22 - 2	31 - 20 - 1
Gross passing yards	266	229
Sacked - yards lost	2 - 14	0 - 0
Net passing yards	252	229
Interceptions - yards	1 - 0	2 - 48
Punts - average	4 - 43.8	1 - 37.0
Punt returns - yards	0 - 0	3 - 32
Kickoff returns - yards	7 - 124	2 - 21
Fumbles - lost	1 - 0	2 - 0
Penalties - yards	7 - 75	4 - 20

NFC Divisional Playoff
Jan. 10, 1988
Soldier Field, Chicago—58,153

Washington	0	14	7	0	–	21
Chicago	7	7	3	0	–	17

Chi - Thomas 2 run (Butler)
Chi - Morris 14 pass from McMahon (Butler)
Was - Rogers 3 run (Haji - Sheikh)
Was - Didier 18 pass from Williams (Haji - Sheikh)
Was - Green 52 punt return (Haji - Sheikh)
Chi - Butler 25 FG

TEAM STATISTICS	Was	Chi
First Downs	17	15
Rushing	4	8
Passing	11	7
Penalty	2	0
Offensive plays - yards	59 - 272	64 - 280
Rushes - yards	29 - 72	30 - 110
Passes	29 - 14 - 1	29 - 15 - 3
Gross passing yards	207	197
Sacked - yards lost	1 - 7	5 - 27
Net passing yards	200	170
Interceptions - yards	3 - 23	1 - 0
Punts - average	4 - 42.3	4 - 36.3
Punt returns - yards	3 - 65	2 - 12
Kickoff returns - yards	4 - 56	3 - 103
Fumbles - lost	1 - 1	1 - 0
Penalties - yards	3 - 20	5 - 50

AFC Divisional Playoff
Jan. 10, 1988
Mile High Stadium, Denver—75,968

Houston	0	3	0	7	–	10
Denver	14	10	3	7	–	34

Den - Lang 1 run (Karlis)
Den - Kay 27 pass from Elway (Karlis)
Den - Karlis 43 FG
Hou - Zendejas 46 FG
Den - Kay 1 pass from Elway (Karlis)
Den - Karlis 23 FG
Hou - Givins 19 pass from Moon (Zendejas)
Den - Elway 3 run (Karlis)

TEAM STATISTICS	Hou	Den
First Downs	20	19
Rushing	5	9
Passing	14	9

Penalty	1	1
Offensive plays - yards	69 - 337	55 - 316
Rushes - yards	26 - 73	29 - 61
Passes	43 - 24 - 2	25 - 14 - 1
Gross passing yards	264	259
Sacked - yards lost	0 - 0	1 - 4
Net passing yards	264	255
Interceptions - yards	1 - 2	2 - 75
Punts - average	3 - 44.7	2 - 46.0
Punt returns - yards	0 - 0	2 - 15
Kickoff returns - yards	3 - 62	2 - 28
Fumbles - lost	2 - 1	0 - 0
Penalties - yards	10 - 73	4 - 35

NFC Championship Game
Jan. 17, 1988
RFK Stadium, Washington—55,212

Minnesota	0	7	0	3	–	10
Washington	7	0	3	7	–	17

Was - Bryant 42 pass from Williams (Haji - Sheikh)
Min - Lewis 23 pass from Wilson (C. Nelson)
Was - Haji - Sheikh 28 FG
Min - C. Nelson 18 FG
Was - Clark 7 pass from Williams (Haji - Sheikh)

TEAM STATISTICS	Min	Was
First Downs	16	11
Rushing	5	7
Passing	10	4
Penalty	1	0
Offensive plays - yards	68 - 259	60 - 280
Rushes - yards	21 - 76	34 - 161
Passes	39 - 19 - 1	26 - 9 - 0
Gross passing yards	243	119
Sacked - yards lost	8 - 60	0 - 0
Net passing yards	183	119
Interceptions - yards	0 - 0	1 - 10
Punts - average	10 - 33.2	8 - 39.1
Punt returns - yards	4 - 57	4 - 10
Kickoff returns - yards	3 - 58	3 - 54
Fumbles - lost	0 - 0	1 - 0
Penalties - yards	2 - 10	3 - 18

AFC Championship Game
Jan. 17, 1988
Mile High Stadium, Denver—75,993

Cleveland	0	3	21	9	–	33
Denver	14	7	10	7	–	38

Den - Nattiel 8 pass from Elway (Karlis)
Den - Sewell 1 run (Karlis)
Cle - Bahr 24 FG
Den - Lang 1 run (Karlis)
Cle - Langhorne 18 pass from Kosar (Bahr)
Den - Jackson 80 pass from Elway (Karlis)
Cle - Byner 32 pass from Kosar (Bahr)
Cle - Byner 4 run (Bahr)
Den - Karlis 38 FG
Cle - Slaughter 4 pass from Kosar (Bahr)
Den - Winder 20 pass from Elway (Karlis)
Cle - Safety, Horan stepped out of end zone

TEAM STATISTICS	Cle	Den
First Downs	25	24

Rushing	8	10
Passing	15	11
Penalty	2	3
Offensive plays - yards	70 - 464	67 - 412
Rushes - yards	27 - 128	39 - 156
Passes	41 - 26 - 1	26 - 14 - 1
Gross passing yards	356	281
Sacked - yards lost	2 - 20	2 - 25
Net passing yards	336	256
Interceptions - yards	1 - 13	1 - 0
Punts - average	2 - 48.0	3 - 33.7
Punt returns - yards	2 - 24	2 - 13
Kickoff returns - yards	5 - 94	3 - 43
Fumbles - lost	3 - 3	2 - 0
Penalties - yards	7 - 59	7 - 44

Super Bowl XXII

Jan. 31, 1988

Jack Murphy Stadium, San Diego–73,302

Washington	0	35	0	7	–	42
Denver	10	0	0	0	–	10

Den - Nattiel 56 pass from Elway (Karlis)
Den - Karlis 24 FG
Was - Sanders 80 pass from Williams (Haji - Sheikh)
Was - Clark 27 pass from Williams (Haji - Sheikh)
Was - Smith 58 run (Haji - Sheikh)
Was - Sanders 50 pass from Williams (Haji - Sheikh)
Was - Didier 8 pass from Williams (Haji - Sheikh)
Was - Smith 4 run (Haji - Sheikh)

MVP: Doug Williams, QB, Washington

TEAM STATISTICS	Was	Den
First Downs	25	18
Rushing	13	6
Passing	11	10
Penalty	1	2
Offensive plays - yards	72 - 602	61 - 327
Rushes - yards	40 - 280	17 - 97
Passes	30 - 18 - 1	39 - 15 - 3
Gross passing yards	340	280
Sacked - yards lost	2 - 18	5 - 50
Net passing yards	322	230
Interceptions - yards	3 - 11	1 - 0
Punts - average	4 - 37.5	7 - 36.1
Punt returns - yards	1 - 0	2 - 18
Kickoff returns - yards	3 - 46	5 - 88
Fumbles - lost	1 - 0	0 - 0
Penalties - yards	6 - 65	5 - 26

AFC Wild Card Game

Dec. 24, 1988

Municipal Stadium, Cleveland–74,977

Houston	0	14	0	10	–	24
Cleveland	3	6	7	7	–	23

Cle - Bahr 33 FG
Hou - Pinkett 14 pass from Moon (Zendejas)
Hou - Pinkett 16 run (Zendejas)
Cle - Bahr 26 FG
Cle - Bahr 28 FG
Cle - Slaughter 14 pass from Pagel (Bahr)

Hou - White 1 run (Zendejas)
Hou - Zendejas 49 FG
Cle - Slaughter 2 pass from Pagel (Bahr)

TEAM STATISTICS	Hou	Cle
First Downs	19	19
Rushing	7	4
Passing	12	11
Penalty	0	4
Offensive plays - yards	62 - 334	54 - 260
Rushes - yards	35 - 129	26 - 68
Passes	26 - 16 - 3	28 - 19 - 1
Gross passing yards	213	192
Sacked - yards lost	1 - 8	0 - 0
Net passing yards	205	192
Interceptions - yards	1 - 0	3 - 49
Punts - average	3 - 37.7	3 - 35.3
Punt returns - yards	0 - 0	3 - 27
Kickoff returns - yards	5 - 72	3 - 75
Fumbles - lost	2 - 0	1 - 1
Penalties - yards	13 - 118	9 - 75

NFC Wild Card Game

Dec. 26, 1988

Metrodome, Minneapolis–57,666

Los Angeles	0	7	3	7	–	17
Minnesota	14	0	7	7	–	28

Min - Anderson 7 run (C. Nelson)
Min - Rice 17 run (C. Nelson)
LA - D. Johnson 3 pass from Everett (Lansford)
Min - Anderson 1 run (C. Nelson)
LA - Lansford 43 FG
Min - Hilton 5 pass from Wilson (C. Nelson)
LA - Holohan 11 pass from Everett (Lansford)

TEAM STATISTICS	LA	Min
First Downs	19	20
Rushing	4	7
Passing	15	11
Penalty	0	2
Offensive plays - yards	70 - 342	66 - 310
Rushes - yards	24 - 107	33 - 103
Passes	45 - 19 - 3	28 - 17 - 0
Gross passing yards	247	253
Sacked - yards lost	1 - 12	5 - 46
Net passing yards	235	207
Interceptions - yards	0 - 0	3 - 40
Punts - average	5 - 48.2	7 - 41.6
Punt returns - yards	5 - 60	2 - 15
Kickoff returns - yards	5 - 106	3 - 58
Fumbles - lost	0 - 0	1 - 0
Penalties - yards	10 - 54	6 - 40

NFC Divisional Playoff

Dec. 31, 1988

Soldier Field, Chicago–65,534

Philadelphia	3	6	3	0	–	12
Chicago	7	10	0	3	–	20

Chi - McKinnon 64 pass from Tomczak (Butler)
Phi - Zendejas 42 FG
Phi - Zendejas 29 FG
Chi - Anderson 4 run (Butler)
Chi - Butler 46 FG
Phi - Zendejas 30 FG

Phi - Zendejas 35 FG
Chi - Butler 27 FG

TEAM STATISTICS	Phi	Chi
First Downs	22	14
Rushing	1	8
Passing	21	6
Offensive plays - yards	75 - 430	57 - 341
Rushes - yards	16 - 52	33 - 164
Passes	55 - 27 - 3	23 - 12 - 3
Gross passing yards	407	185
Sacked - yards lost	4 - 29	1 - 8
Net passing yards	378	177
Interceptions - yards	3 - 24	3 - 98
Punts - average	4 - 32.5	2 - 43.0
Punt returns - yards	1 - 3	1 - 0
Kickoff returns - yards	5 - 101	5 - 86
Fumbles - lost	0 - 0	1 - 1
Penalties - yards	7 - 60	1 - 5

AFC Divisional Playoff

Dec. 31, 1988

Riverfront Stadium, Cincinnati–58,560

Seattle	0	0	0	13	–	13
Cincinnati	7	14	0	0	–	21

Cin - Wilson 3 run (Breech)
Cin - Wilson 3 run (Breech)
Cin - Woods 1 run (Breech)
Sea - Williams 7 pass from Krieg (N. Johnson)
Sea - Krieg 1 run (N. Johnson miss)

TEAM STATISTICS	Sea	Cin
First Downs	19	22
Rushing	1	17
Passing	16	5
Penalty	2	0
Offensive plays - yards	69 - 294	68 - 345
Rushes - yards	17 - 18	47 - 254
Passes	50 - 24 - 2	19 - 7 - 0
Gross passing yards	297	108
Sacked - yards lost	2 - 21	2 - 17
Net passing yards	276	91
Interceptions - yards	0 - 0	2 - 0
Punts - average	6 - 44.2	6 - 46.0
Punt returns - yards	5 - 30	3 - 19
Kickoff returns - yards	3 - 66	3 - 54
Fumbles - lost	1 - 1	3 - 2
Penalties - yards	5 - 45	2 - 29

NFC Divisional Playoff

Jan. 1, 1989

Candlestick Park, San Francisco–61,848

Minnesota	3	0	6	0	–	9
San Francisco	7	14	0	13	–	34

Min - C. Nelson 47 FG
SF - Rice 2 pass from Montana (Cofer)
SF - Rice 4 pass from Montana (Cofer)
SF - Rice 11 pass from Montana (Cofer)
Min - Jones 5 pass from Wilson (C. Nelson miss)
SF - Craig 4 run (Cofer)
SF - Craig 80 run (Cofer miss)

TEAM STATISTICS	Min	SF
First Downs	20	20

Rushing	4	7
Passing	14	11
Penalty	2	2
Offensive plays - yards	66 - 262	62 - 372
Rushes - yards	19 - 54	34 - 201
Passes	47 - 23 - 2	28 - 17 - 1
Gross passing yards	255	177
Sacked - yards lost	6 - 47	1 - 6
Net passing yards	208	171
Interceptions - yards	1 - 0	2 - 10
Punts - average	7 - 39.3	5 - 36.2
Punt returns - yards	3 - 27	2 - 27
Kickoff returns - yards	6 - 96	3 - 39
Fumbles - lost	1 - 1	2 - 1
Penalties - yards	9 - 90	6 - 60

AFC Divisional Playoff
Jan. 1, 1989
Rich Stadium, Orchard Park–79,532

Houston	0	3	0	7	– 10
Buffalo	0	7	7	3	– 17

Buf - Riddick 1 run (Norwood)
Hou - Zendejas 35 FG
Buf - Thomas 11 run (Norwood)
Buf - Norwood 27 FG
Hou - Rozier 1 run (Zendejas)

TEAM STATISTICS	Hou	Buf
First Downs	20	18
Rushing	6	6
Passing	12	9
Penalty	2	3
Offensive plays - yards	61 - 351	63 - 372
Rushes - yards	26 - 125	29 - 135
Passes	33 - 17 - 1	33 - 19 - 1
Gross passing yards	240	244
Sacked - yards lost	2 - 14	1 - 7
Net passing yards	226	237
Interceptions - yards	1 - 0	1 - 28
Punts - average	6 - 37.2	4 - 39.3
Had blocked	1	0
Punt returns - yards	1 - 6	4 - 56
Kickoff returns - yards	4 - 58	3 - 57
Fumbles - lost	5 - 2	1 - 0
Penalties - yards	8 - 60	8 - 57

NFC Championship Game
Jan. 8, 1989
Soldier Field, Chicago–64,830

San Francisco	7	7	7	7	– 28
Chicago	0	3	0	0	– 3

SF - Rice 61 pass from Montana (Cofer)
SF - Rice 27 pass from Montana (Cofer)
Chi - Butler 25 FG
SF - Frank 5 pass from Montana (Cofer)
SF - Rathman 4 run (Cofer)

TEAM STATISTICS	SF	Chi
First Downs	21	15
Rushing	9	8
Passing	12	7
Offensive plays - yards	66 - 406	66 - 267
Rushes - yards	37 - 138	25 - 91
Passes	27 - 17 - 0	41 - 20 - 1
Gross passing yards	288	176

Sacked - yards lost	2 - 20	0 - 0
Net passing yards	268	176
Interceptions - yards	1 - 0	0 - 0
Punts - average	6 - 34.5	7 - 31.4
Punt returns - yards	4 - 24	1 - 1
Kickoff returns - yards	2 - 36	5 - 89
Fumbles - lost	1 - 1	2 - 1
Penalties - yards	0 - 0	3 - 35

AFC Championship Game
Jan. 8, 1989
Riverfront Stadium, Cincinnati–59,747

Buffalo	0	10	0	0	– 10
Cincinnati	7	7	0	7	– 21

Cin - Woods 1 run (Breech)
Buf - Reed 9 pass from Kelly (Norwood)
Cin - Brooks 10 pass from Esiason (Breech)
Buf - Norwood 39 FG
Cin - Woods 1 run (Breech)

TEAM STATISTICS	Buf	Cin
First Downs	10	23
Rushing	2	15
Passing	8	5
Penalty	0	3
Offensive plays - yards	50 - 181	73 - 249
Rushes - yards	17 - 45	50 - 175
Passes	30 - 14 - 3	20 - 11 - 2
Gross passing yards	163	94
Sacked - yards lost	3 - 27	3 - 20
Net passing yards	136	74
Interceptions - yards	2 - 25	3 - 23
Punts - average	6 - 45.1	6 - 36.8
Punt returns - yards	1 - 2	3 - 24
Kickoff returns - yards	3 - 57	3 - 30
Fumbles - lost	0 - 0	2 - 0
Penalties - yards	5 - 50	4 - 45

Super Bowl XXIII
Jan. 22, 1989
Joe Robbie Stadium, Miami–75,129

Cincinnati	0	3	10	3	– 16
San Francisco	3	0	3	14	– 20

SF - Cofer 41 FG
Cin - Breech 34 FG
Cin - Breech 43 FG
SF - Cofer 32 FG
Cin - Jennings 93 kickoff return (Breech)
SF - Rice 14 pass from Montana (Cofer)
Cin - Breech 40 FG
SF - Taylor 10 pass from Montana (Cofer)
MVP: Jerry Rice, WR, San Francisco

TEAM STATISTICS	Cin	SF
First Downs	13	23
Rushing	7	6
Passing	6	16
Penalty	0	1
Offensive plays - yards	58 - 229	67 - 453
Rushes - yards	28 - 106	27 - 112
Passes	25 - 11 - 1	36 - 23 - 0
Gross passing yards	144	357
Sacked - yards lost	5 - 21	4 - 16
Net passing yards	123	341
Interceptions - yards	0 - 0	1 - 0

Punts - average	5 - 44.2	4 - 37.0
Punt returns - yards	2 - 5	3 - 56
Kickoff returns - yards	3 - 132	5 - 77
Fumbles - lost	1 - 0	4 - 1
Penalties - yards	7 - 65	4 - 32

NFC Wild Card Game
Dec. 31, 1989
Veterans Stadium, Philadelphia–57,869

Los Angeles	14	0	0	7	– 21
Philadelphia	0	0	0	7	– 7

LA - Ellard 39 pass from Everett (Lansford)
LA - Johnson 4 pass from Everett (Lansford)
Phi - Toney 1 run (Ruzek)
LA - Bell 7 run (Lansford)

TEAM STATISTICS	LA	Phi
First Downs	19	14
Rushing	6	6
Passing	12	8
Penalty	1	0
Offensive plays - yards	71 - 409	62 - 306
Rushes - yards	36 - 144	20 - 95
Passes	33 - 18 - 2	40 - 24 - 1
Gross passing yards	281	238
Sacked - yards lost	2 - 16	2 - 27
Net passing yards	265	211
Interceptions - yards	1 - 0	2 - 34
Punts - average	7 - 37.0	9 - 36.3
Punt returns - yards	3 - 15	2 - 5
Kickoff returns - yards	2 - 14	4 - 52
Fumbles - lost	1 - 1	6 - 2
Penalties - yards	1 - 5	4 - 35

AFC Wild Card Game
Dec. 31, 1989
Astrodome, Houston–58,306

Pittsburgh	7	3	3	10	3	– 26
Houston	0	6	3	14	0	– 23

Pit - Worley 9 run (Anderson)
Hou - Zendejas 26 FG
Hou - Zendejas 35 FG
Pit - Anderson 25 FG
Hou - Zendejas 26 FG
Pit - Anderson 30 FG
Pit - Anderson 48 FG
Hou - Givins 18 pass from Moon (Zendejas)
Hou - Givins 9 pass from Moon (Zendejas)
Pit - Hoge 2 run (Anderson)
Pit - Anderson 50 FG

TEAM STATISTICS	Pit	Hou
First Downs	17	22
Rushing	8	2
Passing	9	18
Penalty	0	2
Offensive plays - yards	64 - 289	73 - 380
Rushes - yards	30 - 177	25 - 65
Passes	33 - 15 - 0	48 - 29 - 0
Gross passing yards	127	315
Sacked - yards lost	1 - 15	0 - 0
Net passing yards	112	315
Interceptions - yards	0 - 0	0 - 0
Punts - average	6 - 25.3	4 - 33.0
Had blocked	1	1

Punt returns - yards	2 - 20	1 - 0
Kickoff returns - yards	6 - 99	2 - 27
Fumbles - lost	1 - 1	3 - 2
Penalties - yards	5 - 40	8 - 45

NFC Divisional Playoff

Jan. 6, 1990

Candlestick Park, San Francisco–64,585

Minnesota	3	0	3	7	–	13
San Francisco	7	20	0	14	–	41

Min	-	Karlis 38 FG
SF	-	Rice 72 pass from Montana (Cofer)
SF	-	Jones 8 pass from Montana (Cofer)
SF	-	Taylor 8 pass from Montana (Cofer miss)
SF	-	Rice 13 pass from Montana (Cofer)
Min	-	Karlis 44 FG
SF	-	Lott 58 interception return (Cofer)
SF	-	Craig 4 run (Cofer)
Min	-	Fenney 3 run (Karlis)

TEAM STATISTICS	Min	SF
First Downs	25	22
Rushing	7	10
Passing	17	11
Penalty	1	1
Offensive plays - yards	79 - 385	57 - 403
Rushes - yards	21 - 86	32 - 162
Passes	54 - 31 - 4	25 - 17 - 0
Gross passing yards	338	241
Sacked - yards lost	4 - 39	0 - 0
Net passing yards	299	241
Interceptions - yards	0 - 0	4 - 127
Punts - average	5 - 25.6	4 - 30.8
Had blocked	1	0
Punt returns - yards	2 - 18	2 - 6
Kickoff returns - yards	7 - 130	4 - 84
Fumbles - lost	1 - 1	1 - 1
Penalties - yards	4 - 31	9 - 65

AFC Divisional Playoff

Jan. 6, 1990

Municipal Stadium, Cleveland–77,706

Buffalo	7	7	7	9	–	30
Cleveland	3	14	14	3	–	34

Buf	-	Reed 72 pass from Kelly (Norwood)
Cle	-	Bahr 45 FG
Cle	-	Slaughter 52 pass from Kosar (Bahr)
Buf	-	Lofton 33 pass from Kelly (Norwood)
Cle	-	Middleton 3 pass from Kosar (Bahr)
Cle	-	Slaughter 44 pass from Kosar (Bahr)
Buf	-	Thomas 6 pass from Kelly (Norwood)
Cle	-	Metcalf 90 kickoff return (Bahr)
Buf	-	Norwood 30 FG
Cle	-	Bahr 47 FG
Buf	-	Thomas 3 pass from Kelly (Norwood miss)

TEAM STATISTICS	Buf	Cle
First Downs	24	18
Rushing	2	10
Passing	20	8
Penalty	2	0
Offensive plays - yards	73 - 453	61 - 325
Rushes - yards	18 - 49	30 - 90
Passes	54 - 28 - 2	29 - 20 - 0

Gross passing yards	405	251
Sacked - yards lost	1 - 1	2 - 16
Net passing yards	404	235
Interceptions - yards	0 - 0	2 - 0
Punts - average	3 - 41.3	3 - 37.7
Punt returns - yards	1 - 4	1 - 0
Kickoff returns - yards	5 - 105	6 - 180
Fumbles - lost	2 - 1	1 - 1
Penalties - yards	6 - 35	5 - 30

NFC Divisional Playoff

Jan. 7, 1990

Giants Stadium, East Rutherford, N.J.–76,325

Los Angeles	0	7	0	6	6	– 19
New York	6	0	7	0	0	– 13

NY	-	Allegre 35 FG
NY	-	Allegre 41 FG
LA	-	Anderson 20 pass from Everett (Lansford)
NY	-	Anderson 2 run (Allegre)
LA	-	Lansford 31 FG
LA	-	Lansford 22 FG
LA	-	Anderson 30 pass from Everett (no attempt)

TEAM STATISTICS	LA	NY
First Downs	26	20
Rushing	6	11
Passing	18	8
Penalty	2	1
Offensive plays - yards	70 - 448	67 - 344
Rushes - yards	24 - 146	36 - 171
Passes	44 - 25 - 1	30 - 14 - 1
Gross passing yards	315	180
Sacked - yards lost	2 - 13	1 - 7
Net passing yards	302	173
Interceptions - yards	1 - 29	1 - 0
Punts - average	4 - 30.3	5 - 37.2
Punt returns - yards	3 - (- 1)	1 - 0
Kickoff returns - yards	5 - 98	4 - 75
Fumbles - lost	1 - 1	3 - 0
Penalties - yards	5 - 35	4 - 59

AFC Divisional Playoff

Jan. 7, 1990

Mile High Stadium, Denver–75,868

Pittsburgh	3	14	3	3	–	23
Denver	0	10	7	7	–	24

Pit	-	Anderson 32 FG
Pit	-	Hoge 7 run (Anderson)
Den	-	Bratton 1 run (Treadwell)
Pit	-	Lipps 9 pass from Brister (Anderson)
Den	-	Treadwell 43 FG
Den	-	Johnson 37 pass from Elway (Treadwell)
Pit	-	Anderson 35 FG
Pit	-	Anderson 32 FG
Den	-	Bratton 1 run (Treadwell)

TEAM STATISTICS	Pit	Den
First Downs	19	19
Rushing	7	8
Passing	12	9
Penalty	0	2
Offensive plays - yards	61 - 404	52 - 364
Rushes - yards	32 - 175	31 - 138

Passes	29 - 19 - 0	20 - 12 - 1
Gross passing yards	229	239
Sacked - yards lost	0 - 0	1 - 13
Net passing yards	229	226
Interceptions - yards	1 - 26	0 - 0
Punts - average	2 - 43.0	4 - 37.5
Punt returns - yards	0 - 0	1 - 6
Kickoff returns - yards	2 - 33	5 - 119
Fumbles - lost	2 - 2	1 - 0
Penalties - yards	8 - 50	2 - 19

NFC Championship Game

Jan. 14, 1990

Candlestick Park, San Francisco–64,769

Los Angeles	3	0	0	0	–	3
San Francisco	0	21	3	6	–	30

LA	-	Lansford 23 FG
SF	-	Jones 20 pass from Montana (Cofer)
SF	-	Craig 1 run (Cofer)
SF	-	Taylor 18 pass from Montana (Cofer)
SF	-	Cofer 28 FG
SF	-	Cofer 36 FG
SF	-	Cofer 25 FG

TEAM STATISTICS	LA	SF
First Downs	9	29
Rushing	0	12
Passing	9	16
Penalty	0	1
Offensive plays - yards	47 - 156	76 - 442
Rushes - yards	10 - 26	44 - 179
Passes	36 - 16 - 3	31 - 27 - 0
Gross passing yards	141	268
Sacked - yards lost	1 - 11	1 - 5
Net passing yards	130	263
Interceptions - yards	0 - 0	3 - 56
Punts - average	7 - 31.4	2 - 31.0
Punt returns - yards	1 - 10	1 - 2
Kickoff returns - yards	6 - 146	2 - 35
Fumbles - lost	1 - 0	3 - 2
Penalties - yards	1 - 10	4 - 40

AFC Championship Game

Jan. 14, 1990

Mile High Stadium, Denver–76,046

Cleveland	0	0	21	0	–	21
Denver	3	7	14	13	–	37

Den	-	Treadwell 39 FG
Den	-	Young 70 pass from Elway (Treadwell)
Cle	-	Brennan 27 pass from Kosar (Bahr)
Den	-	Mobley 5 pass from Elway (Treadwell)
Den	-	Winder 7 run (Treadwell)
Cle	-	Brennan 10 pass from Kosar (Bahr)
Den	-	Manoa 2 run (Bahr)
Den	-	Winder 39 pass from Elway (Treadwell)
Den	-	Treadwell 34 FG
Den	-	Treadwell 31 FG

TEAM STATISTICS	Cle	Den
First Downs	14	22
Rushing	3	6
Passing	11	14
Penalty	0	2
Offensive plays - yards	62 - 256	76 - 497
Rushes - yards	14 - 66	39 - 120

Passes	44 - 19 - 3	36 - 20 - 0
Gross passing yards	210	385
Sacked - yards lost	4 - 20	1 - 8
Net passing yards	190	377
Interceptions - yards	0 - 0	3 - 14
Punts - average	8 - 42.3	5 - 46.4
Punt returns - yards	1 - 7	4 - 36
Kickoff returns - yards	7 - 130	0 - 0
Fumbles - lost	3 - 0	2 - 2
Penalties - yards	8 - 55	1 - 5

Super Bowl XXIV
Jan. 28, 1990
Louisiana Superdome, New Orleans—72,919

San Francisco	13	14	14	14	– 55
Denver	3	0	7	0	– 10

SF - Rice 20 pass from Montana (Cofer)
Den - Treadwell 42 FG
SF - Jones 7 pass from Montana (Cofer miss)
SF - Rathman 1 run (Cofer)
SF - Rice 38 pass from Montana (Cofer)
SF - Rice 28 pass from Montana (Cofer)
SF - Taylor 35 pass from Montana (Cofer)
Den - Elway 3 run (Treadwell)
SF - Rathman 3 run (Cofer)
SF - Craig 1 run (Cofer)
MVP: Joe Montana, QB, San Francisco

TEAM STATISTICS	SF	Den
First Downs	28	12
Rushing	14	5
Passing	14	6
Penalty	0	1
Offensive plays - yards	77 - 461	52 - 167
Rushes - yards	44 - 144	17 - 64
Passes	32 - 24 - 0	29 - 11 - 2
Gross passing yards	317	136
Sacked - yards lost	1 - 0	6 - 33
Net passing yards	317	103
Interceptions - yards	2 - 42	0 - 0
Punts - average	4 - 39.5	6 - 38.5
Punt returns - yards	3 - 38	2 - 11
Kickoff returns - yards	3 - 49	9 - 196
Fumbles - lost	0 - 0	3 - 2
Penalties - yards	4 - 38	0 - 0

NFC Wild Card Game
Jan. 5, 1991
Veterans Stadium, Philadelphia—65,287

Washington	0	10	10	0	– 20
Philadelphia	3	3	0	0	– 6

Phi - Ruzek 37 FG
Phi - Ruzek 28 FG
Was - Monk 16 pass from Rypien (Lohmiller)
Was - Lohmiller 20 FG
Was - Lohmiller 19 FG
Was - Clark 3 pass from Rypien (Lohmiller)

TEAM STATISTICS	Was	Phi
First Downs	15	16
Rushing	3	6
Passing	12	8
Penalty	0	2
Offensive plays - yards	66 - 299	65 - 318
Rushes - yards	35 - 93	28 - 148

Passes	31 - 15 - 1	32 - 15 - 1
Gross passing yards	206	205
Sacked - yards lost	0 - 0	5 - 35
Net passing yards	206	170
Interceptions - yards	1 - 0	1 - 3
Punts - average	9 - 38.0	7 - 39.1
Punt returns - yards	5 - 41	4 - 33
Kickoff returns - yards	3 - 38	4 - 52
Fumbles - lost	2 - 1	2 - 2
Penalties - yards	3 - 23	4 - 40

AFC Wild Card Game
Jan. 5, 1991
Joe Robbie Stadium, Miami—67,276

Kansas City	3	7	6	0	– 16
Miami	0	3	0	14	– 17

KC - Lowery 27 FG
Mia - Stoyanovich 58 FG
KC - Paige 26 pass from DeBerg (Lowery)
KC - Lowery 25 FG
KC - Lowery 38 FG
Mia - Paige 1 pass from Marino (Stoyanovich)
Mia - Clayton 12 pass from Marino (Stoyanovich)

TEAM STATISTICS	KC	Mia
First Downs	16	23
Rushing	4	7
Passing	11	14
Penalty	1	2
Offensive plays - yards	55 - 364	64 - 311
Rushes - yards	24 - 103	32 - 98
Passes	30 - 17 - 1	30 - 19 - 0
Gross passing yards	269	221
Sacked - yards lost	1 - 5	2 - 8
Net passing yards	261	213
Interceptions - yards	0 - 0	1 - 0
Punts - average	4 - 35.0	2 - 59.5
Punt returns - yards	2 - 16	0 - 0
Kickoff returns - yards	3 - 59	3 - 42
Fumbles - lost	0 - 0	2 - 2
Penalties - yards	4 - 35	2 - 22

NFC Wild Card Game
Jan. 6, 1991
Soldier Field, Chicago—60,767

New Orleans	0	3	0	3	– 6
Chicago	3	7	3	3	– 16

Chi - Butler 19 FG
Chi - Thornton 18 pass from Tomczak (Butler)
NO - Andersen 47 FG
Chi - Butler 22 FG
NO - Andersen 38 FG
Chi - Butler 21 FG

TEAM STATISTICS	NO	Chi
First Downs	11	18
Rushing	2	9
Passing	7	8
Penalty	2	1
Offensive plays - yards	54 - 193	71 - 365
Rushes - yards	18 - 65	43 - 189
Passes	34 - 11 - 3	26 - 13 - 0
Gross passing yards	153	188
Sacked - yards lost	2 - 25	2 - 12

Net passing yards	128	176
Interceptions - yards	0 - 0	3 - 36
Punts - average	3 - 30.0	2 - 27.5
Punt returns - yards	1 - 2	2 - 13
Kickoff returns - yards	5 - 85	1 - 39
Fumbles - lost	1 - 0	2 - 1
Penalties - yards	2 - 10	7 - 57

AFC Wild Card Game
Jan. 6, 1991
Riverfront Stadium, Cincinnati—60,012

Houston	0	0	7	7	– 14
Cincinnati	10	10	14	7	– 41

Cin - Woods 1 run (Breech)
Cin - Breech 27 FG
Cin - Green 2 pass from Esiason (Breech)
Cin - Breech 30 FG
Cin - Ball 3 run (Breech)
Cin - Esiason 10 run (Breech)
Hou - Givins 16 pass from Carlson (Garcia)
Cin - Kattus 9 pass from Esiason (Breech)
Hou - Givins 5 pass from Carlson (Garcia)

TEAM STATISTICS	Hou	Cin
First Downs	13	24
Rushing	4	15
Passing	9	7
Penalty	0	2
Offensive plays - yards	47 - 226	69 - 349
Rushes - yards	13 - 67	44 - 187
Passes	33 - 16 - 1	25 - 15 - 0
Gross passing yards	165	162
Sacked - yards lost	1 - 6	0 - 0
Net passing yards	159	162
Interceptions - yards	0 - 0	1 - 43
Punts - average	6 - 42.7	3 - 45.0
Punt returns - yards	1 - 19	3 - 42
Kickoff returns - yards	6 - 114	3 - 58
Fumbles - lost	2 - 1	1 - 0
Penalties - yards	5 - 33	4 - 40

NFC Divisional Playoff
Jan. 12, 1991
Candlestick Park, San Francisco—65,292

Washington	10	0	0	0	– 10
San Francisco	7	14	0	7	– 28

Was - Monk 31 pass from Rypien (Lohmiller)
SF - Rathman 1 run (Cofer)
Was - Lohmiller 44 FG
SF - Rice 10 pass from Montana (Cofer)
SF - Sherrard 8 pass from Montana (Cofer)
SF - M. Carter 61 interception return (Cofer)

TEAM STATISTICS	Was	SF
First Downs	25	20
Rushing	6	3
Passing	18	16
Penalty	1	1
Offensive plays - yards	72 - 441	58 - 338
Rushes - yards	24 - 80	24 - 46
Passes	48 - 27 - 3	32 - 23 - 1
Gross passing yards	361	302
Sacked - yards lost	0 - 0	2 - 10
Net passing yards	351	292
Interceptions - yards	1 - 15	3 - 61

Punts - average	4 - 33.0	5 - 41.8
Punt returns - yards	3 - 20	1 - (- 4
Kickoff returns - yards	4 - 74	1 - 19
Fumbles - lost	0 - 0	0 - 0
Penalties - yards	1 - 15	4 - 25

AFC Divisional Playoff
Jan. 12, 1991
Rich Stadium, Orchard Park–77,087

Miami	3	14	3	14	–	34
Buffalo	13	14	3	14	–	44

Buf - Reed 40 pass from Kelly (Norwood)
Mia - Stoyanovich 49 FG
Buf - Norwood 24 FG
Buf - Norwood 22 FG
Buf - Thomas 5 run (Norwood)
Mia - Duper 64 pass from Marino (Stoyanovich)
Buf - Lofton 13 pass from Kelly (Norwood)
Mia - Marino 2 run (Stoyanovich)
Mia - Stoyanovich 22 FG
Buf - Norwood 28 FG
Mia - Foster 2 pass from Marino (Stoyanovich)
Buf - Thomas 5 run (Norwood)
Buf - Reed 26 pass from Kelly (Norwood)
Mia - Martin 8 pass from Marino (Stoyanovich)

TEAM STATISTICS	Mia	Buf
First Downs	24	24
Rushing	9	7
Passing	13	16
Penalty	2	1
Offensive plays - yards	76 - 430	66 - 493
Rushes - yards	27 - 107	37 - 154
Passes	49 - 23 - 2	29 - 19 - 1
Gross passing yards	323	339
Sacked - yards lost	0 - 0	0 - 0
Net passing yards	323	339
Interceptions - yards	1 - 0	2 - 9
Punts - average	2 - 40.0	1 - 47.0
Punt returns - yards	1 - 3	2 - 17
Kickoff returns - yards	9 - 151	6 - 116
Fumbles - lost	1 - 1	3 - 1
Penalties - yards	4 - 32	4 - 30

NFC Divisional Playoff
Jan. 13, 1991
Giants Stadium, East Rutherford,
N.J.–77,025

Chicago	0	3	0	0	–	3
New York	10	7	7	7	–	31

NY - Bahr 46 FG
NY - Baker 21 pass from Hostetler (Bahr)
Chi - Butler 33 FG
NY - Cross 5 pass from Hostetler (Bahr)
NY - Hostetler 3 run (Bahr)
NY - Carthon 1 run (Bahr)

TEAM STATISTICS	Chi	NY
First Downs	11	23
Rushing	0	16
Passing	11	7
Offensive plays - yards	52 - 232	65 - 288
Rushes - yards	16 - 27	48 - 194

Passes	36 - 17 - 2	17 - 10 - 0
Gross passing yards	205	112
Sacked - yards lost	0 - 0	3 - 18
Net passing yards	205	94
Interceptions - yards	0 - 0	2 - 48
Punts - average	2 - 42.0	3 - 40.7
Punt returns - yards	2 - 3	1 - 13
Kickoff returns - yards	5 - 112	1 - 18
Fumbles - lost	0 - 0	1 - 1
Penalties - yards	4 - 30	2 - 15

AFC Divisional Playoff
Jan. 13, 1991
Memorial Coliseum, Los Angeles–92,045

Cincinnati	0	3	0	7	–	10
Los Angeles	0	7	3	10	–	20

Cin - Breech 27 FG
LA - Fernandez 13 pass from Schroeder (Jaeger)
LA - Jaeger 49 FG
Cin - Jennings 8 pass from Esiason (Breech)
LA - Horton 41 pass from Schroeder (Jaeger)
LA - Jaeger 25 FG

TEAM STATISTICS	Cin	LA
First Downs	12	20
Rushing	7	11
Passing	5	9
Offensive plays - yards	48 - 182	56 - 389
Rushes - yards	29 - 124	32 - 235
Passes	15 - 8 - 0	21 - 11 - 1
Gross passing yards	104	172
Sacked - yards lost	4 - 46	3 - 18
Net passing yards	58	154
Interceptions - yards	1 - 11	0 - 0
Punts - average	5 - 51.6	2 - 39.5
Punt returns - yards	0 - 0	3 - 40
Kickoff returns - yards	4 - 82	1 - 18
Fumbles - lost	1 - 0	0 - 0
Penalties - yards	1 - 5	0 - 0

NFC Championship Game
Jan. 20, 1991
Candlestick Park, San Francisco–65,750

New York	3	3	3	6	–	15
San Francisco	3	3	7	0	–	13

SF - Cofer 47 FG
NY - Bahr 28 FG
NY - Bahr 42 FG
SF - Cofer 35 FG
SF - Taylor 61 pass from Montana (Cofer)
NY - Bahr 46 FG
NY - Bahr 38 FG
NY - Bahr 42 FG

TEAM STATISTICS	NY	SF
First Downs	20	13
Rushing	8	1
Passing	8	11
Penalty	4	1
Offensive plays - yards	68 - 311	41 - 240
Rushes - yards	36 - 152	11 - 39
Passes	29 - 15 - 0	27 - 19 - 0
Gross passing yards	176	215

Sacked - yards lost	3 - 17	3 - 14
Net passing yards	159	201
Interceptions - yards	0 - 0	0 - 0
Punts - average	3 - 41.3	5 - 40.0
Punt returns - yards	5 - 42	2 - 40
Kickoff returns - yards	3 - 39	4 - 85
Fumbles - lost	0 - 0	3 - 1
Penalties - yards	5 - 45	9 - 63

AFC Championship Game
Jan. 20, 1991
Rich Stadium, Orchard Park–80,324

Los Angeles	3	0	0	0	–	3
Buffalo	21	20	0	10	–	51

Buf - Lofton 13 pass from Kelly (Norwood)
LA - Jaeger 41 FG
Buf - Thomas 12 run (Norwood)
Buf - Talley 27 interception return (Norwood)
Buf - K. Davis 1 run (Norwood miss)
Buf - K. Davis 3 run (Norwood)
Buf - Lofton 8 pass from Kelly (Norwood)
Buf - K. Davis 1 run (Norwood)
Buf - Norwood 39 FG

TEAM STATISTICS	LA	Buf
First Downs	21	30
Rushing	12	14
Passing	8	15
Penalty	1	1
Offensive plays - yards	68 - 320	69 - 502
Rushes - yards	28 - 151	46 - 202
Passes	39 - 15 - 6	23 - 17 - 1
Gross passing yards	176	300
Sacked - yards lost	1 - 7	0 - 0
Net passing yards	169	300
Interceptions - yards	1 - 0	6 - 113
Punts - average	3 - 40.3	2 - 37.5
Punt returns - yards	2 - 22	2 - 30
Kickoff returns - yards	9 - 119	2 - 30
Fumbles - lost	1 - 1	3 - 0
Penalties - yards	2 - 28	6 - 32

Super Bowl XXV
Jan. 27, 1991
Tampa Stadium–73,813

Buffalo	3	9	0	7	–	19
New York Giants	3	7	7	3	–	20

NY - Bahr 28 FG
Buf - Norwood 23 FG
Buf - D. Smith 1 run (Norwood)
Buf - Safety, B. Smith tackled Hostetler in end zone
NY - Baker 14 pass from Hostetler (Bahr)
NY - Anderson 1 run (Bahr)
Buf - Thomas 31 run (Norwood)
NY - Bahr 21 FG

MVP: Ottis Anderson, RB, New York

TEAM STATISTICS	Buf	NY
First Downs	18	24
Rushing	8	10
Passing	9	13
Penalty	1	1
Offensive plays - yards	56 - 371	73 - 386

Rushes - yards	25 - 166	39 - 172
Passes	30 - 18 - 0	32 - 20 - 0
Gross passing yards	212	222
Sacked - yards lost	1 - 7	2 - 8
Net passing yards	205	214
Interceptions - yards	0 - 0	0 - 0
Punts - average	6 - 38.8	4 - 43.8
Punt returns - yards	0 - 0	2 - 37
Kickoff returns - yards	6 - 114	3 - 48
Fumbles - lost	1 - 0	0 - 0
Penalties - yards	6 - 35	5 - 31

AFC Wild Card Game
Dec. 28, 1991
Arrowhead Stadium, Kansas City–75,827

Los Angeles	0	3	3	0	– 6
Kansas City	0	7	0	3	– 10

KC - F. Jones 11 pass from DeBerg (Lowery)
LA - Jaeger 32 FG
LA - Jaeger 26 FG
KC - Lowery 18 FG

TEAM STATISTICS	LA	KC
First Downs	16	16
Rushing	7	10
Passing	7	5
Penalty	2	1
Offensive plays - yards	55 - 276	55 - 204
Rushes - yards	30 - 152	39 - 131
Passes	23 - 12 - 4	14 - 9 - 1
Gross passing yards	140	89
Sacked - yards lost	2 - 16	2 - 16
Net passing yards	124	73
Interceptions - yards	1 - 35	4 - 76
Punts - average	1 - 20.0	2 - 46.0
Punt returns - yards	2 - 23	0 - 0
Kickoff returns - yards	3 - 46	2 - 33
Fumbles - lost	2 - 2	2 - 1
Penalties - yards	9 - 75	3 - 20

NFC Wild Card Game
Dec. 28, 1991
Louisiana Superdome, New Orleans–68,794

Atlanta	0	10	7	10	– 27
New Orleans	7	6	0	7	– 20

NO - Turner 26 pass from Hebert (Andersen)
NO - Andersen 45 FG
Atl - Rison 24 pass from Miller (N. Johnson)
Atl - N. Johnson 44 FG
NO - Andersen 35 FG
Atl - Haynes 20 pass from Miller (N. Johnson)
NO - Hilliard 1 run (Andersen)
Atl - N. Johnson 36 FG
Atl - Haynes 61 pass from Miller (N. Johnson)

TEAM STATISTICS	Atl	NO
First Downs	20	23
Rushing	6	3
Passing	13	16
Penalty	1	4
Offensive plays - yards	57 - 334	67 - 330
Rushes - yards	22 - 79	22 - 65
Passes	30 - 18 - 1	44 - 26 - 2
Gross passing yards	291	273

Sacked - yards lost	5 - 36	1 - 8
Net passing yards	255	265
Interceptions - yards	2 - 31	1 - 0
Punts - average	1 - 42.0	3 - 54.0
Punt returns - yards	1 - 22	0 - 0
Kickoff returns - yards	3 - 32	4 - 98
Fumbles - lost	3 - 1	2 - 1
Penalties - yards	6 - 48	5 - 49

AFC Wild Card Game
Dec. 29, 1991
Astrodome, Houston–61,485

New York	0	10	0	0	– 10
Houston	7	7	0	3	– 17

Hou - Givins 5 pass from Moon (Del Greco)
NY - Toon 10 pass from O'Brien (Allegre)
Hou - Givins 20 pass from Moon (Del Greco)
NY - Allegre 33 FG
Hou - Del Greco 53 FG

TEAM STATISTICS	NY	Hou
First Downs	18	21
Rushing	1	5
Passing	14	15
Penalty	3	1
Offensive plays - yards	55 - 285	64 - 303
Rushes - yards	23 - 71	20 - 71
Passes	31 - 21 - 3	40 - 28 - 1
Gross passing yards	221	271
Sacked - yards lost	1 - 7	4 - 39
Net passing yards	214	232
Interceptions - yards	1 - 0	3 - 32
Punts - average	2 - 36.0	2 - 44.5
Punt returns - yards	0 - 0	0 - 0
Kickoff returns - yards	3 - 54	1 - 0
Fumbles - lost	0 - 0	3 - 1
Penalties - yards	5 - 45	8 - 55

NFC Wild Card Game
Dec. 29, 1991
Soldier Field, Chicago–62,594

Dallas	10	0	7	0	– 17
Chicago	0	3	3	7	– 13

Dal - Willis 27 FG
Dal - E. Smith 1 run (Willis)
Chi - Butler 19 FG
Chi - Butler 43 FG
Dal - Novacek 3 pass from Beuerlein (Willis)
Chi - Waddle 6 pass from Harbaugh (Butler)

TEAM STATISTICS	Dal	Chi
First Downs	15	26
Rushing	6	12
Passing	7	14
Penalty	2	0
Offensive plays - yards	48 - 288	82 - 372
Rushes - yards	30 - 108	34 - 150
Passes	18 - 9 - 0	45 - 23 - 2
Gross passing yards	180	233
Sacked - yards lost	0 - 0	3 - 11
Net passing yards	180	222
Interceptions - yards	2 - 7	0 - 0
Punts - average	3 - 44.7	1 - 0.0
Had blocked	0	1

Punt returns - yards	0 - 0	2 - 5
Kickoff returns - yards	2 - 34	4 - 59
Fumbles - lost	2 - 0	1 - 1
Penalties - yards	2 - 16	4 - 16

AFC Divisional Playoff
Jan. 4, 1992
Mile High Stadium, Denver–75,301

Houston	14	7	0	3	– 24
Denver	6	7	3	10	– 26

Hou - Jeffires 15 pass from Moon (Del Greco)
Hou - Hill 9 pass from Moon (Del Greco)
Den - V. Johnson 10 pass from Elway (Treadwell miss)
Hou - Duncan 6 pass from Moon (Del Greco)
Den - Lewis 1 run (Treadwell)
Den - Treadwell 49 FG
Hou - Del Greco 25 FG
Den - Lewis 1 run (Treadwell)
Den - Treadwell 28 FG

TEAM STATISTICS	Hou	Den
First Downs	23	26
Rushing	7	13
Passing	14	12
Penalty	2	1
Offensive plays - yards	55 - 422	65 - 418
Rushes - yards	19 - 97	31 - 151
Passes	36 - 27 - 1	34 - 20 - 1
Gross passing yards	325	267
Sacked - yards lost	0 - 0	0 - 0
Net passing yards	325	267
Interceptions - yards	1 - 25	1 - 0
Punts - average	1 - 44.0	2 - 40.5
Punt returns - yards	0 - 0	0 - 0
Kickoff returns - yards	6 - 82	4 - 88
Fumbles - lost	0 - 0	3 - 0
Penalties - yards	13 - 85	6 - 70

NFC Divisional Playoff
Jan. 4, 1992
RFK Stadium, Washington–55,181

Atlanta	0	7	0	0	– 7
Washington	0	14	3	7	– 24

Was - Ervins 17 run (Lohmiller)
Was - Riggs 2 run (Lohmiller)
Atl - T. Johnson 1 run (N. Johnson)
Was - Lohmiller 24 FG
Was - Riggs 1 run (Lohmiller)

TEAM STATISTICS	Atl	Was
First Downs	12	22
Rushing	2	10
Passing	9	11
Penalty	1	1
Offensive plays - yards	50 - 193	74 - 332
Rushes - yards	14 - 43	45 - 162
Passes	32 - 17 - 4	29 - 14 - 1
Gross passing yards	178	170
Sacked - yards lost	4 - 28	0 - 0
Net passing yards	150	170
Interceptions - yards	1 - 4	4 - 27
Punts - average	4 - 42.3	4 - 38.8
Punt returns - yards	2 - 11	3 - 28

Kickoff returns - yards	4 - 92	2 - 51
Fumbles - lost	3 - 2	0 - 0
Penalties - yards	3 - 19	4 - 23

AFC Divisional Playoff
Jan. 5, 1992
Rich Stadium, Orchard Park–80,182

Kansas City	0	0	7	7	–	14
Buffalo	7	10	7	13	–	37

Buf - Reed 25 pass from Kelly (Norwood)
Buf - Reed 53 pass from Kelly (Norwood)
Buf - Norwood 33 FG
Buf - Lofton 10 pass from Kelly (Norwood)
KC - Word 3 run (Lowery)
Buf - Norwood 20 FG
Buf - Norwood 47 FG
Buf - K. Davis 5 run (Norwood)
KC - F. Jones 20 pass from Vlasic (Lowery)

TEAM STATISTICS	KC	Buf
First Downs	14	29
Rushing	4	13
Passing	9	12
Penalty	1	4
Offensive plays - yards	54 - 213	82 - 448
Rushes - yards	24 - 77	46 - 180
Passes	29 - 14 - 4	35 - 23 - 3
Gross passing yards	146	273
Sacked - yards lost	1 - 10	1 - 5
Net passing yards	136	268
Interceptions - yards	3 - 28	4 - 6
Punts - average	7 - 40.3	3 - 33.3
Punt returns - yards	1 - 11	4 - 32
Kickoff returns - yards	4 - 48	2 - 24
Fumbles - lost	3 - 0	0 - 0
Penalties - yards	10 - 59	6 - 40

NFC Divisional Playoff
Jan. 5, 1992
Pontiac Silverdome–78,290

Dallas	3	3	0	0	–	6
Detroit	7	10	14	7	–	38

Det - Green 31 pass from Kramer (Murray)
Dal - Willis 28 FG
Det - Jenkins 41 interception return (Murray)
Dal - Willis 28 FG
Det - Murray 36 FG
Det - Green 9 pass from Kramer (Murray)
Det - Moore 7 pass from Kramer (Murray)
Det - B. Sanders 47 run (Murray)

TEAM STATISTICS	Dal	Det
First Downs	16	23
Rushing	4	3
Passing	11	19
Penalty	1	1
Offensive plays - yards	54 - 276	55 - 421
Rushes - yards	22 - 97	16 - 84
Passes	29 - 18 - 2	38 - 29 - 0
Gross passing yards	205	341
Sacked - yards lost	3 - 26	1 - 4
Net passing yards	179	337
Interceptions - yards	0 - 0	2 - 41
Punts - average	5 - 44.8	5 - 46.2

Punt returns - yards	1 - 18	2 - 26
Kickoff returns - yards	6 - 108	3 - 49
Fumbles - lost	3 - 2	0 - 0
Penalties - yards	3 - 19	4 - 39

AFC Championship Game
Jan. 12, 1992
Rich Stadium, Orchard Park–80,272

Denver	0	0	0	7	–	7
Buffalo	0	0	7	3	–	10

Buf - Bailey 11 interception return (Norwood)
Buf - Norwood 44 FG
Den - Kubiak 3 run (Treadwell)

TEAM STATISTICS	Den	Buf
First Downs	20	12
Rushing	6	5
Passing	13	5
Penalty	1	2
Offensive plays - yards	69 - 304	61 - 213
Rushes - yards	32 - 81	35 - 104
Passes	33 - 22 - 1	25 - 13 - 2
Gross passing yards	257	117
Sacked - yards lost	4 - 34	1 - 8
Net passing yards	223	109
Interceptions - yards	2 - 5	1 - 11
Punts - average	6 - 43.7	8 - 38.0
Punt returns - yards	3 - 36	0 - 0
Kickoff returns - yards	3 - 49	1 - 24
Fumbles - lost	4 - 1	0 - 0
Penalties - yards	4 - 20	6 - 35

NFC Championship Game
Jan. 12, 1992
RFK Stadium, Washington–55,585

Detroit	0	10	0	0	–	10
Washington	10	7	10	14	–	41

Was - Riggs 2 run (Lohmiller)
Was - Lohmiller 20 FG
Det - Green 18 pass from Kramer (Murray)
Was - Riggs 3 run (Lohmiller)
Det - Murray 30 FG
Was - Lohmiller 28 FG
Was - Clark 45 pass from Rypien (Lohmiller)
Was - Monk 21 pass from Rypien (Lohmiller)
Was - Green 32 interception return (Lohmiller)

TEAM STATISTICS	Det	Was
First Downs	20	17
Rushing	6	6
Passing	12	10
Penalty	2	1
Offensive plays - yards	65 - 304	52 - 345
Rushes - yards	18 - 72	35 - 117
Passes	42 - 25 - 2	17 - 12 - 0
Gross passing yards	264	228
Sacked - yards lost	5 - 32	0 - 0
Net passing yards	232	228
Interceptions - yards	0 - 0	2 - 70
Punts - average	3 - 47.0	3 - 35.7
Punt returns - yards	3 - 13	1 - 13
Kickoff returns - yards	7 - 170	3 - 59
Fumbles - lost	3 - 1	0 - 0
Penalties - yards	7 - 46	4 - 46

Super Bowl XXVI
Jan. 26, 1992
Metrodome, Minneapolis–63,130

Washington	0	17	14	6	–	37
Buffalo	0	0	10	14	–	24

Was - Lohmiller 34 FG
Was - Byner 10 pass from Rypien (Lohmiller)
Was - Riggs 1 run (Lohmiller)
Was - Riggs 2 run (Lohmiller)
Buf - Norwood 21 FG
Buf - Thomas 1 run (Norwood)
Was - Clark 30 pass from Rypien (Lohmiller)
Was - Lohmiller 25 FG
Was - Lohmiller 39 FG
Buf - Metzelaars 2 pass from Kelly (Norwood)
Buf - Beebe 4 pass from Kelly (Norwood)
MVP: Mark Rypien, QB, Washington

TEAM STATISTICS	Was	Buf
First Downs	24	25
Rushing	10	4
Passing	12	18
Penalty	2	3
Offensive plays - yards	73 - 417	82 - 283
Rushes - yards	40 - 125	18 - 43
Passes	33 - 18 - 1	59 - 29 - 4
Gross passing yards	292	286
Sacked - yards lost	0 - 0	5 - 46
Net passing yards	292	240
Interceptions - yards	4 - 79	1 - 4
Punts - average	4 - 37.5	6 - 35.0
Punt returns - yards	0 - 0	3 - 9
Kickoff returns - yards	1 - 16	4 - 77
Fumbles - lost	1 - 0	6 - 1
Penalties - yards	5 - 82	6 - 50

NFC Wild Card Game
Jan. 2, 1993
Metrodome, Minneapolis–57,353

Washington	3	14	7	0	–	24
Minnesota	7	0	0	0	–	7

Min - Allen 1 run (Reveiz)
Was - Lohmiller 44 FG
Was - Byner 3 run (Lohmiller)
Was - Mitchell 8 run (Lohmiller)
Was - Clark 24 pass from Rypien (Lohmiller)

TEAM STATISTICS	Was	Min
First Downs	24	9
Rushing	12	5
Passing	9	4
Penalty	3	0
Offensive plays - yards	73 - 358	41 - 148
Rushes - yards	47 - 196	17 - 73
Passes	25 - 16 - 1	20 - 6 - 2
Gross passing yards	172	113
Sacked - yards lost	1 - 10	4 - 38
Net passing yards	162	75
Interceptions - yards	2 - 50	1 - 21
Punts - average	3 - 37.0	7 - 43.1
Punt returns - yards	3 - 70	1 - 13
Kickoff returns - yards	2 - 20	5 - 104
Fumbles - lost	0 - 0	1 - 0
Penalties - yards	2 - 15	7 - 53

AFC Wild Card Game
Jan. 2, 1993
Jack Murphy Stadium, San Diego—58,278

Kansas City	0	0	0	0	–	0
San Diego	0	0	10	7	–	17

SD - Butts 54 run (Carney)
SD - Carney 34 FG
SD - Hendrickson 5 run (Carney)

TEAM STATISTICS	KC	SD
First Downs	17	18
Rushing	5	8
Passing	10	7
Penalty	2	3
Offensive plays - yards	60 - 251	63 - 342
Rushes - yards	19 - 61	35 - 192
Passes	34 - 16 - 2	23 - 14 - 0
Gross passing yards	233	199
Sacked - yards lost	7 - 43	5 - 49
Net passing yards	190	150
Interceptions - yards	0 - 0	2 - 43
Punts - average	8 - 45.0	6 - 44.2
Punt returns - yards	2 - 5	4 - 35
Kickoff returns - yards	1 - 5	0 - 0
Fumbles - lost	2 - 1	2 - 1
Penalties - yards	7 - 62	5 - 44

NFC Wild Card Game
Jan. 3, 1993
Louisiana Superdome, New Orleans—68,893

Philadelphia	7	0	3	26	–	36
New Orleans	7	10	3	0	–	20

NO - Heyward 1 run (Andersen)
Phi - Barnett 57 pass from Cunningham (Ruzek)
NO - Andersen 35 FG
NO - Early 7 pass from Hebert (Andersen)
NO - Andersen 42 FG
Phi - Ruzek 40 FG
Phi - Barnett 35 pass from Cunningham (Ruzek)
Phi - Sherman 6 run (Ruzek)
Phi - Safety, White tackled Hebert in end zone
Phi - Ruzek 39 FG
Phi - Allen 18 interception return (Ruzek)

TEAM STATISTICS	Phi	NO
First Downs	19	20
Rushing	10	3
Passing	8	16
Penalty	1	1
Offensive plays - yards	64 - 349	60 - 360
Rushes - yards	28 - 136	20 - 76
Passes	35 - 19 - 0	39 - 23 - 3
Gross passing yards	219	291
Sacked - yards lost	1 - 6	1 - 7
Net passing yards	213	284
Interceptions - yards	3 - 36	0 - 0
Punts - average	5 - 51.2	3 - 45.3
Punt returns - yards	2 - 8	3 - 31
Kickoff returns - yards	3 - 56	3 - 64
Fumbles - lost	1 - 1	1 - 1
Penalties - yards	4 - 37	4 - 35

AFC Wild Card Game
Jan. 3, 1993
Rich Stadium, Orchard Park—75,141

Houston	7	21	7	3	0	–	38
Buffalo	3	0	28	7	3	–	41

Hou - Jeffires 3 pass from Moon (Del Greco)
Buf - Christie 36 FG
Hou - Slaughter 7 pass from Moon (Del Greco)
Hou - Duncan 26 pass from Moon (Del Greco)
Hou - Jeffires 27 pass from Moon (Del Greco)
Hou - McDowell 58 interception return (Del Greco)
Buf - K. Davis 1 run (Christie)
Buf - Beebe 38 pass from Reich (Christie)
Buf - Reed 26 pass from Reich (Christie)
Buf - Reed 18 pass from Reich (Christie)
Buf - Reed 17 pass from Reich (Christie)
Hou - Del Greco 26 FG
Buf - Christie 32 FG

TEAM STATISTICS	Hou	Buf
First Downs	27	19
Rushing	6	5
Passing	18	13
Penalty	3	1
Offensive plays - yards	76 - 429	63 - 366
Rushes - yards	22 - 82	26 - 98
Passes	50 - 36 - 2	34 - 21 - 1
Gross passing yards	371	289
Sacked - yards lost	4 - 24	3 - 21
Net passing yards	347	268
Interceptions - yards	1 - 58	2 - 17
Punts - average	2 - 24.5	2 - 35.0
Punt returns - yards	1 - 7	0 - 0
Kickoff returns - yards	4 - 27	5 - 55
Fumbles - lost	2 - 0	0 - 0
Penalties - yards	4 - 30	4 - 30

NFC Divisional Playoff
Jan. 9, 1993
Candlestick Park, San Francisco—64,991

Washington	3	0	3	7	–	13
San Francisco	7	10	0	3	–	20

SF - Taylor 5 pass from Young (Cofer)
Was - Lohmiller 19 FG
SF - Cofer 23 FG
SF - Jones 16 pass from Young (Cofer)
Was - Lohmiller 32 FG
Was - Rypien 1 run (Lohmiller)
SF - Cofer 33 FG

TEAM STATISTICS	Was	SF
First Downs	20	22
Rushing	4	10
Passing	15	12
Penalty	1	0
Offensive plays - yards	67 - 323	63 - 401
Rushes - yards	21 - 73	31 - 187
Passes	41 - 20 - 2	30 - 20 - 1
Gross passing yards	280	227
Sacked - yards lost	5 - 30	2 - 13
Net passing yards	250	214
Interceptions - yards	1 - 0	2 - 4
Punts - average	2 - 36.0	2 - 40.0

Punt returns - yards	0 - 0	0 - 0
Kickoff returns - yards	5 - 84	2 - 27
Fumbles - lost	3 - 2	4 - 3
Penalties - yards	4 - 23	4 - 35

AFC Divisional Playoff
Jan. 9, 1993
Three Rivers Stadium, Pittsburgh—60,407

Buffalo	0	7	7	10	–	24
Pittsburgh	3	0	0	0	–	3

Pit - Anderson 38 FG
Buf - Frerotte 1 pass from Reich (Christie)
Buf - Lofton 17 pass from Reich (Christie)
Buf - Christie 43 FG
Buf - Gardner 1 run (Christie)

TEAM STATISTICS	Buf	Pit
First Downs	19	18
Rushing	7	7
Passing	11	10
Penalty	1	1
Offensive plays - yards	63 - 325	63 - 240
Rushes - yards	39 - 169	27 - 129
Passes	23 - 16 - 0	29 - 15 - 2
Gross passing yards	160	163
Sacked - yards lost	1 - 4	7 - 52
Net passing yards	156	111
Interceptions - yards	2 - 1	0 - 0
Punts - average	4 - 42.3	3 - 37.3
Punt returns - yards	0 - 0	2 - 14
Kickoff returns - yards	2 - 42	5 - 99
Fumbles - lost	0 - 0	4 - 1
Penalties - yards	4 - 33	2 - 23

NFC Divisional Playoff
Jan. 10, 1993
Texas Stadium, Irving—63,721

Philadelphia	3	0	0	7	–	10
Dallas	7	10	10	7	–	34

Phi - Ruzek 32 FG
Dal - Tennell 1 pass from Aikman (Elliott)
Dal - Novacek 6 pass from Aikman (Elliott)
Dal - Elliott 20 FG
Dal - E. Smith 23 run (Elliott)
Dal - Elliott 43 FG
Dal - Gainer 1 run (Elliott)
Phi - Williams 18 pass from Cunningham (Ruzek)

TEAM STATISTICS	Phi	Dal
First Downs	12	22
Rushing	5	10
Passing	6	11
Penalty	1	1
Offensive plays - yards	52 - 178	65 - 346
Rushes - yards	17 - 63	38 - 160
Passes	30 - 17 - 0	25 - 15 - 0
Gross passing yards	160	200
Sacked - yards lost	5 - 45	2 - 14
Net passing yards	115	186
Interceptions - yards	0 - 0	0 - 0
Punts - average	7 - 40.9	4 - 42.8
Punt returns - yards	4 - 24	2 - 5
Kickoff returns - yards	6 - 110	2 - 60

Fumbles - lost	4 - 2	2 - 1
Penalties - yards	6 - 76	5 - 30

AFC Divisional Playoff
Jan. 10, 1993
Joe Robbie Stadium, Miami–71,224

San Diego	0	0	0	0	– 0
Miami	0	21	0	10	– 31

Mia - Paige 1 pass from Marino (Stoyanovich)
Mia - K. Jackson 9 pass from Marino (Stoyanovich)
Mia - K. Jackson 30 pass from Marino (Stoyanovich)
Mia - Stoyanovich 22 FG
Mia - Craver 25 run (Stoyanovich)

TEAM STATISTICS	SD	Mia
First Downs	10	18
Rushing	3	9
Passing	7	9
Offensive plays - yards	62 - 202	69 - 324
Rushes - yards	16 - 70	40 - 157
Passes	45 - 18 - 4	29 - 17 - 0
Gross passing yards	140	167
Sacked - yards lost	1 - 8	0 - 0
Net passing yards	132	167
Interceptions - yards	0 - 0	4 - 30
Punts - average	7 - 46.3	8 - 41.0
Punt returns - yards	1 - 7	5 - 45
Kickoff returns - yards	6 - 136	1 - 18
Fumbles - lost	3 - 1	3 - 1
Penalties - yards	4 - 39	0 - 0

NFC Championship Game
Jan. 17, 1993
Candlestick Park, San Francisco–64,920

Dallas	3	7	7	13	– 30
San Francisco	7	3	3	7	– 20

Dal - Elliott 20 FG
SF - Young 1 run (Cofer)
Dal - E. Smith 4 run (Elliott)
SF - Cofer 28 FG
Dal - Johnston 3 run (Elliott)
SF - Cofer 42 FG
Dal - E. Smith 16 pass from Aikman (Elliott)
SF - Rice 5 pass from Young (Cofer)
Dal - Martin 6 pass from Aikman (Elliott miss)

TEAM STATISTICS	Dal	SF
First Downs	24	24
Rushing	7	8
Passing	16	16
Penalty	1	0
Offensive plays - yards	68 - 416	59 - 415
Rushes - yards	30 - 121	21 - 114
Passes	34 - 24 - 0	35 - 25 - 2
Gross passing yards	322	313
Sacked - yards lost	4 - 27	3 - 12
Net passing yards	295	301
Interceptions - yards	2 - 35	0 - 0
Punts - average	4 - 35.8	1 - 57.0
Punt returns - yards	1 - 8	3 - 30
Kickoff returns - yards	4 - 73	5 - 114
Fumbles - lost	1 - 0	2 - 2
Penalties - yards	4 - 25	4 - 38

AFC Championship Game
Jan. 17, 1993
Joe Robbie Stadium, Miami–72,703

Buffalo	3	10	10	6	– 29
Miami	3	0	0	7	– 10

Buf - Christie 21 FG
Mia - Stoyanovich 51 FG
Buf - Thomas 17 pass from Kelly (Christie)
Buf - Christie 33 FG
Buf - K. Davis 2 run (Christie)
Buf - Christie 21 FG
Buf - Christie 31 FG
Mia - Duper 15 pass from Marino (Stoyanovich)
Buf - Christie 38 FG

TEAM STATISTICS	Buf	Mia
First Downs	20	15
Rushing	10	1
Passing	8	14
Penalty	2	0
Offensive plays - yards	73 - 358	60 - 276
Rushes - yards	48 - 182	11 - 33
Passes	24 - 17 - 2	45 - 22 - 2
Gross passing yards	177	268
Sacked - yards lost	1 - 1	4 - 25
Net passing yards	176	243
Interceptions - yards	2 - 31	2 - 32
Punts - average	2 - 34.5	4 - 37.0
Punt returns - yards	1 - 16	1 - 14
Kickoff returns - yards	2 - 59	7 - 112
Fumbles - lost	1 - 0	4 - 3
Penalties - yards	3 - 20	5 - 40

Super Bowl XXVII
Jan. 31, 1993
Rose Bowl, Pasadena–98,374

Buffalo	7	3	7	0	– 17
Dallas	14	14	3	21	– 52

Buf - Thomas 2 run (Christie)
Dal - Novacek 23 pass from Aikman (Elliott)
Dal - J. Jones 2 fumble return (Elliott)
Buf - Christie 21 FG
Dal - Irvin 19 pass from Aikman (Elliott)
Dal - Irvin 18 pass from Aikman (Elliott)
Dal - Elliott 20 FG
Buf - Beebe 40 pass from Reich (Christie)
Dal - Harper 45 pass from Aikman (Elliott)
Dal - E. Smith 10 run (Elliott)
Dal - Norton 9 fumble return (Elliott)
MVP: Troy Aikman, QB, Dallas

TEAM STATISTICS	Buf	Dal
First Downs	22	20
Rushing	7	9
Passing	11	11
Penalty	4	0
Offensive plays - yards	71 - 362	60 - 408
Rushes - yards	29 - 108	29 - 137
Passes	38 - 22 - 4	30 - 22 - 0
Gross passing yards	276	273
Sacked - yards lost	4 - 22	1 - 2
Net passing yards	254	271
Interceptions - yards	0 - 0	4 - 35
Punts - average	3 - 45.3	4 - 32.8

Had blocked	0	1
Punt returns - yards	1 - 0	3 - 35
Kickoff returns - yards	4 - 90	4 - 79
Fumbles - lost	8 - 5	4 - 2
Penalties - yards	4 - 30	8 - 53

AFC Wild Card Game
Jan. 8, 1994
Arrowhead Stadium, Kansas City–74,515

Pittsburgh	7	10	0	7	0	– 24
Kansas City	7	0	3	14	3	– 27

Pit - Cooper 10 pass from O'Donnell (Anderson)
KC - Birden 23 pass from Krieg (Lowery)
Pit - Anderson 30 FG
Pit - Mills 26 pass from O'Donnell (Anderson)
KC - Lowery 23 FG
Pit - Green 22 pass from O'Donnell (Anderson)
KC - Barnett 7 pass from Montana (Lowery)
KC - Lowery 32 FG

TEAM STATISTICS	Pit	KC
First Downs	21	28
Rushing	5	7
Passing	15	19
Penalty	1	2
Offensive plays - yards	80 - 373	81 - 401
Rushes - yards	35 - 97	33 - 125
Passes	42 - 23 - 0	44 - 29 - 0
Gross passing yards	286	299
Sacked - yards lost	3 - 10	4 - 23
Net passing yards	276	276
Interceptions - yards	0 - 0	0 - 0
Punts - average	7 - 38.3	6 - 44.8
Had blocked	1	0
Punt returns - yards	3 - 18	4 - 36
Kickoff returns - yards	5 - 97	6 - 127
Fumbles - lost	1 - 0	0 - 0
Penalties - yards	5 - 40	5 - 25

NFC Wild Card Game
Jan. 8, 1994
Pontiac Silverdome–68,479

Green Bay	0	7	14	7	– 28
Detroit	3	7	7	7	– 24

Det - Hanson 47 FG
GB - Sharpe 12 pass from Favre (Jacke)
Det - Perriman 1 pass from Kramer (Hanson)
Det - Jenkins 15 interception return (Hanson)
GB - Sharpe 28 pass from Favre (Jacke)
GB - Teague 101 interception return (Jacke)
Det - D. Moore 5 run (Hanson)
GB - Sharpe 40 pass from Favre (Jacke)

TEAM STATISTICS	GB	Det
First Downs	16	25
Rushing	6	9
Passing	10	14
Penalty	0	2
Offensive plays - yards	51 - 293	64 - 410
Rushes - yards	25 - 89	29 - 175
Passes	26 - 15 - 1	31 - 22 - 2
Gross passing yards	204	248

Sacked - yards lost	0 - 0	4 - 13
Net passing yards	204	235
Interceptions - yards	2 - 101	1 - 15
Punts - average	4 - 40.3	3 - 48.3
Punt returns - yards	2 - 43	1 - 22
Kickoff returns - yards	3 - 89	5 - 64
Fumbles - lost	2 - 0	2 - 0
Penalties - yards	6 - 49	5 - 35

AFC Wild Card Game
Jan. 9, 1994
Memorial Coliseum, Los Angeles–65,314

Denver	7	14	0	3	– 24
Los Angeles	14	7	14	7	– 42

LA - Horton 9 pass from Hostetler (Jaeger)
Den - Sharpe 23 pass from Elway (Elam)
LA - Brown 65 pass from Hostetler (Jaeger)
Den - R. Johnson 16 pass from Elway (Elam)
LA - Jett 54 pass from Hostetler (Jaeger)
Den - Russell 6 pass from Elway (Elam)
LA - McCallum 26 run (Jaeger)
LA - McCallum 2 run (Jaeger)
Den - Elam 33 FG
LA - McCallum 1 run (Jaeger)

TEAM STATISTICS	Den	LA
First Downs	26	19
Rushing	4	6
Passing	18	10
Penalty	4	3
Offensive plays - yards	73 - 387	53 - 427
Rushes - yards	18 - 56	32 - 136
Passes	54 - 32 - 1	19 - 13 - 0
Gross passing yards	336	294
Sacked - yards lost	1 - 5	2 - 3
Net passing yards	331	291
Interceptions - yards	0 - 0	1 - 1
Punts - average	4 - 33.8	4 - 42.5
Punt returns - yards	3 - 38	0 - 0
Kickoff returns - yards	6 - 85	4 - 55
Fumbles - lost	2 - 0	0 - 0
Penalties - yards	10 - 97	17 - 130

AFC Wild Card Game
Jan. 9, 1994
Giants Stadium, East Rutherford, N.J.–75,089

Minnesota	0	10	0	0	– 10
New York	3	0	14	0	– 17

NY - Treadwell 26 FG
Min - C. Carter 40 pass from McMahon (Reveiz)
Min - Reveiz 52 FG
NY - Hampton 51 run (Treadwell)
NY - Hampton 2 run (Treadwell)

TEAM STATISTICS	Min	NY
First Downs	11	17
Rushing	4	10
Passing	6	6
Penalty	1	1
Offensive plays - yards	59 - 260	67 - 270
Rushes - yards	22 - 79	41 - 176
Passes	34 - 15 - 0	26 - 17 - 0
Gross passing yards	192	94

Sacked - yards lost	3 - 11	0 - 0
Net passing yards	181	94
Interceptions - yards	0 - 0	0 - 0
Punts - average	8 - 37.8	7 - 32.0
Punt returns - yards	2 - 22	2 - 5
Kickoff returns - yards	4 - 47	2 - 12
Fumbles - lost	2 - 1	0 - 0
Penalties - yards	6 - 28	2 - 20

AFC Divisional Playoff
Jan. 15, 1994
Rich Stadium, Orchard Park–61,923

Los Angeles	0	17	6	0	– 23
Buffalo	0	13	9	7	– 29

LA - Jaeger 30 FG
Buf - K. Davis 1 run (Christie miss)
LA - McCallum 1 run (Jaeger)
LA - McCallum 1 run (Jaeger)
Buf - Thomas 8 run (Christie)
Buf - Brooks 25 pass from Kelly (Christie miss)
Buf - Christie 29 FG
LA - Brown 86 pass from Hostetler (Jaeger miss)
Buf - Brooks 22 pass from Kelly (Christie)

TEAM STATISTICS	LA	Buf
First Downs	15	25
Rushing	9	7
Passing	6	14
Penalty	0	4
Offensive plays - yards	57 - 325	70 - 355
Rushes - yards	35 - 110	30 - 75
Passes	20 - 14 - 0	37 - 27 - 0
Gross passing yards	230	287
Sacked - yards lost	2 - 15	3 - 7
Net passing yards	215	280
Interceptions - yards	0 - 0	0 - 0
Punts - average	6 - 37.0	3 - 36.3
Punt returns - yards	3 - 7	3 - 7
Kickoff returns - yards	6 - 83	4 - 111
Fumbles - lost	2 - 1	3 - 1
Penalties - yards	9 - 77	2 - 15

NFC Divisional Playoff
Jan. 15, 1994
Candlestick Park, San Francisco–67,143

New York	0	3	0	0	– 3
San Francisco	9	14	14	7	– 44

SF - Watters 1 run (Cofer miss)
SF - Cofer 29 FG
SF - Watters 1 run (Cofer)
SF - Watters 2 run (Cofer)
NY - Treadwell 25 FG
SF - Watters 6 run (Cofer)
SF - Watters 2 run (Cofer)
SF - Logan 2 run (Cofer)

TEAM STATISTICS	NY	SF
First Downs	12	25
Rushing	3	13
Passing	6	11
Penalty	3	1
Offensive plays - yards	58 - 194	65 - 413
Rushes - yards	19 - 41	40 - 178
Passes	35 - 18 - 3	24 - 19 - 0

Gross passing yards	180	241
Sacked - yards lost	4 - 27	1 - 6
Net passing yards	153	235
Interceptions - yards	0 - 0	3 - 21
Punts - average	5 - 39.8	3 - 48.0
Punt returns - yards	1 - 3	2 - 39
Kickoff returns - yards	5 - 105	0 - 0
Fumbles - lost	0 - 0	2 - 1
Penalties - yards	4 - 24	6 - 50

AFC Divisional Playoff
Jan. 16, 1994
Astrodome, Houston–64,011

Kansas City	0	0	7	21	– 28
Houston	10	0	0	10	– 20

Hou - Del Greco 49 FG
Hou - Brown 2 run (Del Greco)
KC - Cash 7 pass from Montana (Lowery)
Hou - Del Greco 43 FG
KC - Birden 11 pass from Montana (Lowery)
KC - Davis 18 pass from Montana (Lowery)
Hou - Givins 7 pass from Moon (Del Greco)
KC - Allen 21 run (Lowery)

TEAM STATISTICS	KC	Hou
First Downs	18	19
Rushing	3	4
Passing	14	14
Penalty	1	1
Offensive plays - yards	58 - 354	66 - 277
Rushes - yards	18 - 71	14 - 39
Passes	38 - 22 - 2	43 - 32 - 1
Gross passing yards	299	306
Sacked - yards lost	2 - 16	9 - 68
Net passing yards	283	238
Interceptions - yards	1 - 12	2 - 14
Punts - average	5 - 45.0	5 - 48.6
Punt returns - yards	4 - 44	1 - 12
Kickoff returns - yards	2 - 38	3 - 50
Fumbles - lost	0 - 0	7 - 2
Penalties - yards	7 - 51	3 - 63

NFC Divisional Playoff
Jan. 16, 1994
Texas Stadium, Irving–64,790

Green Bay	3	0	7	7	– 17
Dallas	0	17	7	3	– 27

GB - Jacke 30 FG
Dal - Harper 25 pass from Aikman (Murray)
Dal - Murray 41 FG
Dal - Novacek 6 pass from Aikman (Murray)
Dal - Irvin 19 pass from Aikman (Murray)
GB - Brooks 13 pass from Favre (Jacke)
Dal - Murray 38 FG
GB - Sharpe 29 pass from Favre (Jacke)

TEAM STATISTICS	GB	Dal
First Downs	19	23
Rushing	2	6
Passing	17	16
Penalty	0	1
Offensive plays - yards	60 - 358	68 - 381
Rushes - yards	13 - 31	27 - 97
Passes	45 - 28 - 2	37 - 28 - 2
Gross passing yards	331	302

Sacked - yards lost	2 - 4	4 - 18
Net passing yards	327	284
Interceptions - yards	2 - 14	2 - 5
Punts - average	3 - 39.0	3 - 43.7
Punt returns - yards	2 - 59	2 - 14
Kickoff returns - yards	6 - 70	2 - 34
Fumbles - lost	3 - 2	2 - 1
Penalties - yards	4 - 30	5 - 39

AFC Championship Game
Jan. 23, 1994
Rich Stadium, Orchard Park–76,642

Kansas City	6	0	7	0	– 13
Buffalo	7	13	0	10	– 30

Buf - Thomas 12 run (Christie)
KC - Lowery 31 FG
KC - Lowery 31 FG
Buf - Thomas 3 run (Christie)
Buf - Christie 23 FG
Buf - Christie 25 FG
KC - Allen 1 run (Lowery)
Buf - Christie 18 FG
Buf - Thomas 3 run (Christie)

TEAM STATISTICS	KC	Buf
First Downs	22	30
Rushing	3	17
Passing	18	9
Penalty	1	4
Offensive plays - yards	77 - 338	73 - 389
Rushes - yards	21 - 52	46 - 229
Passes	52 - 25 - 2	27 - 17 - 0
Gross passing yards	323	160
Sacked - yards lost	4 - 37	0 - 0
Net passing yards	286	160
Interceptions - yards	0 - 0	2 - 15
Punts - average	6 - 40.8	4 - 33.3
Punt returns - yards	1 - 11	5 - 70
Kickoff returns - yards	5 - 89	4 - 68
Fumbles - lost	1 - 0	1 - 1
Penalties - yards	6 - 29	2 - 10

NFC Championship Game
Jan. 23, 1994
Texas Stadium, Irving–64,902

San Francisco	0	7	7	7	– 21
Dallas	7	21	7	3	– 38

Dal - E. Smith 5 run (Murray)
SF - Rathman 7 pass from Young (Cofer)
Dal - Johnston 4 run (Murray)
Dal - E. Smith 11 pass from Aikman (Murray)
Dal - Novacek 19 pass from Aikman (Murray)
SF - Watters 4 run (Cofer)
Dal - Harper 42 pass from Kosar (Murray)
Dal - Murray 50 FG
SF - Young 1 run (Cofer)

TEAM STATISTICS	SF	Dal
First Downs	23	24
Rushing	5	9
Passing	15	15
Penalty	3	0
Offensive plays - yards	70 - 359	63 - 377
Rushes - yards	21 - 84	33 - 124
Passes	45 - 27 - 1	28 - 19 - 0

Gross passing yards	287	260
Sacked - yards lost	4 - 12	2 - 7
Net passing yards	275	253
Interceptions - yards	0 - 0	1 - 14
Punts - average	4 - 45.5	4 - 41.0
Punt returns - yards	1 - 9	1 - 6
Kickoff returns - yards	6 - 82	2 - 29
Fumbles - lost	2 - 0	0 - 0
Penalties - yards	6 - 40	4 - 29

Super Bowl XXVIII
Jan. 30, 1994
Georgia Dome, Atlanta–72,817

Dallas	6	0	14	10	– 30
Buffalo	3	10	0	0	– 13

Dal - Murray 41 FG
Buf - Christie 54 FG
Dal - Murray 24 FG
Buf - Thomas 4 run (Christie)
Buf - Christie 28 FG
Dal - Washington 46 fumble return (Murray)
Dal - E. Smith 15 run (Murray)
Dal - E. Smith 1 run (Murray)
Dal - Murray 20 FG
MVP: Emmitt Smith, RB, Dallas

TEAM STATISTICS	Dal	Buf
First Downs	20	22
Rushing	6	6
Passing	14	15
Penalty	0	1
Offensive plays - yards	64 - 341	80 - 314
Rushes - yards	35 - 137	27 - 87
Passes	27 - 19 - 1	50 - 31 - 1
Gross passing yards	207	260
Sacked - yards lost	2 - 3	3 - 33
Net passing yards	204	227
Interceptions - yards	1 - 12	1 - 41
Punts - average	4 - 43.8	5 - 37.6
Punt returns - yards	1 - 5	1 - 5
Kickoff returns - yards	2 - 72	6 - 144
Fumbles - lost	0 - 0	3 - 2
Penalties - yards	6 - 50	1 - 10

NFC Wild Card Game
Dec. 31, 1994
Lambeau Field, Green Bay–58,125

Detroit	0	0	3	9	– 12
Green Bay	7	3	3	3	– 16

GB - Levens 3 run (Jacke)
GB - Jacke 51 FG
Det - Hanson 38 FG
GB - Jacke 32 FG
Det - Perriman 3 pass from Krieg (Hanson)
GB - Jacke 28 FG
Det - Safety, Hentrich stepped out of end zone

TEAM STATISTICS	Det	GB
First Downs	9	18
Rushing	1	6
Passing	8	11
Penalty	0	1
Offensive plays - yards	54 - 171	74 - 336
Rushes - yards	15 - (-4)	35 - 81
Passes	35 - 17 - 0	38 - 23 - 0

Gross passing yards	199	262
Sacked - yards lost	4 - 24	1 - 7
Net passing yards	175	255
Interceptions - yards	0 - 0	0 - 0
Punts - average	8 - 36.5	5 - 39.0
Punt returns - yards	2 - 17	3 - 15
Kickoff returns - yards	5 - 186	3 - 45
Fumbles - lost	1 - 0	0 - 0
Penalties - yards	4 - 30	3 - 35

AFC Wild Card Game
Dec. 31, 1994
Joe Robbie Stadium, Miami–67,487

Kansas City	14	3	0	0	– 17
Miami	7	10	10	0	– 27

KC - Walker 1 pass from Montana (Elliot)
Mia - Parmalee 1 run (Stoyanovich)
KC - Anders 57 pass from Montana (Elliot)
Mia - Stoyanovich 40 FG
KC - Elliot 21 FG
Mia - R. Williams 1 pass from Marino (Stoyanovich)
Mia - Fryar 7 pass from Marino (Stoyanovich)
Mia - Stoyanovich 40 FG

TEAM STATISTICS	KC	Mia
First Downs	24	22
Rushing	7	7
Passing	17	13
Penalty	0	2
Offensive plays - yards	60 - 414	61 - 381
Rushes - yards	23 - 100	31 - 132
Passes	37 - 26 - 1	29 - 22 - 0
Gross passing yards	314	257
Sacked - yards lost	0 - 0	1 - 8
Net passing yards	314	249
Interceptions - yards	0 - 0	1 - 24
Punts - average	2 - 40.0	3 - 43.3
Punt returns - yards	1 - 7	0 - 0
Kickoff returns - yards	5 - 81	3 - 95
Fumbles - lost	3 - 1	0 - 0
Penalties - yards	4 - 15	6 - 50

NFC Wild Card Game
Jan. 1, 1995
Metrodome, Minneapolis–60,347

Chicago	0	14	7	14	– 35
Minnesota	3	6	3	6	– 18

Min - Reveiz 29 FG
Chi - Tillman 1 run (Butler)
Chi - Jennings 9 pass from Walsh (Butler)
Min - Carter 4 pass from Moon (Moon pass failed)
Chi - Harris 29 run (Butler)
Min - Reveiz 48 FG
Chi - Graham 21 pass from Walsh (Butler)
Min - Lee 11 pass from Moon (Moon pass failed)
Chi - Miniefield 48 fumble return (Butler)

TEAM STATISTICS	Chi	Min
First Downs	18	22
Rushing	5	3
Passing	11	18
Penalty	2	1

Offensive plays - yards	54 - 308	82 - 389
Rushes - yards	30 - 94	19 - 49
Passes	23 - 15 - 1	61 - 33 - 2
Gross passing yards	221	351
Sacked - yards lost	1 - 7	2 - 11
Net passing yards	214	340
Interceptions - yards	2 - 19	1 - 10
Punts - average	3 - 38.7	4 - 32.8
Punt returns - yards	1 - 1	0 - 0
Kickoff returns - yards	3 - 65	6 - 132
Fumbles - lost	1 - 1	3 - 2
Penalties - yards	6 - 30	11 - 85

AFC Wild Card Game
Jan. 1, 1995
Municipal Stadium, Cleveland—77,452

New England	0	10	0	3	– 13
Cleveland	3	7	7	3	– 20

Cle - Stover 30 FG
NE - Thompson 13 pass from Bledsoe (Bahr)
Cle - Carrier 5 pass from Testaverde (Stover)
NE - Bahr 23 FG
Cle - Hoard 10 run (Stover)
Cle - Stover 21 FG
NE - Bahr 33 FG

TEAM STATISTICS	NE	Cle
First Downs	20	22
Rushing	6	8
Passing	14	14
Offensive plays - yards	68 - 303	66 - 379
Rushes - yards	16 - 57	34 - 125
Passes	51 - 22 - 3	30 - 20 - 0
Gross passing yards	256	268
Sacked - yards lost	1 - 10	2 - 14
Net passing yards	246	254
Interceptions - yards	0 - 0	3 - 47
Punts - average	4 - 42.3	3 - 37.7
Punt returns - yards	2 - 5	1 - 1
Kickoff returns - yards	5 - 99	3 - 70
Fumbles - lost	0 - 0	2 - 1
Penalties - yards	3 - 21	4 - 25

NFC Divisional Playoff
Jan. 7, 1995
Candlestick Park, San Francisco—64,644

Chicago	3	0	0	12	– 15
San Francisco	7	23	7	7	– 44

Chi - Butler 39 FG
SF - Floyd 2 run (Brien)
SF - Jones 8 pass from Young (Brien kick failed)
SF - Floyd 4 run (Brien)
SF - Brien 36 FG
SF - Young 6 run (Brien)
SF - Floyd 1 run (Brien)
Chi - Flanigan 2 pass from Kramer (Kramer pass failed)
SF - Walker 1 run (Brien)
Chi - Tillman 1 run (Kramer pass failed)

TEAM STATISTICS	Chi	SF
First Downs	20	27
Rushing	4	13
Passing	13	11

Penalty	3	3
Offensive plays - yards	69 - 247	64 - 330
Rushes - yards	18 - 39	37 - 145
Passes	47 - 29 - 2	26 - 18 - 0
Gross passing yards	239	190
Sacked - yards lost	4 - 31	1 - 5
Net passing yards	208	185
Interceptions - yards	0 - 0	2 - 31
Punts - average	4 - 36.8	2 - 38.5
Punt returns - yards	0 - 0	2 - 6
Kickoff returns - yards	6 - 137	2 - 24
Fumbles - lost	2 - 0	3 - 1
Penalties - yards	4 - 32	3 - 16

AFC Divisional Playoff
Jan. 7, 1995
Three Rivers Stadium, Pittsburgh—58,185

Cleveland	0	3	0	6	– 9
Pittsburgh	3	21	3	2	– 29

Pit - Anderson 39 FG
Pit - Green 2 pass from O'Donnell (Anderson)
Pit - J. Williams 26 run (Anderson)
Cle - Stover 22 FG
Pit - Thigpen 9 pass from O'Donnell (Anderson)
Pit - Anderson 40 FG
Cle - McCardell 20 pass from Testaverde–Testaverde pass failed)
Pit - Safety, Lake tackled Testaverde in end zone

TEAM STATISTICS	Cle	Pit
First Downs	10	23
Rushing	3	14
Passing	6	9
Penalty	1	0
Offensive plays - yards	50 - 186	74 - 424
Rushes - yards	17 - 55	51 - 238
Passes	31 - 13 - 2	23 - 16 - 0
Gross passing yards	144	186
Sacked - yards lost	2 - 13	0 - 0
Net passing yards	131	186
Interceptions - yards	0 - 0	2 - 21
Punts - average	5 - 38.0	5 - 38.2
Punt returns - yards	3 - 40	1 - 0
Kickoff returns - yards	6 - 106	3 - 30
Fumbles - lost	0 - 0	2 - 1
Penalties - yards	2 - 17	4 - 50

NFC Divisional Playoff
Jan. 8, 1995
Texas Stadium, Irving—64,745

Green Bay	3	6	0	0	– 9
Dallas	14	14	0	7	– 35

Dal - E. Smith 5 run (Boniol)
GB - Jacke 50 FG
Dal - Harper 94 pass from Aikman (Boniol)
Dal - B. Thomas 1 run (Boniol)
GB - Bennett 1 run (Favre pass failed)
Dal - Galbraith 1 pass from Aikman (Boniol)
Dal - B. Thomas 2 run (Boniol)

TEAM STATISTICS	GB	Dal
First Downs	18	27
Rushing	6	11

Passing	11	13
Penalty	1	3
Offensive plays - yards	70 - 327	65 - 450
Rushes - yards	23 - 99	32 - 120
Passes	46 - 21 - 1	32 - 23 - 1
Gross passing yards	236	337
Sacked - yards lost	1 - 8	1 - 7
Net passing yards	228	330
Interceptions - yards	1 - 34	1 - 2
Punts - average	4 - 44.0	4 - 45.8
Punt returns - yards	2 - 23	0 - 0
Kickoff returns - yards	6 - 144	3 - 88
Fumbles - lost	0 - 0	1 - 1
Penalties - yards	8 - 43	7 - 46

AFC Divisional Playoff
Jan. 8, 1995
Jack Murphy Stadium, San Diego—63,381

Miami	7	14	0	0	– 21
San Diego	0	6	9	7	– 22

Mia - K. Jackson 8 pass from Marino (Stoyanovich)
SD - Carney 20 FG
Mia - K. Jackson 9 pass from Marino (Stoyanovich)
SD - Carney 21 FG
Mia - M. Williams 16 pass from Marino (Stoyanovich)
SD - Safety, R. Davis tackled Parmalee in end zone
SD - Means 24 run (Carney)
SD - Seay 8 pass from Humphries (Carney)

TEAM STATISTICS	Mia	SD
First Downs	17	28
Rushing	2	12
Passing	12	15
Penalty	3	1
Offensive plays - yards	47 - 282	85 - 466
Rushes - yards	8 - 26	40 - 202
Passes	38 - 24 - 0	43 - 28 - 2
Gross passing yards	262	276
Sacked - yards lost	1 - 6	2 - 12
Net passing yards	256	264
Interceptions - yards	2 - 14	0 - 0
Punts - average	5 - 45.2	2 - 43.5
Punt returns - yards	1 - 14	2 - 14
Kickoff returns - yards	5 - 112	5 - 88
Fumbles - lost	1 - 0	2 - 1
Penalties - yards	7 - 47	5 - 67

NFC Championship Game
Jan. 15, 1995
Candlestick Park, San Francisco—69,125

Dallas	7	7	7	7	– 28
San Francisco	21	10	7	0	– 38

SF - Davis 44 interception return (Brien)
SF - Watters 29 pass from Young (Brien)
SF - Floyd 1 run (Brien)
Dal - Irvin 44 pass from Aikman (Boniol)
SF - Brien 34 FG
Dal - E. Smith 4 run (Boniol)
SF - Rice 28 pass from Young (Brien)
Dal - E. Smith 1 run (Boniol)

SF - Young 3 run (Brien)
Dal - Irvin 10 pass from Aikman (Boniol)

TEAM STATISTICS	Dal	SF
First Downs	29	19
Rushing	8	9
Passing	18	9
Penalty	3	1
Offensive plays - yards	81 - 451	60 - 294
Rushes - yards	24 - 99	31 - 139
Passes	53 - 30 - 3	29 - 13 - 0
Gross passing yards	380	155
Sacked - yards lost	4 - 28	0 - 0
Net passing yards	352	155
Interceptions - yards	0 - 0	3 - 44
Punts - average	1 - 23.0	5 - 35.6
Punt returns - yards	1 - 10	0 - 0
Kickoff returns - yards	7 - 144	5 - 90
Fumbles - lost	2 - 2	1 - 1
Penalties - yards	9 - 98	4 - 30

AFC Championship Game
Jan. 15, 1995
Three Rivers Stadium, Pittsburgh–61,545

San Diego	0	3	7	7	– 17
Pittsburgh	7	3	3	0	– 13

Pit - J. Williams 16 pass from O'Donnell (Anderson)
SD - Carney 20 FG
Pit - Anderson 39 FG
Pit - Anderson 23 FG
SD - Pupunu 43 pass from Humphries (Carney)
SD - Martin 43 pass from Humphries (Carney)

TEAM STATISTICS	SD	Pit
First Downs	13	22
Rushing	4	4
Passing	8	17
Penalty	1	1
Offensive plays - yards	47 - 226	80 - 415
Rushes - yards	24 - 66	26 - 66
Passes	22 - 11 - 1	54 - 32 - 0
Gross passing yards	165	349
Sacked - yards lost	1 - 5	0 - 0
Net passing yards	160	349
Interceptions - yards	0 - 0	1 - 6
Punts - average	5 - 38.4	5 - 44.4
Punt returns - yards	2 - 2	2 - 10
Kickoff returns - yards	3 - 72	4 - 73
Fumbles - lost	0 - 0	3 - 1
Penalties - yards	3 - 15	8 - 111

Super Bowl XXIX
Jan. 29, 1995
Joe Robbie Stadium, Miami–74,107

San Diego	7	3	8	8	– 26
San Francisco	14	14	14	7	– 49

SF - Rice 44 pass from Young (Brien)
SF - Watters 51 pass from Young (Brien)
SD - Means 1 run (Carney)
SF - Floyd 5 pass from Young (Brien)
SF - Watters 8 pass from Young (Brien)
SD - Carney 31 FG
SF - Watters 9 run (Brien)
SF - Rice 15 pass from Young (Brien)

SD - Coleman 98 kickoff return (Seay pass from Humphries)
SF - Rice 7 pass from Young (Brien)
SD - Martin 30 pass from Humphries (Pupunu pass from Humphries)
MVP: Steve Young, QB, San Francisco

TEAM STATISTICS	SD	SF
First Downs	20	28
Rushing	5	10
Passing	14	17
Penalty	1	1
Offensive plays - yards	76 - 354	73 - 455
Rushes - yards	19 - 67	32 - 139
Passes	55 - 27 - 3	38 - 25 - 0
Gross passing yards	305	331
Sacked - yards lost	2 - 18	3 - 15
Net passing yards	287	316
Interceptions - yards	0 - 0	3 - 16
Punts - average	4 - 48.8	5 - 39.8
Punt returns - yards	3 - 1	2 - 12
Kickoff returns - yards	8 - 242	4 - 48
Fumbles - lost	1 - 0	2 - 0
Penalties - yards	6 - 63	3 - 18

AFC Wild Card Game
Dec. 30, 1995
Rich Stadium, Orchard Park–73,103

Miami	0	0	0	22	– 22
Buffalo	10	14	3	10	– 37

Buf - Thomas 1 run (Christie)
Buf - Christie 48 FG
Buf - Holmes 21 run (Christie)
Buf - Tasker 37 pass from Kelly (Christie)
Buf - Christie 23 FG
Mia - McDuffie 5 pass from Marino (Stoyanovich)
Buf - Tindale 44 run (Christie)
Mia - Hill 45 pass from Marino (Stoyanovich)
Buf - Christie 42 FG
Mia - Kirby 1 run (McDuffie pass from Marino)

TEAM STATISTICS	Mia	Buf
First Downs	26	27
Rushing	5	18
Passing	20	9
Penalty	1	0
Offensive plays - yards	80 - 502	74 - 536
Rushes - yards	14 - 70	52 - 341
Passes	66 - 34 - 3	22 - 12 - 2
Gross passing yards	432	195
Sacked - yards lost	0 - 0	0 - 0
Net passing yards	432	195
Interceptions - yards	2 - 26	3 - 5
Punts - average	3 - 38.3	4 - 34.5
Punt returns - yards	1 - 12	0 - 0
Kickoff returns - yards	8 - 137	2 - 37
Fumbles - lost	2 - 1	1 - 0
Penalties - yards	4 - 15	5 - 29

NFC Wild Card Game
Dec. 30, 1995
Veterans Stadium, Philadelphia–66,099

Detroit	7	0	14	16	– 37
Philadelphia	7	31	13	7	– 58

Phi - Garner 15 run (Anderson)
Det - Sloan 32 pass from Mitchell (Hanson)
Phi - Anderson 21 FG
Phi - Barnett 22 pass from Peete (Anderson)
Phi - Wilburn 24 interception return (Anderson)
Phi - Watters 1 run (Anderson)
Phi - Carpenter 43 pass from Peete (Anderson)
Phi - Watters 45 pass from Peete (Anderson)
Phi - Anderson 31 FG
Phi - Anderson 39 FG
Det - Moore 68 pass from Majkowski (Hanson)
Det - Morton 7 pass from Majkowski (Hanson)
Phi - Thomas 30 interception return (Anderson)
Det - Sloan 2 pass from Majkowski (Rivers run)
Det - Rivers 1 run (Moore pass from Majkowski)

TEAM STATISTICS	Det	Phi
First Downs	26	22
Rushing	5	7
Passing	20	12
Penalty	1	3
Offensive plays - yards	70 - 422	69 - 452
Rushes - yards	16 - 72	43 - 189
Passes	52 - 27 - 6	25 - 17 - 0
Gross passing yards	361	270
Sacked - yards lost	2 - 11	1 - 7
Net passing yards	350	263
Interceptions - yards	0 - 0	6 - 119
Punts - average	5 - 37.4	4 - 42.8
Punt returns - yards	0 - 0	2 - 13
Kickoff returns - yards	10 - 148	4 - 25
Fumbles - lost	2 - 1	1 - 1
Penalties - yards	7 - 65	8 - 80

AFC Wild Card Game
Dec. 31, 1995
Jack Murphy Stadium, San Diego–61,182

Indianapolis	0	14	7	14	– 35
San Diego	3	7	7	3	– 20

SD - Carney 54 FG
Ind - Dilger 2 pass from Harbaugh (Blanchard)
SD - Pupunu 6 pass from Humphries (Carney)
Ind - Crockett 33 run (Blanchard)
SD - Jefferson 11 pass from Humphries (Carney)
Ind - Dawkins 42 pass from Harbaugh (Blanchard)
SD - Carney 30 FG
Ind - Crockett 66 run (Blanchard)
Ind - Harbaugh 3 run (Blanchard)

TEAM STATISTICS	Ind	SD
First Downs	19	27
Rushing	10	7
Passing	9	20
Penalty	0	0
Offensive plays - yards	58 - 333	80 - 429
Rushes - yards	29 - 178	32 - 145
Passes	27 - 16 - 1	47 - 23 - 4
Gross passing yards	175	292
Sacked - yards lost	2 - 20	1 - 8
Net passing yards	155	284
Interceptions - yards	4 - 81	1 - 0
Punts - average	5 - 37.4	2 - 54.5

Punt returns - yards	2 - 52	0 - 0
Kickoff returns - yards	5 - 110	6 - 133
Fumbles - lost	2 - 0	0 - 0
Penalties - yards	4 - 30	4 - 24

NFC Wild Card Game
Dec. 31, 1995
Lambeau Field, Green Bay–60,453

Atlanta	7	3	0	10	– 20
Green Bay	14	13	0	10	– 37

Atl - Metcalf 65 pass from George (Andersen)
GB - Bennett 8 run (Jacke)
GB - Brooks 14 pass from Favre (Jacke)
Atl - Andersen 31 FG
GB - Freeman 76 punt return (bad snap)
GB - Chmura 2 pass from Favre (Jacke)
Atl - Birden 27 pass from George (Andersen)
GB - Levens 18 pass from Favre (Jacke)
Atl - Andersen 22 FG
GB - Jacke 25 FG

TEAM STATISTICS	Atl	GB
First Downs	18	23
Rushing	1	6
Passing	17	14
Penalty	0	3
Offensive plays - yards	67 - 360	65 - 307
Rushes - yards	10 - 21	29 - 117
Passes	54 - 30 - 2	35 - 24 - 0
Gross passing yards	366	199
Sacked - yards lost	3 - 27	1 - 9
Net passing yards	339	190
Interceptions - yards	0 - 0	2 - 30
Punts - average	5 - 36.6	4 - 42.5
Punt returns - yards	2 - 6	3 - 72
Kickoff returns - yards	6 - 107	4 - 87
Fumbles - lost	1 - 0	0 - 0
Penalties - yards	5 - 67	5 - 36

AFC Divisional Playoff
Jan. 6, 1996
Three Rivers Stadium, Pittsburgh–59,072

Buffalo	0	7	7	7	– 21
Pittsburgh	7	16	3	14	– 40

Pit - J. Williams 1 run (N. Johnson)
Pit - Mills 10 pass from O'Donnell (N. Johnson)
Pit - N. Johnson 45 FG
Pit - N. Johnson 38 FG
Buf - Thomas 1 run (Christie)
Pit - N. Johnson 34 FG
Pit - N. Johnson 39 FG
Buf - Cline 2 pass from Van Pelt (Christie)
Buf - Thomas 9 pass from Kelly (Christie)
Pit - Morris 13 run (N. Johnson)
Pit - Morris 2 run (N. Johnson)

TEAM STATISTICS	Buf	Pit
First Downs	18	23
Rushing	6	8
Passing	11	15
Penalty	1	0
Offensive plays - yards	62 - 250	78 - 409
Rushes - yards	21 - 94	43 - 147

Passes	39 - 18 - 3	35 - 19 - 2
Gross passing yards	162	262
Sacked - yards lost	2 - 6	0 - 0
Net passing yards	156	262
Interceptions - yards	2 - 22	3 - 12
Punts - average	5 - 39.8	5 - 32.8
Punt returns - yards	3 - 4	2 - 13
Kickoff returns - yards	8 - 133	4 - 71
Fumbles - lost	3 - 1	1 - 0
Penalties - yards	5 - 25	5 - 41

NFC Divisional Playoff
Jan. 6, 1996
3Com Park, San Francisco–69,311

Green Bay	14	7	3	3	– 27
San Francisco	0	3	7	7	– 17

GB - Newsome 31 fumble return (Jacke)
GB - Jackson 3 pass from Favre (Jacke)
GB - Chmura 13 pass from Favre (Jacke)
SF - Wilkins 21 FG
SF - Young 1 run (Wilkins)
GB - Jacke 27 FG
GB - Jacke 26 FG
SF - Loville 2 run (Wilkins)

TEAM STATISTICS	GB	SF
First Downs	18	25
Rushing	3	7
Passing	13	16
Penalty	2	2
Offensive plays - yards	57 - 368	86 - 395
Rushes - yards	28 - 74	18 - 87
Passes	28 - 21 - 0	65 - 32 - 2
Gross passing yards	299	328
Sacked - yards lost	1 - 5	3 - 20
Net passing yards	294	308
Interceptions - yards	2 - 4	0 - 0
Punts - average	5 - 39.2	5 - 44.0
Punt returns - yards	3 - 17	3 - 14
Kickoff returns - yards	3 - 55	3 - 63
Fumbles - lost	0 - 0	2 - 2
Penalties - yards	5 - 35	8 - 72

AFC Divisional Playoff
Jan. 7, 1996
Arrowhead Stadium, Kansas City–77,594

Indianapolis	0	7	3	0	– 10
Kansas City	7	0	0	0	– 7

KC - Dawson 20 pass from Bono (Elliott)
Ind - Turner 5 pass from Harbaugh (Blanchard)
Ind - Blanchard 30 FG

TEAM STATISTICS	Ind	KC
First Downs	16	15
Rushing	7	5
Passing	8	9
Penalty	1	1
Offensive plays - yards	68 - 249	61 - 281
Rushes - yards	39 - 147	28 - 129
Passes	27 - 12 - 1	33 - 16 - 3
Gross passing yards	112	152
Sacked - yards lost	2 - 10	0 - 0
Net passing yards	102	152
Interceptions - yards	3 - 25	1 - 0

Punts - average	6 - 36.5	4 - 36.8
Punt returns - yards	2 - 10	4 - 34
Kickoff returns - yards	2 - 22	3 - 66
Fumbles - lost	4 - 0	1 - 1
Penalties - yards	6 - 38	3 - 29

NFC Divisional Playoff
Jan. 7, 1996
Texas Stadium, Irving–64,371

Philadelphia	0	3	0	8	– 11
Dallas	3	14	6	7	– 30

Dal - Boniol 24 FG
Phi - Anderson 26 FG
Dal - Sanders 21 run (Boniol)
Dal - E. Smith 1 run (Boniol)
Dal - Boniol 18 FG
Dal - Boniol 51 FG
Dal - Irvin 9 pass from Aikman (Boniol)
Phi - Cunningham 4 run (R. Johnson pass from Cunningham)

TEAM STATISTICS	Phi	Dal
First Downs	13	21
Rushing	4	10
Passing	8	11
Penalty	1	0
Offensive plays - yards	58 - 227	63 - 397
Rushes - yards	22 - 74	38 - 153
Passes	31 - 14 - 1	24 - 17 - 1
Gross passing yards	189	253
Sacked - yards lost	5 - 36	1 - 9
Net passing yards	153	244
Interceptions - yards	1 - 34	1 - 12
Punts - average	8 - 41.4	4 - 42.3
Punt returns - yards	2 - 8	2 - 21
Kickoff returns - yards	7 - 63	2 - 45
Fumbles - lost	1 - 0	0 - 0
Penalties - yards	3 - 21	7 - 89

AFC Championship Game
Jan. 14, 1996
Three Rivers Stadium, Pittsburgh–61,062

Indianapolis	3	3	3	7	– 16
Pittsburgh	3	7	3	7	– 20

Ind - Blanchard 34 FG
Pit - N. Johnson 31 FG
Ind - Blanchard 36 FG
Pit - Stewart 5 pass from O'Donnell (N. Johnson)
Ind - Blanchard 37 FG
Pit - N. Johnson 36 FG
Ind - Turner 47 pass from Harbaugh (Blanchard)
Pit - Morris 1 run (N. Johnson)

TEAM STATISTICS	Ind	Pit
First Downs	16	21
Rushing	4	6
Passing	12	12
Penalty	0	3
Offensive plays - yards	60 - 328	66 - 285
Rushes - yards	23 - 83	24 - 80
Passes	34 - 21 - 0	41 - 25 - 1
Gross passing yards	267	205

Sacked - yards lost	3 - 22	1 - 0
Net passing yards	245	205
Interceptions - yards	1 - 17	0 - 0
Punts - average	4 - 50.0	4 - 38.8
Punt returns - yards	1 - 5	3 - 53
Kickoff returns - yards	4 - 70	4 - 96
Fumbles - lost	1 - 0	0 - 0
Penalties - yards	5 - 57	4 - 25

NFC Championship Game
Jan. 14, 1996
Texas Stadium, Irving–65,135

Green Bay	10	7	10	0	–	27
Dallas	14	10	0	14	–	38

GB - Jacke 46 FG
Dal - Irvin 6 pass from Aikman (Boniol)
Dal - Irvin 4 pass from Aikman (Boniol)
GB - R. Brooks 73 pass from Favre (Jacke)
GB - Jackson 24 pass from Favre (Jacke)
Dal - Boniol 34 FG
Dal - E. Smith 1 run (Boniol)
GB - Jacke 37 FG
GB - R. Brooks 1 pass from Favre (Jacke)
Dal - E. Smith 5 run (Boniol)
Dal - E. Smith 16 run (Boniol)

TEAM STATISTICS	GB	Dal
First Downs	17	26
Rushing	3	11
Passing	11	13
Penalty	3	2
Offensive plays - yards	55 - 328	77 - 419
Rushes - yards	12 - 48	43 - 169
Passes	39 - 21 - 2	33 - 21 - 0
Gross passing yards	307	255
Sacked - yards lost	4 - 27	1 - 5
Net passing yards	280	250
Interceptions - yards	0 - 0	2 - 27
Punts - average	3 - 48.0	5 - 36.6
Had blocked	0	1
Punt returns - yards	4 - 54	1 - 6
Kickoff returns - yards	7 - 148	4 - 90
Fumbles - lost	0 - 0	0 - 0
Penalties - yards	11 - 84	6 - 65

Super Bowl XXX
Jan. 28, 1996
Sun Devil Stadium, Tempe–76,347

Dallas	10	3	7	7	–	27
Pittsburgh	0	7	0	10	–	17

Dal - Boniol 42 FG
Dal - Novacek 3 pass from Aikman (Boniol)
Dal - Boniol 35 FG
Pit - Thigpen 6 pass from O'Donnell (N. Johnson)
Dal - E. Smith 1 run (Boniol)
Pit - N. Johnson 46 FG
Pit - Morris 1 run (N. Johnson)
Dal - E. Smith 4 run (Boniol)
MVP: Larry Brown, CB, Dallas

TEAM STATISTICS	Dal	Pit
First Downs	15	25
Rushing	5	9

Passing	10	15
Penalty	0	1
Offensive plays - yards	50 - 254	84 - 310
Rushes - yards	25 - 56	31 - 103
Passes	23 - 15 - 0	49 - 28 - 3
Gross passing yards	209	239
Sacked - yards lost	2 - 11	4 - 32
Net passing yards	198	207
Interceptions - yards	3 - 77	0 - 0
Punts - average	5 - 38.2	4 - 44.8
Punt returns - yards	1 - 11	2 - 18
Kickoff returns - yards	3 - 37	5 - 96
Fumbles - lost	0 - 0	2 - 0
Penalties - yards	4 - 25	2 - 15

AFC Wild Card Game
Dec. 28, 1996
Rich Stadium, Orchard Park–70,213

Jacksonville	10	7	3	10	–	30
Buffalo	14	3	3	7	–	27

Buf - Thomas 7 pass from Kelly (Christie)
Jac - Simmons 20 interception return (Hollis)
Buf - Thomas 2 run (Christie)
Jac - Hollis 27 FG
Jac - Means 30 run (Hollis)
Buf - Christie 33 FG
Buf - Christie 47 FG
Jac - Hollis 24 FG
Buf - Burris 38 interception return (Christie)
Jac - Smith 2 pass from Brunell (Hollis)
Jac - Hollis 45 FG

TEAM STATISTICS	Jac	Buf
First Downs	18	19
Rushing	5	5
Passing	13	14
Penalty	0	0
Offensive plays - yards	70 - 409	68 - 308
Rushes - yards	35 - 184	29 - 92
Passes	33 - 18 - 2	36 - 22 - 1
Gross passing yards	239	246
Sacked - yards lost	2 - 14	3 - 30
Net passing yards	225	216
Interceptions - yards	1 - 20	2 - 38
Punts - average	5 - 50.6	5 - 43.2
Punt returns - yards	2 - 11	5 - 32
Kickoff returns - yards	5 - 99	7 - 172
Fumbles - lost	0 - 0	5 - 2
Penalties - yards	6 - 42	6 - 39

NFC Wild Card Game
Dec. 28, 1996
Texas Stadium, Irving–64,682

Minnesota	0	0	7	8	–	15
Dallas	7	23	7	3	–	40

Dal - Aikman 2 run (Boniol)
Dal - Boniol 28 FG
Dal - E. Smith 37 run (Boniol)
Dal - Teague 29 interception return (Boniol)
Dal - Boniol 31 FG
Dal - Boniol 22 FG
Min - Carter 30 pass from B. Johnson (Sisson)
Dal - E. Smith 1 run (Boniol)
Dal - Boniol 25 FG

Min - B. Johnson 5 run (Carter pass from B. Johnson)

TEAM STATISTICS	Min	Dal
First Downs	12	27
Rushing	3	16
Passing	7	10
Penalty	2	1
Offensive plays - yards	44 - 268	78 - 438
Rushes - yards	15 - 63	46 - 255
Passes	27 - 15 - 2	31 - 21 - 1
Gross passing yards	208	192
Sacked - yards lost	2 - 3	1 - 9
Net passing yards	205	183
Interceptions - yards	1 - 4	2 - 51
Punts - average	2 - 39.5	1 - 43.0
Punt returns - yards	1 - 8	1 - 6
Kickoff returns - yards	8 - 153	1 - 21
Fumbles - lost	4 - 4	2 - 1
Penalties - yards	3 - 15	5 - 54

AFC Wild Card Game
Dec. 29, 1996
Three Rivers Stadium, Pittsburgh–58,078

Indianapolis	0	14	0	0	–	14
Pittsburgh	10	3	8	21	–	42

Pit - N. Johnson 29 FG
Pit - Stewart 1 run (N. Johnson)
Pit - N. Johnson 50 FG
Ind - Daniel 59 interception return (Blanchard)
Ind - Bailey 9 pass from Harbaugh (Blanchard)
Pit - Bettis 1 run (Farquhar pass from Stewart)
Pit - Bettis 1 run (N. Johnson)
Pit - Witman 31 run (N. Johnson)
Pit - Stewart 3 run (N. Johnson)

TEAM STATISTICS	Ind	Pit
First Downs	8	24
Rushing	0	16
Passing	7	7
Penalty	1	1
Offensive plays - yards	52 - 146	73 - 407
Rushes - yards	15 - 41	51 - 231
Passes	33 - 13 - 1	22 - 14 - 2
Gross passing yards	140	176
Sacked - yards lost	4 - 35	0 - 0
Net passing yards	105	176
Interceptions - yards	2 - 59	1 - 0
Punts - average	8 - 42.4	2 - 41.5
Punt returns - yards	1 - 4	5 - 77
Kickoff returns - yards	7 - 127	3 - 67
Fumbles - lost	1 - 1	2 - 1
Penalties - yards	6 - 30	3 - 19

NFC Wild Card Game
Dec. 29, 1996
3Com Park, San Francisco–56,460

Philadelphia	0	0	0	0	–	0
San Francisco	0	7	7	0	–	14

SF - S. Young 9 run (Wilkins)
SF - Rice 3 pass from S. Young (Wilkins)

TEAM STATISTICS	Phi	SF
First Downs	16	17
Rushing	3	9

Passing	13	8
Penalty	0	0
Offensive plays - yards	62 - 283	56 - 279
Rushes - yards	26 - 71	34 - 118
Passes	33 - 19 - 3	21 - 14 - 0
Gross passing yards	225	161
Sacked - yards lost	3 - 13	1 - 0
Net passing yards	212	161
Interceptions - yards	0 - 0	3 - 5
Punts - average	5 - 35.8	6 - 37.2
Punt returns - yards	4 - 17	2 - 10
Kickoff returns - yards	2 - 48	1 - 11
Fumbles - lost	2 - 0	0 - 0
Penalties - yards	3 - 20	4 - 38

AFC Divisional Playoff
Jan. 4, 1997
Mile High Stadium, Denver–75,678

Jacksonville	0	13	7	10	–	30
Denver	12	0	0	15	–	27

Den - Hebron 1 run (Elam miss)
Den - Sharpe 18 pass from Elway (Elway pass failed)
Jac - Hollis 46 FG
Jac - Means 8 run (Hollis)
Jac - Hollis 42 FG
Jac - McCardell 31 pass from Brunell (Hollis)
Jac - Hollis 22 FG
Den - Davis 2 run (Davis run)
Jac - Smith 16 pass from Brunell (Hollis)
Den - McCaffrey 15 pass from Elway (Elam)

TEAM STATISTICS	Jac	Den
First Downs	22	21
Rushing	9	7
Passing	11	13
Penalty	2	1
Offensive plays - yards	67 - 443	60 - 351
Rushes - yards	36 - 203	21 - 126
Passes	29 - 18 - 0	38 - 25 - 0
Gross passing yards	245	226
Sacked - yards lost	2 - 5	1 - 1
Net passing yards	240	225
Interceptions - yards	0 - 0	0 - 0
Punts - average	3 - 39.7	5 - 42.6
Punt returns - yards	1 - 3	2 - 12
Kickoff returns - yards	4 - 75	6 - 123
Fumbles - lost	0 - 0	1 - 0
Penalties - yards	3 - 18	8 - 64

NFC Divisional Playoff
Jan. 4, 1997
Lambeau Field, Green Bay–60,787

San Francisco	0	7	7	0	–	14
Green Bay	14	7	7	7	–	35

GB - Howard 71 punt return (Jacke)
GB - Rison 4 pass from Favre (Jacke)
GB - Bennett 2 run (Jacke)
SF - Kirby 8 pass from Grbac (Wilkins)
SF - Grbac 4 run (Wilkins)
GB - Freeman offensive fumble recovery (Jacke)
GB - Bennett 11 run (Jacke)

TEAM STATISTICS	SF	GB
First Downs	12	15
Rushing	4	10
Passing	8	5
Penalty	0	0
Offensive plays - yards	60 - 196	55 - 210
Rushes - yards	18 - 68	39 - 139
Passes	41 - 21 - 3	15 - 11 - 0
Gross passing yards	133	79
Sacked - yards lost	1 - 5	1 - 8
Net passing yards	128	71
Interceptions - yards	0 - 0	3 - 5
Punts - average	6 - 35.8	6 - 43.2
Punt returns - yards	3 - 23	3 - 117
Kickoff returns - yards	4 - 75	2 - 44
Fumbles - lost	3 - 2	5 - 1
Penalties - yards	6 - 42	1 - 5

AFC Divisional Playoff
Jan. 5, 1997
Foxboro Stadium–60,188

Pittsburgh	0	0	3	0	–	3
New England	14	7	0	7	–	28

NE - Martin 2 run (Vinatieri)
NE - Byars 34 pass from Bledsoe (Vinatieri)
NE - Martin 78 run (Vinatieri)
Pit - N. Johnson 29 FG
NE - Martin 23 run (Vinatieri)

TEAM STATISTICS	Pit	NE
First Downs	12	17
Rushing	7	9
Passing	5	6
Penalty	0	2
Offensive plays - yards	69 - 213	60 - 346
Rushes - yards	27 - 123	32 - 194
Passes	39 - 16 - 2	26 - 15 - 2
Gross passing yards	110	167
Sacked - yards lost	3 - 20	2 - 15
Net passing yards	90	152
Interceptions - yards	2 - 0	2 - 14
Punts - average	9 - 42.0	7 - 43.6
Punt returns - yards	5 - 34	7 - 72
Kickoff returns - yards	5 - 99	2 - 54
Fumbles - lost	0 - 0	0 - 0
Penalties - yards	3 - 15	2 - 21

NFC Divisional Playoff
Jan. 5, 1997
Ericsson Stadium, Charlotte–72,808

Dallas	3	8	3	3	–	17
Carolina	7	10	3	6	–	26

Dal - Boniol 22 FG
Car - Walls 1 pass from Collins (Kasay)
Car - Green 10 pass from Collins (Kasay)
Dal - Johnston 2 pass from Aikman (Aikman pass failed)
Dal - Safety, ball snapped out of end zone
Car - Kasay 24 FG
Dal - Boniol 21 FG
Car - Kasay 40 FG
Car - Kasay 40 FG
Dal - Boniol 21 FG
Car - Kasay 32 FG

AFC Championship Game
Jan. 12, 1997
Foxboro Stadium–60,190

Jacksonville	0	3	3	0	–	6
New England	7	6	0	7	–	20

NE - Martin 1 run (Vinatieri)
Jac - Hollis 32 FG
NE - Vinatieri 29 FG
NE - Vinatieri 20 FG
Jac - Hollis 28 FG
NE - O. Smith 47 fumble return (Vinatieri)

TEAM STATISTICS	Jac	NE
First Downs	18	13
Rushing	6	6
Passing	12	7
Penalty	0	0
Offensive plays - yards	72 - 289	59 - 234
Rushes - yards	33 - 101	24 - 73
Passes	38 - 20 - 2	33 - 20 - 1
Gross passing yards	190	178
Sacked - yards lost	1 - 2	2 - 17
Net passing yards	188	161
Interceptions - yards	1 - 15	2 - 12
Punts - average	5 - 36.4	6 - 39.7
Punt returns - yards	4 - 15	3 - 29
Kickoff returns - yards	4 - 69	3 - 52
Fumbles - lost	3 - 2	2 - 1
Penalties - yards	4 - 23	2 - 5

NFC Championship Game
Jan. 12, 1997
Lambeau Field, Green Bay–60,216

Carolina	7	3	3	0	–	13
Green Bay	0	17	10	3	–	30

Car - Griffith 3 pass from Collins (Kasay)
GB - Levens 29 pass from Favre (Jacke)
Car - Kasay 22 FG
GB - Freeman 6 pass from Favre (Jacke)
GB - Jacke 31 FG
GB - Jacke 32 FG
Car - Kasay 23 FG
GB - Bennett 4 run (Jacke)
GB - Jacke 28 FG

TEAM STATISTICS	Car	GB
First Downs	12	22

Also included in column 3:

TEAM STATISTICS	Dal	Car
First Downs	21	18
Rushing	5	8
Passing	12	7
Penalty	4	3
Offensive plays - yards	62 - 244	59 - 227
Rushes - yards	24 - 96	37 - 127
Passes	36 - 18 - 3	22 - 12 - 1
Gross passing yards	165	100
Sacked - yards lost	2 - 17	0 - 0
Net passing yards	148	100
Interceptions - yards	1 - 0	3 - 122
Punts - average	3 - 51.0	1 - 39.0
Punt returns - yards	0 - 0	2 - 17
Kickoff returns - yards	6 - 101	5 - 155
Fumbles - lost	1 - 0	2 - 1
Penalties - yards	6 - 61	5 - 38

Rushing	1	10
Passing	11	12
Penalty	0	0
Offensive plays - yards	53 - 251	75 - 479
Rushes - yards	14 - 45	45 - 201
Passes	37 - 19 - 2	29 - 19 - 1
Gross passing yards	215	292
Sacked - yards lost	2 - 9	1 - 14
Net passing yards	206	278
Interceptions - yards	1 - 10	2 - 35
Punts - average	5 - 36.0	2 - 36.0
Punt returns - yards	1 - 4	1 - 3
Kickoff returns - yards	7 - 86	4 - 104
Fumbles - lost	2 - 1	2 - 1
Penalties - yards	4 - 25	5 - 45

Super Bowl XXXI

Jan. 26, 1997

Louisiana Superdome, New Orleans–72,301

New England	14	0	7	0	–	21
Green Bay	10	17	8	0	–	35

GB - Rison 54 pass from Favre (Jacke)

GB - Jacke 37 FG

NE - Byars 1 pass from Bledsoe (Vinatieri)

NE - Coates 4 pass from Bledsoe (Vinatieri)

GB - Freeman 81 pass from Favre (Jacke)

GB - Jacke 31 FG

GB - Favre 2 run (Jacke)

NE - Martin 18 run (Vinatieri)

GB - Howard 99 kickoff return (Chmura pass from Favre)

MVP: Desmond Howard, KR, Green Bay

TEAM STATISTICS	NE	GB
First Downs	16	16
Rushing	3	8
Passing	12	6
Penalty	1	2
Offensive plays - yards	66 - 257	68 - 323
Rushes - yards	13 - 43	36 - 115
Passes	48 - 25 - 4	27 - 14 - 0
Gross passing yards	253	246
Sacked - yards lost	5 - 39	5 - 38
Net passing yards	214	208
Interceptions - yards	0 - 0	4 - 24
Punts - average	8 - 45.1	7 - 42.7
Punt returns - yards	4 - 30	6 - 90
Kickoff returns - yards	6 - 135	4 - 154
Fumbles - lost	0 - 0	0 - 0
Penalties - yards	2 - 22	3 - 41

PART SIX

The Yearly Record

The Yearly Record

The Yearly Record contains the final standings, team statistics, and individual leaders for every major pro football league since the formation of the American Professional Football Association in 1920.

THE FINAL STANDINGS

The following sample illustrates a typical listing of final team standings. All teams are listed in their official order of finish.

The first listing is for all league games. The home and road record of each team follows. For a complete list and record of neutral site games, please refer to The Game Scores.

National Football League 1992
AMERICAN FOOTBALL CONFERENCE
Eastern Division

Team	W	L	T	Pct	Pts	Opp	HW	HL	HT	HPct	AW	AL	AT	APct
MIA	11	5	0	.688	340	281	6	2	0	.750	5	3	0	.625
BUF	11	5	0	.688	381	283	6	2	0	.750	5	3	0	.625
IND	9	7	0	.563	216	302	4	4	0	.500	5	3	0	.625
NYJ	4	12	0	.250	220	315	3	5	0	.375	1	7	0	.125
NE	2	14	0	.125	205	363	1	7	0	.125	1	7	0	.125

TEAM	The standard abbreviation for each team.
W	Wins
L	Losses
T	Ties
PCT	Official winning percentage.
	Before 1972, tied games were not counted in the standings. Beginning in 1972, ties were counted as half-wins and half-losses.
	Note: Neutral site games are counted as Road Games.
Pts	Points scored
Opp	Points given up
HW	Home wins
HL	Home losses
HT	Home ties
HPCT	Home winning percentage.
AW	Road wins
AL	Road losses
AT	Road ties
APCT	Road winning percentage.

THE INDIVIDUAL LEADERS

Following the Team Statistics are the Yearly Leaders in each of the nine statistical catgeories. The top five scorers, rushers, passers and pass receivers are listed, as well as the leader in interceptions, punting, punt returns, kickoff returns and sacks.

For each category, the leaders are listed according to the criteria used by each league at the time.

INDIVIDUAL LEADER QUALIFICATIONS

CATEGORY	YEARS	LGE	MINIMUM	METHOD (statistics used)
SCORING	1932–1996	NFL	—	PTS
	1946–1949	AAFC	—	PTS
	1960–1969	AFL	—	PTS
RUSHING	1932–1996	NFL	—	YDS
	1946–1949	AAFC	—	YDS
	1960–1969	AFL	—	YDS
PASSING	1932–1937	NFL	—	YDS
	1938–1939	NFL	—	COM (ties broken by PC%)

	1940–1944	NFL	—	inverse ranking (COM/PC%)
	1945	NFL	32ATT	inverse ranking or 13COM (COM/YDS/TDS)
	1946	NFL	32ATT	inverse ranking or 13COM (COM/PC%/YDS/TD/PI%)
	1946–1948	AAFC	—	inverse ranking (COM/YDS/Efficiency (COM%-IN%)
	1947–1948	NFL	33ATT	inverse ranking or 14COM (COM/PC%/TD/YDS/INT/PI%)
	1949	AAFC	—	Record Percentage (Percentage of "all-time" AAFC record COM/YDS/Efficiency Percentage (COM%-IN%)
	1949	NFL	33ATT	inverse ranking or 14COM (COM/PC%/YDS/TD/PI%)
	1950–1959	NFL	100ATT	AVG
	1960–1965	AFL	140ATT	Efficiency Percentage (inverse ranking of COM/YDS/TD/COM%/PI%/AVG)
	1960	NFL	120ATT	inverse ranking (COM/YDS/TD/PC%/PI%/AVG)
	1961	NFL	140ATT	inverse ranking (COM/YDS/TD/PC%/PI%/AVG)
	1962–1972	NFL	140ATT	inverse ranking (PC%/TD/PI%/AVG)
	1966	AFL	140ATT	inverse ranking (COM/YDS/TD/PC%/PI%/AVG)
	1967–1969	AFL	140ATT	inverse ranking (PC%/TD/PI%/AVG)
	1973–1976	NFL	140ATT	RTG
	1977	NFL	168ATT	RTG
	1978–1983	NFL	192ATT	RTG
	1984	NFL	?	RTG
	1985–1986	NFL	224ATT	RTG
	1987	NFL	210ATT	RTG
	1988–1996	NFL	224ATT	RTG
RECEIVING	1932–1996	NFL	—	NO
	1946–1949	AAFC	—	NO
	1960–1969	AFL	—	NO
INTERCEPTIONS	1940–1996	NFL	—	NO
	1946	AAFC	—	NO
	1947	AAFC	—	NO (ties broken by YDS)
	1948–1949	AAFC	—	NO
	1960–1969	AFL	—	NO
PUNTING	1939	NFL	—	NO (ties broken by AVG)
	1940	NFL	—	AVG (ties broken by NO)
	1941–1944	NFL	?	inverse ranking (NO/AVG)
	1945	NFL	12NO	inverse ranking (NO/AVG)
	1946	NFL	12NO	inverse ranking (NO/AVG)
	1946	AAFC	13NO	inverse ranking (NO/AVG)
	1947–1949	NFL	13NO	inverse ranking (NO/AVG)
	1947–1948	AAFC	?	inverse ranking (NO/AVG)
	1949	AAFC	?	AVG
	1950–1960	NFL	24NO	AVG
	1960–1963	AFL	28NO	AVG
	1961–1965	NFL	28NO	AVG
	1964–1966	AFL	?	AVG
	1966–1968	NFL	42NO	AVG
	1967–1968	AFL	28NO	AVG
	1969–1975	NFL	35NO	AVG
	1969	AFL	35NO	AVG
	1976–1977	NFL	35NO	GAVG
	1978–1981	NFL	40NO	GAVG
	1982	NFL	23NO	GAVG
	1983–1986	NFL	40NO	GAVG
	1987	NFL	38NO	GAVG

	1988–1996	NFL	40NO	GAVG
PUNT RETURNS	1941–1943	NFL	—	NO (ties broken by YDS)
	1944	NFL	?	inverse ranking (NO/AVG)
	1945–1946	NFL	8NO	inverse ranking (NO/AVG)
	1946–1949	AAFC	—	YDS
	1947–1949	NFL	9NO	inverse ranking (NO/AVG)
	1950–1952	NFL	9NO	AVG
	1953–1960	NFL	12NO	AVG
	1960–1964	AFL	10NO	AVG
	1961–1978	NFL	14NO	AVG
	1965	AFL	14NO	AVG
	1966	AFL	10NO	AVG
	1967–1969	AFL	14NO	AVG
	1969	AFL	?	AVG
	1979–1981	NFL	16NO	AVG
	1982	NFL	9NO	AVG
	1983	NFL	16NO	AVG
	1984–1986	NFL	20NO	AVG
	1987	NFL	15NO	AVG
	1988–1996	NFL	20NO	AVG
KICKOFF RETURNS	1941–1943	NFL	—	NO (ties broken by YDS)
	1944–1945	NFL	7NO	inverse ranking (NO/AVG)
	1946	NFL	?	inverse ranking (NO/AVG)
	1946–1949	AAFC	—	YDS
	1947–1949	NFL	9NO	inverse ranking (NO/AVG)
	1950–1952	NFL	9NO	AVG
	1953–1960	NFL	12NO	AVG
	1960–1969	AFL	14NO	AVG
	1961–1977	NFL	14NO	AVG
	1978–1981	NFL	16NO	AVG
	1982	NFL	9NO	AVG
	1983	NFL	16NO	AVG
	1984–1986	NFL	20NO	AVG
	1987	NFL	19NO	AVG
	1988–1996	NFL	20NO	AVG
SACKS	1982–1996	NFL	—	NO

American Professional Football Association 1920

Team	W	L	T	Pct	Pts	Opp	HW	HL	HT	HPct	AW	AL	AT	APct
AKR	6	0	3	1.000	95	7	4	0	0	1.000	2	0	3	.700
DEC	5	1	2	.833	67	14	1	0	1	.750	4	1	1	.750
BUF	4	1	1	.800	74	19	3	1	1	.700	1	0	0	1.000
DAY	4	2	2	.667	127	47	3	1	2	.667	1	1	0	.500
RI	4	2	1	.667	98	35	4	2	1	.643	0	0	0	
CHIC	3	2	1	.600	34	26	2	1	0	.667	1	1	1	.500
CAN	4	3	1	.571	72	44	2	1	0	.667	2	2	1	.500
DET	1	3	0	.250	6	61	1	0	0	1.000	0	3	0	.000
CLE	1	4	2	.200	14	46	1	1	1	.500	0	3	1	.125
CHIT	1	5	1	.167	22	63	1	3	1	.300	0	2	0	.000
ROC	0	1	0	.000	6	17	0	0	0		0	1	0	.000
MUN	0	1	0	.000	0	45	0	0	0		0	1	0	.000
COL	0	5	0	.000	7	107	0	0	0		0	5	0	.000
HAM	0	3	0	.000	7	98	0	0	0		0	3	0	.000

Scoring

	TD	1XP	2XP	FG	SAF	PTS
Frank Bacon, DAY	5	2		0	0	32
Arnie Wyman, RI	5	0		0	0	30
Fritz Pollard, AKR	4	0		0	0	24
Pat Smith, BUF	4	0		0	0	24
seven tied with						18

American Professional Football Association 1921

Team	W	L	T	Pct	Pts	Opp	HW	HL	HT	HPct	AW	AL	AT	APct
DEC	9	1	1	.900	128	53	9	1	1	.864	0	0	0	
BUF	9	1	2	.900	211	29	8	0	2	.900	1	1	0	.500
AKR	8	3	1	.727	148	31	3	1	0	.750	5	2	1	.688
CAN	5	2	3	.714	106	55	1	1	1	.500	4	1	2	.714
RI	4	2	1	.667	65	30	1	0	1	.750	3	2	0	.600
GB	3	2	1	.600	70	55	3	1	0	.750	0	1	1	.250
EVA	3	2	0	.600	89	46	3	1	0	.750	0	1	0	.000
CHIC	3	3	2	.500	54	53	3	3	1	.500	0	0	1	.500
DAY	4	4	1	.500	96	67	4	0	1	.900	0	4	0	.000
ROC	3	3	0	.500	97	76	3	0	0	1.000	0	3	0	.000
WAS	2	2	0	.500	41	50	2	2	0	.500	0	0	0	
CLE	3	5	0	.375	95	58	2	1	0	.667	1	4	0	.200
CIN	1	3	0	.250	14	117	0	0	0		1	3	0	.250
HAM	1	3	1	.250	17	45	0	0	0		1	3	1	.300
MIN	1	3	1	.250	37	41	1	0	0	1.000	0	3	0	.000
DET	1	5	1	.167	19	109	1	2	0	.333	0	3	1	.125
COL	1	8	0	.111	47	222	0	1	0	.000	1	7	0	.125
MUN	0	2	0	.000	0	28	0	1	0	.100	0	1	0	.000
NY	0	2	0	.000	0	72	0	1	0	.000	0	1	0	.000
SYR	0	2	1	.000	7	32	0	0	1	.500	0	2	0	.000
TON	0	1	1	.000	0	45	0	0	0		0	1	1	.250
LOU	0	2	0	.000	0	27	0	1	0	.000	0	1	0	.000

Scoring

	TD	1XP	2XP	FG	SAF	PTS
Elmer Oliphant, BUF	1	26		5	0	47
Ockie Anderson, BUF	7	0		0	0	42
Fritz Pollard, AKR	7	0		0	0	42
Benny Boynton, ROC-WAS	4	12		1	0	39
Carl Cramer, AKR	6	1		0	0	37

National Football League 1922

Team	W	L	T	Pct	Pts	Opp	HW	HL	HT	HPct	AW	AL	AT	APct
CAN	10	0	2	1.000	184	15	6	0	1	.929	4	0	1	.900
CHIB	9	3	0	.750	123	44	7	1	0	.875	2	2	0	.500
CHIC	8	3	0	.727	96	50	8	2	0	.800	0	1	0	.000
TOL	5	2	2	.714	94	59	4	1	1	.750	1	1	1	.500
RI	4	2	1	.667	154	27	4	1	0	.800	0	1	1	.250
RAC	6	4	1	.600	122	56	5	2	1	.688	1	2	0	.333
GB	4	3	3	.571	70	54	3	1	1	.700	1	2	2	.400
DAY	4	3	1	.571	80	54	3	1	1	.700	1	2	0	.333
BUF	5	4	1	.556	87	41	3	1	1	.700	2	3	0	.400
AKR	3	5	2	.375	146	95	3	1	1	.700	0	4	1	.100
MIL	2	4	3	.333	51	71	2	0	2	.750	0	4	1	.100
OOR	3	6	0	.333	69	190	1	0	0	1.000	2	6	0	.250
MIN	1	3	0	.250	19	40	1	0	0	1.000	0	3	0	.000
LOU	1	3	0	.250	13	140	1	0	0	1.000	0	3	0	.000
ROC	0	4	1	.000	13	76	0	1	0	.000	0	3	1	.125
HAM	0	5	1	.000	0	69	0	0	0		0	5	1	.083
COL	0	7	0	.000	24	174	0	1	0	.000	0	6	0	.000
EVA	0	3	0	.000	6	88	0	0	0		0	3	0	.000

Scoring

	TD	1XP	2XP	FG	SAF	PTS
Jimmy Conzelman, RI-MIL	8	1		2	0	55
Hank Gillo, RAC	5	4		6	0	52
Ed Shaw, CAN	5	8		2	0	44
Guy Chamberlin, CAN	7	0		0	0	42
Paddy Driscoll, CHIC	2	5		8	0	41

National Football League 1923

Team	W	L	T	Pct	Pts	Opp	HW	HL	HT	HPct	AW	AL	AT	APct
CAN	11	0	1	1.000	246	19	7	0	0	1.000	4	0	1	.900
CHIB	9	2	2	.818	130	42	7	1	2	.800	2	1	0	.667
GB	7	2	1	.778	85	34	5	1	1	.786	3	0	0	1.000
MIL	7	2	4	.778	107	56	3	1	2	.667	4	1	2	.714
CLE	3	1	3	.750	52	49	3	1	1	.700	0	0	2	.500
CHIC	8	4	0	.667	161	56	8	3	0	.727	0	1	0	.000
DUL	4	3	0	.571	35	363	3	0	0	1.000	1	3	0	.250
COL	5	4	1	.556	119	35	5	2	0	.714	0	2	1	.167
BUF	5	4	3	.556	94	43	3	0	3	.750	2	4	0	.333
TOL	3	3	2	.500	35	66	2	0	0	1.000	1	3	2	.333
RAC	4	4	2	.500	86	76	2	3	1	.417	2	1	1	.625
RI	2	3	3	.400	84	62	2	1	2	.600	0	2	1	.167
MIN	2	5	2	.296	48	81	2	1	1	.625	0	4	1	.100
STL	1	4	2	.200	14	39	1	2	1	.375	0	2	1	.167
HAM	1	5	1	.167	14	59	1	0	0	1.000	5	0	5	.083
DAY	1	6	1	.143	16	95	1	0	0	1.000	0	6	1	.071
AKR	1	6	0	.143	25	74	1	0	0	1.000	0	6	0	.000
OOR	1	10	0	.091	43	257	0	0	0		1	10	0	.091
LOU	0	3	0	.000	0	83	0	1	0	.000	0	2	0	.000
ROC	0	4	0	.000	6	141	0	2	0	.000	0	2	0	.000

Scoring

	TD	1XP	2XP	FG	SAF	PTS
Paddy Driscoll, CHIC	7	6		10		78
Pete Henry, CAN	1	25		9	0	58
Dutch Sternaman, CHIB	5	7		5	0	52
Ben Winkleman, MIL	3	9		6	0	45
Hank Gillo, RAC	2	8		8	0	44

National Football League 1924

Team	W	L	T	Pct	Pts	Opp	HW	HL	HT	HPct	AW	AL	AT	APct
CLE	7	1	1	.875	229	60	5	1	0	.833	2	0	1	.833
CHIB	6	1	4	.857	136	55	5	0	3	.813	1	1	1	.500
FRA	11	2	1	.846	326	109	8	0	1	.944	3	2	0	.600
DUL	5	1	0	.833	56	16	2	0	0	1.000	3	1	0	.750
RI	5	2	2	.714	88	38	4	1	1	.750	1	1	1	.500
GB	7	4	0	.636	108	38	5	0	0	1.000	2	4	0	.333
RAC	4	3	3	.571	69	47	3	1	0	.750	1	2	3	.417
CHIC	5	4	1	.556	90	67	5	3	1	.611	0	1	0	.000
BUF	6	5	0	.545	120	140	5	3	0	.625	1	2	0	.333
COL	4	4	0	.500	91	68	2	0	0	1.000	2	4	0	.333
HAM	2	2	1	.500	18	45	0	0	0		0	5	0	.000
MIL	5	8	0	.385	142	188	3	2	0	.600	2	6	0	.250
AKR	2	6	0	.250	59	132	1	1	0	.500	1	5	0	.167
DAY	2	6	0	.250	45	148	1	1	0	.500	1	5	0	.167
KC	2	7	0	.222	46	124	2	2	0	.500	0	5	0	.000
ROC	0	7	0	.000	7	156	0	3	0	.000	0	4	0	.000
MIN	0	6	0	.000	14	108	0	2	0	.000	0	4	0	.000
KEN	0	4	1	.000	12	117	0	0	1	.500	0	4	0	.000

Scoring

	TD	1XP	2XP	FG	SAF	PTS
Joe Sternaman, CHIB	6	12		9		75
Tex Hamer, FRA	12	0		0	0	72
Benny Boynton, BUF	6	11		4	0	59
Hank Gillo, RAC	3	6		8	0	48
Jack Storer, FRA	8	0		0	0	48

National Football League 1925

Team	W	L	T	Pct	Pts	Opp	HW	HL	HT	HPct	AW	AL	AT	APct
CHIC	11	2	1	.846	229	65	11	2	0	.846	0	0	1	.500
POT	10	2	0	.833	270	45	8	1	0	.889	2	1	0	.667
DET	8	2	2	.800	129	39	8	1	2	.818	0	1	0	.000
NYG	8	4	0	.667	122	67	7	2	0	.778	1	2	0	.333
AKR	4	2	2	.667	65	51	3	0	0	1.000	1	2	2	.400
FRA	13	7	0	.650	190	169	9	3	0	.750	4	4	0	.500
CHIB	9	5	3	.643	158	96	7	1	1	.833	2	4	2	.375
RI	5	3	3	.625	99	58	3	0	3	.750	2	3	0	.400
GB	8	5	0	.615	151	110	6	0	0	1.000	2	5	0	.286
PRO	6	5	1	.545	111	101	4	3	1	.563	2	2	0	.500
CAN	4	4	0	.500	50	73	4	1	0	.800	0	3	0	.000
CLE	5	8	1	.385	75	135	3	1	0	.750	2	7	1	.250
KC	2	5	1	.286	65	97	0	0	0		2	5	1	.313
HAM	1	4	0	.200	23	87	0	0	0		1	4	0	.200
BUF	1	6	2	.143	33	113	1	1	2	.500	0	5	0	.000
ROC	0	6	1	.000	26	111	0	0	0		0	6	1	.071
COL	0	9	0	.000	28	124	0	0	0		0	9	0	.000
DAY	0	7	1	.000	3	84	0	0	0		0	7	1	.063
DUL	0	3	0	.000	6	25	0	2	0	.000	0	1	0	.000
MIL	0	6	0	.000	7	190	0	1	0	.000	0	5	0	.000

Scoring

	TD	1XP	2XP	FG	SAF	PTS
Charlie Berry, POT	6	29		3	0	74
Paddy Driscoll, CHIC	4	10		11		67
Joe Sternaman, CHIB	6	17		3	0	62
Tony Latone, POT	8	0		0	0	48
Tex Hamer, FRA	7	3		0	0	45

American Football League 1926

Team	W	L	T	Pct	Pts	Opp	HW	HL	HT	HPct	AW	AL	AT	APct
PHI	8	2	0	.800	93	52	7	1	0	.875	1	1	0	.500
NY	10	5	0	.667	212	82	5	2	0	.714	5	3	0	.625
CLE	3	2	0	.600	62	46	3	1	0	.750	0	1	0	.000
LA	6	6	2	.500	105	83	0	0	0		6	6	2	.500
CHI	5	6	3	.455	88	69	5	2	2	.667	0	4	1	.100
BOS	2	4	0	.333	20	81	0	2	0	.000	2	2	0	.500
RI	2	6	1	.250	21	126	2	1	0	.667	0	5	1	.083
BKN	1	3	0	.250	25	68	1	2	0	.333	0	1	0	.000
NEW	0	3	2	.000	7	26	0	2	2	.250	0	1	0	.000

Scoring

	TD	1XP	2XP	FG	SAF	PTS
Eddie Tryon, NY	9	12		2	0	72
Joe Sternaman, CHI	3	7		9	0	52
Red Grange, NY	8	2		0	0	50
Al Kreuz, PHI	1	4		8	0	34
Dave Noble, CLE	5	0		0	0	30

National Football League 1926

Team	W	L	T	Pct	Pts	Opp	HW	HL	HT	HPct	AW	AL	AT	APct
FRA	14	1	2	.933	236	49	11	1	2	.857	3	0	0	1.000
CHIB	12	1	3	.923	216	63	10	0	2	.917	2	1	1	.625
POT	10	2	2	.833	155	29	9	0	0	1.000	1	2	2	.400
KC	8	3	0	.727	76	53	2	0	0	1.000	6	3	0	.667
GB	7	3	3	.700	151	61	4	1	2	.714	3	2	1	.583
LA	6	3	1	.667	67	57	0	0	0		6	3	1	.650
NYG	8	4	1	.667	147	51	5	2	1	.688	3	2	0	.600
DUL	6	5	3	.545	113	81	1	0	0	1.000	5	5	3	.500
BUF	4	4	2	.500	53	62	2	2	2	.500	2	2	0	.500
CHIC	5	6	1	.455	74	98	3	2	0	.600	2	4	1	.357
PRO	5	7	1	.417	89	103	4	4	1	.500	1	3	0	.250
DET	4	6	2	.400	107	60	4	3	2	.556	0	3	0	.000
HAR	3	7	0	.300	57	99	3	5	0	.375	0	2	0	.000
BKN	3	8	0	.273	60	150	4	3	0	.571	0	4	0	.000
MIL	2	7	0	.222	41	66	1	5	0	.167	1	2	0	.333
DAY	1	4	1	.200	15	82	0	1	0	.000	1	3	1	.300
RAC	1	4	0	.200	8	92	1	2	0	.333	0	2	0	.000
AKR	1	4	3	.200	23	89	1	0	1	.750	0	4	2	.167
COL	1	6	0	.143	26	93	0	1	0	.000	1	5	0	.167
CAN	1	9	3	.100	46	161	1	3	1	.300	0	6	2	.125
HAM	0	4	0	.000	3	56	0	1	0	.000	0	3	0	.000
LOU	0	4	0	.000	0	108	0	0	0		0	4	0	.000

Scoring

	TD	1XP	2XP	FG	SAF	PTS
Paddy Driscoll, CHIB	6	14		12	0	86
Ernie Nevers, DUL	8	11		4	0	71
Curley Oden, PRO	9	1		0	0	55
Barney Wentz, POT	9	0		0	0	54
Ben Jones, FRA	8	0		0	0	48
Jack McBride, NYG	5	15		1	0	48

National Football League 1927

Team	W	L	T	Pct	Pts	Opp	HW	HL	HT	HPct	AW	AL	AT	APct
NYG	11	1	1	.917	197	20	7	1	0	.875	4	0	1	.900
GB	7	2	1	.778	113	43	6	2	0	.750	1	0	1	.750
CHIB	9	3	2	.750	149	98	7	1	1	.833	2	2	1	.500
CLE	8	4	1	.667	209	107	4	0	1	.900	4	4	0	.500
PRO	8	5	1	.615	105	88	6	3	0	.667	2	2	1	.500
NYY	7	8	1	.467	142	174	2	2	0	.500	5	6	1	.458
FRA	6	9	3	.400	152	166	5	4	3	.542	1	5	0	.167

POT	5	8	0	.385	80	163	4	3	0	.571	1	5	0	.167
CHIC	3	7	1	.300	69	134	2	3	1	.417	1	4	0	.200
DAY	1	6	1	.143	15	57	0	1	0	.000	1	5	1	.214
DUL	1	8	1	.111	68	134	0	0	0		1	8	0	.111
BUF	0	5	0	.000	8	123	0	2	0	.000	0	3	0	.000

Scoring

	TD	1XP	2XP	FG	SAF	PTS
Jack McBride, NYG	6	15		2		57
Al Bloodgood, CLE	6	6		1		45
Eddie Tryon, NYY	6	8		0	0	44
Paddy Driscoll, CHIB	5	7		2		43
Ken Mercer, FRA	2	8		5	1	37

National Football League 1928

Team	W	L	T	Pct	Pts	Opp	HW	HL	HT	HPct	AW	AL	AT	APct
PRO	8	1	2	.889	128	42	6	1	1	.813	2	0	1	.833
FRA	11	3	2	.786	175	84	8	1	1	.850	3	2	1	.583
DET	7	2	1	.778	189	76	3	0	0	1.000	4	2	1	.643
GB	6	4	3	.600	120	92	3	2	2	.571	3	2	1	.583
CHIB	7	5	1	.583	182	85	6	4	0	.600	2	1	0	.667
NYG	4	7	2	.364	79	136	1	2	2	.400	3	5	0	.375
NYY	4	8	1	.333	103	179	2	4	0	.333	2	4	1	.357
POT	2	8	0	.200	74	134	2	3	0	.400	0	5	0	.000
CHIC	1	5	0	.167	7	107	1	1	0	.500	0	4	0	.000
DAY	0	7	0	.000	9	131	0	0	0		0	7	0	.000

Scoring

	TD	1XP	2XP	FG	SAF	PTS
Verne Lewellen, GB	9	0		0	0	54
Benny Friedman, DET	4	19		0	0	43
Tiny Feather, DET	7	0		0	0	42
Gibby Welch, NYY	7	0		0	0	42
Ken Mercer, FRA	6	2		0		38

National Football League 1929

Team	W	L	T	Pct	Pts	Opp	HW	HL	HT	HPct	AW	AL	AT	APct
GB	12	0	1	1.000	198	22	5	0	0	1.000	7	0	1	.938
NYG	13	1	1	.929	312	86	7	1	0	.875	6	0	1	.929
FRA	10	4	5	.714	139	128	7	1	3	.773	3	3	2	.500
CHIC	6	6	1	.500	154	83	3	2	0	.600	3	4	1	.438
BOS	4	4	0	.500	98	73	2	1	0	.667	2	3	0	.400
SI	3	4	3	.429	89	65	3	2	2	.571	0	2	1	.167
PRO	4	6	2	.400	107	117	4	4	1	.500	0	2	1	.167
ORA	3	5	4	.375	35	90	2	1	2	.600	1	4	2	.286
CHIB	4	9	2	.308	119	227	1	5	2	.250	3	4	0	.429
BUF	1	7	1	.125	48	142	0	4	0	.000	1	3	1	.300
MIN	1	9	0	.100	48	185	1	2	0	.333	0	7	0	.000
DAY	0	6	0	.000	7	136	0	0	0		0	6	0	.000

Scoring

	TD	1XP	2XP	FG	SAF	PTS
Ernie Nevers, CHIC	12	10		1		85
Len Sedbrook, NYG	11	0		0	0	66
Tony Plansky, NYG	9	2		2	0	62
Tony Latone, BOS	9	0		0	0	54
Ray Flaherty, NYG	8	1		0	0	49
Verne Lewellen, GB	8	1		0	0	49

National Football League 1930

Team	W	L	T	Pct	Pts	Opp	HW	HL	HT	HPct	AW	AL	AT	APct
GB	10	3	1	.769	234	111	6	0	0	1.000	4	3	1	.563
NYG	13	4	0	.765	308	98	6	2	0	.750	7	2	0	.778
CHIB	9	4	1	.692	169	71	5	2	1	.688	4	2	0	.667
BKN	7	4	1	.636	154	59	3	2	0	.600	4	2	1	.643
PRO	6	4	1	.600	90	125	6	1	1	.813	0	3	0	.000
SI	5	5	1	.500	95	112	3	2	1	.583	2	3	1	.417
POR	5	6	3	.455	176	161	5	1	2	.750	0	5	1	.083
CHIC	5	6	2	.455	128	132	3	2	0	.600	2	4	2	.375
FRA	4	13	0	.235	113	321	3	6	0	.333	1	7	1	.167
MIN	1	7	1	.125	27	165	1	2	1	.375	0	5	0	.000
NEW	1	10	1	.091	51	190	0	5	1	.083	1	5	0	.167

Scoring

	TD	1XP	2XP	FG	SAF	PTS
Jack McBride, BKN	8	8		0	0	56
Verne Lewellen, GB	9	0		0	0	54
Ken Strong, SI	7	8		1	0	53
Benny Friedman, NYG	6	10		1	0	49
Red Grange, CHIB	8	1		0	0	49

National Football League 1931

Team	W	L	T	Pct	Pts	Opp	HW	HL	HT	HPct	AW	AL	AT	APct
GB	12	2	0	.857	291	87	8	0	0	1.000	5	1	0	.833
POR	11	3	0	.796	175	77	7	0	0	1.000	5	2	0	.714
CHIB	8	5	0	.615	145	92	6	3	0	.667	2	2	0	.500
CHIC	5	4	0	.556	120	128	3	0	0	1.000	2	4	0	.333
NYG	7	6	1	.538	154	100	4	2	1	.643	3	4	0	.429
PRO	4	4	3	.500	78	127	3	3	1	.500	1	1	2	.500
SI	4	6	1	.400	79	118	4	1	1	.750	0	5	0	.000
CLE	2	8	0	.200	45	137	1	1	0	.500	1	7	0	.125
BKN	2	12	0	.143	64	199	1	5	0	.167	1	7	0	.125
FRA	1	6	1	.143	13	99	0	3	0	.000	1	3	1	.300

Scoring

	TD	1XP	2XP	FG	SAF	PTS
Johnny Blood, GB	13	0		0	0	78
Ernie Nevers, CHIC	8	15		1	0	66
Dutch Clark, POR	9	6		0	0	60
Ken Strong, SI	7	5		2	0	53
Red Grange, CHIB	7	0		0	0	42

National Football League 1932

Team	W	L	T	Pct	Pts	Opp	HW	HL	HT	HPct	AW	AL	AT	APct
CHIB	7	1	6	.875	160	44	6	1	1	.813	1	0	5	.583
GB	10	3	1	.769	152	63	5	0	1	.917	5	3	0	.625
POR	6	2	4	.750	116	71	3	0	2	.800	3	2	2	.571
BOS	4	4	2	.500	55	79	2	3	1	.417	2	1	1	.625
NYG	4	6	2	.400	93	113	3	2	1	.583	1	4	1	.250
BKN	3	9	0	.250	63	131	1	5	0	.167	2	4	0	.333
CHIC	2	6	2	.250	72	114	1	2	1	.375	1	4	1	.250
SI	2	7	3	.222	77	173	1	3	3	.313	1	4	0	.200

Scoring

	TD	1XP	2XP	FG	SAF	PTS
Dutch Clark, POR	6	10		3	0	55
Red Grange, CHIB	7	0		0		42
Ray Flaherty, NYG	5	0		0		30
Jack Grossman, BKN	5	0		0	0	30
Luke Johnsos, CHIB	4	2		0		26

Rushing

	ATT	YDS	AVG	LG	TD
Cliff Battles, BOS	148	576	3.9		3
Bob Campiglio, SI	104	504	4.8		2
Bronko Nagurski, CHIB	109	486	4.5		4
Dutch Clark, POR	112	461	4.1		3
Ken Strong, SI	96	375	3.9		2

Passing

	ATT	COM	YDS	TD	INT	LG
Arnie Herber, GB	101	37	639	9		9
Keith Molesworth, CHIB	54	22	475	3		6
Jack McBride, BKN-NYG	74	36	463	6		9

Receiving

	NO	YDS	AVG	LG	TD
Ray Flaherty, NYG	21	350	16.7		5
Luke Johnsos, CHIB	19	321	16.9		2

National Football League 1933
Eastern Division

Team	W	L	T	Pct	Pts	Opp	HW	HL	HT	HPct	AW	AL	AT	APct
NYG	11	3	0	.786	244	101	7	0	0	1.000	4	3	0	.571
BKN	5	4	1	.556	93	54	3	2	1	.583	2	2	0	.500
BOS	5	5	2	.500	103	97	4	2	0	.667	1	3	2	.333
PHI	3	5	1	.375	77	158	2	3	1	.417	1	2	0	.333
PIT	3	6	2	.333	67	208	2	3	0	.400	1	3	2	.333

Western Division

Team	W	L	T	Pct	Pts	Opp	HW	HL	HT	HPct	AW	AL	AT	APct
CHIB	10	2	1	.833	133	82	6	0	0	1.000	4	2	1	.643
POR	6	5	0	.545	128	87	4	1	0	.800	2	4	0	.333
GB	5	7	1	.417	170	107	3	2	1	.583	2	5	0	.286
CIN	3	6	1	.333	38	110	2	2	1	.500	2	3	0	.400
CHIC	1	9	1	.100	52	101	0	4	1	.100	1	5	0	.167

Scoring

	TD	1XP	2XP	FG	SAF	PTS
Glen Presnell, POR	6	12		5	0	63
Ken Strong, NYG	5	14		5	0	59
Jim Musick, BOS	5	11		1	0	44
John Kelly, BKN	7	1		0	0	43
Kink Richards, NYG	7	1		0	0	43

Rushing

	ATT	YDS	AVG	LG	TD
Jim Musick, BOS	173	809	4.7		5
Cliff Battles, BOS	146	737	5.0		3
Bronko Nagurski, CHIB	128	533	4.2		1
Glenn Presnell, POR	118	522	4.4		6
Swede Hanson, PHI	133	494	3.7		3

Passing

	ATT	COM	YDS	TD	INT	LG
Harry Newman, NYG	136	53	973	11		17
Glenn Presnell, POR	125	47	774	5		12
Arnie Herber, GB	126	50	656	4		12
Benny Friedman, BKN	80	42	597	5		7
Keith Molesworth, CHIB	50	19	421	4		4

Receiving

	NO	YDS	AVG	LG	TD
John Kelly, BKN	22	246	11.2		3
Bill Hewitt, CHIB	16	274	17.1		2
Roger Grove, GB	15	217	14.5		0
Ray Tesser, PIT	14	274	19.6		0
Lavern Dilweg, GB	14	225	16.1		0

National Football League 1934
Eastern Division

Team	W	L	T	Pct	Pts	Opp	HW	HL	HT	HPct	AW	AL	AT	APct
NYG	8	5	0	.615	147	107	5	1	0	.833	3	4	0	.429
BOS	6	6	0	.500	107	94	4	3	0	.571	2	3	0	.400
BKN	4	7	0	.364	61	153	2	4	0	.333	2	3	0	.400
PHI	4	7	0	.364	127	85	2	4	0	.333	2	3	0	.400
PIT	2	10	0	.167	51	206	1	5	0	.167	1	5	0	.167

Western Division

Team	W	L	T	Pct	Pts	Opp	HW	HL	HT	HPct	AW	AL	AT	APct
CHIB	13	0	0	1.000	286	86	5	0	0	1.000	8	0	0	1.000
DET	10	3	0	.769	238	59	6	2	0	.750	4	1	0	.800
GB	7	6	0	.538	156	112	4	2	0	.667	3	4	0	.429

CHIC	5	6	0	.455	80	84	2	2	0	.500	3	4	0	.429
C-S	1	10	0	.091	37	304	1	3	0	.250	0	7	0	.000

Scoring

	TD	1XP	2XP	FG	SAF	PTS
Jack Manders, CHIB	3	29		10	0	77
Dutch Clark, DET	8	13		4	0	73
Glenn Presnell, DET	7	9		4		63
Ken Strong, NYG	6	7		4		55
Beattie Feathers, CHIB	9	0		0	0	54

Rushing

	ATT	YDS	AVG	LG	TD
Beattie Feathers, CHIB	119	1004	8.4		8
Swede Hanson, PHI	147	805	5.5		7
Dutch Clark, DET	122	763	6.3		8
Bronko Nagurski, CHIB	123	586	4.8		7
Warren Heller, PIT	132	528	4.0		1

Passing

	ATT	COM	YDS	TD	INT	LG
Arnie Herber, GB	115	42	799	8		12
Warren Heller, PIT	112	31	511	2		15
Dutch Clark, DET	49	23	383	0		3
Harry Newman, NYG	91	35	366	1		5
Ed Matesic, PHI	60	20	272	2		5
Harp Vaughan, PIT	39	14	272	2		5

Receiving

	NO	YDS	AVG	LG	TD
Joe Carter, PHI	16	238	14.9		4
Red Badgro, NYG	16	206	12.9		1
Ben Smith, PIT	12	190	15.8		0
Charley Malone, BOS	11	121	11.0		2
Joe Skladany, PIT	10	222	22.2		2

National Football League 1935
Eastern Division

Team	W	L	T	Pct	Pts	Opp	HW	HL	HT	HPct	AW	AL	AT	APct
NYG	9	3	0	.750	180	96	4	2	0	.667	5	1	0	.833
BKN	5	6	1	.455	90	141	3	2	1	.583	2	4	0	.333
PIT	4	8	0	.333	100	209	2	5	0	.286	2	3	0	.400
BOS	2	8	1	.200	65	123	2	5	0	.286	0	3	1	.125
PHI	2	9	0	.182	60	179	0	5	0	.000	2	4	0	.333

Western Division

Team	W	L	T	Pct	Pts	Opp	HW	HL	HT	HPct	AW	AL	AT	APct
DET	7	3	2	.700	191	111	5	0	1	.917	2	3	1	.417
GB	8	4	0	.667	181	96	5	2	0	.714	3	2	0	.600
CHIC	6	4	2	.600	99	97	2	2	0	.500	4	2	2	.625
CHIB	6	4	2	.600	192	106	1	2	2	.400	5	2	0	.714

Scoring

	TD	1XP	2XP	FG	SAF	PTS
Dutch Clark, DET	6	16		1		55
Don Hutson, GB	7	1		0	0	43
Dale Burnett, NYG	6	0		0	0	36
Ernie Caddel, DET	6	0		0		36
Bill Karr, CHIB	6	0		0		36

Rushing

	ATT	YDS	AVG	LG	TD
Doug Russell, CHIC	140	499	3.6		0
Ernie Caddel, DET	87	450	5.2		6
Kink Richards, NYG	149	449	3.0		4
Bill Shepherd, BOS-DET	143	425	3.0		4
Dutch Clark, DET	120	412	3.4		4

Passing

	ATT	COM	YDS	TD	INT	LG
Ed Danowski, NYG	113	57	795	11		9
Arnie Herber, GB	106	40	729	8		6
John Gildea, PIT	95	28	529	2		20
Bernie Masterson, CHIB	44	18	456	7		4
Bob Monnett, GB	65	31	454	2		6

Receiving

	NO	YDS	AVG	LG	TD
Tod Goodwin, NYG	26	432	16.6		4
Johnny Blood, GB	25	404	16.2		3
Bill Smith, CHIC	24	318	13.3		2
Charley Malone, BOS	22	433	19.7		2
Luke Johnsos, CHIB	19	298	15.7		4

National Football League 1936
Eastern Division

Team	W	L	T	Pct	Pts	Opp	HW	HL	HT	HPct	AW	AL	AT	APct
BOS	7	5	0	.583	149	110	4	3	0	.571	3	2	0	.600
PIT	6	6	0	.500	98	187	4	1	0	.800	2	5	0	.286
NYG	5	6	1	.455	115	163	3	3	1	.500	2	3	0	.400
BKN	3	8	1	.273	92	161	2	5	0	.286	1	3	1	.300
PHI	1	11	0	.083	51	206	1	6	0	.143	0	5	0	.000

Western Division

Team	W	L	T	Pct	Pts	Opp	HW	HL	HT	HPct	AW	AL	AT	APct
GB	10	1	1	.909	248	118	5	1	0	.833	5	0	1	.917
CHIB	9	3	0	.750	222	94	3	1	0	.750	6	2	0	.750
DET	8	4	0	.667	235	102	5	1	0	.833	3	3	0	.500
CHIC	3	8	1	.273	74	143	3	1	1	.700	0	7	0	.000

Scoring

	TD	1XP	2XP	FG	SAF	PTS
Dutch Clark, DET	7	19		4		73
Jack Manders, CHIB	4	17		7	0	62
Don Hutson, GB	9	0		0	0	54
Cliff Battles, BOS	7	0		0		42
Bill Hewitt, CHIB	7	0		0	0	42

Rushing

	ATT	YDS	AVG	LG	TD
Tuffy Leemans, NYG	206	830	4.0		2
Ace Gutowsky, DET	191	827	4.3		6
Dutch Clark, DET	123	628	5.1		7
Cliff Battles, BOS	176	614	3.5		5
George Grosvenor, CHIB-CHIC	170	612	3.6		4

Passing

	ATT	COM	YDS	TD	INT	LG
Arnie Herber, GB	173	77	1239	11		13
Ed Matesic, PIT	138	64	850	5		16
Phil Sarboe, CHIC-BKN	114	47	680	3		13
Pug Vaughan, CHIC	79	30	545	3		10
Ed Danowski, NYG	104	47	515	6		10

Receiving

	NO	YDS	AVG	LG	TD
Don Hutson, GB	34	526	15.5		8
Bill Smith, CHIC	20	414	20.7		1
Ernie Caddel, DET	19	150	7.9		1
Wayne Millner, BOS	18	211	11.7		0
Ed Manske, PHI	17	325	19.1		0

National Football League 1937

Eastern Division

Team	W	L	T	Pct	Pts	Opp	HW	HL	HT	HPct	AW	AL	AT	APct
WAS	8	3	0	.727	195	120	4	2	0	.667	4	1	0	.800
NYG	6	3	2	.667	128	109	4	2	1	.643	2	1	1	.625
PIT	4	7	0	.364	122	145	2	4	0	.333	2	3	0	.400
BKN	3	7	1	.300	82	174	1	3	1	.300	2	4	0	.333
PHI	2	8	1	.200	86	177	0	5	1	.083	2	3	0	.400

Western Division

Team	W	L	T	Pct	Pts	Opp	HW	HL	HT	HPct	AW	AL	AT	APct
CHIB	9	1	1	.900	201	100	4	1	0	.800	5	0	1	.917
GB	7	4	0	.636	220	122	3	2	0	.600	4	2	0	.667
DET	7	4	0	.636	180	105	4	2	0	.667	3	2	0	.600
CHIC	5	5	1	.500	135	165	1	3	0	.250	4	2	1	.643
CLE	1	10	0	.091	75	207	0	5	0	.000	1	5	0	.167

Scoring

	TD	1XP	2XP	FG	SAF	PTS
Jack Manders, CHIB	5	15		8	0	69
Clarke Hinkle, GB	7	9		2	0	57
Riley Smith, WAS	3	22		5	0	55
Dutch Clark, DET	6	6		1	0	45
Don Hutson, GB	7	0		0	1	44

Rushing

	ATT	YDS	AVG	LG	TD
Cliff Battles, WAS	216	874	4.0		5
Clarke Hinkle, GB	129	552	4.3		5
John Karcis, PIT	128	511	4.0		3
Dutch Clark, DET	96	468	4.9		5
George Grosvenor, CHIC	137	461	3.4		2

Passing

	ATT	COM	YDS	TD	INT	LG
Sammy Baugh, WAS	171	81	1127	8		14
Ed Danowski, NYG	134	66	814	8		5
Pat Coffee, CHIC	119	52	804	5	95t	11
Arnie Herber, GB	104	47	676	7		10
Bernie Masterson, CHIB	72	26	615	8		7

Receiving

	NO	YDS	AVG	LG	TD
Don Hutson, GB	41	552	13.5		7
Gaynell Tinsley, CHIC	36	675	18.8		5
Charley Malone, WAS	28	419	15.0		4
Jeff Barrett, BKN	20	461	23.1		3
Bill Hewitt, PHI	16	197	12.3		5

National Football League 1938

Eastern Division

Team	W	L	T	Pct	Pts	Opp	HW	HL	HT	HPct	AW	AL	AT	APct
NYG	8	2	1	.800	194	79	6	1	0	.857	2	1	1	.625
WAS	6	3	2	.667	148	154	3	1	1	.700	3	2	1	.583

	W	L	T	Pct		Pts	Opp		HW	HL	HT	HPct		AW	AL	AT	APct
BKN	4	4	3	.500		131	161		2	2	2	.500		2	2	1	.500
PHI	5	6	0	.455		154	164		2	3	0	.400		3	3	0	.500
PIT	2	9	0	.182		79	169		0	5	0	.000		2	4	0	.333

Western Division

Team	W	L	T	Pct		Pts	Opp		HW	HL	HT	HPct		AW	AL	AT	APct
GB	8	3	0	.727		223	118		4	2	0	.667		4	1	0	.800
DET	7	4	0	.636		119	108		4	3	0	.571		3	1	0	.750
CHIB	6	5	0	.545		194	148		2	3	0	.400		4	2	0	.667
CLE	4	7	0	.364		131	215		2	2	0	.500		2	5	0	.286
CHIC	2	9	0	.182		111	168		1	4	0	.200		1	5	0	.167

Scoring

	TD	1XP	2XP	FG	SAF	PTS
Clarke Hinkle, GB	7	7		3	0	58
Don Hutson, GB	9	3		0	0	57
Joe Carter, PHI	8	0		0	0	48
Ward Cuff, NYG	2	18		5	0	45
Andy Farkas, WAS	6	1		0	0	37
Jack Manders, CHIB	3	10		3		37

Rushing

	ATT	YDS	AVG	LG	TD
Whizzer White, PIT	152	567	3.7		4
Tuffy Leemans, NYG	121	463	3.8		4
Bill Shepherd, DET	100	455	4.6		3
Cecil Isbell, GB	85	445	5.2		2
Ace Gutowsky, DET	131	444	3.4		2

Passing

	ATT	COM	YDS	TD	INT	LG
Ed Danowski, NYG	129	70	848	7		8
Sammy Baugh, WAS	128	63	853	5		11
Ace Parker, BKN	148	63	865	5		7
Jack Robbins, CHIC	97	52	577	2		9
Bernie Masterson, CHIB	112	46	848	7		9

Receiving

	NO	YDS	AVG	LG	TD
Gaynell Tinsley, CHIC	41	516	12.6		1
Don Hutson, GB	32	548	17.1		9
Joe Carter, PHI	27	386	14.3		7
Charley Malone, WAS	24	257	10.7		1
Jim Benton, CLE	21	418	19.9		5

National Football League 1939

Eastern Division

Team	W	L	T	Pct		Pts	Opp		HW	HL	HT	HPct		AW	AL	AT	APct
NYG	9	1	1	.900		168	85		6	0	0	1.000		3	1	1	.700
WAS	8	2	1	.800		242	94		5	0	1	.917		3	2	0	.600
BKN	4	6	1	.400		108	219		4	3	0	.571		0	3	1	.125
PHI	1	9	1	.100		105	200		1	3	1	.300		0	6	0	.000
PIT	1	9	1	.100		114	216		1	4	0	.200		0	5	1	.083

Western Division

Team	W	L	T	Pct		Pts	Opp		HW	HL	HT	HPct		AW	AL	AT	APct
GB	9	2	0	.818		233	153		4	1	0	.800		5	1	0	.833
CHIB	8	3	0	.727		298	157		4	1	0	.800		4	2	0	.667
DET	6	5	0	.545		145	150		4	2	0	.667		2	3	0	.400
CLE	5	5	1	.500		195	164		3	2	1	.583		2	3	0	.400
CHIC	1	10	0	.091		84	254		0	4	0	.000		1	6	0	.143

Scoring

	TD	1XP	2XP	FG	SAF	PTS
Andy Farkas, WAS	11	2		0	0	68
Johnny Drake, CLE	9	0		0	0	54
Jack Manders, CHIB	4	17		3	0	50
Jim Benton, CLE	8	0		0	0	48
Bill Osmanski, CHIB	8	0		0	0	48

Rushing

	ATT	YDS	AVG	LG	TD
Bill Osmanski, CHIB	121	699	5.8		7
Andy Farkas, WAS	139	547	3.9		5
Joe Maniaci, CHIB	77	544	7.1		4
Pug Manders, BKN	114	482	4.2		2
Parker Hall, CLE	120	458	3.8		2

Passing

	ATT	COM	YDS	TD	INT	LG
Parker Hall, CLE	208	106	1227	9		13
Davey O'Brien, PHI	201	99	1324	6		17
Ace Parker, BKN	157	72	977	4		13
Arnie Herber, GB	139	57	1107	8		9
Frank Filchock, WAS	89	55	1094	11	99t	7

Receiving

	NO	YDS	AVG	LG	TD
Don Hutson, GB	34	846	24.9		6
Perry Schwartz, BKN	33	550	16.7		3
Vic Spadaccini, CLE	32	292	9.1		1
Red Ramsey, PHI	31	359	11.6		1
Jim Benton, CLE	27	388	14.4		7

Punting

	NO	YDS	AVG	LG	BL
Parker Hall, BKN	58		40.8	80	

National Football League 1940
Eastern Division

Team	W	L	T	Pct	Pts	Opp	HW	HL	HT	HPct	AW	AL	AT	APct
WAS	9	2	0	.818	245	142	6	0	0	1.000	3	2	0	.600
BKN	8	3	0	.727	186	120	5	1	0	.833	3	2	0	.600
NYG	6	4	1	.600	131	133	4	3	0	.571	2	1	1	.625
PIT	2	7	2	.222	60	178	1	2	2	.400	1	5	0	.167
PHI	1	10	0	.091	111	211	1	4	0	.200	0	6	0	.000

Western Division

Team	W	L	T	Pct	Pts	Opp	HW	HL	HT	HPct	AW	AL	AT	APct
CHIB	8	3	0	.727	238	152	5	0	0	1.000	3	3	0	.500
GB	6	4	1	.600	238	155	4	2	0	.667	2	2	1	.500
DET	5	5	0	.500	138	153	3	3	0	.500	2	2	1	.500
CLE	4	6	1	.400	171	191	3	1	1	.700	1	5	0	.167
CHIC	2	7	2	.222	139	222	2	1	1	.625	0	6	1	.071

Scoring

	TD	1XP	2XP	FG	SAF	PTS
Don Hutson, GB	7	15		0	0	57
Johnny Drake, CLE	9	2		0	0	56
Dick Todd, WAS	9	0		0	0	54
Ace Parker, BKN	5	19		0	0	49
Clarke Hinkle, GB	3	3		9	0	48

Rushing

	ATT	YDS	AVG	LG	TD
Whizzer White, DET	146	514	3.5		5
Johnny Drake, CLE	134	480	3.6		9
Tuffy Leemans, NYG	132	474	3.6		1
Banks McFadden, BKN	65	411	6.3		1
Dick Todd, WAS	76	408	5.4		4

Passing

	ATT	COM	YDS	TD	INT	LG
Sammy Baugh, WAS	177	111	1367	12		10
Davey O'Brien, PHI	277	124	1290	5		17
Cecil Isbell, GB	150	68	1037	9		12
Sid Luckman, CHIB	105	48	941	4		9
Ace Parker, BKN	111	49	817	10		7

Receiving

	NO	YDS	AVG	LG	TD
Don Looney, PHI	58	707	12.2		4
Don Hutson, GB	45	664	14.8		7
Jimmy Johnston, WAS	29	350	12.1		3
Jim Benton, CLE	22	351	16.0		3
Vic Spadaccini, CLE	22	276	12.5		2

Interceptions

	NO	YDS	AVG	LG	TD
Ace Parker, BKN	6	146		1	24.3
Kent Ryan, DET	6	65		0	10.8
Don Hutson, GB	6	24		0	4.0

Punting

	NO	YDS	AVG	LG	BL
Sammy Baugh, WAS	34	1799	52.9	85	1

National Football League 1941
Eastern Division

Team	W	L	T	Pct	Pts	Opp	HW	HL	HT	HPct	AW	AL	AT	APct
NYG	8	3	0	.727	238	114	5	2	0	.714	3	1	0	.750
BKN	7	4	0	.636	158	127	5	1	0	.833	2	3	0	.400
WAS	6	5	0	.545	176	174	4	2	0	.667	2	3	0	.400
PHI	2	8	1	.200	119	218	1	4	1	.250	1	4	0	.200
PIT	1	9	1	.100	103	276	1	4	0	.200	0	5	1	.083

Western Division

Team	W	L	T	Pct	Pts	Opp	HW	HL	HT	HPct	AW	AL	AT	APct
CHIB	10	1	0	.909	396	147	5	1	0	.833	5	0	0	1.000
GB	10	1	0	.909	258	120	4	1	0	.800	6	0	0	1.000
DET	4	6	1	.400	121	195	3	2	0	.600	1	4	1	.250
CHIC	3	7	1	.300	127	197	0	3	1	.125	3	4	0	.429
CLE	2	9	0	.182	116	244	1	4	0	.200	1	5	0	.167

Scoring

	TD	1XP	2XP	FG	SAF	PTS
Don Hutson, GB	12	20		1	0	95
George McAfee, CHIB	12	0		0	0	72
Hugh Gallarneau, CHIB	11	0		0	0	66
Clarke Hinkle, GB	6	2		6	0	56
Ward Cuff, NYG	2	19		5	0	46

Rushing

	ATT	YDS	AVG	LG	TD
Pug Manders, BKN	111	486	4.4	46	6
George McAfee, CHIB	65	474	7.3	70	6
Marshall Goldberg, CHIC	117	427	3.6	25	3
Norm Standlee, CHIB	81	414	5.1	46	5
Clarke Hinkle, GB	129	393	3.0	20	5

Passing

	ATT	COM	YDS	TD	INT	LG
Cecil Isbell, GB	206	117	1479	15	56	11
Sammy Baugh, WAS	193	106	1236	10	55	19
Sid Luckman, CHIB	119	68	1181	9	65	6
Tommy Thompson, PHI	162	86	974	8	50	14
Ace Parker, BKN	102	51	642	2	47	8

Receiving

	NO	YDS	AVG	LG	TD
Don Hutson, GB	58	738	12.7	45	10
Dick Humbert, PHI	29	332	11.4	33	3
Bill Dewell, CHIC	28	262	9.4	30	1
Perry Schwartz, BKN	25	362	14.5	36	2
Lou Brock, GB	22	307	14.0	36	2

Interceptions

	NO	YDS	AVG	LG	TD	
Marshall Goldberg, CHIC	7	54	16	0	7.7	
Art Jones, PIT	7	35	12	0	5.0	

Punting

	NO	YDS	AVG	LG	BL
Sammy Baugh, WAS	30	1462	48.7	75	0

Kickoff Returns

	NO	YDS	LG	TD	AVG
Marshall Goldberg, CHIC	12	290	41	0	24.2

Punt Returns

	NO	FC	YDS	LG	TD	AVG
Whizzer White, DET	19		262	64	0	13.8

National Football League 1942
Eastern Division

Team	W	L	T	Pct	Pts	Opp	HW	HL	HT	HPct	AW	AL	AT	APct
WAS	10	1	0	.909	227	102	5	1	0	.833	5	0	0	1.000
PIT	7	4	0	.636	167	119	3	2	0	.600	4	2	0	.667
NYG	5	5	1	.500	155	139	3	2	1	.583	2	3	0	.400
BKN	3	8	0	.273	100	168	1	5	0	.167	2	3	0	.400
PHI	2	9	0	.182	134	239	0	5	0	.000	2	4	0	.333

Western Division

Team	W	L	T	Pct	Pts	Opp	HW	HL	HT	HPct	AW	AL	AT	APct
CHIB	11	0	0	1.000	376	84	6	0	0	1.000	5	0	0	1.000
GB	8	2	1	.800	300	215	4	1	0	.800	4	1	1	.750
CLE	5	6	0	.455	150	207	3	2	0	.600	2	4	0	.333
CHIC	3	8	0	.273	98	209	2	2	0	.500	1	6	0	.143
DET	0	11	0	.000	38	263	0	7	0	.000	0	4	0	.000

Scoring

	TD	1XP	2XP	FG	SAF	PTS
Don Hutson, GB	17	33		1	0	138
Ray McLean, CHIB	9	0		0	0	54
Frank Maznicki, CHIB	2	21		4	0	45
Gary Famiglietti, CHIB	7	0		0	0	42
Hugh Gallarneau, CHIB	7	0		0	0	42

Rushing

	ATT	YDS	AVG	LG	TD
Bill Dudley, PIT	162	696	4.3	66	5
Merl Condit, BKN	129	647	5.0	63	3
Gary Famiglietti, CHIB	118	503	4.3	21	8
Andy Farkas, WAS	125	468	3.7	22	4
Dick Riffle, PIT	115	467	4.1	44	4

Passing

	ATT	COM	YDS	TD	INT	LG
Cecil Isbell, GB	268	146	2021	24	73	14
Sammy Baugh, WAS	225	132	1524	16	53	11
Sid Luckman, CHIB	105	57	1023	10	52	13
Tommy Thompson, PHI	203	95	1410	8	65	16
Bud Schwenk, CHIC	295	126	1350	6	69	27

Receiving

	NO	YDS	AVG	LG	TD
Don Hutson, GB	74	1211	16.4	73	17
Pop Ivy, CHIC	27	259	9.6	18	0
Dante Magnani, CLE	24	276	11.5	67	4
Jim Benton, CLE	23	345	15.0	45	1
Dick Todd, WAS	23	328	14.3	53	4

Interceptions

	NO	YDS	AVG	LG	TD
Bulldog Turner, CHIB	8	96	42	1	12.0

Punting

	NO	YDS	AVG	LG	BL
Sammy Baugh, WAS	37	1725	46.6	74	0

Kickoff Returns

	NO	YDS	LG	TD	AVG
Marshall Goldberg, CHIC	15	393	95	1	26.2

Punt Returns

	NO	FC	YDS	LG	TD	AVG
Merlyn Condit, BKN	21		210	23	0	10.0

National Football League 1943
Eastern Division

Team	W	L	T	Pct	Pts	Opp	HW	HL	HT	HPct	AW	AL	AT	APct
NYG	6	3	1	.667	197	170	4	2	0	.667	2	1	1	.625
WAS	6	3	1	.667	229	137	4	2	0	.667	2	1	1	.625
P-P	5	4	1	.556	225	230	4	1	1	.750	1	3	0	.250
BKN	2	8	0	.200	65	234	2	3	0	.400	0	5	0	.000

Western Division

Team	W	L	T	Pct	Pts	Opp	HW	HL	HT	HPct	AW	AL	AT	APct
CHIB	8	1	1	.889	303	157	5	0	0	1.000	3	1	1	.700

GB	7	2	1	.778	264	172	2	1	1	.625	5	1	0	.833
DET	3	6	1	.333	178	218	2	2	1	.500	1	4	0	.200
CHIC	0	10	0	.000	95	238	0	3	0	.000	0	7	0	.000

Scoring

	TD	1XP	2XP	FG	SAF	PTS
Don Hutson, GB	12	36		3		117
Bill Paschal, NYG	12	0		0		72
Harry Clark, CHIB	10	0		0		60
Andy Farkas, WAS	9	0		0		54
Harry Hopp, DET	9	0		0		54
Wilbur Moore, WAS	9	0		0		54

Rushing

	ATT	YDS	AVG	LG	TD
Bill Paschal, NYG	147	572	3.9	54	10
Jack Hinkle, P-P	116	571	4.9	56	4
Harry Clark, CHIB	120	556	4.6	20	3
Ward Cuff, NYG	80	523	6.5	65	3
Tony Canadeo, GB	94	489	5.2	35	3

Passing

	ATT	COM	YDS	TD	INT	LG
Sammy Baugh, WAS	239	133	1754	23	72	19
Sid Luckman, CHIB	202	110	2194	28	66	12
Irv Comp, GB	92	46	662	7	79	4
Ronnie Cahill, CHIC	109	50	608	3	67	21
Dean McAdams, BKN	75	37	315	0	49	7

Receiving

	NO	YDS	AVG	LG	TD
Don Hutson, GB	47	776	16.5	79	11
Joe Aguirre, WAS	37	420	11.4	44	7
Wilbur Moore, WAS	30	537	17.9	72	7
Ed Rucinski, CHIC	26	398	15.3	47	5
Harry Jacunski, GB	24	528	22.0	86	3

Interceptions

	NO	YDS	AVG	LG	TD
Sammy Baugh, WAS	11	112	23	0	10.2

Punting

	NO	YDS	AVG	LG	BL
Sammy Baugh, WAS	47	2295	48.8	81	3

Kickoff Returns

	NO	YDS	LG	TD	AVG
Ken Heineman, BKN	16	442	69	0	27.6

Punt Returns

	NO	FC	YDS	LG	TD	AVG
Andy Farkas, WAS	15		168	33	0	11.2

National Football League 1944

Eastern Division

Team	W	L	T	Pct	Pts	Opp	HW	HL	HT	HPct	AW	AL	AT	APct
NYG	8	1	1	.889	206	75	5	1	0	.833	3	0	1	.875
PHI	7	1	2	.875	267	131	3	1	2	.667	4	0	0	1.000
WAS	6	3	1	.667	169	180	4	2	0	.667	2	1	1	.625
BOS	2	8	0	.200	82	233	1	3	0	.250	1	5	0	.167
BKN	0	10	0	.000	69	166	0	4	0	.000	0	6	0	.000

Western Division

Team	W	L	T	Pct	Pts	Opp	HW	HL	HT	HPct	AW	AL	AT	APct
GB	8	2	0	.800	238	141	5	0	0	1.000	3	2	0	.600
DET	6	3	1	.667	216	151	4	2	0	.667	2	1	1	.625
CHIB	6	3	1	.667	258	172	4	0	1	.900	2	3	0	.400
CLE	4	6	0	.400	188	224	1	2	0	.333	3	4	0	.429
C-P	0	10	0	.000	108	328	0	5	0	.000	0	5	0	.000

Scoring

	TD	1XP	2XP	FG	SAF	PTS
Don Hutson, GB	9	31		0	0	85
Frankie Sinkwich, DET	6	24		2	0	66
Roy Zimmerman, PHI	3	32		4	0	62
Bill Paschal, NYG	9	0		0		54
Joe Aguirre, WAS	4	15		4	0	51

Rushing

	ATT	YDS	AVG	LG	TD
Bill Paschal, NYG	196	737	3.8	68t	9
John Grigas, C-P	185	610	3.3	29	3
Frank Sinkwich, DET	150	563	3.8	72t	6
Hank Margarita, CHIB	88	463	5.3	47t	4
Steve Van Buren, PHI	80	444	5.6	70t	5

Passing

	ATT	COM	YDS	TD	INT	LG
Frank Filchock, WAS	147	84	1139	13	61	9
Sammy Baugh, WAS	146	82	849	4	71	8
Sid Luckman, CHIB	143	71	1018	11	86	11
Irv Comp, GB	177	80	1159	12	55	21
Albie Reisz, CLE	113	49	777	8	70	10

Receiving

	NO	YDS	AVG	LG	TD
Don Hutson, GB	58	866	14.9	55t	9
Jim Benton, CLE	39	505	12.9	36	6
Joe Aguirre, WAS	34	410	12.1	58t	4
Wilbur Moore, WAS	33	424	12.8	59t	5
three tied with	24				

Interceptions

	NO	YDS	AVG	LG	TD
Howie Livingston, NYG	9	172	40	1	19.1

Punting

	NO	YDS	AVG	LG	BL
Frankie Sinkwich, DET	45	1845	41.0	73	0

Kickoff Returns

	NO	YDS	LG	TD	AVG
Bob Thurbon, C-P	12	291	55	0	24.3

Punt Returns

	NO	FC	YDS	LG	TD	AVG
Steve Van Buren, PHI	15		230	55	1	15.3

National Football League 1945

Eastern Division

Team	W	L	T	Pct	Pts	Opp	HW	HL	HT	HPct	AW	AL	AT	APct
WAS	8	2	0	1.000	209	121	6	0	0	1.000	2	2	0	.500
PHI	7	3	0	.700	272	133	6	0	0	1.000	1	3	0	.250
NYG	3	6	1	.333	179	198	2	4	0	.333	1	2	1	.375
BOS	3	6	1	.333	123	211	2	2	0	.500	1	4	1	.250
PIT	2	8	0	.200	79	220	1	4	0	.200	1	4	0	.200

Western Division

Team	W	L	T	Pct	Pts	Opp	HW	HL	HT	HPct	AW	AL	AT	APct
CLE	9	1	0	.900	244	136	4	0	0	1.000	5	1	0	.833
DET	7	3	0	.700	195	194	4	1	0	.800	3	2	0	.600
GB	6	4	0	.600	258	173	4	1	0	.800	2	3	0	.400
CHIB	3	7	0	.300	192	235	2	3	0	.400	1	4	0	.200
CHIC	1	9	0	.100	98	228	0	3	0	.000	1	6	0	.143

Scoring

	TD	1XP	2XP	FG	SAF	PTS
Steve Van Buren, PHI	18	2		0	0	110
Don Hutson, GB	10	31	2			97
Bob Waterfield, CLE	5	31	1	0		64
Frank Liebel, NYG	10	0		0	0	60
Ted Fritsch, GB	8	0		3		57

Rushing

	ATT	YDS	AVG	LG	TD
Steve Van Buren, PHI	143	832	5.8	69t	15
Frank Akins, WAS	147	797	5.4	45	6
Hank Margarita, CHIB	112	497	4.4	38	3
Fred Gehrke, CLE	74	467	6.3	72t	7
Fred Gillette, CLE	63	390	6.2	52	1

Passing

	ATT	COM	YDS	TD	INT	LG
Sid Luckman, CHIB	217	117	1725	14	65	10
Sammy Baugh, WAS	182	128	1669	11	70	4
Bob Waterfield, CLE	171	88	1509	14	84t	16
Roy Zimmerman, PHI	132	67	991	9	74t	8
Paul Christman, CHIC	219	89	1147	5	70	12

Receiving

	NO	YDS	AVG	LG	TD
Don Hutson, GB	47	834	17.7	75t	9
Jim Benton, CLE	45	1067	23.7	84t	8
Steve Bagarus, WAS	35	623	17.8	70t	5
George Wilson, CHIB	28	259	9.3	18	3
John Greene, DET	26	550	21.2	63t	4

Interceptions

	NO	YDS	AVG	LG	TD	
Roy Zimmerman, PHI	7	90	23	0		12.9

Punting

	NO	YDS	AVG	LG	BL
Roy McKay, GB	44	1813	41.2	73	0

Kickoff Returns

	NO	YDS	LG	TD	AVG
Steve Van Buren, PHI	13	373	98	1	28.7

Punt Returns

	NO	FC	YDS	LG	TD	AVG
Dave Ryan, DET	15		220	58	0	14.7

All-America Football Conference 1946

Eastern Division

Team	W	L	T	Pct	Pts	Opp	HW	HL	HT	HPct	AW	AL	AT	APct
NY	10	3	1	.769	270	192	5	2	0	.714	5	1	1	.786
BKN	3	10	1	.231	226	339	1	5	1	.214	3	4	0	.429
BUF	3	10	1	.231	249	370	2	4	1	.357	1	6	0	.143
MIA	3	11	0	.214	167	378	2	5	0	.286	1	6	0	.143

Western Division

Team	W	L	T	Pct	Pts	Opp	HW	HL	HT	HPct	AW	AL	AT	APct
CLE	12	2	0	.857	423	137	6	1	0	.857	6	1	0	.857
SF	9	5	0	.643	307	189	5	2	0	.714	4	3	0	.571
LA	7	5	2	.583	305	290	4	2	1	.643	3	3	1	.500
CHI	5	6	3	.455	263	315	3	3	1	.500	2	3	2	.429

Scoring

	TD	1XP	2XP	FG	SAF	PTS
Lou Groza, CLE	0	45		13	0	84
Spec Sanders, NY	12	0		0	0	72
Alyn Beals, SF	10	1		0	0	61
Steve Nemeth, CHI	0	32		9	0	59
Joe Aguirre, LA	2	31		4	0	55

Rushing

	ATT	YDS	AVG	LG	TD
Spec Sanders, NY	140	709	5.1		6
Norm Standlee, SF	134	651	4.9		2
Vic Kulbitski, BUF	97	605	6.2		2
Marion Motley, CLE	73	601	8.2		5
Edgar Jones, CLE	77	539	7.0		4

Passing

	ATT	COM	YDS	TD	INT	LG
Glenn Dobbs, BKN	269	135	1886	13		15
Otto Graham, CLE	174	95	1834	17		5
Charlie O'Rourke, LA	182	105	1250	12		14
Frankie Albert, SF	197	104	1404	14		14
Bob Hoernschemeyer, CHI	193	95	1266	14		14

Receiving

	NO	YDS	AVG	LG	TD
Dante Lavelli, CLE	40	843	21.1		8
Alyn Beals, SF	40	586	14.7		10
Saxon Judd, BKN	34	443	13.0		4
Ed King, BUF	30	466	15.5		6
Elroy Hirsch, CHI	27	347	12.9		3

Interceptions

	NO	YDS	AVG	LG	TD
Tom Colella, CLE	10	110	0		11.0

Punting

	NO	YDS	AVG	LG	BL
Glenn Dobbs, BKN	80	3824	47.8	78	2

Kickoff Returns

	NO	YDS	LG	TD	AVG
Chuck Fenenbock, LA	17	479	97t	1	28.2

Punt Returns

	NO	FC	YDS	LG	TD	AVG
Chuck Fenenbock, LA	16		299		0	18.7

National Football League 1946
Eastern Division

Team	W	L	T	Pct	Pts	Opp	HW	HL	HT	HPct	AW	AL	AT	APct
NYG	7	3	1	.700	236	162	5	1	1	.786	2	2	0	.500
PHI	6	5	0	.545	231	220	3	2	0	.600	3	3	0	.500
WAS	5	5	1	.500	171	191	3	2	1	.583	2	3	0	.400
PIT	5	5	1	.500	136	117	4	1	0	.800	1	4	1	.250
BOS	2	8	1	.200	189	273	1	5	0	.167	1	3	1	.300

Western Division

Team	W	L	T	Pct	Pts	Opp	HW	HL	HT	HPct	AW	AL	AT	APct
CHIB	8	2	1	.800	289	193	4	1	1	.750	4	1	0	.800
LA	6	4	1	.600	277	257	3	2	0	.600	3	2	1	.583
CHIC	6	5	0	.545	260	198	2	2	0	.500	4	3	0	.571
GB	6	5	0	.545	148	158	2	3	0	.400	4	2	0	.667
DET	1	10	0	.091	142	310	1	5	0	.167	0	5	0	.000

Scoring

	TD	1XP	2XP	FG	SAF	PTS
Ted Fritsch, GB	10	13		9	0	100
Bob Waterfield, LA	1	37		6	0	61
Ward Cuff, CHIC	2	28		5	0	55
Augie Lio, PHI	1	27		6	0	51
Bill Dudley, PIT	5	12		2	0	48
Hugh Gallarneau, CHIB	8	0		0	0	48

Rushing

	ATT	YDS	AVG	LG	TD
Bill Dudley, PIT	146	604	4.1	41	3
Pat Harder, CHIC	106	545	5.1	55	4
Steve Van Buren, PHI	116	529	4.6	58	5
Hugh Gallarneau, CHIB	112	476	4.3	52t	7
Tony Canadeo, GB	122	476	3.9	27	0

Passing

	ATT	COM	YDS	TD	INT	LG
Bob Waterfield, LA	251	127	1747	18	57	17
Sid Luckman, CHIB	229	110	1826	17	48	16
Paul Governali, BOS	192	83	1293	13	62	10
Paul Christman, CHIC	229	100	1656	13	82	18
Sammy Baugh, WAS	161	87	1163	8	51	17

Receiving

	NO	YDS	AVG	LG	TD
Jim Benton, LA	63	981	15.5	57	6
Hal Crisler, BOS	32	385	12.0	62	5
Steve Bagarus, WAS	31	438	14.1	51t	3
Jack Ferrante, PHI	28	451	16.1	48	4
Bill Dewell, CHIC	27	643	23.8	82t	7
Mal Kutner, CHIC	27	634	23.5	63	5

Interceptions

	NO	YDS	AVG	LG	TD
Bill Dudley, PIT	10	242	80t	1	24.2

Punting

	NO	YDS	AVG	LG	BL
Roy McKay, GB	63	2735	43.4	64	1

Kickoff Returns

	NO	YDS	LG	TD	AVG
Abe Karnofsky, BOS	21	599	97	1	28.5

Punt Returns

	NO	FC	YDS	LG	TD	AVG
Bill Dudley, PIT	27		385	52	0	14.3

All-America Football Conference 1947
Eastern Division

Team	W	L	T	Pct	Pts	Opp	HW	HL	HT	HPct	AW	AL	AT	APct
NY	11	2	1	.846	378	239	6	0	1	.929	5	2	0	.714
BUF	8	4	2	.667	320	288	5	2	0	.714	3	2	2	.571
BKN	3	10	1	.231	181	340	2	4	1	.357	1	5	1	.214
BAL	2	11	1	.154	167	377	2	4	1	.357	0	7	0	.000

Western Division

Team	W	L	T	Pct	Pts	Opp	HW	HL	HT	HPct	AW	AL	AT	APct
CLE	12	1	1	.923	410	185	4	2	1	.643	6	0	1	.929
SF	8	4	2	.667	327	264	3	3	1	.500	5	1	1	.786
LA	7	7	0	.500	328	256	3	4	0	.429	4	3	0	.571
CHI	1	13	0	.071	263	425	1	6	0	.143	0	7	0	.000

Scoring

	TD	1XP	2XP	FG	SAF	PTS
Spec Sanders, NY	19	0		0	0	114
Ben Agajanian, LA	0	39		15	0	84
Chet Mutryn, BUF	12	1		0	0	73
Harvey Johnson, NY	0	49		7	0	70
John Kimbrough, LA	11	0		0	0	66

Rushing

	ATT	YDS	AVG	LG	TD
Spec Sanders, NY	231	1432	6.2		18
John Strzykalski, SF	143	906	6.3		5
Marion Motley, CLE	146	889	6.0		8
Chet Mutryn, BUF	140	868	6.2		9
Buddy Young, NY	116	712	6.1		3

Passing

	ATT	COM	YDS	TD	INT	LG
Otto Graham, CLE	269	163	2753	25		11
Bud Schwenk, BAL	327	168	2236	13		20
Frankie Albert, SF	242	128	1692	18		15
George Ratterman, BUF	244	124	1840	22		20
Spec Sanders, NY	171	93	1442	14		17

Receiving

	NO	YDS	AVG	LG	TD
Mac Speedie, CLE	67	1146	17.1		6
Dante Lavelli, CLE	49	799	16.3		9
Alyn Beals, SF	47	655	13.9		10
Lamar Davis, BAL	46	515	11.2		2
Billy Hillenbrand, BAL	39	702	18.0		7

Interceptions

	NO	YDS	AVG	LG	TD
Tom Colella, CLE	6	130	1		21.7
Bill Kellagher, CHI	6	77	0		12.8
Len Eshmont, SF	6	72	0		12.0

Punting

	NO	YDS	AVG	LG	BL
Mickey Colmer, BKN	56	2504	44.7	69	0

Kickoff Returns

	NO	YDS	LG	TD	AVG
Chet Mutryn, BUF	21	691	87t	1	32.9

Punt Returns

	NO	FC	YDS	LG	TD	AVG
Glenn Dobbs, LA	19		215		0	11.3

National Football League 1947

Eastern Division

Team	W	L	T	Pct	Pts	Opp	HW	HL	HT	HPct	AW	AL	AT	APct
PHI	8	4	0	.667	308	242	6	1	0	.857	2	3	0	.400
PIT	8	4	0	.667	240	259	5	1	0	.833	3	3	0	.500
BOS	4	7	1	.364	168	256	2	3	1	.417	2	4	0	.333
WAS	4	8	0	.333	295	367	4	2	0	.667	0	6	0	.000
NYG	2	8	2	.200	190	309	2	3	1	.417	0	5	1	.083

Western Division

Team	W	L	T	Pct	Pts	Opp	HW	HL	HT	HPct	AW	AL	AT	APct
CHIC	9	3	0	.750	306	231	5	0	0	1.000	4	3	0	.571
CHIB	8	4	0	.667	363	241	4	2	0	.667	4	2	0	.667
GB	6	5	1	.545	274	210	4	2	0	.667	2	3	1	.417
LA	6	6	0	.500	259	214	3	3	0	.500	3	3	0	.500
DET	3	9	0	.250	231	305	2	4	0	.333	1	5	0	.167

Scoring

	TD	1XP	2XP	FG	SAF	PTS
Pat Harder, CHIC	7	39		7	0	102
Dick Poillon, WAS	6	37		4	0	85
Steve Van Buren, PHI	14	0		0	0	84
Ken Kavanaugh, CHIB	13	0		0	0	78
Bill Dudley, DET	11	0		0	0	66

Rushing

	ATT	YDS	AVG	LG	TD
Steve Van Buren, PHI	217	1008	4.6	45	14
Johnny Clement, PIT	129	670	5.2	43	4
Tony Canadeo, GB	103	464	4.5	35	2
Kenny Washington, LA	60	444	7.4	92t	5
Walt Schlinkman, GB	115	439	3.8	20	2

Passing

	ATT	COM	YDS	TD	INT	LG
Sammy Baugh, WAS	354	210	2938	25	74	15
Tommy Thompson, PHI	201	106	1680	16	69	15
Sid Luckman, CHIB	323	176	2712	24	81	31
Jack Jacobs, GB	242	108	1615	16	69	17
Paul Christman, CHIC	301	138	2191	17	80	23

Receiving

	NO	YDS	AVG	LG	TD
Jim Keane, CHIB	64	910	14.2	50	10
Bob Nussbaumer, WAS	47	597	12.7	55t	4
Mal Kutner, CHIC	43	944	22.0	70t	7
Nolan Luhn, GB	42	696	16.6	44	7
Bill Dewell, CHIC	42	576	13.7	46t	4

Interceptions

	NO	YDS	AVG	LG	TD
Frank Reagan, NYG	10	203	71	0	20.3
Frank Seno, BOS	10	100	38	0	10.0

Punting

	NO	YDS	AVG	LG	BL
Jack Jacobs, GB	56	2480	43.5	74	1

Kickoff Returns

	NO	YDS	LG	TD	AVG
Eddie Saenz, WAS	29	797	94t	2	27.5

Punt Returns

	NO	FC	YDS	LG	TD	AVG
Walt Slater, PIT	28		435	33t	0	15.5

All-America Football Conference 1948

Eastern Division

Team	W	L	T	Pct	Pts	Opp	HW	HL	HT	HPct	AW	AL	AT	APct
BUF	7	7	0	.500	360	358	3	4	0	.429	4	3	0	.571
BAL	7	7	0	.500	333	327	4	3	0	.571	3	4	0	.429
NY	6	8	0	.429	265	301	3	4	0	.429	3	4	0	.429
BKN	2	12	0	.143	253	387	1	6	0	.143	1	6	0	.143

Western Division

Team	W	L	T	Pct	Pts	Opp	HW	HL	HT	HPct	AW	AL	AT	APct
CLE	14	0	0	1.000	389	190	7	0	0	1.000	7	0	0	1.000
SF	12	2	0	.857	495	248	6	1	0	.857	6	1	0	.857
LA	7	7	0	.500	258	305	3	4	0	.429	4	3	0	.571
CHI	1	13	0	.071	202	439	1	6	0	.143	0	7	0	.000

Scoring

	TD	1XP	2XP	FG	SAF	PTS
Chet Mutryn, BUF	16	0		0	0	96
Alyn Beals, SF	14	0		0	0	84
Joe Vetrano, SF	1	62		5	0	83
Billy Hillenbrand, BAL	13	0		0	0	78
Lou Groza, CLE	0	51		8	0	75

Rushing

	ATT	YDS	AVG	LG	TD
Marion Motley, CLE	157	964	6.1		5
John Strzykalski, SF	141	915	6.5		4
Chet Mutryn, BUF	147	823	5.6		10
Spec Sanders, NY	169	759	4.5		9
Lou Tomasetti, BUF	134	716	5.3		7

Passing

	ATT	COM	YDS	TD	INT	LG
Otto Graham, CLE	333	173	2713	25		15
Glenn Dobbs, LA	369	185	2403	21		20
Y.A. Tittle, BAL	289	161	2522	16		9
George Ratterman, BUF	335	168	2577	16		22
Frankie Albert, SF	246	154	1990	29		10

Receiving

	NO	YDS	AVG	LG	TD
Mac Speedie, CLE	58	816	14.1		4
Al Baldwin, BUF	54	916	17.0		8
Billy Hillenbrand, BAL	50	970	19.4		6
Fay King, CHI	50	647	12.9		7
Alyn Beals, SF	45	591	13.1		14

Interceptions

	NO	YDS	AVG	LG	TD	
Otto Schnellbacher, NY	11	239	51	1	21.7	

Punting

	NO	YDS	AVG	LG	BL
Glenn Dobbs, LA	65	3336	51.3	80	3

Kickoff Returns

	NO	YDS	LG	TD	AVG
Monk Gafford, BKN	23	559	58	0	24.3

Punt Returns

	NO	FC	YDS	LG	TD	AVG
Herman Wedemeyer, LA	23		368	61	0	16.0

National Football League 1948

Eastern Division

Team	W	L	T	Pct	Pts	Opp	HW	HL	HT	HPct	AW	AL	AT	APct
PHI	9	2	1	.818	376	156	6	0	0	1.000	3	2	1	.583
WAS	7	5	0	.583	291	287	4	2	0	.667	3	3	0	.500
PIT	4	8	0	.333	200	243	4	2	0	.667	0	6	0	.000
NYG	4	8	0	.333	297	388	2	4	0	.333	2	4	0	.333
BOS	3	9	0	.250	174	372	2	4	0	.333	1	5	0	.167

Western Division

Team	W	L	T	Pct	Pts	Opp	HW	HL	HT	HPct	AW	AL	AT	APct
CHIC	11	1	0	.917	395	226	5	1	0	.833	6	0	0	1.000
CHIB	10	2	0	.833	375	151	5	1	0	.833	5	1	0	.833
LA	6	5	1	.545	327	269	3	2	1	.583	3	3	0	.500
GB	3	9	0	.250	154	290	2	4	0	.333	1	5	0	.167
DET	2	10	0	.167	200	407	2	4	0	.333	0	6	0	.000

Scoring

	TD	1XP	2XP	FG	SAF	PTS
Pat Harder, CHIC	6	53		7	0	110
Mal Kutner, CHIC	15	0		0	0	90
Cliff Patton, PHI	0	50		8	0	74
Pete Pihos, PHI	11	0		0	0	66
Dick Poillon, WAS	3	33		5	0	66

Rushing

	ATT	YDS	AVG	LG	TD
Steve Van Buren, PHI	201	945	4.7	29	10
Charley Trippi, CHIC	128	690	5.4	50t	6
Elmer Angsman, CHIC	131	638	4.9	72t	8
Camp Wilson, DET	157	612	3.9	38	2
Tony Canadeo, GB	123	589	4.8	49	4

Passing

	ATT	COM	YDS	TD	INT	LG
Tommy Thompson, PHI	246	141	1965	25	70	11
Jim Hardy, LA	211	112	1390	14	69	7
Charlie Conerly, NYG	299	162	2175	21	65	13
Sammy Baugh, WAS	315	185	2599	22	86	23
Ray Mallouf, CHIC	143	73	1160	13	54	6

Receiving

	NO	YDS	AVG	LG	TD
Tom Fears, LA	51	698	13.7	80t	4
Pete Pihos, PHI	46	766	16.7	48	11
Mal Kutner, CHIC	41	943	23.0	71t	14
Val Jansante, PIT	39	623	16.0	66t	3
Bill Swiacki, NYG	39	550	14.1	65t	10

Interceptions

	NO	YDS	AVG	LG	TD
Dan Sandifer, WAS	13	258	5	2	19.8

Punting

	NO	YDS	AVG	LG	BL
Joe Muha, PHI	57	2692	47.2	82	0

Kickoff Returns

	NO	YDS	LG	TD	AVG
Joe Scott, NYG	20	569	99t	1	28.4

Punt Returns

	NO	FC	YDS	LG	TD	AVG
George McAfee, CHIC	30		417	60t	1	13.9

All-America Football Conference 1949

Team	W	L	T	Pct	Pts	Opp	HW	HL	HT	HPct	AW	AL	AT	APct
CLE	9	1	2	.900	339	171	5	0	1	.917	4	1	1	.750
SF	9	3	0	.750	416	227	6	0	0	1.000	3	3	0	.500
B-NY	8	4	0	.667	196	206	4	2	0	.667	4	2	0	.667
BUF	5	5	2	.500	236	256	3	2	1	.583	2	3	1	.417
CHI	4	8	0	.333	179	268	2	4	0	.333	2	4	0	.333
LA	4	8	0	.333	253	322	2	4	0	.333	2	4	0	.333
BAL	1	11	0	.083	172	341	0	6	0	.000	1	5	0	.167

Scoring

	TD	1XP	2XP	FG	SAF	PTS
Alyn Beals, SF	12	1		0	0	73
Joe Perry, SF	11	0		0	0	66
Joe Vetrano, SF	0	56		3	0	65
Marion Motley, CLE	8	0		0	0	48
Billy Stone, BAL	8	0		0	0	48
Buddy Young, B-NY	8	0		0	0	48

Rushing

	ATT	YDS	AVG	LG	TD
Joe Perry, SF	115	783	6.8		8
Chet Mutryn, BUF	131	696	5.3		5
Marion Motley, CLE	113	570	5.0		8
Ollie Cline, BUF	125	518	4.1		3
Buddy Young, B-NY	76	495	6.5		5

Passing

	ATT	COM	YDS	TD	INT	LG
Otto Graham, CLE	285	161	2785	19		10
Y.A. Tittle, BAL	289	148	2209	14		18
George Ratterman, B-NY	252	146	1777	14		13
Frankie Albert, SF	260	129	1862	27		16
Bob Hoernschemeyer, CHI	167	69	1063	6		11

Receiving

	NO	YDS	AVG	LG	TD
Mac Speedie, CLE	62	1028	16.6		7
Al Baldwin, BUF	53	719	13.6		7
Alyn Beals, SF	44	678	15.4		12
Dan Edwards, CHI	42	573	13.6		3
Lamar Davis, BAL	38	548	14.4		1

Interceptions

	NO	YDS	AVG	LG	TD
Jim Cason, SF	9	152	0		16.9

Punting

	NO	YDS	AVG	LG	BL
Frankie Albert, SF	31	1495	48.2	72	0

Kickoff Returns

	NO	YDS	LG	TD	AVG
Herman Wedemeyer, BAL	30	602	0		20.1

Punt Returns

	NO	FC	YDS	LG	TD	AVG
Jim Cason, SF	21		351	0		16.7

National Football League 1949
Eastern Division

Team	W	L	T	Pct	Pts	Opp	HW	HL	HT	HPct	AW	AL	AT	APct
PHI	11	1	0	.917	364	134	6	0	0	1.000	5	1	0	.833
PIT	6	5	1	.545	224	214	3	2	1	.583	3	3	0	.500
NYG	6	6	0	.500	287	298	2	4	0	.333	4	2	0	.667
WAS	4	7	1	.364	268	339	3	3	0	.500	1	4	1	.250

NYB	1	10	1	.091	153	368	1	4	1	.250	1	5	0	.167	

Western Division

Team	W	L	T	Pct	Pts	Opp	HW	HL	HT	HPct	AW	AL	AT	APct
LA	8	2	2	.800	360	239	5	1	0	.833	3	1	2	.667
CHIB	9	3	0	.750	332	218	5	1	0	.833	4	2	0	.667
CHIC	6	5	1	.545	360	301	2	3	1	.417	4	2	0	.667
DET	4	8	0	.333	237	259	2	4	0	.333	2	4	0	.333
GB	2	10	0	.167	114	329	1	5	0	.167	1	5	0	.167

Scoring

	TD	1XP	2XP	FG	SAF	PTS
Pat Harder, CHIC	8	45		3	0	102
Gene Roberts, NYG	17	0		0	0	102
Bill Dudley, DET	6	30		5	0	81
Bob Waterfield, LA	1	43		9	0	76
Steve Van Buren, PHI	12	0		0	0	72

Rushing

	ATT	YDS	AVG	LG	TD
Steve Van Buren, PHI	263	1146	4.4	41	11
Tony Canadeo, GB	208	1052	5.1	54	4
Elmer Angsman, CHIC	125	674	5.4	82t	6
Gene Roberts, NYG	152	634	4.2	63t	9
Jerry Nuzum, PIT	139	611	4.4	64t	5

Passing

	ATT	COM	YDS	TD	INT	LG
Sammy Baugh, WAS	255	145	1903	18	76	14
Johnny Lujack, CHIB	312	162	2658	23	81	22
Tommy Thompson, PHI	214	116	1727	16	75	11
Bob Waterfield, LA	296	154	2168	17	71	24
Charlie Conerly, NYG	305	151	2138	17	85	20

Receiving

	NO	YDS	AVG	LG	TD
Tom Fears, LA	77	1013	13.2	51t	9
Bob Mann, DET	66	1014	15.4	64t	4
Bill Chipley, NYB	57	631	11.1	69	2
Jim Keane, CHIB	47	696	14.8	39	6
Bill Swiacki, NYG	47	652	13.9	42	4

Interceptions

	NO	YDS	AVG	LG	TD
Bob Nussbaumer, CHIC	12	157	68	0	13.1

Punting

	NO	YDS	AVG	LG	BL
Mike Boyda, NYB	56	2475	44.2	61	0

Kickoff Returns

	NO	YDS	LG	TD	AVG
Don Doll, DET	21	536	56	0	25.5

Punt Returns

	NO	FC	YDS	LG	TD	AVG
Vitamin Smith, LA	27		427	85	1	15.8

National Football League 1950

American Conference

Team	W	L	T	Pct	Pts	Opp	HW	HL	HT	HPct	AW	AL	AT	APct
CLE	10	2	0	.833	310	144	5	1	0	.833	5	1	0	.833
NYG	10	2	0	.833	268	150	5	1	0	.833	5	1	0	.833
PHI	6	6	0	.500	254	141	2	4	0	.333	4	2	0	.667
PIT	6	6	0	.500	180	195	2	4	0	.333	4	2	0	.667
CHIC	5	7	0	.417	233	287	3	3	0	.500	2	4	0	.333
WAS	3	9	0	.250	232	326	1	5	0	.167	2	4	0	.333

National Conference

Team	W	L	T	Pct	Pts	Opp	HW	HL	HT	HPct	AW	AL	AT	APct
LA	9	3	0	.750	466	309	5	1	0	.833	4	2	0	.667
CHIB	9	3	0	.750	279	207	6	0	0	1.000	3	3	0	.500
NYY	7	5	0	.583	366	367	5	1	0	.833	2	4	0	.333
DET	6	6	0	.500	321	285	4	2	0	.667	2	4	0	.333
GB	3	9	0	.250	244	406	3	3	0	.500	0	6	0	.000
SF	3	9	0	.250	213	300	3	3	0	.500	0	6	0	.000
BAL	1	11	0	.083	213	462	1	5	0	.167	0	6	0	.000

Scoring

	TD	1XP	2XP	FG	SAF	PTS
Doak Walker, DET	11	38		8	0	128
Johnny Lujack, CHIB	11	34		3	0	109
Bob Waterfield, LA	1	54		7	0	81
Lou Groza, CLE	1	29		13	0	74
Bob Shaw, CHIC	12	0		0	0	72

Rushing

	ATT	YDS	AVG	LG	TD
Marion Motley, CLE	140	810	5.8	69t	3
Frank Ziegler, PHI	172	733	4.3	52	1
Joe Geri, PIT	188	705	3.8	47	2
Eddie Price, NYG	126	703	5.6	74	4
Joe Perry, SF	124	647	5.2	78t	5

Passing

	ATT	COM	YDS	TD	INT	LG
Norm VanBrocklin, LA	233	127	2061	18	58	14
Otto Graham, CLE	253	137	1943	14	80t	20
Joe Geri, PIT	113	41	866	6	78t	15
George Ratterman, NYY	294	140	2251	22	69t	24
Charlie Conerly, NYG	132	56	1000	8	43	7

Receiving

	NO	YDS	AVG	LG	TD
Tom Fears, LA	84	1116	13.3	53t	7
Dan Edwards, NYY	52	775	14.9	82t	6
Cloyce Box, DET	50	1009	20.2	82t	11
Paul Salata, BAL	50	618	12.4	57t	4
Bob Shaw, CHIC	48	971	20.2	65t	12

Interceptions

	NO	YDS	AVG	LG	TD
Spec Sanders, NYY	13	199	29	0	15.3

Punting

	NO	YDS	AVG	LG	BL
Curly Morrison, CHIB	57	2470	43.3	65	0

Kickoff Returns

	NO	YDS	LG	TD	AVG
Vitamin Smith, LA	22	742	97t	3	33.7

Punt Returns

	NO	FC	YDS	LG	TD	AVG
Herb Rich, BAL	12		276	86	1	23.0

National Football League 1951
American Conference

Team	W	L	T	Pct	Pts	Opp	HW	HL	HT	HPct	AW	AL	AT	APct
CLE	11	1	0	.917	331	152	6	0	0	1.000	5	1	0	.833
NYG	9	2	1	.818	254	161	5	1	0	.833	4	1	1	.750
WAS	5	7	0	.417	183	296	2	4	0	.333	3	3	0	.500
PIT	4	7	1	.364	183	235	1	4	1	.250	3	3	0	.500
PHI	4	8	0	.333	234	264	1	5	0	.167	3	3	0	.500
CHIC	3	9	0	.250	210	287	1	5	0	.167	2	4	0	.333

National Conference

Team	W	L	T	Pct	Pts	Opp	HW	HL	HT	HPct	AW	AL	AT	APct
LA	8	4	0	.667	392	261	5	2	0	.714	3	2	0	.600
SF	7	4	1	.636	255	205	5	1	0	.833	2	3	1	.417
DET	7	4	1	.636	336	259	3	3	1	.500	4	1	0	.800
CHIB	7	5	0	.583	286	282	3	3	0	.500	4	2	0	.667
GB	3	9	0	.250	254	375	2	4	0	.333	1	5	0	.167
NYY	1	9	2	.100	241	382	0	3	1	.125	1	6	1	.188

Scoring

	TD	1XP	2XP	FG	SAF	PTS
Elroy Hirsch, LA	17	0		0	0	102
Bob Waterfield, LA	3	41		13	0	98
Doak Walker, DET	6	43		6	0	97
Bobby Walston, PHI	8	28		6	0	94
Gordie Soltau, SF	7	30		6	0	90

Rushing

	ATT	YDS	AVG	LG	TD
Eddie Price, NYG	271	971	3.6	80t	7
Rob Goode, WAS	208	951	4.6	33	9
Dan Towler, LA	126	854	6.8	79t	6
Bob Hoernschemeyer, DET	132	678	5.1	85t	2
Joe Perry, SF	136	677	5.0	58t	3

Passing

	ATT	COM	YDS	TD	INT	LG
Bob Waterfield, LA	176	88	1566	13	91t	10
Norm Van Brocklin, LA	104	100	1725	13	81t	11
Otto Graham, CLE	265	147	2205	17	81t	16
Steve Romanik, CHIB	101	43	791	3	54t	9
Bob Celeri, NYY	238	102	1797	12	75t	15

Receiving

	NO	YDS	AVG	LG	TD
Elroy Hirsch, LA	66	1495	22.7	91t	17
Gordie Soltau, SF	59	826	14.0	48t	7
Fran Polsfoot, CHIC	57	796	14.0	80t	4
Bob Mann, GB	50	696	13.9	52	8
Dante Lavelli, CLE	43	586	13.6	47	6

Interceptions

	NO	YDS	AVG	LG	TD	
Otto Schnellbacher, NYG	11	194	46t	2		17.6

Punting

	NO	YDS	AVG	LG	BL
Horace Gillom, CLE	73	3321	45.5	66	0

Kickoff Returns

	NO	YDS	LG	TD	AVG
Lynn Chandnois, PIT	12	390	55	0	32.5

Punt Returns

	NO	FC	YDS	LG	TD	AVG
Buddy Young, NYY	12		231	79t	1	19.3

National Football League 1952
American Conference

Team	W	L	T	Pct	Pts	Opp	HW	HL	HT	HPct	AW	AL	AT	APct
CLE	8	4	0	.667	310	213	4	2	0	.667	4	2	0	.667
NYG	7	5	0	.583	234	231	2	4	0	.333	5	1	0	.833
PHI	7	5	0	.583	252	271	4	2	0	.667	3	3	0	.500
PIT	5	7	0	.417	300	273	2	4	0	.333	3	3	0	.500
WAS	4	8	0	.333	240	287	1	5	0	.167	3	3	0	.500
CHIC	4	8	0	.333	172	221	2	4	0	.333	2	4	0	.333

National Conference

Team	W	L	T	Pct	Pts	Opp	HW	HL	HT	HPct	AW	AL	AT	APct
LA	9	3	0	.750	349	234	5	1	0	.833	4	2	0	.667
DET	9	3	0	.750	344	192	6	1	0	.857	3	2	0	.600
SF	7	5	0	.583	285	221	3	3	3	.500	4	2	0	.667
GB	6	6	0	.500	295	312	3	3	0	.500	3	3	0	.500

CHIB	5	7	0	.417	245	326	3	3	0	.500	2	4	0	.333
DAL	1	11	0	.083	182	427	0	4	0	.000	1	7	0	.125

Scoring

	TD	1XP	2XP	FG	SAF	PTS
Gordie Soltau, SF	7	34		6	0	94
Cloyce Box, DET	15	0		0	0	90
Lou Groza, CLE	0	32		19	0	89
Pat Harder, DET	3	34		11	0	85
Bob Waterfield, LA	1	44		11	0	83

Rushing

	ATT	YDS	AVG	LG	TD
Dan Towler, LA	156	894	5.7	44t	10
Eddie Price, NYG	183	748	4.1	75t	5
Joe Perry, SF	158	725	4.6	78t	8
Hugh McElhenny, SF	98	684	7.0	89t	6
Bob Hoernschemeyer, DET	106	457	4.3	41	4

Passing

	ATT	COM	YDS	TD	INT	LG
Norm Van Brocklin, LA	205	113	1736	14	84t	17
Tobin Rote, GB	157	82	1268	13	81t	8
Babe Parilli, GB	177	77	1416	13	90t	17
Otto Graham, CLE	364	181	2816	20	68t	24
Frankie Albert, SF	129	71	964	8	60	10

Receiving

	NO	YDS	AVG	LG	TD
Mac Speedie, CLE	62	911	14.7	50	5
Bud Grant, PHI	56	997	17.8	84t	7
Elbie Nickel, PIT	55	884	16.1	54t	9
Gordie Soltau, SF	55	774	14.1	49t	7
Don Stonesifer, CHIC	54	617	11.4	26	0

Interceptions

	NO	YDS	AVG	LG	TD
Dick (Night Train) Lane, LA	14	298	80t	2	21.3

Punting

	NO	YDS	AVG	LG	BL
Horace Gillom, CLE	60	2787	46.5	73	1

Kickoff Returns

	NO	YDS	LG	TD	AVG
Lynn Chandnois, PIT	17	599	93t	2	35.2

Punt Returns

	NO	FC	YDS	LG	TD	AVG
Jack Christiansen, DET	15		322	79t	2	21.5

National Football League 1953

Eastern Conference

Team	W	L	T	Pct	Pts	Opp	HW	HL	HT	HPct	AW	AL	AT	APct
CLE	11	1	0	.917	348	162	6	0	0	1.000	5	1	0	.833
PHI	7	4	1	.636	352	215	5	0	1	.917	2	4	0	.333
WAS	6	5	1	.545	208	215	3	3	0	.500	3	2	1	.583
PIT	6	6	0	.500	211	263	3	3	0	.500	3	3	0	.500
NYG	3	9	0	.250	179	277	2	4	0	.333	1	5	0	.167
CHIC	1	10	1	.091	190	337	0	5	1	.083	1	5	0	.167

Western Conference

Team	W	L	T	Pct	Pts	Opp	HW	HL	HT	HPct	AW	AL	AT	APct
DET	10	2	0	.833	271	205	5	1	0	.833	5	1	0	.833
SF	9	3	0	.750	372	237	5	1	0	.833	4	2	0	.667
LA	8	3	1	.727	366	236	5	1	0	.833	3	2	1	.583
CHIB	3	8	1	.273	218	262	1	4	1	.250	2	4	0	.333
BAL	3	9	0	.250	182	350	2	4	0	.333	1	5	0	.167
GB	2	9	1	.182	200	338	1	5	0	.167	1	4	1	.250

Scoring

	TD	1XP	2XP	FG	SAF	PTS
Gordie Soltau, SF	6	48		10	0	114
Lou Groza, CLE	0	39		23	0	108
Doak Walker, DET	5	27		12	0	93
Bobby Walston, PHI	5	45		4	0	87
Joe Perry, SF	13	0		0	0	78

Rushing

	ATT	YDS	AVG	LG	TD
Joe Perry, SF	192	1018	5.3	51t	10
Dan Towler, LA	152	879	5.8	73t	7
Skeets Quinlan, LA	97	705	7.3	74t	4
Charlie Justice, WAS	115	616	5.4	43	2
Fran Rogel, PIT	137	527	3.8	58	2

Passing

	ATT	COM	YDS	TD	INT	LG
Otto Graham, CLE	258	167	2722	11	70	9
Norm Van Brocklin, LA	286	156	2393	19	70t	14
Y.A. Tittle, SF	259	149	2121	20	71	16
Bobby Thomason, PHI	304	162	2462	21	62t	20
Bobby Layne, DET	273	125	2088	16	97t	21

Receiving

	NO	YDS	AVG	LG	TD
Pete Pihos, PHI	63	1049	16.7	59	10
Elbie Nickel, PIT	62	743	12.0	40	4
Elroy Hirsch, LA	61	941	15.4	70	4
Don Stonesifer, CHIC	56	684	12.2	46	2
Jim Dooley, CHIB	53	841	15.9	72	4

Interceptions

	NO	YDS	AVG	LG	TD
Jack Christiansen, DET	12	238	92t	1	19.8

Punting

	NO	YDS	AVG	LG	BL
Pat Brady, PIT	80	3752	46.9	64	0

Kickoff Returns

	NO	YDS	LG	TD	AVG
Joe Arenas, SF	16	551	82	0	34.4

Punt Returns

	NO	FC	YDS	LG	TD	AVG
Charley Trippi, CHIC	21		239	38	0	11.4

National Football League 1954
Eastern Conference

Team	W	L	T	Pct	Pts	Opp	HW	HL	HT	HPct	AW	AL	AT	APct
CLE	9	3	0	.750	336	162	5	1	0	.833	4	2	0	.667
PHI	7	4	1	.636	284	230	5	1	0	.833	2	3	1	.417
NYG	7	5	0	.583	293	184	4	2	0	.667	3	3	0	.500
PIT	5	7	0	.417	219	263	4	2	0	.667	1	5	0	.167
WAS	3	9	0	.250	207	432	3	3	0	.500	0	6	0	.000
CHIC	2	10	0	.167	183	347	2	4	0	.333	0	6	0	.000

Western Conference

Team	W	L	T	Pct	Pts	Opp	HW	HL	HT	HPct	AW	AL	AT	APct
DET	9	2	1	.818	337	189	5	0	1	.917	4	2	0	.667
CHIB	8	4	0	.667	301	279	4	2	0	.667	4	2	0	.667
SF	7	4	1	.636	313	251	4	2	0	.667	3	2	1	.583
LA	6	5	1	.545	314	285	3	2	1	.583	3	3	0	.500
GB	4	8	0	.333	234	251	2	4	0	.333	2	4	0	.333
BAL	3	9	0	.250	131	279	2	4	0	.333	1	5	0	.167

Scoring

	TD	1XP	2XP	FG	SAF	PTS
Bobby Walston, PHI	11	36		4	0	114
Doak Walker, DET	5	43		11	0	106
Lou Groza, CLE	0	37		16	0	85
Gordie Soltau, SF	2	31		11	0	76
Ben Agajanian, NYG	0	35		13	0	74

Rushing

	ATT	YDS	AVG	LG	TD
Joe Perry, SF	173	1049	6.1	58	8
John Henry Johnson, SF	129	681	5.3	38t	9
Tank Younger, LA	91	610	6.7	75t	8
Dan Towler, LA	149	599	4.0	24	11
Mo Bassett, CLE	144	588	4.1	22	6

Passing

	ATT	COM	YDS	TD	INT	LG
Norm Van Brocklin, LA	260	130	2637	13	80t	21
Otto Graham, CLE	240	142	2092	11	64t	17
Zeke Bratkowski, CHIB	130	67	1087	8	71t	17
Tom Dublinski, DET	138	77	1073	8	66t	7
Bobby Clatterbuck, NYG	101	50	781	8	72t	7

Receiving

	NO	YDS	AVG	LG	TD
Pete Pihos, PHI	60	872	14.5	34	10
Billy Wilson, SF	60	830	13.8	43	5
Bob Boyd, LA	53	1212	22.9	80t	6
Billy Howton, GB	52	768	14.8	59	2
Dante Lavelli, CLE	47	802	17.1	64	7

Interceptions

	NO	YDS	AVG	LG	TD	
Dick (Night Train) Lane, CHIC	10	181	64	0	18.1	

Punting

	NO	YDS	AVG	LG	BL
Pat Brady, PIT	66	2852	43.2	72	0

Kickoff Returns

	NO	YDS	LG	TD	AVG
Billy Reynolds, CLE	14	413	51	0	29.5

Punt Returns

	NO	FC	YDS	LG	TD	AVG
Veryl Switzer, GB	24		306	93t	1	12.8

National Football League 1955
Eastern Conference

Team	W	L	T	Pct	Pts	Opp	HW	HL	HT	HPct	AW	AL	AT	APct
CLE	9	2	1	.818	349	218	5	1	0	.833	4	1	1	.750
WAS	8	4	0	.667	246	222	3	3	0	.500	5	1	0	.833
NYG	6	5	1	.545	267	223	4	1	1	.750	2	4	0	.333
CHIC	4	7	1	.364	224	252	3	2	1	.583	1	5	0	.167
PHI	4	7	1	.364	248	231	4	2	0	.667	0	5	1	.083
PIT	4	8	0	.333	195	285	3	2	0	.600	1	6	0	.143

Western Conference

Team	W	L	T	Pct	Pts	Opp	HW	HL	HT	HPct	AW	AL	AT	APct
LA	8	3	1	.727	260	231	5	1	0	.833	3	2	1	.583
CHIB	8	4	0	.667	294	251	5	1	0	.833	3	3	0	.500
GB	6	6	0	.500	258	276	5	1	0	.833	1	5	0	.167
BAL	5	6	1	.455	214	239	4	1	1	.750	1	5	0	.167
SF	4	8	0	.333	216	298	2	4	0	.333	2	4	0	.333
DET	3	9	0	.250	230	275	3	4	0	.429	0	5	0	.000

Scoring

	TD	1XP	2XP	FG	SAF	PTS
Doak Walker, DET	7	27		9	0	96
Vic Janowicz, WAS	7	28		6	0	88
George Blanda, CHIB	2	37		11	0	82
Fred Cone, GB	0	30		16	0	78
Lou Groza, CLE	0	44		11	0	77

Rushing

	ATT	YDS	AVG	LG	TD
Alan Ameche, BAL	213	961	4.5	79t	9
Howie Ferguson, GB	192	859	4.5	57	4
Fred Morrison, CLE	156	824	5.3	56	3
Ron Waller, LA	151	716	4.7	55t	7
Joe Perry, SF	156	701	4.5	42	2

Passing

	ATT	COM	YDS	TD	INT	LG
Otto Graham, CLE	185	98	1721	15	61t	8
Ed Brown, CHIB	164	85	1307	9	86t	10
Bobby Thomason, PHI	171	88	1337	10	63t	7
Y.A. Tittle, SF	287	147	2185	17	78t	28
Eddie LeBaron, WAS	178	79	1270	9	70	15

Receiving

	NO	YDS	AVG	LG	TD
Pete Pihos, PHI	62	864	13.9	40t	7
Billy Wilson, SF	53	831	15.7	72t	7
Billy Howton, GB	44	697	15.8	60	5
Dave Middleton, DET	44	663	15.1	77t	3
Tom Fears, LA	44	569	12.9	31	2

Interceptions

	NO	YDS	AVG	LG	TD	
Will Sherman, LA	11	101	36	0	9.2	

Punting

	NO	YDS	AVG	LG	BL
Norm Van Brocklin, LA	60	2676	44.6	61	0

Kickoff Returns

	NO	YDS	LG	TD	AVG
Al Carmichael, GB	14	418	100t	1	29.9

Punt Returns

	NO	FC	YDS	LG	TD	AVG
Ollie Matson, CHIC	13		245	78t	2	18.8

National Football League 1956

Eastern Conference

Team	W	L	T	Pct	Pts	Opp	HW	HL	HT	HPct	AW	AL	AT	APct
NYG	8	3	1	.727	264	197	4	1	1	.750	4	2	0	.667
CHIC	7	5	0	.583	240	182	4	2	0	.667	3	3	0	.500
WAS	6	6	0	.500	183	225	4	2	0	.667	2	4	0	.333
CLE	5	7	0	.417	167	177	1	5	0	.167	4	2	0	.667
PIT	5	7	0	.417	217	250	3	3	0	.500	2	4	0	.333
PHI	3	8	1	.273	143	215	2	3	1	.417	1	5	0	.167

Western Conference

Team	W	L	T	Pct	Pts	Opp	HW	HL	HT	HPct	AW	AL	AT	APct
CHIB	9	2	1	.818	363	246	6	0	0	1.000	3	2	1	.583
DET	9	3	0	.750	300	188	5	1	0	.833	4	2	0	.667
SF	5	6	1	.455	233	284	3	3	0	.500	2	3	1	.417
BAL	5	7	0	.417	270	322	4	2	0	.667	1	5	0	.167
GB	4	8	0	.333	264	342	2	4	0	.333	2	4	0	.333
LA	4	8	0	.333	291	307	4	2	0	.667	0	6	0	.000

Scoring

	TD	1XP	2XP	FG	SAF	PTS
Bobby Layne, DET	5	33		12	0	99
Rick Casares, CHIB	14	0		0	0	84
George Blanda, CHIB	0	45		12	0	81
Fred Cone, GB	4	33		5	0	72
Billy Howton, GB	12	0		0	0	72

Rushing

	ATT	YDS	AVG	LG	TD
Rick Casares, CHIB	234	1126	4.8	68t	12
Ollie Matson, CHIC	192	924	4.8	79t	5
Hugh McElhenny, SF	185	916	5.0	86t	8
Alan Ameche, BAL	178	858	4.8	43	8
Frank Gifford, NYG	159	819	5.2	69	5

Passing

	ATT	COM	YDS	TD	INT	LG
Ed Brown, CHIB	168	96	1667	11	70t	12
Billy Wade, LA	178	91	1461	10	76t	13
Bobby Layne, DET	244	129	1909	9	70	17
Norm Van Brocklin, LA	124	68	966	7	58t	12
Lamar McHan, CHIC	152	72	1159	10	75	8

Receiving

	NO	YDS	AVG	LG	TD
Billy Wilson, SF	60	889	14.8	77t	5
Billy Howton, GB	55	1188	21.6	66t	12
Frank Gifford, NYG	51	603	11.8	48	4
Harlon Hill, CHIB	47	1128	24.0	79t	11
Jim Mutscheller, BAL	44	715	16.3	53t	6

Interceptions

	NO	YDS	AVG	LG	TD
Linden Crow, CHIC	11	170	42	0	15.5

Punting

	NO	YDS	AVG	LG	BL
Norm Van Brocklin, LA	48	2070	43.1	72	0

Kickoff Returns

	NO	YDS	LG	TD	AVG
Tom Wilson, LA	15	477	103t	1	31.8

Punt Returns

	NO	FC	YDS	LG	TD	AVG
Ken Konz, CLE	13		187	65t	1	14.4

National Football League 1957

Eastern Conference

Team	W	L	T	Pct	Pts	Opp	HW	HL	HT	HPct	AW	AL	AT	APct
CLE	9	2	1	.818	269	172	6	0	0	1.000	3	2	1	.583
NYG	7	5	0	.583	254	211	3	3	0	.500	4	2	0	.667
PIT	6	6	0	.500	161	178	4	2	0	.667	2	4	0	.333
WAS	5	6	1	.455	251	230	2	3	1	.417	3	3	0	.500

Team	W	L	T	Pct	Pts	Opp	HW	HL	HT	HPct	AW	AL	AT	APct
PHI	4	8	0	.333	173	230	3	3	0	.500	1	5	0	.167
CHIC	3	9	0	.250	200	299	0	6	0	.000	3	3	0	.500

Western Conference

Team	W	L	T	Pct	Pts	Opp	HW	HL	HT	HPct	AW	AL	AT	APct
DET	8	4	0	.667	251	231	5	1	0	.833	3	3	0	.500
SF	8	4	0	.667	260	264	5	1	0	.833	3	3	0	.500
BAL	7	5	0	.583	303	235	4	2	0	.667	3	3	0	.500
LA	6	6	0	.500	307	278	5	1	0	.833	1	5	0	.167
CHIB	5	7	0	.417	203	211	2	4	0	.333	3	3	0	.500
GB	3	9	0	.250	218	311	1	5	0	.167	2	4	0	.333

Scoring

	TD	1XP	2XP	FG	SAF	PTS
Sam Baker, WAS	1	29		14	0	77
Lou Groza, CLE	0	32		15	0	77
Fred Cone, GB	2	26		12	0	74
George Blanda, CHIB	1	23		14	0	71
Paige Cothren, LA	0	38		11	0	71

Rushing

	ATT	YDS	AVG	LG	TD
Jim Brown, CLE	202	942	4.7	69t	9
Rick Casares, CHIB	204	700	3.4	25t	6
Don Bosseler, WAS	167	673	4.0	28	7
John Henry Johnson, DET	129	621	4.8	62	5
Tommy Wilson, LA	127	616	4.9	46	3

Passing

	ATT	COM	YDS	TD	INT	LG
Tommy O'Connell, CLE	110	63	1229	9	8	65t
Eddie LeBaron, WAS	167	99	1508	11	10	82t
Johnny Unitas, BAL	301	172	2550	24	17	82t
Norm Van Brocklin, LA	265	132	2105	20	21	70t
Lamar McHan, CHIC	200	87	1568	10	15	83t

Receiving

	NO	YDS	AVG	LG	TD
Billy Wilson, SF	52	757	14.6	40	6
Raymond Berry, BAL	47	800	17.0	67t	6
Jack McClairen, PIT	46	630	13.7	48t	2
Frank Gifford, NYG	41	588	14.3	63	4
Lenny Moore, BAL	40	687	17.2	82t	7

Interceptions

	NO	YDS	AVG	LG	TD
Milt Davis, BAL	10	219	21.9	75t	2
Jack Christiansen, DET	10	137	13.7	52	1
Jack Butler, PIT	10	85	8.5	20	0

Punting

	NO	YDS	AVG	LG	BL
Don Chandler, NYG	60	2673	44.5	61	0

Kickoff Returns

	NO	YDS	LG	TD	AVG
Jon Arnett, LA	18	504	98t	1	28.0

Punt Returns

	NO	FC	YDS	LG	TD	AVG
Bert Zagers, WAS	14		217	76t	2	15.5

National Football League 1958

Eastern Conference

Team	W	L	T	Pct	Pts	Opp	HW	HL	HT	HPct	AW	AL	AT	APct
NYG	9	3	0	.750	246	183	5	1	0	.833	4	2	0	.667
CLE	9	3	0	.750	302	217	4	2	0	.667	5	1	0	.833
PIT	7	4	1	.636	261	230	5	1	0	.833	2	3	1	.417
WAS	4	7	1	.364	214	268	3	2	1	.583	1	5	0	.167
CHIC	2	9	1	.182	261	356	1	4	1	.250	1	5	0	.167
PHI	2	9	1	.182	235	306	2	4	0	.333	0	5	1	.083

Western Conference

Team	W	L	T	Pct	Pts	Opp	HW	HL	HT	HPct	AW	AL	AT	APct
BAL	9	3	0	.750	381	203	6	0	0	1.000	3	3	0	.500
CHIB	8	4	0	.667	298	230	5	1	0	.833	3	3	0	.500
LA	8	4	0	.667	344	278	4	2	0	.667	4	2	0	.667
SF	6	6	0	.500	257	324	4	2	0	.667	2	4	0	.333
DET	4	7	1	.364	261	276	2	4	0	.333	2	3	1	.417
GB	1	10	1	.091	193	382	1	4	1	.250	0	6	0	.000

Scoring

	TD	1XP	2XP	FG	SAF	PTS
Jim Brown, CLE	18	0		0	0	108
Paige Cothren, LA	0	42		14	0	84
Lenny Moore, BAL	14	0		0	0	84
Tom Miner, PIT	0	31		14	0	73
Willie Galimore, CHIB	12	0		0	0	72

Rushing

	ATT	YDS	AVG	LG	TD
Jim Brown, CLE	257	1527	5.9	65t	17
Alan Ameche, BAL	171	791	4.6	28	8
Joe Perry, SF	125	758	6.1	73t	4
Tom Tracy, PIT	169	714	4.2	64	5
Jon Arnett, LA	133	683	5.1	57	6

Passing

	ATT	COM	YDS	TD	INT	LG
Eddie LeBaron, WAS	145	79	1365	11	10	71t
Milt Plum, CLE	189	102	1619	11	11	74
Bobby Layne, DET-PIT	294	145	2510	14	12	78t
Billy Wade, LA	341	181	2875	18	22	93t
Johnny Unitas, BAL	263	136	2007	19	7	77t

Receiving

	NO	YDS	AVG	LG	TD
Raymond Berry, BAL	56	794	14.2	54	9
Pete Retzlaff, PHI	56	766	13.7	49	2
Del Shofner, LA	51	1097	21.5	92t	8
Lenny Moore, BAL	50	938	18.8	77t	7
Clyde Conner, SF	49	512	10.4	26	5

Interceptions

	NO	YDS	AVG	LG	TD
Jim Patton, NYG	11	183	16.6	42	0

Punting

	NO	YDS	AVG	LG	BL
Sam Baker, WAS	48	2181	45.4	64	0

Kickoff Returns

	NO	YDS	LG	TD	AVG
Ollie Matson, CHIC	14	497	101t	2	35.5

Punt Returns

	NO	FC	YDS	LG	TD	AVG
Jon Arnett, LA	18		223	58	0	12.4

National Football League 1959

Eastern Conference

Team	W	L	T	Pct	Pts	Opp	HW	HL	HT	HPct	AW	AL	AT	APct
NYG	10	2	0	.833	284	170	5	1	0	.833	5	1	0	.833
CLE	7	5	0	.583	270	214	3	3	0	.500	4	2	0	.667
PHI	7	5	0	.583	268	278	5	1	0	.833	2	4	0	.333
PIT	6	5	1	.545	257	216	3	2	1	.583	3	3	0	.500
WAS	3	9	0	.250	185	350	2	4	0	.333	1	5	0	.167
CHIC	2	10	0	.167	234	324	2	4	0	.333	0	6	0	.000

Western Conference

Team	W	L	T	Pct	Pts	Opp	HW	HL	HT	HPct	AW	AL	AT	APct
BAL	9	3	0	.750	374	251	4	2	0	.667	5	1	0	.833
CHIB	8	4	0	.667	252	196	4	2	0	.667	4	2	0	.667
GB	7	5	0	.583	248	246	4	2	0	.667	3	3	0	.500
SF	7	5	0	.583	255	237	4	2	0	.667	3	3	0	.500
DET	3	8	1	.273	203	275	2	4	0	.333	1	4	1	.250
LA	2	10	0	.167	242	315	0	6	0	.000	2	4	0	.333

Scoring

	TD	1XP	2XP	FG	SAF	PTS
Paul Hornung, GB	7	31		7	0	94
Pat Summerall, NYG	0	30		20	0	90
Raymond Berry, BAL	14	0		0	0	84
Jim Brown, CLE	14	0		0	0	84
Bobby Joe Conrad, CHIC	6	30		6	0	84

Rushing

	ATT	YDS	AVG	LG	TD
Jim Brown, CLE	290	1329	4.6	70t	14
J.D. Smith, SF	207	1036	5.0	73t	10
Ollie Matson, LA	161	863	5.4	50	6
Tom Tracy, PIT	199	794	4.0	51	3
Bobby Mitchell, CLE	131	743	5.7	90t	5

Passing

	ATT	COM	YDS	TD	INT	LG
Charlie Conerly, NYG	194	113	1706	14	77t	4
Earl Morrall, DET	137	65	1102	5	79t	6
Johnny Unitas, BAL	367	193	2899	32	71	14
Norm Van Brocklin, PHI	340	191	2617	16	71	14
Billy Wade, LA	261	153	2001	12	72t	17

Receiving

	NO	YDS	AVG	LG	TD
Raymond Berry, BAL	66	959	14.5	55t	14
Del Shofner, NYG	47	936	19.9	72t	7
Tommy McDonald, PHI	47	846	18.0	71	10
Lenny Moore, BAL	47	846	18.0	71	6
Jim Mutscheller, BAL	44	699	15.9	40t	8

Interceptions

	NO	YDS	AVG	LG	TD
Dean Derby, PIT	7	127	24	0	18.1
Milt Davis, BAL	7	119	57t	1	17.0
Don Shinnick, BAL	7	70	23	0	10.0

Punting

	NO	YDS	AVG	LG	BL
Yale Lary, DET	45	2121	47.1	67	0

Kickoff Returns

	NO	YDS	LG	TD	AVG
Abe Woodson, SF	13	382	105t	1	29.4

Punt Returns

	NO	FC	YDS	LG	TD	AVG
Johnny Morris, CHIB	14		171	78t	1	12.2

American Football League 1960

Eastern Division

Team	W	L	T	Pct	Pts	Opp	HW	HL	HT	HPct	AW	AL	AT	APct
HOU	10	4	0	.714	379	285	6	1	0	.857	4	3	0	.571
NY	7	7	0	.500	382	399	3	4	0	.429	4	3	0	.571
BUF	5	8	1	.385	296	303	3	4	0	.429	2	4	1	.357
BOS	5	9	0	.357	286	349	3	4	0	.429	2	5	0	.286

Western Division

Team	W	L	T	Pct	Pts	Opp	HW	HL	HT	HPct	AW	AL	AT	APct
LA	10	4	0	.714	373	336	5	2	0	.714	5	2	0	.714
DAL	8	6	0	.571	362	253	5	2	0	.714	3	4	0	.429
OAK	6	8	0	.429	319	388	3	4	0	.429	3	4	0	.429
DEN	4	9	1	.308	309	393	2	4	1	.357	2	5	0	.286

Scoring

	TD	1XP	2XP	FG	SAF	PTS
Gene Mingo, DEN	6	33	0	18	0	123
George Blanda, HOU	4	46	0	15	0	115
Jack Spikes, DAL	5	34	0	13	0	103
Bill Shockley, NY	2	47	0	9	0	86
Ben Agajanian, LA	0	46	0	13	0	85

Rushing

	ATT	YDS	AVG	LG	TD
Abner Haynes, DAL	156	875	5.6	57	9
Paul Lowe, LA	136	855	6.3	69	9
Billy Cannon, HOU	152	644	4.2	60	1
Dave Smith, HOU	154	643	4.2	65	5
Tony Teresa, OAK	139	608	4.4	83	6

Passing

	ATT	COM	YDS	TD	INT	LG
Jack Kemp, LA	406	211	3018	20		25
Al Dorow, NY	396	201	2748	26		26
Frank Tripucka, DEN	478	248	3038	24		34
Butch Songin, BOS	392	187	2476	22		15
Cotton Davidson, DAL	379	179	2474	15		16

Receiving

	NO	YDS	AVG	LG	TD
Lionel Taylor, DEN	92	1235	13.4	80	12
Bill Groman, HOU	72	1473	20.5	92t	12
Don Maynard, NY	72	1265	17.6	65	6
Art Powell, NY	69	1167	16.9	76	14
Abner Haynes, DAL	55	576	10.5	34	3

Interceptions

	NO	YDS	AVG	LG	TD
Goose Gonsoulin, DEN	11	98	0	8.9	

Punting

	NO	YDS	AVG	LG	BL
Paul Maguire, LA	43	1743	40.5	61	0

Kickoff Returns

	NO	YDS	LG	TD	AVG
Ken Hall, HOU	19	594	104	1	31.3

Punt Returns

	NO	FC	YDS	LG	TD	AVG
Abner Haynes, DAL	14		215	46	0	15.4

National Football League 1960

Eastern Conference

Team	W	L	T	Pct	Pts	Opp	HW	HL	HT	HPct	AW	AL	AT	APct
PHI	10	2	0	.833	321	246	5	1	0	.833	5	1	0	.833
CLE	8	3	1	.727	362	217	4	2	0	.667	4	1	1	.750
NYG	6	4	2	.600	271	261	1	3	2	.333	5	1	0	.833
STL	6	5	1	.545	288	230	3	2	1	.583	3	3	0	.500
PIT	5	6	1	.455	240	275	4	2	0	.667	1	4	1	.250
WAS	1	9	2	.100	178	309	1	4	1	.250	0	5	1	.083

Western Conference

Team	W	L	T	Pct	Pts	Opp	HW	HL	HT	HPct	AW	AL	AT	APct
GB	8	4	0	.667	332	209	4	2	0	.667	4	2	0	.667
DET	7	5	0	.583	239	212	5	1	0	.833	2	4	0	.333
SF	7	5	0	.583	208	205	3	3	0	.500	4	2	0	.667
BAL	6	6	0	.500	288	234	4	2	0	.667	2	4	0	.333
CHI	5	6	1	.455	194	299	4	2	0	.667	1	4	1	.250
LA	4	7	1	.364	265	297	2	3	1	.417	2	4	0	.333
DAL	0	11	1	.000	177	369	0	6	0	.000	0	5	1	.083

Scoring

	TD	1XP	2XP	FG	SAF	PTS
Paul Hornung, GB	15	41		15	0	176
Bobby Walston, PHI	4	39		14	0	105
Sonny Randle, STL	15	0		0	0	90
Sam Baker, CLE	0	44		12	0	80
three tied with						78

Rushing

	ATT	YDS	AVG	LG	TD
Jim Brown, CLE	215	1257	5.8	71t	9
Jim Taylor, GB	230	1101	4.8	32	11
John David Crow, STL	183	1071	5.9	57	6
Nick Pietrosante, DET	161	872	5.4	57	8
J.D. Smith, SF	174	780	4.5	41	5

Passing

	ATT	COM	YDS	TD	INT	LG
Milt Plum, CLE	250	151	2297	21	80t	5
Norm Van Brocklin, PHI	284	153	2471	24	64t	17
Johnny Unitas, BAL	378	190	3099	25	80t	24
Billy Wade, LA	182	106	1294	12	63	11
Bobby Layne, PIT	209	103	1814	13	70	17

Receiving

	NO	YDS	AVG	LG	TD
Raymond Berry, BAL	74	1298	17.5	70t	10
Sonny Randle, STL	62	893	14.4	57t	15
Jim Phillips, LA	52	883	17.0	61t	8
Jim Gibbons, DET	51	604	11.8	65t	2
Pete Retzlaff, PHI	46	826	18.0	57t	5

Interceptions

	NO	YDS	AVG	LG	TD
Dave Baker, SF	10	96	28	0	9.6
Jerry Norton, STL	10	96	26	0	9.6

Punting

	NO	YDS	AVG	LG	BL
Jerry Norton, STL	39	1777	45.6	62	0

Kickoff Returns

	NO	YDS	LG	TD	AVG
Tom Moore, GB	12	397	84	0	33.1

Punt Returns

	NO	FC	YDS	LG	TD	AVG
Abe Woodson, SF	13		174	48	0	13.4

American Football League 1961

Eastern Division

Team	W	L	T	Pct	Pts	Opp	HW	HL	HT	HPct	AW	AL	AT	APct
HOU	10	3	1	.769	513	242	6	1	0	.857	4	2	1	.643
BOS	9	4	1	.692	413	313	4	2	1	.643	5	2	0	.714
NY	7	7	0	.500	301	390	5	2	0	.714	2	5	0	.286
BUF	6	8	0	.429	294	342	2	5	0	.286	4	3	0	.571

Western Division

Team	W	L	T	Pct	Pts	Opp	HW	HL	HT	HPct	AW	AL	AT	APct
SD	12	2	0	.857	396	219	6	1	0	.857	6	1	0	.857
DAL	6	8	0	.429	334	343	4	3	0	.571	2	5	0	.286
DEN	3	11	0	.214	251	432	2	5	0	.286	1	6	0	.143
OAK	2	12	0	.143	237	458	1	6	0	.143	1	6	0	.143

Scoring

	TD	1XP	2XP	FG	SAF	PTS
Gino Cappelletti, BOS	8	48	0	17	0	147
George Blanda, HOU	0	64	0	16	0	112
Bill Groman, HOU	18	0	0	0	0	108
Billy Cannon, HOU	15	0	0	0	0	90
George Blair, SD	0	42	0	13	0	81

Rushing

	ATT	YDS	AVG	LG	TD
Billy Cannon, HOU	200	948	4.7	61	6
Bill Mathis, NY	202	846	4.2	30	7
Abner Haynes, DAL	179	841	4.7	59	9
Paul Lowe, SD	175	767	4.4	87t	9
Charlie Tolar, HOU	157	577	3.7	28	4

Passing

	ATT	COM	YDS	TD	INT	LG
George Blanda, HOU	362	187	3330	36		22
Tom Flores, OAK	366	190	2176	15		19
Jack Kemp, SD	364	165	2686	15		22
Al Dorow, NY	438	197	2651	19		30
Babe Parilli, BOS	198	104	1314	13		9

Receiving

	NO	YDS	AVG	LG	TD
Lionel Taylor, DEN	100	1176	11.8	52	4
Charley Hennigan, HOU	82	1746	21.3	80	12
Art Powell, NY	71	881	12.4	48	5
Dave Kocourek, SD	55	1055	19.2	76	4
Chris Burford, DAL	51	850	16.7	54	5

Interceptions

	NO	YDS	AVG	LG	TD
Billy Atkins, BUF	10	158	29	0	15.8

Punting

	NO	YDS	AVG	LG	BL
Billy Atkins, BUF	84	3783	45.0	70	

Kickoff Returns

	NO	YDS	LG	TD	AVG
Dave Grayson, DAL	16	453	73	0	28.3

Punt Returns

	NO	FC	YDS	LG	TD	AVG
Dick Christy, NY	18		383	70	2	21.3

National Football League 1961

Eastern Conference

Team	W	L	T	Pct	Pts	Opp	HW	HL	HT	HPct	AW	AL	AT	APct
NYG	10	3	1	.769	368	220	4	2	1	.643	6	1	0	.857
PHI	10	4	0	.714	361	297	5	2	0	.714	5	2	0	.714
CLE	8	5	1	.615	319	270	4	3	0	.571	4	2	1	.643
STL	7	7	0	.500	279	267	3	4	0	.429	4	3	0	.571
PIT	6	8	0	.429	295	287	4	3	0	.571	2	5	0	.286
DAL	4	9	1	.308	236	380	2	4	1	.357	2	5	0	.286
WAS	1	12	1	.077	174	392	1	6	0	.143	0	6	1	.071

Western Conference

Team	W	L	T	Pct	Pts	Opp	HW	HL	HT	HPct	AW	AL	AT	APct
GB	11	3	0	.786	391	223	6	1	0	.857	5	2	0	.714
DET	8	5	1	.615	270	258	2	5	0	.286	6	0	1	.929
BAL	8	6	0	.571	302	307	5	2	0	.714	3	4	0	.429
CHI	8	6	0	.571	326	302	5	2	0	.714	3	4	0	.429
SF	7	6	1	.538	346	272	5	1	1	.786	2	5	0	.286
LA	4	10	0	.286	263	333	4	3	0	.571	0	7	0	.000
MIN	3	11	0	.214	285	407	3	4	0	.429	0	7	0	.000

Scoring

	TD	1XP	2XP	FG	SAF	PTS
Paul Hornung, GB	10	41		15	0	146
Bobby Walston, PHI	2	43		14	0	97
Steve Myhra, BAL	0	33		21	0	96
Jim Taylor, GB	16	0		0	0	96
Lenny Moore, BAL	15	0		0	0	90

Rushing

	ATT	YDS	AVG	LG	TD
Jim Brown, CLE	305	1408	4.6	38	8
Jim Taylor, GB	243	1307	5.4	53	15
Alex Webster, NYG	196	928	4.7	59	2
Nick Pietrosante, DET	201	841	4.2	42	5
J.D. Smith, SF	167	823	4.9	33	8

Passing

	ATT	COM	YDS	TD	INT	LG
Milt Plum, CLE	302	177	2416	18	77	10
Sonny Jurgensen, PHI	416	235	3723	32	69	24
Bart Starr, GB	295	172	2418	16	78t	16
John Brodie, SF	283	155	2588	14	70t	12
Billy Wade, CHI	250	139	2258	22	98t	13

Receiving

	NO	YDS	AVG	LG	TD
Jim Phillips, LA	78	1092	14.0	69t	5
Raymond Berry, BAL	75	873	11.6	44	0
Del Shofner, NYG	68	1125	16.5	46t	11
Tommy McDonald, PHI	64	1144	17.9	66	13
Mike Ditka, CHIB	56	1076	19.2	76t	12

Interceptions

	NO	YDS	AVG	LG	TD	
Dick Lynch, NYG	9	60	36	0	6.7	

Punting

	NO	YDS	AVG	LG	BL
Yale Lary, DET	52	2519	48.4	71	0

Kickoff Returns

	NO	YDS	LG	TD	AVG
Dick Bass, LA	23	698	64	0	30.3

Punt Returns

	NO	FC	YDS	LG	TD	AVG
Willie Wood, GB	14		225	72t	2	16.1

American Football League 1962
Eastern Division

Team	W	L	T	Pct	Pts	Opp	HW	HL	HT	HPct	AW	AL	AT	APct
HOU	11	3	0	.786	387	270	6	1	0	.857	5	2	0	.714
BOS	9	4	1	.692	346	295	6	1	0	.857	3	3	1	.500
BUF	7	6	1	.538	309	272	3	3	1	.500	4	3	0	.571
NY	5	9	0	.357	278	423	2	5	0	.286	3	4	0	.429

Western Division

Team	W	L	T	Pct	Pts	Opp	HW	HL	HT	HPct	AW	AL	AT	APct
DAL	11	3	0	.786	389	233	6	1	0	.857	5	2	0	.714
DEN	7	7	0	.500	353	334	3	4	0	.429	4	3	0	.571
SD	4	10	0	.286	314	392	3	4	0	.429	1	6	0	.143
OAK	1	13	0	.071	213	370	1	6	0	.143	0	7	0	.000

Scoring

	TD	1XP	2XP	FG	SAF	PTS
Gene Mingo, DEN	4	32	0	27	0	137
Gino Cappelletti, BOS	5	38	0	20	0	128
Cookie Gilchrist, BUF	15	14	0	8	0	128
Abner Haynes, DAL	19	0	0	0	0	114
Tommy Brooker, DAL	3	33	0	12	0	87

Rushing

	ATT	YDS	AVG	LG	TD
Cookie Gilchrist, BUF	214	1096	5.1	44	13
Abner Haynes, DAL	221	1049	4.7	71	13
Charlie Tolar, HOU	244	1012	4.1	25	7
Clem Daniels, OAK	161	766	4.8	72	7
Curtis McClinton, DAL	111	604	5.4	69	2

Passing

	ATT	COM	YDS	TD	INT	LG
Len Dawson, DAL	310	189	2759	29	17	
Babe Parilli, BOS	253	140	1988	18	8	
Frank Tripucka, DEN	440	240	2917	17	25	
George Blanda, HOU	418	197	2810	27	42	
Johnny Green, NY	258	128	1741	10	18	

Receiving

	NO	YDS	AVG	LG	TD
Lionel Taylor, DEN	77	908	11.8	45	4
Art Powell, NY	64	1130	17.7	80	8
Dick Christy, NY	62	538	8.7	41	3
Bo Dickinson, DEN	60	554	9.2	33	4
Don Maynard, NY	56	1041	18.6	86	8

Interceptions

	NO	YDS	AVG	LG	TD
Lee Riley, NY	11	122	30	0	11.1

Punting

	NO	YDS	AVG	LG	BL
Jim Fraser, DEN	54	2400	44.4	75	1

Kickoff Returns

	NO	YDS	LG	TD	AVG
Bobby Jancik, HOU	24	726	61	0	30.3

Punt Returns

	NO	FC	YDS	LG	TD	AVG
Dick Christy, NY	15		250	73	2	16.7

National Football League 1962
Eastern Conference

Team	W	L	T	Pct	Pts	Opp	HW	HL	HT	HPct	AW	AL	AT	APct
NYG	12	2	0	.857	398	283	6	1	0	.857	6	1	0	.857
PIT	9	5	0	.643	312	363	4	3	0	.571	5	2	0	.714
CLE	7	6	1	.538	291	257	4	2	1	.643	3	4	0	.429
WAS	5	7	2	.417	305	376	3	4	0	.429	2	3	2	.429
DAL	5	8	1	.385	398	402	2	4	1	.357	3	4	0	.429
STL	4	9	1	.308	287	361	2	4	1	.357	2	5	0	.286
PHI	3	10	1	.231	282	356	2	5	0	.286	1	5	1	.214

Western Conference

Team	W	L	T	Pct	Pts	Opp	HW	HL	HT	HPct	AW	AL	AT	APct
GB	13	1	0	.929	415	148	7	0	0	1.000	6	1	0	.857
DET	11	3	0	.786	315	177	7	0	0	1.000	4	3	0	.571
CHI	9	5	0	.643	321	287	4	3	0	.571	5	2	0	.714
BAL	7	7	0	.500	293	288	3	4	0	.429	4	3	0	.571
SF	6	8	0	.429	282	331	1	6	0	.143	5	2	0	.714
MIN	2	11	1	.154	254	410	1	5	1	.214	1	6	0	.143
LA	1	12	1	.077	220	334	0	7	0	.000	1	5	1	.214

Scoring

	TD	1XP	2XP	FG	SAF	PTS
Jim Taylor, GB	19	0		0	0	114
Lou Michaels, PIT	0	32		26	0	110
Jim Brown, CLE	18	0		0	0	108
Don Chandler, NYG	0	47		19	0	104
John David Crow, STL	17	0		0	0	102

Rushing

	ATT	YDS	AVG	LG	TD
Jim Taylor, GB	272	1474	5.4	51	19
John Henry Johnson, PIT	251	1141	4.5	40	7
Dick Bass, LA	196	1033	5.3	57	6
Jim Brown, CLE	230	996	4.3	31	13
Don Perkins, DAL	222	945	4.3	35	7

Passing

	ATT	COM	YDS	TD	INT	LG
Bart Starr, GB	285	178	2438	12	83t	9
Y.A. Tittle, NYG	375	200	3224	33	69t	20
Eddie LeBaron, DAL	166	95	1436	16	85t	9
Frank Ryan, CLE	194	112	1541	10	65t	7
Sonny Jurgensen, PHI	366	196	3261	22	84	26

Receiving

	NO	YDS	AVG	LG	TD
Bobby Mitchell, WAS	72	1384	19.2	81t	11
Sonny Randle, STL	63	1158	18.4	86t	7
Bobby Joe Conrad, STL	62	954	15.4	72t	4
Jim Phillips, LA	60	875	14.6	65t	5
Tommy McDonald, PHI	58	1146	19.8	60t	10

Interceptions

	NO	YDS	AVG	LG	TD	
Willie Wood, GB	9	132	37	0		14.7

Punting

	NO	YDS	AVG	LG	BL
Tommy Davis, SF	48	2188	45.6	82	0

Kickoff Returns

	NO	YDS	LG	TD	AVG
Abe Woodson, SF	37	1157	79	0	31.3

Punt Returns

	NO	FC	YDS	LG	TD	AVG
Pat Studstill, DET	29	7	457	44	0	15.8

American Football League 1963

Eastern Division

Team	W	L	T	Pct	Pts	Opp	HW	HL	HT	HPct	AW	AL	AT	APct
BOS	7	6	1	.538	327	257	5	1	1	.786	2	5	0	.286
BUF	7	6	1	.538	304	291	4	2	1	.643	3	4	0	.429
HOU	6	8	0	.429	302	372	4	3	0	.571	2	5	0	.286
NY	5	8	1	.385	249	399	4	2	1	.643	1	6	0	.143

Western Division

Team	W	L	T	Pct	Pts	Opp	HW	HL	HT	HPct	AW	AL	AT	APct
SD	11	3	0	.786	399	255	6	1	0	.857	5	2	0	.714
OAK	10	4	0	.714	363	282	6	1	0	.857	4	3	0	.571
KC	5	7	2	.417	347	263	4	3	0	.571	1	4	2	.286
DEN	2	11	1	.154	301	473	2	5	0	.286	0	6	1	.071

Scoring

	TD	1XP	2XP	FG	SAF	PTS
Gino Cappelletti, BOS	2	35	0	22	0	113
Art Powell, OAK	16	0	0	0	0	96
George Blair, SD	0	44	0	17	0	95
Cookie Gilchrist, BUF	14	0	0	0	0	84
Gene Mingo, DEN	0	35	0	16	0	83

Rushing

	ATT	YDS	AVG	LG	TD
Clem Daniels, OAK	215	1099	5.1	74	3
Paul Lowe, SD	177	1010	5.7	66	8
Cookie Gilchrist, BUF	232	979	4.2	32	12
Keith Lincoln, SD	128	826	6.5	76	5
Larry Garron, BOS	179	750	4.2	47	2

Passing

	ATT	COM	YDS	TD	INT	LG
Tobin Rote, SD	286	170	2510	20		17
Tom Flores, OAK	247	113	2101	20		13
Jack Kemp, BUF	384	194	2914	13		20
Len Dawson, KC	352	190	2389	26		19
George Blanda, HOU	423	224	3003	24		25

Receiving

	NO	YDS	AVG	LG	TD
Lionel Taylor, DEN	78	1101	14.1	72	10
Art Powell, OAK	73	1304	17.8	85	16
Bake Turner, NY	71	1007	14.2	53	6
Bill Miller, BUF	69	860	12.5	36	3
Chris Burford, KC	68	824	12.1	69	9

Interceptions

	NO	YDS	AVG	LG	TD	
Fred Glick, HOU	12	180	45	1		15.0

Punting

	NO	YDS	AVG	LG	BL
Jim Fraser, DEN	78	3595	46.1	66	

Kickoff Returns

	NO	YDS	LG	TD	AVG
Bobby Jancik, HOU	45	1317	53	0	29.3

Punt Returns

	NO	FC	YDS	LG	TD	AVG
Hoot Gibson, OAK	26		307	83	2	11.8

National Football League 1963
Eastern Conference

Team	W	L	T	Pct	Pts	Opp	HW	HL	HT	HPct	AW	AL	AT	APct
NYG	11	3	0	.786	448	280	5	2	0	.714	6	1	0	.857
CLE	10	4	0	.714	343	262	5	2	0	.714	5	2	0	.714
STL	9	5	0	.643	341	283	3	4	0	.429	6	1	0	.857
PIT	7	4	3	.636	321	295	5	0	2	.857	2	4	1	.357
DAL	4	10	0	.286	305	378	3	4	0	.429	1	6	0	.143
WAS	3	11	0	.214	279	398	1	6	0	.143	2	5	0	.286
PHI	2	10	2	.167	242	381	1	5	1	.214	1	5	1	.214

Western Conference

Team	W	L	T	Pct	Pts	Opp	HW	HL	HT	HPct	AW	AL	AT	APct
CHI	11	1	2	.917	301	144	6	0	1	.929	5	1	1	.786
GB	11	2	1	.846	369	206	6	1	0	.857	5	1	1	.786
BAL	8	6	0	.571	316	285	4	3	0	.571	4	0	0	.571
MIN	5	8	1	.385	309	390	3	4	0	.429	2	4	1	.357
DET	5	8	1	.385	326	265	3	3	1	.500	2	5	0	.286
LA	5	9	0	.357	210	350	3	4	0	.429	2	5	0	.286
SF	2	12	0	.143	198	391	2	5	0	.286	0	7	0	.000

Scoring

	TD	1XP	2XP	FG	SAF	PTS
Don Chandler, NYG	0	52		18	0	106
Jim Martin, BAL	0	32		24	0	104
Lou Michaels, PIT	0	32		21	0	95
Jerry Kramer, GB	0	43		16	0	91
Jim Brown, CLE	15	0		0	0	90

Rushing

	ATT	YDS	AVG	LG	TD
Jim Brown, CLE	291	1863	6.4	80t	12
Jim Taylor, GB	248	1018	4.1	40t	9
Timmy Brown, PHI	192	841	4.4	34	6
John Henry Johnson, PIT	186	773	4.2	48	4
Tommy Mason, MIN	166	763	4.6	70t	7

Passing

	ATT	COM	YDS	TD	INT	LG
Y.A. Tittle, NYG	367	221	3145	36	70t	14
Johnny Unitas, BAL	410	237	3481	20	64t	12
Earl Morrall, DET	328	174	2621	24	75t	14
Frank Ryan, CLE	256	135	2026	25	83t	13
Charley Johnson, STL	423	222	3280	28	78t	21

Receiving

	NO	YDS	AVG	LG	TD
Bobby Joe Conrad, STL	73	967	13.2	48	10
Bobby Mitchell, WAS	69	1436	20.8	99t	7
Terry Barr, DET	66	1086	16.5	75t	13
Del Shofner, NYG	64	1181	18.5	70t	9
Buddy Dial, PIT	60	1295	21.6	83t	9

Interceptions

	NO	YDS	AVG	LG	TD	
Dick Lynch, NYG	9	251	82t	3	27.9	
Roosevelt Taylor, CHI	9	172	46	1	19.1	

Punting

	NO	YDS	AVG	LG	BL
Yale Lary, DET	35	1713	48.9	73	0

Kickoff Returns

	NO	YDS	LG	TD	AVG
Abe Woodson, SF	29	935	103t	3	32.2

Punt Returns

	NO	FC	YDS	LG	TD	AVG
Dick James, WAS	16	6	214	39	0	13.4

American Football League 1964
Eastern Division

Team	W	L	T	Pct	Pts	Opp	HW	HL	HT	HPct	AW	AL	AT	APct
BUF	12	2	0	.857	400	242	6	1	0	.857	6	1	0	.857
BOS	10	3	1	.769	365	297	4	2	1	.643	6	1	0	.857
NY	5	8	1	.385	278	315	5	1	1	.786	0	7	0	.000
HOU	4	10	0	.296	310	355	3	4	0	.429	1	6	0	.143

Western Division

Team	W	L	T	Pct	Pts	Opp	HW	HL	HT	HPct	AW	AL	AT	APct
SD	8	5	1	.615	341	300	4	3	0	.571	4	2	1	.643
KC	7	7	0	.500	366	306	4	3	0	.571	3	4	0	.429
OAK	5	7	2	.417	303	350	5	2	0	.714	0	5	2	.143
DEN	2	11	1	.154	240	438	2	4	1	.357	0	7	0	.000

Scoring

	TD	1XP	2XP	FG	SAF	PTS
Gino Cappelletti, BOS	7	36	1	25	0	155
Pete Gogolak, BUF	0	45	0	19	0	102
Lance Alworth, SD	15	0	0	0	0	90
Mike Mercer, OAK	0	34	0	15	0	79
George Blanda, HOU	0	37	0	13	0	76

Rushing

	ATT	YDS	AVG	LG	TD
Cookie Gilchrist, BUF	230	981	4.3	67	6
Matt Snell, NY	215	948	4.4	42	5
Clem Daniels, OAK	173	824	4.8	42	2
Sid Blanks, HOU	145	756	5.2	91t	6
Abner Haynes, KC	139	697	5.0	80	4

Passing

	ATT	COM	YDS	TD	INT	LG
Len Dawson, KC	354	199	2879	30		18
Babe Parilli, BOS	473	228	3465	31		27
George Blanda, HOU	505	262	3287	17		27
John Hadl, SD	274	147	2157	18		15
Cotton Davidson, OAK	320	155	2497	21		19

Receiving

	NO	YDS	AVG	LG	TD
Charley Hennigan, HOU	101	1546	15.3	53	8
Art Powell, OAK	76	1361	17.9	77	11
Lionel Taylor, DEN	76	873	11.5	57	7
Frank Jackson, KC	62	943	15.2	72	9
Lance Alworth, SD	61	1235	20.2	82	13

Interceptions

	NO	YDS	AVG	LG	TD
Dainard Paulson, NY	12	157	42	1	13.1

Punting

	NO	YDS	AVG	LG	BL
Jim Fraser, DEN	72	3225	44.7	67	

Kickoff Returns

	NO	YDS	LG	TD	AVG
Bo Roberson, OAK	36	975	59	0	27.1

Punt Returns

	NO	FC	YDS	LG	TD	AVG
Bobby Jancik, HOU	12		220	82	1	18.3

National Football League 1964

Eastern Conference

Team	W	L	T	Pct	Pts	Opp	HW	HL	HT	HPct	AW	AL	AT	APct
CLE	10	3	1	.769	415	293	5	1	1	.786	5	2	0	.714
STL	9	3	2	.750	357	331	4	1	1	.750	5	2	1	.688
PHI	6	8	0	.429	312	313	3	4	0	.429	3	4	0	.429
WAS	6	8	0	.429	307	305	4	3	0	.571	2	5	0	.286
DAL	5	8	1	.385	250	289	2	4	1	.357	3	4	0	.429
PIT	5	9	0	.357	253	315	2	5	0	.286	3	4	0	.429
NYG	2	10	2	.167	241	399	2	5	0	.286	0	5	2	.143

Western Conference

Team	W	L	T	Pct	Pts	Opp	HW	HL	HT	HPct	AW	AL	AT	APct
BAL	12	2	0	.857	428	225	7	1	0	.875	5	1	0	.833
MIN	8	5	1	.615	355	296	4	3	0	.571	4	2	1	.643
GB	8	5	1	.615	342	245	4	3	0	.571	4	2	1	.643
DET	7	5	2	.583	280	260	3	3	1	.500	4	2	1	.643
LA	5	7	2	.417	283	339	3	2	2	.571	2	5	0	.286
CHI	5	9	0	.357	260	379	2	5	0	.286	3	4	0	.429
SF	4	10	0	.286	236	330	3	4	0	.429	1	6	0	.143

Scoring

	TD	1XP	2XP	FG	SAF	PTS
Lenny Moore, BAL	20	0		0	0	120
Jim Bakken, STL	0	40		25	0	115
Lou Groza, CLE	0	49		22	0	115
Paul Hornung, GB	5	41		12	0	107
Lou Michaels, BAL	0	53		17	0	104

Rushing

	ATT	YDS	AVG	LG	TD
Jim Brown, CLE	280	1446	5.2	71	7
Jim Taylor, GB	235	1169	5.0	84t	12
John Henry Johnson, PIT	235	1048	4.5	45t	7
Bill Brown, MIN	226	866	3.8	48	7
Don Perkins, DAL	174	768	4.4	59	6

Passing

	ATT	COM	YDS	TD	INT	LG
Bart Starr, GB	272	163	2144	15	73	4
Fran Tarkenton, MIN	306	171	2506	22	64	11
Sonny Jurgensen, WAS	385	207	2934	24	80t	13
Johnny Unitas, BAL	305	158	2824	19	74t	6
Milt Plum, DET	287	154	2241	18	92t	15

Receiving

	NO	YDS	AVG	LG	TD
Johnny Morris, CHI	93	1200	12.9	63t	10
Mike Ditka, CHI	75	897	12.0	34	5
Frank Clarke, DAL	65	973	15.0	49	5
Bobby Joe Conrad, STL	61	780	12.8	53	6
Bobby Mitchell, WAS	60	904	15.1	60	10

Interceptions

	NO	YDS	AVG	LG	TD
Paul Krause, WAS	12	140	35t	1	11.7

Punting

	NO	YDS	AVG	LG	BL
Bobby Walden, MIN	72	3341	46.4	73	0

Kickoff Returns

	NO	YDS	LG	TD	AVG
Clarence Childs, NYG	34	987	100t	1	29.0

Punt Returns

	NO	FC	YDS	LG	TD	AVG
Tommy Watkins, DET	16	6	238	68t	2	14.9

American Football League 1965
Eastern Division

Team	W	L	T	Pct	Pts	Opp	HW	HL	HT	HPct	AW	AL	AT	APct
BUF	10	3	1	.769	313	226	5	2	0	.714	5	1	1	.786
NY	5	8	1	.385	285	303	3	3	1	.500	2	5	0	.286
BOS	4	8	2	.333	244	302	1	4	2	.286	3	4	0	.429
HOU	4	10	0	.286	298	429	3	4	0	.429	1	6	0	.143

Western Division

Team	W	L	T	Pct	Pts	Opp	HW	HL	HT	HPct	AW	AL	AT	APct
SD	9	2	3	.818	340	227	4	1	2	.714	5	1	1	.786
OAK	8	5	1	.615	298	239	5	2	0	.714	3	3	1	.500
KC	7	5	2	.583	322	285	5	2	0	.714	2	3	2	.429
DEN	4	10	0	.286	303	392	2	5	0	.286	2	5	0	.286

Scoring

	TD	1XP	2XP	FG	SAF	PTS
Gino Cappelletti, BOS	9	27	0	17	0	132
Pete Gogolak, BUF	0	31	0	28	0	115
Herb Travenio, SD	0	40	0	18	0	94
Jim Turner, NY	0	31	0	20	0	91
Lance Alworth, SD	14	0	0	0	0	84
Don Maynard, NY	14	0	0	0	0	84

Rushing

	ATT	YDS	AVG	LG	TD
Paul Lowe, SD	222	1121	5.0	59	7
Cookie Gilchrist, DEN	252	954	3.8	44	6
Clem Daniels, OAK	219	884	4.0	57	5
Matt Snell, NY	169	763	4.5	44	4
Curtis McClinton, KC	175	661	3.8	48	6

Passing

	ATT	COM	YDS	TD	INT	LG
John Hadl, SD	348	174	2798	20	85	21
Len Dawson, KC	305	163	2262	21	67	14
Joe Namath, NY	340	164	2220	18	62	15
Jack Kemp, BUF	391	179	2368	10	78	18
George Blanda, HOU	442	186	2542	20	95	30

Receiving

	NO	YDS	AVG	LG	TD
Lionel Taylor, DEN	85	1131	13.3	63	6
Lance Alworth, SD	69	1602	23.2	85	14
Don Maynard, NY	68	1218	17.9	56	14
Ode Burrell, HOU	55	650	11.8	52	4
Art Powell, OAK	52	800	15.4	66	12

Interceptions

	NO	YDS	AVG	LG	TD	
W.K. Hicks, HOU	9	156	31	0	17.3	

Punting

	NO	YDS	AVG	LG	BL
Jerrel Wilson, KC	68	3132	46.1	64	

Kickoff Returns

	NO	YDS	LG	TD	AVG
Abner Haynes, DEN	34	901	60	0	26.5

Punt Returns

	NO	FC	YDS	LG	TD	AVG
Speedy Duncan, SD	30		464	66	2	15.5

National Football League 1965
Eastern Conference

Team	W	L	T	Pct	Pts	Opp	HW	HL	HT	HPct	AW	AL	AT	APct
CLE	11	3	0	.786	363	325	5	2	0	.714	6	1	0	.857
DAL	7	7	0	.500	325	280	5	2	0	.714	2	5	0	.286
NYG	7	7	0	.500	270	338	3	4	0	.429	4	3	0	.571
WAS	6	8	0	.429	257	301	3	4	0	.429	3	4	0	.429
PHI	5	9	0	.357	363	359	2	5	0	.286	3	4	0	.429
STL	5	9	0	.357	296	309	2	5	0	.286	3	4	0	.429
PIT	2	12	0	.143	202	397	1	6	0	.143	1	6	0	.143

Western Conference

Team	W	L	T	Pct	Pts	Opp	HW	HL	HT	HPct	AW	AL	AT	APct
BAL	10	3	1	.769	389	284	5	2	0	.714	5	1	1	.786
GB	10	3	1	.769	316	224	6	1	0	.857	4	2	1	.643
CHI	9	5	0	.643	409	275	5	2	0	.714	4	3	0	.571
SF	7	6	1	.538	421	402	4	2	1	.643	0	7	0	.000
MIN	7	7	0	.500	383	403	2	5	0	.286	5	2	0	.714
DET	6	7	1	.462	257	295	2	4	1	.357	4	3	0	.571
LA	4	10	0	.286	269	328	3	4	0	.429	1	6	0	.143

Scoring

	TD	1XP	2XP	FG	SAF	PTS
Gale Sayers, CHI	22	0		0	0	132
Jim Brown, CLE	21	0		0	0	126
Fred Cox, MIN	0	44		23	0	113
Tommy Davis, SF	0	52		17	0	103
Lou Michaels, BAL	0	48		17	1	101

Rushing

	ATT	YDS	AVG	LG	TD
Jim Brown, CLE	289	1544	5.3	67	17
Gale Sayers, CHI	166	867	5.2	61t	14
Timmy Brown, PHI	158	861	5.4	54t	6
Ken Willard, SF	189	778	4.1	32	5
Jim Taylor, GB	207	734	3.5	35	4

Passing

	ATT	COM	YDS	TD	INT	LG
Rudy Bukich, CHI	312	176	2641	20	80t	9
Johnny Unitas, BAL	282	164	2530	23	61	12
John Brodie, SF	391	242	3112	30	59t	16
Bart Starr, GB	251	140	2055	16	77t	9
Earl Morrall, NYG	302	155	2446	22	89t	12

Receiving

	NO	YDS	AVG	LG	TD
Dave Parks, SF	80	1344	16.8	53t	12
Tommy McDonald, LA	67	1036	15.5	51	9
Pete Retzlaff, PHI	66	1190	18.0	78	10
Bobby Mitchell, WAS	60	867	14.5	80t	6
Bernie Casey, SF	59	765	13.0	59t	8

Interceptions

	NO	YDS	AVG	LG	TD	
Bobby Boyd, BAL	9	78	24	1	8.7	

Punting

	NO	YDS	AVG	LG	BL
Gary Collins, CLE	65	3035	46.7	71	0

Kickoff Returns

	NO	YDS	LG	TD	AVG
Tommy Watkins, DET	17	584	94	0	34.4

Punt Returns

	NO	FC	YDS	LG	TD	AVG
Leroy Kelly, CLE	17	6	265	67t	2	15.6

American Football League 1966
Eastern Division

Team	W	L	T	Pct	Pts	Opp	HW	HL	HT	HPct	AW	AL	AT	APct
BUF	9	4	1	.692	358	255	4	2	1	.643	5	2	0	.714
BOS	8	4	2	.667	315	283	4	2	1	.643	4	2	1	.643
NY	6	6	2	.500	322	312	4	3	0	.571	2	3	2	.429
HOU	3	11	0	.214	335	396	3	4	0	.429	0	7	0	.000
MIA	3	11	0	.214	213	362	2	5	0	.286	1	6	0	.143

Western Division

Team	W	L	T	Pct	Pts	Opp	HW	HL	HT	HPct	AW	AL	AT	APct
KC	11	2	1	.846	448	276	4	2	1	.643	7	0	0	1.000
OAK	8	5	1	.615	315	288	3	3	1	.500	5	2	0	.714
SD	7	6	1	.538	335	284	5	2	0	.714	2	4	1	.357
DEN	4	10	0	.286	196	381	3	4	0	.429	1	6	0	.143

Scoring

	TD	1XP	2XP	FG	SAF	PTS
Gino Cappelletti, BOS	6	35	0	16	0	119
Booth Lusteg, BUF	0	41	0	19	0	98
Mike Mercer, OAK-KC	0	35	0	21	0	98
Jim Turner, NY	0	34	0	18	0	88
George Blanda, HOU	0	39	0	16	0	87
Dick Van Raaphorst, SD	0	39	0	16	0	87

Rushing

	ATT	YDS	AVG	LG	TD
Jim Nance, BOS	299	1458	4.9	65	11
Mike Garrett, KC	147	801	5.4	77t	6
Clem Daniels, OAK	204	801	3.9	64	7
Bobby Burnett, BUF	187	766	4.1	32	4
Wray Carlton, BUF	156	696	4.5	23	6

Passing

	ATT	COM	YDS	TD	INT	LG
Len Dawson, KC	284	159	2527	26	89	10
John Hadl, SD	375	200	2846	23	78	14
Tom Flores, OAK	306	151	2638	24	78	14
Joe Namath, NY	471	232	3379	19	77	27
Babe Parilli, BOS	382	181	2721	20	63	20

Receiving

	NO	YDS	AVG	LG	TD
Lance Alworth, SD	73	1383	18.9	78	13
George Sauer, NY	63	1079	17.1	77	5
Otis Taylor, KC	58	1297	22.4	89t	8
Chris Burford, KC	58	758	13.1	38	8
Willie Frazier, HOU	57	1129	19.8	79	12

Interceptions

	NO	YDS	AVG	LG	TD
Johnny Robinson, KC	10	136	29	1	13.6
Bobby Hunt, KC	10	113	33	0	11.3

Punting

	NO	YDS	AVG	LG	BL
Bob Scarpitto, DEN	76	3480	45.8	70	

Kickoff Returns

	NO	YDS	LG	TD	AVG
Goldie Sellers, DEN	19	541	100t	2	28.5

Punt Returns

	NO	FC	YDS	LG	TD	AVG
Speedy Duncan, SD	18		238	81	1	13.2

National Football League 1966
Eastern Conference

Team	W	L	T	Pct	Pts	Opp	HW	HL	HT	HPct	AW	AL	AT	APct
DAL	10	3	1	.769	445	239	6	1	0	.857	4	2	1	.643
CLE	9	5	0	.643	403	259	5	2	0	.714	4	3	0	.571
PHI	9	5	0	.643	326	340	5	2	0	.714	4	3	0	.571
STL	8	5	1	.615	264	265	5	1	1	.786	3	4	0	.429
WAS	7	7	0	.500	351	355	4	3	0	.571	3	4	0	.429
PIT	5	8	1	.385	316	347	3	3	1	.500	2	5	0	.286
ATL	3	11	0	.214	204	437	1	6	0	.143	2	5	0	.286
NYG	1	12	1	.077	263	501	1	6	0	.143	0	6	1	.071

Western Conference

Team	W	L	T	Pct	Pts	Opp	HW	HL	HT	HPct	AW	AL	AT	APct
GB	12	2	0	.857	335	163	6	1	0	.857	6	1	0	.857
BAL	9	5	0	.643	314	226	5	2	0	.714	4	3	0	.571

	W	L	T	Pct	Pts	Opp	HW	HL	HT	HPct	AW	AL	AT	APct
LA	8	6	0	.571	289	212	5	2	0	.714	3	4	0	.429
SF	6	6	2	.500	320	325	4	2	1	.643	2	4	1	.357
CHI	5	7	2	.417	234	272	4	1	2	.714	1	6	0	.143
DET	4	9	1	.308	206	317	3	4	0	.429	1	5	1	.214
MIN	4	9	1	.308	292	304	2	5	0	.286	2	4	1	.357

Scoring

	TD	1XP	2XP	FG	SAF	PTS
Bruce Gossett, LA	0	29		28	0	113
Danny Villanueva, DAL	0	56		17	0	107
Charlie Gogolak, WAS	0	39		22	0	105
Lou Michaels, BAL	0	35		21	0	98
Mike Clark, PIT	0	34		21	0	97

Rushing

	ATT	YDS	AVG	LG	TD
Gale Sayers, CHI	229	1231	5.4	58t	8
Leroy Kelly, CLE	209	1141	5.5	70t	15
Dick Bass, LA	248	1090	4.4	50	8
Bill Brown, MIN	251	829	3.3	33t	6
Ken Willard, SF	191	763	4.0	49	5

Passing

	ATT	COM	YDS	TD	INT	LG
Bart Starr, GB	251	156	2257	14	83t	3
Sonny Jurgensen, WAS	436	254	3209	28	86t	19
Frank Ryan, CLE	382	200	2974	29	54	14
Don Meredith, DAL	344	177	2805	24	95t	12
Johnny Unitas, BAL	348	195	2748	22	89t	24

Receiving

	NO	YDS	AVG	LG	TD
Charley Taylor, WAS	72	1119	15.5	86t	12
Pat Studstill, DET	67	1266	18.9	99t	5
Dave Parks, SF	66	974	14.8	65t	5
Bob Hayes, DAL	64	1232	19.3	95t	13
Tom Moore, LA	60	433	7.2	30t	3

Interceptions

	NO	YDS	AVG	LG	TD
Larry Wilson, STL	10	180	91t	2	18.0

Punting

	NO	YDS	AVG	LG	BL
David Lee, BAL	49	2233	45.6	64	0

Kickoff Returns

	NO	YDS	LG	TD	AVG
Gale Sayers, CHI	23	718	93t	2	31.2

Punt Returns

	NO	FC	YDS	LG	TD	AVG
Johnny Roland, STL	20	18	221	86t	1	11.1

American Football League 1967
Eastern Division

Team	W	L	T	Pct	Pts	Opp	HW	HL	HT	HPct	AW	AL	AT	APct
HOU	9	4	1	.692	258	199	5	2	0	.714	4	2	1	.643
NY	8	5	1	.615	371	329	4	2	1	.643	4	3	0	.571
BUF	4	10	0	.286	237	285	2	5	0	.286	2	5	0	.286
MIA	4	10	0	.286	219	407	4	3	0	.571	0	7	0	.000
BOS	3	10	1	.231	280	389	2	4	0	.333	1	6	1	.188

Western Division

Team	W	L	T	Pct	Pts	Opp	HW	HL	HT	HPct	AW	AL	AT	APct
OAK	13	1	0	.929	468	233	7	0	0	1.000	6	1	0	.857
KC	9	5	0	.643	408	254	4	3	0	.571	5	2	0	.714
SD	8	5	1	.615	360	352	5	2	1	.688	3	3	0	.500
DEN	3	11	0	.214	256	409	1	6	0	.143	2	5	0	.286

Scoring

	TD	1XP	2XP	FG	SAF	PTS
George Blanda, OAK	0	56	0	20	0	116
Jan Stenerud, KC	0	45	0	21	0	108
Gino Cappelletti, BOS	3	29	0	16	0	95
Dick Van Raaphorst, SD	0	45	0	15	0	90
Jim Turner, NY	0	36	0	17	0	87

Rushing

	ATT	YDS	AVG	LG	TD
Jim Nance, BOS	269	1216	4.5	53	7
Hoyle Granger, HOU	236	1194	5.1	67	6
Mike Garrett, KC	236	1087	4.6	58	9
Dickie Post, SD	161	663	4.1	67t	7
Brad Hubbert, SD	116	643	5.5	80t	2

Passing

	ATT	COM	YDS	TD	INT	LG
Daryle Lamonica, OAK	425	220	3228	30	72	20
Len Dawson, KC	357	206	2651	24	71t	17
Joe Namath, NY	491	258	4007	26	75t	28
John Hadl, SD	427	217	3365	24	72t	22
Bob Griese, MIA	331	166	2005	15	68t	18

Receiving

	NO	YDS	AVG	LG	TD
George Sauer, NY	75	1189	15.9	61t	6
Don Maynard, NY	71	1434	20.2	75t	10
Jack Clancy, MIA	67	868	13.0	44t	2
Otis Taylor, KC	59	958	16.2	71t	11
Hewritt Dixon, OAK	59	563	9.5	48	2

Interceptions

	NO	YDS	AVG	LG	TD
Miller Farr, HOU	10	264	67	3	26.4
Tom Janik, BUF	10	222	46	2	22.2
Dick Westmoreland, MIA	10	127	29	1	12.7

Punting

	NO	YDS	AVG	LG	BL
Bob Scarpitto, DEN	104	4713	45.3	73	1

Kickoff Returns

	NO	YDS	LG	TD	AVG
Zeke Moore, HOU	14	405	92t	1	28.9

Punt Returns

	NO	FC	YDS	LG	TD	AVG
Floyd Little, DEN	16	6	270	72t	1	16.9

National Football League 1967

EASTERN CONFERENCE
Century Division

Team	W	L	T	Pct	Pts	Opp	HW	HL	HT	HPct	AW	AL	AT	APct
CLE	9	5	0	.643	334	297	6	1	0	.857	3	4	0	.429
NYG	7	7	0	.500	369	379	5	2	0	.714	2	5	0	.286
STL	6	7	1	.462	333	356	3	3	1	.500	3	4	0	.429
PIT	4	9	1	.308	281	320	1	6	0	.143	3	3	1	.500

Capitol Division

Team	W	L	T	Pct	Pts	Opp	HW	HL	HT	HPct	AW	AL	AT	APct
DAL	9	5	0	.643	342	268	7	5	2	.714	4	3	0	.571
PHI	6	7	1	.462	351	409	5	2	0	.714	1	5	1	.214
WAS	5	6	3	.455	347	353	2	4	1	.357	3	2	2	.571
NO	3	11	0	.214	233	279	2	5	0	.286	1	6	0	.143

WESTERN CONFERENCE
Coastal Division

Team	W	L	T	Pct	Pts	Opp	HW	HL	HT	HPct	AW	AL	AT	APct
LA	11	1	2	.917	398	196	5	1	1	.786	6	0	1	.929
BAL	11	1	2	.917	394	198	6	0	1	.929	5	1	1	.786
SF	7	7	0	.500	273	337	3	4	0	.429	4	3	0	.571
ATL	1	12	1	.077	175	422	1	5	1	.214	0	7	0	.000

Central Division

Team	W	L	T	Pct	Pts	Opp	HW	HL	HT	HPct	AW	AL	AT	APct
GB	9	4	1	.692	332	209	4	2	1	.643	5	2	0	.714
CHI	7	6	1	.538	239	218	3	3	1	.500	4	3	0	.571
DET	5	7	2	.417	260	259	3	4	0	.429	2	3	2	.429
MIN	3	8	3	.273	233	294	1	4	2	.286	2	4	1	.357

Scoring

	TD	1XP	2XP	FG	SAF	PTS
Jim Bakken, STL	0	36		27	0	117
Bruce Gossett, LA	0	48		20	0	108
Lou Michaels, BAL	0	46		20	0	106
Don Chandler, GB	0	39		19	0	96
Homer Jones, NYG	14	0		0	0	84

Rushing

	ATT	YDS	AVG	LG	TD
Leroy Kelly, CLE	235	1205	5.1	42t	11
Dave Osborn, MIN	215	972	4.5	73	2
Gale Sayers, CHI	186	880	4.7	70	7
Johnny Roland, STL	234	876	3.7	70	10
Mel Farr, DET	206	860	4.2	57	3

Passing

	ATT	COM	YDS	TD	INT	LG
Sonny Jurgensen, WAS	508	288	3747	31	86t	16
Johnny Unitas, BAL	436	255	3428	20	88t	16
Fran Tarkenton, NYG	377	204	3088	29	70t	19
Roman Gabriel, LA	371	196	2779	25	80t	13
Norm Snead, PHI	434	240	3399	29	87t	24

Receiving

	NO	YDS	AVG	LG	TD
Charley Taylor, WAS	70	990	14.1	86t	9
Jerry Smith, WAS	67	849	12.7	43	12
Willie Richardson, BAL	63	860	13.7	31t	8
Bobby Mitchell, WAS	60	866	14.4	65t	6
Ben Hawkins, PHI	59	1265	21.4	87t	10

Interceptions

	NO	YDS	AVG	LG	TD	
Lem Barney, DET	10	232	71t	3	23.2	
Dave Whitsell, NO	10	178	41t	2	17.8	

Punting

	NO	YDS	AVG	LG	BL
Billy Lothridge, ATL	87	3801	43.7	62	0

Kickoff Returns

	NO	YDS	LG	TD	AVG
Travis Williams, GB	18	739	104t	4	41.1

Punt Returns

	NO	FC	YDS	LG	TD	AVG
Ben Davis, CLE	18	7	229	52t	1	12.7

American Football League 1968

Eastern Division

Team	W	L	T	Pct	Pts	Opp	HW	HL	HT	HPct	AW	AL	AT	APct
NY	11	3	0	.786	419	280	6	1	0	.857	5	2	0	.714
HOU	7	7	0	.500	303	248	3	4	0	.429	4	3	0	.571
MIA	5	8	1	.385	276	355	1	5	1	.214	4	3	0	.571
BOS	4	10	0	.286	229	406	2	5	0	.286	2	5	0	.286
BUF	1	12	1	.077	199	367	1	6	0	.143	0	6	1	.071

Western Division

Team	W	L	T	Pct	Pts	Opp	HW	HL	HT	HPct	AW	AL	AT	APct
KC	12	2	0	.857	371	170	6	1	0	.857	6	1	0	.857
OAK	12	2	0	.857	453	233	6	1	0	.857	6	1	0	.857
SD	9	5	0	.643	382	310	4	3	0	.571	5	2	0	.714
CIN	3	11	0	.214	215	329	2	5	0	.286	1	6	0	.143
DEN	5	9	0	.357	255	404	3	4	0	.429	2	5	0	.286

Scoring

	TD	1XP	2XP	FG	SAF	PTS
Jim Turner, NY	0	43	0	34	0	145
Jan Stenerud, KC	0	39	0	30	0	129
George Blanda, OAK	0	54	0	21	0	117
Dennis Partee, SD	0	40	0	22	0	106
Gino Cappelletti, BOS	2	26	0	15	0	83

Rushing

	ATT	YDS	AVG	LG	TD
Paul Robinson, CIN	238	1023	4.3	87t	8
Robert Holmes, KC	174	866	5.0	76t	7
Hewritt Dixon, OAK	206	865	4.2	28	2
Hoyle Granger, HOU	202	848	4.2	47t	7
Dickie Post, SD	151	758	5.0	62t	3

Passing

	ATT	COM	YDS	TD	INT	LG
Len Dawson, KC	224	131	2109	17	92t	9
Daryle Lamonica, OAK	416	206	3245	25	82	15
Joe Namath, NY	380	187	3147	15	87t	17
Bob Griese, MIA	355	186	2473	21	50t	16
John Hadl, SD	440	208	3473	27	84t	32

Receiving

	NO	YDS	AVG	LG	TD
Lance Alworth, SD	68	1312	19.3	80t	10
George Sauer, NY	66	1141	17.3	43	3
Fred Biletnikoff, OAK	61	1037	17.0	82	6
Karl Noonan, MIA	58	760	13.1	50t	11
Don Maynard, NY	57	1297	22.8	87t	10

Interceptions

	NO	YDS	AVG	LG	TD
Dave Grayson, OAK	10	195	54	1	19.5

Punting

	NO	YDS	AVG	LG	BL
Jerrel Wilson, KC	63	2841	45.1	70	0

Kickoff Returns

	NO	YDS	LG	TD	AVG
George Atkinson, OAK	32	802	60	0	25.1

Punt Returns

	NO	FC	YDS	LG	TD	AVG
Noland Smith, KC	18	10	270	80t	1	15.0

National Football League 1968

EASTERN CONFERENCE
Century Division

Team	W	L	T	Pct	Pts	Opp	HW	HL	HT	HPct	AW	AL	AT	APct
CLE	10	4	0	.714	394	273	5	2	0	.714	5	2	0	.714
STL	9	4	1	.692	325	289	4	2	1	.643	5	2	0	.714
NO	4	9	1	.308	246	327	3	4	0	.429	1	5	1	.214
PIT	2	11	1	.154	244	397	1	6	0	.143	1	5	1	.214

Capitol Division

Team	W	L	T	Pct	Pts	Opp	HW	HL	HT	HPct	AW	AL	AT	APct
DAL	12	2	0	.857	431	186	5	2	0	.714	7	0	0	1.000
NYG	7	7	0	.500	294	325	3	4	0	.429	4	3	0	.571
WAS	5	9	0	.357	249	358	3	4	0	.429	2	5	0	.286
PHI	2	12	0	.143	202	351	1	6	0	.143	1	6	0	.143

WESTERN CONFERENCE
Coastal Division

Team	W	L	T	Pct	Pts	Opp	HW	HL	HT	HPct	AW	AL	AT	APct
BAL	13	1	0	.929	402	144	6	1	0	.857	7	0	0	1.000
LA	10	3	1	.769	312	200	5	2	0	.714	5	1	1	.786
SF	7	6	1	.538	303	310	3	3	1	.500	4	3	0	.571
ATL	2	12	0	.143	170	389	1	6	0	.143	1	6	0	.143

Central Division

Team	W	L	T	Pct	Pts	Opp	HW	HL	HT	HPct	AW	AL	AT	APct
MIN	8	6	0	.571	282	242	4	3	0	.571	4	3	0	.571
CHI	7	7	0	.500	250	333	2	5	0	.286	5	2	0	.714
GB	6	7	1	.462	281	227	2	5	0	.286	4	2	1	.643
DET	4	8	2	.333	207	241	1	4	2	.286	3	4	0	.429

Scoring

	TD	1XP	2XP	FG	SAF	PTS
Leroy Kelly, CLE	20	0		0	0	120
Mike Clark, DAL	0	54		17	0	105
Lou Michaels, BAL	0	48		18	0	102
Don Cockroft, CLE	0	46		18	0	100
Mac Percival, CHI	0	25		25	0	100

Rushing

	ATT	YDS	AVG	LG	TD
Leroy Kelly, CLE	248	1239	5.0	65	16
Ken Willard, SF	227	967	4.3	69t	7
Tom Woodeshick, PHI	217	947	4.4	54t	3
Dick Hoak, PIT	175	858	4.9	77t	3
Gale Sayers, CHI	138	856	6.2	63	2

Passing

	ATT	COM	YDS	TD	INT	LG
Earl Morrall, BAL	317	182	2909	26	84	17
Don Meredith, DAL	309	171	2500	21	65t	12
John Brodie, SF	404	234	3020	22	65t	21
Bart Starr, GB	171	109	1617	15	63t	8
Fran Tarkenton, NYG	337	182	2555	21	84	12

Receiving

	NO	YDS	AVG	LG	TD
Clifton McNeil, SF	71	994	14.0	65t	7
Roy Jefferson, PIT	58	1074	18.5	62	11
Lance Rentzel, DAL	54	1009	18.7	65t	6
Dan Abramowicz, NO	54	890	16.5	47t	7
Bob Hayes, DAL	53	909	17.2	54t	10

Interceptions

	NO	YDS	AVG	LG	TD
Willie Williams, NYG	10	103	24	0	10.3

Punting

	NO	YDS	AVG	LG	BL
Billy Lothridge, ATL	75	3324	44.3	70	0

Kickoff Returns

	NO	YDS	LG	TD	AVG
Preston Pearson, BAL	15	527	102t	2	35.1

Punt Returns

	NO	FC	YDS	LG	TD	AVG
Bob Hayes, DAL	15	10	312	90t	2	20.8

American Football League 1969

Eastern Division

Team	W	L	T	Pct	Pts	Opp	HW	HL	HT	HPct	AW	AL	AT	APct
NY	10	4	0	.714	353	269	5	2	0	.714	5	2	0	.714
HOU	6	6	2	.500	278	279	4	2	1	.643	2	4	1	.357
BUF	4	10	0	.286	230	359	4	3	0	.571	0	7	0	.000
BOS	4	10	0	.286	266	316	2	5	0	.286	2	5	0	.286
MIA	3	10	1	.231	233	332	2	4	1	.357	1	6	0	.143

Western Division

Team	W	L	T	Pct	Pts	Opp	HW	HL	HT	HPct	AW	AL	AT	APct
OAK	12	1	1	.923	377	242	7	0	0	1.000	5	1	1	.786
KC	11	3	0	.786	359	177	6	1	0	.857	5	2	0	.714
SD	8	6	0	.571	288	276	5	2	0	.714	3	4	0	.429
DEN	5	8	1	.385	297	344	4	2	1	.643	1	6	0	.143
CIN	4	9	1	.308	280	367	4	3	0	.571	0	6	1	.071

Scoring

	TD	1XP	2XP	FG	SAF	PTS
Jim Turner, NY	0	33	0	32	0	129
Jan Stenerud, KC	0	38	0	27	0	119
George Blanda, OAK	0	45	0	20	0	105
Roy Gerela, HOU	0	29	0	19	0	86
Warren Wells, OAK	14	0	0	0	0	84

Rushing

	ATT	YDS	AVG	LG	TD
Dickie Post, SD	182	873	4.8	60	6
Jim Nance, BOS	193	750	3.9	43	6
Hoyle Granger, HOU	186	740	4.0	23	3
Mike Garrett, KC	168	732	4.4	34t	6
Floyd Little, DEN	146	729	5.0	48t	6

Passing

	ATT	COM	YDS	TD	INT	LG
Greg Cook, CIN	197	106	1854	15	78t	11
Joe Namath, NY	361	185	2734	19	60t	17
Daryle Lamonica, OAK	426	221	3302	34	80t	25
Mike Livingston, KC	161	84	1123	4	93t	6
John Hadl, SD	324	158	2253	10	76t	11

Receiving

	NO	YDS	AVG	LG	TD
Lance Alworth, SD	64	1003	15.7	76t	4
Fred Biletnikoff, OAK	54	837	15.5	53t	12
Al Denson, DEN	53	809	15.3	62t	10
Alvin Reed, HOU	51	664	13.0	43t	2
Warren Wells, OAK	47	1260	26.8	80t	14

Interceptions

	NO	YDS	AVG	LG	TD
Emmitt Thomas, KC	9	146	45t	1	16.2

Punting

	NO	YDS	AVG	LG	BL
Dennis Partee, SD	71	3169	44.6	62	0

Kickoff Returns

	NO	YDS	LG	TD	AVG
Bill Thompson, DEN	18	513	63	0	28.5

Punt Returns

	NO	FC	YDS	LG	TD	AVG
Bill Thompson, DEN	25	4	288	40	0	11.5

National Football League 1969

EASTERN CONFERENCE
Century Division

Team	W	L	T	Pct	Pts	Opp	HW	HL	HT	HPct	AW	AL	AT	APct
CLE	10	3	1	.769	351	300	5	1	1	.786	5	2	0	.714
NYG	6	8	0	.429	264	298	5	2	0	.714	1	6	0	.143
STL	4	9	1	.308	314	389	3	4	0	.429	1	5	1	.214
PIT	1	13	0	.071	218	404	1	6	0	.143	0	7	0	.000

Capitol Division

Team	W	L	T	Pct	Pts	Opp	HW	HL	HT	HPct	AW	AL	AT	APct
DAL	11	2	1	.846	369	223	6	0	1	.929	5	2	0	.714
WAS	7	5	2	.583	307	319	4	2	1	.643	3	3	1	.500
NO	5	9	0	.357	311	393	3	4	0	.429	2	5	0	.286
PHI	4	9	1	.308	279	377	2	5	0	.286	2	4	1	.357

WESTERN CONFERENCE
Coastal Division

Team	W	L	T	Pct	Pts	Opp	HW	HL	HT	HPct	AW	AL	AT	APct
LA	11	3	0	.786	320	243	5	2	0	.714	6	1	0	.857
BAL	8	5	1	.615	279	268	4	2	1	.643	4	3	0	.571
ATL	6	8	0	.429	276	268	4	3	0	.571	2	5	0	.286
SF	4	8	2	.333	277	319	3	3	1	.500	1	5	1	.214

Central Division

Team	W	L	T	Pct	Pts	Opp	HW	HL	HT	HPct	AW	AL	AT	APct
MIN	12	2	0	.857	379	133	7	0	0	1.000	5	2	0	.714
DET	9	4	1	.692	259	188	5	2	0	.714	4	2	1	.643
GB	8	6	0	.571	269	221	5	2	0	.714	3	4	0	.429
CHI	1	13	0	.071	210	339	1	6	0	.143	0	7	0	.000

Scoring

	TD	1XP	2XP	FG	SAF	PTS
Fred Cox, MIN	0	43		26	0	121
Mike Clark, DAL	0	43		20	0	103
Bruce Gossett, LA	0	36		22	0	102
Errol Mann, DET	0	26		25	0	101
Tom Dempsey, NO	0	33		22	0	99

Rushing

	ATT	YDS	AVG	LG	TD
Gale Sayers, CHI	236	1032	4.4	28	8
Calvin Hill, DAL	204	942	4.6	55	8
Tom Matte, BAL	235	909	3.9	26	11
Larry Brown, WAS	202	888	4.4	57	4
Tom Woodeshick, PHI	186	831	4.5	21	4

Passing

	ATT	COM	YDS	TD	INT	LG
Sonny Jurgensen, WAS	442	274	3102	22	88t	15
Bart Starr, GB	148	92	1161	9	51	6
Fran Tarkenton, NYG	409	220	2918	23	65	8
Roman Gabriel, LA	399	217	2549	24	93t	7
Craig Morton, DAL	302	162	2619	21	67t	15

Receiving

	NO	YDS	AVG	LG	TD
Dan Abramowicz, NO	73	1015	13.9	49t	7
Charley Taylor, WAS	71	883	12.4	88t	8
Roy Jefferson, PIT	67	1079	16.1	63	9
Harold Jackson, PHI	65	1116	17.2	65t	9
Dave Williams, STL	56	702	12.5	61	7

Interceptions

	NO	YDS	AVG	LG	TD	
Mel Renfro, DAL	10	118	41	0		11.8

Punting

	NO	YDS	AVG	LG	BL
David Lee, BAL	57	2580	45.3	66	0

Kickoff Returns

	NO	YDS	LG	TD	AVG
Bobby Williams, DET	17	563	96t	1	33.1

Punt Returns

	NO	FC	YDS	LG	TD	AVG
Alvin Haymond, LA	33	8	435	52	0	13.2

National Football League 1970

AMERICAN FOOTBALL CONFERENCE
Eastern Division

Team	W	L	T	Pct	Pts	Opp	HW	HL	HT	HPct	AW	AL	AT	APct
BAL	11	2	1	.846	321	234	5	1	1	.786	6	1	0	.857
MIA	10	4	0	.714	297	228	6	1	0	.857	4	3	0	.571
NYJ	4	10	0	.286	255	286	2	5	0	.286	2	5	0	.286

Team	W	L	T	Pct	Pts	Opp	HW	HL	HT	HPct	AW	AL	AT	APct
BUF	3	10	1	.231	204	337	1	6	0	.143	2	4	1	.357
BOS	2	12	0	.143	149	361	1	6	0	.143	1	6	0	.143

Central Division

Team	W	L	T	Pct	Pts	Opp	HW	HL	HT	HPct	AW	AL	AT	APct
CIN	8	6	0	.571	312	255	5	2	0	.714	3	4	0	.429
CLE	7	7	0	.500	286	265	4	3	0	.571	3	4	0	.429
PIT	5	9	0	.357	210	272	4	3	0	.571	1	6	0	.143
HOU	3	10	1	.231	217	352	1	6	0	.143	2	4	1	.357

Western Division

Team	W	L	T	Pct	Pts	Opp	HW	HL	HT	HPct	AW	AL	AT	APct
OAK	8	4	2	.667	300	293	6	1	0	.857	2	3	2	.429
KC	7	5	2	.583	272	244	4	1	2	.714	3	4	0	.429
SD	5	6	3	.455	282	278	2	3	2	.429	3	3	1	.500
DEN	5	8	1	.385	253	264	3	3	1	.500	2	5	0	.286

NATIONAL FOOTBALL CONFERENCE
Eastern Division

Team	W	L	T	Pct	Pts	Opp	HW	HL	HT	HPct	AW	AL	AT	APct
DAL	10	4	0	.714	299	221	6	1	0	.857	4	3	0	.571
NYG	9	5	0	.643	301	270	5	2	0	.714	4	3	0	.571
STL	8	5	1	.615	325	228	6	1	0	.857	2	4	1	.357
WAS	6	8	0	.429	297	314	4	3	0	.571	2	5	0	.286
PHI	3	10	1	.231	241	332	3	3	1	.500	0	7	0	.000

Central Division

Team	W	L	T	Pct	Pts	Opp	HW	HL	HT	HPct	AW	AL	AT	APct
MIN	12	2	0	.857	335	143	7	0	0	1.000	5	2	0	.714
DET	10	4	0	.714	347	202	6	1	0	.857	4	3	0	.571
GB	6	8	0	.429	196	293	4	3	0	.571	2	5	0	.286
CHI	6	8	0	.429	256	261	3	4	0	.429	3	4	0	.429

Western Division

Team	W	L	T	Pct	Pts	Opp	HW	HL	HT	HPct	AW	AL	AT	APct
SF	10	3	1	.789	352	267	5	1	1	.786	5	2	0	.714
LA	9	4	1	.692	325	202	3	3	1	.500	6	1	0	.857
ATL	4	8	2	.333	206	261	3	4	0	.429	1	4	2	.286
NO	2	11	1	.154	172	347	2	5	0	.286	0	6	1	.071

Scoring

	TD	1XP	2XP	FG	SAF	PTS
Fred Cox, MIN	0	35		30	0	125
David Ray, LA	0	34		29	0	121
Jan Stenerud, KC	0	26		30	0	116
Horst Muhlmann, CIN	0	33		25	0	108
Pete Gogolak, NYG	0	32		25	0	107

Rushing

	ATT	YDS	AVG	LG	TD
Larry Brown, WAS	237	1125	4.7	75t	5
Ron Johnson, NYG	263	1027	3.9	68t	8
MacArthur Lane, STL	206	977	4.7	75	11
Floyd Little, DEN	209	901	4.3	80t	3
Larry Csonka, MIA	193	874	4.5	53	6

Passing

	ATT	COM	YDS	TD	INT	LG
John Brodie, SF	378	223	2941	24	79t	10
Sonny Jurgensen, WAS	337	202	2354	23	66t	10
Fran Tarkenton, NYG	389	219	2777	19	59	12
Daryle Lamonica, OAK	356	179	2516	22	60t	15
Craig Morton, DAL	207	102	1819	15	89t	7

Receiving

	NO	YDS	AVG	LG	TD
Dick Gordon, CHI	71	1026	14.5	69t	13
Marlin Briscoe, BUF	57	1036	18.2	48	8
Dan Abramowicz, NO	55	906	16.5	48	5
Gene Washington, SF	53	1100	20.8	79t	12
Jack Snow, LA	51	859	16.8	71	7

Interceptions

	NO	YDS	AVG	LG	TD	
Johnny Robinson, KC	10	155	57	0	15.5	

Punting

	NO	YDS	AVG	LG	BL
Dave Lewis, CIN	79	3651	46.2	63	0

Kickoff Returns

	NO	YDS	LG	TD	AVG
Jim Duncan, BAL	20	707	99t	1	35.4

Punt Returns

	NO	FC	YDS	LG	TD	AVG
Ed Podolak, KC	23	21	311	60	0	13.5

National Football League 1971
AMERICAN FOOTBALL CONFERENCE
Eastern Division

Team	W	L	T	Pct	Pts	Opp	HW	HL	HT	HPct	AW	AL	AT	APct
MIA	10	3	1	.769	315	174	6	1	0	.857	4	2	1	.643
BAL	10	4	0	.714	313	140	5	2	0	.714	5	2	0	.714
NE	6	8	0	.429	238	325	5	2	0	.714	1	6	0	.143
NYJ	6	8	0	.429	212	299	4	3	0	.571	2	5	0	.286
BUF	1	13	0	.071	184	394	1	6	0	.143	0	7	0	.000

Central Division

Team	W	L	T	Pct	Pts	Opp	HW	HL	HT	HPct	AW	AL	AT	APct
CLE	9	5	0	.643	285	273	4	3	0	.571	5	2	0	.714
PIT	6	8	0	.429	246	292	5	2	0	.714	1	6	0	.143
HOU	4	9	1	.308	251	330	3	3	1	.500	1	6	0	.143
CIN	4	10	0	.286	284	265	3	4	0	.429	1	6	0	.143

Western Division

Team	W	L	T	Pct	Pts	Opp	HW	HL	HT	HPct	AW	AL	AT	APct
KC	10	3	1	.769	302	208	7	0	0	1.000	3	3	1	.500
OAK	8	4	2	.667	344	278	5	1	1	.786	3	3	1	.500
SD	6	8	0	.429	311	341	6	1	0	.857	0	7	0	.000
DEN	4	9	1	.308	203	275	2	4	1	.357	2	5	0	.286

NATIONAL FOOTBALL CONFERENCE
Eastern Division

Team	W	L	T	Pct	Pts	Opp	HW	HL	HT	HPct	AW	AL	AT	APct
DAL	11	3	0	.786	406	222	6	1	0	.857	5	2	0	.714
WAS	9	4	1	.692	276	190	4	2	1	.643	5	2	0	.714
PHI	6	7	1	.462	221	302	3	4	0	.429	3	3	1	.500
STL	4	9	1	.308	231	279	1	5	1	.214	3	4	0	.429
NYG	4	10	0	.286	228	362	1	6	0	.143	3	4	0	.429

Central Division

Team	W	L	T	Pct	Pts	Opp	HW	HL	HT	HPct	AW	AL	AT	APct
MIN	11	3	0	.786	245	139	5	2	0	.714	6	1	0	.857
DET	7	6	1	.538	341	286	3	4	0	.429	4	2	1	.643
CHI	6	8	0	.429	185	276	4	3	0	.571	2	5	0	.286
GB	4	8	2	.333	274	298	3	3	1	.500	1	5	1	.214

Western Division

Team	W	L	T	Pct	Pts	Opp	HW	HL	HT	HPct	AW	AL	AT	APct
SF	9	5	0	.643	300	216	4	3	0	.571	5	2	0	.714
LA	8	5	1	.615	313	260	4	2	1	.643	4	3	0	.571
ATL	7	6	1	.538	274	277	4	3	0	.571	3	3	1	.500
NO	4	8	2	.333	266	347	2	4	1	.357	2	4	1	.357

Scoring

	TD	1XP	2XP	FG	SAF	PTS
Garo Yepremian, MIA	0	33		28	0	117
Curt Knight, WAS	0	27		29	0	114
Jan Stenerud, KC	0	32		26	0	110
Errol Mann, DET	0	37		22	0	103
Bruce Gossett, SF	0	32		23	0	101

Rushing

	ATT	YDS	AVG	LG	TD
Floyd Little, DEN	284	1133	4.0	40	6
John Brockington, GB	216	1105	5.1	52t	4
Larry Csonka, MIA	195	1051	5.4	28	7
Steve Owens, DET	246	1035	4.2	23	8
Willie Ellison, LA	211	1000	4.7	80t	4

Passing

	ATT	COM	YDS	TD	INT	LG
Roger Staubach, DAL	211	126	1882	15	85t	4
Bob Griese, MIA	263	145	2089	19	86t	9
Len Dawson, KC	301	167	2504	15	82	13
Virgil Carter, CIN	222	138	1624	10	90t	7
Greg Landry, DET	261	136	2237	16	76t	13

Receiving

	NO	YDS	AVG	LG	TD
Fred Biletnikoff, OAK	61	929	15.2	49	9
Bob Tucker, NYG	59	791	13.4	63t	4
Otis Taylor, KC	57	1110	19.5	82	7
Ted Kwalick, SF	52	664	12.8	42t	5
Randy Vataha, NE	51	872	17.1	88t	9

Interceptions

	NO	YDS	AVG	LG	TD	
Bill Bradley, PHI	11	248	51	0		22.5

Punting

	NO	YDS	AVG	LG	BL
Dave Lewis, CIN	72	3229		56	0
	72		44.8		

Kickoff Returns

	NO	YDS	LG	TD	AVG
Travis Williams, LA	25	743	105t	1	29.7

Punt Returns

	NO	FC	YDS	LG	TD	AVG
Speedy Duncan, WAS	22	9	233	33	0	10.6

National Football League 1972

AMERICAN FOOTBALL CONFERENCE
Eastern Division

Team	W	L	T	Pct	Pts	Opp	HW	HL	HT	HPct	AW	AL	AT	APct
MIA	14	0	0	1.000	385	171	7	0	0	1.000	7	0	0	1.000
NYJ	7	7	0	.500	367	324	4	3	0	.571	3	4	0	.429
BAL	5	9	0	.429	235	252	2	5	0	.286	3	4	0	.429
BUF	4	9	1	.321	257	377	2	4	1	.357	2	5	0	.286
NE	3	11	0	.214	192	446	2	5	0	.286	1	6	0	.143

Central Division

Team	W	L	T	Pct	Pts	Opp	HW	HL	HT	HPct	AW	AL	AT	APct
PIT	11	3	0	.786	343	175	7	0	0	1.000	4	3	0	.571
CLE	10	4	0	.714	268	249	4	3	0	.571	6	1	0	.857
CIN	8	6	0	.571	299	229	4	3	0	.571	4	3	0	.571
HOU	1	13	0	.071	164	380	1	6	0	.143	0	7	0	.000

Western Division

Team	W	L	T	Pct	Pts	Opp	HW	HL	HT	HPct	AW	AL	AT	APct
OAK	10	3	1	.750	365	248	5	1	1	.786	5	2	0	.714
KC	8	6	0	.571	287	254	3	4	0	.429	5	2	0	.714
DEN	5	9	0	.357	325	350	3	4	0	.429	2	5	0	.286
SD	4	9	1	.321	264	344	2	5	0	.286	2	4	1	.357

NATIONAL FOOTBALL CONFERENCE
Eastern Division

Team	W	L	T	Pct	Pts	Opp	HW	HL	HT	HPct	AW	AL	AT	APct
WAS	11	3	0	.786	336	218	6	1	0	.857	5	2	0	.714
DAL	10	4	0	.714	319	240	5	2	0	.714	5	2	0	.714
NYG	8	6	0	.571	331	247	4	3	0	.571	4	3	0	.571
STL	4	9	1	.321	193	303	2	5	0	.286	2	4	1	.357
PHI	2	11	1	.179	145	352	0	6	1	.071	2	5	0	.286

Central Division

Team	W	L	T	Pct	Pts	Opp	HW	HL	HT	HPct	AW	AL	AT	APct
GB	10	4	0	.714	304	226	4	3	0	.571	6	1	0	.857
DET	8	5	1	.607	339	290	5	2	0	.714	3	3	1	.500
MIN	7	7	0	.500	301	252	3	4	0	.429	4	3	0	.571
CHI	4	9	1	.321	225	275	1	5	1	.214	3	4	0	.429

Western Division

Team	W	L	T	Pct	Pts	Opp	HW	HL	HT	HPct	AW	AL	AT	APct
SF	8	5	1	.607	353	249	4	2	1	.643	4	3	0	.571
ATL	7	7	0	.500	269	274	4	3	0	.571	3	4	0	.429
LA	6	7	1	.464	291	286	4	3	0	.571	2	4	1	.357
NO	2	11	1	.179	215	361	2	5	0	.286	0	6	1	.071

Scoring

	TD	1XP	2XP	FG	SAF	PTS
Chester Marcol, GB	0	29		33	0	128
Bobby Howfield, NYJ	0	40		27	0	121
Roy Gerela, PIT	0	35		28	0	119
Garo Yepremian, MIA	0	43		24	0	115
Horst Muhlmann, CIN	0	30		27	0	111

Rushing

	ATT	YDS	AVG	LG	TD
O.J. Simpson, BUF	292	1251	4.3	94t	6
Larry Brown, WAS	285	1216	4.3	38t	8
Ron Johnson, NYG	298	1182	4.0	35t	9
Larry Csonka, MIA	213	1117	5.2	45	6
Marv Hubbard, OAK	219	1100	5.0	39	4

Passing

	ATT	COM	YDS	TD	INT	LG
Norm Snead, NYG	325	196	2307	17	94t	12
Earl Morrall, MIA	150	83	1360	11	49	7
Fran Tarkenton, MIN	378	215	2651	18	76t	13
Bob Berry, ATL	277	154	2158	13	57t	12
Billy Kilmer, WAS	225	120	1648	19	89t	11

Receiving

	NO	YDS	AVG	LG	TD
Harold Jackson, PHI	62	1048	16.9	77t	4
Fred Biletnikoff, OAK	58	802	13.8	39t	7
Otis Taylor, KC	57	821	14.4	44	6
Chip Myers, CIN	57	792	13.9	42	3
Bob Tucker, NYG	55	764	13.9	39	4

Interceptions

	NO	YDS	AVG	LG	TD	
Bill Bradley, PHI	9	73	21	0		8.1

Punting

	NO	YDS	AVG	LG	BL
Jerrel Wilson, KC	65	2960	45.5	69	1

Kickoff Returns

	NO	YDS	LG	TD	AVG
Ron Smith, CHI	30	924	94t	1	30.8

Punt Returns

	NO	FC	YDS	LG	TD	AVG
Ken Ellis, GB	14	1	215	80t	1	15.4

National Football League 1973

AMERICAN FOOTBALL CONFERENCE
Eastern Division

Team	W	L	T	Pct	Pts	Opp	HW	HL	HT	HPct	AW	AL	AT	APct
MIA	12	2	0	.857	343	150	7	0	0	1.000	5	2	0	.714
BUF	9	5	0	.643	259	230	5	2	0	.714	4	3	0	.571
NE	5	9	0	.357	258	300	3	4	0	.429	2	5	0	.286
BAL	4	10	0	.286	226	341	3	4	0	.429	1	6	0	.143
NYJ	4	10	0	.286	240	306	2	4	0	.333	2	6	0	.250

Central Division

Team	W	L	T	Pct	Pts	Opp	HW	HL	HT	HPct	AW	AL	AT	APct
CIN	10	4	0	.714	286	231	7	0	0	1.000	3	4	0	.429
PIT	10	4	0	.714	347	210	7	1	0	.875	3	3	0	.500
CLE	7	5	2	.571	234	255	5	1	1	.786	2	4	1	.357
HOU	1	13	0	.071	199	447	0	7	0	.000	1	6	0	.143

Western Division

Team	W	L	T	Pct	Pts	Opp	HW	HL	HT	HPct	AW	AL	AT	APct
OAK	9	4	1	.679	292	175	5	2	0	.714	4	2	1	.643
DEN	7	5	2	.571	354	296	3	3	1	.500	4	2	1	.643
KC	7	5	2	.571	231	192	5	1	1	.786	2	4	1	.357
SD	2	11	1	.179	188	386	2	5	0	.286	0	6	1	.071

NATIONAL FOOTBALL CONFERENCE
Eastern Division

Team	W	L	T	Pct	Pts	Opp	HW	HL	HT	HPct	AW	AL	AT	APct
DAL	10	4	0	.714	382	203	6	1	0	.857	4	3	0	.571
WAS	10	4	0	.714	325	198	7	0	0	1.000	3	4	0	.429
PHI	5	8	1	.393	310	393	4	3	0	.571	1	5	1	.214
STL	4	9	1	.321	286	365	2	4	1	.357	2	5	0	.286
NYG	2	11	1	.179	226	362	2	4	1	.357	0	7	0	.000

Central Division

Team	W	L	T	Pct	Pts	Opp	HW	HL	HT	HPct	AW	AL	AT	APct
MIN	12	2	0	.857	296	168	7	0	0	1.000	5	2	0	.714
DET	6	7	1	.464	271	247	4	3	0	.571	2	4	1	.357
GB	5	7	2	.429	202	259	3	2	2	.571	2	5	0	.286
CHI	3	11	0	.214	195	334	1	6	0	.143	2	5	0	.286

Western Division

Team	W	L	T	Pct	Pts	Opp	HW	HL	HT	HPct	AW	AL	AT	APct
LA	12	2	0	.857	388	178	7	0	0	1.000	5	2	0	.714
ATL	9	5	0	.643	318	223	4	3	0	.571	5	2	0	.714
NO	5	9	0	.357	163	312	5	2	0	.714	0	7	0	.000
SF	5	9	0	.357	262	319	3	4	0	.429	2	5	0	.286

Scoring

	TD	1XP	2XP	FG	SAF	PTS
David, Ray, LA	0	40		30	0	130
Roy Gerela, PIT	0	36		29	0	123
Garo Yepremian, MIA	0	38		25	0	113
Nick Mike-Mayer, ATL	0	34		26	0	112
Tom Dempsey, PHI	0	34		24	0	106
Jim Turner, DEN	0	40		22	0	106

Rushing

	ATT	YDS	AVG	LG	TD
O.J. Simpson, BUF	332	2003	6.0	80t	12
John Brockington, GB	265	1144	4.3	53	3
Calvin Hill, DAL	273	1142	4.2	21	6
Lawrence McCutcheon, LA	210	1097	5.2	37	2
Larry Csonka, MIA	219	1003	4.6	25	5

Passing

	ATT	COM	YDS	TD	INT	LG
Roger Staubach, DAL	286	179	2428	23	53	15
Ken Stabler, OAK	260	163	1997	14	80t	10
John Hadl, LA	258	135	2008	22	69t	11
Fran Tarkenton, MIN	274	169	2113	15	54t	7
Roman Gabriel, PHI	460	270	3219	23	80t	12
Bob Griese, MIA	218	116	1422	17	46	8
Ken Anderson, CIN	329	179	2428	18	78t	12

Receiving

	NO	YDS	AVG	LG	TD
Harold Carmichael, PHI	67	1116	16.7	73	9
Charley Taylor, WAS	59	801	13.6	53	7
Fred Willis, HOU	57	371	6.5	50	1
Charle Young, PHI	55	854	15.5	80t	6
Ed Podolak, KC	55	445	8.1	25	0

Interceptions

	NO	YDS	AVG	LG	TD	
Dick Anderson, MIA	8	163	38t	2	20.4	
Mike Wagner, PIT	8	134	38	0	16.8	

Punting

	NO	YDS	AVG	LG	BL
Jerrel Wilson, KC	79	3642	46.1	68	1

Kickoff Returns

	NO	YDS	LG	TD	AVG
Carl Garrett, CHI	16	486	67	0	30.4

Punt Returns

	NO	FC	YDS	LG	TD	AVG
Bruce Taylor, SF	15	6	207	61	0	13.8

National Football League 1974
AMERICAN FOOTBALL CONFERENCE
Eastern Division

Team	W	L	T	Pct	Pts	Opp	HW	HL	HT	HPct	AW	AL	AT	APct
MIA	11	3	0	.786	327	216	7	0	0	1.000	4	3	0	.571
BUF	9	5	0	.643	264	244	5	2	0	.714	4	3	0	.571
NE	7	7	0	.500	348	298	3	4	0	.429	4	3	0	.571
NYJ	7	7	0	.500	279	300	3	4	0	.429	4	3	0	.571
BAL	2	12	0	.143	190	329	0	7	0	.000	2	5	0	.286

Central Division

Team	W	L	T	Pct	Pts	Opp	HW	HL	HT	HPct	AW	AL	AT	APct
PIT	10	3	1	.750	305	189	5	2	0	.714	5	1	1	.786
CIN	7	7	0	.500	283	259	4	3	0	.571	3	4	0	.429
HOU	7	7	0	.500	236	282	3	4	0	.429	4	3	0	.571
CLE	4	10	0	.286	251	344	3	4	0	.429	1	6	0	.143

Western Division

Team	W	L	T	Pct	Pts	Opp	HW	HL	HT	HPct	AW	AL	AT	APct
OAK	12	2	0	.857	355	228	6	1	0	.857	6	1	0	.857
DEN	7	6	1	.536	302	294	3	3	1	.500	4	3	0	.571
KC	5	9	0	.357	233	293	1	6	0	.143	4	3	0	.571
SD	5	9	0	.357	212	285	3	4	0	.429	2	5	0	.286

NATIONAL FOOTBALL CONFERENCE
Eastern Division

Team	W	L	T	Pct	Pts	Opp	HW	HL	HT	HPct	AW	AL	AT	APct
STL	10	4	0	.714	285	218	5	2	0	.714	5	2	0	.714
WAS	10	4	0	.714	320	196	6	1	0	.857	4	3	0	.571
DAL	8	6	0	.571	297	235	5	2	0	.714	3	4	0	.429
PHI	7	7	0	.500	242	217	5	2	0	.714	2	5	0	.286
NYG	2	12	0	.143	195	299	0	7	0	.000	2	5	0	.286

Central Division

Team	W	L	T	Pct	Pts	Opp	HW	HL	HT	HPct	AW	AL	AT	APct
MIN	10	4	0	.714	310	195	4	3	0	.571	6	1	0	.857
DET	7	7	0	.500	256	270	5	2	0	.714	2	5	0	.286
GB	6	8	0	.429	210	206	4	3	0	.571	2	5	0	.286
CHI	4	10	0	.286	152	279	4	3	0	.571	0	7	0	.000

Western Division

Team	W	L	T	Pct	Pts	Opp	HW	HL	HT	HPct	AW	AL	AT	APct
LA	10	4	0	.714	263	181	6	1	0	.857	4	3	0	.571
SF	6	8	0	.429	226	236	3	4	0	.429	3	4	0	.429
NO	5	9	0	.357	166	263	4	3	0	.571	1	6	0	.143
ATL	3	11	0	.214	111	271	2	5	0	.286	1	6	0	.143

Scoring

	TD	1XP	2XP	FG	SAF	PTS
Chester Marcol, GB	0	19		25	0	94
Roy Gerela, PIT	0	33		20	0	93
Errol Mann, DET	0	23		23	0	92
Chuck Foreman, MIN	15	0		0	0	90
John Smith, NE	0	42		16	0	90

Rushing

	ATT	YDS	AVG	LG	TD
Otis Armstrong, DEN	263	1407	5.3	43	9
Don Woods, SD	227	1162	5.1	56t	7
O.J. Simpson, BUF	270	1125	4.2	41t	3
Lawrence McCutcheon, LA	236	1109	4.7	23t	3
Franco Harris, PIT	208	1006	4.8	54	5

Passing

	ATT	COM	YDS	TD	INT	LG
Ken Anderson, CIN	328	213	2667	18	77t	10
Ken Stabler, OAK	310	178	2469	26	67t	12
Sonny Jurgensen, WAS	167	107	1185	11	44	5
James Harris, LA	198	106	1544	11	50t	6
Bob Griese, MIA	253	152	1968	16	54	15
Charley Johnson, DEN	244	136	1969	13	73t	9

Receiving

	NO	YDS	AVG	LG	TD
Lydell Mitchell, BAL	72	544	7.6	24	2
Charle Young, PHI	63	696	11.0	29	3
Drew Pearson, DAL	62	1087	17.5	50t	2
Cliff Branch, OAK	60	1092	18.2	67t	13
Harold Carmichael, PHI	56	649	11.6	39	8

Interceptions

	NO	YDS	AVG	LG	TD	
Emmitt Thomas, KC	12	214	73t	2	17.8	

Punting

	NO	YDS	AVG	LG	BL
Ray Guy, OAK	74	3124	42.2	66	0

Kickoff Returns

	NO	YDS	LG	TD	AVG
Terry Metcalf, STL	20	623	94t	1	31.1

Punt Returns

	NO	FC	YDS	LG	TD	AVG
Lemar Parrish, CIN	18	1	338	90t	2	18.8

National Football League 1975

AMERICAN FOOTBALL CONFERENCE
Eastern Division

Team	W	L	T	Pct	Pts	Opp	HW	HL	HT	HPct	AW	AL	AT	APct
BAL	10	4	0	.714	395	269	5	2	0	.714	5	2	0	.714
MIA	10	4	0	.714	357	222	5	2	0	.714	5	2	0	.714
BUF	8	6	0	.571	420	355	3	4	0	.429	5	2	0	.714
NE	3	11	0	.214	258	358	2	5	0	.286	1	6	0	.143
NYJ	3	11	0	.214	258	433	1	6	0	.143	2	5	0	.286

Central Division

Team	W	L	T	Pct	Pts	Opp	HW	HL	HT	HPct	AW	AL	AT	APct
PIT	12	2	0	.857	373	162	6	1	0	.857	6	1	0	.857
CIN	11	3	0	.786	340	246	6	1	0	.857	5	2	0	.704
HOU	10	4	0	.714	293	226	5	2	0	.714	5	2	0	.714
CLE	3	11	0	.214	218	372	3	4	0	.429	0	7	0	.000

Western Division

Team	W	L	T	Pct	Pts	Opp	HW	HL	HT	HPct	AW	AL	AT	APct
OAK	11	3	0	.786	375	255	6	1	0	.857	5	2	0	.714
DEN	6	8	0	.429	254	307	5	2	0	.714	1	6	0	.143
KC	5	9	0	.357	282	341	3	4	0	.429	2	5	0	.286
SD	2	12	0	.143	189	345	1	6	0	.143	1	6	0	.143

NATIONAL FOOTBALL CONFERENCE
Eastern Division

Team	W	L	T	Pct	Pts	Opp	HW	HL	HT	HPct	AW	AL	AT	APct
STL	11	3	0	.786	356	276	6	1	0	.857	5	2	0	.714
DAL	10	4	0	.714	350	268	5	2	0	.714	5	2	0	.714
WAS	8	6	0	.571	325	276	5	2	0	.714	3	4	0	.429
NYG	5	9	0	.357	216	306	2	5	0	.286	3	4	0	.429
PHI	4	10	0	.286	225	302	2	5	0	.286	2	5	0	.286

Central Division

Team	W	L	T	Pct	Pts	Opp	HW	HL	HT	HPct	AW	AL	AT	APct
MIN	12	2	0	.857	377	180	7	0	0	1.000	5	2	0	.714
DET	7	7	0	.500	245	262	4	3	0	.571	3	4	0	.429
CHI	4	10	0	.286	191	379	3	4	0	.429	1	6	0	.143
GB	4	10	0	.286	226	285	3	4	0	.429	1	6	0	.143

Western Division

Team	W	L	T	Pct	Pts	Opp	HW	HL	HT	HPct	AW	AL	AT	APct
LA	12	2	0	.857	312	135	6	1	0	.857	6	1	0	.857
SF	5	9	0	.357	255	286	2	5	0	.286	3	4	0	.429
ATL	4	10	0	.286	240	289	3	4	0	.429	1	6	0	.143
NO	2	12	0	.143	165	360	2	5	0	.286	0	7	0	.000

Scoring

	TD	1XP	2XP	FG	SAF	PTS
O.J. Simpson, BUF	23	0		0	0	138
Chuck Foreman, MIN	22	0		0	0	132
Toni Fritsch, DAL	0	38		22	0	104
Jim Bakken, STL	0	40		19	0	97
Pete Banaszak, OAK	16	0		0	0	96
Jan Stenerud, KC	0	30		22	0	96

Rushing

	ATT	YDS	AVG	LG	TD
O.J. Simpson, BUF	329	1817	5.5	88t	16
Franco Harris, PIT	262	1246	4.8	36	10
Lydell Mitchell, BAL	289	1193	4.1	70t	11
Jim Otis, STL	269	1076	4.0	30	5
Chuck Foreman, MIN	280	1070	3.8	31t	13

Passing

	ATT	COM	YDS	TD	INT	LG
Ken Anderson, CIN	377	228	3169	21	55	11
Fran Tarkenton, MIN	425	273	2994	25	46	13
Len Dawson, KC	140	93	1095	5	51	4
Bert Jones, BAL	344	203	2483	18	90t	8
Terry Bradshaw, PIT	286	165	2055	18	59	9

Receiving

	NO	YDS	AVG	LG	TD
Chuck Foreman, MIN	73	691	9.5	33	9
Reggie Rucker, CLE	60	770	12.8	40t	3
Lydell Mitchell, BAL	60	544	9.1	35t	4
Ken Payne, GB	58	766	13.2	54	0
Bob Chandler, BUF	55	746	13.6	35	6

Interceptions

	NO	YDS	AVG	LG	TD	
Mel Blount, PIT	11	121	47	0		11.0

Punting

	NO	YDS	AVG	LG	BL
Ray Guy, OAK	68	2979	43.8	64	0

Kickoff Returns

	NO	YDS	LG	TD	AVG
Walter Payton, CHI	14	444	70	0	31.7

Punt Returns

	NO	FC	YDS	LG	TD	AVG
Billy Johnson, HOU	40	1	612	83t	3	15.3

National Football League 1976
AMERICAN FOOTBALL CONFERENCE
Eastern Division

Team	W	L	T	Pct	Pts	Opp	HW	HL	HT	HPct	AW	AL	AT	APct
BAL	11	3	0	.786	417	246	6	1	0	.857	5	2	0	.714
NE	11	3	0	.786	376	236	6	1	0	.857	5	2	0	.714
MIA	6	8	0	.429	263	264	3	4	0	.429	3	4	0	.429
NYJ	3	11	0	.214	169	383	2	5	0	.286	1	6	0	.143
BUF	2	12	0	.143	245	363	1	6	0	.143	1	6	0	.143

Central Division

Team	W	L	T	Pct	Pts	Opp	HW	HL	HT	HPct	AW	AL	AT	APct
PIT	10	4	0	.714	342	138	6	1	0	.857	4	3	0	.571
CIN	10	4	0	.714	335	210	6	1	0	.857	4	3	0	.571
CLE	9	5	0	.643	267	287	6	1	0	.857	3	4	0	.429
HOU	5	9	0	.357	222	273	3	4	0	.429	2	5	0	.286

Western Division

Team	W	L	T	Pct	Pts	Opp	HW	HL	HT	HPct	AW	AL	AT	APct
OAK	13	1	0	.929	350	237	7	0	0	1.000	6	1	0	.857
DEN	9	5	0	.643	315	206	6	1	0	.857	3	4	0	.429
SD	6	8	0	.429	248	285	3	4	0	.429	3	4	0	.429
KC	5	9	0	.357	290	376	1	6	0	.143	4	3	0	.571
TB	0	14	0	.000	125	412	0	7	0	.000	0	7	0	.000

NATIONAL FOOTBALL CONFERENCE
Eastern Division

Team	W	L	T	Pct	Pts	Opp	HW	HL	HT	HPct	AW	AL	AT	APct
DAL	11	3	0	.786	296	194	6	1	0	.857	5	2	0	.714
WAS	10	4	0	.714	291	217	5	2	0	.714	5	2	0	.714
STL	10	4	0	.714	309	267	6	1	0	.857	4	3	0	.571
PHI	4	10	0	.286	165	286	2	5	0	.286	2	5	0	.286
NYG	3	11	0	.214	170	250	3	4	0	.429	0	7	0	.000

Central Division

Team	W	L	T	Pct	Pts	Opp	HW	HL	HT	HPct	AW	AL	AT	APct
MIN	11	2	1	.821	305	176	6	0	1	.929	5	2	0	.714
CHI	7	7	0	.500	253	216	4	3	0	.571	3	4	0	.429
DET	6	8	0	.429	262	220	5	2	0	.714	1	6	0	.143
GB	5	9	0	.357	218	299	4	3	0	.571	1	6	0	.143

Western Division

Team	W	L	T	Pct	Pts	Opp	HW	HL	HT	HPct	AW	AL	AT	APct
LA	10	3	1	.750	351	190	5	2	0	.714	5	1	1	.786
SF	8	6	0	.571	270	190	4	3	0	.571	4	3	0	.571
ATL	4	10	0	.286	172	312	3	4	0	.429	1	6	0	.143
NO	4	10	0	.286	253	346	2	5	0	.286	2	5	0	.286
SEA	2	12	0	.143	229	429	1	6	0	.143	1	6	0	.143

Scoring

	TD	1XP	2XP	FG	SAF	PTS
Toni Linhart, BAL	0	49		20	0	109
Mark Moseley, WAS	0	31		22	0	97
Jim Bakken, STL	0	33		20	0	93
Jan Stenerud, KC	0	27		21	0	90
Fred Cox, MIN	0	32		19	0	89

Rushing

	ATT	YDS	AVG	LG	TD
O.J. Simpson, BUF	290	1503	5.2	75t	8
Walter Payton, CHI	311	1390	4.5	60	13
Delvin Williams, SF	248	1203	4.9	80t	7
Lydell Mitchell, BAL	289	1200	4.2	43	5
Lawrence McCutcheon, LA	291	1168	4.0	40	9

Passing

	ATT	COM	YDS	TD	INT	LG
Joe Ferguson, BUF	151	74	1086	9	58t	1
James Harris, LA	158	91	1460	8	80t	6
Greg Landry, DET	291	168	2191	17	74t	8
Fran Tarkenton, MIN	412	255	2961	17	56t	8
Jim Hart, STL	388	218	2946	18	77t	13

Receiving

	NO	YDS	AVG	LG	TD
MacArthur Lane, KC	66	686	10.4	44	1
Bob Chandler, BUF	61	824	13.5	58t	10
Lydell Mitchell, BAL	60	555	9.3	40t	3
Drew Pearson, DAL	58	806	13.9	40t	6
Chuck Foreman, MIN	55	567	10.3	41t	1

Interceptions

	NO	YDS	AVG	LG	TD
Monte Jackson, LA	10	173	46t	3	17.3

Punting

	NO	YDS	AVG	LG	BL
Marv Bateman, BUF	86	3678	42.8	78	1

Kickoff Returns

	NO	YDS	LG	TD	AVG
Duriel Harris, MIA	17	559	69	0	32.9

Punt Returns

	NO	FC	YDS	LG	TD	AVG
Rick Upchurch, DEN	39	3	536	92t	4	13.7

National Football League 1977

AMERICAN FOOTBALL CONFERENCE
Eastern Division

Team	W	L	T	Pct	Pts	Opp	HW	HL	HT	HPct	AW	AL	AT	APct
BAL	10	4	0	.714	295	221	6	1	0	.857	4	3	0	.571
MIA	10	4	0	.714	313	197	6	1	0	.857	4	3	0	.571
NE	9	5	0	.643	278	217	6	1	0	.857	3	4	0	.429
NYJ	3	11	0	.214	191	300	1	6	0	.143	2	5	0	.286
BUF	3	11	0	.214	160	313	1	6	0	.143	2	5	0	.286

Central Division

Team	W	L	T	Pct	Pts	Opp	HW	HL	HT	HPct	AW	AL	AT	APct
PIT	9	5	0	.643	283	243	6	1	0	.857	3	4	0	.429
CIN	8	6	0	.571	238	235	5	2	0	.714	3	4	0	.429
HOU	8	6	0	.571	299	230	5	2	0	.714	3	4	0	.429
CLE	6	8	0	.429	269	267	2	5	0	.286	4	3	0	.571

Western Division

Team	W	L	T	Pct	Pts	Opp	HW	HL	HT	HPct	AW	AL	AT	APct
DEN	12	2	0	.857	274	148	6	1	0	.857	6	1	0	.857
OAK	11	3	0	.786	351	230	6	1	0	.857	5	2	0	.714
SD	7	7	0	.500	222	205	3	4	0	.429	4	3	0	.571
SEA	5	9	0	.357	282	373	3	4	0	.429	2	5	0	.286
KC	2	12	0	.143	225	349	1	6	0	.143	1	6	0	.143

NATIONAL FOOTBALL CONFERENCE
Eastern Division

Team	W	L	T	Pct	Pts	Opp	HW	HL	HT	HPct	AW	AL	AT	APct
DAL	12	2	0	.857	345	212	6	1	0	.857	6	1	0	.857
WAS	9	5	0	.643	196	189	5	2	0	.714	4	3	0	.571
STL	7	7	0	.500	272	287	4	3	0	.571	3	4	0	.429
NYG	5	9	0	.357	181	265	3	4	0	.429	2	5	0	.286
PHI	5	9	0	.357	220	207	4	3	0	.571	1	6	0	.143

Central Division

Team	W	L	T	Pct	Pts	Opp	HW	HL	HT	HPct	AW	AL	AT	APct
MIN	9	5	0	.643	231	227	5	2	0	.714	4	3	0	.571
CHI	9	5	0	.643	255	253	5	2	0	.714	4	3	0	.571
DET	6	8	0	.429	183	252	5	2	0	.714	1	6	0	.143
GB	4	10	0	.286	134	219	2	5	0	.286	2	5	0	.286
TB	2	12	0	.143	103	223	1	6	0	.143	1	6	0	.143

Western Division

Team	W	L	T	Pct	Pts	Opp	HW	HL	HT	HPct	AW	AL	AT	APct
LA	10	4	0	.714	302	146	7	0	0	1.000	3	4	0	.429
ATL	7	7	0	.500	179	129	4	3	0	.571	3	4	0	.429
SF	5	9	0	.357	220	260	3	4	0	.429	2	5	0	.286
NO	3	11	0	.214	232	336	2	5	0	.286	1	6	0	.143

Scoring

	TD	1XP	2XP	FG	SAF	PTS
Errol Mann, OAK	0	39		20	0	99
Walter Payton, CHI	16	0		0	0	96
Efren Herrera, DAL	0	39		18	0	93
Rafael Septien, LA	0	32		18	0	86
Toni Linhart, BAL	0	32		17	0	83

Rushing

	ATT	YDS	AVG	LG	TD
Walter Payton, CHI	339	1852	5.5	73	14
Mark van Eeghen, OAK	324	1273	3.9	27	7
Lawrence McCutcheon, LA	294	1238	4.2	48	7
Franco Harris, PIT	300	1162	3.9	61t	11
Lydell Mitchell, BAL	301	1159	3.9	64t	3

Passing

	ATT	COM	YDS	TD	INT	LG
Bob Griese, MIA	307	180	2252	22	73t	13
Roger Staubach, DAL	361	210	2620	18	67	9
Pat Haden, LA	216	122	1551	11	58	6
Craig Morton, DEN	254	131	1929	14	81t	8
Bert Jones, BAL	393	224	2686	17	78t	11

Receiving

	NO	YDS	AVG	LG	TD
Lydell Mitchell, BAL	71	620	8.7	38	4
Bob Chandler, BUF	60	745	12.4	31	4
Clark Gaines, NYJ	55	469	8.5	31	1
Nat Moore, MIA	52	765	14.7	73t	12
Ahmad Rashad, MIN	51	681	13.4	48t	2
Don McCauley, BAL	51	495	9.7	34t	2

Interceptions

	NO	YDS	AVG	LG	TD	
Lyle Blackwood, BAL	10	163	37	0		16.3

Punting

	NO	YDS	AVG	LG	BL
Ray Guy, OAK	59	2552	43.3	74	0

Kickoff Returns

	NO	YDS	LG	TD	AVG
Raymond Clayborn, NE	28	869	101t	3	31.0

Punt Returns

	NO	FC	YDS	LG	TD	AVG
Billy Johnson, HOU	35	8	539	87t	2	15.4

National Football League 1978

AMERICAN FOOTBALL CONFERENCE
Eastern Division

Team	W	L	T	Pct	Pts	Opp	HW	HL	HT	HPct	AW	AL	AT	APct
NE	11	5	0	.688	358	286	5	3	0	.625	6	2	0	.750
MIA	11	5	0	.688	372	254	7	1	0	.875	4	4	0	.500
NYJ	8	8	0	.500	359	364	4	4	0	.500	4	4	0	.500
BAL	5	11	0	.313	239	421	2	6	0	.250	3	5	0	.375
BUF	5	11	0	.313	302	354	4	4	0	.500	1	7	0	.125

Central Division

Team	W	L	T	Pct	Pts	Opp	HW	HL	HT	HPct	AW	AL	AT	APct
PIT	14	2	0	.875	356	195	7	1	0	.875	7	1	0	.875
HOU	10	6	0	.625	283	298	5	3	0	.625	5	3	0	.625
CLE	8	8	0	.500	334	356	5	3	0	.625	3	5	0	.375
CIN	4	12	0	.250	252	284	3	5	0	.375	1	7	0	.125

Western Division

Team	W	L	T	Pct	Pts	Opp	HW	HL	HT	HPct	AW	AL	AT	APct
DEN	10	6	0	.625	282	198	6	2	0	.750	4	4	0	.500
OAK	9	7	0	.563	311	283	4	4	0	.500	5	3	0	.625
SD	9	7	0	.563	355	309	5	3	0	.625	4	4	0	.500
SEA	9	7	0	.563	345	358	5	3	0	.625	4	4	0	.500
KC	4	12	0	.250	243	327	3	5	0	.375	1	7	0	.125

NATIONAL FOOTBALL CONFERENCE
Eastern Division

Team	W	L	T	Pct	Pts	Opp	HW	HL	HT	HPct	AW	AL	AT	APct
DAL	12	4	0	.750	384	208	7	1	0	.875	5	3	0	.625
PHI	9	7	0	.563	270	250	5	3	0	.625	4	4	0	.500
WAS	8	8	0	.500	273	283	5	3	0	.625	3	5	0	.375
NYG	6	10	0	.375	264	298	5	3	0	.625	1	7	0	.125
STL	6	10	0	.375	248	296	3	5	0	.375	3	5	0	.375

Central Division

Team	W	L	T	Pct	Pts	Opp	HW	HL	HT	HPct	AW	AL	AT	APct
MIN	8	7	1	.531	294	306	5	3	0	.625	3	4	1	.438
GB	8	7	1	.531	249	269	5	2	1	.688	3	5	0	.375
CHI	7	9	0	.438	253	274	4	4	0	.500	3	5	0	.375
DET	7	9	0	.438	290	300	5	3	0	.625	2	6	0	.250
TB	5	11	0	.313	241	259	3	5	0	.375	2	6	0	.250

Western Division

Team	W	L	T	Pct	Pts	Opp	HW	HL	HT	HPct	AW	AL	AT	APct
LA	12	4	0	.750	316	245	6	2	0	.750	6	2	0	.750
ATL	9	7	0	.563	240	290	7	1	0	.875	2	6	0	.250
NO	7	9	0	.438	281	298	3	5	0	.375	4	4	0	.500
SF	2	14	0	.125	219	350	2	6	0	.250	0	8	0	.000

Scoring

	TD	1XP	2XP	FG	SAF	PTS
Frank Corral, LA	0	31		29	0	118
Pat Leahy, NYJ	0	41		22	0	107
Garo Yepremian, MIA	0	41		19	0	98
Don Cockroft, CLE	0	37		19	0	94
Rafael Septien, DAL	0	46		16	0	94

Rushing

	ATT	YDS	AVG	LG	TD
Earl Campbell, HOU	302	1450	4.8	81t	13
Walter Payton, CHI	333	1395	4.2	76	11
Tony Dorsett, DAL	290	1325	4.6	63	7
Delvin Williams, MIA	272	1258	4.6	58	8
Wilbert Montgomery, PHI	259	1220	4.7	47	9

Passing

	ATT	COM	YDS	TD	INT	LG
Roger Staubach, DAL	413	231	3190	25	91t	16
Terry Bradshaw, PIT	368	207	2915	28	70	20
Dan Fouts, SD	381	224	2999	24	55t	20
Bob Griese, MIA	235	148	1791	11	63t	11
Archie Manning, NO	471	291	3416	17	71t	16

Receiving

	NO	YDS	AVG	LG	TD
Rickey Young, MIN	88	704	8.0	48	5
Tony Galbreath, NO	74	582	7.9	35	2
Steve Largent, SEA	71	1168	16.5	57t	8
Ahmad Rashad, MIN	66	769	11.7	58t	8
Pat Tilley, STL	62	900	14.5	43	3
Dave Casper, OAK	62	852	13.7	44	9

Interceptions

	NO	YDS	AVG	LG	TD
Thom Darden, CLE	10	200	46	0	20.0

Punting

	NO	YDS	AVG	LG	BL
Pat McInally, CIN	91	3919	43.1	65	0

Kickoff Returns

	NO	YDS	LG	TD	AVG
Steve Odom, GB	25	677	95t	1	27.1

Punt Returns

	NO	FC	YDS	LG	TD	AVG
Rick Upchurch, DEN	36	2	493	75t	1	13.7

National Football League 1979

AMERICAN FOOTBALL CONFERENCE
Eastern Division

Team	W	L	T	Pct	Pts	Opp	HW	HL	HT	HPct	AW	AL	AT	APct
MIA	10	6	0	.625	341	257	6	2	0	.750	4	4	0	.500
NE	9	7	0	.563	411	326	6	2	0	.750	3	5	0	.375
NYJ	8	8	0	.500	337	383	6	2	0	.750	2	6	0	.250
BUF	7	9	0	.438	268	279	3	5	0	.375	4	4	0	.500
BAL	5	11	0	.313	271	351	3	5	0	.375	2	6	0	.250

Central Division

Team	W	L	T	Pct	Pts	Opp	HW	HL	HT	HPct	AW	AL	AT	APct
PIT	12	4	0	.750	416	262	8	0	0	1.000	4	4	0	.500
HOU	11	5	0	.688	362	331	6	2	0	.750	5	3	0	.625
CLE	9	7	0	.563	359	352	5	3	0	.625	4	4	0	.500
CIN	4	12	0	.250	337	421	4	4	0	.500	0	8	0	.000

Western Division

Team	W	L	T	Pct	Pts	Opp	HW	HL	HT	HPct	AW	AL	AT	APct
SD	12	4	0	.750	411	246	7	1	0	.875	5	3	0	.625
DEN	10	6	0	.625	289	262	6	2	0	.750	4	4	0	.500
SEA	9	7	0	.563	378	372	5	3	0	.625	4	4	0	.500
OAK	9	7	0	.563	365	337	6	2	0	.750	3	5	0	.375
KC	7	9	0	.438	238	262	3	5	0	.375	4	4	0	.500

NATIONAL FOOTBALL CONFERENCE
Eastern Division

Team	W	L	T	Pct	Pts	Opp	HW	HL	HT	HPct	AW	AL	AT	APct
DAL	11	5	0	.688	371	313	6	2	0	.750	5	3	0	.625
PHI	11	5	0	.688	339	282	5	3	0	.625	6	2	0	.750
WAS	10	6	0	.625	348	295	6	2	0	.750	4	4	0	.500
NYG	6	10	0	.375	237	323	4	4	0	.500	2	6	0	.250
STL	5	11	0	.313	307	358	3	5	0	.375	2	6	0	.250

Central Division

Team	W	L	T	Pct	Pts	Opp	HW	HL	HT	HPct	AW	AL	AT	APct
TB	10	6	0	.625	273	237	5	3	0	.625	5	3	0	.625
CHI	10	6	0	.625	306	249	6	2	0	.750	4	4	0	.500
MIN	7	9	0	.438	259	337	5	3	0	.625	2	6	0	.250
GB	5	11	0	.313	246	316	4	4	0	.500	1	7	0	.125
DET	2	14	0	.125	219	365	2	6	0	.250	0	8	0	.000

Western Division

Team	W	L	T	Pct	Pts	Opp	HW	HL	HT	HPct	AW	AL	AT	APct
LA	9	7	0	.563	323	309	4	4	0	.500	5	3	0	.625
NO	8	8	0	.500	370	360	3	5	0	.375	5	3	0	.625
ATL	6	10	0	.375	300	388	3	5	0	.375	3	5	0	.375
SF	2	14	0	.125	308	416	2	6	0	.250	0	8	0	.000

Scoring

	TD	1XP	2XP	FG	SAF	PTS
John Smith, NE	0	46		23	0	115
Earl Campbell, HOU	19	0		0	0	114
Mark Moseley, WAS	0	39		25	0	114
Tony Franklin, PHI	0	36		23	0	105
Matt Bahr, PIT	0	50		18	0	104
Toni Fritsch, HOU	0	41		21	0	104

Rushing

	ATT	YDS	AVG	LG	TD
Earl Campbell, HOU	368	1697	4.6	61t	19
Walter Payton, CHI	369	1610	4.4	43t	14
Ottis Anderson, STL	331	1605	4.8	76t	8
Wilbert Montgomery, PHI	338	1512	4.5	62t	9
Mike Pruitt, CLE	264	1294	4.9	77t	9

Passing

	ATT	COM	YDS	TD	INT	LG
Roger Staubach, DAL	461	267	3586	27	75t	11
Joe Theismann, WAS	395	233	2797	20	62	13
Dan Fouts, SD	530	332	4082	24	65t	24
Ken Stabler, OAK	498	304	3615	26	66t	22
Ken Anderson, CIN	339	189	2340	16	73t	10

Receiving

	NO	YDS	AVG	LG	TD
Joe Washington, BAL	82	750	9.1	43t	3
Ahmad Rashad, MIN	80	1156	14.5	52t	9
Wallace Francis, ATL	74	1013	13.7	42	8
Charlie Joiner, SD	72	1008	14.0	39	4
Rickey Young, MIN	72	519	7.2	18	4

Interceptions

	NO	YDS	AVG	LG	TD	
Mike Reinfeldt, HOU	12	205	39	0	17.1	

Punting

	NO	YDS	AVG	LG	BL
Bob Grupp, KC	89	3883	43.6	74	1

Kickoff Returns

	NO	YDS	LG	TD	AVG
Larry Brunson, OAK	17	441	89	0	25.9

Punt Returns

	NO	FC	YDS	LG	TD	AVG
John Sciarra, PHI	16	0	182	38	0	11.4

National Football League 1980

AMERICAN FOOTBALL CONFERENCE
Eastern Division

Team	W	L	T	Pct	Pts	Opp	HW	HL	HT	HPct	AW	AL	AT	APct
BUF	11	5	0	.688	320	260	6	2	0	.750	5	3	0	.625
NE	10	6	0	.625	441	325	6	2	0	.750	4	4	0	.500
MIA	8	8	0	.500	266	305	5	3	0	.625	3	5	0	.375
BAL	7	9	0	.438	355	387	2	6	0	.250	5	3	0	.625
NYJ	4	12	0	.250	302	395	2	6	0	.250	2	6	0	.250

Central Division

Team	W	L	T	Pct	Pts	Opp	HW	HL	HT	HPct	AW	AL	AT	APct
CLE	11	5	0	.688	357	310	6	2	0	.750	5	3	0	.625
HOU	11	5	0	.688	295	251	6	2	0	.750	5	3	0	.625
PIT	9	7	0	.563	352	313	6	2	0	.750	3	5	0	.375
CIN	6	10	0	.375	244	312	3	5	0	.375	3	5	0	.375

Western Division

Team	W	L	T	Pct	Pts	Opp	HW	HL	HT	HPct	AW	AL	AT	APct
SD	11	5	0	.688	418	227	6	2	0	.750	5	3	0	.625
OAK	11	5	0	.688	364	306	6	2	0	.750	5	3	0	.625
DEN	8	8	0	.500	310	323	4	4	0	.500	4	4	0	.500
KC	8	8	0	.500	319	336	3	5	0	.375	5	3	0	.625
SEA	4	12	0	.250	291	408	0	8	0	.000	4	4	0	.500

NATIONAL FOOTBALL CONFERENCE
Eastern Division

Team	W	L	T	Pct	Pts	Opp	HW	HL	HT	HPct	AW	AL	AT	APct
PHI	12	4	0	.750	384	222	7	1	0	.875	5	3	0	.625
DAL	12	4	0	.750	454	311	8	0	0	1.000	4	4	0	.500
WAS	6	10	0	.375	261	293	4	4	0	.500	2	6	0	.250
STL	5	11	0	.313	299	350	2	6	0	.250	3	5	0	.375
NYG	4	12	0	.250	249	425	2	6	0	.250	2	6	0	.250

Central Division

Team	W	L	T	Pct	Pts	Opp	HW	HL	HT	HPct	AW	AL	AT	APct
MIN	9	7	0	.563	317	308	5	3	0	.625	4	4	0	.500
DET	9	7	0	.563	334	272	6	2	0	.750	3	5	0	.375
CHI	7	9	0	.438	304	264	5	3	0	.625	2	6	0	.250
GB	5	10	1	.344	231	371	4	4	0	.500	1	6	1	.188
TB	5	10	1	.344	271	341	2	5	1	.313	3	5	0	.375

Western Division

Team	W	L	T	Pct	Pts	Opp	HW	HL	HT	HPct	AW	AL	AT	APct
ATL	12	4	0	.750	405	272	6	2	0	.750	6	2	0	.750
LA	11	5	0	.688	424	289	6	2	0	.750	5	3	0	.625
SF	6	10	0	.375	320	415	4	4	0	.500	2	6	0	.250
NO	1	15	0	.063	291	487	0	8	0	.000	1	7	0	.125

Scoring

	TD	1XP	2XP	FG	SAF	PTS
John Smith, NE	0	51		26	0	129
Rolf Benirschke, SD	0	46		24	0	118
Eddie Murray, DET	0	35		27	0	116
Fred Steinfort, DEN	0	32		26	0	110
Tim Mazzetti, ATL	0	46		19	0	103

Rushing

	ATT	YDS	AVG	LG	TD
Earl Campbell, HOU	373	1934	5.2	55t	13
Walter Payton, CHI	317	1460	4.6	69t	6
Ottis Anderson, STL	301	1352	4.5	52	9
William Andrews, ATL	265	1308	4.9	33	4
Billy Sims, DET	313	1303	4.2	52	13

Passing

	ATT	COM	YDS	TD	INT	LG
Brian Sipe, CLE	554	337	4132	30	65	14
Ron Jaworski, PHI	451	257	3529	27	56t	12
Vince Ferragamo, LA	404	240	3199	30	74t	19
Steve Bartkowski, ATL	463	257	3544	31	81t	16
Joe Montana, SF	273	176	1795	15	71t	9

Receiving

	NO	YDS	AVG	LG	TD
Kellen Winslow, SD	89	1290	14.5	65	9
Earl Cooper, SF	83	567	6.8	66t	4
John Jefferson, SD	82	1340	16.3	58t	13
Dwight Clark, SF	82	991	12.1	71t	8
James Lofton, GB	71	1226	17.3	47	4
Charlie Joiner, SD	71	1132	15.9	51	4

Interceptions

	NO	YDS	AVG	LG	TD
Lester Hayes, OAK	13	273	62	1	21.0

Punting

	NO	YDS	AVG	LG	BL
Dave Jennings, NYG	94	4211	44.8	63	0

Kickoff Returns

	NO	YDS	LG	TD	AVG
Horace Ivory, NE	36	992	98t	1	27.6

Punt Returns

	NO	FC	YDS	LG	TD	AVG
J.T. Smith, KC	40	8	581	75t	2	14.5

National Football League 1981

AMERICAN FOOTBALL CONFERENCE
Eastern Division

Team	W	L	T	Pct	Pts	Opp	HW	HL	HT	HPct	AW	AL	AT	APct
MIA	11	4	1	.719	345	275	6	1	1	.813	5	3	0	.625
NYJ	10	5	1	.656	355	287	6	2	0	.750	4	3	1	.563
BUF	10	6	0	.625	311	276	7	1	0	.875	3	5	0	.375
BAL	2	14	0	.125	259	533	1	7	0	.125	1	7	0	.125
NE	2	14	0	.125	322	370	2	6	0	.250	0	8	0	.000

Central Division

Team	W	L	T	Pct	Pts	Opp	HW	HL	HT	HPct	AW	AL	AT	APct
CIN	12	4	0	.750	421	304	6	2	0	.750	6	2	0	.750
PIT	8	8	0	.500	356	297	5	3	0	.625	3	5	0	.375
HOU	7	9	0	.438	281	355	5	3	0	.625	2	6	0	.250
CLE	5	11	0	.313	276	375	3	5	0	.375	2	6	0	.250

Western Division

Team	W	L	T	Pct	Pts	Opp	HW	HL	HT	HPct	AW	AL	AT	APct
SD	10	6	0	.625	478	390	5	3	0	.625	5	3	0	.625
DEN	10	6	0	.625	321	289	8	0	0	1.000	2	6	0	.250
KC	9	7	0	.563	343	290	5	3	0	.625	4	4	0	.500
OAK	7	9	0	.438	273	343	4	4	0	.500	3	5	0	.375
SEA	6	10	0	.375	322	388	5	3	0	.625	1	7	0	.125

NATIONAL FOOTBALL CONFERENCE
Eastern Division

Team	W	L	T	Pct	Pts	Opp	HW	HL	HT	HPct	AW	AL	AT	APct
DAL	12	4	0	.750	367	277	8	0	0	1.000	4	4	0	.500
PHI	10	6	0	.625	368	221	6	2	0	.750	4	4	0	.500
NYG	9	7	0	.563	295	257	4	4	0	.500	5	3	0	.625
WAS	8	8	0	.500	347	349	5	3	0	.625	3	5	0	.375
STL	7	9	0	.438	315	408	5	3	0	.625	2	6	0	.250

Central Division

Team	W	L	T	Pct	Pts	Opp	HW	HL	HT	HPct	AW	AL	AT	APct
TB	9	7	0	.563	315	268	6	2	0	.750	3	5	0	.375
DET	8	8	0	.500	397	322	7	1	0	.875	1	7	0	.125
GB	8	8	0	.500	324	361	4	4	0	.500	4	4	0	.500
MIN	7	9	0	.438	325	369	5	3	0	.625	2	6	0	.250
CHI	6	10	0	.375	253	324	4	4	0	.500	2	6	0	.250

Western Division

Team	W	L	T	Pct	Pts	Opp	HW	HL	HT	HPct	AW	AL	AT	APct
SF	13	3	0	.813	357	250	7	1	0	.875	6	2	0	.750
ATL	7	9	0	.438	426	355	4	4	0	.500	3	5	0	.375
LA	6	10	0	.375	303	351	4	4	0	.500	2	6	0	.250
NO	4	12	0	.250	207	378	2	6	0	.250	2	6	0	.250

Scoring

	TD	1XP	2XP	FG	SAF	PTS
Eddie Murray, DET	0	46		25	0	121
Rafael Septien, DAL	0	40		27	0	121
Jim Breech, CIN	0	49		22	0	115
Nick Lowery, KC	0	37		26	0	115
Mick Luckhurst, ATL	0	51		21	0	114
Chuck Muncie, SD	19	0		0	0	114

Rushing

	ATT	YDS	AVG	LG	TD
George Rogers, NO	378	1674	4.4	79t	13
Tony Dorsett, DAL	342	1646	4.8	75t	4
Billy Sims, DET	296	1437	4.9	51	13
Wilbert Montgomery, PHI	286	1402	4.9	41	8
Ottis Anderson, STL	328	1376	4.2	28	9
Earl Campbell, HOU	361	1376	3.8	43	10

Passing

	ATT	COM	YDS	TD	INT	LG
Ken Anderson, CIN	479	300	3754	29	74t	10
Craig Morton, DEN	376	225	3195	21	95t	14
Dan Fouts, SD	609	360	4802	33	67t	17
Joe Montana, SF	488	311	3565	19	78t	12
Danny White, DAL	391	223	3098	22	73t	13

Receiving

	NO	YDS	AVG	LG	TD
Kellen Winslow, SD	88	1075	12.2	67t	10
Dwight Clark, SF	85	1105	13.0	78t	4
Ted Brown, MIN	83	694	8.4	63	2
William Andrews, ATL	81	735	9.1	70t	2
Joe Senser, MIN	79	1004	12.7	53	8

Interceptions

	NO	YDS	AVG	LG	TD	
Everson Walls, DAL	11	133	33	0		12.1

Punting

	NO	YDS	AVG	LG	BL
Pat McInally, CIN	72	3272	45.4	62	1

Kickoff Returns

	NO	YDS	LG	TD	AVG
Mike Nelms, WAS	37	1099	84	0	29.7

Punt Returns

	NO	FC	YDS	LG	TD	AVG
LeRoy Irvin, LA	46	6	615	84t	3	13.4

National Football League 1982

AMERICAN FOOTBALL CONFERENCE

Team	W	L	T	Pct	Pts	Opp	HW	HL	HT	HPct	AW	AL	AT	APct
LARI	8	1	0	.889	260	200	4	0	0	1.000	4	1	0	.800
MIA	7	2	0	.778	198	131	4	0	0	1.000	3	2	0	.600
CIN	7	2	0	.778	232	177	4	0	0	1.000	3	2	0	.600
PIT	6	3	0	.667	204	146	4	0	0	1.000	2	3	0	.400
SD	6	3	0	.667	288	221	3	1	0	.750	3	2	0	.600
NYJ	6	3	0	.667	245	166	3	1	0	.750	3	2	0	.600
NE	5	4	0	.556	143	157	3	1	0	.750	2	3	0	.400
CLE	4	5	0	.444	140	182	2	2	0	.500	2	3	0	.400
BUF	4	5	0	.444	150	154	4	1	0	.800	0	4	0	.000
SEA	4	5	0	.444	127	147	3	2	0	.600	1	3	0	.250
KC	3	6	0	.333	176	184	2	2	0	.500	1	4	0	.200
DEN	2	7	0	.222	148	226	1	4	0	.200	1	3	0	.250
HOU	1	8	0	.111	136	245	1	4	0	.200	0	4	0	.000
BAL	0	8	1	.056	113	236	0	3	1	.125	0	5	0	.000

NATIONAL FOOTBALL CONFERENCE

Team	W	L	T	Pct	Pts	Opp	HW	HL	HT	HPct	AW	AL	AT	APct
WAS	8	1	0	.889	190	128	3	1	0	.750	5	0	0	1.000
DAL	6	3	0	.667	226	145	3	2	0	.600	3	1	0	.750
GB	5	3	1	.611	226	169	3	1	0	.750	2	2	1	.500
MIN	5	4	0	.556	187	198	4	1	0	.800	1	3	0	.250
ATL	5	4	0	.556	183	199	2	3	0	.400	3	1	0	.750
STL	5	4	0	.556	135	170	1	3	0	.250	4	1	0	.800
TB	5	4	0	.556	158	178	4	1	0	.800	1	3	0	.250

Team	W	L	T	Pct	Pts	Opp	HW	HL	HT	HPct	AW	AL	AT	APct
DET	4	5	0	.444	181	176	2	3	0	.400	2	2	0	.500
NO	4	5	0	.444	129	160	2	3	0	.400	2	2	0	.500
NYG	4	5	0	.444	164	160	2	3	0	.400	2	2	0	.500
SF	3	6	0	.333	209	206	0	5	0	.000	3	1	0	.750
CHI	3	6	0	.333	141	174	2	2	0	.500	1	4	0	.200
PHI	3	6	0	.333	191	195	1	4	0	.200	2	2	0	.500
LARM	2	7	0	.222	200	250	1	4	0	.200	1	3	0	.250

Scoring

	TD	1XP	2XP	FG	SAF	PTS
Marcus Allen, LARI	14	0		0	0	84
Rolf Benirschke, SD	0	32		16	0	80
Wendell Tyler, LARM	13	0		0	0	78
Mark Moseley, WAS	0	16		20	0	76
Nick Lowery, KC	0	17		19	0	74

Rushing

	ATT	YDS	AVG	LG	TD
Freeman McNeil, NYJ	151	786	5.2	48	6
Tony Dorsett, DAL	177	745	4.2	99t	5
Andra Franklin, MIA	177	701	4.0	25t	7
Marcus Allen, LARI	160	697	4.4	53	11
Billy Sims, DET	172	639	3.7	29	4

Passing

	ATT	COM	YDS	TD	INT	LG
Ken Anderson, CIN	309	218	2495	12	56t	9
Dan Fouts, SD	330	204	2883	17	44t	11
Joe Theismann, WAS	252	161	2033	13	78t	9
Danny White, DAL	247	156	2079	16	49	12
Joe Montana, SF	346	213	2613	17	55	11

Receiving

	NO	YDS	AVG	LG	TD
Dwight Clark, SF	60	913	15.2	51	5
Kellen Winslow, SD	54	721	13.4	40	6
James Wilder, TB	53	466	8.8	32	1
Wes Chandler, SD	49	1032	21.1	66t	9
Cris Collinsworth, CIN	49	700	14.3	50	1
Ozzie Newsome, CLE	49	633	12.9	54	3

Interceptions

	NO	YDS	AVG	LG	TD
Everson Walls, DAL	7	61	37	0	8.7

Punting

	NO	YDS	AVG	LG	BL
Luke Prestridge, DEN	45	2026	45.0	65	0

Sacks

	NO
Doug Martin, MIN	11.5

Kickoff Returns

	NO	YDS	LG	TD	AVG
Mike Mosley, BUF	18	487	66	0	27.1

Punt Returns

	NO	FC	YDS	LG	TD	AVG
Rick Upchurch, DEN	15	3	242	78t	2	16.1

National Football League 1983

AMERICAN FOOTBALL CONFERENCE
Eastern Division

Team	W	L	T	Pct	Pts	Opp	HW	HL	HT	HPct	AW	AL	AT	APct
MIA	12	4	0	.750	389	250	7	1	0	.875	5	3	0	.625
BUF	8	8	0	.500	283	351	3	5	0	.375	5	3	0	.625
NE	8	8	0	.500	274	289	5	3	0	.625	3	5	0	.375
NYJ	7	9	0	.438	313	331	2	6	0	.250	5	3	0	.625
BAL	7	9	0	.438	264	354	3	5	0	.375	4	4	0	.500

Central Division

Team	W	L	T	Pct	Pts	Opp	HW	HL	HT	HPct	AW	AL	AT	APct
PIT	10	6	0	.625	355	303	4	4	0	.500	6	2	0	.750
CLE	9	7	0	.563	356	342	6	2	0	.750	3	5	0	.375
CIN	7	9	0	.438	346	302	4	4	0	.500	3	5	0	.375
HOU	2	14	0	.125	288	460	2	6	0	.250	0	8	0	.000

Western Division

Team	W	L	T	Pct	Pts	Opp	HW	HL	HT	HPct	AW	AL	AT	APct
LARI	12	4	0	.750	442	338	6	2	0	.750	6	2	0	.750
DEN	9	7	0	.563	302	327	6	2	0	.750	3	5	0	.375
SEA	9	7	0	.563	403	397	5	3	0	.625	4	4	0	.500
KC	6	10	0	.375	386	367	5	3	0	.625	1	7	0	.125
SD	6	10	0	.375	358	462	4	4	0	.500	2	6	0	.250

NATIONAL FOOTBALL CONFERENCE
Eastern Division

Team	W	L	T	Pct	Pts	Opp	HW	HL	HT	HPct	AW	AL	AT	APct
WAS	14	2	0	.875	541	332	7	1	0	.875	7	1	0	.875
DAL	12	4	0	.750	479	360	6	2	0	.750	6	2	0	.750
STL	8	7	1	.531	374	428	4	3	1	.563	4	4	0	.500
PHI	5	11	0	.313	233	322	1	7	0	.125	4	4	4	.500
NYG	3	12	1	.219	267	347	1	7	0	.125	2	5	1	.313

Central Division

Team	W	L	T	Pct	Pts	Opp	HW	HL	HT	HPct	AW	AL	AT	APct
DET	9	7	0	.553	347	286	6	2	0	.750	3	5	0	.375
CHI	8	8	0	.500	311	301	5	3	0	.625	3	5	0	.375
GB	8	8	0	.500	429	439	5	3	0	.625	3	5	0	.375
MIN	8	8	0	.500	316	348	3	5	0	.375	5	3	0	.625
TB	2	14	0	.125	241	380	1	7	0	.125	1	7	0	.125

Western Division

Team	W	L	T	Pct	Pts	Opp	HW	HL	HT	HPct	AW	AL	AT	APct
SF	10	6	0	.625	432	293	4	4	0	.500	6	2	0	.750
LARM	9	7	0	.563	361	344	5	3	0	.625	4	4	0	.500
NO	8	8	0	.500	319	337	5	3	0	.625	3	5	0	.375
ATL	7	9	0	.438	370	389	4	4	0	.500	3	5	0	.375

Scoring

	TD	1XP	2XP	FG	SAF	PTS
Mark Moseley, WAS	0	62		33	0	161
John Riggins, WAS	24	0		0	0	144
Ali Haji-Sheikh, NYG	0	22		35	0	127
Ray Wersching, SF	0	51		25	0	126
Rafael Septien, DAL	0	57		22	0	123

Rushing

	ATT	YDS	AVG	LG	TD
Eric Dickerson, LARM	390	1808	4.6	85t	18
William Andrews, ATL	331	1567	4.7	27	7
Curt Warner, SEA	335	1449	4.3	60	13
Walter Payton, CHI	314	1421	4.5	49t	6
John Riggins, WAS	375	1347	3.6	44	24

Passing

	ATT	COM	YDS	TD	INT	LG
Steve Bartkowski, ATL	432	274	3167	22	76t	5
Joe Theismann, WAS	459	276	3714	29	84	11
Dan Marino, MIA	296	173	2210	20	85t	6
Dave Krieg, SEA	243	147	2139	18	50t	11
Joe Montana, SF	515	332	3910	26	77t	12

Receiving

	NO	YDS	AVG	LG	TD
Todd Christensen, LARI	92	1247	13.6	45	12
Ozzie Newsome, CLE	89	970	10.9	66t	6
Kellen Winslow, SD	88	1172	13.3	46	8
Tim Smith, HOU	83	1176	14.2	47t	6
Carlos Carson, KC	80	1351	16.9	50t	7

Interceptions

	NO	YDS	AVG	LG	TD	
Mark Murphy, WAS	9	127	48	0		14.1

Punting

	NO	YDS	AVG	LG	BL
Rohn Stark, BAL	91	4124	45.3	68	0

Sacks

	NO	
Mark Gastineau, NYJ	19	

Kickoff Returns

	NO	YDS	LG	TD	AVG
Fulton Walker, MIA	36	962	78	0	26.7

Punt Returns

	NO	FC	YDS	LG	TD	AVG
Henry Ellard, LARM	16	4	217	72t	1	13.6

National Football League 1984

AMERICAN FOOTBALL CONFERENCE
Eastern Division

Team	W	L	T	Pct	Pts	Opp	HW	HL	HT	HPct	AW	AL	AT	APct
MIA	14	2	0	.875	513	298	7	1	0	.875	7	1	0	.875
NE	9	7	0	.563	362	352	5	3	0	.625	4	4	0	.500
NYJ	7	9	0	.438	332	364	3	5	0	.375	4	4	0	.500
IND	4	12	0	.250	239	414	2	6	0	.250	2	6	0	.250
BUF	2	14	0	.125	250	454	2	6	0	.250	0	8	0	.000

Central Division

Team	W	L	T	Pct	Pts	Opp	HW	HL	HT	HPct	AW	AL	AT	APct
PIT	9	7	0	.563	387	310	6	2	0	.750	3	5	0	.375
CIN	8	8	0	.500	339	339	5	3	0	.625	3	5	0	.375
CLE	5	11	0	.313	250	297	2	6	0	.250	3	5	0	.375
HOU	3	13	0	.188	240	437	2	6	0	.250	1	7	0	.125

Western Division

Team	W	L	T	Pct	Pts	Opp	HW	HL	HT	HPct	AW	AL	AT	APct
DEN	13	3	0	.813	353	241	7	1	0	.875	6	2	0	.750
SEA	12	4	0	.750	418	282	7	1	0	.875	5	3	0	.625
LARI	11	5	0	.688	368	278	6	2	0	.750	5	3	0	.625
KC	8	8	0	.500	314	324	5	3	0	.625	3	5	0	.375
SD	7	9	0	.438	394	413	4	4	0	.500	3	5	0	.375

NATIONAL FOOTBALL CONFERENCE
Eastern Division

Team	W	L	T	Pct	Pts	Opp	HW	HL	HT	HPct	AW	AL	AT	APct
WAS	11	5	0	.688	426	310	7	1	0	.875	4	4	0	.500
NYG	9	7	0	.563	299	301	6	2	0	.750	3	5	0	.375
PHI	6	9	1	.406	278	320	5	3	0	.625	1	6	1	.188
STL	9	7	0	.563	423	345	5	3	0	.625	4	4	0	.500
DAL	9	7	0	.563	308	308	5	3	0	.625	4	4	0	.500

Central Division

Team	W	L	T	Pct	Pts	Opp	HW	HL	HT	HPct	AW	AL	AT	APct
CHI	10	6	0	.625	325	248	6	2	0	.750	4	4	0	.500
GB	8	8	0	.500	390	309	5	3	0	.625	3	5	0	.375
TB	6	10	0	.375	335	380	6	2	0	.750	0	8	0	.000
DET	4	11	1	.281	283	408	2	5	1	.313	2	6	0	.250
MIN	3	13	0	.188	276	484	2	6	0	.250	1	7	0	.125

Western Division

Team	W	L	T	Pct	Pts	Opp	HW	HL	HT	HPct	AW	AL	AT	APct
SF	15	1	0	.938	475	227	7	1	0	.875	8	0	0	1.000
LARM	10	6	0	.625	346	316	5	3	0	.625	5	3	0	.625
NO	7	9	0	.438	298	361	3	5	0	.375	4	4	0	.500
ATL	4	12	0	.250	281	382	2	6	0	.250	2	6	0	.250

Scoring

	TD	1XP	2XP	FG	SAF	PTS
Ray Wersching, SF	0	56		25	0	131
Mark Moseley, WAS	0	48		24	0	120
Gary Anderson, PIT	0	45		24	0	117
Neil O'Donoghue, STL	0	48		23	0	117
Paul McFadden, PHI	0	26		30	0	116

Rushing

	ATT	YDS	AVG	LG	TD
Eric Dickerson, LARM	379	2105	5.6	66	14
Walter Payton, CHI	381	1684	4.4	72t	11
James Wilder, TB	407	1544	3.8	37	13
Gerald Riggs, ATL	353	1486	4.2	57	13
Wendell Tyler, SF	246	1262	5.1	40	7

Passing

	ATT	COM	YDS	TD	INT	LG
Tony Eason, NE	431	259	3228	23	76t	8
Neil Lomax, STL	560	345	4614	28	83t	16
Steve Bartkowski, ATL	269	181	2158	11	61	10
Joe Theismann, WAS	477	283	3391	24	80t	13
Lynn Dickey, GB	401	237	3195	25	79t	19

Receiving

	NO	YDS	AVG	LG	TD
Art Monk, WAS	106	1372	12.9	72	7
Ozzie Newsome, CLE	89	1001	11.2	52	5
James Wilder, TB	85	685	8.1	50	0
John Stallworth, PIT	80	1395	17.4	51	11
Todd Christensen, LARI	80	1007	12.6	38	7

Interceptions

	NO	YDS	AVG	LG		TD
Kenny Easley, SEA	10	126	58t	2		12.6

Punting

	NO	YDS	AVG	LG	BL
Jim Arnold, KC	98	4397	44.9	63	0

Sacks

	NO
Mark Gastineau, NYJ	22

Kickoff Returns

	NO	YDS	LG	TD	AVG
Bobby Humphery, NYJ	22	675	97t	1	30.7

Punt Returns

	NO	FC	YDS	LG	TD	AVG
Mike Martin, CIN	24	5	376	55	0	15.7

National Football League 1985

AMERICAN FOOTBALL CONFERENCE
Eastern Division

Team	W	L	T	Pct	Pts	Opp	HW	HL	HT	HPct	AW	AL	AT	APct
MIA	12	4	0	.750	428	320	8	0	0	1.000	4	4	0	.500
NYJ	11	5	0	.688	393	264	7	1	0	.625	4	4	0	.500
NE	11	5	0	.688	362	290	7	1	0	.875	4	4	0	.500
IND	5	11	0	.313	320	386	4	4	0	.500	1	7	0	.125
BUF	2	14	0	.125	200	381	2	6	0	.250	0	8	0	.000

Central Division

Team	W	L	T	Pct	Pts	Opp	HW	HL	HT	HPct	AW	AL	AT	APct
CLE	8	8	0	.500	287	294	5	3	0	.625	3	5	0	.375
CIN	7	9	0	.438	441	437	5	3	0	.625	2	6	0	.250
PIT	7	9	0	.438	379	355	5	3	0	.625	2	6	0	.250
HOU	5	11	0	.313	284	412	4	4	0	.500	1	7	0	.125

Western Division

Team	W	L	T	Pct	Pts	Opp	HW	HL	HT	HPct	AW	AL	AT	APct
LARI	12	4	0	.750	354	308	7	1	0	.875	5	3	0	.625

	W	L	T	Pct	Pts	Opp	HW	HL	HT	HPct	AW	AL	AT	APct
DEN	11	5	0	.688	380	329	6	2	0	.750	5	3	0	.625
SD	8	8	0	.500	467	435	6	2	0	.750	2	6	0	.250
SEA	8	8	0	.500	349	303	5	3	0	.625	3	5	0	.375
KC	6	10	0	.375	317	360	5	3	0	.625	1	7	0	.125

NATIONAL FOOTBALL CONFERENCE
Eastern Division

Team	W	L	T	Pct	Pts	Opp	HW	HL	HT	HPct	AW	AL	AT	APct
DAL	10	6	0	.625	357	333	7	1	0	.875	3	5	0	.375
NYG	10	6	0	.625	399	283	6	2	0	.750	4	4	0	.500
WAS	10	6	0	.625	297	312	5	3	0	.625	5	3	0	.625
PHI	7	9	0	.438	286	310	4	4	0	.500	3	5	0	.375
STL	5	11	0	.313	278	414	4	4	0	.500	1	7	0	.125

Central Division

Team	W	L	T	Pct	Pts	Opp	HW	HL	HT	HPct	AW	AL	AT	APct
CHI	15	1	0	.938	456	198	8	0	0	1.000	7	1	0	.875
GB	8	8	0	.500	337	355	5	3	0	.625	3	5	0	.375
DET	7	9	0	.438	307	366	6	2	0	.750	1	7	0	.125
MIN	7	9	0	.438	346	359	4	4	0	.500	3	5	0	.375
TB	2	14	0	.125	294	448	2	6	0	.250	0	8	0	.000

Western Division

Team	W	L	T	Pct	Pts	Opp	HW	HL	HT	HPct	AW	AL	AT	APct
LARM	11	5	0	.688	340	277	6	2	0	.750	5	3	0	.625
SF	10	6	0	.625	411	263	5	3	0	.625	5	3	0	.625
NO	5	11	0	.313	294	401	3	5	0	.375	2	6	0	.250
ATL	4	12	0	.250	282	452	3	5	0	.375	1	7	0	.125

Scoring
	TD	1XP	2XP	FG	SAF	PTS
Kevin Butler, CHI	0	51		31	0	144
Gary Anderson, PIT	0	40		33	0	139
Joe Morris, NYG	21	0		0	0	126
Pat Leahy, NYJ	0	43		26	0	121
Morten Andersen, NO	0	27		31	0	120
Jim Breech, CIN	0	48		24	0	120

Rushing
	ATT	YDS	AVG	LG	TD
Marcus Allen, LARI	380	1759	4.6	61t	11
Gerald Riggs, ATL	397	1719	4.3	50	10
Walter Payton, CHI	324	1551	4.8	40t	9
Joe Morris, NYG	294	1336	4.5	65t	21
Freeman McNeil, NYJ	294	1331	4.5	69	3

Passing
	ATT	COM	YDS	TD	INT	LG
Ken O'Brien, NYJ	488	297	3888	25	96t	8
Boomer Esiason, CIN	431	251	3443	27	68t	12
Joe Montana, SF	494	303	3653	27	73	13
Dan Fouts, SD	430	254	3638	27	75t	20
Dan Marino, MIA	567	336	4137	30	73	21

Receiving
	NO	YDS	AVG	LG	TD
Roger Craig, SF	92	1016	11.0	73	6
Art Monk, WAS	91	1226	13.5	53	2
Lionel James, SD	86	1027	11.9	67t	6
Todd Christensen, LARI	82	987	12.0	48	6
Butch Woolfolk, HOU	80	814	10.2	80t	4

Interceptions
	NO	YDS	AVG	LG	TD
Everson Walls, DAL	9	31	19	0	3.4

Punting
	NO	YDS	AVG	LG	BL
Rohn Stark, IND	78	3584	45.9	68	2

Sacks
	NO
Richard Dent, CHI	17

Kickoff Returns
	NO	YDS	LG	TD	AVG
Ron Brown, LARM	28	918	98t	3	32.8

Punt Returns
	NO	FC	YDS	LG	TD	AVG
Irving Fryar, NE	37	15	520	85t	2	14.1

National Football League 1986
AMERICAN FOOTBALL CONFERENCE
Eastern Division

Team	W	L	T	Pct	Pts	Opp	HW	HL	HT	HPct	AW	AL	AT	APct
NE	11	5	0	.688	412	307	4	4	0	.500	7	1	0	.875
NYJ	10	6	0	.625	364	386	5	3	0	.625	5	3	0	.625
MIA	8	8	0	.500	430	405	4	4	0	.500	4	4	0	.500
BUF	4	12	0	.250	287	348	3	5	0	.375	1	7	0	.125
IND	3	13	0	.188	229	400	1	7	0	.125	2	6	0	.250

Central Division

Team	W	L	T	Pct	Pts	Opp	HW	HL	HT	HPct	AW	AL	AT	APct
CLE	12	4	0	.750	391	310	6	2	0	.750	6	2	0	.750

	W	L	T	Pct	Pts	Opp	HW	HL	HT	HPct	AW	AL	AT	APct
CIN	10	6	0	.625	409	394	6	2	0	.750	4	4	0	.500
PIT	6	10	0	.375	307	336	4	4	0	.500	2	6	0	.250
HOU	5	11	0	.313	274	329	4	4	0	.500	1	7	0	.125

Western Division

Team	W	L	T	Pct	Pts	Opp	HW	HL	HT	HPct	AW	AL	AT	APct
DEN	11	5	0	.688	378	327	7	1	0	.875	4	4	0	.500
KC	10	6	0	.625	358	326	6	2	0	.750	4	4	0	.500
SEA	10	6	0	.625	366	293	7	1	0	.875	3	5	0	.375
LARI	8	8	0	.500	323	346	3	5	0	.375	5	3	0	.625
SD	4	12	0	.250	335	396	2	6	0	.250	2	6	0	.250

NATIONAL FOOTBALL CONFERENCE
Eastern Division

Team	W	L	T	Pct	Pts	Opp	HW	HL	HT	HPct	AW	AL	AT	APct
NYG	14	2	0	.875	371	236	8	0	0	1.000	6	2	0	.750
WAS	12	4	0	.750	368	296	7	1	0	.875	5	3	0	.625
DAL	7	9	0	.438	346	337	3	5	0	.375	4	4	0	.500
PHI	5	10	1	.344	256	312	2	5	1	.313	3	5	0	.375
STL	4	11	1	.281	218	351	3	5	0	.375	1	6	1	.188

Central Division

Team	W	L	T	Pct	Pts	Opp	HW	HL	HT	HPct	AW	AL	AT	APct
CHI	14	2	0	.875	352	187	7	1	0	.875	7	1	0	.875
MIN	9	7	0	.563	398	273	5	3	0	.625	4	4	0	.500
DET	5	11	0	.313	277	326	1	7	0	.125	4	4	0	.500
GB	4	12	0	.250	254	418	1	7	0	.125	3	5	0	.375
TB	2	14	0	.125	239	473	1	7	0	.125	1	7	0	.125

Western Division

Team	W	L	T	Pct	Pts	Opp	HW	HL	HT	HPct	AW	AL	AT	APct
SF	10	5	1	.656	374	247	6	2	0	.750	4	3	1	.563
LARM	10	6	0	.625	309	267	6	2	0	.750	4	4	0	.500
ATL	7	8	1	.469	280	280	2	5	1	.313	5	3	0	.625
NO	7	9	0	.438	288	287	4	4	0	.500	3	5	0	.375

Scoring

	TD	1XP	2XP	FG	SAF	PTS
Tony Franklin, NE	0	44		32	0	140
Kevin Butler, CHI	0	36		28	0	120
Ray Wersching, SF	0	41		25	0	116
Chuck Nelson, MIN	0	44		22	0	110

Rushing

	ATT	YDS	AVG	LG	TD
Eric Dickerson, LARM	404	1821	4.5	42t	11
Joe Morris, NYG	341	1516	4.4	54	14
Curt Warner, SEA	319	1481	4.6	60t	13
Rueben Mayes, NO	286	1353	4.7	50	8
Walter Payton, CHI	321	1333	4.2	41	8

Passing

	ATT	COM	YDS	TD	INT	LG
Tommy Kramer, MIN	372	208	3000	24	76t	10
Dan Marino, MIA	623	378	4746	44	85t	23
Dave Krieg, SEA	375	225	2921	21	72	11
Tony Eason, NE	448	276	3328	19	49	10
Boomer Esiason, CIN	469	273	3959	24	57	17

Receiving

	NO	YDS	AVG	LG	TD
Todd Christensen, LARI	95	1153	12.1	35	8
Jerry Rice, SF	86	1570	18.3	66t	15
Al Toon, NYJ	85	1176	13.8	62t	8
Stanley Morgan, NE	84	1491	17.8	44t	10
Roger Craig, SF	81	624	7.7	48	0

Interceptions

	NO	YDS	AVG	LG	TD	
Ronnie Lott, SF	10	134	57t	1		13.4

Punting

	NO	YDS	AVG	LG	BL
Rohn Stark, IND	76	3432	45.2	63	0

Sacks

	NO
Lawrence Taylor, NYG	20.5

Kickoff Returns

	NO	YDS	LG	TD	AVG
Dennis Gentry, CHI	20	576	91t	1	28.8

Punt Returns

	NO	FC	YDS	LG	TD	AVG
Bobby Joe Edmonds, SEA	34	14	419	75t	1	12.3

National Football League 1987
AMERICAN FOOTBALL CONFERENCE
Eastern Division

Team	W	L	T	Pct	Pts	Opp	HW	HL	HT	HPct	AW	AL	AT	APct
IND	9	6	0	.600	300	238	4	4	0	.500	5	2	0	.714

MIA	8	7	0	.533	362	335	4	3	0	.571	4	4	0	.500
NE	8	7	0	.533	320	293	5	3	0	.625	3	4	0	.429
BUF	7	8	0	.467	270	305	4	4	0	.500	3	4	0	.429
NYJ	6	9	0	.400	334	360	4	4	0	.500	2	5	0	.286

Central Division

Team	W	L	T	Pct	Pts	Opp	HW	HL	HT	HPct	AW	AL	AT	APct
CLE	10	5	0	.667	390	239	5	2	0	.714	5	3	0	.625
HOU	9	6	0	.600	345	349	5	2	0	.714	4	4	0	.500
PIT	8	7	0	.533	285	299	4	3	0	.571	4	4	0	.500
CIN	4	11	0	.267	285	370	1	7	0	.125	3	4	0	.429

Western Division

Team	W	L	T	Pct	Pts	Opp	HW	HL	HT	HPct	AW	AL	AT	APct
DEN	10	4	1	.700	379	288	7	1	0	.875	3	3	1	.500
SEA	9	6	0	.600	371	314	6	2	0	.750	3	4	0	.429
SD	8	7	0	.533	253	317	4	3	0	.571	4	4	0	.500
LARI	5	10	0	.333	301	289	3	5	0	.375	2	5	0	.286
KC	4	11	0	.267	273	388	3	4	0	.429	1	7	0	.125

NATIONAL FOOTBALL CONFERENCE
Eastern Division

Team	W	L	T	Pct	Pts	Opp	HW	HL	HT	HPct	AW	AL	AT	APct
WAS	11	4	0	.733	379	285	6	1	0	.857	5	3	0	.625
DAL	7	8	0	.467	340	348	3	4	0	.429	4	4	0	.500
STL	7	8	0	.467	362	368	4	3	0	.571	3	5	0	.375
PHI	7	8	0	.467	337	380	4	4	0	.500	3	4	0	.429
NYG	6	9	0	.400	280	312	5	3	0	.625	1	6	0	.143

Central Division

Team	W	L	T	Pct	Pts	Opp	HW	HL	HT	HPct	AW	AL	AT	APct
CHI	11	4	0	.733	356	282	6	2	0	.750	5	2	0	.714
MIN	8	7	0	.533	336	335	5	3	0	.625	3	4	0	.429
GB	5	9	1	.367	255	300	2	5	1	.313	3	4	0	.429
DET	4	11	0	.267	269	384	1	6	0	.143	3	5	0	.375
TB	4	11	0	.267	286	360	2	5	0	.286	2	6	0	.250

Western Division

Team	W	L	T	Pct	Pts	Opp	HW	HL	HT	HPct	AW	AL	AT	APct
SF	13	2	0	.867	459	253	6	1	0	.857	7	1	0	.875
NO	12	3	0	.800	422	283	6	1	0	.857	6	2	0	.750
LARM	6	9	0	.400	317	361	3	4	0	.429	3	5	0	.375
ATL	3	12	0	.200	205	436	2	6	0	.250	1	6	0	.143

Scoring

	TD	1XP	2XP	FG	SAF	PTS
Jerry Rice, SF	23	0		0	0	138
Morten Andersen, NO	0	37		28	0	121
Jim Breech, CIN	0	25		24	0	97
Dean Biasucci, IND	0	24		24	0	96
Roger Ruzek, DAL	0	26		22	0	92
Tony Zendejas, HOU	0	32		20	0	92

Rushing

	ATT	YDS	AVG	LG	TD
Charles White, LARM	324	1374	4.2	58	11
Eric Dickerson, LARM-IND	283	1288	4.6	57	6
Curt Warner, SEA	234	985	4.2	57t	8
Mike Rozier, HOU	229	957	4.2	41	3
Rueben Mayes, NO	243	917	3.8	38	5

Passing

	ATT	COM	YDS	TD	INT	LG
Bernie Kosar, CLE	389	241	3033	22	54t	9
Phil Simms, NYG	282	163	2230	17	50t	9
Dan Marino, MIA	444	263	3245	26	59t	13
Neil Lomax, STL	463	275	3387	24	57	12
Dave Krieg, SEA	294	178	2131	23	75t	15

Receiving

	NO	YDS	AVG	LG	TD
J.T. Smith, STL	91	1117	12.3	38	8
Al Toon, NYJ	68	976	14.4	58t	5
Roger Craig, SF	66	492	7.5	35t	1
Jerry Rice, SF	65	1078	16.6	57t	22
Herschel Walker, DAL	60	715	11.9	44	1

Interceptions

	NO	YDS	AVG	LG	TD
Barry Wilburn, WAS	9	135	100t	1	15.0

Punting

	NO	YDS	AVG	LG	BL
Rick Donnelly, ATL	61	2686	44.0	62	2

Sacks

	NO
Reggie White, PHI	21

Kickoff Returns

	NO	YDS	LG	TD	AVG
Sylvester Stamps, ATL	24	660	97t	1	27.5

Punt Returns

	NO	FC	YDS	LG	TD	AVG
Mel Gray, NO	24	5	352	80	0	14.7

National Football League 1988
AMERICAN FOOTBALL CONFERENCE
Eastern Division

Team	W	L	T	Pct	Pts	Opp	HW	HL	HT	HPct	AW	AL	AT	APct
BUF	12	4	0	.750	329	237	8	0	0	1.000	4	4	0	.500
IND	9	7	0	.563	354	315	6	2	0	.750	3	5	0	.375
NE	9	7	0	.563	250	284	7	1	0	.875	2	6	0	.250
NYJ	8	7	1	.531	372	354	5	2	1	.688	3	5	0	.375
MIA	6	10	0	.375	319	380	4	4	0	.500	2	6	0	.250

Central Division

Team	W	L	T	Pct	Pts	Opp	HW	HL	HT	HPct	AW	AL	AT	APct
CIN	12	4	0	.750	448	329	8	0	0	1.000	4	4	0	.500
CLE	10	6	0	.625	304	288	6	2	0	.750	4	4	0	.500
HOU	10	6	0	.625	424	365	7	1	0	.875	3	5	0	.375
PIT	5	11	0	.313	336	421	4	4	0	.500	1	7	0	.125

Western Division

Team	W	L	T	Pct	Pts	Opp	HW	HL	HT	HPct	AW	AL	AT	APct
SEA	9	7	0	.563	339	329	5	3	0	.625	4	4	0	.500
DEN	8	8	0	.500	327	352	6	2	0	.750	2	6	0	.250
LARI	7	9	0	.438	325	369	3	5	0	.375	4	4	0	.500
SD	6	10	0	.375	231	332	3	5	0	.375	3	5	0	.375
KC	4	11	1	.281	254	320	4	4	0	.500	0	7	1	.063

NATIONAL FOOTBALL CONFERENCE
Eastern Division

Team	W	L	T	Pct	Pts	Opp	HW	HL	HT	HPct	AW	AL	AT	APct
PHI	10	6	0	.625	379	319	5	3	0	.625	5	3	0	.625
NYG	10	6	0	.625	359	304	5	3	0	.625	5	3	0	.625
PHX	7	9	0	.438	344	398	4	4	0	.500	3	5	0	.375
WAS	7	9	0	.438	345	387	4	4	0	.500	3	5	0	.625
DAL	3	13	0	.188	265	381	1	7	0	.125	2	6	0	.250

Central Division

Team	W	L	T	Pct	Pts	Opp	HW	HL	HT	HPct	AW	AL	AT	APct
CHI	12	4	0	.750	312	215	7	1	0	.875	5	3	0	.625
MIN	11	5	0	.688	406	233	7	1	0	.875	4	4	0	.500
TB	5	11	0	.313	261	350	3	5	0	.375	2	6	0	.250
DET	4	12	0	.250	220	313	2	6	0	.250	2	6	0	.250
GB	4	12	0	.250	240	315	2	6	0	.250	2	6	0	.250

Western Division

Team	W	L	T	Pct	Pts	Opp	HW	HL	HT	HPct	AW	AL	AT	APct
SF	10	6	0	.625	369	294	4	4	0	.500	6	2	0	.750
LARM	10	6	0	.625	407	293	4	4	0	.500	6	2	0	.750
NO	10	6	0	.625	312	283	5	3	0	.625	5	3	0	.625
ATL	5	11	0	.313	244	315	2	6	0	.250	3	5	0	.375

Scoring

	TD	1XP	2XP	FG	SAF	PTS
Scott Norwood, BUF	0	33		32	0	129
Mike Cofer, SF	0	40		27	0	121
Gary Anderson, PIT	0	34		28	0	118
Mike Lansford, LARM	0	45		24	0	117
Dean Biasucci, IND	0	39		25	0	114
Tony Zendejas, HOU	0	48		22	0	114

Rushing

	ATT	YDS	AVG	LG	TD
Eric Dickerson, IND	388	1659	4.3	41t	14
Herschel Walker, DAL	361	1514	4.2	38	5
Roger Craig, SF	310	1502	4.8	46t	9
Greg Bell, LARM	288	1212	4.2	44	16
John Stephens, NE	297	1168	3.9	52	4

Passing

	ATT	COM	YDS	TD	INT	LG
Boomer Esiason, CIN	388	223	3572	28	86t	14
Dave Krieg, SEA	228	134	1741	18	75t	8
Wade Wilson, MIN	332	204	2746	15	68t	9
Jim Everett, LARM	517	308	3964	31	69t	18
Warren Moon, HOU	294	160	2327	17	57t	8

Receiving

	NO	YDS	AVG	LG	TD
Al Toon, NYJ	93	1067	11.5	42	5
Henry Ellard, LARM	86	1414	16.4	68	10
Mark Clayton, MIA	86	1129	13.1	45t	14
Eric Martin, NO	85	1083	12.7	40t	7
J.T. Smith, PHX	83	986	11.9	29	5

Interceptions

	NO	YDS	AVG	LG	TD	
Scott Case, ATL	10	47	12	0	4.7	

Punting

	NO	YDS	AVG	LG	BL
Harry Newsome, PIT	65	2950	45.4	62	6

Sacks	NO
Reggie White, PHI	18

Kickoff Returns	NO	YDS	LG	TD	AVG
Tim Brown, LARI	41	1098	97t	1	26.8

Punt Returns	NO	FC	YDS	LG	TD	AVG
John Taylor, SF	44	7	556	95t	2	12.6

National Football League 1989

AMERICAN FOOTBALL CONFERENCE

Eastern Division

Team	W	L	T	Pct	Pts	Opp	HW	HL	HT	HPct	AW	AL	AT	APct
BUF	9	7	0	.563	409	317	6	2	0	.750	3	5	0	.375
IND	8	8	0	.500	298	301	6	2	0	.750	2	6	0	.250
MIA	8	8	0	.500	331	379	4	4	0	.500	4	4	0	.500
NE	5	11	0	.313	297	391	3	5	0	.375	2	6	0	.250
NYJ	4	12	0	.250	253	411	1	7	0	.125	3	5	0	.375

Central Division

Team	W	L	T	Pct	Pts	Opp	HW	HL	HT	HPct	AW	AL	AT	APct
CLE	9	6	1	.594	334	254	5	2	1	.688	4	4	0	.500
HOU	9	7	0	.563	365	412	6	2	0	.750	3	5	0	.375
PIT	9	7	0	.563	265	326	4	4	0	.500	5	3	0	.625
CIN	8	8	0	.500	404	285	5	3	0	.625	3	5	0	.375

Western Division

Team	W	L	T	Pct	Pts	Opp	HW	HL	HT	HPct	AW	AL	AT	APct
DEN	11	5	0	.688	362	226	6	2	0	.750	5	3	0	.625
KC	8	7	1	.531	318	286	5	3	0	.625	3	4	1	.438
LARI	8	8	0	.500	315	297	7	1	0	.875	1	7	0	.125
SEA	7	9	0	.438	241	327	3	5	0	.375	4	4	0	.500
SD	6	10	0	.375	266	290	4	4	0	.500	2	6	0	.250

NATIONAL FOOTBALL CONFERENCE

Eastern Division

Team	W	L	T	Pct	Pts	Opp	HW	HL	HT	HPct	AW	AL	AT	APct
NYG	12	4	0	.750	348	252	7	1	0	.875	5	3	0	.625
PHI	11	5	0	.688	342	274	6	2	0	.750	5	3	0	.625
WAS	10	6	0	.625	386	308	4	4	0	.500	6	2	0	.750
PHX	5	11	0	.313	258	377	2	6	0	.250	3	5	0	.375
DAL	1	15	0	.063	204	393	0	8	0	.000	1	7	0	.125

Central Division

Team	W	L	T	Pct	Pts	Opp	HW	HL	HT	HPct	AW	AL	AT	APct
MIN	10	6	0	.625	351	275	8	0	0	1.000	2	6	0	.250
GB	10	6	0	.625	362	356	6	2	0	.750	4	4	0	.500
DET	7	9	0	.438	312	364	4	4	0	.500	3	5	0	.375
CHI	6	10	0	.375	358	377	4	4	0	.500	2	6	0	.250
TB	5	11	0	.313	320	419	2	6	0	.250	3	5	0	.375

Western Division

Team	W	L	T	Pct	Pts	Opp	HW	HL	HT	HPct	AW	AL	AT	APct
SF	14	2	0	.875	442	253	6	2	0	.750	8	0	0	1.000
LARM	11	5	0	.688	426	344	6	2	0	.750	5	3	0	.625
NO	9	7	0	.563	386	301	5	3	0	.625	4	4	0	.500
ATL	3	13	0	.188	279	437	3	5	0	.375	0	8	0	.000

Scoring	TD	1XP	2XP	FG	SAF	PTS
Mike Cofer, SF	0	49		29	0	136
Chip Lohmiller, WAS	0	41		29	0	128
Rich Karlis, MIN	0	27		31	0	120
Mike Lansford, LARM	0	51		23	0	120
David Treadwell, DEN	0	39		27	0	120

Rushing	ATT	YDS	AVG	LG	TD
Christian Okoye, KC	370	1480	4.0	59	12
Barry Sanders, DET	280	1470	4.3	34	14
Eric Dickerson, IND	314	1311	4.2	21t	7
Neal Anderson, CHI	274	1275	4.7	73	11
Dalton Hilliard, NO	344	1262	3.7	40	13

Passing	ATT	COM	YDS	TD	INT	LG
Boomer Esiason, CIN	455	258	3525	28	74t	11
Jim Everett, LARM	518	304	4310	29	78t	17
Warren Moon, HOU	464	280	3631	23	55	14
Mark Rypien, WAS	476	280	3768	22	80t	13
Jim Kelly, BUF	391	228	3130	25	78t	18

Receiving

	NO	YDS	AVG	LG	TD
Sterling Sharpe, GB	90	1423	15.8	79t	12
Andre Reed, BUF	88	1312	14.9	78t	9
Mark Carrier, TB	86	1422	16.5	78t	9
Art Monk, WAS	86	1186	13.8	60t	8
Jerry Rice, SF	82	1483	18.1	68t	17

Interceptions

	NO	YDS	AVG	LG	TD
Felix Wright, CLE	9	91	27t	1	10.1

Punting

	NO	YDS	AVG	LG	BL
Rich Camarillo, PHX	76	3298	43.4	58	0

Sacks

	NO
Chris Doleman, MIN	21

Kickoff Returns

	NO	YDS	LG	TD	AVG
Rod Woodson, PIT	36	982	84t	1	27.3

Punt Returns

	NO	FC	YDS	LG	TD	AVG
Walter Stanley, DET	36	5	496	74	0	13.8

National Football League 1990

AMERICAN FOOTBALL CONFERENCE
Eastern Division

Team	W	L	T	Pct	Pts	Opp	HW	HL	HT	HPct	AW	AL	AT	APct
BUF	13	3	0	.813	428	263	8	0	0	1.000	5	3	0	.625
MIA	12	4	0	.750	336	242	7	1	0	.875	5	3	0	.625
IND	7	9	0	.438	281	353	3	5	0	.375	4	4	0	.500
NYJ	6	10	0	.375	295	345	3	5	0	.375	3	5	0	.375
NE	1	15	0	.063	181	446	0	8	0	.000	1	7	0	.125

Central Division

Team	W	L	T	Pct	Pts	Opp	HW	HL	HT	HPct	AW	AL	AT	APct
CIN	9	7	0	.563	360	352	5	3	0	.625	4	4	0	.500
HOU	9	7	0	.563	405	307	6	2	0	.750	3	5	0	.375
PIT	9	7	0	.563	292	240	6	2	0	.750	3	5	0	.375
CLE	3	13	0	.188	228	462	2	6	0	.250	1	7	0	.125

Western Division

Team	W	L	T	Pct	Pts	Opp	HW	HL	HT	HPct	AW	AL	AT	APct
LARI	12	4	0	.750	337	268	6	2	0	.750	6	2	0	.750
KC	11	5	0	.688	369	257	6	2	0	.750	5	3	0	.625
SEA	9	7	0	.563	306	286	5	3	0	.625	4	4	0	.500
SD	6	10	0	.375	315	281	3	5	0	.375	3	5	0	.375
DEN	5	11	0	.313	331	374	4	4	0	.500	1	7	0	.125

NATIONAL FOOTBALL CONFERENCE
Eastern Division

Team	W	L	T	Pct	Pts	Opp	HW	HL	HT	HPct	AW	AL	AT	APct
NYG	13	3	0	.813	335	211	7	1	0	.875	6	2	0	.750
PHI	10	6	0	.625	396	299	6	2	0	.750	4	4	0	.500
WAS	10	6	0	.625	381	301	7	1	0	.875	3	5	0	.375
DAL	7	9	0	.438	244	308	5	3	0	.625	2	6	0	.250
PHX	5	11	0	.313	268	396	3	5	0	.375	2	6	0	.250

Central Division

Team	W	L	T	Pct	Pts	Opp	HW	HL	HT	HPct	AW	AL	AT	APct
CHI	11	5	0	.688	348	280	7	1	0	.875	4	4	0	.500
TB	6	10	0	.375	264	367	4	4	0	.500	2	6	0	.250
DET	6	10	0	.375	373	413	3	5	0	.375	3	5	0	.375
GB	6	10	0	.375	271	347	3	5	0	.375	3	5	0	.375
MIN	6	10	0	.375	351	326	4	4	0	.500	2	6	0	.250

Western Division

Team	W	L	T	Pct	Pts	Opp	HW	HL	HT	HPct	AW	AL	AT	APct
SF	14	2	0	.875	353	239	6	2	0	.750	8	0	0	1.000
NO	8	8	0	.500	274	275	5	3	0	.625	3	5	0	.375
LARM	5	11	0	.313	345	412	2	6	0	.250	3	5	0	.375
ATL	5	11	0	.313	348	365	5	3	0	.625	0	8	0	.000

Scoring

	TD	1XP	2XP	FG	SAF	PTS
Nick Lowery, KC	0	37		34	0	139
Chip Lohmiller, WAS	0	41		30	0	131
Kevin Butler, CHI	0	36		26	0	114
Mike Cofer, SF	0	39		24	0	111
Scott Norwood, BUF	0	50		20	0	110

Rushing

	ATT	YDS	AVG	LG	TD
Barry Sanders, DET	255	1304	5.1	45t	13
Thurman Thomas, BUF	271	1297	4.8	80t	11
Marion Butts, SD	265	1225	4.6	52	8
Earnest Byner, WAS	297	1219	4.1	22	6
Bobby Humphrey, DEN	288	1202	4.2	37t	7

Passing

	ATT	COM	YDS	TD	INT	LG
Warren Moon, HOU	584	362	4689	33	87t	13
Steve DeBerg, KC	444	258	3444	23	90t	4
Phil Simms, NYG	311	184	2284	15	80t	4
Randall Cunningham, PHI	465	271	3466	30	95t	13
Schroeder, Jay, LARI	334	182	2849	19	68t	9

Receiving

	NO	YDS	AVG	LG	TD
Jerry Rice, SF	100	1502	15.0	64t	13
Andre Rison, ATL	82	1208	14.7	75t	10
Keith Byars, PHI	81	819	10.1	54	3
Henry Ellard, LARM	76	1294	17.0	50t	4
Gary Clark, WAS	75	1112	14.8	53t	8

Interceptions

	NO	YDS	AVG	LG	TD	
Mark Carrier, CHI	10	39	14	0	3.9	

Punting

	NO	YDS	AVG	LG	BL
Mike Horan, DEN	58	2575	44.4	67	1

Sacks

	NO
Derrick Thomas, KC	20

Kickoff Returns

	NO	YDS	LG	TD	AVG
Kevin Clark, DEN	20	505	75	0	25.3

Punt Returns

	NO	FC	YDS	LG	TD	AVG
Clarence Verdin, IND	31	3	396	36	0	12.8

National Football League 1991

AMERICAN FOOTBALL CONFERENCE
Eastern Division

Team	W	L	T	Pct	Pts	Opp	HW	HL	HT	HPct	AW	AL	AT	APct
BUF	13	3	0	.813	458	318	7	1	0	.875	6	2	0	.750
NYJ	8	8	0	.500	314	293	4	4	0	.500	4	4	0	.500
MIA	8	8	0	.500	343	349	5	3	0	.625	3	5	0	.375
NE	6	10	0	.375	211	305	4	4	0	.500	2	6	0	.250
IND	1	15	0	.063	143	381	0	8	0	.000	1	7	0	.125

Central Division

Team	W	L	T	Pct	Pts	Opp	HW	HL	HT	HPct	AW	AL	AT	APct
HOU	11	5	0	.688	386	251	7	1	0	.875	4	4	0	.500
PIT	7	9	0	.438	292	344	5	3	0	.625	2	6	0	.250
CLE	6	10	0	.375	293	298	3	5	0	.375	3	5	0	.375
CIN	3	13	0	.188	263	435	3	5	0	.375	0	8	0	.000

Western Division

Team	W	L	T	Pct	Pts	Opp	HW	HL	HT	HPct	AW	AL	AT	APct
DEN	12	4	0	.750	304	235	7	1	0	.875	5	3	0	.625
KC	10	6	0	.625	322	252	6	2	0	.750	4	4	0	.500
LARI	9	7	0	.563	298	297	5	3	0	.625	4	4	0	.500
SEA	7	9	0	.438	276	261	5	3	0	.625	2	6	0	.250
SD	4	12	0	.250	274	342	3	5	0	.375	1	7	0	.125

NATIONAL FOOTBALL CONFERENCE
Eastern Division

Team	W	L	T	Pct	Pts	Opp	HW	HL	HT	HPct	AW	AL	AT	APct
WAS	14	2	0	.875	485	224	7	1	0	.875	7	1	0	.875
DAL	11	5	0	.688	342	310	6	2	0	.750	5	3	0	.625
PHI	10	6	0	.625	285	244	4	4	0	.500	6	2	0	.750
NYG	8	8	0	.500	281	297	5	3	0	.625	3	5	0	.375
PHX	4	12	0	.250	196	344	2	6	0	.250	2	6	0	.250

Central Division

Team	W	L	T	Pct	Pts	Opp	HW	HL	HT	HPct	AW	AL	AT	APct
DET	12	4	0	.750	339	295	8	0	0	1.000	4	4	0	.500
CHI	11	5	0	.688	299	269	6	2	0	.750	5	3	0	.625
MIN	8	8	0	.500	301	306	4	4	0	.500	4	4	0	.500
GB	4	12	0	.250	273	313	2	6	0	.250	2	6	0	.250
TB	3	13	0	.188	199	365	3	5	0	.375	0	8	0	.000

Western Division

Team	W	L	T	Pct	Pts	Opp	HW	HL	HT	HPct	AW	AL	AT	APct
NO	11	5	0	.688	341	211	6	2	0	.750	5	3	0	.625
ATL	10	6	0	.625	361	338	6	2	0	.750	4	4	0	.500
SF	10	6	0	.625	393	239	7	1	0	.875	3	5	0	.375
LARM	3	13	0	.188	234	390	2	6	0	.250	1	7	0	.125

Scoring

	TD	1XP	2XP	FG	SAF	PTS
Chip Lohmiller, WAS	0	56		31	0	149
Pete Stoyanovich, MIA	0	28		31	0	121
Ken Willis, DAL	0	37		27	0	118
Jeff Jaeger, LARI	0	29		29	0	116
Morten Andersen, NO	0	38		25	0	113

Rushing

	ATT	YDS	AVG	LG	TD
Thurman Thomas, BUF	288	1407	4.9	33	7
Emmitt Smith, DAL	365	1563	4.3	75t	12
Gaston Green, DEN	261	1037	4.0	63t	4
Barry Sanders, DET	342	1548	4.5	69t	16
Rodney Hampton, NYG	256	1059	4.1	44	10
Christian Okoye, KC	225	1031	4.6	48	9
Leonard Russell, NE	266	959	3.6	24	4
Earnest Byner, WAS	274	1048	3.8	32	5
Mark Higgs, MIA	231	905	3.9	24	4
Herschel Walker, MIN	198	825	4.2	71t	10

Passing

	ATT	COM	YDS	TD	INT	LG
Mark Rypien, WAS	421	249	3564	28	82t	11
Jim Kelly, BUF	474	304	3844	33	77t	17
Steve Bono, SF	237	141	1617	11	78	4
Bernie Kosar, CLE	494	307	3487	18	71t	9
Troy Aikman, DAL	363	237	2754	11	61	10

Receiving

	NO	YDS	AVG	LG	TD
Haywood Jeffires, HOU	100	1181	11.8	44	7
Michael Irvin, DAL	93	1523	16.4	66t	8
Drew Hill, HOU	90	1109	12.3	61t	4
Marv Cook, NE	82	808	9.9	49	3
Andre Reed, BUF	81	1113	13.7	55	10
Andre Rison, ATL	81	976	12.0	39t	12

Interceptions

	NO	YDS	AVG	LG	TD	
Ronnie Lott, LARI	8	52	27	0		6.5

Punting

	NO	YDS	AVG	LG	BL
Reggie Roby, MIA	54	2466	45.7	64	1

Sacks

	NO
Pat Swilling, NO	17

Kickoff Returns

	NO	YDS	LG	TD	AVG
Mel Gray, DET	36	929	71	0	25.8

Punt Returns

	NO	FC	YDS	LG	TD	AVG
Mel Gray, DET	25	14	385	78t	1	15.4

National Football League 1992

AMERICAN FOOTBALL CONFERENCE
Eastern Division

Team	W	L	T	Pct	Pts	Opp	HW	HL	HT	HPct	AW	AL	AT	APct
MIA	11	5	0	.688	340	281	6	2	0	.750	5	3	0	.625
BUF	11	5	0	.688	381	283	6	2	0	.750	5	3	0	.625
IND	9	7	0	.563	216	302	4	4	0	.500	5	3	0	.625
NYJ	4	12	0	.250	220	315	3	5	0	.375	1	7	0	.125
NE	2	14	0	.125	205	363	1	7	0	.125	1	7	0	.125

Central Division

Team	W	L	T	Pct	Pts	Opp	HW	HL	HT	HPct	AW	AL	AT	APct
PIT	11	5	0	.688	299	225	7	1	0	.875	4	4	0	.500
HOU	10	6	0	.625	352	258	5	3	0	.625	5	3	0	.625
CLE	7	9	0	.438	272	275	4	4	0	.500	3	5	0	.375
CIN	5	11	0	.313	274	364	3	5	0	.375	2	6	0	.250

Western Division

Team	W	L	T	Pct	Pts	Opp	HW	HL	HT	HPct	AW	AL	AT	APct
SD	11	5	0	.688	335	241	6	2	0	.750	5	3	0	.625
KC	10	6	0	.625	348	282	7	1	0	.875	3	5	0	.375
DEN	8	8	0	.500	262	329	7	1	0	.875	1	7	0	.125
LARI	7	9	0	.438	249	281	5	3	0	.625	2	6	0	.250
SEA	2	14	0	.125	140	312	1	7	0	.125	1	7	0	.125

NATIONAL FOOTBALL CONFERENCE
Eastern Division

Team	W	L	T	Pct	Pts	Opp	HW	HL	HT	HPct	AW	AL	AT	APct
DAL	13	3	0	.813	409	243	7	1	0	.875	6	2	0	.750

	W	L	T	Pct	Pts	Opp	HW	HL	HT	HPct	AW	AL	AT	APct
PHI	11	5	0	.688	354	245	8	0	0	1.000	3	5	0	.375
WAS	9	7	0	.563	300	255	6	2	0	.750	3	5	0	.375
NYG	6	10	0	.375	306	367	4	4	0	.500	2	6	0	.250
PHX	4	12	0	.250	243	332	3	5	0	.375	1	7	0	.125

Central Division

Team	W	L	T	Pct	Pts	Opp	HW	HL	HT	HPct	AW	AL	AT	APct
MIN	11	5	0	.688	374	249	5	3	0	.625	6	2	0	.750
GB	9	7	0	.563	276	296	2	6	0	.250	2	6	0	.250
TB	5	11	0	.313	267	365	3	5	0	.375	2	6	0	.250
CHI	5	11	0	.313	295	361	4	4	0	.500	1	7	0	.125
DET	5	11	0	.313	273	332	3	5	0	.375	2	6	0	.250

Western Division

Team	W	L	T	Pct	Pts	Opp	HW	HL	HT	HPct	AW	AL	AT	APct
SF	14	2	0	.875	431	236	7	1	0	.875	7	1	0	.875
NO	12	4	0	.750	330	202	6	2	0	.750	6	2	0	.750
ATL	6	10	0	.375	327	414	5	3	0	.625	1	7	0	.125
LARM	6	10	0	.375	313	383	4	4	0	.500	2	6	0	.250

Scoring

	TD	1XP	2XP	FG	SAF	PTS
Pete Stoyanovich, MIA	0	34		30	0	124
Morten Andersen, NO	0	33		29	0	120
Chip Lohmiller, WAS	0	30		30	0	120
Lin Elliott, DAL	0	47		24	0	119
Steve Christie, BUF	0	43		24	0	115

Rushing

	ATT	YDS	AVG	LG	TD
Emmitt Smith, DAL	373	1713	4.6	68t	18
Barry Foster, PIT	390	1690	4.3	69	11
Thurman Thomas, BUF	312	1487	4.8	44	9
Barry Sanders, DET	312	1352	4.3	55t	9
Lorenzo White, HOU	265	1226	4.6	44	7

Passing

	ATT	COM	YDS	TD	INT	LG
Chris Miller, ATL	253	152	1739	15	89t	6
Troy Aikman, DAL	473	302	3445	23	87t	14
Warren Moon, HOU	346	224	2521	18	72	12
Randall Cunningham, PHI	384	233	2775	19	75t	11
Brett Favre, GB	471	302	3227	18	76t	13

Receiving

	NO	YDS	AVG	LG	TD
Sterling Sharpe, GB	108	1461	13.5	76t	13
Andre Rison, ATL	93	1119	12.0	71t	11
Haywood Jeffires, HOU	90	913	10.1	47	9
Jerry Rice, SF	84	1201	14.3	80t	10
Curtis Duncan, HOU	82	954	11.6	72	1

Interceptions

	NO	YDS	AVG	LG	TD
Henry Jones, BUF	8	263	82t	2	32.9
Audray McMillan, MIN	8	157	51t	2	19.6

Punting

	NO	YDS	AVG	LG	BL
Greg Montgomery, HOU	53	2487	46.9	66	2

Sacks

	NO
Clyde Simmons, PHI	19

Kickoff Returns

	NO	YDS	LG	TD	AVG
Jon Vaughn, NE	20	564	100t	1	28.2

Punt Returns

	NO	FC	YDS	LG	TD	AVG
Johnny Bailey, PHX	20	8	263	65	0	13.2

National Football League 1993

AMERICAN FOOTBALL CONFERENCE
Eastern Division

Team	W	L	T	Pct	Pts	Opp	HW	HL	HT	HPct	AW	AL	AT	APct
BUF	12	4	0	.750	329	242	6	2	0	.750	6	2	0	.750
MIA	9	7	0	.563	349	351	4	4	0	.500	5	3	0	.625
NYJ	8	8	0	.500	270	247	3	5	0	.375	5	3	0	.625
NE	5	11	0	.313	238	286	3	5	0	.375	2	6	0	.250
IND	4	12	0	.250	189	378	2	6	0	.250	2	6	0	.250

Central Division

Team	W	L	T	Pct	Pts	Opp	HW	HL	HT	HPct	AW	AL	AT	APct
HOU	12	4	0	.750	368	238	7	1	0	.875	5	3	0	.625
PIT	9	7	0	.563	308	281	6	2	0	.750	3	5	0	.375
CLE	7	9	0	.438	304	307	4	4	0	.500	3	5	0	.375
CIN	3	13	0	.188	187	319	3	5	0	.375	0	8	0	.000

Western Division

Team	W	L	T	Pct	Pts	Opp	HW	HL	HT	HPct	AW	AL	AT	APct
KC	11	5	0	.688	328	291	7	1	0	.875	4	4	0	.500
LARI	10	6	0	.625	306	326	5	3	0	.625	5	3	0	.625
DEN	9	7	0	.563	373	284	5	3	0	.625	4	4	0	.500

	W	L	T	Pct	Pts	Opp								
SD	8	8	0	.500	322	290	4	4	0	.500	4	4	0	.500
SEA	6	10	0	.375	280	314	4	4	0	.500	2	6	0	.250

NATIONAL FOOTBALL CONFERENCE
Eastern Division

Team	W	L	T	Pct	Pts	Opp	HW	HL	HT	HPct	AW	AL	AT	APct
DAL	12	4	0	.750	376	229	6	2	0	.750	6	2	0	.750
NYG	11	5	0	.688	288	205	6	2	0	.750	5	3	0	.625
PHI	8	8	0	.500	293	315	3	5	0	.375	5	3	0	.625
PHX	7	9	0	.438	326	269	4	4	0	.500	3	5	0	.375
WAS	4	12	0	.250	230	345	3	5	0	.375	1	7	0	.125

Central Division

Team	W	L	T	Pct	Pts	Opp	HW	HL	HT	HPct	AW	AL	AT	APct
DET	10	6	0	.625	298	292	5	3	0	.625	5	3	0	.625
MIN	9	7	0	.563	277	290	4	4	0	.500	5	3	0	.625
GB	9	7	0	.563	340	282	6	2	0	.750	3	5	0	.375
CHI	7	9	0	.438	234	230	3	5	0	.375	4	4	0	.500
TB	5	11	0	.313	237	376	3	5	0	.375	2	6	0	.250

Western Division

Team	W	L	T	Pct	Pts	Opp	HW	HL	HT	HPct	AW	AL	AT	APct
SF	10	6	0	.625	473	295	6	2	0	.750	4	4	0	.500
NO	8	8	0	.500	317	343	4	4	0	.500	4	4	0	.500
ATL	6	10	0	.375	316	385	4	4	0	.500	2	6	0	.250
LARM	5	11	0	.313	221	367	3	5	0	.375	2	6	0	.250

Scoring

	TD	1XP	2XP	FG	SAF	PTS
Jeff Jaeger, LARI	0	27		35	0	132
Jason Hanson, DET	0	28		34	0	130
Chris Jacke, GB	0	35		31	0	128
Al Del Greco, HOU	0	39		29	0	126
John Carney, SD	0	31		31	0	124

Rushing

	ATT	YDS	AVG	LG	TD
Emmitt Smith, DAL	283	1486	5.3	62t	9
Jerome Bettis, LARM	294	1429	4.9	71t	7
Thurman Thomas, BUF	355	1315	3.7	27	6
Erric Pegram, ATL	292	1185	4.1	29	3
Barry Sanders, DET	243	1115	4.6	42	3

Passing

	ATT	COM	YDS	TD	INT	LG
Troy Aikman, DAL	392	271	3100	15	80t	6
John Elway, DEN	551	348	4030	25	63	10
Phil Simms, NYG	400	247	3038	15	62	9
Joe Montana, KC	298	181	2144	13	50t	7
Vinny Testaverde, CLE	230	130	1797	14	62t	9

Receiving

	NO	YDS	AVG	LG	TD
Sterling Sharpe, GB	112	1274	11.4	54	11
Jerry Rice, SF	98	1503	15.3	80t	15
Michael Irvin, DAL	88	1330	15.1	61t	7
Andre Rison, ATL	86	1242	14.4	53t	15
Cris Carter, MIN	86	1071	12.5	58	9

Interceptions

	NO	YDS	AVG	LG	TD	
Eugene Robinson, SEA	9	80	28	0		8.9
Nate Odomes, BUF	9	65	25	0		7.2

Punting

	NO	YDS	AVG	LG	BL
Greg Montgomery, HOU	54	2462	45.6	77	0

Sacks

	NO
Neil Smith, KC	15

Kickoff Returns

	NO	YDS	LG	TD	AVG
Robert Brooks, GB	23	611	95t	1	26.6

Punt Returns

	NO	FC	YDS	LG	TD	AVG
Tyrone Hughes, NO	37	21	503	83t	2	13.6

National Football League 1994
AMERICAN FOOTBALL CONFERENCE
Eastern Division

Team	W	L	T	Pct	Pts	Opp	HW	HL	HT	HPct	AW	AL	AT	APct
MIA	10	6	0	.625	389	327	6	2	0	.750	4	4	0	.500
NE	10	6	0	.625	351	312	5	3	0	.625	5	3	0	.625
IND	8	8	0	.500	307	320	5	3	0	.625	3	5	0	.375
BUF	7	9	0	.438	340	356	4	4	0	.500	3	5	0	.375
NYJ	6	10	0	.375	264	320	4	4	0	.500	2	6	0	.250

Central Division

Team	W	L	T	Pct	Pts	Opp	HW	HL	HT	HPct	AW	AL	AT	APct
PIT	12	4	0	.750	316	234	7	1	0	.875	5	3	0	.625
CLE	11	5	0	.688	340	204	6	2	0	.750	5	3	0	.625

CIN	3	13	0	.188	276	406	2	6	0	.250	1	7	0	.125
HOU	2	14	0	.125	226	352	2	6	0	.250	0	8	0	.000

Western Division

Team	W	L	T	Pct	Pts	Opp	HW	HL	HT	HPct	AW	AL	AT	APct
SD	11	5	0	.688	381	306	5	3	0	.625	6	2	0	.750
KC	9	7	0	.563	319	298	5	3	0	.625	4	4	0	.500
LARI	9	7	0	.563	303	327	4	4	0	.500	5	3	0	.625
DEN	7	9	0	.438	347	396	4	4	0	.500	3	5	0	.375
SEA	6	10	0	.375	287	323	3	5	0	.375	3	5	0	.375

NATIONAL FOOTBALL CONFERENCE
Eastern Division

Team	W	L	T	Pct	Pts	Opp	HW	HL	HT	HPct	AW	AL	AT	APct
DAL	12	4	0	.750	414	248	6	2	0	.750	6	2	0	.750
NYG	9	7	0	.563	279	305	4	4	0	.500	5	3	0	.625
ARI	8	8	0	.500	235	267	5	3	0	.625	3	5	0	.375
PHI	7	9	0	.438	308	308	5	3	0	.625	2	6	0	.250
WAS	3	13	0	.188	320	412	0	8	0	.000	3	5	0	.375

Central Division

Team	W	L	T	Pct	Pts	Opp	HW	HL	HT	HPct	AW	AL	AT	APct
MIN	10	6	0	.625	356	314	6	2	0	.750	4	4	0	.500
GB	9	7	0	.563	382	287	7	1	0	.875	2	6	0	.250
DET	9	7	0	.563	357	342	6	2	0	.750	3	5	0	.375
CHI	9	7	0	.563	271	307	5	3	0	.625	4	4	0	.500
TB	6	10	0	.375	251	351	4	4	0	.500	2	6	0	.250

Western Division

Team	W	L	T	Pct	Pts	Opp	HW	HL	HT	HPct	AW	AL	AT	APct
SF	13	3	0	.813	505	296	7	1	0	.875	6	2	0	.750
NO	7	9	0	.438	348	407	3	5	0	.375	4	4	0	.500
ATL	7	9	0	.438	317	385	5	3	0	.625	2	6	0	.250
LARM	4	12	0	.250	286	365	3	5	0	.375	1	7	0	.125

Scoring

	TD	1XP	2XP	FG	SAF	PTS
John Carney, SD	0	33	0	34	0	135
Fuad Reveiz, MIN	0	30	0	34	0	132
Emmitt Smith, DAL	22	0	0	0	0	132
Jason Elam, DEN	0	29	0	30	0	119
Matt Bahr, NE	0	36	0	27	0	117

Rushing

	ATT	YDS	AVG	LG	TD
Barry Sanders, DET	331	1883	5.7	85	7
Chris Warren, SEA	333	1545	4.6	41	9
Emmitt Smith, DAL	368	1484	4.0	46	21
Natrone Means, SD	343	1350	3.9	25	12
Marshall Faulk, IND	314	1282	4.1	52	11

Passing

	ATT	COM	YDS	TD	INT	LG
Brett Favre, GB	582	363	3882	33	49	14
Dan Marino, MIA	615	385	4453	30	64t	17
John Elway, DEN	494	307	3490	16	63	10
Jim Everett, NO	540	346	3855	22	78t	18
Troy Aikman, DAL	361	233	2676	13	90	12

Receiving

	NO	YDS	AVG	LG	TD
Cris Carter, MIN	122	1256	10.3	65t	7
Jerry Rice, SF	112	1499	13.4	69t	13
Terance Mathis, ATL	111	1342	12.1	81	11
Ben Coates, NE	96	1174	12.2	62t	7
Sterling Sharpe, GB	94	1119	11.9	49	18

Interceptions

	NO	YDS	AVG	LG	TD	
Eric Turner, CLE	9	199	93t	1	22.1	
Aeneas Williams, ARI	9	89	43	0	9.9	

Punting

	NO	YDS	AVG	LG	BL
Sean Landeta, LARM	78	3494	44.8	62	0

Sacks

	NO
Kevin Greene, PIT	14

Kickoff Returns

	NO	YDS	LG	TD	AVG
Mel Gray, DET	45	1276	102t	3	28.4

Punt Returns

	NO	FC	YDS	LG	TD	AVG
Brian Mitchell, WAS	32	24	452	78t	2	14.1

National Football League 1995
AMERICAN FOOTBALL CONFERENCE
Eastern Division

Team	W	L	T	Pct	Pts	Opp	HW	HL	HT	HPct	AW	AL	AT	APct
BUF	10	6	0	.625	350	335	6	2	0	.750	4	4	0	.500
IND	9	7	0	.563	331	316	5	3	0	.625	4	4	0	.500
MIA	9	7	0	.563	398	332	5	3	0	.625	4	4	0	.500

Team	W	L	T	Pct	Pts	Opp	HW	HL	HT	HPct	AW	AL	AT	APct
NE	6	10	0	.375	294	377	3	5	0	.375	3	5	0	.375
NYJ	3	13	0	.188	233	384	2	6	0	.250	1	7	0	.125

Central Division

Team	W	L	T	Pct	Pts	Opp	HW	HL	HT	HPct	AW	AL	AT	APct
PIT	11	5	0	.688	407	327	6	2	0	.750	5	3	0	.625
CIN	7	9	0	.438	349	374	3	5	0	.375	4	4	0	.500
HOU	7	9	0	.438	348	324	3	5	0	.375	4	4	0	.500
CLE	5	11	0	.313	289	356	3	5	0	.375	2	6	0	.250
JAC	4	12	0	.250	275	404	2	6	0	.250	2	6	0	.250

Western Division

Team	W	L	T	Pct	Pts	Opp	HW	HL	HT	HPct	AW	AL	AT	APct
KC	13	3	0	.813	358	241	8	0	0	1.000	5	3	0	.625
SD	9	7	0	.563	321	323	5	3	0	.625	4	4	0	.500
DEN	8	8	0	.500	388	345	6	2	0	.750	2	6	0	.250
OAK	8	8	0	.500	348	332	4	4	0	.500	4	4	0	.500
SEA	8	8	0	.500	363	366	5	3	0	.625	3	5	0	.375

NATIONAL FOOTBALL CONFERENCE
Eastern Division

Team	W	L	T	Pct	Pts	Opp	HW	HL	HT	HPct	AW	AL	AT	APct
DAL	12	4	0	.750	435	291	6	2	0	.750	6	2	0	.750
PHI	10	6	0	.625	318	338	6	2	0	.750	4	4	0	.500
WAS	6	10	0	.375	326	359	4	4	0	.500	2	6	0	.250
NYG	5	11	0	.313	290	340	3	5	0	.375	2	6	0	.250
ARI	4	12	0	.250	275	422	3	5	0	.375	1	7	0	.125

Central Division

Team	W	L	T	Pct	Pts	Opp	HW	HL	HT	HPct	AW	AL	AT	APct
GB	11	5	0	.688	404	314	7	1	0	.875	4	4	0	.500
DET	10	6	0	.625	436	336	7	1	0	.875	3	5	0	.375
CHI	9	7	0	.563	392	360	5	3	0	.625	4	4	0	.500
MIN	8	8	0	.500	412	385	6	2	0	.750	2	6	0	.250
TB	7	9	0	.438	238	335	5	3	0	.625	2	6	0	.250

Western Division

Team	W	L	T	Pct	Pts	Opp	HW	HL	HT	HPct	AW	AL	AT	APct
SF	11	5	0	.688	457	258	6	2	0	.750	5	3	0	.625
ATL	9	7	0	.563	362	349	7	1	0	.875	2	6	0	.250
CAR	7	9	0	.438	289	325	5	3	0	.625	2	6	0	.250
NO	7	9	0	.438	319	348	4	4	0	.500	3	5	0	.375
STL	7	9	0	.438	309	418	4	4	0	.500	3	5	0	.375

Scoring

	TD	1XP	2XP	FG	SAF	PTS
Emmitt Smith, DAL	25	0	0	0	0	150
Norm Johnson, PIT	0	39	0	34	0	141
Jason Elam, DEN	0	39	0	31	0	132
Jason Hanson, DET	0	48	0	28	0	132
Chris Boniol, DAL	0	46	0	27	0	127

Rushing

	ATT	YDS	AVG	LG	TD
Emmitt Smith, DAL	377	1773	4.7	60t	25
Barry Sanders, DET	314	1500	4.8	75t	11
Curtis Martin, NE	368	1487	4.0	49	14
Chris Warren, SEA	310	1346	4.3	52	15
Terry Allen, WAS	338	1309	3.9	28	10

Passing

	ATT	COM	YDS	TD	INT	LG
Brett Favre, GB	570	359	4413	38	99t	13
Troy Aikman, DAL	432	280	3304	16	50	7
Erik Kramer, CHI	522	315	3838	29	76t	10
Steve Young, SF	447	299	3200	20	57	11
Scott Mitchell, DET	583	346	4338	32	91t	12

Receiving

	NO	YDS	AVG	LG	TD
Herman Moore, DET	123	1686	13.7	69t	14
Jerry Rice, SF	122	1848	15.1	81t	15
Cris Carter, MIN	122	1371	11.2	60t	17
Isaac Bruce, STL	119	1781	15.0	72	13
Michael Irvin, DAL	111	1603	14.4	50	10

Interceptions

	NO	YDS	AVG	LG	TD	
Orlando Thomas, MIN	9	108	45t	1	12.0	

Punting

	NO	YDS	AVG	LG	BL
Rick Tuten, SEA	83	3735	45.0	73	0

Sacks			**Kickoff Returns**						**Punt Returns**						
	NO			NO	YDS	LG	TD	AVG		NO	FC	YDS	LG	TD	AVG
Bryce Paup, BUF	17.5		Ron Carpenter, NYJ	20	553	58	0	27.6	David Palmer, MIN	26	13	342	74t	1	13.2

National Football League 1996

AMERICAN FOOTBALL CONFERENCE
Eastern Division

Team	W	L	T	Pct	Pts	Opp	HW	HL	HT	HPct	AW	AL	AT	APct
NE	11	5	0	.688	418	313	6	2	0	.750	5	3	0	.625
BUF	10	6	0	.625	319	266	7	1	0	.875	3	5	0	.375
IND	9	7	0	.563	317	334	6	2	0	.750	3	5	0	.375
MIA	8	8	0	.500	339	325	4	4	0	.500	4	4	0	.500
NYJ	1	15	0	.063	279	454	0	8	0	.000	1	7	0	.125

Central Division

Team	W	L	T	Pct	Pts	Opp	HW	HL	HT	HPct	AW	AL	AT	APct
PIT	10	6	0	.625	344	257	7	1	0	.875	3	5	0	.375
JAC	9	7	0	.563	325	335	7	1	0	.875	2	6	0	.250
CIN	8	8	0	.500	372	369	6	2	0	.750	2	6	0	.250
HOU	8	8	0	.500	345	319	2	6	0	.250	6	2	0	.750
BAL	4	12	0	.250	371	441	4	4	0	.500	0	8	0	.000

Western Division

Team	W	L	T	Pct	Pts	Opp	HW	HL	HT	HPct	AW	AL	AT	APct
DEN	13	3	0	.813	391	275	8	0	0	1.000	5	3	0	.625
KC	9	7	0	.563	297	300	5	3	0	.625	4	4	0	.500
SD	8	8	0	.500	310	376	5	3	0	.625	3	5	0	.375
OAK	7	9	0	.438	340	293	4	4	0	.500	3	5	0	.375
SEA	7	9	0	.438	317	376	4	4	0	.500	3	5	0	.375

NATIONAL FOOTBALL CONFERENCE
Eastern Division

Team	W	L	T	Pct	Pts	Opp	HW	HL	HT	HPct	AW	AL	AT	APct
DAL	10	6	0	.625	286	250	6	2	0	.750	4	4	0	.500
PHI	10	6	0	.625	363	341	5	3	0	.625	5	3	0	.625
WAS	9	7	0	.563	364	312	5	3	0	.625	4	4	0	.500
ARI	7	9	0	.438	300	397	5	3	0	.625	2	6	0	.250
NYG	6	10	0	.375	242	297	3	5	0	.375	3	5	0	.375

Central Division

Team	W	L	T	Pct	Pts	Opp	HW	HL	HT	HPct	AW	AL	AT	APct
GB	13	3	0	.813	456	210	8	0	0	1.000	5	3	0	.625
MIN	9	7	0	.563	298	315	5	3	0	.625	4	4	0	.500
CHI	7	9	0	.438	283	305	6	2	0	.750	1	7	0	.125
TB	6	10	0	.375	221	293	5	3	0	.625	1	7	0	.125
DET	5	11	0	.313	302	368	4	4	0	.500	1	7	0	.125

Western Division

Team	W	L	T	Pct	Pts	Opp	HW	HL	HT	HPct	AW	AL	AT	APct
CAR	12	4	0	.750	367	218	8	0	0	1.000	4	4	0	.500
SF	12	4	0	.750	398	257	6	2	0	.750	6	2	0	.750
STL	6	10	0	.375	303	409	4	4	0	.500	2	6	0	.250
ATL	3	13	0	.188	309	465	2	6	0	.250	1	7	0	.125
NO	3	13	0	.188	229	339	2	6	0	.250	1	7	0	.125

Scoring

	TD	1XP	2XP	FG	SAF	PTS
John Kasay, CAR	0	34	0	37	0	145
Cary Blanchard, IND	0	27	0	36	0	135
Al Del Greco, HOU	0	35	0	32	0	131
Jeff Wilkins, SF	0	40	0	30	0	130
Terry Allen, WAS	21	0	0	0	0	126

Rushing

	ATT	YDS	AVG	LG	TD
Barry Sanders, DET	307	1553	5.1	54t	11
Terrell Davis, DEN	345	1538	4.5	71t	13
Jerome Bettis, PIT	320	1431	4.5	50t	11
Ricky Watters, PHI	353	1411	4.0	56t	13
Eddie George, HOU	335	1368	4.1	76	8

Passing

	ATT	COM	YDS	TD	INT	LG
Steve Young, SF	316	214	2410	14	52	6
Brett Favre, GB	543	325	3899	39	80t	13
Brad Johnson, MIN	311	195	2258	17	82t	10
John Elway, DEN	466	287	3328	26	51	14
Vinny Testaverde, CLE	549	325	4177	33	86t	19

Receiving

	NO	YDS	AVG	LG	TD
Jerry Rice, SF	108	1254	11.6	39	8
Herman Moore, DET	106	1296	12.2	50t	9
Carl Pickens, CIN	100	1180	11.8	61t	12
Larry Centers, ARI	99	766	7.7	39	7
Cris Carter, MIN	96	1163	12.1	43t	10

Interceptions

	NO	YDS	AVG	LG	TD
Keith Lyle, STL	9	152	68	0	16.9
Tyrone Braxton, DEN	9	128	69t	1	14.2

Punting

	NO	YDS	AVG	LG	BL
John Kidd, MIA	78	3611	46.3	63	0

Sacks

	NO
Kevin Greene, CAR	14.5

Kickoff Returns

	NO	YDS	LG	TD	AVG
Michael Bates, CAR	33	998	93t	1	30.2

Punt Returns

	NO	FC	YDS	LG	TD	AVG
Desmond Howard, GB	58	16	875	92t	3	15.1

Part Seven

Player Register

Key

Year Team	Games	Pos.

Ed Rate
RATE, EDWIN S. (Speedy)
B. May 27, 1899
Deceased
Purdue 5'9" 165 lbs.

1923	**MIL**	N	1	HB

Player Information

Ed Rate—This shortened version of the player's full name is the name most familiar to fans.

Edwin S. Rate—Player's full name.

(Speedy)—Player's nickname.

B. May 27, 1899—Player's date and place of birth.

Deceased—Player's date and place of death. If Deceased is used, more specific information is not known.

Purdue—College attended.

5'9" 165lbs.—Player's average playing height and weight.

1923 MIL N—Year, team, and league played for.

1—Games played that particular year

HB—Player's position

Year	Team		Games	Pos.

Joe Abbey
ABBEY, JOSEPH
B. May 21, 1925, Denton, TX
Texas/North Texas State 6'1" 200 lbs.

Year	Team		Games	Pos.
1948	CHIB	N	12	E
1949	NYB	N	6	E
2 yrs.	18 games			

Fay Abbott
ABBOTT, LAFAYETTE (Hack)
B. Aug. 16, 1895
D. Jan, 1965, Dayton, OH
Syracuse 5'8" 185 lbs.

Year	Team		Games	Pos.
1921	DAY	A	8	QB, HB
1922	DAY	N	6	QB, HB
1923			8	QB
1924			7	QB, E
1925			8	QB
1926			6	FB, HB
1927			6	HB, FB, QB
1928			5	QB, HB
1929			1	FB, HB
9 yrs.	55 games			

Vince Abbott
ABBOTT, VINCENT STEVEN
B. May 31, 1958, London, England
Washington/Fullerton State 5'11" 195 lbs.

Year	Team		Games	Pos.
1987	SD	N	12	K
1988			11	K
2 yrs.	23 games			

Lou Abbruzzi
ABBRUZZI, LOUIS J. (Duke)
B. 1921
Rhode Island 5'10" 175 lbs.

Year	Team		Games	Pos.
1946	BOS	N	3	HB, DB

Frank Abbruzzino
ABBRUZZINO, FRANK
B. Jan. 22, 1908
D. Jun, 1986, Fort Lauderdale, FL
Colgate 6'0" 190 lbs.

Year	Team		Games	Pos.
1931	BKN	N	13	G, QB, HB, E, C
1933	CIN	N	9	C, QB, E, HB
2 yrs.	22 games			

Karim Abdul-Jabbar
Born SHARMON SHAH
B. Jun. 28, 1974, Los Angeles, CA
UCLA 5'10" 194 lbs.

Year	Team		Games	Pos.
1996	MIA	N	16	RB

Fred Abel
ABEL, FREDERICK
B. Jul. 17, 1903
D. Aug, 1980, Port Townsend, WA
Washington 5'10" 175 lbs.

Year	Team		Games	Pos.
1926	MIL	N	3	QB, HB

Bud Abell
ABELL, HARRY E.
B. Dec. 21, 1940, Kansas City, MO
Missouri 6'3" 220 lbs.

Year	Team		Games	Pos.
1966	KC	A	14	LB
1967			14	LB
1968			12	LB
3 yrs.	40 games			

Walter Abercrombie
ABERCROMBIE, WALTER AUGUSTUS
B. Sep. 26, 1959, Waco, TX
Baylor 6'0" 210 lbs.

Year	Team		Games	Pos.
1982	PIT	N	6	RB

Walter Abercrombie cont.

Year	Team		Games	Pos.
1983			15	RB
1984			14	RB
1985			16	RB
1986			16	RB
1987			12	RB
1988	PHI	N	5	RB
7 yrs.	84 games			

Cliff Aberson
ABERSON, CLIFFORD ALEXANDER (Kif)
B. Aug. 28, 1921, Chicago, IL
D. Jul. 23, 1973, Vallejo, CA
None 6'0" 195 lbs.

Year	Team		Games	Pos.
1946	GB	N	10	HB, DB

Clifton Abraham
ABRAHAM, CLIFTON EUGENE
B. Dec. 9, 1971, Dallas, TX
Florida State 5'9" 184 lbs.

Year	Team		Games	Pos.
1995	TB	N	6	CB, S
1996	CHI	N	2	CB
2 yrs.	8 games			

Donnie Abraham
ABRAHAM, DONNIE
B. Oct. 8, 1973, Orangeburg, SC
East Tennessee State 5'10" 181 lbs.

Year	Team		Games	Pos.
1996	TB	N	16	CB

Robert Abraham
ABRAHAM, ROBERT
B. Jul. 13, 1960, Myrtle Beach, SC
North Carolina State 6'1" 236 lbs.

Year	Team		Games	Pos.
1982	HOU	N	9	LB
1983			16	LB
1984			16	LB
1985			16	LB
1986			16	LB
1987			2	LB
6 yrs.	73 games			

Danny Abramowicz
ABRAMOWICZ, DANIEL
B. Jul. 13, 1945, Steubenville, OH
Xavier (Ohio) 6'1" 195 lbs.

Year	Team		Games	Pos.
1967	NO	N	14	FL
1968			14	OE
1969			14	WR
1970			14	WR
1971			14	WR
1972			13	WR
1973			2	WR
1973	SF	N	12	WR
1974			14	WR
8 yrs.	111 games			

Sid Abramowitz
ABRAMOWITZ, SIDNEY
B. May 21, 1960, Culver City, CA
Air Force/Tulsa 6'6" 280 lbs.

Year	Team		Games	Pos.
1983	BAL	N	14	OT
1984	SEA	N	4	OT
1985	NYJ	N	1	OT
1987	IND	N	3	OT
4 yrs.	22 games			

Bobby Abrams
ABRAMS, BOBBY E.
B. Apr. 12, 1967, Detroit, MI
Michigan 6'3" 230 lbs.

Year	Team		Games	Pos.
1990	NYG	N	16	LB
1991			16	LB
1992	DAL	N	3	LB
1992	CLE	N	3	LB
1992	NYG	N	1	LB

Bobby Abrams continued

Year	Team		Games	Pos.
1993	DAL	N	5	LB
1993	MIN	N	4	LB
1994			16	LB
1995	NE	N	9	LB
6 yrs.	73 games			

Nate Abrams
ABRAMS, NATHAN
B. Dec., 1897
D. May, 1941, Green Bay, WI
None 5'4" 145 lbs.

Year	Team		Games	Pos.
1921	GB	A	1	E

George Abramson
ABRAMSON, GEORGE N.
B. May 13, 1903, Eveleth, MN
D. Mar. 15, 1985, Beverly Hills, CA
Minnesota 5'7" 198 lbs.

Year	Team		Games	Pos.
1925	GB	N	10	G, T

Dick Abrell
ABRELL, RICHARD T.
B. May 15, 1892
D. May 5, 1973, St. Cloud, MN
Purdue 5'10" 172 lbs.

Year	Team		Games	Pos.
1920	DAY	A	5	QB, HB

Ray Abruzzese
ABRUZZESE, RAYMOND LEWIS, JR.
B. Oct. 27, 1937, Philadelphia, PA
Alabama 6'1" 194 lbs.

Year	Team		Games	Pos.
1962	BUF	A	12	DB
1963			14	DB
1964			9	DB
1965	NY	A	12	DB
1966			14	DB
5 yrs.	61 games			

Dick Absher
ABSHER, RICHARD ALFRED
B. Apr. 19, 1944, Washington, DC
Maryland 6'4" 243 lbs.

Year	Team		Games	Pos.
1967	WAS	N	1	LB
1967	ATL	N	2	LB, K
1968			10	LB
1969	NO	N	14	LB
1970			10	LB
1971			14	LB
1972	PHI	N	8	LB
6 yrs.	59 games			

Steve Ache
ACHE, STEVE
B. Mar. 16, 1962, Syracuse, NY
Southwest Missouri State 6'3" 229 lbs.

Year	Team		Games	Pos.
1987	MIN	N	3	LB

George Achicha
ACHICHA, GEORGE
B. Dec. 19, 1961, American Samoa
Southern California 6'5" 260 lbs.

Year	Team		Games	Pos.
1985	IND	N	4	NT

Walt Achui
ACHUI, WALTER (Sneeze)
B. Aug. 3, 1902
D. Mar. 21, 1989, Eugene, OR
Hawaii/Dayton 5'8" 170 lbs.

Year	Team		Games	Pos.
1927	DAY	N	7	HB
1928			4	HB, E, FB, QB
2 yrs.	11 games			

Bill Acker
ACKER, WILLIAM
B. Nov. 7, 1956, Freer, TX
Texas 6'3" 255 lbs.

Year	Team		Games	Pos.
1980	STL	N	16	DT
1981			8	DT
1982	KC	N	3	NT
1983	BUF	N	11	NT
1984			15	NT
1987	KC	N	2	NT
6 yrs.	55 games			

Rick Ackerman
ACKERMAN, RICHARD CARL
B. Jun. 16, 1959, La Grange, IL
Memphis State 6'4" 250 lbs.

Year	Team		Games	Pos.
1982	SD	N	9	DT
1983			15	DT
1984			9	NT
1984	LARI	N	6	NT
1987			3	DT
4 yrs.	42 games			

Tom Ackerman
ACKERMAN, TOM
B. Sep. 6, 1972, Bellingham, WA
Eastern Washington 6'3" 290 lbs.

Year	Team		Games	Pos.
1996	NO	N	2	C

Ron Acks
ACKS, RONALD WILLIAM
B. Oct. 3, 1944, Herrin, IL
Illinois 6'2" 210 lbs.

Year	Team		Games	Pos.
1968	ATL	N	1	LB
1969			14	LB
1970			8	LB
1971			14	LB
1972	NE	N	14	LB
1973			14	LB
1974	GB	N	13	LB
1975			14	LB
1976			13	LB
9 yrs.	105 games			

Fred Acorn
ACORN, FREDERICK EARL
B. Mar. 17, 1961, Rotan, TX
Texas 5'10" 180 lbs.

Year	Team		Games	Pos.
1984	TB	N	16	CB

Ed Adamchik
ADAMCHIK, EDWARD
B. Nov. 2, 1941, Johnstown, PA
Pittsburgh 6'2" 235 lbs.

Year	Team		Games	Pos.
1965	NYG	N	2	C
1965	PIT	N	4	C
1 yr.	6 games			

Mike Adamle
ADAMLE, MICHAEL DAVID
B. Oct. 4, 1949, Kent, OH
Northwestern 5'9" 197 lbs.

Year	Team		Games	Pos.
1971	KC	N	8	RB
1972			14	RB
1973	NYJ	N	14	RB
1974			12	RB
1975	CHI	N	14	RB
1976			14	RB
6 yrs.	76 games			

Tony Adamle
ADAMLE, ANTHONY
B. May 15, 1924, Fairmont, WV
Ohio State 6'0" 210 lbs.

Year	Team		Games	Pos.
1947	CLE	AA	14	B
1948			14	B
1949			12	B

315

Year	Team		Games	Pos.

Tony Adamle *continued*
1950	CLE	N	12	FB, LB
1951			12	LB
1954			11	LB

6 yrs. 75 games

Bill Adams
ADAMS, WILLIAM JOSEPH
B. Feb. 4, 1950, Lynn, MA
Holy Cross 6'2" 250 lbs.
1972	BUF	N	6	G
1974			8	G
1975			6	G
1976			11	G
1977			9	G, OT
1978			6	G

6 yrs. 46 games

Bob Adams
ADAMS, ROBERT BRUCE
B. Aug. 15, 1946, San Francisco, CA
Pacific 6'2" 225 lbs.
1969	PIT	N	14	TE
1970			14	TE
1971			14	TE
1973	NE	N	11	TE
1974			14	TE
1975	DEN	N	2	TE
1976	ATL	N	13	TE

7 yrs. 82 games

Brent Adams
ADAMS, DAVID BRENT
B. Jun. 26, 1952, Elberton, GA
Tennessee-Chattanooga 6'5" 256 lbs.
1975	ATL	N	13	OT
1976			14	OT
1977			14	OT

3 yrs. 41 games

Chet Adams
ADAMCZYK, CHESTER FRANK
B. Oct. 24, 1915, Cleveland, OH
D. Oct. 28, 1990, Cleveland, OH
Ohio University 6'3" 240 lbs.
1939	CLE	N	9	T, B
1940			11	T, E
1941			11	T
1942			11	T
1943	GB	N	10	T
1946	CLE	AA	14	T
1947			13	T
1948			14	T
1949	BUF	AA	12	T
1950	NYY	N	12	T

10 yrs. 117 games

Curtis Adams
ADAMS, CURTIS LANDON
B. Apr. 30, 1962, Muskegon, MI
Central Michigan 6'0" 194 lbs.
1985	SD	N	1	RB
1986			7	RB
1987			12	RB
1988			7	RB

4 yrs. 27 games

David Adams
ADAMS, DAVID D.
B. Jun. 24, 1964, Tucson, AZ
Arizona 5'6" 170 lbs.
| 1987 | DAL | N | 3 | RB |

Doug Adams
ADAMS, DOUGLAS O.
B. Nov. 3, 1949, Xenia, OH
Ohio State 6'0" 223 lbs.
| 1971 | CIN | N | 11 | LB |

Doug Adams *continued*
1972			14	LB
1973			12	LB
1974			12	LB

4 yrs. 49 games

Earnest Adams
ADAMS, EARNEST
B. Mar. 12, 1959, Fort Lauderdale, FL
Illinois 6'3" 225 lbs.
| 1987 | DET | N | 3 | LB |

George Adams
ADAMS, GEORGE WALLACE
B. Dec. 22, 1962, Lexington, KY
Kentucky 6'1" 225 lbs.
1985	NYG	N	16	RB
1987			12	RB
1988			16	RB
1989			14	RB
1990	NE	N	16	RB
1991			2	RB

6 yrs. 76 games

Hank Adams
ADAMS, HENRY (Heinie)
B. Dec. 24, 1915, California, PA
Pittsburgh 6'1" 190 lbs.
| 1939 | CHIC | N | 2 | C |

John Adams
ADAMS, JOHN
B. Nov. 28, 1937, San Diego, CA
Los Angeles State 6'3" 235 lbs.
1959	CHIB	N	12	FB
1960	CHI		12	FB
1961			13	FB
1962			14	FB
1963	LA		13	OE

5 yrs. 64 games

John Adams
ADAMS, JOHN WILLIAM (Tree)
B. Sep. 22, 1921, Carthage, AR
D. Aug. 20, 1969, Bethesda, MD
Notre Dame 6'7" 245 lbs.
1945	WAS	N	10	T
1946			11	T
1947			10	T
1948			12	T
1949			12	T

5 yrs. 55 games

Julius Adams
ADAMS, JULIUS THOMAS (Jewel)
B. Apr. 26, 1948, Macon, GA
Texas Southern 6'3" 262 lbs.
1971	NE	N	14	DT
1972			11	DT
1973			14	DT
1974			14	DT
1975			9	DE
1976			14	DE
1977			14	DE
1978			1	DE
1979			16	DE
1980			16	DE
1981			16	DE
1982			9	DE
1983			16	DE
1984			16	DE
1985			16	DE
1987			10	DE

16 yrs. 206 games

Mike Adams
ADAMS, MICHAEL
B. Apr. 5, 1964, Shelby, MS

Mike Adams *continued*
Arkansas State 5'9" 206 lbs.
1987	NO	N	7	CB
1988			5	CB, S
1989	PHX	N	3	CB

3 yrs. 15 games

O'Neal Adams
ADAMS, HOWARD O'NEAL
B. Jan. 21, 1919, El Paso, AR
Arkansas 6'3" 195 lbs.
1942	NYG	N	11	E
1943			8	E
1944			10	E
1946	BKN	AA	13	E
1947			1	E

5 yrs. 43 games

Pete Adams
ADAMS, PETER ANTHONY
B. May 4, 1951, San Diego, CA
Southern California 6'4" 260 lbs.
| 1974 | CLE | N | 12 | G |
| 1976 | | | 13 | G |

2 yrs. 25 games

Sam Adams
ADAMS, SAM AARON
B. Jun. 13, 1973, Houston, TX
Texas A&M 6'3" 285 lbs.
1994	SEA	N	12	DE, DT
1995			16	DT
1996			16	DT

3 yrs. 44 games

Sam Adams
ADAMS, SAM EDWARD
B. Sep. 20, 1948, Jasper, TX
Prairie View A&M 6'3" 260 lbs.
1972	NE	N	7	G
1973			13	G
1974			14	G
1975			14	G
1976			14	G
1977			14	G
1978			16	G
1979			15	G
1980			15	G
1981	NO	N	16	G

10 yrs. 138 games

Scott Adams
ADAMS, SCOTT ALEXANDER
B. Sep. 28, 1966, Lake City, FL
Georgia 6'5" 281 lbs.
1992	MIN	N	15	G
1993			15	G, OT
1994	NO	N	11	G
1995	CHI	N	4	OT
1996	TB	N	7	G

5 yrs. 52 games

Stan Adams
ADAMS, STANLEY EARL
B. May 22 1960, Marion, AR
Memphis State 6'2" 220 lbs.
| 1984 | LARI | N | 4 | LB |

Stefon Adams
ADAMS, STEFON LEE
B. Aug. 11, 1963, High Point, NC
East Carolina 5'10" 190 lbs.
1986	LARI	N	16	CB
1987			9	S
1988			14	S
1989			14	S
1990	CLE	N	10	CB
1990	MIA	N	2	S

5 yrs. 65 games

Theo Adams
ADAMS, THEO
B. Apr. 24, 1966, San Francisco, CA
Hawaii 6'4" 282 lbs.
1992	SEA	N	10	OT
1993	TB	N	7	OT
1995	PHI	N	18	G

3 yrs. 35 games

Tom Adams
ADAMS, TOM
B. Apr. 26, 1940, Keewatin, MN
Minnesota-Duluth 6'5" 210 lbs.
| 1962 | MIN | N | 6 | OE |

Tony Adams
ADAMS, ANTHONY LEE
B. Mar. 19, 1950, San Antonio, TX
Texas/Utah State 6'0" 190 lbs.
1975	KC	N	6	QB
1976			14	QB
1977			14	QB
1978			7	QB
1987	MIN	N	3	QB

5 yrs. 44 games

Vashone Adams
ADAMS, VASHONE LAREY
B. Sep. 12, 1973, Aurora, CO
Fort Hays/Eastern Michigan 5'10" 196 lbs.
| 1995 | CLE | N | 8 | S |
| 1996 | BAL | N | 16 | S |

2 yrs. 24 games

Verlin Adams
ADAMS, VERLIN T. (Sparky)
B. Jun. 14, 1918, Burnwell, KY
D. Mar. 30, 1985, Charleston, WV
Morris Harvey 6'0" 205 lbs.
1943	NYG	N	4	E
1944			10	E
1945			9	E

3 yrs. 23 games

Willie Adams
ADAMS, WILLIE JAMES (Hawk)
B. Dec. 12, 1941, Corpus Christi, TX
New Mexico State 6'2" 245 lbs.
| 1965 | WAS | N | 14 | LB |
| 1966 | | | 14 | LB |

2 yrs. 28 games

Willis Adams
ADAMS, WILLIS DEAN
B. Aug. 22, 1956, Weimar, TX
Houston 6'2" 200 lbs.
1979	CLE	N	16	WR
1980			16	WR
1981			7	WR
1982			1	WR
1983			16	WR
1984			16	WR
1985			3	WR

7 yrs. 75 games

Ken Adamson
ADAMSON, KENNETH
B. Oct. 12, 1938
Notre Dame 6'2" 222 lbs.
1960	DEN	A		G
1961			14	G
1962			4	G

3 yrs. 18 games

Abe Addams
ADDAMS, ABE B.

Year	Team		Games	Pos.

Abe Addams *continued*
B. Jul. 12, 1926, Louisville, KY
Indiana 6'2" 220 lbs.

1949	DET	N	5	DE

Herb Adderley
ADDERLEY, HERBERT B.
B. Jun. 8, 1939, Philadelphia, PA
Michigan State 6'0" 200 lbs.

1961	GB		14	DB
1962			14	DB
1963			14	DB
1964			13	DB
1965			14	DB
1966			14	DB
1967			14	DB
1968			14	DB
1969			14	CB
1970	DAL	N	14	CB
1971			12	CB
1972			13	CB

12 yrs.   164 games

Tom Addison
ADDISON, THOMAS MARION
B. Apr. 12, 1936, Lancaster, SC
South Carolina 6'2" 225 lbs.

1960	BOS	A	13	LB
1961			14	LB
1962			14	LB
1963			14	LB
1964			14	LB
1965			14	LB
1966			14	LB
1967			11	LB

8 yrs.   108 games

Nick Adducci
ADDUCCI, NICHOLAS FRANK
B. Jul. 12, 1929, Chicago, IL
Nebraska 5'10" 203 lbs.

| 1954 | WAS | N | 10 | HB |
| 1955 | | | 12 | FB |

2 yrs.   22 games

Samaji Adi Akili
Born SAMUEL CHARLES WILLIAMS
Played as SAM WILLIAMS 1974-75
B. Jul. 22, 1952, Cameron, TX
New Mexico Highlands/California 6'2" 190 lbs.

1974	SD	N	13	S
1975			11	CB
1976	HOU	N	4	DB

3 yrs.   28 games

John Adickes
ADICKES, JOHN M.
B. Jun. 29, 1964, St. Albans, NY
Baylor 6'3" 264 lbs.

1987	CHI	N	6	C
1988			16	C
1989	MIN	N	1	C

3 yrs.   23 games

Mark Adickes
ADICKES, MARK STEPHEN
B. Apr. 22, 1961, Bad Constadt, Germany
Baylor 6'5" 278 lbs.

1986	KC	N	15	G
1987			12	G
1988			10	G
1989			16	G
1990	WAS	N	8	G
1991			16	G

6 yrs.   77 games

Bob Adkins
ADKINS, ROBERT GRANT
B. Feb. 7, 1917, Point Pleasant, WV
Marshall 6'1" 210 lbs.

1940	GB	N	10	QB, E, HB
1941			7	QB
1945			4	QB

3 yrs.   21 games

Kevin Adkins
ADKINS, KEVIN
B. 1964
Oklahoma 6'1" 250 lbs.

| 1987 | KC | N | 2 | C |

Margene Adkins
ADKINS, MARGENE
B. Apr. 30, 1947, Fort Worth, TX
Henderson JC 5'10" 183 lbs.

1970	DAL	N	5	WR
1971			3	WR
1972	NO	N	14	WR
1973	NYJ	N	13	WR

4 yrs.   35 games

Sam Adkins
ADKINS, SAM
B. May 21, 1955, Van Nuys, CA
Wichita State 6'2" 214 lbs.

1977	SEA	N	1	QB
1979			3	QB
1980			4	QB
1981			3	QB

4 yrs.   11 games

Erik Affholter
AFFHOLTER, ERIK CONRAD
B. Apr. 10, 1966, Detroit, MI
Southern California 6'0" 183 lbs.

| 1991 | GB | N | 4 | WR |

Dick Afflis
AFFLIS, WILLIAM RICHARD
(Bruiser)
B. Jun. 27, 1929, Lafayette, IN
D. Nov. 10, 1991, Indianapolis, IN
Nevada-Reno 5'11" 250 lbs.

1951	GB	N	12	G
1952			12	T
1953			12	T
1954			12	G

4 yrs.   48 games

Ben Agajanian
AGAJANIAN, BENJAMIN JAMES
(The Toeless Wonder)
B. Aug. 28, 1919, Santa Ana, CA
New Mexico 6'0" 195 lbs.

1945	PHI	N	1	G
1945	PIT	N	5	K
1947	LA	AA	13	K
1948			13	K
1949	NYG	N	12	K
1953	LA	N	10	K
1954	NYG	N	12	K
1955			12	K
1956			10	K
1957			12	K
1960	LA	A		K
1961	DAL	A	3	K
1961	GB	N	3	K
1962	OAK	A	6	K
1964	SD	A	3	K

13 yrs.   115 games

Alex Agase
AGASE, ALEXANDER ARRASI
B. Mar. 27, 1922, Evanston, IL

Alex Agase *continued*
Illinois/Purdue/Illinois 5'10" 210 lbs.

1947	LA	AA	3	G
1947	CHI	AA	11	G
1948	CLE	AA	13	G
1949			11	G
1950	CLE	N	11	G
1951			11	G
1953	BAL	N	10	G

6 yrs.   70 games

Louis Age
AGE, LOUIS THEODORE, III
B. Feb. 1, 1970, New Orleans, LA
Southwestern Louisiana 6'7" 350 lbs.

| 1992 | CHI | N | 6 | OT |

Mel Agee
AGEE, MEL
B. Nov. 22, 1968, Chicago, IL
Illinois 6'5" 294 lbs.

1991	IND	N	16	DE
1992			1	DE
1993	ATL	N	11	DE
1994			16	DT, DE
1995			10	DT

5 yrs.   54 games

Sam Agee
AGEE, SAMUEL WEBSTER
B. Oct. 21, 1915, Courtland, AL
Vanderbilt 6'1" 218 lbs.

| 1938 | CHIC | N | 9 | FB |
| 1939 | | | 11 | FB, HB |

2 yrs.   20 games

Tommie Agee
AGEE, TOMMIE LEE
B. Feb. 22, 1964, Chilton, AL
Auburn 6'0" 218 lbs.

1988	SEA	N	16	RB
1989	KC	N	9	RB
1990	DAL	N	16	RB
1991			16	RB
1992			16	RB
1993			12	RB
1994			15	RB

7 yrs.   100 games

Bob Agler
AGLER, ROBERT
B. Mar. 13, 1924, Columbus, OH
Otterbein 6'1" 205 lbs.

| 1948 | LA | N | 8 | HB |
| 1949 | | | 8 | FB |

2 yrs.   16 games

Ray Agnew
AGNEW, RAYMOND MITCHELL
B. Dec. 9, 1967, Winston-Salem, NC
North Carolina State 6'3" 272 lbs.

1990	NE	N	12	DE
1991			13	DE
1992			14	DE
1993			16	DE
1994			11	DE, NT
1995	NYG	N	16	DT
1996			13	DE

7 yrs.   95 games

Louie Aguiar
AGUIAR, LOUIE
B. Jun. 30, 1966, Livermore, CA
Utah State 6'2" 200 lbs.

1991	NYJ	N	16	P
1992			16	P
1993			16	P
1994	KC	N	16	P

Louie Aguiar *continued*

| 1995 | | | 16 | P |
| 1996 | | | 16 | P |

6 yrs.   96 games

Joe Aguirre
AGUIRRE, JOSEPH (Jude)
B. Oct. 17, 1918, Rock Springs, WY
St. Mary's (California) 6'3.5" 225 lbs.

1941	WAS	N	10	E, B
1943			10	E
1944			10	E
1945			10	E
1946	LA	AA	14	E
1947			12	E
1948			13	E
1949			4	E

8 yrs.   83 games

Chidi Ahanotu
AHANOTU, CHIDI OBIOMA
B. Oct. 11, 1970, Modesto, CA
California 6'2" 280 lbs.

1993	TB	N	16	DE, DT
1994			16	DE, DT
1995			16	DE
1996			13	DE

4 yrs.   61 games

Dan Ahern
AHERN, DANIEL F.
B. Feb. 15, 1898, Manchester, NH
Deceased
Georgetown (DC) 6'2" 195 lbs.

| 1921 | WAS | N | 4 | T, G |

Dave Ahrens
AHRENS, DAVID IVER
B. Dec. 5, 1958, Cedar Falls, IA
Wisconsin 6'3" 238 lbs.

1981	STL	N	16	LB
1982			9	LB
1983			16	LB
1984			16	LB
1985	IND	N	16	LB
1986			16	LB
1987			12	LB
1988	DET	N	8	LB
1989	MIA	N	11	LB
1990	SEA	N	10	LB

10 yrs.   130 games

Tony Aiello
AIELLO, ANTHONY
B. Apr. 29, 1921, Monongahela, PA
Youngstown State 5'6.5" 165 lbs.

| 1944 | DET | N | 4 | B |
| 1944 | BKN | N | 1 | B |

1 yr.   5 games

Carl Aikens
AIKENS, CARL
B. Jun. 5, 1962, Great Lakes, IL
Northern Illinois 6'1" 187 lbs.

| 1987 | LARI | N | 3 | WR |

Troy Aikman
AIKMAN, TROY KENNETH
B. Nov. 21, 1966, West Covina, CA
UCLA 6'4" 216 lbs.

1989	DAL		11	QB
1990			15	QB
1991			12	QB
1992			16	QB
1993			14	QB
1994			14	QB
1995			16	QB

Year	Team	Games	Pos.

Troy Aikman continued

1996		15	QB
8 yrs.	113 games		

Jim Ailinger

AILINGER, JAMES J.
B. Jul. 10, 1901, Buffalo, NY
Deceased
Buffalo State 5'11" 185 lbs.

1924	BUF	N	7	G, T

Charlie Aiu

AIU, CHARLES KAHOALII
B. May 22, 1954, Honolulu, HI
Hawaii 6'2" 250 lbs.

1976	SD	N	12	G
1977			14	G
1978			6	G
1978	SEA	N	1	G
3 yrs.	33 games			

Harold Akin

AKIN, HAROLD DWAYNE (Horse)
B. Jan. 11, 1945, McAlester, OK
Oklahoma State 6'5" 261 lbs.

1967	SD	A	3	OT
1968			11	OT
2 yrs.	14 games			

Len Akin

AKIN, LEONARD R. (Tex)
B. Apr. 8, 1916, McKinney, TX
D. Mar, 1987, Irving, TX
Baylor 5'11" 207 lbs.

1942	CHIB	N	11	G

Al Akins

AKINS, ALBERT GEORGE
B. Jun. 13, 1921, Spokane, WA
Washington/Washington State 6'1" 195 lbs.

1946	CLE	AA	4	HB, DB
1947	BKN	AA	13	HB, DB
1948			3	HB, DB
1948	BUF	AA	5	HB, DB
3 yrs.	25 games			

Frank Akins

AKINS, FRANK SCOTT
B. Mar. 31, 1919, Dutton, MT
D. Jul. 6, 1992
Washington State 5'10" 215 lbs.

1943	WAS	N	6	B
1944			6	FB
1945			10	FB
1946			8	FB
4 yrs.	30 games			

Mike Akiu

AKIU, MIKE
B. Feb. 12, 1962, Kailua, HI
Washington State/Hawaii 5'9" 182 lbs.

1985	HOU	N	9	WR
1986			1	WR
2 yrs.	10 games			

Dick Alban

ALBAN, RICHARD HERBERT
B. Jan. 17, 1929, Hanover, PA
Northwestern 6'0" 193 lbs.

1952	WAS	N	12	DB
1953			12	DB
1954			12	DB
1955			12	DB
1956	PIT	N	12	DB
1957			12	DB

Dick Alban continued

1958		12	DB
1959		12	DB
8 yrs.	96 games		

Dom Albanese

ALBANESE, DOMINIC
B. Sep. 9, 1903
D. Mar. 17, 1992, Millersport, OH
Aquinas 190 lbs.

1925	COL	N	3	E, FB, QB

Vannie Albanese

ALBANESE, VANNIE M.
B. 1913
D. Sep. 2, 1984, Canandaigua, NY
Syracuse 6'0" 185 lbs.

1937	BKN	N	10	FB, HB
1938			8	B
2 yrs.	18 games			

Frankie Albert

ALBERT, FRANK CULLEN
B. Jan. 27, 1920, Chicago, IL
Stanford 5'10" 160 lbs.

1946	SF	AA	14	QB
1947			14	QB
1948			14	QB
1949			12	QB
1950	SF	N	12	QB
1951			12	QB
1952			12	QB
7 yrs.	90 games			

Sergio Albert

ALBERT, SERGIO
B. Oct. 28, 1951, Mexico City, Mexico
U.S. International 6'3" 200 lbs.

1974	STL	N	12	K

Trev Alberts

ALBERTS, TREV
B. Aug. 8, 1970, Cedar Falls, IA
Nebraska 6'4" 242 lbs.

1994	IND	N	5	LB
1995			15	LB
1996			9	LB
3 yrs.	29 games			

Art Albrecht

ALBRECHT, ARTHUR
B. Dec. 29, 1921, Manitowoc, WI
Wisconsin 6'1" 200 lbs.

1942	PIT	N	3	C
1943	CHIC	N	6	T
1944	BOS	N	5	T, C
3 yrs.	14 games			

Ted Albrecht

ALBRECHT, THEODORE CARL
B. Oct. 8, 1954, Harvey, IL
California 6'4" 250 lbs.

1977	CHI	N	14	OT, G
1978			15	OT, G
1979			16	OT, G
1980			16	OT, G
1981			16	OT, G
5 yrs.	77 games			

Bill Albright

ALBRIGHT, WILLIAM
B. Apr. 4, 1929
Wisconsin 6'1" 245 lbs.

1951	NYG	N	11	T
1952			12	G

Bill Albright continued

1953		12	G
1954		12	G
4 yrs.	47 games		

Ethan Albright

ALBRIGHT, LAWRENCE ETHAN
B. May 1, 1971, Greensboro, NC
North Carolina 6'5" 292 lbs.

1995	MIA	N	10	OT, G
1996	BUF	N	16	OT
2 yrs.	26 games			

Ira Albright

ALBRIGHT, IRA LADOL
B. Jan. 2, 1959, Dallas, TX
Northeastern Oklahoma 5'11" 260 lbs.

1987	BUF	N	3	NT, RB

Vince Albritton

ALBRITTON, VINCE DENADER
B. Jul. 23, 1962, Oakland, CA
Washington 6'2" 215 lbs.

1984	DAL	N	16	S
1985			7	S
1986			16	S
1987			11	S
1988			6	S
1989			16	S
1990			8	S
1991			6	S
8 yrs.	86 games			

Grady Alderman

ALDERMAN, GRADY CHARLES
B. Dec. 10, 1938, Detroit, MI
Detroit 6'2" 242 lbs.

1960	DET	N	11	G
1961	MIN	N	14	OT
1962			14	OT
1963			14	OT
1964			14	OT
1965			13	OT
1966			14	OT
1967			14	OT
1968			14	OT
1969			14	OT
1970			14	OT
1971			13	OT
1972			14	OT
1973			14	OT
1974			13	OT
15 yrs.	204 games			

John Alderton

ALDERTON, JOHN
B. Sep. 5, 1931
Maryland 6'1" 200 lbs.

1953	PIT	N	10	DE

Ki Aldrich

ALDRICH, CHARLES C.
B. Jun. 1, 1916, Rogers, TX
D. Mar. 12, 1983, Temple, TX
Texas Christian 6'0" 215 lbs.

1939	CHIC	N	11	C
1940			11	C
1941	WAS	N	11	C
1942			11	C
1945			6	C
1946			11	C
1947			12	C, G
7 yrs.	73 games			

Allen Aldridge

ALDRIDGE, ALLEN

Allen Aldridge continued

B. May 30, 1972, Houston, TX
Houston 6'1" 243 lbs.

1994	DEN	N	16	LB
1995			16	LB
1996			16	LB
3 yrs.	48 games			

Allen Aldridge

ALDRIDGE, ALLEN RAY
B. Apr. 27, 1945, Galveston, TX
Prairie View A&M 6'6" 240 lbs.

1971	HOU	N	13	DE
1972			8	DE
1974	CLE	N	14	DT
3 yrs.	35 games			

Bennie Aldridge

ALDRIDGE, BENNIE LEO (Lefty)
B. Oct. 24, 1926, Duncan, OK
Deceased
Oklahoma A&M 6'0" 195 lbs.

1950	NYY	N	11	B
1951			12	B
1952	DAL	N	1	HB
1952	SF	N	11	HB
1953	GB	N	8	HB
4 yrs.	43 games			

Jerry Aldridge

ALDRIDGE, JERRY CHARLES
B. Sep. 1, 1956, Jacksonville, TX
Angelo State 6'2" 215 lbs.

1980	SF	N	1	RB

Lionel Aldridge

ALDRIDGE, LIONEL
B. Dec. 14, 1941, Evergreen, LA
Utah State 6'4" 245 lbs.

1963	GB	N	14	DE
1964			14	DE
1965			14	DE
1966			13	DE
1967			12	DE
1968			14	DE
1969			14	DE
1970			14	DE
1971			14	DE
1972	SD	N	14	DE
1973			10	DE
11 yrs.	147 games			

Melvin Aldridge

ALDRIDGE, MELVIN KEITH
B. Jul. 22, 1970, Pittsburg, TX
Murray State 6'2" 195 lbs.

1993	HOU	N	1	S
1995	ARI	N	2	S
2 yrs.	3 games			

Arnold Ale

ALE, ARNOLD TAUESE
B. Jun. 17, 1970, San Pedro, CA
UCLA 6'2" 230 lbs.

1994	KC	N	3	LB
1996	SD	N	7	LB
2 yrs.	10 games			

Keith Alex

ALEX, HIRAM KEITH
B. Jun. 9, 1969, Kountze, TX
Texas A&M 6'4" 307 lbs.

1993	ATL	N	14	G
1995	MIN	N	1	G
2 yrs.	15 games			

Year	Team	Games	Pos.

Steve Alexakos
ALEXAKOS, STEVE
B. Dec. 15, 1946, Lowell, MA
San Jose State 6'2" 260 lbs.

Year	Team		Games	Pos.
1970	DEN	N	8	G
1971	NYG	N	10	G
2 yrs.	18 games			

Brent Alexander
ALEXANDER, BRENT
B. Jul. 10, 1970, Gallatin, TN
Tennessee State 5'10" 184 lbs.

1994	ARI	N	16	CB
1995			16	S, CB
1996			16	S
3 yrs.	48 games			

Bruce Alexander
ALEXANDER, BRUCE EDWARD
B. Sep. 17, 1965, Lufkin, TX
Stephen F. Austin 5'9" 171 lbs.

1989	DET	N	8	CB, S
1990			1	CB
1991			9	CB
1992	MIA	N	12	CB
1993			14	CB
5 yrs.	44 games			

Charles Alexander
ALEXANDER, CHARLES FRED, JR.
B. Jul. 28, 1957, Galveston, TX
Louisiana State 6'1" 225 lbs.

1979	CIN	N	16	RB
1980			16	RB
1981			15	RB
1982			9	RB
1983			14	RB
1984			16	RB
1985			16	RB
7 yrs.	102 games			

Dan Alexander
ALEXANDER, DAN LAMARR
B. Jun. 17, 1955, Houston, TX
Louisiana State 6'4" 270 lbs.

1977	NYJ	N	14	G
1978			16	G
1979			16	G
1980			16	G
1981			16	G
1982			9	G
1983			16	G
1984			16	G
1985			16	G
1986			16	G
1987			12	G, T
1988			14	G
1989			14	G
13 yrs.	191 games			

David Alexander
ALEXANDER, DAVID
B. Jul. 28, 1964, Silver Spring, MD
Tulsa 6'3" 275 lbs.

1987	PHI	N	12	OT
1988			16	OT
1989			16	C, G
1990			16	C, OT
1991			16	C
1992			16	C
1993			16	C
1994			16	C
1996	NYJ	N	7	C
9 yrs.	131 games			

Derrick Alexander
ALEXANDER, DERRICK

Derrick Alexander cont.
B. Nov. 3, 1973, Jacksonville, FL
Florida State 6'4" 276 lbs.

1995	MIN	N	15	DE
1996			12	DE
2 yrs.	27 games			

Derrick Alexander
ALEXANDER, DERRICK SCOTT
B. Nov. 6, 1971, Detroit, MI
Michigan 6'2" 195 lbs.

1994	CLE	N	14	WR
1995			14	WR
1996	BAL	N	15	WR
3 yrs.	43 games			

Elijah Alexander
ALEXANDER, ELIJAH ALFRED III
B. Aug. 8, 1970, Fort Worth, TX
Kansas State 6'2" 230 lbs.

1992	TB	N	12	LB
1993	DEN	N	16	LB
1994			16	LB
1995			9	LB
1996	IND	N	14	LB
5 yrs.	67 games			

Glenn Alexander
ALEXANDER, GLENN ELLIOTT
B. Jun. 3, 1947, New Orleans, LA
Grambling State 6'3" 205 lbs.

| 1970 | BUF | N | 13 | WR |

Harold Alexander
ALEXANDER, HAROLD DONALD, II
B. Oct. 20, 1970, Pickens, SC
Appalachian State 6'2" 224 lbs.

1993	ATL	N	16	P
1994			15	P
2 yrs.	31 games			

Jeff Alexander
ALEXANDER, JEFFREY O'NEAL
B. Jan. 15, 1965, Baton Rouge, LA
Southern University 6'0" 232 lbs.

1989	DEN	N	14	RB
1992	DEN	N	7	RB
2 yrs.	21 games			

Joe Alexander
ALEXANDER, JOSEPH A. (Doc)
B. Apr. 1, 1898, Silver Creek, NY
D. Sep. 12, 1975, New York, NY
Syracuse 5'11" 221 lbs.

1921	SYR	A	1	C
1921	ROC		5	C, T, G
1922	ROC	N	3	C
1924			2	T
1925	NYG	N	12	C
1926			13	G, C, T
1927			4	G, E
6 yrs.	40 games			

John Alexander
ALEXANDER, JOHN
B. Jul. 4, 1897
D. Aug. 5, 1986, Edison, NJ
Rutgers/Fordham 6'3" 248 lbs.

1922	MIL	N	7	T, E, G
1926	NYG	N	9	T, E
2 yrs.	16 games			

John Alexander
ALEXANDER, JOHN

John Alexander continued
B. Nov. 12, 1955, Hattiesburg, MS
Rutgers 6'2" 250 lbs.

1977	MIA	N	14	DE
1978			8	DE
2 yrs.	22 games			

Kermit Alexander
ALEXANDER, KERMIT JOSEPH
B. Jan. 4, 1941, New Iberia, LA
UCLA 5'11" 185 lbs.

1963	SF	N	14	HB, DB
1964			14	DB
1965			14	DB
1966			14	DB
1967			13	DB
1968			14	DB
1969			11	CB
1970	LA	N	14	CB
1971			14	CB
1972	PHI	N	7	S
1973			14	S
11 yrs.	143 games			

Kevin Alexander
ALEXANDER, KEVIN
B. Jan. 23, 1975, Denver, CO
Utah State 5'9" 184 lbs.

| 1996 | NYG | N | 4 | WR |

Mike Alexander
ALEXANDER, MICHAEL FITZGERALD
B. Mar. 19, 1965, Manhattan, NY
Penn State 6'3" 195 lbs.

1989	LARI	N	16	WR
1991	BUF	N	3	WR
2 yrs.	19 games			

Patrise Alexander
ALEXANDER, PATRISE
B. Oct. 23, 1972, Galveston, TX
Southwestern Louisiana 6'1" 248 lbs.

| 1996 | WAS | N | 16 | LB |

Ray Alexander
ALEXANDER, VERNEST RAYNARD
B. Jul. 8, 1962, Miami, FL
Florida A&M 6'4" 195 lbs.

1984	DEN	N	8	WR
1988	DAL	N	16	WR
1989			2	WR
3 yrs.	26 games			

Robert Alexander
ALEXANDER, ROBERT
B. Apr. 21, 1958, Charleston, WV
West Virginia 6'0" 185 lbs.

1982	LARM	N	9	RB
1983			15	RB
2 yrs.	24 games			

Rogers Alexander
ALEXANDER, ROGERS
B. Aug. 11, 1964, Washington, DC
Penn State 6'3" 222 lbs.

1986	NYJ	N	1	LB
1987	NE	N	3	LB
2 yrs.	4 games			

Vincent Alexander
ALEXANDER, VINCENT
B. Mar. 11, 1964
Southern Mississippi 5'10" 205 lbs.

| 1987 | NO | N | 1 | RB |

Willie Alexander
ALEXANDER, WILLIE JAMES
B. Sep. 21, 1949, Montgomery, AL
Alcorn State 6'2" 194 lbs.

1971	HOU	N	14	CB
1972			14	CB
1973			11	CB
1974			14	CB
1975			14	CB
1976			12	CB
1977			14	CB
1978			16	CB
1979			13	CB
9 yrs.	122 games			

Alton Alexis
ALEXIS, ALTON
B. Nov. 16, 1957, New Iberia, LA
Tulane 6'0" 184 lbs.

| 1980 | CIN | N | 1 | WR |

Ted Alfen
ALFEN, THEODORE
B. Jan. 3, 1947, Dunsmuir, CA
Springfield 6'0" 195 lbs.

| 1969 | DEN | A | 4 | RB |

Julie Alfonse
ALFONSE, JULIUS
B. 1914
Minnesota 5'8" 180 lbs.

1937	CLE	N	10	HB
1938			10	HB
2 yrs.	20 games			

Bruce Alford
ALFORD, HERBERT BRUCE, SR.
B. Sep. 12, 1922, Waco, TX
Texas Christian 6'0" 190 lbs.

1946	NY	AA	13	E
1947			13	E
1948			14	E
1949	B, NY	AA	11	E
1950	NYY	N	12	E
1951			12	E
6 yrs.	75 games			

Bruce Alford
ALFORD, HERBERT BRUCE, JR.
B. Apr. 21, 1945, Fort Worth, TX
Texas Christian 6'0" 185 lbs.

1967	WAS	N	2	K
1968	BUF	A	11	K
1969			14	K
3 yrs.	27 games			

Gene Alford
ALFORD, EUGENE
B. 1906
Texas Tech 5'9" 180 lbs.

1931	POR	N	14	HB, QB
1932			10	HB
1933			10	HB, QB
1934	C, S	N	4	HB
4 yrs.	38 games			

Lynwood Alford
ALFORD, LYNWOOD
B. Aug. 22, 1963
Syracuse 6'3" 220 lbs.

| 1987 | NYJ | N | 1 | LB |

Mike Alford
ALFORD, MICHAEL DEAL
B. Jun. 19, 1943, De Funiak Springs, FL

Year	Team		Games	Pos.

Mike Alford continued
Auburn 6'3" 233 lbs.

Year	Team		Games	Pos.
1965	STL	N	13	C
1966	DET	N	12	C
2 yrs.	25 games			

Warren Alfson
ALFSON, WARREN FRANK
B. May 10, 1915, Wisner, NE
Nebraska 6'0" 198 lbs.

1941	BKN	N	11	G

Tuineau Alipate
ALIPATE, TUINEAU
B. Aug. 21, 1967, Union City, CA
Washington State 6'1" 245 lbs.

1994	NYJ	N	9	LB
1995	MIN	N	16	LB
2 yrs.	25 games			

Don Allard
ALLARD, DONALD
B. 1936
Boston College 6'0" 189 lbs.

1961	NY	A	1	QB
1962	BOS	A	4	QB
2 yrs.	5 games			

Raul Allegre
ALLEGRE, RAUL ENRIQUE
B. Jun. 15, 1959, Torreon, Mexico
Montana/Texas 5'10" 167 lbs.

1983	BAL	N	16	K
1984	IND	N	12	K
1985			16	K
1986	NYG	N	13	K
1987			12	K
1988			6	K
1989			10	K
1990			3	K
1991			3	K
1991	NYJ	N	1	K
9 yrs.	92 games			

Anthony Allen
ALLEN, ANTHONY DERRICK
B. Jun. 29, 1959, McComb, MS
Washington 5'11" 182 lbs.

1985	ATL	N	16	WR
1986			5	WR
1987	WAS	N	3	WR
1988			14	WR
1989	SD	N	7	WR
5 yrs.	45 games			

Buddy Allen
ALLEN, ELIHU, JR.
B. Jul. 11, 1937
Oklahoma City/Utah State 5'10" 190 lbs.

1961	DEN	A	1	HB

Carl Allen
ALLEN, CARL
B. 1921
Ouachita Baptist 6'0" 175 lbs.

1948	BKN	AA	13	B

Carl Allen
ALLEN, CARL
B. Dec. 21, 1955, Hattiesburg, MS
Southern Mississippi 6'0" 186 lbs.

1977	STL	N	14	CB
1978			15	CB
1979			15	CB

Carl Allen continued

1980			16	CB
1981			10	CB
1982			9	CB
6 yrs.	79 games			

Chuck Allen
ALLEN, CHARLES R.
B. Sep. 7, 1939, Cle Elum, WA
Washington 6'1" 224 lbs.

1961	SD	A	9	LB
1962			14	LB
1963			14	LB
1964			14	LB
1965			14	LB
1966			5	LB
1967			12	LB
1968			11	LB
1969			14	LB
1970	PIT	N	14	LB
1971			10	LB
1972	PHI	N	12	LB
12 yrs.	143 games			

Dalva Allen
ALLEN, DALVA
B. Jan. 13, 1935, Gonzales, TX
Houston 6'5" 224 lbs.

1960	HOU	A		DE
1961			14	DE
1962	OAK	A	14	DE
1963			14	DE
1964			14	DE
4 yrs.	56 games			

Derek Allen
ALLEN, DEREK
B. Jan. 30, 1971, Geneseo, IL
Illinois 6'4" 290 lbs.

1995	NYG	N	1	G

Don Allen
ALLEN, DON RAY
B. 1937
Texas 6'0" 200 lbs.

1960	DEN	A		FB

Doug Allen
ALLEN, DOUGLAS
B. Nov. 13, 1951, West Corning, NY
Penn State 6'2" 228 lbs.

1974	BUF	N	14	LB
1975			14	LB
2 yrs.	28 games			

Duane Allen
ALLEN, DUANE DOUGLAS
B. Oct. 21, 1937, Alhambra, CA
Mt. San Antonio JC/Santa Ana JC 6'4" 221 lbs.

1961	LA	N	10	OE, DB
1962			7	OE
1963			7	OE
1964			7	OE
1965	PIT	N	2	OE
1965	BAL	N	2	OE
1966	CHI	N	11	TE
1967			5	TE
7 yrs.	51 games			

Earl Allen
ALLEN, EARL
B. Oct. 24, 1961
Michigan/Houston 5'11" 193 lbs.

1987	HOU	N	1	CB

Ed Allen
ALLEN, EDMUND
B. Jun. 5, 1901
D. Feb. 20, 1943
Creighton 175 lbs.

1928	CHIC	N	2	E

Eddie Allen
ALLEN, EDWARD
B. May 5, 1920, Danville, NY
Pennsylvania 6'1" 200 lbs.

1947	CHIB	N	9	FB

Egypt Allen
ALLEN, EGYPT TYRONE
B. Jul. 28, 1964, Dallas, TX
Texas Christian 6'3" 203 lbs.

1987	CHI	N	6	DB

Eric Allen
ALLEN, ERIC ANDRE
B. Nov. 22, 1965, San Diego, CA
Arizona State 5'10" 181 lbs.

1988	PHI	N	16	CB
1989			15	CB
1990			16	CB
1991			16	CB
1992			16	CB
1993			16	CB
1994			16	CB
1995	NO	N	16	CB
1996			16	CB
9 yrs.	143 games			

Ermal Allen
ALLEN, ERMAL G.
B. Dec. 25, 1920, Sneedville, TN
D. Feb. 9, 1988, Dallas, TX
Kentucky 5'11" 165 lbs.

1947	CLE	AA	12	B

Gary Allen
ALLEN, GARY
B. Apr. 23, 1960, Baldwin Park, CA
Hawaii 5'10" 183 lbs.

1982	HOU	N	7	RB
1983			1	RB
1983	DAL	N	6	RB
1984			16	RB
3 yrs.	30 games			

George Allen
ALLEN, GEORGE ROBERT
B. April 4, 1944, Longview, TX
West Texas A&M 6'7" 270 lbs.

1966	HOU	A	9	OT

Grady Allen
ALLEN, GRADY L.
B. Jan. 1, 1946, San Augustine, TX
Texas A&M 6'3" 226 lbs.

1968	ATL	N	14	LB
1969			14	LB
1970			14	LB
1971			3	LB
1972			14	LB
5 yrs.	59 games			

Greg Allen
ALLEN, GREG
B. Jun. 4, 1963, Milton, FL
Florida State 5'11" 200 lbs.

1985	CLE	N	7	RB
1986	TB	N	2	RB
2 yrs.	9 games			

Harvey Allen
ALLEN, HARVEY J.
B. Oct. 2, 1962
Nevada-Las Vegas 6'3" 215 lbs.

1987	SEA	N	2	S

Jackie Allen
ALLEN, JACK FRANKLIN
B. Sep. 24, 1947, Lawton, OK
Baylor 6'1" 187 lbs.

1969	OAK	A	5	CB
1970	BUF	N	14	CB
1971	BUF	N	14	CB
1972	PHI	N	1	DB
4 yrs.	34 games			

Jeff Allen
ALLEN, JEFFREY
B. Aug. 27, 1948, Chicago, IL
Iowa State 5'11" 190 lbs.

1971	STL	N	1	CB

Jeff Allen
ALLEN, JEFFREY
B. Jul. 1, 1958, Richmond, IN
California, Davis 5'11" 185 lbs.

1980	MIA	N	16	CB
1982	SD	N	9	CB
2 yrs.	25 games			

Jerry Allen
ALLEN, GERALD
B. Jun. 26, 1941, Canton, OH
Nebraska-Omaha 6'1" 204 lbs.

1966	BAL	N	4	RB
1967	WAS	N	11	RB
1968			11	RB
1969			2	RB
4 yrs.	28 games			

Jimmy Allen
ALLEN, JAMES LEE
B. Mar. 6, 1952, Clearwater, FL
UCLA 6'2" 194 lbs.

1974	PIT	N	14	DB
1975			14	CB
1976			10	CB
1977			12	CB
1978	DET	N	14	S
1979			16	S
1980			15	S
1981			15	S
8 yrs.	110 games			

Johnny Allen
ALLEN, JOHN MCKEE
B. Jun. 4, 1933, Monmouth, IL
Purdue 6'2" 224 lbs.

1955	WAS	N	12	C, LB
1956			12	C, LB
1957			12	C, LB
1958			12	C, LB
4 yrs.	48 games			

Kevin Allen
ALLEN, KEVIN E.
B. Jun. 21, 1963, Cincinnati, OH
Indiana 6'5" 284 lbs.

1985	PHI	N	16	OT

Larry Allen
ALLEN, LARRY CHRISTOPHER
B. Nov. 27, 1971, Los Angeles, CA
Sonoma State 6'3" 315 lbs.

1994	DAL	N	16	OT

Year	Team	Games	Pos.

Larry Allen *continued*

Year	Team		Games	Pos.
1995			16	G
1996			16	OT
3 yrs.	48 games			

Lou Allen
ALLEN, LOUIS
B. Jul. 12, 1924, Gadsden, AL
Duke 6'3" 215 lbs.

1950	PIT	N	12	T
1951			12	T
2 yrs.	24 games			

Marcus Allen
ALLEN, MARCUS
B. Mar. 26, 1960, San Diego, CA
Southern California 6'2" 205 lbs.

1982	LARI	N	9	RB
1983			16	RB
1984			16	RB
1985			16	RB
1986			13	RB
1987			12	RB
1988			15	RB
1989			8	RB
1990			16	RB
1991			8	RB
1992			16	RB
1993	KC	N	16	RB
1994			13	RB
1995			16	RB
1996			16	RB
15 yrs.	206 games			

Marvin Allen
ALLEN, MARVIN RAY
B. Nov. 23, 1965, Wichita Falls, TX
Tulane 5'10" 215 lbs.

1988	NE	N	11	RB
1989			3	RB
1990			8	RB
1991			15	RB
4 yrs.	37 games			

Nate Allen
ALLEN, NATHAN SHERALDTON
B. May 13, 1948, Georgetown, SC
Texas Southern 5'10" 172 lbs.

1971	KC	N	4	CB
1972			14	CB
1973			14	CB
1974			12	CB
1975	SF	N	14	CB
1976	MIN	N	12	CB
1977			14	CB
1978			16	CB
1979			5	CB
1979	DET	N	3	CB
9 yrs.	108 games			

Patrick Allen
ALLEN, LLOYD PATRICK
B. Aug. 26, 1961, Seattle, WA
Utah State 5'10" 179 lbs.

1984	HOU	N	16	CB
1985			16	CB
1986			16	CB
1987			11	CB
1988			15	CB
1989			16	CB
1990			16	CB, S
7 yrs.	106 games			

Terry Allen
ALLEN, TERRY THOMAS, JR.
B. Feb. 21, 1968, Commerce, GA

Terry Allen *continued*
Clemson 5'10" 189 lbs.

1991	MIN	N	15	RB
1992			16	RB
1994			16	RB
1995	WAS	N	16	RB
1996			16	RB
5 yrs.	79 games			

Kurt Allerman
ALLERMAN, KURT DANIEL
B. Aug. 30, 1955, Glen Ridge, NJ
Penn State 6'3" 222 lbs.

1977	STL	N	14	LB
1978			15	LB
1979			16	LB
1980	GB	N	13	LB
1981			16	LB
1982	STL	N	9	LB
1983			16	LB
1984			16	LB
1985	DET	N	10	LB
9 yrs.	125 games			

Ty Allert
ALLERT, TY HUNTER
B. Jul. 7, 1963, Rosenberg, TX
Texas 6'2" 233 lbs.

1986	SD	N	16	LB
1987			3	LB
1987	PHI	N	7	LB
1988			10	LB
1989			7	LB
1990	DEN	N	7	LB
1990	SEA	N	1	LB
5 yrs.	51 games			

Don Alley
ALLEY, DONALD
B. Apr. 21, 1945, Cheyenne, WY
Adams State 6'2" 200 lbs.

1967	BAL	N	10	RB
1969	PIT	N	6	LB
2 yrs.	16 games			

Hank Allison
ALLISON, HENRY HENDERSON
B. Feb. 11, 1947, Stevenson, AL
San Diego State 6'3" 257 lbs.

1971	PHI	N	14	G
1972			6	G
1975	STL	N	14	G
1976			10	G, OT
1977			8	G, OT
1977	DEN	N	3	OT
5 yrs.	55 games			

Jim Allison
ALLISON, JAMES RUSSELL
B. Mar. 2, 1943, Richmond, CA
San Diego State 6'0" 220 lbs.

1965	SD	A	14	FB
1966			14	FB
1967			3	RB
1968			13	RB
4 yrs.	44 games			

Neely Allison
ALLISON, JAMES NEELY
B. May 14, 1902
D. Feb, 1970, Houston, TX
Texas A&M 6'0" 190 lbs.

1926	BUF	N	9	E
1927			2	E
1928	NYG	N	13	E
3 yrs.	24 games			

Vaughn Alliston
ALLISTON, VAUGHN S., JR.
(Buddy)
B. 1934
Mississippi 6'0" 218 lbs.

1960	DEN	A		LB

Bob Allman
ALLMAN, ROBERT M.
B. 1914
Michigan State 6'0" 198 lbs.

1936	CHIB	N	1	E

Brian Allred
ALLRED, BRIAN MCCRAY
B. Mar. 16, 1969, Washington, DC
Sacramento State 5'10" 175 lbs.

1993	SEA	N	4	CB

Joe Allton
ALLTON, JOSEPH J.
B. Sep. 7, 1920, Claremore, OK
Oklahoma 6'2" 235 lbs.

1942	CHIC	N	11	T, C

Jeff Alm
ALM, JEFFREY LAWRENCE
B. Mar. 31, 1968, New York, NY
D. Dec. 13, 1993, Houston, TX
Notre Dame 6'6" 284 lbs.

1990	HOU	N	16	NT
1991			12	DT
1992			14	DT
1993			2	DT
4 yrs.	44 games			

Beau Almodobar
ALMODOBAR, BEAU
B. Oct. 25, 1962
Norwich 5'9" 180 lbs.

1987	NYG	N	2	WR

Gerald Alphin
ALPHIN, GERALD
B. May 21, 1964, Portland, OR
Kansas State 6'3" 220 lbs.

1990	NO	N	11	WR
1991			5	WR
2 yrs.	16 games			

Lyneal Alston
ALSTON, LYNEAL
B. Jul. 23, 1964, Mobile, AL
Southern Mississippi 6'1" 205 lbs.

1987	PIT	N	3	WR

Mack Alston
ALSTON, MACK, JR.
B. Apr. 27, 1947, Georgetown, SC
Maryland-Eastern Shore 6'2" 231 lbs.

1970	WAS	N	8	TE
1971			12	TE
1972			14	TE
1973	HOU	N	14	TE
1974			12	TE
1975			13	TE
1976			14	TE
1977	BAL	N	14	TE
1978			16	TE
1979			14	TE
1980			13	TE
11 yrs.	144 games			

O'Brien Alston
ALSTON, O'BRIEN DARWIN
B. Dec. 21, 1965, New Haven, CT
Maryland 6'6" 246 lbs.

1988	IND	N	15	LB
1989			4	LB
2 yrs.	19 games			

Mike Alstott
ALSTOTT, MIKE JOSEPH
B. Dec. 21, 1973, Joliet, IL
Purdue 6'0" 240 lbs.

1996	TB	N	16	RB

John Alt
ALT, JOHN MICHAEL
B. May 30, 1962, Stuttgart, Germany
Iowa 6'7" 282 lbs.

1984	KC	N	15	OT
1985			13	OT
1986			7	OT
1987			9	OT
1988			14	OT
1989			16	OT
1990			16	OT
1991			16	OT
1992			16	OT
1993			16	OT
1994			13	OT
1995			16	OT
1996			12	OT
13 yrs.	179 games			

Jim Althoff
ALTHOFF, JIM
B. Sep. 27, 1961, McHenry, IL
Winona State 6'3" 278 lbs.

1987	CHI	N	4	DT

Wilson Alvarez
ALVAREZ, WILSON
B. Mar. 22, 1957, Santa Cruz, Bolivia
Southeastern Louisiana 6'0" 165 lbs.

1981	SEA	N	4	K

Steve Alvers
ALVERS, STEVE DEAN
B. Apr. 4, 1958, West Palm Beach, FL
Miami (Florida) 6'4" 240 lbs.

1981	BUF	N	16	TE
1982	NYJ	N	3	TE, C
2 yrs.	19 games			

Steve Alvord
ALVORD, STEVEN LEE
B. Oct. 2, 1964, Bellingham, WA
Washington 6'5" 248 lbs.

1987	STL	N	12	DT
1988	PHX	N	15	DT
2 yrs.	27 games			

Tom Alward
ALWARD, THOMAS LAVERN
B. Oct. 13, 1952, Flint, MI
Nebraska 6'4" 255 lbs.

1976	TB	N	14	G

Lance Alworth
ALWORTH, LANCE DWIGHT
(Bambi)
B. Aug. 3, 1940, Houston, TX
Arkansas 6'0" 182 lbs.

1962	SD	A	8	OE
1963			14	OE
1964			14	FL

Year	Team		Games	Pos.

Lance Alworth continued

Year	Team		Games	Pos.
1965			14	FL
1966			14	FL
1967			11	FL
1968			14	FL
1969			14	WR
1970	SD	N	14	WR
1971	DAL	N	12	WR
1972			14	WR

11 yrs.   143 games

Lyle Alzado
ALZADO, LYLE MARTIN
B. Apr. 3, 1949, Brooklyn, NY
D. May 14, 1992, Portland, OR
Yankton 6'3" 254 lbs.

Year	Team		Games	Pos.
1971	DEN	N	12	DE
1972			14	DE
1973			14	DE
1974			14	DE
1975			14	DE
1976			1	DE
1977			14	DE
1978			16	DE
1979	CLE	N	15	DE
1980			16	DE
1981			15	DE
1982	LARI	N	9	DE
1983			15	DE
1984			16	DE
1985			11	DE

15 yrs.   196 games

John Amberg
AMBERG, JOHN
B. Mar. 6, 1928
Kansas 5'11" 195 lbs.

Year	Team		Games	Pos.
1951	NYG	N	12	HB, DB
1952			12	HB, DB

2 yrs.   24 games

Ashley Ambrose
AMBROSE, ASHLEY AVERY
B. Sep. 17, 1970, New Orleans, LA
Mississippi Valley State 5'10" 177 lbs.

Year	Team		Games	Pos.
1992	IND	N	10	CB, S
1993			14	CB, S
1994			16	CB
1995			16	CB
1996	CIN	N	16	CB

5 yrs.   72 games

Dick Ambrose
AMBROSE, RICHARD JOHN
(Bam-Bam)
B. Jan. 17, 1953, New Rochelle, NY
Virginia 6'0" 233 lbs.

Year	Team		Games	Pos.
1975	CLE	N	14	LB
1976			10	LB
1977			14	LB
1978			16	LB
1979			15	LB
1980			16	LB
1981			16	LB
1982			9	LB
1983			6	LB

9 yrs.   116 games

John Ambrose
AMBROSE, JOHN VINCENT
(Whitey)
B. Mar. 24, 1910, Three Rivers, MA
Catholic 6'0" 185 lbs.

Year	Team		Games	Pos.
1932	BKN	N	4	C

Walt Ambrose
AMBROSE, WALTER
B. Aug. 7, 1905

Walt Ambrose continued
Carroll (Wisconsin) 5'11" 210 lbs.

Year	Team		Games	Pos.
1930	POR	N	1	E

Alan Ameche
AMECHE, ALAN DANTE (The Horse)
B. Jun. 1, 1933, Kenosha, WI
D. Aug. 8, 1988, Houston, TX
Wisconsin 6'0" 218 lbs.

Year	Team		Games	Pos.
1955	BAL	N	12	FB
1956			12	FB
1957			12	FB
1958			12	FB
1959			12	FB
1960			10	FB

6 yrs.   70 games

Glen Amerson
AMERSON, GLEN DOUGLAS
B. Nov. 24, 1938
Texas Tech 6'1" 186 lbs.

Year	Team		Games	Pos.
1961	PHI	N	14	DB

Dave Ames
AMES, DAVID
B. 1937
Richmond 6'0" 185 lbs.

Year	Team		Games	Pos.
1961	NY	A	5	DB
1961	DEN	A	7	HB

1 yr.   12 games

Dick Amman
AMMAN, RICHARD DALE
B. Sep. 21, 1950, Seattle, WA
Florida State 6'5" 242 lbs.

Year	Team		Games	Pos.
1972	BAL	N	14	DE
1973			14	DE

2 yrs.   28 games

Marty Amsler
AMSLER, C. MARTIN
B. Oct. 26, 1942, Evansville, IN
Indiana/Evansville 6'5" 257 lbs.

Year	Team		Games	Pos.
1967	CHI	N	14	DE
1969			11	DE
1970	GB	N	9	DE
1970	CIN	N	3	DE

3 yrs.   37 games

Joe Amstutz
AMSTUTZ, GERALD JOSEPH
B. Oct. 12, 1934, Toledo, OH
Indiana 6'5" 264 lbs.

Year	Team		Games	Pos.
1957	CLE	N	11	C

Norm Amundsen
AMUNDSEN, NORMAN
B. Sep. 28, 1932, Chicago, IL
Wisconsin 5'11" 245 lbs.

Year	Team		Games	Pos.
1957	GB	N	12	G

George Amundson
AMUNDSON, GEORGE
B. Mar. 31, 1951, Pendleton, OR
Iowa State 6'3" 215 lbs.

Year	Team		Games	Pos.
1973	HOU	N	9	RB
1974			14	RB
1975	PHI	N	6	RB

3 yrs.   29 games

Vito Ananis
ANANIS, VITO FRANCIS
B. 1915, Cambridge, MA
D. Sep. 3, 1944, Wayland, MA

Vito Ananis continued
Boston College 5'10" 195 lbs.

Year	Team		Games	Pos.
1945	WAS	N	1	HB

Rudy Andabaker
ANDABAKER, RUDOLPH
B. Apr. 13, 1929, Donora, PA
Pittsburgh 6'0" 208 lbs.

Year	Team		Games	Pos.
1952	PIT	N	6	G
1954			4	G

2 yrs.   10 games

Kimble Anders
ANDERS, KIMBLE LYNARD
B. Sep. 10, 1966, Galveston, TX
Houston 5'11" 219 lbs.

Year	Team		Games	Pos.
1991	KC	N	2	RB
1992			11	RB
1993			16	RB
1994			16	RB
1995			16	RB
1996			16	RB

6 yrs.   77 games

Morten Andersen
ANDERSEN, MORTEN
B. Aug. 19, 1960, Struer, Denmark
Michigan State 6'2" 210 lbs.

Year	Team		Games	Pos.
1982	NO	N	8	K
1983			16	K
1984			16	K
1985			16	K
1986			16	K
1987			12	K
1988			16	K
1989			16	K
1990			16	K
1991			16	K
1992			16	K
1993			16	K
1994			16	K
1995	ATL	N	16	K
1996			16	K

15 yrs.   228 games

Stan Andersen
ANDERSEN, STANLEY
B. Sep. 14, 1917, Portland, OR
Stanford 6'2" 218 lbs.

Year	Team		Games	Pos.
1940	CLE	N	11	T
1941			5	E, T
1941	DET	N	6	E, T

2 yrs.   22 games

Anderson
ANDERSON

Year	Team		Games	Pos.
1922	HAM		1	HB

Anderson
ANDERSON
None 230 lbs.

Year	Team		Games	Pos.
1922	MIN	N	2	C, G

Alex Anderson
ANDERSON, ALEX
B. May 15, 1893
D. Oct, 1975, Hadley, MA
Boston College/Holy Cross/Georgetown (DC) 5'8" 166 lbs.

Year	Team		Games	Pos.
1921	WAS	A	1	G

Alfred Anderson
ANDERSON, ALFRED ANTHONY
B. Aug. 4, 1961, Waco, TX
Baylor 6'1" 220 lbs.

Year	Team		Games	Pos.
1984	MIN	N	16	RB

Alfred Anderson continued

Year	Team		Games	Pos.
1985			12	RB
1986			16	RB
1987			10	RB
1988			16	RB
1989			11	RB
1990			11	RB
1991			16	RB

8 yrs.   108 games

Anthony Anderson
ANDERSON, ANTHONY EUGENE
B. Sep. 27, 1956, Wilmington, DE
Temple 6'0" 197 lbs.

Year	Team		Games	Pos.
1979	PIT	N	16	RB
1980	ATL	N	16	RB

2 yrs.   32 games

Anthony Anderson
ANDERSON, ANTHONY RAY
B. Oct. 24, 1964, Ruston, LA
Grambling State 6'2" 205 lbs.

Year	Team		Games	Pos.
1987	SD	N	3	S

Aric Anderson
ANDERSON, ARIC
B. Apr. 9, 1965
Millikin 6'2" 220 lbs.

Year	Team		Games	Pos.
1987	GB	N	3	LB

Art Anderson
ANDERSON, ARTHUR
B. Oct. 9, 1937, Wahpeton, ND
Idaho 6'3" 244 lbs.

Year	Team		Games	Pos.
1961	CHI	N	14	OT
1962			14	OT
1963	PIT	N	13	OT

3 yrs.   41 games

Bill Anderson
ANDERSON, WALTER WILLIAM
B. Jul. 16, 1936, Hendersonville, NC
Tennessee 6'3" 211 lbs.

Year	Team		Games	Pos.
1958	WAS	N	12	E
1959			11	E
1960			12	E
1961			14	OE
1962			12	OE
1963			13	OE
1965	GB	N	14	OE
1966			10	TE

8 yrs.   98 games

Bill Anderson
ANDERSON, WILLIAM
B. Jan. 6, 1921, Triadelphia, WV
D. Apr, 1984, Wheeling, WV
West Virginia 6'2" 190 lbs.

Year	Team		Games	Pos.
1945	BOS	N	6	E

Billy Anderson
ANDERSON, BILL GUY
B. Feb. 17, 1942, Palme, TX
Tulsa 6'1" 195 lbs.

Year	Team		Games	Pos.
1967	HOU	A	8	QB

Billy Anderson
ANDERSON, WILLIAM
B. Mar. 3, 1929, Los Angeles, CA
Compton JC 6'0" 198 lbs.

Year	Team		Games	Pos.
1953	CHIB	N	12	HB, DB
1954			7	HB, DB

2 yrs.   19 games

Year	Team	Games	Pos.

Bob Anderson
ANDERSON, ROBERT P.
B. Mar. 31, 1938, Elizabeth, NJ
Army 6'2" 210 lbs.

Year	Team		Games	Pos.
1963	**NYG**	N	1	HB

Bobby Anderson
ANDERSON, ROBERT CONRAD
B. Oct. 11, 1947, Midland, MI
Colorado 6'0" 208 lbs.

Year	Team		Games	Pos.
1970	**DEN**	N	14	RB
1971			13	RB
1972			9	RB
1973			12	RB
1975	**NE**	N	5	RB
1975	**WAS**	N	1	RB

5 yrs.   54 games

Brad Anderson
ANDERSON, BRADLEY STEWART
B. Jan. 21, 1961, Glendale, AZ
Brigham Young/Arizona 6'2" 196 lbs.

Year	Team		Games	Pos.
1984	**CHI**	N	13	WR
1985			14	WR

2 yrs.   27 games

Bruce Anderson
ANDERSON, BRUCE ALBERT
B. Jan. 18, 1944, Coos Bay, OR
Willamette 6'4" 246 lbs.

Year	Team		Games	Pos.
1966	**LA**	N	7	DE
1967	**NYG**	N	14	DT
1968			14	DT
1969			10	DE
1970	**WAS**	N	14	DE

5 yrs.   59 games

Charlie Anderson
ANDERSON, CHARLES
B. Sep. 2, 1933, Atlanta, AR
Louisiana Tech 6'0" 230 lbs.

Year	Team		Games	Pos.
1956	**CHIC**	N	2	E

Chet Anderson
ANDERSON, CHESTER LEONARD, JR.
B. Mar. 14, 1945, Duluth, MN
Minnesota 6'3" 245 lbs.

Year	Team		Games	Pos.
1967	**PIT**	N	14	TE

Cliff Anderson
ANDERSON, CLIFTON, JR. (Doc)
B. Nov. 25, 1929, Cape May, NJ
D. Mar. 16, 1979, Princess Anne, MD
Indiana 6'2" 215 lbs.

Year	Team		Games	Pos.
1952	**CHIC**	N	12	E
1953			1	E
1953	**NYG**	N	7	E

2 yrs.   20 games

Curtis Anderson
ANDERSON, CURTIS LEE
B. May 16, 1957, Cincinnati, OH
Central State (Ohio) 6'6" 250 lbs.

Year	Team		Games	Pos.
1979	**KC**	N	6	DE

Darren Anderson
ANDERSON, DARREN HUNTER
B. Jan. 11, 1969, Cincinnati, OH
Toledo 5'10" 180 lbs.

Year	Team		Games	Pos.
1992	**NE**	N	1	CB
1992	**TB**	N	1	CB
1993			14	CB
1994	**KC**	N	15	CB
1995			16	CB

Darren Anderson continued

Year	Team		Games	Pos.
1996			11	CB

5 yrs.   58 games

Dick Anderson
ANDERSON, RICHARD JOSEPH
B. Jan. 26, 1944, Massillon, OH
Ohio State 6'5" 245 lbs.

Year	Team		Games	Pos.
1967	**NO**	N	2	OT

Dick Anderson
ANDERSON, RICHARD PAUL
B. Feb. 10, 1946, Midland, MI
Colorado 6'2" 198 lbs.

Year	Team		Games	Pos.
1968	**MIA**	A	14	DB
1969			14	DB, P
1970	**MIA**	N	14	S
1971			14	S
1972			14	S, P
1973			14	S
1974			14	S
1976			9	S
1977			14	S

9 yrs.   121 games

Don Anderson
ANDERSON, DONALD CORTEZ
B. Jul. 8, 1963, Detroit, MI
Purdue 5'10" 197 lbs.

Year	Team		Games	Pos.
1985	**IND**	N	5	S
1987	**TB**	N	11	CB

2 yrs.   16 games

Donny Anderson
ANDERSON, GARRY DONNY
B. May 16, 1943, Borger, TX
Texas Tech 6'3" 212 lbs.

Year	Team		Games	Pos.
1966	**GB**		14	HB, P
1967			14	RB, P
1968			14	RB, P
1969			14	RB, P
1970			14	RB, P
1971			14	RB, P
1972	**STL**	N	14	RB, P
1973			14	RB,
1974			14	RB

9 yrs.   126 games

Dunstan Anderson
ANDERSON, DUNSTAN EVRETTE
B. Dec. 31, 1970, Fort Worth, TX
Tulsa 6'4" 260 lbs.

Year	Team		Games	Pos.
1994	**ATL**	N	1	DE

Dwayne Anderson
ANDERSON, DWAYNE EVERETT
B. Dec. 7, 1961, St. Louis, MO
Southern Methodist 6'0" 205 lbs.

Year	Team		Games	Pos.
1987	**STL**	N	1	S

Eddie Anderson
ANDERSON, EDDIE LEE, JR.
B. Jul. 22, 1963, Warner Robins, GA
Fort Valley State 6'1" 199 lbs.

Year	Team		Games	Pos.
1986	**SEA**	N	5	S
1987	**LARI**	N	13	S
1988			16	S
1989			15	S
1990			16	S
1991			16	S
1992			16	S
1993			16	S
1994			14	S
1995	**OAK**	N	14	S
1996			7	S

11 yrs.   148 games

Eddie Anderson
ANDERSON, EDWARD NICHOLAS
B. Nov. 13, 1900, Mason City, IA
D. Apr. 26, 1974, Clearwater, FL
Notre Dame 5'10" 176 lbs.

Year	Team		Games	Pos.
1922	**ROC**	N	3	E
1922	**CHIC**	N	7	E
1923			11	E
1924			9	E
1925			13	E
1926	**CHI**	A	10	E, G

5 yrs.   53 games

Erick Anderson
ANDERSON, ERICK SCOTT
B. Oct. 7, 1968, Long Beach, CA
Michigan 6'1" 235 lbs.

Year	Team		Games	Pos.
1993	**KC**	N	8	LB
1994	**WAS**	N	2	LB

2 yrs.   10 games

Ezz Anderson
ANDERSON, EZZRETT (Sugarfoot)
B. Feb. 10, 1920, Nashville, AR
Kentucky State 6'4" 215 lbs.

Year	Team		Games	Pos.
1947	**LA**	AA	13	E

Flipper Anderson
ANDERSON, WILLIE LEE, JR.
B. Mar. 7, 1965, Philadelphia, PA
UCLA 6'0" 169 lbs.

Year	Team		Games	Pos.
1988	**LARM**	N	16	WR
1989			16	WR
1990			16	WR
1991			12	WR
1992			15	WR
1993			15	WR
1994			16	WR
1995	**IND**	N	2	WR
1996	**WAS**	N	2	WR

9 yrs.   110 games

Fred Anderson
ANDERSON, FREDELL LAMONT
B. Oct. 30, 1954, Toppenish, WA
Oregon State/PrairieView A&M 6'4" 240 lbs.

Year	Team		Games	Pos.
1978	**PIT**	N	16	DL
1980	**SEA**	N	7	DE
1981			14	DE
1982			1	DE

4 yrs.   38 games

Gary Anderson
ANDERSON, GARY ALAN
B. Sep. 22, 1955, Fairfield, CA
Stanford 6'3" 253 lbs.

Year	Team		Games	Pos.
1977	**DET**	N	13	G
1978			2	G
1978	**NO**	N	2	G
1980	**WAS**	N	5	G

3 yrs.   22 games

Gary Anderson
ANDERSON, GARY ALLAN
B. Jul. 16, 1959, Parys, South Africa
Syracuse 5'11" 166 lbs.

Year	Team		Games	Pos.
1982	**PIT**	N	9	K
1983			16	K
1984			16	K
1985			16	K
1986			16	K
1987			12	K
1988			16	K
1989			16	K
1990			16	K

Gary Anderson continued

Year	Team		Games	Pos.
1991			16	K
1992			16	K
1993			16	K
1994			16	K
1995	**PHI**	N	16	K
1996			16	K

15 yrs.   229 games

Gary Anderson
ANDERSON, GARY WAYNE
B. Apr. 18, 1961, Columbia, MO
Arkansas 6'0" 180 lbs.

Year	Team		Games	Pos.
1985	**SD**	N	12	RB
1986			16	RB
1987			12	RB, WR
1988			14	RB
1990	**TB**	N	16	RB
1991			16	RB
1992			15	RB
1993			6	RB
1993	**DET**	N	4	RB

8 yrs.   111 games

Herbie Anderson
ANDERSON, HERBERT JAMES
B. Nov. 19, 1968, Port Arthur, TX
Texas A&I-Kingsville 5'9" 183 lbs.

Year	Team		Games	Pos.
1991	**HOU**	N	1	CB

Hunk Anderson
ANDERSON, HEARTLEY WILLIAM
B. Sep. 22, 1898, Calumet, MI
D. Apr. 24, 1978, West Palm Beach, FL
Notre Dame 5'11" 191 lbs.

Year	Team		Games	Pos.
1922	**CHIB**	N	10	G, E
1923			1	E
1923	**CLE**	N	1	G
1923	**CHIB**	N	10	G, C
1924			10	G
1925			6	G, C

4 yrs.   38 games

Jamal Anderson
ANDERSON, JAMAL SHARIF
B. Mar. 6, 1972, Woodland Hills, CA
Utah 5'10" 246 lbs.

Year	Team		Games	Pos.
1994	**ATL**	N	4	RB
1995			16	RB
1996			16	RB

3 yrs.   36 games

Jerry Anderson
ANDERSON, JERRY O.
B. Oct. 27, 1953, Murfreesboro, TN
D. May 27, 1989, Murfreesboro, TN
Oklahoma 5'11" 196 lbs.

Year	Team		Games	Pos.
1977	**CIN**	N	14	CB
1978	**TB**	N	1	S

2 yrs.   15 games

Jesse Anderson
ANDERSON, JESSE LEMOND
B. Jul. 26, 1966, West Point, MS
Mississippi State 6'2" 245 lbs.

Year	Team		Games	Pos.
1990	**TB**	N	16	TE
1991			15	TE
1992	**TB**	N	1	TE
1992	**PIT**	N	2	TE
1993	**NO**	N	1	TE

4 yrs.   35 games

John Anderson
ANDERSON, ROGER JOHN
B. Feb. 14, 1956, Waukesha, WI

Year	Team	Games	Pos.

John Anderson continued
Michigan 6'3" 221 lbs.

Year	Team		Games	Pos.
1978	GB	N	13	LB
1979			7	LB
1980			9	LB
1981			16	LB
1982			9	LB
1983			16	LB
1984			16	LB
1985			16	LB
1986			4	LB
1987			12	LB
1988			14	LB
1989			14	LB
12 yrs.	146 games			

Ken Anderson
ANDERSON, KENNETH ALLAN
B. Feb. 15, 1949, Batavia, IL
Augustana (Illinois) 6'3" 212 lbs.

Year	Team		Games	Pos.
1971	CIN	N	11	QB
1972			13	QB
1973			14	QB
1974			13	QB
1975			13	QB
1976			14	QB
1977			14	QB
1978			12	QB
1979			15	QB
1980			13	QB
1981			16	QB
1982			9	QB
1983			13	QB
1984			11	QB
1985			3	QB
1986			8	QB
16 yrs.	192 games			

Kim Anderson
ANDERSON, KIM SHERWOOD
B. Jul. 19, 1957, Pasadena, CA
Arizona State 5'11" 183 lbs.

Year	Team		Games	Pos.
1980	BAL	N	16	CB, S
1981			14	CB
1982			9	CB
1983			16	CB
1984	IND	N	1	S
5 yrs.	56 games			

Larry Anderson
ANDERSON, LAWRENCE ANDREW
B. Sep. 25, 1956, West Monroe, LA
Louisiana Tech 5'11" 177 lbs.

Year	Team		Games	Pos.
1978	PIT	N	16	CB
1979			16	CB
1980			4	CB
1981			16	CB
1982	BAL	N	9	S
1983			9	S
1984	IND	N	12	S
7 yrs.	82 games			

Marcus Anderson
ANDERSON, MARQUES JAMES
B. Jun. 12, 1959, Port Arthur, TX
Tulane 6'0" 178 lbs.

Year	Team		Games	Pos.
1981	CHI	N	12	WR

Max Anderson
ANDERSON, MAX ARTHUR
(Mouse, Mini Max)
B. Jun. 6, 1945, Stockton, CA
Arizona State 5'8" 180 lbs.

Year	Team		Games	Pos.
1968	BUF	A	14	RB
1969			11	RB
2 yrs.	25 games			

Melvin Anderson
ANDERSON, MELVIN A.
B. Aug. 29, 1965
Minnesota 5'11" 175 lbs.

Year	Team		Games	Pos.
1987	PIT	N	2	WR

Neal Anderson
ANDERSON, CHARLES NEAL
B. Aug. 14, 1964, Graceville, FL
Florida 5'11" 210 lbs.

Year	Team		Games	Pos.
1986	CHI	N	14	RB
1987			11	RB
1988			16	RB
1989			16	RB
1990			15	RB
1991			13	RB
1992			16	RB
1993			15	RB
8 yrs.	116 games			

Ockie Anderson
ANDERSON, OSCAR C.
B. 1894
D. Jan. 25, 1962
Colgate 5'9" 165 lbs.

Year	Team		Games	Pos.
1920	BUF	A	6	HB, QB
1921			11	HB
1922	BUF	N	7	HB, QB
3 yrs.	24 games			

O.J. Anderson
ANDERSON, OTTIS JEROME
B. Jan. 19, 1957, West Palm Beach, FL
Miami (Florida) 6'2" 225 lbs.

Year	Team		Games	Pos.
1979	STL	N	16	RB
1980			16	RB
1981			16	RB
1982			8	RB
1983			15	RB
1984			15	RB
1985			9	RB
1986			4	RB
1986	NYG	N	8	RB
1987			4	RB
1988			16	RB
1989			16	RB
1990			16	RB
1991			10	RB
1992			13	RB
14 yrs.	182 games			

Paul Anderson
ANDERSON, PAUL T.
B. Feb. 6, 1901
Deceased
Illinois 6'0" 190 lbs.

Year	Team		Games	Pos.
1925	RI	N	1	G

Preston Anderson
ANDERSON, PRESTON
B. Sep. 30, 1951, Bonham, TX
Rice 6'1" 183 lbs.

Year	Team		Games	Pos.
1974	CLE	N	14	CB

Ralph Anderson
ANDERSON, RALPH EDWARD
(Sticks)
B. Apr. 3, 1949, Dallas, TX
West Texas State 6'2" 180 lbs.

Year	Team		Games	Pos.
1971	PIT	N	6	DB
1972			14	DB
1973	NE	N	13	S
3 yrs.	33 games			

Ralph Anderson
ANDERSON, RALPH M.

Ralph Anderson continued
B. Jan. 1, 1937, Long Beach, CA
D. Nov. 26, 1960, Los Angeles County, CA
Los Angeles State 6'4" 223 lbs.

Year	Team		Games	Pos.
1958	CHIB	N	12	HB
1960	LA	A		OE
2 yrs.	12 games			

Richie Anderson
ANDERSON, RICHARD DARNOLL
B. Sep. 13, 1971, Sandy Spring, MD
Penn State 6'2" 215 lbs.

Year	Team		Games	Pos.
1993	NYJ	N	7	RB
1994			13	RB
1995			10	RB
1996			16	RB
4 yrs.	46 games			

Rickey Anderson
ANDERSON, RICKEY RECARDO
B. May 21, 1953, Kingsland, GA
South Carolina State 6'1" 211 lbs.

Year	Team		Games	Pos.
1978	SD	N	16	RB

Roger Anderson
ANDERSON, ROGER COLE
B. Dec. 11, 1942, Bedford, VA
Virginia Union 6'5" 263 lbs.

Year	Team		Games	Pos.
1964	NYG	N	11	OT
1965			8	DT
1967			4	DT
1968			14	DT
4 yrs.	37 games			

Scott Anderson
ANDERSON, DONALD SCOTT
B. Feb. 13, 1951, Benton, IL
Missouri 6'4" 242 lbs.

Year	Team		Games	Pos.
1974	MIN	N	5	C
1976			1	C
2 yrs.	6 games			

Stevie Anderson
ANDERSON, STEVIE
B. May 12, 1970, Monroe, LA
Grambling State 6'5" 205 lbs.

Year	Team		Games	Pos.
1994	NYJ	N	10	WR
1995	ARI	N	6	WR
1996			8	WR
3 yrs.	24 games			

Stuart Anderson
ANDERSON, STUART NOEL
B. Dec. 25, 1959, Mathews, VA
Virginia 6'1" 235 lbs.

Year	Team		Games	Pos.
1982	WAS	N	2	LB
1983			16	LB
1984			2	LB
1984	CLE	N	4	LB
1985	WAS	N	16	LB
4 yrs.	40 games			

Taz Anderson
ANDERSON, TAZWELL LEIGH, JR.
B. Nov. 15, 1938, Savannah, GA
Georgia Tech 6'2" 208 lbs.

Year	Team		Games	Pos.
1961	STL	N	14	OE
1962			14	OE
1963			5	OE
1964			13	OE
1966	ATL	N	8	TE
1967			8	TE
6 yrs.	62 games			

Terry Anderson
ANDERSON, TERRY C.
B. Jan. 10, 1955, Eastover, SC
Bethune-Cookman 5'9" 182 lbs.

Year	Team		Games	Pos.
1977	MIA	N	11	WR
1978			4	WR
1978	WAS	N	10	WR
1980	SF	N	4	WR
3 yrs.	29 games			

Tim Anderson
ANDERSON, WILLIAM T.
B. Aug. 1, 1949, Colliers, WV
Ohio State 6'0" 193 lbs.

Year	Team		Games	Pos.
1975	SF	N	13	CB, S
1976	BUF	N	2	DB
2 yrs.	15 games			

Vickey Ray Anderson
ANDERSON, VICKEY RAY
B. May 3, 1956, Oklahoma City, OK
Oklahoma 6'0" 205 lbs.

Year	Team		Games	Pos.
1980	GB	N	7	RB

Warren Anderson
ANDERSON, WARREN
B. Jul. 3, 1955, Williamsburg, VA
West Virginia State 6'2" 195 lbs.

Year	Team		Games	Pos.
1977	HOU	N	8	WR
1978	STL	N	2	WR
2 yrs.	10 games			

Will Anderson
ANDERSON, WILLARD
B. May 5, 1897
D. Apr. 1982, Rochester, NY
Syracuse 5'10" 173 lbs.

Year	Team		Games	Pos.
1923	ROC	N	1	FB
1924			3	HB, FB
2 yrs.	4 games			

Willie Anderson
ANDERSON, WILLIE AARON
B. Jul. 11, 1975, Mobile, AL
Auburn 6'5" 325 lbs.

Year	Team		Games	Pos.
1996	CIN	N	16	OT

Winnie Anderson
ANDERSON, WINSTON D.
B. May 23, 1914
D. Aug. 1984, Pickerington, OH
Colgate 6'0" 185 lbs.

Year	Team		Games	Pos.
1936	NYG	N	5	E

Eric Andolsek
ANDOLSEK, ERIC THOMAS
B. Aug. 22, 1966, Thibodaux, LA
D. Jun. 23, 1992, Thibodaux, LA
Louisiana State 6'2" 277 lbs.

Year	Team		Games	Pos.
1988	DET	N	13	G
1989			16	G
1990			16	G
1991			16	G
4 yrs.	61 games			

Steve Andrako
ANDREJKO, STEVEN F.
B. Sep. 11, 1915, Braddock, PA
D. Nov. 30, 1980, Half Moon Bay, CA
Ohio State 6'0" 210 lbs.

Year	Team		Games	Pos.
1940	WAS	N	5	C, LB

Lew Andreas
ANDREAS, LEWIS P.

Year	Team	Games	Pos.

Lew Andreas continued

Syracuse

1921	SYR	A	2	E

Al Andrews
ANDREWS, AL
B. Jun. 10, 1945, Richmond, CA
New Mexico State 6'3" 216 lbs.

1970	BUF	N	8	LB
1971			14	LB

2 yrs.   22 games

Billy Andrews
ANDREWS, WILLIAM DOUGHTY, JR.
B. Jun. 10, 1945, Clinton, LA
Southeastern Louisiana 6'0" 223 lbs.

1967	CLE	N	14	LB
1968			14	LB
1969			14	LB
1970			14	LB
1971			14	LB
1972			14	LB
1973			5	LB
1974			11	LB
1975	SD	N	14	LB
1976	KC	N	14	LB
1977			14	LB

11 yrs.   142 games

George Andrews
ANDREWS, GEORGE ELDON, II
B. Nov. 28, 1955, Omaha, NE
Nebraska 6'3" 223 lbs.

1979	LA	N	16	LB
1980			13	LB
1981			15	LB
1982	LARM	N	9	LB
1983			16	LB
1984			11	LB

6 yrs.   80 games

Jabby Andrews
ANDREWS, J.B.
Texas Western 200 lbs.

1934	C, S	N	3	B

John Andrews
ANDREWS, JOHN MILTON
B. Nov. 2, 1948, Indianapolis, IN
Indiana 6'3" 222 lbs.

1972	SD	N	1	LB
1973	BAL	N	8	TE
1974			14	TE

3 yrs.   23 games

John Andrews
ANDREWS, JOHN V., JR. (Tiny)
B. Nov. 7, 1951, Detroit, MI
Morgan State 6'6" 251 lbs.

1975	MIA	N	14	DT
1976			14	DT

2 yrs.   28 games

Mitch Andrews
ANDREWS, MITCHELL DEAN
B. Mar. 4, 1964, Houma, LA
Louisiana State 6'2" 239 lbs.

1987	DEN	N	8	TE

Ricky Andrews
ANDREWS, RICHARD GUY
B. Apr. 14, 1966, Western Samoa
Washington 6'2" 236 lbs.

1990	SEA	N	15	LB

Roy Andrews
ANDREWS, LEROY (Bull)
B. Jun., 1896, Osage Township, KS
Deceased
Pittsburg State 6'0" 226 lbs.

1923	STL	N	4	G
1924	KC	N	7	T, G, HB
1925			7	G, QB, HB, T
1926			8	T, QB, HB, G, E
1927	CLE	N	1	T

5 yrs.   27 games

Tom Andrews
ANDREWS, THOMAS EDWARD
B. Jan. 11, 1962, Parma, OH
Louisville 6'4" 267 lbs.

1984	CHI	N	7	OT, C
1985			14	C
1987	SEA	N	2	C

3 yrs.   23 games

William Andrews
ANDREWS, WILLIAM L.
B. Dec. 25, 1955, Thomasville, GA
Auburn 6'0" 210 lbs.

1979	ATL	N	15	RB
1980			16	RB
1981			16	RB
1982			9	RB
1983			16	RB
1986			15	RB

6 yrs.   87 games

George Andrie
ANDRIE, GEORGE JOSEPH
B. Apr. 20, 1940, Grand Rapids, MI
Marquette 6'7" 252 lbs.

1962	DAL	N	14	OT, DE
1963			12	DE
1964			14	DE
1965			14	DE
1966			14	DE
1967			14	DE
1968			14	DE
1969			14	DE
1970			14	DE
1971			14	DE
1972			3	DE

11 yrs.   141 games

Plato Andros
ANDROS, PLATO
B. Nov. 28, 1921, Oklahoma City, OK
Oklahoma 6'0" 240 lbs.

1947	CHIC	N	12	G
1948			12	G
1949			12	G
1950			9	G, T

4 yrs.   45 games

Teddy Andrulewicz
ANDRULEWICZ, THEODORE S. (Tuffy)
B. 1904
Villanova 5'11" 175 lbs.

1930	NEW	N	8	HB, FB

Lou Andrus
ANDRUS, LOUIS
B. Jul. 10, 1943, Salt Lake City, UT
Brigham Young 6'6" 255 lbs.

1967	DEN	A	7	DE

Sheldon Andrus
ANDRUS, SHELDON JAMES, JR.
B. Oct. 5, 1962, Lafayette, LA

Sheldon Andrus continued

Nicholls State 6'1" 271 lbs.

1986	NO	N	1	NT
1987			3	NT

2 yrs.   4 games

Sig Andrusking
ANDRUSKING, SIGMUND
B. 1914
Detroit 5'8" 187 lbs.

1937	BKN	N	8	G

Zenon Andrusyshyn
ANDRUSYSHYN, ZENON
B. Feb. 25, 1947, Gunsburg, Germany
UCLA 6'2" 210 lbs.

1978	KC	N	16	P

Charlie Ane
ANE, CHARLES TEETAI, SR.
B. Jan. 25, 1931, Honolulu, HI
Southern California 6'2" 260 lbs.

1953	DET	N	12	C, T
1954			12	T
1955			12	T
1956			12	C
1957			12	T
1958			12	C, T
1959			11	C, T

7 yrs.   83 games

Charlie Ane
ANE, CHARLES TEETAI, JR.
B. Aug. 12, 1952, Los Angeles, CA
Michigan State 6'1" 234 lbs.

1975	KC	N	14	C
1976			14	C
1977			14	C
1978			16	C
1979			16	C
1980			16	C
1981	GB	N	16	C

7 yrs.   106 games

Jim Angelo
ANGELO, JAMES
B. Aug. 23, 1963
Indiana (Pennsylvania) 6'3" 275 lbs.

1987	PHI	N	1	G

Elmer Angsman
ANGSMAN, ELMER JOSEPH, JR.
B. Dec 11, 1925, Chicago, IL
Notre Dame 5'11" 200 lbs.

1946	CHIC	N	11	HB
1947			12	HB
1948			12	HB
1949			12	HB
1950			12	B
1951			12	B
1952			10	B

7 yrs.   81 games

Scott Ankrom
ANKROM, SCOTT RANDALL
B. Jan. 4, 1966, San Antonio, TX
Texas Christian 6'1" 194 lbs.

1989	DAL	N	10	DB

Dunc Annan
ANNAN, DUNCAN COLIN
B. Aug. 10, 1895
D. Jun, 1981, Fort Pierce, FL
Brown/Chicago 5'10" 178 lbs.

1920	CHIT	A	7	HB

Dunc Annan continued

1922	TOL	N	9	HB, FB
1923	HAM	N	2	HB, QB
1924			5	HB, E, FB
1925			1	HB
1925	AKR	N	8	HB, FB
1925	HAM	N	1	HB
1926			3	HB, QB
1926	AKR	N	4	HB

6 yrs.   40 games

Sam Anno
AONO, SAM
B. Jan. 26, 1965, Silver Spring, MD
Southern California 6'2" 230 lbs.

1987	LARM	N	3	LB
1987	MIN	N	6	LB
1988			16	LB
1989	TB	N	16	LB
1990			16	LB
1991			16	LB
1992	SD	N	16	LB
1993			16	LB

7 yrs.   105 games

Charles Anthony
ANTHONY, CHARLES
B. Jul. 10, 1952, Houston, TX
Southern California 6'1" 230 lbs.

1974	SD	N	13	LB

Terrence Anthony
ANTHONY, TERRENCE EVERETT
B. Jan. 17, 1965, East St. Louis, IL
Iowa State 5'10" 183 lbs.

1987	STL	N	1	DB

Terry Anthony
ANTHONY, TERRENCE
B. Mar. 9, 1968, Daytona Beach, FL
Florida State 6'0" 200 lbs.

1990	TB	N	1	WR
1991			9	WR

2 yrs.   10 games

Tyrone Anthony
ANTHONY, TYRONE
B. Mar. 3, 1962, Winston, Salem, NC
North Carolina 5'11" 200 lbs.

1984	NO	N	15	RB
1985			16	RB

2 yrs.   31 games

Lionel Antoine
ANTOINE, LIONEL SYLVESTER
B. Aug. 31, 1950, Biloxi, MS
Southern Illinois 6'6" 262 lbs.

1972	CHI	N	5	OT
1973			13	OT
1974			14	OT
1975			14	OT
1976			13	OT
1978			9	OT

6 yrs.   68 games

Glenn Antrum
ANTRUM, GLENN
B. Feb. 3, 1966, Derby, CT
Connecticut 5'11" 175 lbs.

1989	NE	N	1	WR

Houston Antwine
ANTWINE, HOUSTON
B. Apr. 11, 1939, Louise, MS

Year	Team		Games	Pos.

Houston Antwine continued
Southern Illinois 6'0" 265 lbs.

Year	Team		Games	Pos.
1961	**BOS**	A	9	DT
1962			14	DT
1963			14	DT
1964			14	DT
1965			14	DT
1966			14	DT
1967			13	DT
1968			14	DT
1969			14	DT
1970	**BOS**	N	14	DT
1971	**NE**	N	3	DT
1972	**PHI**	N	14	DT

12 yrs.   151 games

Steve Apke
APKE, STEVE
B. Aug. 3, 1965
Pittsburgh 6'1" 222 lbs.

Year	Team		Games	Pos.
1987	**PIT**	N	3	LB

Chuck Apolskis
APOLSKIS, CHARLES
B. 1916
Deceased
DePaul 6'2" 207 lbs.

Year	Team		Games	Pos.
1938	**CHIB**	N	1	E
1939			1	E

2 yrs.   2 games

Ray Apolskis
APOLSKIS, RAYMOND EDWARD
B. Oct. 19, 1918, Cicero, IL
Marquette 5'11" 206 lbs.

Year	Team		Games	Pos.
1941	**CHIC**	N	11	C
1942			11	C
1945			5	C
1946			6	G
1947			12	G
1948			12	G
1949			8	G
1950			9	G

8 yrs.   74 games

Jim Apple
APPLE, JAMES
B. 1939
Upsala 6'0" 200 lbs.

Year	Team		Games	Pos.
1961	**NY**	A	3	HB

Clarence Applegran
APPLEGRAN, CLARENCE O.
B. Nov., 1893, Chicago, IL
D. May, 1960
Illinois 6'2" 200 lbs.

Year	Team		Games	Pos.
1920	**DET**	A	2	G

Scott Appleton
APPLETON, GORDON SCOTT
B. Feb. 20, 1942, Brady, TX
Texas 6'3" 254 lbs.

Year	Team		Games	Pos.
1964	**HOU**	A	14	DE
1965			14	DT
1966			14	DT
1967	**SD**	A	14	DT
1968			14	DT

5 yrs.   70 games

Megs Apsit
APSIT, MARGER
B. Jun. 5, 1909
D. Dec. 22, 1988, Bakersfield, CA
Southern California 5'11" 200 lbs.

Year	Team		Games	Pos.
1931	**FRA**	N	6	HB, QB, FB
1931	**BKN**	N	3	HB
1932	**GB**	N	2	HB

Megs Apsit continued

Year	Team		Games	Pos.
1933	**BOS**	N	12	QB, FB

3 yrs.   23 games

Ben Apuna
APUNA, BEN CALVIN
B. Jun. 26, 1957, Honolulu, HI
Arizona State 6'1" 222 lbs.

Year	Team		Games	Pos.
1980	**NYG**	N	10	LB

Leo Araguz
ARAGUZ, LEO
B. Jan. 18, 1970
Stephen F. Austin 6'0" 185 lbs.

Year	Team		Games	Pos.
1996	**OAK**	N	3	P

Evan Arapostathis
ARAPOSTATHIS, EVAN ANTHONY
B. Oct. 30, 1963, San Diego, CA
Michigan State 5'9" 160 lbs.

Year	Team		Games	Pos.
1986	**STL**	N	5	P

Fred Arbanas
ARBANAS, FREDERICK VINCENT
B. Jan. 14, 1939, Detroit, MI
Michigan State 6'3" 240 lbs.

Year	Team		Games	Pos.
1962	**DAL**	A	14	OE
1963	**KC**	A	14	OE
1964			14	OE
1965			14	OE
1966			14	OE
1967			14	TE
1968			14	TE
1969			14	TE, OT
1970	**KC**	N	6	TE

9 yrs.   118 games

Hasson Arbubakrr
ARBUBAKRR, HASSON
B. Dec. 9, 1960, Newark, NJ
Texas Tech 6'4" 250 lbs.

Year	Team		Games	Pos.
1983	**TB**	N	16	DE
1984	**MIN**	N	4	DE

2 yrs.   20 games

Charles Arbuckle
ARBUCKLE, CHARLES EDWARD
B. Sep. 13, 1968, Beaumont, TX
UCLA 6'2" 248 lbs.

Year	Team		Games	Pos.
1992	**IND**	N	16	TE
1993			16	TE
1994			7	TE
1995			3	TE

4 yrs.   42 games

Lester Archambeau
ARCHAMBEAU, LESTER MILWARD
B. Jun. 27, 1967, Montville, NJ
Stanford 6'4" 274 lbs.

Year	Team		Games	Pos.
1990	**GB**	N	4	DE
1991			16	DE
1992			16	DE
1993	**ATL**	N	15	DE
1994			16	DE
1995			16	DE, DT
1996			15	DE

7 yrs.   98 games

Dan Archer
ARCHER, DAN
B. Sep. 9, 1944, Grand Rapids, MI
Oregon 6'5" 245 lbs.

Year	Team		Games	Pos.
1967	**OAK**	A	14	G, OT

Dan Archer continued

Year	Team		Games	Pos.
1968	**CIN**	A	8	G, OT

2 yrs.   22 games

David Archer
ARCHER, DAVID
B. Feb. 15, 1962, Fayetteville, NC
Iowa State 6'2" 208 lbs.

Year	Team		Games	Pos.
1984	**ATL**	N	2	QB
1985			16	QB
1986			11	QB
1987			9	QB
1988	**WAS**	N	1	QB
1989	**SD**	N	16	QB

6 yrs.   55 games

Troy Archer
ARCHER, JAMES TROY
B. Jan. 16, 1955, Glendale, CA
D. Jun. 22, 1979, North Bergen, NJ
Colorado 6'4" 250 lbs.

Year	Team		Games	Pos.
1976	**NYG**	N	14	DE
1977			14	DT
1978			10	DT

3 yrs.   38 games

Mike Archie
ARCHIE, MICHAEL LAMONT
B. Oct. 14, 1972, Sharon, PA
Penn State 5'8" 205 lbs.

Year	Team		Games	Pos.
1996	**HOU**	N	2	RB

Julie Archoska
ARCHOSKA, JULIUS
B. Mar. 13, 1905
D. Mar, 1972, Lynn, MA
Syracuse 5'11" 180 lbs.

Year	Team		Games	Pos.
1930	**SI**	N	4	E

Billy Ard
ARD, WILLIAM DONOVAN
B. Mar. 12, 1959, East Orange, NJ
Wake Forest 6'3" 270 lbs.

Year	Team		Games	Pos.
1981	**NYG**	N	13	G
1982			9	G
1983			16	G
1984			15	G
1985			16	G
1986			16	G
1987			12	G
1988			16	G
1989	**GB**	N	15	G
1990			15	G
1991			5	G

11 yrs.   148 games

Tony Ardizzone
ARDIZZONE, ANTHONY ALLEN
B. Dec. 19, 1956, La Grange, IL
Northwestern 6'3" 241 lbs.

Year	Team		Games	Pos.
1979	**CHI**	N	16	C

Tony Arena
ARENA, ANTHONY GERALD
B. Jul. 2, 1918, Detroit, MI
Michigan State 6'0" 200 lbs.

Year	Team		Games	Pos.
1942	**DET**	N	1	C

Joe Arenas
ARENAS, LUPE JOSEPH
B. Dec. 12, 1925, Cedar Rapids, IA
Nebraska-Omaha 5'11" 180 lbs.

Year	Team		Games	Pos.
1951	**SF**	N	12	HB
1952			12	HB
1953			12	HB
1954			12	HB

Joe Arenas continued

Year	Team		Games	Pos.
1955			12	HB
1956			12	HB
1957			12	HB

7 yrs.   84 games

Arnie Arenz
ARENZ, ARNOLD
B. Oct. 13, 1911
D. Jan, 1985, Olympia, WA
St. Louis 6'1" 215 lbs.

Year	Team		Games	Pos.
1934	**BOS**	N	3	QB

Bob Argus
ARGUS, ROBERT
B. Jan., 1894
Deceased
None 5'10" 195 lbs.

Year	Team		Games	Pos.
1920	**ROC**	A	1	FB, HB
1921			5	HB
1922	**ROC**	N	5	HB, FB
1923			4	HB
1924			7	FB, HB, QB
1925			5	FB, QB

6 yrs.   27 games

David Ariail
ARIAIL, DAVID (Gump)
B. 1912
Auburn 5'11" 205 lbs.

Year	Team		Games	Pos.
1934	**BKN**	N	1	E
1934	**C, S**		1	E

Mike Ariey
ARIEY, MIKE A.
B. Mar. 12, 1964, Bakersfield, CA
San Diego State 6'5" 285 lbs.

Year	Team		Games	Pos.
1989	**SI**	N	1	OT

Obed Ariri
ARIRI, OBED CHUKWUMA
B. Apr. 7, 1956, Owerri, Nigeria
Clemson 5'8" 170 lbs.

Year	Team		Games	Pos.
1984	**TB**	N	16	K
1987	**WAS**	N	2	K

2 yrs.   18 games

Justin Armour
ARMOUR, JUSTIN
B. Jan. 1, 1973, Colorado Springs, CO
Stanford 6'4" 221 lbs.

Year	Team		Games	Pos.
1995	**BUF**	N	15	WR

Lloyd Arms
ARMS, LLOYD
B. Sep. 24, 1919, Sulphur, OK
Oklahoma State 6'1" 215 lbs.

Year	Team		Games	Pos.
1946	**CHIC**	N	8	G
1947			12	G
1948			7	G

3 yrs.   27 games

Jessie Armstead
ARMSTEAD, JESSIE
B. Oct. 26, 1970, Dallas, TX
Miami (Florida) 6'1" 238 lbs.

Year	Team		Games	Pos.
1993	**NYG**	N	16	LB
1994			16	LB
1995			16	LB
1996			16	LB

4 yrs.   64 games

Adger Armstrong
ARMSTRONG, ADGER
B. Jun. 21, 1957, Houston, TX

Year	Team	Games	Pos.

Adger Armstrong continued
Texas A&M 6'0" 220 lbs.

1980	HOU	N	16	RB
1981			16	RB
1982	TB	N	6	RB
1983	TB	N	11	RB
1984			15	RB
1985			16	RB

6 yrs. 80 games

Antonio Armstrong
SHORTER, ANTONIO DONNELL
B. Oct. 15, 1973, Houston, TX
Texas A&M 6'1" 234 lbs.

| 1995 | MIA | N | 4 | LB |

Bill Armstrong
ARMSTRONG, WILLIAM
B. 1920
UCLA 6'1" 210 lbs.

| 1943 | BKN | N | 4 | G, T |

Bob Armstrong
ARMSTRONG, ROBERT, JR.
B. Feb. 16, 1909
Missouri 5'11" 221 lbs.

| 1931 | POR | N | 13 | T, G, C |
| 1932 | | | 6 | T, E |

2 yrs. 19 games

Bruce Armstrong
ARMSTRONG, BRUCE
B. Sep. 7, 1965, Miami, FL
Louisville 6'4" 284 lbs.

1987	NE	N	12	OT
1988			16	OT
1989			16	OT
1990			16	OT
1991			16	OT
1992			8	OT
1993			16	OT
1994			16	OT
1995			16	OT
1996			16	OT

10 yrs. 148 games

Charlie Armstrong
ARMSTRONG, CHARLES A.
B. 1919
Mississippi College 5'10" 180 lbs.

| 1941 | CHIC | N | 1 | HB |
| 1946 | BKN | AA | 10 | HB |

2 yrs. 11 games

Graham Armstrong
ARMSTRONG, GRAHAM LEO
B. May 30, 1918, Cleveland, OH
D. 1985
John Carroll 6'4" 230 lbs.

1941	CLE	N	8	T
1945			1	T
1947	BUF	AA	14	T
1948			13	T

4 yrs. 36 games

Harvey Armstrong
ARMSTRONG, HARVEY LEE
B. Dec. 29, 1959, Houston, TX
Southern Methodist 6'3" 260 lbs.

1982	PHI	N	8	NT
1983			16	NT
1984			16	NT
1986	IND	N	16	NT
1987			11	NT
1988			16	NT
1989			16	NT
1990			12	NT

8 yrs. 111 games

Year	Team	Games	Pos.

Jimmy Armstrong
ARMSTRONG, JAMES
B. Jun. 18, 1962
Appalachian State 5'8" 166 lbs.

| 1987 | DAL | N | 2 | CB |

John Armstrong
ARMSTRONG, JOHN
B. Jul. 7, 1963, Calhoun City, MS
Richmond 5'9" 190 lbs.

| 1987 | BUF | N | 3 | CB |

Johnny Armstrong
ARMSTRONG, JOHN A.
B. 1894
Deceased
Dubuque 5'8" 175 lbs.

1923	RI	N	8	QB
1924			9	QB, HB
1925			11	QB, HB
1926	RI	A	7	QB, FB

4 yrs. 35 games

Neill Armstrong
ARMSTRONG, NEILL FORD
(Bird)
B. Mar. 9, 1926, Tishomingo, OK
Oklahoma A&M 6'2" 189 lbs.

1947	PHI	N	12	E
1948			12	E
1949			12	E
1950			12	E
1951			6	E

5 yrs. 54 games

Norris Armstrong
ARMSTRONG, P. NORRIS
B. Sep. 15, 1898, Fort Smith, AR
D. Oct. 11, 1981, Danville, KY
Centre 5'10" 165 lbs.

| 1922 | MIL | N | 1 | FB |

Otis Armstrong
ARMSTRONG, OTIS
B. Nov. 15, 1950, Chicago, IL
Purdue 5'10" 196 lbs.

1973	DEN	N	14	RB
1974			14	RB
1975			4	RB
1976			14	RB
1977			10	RB
1978			16	RB
1979			15	RB
1980			9	RB

8 yrs. 96 games

Ray Armstrong
ARMSTRONG, RAMON
B. 1938
Texas Christian 6'1" 235 lbs.

| 1960 | OAK | A | | DT |

Trace Armstrong
ARMSTRONG, RAYMOND LESTER
B. Oct. 5, 1965, Bethesda, MD
Arizona State/Florida 6'4" 270 lbs.

1989	CHI	N	15	DE
1990			16	DE
1991			12	DE
1992			14	DE
1993			16	DE
1994			15	DE
1995	MIA	N	15	DE
1996			16	DE

8 yrs. 119 games

Year	Team	Games	Pos.

Tyji Armstrong
ARMSTRONG, TYJI DONRAPHEAL
B. Oct. 3, 1970, Inkster, MI
Mississippi 6'4" 255 lbs.

1992	TB	N	15	TE
1993			12	TE
1994			16	TE
1995			16	TE
1996	DAL	N	16	TE

5 yrs. 75 games

Al Arndt
ARNDT, ALFRED HERMAN
B. Jul. 15, 1911, Comfrey, MN
Deceased
South Dakota State 5'11" 205 lbs.

| 1935 | PIT | N | 7 | G |

Dick Arndt
ARNDT, RICHARD LEE
B. Mar. 12, 1944, Bonners Ferry, ID
Stanford/Idaho 6'5" 265 lbs.

1967	PIT	N	14	DT
1968			3	DT
1969			3	DT
1970			14	DT

4 yrs. 34 games

Jim Arneson
ARNESON, JAMES A.
B. Jan. 7, 1951, Iowa City, IA
Arizona 6'3" 247 lbs.

1973	DAL	N	12	G, C
1974			14	G, C
1975	WAS	N	7	G, C

3 yrs. 33 games

Mark Arneson
ARNESON, MARK EDWARD
B. Sep. 9, 1949, Iowa City, IA
Arizona 6'2" 222 lbs.

1972	STL	N	14	LB
1973			14	LB
1974			14	LB
1975			14	LB
1976			14	LB
1977			14	LB
1978			16	LB
1979			11	LB
1980			16	LB

9 yrs. 127 games

Jon Arnett
ARNETT, JON DWANE
(The Jaguar)
B. Apr. 20, 1935, Los Angeles, CA
Southern California 5'11" 197 lbs.

1957	LA	N	12	E, HB
1958			12	HB
1959			12	HB
1960			12	HB
1961			14	HB
1962			10	HB
1963			9	HB
1964	CHI	N	14	HB
1965			14	HB
1966			14	HB

10 yrs. 123 games

David Arnold
ARNOLD, DAVID PAUL
B. Nov. 21, 1966, Warren, OH
Michigan 6'3" 208 lbs.

| 1989 | PIT | N | 15 | CB |

Year	Team	Games	Pos.

Francis Arnold
ARNOLD, LEFRANCIS
B. Nov. 24, 1952, Los Angeles, CA
Oregon 6'3" 295 lbs.

| 1974 | DEN | N | 2 | G |

Jahine Arnold
ARNOLD, JAHINE
B. Jun. 19, 1973, Rockville, CT
Fresno State 6'0" 187 lbs.

| 1996 | PIT | N | 9 | WR |

Jay Arnold
ARNOLD, JAY
B. Sep. 9, 1913, Rogers, TX
Deceased
Texas 6'1" 210 lbs.

1937	PHI	N	10	HB, QB
1938			11	HB
1939			10	HB, FB
1940			9	HB, FB
1941	PIT	N	10	HB, QB

5 yrs. 50 games

Jim Arnold
ARNOLD, JAMES EDWARD
B. Jan. 31, 1961, Dalton, GA
Vanderbilt 6'2" 220 lbs.

1983	KC	N	16	P
1984			16	P
1985			16	P
1986	DET	N	7	P
1987			11	P
1988			16	P
1989			16	P
1990			16	P
1991			16	P
1992			16	P
1993			16	P
1994	MIA	N	12	P

12 yrs. 174 games

John Arnold
ARNOLD, JOHN RICHARD
B. Oct. 5, 1955, Shizuoka, Japan
Wyoming 5'10" 175 lbs.

| 1979 | DET | N | 7 | WR |
| 1980 | | | 10 | WR |

2 yrs. 17 games

Walt Arnold
ARNOLD, WALTER HENSLEE
B. Aug. 31, 1958, Galveston, TX
New Mexico 6'3" 225 lbs.

1980	LA	N	16	TE
1981			16	TE
1982	HOU	N	9	TE
1983			13	TE
1984	WAS	N	4	TE
1984	KC	N	10	TE
1985			16	TE
1986			16	TE
1987			5	TE

8 yrs. 105 games

Doug Aronson
ARONSON, DOUGLAS
B. Aug. 14, 1964, San Francisco, CA
San Diego State 6'3" 290 lbs.

| 1987 | CIN | N | 2 | G |

John Arp
ARP, JOHN
B. Aug. 15, 1965
Lincoln 6'5" 275 lbs.

| 1987 | CHI | N | 3 | OT |

Year	Team	Games	Pos.

Rick Arrington
ARRINGTON, RICHARD CAMERON
B. Feb. 26, 1947, Charlotte, NC
Georgia/Tulsa 6'2" 187 lbs.

Year	Team		Games	Pos.
1970	PHI	N	6	QB
1971			10	QB
1972			1	QB
3 yrs.	17 games			

Chuck Arrobio
ARROBIO, CHARLES AUGUSTUS
B. Jul. 9, 1944, Los Angeles, CA
Southern California 6'4" 250 lbs.

1966	MIN	N	11	OT

Arrowhead
ARROWHEAD
None

1923	OOR	N	4	E, T

Elmer Arterburn
ARTERBURN, ELMER F.
B. Jun. 15, 1929, Ranger, TX
Texas Tech 5'10" 175 lbs.

1954	CHIC	N	1	B

Gary Arthur
ARTHUR, GARY PATRICK
B. Jan. 9, 1948, Dayton, OH
Miami (Ohio) 6'5" 254 lbs.

1970	NYJ	N	7	TE
1971			14	TE
2 yrs.	21 games			

Mike Arthur
ARTHUR, MICHAEL SCOT
B. May 7, 1968, Minneapolis, MN
Texas A&M 6'3" 277 lbs.

1991	CIN	N	7	C
1992			16	C
1993	NE	N	13	C
1994			12	C
1995	GB	N	11	C
1996			5	C
6 yrs.	64 games			

Corrie Artman
ARTMAN, CORWIN W. (Whitey, Chang)
B. Jan. 8, 1907
D. Mar, 1970, Long Beach, CA
Stanford 6'2" 240 lbs.

1931	NYG	N	10	T, G
1932	BOS	N	1	T, G
1933	PIT	N	10	T
3 yrs.	21 games			

Lee Artoe
ARTOE, LEE R.
B. Mar. 2, 1916, Tacoma, WA
Santa Clara/California 6'3" 234 lbs.

1940	CHIB	N	11	T
1941			11	T
1942			11	T
1945			9	T
1946	LA	AA	14	T
1947			14	T
1948	BAL	AA	14	T
7 yrs.	84 games			

Herman Arvie
ARVIE, HERMAN JOSEPH
B. Oct. 12, 1970, Opelousas, LA
Grambling State 6'4" 320 lbs.

1993	CLE	N	16	OT

Herman Arvie continued

1994			16	OT, G
1995			15	OT, G
1996	BAL	N	14	G
4 yrs.	61 games			

Doug Asad
ASAD, DOUGLAS S.
B. 1938
Northwestern 6'3" 203 lbs.

1960	OAK	A		OE
1961			14	OE
2 yrs.	14 games			

Willie Asbury
ASBURY, WILLIAM WESLEY
B. Feb. 22, 1943, Crawfordville, GA
Kent State 6'1" 230 lbs.

1966	PIT	N	14	RB
1967			12	RB
1968			7	RB
3 yrs.	33 games			

Darrell Aschbacher
ASCHBACHER, DARREL G.
B. Jun. 2, 1935
Oregon 6'1" 220 lbs.

1959	PHI	N	11	G

Frank Aschenbrenner
ASCHENBRENNER, FRANK XAVIER
B. 1925, Heibuhl, Germany
Marquette/Northwestern 5'10" 188 lbs.

1949	CHI	AA	6	B

Juddy Ash
ASH, JULIAN
B. 1900
Deceased
Oregon State 6'2" 205 lbs.

1926	LA	N	2	G

John Ashbaugh
ASHBAUGH, JOHN (Bill)
St. Thomas (Minnesota) 185 lbs.

1924	RI	N	1	FB

Cliff Ashburn
ASHBURN, CLIFFORD
B. Nov. 21, 1905
D. Nov. 9, 1989
Nebraska 5'11" 190 lbs.

1929	NYG	N	12	G, T, E

Richard Ashe
ASHE, RICHARD ANTHONY
B. Mar. 14, 1967, Chicago, IL
Humboldt State 6'4" 260 lbs.

1990	LARM	N	1	DE

Bob Asher
ASHER, ROBERT DABNEY
B. Jun. 13, 1948, Arlington, VA
Vanderbilt 6'5" 254 lbs.

1970	DAL	N	6	OT
1972	CHI	N	14	OT, G
1973			13	OT
1974			14	OT
1975			11	OT
5 yrs.	58 games			

Jamie Asher
ASHER, JAMIE

Jamie Asher continued
B. Oct. 31, 1972, Indianapolis, IN
Louisville 6'3" 243 lbs.

1995	WAS	N	7	TE
1996			16	TE
2 yrs.	23 games			

Walker Lee Ashley
ASHLEY, WALKER LEE
B. Jul. 28, 1960, Bayonne, NJ
Penn State 6'0" 240 lbs.

1983	MIN	N	15	LB
1984			15	LB
1986			16	LB
1987			12	LB
1988			16	LB
1989	KC	N	16	LB
1990	MIN	N	4	LB
7 yrs.	94 games			

Darryl Ashmore
ASHMORE, DARRYL ALLAN
B. Nov. 1, 1969, Peoria, IL
Northwestern 6'7" 300 lbs.

1993	LARM	N	9	OT
1994			11	OT, G
1995	STL	N	16	OT
1996			6	OT
1996	WAS	N	5	OT
4 yrs.	47 games			

Marion Ashmore
ASHMORE, MARION ROGER (Bert)
B. 1903
Deceased
Gonzaga 6'0" 215 lbs.

1926	MIL	N	9	T
1927	DUL	N	9	T, G
1928	GB	N	13	T, C, E
1929			8	T
4 yrs.	39 games			

Josh Ashton
ASHTON, JOSHUA, JR.
B. Aug. 24, 1949, Eagle Lake, TX
Tulsa 6'1" 204 lbs.

1972	NE	N	14	RB
1973			13	RB
1974			12	RB
1975	STL	N	2	RB
4 yrs.	41 games			

Joe Aska
ASKA, JOE
B. Jul. 14, 1972, St. Croix, Virgin Islands
Central Oklahoma 5'10" 230 lbs.

1995	OAK	N	1	RB
1996			14	RB
2 yrs.	15 games			

Mike Askea
ASKEA, MICHAEL V.
B. Jan. 7, 1951, Visalia, CA
Stanford 6'4" 260 lbs.

1973	DEN	N	4	OT

Bert Askson
ASKSON, BERT
B. Dec. 16, 1945, Houston, TX
Texas Southern 6'3" 223 lbs.

1971	PIT	N	11	DE
1973	NO	N	1	TE
1975	GB	N	14	TE
1976			14	TE

Bert Askson continued

1977			14	TE
5 yrs.	54 games			

Jim Asmus
ASMUS, JAMES VICTOR DANIEL
B. Dec. 2, 1958, Meppel, Netherlands
Hawaii 6'2" 195 lbs.

1987	SF	N	3	K

Ed Aspatore
ASPATORE, EDWARD
B. Jun. 23, 1909
D. Mar, 1986, Louisville, KY
Marquette 6'1" 220 lbs.

1934	C, S	N	6	G, T

Les Asplundh
ASPLUNDH, LESTER
B. May 3, 1901
D. May, 1984, Bryn Athyn, PA
Swarthmore 6'3" 213 lbs.

1925	BUF	N	1	FB
1926	PHI	A	5	FB, QB, HB
2 yrs.	6 games			

Jack Atchason
ATCHASON, JOHN
B. 1937, Springfield, IL
Western Illinois 6'4" 215 lbs.

1960	BOS	A		OE
1960	HOU	A		OE

Burl Atcheson
ATCHESON, BURL
B. 1901
None

1922	COL	N	1	E

Bill Atessis
ATESSIS, WILLIAM JAMES
B. Jul. 16, 1949, Houston, TX
Texas 6'3" 240 lbs.

1971	NE	N	5	DE, DT

Pete Athas
ATHAS, PETER
B. Sep. 15, 1947, Hackensack, NJ
Tennessee 5'11" 185 lbs.

1971	NYG	N	13	DB
1972			14	S
1973			14	CB
1974			14	CB
1975	CLE	N	6	DB
1975	MIN	N	5	CB
1976	NO	N	13	DB
6 yrs.	79 games			

Dale Atkeson
ATKESON, DALE WAYNE
B. Dec. 24, 1930, Lomita, CA
None 6'2" 211 lbs.

1954	WAS	N	10	FB
1955			11	FB
1956			5	FB
3 yrs.	26 games			

Billy Atkins
ATKINS, WILLIAM E.
B. Nov. 19, 1934, Millport, AL
D. Nov, 1991, El Paso, TX
Auburn 6'1" 196 lbs.

1958	SF	N	12	HB
1959			11	HB

Year	Team	Games	Pos.

Billy Atkins *continued*

Year	Team	Games	Pos.
1960	BUF	A	DB
1961		14	DB
1962	NY	A 7	DB
1963		2	DB
1963	BUF	A 1	DB
1964	DEN	A 3	DB

7 yrs. 50 games

Bob Atkins
ATKINS, ROBERT
B. Apr. 2, 1946, Atlanta, GA
Grambling State 6'3" 211 lbs.

1968	STL	N 14	DB
1969		11	CB
1970	HOU	N 14	S
1971		12	S
1972		14	S
1973		5	S
1974		14	S
1975		14	S
1976		14	S

9 yrs. 112 games

Dave Atkins
ATKINS, DAVID CHALES
B. May 18, 1949, Victoria, TX
Texas-El Paso 6'1" 205 lbs.

1973	SF	N 5	RB
1974		1	RB
1975	SD	N 3	RB

3 yrs. 9 games

Doug Atkins
ATKINS, DOUGLAS LEON
B. May 8, 1930, Humboldt, TN
Tennessee 6'8" 257 lbs.

1953	CLE	N 8	E
1954		12	E
1955	CHIB	N 12	E
1956		6	E
1957		12	E
1958		12	E
1959		12	E
1960	CHI	N 12	E
1961		14	DE
1962		14	DE
1963		14	DE
1964		12	DE
1965		14	DE
1966		12	DE
1967	NO	N 14	DE
1968		11	DE
1969		14	DE

17 yrs. 205 games

Gene Atkins
ATKINS, GENE REYNARD
B. Nov. 22, 1964, Tallahassee, FL
Florida A&M 6'1" 200 lbs.

1987	NO	N 13	DB
1988		16	CB, S
1989		14	CB, S
1990		16	S
1991		16	S
1992		16	S
1993		16	S
1994	MIA	N 15	S
1995		16	S
1996		5	S

10 yrs. 143 games

George Atkins
ATKINS, GEORGE A.
B. Apr. 10, 1932, Birmingham, AL
Auburn 6'1" 210 lbs.

1955	DET	N 12	G

James Atkins
ATKINS, JAMES
B. Jan. 28, 1970, Amite, LA
Southwestern Louisiana 6'6" 291 lbs.

1994	SEA	N 4	OT, G
1995		16	OT
1996		16	OT

3 yrs. 36 games

Kelvin Atkins
ATKINS, KELVIN LAMAR (Kal)
B. Jun. 3, 1960, Orlando, FL
Illinois 6'3" 235 lbs.

1983	CHI	N 13	LB

Pervis Atkins
ATKINS, PERVIS R.
B. Nov. 24, 1935, Ruston, LA
New Mexico State 6'1" 200 lbs.

1961	LA	N 14	HB
1962		14	HB
1963		14	HB
1964	WAS	N 13	HB
1965		4	HB
1965	OAK	A 5	OE
1966		14	OE

6 yrs. 78 games

Steve Atkins
ATKINS, STEVE E.
B. Jun. 22, 1956, Spotsylvania, PA
Maryland 6'0" 216 lbs.

1979	GB	N 7	RB
1980		9	RB
1981		3	RB
1981	PHI	N 1	RB

3 yrs. 20 games

Al Atkinson
ATKINSON, ALLEN EDWARD
B. Jul. 28, 1943, Philadelphia, PA
Villanova 6'1" 229 lbs.

1965	NY	A 14	LB
1966		14	LB
1967		14	LB
1968		12	LB
1969		10	LB
1970	NYJ	N 14	LB
1971		11	LB
1972		14	LB
1973		5	LB
1974		14	LB

10 yrs. 122 games

Frank Atkinson
ATKINSON, FRANKLIN R.
B. Dec. 13, 1941
Stanford 6'3" 240 lbs.

1963	PIT	N 14	DT

George Atkinson
ATKINSON, GEORGE HENRY (Butch)
B. Jan. 4, 1947, Savannah, GA
Morris Brown 6'0" 182 lbs.

1968	OAK	A 14	DB
1969		14	CB
1970	OAK	N 14	CB
1971		14	DB
1972		14	S
1973		14	S
1974		14	DB
1975		14	S
1976		14	S
1977		12	S
1979	DEN	N 6	DB

11 yrs. 144 games

Jess Atkinson
ATKINSON, JESS GERALD
B. Dec. 11, 1961, Ann Arbor, MI
Maryland 5'9" 168 lbs.

1985	NYG	N 6	K
1985	STL	N 2	K
1986	WAS	N 1	K
1987		1	K
1988	IND	N 1	K

4 yrs. 11 games

Ricky Atkinson
ATKINSON, RICHARD
B. Aug. 28, 1965
Southern Connecticut State 6'0" 175 lbs.

1987	NE	N 1	CB

Reggie Attache
ATTACHE, REGGIE (LAUGHING GAS)
Sherman 5'9" 185 lbs.

1922	OOR	N 7	HB, FB

Alex Atty
ATTY, ALEXANDER GEORGE
B. Dec. 8, 1916, Johnstown, PA
D. May 2, 1973, Pottsville, PA
West Virginia 5'8" 216 lbs.

1939	CLE	N 3	G

Steve Atwater
ATWATER, STEPHEN DENNIS
B. Oct. 28, 1966, Chicago, IL
Arkansas 6'3" 217 lbs.

1989	DEN	N 16	S
1990		15	S
1991		16	S
1992		15	S
1993		16	S
1994		15	S
1995		16	S
1996		16	S

8 yrs. 125 games

John Atwood
ATWOOD, JOHN
B. 1925
Wisconsin 5'11" 185 lbs.

1948	NYG	N 8	HB

Earl Audet
AUDET, EARL TOUSSAINT (Streaky)
B. May 14, 1921, Providence, RI
Georgetown/Southern California 6'2" 252 lbs.

1945	WAS	N 10	T
1946	LA	AA 13	T
1947		14	T
1948		14	T

4 yrs. 51 games

Dan Audick
AUDICK, DANIEL JAMES BARTHOLOMEW
B. Nov. 15, 1954, San Bernardino, CA
Hawaii 6'3" 253 lbs.

1977	STL	N 2	G
1978	SD	N 1	G
1979		16	G
1980		15	G
1981	SF	N 16	OT
1982		7	G, OT
1983	STL	N 12	G, OT
1984		7	G

8 yrs. 76 games

Howie Auer
AUER, HOWARD JOSEPH
B. Jan. 9, 1908
D. Nov. 12, 1985, FL
Michigan 6'1" 205 lbs.

1933	PHI	N 2	T

Jim Auer
AUER, JAMES ROBERT
B. Jan. 4, 1962, Philadelphia, PA
Georgia 6'7" 275 lbs.

1987	PHI	N 1	DE

Joe Auer
AUER, JOSEPH
B. Oct. 11, 1941, Trenton, NJ
Miami (Florida)/Georgia Tech 6'1" 204 lbs.

1964	BUF	A 12	HB
1965		5	HB
1966	MIA	A 14	HB
1967		13	RB
1968	ATL	N 7	RB

5 yrs. 51 games

Scott Auer
AUER, SCOTT EUGENE
B. Oct. 4, 1961, Fort Wayne, IN
Michigan State 6'5" 255 lbs.

1984	KC	N 16	G, OT
1985		7	G, OT

2 yrs. 23 games

Todd Auer
AUER, TODD
B. Jan. 8, 1965
Western Illinois 6'1" 230 lbs.

1987	GB	N 3	LB

Dowe Aughtman
AUGHTMAN, LORENZO DOWE
B. Jan. 28, 1961, Brewton, AL
Auburn 6'3" 260 lbs.

1984	DAL	N 7	DT, DE

Sky August
AUGUST, EDWARD W.
B. Jan. 10, 1908
D. Oct. 15, 1993, Mahanoy City, PA
Villanova 5'11" 180 lbs.

1931	PRO	N 6	HB, QB

Steve August
AUGUST, STEVE PAUL
B. Sep. 4, 1954, Jeannette, PA
Tulsa 6'5" 254 lbs.

1977	SEA	N 6	G
1978		14	OT
1979		16	OT
1980		16	OT
1981		16	OT
1982		8	OT
1983		15	OT
1984		6	OT
1984	PIT	N 5	OT

8 yrs. 102 games

Gene Augusterfer
AUGUSTERFER, EUGENE
B. 1912
Deceased
Catholic 5'9" 180 lbs.

1935	PIT	N 1	QB

Mike Augustyniak
AUGUSTYNIAK, MICHAEL EUGENE
B. Jul. 17, 1956, Fort Wayne, IN
Purdue 5'11" 220 lbs.

Year	Team		Games	Pos.
1981	NYJ	N	10	RB
1982			9	RB
1983			8	RB
3 yrs.	27 games			

Chalmers Ault
AULT, CHALMERS
B. Jul. 10, 1900
D. May, 1979, Buckhannon, WV
West Virginia Wesleyan 5'9" 195 lbs.

Year	Team		Games	Pos.
1924	CLE	N	2	G
1925			1	T
2 yrs.	3 games			

David Aupiu
AUPIU, LOTOPUE DAVID
B. Feb. 10, 1961, Honolulu, HI
Brigham Young 6'2" 235 lbs.

Year	Team		Games	Pos.
1987	LARM	N	1	LB

Bill Austin
AUSTIN, WILLIAM LEE
B. Oct. 28, 1928, San Pedro, CA
Oregon State 6'1" 223 lbs.

Year	Team		Games	Pos.
1949	NYG	N	9	T
1950			12	G
1953			12	G
1954			11	G
1955			12	G
1956			8	G
1957			11	G
7 yrs.	75 games			

Cliff Austin
AUSTIN, CLIFF
B. Mar. 2, 1960, Atlanta, GA
Clemson 6'1" 210 lbs.

Year	Team		Games	Pos.
1983	NO	N	11	RB
1984	ATL	N	15	RB
1985			14	RB
1986			15	RB
1987	TB	N	3	RB
5 yrs.	58 games			

Darrell Austin
AUSTIN, KENNETH DARRELL
B. Nov. 6, 1951, Union, SC
South Carolina 6'4" 252 lbs.

Year	Team		Games	Pos.
1975	NYJ	N	12	OL
1976			11	G, OT
1977			9	C, G
1978			13	G
1979	TB	N	16	G, C
1980			8	G, OT, C
6 yrs.	69 games			

Eric Austin
AUSTIN, ERIC
B. Jun. 7, 1973, Moss Point, MS
Jackson State 5'10" 217 lbs.

Year	Team		Games	Pos.
1996	TB	N	2	S

Hise Austin
AUSTIN, HISE
B. Sep. 8, 1950, Houston, TX
Prairie View A&M 6'4" 191 lbs.

Year	Team		Games	Pos.
1973	GB	N	9	DB
1975	KC	N	3	CB
2 yrs.	12 games			

Jim Austin
AUSTIN, JAMES L.
B. Sep. 10, 1913, Omaha, NE
D. Oct, 1975, La Jolla, CA
St. Mary's 6'2" 199 lbs.

Year	Team		Games	Pos.
1937	BKN	N	7	E
1938			11	E
1939	DET	N	10	E
3 yrs.	28 games			

Kent Austin
AUSTIN, RICHARD KENT
B. Jun. 25, 1963, Natick, MA
Mississippi 6'1" 195 lbs.

Year	Team		Games	Pos.
1986	STL	N	16	QB

Ocie Austin
AUSTIN, OCIE MOORE
B. Jan. 8, 1947, Norfolk, VA
Utah State 6'3" 200 lbs.

Year	Team		Games	Pos.
1968	BAL	N	14	DB
1969			14	S, CB
1970	PIT	N	7	CB
1971			14	S
4 yrs.	49 games			

Billy Autrey
AUTREY, WILLIAM
B. Jan. 17, 1933, Ridge, TX
Austin 6'3" 220 lbs.

Year	Team		Games	Pos.
1953	CHIB	N	7	C

Hank Autry
AUTRY, MELVIN HENRY
B. May 2, 1947, Hattiesburg, MS
Southern Mississippi 6'3" 233 lbs.

Year	Team		Games	Pos.
1969	HOU	A	14	C
1970	HOU	A	14	C
2 yrs.	28 games			

Troy Auzenne
AUZENNE, TROY ANTHONY
B. Jun. 26, 1969, El Monte, CA
California 6'7" 286 lbs.

Year	Team		Games	Pos.
1992	CHI	N	16	OT
1993			11	OT
1994			10	OT
1995			12	OT
1996	IND	N	12	OT
5 yrs.	61 games			

Chuck Avedisian
AVEDISIAN, CHARLES T.
B. Sep. 19, 1917, West Hoboken, NJ
D. Aug. 26, 1983, New Britain, CT
Providence 5'9" 203 lbs.

Year	Team		Games	Pos.
1942	NYG	N	10	G
1943			10	G
1944			9	G
3 yrs.	29 games			

Bob Avellini
AVELLINI, ROBERT HAYDEN
B. Aug. 28, 1953, New York, NY
Maryland 6'2" 207 lbs.

Year	Team		Games	Pos.
1975	CHI	N	8	QB
1976			14	QB
1977			14	QB
1978			13	QB
1979			7	QB
1981			9	QB
1982			2	QB
1983			2	QB
1984			4	QB
9 yrs.	73 games			

John Aveni
AVENI, JOHN P.
B. Mar. 17, 1935, Glassboro, NJ
Indiana 6'3" 212 lbs.

Year	Team		Games	Pos.
1959	CHIB	N	12	K, E
1960	CHI	N	12	K, E
1961	WAS	N	14	K, E
3 yrs.	38 games			

Sisto Averno
AVERNO, SISTO J. (Joe)
B. May 12, 1926, Paterson, NJ
Muhlenberg 5'11" 237 lbs.

Year	Team		Games	Pos.
1950	BAL	N	12	G
1951	NYY	N	12	G
1952	DAL	N	12	G
1953	BAL	N	12	G
1954	BAL	N		G
5 yrs.	48 games			

Don Avery
AVERY, DONALD
B. Feb. 10, 1921, Los Angeles, CA
Alabama/Southern California 6'4" 254 lbs.

Year	Team		Games	Pos.
1946	WAS	N	11	T
1947			10	T
1948	LA	AA	1	T
3 yrs.	22 games			

Jim Avery
AVERY, JAMES
B. Jul. 11, 1944, Grand Rapids, MI
Northern Illinois 6'2" 235 lbs.

Year	Team		Games	Pos.
1966	WAS	N	1	TE

Ken Avery
AVERY, KENNETH WILLIAM
B. May 23, 1944, New York, NY
Southern Mississippi 6'1" 225 lbs.

Year	Team		Games	Pos.
1967	NYG	N	13	LB
1968			14	LB
1969	CIN	A	14	LB
1970	CIN	N	14	LB
1971			14	LB
1972			13	LB
1973			14	LB
1974			13	LB
1975	KC	N	14	LB
9 yrs.	123 games			

Steve Avery
AVERY, STEVEN GEORGE
B. Aug. 18, 1966, Milwaukee, WI
Northern Michigan 6'1" 216 lbs.

Year	Team		Games	Pos.
1989	HOU	N	1	RB
1991	GB	N	1	RB
1994	PIT	N	14	RB
1995			12	RB
4 yrs.	28 games			

Joe Avezzano
AVEZZANO, JOSEPH
B. Nov. 17, 1943, Yonkers, NY
Florida State 6'2" 235 lbs.

Year	Team		Games	Pos.
1966	BOS	A	3	C

Clarence Avinger
AVINGER, CLARENCE EDMUND (Butch)
B. Dec. 15, 1928, Beatrice, AL
Alabama 6'1" 215 lbs.

Year	Team		Games	Pos.
1953	NYG	N	12	FB

Rob Awalt
AWALT, ROBERT MITCHELL
B. Apr. 9, 1964, Landstuhl, Germany
Nevada-Reno/San Diego State 6'5" 248 lbs.

Year	Team		Games	Pos.
1987	STL	N	12	TE
1988	PHX	N	16	TE
1989			16	TE
1990	DAL	N	13	TE
1991			12	TE
1992	BUF	N	14	TE
1993			12	TE
7 yrs.	95 games			

Buddy Aydelette
AYDELETTE, WILLIAM LESLIE
B. Aug. 19, 1956, Mobile, AL
Alabama 6'4" 260 lbs.

Year	Team		Games	Pos.
1980	GB	N	9	OT
1987	PIT	N	12	OT, C
2 yrs.	21 games			

John Ayers
AYERS, JOHN MILTON
B. Apr. 4, 1953, Carrizo Springs, TX
D. Oct. 2, 1995, Canyon, TX
Texas/West Texas State 6'5" 260 lbs.

Year	Team		Games	Pos.
1977	SF	N	14	OT
1978			16	OT
1979			16	OT, G
1980			16	G
1981			16	G
1982			8	G
1983			16	G
1984			16	G
1985			16	G
1986			14	G
1987	DEN	N	9	G
11 yrs.	157 games			

Marvin Ayers
AYERS, MARVIN
B. Sep. 12, 1963
Southern Methodist/Grambling State 6'5" 265 lbs.

Year	Team		Games	Pos.
1987	PHI	N	2	DE

Joe Azelby
AZELBY, JOSEPH K.
B. Mar. 5, 1962, New York, NY
Harvard 6'1" 225 lbs.

Year	Team		Games	Pos.
1984	BUF	N	14	LB

Mike Baab
BAAB, MICHAEL JAMES
B. Dec. 6, 1959, Fort Worth, TX
Texas 6'4" 279 lbs.

Year	Team		Games	Pos.
1982	CLE	N	7	C
1983			15	C
1984			16	C
1985			16	C
1986			12	C
1988	NE	N	15	C
1989			16	C
1990	CLE	N	16	C
1991			16	C
1992	KC	N	3	C
11 yrs.	148 games			

Steve Baack
BAACK, STEVEN WILLIAM
B. Nov. 16, 1960, Ames, IA
Oregon 6'4" 265 lbs.

Year	Team		Games	Pos.
1984	DET	N	16	DE, DT
1985			16	DE, DT

Year	Team		Games	Pos.

Steve Baack *continued*

Year	Team		Games	Pos.
1986			16	NT, DE
1987			7	G
4 yrs.	55 games			

Al Babartsky
BABARTSKY, ALBERT J.
B. Apr. 19, 1915, Shenandoah, PA
Fordham 6'0" 223 lbs.

Year	Team		Games	Pos.
1938	CHIC	N	7	T
1939			11	T
1941			11	T
1943	CHIB	N	9	T
1944			10	T
1945			8	T
6 yrs.	56 games			

Charlie Babb
BABB, CHARLES DAVID
B. Feb. 4, 1950, Sikeston, MO
Memphis State 6'0" 190 lbs.

Year	Team		Games	Pos.
1972	MIA	N	14	DB
1973			14	S
1974			14	S
1975			14	S
1976			14	S
1977			6	S
1978			16	S
1979			5	S
8 yrs.	97 games			

Gene Babb
BABB, GENE WALTER
B. Dec. 27, 1934, El Paso, TX
Austin 6'3" 216 lbs.

Year	Team		Games	Pos.
1957	SF	N	12	FB
1958			12	FB
1960	DAL	N	10	FB
1961			14	LB
1962	HOU	A	14	FB, LB
1963			14	FB, LB
6 yrs.	76 games			

Harry Babcock
BABCOCK, HARRY
B. Aug. 12, 1930, West Nyack, NY
Georgia 6'2" 193 lbs.

Year	Team		Games	Pos.
1953	SF	N	10	E
1954			12	E
1955			8	E
3 yrs.	30 games			

Sam Babcock
BABCOCK, WHITEMORE
B. Nov. 5, 1901
D. Jul, 1970, San Diego, CA
Syracuse 5'6" 168 lbs.

Year	Team		Games	Pos.
1926	CAN	N	8	HB, FB, QB

Bob Babich
BABICH, ROBERT (Bluto)
B. May 5, 1947, Youngstown, OH
Miami (Ohio) 6'2" 231 lbs.

Year	Team		Games	Pos.
1970	SD	N	14	LB
1971			14	LB
1972			14	LB
1973	CLE	N	14	LB
1974			14	LB
1975			11	LB
1976			14	LB
1977			14	LB
1978			16	LB
9 yrs.	125 games			

John Babinecz
BABINECZ, JOHN MICHAEL

John Babinecz *continued*
B. Jul. 27, 1950, Pittsburgh, PA
Villanova 6'1" 222 lbs.

Year	Team		Games	Pos.
1972	DAL	N	14	LB
1973			12	LB
1975	CHI	N	14	LB
3 yrs.	40 games			

Marty Baccaglio
BACCAGLIO, MARTIN
B. Aug. 28, 1944, Novato, CA
San Jose State 6'3" 245 lbs.

Year	Team		Games	Pos.
1968	SD	A	9	DE
1968	CIN	A	2	DE
1969			14	DE
1970	CIN	N	14	DE
3 yrs.	39 games			

Carl Bacchus
BACCHUS, ROBERT CARL
B. Jul. 31, 1904
D. Mar, 1985, Kansas City, MO
Missouri 6'0" 205 lbs.

Year	Team		Games	Pos.
1927	CLE	N	10	E
1928	DET	N	9	E
2 yrs.	19 games			

Joe Bachmaier
BACHMAIER, JOSEPH W. (Buck)
B. Nov. 18, 1895, New York State
D. Jan, 1974, Rochester, NY
None 5'9" 175 lbs.

Year	Team		Games	Pos.
1920	ROC	A	1	C
1921			4	G, C, E
1922	ROC	N	3	T, G
1923			2	G, C
1924			3	G
5 yrs.	13 games			

Jay Bachman
BACHMAN, JAY LANCE
B. Dec. 8, 1945, Hamilton, OH
Cincinnati 6'3" 250 lbs.

Year	Team		Games	Pos.
1968	DEN	A	6	C
1969			14	C
1970	DEN	N	11	C
1971	DEN	N	14	C
4 yrs.	45 games			

Ted Bachman
BACHMAN, TED L.
B. Jan. 19, 1952, Pensacola, FL
New Mexico State 6'0" 190 lbs.

Year	Team		Games	Pos.
1976	SEA	N	5	CB
1976	MIA	N	8	CB
1 yr.	13 games			

Ludwig Bachor
BACHOR, LUDWIG A. (Rip)
B. 1901
D. Dec 11, 1959
Detroit 6'0" 215 lbs.

Year	Team		Games	Pos.
1928	DET	N	2	T

Coy Bacon
BACON, LANDER MCCOY
B. Aug. 30, 1942, Cadiz, KY
Jackson State 6'4" 269 lbs.

Year	Team		Games	Pos.
1968	LA	N	7	DE
1969			14	DE
1970			14	DT
1971			14	DE, DT
1972			14	DT
1973	SD	N	12	DT
1974			14	DE

Coy Bacon *continued*

Year	Team		Games	Pos.
1975			14	DE
1976	CIN	N	14	DE
1977			12	DE
1978	WAS	N	16	DE
1979			16	DE
1980			16	DE
1981			3	DE
14 yrs.	180 games			

Frank Bacon
BACON, FRANCIS WILLIAM
B. Jan. 11, 1894, South Bend, IN
D. Aug, 1977, Port Clinton, OH
Wabash 5'11" 182 lbs.

Year	Team		Games	Pos.
1920	DAY	A	8	HB
1921			9	HB, FB
1922	DAY	N	6	HB, FB
1923			8	HB
1923	AKR	N	1	HB
1924	DAY	N	8	E, HB, FB
1925			6	HB, FB
6 yrs.	46 games			

Rick Badanjek
BADANJEK, RICHARD ALAN
B. Apr. 25, 1962, Warren, OH
Maryland 5'8" 217 lbs.

Year	Team		Games	Pos.
1986	WAS	N	6	RB
1987	ATL	N	2	RB
1988			6	RB
3 yrs.	14 games			

John Badaczewski
BADACZEWSKI, JOHN WALTER
B. Jan. 17, 1923, Johnstown, PA
Case Western Reserve 6'1" 239 lbs.

Year	Team		Games	Pos.
1946	BOS	N	11	G
1947			12	G
1948			6	G
1949	WAS	N	12	G
1950			12	G
1951			12	G
1953	CHIB	N	12	G
7 yrs.	77 games			

Rich Badar
BADAR, RICH
B. 1943
Indiana 6'1" 190 lbs.

Year	Team		Games	Pos.
1967	PIT	N	1	QB

Red Badgro
BADGRO, MORRIS HIRAM
B. Dec. 1, 1902, Orillia, WA
Southern California 6'0" 191 lbs.

Year	Team		Games	Pos.
1927	NYY	N	13	E
1928			1	G
1930	NYG	N	16	E
1931			13	E
1932			12	E
1933			12	E
1934			13	E
1935			5	E
1936	BKN	N	9	E
9 yrs.	94 games			

Steve Bagarus
BAGARUS, STEPHEN MICHAEL
B. Sep. 19, 1919, South Bend, IN
D. Oct. 17, 1981, Gaithersburg, MD
Notre Dame 6'0" 173 lbs.

Year	Team		Games	Pos.
1945	WAS	N	10	HB, DB
1946			11	HB, DB
1947	LA	N	2	HB, DB
1948	WAS	N	5	HB, DB
4 yrs.	28 games			

Herm Bagby
BAGBY, HERMAN
B. Feb. 21, 1903
D. Feb, 1980, Lake Village, AR
Arkansas 5'9" 175 lbs.

Year	Team		Games	Pos.
1926	BKN	N	8	HB, QB
1927	CLE	N	4	HB, FB
2 yrs.	12 games			

Eddie Bagdon
BAGDON, EDWARD
B. 1926, Dearborn, MI
D. Oct. 25, 1990, Hesperia, CA
Michigan State 5'10" 204 lbs.

Year	Team		Games	Pos.
1950	CHIC	N	12	G, LB
1951			12	G, LB
1952	WAS	N	3	G, LB
3 yrs.	27 games			

Billy Baggett
BAGGETT, WILLIAM
B. 1929
Louisiana State 5'11" 175 lbs.

Year	Team		Games	Pos.
1952	DAL	N	12	HB

Curt Baham
BAHAM, CURTIS
B. Mar. 2, 1963
Tulane 5'11" 180 lbs.

Year	Team		Games	Pos.
1987	SEA	N	3	CB

Pete Bahan
BAHAN, LEONARD F.
B. Feb. 18, 1898
D. May, 1977, Fort Worth, TX
Notre Dame/Detroit 5'9" 160 lbs.

Year	Team		Games	Pos.
1923	CLE	N	7	QB
1923	BUF	N	1	HB
1 yr.	8 games			

Ken Bahnsen
BAHNSEN, KENNETH ANTONE
B. Feb. 19, 1930, Vinton, LA
North Texas State 5'10" 200 lbs.

Year	Team		Games	Pos.
1953	SF	N	5	FB

Chris Bahr
BAHR, CHRIS
B. Feb. 3, 1953, State College, PA
Penn State 5'10" 170 lbs.

Year	Team		Games	Pos.
1976	CIN	N	14	K
1977			14	K, P
1978			16	K, P
1979			16	K
1980	OAK	N	16	K
1981			16	K, P
1982	LARI	N	9	K
1983			16	K
1984			16	K
1985			16	K
1986			13	K
1987			16	K
1988			16	K
1989	SD	N	16	K
14 yrs.	210 games			

Matt Bahr
BAHR, MATTHEW DAVID
B. Jul. 6, 1956, Philadelphia, PA
Penn State 5'10" 185 lbs.

Year	Team		Games	Pos.
1979	PIT	N	16	K
1980			16	K
1981	SF	N	4	K
1981	CLE	N	11	K
1982			9	K

Year	Team		Games	Pos.

Matt Bahr continued

Year	Team		Games	Pos.
1983			16	K
1984			16	K
1985			16	K
1986			12	K
1987			3	K
1988			16	K
1989			16	K
1990	NYG	N	13	K
1991			13	K
1992			12	K
1993	PHI	N	11	K
1993	NE		3	K
1994			16	K
1995			16	K, P

17 yrs.   235 games

Aaron Bailey

BAILEY, AARON
B. Oct. 24, 1971, Ann Arbor, MI
Louisville 5'10" 184 lbs.

Year	Team		Games	Pos.
1994	IND	N	12	WR
1995			15	WR
1996			14	WR

3 yrs.   41 games

Bill Bailey

BAILEY, BILL (Teddy)
B. Aug. 12, 1944, Cincinnati, OH
Cincinnati 6'0" 210 lbs.

Year	Team		Games	Pos.
1967	BUF	A	1	RB
1969	BOS	A	2	RB

2 yrs.   3 games

Bill Bailey

BAILEY, EDGAR WILLIAM
B. Apr. 12, 1916, Thomasville, NC
D. Apr. 9, 1990, Winston-Salem, NC
Duke 6'2" 213 lbs.

Year	Team		Games	Pos.
1940	BKN	N	11	E
1941			6	E

2 yrs.   17 games

By Bailey

BAILEY, BYRON LEDARE
B. Oct. 12, 1930, Omaha, NE
Washington State 5'10" 192 lbs.

Year	Team		Games	Pos.
1952	DET	N	8	HB
1953	GB	N	9	HB

2 yrs.   17 games

Carlton Bailey

BAILEY, CARLTON WILSON
B. Dec. 15, 1964, Baltimore, MD
North Carolina 6'2" 240 lbs.

Year	Team		Games	Pos.
1988	BUF	N	6	LB
1989			16	LB
1990			16	LB
1991			16	LB
1992			16	LB
1993	NYG	N	16	LB
1994			16	LB
1995	CAR	N	16	LB
1996			16	LB

9 yrs.   134 games

Clarence Bailey

BAILEY, CLARENCE
B. Mar. 7, 1963, Milford, DE
Hampton Institute 5'11" 220 lbs.

Year	Team		Games	Pos.
1987	MIA	N	3	RB

David Bailey

BAILEY, DAVID
B. Sep. 3, 1965, Coatesville, PA
Oklahoma State 6'4" 240 lbs.

Year	Team		Games	Pos.
1990	PHI	N	13	DE

Don Bailey

BAILEY, WILLIAM DONALD
B. Mar. 24, 1961, Miami, FL
Miami (Florida) 6'3" 260 lbs.

Year	Team		Games	Pos.
1984	IND	N	10	C
1985			12	C

2 yrs.   22 games

Edwin Bailey

BAILEY, EDWIN RAYMOND
B. May 15, 1959, Savannah, GA
South Carolina State 6'4" 270 lbs.

Year	Team		Games	Pos.
1981	SEA	N	16	G
1982			9	G
1983			16	G
1984			12	G
1985			16	G
1986			12	G
1987			12	G
1988			16	G
1989			16	G
1990			11	G
1991			3	G

11 yrs.   139 games

Elmer Bailey

BAILEY, ELMER FRANCIS
B. Dec. 13, 1957, Evanston, IL
Lincoln (Missouri)/Macalester/Minnesota 6'0" 195 lbs.

Year	Team		Games	Pos.
1980	MIA	N	14	WR
1981			16	WR
1982	BAL	N	1	WR

3 yrs.   31 games

Eric Bailey

BAILEY, ERIC R.
B. May 12, 1963, Fort Worth, TX
Kansas State 6'5" 240 lbs.

Year	Team		Games	Pos.
1987	PHI	N	3	TE

Harold Bailey

BAILEY, HAROLD
B. Apr. 2, 1957, Houston, TX
Oklahoma State 6'2" 197 lbs.

Year	Team		Games	Pos.
1981	HOU	N	11	WR
1982			9	WR

2 yrs.   20 games

Henry Bailey

BAILEY, HENRY
B. Feb. 28, 1973, Chicago, IL
Nevada-Las Vegas 5'9" 183 lbs.

Year	Team		Games	Pos.
1996	NYJ	N	8	WR

Howard Bailey

BAILEY, HOWARD HENRY
(Screeno)
B. Jan. 10, 1913, Birmingham, AL
D. Aug, 1966
Tennessee 6'0" 205 lbs.

Year	Team		Games	Pos.
1935	PHI	N	1	T

Jim Bailey

BAILEY, JAMES A.
B. 1927
West Virginia State 6'2" 215 lbs.

Year	Team		Games	Pos.
1949	CHI	AA	7	G

Jim Bailey

BAILEY, JAMES RANDALL
B. Jun. 9, 1948, Kansas City, MO
Kansas 6'4" 253 lbs.

Year	Team		Games	Pos.
1970	BAL	N	10	DT
1971			13	DT
1972			14	DT

Jim Bailey continued

Year	Team		Games	Pos.
1973			14	DT
1974			14	DT
1975	NYJ	N	14	DT
1976	ATL	N	7	DE
1977			14	DE
1978			16	DE

9 yrs.   116 games

Johnny Bailey

BAILEY, JOHNNY LEE
B. Mar. 17, 1967, Houston, TX
Texas A&I-Kingsville 5'8" 180 lbs.

Year	Team		Games	Pos.
1990	CHI	N	16	RB
1991			14	RB
1992	PHX	N	12	RB
1993			13	RB
1994	LARM	N	14	RB
1995	STL	N	12	RB

6 yrs.   81 games

Larry Bailey

BAILEY, LARRY
B. May 10, 1952, San Mateo, CA
Pacific 6'4" 238 lbs.

Year	Team		Games	Pos.
1974	ATL	N	1	DT

Mark Bailey

BAILEY, MARK
B. Dec. 13, 1954, Lynwood, CA
California/Long Beach State 6'3" 237 lbs.

Year	Team		Games	Pos.
1977	KC	N	14	RB
1978			13	RB

2 yrs.   27 games

Monk Bailey

BAILEY, CLARON
B. Apr. 22, 1938, Utah
Utah 6'0" 178 lbs.

Year	Team		Games	Pos.
1964	STL	N	12	DB
1965			11	DB

2 yrs.   23 games

Robert Bailey

BAILEY, ROBERT MARTIN
B. Sep. 3, 1968, Miami, FL
Miami (Florida) 5'9" 176 lbs.

Year	Team		Games	Pos.
1991	LARM	N	6	CB
1992			16	CB
1993			9	CB
1994			16	CB, S
1995	WAS	N	4	CB
1995	DAL	N	9	CB
1996	MIA	N	14	CB

6 yrs.   74 games

Russ Bailey

BAILEY, RUSSELL BROOKS
B. Sep. 3, 1899, Weston, WV
D. Sep. 15, 1949, Wheeling, WV
West Virginia 5'11" 183 lbs.

Year	Team		Games	Pos.
1920	AKR	A	9	C
1921			12	C

2 yrs.   21 games

Stacey Bailey

BAILEY, STACEY DWAYNE
B. Feb. 10, 1960, San Rafael, CA
San Jose State 6'0" 160 lbs.

Year	Team		Games	Pos.
1982	ATL	N	5	WR
1983			14	WR
1984			16	WR
1985			15	WR
1986			6	WR
1987			7	WR
1988			10	WR

Stacey Bailey continued

Year	Team		Games	Pos.
1989			15	WR
1990			3	WR

9 yrs.   91 games

Thomas Bailey

BAILEY, THOMAS
B. Dec. 6, 1971, Dallas, TX
Auburn 6'0" 196 lbs.

Year	Team		Games	Pos.
1995	CIN	N	1	WR

Tom Bailey

BAILEY, GEORGE THOMAS
B. Feb. 2, 1949, Gainesville, FL
Florida State 6'2" 211 lbs.

Year	Team		Games	Pos.
1971	PHI	N	13	RB
1972			13	RB
1973			12	RB
1974			11	RB

4 yrs.   49 games

Victor Bailey

BAILEY, VICTOR
B. Jul. 30, 1970, Fort Worth, TX
Texas-El Paso/Missouri 6'2" 196 lbs.

Year	Team		Games	Pos.
1993	PHI	N	16	WR
1994			16	WR
1996	KC	N	2	WR

3 yrs.   34 games

Bill Bain

BAIN, WILLIAM ERNEST
B. Aug. 9, 1952, Los Angeles, CA
Colorado/Southern California 6'4" 270 lbs.

Year	Team		Games	Pos.
1975	GB	N	14	G
1976	DEN	N	14	OT
1978			1	OT
1979	LA	N	8	OT
1980			16	G
1981			16	G
1982	LARM	N	9	G
1983			16	G
1984			16	OT
1985			15	OT
1986	NYJ	N	4	OT
1986	NE	N	3	OT

11 yrs.   132 games

Bill Baird

BAIRD, WILLIAM ARTHUR
B. Mar. 1, 1939, Lindsay, CA
San Francisco State 5'10" 180 lbs.

Year	Team		Games	Pos.
1963	NY	A	14	DB
1964			14	DB
1965			14	DB
1966			14	DB
1967			14	DB
1968			14	DB
1969			14	DB

7 yrs.   98 games

Al Baisi

BAISI, ALBERT FRANK
B. Sep. 6, 1917, Norton, WV
West Virginia 6'0" 217 lbs.

Year	Team		Games	Pos.
1940	CHIB	N	7	G
1941			10	G
1946			8	G, T
1947	PHI	N	2	G

4 yrs.   27 games

Art Baker

BAKER, ARTHUR L.
B. Dec. 31, 1937, Erie, PA
Syracuse 6'0" 220 lbs.

Year	Team		Games	Pos.
1961	BUF	A	14	FB

Year	Team	Games	Pos.

Art Baker continued

Year	Team	Games	Pos.
1962		3	FB
2 yrs.	17 games		

Bubba Baker
BAKER, JAMES ALBERT LONDON
B. Dec. 9, 1956, Jacksonville, FL
Colorado State 6'6" 264 lbs.

Year	Team		Games	Pos.
1978	DET	N	16	DE
1979			16	DE
1980			15	DE
1981			11	DE
1982			9	DE
1983	STL	N	16	DE
1984			15	DE
1985			16	DE
1986			16	DE
1987	CLE	N	12	DE
1988	MIN	N	14	DE
1989	CLE	N	16	DE
1990			9	DE
13 yrs.	181 games			

Bullet Baker
BAKER, ROY
B. 1900
Deceased
Southern California 5'8" 178 lbs.

Year	Team		Games	Pos.
1926	NY	A	13	HB, QB, FB
1927	NYY	N	13	HB, QB, FB
1928	GB	N	12	HB, QB, FB
1929			2	HB
1929	CHIC	N	4	HB, QB
1930			10	QB, HB
1931	SI	N	7	QB, HB, FB
6 yrs.	61 games			

Charlie Baker
BAKER, CHARLES EDWARD
B. Sep. 26, 1957, Mount Pleasant, TX
New Mexico 6'2" 230 lbs.

Year	Team		Games	Pos.
1980	STL	N	16	LB
1981			14	LB
1982			9	LB
1983			16	LB
1984			9	LB
1985			15	LB
1986			16	LB
1987			14	LB
8 yrs.	109 games			

Conway Baker
BAKER, CONWAY
B. Sep. 9, 1911, Marlin, TX
Deceased
Centenary 5'11" 228 lbs.

Year	Team		Games	Pos.
1936	CHIC	N	9	T
1937			6	T
1938			11	T
1939			10	T
1940			11	T
1941			11	T
1942			11	G
1943			10	G
1944	C, P	N	10	G, T
1945	CHIC	N	8	G
10 yrs.	97 games			

Dave Baker
BAKER, DAVID L.
B. Jul. 30, 1937, Coffeyville, KS
Oklahoma 6'0" 192 lbs.

Year	Team		Games	Pos.
1959	SF	N	12	HB
1960			12	HB
1961			14	DB
3 yrs.	38 games			

Ed Baker
BAKER, EDWARD
B. May 29, 1948, East Orange, NJ
Lafayette 6'2" 198 lbs.

Year	Team		Games	Pos.
1972	HOU	N	1	QB

Frank Baker
BAKER, FRANK L. (Moon)
B. 1909
Northwestern 6'2" 182 lbs.

Year	Team		Games	Pos.
1931	GB	N	2	E

Jerry Baker
BAKER, JERRY EUGENE
B. Mar. 6, 1960, Bartow, FL
Tulane 6'2" 297 lbs.

Year	Team		Games	Pos.
1983	DEN	N	5	NT

Jesse Baker
BAKER, JESSE
B. Jul. 10, 1957, Conyers, GA
Jacksonville State 6'5" 270 lbs.

Year	Team		Games	Pos.
1979	HOU	N	16	DE
1980			16	DE
1981			16	DE
1982			9	DE
1983			16	DE
1984			16	DE
1985			16	DE
1986	DAL	N	3	DE
1986	HOU	N	11	DE
1987			9	DE
9 yrs.	128 games			

John Baker
BAKER, JOHN HAYWOOD
B. Jun. 10, 1935, Raleigh, NC
North Carolina Central 6'6" 279 lbs.

Year	Team		Games	Pos.
1958	LA	N	12	T
1959			12	E, T
1960			12	T
1961			13	DT
1962	PHI	N	14	DE
1963	PIT	N	14	DE
1964			14	DE
1965			14	DE
1966			7	DE
1967			13	DE
1968	DET	N	13	DE
11 yrs.	138 games			

John Baker
BAKER, JOHN WILLEY ALEXANDER
B. Aug. 15, 1944, Suffolk, VA
Virginia Union/Norfolk State 6'5" 260 lbs.

Year	Team		Games	Pos.
1970	NYG	N	14	DE

Johnny Baker
BAKER, JOHNNY
B. Mar. 15, 1941, Meridian, MS
Mississippi State 6'3" 229 lbs.

Year	Team		Games	Pos.
1963	HOU	A	6	DE, LB
1964			14	LB
1965			7	LB
1966			14	LB
1967	SD	A	10	LB
5 yrs.	51 games			

Jon Baker
BAKER, JON
B. Jun. 14, 1923
D. 1992
California 6'2" 214 lbs.

Year	Team		Games	Pos.
1949	NYG	N	10	G
1950			12	G
1951			12	G
1952			12	G
4 yrs.	46 games			

Jon Baker
BAKER, JONATHON DAVID
B. Aug. 13, 1972, Orange, CA
Arizona State 6'1" 170 lbs.

Year	Team		Games	Pos.
1995	DAL	N	3	K

Keith Baker
BAKER, KEITH LEONARD
B. Jun. 4, 1957, Dallas, TX
Texas A&M/Texas Southern 5'10" 185 lbs.

Year	Team		Games	Pos.
1985	PHI	N	8	WR

Larry Baker
BAKER, LAWRENCE
B. 1937
Bowling Green 6'2" 240 lbs.

Year	Team		Games	Pos.
1960	NY	A		OT

Melvin Baker
BAKER, MELVIN
B. Aug. 12, 1950, Beaumont, TX
Texas Southern 6'0" 189 lbs.

Year	Team		Games	Pos.
1974	MIA	N	9	WR
1975	NO	N	2	WR
1975	NE	N	1	WR
1975	SD	N	1	WR
1976	HOU	N	8	WR
1977	BUF	N		WR
4 yrs.	21 games			

Myron Baker
BAKER, MYRON TOBIAS
B. Jan. 6, 1971, Haughton, LA
Louisiana Tech 6'1" 228 lbs.

Year	Team		Games	Pos.
1993	CHI	N	16	LB
1994			16	LB
1995			16	LB
1996	CAR	N	16	LB
4 yrs.	64 games			

Ralph Baker
BAKER, RALPH ROBERT
B. Aug. 25, 1942, Lewiston, PA
Penn State 6'3" 232 lbs.

Year	Team		Games	Pos.
1964	NY	A	14	LB
1965			14	LB
1966			11	LB
1967			14	LB
1968			14	LB
1969			10	LB
1970	NYJ	N	14	LB
1971			12	LB
1972			10	LB
1973			14	LB
1974			14	LB
11 yrs.	141 games			

Ron Baker
BAKER, RONALD
B. Nov. 19, 1954, Gary, IN
Oklahoma State 6'4" 270 lbs.

Year	Team		Games	Pos.
1978	BAL	N	16	G
1979			16	G
1980	PHI	N	16	G
1981			16	G
1982			9	G
1983			16	G
1984			16	G
1985			15	G
1986			16	G
1987			10	G

Ron Baker continued

Year	Team		Games	Pos.
1988			9	G
11 yrs.	155 games			

Sam Baker
BAKER, LORIS HOSKINS
B. Nov. 12, 1930, San Francisco, CA
Oregon State 6'2" 217 lbs.

Year	Team		Games	Pos.
1953	WAS	N	11	FB, P
1956			12	FB, K, P
1957			12	FB, K, P
1958			12	K, P
1959			12	FB, K, P
1960	CLE	N	12	K, P
1961			14	P
1962	DAL	N	14	K, P
1963			14	K, P
1964	PHI	N	14	K, P
1965			12	K, P
1966			14	K, P
1967			14	K, P
1968			14	K, P
1969			14	K, P
15 yrs.	195 games			

Shannon Baker
BAKER, SHANNON MAURICE
B. Jul. 20, 1971, Lakeland, FL
Florida State 5'9" 185 lbs.

Year	Team		Games	Pos.
1994	IND	N	4	WR

Stephen Baker
BAKER, STEPHEN (The Touchdown Maker)
B. Aug. 30, 1964, San Antonio, TX
Fresno State 5'8" 160 lbs.

Year	Team		Games	Pos.
1987	NYG	N	12	WR
1988			16	WR
1989			15	WR
1990			16	WR
1991			15	WR
1992			16	WR
6 yrs.	90 games			

Terry Baker
BAKER, TERRY
B. May 5, 1941, Pine River, MN
Oregon State 6'3" 198 lbs.

Year	Team		Games	Pos.
1963	LA	N	4	QB
1964			5	HB
1965			9	HB
3 yrs.	18 games			

Tony Baker
BAKER, TONY FERRINO
B. Jun. 11, 1964, High Point, SC
East Carolina 5'10" 175 lbs.

Year	Team		Games	Pos.
1986	ATL	N	2	RB
1986	CLE	N	2	RB
1988			4	RB
1989	PHX	N	10	RB
3 yrs.	18 games			

Tony Baker
BAKER, VERNON ANTHONY
B. Feb. 16, 1945, Fort Madison, IA
Iowa State 5'11" 224 lbs.

Year	Team		Games	Pos.
1968	NO	N	1	RB
1969			14	RB
1970			8	RB
1971	NO	N		RB
1971	PHI	N	5	RB
1972			5	RB
1973	LA	N	14	RB
1974			14	RB
1975	SD	N	13	RB
8 yrs.	74 games			

Year	Team		Games	Pos.

Wayne Baker
BAKER, WAYNE
B. Jul. 7, 1953, Sandpoint, ID
Brigham Young 6'6" 270 lbs.

Year	Team		Games	Pos.
1975	SF	N	14	DT

Jim Bakken
BAKKEN, JAMES LEROY
B. Nov. 2, 1940, Madison, WI
Wisconsin 6'0" 199 lbs.

1962	STL	N	8	K
1963			14	K
1964			14	K
1965			14	K, P
1966			14	K, P
1967			14	K
1968			14	K
1969			14	K
1970			14	K
1971			14	K, P
1972			14	K, P
1973			14	K
1974			14	K
1975			14	K
1976			14	K
1977			14	K
1978			16	K
17 yrs.	234 games			

Ed Balatti
BALATTI, EDWARD T.
B. Apr. 8, 1924
D. Aug. 28, 1990, Novato, CA
None 6'1" 195 lbs.

1946	SF	AA	14	E
1947			14	E
1948			1	E
1948	NY	AA	2	E
1948	BUF	AA	7	E
3 yrs.	38 games			

Frank Balazs
BALAZS, FRANK
B. Jan. 23, 1918, Chicago, IL
Deceased
Iowa 6'2" 212 lbs.

1939	GB	N	5	B
1940			7	FB
1941			1	B
1941	CHIC	N	7	FB
1945			2	FB
4 yrs.	22 games			

Lou Baldacci
BALDACCI, LOUIS G.
B. 1934
Michigan 6'2" 200 lbs.

1956	PIT	N	12	HB

Mike Baldassin
BALDASSIN, MICHAEL ROBERT
B. Jul. 26, 1955, Tacoma, WA
Washington 6'1" 218 lbs.

1977	SF	N	14	LB
1978			16	LB
2 yrs.	30 games			

Brian Baldinger
BALDINGER, BRIAN D.
B. Jan. 7, 1959, Pittsburgh, PA
Duke 6'4" 260 lbs.

1982	DAL	N	4	C, G
1983			16	C, G
1984			16	G
1986			16	G
1987			3	OT, G
1988	IND	N	16	G
1989			16	G

Brian Baldinger continued

1990			16	G
1991			16	G
1992	PHI	N	12	C, OT
1993			12	G, OT
11 yrs.	143 games			

Gary Baldinger
BALDINGER, GARY THOMAS
B. Oct. 4, 1963, Philadelphia, PA
Wake Forest 6'2" 260 lbs.

1986	KC	N	5	NT, DE
1987			7	DE
1988			11	NT, DE
1990	IND	N	1	NT
1990	BUF		9	NT
1991			7	NT
1992			4	NT
6 yrs.	44 games			

Rich Baldinger
BALDINGER, RICHARD L.
B. Dec. 31, 1959, Camp Lejeune, NC
Wake Forest 6'4" 280 lbs.

1982	NYG	N	1	OT
1983			2	OT
1983	KC	N	6	OT, G
1984			14	OT, G
1985			16	OT, G
1986			16	G, OT
1987			14	G, OT
1988			14	G, OT
1989			16	G, OT
1990			16	G, OT
1991			16	G
1992			13	G
1993	NE	N	15	G
12 yrs.	157 games			

Karl Baldischwiler
BALDISCHWILER, JOHN KARL
B. Jan. 19, 1956, Okmulgee, OK
Oklahoma 6'5" 270 lbs.

1978	DET	N	16	OT
1979			16	OT
1980			16	OT
1981			16	OT
1982			9	OT
1983	BAL	N	14	OT
1985	IND	N	16	OT
1986			15	OT
8 yrs.	118 games			

Al Baldwin
BALDWIN, ALTON (Legs)
B. Apr. 16, 1923, Hot Springs, AR
Arkansas 6'2" 201 lbs.

1947	BUF	AA	14	E
1948			14	B
1949			12	E
1950	GB	N	12	E
4 yrs.	52 games			

Bob Baldwin
BALDWIN, ROBERT
B. Jul. 7, 1943, Baltimore, MD
Clemson 6'1" 225 lbs.

1966	BAL	N	9	LB

Burr Baldwin
BALDWIN, BURR BROWNING
B. Jun. 13, 1922, Bakersfield, CA
UCLA 6'1" 197 lbs.

1947	LA	AA	13	E
1948			12	E
1949			9	E
3 yrs.	34 games			

Cliff Baldwin
BALDWIN, CLIFFORD (Kip)
B. Sep. 22, 1899, Indiana
D. Jan, 1979, Muncie, IN
None 5'10" 172 lbs.

1920	MUN	A	1	HB
1921			2	HB, QB
2 yrs.	3 games			

Don Baldwin
BALDWIN, DONALD WAYNE
B. Jul. 9, 1964, St. Charles, MO
Purdue 6'3" 263 lbs.

1987	NYJ	N	8	DE

George Baldwin
BALDWIN, GEORGE W.E.
B. May 3, 1902
D. Jun. 13, 1971, Spring Lake, NJ
Virginia 5'11" 190 lbs.

1925	CLE	N	9	E, T
1926	BKN	A	1	G
2 yrs.	10 games			

Jack Baldwin
BALDWIN, JOHN D.
B. Jul. 31, 1921, Clyde, TX
Centenary 6'3" 223 lbs.

1946	NY	AA	7	C
1947			2	C
1947	SF	AA	3	C
1948	BUF	AA		C
3 yrs.	12 games			

Keith Baldwin
BALDWIN, KEITH MANNING
B. Oct. 13, 1960, Houston, TX
Texas A&M 6'5" 265 lbs.

1982	CLE	N	9	DE
1983			16	DE
1984			16	DE
1985			10	DE
1987	SD	N	6	DE
1988			6	DE
6 yrs.	63 games			

Randy Baldwin
BALDWIN, RANDY CHADWICK
B. Aug. 19, 1967, Griffin, GA
Mississippi 5'10" 216 lbs.

1991	MIN	N	4	RB
1992	CLE	N	15	RB
1993			14	RB
1994			16	RB
1995	CAR	N	7	RB
1996	BAL	N	9	RB
6 yrs.	65 games			

Tom Baldwin
BALDWIN, THOMAS BURKE
B. May 13, 1961, Evergreen Park, IL
Wisconsin/Tulsa 6'4" 270 lbs.

1984	NYJ	N	16	DT
1985			16	DT
1986			16	DT
1988			16	DE
4 yrs.	64 games			

Eric Ball
BALL, ERIC CLINTON
B. Jul. 1, 1966, Cleveland, OH
UCLA 6'2" 215 lbs.

1989	CIN	N	15	RB
1990			13	RB
1991			6	RB
1992			16	RB
1993			15	RB

Eric Ball continued

1994			16	RB
1995	OAK	N	16	RB
7 yrs.	97 games			

Jerry Ball
BALL, JERRY LEE
B. Dec. 15, 1964, Beaumont, TX
Southern Methodist 6'1" 283 lbs.

1987	DET	N	12	NT
1988			16	NT
1989			16	NT
1990			15	NT
1991			13	NT
1992			12	NT
1993	CLE	N	16	DT
1994	LARI	N	16	DT
1995	OAK	N	15	DT
1996			16	DT
10 yrs.	147 games			

Larry Ball
BALL, LARRY LAUREN
B. Sep. 27, 1949, Iowa City, IA
Louisville 6'6" 232 lbs.

1972	MIA	N	10	LB
1973			14	LB
1974			14	LB
1975	DET	N	14	LB
1976	TB	N	13	LB
1977	MIA	N	8	LB
1978				LB
7 yrs.	73 games			

Michael Ball
BALL, MICHAEL, JR.
B. Aug. 5, 1964, New Orleans, LA
Southern University 6'0" 216 lbs.

1988	IND	N	16	CB, S
1989			16	CB, S
1990			16	CB, S
1991			15	CB, S
1992			16	CB, S
1993			5	CB, S
6 yrs.	84 games			

Sam Ball
BALL, SAM DAVIS
B. Jun. 7, 1944, Henderson, KY
Kentucky 6'4" 240 lbs.

1966	BAL	N	7	OT
1967			14	OT
1968			14	OT
1969			14	OT
1970			12	OT
5 yrs.	61 games			

Pat Ballage
BALLAGE, PATRICK FITZGERALD
B. Apr. 8, 1964, Fort Hood, TX
Notre Dame 6'1" 200 lbs.

1986	IND	N	2	CB, S
1987			3	CB, S
2 yrs.	5 games			

Howard Ballard
BALLARD, HOWARD LOUIS (House)
B. Nov. 3, 1963, Ashland, AL
Alabama A&M 6'6" 300 lbs.

1988	BUF	N	16	OT
1989			16	OT
1990			16	OT
1991			16	OT
1992			16	OT
1993			16	OT
1994	SEA	N	16	OT

Year	Team		Games	Pos.

Howard Ballard continued

Year	Team		Games	Pos.
1995			16	OT
1996			16	OT
9 yrs.	144 games			

Quinton Ballard
BALLARD, QUINTON MCCOY
B. Nov. 18, 1960, Ahoskie, NC
Elon 6'3" 289 lbs.

Year	Team		Games	Pos.
1983	**BAL**	N	15	NT

Gary Ballman
BALLMAN, GARY JOHN
B. Jul. 6, 1940, Detroit, MI
Michigan State 6'0" 203 lbs.

Year	Team		Games	Pos.
1962	**PIT**	N	3	HB
1963			14	HB
1964			13	FL
1965			14	OE, FL
1966			13	OE
1967	**PHI**	N	12	FL, OE
1968			12	FL, OE
1969			14	WR
1970			14	WR
1971			6	TE
1972			8	TE
1973	**NYG**	N	5	TE
1973	**MIN**	N	3	TE
12 yrs.	131 games			

Mike Ballou
BALLOU, MICHAEL RUDOLPH
B. Sep. 11, 1947, Los Angeles, CA
UCLA 6'3" 235 lbs.

Year	Team		Games	Pos.
1970	**BOS**	N	14	LB

Bob Balog
BALOG, ROBERT S.
B. Nov. 21, 1924
Denver 6'2" 225 lbs.

Year	Team		Games	Pos.
1949	**PIT**	N	7	C, LB
1950			9	C, LB
2 yrs.	16 games			

Vic Baltzell
BALTZELL, VICTOR LEROY
B. Jun. 22, 1912, Soda Springs, ID
Southwestern (Kansas) 5'11" 205 lbs.

Year	Team		Games	Pos.
1935	**BOS**	N	2	HB, FB

Steve Banas
BANAS, STEPHEN PETER
B. 1910, East Chicago, IL
D. 1974
Notre Dame 6'0" 190 lbs.

Year	Team		Games	Pos.
1935	**DET**	N	1	FB
1935	**PHI**	N	2	FB, QB
1 yr.	3 games			

John Banaszak
BANASZAK, JOHN ARTHUR
B. Aug. 24, 1950, Cleveland, OH
Eastern Michigan 6'3" 242 lbs.

Year	Team		Games	Pos.
1975	**PIT**	N	14	DE
1976			13	DE
1977			8	DE
1978			16	DE
1979			16	DE, DT
1980			12	DE, DT
1981			12	DE
7 yrs.	91 games			

Pete Banaszak
BANASZAK, PETER ANDREW
B. May 21, 1944, Crivitz, WI

Pete Banaszak continued
Miami (Florida) 5'11" 206 lbs.

Year	Team		Games	Pos.
1966	**OAK**	A	14	RB
1967			10	RB
1968			13	RB
1969			12	RB
1970	**OAK**	N	10	RB
1971			14	RB
1972			14	RB
1973			14	RB
1974			14	RB
1975			14	RB
1976			14	RB
1977			14	RB
1978			16	RB
13 yrs.	173 games			

Cas Banaszek
BANASZEK, CASIMIR JOSEPH, II
B. Dec. 24, 1945, Chicago, IL
Northwestern 6'3" 249 lbs.

Year	Team		Games	Pos.
1968	**SF**	N	14	TE
1969			14	OT
1970			13	OT
1971			14	OT
1972			13	OT
1973			9	OT
1974			14	OT
1975			14	OT
1976			9	OT
1977			6	OT
10 yrs.	120 games			

Hugh Bancroft
BANCROFT, HUGH
B. Aug. 4, 1894
D. Oct, 1974, Bradenton, FL
None

Year	Team		Games	Pos.
1923	**ROC**	N	2	E

Romeo Bandison
BANDISON, ROMEO
B. Feb. 12, 1971, The Hague, Netherlands
Oregon 6'5" 290 lbs.

Year	Team		Games	Pos.
1995	**WAS**	N	4	DT
1996			10	DT
2 yrs.	14 games			

Bruno Banducci
BANDUCCI, BRUNO
B. Nov. 11, 1921, Tasignano, Italy
D. Sep. 15, 1985, Sonoma, CA
Stanford 5'11" 216 lbs.

Year	Team		Games	Pos.
1944	**PHI**	N	10	G, T
1945			9	G
1946	**SF**	AA	14	G
1947			10	G
1948			8	G
1949			12	G
1950	**SF**	N	12	G
1951			12	G
1952			12	G
1953			12	G
1954			11	G
11 yrs.	122 games			

John Bandura
BANDURA, JOHN
B. 1919
Southwestern Louisiana 6'0" 206 lbs.

Year	Team		Games	Pos.
1943	**BKN**	N	1	E

Don Bandy
BANDY, DONALD S.
B. Jul. 1, 1945, Southgate, CA
Tulsa 6'3" 250 lbs.

Year	Team		Games	Pos.
1967	**WAS**	N	14	OT

Don Bandy continued

Year	Team		Games	Pos.
1968			12	G
2 yrs.	26 games			

Joey Banes
BANES, JOEY
B. Apr. 7, 1967, Houston, TX
Houston 6'7" 282 lbs.

Year	Team		Games	Pos.
1990	**IND**	N	1	OT

Herb Banet
BANET, HERBERT
B. Sep. 6, 1911
D. Jan, 1981, Floyds Knobs, IN
Manchester 6'2" 200 lbs.

Year	Team		Games	Pos.
1937	**GB**	N	6	HB

Tony Banfield
BANFIELD, JAMES ANTHONY
B. 1939
Oklahoma State 6'1" 185 lbs.

Year	Team		Games	Pos.
1960	**HOU**	A		DB
1961			14	DB
1962			14	DB
1963			14	DB
1965			14	DB
5 yrs.	56 games			

Ben Bangs
BANGS, BENTON M. (Biff)
B. Sep. 5, 1893
D. Jun. 7, 1970, Wenatchee, WA
Washington State 5'10" 180 lbs.

Year	Team		Games	Pos.
1926	**LA**	N	1	E

Emil Banjavic
BANJAVIC, EMIL T.
B. Sep. 9, 1918, Staunton, IL
Arizona 6'1" 194 lbs.

Year	Team		Games	Pos.
1942	**DET**	N	10	HB

Ted Banker
BANKER, TED
B. Feb. 17, 1961, Belleville, IL
Southeast Missouri State 6'2" 270 lbs.

Year	Team		Games	Pos.
1984	**NYJ**	N	4	C
1985			16	G, C
1986			15	OT, G, C
1987			13	OL
1988			11	G
1989	**CLE**	N	16	G
6 yrs.	75 games			

Carl Banks
BANKS, CARL E.
B. Aug. 29, 1962, Flint, MI
Michigan State 6'4" 235 lbs.

Year	Team		Games	Pos.
1984	**NYG**	N	16	LB
1985			12	LB
1986			16	LB
1987			12	LB
1988			14	LB
1989			16	LB
1990			9	LB
1991			16	LB
1992			15	LB
1993	**WAS**	N	15	LB
1994	**CLE**	N	14	LB
1995			16	LB
12 yrs.	173 games			

Chip Banks
BANKS, WILLIAM CHIP
B. Sep. 18, 1959, Fort Lawton, OK
Southern California 6'4" 233 lbs.

Year	Team		Games	Pos.
1982	**CLE**	N	9	LB

Chip Banks continued

Year	Team		Games	Pos.
1983			16	LB
1984			16	LB
1985			16	LB
1986			16	LB
1987	**SD**	N	12	LB
1989	**IND**	N	10	LB
1990			16	LB
1991			11	LB
1992			12	LB
10 yrs.	138 games			

Chuck Banks
BANKS, CHUCK EDWARD
B. Jan. 4, 1964, Baltimore, MD
West Virginia Tech 6'2" 225 lbs.

Year	Team		Games	Pos.
1986	**HOU**	N	13	RB
1987	**IND**	N	3	RB
2 yrs.	16 games			

Estes Banks
BANKS, ESTES
B. Dec. 18, 1945, Los Angeles, CA
Colorado 6'1" 210 lbs.

Year	Team		Games	Pos.
1967	**OAK**	A	9	RB
1968	**CIN**	A	14	HB
2 yrs.	23 games			

Fred Banks
BANKS, FREDERICK RAY
B. May 26, 1962, Columbus, GA
Liberty 5'10" 177 lbs.

Year	Team		Games	Pos.
1985	**CLE**	N	10	WR
1987	**MIA**	N	3	WR
1988			11	WR
1989			15	WR
1990			8	WR
1991			7	WR
1992			16	WR
1993			2	WR
1993	**CHI**	N	8	WR
8 yrs.	80 games			

Gordon Banks
BANKS, GORDON GERARD
B. Mar. 12, 1958, Los Angeles, CA
Stanford 5'10" 173 lbs.

Year	Team		Games	Pos.
1980	**NO**	N	7	WR
1981			6	WR
1985	**DAL**	N	2	WR
1986			16	WR
1987			5	WR
5 yrs.	36 games			

Robert Banks
BANKS, ROBERT NATHAN
B. Dec. 10, 1963, Williamsburg, VA
Notre Dame 6'5" 263 lbs.

Year	Team		Games	Pos.
1988	**HOU**	N	14	DE
1989	**CLE**	N	15	DE
1990			15	DE
3 yrs.	44 games			

Roy Banks
BANKS, ROY F.
B. Feb. 19, 1965, Detroit, MI
Eastern Illinois 5'10" 190 lbs.

Year	Team		Games	Pos.
1987	**IND**	N	1	WR
1988			14	WR
2 yrs.	15 games			

Tom Banks
BANKS, THOMAS SIDNEY, JR.
B. Aug. 20, 1948, Birmingham, AL
Auburn 6'1" 243 lbs.

Year	Team		Games	Pos.
1971	**STL**	N	9	C
1972			4	C

Year	Team		Games	Pos.

Tom Banks *continued*

Year	Team		Games	Pos.
1973			14	G, C
1974			1	G, C
1975			14	C, G
1976			14	C, G
1977			14	C
1978			16	C, G
1979			14	C, G
1980			6	C
10 yrs.	116 games			

Tony Banks
BANKS, TONY
B. Apr. 5, 1973, San Diego, CA
Michigan State 6'4" 220 lbs.

1996	STL	N	14	QB

Willie Banks
BANKS, WILLIE GREEN
B. Mar. 17, 1946, Greenville, TX
Alcorn State 6'2" 240 lbs.

1968	WAS	N	10	G
1969			9	G
1970	NYG	N	5	G
1973	NE	N	13	G
4 yrs.	37 games			

Michael Bankston
BANKSTON, MICHAEL
B. Mar. 12, 1970, East Bernard, TX
Sam Houston State 6'2" 285 lbs.

1992	PHX	N	16	NT
1993			16	DE, DT
1994	ARI	N	16	DE, DT
1995			16	DE, DT
1996			16	DE
5 yrs.	80 games			

Warren Bankston
BANKSTON, WARREN STEPHEN
B. Jul. 22, 1947, Baton Rouge, LA
Tulane 6'4" 233 lbs.

1969	PIT	N	14	RB
1970			4	RB
1971			14	RB
1972			7	RB
1973	OAK	N	11	TE
1974			14	TE
1975			14	TE, RB
1976			14	TE
1977			14	TE
1978			8	TE
10 yrs.	114 games			

Bruce Bannon
BANNON, BRUCE
B. Mar. 11, 1951, Rockaway, NJ
Penn State 6'3" 225 lbs.

1973	MIA	N	14	LB
1974			14	LB
2 yrs.	28 games			

Vincent Banonis
BANONIS, VINCENT JOSEPH
B. Apr. 9, 1921, Detroit, MI
Detroit 6'1" 230 lbs.

1942	CHIC	N	11	C, T
1944	C, P	N	1	C
1946	CHIC	N	11	C
1947			12	C
1948			12	C
1949			12	C
1950			11	C
1951	DET	N	12	C
1952			12	C
1953			12	C
10 yrs.	106 games			

Al Bansavage
BANSAVAGE, ALBERT A.
B. Jan. 9, 1938, New Jersey
The Citadel/Southern California 6'2" 225 lbs.

1960	LA	A		LB
1961	OAK	A	14	LB
2 yrs.	14 games			

Bradford Banta
BANTA, DENNIS BRADFORD
B. Dec. 14, 1970, Baton Rouge, LA
Southern California 6'6" 255 lbs.

1994	IND	N	16	TE
1995			16	TE
1996			13	TE
3 yrs.	45 games			

Jack Banta
BANTA, HERBERT JACK
B. Nov. 19, 1917, Los Angeles, CA
D. Feb. 22, 1977, Newport Beach, CA
Southern California 5'11" 191 lbs.

1941	WAS	N	1	B
1941	PHI	N	5	HB
1944			7	HB
1945			5	HB
1946	LA	N	10	HB
1947			12	HB
1948			12	HB
6 yrs.	52 games			

Gary Barbaro
BARBARO, GARY WAYNE
B. Feb. 11, 1954, New Orleans, LA
Nicholls State 6'4" 201 lbs.

1976	KC	N	14	S
1977			14	S
1978			16	S
1979			16	S
1980			16	S
1981			16	S
1982			9	S
7 yrs.	101 games			

Roland Barbay
BARBAY, ROLAND ANTHONY, JR.
B. Oct. 1, 1964, New Orleans, LA
Louisiana State 6'2" 260 lbs.

1987	SEA	N	5	NT

Joe Barbee
BARBEE, JOSEPH A.
B. 1935
D. Aug. 12, 1969, Cleveland, OH
Kent State 6'3" 250 lbs.

1960	OAK	A		DT

Ben Barber
BARBER, BENJAMIN
B. Apr. 8, 1904
D. Sep, 1984, Greenville, SC
Virginia Military Institute 6'3" 235 lbs.

1925	BUF	N	7	T, G, HB

Bob Barber
BARBER, ROBERT
B. Dec. 26, 1951, Ferriday, LA
Grambling State 6'3" 240 lbs.

1976	GB	N	14	DE
1977			14	DE
1978			16	DE
1979			16	DE
4 yrs.	60 games			

Chris Barber
BARBER, CHRISTOPHER EDGAR
B. Jan. 15, 1964, Fort Bragg, NC
North Carolina A&T 6'0" 187 lbs.

1987	CIN	N	3	S
1989			8	S
1992	TB	N	3	CB
3 yrs.	14 games			

Ernie Barber
BARBER, ERNEST
B. Apr. 18, 1914, Manteca, CA
D. Jun. 5, 1989, Manteca, CA
San Francisco 6'1" 225 lbs.

1945	WAS	N	3	C

Jim Barber
BARBER, JAMES PATRICK
B. Jul. 21, 1912, Nashville, TN
San Francisco 6'3" 223 lbs.

1935	BOS	N	9	T
1936			11	T
1937	WAS	N	11	T
1938			11	T
1939			10	T
1940			11	T
1941			11	T
7 yrs.	74 games			

Kurt Barber
BARBER, KURT
B. Jan. 5, 1969, Paducah, KY
Southern California 6'4" 241 lbs.

1992	NYJ	N	16	LB
1993			13	LB
1994			15	LB, DE
1995			6	DE
4 yrs.	50 games			

Marion Barber
BARBER, MARION S.
B. Dec. 6, 1959, Fort Lauderdale, FL
Minnesota 6'3" 228 lbs.

1982	NYJ	N	6	RB
1983			14	RB
1984			14	FB
1985			9	FB
1986			15	RB
1987			12	FB
1988			16	RB
7 yrs.	86 games			

Mark Barber
BARBER, MARK E.
B. May 9, 1915
D. Feb, 1975
South Dakota State 5'11" 192 lbs.

1937	CLE	N	5	FB

Michael Barber
BARBER, MICHAEL
B. Nov. 9, 1971, Edgemoor, SC
Clemson 6'1" 247 lbs.

1995	SEA	N	2	LB
1996			13	LB
2 yrs.	15 games			

Mike Barber
BARBER, MICHAEL DALE
B. Jun. 19, 1967, Winfield, WV
Marshall 5'10" 172 lbs.

1989	SF	N	8	WR
1990	CIN	N	16	WR
1991			15	WR
1992	TB	N	2	WR
4 yrs.	41 games			

Mike Barber
BARBER, MIKE
B. Jun. 4, 1953, Marshall, TX
Louisiana Tech 6'3" 235 lbs.

1977	HOU	N	13	TE
1978			16	TE
1979			15	TE
1980			16	TE
1981			16	TE
1982	LARM	N	9	TE
1983			16	TE
1984			11	TE
1985			5	TE
1985	DEN	N	10	TE
9 yrs.	127 games			

Rudy Barber
BARBER, RUDOLPH
B. Dec. 24, 1944, Auburndale, FL
Bethune, Cookman 6'1" 255 lbs.

1968	MIA	A	2	DT

Stew Barber
BARBER, STEWART C.
B. Jun. 14, 1939, Bradford, PA
Penn State 6'3" 247 lbs.

1961	BUF	A	14	OT, LB
1962			14	OT
1963			14	OT
1964			14	OT
1965			14	OT
1966			14	OT
1967			14	OT
1968			14	OT
1969			12	OT
9 yrs.	124 games			

Pete Barbolak
BARBOLAK, PETER
B. 1926
Purdue 6'3" 235 lbs.

1949	PIT	N	10	T

Elmer Barbour
BARBOUR, WESLEY ELMER, II
B. 1922
D. Feb. 9, 1993
Wake Forest 6'1" 200 lbs.

1945	NYG	N	3	QB

Johnny Barefield
BAREFIELD, JOHN GLENN
B. Mar. 23, 1955, Victoria, TX
Texas A&I-Kingsville 6'2" 224 lbs.

1978	STL	N	9	LB
1979			15	LB
1980			6	LB
3 yrs.	30 games			

Ken Barefoot
BAREFOOT, KEN
B. Oct. 11, 1945, Portsmouth, VA
Virginia Tech 6'5" 228 lbs.

1968	WAS	N	8	OE

Ken Barfield
BARFIELD, KENNETH A.
B. Jul. 19, 1929, Sunnyside, GA
Mississippi 6'5" 238 lbs.

1954	WAS	N	8	T

Adrian Baril
BARIL, ADRIAN (Barrel)
B. Jun. 4, 1898
Deceased

Year	Team		Games	Pos.

Adrian Baril continued

St. Thomas (Minnesota) 5'11" 210 lbs.

Year	Team		Games	Pos.
1923	MIN	N	8	T
1924			4	T, G
1925	MIL	N	2	T
3 yrs.	14 games			

Carl Barisich
BARISICH, CARL JOHN
B. Jul. 12, 1951, Jersey City, NJ
Princeton 6'4" 255 lbs.

Year	Team		Games	Pos.
1973	CLE	N	14	DT
1974			13	DT
1975			14	DT
1976	SEA	N	14	DT
1977	MIA	N	3	DT
1978			16	DT
1979			11	DT
1980			15	DT
1981	NYG	N	2	NT
9 yrs.	102 games			

Bryan Barker
BARKER, BRYAN CHRISTOPHER
B. Jun. 28, 1964, Jacksonville Bch., FL
Santa Clara 6'1" 187 lbs.

Year	Team		Games	Pos.
1990	KC	N	13	P
1991			16	P
1992			15	P
1993			16	P
1994	PHI	N	11	P
1995	JAC	N	16	P
1996			16	P
7 yrs.	103 games			

Dick Barker
BARKER, RICHARD WILLIAM
B. Jan. 6, 1897, Sedalia, MO
D. Dec. 17, 1964
Iowa State 5'9" 180 lbs.

Year	Team		Games	Pos.
1921	DEC	A	2	G
1921	RI	A	2	G
1 yr.	4 games			

Ed Barker
BARKER, EDWARD R.
B. May 31, 1931, Dillon, MT
Washington State 6'3" 196 lbs.

Year	Team		Games	Pos.
1953	PIT	N	6	E
1954	WAS	N	12	E
2 yrs.	18 games			

Hub Barker
BARKER, HUBERT LYLE
B. Nov. 12, 1918, Welch, OK
Arkansas 5'10" 193 lbs.

Year	Team		Games	Pos.
1943	NYG	N	2	B
1944			10	B
1945			4	B
3 yrs.	16 games			

Leo Barker
BARKER, LEO
B. Nov. 7, 1959, Cristobal, Panama
New Mexico State 6'2" 221 lbs.

Year	Team		Games	Pos.
1984	CIN	N	16	LB
1985			16	LB
1986			16	LB
1987			12	LB
1988			16	LB
1989			16	LB
1990			14	LB
1991			16	LB
8 yrs.	122 games			

Roy Barker
BARKER, ROY

Roy Barker continued

B. Feb. 14, 1969, New York, NY
North Carolina 6'4" 286 lbs.

Year	Team		Games	Pos.
1992	MIN	N	8	DT
1993			16	DT
1994			16	DE, LB
1995			16	DE
1996	SF	N	16	DE
5 yrs.	72 games			

Tony Barker
BARKER, ANTHONY RAY
B. Sep. 7, 1968, Wichita, KS
Rice 6'2" 230 lbs.

Year	Team		Games	Pos.
1992	WAS	N	8	LB

Ralph Barkman
BARKMAN, RALPH
B. 1907, New Jersey
Schuylkill 5'8" 165 lbs.

Year	Team		Games	Pos.
1929	ORA	N	7	HB, FB, QB, T

Rod Barksdale
BARKSDALE, ROD DEAN
B. Sep. 8, 1962, Los Angeles, CA
Arizona 6'0" 180 lbs.

Year	Team		Games	Pos.
1986	LARI	N	16	WR
1987	DAL	N	12	WR
2 yrs.	28 games			

Jerome Barkum
BARKUM, JEROME PHILLIP
B. Jul. 18, 1950, Gulfport, MS
Jackson State 6'3" 218 lbs.

Year	Team		Games	Pos.
1972	NYJ	N	14	WR
1973			14	WR
1974			14	WR
1975			13	WR
1976			4	WR
1977			14	WR
1978			16	TE
1979			13	TE
1980			16	TE
1981			16	TE
1982			9	TE
1983			15	TE
12 yrs.	158 games			

Lou Barle
BARLE, LOUIS PETER (Fats)
B. Jun. 23, 1916, Gilbert, MN
Minnesota-Duluth 6'1" 205 lbs.

Year	Team		Games	Pos.
1938	DET	N	1	HB
1939	CLE	N	3	QB
2 yrs.	4 games			

Corey Barlow
BARLOW, COREY ANTONIO
B. Nov. 1, 1970, Atlanta, GA
Auburn 5'9" 182 lbs.

Year	Team		Games	Pos.
1993	PHI	N	10	CB

Reggie Barlow
BARLOW, REGGIE DEVON
B. Jan. 22, 1973, Montgomery, AL
Alabama State 5'11" 187 lbs.

Year	Team		Games	Pos.
1996	JAC	N	7	WR

George Barna
BARNA, GEORGE
B. Mar. 23, 1908
D. Nov. 1972, Buffalo, NY
Hobart 6'1" 198 lbs.

Year	Team		Games	Pos.
1929	FRA	N	17	E

Hap Barnard
BARNARD, W.C. (Happy)
B. Jul. 27, 1915
D. Nov. 1968
Central Oklahoma 6'2" 190 lbs.

Year	Team		Games	Pos.
1938	NYG	N	5	E

Tom Barndt
BARNDT, TOM
B. Mar. 14, 1972
Pittsburgh 6'3" 285 lbs.

Year	Team		Games	Pos.
1996	KC	N	13	G

Al Barnes
BARNES, AL MARVIN
B. Jul. 4, 1949, Los Angeles, CA
New Mexico State 6'1" 170 lbs.

Year	Team		Games	Pos.
1972	DET	N	9	WR
1973			11	WR
2 yrs.	20 games			

Benny Barnes
BARNES, BENNY JEWELL
B. Mar. 3, 1951, Lufkin, TX
Stanford 6'1" 192 lbs.

Year	Team		Games	Pos.
1972	DAL	N	4	DB
1973			14	CB
1974			14	CB, S
1975			14	CB
1976			14	CB
1977			14	CB
1978			14	CB
1979			15	CB
1980			11	CB
1981			16	CB
1982			9	CB
11 yrs.	139 games			

Billy Ray Barnes
BARNES, BILLY RAY (Bullet)
B. May 14, 1935, Landis, NC
Wake Forest 5'11" 201 lbs.

Year	Team		Games	Pos.
1957	PHI	N	12	HB
1958			12	HB
1959			12	HB
1960			12	HB
1961			12	HB
1962	WAS	N	10	HB
1963			14	HB
1965	MIN	N	14	HB
1966			2	HB
9 yrs.	100 games			

Bruce Barnes
BARNES, BRUCE FRANCIS
B. Jun. 21, 1951, Coshocton, OH
UCLA 5'11" 214 lbs.

Year	Team		Games	Pos.
1973	NE	N	14	P
1974			9	P
2 yrs.	23 games			

Charlie Barnes
BARNES, CHARLES
B. 1940
Northeast Louisiana 6'5" 230 lbs.

Year	Team		Games	Pos.
1961	DAL	A	4	OE

Earnest Barnes
BARNES, EARNEST
B. Feb. 10, 1961, Moss Point, MS
Mississippi State 6'4" 260 lbs.

Year	Team		Games	Pos.
1983	BAL	N	7	NT

Emery Barnes
BARNES, EMERY O.

Emery Barnes continued

B. Dec. 15, 1929, Hermiston, OR
Oregon 6'6" 235 lbs.

Year	Team		Games	Pos.
1956	GB	N	2	E

Erich Barnes
BARNES, ERICH THEODORE
B. Jul. 4, 1935, Elkhart, IN
Purdue 6'2" 201 lbs.

Year	Team		Games	Pos.
1958	CHIB	N	12	DB
1959			12	DB
1960	CHI	N	12	DB
1961	NYG	N	14	DB
1962			14	DB
1963			14	DB
1964			14	DB
1965	CLE	N	13	DB
1966			14	DB
1967			13	DB
1968			14	DB
1969			14	CB
1970			14	CB
1971			5	CB
14 yrs.	179 games			

Ernie Barnes
BARNES, ERNEST
B. Jul. 15, 1938, Durham, NC
North Carolina Central 6'3" 250 lbs.

Year	Team		Games	Pos.
1960	NY	A		OT
1961	SD	A	10	G
1962			3	G
1963	DEN	A	14	G
1964			11	G
5 yrs.	38 games			

Gary Barnes
BARNES, GARY MARSHALL
B. Sep. 13, 1939, Fairfax, AL
Clemson 6'4" 210 lbs.

Year	Team		Games	Pos.
1962	GB	N	13	OE
1963	DAL	N	12	OE
1964	CHI	N	13	OE
1966	ATL	N	9	OE
1967			13	OE
5 yrs.	60 games			

Jeff Barnes
BARNES, JEFF
B. Mar. 1, 1955, Philadelphia, PA
California 6'2" 226 lbs.

Year	Team		Games	Pos.
1977	OAK	N	14	LB
1978			16	LB
1979			16	LB
1980			16	LB
1981			15	LB
1982	LARI	N	9	LB
1983			16	LB
1984			16	LB
1985			16	LB
1986			16	LB
1987			7	LB
11 yrs.	157 games			

Joe Barnes
BARNES, JOSEPH WILLIAM
B. Dec. 18, 1951, Fort Worth, TX
Texas Tech 5'11" 196 lbs.

Year	Team		Games	Pos.
1974	CHI	N	2	QB

Johnnie Barnes
BARNES, JOHNNIE DARNELL
B. Jul. 21, 1968, Suffolk, VA
Hampton Institute 6'1" 180 lbs.

Year	Team		Games	Pos.
1992	SD	N	1	WR
1993			14	WR
1994			11	WR

Johnnie Barnes continued

Year	Team		Games	Pos.
1995	PIT	N	3	WR
4 yrs.	29 games			

Larry Barnes
BARNES, LARRY E.
B. 1933, Sterling, CO
Colorado State 6'1" 228 lbs.

Year	Team		Games	Pos.
1957	SF	N	10	FB
1960	OAK	A	14	DE, LB
2 yrs.	24 games			

Larry Barnes
BARNES, LAWRENCE
B. Jul. 17, 1954, Bessemer, AL
Tennessee State 5'11" 220 lbs.

Year	Team		Games	Pos.
1977	SD	N	5	RB
1978			4	RB
1978	STL	N	2	RB
1978	PHI	N	7	RB
1979			16	FB
3 yrs.	34 games			

Lew Barnes
BARNES, LEW ERIC
B. Dec. 27, 1962, Long Beach, CA
Oregon 5'8" 163 lbs.

Year	Team		Games	Pos.
1986	CHI	N	16	WR
1988	ATL	N	13	WR
1989	KC	N	2	WR
3 yrs.	31 games			

Mike Barnes
BARNES, MIKE
B. Dec. 30, 1944, Denison, TX
Texas-Arlington 6'3" 205 lbs.

Year	Team		Games	Pos.
1967	STL	N	3	DB
1968			14	DB
2 yrs.	17 games			

Mike Barnes
BARNES, MICHAEL JOSEPH
B. Dec. 24, 1950, Pittsburgh, PA
Miami (Florida) 6'6" 256 lbs.

Year	Team		Games	Pos.
1973	BAL	N	14	DE
1974			11	DE
1975			14	DE
1976			14	DT
1977			14	DT
1978			10	DT
1979			14	DT
1980			16	DT
1981			6	DT
9 yrs.	113 games			

Pete Barnes
BARNES, PETER G.
B. Aug. 31, 1945, Longview, TX
Southern University 6'3" 242 lbs.

Year	Team		Games	Pos.
1967	HOU	A	8	LB
1968			14	LB
1969	SD	A	13	LB
1970	SD	N	14	LB
1971			14	LB
1972			14	LB
1973	STL	N	12	LB
1974			14	LB
1975			14	LB
1976	NE	N	13	LB
1977			12	LB
11 yrs.	142 games			

Reggie Barnes
BARNES, REGINALD KEITH
B. Oct. 23, 1969, Arlington, TX
Oklahoma 6'1" 235 lbs.

Year	Team		Games	Pos.
1993	PIT	N	16	LB

Reggie Barnes continued

Year	Team		Games	Pos.
1995	DAL	N	7	LB
2 yrs.	23 games			

Rodrigo Barnes
BARNES, RODRIGO DETRIANA
B. Feb. 10, 1950, Waco, TX
Rice 6'1" 215 lbs.

Year	Team		Games	Pos.
1973	DAL	N	14	LB
1974			5	LB
1974	NE	N	5	LB
1975			1	
1975	MIA	N	5	LB
1976	OAK	N	5	LB
4 yrs.	35 games			

Roosevelt Barnes
BARNES, ROOSEVELT
B. Aug. 3, 1958, Fort Wayne, IN
Purdue 6'2" 226 lbs.

Year	Team		Games	Pos.
1982	DET	N	9	LB
1983			16	LB
1984			16	LB
1985			16	LB
4 yrs.	57 games			

Tomur Barnes
BARNES, TOMUR
B. Sep. 8, 1970, McNair, TX
North Texas State 5'10" 188 lbs.

Year	Team		Games	Pos.
1994	HOU	N	1	CB
1995			15	CB
1996			5	CB
1996	MIN	N	2	CB
1996	WAS	N	3	CB
3 yrs.	26 games			

Walt Barnes
BARNES, WALTER (Piggy)
B. Jan. 26, 1918, Parkersburg, WV
Louisiana State 6'1" 238 lbs.

Year	Team		Games	Pos.
1948	PHI	N	11	G
1949			12	G
1950			12	G
1951			12	G
4 yrs.	47 games			

Walt Barnes
BARNES, WALTER CHARLES
B. Jan. 19, 1944, Chicago, IL
Nebraska 6'3" 250 lbs.

Year	Team		Games	Pos.
1966	WAS	N	14	DT
1967			14	DT
1968			14	DT
1969	DEN	A	9	DE
1970	DEN	N	5	DE
1971			4	DE
6 yrs.	60 games			

Bill Barnett
BARNETT, WILLIAM PERRY
B. May 10, 1956, St. Paul, MN
Nebraska 6'4" 256 lbs.

Year	Team		Games	Pos.
1980	MIA	N	16	DE
1981			9	DE
1982			5	DE
1983			15	DE
1984			16	DE
1985			16	DE
6 yrs.	77 games			

Buster Barnett
BARNETT, BUSTER
B. Nov. 24, 1958, Brooksville, MS
Jackson State 6'5" 230 lbs.

Year	Team		Games	Pos.
1981	BUF	N	16	TE
1982			9	TE

Buster Barnett continued

Year	Team		Games	Pos.
1983			15	TE
1984			16	TE
4 yrs.	56 games			

Dean Barnett
BARNETT, DONALD DEAN
B. Jun. 6, 1957, Long Beach, CA
Nevada-Las Vegas 6'2" 225 lbs.

Year	Team		Games	Pos.
1983	DEN	N	8	TE

Doug Barnett
BARNETT, DOUGLAS SHIRL, JR.
B. Apr. 12, 1960, Montebello, CA
Azusa Pacific 6'3" 250 lbs.

Year	Team		Games	Pos.
1982	LARM	N	9	DE
1983			16	DE, C
1985	WAS	N	2	DE
1987	ATL	N	10	C
4 yrs.	37 games			

Fred Barnett
BARNETT, FRED LEE
B. Jun. 17, 1966, Shelby, MS
Arkansas State 6'0" 203 lbs.

Year	Team		Games	Pos.
1990	PHI	N	16	WR
1991			15	WR
1992			16	WR
1993			4	WR
1994			16	WR
1995			14	WR
1996	MIA	N	9	WR
7 yrs.	90 games			

Harlon Barnett
BARNETT, HARLON
B. Jan. 2, 1967, Cincinnati, OH
Michigan State 5'11" 200 lbs.

Year	Team		Games	Pos.
1990	CLE	N	6	S
1991			16	S
1992			16	S
1993	NE	N	14	S
1994			16	S
1995	MIN	N	15	S
1996			16	S
7 yrs.	99 games			

Oliver Barnett
BARNETT, OLIVER WESLEY
B. Apr. 9, 1966, Louisville, KY
Kentucky 6'3" 288 lbs.

Year	Team		Games	Pos.
1990	ATL	N	15	NT
1991			15	NT
1992			16	DE
1993	BUF	N	16	DE
1994			16	DE, LB
1995	SF	N	6	DE
6 yrs.	84 games			

Solon Barnett
BARNETT, SOLON S., JR. (Bobo)
B. Mar. 29, 1921
Baylor 6'1" 235 lbs.

Year	Team		Games	Pos.
1945	GB	N	4	T
1946			10	G
2 yrs.	14 games			

Steve Barnett
BARNETT, JERRY STEPHEN
B. Jun. 4, 1941, Sand Springs, OK
Oregon 6'1" 255 lbs.

Year	Team		Games	Pos.
1963	CHI	N	13	OT
1964	WAS	N	14	OT
2 yrs.	27 games			

Tim Barnett
BARNETT, TIM ANDRE
B. Apr. 19, 1968, Gunnison, MS
Jackson State 6'1" 209 lbs.

Year	Team		Games	Pos.
1991	KC	N	16	WR
1992			12	WR
1993			16	WR
3 yrs.	44 games			

Tom Barnett
BARNETT, THOMAS
B. Jul. 11, 1937, Alliance, OH
Purdue 5'11" 190 lbs.

Year	Team		Games	Pos.
1959	PIT	N	12	HB
1960			12	HB
2 yrs.	24 games			

Troy Barnett
BARNETT, TROY ANTHONY
B. May 24, 1971, Jacksonville, NC
North Carolina 6'4" 280 lbs.

Year	Team		Games	Pos.
1994	NE	N	14	NT, DE
1995			16	DE
1996			1	DT
1996	WAS	N	3	DT
3 yrs.	34 games			

Vince Barnett
BARNETT, VINCENT
B. Feb. 19, 1965
Arkansas State 6'0" 200 lbs.

Year	Team		Games	Pos.
1987	CLE	N	3	S, CB

Eppie Barney
BARNEY, EPPIE
B. Mar. 20, 1944, Birmingham, AL
Iowa State 6'0" 201 lbs.

Year	Team		Games	Pos.
1967	CLE	N	14	FL
1968			11	FL
2 yrs.	25 games			

Lem Barney
BARNEY, LEMUEL JACKSON
B. Sep. 8, 1945, Gulfport, MS
Jackson State 6'1" 189 lbs.

Year	Team		Games	Pos.
1967	DET	N	14	DB, P
1968			14	DB
1969			13	CB, P
1970			13	CB
1971			9	CB
1972			14	CB
1973			14	CB
1974			13	CB
1975			10	CB
1976			14	CB
1977			12	CB
11 yrs.	140 games			

Milton Barney
BARNEY, MILTON
B. Dec. 23, 1963
Alcorn State 5'9" 156 lbs.

Year	Team		Games	Pos.
1987	ATL	N	3	WR

Tommy Barnhardt
BARNHARDT, TOMMY RAY
B. Jun. 11, 1963, Salisbury, NC
East Carolina/North Carolina 6'3" 205 lbs.

Year	Team		Games	Pos.
1987	NO	N	3	P
1987	CHI	N	2	P
1988	WAS	N	4	P
1989	NO	N	11	P
1990			16	P
1991			16	P
1992			16	P
1993			16	P

Year	Team		Games	Pos.

Tommy Barnhardt *continued*

Year	Team		Games	Pos.
1994			16	P
1995	CAR	N	16	P
1996	TB	N	16	P
10 yrs.	132 games			

Dan Barnhart
BARNHART, DANIEL HIGH
B. Jun. 27, 1912, Chickasha, OK
D. Jun, 1965
St. Mary's/Centenary 6'0" 200 lbs.

1934	PHI	N	1	HB

Roy Barni
BARNI, ROY B.
B. Feb. 15, 1927, San Francisco, CA
D. Jun. 22, 1957, San Francisco, CA
San Francisco 5'11" 185 lbs.

1952	CHIC	N	12	DB
1953			8	DB
1954	PHI	N	10	DB
1955			4	DB
1955	WAS	N	8	DB
1956			12	DB
5 yrs.	54 games			

Eddie Barnikow
BARNIKOW, EDWARD JOHN
B. Dec. 18, 1897, Meriden, CT
D. Dec. 1, 1953, Schenectady, NY
None

1926	HAR	N	2	FB

Len Barnum
BARNUM, LEONARD WARNER
(Feets, Bear Tracks)
B. Sep. 18, 1912, Parkersburg, WV
West Virginia Wesleyan 6'0" 200 lbs.

1938	NYG	N	10	FB
1939			10	HB
1940			10	FB
1941	PHI	N	10	QB, HB, FB
1942			10	HB, QB
5 yrs.	50 games			

Pete Barnum
BARNUM, ROBERT LEROY
B. 1901, Pennsylvania
Deceased
West Virginia 5'10" 195 lbs.

1926	COL	N	6	HB, FB, G

Malcolm Barnwell
BARNWELL, MALCOLM
B. Jun. 28, 1958, Charleston, SC
Virginia Union 5'11" 180 lbs.

1981	OAK	N	16	WR
1982	LARI	N	9	WR
1983			16	WR
1984			16	WR
1985	WAS	N	7	WR
1985	NO	N	2	WR
5 yrs.	66 games			

Dave Barr
BARR, DAVE
B. May 9, 1972, Oakland, CA
California 6'3" 205 lbs.

1995	STL	N	2	QB

Shorty Barr
BARR, WALLACE C.
B. May 28, 1896
D. Mar, 1980, Chenequa, WI
Wisconsin 5'8" 195 lbs.

1923	RAC	N	10	QB

Shorty Barr *continued*

1924			9	FB, QB, HB
1925	MIL	N	4	QB
1926	RAC	N	3	QB, FB, HB
4 yrs.	26 games			

Terry Barr
BARR, TERRY ALBERT
B. Aug. 10, 1935, Grand Rapids, MI
Michigan 6'0" 189 lbs.

1957	DET	N	12	DB
1958			12	DB
1959			11	HB, DB
1960			12	RB
1961			14	FL
1962			6	FL
1963			14	FL
1964			14	FL
1965			7	FL
9 yrs.	102 games			

Bob Barrabee
BARRABEE, ROBERT S.
B. Jan. 23, 1905
D. Jun, 1984, Elberon Park, NJ
New York University 5'9" 190 lbs.

1931	SI	N	7	E

Nate Barragar
BARRAGAR, NATHAN
B. Jun. 3, 1907
D. Aug. 10, 1985, Pacific Palisades, CA
Southern California 6'0" 212 lbs.

1930	MIN	N	8	C
1930	FRA	N	5	C
1931	FRA	N	6	C
1931	GB	N	7	C, G
1932			11	C
1934			12	C, G
1935			10	C
5 yrs.	59 games			

Napoleon Barrel
BARREL, NAPOLEON
B. Dec. 25, 1885
D. Dec, 1964
Carlisle 5'8" 200 lbs.

1923	OOR	N	7	C, QB

Bob Barrett
BARRETT, ROBERT
B. 1936
Baldwin-Wallace 6'3" 200 lbs.

1960	BUF	A		OE

Dave Barrett
BARRETT, DAVID EARL
B. Sep. 9, 1959, Corpus Christi, TX
Houston 6'0" 230 lbs.

1982	TB	N	7	RB

Emmett Barrett
BARRETT, EMMETT E.
B. Nov. 7, 1918, Sioux City, IA
Portland 6'2" 192 lbs.

1942	NYG	N	11	C

Jan Barrett
BARRETT, JAN
B. Nov. 13, 1939, Santa Barbara, CA
D. Oct. 7, 1973, Lake Ming, CA
Fresno State 6'3" 226 lbs.

1963	GB	N	3	OE
1963	OAK	A	3	OE
1964			14	OE
2 yrs.	20 games			

Jean Barrett
BARRETT, JEAN MARTIN, JR.
B. May 24, 1951, Fort Worth, TX
Tulsa 6'6" 251 lbs.

1973	SF	N	14	OT
1974			14	C, OT
1975			9	OT, C
1976			14	G, C
1977			14	OT
1979			13	OT
1980			15	OT
7 yrs.	93 games			

Jeff Barrett
BARRETT, W. JEFFREY
B. 1913
Louisiana State 6'1" 182 lbs.

1936	BKN	N	12	E
1937	BKN	N	11	E
1938			11	E, B
3 yrs.	34 games			

John Barrett
BARRETT, JOHN P. (Bunny)
B. Feb. 25, 1899
D. Sep, 1966, Detroit, MI
Detroit 5'6" 170 lbs.

1924	AKR	N	5	C, E
1925			7	C
1926	DET	N	11	C
1927	POT	N	5	C
1928	DET	N	6	C, T
5 yrs.	34 games			

Johnny Barrett
BARRETT, JOHN F.
B. Aug. 29, 1895
D. Mar, 1974, Montvale, NJ
Washington & Lee 5'9" 195 lbs.

1920	CHIT	A	6	HB, E

Reggie Barrett
BARRETT, AARON REGINALD
B. Aug. 14, 1969, Corpus Christi, TX
Texas-El Paso 6'3" 215 lbs.

1991	DET	N	2	WR
1992			8	WR
1993			13	WR
3 yrs.	23 games			

Sebastian Barrie
BARRIE, SEBASTIAN
B. May 26, 1970, Dallas, TX
Prairie View A&M/Liberty 6'2" 270 lbs.

1992	GB	N	3	DE
1994	ARI	N	10	DT, DE
1995	SD	N	7	DT
3 yrs.	20 games			

Tom Barrington
BARRINGTON, GEORGE THOMAS
B. Jan. 29, 1944, Lima, OH
Ohio State 6'1" 214 lbs.

1966	WAS	N	6	RB
1967	NO	N	14	RB
1968			14	RB
1969			11	RB
1970			12	RB
5 yrs.	57 games			

Jim Barron
BARRON, JAMES MARTIN
(Botchy)
B. Nov. 10, 1890
D. Feb. 6, 1936, Boston, MA

Jim Barron *continued*
Georgetown (DC) 6'0" 195 lbs.

1921	ROC	A	5	T

Micheal Barrow
BARROW, MICHEAL CALVIN
B. Apr. 19, 1970, Homestead, FL
Miami (Florida) 6'1" 236 lbs.

1993	HOU	N	16	LB
1994			16	LB
1995			13	LB
1996			16	LB
4 yrs.	61 games			

Scott Barrows
BARROWS, SCOTT MARTIN
B. Mar. 31, 1963, Marietta, OH
West Virginia 6'2" 278 lbs.

1986	DET	N	16	G
1987			12	G, C
1988			16	G, C
3 yrs.	44 games			

Al Barry
BARRY, ALLEN
B. Dec. 24, 1930, Los Angeles, CA
Southern California 6'2" 230 lbs.

1954	GB	N	12	G
1957			12	G
1958	NYG	N	12	G
1959			12	G
1960	LA	A		G
5 yrs.	48 games			

Fred Barry
BARRY, FRED
B. Jul. 31, 1948, Washington, PA
Boston University 5'10" 184 lbs.

1970	PIT	N	9	CB

Norm Barry
BARRY, NORMAN CHRISTOPHER
B. Dec. 25, 1897, Chicago, IL
D. Oct. 12, 1988, Chicago, IL
Notre Dame 5'10" 170 lbs.

1921	CHIC	A	3	HB
1921	GB	A	3	HB
1 yr.	8 games			

Odell Barry
BARRY, ODELL CARL
B. Oct. 10, 1941, Memphis, TN
Findlay 5'10" 180 lbs.

1964	DEN	A	14	OE
1965			12	OE
2 yrs.	26 games			

Paul Barry
BARRY, PAUL F.
B. Aug. 7, 1926, El Paso, TX
Tulsa 6'0" 208 lbs.

1950	LA	N	12	HB
1952			6	HB
1953	WAS	N	12	HB
1954	CHIC	N	12	B
4 yrs.	42 games			

Steve Bartalo
BARTALO, STEPHEN JAMES
B. Jul. 15, 1964, Limestone, ME
Colorado State 5'9" 200 lbs.

1987	TB	N	9	RB
1988	SF	N	16	RB
2 yrs.	25 games			

Year	Team		Games	Pos.

Sam Bartholomew
BARTHOLOMEW, SAMUEL WILSON
B. Apr. 10, 1917, Charleston, WV
Tennessee 5'11" 188 lbs.

Year	Team		Games	Pos.
1941	PHI	N	8	FB

Steve Bartkowski
BARTKOWSKI, STEVEN JOSEPH
B. Nov. 12, 1952, Des Moines, IA
California 6'4" 216 lbs.

Year	Team		Games	Pos.
1975	ATL	N	11	QB
1976			5	QB
1977			8	QB
1978			14	QB
1979			14	QB
1980			16	QB
1981			16	QB
1982			9	QB
1983			14	QB
1984			11	QB
1985			5	QB
1986	LARM	N	6	QB
12 yrs.	129 games			

Doug Bartlett
BARTLETT, DOUGLAS WILLIAM
B. May 22, 1963, Springfield, IL
Northern Illinois 6'2" 239 lbs.

Year	Team		Games	Pos.
1988	PHI	N	10	DT, DE

Earl Bartlett
BARTLETT, EARL (Cowboy)
B. Sep. 27, 1911
D. Jan, 1985, Grafton, WV
Centre 6'0" 200 lbs.

Year	Team		Games	Pos.
1939	PIT	N	1	B

Rich Bartlewski
BARTLEWSKI, RICHARD STANLEY, JR.
B. Aug. 15, 1967, Butler, PA
Fresno State 6'5" 250 lbs.

Year	Team		Games	Pos.
1990	LARI	N	4	TE
1991	ATL	N	1	TE
2 yrs.	5 games			

Ephesians Bartley
BARTLEY, EPHESIANS ALEXANDER, JR.
B. Aug. 9, 1969, Jacksonville, FL
Florida 6'2" 213 lbs.

Year	Team		Games	Pos.
1992	PHI	N	6	LB

Don Barton
BARTON, DON REID
B. May 29, 1930, Cisco, TX
Texas 5'11" 175 lbs.

Year	Team		Games	Pos.
1953	GB	N	5	HB, DB

Greg Barton
BARTON, GREGORY
B. Jul. 14, 1946, Long Beach, CA
Tulsa 6'2" 195 lbs.

Year	Team		Games	Pos.
1969	DET	N	1	QB

Harris Barton
BARTON, HARRIS SCOTT
B. Apr. 19, 1964, Atlanta, GA
North Carolina 6'4" 280 lbs.

Year	Team		Games	Pos.
1987	SF	N	12	OT
1989			16	OT
1990			16	OT
1991			16	G
1992			13	G
1993			15	G

Harris Barton continued

Year	Team		Games	Pos.
1994			9	OT
1995			12	OT
1996			13	OT
9 yrs.	122 games			

Jim Barton
BARTON, JAMES EDWARD
B. Jun. 12, 1935, Kirbyville, PA
Marshall 6'5" 250 lbs.

Year	Team		Games	Pos.
1960	DAL	A	14	C
1961	DEN	A	14	C
1962			14	C
3 yrs.	42 games			

Hank Bartos
BARTOS, HENRY
B. May 20, 1914, Westmoreland, PA
D. 1987
North Carolina 6'1" 216 lbs.

Year	Team		Games	Pos.
1938	WAS	N	7	G

Joe Bartos
BARTOS, JOSEPH S., JR.
B. Nov. 18, 1926, Lorain, OH
D. Mar. 11, 1989, Bridgeport, CT
Navy 6'2" 194 lbs.

Year	Team		Games	Pos.
1950	WAS	N	12	HB

Mike Bartrum
BARTRUM, MICHAEL WELDON
B. Jun. 23, 1970, Gallipolis, OH
Marshall 6'4" 234 lbs.

Year	Team		Games	Pos.
1993	KC	N	3	TE
1995	GB	N	4	TE
1996	NE	N	16	TE
3 yrs.	23 games			

Dick Barwegan
BARWEGAN, RICHARD J.
B. Dec. 25, 1921, Chicago, IL
D. Sep. 3, 1966, Baltimore, MD
Purdue 6'1" 227 lbs.

Year	Team		Games	Pos.
1947	NY	AA	14	G
1948	BAL	AA	12	G
1949			12	G
1950	CHIB	N	11	G
1951			12	G
1952			11	G
1953	BAL	N	11	G
1954			9	G
8 yrs.	92 games			

Carl Barzilauskas
BARZILAUSKAS, CARL JOSEPH
B. Mar. 19, 1951, Waterbury, CT
Indiana 6'6" 271 lbs.

Year	Team		Games	Pos.
1974	NYJ	N	14	DT
1975			14	DT
1976			12	DT
1977			9	DT
1978	GB	N	16	DT
1979			5	DT
6 yrs.	70 games			

Fritz Barzilauskas
BARZILAUSKAS, FRANCIS DANIEL
B. Jun. 13, 1921, Waterbury, CT
D. Nov. 30, 1990
Holy Cross/Yale 6'1" 230 lbs.

Year	Team		Games	Pos.
1947	BOS	N	5	G
1948			12	G
1949	NYB	N	12	G
1951	NYG	N	7	G
4 yrs.	36 games			

Mike Basca
BASCA, MICHAEL M.
B. Dec. 4, 1916, Phoenixville, PA
D. Nov. 11, 1944, France
Villanova 5'8" 170 lbs.

Year	Team		Games	Pos.
1941	PHI	N	11	B

Brian Baschnagel
BASCHNAGEL, BRIAN DALE
B. Jan. 8, 1954, Kingston, NY
Ohio State 5'11" 187 lbs.

Year	Team		Games	Pos.
1976	CHI	N	14	S, WR
1977			10	WR
1978			16	WR
1979			16	WR
1980			16	WR
1981			16	WR
1982			9	WR
1983			16	WR
1984			16	WR
9 yrs.	129 games			

Mose Bashaw
BASHAW, MOSE
B. Jan., 1888
Deceased
None 5'9" 200 lbs.

Year	Team		Games	Pos.
1920	HAM	A	3	T

Myrt Basing
BASING, MYRTON NATHAN (Biff)
B. Oct. 29, 1900
Deceased
Lawrence 5'9" 190 lbs.

Year	Team		Games	Pos.
1923	GB	N	10	HB, E
1924			11	HB, E
1925			13	FB, HB
1926			5	E, HB, FB, QB
1927			3	FB
5 yrs.	42 games			

Mike Basinger
BASINGER, MIKE
B. Dec. 11, 1951, Merced, CA
California-Riverside 6'3" 258 lbs.

Year	Team		Games	Pos.
1974	GB	N	1	DE

Rick Baska
BASKA, RICHARD PAUL
B. Feb. 19, 1952, Bismarck, ND
UCLA 6'3" 225 lbs.

Year	Team		Games	Pos.
1976	DEN	N	14	LB
1977			4	LB
2 yrs.	18 games			

Mike Basrak
BASRAK, MICHAEL
B. Nov. 23, 1912
D. Dec. 18, 1974, Skokie, IL
Duquesne 6'2" 220 lbs.

Year	Team		Games	Pos.
1937	PIT	N	11	C
1938			5	C
2 yrs.	16 games			

Billy Bass
BASS, WILLIAM T.
B. 1922, Greensboro, NC
Tennessee State/Nevada-Reno 5'10" 180 lbs.

Year	Team		Games	Pos.
1947	CHI	AA	14	B

Dick Bass
BASS, RICHARD (The Scooter)
B. Mar. 15, 1937, Georgetown, MA

Dick Bass continued
Pacific 5'10" 197 lbs.

Year	Team		Games	Pos.
1960	LA	N	12	HB
1961			14	HB
1962			14	FB
1963			12	HB, FB
1964			9	FB
1965			12	FB
1966			14	FB
1967			14	RB
1968			10	RB
1969			1	RB
10 yrs.	112 games			

Don Bass
BASS, DON
B. Mar. 11, 1956, Fort Worth, TX
D. Oct. 26, 1989, Waxahachie, TX
Houston 6'2" 219 lbs.

Year	Team		Games	Pos.
1978	CIN	N	16	TE
1979			16	TE
1980			14	TE
1981			6	WR, TE
1982	NO	N	3	TE
5 yrs.	55 games			

Glenn Bass
BASS, GLENN
B. Apr. 12, 1939, Wilson, NC
East Carolina 6'2" 202 lbs.

Year	Team		Games	Pos.
1961	BUF	A	14	OE
1962			14	OE
1963			9	OE
1964			14	OE
1965			4	OE
1966			14	OE
1967	HOU	A	7	FL
1968			3	FL
8 yrs.	79 games			

Mike Bass
BASS, MICHAEL THOMAS
B. Mar. 31, 1945, Ypsilanti, MI
Michigan 6'0" 190 lbs.

Year	Team		Games	Pos.
1967	DET	N	2	DB
1969	WAS	N	14	CB
1970			14	CB
1971			14	CB
1972			14	CB
1973			14	CB
1974			14	CB
1975			14	CB
8 yrs.	100 games			

Norm Bass
BASS, NORMAN DELANEY
B. Jan. 21, 1939, Laurel, MS
Pacific 6'3" 210 lbs.

Year	Team		Games	Pos.
1964	DEN	A	1	DB

Robert Bass
BASS, ROBERT
B. Nov. 10, 1970, Brooklyn, NY
Miami (Florida) 6'1" 239 lbs.

Year	Team		Games	Pos.
1995	CHI	N	2	LB

Henry Bassett
BASSETT, HENRY H.
B. Sep. 1, 1899
D. Feb, 1973
Nebraska 6'2" 215 lbs.

Year	Team		Games	Pos.
1924	KC	N	7	T, G

Mo Bassett
BASSETT, MAURICE L.
B. Apr. 26, 1931
D. May 24, 1991, Springfield, OH

Year	Team	Games	Pos.

Mo Bassett continued

Langston 6'1" 231 lbs.

1954	CLE	N	12	FB
1955		12	FB
1956		12	FB

3 yrs.   36 games

Dick Bassi
BASSI, RICHARD J.
B. Jan. 1, 1915, San Luis Obispo, CA
D. Aug. 12, 1973, San Francisco, CA
Santa Clara 5'11" 214 lbs.

1938	CHIB	N	7	G
1939		10	G
1940	PHI	N	11	G
1941	PIT	N	11	G
1946	SF	AA	8	G
1947		8	G

6 yrs.   55 games

Reds Bassman
BASSMAN, HERMAN
B. Feb. 25, 1913, Philadelphia, PA
Ursinus 5'11" 180 lbs.

1936	PHI	N	8	HB

Max Bastian
BASTIAN, MAX
None

1926	AKR	N	1	QB

Bert Baston
BASTON, ALBERT PRESTON
B. Dec. 3, 1894, St. Louis Park, MN
D. Nov. 16, 1979, St. Cloud, MN
Minnesota 6'1" 170 lbs.

1920	CLE	A	7	E

Don Batchellor
BATCHELLOR, DONALD
B. 1895
Deceased
Ohio Northern/Grove City 6'3" 225 lbs.

1922	CAN	N	1	T
1923	TOL	N	2	T

2 yrs.   3 games

Marv Bateman
BATEMAN, MARVIN F.
B. Apr. 5, 1950, Salt Lake City, UT
Utah 6'4" 213 lbs.

1972	DAL	N	14	P, K
1973		13	P, K
1974		7	P
1974	BUF	N	5	P
1975		14	P
1976		14	P
1977		14	P

6 yrs.   81 games

Bill Bates
BATES, WILLIAM FREDERICK
B. Jun. 6, 1961, Knoxville, TN
Tennessee 6'1" 200 lbs.

1983	DAL	N	16	S
1984		12	S
1985		16	S
1986		15	S
1987		12	S
1988		16	S
1989		16	S
1990		16	S
1991		16	S
1992		5	S
1993		16	S
1994		15	S
1995		16	S

Bill Bates continued

1996			14	S

14 yrs.   201 games

Mario Bates
BATES, MARIO
B. Jan. 16, 1973, Tucson, AZ
Arizona State 6'1" 217 lbs.

1994	NO	N	11	RB
1995		16	RB
1996		14	RB

3 yrs.   41 games

Michael Bates
BATES, MICHAEL D.
B. Dec. 19, 1969, Tucson, AZ
Arizona 5'10" 189 lbs.

1993	SEA	N	16	WR
1994		15	WR
1995	CLE	N	13	WR
1996	CAR	N	14	WR

4 yrs.   58 games

Patrick Bates
BATES, PATRICK JAMES
B. Nov. 27, 1970, Galveston, TX
Texas A&M 6'3" 220 lbs.

1993	LARI	N	13	S
1994		16	S
1996	ATL	N	15	S

3 yrs.   44 games

Ted Bates
BATES, TED DOUGLAS
B. Sep. 22, 1936, Baytown, TX
Oregon State 6'3" 219 lbs.

1959	CHIC	N	12	LB
1960	STL	N	12	LB
1961		14	LB
1962		8	LB
1963	NY	A	8	LB

5 yrs.   54 games

Stan Batinski
BATINSKI, STANLEY
B. Mar. 4, 1917, Greenfield, MA
D. Jan. 29, 1990, Greenfield, MA
Temple 5'10" 215 lbs.

1941	DET	N	7	G
1943		8	G, T
1944		8	G, T
1945		10	G
1946		11	G
1947		12	G
1948	BOS		12	G
1949	NYB	N	12	G

8 yrs.   80 games

Michael Batiste
BATISTE, MICHAEL
B. Dec. 24, 1970, Beaumont, TX
Tulane 6'3" 295 lbs.

1995	DAL	N	2	G

John Batorski
BATORSKI, JOHN MICHAEL
B. Sep. 27, 1920, Lackawanna, NY
D. Nov. 16, 1982, Old Field, NY
Colgate 6'2" 238 lbs.

1946	BUF	AA	8	E

Marco Battaglia
BATTAGLIA, MARCO
B. Jan. 25, 1973, Howard Beach, NY
Rutgers 6'3" 250 lbs.

1996	CIN	N	16	TE

Matt Battaglia
BATTAGLIA, MATT MARTIN
B. Sep. 25, 1965
Louisville 6'2" 225 lbs.

1987	PHI	N	3	LB

Pat Batten
BATTEN, PAT
B. Dec. 5, 1941, Indianola, IA
Hardin-Simmons 6'2" 225 lbs.

1964	DET	N	3	FB

Jim Battle
BATTLE, JAMES
B. Feb. 20, 1938, Bartow, FL
Southern Illinois 6'1" 240 lbs.

1963	MIN	N	14	DE

Jim Battle
BATTLES, JAMES
B. Sep. 18, 1941, Shreveport, LA
Southern University 6'4" 235 lbs.

1966	CLE	N	6	OT

Mike Battle
BATTLE, MICHAEL LEONARD
B. Jul. 9, 1946, South Gate, CA
Southern California 6'1" 175 lbs.

1969	NY	A	14	S
1970	NYJ	N	14	S

2 yrs.   28 games

Ralph Battle
BATTLE, RALPH KEITH
B. Jun. 15, 1961, Huntsville, AL
Jacksonville State 6'2" 205 lbs.

1984	CIN	N	3	S

Ron Battle
BATTLE, RON JEROME
B. Mar. 27, 1959, Shreveport, LA
North Texas State 6'3" 220 lbs.

1981	LA	N	4	TE
1982	LARM	N	9	TE

2 yrs.   13 games

Cliff Battles
**BATTLES, CLIFFORD
FRANKLYN (Gyp)**
B. May 1, 1910, Akron, OH
D. Apr. 28, 1981, Clearwater, FL
West Virginia Wesleyan 6'1" 195 lbs.

1932	BOS	N	8	QB, FB, HB
1933		12	HB
1934		12	HB
1935		6	HB
1936		11	HB
1937	WAS	N	10	HB, FB

6 yrs.   59 games

Bobby Batton
BATTON, BOBBY JOE
B. Mar. 17, 1957, Yazoo City, MS
Nevada-Las Vegas 5'11" 185 lbs.

1980	NYJ	N	8	RB

Greg Baty
BATY, GREGORY JAMES
B. Aug. 28, 1964, Hastings, MI
Stanford 6'5" 241 lbs.

1986	NE	N	16	TE
1987		5	TE
1987	LARM	N	4	TE
1988	PHX	N	1	TE
1990	MIA	N	12	TE

Greg Baty continued

1991		16	TE
1992		16	TE
1993		16	TE
1994		16	TE

8 yrs.   102 games

Bauer
BAUER
None

1925	KC	N	1	FB

Hank Bauer
BAUER, HENRY JOHN
B. Jul. 15, 1954, Scottsbluff, NE
California Lutheran 5'10" 200 lbs.

1977	SD	N	13	RB
1978		16	RB
1979		16	RB
1980		16	RB
1981		16	RB
1982		9	RB

6 yrs.   86 games

Herb Bauer
BAUER, HERBERT
B. Oct. 13, 1906
D. Jul. 30, 1980
Baldwin-Wallace 5'10" 190 lbs.

1925	CLE	N	2	E

John Bauer
BAUER, JOHN RICHARD
B. Mar. 11, 1932, Benton, IL
Illinois 6'3" 235 lbs.

1954	NYG	N	2	G

Sammy Baugh
**BAUGH, SAMUEL ADRIAN
(Slingin' Sam)**
B. Mar. 17, 1914, Temple, TX
Texas Christian 6'2" 182 lbs.

1937	WAS	N	11	QB, DB
1938		9	QB, DB
1939		9	QB, DB
1940		11	QB, DB
1941		11	QB, DB
1942		11	QB, DB
1943		10	QB, DB
1944		8	QB, DB
1945		8	QB, DB
1946		11	QB
1947		12	QB
1948		12	QB
1949		12	QB
1950		11	QB
1951		12	QB
1952		7	QB

16 yrs.   165 games

Tom Baugh
BAUGH, THOMAS ANTHONY
B. Dec. 1, 1963, Chicago, IL
Southern Illinois 6'3" 274 lbs.

1986	KC	N	5	C
1987		12	C
1988		12	C
1989	CLE	N	16	C

4 yrs.   45 games

Maxie Baughan
**BAUGHAN, MAXIE CALLOWAY,
JR.**
B. Aug. 3, 1938, Forkland, AL
Georgia Tech 6'1" 227 lbs.

1960	PHI	N	12	LB
1961		14	LB

Year	Team		Games	Pos.

Maxie Baughan *continued*

Year	Team		Games	Pos.
1962			14	LB
1963			14	LB
1964			14	LB
1965			12	LB
1966	LA	N	14	LB
1967			14	LB
1968			14	LB
1969			13	LB
1970			10	LB
1974	WAS	N	1	LB

12 yrs.   146 games

Harry Baujan
BAUJAN, HARRY CLIFFORD
B. May 24, 1984, Beardstown, IL
D. Dec, 1976, Dayton, OH
Notre Dame 5'8" 170 lbs.

1920	CLE	A	6	E
1921			4	E

2 yrs.   10 games

Alf Bauman
BAUMAN, ALFRED E.
B. Jan. 3, 1920, Chicago, IL
D. May 20, 1980
Northwestern 6'2" 228 lbs.

1947	CHI	AA	3	T
1947	PHI	N	2	T
1948	CHIB	N	5	T
1949			12	T
1950			12	T

4 yrs.   34 games

Buddy Baumann
BAUMANN, CARL
B. 1900, Wisconsin
Deceased
None 6'1" 190 lbs.

1922	RAC	N	4	T, G

Charlie Baumann
BAUMANN, CHARLIE
B. Aug. 25, 1967, Erie, PA
West Virginia 6'1" 203 lbs.

1991	MIA	N	2	K
1991	NE	N	7	K
1992			16	K

2 yrs.   25 games

Bill Baumgartner
BAUMGARTNER, WILLIAM R.
B. Apr. 17, 1921, Duluth, MN
Minnesota 6'3" 202 lbs.

1947	BAL	AA	2	E

Steve Baumgartner
BAUMGARTNER, STEVEN JOHN
B. Mar. 26, 1951, Chicago, IL
Purdue 6'7" 256 lbs.

1973	NO	N	14	DE
1974			14	DE
1975			14	DE
1976			14	DE
1977			5	DE, DT
1977	HOU	N	6	DE, DT
1978			16	DE, LB
1979			12	LB

7 yrs.   95 games

Bob Baumhower
BAUMHOWER, ROBERT GLENN
B. Aug. 4, 1955, Portsmouth, VA
Alabama 6'5" 265 lbs.

1977	MIA	N	14	DT
1978			16	DT

Bob Baumhower *continued*

Year	Team		Games	Pos.
1979			16	DT
1980			16	DT
1981			16	NT
1982			9	NT
1983			16	NT
1984			15	NT
1986			12	NT

9 yrs.   130 games

Frank Bausch
BAUSCH, FRANK J. (Pete)
B. Jun. 14, 1908, Marion, SD
D. Apr. 6, 1976, Wichita, KS
Kansas 6'3" 220 lbs.

1934	BOS	N	11	C
1935			10	C
1936			12	C
1937	CHIB	N	9	C
1938			11	C
1939			11	C
1940			10	C
1941	PHI	N	4	C

8 yrs.   78 games

Jim Bausch
BAUSCH, JAMES ALOYSIUS
B. Mar. 28, 1906, Marion, SD
Deceased
Wichita State/Kansas 6'1" 200 lbs.

1933	CHIC	N	2	FB
1933	CIN	N	4	HB

1 yr.   6 games

David Bavaro
BAVARO, DAVID ANTHONY
B. Mar. 27, 1967, Danvers, MA
Syracuse 6'0" 234 lbs.

1990	PHX	N	14	LB
1991	BUF	N	2	LB
1992	MIN	N	5	LB
1993	NE	N	12	LB
1994			9	LB

5 yrs.   42 games

Mark Bavaro
BAVARO, MARK
B. Apr. 28, 1963, Winthrop, MA
Notre Dame 6'4" 245 lbs.

1985	NYG	N	16	TE
1986			16	TE
1987			12	TE
1988			16	TE
1989			7	TE
1990			15	TE
1992	CLE	N	16	TE
1993	PHI	N	16	TE
1994			12	TE

9 yrs.   126 games

Bibbles Bawel
BAWEL, EDWARD RAY
B. Nov. 21, 1930, Boonville, IN
Evansville 6'1" 185 lbs.

1952	PHI	N	12	HB
1955			12	HB
1956			12	HB

3 yrs.   36 games

Carl Bax
BAX, CARL WILLIAM
B. Jan. 5, 1966, St. Charles, MO
Missouri 6'4" 290 lbs.

1989	TB	N	6	OT, G
1990			9	G

2 yrs.   15 games

Rob Baxley
BAXLEY, ROB
B. Mar. 14, 1969, Oswego, IL
Iowa 6'5" 287 lbs.

1992	PHX	N	6	OT

Brad Baxter
BAXTER, HERMAN BRADLEY
B. May 5, 1967, Dothan, AL
Alabama State 6'1" 233 lbs.

1989	NYJ	N	1	RB
1990			16	RB
1991			16	RB
1992			15	RB
1993			16	RB
1994			15	RB
1995			15	RB

7 yrs.   94 games

Fred Baxter
BAXTER, FREDERICK DENARD
B. Jun. 14, 1971, Brundidge, AL
Auburn 6'3" 250 lbs.

1993	NYJ	N	7	TE
1994			12	TE
1995			15	TE
1996			16	TE

4 yrs.   50 games

Jimmy Baxter
BAXTER, JAMES
B. Jul. 19, 1892, Ohio
D. Apr, 1973, South Bend, IN
None 5'7" 173 lbs.

1923	RAC	N	1	HB
1924	KEN	N	3	HB, E

2 yrs.   4 games

Lloyd Baxter
BAXTER, LLOYD T.
B. Jan. 18, 1923, Howe, TX
Southern Methodist 6'2" 210 lbs.

1948	GB	N	11	C

Martin Bayless
BAYLESS, MARTIN
B. Oct. 11, 1962, Dayton, OH
Bowling Green 6'2" 195 lbs.

1984	STL	N	3	S
1984	BUF	N	13	S
1985			12	S
1986			16	S
1987	SD	N	12	S
1988			15	S
1989			16	S
1990			14	S
1991			16	S
1992	KC	N	16	S
1993			16	S
1994	WAS	N	16	S
1995	KC	N	12	S
1996			16	S

13 yrs.   193 games

Rick Bayless
BAYLESS, RICK
B. 1965
Iowa 6'0" 202 lbs.

1989	MIN	N	1	RB

Tom Bayless
BAYLESS, THOMAS MCDOWELL
B. Dec. 17, 1947, Knob Lick, MO
Purdue 6'3" 240 lbs.

1970	NYJ	N	2	G

John Bayley
BAYLEY, JOHN M.
B. Nov. 10, 1903
D. Apr. 5, 1969, Massena, NY
Syracuse 5'11" 180 lbs.

1927	NYY	N	7	T

John Baylor
BAYLOR, JOHN MARTIN
B. Mar. 5, 1965, Meridian, MS
Southern Mississippi 6'0" 203 lbs.

1989	IND	N	16	CB, S
1990			10	CB, S
1991			16	CB, S
1992			16	CB, S
1993			16	CB, S

5 yrs.   74 games

Ray Baylor
BAYLOR, RAYMOND
B. Mar. 7, 1947, Houston, TX
Texas Southern 6'5" 263 lbs.

1974	SD	N	1	DE

Tim Baylor
BAYLOR, TIM
B. May 23, 1954, Washington, DC
Morgan State 6'6" 195 lbs.

1976	BAL	N	14	DB
1977			13	S
1978			16	S
1979	MIN	N	16	S

4 yrs.   59 games

Craig Baynham
BAYNHAM, GORDON CRAIG
B. Jul. 24, 1944, Casper, WY
Georgia Tech 6'1" 204 lbs.

1967	DAL	N	14	RB
1968			14	RB
1969			10	RB
1970	CHI	N	5	RB
1972	STL	N	7	RB

5 yrs.   50 games

Reeves Baysinger
BAYSINGER, REEVES S., SR.
(Ribs)
B. 1901
Deceased
Syracuse 6'0" 180 lbs.

1924	ROC	N	1	E

Winnie Baze
BAZE, WINFORD EASON
B. Jul. 14, 1914, Robert Lee, TX
Schreiner Institute/Texas Tech 5'11" 190 lbs.

1937	PHI	N	10	HB, QB

Pat Beach
BEACH, PATRICK JESSE
B. Dec. 28, 1959, Grant's Pass, OR
Washington State 6'4" 244 lbs.

1982	BAL	N	9	TE
1983			16	TE
1985	IND	N	16	TE
1986			16	TE
1987			12	TE
1988			16	TE
1989			16	TE
1990			16	TE
1991			12	TE
1992	PHI	N	16	TE
1993	PHX	N	15	TE

11 yrs.   160 games

Year	Team		Games	Pos.

Sanjay Beach
BEACH, SANJAY RAGIV
B. Feb. 21, 1966, Clark AFB, Philippines
Colorado State 6'0" 189 lbs.

Year	Team		Games	Pos.
1989	NYJ	N	1	WR
1991	SF	N	16	WR
1992	GB	N	16	WR
1993	SF	N	9	WR
4 yrs.	42 games			

Walter Beach
BEACH, WALTER, III
B. Jan. 31, 1935, Pontiac, MI
Central Michigan 6'0" 184 lbs.

Year	Team		Games	Pos.
1960	BOS	A	14	HB
1961			12	DB
1963	CLE	N	2	DB
1964			14	DB
1965			10	DB
1966			5	DB
6 yrs.	57 games			

Norm Beal
BEAL, NORMAN L.
B. 1940, St. Louis, MO
Missouri 5'11" 170 lbs.

Year	Team		Games	Pos.
1962	STL	N	7	DB

Alyn Beals
BEALS, ALYN R.
B. Apr. 27, 1921, Marysville, CA
D. Aug. 11, 1993, Redwood City, CA
Santa Clara 6'0" 188 lbs.

Year	Team		Games	Pos.
1946	SF	AA	14	E
1947			13	E
1948			14	E
1949			12	E
1950	SF	N	12	E
1951			12	E
6 yrs.	77 games			

Shawn Beals
BEALS, SHAWN
B. Aug. 16, 1966, Pittsburg, CA
Idaho State 5'10" 178 lbs.

Year	Team		Games	Pos.
1988	PHI	N	13	WR

Bill Bealles
BEALLES, WILLIAM
B. Jun. 11, 1963, Steubenville, OH
Northern Iowa 6'7" 290 lbs.

Year	Team		Games	Pos.
1987	MIA	N	3	OT

Tim Beamer
BEAMER, TIMOTHY CARL
B. Apr. 6, 1948, Galax, VA
Illinois/Johnson C. Smith 5'11" 185 lbs.

Year	Team		Games	Pos.
1971	BUF	N	12	CB

Autry Beamon
BEAMON, AUTRY, JR.
B. Nov. 12, 1953, Terrell, TX
East Texas State 6'1" 190 lbs.

Year	Team		Games	Pos.
1975	MIN	N	14	S
1976			14	S
1977	SEA	N	14	S
1978			16	S
1979			15	S
1980	CLE	N	13	S
6 yrs.	86 games			

Willie Beamon
BEAMON, WILLIE
B. Jun. 14, 1970, Belle Glade, FL

Willie Beamon continued
Northern Iowa 5'11" 170 lbs.

Year	Team		Games	Pos.
1993	NYG	N	13	CB, S
1994			15	CB
1995			16	CB
1996			5	CB
4 yrs.	49 games			

Byron Beams
BEAMS, BYRON
B. 1934
Notre Dame/East Central Oklahoma 6'6" 249 lbs.

Year	Team		Games	Pos.
1959	PIT	N	6	T
1960			3	T
1961	HOU	A	7	DT
3 yrs.	16 games			

Bubba Bean
BEAN, EARNEST RAY
B. Jan. 26, 1954, Kirbyville, TX
Texas A&M 5'11" 195 lbs.

Year	Team		Games	Pos.
1976	ATL	N	14	RB
1978			15	RB
1979			11	RB
3 yrs.	40 games			

Bear Behind
BEAR BEHIND
None 190 lbs.

Year	Team		Games	Pos.
1923	OOR	N	1	E

Ed Beard
BEARD, EDWARD LEROY
B. Dec. 9, 1939, Chesapeake, VA
Tennessee 6'2" 225 lbs.

Year	Team		Games	Pos.
1965	SF	N	12	LB
1966			12	LB
1967			14	LB
1968			14	LB
1969			3	LB
1970			14	LB
1971			14	LB
1972			14	LB
8 yrs.	97 games			

Tom Beard
BEARD, THOMAS LEROY, JR.
B. Jun. 10, 1948, Findlay, OH
Michigan State 6'6" 280 lbs.

Year	Team		Games	Pos.
1972	BUF	N	8	C

Aaron Beasley
BEASLEY, AARON
B. Jul. 7, 1973, Pottstown, PA
West Virginia 6'0" 194 lbs.

Year	Team		Games	Pos.
1996	JAC	N	9	CB

Emil Beasley
BEASLEY, EMIL
None 162 lbs.

Year	Team		Games	Pos.
1924	GB	N	1	FB

John Beasley
BEASLEY, JOHN
B. Feb. 14, 1897
D. Nov, 1964
Earlham 230 lbs.

Year	Team		Games	Pos.
1923	DAY	N	4	G

John Beasley
BEASLEY, JOHN WALTER
B. Apr. 6, 1945, Buena Park, CA
California 6'3" 229 lbs.

Year	Team		Games	Pos.
1967	MIN	N	14	TE

John Beasley continued

Year	Team		Games	Pos.
1968			14	TE
1969			14	TE
1970			14	TE
1972			14	TE
1973			3	TE
1973	NO	N	8	TE
1974			14	TE
7 yrs.	95 games			

Terry Beasley
BEASLEY, TERRY PAUL
B. Feb. 5, 1950, Montgomery, AL
Auburn 5'10" 183 lbs.

Year	Team		Games	Pos.
1972	SF	N	8	WR
1974			13	WR
1975			8	WR
3 yrs.	29 games			

Tom Beasley
BEASLEY, THOMAS LYNN
B. Aug. 11, 1954, Bluefield, WV
Virginia Tech 6'5" 250 lbs.

Year	Team		Games	Pos.
1978	PIT	N	15	DT
1979			13	DT
1980			15	DT
1981			13	DT, DE
1982			7	DT
1983			16	DE, NT
1984	WAS	N	13	DE
1985			12	DE
1986			1	DE
9 yrs.	105 games			

Pete Beathard
BEATHARD, PETER FRANK
B. Mar. 7, 1942, Hermosa Beach, CA
Southern California 6'2" 205 lbs.

Year	Team		Games	Pos.
1964	KC	A	14	QB
1965			14	QB
1966			14	QB
1967			1	QB
1967	HOU	A	11	QB
1968			9	QB
1969			12	QB
1970	STL	N	4	QB
1971			9	QB
1972	LA	N	14	QB
1973	KC	N	9	QB
10 yrs.	111 games			

Bob Beattie
BEATTIE, ROBERT W.
B. Oct. 16, 1902
D. Jun, 1983, Orangeburg, NY
Princeton 6'3" 230 lbs.

Year	Team		Games	Pos.
1926	PHI	A	4	HB, E
1927	NYY	N	1	T
1929	ORA	N	11	T, G
1930	NEW	N	5	T, G
4 yrs.	21 games			

Chuck Beatty
BEATTY, CHARLES
B. Feb. 8, 1946, Waxahachie, TX
North Texas State 6'2" 203 lbs.

Year	Team		Games	Pos.
1969	PIT	N	7	DB
1970			12	S
1971			3	S
1972			8	S
1972	STL	N	4	S
4 yrs.	34 games			

Ed Beatty
BEATTY, EDWARD MARSHALL, JR.
B. Apr. 6, 1932, Clarksdale, MS

Ed Beatty continued
Mississippi 6'3" 229 lbs.

Year	Team		Games	Pos.
1955	SF	N	6	C
1956			12	C
1957	PIT	N	12	C
1958			12	C
1959			12	C
1960			12	C
1961	WAS	N	11	C
7 yrs.	77 games			

Al Beauchamp
BEAUCHAMP, ALFRED
B. Jun. 25, 1944, Baton Rouge, LA
Southern University 6'2" 235 lbs.

Year	Team		Games	Pos.
1968	CIN	A	14	LB
1969			13	LB
1970	CIN	N	14	LB
1971			14	LB
1972			14	LB
1973			14	LB
1974			14	LB
1975			14	LB
1976	STL	N	14	LB
9 yrs.	125 games			

Joe Beauchamp
BEAUCHAMP, JOSEPH SCOTT
B. Apr. 11, 1944, Chicago, IL
Iowa 6'0" 185 lbs.

Year	Team		Games	Pos.
1966	SD	A	8	DB
1967			14	DB
1968			14	DB
1969			14	S
1970	SD	N	13	CB
1971			13	CB
1972			14	CB
1973			9	S
1974			10	S
1975			8	S
10 yrs.	117 games			

Doug Beaudoin
BEAUDOIN, DOUGLAS LEE
B. May 15, 1954, Dickinson, ND
Minnesota 6'1" 193 lbs.

Year	Team		Games	Pos.
1976	NE	N	9	S
1977			11	S
1978			15	S
1979			10	S
1980	MIA	N	10	S
1981	SD	N	4	S
6 yrs.	59 games			

Clayton Beauford
BEAUFORD, CLAYTON MAURICE
B. Mar. 1, 1963, Palatka, FL
Auburn 5'11" 190 lbs.

Year	Team		Games	Pos.
1987	CLE	N	1	WR

Jim Beaver
BEAVER, JAMES EDWARD
B. May 18, 1938
Florida 6'1" 235 lbs.

Year	Team		Games	Pos.
1962	PHI	N	1	DT

Aubrey Beavers
BEAVERS, AUBREY TOD
B. Aug. 31, 1971, Houston, TX
Oklahoma 6'3" 233 lbs.

Year	Team		Games	Pos.
1994	MIA	N	16	LB
1995			16	LB
1996	NYJ	N	7	LB
3 yrs.	39 games			

Year	Team	Games	Pos.

Scott Beavers
BEAVERS, SCOTT TRAVIS
B. Feb. 17, 1967, Atlanta, GA
Georgia Tech 6'4" 277 lbs.

Year	Team	Games	Pos.
1990	DEN N	2	G

Gary Beban
BEBAN, GARY JOSEPH
B. Aug. 5, 1946, Redwood City, CA
UCLA 6'1" 195 lbs.

Year	Team	Games	Pos.
1968	WAS N	4	RB
1969		1	WR
2 yrs.	5 games		

Nick Bebout
BEBOUT, NICK
B. May 5, 1951, Riverton, WI
Wyoming 6'5" 261 lbs.

Year	Team	Games	Pos.
1973	ATL N	13	OT
1974		13	OT
1975		14	OT
1976	SEA N	14	OT
1977		12	OT
1978		16	OT
1979		13	OT
1980	MIN N	1	OT
8 yrs.	96 games		

Hub Bechtol
BECHTOL, HUBERT E. (Big Boy)
B. Apr. 20, 1926, Amarillo, TX
Texas 6'3" 202 lbs.

Year	Team	Games	Pos.
1947	BAL AA	14	E
1948		12	E
1949		12	E
3 yrs.	38 games		

Braden Beck
BECK, BRADEN W.
B. Jan. 12, 1944, Oakland, CA
Stanford 6'2" 200 lbs.

Year	Team	Games	Pos.
1971	HOU N		K

Carl Beck
BECK, CARL
B. 1900, Harrisburg, PA
D. Harrisburg, PA
Bucknell/Lafayette/West Virginia 5'11" 195 lbs.

Year	Team	Games	Pos.
1921	BUF A	6	HB, FB, T, E

Clarence Beck
BECK, CLARENCE
B. Oct. 3, 1894, Harrisburg, PA
D. Oct, 1970, Grampian, PA
Penn State 5'11" 200 lbs.

Year	Team	Games	Pos.
1925	POT N	7	T, G

Ken Beck
BECK, KENNETH
B. Aug. 3, 1936, Minden, LA
Texas A&M 6'2" 245 lbs.

Year	Team	Games	Pos.
1959	GB N	12	T
1960		12	E
2 yrs.	24 games		

Marty Beck
BECK, MARTIN
B. Jan. 2, 1900
D. Jun, 1968, New York, NY
None 5'9" 175 lbs.

Year	Team	Games	Pos.
1921	AKR A	6	HB
1922	AKR N	1	HB
1924		1	HB
3 yrs.	8 games		

Ray Beck
BECK, RAY M.
B. Mar. 7, 1932
Georgia Tech 6'2" 224 lbs.

Year	Team	Games	Pos.
1952	NYG N	12	G
1955		12	G
1956		10	G
1957		12	G
4 yrs.	46 games		

Dave Becker
BECKER, DAVID PAUL
B. Jan. 15, 1957, Atlantic, IA
Iowa 6'2" 190 lbs.

Year	Team	Games	Pos.
1980	CHI N	11	S

Doug Becker
BECKER, DOUGLAS JAMES
B. Jun. 27, 1956, Hamilton, OH
Notre Dame 6'0" 222 lbs.

Year	Team	Games	Pos.
1978	CHI N	1	LB
1978	BUF N	8	LB
1 yrs.	9 games		

Johnnie Becker
BECKER, JOHN W.
B. Feb. 10, 1903
D. Sep. 17, 1947
Denison 5'11" 208 lbs.

Year	Team	Games	Pos.
1926	DAY N	5	T, G, HB
1927		7	T
1928		5	T
1929		1	T
4 yrs.	18 games		

Kurt Becker
BECKER, KURT FRANK
B. Dec. 22, 1958, Aurora, IL
Michigan 6'5" 275 lbs.

Year	Team	Games	Pos.
1982	CHI N	5	G
1983		16	G
1984		16	G
1985		3	G
1986		14	G
1987		12	G
1988		16	G
1989	LARM N	2	G
1990	CHI N	10	G, OT
9 yrs.	94 games		

Wayland Becker
BECKER, WAYLAND
B. Nov. 2, 1910, Soperton, WI
D. Dec, 1984, Lena, WI
Marquette 6'0" 198 lbs.

Year	Team	Games	Pos.
1934	CHIB N	1	E
1934	BKN N	9	E
1935	BKN N	11	E
1936	GB N	12	E
1937		9	E
1938		11	E
1939	PIT N	2	E
6 yrs.	55 games		

Jack Beckett
BECKETT, JOHN W.
B. Jan. 5, 1892
D. Jul. 26, 1981, San Diego, CA
Oregon 6'1" 200 lbs.

Year	Team	Games	Pos.
1920	BUF A	2	T
1922	COL N	1	G
2 yrs.	3 games		

Ian Beckles
BECKLES, IAN HAROLD
B. Jul. 20, 1967, Montreal, Que.

Ian Beckles *continued*
Indiana 6'1" 295 lbs.

Year	Team	Games	Pos.
1990	TB N	16	G
1991		16	G
1992		11	G
1993		14	G
1994		16	G
1995		15	G
1996		14	G
7 yrs.	102 games		

Art Beckley
BECKLEY, ARTHUR K.
B. Sep. 1, 1901
Michigan State 5'10" 180 lbs.

Year	Team	Games	Pos.
1926	DAY N	5	HB

Brad Beckman
BECKMAN, BRADLEY SCOTT
B. Dec. 31, 1964, Lincoln, NE
D. Dec. 18, 1989
Nebraska-Omaha 6'2" 236 lbs.

Year	Team	Games	Pos.
1988	NYG N	9	TE
1989	ATL N	15	TE
2 yrs.	24 games		

Ed Beckman
BECKMAN, EDWIN JAY
B. Jan. 2, 1955, Key West, FL
Florida State 6'4" 232 lbs.

Year	Team	Games	Pos.
1977	KC N	14	TE
1978		16	TE
1979		9	TE
1980		16	TE
1981		15	TE
1982		9	TE
1983		15	TE
1984		13	TE
8 yrs.	107 games		

Tom Beckman
BECKMAN, THOMAS CLARE
B. Sep. 21, 1950, Saginaw, MI
Michigan 6'5" 250 lbs.

Year	Team	Games	Pos.
1972	STL N	2	DE

John Beckwith
BECKWITH, JOHN
B. 1895
Deceased
None 150 lbs.

Year	Team	Games	Pos.
1920	COL A	1	HB

Gene Bedford
**BEDFORD, WILLIAM EUGENE
(Blink)**
B. Dec. 2, 1896, Dallas, TX
D. Oct. 6, 1977, San Antonio, TX
Centre/Southern Methodist 5'9" 165 lbs.

Year	Team	Games	Pos.
1925	ROC N	2	E

Chuck Bednarik
BEDNARIK, CHARLES PHILIP
B. Mar. 1, 1925, Bethlehem, PA
Pennsylvania 6'3" 233 lbs.

Year	Team	Games	Pos.
1949	PHI N	10	C, LB
1950		12	C, LB
1951		12	C, LB
1952		12	C, LB
1953		12	C, LB
1954		12	C, LB
1955		12	C, LB
1956		12	LB
1957		11	C, LB
1958		12	C
1959		12	C
1960		12	C, LB

Chuck Bednarik *continued*

Year	Team	Games	Pos.
1961		14	LB
1962		14	LB
14 yrs.	169 games		

Al Bedner
BEDNER, ALBERT
B. Jul. 9, 1898
D. Jul. 12, 1988, Wilkes, Barre, PA
Lafayette 5'10" 193 lbs.

Year	Team	Games	Pos.
1924	FRA N	3	G
1925	NYG N	9	G, T
1926		7	G, C
3 yrs.	19 games		

Tom Bedore
BEDORE, THOMAS
B. Nov. 14, 1925, Faust, NY
None 5'11" 193 lbs.

Year	Team	Games	Pos.
1944	WAS N	2	G, LB

Hal Bedsole
BEDSOLE, HAROLD JAY
B. Dec. 21, 1941, Chicago, IL
Southern California 6'4" 230 lbs.

Year	Team	Games	Pos.
1964	MIN N	14	OE
1965		9	OE
1966		1	TE
3 yrs.	24 games		

Don Beebe
BEEBE, DON LEE
B. Dec. 18, 1964, Aurora, IL
Western Illinois/Aurora/Chadron State 5'11" 177 lbs.*

Year	Team	Games	Pos.
1989	BUF N	14	WR
1990		12	WR
1991		11	WR
1992		12	WR
1993		14	WR
1994		13	WR
1995	CAR N	14	WR
1996	GB N	16	WR
8 yrs.	106 games		

Keith Beebe
BEEBE, HIRAM KEITH
B. Mar. 16, 1921, Anaheim, CA
Occidental 5'9" 180 lbs.

Year	Team	Games	Pos.
1944	NYG N	6	B

Earl Beecham
BEECHAM, EARL
B. Sep. 8, 1965, Brooklyn, NY
Bucknell 5'8" 180 lbs.

Year	Team	Games	Pos.
1987	NYG N	1	RB

Willie Beecher
BEECHER, WILLIAM WEIGEL
B. Apr. 14, 1963, El Paso, TX
Utah State 5'10" 170 lbs.

Year	Team	Games	Pos.
1987	MIA N	3	K

Frank Beede
BEEDE, FRANK
B. May 1, 1973, Antioch, CA
Panhandle State 6'4" 292 lbs.

Year	Team	Games	Pos.
1996	SEA N	14	C

Bruce Beekley
BEEKLEY, BRUCE EDWARD
B. Dec. 15, 1956, Cincinnati, OH
Oregon 6'2" 225 lbs.

Year	Team	Games	Pos.
1980	GB N	15	LB

Year	Team	Games	Pos.

Ferris Beekley
BEEKLEY, FERRIS EUGENE
B. Feb. 27, 1897, Butler County, OH
D. Jun. 15, 1986, Cincinnati, OH
Miami (Ohio) 5'8" 185 lbs.

Year	Team	Games	Pos.
1921	**CIN** A	3	G, HB

Beeming
BEEMING
None

1924	**DAY** N	1	G

Tom Beer
BEER, THOMAS
B. Mar. 27, 1969, Bay Port, MI
Saginaw Valley State/Wayne State (Michigan) 6'2" 237 lbs.

Year	Team	Games	Pos.
1994	**DET** N	9	LB
1995		16	LB
1996		16	LB
3 yrs.	41 games		

Tom Beer
BEER, THOMAS JOHN
B. Dec. 21, 1944, Detroit, MI
Detroit/Houston 6'4" 232 lbs.

Year	Team	Games	Pos.
1967	**DEN** A	14	OE
1968		14	TE
1969		7	TE
1970	**BOS** N	14	TE
1971	**NE** N	14	G, TE
1972		14	TE
6 yrs.	77 games		

Terry Beeson
BEESON, TERRY EUGENE
B. Sep. 19, 1955, Coffeyville, KS
Kansas 6'3" 239 lbs.

Year	Team	Games	Pos.
1977	**SEA** N	14	LB
1978		16	LB
1979		16	LB
1980		16	LB
1981		15	LB
1982	**SF** N	5	LB
6 yrs.	82 games		

Charlie Behan
BEHAN, CHARLES EDWIN (Ed)
B. Aug. 4, 1920, Crystal Lake, IL
D. May 18, 1945, Okinawa
Northern Illinois 6'3" 195 lbs.

Year	Team	Games	Pos.
1942	**DET** N	9	E

Norty Behm
BEHM, NORTON (Mope)
B. 1901
D. 1980
Iowa State 5'7" 150 lbs.

Year	Team	Games	Pos.
1926	**CLE** A	5	E, FB, HB

Bull Behman
BEHMAN, RUSSELL J.
B. Jan. 15, 1900, Steelton, PA
D. Mar. 24, 1950, Harrisburg, PA
Lebanon Valley/Dickinson 5'10" 214 lbs.

Year	Team	Games	Pos.
1924	**FRA** N	13	T, G
1925		16	T, C
1926	**PHI** A	10	T
1927	**FRA** N	11	T, E
1928		16	T, G
1929		18	T
1930		5	T
1931		7	T, G
8 yrs.	96 games		

Mark Behning
BEHNING, MARK GERALD
B. Sep. 26, 1961, Alpena, MI
Nebraska 6'6" 290 lbs.

Year	Team	Games	Pos.
1986	**PIT** N	16	OT

Dave Behrman
BEHRMAN, DAVID WESLEY
B. Nov. 9, 1941, Dowagiac, MI
Michigan State 6'5" 260 lbs.

Year	Team	Games	Pos.
1963	**BUF** A	14	OT
1965		14	C
1967	**DEN** A	11	OT
3 yrs.	39 games		

Tom Beier
BEIER, THOMAS EUGENE
B. Jun. 23, 1945, Fremont, OH
Detroit/Miami (Florida) 5'11" 198 lbs.

Year	Team	Games	Pos.
1967	**MIA** A	14	DB, FL
1969		14	S
2 yrs.	28 games		

Larry Beil
BEIL, LAWRENCE
B. 1924
Portland 6'2" 235 lbs.

Year	Team	Games	Pos.
1948	**NYG** N	9	T

Ed Beinor
BEINOR, JOSEPH EDWARD
B. Nov. 16, 1917, Harvey, IL
Deceased
Notre Dame 6'2" 222 lbs.

Year	Team	Games	Pos.
1940	**CHIC** N	11	T
1941		8	T
1941	**WAS** N	4	T, G
1942		11	T
3 yrs.	34 games		

Jim Beirne
BEIRNE, JAMES PATRICK
B. Oct. 15, 1946, McKeesport, PA
Purdue 6'2" 198 lbs.

Year	Team	Games	Pos.
1968	**HOU** A	14	OE
1969		14	WR
1970	**HOU** N	14	WR
1971		14	WR
1972		10	WR, TE
1973		1	WR
1974	**SD** N	14	WR
1975	**HOU** N	6	WR
1976		7	WR
9 yrs.	94 games		

Randy Beisler
BEISLER, RANDALL LEE
B. Oct. 24, 1944, Gary, IN
Indiana 6'4" 249 lbs.

Year	Team	Games	Pos.
1966	**PHI** N	14	DE
1967		14	DE
1968		8	OT, DE
1969	**SF** N	14	OT
1970		14	OT
1971		14	G
1972		14	G
1973		14	G
1974		10	G
1975	**KC** N	3	G
10 yrs.	119 games		

Bill Belanich
BELANICH, FRANK WILLIAM
B. May 19, 1903
D. Aug, 1960
Dayton 6'0" 205 lbs.

Year	Team	Games	Pos.
1927	**DAY** N	8	T

Bill Belanich *continued*

Year	Team	Games	Pos.
1928		7	T, E
1929		4	T
3 yrs.	19 games		

Kevin Belcher
BELCHER, KEVIN
B. Feb. 23, 1961, Detroit, MI
Texas-El Paso 6'3" 270 lbs.

Year	Team	Games	Pos.
1983	**NYG** N	16	G
1984		16	G
2 yrs.	32 games		

Kevin Belcher
BELCHER, KEVIN LEANDER
B. Nov. 9, 1961, Bridgeport, CT
Wisconsin 6'6" 310 lbs.

Year	Team	Games	Pos.
1985	**LARI** N	4	OT
1987	**DEN** N	1	OT
2 yrs.	5 games		

Bunny Belden
BELDEN, CHARLES
B. Dec. 7, 1900
D. Nov, 1976, Skokie, IL
None 5'8" 173 lbs.

Year	Team	Games	Pos.
1927	**DUL** N	5	QB, E, FB, HB
1930	**CHIC** N	11	HB, QB, FB
1931		7	HB, FB
3 yrs.	23 games		

Les Belding
BELDING, LESTER COIT
B. Dec. 5, 1900, Mason City, IA
Deceased
Upper Iowa/Iowa 5'11" 195 lbs.

Year	Team	Games	Pos.
1925	**RI** N	1	E, HB

Steve Belichick
BELICHICK, STEPHEN N.
B. Jan. 7, 1919, Monessen, PA
Case Western Reserve 5'8" 190 lbs.

Year	Team	Games	Pos.
1941	**DET** N	6	FB

Chuck Belin
BELIN, CHARLES EDWARD
B. Oct. 27, 1970, Milwaukee, WI
Wisconsin 6'2" 312 lbs.

Year	Team	Games	Pos.
1994	**LARM** N	14	G
1995	**STL** N	6	G
1996		2	G
3 yrs.	22 games		

Bill Belk
BELK, WILLIAM ARTHUR
B. Feb. 19, 1946, Lancaster, NC
Maryland-Eastern Shore 6'3" 248 lbs.

Year	Team	Games	Pos.
1968	**SF** N	10	DE
1969		14	DE
1970		14	DE
1971		8	DE
1972		14	DE
1973		13	DE
1974		14	DT, DE
7 yrs.	87 games		

Rocky Belk
BELK, ANTHONY LOVETT
B. Jun. 20, 1960, Alexandria, VA
Miami (Florida) 6'0" 187 lbs.

Year	Team	Games	Pos.
1983	**CLE** N	10	WR

Veno Belk
BELK, VENO L.
B. Mar. 7, 1963, Tifton, GA

Veno Belk *continued*
Michigan State 6'3" 233 lbs.

Year	Team	Games	Pos.
1987	**BUF** N	2	TE

Albert Bell
BELL, ALBERT, II
B. Apr. 23, 1964, Birmingham, AL
Alabama 6'0" 170 lbs.

Year	Team	Games	Pos.
1988	**GB** N	5	WR

Anthony Bell
BELL, ANTHONY DEWITT
B. Jul. 2, 1964, Miami, FL
Michigan State 6'3" 231 lbs.

Year	Team	Games	Pos.
1986	**STL** N	16	LB
1987		12	LB
1988	**PHX** N	16	LB
1989		16	LB
1990		16	LB
1991	**DET** N	10	LB
1992	**LARI** N	16	LB
7 yrs.	102 games		

Bill Bell
BELL, WILLIAM STEPHEN
B. Dec. 9, 1949, Fort Knox, KY
Kansas 6'1" 191 lbs.

Year	Team	Games	Pos.
1971	**ATL** N	14	K
1972		14	K
1973	**NE** N	3	K
3 yrs.	31 games		

Billy Bell
BELL, BILLY RAY
B. Jan. 16, 1961, Dayton, TX
Lamar 5'10" 170 lbs.

Year	Team	Games	Pos.
1989	**HOU** N	4	CB
1991	**KC** N	8	CB
2 yrs.	12 games		

Bob Bell
BELL, ROBERT FRANCIS
B. Jan. 25, 1948, Philadelphia, PA
Cincinnati 6'4" 252 lbs.

Year	Team	Games	Pos.
1971	**DET** N	14	DT
1972		14	DT
1973		13	DT
1974	**STL** N	10	DE
1975		14	DE
1976		14	DE
1977		7	DE
1978		15	DE
8 yrs.	101 games		

Bobby Bell
BELL, ROBERT LEE, SR.
B. Jun. 17, 1940, Shelby, NC
Minnesota 6'4" 228 lbs.

Year	Team	Games	Pos.
1963	**KC** A	14	LB
1964		14	LB
1965		14	DE, LB
1966		14	DE, LB
1967		14	LB
1968		14	LB
1969		14	LB
1970	**KC** N	14	LB
1971		14	LB
1972		14	LB
1973		14	LB
1974		14	LB
12 yrs.	168 games		

Bobby Bell
BELL, ROBERT LEE, JR.
B. Feb. 7, 1962, St. Paul, MN
Missouri 6'3" 217 lbs.

Year	Team	Games	Pos.
1984	**NYJ** N	15	LB

Year	Team	Games	Pos.

Bobby Bell continued

Year	Team	Games	Pos.
1987	CHI	N 3	LB
2 yrs.	18 games		

Carlos Bell
BELL, CARLOS
B. Sep. 21, 1947, Clinton, OK
Houston 6'5" 238 lbs.

Year	Team	Games	Pos.
1971	NO	N 1	TE

Coleman Bell
BELL, COLEMAN
B. Apr. 22, 1970, Tampa, FL
Miami (Florida) 6'2" 232 lbs.

Year	Team	Games	Pos.
1995	WAS	N 11	TE

Ed Bell
BELL, EDWARD
B. Sep. 20, 1921, Chicago, IL
D. Dec. 6, 1990, South Bend, IN
Indiana 6'6" 227 lbs.

Year	Team	Games	Pos.
1946	MIA	AA 7	G
1947	GB	N 11	G
1948		12	T
1949		12	T
4 yrs.	42 games		

Eddie Bell
BELL, EDWARD ALLEN
B. Sep. 13, 1947, Waco, TX
Idaho State 5'10" 160 lbs.

Year	Team	Games	Pos.
1970	NYJ	N 14	WR
1971		13	WR
1972		13	WR
1973		13	WR
1974		13	WR
1975		14	WR
1976	SD	N 5	WR
7 yrs.	85 games		

Eddie Bell
BELL, EDWARD B.
B. Mar. 25, 1931, Philadelphia, PA
Pennsylvania 6'1" 212 lbs.

Year	Team	Games	Pos.
1955	PHI	N 12	DB
1956		12	DB
1957		12	DB
1958		12	DB
1960	NY	A	DB
5 yrs.	48 games		

Gordon Bell
BELL, GORDON
B. Dec. 25, 1953, Troy, OH
Michigan 5'9" 180 lbs.

Year	Team	Games	Pos.
1976	NYG	N 14	RB
1977		10	RB
1978	STL	N 6	RB
3 yrs.	30 games		

Greg Bell
BELL, GREG LEON
B. Aug. 1, 1962, Columbus, OH
Notre Dame 5'10" 210 lbs.

Year	Team	Games	Pos.
1984	BUF	N 16	RB
1985		16	RB
1986		6	RB
1987		2	RB
1987	LARM	N 2	RB
1988		16	RB
1989		16	RB
1990	LARI	N 6	RB
7 yrs.	80 games		

Henry Bell
BELL, HENRY

Henry Bell continued
B. 1937
none 5'10" 210 lbs.

Year	Team	Games	Pos.
1960	DEN	A	HB

Jerry Bell
BELL, GERALD ALFRED
B. Mar. 7, 1959, Derby, CT
Arizona State 6'5" 230 lbs.

Year	Team	Games	Pos.
1982	TB	N 9	TE
1983		16	TE
1984		16	TE
1985		9	TE
1986		10	TE
5 yrs.	60 games		

Joe Bell
BELL, JOSEPH
B. Apr. 20, 1956
Norfolk State 6'3" 250 lbs.

Year	Team	Games	Pos.
1979	OAK	N 1	DE

Kay Bell
BELL, KAY
B. Oct. 14, 1914, Pullman, WA
D. Oct. 27, 1994, Redmond, WA
Washington State 6'2" 220 lbs.

Year	Team	Games	Pos.
1937	CHIB	N 10	G
1942	NYG	N 11	T
2 yrs.	21 games		

Ken Bell
BELL, KENNETH SHAWN
B. Nov. 16, 1964, Greenwich, CT
Boston College 5'10" 190 lbs.

Year	Team	Games	Pos.
1986	DEN	N 16	RB
1987		12	RB
1988		16	RB
1989		15	RB
4 yrs.	59 games		

Kerwin Bell
BELL, KERWIN DOUGLAS
B. Jun. 15, 1965, Live Oak, FL
Florida 6'2" 205 lbs.

Year	Team	Games	Pos.
1996	IND	N 2	QB

Kevin Bell
BELL, KEVIN ABRAHAM
B. Mar. 14, 1955, Beaumont, TX
Lamar 5'10" 180 lbs.

Year	Team	Games	Pos.
1978	NYJ	N 9	WR

Leonard Bell
BELL, LEONARD CHARLES
B. Mar. 14, 1964, Rockford, IL
Indiana 5'11" 201 lbs.

Year	Team	Games	Pos.
1987	CIN	N 1	S

Mark Bell
BELL, MARK E.
B. Aug. 30, 1957, Wichita, KS
Colorado State 6'5" 240 lbs.

Year	Team	Games	Pos.
1979	SEA	N 16	TE
1980		16	TE
1982		9	DE
1983	BAL	N 7	DE
1984	IND	N 16	DE
5 yrs.	64 games		

Mark Bell
BELL, MARK R.
B. Jun. 14, 1957, Jamestown, OH
Colorado State 5'9" 175 lbs.

Year	Team	Games	Pos.
1980	STL	N 11	WR

Mark Bell continued

Year	Team	Games	Pos.
1981		1	WR
2 yrs.	12 games		

Mike Bell
BELL, MIKE J.
B. Aug. 30, 1957, Wichita, KS
Colorado State 6'4" 255 lbs.

Year	Team	Games	Pos.
1979	KC	N 11	DE
1980		2	DE
1981		16	DE
1982		6	DE
1983		16	DE
1984		15	DE
1985		11	DE
1987		12	DE
1988		15	DE
1989		15	DE
1990		16	DE
1991		8	DE
12 yrs.	140 games		

Myron Bell
BELL, MYRON
B. Sep. 15, 1971, Toledo, OH
Michigan State 5'11" 203 lbs.

Year	Team	Games	Pos.
1994	PIT	N 15	S
1995		16	S
1996		16	S
3 yrs.	47 games		

Nick Bell
BELL, H. NICKOLAS
B. Aug. 19, 1968, Las Vegas, NV
Iowa 6'2" 255 lbs.

Year	Team	Games	Pos.
1991	LARI	N 9	RB
1992		16	RB
1993		10	RB
3 yrs.	35 games		

Richard Bell
BELL, RICHARD ARRON
B. May 3, 1967, Los Angeles, CA
Nebraska 6'2" 200 lbs.

Year	Team	Games	Pos.
1990	PIT	N 16	RB

Rick Bell
BELL, RICHARD THOMAS
B. Oct 18, 1960, St. Cloud, MN
St. John's 6'0" 205 lbs.

Year	Team	Games	Pos.
1983	MIN	N 14	RB

Ricky Bell
BELL, RICKY
B. Oct. 2, 1974, Columbia, SC
North Carolina State 5'10" 186 lbs.

Year	Team	Games	Pos.
1996	JAC	N 12	CB

Ricky Bell
BELL, RICKY LYNN
B. Apr. 8, 1955, Houston, TX
Southern California 6'2" 218 lbs.

Year	Team	Games	Pos.
1977	TB	N 11	RB
1978		12	RB
1979		16	RB
1980		14	RB
1981		16	RB
1982	SD	N 4	RB
6 yrs.	73 games		

Theo Bell
BELL, THEOPOLIS, JR. (T)
B. Dec. 21, 1953, Bakersfield, CA
Arizona 6'0" 185 lbs.

Year	Team	Games	Pos.
1976	PIT	N 13	WR
1978		16	WR

Theo Bell continued

Year	Team	Games	Pos.
1979		13	WR
1980		14	WR
1981	TB	N 7	WR
1982		9	WR
1983		16	WR
1984		15	WR
1985		15	WR
9 yrs.	118 games		

Todd Bell
BELL, TODD ANTHONY
B. Nov. 28, 1958, Middletown, OH
Ohio State 6'1" 207 lbs.

Year	Team	Games	Pos.
1981	CHI	N 16	CB
1982		9	S
1983		15	S
1984		15	S
1986		15	S
1987		12	S
1988	PHI	N 16	S
1989		4	S
8 yrs.	103 games		

William Bell
BELL, WILLIAM
B. Jul. 22, 1971, Miami, OH
Georgia Tech 5'11" 203 lbs.

Year	Team	Games	Pos.
1994	WAS	N 8	RB
1995		16	RB
1996		16	RB
3 yrs.	40 games		

Jay Bellamy
BELLAMY, JOHN LEE
B. Jul. 8, 1972, Perth Amboy, NJ
Rutgers 5'11" 177 lbs.

Year	Team	Games	Pos.
1994	SEA	N 3	S
1995		14	S
1996		16	S
3 yrs.	33 games		

Mike Bellamy
BELLAMY, MICHAEL SINCLAIR
B. Jun. 28, 1966, New York, NY
Illinois 6'0" 195 lbs.

Year	Team	Games	Pos.
1990	PHI	N 6	WR

Vic Bellamy
BELLAMY, VICTOR
B. Jun. 2, 1963, Philadelphia, PA
Syracuse 6'1" 195 lbs.

Year	Team	Games	Pos.
1987	PHI	N 3	CB

Bob Bellinger
BELLINGER, ROBERT
B. Jan. 20, 1913, Spokane, WA
Deceased
Gonzaga 5'11" 216 lbs.

Year	Team	Games	Pos.
1934	NYG	N 10	G
1935		9	G
2 yrs.	19 games		

Rodney Bellinger
BELLINGER, RODNEY CARWELL
B. Jun. 4, 1962, Miami, FL
Miami (Florida) 5'8" 188 lbs.

Year	Team	Games	Pos.
1984	BUF	N 10	CB
1985		16	CB
1986		16	CB
3 yrs.	42 games		

Mark Bellini
BELLINI, MARK JOSEPH
B. Jan. 19, 1964, San Leandro, CA

Year	Team	Games	Pos.

Mark Bellini continued

Brigham Young 5'11" 185 lbs.

Year	Team		Games	Pos.
1987	IND	N	10	WR
1988			15	WR

2 yrs. 25 games

Joe Bellino

BELLINO, JOSEPH MICHAEL
B. Mar. 13, 1938, Winchester, MA
Navy 5'9" 186 lbs.

Year	Team		Games	Pos.
1965	BOS	A	10	HB
1966			11	HB
1967			14	HB

3 yrs. 35 games

Beloit

BELOIT
None

Year	Team		Games	Pos.
1926	HAM	N	1	G

George Belotti

BELOTTI, D. GEORGE
B. 1935
Southern California 6'4" 253 lbs.

Year	Team		Games	Pos.
1960	HOU	A		C
1961			2	C
1961	SD	A	2	C

2 yrs. 4 games

Caesar Belser

BELSER, CAESAR EDWARD
B. Sep. 13, 1944, Montgomery, AL
Arkansas, Pine Bluff 6'0" 211 lbs.

Year	Team		Games	Pos.
1968	KC	A	14	DB
1969			14	S
1970	KC	N	14	S
1971			14	S
1974	SF	N	3	DB

5 yrs. 59 games

Jason Belser

BELSER, JASON
B. May 28, 1970, Kansas City, MO
Oklahoma 5'9" 187 lbs.

Year	Team		Games	Pos.
1992	IND	N	16	CB, S
1993			16	CB, S
1994			13	S
1995			16	S
1996			16	S

5 yrs. 77 games

Horace Belton

BELTON, HORACE
B. Jul. 16, 1955, Baton Rouge, LA
Southeastern Louisiana 5'8" 200 lbs.

Year	Team		Games	Pos.
1978	KC	N	16	RB
1979			16	RB
1980			14	RB

3 yrs. 46 games

Willie Belton

BELTON, WILLIE DAVIS
B. Dec. 12, 1948, Greenville, SC
Maryland-Eastern Shore 5'11" 198 lbs.

Year	Team		Games	Pos.
1971	ATL	N	14	RB
1972			14	RB
1973	STL	N	3	RB
1974			5	RB

4 yrs. 36 games

Brian Belway

BELWAY, BRIAN
B. May 28, 1963, Ottawa, Ont.
Calgary 6'6" 265 lbs.

Year	Team		Games	Pos.
1987	LARI	N	1	DE

Al Bemiller

BEMILLER, ALBERT DELANE
(Tombstone)
B. Apr. 18, 1939, Hanover, PA
Syracuse 6'3" 243 lbs.

Year	Team		Games	Pos.
1961	BUF	A	14	C
1962			14	C
1963			14	C
1964			14	C
1965			14	G
1966			14	G
1967			13	C, G
1968			14	C
1969			14	C

9 yrs. 125 games

Carey Bender

BENDER, CAREY WAYNE
B. Jan. 28, 1972, Marion, IA
Coe 5'8" 185 lbs.

Year	Team		Games	Pos.
1996	BUF	N	1	RB

Wes Bender

BENDER, WES
B. Aug. 2, 1970, Van Nuys, CA
Southern California 5'10" 235 lbs.

Year	Team		Games	Pos.
1994	LARI	N	9	RB

Jesse Bendross

BENDROSS, JESSE JAMES
B. Jul. 19, 1962, Hollywood, FL
Alabama 6'0" 196 lbs.

Year	Team		Games	Pos.
1984	SD	N	16	WR
1985			16	WR
1987	PHI	N	3	WR

3 yrs. 35 games

Daved Benefield

BENEFIELD, DAVED
B. Feb. 16, 1968, Los Angeles, CA
Northridge State 6'4" 231 lbs.

Year	Team		Games	Pos.
1996	SF	N	14	LB

Lou Benfatti

BENFATTI, LEWIS VINCENT
B. Mar. 9, 1971, Green Pond, NJ
Penn State 6'2" 278 lbs.

Year	Team		Games	Pos.
1994	NYJ	N	7	DT
1995			12	DT

2 yrs. 19 games

Brant Bengen

BENGEN, BRANT
B. Mar. 30, 1964
British Columbia/Idaho 5'8" 172 lbs.

Year	Team		Games	Pos.
1987	SEA	N	3	WR

Rolf Benirschke

BENIRSCHKE, ROLF JOACHIM
B. Feb. 7, 1955, Boston, MA
California-Davis 6'0" 171 lbs.

Year	Team		Games	Pos.
1977	SD	N	14	K
1978			15	K
1979			4	K
1980			16	K
1981			16	K
1982			9	K
1983			16	K
1984			14	K
1985			1	K
1986			16	K

10 yrs. 121 games

Dan Benish

BENISH, DAN
B. Nov. 21, 1961, Youngstown, OH

Dan Benish continued

Clemson 6'5" 280 lbs.

Year	Team		Games	Pos.
1983	ATL	N	16	DE
1984			15	DT
1985			16	DT
1986			5	DT
1987	WAS	N	3	DT

5 yrs. 55 games

Bill Benjamin

BENJAMIN, WILLIAM JOSEPH
B. Sep. 14, 1958, Indianapolis, IN
San Jose State 6'3" 226 lbs.

Year	Team		Games	Pos.
1987	NO	N		LB

Guy Benjamin

BENJAMIN, GUY EMORY
B. Jun. 27, 1955, Hollywood, CA
Stanford 6'4" 210 lbs.

Year	Team		Games	Pos.
1978	MIA	N	3	QB
1979			4	QB
1980	NO	N	2	QB
1981	SF	N	4	QB
1982			2	QB
1983			4	QB

6 yrs. 19 games

Ryan Benjamin

BENJAMIN, RYAN LAMONT
B. Apr. 23, 1970, Pixley, CA
Pacific 5'7" 183 lbs.

Year	Team		Games	Pos.
1993	CIN	N	1	RB

Tony Benjamin

BENJAMIN, TONY
B. Oct. 27, 1955, Monessen, PA
Duke 6'3" 225 lbs.

Year	Team		Games	Pos.
1977	SEA	N	6	RB
1978			6	RB
1979			16	FB

3 yrs. 28 games

Heinie Benkert

BENKERT, HENRY W.
B. Jun. 30, 1901, Newark, NJ
D. Jul. 15, 1972, Orange, NJ
Rutgers 5'9" 169 lbs.

Year	Team		Games	Pos.
1925	NYG	N	11	HB
1926	POT	N	5	HB
1929	ORA	N	8	HB, FB, QB
1930	NEW	N	4	HB, FB

4 yrs. 28 games

Fred Benners

BENNERS, FREDERICK H.
B. 1930
Sewanee/Southern Methodist 6'3" 196 lbs.

Year	Team		Games	Pos.
1952	NYG	N	6	QB

Bennett

BENNETT
None

Year	Team		Games	Pos.
1936	CHIB	N	1	B

Antoine Bennett

BENNETT, ANTOINE
B. Nov. 29, 1967, Miami, FL
Florida A&M 5'11" 185 lbs.

Year	Team		Games	Pos.
1991	CIN	N	3	CB
1992			11	CB, S

2 yrs. 14 games

Barry Bennett

BENNETT, BARRY

Barry Bennett continued

B. Dec. 10, 1955, St. Paul, MN
Concordia (Minnesota) 6'4" 260 lbs.

Year	Team		Games	Pos.
1978	NO	N	16	DE
1979			16	DT
1980			15	DT
1981			3	NT
1982	NYJ	N	7	DT, DE
1983			13	DT, DE
1984			15	DT, DE
1985			16	DT
1986			16	DE, DT
1987			13	DE
1988	MIN	N	1	DE

11 yrs. 132 games

Ben Bennett

BENNETT, BEN
B. May 5, 1962, Greensboro, NC
Duke 6'1" 200 lbs.

Year	Team		Games	Pos.
1987	CIN	N	1	QB

Charles Bennett

BENNETT, CHARLES A.
B. Feb. 9, 1963, Alligator, MS
Southwestern Louisiana 6'5" 257 lbs.

Year	Team		Games	Pos.
1987	MIA	N	3	DE

Chuck Bennett

BENNETT, CHARLES H.
B. Aug. 9, 1907
D. Jun. 9, 1973, Countryside, IL
Indiana 5'9" 193 lbs.

Year	Team		Games	Pos.
1930	POR	N	14	HB, QB, FB
1933	CHIC	N	2	B

2 yrs. 16 games

Cornelius Bennett

BENNETT, CORNELIUS O'LANDA (Biscuit)
B. Aug. 25, 1966, Birmingham, AL
Alabama 6'2" 235 lbs.

Year	Team		Games	Pos.
1987	BUF	N	8	LB
1988			16	LB
1989			12	LB
1990			16	LB
1991			16	LB
1992			15	LB
1993			16	LB
1994			16	LB
1995			14	LB
1996	ATL	N	13	LB

10 yrs. 142 games

Darren Bennett

BENNETT, DARREN
B. Jan. 9, 1965, Sydney, Australia
none 6'5" 235 lbs.

Year	Team		Games	Pos.
1995	SD	N	16	P
1996			16	P

2 yrs. 32 games

Donnell Bennett

BENNETT, DONNELL
B. Sep. 14, 1972, Fort Lauderdale, FL
Miami (Florida) 5'11" 241 lbs.

Year	Team		Games	Pos.
1994	KC	N	15	RB
1995			3	RB
1996			16	RB

3 yrs. 34 games

Earl Bennett

BENNETT, EARL C., JR.
B. Feb. 27, 1920
Hardin-Simmons 5'8" 188 lbs.

Year	Team		Games	Pos.
1946	GB	N	3	G

Year	Team		Games	Pos.

Edgar Bennett
BENNETT, EDGAR
B. Feb. 15, 1969, Jacksonville, FL
Florida State 6'0" 223 lbs.

Year	Team		Games	Pos.
1992	**GB**	N	16	RB
1993			16	RB
1994			16	RB
1995			16	RB
1996			16	RB
5 yrs.	80 games			

Lewis Bennett
BENNETT, LEWIS
B. Aug. 4, 1963, Jacksonville, FL
Florida A&M 5'11" 175 lbs.

Year	Team		Games	Pos.
1987	**NYG**	N	3	WR

Monte Bennett
BENNETT, MONTE LEWIS
B. Apr. 27, 1959, Sterling, KS
Kansas State 6'5" 270 lbs.

Year	Team		Games	Pos.
1981	**NO**	N	16	DT
1987	**SD**	N	3	DE
2 yrs.	19 games			

Phil Bennett
BENNETT, PHIL
B. 1935
Miami (Florida) 6'3" 225 lbs.

Year	Team		Games	Pos.
1960	**BOS**	A		LB

Roy Bennett
BENNETT, ROY
B. Jul. 5, 1961, Birmingham, AL
Jackson State 6'2" 195 lbs.

Year	Team		Games	Pos.
1988	**SD**	N	16	CB, S
1989			16	CB
2 yrs.	32 games			

Sid Bennett
BENNETT, SYDNEY C.
B. Feb. 2, 1895
D. Dec, 1971, Elgin, IL
Northwestern 5'9" 194 lbs.

Year	Team		Games	Pos.
1920	**CHIT**	A	6	T
1922	**MIL**	N	1	G
2 yrs.	7 games			

Tommy Bennett
BENNETT, TOMMY
B. Feb. 19, 1973, Las Vegas, NV
UCLA 6'1" 204 lbs.

Year	Team		Games	Pos.
1996	**ARI**	N	16	S

Tony Bennett
BENNETT, TONY LYDELL
B. Jul. 1, 1967, Alligator, MS
Mississippi 6'2" 240 lbs.

Year	Team		Games	Pos.
1990	**GB**	N	14	LB
1991			16	LB
1992			16	LB
1993			10	LB
1994	**IND**	N	16	DE
1995			16	DE
1996			14	LB
7 yrs.	102 games			

Woody Bennett
BENNETT, WOODROW, JR.
B. Mar. 24, 1955, York, PA
Miami (Florida) 6'2" 220 lbs.

Year	Team		Games	Pos.
1979	**NYJ**	N	15	RB
1980			10	RB
1980	**MIA**	N	4	FB
1981			3	FB
1982			1	FB

Woody Bennett *continued*

Year	Team		Games	Pos.
1983			16	FB
1984			16	FB
1985			16	FB
1986			16	FB
1987			12	FB
1988			16	FB
10 yrs.	125 games			

Brad Benson
BENSON, BRADLEY WILLIAM
B. Nov. 25, 1955, Altoona, PA
Penn State 6'3" 270 lbs.

Year	Team		Games	Pos.
1978	**NYG**	N	16	C
1979			10	C
1980			15	OT
1981			11	OT
1982			9	OT
1983			16	OT
1984			16	OT
1985			16	OT
1986			16	OT
1987			12	OT
10 yrs.	137 games			

Charles Benson
BENSON, CHARLES HENRY
B. Nov. 21, 1960, Houston, TX
Baylor 6'3" 267 lbs.

Year	Team		Games	Pos.
1983	**MIA**	N	8	DE
1984			16	DE
1985	**IND**	N	1	DE
1987	**DET**	N	3	DE
4 yrs.	28 games			

Cliff Benson
BENSON, CLIFFORD ANTHONY
B. Aug. 28, 1961, Chicago, IL
Purdue 6'4" 234 lbs.

Year	Team		Games	Pos.
1984	**ATL**	N	16	TE
1985			16	TE
1987	**WAS**	N	2	TE
1987	**NO**	N	8	TE
1988			7	TE
4 yrs.	49 games			

Darren Benson
BENSON, DARREN
B. Aug. 25, 1974, Memphis, TN
Trinity Valley CC 6'7" 305 lbs.

Year	Team		Games	Pos.
1995	**DAL**	N	6	DT

Duane Benson
BENSON, DUANE DEAN
B. Aug. 5, 1945, Belmond, IA
Hamline 6'2" 217 lbs.

Year	Team		Games	Pos.
1967	**OAK**	A	8	LB
1968			12	LB
1969			14	LB
1970	**OAK**	N	14	LB
1971			14	LB
1972	**ATL**	N	14	LB
1973			14	LB
1974	**HOU**	N	13	LB
1975			4	LB
1976			14	LB
10 yrs.	121 games			

George Benson
BENSON, GEORGE NATHAN
B. May 7, 1919, Madison, IN
Northwestern 6'1" 205 lbs.

Year	Team		Games	Pos.
1947	**BKN**	AA	1	B

Harry Benson
BENSON, HARRY
B. 1910, Baltimore, MD

Harry Benson *continued*
Western Maryland 5'10" 218 lbs.

Year	Team		Games	Pos.
1935	**PHI**	N	7	G

Mitchell Benson
BENSON, MITCHELL OSWELL
B. May 30, 1967, Fort Worth, TX
Texas Christian 6'4" 302 lbs.

Year	Team		Games	Pos.
1989	**IND**	N	16	DT
1990			11	NT
1991	**SD**	N	16	DT
3 yrs.	43 games			

Tom Benson
BENSON, THOMAS CARL
B. Sep. 6, 1961, Ardmore, OK
Oklahoma 6'2" 235 lbs.

Year	Team		Games	Pos.
1984	**ATL**	N	16	LB
1985			16	LB
1986	**SD**	N	16	LB
1987			11	LB
1988	**NE**	N	12	LB
1989	**LARI**	N	16	LB
1990			16	LB
1991			16	LB
1992			1	LB
9 yrs.	120 games			

Troy Benson
BENSON, TROY B.
B. Jul. 30, 1963, Altoona, PA
Pittsburgh 6'2" 235 lbs.

Year	Team		Games	Pos.
1986	**NYJ**	N	15	LB
1987			11	LB
1988			16	LB
1989			16	LB
4 yrs.	58 games			

Albert Bentley
BENTLEY, ALBERT TIMOTHY
B. Aug. 15, 1960, Naples, FL
Miami (Florida) 5'11" 200 lbs.

Year	Team		Games	Pos.
1985	**IND**	N	15	RB
1986			12	RB
1987			12	RB
1988			16	RB
1989			16	RB
1990			16	RB
1991			1	RB
1992	**PIT**	N	2	RB
8 yrs.	90 games			

Ray Bentley
BENTLEY, RAY RUSSELL
B. Nov. 25, 1960, Grand Rapids, MI
Central Michigan 6'2" 250 lbs.

Year	Team		Games	Pos.
1986	**BUF**	N	13	LB
1987			9	LB
1988			16	LB
1989			15	LB
1990			16	LB
1991			16	LB
1992	**CIN**	N	2	LB
7 yrs.	87 games			

Jim Benton
BENTON, JAMES W. (Big Jim)
B. Sep. 25, 1916, Carthage, AR
Arkansas 6'3" 200 lbs.

Year	Team		Games	Pos.
1938	**CLE**	N	11	E
1939			11	E
1940			10	E
1942			9	E
1943	**CHIB**	N	9	E
1944	**CLE**	N	10	E
1945			9	E
1946	**LA**	N	11	E

Jim Benton *continued*

Year	Team		Games	Pos.
1947			11	E
9 yrs.	91 games			

Benton
BENTON
None

Year	Team		Games	Pos.
1922	**ROC**	N	1	E

Chris Bentz
BENTZ, CHRISTIAN
B. Dec. 20, 1891
D. Jan, 1981, Spokane, WA
Montana 6'1" 215 lbs.

Year	Team		Games	Pos.
1920	**DET**	A	1	T

Roman Bentz
BENTZ, ROMAN WALTER
B. Sep. 1, 1919, Iron Ridge, WI
Deceased
Tulane 6'2" 230 lbs.

Year	Team		Games	Pos.
1946	**NY**	AA	12	T
1947			13	G
1948			5	G
1948	**SF**	AA	4	G
3 yrs.	34 games			

Al Bentzin
BENTZIN, ALFRED (Mike)
B. Mar. 7, 1902
D. Jan. 1, 1979, Watertown, WI
Marquette 6'0" 188 lbs.

Year	Team		Games	Pos.
1924	**RAC**	N	9	G

George Benyola
BENYOLA, GEORGE
B. Sep. 17, 1964
Louisiana Tech 5'10" 195 lbs.

Year	Team		Games	Pos.
1987	**NYG**	N	3	K

Larry Benz
BENZ, LARRY W.
B. Jan. 28, 1941, Chattanooga, TN
Northwestern 5'11" 185 lbs.

Year	Team		Games	Pos.
1963	**CLE**	N	14	S
1964			13	DB
1965			14	DB
3 yrs.	41 games			

Bob Bercich
BERCICH, ROBERT E.
B. Nov. 9, 1936
Michigan State 6'1" 198 lbs.

Year	Team		Games	Pos.
1960	**DAL**	N	12	DB
1961			6	S
2 yrs.	18 games			

Pete Bercich
BERCICH, PETER JAMES
B. Dec. 23, 1971, Joliet, IL
Notre Dame 6'1" 240 lbs.

Year	Team		Games	Pos.
1995	**MIN**	N	9	LB
1996			15	LB
2 yrs.	24 games			

Paul Berezney
BEREZNEY, PAUL LAWRENCE
B. Apr. 25, 1916, Jersey City, NJ
D. 1991, Columbus, GA
Fordham 6'2" 221 lbs.

Year	Team		Games	Pos.
1942	**GB**	N	11	T
1943			10	T
1944			10	T
1946	**MIA**	AA	1	T
4 yrs.	32 games			

Year	Team		Games	Pos.

Pete Berezney
BEREZNEY, PETER JOHN, JR.
B. Nov. 14, 1923, Jersey City, NJ
Notre Dame 6'2" 240 lbs.

Year	Team		Games	Pos.
1947	**LA**	**AA**	12	T
1948	**BAL**	**AA**	13	T
2 yrs.	25 games			

Bergen
BERGEN
None

Year	Team		Games	Pos.
1926	**MIL**	**N**	5	HB, QB

Mitch Berger
BERGER, MITCH
B. Jun. 24, 1972, Kamloops, B.C.
Colorado 6'2" 231 lbs.

Year	Team		Games	Pos.
1994	**PHI**	**N**	5	P
1996	**MIN**	**N**	16	P
2 yrs.	21 games			

Ron Berger
BERGER, RONALD
B. Sep. 30, 1943, Detroit, MI
Wayne State (Michigan) 6'8" 278 lbs.

Year	Team		Games	Pos.
1969	**BOS**	**A**	7	DE
1970	**BOS**	**N**	14	DE
1971	**NE**	**N**	14	DE, DT
1972			8	DE
4 yrs.	43 games			

Gil Bergerson
BERGERSON, GILBERT C.
B. Jul. 19, 1910
Deceased
Oregon State 6'6" 245 lbs.

Year	Team		Games	Pos.
1932	**CHIB**	**N**	12	G
1933			2	G
1933	**CHIC**	**N**	8	G
1935	**BKN**	**N**	12	G, T
1936			5	G
4 yrs.	39 games			

Eric Bergeson
BERGESON, ERIC SCOTT
B. Jan. 1, 1966, Salt Lake City, UT
Brigham Young 5'11" 192 lbs.

Year	Team		Games	Pos.
1990	**ATL**	**N**	13	CB

Bill Bergey
BERGEY, WILLIAM EARL
B. Feb. 9, 1945, Lyons, NY
Arkansas State 6'2" 245 lbs.

Year	Team		Games	Pos.
1969	**CIN**	**A**	14	LB
1970	**CIN**	**N**	14	LB
1971			14	LB
1972			12	LB
1973			14	LB
1974	**PHI**	**N**	14	LB
1975			14	LB
1976			14	LB
1977			14	LB
1978			16	LB
1979			3	LB
1980			16	LB
12 yrs.	159 games			

Bruce Bergey
BERGEY, BRUCE
B. Aug. 8, 1946, South Dayton, NY
UCLA 6'4" 240 lbs.

Year	Team		Games	Pos.
1971	**KC**	**N**	6	DE

Scott Bergold
BERGOLD, SCOTT M.
B. Nov. 19, 1961, Milwaukee, WI

Scott Bergold continued
Wisconsin 6'7" 263 lbs.

Year	Team		Games	Pos.
1985	**STL**	**N**	16	OT

Chuck Bernard
BERNARD, JOSEPH CHARLES
B. Aug. 29, 1911
D. Mar, 1962
Michigan 6'3" 225 lbs.

Year	Team		Games	Pos.
1934	**DET**	**N**	10	C

Dave Bernard
BERNARD, DAVID (King)
B. Sep. 26, 1912, Jefferson, SD
D. Jul. 17, 1973, Montgomery, AL
Mississippi 5'10" 194 lbs.

Year	Team		Games	Pos.
1944	**CLE**	**N**	6	B
1945			7	FB
2 yrs.	13 games			

George Bernard
BERNARD, GEORGE
None

Year	Team		Games	Pos.
1926	**RAC**	**N**	4	G, T

Karl Bernard
BERNARD, GREGORY KARL
B. Oct. 12, 1964, New Orleans, LA
Louisiana State/Southwestern Louisiana 5'11" 205 lbs.

Year	Team		Games	Pos.
1987	**DET**	**N**	8	RB

Frank Bernardi
BERNARDI, FRANK V.
B. Jun. 17, 1933, Highland Park, IL
Colorado 5'9" 181 lbs.

Year	Team		Games	Pos.
1955	**CHIC**	**N**	11	HB, DB
1956			12	HB, DB
1957			12	HB, DB
1960	**DEN**	**A**		DB
4 yrs.	35 games			

Mil Berner
BERNER, MILFORD C.
B. 1906
Syracuse 6'2" 204 lbs.

Year	Team		Games	Pos.
1933	**CIN**	**N**	1	C

Ed Bernet
BERNET, EDWARD NELSON
B. Oct. 24, 1933, Dallas, TX
Southern Methodist 6'2" 203 lbs.

Year	Team		Games	Pos.
1955	**PIT**	**N**	12	E
1960	**DAL**	**A**		OE
2 yrs.	12 games			

Lee Bernet
BERNET, LEE ANTHONY
B. Jan. 24, 1944, Chicago, IL
Wisconsin 6'2" 245 lbs.

Year	Team		Games	Pos.
1965	**DEN**	**A**	14	OT
1966			14	OT
2 yrs.	28 games			

George Bernhardt
BERNHARDT GEORGE W.
B. Jun. 15, 1920
D. Dec, 1987
Illinois 5'10" 213 lbs.

Year	Team		Games	Pos.
1946	**BKN**	**AA**	14	G
1947			2	G
1948			3	G
1948	**CHI**	**AA**	11	G
3 yrs.	30 games			

Roger Bernhardt
BERNHARDT, ROGER ERNEST
B. Oct. 14, 1949, Lyons, NY
Kansas 6'4" 244 lbs.

Year	Team		Games	Pos.
1974	**NYJ**	**N**	14	G
1975	**KC**	**N**	4	G
2 yrs.	18 games			

Ken Bernich
BERNICH, KENNETH
B. Sep. 6, 1951, Biloxi, MS
Auburn 6'2" 250 lbs.

Year	Team		Games	Pos.
1975	**NYJ**	**N**	5	LB

Dan Bernoske
BERNOSKE, DANIEL G.
B. Jul. 20, 1905
D. Jul, 1979, Indianapolis, IN
Indiana 5'10" 190 lbs.

Year	Team		Games	Pos.
1926	**LOU**	**N**	2	G

Bobby Berns
BERNS, ROBERT F.
B. Dec. 10, 1895
D. Apr. 30, 1974
Purdue 6'1" 200 lbs.

Year	Team		Games	Pos.
1920	**MUN**	**A**	1	T
1922	**DAY**	**N**	6	G
1923			8	G
1924			2	G
4 yrs.	17 games			

Rick Berns
BERNS, RICHARD R.
B. Feb. 5, 1956, Okinawa, Japan
Nebraska 6'2" 203 lbs.

Year	Team		Games	Pos.
1979	**TB**	**N**	16	RB
1980			16	RB
1982	**LARI**	**N**	9	RB
1983			16	RB
4 yrs.	57 games			

Rod Bernstine
BERNSTINE, ROD EARL
B. Feb. 8, 1965, Fairfield, CA
Texas A&M 6'3" 235 lbs.

Year	Team		Games	Pos.
1987	**SD**	**N**	10	TE
1988			14	TE
1989			5	TE
1990			12	TE, RB
1991			13	RB
1992			9	RB
1993	**DEN**	**N**	15	RB
1994			3	RB
1995			3	RB
9 yrs.	84 games			

Jay Berquist
BERQUIST, JAY
B. 1902
Deceased
Nebraska 6'3" 253 lbs.

Year	Team		Games	Pos.
1924	**KC**	**N**	9	G
1926			9	G
1927	**CHIC**	**N**	2	G
3 yrs.	20 games			

Tim Berra
BERRA, TIMOTHY T.
B. Sep. 23, 1951, Montclair, NJ
Massachusetts 5'11" 185 lbs.

Year	Team		Games	Pos.
1974	**BAL**	**N**	14	WR

Eddie Berrang
BERRANG, EDWARD
B. Oct. 14, 1924, New Philadelphia, PA

Eddie Berrang continued
Villanova 6'2" 205 lbs.

Year	Team		Games	Pos.
1949	**WAS**	**N**	11	E
1950			11	E
1951			2	E
1951	**DET**	**N**	10	E
1952	**WAS**	**N**	7	E
4 yrs.	41 games			

Bill Berrehsem
BERREHSEM, WILLIAM S.
B. Apr. 25, 1903
D. Nov. 6, 1968, Baldwin, PA
Washington & Jefferson 5'10" 195 lbs.

Year	Team		Games	Pos.
1926	**COL**	**N**	6	T

Bob Berry
BERRY, ROBERT CHADWICK
B. Mar. 10, 1942, San Jose, CA
Oregon 5'11" 189 lbs.

Year	Team		Games	Pos.
1965	**MIN**	**N**	2	QB
1966			3	QB
1967			2	QB
1968	**ATL**	**N**	10	QB
1969			7	QB
1970			12	QB
1971			11	QB
1972			14	QB
1973	**MIN**	**N**	6	QB
1974			9	QB
1975			1	QB
11 yrs.	77 games			

Charlie Berry
BERRY, CHARLES FRANCIS
B. Oct. 18, 1902, Phillipsburg, NJ
D. Sep. 6, 1972, Evanston, IL
Lafayette 6'0" 185 lbs.

Year	Team		Games	Pos.
1925	**POT**	**N**	10	E
1926			10	E
2 yrs.	20 games			

Connie Mack Berry
BERRY, CONNIE MACK
B. Apr. 19, 1915, Spartanburg, SC
D. Jun. 24, 1980, Fayetteville, NC
North Carolina State 6'3" 215 lbs.

Year	Team		Games	Pos.
1939	**DET**	**N**	3	E
1940	**CLE**	**N**	3	E
1942	**CHIB**	**N**	10	E
1943			10	E
1944			10	E
1945			7	E
1946			8	E
1947	**CHI**	**AA**	1	E
8 yrs.	52 games			

Ed Berry
BERRY, EDWARD, JR.
B. Sep. 28, 1963, San Francisco, CA
Utah State 5'10" 183 lbs.

Year	Team		Games	Pos.
1986	**GB**	**N**	16	CB, S
1987	**SD**	**N**	2	CB
2 yrs.	18 games			

George Berry
BERRY, GEORGE W.
B. Mar. 18, 1900, Milwaukee, WI
D. Feb. 25, 1986, Half Moon Bay, CA
None 5'11" 208 lbs.

Year	Team		Games	Pos.
1922	**RAC**	**N**	2	T
1922	**HAM**	**N**	4	T, G
1923			7	G
1924	**HAM**	**N**	5	G, T
1924	**AKR**	**N**	3	G, T
1925			5	G, T
1926			7	C, G
5 yrs.	33 games			

349

Year	Team	Games	Pos.

Gil Berry
BERRY, GILBERT IRWIN
B. Mar. 21, 1911, Lewistown, IL
D. Apr, 1974, Indianapolis, IN
Illinois 5'10" 178 lbs.

Year	Team	Games	Pos.
1935	**CHIC** N	5	HB

Howard Berry
BERRY, JOSEPH HOWARD, JR.
(Nig)
B. Dec. 31, 1894, Philadelphia, PA
D. Apr. 29, 1976, Philadelphia, PA
Muhlenberg/Pennsylvania 5'11" 165 lbs.

Year	Team	Games	Pos.
1921	**ROC** A	4	HB

Latin Berry
BERRY, LATIN DAFONSO
B. Jan. 13, 1967, Lakeview Terrace, CA
Oregon 5'10" 196 lbs.

Year	Team	Games	Pos.
1990	**LARM** N	16	CB
1991	**CLE** N	15	DB
1992		1	CB, S
3 yrs.	32 games		

Louis Berry
BERRY, LOUIS
B. Jul. 21, 1965
Florida State 6'0" 193 lbs.

Year	Team	Games	Pos.
1987	**ATL** N	2	P

Ray Berry
BERRY, RAYMOND LEON
B. Oct. 28, 1963, Lovington, NM
Baylor 6'2" 230 lbs.

Year	Team	Games	Pos.
1987	**MIN** N	11	LB
1988		15	LB
1989		16	LB
1990		16	LB
1991		16	LB
1992		8	LB
1993	**SEA** N	7	LB
7 yrs.	89 games		

Raymond Berry
BERRY, RAYMOND EMMETT
B. Feb. 27, 1933, Corpus Christi, TX
Southern Methodist 6'2" 189 lbs.

Year	Team	Games	Pos.
1955	**BAL** N	12	E
1956		12	E
1957		12	E
1958		12	E
1959		12	E
1960		12	E
1961		12	OE
1962		14	OE
1963		9	OE
1964		12	OE
1965		14	OE
1966		14	OE
1967		7	OE
13 yrs.	154 games		

Reggie Berry
BERRY, REGINALD DENNIS
B. Mar. 13, 1950, Minneapolis, MN
Long Beach State 6'0" 188 lbs.

Year	Team	Games	Pos.
1972	**SD** N	9	S
1973		8	S
1974		13	S
3 yrs.	30 games		

Rex Berry
BERRY, CHARLES REX
B. Feb. 9, 1924, Moab, UT
Brigham Young 5'11" 181 lbs.

Year	Team	Games	Pos.
1951	**SF** N	10	HB, DB
1952		12	HB, DB

Rex Berry continued

Year	Team	Games	Pos.
1953		12	DB
1954		8	DB
1955		12	DB
1956		12	DB
6 yrs.	66 games		

Royce Berry
BERRY, ROYCE E.
B. Apr. 19, 1946, Odessa, TX
Houston 6'3" 247 lbs.

Year	Team	Games	Pos.
1969	**CIN** A	13	DE
1970	**CIN**	14	DE
1971		14	DE
1972		14	DE
1973		13	DE
1974		14	DE
1976	**CHI** N	12	DE
7 yrs.	94 games		

Wayne Berry
BERRY, WAYNE L.
B. Aug. 2, 1932
Washington State 6'0" 175 lbs.

Year	Team	Games	Pos.
1954	**NYG** N	10	HB

Marv Berschet
BERSCHET, MARVIN (Moose)
B. Dec. 28, 1929, Arlington Heights, IL
Illinois 6'2" 220 lbs.

Year	Team	Games	Pos.
1954	**WAS** N	12	G, DE
1955		4	G, DE
2 yrs.	16 games		

Libero Bertagnolli
BERTAGNOLLI, LIBERO LORENZ
B. Nov. 13, 1914, Benld, IL
D. Sep. 14, 1992, Bloomington, IL
Washington (Missouri) 5'9" 189 lbs.

Year	Team	Games	Pos.
1942	**CHIC** N	10	G

Angelo Bertelli
BERTELLI, ANGELO BORTOLO
(The Springfield Rifle)
B. Jun. 18, 1921, Springfield, MA
Notre Dame 6'1" 190 lbs.

Year	Team	Games	Pos.
1946	**LA** AA	12	QB
1947	**CHI** AA	1	QB
1948		3	QB
3 yrs.	16 games		

Jim Bertelsen
BERTELSEN, JAMES ALLEN
B. Feb. 26, 1950, St. Paul, MN
Texas 5'11" 205 lbs.

Year	Team	Games	Pos.
1972	**LA** N	14	RB
1973		14	RB
1974		13	RB
1975		13	RB
1976		14	RB
5 yrs.	68 games		

Bill Berthusen
BERTHUSEN, BILL
B. Jun. 26, 1964, Grinnell, IA
Iowa State 6'5" 290 lbs.

Year	Team	Games	Pos.
1987	**CIN** N	3	NT
1987	**NYG** N	1	NTB
1 yr.	4 games		

Tony Berti
BERTI, CHARLES ANTON, JR.
B. Jun. 21, 1972, Rock Springs, WY

Tony Berti continued
Colorado 6'5" 287 lbs.

Year	Team	Games	Pos.
1995	**SD** N	1	OT
1996		16	OT
2 yrs.	17 games		

Jim Bertoglio
BERTOGLIO, JAMES E.
B. Sep. 1, 1905
D. Jan, 1976, Butte, MT
Creighton 5'9" 187 lbs.

Year	Team	Games	Pos.
1926	**COL** N	7	FB

Tony Bertuca
BERTUCA, ANTHONY FRANCIS
B. Jan. 4, 1950, Chicago, IL
Chico State 6'2" 225 lbs.

Year	Team	Games	Pos.
1974	**BAL** N	14	LB

Ed Berwick
BERWICK, EDWIN J.
B. Dec. 27, 1904
D. Mar, 1977, High Island, TX
Loyola (Illinois) 6'0" 185 lbs.

Year	Team	Games	Pos.
1926	**LOU** N	4	C, E

Willie Berzinski
BERZINSKI, WILLIAM
B. Jul. 18, 1934
D. Aug, 1994
Wisconsin-La Crosse 6'2" 195 lbs.

Year	Team	Games	Pos.
1956	**PHI** N	4	HB

Warren Beson
BESON, WARREN
B. Nov. 16, 1923, Minneapolis, MN
Minnesota 6'0" 205 lbs.

Year	Team	Games	Pos.
1949	**BAL** AA	3	C

Gerald Bess
BESS, GERALD
B. Apr. 24, 1959, Pensacola, FL
Tuskegee Institute 6'0" 188 lbs.

Year	Team	Games	Pos.
1987	**BUF** N	2	CB

Rufus Bess
BESS, RUFUS T., JR.
B. Sep. 13, 1956, Hartsville, SC
South Carolina State 5'9" 189 lbs.

Year	Team	Games	Pos.
1979	**OAK** N	16	CB
1980	**BUF** N	16	CB
1981		16	CB
1982	**MIN** N	8	CB
1983		14	CB
1984		16	CB
1985		11	CB
1986		16	CB
1987		3	CB
9 yrs.	116 games		

Don Bessillieu
BESSILLIEU, DONALD ANDREW
B. May 4, 1956, Fort Benning, GA
Georgia Tech 6'1" 200 lbs.

Year	Team	Games	Pos.
1979	**MIA** N	16	S
1980		16	S
1981		16	S
1982	**STL** N	3	DB
1983	**LARI** N	4	S
1985		4	S
6 yrs.	59 games		

Art Best
BEST, ARTHUR
B. Mar. 18, 1953, Camden, NJ

Art Best continued
Notre Dame/Kent State 6'1" 205 lbs.

Year	Team	Games	Pos.
1977	**CHI** N	14	RB
1978		16	RB
1980	**NYG** N	1	RB
3 yrs.	31 games		

Greg Best
BEST, GREGORY LEE
B. Jan. 14, 1960, New Brighton, PA
Kansas State 5'10" 185 lbs.

Year	Team	Games	Pos.
1983	**PIT** N	13	S
1984	**CLE** N	5	S
2 yrs.	18 games		

Keith Best
BEST, KEITH A.
B. Aug. 21, 1950, Canton, OH
Kansas State 6'3" 220 lbs.

Year	Team	Games	Pos.
1972	**KC** N	6	LB

Teddy Besta
BESTA, CHARLES
B. Jul., 1896
Deceased
None

Year	Team	Games	Pos.
1922	**HAM** N	1	B
1924		2	HB
2 yrs.	3 games		

Elvin Bethea
BETHEA, ELVIN LAMONT
B. Mar. 1, 1946, Trenton, NJ
North Carolina A&T 6'3" 255 lbs.

Year	Team	Games	Pos.
1968	**HOU** A	14	DE
1969		14	DE
1970	**HOU** N	14	DE
1971		14	DE
1972		14	DE
1973		14	DE
1974		14	DE
1975		14	DE
1976		14	DE
1977		9	DE
1978		16	DE
1979		14	DE
1980		14	DE
1981		16	DE
1982		9	DE
1983		7	DE
16 yrs.	211 games		

Larry Bethea
BETHEA, LARRY
B. Jul. 21, 1956, Florence, SC
D. Apr. 23, 1987, Hampton, VA
Michigan State 6'5" 254 lbs.

Year	Team	Games	Pos.
1978	**DAL** N	16	DE
1979		16	DE
1980		11	DT
1981		16	DT
1982		8	DT
1983		14	DT
6 yrs.	81 games		

Bobby Bethune
BETHUNE, ROBERT
B. 1939
Mississippi State 5'11" 190 lbs.

Year	Team	Games	Pos.
1962	**SD** A	10	DB

George Bethune
BETHUNE, GEORGE EDWARD
B. Mar. 30, 1967, Fort Walton Beach, FL
Alabama 6'4" 240 lbs.

Year	Team	Games	Pos.
1989	**LARM** N	16	LB

George Bethune *continued*

Year	Team	Games	Pos.
1990		16	LB
2 yrs.	32 games		

Larry Bettencourt
BETTENCOURT, LAWRENCE JOSEPH
B. Sep. 22, 1905, Newark, CA
D. Sep. 15, 1978, New Orleans, LA
St. Mary's (California) 5'11" 205 lbs.

Year	Team	Games	Pos.
1933	GB N	2	C

Doug Betters
BETTERS, DOUGLAS LLOYD
B. Jun. 11, 1956, Lincoln, NE
Montana/Nevada-Reno 6'7" 260 lbs.

Year	Team	Games	Pos.
1978	MIA N	16	DE
1979		16	DE
1980		16	DE
1981		15	DE
1982		9	DE
1983		16	DE
1984		16	DE
1985		14	DE
1986		16	DE
1987		12	DE
10 yrs.	146 games		

James Betterson
BETTERSON, JAMES THOMAS
B. Aug. 20, 1954, Blackshear, GA
North Carolina 6'0" 210 lbs.

Year	Team	Games	Pos.
1977	PHI N	14	RB
1978		9	RB
2 yrs.	23 games		

Mike Bettiga
BETTIGA, MICHAEL
B. Sep. 19, 1950, Scotia, CA
Humboldt State 6'3" 193 lbs.

Year	Team	Games	Pos.
1974	SF N	10	WR

Jerome Bettis
BETTIS, JEROME ABRAM
(The Bus)
B. Feb. 16, 1972, Detroit, MI
Notre Dame 5'11" 243 lbs.

Year	Team	Games	Pos.
1993	LARM N	16	RB
1994		16	RB
1995	STL N	15	RB
1996	PIT N	16	RB
4 yrs.	63 games		

Tom Bettis
BETTIS, THOMAS W.
B. Mar. 17, 1933, Chicago, IL
Purdue 6'2" 228 lbs.

Year	Team	Games	Pos.
1955	GB N	12	LB
1956		12	LB
1957		12	LB
1958		12	LB
1959		12	LB
1960		12	LB
1961		12	LB
1962	PIT N	11	LB
1963	CHI N	14	LB
9 yrs.	109 games		

Ed Bettridge
BETTRIDGE, EDWARD
B. Sep. 16, 1940, Sandusky, OH
Bowling Green 6'1" 235 lbs.

Year	Team	Games	Pos.
1964	CLE N	3	LB

John Bettridge
BETTRIDGE, JOHN W.

John Bettridge *continued*
B. Mar. 19, 1910
D. Dec. 10, 1975, Sandusky, OH
Ohio State 5'10" 188 lbs.

Year	Team	Games	Pos.
1937	CHIB N	3	HB
1937	CLE N	6	HB, FB
1 yr.	9 games		

Steve Beuerlein
BEUERLEIN, STEPHEN TAYLOR
B. Mar. 7, 1965, Hollywood, CA
Notre Dame 6'2" 205 lbs.

Year	Team	Games	Pos.
1988	LARI N	10	QB
1989		10	QB
1991	DAL N	8	QB
1992		16	QB
1993	PHX N	16	QB
1994	ARI N	9	QB
1995	JAC N	7	QB
1996	CAR N	8	QB
8 yrs.	84 games		

Tom Beutler
BEUTLER, THOMAS JOSEPH
(Bullets)
B. Sep. 29, 1946, Bluffton, OH
Toledo 6'1" 232 lbs.

Year	Team	Games	Pos.
1970	CLE N	4	LB
1971	BAL N	4	LB
2 yrs.	8 games		

David Beverly
BEVERLY, DAVID EDWARD
B. Aug. 19, 1950, Selma, AL
Auburn 6'2" 180 lbs.

Year	Team	Games	Pos.
1974	HOU N	14	P
1975		2	P
1975	GB N	10	P
1976		14	P
1977		14	P
1978		16	P
1979		16	P
1980		16	P
7 yrs.	102 games		

Dwight Beverly
BEVERLY, DWIGHT
B. Dec. 5, 1961, Long Beach, CA
Illinois 5'11" 205 lbs.

Year	Team	Games	Pos.
1987	NO N	3	RB

Ed Beverly
BEVERLY, EDWARD LOUIS
B. Sep. 27, 1949, Harrisburg, PA
Arizona State 5'11" 168 lbs.

Year	Team	Games	Pos.
1973	SF N	2	WR

Randy Beverly
BEVERLY, RANDOLPH
B. Apr. 3, 1944, Wildwood, NJ
Colorado State 5'11" 189 lbs.

Year	Team	Games	Pos.
1967	NY A	14	DB
1968		13	DB
1969		13	CB
1970	BOS N	13	CB
1971	NE N	8	CB
5 yrs.	61 games		

George Beyers
BEYERS, GEORGE
None 168 lbs.

Year	Team	Games	Pos.
1921	WAS A	4	HB, QB, FB

Tim Biakabutuka
BIAKABUTUKA, TSHIMANGA

Tim Biakabutuka *continued*
B. Jan. 24, 1974, Zaire
Michigan 6'0" 210 lbs.

Year	Team	Games	Pos.
1996	CAR N	4	RB

Frank Bianchini
BIANCHINI, FRANK
B. May 27, 1961
Hofstra 5'8" 190 lbs.

Year	Team	Games	Pos.
1987	NE N	1	RB

Johnny Biancone
BIANCONE, JOHN L.
B. Dec. 5, 1911, Portland, OR
Oregon State 5'6" 165 lbs.

Year	Team	Games	Pos.
1936	BKN N	5	HB

Dean Biasucci
BIASUCCI, DEAN
B. Jul. 25, 1962, Niagara Falls, NY
Western Carolina 6'0" 198 lbs.

Year	Team	Games	Pos.
1984	IND N	15	K
1986		16	K
1987		12	K
1988		16	K
1989		16	K
1990		16	K
1991		16	K
1992		16	K
1993		16	K
1994		16	K
1995	STL N	8	K
11 yrs.	163 games		

Duane Bickett
BICKETT, DUANE CLAIR
B. Dec. 1, 1962, Los Angeles, CA
Southern California 6'5" 241 lbs.

Year	Team	Games	Pos.
1985	IND N	16	LB
1986		16	LB
1987		12	LB
1988		16	LB
1989		16	LB
1990		15	LB
1991		16	LB
1992		15	LB
1993		15	LB
1994	SEA N	7	LB
1995		13	LB
1996	CAR N	16	LB
12 yrs.	173 games		

Adolph Bieberstein
BIEBERSTEIN, ADOLPH JOSEPH
B. Dec. 17, 1902, Phillips, WI
D. Dec, 1981, Madison, WI
Wisconsin 5'10" 205 lbs.

Year	Team	Games	Pos.
1926	RAC N	5	G
1926	GB N	1	G
1 yr.	6 games		

Leo Biedermann
BIEDERMANN, LEO GEORGE
B. Oct. 19, 1955, Omaha, NE
California 6'7" 254 lbs.

Year	Team	Games	Pos.
1978	CLE N	16	OT

Greg Biekert
BIEKERT, GREG
B. Mar. 14, 1969, Iowa City, IA
Colorado 6'2" 235 lbs.

Year	Team	Games	Pos.
1993	LARI N	16	LB
1994		16	LB
1995	OAK N	16	LB
1996		16	LB
4 yrs.	64 games		

Dick Bielski
BIELSKI, RICHARD ADAM
B. Sep. 7, 1932, Baltimore, MD
Maryland 6'1" 224 lbs.

Year	Team	Games	Pos.
1955	PHI N	12	FB, K
1956		12	FB
1957		12	E, FB
1958		12	E
1959		12	E
1960	DAL N	12	OE
1961		14	OE, K
1962	BAL N	14	OE
1963		14	OE
9 yrs.	114 games		

Tom Bienemann
BIENEMANN, THOMAS JEROME
(Beans)
B. Jan. 18, 1928, Kenosha, WI
Drake 6'3" 221 lbs.

Year	Team	Games	Pos.
1951	CHIC N	12	E
1952		12	E
1953		12	E
1954		11	E
1955		10	E
1956		8	E
6 yrs.	65 games		

Eric Bieniemy
BIENIEMY, ERIC
B. Aug. 15, 1969, New Orleans, LA
Colorado 5'7" 210 lbs.

Year	Team	Games	Pos.
1991	SD N	15	RB
1992		15	RB
1993		16	RB
1994		16	RB
1995	CIN N	16	RB
1996		16	RB
6 yrs.	94 games		

Scotty Bierce
BIERCE, BRUCE W.
B. Sep. 3, 1896, Kearney, NE
D. Apr. 26, 1982, Medina, OH
Akron 5'9" 163 lbs.

Year	Team	Games	Pos.
1920	AKR A	8	E
1921		12	E
1922	AKR N	4	E
1923	CLE N	7	E
1923	BUF N	3	E
1924	CLE N	4	E
1925	AKR N	7	E, T
6 yrs.	45 games		

Big Bear
BIG BEAR
None 6'4" 215 lbs.

Year	Team	Games	Pos.
1922	OOR N	1	T
1923		5	T, E
2 yrs.	6 games		

Lyle Bigbee
BIGBEE, LYLE RANDOLPH (Al)
B. Aug. 22, 1893, Sweet Home, OR
D. Aug. 5, 1942, Portland, OR
Oregon 6'0" 200 lbs.

Year	Team	Games	Pos.
1922	MIL N	2	HB, E

Keiron Bigby
BIGBY, KEIRON
B. Feb. 27, 1966
Brown 5'10" 177 lbs.

Year	Team	Games	Pos.
1987	WAS N	1	WR

Riley Biggs
BIGGS, RILEY E.
B. Mar. 24, 1900

Year	Team	Games	Pos.

Riley Biggs continued

D. Nov, 1971, Ames, TX
Baylor 6'2" 230 lbs.

Year	Team		Games	Pos.
1926	RI	A	5	C, G
1926	NYG	N	3	C, G
1927			9	C, G
2 yrs.	17 games			

Verlon Biggs

BIGGS, VERLON MARION
B. Mar. 16, 1943, Moss Point, MS
D. Jun 7, 1994, Moss Point, MS
Jackson State 6'4" 267 lbs.

Year	Team		Games	Pos.
1965	NY	A	14	DE, DT
1966			14	DE, DT
1967			14	DE
1968			13	DE
1969			12	DE
1970	NYJ	N	13	DE
1971	WAS	N	13	DE
1972			14	DE
1973			14	DE
1974			14	DE
10 yrs.	135 games			

Jack Bighead

BIGHEAD, JOHN
B. Apr. 23, 1930
D. Apr. 28, 1993
Pepperdine 6'3" 215 lbs.

Year	Team		Games	Pos.
1954	BAL	N	11	E
1955	LA	N	2	E
2 yrs.	13 games			

Chief Big Twig

McCOMBS, NAT (Spiecha)
B. Dec. 18, 1904, Oklahoma
D. Jul, 1965
Haskell 5'11" 226 lbs.

Year	Team		Games	Pos.
1929	BUF	N	9	G, T

Jon Bilbo

BILBO, JONATHAN PAYNE
B. Oct. 17, 1914, Talisheek, LA
Mississippi 6'0" 195 lbs.

Year	Team		Games	Pos.
1938	CHIC	N	8	G
1939			1	G
2 yrs.	9 games			

Dick Bilda

BILDA, RICHARD F.
B. May 17, 1919, Milwaukee, WI
Marquette 6'0" 200 lbs.

Year	Team		Games	Pos.
1944	GB	N	2	B

Fred Biletnikoff

BILETNIKOFF, FREDERICK
B. Mar. 23, 1943, Erie, PA
Florida State 6'1" 190 lbs.

Year	Team		Games	Pos.
1965	OAK	A	14	FL
1966			10	FL
1967			14	FL
1968			14	OE
1969			14	WR
1970	OAK	N	14	WR
1971			14	WR
1972			14	WR
1973			14	WR
1974			14	WR
1975			11	WR
1976			13	WR
1977			14	WR
1978			16	WR
14 yrs.	190 games			

Ron Billingsley

BILLINGSLEY, RONALD SMITH

Ron Billingsley continued

B. Apr. 6, 1945, Florence, AL
Wyoming 6'8" 278 lbs.

Year	Team		Games	Pos.
1967	SD	A	13	DE
1968			14	DT
1969			9	DE
1970	SD	N	9	DE
1971	HOU	N	13	DT
1972			4	DT
6 yrs.	62 games			

John Billman

BILLMAN, JOHN A.
B. Dec. 1, 1919, Minneapolis, MN
Minnesota 6'1" 202 lbs.

Year	Team		Games	Pos.
1946	BKN	AA	3	G
1947	CHI	AA	2	G
2 yrs.	5 games			

Frank Billock

BILLOCK, FRANK
B. May 20, 1912
D. Oct, 1964
St. Mary's (Minnesota) 6'0" 230 lbs.

Year	Team		Games	Pos.
1937	PIT	N	2	G, T

Lewis Billups

BILLUPS, LEWIS KENNETH
B. Oct. 10, 1963, Tampa, FL
D. Apr. 9, 1994 Orlando, FL
North Alabama 5'11" 190 lbs.

Year	Team		Games	Pos.
1986	CIN	N	12	CB
1987			11	CB
1988			16	CB
1989			16	CB
1990			15	CB
1991			13	CB
1992	GB	N	5	CB
7 yrs.	88 games			

Les Bingaman

BINGAMAN, LESTER ALONZA
B. Feb. 3, 1926, McKenzie, TN
D. Nov. 20, 1970, Miami, FL
Illinois 6'3" 272 lbs.

Year	Team		Games	Pos.
1948	DET	N	12	G
1949			12	G
1950			12	G
1951			6	G
1952			12	G
1953			12	G
1954			12	G
7 yrs.	78 games			

Craig Bingham

BINGHAM, CRAIG MARLON
B. Sep. 29, 1959, Kingston, Jamaica
Syracuse 6'2" 220 lbs.

Year	Team		Games	Pos.
1982	PIT	N	7	LB
1983			12	LB
1984			11	LB
1985	SD	N	8	LB
1987	PIT	N	3	LB
5 yrs.	41 games			

Don Bingham

BINGHAM, DONALD DEAN
B. Nov. 7, 1929, Shattuck, OK
Sul Ross 6'0" 185 lbs.

Year	Team		Games	Pos.
1956	CHIB	N	12	HB

Dwight Bingham

BINGHAM, DWIGHT
B. Aug. 5, 1961, Kingston, Jamaica
Mississippi 6'6" 265 lbs.

Year	Team		Games	Pos.
1987	ATL	N	3	DE

Gregg Bingham

BINGHAM, GREGORY RALEIGH
B. Mar. 13, 1951, Evanston, IL
Purdue 6'1" 230 lbs.

Year	Team		Games	Pos.
1973	HOU	N	14	LB
1974			14	LB
1975			14	LB
1976			14	LB
1977			14	LB
1978			16	LB
1979			16	LB
1980			16	LB
1981			16	LB
1982			7	LB
1983			16	LB
1984			16	LB
12 yrs.	173 games			

Guy Bingham

BINGHAM, GUY RICHARD
B. Feb. 25, 1958, Koizuma Gumma
Ken, Japan
Montana 6'3" 260 lbs.

Year	Team		Games	Pos.
1980	NYJ	N	16	C
1981			16	C, OT, G
1982			7	C, G, OT
1983			16	C, G, OT
1984			16	C, G, OT
1985			16	C, G, OT
1986			16	OT, G, C
1987			12	C, G
1988			10	C, G
1989	ATL	N	16	C, G
1990			16	C, G
1991			13	C
1992	WAS	N	15	C
1993			14	C
14 yrs.	199 games			

Shep Bingham

BINGHAM, JOHN SHEPARD D.
B. Dec. 16, 1902
D. May, 1969, Cape Coral, FL
Yale 6'0" 180 lbs.

Year	Team		Games	Pos.
1926	BKN	A	4	E

Dave Binn

BINN, DAVID AARON
B. Feb. 6, 1972, San Mateo, CA
California 6'3" 234 lbs.

Year	Team		Games	Pos.
1994	SD	N	16	TE
1995			16	TE
1996			16	TE
3 yrs.	48 games			

John Binotto

BINOTTO, JOHN
B. Nov. 24, 1919, Lawrence, PA
Duquesne 5'10" 185 lbs.

Year	Team		Games	Pos.
1942	PIT	N	6	HB
1942	PHI	N	2	B
1 yr.	8 games			

Denny Biodrowski

BIODROWSKI, DENNIS
B. Jun. 27, 1940, Gary, IN
Memphis State 6'1" 255 lbs.

Year	Team		Games	Pos.
1963	KC	A	2	G
1964			1	G
1965			8	G
1966			14	G
1967			7	G
5 yrs.	32 games			

Rodger Bird

BIRD, RODGER PAUL
B. Jul. 2, 1943, Corbin, KY

Rodger Bird continued

Kentucky 5'11" 195 lbs.

Year	Team		Games	Pos.
1966	OAK	A	14	DB
1967			14	DB
1968			10	DB
3 yrs.	38 games			

Steve Bird

BIRD, STEVE L.
B. Oct. 20, 1960, Indianapolis, IN
Eastern Kentucky 5'11" 171 lbs.

Year	Team		Games	Pos.
1983	STL	N	14	WR
1984			8	WR
1984	SD	N	1	WR
2 yrs.	23 games			

J.J. Birden

BIRDEN, J.J.
B. Jun. 16, 1965, Portland, OR
Oregon 5'9" 160 lbs.

Year	Team		Games	Pos.
1990	KC	N	11	WR
1991			15	WR
1992			16	WR
1993			16	WR
1994			13	WR
1995	ATL	N	10	WR
1996			12	WR
7 yrs.	93 games			

Carl Birdsong

BIRDSONG, CARL
B. Jan. 1, 1959, Kaufman, TX
Southwestern Oklahoma State 6'0" 192 lbs.

Year	Team		Games	Pos.
1981	STL	N	16	P
1982			9	P
1983			16	P
1984			16	P
1985			16	P
5 yrs.	73 games			

Craig Birdsong

BIRDSONG, CRAIG
B. Aug. 16, 1964, Kaufman, TX
North Texas State 6'2" 217 lbs.

Year	Team		Games	Pos.
1987	HOU	N	8	S

Danny Birdwell

BIRDWELL, DANIEL LEE
B. Oct. 14, 1940, Big Spring, TX
Houston 6'4" 247 lbs.

Year	Team		Games	Pos.
1962	OAK	A	14	DE
1963			10	DE
1964			14	DT
1965			14	DT
1966			14	DT
1967			14	DT
1968			14	DT
1969			2	DT
8 yrs.	96 games			

Keith Birlem

BIRLEM, KEITH
B. May 4, 1915, San Jose, CA
D. May 7, 1943, England
San Jose State 5'11" 198 lbs.

Year	Team		Games	Pos.
1939	CHIC	N	6	E
1939	WAS	N	3	B
1 yr.	9 games			

Tom Birney

BIRNEY, THOMAS FRANCIS
B. Aug. 11, 1956, Bellshill, Scotland
Michigan State 6'4" 220 lbs.

Year	Team		Games	Pos.
1979	GB	N	6	K
1980			7	K
2 yrs.	13 games			

Joe Biscaha
BISCAHA, JOSEPH DANIEL
B. Jun. 1, 1937, Clifton, NJ
Richmond 6'1" 190 lbs.

Year	Team		Games	Pos.
1959	NYG	N	8	E
1960	BOS	A		OE
2 yrs.	8 games			

Bill Bishop
BISHOP, BILL E.
B. May 8, 1931, Borger, TX
North Texas State 6'4" 248 lbs.

Year	Team		Games	Pos.
1952	CHIB	N	12	DT
1953			12	DT
1954			12	DT
1955			12	DT
1956			12	DT
1957			11	DT
1958			12	DT
1959	CHI	N	12	DT
1960			12	DT
1961	MIN	N	10	DT
10 yrs.	117 games			

Blaine Bishop
BISHOP, BLAINE ELWOOD
B. Jul. 24, 1970, Indianapolis, IN
St. Joseph's (Indiana)/Ball State 5'8" 197 lbs.

Year	Team		Games	Pos.
1993	HOU	N	16	CB
1994			16	S, CB
1995			16	S
1996			15	S
4 yrs.	63 games			

Don Bishop
BISHOP, DONALD
B. Jul. 1, 1934, Los Angeles, CA
Los Angeles CC 6'2" 209 lbs.

Year	Team		Games	Pos.
1958	PIT	N	12	DB, FL
1959			2	DB
1959	CHIB	N	1	DB
1960	DAL	N	12	DB
1961			14	DB
1962			14	DB
1963			13	DB
1964			14	DB
1965			14	DB
8 yrs.	96 games			

Greg Bishop
BISHOP, GREGORY LAWRENCE
B. May 2, 1971, Stockton, CA
Pacific 6'5" 298 lbs.

Year	Team		Games	Pos.
1993	NYG	N	8	OT
1994			16	OT
1995			16	OT
1996			16	OT
4 yrs.	56 games			

Harold Bishop
BISHOP, HAROLD LUCIUS
B. Apr. 8, 1970, Tuscaloosa, AL
Louisiana State 6'4" 250 lbs.

Year	Team		Games	Pos.
1994	TB	N	7	TE
1995	CLE	N	13	TE
1996	BAL	N	8	TE
3 yrs.	28 games			

Keith Bishop
BISHOP, KEITH BRYAN
B. Mar. 10, 1957, San Diego, CA
Nebraska/Baylor 6'3" 265 lbs.

Year	Team		Games	Pos.
1980	DEN	N	16	C
1982			9	C, G
1983			16	C, G
1984			16	C, G
1985			14	G, C

Keith Bishop *continued*

Year	Team		Games	Pos.
1986			16	C, G
1987			12	C, G
1988			16	C, G
1989			14	C, G
9 yrs.	129 games			

Richard Bishop
BISHOP, RICHARD ALLEN
B. Mar. 23, 1950, Cleveland, OH
Louisville 6'1" 265 lbs.

Year	Team		Games	Pos.
1976	NE	N	14	DT
1977			12	NT
1978			16	NT
1979			14	NT, DE
1980			13	DE, NT
1981			16	NT, DE
1982	MIA	N	2	NT
1983	LARM	N	2	NT
8 yrs.	89 games			

Sonny Bishop
BISHOP, ERWIN WILFRED
B. Oct. 1, 1939, Winner, SD
Fresno State 6'2" 243 lbs.

Year	Team		Games	Pos.
1962	DAL	A	14	G
1963	OAK	A	14	G
1964	HOU	A	14	G
1965			14	G
1966			14	G
1967			12	G
1968			14	G
1969			14	G
8 yrs.	110 games			

Frank Bissell
BISSELL, FRANK
Fordham 6'1" 180 lbs.

Year	Team		Games	Pos.
1925	AKR	N	8	E
1926			8	E
2 yrs.	16 games			

Don Bitterlich
BITTERLICH, DONALD
B. Jan. 5, 1954, Philadelphia, PA
Temple 5'7" 166 lbs.

Year	Team		Games	Pos.
1976	SEA	N	3	K

Charlie Bivins
BIVINS, CHARLES LOUIS
B. Oct. 16, 1938, Atlanta, GA
D. Mar 11, 1994
Morris Brown 6'2" 212 lbs.

Year	Team		Games	Pos.
1960	CHI	N	12	HB
1961			14	HB
1962			12	HB
1963			14	HB
1964			11	HB
1965			14	HB
1966			14	HB
1967	PIT	N	2	HB
1967	BUF	A	9	HB
8 yrs.	102 games			

Herb Bizer
BIZER, HERBERT
B. Aug. 3, 1906
D. Dec, 1974, Iron Mountain, MI
Carroll (Wisconsin) 5'11" 205 lbs.

Year	Team		Games	Pos.
1929	BUF	N	8	FB, E

Del Bjork
BJORK, DELBERT L.
B. Jun. 27, 1914
D. Aug. 26, 1988, Astoria, OR
Oregon 6'1" 218 lbs.

Year	Team		Games	Pos.
1937	CHIB	N	11	T

Del Bjork *continued*

Year	Team		Games	Pos.
1938			9	T
2 yrs.	20 games			

Bob Bjorklund
BJORKLUND, ROBERT J.
B. Jun. 12, 1918, Minneapolis, MN
D. Jan. 29, 1994, Hopkins, MN
Minnesota 6'2" 225 lbs.

Year	Team		Games	Pos.
1941	PHI	N	7	C

Hank Bjorklund
BJORKLUND, JOHN HENRY
B. Jun. 5, 1950, Glen Head, NY
Princeton 6'1" 200 lbs.

Year	Team		Games	Pos.
1972	NYJ	N	7	RB
1973			10	RB
1974			13	RB
3 yrs.	30 games			

Eric Bjornson
BJORNSON, ERIC
B. Dec. 15, 1971, San Francisco, CA
Washington 6'4" 215 lbs.

Year	Team		Games	Pos.
1995	DAL	N	14	TE
1996			14	TE
2 yrs.	28 games			

Barry Black
BLACK, BARRY
B. Mar. 7, 1965
Boise State 6'2" 280 lbs.

Year	Team		Games	Pos.
1987	LARI	N	3	G

Blondy Black
BLACK, JOHN T.
B. Aug. 20, 1920, Philadelphia, MS
Mississippi State 5'11" 195 lbs.

Year	Team		Games	Pos.
1946	BUF	AA	4	FB
1947	BAL	AA	5	B
2 yrs.	9 games			

Charlie Black
BLACK, CHARLES T.
B. Jan. 5, 1901, Alton, IL
D. Dec. 14, 1988
Kansas 5'9" 160 lbs.

Year	Team		Games	Pos.
1925	DUL	N	1	E

Eddie Black
BLACK, EDWARD J.
B. Sep. 14, 1904
D. Jan, 1986, Lakeland, FL
Muhlenberg 5'10" 175 lbs.

Year	Team		Games	Pos.
1926	NEW	A	3	E

James Black
BLACK, JAMES
B. Apr. 3, 1962, Lima, OH
Akron 5'11" 198 lbs.

Year	Team		Games	Pos.
1984	CLE	N	2	RB

James Black
BLACK, JAMES R., III
B. Nov. 4, 1956, Xenia, OH
South Carolina State 6'4" 280 lbs.

Year	Team		Games	Pos.
1987	KC	N	1	DE

Mel Black
BLACK, MEL
B. Feb. 7, 1962, New Haven, CT
Eastern Illinois 6'2" 228 lbs.

Year	Team		Games	Pos.
1986	NE	N	3	LB

Mel Black *continued*

Year	Team		Games	Pos.
1987			3	LB
2 yrs.	6 games			

Mike Black
BLACK, MICHAEL DAVID
B. Aug. 24, 1964, Auburn, CA
Sacramento State 6'4" 290 lbs.

Year	Team		Games	Pos.
1986	PHI	N	1	OT, G
1987	NYG	N	2	OT
2 yrs.	3 games			

Mike Black
BLACK, PETER MICHAEL
B. Jan. 18, 1961, Glendale, CA
Arizona State 6'1" 197 lbs.

Year	Team		Games	Pos.
1983	DET	N	16	P
1984			16	P
1985			16	P
1986			9	P
1987			1	P
5 yrs.	58 games			

Stan Black
BLACK, STANLEY ROSS
B. Nov. 12, 1955, Greenville, MS
Mississippi State 6'0" 196 lbs.

Year	Team		Games	Pos.
1977	SF	N	13	S

Tim Black
BLACK, TIM A.
B. Jan. 3, 1955, Amarillo, TX
Baylor 6'2" 215 lbs.

Year	Team		Games	Pos.
1977	STL	N	4	LB

Todd Black
BLACK, TODD
B. Apr. 12, 1964
Concordia (Illinois) 5'11" 174 lbs.

Year	Team		Games	Pos.
1987	CHI	N	1	WR

Bill Blackburn
BLACKBURN, WILLIAM WHITFORD, JR.
B. Feb. 5, 1923, Weleetka, OK
Rice 6'6" 228 lbs.

Year	Team		Games	Pos.
1946	CHIC	N	11	C
1947			12	C
1948			12	C
1949			12	C
1950			11	C
5 yrs.	58 games			

Todd Blackledge
BLACKLEDGE, TODD ALAN
B. Feb. 25, 1961, Canton, OH
Penn State 6'3" 223 lbs.

Year	Team		Games	Pos.
1983	KC	N	4	QB
1984			11	QB
1985			12	QB
1986			10	QB
1987			3	QB
1988	PIT	N	3	QB
1989			3	QB
7 yrs.	46 games			

Hugh Blacklock
BLACKLOCK, HUGH M.
B. Jan., 1893
D. May 18, 1954
Michigan State 6'0" 220 lbs.

Year	Team		Games	Pos.
1920	DEC	A	8	T
1921			11	T
1922	CHIB	N	11	T
1923			4	T
1924			11	T

Year	Team	Games	Pos.

Hugh Blacklock *continued*

Year	Team	Games	Pos.
1925		3	T
1926	BKN	N	5	T
7 yrs.	53 games		

Ken Blackman
BLACKMAN, KEN
B. Nov. 8, 1972, Abilene, TX
Illinois 6'6" 315 lbs.

| 1996 | CIN | N | 13 | G |

Stub Blackman
BLACKMAN, HAROLD LENNON
B. Feb. 1, 1907
Tulsa 5'11" 195 lbs.

1930	CHIB	N	1	FB
1933	CHIC	N	1	QB
2 yrs.	2 games		

Don Blackmon
BLACKMON, DONALD KIRK
B. Mar. 14, 1958, Pompano Beach, FL
Tulsa 6'3" 235 lbs.

1981	NE	N	16	LB
1982		9	LB
1983		15	LB
1984		16	LB
1985		14	LB
1986		15	LB
1987		4	LB
7 yrs.	89 games		

Robert Blackmon
BLACKMON, ROBERT JAMES
B. May 12, 1967, Bay City, TX
Baylor 6'0" 198 lbs.

1990	SEA	N	15	S
1991		16	S
1992		15	S
1993		16	S
1994		15	S
1995		13	S
1996		16	S
7 yrs.	106 games		

Richard Blackmore
BLACKMORE, RICHARD EARL
B. Aug. 14, 1956, Vicksburg, MS
Mississippi State 5'10" 174 lbs.

1979	PHI	N	16	CB
1980		16	CB
1981		16	CB
1982		4	CB
1983	SF	N	11	CB
5 yrs.	63 games		

Jeff Blackshear
BLACKSHEAR, JEFF
B. Mar. 29, 1969, Fort Pierce, FL
Northeast Louisiana 6'6" 325 lbs.

1993	SEA	N	15	G
1994		16	G
1995		16	G
1996	BAL	N	16	G
4 yrs.	63 games		

Alois Blackwell
BLACKWELL, ALOIS STERLING
B. Nov. 12, 1954, Cuero, TX
Houston 5'10" 195 lbs.

1978	DAL	N	13	RB
1979		6	RB
2 yrs.	19 games		

Hal Blackwell
BLACKWELL, CARROLL

Hal Blackwell *continued*

Year	Team	Games	Pos.
B. 1919			

South Carolina 6'1" 205 lbs.

| 1945 | CHIC | N | 2 | HB |

Kelly Blackwell
BLACKWELL, KELLY REARDON
B. Feb. 13, 1969, Blytheville, TX
Texas Christian 6'1" 255 lbs.

1992	CHI	N	16	TE
1993	DAL	N	2	TE
2 yrs.	18 games		

Hal Blackwood
BLACKWOOD, HOWARD C.
B. May 9, 1898
D. Feb. 19, 1983, Fort Lauderdale, FL
Chicago/Northwestern 6'2" 250 lbs.

| 1926 | CHI | A | 1 | G |

Glenn Blackwood
BLACKWOOD, GLENN ALLEN
B. Feb. 23, 1957, San Antonio, TX
Texas 6'0" 190 lbs.

1979	MIA	N	11	CB
1980		16	S
1981		16	S
1982		9	S
1983		16	S
1984		16	S
1985		14	S
1986		10	S
1987		10	S
9 yrs.	118 games		

Lyle Blackwood
BLACKWOOD, LYLE VERNON, JR.
B. May 24, 1951, San Antonio, TX
Texas Christian 6'1" 190 lbs.

1973	CIN	N	7	S
1974		13	S
1975		14	S
1976	SEA	N	11	S
1977	BAL	N	14	S
1978		16	S
1979		16	S
1980		11	S
1981	MIA	N	12	S
1982		9	S
1983		16	S
1984		16	S
1985		16	S
1986		5	S
14 yrs.	176 games		

Bennie Blades
BLADES, HORATIO BENEDICT
B. Sep. 3, 1966, Fort Lauderdale, FL
Miami (Florida) 6'1" 221 lbs.

1988	DET	N	15	CB, S
1989		16	CB, S
1990		16	S
1991		16	S
1992		16	S
1993		4	S
1994		16	S
1995		16	S
1996		15	S
9 yrs.	126 games		

Brian Blades
BLADES, BRIAN KEITH
B. Jul. 24, 1965, Fort Lauderdale, FL
Miami (Florida) 5'11" 182 lbs.

1988	SEA	N	16	WR
1989		16	WR
1990		16	WR

Brian Blades *continued*

Year	Team	Games	Pos.
1991		16	WR
1992		6	WR
1993		16	WR
1994		16	WR
1995		16	WR
1996		11	WR
9 yrs.	129 games		

Brian Blados
BLADOS, BRIAN TIMOTHY
B. Jan. 11, 1962, Arlington, VA
North Carolina 6'5" 300 lbs.

1984	CIN	N	16	OT, G
1985		16	OT
1986		16	OT
1987		11	G
1988		16	G
1989		13	G
1990		4	G
1991		6	G
1991	IND	N	7	G
1992	TB	N	2	G
9 yrs.	107 games		

Joe Blahak
BLAHAK, JOSEPH PHILLIP
B. Aug. 29, 1950, Columbus, NE
Nebraska 5'9" 187 lbs.

1973	HOU	N	12	CB
1974	MIN	N	7	DB
1975		8	DB
1976	TB	N	2	DB
1976	NE	N	2	DB
1977	MIN	N	12	CB
5 yrs.	43 games		

Russ Blailock
BLAILOCK, WILLIAM RUSSELL
B. Jun. 29, 1902
D. Jan, 1972, Dallas, TX
Baylor 5'11" 230 lbs.

1923	MIL	N	12	T
1925	AKR	N	7	G, T
2 yrs.	19 games		

Ed Blaine
BLAINE, EDWARD HOMER
B. Jan. 30, 1940, Farmington, MO
Missouri 6'2" 240 lbs.

1962	GB	N	14	G
1963	PHI	N	14	G
1964		14	G
1965		14	G
1966		14	G
5 yrs.	70 games		

George Blair
BLAIR, GEORGE L.
B. May 10, 1938, Pascagoula, MS
Mississippi 5'11" 194 lbs.

1961	SD	A	14	DB
1962		14	DB
1963		14	DB
1964		4	DB
4 yrs.	46 games		

Matt Blair
BLAIR, ALBERT MATTHEW
B. Sep. 20, 1950, Hilo, HI
Iowa State 6'5" 240 lbs.

1974	MIN	N	14	LB
1975		14	LB
1976		14	LB
1977		14	LB
1978		16	LB
1979		16	LB
1980		14	LB

Matt Blair *continued*

Year	Team	Games	Pos.
1981		16	LB
1982		9	LB
1983		16	LB
1984		11	LB
1985		6	LB
12 yrs.	160 games		

Paul Blair
BLAIR, PAUL KEVIN
B. Aug. 3, 1963, Edmond, OK
Oklahoma State 6'4" 295 lbs.

1986	CHI	N	14	OT
1987		10	OT
1990	MIN	N	2	OT
3 yrs.	26 games		

Stanley Blair
BLAIR, STANLEY R.
B. Jul. 4, 1964, Pine Bluff, AR
Oklahoma State/Southeastern Oklahoma State 6'0" 192 lbs.

| 1990 | PHX | N | 5 | CB |

T.C. Blair
BLAIR, THOMAS CALVIN
B. Aug. 4, 1951, Ann Arbor, MI
Tulsa 6'4" 220 lbs.

| 1974 | DET | N | 11 | TE |

Jeff Blake
BLAKE, JEFF
B. Dec. 4, 1970, Daytona Beach, FL
East Carolina 6'0" 202 lbs.

1992	NYJ	N	3	QB
1994	CIN	N	10	QB
1995		16	QB
1996		16	QB
4 yrs.	45 games		

Ricky Blake
BLAKE, RICKY DARNELL
B. Jul. 15, 1967, Fayetteville, TN
Alabama A&M 6'2" 244 lbs.*

| 1991 | DAL | N | 2 | RB |

Tom Blake
BLAKE, THOMAS
B. 1926
Cincinnati 6'2" 220 lbs.

| 1949 | NYB | N | 5 | T |

Cary Blanchard
BLANCHARD, CARY
B. Nov. 5, 1968, Fort Worth, TX
Oklahoma State 6'1" 235 lbs.

1992	NYJ	N	11	K
1993		16	K
1995	IND	N	12	K
1996		16	K
4 yrs.	55 games		

Dick Blanchard
BLANCHARD, RICHARD
B. Jan. 17, 1949, Waukesha, WI
Tulsa 6'3" 225 lbs.

| 1972 | NE | N | 14 | LB |

Tom Blanchard
BLANCHARD, THOMAS RICHARD
B. May 28, 1949, Grant's Pass, OR
Oregon 6'0" 185 lbs.

| 1971 | NYG | N | 14 | P |
| 1972 | | 14 | P |

Year	Team		Games	Pos.

Tom Blanchard continued

Year	Team		Games	Pos.
1973			14	P
1974	NO	N	13	P
1975			14	P
1976			14	P
1977			14	P
1978			16	P
1979	TB	N	16	P
1980			16	P
1981			3	P
11 yrs.	148 games			

Carl Bland
BLAND, CARL NATHANIEL
B. Aug. 17, 1961, Fluvanna County, VA
Virginia Union 5'11" 181 lbs.

Year	Team		Games	Pos.
1984	DET	N	3	WR
1985			8	WR
1986			16	WR
1987			10	WR
1988			14	WR
1989	GB	N	16	WR
1990			14	WR
7 yrs.	81 games			

George Blanda
BLANDA, GEORGE FREDERICK
B. Sep. 17, 1927, Youngwood, PA
Kentucky 6'1" 210 lbs.

Year	Team		Games	Pos.
1949	CHIB	N	12	QB, DB, K, P
1950	BAL	N	1	DB
1950	CHIB	N	12	QB, DB, K, P
1951			11	DB, K
1952			12	QB, DB, K
1953			12	QB, K
1954			8	QB, K
1955			12	QB, K
1956			12	QB, K
1957			12	QB, K
1958			12	QB, K
1960	HOU	A	14	QB, K
1961			14	QB, K
1962			14	QB, K
1963			14	QB, K
1964			14	QB, K
1965			14	QB, K
1966			14	QB, K
1967	OAK	A	14	QB, K
1968			14	QB, K
1969			14	QB, K
1970	OAK	N	14	QB, K
1971			14	QB, K
1972			14	QB, K
1973			14	QB, K
1974			14	QB, K
1975			14	QB, K
26 yrs.	340 games			

Ernie Blandin
BLANDIN, ERNEST C.
B. Jun. 21, 1919, Augusta, KS
D. Sep, 1968
Tulane 6'4" 248 lbs.

Year	Team		Games	Pos.
1946	CLE	AA	14	T
1947			12	T
1948	BAL	AA	14	T
1949			10	T
1950	BAL	N	12	T
1953			9	T
6 yrs.	71 games			

Brian Blankenship
BLANKENSHIP, BRIAN PATRICK
B. Apr. 7, 1963, Omaha, NE
Nebraska-Omaha/Nebraska 6'1" 275 lbs.

Year	Team		Games	Pos.
1987	PIT	N	13	OL
1988			13	G, C
1989			16	G, C
1990			16	G, C

Brian Blankenship cont.

Year	Team		Games	Pos.
1991			3	G
5 yrs.	61 games			

Greg Blankenship
BLANKENSHIP, GREGORY
B. Mar. 24, 1954, Vallejo, CA
Hayward State 6'1" 212 lbs.

Year	Team		Games	Pos.
1976	OAK	N	4	LB
1976	PIT	N	6	LB
1 yr.	10 games			

Sid Blanks
BLANKS, SIDNEY
B. Apr. 29, 1940, Del Rio, TX
Texas A&I-Kingsville 6'0" 206 lbs.

Year	Team		Games	Pos.
1964	HOU	A	14	RB
1966			14	RB
1967			13	RB
1968			14	RB
1969	BOS	A	14	RB
1970	BOS	N	14	RB
6 yrs.	83 games			

Jerry Blanton
BLANTON, GERALD
B. Dec. 20, 1956, Toledo, OH
Kentucky 6'1" 225 lbs.

Year	Team		Games	Pos.
1979	KC	N	16	LB
1980			16	LB
1981			9	LB
1982			9	LB
1983			16	LB
1984			10	LB
1985			16	LB
7 yrs.	92 games			

Scott Blanton
BLANTON, SCOTT
B. Jul. 1, 1973, Norman, OK
Oklahoma 6'2" 218 lbs.

Year	Team		Games	Pos.
1996	WAS	N	16	K

Anthony Blaylock
BLAYLOCK, ANTHONY DARIUS
B. Feb. 21, 1965, Raleigh, NC
Winston-Salem State 5'11" 190 lbs.

Year	Team		Games	Pos.
1988	CLE	N	12	CB
1989			16	CB
1990			16	CB
1991			5	CB
1991	SD	N	2	CB
1992			11	CB
1993	CHI	N	9	CB
6 yrs.	71 games			

Phil Blazer
BLAZER, PHIL
B. 1936
North Carolina 6'1" 235 lbs.

Year	Team		Games	Pos.
1960	BUF	A		G

Tony Blazine
BLAZINE, ANTHONY
B. Jan. 2, 1912, Canton, IL
D. Jul. 3, 1963
Illinois Wesleyan 6'0" 232 lbs.

Year	Team		Games	Pos.
1935	CHIC	N	12	T
1936			11	T
1937			11	T
1938			11	T
1939			11	T
1940			7	T
1941	NYG	N	11	T, E
7 yrs.	74 games			

Jeff Bleamer
BLEAMER, JEFFREY HARRISON
B. Jun. 22, 1953, Allentown, PA
Penn State 6'4" 253 lbs.

Year	Team		Games	Pos.
1975	PHI	N	14	OT
1976			10	OT, G
1977	NYJ	N	8	OT, G
3 yrs.	32 games			

Curtis Bledsoe
BLEDSOE, CURTIS KEMP
B. Mar. 19, 1957, Odessa, TX
San Diego State 5'11" 215 lbs.

Year	Team		Games	Pos.
1981	KC	N	13	RB
1982			3	RB
2 yrs.	16 games			

Drew Bledsoe
BLEDSOE, DREW
B. Feb. 14, 1972, Ellensburg, WA
Washington State 6'5" 233 lbs.

Year	Team		Games	Pos.
1993	NE	N	13	QB
1994			16	QB
1995			15	QB
1996			16	QB
4 yrs.	60 games			

Mal Bleeker
BLEEKER, MALCOLM
B. 1907
Columbia 6'0" 205 lbs.

Year	Team		Games	Pos.
1930	BKN	N	3	E, G, C

Mel Bleeker
BLEEKER, MELVIN
B. Aug. 20, 1920, Los Angeles, CA
Southern California 5'11" 189 lbs.

Year	Team		Games	Pos.
1944	PHI	N	9	HB, FB
1945			4	HB
1946			4	HB
1947	LA	N	11	HB
4 yrs.	28 games			

Tom Bleick
BLEICK, THOMAS W.
B. Mar. 21, 1943, Talladega, AL
Georgia Tech 6'2" 200 lbs.

Year	Team		Games	Pos.
1966	BAL	N	7	DB
1967	ATL	N	2	DB
2 yrs.	9 games			

Bob Bleier
BLEIER, ROBERT
B. Jun. 1, 1964
Richmond 6'3" 210 lbs.

Year	Team		Games	Pos.
1987	NE	N	3	QB

Johnny Bleier
BLEIER, JOHN L.
B. Aug. 25, 1891, Ohio
D. Apr. 13, 1981, Hyattsville, MD
None 153 lbs.

Year	Team		Games	Pos.
1921	WAS	A	4	HB, E, QB

Rocky Bleier
BLEIER, ROBERT PATRICK
B. Mar. 5, 1946, Appleton, WI
Notre Dame 5'11" 207 lbs.

Year	Team		Games	Pos.
1968	PIT	N	10	RB
1971			6	RB
1972			14	RB
1973			12	RB
1974			12	RB
1975			11	RB
1976			14	RB
1977			13	RB

Rocky Bleier continued

Year	Team		Games	Pos.
1978			16	RB
1979			16	RB
1980			16	RB
11 yrs.	140 games			

Paul Blessing
BLESSING, PAUL
B. Jan. 16, 1919, Ord, NE
Kearney State 6'4" 215 lbs.

Year	Team		Games	Pos.
1944	DET	N	7	E

Dennis Bligen
BLIGEN, DENNIS
B. Mar. 3, 1962, New York, NY
St. John's (New York) 5'11" 210 lbs.

Year	Team		Games	Pos.
1984	NYJ	N	1	RB
1985			9	RB
1986			4	RB
1986	TB	N	1	RB
1987	NYJ	N	6	RB
4 yrs.	21 games			

Stan Blinka
BLINKA, STANLEY JOHN
B. Apr. 29, 1957, Columbus, OH
Sam Houston State 6'2" 230 lbs.

Year	Team		Games	Pos.
1979	NYJ	N	16	LB
1980			16	LB
1981			16	LB
1982			8	LB
1983			16	LB
5 yrs.	72 games			

Harry Bliss
BLISS, HAROLD W.
B. Jun. 17, 1897
D. May, 1967, Shelby, OH
Ohio State 5'8" 155 lbs.

Year	Team		Games	Pos.
1921	COL	A	9	QB, HB

Homer Bliss
BLISS, HOMER C.
B. Aug. 16, 1904
D. Mar, 1970, Detroit, MI
Washington & Jefferson 5'11" 195 lbs.

Year	Team		Games	Pos.
1928	CHIC	N	1	G

Tom Blondin
BLONDIN, THOMAS ALBERT
B. Oct. 25, 1910, Williamson, WV
D. Dec, 1978, Parkersburg, WV
West Virginia Wesleyan 6'0" 195 lbs.

Year	Team		Games	Pos.
1933	CIN	N	3	G

Johnny Blood
MCNALLY, JOHN VICTOR
B. Nov. 27, 1903, New Richmond, WI
D. Nov. 28, 1985, Palm Springs, CA
Wisconsin-River Falls/St. John's (Minnesota) 6'1" 188 lbs.

Year	Team		Games	Pos.
1925	MIL	N	5	HB
1926	DUL	N	12	HB, FB, QB
1927			9	HB
1928	POT	N	10	HB, FB
1929	GB	N	12	HB, QB
1930			10	HB
1931			12	HB
1932			13	HB, QB, FB
1933			9	QB, HB
1934	PIT	N	5	HB
1935	GB	N	9	HB
1936			7	HB, QB
1937	PIT	N	9	HB
1938			10	QB, FB, HB
14 yrs.	132 games			

Year	Team		Games	Pos.

Al Bloodgood
BLOODGOOD, ELBERT L.
B. 1902
D. 1947
DePauw/Nebraska 5'8" 153 lbs.

Year	Team		Games	Pos.
1925	KC	N	6	QB, HB
1926			11	QB, HB
1927	CLE	N	10	QB, HB
1928	NYG	N	5	QB, HB
1930	GB	N	2	QB
5 yrs.		34 games		

Alvin Blount
BLOUNT, ALVIN
B. Feb. 12, 1965
Maryland 5'9" 197 lbs.

1987	DAL	N	2	RB

Ed Blount
BLOUNT, ED
B. Feb. 26, 1964, Los Angeles, CA
Washington State 6'0" 195 lbs.

1987	SF	N	1	QB

Eric Blount
BLOUNT, ERIC LAMONT
B. Sep. 22, 1970, Ayden, NC
North Carolina 5'9" 190 lbs.

1992	PHX	N	4	WR
1993			6	RB
2 yrs.		10 games		

Jeb Blount
BLOUNT, JOHN EUGENE
B. Jul. 12, 1954, Tyler, TX
Tulsa 6'3" 200 lbs.

1977	TB	N	5	QB

Lamar Blount
BLOUNT, LLOYD LAMAR (Pappy)
B. Apr. 11, 1920, Decatur, MS
Mississippi State 6'1" 190 lbs.

1946	MIA	AA	12	E
1947	BUF	AA	5	E
1947	BAL	AA	5	E
2 yrs.		22 games		

Mel Blount
BLOUNT, MELVIN CORNELL
B. Apr. 10, 1948, Vidalia, GA
Southern University 6'3" 205 lbs.

1970	PIT	N	14	CB
1971			14	CB
1972			14	CB
1973			14	CB
1974			13	CB
1975			14	CB
1976			14	CB
1977			14	CB
1978			16	CB
1979			16	CB
1980			16	CB
1981			16	CB
1982			9	CB
1983			16	CB
14 yrs.		200 games		

Tony Blount
BLOUNT, ANTHONY URBAN
B. Nov. 5, 1958, Atlanta, GA
Virginia 6'1" 195 lbs.

1980	NYG	N	3	S

Al Blozis
BLOZIS, ALBERT C. (The Human Howitzer)

Al Blozis continued
B. Jan. 5, 1919, Garfield, NJ
D. Jan. 31, 1945, Vosges Mountains, France
Georgetown (DC) 6'6" 250 lbs.

1942	NYG	N	11	T
1943			10	T
1944			3	T, FB
3 yrs.		24 games		

Anthony Blue
BLUE, ANTHONY ALLEN
B. Sep. 19, 1964
Nevada-Las Vegas 5'9" 185 lbs.

1987	SEA	N	3	CB

Forrest Blue
BLUE, FORREST MURRELL, JR.
B. Sep. 7, 1945, Marfa, TX
Auburn 6'5" 259 lbs.

1968	SF	N	14	C
1969			14	C
1970			14	C
1971			14	C
1972			14	C
1973			14	C
1974			12	C
1975	BAL		11	C
1976			14	C
1977			14	C
1978			13	C
11 yrs.		148 games		

Luther Blue
BLUE, LUTHER
B. Oct. 21, 1954, Valdosta, GA
Iowa State 5'11" 185 lbs.

1977	DET	N	14	WR
1978			16	WR
1979			9	WR
1980	PHI	N	3	WR
4 yrs.		42 games		

Jimmy Blumenstock
BLUMENSTOCK, JAMES
B. 1919
D. 1963
Fordham 5'11" 190 lbs.

1947	NYG	N	10	FB

Herb Blumer
BLUMER, HERBERT
B. Mar. 7, 1900
D. Apr, 1987, Danville, CA
Missouri 6'1" 200 lbs.

1925	CHIC	N	9	E, T
1926			12	E, QB
1927			9	E, T, G, C
1928			6	E, C, T
1929			10	G
1930			12	G, E
1933			1	G
7 yrs.		59 games		

Matt Blundin
BLUNDIN, MATTHEW BRENT
B. Mar. 7, 1969, Darby, PA
Virginia 6'6" 230 lbs.

1993	KC	N	1	QB
1994			1	QB
2 yrs.		2 games		

Ronnie Blye
BLIEY, RONNIE
B. Dec. 29, 1943, Clearwater, FL
Florida A&M 5'11" 185 lbs.

1968	NYG	N	13	RB

Ronnie Blye continued

1969	PHI	N	14	RB
2 yrs.		27 games		

Dwaine Board
BOARD, DWAINE P. (Pee Wee)
B. Nov. 29, 1956, Union Hall, VA
North Carolina A&T 6'5" 246 lbs.

1979	SF	N	16	DE
1980			3	DE
1981			16	DE
1982			1	DE
1983			16	DE
1984			16	DE
1985			16	DE
1986			14	DE
1987			3	DE
1988	NO	N	4	DE
10 yrs.		121 games		

Mack Boatner
BOATNER, MACK ERNEST
B. Oct. 4, 1958, Baton Rouge, LA
Southeastern Louisiana 6'0" 220 lbs.

1986	TB		7	RB

Harry Boatswain
BOATSWAIN, HARRY KWANE
B. Jun. 26, 1969, Brooklyn, NY
New Haven 6'4" 295 lbs.

1992	SF		16	OT
1993			16	OT
1994			13	OT
1995	PHI	N	13	G, OT
1996	NYJ	N	16	OT
5 yrs.		74 games		

Bon Boatwright
BOATWRIGHT, BON LOVELL
B. Oct. 28, 1951, Henderson, TX
Oklahoma State 6'5" 262 lbs.

1974	SD	N	10	DT

Adam Bob
BOB, ADAM, JR.
B. Oct. 30, 1967, Milwaukee, WI
Texas A&M 6'2" 240 lbs.

1989	NYJ	N	5	LB

E. Bobadash
BOBADASH, E.
None

1922	OOR	N	1	E

Hubert Bobo
BOBO, HUBERT L.
B. Jul. 2, 1934
Ohio State 6'1" 217 lbs.

1960	LA	A		LB
1961	NY	A	14	LB
1962			14	LB
3 yrs.		28 games		

Joe Bock
BOCK, JOSEPH ALAN
B. Jul. 21, 1959, Rochester, NY
Virginia 6'4" 254 lbs.

1987	BUF	N	1	C
1987	STL	N	1	G
1 yr.		2 games		

John Bock
BOCK, JOHN MATTHEW
B. Feb. 11, 1971, Crystal Lake, IL

John Bock continued
Louisville/Indiana State 6'3" 275 lbs.

1995	NYJ	N	10	C, G
1996	MIA	N	2	C, G
2 yrs.		12 games		

Wayne Bock
BOCK, WAYNE, JR.
B. May 28, 1934, St. Paul, MN
Illinois 6'4" 250 lbs.

1957	CHIC	N	4	T

Tony Boddie
BODDIE, TONY L.
B. Nov. 11, 1960, Portsmouth, VA
Montana State 5'11" 198 lbs.

1986	DEN	N	1	RB
1987			5	RB
2 yrs.		6 games		

Lynn Boden
BODEN, LYNN RAY
B. Jun. 5, 1953, Stromsburg, NE
South Dakota State 6'5" 266 lbs.

1975	DET	N	14	G
1976			14	G
1977			13	G
1978			16	G
1979	CHI	N	9	G
5 yrs.		66 games		

Maury Bodenger
BODENGER, MORRIS
B. Jul. 31, 1909, New Orleans, LA
Deceased
Tulane 5'10" 214 lbs.

1931	POR	N	13	G
1932			12	G, T
1933			11	G
1934	DET	N	12	G
4 yrs.		48 games		

Ping Bodie
BODIE, PING
B. May 10, 1897
D. Dec, 1981, Stockton, CA
None

1921	CHIC	A	2	HB, FB

Billy Boedecker
BOEDECKER, WILLIAM HENRY
B. Mar. 7, 1924, Milwaukee, WI
DePaul/Kalamazoo 5'11" 192 lbs.*

1946	CHI	AA	12	HB
1947	CLE	AA	12	HB
1948			14	HB
1949			12	HB
1950	GB	N	12	HB
1950	PHI	N	1	HB
5 yrs.		63 games		

Jim Boeke
BOEKE, JAMES FREDERICK
B. Sep. 11, 1938, Akron, OH
Heidelberg 6'5" 250 lbs.

1960	LA	N	12	OT
1961			14	OT
1962			14	OT
1963			14	OT
1964	DAL	N	14	OT
1965			14	OT
1966			10	OT
1967			14	OT
1968	NO	N	13	OT
9 yrs.		119 games		

Year	Team		Games	Pos.

Fred Boensch
BOENSCH, FREDERICK MAX
B. Sep. 27, 1920, Portland, OR
Stanford/California/Stanford 6'4" 228 lbs.

Year	Team		Games	Pos.
1947	**WAS**	N	12	G
1948			12	G
2 yrs.	24 games			

Raymond Boettcher
BOETTCHER, RAYMOND (Champ)
B. Sep. 18, 1900
D. Dec, 1965
Lawrence 5'10" 198 lbs.

1926	**RAC**	N	3	FB, HB

Rex Boggan
BOGGAN, REX REED
B. Mar. 27, 1930
D. Dec. 8, 1985
Mississippi 6'3" 245 lbs.

1955	**NYG**	N	11	T

Mark Boggs
BOGGS, MARK ALLEN
B. May 7, 1964, Kankakee, IL
Ball State 6'5" 301 lbs.

1987	**IND**	N	1	OT

George Bogue
BOGUE, GEORGE RICHARDSON
B. Feb. 10, 1906, Omaha, NE
D. Oct, 1972, Pasadena, CA
Stanford 6'0" 210 lbs.

1930	**CHIC**	N	3	HB, QB
1930	**NEW**	N	3	HB, FB
1 yr.	6 games			

Fred Bohannon
BOHANNON, FREDERICK JEROME
B. May 31, 1958, Birmingham, AL
Mississippi Valley State 6'0" 201 lbs.

1982	**PIT**	N	7	DB

Dewey Bohling
BOHLING, DEWEY
B. 1939
Hardin-Simmons 5'11" 190 lbs.

1960	**NY**	A	14	HB
1961			5	HB
1961	**BUF**	A	7	HB
2 yrs.	26 games			

Frank Bohlmann
BOHLMANN, FRANK
B. Jan. 26, 1917, Milwaukee, WI
Marquette 5'11" 212 lbs.

1942	**CHIC**	N	5	G, T

Ron Bohm
BOHM, RON
B. Sep. 3, 1964
Illinois 6'3" 250 lbs.

1987	**STL**	N	3	DT

Reed Bohovich
BOHOVICH, GEORGE REED
B. Nov. 28, 1941, Buffalo, NY
Lehigh 6'3" 260 lbs.

1962	**NYG**	N	10	G, OT

Karl Bohren
BOHREN, KARL W. (Jake)
B. May 26, 1902
D. Mar, 1987, Clairton, PA
Pittsburgh 5'8" 180 lbs.

1927	**BUF**	N	2	FB, HB

Novo Bojovic
BOJOVIC, NOVO
B. Nov. 2, 1959, Titograd, Yugoslavia
Central Michigan 5'10" 172 lbs.

1985	**STL**	N	6	K

Kim Bokamper
BOKAMPER, KIM
B. Sep. 25, 1954, San Diego, CA
Concordia/San Jose State 6'6" 250 lbs.

1977	**MIA**	N	14	LB
1978			16	LB
1979			14	LB
1980			16	LB
1981			16	LB
1982			9	DE
1983			15	DE
1984			11	DE
1985			16	DE
9 yrs.	127 games			

George Bolan
BOLAN, GEORGE
B. Apr., 1897
D. 1940
Purdue 5'11" 203 lbs.

1921	**DEC**	A	5	FB, HB
1922	**CHIB**	N	10	FB, HB
1923			10	FB, HB
1924			1	FB
4 yrs.	26 games			

Ned Bolcar
BOLCAR, NED FRANCIS
B. Jan. 12, 1967, Phillipsburg, NJ
Notre Dame 6'1" 240 lbs.

1990	**SEA**	N	5	LB
1991	**MIA**	N	8	LB
2 yrs.	13 games			

Gary Bolden
BOLDEN, GARY (The Mule)
B. Feb. 13, 1962
Southwestern Oklahoma State 6'1" 250 lbs.

1987	**PHI**	N	2	DT

Juran Bolden
BOLDEN, JURAN
B. Jun. 27, 1974, Tampa, FL
Mississippi Delta CC 6'2" 201 lbs.

1996	**ATL**	N	9	CB

Leroy Bolden
BOLDEN, LEROY, JR.
B. Aug. 24, 1932, Wabash, AR
Michigan State 5'8" 170 lbs.

1958	**CLE**	N	11	HB
1959			12	HB
2 yrs.	23 games			

Rickey Bolden
BOLDEN, RICKEY ALLEN
B. Sep. 8, 1961, Dallas, TX
Southern Methodist 6'6" 280 lbs.

1984	**CLE**	N	12	TE
1985			16	OT
1986			7	OT, G
1987			5	OT

Rickey Bolden continued

1988			16	OT
1989			6	OT
6 yrs.	62 games			

Chase Boldt
BOLDT, STEPHEN CHASE
B. May 7, 1900
D. May, 1973, Pewee Valley, KY
None 5'6" 145 lbs.

1921	**LOU**	A	2	QB, HB
1922	**LOU**	N	4	QB, E, T
1923			2	QB, HB
3 yrs.	8 games			

Jim Bolger
BOLGER, JAMES L.
B. Dec. 21, 1902
D. Dec, 1968, Brooklyn, NY
St. Mary's/St. Bonaventure 6'0" 175 lbs.

1926	**BKN**	A	4	HB

Bookie Bolin
BOLIN, TREVA GENE
B. Jun. 17, 1940, Hamilton, AL
Mississippi 6'2" 240 lbs.

1962	**NYG**	N	9	G
1963			13	G
1964			14	G
1965			14	G
1966			14	G
1967			13	G
1968	**MIN**		6	G
1969			6	G
8 yrs.	89 games			

Russ Bolinger
BOLINGER, RUSSELL DEAN
B. Sep. 10, 1954, Wichita, KS
California-Riverside/Long Beach State 6'5" 254 lbs.

1976	**DET**	N	12	OT
1977			14	G
1979			16	OT
1980			16	G
1981			16	G
1982			9	G
1983	**LARM**	N	16	G
1984			16	G
1985			6	G
9 yrs.	121 games			

Nick Bolkovac
BOLKOVAC, NICHOLAS F.
B. Mar. 20, 1928, McKees Rocks, PA
Pittsburgh 6'1" 230 lbs.

1953	**PIT**	N	12	T
1954			5	T
2 yrs.	17 games			

Don Boll
BOLL, DONALD E.
B. Jul. 16, 1927, Scribner, NE
D. Mar, 1962
Nebraska 6'2" 270 lbs.

1953	**WAS**	N	12	T
1954			12	T
1955			12	T
1956			12	T
1957			12	T
1958			9	T
1959			12	G, T
1960	**NYG**	N	11	T
8 yrs.	92 games			

Brian Bollinger
BOLLINGER, BRIAN REID

Brian Bollinger continued
B. Nov. 21, 1968, Indialantic, FL
North Carolina 6'5" 285 lbs.

1992	**SF**	N	16	G
1993			16	G
1994			7	G
3 yrs.	39 games			

Eddie Bollinger
BOLLINGER, EDWARD E.
B. Jul. 9, 1906, Northumberland, PA
D. Jul. 14, 1984, Lancaster, PA
Bucknell 6'1" 215 lbs.

1930	**FRA**	N	4	T, G

Andy Bolton
BOLTON, ANDREW
B. May 23, 1954, Memphis, TN
Fisk 6'1" 205 lbs.

1976	**SEA**	N	5	RB
1976	**DET**	N	7	RB
1977			14	RB
1978			6	RB
3 yrs.	32 games			

Ron Bolton
BOLTON, RONALD CLIFTON
B. Apr. 16, 1950, Petersburg, VA
Norfolk State 6'2" 170 lbs.

1972	**NE**	N	14	K, DB
1973			14	CB
1974			14	CB
1975			13	CB
1976	**CLE**	N	14	CB
1977			14	CB
1978			10	CB
1979			16	CB
1980			16	CB
1981			16	CB
1982			4	CB
11 yrs.	145 games			

Scott Bolton
BOLTON, SCOTT ALLEN
B. Jan. 4, 1965, Mobile, AL
Auburn 6'0" 188 lbs.

1988	**GB**	N	4	WR

Lynn Bomar
BOMAR, ROBERT LYNN
B. Jan. 21, 1901, Gallatin, TX
D. Jun. 11, 1964
Vanderbilt 6'1" 210 lbs.

1925	**NYG**	N	12	E
1926			8	E
2 yrs.	20 games			

Jack Bonadies
BONADIES, JOHN
B. Dec. 2, 1892
D. Oct, 1965
None 208 lbs.

1926	**HAR**	N	4	G, T

Chuck Bond
BOND, CHARLES E.
B. Jan. 5, 1914, Fairland, WA
D. Sep. 24, 1989, Puyallup, WA
Washington 6'2" 236 lbs.

1937	**WAS**	N	11	T
1938			11	T
2 yrs.	22 games			

Jim Bond
BOND, JAMES
B. Feb., 1894, Pittsburgh, PA

Year	Team	Games	Pos.

Jim Bond *continued*
Pittsburgh 5'9" 200 lbs.

1926	**BKN**	N	2	G

Rink Bond
BOND, RANDALL E.
B. Jun. 3, 1917, Fairland, WA
Washington 5'10" 200 lbs.

1938	**WAS**	N	2	T, QB
1939	**PIT**	N	11	QB
2 yrs.	13 games			

Bourbon Bondurant
BONDURANT, BOURBON PATCH (Sandy)
B. Feb. 18, 1898, Kentucky
D. Sep. 4, 1971, Scottsdale, AZ
DePauw 6'1" 198 lbs.

1921	**EVA**	A	5	T, E
1922	**EVA**	N	2	T
1922	**CHIB**	N	1	G
2 yrs.	8 games			

Warren Bone
BONE, WARREN JAMES
B. Nov. 4, 1964, Fairfield, AL
Texas Southern 6'4" 260 lbs.

1987	**GB**	N	1	DE

Ernie Bonelli
BONELLI, EARNEST
B. Jul. 27, 1919, Russellton, PA
Pittsburgh 5'11" 194 lbs.

1945	**CHIC**	N	7	FB
1946	**PIT**	N	3	HB
2 yrs.	10 games			

Shane Bonham
BONHAM, STEVEN SHANE
B. Oct. 18, 1970, Fairbanks, AK
Air Force/Tennessee 6'4" 260 lbs.

1994	**DET**	N	15	DE, DT
1995			15	DT, DE
1996			15	DT
3 yrs.	45 games			

Chris Boniol
BONIOL, CHRIS
B. Dec. 9, 1971, Alexandria, LA
Louisiana Tech 5'11" 159 lbs.

1994	**DAL**	N	16	K
1995			16	K
1996			16	K
3 yrs.	48 games			

Brian Bonner
BONNER, BRIAN
B. Oct. 9, 1965, Minneapolis, MN
Wisconsin/Minnesota 6'2" 225 lbs.

1989	**WAS**	N	6	LB

Glen Bonner
BONNER, GLEN
B. May 5, 1952, Bremerton, WA
Washington 6'2" 202 lbs.

1974	**SD**	N	12	RB
1975			9	RB
2 yrs.	21 games			

Melvin Bonner
BONNER, MELVIN
B. Feb. 18, 1970, Hempstead, TX
Baylor 6'3" 207 lbs.

1993	**DEN**	N	3	WR

Rik Bonness
BONNESS, RIK
B. Mar. 20, 1954, Borger, TX
Nebraska 6'5" 219 lbs.

1976	**OAK**	N	14	LB
1977	**TB**	N	13	LB
1978			16	LB
1979			16	LB
4 yrs.	59 games			

Steve Bono
BONO, STEVEN CHRISTOPHER
B. May 11, 1962, Norristown, PA
UCLA 6'3" 211 lbs.

1985	**MIN**	N	1	QB
1986			1	QB
1987	**PIT**	N	3	QB
1988			2	QB
1989	**SF**	N	1	QB
1991			9	QB
1992			16	QB
1993			8	QB
1994	**KC**	N	7	QB
1995			16	QB
1996			14	QB
11 yrs.	78 games			

Elliott Bonowitz
BONOWITZ, ELLIOTT
B. 1899
Deceased
Wilmington 6'4" 218 lbs.

1923	**COL**	N	5	HB, QB, T, C
1924	**DAY**	N	8	G, E, C
1925			6	G
3 yrs.	19 games			

Vaughn Booker
BOOKER, VAUGHN JAMEL
B. Feb. 24, 1968, Cincinnati, OH
Cincinnati 6'5" 283 lbs.

1994	**KC**	N	15	DE
1995			16	DE
1996			14	DE
3 yrs.	45 games			

Johnny Bookman
BOOKMAN, JOHN DOLAN
B. Sep. 6, 1934, Baton Rouge, LA
Miami (Florida) 5'11" 182 lbs.

1957	**NYG**	N	11	DB
1960	**DAL**	A		DB
1961	**NY**	A	8	DB
3 yrs.	19 games			

Billy Bookout
BOOKOUT, BILLY PAUL
B. Jun. 1, 1932, Choice, TX
Oklahoma/Austin 5'11" 180 lbs.

1955	**GB**	N	12	B
1956			7	HB
2 yrs.	19 games			

Bob Books
BOOKS, ROBERT C.
B. 1902
Deceased
Dickinson 5'11" 190 lbs.

1926	**FRA**	N	3	FB, HB

Dave Boone
BOONE, H. DAVID
B. Oct. 30, 1951, Detroit, MI
Eastern Michigan 6'3" 248 lbs.

1974	**MIN**	N	5	DE

Greg Boone
BOONE, GREGORY JOEL
B. Jan. 8, 1962, Aberdeen, MA
Duke 5'9" 196 lbs.

1987	**TB**	N	2	RB

Jack Boone
BOONE, ROBERT LEE
B. May 28, 1918, Roanoke Rapids, NC
D. Feb. 6, 1984, Greenville, NC
Elon 5'11" 175 lbs.

1942	**CLE**	N	2	HB

J.R. Boone
BOONE, J.R. (Junior)
B. Jul. 28, 1925, Clinton, OK
Tulsa 5'8" 162 lbs.

1948	**CHIB**	N	11	HB
1949			12	HB
1950			10	HB
1951			10	HB
1952	**SF**	N	12	HB
1953	**GB**	N	8	HB
6 yrs.	63 games			

Clarence Booth
BOOTH, CLARENCE E.
B. Sep. 4, 1919, Childress, TX
Southern Methodist 6'0" 223 lbs.

1943	**CHIC**	N	6	T
1944	**C, P**		5	T, G
2 yrs.	11 games			

Dick Booth
BOOTH, RICHARD
B. Jul. 13, 1918, Newell, WV
Case Western Reserve 6'1" 190 lbs.

1941	**DET**	N	11	HB, DB
1945			4	HB, DB
2 yrs.	15 games			

Isaac Booth
BOOTH, ISAAC RAMOUN
B. May 23, 1971, Indianapolis, IN
California 6'3" 183 lbs.

1994	**CLE**	N	16	CB
1995			9	CB
1996	**BAL**	N	11	CB
3 yrs.	36 games			

John Booty
BOOTY, JOHN FITZGERALD
B. Oct. 9, 1965, De Berry, TX
Texas Christian 6'0" 179 lbs.

1988	**NYJ**	N	16	CB
1989			9	CB, S
1990			13	CB, S
1991	**PHI**	N	13	CB, S
1992			16	CB, S
1993	**PHX**	N	12	S
1994	**NYG**	N	16	S
1995	**TB**	N	8	S
8 yrs.	103 games			

Emerson Boozer
BOOZER, EMERSON, JR.
B. Jul. 4, 1943, Augusta, GA
Maryland-Eastern Shore 5'11" 203 lbs.

1966	**NY**	A	14	RB
1967			8	RB
1968			12	RB
1969			14	RB
1970	**NYJ**	N	10	RB
1971			14	RB
1972			11	RB
1973			13	RB

Emerson Boozer *continued*

1974			13	RB
1975			9	RB
10 yrs.	118 games			

Tony Borak
BORAK, ANTHONY (Fritz)
B. 1913
Creighton 6'1" 190 lbs.

1938	**GB**	N	1	E

Jon Borchardt
BORCHARDT, JON L.
B. Aug. 13, 1957, Minneapolis, MN
Montana State 6'5" 265 lbs.

1979	**BUF**	N	16	OT
1980			16	OT
1981			16	OT
1982			9	OT
1983			16	OT
1984			16	G
1985	**SEA**	N	14	G
1986			16	G
1987			12	G
9 yrs.	131 games			

Kenny Bordelon
BORDELON, KENNY P.
B. Aug. 26, 1954, New Orleans, LA
Louisiana State 6'4" 228 lbs.

1976	**NO**	N	12	LB
1977			14	LB
1979			16	LB
1980			16	LB
1981			15	LB
1982			9	LB
6 yrs.	82 games			

Les Borden
BORDEN, LESTER
B. Apr. 8, 1910
D. May, 1981, King of Prussia, PA
Fordham 6'0" 185 lbs.

1935	**NYG**	N	1	E

Nate Borden
BORDEN, NATHANIEL
B. Sep. 22, 1932, Detroit, MI
D. Sep. 30, 1992, Las Vegas, NV
Indiana 6'0" 234 lbs.

1955	**GB**	N	12	DE
1956			12	DE
1957			9	DE
1958			12	DE
1959			12	DE
1960	**DAL**	N	12	DE
1961			14	DE
1962	**BUF**	A	9	DE
8 yrs.	92 games			

Nate Borders
BORDERS, NATHAN
B. Jun. 11, 1963
Indiana 5'10" 190 lbs.

1987	**CIN**	N	3	S

Nick Borelli
BORELLI, NICHOLAS
B. Mar. 2, 1905
Muhlenberg 5'10" 175 lbs.

1930	**NEW**	N	10	HB, FB, QB

Jocelyn Borgella
BORGELLA, JOCELYN KENZA
B. Aug. 26, 1971, Nassau, Bahamas

Jocelyn Borgella continued

Cincinnati 5'10" 182 lbs.

Year	Team		Games	Pos.
1994	DET	N	4	CB
1995			1	CB
1996			11	CB
3 yrs.	16 games			

Dirk Borgognone

BORGOGNONE, DIRK RONALD
B. Jan. 9, 1968, Elko, NV
Tennessee/Pacific 6'2" 221 lbs.

Year	Team		Games	Pos.
1995	GB	N	2	K

Kyle Borland

BORLAND, KYLE CRAIG
B. Jul. 5, 1961, Denison, IA
Wisconsin 6'3" 232 lbs.

Year	Team		Games	Pos.
1987	LARM	N	2	LB

Rich Borresen

BORRESEN, RICH
B. Mar. 16, 1964, Queens, NY
Northwestern 6'5" 252 lbs.

Year	Team		Games	Pos.
1987	DAL	N	3	TE

John Borton

BORTON, JOHN R.
B. Dec. 14, 1932, Alliance, OH
Ohio State 6'0" 208 lbs.

Year	Team		Games	Pos.
1957	CLE	N	5	QB

Mark Bortz

BORTZ, MARK STEVEN
B. Feb. 12, 1961, Pardeeville, WI
Iowa 6'6" 269 lbs.

Year	Team		Games	Pos.
1983	CHI	N	16	G
1984			15	G
1985			16	G
1986			15	G
1987			12	G
1988			16	G
1989			16	G
1990			16	G
1991			9	G
1992			12	G
1993			16	G
1994			12	G
12 yrs.	171 games			

Mike Boryla

BORYLA, MICHAEL JAY
B. Mar. 6, 1951, Long Island, NY
Stanford 6'3" 200 lbs.

Year	Team		Games	Pos.
1974	PHI	N	4	QB
1975			7	QB
1976			11	QB
1978	TB	N	1	QB
4 yrs.	23 games			

John Bosa

BOSA, JOHN WILFRED
B. Jan. 10, 1964, Keene, NH
Boston College 6'4" 263 lbs.

Year	Team		Games	Pos.
1987	MIA	N	12	DE
1988			6	DE
1989			13	DE
3 yrs.	31 games			

Wade Bosarge

BOSARGE, WADE
B. Sep. 14, 1955, Bayou LaBatre, LA
Tulsa 5'10" 175 lbs.

Year	Team		Games	Pos.
1977	MIA	N	5	S
1977	NO	N	5	S
1 yr.	10 games			

Frank Bosch

BOSCH, FRANK WILLIAM
B. Oct. 24, 1945, Bremerton, WA
Colorado 6'4" 246 lbs.

Year	Team		Games	Pos.
1968	WAS	N	14	DT
1969			14	DT
1970			11	DT
3 yrs.	39 games			

John Bosdett

BOSDETT, JOHN
B. Nov. 4, 1895
D. Sep, 1980, Oklahoma City, OK
None

Year	Team		Games	Pos.
1920	CHIT	A	6	E

Tony Boselli

BOSELLI, DON ANTHONY, JR.
B. Apr. 17, 1972, Boulder, CO
Southern California 6'7" 323 lbs.

Year	Team		Games	Pos.
1995	JAC	N	13	OT
1996			16	OT
2 yrs.	29 games			

Bruce Bosley

BOSLEY, BRUCE LEE
B. Nov. 5, 1933, Fresno, CA
D. Apr. 26, 1995, San Francisco, CA
West Virginia 6'2" 241 lbs.

Year	Team		Games	Pos.
1956	SF		12	T, E
1957			6	G
1958			12	G
1959			12	G
1960			12	G
1961			12	G
1962			13	G
1963			14	G
1964			14	C, G
1965			14	C
1966			14	C
1967			14	C
1968			14	C
1969	ATL	N	12	C
14 yrs.	175 games			

Keith Bosley

BOSLEY, KEITH
B. Jun. 19, 1963
Eastern Kentucky 6'5" 320 lbs.

Year	Team		Games	Pos.
1987	CLE	N	3	OT

Cap Boso

BOSO, CASPER N.
B. Sep. 10, 1963, Kansas City, MO
Illinois 6'3" 224 lbs.

Year	Team		Games	Pos.
1986	STL	N	2	TE
1987	CHI	N	12	TE
1988			6	TE
1989			16	TE
1990			13	TE
1991			6	TE
6 yrs.	55 games			

Don Bosseler

BOSSELER, DONALD JOHN
B. Jan. 24, 1936, Batavia, NY
Miami (Florida) 6'1" 212 lbs.

Year	Team		Games	Pos.
1957	WAS	N	12	FB
1958			10	FB
1959			12	FB
1960			11	FB
1961			12	FB
1962			14	FB
1963			14	FB
1964			11	FB
8 yrs.	96 games			

Jeff Bostic

BOSTIC, JEFF
B. Sep. 18, 1958, Greensboro, NC
Clemson 6'2" 256 lbs.

Year	Team		Games	Pos.
1980	WAS	N	16	C
1981			16	C
1982			9	C
1983			16	C
1984			8	C
1985			10	C
1986			16	C
1987			12	C
1988			13	C
1989			16	C
1990			16	C
1991			16	C
1992			4	C
1993			16	C
14 yrs.	184 games			

Joe Bostic

BOSTIC, JOE EARL, JR.
B. Apr. 20, 1957, Greensboro, NC
Clemson 6'3" 268 lbs.

Year	Team		Games	Pos.
1979	STL	N	16	G
1980			16	OT
1981			14	G
1982			8	G
1983			14	G
1984			16	G
1985			16	G
1986			13	G
1987			9	G
1988	PHX	N	10	G
10 yrs.	132 games			

John Bostic

BOSTIC, JOHN
B. Oct. 6, 1962, Titusville, FL
Bethune-Cookman 5'10" 178 lbs.

Year	Team		Games	Pos.
1985	DET	N	13	CB
1986			13	CB
1987			3	CB
3 yrs.	29 games			

Keith Bostic

BOSTIC, KEITH
B. Jan. 17, 1961, Ann Arbor, MI
Michigan 6'1" 223 lbs.

Year	Team		Games	Pos.
1983	HOU	N	16	S
1984			16	S
1985			16	S
1986			16	S
1987			12	S
1988			16	S
1990	CLE	N	4	S
7 yrs.	96 games			

Lew Bostick

BOSTICK, LEWIS TOWNLEY
B. Oct. 3, 1916, Birmingham, AL
Alabama 6'0" 197 lbs.

Year	Team		Games	Pos.
1939	CLE	N	7	G, T

McKinley Boston

BOSTON, MCKINLEY, JR.
B. Nov. 5, 1946, Elizabeth City, NC
Minnesota 6'2" 245 lbs.

Year	Team		Games	Pos.
1968	NYG	N	13	DT, DE
1969			14	DE
2 yrs.	27 games			

Ben Boswell

BOSWELL, BENJAMIN
B. Nov. 24, 1910
D. May, 1981, Momence, IL
Texas Christian 6'0" 245 lbs.

Year	Team		Games	Pos.
1933	POR	N	1	T

Ben Boswell continued

Year	Team		Games	Pos.
1934	BOS	N	10	T
2 yrs.	11 games			

Brian Bosworth

BOSWORTH, BRIAN KEITH (Boz)
B. Mar. 9, 1965, Oklahoma City, OK
Oklahoma 6'2" 248 lbs.

Year	Team		Games	Pos.
1987	SEA	N	12	LB
1988			10	LB
1989			2	LB
3 yrs.	24 games			

Ron Botchan

BOTCHAN, RON
B. 1935
Occidental 6'1" 234 lbs.

Year	Team		Games	Pos.
1960	LA	A		LB
1961	HOU	A	14	LB
2 yrs.	14 games			

Kirk Botkin

BOTKIN, KIRK
B. Mar. 19, 1971, Baytown, TX
Arkansas 6'2" 233 lbs.

Year	Team		Games	Pos.
1994	NO	N	3	TE
1995			16	TE
1996	PIT	N	16	TE
3 yrs.	35 games			

Scott Boucher

BOUCHER, SCOTT ALLEN
B. Sep. 15, 1958, Houston, TX
Northeast Louisiana 6'3" 260 lbs.

Year	Team		Games	Pos.
1987	HOU	N	2	G

Jim Boudreaux

BOUDREAUX, JAMES LEE
B. Apr. 15, 1945, Ville Platte, LA
Louisiana Tech 6'4" 245 lbs.

Year	Team		Games	Pos.
1966	BOS	A	4	DE
1967			5	OT
1968			3	OT
3 yrs.	12 games			

Lee Bouggess

BOUGGESS, LEE EDWARD
B. Jan. 18, 1948, Louisville, KY
Louisville 6'2" 210 lbs.

Year	Team		Games	Pos.
1970	PHI	N	14	RB
1971			10	RB
1973			8	RB
3 yrs.	32 games			

Kevin Bouie

BOUIE, KEVIN LAMOUNT
B. Aug. 18, 1971, Pahokee, FL
Mississippi State 6'1" 230 lbs.

Year	Team		Games	Pos.
1996	SD	N	1	RB

Tony Bouie

BOUIE, TONY VANDERSON
B. Aug. 7, 1972, New Orleans, LA
Arizona 5'10" 187 lbs.

Year	Team		Games	Pos.
1995	TB	N	9	S
1996			16	S
2 yrs.	25 games			

Gil Bouley

BOULEY, GILBERT
B. Nov. 15, 1921, Plainfield, CT
Boston College 6'2" 235 lbs.

Year	Team		Games	Pos.
1945	CLE	N	6	T
1946	LA	N	1	T

Year	Team	Games	Pos.

Gil Bouley continued

1947		12	T
1948		12	T
1949		12	T
1950		11	T
6 yrs.	64 games		

Emil Boures

BOURES, EMIL NICHOLAS
B. Jan. 29, 1960, Bridgeport, PA
Pittsburgh 6'1" 258 lbs.

1982	PIT	N	4	C
1983			16	C, G
1984			8	G, C
1985			6	G, OT
4 yrs.	34 games			

Marc Boutte

BOUTTE, MARC ANTHONY
B. Jul. 25, 1969, Lake Charles, LA
Louisiana State 6'4" 296 lbs.

1992	LARM	N	16	DT, DE
1993			16	DT
1994	WAS	N	10	DT
1995			16	DT
1996			10	DT
5 yrs.	68 games			

Lo Boutwell

BOUTWELL, LEON
(Little Cyclone)
B. Oct. 3, 1892
D. Oct, 1969, Mechanicsburg, OH
Carlisle 5'7" 188 lbs.

1922	OOR	N	7	QB
1923			7	QB, HB, FB
2 yrs.	14 games			

Tommy Boutwell

BOUTWELL, THOMAS
B. Dec. 31, 1946, McComb, MS
Southern Mississippi 6'2" 205 lbs.

| 1969 | MIA | A | 7 | QB |

Shawn Bouwens

BOUWENS, SHAWN
B. May 25, 1968, Lincoln, NE
Nebraska Wesleyan 6'4" 290 lbs.

1991	DET	N	16	G
1992			16	G
1993			15	G
1994			16	G
1995	JAC	N	10	G
5 yrs.	73 games			

Willie Bouyer

BOUYER, WILLIE LOUIS
B. Sep. 24, 1966, Detroit, MI
Michigan State 6'3" 200 lbs.

1989	SEA	N	1	WR
1990			1	WR
2 yrs.	2 games			

Matt Bouza

BOUZA, MATTHEW KYLE
B. Apr. 8, 1959, San Jose, CA
California 6'2" 205 lbs.

1981	SF	N	1	WR
1982	BAL	N	9	WR
1983			11	WR
1984	IND	N	16	WR
1985			12	WR
1986			16	WR
1987			12	WR
1988			15	WR
1989			2	WR
9 yrs.	94 games			

Tony Bova

BOVA, ANTHONY J.
B. Aug. 21, 1917, Pittsburgh, PA
D. Oct. 16, 1973, Pittsburgh, PA
St. Francis (Pennsylvania) 6'1" 190 lbs.

1942	PIT	N	11	E
1943	P, P	N	10	E
1944	C, P	N	9	E
1945	PIT	N	10	E
1946			11	E
1947			10	E
6 yrs.	61 games			

Pete Bove

BOVE, PETE A.
B. Sep. 21, 1906
D. Jul, 1974, Christiansted, St. Croix,
Virgin Islands
Holy Cross 5'10" 187 lbs.

| 1930 | NEW | N | 3 | G, T |

Gordon Bowdell

BOWDELL, GORDON
BENNETT, III
B. Oct. 9, 1948, Detroit, MI
Michigan State 6'2" 203 lbs.

| 1971 | DEN | N | 2 | WR |

Joe Bowden

BOWDEN, JOSEPH TARROD
B. Feb. 25, 1970, Dallas, TX
Oklahoma 5'11" 229 lbs.

1992	HOU	N	14	LB
1993			16	LB
1994			13	LB
1995			16	LB
1996			16	LB
5 yrs.	75 games			

Jim Bowdoin

BOWDOIN, JAMES L. (Goofy)
B. Jan. 15, 1904
D. May, 1969, Chickasaw, AL
Alabama 6'1" 227 lbs.

1928	GB	N	10	G
1929			12	G
1930			9	G
1931			13	G
1932	BKN	N	6	G
1932	NYG	N	6	G
1933	POR	N	7	G
1934	BKN	N	11	G
7 yrs.	74 games			

Kenny Bowen

BOWEN, KEN
B. Nov. 15, 1962
East Tennessee State 6'1" 220 lbs.

| 1987 | ATL | N | 1 | LB |

Tim Bowens

BOWENS, TIM
B. Feb. 7, 1973, Okolona, MS
Mississippi 6'4" 315 lbs.

1994	MIA	N	16	DT
1995			16	DT
1996			16	DT
3 yrs.	48 games			

Phil Bower

BOWER, JAMES PHILIP
B. Oct. 22, 1894
Deceased
Dartmouth 5'8" 160 lbs.

| 1921 | CLE | A | 5 | QB, HB |

Bill Bowers

BOWERS, WILLIAM
B. 1931
Southern California 6'0" 198 lbs.

| 1954 | LA | N | 8 | HB |

Sam Bowers

BOWERS, SAM TYRONE
B. Dec. 22, 1957, White Plains, NY
Tennessee State/Fordham 6'4" 250 lbs.*

| 1987 | CHI | N | 3 | TE |

Tony Bowick

BOWICK, VANTONIO BERNARD
B. Oct. 3, 1966, Dothan, AL
Tennessee, Chattanooga 6'2" 265 lbs.

| 1989 | ATL | N | 12 | NT |

Larry Bowie

BOWIE, LAWRENCE GLEN
B. Oct. 13, 1939, Pike, WV
Purdue 6'2" 247 lbs.

1962	MIN	N	14	G
1963			14	G
1964			14	G
1965			14	G
1966			14	G
1967			14	G
1968			8	G
7 yrs.	92 games			

Larry Bowie

BOWIE, LARRY
B. Mar. 21, 1973, Anniston, AL
Georgia 6'0" 224 lbs.

| 1996 | WAS | N | 3 | RB |

Todd Bowles

BOWLES, TODD ROBERT
B. Nov. 18, 1963, Elizabeth, NJ
Temple 6'2" 203 lbs.

1986	WAS	N	15	S
1987			12	S
1988			16	S
1989			16	S
1990			16	S
1991	SF	N	16	S
1992	WAS	N	16	S
1993			10	S
8 yrs.	117 games			

Andy Bowling

BOWLING, ANDY
B. Sep. 25, 1945
Virginia Tech 6'3" 235 lbs.

| 1967 | ATL | N | 6 | LB |

Barry Bowman

BOWMAN, BARRY
B. Dec. 18, 1964
Louisiana Tech 5'11" 180 lbs.

| 1987 | SEA | N | 1 | P |

Bill Bowman

BOWMAN, WILLIAM E., JR.
B. Sep. 22, 1931
William & Mary 6'2" 215 lbs.

1954	DET	N	12	FB
1956			6	FB
1957	PIT	N	5	FB
3 yrs.	23 games			

Jim Bowman

BOWMAN, JAMES EDWIN
B. Oct. 26, 1963, Cadillac, MI

Jim Bowman continued

Central Michigan 6'2" 210 lbs.

1985	NE	N	16	S
1986			16	S
1987			12	S
1988			16	S
1989			13	S
5 yrs.	73 games			

Ken Bowman

BOWMAN, KENNETH BRIAN
B. Dec. 15, 1942, Milan, IL
Wisconsin 6'3" 230 lbs.

1964	GB	N	14	C
1965			14	C
1966			4	C
1967			13	C
1968			12	C
1969			14	C
1970			14	C
1971			14	C
1972			14	C
1973			14	C
10 yrs.	127 games			

Kevin Bowman

BOWMAN, KEVIN GERARD
B. Feb. 23, 1962, Sacramento, CA
San Jose State 6'3" 205 lbs.

| 1987 | PHI | N | 3 | WR |

Steve Bowman

BOWMAN, STEVEN E.
B. Nov. 30, 1944, Pascagoula, MS
Alabama 6'0" 195 lbs.

| 1966 | NYG | N | 4 | HB |

Fabien Bownes

BOWNES, FABIEN
B. Feb. 29, 1972, Aurora, IL
Western Illinois 5'11" 180 lbs.

| 1995 | CHI | N | 1 | WR |

Arda Bowser

BOWSER, ARDA CRAWFORD
B. Jan. 9, 1899, Danville, PA
D. Sep. 7, 1996, Winter Park, FL
*Bethany (West Virginia)/Bucknell 6'2"
210 lbs.*

1922	CAN	N	5	FB, H, E
1923	CLE	N	3	FB
2 yrs.	8 games			

Charles Bowser

BOWSER, CHARLES EMANUEL
B. Oct. 2, 1959, Plymouth, NC
Duke 6'3" 232 lbs.

1982	MIA	N	9	LB
1983			16	LB
1984			15	LB
1985			2	LB
4 yrs.	42 games			

Walt Bowyer

**BOWYER, WALTER NATHANIEL,
JR.**
B. Sep. 8, 1960, Pittsburgh, PA
Arizona State 6'4" 260 lbs.

1983	DEN	N	14	DE
1984			16	DE
1987			15	DE
1988			16	DE
4 yrs.	61 games			

Cloyce Box

BOX, CLOYCE KENNEDY

Year	Team	Games	Pos.

Cloyce Box continued

B. Aug. 24, 1923, Gatesville, TX
D. Oct. 24, 1993, Frisco, TX
West Texas State 6'4" 220 lbs.

Year	Team		Games	Pos.
1949	DET	N	10	HB
1950			12	E
1952			12	E
1953			12	E
1954			11	E

5 yrs. 57 games

Jerry Boyarsky
BOYARSKY, GERARD MARK JOSEPH
B. May 15, 1959, Scranton, PA
Pittsburgh 6'3" 290 lbs.

Year	Team		Games	Pos.
1981	NO	N	11	DT
1982	CIN	N	2	NT
1983			15	NT
1984			15	NT
1985			16	NT
1986	BUF	N	10	NT
1986	GB	N	2	NT
1987			12	NT
1988			2	NT
1989			13	NT

9 yrs. 98 games

Bill Boyd
BOYD, WILLIAM ALVIN
B. 1907
Westminster (Missouri) 5'11" 175 lbs.

Year	Team		Games	Pos.
1930	CHIC	N	11	HB, QB
1931			4	HB

2 yrs. 15 games

Bob Boyd
BOYD, ROBERT B.
B. Mar. 7, 1928, Riverside, CA
Loyola (California) 6'2" 201 lbs.

Year	Team		Games	Pos.
1950	LA	N	12	E
1951			12	E, DB
1953			12	E, DB
1954			12	E
1955			6	E
1956			12	E
1957			12	E

7 yrs. 78 games

Bobby Boyd
BOYD, ROBERT DEAN
B. Dec. 3, 1937, Garland, TX
Oklahoma 5'10" 190 lbs.

Year	Team		Games	Pos.
1960	BAL	N	11	DB
1961			14	DB
1962			14	DB
1963			12	DB
1964			14	DB
1965			14	DB
1966			14	DB
1967			14	DB
1968			14	DB

9 yrs. 121 games

Brent Boyd
BOYD, BRENT VARNER
B. Mar. 23, 1957, Downey, CA
UCLA 6'3" 270 lbs.

Year	Team		Games	Pos.
1980	MIN	N	16	G, C
1981			3	G
1982			4	G
1983			16	G
1985			15	G
1986			5	G

6 yrs. 59 games

Dennis Boyd
BOYD, DENNIS

Dennis Boyd continued

B. Nov. 5, 1955, Washington, DC
Oregon State 6'6" 255 lbs.

Year	Team		Games	Pos.
1977	SEA	N	14	DE
1978			16	DT
1979			11	DT
1981			16	OT
1982			2	OT

5 yrs. 59 games

Elmo Boyd
BOYD, ELMO DAVID
B. Jun. 15, 1954, Muleshoe, TX
Eastern Kentucky 6'0" 188 lbs.

Year	Team		Games	Pos.
1978	SF	N	9	WR
1978	GB	N	2	WR

1 yr. 11 games

Greg Boyd
BOYD, GREGORY
B. Dec. 30, 1950, Scottsdale, AZ
Arizona 6'2" 201 lbs.

Year	Team		Games	Pos.
1973	NE	N	2	S
1974	NO	N	4	S

2 yrs. 6 games

Greg Boyd
BOYD, GREGORY EARL
B. Sep. 15, 1952, Merced, CA
San Diego State 6'6" 274 lbs.

Year	Team		Games	Pos.
1977	NE	N	13	DE
1978			10	DE
1980	DEN	N	16	DE
1981			15	DE
1982			9	DE
1983	GB	N	12	DE
1984	SF	N	2	DE
1984	LARI	N	5	NT

7 yrs. 82 games

Malik Boyd
BOYD, MALIK
B. Nov. 5, 1970, Houston, TX
Southern University 5'10" 175 lbs.

Year	Team		Games	Pos.
1994	MIN	N	15	CB

Sam Boyd
BOYD, SAM B.
B. 1914
Baylor 6'1" 188 lbs.

Year	Team		Games	Pos.
1939	PIT	N	11	E
1940			3	E

2 yrs. 14 games

Sean Boyd
BOYD, SEAN LEFELL
B. Dec. 19, 1972, Gastonia, NC
North Carolina 6'3" 206 lbs.

Year	Team		Games	Pos.
1996	ATL	N	2	S

Stephen Boyd
BOYD, STEPHEN GERARD
B. Aug. 22, 1972, Valley Stream, NY
Boston College 6'1" 247 lbs.

Year	Team		Games	Pos.
1995	DET	N	16	LB
1996			8	LB

2 yrs. 24 games

Thomas Boyd
BOYD, THOMAS TAYLOR
B. Nov. 24, 1959, Huntsville, AL
Alabama 6'3" 210 lbs.

Year	Team		Games	Pos.
1987	DET	N	4	LB

Mike Boyda
BOYDA, MICHAEL
B. Nov. 22, 1921, Jenners, PA
Washington & Lee 6'1" 205 lbs.

Year	Team		Games	Pos.
1949	NYB	N	9	FB, LB

Max Boydston
BOYDSTON, MAX
B. Jan. 22, 1932, Ardmore, OK
Oklahoma 6'2" 210 lbs.

Year	Team		Games	Pos.
1955	CHIC	N	3	OE
1956			12	OE
1957			12	OE
1958			10	OE
1960	DAL	A		OE
1961			11	OE
1962	OAK	A	14	OE

7 yrs. 62 games

Brant Boyer
BOYER, BRANT
B. Jun. 27, 1971, Ogden, UT
Arizona 6'0" 233 lbs.

Year	Team		Games	Pos.
1994	MIA	N	14	LB
1995	JAC	N	2	LB
1996			12	LB

3 yrs. 28 games

Mark Boyer
BOYER, MARK HEARN
B. Sep. 16, 1962, Huntington Beach, CA
Southern California 6'4" 239 lbs.

Year	Team		Games	Pos.
1985	IND	N	16	TE
1986			16	TE
1987			7	TE
1988			16	TE
1989			16	TE
1990	NYJ	N	16	TE
1991			11	TE
1992			12	TE

8 yrs. 110 games

Verdi Boyer
BOYER, VERDI E., JR.
B. Sep. 2, 1911, San Francisco, CA
UCLA 5'10" 195 lbs.

Year	Team		Games	Pos.
1936	BKN	N	11	G

Lon Boyett
BOYETT, LON
B. Dec. 24, 1953, Lancaster, CA
Northridge State 6'6" 240 lbs.

Year	Team		Games	Pos.
1978	SF	N	3	TE

Garland Boyette
BOYETTE, GARLAND DEAN
B. Mar. 22, 1940, Orange, TX
Grambling State 6'1" 237 lbs.

Year	Team		Games	Pos.
1962	STL	N	14	LB
1963			9	LB
1966	HOU	A	14	LB
1967			14	LB
1968			14	LB
1969			14	LB
1970	HOU	N	13	LB
1971			14	LB
1972			14	LB

9 yrs. 120 games

Deral Boykin
BOYKIN, DERAL LAMONT
B. Sep. 2, 1970, Kent, OH
Louisville 5'11" 196 lbs.

Year	Team		Games	Pos.
1993	LARM	N	16	S
1994	WAS	N	12	S
1995	JAC	N	5	S

Deral Boykin continued

Year	Team		Games	Pos.
1996	PHI	N	10	S

4 yrs. 43 games

Greg Boykin
BOYKIN, GREG
B. Dec. 8, 1953, Ravenna, OH
Northwestern 6'0" 225 lbs.

Year	Team		Games	Pos.
1977	NO	N	14	RB
1978	SF	N	16	RB

2 yrs. 30 games

Jim Boylan
BOYLAN, JAMES
B. 1939
Washington State 6'1" 185 lbs.

Year	Team		Games	Pos.
1963	MIN	N	3	DB

Bill Boyle
BOYLE, WILLIAM (Knuckles)
B. 1909
None 5'11" 232 lbs.

Year	Team		Games	Pos.
1934	NYG	N	1	T

Jack Boyle
BOYLE, JOHN C.
B. Jan. 4, 1904, Illinois
D. Dec., 1966
Loras 195 lbs.

Year	Team		Games	Pos.
1926	CHI	A	1	E

Jim Boyle
BOYLE, JAMES ROBERT
B. Jul. 27, 1962, Cincinnati, OH
Tulane 6'5" 270 lbs.

Year	Team		Games	Pos.
1987	PIT	N	3	OT
1988			6	OT

2 yrs. 9 games

Benny Boynton
BOYNTON, BEN LEE (The Purple Streak)
B. Dec. 6, 1898, Waco, TX
D. Jan. 24, 1963
Williams 5'9" 170 lbs.

Year	Team		Games	Pos.
1921	WAS	A	2	HB, QB
1921	ROC	A	4	QB
1922	ROC	N	1	QB
1924			1	HB
1924	BUF	N	9	QB, HB

3 yrs. 17 games

George Boynton
BOYNTON, GEORGE
B. 1938
East Texas State 5'11" 190 lbs.

Year	Team		Games	Pos.
1962	OAK	A	3	DB

John Boynton
BOYNTON, JOHN
B. Mar. 28, 1946, Pikeville, TN
Tennessee 6'4" 255 lbs.

Year	Team		Games	Pos.
1969	MIA	A	14	OT

Ordell Braase
BRAASE, ORDELL WAYNE
B. Mar. 13, 1932, Mitchell, SD
South Dakota 6'4" 240 lbs.

Year	Team		Games	Pos.
1957	BAL	N	12	DE
1958			12	DE
1959			12	DE
1960			12	DE
1961			14	DE
1962			14	DE
1963			14	DE

Year	Team	Games	Pos.

Ordell Braase *continued*

Year	Team		Games	Pos.
1964			14	DE
1965			12	DE
1966			14	DE
1967			14	DE
1968			14	DE
12 yrs.	156 games			

Tom Braatz
BRAATZ, THOMAS
B. 1933, Kenosha, WI
Marquette 6'1" 216 lbs.

1957	WAS	N	10	E
1958	LA	N	1	E
1958	WAS	N	3	E
1959			12	E
1960	DAL	N	12	LB
4 yrs.	38 games			

Cary Brabham
BRABHAM, CARY
B. Aug. 11, 1970, Longview, TX
Southern Methodist 6'0" 195 lbs.

| 1994 | LARI | N | 7 | S |

Danny Brabham
BRABHAM, DANIEL EDWARD
B. Feb. 25, 1941, Magnolia, MS
Arkansas 6'4" 236 lbs.

1963	HOU	A	14	FB
1964			13	LB
1965			14	LB
1966			3	LB
1967			12	LB
1968	CIN	A	9	LB
6 yrs.	65 games			

Bill Brace
BRACE, GEORGE WELLS
B. Nov. 19, 1895
D. Jan., 1972, Lakewood, NY
Brown 6'0" 180 lbs.

1920	BUF	A	6	G
1921			11	G, C
1922	BUF	N	10	G
3 yrs.	27 games			

Greg Bracelin
BRACELIN, GREGORY LEE
B. Apr. 16, 1957, Lawrence, KS
California 6'1" 218 lbs.

1980	DEN	N	12	LB
1981	OAK	N	15	LB
1982	BAL	N	9	LB
1983			16	LB
1984	IND	N	16	LB
5 yrs.	68 games			

Don Bracken
BRACKEN, DONALD CRAIG
B. Feb. 16, 1962, Coalinga, CA
Michigan 6'0" 205 lbs.

1985	GB	N	7	P
1986			13	P
1987			12	P
1988			16	P
1989			16	P
1990			16	P
1992	LARM	N	16	P
1993			3	P
8 yrs.	99 games			

Tony Brackens
BRACKENS, TONY
B. Dec. 26, 1974, Fairfield, TX
Texas 6'4" 260 lbs.

| 1996 | JAC | N | 16 | DE |

M.L. Brackett
BRACKETT, M.L.
B. Jul. 4, 1933, Etowah County, AL
Auburn 6'5" 248 lbs.

1956	CHIB	N	12	T
1957			8	T
1958	NYG	N	12	T
3 yrs.	32 games			

Charlie Brackins
BRACKINS, CHARLES
B. Jan. 12, 1932, Dallas, TX
Prairie View A&M 6'2" 202 lbs.

| 1955 | GB | N | 7 | QB |

Dave Braden
BRADEN, DAVID E.T.
B. Sep. 27, 1917
D. Aug., 1980, Milwaukee, WI
Marquette 6'0" 210 lbs.

| 1945 | CHIC | N | 1 | G |

Ronnie Bradford
BRADFORD, RON
B. Oct. 1, 1970, Minot, ND
Colorado 5'10" 188 lbs.

1993	DEN	N	10	CB
1994			12	CB
1995			4	CB
1996	ARI	N	15	CB
4 yrs.	41 games			

Byron Bradfute
BRADFUTE, BYRON
B. 1938, Beeville, TX
Abilene Christian/Southern Mississippi 6'3" 243 lbs.

1960	DAL	N	12	OT
1961			5	OT
2 yrs.	17 games			

Bill Bradley
BRADLEY, WILLIAM CALVIN
B. Jun. 24, 1947, Palestine, TX
Texas 5'11" 190 lbs.

1969	PHI	N	14	P, S
1970			12	P, S
1971			14	P, S
1972			14	P, S
1973			14	S, P
1974			14	S, P
1975			14	S
1976			14	S
1977	STL	N	4	S
9 yrs.	114 games			

Carlos Bradley
BRADLEY, CARLOS HUMBERTO
B. Apr. 27, 1960, Philadelphia, PA
Wake Forest 6'0" 221 lbs.

1981	SD	N	8	LB
1982			9	LB
1983			16	LB
1984			8	LB
1985			10	LB
1987	PHI	N	3	LB
6 yrs.	54 games			

Chuck Bradley
BRADLEY, CHARLES JOHN
B. Oct. 13, 1950, Hinsdale, IL
Oregon 6'6" 243 lbs.

1975	SD	N	4	TE
1976			7	TE
1977			1	TE
1977	CHI	N	7	TE
3 yrs.	19 games			

Chuck Bradley
BRADLEY, CHARLES WARREN, II
B. Apr. 9, 1970, Covington, KY
Kentucky 6'5" 296 lbs.

| 1993 | CIN | N | 1 | LB |

Danny Bradley
BRADLEY, DANNY L.
B. Mar. 2, 1963, Pine Bluff, AR
Oklahoma 5'9" 175 lbs.

| 1987 | DET | N | 3 | WR |

Dave Bradley
BRADLEY, DAVID
B. Feb. 13, 1947, Burnham, PA
Penn State 6'4" 245 lbs.

1969	GB	N	4	G
1970			4	G
1971			6	G
1972	STL	N	1	G
4 yrs.	15 games			

Ed Bradley
BRADLEY, EDWARD WILLIAM, II
(Strong Man)
B. Sep. 16, 1926, Stratford, CT
Wake Forest 6'0" 212 lbs.

1950	CHIB	N	3	DE
1952			8	G
2 yrs.	11 games			

Ed Bradley
BRADLEY, EDWARD WILLIAM
B. Apr. 22, 1950, Bridgeport, CT
Wake Forest 6'2" 234 lbs.

1972	PIT	N	12	LB
1973			14	LB
1974			10	LB
1975			13	LB
1976	SEA	N	14	LB
1977	SF	N	14	LB
1978			16	LB
7 yrs.	93 games			

Freddie Bradley
BRADLEY, FREDDIE
B. Jun. 12, 1970, Helena, AR
Arkansas/Sonoma State 5'10" 208 lbs.

| 1996 | SD | N | 10 | RB |

Hal Bradley
BRADLEY, HAROLD
B. Nov. 23, 1913, Winston-Salem, NC
Elon 6'4" 205 lbs.

1938	WAS	N	7	E
1939			1	E
1939	CHIC	N	3	E
2 yrs.	11 games			

Hal Bradley
BRADLEY, HAROLD H.
B. 1905
None 185 lbs.

| 1928 | CHIC | N | 2 | G |

Harold Bradley
BRADLEY, HAROLD W.
B. Oct. 13, 1929
Iowa 6'2" 230 lbs.

1954	CLE	N	12	G
1955			12	G
1956			11	G
1958	PHI	N	12	G
4 yrs.	47 games			

Henry Bradley
BRADLEY, HENRY AVERSON
B. Sep. 4, 1953, St. Joseph, PA
Alcorn State 6'2" 262 lbs.

1979	CLE	N	5	DT
1980			16	DT
1981			16	DT
1982			6	NT
4 yrs.	43 games			

Luther Bradley
BRADLEY, LUTHER ALEXANDER
B. May 7, 1955, Florence, SC
Notre Dame 6'2" 194 lbs.

1978	DET	N	16	CB
1979			16	CB
1980			8	CB
1981			16	S
4 yrs.	56 games			

Steve Bradley
BRADLEY, STEVE
B. Jul. 16, 1963
Indiana 6'2" 216 lbs.

| 1987 | CHI | N | 1 | QB |

Charlie Bradshaw
BRADSHAW, CHARLES MARVIN
B. Mar. 13, 1936, Center, TX
Baylor 6'6" 255 lbs.

1958	LA	N	12	OT
1959			12	OT
1960			12	OT
1961	PIT	N	12	OT
1962			14	OT
1963			14	OT
1964			14	OT
1965			14	OT
1966			14	OT
1967	DET	N	14	OT
1968			13	OT
11 yrs.	145 games			

Craig Bradshaw
BRADSHAW, CRAIG
B. Aug. 14, 1957, Shreveport, LA
Louisiana Tech/Utah State 6'5" 215 lbs.

| 1980 | HOU | N | 2 | QB |

Jim Bradshaw
BRADSHAW, JAMES (Rabbit)
B. Jun. 23, 1898, Green County, MO
D. Jul. 6, 1987, Monterey, CA
Illinois/Nevada-Reno 5'6" 145 lbs.

1924	KC	N	1	HB
1926	LA	A	10	QB
2 yrs.	11 games			

Jim Bradshaw
BRADSHAW, JAMES ALFRED
B. Jan. 13, 1939, St. Clairsville, OH
Tennessee-Chattanooga 6'1" 199 lbs.

1963	PIT	N	14	DB
1964			14	DB
1965			12	DB
1966			9	DB
1967			13	DB
5 yrs.	62 games			

Morris Bradshaw
BRADSHAW, MORRIS, JR.
B. Oct. 19, 1952, Highland, IL
Ohio State 6'0" 196 lbs.

| 1974 | OAK | N | 12 | WR |

Year	Team		Games	Pos.

Morris Bradshaw continued

Year	Team		Games	Pos.
1975			14	WR
1976			14	WR
1977			14	WR
1978			16	WR
1979			3	WR
1980			16	WR
1981			15	WR
1982	NE	N	8	WR
9 yrs.		112 games		

Terry Bradshaw
BRADSHAW, TERRY PAXTON
B. Sep. 2, 1948, Shreveport, LA
Louisiana Tech 6'3" 215 lbs.

1970	PIT	N	13	QB
1971			14	QB
1972			14	QB
1973			10	QB
1974			8	QB
1975			14	QB
1976			10	QB
1977			14	QB
1978			16	QB
1979			16	QB
1980			15	QB
1981			14	QB
1982			9	QB
1983			1	QB
14 yrs.		168 games		

Wes Bradshaw
BRADSHAW, WESLEY W.
B. Nov. 26, 1898
Trinity (Texas)/Baylor 5'11" 175 lbs.

1924	RI	N	7	HB, QB
1926	RI	A	8	HB, QB
1926	BUF	N	1	HB, QB
2 yrs.		16 games		

Donny Brady
BRADY, DONNY
B. Nov. 24, 1973, North Bellmore, NY
Wisconsin 6'2" 195 lbs.

1995	CLE	N	2	DB
1996	BAL	N	16	CB
2 yrs.		18 games		

Ed Brady
BRADY, ED JOHN
B. Jun. 17, 1960, Morris, IL
Illinois 6'2" 235 lbs.

1984	LARM	N	16	LB
1985			16	LB
1986	CIN	N	16	LB
1987			12	LB
1988			16	LB
1989			16	LB
1990			16	LB
1991			16	LB
1992	TB	N	16	LB
1993			16	LB
1994			16	LB
1995			16	LB
12 yrs.		188 games		

Jeff Brady
BRADY, JEFFREY THOMAS
B. Nov. 9, 1968, Cincinnati, OH
Kentucky 6'1" 224 lbs.

1991	PIT	N	16	LB
1992	GB	N	8	LB
1993	LARM	N	6	LB
1993	SD	N	3	LB
1994	TB	N	16	LB
1995	MIN	N	16	LB
1996			16	LB
6 yrs.		81 games		

Kerry Brady
BRADY, KERRY
B. Aug. 27, 1963, Vancouver, WA
Hawaii 6'1" 205 lbs.

1987	DAL	N	1	K
1988	IND	N	2	K
1989	BUF	N	3	K
3 yrs.		6 games		

Kyle Brady
BRADY, KYLE JAMES
B. Jan. 14, 1972, New Cumberland, PA
Penn State 6'6" 260 lbs.

1995	NYJ	N	15	TE
1996			16	TE
2 yrs.		31 games		

Pat Brady
BRADY, PATRICK
B. Sep. 7, 1928, Seattle, WA
Nevada-Reno/Bradley 6'1" 195 lbs.

1952	PIT	N	12	QB, P
1953			12	QB, P
1954			12	QB, P
3 yrs.		36 games		

Phil Brady
BRADY, PHILIP
B. Apr. 22, 1943, Mesa, AZ
Brigham Young 6'2" 211 lbs.

1969	DEN	A	4	S

Rickey Brady
BRADY, RICKEY LEE
B. Nov. 19, 1970, Oklahoma City, OK
Oklahoma 6'4" 242 lbs.

1994	LARM	N	1	TE

Mike Bragg
BRAGG, MICHAEL EDWARD
B. Sep. 26, 1946, Richmond, VA
Richmond 5'11" 186 lbs.

1968	WAS	N	14	P
1969			14	P
1970			14	P
1971			14	P
1972			14	P
1973			14	P
1974			14	P
1975			14	P
1976			14	P
1977			14	P
1978			16	P
1979			16	P
1980	BAL	N	16	P
13 yrs.		188 games		

Byron Braggs
BRAGGS, BYRON C.
B. Oct. 10, 1959, Montgomery, AL
Alabama 6'4" 290 lbs.

1981	GB	N	16	DE
1982			9	DE
1983			16	DE
1984	TB	N	14	DE
4 yrs.		55 games		

Stephen Braggs
BRAGGS, STEPHEN
B. Aug. 29, 1965, Houston, TX
Texas 5'9" 173 lbs.

1987	CLE	N	12	CB, S
1988			16	CB, S
1989			7	CB
1990			15	CB
1991			16	CB
1992	MIA	N	6	CB

Stephen Braggs continued

1993			11	S, CB
7 yrs.		83 games		

Dennis Bragonier
BRAGONIER, DENNIS
Stanford

1974	SF	N	2	DB

Rich Braham
BRAHAM, RICH
B. Nov. 6, 1970, Morgantown, WV
West Virginia 6'4" 290 lbs.

1994	CIN	N	3	OT
1996			16	G
2 yrs.		19 games		

Tom Brahaney
BRAHANEY, THOMAS FRANK
B. Oct. 23, 1951, Midland, TX
Oklahoma 6'2" 245 lbs.

1973	STL	N	14	C
1974			14	C
1975			14	C
1976			14	C
1977			14	C
1978			16	C
1979			16	C
1980			16	C
1981			16	C
9 yrs.		134 games		

Larry Brahm
BRAHM, LAWRENCE
B. Aug. 12, 1916, Bayonne, NJ
D. Jul., 1959
Temple 5'10" 204 lbs.

1942	CLE	N	11	G

Chuck Braidwood
BRAIDWOOD, CHARLES
B. 1905
D. 1944-1945, South Pacific
Loyola (Illinois)/Tennessee-Chattanooga 6'0" 199 lbs.

1930	POR	N	9	E, G
1931	CLE	N	8	E
1932	CHIC	N	1	E
1933	CIN	N	6	E
4 yrs.		24 games		

Art Braman
BRAMAN, ARTHUR H. (Bull)
B. Aug. 4, 1897
D. Aug. 12, 1967, Carmel Highlands, CA
Yale 6'0" 215 lbs.

1922	RAC	N	8	T
1923			6	T
2 yrs.		14 games		

Don Bramlett
BRAMLETT, DON
B. Oct. 5, 1962, Memphis, TN
Memphis State/Carson-Newman 6'2" 270 lbs.

1987	MIN	N	3	DT

John Bramlett
BRAMLETT, JOHN CAMERON
B. Jul. 7, 1941, Memphis, TN
Memphis State 6'2" 216 lbs.

1965	DEN	A	14	LB
1966			14	LB
1967	MIA	A	14	LB
1968			13	LB

John Bramlett continued

1969	BOS	A	12	LB
1970	BOS	N	12	LB
1971	ATL	N	7	LB
7 yrs.		86 games		

Mark Brammer
BRAMMER, MARK D.
B. May 3, 1958, Traverse City, MI
Michigan State 6'3" 236 lbs.

1980	BUF	N	16	TE
1981			16	TE
1982			9	TE
1983			12	TE
1984			12	TE
5 yrs.		65 games		

George Brancato
BRANCATO, GEORGE
B. May 27, 1931, Brooklyn, NY
Louisiana State 5'9" 177 lbs.

1954	CHIC	N	5	B

Cliff Branch
BRANCH, CLIFFORD
B. Aug. 1, 1948, Houston, TX
Colorado 5'11" 170 lbs.

1972	OAK	N	14	WR
1973			13	WR
1974			13	WR
1975			14	WR
1976			14	WR
1977			13	WR
1978			16	WR
1979			16	WR
1980			16	WR
1981			16	WR
1982	LARI	N	9	WR
1983			12	WR
1984			14	WR
1985			4	WR
14 yrs.		182 games		

Mel Branch
BRANCH, MELVIN LEROY
B. Feb. 15, 1937, Leesville, LA
Louisiana State 6'2" 231 lbs.

1960	DAL	A	14	DE
1961			14	DE
1962			14	DE
1963	KC	A	14	DE
1964			14	DE
1965			14	DE
1966	MIA	A	14	DE
1967			14	DE
1968			14	DE
9 yrs.		126 games		

Reggie Branch
BRANCH, REGINALD ETOY
B. Oct. 22, 1962, Sanford, FL
West Virginia State/East Carolina 5'11" 227 lbs.

1985	WAS	N	8	RB
1986			1	RB
1987			12	RB
1988			7	RB
1989			10	RB
5 yrs.		38 games		

Art Brandau
BRANDAU, ARTHUR ALBERT
B. Jun. 23, 1922, Baltimore, MD
Tennessee 6'2" 210 lbs.

1945	PIT	N	1	C, LB
1946			5	C, LB
2 yrs.		6 games		

Year	Team	Games	Pos.

Butch Brandau
BRANDAU, ARTHUR FRANK
B. Dec. 5, 1897
D. Jul., 1973, Detroit, MI
None 192 lbs.

Year	Team		Games	Pos.
1921	DET	A	4	HB, FB, C

John Brandes
BRANDES, JOHN WESLEY
B. Apr. 2, 1964, Fort Riley, KS
Cameron 6'2" 237 lbs.

Year	Team		Games	Pos.
1987	IND	N	12	TE
1988			16	TE
1989			16	TE
1990	WAS	N	16	TE
1991			16	TE
1992			1	TE
1992	NYG	N	4	TE
1993	SF	N	9	TE

7 yrs.   90 games

David Brandon
BRANDON, DAVID SHERROD
B. Feb. 9, 1965, Memphis, TN
Memphis State 6'4" 225 lbs.

Year	Team		Games	Pos.
1987	SD	N	8	LB
1988			8	LB
1989			13	LB
1991	CLE	N	16	LB
1992			16	LB
1993			6	LB
1993	SEA	N	7	LB
1994			13	LB
1995	SD	N	15	LB
1996	ATL	N	16	LB

9 yrs.   118 games

Michael Brandon
BRANDON, MICHAEL BREON
B. Jul. 30, 1968, Perry, FL
Florida 6'4" 290 lbs.

Year	Team		Games	Pos.
1993	IND	N	15	DE
1994	ARI	N	1	DE
1995	SF	N	12	DE
1996			3	DE

4 yrs.   31 games

Jim Brandt
BRANDT, JAMES
B. May 19, 1929, Fargo, ND
St. Thomas (Minnesota) 6'1" 200 lbs.

Year	Team		Games	Pos.
1952	PIT	N	12	HB
1953			12	HB
1954			12	HB

3 yrs.   36 games

Speed Braney
BREHENEY, JOSEPH P.
B. Aug. 19, 1892
D. Dec., 1967, Boston, MA
Syracuse/Fordham 6'0" 188 lbs.

Year	Team		Games	Pos.
1925	PRO	N	6	G
1926			7	G, T, C

2 yrs.   13 games

Solomon Brannan
BRANNAN, SOLOMON EMBRA
B. Sep. 5, 1942, Savannah, GA
Morris Brown 6'1" 188 lbs.

Year	Team		Games	Pos.
1965	KC	A	10	HB
1966			3	DB
1967	NY	A	12	DB

3 yrs.   25 games

Robert Brannon
BRANNON, ROBERT
B. Mar. 26, 1961, Charleston, SC

Robert Brannon continued
Arkansas 6'7" 245 lbs.

Year	Team		Games	Pos.
1987	CLE	N	1	DE
1987	NO	N	1	DE

1 yr.   2 games

Kent Bransletter
BRANSLETTER, KENT WAYNE
B. Feb. 3, 1949, Galveston, TX
Houston 6'3" 260 lbs.

Year	Team		Games	Pos.
1973	GB	N	9	OT

Chris Brantley
BRANTLEY, CHRISTOPHER CHARLES
B. Dec. 12, 1970, Rahway, NJ
Rutgers 5'10" 175 lbs.

Year	Team		Games	Pos.
1994	LARM	N	13	WR
1996	BUF	N	9	WR

2 yrs.   22 games

John Brantley
BRANTLEY, JOHN PHILLIP
B. Oct. 23, 1965, Ocala, FL
Georgia 6'2" 245 lbs.

Year	Team		Games	Pos.
1989	HOU	N	8	LB
1992	WAS	N	12	LB

2 yrs.   20 games

Scot Brantley
BRANTLEY, SCOT EUGENE
B. Feb. 24, 1958, Chester, SC
Florida 6'2" 230 lbs.

Year	Team		Games	Pos.
1980	TB	N	16	LB
1981			16	LB
1982			9	LB
1983			16	LB
1984			16	LB
1985			13	LB
1986			16	LB
1987			12	LB

8 yrs.   114 games

Gene Branton
BRANTON, RHEUGENE JAMES
B. Nov. 23, 1960, Tampa, FL
Texas Southern 6'4" 210 lbs.

Year	Team		Games	Pos.
1983	TB	N	1	WR
1985			3	TE

2 yrs.   4 games

Zeke Bratkowski
BRATKOWSKI, EDMUND RAYMOND
B. Oct. 20, 1931, Danville, IL
Georgia 6'4" 204 lbs.

Year	Team		Games	Pos.
1954	CHIB	N	12	QB
1957			12	QB
1958			12	QB
1959			12	QB
1960	CHI		11	QB
1961	LA		13	QB
1962			13	QB
1963			4	QB
1963	GB	N	6	QB
1964			5	QB
1965			6	QB
1966			8	QB
1967			6	QB
1968			10	QB
1971			6	QB

14 yrs.   136 games

Jason Bratton
BRATTON, JASON
B. Oct. 19, 1972

Jason Bratton continued
Grambling State 6'1" 252 lbs.

Year	Team		Games	Pos.
1996	BUF	N	2	RB

Melvin Bratton
BRATTON, MELVIN TORRANCE
B. Feb. 2, 1965, Miami, FL
Miami (Florida) 6'1" 225 lbs.

Year	Team		Games	Pos.
1989	DEN	N	16	RB
1990			16	RB

2 yrs.   32 games

Chad Bratzke
BRATZKE, CHAD ALLEN
B. Sep. 15, 1971, Brandon, FL
Eastern Kentucky 6'4" 262 lbs.

Year	Team		Games	Pos.
1994	NYG	N	2	DE
1995			6	DE
1996			16	DE

3 yrs.   24 games

Alex Bravo
BRAVO, ALEXANDER
B. Jul. 27, 1930
California Poly 6'0" 190 lbs.

Year	Team		Games	Pos.
1957	LA	N	12	DB
1958			3	DB
1960	OAK	A		DB
1961			14	DB

4 yrs.   29 games

Jack Bravyak
BRAVYAK, JOHN
B. Sep. 10, 1959
Temple 6'3" 255 lbs.

Year	Team		Games	Pos.
1987	BUF	N	1	DE

Ed Brawley
BRAWLEY, E.F.
B. Jul., 1892
Deceased
Holy Cross 5'9" 175 lbs.

Year	Team		Games	Pos.
1921	NY	A	1	G
1921	CLE	A	4	G

1 yr.   5 games

David Braxton
BRAXTON, DAVID HAROLD
B. May 26, 1965, Omaha, NE
Wake Forest 6'1" 236 lbs.

Year	Team		Games	Pos.
1989	MIN	N	3	LB
1990				LB
1990	PHX	N	11	LB
1991			16	LB
1992			16	LB
1993			16	LB
1994	CIN		8	LB

6 yrs.   71 games

Hez Braxton
BRAXTON, HEZEKIAH
B. 1936
Virginia Union 6'2" 227 lbs.

Year	Team		Games	Pos.
1962	SD	A	8	FB
1963	BUF	A	1	HB

2 yrs.   9 games

Jim Braxton
BRAXTON, JAMES ROBERT
B. May 23, 1949, Vanderbilt, PA
D. Jun. 28, 1986, Buffalo, NY
West Virginia 6'2" 238 lbs.

Year	Team		Games	Pos.
1971	BUF	N	13	FB
1972			12	FB
1973			6	FB
1974			12	FB

Jim Braxton continued

Year	Team		Games	Pos.
1975			14	FB
1976			1	FB
1977			14	FB
1978			6	FB
1978	MIA	N	10	FB

8 yrs.   88 games

Tyrone Braxton
BRAXTON, TYRONE SCOTT
B. Dec. 12, 1964, Madison, WI
North Dakota State 5'11" 174 lbs.

Year	Team		Games	Pos.
1987	DEN	N	2	S
1988			16	S
1989			16	S
1990			3	CB
1991			16	CB
1992			16	CB
1993			16	CB
1994	MIA	N	16	CB, S
1995	DEN	N	16	S
1996			16	S

10 yrs.   133 games

Mule Bray
BRAY, ANDREW MAURICE
B. Aug. 27, 1909, Paducah, TX
D. Dec. 9, 1966
Southern Methodist 6'2" 220 lbs.

Year	Team		Games	Pos.
1935	PIT	N	12	T
1936			11	T

2 yrs.   23 games

Ray Bray
BRAY, RAYMOND ROBERT
(Muscles)
B. Feb. 1, 1917, Caspian, MI
D. Dec. 26, 1993, Mesa, AZ
Western Michigan 6'0" 237 lbs.

Year	Team		Games	Pos.
1939	CHIB	N	11	G, T
1940			6	G
1941			11	G
1942			10	G
1946			11	G
1947			12	G
1948			12	G
1949			12	G
1950			12	G
1951			12	G
1952	GB	N	12	G

11 yrs.   121 games

Carl Brazell
BRAZELL, CARL
B. Jul. 20, 1917
D. May, 1978, Parkersburg, WV
Baylor 5'10" 195 lbs.

Year	Team		Games	Pos.
1938	CLE	N	11	QB

Larry Braziel
BRAZIEL, LARRY
B. Sep. 25, 1954, Fort Worth, TX
Southern California 6'0" 190 lbs.

Year	Team		Games	Pos.
1979	BAL	N	16	CB, S
1980			15	CB
1981			16	CB
1982	CLE	N	6	CB
1983			13	CB
1984			13	CB
1985			16	CB

7 yrs.   95 games

Robert Brazile
BRAZILE, ROBERT LORENZO, JR.
B. Feb. 7, 1953, Mobile, AL
Jackson State 6'4" 238 lbs.

Year	Team		Games	Pos.
1975	HOU	N	14	LB

Year	Team		Games	Pos.

Robert Brazile *continued*

Year	Team		Games	Pos.
1976			14	LB
1977			14	LB
1978			16	LB
1979			16	LB
1980			16	LB
1981			16	LB
1982			9	LB
1983			16	LB
1984			16	LB
10 yrs.	147 games			

Sam Brazinsky
BRAZINSKY, SAMUEL J.
B. Jan. 9, 1921, Kulpmont, PA
Villanova 6'1" 215 lbs.

1946	BUF	AA	5	B, C

Carl Brazley
BRAZLEY, CARL
B. Sep. 5, 1957, Louisville, KY
Western Kentucky 6'0" 180 lbs.

1987	SD	N	2	CB

Don Breaux
BREAUX, DONALD
B. Aug. 3, 1940, Jennings, LA
McNeese State 6'1" 203 lbs.

1963	DEN	A	9	QB
1965	SD	A	14	QB
2 yrs.	23 games			

Bill Bredde
BREDDE, WILLIAM
B. Dec. 31, 1932, Shawnee, OK
Oklahoma A&M 6'1" 195 lbs.

1954	CHIC	N	12	B

John Bredice
BREDICE, JOHN J.
B. Jun. 23, 1964
Boston University 6'1" 213 lbs.

1956	PHI	N	12	E

Ed Breding
BREDING, EDWARD VINCENT
B. Nov. 3, 1944, Billings, MT
Texas A&M 6'4" 235 lbs.

1967	WAS	N	14	LB
1968			14	LB
2 yrs.	28 games			

Jim Breech
BREECH, JAMES THOMAS
B. Apr. 11, 1956, Sacramento, CA
California 5'6" 160 lbs.

1979	OAK	N	16	K
1980	CIN	N	4	K
1981			16	K
1982			9	K
1983			16	K
1984			16	K
1985			16	K
1986			16	K
1987			12	K
1988			16	K
1989			12	K
1990			16	K
1991			16	K
1992			16	K
14 yrs.	197 games			

Bill Breeden
BREEDEN, J.W.
B. 1915
D. Dec. 16, 1982, Dallas, TX

Bill Breeden *continued*
Oklahoma 6'1" 210 lbs.

1937	PIT	N	9	E, B

Louis Breeden
BREEDEN, LOUIS EVERETT
B. Oct. 26, 1953, Hamlet, NC
North Carolina Central 5'11" 185 lbs.

1978	CIN	N	16	CB
1979			10	CB
1980			16	CB
1981			16	CB
1982			6	CB
1983			14	CB
1984			16	CB
1985			16	CB
1986			16	CB
1987			8	CB
10 yrs.	134 games			

Rod Breedlove
BREEDLOVE, RODNEY WINSTON
B. Mar. 10, 1938, Cumberland, MD
Maryland 6'2" 225 lbs.

1960	WAS	N	11	LB
1961			11	LB
1962			14	LB
1963			14	LB
1964			12	LB
1965	PIT	N	14	LB
1966			11	LB
1967			14	LB
8 yrs.	101 games			

Adrian Breen
BREEN, ADRIAN
B. Jan. 11, 1965
Morehead State 6'4" 183 lbs.

1987	CIN	N		QB

Gene Breen
BREEN, JOSEPH EUGENE
B. Jun. 21, 1941, Crafton, PA
Virginia Tech 6'2" 229 lbs.

1964	GB	N	6	LB
1965	PIT	N	14	LB
1966			2	LB
1967	LA	N	7	LB
1968			3	LB
5 yrs.	32 games			

Jeff Bregel
BREGEL, JEFFERY BRYAN
B. May 1, 1964, Redondo Beach, CA
Southern California 6'4" 280 lbs.

1987	SF	N	5	G
1988			13	G
1989			3	G
3 yrs.	21 games			

Bob Breitenstein
BREITENSTEIN, ROBERT CORR
B. Apr. 8, 1943, Buenos Aires, Argentina
Tulsa 6'3" 264 lbs.

1965	DEN	A	14	OT
1966			14	OT
1967			2	OT
1968	MIN	N	11	OT
1969	ATL	N	10	G
1970			7	G, OT
5 yrs.	58 games			

Wayne Brenkert
BRENKERT, WAYNE D.
B. Mar. 5, 1898

Wayne Brenkert *continued*
D. Aug. 1, 1979, Altamonte Springs, FL
Washington & Jefferson 5'10" 160 lbs.

1923	AKR	N	7	HB, QB
1924			8	QB, HB
2 yrs.	15 games			

Brian Brennan
BRENNAN, BRIAN MICHAEL
B. Feb. 15, 1962, Bloomfield, MI
Boston College 5'9" 178 lbs.

1984	CLE	N	15	WR
1985			12	WR
1986			16	WR
1987			13	WR
1988			16	WR
1989			14	WR
1990			16	WR
1991			15	WR
1992	CIN	N	9	WR
1992	SD	N	5	WR
9 yrs.	131 games			

Jack Brennan
BRENNAN, JOHN
B. Sep. 28, 1913
D. Mar., 1975
Michigan 6'1" 204 lbs.

1939	GB	N	2	G

Leo Brennan
BRENNAN, LEO
B. Sep. 19, 1919, Boston, MA
Holy Cross 6'0" 210 lbs.

1942	PHI	N	10	T, G

Matt Brennan
BRENNAN, MATTHEW
B. Nov. 4, 1897
D. Oct., 1971, Delmar, NY
Villanova/Fordham/Lafayette 6'1" 183 lbs.

1925	NYG	N	6	HB, QB, FB
1926	BKN	N	10	QB, HB
2 yrs.	16 games			

Mike Brennan
BRENNAN, MICHAEL SEAN
B. Mar. 22, 1967, Los Angeles, CA
Notre Dame 6'5" 274 lbs.

1990	CIN	N	16	OT
1991			3	OT
2 yrs.	19 games			

Paul Brennan
BRENNAN, PAUL P. (Red)
B. 1902
Fordham 5'10" 180 lbs.

1926	BKN	A	2	G, C

Phil Brennan
BRENNAN, PHILIP
B. 1903
Deceased
Loyola (Illinois) 5'11" 165 lbs.

1930	NEW	N	1	E

Phil Brennan
BRENNAN, PHILIP J.
B. 1898
D. Nov. 22, 1970, Montego Bay, Jamaica
Holy Cross 6'0" 200 lbs.

1925	CLE	N	1	T

Willie Brennan
BRENNAN, WILLIS
B. Feb., 1894
Deceased
None 214 lbs.

1920	CHIC	A	6	T
1921	CHIC	A	6	G, T
1922	CHIC	N	8	G
1923			10	G, T
1924			10	G, T
1925			13	G
1926			11	G, T
1927			11	G
8 yrs.	75 games			

Al Brenner
BRENNER, ALLEN R.
B. Nov. 13, 1947, Benton Harbor, MI
Michigan State 6'1" 200 lbs.

1969	NYG	N	6	CB
1970			1	DB
2 yrs.	7 games			

Hoby Brenner
BRENNER, HOBY F.J.
B. Jun. 2, 1959, Linwood, CA
Southern California 6'4" 244 lbs.

1981	NO	N	9	TE
1982			8	TE
1983			16	TE
1984			16	TE
1985			16	TE
1986			15	TE
1987			12	TE
1988			16	TE
1989			16	TE
1990			16	TE
1991			16	TE
1992			15	TE
1993			10	TE
13 yrs.	175 games			

Ray Brenner
BRENNER, RAYMOND
B. Mar. 18, 1898
D. Jun., 1975, Massillon, OH
None 5'4" 145 lbs.

1925	CAN	N	2	HB

Monte Brethauer
BRETHAUER, MONTE L.
B. Apr. 8, 1931, Portland, OR
Oregon 6'1" 178 lbs.

1953	BAL	N	12	E
1955			12	HB
2 yrs.	24 games			

Jeep Brett
BRETT, EDWIN
B. Mar. 20, 1914, Lewiston, ID
Washington State 6'2" 203 lbs.

1936	CHIC	N	1	E
1936	PIT	N	8	E
1937			10	E
2 yrs.	19 games			

Carl Brettschneider
BRETTSCHNEIDER, CARL
B. Dec. 2, 1931, Dundee, IL
Iowa State 6'1" 223 lbs.

1956	CHIC	N	12	LB
1957			12	LB
1958			10	LB
1959			12	LB
1960	DET	N	12	LB
1961			12	LB
1962			14	LB

Year	Team	Games	Pos.

Carl Brettschneider cont.

Year	Team	Games	Pos.
1963		5	LB
8 yrs.	89 games		

Bob Breunig
BREUNIG, ROBERT PAUL
B. Jul. 4, 1953, Inglewood, CA
Arizona State 6'2" 226 lbs.

1975	DAL	N	10	LB
1976			14	LB
1977			14	LB
1978			16	LB
1979			16	LB
1980			16	LB
1981			16	LB
1982			9	LB
1983			16	LB
1984			8	LB
10 yrs.	135 games		

Dorian Brew
BREW, DORIAN
B. Jul. 19, 1974, St. Louis, MO
Kansas 5'10" 182 lbs.

| 1996 | BAL | N | 7 | CB |

Billy Brewer
BREWER, WILLIAM E.
B. Oct. 8, 1934, Columbus, MS
Mississippi 6'0" 190 lbs.

| 1960 | WAS | N | 11 | HB |

Untz Brewer
BREWER, EDWARD BROOKE
B. Nov. 21, 1894, Washington, DC
D. Feb., 1970, Rockville, MD
Maryland 5'6" 160 lbs.

| 1922 | AKR | | 8 | HB, FB |

Chris Brewer
BREWER, CHRISTOPHER
B. Jan. 23, 1962, Denver, CO
Arizona 6'1" 203 lbs.

1984	DEN	N	13	RB
1987	CHI	N	3	RB
2 yrs.	16 games		

Dewell Brewer
BREWER, DEWELL
B. May 22, 1970, Lawton, OK
Oklahoma 5'8" 199 lbs.

| 1994 | IND | N | 16 | RB |

John Brewer
BREWER, JOHN
B. Aug. 26, 1928, Twin Branch, WV
Louisville 6'4" 230 lbs.

1952	PHI	N	12	FB
1953			6	FB
2 yrs.	18 games		

John Brewer
BREWER, JOHN M.
B. Mar. 7, 1906
D. Sep., 1974, Monroe, NC
Georgia Tech 6'0" 185 lbs.

| 1929 | DAY | N | 6 | HB |

Johnny Brewer
BREWER, JOHN LEE
B. Mar. 8, 1937, Vicksburg, MS
Mississippi 6'4" 233 lbs.

| 1961 | CLE | N | 14 | DE |
| 1962 | | | 14 | OE |

Johnny Brewer continued

Year	Team	Games	Pos.
1963		14	OE
1964		14	OE
1965		14	TE
1966		14	LB
1967		14	LB
1968	NO	N	14	LB
1969		14	LB
1970		9	LB
10 yrs.	135 games		

Jim Brewington
BREWINGTON, JAMES
B. Feb. 25, 1939, Greenville, NC
North Carolina Central 6'6" 280 lbs.

| 1961 | OAK | A | 14 | OT |

Darrel Brewster
BREWSTER, DARREL P. (Pete)
B. Sep. 1, 1930, Portland, IN
Purdue 6'3" 210 lbs.

1952	CLE	N	12	E
1953			12	E
1954			12	E
1955			12	E
1956			12	E
1957			12	E
1958			11	E
1959	PIT	N	9	E
1960			12	E
9 yrs.	104 games		

Jim Brewster
BREWSTER, J.D.
B. Jan. 9, 1902
Deceased
Georgia Tech 5'7" 155 lbs.

| 1926 | NEW | A | 4 | QB |

Walt Brewster
BREWSTER, WALTER S.
B. 1906, Lewisburg, WV
West Virginia 6'1" 195 lbs.

| 1929 | BUF | | 8 | T |

Bobby Brezina
BREZINA, ROBERT
B. 1942
Houston 6'0" 200 lbs.

| 1963 | HOU | A | 1 | HB |

Greg Brezina
BREZINA, GREGORY
B. Jan. 7, 1946, Sinton, TX
Houston 6'2" 222 lbs.

1968	ATL	N	11	LB
1969			14	LB
1971			14	LB
1972			14	LB
1973			14	LB
1974			14	LB
1975			14	LB
1976			14	LB
1977			14	LB
1978			16	LB
1979			16	LB
11 yrs.	155 games		

Bill Brian
BRIAN, WILLIAM LAWSON
B. Oct. 12, 1912, Lincoln, NE
Gonzaga 6'2" 210 lbs.

1935	PHI	N	9	T
1936			9	T
2 yrs.	18 games		

Harry Brian
HITE, HAROLD BRIAN
B. Jan. 24, 1903
D. Apr., 1980, Media, PA
Grove City 6'0" 180 lbs.

| 1926 | HAR | N | 4 | HB |

Frank Briante
BRIANTE, FRANK XAVIER
(Bullet)
B. Mar. 5, 1905, White Plains, NY
Deceased
New York University 5'10" 185 lbs.

1929	SI	N	8	HB, QB, FB
1930	NEW	N	4	FB, HB
2 yrs.	12 games		

Alundis Brice
BRICE, ALUNDIS
B. May 1, 1970, Brookhaven, MA
Mississippi 5'10" 178 lbs.

1995	DAL	N	11	CB
1996			14	CB
2 yrs.	25 games		

Shirley Brick
BRICK, SHIRLEY E.
B. 1898
D. 1929
Rice 5'8" 165 lbs.

| 1920 | BUF | A | 1 | E |

George Brickley
BRICKLEY, GEORGE VINCENT
B. Jul. 19, 1894
D. Feb. 3, 1947
Trinity (Connecticut) 5'10" 190 lbs.

1920	CLE	A	4	HB
1921	NY	A	2	FB, HB
2 yrs.	6 games		

Lane Bridgeford
BRIDGEFORD, LANE
B. Aug. 11, 1898
D. Jul. 12, 1973, Northridge, CA
Knox 6'0" 180 lbs.

1921	RI	A	4	HB
1922	RI	N	3	HB, FB
2 yrs.	7 games		

Tom Briehl
BRIEHL, TOM M.
B. Sep. 8, 1962, Phoenix, AZ
Stanford 6'3" 247 lbs.

1985	HOU	N	16	LB
1987			3	LB
2 yrs.	19 games		

Doug Brien
BRIEN, DOUGLAS ROBERT ZACHARIAH
B. Nov. 24, 1970, Bloomfield, NJ
California 5'11" 179 lbs.

1994	SF	N	16	K
1995			6	K
1995	NO	N	8	K
1996			16	K
3 yrs.	46 games		

O.J. Brigance
BRIGANCE, ORENTHAL JAMES
B. Sep. 29, 1969, Louisville, KY
Rice 6'0" 223 lbs.

| 1996 | MIA | N | 12 | LB |

Bill Briggs
BRIGGS, WILLIAM JOHN
B. Dec. 25, 1943, Sanford, NC
Iowa 6'3" 250 lbs.

1966	WAS	N	9	DE
1967			14	DE
2 yrs.	23 games		

Bob Briggs
BRIGGS, ROBERT JAMES
B. Apr. 28, 1945, Toledo, OH
Heidelberg 6'4" 267 lbs.

1968	SD	A	14	DT
1969			14	DT
1970	SD	N	10	DT
1971	CLE	N	14	DE
1972			13	DE, DT
1973			12	DE, DT
1974	KC	N	7	DE
7 yrs.	84 games		

Bob Briggs
BRIGGS, ROBERT L.
B. Jan. 12, 1941, Amarillo, TX
Central Oklahoma 6'1" 228 lbs.

| 1965 | WAS | N | 7 | FB |

Greg Briggs
BRIGGS, GREG
B. Oct. 1, 1968, Meadville, MS
Arkansas-Pine Bluff/Texas Southern 6'3" 212 lbs.

1995	DAL	N	11	S
1996	CHI	N	14	S, LB
2 yrs.	25 games		

Paul Briggs
BRIGGS, PAUL H.
B. 1920, Providence, RI
Colorado 6'4" 248 lbs.

| 1948 | DET | N | 12 | T |

Walter Briggs
BRIGGS, WALTER
B. Aug. 6, 1965
Montclair State 6'1" 205 lbs.

| 1987 | NYJ | N | 1 | QB |

Hi Brigham
BRIGHAM, HAVEN A.
B. Jul., 1892, Bowling Green, OH
D. Oct. 6, 1987, Toledo, OH
Ohio State 5'11" 185 lbs.

| 1920 | COL | A | 1 | G |

Greg Bright
BRIGHT, GREGORY KEITH
B. Aug. 2, 1957, Fort Campbell, KY
Morehead State 6'0" 208 lbs.

1980	CIN	N	16	CB, S
1981			4	S
1981	OAK	N	1	S
2 yrs.	21 games		

Leon Bright
BRIGHT, LEON
B. May 19, 1955, Starke, FL
Florida State 5'9" 192 lbs.

1981	NYG	N	15	RB
1982			8	RB
1983			7	RB
1984	TB	N	12	RB
1985			8	RB
5 yrs.	50 games		

Year	Team		Games	Pos.

Hal Brill
BRILL, HAROLD E.
B. Mar. 26, 1914
D. Sep. 2, 1980, Wichita, KS
Wichita State 5'10" 175 lbs.

Year	Team		Games	Pos.
1939	DET	N	2	HB

Darrick Brilz
BRILZ, DARRICK JOSEPH
B. Feb. 14, 1964, Richmond, CA
Oregon State 6'3" 264 lbs.

Year	Team		Games	Pos.
1987	WAS	N	7	G
1988	SD	N	14	OL
1989	SEA	N	14	G
1990			16	G
1991			16	G
1992			16	G
1993			16	G
1994	CIN	N	15	C
1995			16	C
1996			13	C
10 yrs.		143 games		

James Brim
BRIM, JAMES
B. Feb. 28, 1963, Mount Airy, NC
Wake Forest 6'3" 187 lbs.

Year	Team		Games	Pos.
1987	MIN	N	3	WR

Mike Brim
BRIM, MICHAEL ANRTHONY
B. Jan. 23, 1966, Danville, VA
Virginia Union 6'0" 186 lbs.

Year	Team		Games	Pos.
1988	PHX	N	4	CB
1989	DET	N	2	CB
1989	MIN	N	7	CB
1990			16	CB
1991	NYJ	N	16	CB
1992			16	CB, S
1993	CIN	N	16	CB
1994			16	CB
1995			1	CB
8 yrs.		94 games		

Walt Brindley
BRINDLEY, WALTER
B. May 24, 1895
Drake 5'10" 180 lbs.

Year	Team		Games	Pos.
1921	RI	A	2	HB, QB
1922	RI	N	3	QB, FB
2 yrs.		5 games		

Larry Brink
BRINK, LAWRENCE
B. Sep. 12, 1923, Milaca, MN
Northern Illinois 6'5" 235 lbs.

Year	Team		Games	Pos.
1948	LA	N	11	E
1949			11	E
1950			12	E
1951			12	E
1952			12	E
1953			12	E
1954	CHIB	N	12	E
7 yrs.		82 games		

Lester Brinkley
BRINKLEY, LESTER L.
B. May 16, 1965, Ruleville, MS
Mississippi 6'6" 270 lbs.

Year	Team		Games	Pos.
1990	DAL	N	6	DE

Dana Brinson
BRINSON, DANA DEMONE
B. Apr. 10, 1965, Valdosta, GA
Nebraska 5'9" 167 lbs.

Year	Team		Games	Pos.
1989	SD	N	10	RB

Larry Brinson
BRINSON, LARRY SYLVESTA
B. Jun. 6, 1954, Opa-Locka, FL
Florida 6'0" 214 lbs.

Year	Team		Games	Pos.
1977	DAL	N	14	RB
1978			10	RB
1979			14	RB
1980	SEA	N	7	RB
4 yrs.		45 games		

Vincent Brisby
BRISBY, VINCENT COLE
B. Jan. 25, 1971, Lake Charles, LA
Northeast Louisiana 6'1" 186 lbs.

Year	Team		Games	Pos.
1993	NE	N	16	WR
1994			14	WR
1995			16	WR
1996			3	WR
4 yrs.		49 games		

Marlin Briscoe
BRISCOE, MARLIN
B. Sep. 10, 1945, Oakland, CA
Nebraska-Omaha 5'10" 178 lbs.

Year	Team		Games	Pos.
1968	DEN	A	11	QB
1969	BUF	A	14	WR
1970	BUF	N	14	WR
1971			14	WR
1972	MIA	N	10	WR
1973			14	WR
1974			14	WR
1975	SD	N	3	WR
1975	DET	N	8	WR
1976	NE	N	14	WR
9 yrs.		116 games		

Bubby Brister
BRISTER, WALTER ANDREW, III
B. Aug. 15, 1962, Alexandria, LA
Tulane/Northeast Louisiana 6'2" 184 lbs.

Year	Team		Games	Pos.
1986	PIT	N	2	QB
1987			2	QB
1988			13	QB
1989			14	QB
1990			16	QB
1991			8	QB
1992			6	QB
1993	PHI	N	10	QB
1994			8	QB
1995	NYJ	N	9	QB
10 yrs.		88 games		

Willie Brister
BRISTER, WILLIE
B. Jan. 28, 1952, Tylertown, MS
Southern University 6'4" 236 lbs.

Year	Team		Games	Pos.
1974	NYJ	N	12	TE
1975			12	TE
2 yrs.		24 games		

John Bristor
BRISTOR, JOHN ROLLINS
B. Nov. 25, 1955, Waynesburg, PA
California (Pennsylvania)/Waynesburg 6'0" 188 lbs.

Year	Team		Games	Pos.
1979	SF	N	1	CB

Obie Bristow
BRISTOW, J. GORDON
B. 1902, Ardmore, OK
D. Dec. 24, 1969
Central Oklahoma/Oklahoma 6'2" 210 lbs.

Year	Team		Games	Pos.
1925	KC	N	8	FB, HB, T
1925	CLE	N	1	HB
1926	KC	N	8	HB, FB
2 yrs.		17 games		

Gene Brito
BRITO, GENERO HERMAN
B. Oct. 23, 1925, Los Angeles, CA
D. Jun. 8, 1985, Los Angeles County, CA
Loyola (California) 6'1" 226 lbs.

Year	Team		Games	Pos.
1951	WAS	N	12	E
1952			12	E
1953			12	E
1955			12	E
1956			12	E
1957			12	E
1958			12	E
1959	LA	N	2	E
1960			11	E
9 yrs.		97 games		

Charley Britt
BRITT, CHARLES
B. Mar. 20, 1938, Augusta, GA
Georgia 6'2" 183 lbs.

Year	Team		Games	Pos.
1960	LA	N	12	DB
1961			11	DB
1962			11	DB
1963			10	DB
1964	MIN	N	5	DB
1964	SF	N	10	DB
5 yrs.		59 games		

Eddie Britt
BRITT, EDWARD J.
B. Jul. 19, 1912, Lexington, MA
D. Nov., 1978, Pelham, NH
Holy Cross 6'2" 205 lbs.

Year	Team		Games	Pos.
1936	BOS	N	10	FB, DB
1937	WAS	N	4	FB, DB
1938	BKN	N	1	DB
3 yrs.		15 games		

James Britt
BRITT, JAMES E.
B. Sep. 12, 1960, Minden, LA
Louisiana State 6'0" 185 lbs.

Year	Team		Games	Pos.
1983	ATL	N	14	CB, S
1984			16	S
1985			2	CB
1986			16	CB
1987			12	CB
5 yrs.		60 games		

Jessie Britt
BRITT, JESSIE LOFTIN, JR.
B. Mar. 3, 1963, Suffolk, VA
North Carolina A&T 6'4" 198 lbs.

Year	Team		Games	Pos.
1986	PIT	N	8	WR

Maury Britt
BRITT, MAURICE LEE, JR.
B. Jun. 29, 1919, Carlisle, AR
Arkansas 6'4" 210 lbs.

Year	Team		Games	Pos.
1941	DET	N	9	E

Oscar Britt
BRITT, OSCAR
B. Jun. 18, 1919, Brookhaven, MS
Mississippi 5'11" 193 lbs.

Year	Team		Games	Pos.
1946	WAS	N	1	G

Ralph Britt
BRITT, JAMES RALPH, JR.
B. Aug. 18, 1965, Goldsboro, NC
North Carolina State 6'3" 240 lbs.

Year	Team		Games	Pos.
1987	PIT	N	3	TE

Rankin Britt
BRITT, A. RANKIN
B. 1915
Texas A&M 6'2" 206 lbs.

Year	Team		Games	Pos.
1939	PHI	N	1	E

Jon Brittenum
BRITTENUM, JON ROGER
B. May 27, 1944, Brinkley, AR
Arkansas 6'0" 185 lbs.

Year	Team		Games	Pos.
1968	SD	A	14	QB, DB

Earl Britton
BRITTON, EARL T.
B. Jul. 15, 1903
D. Oct., 1973, Elgin, IL
Illinois 6'0" 212 lbs.

Year	Team		Games	Pos.
1925	CHIB	N	4	FB, HB
1926	BKN	A	4	FB, HB
1926	BKN	N	3	FB, HB
1927	DAY	N	8	FB
1927	FRA	N	6	FB, HB
1928	DAY	N	7	FB, HB
1929	CHIC	N	2	QB, FB
5 yrs.		34 games		

Max Broadhurst
BROADHURST, ARTHUR
B. Aug. 9, 1896, Wisconsin
D. Oct., 1964, Oregon
None 6'0" 220 lbs.

Year	Team		Games	Pos.
1920	DAY	A	1	T

Karl Broadley
BROADLEY, KARL T.
B. Nov. 10, 1895, Fort Worth, TX
D. Apr., 1967, St. Petersburg, FL
Bethany (West Virginia) 6'4" 185 lbs.

Year	Team		Games	Pos.
1925	CLE	N	4	G

Jerry Broadnax
BROADNAX, JERRY L.
B. Aug. 19, 1951, Dallas, TX
Southern University 6'2" 225 lbs.

Year	Team		Games	Pos.
1974	HOU	N	8	TE

Marion Broadstone
BROADSTONE, MARION G.
B. Jun. 24, 1906
D. Apr. 10, 1972, San Jose, CA
Nebraska 6'2" 210 lbs.

Year	Team		Games	Pos.
1931	NYG	N	2	G

Charley Brock
BROCK, CHARLES J. (Ears)
B. Mar. 15, 1916, Columbus, NE
D. May 25, 1987, Green Bay, WI
Nebraska 6'2" 207 lbs.

Year	Team		Games	Pos.
1939	GB	N	10	C
1940			11	C
1941			11	C
1942			11	C
1943			6	C
1944			10	C
1945			10	C
1946			11	C
1947			12	C
9 yrs.		92 games		

Clyde Brock
BROCK, CLYDE
B. Aug. 30, 1940
Utah State 6'5" 268 lbs.

Year	Team		Games	Pos.
1962	DAL	N	14	OT
1963			4	OT

Year	Team	Games	Pos.

Clyde Brock continued

Year	Team	Games	Pos.
1963	SF N	11	OT
2 yrs.	29 games		

Dieter Brock
BROCK, RALPH DIETER
B. Feb. 12, 1951, Birmingham, AL
Auburn/Jacksonville State 6'0" 195 lbs.

1985	LARM N	15	QB

Lou Brock
BROCK, JAMES LOUIS
B. Dec. 9, 1917, Stafford, KS
D. May 7, 1989, Wichita, KS
Purdue 6'0" 195 lbs.

1940	GB	11	HB, QB
1941		10	HB
1942		11	FB, HB
1943		10	HB
1944		6	HB
1945		10	HB
6 yrs.	58 games		

Lou Brock
BROCK, LOUIS CLARK, JR.
B. May 8, 1964, Chicago, IL
Southern California 5'11" 175 lbs.

1987	SD N	1	CB
1988	SEA N	1	CB
1988	DET N	2	CB, S
2 yrs.	4 games		

Matt Brock
BROCK, MATTHEW LEE
B. Jan. 14, 1966, Ogden, UT
Oregon 6'5" 284 lbs.

1989	GB N	7	DE
1990		16	DE
1991		16	DE, NT
1992		16	DE
1993		16	DE
1994		5	DT
1995	NYJ N	16	DT
1996		16	DT
8 yrs.	108 games		

Pete Brock
BROCK, PETER ANTHONY
B. Jul. 14, 1954, Portland, OR
Colorado 6'5" 270 lbs.

1976	NE N	14	C, TE
1977		14	C, G
1978		15	C
1979		16	C, OT, G
1980		16	C, OT
1981		16	C
1982		9	C
1983		13	C
1984		12	C
1985		9	C
1986		16	C
1987		4	C
12 yrs.	154 games		

Stan Brock
BROCK, STANLEY JAMES
B. Jun. 8, 1958, Portland, OR
Colorado 6'6" 290 lbs.

1980	NO N	16	OT
1981		16	OT
1982		9	OT
1983		16	OT
1984		14	OT
1985		16	OT
1986		16	OT
1987		12	OT
1988		7	OT
1989		16	OT

Stan Brock continued

Year	Team	Games	Pos.
1990		16	OT
1991		16	OT
1992		16	OT
1993	SD N	16	OT
1994		16	OT
1995		16	OT
16 yrs.	234 games		

Willie Brock
BROCK, WILLIE
B. Sep. 20, 1955, Vancouver, WA
Colorado 6'3" 246 lbs.

1978	DET N		C

Jeff Brockhaus
BROCKHAUS, JEFF JEROME
B. Apr. 15, 1959, Fort Lauderdale, FL
Missouri 6'2" 212 lbs.

1987	SF N	3	K

John Brockington
BROCKINGTON, JOHN STANLEY
B. Sep. 7, 1948, Brooklyn, NY
Ohio State 6'1" 225 lbs.

1971	GB N	14	FB
1972		14	FB
1973		14	FB
1974		14	FB
1975		14	FB
1976		14	FB
1977		1	FB
1977	KC N	10	FB
7 yrs.	95 games		

Blake Brockermeyer
BROCKERMEYER, BLAKE
B. Apr. 11, 1973, Fort Worth, TX
Texas 6'4" 305 lbs.

1995	CAR N	16	OT
1996		12	OT
2 yrs.	28 games		

Hal Broda
BRODA, HAROLD A.
B. Jul. 27, 1905
D. Feb. 13, 1989, Canton, OH
Brown 6'1" 180 lbs.

1927	CLE N	3	E

Bob Brodhead
BRODHEAD, ROBERT
B. Dec. 20, 1936, Kittanning, PA
Duke 6'2" 207 lbs.

1960	BUF A		QB

John Brodie
BRODIE, JOHN RILEY
B. Aug. 14, 1935, San Francisco, CA
Stanford 6'1" 198 lbs.

1957	SF N	5	QB
1958		12	QB
1959		12	QB
1960		11	QB
1961		14	QB
1962		14	QB
1963		3	QB
1964		14	QB
1965		13	QB
1966		14	QB
1967		14	QB
1968		14	QB
1969		12	QB
1970		14	QB
1971		14	QB
1972		6	QB

John Brodie continued

Year	Team	Games	Pos.
1973		14	QB
17 yrs.	200 games		

J.W. Brodnax
BRODNAX, JOHN W. (Red)
B. 1937
Louisiana State 6'0" 208 lbs.

1960	DEN	A		FB

Chuck Brodnicki
BRODNICKI, CHARLES T.
B. 1911
Villanova 6'2" 225 lbs.

1934	BKN N	1	T

Jeff Brohm
BROHM, JEFF
B. Apr. 24, 1971, Louisville, KY
Louisville 6'1" 205 lbs.

1996	SF N	4	QB

Fred Broker
BROKER, FRED
None 5'9" 175 lbs.

1922	OOR N	1	T, QB

Ben Bronson
BRONSON, BEN
B. Sep. 9, 1972, Jasper, TX
Baylor 5'10" 165 lbs.

1995	IND N	9	WR

Tommy Brooker
BROOKER, WILLIAM THOMAS
B. Oct. 31, 1939, Demopolis, AL
Alabama 6'2" 230 lbs.

1962	DAL A	14	OE, K
1963	KC A	9	OE, K
1964		14	OE, K
1965		14	OE, K
1966		4	OE, K
5 yrs.	55 games		

Mitchell Brookins
BROOKINS, MITCHELL EUGENE
B. Dec. 10, 1960, Chicago, IL
Illinois 5'11" 196 lbs.

1984	BUF N	16	WR
1985		5	WR
2 yrs.	21 games		

Barrett Brooks
BROOKS, BARRETT
B. May 5, 1972, St. Louis, MO
Kansas State 6'4" 309 lbs.

1995	PHI N	16	OT
1996		16	OT
2 yrs.	32 games		

Bill Brooks
BROOKS, WILLIAM, JR.
B. Apr. 6, 1964, Boston, MA
Boston University 5'11" 190 lbs.

1986	IND N	16	WR
1987		12	WR
1988		16	WR
1989		16	WR
1990		16	WR
1991		16	WR
1992		14	WR
1993	BUF N	16	WR
1994		16	WR
1995		15	WR

Bill Brooks continued

Year	Team	Games	Pos.
1996	WAS N	16	WR
11 yrs.	169 games		

Billy Brooks
BROOKS, WILLIAM MCKINLEY, III
B. Aug. 20, 1953, Houston, TX
Oklahoma 6'3" 204 lbs.

1976	CIN N	12	WR
1977		14	WR
1978		15	WR
1979		4	WR
1981	SD N	7	WR
1981	HOU N	3	WR
5 yrs.	55 games		

Bob Brooks
BROOKS, ROBERT
B. 1940
Ohio Univeristy 6'0" 215 lbs.

1961	NY A	14	FB

Bobby Brooks
BROOKS, BOBBY DANIEL
B. Feb. 24, 1951, Dallas, TX
Bishop 6'1" 195 lbs.

1974	NYG N	14	CB, S
1975		14	CB
1976		4	CB
3 yrs.	32 games		

Bucky Brooks
BROOKS, WILLIAM ELDRIDGE, JR.
B. Jan. 22, 1971, Raleigh, NC
North Carolina 5'11" 186 lbs.

1994	BUF N	3	CB
1996	GB N	2	CB
1996	JAC N	6	CB
2 yrs.	11 games		

Carlos Brooks
BROOKS, CARLOS
B. May 8, 1971, Hamilton, OH
Bowling Green 6'0" 200 lbs.

1995	ARI N	7	CB

Chet Brooks
BROOKS, TERRENCE DONNELL
B. Jan. 1, 1966, Midland, TX
Texas A&M 5'11" 191 lbs.

1988	SF N	10	CB
1989		15	CB
1990		8	S
3 yrs.	33 games		

Cliff Brooks
BROOKS, CLIFFORD
B. Jun. 21, 1949, Pineland, TX
Tennessee State 6'1" 190 lbs.

1972	CLE N	14	CB
1973		14	CB
1974		13	CB
1975	PHI N	14	CB
1976		1	CB
1976	NYJ N	1	S
1976	BUF N	1	S
5 yrs.	58 games		

Derrick Brooks
BROOKS, DERRICK
B. Apr. 18, 1973, Pensacola, FL
Florida State 6'0" 229 lbs.

1995	TB N	16	LB

Year	Team	Games	Pos.

Derrick Brooks continued

Year	Team	Games	Pos.
1996		16	LB
2 yrs.	32 games		

Ethan Brooks
BROOKS, ETHAN
B. Apr. 27, 1972, Simsbury, CT
Williams 6'6" 270 lbs.

Year	Team	Games	Pos.
1996	ATL N	1	OT

James Brooks
BROOKS, JAMES ROBERT
B. Dec. 28, 1958, Warner Robins, GA
Auburn 5'10" 182 lbs.

Year	Team	Games	Pos.
1981	SD N	14	RB
1982		9	RB
1983		15	RB
1984	CIN N	15	RB
1985		16	RB
1986		16	RB
1987		9	RB
1988		15	RB
1989		16	RB
1990		16	RB
1991		15	RB
1992	CLE N	4	RB
1992	TB N	2	RB
12 yrs.	162 games		

Jon Brooks
BROOKS, JONATHAN
B. Jun. 22, 1957, Saluda, SC
Clemson 6'2" 215 lbs.

Year	Team	Games	Pos.
1979	DET N	15	LB
1980	ATL N	4	LB
1980	STL N	1	LB
2 yrs.	20 games		

Kevin Brooks
BROOKS, KEVIN CRAIG
B. Feb. 9, 1963, Detroit, MI
Michigan 6'6" 273 lbs.

Year	Team	Games	Pos.
1985	DAL N	11	DE
1986		9	DE
1987		13	DL
1988		15	DE
1989	DET N	15	DE, NT
1990		6	DE
6 yrs.	69 games		

Larry Brooks
BROOKS, LAWRENCE LEE, SR.
B. Jun. 10, 1950, Prince George, VA
Virginia State 6'3" 255 lbs.

Year	Team	Games	Pos.
1972	LA N	8	DT
1973		14	DT
1974		13	DT
1975		8	DT
1976		14	DT
1977		14	DT
1978		14	DT
1979		16	DT
1980		8	DT
1981		8	DT
1982	LARM N	6	DT
11 yrs.	131 games		

Leo Brooks
BROOKS, LEONARD LEO, JR.
B. Dec. 12, 1947, Kermit, TX
Texas 6'5" 256 lbs.

Year	Team	Games	Pos.
1970	HOU N	13	DT
1971		11	DT
1972		12	DT
1973	STL N	13	DL
1974		14	DT, DE
1975		8	DT

Leo Brooks continued

Year	Team	Games	Pos.
1976		8	DT
7 yrs.	79 games		

Michael Brooks
BROOKS, MICHAEL
B. Oct. 2, 1964, Ruston, LA
Louisiana State 6'1" 235 lbs.

Year	Team	Games	Pos.
1987	DEN N	12	LB
1988		16	LB
1989		16	LB
1990		16	LB
1991		14	LB
1992		15	LB
1993	NYG N	13	LB
1994		16	LB
1995		16	LB
1996	DET N	4	LB
10 yrs.	138 games		

Michael Brooks
BROOKS, MICHAEL ANTONIO
B. Mar. 12, 1967, Greensboro, NC
North Carolina State 6'0" 195 lbs.

Year	Team	Games	Pos.
1989	SD N	16	S
1990		1	S
1990	DAL N	3	CB
2 yrs.	20 games		

Perry Brooks
BROOKS, PERRY
B. Dec. 4, 1954, Bogalusa, LA
Southern University 6'3" 265 lbs.

Year	Team	Games	Pos.
1978	WAS N	16	DT, DE
1979		12	DT
1980		12	DT
1981		15	DT
1982		5	DT
1983		16	DT
1984		16	DT
7 yrs.	92 games		

Reggie Brooks
BROOKS, REGINALD ARTHUR
B. Jan. 19, 1971, Tulsa, OK
Notre Dame 5'8" 202 lbs.

Year	Team	Games	Pos.
1993	WAS N	16	RB
1994		12	RB
1995		1	RB
1996	TB N	11	RB
4 yrs.	40 games		

Robert Brooks
BROOKS, ROBERT DARREN
B. Jun. 23, 1970, Greenwood, SC
South Carolina 6'0" 171 lbs.

Year	Team	Games	Pos.
1992	GB N	16	WR
1993		14	WR
1994		16	WR
1995		16	WR
1996		7	WR
5 yrs.	69 games		

Steve Brooks
BROOKS, STEVE
B. Jun. 2, 1971, Ventura, CA
*California-Santa Barbara/Occidental
6'5" 245 lbs.*

Year	Team	Games	Pos.
1996	DET N	1	TE

Tony Brooks
BROOKS, RAYMOND ANTHONY
B. Aug. 17, 1969, Tulsa, OK
Notre Dame 6'0" 230 lbs.

Year	Team	Games	Pos.
1992	PHI N	5	RB

Tom Brookshier
BROOKSHIER, THOMAS J.
B. Dec. 16, 1931, Aurora, CO
Colorado 6'0" 196 lbs.

Year	Team	Games	Pos.
1953	PHI N	11	DB
1956		11	DB
1957		12	DB
1958		11	DB
1959		12	DB
1960		12	DB
1961		7	DB
7 yrs.	76 games		

Jay Brophy
BROPHY, JAMES JAY
B. Jul. 27, 1960, Akron, OH
Miami (Florida) 6'3" 233 lbs.

Year	Team	Games	Pos.
1984	MIA N	11	LB
1985		16	LB
1986		4	LB
1987	NYJ N	3	LB
4 yrs.	34 games		

Al Brosky
BROSKY, ALFRED E.
B. Jun. 9, 1930, Chicago, IL
Illinois 5'11" 175 lbs.

Year	Team	Games	Pos.
1954	CHIC N	9	B

Bern Brostek
BROSTEK, BERN
B. Sep. 11, 1966, Honolulu, HI
Washington 6'3" 300 lbs.

Year	Team	Games	Pos.
1990	LARM N	16	C
1991		14	G, C
1992		16	C, G
1993		16	C
1994		11	C
1995	STL N	16	C
1996		16	C
7 yrs.	105 games		

Mal Bross
BROSS, MALCOLM
B. Dec. 7, 1904
Gonzaga 5'9" 170 lbs.

Year	Team	Games	Pos.
1926	LA A	12	QB, HB
1927	GB N	2	HB
2 yrs.	14 games		

Bob Brotzki
BROTZKI, ROBERT JOHN
B. Dec. 24, 1962, Sandusky, OH
Syracuse 6'5" 269 lbs.

Year	Team	Games	Pos.
1986	IND N	2	OT
1987		11	OT
1988		1	C
1988	DAL N	7	OT
3 yrs.	21 games		

Walter Broughton
BROUGHTON, WALTER CRAIG
B. Oct. 20, 1960, Brewton, AL
Jacksonville State 5'10" 180 lbs.

Year	Team	Games	Pos.
1986	BUF N	8	WR
1987		9	WR
1988		1	WR
3 yrs.	18 games		

Willie Broughton
BROUGHTON, WILLIE LEE
B. Sep. 9, 1964, Fort Pierce, FL
Miami (Florida) 6'5" 277 lbs.

Year	Team	Games	Pos.
1985	IND N	15	DE
1986		15	DE
1989	DAL N	16	DT
1990		4	DT

Willie Broughton continued

Year	Team	Games	Pos.
1992	LARI N	16	DT
1993		15	DT
1995	NO N	16	NT, DE
1996		14	NT
8 yrs.	111 games		

Fred Broussard
BROUSSARD, FRED E.
B. 1933
*Texas A&M/Northwestern State
(Louisiana) 6'3" 235 lbs.*

Year	Team	Games	Pos.
1955	PIT N	6	C
1955	NYG N		C
1 yr.	6 games		

Steve Broussard
BROUSSARD, JOHN STEVE
B. Jul. 19, 1949, McComb, MS
*Auburn/Southern Mississippi 6'0"
200 lbs.*

Year	Team	Games	Pos.
1975	GB N	4	P

Steve Broussard
BROUSSARD, STEVE
B. Feb. 22, 1967, Los Angeles, CA
Washington State 5'7" 201 lbs.

Year	Team	Games	Pos.
1990	ATL N	13	RB
1991		14	RB
1992		15	RB
1993		8	RB
1994	CIN N	14	RB
1995	SEA N	15	RB
1996		12	RB
7 yrs.	91 games		

Angie Brovelli
BROVELLI, ANGELO ANDREW
B. Aug. 21, 1910, Porterville, CA
St. Mary's (California) 6'0" 193 lbs.

Year	Team	Games	Pos.
1933	PIT N	8	HB, QB
1934		5	FB, HB
2 yrs.	13 games		

Aaron Brown
BROWN, AARON CEDRIC
B. Jan. 13, 1956, Warren, OH
Ohio State 6'2" 238 lbs.

Year	Team	Games	Pos.
1978	TB N	16	LB
1979		12	LB
1980		16	LB
1985	PHI N	7	LB
1986	ATL N	16	LB
1987		6	LB
6 yrs.	73 games		

Aaron Brown
BROWN, AARON LEWIS, JR.
B. Nov. 16, 1943, Port Arthur, TX
Minnesota 6'5" 263 lbs.

Year	Team	Games	Pos.
1966	KC A	14	DE
1968		14	DE
1969		14	DE
1970	KC N	13	DE
1971		13	DE
1972		14	DE
1973	GB N	8	DE
1974		2	DE
8 yrs.	92 games		

A.B. Brown
BROWN, ANTHONY JAMES
B. Dec. 4, 1965, Salem, NJ
Pittsburgh/West Virginia 5'9" 212 lbs.

Year	Team	Games	Pos.
1989	NYJ N	16	RB
1990		1	RB
1991			RB

Year	Team	Games	Pos.

A.B. Brown continued

Year	Team	Games	Pos.
1992		7	RB
4 yrs.	33 games		

Allen Brown
BROWN, ALLEN
B. Mar. 2, 1943, Natchez, MS
Mississippi 6'5" 238 lbs.

Year	Team	Games	Pos.
1966	GB	N	5	TE
1967			14	TE
2 yrs.	19 games		

Andre Brown
BROWN, ANDRE L.
B. Aug. 21, 1966, Chicago, IL
Miami (Florida) 6'3" 210 lbs.

Year	Team	Games	Pos.
1989	MIA	N	16	WR
1990			6	WR
2 yrs.	22 games		

Anthony Brown
BROWN, ANTHONY
B. Nov. 6, 1972, Okinawa, Japan
Utah 6'5" 310 lbs.

Year	Team	Games	Pos.
1995	CIN	N	6	OT, G
1996			7	OT
2 yrs.	13 games		

Arnold Brown
BROWN, ARNOLD LEE
B. Aug. 27, 1962, Wilmington, NC
North Carolina Central 5'11" 185 lbs.

Year	Team	Games	Pos.
1985	DET	N	7	CB
1987	SEA	N	2	CB
2 yrs.	9 games		

Barry Brown
BROWN, BARRY
B. Apr. 17, 1943, Boston, MA
Florida 6'3" 228 lbs.

Year	Team	Games	Pos.
1966	BAL	N	10	LB
1967			14	LB
1968	NYG	N	12	LB
1969	BOS	A	7	LB, TE
1970	BOS	N	14	LB, TE
5 yrs.	57 games		

Bill Brown
BROWN, WILLIAM
B. 1937
Syracuse 6'1" 230 lbs.

Year	Team	Games	Pos.
1960	BOS	A		LB

Bill Brown
BROWN, WILLIAM DORSEY
B. Jun. 29, 1938, Mendota, IL
Illinois 5'11" 225 lbs.

Year	Team	Games	Pos.
1961	CHI	N	14	FB
1962	MIN	N	14	FB
1963			14	FB
1964			14	FB
1965			14	FB
1966			14	FB
1967			14	FB
1968			14	FB
1969			12	FB
1970			14	FB
1971			14	FB
1972			14	FB
1973			14	FB
1974			14	FB
14 yrs.	194 games		

Bill Brown
BROWN, WILLIAM L., JR.

Bill Brown continued
B. Jun. 1, 1917, McKeesport, PA
Texas Tech 6'0" 202 lbs.

Year	Team	Games	Pos.
1943	BKN	N	4	QB, DB
1944			9	QB, LB
1945	PIT	N	1	QB, DB
3 yrs.	14 games		

Bob Brown
BROWN, ROBERT EARL
B. Jan. 1, 1943, Pace, MS
Alcorn State 6'3" 225 lbs.

Year	Team	Games	Pos.
1969	STL	N	12	TE
1970			14	TE
1971	MIN	N	8	TE
1972	NO	N	14	TE
1973			5	TE
5 yrs.	53 games		

Bob Brown
BROWN, ROBERT EDDIE
B. Feb. 22, 1940, Bonita, LA
Arkansas-Pine Bluff 6'5" 268 lbs.

Year	Team	Games	Pos.
1966	GB	N	14	DE
1967			14	DE
1968			6	DE
1969			14	DT
1970			14	DT
1971			14	DE
1972			14	DE
1973			14	DT
1974	SD	N	14	DT
1975	CIN	N	14	DT
1976			14	DT
11 yrs.	146 games		

Bob Brown
BROWN, ROBERT STANFORD
B. Dec. 8, 1941, Cleveland, OH
Nebraska 6'4" 284 lbs.

Year	Team	Games	Pos.
1964	PHI	N	14	OT
1965			14	OT
1966			14	OT
1967			8	OT
1968			14	OT
1969	LA	N	14	OT
1970			14	OT
1971	OAK	N	10	OT
1972			14	OT
1973			10	OT
10 yrs.	126 games		

Booker Brown
BROWN, BOOKER TAYLOR
B. Sep. 25, 1952, Desson, MS
Southern California 6'2" 257 lbs.

Year	Team	Games	Pos.
1975	SD	N	11	G
1977			6	OT
2 yrs.	17 games		

Boyd Brown
BROWN, BOYD
B. May 24, 1952, Crosby, MS
Alcorn State 6'4" 216 lbs.

Year	Team	Games	Pos.
1974	DEN	N	14	TE
1975			12	TE
1976			14	TE
1977	NYG	N	6	TE
4 yrs.	46 games		

Bud Brown
BROWN, CHARLES LEE
B. Apr. 19, 1961, De Kalb, MS
Southern Mississippi 6'0" 194 lbs.

Year	Team	Games	Pos.
1984	MIA	N	16	CB, S
1985			16	S

Bud Brown continued

Year	Team	Games	Pos.
1986			16	S
1987			9	S
1988			16	S
5 yrs.	73 games		

Buddy Brown
BROWN, WILLIAM
B. Oct. 19, 1926, Wynne, AR
Arkansas 6'1" 220 lbs.

Year	Team	Games	Pos.
1951	WAS	N	12	G
1952			12	G
1953	GB	N	11	G
1954			12	G
1955			12	G
1956			12	G
6 yrs.	71 games		

Carlos Brown
BROWN, CARLOS ALLEN
B. Jul. 31, 1952, Shreveport, LA
Pacific 6'3" 210 lbs.

Year	Team	Games	Pos.
1975	GB	N	14	QB
1976			13	QB
2 yrs.	27 games		

Cedric Brown
BROWN, CEDRIC WALLACE
B. May 6, 1954, Columbus, OH
Kent State 6'1" 199 lbs.

Year	Team	Games	Pos.
1977	TB	N	14	S
1978			13	S
1979			16	S
1980			13	S
1981			16	S
1982			9	S
1983			8	S
1984			9	S
8 yrs.	98 games		

Cedrick Brown
BROWN, CEDRICK
B. Sep. 6, 1964, Compton, CA
Washington State 5'10" 182 lbs.

Year	Team	Games	Pos.
1987	PHI	N	12	CB

Chad Brown
BROWN, CHADRICK CHICO
B. Jul. 9, 1971, Thomasville, GA
Mississippi 6'7" 265 lbs.

Year	Team	Games	Pos.
1993	PHX	N	5	DE
1994	ARI	N	8	DE
1995			6	DE
3 yrs.	19 games		

Chad Brown
BROWN, CHADWICK EVERETT
B. Jul. 12, 1970, Pasadena, CA
Colorado 6'2" 240 lbs.

Year	Team	Games	Pos.
1993	PIT	N	16	LB
1994			16	LB
1995			10	LB
1996			14	LB
4 yrs.	56 games		

Charlie Brown
BROWN, CHARLIE
B. Oct. 29, 1958, Charleston, SC
South Carolina State 5'10" 182 lbs.

Year	Team	Games	Pos.
1982	WAS	N	9	WR
1983			15	WR
1984			9	WR
1985	ATL	N	13	WR
1986			16	WR
1987			6	WR
6 yrs.	68 games		

Charlie Brown
BROWN, CHARLIE E.
B. 1937
Houston 6'4" 245 lbs.

Year	Team	Games	Pos.
1962	OAK	A	14	OT

Charlie Brown
BROWN, CHARLES E.
B. Sep. 13, 1942, Heflin, AL
Syracuse 6'1" 194 lbs.

Year	Team	Games	Pos.
1966	CHI	N	14	DB
1967			8	DB
1968	BUF	A	8	DB
3 yrs.	30 games		

Charlie Brown
BROWN, CHARLES KELLY
B. Oct. 13, 1948, Oakland, CA
Northern Arizona 6'2" 195 lbs.

Year	Team	Games	Pos.
1970	DET	N	14	WR

Charlie Brown
BROWN, CHARLES ROBERT
B. Oct. 16, 1945, Jefferson City, MO
Missouri 5'10" 187 lbs.

Year	Team	Games	Pos.
1967	NO	N	3	RB
1968			3	RB
2 yrs.	6 games		

Chris Brown
BROWN, CHRIS
B. Jul. 13, 1963
Lamar 6'1" 295 lbs.

Year	Team	Games	Pos.
1987	NYJ	N	1	OT

Chris Brown
BROWN, CHRISTOPHER DUKE
B. Apr. 11, 1962, Owensboro, KY
Notre Dame 6'0" 200 lbs.

Year	Team	Games	Pos.
1984	PIT	N	16	S, CB
1985			6	CB, S
2 yrs.	22 games		

Chuck Brown
BROWN, CHARLES EDWARD
B. Mar. 15, 1957, Houston, TX
Houston 6'1" 235 lbs.

Year	Team	Games	Pos.
1979	STL	N	4	C, G

Clay Brown
BROWN, CLAYTON LEE
B. Sep. 20, 1958, Los Angeles, CA
Brigham Young 6'3" 225 lbs.

Year	Team	Games	Pos.
1982	ATL	N	1	TE
1983	DEN	N	3	TE
2 yrs.	4 games		

Corwin Brown
BROWN, CORWIN ALAN
B. Apr. 25, 1970, Chicago, IL
Michigan 6'0" 192 lbs.

Year	Team	Games	Pos.
1993	NE	N	15	CB
1994			16	CB, S
1995			16	S
1996			14	S
4 yrs.	61 games		

Curtis Brown
BROWN, CURTIS JEROME
B. Dec. 7, 1954, St. Louis, MO
Missouri 5'10" 203 lbs.

Year	Team	Games	Pos.
1977	BUF	N	7	RB
1978			15	RB
1979			15	FB

Year	Team		Games	Pos.

Curtis Brown *continued*

Year	Team		Games	Pos.
1980			16	FB
1981			14	FB
1982			9	RB
1983	HOU	N	2	RB

7 yrs. 78 games

Danny Brown
BROWN, DANIEL JOSEPH
B. Aug. 26, 1925, Philadelphia, PA
D. Jun., 1995
Villanova 6'1" 200 lbs.

1950	WAS	N	11	E

Dave Brown
BROWN, DAVID
B. Jan. 17, 1964, Dayton, OH
Miami (Ohio) 6'2" 215 lbs.

1987	PHI	N	1	LB

Dave Brown
BROWN, DAVID ALEXANDER
B. 1919
Alabama 5'11" 190 lbs.

1943	NYG	N	10	FB, HB
1946			7	HB
1947			7	HB

3 yrs. 24 games

Dave Brown
BROWN, DAVID MICHAEL
B. Feb. 25, 1970, Summit, NJ
Duke 6'5" 215 lbs.

1992	NYG	N	2	QB
1993			1	QB
1994			15	QB
1995			16	QB
1996			16	QB

5 yrs. 50 games

Dave Brown
BROWN, DAVID STEVEN
B. Jan. 16, 1953, Akron, OH
Michigan 6'1" 195 lbs.

1975	PIT	N	13	S
1976	SEA	N	14	DB
1977			14	S
1978			16	CB
1979			16	CB
1980			16	CB
1981			10	CB
1982			9	CB
1983			16	CB
1984			16	CB
1985			16	CB
1986			16	CB
1987	GB	N	12	CB
1988			16	CB
1989			16	CB, S

15 yrs. 216 games

Dean Brown
BROWN, DEAN
B. Oct. 6, 1944, McDonough, GA
Fort Valley State 5'10" 170 lbs.

1969	CLE	N	5	S
1970	MIA	N	5	DB

2 yrs. 10 games

Dennis Brown
BROWN, DENNIS TRAMMEL
B. Nov. 6, 1967, Los Angeles, CA
Washington 6'4" 290 lbs.

1990	SF	N	15	DE
1991			16	DE

Dennis Brown *continued*

Year	Team		Games	Pos.
1992			16	DE
1993			16	DE
1994			16	DE
1995			16	DE
1996			14	DE

7 yrs. 109 games

Derek Brown
BROWN, DEREK DARNELL
B. Apr. 15, 1971, Banning, CA
Nebraska 5'9" 186 lbs.

1993	NO	N	13	RB
1994			16	RB
1995			16	RB
1996			11	RB

4 yrs. 56 games

Derek Brown
BROWN, DEREK VERNON
B. Mar. 31, 1970, Fairfax, VA
Notre Dame 6'6" 252 lbs.

1992	NYG	N	16	TE
1993			16	TE
1994			13	TE
1996	JAC	N	16	TE

4 yrs. 61 games

Dick Brown
BROWN, RICHARD M.
B. 1907
Iowa 6'1" 220 lbs.

1930	POR	N	11	C

Don Brown
BROWN, DONALD
B. Aug. 20, 1937, Dayton, TX
Houston 6'1" 205 lbs.

1960	HOU	A		HB

Don Brown
BROWN, DONALD
B. Nov. 28, 1963, Annapolis, MD
Oklahoma/Maryland 5'11" 189 lbs.

1986	SD	N	13	CB
1986	MIA	N	2	CB
1987	NYG	N	3	CB

2 yrs. 18 games

Don Brown
BROWN, DONALD COLBY
B. Apr. 2, 1959, San Jose, CA
Santa Clara 6'6" 262 lbs.

1983	SD	N	13	OT

Doug Brown
BROWN, DOUGLAS PAT
B. 1940
Fresno State 6'4" 250 lbs.

1964	OAK	A	12	OT

Ed Brown
BROWN, CHARLES EDWARD
B. Oct. 26, 1928, San Luis Obispo, CA
San Francisco 6'2" 209 lbs.

1954	CHIB	N	12	QB, P
1955			12	QB, P
1956			12	QB, P
1957			12	QB, P
1958			12	QB, P
1959			12	QB, P
1960	CHI	N	12	QB, P
1961			14	QB, P
1962	PIT	N	14	QB, P

Ed Brown *continued*

Year	Team		Games	Pos.
1963			14	QB, P
1964			14	QB, P
1965			13	QB, P
1965	BAL	N	1	QB

12 yrs. 154 games

Eddie Brown
BROWN, EDDIE LEE
B. Dec. 17, 1962, Miami, FL
Miami (Florida) 6'0" 185 lbs.

1985	CIN	N	16	WR
1986			16	WR
1987			12	WR
1988			16	WR
1989			15	WR
1990			14	WR
1991			13	WR

7 yrs. 102 games

Eddie Brown
BROWN, PAUL EDWARD
B. Feb. 19, 1952, Jasper, TN
Tennessee 5'11" 187 lbs.

1974	CLE	N	13	S
1975			3	S
1975	WAS	N	11	S
1976			14	S
1977			14	S
1978	LA	N	1	S
1979			16	S

6 yrs. 72 games

Eric Brown
BROWN, ERIC
B. Sep. 7, 1964
Tulsa 6'2" 180 lbs.

1987	KC	N	2	WR

Eric Brown
BROWN, ERIC
B. Apr. 12, 1967
Savannah State 5'11" 177 lbs.

1989	DAL	N	1	CB, S

Fred Brown
BROWN, FRED RICHARD
B. May 4, 1943, Honolulu, HI
Miami (Florida) 6'5" 231 lbs.

1965	LA	N	14	LB
1967	PHI	N	13	LB
1968			7	LB
1969			6	TE

4 yrs. 40 games

Fred Brown
BROWN, FREDERICK
B. Dec. 9, 1905
D. Jul., 1973, Brooklyn, NY
New York University 6'2" 195 lbs.

1930	SI	N	6	G

Fred Brown
BROWN, FREDERICK
B. Dec. 22, 1938, Atlanta, GA
Georgia 5'11" 189 lbs.

1961	BUF	A	5	HB
1963			4	HB

2 yrs. 9 games

Gary Brown
BROWN, GARY LEE
B. Jun. 25, 1971, Amityville, NY
Georgia Tech 6'4" 288 lbs.

1994	GB	N	1	OT

Gary Brown *continued*

Year	Team		Games	Pos.
1995			16	OT
1996			8	OT

3 yrs. 25 games

Gary Brown
BROWN, GARY LEROY
B. Jul. 1, 1969, Williamsport, PA
Penn State 5'11" 227 lbs.

1991	HOU	N	11	RB
1992			16	RB
1993			16	RB
1994			12	RB
1995			9	RB

5 yrs. 64 games

George Brown
BROWN, GEORGE T.
B. Jul. 13, 1894, Ohio
D. Mar. 24, 1973, Youngstown, OH
None 190 lbs.

1923	AKR	N	2	T, E

George Brown
BROWN, GEORGE WILLIAM
B. Sep. 23, 1923, Boyd, TX
Texas Christian 6'2" 222 lbs.

1949	B, NY	AA	8	G
1950	NYY	N	12	G

2 yrs. 20 games

Gilbert Brown
BROWN, GILBERT JESSE
B. Feb. 22, 1971, Farmington, MI
Kansas 6'2" 330 lbs.

1993	GB	N	2	NT
1994			13	NT, DE
1995			13	DT
1996			16	NT

4 yrs. 44 games

Gordon Brown
BROWN, GORDON S.
B. Mar. 19, 1963, Philadelphia, PA
Tulsa 5'11" 220 lbs.

1987	IND	N	3	RB

Greg Brown
BROWN, GREGORY LEE
B. Jan. 5, 1957, Washington, DC
Kansas State/Eastern Illinois 6'5" 260 lbs.

1981	PHI	N	16	DE
1982			9	DE
1983			16	DE
1984			16	DE
1985			16	DE
1986			16	DE
1987	ATL	N	12	DE
1988			16	DE

8 yrs. 117 games

Guy Brown
BROWN, GUY, III
B. Jun. 1, 1955, Palestine, TX
Houston 6'4" 223 lbs.

1977	DAL	N	14	LB
1978			15	LB
1979			15	LB
1980			16	LB
1981			16	LB
1982			9	LB

6 yrs. 85 games

Year	Team	Games	Pos.

Hardy Brown
BROWN, HARDY (Thumper)
B. May 8, 1924, Childress, TX
D. Nov. 8, 1991, Stockton, CA
Southern Methodist/Tulsa 6'0" 193 lbs.

Year	Team		Games	Pos.
1948	BKN	AA	11	RB, DB
1949	CHI	AA	12	RB, DB
1950	BAL	N	4	DB
1950	WAS	N	8	DB
1951	SF	N	12	LB
1952			12	LB
1953			12	LB
1954			11	LB
1955			12	LB
1956	CHIC	N	8	LB
1960	DEN	A		LB

10 yrs. 102 games

Howie Brown
BROWN, HOWARD KENNETH
B. Jan. 26, 1922, Dayton, OH
D. Apr. 4, 1975, Bloomington, IN
Indiana 5'11" 215 lbs.

Year	Team		Games	Pos.
1948	DET	N	12	G
1949			12	T, G
1950			12	G

3 yrs. 36 games

Ivory Lee Brown
BROWN, IVORY LEE
B. Aug. 17, 1969, Palestine, TX
Arkansas-Pine Bluff 6'2" 245 lbs.

Year	Team		Games	Pos.
1992	PHX	N	7	RB

Jack Brown
BROWN, JACK R.
B. Oct. 24, 1902
D. Nov. 25, 1987, Dayton, OH
Dayton 6'0" 191 lbs.

Year	Team		Games	Pos.
1926	DAY	N	2	C, G
1927			3	C
1928			4	C, E, T
1929			4	C, G

4 yrs. 13 games

James Brown
BROWN, JAMES LAMONT
B. Jan. 3, 1970, Philadelphia, PA
Virginia State 6'6" 321 lbs.

Year	Team		Games	Pos.
1993	NYJ	N	14	OT
1994			16	OT
1995			14	OT
1996	MIA	N	16	OT

4 yrs. 60 games

Jamie Brown
BROWN, JAMIE
B. Apr. 24, 1972, Miami, FL
Florida A&M 6'8" 320 lbs.

Year	Team		Games	Pos.
1995	DEN	N	6	OT
1996			12	OT

2 yrs. 18 games

J.B. Brown
BROWN, JAMES HAROLD
B. Jan. 5, 1967, Washington, DC
Maryland 6'0" 192 lbs.

Year	Team		Games	Pos.
1989	MIA	N	16	CB
1990			16	CB
1991			15	CB
1992			16	CB
1993			16	CB
1994			16	CB
1995			13	CB
1996			13	CB

8 yrs. 121 games

Jerome Brown
BROWN, JEROME
B. Feb. 4, 1965, Brooksville, FL
D. Jun. 25, 1992, Brooksville, FL
Miami (Florida) 6'2" 288 lbs.

Year	Team		Games	Pos.
1987	PHI	N	12	DT
1988			16	DT
1989			16	DT
1990			16	DT
1991			16	DT

5 yrs. 76 games

Jesse Brown
BROWN, JESSE J.
B. Nov. 6, 1902
D. Nov., 1987, Ellwood City, CA
Pittsburgh 5'10" 180 lbs.

Year	Team		Games	Pos.
1926	POT	N	13	HB

Jim Brown
BROWN, JAMES NATHANIEL
B. Feb. 17, 1936, St. Simons, GA
Syracuse 6'2" 228 lbs.

Year	Team		Games	Pos.
1957	CLE	N	12	FB
1958			12	FB
1959			12	FB
1960			12	FB
1961			14	FB
1962			14	FB
1963			14	FB
1964			14	FB
1965			14	FB

9 yrs. 118 games

John Brown
BROWN, JOHN C.
B. Jun. 9, 1939, Camden, NJ
Syracuse 6'2" 250 lbs.

Year	Team		Games	Pos.
1962	CLE	N	14	OT
1963			14	OT
1964			11	OT
1965			14	OT
1966			14	OT
1967	PIT	N	14	OT
1968			13	OT
1969			14	OT
1970			14	OT
1971			14	OT

10 yrs. 136 games

John Brown
BROWN, JOHN E. (The Body)
B. Apr. 9, 1922, Belen, MI
North Carolina Central 6'4" 230 lbs.

Year	Team		Games	Pos.
1947	LA	AA	14	C
1948			14	C
1949			12	C

3 yrs. 40 games

Ken Brown
BROWN, KEN
B. Nov. 8, 1945, Holdenville, OK
none 5'10" 204 lbs.

Year	Team		Games	Pos.
1970	CLE	N	11	RB
1971			10	RB
1972			14	RB
1973			14	RB
1974			14	RB
1975			14	RB

6 yrs. 77 games

Ken Brown
BROWN, KENNETH
B. Mar. 10, 1965
Southern Arkansas 5'8" 175 lbs.

Year	Team		Games	Pos.
1987	CIN	N	3	WR

Ken Brown
BROWN, KENNETH ANDERSON
B. May 5, 1971, Wiesbaden, Germany
Virginia Tech 6'1" 235 lbs.

Year	Team		Games	Pos.
1995	DEN	N	2	LB

Ken Brown
BROWN, KENNETH E.
B. Apr. 19, 1954, Saginaw, MI
New Mexico 6'1" 245 lbs.

Year	Team		Games	Pos.
1979	DEN	N	16	C
1980	GB	N	6	C

2 yrs. 22 games

Kevin Brown
BROWN, KEVIN
B. Jan. 11, 1963
West Texas State 6'2" 178 lbs.

Year	Team		Games	Pos.
1987	CHI	N	3	P

Lance Brown
BROWN, LANCE
B. Feb. 2, 1972, Jacksonville, FL
Indiana 6'0" 200 lbs.

Year	Team		Games	Pos.
1995	ARI	N	11	CB
1996			1	CB

2 yrs. 12 games

Laron Brown
BROWN, LARON
B. Nov. 10, 1963
Texas 5'9" 172 lbs.

Year	Team		Games	Pos.
1987	DEN	N	3	WR

Larry Brown
BROWN, LARRY
B. Jun. 16, 1949, Jacksonville, FL
Kansas 6'4" 260 lbs.

Year	Team		Games	Pos.
1971	PIT	N	13	TE
1972			9	TE
1973			14	TE
1974			14	TE
1975			14	TE
1976			13	TE
1977			14	TE, OT
1978			8	OT
1979			15	OT
1980			16	OT
1981			14	OT
1982			8	OT
1983			8	OT
1984			7	OT

14 yrs. 167 games

Larry Brown
BROWN, LARRY
B. Sep. 4, 1963, Miami, FL
Mankato State 5'11" 180 lbs.

Year	Team		Games	Pos.
1987	MIN	N	1	WR

Larry Brown
BROWN, LARRY
B. Nov. 30, 1969, Miami, FL
Texas Christian 5'11" 184 lbs.

Year	Team		Games	Pos.
1991	DAL	N	16	CB
1992			16	CB
1993			16	CB
1994			15	CB
1995			16	CB
1996	OAK	N	8	CB

6 yrs. 87 games

Larry Brown
BROWN, LARRY DONELL
B. Jun. 4, 1955, Jacksonville, FL

Larry Brown continued
Miami (Florida) 6'5" 262 lbs.

Year	Team		Games	Pos.
1978	KC	N	1	OT
1979			4	OT

2 yrs. 5 games

Larry Brown
BROWN, LAWRENCE
B. Sep. 19, 1947, Clairton, PA
Kansas State 5'11" 195 lbs.

Year	Team		Games	Pos.
1969	WAS	N	14	RB
1970			13	RB
1971			13	RB
1972			12	RB
1973			14	RB
1974			11	RB
1975			14	RB
1976			11	RB

8 yrs. 102 games

Lomas Brown
BROWN, LOMAS, JR.
B. Mar. 30, 1963, Miami, FL
Florida 6'4" 282 lbs.

Year	Team		Games	Pos.
1985	DET	N	16	OT
1986			16	OT
1987			11	OT
1988			16	OT
1989			16	OT
1990			16	OT
1991			15	OT
1992			16	OT
1993			11	OT
1994			16	OT
1995			15	OT
1996	ARI	N	16	OT

12 yrs. 180 games

Marc Brown
BROWN, MARC STACY
B. May 7, 1961, Nyack, NY
Towson State 6'2" 195 lbs.

Year	Team		Games	Pos.
1987	BUF	N	3	WR

Mark Brown
BROWN, MARK ANTHONY
B. Jul. 18, 1961, Los Angeles, CA
Purdue 6'2" 230 lbs.

Year	Team		Games	Pos.
1983	MIA	N	14	LB
1984			16	LB
1985			15	LB
1986			14	LB
1987			12	LB
1988			13	LB
1989	DET	N	6	LB
1990			15	LB
1991			2	LB

9 yrs. 107 games

Marv Brown
BROWN, MARVIN C.
B. Aug. 15, 1932, Dallas, TX
East Texas State 5'8" 150 lbs.

Year	Team		Games	Pos.
1957	DET	N	4	HB

Monty Brown
BROWN, MONTY
B. Apr. 13, 1970, Bridgeport, MI
Ferris State 6'0" 228 lbs.

Year	Team		Games	Pos.
1993	BUF	N	13	LB
1994			3	LB
1995			16	LB
1996	NE	N	11	LB

4 yrs. 43 games

Norris Brown
BROWN, WILLIE NORRIS

Year	Team	Games	Pos.

Norris Brown *continued*
B. Jul. 10, 1961, Laurens, SC
Georgia 6'3" 220 lbs.

Year	Team	Games	Pos.
1983	**MIN** N	2	TE

Orlando Brown
BROWN, ORLANDO CLAUDE
B. Dec. 12, 1970, Washington, DC
Central State (Ohio)/South Carolina State 6'7" 325 lbs.

Year	Team	Games	Pos.
1994	**CLE** N	14	OT
1995		16	OT
1996	**BAL** N	16	OT
3 yrs.	46 games		

Otto Brown
BROWN, OTTO
B. Jan. 12, 1947, Tallahassee, FL
Prairie View A&M 6'1" 187 lbs.

Year	Team	Games	Pos.
1969	**DAL** N	14	S
1970	**NYG** N	13	CB
1971		12	CB
1972		13	CB
1973		11	CB
5 yrs.	63 games		

Pete Brown
BROWN, SAMUEL
B. 1931, Rossville, GA
Georgia Tech 6'2" 210 lbs.

Year	Team	Games	Pos.
1953	**SF** N	10	C, LB
1954		12	C, LB
2 yrs.	22 games		

Preston Brown
BROWN, PRESTON MELVILLE
B. Mar. 2, 1958, Nashville, TN
Vanderbilt 5'10" 184 lbs.

Year	Team	Games	Pos.
1980	**NE** N	5	WR
1982		9	WR
1983	**NYJ** N	16	WR
1984	**CLE** N	2	WR
4 yrs.	32 games		

Ray Brown
BROWN, LEONARD RAY, JR.
B. Dec. 12, 1962, West Memphis, AR
Arkansas State 6'5" 257 lbs.

Year	Team	Games	Pos.
1986	**STL** N	11	G, OT
1987		7	OT, G
1988	**PHX** N	15	G, OT
1989	**WAS** N	7	G, OT
1992		16	OT
1993		16	OT
1994		16	G, OT
1995		16	G
1996	**SF** N	16	G
9 yrs.	120 games		

Ray Brown
BROWN, RAYMOND LLOYD
B. Jul. 7, 1936, Clarksdale, MS
Mississippi 6'2" 195 lbs.

Year	Team	Games	Pos.
1958	**BAL** N	12	QB, DB, P
1959		12	QB, DB, P
1960		12	QB, DB, P
3 yrs.	36 games		

Ray Brown
BROWN, RAYMOND MADISON
B. Jan. 12, 1949, Fort Worth, TX
West Texas State 6'2" 203 lbs.

Year	Team	Games	Pos.
1971	**ATL** N	10	CB, S
1972		14	S
1973		14	S
1974		14	S

Ray Brown *continued*

Year	Team	Games	Pos.
1975		14	S
1976		14	S
1977		14	S
1978	**NO** N	16	S
1979		12	S
1980		15	S
10 yrs.	137 games		

Ray Brown
BROWN, RAYNARD
B. Jul. 25, 1965
South Carolina 5'9" 185 lbs.

Year	Team	Games	Pos.
1987	**SF** N	1	RB

Reggie Brown
BROWN, REGGIE
B. Jun. 26, 1973, Detroit, TX
Fresno State 6'0" 233 lbs.

Year	Team	Games	Pos.
1996	**SEA** N	7	FB

Reggie Brown
BROWN, REGGIE VAN
B. Mar. 12, 1960, Dendron, VA
Oregon 5'11" 211 lbs.

Year	Team	Games	Pos.
1982	**ATL** N	8	RB
1983		2	RB
1987	**PHI** N	3	RB
3 yrs.	13 games		

Reggie Brown
BROWN, REGINALD ALONZO
B. May 5, 1970, Miami, FL
Alabama State 6'1" 195 lbs.

Year	Team	Games	Pos.
1993	**HOU** N	4	WR
1994		3	WR
2 yrs.	7 games		

Reggie Brown
BROWN, REGINALD DWAYNE
B. Sep. 28, 1974, Austin, TX
Texas A&M 6'2" 241 lbs.

Year	Team	Games	Pos.
1996	**DET** N	10	LB

Richard Brown
BROWN, RICHARD SOLOMON
B. Sep. 21, 1965, Western Samoa
San Diego State 6'3" 240 lbs.

Year	Team	Games	Pos.
1987	**LARM** N	8	LB
1989		13	LB
1990	**SD** N	11	LB
1991	**CLE** N	16	LB
1992		10	LB
1994	**MIN** N	3	LB
1995		16	LB
1996		14	LB
8 yrs.	91 games		

Robert Brown
BROWN, ROBERT LEE
B. May 21, 1960, Edenton, NC
Virginia Tech 6'2" 268 lbs.

Year	Team	Games	Pos.
1982	**GB** N	8	DE
1983		16	DE
1984		16	DE
1985		16	DE
1986		16	DE
1987		12	DE
1988		16	DE
1989		16	DE
1990		16	DE
1991		16	DE
1992		16	DE
11 yrs.	164 games		

Roger Brown
BROWN, ROGER
B. Dec. 16, 1966, Baltimore, MD
Virginia Tech 6'0" 196 lbs.

Year	Team	Games	Pos.
1990	**NYG** N	5	CB
1991		16	CB
1992	**NE** N	16	S
3 yrs.	37 games		

Roger Brown
BROWN, ROGER LEE
B. May 1, 1937, Surry County, VA
Maryland-Eastern Shore 6'5" 298 lbs.

Year	Team	Games	Pos.
1960	**DET** N	12	T
1961		14	DT
1962		14	DT
1963		14	DT
1964		14	DT
1965		14	DT
1966		14	DT
1967	**LA** N	14	DT
1968		14	DT
1969		14	DT
10 yrs.	138 games		

Ron Brown
BROWN, RONALD
B. Apr. 28, 1964, Oroville, CA
Southern California 6'4" 215 lbs.

Year	Team	Games	Pos.
1987	**LARI** N	3	DE
1988		16	DE
2 yrs.	19 games		

Ron Brown
BROWN, RONALD
B. Jan. 11, 1963, Long Island, NY
Colorado 5'10" 186 lbs.

Year	Team	Games	Pos.
1987	**STL** N	3	WR

Ron Brown
BROWN, RONALD JAMES
B. Mar. 31, 1961, Los Angeles, CA
Arizona State 5'11" 181 lbs.

Year	Team	Games	Pos.
1984	**LARM** N	16	WR
1985		13	WR
1986		14	WR
1987		12	WR
1988		7	WR
1989		16	WR
1990	**LARI** N	16	CB
1991	**LARM** N	6	WR
8 yrs.	100 games		

Rosey Brown
BROWN, ROOSEVELT, JR.
B. Oct. 20, 1932, Charlottesville, VA
Morgan State 6'3" 249 lbs.

Year	Team	Games	Pos.
1953	**NYG** N	12	OT
1954		12	OT
1955		12	OT
1956		12	OT
1957		11	OT
1958		12	OT
1959		12	OT
1960		12	OT
1961		14	OT
1962		14	OT
1963		13	OT
1964		13	OT
1965		14	OT
13 yrs.	163 games		

Ruben Brown
BROWN, RUBEN PERNELL
B. Feb. 13, 1972, Lynchburg, VA
Pittsburgh 6'3" 304 lbs.

Year	Team	Games	Pos.
1995	**BUF** N	16	G

Ruben Brown *continued*

Year	Team	Games	Pos.
1996		14	G
2 yrs.	30 games		

Rufus Brown
BROWN, RUFUS BERNARD
B. May 19, 1962, Bartow, FL
Florida A&M 6'2" 295 lbs.

Year	Team	Games	Pos.
1987	**TB** N	2	G

Rush Brown
BROWN, RUSH, JR.
B. Jun. 27, 1954, Laurinburg, NC
Ball State 6'2" 257 lbs.

Year	Team	Games	Pos.
1980	**STL** N	16	DT
1981		16	DT
1982		9	DT
1983		6	DE
4 yrs.	47 games		

Selwyn Brown
BROWN, SELWYN G.
B. Sep. 28, 1965, St. Petersburg, FL
Miami (Florida) 5'11" 205 lbs.

Year	Team	Games	Pos.
1988	**TB** N	4	CB, S

Sidney Brown
BROWN, SIDNEY LOUIS, JR.
B. Jan. 27, 1956, New Orleans, LA
Oklahoma 6'0" 186 lbs.

Year	Team	Games	Pos.
1978	**NE** N	16	CB

Sonny Brown
BROWN, CLIFTON D.
B. Nov. 12, 1963, Tinker Air Force Base, OK
Oklahoma 6'2" 200 lbs.

Year	Team	Games	Pos.
1987	**HOU** N	2	S

Stan Brown
BROWN, BYRON STANLEY
B. Aug. 4, 1949, Martinez, CA
Purdue 5'9" 184 lbs.

Year	Team	Games	Pos.
1971	**CLE** N	6	WR

Steve Brown
BROWN, STEVE
B. Mar. 20, 1960, Sacramento, CA
Oregon 5'11" 188 lbs.

Year	Team	Games	Pos.
1983	**HOU** N	16	CB
1984		16	CB
1985		15	CB
1986		16	CB
1987		10	CB
1988		14	CB
1989		16	CB
1990		16	CB
8 yrs.	119 games		

Ted Brown
BROWN, THOMAS EDWARD
B. Feb. 15, 1957, High Point, NC
North Carolina State 5'10" 210 lbs.

Year	Team	Games	Pos.
1979	**MIN** N	14	RB
1980		16	RB
1981		16	RB
1982		8	RB
1983		10	RB
1984		13	RB
1985		14	RB
1986		13	RB
8 yrs.	104 games		

Year	Team		Games	Pos.

Terry Brown
BROWN, TERRY LYNN
B. Jan. 9, 1947, Walters, OK
Oklahoma State 6'1" 206 lbs.

Year	Team		Games	Pos.
1969	STL	N	14	CB
1970			10	S
1972	MIN	N	8	DB
1973			14	CB, S
1974			14	S
1975			13	S
1976	CLE	N	12	S
7 yrs.	85 games			

Theotis Brown
BROWN, THEOTIS, II
B. Apr. 20, 1957, Chicago, IL
UCLA 6'3" 225 lbs.

Year	Team		Games	Pos.
1979	STL	N	16	RB
1980			16	RB
1981			4	RB
1981	SEA	N	9	RB
1982			9	RB
1983			3	RB
1983	KC		12	RB
1984			14	RB
6 yrs.	83 games			

Thomas Brown
BROWN, THOMAS W.
B. Jul. 8, 1957, Galveston, TX
Baylor 6'4" 243 lbs.

Year	Team		Games	Pos.
1980	PHI	N	16	DE
1981	CLE	N	16	DE
1983			16	DE
3 yrs.	48 games			

Tim Brown
BROWN, TIMOTHY DONELL
B. Jul. 22, 1966, Dallas, TX
Notre Dame 6'0" 195 lbs.

Year	Team		Games	Pos.
1988	LARI	N	16	WR
1989			1	WR
1990			16	WR
1991			16	WR
1992			15	WR
1993			16	WR
1994			16	WR
1995	OAK	N	16	WR
1996			16	WR
9 yrs.	128 games			

Timmy Brown
BROWN, THOMAS ALLEN
B. May 24, 1937, Richmond, IN
Ball State 5'10" 195 lbs.

Year	Team		Games	Pos.
1959	GB	N	1	HB
1960	PHI	N	12	HB
1961			14	HB
1962			14	HB
1963			14	HB
1964			10	HB
1965			13	HB
1966			13	RB
1967			7	RB
1968	BAL	N	11	RB
10 yrs.	109 games			

Tom Brown
BROWN, THOMAS
B. Dec. 24, 1963
Augustana (South Dakota) 6'4" 190 lbs.

Year	Team		Games	Pos.
1987	CIN	N	2	WR

Tom Brown
BROWN, THOMAS M.
B. May 22, 1921, Pittsburgh, PA
William & Mary 6'2" 216 lbs.

Year	Team		Games	Pos.
1942	PIT	N	7	E

Tom Brown
BROWN, THOMAS MARTIN
B. Nov. 20, 1964, Ridgway, PA
Pittsburgh 6'1" 218 lbs.

Year	Team		Games	Pos.
1987	MIA	N	1	RB
1989			16	RB
2 yrs.	17 games			

Tom Brown
BROWN, THOMAS WILLIAM
B. Dec. 12, 1940, Lauderdale, PA
Maryland 6'1" 191 lbs.

Year	Team		Games	Pos.
1964	GB	N	14	DB
1965			14	DB
1966			14	DB
1967			14	DB
1968			14	DB
1969	WAS	N	1	S
6 yrs.	71 games			

Tony Brown
BROWN, ANTHONY LAMAR
B. May 15, 1970, Bangkok, Thailand
Fresno State 5'9" 183 lbs.

Year	Team		Games	Pos.
1992	HOU	N	12	CB
1993			16	CB
1994	SEA	N	13	CB
1995			16	CB
4 yrs.	57 games			

Tony Brown
BROWN, TONY
B. Jul. 11, 1964, Stamford, CT
Pittsburgh 6'5" 285 lbs.

Year	Team		Games	Pos.
1987	BUF	N	2	OT

Troy Brown
BROWN, TROY FITZGERALD
B. Jul. 2, 1971, Blackville, SC
Marshall 5'9" 183 lbs.

Year	Team		Games	Pos.
1993	NE	N	12	WR
1994			9	WR
1995			16	WR
1996			16	WR
4 yrs.	53 games			

Tyrone Brown
BROWN, TYRONE
B. Jan. 3, 1973, Cincinnati, OH
Toledo 5'11" 164 lbs.

Year	Team		Games	Pos.
1995	ATL	N	6	WR
1996			9	WR
2 yrs.	15 games			

Vincent Brown
BROWN, VINCENT BERNARD
B. Jan. 9, 1965, Atlanta, GA
Mississippi Valley State 6'2" 245 lbs.

Year	Team		Games	Pos.
1988	NE	N	16	LB
1989			14	LB
1990			16	LB
1991			16	LB
1992			13	LB
1993			16	LB
1994			16	LB
1995			16	LB
8 yrs.	123 games			

Willie Brown
BROWN, WILLIAM FERDIE
B. Dec. 2, 1940, Yazoo City, MS
Grambling State 6'1" 194 lbs.

Year	Team		Games	Pos.
1963	DEN	A	8	DB
1964			14	DB
1965			14	DB
1966			14	DB
1967	OAK	A	14	DB

Willie Brown continued

Year	Team		Games	Pos.
1968			14	DB
1969			14	CB
1970	OAK	N	9	CB
1971			14	DB
1972			14	CB
1973			14	CB
1974			9	DB
1975			12	DB
1976			14	CB
1977			14	CB
1978			13	CB
16 yrs.	205 games			

Willie Brown
BROWN, WILLIE F.
B. Mar. 21, 1942, Tuscaloosa, AL
Southern California 6'0" 185 lbs.

Year	Team		Games	Pos.
1964	LA	N	9	OE, FL
1965			14	FL
1966	PHI	N	7	FL
3 yrs.	30 games			

Gordie Browne
BROWNE, GORDON WAYLAND, JR.
B. Dec. 5, 1951, Franklin, MA
Boston College 6'5" 265 lbs.

Year	Team		Games	Pos.
1974	NYJ	N	10	OT
1975			13	OT
2 yrs.	23 games			

Jim Browne
BROWNE, JAMES
B. Mar. 16, 1962
Boston College 6'1" 215 lbs.

Year	Team		Games	Pos.
1987	LARI	N	2	RB

Jim Browner
BROWNER, JIMMIE LEE
B. Dec. 4, 1955, Warren, OH
Notre Dame 6'1" 208 lbs.

Year	Team		Games	Pos.
1979	CIN	N	16	S
1980			2	S
2 yrs.	18 games			

Joey Browner
BROWNER, JOEY MATTHEW
B. May 15, 1960, Warren, OH
Southern California 6'2" 210 lbs.

Year	Team		Games	Pos.
1983	MIN	N	16	CB, S
1984			16	CB, S
1985			16	S
1986			16	S
1987			12	DB
1988			16	S
1989			16	S
1990			16	S
1991			14	S
1992	TB	N	7	S
10 yrs.	145 games			

Keith Browner
BROWNER, KEITH TELLUS
B. Jan. 24, 1962, Warren, OH
Southern California 6'6" 245 lbs.

Year	Team		Games	Pos.
1984	TB	N	16	LB
1985			16	LB
1986			15	LB
1987	SF	N	1	LB
1987	LARI	N	1	LB
1988	SD	N	16	LB
5 yrs.	65 games			

Ross Browner
BROWNER, ROSS
B. Mar. 22, 1954, Warren, OH

Ross Browner continued
Notre Dame 6'3" 265 lbs.

Year	Team		Games	Pos.
1978	CIN	N	11	DT
1979			16	DE
1980			15	DE
1981			16	DE
1982			9	DE
1983			12	DE
1984			16	DE
1985			16	DE
1986			16	DE
1987	GB	N	11	DE
10 yrs.	138 games			

Charlie Browning
BROWNING, CHARLES
B. Jul. 28, 1943
Washington 6'0" 220 lbs.

Year	Team		Games	Pos.
1965	NY	A	1	HB

Dave Browning
BROWNING, DAVID
B. Aug. 18, 1956, Spokane, WA
Washington 6'5" 245 lbs.

Year	Team		Games	Pos.
1978	OAK	N	12	DE
1979			16	DE
1980			16	DE
1981			16	DE
1982	LARI	N	5	DE
1983	NE	N	12	DE
6 yrs.	77 games			

Greg Browning
BROWNING, GREGG, JR.
B. 1922
Denver 6'0" 190 lbs.

Year	Team		Games	Pos.
1947	NYG	N	2	E

John Browning
BROWNING, JOHN
B. Sep. 30, 1973, Miami, FL
West Virginia 6'4" 264 lbs.

Year	Team		Games	Pos.
1996	KC	N	13	DE

Claude Brownlee
BROWNLEE, CLAUDE
B. Aug. 4, 1944, Atlanta, GA
Benedict 6'4" 265 lbs.

Year	Team		Games	Pos.
1967	MIA	A	3	DT

Darrick Brownlow
BROWNLOW, DARRICK DEWAYNE
B. Dec. 28, 1968, Indianapolis, IN
Illinois 5'10" 237 lbs.

Year	Team		Games	Pos.
1991	DAL	N	16	LB
1992	TB	N	16	LB
1993			15	LB
1994	DAL	N	16	LB
1995	WAS	N	16	LB
1996			16	LB
6 yrs.	95 games			

Dick Brubaker
BRUBAKER, CARL RICHARD
B. Jan. 2, 1932, Cleveland, OH
D. Jun. 14, 1978
Ohio State 6'0" 202 lbs.

Year	Team		Games	Pos.
1955	CHIC	N	10	E
1957			3	E
1960	BUF	A		OE
3 yrs.	13 games			

Bruce
BRUCE
None

Year	Team		Games	Pos.
1921	SYR	A	1	E

Year	Team	Games	Pos.

Aundray Bruce
BRUCE, AUNDRAY
B. Apr. 30, 1966, Montgomery, AL
Auburn 6'5" 245 lbs.

Year	Team		Games	Pos.
1988	ATL	N	16	LB
1989			16	LB
1990			16	LB
1991			14	LB
1992	LARI	N	16	LB
1993			16	TE
1994			16	TE
1995	OAK	N	14	TE
1996			16	TE
9 yrs.	140 games			

Gail Bruce
BRUCE, GAIL ROBERT
B. Sep. 29, 1923, Puyallup, WA
Washington 6'1" 206 lbs.

Year	Team		Games	Pos.
1948	SF	AA	14	E
1949			12	E
1950	SF	N	12	E
1951			12	E
4 yrs.	50 games			

Isaac Bruce
BRUCE, ISAAC ISIDORE
B. Nov. 10, 1972, Fort Lauderdale, FL
Memphis State 6'0" 178 lbs.

Year	Team		Games	Pos.
1994	LARM	N	12	WR
1995	STL	N	16	WR
1996			16	WR
3 yrs.	44 games			

Les Bruckner
BRUCKNER, LESLIE C.
B. Apr. 16, 1918, Milan, MI
Michigan State 6'1" 195 lbs.

Year	Team		Games	Pos.
1945	CHIC	N	2	FB

Nick Bruckner
BRUCKNER, NICHOLAS, JR.
B. May 19, 1961, Astoria, NY
Syracuse 5'11" 185 lbs.

Year	Team		Games	Pos.
1983	NYJ	N	7	WR
1984			16	WR
1985			9	WR
3 yrs.	32 games			

Hank Bruder
BRUDER, HENRY GEORGE, JR.
B. Nov. 22, 1907, Pekin, IL
D. Jun. 29, 1970, Mattoon, IL
Northwestern 6'0" 199 lbs.

Year	Team		Games	Pos.
1931	GB	N	13	HB, QB
1932			13	HB, FB, QB
1933			9	HB
1934			13	QB, FB, HB
1935			10	HB, FB, QB
1936			11	QB, FB
1937			10	QB, HB
1938			8	QB
1939			10	QB, HB
1940	PIT	N	8	QB
10 yrs.	105 games			

Woody Bruder
BRUDER, WOODRUFF HARLAN
(Doc)
B. 1902, Houston, TX
D. Nov. 13, 1953, Houston, TX
Pittsburgh/West Virginia 5'11" 178 lbs.

Year	Team		Games	Pos.
1925	BUF	N	5	HB, FB
1925	FRA	N	4	HB, FB
1926			13	HB, FB, QB
2 yrs.	22 games			

Bob Brudzinski
BRUDZINSKI, ROBERT LOUIS
B. Jan. 1, 1955, Fremont, OH
Ohio State 6'4" 225 lbs.

Year	Team		Games	Pos.
1977	LA	N	14	LB
1978			16	LB
1979			16	LB
1980			9	LB
1981	MIA	N	16	LB
1982			9	LB
1983			16	LB
1984			16	LB
1985			14	LB
1986			16	LB
1987			12	LB
1988			16	LB
1989			10	LB
13 yrs.	180 games			

Charlie Brueckman
BRUECKMAN, CHARLES WILLIAM
B. Nov. 23, 1935, McKees Rocks, PA
Pittsburgh 6'2" 223 lbs.

Year	Team		Games	Pos.
1958	WAS	N	9	C
1960	LA	A		LB
2 yrs.	9 games			

Mark Bruener
BRUENER, MARK
B. Sep. 16, 1972, Olympia, WA
Washington 6'4" 250 lbs.

Year	Team		Games	Pos.
1995	PIT	N	16	TE
1996			12	TE
2 yrs.	28 games			

Bob Bruer
BRUER, ROBERT ANTHONY
B. May 22, 1953, Madison, WI
Mankato State 6'5" 234 lbs.

Year	Team		Games	Pos.
1979	SF	N	16	TE
1980			1	TE
1980	MIN	N	12	TE
1981			15	TE
1982			8	TE
1983			16	TE
5 yrs.	68 games			

Bob Bruggers
BRUGGERS, ROBERT EUGENE
B. Apr. 20, 1944, Lincoln, NE
Minnesota 6'1" 226 lbs.

Year	Team		Games	Pos.
1966	MIA	A	14	LB
1967			4	LB
1968			6	LB
1968	SD	A	10	LB
1969			12	LB
1970	SD	N	13	LB
1971			3	LB
6 yrs.	62 games			

John Bruhin
BRUHIN, JOHN GLENN
B. Dec. 9, 1964, Knoxville, TN
Tennessee 6'3" 280 lbs.

Year	Team		Games	Pos.
1988	TB	N	16	G
1989			9	G
1990			14	G
1991			10	G
4 yrs.	49 games			

Boyd Brumbaugh
BRUMBAUGH, BOYD
B. Aug. 24, 1915, Springdale, PA
Deceased
Duquesne 5'11" 195 lbs.

Year	Team		Games	Pos.
1938	BKN	N	7	FB
1939			5	FB, QB

Boyd Brumbaugh continued

Year	Team		Games	Pos.
1939	PIT	N	5	FB, HB
1940			8	FB
1941			10	HB, FB, QB
4 yrs.	35 games			

Carl Brumbaugh
BRUMBAUGH, CARL L.
B. Sep. 22, 1906, West Milton, OH
D. Oct. 25, 1969, West Milton, OH
Ohio State/Florida 5'10" 170 lbs.

Year	Team		Games	Pos.
1930	CHIB	N	14	QB
1931			12	QB
1932			12	QB, HB
1933			13	QB
1934			13	QB
1936			12	QB
1937	CLE	N	5	QB
1937	BKN	N	4	QB
1937	CHIB	N	1	QB
1938			6	QB, HB
8 yrs.	92 games			

Justin Brumbaugh
BRUMBAUGH, JUSTIN J.
B. 1905, Springdale, PA
D. Jul. 3, 1951, Rochester, MN
Bucknell 6'0" 205 lbs.

Year	Team		Games	Pos.
1931	FRA	N	8	HB, QB, FB

Jack Brumfield
BRUMFIELD, JACKSON
B. 1932
Southern Mississippi 6'2" 215 lbs.

Year	Team		Games	Pos.
1954	SF	N	12	E

Jim Brumfield
BRUMFIELD, JAMES
B. Sep. 4, 1947, Osyka, MS
Indiana State 6'1" 195 lbs.

Year	Team		Games	Pos.
1971	PIT	N	14	RB

Scott Brumfield
BRUMFIELD, SCOTT
B. Aug. 19, 1970, Salt Lake City, UT
Brigham Young 6'8" 320 lbs.

Year	Team		Games	Pos.
1993	CIN	N	16	OT
1994			2	OT
1995			13	G, OT
1996			9	OT
4 yrs.	40 games			

Bob Brumley
BRUMLEY, ROBERT L.
B. 1922
Rice 6'0" 200 lbs.

Year	Team		Games	Pos.
1945	DET	N	1	HB

Don Brumm
BRUMM, DONALD DWAIN
B. Oct. 4, 1941, Chicago Heights, IL
Purdue 6'3" 243 lbs.

Year	Team		Games	Pos.
1963	STL	N	11	DE
1964			14	DE
1965			14	DE
1966			14	DE
1967			10	DB
1968			14	DE
1969			4	DE
1970	PHI	N	7	DE
1971			9	DE
1972	STL	N	14	DE
10 yrs.	111 games			

Fred Brumm
BRUMM, FREDERICK, JR.

Fred Brumm continued
B. Nov., 1887, Tonawanda, NY
Deceased
None

Year	Team		Games	Pos.
1921	TON	A	1	T, C

Kibo Brumm
BRUMM, ROMAN HENRY
B. Mar. 5, 1898, Dane County, WI
D. 1981
Wisconsin-La Crosse/Wisconsin-Eau Claire/Wisconsin 6'0" 182 lbs.

Year	Team		Games	Pos.
1924	RAC	N	9	E, G
1925	MIL	N	5	T, E, G
1926	RAC	N	4	C, G
3 yrs.	18 games			

Dewey Brundage
BRUNDAGE, JOHN DEWEY
B. Oct. 1, 1931
Brigham Young 6'3" 210 lbs.

Year	Team		Games	Pos.
1954	PIT	N	11	E

Bill Brundige
BRUNDIGE, WILLIAM GLENN
B. Nov. 13, 1948, Holyoke, CO
Colorado 6'5" 270 lbs.

Year	Team		Games	Pos.
1970	WAS	N	14	DE
1971			14	DE
1972			11	DE
1973			14	DT
1974			14	DT
1975			14	DT
1976			14	DT
1977			12	DT
8 yrs.	107 games			

Larry Brune
BRUNE, LARRY
B. May 4, 1953, San Diego, CA
Rice 6'2" 202 lbs.

Year	Team		Games	Pos.
1980	MIN	N	16	S

Mark Brunell
BRUNELL, MARK ALLEN
B. Sep. 17, 1970, Los Angeles, CA
Washington 6'1" 208 lbs.

Year	Team		Games	Pos.
1994	GB	N	2	QB
1995	JAC	N	13	QB
1996			16	QB
3 yrs.	31 games			

Sam Brunelli
BRUNELLI, SAMUEL ALDINO
B. Feb. 13, 1943, Fort Morgan, CO
Colorado State 6'1" 263 lbs.

Year	Team		Games	Pos.
1966	DEN	A	2	G
1967			12	G
1968			14	OT
1969			14	OT
1970	DEN	N	13	OT
1971			5	OT
6 yrs.	60 games			

Bob Brunet
BRUNET, ROBERT PAUL
B. Jul. 29, 1946, Larose, LA
Louisiana Tech 6'1" 205 lbs.

Year	Team		Games	Pos.
1968	WAS	N	7	RB
1970			7	RB
1971			7	RB
1972			14	RB
1973			14	RB
1975			14	RB
1976			14	RB
1977				RB
8 yrs.	77 games			

Year	Team		Games	Pos.

Fred Bruney
BRUNEY, FREDERICK K.
B. Dec. 30, 1931, Martins Ferry, OH
Ohio State 5'10" 184 lbs.

Year	Team		Games	Pos.
1953	SF	N	12	DB
1956			2	DB
1956	PIT	N	5	DB
1957			12	DB
1958	LA	N	3	DB
1960	BOS	A		DB
1961			14	DB
1962			14	DB
7 yrs.		62 games		

Austin Brunklacher
BRUNKLACHER, N. AUSTIN
B. 1898, Kentucky
Deceased
None 193 lbs.

Year	Team		Games	Pos.
1921	LOU	A	1	G
1922	LOU	N	3	G
1923			2	G
3 yrs.		6 games		

Scott Brunner
BRUNNER, SCOTT LEE
B. Mar. 24, 1957, Sellersville, PA
Delaware 6'5" 210 lbs.

Year	Team		Games	Pos.
1980	NYG	N	16	QB
1981			16	QB
1982			9	QB
1983			16	QB
1985	STL	N	16	QB
5 yrs.		73 games		

Dave Bruno
BRUNO, DAVE
B. Mar. 19, 1963, Chicago, IL
Moraine Valley CC 6'1" 235 lbs.

Year	Team		Games	Pos.
1987	MIN	N	2	P

John Bruno
BRUNO, JOHN, JR.
B. Sep. 10, 1964, Jeannette, PA
Penn State 6'2" 190 lbs.

Year	Team		Games	Pos.
1987	PIT	N	3	P

Larry Brunson
BRUNSON, LARRY R.
B. Aug. 11, 1949, Little Rock, AR
Colorado 5'11" 180 lbs.

Year	Team		Games	Pos.
1974	KC	N	14	WR
1975			14	WR
1976			14	WR
1977			11	WR
1978	OAK	N	2	WR
1979			11	WR
1980	DEN	N	13	WR
7 yrs.		79 games		

Mike Brunson
BRUNSON, MICHAEL S.
B. Jul. 30, 1947, Little Rock, AR
Arizona State 6'1" 187 lbs.

Year	Team		Games	Pos.
1970	ATL	N	8	WR

Brunswick
BRUNSWICK
None 5'10" 182 lbs.

Year	Team		Games	Pos.
1920	HAM	A	1	G

Ross Brupbacher
BRUPBACHER, ROSS ALAN
B. Apr. 7, 1948, Lafayette, LA
Texas A&M 6'3" 216 lbs.

Year	Team		Games	Pos.
1970	CHI	N	14	LB

Ross Brupbacher continued

Year	Team		Games	Pos.
1971			14	LB
1972			14	LB
1976			14	LB
4 yrs.		56 games		

Tedy Bruschi
BRUSCHI, TEDY LACAP
B. Jun. 9, 1973, San Francisco, CA
Arizona 6'0" 245 lbs.

Year	Team		Games	Pos.
1996	NE	N	16	LB

Jim Brutz
BRUTZ, JAMES CHARLES
B. Feb. 12, 1919, Niles, OH
Notre Dame 6'0" 230 lbs.

Year	Team		Games	Pos.
1946	CHI	AA	14	T
1948			9	T
2 yrs.		23 games		

Billy Bryan
BRYAN, WILLIAM KIRBY
B. Jun. 21, 1955, Burlington, NC
Duke 6'2" 255 lbs.

Year	Team		Games	Pos.
1978	DEN	N	13	C
1979			16	C
1980			16	C
1981			14	C
1982			9	C
1983			16	C
1984			16	C
1985			16	C
1986			16	C
1987			16	C
1988			16	C
11 yrs.		152 games		

Johnny Bryan
BRYAN, JOHN FREDERICK (Red)
B. Feb. 28, 1897, Chicago, IL
D. Jul. 1, 1966, Fort Collins, CO
Dartmouth/Chicago 5'7" 170 lbs.

Year	Team		Games	Pos.
1922	CHIC	N	9	HB, QB, FB
1923	CHIB	N	13	QB, HB
1924			11	HB
1925			3	HB
1925	MIL	N	5	HB
1926			4	HB, QB
1926	CHIB	N	3	HB, QB
1927			1	QB
6 yrs.		49 games		

Rick Bryan
BRYAN, RICK DON
B. Mar. 20, 1962, Coweta, OK
Oklahoma 6'4" 265 lbs.

Year	Team		Games	Pos.
1984	ATL	N	16	DT
1985			16	DE
1986			16	DE
1987			9	DE
1988			16	DE
1989			2	DE
1990			16	DE
1991			16	DE
1993			2	DE
9 yrs.		109 games		

Steve Bryan
BRYAN, STEVEN RAY
B. May 6, 1964, Wagoner, OK
Oklahoma 6'2" 256 lbs.

Year	Team		Games	Pos.
1987	DEN	N	4	NT
1988			8	NT
2 yrs.		12 games		

Beno Bryant
BRYANT, BENO

Beno Bryant continued
B. Jan. 1, 1971, Los Angeles, CA
Washington 5'9" 170 lbs.

Year	Team		Games	Pos.
1994	SEA	N	2	RB

Bill Bryant
BRYANT, WILLIAM, JR. (Boone)
B. Jan. 15, 1951, Shreveport, LA
Grambling State 5'11" 195 lbs.

Year	Team		Games	Pos.
1976	NYG	N	14	DB
1977			14	CB
1978			10	CB
1978	PHI	N	3	CB
3 yrs.		41 games		

Bob Bryant
BRYANT, ROBERT E.
B. 1937
Texas 6'5" 230 lbs.

Year	Team		Games	Pos.
1960	DAL	A		OE

Bob Bryant
BRYANT, ROBERT R.
B. Jun. 14, 1919
Texas Tech 6'3" 226 lbs.

Year	Team		Games	Pos.
1946	SF	AA	14	T
1947			14	T
1948			14	T
1949			5	T
4 yrs.		47 games		

Bobby Bryant
BRYANT, BOBBY LEE
B. Jan. 24, 1944, Macon, GA
South Carolina 6'0" 171 lbs.

Year	Team		Games	Pos.
1968	MIN	N	14	DB
1969			10	CB
1970			11	CB
1971			13	CB
1972			14	CB
1973			14	CB
1974			1	CB
1975			14	CB
1976			12	CB
1977			14	CB
1978			16	CB
1979			14	CB
1980			14	CB
13 yrs.		161 games		

Charlie Bryant
BRYANT, CHARLES LIMAR
B. Mar. 7, 1941, Lakeview, SC
Allen 6'1" 207 lbs.

Year	Team		Games	Pos.
1966	STL	N	4	FB
1967			14	RB
1968	ATL	N	3	RB
1969			14	RB
4 yrs.		35 games		

Chuck Bryant
BRYANT, CHARLES S.
B. 1941
Ohio State 6'2" 220 lbs.

Year	Team		Games	Pos.
1962	STL	N	13	OE

Cullen Bryant
BRYANT, WILLIAM CULLEN
B. May 20, 1951, Fort Sill, OK
Colorado 6'1" 230 lbs.

Year	Team		Games	Pos.
1973	LA	N	13	S, CB
1974			14	RB
1975			14	RB
1976			14	RB
1977			14	RB
1978			16	RB
1979			16	FB

Cullen Bryant continued

Year	Team		Games	Pos.
1980			16	RB
1981			13	FB
1982	LARM	N	1	RB
1983	SEA	N	10	RB
1984			9	FB
1987	LARM	N	3	RB
13 yrs.		153 games		

Domingo Bryant
BRYANT, DOMINGO GARCIA
B. Dec. 8, 1963, Nacogdoches, TX
Texas A&M 6'4" 175 lbs.

Year	Team		Games	Pos.
1987	HOU	N	13	S
1988			14	S
2 yrs.		27 games		

Hubie Bryant
BRYANT, HUBERT L.
B. Feb. 10, 1946, Pittsburgh, PA
Minnesota 5'10" 170 lbs.

Year	Team		Games	Pos.
1970	PIT	N	14	WR
1971	NE	N	11	WR
1972			2	WR
3 yrs.		27 games		

Jeff Bryant
BRYANT, JEFFREY DWIGHT
B. May 22, 1960, Atlanta, GA
Clemson 6'5" 268 lbs.

Year	Team		Games	Pos.
1982	SEA	N	9	DE
1983			16	DE
1984			16	DE
1985			16	DE
1986			12	DE
1987			12	DE
1988			16	DE
1989			15	DE
1990			15	DE
1991			16	DE, DT
1992			16	DE
1993			16	DE
12 yrs.		175 games		

Jim Bryant
BRYANT, JAMES G.
B. Jul. 12, 1894, Toronto, Ont.
D. Apr. 18, 1972, Sacramento, CA
Pennsylvania/George Washington 5'6" 155 lbs.

Year	Team		Games	Pos.
1920	CLE	A	3	QB, HB

Junior Bryant
BRYANT, EDWARD E., JR.
B. Jan. 16, 1971, Omaha, NE
Notre Dame 6'4" 275 lbs.

Year	Team		Games	Pos.
1995	SF	N	16	DE, DT
1996			16	DE
2 yrs.		32 games		

Kelvin Bryant
BRYANT, KELVIN LEROY
B. Sep. 26, 1960, Tarboro, NC
North Carolina 6'2" 195 lbs.

Year	Team		Games	Pos.
1986	WAS	N	10	RB
1987			11	RB
1988			10	RB
1990			15	RB
4 yrs.		46 games		

Steve Bryant
BRYANT, STEPHEN
B. Oct. 10, 1959, Los Angeles, CA
Purdue 6'2" 196 lbs.

Year	Team		Games	Pos.
1982	HOU	N	7	WR
1983			16	WR
1984			14	WR

Steve Bryant continued

Year	Team	Games	Pos.
1985		4	WR
1987	IND N	1	WR
5 yrs.	42 games		

Tim Bryant

BRYANT, TIMOTHY CRAIG
B. May 5, 1962, Nashville, TN
Vanderbilt/Southern Mississippi 6'1" 217 lbs.

Year	Team	Games	Pos.
1987	MIN N	1	LB

Trent Bryant

BRYANT, TRENT BARON
B. Aug. 14, 1959, Arkadelphia, AR
Arkansas 5'10" 180 lbs.

Year	Team	Games	Pos.
1981	WAS N	4	CB
1982	KC N	9	CB
1983		16	CB
1987		3	CB
4 yrs.	32 games		

Walter Bryant

BRYANT, WALTER
B. 1933
Texas Tech 6'1" 185 lbs.

Year	Team	Games	Pos.
1955	BAL N	10	HB

Warren Bryant

BRYANT, WARREN
B. Nov. 11, 1955, Miami, FL
Kentucky 6'7" 275 lbs.

Year	Team	Games	Pos.
1977	ATL N	14	OT
1978		13	OT
1979		16	OT
1980		16	OT
1981		11	OT
1982		9	OT
1983		16	OT
1984		4	OT
1984	LARI N	5	OT
8 yrs.	104 games		

Waymond Bryant

BRYANT, WAYMOND
B. Jul. 7, 1952, Dallas, TX
Tennessee State 6'3" 235 lbs.

Year	Team	Games	Pos.
1974	CHI N	14	LB
1975		13	LB
1976		14	LB
1977		13	LB
4 yrs.	54 games		

Mark Buben

BUBEN, MARK MICHAEL
B. Mar. 23, 1957, Auburn, MA
Tufts 6'3" 260 lbs.

Year	Team	Games	Pos.
1979	NE N	16	DE, NT
1981		16	DE
1982	CLE N	3	NT
3 yrs.	35 games		

Mike Bucchianeri

BUCCHIANERI, AMADEO ROGER
B. Jan. 9, 1917, Van Voorhis, PA
D. Feb. 9, 1992, Ocala, FL
Indiana 5'10" 212 lbs.

Year	Team	Games	Pos.
1941	GB N	1	G
1944		7	G
1945		5	G
3 yrs.	13 games		

Ray Bucek

BUCEK, FELIX A.
B. Jan. 30, 1922

Ray Bucek continued

D. Aug., 1965
Texas A&M 6'0" 186 lbs.

Year	Team	Games	Pos.
1946	PIT N	11	G

Buck Buchanan

BUCHANAN, JUNIOUS
B. Sep. 10, 1940, Gainesville, AL
D. Jul. 16, 1992, Kansas City, MO
Grambling State 6'7" 279 lbs.

Year	Team	Games	Pos.
1963	KC A	14	DT
1964		14	DT
1965		14	DT
1966		14	DT
1967		14	DT
1968		14	DT
1969		14	DT
1970	KC N	14	DT
1971		14	DT
1972		14	DT
1973		14	DT
1974		13	DT
1975		14	DE
13 yrs.	181 games		

Charles Buchanan

BUCHANAN, CHARLES HARRISON
B. Sep. 20, 1964, Memphis, TN
Tennessee State 6'3" 245 lbs.

Year	Team	Games	Pos.
1988	CLE N	9	DE

Ray Buchanan

BUCHANAN, RAYMOND LOUIS
B. Sep. 29, 1971, Chicago, IL
Louisville 5'9" 193 lbs.

Year	Team	Games	Pos.
1993	IND N	16	CB, S
1994		16	S, CB
1995		16	CB
1996		13	S
4 yrs.	61 games		

Richard Buchanan

BUCHANAN, RICHARD LAWRENCE
B. May 8, 1969, Chicago, IL
Northwestern 5'10" 178 lbs.

Year	Team	Games	Pos.
1993	LARM N	5	WR
1994		3	WR
2 yrs.	8 games		

Steve Buchanan

BUCHANAN, STEPHEN
B. Mar., 1903
Miami (Ohio) 5'8" 160 lbs.

Year	Team	Games	Pos.
1929	DAY N	5	QB

Tim Buchanan

BUCHANAN, TIMOTHY
B. May 26, 1946, Pasadena, CA
Hawaii 6'0" 233 lbs.

Year	Team	Games	Pos.
1969	CIN A	14	LB

Willie Buchanon

BUCHANON, WILLIE JAMES
B. Nov. 4, 1950, Oceanside, CA
San Diego State 6'0" 189 lbs.

Year	Team	Games	Pos.
1972	GB N	14	CB
1973		6	CB
1974		14	CB
1975		2	CB
1976		14	CB
1977		14	CB
1978		16	CB
1979	SD N	16	CB
1980		16	CB
1981		16	CB

Willie Buchanon continued

Year	Team	Games	Pos.
1982		9	CB
11 yrs.	137 games		

Bill Bucher

BUCHER, WILLIAM
B. Apr. 23, 1903
D. May, 1976, Detroit, MI
Clarkson 5'10" 180 lbs.

Year	Team	Games	Pos.
1925	DET N	1	E

Frank Bucher

BUCHER, FRANK H. (Butcher)
B. Dec. 19, 1900, Fairport, NY
D. Mar. 20, 1971, Brighton, MI
Detroit 5'11" 190 lbs.

Year	Team	Games	Pos.
1925	POT N	10	E
1926		13	E
2 yrs.	23 games		

Howard Buck

BUCK, HOWARD (Cub)
B. Aug. 7, 1892
D. Sep., 1966, Rock Island, IL
Wisconsin 6'0" 259 lbs.

Year	Team	Games	Pos.
1920	CAN A	8	T
1921	GB A	6	T
1922	GB N	10	T
1923		10	T
1924		11	T
1925		12	T
6 yrs.	57 games		

Jason Buck

BUCK, JASON OGDEN
B. Jul. 27, 1963, Moses Lake, WA
Brigham Young 6'5" 264 lbs.

Year	Team	Games	Pos.
1987	CIN N	12	DE
1988		16	DE
1989		16	DE
1990		16	DE
1991	WAS N	8	DE
1992		16	DE
1993		13	DE
7 yrs.	97 games		

Mike Buck

BUCK, MIKE ERIC
B. Apr. 22, 1967, Long Island, NY
Maine 6'3" 227 lbs.

Year	Team	Games	Pos.
1991	NO N	2	QB
1992		2	QB
1993		4	QB
1995	ARI N	6	QB
4 yrs.	14 games		

Vince Buck

BUCK, VINCENT LAMONT
B. Jan. 12, 1968, Owensboro, KY
Central State (Ohio) 6'0" 198 lbs.

Year	Team	Games	Pos.
1990	NO N	16	DB
1991		13	CB
1992		10	CB
1993		16	CB
1994		16	S
1995		13	S
6 yrs.	84 games		

Don Buckey

BUCKEY, DONALD
B. Nov. 9, 1953, Akron, OH
North Carolina State 5'11" 180 lbs.

Year	Team	Games	Pos.
1976	NYJ N	4	WR

Jeff Buckey

BUCKEY, JEFF

Jeff Buckey continued

B. Aug. 7, 1974, Bakersfield, CA
Stanford 6'5" 300 lbs.

Year	Team	Games	Pos.
1996	MIA N	15	G

Garland Buckeye

BUCKEYE, GARLAND MAIERS (Gob)
B. Oct. 16, 1897, Heron Lake, MN
D. Nov. 14, 1975, Stone Lake, WI
None 6'0" 238 lbs.

Year	Team	Games	Pos.
1920	CHIT A	5	G
1921	CHIC A	5	G, C
1922	CHIC N	11	G
1923		10	G
1924		9	G
1926	CHI N	11	G, E
6 yrs.	51 games		

Bill Buckler

BUCKLER, WILLIAM EARL
B. Apr. 29, 1901
D. Jun. 20, 1979, Wood River, IL
Alabama 6'0" 224 lbs.

Year	Team	Games	Pos.
1926	CHIB N	15	G
1927		12	G
1928		13	G, C
1931		13	G, T
1932		14	G, T
1933		9	G, T, E
6 yrs.	76 games		

Phil Bucklew

BUCKLEW, PHILIP
B. 1915
Xavier (Ohio) 6'1" 205 lbs.

Year	Team	Games	Pos.
1937	CLE N	11	E
1938		1	E
2 yrs.	12 games		

Curtis Buckley

BUCKLEY, CURTIS LADONN
B. Sep. 25, 1970, Oakdale, CA
East Texas State 6'0" 185 lbs.

Year	Team	Games	Pos.
1993	TB N	10	DB
1994		13	S, CB
1995		15	S
1996	SF N	15	S
4 yrs.	53 games		

Marcus Buckley

BUCKLEY, MARCUS WAYNE
B. Feb. 3, 1971, Fort Worth, TX
Texas A&M 6'3" 235 lbs.

Year	Team	Games	Pos.
1993	NYG N	16	LB
1994		16	LB
1995		16	LB
1996		15	LB
4 yrs.	63 games		

Ralph Buckley

BUCKLEY, RALPH J.
B. Mar. 18, 1907
D. Jul. 13, 1979, Dunedin, FL
Fordham 5'8" 175 lbs.

Year	Team	Games	Pos.
1930	SI N	7	QB, HB, FB

Terrell Buckley

BUCKLEY, DOUGLAS TERRELL
B. Jun. 7, 1971, Pascagoula, MS
Florida State 5'9" 174 lbs.

Year	Team	Games	Pos.
1992	GB N	14	CB
1993		16	CB
1994		16	CB
1995	MIA N	16	CB
1996		16	CB
5 yrs.	78 games		

Year	Team		Games	Pos.

Ted Bucklin
BUCKLIN, THOMAS C.
B. Apr. 5, 1900
D. Sep., 1972, Twin Falls, ID
Idaho 6'0" 197 lbs.

1926	LA	A	13	FB, HB, QB
1927	CHIC		9	FB
1931	NYG	N	4	FB, HB, G

3 yrs. 26 games

Tom Buckman
BUCKMAN, THOMAS
B. Mar. 7, 1947, Fort Worth, TX
Texas A&M 6'4" 230 lbs.

1969	DEN	A	7	TE

Brentson Buckner
BUCKNER, BRENTSON ANDRE
B. Sep. 30, 1971, Columbus, GA
Clemson 6'2" 305 lbs.

1994	PIT	N	12	DE
1995			16	DE, NT
1996			14	DE

3 yrs. 42 games

Bob Buczkowski
BUCZKOWSKI, JOHN ROBERT
B. May 5, 1964, Pittsburgh, PA
Pittsburgh 6'5" 260 lbs.

1987	LARI	N	2	DE
1989	PHX	N	4	DE
1990	CLE	N	15	DE

3 yrs. 21 games

Carl Buda
BUDA, CARL JOSEPH
B. 1919
D. Jun 11, 1994 Omaha, NE
Creighton/Tulsa 5'11" 220 lbs.

1945	PIT	N	3	G

Frank Budd
BUDD, FRANCIS JOSEPH
B. Jul. 20, 1939
Villanova 5'10" 187 lbs.*

1962	PHI	N	13	OE
1963	WAS	N	14	OE

2 yrs. 27 games

Johnny Budd
BUDD, JOHN
B. 1899
Deceased
Lafayette 5'11" 246 lbs.

1926	FRA	N	16	T, G
1927	POT	N	13	G, T, C
1928			10	T

3 yrs. 39 games

Brad Budde
BUDDE, BRAD EDWARD
B. May 9, 1958, Detroit, MI
Southern California 6'4" 265 lbs.

1980	KC	N	16	G
1981			16	G
1982			9	G
1983			12	G
1984			16	G
1985			7	G
1986			16	G

7 yrs. 92 games

Ed Budde
BUDDE, EDWARD LEON
B. Nov. 2, 1940, Highland Park, MI
Michigan State 6'5" 261 lbs.

1963	KC	A	14	G

Ed Budde *continued*

1964			14	G
1965			14	G
1966			14	G
1967			14	G
1968			14	G
1969			14	G
1970	KC	N	14	G
1971			14	G
1972			13	G
1973			12	G
1974			14	G
1975			1	G
1976			11	G

14 yrs. 177 games

Frank Budka
BUDKA, FRANK
B. Mar. 20, 1942, Cleveland, OH
Notre Dame 6'0" 195 lbs.

1964	LA	N	14	DB

Bill Budness
BUDNESS, WILLIAM WALTER
B. Jan. 30, 1943, Chicopee, MA
Boston University 6'1" 215 lbs.

1964	OAK	A	9	LB
1965			14	LB
1966			14	LB
1967			13	LB
1968			14	LB
1969			14	LB
1970	OAK	N	14	LB

7 yrs. 92 games

Tom Budrewicz
BUDREWICZ THOMAS P.
B. 1937
Brown 6'2" 245 lbs.

1961	NY	A	2	G

George Buehler
BUEHLER, GEORGE SIEGRIST
B. Aug. 10, 1947, Whittier, CA
Stanford 6'2" 264 lbs.

1969	OAK	A	2	G
1970	OAK	N	14	G
1971			14	G
1972			14	G
1973			14	G
1974			14	G
1975			14	G
1976			14	G
1977			14	G
1978			1	G
1978	CLE	N	11	G
1979			11	G

11 yrs. 137 games

Bart Buetow
BUETOW, BARTON MAX (The Mad Scientist)
B. Oct. 28, 1950, Minneapolis, MN
Minnesota 6'5" 250 lbs.

1973	NYG	N	7	OT
1976	MIN	N	2	OT

2 yrs. 9 games

Ted Buffalo
BUFFALO, TED
B. 1900, Wisconsin
Deceased
Haskell 6'0" 190 lbs.

1923	OOR	N	9	T, E, G

Harry Buffington
BUFFINGTON, HARRY WEBSTER

Harry Buffington *continued*
B. Jul. 27, 1919, Pryor, OK
Oklahoma A&M 6'0" 206 lbs.

1942	NYG	N	10	G
1946	BKN	AA	12	G
1947			14	G
1948			10	G

4 yrs. 46 games

Doug Buffone
BUFFONE, DOUGLAS JOHN
B. Jul. 27, 1944, Yatesboro, PA
Louisville 6'1" 227 lbs.

1966	CHI	N	14	LB
1967			14	LB
1968			14	LB
1969			14	LB
1970			14	LB
1971			14	LB
1972			14	LB
1973			14	LB
1974			14	LB
1975			14	LB
1976			2	LB
1977			13	LB
1978			15	LB
1979			16	LB

14 yrs. 186 games

Maury Buford
BUFORD, MAURY ANTHONY
B. Feb. 18, 1960, Mount Pleasant, TX
Texas Tech 6'1" 191 lbs.

1982	SD	N	9	P
1983			16	P
1984			16	P
1985	CHI	N	16	P
1986			16	P
1988	NYG	N	15	P
1989	CHI	N	16	P
1990			16	P
1991			16	P

9 yrs. 136 games

Tony Buford
BUFORD, TONY
B. Apr. 21, 1964
Tulsa 6'2" 222 lbs.

1987	STL	N	2	LB

Gary Bugenhagen
BUGENHAGEN, GARY ALAN
B. Feb. 6, 1945, Buffalo, NY
Syracuse 6'2" 249 lbs.

1967	BUF	A	14	G
1970	BOS	N	10	OT, G

2 yrs. 24 games

Danny Buggs
BUGGS, DANIEL
B. Apr. 22, 1953, Duluth, GA
West Virginia 6'2" 185 lbs.

1975	NYG	N	14	WR
1976			5	WR
1976	WAS	N	6	WR
1977			14	WR
1978			13	WR
1979			16	WR

5 yrs. 68 games

Larry Buhler
BUHLER, LAWRENCE ABRAHAM
B. May 28, 1917, Windom, MN
D. Aug. 21, 1990, Rochester, MN
Minnesota 6'2" 210 lbs.

1939	GB	N	3	HB
1940			7	HB, FB
1941			11	QB

3 yrs. 21 games

Drew Buie
BUIE, LESLIE DREW
B. Jul. 12, 1947, Council, NC
Catawba 6'2" 180 lbs.

1969	OAK	A	14	WR
1970	OAK	N	14	WR
1971			14	WR
1972	CIN	N	4	WR

4 yrs. 46 games

Ray Buivid
BUIVID, RAYMOND (Buzz)
B. Aug. 15, 1915
D. Jul. 5, 1972, Cherry Hill, NJ
Marquette 6'1" 195 lbs.

1937	CHIB	N	6	HB
1938			10	QB, HB, E

2 yrs. 16 games

Glenn Bujnoch
BUJNOCH, GLENN
B. Dec. 20, 1953, Houston, TX
Texas A&M 6'5" 258 lbs.

1976	CIN	N	14	G
1977			13	G
1978			16	G
1979			15	G
1980			16	G
1981			6	G
1982			9	G
1983	TB	N	6	G
1984			8	G

9 yrs. 103 games

Joe Bukant
BUKANT, JOSEPH (Buckin' Joe)
B. Oct. 31, 1915, Divernon, IL
Washington (Missouri) 6'0" 216 lbs.

1938	PHI	N	11	HB, FB
1939			11	FB, HB
1940			11	HB, FB
1942	CHIC	N	9	FB
1943			8	HB, FB

5 yrs. 50 games

Fred Bukaty
BUKATY, FRED FRANCIS
B. Feb. 13, 1936
Kansas 5'11" 195 lbs.

1961	DEN	A	14	FB

Rudy Bukich
BUKICH, RUDOLPH ANDREW
B. Dec. 15, 1932, St. Louis, MO
Iowa/Southern California 6'1" 202 lbs.

1953	LA	N	8	QB
1956			3	QB
1957	WAS	N	7	QB
1958			3	QB
1958	CHIB	N	1	QB
1959			5	QB
1960	PIT	N	12	QB
1961			11	QB
1962	CHI	N	5	QB
1963			9	QB
1964			9	QB
1965			14	QB
1966			14	QB
1967			3	QB
1968			2	QB

14 yrs. 103 games

George Buksar
BUKSAR, GEORGE BENJAMIN
B. Aug. 12, 1926, Whiting, IN
San Francisco 6'0" 206 lbs.

1949	CHI	AA	6	FB, LB
1950	BAL	N	10	FB
1951	WAS	N	11	FB

Year	Team	Games	Pos.

George Buksar *continued*

Year	Team	Games	Pos.
1952		10	FB
4 yrs.	37 games		

Norm Bulaich
BULAICH, NORMAN BATTON
B. Dec. 25, 1946, Galveston, TX
Texas Christian 6'1" 217 lbs.

Year	Team	Games	Pos.
1970	**BAL** N	12	RB
1971		13	RB
1972		5	RB
1973	**PHI** N	14	RB
1974		11	RB
1975	**MIA** N	14	RB
1976		11	RB
1977		14	RB
1978		16	RB
1979		9	RB
10 yrs.	119 games		

Walt Buland
BULAND, WALTER (Big Boy)
B. 1892
Deceased
None 6'1" 213 lbs.

Year	Team	Games	Pos.
1920	**RI** A	3	T
1921		4	T
1924	**GB** N	1	T
1924	**RI** N	5	G, T
1926	**DUL** N	2	T
4 yrs.	15 games		

Chet Bulger
BULGER, CHESTER NOYES
B. Sep. 18, 1917, Rumford, ME
Auburn 6'3" 239 lbs.

Year	Team	Games	Pos.
1942	**CHIC** N	6	T
1943		10	T
1944	**C-P** N	10	T
1945	**CHIC** N	10	T
1946		6	T
1947		12	T
1948		12	T
1949		9	T
1950	**DET** N	12	T
9 yrs.	87 games		

Ronnie Bull
BULL, RONALD DAVID
B. Feb. 2, 1940, Kingsville, TX
Baylor 6'0" 200 lbs.

Year	Team	Games	Pos.
1962	**CHI** N	14	HB
1963		13	HB
1964		13	HB
1965		13	HB
1966		14	HB
1967		12	RB
1968		13	RB
1969		6	RB
1970		12	RB
1971	**PHI** N	13	RB
10 yrs.	123 games		

Scott Bull
BULL, JOHN SCOTT
B. Jun. 8, 1953, Camden, AR
Arkansas 6'5" 212 lbs.

Year	Team	Games	Pos.
1976	**SF** N	14	QB
1977		6	QB
1978		16	QB
3 yrs.	36 games		

Kendricke Bullard
BULLARD, KENDRICKE BERNARD
B. Apr. 30, 1972, San Diego, CA
Arkansas State 6'1" 183 lbs.

Year	Team	Games	Pos.
1996	**JAC** N	12	WR

Louis Bullard
BULLARD, LOUIS EUGENE
B. May 6, 1956, Hernando, MS
Jackson State 6'6" 265 lbs.

Year	Team	Games	Pos.
1978	**SEA** N	16	OT
1979		3	OT
1980		16	OT
3 yrs.	35 games		

Gale Bullman
BULLMAN, DELMAR GALE
B. Aug. 18, 1902, Sisterville, WV
D. Jun. 24, 1977, Rolla, MO
West Virginia Wesleyan 6'0" 182 lbs.

Year	Team	Games	Pos.
1925	**COL** N	2	E

Brian Bullock
BULLOCK, BRIAN
B. Oct. 29, 1965
North Carolina State 6'3" 236 lbs.

Year	Team	Games	Pos.
1987	**IND** N	2	LB

Amos Bullocks
BULLOCKS, AMOS L.
B. Feb. 7, 1939, Chicago, IL
Southern Illinois 6'1" 201 lbs.

Year	Team	Games	Pos.
1962	**DAL** N	11	HB
1963		14	HB
1964		1	HB
1966	**PIT** N	8	RB
4 yrs.	34 games		

Chuck Bullough
BULLOUGH, CHUCK
B. Mar. 3, 1969, Orchard Park, NY
Michigan State 6'1" 238 lbs.

Year	Team	Games	Pos.
1993	**MIA** N	3	LB
1994		2	LB
2 yrs.	5 games		

Hank Bullough
BULLOUGH, HENRY CHARLES
B. Jan. 24, 1934, Scranton, PA
Michigan State 6'0" 230 lbs.

Year	Team	Games	Pos.
1955	**GB** N	12	G
1958		8	G
2 yrs.	20 games		

Art Bultman
BULTMAN, ARTHUR (Red)
B. Sep. 16, 1907
D. Feb., 1967
Marquette 6'2" 201 lbs.

Year	Team	Games	Pos.
1931	**BKN** N	11	C
1932	**GB** N	13	C
1933		13	C, G
1934		10	C
4 yrs.	47 games		

Max Bumgardner
BUMGARDNER, MAX ANDREW
B. 1924
Texas 6'2" 190 lbs.

Year	Team	Games	Pos.
1948	**DET** N	10	E

Rex Bumgardner
BUMGARDNER, REX KEITH
B. Sep. 6, 1923, Clarksburg, WV
West Virginia 5'11" 193 lbs.

Year	Team	Games	Pos.
1948	**BUF** AA	13	B
1949		10	B
1950	**CLE** N	10	HB
1951		10	HB
1952		11	HB
5 yrs.	54 games		

Derek Bunch
BUNCH, DEREK C.
B. Oct. 28, 1961, Fort Sill, OK
Michigan State 6'3" 215 lbs.

Year	Team	Games	Pos.
1987	**WAS** N	3	LB

Jarrod Bunch
BUNCH, JARROD R.
B. Aug. 8, 1968, Ashtabula, OH
Michigan 6'2" 248 lbs.

Year	Team	Games	Pos.
1991	**NYG** N	16	RB
1992		16	RB
1993		13	RB
1994	**LARI** N	2	RB
4 yrs.	47 games		

Frank Buncom
BUNCOM, FRANK JAMES
B. Nov. 2, 1939, Shreveport, LA
D. Sep. 14, 1969, Cincinnati, OH
Southern California 6'1" 236 lbs.

Year	Team	Games	Pos.
1962	**SD** A	14	LB
1963		14	LB
1964		14	LB
1966		14	LB
1967		14	LB
1968	**CIN** A	12	LB
7 yrs.	96 games		

Mike Bundra
BUNDRA, MIKE P.
B. Jun. 24, 1939, Coplay, PA
Southern California 6'3" 258 lbs.

Year	Team	Games	Pos.
1962	**DET** N	12	DT
1963		14	DT
1964	**MIN** N	4	DT
1964	**CLE** N	13	DT
1965	**NYG** N	8	DT
4 yrs.	51 games		

Ken Bungarda
BUNGARDA, KESTUTIS JOHN
B. Jan. 25, 1957, Hartford, CT
Missouri 6'6" 270 lbs.

Year	Team	Games	Pos.
1980	**SF** N	15	OT

John Bunting
BUNTING, JOHN STEPHEN
B. Jul. 15, 1950, Portland, ME
North Carolina 6'1" 220 lbs.

Year	Team	Games	Pos.
1972	**PHI** N	14	LB
1973		7	LB
1974		14	LB
1975		14	LB
1976		14	LB
1977		14	LB
1978		6	LB
1979		15	LB
1980		16	LB
1981		9	LB
1982		9	LB
11 yrs.	132 games		

John Bunyan
BUNYAN, JOHN (Moose)
B. 1906
New York University 5'10" 215 lbs.

Year	Team	Games	Pos.
1929	**SI** N	5	G
1930		11	G, T, C
1932		6	G
1932	**BKN** N	1	E
3 yrs.	23 games		

Dan Bunz
BUNZ, DAN
B. Oct. 7, 1955, Roseville, CA

Dan Bunz *continued*
California-Riverside/Long Beach State 6'4" 227 lbs.

Year	Team	Games	Pos.
1978	**SF** N	16	LB
1979		14	LB
1980		16	LB
1981		14	LB
1982		1	LB
1983		9	LB
1984		16	LB
1985	**DET** N	2	LB
8 yrs.	88 games		

Nick Buoniconti
BUONICONTI, NICHOLAS
B. Dec. 15, 1940, Springfield, MA
Notre Dame 5'11" 220 lbs.

Year	Team	Games	Pos.
1962	**BOS** A	14	LB
1963		14	LB
1964		14	LB
1965		14	LB
1966		13	LB
1967		8	LB
1969	**MIA** A	13	LB
1970	**MIA** N	14	LB
1971		14	LB
1972		14	LB
1973		13	LB
1974		13	LB
1976		11	LB
14 yrs.	183 games		

Cornell Burbage
BURBAGE, CORNELL RODNEY
B. Feb. 22, 1965, Lexington, KY
Kentucky 5'10" 181 lbs.

Year	Team	Games	Pos.
1987	**DAL** N	3	WR
1988		10	WR
1989		10	WR
3 yrs.	23 games		

Jerry Burch
BURCH, GERALD T.
B. 1940
Georgia Tech 6'1" 195 lbs.

Year	Team	Games	Pos.
1961	**OAK** A	14	OE

Don Burchfield
BURCHFIELD, DONALD LEE
B. Mar. 17, 1949, Indianapolis, IN
Ball State 6'2" 227 lbs.

Year	Team	Games	Pos.
1971	**NO** N	14	TE

Lloyd Burdick
**BURDICK, LLOYD SUMNER
(Tiny, Shorty)**
B. Aug. 8, 1909, Assumption, IL
Deceased
Illinois 6'4" 248 lbs.

Year	Team	Games	Pos.
1931	**CHIB** N	9	T
1932		12	T
1933	**CIN** N	10	T
3 yrs.	31 games		

Chris Burford
BURFORD, CHRISTOPHER WILLIAM, III
B. Jan. 31, 1938, Oakland, CA
Stanford 6'3" 211 lbs.

Year	Team	Games	Pos.
1960	**DAL** A	14	OE
1961		14	OE
1962		11	OE
1963	**KC** A	14	OE
1964		12	OE
1965		11	OE
1966		14	OE
1967		12	OE
8 yrs.	102 games		

Year	Team	Games	Pos.

Glen Burgeis
BURGEIS, GLEN
B. 1922
Tulsa 6'1" 220 lbs.

Year	Team	Games	Pos.
1945	**CHIB** N	3	T

Todd Burger
BURGER, TODD
B. Mar. 20, 1970, Clark, NJ
Penn State 6'3" 296 lbs.

Year	Team	Games	Pos.
1994	**CHI** N	4	G
1995		16	G
1996		11	G
3 yrs.	31 games		

Charlie Burgess
BURGESS, CHARLES
B. Dec. 29, 1962
Carson-Newman 6'0" 230 lbs.

Year	Team	Games	Pos.
1987	**NYG** N	2	LB

Fernanza Burgess
BURGESS, FERNANZA
B. Mar. 6, 1960, Miami, FL
Morris Brown 6'1" 210 lbs.

Year	Team	Games	Pos.
1984	**NYJ** N	11	WR
1984	**MIA** N	3	WR
1 yr.	14 games		

Carvell Burgess
BURGESS, MARVELL, JR.
B. Oct. 7, 1965, Miami, FL
Henderson State 6'3" 195 lbs.

Year	Team	Games	Pos.
1987	**MIA** N	1	S

Ronnie Burgess
BURGESS, RONNIE
B. Mar. 7, 1963, Sumter, SC
Wake Forest 5'11" 175 lbs.

Year	Team	Games	Pos.
1985	**GB** N	16	DB

Al Burgin
BURGIN, ALBERT
B. Apr. 13, 1894
D. Jul., 1978, San Francisco, CA
None 6'0" 200 lbs.

Year	Team	Games	Pos.
1922	**TOL** N	1	G

Ted Burgmeier
BURGMEIER, TED JOSEPH
B. Nov. 8, 1955, Dubuque, IA
Notre Dame 5'10" 185 lbs.

Year	Team	Games	Pos.
1978	**KC** N	8	S

Earl Burgner
BURGNER, EARL W. (Puss)
B. May 19, 1900
D. Jan. 11, 1970, Dayton, OH
Wittenberg 5'6" 165 lbs.

Year	Team	Games	Pos.
1923	**DAY** N	2	QB, HB

Adrian Burk
BURK, ADRIAN MATTHEW
B. Dec. 14, 1927, Mexia, TX
Baylor 6'2" 190 lbs.

Year	Team	Games	Pos.
1950	**BAL** N	12	QB, P
1951	**PHI** N	12	QB, P
1952		12	QB, P
1953		10	QB, P
1954		12	QB, P
1955		12	QB, P
1956		12	QB, P
7 yrs.	82 games		

Scott Burk
BURK, MARSHALL SCOTT
B. Aug. 2, 1956, Houston, TX
Oklahoma State 6'2" 193 lbs.

Year	Team	Games	Pos.
1979	**CIN** N	16	S

Anthony Burke
BURKE, ANTHONY H.
B. Sep. 2, 1964
Minnesota 6'3" 262 lbs.

Year	Team	Games	Pos.
1987	**STL** N	1	DT

Charlie Burke
BURKE, CHARLES F. (Chick)
B. May 30, 1901
D. Aug., 1965, Dedham, MA
Dartmouth 5'9" 165 lbs.

Year	Team	Games	Pos.
1925	**PRO** N	5	HB

Don Burke
BURKE, DONALD
B. 1926, Chico, CA
Southern California 6'0" 235 lbs.

Year	Team	Games	Pos.
1950	**SF** N	6	LB
1951		9	G, LB
1952		12	G, LB
1953		10	G, LB
1954		2	G, LB
5 yrs.	39 games		

Joe Burke
BURKE, JOE
B. Feb. 9, 1961
Rutgers 6'0" 200 lbs.

Year	Team	Games	Pos.
1987	**NYJ** N	2	RB

John Burke
BURKE, JOHN RICHARD
B. Sep. 7, 1971, Elizabeth, NJ
Virginia Tech 6'3" 258 lbs.

Year	Team	Games	Pos.
1994	**NE** N	16	TE
1995		16	TE
1996		11	TE
3 yrs.	43 games		

Mark Burke
BURKE, MARK
B. Jun. 10, 1954, Marietta, OH
West Virginia 6'1" 175 lbs.

Year	Team	Games	Pos.
1976	**PHI** N		DB

Mike Burke
BURKE, MICHAEL DENNIS
B. Jul. 28, 1950, Sacramento, CA
Oregon State/Miami (Florida) 5'10" 175 lbs.

Year	Team	Games	Pos.
1974	**LA** N	8	P, K

Randy Burke
BURKE, RANDALL WILLIAM
B. May 26, 1955, Miami, FL
Kentucky 6'2" 190 lbs.

Year	Team	Games	Pos.
1978	**BAL** N	15	WR
1979		16	WR
1980		10	WR
1981		16	WR
4 yrs.	57 games		

Vern Burke
BURKE, VERNON
B. Apr. 30, 1941, San Luis Obispo, CA
Oregon State 6'4" 201 lbs.

Year	Team	Games	Pos.
1965	**SF** N	3	OE
1966	**ATL** N	14	TE

Vern Burke continued

Year	Team	Games	Pos.
1967	**NO** N	7	TE
3 yrs.	24 games		

Chris Burkett
BURKETT, CHRIS
B. Aug. 21, 1962, Collins, MS
Jackson State 6'4" 198 lbs.

Year	Team	Games	Pos.
1985	**BUF** N	16	WR
1986		14	WR
1987		12	WR
1988		11	WR
1989		2	WR
1989	**NYJ** N	13	WR
1990		16	WR
1991		15	WR
1992		16	WR
1993		16	WR
9 yrs.	131 games		

Jackie Burkett
BURKETT, WALTER JACKSON
B. Dec. 16, 1936, Thorsby, AL
Auburn 6'4" 229 lbs.

Year	Team	Games	Pos.
1961	**BAL** N	14	C, LB
1962		14	LB, C
1963		14	LB
1964		12	LB
1965		11	LB
1966		14	LB
1967	**NO** N	14	LB
1968	**DAL** N	3	LB
1969		11	LB
1970	**NO** N	14	LB
10 yrs.	121 games		

Jeff Burkett
BURKETT, JEFFERSON DAVIS
B. Jul. 15, 1921, Hattiesburg, MS
D. Oct. 24, 1947, Bryce Canyon, UT
Louisiana State 6'1" 190 lbs.

Year	Team	Games	Pos.
1947	**CHIC** N	3	E

Joe Burks
BURKS, JOSEPH (Flyweight)
B. Jul. 8, 1899
D. Nov., 1969, Chicago, IL
Washington State 5'10" 171 lbs.

Year	Team	Games	Pos.
1926	**MIL** N	9	C

Randy Burks
BURKS, RANDALL
B. Aug. 22, 1953, Garvin, OK
Southeastern Oklahoma State 5'11" 170 lbs.

Year	Team	Games	Pos.
1976	**CHI** N	1	WR

Ray Burks
BURKS, RAYMOND CHARLES
B. Mar. 9, 1955, Gardena, CA
UCLA 6'3" 217 lbs.

Year	Team	Games	Pos.
1977	**KC** N	13	LB

Shawn Burks
BURKS, SHAWN SPENCER
B. Feb. 10, 1963, Baton Rouge, LA
Louisiana State 6'1" 230 lbs.

Year	Team	Games	Pos.
1986	**WAS** N	15	LB

Steve Burks
BURKS, STEVEN BRUCE
B. Aug. 6, 1953, Little Rock, AR
Arkansas State 6'5" 211 lbs.

Year	Team	Games	Pos.
1975	**NE** N	13	WR
1976		8	WR

Steve Burks continued

Year	Team	Games	Pos.
1977		13	WR
3 yrs.	34 games		

Alex Burl
BURL, ALEX, JR.
B. Aug. 8, 1931, Warren, AR
Colorado State 5'10" 165 lbs.

Year	Team	Games	Pos.
1956	**CHIC** N	8	HB

John Burleson
BURLESON, JOHN C. (Tex)
B. Aug. 21, 1909
D. Oct., 1983, Clyde, TX
Southern Methodist 6'2" 237 lbs.

Year	Team	Games	Pos.
1933	**POR** N	1	G
1933	**PIT** N	3	T, G
1933	**CIN** N	2	T
1 yr.	6 games		

Gary Burley
BURLEY, GARY
B. Dec. 8, 1952, Urbancrest, OH
Pittsburgh 6'3" 267 lbs.

Year	Team	Games	Pos.
1976	**CIN** N	14	DE
1977		14	DE
1978		16	DE
1979		16	DE
1980		11	DE
1981		16	DE
1982		4	DE
1983		14	DE
1984	**ATL** N	12	DT
9 yrs.	117 games		

George Burman
BURMAN, GEORGE ROBERT
B. Dec. 1, 1942, Chicago, IL
Northwestern 6'3" 253 lbs.

Year	Team	Games	Pos.
1964	**CHI** N	14	OT
1967	**LA** N	14	C, G
1968		1	C, G
1969		13	C, G
1970		14	C, G
1971	**WAS** N	14	C, G
1972		14	C, G
7 yrs.	84 games		

Danny Burmeister
BURMEISTER, DAN
B. Sep. 13, 1963
North Carolina 6'2" 201 lbs.

Year	Team	Games	Pos.
1987	**WAS** N	3	S

Forrest Burmeister
BURMEISTER, FORREST
B. 1913
Purdue 6'3" 215 lbs.

Year	Team	Games	Pos.
1937	**CLE** N	11	G, T
1938		1	G
2 yrs.	12 games		

Max Burnell
BURNELL, HERMAN JOSEPH
B. 1915, Duluth, MN
Notre Dame 5'11" 180 lbs.

Year	Team	Games	Pos.
1944	**CHIB** N	1	B

Bobby Burnett
BURNETT, ROBERT CLELL
B. Jan. 4, 1943, Clinton, AR
Arkansas 6'2" 208 lbs.

Year	Team	Games	Pos.
1966	**BUF** A	14	HB
1967		8	RB

Year	Team	Games	Pos.

Bobby Burnett *continued*

Year	Team	Games	Pos.
1969	**DEN**	A	3	RB

3 yrs.   25 games

Dale Burnett
BURNETT, DALE
B. Jan. 23, 1909, Larned, KS
Emporia State 6'1" 187 lbs.

Year	Team	Games	Pos.
1930	**NYG**	**N**	13	HB, FB
1931			14	HB, QB, FB
1932			12	HB, FB
1933			14	HB
1934			10	HB
1935			8	HB
1936			12	HB
1937			9	HB
1938			11	B
1939			11	HB

10 yrs.   114 games

Len Burnett
BURNETT, LEONARD
B. Aug. 29, 1939, San Antonio, TX
Oregon 6'1" 195 lbs.

Year	Team	Games	Pos.
1961	**PIT**	**N**	4	DB

Ray Burnett
BURNETT, RAYMOND
B. Jan. 29, 1914
Arkansas Tech/Central Arkansas

Year	Team	Games	Pos.
1938	**CHIC**	**N**	1	HB

Rob Burnett
BURNETT, ROBERT BARRY
B. Aug. 27, 1967, Livingston, NJ
Syracuse 6'4" 275 lbs.

Year	Team	Games	Pos.
1990	**CLE**	**N**	16	DE, NT
1991			13	DT, DE
1992			16	DE, DT
1993			16	DE
1994			16	DE
1995			16	DE
1996	**BAL**	**N**	6	DE

7 yrs.   99 games

Victor Burnett
BURNETT, VICTOR
B. Oct. 5, 1962
Fresno State 6'5" 250 lbs.

Year	Team	Games	Pos.
1987	**STL**	**N**	3	DT

Dave Burnette
BURNETTE, DAVID
B. Mar. 24, 1961, Parkin, AR
Central Arkansas 6'6" 278 lbs.

Year	Team	Games	Pos.
1987	**DAL**	**N**	1	OT

Reggie Burnette
BURNETTE, REGGIE
B. Oct. 4, 1968, Rayville, LA
Houston 6'2" 240 lbs.

Year	Team	Games	Pos.
1991	**TB**	**N**	3	LB
1992			15	LB
1993			5	LB

3 yrs.   23 games

Tom Burnette
BURNETTE, THOMAS DENMARK
B. Sep. 14, 1915, Fremont, NC
D. Apr., 1989, Canton, NC
North Carolina 6'1" 194 lbs.

Year	Team	Games	Pos.
1938	**PIT**	**N**	6	HB, QB
1938	**PHI**	**N**	7	HB

1 yr.   13 games

Lem Burnham
BURNHAM, LEM
B. Aug. 30, 1947, Winter Haven, FL
U.S. International 6'4" 236 lbs.

Year	Team	Games	Pos.
1977	**PHI**	**N**	14	DE
1978			15	DE
1979			16	DE

3 yrs.   45 games

Stan Burnham
BURNHAM, STANLEY
B. 1897
Deceased
Harvard 5'10" 175 lbs.

Year	Team	Games	Pos.
1925	**FRA**	**N**	4	HB, QB

Tim Burnham
BURNHAM, TIMOTHY SCOTT
B. May 6, 1963, Redding, CA
Washington 6'5" 280 lbs.

Year	Team	Games	Pos.
1987	**SEA**	**N**	3	OT

Hank Burnine
BURNINE, HAROLD HENRY
B. Nov. 9, 1932
Missouri 6'2" 188 lbs.

Year	Team	Games	Pos.
1956	**NYG**	**N**	1	E
1956	**PHI**	**N**	7	E
1957			7	E

2 yrs.   15 games

Bob Burns
BURNS, ROBERT
B. Jan. 12, 1952, Tampa, FL
Georgia 6'3" 212 lbs.

Year	Team	Games	Pos.
1974	**NYJ**	**N**	14	RB

Ed Burns
BURNS, ED
B. Dec. 7, 1954, Council Bluffs, IA
Nebraska 6'3" 210 lbs.

Year	Team	Games	Pos.
1979	**NO**	**N**	16	QB
1980			2	QB

2 yrs.   18 games

Jason Burns
BURNS, JASON
B. Nov. 27, 1972, Chicago, IL
Wisconsin 5'7" 185 lbs.

Year	Team	Games	Pos.
1995	**CIN**	**N**	1	RB

Keith Burns
BURNS, KEITH BERNARD
B. May 16, 1972, Greeleyville, SC
Oklahoma State 6'1" 233 lbs.

Year	Team	Games	Pos.
1994	**DEN**	**N**	12	LB
1995			16	LB
1996			16	LB

3 yrs.   44 games

Leon Burns
BURNS, LEON KEITH
B. Sep. 15, 1944, Oakland, CA
D. Dec. 22, 1984, Los Angeles, CA
Long Beach State 6'2" 229 lbs.

Year	Team	Games	Pos.
1971	**SD**	**N**	14	RB
1972	**STL**	**N**	14	RB

2 yrs.   28 games

Mike Burns
BURNS, MICHAEL WAYNE
B. Apr. 6, 1954, Oakland, CA
Southern California 6'0" 180 lbs.

Year	Team	Games	Pos.
1977	**SF**	**N**	14	CB

Mike Burns *continued*

Year	Team	Games	Pos.
1978	**DET**	**N**	15	S

2 yrs.   29 games

George Burnside
BURNSIDE, GEORGE HARRISON
B. Jan. 21, 1899, Oconto Falls, WI
D. Nov., 1962
Wisconsin/South Dakota/Wisconsin 5'9" 153 lbs.

Year	Team	Games	Pos.
1926	**RAC**	**N**	2	QB

Clinton Burrell
BURRELL, CLINTON BLANE
B. Sep. 4, 1956, Franklin, LA
Louisiana State 6'2" 192 lbs.

Year	Team	Games	Pos.
1979	**CLE**	**N**	16	CB
1980			15	CB
1981			2	S
1982			9	S
1983			12	S
1984			13	S

6 yrs.   67 games

George Burrell
BURRELL, GEORGE
B. Jan. 1, 1948, Camden, NJ
Pennsylvania 5'10" 180 lbs.

Year	Team	Games	Pos.
1969	**DEN**	A	14	S

Johnny Burrell
BURRELL, JOHN
B. Nov. 22, 1940, Fort Worth, TX
Rice 6'3" 191 lbs.

Year	Team	Games	Pos.
1962	**PIT**	**N**	14	OE
1963			14	OE
1964			14	OE
1966	**WAS**	**N**	4	FL
1967			10	FL

5 yrs.   56 games

Ode Burrell
BURRELL, ODE, JR.
B. Sep. 15, 1939, Goodman, MS
Mississippi State 6'0" 189 lbs.

Year	Team	Games	Pos.
1964	**HOU**	A	12	FL
1965			14	HB
1966			14	HB
1967			11	RB
1968			1	FL
1969			14	RB

6 yrs.   66 games

Bo Burris
BURRIS, JAMES ENGLAND, JR.
B. Oct. 16, 1944, Luling, TX
Houston 6'3" 195 lbs.

Year	Team	Games	Pos.
1967	**NO**	**N**	14	DB
1968			14	DB
1969			12	S

3 yrs.   40 games

Buddy Burris
BURRIS, PAUL B.
B. Jan. 20, 1923, Claremore, OK
Oklahoma 5'11" 215 lbs.

Year	Team	Games	Pos.
1949	**GB**	**N**	10	G, LB
1950			9	LB
1951			7	G, LB

3 yrs.   26 games

Jeff Burris
BURRIS, JEFFREY LAMAR
B. Jun. 7, 1972, York, SC

Jeff Burris *continued*
Notre Dame 5'10" 204 lbs.

Year	Team	Games	Pos.
1994	**BUF**	**N**	16	CB
1995			9	CB
1996			15	CB

3 yrs.   40 games

John Burrough
BURROUGH, JOHN
B. May 17, 1972, Laramie, WY
Wyoming 6'5" 265 lbs.

Year	Team	Games	Pos.
1995	**ATL**	**N**	16	DT, DE
1996			16	DT

2 yrs.   32 games

Ken Burrough
BURROUGH, KENNETH OTHELL (Double Zero)
B. Jul. 14, 1948, Jacksonville, FL
Texas Southern 6'4" 210 lbs.

Year	Team	Games	Pos.
1970	**NO**	**N**	12	WR
1971	**HOU**	**N**	13	WR
1972			14	WR
1973			14	WR
1974			11	WR
1975			14	WR
1976			14	WR
1977			14	WR
1978			16	WR
1979			16	WR
1980			2	WR
1981			16	WR

12 yrs.   156 games

Derrick Burroughs
BURROUGHS, DERRICK D.
B. May 18, 1962, Mobile, AL
Memphis State 6'1" 180 lbs.

Year	Team	Games	Pos.
1985	**BUF**	**N**	14	CB
1986			15	CB
1987			12	CB
1988			14	CB
1989			3	CB

5 yrs.   58 games

Don Burroughs
BURROUGHS, DONALD E. (Blade)
B. Aug. 19, 1931, Los Angeles, CA
Colorado State 6'4" 185 lbs.

Year	Team	Games	Pos.
1955	**LA**	**N**	12	DB
1956			12	DB
1957			12	DB
1958			12	DB
1959			10	DB
1960	**PHI**	**N**	12	DB
1961			13	DB
1962			12	DB
1963			13	DB
1964			14	DB

10 yrs.   122 games

Jim Burroughs
BURROUGHS, JAMES E.
B. Jan. 21, 1958, Pahokee, FL
Michigan State 6'1" 192 lbs.

Year	Team	Games	Pos.
1982	**BAL**	**N**	8	CB
1983			16	CB
1984	**IND**	**N**	6	CB

3 yrs.   30 games

Sammie Burroughs
BURROUGHS, SAMMIE
B. Jun. 21, 1973, Pomona, CA
Portland State 6'0" 215 lbs.

Year	Team	Games	Pos.
1996	**IND**	**N**	16	LB

Year	Team		Games	Pos.

Curtis Burrow

BURROW, CURTIS D.
B. Dec. 11, 1962, Brinkley, AR
Central Arkansas 5'11" 185 lbs.

Year	Team		Games	Pos.
1988	**GB**	N	1	K

Jim Burrow

BURROW, JAMES
B. Nov. 29, 1953, Amory, MS
Nebraska 5'11" 181 lbs.

Year	Team		Games	Pos.
1976	**GB**	N	3	S

Ken Burrow

BURROW, KENNETH ROBERT
B. Mar. 29, 1948, Richmond, CA
Utah State/San Diego State 6'0" 190 lbs.

Year	Team		Games	Pos.
1971	**ATL**	N	14	WR
1972			14	WR
1973			9	WR
1974			14	WR
1975			13	WR
5 yrs.	64 games			

Harry Burrus

BURRUS, HARRY CLIFTON, JR.
B. Apr. 6, 1921, Slaton, TX
Hardin-Simmons 6'1" 195 lbs.

Year	Team		Games	Pos.
1946	**NY**	AA	11	E
1947			14	E, B
1948	**CHI**	AA	1	E, B
1948	**BKN**	AA	12	E
3 yrs.	38 games			

Lloyd Burruss

BURRUSS, LLOYD EARL, JR.
B. Oct. 31, 1957, Charlottesville, VA
Maryland 6'0" 209 lbs.

Year	Team		Games	Pos.
1981	**KC**	N	16	S
1982			9	S
1983			12	S
1984			16	S
1985			15	S
1986			15	S
1987			11	S
1988			10	S
1989			9	S
1990			16	S
1991			16	S
11 yrs.	145 games			

Tony Burse

BURSE, TONY LEE
B. Apr. 4, 1965, Lafayette, GA
Middle Tennessee State 6'0" 220 lbs.

Year	Team		Games	Pos.
1987	**SEA**	N	12	RB

Jimmy Burson

BURSON, JAMES OERTELL
B. Oct. 13, 1940, La Grange, GA
Auburn 6'0" 181 lbs.

Year	Team		Games	Pos.
1963	**STL**	N	14	DB
1964			14	DB
1965			12	DB
1966			11	DB
1967			13	DB
1968	**ATL**	N	14	DB
6 yrs.	65 games			

Hal Burt

BURT, HAROLD
B. Jun. 28, 1899
D. Oct., 1973, Lost Nation, IA
Kansas 5'10" 175 lbs.

Year	Team		Games	Pos.
1924	**CLE**	N	2	G

Jim Burt

BURT, JAMES P.
B. Jun. 7, 1959, Buffalo, NY
Miami (Florida) 6'1" 260 lbs.

Year	Team		Games	Pos.
1981	**NYG**	N	13	DT
1982			4	NT
1983			7	NT
1984			16	NT
1985			16	NT
1986			13	NT
1987			8	NT
1988			16	NT
1989	**SF**	N	8	NT
1990			11	NT
1991			4	NT
11 yrs.	116 games			

Russ Burt

BURT, RUSSELL EDWARD
(Peanuts)
B. Dec. 15, 1900
D. Apr. 7, 1978
Canisius 5'7" 160 lbs.

Year	Team		Games	Pos.
1924	**BUF**	N	1	HB
1925			1	FB
2 yrs.	2 games			

Joe Burten

BERNSTEIN, JOE
B. Oct. 6, 1893
Deceased
Louisiana State 6'0" 210 lbs.

Year	Team		Games	Pos.
1921	**NY**	A	1	HB
1923	**RI**	N	3	G, T
1924			5	G
3 yrs.	9 games			

Burton

BURTON
None

Year	Team		Games	Pos.
1924	**HAM**	N	1	FB

Al Burton

BURTON, ALBERT, III
B. Mar. 30, 1962, Daytona Beach, FL
Bethune-Cookman 6'5" 267 lbs.

Year	Team		Games	Pos.
1976	**HOU**	N	12	DT
1977			6	DE
2 yrs.	18 games			

Derek Burton

BURTON, DEREK
B. Aug. 10, 1963, Okmulgee, OK
Oklahoma State 6'2" 270 lbs.

Year	Team		Games	Pos.
1987	**MIN**	N	3	OT

James Burton

BURTON, JAMES
B. Apr. 22, 1971, Torrance, CA
Fresno State 5'9" 181 lbs.

Year	Team		Games	Pos.
1994	**CHI**	N	13	CB
1995			11	CB
1996			16	CB
3 yrs.	40 games			

Kendrick Burton

BURTON, KENDRICK
B. Sep. 7, 1973, Decatur, AL
Alabama 6'5" 288 lbs.

Year	Team		Games	Pos.
1996	**HOU**	N	3	DE

Larry Burton

BURTON, LAWRENCE GODFREY, JR.
B. Dec. 15, 1951, Northampton, VA

Larry Burton continued

Purdue 6'1" 192 lbs.

Year	Team		Games	Pos.
1975	**NO**	N	13	WR
1976			14	WR
1977			1	WR
1978	**SD**	N	3	WR
1979			12	WR
5 yrs.	43 games			

Leon Burton

BURTON, LEON (Jet)
B. 1935
Arizona State 5'9" 172 lbs.

Year	Team		Games	Pos.
1960	**NY**	A		HB

Leonard Burton

BURTON, LEONARD BERNARD
B. Jun. 18, 1964, Memphis, TN
South Carolina 6'3" 265 lbs.

Year	Team		Games	Pos.
1986	**BUF**	N	14	C
1987			12	C
1988			16	OT
1989			6	OT
1992	**DET**	N	2	C
5 yrs.	50 games			

Lyle Burton

BURTON, LYLE
Depauw 6' 195 lbs.

Year	Team		Games	Pos.
1925	**RI**	N	7	G, T

Ron Burton

BURTON, RONALD E.
B. 1937, Springfield, OH
Northwestern 5'10" 190 lbs.

Year	Team		Games	Pos.
1960	**BOS**	A		HB
1961			14	HB
1962			14	HB
1964			14	HB
1965			14	HB
5 yrs.	56 games			

Ron Burton

BURTON, RONALD LEON
B. May 2, 1964, Richmond, VA
North Carolina 6'1" 245 lbs.

Year	Team		Games	Pos.
1987	**DAL**	N	12	LB
1988			16	LB
1989			6	LB
1989	**PHX**	N	10	LB
1990	**LARI**	N	5	LB
4 yrs.	49 games			

Shane Burton

BURTON, FRANKLIN SHANE
B. Jan. 18, 1974, Catawba, NC
Tennessee 6'6" 300 lbs.

Year	Team		Games	Pos.
1996	**MIA**	N	16	DT

Sherrill Busby

BUSBY, SHERRILL
B. 1918
Troy State 6'2" 200 lbs.

Year	Team		Games	Pos.
1940	**BKN**	N	2	E

Elmer Busch

BUSCH, ELMER E. (Pete)
B. 1889
Deceased
Sherman/Carlisle 5'10" 200 lbs.

Year	Team		Games	Pos.
1922	**OOR**	N	9	G

Mike Busch

BUSCH, MIKE

Mike Busch continued

B. Feb. 8, 1963
Idaho State/South Dakota State 6'4" 214 lbs.

Year	Team		Games	Pos.
1987	**NYG**	N	2	QB

Nick Busch

BUSCH, NICHOLAS J.
B. Jul. 26, 1898
D. Nov., 1972, Lewiston, ID
Gonzaga/Georgetown (DC) 5'10" 181 lbs.

Year	Team		Games	Pos.
1926	**LA**	A	12	G

Blair Bush

BUSH, BLAIR WALTER
B. Nov. 25, 1956, Fort Hood, TX
Washington 6'3" 262 lbs.

Year	Team		Games	Pos.
1978	**CIN**	N	16	C
1979			12	C
1980			16	C
1981			16	C
1982			8	C
1983	**SEA**	N	16	C
1984			16	C
1985			16	C
1986			7	C
1987			11	C
1988			16	C
1989	**GB**	N	16	C
1990			16	C
1991			16	C
1992	**LARM**	N	16	C
1993			16	C
1994			16	C
17 yrs.	246 games			

Devin Bush

BUSH, DEVIN
B. Jul. 3, 1973, Miami, FL
Florida State 5'11" 205 lbs.

Year	Team		Games	Pos.
1995	**ATL**	N	11	S
1996			16	S
2 yrs.	27 games			

Frank Bush

BUSH, FRANK EVERETT
B. Jan. 10, 1962, Athens, GA
North Carolina State 6'1" 218 lbs.

Year	Team		Games	Pos.
1985	**HOU**	N	16	LB
1986			3	LB
2 yrs.	19 games			

Lewis Bush

BUSH, LEWIS FITZGERALD
B. Dec. 2, 1969, Atlanta, GA
Washington State 6'2" 245 lbs.

Year	Team		Games	Pos.
1993	**SD**	N	16	LB
1994			16	LB
1995			16	LB
1996			16	LB
4 yrs.	64 games			

Ray Bush

BUSH, RAYMOND M.
B. 1902
Deceased
Loyola (Illinois) 5'8" 180 lbs.

Year	Team		Games	Pos.
1926	**LOU**	N	4	E, HB

Tom Bushby

BUSHBY, THOMAS B.
B. Dec. 30, 1911, Munden, KS
D. Oct., 1983, Northridge, CA
Kansas State 5'10" 200 lbs.

Year	Team		Games	Pos.
1934	**C, S**	N	6	HB, FB

Sam Busich
BUSICH, SAMUEL
B. 1913, Lorain, OH
Ohio State 6'3" 189 lbs.

Year	Team		Games	Pos.
1936	BOS	N	11	E
1937	CLE	N	10	E
1943	DET	N	1	E
3 yrs.			22 games	

Steve Busick
BUSICK, STEVE RAY
B. Dec. 10, 1958, Los Angeles, CA
Southern California 6'4" 227 lbs.

Year	Team		Games	Pos.
1981	DEN	N	16	LB
1982			9	LB
1983			16	LB
1984			16	LB
1985			16	LB
1986	LARM	N	4	LB
1987	SD	N	1	LB
7 yrs.			78 games	

Ray Busler
BUSLER, RAYMOND
B. Jan. 16, 1915, Watertown, WI
D. Oct. 9, 1969, Granite City, IL
Marquette 6'1" 222 lbs.

Year	Team		Games	Pos.
1940	CHIC	N	11	T
1941			7	T
1945			1	T
3 yrs.			19 games	

Art Buss
BUSS, ARTHUR T.
B. Jul. 14, 1911, St. Joseph, MI
Michigan State 6'3" 219 lbs.

Year	Team		Games	Pos.
1934	CHIB	N	13	T
1935			11	T
1936	PHI	N	12	T
1937			11	T
4 yrs.			47 games	

Gerry Bussell
BUSSELL, GERALD W.
B. Sep. 7, 1943, Middlesboro, KY
Georgia Tech 6'0" 185 lbs.

Year	Team		Games	Pos.
1965	DEN	A	6	DB

Barney Bussey
BUSSEY, BARNEY A.
B. May 20, 1962, Lincolnton, GA
South Carolina State 6'0" 195 lbs.

Year	Team		Games	Pos.
1986	CIN	N	16	S
1987			12	S
1988			16	S
1989			16	S
1990			16	S
1991			12	S
1992			16	S
1993	TB	N	16	S
1994			16	S
1995			8	S
10 yrs.			144 games	

Dexter Bussey
BUSSEY, DEXTER MANLEY
B. Mar. 11, 1952, Dallas, TX
Oklahoma/Texas-Arlington 6'1" 205 lbs.

Year	Team		Games	Pos.
1974	DET	N	11	RB
1975			13	RB
1976			14	RB
1977			8	RB
1978			16	RB
1979			16	RB
1980			16	RB
1981			16	RB
1982			9	RB

Dexter Bussey continued

Year	Team		Games	Pos.
1983			15	RB
1984			16	RB
11 yrs.			150 games	

Young Bussey
BUSSEY, YOUNG
B. Oct. 4, 1917, Timpson, TX
D. Oct., 1944, Lingayen, Philippines
Louisiana State 5'9" 184 lbs.

Year	Team		Games	Pos.
1941	CHIB	N	9	B

Paul Butcher
BUTCHER, PAUL MARTIN
B. Nov. 8, 1963, Detroit, MI
Wayne State (Michigan) 6'0" 219 lbs.

Year	Team		Games	Pos.
1986	DET	N	12	LB
1987			12	LB
1988			16	LB
1990	LARM	N	16	LB
1991			16	LB
1992			1	LB
1993	IND	N	16	LB
1994			13	LB
1995	CAR	N	16	LB
1996	OAK	N	16	LB
10 yrs.			134 games	

Wendell Butcher
BUTCHER, WENDELL RALPH
B. Mar. 24, 1914, Worthington, MN
D. Dec. 18, 1988, Memphis, TN
Gustavus Adolphus 6'1" 197 lbs.

Year	Team		Games	Pos.
1938	BKN	N	9	HB, LB
1939			10	HB, QB, LB
1940			5	QB, LB
1941			10	QB, LB
1942			11	QB, LB
5 yrs.			45 games	

Carl Butkus
BUTKUS, CARL T.
B. Dec. 26, 1922, Scranton, PA
D. Aug. 3, 1978, Washington, DC
George Washington 6'1" 245 lbs.

Year	Team		Games	Pos.
1948	WAS	N	9	T
1948	NY	AA	4	T
1949	NYG	N	11	T
2 yrs.			24 games	

Dick Butkus
BUTKUS, RICHARD MARVIN
B. Dec. 9, 1942, Chicago, IL
Illinois 6'3" 244 lbs.

Year	Team		Games	Pos.
1965	CHI	N	14	LB
1966			14	LB
1967			14	LB
1968			14	LB
1969			13	LB
1970			14	LB
1971			14	LB
1972			14	LB
1973			9	LB
9 yrs.			120 games	

Bill Butler
BUTLER, WILLIAM
B. Jul. 10, 1937, Berlin, WI
Tennessee-Chattanooga 5'10" 189 lbs.

Year	Team		Games	Pos.
1959	GB	N	11	HB
1960	DAL	N	12	DB
1961	PIT	N	10	DB
1962	MIN	N	14	DB
1963			14	HB
1964			14	HB
6 yrs.			75 games	

Bill Butler
BUTLER, WILLIAM
B. Aug. 4, 1947, Reseda, CA
Northridge State 6'4" 226 lbs.

Year	Team		Games	Pos.
1970	DEN	N	14	LB

Bill Butler
BUTLER, WILLIAM EDWARD
B. Aug. 12, 1950, Leaksville, NC
Kansas State 6'2" 212 lbs.

Year	Team		Games	Pos.
1972	NO	N	14	RB
1973			13	RB
1974			14	RB
3 yrs.			41 games	

Bob Butler
BUTLER, ROBERT DOUGLAS
B. Oct. 27, 1940
Kentucky 6'1" 233 lbs.

Year	Team		Games	Pos.
1962	PHI	N	3	G
1963	NY	A	1	G
2 yrs.			4 games	

Bobby Butler
BUTLER, ROBERT CALVIN
B. May 28, 1959, Boynton Beach, FL
Florida State 5'11" 180 lbs.

Year	Team		Games	Pos.
1981	ATL	N	16	CB
1982			9	CB
1983			16	CB
1984			15	CB
1985			16	CB
1986			7	CB
1987			12	CB
1988			16	CB
1989			16	CB
1990			16	CB
1991			15	CB
1992			15	CB
12 yrs.			169 games	

Chuck Butler
BUTLER, CHARLES WALLACE
B. Dec. 18, 1961, New Haven, CT
Utah State/Boise State 6'0" 220 lbs.

Year	Team		Games	Pos.
1984	SEA	N	8	LB

Dave Butler
BUTLER, DAVID
B. Jul. 17, 1965
Notre Dame 6'4" 225 lbs.

Year	Team		Games	Pos.
1987	CLE	N	1	LB

Frank Butler
BUTLER, FRANK JOHN
B. May 3, 1909, Bloomington, IL
Michigan State 6'3" 237 lbs.

Year	Team		Games	Pos.
1934	GB	N	3	C
1935			7	C
1936			9	C
1938			8	T
4 yrs.			27 games	

Gary Butler
BUTLER, GARY BERNARD
B. Jan. 11, 1951, Houston, TX
Rice 6'3" 235 lbs.

Year	Team		Games	Pos.
1973	KC	N	14	TE
1975	CHI	N	8	TE
1977	TB	N	4	TE
3 yrs.			26 games	

Jack Butler
BUTLER, JOHN B.
B. Nov. 12, 1927, Pittsburgh, PA

Jack Butler continued
St. Bonaventure 6'0" 195 lbs.

Year	Team		Games	Pos.
1951	PIT	N	12	DB
1952			12	OE, DB
1953			12	OE, DB
1954			12	OE, DB
1955			12	DB
1956			12	DB
1957			12	DB
1958			12	DB
1959			7	DB
9 yrs.			103 games	

Jerry Butler
BUTLER, JERRY
B. Dec. 7, 1961
East Tennessee State 5'11" 193 lbs.

Year	Team		Games	Pos.
1987	ATL	N	1	RB

Jerry Butler
BUTLER, JERRY O'DELL
B. Oct. 2, 1957, Ware Shoals, SC
Clemson 6'0" 178 lbs.

Year	Team		Games	Pos.
1979	BUF	N	13	WR
1980			16	WR
1981			16	WR
1982			7	WR
1983			9	WR
1985			16	WR
1986			11	WR
7 yrs.			88 games	

Jim Butler
BUTLER, JAMES (Cannonball)
B. May 4, 1943, Quincy, FL
Edward Waters 5'10" 191 lbs.

Year	Team		Games	Pos.
1965	PIT	N	14	HB
1966			14	HB
1967			11	HB
1968	ATL	N	12	RB
1969			14	RB
1970			14	RB
1971			14	RB
1972	STL	N	5	RB
8 yrs.			98 games	

John Butler
BUTLER, JOHN
B. Apr. 13, 1965
Principia 6'1" 200 lbs.

Year	Team		Games	Pos.
1987	SF	N	3	S

Johnny Butler
BUTLER, JOHNNY W.
B. Sep. 10, 1918, Knoxville, TN
Tennessee 5'10" 185 lbs.

Year	Team		Games	Pos.
1943	P, P	N	10	HB
1944	C, P	N	3	HB
1944	BKN	N	6	HB
1945	PHI	N	7	HB
3 yrs.			26 games	

Keith Butler
BUTLER, JOHN KEITH
B. May 16, 1966, Anniston, AL
Memphis State 6'4" 235 lbs.

Year	Team		Games	Pos.
1978	SEA	N	16	LB
1979			14	LB
1980			16	LB
1981			16	LB
1982			8	LB
1983			16	LB
1984			16	LB
1985			16	LB
1986			16	LB
1987			12	LB
10 yrs.			146 games	

Year	Team	Games	Pos.

Kevin Butler
BUTLER, KEVIN GREGORY
B. Jul. 24, 1962, Savannah, GA
Georgia 6'1" 195 lbs.

Year	Team		Games	Pos.
1985	CHI	N	16	K
1986			16	K
1987			12	K
1988			16	K
1989			16	K
1990			16	K
1991			16	K
1992			16	K
1993			16	K
1994			15	K
1995			16	K
1996	ARI	N	7	K

12 yrs. 178 games

LeRoy Butler
BUTLER, LEROY
B. Jul. 19, 1968, Jacksonville, FL
Florida State 6'0" 192 lbs.

Year	Team		Games	Pos.
1990	GB	N	16	CB
1991			16	CB
1992			15	CB
1993			16	S
1994			13	S
1995			16	S
1996			16	S

7 yrs. 108 games

Mike Butler
BUTLER, MICHAEL ANTHONY
B. Apr. 4, 1954, Washington, DC
Kansas 6'5" 265 lbs.

Year	Team		Games	Pos.
1977	GB	N	14	DE
1978			16	DE
1979			14	DE
1980			16	DE
1981			16	DE
1982			9	DE
1985			11	DE

7 yrs. 96 games

Ray Butler
BUTLER, RAYMOND LEONARD
B. Jun. 28, 1956, Port Lavaca, TX
Southern California 6'3" 200 lbs.

Year	Team		Games	Pos.
1980	BAL	N	16	WR
1981			16	WR
1982			9	WR
1983			11	WR
1984	IND	N	16	WR
1985			11	WR
1985	SEA	N	2	WR
1986			16	WR
1987			12	WR
1988			12	WR

9 yrs. 121 games

Skip Butler
BUTLER, WILLIAM FOSTER
B. Oct. 21, 1947, Gladewater, TX
Texas-Arlington 6'2" 200 lbs.

Year	Team		Games	Pos.
1971	NO	N	2	K
1971	NYG	N	1	K
1972	HOU	N	13	K
1973			14	K
1974			14	K
1975			14	K
1976			14	K
1977			1	K

7 yrs. 73 games

Sol Butler
BUTLER, EDWARD
B. Jul. 26, 1897
D. Nov. 6, 1988, Chicago, IL

Sol Butler *continued*
Dubuque 5'8" 184 lbs.

Year	Team		Games	Pos.
1923	RI	N	3	HB, FB
1923	HAM	N	3	HB
1924			4	HB
1924	AKR	N	1	HB
1925	HAM	N	1	HB
1926	CAN	N	8	QB, HB, FB
1926	HAM	N	1	HB

4 yrs. 21 games

Harry Butsko
BUTSKO, HARRY
B. Feb. 2, 1941, Pottsville, PA
Maryland 6'3" 220 lbs.

Year	Team		Games	Pos.
1963	WAS	N	4	LB

Greg Buttle
BUTTLE, GREGORY ELLIS
B. Jun. 20, 1954, Atlantic City, NJ
Penn State 6'3" 232 lbs.

Year	Team		Games	Pos.
1976	NYJ	N	14	LB
1977			13	LB
1978			8	LB
1979			16	LB
1980			14	LB
1981			15	LB
1982			7	LB
1983			9	LB
1984			14	LB

9 yrs. 110 games

Eddie Butts
BUTTS, EDWARD CARMACK
B. 1903
Deceased
Chico State 190 lbs.

Year	Team		Games	Pos.
1929	CHIC	N	9	HB, QB, FB, G

Marion Butts
BUTTS, MARION STEVENSON, JR.
B. Aug. 1, 1966, Sylvester, GA
Florida State 6'1" 248 lbs.

Year	Team		Games	Pos.
1989	SD	N	15	RB
1990			14	RB
1991			16	RB
1992			15	RB
1993			16	RB
1994	NE	N	16	RB
1995	HOU	N	12	RB

7 yrs. 104 games

Dave Butz
BUTZ, DAVID ROY
B. Jun. 23 1950, Lafayette, AL
Purdue 6'7" 295 lbs.

Year	Team		Games	Pos.
1973	STL	N	12	DT
1974			1	DT
1975	WAS	N	14	DE
1976			14	DT
1977			12	DT
1978			16	DT
1979			15	DT
1980			16	DT
1981			16	DT
1982			9	DT
1983			16	DT
1984			15	DT
1985			16	DT
1986			16	DT
1987			12	DT
1988			16	DT

16 yrs. 216 games

Rich Buzin
BUZIN, RICHARD LAWRENCE

Rich Buzin *continued*
B. Jan. 25, 1946, Youngstown, OH
Penn State 6'4" 250 lbs.

Year	Team		Games	Pos.
1968	NYG	N	14	OT
1969			14	OT
1970			14	OT
1971	LA	N	5	OT
1972	CHI	N	2	OT

5 yrs. 49 games

Bernie Buzyniski
BUZYNISKI, BERNARD
B. 1938
Holy Cross 6'3" 228 lbs.

Year	Team		Games	Pos.
1960	BUF	A		LB

Keith Byars
BYARS, KEITH
B. Oct. 14, 1963, Dayton, OH
Ohio State 6'1" 230 lbs.

Year	Team		Games	Pos.
1986	PHI		16	RB
1987			10	RB
1988			16	RB
1989			16	RB
1990			16	RB
1991			16	RB
1992			15	RB
1993	MIA	N	16	RB
1994			9	RB
1995			16	RB
1996			4	FB, TE
1996	NE	N	10	FB

11 yrs. 160 games

Rick Byas
BYAS, RICHARD REESE, JR.
B. Oct. 19, 1950, Detroit, MI
Eastern Michigan/Wayne State 5'9" 179 lbs.

Year	Team		Games	Pos.
1974	ATL	N	14	DB
1975			14	DB
1976			14	CB, S
1977			14	S
1978			16	S
1979			16	S
1980			15	S

7 yrs. 103 games

Ken Byers
BYERS, KEN
B. Apr. 6, 1940, Logan, OH
Cincinnati 6'1" 240 lbs.

Year	Team		Games	Pos.
1962	NYG	N	14	G
1963			14	DE
1964			8	DE, G
1964	MIN	N	6	G
1965			14	G

4 yrs. 56 games

Scotty Byers
BYERS, NORMAN SCOTT
B. Jul. 3, 1958, Bayonne, NJ
Long Beach State 5'11" 170 lbs.

Year	Team		Games	Pos.
1984	SD	N	6	CB, S

Frank Bykowski
BYKOWSKI, FRANK PETER
B. Mar. 24, 1915
D. May 1, 1985, Bradenton, FL
Purdue 6'0" 205 lbs.

Year	Team		Games	Pos.
1940	PIT	N	1	G

Joe Byler
BYLER, JOSEPH (Big Boy)
B. 1923

Joe Byler *continued*
Nebraska 6'5" 240 lbs.

Year	Team		Games	Pos.
1946	NYG	N	7	T

Earnest Byner
BYNER, EARNEST ALEXANDER
B. Sep. 15, 1962, Milledgeville, GA
East Carolina 5'10" 215 lbs.

Year	Team		Games	Pos.
1984	CLE	N	16	FB
1985			16	RB
1986			7	RB
1987			12	RB
1988			16	RB
1989	WAS	N	16	RB
1990			16	RB
1991			16	RB
1992			16	RB
1993			16	RB
1994	CLE	N	16	RB
1995			16	RB
1996	BAL	N	16	RB

13 yrs. 195 games

Butler By'Not'e
BY'NOT'E, BUTLER
B. Sep. 29, 1972, St. Louis, MO
Ohio State 5'9" 188 lbs.

Year	Team		Games	Pos.
1994	DEN	N	10	CB
1995	CAR	N	7	CB

2 yrs. 17 games

Reggie Bynum
BYNUM, REGINALD DESHAIN
B. Feb. 10, 1964, Greenville, MS
Oregon State 6'1" 185 lbs.

Year	Team		Games	Pos.
1987	BUF	N	1	WR

Boris Byrd
BYRD, BORIS
B. Apr. 15, 1962, Warren County, KY
Austin Peay 6'0" 210 lbs.

Year	Team		Games	Pos.
1987	NYG	N	3	DB

Butch Byrd
BYRD, GEORGE EDWARD
B. Sep. 20, 1941, Watervliet, NY
Boston University 6'0" 203 lbs.

Year	Team		Games	Pos.
1964	BUF	A	14	DB
1965			14	DB
1966			14	DB
1967			14	DB
1968			14	CB
1969			14	CB
1970	BUF	N	14	CB
1971	DEN	N	14	CB

8 yrs. 112 games

Darryl Byrd
BYRD, DARRYL TERRENCE
B. Sep. 3, 1960, San Diego, CA
Illinois 6'1" 220 lbs.

Year	Team		Games	Pos.
1983	LARI	N	16	LB
1984			16	LB
1987			3	LB

3 yrs. 35 games

Dennis Byrd
BYRD, DENNIS
B. Feb. 14, 1945, Lincolnton, NC
North Carolina State 6'4" 260 lbs.

Year	Team		Games	Pos.
1968	BOS	A	14	DT, DE

Dennis Byrd
BYRD, DENNIS DEWAYNE
B. Oct. 5, 1966, Oklahoma City, OK

Year	Team	Games	Pos.

Dennis Byrd continued

Tulsa 6'5" 270 lbs.

Year	Team		Games	Pos.
1989	**NYJ**	**N**	16	DE
1990			16	DE
1991			16	DE
1992			7	DE

4 yrs.   55 games

Gill Byrd
BYRD, GILL ARNETTE
B. Feb. 20, 1961, San Francisco, CA
San Jose State 5'11" 194 lbs.

1983	**SD**	**N**	14	CB
1984			13	CB
1985			16	CB
1986			15	S
1987			12	CB, S
1988			16	CB, S
1989			16	CB
1990			16	CB
1991			15	CB, S
1992			16	CB, S

10 yrs.   149 games

Israel Byrd
BYRD, ISRAEL
B. Feb. 1, 1971, St. Louis, MO
Utah State 5'11" 184 lbs.

1994	**NO**	**N**	3	CB
1995			4	CB

2 yrs.   7 games

Mack Byrd
BYRD, MACARTHUR
B. 1943
Southern California 6'0" 215 lbs.

1965	**LA**	**N**	2	LB

Richard Byrd
BYRD, RICHARD
B. Mar. 20, 1962, Natchez, MS
Southern Mississippi 6'3" 264 lbs.

1985	**HOU**	**N**	15	DE
1986			16	NT
1987			12	DE
1988			16	DE
1989			16	NT

5 yrs.   75 games

Sylvester Byrd
BYRD, SYLVESTER
B. May 1, 1963
Kansas 6'2" 225 lbs.

1987	**ATL**	**N**		TE

Bill Byrne
BYRNE, WILLIAM JOSEPH
B. Nov. 19, 1940
Boston College 6'0" 240 lbs.

1963	**PHI**	**N**	12	G

Carl Byrum
BYRUM, CARL EDWARD
B. Jun. 29, 1963, Olive Branch, MS
Mississippi Valley State 6'0" 232 lbs.

1986	**BUF**	**N**	13	FB
1987			13	FB
1988			15	RB

3 yrs.   41 games

Brian Cabral
**CABRAL, BRIAN DAVID
(KEALIIHAAHEO)**
B. Jun. 23, 1956, Fort Benning, GA

Brian Cabral continued

Colorado 6'1" 232 lbs.

1979	**ATL**	**N**	3	LB
1980	**GB**	**N**	7	LB
1981	**CHI**	**N**	16	LB
1982			8	LB
1983			16	LB
1984			16	LB
1985			1	LB
1986			3	LB

8 yrs.   70 games

Larry Cabrelli
CABRELLI, LAWRENCE A.
B. Mar. 30, 1917, Newark, NJ
D. Jun. 5, 1974, Bryn Mawr, PA
Colgate 5'11" 194 lbs.

1941	**PHI**	**N**	8	E
1942			11	E
1943	**P, P**	**N**	10	E
1944	**PHI**	**N**	9	E
1945			10	E
1946			8	E
1947			6	E

7 yrs.   62 games

Augie Cabrinha
CABRINHA, AUGUST
B. Apr. 13, 1902
D. Mar., 1979, Kahaluu, HI
Dayton 5'9" 170 lbs.

1927	**DAY**	**N**	3	HB, QB

Ernie Caddel
CADDEL, ERNEST WILEY, JR.
B. Mar. 12, 1911, Granite, OK
D. Mar. 28, 1992, Roseville, CA
Stanford 6'2" 199 lbs.

1933	**POR**	**N**	11	HB, FB
1934	**DET**	**N**	12	HB
1935			12	HB
1936			11	HB
1937			11	HB
1938			7	HB

6 yrs.   64 games

Eddie Cade
CADE, EDDIE RAY
B. Aug. 4, 1973, Casa Grande, AZ
Arizona State 6'1" 206 lbs.

1995	**NE**	**N**	10	S

Mossy Cade
CADE, TOMMORIES
B. Dec. 26, 1961, Eloy, AZ
Texas 6'1" 198 lbs.

1985	**GB**	**N**	12	CB
1986			16	CB

2 yrs.   28 games

Dave Cadigan
CADIGAN, DAVE
B. Apr. 6, 1965, Needham, MA
Southern California 6'4" 285 lbs.

1988	**NYJ**	**N**	5	OT
1989			13	OT, G
1990			5	G, OT
1991			15	G, OT
1992			15	G
1993			16	G
1994	**CIN**	**N**	13	G

7 yrs.   82 games

Jim Cadile
CADILE, JAMES D.
B. Jul. 16, 1940, San Jose, CA

Jim Cadile continued

San Jose State 6'3" 239 lbs.

1962	**CHI**	**N**	4	OT
1963			13	OT
1964			14	G
1965			14	G
1966			14	G
1967			10	G
1968			14	G
1969			14	G
1970			12	G
1971			13	G
1972			6	G

11 yrs.   128 games

Glenn Cadrez
CADREZ, GLENN
B. Jan. 20, 1970, El Centro, CA
Houston 6'3" 240 lbs.

1992	**NYJ**	**N**	16	LB
1993			16	LB
1994			16	LB
1995			1	LB
1995	**DEN**	**N**	10	LB
1996			16	LB

5 yrs.   75 games

John Cadwell
CADWELL, JOHN
B. 1939
Oregon State 6'3" 230 lbs.

1961	**DAL**	**A**	4	G

Ivan Caesar
CAESAR, IVAN O.J., II
B. Jan. 7, 1967, St. Thomas, Virgin Islands
Boston College 6'1" 241 lbs.

1991	**MIN**	**N**	14	LB

George Cafego
CAFEGO, GEORGE (Bad News)
B. Aug. 27, 1915, Scarbro, WV
Deceased
Tennessee 5'10" 183 lbs.

1940	**BKN**	**N**	10	HB
1943			5	HB
1943	**WAS**	**N**	4	HB
1944	**BOS**	**N**	9	FB, QB
1945			7	HB

4 yrs.   35 games

Lee Roy Caffey
CAFFEY, LEE ROY
B. Jun. 3, 1941, Thorndale, TX
D. Jan. 18, 1994, Houston, TX
Texas A&M 6'3" 247 lbs.

1963	**PHI**	**N**	14	LB
1964	**GB**	**N**	14	LB
1965			14	LB
1966			14	LB
1967			13	LB
1968			14	LB
1969			14	LB
1970	**CHI**	**N**	14	LB
1971	**DAL**	**N**	6	LB
1972	**SD**	**N**	12	LB

10 yrs.   129 games

Chris Cagle
**CAGLE, CHRISTIAN KEENER
(Red)**
B. May 1, 1905, De Ridder, LA
D. Dec. 23, 1942, Queens, NY
Southwestern Louisiana/Army 5'10" 174 lbs.

1930	**NYG**	**N**	4	HB, QB

Chris Cagle continued

1931			13	HB
1932			10	HB, QB
1933	**BKN**	**N**	10	QB, HB
1934			10	QB, HB

5 yrs.   47 games

Jim Cagle
CAGLE, JAMES COLQUITT
B. Jan. 15, 1952, Jacksonville, FL
Georgia 6'5" 255 lbs.

1974	**PHI**	**N**	14	DT

Johnny Cagle
CAGLE, JOHN
B. Mar. 26, 1947, Anderson, SC
Clemson 6'3" 260 lbs.

1969	**BOS**	**A**	6	DE

Bill Cahill
CAHILL, WILLIAM
B. May 5, 1951, Bellevue, WA
Washington 5'11" 175 lbs.

1973	**BUF**	**N**	5	S
1974			14	S

2 yrs.   19 games

Dave Cahill
CAHILL, DAVID ALLEN
B. Jul. 26, 1942, Stanley, WI
Arizona State 6'3" 240 lbs.

1966	**PHI**	**N**	14	DT
1967	**LA**	**N**	14	DT, DE
1969	**ATL**	**N**	11	DT

3 yrs.   39 games

Ronnie Cahill
CAHILL, RONALD (Butch)
B. 1917
D. Sep. 6, 1992, Leominster, PA
Holy Cross 5'8" 170 lbs.

1943	**CHIC**	**N**	10	HB

Tiny Cahoon
CAHOON, IVAN W.
B. May 22, 1900
D. Feb. 3, 1973, Concord, CA
Montana/Gonzaga 6'2" 235 lbs.

1926	**GB**	**N**	11	T
1927			8	T
1928			10	T
1929			2	T

4 yrs.   31 games

Jim Cain
CAIN, JAMES EDGAR (Sugar)
B. Oct. 1, 1927, Eudora, AR
Deceased
Alabama 6'1" 202 lbs.

1949	**CHIC**	**N**	12	E
1950	**DET**	**N**	12	E
1953			12	E
1954			12	E
1955			12	E

5 yrs.   60 games

Joe Cain
CAIN, JOSEPH HARRISON, JR.
B. Jun. 11, 1965, Los Angeles, CA
Stanford/Oregon Tech 6'1" 231 lbs.

1989	**SEA**	**N**	9	LB
1990			16	LB
1991			16	LB
1992			16	LB
1993	**CHI**	**N**	15	LB

Year	Team	Games	Pos.

Joe Cain *continued*

Year	Team	Games	Pos.
1994		16	LB
1995		16	LB
1996		16	LB

8 yrs.   120 games

J.V. Cain
CAIN, JAMES VICTOR
B. Jul. 22, 1951, Houston, TX
D. Jul. 22, 1979, St. Louis, MO
Colorado 6'4" 224 lbs.

Year	Team		Games	Pos.
1974	STL	N	14	TE
1975			14	WR
1976			14	TE, WR
1977			13	TE

4 yrs.   55 games

Lynn Cain
CAIN, LYNN DWIGHT
B. Oct. 16, 1955, Los Angeles, CA
Southern California 6'1" 205 lbs.

Year	Team		Games	Pos.
1979	ATL	N	10	RB
1980			16	RB
1981			16	RB
1982			9	RB
1983			16	RB
1984			15	RB
1985	LARM	N	7	RB

7 yrs.   89 games

Pat Cain
CAIN, PATRICK
B. Oct. 1, 1962
Wichita State 6'2" 260 lbs.

Year	Team		Games	Pos.
1987	DET	N	3	C

Pete Calac
CALAC, PETER
B. May 13, 1892, San Diego, CA
D. Jan. 13, 1968, Canton, OH
*Sherman/Carlisle/West Virginia Wesleyan
5'10" 196 lbs.*

Year	Team		Games	Pos.
1920	CAN	A	8	FB
1921	CLE	A	8	FB
1921	WAS	A	1	FB
1922	OOR	N	9	E, FB, HB
1923			10	FB, E, HB, T
1924	BUF	N	11	FB, E, T
1925	CAN	N	7	FB, HB
1926			9	FB, HB

7 yrs.   63 games

Ralph Calacagni
CALACAGNI, CLEO RALPH
B. 1922
D. 1948
Pennsylvania/Cornell 6'3" 230 lbs.

Year	Team		Games	Pos.
1946	BOS	N	11	T
1947	PIT	N	9	T

2 yrs.   20 games

Alan Caldwell
CALDWELL, ALAN LORENZO
B. May 22, 1956, Winston-Salem, NC
North Carolina 6'0" 176 lbs.

Year	Team		Games	Pos.
1979	NYG	N	16	CB, S

Bruce Caldwell
CALDWELL, BRUCE
B. Feb. 8, 1906, Ashton, RI
D. Feb. 15, 1959, West Haven, CT
Brown/Yale 6'0" 190 lbs.

Year	Team		Games	Pos.
1928	NYG	N	10	HB, FB

Bryan Caldwell
CALDWELL, BRYAN CRAIG

Bryan Caldwell *continued*
B. May 6, 1960, Oakland, CA
Arizona State 6'4" 248 lbs.

Year	Team		Games	Pos.
1984	HOU	N	8	DE

Darryl Caldwell
CALDWELL, DARRYL
B. Feb. 2, 1960, Birmingham, AL
Tennessee State 6'5" 245 lbs.

Year	Team		Games	Pos.
1983	BUF	N	14	G

David Caldwell
CALDWELL, DAVID A.
B. Feb. 28, 1965, Bay City, TX
Texas Christian 6'1" 261 lbs.

Year	Team		Games	Pos.
1987	GB	N	3	NT

Mike Caldwell
CALDWELL, MIKE
B. Mar. 28, 1971, Cleveland, OH
California 6'2" 200 lbs.

Year	Team		Games	Pos.
1995	SF	N	2	WR
1996			1	WR

2 yrs.   3 games

Mike Caldwell
CALDWELL, MIKE ISIAH
B. Aug. 31, 1971, Oak Ridge, TN
Middle Tennessee State 6'2" 222 lbs.

Year	Team		Games	Pos.
1993	CLE	N	15	LB
1994			16	LB
1995			16	LB
1996	BAL	N	9	LB

4 yrs.   56 games

Ravin Caldwell
CALDWELL, RAVIN, JR.
B. Aug. 4, 1963, Port Arthur, TX
Arkansas 6'3" 229 lbs.

Year	Team		Games	Pos.
1987	WAS	N	12	LB
1988			16	LB
1989			15	LB
1990			16	LB
1991			16	LB
1992			4	LB

6 yrs.   79 games

Scotty Caldwell
CALDWELL, SCOTT
B. Feb. 8, 1963, Dallas, TX
Texas-Arlington 5'10" 196 lbs.

Year	Team		Games	Pos.
1987	DEN	N	3	RB

Tony Caldwell
CALDWELL, ANTHONY
B. Apr. 1, 1961, Los Angeles, CA
Washington 6'1" 225 lbs.

Year	Team		Games	Pos.
1983	LARI	N	16	LB
1984			16	LB
1985			3	LB
1987	SEA	N	1	LB

4 yrs.   36 games

Jamie Caleb
CALEB, JAMIE
B. Oct. 29, 1936, Calhoun, LA
Grambling State 6'1" 210 lbs.

Year	Team		Games	Pos.
1960	CLE	N	12	HB
1961	MIN	N	10	HB
1965	CLE	N	4	HB

3 yrs.   26 games

Don Calhoun
CALHOUN, DONALD C.
B. Apr. 29, 1952, Sumner, OK

Don Calhoun *continued*
Kansas State 6'0" 207 lbs.

Year	Team		Games	Pos.
1974	BUF	N	14	RB
1975			6	RB
1975	NE	N	5	RB
1976			14	RB
1977			14	RB
1978			14	RB
1979			16	RB
1980			16	RB
1981			14	RB
1982	PHI	N	1	RB

9 yrs.   114 games

Eric Calhoun
CALHOUN, ERIC V. (Enoch)
B. Aug. 1, 1900
D. Sep., 1974, South Euclid, OH
Denison 5'9" 210 lbs.

Year	Team		Games	Pos.
1926	DAY	N	6	T

Mike Calhoun
CALHOUN, MICHAEL EDWARD
B. May 6, 1957, Youngstown, OH
Notre Dame 6'4" 260 lbs.

Year	Team		Games	Pos.
1980	TB	N	3	DE
1980	SF	N	4	DT

1 yr.   7 games

Rick Calhoun
CALHOUN, RICK
B. Jun. 30, 1963, Montgomery, AL
Fullerton State 5'7" 190 lbs.

Year	Team		Games	Pos.
1987	LARI	N	3	RB

Dean Caliguire
CALIGUIRE, DEAN PATRICK
B. Mar. 2, 1967, Pittsburgh, PA
Pittsburgh 6'2" 290 lbs.

Year	Team		Games	Pos.
1991	SF	N	2	C
1991	PIT	N	7	C, G

1 yr.   9 games

Jack Call
CALL, JOHN A.
B. Jul. 30, 1935, Cortland, NY
Colgate 6'1" 200 lbs.

Year	Team		Games	Pos.
1957	BAL	N	12	HB
1958			12	HB
1959	PIT	N	4	HB

3 yrs.   28 games

Kevin Call
CALL, KEVIN BRADLEY
B. Nov. 13, 1961, Boulder, CO
Colorado State 6'7" 292 lbs.

Year	Team		Games	Pos.
1984	IND	N	15	OT
1985			13	OT
1986			16	OT
1987			12	OT
1988			8	OT
1989			15	OT
1990			8	OT
1991			16	OT
1992			16	OT
1993			10	OT

10 yrs.   129 games

Bill Callahan
CALLAHAN, WILLIAM
B. Apr. 11, 1964, New Kensington, PA
Pittsburgh 6'0" 200 lbs.

Year	Team		Games	Pos.
1987	BUF	N	1	S

Bob Callahan
CALLAHAN, ROBERT FRANCIS

Bob Callahan *continued*
B. Sep. 26, 1923, St. Louis, MO
Missouri/Michigan 6'0" 205 lbs.

Year	Team		Games	Pos.
1948	BUF	AA	7	C

Dan Callahan
CALLAHAN, DANIEL
B. 1938
Wooster 6'0" 230 lbs.

Year	Team		Games	Pos.
1960	NY	A		G

Jim Callahan
CALLAHAN, JAMES ROSS (J.R.)
B. Dec. 19, 1920, El Paso, TX
Texas Tech/Texas 5'11" 185 lbs.

Year	Team		Games	Pos.
1946	DET	N	9	HB

Lee Calland
CALLAND, LEE
B. Sep. 14, 1941, Louisville, KY
Louisville 6'0" 190 lbs.

Year	Team		Games	Pos.
1963	MIN	N	14	DB
1964			1	DB
1965			5	DB
1966	ATL	N	14	DB
1967			14	DB
1968			7	DB
1969	CHI	N	4	CB
1969	PIT	N	8	CB
1970			14	CB
1971			13	CB
1972			7	CB

10 yrs.   101 games

Ken Callicut
CALLICUT, KEN BYRON
B. Aug. 20, 1955, Chester, SC
Clemson 6'1" 191 lbs.

Year	Team		Games	Pos.
1978	DET	N	13	RB
1979			16	RB
1980			13	RB
1981			16	RB
1982			8	RB

5 yrs.   66 games

Len Calligaro
CALLIGARO, LEONARD J.
B. Jun. 24, 1921, Hurley, WI
Wisconsin 5'11" 190 lbs.

Year	Team		Games	Pos.
1944	NYG	N	10	QB

Bill Callihan
CALLIHAN, WILLIAM E.
B. May 15, 1916, Paxton, NE
D. Aug. 23, 1986, Columbus, NE
Nebraska 6'3" 217 lbs.

Year	Team		Games	Pos.
1940	DET	N	10	B
1941			11	B
1942			11	B
1943			10	B
1944			10	B
1945			10	B

6 yrs.   62 games

Chris Calloway
CALLOWAY, CHRISTOPHER FITZPATRICK
B. Mar. 29, 1968, Chicago, IL
Michigan 5'10" 185 lbs.

Year	Team		Games	Pos.
1990	PIT	N	16	WR
1991			12	WR
1992	NYG	N	16	WR
1993			16	WR
1994			16	WR
1995			16	WR
1996			16	WR

7 yrs.   108 games

Ernie Calloway
CALLOWAY, ERNEST HENRY
B. Jan. 1, 1948, Orlando, FL
Texas Southern 6'6" 244 lbs.

Year	Team		Games	Pos.
1969	PHI	N	14	DT
1970			14	DT
1971			14	DE
1972			5	DT

4 yrs. 47 games

Tony Calvelli
CALVELLI, ANTHONY J.
B. 1916
Deceased
Stanford 5'10" 189 lbs.

Year	Team		Games	Pos.
1939	DET	N	7	G, C, T
1940			11	C
1947	SF	AA	13	C

3 yrs. 31 games

Tom Calvin
CALVIN, THOMAS MARVIN
B. Jun. 13, 1926, Athens, AL
Alabama 6'0" 200 lbs.

Year	Team		Games	Pos.
1952	PIT	N	12	HB
1953			10	HB
1954			6	HB

3 yrs. 28 games

Rich Camarillo
CAMARILLO, RICHARD JON
B. Nov. 29, 1959, Whittier, CA
Washington 5'11" 185 lbs.

Year	Team		Games	Pos.
1981	NE	N	9	P
1982			9	P
1983			16	P
1984			7	P
1985			16	P
1986			16	P
1987			12	P
1988	LARM	N	9	P
1989	PHX	N	15	P
1990			16	P
1991			16	P
1992			15	P
1993			16	P
1994	HOU	N	16	P
1995			16	P
1996	OAK	N	1	P

16 yrs. 205 games

Dennis Cambal
CAMBAL, DENNIS HAYDEN
B. Jan. 27, 1949, Waltham, MA
William & Mary 6'3" 228 lbs.

Year	Team		Games	Pos.
1973	NYJ	N	8	TE

Glenn Cameron
CAMERON, GLENN SCOTT
B. Feb. 21, 1953, Miami, FL
Florida 6'2" 226 lbs.

Year	Team		Games	Pos.
1975	CIN	N	14	LB
1976			14	LB
1977			14	LB
1978			15	LB
1979			15	LB
1980			14	LB
1981			16	LB
1982			9	LB
1983			16	LB
1984			16	LB
1985			16	LB

11 yrs. 159 games

Jack Cameron
CAMERON, JACK LYNDEN
B. Nov. 5, 1961, Roxboro, NC

Jack Cameron continued
Winston-Salem State 6'0" 182 lbs.

Year	Team		Games	Pos.
1984	CHI	N	16	WR

John Cameron
CAMERON, JOHN L., JR.
B. 1902
Deceased
Western Michigan 175 lbs.

Year	Team		Games	Pos.
1926	DET	N	7	G, T

Paul Cameron
CAMERON, PAUL
B. Aug. 17, 1932, Burbank, CA
UCLA 6'0" 185 lbs.

Year	Team		Games	Pos.
1954	PIT	N	12	HB

Jim Camp
CAMP, JAMES VERNON
B. Aug. 8, 1924, Union, SC
North Carolina 6'0" 170 lbs.

Year	Team		Games	Pos.
1948	BKN	AA	12	B

Reggie Camp
CAMP, REGGIE LOUIS
B. Feb. 28, 1961, San Francisco, CA
California 6'4" 274 lbs.

Year	Team		Games	Pos.
1983	CLE	N	16	DE
1984			16	DE
1985			16	DE
1986			16	DE
1987			6	DE
1988	ATL	N	6	DE

6 yrs. 76 games

Al Campana
CAMPANA, ALBERT
B. Feb. 25, 1926, Youngstown, OH
Youngstown State 5'11" 181 lbs.

Year	Team		Games	Pos.
1950	CHIB	N	9	HB, DB
1951			2	HB, DB
1952			12	HB, DB
1953	CHIC	N	8	HB, DB

4 yrs. 31 games

Joe Campanella
CAMPANELLA, JOSEPH A.
B. Sep. 3, 1930
D. Feb. 15, 1967, Baltimore, MD
Ohio State 6'2" 242 lbs.

Year	Team		Games	Pos.
1952	DAL	N	12	T, G
1953	BAL	N	12	T
1954			12	G
1955			11	G
1956			10	G
1957			11	T

6 yrs. 68 games

Arnold Campbell
CAMPBELL, ARNOLD
B. Nov. 13, 1962, Charleston, MS
Alcorn State 6'3" 260 lbs.

Year	Team		Games	Pos.
1987	BUF	N	3	DE

Bill Campbell
CAMPBELL, WILLIAM ROSCOE
B. Aug. 6, 1920, Pawhuska, OK
Oklahoma 6'0" 195 lbs.

Year	Team		Games	Pos.
1945	CHIC	N	6	HB
1946			11	C
1947			4	C
1948			7	C
1949			6	C
1949	NYB	N	4	C

5 yrs. 38 games

Bob Campbell
CAMPBELL, ROBERT
B. Apr. 18, 1947, Johnson City, NY
Penn State 6'0" 195 lbs.

Year	Team		Games	Pos.
1969	PIT	N	14	RB

Carter Campbell
CAMPBELL, CARTER BRADFORD
B. Sep. 29, 1947, Mobile, AL
Weber State 6'3" 232 lbs.

Year	Team		Games	Pos.
1970	SF	N	1	LB
1971	DEN	N	14	LB
1972	NYG	N	14	LB
1973			14	DE

4 yrs. 43 games

Dick Campbell
CAMPBELL, RICHARD
B. Jul. 17, 1935, Green Bay, WI
Marquette 6'1" 227 lbs.

Year	Team		Games	Pos.
1958	PIT	N	12	C, LB
1959			12	C, LB
1960			12	LB

3 yrs. 36 games

Don Campbell
CAMPBELL, DONALD C. (Pop)
B. Nov. 25, 1916
D. Sep. 1, 1991, Philadelphia, PA
Carnegie-Mellon 6'0" 225 lbs.

Year	Team		Games	Pos.
1939	PIT	N	11	T
1940			11	T, E

2 yrs. 22 games

Earl Campbell
CAMPBELL, EARL CHRISTIAN (The Tyler Rose)
B. Mar. 29, 1955, Tyler, TX
Texas 5'11" 230 lbs.

Year	Team		Games	Pos.
1978	HOU	N	16	RB
1979			16	RB
1980			15	RB
1981			16	RB
1982			9	RB
1983			14	RB
1984			6	RB
1984	NO	N	8	RB
1985			16	RB

8 yrs. 116 games

Gary Campbell
CAMPBELL, GARY KALANI
B. Mar. 4, 1952, Honolulu, HI
Colorado 6'1" 219 lbs.

Year	Team		Games	Pos.
1977	CHI	N	14	LB
1978			16	LB
1979			16	LB
1980			16	LB
1981			16	LB
1982			9	LB
1983			6	LB

7 yrs. 93 games

Glenn Campbell
CAMPBELL, GLENN R. (Turtle, Flash)
B. Apr. 20, 1904
D. Sep. 16, 1973, Topeka, KS
Emporia State 5'11" 199 lbs.

Year	Team		Games	Pos.
1929	NYG	N	15	E
1930			17	E
1931			13	E
1932			9	E
1933			11	E
1935	PIT	N	1	E

6 yrs. 66 games

Jack Campbell
CAMPBELL, JACK CARTER
B. Dec. 16, 1958, Los Angeles, CA
Southern California/Utah 6'5" 277 lbs.

Year	Team		Games	Pos.
1982	SEA	N	1	OT

Jeff Campbell
CAMPBELL, JEFF
B. Mar. 2, 1968, Denver, CO
Colorado 5'8" 169 lbs.

Year	Team		Games	Pos.
1990	DET	N	16	WR
1991			14	WR
1992			15	WR
1993			10	WR
1994	DEN	N	16	WR

5 yrs. 71 games

Jesse Campbell
CAMPBELL, JESSE
B. Apr. 11, 1969, Washington, NC
North Carolina State 6'1" 215 lbs.

Year	Team		Games	Pos.
1992	NYG	N	11	S
1993			16	S
1994			14	S
1995			16	S
1996			16	S

5 yrs. 73 games

Jimmy Campbell
CAMPBELL, JAMES
B. Jan. 1, 1946, Odessa, TX
West Texas State 6'3" 218 lbs.

Year	Team		Games	Pos.
1969	SD	A	1	LB

Joe Campbell
CAMPBELL, JOSEPH, JR.
B. Dec. 28, 1966, Chandler, AZ
New Mexico State 6'4" 245 lbs.

Year	Team		Games	Pos.
1988	SD	N	16	DE, NT
1989			9	LB

2 yrs. 25 games

Joe Campbell
CAMPBELL, JOSEPH PATRICK
B. May 8, 1955, Wilmington, DE
Maryland 6'6" 253 lbs.

Year	Team		Games	Pos.
1977	NO	N	14	DE
1978			16	DE
1979			10	DE
1980			5	DE
1980	OAK	N	10	DE
1981			3	DE
1981	TB	N	7	DE

5 yrs. 65 games

John Campbell
CAMPBELL, JOHN WILLIAM
B. Oct. 7, 1938, Wadena, MN
Minnesota 6'3" 222 lbs.

Year	Team		Games	Pos.
1963	MIN	N	14	LB
1964			14	LB
1965	PIT	N	14	LB
1966			13	LB
1967			14	LB
1968			8	LB
1969			3	LB
1969	BAL	N	8	LB

7 yrs. 88 games

Ken Campbell
CAMPBELL, KEN
B. 1939
West Chester State 6'1" 213 lbs.

Year	Team		Games	Pos.
1960	NY	A		OE

Year	Team	Games	Pos.

Leon Campbell
CAMPBELL, LEON (Muscles)
B. Jul. 1, 1927, Bauxite, AR
Arkansas 6'0" 199 lbs.

Year	Team		Games	Pos.
1950	BAL	N	5	FB
1952	CHIB	N	8	FB
1953			11	FB
1954			6	FB
1955	PIT	N	12	FB
5 yrs.	42 games			

Marion Campbell
CAMPBELL, FRANCIS MARION
B. May 25, 1959, Chester, SC
Georgia 6'3" 250 lbs.

Year	Team		Games	Pos.
1954	SF	N	12	T
1955			11	T
1956	PHI	N	12	T
1957			10	T
1958			11	T
1959			12	T
1960			12	T
1961			14	DE
8 yrs.	94 games			

Matthew Campbell
CAMPBELL, MATTHEW
B. Jul. 14, 1972, North Augusta, SC
South Carolina 6'4" 270 lbs.

Year	Team		Games	Pos.
1995	CAR	N	10	TE
1996			9	OT
2 yrs.	19 games			

Mike Campbell
CAMPBELL, MICHAEL
B. May 29, 1945, Altavista, VA
Lenoir-Rhyne 5'11" 200 lbs.

Year	Team		Games	Pos.
1968	DET	N	3	RB

Milt Campbell
CAMPBELL, MILTON G.
B. Dec. 9, 1933, Plainfield, NJ
Indiana 6'3" 217 lbs.

Year	Team		Games	Pos.
1957	CLE	N	9	HB

Rich Campbell
CAMPBELL, RICARD DELANO
B. Dec. 21, 1958, Miami, FL
California 6'4" 224 lbs.

Year	Team		Games	Pos.
1981	GB	N	2	QB
1982			1	QB
1983			1	QB
1984			3	QB
4 yrs.	7 games			

Russ Campbell
CAMPBELL, RUSSELL LEE
B. Apr. 2, 1969, Columbus, OH
Kansas State 6'5" 259 lbs.

Year	Team		Games	Pos.
1992	PIT	N	7	TE

Scott Campbell
CAMPBELL, ROBERT SCOTT
B. Apr. 15, 1962, Hershey, PA
Purdue 6'0" 195 lbs.

Year	Team		Games	Pos.
1984	PIT	N	5	QB
1985			16	QB
1986			3	QB
1986	ATL	N	1	QB
1987			12	QB
1989			1	QB
1990			7	QB
6 yrs.	45 games			

Sonny Campbell
CAMPBELL, SONNY

Sonny Campbell *continued*
B. Mar. 5, 1948, Marana, AZ
Northern Arizona 5'11" 192 lbs.

Year	Team		Games	Pos.
1970	ATL	N	11	RB
1971			14	RB
2 yrs.	25 games			

Stan Campbell
CAMPBELL, STANLEY
B. Aug. 26, 1930, Rochelle, IL
Iowa State 6'0" 226 lbs.

Year	Team		Games	Pos.
1952	DET	N	3	G
1955			7	G
1956			7	G
1957			12	G
1958			12	G
1959	PHI	N	12	G
1960			12	G
1962	OAK	A	14	G
8 yrs.	79 games			

Tommy Campbell
CAMPBELL, GEORGE THOMAS
B. Dec. 30, 1949, New York, NY
Iowa State 6'0" 188 lbs.

Year	Team		Games	Pos.
1976	PHI	N	14	CB

Woody Campbell
CAMPBELL, WOODROW LAMAR
B. Sep. 26, 1944, Mount Pleasant, FL
Northwestern 5'11" 205 lbs.

Year	Team		Games	Pos.
1967	HOU	A	14	RB
1968			14	RB
1969			4	RB
1970	HOU	N	6	RB
1971			12	RB
5 yrs.	50 games			

James Campen
CAMPEN, JAMES F.
B. Jun. 11, 1964, Sacramento, CA
Tulane 6'3" 260 lbs.

Year	Team		Games	Pos.
1987	NO	N	3	C
1988			12	C
1989	GB	N	15	C
1990			16	C
1991			13	C
1992			13	C
1993			4	C
7 yrs.	76 games			

Billy Campfield
CAMPFIELD, WILLIAM
B. Aug. 20, 1956, Las Vegas, NV
Kansas 5'11" 200 lbs.

Year	Team		Games	Pos.
1978	PHI	N	16	RB
1979			16	RB
1980			15	RB
1981			16	RB
1982			6	RB
1983	NYG	N	4	RB
6 yrs.	73 games			

Bob Campiglio
CAMPIGLIO, ROBERT F.
B. 1908
West Liberty State 6'1" 183 lbs.

Year	Team		Games	Pos.
1932	SI	N	11	QB
1933	BOS	N	5	HB
2 yrs.	16 games			

T.G. Campion
CAMPION, THOMAS G.
B. 1921
Southeastern Louisiana 6'2" 235 lbs.

Year	Team		Games	Pos.
1947	PHI	N	5	T

Nick Campofreda
CAMPOFREDA, NICHOLAS
B. Jan. 14, 1914, Baltimore, MD
D. Jun., 1959
Western Maryland 6'1" 240 lbs.

Year	Team		Games	Pos.
1944	WAS	N	3	C, T, G

Don Campora
CAMPORA, DONALD CARLO
B. Aug. 30, 1927
D. Jun. 5, 1978, San Bernardino, CA
Pacific 6'3" 268 lbs.

Year	Team		Games	Pos.
1950	SF	N	12	T
1952			8	T
1953	WAS	N	5	T
3 yrs.	25 games			

Alan Campos
CAMPOS, ALAN
B. Mar. 3, 1973, Miami, FL
Louisville 6'3" 236 lbs.

Year	Team		Games	Pos.
1996	DAL	N	15	LB

Larry Canada
CANADA, LAWRENCE L.
B. Dec. 16, 1954, Chicago, IL
Wisconsin 6'2" 233 lbs.

Year	Team		Games	Pos.
1978	DEN	N	16	FB
1979			16	FB
1981			16	RB
3 yrs.	48 games			

Tony Canadeo
CANADEO, ANTHONY ROBERT
(The Gray Ghost of Gonzaga)
B. May 5, 1919, Chicago, IL
Gonzaga 5'11" 190 lbs.

Year	Team		Games	Pos.
1941	GB	N	10	HB
1942			11	HB
1943			10	HB
1944			3	HB
1946			11	HB
1947			12	HB
1948			12	HB
1949			12	HB
1950			12	HB
1951			12	HB
1952			12	HB
11 yrs.	117 games			

Jim Canady
CANADY, JAMES MAURICE
B. Jan. 14, 1926, Austin, TX
Texas/Arkansas-Monticello/Texas 5'10" 178 lbs.

Year	Team		Games	Pos.
1948	CHIB	N		B
1949	CHIB	N		B
1949	NYB	N	7	B
2 yrs.	7 games			

Justin Canale
CANALE JUSTIN DOMINIC
B. Apr. 11, 1943, Memphis, TN
Mississippi State 6'2" 242 lbs.

Year	Team		Games	Pos.
1965	BOS	A	14	G
1966			14	G
1967			14	G
1968			13	G
1969	CIN	A	8	G
5 yrs.	63 games			

Rocco Canale
CANALE, ROCCO P.
B. May 1, 1917, Boston, MA
Boston College 5'11" 240 lbs.

Year	Team		Games	Pos.
1943	P, P		3	G
1944	PHI	N	9	T

Rocco Canale *continued*

Year	Team		Games	Pos.
1945			3	T
1946	BOS	N	11	G
1947			10	T
5 yrs.	36 games			

Whit Canale
CANALE, WHIT
B. Dec. 27, 1941
Tennessee 6'3" 145 lbs.

Year	Team		Games	Pos.
1966	MIA	A	3	DE

Phil Cancik
CANCIK, PHILLIP
B. Apr. 19, 1957, South Bend, IN
Northern Arizona 6'1" 228 lbs.

Year	Team		Games	Pos.
1980	NYG	N	5	LB
1981	KC	N	15	LB
2 yrs.	20 games			

Sheldon Canley
CANLEY, SHELDON LAVELL
B. Apr. 19, 1968, Santa Barbara, CA
San Jose State 5'9" 195 lbs.

Year	Team		Games	Pos.
1992	NYJ	N	1	RB

John Cannady
CANNADY, JOHN HANLEY
B. May 9, 1924
Indiana 6'2" 227 lbs.

Year	Team		Games	Pos.
1947	NYG	N	11	B, LB
1948			12	C, LB
1949			12	LB
1950			11	LB
1951			12	LB
1952			12	LB
1953			12	LB
1954			10	LB
8 yrs.	92 games			

Pat Cannamela
CANNAMELA, PATTERSON N.
B. Apr. 27, 1929
D. Jan. 28, 1973, Hollywood, CA
Southern California 6'0" 195 lbs.

Year	Team		Games	Pos.
1952	DAL	N	11	G, FB, C

Tony Cannava
CANNAVA, ANTHONY LOUIS
B. May 24, 1924, Boston, MA
Boston College 5'10" 180 lbs.

Year	Team		Games	Pos.
1950	GB	N	1	HB

Joe Cannavino
CANNAVINO, JOSEPH P.
B. Jan. 20, 1935, Cleveland, OH
Ohio State 5'11" 186 lbs.

Year	Team		Games	Pos.
1960	OAK	A		DB
1961			14	DB
1962	BUF	A	4	DB
3 yrs.	18 games			

John Cannella
CANNELLA, JOHN M.
B. Apr. 6, 1908
D. Mar. 8, 1989, Queens, NY
Fordham 6'1" 199 lbs.

Year	Team		Games	Pos.
1933	NYG	N	10	G, C
1934			2	G, T
1934	BKN	N	1	T
2 yrs.	13 games			

Billy Cannon
CANNON, WILLIAM ABB
B. Aug. 2, 1937, Philadelphia, MS

Year	Team		Games	Pos.

Billy Cannon *continued*
Louisiana State 6'1" 216 lbs.

Year	Team		Games	Pos.
1960	**HOU**	A	14	HB
1961			14	HB
1962			14	HB
1963			6	HB
1964	**OAK**	A	14	HB, FB
1965			10	OE
1966			14	TE
1967			14	TE
1968			14	TE
1969			13	TE
1970	**KC**	A		TE

11 yrs.　127 games

Billy Cannon
CANNON, BILLY
B. Oct. 8, 1961, Baton Rouge, LA
Texas A&M 6'4" 231 lbs.

1984	**DAL**	N	8	LB

John Cannon
CANNON, JOHN RAYMOND
B. Jul. 30, 1960, Long Branch, NJ
William & Mary 6'5" 260 lbs.

1982	**TB**	N	9	DE
1983			14	DE
1984			16	DE
1985			16	DE
1986			9	DE
1987			11	DE
1988			16	DE
1989			16	DE
1990			15	DE

9 yrs.　122 games

Mark Cannon
CANNON, MARK MAIDA
B. Jun. 14, 1962, Whittier, CA
Texas-Arlington 6'3" 268 lbs.

1984	**GB**	N	16	C
1985			14	C
1986			7	C
1987			12	C
1988			16	C
1989			4	C
1989	**KC**	N	11	C
1991	**IND**	N	4	C

7 yrs.　84 games

Leo Cantor
CANTOR, LEO
B. Feb. 28, 1919, Chicago, IL
UCLA 6'0" 195 lbs.

1942	**NYG**	N	10	FB
1945	**CHIC**	N	10	HB

2 yrs.　20 games

Bill Capece
CAPECE, WILLIAM GEORGE
B. Apr. 1, 1959, Miami, FL
Florida State 5'7" 170 lbs.

1981	**TB**	N	13	K
1982			9	K
1983			15	K

3 yrs.　37 games

James Capers
CAPERS, JAMES
B. Jun. 14, 1958, Kalamazoo, MI
Central Michigan 6'4" 232 lbs.

1987	**CLE**	N	3	DE, LB

Wayne Capers
CAPERS, WAYNE ERWIN
B. May 17, 1961, Miami, FL

Year	Team		Games	Pos.

Wayne Capers *continued*
Kansas 6'2" 193 lbs.

Year	Team		Games	Pos.
1983	**PIT**	N	11	WR
1984			16	WR
1985	**IND**	N	14	WR
1986			6	WR

4 yrs.　47 games

Warren Capone
CAPONE, WARREN SAMUEL
B. Aug. 14, 1951, Baton Rouge, LA
Louisiana State 6'1" 218 lbs.

1975	**DAL**	N	5	LB
1976	**NO**	N	7	LB

2 yrs.　12 games

Dick Capp
CAPP, RICHARD FRANCIS
B. Apr. 9, 1944, Portland, ME
Boston College 6'3" 235 lbs.

1967	**GB**	N	2	TE
1968	**PIT**	N	14	LB

2 yrs.　16 games

Bob Cappadona
CAPPADONA, ROBERT JOSEPH
B. Dec. 13, 1942, Watertown, MA
Northeastern 6'1" 230 lbs.

1966	**BOS**	A	14	FB
1967			13	FB
1968	**BUF**	A	14	FB

3 yrs.　41 games

Gino Cappelletti
CAPPELLETTI, GINO (Duke)
B. Mar. 26, 1934, Keewatin, MN
Minnesota 6'0" 190 lbs.

1960	**BOS**	A	14	DB, K
1961			14	OE, K
1962			14	OE, K
1963			14	OE, K
1964			14	OE, K
1965			14	OE, K
1966			14	FL, K
1967			14	FL, K
1968			14	WR, K
1969			14	WR, K
1970	**BOS**	N	13	WR, K

11 yrs.　153 games

John Cappelletti
CAPPELLETTI, JOHN RAYMOND
B. Aug. 9, 1952, Philadelphia, PA
Penn State 6'1" 219 lbs.

1974	**LA**	N	14	RB
1975			13	RB
1976			14	RB
1977			14	RB
1978			14	RB
1980	**SD**	N	10	RB
1981			16	RB
1982			9	RB
1983			1	RB

9 yrs.　105 games

Bill Cappelman
CAPPELMAN, GEORGE WILLIAM
B. Mar. 12, 1947, Brooksville, FL
Florida State 6'3" 210 lbs.

1970	**MIN**	N	1	QB
1973	**DET**	N	7	QB

2 yrs.　8 games

Tom Capps
CAPPS, THOMAS WILBORN (Bill)

Year	Team		Games	Pos.

Tom Capps *continued*
B. Jun. 23, 1904, Coalville, OK
East Central State (Oklahoma) 6'1" 233 lbs.

Year	Team		Games	Pos.
1929	**FRA**	N	5	T, G
1930			8	T, G
1930	**MIN**	N	1	T

2 yrs.　14 games

Carl Capria
CAPRIA, CARL DANIEL
B. Jun. 8, 1952, New York, NY
Purdue 6'3" 185 lbs.

1974	**DET**	N	12	S
1975	**NYJ**	N	1	S

2 yrs.　13 games

Ralph Capron
CAPRON, RALPH EARL
B. Jun. 16, 1889, Minneapolis, MN
D. Sep. 19, 1980, Los Angeles, CA
Minnesota 5'11" 165 lbs.

1920	**CHIT**	A	1	HB

Jim Capuzzi
CAPUZZI, JAMES
B. Mar. 12, 1932, Niles, OH
Cincinnati 6'0" 190 lbs.

1955	**GB**	N	3	DB
1956			7	DB

2 yrs.　10 games

Dom Cara
CARA, DOMINIC (Mac)
B. 1914
North Carolina State 5'10" 193 lbs.

1937	**PIT**	N	10	E
1938			8	E

2 yrs.　18 games

Roland Caranci
CARANCI, ROLAND
B. Mar. 4, 1921, Marshall, CO
Colorado 6'1" 227 lbs.

1944	**NYG**	N	2	G, T

Glenn Carano
CARANO, GLENN THOMAS
B. Nov. 18, 1955, San Pedro, CA
Nevada-Las Vegas 6'3" 199 lbs.

1978	**DAL**	N	2	QB
1979			3	QB
1980			3	QB
1981			5	QB
1982			7	QB
1983			16	QB

6 yrs.　36 games

Al Carapella
CARAPELLA, ALFRED RICHARD
B. Apr. 26, 1927, Tuckahoe, NY
Miami (Florida) 6'0" 235 lbs.

1951	**SF**	N	12	T
1952			12	T
1953			12	T
1954			12	T
1955			12	T

5 yrs.　60 games

Joe Caravello
CARAVELLO, JOSEPH J.
B. Jun. 6, 1963, Santa Monica, CA
Tulane 6'3" 270 lbs.

1987	**WAS**	N	11	TE
1988			12	TE
1989	**SD**	N	12	TE

Year	Team		Games	Pos.

Joe Caravello *continued*

Year	Team		Games	Pos.
1990			7	TE

4 yrs.　42 games

Glen Carberry
CARBERRY, GLENN M. (Judge)
B. Apr. 10, 1896, Ames, IA
D. Feb. 19, 1976, New York, NY
Army/Notre Dame 6'0" 190 lbs.

1923	**BUF**	N	10	E, T
1924			2	E
1925	**CLE**	N	1	E

3 yrs.　13 games

Harper Card
CARD, J. HARPER
B. 1903
Deceased
None 6'1" 183 lbs.

1921	**LOU**	A	1	T
1922	**LOU**	N	4	T, G

2 yrs.　5 games

Carl Cardarelli
CARDARELLI, CARLO (Squash)
B. Sep. 8, 1895
D. Aug. 11, 1969, San Jose, CA
None 5'9" 170 lbs.

1924	**AKR**	N	2	C
1925	**CLE**	N	1	C

2 yrs.　3 games

Fred Cardinal
CARDINAL, FREDERICK
B. Feb. 12, 1925, Dover, OH
Baldwin-Wallace 5'11" 220 lbs.

1947	**NY**	AA	1	B

Joe Cardwell
CARDWELL, JOSEPH T.
B. 1914
D. Jul. 6, 1957
Duke 6'3" 235 lbs.

1937	**PIT**	N	6	T, E, G
1938			11	T, G

2 yrs.　17 games

John Cardwell
CARDWELL, JOHN
B. Jul. 28, 1893
D. May, 1974, Wilmington, OH
None 5'9" 170 lbs.

1923	**STL**	N	2	QB, HB

Lloyd Cardwell
CARDWELL, LLOYD R.
B. Apr. 19, 1913, Republic, KS
Nebraska 6'2" 195 lbs.

1937	**DET**	N	9	WB, DB
1938			10	WB, DB
1939			10	WB, DB
1940			10	WB, DB
1941			4	WB, DB
1942			7	WB, DB
1943			7	WB, DB

7 yrs.　57 games

Bob Carey
CAREY, ROBERT W.
B. Feb. 8, 1930, Charleroi, MI
D. Oct. 25, 1988, Cincinnati, OH
Michigan State 6'5" 219 lbs.

1952	**LA**	N	12	E
1954			2	E
1956			7	E

Year	Team		Games	Pos.

Bob Carey continued

Year	Team		Games	Pos.
1958	CHIB	N	11	E
4 yrs.	32 games			

Brian Carey
CAREY, BRIAN
B. Nov. 6, 1963
American International 6'0" 200 lbs.

Year	Team		Games	Pos.
1987	NE	N	2	WR

Dana Carey
CAREY, H. DANA
B. 1903
Deceased
California 6'2" 200 lbs.

Year	Team		Games	Pos.
1926	LA	A	3	G

Joe Carey
CAREY, JOSEPH
B. Nov., 1895
D. Jul. 22, 1962
Illinois Tech 6'2" 170 lbs.

Year	Team		Games	Pos.
1920	CHIC	A	4	T, G
1921	GB	A	6	G
2 yrs.	10 games			

Richard Carey
CAREY, RICHARD ANDRE
B. May 6, 1968, Seattle, WA
Idaho 5'9" 185 lbs.

Year	Team		Games	Pos.
1989	CIN	N	7	CB
1990	BUF	N	3	CB, S
2 yrs.	10 games			

Harland Carl
CARL, HARLAND
B. Oct. 1, 1931, Greenwood, WI
Wisconsin 6'0" 195 lbs.

Year	Team		Games	Pos.
1956	CHIB	N	9	HB

Carlson
CARLSON
None

Year	Team		Games	Pos.
1926	LOU	N	1	E

Cody Carlson
CARLSON, MATTHEW CODY
B. Nov. 5, 1963, Dallas, TX
Baylor 6'3" 203 lbs.

Year	Team		Games	Pos.
1988	HOU	N	6	QB
1989			6	QB
1990			6	QB
1991			3	QB
1992			11	QB
1993			8	QB
1994			6	QB
7 yrs.	46 games			

Dean Carlson
CARLSON, DEAN PAUL
B. Aug. 1, 1950, Rushford, MA
Iowa State 6'3" 210 lbs.

Year	Team		Games	Pos.
1974	KC	N	1	QB

Hal Carlson
CARLSON, HAROLD
B. 1915
Northwestern/DePaul 6'3" 220 lbs.

Year	Team		Games	Pos.
1937	CHIC	N	1	T

Irv Carlson
CARLSON, IRVING G.
B. Aug., 1896

Irv Carlson continued

Deceased
St. John's (Minnesota)/Wisconsin 5'8" 170 lbs.

Year	Team		Games	Pos.
1924	KEN	N	2	HB, QB

Jeff Carlson
CARLSON, JEFFREY ALLEN
B. May 23, 1966, Long Beach, CA
Weber State 6'3" 215 lbs.

Year	Team		Games	Pos.
1990	TB	N	1	QB
1991			3	QB
1992	NE	N	3	QB
3 yrs.	7 games			

Mark Carlson
CARLSON, MARK
B. Jun. 6, 1963, Milford, CT
Southern Connecticut State 6'6" 284 lbs.

Year	Team		Games	Pos.
1987	WAS	N	3	OT

Oke Carlson
CARLSON, EUGENE (Curly)
B. Dec. 10, 1897
D. Apr., 1977, Battle Lake, MN
None 6'1" 203 lbs.

Year	Team		Games	Pos.
1924	DUL	N	3	T, G
1925			2	G, T
1926			11	G, C, T
3 yrs.	16 games			

Roy Carlson
CARLSON, ROY H.
B. May 8, 1906, Chicago, IL
D. Sep. 10, 1984, Phoenix, AZ
Bradley 5'9" 178 lbs.

Year	Team		Games	Pos.
1928	CHIB	N	10	E
1929	DAY		6	E, G
2 yrs.	16 games			

Wes Carlson
CARLSON, WESLEY (Brute)
B. Jul. 24, 1901, Michigan
D. Jul. 12, 1989, Benton Harbor, MI
Detroit 6'1" 210 lbs.

Year	Team		Games	Pos.
1926	GB	N	4	G, T

Zuck Carlson
CARLSON, JULES ED
B. Nov. 4, 1904, Isaca, ID
D. Jan. 21, 1986, Chicago, IL
Oregon State 6'0" 208 lbs.

Year	Team		Games	Pos.
1929	CHIB	N	14	G
1930			13	G
1931			11	G, T
1932			12	G
1933			11	G
1934			12	G
1935			11	G, T
1936			9	G
8 yrs.	93 games			

Darryl Carlton
CARLTON, DARRYL
B. Jun. 24, 1953, Barrstow, FL
Deceased
Tampa 6'6" 271 lbs.

Year	Team		Games	Pos.
1975	MIA	N	14	OT
1976			14	OT
1977	TB	N	14	OT
1978			13	OT
1979			16	OT
5 yrs.	71 games			

Wray Carlton
CARLTON, LINWOOD WRAY

Wray Carlton continued

B. Jun. 18, 1937, Wallace, NC
Duke 6'2" 218 lbs.

Year	Team		Games	Pos.
1960	BUF	A	14	FB
1961			14	HB
1962			11	FB
1963			4	FB
1964			4	HB
1965			14	HB
1966			14	HB
1967			12	RB
8 yrs.	87 games			

Charlie Carman
CARMAN, W. CHARLES (Chili)
B. Jan. 6, 1897
D. Nov., 1975, McAllen, TX
Vanderbilt 5'10" 215 lbs.

Year	Team		Games	Pos.
1921	DET	A	6	G

Ed Carman
CARMAN, EDMUND R. (Zeb)
B. Jan. 21, 1894
Deceased
Purdue 5'11" 199 lbs.

Year	Team		Games	Pos.
1922	HAM	N	5	E, T
1925	BUF	N	1	T
1925	HAM		4	T, G
2 yrs.	10 games			

Al Carmichael
CARMICHAEL, ALBERT REINHOLD
B. Nov. 10, 1928, Boston, MA
Southern California 6'1" 192 lbs.

Year	Team		Games	Pos.
1953	GB	N	12	HB
1954			10	HB
1955			12	HB
1956			12	HB
1957			12	HB
1958			12	HB
1960	DEN	A	9	HB
1961			6	HB
8 yrs.	85 games			

Harold Carmichael
CARMICHAEL, LEE HAROLD
B. Sep. 22, 1949, Jacksonville, FL
Southern University 6'7" 255 lbs.

Year	Team		Games	Pos.
1971	PHI	N	9	WR
1972			14	WR
1973			14	WR
1974			14	WR
1975			14	WR
1976			14	WR
1977			14	WR
1978			16	WR
1979			16	WR
1980			16	WR
1981			16	WR
1982			9	WR
1983			15	WR
1984	DAL	N	2	WR
14 yrs.	183 games			

Paul Carmichael
CARMICHAEL, PAUL HAROLD
B. Sep. 7, 1943, Middlesboro, KY
El Camino JC 6'0" 200 lbs.

Year	Team		Games	Pos.
1965	DEN	A	3	HB

Ray Carnelly
CARNELLY, RAYMOND HARRY
B. Aug. 11, 1917, Beaver Falls, PA
Carnegie-Mellon 6'2" 187 lbs.

Year	Team		Games	Pos.
1939	BKN	N	9	HB

Art Carney
CARNEY, ARTHUR G.
B. 1900
Deceased
Navy 6'2" 230 lbs.

Year	Team		Games	Pos.
1925	NYG	N	9	G
1926			8	E, G
2 yrs.	17 games			

Chuck Carney
CARNEY, CHARLES R.
B. Aug. 25, 1900, Chicago, IL
D. Sep. 5, 1984, Manchester, MA
Illinois 6'1" 190 lbs.

Year	Team		Games	Pos.
1922	COL	N	3	T, G

John Carney
CARNEY, JOHN MICHAEL
B. Apr. 20, 1964, Hartford, CT
Notre Dame 5'11" 160 lbs.

Year	Team		Games	Pos.
1988	TB	N	4	K
1989			1	K
1990	LARM		1	K
1990	SD	N	12	K
1991			16	K
1992			16	K
1993			16	K
1994			16	K
1995			16	K
1996			16	K
9 yrs.	114 games			

Brett Carolan
CAROLAN, BRETT
B. Mar. 16, 1971, San Rafael, CA
Washington State 6'3" 241 lbs.

Year	Team		Games	Pos.
1994	SF	N	5	TE
1995			14	TE
1996	MIA	N	6	TE
3 yrs.	25 games			

Reg Carolan
CAROLAN, REGINALD HOWARD
B. Oct. 25, 1939, San Rafael, CA
Idaho 6'6" 235 lbs.

Year	Team		Games	Pos.
1962	SD	A	14	OE
1963			4	OE
1964	KC	A	6	OE
1965			14	OE
1966			14	OE
1967			14	OE
1968			14	TE
7 yrs.	80 games			

J.C. Caroline
CAROLINE, JAMES C.
B. Jan. 17, 1933, Columbia, SC
Illinois 6'1" 190 lbs.

Year	Team		Games	Pos.
1956	CHIB	N	12	RB, DB
1957			12	RB, DB
1958			12	RB, DB
1959			12	DB
1960	CHI	N	12	DB
1961			14	DB
1962			14	DB
1963			14	DB
1964			14	DB
1965			2	DB
10 yrs.	118 games			

Joe Carollo
CAROLLO, JOSEPH PAUL
B. Mar. 25, 1940, Wyandotte, MI
Notre Dame 6'2" 262 lbs.

Year	Team		Games	Pos.
1962	LA	N	13	OT
1963			14	OT
1964			14	OT
1965			14	OT

Joe Carollo continued

Year	Team		Games	Pos.
1966			14	OT
1967			14	OT
1968			14	OT
1969	**PHI**	**N**	14	OT
1970			14	OT
1971	**LA**	**N**	11	OT
1972	**CLE**	**N**	4	OT
1973			12	OT

12 yrs. 152 games

Roger Caron
CARON, ROGER EUGENE
B. Jun. 3, 1962, Boston, MA
Harvard 6'5" 275 lbs.

Year	Team		Games	Pos.
1985	**IND**	**N**	7	OT
1986			3	OT

2 yrs. 10 games

Don Carothers
CAROTHERS, DON
B. May 13, 1934, Moline, IL
Bradley 6'5" 225 lbs.

Year	Team		Games	Pos.
1960	**DEN**	**A**		OE

Joe Carpe
CARPE, JOSEPH
B. Jan. 23, 1903
D. Nov. 4, 1977, Boston, MA
Millikin 6'0" 197 lbs.

Year	Team		Games	Pos.
1926	**FRA**	**N**	5	T, HB, E-G
1927	**POT**	**N**	3	T, G-E
1928			9	T
1929	**BOS**	**N**	6	T
1933	**PHI**	**N**	2	T

5 yrs. 25 games

Brian Carpenter
CARPENTER, BRIAN MILTON
B. Nov. 27, 1960, Flint, MI
Michigan 5'10" 167 lbs.

Year	Team		Games	Pos.
1982	**NYG**	**N**	4	DB
1983	**WAS**	**N**	15	DB
1984			3	CB
1984	**BUF**	**N**	13	CB

3 yrs. 35 games

Jack Carpenter
CARPENTER, JOHN C.
B. Jul. 29, 1923, Kansas City, MO
Columbia/Missouri/Michigan 6'0" 240 lbs.

Year	Team		Games	Pos.
1947	**BUF**	**AA**	13	T
1948			12	T
1949			8	T
1949	**SF**	**AA**	3	T

3 yrs. 36 games

Ken Carpenter
CARPENTER, KENNETH
B. Feb. 26, 1926, Seaside, OR
Oregon State 6'0" 195 lbs.

Year	Team		Games	Pos.
1950	**CLE**	**N**	12	HB
1951			11	HB
1952			8	HB
1953			12	HB
1960	**DEN**	**A**	6	OE

5 yrs. 49 games

Lew Carpenter
CARPENTER, LEWIS GLENN
B. Jan. 12, 1932, Hayti, MO
Arkansas 6'1" 209 lbs.

Year	Team		Games	Pos.
1953	**DET**	**N**	12	HB
1954			11	HB
1955			12	HB
1957	**CLE**	**N**	10	HB

Lew Carpenter continued

Year	Team		Games	Pos.
1958			12	HB
1959	**GB**	**N**	12	FB
1960			12	HB
1961			14	HB
1962			14	HB
1963			14	HB

10 yrs. 123 games

Preston Carpenter
CARPENTER, VERDA PRESTON
B. Jan. 24, 1934, Hayti, MO
Arkansas 6'2" 197 lbs.

Year	Team		Games	Pos.
1956	**CLE**	**N**	12	HB
1957			12	E
1958			12	E
1959			12	E
1960	**PIT**	**N**	12	E
1961			13	OE
1962			13	OE
1963			14	OE
1964	**WAS**	**N**	14	OE
1965			9	OE
1966			1	OE
1966	**MIN**	**N**	13	TE
1967	**MIA**	**A**	13	TE

12 yrs. 150 games

Rob Carpenter
CARPENTER, ROBERT G.
B. Aug. 1, 1968, Amityville, NY
Syracuse 6'2" 215 lbs.

Year	Team		Games	Pos.
1991	**NE**	**N**	8	WR
1992	**NYJ**	**N**	16	WR
1993			16	WR
1994			3	WR
1995	**PHI**	**N**	16	WR

5 yrs. 59 games

Rob Carpenter
CARPENTER, ROBERT J., JR.
B. Apr. 20, 1955, Lancaster, OH
Miami (Ohio) 6'1" 220 lbs.

Year	Team		Games	Pos.
1977	**HOU**	**N**	11	RB
1978			11	RB
1979			16	RB
1980			15	RB
1981			4	RB
1981	**NYG**	**N**	10	RB
1982			5	RB
1983			10	RB
1984			16	RB
1985			14	RB
1986	**LARM**	**N**	6	RB

10 yrs. 118 games

Ron Carpenter
CARPENTER, RON
B. Jan. 20, 1970, Cincinnati, OH
Miami (Ohio) 6'1" 188 lbs.

Year	Team		Games	Pos.
1993	**MIN**	**N**	7	S
1993	**CIN**	**N**	6	S
1995	**NYJ**	**N**	13	S
1996			2	S

3 yrs. 28 games

Ron Carpenter
CARPENTER, RONALD NELSON
B. Jun. 24, 1958, High Point, NC
North Carolina State 6'4" 261 lbs.

Year	Team		Games	Pos.
1970	**CIN**	**N**	14	DE
1971			14	DE
1972			14	DE
1973			13	DT
1974			14	DT
1975			14	DT
1976			14	DT

7 yrs. 97 games

Ronnie Carpenter
CARPENTER, RONNIE D.
B. Sep. 2, 1941, Marshall, TX
Texas A&M 6'2" 230 lbs.

Year	Team		Games	Pos.
1964	**SD**	**A**	12	LB
1965			6	LB

2 yrs. 18 games

Steve Carpenter
CARPENTER, STEVE
B. Jan. 22, 1958, Staunton, IL
Western Illinois 6'2" 195 lbs.

Year	Team		Games	Pos.
1980	**NYJ**	**N**	3	S
1981	**STL**	**N**	1	CB

2 yrs. 4 games

Carl Carr
CARR, CARL
B. Mar. 26, 1964, South Boston, VA
North Carolina 6'3" 230 lbs.

Year	Team		Games	Pos.
1987	**DET**	**N**	3	LB

Chetti Carr
CARR, CHETTI
B. Jan. 1, 1963
Northwestern Oklahoma State 5'9" 185 lbs.

Year	Team		Games	Pos.
1987	**LARI**	**N**	2	CB

Earl Carr
CARL, EARL
B. Jan. 2, 1955, Tallassee, AL
Florida 6'0" 224 lbs.

Year	Team		Games	Pos.
1978	**SF**	**N**	14	RB
1979	**PHI**	**N**	1	RB

2 yrs. 15 games

Ed Carr
CARR, EDWIN FORREST
B. Apr. 27, 1927
none 6'0" 185 lbs.

Year	Team		Games	Pos.
1947	**SF**	**AA**	10	B
1948			13	B
1949			7	B

3 yrs. 30 games

Freddie Carr
CARR, FRED ALTON
B. Aug. 19, 1946, Phoenix, AZ
Texas-El Paso 6'5" 239 lbs.

Year	Team		Games	Pos.
1968	**GB**	**N**	14	LB
1969			14	LB
1970			14	LB
1971			14	LB
1972			14	LB
1973			14	LB
1974			14	LB
1975			14	LB
1976			14	LB
1977			14	LB

10 yrs. 140 games

Gregg Carr
CARR, GREGG KEVIN
B. Mar. 31, 1962, Birmingham, AL
Auburn 6'1" 220 lbs.

Year	Team		Games	Pos.
1985	**PIT**	**N**	16	LB
1986			16	LB
1987			12	LB
1988			13	LB

4 yrs. 57 games

Harlan Carr
CARR, HARLAN B. (Whippety, Gotch)
B. Apr. 30, 1903

Harlan Carr continued
D. Oct. 24, 1970, Auburn, NY
Syracuse 5'10" 165 lbs.

Year	Team		Games	Pos.
1927	**BUF**	**N**	5	HB, QB
1927	**POT**	**N**	6	HB

1 yr. 11 games

Henry Carr
CARR, HENRY JOSEPH
B. Nov. 27, 1942, Detroit, MI
Arizona State 6'3" 198 lbs.

Year	Team		Games	Pos.
1965	**NYG**	**N**	14	DB
1966			14	DB
1967			9	DB

3 yrs. 37 games

Jimmy Carr
CARR, JIMMY
B. Mar. 25, 1933, Kayford, WV
Charleston 6'1" 206 lbs.

Year	Team		Games	Pos.
1955	**CHIC**	**N**	12	RB, DB
1957			6	DB
1959	**PHI**	**N**	12	DB
1960			10	DB
1961			13	DB
1962			14	DB
1963			14	DB
1964	**WAS**	**N**	14	DB
1965			13	LB

9 yrs. 108 games

Lee Carr
CARR, CLYTUS HENRY
B. Jan. 21, 1904, Otsego, MI
D. Nov. 1, 1976, Marshall, MI
Western Michigan 5'10" 175 lbs.

Year	Team		Games	Pos.
1926	**HAM**	**N**	2	FB, HB

Levert Carr
CARR, LEVERT
B. Jun. 30, 1944, Birmingham, AL
North Central (Illinois) 6'5" 258 lbs.

Year	Team		Games	Pos.
1969	**SD**	**A**	7	DT
1970	**BUF**	**N**	6	OT
1971			14	OT, G
1972	**HOU**	**N**	14	OT
1973			13	OT

5 yrs. 54 games

Lydell Carr
CARR, LYDELL
B. May 27, 1965, Enid, OK
Oklahoma 6'1" 228 lbs.

Year	Team		Games	Pos.
1989	**PHX**	**N**	5	RB

Paul Carr
CARR, PAUL (Rock)
B. 1932, Los Angeles, CA
Houston 6'0" 205 lbs.

Year	Team		Games	Pos.
1955	**SF**	**N**	10	FB, LB
1956			12	HB, LB
1957			8	LB

3 yrs. 30 games

Reggie Carr
CARR, REGINALD
B. Feb. 17, 1963
Jackson State 6'3" 300 lbs.

Year	Team		Games	Pos.
1987	**NYG**	**N**	3	DE

Roger Carr
CARR, ROGER DALE
B. Jul. 1, 1952, Seminole, OK
Louisiana Tech 6'3" 196 lbs.

Year	Team		Games	Pos.
1974	**BAL**	**N**	11	WR
1975			14	WR

Roger Carr continued

Year	Team		Games	Pos.
1976			14	WR
1977			7	WR
1978			16	WR
1979			9	WR
1980			16	WR
1981			15	WR
1982	SEA	N	9	WR
1983	SD	N	4	WR
10 yrs. 115 games				

Tom Carr
CARR, THOMAS WINTHER
B. Apr. 4, 1942, Philadelphia, PA
Morgan State 6'3" 267 lbs.

Year	Team		Games	Pos.
1968	NO	N	4	DT

Alphonso Carreker
CARREKER, ALPHONSO
B. May 25, 1962, Columbus, OH
Florida State 6'6" 270 lbs.

Year	Team		Games	Pos.
1984	GB	N	14	DE
1985			16	DE
1986			16	DE
1987			12	DE
1988			14	DE
1989	DEN	N	16	DE
1991			6	DE
7 yrs. 94 games				

Vince Carreker
CARREKER, VINCENT
B. Aug. 21, 1963
Central State (Ohio)/Cincinnati 6'0" 183 lbs.

Year	Team		Games	Pos.
1987	CLE	N	2	S, CB

Duane Carrell
CARRELL, DUANE BLORE
B. Oct. 3, 1949, Washington, DC
Florida State 5'10" 184 lbs.

Year	Team		Games	Pos.
1974	DAL	N	7	P
1975	LA	N	14	P
1976	NYJ	N	14	P
1977			2	P
1977	STL	N	10	P
4 yrs. 47 games				

John Carrell
CARRELL, JOHN
B. Dec. 19, 1942
Texas Tech 6'3" 227 lbs.

Year	Team		Games	Pos.
1966	HOU	A	8	LB

Mark Carrier
CARRIER, JOHN MARK
B. Oct. 28, 1965, Lafayette, LA
Nicholls State 6'0" 182 lbs.

Year	Team		Games	Pos.
1987	TB	N	10	WR
1988			16	WR
1989			16	WR
1990			16	WR
1991			16	WR
1992			14	WR
1993	CLE	N	16	WR
1994			16	WR
1995	CAR	N	16	WR
1996			16	WR
10 yrs. 152 games				

Mark Carrier
CARRIER, MARK ANTHONY
B. Apr. 28, 1968, Lake Charles, LA
Southern California 6'1" 188 lbs.

Year	Team		Games	Pos.
1990	CHI	N	16	S
1991			16	S
1992			16	S

Mark Carrier continued

Year	Team		Games	Pos.
1993			16	S
1994			16	S
1995			16	S
1996			13	S
7 yrs. 109 games				

Darren Carrington
CARRINGTON, DARREN RUSSELL
B. Oct. 10, 1966, Bronx, NY
Northern Arizona 6'1" 189 lbs.

Year	Team		Games	Pos.
1989	DEN	N	16	CB
1990	DET	N	12	CB
1991	SD	N	16	CB, S
1992			16	S
1993			16	S
1994			16	S
1995	JAC	N	6	S
1996	OAK	N	15	S
8 yrs. 113 games				

Ed Carrington
CARRINGTON, EDWARD
B. Sep. 1, 1944, Beaumont, TX
Virginia 6'4" 225 lbs.

Year	Team		Games	Pos.
1969	HOU	A	14	TE

Russ Carroccio
CARROCCIO, RUSSELL
B. Apr. 28, 1931
Virginia 6'1" 235 lbs.

Year	Team		Games	Pos.
1954	NYG	N	9	G
1955			5	G
1955	PHI	N	7	G, T
2 yrs. 21 games				

Bart Carroll
CARROLL, BART J.
B. Dec. 29, 1893
D. Aug. 1, 1967, Schenectady, NY
Colgate 5'11" 180 lbs.

Year	Team		Games	Pos.
1920	ROC	A	1	T

Bird Carroll
CARROLL, ELMER E.
B. Jul. 25, 1896
D. Aug. 6, 1982, Winter Park, FL
Washington & Jefferson 5'8" 185 lbs.

Year	Team		Games	Pos.
1921	CAN	A	5	E
1922	CAN	N	12	E
1923			9	E
1925			7	E
4 yrs. 33 games				

Gene Carroll
CARROLL, HARRY EUGENE
B. Jul., 1897, Wood County, WV
Deceased
Marietta (Freshmen) 5'10" 170 lbs.

Year	Team		Games	Pos.
1922	COL	N	4	E, G, T

Herman Carroll
CARROLL, HERMAN
B. Jun. 20, 1971, Natchez, MS
Mississippi State 6'4" 265 lbs.

Year	Team		Games	Pos.
1994	NO	N	5	DE

Jay Carroll
CARROLL, JAY TIMOTHY
B. Nov. 8, 1961, Winona, MN
Minnesota 6'4" 230 lbs.

Year	Team		Games	Pos.
1984	TB	N	16	TE
1985	MIN	N	16	TE
2 yrs. 32 games				

Jim Carroll
CARROLL, JAMES S.
B. May 6, 1943, Jonesboro, AR
Notre Dame 6'1" 229 lbs.

Year	Team		Games	Pos.
1965	NYG	N	14	LB
1966			1	LB
1966	WAS	N	13	LB
1967			14	LB
1968			14	LB
1969	NY	A	6	LB
5 yrs. 62 games				

Joe Carroll
CARROLL, JOSEPH WALKER
B. May 29, 1950, Warren, OH
Pittsburgh 6'1" 220 lbs.

Year	Team		Games	Pos.
1972	OAK	N	13	LB
1973			9	LB
2 yrs. 22 games				

Leo Carroll
CARROLL, LEO
B. Feb. 16, 1944, Alhambra, CA
Tulsa/San Diego State 6'7" 250 lbs.

Year	Team		Games	Pos.
1968	GB	N	6	DE
1969	WAS	N	14	DE
1970			7	DE
3 yrs. 27 games				

Ronnie Carroll
CARROLL, RONNIE
B. Apr. 11, 1949, Galveston, TX
Sam Houston State 6'2" 265 lbs.

Year	Team		Games	Pos.
1974	HOU	N	14	G

Vic Carroll
CARROLL, VICTOR E.
B. Nov. 19, 1912, Alhambra, CA
D. Jul., 1986, Mission Viejo, CA
Nevada-Reno 6'4" 231 lbs.

Year	Team		Games	Pos.
1936	BOS	N	6	T, G
1937	WAS	N	10	G, T, C
1938			10	C
1939			11	C
1940			11	C
1941			10	G
1942			4	G
1943	NYG	N	10	T, G
1944			9	T
1945			2	T
1946			6	T
1947			11	E
12 yrs. 100 games				

Wesley Carroll
CARROLL, WESLEY
B. Sep. 6, 1967, Cleveland, OH
Miami (Florida) 6'0" 183 lbs.

Year	Team		Games	Pos.
1991	NO	N	12	WR
1992			16	WR
1993	CIN	N	12	WR
3 yrs. 40 games				

Paul Ott Carruth
CARRUTH, PAUL OTT
B. Jul. 12, 1961, Hattiesburg, MS
Alabama 6'1" 220 lbs.

Year	Team		Games	Pos.
1986	GB	N	16	RB
1987			12	RB
1988			15	RB
1989	KC	N	2	RB
4 yrs. 45 games				

Carlos Carson
CARSON, CARLOS A.
B. Dec. 28, 1958, Lake Worth, FL

Carlos Carson continued

Louisiana State 5'11" 184 lbs.

Year	Team		Games	Pos.
1980	KC	N	16	WR
1981			5	WR
1982			9	WR
1983			16	WR
1984			16	WR
1985			15	WR
1986			10	WR
1987			12	WR
1988			14	WR
1989			7	WR
1989	PHI	N	6	WR
10 yrs. 126 games				

Harry Carson
CARSON, HAROLD DONALD
B. Nov. 26, 1953, Florence, SC
South Carolina State 6'2" 240 lbs.

Year	Team		Games	Pos.
1976	NYG	N	12	LB
1977			14	LB
1978			16	LB
1979			16	LB
1980			8	LB
1981			16	LB
1982			9	LB
1983			10	LB
1984			16	LB
1985			16	LB
1986			16	LB
1987			12	LB
1988			12	LB
13 yrs. 173 games				

Howard Carson
CARSON, HUELAND HOWARD
B. Feb. 11, 1957, Hico, TX
Howard Payne 6'2" 233 lbs.

Year	Team		Games	Pos.
1981	LA	N	10	LB
1982	LARM	N	2	LB
1983			16	LB
3 yrs. 28 games				

Howie Carson
CARSON, HOWARD W.
B. 1915
D. Jan. 14, 1980
Illinois 6'0" 190 lbs.

Year	Team		Games	Pos.
1944	CLE	N	1	T

Johnny Carson
CARSON, JOHNNY RICHARD
B. Jan. 31, 1930, Atlanta, GA
Georgia 6'3" 202 lbs.

Year	Team		Games	Pos.
1954	WAS	N	12	E
1955			12	E
1956			12	E
1957			12	E
1958			4	E
1959			5	E
1960	HOU	A		OE
7 yrs. 57 games				

Kern Carson
CARSON, KERN
B. 1942
San Diego State 6'0" 202 lbs.

Year	Team		Games	Pos.
1965	SD	A	3	HB
1965	NY	A	10	HB
1 yr. 13 games				

Malcolm Carson
CARSON, MALCOLM DARRYL
B. Nov. 1, 1959, Birmingham, AL
Tennessee-Chattanooga 6'2" 260 lbs.

Year	Team		Games	Pos.
1984	MIN	N	1	G

Year	Team	Games	Pos.

Dwayne Carswell
CARSWELL, DWAYNE
B. Jan. 18, 1972, Jacksonville, FL
Liberty 6'3" 261 lbs.

Year	Team		Games	Pos.
1994	DEN	N	4	TE
1995			9	TE
1996			16	TE

3 yrs. 29 games

Alex Carter
CARTER, ALEX
B. Sep. 6, 1963, Miami, FL
Tennessee State 6'3" 255 lbs.

Year	Team		Games	Pos.
1987	CLE	N	3	DE

Allen Carter
CARTER, ALLEN
B. Dec. 12, 1952, Pomona, CA
Southern California 5'11" 208 lbs.

Year	Team		Games	Pos.
1975	NE	N	14	FB
1976			1	FB

2 yrs. 15 games

Anthony Carter
CARTER, ANTHONY
B. Sep. 17, 1960, Riviera Beach, FL
Michigan 5'11" 175 lbs.

Year	Team		Games	Pos.
1985	MIN	N	16	WR
1986			12	WR
1987			12	WR
1988			16	WR
1989			16	WR
1990			15	WR
1991			15	WR
1992			16	WR
1993			15	WR
1994	DET	N	4	WR
1995			3	WR

11 yrs. 140 games

Bernard Carter
CARTER, EDWIN BERNARD
B. Aug. 22, 1971, Tallahassee, FL
East Carolina 6'2" 245 lbs.

Year	Team		Games	Pos.
1995	JAC	N	5	LB

Blanchard Carter
CARTER, BLANCHARD
B. Jun. 3, 1955, Stockton, CA
Nevada-Las Vegas 6'4" 250 lbs.

Year	Team		Games	Pos.
1977	TB	N	13	OT

Carl Carter
CARTER, CARL ANTHONY
B. Mar. 7, 1964, Fort Worth, TX
Texas Tech 5'11" 180 lbs.

Year	Team		Games	Pos.
1986	STL	N	14	CB
1987			12	CB
1988	PHX	N	16	CB
1989			15	CB
1990	CIN	N	15	CB
1991	TB	N	11	CB
1992	GB	N	7	CB

7 yrs. 90 games

Cris Carter
CARTER, CRIS
B. Nov. 25, 1965, Middletown, OH
Ohio State 6'3" 194 lbs.

Year	Team		Games	Pos.
1987	PHI	N	9	WR
1988			16	WR
1989			16	WR
1990	MIN	N	16	WR
1991			16	WR
1992			12	WR
1993			16	WR
1994			16	WR

Cris Carter continued

Year	Team	Games	Pos.
1995		16	WR
1996		16	WR

10 yrs. 149 games

Dale Carter
CARTER, DALE LAVELLE
B. Nov. 28, 1969, Covington, GA
Tennessee 6'1" 188 lbs.

Year	Team		Games	Pos.
1992	KC	N	16	CB, S
1993			15	CB
1994			16	CB
1995			16	CB
1996			14	CB

5 yrs. 77 games

David Carter
CARTER, DAVID
B. Nov. 27, 1953, Vincennes, IN
Western Kentucky 6'2" 236 lbs.

Year	Team		Games	Pos.
1977	HOU	N	14	C
1978			16	C
1979			16	C
1980			16	C
1981			16	G, C
1982			9	G, C
1983			16	C
1984			7	C
1984	NO	N	7	C
1985			4	C, G

9 yrs. 121 games

Dexter Carter
CARTER, DEXTER ANTHONY
B. Sep. 15, 1967, Baxley, GA
Florida State 5'9" 170 lbs.

Year	Team		Games	Pos.
1990	SF	N	16	RB
1991			16	RB
1992			3	RB
1993			16	RB
1994			16	RB
1995	NYJ	N	10	RB
1995	SF	N	7	RB
1996			16	RB

7 yrs. 100 games

Gerald Carter
CARTER, GERALD LOUIS
B. Jun. 19, 1957, Bryan, TX
Texas A&M 6'1" 190 lbs.

Year	Team		Games	Pos.
1980	NYJ	N	3	WR
1981	TB	N	16	WR
1982			9	WR
1983			16	WR
1984			16	WR
1985			16	WR
1986			15	WR
1987			12	WR

8 yrs. 103 games

Jim Carter
CARTER, JAMES CHARLES
B. Oct. 18, 1948, St. Paul, MN
Minnesota 6'3" 240 lbs.

Year	Team		Games	Pos.
1970	GB	N	10	LB
1971			10	LB
1972			14	LB
1973			14	LB
1974			14	LB
1975			14	LB
1977			14	LB
1978			14	LB

8 yrs. 104 games

Jimmie Carter
CARTER, JIMMIE
B. Jul. 26, 1961, Weimar, TX
New Mexico 6'1" 220 lbs.

Year	Team		Games	Pos.
1987	STL	N	1	LB

Joe Carter
CARTER, JOSEPH THOMAS
B. Jun. 23, 1962, Starkville, MS
Alabama 5'11" 198 lbs.

Year	Team		Games	Pos.
1984	MIA	N	13	RB
1985			10	RB
1986			7	RB

3 yrs. 30 games

Joe Carter
CARTER, WILLIAM JOSEPH
B. Jul. 23, 1910, Dalhart, TX
Austin 6'1" 201 lbs.

Year	Team		Games	Pos.
1933	PHI	N	8	E
1934			11	E
1935			11	E
1936			9	E
1937			10	E
1938			11	E
1939			11	E
1940			6	E
1942	GB	N	11	E
1944	BKN	N	10	E
1945	CHIC	N	10	E

11 yrs. 108 games

Jon Carter
CARTER, JON S.
B. Mar. 12, 1965, Los Angeles, CA
Pittsburgh 6'4" 273 lbs.

Year	Team		Games	Pos.
1989	DAL	N	13	DT

Kent Carter
CARTER, KENT ALEXANDER
B. May 25, 1950, Los Angeles, CA
Southern California 6'3" 235 lbs.

Year	Team		Games	Pos.
1974	NE	N	3	LB

Kevin Carter
CARTER, KEVIN LOUIS
B. Sep. 21, 1973, Tallahassee, FL
Florida 6'5" 275 lbs.

Year	Team		Games	Pos.
1995	STL	N	16	DE
1996			16	DE

2 yrs. 32 games

Ki-Jana Carter
CARTER, KENNETH LEONARD
B. Sep. 12, 1973, Westerville, OH
Penn State 5'10" 227 lbs.

Year	Team		Games	Pos.
1996	CIN	N	16	RB

Louis Carter
CARTER, LOUIS EDWARD
B. Feb. 6, 1953, Laurel, MD
Maryland 5'11" 207 lbs.

Year	Team		Games	Pos.
1975	OAK	N	8	RB
1976	TB	N	14	RB
1977			14	RB
1978			16	RB

4 yrs. 52 games

Marty Carter
CARTER, MARTY LAVINCENT
B. Dec. 17, 1969, La Grange, GA
Middle Tennessee State 6'1" 200 lbs.

Year	Team		Games	Pos.
1991	TB	N	14	S
1992			16	S
1993			16	S
1994			16	S
1995	CHI	N	16	S
1996			16	S

6 yrs. 94 games

Michael Carter
CARTER, MICHAEL D'ANDREA

Michael Carter continued
B. Oct. 29, 1960, Dallas, TX
Southern Methodist 6'2" 285 lbs.

Year	Team		Games	Pos.
1984	SF	N	16	NT
1985			12	NT
1986			15	NT
1987			12	NT
1988			16	NT
1989			8	NT
1990			15	NT
1991			15	NT
1992			12	NT

9 yrs. 121 games

Mike Carter
CARTER, MICHAEL NORMAN
B. Feb. 18, 1948, Little Rock, AR
Sacramento State 6'1" 210 lbs.

Year	Team		Games	Pos.
1970	GB	N	3	WR
1972	SD	N	5	WR

2 yrs. 8 games

M.L. Carter
CARTER, MILTON LOUIS
B. Dec. 9, 1955, Beaufort, SC
Fullerton State/San Jose State 5'9" 173 lbs.

Year	Team		Games	Pos.
1979	KC	N	1	CB
1980			7	CB
1981			10	CB

3 yrs. 18 games

Pat Carter
CARTER, WENDELL PATRICK
B. Aug. 1, 1966, Sarasota, FL
Florida State 6'4" 250 lbs.

Year	Team		Games	Pos.
1988	DET	N	15	TE
1989	LARM	N	16	TE
1990			16	TE
1991			16	TE
1992			16	TE
1993			11	TE
1994	HOU	N	16	TE
1995	STL	N	16	TE
1996	ARI	N	16	TE

9 yrs. 138 games

Perry Carter
CARTER, PERRY LYNN
B. Aug. 15, 1971, McComb, MS
Southern Mississippi 5'11" 206 lbs.

Year	Team		Games	Pos.
1995	KC	N	2	CB
1996	OAK	N	4	CB

2 yrs. 6 games

Rodney Carter
CARTER, RODNEY CARL
B. Oct. 30, 1964, Elizabeth, NJ
Purdue 6'0" 222 lbs.

Year	Team		Games	Pos.
1987	PIT	N	11	RB
1988			14	RB
1989			15	RB

3 yrs. 40 games

Ross Carter
CARTER, ROSCOE C. (Timber Beast)
B. 1914
Oregon 6'0" 238 lbs.

Year	Team		Games	Pos.
1936	CHIC	N	11	G
1937			11	G
1938			11	G
1939			10	G, C

4 yrs. 43 games

Rubin Carter
CARTER, RUBIN

Year	Team		Games	Pos.

Rubin Carter *continued*

B. Dec. 12, 1952, Pompano Beach, FL
Miami (Florida) 6'0" 254 lbs.

Year	Team		Games	Pos.
1975	DEN	N	14	DT
1976			14	DT
1977			14	DT
1978			16	DT
1979			15	DT
1980			16	DT
1981			16	NT
1982			9	NT
1983			16	NT
1984			15	NT
1985			16	NT
1986			5	NT
12 yrs.			166 games	

Russell Carter

CARTER, RUSSELL EDMONDS, JR.
B. Feb. 10, 1962, Philadelphia, PA
Southern Methodist 6'2" 195 lbs.

Year	Team		Games	Pos.
1984	NYJ	N	11	CB, S
1985			8	CB, S
1986			13	CB, S
1987			8	CB
1988	LARI	N	15	CB, S
1989			9	S
6 yrs.			64 games	

Steve Carter

CARTER, STEVE
B. Sep. 12, 1962, New York, NY
Albany State 5'10" 170 lbs.

Year	Team		Games	Pos.
1987	TB	N	3	WR

Tom Carter

CARTER, TOM
B. Sep. 5, 1972, St. Petersburg, FL
Notre Dame 5'11" 181 lbs.

Year	Team		Games	Pos.
1993	WAS	N	14	CB
1994			16	CB
1995			16	CB
1996			16	CB
4 yrs.			62 games	

Tony Carter

CARTER, ANTONIO
B. Aug. 23, 1972, Columbus, OH
Minnesota 5'11" 232 lbs.

Year	Team		Games	Pos.
1994	CHI	N	14	RB
1995			16	RB
1996			16	RB
3 yrs.			46 games	

Virgil Carter

CARTER, VIRGIL R.
B. Nov. 9, 1945, Provo, UT
Brigham Young 6'1" 192 lbs.

Year	Team		Games	Pos.
1968	CHI	N	7	QB
1969			3	QB
1970	CIN	N	13	QB
1971			10	QB
1972			10	QB
1975	SD	N	1	QB
1976	CHI	N	8	QB
7 yrs.			52 games	

Walter Carter

CARTER, WALTER BURKE
B. Dec. 19, 1957, Richmond, VA
Florida State 6'4" 276 lbs.

Year	Team		Games	Pos.
1987	TB	N	2	DE

Willie Carter

CARTER, WILLIE
B. 1931

Willie Carter *continued*

Tennessee State 5'11" 198 lbs.

Year	Team		Games	Pos.
1953	CHIC	N	6	B

Jason Carthen

CARTHEN, JASON
B. Nov. 16, 1970, Toledo, OH
Ohio University 6'3" 255 lbs.

Year	Team		Games	Pos.
1993	NE	N	5	LB
1994			1	LB
2 yrs.			6 games	

Milt Carthens

CARTHENS, MILTON
B. Dec. 22, 1960
Michigan 6'4" 305 lbs.

Year	Team		Games	Pos.
1987	IND	N	1	OT

Maurice Carthon

CARTHON, MAURICE
B. Apr. 24, 1961, Chicago, IL
Arkansas State 6'1" 225 lbs.

Year	Team		Games	Pos.
1985	NYG	N	16	RB
1986			16	RB
1987			11	RB
1988			16	RB
1989			16	RB
1990			16	RB
1991			16	RB
1992	IND	N	16	RB
8 yrs.			123 games	

Charlie Cartin

CARTIN, CHARLES
B. 1902
D. Jun. 9, 1951
Holy Cross 5'10" 195 lbs.

Year	Team		Games	Pos.
1925	FRA	N	12	E, T, G, C
1926	PHI	A	1	T
2 yrs.			13 games	

Dale Carver

CARVER, DALE K.
B. Mar. 5, 1961, Melbourne, FL
Georgia 6'2" 225 lbs.

Year	Team		Games	Pos.
1983	CLE	N	16	LB

Mel Carver

CARVER, MELVIN
B. Jul. 14, 1959, Pensacola, FL
Nevada-Las Vegas 5'11" 215 lbs.

Year	Team		Games	Pos.
1982	TB	N	9	RB
1983			16	RB
1984			5	RB
1985			2	RB
1987	IND	N	1	RB
5 yrs.			33 games	

Shante Carver

CARVER, SHANTE
B. Feb. 12, 1971, Stockton, CA
Arizona State 6'5" 240 lbs.

Year	Team		Games	Pos.
1994	DAL	N	7	DE
1995			15	DE
1996			10	DE
3 yrs.			32 games	

Larry Carwell

CARWELL, LARRY NEIL
B. Aug. 5, 1944, Vada, GA
D. Oct. 28, 1984, Bahamas
Iowa State 6'1" 191 lbs.

Year	Team		Games	Pos.
1967	HOU	A	9	DB
1968			14	DB
1969	BOS	A	13	DB
1970	BOS	N	10	CB

Larry Carwell *continued*

Year	Team		Games	Pos.
1971	NE	N	14	CB
1972			14	CB
6 yrs.			74 games	

Ken Casanega

CASANEGA, KENNETH T.
B. 1921
Santa Clara 5'11" 175 lbs.

Year	Team		Games	Pos.
1946	SF	AA	14	HB, DB
1948			1	HB, DB
2 yrs.			15 games	

Tommy Casanova

CASANOVA, THOMAS H.
B. Jul. 29, 1950, New Orleans, LA
Louisiana State 6'2" 197 lbs.

Year	Team		Games	Pos.
1972	CIN	N	14	DB
1973			10	S
1974			14	S
1975			11	S
1976			11	S
1977			11	S
6 yrs.			71 games	

Rick Casares

CASARES, RICARDO JOSE
B. Jul. 4, 1931, Tampa, FL
Florida 6'2" 226 lbs.

Year	Team		Games	Pos.
1955	CHIB	N	12	FB
1956			12	FB
1957			12	FB
1958			12	FB
1959			12	FB
1960	CHI	N	12	FB
1961			13	FB
1962			14	FB
1963			10	FB
1964			13	FB
1965	WAS	N	3	FB
1966	MIA	A	6	FB
12 yrs.			131 games	

Chad Cascadden

CASCADDEN, CHAD
B. May 14, 1972, Chippewa Falls, WI
Wisconsin 6'1" 225 lbs.

Year	Team		Games	Pos.
1995	NYJ	N	12	LB
1996			16	LB
2 yrs.			28 games	

Ernie Case

CASE, ERNEST FRANCIS
B. Nov. 23, 1919, Case, TX
UCLA 5'10" 170 lbs.

Year	Team		Games	Pos.
1947	BAL	AA	14	B

Frank Case

CASE, FRANCIS
B. Aug. 14, 1958, Jacksonville, NC
Penn State 6'4" 243 lbs.

Year	Team		Games	Pos.
1981	KC	N	6	DE

Pete Case

CASE, RONALD LEE
B. Dec. 27, 1940, Dayton, OH
Georgia 6'3" 242 lbs.

Year	Team		Games	Pos.
1962	PHI	N	14	G
1963			13	G
1964			14	G
1965	NYG	N	14	G
1966			14	G
1967			14	G
1968			14	G
1969			14	G
1970			7	G
9 yrs.			118 games	

Scott Case

CASE, JEFFREY SCOTT
B. May 17, 1962, Waynoka, OK
Oklahoma 6'0" 178 lbs.

Year	Team		Games	Pos.
1984	ATL	N	16	CB, S
1985			14	S
1986			16	S
1987			11	CB
1988			16	CB
1989			14	CB
1990			16	CB
1991			16	S
1992			12	S
1993			16	S
1994			14	S
1995	DAL	N	15	S
12 yrs.			176 games	

Stoney Case

CASE, STONEY JARROD
B. Jul. 7, 1972, Odessa, TX
New Mexico 6'2" 206 lbs.

Year	Team		Games	Pos.
1995	ARI	N	3	QB
1996			1	QB
2 yrs.			4 games	

Al Casey

CASEY, ALBERT (Pete)
B. Dec., 1895, Missouri
Deceased
None 180 lbs.

Year	Team		Games	Pos.
1923	STL	N	7	HB, FB

Alvro Casey

CASEY, ALVRO (RUNNING WOLF)
B. Mar. 29, 1903, Oklahoma
D. Oct., 1971, Denver City, TX
Haskell/Northeastern Oklahoma 6'0" 215 lbs.

Year	Team		Games	Pos.
1926	AKR	N	4	T

Bernie Casey

CASEY, BERNARD TERRY
B. Jun. 8, 1939, Wyco, WV
Bowling Green 6'4" 213 lbs.

Year	Team		Games	Pos.
1961	SF	N	12	OE
1962			13	OE
1963			14	FL
1964			14	FL
1965			14	FL
1966			13	FL
1967	LA	N	14	FL
1968			12	FL
8 yrs.			105 games	

Tim Casey

CASEY, TIM
B. Feb. 29, 1944, Portland, OR
Oregon 6'1" 225 lbs.

Year	Team		Games	Pos.
1969	CHI	N	3	LB
1969	DEN	A	2	LB
1 yr.			5 games	

Tom Casey

CASEY, THOMAS R. (Citation)
B. Jul. 30, 1924, Wellsville, OH
Hampton Institute 5'11" 175 lbs.

Year	Team		Games	Pos.
1948	NY	AA	11	B

John Cash

CASH, JOHN LEWIS
B. Aug. 5, 1936, Brunswick, GA
Allen 6'3" 235 lbs.

Year	Team		Games	Pos.
1961	DEN	A	14	DE
1962			14	DE
2 yrs.			28 games	

Year	Team		Games	Pos.

Keith Cash
CASH, KEITH LOVELL
B. Aug. 7, 1969, San Antonio, TX
Texas 6'4" 235 lbs.

Year	Team		Games	Pos.
1991	PIT	N	5	TE
1992	KC	N	15	TE
1993			15	TE
1994			6	TE
1995			14	TE
1996			9	TE
6 yrs.		64 games		

Kerry Cash
CASH, KERRY LENARD
B. Aug. 7, 1969, San Antonio, TX
Texas 6'4" 247 lbs.

Year	Team		Games	Pos.
1991	IND	N	4	TE
1992			16	TE
1993			16	TE
1994			16	TE
1995	OAK	N	16	TE
1996	CHI	N	3	TE
6 yrs.		71 games		

Rick Cash
CASH, RICHARD FRANCIS
B. Jul. 1, 1945, St. Louis, MO
Missouri/Northeast Missouri State 6'5" 260 lbs.

Year	Team		Games	Pos.
1968	ATL	N	14	DE
1969	LA	N	13	DE
1970			8	DE
1972	NE	N	14	DT
1973			14	DT
5 yrs.		63 games		

Tony Casillas
CASILLAS, TONY STEVEN
B. Oct. 26, 1963, Tulsa, OK
Oklahoma 6'3" 280 lbs.

Year	Team		Games	Pos.
1986	ATL	N	16	NT
1987			9	NT
1988			16	NT
1989			16	NT
1990			9	NT
1991	DAL	N	16	DT
1992			15	DT
1993			15	DT
1994	NYJ	N	13	DT
1995			11	DT
1996	DAL	N	16	DT
11 yrs.		152 games		

Ken Casner
CASNER, KENNETH
B. 1930
Baylor 6'2" 245 lbs.

Year	Team		Games	Pos.
1952	LA	N	12	T

Jim Cason
CASON, JAMES A.
B. Jul. 25, 1927, Sondheimer, LA
Louisiana State 6'0" 171 lbs.

Year	Team		Games	Pos.
1948	SF	AA	13	B
1949			12	B
1950	SF	N	9	HB
1951			12	HB
1952			10	HB
1954			9	HB
1955	LA	N	12	HB
1956			12	HB
8 yrs.		89 games		

Wendell Cason
CASON, WENDELL B.
B. Jan. 22, 1963, Lakewood, CA
Oregon 5'11" 197 lbs.

Year	Team		Games	Pos.
1985	ATL	N	14	CB

Wendell Cason continued

Year	Team		Games	Pos.
1986			16	CB
1987			3	S
3 yrs.		33 games		

Cy Casper
CASPER, CHARLES
B. May 28, 1912, Memphis, TN
D. Mar. 7, 1968, Fort Worth, TX
Texas Christian 6'0" 190 lbs.

Year	Team		Games	Pos.
1934	GB	N	1	QB
1934	C, S	N	3	HB
1935	PIT	N	10	QB, HB
2 yrs.		14 games		

Dave Casper
CASPER, DAVID JOHN
B. Sep. 26, 1951, Bemidji, MN
Notre Dame 6'4" 232 lbs.

Year	Team		Games	Pos.
1974	OAK	N	14	TE
1975			14	TE
1976			13	TE
1977			14	TE
1978			14	TE
1979			15	TE
1980			6	TE
1980	HOU	N	10	TE
1981			16	TE
1982			9	TE
1983			3	TE
1983	MIN	N	10	TE
1984	LARI	N	7	TE
11 yrs.		147 games		

Craig Cassady
CASSADY, CRAIG
B. Dec. 21, 1953, Columbus, OH
Ohio State 5'11" 175 lbs.

Year	Team		Games	Pos.
1977	NO	N	12	S

Howard Cassady
CASSADY, HOWARD A. (Hopalong)
B. Mar. 2, 1934, Columbus, OH
Ohio State 5'10" 183 lbs.

Year	Team		Games	Pos.
1956	DET	N	12	HB
1957			12	HB
1958			10	HB
1959			12	HB
1960			12	HB
1961			14	HB
1962	CLE	N	5	FL
1962	PHI	N	10	FL
1963	DET	N	2	HB
8 yrs.		89 games		

Frank Cassara
CASSARA, FRANK
B. Mar. 22, 1928, San Fernando, CA
St. Mary's (California) 6'0" 215 lbs.

Year	Team		Games	Pos.
1954	SF		6	FB

Tom Cassese
CASSESE, THOMAS LEE
B. Apr. 7, 1946, Bayside, NY
C.W. Post 6'1" 197 lbs.

Year	Team		Games	Pos.
1967	DEN	A	14	OE

Dick Cassiano
CASSIANO, RICHARD P.
B. Oct. 7, 1917
D. May 28, 1980, Guilderland, NY
Pittsburgh 5'11" 175 lbs.

Year	Team		Games	Pos.
1940	BKN	N	10	HB

Cassidy
CASSIDY

Cassidy continued

Year	Team		Games	Pos.
None				
1921	TON	A	1	QB

Ron Cassidy
CASSIDY, RONALD G.
B. Jul. 23, 1957, Ventura, CA
Utah State 6'0" 185 lbs.

Year	Team		Games	Pos.
1979	GB	N	8	WR
1980			15	WR
1981			11	WR
1983			16	WR
1984			15	WR
5 yrs.		65 games		

Walt Cassidy
CASSIDY, WALTER
B. Dec. 16, 1899
D. Oct., 1974, Cleveland, OH
Detroit 5'10" 200 lbs.

Year	Team		Games	Pos.
1924	KEN	N	5	E

Mike Casteel
CASTEEL, MILES
B. Dec. 30, 1895, Elmira, NY
D. Mar. 27, 1977, Phoenix, AZ
Kalamazoo 5'11" 160 lbs.

Year	Team		Games	Pos.
1922	RI	N	6	QB, HB

Rich Caster
CASTER, RICHARD C.
B. Oct. 16, 1948, Mobile, AL
Jackson State 6'5" 228 lbs.

Year	Team		Games	Pos.
1970	NYJ	N	14	WR
1971			14	WR
1972			14	WR, TE
1973			14	TE
1974			13	TE
1975			14	TE
1976			14	TE
1977			10	TE
1978	HOU	N	14	WR
1979			16	WR
1980			16	WR
1981	NO	N	4	TE
1981	WAS	N	3	TE
1982			1	TE
13 yrs.		161 games		

Jesse Castete
CASTETE, JESSE
B. 1935
McNeese State 5'11" 178 lbs.

Year	Team		Games	Pos.
1956	CHIB	N	3	DB
1956	LA	N	3	DB
1957			11	DB
2 yrs.		17 games		

Jim Castiglia
CASTIGLIA, JAMES VINCENT
B. Sep. 30, 1918, Passaic, NJ
Georgetown (DC) 5'11" 208 lbs.

Year	Team		Games	Pos.
1941	PHI	N	11	FB
1945			1	FB
1946			11	FB
1947	BAL	AA	2	FB
1947	WAS	N	7	FB
1948			10	FB
5 yrs.		42 games		

Jeremiah Castille
CASTILLE, JEREMIAH
B. Jan. 15, 1961, Columbus, GA
Alabama 5'10" 175 lbs.

Year	Team		Games	Pos.
1983	TB	N	15	CB, S
1984			16	CB
1985			16	CB

Jeremiah Castille continued

Year	Team		Games	Pos.
1986			13	CB
1987	DEN	N	11	DB
1988			16	CB, S
6 yrs.		87 games		

Eric Castle
CASTLE, ERIC DEAN
B. Mar. 15, 1970, Longview, WA
Oregon 6'3" 212 lbs.

Year	Team		Games	Pos.
1993	SD	N	5	S
1994			16	S
1995			16	S
1996			16	S
4 yrs.		53 games		

Toby Caston
CASTON, SEBASTIAN TOBIAS
B. Jul. 17, 1965, Monroe, LA
D. Oct. 2, 1994, Dallas, TX
Louisiana State 6'1" 235 lbs.

Year	Team		Games	Pos.
1987	HOU	N	6	LB
1988			16	LB
1989	DET	N	16	LB
1990			12	LB
1991			16	LB
1992			15	LB
1993			9	LB
7 yrs.		90 games		

Chris Castor
CASTOR, CHRIS
B. Aug. 13, 1960, Burlington, NC
Duke 6'0" 170 lbs.

Year	Team		Games	Pos.
1983	SEA	N	8	WR
1984			15	WR
2 yrs.		23 games		

Tony Catalano
CATALANO, ANTHONY E.
B. Apr. 13, 1895, Indianapolis, IN
D. Jul. 25, 1980, Boise, ID
None

Year	Team		Games	Pos.
1920	HAM	A	1	G

Alcides Catanho
CATANHO, ALCIDES
B. Jan. 20, 1972, Elizabeth, NJ
Rutgers 6'3" 216 lbs.

Year	Team		Games	Pos.
1995	NE	N	12	LB
1996	WAS	N	15	LB
2 yrs.		27 games		

Mark Catano
CATANO, MARK
B. Jan. 26, 1962, Yonkers, NY
Valdosta State 6'3" 265 lbs.

Year	Team		Games	Pos.
1984	PIT	N	16	G
1985			15	DE
1986	BUF	N	1	NT
3 yrs.		32 games		

Toney Catchings
CATCHINGS, TONEY
B. Aug. 11, 1965, Jackson, MS
Cincinnati 6'3" 236 lbs.

Year	Team		Games	Pos.
1987	CIN	N	3	LB

Greg Cater
CATER, GREGORY WAYNE
B. Apr. 17, 1957, La Grange, GA
Tennessee-Chattanooga 6'1" 191 lbs.

Year	Team		Games	Pos.
1980	BUF	N	16	P
1981			16	P
1982			9	P
1983			16	P

Year	Team		Games	Pos.

Greg Cater continued

Year	Team		Games	Pos.
1986	STL	N	11	P
1987			9	P
6 yrs.	77 games			

Mike Caterbone
CATERBONE, MICHAEL THOMAS
B. Feb. 17, 1962, Lancaster, PA
Franklin & Marshall 5'11" 175 lbs.

Year	Team		Games	Pos.
1987	MIA	N	3	WR

Tom Caterbone
CATERBONE, TOM
B. Jun. 29, 1964
Franklin & Marshall 5'8" 175 lbs.

Year	Team		Games	Pos.
1987	PHI	N	2	CB

Royal Cathcart
CATHCART, ROYAL JENSEN
B. Apr. 8, 1926, Canute, OK
California-Santa Barbara 6'0" 185 lbs.

Year	Team		Games	Pos.
1950	SF	N	2	HB

Sam Cathcart
CATHCART, SAMUEL WOODROW
B. Jul. 7, 1924, Canute, OK
California-Santa Barbara 6'0" 175 lbs.

Year	Team		Games	Pos.
1949	SF	AA	12	HB, DB
1950	SF	N	12	HB, DB
1952			12	HB, DB
3 yrs.	36 games			

Tom Catlin
CATLIN, TOM A.
B. Sep. 8, 1931, Ponca City, OK
Oklahoma 6'1" 213 lbs.

Year	Team		Games	Pos.
1953	CLE	N	12	C, LB
1954			11	C, LB
1957			4	LB
1958			12	LB
1959	PHI	N	12	LB
5 yrs.	51 games			

Daryl Cato
CATO, RALPH DARYL
B. Jan. 8, 1920, Lonoke, AR
D. Oct. 3, 1970
Arkansas 6'2" 195 lbs.

Year	Team		Games	Pos.
1946	MIA	AA	12	C

Knute Cauldwell
CAULDWELL, HAROLD
B. 1895
Deceased
Wabash 6'1" 210 lbs.

Year	Team		Games	Pos.
1925	AKR	N	6	T
1926			7	T
2 yrs.	13 games			

Carmen Cavalli
CAVALLI, CARMEN
B. 1938
Richmond 6'4" 245 lbs.

Year	Team		Games	Pos.
1960	OAK	A		DE

Matt Cavanaugh
CAVANAUGH, MATTHEW ANDREW
B. Oct. 27, 1956, Youngstown, OH
Pittsburgh 6'2" 212 lbs.

Year	Team		Games	Pos.
1979	NE	N	13	QB
1980			16	QB
1981			16	QB

Matt Cavanaugh continued

Year	Team		Games	Pos.
1982			7	QB
1983	SF	N	5	QB
1984			8	QB
1985			16	QB
1986	PHI	N	10	QB
1987			3	QB
1988			5	QB
1989			9	QB
1991	NYG	N	4	QB
12 yrs.	112 games			

Ronnie Caveness
CAVENESS, RONALD GLEN
B. Mar. 6, 1943, Houston, TX
Arkansas 6'1" 223 lbs.

Year	Team		Games	Pos.
1965	KC	A	7	LB
1966	HOU	A	14	LB
1967			14	LB
1968			11	LB
4 yrs.	46 games			

James Caver
CAVER, JAMES
B. Sep. 28, 1960, Birmingham, AL
Missouri 5'9" 175 lbs.

Year	Team		Games	Pos.
1983	DET	N	2	S

Grady Cavness
CAVNESS, GRADY C.
B. Mar. 1, 1947, Houston, TX
Texas-El Paso 5'11" 190 lbs.

Year	Team		Games	Pos.
1969	DEN	A	14	CB
1970	ATL	N	4	CB
2 yrs.	18 games			

John Cavosie
CAVOSIE, JOHN C.
B. 1908
Butler 6'0" 207 lbs.

Year	Team		Games	Pos.
1931	POR	N	10	FB, HB
1932			11	FB, HB
1933			9	E, HB, FB
3 yrs.	30 games			

Lowell Caylor
CAYLOR, LOWELL
B. Jun. 17, 1941, Dayton, OH
Miami (Ohio) 6'3" 205 lbs.

Year	Team		Games	Pos.
1964	CLE	N	13	DB

Les Caywood
CAYWOOD, LESTER (Wimpy)
B. Aug. 18, 1903
D. Feb., 1986, Oakwood, OK
St. John's (New York) 6'0" 231 lbs.

Year	Team		Games	Pos.
1926	BUF	N	6	T
1927	POT	N	5	T, G
1927	NYG	N	1	G
1927	CLE	N	2	T
1928	DET	N	9	G, T
1929	NYG	N	12	G, T
1930			15	G, T
1931	CHIC	N	1	G
1931	NYG	N	11	G
1932			7	G
1932	BKN	N	2	G, E
1933	CIN	N	10	G
1934	C, S	N	8	G, C
9 yrs.	89 games			

Lloyd Cearing
CEARING, LLOYD
B. Nov. 3, 1900
Deceased
Valparaiso 185 lbs.

Year	Team		Games	Pos.
1922	HAM	N	6	HB, QB

Lloyd Cearing continued

Year	Team		Games	Pos.
1923			7	HB
2 yrs.	13 games			

Curtis Ceaser
CEASER, CURTIS
B. Aug. 11, 1972, Lincoln, NE
Grambling State 6'2" 190 lbs.

Year	Team		Games	Pos.
1995	NYJ	N	4	WR

Chuck Cecil
CECIL, CHARLES DOUGLAS
B. Nov. 8, 1964, Red Bluff, CA
Arizona 6'0" 184 lbs.

Year	Team		Games	Pos.
1988	GB	N	16	S
1989			9	S
1990			16	S
1991			16	S
1992			16	S
1993	PHX	N	15	S
1995	HOU	N	14	S
7 yrs.	95 games			

Jimmy Cefalo
CEFALO, JAMES CARMEN
B. Oct. 6, 1956, Pittston, PA
Penn State 5'11" 189 lbs.

Year	Team		Games	Pos.
1978	MIA	N	16	WR
1979			16	WR
1980			16	WR
1981			16	WR
1982			9	WR
1983			1	WR
1984			16	WR
7 yrs.	90 games			

Bob Celeri
CELERI, ROBERT L.
B. Jun. 1, 1927
D. Mar. 9, 1975, Buffalo, NY
California 5'10" 180 lbs.

Year	Team		Games	Pos.
1951	NYY	N	11	QB, P
1952	DAL	N	8	QB, P
2 yrs.	19 games			

Mario Celotto
CELOTTO, MARIO R.
B. Aug. 23, 1956, Palos Verdes, CA
Southern California 6'3" 228 lbs.

Year	Team		Games	Pos.
1978	BUF	N	4	LB
1980	OAK	N	11	LB
1981			7	LB
1981	LA	N	3	LB
3 yrs.	25 games			

Tony Cemore
CEMORE, ANTHONY S.
B. Aug. 8, 1917, Omaha, NE
D. Mar., 1981
Creighton 6'0" 210 lbs.

Year	Team		Games	Pos.
1941	PHI	N	9	G

John Cenci
CENCI, JOHN
B. 1934
Pittsburgh 6'0" 215 lbs.

Year	Team		Games	Pos.
1956	PIT	N	7	C

Larry Centers
CENTERS, LARRY
B. Jun. 1, 1968, Tatum, TX
Stephen F. Austin 5'11" 209 lbs.

Year	Team		Games	Pos.
1990	PHX	N	6	RB
1991			9	RB
1992			16	RB
1993			16	RB

Larry Centers continued

Year	Team		Games	Pos.
1994	ARI	N	16	RB
1995			16	RB
1996			16	RB
7 yrs.	95 games			

Frank Cephous
CEPHOUS, FRANK, III
B. Jul. 4, 1961, Philadelphia, PA
UCLA 5'10" 205 lbs.

Year	Team		Games	Pos.
1984	NYG	N	16	RB

Gene Ceppetelli
CEPPETELLI, EUGENE C.
B. Jul. 28, 1942, Sudbury, Ont.
Villanova 6'2" 247 lbs.

Year	Team		Games	Pos.
1968	PHI	N	14	C
1969			7	C
1969	NYG	N	6	C
2 yrs.	27 games			

Gordy Ceresino
CERESINO, GORDON JOSEPH
B. Oct. 26, 1957, Thunder Bay, Ont.
Stanford 6'0" 224 lbs.

Year	Team		Games	Pos.
1979	SF	N	16	LB

Joe Cerne
CERNE, JOSEPH
B. Apr. 26, 1942, Chronomlj, Yugoslavia
Northwestern 6'2" 238 lbs.

Year	Team		Games	Pos.
1965	SF	N	11	C
1966			14	C
1967			14	C
1968	ATL	N	6	C
4 yrs.	45 games			

Billy Cesare
CESARE, WILLIAM JOSEPH
B. Jun. 2, 1955, New York, NY
Memphis State/Miami (Florida) 5'11" 191 lbs.

Year	Team		Games	Pos.
1978	TB	N	10	DB
1979			16	CB
1980	MIA	N	2	S
1981	TB	N	16	S
1982	DET	N	2	S
5 yrs.	46 games			

Sal Cesario
CESARIO, SAL J.
B. Jul. 4, 1963, Stockton, CA
California Poly (San Luis Obispo) 6'4" 255 lbs.

Year	Team		Games	Pos.
1987	DAL	N	3	G

Jeff Chadwick
CHADWICK, JEFFREY ALLAN
B. Dec. 16, 1960, Detroit, MI
Grand Valley State 6'3" 185 lbs.

Year	Team		Games	Pos.
1983	DET	N	16	WR
1984			16	WR
1985			7	WR
1986			15	WR
1987			8	WR
1988			10	WR
1989			1	WR
1989	SEA	N	12	WR
1990			16	WR
1991			16	WR
1992	LARM	N	16	WR
10 yrs.	129 games			

Pat Chaffey
CHAFFEY, PAT

Pat Chaffey continued
B. Apr. 19, 1967, McMinnville, OR
Oregon State 6'1" 218 lbs.

Year	Team		Games	Pos.
1991	ATL	N	14	RB
1992	NYJ	N	14	RB
1993			3	RB

3 yrs.   31 games

Mike Chalenski
CHALENSKI, MICHAEL
B. Jan. 28, 1970, Elizabeth, NJ
Pittsburgh/UCLA 6'4" 260 lbs.

Year	Team		Games	Pos.
1993	PHI	N	15	DE, DT
1995			9	DT, DE
1996	NYJ	N	15	DT

3 yrs.   39 games

George Chalmers
CHALMERS, GEORGE
B. Oct. 19, 1908
D. Aug. 7, 1988, Los Angeles, CA
New York University 6'0" 196 lbs.

Year	Team		Games	Pos.
1933	BKN	N	7	C

Byron Chamberlain
CHAMBERLAIN, BYRON
B. Oct. 17, 1971, Honolulu, HI
Missouri/Wayne State (Nebraska) 6'1" 225 lbs.

Year	Team		Games	Pos.
1995	DEN	N	5	TE
1996			11	TE

2 yrs.   16 games

Dan Chamberlain
CHAMBERLAIN, DAN
B. Aug. 26, 1937, Grand Rapids, MI
Sacramento State 6'4" 200 lbs.

Year	Team		Games	Pos.
1960	BUF	A		OE
1961			3	HB

2 yrs.   3 games

Garth Chamberlain
CHAMBERLAIN, GARTH G.
B. May 20, 1920, Alton, UT
D. Dec. 21, 1988, Chandler, AZ
Brigham Young 6'0" 215 lbs.

Year	Team		Games	Pos.
1945	PIT	N	3	G

Guy Chamberlin
CHAMBERLIN, BERLIN GUY
(Champ)
B. Jan. 16, 1894, Blue Springs, NE
D. Apr. 4, 1967, Lincoln, NE
Nebraska Wesleyan/Nebraska 6'2" 191 lbs.

Year	Team		Games	Pos.
1920	DEC	A	8	E
1921			11	E
1922	CAN	N	12	E, HB
1923			12	E
1924	CLE	N	9	E
1925	FRA	N	14	E
1926			17	E
1927	CHIC	N	6	E

8 yrs.   89 games

Bill Chambers
CHAMBERS, WILLIAM J.
B. 1923
Alabama/Georgia Tech/UCLA 6'2" 230 lbs.

Year	Team		Games	Pos.
1948	NY	AA	13	T
1949	B, NY	AA	12	G

2 yrs.   25 games

Rusty Chambers
CHAMBERS, RUSSELL FRANCIS

Rusty Chambers continued
B. Nov. 10, 1953, Amite, LA
D. Jul. 1, 1981, Hammond, LA
Tulane 6'1" 218 lbs.

Year	Team		Games	Pos.
1975	NO	N	12	LB
1976			4	LB
1976	MIA	N	10	LB
1977			14	LB
1978			16	LB
1979			16	LB
1980			16	LB

6 yrs.   88 games

Wally Chambers
CHAMBERS, WALLACE
B. May 15, 1951, Phenix City, AL
Eastern Kentucky 6'6" 253 lbs.

Year	Team		Games	Pos.
1973	CHI	N	14	DE
1974			14	DT
1975			14	DT
1976			14	DT
1977			4	DT
1978	TB	N	12	DT, DE
1979			16	DE

7 yrs.   88 games

Al Chamblee
CHAMBLEE, ALDRIC DORAN
B. Nov. 17, 1968, Virginia Beach, VA
Virginia Tech 6'1" 240 lbs.

Year	Team		Games	Pos.
1991	TB	N	9	DE
1992			13	DE

2 yrs.   22 games

Ed Champagne
CHAMPAGNE, EDWARD
B. Dec. 4, 1922, New Orleans, LA
Louisiana State 6'3" 236 lbs.

Year	Team		Games	Pos.
1947	LA	N	4	T
1948			12	T
1949			12	T
1950			11	T

4 yrs.   39 games

Jim Champion
CHAMPION, JAMES HENRY
B. Jan. 11, 1926, Tillatoba, MS
Mississippi State 6'0" 238 lbs.

Year	Team		Games	Pos.
1950	NYY	N	7	G
1951			12	T

2 yrs.   19 games

Al Chandler
CHANDLER, ALBERT MORRIS
B. Nov. 18, 1950, Oklahoma City, OK
Oklahoma 6'2" 229 lbs.

Year	Team		Games	Pos.
1973	CIN	N	13	TE
1974			14	TE
1976	NE	N	14	TE
1977			14	TE
1978			4	TE
1978	STL	N	11	TE
1979			8	TE
1979	NE	N	7	TE

6 yrs.   85 games

Bob Chandler
CHANDLER, ROBERT DONALD
B. Apr. 24, 1949, Long Beach, CA
D. Jan. 27, 1995, Los Angeles, CA
Southern California 6'0" 180 lbs.

Year	Team		Games	Pos.
1971	BUF	N	14	WR
1972			14	WR
1973			14	WR
1974			14	WR
1975			14	WR
1976			14	WR
1977			14	WR

Bob Chandler continued

Year	Team		Games	Pos.
1978			16	WR
1979			10	WR
1980	OAK	N	16	WR
1981			11	WR
1982	LARI	N	2	WR

12 yrs.   153 games

Chris Chandler
CHANDLER, CHRISTOPHER MARK
B. Oct. 12, 1965, Everett, WA
Washington 6'4" 210 lbs.

Year	Team		Games	Pos.
1988	IND	N	15	QB
1989			3	QB
1990	TB	N	7	QB
1991			6	QB
1991	PHX	N	3	QB
1992			15	QB
1993			4	QB
1994	LARM	N	12	QB
1995	HOU	N	13	QB
1996			12	QB

9 yrs.   90 games

Don Chandler
CHANDLER, DONALD G. (Babe)
B. Sep. 5, 1934, Council Bluffs, IA
Florida 6'2" 208 lbs.

Year	Team		Games	Pos.
1956	NYG	N	12	HB, P, K
1957			12	HB, P
1958			12	HB, P
1959			12	HB, P
1960			8	HB, P
1961			14	HB, P
1962			14	P, K
1963			14	P, K
1964			14	P, K
1965	GB	N	14	P, K
1966			14	P, K
1967			14	P, K

12 yrs.   154 games

Edgar Chandler
CHANDLER, EDGAR, JR.
B. Aug. 31, 1946, Cedartown, GA
Georgia 6'3" 227 lbs.

Year	Team		Games	Pos.
1968	BUF	A	13	LB
1969			14	LB
1970	BUF	N	14	LB
1971			13	LB
1972			1	LB
1973	NE	N	12	LB

6 yrs.   67 games

Karl Chandler
CHANDLER, KARL VICTOR
B. Feb. 15, 1952, Delaware County, PA
Princeton 6'5" 250 lbs.

Year	Team		Games	Pos.
1974	NYG	N	14	C
1975			14	C
1976			12	C, G
1977			14	C
1978	DET	N	11	C
1979			1	C

6 yrs.   66 games

Thornton Chandler
CHANDLER, THORNTON GREENE
B. Nov. 27, 1963, Jacksonville, FL
Florida A&M/Alabama 6'5" 245 lbs.

Year	Team		Games	Pos.
1986	DAL	N	15	TE
1987			12	TE
1988			16	TE
1989			6	TE

4 yrs.   49 games

Wes Chandler
CHANDLER, WESLEY SANDY
B. Aug. 22, 1956, New Smyrna Beach, FL
Florida 6'0" 186 lbs.

Year	Team		Games	Pos.
1978	NO	N	16	WR
1979			16	WR
1980			16	WR
1981			4	WR
1981	SD	N	12	WR
1982			8	WR
1983			16	WR
1984			15	WR
1985			15	WR
1986			16	WR
1987			12	WR
1988	SF	N	4	WR

11 yrs.   150 games

Lynn Chandnois
CHANDNOIS, LYNN EVERETT
B. Feb. 24, 1925, Flint, MI
Michigan State 6'2" 198 lbs.

Year	Team		Games	Pos.
1950	PIT	N	12	HB
1951			12	HB
1952			12	HB
1953			12	HB
1954			11	HB
1955			8	HB
1956			5	HB

7 yrs.   72 games

Clarence Chapman
CHAPMAN, CLARENCE
B. Dec. 10, 1953, Detroit, MI
Eastern Michigan 5'10" 165 lbs.

Year	Team		Games	Pos.
1976	NO	N	1	CB
1977			14	CB
1978			14	CB
1979			16	CB
1980			12	CB
1981	CIN	N	5	CB
1985	DET	N	3	CB, S

7 yrs.   65 games

Gil Chapman
CHAPMAN, GIL
B. Aug. 23, 1953, Elizabeth, NJ
Michigan 5'9" 180 lbs.

Year	Team		Games	Pos.
1975	NO	N	9	WR

Mike Chapman
CHAPMAN, MICHAEL GEORGE
B. Feb. 10, 1961, Laredo, TX
Texas 6'4" 250 lbs.

Year	Team		Games	Pos.
1984	ATL	N	4	OL

Ted Chapman
CHAPMAN, TED
B. Apr. 5, 1964
Maryland 6'3" 260 lbs.

Year	Team		Games	Pos.
1987	LARI	N	2	DE

Leo Chappell
CHAPPELL, LEO
None 6'2" 205 lbs.

Year	Team		Games	Pos.
1920	CHIC	A	6	G
1921			1	G

2 yrs.   7 games

Dave Chapple
CHAPPLE, DAVID
B. Mar. 30, 1947, Arcadia, CA
California-Santa Barbara 6'0" 184 lbs.

Year	Team		Games	Pos.
1971	BUF	N	1	P
1972	LA	N	14	P, K
1973			14	P, K

Year Team	Games	Pos.

Dave Chapple continued
DePaul 6'0" 230 lbs. (not applicable)

Year Team	Games	Pos.
1974	6	P
1974 **NE** N	5	P
4 yrs. 40 games		

Jack Chapple
CHAPPLE, JOHN LOUIS
B. Jul. 23, 1943, Daytona Beach, FL
D. Oct. 19, 1979, Palo Alto, CA
Stanford 6'2" 227 lbs.

1965 **SF** N	14	LB

Bob Chappuis
CHAPPUIS, ROBERT RICHARD
B. Feb. 24, 1923, Toledo, OH
Michigan 6'0" 190 lbs.

1948 **BKN** AA	13	B
1949 **CHI** AA	6	B
2 yrs. 19 games		

Dick Chapura
CHAPURA, RICHARD HARRY, JR.
B. Jun. 15, 1954, Sarasota, FL
Missouri 6'3" 280 lbs.

1987 **CHI** N	2	DL
1988	15	DT
1989	16	DT
1990 **PHX** N	3	DT
1990 **PHI** N	7	DT
4 yrs. 43 games		

John Charles
CHARLES, JOHN
B. May 9, 1944, Newark, NJ
Purdue 6'1" 199 lbs.

1967 **BOS** A	14	DB
1968	12	DB
1969	13	S
1970 **MIN** N	8	S
1971 **HOU** N	14	S
1972	13	S
1973	4	S
1974	1	S
8 yrs. 79 games		

Mike Charles
CHARLES, MICHAEL WILLIAM
B. Sep. 23, 1962, Newark, NJ
Syracuse 6'4" 287 lbs.

1983 **MIA** N	16	NT
1984	10	NT
1985	16	NT
1986	9	NT
1987 **SD** N	11	NT
1988	16	NT
1989	6	NT
1990 **LARI** N	10	DT
1991 **LARM** N	7	DT
9 yrs. 101 games		

Win Charles
CHARLES, WINSTON HOLT
(Speed)
B. 1904
D. Jan. 29, 1949
William & Mary 5'9" 160 lbs.

1928 **DAY** N	5	HB, QB

Clifford Charlton
CHARLTON, CLIFFORD TYRONE
B. Feb. 16, 1965, Tallahassee, FL
Florida 6'3" 240 lbs.

1988 **CLE** N	16	LB
1989	15	LB
2 yrs. 31 games		

Carl Charon
CHARON, CARL H.
B. Mar. 17, 1940, Boyne City, MI
Michigan State 5'10" 190 lbs.

1962 **BUF** A	14	DB
1963	12	DB
2 yrs. 26 games		

Len Charpier
CHARPIER, LEONARD L. (Tark)
B. Feb. 17, 1897
D. Oct. 3, 1947
Illinois 5'10" 200 lbs.

1920 **CHIC** A	1	FB

Ben Chase
CHASE, BENJAMIN S., III
B. 1923, Bisbee, AZ
Navy 6'3" 235 lbs.

1947 **DET** N	11	G

Ralph Chase
CHASE, RALPH E.
B. Dec. 19, 1902
D. Oct. 24, 1989, Gillett, PA
Pittsburgh 6'3" 219 lbs.

1926 **AKR** N	5	T

Cliff Chatman
CHATMAN, CLIFFORD
B. Mar. 13, 1959, Clinton, OK
Central Oklahoma 6'2" 225 lbs.

1982 **NYG** N	6	RB

Ricky Chatman
CHATMAN, RICKY L.
B. Jan. 4, 1962, Jonesboro, AR
Louisiana State 6'2" 230 lbs.

1987 **IND** N	3	LB

Laz Chavez
CHAVEZ, LAZ
B. Dec. 20, 1963
Iona 6'0" 220 lbs.

1987 **MIA** N	3	LB

Eddie Chavis
CHAVIS, EDDIE
B. Jul. 12, 1963
Montclair State 6'0" 182 lbs.

1987 **MIA** N	3	WR

Barney Chavous
CHAVOUS, BARNEY LEWIS
B. Mar. 22, 1951, Aiken, SC
South Carolina State 6'3" 254 lbs.

1973 **DEN** N	14	DE
1974	14	DE
1975	9	DE
1976	13	DE
1977	13	DE
1978	16	DE
1979	16	DE
1980	16	DE
1981	16	DE
1982	9	DE
1983	15	DE
1984	15	DE
1985	16	DE
13 yrs. 182 games		

Ernie Cheatham
CHEATHAM, ERNEST CLIFFORD, JR.
B. Jul. 26, 1929, Long Beach, CA

Ernie Cheatham continued
Loyola (California) 6'4" 245 lbs.

1954 **PIT** N	4	T
1954 **BAL** N	2	T
1 yr. 6 games		

Lloyd Cheatham
CHEATHAM, HILLIARD LLOYD
B. Mar. 20, 1919, Navtoo, OK
D. Jun. 11, 1989, Charlotte, NC
Auburn 6'2" 211 lbs.

1942 **CHIC** N	11	WB, DB
1946 **NY** AA	13	B, LB
1947	14	B
1948	12	B
4 yrs. 50 games		

Coonie Checkaye
CHECKAYE, SEVERIN J.
B. Jan. 6, 1893, Muncie, IN
D. Nov. 18, 1970, Muncie, IN
None 5'9" 185 lbs.

1920 **MUN** A	1	QB
1921	2	QB
2 yrs. 3 games		

Louis Cheek
CHEEK, LOUIS RAY, JR.
B. Oct. 6, 1964, Galveston, TX
Texas A&M 6'6" 295 lbs.

1988 **MIA** N	15	OT
1989	13	OT
1990 **DAL** N	4	OT
1990 **PHI** N	1	OL
1991 **GB** N	12	G, OT
4 yrs. 45 games		

Richard Cheek
CHEEK, RICHARD
B. Jan. 19, 1948, Panama City, FL
Auburn 6'3" 266 lbs.

1970 **BUF** N	14	G

B.W. Cheeks
CHEEKS, B.W.
B. 1942
Texas Southern 6'1" 230 lbs.

1965 **HOU** A	2	HB

Michael Cheever
CHEEVER, MICHAEL JOHN
B. Jun. 24, 1973, Newnan, GA
Georgia Tech 6'3" 296 lbs.

1996 **JAC** N	11	C

Don Chelf
CHELF, DONALD
B. Mar. 25, 1933, West Liberty, IA
Iowa 6'3" 235 lbs.

1960 **BUF** A		G
1961	14	OT
2 yrs. 14 games		

Red Chenoweth
CHENOWETH, FRED MYER
B. Aug. 26, 1893, Fairmont, WV
D. Jun. 24, 1965, Weston, WV
West Virginia 5'6" 150 lbs.

1921 **LOU** A	2	HB

Hal Cherne
CHERNE, HAROLD T.
B. Mar. 7, 1907
D. Jan. 31, 1983, Salinas, CA

Hal Cherne continued
DePaul 6'0" 230 lbs.

1933 **BOS** N	4	T, G, C

George Cheroke
CHEROKE, GEORGE
B. Jan. 2, 1921, Jenners, PA
Ohio State 5'9" 195 lbs.

1946 **CLE** AA	11	G

Bill Cherry
CHERRY, WILLIAM KIMBLE
B. Jan. 5, 1961, De Land, FL
Middle Tennessee State 6'4" 277 lbs.

1986 **GB** N	16	C, G
1987	12	C, G
2 yrs. 28 games		

Deron Cherry
CHERRY, DERON LEIGH
B. Sep. 12, 1959, Riverside, NJ
Rutgers 5'11" 196 lbs.

1981 **KC** N	13	S
1982	7	S
1983	16	S
1984	16	S
1985	16	S
1986	16	S
1987	8	S
1988	16	S
1989	15	S
1990	9	S
1991	16	S
11 yrs. 148 games		

Ed Cherry
CHERRY, EDGAR
B. Jul. 6, 1913
D. Nov., 1985, Big Spring, TX
Hardin-Simmons 6'0" 208 lbs.

1938 **CHIC** N	2	FB
1939	4	HB, FB
1939 **PIT** N	2	B
2 yrs. 8 games		

Je'Rod Cherry
CHERRY, JE'ROD
B. May 30, 1973, Charlotte, NC
California 6'0" 196 lbs.

1996 **NO** N	13	S

Raphel Cherry
CHERRY, RAPHEL JEROME
B. Dec. 19, 1961, Little Rock, AR
Hawaii 6'0" 194 lbs.

1985 **WAS** N	16	CB
1987 **DET** N	10	S
1988	16	S
3 yrs. 42 games		

Stan Cherry
CHERRY, STANLEY D.
B. Nov. 2, 1950, Baltimore, MD
Morgan State 6'5" 200 lbs.

1973 **BAL** N	3	LB

Tony Cherry
CHERRY, ANTHONY EARL
B. Feb. 8, 1963, Tripoli, Libya
Oregon 5'7" 187 lbs.

1986 **SF** N	5	RB
1987	1	RB
2 yrs. 6 games		

Year	Team		Games	Pos.

Chuck Cherundolo
CHERUNDOLO, CHARLES
B. Aug. 8, 1916, Old Forge, PA
Penn State 6'1" 215 lbs.

Year	Team		Games	Pos.
1937	CLE	N	11	C
1938			11	C
1939			10	C
1940	PHI	N	11	C
1941	PIT	N	11	C
1942			11	C
1945			6	C
1946			11	C
1947			12	C
1948			12	C
10 yrs.	106 games			

Red Chesbro
CHESBRO, MARCEL M.
B. Aug. 22, 1914
D. Mar. 11, 1970, Hamilton, NY
Colgate 5'11" 190 lbs.

Year	Team		Games	Pos.
1938	CLE	N	7	G

Al Chesley
CHESLEY, ALBERT CORNELL
B. Aug. 23, 1957, Washington, DC
Pittsburgh 6'3" 240 lbs.

Year	Team		Games	Pos.
1979	PHI	N	16	LB
1980			16	LB
1981			16	LB
1982			4	LB
1982	CHI	N	4	LB
4 yrs.	56 games			

Frank Chesley
CHESLEY, FRANCIS MICHAEL
B. Jul. 14, 1955, Washington, DC
Wyoming 6'3" 219 lbs.

Year	Team		Games	Pos.
1978	GB	N	1	LB

John Chesley
CHESLEY, JOHN
B. Jul. 2, 1962, Washington, DC
Oklahoma State 6'5" 225 lbs.

Year	Team		Games	Pos.
1984	MIA	N	1	TE

Chet Chesney
CHESNEY, CHESTER A.
B. Mar. 9, 1916
D. Sep. 20, 1986, Marco Island, FL
DePaul 6'2" 227 lbs.

Year	Team		Games	Pos.
1939	CHIB	N	6	C
1940			3	C, G
2 yrs.	9 games			

George Chesser
CHESSER, GEORGE ALLEN
B. Sep. 11, 1942, Starkville, MS
Mississippi/Delta State 6'2" 223 lbs.

Year	Team		Games	Pos.
1966	MIA	A	14	FB
1967			4	RB
2 yrs.	18 games			

Wes Chesson
CHESSON, WESLEY MERRITT, III
B. Jan. 15, 1949, Edenton, NC
Duke 6'2" 192 lbs.

Year	Team		Games	Pos.
1971	ATL	N	14	WR
1972			13	WR
1973			2	WR
1974	PHI	N	12	WR
4 yrs.	41 games			

Raymond Chester
CHESTER, RAYMOND THOMAS

Raymond Chester continued
B. Jun. 28, 1948, Cambridge, MD
Morgan State 6'3" 232 lbs.

Year	Team		Games	Pos.
1970	OAK	N	14	TE
1971			14	TE
1972			13	TE
1973	BAL	N	13	TE
1974			14	TE
1975			14	TE
1976			14	TE
1977			14	TE
1978	OAK	N	16	TE
1979			14	TE
1980			16	TE
1981			16	TE
12 yrs.	172 games			

Joe Chetti
CHETTI, JOE
B. Nov. 19, 1963, Bay Shore, NY
C.W. Post 5'9" 205 lbs.

Year	Team		Games	Pos.
1987	BUF	N	2	RB

George Cheverko
CHEVERKO, GEORGE F.
B. 1921
Fordham 6'1" 195 lbs.

Year	Team		Games	Pos.
1947	NYG	N	9	HB
1948	WAS	N	2	HB
1948	NYG	N	8	HB
2 yrs.	19 games			

Jim Cheyunski
CHEYUNSKI, JAMES M.
B. Dec. 29, 1945, Bridgewater, MA
Syracuse 6'2" 222 lbs.

Year	Team		Games	Pos.
1968	BOS	A	13	LB
1969			14	LB
1970	BOS	N	11	LB
1971	NE	N	14	LB
1972			14	LB
1973	BUF	N	13	LB
1974			14	LB
1975	BAL	N	14	LB
1976			14	LB
1977	GB	N		LB
10 yrs.	121 games			

Fred Chicken
CHICKEN, FRED S.
B. Apr. 5, 1888, Minnesota
D. Nov., 1969, La Crosse, WI
None 5'10" 183 lbs.

Year	Team		Games	Pos.
1920	RI	A	5	HB

John Chickerneo
CHICKERNEO, JOHN
B. Mar. 13, 1917, Gary, IN
Pittsburgh 6'1" 205 lbs.

Year	Team		Games	Pos.
1942	NYG	N	4	QB

Nick Chickillo
CHICKILLO, NICHOLAS A.
B. Oct. 17, 1930, Scranton, PA
Miami (Florida) 5'11" 220 lbs.

Year	Team		Games	Pos.
1953	CHIC	N	12	G

Tony Chickillo
CHICKILLO, ANTHONY PAUL
B. Jul. 8, 1960, Miami, FL
Miami (Florida) 6'2" 265 lbs.

Year	Team		Games	Pos.
1984	SD	N	1	NT
1985			4	NT
1987	NYJ	N	2	DE
3 yrs.	7 games			

Freddie Childress
CHILDRESS, FREDDIE LEE
B. Sep. 17, 1966, Little Rock, AR
Arkansas 6'4" 331 lbs.

Year	Team		Games	Pos.
1991	NE	N	15	G
1992	CLE	N	16	OT
2 yrs.	31 games			

Joe Childress
CHILDRESS, JOSEPH
B. Dec. 26, 1933, Robertsdale, AL
D. May 5, 1986, Robertsdale, AL
Auburn 6'0" 202 lbs.

Year	Team		Games	Pos.
1956	CHIC	N	11	FB
1957			12	HB
1958			10	HB
1959			9	HB
1960	STL	N	12	HB
1962			14	HB
1963			14	HB
1964			9	HB
1965			5	HB
9 yrs.	96 games			

Ray Childress
CHILDRESS, RAY
B. Oct. 20, 1962, Memphis, TN
Texas A&M 6'6" 276 lbs.

Year	Team		Games	Pos.
1985	HOU	N	16	DE
1986			16	DE
1987			13	DE
1988			16	DE
1989			14	DE
1990			16	NT, DE
1991			15	DT, DE
1992			16	DT, DE
1993			16	DT, DE
1994			16	DT
1995			6	DT
1996	DAL	N	3	DT
12 yrs.	163 games			

Clarence Childs
CHILDS, CLARENCE NORRIS
B. Jan. 13, 1938, Lakeland, FL
Florida A&M 6'0" 180 lbs.

Year	Team		Games	Pos.
1964	NYG	N	13	HB
1965			14	DB
1966			14	DB
1967			14	DB
1968	CHI	N	4	DB
5 yrs.	59 games			

Henry Childs
CHILDS, HENRY
B. Apr. 16, 1951, Thomasville, GA
Kansas State 6'2" 222 lbs.

Year	Team		Games	Pos.
1974	ATL	N	6	TE
1974	NO	N	1	TE
1975			14	TE
1976			14	TE
1977			13	TE
1978			16	TE
1979			16	TE
1980			13	TE
1981	LA	N	7	TE
1984	GB	N	3	TE
9 yrs.	103 games			

Jimmy Childs
CHILDS, JIMMY JOE
B. Aug. 9, 1956, El Dorado, AR
California Poly (San Luis Obispo) 6'2" 194 lbs.

Year	Team		Games	Pos.
1978	STL	N	8	WR
1979			13	WR
2 yrs.	21 games			

Ron Childs
CHILDS, RON LEE
B. Sep. 18, 1971, Kennewick, WA
Washington State 5'11" 212 lbs.

Year	Team		Games	Pos.
1995	NO	N	9	LB

Gene Chilton
CHILTON, GENE ALAN
B. Mar. 27, 1964, Houston, TX
Texas 6'3" 271 lbs.

Year	Team		Games	Pos.
1986	STL	N	16	C
1987			11	C
1989	KC	N	16	C, G
1990	NE	N	4	C
1991			16	C
1992			16	C
6 yrs.	79 games			

Bill Chipley
CHIPLEY, WILLIAM ALLEN
B. Jul. 2, 1920, Lynchburg, VA
Clemson/Washington & Lee 6'3" 199 lbs.

Year	Team		Games	Pos.
1947	BOS	N	6	E, DB
1948			12	E, DB
1949	NYB	N	12	E, DB
3 yrs.	30 games			

John Chirico
CHIRICO, JOHN
B. Aug. 15, 1965
Columbia 6'0" 220 lbs.

Year	Team		Games	Pos.
1987	NYJ	N	3	RB

Andy Chisick
CHISICK, ANDREW
B. Jun. 10, 1916, Sagamore, PA
D. Mar., 1986, Somerset, KY
Villanova 6'1" 207 lbs.

Year	Team		Games	Pos.
1940	CHIC	N	11	C
1941			11	C
2 yrs.	22 games			

Ed Chlebek
CHLEBEK, ED
B. 1941
Western Michigan 5'11" 175 lbs.

Year	Team		Games	Pos.
1963	NY	A	2	QB

Mark Chmura
CHMURA, MARK WILLIAM
B. Feb. 22, 1969, Deerfield, MA
Boston College 6'5" 242 lbs.

Year	Team		Games	Pos.
1993	GB	N	14	TE
1994			15	TE
1995			16	TE
1996			13	TE
4 yrs.	58 games			

Putt Choate
CHOATE, MARK PUTNAM
B. Dec. 11, 1956, Big Spring, TX
Southern Methodist 6'0" 225 lbs.

Year	Team		Games	Pos.
1987	GB	N	2	LB

Max Choboian
CHOBOIAN, MAX JOHN
B. Mar. 17, 1942, Tulare, CA
D. Jan. 2, 1977, Fresno, CA
Oregon/San Francisco State 6'4" 205 lbs.

Year	Team		Games	Pos.
1966	DEN	A	14	QB

John Choma
CHOMA, JOHN GREGORY
B. Feb. 9, 1955, Cleveland, OH

Year	Team		Games	Pos.

John Choma continued

Virginia 6'5" 251 lbs.

1981	SF	N	14	G, C
1982			7	G, C
1983			6	G

3 yrs. 27 games

Steve Chomyszak

CHOMYSZAK, STEPHEN JOHN
B. Feb. 27, 1944, Johnson City, NY
D. Jan. 25, 1984, Binghamton, NY
Syracuse 6'5" 270 lbs.

1966	NY	A	2	C, OT
1968	CIN		10	DT
1969			14	DT
1970	CIN	N	14	DT
1971			14	DT
1972			13	DT
1973			12	DT

7 yrs. 79 games

Dick Chorovich

CHOROVICH, RICHARD
B. Nov. 29, 1933, St. Clairsville, OH
Miami (Ohio) 6'4" 260 lbs.

1955	BAL	N	7	T
1956			3	T
1960	LA	A		OT

3 yrs. 10 games

Joe Chrape

CHRAPE, JOSEPH
B. 1910, Minnesota
Hibbing CC 210 lbs.

| 1929 | MIN | N | 9 | G, T, C |

Wayne Chrebet

CHREBET, WAYNE
B. Aug. 14, 1973, Garfield, NJ
Hofstra 5'10" 180 lbs.

| 1995 | NYJ | N | 16 | WR |
| 1996 | | | 16 | WR |

2 yrs. 32 games

Erik Christensen

CHRISTENSEN, ERIK ROBERT, JR.
B. Oct. 30, 1931, Elizabeth, NJ
Richmond 6'3" 235 lbs.

| 1956 | WAS | N | 2 | E |

Frank Christensen

CHRISTENSEN, FRANK L.
B. Jun. 1, 1910, Salt Lake City, UT
Utah 6'1" 199 lbs.

1934	DET	N	11	FB, HB
1935			12	HB
1936			11	HB, FB
1937			8	HB

4 yrs. 42 games

George Christensen

CHRISTENSEN, GEORGE WASHINGTON (Tarzan)
B. Dec. 13, 1909, Pendleton, OR
D. Jul. 1, 1968, Detroit, MI
Oregon 6'2" 238 lbs.

1931	POR	N	14	T, G
1932			12	T
1933			11	T
1934	DET	N	13	T
1935			12	T
1936			12	T
1937			10	T, G
1938			11	T

8 yrs. 95 games

Jeff Christensen

CHRISTENSEN, JEFFREY BRUCE
B. Jan. 8, 1961, Gibson City, IL
Eastern Illinois 6'3" 202 lbs.

1983	CIN	N	1	QB
1985	PHI	N	1	QB
1987	CLE	N	3	QB

3 yrs. 5 games

Koester Christensen

CHRISTENSEN, KOESTER L.
B. 1905
Michigan State 5'10" 195 lbs.

| 1930 | POR | N | 1 | E |

Todd Christensen

CHRISTENSEN, TODD JAY
B. Aug. 3, 1956, Bellefonte, PA
Brigham Young 6'3" 230 lbs.

1979	NYG	N	1	RB
1979	OAK	N	12	RB
1980			16	RB
1981			16	TE, RB
1982	LARI	N	9	TE, RB
1983			16	TE, RB
1984			16	TE
1985			16	TE
1986			16	TE
1987			12	TE
1988			7	TE

10 yrs. 137 games

Bob Christian

CHRISTIAN, ROBERT DOUGLAS
B. Nov. 14, 1968, St. Louis, MO
Northwestern 5'10" 220 lbs.

1992	CHI	N	2	RB
1993			14	RB
1994			12	RB
1995	CAR	N	14	RB

4 yrs. 42 games

Bob Christiansen

CHRISTIANSEN, ROBERT SCOTT
B. May 8, 1949, Marshalltown, IA
UCLA 6'4" 230 lbs.

| 1972 | BUF | N | 4 | TE |

Jack Christiansen

CHRISTIANSEN, JOHN LEROY
B. Dec. 20, 1928, Sublette, KS
D. Jun. 29, 1986, Stanford, CA
Colorado State 6'1" 190 lbs.

1951	DET	N	12	DB
1952			11	DB
1953			12	DB
1954			11	DB
1955			9	DB
1956			12	DB
1957			12	DB
1958			10	DB

8 yrs. 89 games

Marty Christiansen

CHRISTIANSEN, MARTIN A.
B. Apr. 23, 1917, Minneapolis, MN
D. Apr., 1984, El Cajon, CA
Minnesota 6'0" 200 lbs.

| 1940 | CHIC | N | 6 | FB |

Oscar Christianson

CHRISTIANSON, OSCAR (Bully)
B. Apr. 2, 1899
D. May, 1972, St. Anthony, MN
None 5'10" 186 lbs.

| 1921 | MIN | A | 4 | E |

Oscar Christianson cont.

1922	MIN	N	4	E, HB
1923			6	E
1924			6	E

4 yrs. 20 games

Steve Christie

CHRISTIE, GEOFFREY STEPHEN
B. Nov. 13, 1967, Oakville, Ont.
William & Mary 6'0" 180 lbs.

1990	TB	N	16	K
1991			16	K
1992	BUF	N	16	K
1993			16	K
1994			16	K
1995			16	K
1996			16	K

7 yrs. 112 games

Floyd Christman

CHRISTMAN, FLOYD F.
B. Oct. 14, 1902, Greenville, PA
D. Jan. 24, 1971, Rock Creek, OH
Thiel 5'11" 180 lbs.

| 1925 | BUF | N | 9 | FB, HB |

Paul Christman

CHRISTMAN, PAUL JOSEPH (Pitchin' Paul)
B. Mar. 5, 1918, St. Louis, MO
D. Mar. 2, 1970, Lake Forest, IL
Missouri 6'0" 210 lbs.

1945	CHIC	N	8	QB
1946			11	QB
1947			12	QB
1948			7	QB
1949			12	QB
1950	GB	N	11	QB

6 yrs. 61 games

Herb Christopher

CHRISTOPHER, HERBERT
B. Apr. 7, 1954, Thomasville, GA
Morris Brown 5'10" 194 lbs.

1979	KC	N	16	CB
1980			16	S
1981			16	S
1982			9	S

4 yrs. 57 games

Jim Christopherson

CHRISTOPHERSON, JIM
B. Feb. 17, 1938, Wadena, Minnesota
Concordia-Minnesota 6'0" 215 lbs.

| 1962 | MIN | N | 14 | LB |

Ryan Christopherson

CHRISTOPHERSON, RYAN
B. Jul. 26, 1972, Sioux Falls, SD
Wyoming 5'11" 237 lbs.

1995	JAC	N	11	RB
1996			2	FB
1996	ARI	N	6	RB

2 yrs. 19 games

Dick Christy

CHRISTY, RICHARD
B. Nov. 24, 1935, Chester, PA
D. Aug. 7, 1966
North Carolina State 5'10" 191 lbs.

1958	PIT	N	12	HB
1960	BOS	A		HB
1961	NY	A	14	HB
1962			14	HB
1963			11	HB

5 yrs. 51 games

Earl Christy

CHRISTY, EARL OLIVER
B. Mar. 19, 1943, Perryman, MD
Maryland-Eastern Shore 5'11" 193 lbs.

1966	NY	A	6	HB
1967			10	RB
1968			14	RB

3 yrs. 30 games

Greg Christy

CHRISTY, GREG A.
B. Apr. 29, 1962, Freeport, PA
Pittsburgh 6'4" 285 lbs.

| 1985 | BUF | N | 7 | OT |

Jeff Christy

CHRISTY, JEFFREY ALAN
B. Feb. 3, 1969, Natrona Heights, PA
Pittsburgh 6'3" 277 lbs.

1993	MIN	N	9	C
1994			16	C
1995			16	C
1996			16	C

4 yrs. 57 games

Eugene Chung

CHUNG, YON EUGENE
B. Jun. 14, 1969, Prince George's Co., MD
Virginia Tech 6'4" 295 lbs.

1992	NE	N	16	G
1993			16	OT
1994			4	G
1995	JAC	N	11	G, OT

4 yrs. 47 games

Ricky Churchman

CHURCHMAN, RICKY
B. Mar. 14, 1958, Pearland, TX
Texas 6'1" 193 lbs.

| 1980 | SF | N | 16 | S |
| 1981 | | | 3 | S |

2 yrs. 19 games

Don Churchwell

CHURCHWELL, HANSON (Bull)
B. May 11, 1936, Leakesville, MS
Mississippi 6'1" 253 lbs.

| 1959 | WAS | N | 10 | T |
| 1960 | OAK | A | | OT |

2 yrs. 10 games

Don Chuy

CHUY, DONALD JOHN
B. Jul. 20, 1941, Newark, NJ
Clemson 6'1" 255 lbs.

1963	LA	N	14	G
1964			12	G
1965			11	G
1966			9	G
1967			14	G
1968			14	G
1969	PHI	N	8	G

7 yrs. 82 games

Joe Cibulas

CIBULAS, JOSEPH J.
B. May 31, 1921, Whitney, PA
Duquesne 6'0" 220 lbs.

| 1945 | PIT | N | 5 | T |

Mike Ciccolella

CICCOLELLA, MIKE EUGENE
B. Oct. 19, 1943, Follansbee, WV
Dayton 6'1" 235 lbs.

| 1966 | NYG | N | 14 | LB |

Year	Team		Games	Pos.

Mike Ciccolella continued

Year	Team		Games	Pos.
1967			7	LB
1968			14	LB
3 yrs.	35 games			

Ben Ciccone
CICCONE, BENJAMIN M. (Scaggie)
B. Oct. 10, 1909, New Castle, PA
Duquesne 5'10" 207 lbs.

Year	Team		Games	Pos.
1934	PIT	N	10	C
1935			12	C
1942	CHIC	N	2	C
3 yrs.	24 games			

Gene Cichowski
CICHOWSKI, EUGENE W.
B. May 20, 1934, Chicago, IL
Indiana 6'0" 195 lbs.

Year	Team		Games	Pos.
1957	PIT	N	12	DB
1958	WAS	N	1	DB
1959			1	DB
3 yrs.	14 games			

Tom Cichowski
CICHOWSKI, THOMAS
B. Jun. 13, 1944, New Britain, CT
Maryland 6'4" 250 lbs.

Year	Team		Games	Pos.
1967	DEN	A	11	OT
1968			2	OT
2 yrs.	13 games			

Gus Cifelli
CIFELLI, AUGUST BLASE
B. Feb. 3, 1926, Philadelphia, PA
Notre Dame 6'4" 244 lbs.

Year	Team		Games	Pos.
1950	DET	N	12	T
1951			12	T
1952			12	T
1953	GB	N	12	T
1954	PHI	N	7	T
1954	PIT	N	5	T
5 yrs.	60 games			

Bob Cifers
CIFERS, ROBERT GALE
B. Sep. 5, 1921, Church Hill, TN
Tennessee 5'11" 201 lbs.

Year	Team		Games	Pos.
1946	DET	N	11	QB
1947	PIT	N	10	HB
1948			12	HB
1949	GB	N	9	HB
4 yrs.	42 games			

Ed Cifers
CIFERS, EDWARD C.
B. Jul. 18, 1916, Church Hill, TN
Tennessee 6'2" 227 lbs.

Year	Team		Games	Pos.
1941	WAS	N	11	E
1942			11	E
1946			11	E
1947	CHIB	N	11	E
1948			12	E
5 yrs.	56 games			

Ralph Cindrich
CINDRICH, RALPH EDWARD
B. Oct. 29, 1949, Washington, PA
Pittsburgh 6'1" 229 lbs.

Year	Team		Games	Pos.
1972	NE	N	13	LB
1973	HOU	N	13	LB
1974			6	LB
1974	DEN	N	1	LB
1975	HOU	N	4	LB
4 yrs.	37 games			

Larry Cipa
CIPA, LARRY
B. Oct. 5, 1951, Detroit, MI
Michigan 6'3" 209 lbs.

Year	Team		Games	Pos.
1974	NO	N	4	QB
1975			4	QB
2 yrs.	8 games			

Steve Cisowski
CISOWSKI, STEVE
B. Jan. 23, 1963, Campbell, CA
Santa Clara 6'5" 275 lbs.

Year	Team		Games	Pos.
1987	DAL	N	3	OT

Frank Civiletto
CIVILETTO, FRANK
B. Sep. 11, 1896
D. Feb., 1970, Cleveland Heights, OH
Case Western Reserve/Springfield 5'9" 170 lbs.

Year	Team		Games	Pos.
1923	CLE	N	4	HB

Neil Clabo
CLABO, NEIL
B. Nov. 18, 1952, Miami Beach, FL
Tennessee 6'2" 200 lbs.

Year	Team		Games	Pos.
1975	MIN	N	14	P
1976			13	P
1977			14	P
3 yrs.	41 games			

Darryl Clack
CLACK, DARRYL E.
B. Oct. 29, 1963, San Antonio, TX
Arizona State 5'10" 218 lbs.

Year	Team		Games	Pos.
1986	DAL	N	16	RB
1987			12	RB
1988			15	RB
1989			8	RB
4 yrs.	51 games			

Jim Clack
CLACK, JAMES THOMAS
B. Oct. 26, 1947, Rocky Mount, NC
Wake Forest 6'3" 250 lbs.

Year	Team		Games	Pos.
1971	PIT	N	14	C
1972			14	C
1973			12	C
1974			13	C
1975			14	G, C
1976			11	G, C
1977			14	C
1978	NYG	N	16	G, C
1979			16	C
1980			16	C
1981			6	C
11 yrs.	146 games			

Walt Clago
CLAGO, WALTER
B. Jun., 1899
Deceased
Detroit 6'0" 195 lbs.

Year	Team		Games	Pos.
1921	DET	A	6	E
1922	RI	N	7	E
2 yrs.	13 games			

Robert Claiborne
CLAIBORNE, ROBERT
B. Jul. 10, 1967, New Orleans, LA
San Diego State 5'10" 175 lbs.

Year	Team		Games	Pos.
1992	SD	N	9	WR
1993	TB	N	5	WR
2 yrs.	14 games			

Frank Clair
CLAIR, FRANK J.
B. May 12, 1917, Hamilton, OH
Ohio State 6'1" 204 lbs.

Year	Team		Games	Pos.
1941	WAS	N	6	E

Rickey Claitt
CLAITT, RICKEY
B. Apr. 12, 1957, Sylvester, GA
Bethune-Cookman 5'10" 206 lbs.

Year	Team		Games	Pos.
1980	WAS	N	15	RB
1981			13	RB
2 yrs.	28 games			

Jack Clancy
CLANCY, JOHN DAVID
B. Jun. 18, 1944, Humboldt, IA
Michigan 6'1" 295 lbs.

Year	Team		Games	Pos.
1967	MIA	A	14	FL
1969			8	WR
1970	GB	N	14	WR
3 yrs.	36 games			

Sam Clancy
CLANCY, SAM
B. May 29, 1958, Pittsburgh, PA
Pittsburgh 6'7" 260 lbs.

Year	Team		Games	Pos.
1983	SEA	N	13	DE
1985	CLE	N	14	DE
1986			16	DE
1987			13	DE
1988			16	DE
1989	IND	N	16	DE
1990			16	DE
1991			16	DE
1992			16	DE
1993			16	DE
10 yrs.	152 games			

Sean Clancy
CLANCY, SEAN MATTHEW
B. Oct. 22, 1956, Manhasset, NY
Amherst 6'4" 218 lbs.

Year	Team		Games	Pos.
1978	MIA	N	16	LB
1979	STL	N	10	LB
2 yrs.	26 games			

Stu Clancy
CLANCY, JOSEPH STUART
B. Jun. 6, 1906, Branford, CT
D. Sep., 1965
Holy Cross 5'10" 189 lbs.

Year	Team		Games	Pos.
1930	NEW	N	2	FB
1931	SI	N	10	HB, FB
1932			8	HB, FB
1932	NYG	N	3	HB, QB
1933			10	QB, FB
1934			9	HB, QB
1935			5	HB, QB, FB
6 yrs.	47 games			

Chuck Clanton
CLANTON, CLEVELAND E.
B. Jul. 15, 1962, Richmond, VA
Auburn 5'11" 192 lbs.

Year	Team		Games	Pos.
1985	GB	N	16	CB, S

Sam Claphan
CLAPHAN, SAM JACK
B. Oct. 10, 1956, Tahlequah, OK
Oklahoma 6'7" 285 lbs.

Year	Team		Games	Pos.
1981	SD	N	16	OT
1982			2	OT
1983			16	OT
1984			16	OT
1985			12	OT
1986			16	OT

Sam Claphan continued

Year	Team		Games	Pos.
1987			9	OT
7 yrs.	87 games			

Dennis Claridge
CLARIDGE, DENNIS
B. Aug. 18, 1941, Phoenix, AZ
Nebraska 6'3" 225 lbs.

Year	Team		Games	Pos.
1965	GB	N	1	QB
1966	ATL	N	7	QB
2 yrs.	8 games			

Al Clark
CLARK, AL
B. Feb. 29, 1948, Bogalusa, LA
Grambling St./Northern Arizona/Eastern Mich. 6'0" 183 lbs.

Year	Team		Games	Pos.
1971	DET	N	9	DB
1972	LA	N	14	CB
1973			14	CB
1974			14	CB
1975			4	CB
1976	PHI	N	14	CB
6 yrs.	69 games			

Algy Clark
CLARK, MYERS ALGERNON
B. 1904
Ohio State 6'0" 188 lbs.

Year	Team		Games	Pos.
1930	BKN	N	7	QB, HB, FB
1931	CLE	N	8	HB, QB
1932	BOS	N	8	HB, QB, FB
1933	CIN	N	10	QB
1934	C, S	N	7	QB, T
1934	PHI	N	3	QB
5 yrs.	43 games			

Allan Clark
CLARK, ALLAN VINCENT
B. Jun. 8, 1957, Grand Rapids, MI
Northern Arizona 5'10" 186 lbs.

Year	Team		Games	Pos.
1979	NE	N	16	RB
1980			11	RB
1982	BUF	N	1	RB
1982	GB	N	5	RB
3 yrs.	33 games			

Babe Clark
CLARK, BABE
None

Year	Team		Games	Pos.
1922	ROC	N	1	QB

Bernard Clark
CLARK, BERNARD
B. Jan. 12, 1967, Tampa, FL
Miami (Florida) 6'2" 248 lbs.

Year	Team		Games	Pos.
1990	CIN	N	14	LB
1991			12	LB
1991	SEA	N	2	LB
2 yrs.	28 games			

Beryl Clark
CLARK, BERYL
B. Oct. 13, 1917, Cherokee, OK
Oklahoma 6'0" 200 lbs.

Year	Team		Games	Pos.
1940	CHIC	N	9	HB

Bill Clark
CLARK, WILLIAM
None 6'2" 170 lbs.

Year	Team		Games	Pos.
1920	CHIC	A	3	C, G

Bill Clark
CLARK, WILLIAM D.
B. Aug. 12, 1891, TN

Year	Team		Games	Pos.

Bill Clark continued
D. Jan., 1973, Cleveland, OH
None 5'11" 194 lbs.

Year	Team		Games	Pos.
1920	**DAY**	**A**		2 G

Boobie Clark
CLARK, CHARLES L.
B. Nov. 8, 1950, Jacksonville, FL
D. Oct. 25, 1988, Jacksonville, FL
Bethune-Cookman 6'2" 245 lbs.

Year	Team		Games	Pos.
1973	**CIN**	**N**	14	RB
1974			8	RB
1975			14	RB
1976			13	RB
1977			10	RB
1978			14	RB
1979	**HOU**	**N**	15	RB
1980			6	RB

8 yrs.   94 games

Bret Clark
CLARK, BRET
B. Feb. 24, 1961, Nebraska City, NE
Nebraska 6'3" 198 lbs.

Year	Team		Games	Pos.
1986	**ATL**	**N**	16	S
1987			1	S
1988			12	S

3 yrs.   29 games

Brian Clark
CLARK, BRIAN MATTHEW
B. Jun. 28, 1958, Canton, OH
Florida 6'2" 190 lbs.

Year	Team		Games	Pos.
1982	**TB**	**N**	1	K

Bruce Clark
CLARK, BRUCE
B. Mar. 31, 1958, New Castle, PA
Penn State 6'3" 270 lbs.

Year	Team		Games	Pos.
1982	**NO**	**N**	9	DE
1983			15	DE
1984			15	DE
1985			16	DE
1986			16	DE
1987			15	DE
1988			16	DE
1989	**KC**	**N**	11	DE

8 yrs.   113 games

Bryan Clark
CLARK, MONTE BRYAN
B. Jul. 27, 1960, Redwood City, CA
Michigan State 6'2" 196 lbs.

Year	Team		Games	Pos.
1984	**CIN**	**N**	1	QB

Charlie Clark
CLARK, CHARLES ARTHUR
B. Feb. 15, 1898, Somerville, MA
Deceased
Harvard 5'10" 205 lbs.

Year	Team		Games	Pos.
1924	**CHIC**	**N**	4	G

Danny Clark
CLARK, DANNY
B. May 21, 1964, Zoma, Japan
San Jose State 6'2" 233 lbs.

Year	Team		Games	Pos.
1987	**LARM**	**N**	1	LB

Darryl Clark
CLARK, DARRYL WADE
B. Aug. 9, 1961, Houston, TX
Texas 5'11" 204 lbs.

Year	Team		Games	Pos.
1987	**CHI**	**N**	3	RB

Derrick Clark
CLARK, DERRICK
B. May 4, 1971, Apopka, FL
Evangel 6'1" 235 lbs.

Year	Team		Games	Pos.
1994	**DEN**	**N**	16	RB

Dexter Clark
CLARK, DEXTER DEWAYNE
B. May 5, 1964
Toledo 6'0" 190 lbs.

Year	Team		Games	Pos.
1987	**DET**	**N**	2	CB, S

Don Clark
CLARK, DONALD REX
B. Dec. 22, 1923
D. Aug. 6, 1989, Huntington Beach, CA
Southern California 5'11" 197 lbs.

Year	Team		Games	Pos.
1948	**SF**	**AA**	14	G
1949			12	G

2 yrs.   26 games

Dutch Clark
CLARK, EARL HARRY
B. Oct. 11, 1906, Fowler, CO
D. Aug. 5, 1978, Canon City, CO
Colorado College 6'0" 182 lbs.

Year	Team		Games	Pos.
1931	**POR**	**N**	11	QB, HB
1932			10	QB
1934	**DET**	**N**	12	QB
1935			12	QB, HB
1936			10	QB, HB
1937			11	QB
1938			6	QB

7 yrs.   72 games

Dwight Clark
CLARK, DWIGHT EDWARD
B. Jan. 8, 1957, Kinston, NC
Clemson 6'4" 215 lbs.

Year	Team		Games	Pos.
1979	**SF**	**N**	12	WR
1980			16	WR
1981			16	WR
1982			9	WR
1983			16	WR
1984			16	WR
1985			16	WR
1986			16	WR
1987			13	WR

9 yrs.   134 games

Ernie Clark
CLARK, ERNEST ROBERT
B. Aug. 11, 1937, Arcadia, FL
Michigan State 6'1" 222 lbs.

Year	Team		Games	Pos.
1963	**DET**	**N**	14	LB
1964			14	LB
1965			14	LB
1966			14	LB
1967			12	LB
1968	**STL**	**N**	14	LB

6 yrs.   82 games

Gail Clark
CLARK, GAIL A.
B. Apr. 14, 1951, Bellefontaine, OH
Michigan State 6'2" 226 lbs.

Year	Team		Games	Pos.
1973	**CHI**	**N**	11	LB
1974	**NE**	**N**	8	LB

2 yrs.   19 games

Gary Clark
CLARK, GARY C.
B. May 1, 1962, Radford, VA
James Madison 5'9" 173 lbs.

Year	Team		Games	Pos.
1985	**WAS**	**N**	16	WR
1986			16	WR

Gary Clark continued

Year	Team		Games	Pos.
1987			12	WR
1988			16	WR
1989			15	WR
1990			16	WR
1991			16	WR
1992			16	WR
1993	**PHX**	**N**	14	WR
1994	**ARI**	**N**	15	WR
1995	**MIA**	**N**	16	WR

11 yrs.   167 games

Greg Clark
CLARK, GREGORY KLONDIKE
B. Mar. 5, 1965, Los Angeles, CA
Arizona State 6'0" 221 lbs.

Year	Team		Games	Pos.
1988	**CHI**	**N**	15	LB
1989	**MIA**	**N**	16	LB
1990	**LARM**	**N**	11	LB
1991	**GB**	**N**	2	LB
1991	**SD**	**N**	14	LB
1992	**SEA**	**N**	12	LB

5 yrs.   70 games

Hal Clark
CLARK, HAROLD E. (Butch)
B. Oct. 25, 1893, New York State
D. Jul., 1973, Rochester, NY
None 5'10" 195 lbs.

Year	Team		Games	Pos.
1920	**ROC**	**A**	1	E
1922	**ROC**	**N**	1	E
1923			3	E
1924			7	E
1925			5	E

5 yrs.   17 games

Harry Clark
CLARK, HARRY CHARLES (Flash)
B. Dec. 1, 1917, Cumberland, MD
West Virginia 6'0" 186 lbs.

Year	Team		Games	Pos.
1940	**CHIB**	**N**	11	HB
1941			10	HB
1942			11	HB
1943			10	HB
1946	**LA**	**AA**	14	HB
1947			12	B
1948			12	B
1948	**CHI**	**AA**	5	B

7 yrs.   75 games

Herman Clark
CLARK, HERMAN P.
B. Nov. 30, 1930, Honolulu, HI
Deceased
Oregon State 6'3" 258 lbs.

Year	Team		Games	Pos.
1952	**CHIB**	**N**	12	G
1954			5	G
1955			11	G
1956			12	G
1957			12	G

5 yrs.   52 games

Howard Clark
CLARK, HOWARD
B. 1935
Tennessee-Chattanooga 6'2" 210 lbs.

Year	Team		Games	Pos.
1960	**LA**	**A**		OE
1961	**SD**	**A**	10	OE

2 yrs.   10 games

Jessie Clark
CLARK, JESSIE L.
B. Jan. 3, 1960, Thebes, AR
Louisiana Tech/Arkansas 6'0" 233 lbs.

Year	Team		Games	Pos.
1983	**GB**	**N**	16	RB
1984			11	FB
1985			3	FB
1986			5	RB

Jessie Clark continued

Year	Team		Games	Pos.
1987			12	FB
1988	**DET**	**N**	5	RB
1988	**PHX**	**N**	4	RB
1989			11	RB
1989	**MIN**	**N**	3	RB
1990			5	RB

8 yrs.   75 games

Jim Clark
CLARK, JAMES
B. Jul. 28, 1929, Honolulu, HI
Oregon State 6'1" 230 lbs.

Year	Team		Games	Pos.
1952	**WAS**	**N**	8	G
1953			12	T, G

2 yrs.   20 games

Jimmy Clark
CLARK, JAMES
B. 1909
Pittsburgh 5'9" 174 lbs.

Year	Team		Games	Pos.
1933	**PIT**	**N**	10	HB, FB
1934			9	HB, FB

2 yrs.   19 games

Jon Clark
CLARK, JON
B. Apr. 11, 1973, Philadelphia, PA
Temple 6'6" 339 lbs.

Year	Team		Games	Pos.
1996	**CHI**	**N**	2	OT

Kelvin Clark
CLARK, KELVIN
B. Jan. 30, 1956, Odessa, TX
Nebraska 6'3" 260 lbs.

Year	Team		Games	Pos.
1979	**DEN**	**N**	15	OT
1980			14	OT
1981			16	OT
1982	**NO**	**N**	9	G
1983			16	G
1984			16	G
1985			2	G

7 yrs.   88 games

Ken Clark
CLARK, KEN
B. Jun. 11, 1966, Evergreen, AL
Nebraska 5'9" 203 lbs.

Year	Team		Games	Pos.
1990	**IND**	**N**	5	RB
1991			16	RB
1992			13	RB

3 yrs.   34 games

Ken Clark
CLARK, KENNETH LAWRENCE
B. May 26, 1948, Southampton, England
St. Mary's (Nova Scotia) 6'2" 197 lbs.

Year	Team		Games	Pos.
1979	**LA**	**N**	16	P

Kevin Clark
CLARK, KEVIN RANDALL (K.C.)
B. Jun. 8, 1964, Sacramento, CA
San Jose State 5'10" 185 lbs.

Year	Team		Games	Pos.
1987	**DEN**	**N**	11	S
1988			3	S
1990			8	DB
1991			4	CB, S

4 yrs.   26 games

Leroy Clark
CLARK, LEROY
B. Jan. 16, 1950, College Station, TX
Prairie View A&M 5'11" 200 lbs.

Year	Team		Games	Pos.
1976	**HOU**	**N**		P

Year	Team	Games	Pos.

Louis Clark
CLARK, LOUIS STEVEN
B. Jul. 3, 1964, Shannon, MS
Mississippi State 6'0" 206 lbs.

Year	Team		Games	Pos.
1987	SEA	N	2	WR
1988			7	WR
1989			16	WR
1990			4	WR
1991			16	WR
1992			10	WR
6 yrs.	55 games			

Mario Clark
CLARK, MARIO SEAN
B. Mar. 29, 1954, Pasadena, CA
Oregon 6'2" 193 lbs.

Year	Team		Games	Pos.
1976	BUF	N	14	DB
1977			14	CB
1978			16	CB
1979			16	CB
1980			16	CB
1981			16	CB
1982			9	CB
1983			14	CB
1984	SF	N	11	CB
9 yrs.	126 games			

Mike Clark
CLARK, MICHAEL HUGH
B. Mar. 30, 1959, Dothan, AL
Florida 6'4" 240 lbs.

Year	Team		Games	Pos.
1981	WAS	N	5	DE
1982	SF	N	6	DE
1987	TB	N	3	DE
3 yrs.	14 games			

Mike Clark
CLARK, MICHAEL VINCENT
B. Nov. 7, 1940, Marshall, TX
Texas A&M 6'1" 203 lbs.

Year	Team		Games	Pos.
1963	PHI	N	14	K
1964	PIT	N	14	K
1965			14	K
1966			14	K
1967			14	K
1968	DAL	N	14	K
1969			14	K
1970			14	K
1971			12	K
1973			4	K
10 yrs.	128 games			

Mike Clark
CLARK, MIKE (Spark)
B. May 22, 1965
Akron 5'7" 182 lbs.

Year	Team		Games	Pos.
1987	PIT	N	1	RB

Monte Clark
CLARK, MONTE DALE
B. Jan. 24, 1937, Fillmore, CA
Southern California 6'6" 260 lbs.

Year	Team		Games	Pos.
1959	SF	N	12	T
1960			12	T
1961			12	DT
1962	DAL	N	14	OT
1963	CLE	N	8	OT
1964			14	OT
1965			14	OT
1966			12	OT
1967			13	OT
1968			14	OT
1969			14	OT
11 yrs.	139 games			

Phil Clark
CLARK, PHILIP EUGENE
B. Apr. 28, 1945, Burlington, KY

Phil Clark continued
Northwestern 6'2" 209 lbs.

Year	Team		Games	Pos.
1967	DAL	N	11	DB
1968			13	DB
1969			14	CB
1970	CHI	N	13	S
1971	NE	N	2	DB
5 yrs.	53 games			

Randy Clark
CLARK, RANDALL BYRON
B. Jul. 27, 1957, Chicago, IL
Northern Illinois 6'3" 264 lbs.

Year	Team		Games	Pos.
1980	STL	N	8	OL
1981			16	G, C
1982			9	C, G
1983			14	C
1984			16	C
1985			16	C
1986			12	C
1987	ATL	N	3	G
8 yrs.	94 games			

Randy Clark
CLARK, RANDY CHARLES
B. Feb. 18, 1962, Marshall, MI
Florida 6'0" 204 lbs.

Year	Team		Games	Pos.
1984	TB	N	2	CB, S

Reggie Clark
CLARK, REGGIE
B. Oct. 17, 1967, Charlotte, NC
North Carolina 6'2" 226 lbs.

Year	Team		Games	Pos.
1994	PIT	N	5	LB
1995	JAC	N	5	LB
1996			5	LB
3 yrs.	15 games			

Robert Clark
CLARK, ROBERT
B. Aug. 8, 1965, Brooklyn, NY
North Carolina Central 5'11" 175 lbs.

Year	Team		Games	Pos.
1987	NO	N	2	WR
1988			16	WR
1989	DET	N	16	WR
1990			16	WR
1991			14	WR
1992	MIA	N	3	WR
6 yrs.	67 games			

Russ Clark
CLARK, RUSSELL
B. Oct. 3, 1903
D. May 9, 1977, Cape May, NJ
Muhlenberg 5'11" 190 lbs.

Year	Team		Games	Pos.
1926	NEW	A	3	G, T

Sedric Clark
CLARK, SEDRIC
B. Jan. 28, 1973, Missouri City, TX
Tulsa 6'1" 248 lbs.

Year	Team		Games	Pos.
1996	BAL	N	6	LB

Steve Clark
CLARK, STEPHAN SPENCE
B. Aug. 20, 1960, Salt Lake City, UT
Utah 6'4" 260 lbs.

Year	Team		Games	Pos.
1982	MIA	N	2	DE
1983			11	NT
1984			12	NT
1985			16	G
4 yrs.	41 games			

Steve Clark
CLARK, STEVAN DION
B. Oct. 29, 1959, Chattanooga, TN

Steve Clark continued
Kansas State 6'5" 258 lbs.

Year	Team		Games	Pos.
1981	NE	N	7	DE

Steve Clark
CLARK, STEVE
B. Dec. 14, 1962, Arlington, VA
Liberty 6'2" 190 lbs.

Year	Team		Games	Pos.
1987	BUF	N	3	S

Torin Clark
CLARK, TORIN
B. Dec. 31, 1963
West Virginia State 6'1" 175 lbs.

Year	Team		Games	Pos.
1987	TB	N	2	CB, S

Vinnie Clark
CLARK, VINCENT EUGENE
B. Jan. 22, 1969, Cincinnati, OH
Ohio State 6'0" 194 lbs.

Year	Team		Games	Pos.
1991	GB	N	16	CB
1992			16	CB
1993	ATL	N	15	CB
1994			11	CB
1994	NO	N	5	CB
1995	JAC	N	16	CB
1996			4	CB
6 yrs.	83 games			

Wayne Clark
CLARK, WAYNE
B. Apr. 13, 1918, Los Angeles, CA
Deceased
Utah 6'3" 210 lbs.

Year	Team		Games	Pos.
1944	DET	N	8	E

Wayne Clark
CLARK, WAYNE MAURICE
B. May 30, 1947, Oskaloosa, IA
U.S. International 6'2" 203 lbs.

Year	Team		Games	Pos.
1970	SD	N	1	QB
1972			13	QB
1973			11	QB
1974	CIN	N	14	QB
4 yrs.	39 games			

Willie Clark
CLARK, WILLIE CALVIN
B. Jan. 6, 1972, New Haven, CT
Notre Dame 5'10" 186 lbs.

Year	Team		Games	Pos.
1994	SD	N	6	CB
1995			16	CB
1996			16	CB
3 yrs.	38 games			

Frank Clarke
CLARKE, FRANK D.
B. Mar. 7, 1934, Beloit, WI
Colorado 6'0" 211 lbs.

Year	Team		Games	Pos.
1957	CLE	N	12	E
1958			12	E
1959			12	E
1960	DAL	N	8	OE
1961			14	OE
1962			12	HB
1963			14	HB
1964			14	FL
1965			14	FL
1966			14	OE
1967			14	TE
11 yrs.	140 games			

Hagood Clarke
CLARKE, HAGOOD
B. Jun. 14, 1942, Atlanta, GA

Hagood Clarke continued
Florida 6'0" 193 lbs.

Year	Team		Games	Pos.
1964	BUF	A	14	DB
1965			14	DB
1966			14	DB
1967			11	DB
1968			14	DB
5 yrs.	67 games			

Ken Clarke
CLARKE, KENNETH MAURICE
B. Aug. 28, 1956, Savannah, GA
Syracuse 6'2" 280 lbs.

Year	Team		Games	Pos.
1978	PHI	N	16	NT
1979			16	NT
1980			16	NT
1981			16	NT
1982			9	NT
1983			16	NT
1984			16	NT
1985			16	NT
1986			16	DT
1987			11	DT
1988	SEA	N	16	NT
1989	MIN	N	11	DT
1990			16	DT
1991			16	DT
14 yrs.	203 games			

Leon Clarke
CLARKE, LEON T.
B. Jan. 10, 1933, Los Angeles, CA
Southern California 6'4" 232 lbs.

Year	Team		Games	Pos.
1956	LA	N	12	E
1957			9	E
1958			11	E
1959			11	E
1960	CLE	N	9	E
1961			13	OE
1962			11	OE
1963	MIN	N	3	OE
8 yrs.	79 games			

Potsy Clarke
CLARKE, ALFRED C.
B. Dec. 11, 1900
D. Sep., 1973, Ontario, CA
Nevada-Reno 5'7" 180 lbs.

Year	Team		Games	Pos.
1927	FRA	N	1	T
1927	DUL	N	5	HB, QB
1 yr.	6 games			

Bill Clarken
CLARKEN, WILLIAM
B. Sep. 11, 1899, New Jersey
D. Dec., 1982, Kissimmee, FL
None 6'0" 240 lbs.

Year	Team		Games	Pos.
1929	ORA	N	5	G, QB, T

Conrad Clarks
CLARKS, CONRAD
B. Apr. 21, 1969, Franklin, LA
Northeast Louisiana 5'10" 212 lbs.

Year	Team		Games	Pos.
1995	IND	N	6	S

Stu Clarkson
CLARKSON, STUART
B. Jul. 4, 1919, Corpus Christi, TX
D. Oct., 1957
Texas A&I-Kingsville 6'2" 217 lbs.

Year	Team		Games	Pos.
1942	CHIB	N	7	C, LB
1946			9	C, LB
1947			12	C, LB
1948			10	C, LB
1949			12	C, LB
1950			11	C, LB
1951			11	C, LB
7 yrs.	72 games			

Year	Team	Games	Pos.

Bob Clasby
CLASBY, ROBERT JAMES
B. Sep. 28, 1960, Milton, MA
Notre Dame 6'5" 260 lbs.

Year	Team		Games	Pos.
1986	STL	N	16	DE
1987			12	DE
1988	PHX	N	16	DT
1989			4	DT
1990			1	DT
5 yrs.	49 games			

Corwin Clatt
CLATT, CORWIN SAMUEL
(Cornie)
B. Feb. 5, 1924, Des Moines, IA
Notre Dame 6'0" 210 lbs.

Year	Team		Games	Pos.
1948	CHIC	N	12	FB
1949			12	FB
2 yrs.	24 games			

Bobby Clatterbuck
CLATTERBUCK, ROBERT
B. Jul. 3, 1931
Houston 6'3" 195 lbs.

Year	Team		Games	Pos.
1954	NYG	N	9	QB
1955			3	QB
1956			2	QB
1957			1	QB
1960	LA	A		QB
5 yrs.	15 games			

Shannon Clavelle
CLAVELLE, SHANNON
B. Dec. 12, 1973, Lafayette, LA
Colorado 6'2" 283 lbs.

Year	Team		Games	Pos.
1995	GB	N	1	DE
1996			8	DE
2 yrs.	9 games			

Billy Clay
CLAY, WILLIAM F.
B. Apr. 28, 1944, Oxford, MS
Mississippi 6'1" 192 lbs.

Year	Team		Games	Pos.
1966	WAS	N	6	DB

Boyd Clay
CLAY, BOYD D.
B. May 5, 1913, Hohenwald, TN
Tennessee 6'1" 220 lbs.

Year	Team		Games	Pos.
1940	CLE	N	11	T
1941			11	T
1942			8	T
1944			6	T
4 yrs.	36 games			

Hayward Clay
CLAY, HAYWARD JOHN
B. Jul. 25, 1973, Snyder, TX
Texas 6'4" 256 lbs.

Year	Team		Games	Pos.
1996	STL	N	10	TE

John Clay
CLAY, JOHN GREGORY
B. May 1, 1964, St. Louis, MO
Missouri 6'5" 305 lbs.

Year	Team		Games	Pos.
1987	LARI	N	10	OT
1988	SD	N	2	OT
2 yrs.	12 games			

Ozzie Clay
CLAY, OSWALD
B. Sep. 10, 1941, Hickory, NC
Iowa State 6'0" 190 lbs.

Year	Team		Games	Pos.
1964	WAS	N	14	FL

Randy Clay
CLAY, RANDALL
B. 1928
Texas 6'0" 188 lbs.

Year	Team		Games	Pos.
1950	NYG	N	12	B
1953			12	HB
2 yrs.	24 games			

Walt Clay
CLAY, WALTER E. (Hatchet)
B. Jan. 8, 1924, Erie, CO
Colorado 5'11" 196 lbs.

Year	Team		Games	Pos.
1946	CHI	AA	13	HB
1947			3	B
1947	LA	AA	8	B
1948			13	B
1949			10	B
4 yrs.	47 games			

Willie Clay
CLAY, WILLIE JAMES
B. Sep. 5, 1970, Pittsburgh, PA
Georgia Tech 5'9" 184 lbs.

Year	Team		Games	Pos.
1992	DET	N	6	CB
1993			16	CB
1994			16	S
1995			16	S
1996	NE	N	16	S
5 yrs.	70 games			

Raymond Clayborn
CLAYBORN, RAYMOND DEWAYNE
B. Jan. 2, 1955, Fort Worth, TX
Texas 6'0" 189 lbs.

Year	Team		Games	Pos.
1977	NE	N	14	DB
1978			16	CB
1979			16	CB
1980			16	CB
1981			16	CB
1982			9	CB
1983			16	CB
1984			16	CB
1985			16	CB
1986			16	CB
1987			10	CB
1988			16	CB
1989			14	CB
1990	CLE	N	16	CB
1991			1	CB
15 yrs.	208 games			

Ralph Claypool
CLAYPOOL, RALPH L.
B. Dec. 15, 1898
D. Nov. 17, 1989
Purdue 5'11" 191 lbs.

Year	Team		Games	Pos.
1925	CHIC	N	13	C, G
1926			11	C, G
1927			2	C
1928			4	C
4 yrs.	30 games			

Harvey Clayton
CLAYTON, HARVEY JEROME
B. Apr. 4, 1961, Kendall, FL
Florida State 5'9" 175 lbs.

Year	Team		Games	Pos.
1983	PIT	N	14	CB
1984			14	CB
1985			14	CB
1986			15	CB
1987	NYG	N	2	CB
5 yrs.	59 games			

Mark Clayton
CLAYTON, MARK GREGORY
B. Apr. 8, 1961, Indianapolis, IN

Mark Clayton continued
Louisville 5'9" 175 lbs.

Year	Team		Games	Pos.
1983	MIA	N	15	WR
1984			15	WR
1985			16	WR
1986			15	WR
1987			12	WR
1988			16	WR
1989			15	WR
1990			10	WR
1991			16	WR
1992			13	WR
1993	GB	N	16	WR
11 yrs.	159 games			

Ralph Clayton
CLAYTON, RALPH
B. Sep. 29, 1958, Highland Park, MI
Michigan 6'3" 222 lbs.

Year	Team		Games	Pos.
1981	STL	N	7	WR

Stan Clayton
CLAYTON, STANLEY DAVID
B. Jan. 31, 1965, Philadelphia, PA
Penn State 6'3" 265 lbs.

Year	Team		Games	Pos.
1988	ATL	N	2	OT
1989			13	OT, G
1990	NE	N	11	OT, G
3 yrs.	26 games			

Paul Cleary
CLEARY, PAUL H.
B. 1922
Southern California 6'1" 196 lbs.

Year	Team		Games	Pos.
1948	NY	AA	13	E
1949	CHI	AA	10	E
2 yrs.	23 games			

Bob Clemens
CLEMENS, ROBERT
B. Aug. 27, 1939, North Braddock, PA
Pittsburgh 6'1" 208 lbs.

Year	Team		Games	Pos.
1962	BAL	N	9	RB

Bob Clemens
CLEMENS, ROBERT N.
B. Aug. 3, 1933, Scottsboro, AL
Georgia 6'2" 200 lbs.

Year	Team		Games	Pos.
1955	GB	N	2	FB

Cal Clemens
CLEMENS, CALVIN, JR.
B. Jul. 7, 1909, Oklahoma City, OK
D. May, 1966
Southern California 6'1" 195 lbs.

Year	Team		Games	Pos.
1936	GB	N	9	QB, HB

Alex Clement
CLEMENT, ALEXANDER M.
B. Feb. 11, 1904
D. Jan. 13, 1970, Plymouth, MA
Williams 5'10" 170 lbs.

Year	Team		Games	Pos.
1925	FRA	N	3	HB

Johnny Clement
CLEMENT, JOHN LOUIS (Mr. Zero)
B. Oct. 31, 1919, Stonebluff, OK
D. Dec., 1969
Southern Methodist 6'0" 189 lbs.

Year	Team		Games	Pos.
1941	CHIC	N	9	FB, HB
1946	PIT	N	11	HB
1947			10	HB
1948			5	HB
1949	CHI	AA	12	B
5 yrs.	47 games			

Skip Clement
CLEMENT, HENRY
B. Jun. 15, 1939
North Carolina 6'2" 200 lbs.

Year	Team		Games	Pos.
1961	PIT	N	14	OE

Chase Clements
CLEMENTS, GEORGE CHASE
B. Dec. 31, 1901
D. Aug. 8, 1971, Toledo, OH
Washington & Jefferson 6'3" 205 lbs.

Year	Team		Games	Pos.
1925	AKR	N	2	T

Tom Clements
CLEMENTS, THOMAS ALBERT
B. Jun. 18, 1953, McKees Rocks, PA
Notre Dame 6'0" 183 lbs.

Year	Team		Games	Pos.
1980	KC			QB

Vin Clements
CLEMENTS, VINCENT ANTHONY, JR.
B. Jan. 4, 1949, Southington, CT
Connecticut 6'3" 213 lbs.

Year	Team		Games	Pos.
1972	NYG	N	4	RB
1973			12	RB
2 yrs.	16 games			

Craig Clemons
CLEMONS, CRAIG LYNN
B. Jun. 1, 1949, Sidney, OH
Iowa 5'11" 195 lbs.

Year	Team		Games	Pos.
1972	CHI	N	14	DB
1973			14	CB
1974			14	S
1975			14	S
1976			14	S
1977			13	S
6 yrs.	83 games			

Duane Clemons
CLEMONS, DUANE
B. May 23, 1974, Riverside, CA
California 6'5" 261 lbs.

Year	Team		Games	Pos.
1996	MIN	N	13	LB

Michael Clemons
CLEMONS, MICHAEL LUTRELL
B. Jan. 15, 1965, Clearwater, FL
William & Mary 5'5" 166 lbs.

Year	Team		Games	Pos.
1987	KC	N	6	RB

Ray Clemons
CLEMONS, NORVILLE RAYMOND (Duke)
B. Jun. 4, 1912
D. Dec. 11, 1980, Lincoln Park, MI
Central Oklahoma 6'0" 215 lbs.

Year	Team		Games	Pos.
1939	DET	N	6	G

Ray Clemons
CLEMONS, RAYMOND G.
B. Apr. 2, 1921, Roseville, CA
St. Mary's (California) 5'10" 220 lbs.

Year	Team		Games	Pos.
1947	GB	N	9	G

Topper Clemons
CLEMONS, ORMAN WENDELL
B. Sep. 16, 1963
Wake Forest 5'11" 205 lbs.

Year	Team		Games	Pos.
1987	PHI	N	3	RB

Mike Clendenen
CLENDENEN, MICHAEL

Year	Team	Games	Pos.

Mike Clendenen *continued*
B. Jun. 12, 1963
Houston 5'11" 191 lbs.

1987	DEN	N	3	K

Einar Cleve
CLEVE, ALBERT
B. Oct., 1896
Deceased
None 5'9" 175 lbs.

1921	MIN	A	3	E, HB
1922	MIN	A	4	HB
1923			8	HB
1924			4	HB, QB

4 yrs. 19 games

Greg Cleveland
CLEVELAND, GREG
B. Aug. 19, 1964
Florida 6'5" 295 lbs.

1987	MIA	N	2	OT

Greg Clifton
CLIFTON, GREG
B. Feb. 6, 1968, Charlotte, NC
Virginia Military Institute/Johnson C. Smith 5'11" 175 lbs.

1993	WAS	N	2	WR

Kyle Clifton
CLIFTON, KYLE
B. Aug. 23, 1962, Olney, TX
Texas Christian 6'4" 230 lbs.

1984	NYJ	N	16	LB
1985			16	LB
1986			16	LB
1987			12	LB
1988			16	LB
1989			16	LB
1990			16	LB
1991			16	LB
1992			16	LB
1993			16	LB
1994			16	LB
1995			16	LB
1996			16	LB

13 yrs. 204 games

Ben Clime
CLIME, BENJAMIN
B. Oct. 14, 1891
D. Jan. 13, 1973, Fort Lauderdale, FL
Swarthmore 5'11" 190 lbs.

1920	ROC	A	1	E
1921			2	E, FB

2 yrs. 3 games

Doug Cline
CLINE, DOUG
B. 1939
Clemson 6'2" 225 lbs.

1960	HOU	A	14	FB
1961			14	LB
1962			14	LB
1963			14	LB
1964			14	LB
1965			14	LB
1966			9	LB
1966	SD	A	2	LB

7 yrs. 95 games

Jackie Cline
CLINE, JACKIE WAYNE
B. Mar. 13, 1960, Kansas City, MO
Alabama 6'5" 276 lbs.

1987	PIT	N	1	DE
1987	MIA	N	7	NT

Jackie Cline *continued*

1988			14	NT
1989			15	DE
1990	DET	N	5	DE

4 yrs. 42 games

Ollie Cline
CLINE, OLIVER M.
B. Dec. 31, 1925, Mount Vernon, OH
Ohio State 6'0" 200 lbs.

1948	CLE	AA	11	B
1949	BUF	AA	11	B
1950	DET		10	FB
1951			12	FB
1952			7	FB
1953			12	FB

6 yrs. 63 games

Tony Cline
CLINE, ANTHONY FRANCIS
B. Jul. 25, 1948, Hammond, IN
Miami (Florida) 6'2" 239 lbs.

1970	OAK	N	14	LB
1971			13	DE
1972			14	DE
1973			14	DE
1974			5	DE
1975			12	DE
1976	SF		7	DE
1977			14	DE

8 yrs. 93 games

Tony Cline
CLINE, TONY
B. Nov. 24, 1971, Davis, CA
Stanford 6'4" 251 lbs.

1995	BUF	N	16	TE
1996			16	TE

2 yrs. 32 games

Dextor Clinkscale
CLINKSCALE, FREDERICK DEXTOR
B. Apr. 13, 1958, Greenville, SC
South Carolina State 5'11" 195 lbs.

1980	DAL	N	16	S
1982			9	S
1983			15	S
1984			15	S
1985			16	S
1986	IND	N	5	S

6 yrs. 76 games

Joey Clinkscales
CLINKSCALES, WILLIAM JOSEPH
B. May 21, 1964, Asheville, NC
Tennessee 6'0" 199 lbs.

1987	PIT	N	7	WR
1988			4	WR
1988	TB	N	3	WR

2 yrs. 14 games

Charles Clinton
CLINTON, CHARLES
B. 1962
5'8" 170 lbs.

1987	HOU	N	2	CB

Jack Cloud
CLOUD, JOHN (Flying)
B. Jan. 1, 1925, Britton, OK
William & Mary 5'10" 220 lbs.

1950	GB	N	9	FB
1951			4	FB
1952	WAS	N	8	FB

Jack Cloud *continued*

1953			12	FB

4 yrs. 33 games

Dave Cloutier
CLOUTIER, DAVID
B. 1939
South Carolina/Maine 6'0" 195 lbs.

1964	BOS	A	12	DB

Herb Clow
CLOW, HERBERT W.
B. May 7, 1899
D. Nov., 1977, Beaver Bay, MN
Wisconsin-Superior 5'4" 180 lbs.

1924	DUL	N	1	QB

John Clowes
CLOWES, JOHN ALEXANDER
B. Dec. 15, 1921, Williamsburg, VA
D. Feb. 13, 1978, Norfolk, VA
William & Mary 6'1" 240 lbs.

1948	BKN	AA	14	T
1949	CHI	AA	12	T
1950	NYY	N	11	G
1951			12	T

4 yrs. 49 games

Don Clune
CLUNE, DONALD ANDREW
B. Jul. 31, 1952, Havertown, PA
Pennsylvania 6'3" 195 lbs.

1974	NYG	N	4	WR
1975			14	WR
1976	SEA	N	10	WR

3 yrs. 28 games

Rich Coady
COADY, RICH
B. Dec. 12, 1944, Chicago, IL
Memphis State 6'3" 240 lbs.

1970	CHI	N	14	TE, C
1971			14	C
1972			14	C
1973			14	C
1974			11	C

5 yrs. 67 games

Johnny Coaker
COAKER, JOHN
B. Oct. 22, 1902, New York State
D. Feb., 1982
None

1924	ROC	N	3	T

Bert Coan
COAN, ELROY BERT
B. Jul. 2, 1940, Timpson, TX
Kansas 6'4" 219 lbs.

1962	SD	A	4	HB
1963	KC	A	8	HB
1964			8	HB
1965			14	HB
1966			14	HB
1967			12	RB
1968			12	RB

7 yrs. 72 games

Ben Coates
COATES, BEN
B. Aug. 16, 1969, Greenwood, NC
Livingstone 6'4" 245 lbs.

1991	NE	N	16	TE
1992			16	TE
1993			16	TE
1994			16	TE

Ben Coates *continued*

1995			16	TE
1996			16	TE

6 yrs. 96 games

Ray Coates
COATES, RAYMOND
B. 1924
Louisiana State 6'1" 195 lbs.

1948	NYG	N	9	HB
1949			12	B

2 yrs. 21 games

Alf Cobb
COBB, ALFRED R. (Ty)
B. Jun., 1892
D. Apr. 7, 1974
Syracuse 5'11" 210 lbs.

1920	AKR	A	9	G
1921			1	T
1925	CLE		9	T, G

3 yrs. 19 games

Bob Cobb
COBB, ROBERT LEWIS
B. Oct. 12, 1957, Cincinnati, OH
Cincinnati/Arizona 6'4" 248 lbs.

1981	LA	N	6	DE
1982	TB	N	3	DE
1984	MIN	N	2	DE

3 yrs. 11 games

Garry Cobb
COBB, GARRY WILBERT
B. Mar. 16, 1957, Carthage, NC
Southern California 6'2" 230 lbs.

1979	DET	N	8	LB
1980			16	LB
1981			16	LB
1982			6	LB
1983			15	LB
1984			16	LB
1985	PHI		16	LB
1986			16	LB
1987			12	LB
1988	DAL		16	LB
1989			3	LB

11 yrs. 140 games

Marvin Cobb
COBB, MARVIN LAWRENCE
B. Aug. 6, 1953, Detroit, MI
Southern California 6'0" 189 lbs.

1975	CIN	N	13	DB
1976			14	CB
1977			14	S, CB
1978			16	S
1979			16	S
1980	PIT	N	6	S
1980	MIN	N	2	S

6 yrs. 79 games

Mike Cobb
COBB, MICHAEL
B. Dec. 20, 1955, Youngstown, OH
Michigan State 6'5" 244 lbs.

1977	CIN	N	13	TE
1978	CHI	N	13	TE
1979			16	TE
1980			4	TE
1981			16	TE

5 yrs. 62 games

Reggie Cobb
COBB, REGINALD JOHN
B. Jul. 7, 1968, Knoxville, TN

Year	Team		Games	Pos.

Reggie Cobb *continued*

Tennessee 6'0" 225 lbs.

Year	Team		Games	Pos.
1990	TB	N	16	RB
1991			16	RB
1992			16	RB
1993			12	RB
1994	GB	N	16	RB
1995	JAC	N	1	RB
1996	NYJ	N	15	RB

7 yrs.   92 games

Tom Cobb
COBB, THOMAS
B. Nov. 29, 1903
D. Dec., 1978, Prairie, MO
St. John's (New York) 5'11" 250 lbs.

Year	Team		Games	Pos.
1926	KC	N	11	T
1927	CLE	N	12	T
1928	DET	N	9	T
1931	CHIC	N	5	T, G

4 yrs.   37 games

Trevor Cobb
COBB, TREVOR SEBASTIAN
B. Nov. 20, 1970, Houston, TX
Rice 5'9" 209 lbs.

Year	Team		Games	Pos.
1994	CHI	N	1	RB

Eric Cobble
COBBLE, ERIC
B. Apr. 11, 1964
Southwest Texas State 5'10" 205 lbs.

Year	Team		Games	Pos.
1987	HOU	N	3	RB

Duffy Cobbs
COBBS, DUFFY
B. Jan. 17, 1964
Penn State 5'11" 178 lbs.

Year	Team		Games	Pos.
1987	NE	N	3	S

Mark Cochran
COCHRAN, MARK
B. May 6, 1963
Baylor 6'5" 285 lbs.

Year	Team		Games	Pos.
1987	SF	N	3	OT

Moose Cochran
COCHRAN, STEWART W.
B. 1896
Deceased
Chicago 5'11" 195 lbs.

Year	Team		Games	Pos.
1922	MIL	N	2	E, G

Red Cochran
COCHRAN, JOHN THURMAN, JR.
B. Aug. 2, 1922, Fairfield, AL
Wake Forest 6'0" 193 lbs.

Year	Team		Games	Pos.
1947	CHIC	N	12	FB
1948			12	HB
1949			12	HB

3 yrs.   36 games

Tom Cochran
COCHRAN, LEON THOMAS
B. Apr. 13, 1924, Birmingham, AL
Auburn 6'0" 209 lbs.

Year	Team		Games	Pos.
1949	WAS	N	11	FB

Gene Cockrell
COCKRELL, GENE
B. Jan. 10, 1934, Pampa, TX
Oklahoma/Hardin-Simmons 6'3" 247 lbs.

Year	Team		Games	Pos.
1960	NY	A		OT

Gene Cockrell *continued*

Year	Team		Games	Pos.
1961			14	OT
1962			14	DE, OT

3 yrs.   28 games

Don Cockroft
COCKROFT, DONALD LEE
B. Feb. 6, 1945, Cheyenne, WY
Adams State 6'1" 193 lbs.

Year	Team		Games	Pos.
1968	CLE	N	14	K, P
1969			14	K, P
1970			14	K, P
1971			14	K, P
1972			14	K, P
1973			14	K, P
1974			14	K, P
1975			14	K, P
1976			14	K, P
1977			14	K
1978			16	K
1979			16	K
1980			16	K

13 yrs.   188 games

Joe Cocozzo
COCOZZO, JOSEPH RAMOND
B. Aug. 7, 1970, Mechanicville, NY
Michigan 6'4" 300 lbs.

Year	Team		Games	Pos.
1993	SD	N	16	G
1994			13	G
1995			15	G
1996			16	G

4 yrs.   60 games

Sherman Cocroft
COCROFT, SHERMAN
B. Aug. 29, 1961, Watsonville, CA
San Jose State 6'1" 195 lbs.

Year	Team		Games	Pos.
1985	KC	N	16	S
1986			16	S
1987			12	S, CB
1988	BUF	N	12	CB, S
1989	TB	N	10	S

5 yrs.   66 games

Ron Coder
CODER, WILLIAM
B. May 24, 1954, Savannah, GA
Penn State 6'4" 250 lbs.

Year	Team		Games	Pos.
1976	SEA	N	13	G
1977			14	G
1979			15	G
1980	STL	N	11	G

4 yrs.   53 games

Bill Cody
CODY, WILLIAM EUGENE
B. Aug. 2, 1944, Greenwood, MS
Auburn 6'1" 225 lbs.

Year	Team		Games	Pos.
1966	DET	N	1	LB
1967	NO	N	9	LB
1968			14	LB
1969			3	LB
1970			14	LB
1972	PHI	N	11	LB

6 yrs.   52 games

Ed Cody
CODY, EDWARD J. (Catfoot)
B. Feb. 27, 1923, Newington, CT
Purdue 5'10" 191 lbs.

Year	Team		Games	Pos.
1947	GB	N	10	FB
1948			10	FB
1949	CHIB	N	8	FB
1950			10	FB

4 yrs.   38 games

Stan Cofall
COFALL, STANLEY BINGHAM
B. May 5, 1894, Cleveland, OH
D. Sep. 21, 1961, Cleveland, OH
Notre Dame 5'11" 190 lbs.

Year	Team		Games	Pos.
1920	CLE	A	3	HB

Joe Cofer
COFER, JOE
B. Mar. 5, 1963
Tennessee 6'0" 200 lbs.

Year	Team		Games	Pos.
1987	WAS	N	3	S

Mike Cofer
COFER, JAMES MICHAEL
B. Jan. 19, 1964, Columbia, SC
North Carolina State 6'2" 197 lbs.

Year	Team		Games	Pos.
1987	NO	N	2	K
1988	SF	N	16	K
1989			16	K
1990			16	K
1991			16	K
1992			16	K
1993			16	K
1995	IND	N	4	K

8 yrs.   102 games

Mike Cofer
COFER, MICHAEL LYNN
B. Apr. 7, 1960, Knoxville, TN
Tennessee 6'5" 245 lbs.

Year	Team		Games	Pos.
1983	DET	N	16	DE
1984			16	DE
1985			7	DE
1986			16	LB
1987			11	LB
1988			16	LB
1989			15	LB
1990			16	LB
1991			2	LB
1992			8	LB

10 yrs.   123 games

Pat Coffee
COFFEE, JAMES
B. Jan. 9, 1914
D. Mar., 1968, Lawrenceville, GA
Louisiana State 5'11" 183 lbs.

Year	Team		Games	Pos.
1937	CHIC	N	9	HB, QB
1938			10	HB

2 yrs.   19 games

Don Coffey
COFFEY, DONALD
B. 1940
Memphis State 6'3" 190 lbs.

Year	Team		Games	Pos.
1963	DEN	A	3	FL

Junior Coffey
COFFEY, JUNIOR LEE
B. Mar. 21, 1942, Kyle, TX
Washington 6'1" 211 lbs.

Year	Team		Games	Pos.
1965	GB	N	13	HB
1966	ATL	N	14	RB
1967			14	RB
1969			6	RB
1969	NYG	N	12	RB
1971			6	RB

5 yrs.   65 games

Ken Coffey
COFFEY, KEN
B. Nov. 7, 1960, Rantoul, IL
Southwest Texas State 6'0" 198 lbs.

Year	Team		Games	Pos.
1983	WAS	N	13	CB, S
1984			12	S

Ken Coffey *continued*

Year	Team		Games	Pos.
1986			16	S

3 yrs.   41 games

Wayne Coffey
COFFEY, WAYNE
B. May 30, 1964
Southwest Texas State 5'7" 158 lbs.

Year	Team		Games	Pos.
1987	NE	N	3	WR

Randy Coffield
COFFIELD, RANDALL
B. Dec. 12, 1953, Miami, FL
Florida State 6'3" 215 lbs.

Year	Team		Games	Pos.
1976	SEA	N	13	LB
1978	NYG	N	2	LB
1979			9	LB

3 yrs.   24 games

Paul Coffman
COFFMAN, PAUL RANDOLPH
B. Mar. 29, 1956, St. Louis, MO
Kansas State 6'3" 225 lbs.

Year	Team		Games	Pos.
1978	GB	N	16	TE
1979			16	TE
1980			16	TE
1981			16	TE
1982			9	TE
1983			16	TE
1984			14	TE
1985			16	TE
1986	KC	N	15	TE
1987			12	TE
1988	MIN	N	8	TE

11 yrs.   154 games

Tim Cofield
COFIELD, TIMMY LEE
B. May 18, 1963, Murfreesboro, NC
Elizabeth City State 6'2" 245 lbs.

Year	Team		Games	Pos.
1986	KC	N	15	LB
1987			12	LB
1988			16	LB
1989	NYJ	N	6	LB
1989	BUF	N	5	LB

4 yrs.   54 games

Gail Cogdill
COGDILL, GAIL ROSS
B. Apr. 7, 1937, Worland, WY
Washington State 6'2" 195 lbs.

Year	Team		Games	Pos.
1960	DET	N	12	E
1961			14	OE
1962			14	OE
1963			14	OE
1964			11	OE
1965			9	OE
1966			14	OE
1967			12	OE
1968			3	OE
1968	BAL	N	8	OE
1969	ATL	N	13	WR
1970			6	WR

11 yrs.   130 games

Art Coglizer
COGLIZER, WILLIAM ARTHUR (Cowboy)
B. Sep. 18, 1902
Deceased
Missouri 5'11" 180 lbs.

Year	Team		Games	Pos.
1926	NY	A	13	E

Abe Cohen
COHEN, ABE
B. 1934

Year	Team	Games	Pos.

Abe Cohen continued
Tennessee-Chattanooga 5'11" 230 lbs.

Year	Team	Games	Pos.
1960	BOS	A	G

Angelo Coia
COIA, ANGELO
B. Apr. 21, 1938, Philadelphia, PA
Southern California 6'2" 202 lbs.

Year	Team	Games	Pos.
1960	CHI	N 12	HB
1961		11	OE
1962		9	OE
1963		12	OE
1964	WAS	N 14	OE
1965		13	OE
1966	ATL	N 6	OE
7 yrs.	77 games		

Will Cokeley
COKELEY, WILL H.
B. Dec. 6, 1960, Topeka, KS
Kansas State 6'2" 220 lbs.

Year	Team	Games	Pos.
1987	BUF	N 3	LB

John Colahan
COLAHAN, JOHN
B. Feb. 5, 1905
D. Jul., 1973, Las Vegas, NV
Colorado Mines 6'3" 212 lbs.

Year	Team	Games	Pos.
1928	NYY	N 2	T

Steve Colavito
COLAVITO, STEVE MICHAEL
B. Aug. 9, 1951, Bronx, NY
Wake Forest 6'0" 225 lbs.

Year	Team	Games	Pos.
1975	PHI	N 4	LB

Danny Colbert
COLBERT, DANNY JOEL
B. Dec. 15, 1950, Corsicana, TX
Tulsa 5'11" 175 lbs.

Year	Team	Games	Pos.
1974	SD	N 6	DB
1975		13	S
1976		13	CB
3 yrs.	32 games		

Darrell Colbert
COLBERT, DARRELL RAY
B. Nov. 16, 1964, Beaumont, TX
Texas Southern 5'10" 174 lbs.

Year	Team	Games	Pos.
1987	KC	N 12	WR
1988		3	WR
2 yrs.	15 games		

Lewis Colbert
COLBERT, LEWIS WELTON
B. Aug. 23, 1963, Phenix City, AL
Auburn 5'11" 180 lbs.

Year	Team	Games	Pos.
1986	KC	N 16	P
1987		2	P
1989	SD	N 2	P
3 yrs.	20 games		

Rondy Colbert
COLBERT, RONDY ESTES
B. Jan. 7, 1954, Corsicana, TX
Lamar 5'9" 185 lbs.

Year	Team	Games	Pos.
1975	NYG	N 14	CB
1976		14	CB
1977	STL	N 4	CB
3 yrs.	32 games		

Dan Colchico
COLCHICO, DANIEL MAMETTA
B. May 27, 1935, Port Chicago, CA

Dan Colchico continued
San Jose State 6'4" 240 lbs.

Year	Team	Games	Pos.
1960	SF	N 12	DE
1961		14	DE
1962		14	DE
1963		14	DE
1964		14	DE
1965		1	DE
1969	NO	N 9	DE
7 yrs.	78 games		

Jim Colclough
COLCLOUGH, JAMES MICHAEL
B. Mar. 31, 1936, Medford, MA
Boston College 6'0" 185 lbs.

Year	Team	Games	Pos.
1960	BOS	A 14	OE
1961		14	OE
1962		14	OE
1963		14	OE
1964		14	FL
1965		14	HB
1966		14	HB
1967		14	OE
1968		14	OE
9 yrs.	126 games		

Eddie Cole
COLE, EDDIE LEE
B. Dec. 16, 1956, Clarkside, MS
Mississippi 6'2" 235 lbs.

Year	Team	Games	Pos.
1979	DET	N 15	LB
1980		13	LB
2 yrs.	28 games		

Emerson Cole
COLE, EMERSON ELVIN
B. Dec. 10, 1927, Carrier Mills, IL
Toledo 6'2" 215 lbs.

Year	Team	Games	Pos.
1950	CLE	N 12	FB
1951		12	FB
1952		6	FB
1952	CHIB		OT, FB
3 yrs.	30 games		

Fred Cole
COLE, FRED
B. 1937
Maryland 5'11" 226 lbs.

Year	Team	Games	Pos.
1960	LA	A	G

John Cole
COLE, JOHN (King)
B. 1915
Deceased
St. Joseph's (Pennsylvania) 5'9" 197 lbs.

Year	Team	Games	Pos.
1938	PHI	N 11	HB, QB
1940		7	FB, HB
2 yrs.	18 games		

Larry Cole
COLE, LARRY RUDOLPH
B. Nov. 15, 1946, Clarkfield, MN
Air Force/Hawaii 6'4" 252 lbs.

Year	Team	Games	Pos.
1968	DAL	N 14	DE
1969		14	DE
1970		10	DE
1971		14	DE
1972		9	DE
1973		14	DE
1974		14	DE
1975		13	DE, DT
1976		14	DT
1977		12	DT
1978		16	DE, DT
1979		16	DE, DT
1980		16	DE
13 yrs.	176 games		

Lee Cole
COLE, LEE
B. Jun. 25, 1974, Riverside, CA
Arizona State 5'11" 188 lbs.

Year	Team	Games	Pos.
1996	HOU	N 2	CB

Linzy Cole
COLE, LINZY
B. Apr. 21, 1948, Dallas, TX
Texas Christian 5'11" 170 lbs.

Year	Team	Games	Pos.
1970	CHI	N 7	WR
1971	HOU	N 14	WR
1972		2	WR
1972	BUF	N 8	WR
3 yrs.	31 games		

Pete Cole
COLE, PETER
B. 1916
Trinity (Texas) 5'11" 222 lbs.

Year	Team	Games	Pos.
1937	NYG	N 2	G
1938		9	G, T
1939		10	G, T
1940		9	G
4 yrs.	30 games		

Robin Cole
COLE, ROBIN
B. Sep. 11, 1955, Los Angeles, CA
New Mexico 6'2" 225 lbs.

Year	Team	Games	Pos.
1977	PIT	N 8	LB
1978		16	LB
1979		13	LB
1980		14	LB
1981		14	LB
1982		9	LB
1983		16	LB
1984		16	LB
1985		16	LB
1986		16	LB
1987		12	LB
1988	NYJ	N 16	LB
12 yrs.	166 games		

Terry Cole
COLE, TERRY
B. Jul. 7, 1945, Dallas, TX
Indiana 6'1" 220 lbs.

Year	Team	Games	Pos.
1968	BAL	N 14	RB
1969		9	RB
1970	PIT	N 10	RB
1971	MIA	N 4	RB
4 yrs.	37 games		

Tom Colella
COLELLA, THOMAS A.
B. Jul. 3, 1918, Albion, NY
D. May 15, 1992, Hamburg, NY
Canisius 6'0" 187 lbs.

Year	Team	Games	Pos.
1942	DET	N 9	HB
1943		7	B
1944	CLE	N 10	HB
1945		10	HB
1946	CLE	AA 14	HB
1947		14	B
1948		13	B
1949	BUF	AA 11	B
8 yrs.	88 games		

Al Coleman
COLEMAN, ALVIN M.
B. Dec. 27, 1944, Gulfport, MS
Jackson State/Tennessee State 6'1" 185 lbs.

Year	Team	Games	Pos.
1967	MIN	N 2	DB
1969	CIN	A 14	CB
1970	CIN	N 11	S

Al Coleman continued

Year	Team	Games	Pos.
1971		4	S
1972	PHI	N 12	S
1973		14	S
6 yrs.	57 games		

Andre Coleman
COLEMAN, ANDRE
CLINTONIAN
B. Jan. 18, 1971, Hermitage, PA
Kansas State 5'9" 165 lbs.

Year	Team	Games	Pos.
1994	SD	N 13	WR
1995		15	WR
1996		16	WR
3 yrs.	44 games		

Anthony Coleman
COLEMAN, ANTHONY
B. Aug. 30, 1964
Baylor 6'0" 185 lbs.

Year	Team	Games	Pos.
1987	DAL	N 3	CB, S

Ben Coleman
COLEMAN, BENJAMIN LEON
B. May 18, 1971, South Hill, VA
Wake Forest 6'6" 335 lbs.

Year	Team	Games	Pos.
1993	PHX	N 12	OT
1994	ARI	N 15	G, OT
1995		3	G
1995	JAC	N 10	G, OT
1996		16	G
4 yrs.	56 games		

Bill Coleman
COLEMAN, WILLIAM THOMAS
B. Feb. 7, 1902, Elmira, NY
D. Aug., 1969, Rochester, NY
Pennsylvania 6'0" 200 lbs.

Year	Team	Games	Pos.
1926	PHI	A 6	G

Charles Coleman
COLEMAN, CHARLES
B. Sep. 16, 1963
Alcorn State 6'4" 222 lbs.

Year	Team	Games	Pos.
1987	NYG	N 3	TE

Daniel Coleman
COLEMAN, DANIEL
B. Aug. 14, 1962, Lansing, MI
Murray State 6'4" 249 lbs.

Year	Team	Games	Pos.
1987	MIN	N 3	DE

Dennis Coleman
COLEMAN, DENNIS F.
B. Dec. 19, 1948, Aberdeen, MS
Mississippi 6'3" 225 lbs.

Year	Team	Games	Pos.
1971	NE	N 9	LB

Don Coleman
COLEMAN, DONALD ALVIN
B. Jan. 11, 1952, Toledo, OH
Michigan 6'2" 220 lbs.

Year	Team	Games	Pos.
1974	NO	N 14	LB
1975		13	LB
2 yrs.	27 games		

Eric Coleman
COLEMAN, ERIC GERARD
B. Dec. 27, 1966, Denver, CO
Wyoming 6'0" 190 lbs.

Year	Team	Games	Pos.
1989	NE	N 8	CB
1990		7	CB
2 yrs.	15 games		

Year	Team	Games	Pos.

Fred Coleman
COLEMAN, FRED
B. Jun. 26, 1953, Greenville, MS
Northeast Louisiana 6'4" 240 lbs.

Year	Team		Games	Pos.
1976	BUF	N	7	TE

Greg Coleman
COLEMAN, GREG JEROME
B. Sep. 9, 1954, Jacksonville, FL
Florida A&M 6'0" 182 lbs.

Year	Team		Games	Pos.
1977	CLE	N	14	P
1978	MIN	N	9	P
1979			16	P
1980			16	P
1981			15	P
1982			9	P
1983			16	P
1984			16	P
1985			16	P
1986			16	P
1987			9	P
1988	WAS	N	10	P
12 yrs.	162 games			

Herb Coleman
COLEMAN, HERBERT EDWARD
B. Jun. 18, 1923, Chester, WV
D. Jan. 1, 1985, Northville, MI
Notre Dame 6'0" 200 lbs.

Year	Team		Games	Pos.
1946	CHI	AA	14	C
1947			13	C
1948			9	C
1948	BAL	AA	1	C
3 yrs.	37 games			

Keo Coleman
COLEMAN, KEO
B. May 1, 1970, Los Angeles, CA
Mississippi State 6'1" 255 lbs.

Year	Team		Games	Pos.
1992	NYJ	N	6	LB
1993	GB	N	12	LB
2 yrs.	18 games			

Leonard Coleman
COLEMAN, LEONARD DAVID
B. Jan. 30, 1962, Boynton Beach, FL
Vanderbilt 6'2" 197 lbs.

Year	Team		Games	Pos.
1985	IND	N	12	S
1986			16	S
1987			4	S
1988	SD	N	16	S
1989			1	S
5 yrs.	49 games			

Lincoln Coleman
COLEMAN, LINCOLN CALES
B. Aug. 12, 1969, Dallas, TX
Notre Dame/Baylor 6'1" 249 lbs.

Year	Team		Games	Pos.
1993	DAL	N	7	RB
1994			11	RB
2 yrs.	18 games			

Marco Coleman
COLEMAN, MARCO DARNELL
B. Dec. 18, 1969, Dayton, OH
Georgia Tech 6'3" 261 lbs.

Year	Team		Games	Pos.
1992	MIA	N	16	LB
1993			15	DE
1994			16	DE
1995			16	DE
1996	SD	N	16	DE
5 yrs.	79 games			

Marcus Coleman
COLEMAN, MARCUS
B. May 24, 1974, Dallas, TX

Marcus Coleman continued
Texas Tech 6'2" 208 lbs.

Year	Team		Games	Pos.
1996	NYJ	N	13	S

Monte Coleman
COLEMAN, MONTE
B. Nov. 4, 1957, Pine Bluff, AR
Central Arkansas 6'3" 227 lbs.

Year	Team		Games	Pos.
1979	WAS	N	16	LB
1980			16	LB
1981			12	LB
1982			8	LB
1983			10	LB
1984			16	LB
1985			11	LB
1986			11	LB
1987			12	LB
1988			13	LB
1989			15	LB
1990			15	LB
1991			16	LB
1992			16	LB
1993			14	LB
1994			16	LB
16 yrs.	217 games			

Ned Coleman
COLEMAN, EDWARD
B. Jul. 8, 1902
D. Apr., 1973, Springfield, MA
Holy Cross 5'10" 175 lbs.

Year	Team		Games	Pos.
1926	BOS	A	5	G, E

Pat Coleman
COLEMAN, PATRICK DARRYL
B. Apr. 8, 1967, Cleveland, MS
Mississippi 5'7" 173 lbs.

Year	Team		Games	Pos.
1990	NE	N	1	WR
1991	HOU	N	14	WR
1992			14	WR
1993			13	WR
1994			10	WR
5 yrs.	52 games			

Ronnie Coleman
COLEMAN, RONNIE L.
B. Jul. 9, 1951, Jasper, AL
Alabama A&M 5'10" 197 lbs.

Year	Team		Games	Pos.
1974	HOU	N	13	RB
1975			14	RB
1976			13	RB
1977			14	RB
1978			15	RB
1979			14	RB
1980			14	RB
1981			16	RB
8 yrs.	113 games			

Ralph Coleman
COLEMAN, RALPH DONNELL
B. Aug. 31, 1950, Spartanburg, SC
North Carolina A&T 6'4" 216 lbs.

Year	Team		Games	Pos.
1972	DAL	N	1	LB

Sidney Coleman
COLEMAN, SIDNEY
B. Jan. 14, 1964, Gulfport, MS
Southern Mississippi 6'2" 250 lbs.

Year	Team		Games	Pos.
1988	TB	N	16	LB
1989			4	LB
1990			16	LB
1991	PHX	N	16	LB
1992	TB	N	1	LB
5 yrs.	53 games			

Steve Coleman
COLEMAN, STEVE

Steve Coleman continued
B. Aug. 8, 1950, Philadelphia, PA
Delaware State 6'4" 252 lbs.

Year	Team		Games	Pos.
1974	DEN	N	2	DE

James Coley
COLEY, JAMES LESTER
B. Apr. 13, 1967, Jacksonville, FL
Clemson 6'3" 270 lbs.

Year	Team		Games	Pos.
1990	CHI	N	16	TE
1991	IND	N	7	TE
2 yrs.	23 games			

Jake Colhouer
COLHOUER, JACOB C.
B. Jan. 15, 1922, Altus, OK
Oklahoma A&M 6'1" 211 lbs.

Year	Team		Games	Pos.
1946	CHIC	N	9	G
1947			12	G
1948			11	G
1949	NYG	N	8	G
4 yrs.	40 games			

Elmer Collett
COLLETT, CHARLES ELMER
B. Nov. 7, 1944, Oakland, CA
San Francisco State 6'4" 231 lbs.

Year	Team		Games	Pos.
1967	SF	N	14	G
1968			14	G
1969			14	G
1970			14	G
1971			14	G
1972			14	G
1973	BAL	N	14	G
1974			14	G
1975			14	G
1976			14	G
1977			5	G
11 yrs.	145 games			

Bruce Collie
COLLIE, BRUCE STOKES
B. Jun. 27, 1962, Nuremberg, Germany
Texas-Arlington 6'6" 275 lbs.

Year	Team		Games	Pos.
1985			16	OT
1986			16	OT
1987			11	OT, G
1988			15	OT, G
1989			16	G, OT
1990	PHI	N	12	G
1991			5	G
7 yrs.	91 games			

Bobby Collier
COLLIER, BOBBY F.
B. 1930
Southern Methodist 6'3" 230 lbs.

Year	Team		Games	Pos.
1951	LA	N	11	T

Floyd Collier
COLLIER, FLOYD LEE
B. 1924, Fresno, CA
San Jose State/Fresno State/Southern California 6'1" 215 lbs.

Year	Team		Games	Pos.
1948	SF	AA	12	T

Jimmy Collier
COLLIER, JAMES
B. May 18, 1939, Van Buren, AR
Arkansas 6'2" 195 lbs.

Year	Team		Games	Pos.
1962	NYG	N	13	OE
1963	WAS	N	14	OE
2 yrs.	27 games			

Mike Collier
COLLIER, MICHAEL J.

Mike Collier continued
B. Sep. 21, 1953, Baltimore, MD
Morgan State 5'11" 200 lbs.

Year	Team		Games	Pos.
1975	PIT	N	14	RB
1977	BUF	N	6	RB
1979			16	RB
3 yrs.	36 games			

Reggie Collier
COLLIER, REGINALD C.
B. May 14, 1961, Biloxi, MS
Southern Mississippi 6'3" 207 lbs.

Year	Team		Games	Pos.
1986	DAL	N	4	QB
1987	PIT	N	2	QB
2 yrs.	6 games			

Steve Collier
COLLIER, STEVEN ANDRE
B. Apr. 19, 1963, Chicago, IL
Illinois/Bethune-Cookman 6'7" 342 lbs.

Year	Team		Games	Pos.
1987	GB	N	10	OT

Tim Collier
COLLIER, TIMOTHY
B. May 31, 1954, Dallas, TX
East Texas State 6'0" 170 lbs.

Year	Team		Games	Pos.
1976	KC	N	13	CB
1977			9	CB
1978			15	CB
1979			14	CB
1980	STL	N	12	CB
1981			14	CB
1982			2	CB
1982	SF	N	2	CB
1983			10	CB
8 yrs.	93 games			

Collins
COLLINS
None

Year	Team		Games	Pos.
1922	MIL	N	3	E

Andre Collins
COLLINS, ANDRE PIERRE
B. May 4, 1968, Riverside, NJ
Penn State 6'1" 232 lbs.

Year	Team		Games	Pos.
1990	WAS	N	16	LB
1991			16	LB
1992			14	LB
1993			13	LB
1994			16	LB
1995	CIN	N	16	LB
1996			14	LB
7 yrs.	105 games			

Bill Collins
COLLINS, WILLIAM HAROLD
(Spot)
B. Mar. 4, 1922, Breckenridge, TX
Texas/Southwestern/Texas 5'8" 195 lbs.

Year	Team		Games	Pos.
1947	BOS	N	12	G

Brett Collins
COLLINS, BRETT WILLIAM
B. Oct. 8, 1968, Sheridan, WY
Washington 6'1" 226 lbs.

Year	Team		Games	Pos.
1992	GB	N	11	LB
1993			4	LB
1993	LARM	N	10	LB
1994			2	LB
3 yrs.	27 games			

Clarence Collins
COLLINS, CLARENCE R.
B. Feb. 1, 1962, St. Louis, MO

Year	Team	Games	Pos.

Clarence Collins continued

Illinois State 6'1" 180 lbs.

Year	Team	Games	Pos.
1987	STL	N	1	WR

Dwight Collins

COLLINS, DWIGHT DEAN
B. Aug. 23, 1961, Rochester, NY
Pittsburgh 6'1" 215 lbs.

Year	Team	Games	Pos.
1984	MIN	N	16	WR

Fabray Collins

COLLINS, FABRAY
B. Sep. 16, 1961, Chicago, IL
Southern Illinois 6'2" 215 lbs.

Year	Team	Games	Pos.
1987	MIN	N	3	LB

Gary Collins

COLLINS, GARY JAMES
B. Aug. 20, 1940, Williamstown, PA
Maryland 6'4" 211 lbs.

Year	Team	Games	Pos.
1962	CLE	N	14	OE, P
1963			14	OE, P
1964			14	FL, P
1965			14	FL, P
1966			14	FL, P
1967			13	FL, P
1968			4	FL, P
1969			14	WR, P
1970			12	WR
1971			13	WR, P
10 yrs.		126 games	

George Collins

COLLINS, GEORGE FRANCIS, III
B. Dec. 9, 1955, Macon, GA
Georgia 6'2" 270 lbs.

Year	Team	Games	Pos.
1978	STL	N	13	G
1979			15	G
1980			16	G, OT
1981			16	G, OT
1982			9	G, OT
5 yrs.		69 games	

Gerald Collins

COLLINS, GERALD
B. Feb. 13, 1971, St. Louis, MO
Vanderbilt 6'3" 250 lbs.

Year	Team	Games	Pos.
1995	CIN	N	3	LB

Glen Collins

COLLINS, GLEN LEON
B. Jul. 10, 1959, Jackson, MS
Mississippi State 6'6" 260 lbs.

Year	Team	Games	Pos.
1982	CIN	N	7	DE
1983			16	DE
1984			16	DE
1985			16	DE
1987	SF	N	3	DE
5 yrs.		58 games	

Greg Collins

COLLINS, GREGORY VINCENT
B. Dec. 8, 1952, Troy, MI
Notre Dame 6'3" 229 lbs.

Year	Team	Games	Pos.
1975	SF	N	14	LB
1976	SEA	N	13	LB
1977	BUF	N	11	LB
3 yrs.		38 games	

Harry Collins

COLLINS, HARRY
B. Jan. 8, 1900
D. Jan., 1983, Fort Myers, FL
Canisius 5'11" 190 lbs.

Year	Team	Games	Pos.
1924	BUF	N	10	G, C

Jerry Collins

COLLINS, JERALD EZRA
B. Feb. 1, 1947, Muskegon, MI
Western Michigan 6'1" 220 lbs.

Year	Team	Games	Pos.
1969	BUF	A	9	LB
1970	BUF	N	3	LB
2 yrs.		12 games	

Jim Collins

COLLINS, JAMES BRIAN
B. Jun. 11, 1958, Orange, NJ
Syracuse 6'2" 230 lbs.

Year	Team	Games	Pos.
1981	LA	N	7	LB
1982	LARM	N	6	LB
1983			16	LB
1984			16	LB
1985			16	LB
1987			15	LB
1988			4	LB
1989	SD	N	13	LB
8 yrs.		93 games	

Kerry Collins

COLLINS, KERRY MICHAEL
B. Dec. 30, 1972, West Lawn, PA
Penn State 6'5" 240 lbs.

Year	Team	Games	Pos.
1995	CAR	N	15	QB
1996			13	QB
2 yrs.		28 games	

Kirk Collins

COLLINS, EDWARD KIRK
B. Jul. 18, 1958, San Antonio, TX
D. Feb. 22, 1984, Anaheim, CA
Baylor 5'11" 179 lbs.

Year	Team	Games	Pos.
1981	LA	N	16	CB
1982	LARM	N	9	CB
1983			4	CB
3 yrs.		29 games	

Larry Collins

COLLINS, LARRY
B. Aug. 8, 1955, San Antonio, TX
Texas A&I-Kingsville 5'11" 190 lbs.

Year	Team	Games	Pos.
1978	CLE	N	15	RB
1980	NO	N	8	RB
2 yrs.		23 games	

Mark Collins

COLLINS, MARK
B. Jan. 16, 1964, San Bernardino, CA
Fullerton State 5'10" 190 lbs.

Year	Team	Games	Pos.
1986	NYG	N	15	CB
1987			11	CB
1988			11	CB
1989			16	CB
1990			13	CB
1991			16	CB
1992			14	CB
1993			16	CB
1994	KC	N	14	CB
1995			16	S, CB
1996			16	CB
11 yrs.		158 games	

Patrick Collins

COLLINS, PATRICK
B. Aug. 4, 1966, Tulsa, OK
Oklahoma 5'9" 197 lbs.

Year	Team	Games	Pos.
1988	GB	N	6	RB

Paul Collins

COLLINS, PAUL
B. 1923
Missouri 5'11" 178 lbs.

Year	Team	Games	Pos.
1945	CHIC	N	3	QB

Paul Collins

COLLINS, PAUL ANDREW (Rip)
B. Oct. 31, 1907, Danbury, IA
D. Sep. 25, 1988
Pittsburgh 6'1" 198 lbs.

Year	Team	Games	Pos.
1932	BOS	N	10	E
1933			12	E
1934			12	E
1935			10	E
4 yrs.		44 games	

Ray Collins

COLLINS, RAYMOND
B. 1928, Texas
Louisiana State 5'11" 238 lbs.

Year	Team	Games	Pos.
1950	SF	N	12	T
1951			12	T
1952			8	T
1954	NYG	N	12	T
1960	DAL	A		DT
1961			13	DT
6 yrs.		57 games	

Rip Collins

COLLINS, ALBIN HARRELL
B. Sep. 27, 1927, Baton Rouge, LA
Louisiana State 6'0" 190 lbs.

Year	Team	Games	Pos.
1949	CHI	AA	12	B
1950	BAL	N	11	HB
1951	GB	N	7	HB
3 yrs.		30 games	

Roosevelt Collins

COLLINS, ROOSEVELT
B. Jan. 25, 1968, Shreveport, LA
Texas Christian 6'4" 235 lbs.

Year	Team	Games	Pos.
1992	MIA	N	10	LB

Shane Collins

COLLINS, SHANE WILLIAM
B. Apr. 11, 1969, Roundup, MT
Arizona State 6'3" 267 lbs.

Year	Team	Games	Pos.
1992	WAS	N	16	DE
1993			7	DE
1994			7	DE
3 yrs.		30 games	

Shawn Collins

COLLINS, SHAWN
B. Feb. 20, 1967, San Diego, CA
Northern Arizona 6'2" 207 lbs.

Year	Team	Games	Pos.
1989	ATL	N	16	WR
1990			16	WR
1991			4	WR
1992	CLE	N	9	WR
1993	GB	N	4	WR
5 yrs.		49 games	

Sonny Collins

COLLINS, SONNY
B. Jan. 17, 1953, Madisonville, KY
Kentucky 6'1" 196 lbs.

Year	Team	Games	Pos.
1976	ATL	N	11	RB

Todd Collins

COLLINS, TODD
B. Nov. 5, 1971, Walpole, MA
Michigan 6'4" 224 lbs.

Year	Team	Games	Pos.
1995	BUF	N	7	QB
1996			7	QB
2 yrs.		14 games	

Todd Collins

COLLINS, TODD FRANKLIN
B. May 27, 1970, New Market, TN

Todd Collins continued

Georgia/Tennessee*/Carson-Newman
6'2" 242 lbs.*

Year	Team	Games	Pos.
1992	NE	N	10	LB
1993			16	LB
1994			7	LB
1996			16	LB
4 yrs.		49 games	

Tony Collins

COLLINS, ANTHONY
B. May 27, 1959, Sanford, FL
East Carolina 5'11" 210 lbs.

Year	Team	Games	Pos.
1981	NE	N	16	RB
1982			9	RB
1983			16	RB
1984			16	RB
1985			16	RB
1986			16	RB
1987			13	RB
1990	MIA	N	1	RB
8 yrs.		103 games	

Trent Collins

COLLINS, TRENT
B. May 18, 1961, New Orleans, LA
San Diego State 6'1" 187 lbs.

Year	Team	Games	Pos.
1987	NYJ	N	3	S

Cris Collinsworth

COLLINSWORTH, ANTHONY CRIS
B. Jan. 17, 1959, Dayton, OH
Florida 6'5" 192 lbs.

Year	Team	Games	Pos.
1981	CIN	N	16	WR
1982			9	WR
1983			14	WR
1984			15	WR
1985			16	WR
1986			16	WR
1987			8	WR
1988			13	WR
8 yrs.		107 games	

Ferric Collons

COLLONS, FERRIC JASON
B. Dec. 4, 1969, Scott Air Force Base, IL
California 6'6" 295 lbs.

Year	Team	Games	Pos.
1995	NE	N	16	DE, DT
1996			15	DE
2 yrs.		31 games	

Doug Colman

COLMAN, DOUG
B. Jun. 4, 1973, Somers Point, NJ
Nebraska 6'2" 252 lbs.

Year	Team	Games	Pos.
1996	NYG	N	13	LB

Wayne Colman

COLMAN, WAYNE CHARLES
B. Apr. 13, 1946, Ventnor, NJ
Temple 6'1" 227 lbs.

Year	Team	Games	Pos.
1968	PHI	N	14	LB
1969			5	LB
1969	NO	N	4	LB
1970			14	LB
1971			14	LB
1972			14	LB
1973			12	LB
1974			14	LB
1976			7	LB
8 yrs.		98 games	

Mickey Colmer

COLMER, JOHN F.
B. Oct. 23, 1918

Mickey Colmer *continued*

Miramonte JC 6'2" 219 lbs.

Year	Team		Games	Pos.
1946	**BKN**	**AA**	12	HB
1947			14	B
1948			14	B
1949	**B, NY**	**AA**	8	B
4 yrs.	48 games			

Don Colo

COLO, DONALD RICHARD
B. Jan. 5, 1925
Brown 6'3" 252 lbs.

Year	Team		Games	Pos.
1950	**BAL**	**N**	12	T
1951	**NYY**	**N**	12	T
1952	**DAL**	**N**	4	T
1953	**CLE**	**N**	12	T
1954			12	T
1955			12	T
1956			12	T
1957			12	T
1958			12	T
9 yrs.	100 games			

Harry Colon

COLON, HARRY
B. Feb. 14, 1969, Kansas City, KS
Missouri 5'11" 203 lbs.

Year	Team		Games	Pos.
1991	**NE**	**N**	16	S
1992	**DET**	**N**	16	S
1993			15	S
1994			16	S, CB
1995	**JAC**	**N**	16	S
5 yrs.	79 games			

Tony Colorito

COLORITO, ANTHONY IVAR
B. Sep. 8, 1964, Brooklyn, NY
Southern California 6'5" 260 lbs.

Year	Team		Games	Pos.
1986	**DEN**	**N**	15	NT

Craig Colquitt

COLQUITT, JOSEPH CRAIG
B. Sep. 9, 1954, Knoxville, TN
Tennessee 6'2" 183 lbs.

Year	Team		Games	Pos.
1978	**PIT**	**N**	16	P
1979			16	P
1980			16	P
1981			16	P
1983			16	P
1984			16	P
6 yrs.	96 games			

Jimmy Colquitt

COLQUITT, JAMES MICHAEL
B. Jan. 17, 1963, Knoxville, TN
Tennessee 6'4" 208 lbs.

Year	Team		Games	Pos.
1985	**SEA**	**N**	2	P

Tim Colston

COLSTON, TIM
B. Dec. 18, 1973, Tampa, FL
Kansas State 6'0" 275 lbs.

Year	Team		Games	Pos.
1996	**CAR**	**N**	1	DE

Jeff Colter

COLTER, JEFFREY
B. Apr. 23, 1961, Tucson, AZ
Kansas 5'10" 164 lbs.

Year	Team		Games	Pos.
1984	**MIN**	**N**	16	CB
1987	**KC**	**N**	1	CB
2 yrs.	17 games			

Lloyd Colteryahn

COLTERYAHN, LLOYD KENNETH
B. Aug. 26, 1931, Brentwood, PA

Lloyd Colteryahn *continued*

Maryland 6'2" 220 lbs.

Year	Team		Games	Pos.
1954	**BAL**	**N**	12	E
1955			12	E
1956			3	E
3 yrs.	27 games			

George Colton

COLTON, GEORGE CURTIS
B. Jul. 28, 1963, Lindenhurst, NY
Maryland 6'4" 279 lbs.

Year	Team		Games	Pos.
1987	**NE**	**N**	3	OT

Jim Colvin

COLVIN, JAMES R.
B. Nov. 30, 1937, Monahans, TX
Houston 6'2" 250 lbs.

Year	Team		Games	Pos.
1960	**BAL**	**N**	12	G, DE
1961			13	G, DE, DT
1962			14	DT
1963			14	DT
1964	**DAL**	**N**	14	DT
1965			14	DT
1966			14	DT
1967	**NYG**	**N**	8	DT
8 yrs.	103 games			

Neal Colzie

COLZIE, CORNELIUS CONNIE
B. Feb. 28, 1954, Fitzgerald, FL
Ohio State 6'2" 200 lbs.

Year	Team		Games	Pos.
1975	**OAK**	**N**	13	DB
1976			14	CB
1977			13	CB
1978			16	CB
1979	**MIA**	**N**	16	S
1980	**TB**	**N**	16	S
1981			16	S
1982			9	S
1983			5	S
9 yrs.	118 games			

Bill Combs

COMBS, L. WILLIAM (Loyal)
B. Jun. 29, 1920, Holder, IL
Purdue 5'11" 183 lbs.

Year	Team		Games	Pos.
1942	**PHI**	**N**	8	E

Chris Combs

COMBS, CHRIS A.
B. Mar. 17, 1958, National City, CA
New Mexico 6'4" 238 lbs.

Year	Team		Games	Pos.
1980	**STL**	**N**	16	TE
1981			16	TE
2 yrs.	32 games			

Darren Comeaux

COMEAUX, DARREN
B. Apr. 15, 1960, San Diego, CA
Arizona State 6'1" 227 lbs.

Year	Team		Games	Pos.
1982	**DEN**	**N**	3	LB
1983			14	LB
1984			16	LB
1985			11	LB
1986			16	LB
1987	**SF**	**N**	8	LB
1988	**SEA**	**N**	9	LB
1989			16	LB
1990			9	LB
1991			16	LB
10 yrs.	118 games			

John Comer

COMER, JOHN S., JR. (Hook)
B. Oct., 1898
Deceased

John Comer *continued*

None 180 lbs.

Year	Team		Games	Pos.
1926	**CAN**	**N**	1	FB, HB

Marty Comer

COMER, MARTIN F.
B. Oct. 28, 1917, Indianapolis, IN
Tulane 6'0" 203 lbs.

Year	Team		Games	Pos.
1946	**BUF**	**AA**	6	E
1947			14	E
1948			7	E
3 yrs.	27 games			

Vince Commisa

COMMISA, VINCENT JOHN
B. Nov. 1, 1921, Newark, NJ
D. Mar. 5, 1990
Notre Dame 5'9" 190 lbs.

Year	Team		Games	Pos.
1944	**BOS**	**N**	1	G

Chuck Commiskey

COMMISKEY, CHARLES EDWARD
B. Mar. 2, 1958, Killeen, TX
Mississippi 6'4" 290 lbs.

Year	Team		Games	Pos.
1986	**NO**	**N**	16	G
1987			12	G
1988			6	C
3 yrs.	34 games			

Irv Comp

COMP, IRVIN H., JR.
B. May 17, 1919, Milwaukee, WI
D. Jul. 11, 1989, Woodruff, WI
St. Benedict's (Kansas) 6'2" 204 lbs.

Year	Team		Games	Pos.
1943	**GB**	**N**	9	HB, DB
1944			10	HB, DB
1945			9	HB, DB
1946			11	HB, DB
1947			12	QB, DB
1948			11	QB, DB
1949			7	DB
7 yrs.	69 games			

Tony Compagno

COMPAGNO, ANTHONY
B. Jan. 19, 1921
D. Apr., 1971
St. Mary's (California) 5'11" 199 lbs.

Year	Team		Games	Pos.
1946	**PIT**	**N**	10	FB
1947			12	FB
1948			12	FB
3 yrs.	34 games			

Chuck Compton

COMPTON, CHARLES
B. 1965
Boise State 5'1" 190 lbs.

Year	Team		Games	Pos.
1987	**GB**	**N**	2	CB, S

Dick Compton

COMPTON, RICHARD LEE
B. Apr. 16, 1940, Colorado City, TX
McMurry 6'1" 195 lbs.

Year	Team		Games	Pos.
1962	**DET**	**N**	10	HB
1963			13	HB, DB
1964			12	HB, DB
1965	**HOU**	**A**	3	OE
1967	**PIT**	**N**	12	OE
1968			7	OE
6 yrs.	57 games			

Mike Compton

COMPTON, MICHAEL EUGENE
B. Sep. 18. 1970, Richlands, VA

Mike Compton *continued*

West Virginia 6'6" 297 lbs.

Year	Team		Games	Pos.
1993	**DET**	**N**	8	C, G
1994			3	G, C
1995			16	G, OT
1996			15	C
4 yrs.	42 games			

Ogden Compton

COMPTON, OGDEN BINGHAM
B. Aug. 25, 1932, Ithaca, NY
Hardin-Simmons 6'1" 180 lbs.

Year	Team		Games	Pos.
1955	**CHIC**	**N**	9	QB

Ed Comstock

COMSTOCK, ELWYN C. (Ellie)
B. 1904
West Virginia Wesleyan/Washington (MO) 6'2" 205 lbs.

Year	Team		Games	Pos.
1929	**BUF**	**N**	9	G, T, E
1930	**BKN**	**N**	5	G, HB
1931	**SI**	**N**	8	T
3 yrs.	22 games			

Rudy Comstock

COMSTOCK, RUDOLPH (Bud)
B. 1901
Deceased
Georgetown (DC) 5'10" 209 lbs.

Year	Team		Games	Pos.
1923	**CAN**	**N**	12	G, T
1924	**CLE**	**N**	9	G
1925	**CAN**	**N**	8	G, T
1926	**FRA**	**N**	17	G
1927			18	G
1928			16	G
1929			15	G, C
1930	**NYG**	**N**	14	G, T
1931	**GB**	**N**	14	G, T
1932			13	G, T
1933			13	G
11 yrs.	149 games			

Jack Concannon

CONCANNON, JOHN JOSEPH, JR.
B. Feb. 25, 1943, Boston, MA
Boston College 6'3" 201 lbs.

Year	Team		Games	Pos.
1964	**PHI**	**N**	4	QB
1965			3	QB
1966			11	QB
1967	**CHI**	**N**	13	QB
1968			7	QB
1969			14	QB
1970			14	QB
1971			3	QB
1974	**GB**	**N**	14	QB
1975	**DET**	**N**	7	QB
10 yrs.	90 games			

Rick Concannon

CONCANNON, E.
B. Jan. 12, 1909, Waltham, MA
D. Jun., 1986, Bradenton, FL
New York University 6'0" 217 lbs.

Year	Team		Games	Pos.
1934	**BOS**	**N**	10	G
1935			11	G
1936			3	G
3 yrs.	24 games			

Merl Condit

CONDIT, MERLYN E. (Merlyn the Magician)
B. Mar. 21, 1917, Belle Vernon, PA
D. Oct. 18, 1992
West Virginia/Carnegie-Mellon 5'11" 187 lbs.

Year	Team		Games	Pos.
1940	**PIT**	**N**	10	HB
1941	**BKN**	**N**	11	HB

Year	Team	Games	Pos.

Merl Condit continued

Year	Team		Games	Pos.
1942			11	HB
1943			8	HB
1945	WAS	N	5	HB
1946	PIT	N	9	HB
6 yrs.	54 games			

Tom Condon
CONDON, THOMAS JOSEPH
B. Oct. 26, 1952, Derby, CT
Boston College 6'3" 265 lbs.

Year	Team		Games	Pos.
1974	KC	N	14	G
1975			9	G
1976			14	G
1977			14	G
1978			16	G
1979			16	G
1980			16	G
1981			16	G
1982			7	G
1983			9	G
1984			16	G
1985	NE	N	1	G
12 yrs.	148 games			

Glen Condren
CONDREN, GLEN PAIGE
B. Jun. 10, 1942, Fort Smith, AR
Oklahoma 6'2" 248 lbs.

Year	Team		Games	Pos.
1965	NYG	N	8	DE
1966			13	DE
1967			13	DE
1969	ATL	N	9	DE
1970			14	DT
1971			12	DT
1972			10	DT
7 yrs.	79 games			

Fred Cone
CONE, FRED
B. Jun. 21, 1926, Pine Apple, AL
Clemson 5'11" 199 lbs.

Year	Team		Games	Pos.
1951	GB	N	12	FB, K
1952			10	FB, K
1953			12	FB, K
1954			12	FB, K
1955			12	FB, K
1956			12	FB, K
1957			12	FB, K
1960	DAL	N	12	FB, K
8 yrs.	94 games			

Charlie Conerly
CONERLY, CHARLES ALBERT, JR.
B. Sep. 19, 1923, Clarksdale, MS
D. Feb. 13, 1996, Memphis, TN
Mississippi 6'1" 185 lbs.

Year	Team		Games	Pos.
1948	NYG	N	12	QB
1949			12	QB
1950			11	QB
1951			12	QB
1952			11	QB
1953			10	QB
1954			12	QB
1955			12	QB
1956			12	QB
1957			12	QB
1958			10	QB
1959			10	QB
1960			12	QB
1961			13	QB
14 yrs.	161 games			

Mel Conger
CONGER, MELVIN REESE
B. Jun. 4, 1919, Atlanta, GA
Georgia 6'2" 225 lbs.

Year	Team		Games	Pos.
1946	NY	AA	7	E

Mel Conger continued

Year	Team		Games	Pos.
1947	BKN	AA	2	E
2 yrs.	9 games			

Larry Conjar
CONJAR, LAWRENCE WAYNE
B. Oct. 28, 1945, Harrisburg, PA
Notre Dame 6'0" 214 lbs.

Year	Team		Games	Pos.
1967	CLE	N	12	RB
1968	PHI	N	14	RB
1969	BAL	N	6	RB
1970			2	RB
4 yrs.	34 games			

Cary Conklin
CONKLIN, CARY
B. Feb. 29, 1968, Yakima, WA
Washington 6'4" 220 lbs.

Year	Team		Games	Pos.
1992	WAS	N	1	QB
1993			4	QB
1995	SF	N	3	QB
3 yrs.	8 games			

Bill Conkright
CONKRIGHT, BILL (Red)
B. Apr. 17, 1914, Beggs, OK
D. Oct. 27, 1980, Houston, TX
Oklahoma 6'1" 203 lbs.

Year	Team		Games	Pos.
1937	CHIB	N	8	C, LB
1938			8	C, LB, E
1939	CLE	N	11	C, LB
1940			2	C, LB
1941			11	C, LB
1942			11	C, LB
1943	WAS	N	2	C, LB
1943	BKN	N	7	C, LB
1944	CLE	N	1	C, LB
8 yrs.	61 games			

Shane Conlan
CONLAN, SHANE PATRICK
B. Apr. 3, 1964, Frewsburg, NY
Penn State 6'3" 230 lbs.

Year	Team		Games	Pos.
1987	BUF	N	12	LB
1988			13	LB
1989			10	LB
1990			16	LB
1991			16	LB
1992			13	LB
1993	LARM	N	12	LB
1994			15	LB
1995	STL	N	13	LB
9 yrs.	120 games			

Gerry Conlee
CONLEE, GERRY RUSSELL
B. 1916
St. Mary's (California) 5'11" 203 lbs.

Year	Team		Games	Pos.
1938	CLE	N	7	G, C
1943	DET	N	10	C
1946	SF	AA	10	C
1947			13	C
4 yrs.	40 games			

John Conley
CONLEY, JOHN (Zip)
B. 1889
Deceased
None 5'11" 205 lbs.

Year	Team		Games	Pos.
1922	COL	N	5	T, G
1926			5	T, G, HB
2 yrs.	10 games			

Steve Conley
CONLEY, STEPHEN CRAIG
B. Sep. 3, 1949, Chicago, IL

Steve Conley continued

Kansas 6'2" 225 lbs.

Year	Team		Games	Pos.
1972	STL	N	7	LB

Steve Conley
CONLEY, STEVEN
B. Jan. 18, 1972, Chicago, IL
Arkansas 6'1" 231 lbs.

Year	Team		Games	Pos.
1996	PIT	N	2	LB

Chris Conlin
CONLIN, CHRISTOPHER HOWARD
B. Jun. 7, 1965, Philadelphia, PA
Penn State 6'4" 290 lbs.

Year	Team		Games	Pos.
1987	MIA	N	3	G
1990	IND	N	16	G
1991			8	G
3 yrs.	27 games			

Ray Conlin
CONLIN, RAYMOND
B. Jun. 7, 1962
Ohio State 6'2" 258 lbs.

Year	Team		Games	Pos.
1987	PHI	N	1	DT

Dick Conn
CONN, RICHARD RAYMOND
B. Jan. 9, 1951, Louisville, KY
Georgia 6'0" 183 lbs.

Year	Team		Games	Pos.
1974	PIT	N	12	S
1975	NE	N	3	S
1976			13	S
1977			14	S
1978			15	S
1979			1	S
6 yrs.	58 games			

George Conn
CONN, GEORGE W. (Tuffy)
B. Feb. 22, 1895, Illinois
D. Aug. 2, 1973, Laguna Beach, CA
Oregon State 5'6" 155 lbs.

Year	Team		Games	Pos.
1920	CLE	A	6	HB
1920	AKR	A	3	HB
1 yr.	9 games			

Vaughn Connally
CONNALLY, VAUGHN
B. Aug. 25, 1902
D. Apr. 18, 1991, McLean, VA
Georgia Tech 5'8" 170 lbs.

Year	Team		Games	Pos.
1926	NEW	A	3	FB, HB

Babe Connaughton
CONNAUGHTON, HARRY (Pud, Gunboat)
B. Jun., 1905
Georgetown (DC) 6'2" 285 lbs.

Year	Team		Games	Pos.
1927	FRA	N	16	G

Mike Connell
CONNELL, MIKE
B. Mar. 15, 1956, Sharon, PA
Cincinnati 6'1" 200 lbs.

Year	Team		Games	Pos.
1978	SF	N	16	P
1980	WAS	N	16	P
1981			16	P
3 yrs.	48 games			

Ward Connell
CONNELL, WALTER J. (Doc)
B. May, 1899, Menominee Falls, WI
Deceased

Ward Connell continued

Notre Dame 5'10" 173 lbs.

Year	Team		Games	Pos.
1926	CHIC	N	2	FB, HB
1926	CHI	A	1	HB
1 yr.	3 games			

Mike Connelly
CONNELLY, MICHAEL JAMES
B. Oct. 16, 1935, Monrovia, CA
Washington State/Utah State 6'3" 242 lbs.

Year	Team		Games	Pos.
1960	DAL	N	12	C
1961			14	C
1962			14	C
1963			14	C
1964			14	C
1965			10	C
1966			14	C
1967			14	G, OT
1968	PIT	N	14	C
9 yrs.	120 games			

Clyde Conner
CONNER, CLYDE RAYMOND
B. May 18, 1933, Oklahoma City, OK
Pacific 6'2" 193 lbs.

Year	Team		Games	Pos.
1956	SF	N	12	E
1957			8	E
1958			12	E
1959			9	E
1960			10	E
1961			5	OE
1962			13	OE
1963			11	OE
8 yrs.	80 games			

Darion Conner
CONNER, DARION
B. Sep. 28, 1967, Macon, GA
Jackson State 6'2" 250 lbs.

Year	Team		Games	Pos.
1990	ATL	N	16	LB
1991			15	LB
1992			16	LB
1993			14	LB
1994	NO	N	16	LB
1995	CAR	N	16	LB
1996	PHI	N	7	LB
7 yrs.	100 games			

Dan Conners
CONNERS, DANIEL JOSEPH
B. Feb. 6, 1941, St. Mary's, PA
Miami (Florida) 6'1" 231 lbs.

Year	Team		Games	Pos.
1964	OAK	A	5	LB
1965			14	LB
1966			14	LB
1967			14	LB
1968			14	LB
1969			14	LB
1970	OAK	N	10	LB
1971			14	LB
1972			14	LB
1973			14	LB
1974			14	LB
11 yrs.	141 games			

Harry Connolly
CONNOLLY, HARRY WILLIAM
B. Jul. 16, 1920, Norwalk, CT
Boston College 5'11" 190 lbs.

Year	Team		Games	Pos.
1946	BKN	AA	3	HB

Ted Connolly
CONNOLLY, THEODORE WILLIAM
B. Dec. 5, 1931, Oakland, CA
Santa Clara/Tulsa 6'3" 240 lbs.

Year	Team		Games	Pos.
1954	SF	N	8	G

Year	Team		Games	Pos.

Ted Connolly *continued*

1956			5	G
1957			10	G
1958			12	G
1959			12	G
1960			4	G
1961			14	G
1962			13	G
1963	CLE	N	10	G
9 yrs.	88 games			

Dutch Connor
CONNOR, STAFFORD JOSEPH
B. Apr. 16, 1895, Exeter, NH
D. Nov., 1978, Alamo Heights, TX
New Hampshire 6'0" 190 lbs.

1925	PRO	N	3	FB, HB
1926	BKN	N	1	HB
2 yrs.	4 games			

George Connor
CONNOR, GEORGE L. (Moose)
B. Jan. 1, 1925, Chicago, IL
Holy Cross/Notre Dame 6'3" 240 lbs.

1948	CHIB	N	11	T
1949			12	T
1950			11	T
1951			12	T
1952			12	T
1953			12	T
1954			5	T
1955			12	T
8 yrs.	87 games			

Bill Connors
CONNORS, WILLIAM JOSEPH
B. Apr. 8, 1899
D. Dec., 1980, Jewett City, CT
Providence/Catholic 6'1" 240 lbs.

1929	BOS	N	7	G, T
1930	NEW	N	1	G
2 yrs.	8 games			

Ham Connors
CONNORS, HAMILTON
B. Feb. 22, 1898
D. Feb. 27, 1967, East Rochester, NY
None 190 lbs.

| 1925 | ROC | N | 1 | E |

Bill Conoly
CONOLY, WILLIAM ZUEHL
B. Sep. 13, 1920, San Antonio, TX
Texas 6'0" 227 lbs.

| 1946 | CHIC | | 9 | G |

Frank Conover
CONOVER, FRANK J.
B. Apr. 6, 1968, Monmouth County, NJ
Syracuse 6'5" 317 lbs.

| 1991 | CLE | N | 4 | DT |

Larry Conover
CONOVER, LAWRENCE (Atlantic City Airedale)
B. Mar., 1894
Deceased
Penn State 5'10" 190 lbs.

1921	CAN	A	1	G
1923	CAN	N	12	C
1925	CLE	N	11	C
1926	FRA	N	1	C
4 yrs.	25 games			

Scott Conover
CONOVER, KELSEY SCOTT

Scott Conover *continued*
B. Sep. 27, 1968, Neptune, NJ
Purdue 6'4" 285 lbs.

1991	DET	N	16	OT
1992			15	OT
1993			1	OT
1994			12	OT
1995			14	OT
1996			10	OT
6 yrs.	68 games			

Bobby Joe Conrad
CONRAD, BOBBY JOE
B. Nov. 17, 1935, Clifton, TX
Texas A&M 6'0" 194 lbs.

1958	CHIC	N	12	HB
1959			12	HB
1960	STL	N	12	HB
1961			14	HB
1962			14	HB
1963			14	HB
1964			14	FL
1965			14	FL
1966			14	FL
1967			14	FL
1968			14	FL
1969	DAL	N	8	WR
12 yrs.	156 games			

Marty Conrad
CONRAD, MARTIN
B. Nov. 30, 1895
Deceased
Kalamazoo 6'1" 240 lbs.

1922	TOL		8	C
1923			8	C
1924	KEN	N	3	C
1925	AKR	N	3	G, E
4 yrs.	22 games			

Irv Constantine
CONSTANTINE, IRVING (Murphy)
B. Jan. 18, 1907
D. May, 1966
Syracuse 5'9" 200 lbs.

| 1931 | SI | N | 1 | HB |

Enio Conti
CONTI, ENIO EDWARD
B. Feb. 15, 1913, Naples, Italy
Bucknell 5'11" 204 lbs.

1941	PHI	N	8	G
1942			11	G
1943	P, P		10	G
1944	PHI		8	G
1945			2	G
5 yrs.	39 games			

John Contoulis
CONTOULIS, JOHN
B. Oct. 9, 1940, New London, CT
Connecticut 6'4" 260 lbs.

| 1964 | NYG | N | 12 | HB |

Bill Contz
CONTZ, WILLIAM
B. May 12, 1961, Belle Vernon, PA
Penn State 6'5" 265 lbs.

1983	CLE	N	16	OT
1984			15	OT
1985			5	OT
1986			1	OT
1986	NO	N	13	OT
1987			3	OT
1988			11	OT
6 yrs.	64 games			

Curtis Conway
CONWAY, CURTIS LAMONT
B. Jan. 13, 1971, Los Angeles, CA
Southern California 6'0" 185 lbs.

1993	CHI	N	16	WR
1994			13	WR
1995			16	WR
1996			16	WR
4 yrs.	61 games			

Dave Conway
CONWAY, DAVID
B. Jan. 6, 1945, Baytown, TX
Texas 6'0" 195 lbs.

| 1971 | GB | N | 1 | K |

Ernie Conwell
CONWELL, ERNIE
B. Aug. 17, 1972, Renton, WA
Washington 6'1" 253 lbs.

| 1996 | STL | N | 10 | TE |

Joe Conwell
CONWELL, JOSEPH STANISLAUS
B. Feb. 24, 1961, Philadelphia, PA
North Carolina 6'5" 280 lbs.

1986	PHI	N	16	OT
1987			12	OT
2 yrs.	28 games			

Jimmy Conzelman
CONZELMAN, JAMES GLEASON
B. Mar. 6, 1898, St. Louis, MO
D. Jul. 31, 1970, St. Louis, MO
Washington (Missouri) 6'0" 175 lbs.

1920	DEC	A	7	HB
1921	RI	A	7	QB, HB
1922	RI	N	7	QB, HB
1922	MIL	N	3	HB, QB
1923			13	QB
1924			13	HB
1925	DET	N	12	QB, HB
1926			12	HB, QB
1927	PRO	N	14	QB, HB, E
1928			4	QB, FB, HB
1929			9	QB, HB, E, T, FB
10 yrs.	101 games			

Anthony Cook
COOK, ANTHONY
B. May 30, 1972, Bennettsville, SC
South Carolina State 6'3" 293 lbs.

1995	HOU	N	11	DE
1996			12	DT
2 yrs.	23 games			

Charles Cook
COOK, CHARLES MCKINLEY
B. May 13, 1959, Gainesville, FL
Miami (Florida) 6'3" 255 lbs.

| 1983 | NYG | N | 4 | NT |

Clair Cook
COOK, CLAIR
B. Jan. 7, 1909
D. Nov., 1983, Bellaire, MI
None 5'9" 170 lbs.

| 1928 | DAY | N | 5 | HB, FB |

Dave Cook
COOK, DAVID F.
B. Jan. 1, 1912, Elgin, IL
Deceased
Illinois 6'2" 203 lbs.

| 1934 | CHIC | N | 9 | HB |

Dave Cook *continued*
1935			10	HB
1936			2	FB
1936	BKN	N	3	B
3 yrs.	24 games			

Ed Cook
COOK, EDWARD JOSEPH
B. Jun. 29, 1932, Philadelphia, PA
Notre Dame 6'2" 245 lbs.

1958	CHIC	N	8	T
1959			12	G
1960	STL	N	11	T
1961			13	OT
1962			7	OT
1963			13	OT
1964			14	OT, G
1965			14	G
1966	ATL	N	14	G
1967			4	G
10 yrs.	110 games			

Fred Cook
COOK, FRED HARRISON, III
B. Apr. 15, 1952, Pascagoula, MS
Southern Mississippi 6'3" 244 lbs.

1974	BAL	N	14	DE
1975			14	DE
1976			14	DE
1977			14	DE
1978			16	DE
1979			16	DE
1980			16	DE
7 yrs.	104 games			

Gene Cook
COOK, EUGENE
B. Jan. 11, 1934, Greenfield, TN
Toledo 6'3" 215 lbs.

| 1959 | DET | N | 1 | E |

Greg Cook
COOK, GREGORY LYNN
B. Nov. 20, 1946, Dayton, OH
Cincinnati 6'3" 214 lbs.

1969	CIN	A	11	QB
1973	CIN	N	1	QB
2 yrs.	12 games			

Jim Cook
COOK, JAMES C.
B. Nov. 27, 1888, Green Bay, WI
D. Aug. 21, 1979, Green Bay, WI
None 6'3" 220 lbs.

| 1921 | GB | A | 2 | G |

Kelly Cook
COOK, KELLY EDWARD
B. Aug. 20, 1962, Cushing, OK
Oklahoma State 5'11" 225 lbs.

| 1987 | GB | N | 11 | RB |

Leon Cook
COOK, LEON S.
B. Mar. 17, 1920, Enid, OK
Northwestern 5'11" 220 lbs.

| 1942 | PHI | N | 1 | T |

Marv Cook
COOK, MARVIN EUGENE
B. Feb. 24, 1966, Iowa City, IA
Iowa 6'4" 234 lbs.

1989	NE	N	16	TE
1990			16	TE
1991			16	TE
1992			16	TE

Marv Cook *continued*

Year	Team		Games	Pos.
1993			16	TE
1994	CHI	N	16	TE
1995	STL	N	16	TE
7 yrs.	112 games			

Ted Cook
COOK, THEODORE WALTER
B. Apr. 15, 1921, Birmingham, AL
D. May 2, 1990, Birmingham, AL
Alabama 6'2" 195 lbs.

Year	Team		Games	Pos.
1947	DET	N	11	E
1948	GB	N	12	E
1949			11	E
1950			12	E
4 yrs.	46 games			

Toi Cook
COOK, TOI FITZGERALD
B. Dec. 3, 1964, Chicago, IL
Stanford 5'11" 188 lbs.

Year	Team		Games	Pos.
1987	NO	N	7	S
1988			16	S
1989			16	S
1990			16	CB
1991			14	CB
1992			16	CB
1993			16	CB
1994	SF	N	16	CB
1995			2	CB
1996	CAR	N	15	CB
10 yrs.	134 games			

Bill Cooke
COOKE, WILLIAM MORRILL
B. Feb. 26, 1951, Lowell, MA
Connecticut/Massachusetts 6'5" 249 lbs.

Year	Team		Games	Pos.
1975	GB	N	5	OT, DE
1976	SF	N	9	DE
1977			14	DE
1978	SEA	N	4	DE, DT
1978	DET	N	12	DT
1979	SEA	N	15	DT
1980			16	DT
6 yrs.	75 games			

Ed Cooke
COOKE, EDWARD GREY
B. May 3, 1935, Norfolk, VA
Maryland 6'4" 248 lbs.

Year	Team		Games	Pos.
1958	PHI	N	7	E
1960	NY	A		DE
1961			14	DE
1962			14	LB
1963			9	LB, DE
1964	DEN	A	14	DE
1965			14	DE
1966	MIA	A	14	DE
1967			13	DE
9 yrs.	99 games			

Johnie Cooks
COOKS, JOHNIE EARL
B. Nov. 23, 1958, Leland, MS
Mississippi State 6'4" 251 lbs.

Year	Team		Games	Pos.
1982	BAL	N	9	LB
1983			16	LB
1984	IND	N	16	LB
1985			16	LB
1986			15	LB
1987			10	LB
1988				LB
1988	NYG	N	13	LB
1989			16	LB
1990			14	LB
1991	CLE	N	2	LB
10 yrs.	129 games			

Rayford Cooks
COOKS, RAYFORD E.
B. Aug. 25, 1962, Dallas, TX
North Texas State 6'3" 245 lbs.

Year	Team		Games	Pos.
1987	HOU	N	10	DE

Terrence Cooks
COOKS, TERRENCE
B. Oct. 25, 1966, New Orleans, LA
Nicholls State 6'0" 230 lbs.

Year	Team		Games	Pos.
1989	NE	N	3	LB

Bob Coolbaugh
COOLBAUGH, ROBERT
B. 1940
Richmond 6'3" 200 lbs.

Year	Team		Games	Pos.
1961	OAK	A	14	OE

Larry Coombs
COOMBS, LARRY
B. Aug. 9, 1957, Eureka, CA
Idaho 6'4" 260 lbs.

Year	Team		Games	Pos.
1980	NO	N	1	C

Tom Coombs
COOMBS, THOMAS BARTON
B. May 31, 1959, Eureka, CA
Puget Sound/Idaho 6'3" 236 lbs.

Year	Team		Games	Pos.
1982	NYJ	N	3	TE
1983			12	TE
2 yrs.	15 games			

Joe Coomer
COOMER, JOSEPH D.
B. Sep. 11, 1918, Greenville, TX
D. Oct. 18, 1979, Whitehurst, TX
Austin 6'6" 281 lbs.

Year	Team		Games	Pos.
1941	PIT	N	10	T
1945			9	T
1946			7	T
1947	CHIC	N	12	T
1948			12	T
1949			12	T
6 yrs.	62 games			

Ty Coon
COON, EDWARD H., JR.
B. Jul. 26, 1915, White Plains, NY
D. Jan. 9, 1992, Watertown, CT
North Carolina State 6'0" 215 lbs.

Year	Team		Games	Pos.
1940	BKN	N	9	G

Mark Cooney
COONEY, MARK JOSEPH
B. Jun. 2, 1951, Denver, CO
Colorado 6'4" 230 lbs.

Year	Team		Games	Pos.
1974	GB	N	13	LB

Rob Coons
COONS, ROBERT ALLEN
B. Sep. 18, 1969, Brea, CA
Pittsburgh 6'5" 249 lbs.

Year	Team		Games	Pos.
1995	BUF	N	4	TE
1996			16	TE
2 yrs.	20 games			

Adrian Cooper
COOPER, ADRIAN
B. Apr. 27, 1968, Denver, CO
Oklahoma 6'5" 259 lbs.

Year	Team		Games	Pos.
1991	PIT	N	16	TE
1992			16	TE
1993			14	TE
1994	MIN	N	12	TE
1995			13	TE

Adrian Cooper *continued*

Year	Team		Games	Pos.
1996	SF	N	6	TE
6 yrs.	77 games			

Bert Cooper
COOPER, BERT
B. Aug. 24, 1952, Tallahassee, FL
Florida State 6'1" 242 lbs.

Year	Team		Games	Pos.
1976	TB	N	11	LB

Bill Cooper
COOPER, WILLIAM (Bud)
B. 1914
Penn State 6'1" 204 lbs.

Year	Team		Games	Pos.
1937	CLE	N	5	FB

Bill Cooper
COOPER, WILLIAM A.
B. Jul. 12, 1939, Carrollton, OH
Muskingum 6'1" 215 lbs.

Year	Team		Games	Pos.
1961	SF	N	12	FB
1963			14	LB
1964			2	LB
3 yrs.	28 games			

Earl Cooper
COOPER, MARION EARL
B. Sep. 17, 1957, Giddings, TX
Rice 6'2" 227 lbs.

Year	Team		Games	Pos.
1980	SF	N	16	RB
1981			16	FB
1982			9	RB
1983			16	RB
1984			16	TE, RB
1985			15	TE
1986	LARI	N	5	TE
7 yrs.	93 games			

Evan Cooper
COOPER, EVAN
B. Jun. 28, 1962, Miami, FL
Michigan 5'11" 184 lbs.

Year	Team		Games	Pos.
1984	PHI	N	16	CB, S
1985			16	CB
1986			16	CB, S
1987			12	CB
1988	ATL	N	9	CB, S
1989			16	S
6 yrs.	85 games			

George Cooper
COOPER, GEORGE JUNIOUS
B. Dec. 24, 1958, Detroit, MI
Michigan State 6'2" 225 lbs.

Year	Team		Games	Pos.
1987	SF	N	10	LB

Hal Cooper
COOPER, HAROLD W.
B. 1914
Deceased
Detroit 5'10" 207 lbs.

Year	Team		Games	Pos.
1937	DET	N	8	C, G

Jim Cooper
COOPER, JAMES ALBERT
B. Sep. 28, 1955, Philadelphia, PA
Temple 6'5" 265 lbs.

Year	Team		Games	Pos.
1977	DAL	N	14	OT
1978			14	G
1979			16	C
1980			15	OT
1981			16	OT
1982			9	OT
1983			16	OT
1984			7	OT
1985			15	OT

Jim Cooper *continued*

Year	Team		Games	Pos.
1986			12	OT
10 yrs.	134 games			

Jim Cooper
COOPER, JAMES PAUL
B. Jun. 28, 1924, Colorado City, TX
Texas Christian/North Texas State 6'0" 205 lbs.

Year	Team		Games	Pos.
1948	BKN	AA	1	C

Joe Cooper
COOPER, JOSEPH DONALD
B. Oct. 30, 1960, Fresno, CA
California 5'10" 175 lbs.

Year	Team		Games	Pos.
1984	HOU	N	7	K
1986	NYG	N	2	K
2 yrs.	9 games			

Ken Cooper
COOPER, KENNETH ROUSSEAU
B. Feb. 26, 1923, Rogersville, AL
Vanderbilt 6'1" 205 lbs.

Year	Team		Games	Pos.
1949	BAL	AA	12	G
1950	BAL	N	12	G
2 yrs.	24 games			

Louis Cooper
COOPER, ALEXANDER LOUIS
B. Aug. 5, 1963, Marion, SC
West Carolina 6'2" 235 lbs.

Year	Team		Games	Pos.
1985	KC	N	8	LB
1986			16	LB
1987			12	LB
1988			11	LB
1989			16	LB
1990			16	LB
1991	MIA	N	12	LB
1993	PHI	N	11	LB
8 yrs.	102 games			

Mark Cooper
COOPER, MARK SAMUEL
B. Feb. 14, 1960, Camden, NJ
Miami (Florida) 6'5" 275 lbs.

Year	Team		Games	Pos.
1983	DEN	N	10	OT
1984			15	G
1985			15	G
1986			8	G, OT
1987			5	G
1987	TB	N	4	OT
1988			15	OT
1989			6	OT
7 yrs.	78 games			

Norm Cooper
COOPER, NORMAN
B. Feb. 2, 1913
D. Jan., 1978, Paulsboro, NJ
Samford 6'4" 210 lbs.

Year	Team		Games	Pos.
1937	BKN	N	9	C
1938			10	C
2 yrs.	19 games			

Reggie Cooper
COOPER, REGINALD JOHN
B. Jul. 11, 1968, Bogalusa, LA
Nebraska 6'2" 215 lbs.

Year	Team		Games	Pos.
1991	DAL	N	2	LB

Richard Cooper
COOPER, RICHARD WARREN
B. Nov. 1, 1964, Memphis, TN
Tennessee 6'4" 288 lbs.

Year	Team		Games	Pos.
1990	NO	N	2	OT
1991			15	OT

Year	Team		Games	Pos.

Richard Cooper *continued*

Year	Team		Games	Pos.
1992			16	OT
1993			16	OT
1994			14	OT
1995			14	OT
1996	PHI	N	16	OT
7 yrs.	93 games			

Sam Cooper
COOPER, SAMUEL
B. 1909
Geneva 6'0" 200 lbs.

Year	Team		Games	Pos.
1933	PIT	N	1	T

Thurlow Cooper
COOPER, THURLOW
B. Mar. 18, 1933, Augusta, ME
Maine 6'4" 228 lbs.

Year	Team		Games	Pos.
1960	NY	A		OE, DE
1961			14	OE
1962			14	OE
3 yrs.	28 games			

Frank Cope
COPE, FRANK W.
B. Nov. 19, 1915, Anaconda, MT
D. Oct. 8, 1990, San Jose, CA
Santa Clara 6'2" 225 lbs.

Year	Team		Games	Pos.
1938	NYG	N	9	T
1939			11	T, G
1940			11	T
1941			11	T
1942			11	T
1943			10	T
1944			10	T
1945			9	T
1946			11	T
1947			5	T
10 yrs.	98 games			

Jim Cope
COPE, JAMES
B. Jun. 23, 1953, Oil City, PA
Ohio State 6'1" 235 lbs.

Year	Team		Games	Pos.
1976	ATL	N	6	LB

Anthony Copeland
COPELAND, ANTHONY
B. Apr. 14, 1963
Wichita State/Louisville 6'2" 250 lbs.

Year	Team		Games	Pos.
1987	WAS	N	3	LB

Danny Copeland
COPELAND, DANNY LAMAR
B. Jan. 24, 1966, Camilla, GA
Eastern Kentucky 6'2" 210 lbs.

Year	Team		Games	Pos.
1989	KC	N	16	S, CB
1990			14	CB
1991	WAS	N	16	S, CB
1992			13	S
1993			14	S
5 yrs.	73 games			

Horace Copeland
COPELAND, HORACE NATHANIEL
B. Jan. 2, 1971, Orlando, FL
Miami (Florida) 6'2" 195 lbs.

Year	Team		Games	Pos.
1993	TB	N	14	WR
1994			16	WR
1995			15	WR
3 yrs.	45 games			

Jim Copeland
COPELAND, WYATTE JAMES, JR.
B. Mar. 5, 1945, Charlottesville, VA

Jim Copeland *continued*
Virginia 6'2" 242 lbs.

Year	Team		Games	Pos.
1967	CLE	N	14	G
1968			14	G
1969			8	G
1970			14	G
1971			14	G
1972			1	C, G
1973			14	C
1974			2	C, G
8 yrs.	81 games			

John Copeland
COPELAND, JOHN
B. Sep. 20, 1970, Lanett, AL
Alabama 6'3" 286 lbs.

Year	Team		Games	Pos.
1993	CIN	N	14	NT
1994			12	DE
1995			16	DE
1996			13	DE
4 yrs.	55 games			

Ron Copeland
COPELAND, RONALD
B. Oct. 3, 1946, Los Angeles, CA
UCLA 6'4" 196 lbs.

Year	Team		Games	Pos.
1969	CHI	N	6	WR

Russell Copeland
COPELAND, RUSSELL
B. Nov. 4, 1971, Tupelo, MS
Memphis State 6'0" 200 lbs.

Year	Team		Games	Pos.
1993	BUF	N	16	WR
1994			15	WR
1995			16	WR
1996			11	WR
4 yrs.	58 games			

Charlie Copley
COPLEY, CHARLES F.
B. May 11, 1888
D. Mar., 1982, Wellsboro, PA
Muhlenberg/Missouri-Rolla 5'9" 191 lbs.

Year	Team		Games	Pos.
1920	AKR	A	9	T
1921			12	T
1922	AKR	N	3	T, G
1922	MIL	N	4	E, T, G
3 yrs.	28 games			

Al Coppage
COPPAGE, ALTON M.
B. Feb. 8, 1916, Hollis, OK
D. Jan. 9, 1992, Hollis, OK
Oklahoma 6'1" 195 lbs.

Year	Team		Games	Pos.
1940	CHIC	N	11	E
1941			7	E
1942			11	E
1946	CLE	AA	14	E
1947	BUF	AA	13	E
5 yrs.	56 games			

Gus Coppens
COPPENS, AUGUST RICHARD
B. Feb. 7, 1955, Lynwood, CA
UCLA 6'5" 270 lbs.

Year	Team		Games	Pos.
1979	NYG	N	9	OT

George Corbett
CORBETT, GEORGE BURDETTE
B. Jun. 14, 1908, Dix, IL
D. Oct. 11, 1990, Springfield, IL
Millikin 5'9" 179 lbs.

Year	Team		Games	Pos.
1932	CHIB	N	11	HB, QB
1933			5	HB
1934			7	HB
1935			4	HB

George Corbett *continued*

Year	Team		Games	Pos.
1936			9	HB
1937			2	B
1938			7	QB
7 yrs.	45 games			

Jim Corbett
CORBETT, JIM
B. Feb. 22, 1955, Brockton, MA
Pittsburgh 6'4" 218 lbs.

Year	Team		Games	Pos.
1977	CIN	N	14	TE
1978			16	TE
1979			10	TE
1980			4	TE
4 yrs.	44 games			

Steve Corbett
CORBETT, STEPHEN PAUL
B. Aug. 11, 1951, Dover, NH
Boston College 6'4" 248 lbs.

Year	Team		Games	Pos.
1975	NE	N	14	G

Don Corbitt
CORBITT, DONALD OLIVER
B. Apr. 1, 1924, Creston, IA
D. Sep. 3, 1993, Phoenix, AZ
Arizona 6'4" 224 lbs.

Year	Team		Games	Pos.
1948	WAS	N	3	C

Tom Corbo
CORBO, THOMAS J.
B. Jan. 11, 1918, Altoona, PA
Duquesne 5'11" 210 lbs.

Year	Team		Games	Pos.
1944	CLE	N	10	G

Art Corcoran
CORCORAN, ARTHUR (Bunny, Buddy)
B. 1895
Deceased
Georgetown (DC)/Fordham 5'11" 184 lbs.

Year	Team		Games	Pos.
1920	CAN	A	6	E
1921	CLE	A	8	E
1921	AKR	A	1	E
1922	AKR	N	9	E
1923	BUF	N	1	HB
4 yrs.	25 games			

Jack Corcoran
CORCORAN, JOHN
B. 1906
St. Thomas/St. Louis 180 lbs.

Year	Team		Games	Pos.
1930	MIN	N	5	C, G

King Corcoran
CORCORAN, JAMES SEAN PATRICK
B. Jul. 6, 1943, Jersey City, NJ
Maryland 6'0" 200 lbs.

Year	Team		Games	Pos.
1968	BOS	A	1	QB

Lou Cordileone
CORDILEONE, LOU ANTHONY
B. Aug. 4, 1938, Jersey City, NJ
Clemson 6'0" 247 lbs.

Year	Team		Games	Pos.
1960	NYG	N	11	G
1961	SF	N	12	DE
1962	LA	N	2	DE
1962	PIT	N	14	DE
1963			14	DT
1967	NO	N	11	DT
1968			12	DT
6 yrs.	76 games			

Ollie Cordill
CORDILL, OLIVER
B. Jun. 20, 1943, Houston, TX
Memphis State 6'2" 180 lbs.

Year	Team		Games	Pos.
1967	SD	A	3	OE
1968	ATL	N	1	DB
1969	NO	N	12	DB
3 yrs.	16 games			

Ollie Cordill
CORDILL, OLIVER S.
B. Apr. 28, 1916
D. Nov. 14, 1988, Spicewood, TX
Rice 6'2" 190 lbs.

Year	Team		Games	Pos.
1940	CLE	N	10	HB

Sam Cordovano
CORDOVANO, SAMUEL S.
B. 1907
Georgetown (DC) 5'11" 185 lbs.

Year	Team		Games	Pos.
1930	NEW	N	8	G, C

Walt Corey
COREY, WALTER M.
B. May 9, 1938, Latrobe, PA
Miami (Florida) 6'0" 229 lbs.

Year	Team		Games	Pos.
1960	DAL	A	14	LB
1962			14	LB
1963	KC	A	12	LB
1964			13	LB
1965			7	LB
1966			9	LB
6 yrs.	69 games			

Chuck Corgan
CORGAN, CHARLES HOWARD
B. Dec. 4, 1902, Wagoner, OK
D. Jun. 13, 1928, Wagoner, OK
Arkansas 6'0" 183 lbs.

Year	Team		Games	Pos.
1924	KC	N	9	QB, E, HB
1925			2	QB, HB
1926	HAR	N	7	QB, HB
1926	KC	N	1	HB, QB
1927	NYG	N	11	E
4 yrs.	30 games			

Mike Corgan
CORGAN, MICHAEL HENRY
B. Oct. 26, 1918, Olongpo, Philippines
D. May 28, 1989, Lincoln, NE
Notre Dame 5'10" 188 lbs.

Year	Team		Games	Pos.
1943	DET	N	4	FB

John Corker
CORKER, JOHN
B. Dec. 29, 1958, Miami, FL
Oklahoma State 6'5" 240 lbs.

Year	Team		Games	Pos.
1980	HOU	N	16	LB
1981			11	LB
1982			3	LB
1988	GB	N	2	LB
4 yrs.	32 games			

Anthony Corley
CORLEY, ANTHONY GEORGE
B. Aug. 10, 1960, Reno, NV
Nevada-Reno 6'0" 210 lbs.

Year	Team		Games	Pos.
1984	PIT	N	14	RB
1985	SD	N	4	RB
2 yrs.	18 games			

Bert Corley
CORLEY, ELBERT E. (Mule)
B. Sep. 9, 1920, Okolona, MS
Deceased

Year Team	Games	Pos.

Bert Corley *continued*
Mississippi State 6'2" 210 lbs.

Year	Team		Games	Pos.
1947	BUF	AA	13	C
1948	BAL	AA	9	C
2 yrs.	22 games			

Chris Corley
CORLEY, CHRIS
B. Oct. 24, 1963
South Carolina 6'4" 285 lbs.

1987	SEA	N	1	TE

Joe Cormier
CORMIER, JOSEPH DAILY
B. May 3, 1963, Los Angeles, CA
Southern California 6'6" 230 lbs.

1987	LARI	N	2	LB

Joe Corn
CORN, JOSEPH
B. 1922
None 5'6" 168 lbs.

1948	LA	N	9	HB

Jerry Cornelison
CORNELISON, JERRY G.
B. Sep. 13, 1936
Southern Methodist 6'3" 250 lbs.

1960	DAL	A		OT
1961			14	OT
1962			14	OT
1964	KC	A	14	OT
1965			14	OT
5 yrs.	56 games			

Charles Cornelius
CORNELIUS, CHARLES
B. Jul. 27, 1952, Boynton Beach, FL
Bethune-Cookman 5'9" 178 lbs.

1977	MIA	N	13	CB
1978			16	CB
1979	SF	N	16	CB
1980			16	CB
4 yrs.	61 games			

Bo Cornell
CORNELL, ROBERT PAUL
B. Mar. 7, 1949, Seattle, WA
Washington 6'1" 217 lbs.

1971	CLE	N	14	RB
1972			14	RB
1973	BUF	N	14	RB
1974			14	RB, LB
1975			14	LB
1976			14	LB
1977			12	LB
7 yrs.	96 games			

Martin Cornelson
CORNELSON, MARTIN
B. Jun. 4, 1961
North Carolina State 6'1" 230 lbs.

1987	NYJ	N	3	C

Frank Cornish
CORNISH, FRANK EDGAR, III
B. Jun. 20, 1944, New Orleans, LA
Grambling State 6'6" 285 lbs.

1966	CHI		14	DT
1967			14	DT
1968			13	DT
1969			14	DT
1970	CIN	N	2	DT
1970	MIA	N	12	DT
1971			10	DT

Frank Cornish *continued*

1972	BUF	N	6	DT
7 yrs.	85 games			

Frank Cornish
CORNISH, FRANK EDGAR
B. Sep. 24, 1967, Chicago, IL
UCLA 6'4" 292 lbs.

1990	SD	N	16	C, G
1991			16	C
1992	DAL	N	11	C, G
1993			14	C, G
1994	MIN	N	7	C
1995	JAC	N	3	C
1995	PHI	N	2	C
6 yrs.	69 games			

Al Cornsweet
CORNSWEET, ALBERT CHARLES
B. Jul. 16, 1906
D. Oct. 16, 1991, Arlington, VA
Brown 5'7" 180 lbs.

1931	CLE	N	4	FB, HB

Fred Cornwell
CORNWELL, FREDERICK KEITH
B. Aug. 7, 1961, Osborne, KS
Southern California 6'6" 233 lbs.

1984	DAL	N	14	TE
1985			16	TE
2 yrs.	30 games			

Bobby Coronado
CORONADO, ROBERT
B. May 22, 1936, Vallejo, CA
Pacific 6'1" 195 lbs.

1961	PIT	N	5	OE

Frank Corral
CORRAL, JOHN FRANK
B. Jun. 16, 1955, Chihuahua, Mexico
UCLA 6'2" 224 lbs.

1978	LA	N	16	K
1979			16	K
1980			16	K, P
1981			16	K, P
4 yrs.	64 games			

Chuck Correal
CORREAL, CHUCK
B. May 17, 1956, Uniontown, PA
Penn State 6'3" 247 lbs.

1980	ATL	N	16	C

Phil Corrigan
CORRIGAN, PHILIP
B. Apr. 28, 1898
Deceased
Boston College 5'7" 160 lbs.

1926	BOS	A	4	QB, FB, HB

Kip Corrington
CORRINGTON, KIP ALAN
B. Apr. 12, 1965, Ames, IA
Texas A&M 6'0" 175 lbs.

1989	DEN	N	16	S
1990			16	S
2 yrs.	32 games			

Rico Corsetti
CORSETTI, RICO
B. Jan. 13, 1963

Rico Corsetti *continued*
Bates 6'1" 225 lbs.

1987	NE	N	2	LB

Chris Cortemeglia
CORTEMEGLIA, CHRISTOPHER
B. Sep. 21, 1903, Bryan, TX
D. Mar. 14, 1989, Houston, TX
Southern Methodist 6'0" 210 lbs.

1927	FRA	N	1	QB

Julio Cortes
CORTES, JULIO
B. Aug. 13, 1962, New York, NY
Miami (Florida) 6'0" 226 lbs.

1987	SEA	N	3	LB

Bruce Cortez
CORTEZ, BRUCE FORD
B. Oct. 29, 1945, Carthage, MO
Parsons 6'0" 175 lbs.

1967	NO	N	1	DB

Anthony Corvino
CORVINO, ANTHONY
B. Sep. 15, 1965
Southern Connecticut State 6'1" 262 lbs.

1987	NYJ	N	2	G, OT

Quentin Coryatt
CORYATT, QUENTIN JOHN
B. Aug. 1, 1970, St. Croix, Virgin Islands
Texas A&M 6'3" 250 lbs.

1992	IND	N	7	LB
1993			16	LB
1994			16	LB
1995			16	LB
1996			8	LB
5 yrs.	63 games			

Red Corzine
CORZINE, LESTER HOWARD (Lefty)
B. Jan. 19, 1909, Balcom, IL
Davis & Elkins 6'0" 213 lbs.

1933	CIN	N	9	FB
1934	C, S	N	10	FB
1935	NYG	N	11	FB
1936			10	FB
1937			11	FB, QB
5 yrs.	51 games			

Doug Cosbie
COSBIE, DOUGLAS DURANT
B. Mar. 27, 1956, Palo Alto, CA
Santa Clara 6'6" 236 lbs.

1979	DAL	N	16	TE
1980			16	TE
1981			16	TE
1982			9	TE
1983			16	TE
1984			16	TE
1985			16	TE
1986			16	TE
1987			12	TE
1988			11	TE
10 yrs.	144 games			

Bruce Coslet
COSLET, BRUCE NOEL
B. Aug. 5, 1946, Oakdale, CA
Pacific 6'3" 228 lbs.

1969	CIN	A	8	TE
1970	CIN	N	14	TE
1971			14	TE

Bruce Coslet *continued*

1972			10	TE
1973			13	TE
1974			14	TE
1975			14	TE
1976			14	TE
8 yrs.	101 games			

Don Cosner
COSNER, DONALD
B. 1917
Montana State 6'2" 200 lbs.

1939	CHIC	N	1	HB

Eric Coss
COSS, ERIC
B. Jun. 12, 1963
Temple 6'3" 270 lbs.

1987	NYJ	N	3	G, C

Dave Costa
COSTA, DAVID JOSEPH
B. Oct. 27, 1941, Yonkers, NY
Utah 6'2" 257 lbs.

1963	OAK	A	14	DT
1964			14	DT
1965			14	DT
1966	BUF	A	14	DT
1967	DEN	A	14	DT
1968			14	DT
1969			14	DT
1970	DEN	N	14	DT
1971			14	DT
1972	SD	N	14	DT
1973			14	DT
1974	BUF	N	14	DT
12 yrs.	168 games			

Paul Costa
COSTA, S. PAUL
B. Dec. 7, 1941, Port Chester, NY
Notre Dame 6'4" 252 lbs.

1965	BUF	A	10	OE
1966			14	TE
1967			14	TE
1968			14	TE, OT
1969			14	OT
1970	BUF	N	14	OT
1971			11	OT
1972			9	OT
8 yrs.	100 games			

Joe Costello
COSTELLO, JOSEPH PATRICK, JR.
B. Jun. 1, 1960, New York, NY
Central Connecticut State 6'3" 250 lbs.

1986	ATL	N	14	LB
1987			9	LB
1988			6	LB
1989	LARI	N	2	LB
4 yrs.	31 games			

Tom Costello
COSTELLO, THOMAS
B. May 23, 1941, Flushing, NY
Miami/Dayton 6'3" 220 lbs.

1964	NYG	N	2	LB
1965			8	LB
2 yrs.	10 games			

Vince Costello
COSTELLO, VINCE
B. Aug. 4, 1932, Magnolia, OH
Ohio University 6'0" 228 lbs.

1957	CLE	N	12	G
1958			12	G

Year	Team	Games	Pos.

Vince Costello *continued*

Year	Team		Games	Pos.
1959			12	G
1960			12	G
1961			14	G
1962			13	LB
1963			14	LB
1964			14	LB
1965			13	LB
1966			14	LB
1967	NYG	N	14	LB
1968			2	LB
12 yrs.	146 games			

Ray Costict
COSTICT, RAY CHARLES
B. May 19, 1955, Moss Point, MS
Mississippi State 6'0" 217 lbs.

Year	Team		Games	Pos.
1977	NE	N	14	LB
1978			16	LB
1979			16	LB
3 yrs.	46 games			

Zed Coston
COSTON, FRED M.
B. 1916
Texas A&M 6'2" 222 lbs.

Year	Team		Games	Pos.
1939	PHI	N	1	C

Chad Cota
COTA, CHAD GARRETT
B. Aug. 13, 1971, Ashland, OR
Oregon 6'1" 195 lbs.

Year	Team		Games	Pos.
1995	CAR	N	16	S
1996			16	S
2 yrs.	32 games			

Jeff Cothran
COTHRAN, JEFF
B. Jun. 28, 1971, Middletown, OH
Ohio State 6'2" 231 lbs.

Year	Team		Games	Pos.
1994	CIN	N	14	RB
1995			15	RB
1996			12	FB
3 yrs.	41 games			

Paige Cothren
COTHREN, JENNINGS PAIGE
B. Jul. 12, 1935, Natchez, MS
Mississippi 5'11" 201 lbs.

Year	Team		Games	Pos.
1957	LA	N	12	K
1958			12	K
1959	PHI	N	7	K
3 yrs.	31 games			

Mark Cotney
COTNEY, JOHN MARK
B. Jun. 26, 1952, Altus, OK
Cameron 6'0" 204 lbs.

Year	Team		Games	Pos.
1975	HOU	N	14	S
1976	TB	N	14	DB
1977			14	S
1978			16	S
1979			16	S
1980			16	S
1982			9	S
1983			12	S
1984			16	S
9 yrs.	127 games			

Barney Cotton
COTTON, BARNEY T.
B. Sep. 30, 1956, Omaha, NE
Nebraska 6'5" 264 lbs.

Year	Team		Games	Pos.
1979	CIN	N	13	G
1980	STL	N	16	G
1981			16	G
3 yrs.	45 games			

Craig Cotton
COTTON, CRAIG LEE (Monk)
B. Jul. 7, 1947, Elizabeth, PA
Youngstown State 6'4" 222 lbs.

Year	Team		Games	Pos.
1969	DET	N	13	TE
1970			14	TE
1971			14	TE
1972			14	TE
1973	CHI	N	13	TE
5 yrs.	68 games			

Fod Cotton
COTTON, FORREST G.
B. Jan. 14, 1901, IL
D. Mar., 1967, Kansas City, MO
Notre Dame 6'1" 190 lbs.

Year	Team		Games	Pos.
1923	RI	N	7	T
1925			6	T
2 yrs.	13 games			

Marcus Cotton
COTTON, MARCUS GLENN
B. Aug. 11, 1966, Los Angeles, CA
Southern California 6'3" 225 lbs.

Year	Team		Games	Pos.
1988	ATL	N	11	LB
1989			16	LB
1990			7	LB
1990	CLE	N	7	LB
1991	SEA	N	3	LB
4 yrs.	44 games			

Russ Cotton
COTTON, RUSSELL
B. May 24, 1915, Palestine, TX
Texas Western 6'1" 196 lbs.

Year	Team		Games	Pos.
1941	BKN	N	1	B
1942	PIT	N	11	B
2 yrs.	12 games			

Bill Cottrell
COTTRELL, WILLIAM HENRY
B. Sep. 18, 1944, Chester, PA
Delaware Valley 6'3" 255 lbs.

Year	Team		Games	Pos.
1967	DET	N	14	C
1968			14	OT
1969			14	OT
1970			10	C, G
1972	DEN	N	11	G
5 yrs.	63 games			

Ted Cottrell
COTTRELL, THEODORE JOHN
B. Jun. 13, 1947, Chester, PA
Delaware Valley 6'1" 233 lbs.

Year	Team		Games	Pos.
1969	ATL	N	10	LB
1970			14	LB
2 yrs.	24 games			

Danny Coughlin
COUGHLIN, DANIEL M.
B. Jun., 1897
Deceased
St. Thomas/Notre Dame 5'9" 175 lbs.

Year	Team		Games	Pos.
1923	MIN	N	2	HB

Frank Coughlin
COUGHLIN, FRANK E.
B. Mar., 1896
Deceased
Notre Dame 6'3" 200 lbs.

Year	Team		Games	Pos.
1921	GB	A	5	T
1921	RI	A	3	T
1921	DET	A	2	T
1 yr.	10 games			

Tex Coulter
COULTER, DEWITT E.
B. Oct. 26, 1926, Fort Worth, TX
Army 6'4" 250 lbs.

Year	Team		Games	Pos.
1946	NYG	N	9	T
1947			12	T, E
1948			12	T
1949			12	C
1951			12	T
1952			12	T, C
6 yrs.	69 games			

Ulysses Coumier
COUMIER, ULYSSES
B. 1905
None 5'10" 195 lbs.

Year	Team		Games	Pos.
1929	BUF	N	3	HB, FB

Johnny Counts
COUNTS, JOHN E.
B. Feb. 28, 1939, Mount Pleasant, NY
Illinois 5'10" 170 lbs.

Year	Team		Games	Pos.
1962	NYG	N	14	HB
1963			3	HB
2 yrs.	17 games			

Al Couppee
COUPPEE, ALBERT WALLACE
B. Jun. 4, 1920, Council Bluffs, IA
Iowa 6'0" 225 lbs.

Year	Team		Games	Pos.
1946	WAS	N	7	G

Steve Courson
COURSON, STEPHEN PAUL
B. Oct. 1, 1955, Philadelphia, PA
South Carolina 6'1" 275 lbs.

Year	Team		Games	Pos.
1978	PIT	N	16	G
1979			16	G
1980			8	G
1981			16	G
1982			8	G
1983			9	G
1984	TB	N	14	G
1985			16	G
8 yrs.	103 games			

Gerry Courtney
COURTNEY, GERALD
B. Mar. 2, 1918, Tulsa, OK
Syracuse 6'0" 195 lbs.

Year	Team		Games	Pos.
1942	BKN	N	5	B

Matt Courtney
COURTNEY, MATTHEW CARTER
B. Dec. 21, 1961, Greeley, CO
Idaho State 5'11" 194 lbs.

Year	Team		Games	Pos.
1987	SF	N	3	CB

Vince Courville
COURVILLE, VINCENT ERIC
B. Dec. 5, 1959, Galveston, TX
Texas Southern/Rice 5'9" 170 lbs.

Year	Team		Games	Pos.
1987	DAL	N	2	WR

Tom Cousineau
COUSINEAU, TOM
B. May 6, 1957, Fairview Park, OH
Ohio State 6'3" 225 lbs.

Year	Team		Games	Pos.
1982	CLE	N	9	LB
1983			16	LB
1984			16	LB
1985			16	LB
1986	SF	N	5	LB
1987			4	LB
6 yrs.	66 games			

Brad Cousino
COUSINO, BRADLEY GENE
B. Apr. 5, 1953, Toledo, OH
Miami (Ohio) 6'0" 218 lbs.

Year	Team		Games	Pos.
1975	CIN	N	14	LB
1976	NYG	N	6	LB
1977	PIT	N	3	LB
3 yrs.	23 games			

Larry Coutre
COUTRE, LAWRENCE E.
B. Apr. 11, 1928, Chicago, IL
Notre Dame 5'10" 175 lbs.

Year	Team		Games	Pos.
1950	GB	N	12	HB
1953			7	HB
1953	BAL	N	10	HB
2 yrs.	29 games			

Jim Covert
COVERT, JAMES PAUL (Jimbo)
B. Mar. 22, 1960, Conway, PA
Pittsburgh 6'4" 275 lbs.

Year	Team		Games	Pos.
1983	CHI	N	16	OT
1984			16	OT
1985			15	OT
1986			16	OT
1987			9	OT
1988			9	OT
1989			15	OT
1990			15	OT
8 yrs.	111 games			

Damien Covington
COVINGTON, DAMIEN
B. Dec. 4, 1972, Berlin, NJ
North Carolina State 5'11" 236 lbs.

Year	Team		Games	Pos.
1995	BUF	N	12	LB
1996			9	LB
2 yrs.	21 games			

Jamie Covington
COVINGTON, JAMIE
B. Dec. 12, 1962, Flushing, NY
Syracuse 6'1" 234 lbs.

Year	Team		Games	Pos.
1987	NYG	N	2	RB

John Covington
COVINGTON, JOHN SHAFT
B. Apr. 22, 1972, Winter Haven, FL
Notre Dame 6'0" 198 lbs.

Year	Team		Games	Pos.
1994	IND	N	3	S

Tony Covington
COVINGTON, ANTHONY LAVONNE
B. Dec. 26, 1967, Winston-Salem, NC
Virginia 5'11" 190 lbs.

Year	Team		Games	Pos.
1991	TB	N	16	S
1992			1	S
1994			13	S
1995	SEA	N	11	S
4 yrs.	41 games			

Bob Cowan
COWAN, ROBERT GEORGE
B. Jan. 2, 1923, Fort Wayne, IN
Michigan/Indiana 5'11" 185 lbs.

Year	Team		Games	Pos.
1947	CLE	AA	10	HB, DB
1948			14	HB, DB
1949	BAL	AA	9	HB, DB
3 yrs.	33 games			

Charlie Cowan
COWAN, CHARLES EDWARD
B. Jun. 19, 1938, Braeholm, WV

Year	Team		Games	Pos.

Charlie Cowan *continued*
New Mexico Highlands 6'4" 264 lbs.

Year	Team		Games	Pos.
1961	**LA**	N	14	OT
1962			14	G
1963			14	G
1964			14	G
1965			13	G, OT
1966			14	OT
1967			14	OT
1968			13	OT
1969			14	OT
1970			14	OT
1971			14	OT
1972			13	OT
1973			14	OT
1974			14	OT

14 yrs.   193 games

Larry Cowan
COWAN, LARRY DONNELL
B. Jul. 11, 1960, Mobile, AL
Jackson State 5'11" 194 lbs.

Year	Team		Games	Pos.
1982	**MIA**	N	2	RB
1982	**NE**	N	6	RB

1 yr.   8 games

Les Cowan
COWAN, LESLIE L.
B. Dec. 24, 1925, Stamford, TX
McMurry 6'5" 235 lbs.

Year	Team		Games	Pos.
1951	**CHIB**	N	9	DE, DT

Bill Cowher
COWHER, WILLIAM LAIRD
B. May 8, 1957, Pittsburgh, PA
North Carolina State 6'3" 225 lbs.

Year	Team		Games	Pos.
1980	**CLE**	N	16	LB
1982			9	LB
1983	**PHI**	N	16	LB
1984			4	LB

4 yrs.   45 games

Gerry Cowhig
COWHIG, GERALD FINBAR
B. Jul. 5, 1922, Dorchester, MA
Notre Dame 6'2" 215 lbs.

Year	Team		Games	Pos.
1947	**LA**	N	8	FB, LB
1948			12	FB, DB
1949			11	FB, DB
1950	**CHIC**	N	11	LB
1951	**PHI**	N	11	LB

5 yrs.   53 games

Al Cowlings
COWLINGS, ALLEN G. (A.C.)
B. Jun. 16, 1947, San Francisco, CA
Southern California 6'5" 247 lbs.

Year	Team		Games	Pos.
1970	**BUF**	N	13	DE
1971			14	DE
1972			14	DE
1973	**HOU**	N	14	DE
1974			14	DT
1975	**LA**	N	5	DE
1977	**LA**	N	14	DE, DT
1979	**SF**	N	16	DE

8 yrs.   104 games

John Cowne
COWNE, JOHN
B. May 23, 1962
Virginia Tech 6'2" 245 lbs.

Year	Team		Games	Pos.
1987	**WAS**	N	3	C

Aaron Cox
COX, AARON DION
B. Mar. 13, 1965, Los Angeles, CA

Aaron Cox *continued*
Arizona State 5'9" 174 lbs.

Year	Team		Games	Pos.
1988	**LARM**	N	16	WR
1989			16	WR
1990			14	WR
1991			15	WR
1992			10	WR
1993	**IND**	N	11	WR

6 yrs.   82 games

Arthur Cox
COX, ARTHUR DEAN
B. Feb. 5, 1961, Plant City, FL
Texas Southern 6'3" 260 lbs.

Year	Team		Games	Pos.
1983	**ATL**	N	16	TE
1984			16	TE
1985			16	TE
1986			16	TE
1987			12	TE
1988	**SD**	N	16	TE
1989			16	TE
1990			16	TE
1991			8	TE
1991	**MIA**	N	2	TE
1991	**CLE**	N	2	TE

9 yrs.   136 games

Billy Cox
COX, WILLIAM B.
B. Jun. 17, 1929, Mount Airy, NC
Duke 6'3" 189 lbs.

Year	Team		Games	Pos.
1951	**WAS**	N	10	HB, DB
1952			10	HB, DB
1955			4	E

3 yrs.   24 games

Bryan Cox
COX, BRYAN KEITH
B. Feb. 17, 1968, St. Louis, MO
Western Illinois 6'3" 239 lbs.

Year	Team		Games	Pos.
1991	**MIA**	N	13	LB
1992			16	LB
1993			16	LB
1994			16	LB
1995			16	LB
1996	**CHI**	N	9	LB

6 yrs.   86 games

Fred Cox
COX, FREDERICK WILLIAM
B. Dec. 11, 1958, Monongahela, PA
Pittsburgh 5'10" 200 lbs.

Year	Team		Games	Pos.
1963	**MIN**	N	14	K, P
1964			14	K
1965			14	K
1966			14	K
1967			14	K
1968			14	K
1969			14	K
1970			14	K
1971			14	K
1972			14	K
1973			14	K
1974			14	K
1975			14	K
1976			14	K
1977			14	K

15 yrs.   210 games

Greg Cox
COX, GREGORY MARK
B. Jan. 6, 1965, Niagara Falls, NY
San Jose State 6'0" 223 lbs.

Year	Team		Games	Pos.
1988	**SF**	N	15	S
1989	**NYG**	N	16	S
1990	**SF**	N	13	S
1991			11	S

4 yrs.   55 games

Jim Cox
COX, JAMES
B. Dec. 21, 1946, Baltimore, MD
Miami (Florida) 6'2" 227 lbs.

Year	Team		Games	Pos.
1968	**MIA**	A	13	TE

Jim Cox
COX, JAMES ELLINGSON
B. 1921
Stanford 6'1" 208 lbs.

Year	Team		Games	Pos.
1948	**SF**	AA	14	G, LB

Larry Cox
COX, LARRY DONALD
B. Nov. 12, 1943, Anson, TX
Abilene Christian 6'2" 250 lbs.

Year	Team		Games	Pos.
1966	**DEN**	A	11	DT
1967			13	DT
1968			9	DT

3 yrs.   33 games

Norm Cox
COX, NORMAN L.
B. Sep. 22, 1925, Stamford, TX
Texas Christian 6'2" 210 lbs.

Year	Team		Games	Pos.
1946	**CHI**	AA	3	QB
1947			2	B

2 yrs.   5 games

Ron Cox
COX, RON
B. Feb. 2, 1968, Fresno, CA
Fresno State 6'2" 240 lbs.

Year	Team		Games	Pos.
1990	**CHI**	N	13	LB
1991			6	LB
1992			16	LB
1993			16	LB
1994			15	LB
1995			16	LB
1996	**GB**	N	16	LB

7 yrs.   98 games

Steve Cox
COX, STEVE
B. May 11, 1958, Shreveport, LA
Arkansas 6'4" 195 lbs.

Year	Team		Games	Pos.
1981	**CLE**	N	16	P, K
1982			9	P, K
1983			7	P, K
1984			16	P, K
1985	**WAS**	N	12	P
1986			16	P, K
1987			12	P, K
1988			1	P

8 yrs.   89 games

Tom Cox
COX, TOM
B. Dec. 4, 1962
Southern California 6'5" 260 lbs.

Year	Team		Games	Pos.
1987	**LARM**	N	3	OT

Eric Coyle
COYLE, ERIC
B. Oct. 26, 1963, Longmont, CO
Colorado 6'3" 260 lbs.

Year	Team		Games	Pos.
1987	**WAS**	N	3	C

Frank Coyle
COYLE, FRANCIS J.
B. Nov. 29, 1899
D. Feb., 1987, Moline, IL
Detroit 6'0" 180 lbs.

Year	Team		Games	Pos.
1926	**RI**	A	6	E

Russ Coyle
COYLE, RUSSELL
B. 1937
Oklahoma 6'2" 195 lbs.

Year	Team		Games	Pos.
1961	**LA**	N	13	DB

Claude Crabb
CRABB, CLAUDE CLARENCE
B. Mar. 8, 1940, Monterey, CA
Colorado 6'0" 193 lbs.

Year	Team		Games	Pos.
1962	**WAS**	N	13	DB
1963			13	DB
1964	**PHI**	N	13	DB, FL
1965			10	DB, FL
1966	**LA**	N	14	DB, FL
1967			14	DB
1968			3	DB

7 yrs.   80 games

Bob Crable
CRABLE, ROBERT EDWARD
B. Sep. 22, 1959, Cincinnati, OH
Notre Dame 6'3" 230 lbs.

Year	Team		Games	Pos.
1982	**NYJ**	N	9	LB
1983			14	LB
1984			5	LB
1985			10	LB
1986			16	LB
1987			12	LB

6 yrs.   66 games

Clem Crabtree
CRABTREE, CLEMENT GURLEY
B. Nov. 11, 1918, Durham, NC
D. Jan., 1981
Wake Forest 6'3" 225 lbs.

Year	Team		Games	Pos.
1940	**DET**	N	9	G, T
1941			9	T

2 yrs.   18 games

Clyde Crabtree
CRABTREE, CLYDE (Cannonball)
B. Oct. 11, 1907
D. Apr. 20, 1994, Miami, FL
Northwestern/Florida 5'8" 160 lbs.

Year	Team		Games	Pos.
1930	**FRA**	N	13	QB, HB
1930	**MIN**	N	1	HB

1 yr.   14 games

Eric Crabtree
CRABTREE, ERIC LESLIE
B. Nov. 3, 1944, Monessen, PA
Pittsburgh 5'11" 184 lbs.

Year	Team		Games	Pos.
1966	**DEN**	A	14	DB, OE
1967			14	OE
1968			14	OE
1969	**CIN**	A	14	WR
1970	**CIN**	N	14	WR
1971			7	WR
1971	**NE**	N	6	WR

6 yrs.   83 games

Nat Craddock
CRADDOCK, NAT
B. Dec. 3, 1940
Parsons 6'0" 220 lbs.

Year	Team		Games	Pos.
1963	**BAL**	N	3	FB

Donnie Craft
CRAFT, DONNIE
B. Nov. 19, 1959, Panama City, FL
Louisville 6'0" 209 lbs.

Year	Team		Games	Pos.
1982	**HOU**	N	9	RB
1983			15	RB
1984			1	RB

3 yrs.   25 games

Year	Team	Games	Pos.

Russ Craft
CRAFT, WILLIAM RUSSELL
B. Oct. 15, 1919, McEwen, TN
Alabama 5'9" 174 lbs.

Year	Team		Games	Pos.
1946	PHI	N	9	HB
1947			10	HB
1948			12	HB
1949			10	HB
1950			12	HB
1951			12	HB
1952			12	HB
1953			12	HB
1954	PIT	N	11	HB
9 yrs.		100 games		

Jerry Crafts
CRAFTS, JERRY WAYNE
B. Jan. 6, 1968, Tulsa, OK
Oklahoma/Louisville 6'6" 341 lbs.

Year	Team		Games	Pos.
1992	BUF	N	6	OT
1993			16	OT
1994			16	OT, G
3 yrs.		38 games		

Clark Craig
CRAIG, CLARK
B. Jun. 19, 1902
D. Nov., 1977, Shawnee, OK
Pennsylvania 5'9" 180 lbs.

Year	Team		Games	Pos.
1925	FRA	N	2	E

Dobie Craig
CRAIG, DOBIE
B. 1939
Baylor/Howard Payne 6'4" 200 lbs.

Year	Team		Games	Pos.
1962	OAK	A	14	HB
1963			12	HB
1964	HOU	A	7	OE
3 yrs.		33 games		

Larry Craig
CRAIG, LAWRENCE GANTT
(Superman)
B. Jun. 27, 1916, Central, SC
D. Jun. 1, 1992, Ninety Six, SC
South Carolina 6'1" 211 lbs.

Year	Team		Games	Pos.
1939	GB	N	10	QB, E
1940			11	QB
1941			10	QB, E
1942			11	QB, E
1943			10	QB
1944			10	QB
1945			10	QB
1946			11	QB
1947			12	E
1948			12	E
1949			12	E
11 yrs.		119 games		

Neal Craig
CRAIG, CORNELIUS, JR.
B. Apr. 21, 1948, Cincinnati, OH
Fisk 6'1" 189 lbs.

Year	Team		Games	Pos.
1971	CIN	N	12	DB
1972			14	S
1973			14	S
1974	BUF	N	14	S
1975	CLE	N	11	S
1976			14	S
6 yrs.		79 games		

Paco Craig
CRAIG, FRANCISCO LUIS
B. Feb. 2, 1965, Santa Maria, CA
UCLA 5'10" 170 lbs.

Year	Team		Games	Pos.
1988	DET	N	8	WR

Reggie Craig
CRAIG, REGGIE
B. Jun. 10, 1953, Baytown, TX
Arkansas 6'0" 188 lbs.

Year	Team		Games	Pos.
1975	KC	N	14	WR
1976			1	WR
1977	CLE	N	5	WR
1977	BUF	N	4	WR
3 yrs.		24 games		

Roger Craig
CRAIG, ROGER TIMOTHY
B. Jul. 10, 1960, Davenport, IA
Nebraska 6'0" 224 lbs.

Year	Team		Games	Pos.
1983	SF	N	16	RB
1984			16	FB
1985			16	FB
1986			16	RB
1987			14	FB
1988			16	RB
1989			16	RB
1990			11	RB
1991	LARI	N	15	RB
1992	MIN	N	15	RB
1993			14	RB
11 yrs.		165 games		

Steve Craig
CRAIG, STEVE A.
B. Mar. 13, 1951, Cleveland, OH
Northwestern 6'3" 231 lbs.

Year	Team		Games	Pos.
1974	MIN	N	14	TE
1975			14	TE
1976			14	TE
1977			14	TE
1978			16	TE
5 yrs.		72 games		

Milt Crain
CRAIN, MILTON
B. Dec. 25, 1920, San Antonio, TX
Baylor 6'2" 225 lbs.

Year	Team		Games	Pos.
1944	BOS	N	10	FB, QB

Joe Crakes
CRAKES, JOSEPH
B. Dec. 29, 1907
D. Mar., 1976, Victorville, CA
South Dakota 6'1" 205 lbs.

Year	Team		Games	Pos.
1932	CHIC	N	4	E
1933	CIN	N	8	E
2 yrs.		12 games		

Cramer
CRAMER
None

Year	Team		Games	Pos.
1926	COL	N	1	E

Carl Cramer
CRAMER, CARL (Curley)
B. Dec. 20, 1897
D. Feb., 1978, Canal Fulton, OH
Hamline 5'11" 184 lbs.

Year	Team		Games	Pos.
1920	CLE	A	6	FB, HB
1921	AKR	A	11	HB, FB
1922	AKR	N	10	HB, FB
1923			7	HB, FB
1924			8	HB, FB
1925			4	FB, HB, QB
1926			8	FB
7 yrs.		54 games		

Dennis Crane
CRANE, DENNIS WALTER
B. Feb. 23, 1945, San Bernardino, CA
Southern California 6'6" 260 lbs.

Year	Team		Games	Pos.
1968	WAS	N	14	DT

Dennis Crane *continued*

Year	Team		Games	Pos.
1969			10	DT
1970	NYG	N	9	OT
3 yrs.		33 games		

Paul Crane
CRANE, PAUL EDWARD
B. Jan. 29, 1944, Pascagoula, MS
Alabama 6'2" 208 lbs.

Year	Team		Games	Pos.
1966	NY	A	14	LB, C
1967			11	LB
1968			13	LB
1969			14	LB, C
1970	NYJ	N	14	LB, C
1971			14	LB, C
1972			8	LB, C
7 yrs.		88 games		

Jack Crangle
CRANGLE, WALTER F.
B. Jun. 8, 1899
Deceased
Illinois 6'1" 200 lbs.

Year	Team		Games	Pos.
1923	CHIC	N	9	FB, HB

Mike Crangle
CRANGLE, MICHAEL
B. Feb. 3, 1947, Chicago, IL
Tennessee-Martin 6'4" 243 lbs.

Year	Team		Games	Pos.
1972	NO		13	DE

Bill Crass
CRASS, WILLIAM
B. 1914
Louisiana State 6'0" 205 lbs.

Year	Team		Games	Pos.
1937	CHIC	N	3	B

Bill Craven
CRAVEN, WILLIAM MOTEN
B. Dec. 18, 1951, Ranson, WV
Harvard 5'11" 190 lbs.

Year	Team		Games	Pos.
1976	CLE	N	13	DB

Aaron Craver
CRAVER, AARON LERENZE
B. Dec. 18, 1968, Los Angeles, CA
Fresno State 5'11" 215 lbs.

Year	Team		Games	Pos.
1991	MIA	N	14	RB
1992			6	RB
1994			8	RB
1995	DEN	N	16	RB
1996			15	RB
5 yrs.		59 games		

Bill Crawford
CRAWFORD, WILLIAM
B. Jul. 17, 1937, Canada
British Columbia 6'1" 235 lbs.

Year	Team		Games	Pos.
1960	NYG	N	4	G

Charles Crawford
CRAWFORD, CHARLES
B. Mar. 8, 1964, Bristow, OK
Oklahoma State 6'2" 235 lbs.

Year	Team		Games	Pos.
1986	PHI	N	16	RB
1987			2	RB
2 yrs.		18 games		

Denver Crawford
CRAWFORD, DENVER J.
B. Jun. 16, 1921, Kingsport, TN
Tennessee 6'0" 210 lbs.

Year	Team		Games	Pos.
1948	NY	AA	8	T

Derrick Crawford
CRAWFORD, DERRICK LORENZO
B. Sep. 3, 1960, Memphis, TN
Memphis State 5'10" 185 lbs.

Year	Team		Games	Pos.
1986	SF	N	10	WR

Eddie Crawford
CRAWFORD, EDWARD S., III
B. Jul. 25, 1934
Mississippi 6'3" 185 lbs.

Year	Team		Games	Pos.
1957	NYG	N	12	E, DB

Elbert Crawford
CRAWFORD, ELBERT
B. Jun. 20, 1966, Chicago, IL
Arkansas 6'3" 280 lbs.

Year	Team		Games	Pos.
1990	NE	N	14	OT, G
1991	NE	N	16	G
2 yrs.		30 games		

Fred Crawford
CRAWFORD, FREDERICK EUGENE
B. Jul. 27, 1910, Waynesville, NC
D. Mar. 5, 1974, Tallahassee, FL
Duke 6'2" 200 lbs.

Year	Team		Games	Pos.
1935	CHIB	N	6	E, T

Hilton Crawford
CRAWFORD, HILTON
B. Feb. 2, 1945, Converse, LA
Grambling State 6'0" 198 lbs.

Year	Team		Games	Pos.
1969	BUF	A	7	S

Jim Crawford
CRAWFORD, JAMES
B. 1936, Greybull, WY
Wyoming 6'1" 203 lbs.

Year	Team		Games	Pos.
1960	BOS	A		FB
1961			10	FB
1962			14	HB
1963			14	HB
1964			2	FB
5 yrs.		40 games		

Keith Crawford
CRAWFORD, KEITH
B. Nov. 21, 1970, Palestine, TX
Howard Payne 6'2" 180 lbs.

Year	Team		Games	Pos.
1993	NYG	N	7	WR
1995	GB	N	13	CB
1996	STL	N	16	CB
3 yrs.		36 games		

Ken Crawford
CRAWFORD, KENNETH
B. Sep., 1898
D. Mar. 9, 1957
Miami (Ohio) 5'11" 193 lbs.

Year	Team		Games	Pos.
1920	AKR	A	5	HB, FB
1921	HAM	A	1	HB
1921	CIN	A	3	HB
1923	DAY	N	2	FB, HB
3 yrs.		11 games		

Mike Crawford
CRAWFORD, MICHAEL GERARD
B. Jan. 1, 1964, San Fernando, CA
Arizona State 5'10" 215 lbs.

Year	Team		Games	Pos.
1987	CLE	N	3	RB

Mush Crawford
CRAWFORD, WALTER C.
B. Dec. 23, 1898

Year	Team	Games	Pos.

Mike Crawford *continued*
D. Dec., 1966
Beloit/Lake Forest/Illinois 6'0" 202 lbs.

Year	Team	Games	Pos.
1925	HAM	N	1	C
1925	CHIB	N	3	G
1926	CHI	A	11	G, T, E
1927	NYY	N	8	T, G, HB

3 yrs. 23 games

Rufus Crawford
CRAWFORD, RUFUS
B. May 21, 1955, Gastonia, NC
Virginia State 5'10" 180 lbs.

| 1978 | SEA | N | 16 | RB |

Tim Crawford
CRAWFORD, TIM
B. Dec. 17, 1962, Houston, TX
Texas Tech 6'4" 245 lbs.

| 1987 | CLE | N | 3 | LB |

Dick Crayne
CRAYNE, RICHARD (Baldy)
B. Apr. 24, 1913, West Chester, IA
D. Aug., 1985, Le Mars, IA
Iowa 6'0" 205 lbs.

| 1936 | BKN | N | 12 | FB |
| 1937 | | | 10 | FB |

2 yrs. 22 games

Bob Creech
CREECH, ROBERT
B. Jan. 26, 1949, Corpus Christi, TX
Texas Christian 6'3" 226 lbs.

1971	PHI	N	3	LB
1972			13	LB
1973	NO	N	2	LB

3 yrs. 18 games

Lou Creekmur
CREEKMUR, LOUIS
B. Jan. 22, 1927, Hopelawn, NJ
William & Mary 6'4" 246 lbs.

1950	DET	N	12	G
1951			12	G
1952			12	G, T
1953			12	T
1954			12	T
1955			12	T
1956			12	T
1957			12	T
1958			12	T
1959			8	T

10 yrs. 116 games

Bill Cregar
CREGAR, WILLIAM
B. 1925
Holy Cross 5'11" 195 lbs.

| 1947 | PIT | N | 11 | G, LB |
| 1948 | | | 12 | G, LB |

2 yrs. 23 games

Milan Creighton
CREIGHTON, MILAN S.
B. Jan. 21, 1908, Gothenburg, NE
Arkansas 6'0" 190 lbs.

1931	CHIC	N	8	E, HB
1932			8	E, T
1933			11	E, HB
1934			9	E
1935			8	E
1936			5	E
1937			2	E

7 yrs. 51 games

Ted Cremer
CREMER, THEODORE ROOSEVELT
B. Mar. 16, 1919, Corbin, KY
D. Nov., 1980
Auburn 6'2" 209 lbs.

1946	DET	N	11	E
1947			12	E
1948	GB	N	3	E

3 yrs. 26 games

Carl Crennel
CRENNEL, CARL
B. Sep. 14, 1948, Lynchburg, VA
West Virginia 6'1" 230 lbs.

| 1970 | PIT | N | 3 | LB |

Leon Crenshaw
CRENSHAW, LEON
B. Jul. 14, 1943, Greenville, AL
Tuskegee Institute 6'6" 280 lbs.

| 1968 | GB | N | 10 | DT |

Willis Crenshaw
CRENSHAW, WILLIS CLARENCE
B. Jul. 16, 1941, St. Louis, MO
Kansas State 6'2" 228 lbs.

1964	STL	N	14	FB
1965			14	FB
1966			14	FB
1967			14	RB
1968			14	RB
1969			14	RB
1970	DEN	N	12	RB

7 yrs. 96 games

Bobby Crespino
CRESPINO, ROBERT
B. Jan. 11, 1938, Duncan, MS
Mississippi 6'4" 223 lbs.

1961	CLE	N	13	OE
1962			14	OE
1963			14	OE
1964	NYG	N	13	FL
1965			14	OE
1966			14	TE
1967			14	TE
1968			11	WR

8 yrs. 107 games

Smiley Creswell
CRESWELL, SMILEY LAWRENCE, III
B. Dec. 11, 1959, Monroe, WA
Michigan State 6'4" 250 lbs.

| 1985 | PHI | N | 3 | DE |

Ron Crews
CREWS, RON
B. Oct. 9, 1956, Springfield, IL
Notre Dame/Nevada-Las Vegas 6'3" 256 lbs.

| 1980 | CLE | N | 16 | DE |

Terry Crews
CREWS, TERRY
B. Jul. 30, 1968, Flint, MI
Western Michigan 6'2" 244 lbs.

1991	LARM	N	6	LB
1993	SD	N	10	LB
1995	WAS	N	16	DE

3 yrs. 32 games

James Cribbs
CRIBBS, JAMES
B. Jul. 10, 1966, Memphis, TN

James Cribbs *continued*
Memphis State 6'3" 269 lbs.

| 1989 | DET | N | 8 | DE |

Joe Cribbs
CRIBBS, JOE STANIER
B. Jan. 5, 1958, Sulligent, AL
Auburn 5'11" 192 lbs.

1980	BUF	N	16	RB
1981			15	RB
1982			7	RB
1983			16	RB
1985			10	RB
1986	SF	N	14	RB
1987			11	RB
1988	IND	N	1	RB
1988	MIA	N	12	RB

8 yrs. 102 games

Bernie Crimmins
CRIMMINS, BERNARD ANTHONY
B. Apr. 19, 1919, Louisville, KY
D. Mar. 19, 1993, West Lafayette, IN
Notre Dame 5'11" 195 lbs.

| 1945 | GB | N | 6 | G |

Hal Crisler
CRISLER, HAROLD JAMES
B. Dec. 31, 1923, Richmond, CA
Deceased
San Jose State/Iowa State 6'4" 213 lbs.

1946	BOS	N	11	E
1947			10	E
1948	WAS	N	11	E
1949			11	E
1950	BAL	N	10	E

5 yrs. 53 games

Joel Crisman
CRISMAN, JOEL
B. Feb. 3, 1971, Cherokee, IA
Southern California 6'5" 302 lbs.

| 1996 | TB | N | 9 | G |

Cris Crissy
CRISSY, WILLIAM ROBERT
B. Feb. 3, 1959, Penn Yan, NY
Princeton 5'11" 195 lbs.

| 1981 | WAS | N | 1 | DB |

Chuck Crist
CRIST, CHARLES THOMAS
B. Jan. 16, 1951, Salamanca, NY
Penn State 6'2" 205 lbs.*

1972	NYG	N	14	S
1973			14	S
1974			13	S
1975	NO	N	8	S
1976			14	S
1977			14	S
1978	SF	N	15	S

7 yrs. 92 games

Jeff Criswell
CRISWELL, JEFFREY L.
B. Mar. 7, 1964, Grinnell, IA
Graceland 6'7" 265 lbs.

1987	IND	N	3	G
1988	NYJ	N	15	OL
1989			16	OT, G
1990			16	OT
1991			16	OT
1992			14	OT
1993			16	OT
1994			15	OT
1995	KC	N	15	OT

Jeff Criswell *continued*

| 1996 | | | 15 | OT |

10 yrs. 141 games

Kirby Criswell
CRISWELL, KIRBY LYNN
B. Aug. 31, 1957, Grinnell, IA
Kansas 6'5" 238 lbs.

| 1980 | STL | N | 4 | LB |
| 1981 | | | 2 | DE |

2 yrs. 6 games

Ray Criswell
CRISWELL, RAYMOND
B. Aug. 16, 1963, Lake City, FL
Florida 6'0" 189 lbs.

| 1987 | TB | N | 3 | P |
| 1988 | TB | N | 16 | P |

2 yrs. 19 games

Hank Critchfield
CRITCHFIELD, HENRY B. (Biff)
B. Jun. 14, 1905
D. Jul., 1980, Wooster, OH
Wooster 5'10" 207 lbs.

| 1931 | CLE | N | 9 | C |

Larry Critchfield
CRITCHFIELD, LAWRENCE K.
B. Jan. 6, 1908, Pennsylvania
D. Jun., 1965
Grove City 5'11" 195 lbs.

| 1933 | PIT | N | 11 | G |

Ken Criter
CRITER, KENNETH WILLIAM
B. Feb. 17, 1947, Fond du Lac, WI
Wisconsin 5'11" 223 lbs.

1969	DEN	A	14	LB
1970	DEN	N	14	LB
1971			11	LB
1972			8	LB
1973			14	LB
1974			14	LB

6 yrs. 75 games

Ray Crittenden
CRITTENDEN, RAY
B. Mar. 1, 1970, Washington, DC
Virginia Tech 6'0" 188 lbs.

| 1993 | NE | N | 16 | WR |
| 1994 | | | 16 | WR |

2 yrs. 32 games

Jack Crittendon
CRITTENDON, JOHN
B. 1930, Ferndale, MI
D. Feb. 2, 1993, Toronto, Ont.
Wayne State 6'1" 190 lbs.

| 1954 | CHIC | N | 10 | E |

Jim Crocicchia
CROCICCHIA, JAMES F.
B. Feb. 19, 1964 Waterbury, CT
Pennsylvania 6'2" 209 lbs.

| 1987 | NYG | N | 1 | QB |

Bobby Crockett
CROCKETT, ROBERT PAUL
B. Apr. 3, 1943, Briggsville, AR
Arkansas 6'0" 198 lbs.

1966	BUF	A	14	OE
1968			9	OE
1969			5	WR

3 yrs. 28 games

Year	Team	Games	Pos.

Monte Crockett
CROCKETT, MONTE
B. Jul. 14, 1938, Talcott, WV
New Mexico Highlands 6'3" 213 lbs.

Year	Team	Games	Pos.
1960	**BUF** **A**		OE
1961		14	OE
1962		12	OE
3 yrs.	26 games		

Ray Crockett
CROCKETT, DONALD RAY
B. Jan. 5, 1967, Dallas, TX
Baylor 5'9" 181 lbs.

Year	Team	Games	Pos.
1989	**DET** **N**	16	CB, S
1990		16	CB
1991		16	CB
1992		15	CB
1993		16	CB
1994	**DEN** **N**	14	CB
1995		16	CB
1996		15	CB
8 yrs.	124 games		

Willis Crockett
CROCKETT, WILLIS ROBERT
B. Aug. 25, 1966, Douglas, GA
Georgia Tech 6'3" 234 lbs.

Year	Team	Games	Pos.
1990	**DAL** **N**	13	LB

Zack Crockett
CROCKETT, ZACK
B. Dec. 2, 1972, Pompano Beach, CA
Florida State 6'2" 241 lbs.

Year	Team	Games	Pos.
1995	**IND** **N**	16	RB
1996		5	RB
2 yrs.	21 games		

Mike Croel
CROEL, MIKE
B. Jun. 6, 1969, Detroit, MI
Nebraska 6'3" 231 lbs.

Year	Team	Games	Pos.
1991	**DEN** **N**	13	LB
1992		16	LB
1993		16	LB
1994		13	LB
1995	**NYG** **N**	16	LB
1996	**BAL** **N**	16	LB
6 yrs.	90 games		

Abe Croft
CROFT, ABRAHAM
B. Mar. 12, 1922, Houston, TX
Southern Methodist 6'0" 183 lbs.

Year	Team	Games	Pos.
1944	**CHIB** **N**	10	E
1945		1	
2 yrs.	11 games		

Don Croft
CROFT, DONALD THOMAS
B. Jan. 7, 1949, Temple, TX
Texas-El Paso 6'3" 256 lbs.

Year	Team	Games	Pos.
1972	**BUF** **N**	14	DT
1974		6	DT
1975		13	DT
1976	**DET** **N**	1	DT
4 yrs.	34 games		

Harrison Croft
CROFT, HARRISON
B. Aug. 16, 1899
Deceased
Wisconsin-Platteville 6'1" 190 lbs.

Year	Team	Games	Pos.
1924	**RAC** **N**	1	G

Tiny Croft
CROFT, MILBURN R.

Tiny Croft *continued*
B. Nov. 7, 1920, Chicago, IL
D. Jan., 1977
Ripon 6'3" 287 lbs.

Year	Team	Games	Pos.
1942	**GB** **N**	7	T
1943		4	T
1944		10	T
1945		9	T
1946		11	T
1947		10	T
6 yrs.	51 games		

Win Croft
CROFT, WINFIELD SCOTT
B. Feb. 28, 1910, Cowley, WY
D. Jul. 8, 1993
Utah 5'11" 235 lbs.

Year	Team	Games	Pos.
1935	**BKN** **N**	11	G
1936	**PIT** **N**	9	G
2 yrs.	20 games		

Don Croftcheck
CROFTCHECK, DONALD
B. Sep. 12, 1942, Allison, PA
Indiana 6'1" 230 lbs.

Year	Team	Games	Pos.
1965	**WAS** **N**	14	LB
1966		12	LB, G
1967	**CHI** **N**	9	G
3 yrs.	35 games		

Nolan Cromwell
CROMWELL, NOLAN NEIL
B. Jan. 30, 1955, Smith Center, KS
Kansas 6'1" 199 lbs.

Year	Team	Games	Pos.
1977	**LA** **N**	14	S
1978		16	S
1979		16	S
1980		16	S
1981		16	S
1982	**LARM** **N**	9	S
1983		16	S
1984		11	S
1985		16	S
1986		16	S
1987		15	S
11 yrs.	161 games		

Pete Cronan
CRONAN, PETER JOSEPH
B. Jan. 13, 1955, Bourne, MA
Boston College 6'2" 238 lbs.

Year	Team	Games	Pos.
1977	**SEA** **N**	14	LB
1978		15	LB
1979		16	LB
1980		5	LB
1981	**WAS** **N**	10	LB
1982		7	LB
1983		16	LB
1984		3	LB
1985		4	LB
8 yrs.	90 games		

Bill Cronin
CRONIN, WILLIAM
B. Apr. 18, 1901
D. Apr., 1948
Boston College 5'10" 182 lbs.

Year	Team	Games	Pos.
1926	**BOS** **A**	5	HB
1927	**PRO** **N**	10	HB, FB, QB
1928		9	FB, HB, QB, E, T
1929		9	E, FB, HB
4 yrs.	33 games		

Bill Cronin
CRONIN, WILLIAM F., JR.
B. Nov. 20, 1943

Bill Cronin *continued*
Boston College 6'4" 225 lbs.

Year	Team	Games	Pos.
1965	**PHI** **N**	2	TE
1966	**MIA** **A**	14	TE
2 yrs.	16 games		

Gene Cronin
CRONIN, EUGENE EDWARD
B. Nov. 20, 1933, Spalding, NE
Pacific 6'2" 229 lbs.

Year	Team	Games	Pos.
1956	**DET** **N**	12	G
1957		12	G
1958		12	E
1959		12	E
1960	**DAL** **N**	11	DE
1961	**WAS** **N**	14	DE
1962		14	LB, DE
7 yrs.	87 games		

Jack Cronin
CRONIN, JOHN
B. Aug. 29, 1903
D. Dec., 1965
Boston College 5'11" 178 lbs.

Year	Team	Games	Pos.
1927	**PRO** **N**	13	HB, QB, FB
1928		7	HB, E
1929		12	HB, QB, FB, E
1930		10	HB, QB, FB
4 yrs.	42 games		

Lawrence Cronin
CRONIN, LAWRENCE (Fritz)
St. Mary's (Minnesota) 5'11" 182 lbs.

Year	Team	Games	Pos.
1927	**DUL** **N**	8	E, G

Jerry Cronin
CRONIN, GERALD
B. 1910
Rutgers 6'0" 198 lbs.

Year	Team	Games	Pos.
1932	**BKN** **N**	3	E

Paddy Cronin
CRONIN, TOMMY
Loras/Marquette 5'9" 170 lbs.

Year	Team	Games	Pos.
1922	**GB** **N**	5	HB

Doc Cronkhite
CRONKHITE, HENRY O.
B. 1911
D. Dec. 26, 1949
Kansas State 6'5" 210 lbs.

Year	Team	Games	Pos.
1934	**BKN** **N**	6	E

Al Crook
CROOK, ALFRED J.
B. Nov. 20, 1897
D. Dec. 17, 1958
Washington & Jefferson 5'10" 190 lbs.

Year	Team	Games	Pos.
1925	**DET** **N**	8	C, G, T
1926		8	G
2 yrs.	16 games		

Corey Croom
CROOM, COREY VINCENT
B. May 22, 1971, Sandusky, OH
Ball State 5'11" 212 lbs.

Year	Team	Games	Pos.
1993	**NE** **N**	14	RB
1994		16	RB
1995		13	RB
3 yrs.	43 games		

Sylvester Croom
CROOM, SYLVESTER
B. Sep. 25, 1954, Tuscaloosa, AL

Sylvester Croom *continued*
Alabama 6'0" 235 lbs.

Year	Team	Games	Pos.
1975	**NO** **N**	1	C

Chris Crooms
CROOMS, CHRIS DALE
B. Feb. 4, 1969, Houston, TX
Texas A&M 6'2" 211 lbs.

Year	Team	Games	Pos.
1992	**LARM** **N**	16	S

Marshall Cropper
CROPPER, MARSHALL JOSEPH
B. Apr. 1, 1944, Wattsville, VA
Maryland-Eastern Shore 6'3" 207 lbs.

Year	Team	Games	Pos.
1967	**PIT** **N**	7	OE
1968		5	OE
1969		4	WR
3 yrs.	16 games		

Cleveland Crosby
CROSBY, CLEVELAND PITTSBURGH
B. Apr. 3, 1956, West Point, MS
Purdue/Arizona 6'4" 252 lbs.

Year	Team	Games	Pos.
1982	**BAL** **N**	9	DE

Ron Crosby
CROSBY, RON
B. Mar. 2, 1955, McKeesport, PA
Penn State 6'2" 223 lbs.

Year	Team	Games	Pos.
1978	**NO** **N**	14	LB
1979	**NYJ** **N**	12	LB
1980		16	LB
1981		16	LB
1982		9	LB
1983		16	LB
6 yrs.	83 games		

Steve Crosby
CROSBY, STEVEN K.
B. Jul. 3, 1950, Great Bend, KS
Fort Hays State 5'11" 205 lbs.

Year	Team	Games	Pos.
1974	**NYG** **N**	9	RB
1975		4	RB
1976		2	RB
3 yrs.	15 games		

Billy Cross
CROSS, BILL J.
B. May 3, 1929, Canadian, TX
West Texas State 5'6" 151 lbs.

Year	Team	Games	Pos.
1951	**CHIC** **N**	12	B
1952		12	B
1953		12	B
3 yrs.	36 games		

Bobby Cross
CROSS, ROBERT
B. Jul. 4, 1931, Ranger, TX
Deceased
Stephen F. Austin 6'4" 248 lbs.

Year	Team	Games	Pos.
1952	**CHIB** **N**	12	T
1954	**LA** **N**	12	T
1955		12	T
1956	**SF** **N**	12	T
1957		12	T
1958	**CHIC** **N**	12	T
1959		11	T
1960	**BOS** **A**		OT
8 yrs.	83 games		

Howard Cross
CROSS, HOWARD
B. Aug. 8, 1967, Huntsville, AL
Alabama 6'5" 245 lbs.

Year	Team	Games	Pos.
1989	**NYG** **N**	16	TE

Year	Team	Games	Pos.

Howard Cross *continued*

Year	Team		Games	Pos.
1990			16	TE
1991			16	TE
1992			16	TE
1993			16	TE
1994			16	TE
1995			15	TE
1996			16	TE

8 yrs.   127 games

Irv Cross
CROSS, IRVIN ACIE
B. Jul. 27, 1939, Hammond, IN
Northwestern 6'1" 192 lbs.

1961	PHI	N	13	DB
1962			14	DB
1963			14	DB
1964			14	DB
1965			14	DB
1966	LA	N	14	DB
1967			14	DB
1968			14	DB
1969	PHI	N		DB

9 yrs.   111 games

Jeff Cross
CROSS, JEFFREY ALLEN
B. Mar. 25, 1966, Riverside, CA
Missouri 6'4" 270 lbs.

1988	MIA	N	16	DE
1989			16	DE
1990			16	DE
1991			16	DE
1992			16	DE
1993			16	DE
1994			13	DE
1995			16	DE

8 yrs.   125 games

Justin Cross
CROSS, JUSTIN ALLEN
B. Apr. 29, 1959, Montreal, Que.
Western State (Colorado) 6'6" 265 lbs.

1982	BUF	N	9	OT
1983			15	OT
1984			7	OT
1985			3	OT
1986			10	OT

5 yrs.   44 games

Randy Cross
CROSS, RANDALL LAUREAT
B. Apr. 25, 1954, Brooklyn, NY
UCLA 6'3" 262 lbs.

1976	SF	N	14	C, G
1977			14	C
1978			9	C
1979			16	C
1980			16	G
1981			16	G
1982			8	G
1983			16	G
1984			16	G
1985			15	G
1986			16	G
1987			12	G
1988			16	C

13 yrs.   184 games

Dave Crossan
CROSSAN, DAVID
B. Jun. 8, 1940, Philadelphia, PA
Maryland 6'3" 245 lbs.

1965	WAS	N	14	C
1966			14	C
1967			10	C
1968			14	C

4 yrs.   52 games

Leon Crosswhite
CROSSWHITE, LEON MAC
B. Apr. 28, 1951, Hennessey, OK
Oklahoma 6'2" 215 lbs.

1973	DET	N	7	RB
1974			14	RB

2 yrs.   21 games

Dave Croston
CROSTON, DAVID CHARLES
B. Nov. 10, 1963, Sioux City, IA
Iowa 6'5" 280 lbs.

1988	GB	N	16	OT

Jim Crotty
CROTTY, JAMES R.
B. Mar. 3, 1938, Storm Lake, IA
Notre Dame 5'11" 192 lbs.

1960	WAS	N	9	DB
1961	BUF	A	5	DB
1962			3	DB

3 yrs.   17 games

Billy Crouch
CROUCH, WILLIAM BUTLER
B. Nov. 4, 1898, Cartersville, GA
D. Feb. 23, 1934, Washington, DC
Davidson 6'0" 187 lbs.

1921	WAS	A	4	C

Terry Crouch
CROUCH, TERRY WAYNE
B. Jul. 6, 1959, Dallas, TX
Oklahoma 6'2" 278 lbs.

1982	BAL	N	9	G

David Croudip
CROUDIP, DAVID RODNEY
B. Jan. 25, 1959, Indianapolis, IN
D. Oct. 10, 1988
San Diego State 5'8" 185 lbs.

1984	LARM	N	16	CB, S
1985	SD	N	2	CB, S
1985	ATL	N	11	DB
1986			15	CB, S
1987			12	CB
1988			6	CB

5 yrs.   62 games

Ray Crouse
CROUSE, MARLON RAY
B. Mar. 16, 1959, Oakland, CA
Nevada-Las Vegas 5'11" 214 lbs.

1984	GB	N	16	RB

Jake Crouthamel
CROUTHAMEL, JAKE
B. 1938
Dartmouth 5'11" 195 lbs.

1960	BOS	A		HB

Al Crow
CROW, ALBERT
B. 1933
William & Mary 6'6" 260 lbs.

1960	BOS	A		DT

John David Crow
CROW, JOHN DAVID
B. Jul. 8, 1935, Springhill, LA
Texas A&M 6'2" 218 lbs.

1958	CHIC	N	6	HB
1959			12	HB
1960	STL	N	12	HB
1961			8	HB

John David Crow *continued*

1962			14	HB
1963			3	HB
1964			13	HB
1965	SF	N	14	HB, FB
1966			14	HB
1967			14	RB
1968			14	RB, TE

11 yrs.   124 games

Lindon Crow
CROW, LINDON
B. Apr. 4, 1933, Denison, TX
Southern California 6'1" 195 lbs.

1955	CHIC	N	12	DB
1956			12	DB
1957			12	DB
1958	NYG	N	12	DB
1959			12	DB
1960			12	DB
1961	LA	N	14	DB
1962			14	DB
1963			14	DB
1964			9	DB

10 yrs.   123 games

Orien Crow
CROW, JOHN ORIEN
B. Sep. 7, 1912, Salem, MO
Haskell 6'0" 220 lbs.

1933	BOS	N	11	C
1934			10	C

2 yrs.   21 games

Wayne Crow
CROW, WAYNE
B. May 5, 1938, Coolidge, AZ
California 6'0" 205 lbs.

1960	OAK	A		DB
1961			14	HB
1962	BUF	A	14	HB
1963			5	HB

4 yrs.   33 games

Earl Crowder
CROWDER, EARL F.
B. Jan. 21, 1915
D. Feb. 6, 1984, Cherokee, OK
Oklahoma 6'0" 198 lbs.

1939	CHIC	N	6	QB, HB
1940	CLE	N	3	QB

2 yrs.   9 games

Randy Crowder
CROWDER, RANDOLPH CHANNING (Sugar Bear)
B. Jul. 30, 1952, Farrell, PA
Penn State 6'2" 242 lbs.

1974	MIA	N	12	DT
1975			13	DT
1976			14	DT
1978	TB	N	14	DT, DE
1979			16	DT, DE
1980			2	DT

6 yrs.   71 games

Larry Crowe
CROWE, LARRY DARNELL
B. Oct. 23, 1950, Diana, TX
Texas Southern 6'1" 198 lbs.

1972	PHI	N	1	RB
1975	ATL	N	5	RB

2 yrs.   6 games

Paul Crowe
CROWE, PAUL JAMES
B. Oct. 23, 1923, Chino, CA

Paul Crowe *continued*

Deceased
St. Mary's (California) 6'1" 195 lbs.

1948	SF	AA	14	B
1949			2	B
1949	LA	AA	7	B
1951	NYY	N	9	B

3 yrs.   32 games

Odis Crowell
CROWELL, ODIS LEONARD
B. 1924
Hardin-Simmons 6'2" 220 lbs.

1947	SF	AA	2	T

Dick Crowl
CROWL, RICHARD
B. 1908
Rutgers 5'10" 185 lbs.

1930	BKN	N	2	G, C

Jim Crowley
CROWLEY, JAMES HAROLD (Sleepy Jim)
B. Sep. 10, 1902, Chicago, IL
D. Jan. 15, 1986, Scranton, PA
Notre Dame 5'9" 165 lbs.

1925	GB	N	2	QB, HB
1925	PRO		1	HB

1 yr.   3 games

Joe Crowley
CROWLEY, JOSEPH A.
B. Apr. 6, 1919, Brighton, MA
Dartmouth 6'0" 194 lbs.

1944	BOS	N	10	E
1945			9	E

2 yrs.   19 games

Rae Crowther
CROWTHER, RAE
B. Dec. 11, 1902
D. Nov. 3, 1980, Haddonfield, NJ
Penn State/Colgate 5'11" 175 lbs.

1925	FRA	N	19	E
1926			14	E

2 yrs.   33 games

Saville Crowther
CROWTHER, SAVILLE E.
B. Jul. 10, 1901
D. Jul., 1962
Penn State/Colgate 6'1" 220 lbs.

1925	FRA	N	2	T, G
1926	PHI	A	6	G

2 yrs.   8 games

Phil Croyle
CROYLE, PHIL
B. Oct. 30, 1947, San Lorenzo, CA
California 6'3" 220 lbs.

1971	HOU	N	14	LB
1972			12	LB
1973			1	LB
1973	BUF	N	4	LB

3 yrs.   31 games

Derrick Crudup
CRUDUP, DERRICK
B. Feb. 15, 1965, Delray Beach, FL
Florida/Oklahoma 6'2" 225 lbs.

1989	LARI	N	4	S
1991			16	S

2 yrs.   20 games

Bob Crum
CRUM, ROBERT H.
B. Jun. 28, 1951, Phoenix, AZ
Arizona 6'5" 240 lbs.

Year	Team		Games	Pos.
1974	STL	N	14	DE

Dwayne Crump
CRUMP, DWAYNE ANTHONY
B. Aug. 9, 1950, Madera, CA
Fresno State 5'11" 180 lbs.

Year	Team		Games	Pos.
1973	STL	N	14	CB
1974			14	CB
1975			14	CB, S
1976			13	CB
4 yrs.			55 games	

George Crump
CRUMP, GEORGE STANLEY
B. Jul. 22, 1959, Portsmouth, VA
East Carolina 6'4" 260 lbs.

Year	Team		Games	Pos.
1982	NE	N	9	DE

Harry Crump
CRUMP, HARRY
B. 1941
Boston College 6'0" 205 lbs.

Year	Team		Games	Pos.
1963	BOS	A	14	FB

Carlester Crumpler
CRUMPLER, CARLESTER
B. Sep. 5, 1971, Greenville, NC
East Carolina 6'6" 255 lbs.

Year	Team		Games	Pos.
1994	SEA	N	9	TE
1995			16	TE
1996			16	TE
3 yrs.			41 games	

Doug Crusan
CRUSAN, DOUGLAS GORDON, JR.
B. Jul. 26, 1946, Monessen, PA
Indiana 6'5" 253 lbs.

Year	Team		Games	Pos.
1968	MIA	A	14	OT
1969			14	OT
1970	MIA	N	14	OT
1971			14	OT
1972			11	OT
1973			14	OT
1974			1	OT
7 yrs.			82 games	

Tommy Crutcher
CRUTCHER, THOMAS JOE
B. Aug. 10, 1941, McKinney, TX
Texas Christian 6'3" 229 lbs.

Year	Team		Games	Pos.
1964	GB	N	14	LB, FB
1965			14	LB
1966			14	LB
1967			14	LB
1968	NYG	N	14	LB
1969			14	LB
1971	GB	N	14	LB
1972			12	LB
8 yrs.			110 games	

Dwayne Crutchfield
CRUTCHFIELD, DWAYNE
B. Sep. 30, 1959, Cincinnati, OH
Iowa State 6'0" 240 lbs.

Year	Team		Games	Pos.
1982	NYJ	N	6	RB
1983			11	RB
1983	HOU	N	2	RB
1984	LARM	N	15	RB
3 yrs.			34 games	

Bob Cryder
CRYDER, ROBERT JOSEPH
B. Sep. 7, 1956, O'Fallon, IL
Alabama 6'4" 275 lbs.

Year	Team		Games	Pos.
1978	NE	N	5	G
1979			16	G
1980			16	G
1981			15	G
1982			9	G
1983			14	G
1984	SEA	N	16	OT
1985			16	OT
1986			1	OT
9 yrs.			108 games	

Larry Csonka
CSONKA, LAWRENCE RICHARD
B. Dec. 15, 1946, Stow, OH
Syracuse 6'3" 238 lbs.

Year	Team		Games	Pos.
1968	MIA	A	11	FB
1969			11	FB
1970	MIA	N	14	FB
1971			14	FB
1972			14	FB
1973			14	FB
1974			12	FB
1976	NYG	N	12	FB
1977			14	FB
1978			16	FB
1979	MIA	N	16	FB
11 yrs.			148 games	

Paul Cuba
CUBA, PAUL J.
B. Jun. 12, 1908, New Castle, PA
D. Aug. 12, 1990, New Castle, PA
Pittsburgh 6'0" 212 lbs.

Year	Team		Games	Pos.
1933	PHI	N	8	T
1934			9	T
1935			10	T
3 yrs.			27 games	

Walt Cudzik
CUDZIK, WALTER J.
B. Feb. 21, 1932, Chicago, IL
Purdue 6'2" 231 lbs.

Year	Team		Games	Pos.
1954	WAS	N	1	C
1960	BOS	A		C
1961			14	C
1962			14	C
1963			14	C
1964	BUF	A	14	C
6 yrs.			57 games	

Ward Cuff
CUFF, WARD L.
B. Aug. 13, 1913, Redwood Falls, MN
Marquette 6'1" 192 lbs.

Year	Team		Games	Pos.
1937	NYG	N	11	HB, FB
1938			11	HB
1939			9	HB, FB
1940			8	HB
1941			11	HB, K
1942			11	HB, K
1943			10	HB, K
1944			10	HB
1945			9	HB
1946	CHIC	N	10	HB, K
1947	GB	N	10	HB, K
11 yrs.			110 games	

Jim Culbreath
CULBREATH, JAMES C., JR.
B. Oct. 21, 1952, Yeadon, PA
Oklahoma 6'0" 210 lbs.

Year	Team		Games	Pos.
1977	GB	N	13	RB
1978			12	RB
1979			4	RB

Jim Culbreath continued

Year	Team		Games	Pos.
1980	PHI	N	2	RB
1980	NYG	N	10	RB
4 yrs.			41 games	

Willie Cullars
CULLARS, WILLIE EDWARD
B. Aug. 4, 1951, Washington, GA
Kansas State 6'5" 250 lbs.

Year	Team		Games	Pos.
1974	PHI	N	13	DE

Dave Cullen
CULLEN, DAVID (Jack)
B. Mar. 18, 1905
D. May 15, 1982, Butler, PA
Geneva 5'10" 225 lbs.

Year	Team		Games	Pos.
1931	CLE	N	2	G, T

Ron Cullen
CULLEN, RONALD J. (Fat)
B. 1897
Deceased
Oklahoma 5'9" 180 lbs.

Year	Team		Games	Pos.
1922	MIL	N	1	E

Dave Cullity
CULLITY, DAVID RICHARD
B. Jun. 15, 1964, La Mirada, CA
Utah 6'7" 275 lbs.

Year	Team		Games	Pos.
1989	SF	N	2	OT

Jim Cullom
CULLOM, JIM
B. 1926
California 5'11" 235 lbs.

Year	Team		Games	Pos.
1951	NYY	N	3	G

Curley Culp
CULP, CURLEY
B. Oct. 10, 1946, Yuma, AZ
Arizona State 6'1" 265 lbs.

Year	Team		Games	Pos.
1968	KC	A	9	G
1969			14	G
1970	KC	N	14	DT
1971			14	DT
1972			14	DT
1973			13	DT
1974			4	DT
1974	HOU	N	8	G
1975			14	G, DT
1976			14	DT
1977			14	NT
1978			16	NT
1979			16	NT
1980			10	NT
1980	DET	N	3	DT
1981			2	DT
14 yrs.			179 games	

Brad Culpepper
CULPEPPER, JOHN BROWARD
B. May 8, 1968, Tallahassee, FL
Florida 6'1" 264 lbs.

Year	Team		Games	Pos.
1992	MIN	N	11	DT
1993			15	DT
1994	TB	N	16	DT
1995			16	DT
1996			13	DT
5 yrs.			71 games	

Ed Culpepper
CULPEPPER, EDWARD
B. Jan. 21, 1934, Bradenton, FL
Alabama 6'1" 255 lbs.

Year	Team		Games	Pos.
1958	CHIC	N	11	DT

Ed Culpepper continued

Year	Team		Games	Pos.
1959			11	DT
1960	STL	N	10	DT
1961	MIN	N	14	DT
1962	HOU	A	14	DT
1963			14	DT
6 yrs.			74 games	

Willie Culpepper
CULPEPPER, WILLIE JAMES
B. Mar. 27, 1967, Jacksonville, FL
Southwestern Louisiana 5'11" 155 lbs.

Year	Team		Games	Pos.
1992	TB	N	3	WR

Al Culver
CULVER, ALVIN S.
B. Jun. 11, 1908, Wilmette, IL
D. Feb., 1982, Plymouth, IN
St. Thomas/Notre Dame 6'2" 212 lbs.

Year	Team		Games	Pos.
1932	CHIB	N	2	T
1932	GB	N	1	T
1 yr.			3 games	

Frank Culver
CULVER, FRANK Z.
B. Apr. 24, 1897
D. Jan. 13, 1969, Hastings-on-Hudson, NY
Syracuse 5'11" 175 lbs.

Year	Team		Games	Pos.
1923	BUF	N	12	C
1924			8	C
1924	ROC	N	1	E
1925	CAN	N	8	C, E
3 yrs.			29 games	

Rodney Culver
CULVER, RODNEY DWAYNE
B. Dec. 23, 1969, Detroit, MI
D. May 11, 1996, Dade County, FL
Notre Dame 5'9" 224 lbs.

Year	Team		Games	Pos.
1992	IND	N	16	RB
1993			16	RB
1994	SD	N	3	RB
1995			8	RB
4 yrs.			43 games	

George Cumby
CUMBY, GEORGE EDWARD
B. Jul. 5, 1956, Gorman, TX
Oklahoma 6'0" 224 lbs.

Year	Team		Games	Pos.
1980	GB	N	9	LB
1981			16	LB
1982			9	LB
1983			15	LB
1984			16	LB
1985			16	LB
1986	BUF	N	11	LB
1987	PHI	N	1	LB
8 yrs.			93 games	

Frank Cumiskey
CUMISKEY, FRANK STEVEN (Red)
B. Jul. 24, 1911, Youngstown, OH
D. Jul. 16, 1982, Sun City, AZ
Ohio State 6'2" 205 lbs.

Year	Team		Games	Pos.
1937	BKN	N	9	E

Ed Cummings
CUMMINGS, EDWARD A.
B. 1941, Anaconda, MT
Stanford 6'2" 230 lbs.

Year	Team		Games	Pos.
1964	NY	N	11	LB
1965	DEN	A	14	LB
2 yrs.			25 games	

Year	Team	Games	Pos.

Joe Cummings
CUMMINGS, JOE
B. Jun. 8, 1972, Stevensville, MT
Wyoming 6'2" 242 lbs.

Year	Team	Games	Pos.
1996	SD	N	3	LB

Mack Cummings
CUMMINGS, MACK
B. Mar. 3, 1959, Gainesville, FL
East Tennessee State 6'0" 195 lbs.

| 1987 | NYG | N | 1 | WR |

Ernie Cuneo
CUNEO, ERNEST
B. May 27, 1905
D. Mar. 1, 1988, Arlington, VA
Columbia 5'9" 192 lbs.

1929	ORA	N	11	G, C
1930	BKN	N	6	G, T
2 yrs.	17 games

Cunningham
CUNNINGHAM
None

| 1926 | RI | A | 1 | HB |

Bennie Cunningham
CUNNINGHAM, BENNIE LEE, JR.
B. Dec. 23, 1954, Laurens, SC
Clemson 6'4" 260 lbs.

1976	PIT	N	12	TE
1977			12	TE
1978			6	TE
1979			15	TE
1980			15	TE
1981			15	TE
1982			9	TE
1983			16	TE
1984			7	TE
1985			11	TE
10 yrs.	118 games

Carl Cunningham
CUNNINGHAM, CARL MADISON
B. Jul. 23, 1944, Houston, TX
Houston 6'3" 240 lbs.

1967	DEN	A	13	LB
1968			14	LB
1969			14	LB
1970	DEN	N	14	LB
1971	NO	N	13	LB
5 yrs.	68 games

Cookie Cunningham
CUNNINGHAM, HAROLD B.
B. Feb. 4, 1905, Mount Vernon, OH
Ohio State 6'3" 210 lbs.

1926	CLE	A	5	E
1927	CLE	A	5	E
1929	CHIB	N	10	E
1931	SI	N	10	E
4 yrs.	30 games

Dick Cunningham
CUNNINGHAM, RICHARD K.
B. Oct. 12, 1944, Boston, MA
Arkansas 6'2" 238 lbs.

1967	BUF	A	14	G
1968			14	OT
1970	BUF	N	14	C, LB
1971			5	LB
1972			9	LB
1973	PHI	N	9	LB
1973	HOU	N	1	LB
6 yrs.	66 games

Doug Cunningham
CUNNINGHAM, DOUGLAS SCOTT
B. Nov. 14, 1955, San Antonio, TX
Rice 6'2" 195 lbs.

| 1979 | MIN | N | 6 | WR |

Doug Cunningham
CUNNINGHAM, JULIAN DOUGLAS
B. Sep. 14, 1945, Louisville, MS
Mississippi 5'11" 191 lbs.

1967	SF	N	14	RB
1968			10	RB
1969			14	RB
1970			12	RB
1971			14	RB
1972			4	RB
1973			14	RB
1974	WAS	N	2	RB
8 yrs.	84 games

Ed Cunningham
CUNNINGHAM, ED
B. Aug. 17, 1969, Washington, DC
Washington 6'3" 290 lbs.

1992	PHX	N	10	C
1993			15	C
1994	ARI	N	16	C
1995			9	C
1996	SEA	N	11	C
5 yrs.	61 games

Eric Cunningham
CUNNINGHAM, ERIC ALAN
B. Mar. 16, 1957, Akron, OH
Penn State 6'3" 257 lbs.

1979	NYJ	N	11	G
1980			6	G
2 yrs.	17 games

Jay Cunningham
CUNNINGHAM, JAY
B. Oct. 9, 1943, Youngstown, OH
Bowling Green 5'10" 180 lbs.

1965	BOS	A	14	DB
1966			14	DB
1967			12	DB
3 yrs.	40 games

Jim Cunningham
CUNNINGHAM, JAMES WALTER
B. Mar. 11, 1939, Connellsville, PA
Pittsburgh 5'11" 221 lbs.

1961	WAS	N	14	FB
1962			14	FB
1963			14	FB
3 yrs.	42 games

Leon Cunningham
CUNNINGHAM, LEON
B. 1931
South Carolina 6'2" 215 lbs.

| 1955 | DET | N | 8 | C, LB |

Pat Cunningham
CUNNINGHAM, PATRICK DANTE ROSS
B. Jan. 4, 1967, Los Angeles, CA
Texas A&M 6'6" 312 lbs.

| 1990 | IND | N | 2 | OT |

Randall Cunningham
CUNNINGHAM, RANDALL
B. Mar. 27, 1963, Santa Barbara, CA

Randall Cunningham cont.
Nevada-Las Vegas 6'4" 192 lbs.

1985	PHI	N	6	QB
1986			15	QB, P
1987			12	QB
1988			16	QB, P
1989			16	QB, P
1990			16	QB
1991			1	QB
1992			15	QB
1993			4	QB
1994			14	QB, P
1995			7	QB
11 yrs.	122 games

Rick Cunningham
CUNNINGHAM, PATRICK DANTE ROSS
B. Jan. 4, 1967, Los Angeles, CA
Texas A&M 6'7" 320 lbs.

1992	PHX	N	8	OT
1993			16	OT
1994	ARI	N	12	OT
1995	MIN	N	11	OT
1996	OAK	N	12	OT
5 yrs.	59 games

Sam Cunningham
CUNNINGHAM, SAMUEL LEWIS, JR. (Sam the Bam)
B. Aug. 15, 1950, Santa Barbara, CA
Southern California 6'3" 226 lbs.

1973	NE	N	14	RB
1974			10	RB
1975			13	RB
1976			11	RB
1977			14	RB
1978			16	RB
1979			12	RB
1981			11	RB
1982				RB
9 yrs.	101 games

T.J. Cunningham
CUNNINGHAM, T.J.
B. Oct. 24, 1972, Aurora, CO
Colorado 6'0" 191 lbs.

| 1996 | SEA | N | 3 | S |

Gary Cuozzo
CUOZZO, GARY SAMUEL
B. Apr. 26, 1941, Montclair, NJ
Virginia 6'1" 195 lbs.

1963	BAL	N	5	QB
1964			9	QB
1965			7	QB
1966			7	QB
1967	NO	N	13	QB
1968	MIN	N	4	QB
1969			9	QB
1970			12	QB
1971			8	QB
1972	STL	N	8	QB
10 yrs.	82 games

Keith Cupp
CUPP, KEITH
B. Jun. 20, 1964
Findlay 6'6" 301 lbs.

| 1987 | CIN | N | 3 | OT |

Bree Cuppoletti
CUPPOLETTI, BREE RUDOLPH
B. Jun. 19, 1910, Virginia, MN
D. Sep., 1960
Oregon 5'10" 200 lbs.

| 1934 | CHIC | N | 11 | G, T |

Bree Cuppoletti continued

1935			12	G
1936			12	G
1937			10	G
1938			11	G, T
1939	PHI	N	10	G
6 yrs.	66 games

Jeff Curchin
CURCHIN, JEFF M.
B. Dec. 17, 1947, Binghamton, NY
Florida State 6'6" 256 lbs.

1970	CHI	N	14	OT
1971			12	OT
1972	BUF	N	1	G
3 yrs.	27 games

Tony Curcillo
CURCILLO, ANTHONY, JR.
B. May 27, 1931, Long Branch, NJ
Ohio State 6'1" 200 lbs.

| 1953 | CHIC | N | 12 | B |

Mike Curcio
CURCIO, MICHAEL A.
B. Jan. 24, 1957, Hudson, NY
Temple 6'1" 237 lbs.

1981	PHI	N	16	LB
1982			5	LB
1982	NYG	N	1	LB
1983	GB	N	14	LB
3 yrs.	36 games

Armand Cure
CURE, ARMAND A.
B. Aug. 7, 1919, New Bedford, MA
Rhode Island 6'0" 198 lbs.

| 1947 | BAL | AA | 1 | B |

Will Cureton
CURETON, WILL
B. Feb. 2, 1950, Meridian, TX
East Texas State 6'3" 200 lbs.

| 1975 | CLE | N | 1 | QB |

August Curley
CURLEY, AUGUST ONORATO
B. Jan. 24, 1960, Little Rock, AR
Southern California 6'3" 222 lbs.

1983	DET	N	10	LB
1984			8	LB
1985			16	LB
1986			4	LB
4 yrs.	38 games

Harry Curran
CURRAN, HARRY
B. Jun. 2, 1894, Illinois
D. Jun., 1976, St. Petersburg, FL
None 5'10" 180 lbs.

1920	CHIC	A	6	HB
1921			1	HB
2 yrs.	7 games

Pat Curran
CURRAN, PATRICK MICHAEL
B. Sep. 21, 1945, Milwaukee, WI
Iowa State/Lakeland 6'3" 238 lbs.

1969	LA	N	1	TE
1970			14	TE
1971			14	TE
1972			10	TE
1973			14	TE
1974			14	TE
1975	SD	N	14	TE

Year	Team		Games	Pos.

Pat Curran continued

Year	Team		Games	Pos.
1976			14	TE
1977			14	TE
1978			14	TE
10 yrs.	123 games			

Willie Curran
CURRAN, WILLIAM
B. Dec. 30, 1959, Inglewood, CA
UCLA 5'10" 175 lbs.

Year	Team		Games	Pos.
1982	ATL	N	7	WR
1983			16	WR
1984			14	WR
3 yrs.	37 games			

Mike Current
CURRENT, MICHAEL WAYNE
B. Sep. 17, 1945, Lima, OH
Ohio State 6'4" 267 lbs.

Year	Team		Games	Pos.
1967	MIA	A	2	OT
1967	DEN	A	4	OT
1968			14	OT
1969			14	OT
1970	DEN	N	14	OT
1971			14	OT
1972			14	OT
1973			14	OT
1974			14	OT
1975			7	OT
1976	TB	N	14	OT
1977	MIA	N	14	OT
1978			16	OT
1979			16	OT
13 yrs.	171 games			

Dan Currie
CURRIE, DANIEL GEORGE
B. Jun. 27, 1935, Detroit, MI
Michigan State 6'3" 239 lbs.

Year	Team		Games	Pos.
1958	GB	N	12	LB
1959			12	LB
1960			12	LB
1961			14	LB
1962			12	LB
1963			14	LB
1964			14	LB
1965	LA	N	14	LB
1966			14	LB
9 yrs.	118 games			

Herschel Currie
CURRIE, HERSCHEL LAMONT
B. Aug. 8, 1965, Chicago, IL
Oregon State 6'1" 190 lbs.

Year	Team		Games	Pos.
1994	ARI	N	1	CB

Bill Currier
CURRIER, WILLIAM FRANK
B. Jan. 5, 1955, Glen Burnie, MD
South Carolina 6'0" 193 lbs.

Year	Team		Games	Pos.
1977	HOU	N	14	DB
1978			14	S
1979			16	S
1980	NE	N	16	S
1981	NYG	N	16	S
1982			9	S
1983			15	S
1984			9	CB, S
1985			2	S
9 yrs.	111 games			

Don Currivan
CURRIVAN, DONALD F.
B. Mar. 6, 1920, Mansfield, MA
D. May, 1956
Boston College 6'0" 193 lbs.

Year	Team		Games	Pos.
1943	CHIC	N	7	E
1944	C, P	N	10	E

Don Currivan continued

Year	Team		Games	Pos.
1945	BOS	N	10	E
1946			11	E
1947			12	E
1948			3	E
1948	LA	N	10	E
1949			12	E
7 yrs.	75 games			

Bill Curry
CURRY, WILLIAM ALEXANDER
B. Oct. 21, 1942, College Park, GA
Georgia Tech 6'2" 235 lbs.

Year	Team		Games	Pos.
1965	GB	N	14	C, LB
1966			14	C
1967	BAL	N	11	C, LB
1968			14	LB, C
1969			14	C
1970			13	C
1971			14	C
1972			14	C
1973	HOU	N	4	C
1974	LA	N	10	C
10 yrs.	122 games			

Buddy Curry
CURRY, GEORGE JESSEL
B. Jun. 4, 1958, Greenville, NC
North Carolina 6'4" 221 lbs.

Year	Team		Games	Pos.
1980	ATL	N	16	LB
1981			16	LB
1982			9	LB
1983			16	LB
1984			16	LB
1985			16	LB
1986			16	LB
1987			4	LB
8 yrs.	109 games			

Craig Curry
CURRY, CRAIG ANTHONY
B. Jul. 20, 1961, Houston, TX
Texas 6'0" 190 lbs.

Year	Team		Games	Pos.
1984	TB	N	5	S
1985			16	S
1986			16	S
1987	IND	N	3	CB, S
4 yrs.	40 games			

Eric Curry
CURRY, ERIC FELECE
B. Feb. 3, 1970, Thomasville, GA
Alabama 6'5" 270 lbs.

Year	Team		Games	Pos.
1993	TB	N	10	DE
1994			15	DE
1995			16	DE
1996			12	DE
4 yrs.	53 games			

Ivory Curry
CURRY, IVORY
B. Feb. 6, 1961, Miami, FL
D. Aug. 22, 1989, Brandon, FL
Florida 5'11" 185 lbs.

Year	Team		Games	Pos.
1987	TB	N	3	CB

Roy Curry
CURRY, ROY
B. Nov. 9, 1939
Jackson State 6'1" 195 lbs.

Year	Team		Games	Pos.
1963	PIT	N	6	FL

Shane Curry
CURRY, SHANE CLIFTON
B. Apr. 7, 1968, Cincinnati, OH
D. May 3, 1992, Cincinnati, OH

Shane Curry continued
Georgia Tech/Miami (Florida) 6'5" 270 lbs.

Year	Team		Games	Pos.
1991	IND	N	9	DE

Don Curtin
CURTIN, DONALD (Red)
B. 1902
Deceased
Marquette 5'8" 155 lbs.

Year	Team		Games	Pos.
1926	MIL	N	3	QB

Bobby Curtis
CURTIS, BOBBY
B. Oct. 23, 1964, Macon, GA
Savannah State 6'3" 235 lbs.

Year	Team		Games	Pos.
1987	WAS	N	3	LB

Isaac Curtis
CURTIS, ISAAC FISHER
B. Oct. 20, 1950, Santa Ana, CA
California/San Diego State 6'0" 192 lbs.

Year	Team		Games	Pos.
1973	CIN	N	14	WR
1974			14	WR
1975			14	WR
1976			14	WR
1977			8	WR
1978			16	WR
1979			16	WR
1980			1	WR
1981			15	WR
1982			9	WR
1983			16	WR
1984			16	WR
12 yrs.	153 games			

Mike Curtis
CURTIS, JAMES MICHAEL (Mad Dog)
B. Mar. 27, 1943, Washington, DC
Duke 6'2" 232 lbs.

Year	Team		Games	Pos.
1965	BAL	N	14	LB
1966			12	LB
1967			3	LB
1968			14	LB
1969			14	LB
1970			14	LB
1971			13	LB
1972			14	LB
1973			7	LB
1974			14	LB
1975			6	LB
1976	SEA	N	14	LB
1977	WAS	N	12	LB
1978			13	LB
14 yrs.	164 games			

Scott Curtis
CURTIS, ALSTON SCOTT
B. Dec. 26, 1964, Burlington, VT
New Hampshire 6'1" 230 lbs.

Year	Team		Games	Pos.
1988	PHI	N	16	LB
1989	DEN	N	16	LB
1990			9	LB
3 yrs.	41 games			

Tom Curtis
CURTIS, THOMAS NEWTON
B. Nov. 1, 1947, Cleveland, OH
Michigan 6'1" 196 lbs.

Year	Team		Games	Pos.
1970	BAL	N	10	S
1971			14	S
2 yrs.	24 games			

Travis Curtis
CURTIS, TRAVIS FENNELL
B. Sep. 27, 1965, Washington, DC

Travis Curtis continued
West Virginia 5'10" 180 lbs.

Year	Team		Games	Pos.
1987	STL	N	13	S
1988	PHX	N	12	S
1988	WAS	N	1	S
1989	MIN	N	16	S
1990	NYJ	N	14	S
1991	WAS	N	1	S
5 yrs.	57 games			

Harry Curzon
CURZON, HENRY M.
B. Nov. 12, 1895
D. Apr., 1966, Vero Beach, FL
None 6'0" 185 lbs.

Year	Team		Games	Pos.
1925	HAM	N	3	E, HB, FB
1925	BUF	N	5	E
1926	HAM	N	4	HB, E, FB
1928	CHIC	N	1	FB
3 yrs.	13 games			

Pete Cusick
CUSICK, PETER MARTIN
B. Oct. 27, 1952, San Bernardino, CA
Ohio State 6'1" 255 lbs.

Year	Team		Games	Pos.
1975	NE	N	13	DT

Randy Cuthbert
CUTHBERT, RANDY ALAN
B. Jan. 16, 1970, Lansdale, PA
Duke 6'3" 225 lbs.

Year	Team		Games	Pos.
1993	PIT	N	10	RB
1994			1	RB
2 yrs.	11 games			

Cutler
CUTLER
None

Year	Team		Games	Pos.
1920	BUF	A	1	HB

Harry Cutler
CUTLER, HARRY
B. Mar., 1890
Deceased
None 6'2" 190 lbs.

Year	Team		Games	Pos.
1920	DAY	A	6	T

Gary Cutsinger
CUTSINGER, GARY L.
B. Feb. 4, 1940, Perry, OK
Oklahoma State 6'4" 244 lbs.

Year	Team		Games	Pos.
1962	HOU	A	14	DE
1963			14	DE
1964			14	DE
1965			14	DE
1966			14	DE
1968			14	DE
6 yrs.	84 games			

Andy Cvercko
CVERCKO, ANDREW B.
B. Nov. 6, 1937, Campbell, OH
Northwestern 6'0" 242 lbs.

Year	Team		Games	Pos.
1960	GB	N	12	G
1961	DAL	N	11	G
1962			14	G
1963	CLE	N	1	G
1963	WAS	N	10	G
4 yrs.	48 games			

Hec Cyre
CYRE, HECTOR J.
B. Oct. 5, 1901
D. Aug. 5, 1971, Langley, WA
Gonzaga 6'2" 215 lbs.

Year	Team		Games	Pos.
1926	GB	N	10	T, E, G

Year	Team	Games	Pos.

Hec Cyre *continued*

1928	**NYY**	N	3	T, G
2 yrs.	13 games			

Ziggy Czarobski

CZAROBSKI, ZYGMONT PIERRE
B. Sep. 11, 1922, Chicago, IL
D. Jul. 1, 1984, Chicago, IL
Notre Dame 6'0" 230 lbs.

1948	**CHI**	**AA**	14	T
1949			12	T
2 yrs.	26 games			

Jerry Daanen

DAANEN, JEROME
B. Dec. 15, 1944, De Pere, WI
Miami (Florida) 6'0" 190 lbs.

1968	**STL**	N	14	OE
1969			9	WR
1970			13	WR
3 yrs.	36 games			

Carlton Dabney

DABNEY, CARLTON
B. Jan. 26, 1947, Richmond, VA
Morgan State 6'5" 250 lbs.

1968	**ATL**	N	14	DT, DE

Bill Daddio

DADDIO, LOUIS S.
B. Apr. 26, 1916, Meadville, PA
D. Jul. 5, 1989, Mount Lebanon, PA
Pittsburgh 5'11" 207 lbs.

1941	**CHIC**	N	11	E
1942			11	E
1946	**BUF**	**AA**	3	E
3 yrs.	25 games			

Dave D'Addio

D'ADDIO, DAVID JOHN
B. Jul. 13, 1961, Newark, NJ
Maryland 6'2" 235 lbs.

1984	**DET**	N	16	FB

Harrie Dadmun

DADMUN, HARRIE HOLLAND
(Hal)
B. Jun. 25, 1894, Cambridge, MA
D. Sep. 15, 1980, Concord, MN
Tufts/Harvard 6'0" 235 lbs.

1920	**CAN**	A	3	G
1921	**NY**	A	1	G
2 yrs.	4 games			

Ted Daffer

DAFFER, TERRELL EDWIN
B. Sep. 24, 1929, Norfolk, VA
Tennessee 6'0" 198 lbs.

1954	**CHIB**	N	12	DE

Bernard Dafney

DAFNEY, BERNARD EUGENE
B. Nov. 1, 1968, Los Angeles, CA
Tennessee 6'5" 324 lbs.

1992	**MIN**	N	2	G
1993			16	G
1994			16	G
1995	**ARI**	N	12	G, OT
1996	**PIT**	N	13	OT
5 yrs.	59 games			

Frank D'Agostino

D'AGOSTINO, FRANK JOSEPH
B. Mar. 11, 1934, Philadelphia, PA

Year	Team	Games	Pos.

Frank D'Agostino *continued*

Auburn 6'1" 245 lbs.

1956	**PHI**	N	12	G
1960	**NY**	A		G
2 yrs.	12 games			

Lou D'Agostino

D'AGOSTINO, LOU
B. Dec. 12, 1973, Brooklyn, NY
Hofstra/Rhode Island 6'0" 235 lbs.

1996	**NYJ**	N	9	FB

Bob Dahl

DAHL, ROBERT ALLEN
B. Nov. 5, 1968, Chicago, IL
Notre Dame 6'5" 293 lbs.

1992	**CLE**	N	9	OT
1993			16	G, OT
1994			15	G
1995			16	G
1996	**WAS**	N	15	G
5 yrs.	71 games			

George Dahlgren

DAHLGREN, GEORGE (Swede)
B. Apr. 17, 1887
Deceased
Beloit 5'10" 200 lbs.

1924	**KEN**	N	4	G
1925	**HAM**	N	3	G
1925	**RI**	N	1	G
1926	**HAM**	N	3	T
3 yrs.	11 games			

Tom Dahms

DAHMS, THOMAS
B. Apr. 19, 1927, San Diego, CA
D. Dec. 1, 1988, San Diego, CA
San Diego State 6'5" 242 lbs.

1951	**LA**	N	12	T
1952			12	T
1953			12	T
1954			12	T
1955	**GB**	N	12	T
1956	**CHIC**	N	12	T
1957	**SF**	N	8	T
7 yrs.	80 games			

Anthony Daigle

DAIGLE, ANTHONY JOHN
B. Apr. 5, 1970, San Francisco, CA
Arizona State//Fresno State 5'10" 198 lbs.

1994	**PIT**	N	1	RB

Ted Dailey

DAILEY, THEODORE
B. 1910
D. Oct. 3, 1992, Syracuse, NY
Pittsburgh 5'9" 170 lbs.

1933	**PIT**	N	10	E

Fred Dakata

DAKATA, FRED
None

1931	**PRO**	N	1	FB

Dave Dalby

DALBY, DAVID MERLE
B. Oct. 19, 1950, Alexandria, MN
UCLA 6'3" 247 lbs.

1972	**OAK**	N	14	C
1973			14	C
1974			14	C, G
1975			14	C, G

Year	Team	Games	Pos.

Dave Dalby *continued*

1976			14	C
1977			14	C
1978			16	C
1979			16	C
1980			16	C
1981			16	C
1982	**LARI**	N	9	C
1983			16	C
1984			16	C
1985			16	C
14 yrs.	205 games			

Carroll Dale

DALE, CARROLL WAYNE
B. Apr. 24, 1938, Wise, VA
Virginia Tech 6'1" 198 lbs.

1960	**LA**	N	12	E
1961			14	OE
1962			14	OE
1963			12	OE
1964			13	OE
1965	**GB**	N	13	FL
1966			14	FL
1967			14	FL
1968			14	FL
1969			14	WR
1970			14	WR
1971			14	WR
1972			14	WR
1973	**MIN**	N	13	WR
14 yrs.	189 games			

Jeff Dale

DALE, JEFFERY DWAYNE
B. Oct. 6, 1962, Pineville, LA
Louisiana State 6'3" 213 lbs.

1985	**SD**	N	16	S
1986			16	S
1988			10	S
3 yrs.	42 games			

Roland Dale

DALE, ROLAND H.
B. Oct. 30, 1927, Magee, MS
Mississippi 6'3" 210 lbs.

1950	**WAS**	N	11	DE

Bill Daley

DALEY, WILLIAM E. (Bullet)
B. 1921
Minnesota/Michigan 6'2" 210 lbs.

1946	**BKN**	**AA**	2	FB
1946	**MIA**	**AA**	1	FB
1947	**CHI**	**AA**	14	B
1948	**NY**	**AA**	7	B
3 yrs.	24 games			

Ken Dallafior

DALLAFIOR, KENNETH RAY
B. Aug. 26, 1959, Royal Oak, MI
Minnesota 6'4" 277 lbs.

1985	**SD**	N	3	G
1986			12	G
1987			9	G
1988			13	G, OT
1989	**DET**	N	16	G
1990			16	G
1991			6	G, C
1992			12	G
8 yrs.	87 games			

Dilly Dally

DALLY, DILLY
None

1926	**HAR**	N	5	G, T

Year	Team	Games	Pos.

Chris Dalman

DALMAN, CHRIS WILLIAM
B. Mar. 15, 1970, Salinas, CA
Stanford 6'3" 285 lbs.

1993	**SF**	N	15	G, C
1994			16	C, G
1995			15	G, C
1996			16	G
4 yrs.	62 games			

Pete D'Alonzo

D'ALONZO, PETER JOSEPH
B. 1930, Orange, NJ
Villanova 5'10" 210 lbs.

1951	**DET**	N	12	FB
1952	**DET**	N		FB
2 yrs.	12 games			

Bob Dalrymple

DALRYMPLE, ROBERT (Slats)
B. Jul. 15, 1896
D. May, 1978, Dublin, GA
Wabash 6'2" 210 lbs.

1922	**EVA**	N	1	C

Leather Dalton

DALTON, MAURICE (Jack, Moxie)
B. Sep., 1894, Janesville, WI
D. Feb. 9, 1954
Carroll (Wisconsin)/Loras 5'6" 160 lbs.

1922	**RAC**	N	5	QB, FB

Oakley Dalton

DALTON, OAKLEY
B. Jul. 18, 1952, Welch, WV
Jackson State 6'6" 285 lbs.

1977	**NO**	N	1	DT

Brad Daluiso

DALUISO, BRADLEY WILLIAM
B. Dec. 31, 1967, San Diego, CA
San Diego State/UCLA 6'2" 208 lbs.

1991	**ATL**	N	2	K
1991	**BUF**	N	14	K
1992	**DEN**	N	16	K, P
1993	**NYG**	N	15	K
1994			16	K
1995			16	K
1996			16	K
6 yrs.	95 games			

Frank Damiani

DAMIANI, FRANK ANTHONY
B. Jul. 27, 1922, Carnegie, PA
Manhattan 6'1" 225 lbs.

1944	**NYG**	N	2	T, G

Mike D'Amato

D'AMATO, MIKE
B. Mar. 3, 1943, Brooklyn, NY
Hofstra 6'2" 204 lbs.

1968	**NY**	A	13	DB

Maury Damkroger

DAMKROGER, MAURICE A.
B. Jan. 8, 1952, Cambridge, NE
Nebraska 6'2" 230 lbs.

1974	**NE**	N	11	LB
1975			2	LB
2 yrs.	13 games			

John Damore

DAMORE, JOHN L.
B. Oct. 20, 1933, Riverside, IL

Year	Team		Games	Pos.

John Damore continued

Northwestern 6'0" 228 lbs.

Year	Team		Games	Pos.
1957	CHIB	N	4	G
1959			8	G, C
2 yrs.	12 games			

Boley Dancewicz

DANCEWICZ, FRANCIS JOSEPH
B. Oct. 3, 1924
D. Jun. 26, 1985, Boston, MA
Notre Dame 5'10" 187 lbs.

Year	Team		Games	Pos.
1946	BOS	N	8	QB
1947			12	QB
1948			3	QB
3 yrs.	23 games			

Dick Danehe

DANEHE, RICHARD M.
B. Sep. 10, 1920, Memphis, TN
Southern California 6'2" 235 lbs.

Year	Team		Games	Pos.
1947	LA	AA	11	T
1948			5	T
2 yrs.	16 games			

Joe Danelo

DANELO, JOSEPH PETER
B. Sep. 2, 1953, Spokane, WA
Washington State 5'9" 165 lbs.

Year	Team		Games	Pos.
1975	GB	N	12	K
1976	NYG	N	14	K
1977			14	K
1978			16	K
1979			16	K
1980			16	K
1981			16	K
1982			9	K
1983	BUF	N	14	K
1984			9	K
10 yrs.	136 games			

Bill Danenhauer

DANENHAUER, WILLIAM
B. Jun. 3, 1934, Clay Center, KS
Emporia State 6'4" 245 lbs.

Year	Team		Games	Pos.
1960	DEN	A		DE
1960	BOS	A		DE

Eldon Danenhauer

DANENHAUER, ELDON
B. Oct. 4, 1935, Clay Center, KS
Pittsburg State 6'4" 242 lbs.

Year	Team		Games	Pos.
1960	DEN	A		OT
1961			14	OT
1962			14	OT
1963			9	OT
1964			14	OT
1965			14	OT
6 yrs.	65 games			

George Daney

DANEY, GEORGE ANTHONY
B. Sep. 2, 1946, Washington, PA
Detroit/Texas-El Paso 6'3" 240 lbs.

Year	Team		Games	Pos.
1968	KC	A	14	G
1969			14	G
1970	KC	N	14	G
1971			14	G
1972			14	G
1973			13	DE
1974			13	G
7 yrs.	96 games			

Eugene Daniel

DANIEL, EUGENE, JR.
B. May 4, 1961, Baton Rouge, LA
Louisiana State 6'0" 180 lbs.

Year	Team		Games	Pos.
1984	IND	N	15	CB

Eugene Daniel continued

Year	Team		Games	Pos.
1985			16	CB
1986			15	CB
1987			12	CB
1988			16	CB
1989			15	CB
1990			15	CB
1991			16	CB, S
1992			14	CB, S
1993			16	CB, S
1994			16	CB
1995			16	CB
1996			16	CB
13 yrs.	198 games			

Kenny Daniel

DANIEL, KENNETH RAY
B. Jun. 1, 1960, Martinez, CA
San Jose State 5'10" 180 lbs.

Year	Team		Games	Pos.
1984	NYG	N	15	CB
1986	IND	N	15	CB
1987			2	CB
3 yrs.	32 games			

Willie Daniel

DANIEL, WILLIAM PAUL
B. Nov. 10, 1937, New Albany, MS
Mississippi State 5'11" 187 lbs.

Year	Team		Games	Pos.
1961	PIT	N	14	DB
1962			13	DB
1963			13	DB
1964			14	DB
1965			9	DB
1966			12	DB
1967	LA	N	14	DB
1968			14	DB
1969			10	CB
9 yrs.	113 games			

Av Daniell

DANIELL, AVERELL EDWARD
B. Nov. 6, 1914, Pittsburgh, PA
Pittsburgh 6'3" 215 lbs.

Year	Team		Games	Pos.
1937	GB	N	5	T
1937	BKN	N	4	T
1 yr.	9 games			

Jim Daniell

DANIELL, JAMES L.
B. Apr. 10, 1918, Pittsburgh, PA
D. Dec. 13, 1983, Pittsburgh, PA
Ohio State 6'2" 230 lbs.

Year	Team		Games	Pos.
1945	CHIB	N	7	T
1946	CLE	AA	14	T
2 yrs.	21 games			

Calvin Daniels

DANIELS, CALVIN RICHARD
B. Dec. 26, 1958, Morehead City, NC
North Carolina 6'3" 240 lbs.

Year	Team		Games	Pos.
1982	KC	N	9	LB
1983			16	LB
1984			16	LB
1985			16	LB
1986	WAS	N	13	LB
5 yrs.	70 games			

Clem Daniels

DANIELS, CLEMON
B. Jul. 9, 1937, McKinney, TX
Prairie View A&M 6'1" 219 lbs.

Year	Team		Games	Pos.
1960	DAL	A	14	DB
1961	OAK	A	8	HB
1962			14	HB
1963			14	HB
1964			14	HB
1965			14	HB
1966			14	HB

Clem Daniels continued

Year	Team		Games	Pos.
1967			9	HB
1968	SF	N	9	HB
9 yrs.	110 games			

Dave Daniels

DANIELS, DAVID
B. Apr. 5, 1941, East Palatka, FL
Florida A&M 6'3" 245 lbs.

Year	Team		Games	Pos.
1966	OAK	A	14	DT

David Daniels

DANIELS, DAVID
B. Sep. 16, 1969, Sarasota, FL
Penn State 6'1" 190 lbs.

Year	Team		Games	Pos.
1991	SEA	N	16	WR
1992			13	WR
2 yrs.	29 games			

Dexter Daniels

DANIELS, DEXTER
B. Dec. 8, 1973, Valdosta, GA
Florida 6'1" 241 lbs.

Year	Team		Games	Pos.
1996	BAL	N	4	LB

Dick Daniels

DANIELS, RICHARD B.
B. Oct. 19, 1945, Portland, OR
Pacific (Oregon) 5'9" 180 lbs.

Year	Team		Games	Pos.
1966	DAL	N	4	DB
1967			14	DB
1968			14	DB
1969	CHI	N	8	S
1970			13	S
5 yrs.	53 games			

Jack Daniels

DANIELS, JOHN
B. 1907, Michigan
None 135 lbs.

Year	Team		Games	Pos.
1925	MIL	N	1	QB

Phillip Daniels

DANIELS, PHILLIP BERNARD
B. Mar. 4, 1973, Donalsonville, GA
Georgia 6'5" 263 lbs.

Year	Team		Games	Pos.
1996	SEA	N	15	DE

Gary Danielson

DANIELSON, GARY DENNIS
B. Sep. 10, 1951, Detroit, MI
Purdue 6'2" 195 lbs.

Year	Team		Games	Pos.
1976	DET	N	1	QB
1977			12	QB
1978			16	QB
1979			16	QB
1980			6	QB
1981			8	QB
1982			10	QB
1983			15	QB
1985	CLE	N	8	QB
1987			6	QB
1988			2	QB
11 yrs.	100 games			

Ernie Danjean

DANJEAN, ERNEST J.
B. Mar. 5, 1934, New Orleans, LA
Auburn 6'0" 230 lbs.

Year	Team		Games	Pos.
1957	GB	N	12	LB

Rick Danmeier

DANMEIER, RICHARD CRAIG
B. Apr. 8, 1952, St. Paul, MN

Rick Danmeier continued

Sioux Falls College 6'0" 188 lbs.

Year	Team		Games	Pos.
1978	MIN	N	16	K
1979			16	K
1980			16	K
1981			16	K
1982			9	K
5 yrs.	73 games			

Ed Danowski

DANOWSKI, EDWARD FRANK
B. Sep. 30, 1911, Jamesport, NY
D. Feb. 1, 1997, East Patchogue, NY
Fordham 6'1" 198 lbs.

Year	Team		Games	Pos.
1934	NYG	N	8	QB, HB
1935			12	QB, HB
1936			12	QB, HB
1937			11	HB
1938			11	QB, HB
1939			11	QB
1941			6	B
7 yrs.	71 games			

Fred Danziger

DANZIGER, FRED W.
B. Jan. 12, 1906
D. Oct., 1948
Michigan State 5'11" 175 lbs.

Year	Team		Games	Pos.
1931	CLE	N	1	FB

Jerry DaPrato

DAPRATO, NENO J.
B. Jan. 14, 1893
D. Apr. 29, 1984, Parkesburg, PA
Michigan State 5'10" 180 lbs.

Year	Team		Games	Pos.
1921	DET	A	6	FB

Alvis Darby

DARBY, ALVIS RUSSELL
B. Sep. 14, 1954, Miami, FL
Florida 6'5" 221 lbs.

Year	Team		Games	Pos.
1976	SEA	N	1	TE
1976	HOU	N	2	TE
1978	TB	N	6	TE
2 yrs.	9 games			

Byron Darby

DARBY, BYRON
B. Jun. 4, 1960, Los Angeles, CA
Southern California 6'4" 260 lbs.

Year	Team		Games	Pos.
1983	PHI	N	16	DE
1984			16	DE
1985			10	DE
1986			16	DE
1987	IND	N	12	DE
1988			16	NT
1989	DET	N	1	DE
7 yrs.	87 games			

Matt Darby

DARBY, MATTHEW LAMONT
B. Nov. 19, 1968, Virginia Beach, VA
UCLA 6'1" 200 lbs.

Year	Team		Games	Pos.
1992	BUF	N	16	S
1993			16	S
1994			16	S
1995			7	S
1996	ARI	N	15	S
5 yrs.	70 games			

Paul Darby

DARBY, PAUL WILLIE, JR.
B. Oct. 22, 1956, Buda, TX
Southwest Texas State 5'10" 192 lbs.

Year	Team		Games	Pos.
1979	NYJ	N	15	WR
1980			8	WR
2 yrs.	23 games			

Year	Team	Games	Pos.

Kirby Dar Dar
DAR DAR, KIRBY DAVID
B. Mar. 27, 1972, Morgan City, LA
Syracuse 5'9" 183 lbs.

Year	Team		Games	Pos.
1995	**MIA**	**N**	1	WR
1996			11	WR
2 yrs.	12 games			

Ramsey Dardar
DARDAR, J. RAMSEY
B. Oct. 3, 1959, Cecilia, LA
Louisiana State 6'2" 264 lbs.

Year	Team		Games	Pos.
1984	**STL**	**N**	16	OT, G

Thom Darden
DARDEN, THOMAS VINCENT
B. Aug. 28, 1950, Sandusky, OH
Michigan 6'2" 193 lbs.

Year	Team		Games	Pos.
1972	**CLE**	**N**	14	CB
1973			11	CB
1974			14	CB
1976			14	S
1977			14	S
1978			16	S
1979			16	S
1980			16	S
1981			13	S
9 yrs.	128 games			

Bernie Darling
DARLING, BERNARD E. (Boob)
B. Nov. 18, 1903, Winnebago County, WI
D. Mar. 5, 1968, Green Bay, WI
Wisconsin/Ripon/Beloit 5'11" 206 lbs.

Year	Team		Games	Pos.
1927	**GB**	**N**	2	C
1928			8	C
1929			10	C
1930			12	C
1931			4	C
5 yrs.	36 games			

Bill Darnall
DARNALL, WILLIAM CARLYLE
B. Apr. 21, 1944, Washington, DC
North Carolina 6'2" 197 lbs.

Year	Team		Games	Pos.
1968	**MIA**	**A**	11	WR
1969			2	WR
2 yrs.	13 games			

Phil Darns
DARNS, PHILLIP
B. Jul. 27, 1959, Tampa, FL
Mississippi Valley State 6'3" 245 lbs.

Year	Team		Games	Pos.
1984	**TB**	**N**	2	DE

Dan Darragh
DARRAGH, DANIEL MEYER
B. Nov. 28, 1946, Pittsburgh, PA
William & Mary 6'3" 196 lbs.

Year	Team		Games	Pos.
1968	**BUF**	**A**	11	QB
1969			3	QB
1970	**BUF**	**N**	3	QB
3 yrs.	17 games			

Bernie Darre
DARRE, BERNARD JOHN
B. Nov. 8, 1939, New Orleans, LA
Tulane 6'2" 230 lbs.

Year	Team		Games	Pos.
1961	**WAS**	**N**	12	G

Chris Darrington
DARRINGTON, CHRIS
B. Jul. 13, 1964
Weber State 5'10" 180 lbs.

Year	Team		Games	Pos.
1987	**HOU**	**N**	3	WR

Barry Darrow
DARROW, BARRY WAYNE
B. Jun. 27, 1950, Peoria, IL
Western Montana/Montana 6'7" 260 lbs.

Year	Team		Games	Pos.
1974	**CLE**	**N**	13	OT
1975			14	OT
1976			14	OT
1977			14	OT
1978			16	OT
5 yrs.	71 games			

Matt Darwin
DARWIN, MATTHEW WAYNE
B. Mar. 11, 1963, Houston, TX
Texas A&M 6'4" 270 lbs.

Year	Team		Games	Pos.
1986	**PHI**	**N**	16	C
1987			12	C
1988			16	OT
1989			15	OT
1990			2	OT
5 yrs.	61 games			

Harry Dasstling
DASSTLING, HARRY (Dane)
B. 1894
Deceased
None 6'0" 190 lbs.

Year	Team		Games	Pos.
1921	**CIN**	**A**	4	G, T

Bob Daugherty
DAUGHERTY, ROBERT
B. 1942
Tulsa 6'2" 205 lbs.

Year	Team		Games	Pos.
1966	**SF**	**N**	4	HB

Dick Daugherty
DAUGHERTY, RICHARD
B. Mar. 29, 1930
Oregon 6'1" 219 lbs.

Year	Team		Games	Pos.
1951	**LA**	**N**	12	G
1952			12	G
1953			12	G
1956			12	C
1957			9	C, LB
1958			12	LB
6 yrs.	69 games			

Ron Daugherty
DAUGHTERY, RONALD
B. Mar. 17, 1958, Chicago, IL
Northeastern 6'3" 185 lbs.

Year	Team		Games	Pos.
1987	**MIN**	**N**	3	WR

Russ Daugherty
DAUGHERTY, RUSSELL S. (Pug)
B. Jan. 31, 1902
Deceased
Illinois 5'10" 175 lbs.

Year	Team		Games	Pos.
1927	**FRA**	**N**	2	HB

Lou Daukas
DAUKAS, LOUIS J.
B. 1921, Nashua, NH
Cornell 6'0" 203 lbs.

Year	Team		Games	Pos.
1947	**BKN**	**AA**	4	C

Nick Daukas
DAUKAS, NICHOLAS J.
B. Dec. 11, 1922, Nashua, NH
Dartmouth 6'4" 225 lbs.

Year	Team		Games	Pos.
1946	**BKN**	**AA**	8	T
1947			7	T
2 yrs.	15 games			

Mitch Daum
DAUM, MITCH
B. Nov. 13, 1963
Wyoming 6'5" 250 lbs.

Year	Team		Games	Pos.
1987	**HOU**	**N**	2	TE

Red Daum
DAUM, CARL V.
B. Sep. 18, 1898, Akron, OH
D. Jun. 30, 1959, Akron, OH
Akron 5'7" 165 lbs.

Year	Team		Games	Pos.
1922	**AKR**	**N**	9	E, QB, HB
1923			7	E, T
1924			8	E
1925			5	E
1926			8	E
5 yrs.	37 games			

Charles Davenport
DAVENPORT, CHARLES DONALD, JR.
B. Nov. 22, 1968, Fayetteville, NC
North Carolina State 6'3" 210 lbs.

Year	Team		Games	Pos.
1992	**PIT**	**N**	15	WR
1993			16	WR
1994			7	WR
3 yrs.	38 games			

Ron Davenport
DAVENPORT, RONALD DONOVAN
B. Dec. 22, 1962, Somerset, Bermuda
Louisville 6'2" 230 lbs.

Year	Team		Games	Pos.
1985	**MIA**	**N**	16	FB
1986			16	RB
1987			10	FB
1988			16	RB
1989			9	RB
5 yrs.	67 games			

Wayne Davenport
DAVENPORT, WAYNE (Bill)
B. Dec. 16, 1906
Hardin-Simmons 187 lbs.

Year	Team		Games	Pos.
1931	**GB**	**N**	2	HB, E

Don Davey
DAVEY, DONALD VINCENT
B. Apr. 8, 1968, Scottsville, NY
Wisconsin 6'4" 276 lbs.

Year	Team		Games	Pos.
1991	**GB**	**N**	16	DE
1992			9	DE
1993			9	DE
1994			16	DE, DT
1995	**JAC**	**N**	16	DT, DE
1996			16	DT
6 yrs.	82 games			

Bob David
DAVID, ROBERT
B. 1922
Villanova 6'0" 219 lbs.

Year	Team		Games	Pos.
1947	**LA**	**N**	8	G
1948			3	G
1948	**CHI**	**AA**	4	G
2 yrs.	15 games			

Jimmy David
DAVID, JAMES T. (Hatchet)
B. Dec. 2, 1927, Florence, SC
Colorado State 5'11" 178 lbs.

Year	Team		Games	Pos.
1952	**DET**	**N**	12	DB
1953			12	DB
1954			12	DB
1955			12	DB
1956			12	DB
1957			12	DB

Jimmy David continued

Year	Team		Games	Pos.
1958			12	DB
1959			12	DB
8 yrs.	96 games			

Stan David
DAVID, STANLEY CHAUNCE
B. Feb. 17, 1962, North Platte, NE
Texas Tech 6'3" 210 lbs.

Year	Team		Games	Pos.
1984	**BUF**	**N**	16	LB

Ben Davidson
**DAVIDSON, BENJAMIN EARL
(The Tree)**
B. Jun. 14, 1940, Los Angeles, CA
Washington 6'8" 272 lbs.

Year	Team		Games	Pos.
1961	**GB**	**N**	14	DE
1962	**WAS**	**N**	14	DT
1963			14	DT
1964	**OAK**	**A**	12	DE
1965			14	DE
1966			14	DE
1967			14	DE
1968			14	DE
1969			14	DE
1970	**OAK**	**N**	14	DE
1971			14	DE
11 yrs.	152 games			

Bill Davidson
DAVIDSON, WILLIAM
B. Jun. 15, 1915
D. Aug., 1970
Temple 6'0" 182 lbs.

Year	Team		Games	Pos.
1937	**PIT**	**N**	11	HB
1938			9	HB, QB, E
1939			7	HB
3 yrs.	27 games			

Chy Davidson
DAVIDSON, CHY
B. May 9, 1959, Queens Village, NY
Rhode Island 5'11" 175 lbs.

Year	Team		Games	Pos.
1984	**NYJ**	**N**	3	WR
1985			1	WR
2 yrs.	4 games			

Cotton Davidson
DAVIDSON, FRANCIS MARION
B. Nov. 30, 1931, Gatesville, TX
Baylor 6'1" 182 lbs.

Year	Team		Games	Pos.
1954	**BAL**	**N**	12	QB
1957			12	QB
1960	**DAL**	**A**	14	QB
1961			14	QB
1962			1	QB
1962	**OAK**	**A**	13	QB
1963			14	QB
1964			14	QB
1965			2	QB
1966			14	QB
1968			1	QB
10 yrs.	111 games			

Greg Davidson
DAVIDSON, GREGORY
B. Apr. 24, 1958, Independence, IA
North Texas State 6'2" 250 lbs.

Year	Team		Games	Pos.
1980	**HOU**	**N**	14	C
1981			16	C
1982			9	C
3 yrs.	39 games			

Jeff Davidson
DAVIDSON, JEFFREY JOHN
B. Oct. 3, 1967, Akron, OH

Year	Team		Games	Pos.

Jeff Davidson continued
Ohio State 6'5" 309 lbs.

1990	DEN	N	12	G
1991			16	G
1992			16	G

3 yrs. 44 games

Joe Davidson
DAVIDSON, JOSEPH BURL
B. Jan. 24, 1903
D. May 14, 1982, Dallas, TX
Colgate/Oklahoma State 6'0" 200 lbs.

| 1928 | CHIC | N | 6 | G |
| 1930 | NEW | N | 6 | C, G |

2 yrs. 12 games

Kenny Davidson
DAVIDSON, KENNETH DARRELL
B. Aug. 17, 1967, Shreveport, LA
Louisiana State 6'5" 272 lbs.

1990	PIT	N	14	DE
1991			13	DE
1992			16	DE
1993			16	DE
1994	HOU	N	16	DE
1995			15	DE, DT
1996	CIN	N	3	DE

7 yrs. 93 games

Pete Davidson
DAVIDSON, PETER
B. 1934
The Citadel 6'5" 255 lbs.

| 1960 | HOU | A | | DT |

Davies
DAVIES
None

| 1922 | HAM | N | 1 | HB |

Davis
DAVIS
Chicago 185 lbs.

| 1920 | HAM | A | 3 | G |

Al Davis
DAVIS, ALBERT LEE (Sonny)
B. Jan. 16, 1948, Alcoa, TN
Tennessee State 5'11" 215 lbs.

| 1971 | PHI | N | 14 | RB |

Andre Davis
DAVIS, ANDRE
B. Oct. 7, 1975, Baton Rouge, LA
Southern University 6'3" 330 lbs.

| 1996 | JAC | N | 2 | DT |

Andy Davis
DAVIS, ANDREW N.
B. Jul. 28, 1927, Washington, DC
George Washington 6'0" 188 lbs.

| 1952 | WAS | N | 8 | DB |

Anthony Davis
DAVIS, ANTHONY
B. Mar. 7, 1969, Pasco, WA
Utah 6'0" 231 lbs.

1993	SEA	N	10	LB
1994	KC	N	5	LB
1995			16	LB
1996			16	LB

4 yrs. 47 games

Year	Team		Games	Pos.

Anthony Davis
DAVIS, ANTHONY (A.D.)
B. Sep. 8, 1952, Huntsville, TX
Southern California 5'10" 190 lbs.

1977	TB	N	11	RB
1978	HOU	N	2	RB
1978	LA	N	2	RB

2 yrs. 15 games

Antone Davis
DAVIS, ANTONE EUGENE
B. Feb. 28, 1967, Sweetwater, TN
Tennessee 6'4" 325 lbs.

1991	PHI	N	16	OT
1992			15	OT
1993			16	OT
1994			16	G, OT
1995			15	OT
1996	ATL	N	16	OT

6 yrs. 94 games

Art Davis
DAVIS, ARTHUR
B. Dec. 19, 1929, Montgomery, AL
Alabama State 6'2" 235 lbs.

| 1953 | CHIB | N | 2 | T |

Art Davis
DAVIS, ARTHUR
B. 1934
Mississippi State 6'1" 195 lbs.

| 1956 | PIT | N | 9 | HB |

Ben Davis
DAVIS, BENJAMIN FRANK
B. Oct. 30, 1945, Birmingham, AL
Defiance 5'11" 183 lbs.

1967	CLE	N	14	DB
1968			14	DB
1970			7	CB
1971			13	CB
1972			14	CB
1973			13	CB
1974	DET	N	10	CB
1975			11	CB
1976			14	CB

9 yrs. 110 games

Bill Davis
DAVIS, WILLIAM D.
B. Nov. 10, 1916, Grapevine, TX
D. Sep., 1973
Texas Tech 6'1" 234 lbs.

1940	CHIC	N	10	T
1941			9	T
1943	BKN	N	9	T
1946	MIA	AA	12	T

4 yrs. 40 games

Billy Davis
DAVIS, WILLIAM AUGUSTA, III
B. Jul. 6, 1972, El Paso, TX
Pittsburgh 6'1" 199 lbs.

| 1995 | DAL | N | 16 | WR |
| 1996 | | | 13 | WR |

2 yrs. 29 games

Billy Davis
DAVIS, WILLIAM HENRY, JR.
B. Dec. 6, 1961, Alexandria, VA
Clemson 6'4" 200 lbs.

| 1984 | STL | N | 1 | LB |

Bob Davis
DAVIS, JAMES ROBERT, JR.
(Twenty Grand)

Year	Team		Games	Pos.

Bob Davis continued
B. May 4, 1914, Greenup, KY
D. Jul., 1969, FL
Kentucky 6'0" 185 lbs.

1938	CLE	N	6	HB
1942	PHI	N	10	HB
1944	BOS	N	10	HB, QB
1945			10	HB
1946			11	HB

5 yrs. 47 games

Bob Davis
DAVIS, ROBERT
B. Sep. 26, 1961, Monongahela, PA
Penn State 5'11" 192 lbs.

1946	PIT	N	11	E
1947			11	E
1948			12	E
1949			11	E
1950			10	E

5 yrs. 55 games

Bob Davis
DAVIS, ROBERT E., JR.
B. Sep. 15, 1945, Neptune, NJ
Virginia 6'3" 205 lbs.

1967	HOU	A	2	QB
1968			6	QB
1969			2	QB
1970	NYJ	N	1	QB
1971			12	QB
1972			14	QB
1973	NO	N	2	QB

7 yrs. 39 games

Bob Davis
DAVIS, ROBERT THOMAS, JR.
B. May 3, 1927, Columbus, GA
Georgia Tech 6'4" 235 lbs.

| 1948 | BOS | N | 12 | T |

Brad Davis
DAVIS, BRAD
B. Feb. 9, 1953, Hammond, LA
Louisiana State 5'10" 204 lbs.

| 1975 | ATL | N | 3 | RB |
| 1976 | | | 1 | RB |

2 yrs. 4 games

Brian Davis
DAVIS, BRIAN
B. Aug. 31, 1963, Phoenix, AZ
Nebraska 6'2" 190 lbs.

1987	WAS	N	7	CB
1988			9	CB
1989			15	CB
1990			7	CB
1991	SEA	N	16	CB
1992			13	CB
1993	SD	N	11	CB
1994	MIN	N	9	CB

8 yrs. 87 games

Bruce Davis
DAVIS, BRUCE EDWARD
B. Jun. 21, 1956, Rutherfordton, NC
UCLA 6'6" 285 lbs.

1979	OAK	N	12	OT
1980			16	OT
1981			16	G
1982	LARI	N	9	OT
1983			16	OT
1984			16	OT
1985			16	OT
1986			16	OT
1987			4	OT
1987	HOU	N	7	OT
1988			16	OT

Year	Team		Games	Pos.

Bruce Davis continued

| 1989 | | | 16 | OT |

11 yrs. 160 games

Bruce Davis
DAVIS, BRUCE E.
B. Feb. 25, 1963, Dallas, TX
Baylor 5'8" 160 lbs.

| 1984 | CLE | N | 14 | WR |

Butch Davis
DAVIS, JOHN CHARLES
B. Jul. 3, 1948, La Jolla, CA
Missouri 5'11" 183 lbs.

| 1970 | CHI | N | 9 | CB |

Carl Davis
DAVIS, CARL LOUIS
B. 1903, Charleston, WV
Michigan/West Virginia 6'0" 194 lbs.

| 1926 | NEW | A | 2 | T |
| 1927 | FRA | N | 8 | E, T, C, G |

2 yrs. 10 games

Charlie Davis
DAVIS, CHARLES
B. Jan. 6, 1952, West Columbia, TX
Colorado 5'11" 200 lbs.

| 1974 | CIN | N | 14 | RB |
| 1976 | TB | N | 6 | RB |

2 yrs. 20 games

Charlie Davis
DAVIS, CHARLES MACK
B. Nov. 17, 1951, Wortham, TX
Texas Christian 6'1" 269 lbs.

1974	PIT	N	14	DT
1975	STL	N	14	DT
1976			14	DT
1977			14	DT
1978			1	DT
1979			16	DT
1980	HOU	N	1	DT

7 yrs. 74 games

Chris Davis
DAVIS, CHRISTOPHER WELDON
B. Jul. 26, 1963, Rahway, NJ
Purdue/San Diego State 6'1" 225 lbs.

| 1987 | NYG | N | 3 | LB |

Clarence Davis
DAVIS, CLARENCE EUGENE
B. Jun. 28, 1949, Birmingham, AL
Southern California 5'10" 191 lbs.

1971	OAK	N	14	RB
1972			11	RB
1973			14	RB
1974			11	RB
1975			11	RB
1976			12	RB
1977			14	RB
1978			2	RB

8 yrs. 89 games

Corby Davis
DAVIS, RICHARD CORBETT
B. Dec. 8, 1914, Lowell, IN
D. May, 1968
Indiana 5'11" 212 lbs.

1938	CLE	N	10	FB
1939			10	FB, QB
1941			8	QB, HB, FB
1942			9	FB

4 yrs. 37 games

Year	Team	Games	Pos.

Darrell Davis
DAVIS, DARRELL O.
B. Mar. 10, 1966, Houston, TX
Texas Christian 6'2" 258 lbs.

Year	Team	Games	Pos.
1990	**NYJ** N	15	DE
1991		13	DE
2 yrs.	28 games		

Dave Davis
DAVIS, DAVE
B. Jul. 5, 1948, Alcoa, TN
Tennessee State 6'0" 175 lbs.

Year	Team	Games	Pos.
1971	**GB** N	14	WR
1972		14	WR
1973	**PIT** N	2	WR
1974	**NO** N	6	WR
4 yrs.	36 games		

Dexter Davis
DAVIS, DEXTER WENDELL
B. Mar. 20, 1970, Brooklyn, NY
Clemson 5'10" 190 lbs.

Year	Team	Games	Pos.
1991	**PHX** N	11	CB
1992		16	CB
1993		6	CB
1993	**LARM** N	6	CB
1994		4	CB
1995	**STL** N	16	CB
5 yrs.	59 games		

Dick Davis
DAVIS, RICHARD
B. 1939
Kansas 6'2" 230 lbs.

Year	Team	Games	Pos.
1962	**DAL** A	12	DE

Dick Davis
DAVIS, RICHARD
B. Nov. 28, 1946, Omaha, NE
Nebraska 5'11" 215 lbs.

Year	Team	Games	Pos.
1970	**DEN** N	2	RB
1970	**NO** N	4	RB
1 yr.	6 games		

Don Davis
DAVIS, DON
B. Dec. 17, 1972, Olathe, KS
Kansas 6'1" 239 lbs.

Year	Team	Games	Pos.
1996	**NO** N	11	LB

Don Davis
DAVIS, DONALD
B. Dec. 16, 1943, Santa Ana, CA
Los Angeles State 6'6" 260 lbs.

Year	Team	Games	Pos.
1966	**NYG** N	14	DT

Donnie Davis
DAVIS, DONNIE RAY
B. Sep. 18, 1940, Opelousas, LA
Southern University 6'4" 220 lbs.

Year	Team	Games	Pos.
1962	**DAL** N	10	FL
1970	**HOU** N	14	TE
2 yrs.	24 games		

Doug Davis
DAVIS, DOUGLAS SHERONE
B. Jul. 2, 1944, Elkton, MD
Kentucky 6'4" 250 lbs.

Year	Team	Games	Pos.
1966	**MIN** N	13	OT
1967		11	OT
1968		14	OT
1969		10	OT
1970		12	OT
1971		14	OT
1972		5	OT
7 yrs.	79 games		

Ed Davis
DAVIS, EDWARD (Doc)
B. Feb. 13, 1889
D. Jul., 1963
Indiana 5'10" 187 lbs.

Year	Team	Games	Pos.
1920	**MUN** A	1	T
1920	**DAY** A	6	G, T
1922	**COL** N	1	G
2 yrs.	8 games		

Elgin Davis
DAVIS, ELGIN
B. Oct. 23, 1965, Jacksonville, FL
Central Florida 5'10" 192 lbs.

Year	Team	Games	Pos.
1987	**NE** N	4	RB
1988		5	RB
2 yrs.	9 games		

Eric Davis
DAVIS, ERIC WAYNE
B. Jan. 26, 1968, Anniston, AL
Jacksonville State 5'11" 178 lbs.

Year	Team	Games	Pos.
1990	**SF** N	16	CB
1991		2	CB
1992		16	CB
1993		16	CB
1994		16	CB
1995		15	CB
1996	**CAR** N	16	CB
7 yrs.	97 games		

Fred Davis
DAVIS, FRED
B. Jul. 18, 1964
Western Carolina 5'10" 182 lbs.

Year	Team	Games	Pos.
1987	**SEA** N	1	CB

Fred Davis
DAVIS, FREDERICK L.
B. Feb. 15, 1918, Louisville, KY
Alabama 6'3" 244 lbs.

Year	Team	Games	Pos.
1941	**WAS** N	11	T
1942		11	T
1945		4	T
1946	**CHIB** N	11	T
1947		12	T
1948		12	T
1949		12	T
1950		12	T
1951		12	T
9 yrs.	97 games		

Gaines Davis
DAVIS, GAINES
B. 1913
Texas Tech 5'11" 230 lbs.

Year	Team	Games	Pos.
1936	**NYG** N	6	G

Gary Davis
DAVIS, GARY CURTIS
B. Sep. 7, 1954, Pomona, CA
California Poly (San Luis Obispo) 5'10" 203 lbs.

Year	Team	Games	Pos.
1976	**MIA** N	14	RB
1977		14	RB
1978		14	RB
1979		16	RB
1980	**TB** N	15	RB
1981		7	RB
6 yrs.	80 games		

Glenn Davis
DAVIS, GLENN
B. Sep. 12, 1934
Ohio State 6'0" 180 lbs.*

Year	Team	Games	Pos.
1960	**DET** N	4	OE

Glenn Davis *continued*

Year	Team	Games	Pos.
1961		8	OE
2 yrs.	12 games		

Glenn Davis
DAVIS, GLENN WOODWARD (Junior)
B. Dec. 26, 1924, Burbank, CA
Army 5'11" 170 lbs.

Year	Team	Games	Pos.
1950	**LA** N	12	HB
1951		11	HB
2 yrs.	23 games		

Greg Davis
DAVIS, GREGORY BRIAN
B. Oct. 29, 1965, Rome, GA
The Citadel 5'11" 17 lbs.

Year	Team	Games	Pos.
1987	**ATL** N	3	K, P
1988		16	K
1989	**NE** N	9	K
1989	**ATL** N	6	K
1990		16	K
1991	**PHX** N	16	K
1992		16	K, P
1993		16	K
1994	**ARI** N	14	K
1995		16	K
1996		9	K
10 yrs.	137 games		

Harper Davis
DAVIS, JULIUS HARPER (Julie)
B. Dec. 11, 1925, Clarksdale, MS
Mississippi State 5'11" 173 lbs.

Year	Team	Games	Pos.
1949	**LA** AA	11	HB, DB
1950	**CHIB** N	12	HB, DB
1951	**GB** N	12	HB, DB
3 yrs.	35 games		

Harrison Davis
DAVIS, HARRISON PAUL, III
B. Feb. 20, 1952, Salisbury, NC
Virginia 6'4" 220 lbs.

Year	Team	Games	Pos.
1974	**SD** N	12	WR

Henry Davis
DAVIS, HENRY LOUIS
B. Dec. 8, 1942, Slaughter, LA
Grambling State 6'3" 235 lbs.

Year	Team	Games	Pos.
1968	**NYG** N	14	LB
1969		14	LB
1970	**PIT** N	14	LB
1971		14	LB
1972		14	LB
1973		14	LB
6 yrs.	84 games		

Herb Davis
DAVIS, HERBERT E.
B. Apr. 2, 1899
D. Jan. 1, 1986, San Lorenzo, CA
Xavier (Ohio) 5'10" 175 lbs.

Year	Team	Games	Pos.
1925	**COL** N	4	E, HB, QB
1926		6	QB, HB
2 yrs.	10 games		

Isaac Davis
DAVIS, JOHN ISAAC
B. Apr. 8, 1972, Malvern, AR
Arkansas 6'3" 325 lbs.

Year	Team	Games	Pos.
1994	**SD** N	13	G
1995		16	G
1996		14	G
3 yrs.	43 games		

Jack Davis
DAVIS, JACK
B. 1932
Maryland 6'0" 226 lbs.

Year	Team	Games	Pos.
1960	**DEN** A		G

Jack Davis
DAVIS, JACK OWEN
B. Feb. 19, 1933, Heavener, OK
Arizona 6'2" 235 lbs.

Year	Team	Games	Pos.
1960	**BOS** A		G

James Davis
DAVIS, JAMES STEVEN
B. Jun. 12, 1957, Los Angeles, CA
Southern University 6'0" 190 lbs.

Year	Team	Games	Pos.
1982	**LARI** N	9	CB
1983		16	CB
1984		15	CB
1985		15	CB
1986		16	CB
1987		12	CB
6 yrs.	83 games		

Jeff Davis
DAVIS, JEFFREY EUGENE
B. Jan. 26, 1960, Greensboro, NC
Clemson 6'0" 230 lbs.

Year	Team	Games	Pos.
1982	**TB** N	9	LB
1983		15	LB
1984		16	LB
1985		16	LB
1986		16	LB
1987		11	LB
6 yrs.	83 games		

Jerome Davis
DAVIS, JEROME
B. Feb. 27, 1962
Ball State 6'1" 260 lbs.

Year	Team	Games	Pos.
1987	**DET** N	3	NT

Jerry Davis
DAVIS, JEROME W. (Weasel)
B. Jan. 5, 1924, Savannah, GA
Southeastern Louisiana 5'10" 178 lbs.

Year	Team	Games	Pos.
1948	**CHIC** N	11	HB, DB
1949		9	DB
1950		11	DB
1951		8	DB
1952	**DAL** N	7	DB
5 yrs.	46 games		

Jerry Davis
DAVIS, JERRY WAYNE
B. Feb. 5, 1951, Macon, GA
Morris Brown 5'11" 182 lbs.

Year	Team	Games	Pos.
1975	**NYJ** N	6	CB

Joe Davis
DAVIS, JOSEPH A.
B. 1921
Southern California 6'2" 195 lbs.

Year	Team	Games	Pos.
1946	**BKN** AA	14	E

John Davis
DAVIS, JOHN
B. 1896
Deceased
None

Year	Team	Games	Pos.
1920	**COL** A	4	HB, FB, QB

John Davis
DAVIS, JOHN HENRY
B. Aug. 22, 1965, Ellijay, GA

Year	Team	Games	Pos.

John Davis continued

Georgia Tech 6'4" 304 lbs.

Year	Team		Games	Pos.
1987	HOU	N	6	OL
1988			13	OT
1989	BUF	N	16	C, OT
1990			16	OT
1991			12	OT
1992			9	G
1993			16	G
1994			16	G
8 yrs.	104 games			

Johnny Davis

DAVIS, JOHNNY LEE
B. Jul. 17, 1956, Montgomery, AL
Alabama 6'1" 235 lbs.

Year	Team		Games	Pos.
1978	TB	N	16	RB
1979			16	FB
1980			14	RB
1981	SF	N	16	RB
1982	CLE	N	2	RB
1983			16	RB
1984			16	RB
1985			16	FB
1986			6	RB
1987			1	RB
10 yrs.	119 games			

Kelvin Davis

DAVIS, KELVIN
B. Feb. 7, 1963
Johnson C. Smith 6'2" 260 lbs.

Year	Team		Games	Pos.
1987	NYG	N	1	G

Kenneth Davis

DAVIS, KENNETH EARL (The Texas Twister)
B. Apr. 16, 1962, Williamson County, TX
Texas Christian 5'10" 209 lbs.

Year	Team		Games	Pos.
1986	GB	N	16	RB
1987			10	RB
1988			9	RB
1989	BUF	N	16	RB
1990			16	RB
1991			16	RB
1992			16	RB
1993			16	RB
1994			16	RB
9 yrs.	131 games			

Kyle Davis

DAVIS, KYLE
B. Oct. 1, 1952, Cordell, OK
Oklahoma 6'4" 240 lbs.

Year	Team		Games	Pos.
1975	DAL	N	14	C
1978	SF	N	7	C
2 yrs.	21 games			

Lamar Davis

DAVIS, R. LAMAR (Racehorse)
B. Jun. 15, 1921, Brunswick, GA
Georgia 6'1" 185 lbs.

Year	Team		Games	Pos.
1946	MIA	AA		E, DB
1947	BAL	AA	13	E, DB
1948			14	E, DB
1949			12	E, DB
4 yrs.	39 games			

Lee Davis

DAVIS, LEE ANDREW
B. Dec. 18, 1962, Okolona, MS
Mississippi 5'11" 198 lbs.

Year	Team		Games	Pos.
1985	CIN	N	7	CB
1987	IND	N	3	S, CB
2 yrs.	10 games			

Lorenzo Davis

DAVIS, LORENZO EDWARD
B. Feb. 12, 1968, Fort Lauderdale, FL
Youngstown State 5'11" 185 lbs.

Year	Team		Games	Pos.
1990	PIT	N	4	WR

Marvin Davis

DAVIS, MARVIN
B. May 25, 1952, Shreveport, LA
Southern University 6'4" 235 lbs.

Year	Team		Games	Pos.
1974	HOU	N	13	LB

Marvin Davis

DAVIS, MARVIN DANIEL (Butch)
B. Jun. 6, 1943, Jacksonville, FL
Wichita State 6'4" 252 lbs.

Year	Team		Games	Pos.
1966	DEN	A	1	DE

Mike Davis

DAVIS, MICHAEL ALLEN
B. Jan. 14, 1972, Springfield, OH
Cincinnati 6'1" 192 lbs.

Year	Team		Games	Pos.
1994	HOU	N	16	CB
1995	CLE	N	3	CB
2 yrs.	19 games			

Mike Davis

DAVIS, MICHAEL LEONARD
B. Apr. 15, 1956, Los Angeles, CA
Colorado 6'3" 200 lbs.

Year	Team		Games	Pos.
1978	OAK	N	16	CB
1979			16	S
1980			16	S
1981			7	S
1982	LARI	N	9	S
1983			16	S
1984			16	S
1985			11	S
1987	SD	N	8	S
9 yrs.	115 games			

Milt Davis

DAVIS, MILTON E.
B. May 31, 1929, Los Angeles, CA
UCLA 6'1" 188 lbs.

Year	Team		Games	Pos.
1957	BAL	N	12	DB
1958			10	DB
1959			11	DB
1960			12	DB
4 yrs.	45 games			

Norm Davis

DAVIS, NORMAN
B. Aug. 8, 1945, Cocoa, FL
Grambling State 6'3" 247 lbs.

Year	Team		Games	Pos.
1967	BAL	N	14	G
1969	NO	N	12	G
1970	PHI	N	14	G
3 yrs.	40 games			

Oliver Davis

DAVIS, OLIVER JAMES
B. Aug. 29, 1954, Columbus, GA
Tennessee State 5'11" 203 lbs.

Year	Team		Games	Pos.
1977	CLE	N	14	S
1978			15	CB
1979			16	CB
1980			15	CB
1981	CIN	N	10	S
1982			9	S
6 yrs.	79 games			

Pahl Davis

DAVIS, PAHL
B. Mar. 4, 1897
D. Oct., 1971, Hemet, CA

Pahl Davis continued

Marquette 5'9" 185 lbs.

Year	Team		Games	Pos.
1922	GB	N	6	G, FB, E

Paschall Davis

DAVIS, PASCHALL TEDERALL
B. Jun. 5, 1969, Bryan, TX
Texas A&M-Kingsville 6'2" 225 lbs.

Year	Team		Games	Pos.
1995	STL	N	3	LB
1996			11	LB
2 yrs.	14 games			

Paul Davis

DAVIS, PAUL
B. 1925
Otterbein 6'1" 188 lbs.

Year	Team		Games	Pos.
1947	PIT	N	5	FB, DB
1948			6	FB, DB
2 yrs.	11 games			

Paul Davis

DAVIS, PAUL CALVIN
B. Jul. 10, 1958, Appalachia, VA
North Carolina 6'2" 214 lbs.

Year	Team		Games	Pos.
1981	ATL	N	13	LB
1982			9	LB
1983	NYG	N	3	LB
1983	STL	N	6	LB
3 yrs.	31 games			

Preston Davis

DAVIS, PRESTON
B. Mar. 10, 1962, Lubbock, TX
Baylor 5'11" 173 lbs.

Year	Team		Games	Pos.
1984	IND	N	12	CB
1985			16	CB
1986			8	CB
3 yrs.	36 games			

Ralph Davis

DAVIS, RALPH G.
B. May 30, 1922, Seymour, WI
Wisconsin 5'11" 205 lbs.

Year	Team		Games	Pos.
1947	GB	N	11	G
1948			11	G
2 yrs.	22 games			

Ray Davis

DAVIS, RAYMOND L.
B. 1910
Samford 6'1" 196 lbs.

Year	Team		Games	Pos.
1932	POR	N	11	C, T
1933			4	G, E
1936	CHIC	N	2	E
3 yrs.	17 games			

Red Davis

DAVIS, SYLVESTER
B. 1908
D. Aug., 1988
Geneva College 5'11" 195 lbs.

Year	Team		Games	Pos.
1933	PHI	N	7	HB, FB

Reuben Davis

DAVIS, REUBEN CORDELL
B. May 7, 1965, Greensboro, NC
North Carolina 6'4" 290 lbs.

Year	Team		Games	Pos.
1988	TB	N	16	DE
1989			16	DE
1990			16	DE
1991			12	DE
1992			3	DE, NT
1992	PHX	N	11	DE
1993			16	DE
1994	SD	N	16	DT
1995			16	DT

Reuben Davis continued

Year	Team		Games	Pos.
1996			15	DT
9 yrs.	137 games			

Ricky Davis

DAVIS, RICHARD TERRELL
B. May 18, 1953, Birmingham, AL
Alabama 6'1" 180 lbs.

Year	Team		Games	Pos.
1975	CIN	N	14	S
1976	TB	N	14	DB
1977	KC	N	13	CB
3 yrs.	41 games			

Robert Davis

DAVIS, ROBERT EMMETT
B. Dec. 10, 1968, Washington, DC
Shippensburg 6'2" 270 lbs.

Year	Team		Games	Pos.
1996	CHI	N	16	DT

Roger Davis

DAVIS, ROGER W.
B. Jun. 23, 1938, Cleveland, OH
Syracuse 6'3" 236 lbs.

Year	Team		Games	Pos.
1960	CHI	N	12	G
1961			14	G
1962			9	G
1963			13	G
1964	LA	N	11	G
1965	NYG	N	3	G
1966			10	G
7 yrs.	72 games			

Ron Davis

DAVIS, RONALD ROZELLE
B. Feb. 24, 1972, Bartlett, TN
Tennessee 5'10" 190 lbs.

Year	Team		Games	Pos.
1995	ATL	N	12	CB

Ron Davis

DAVIS, RONALD WILLARD
B. Sep. 16, 1950, Camden, NJ
Virginia State 6'2" 235 lbs.

Year	Team		Games	Pos.
1973	STL	N	2	G

Rosey Davis

DAVIS, ROOSEVELT
B. Nov. 29, 1941, Jackson, MS
Tennessee State 6'5" 260 lbs.

Year	Team		Games	Pos.
1965	NYG	N	14	DE
1966			7	DE
1967			1	DE
3 yrs.	22 games			

Russell Davis

DAVIS, RUSSELL, III
B. Sep. 15, 1956, Millen, GA
Michigan 6'1" 228 lbs.

Year	Team		Games	Pos.
1980	PIT	N	14	RB
1981			16	RB
1982			7	RB
1983			5	RB
4 yrs.	42 games			

Sam Davis

DAVIS, SAMUEL RUEL
B. Jul. 5, 1944, Jacksonville, FL
Allen 6'1" 251 lbs.

Year	Team		Games	Pos.
1967	PIT	N	14	G, OT
1968			14	G, OT
1969			12	G
1970			14	G
1971			12	G
1972			11	G
1973			12	G
1974			11	G
1975			14	G

Year	Team	Games	Pos.

Sam Davis continued

Year	Team	Games	Pos.
1976		13	G
1977		11	G
1978		16	G
1979		13	G
13 yrs.	167 games		

Scott Davis

DAVIS, SCOTT
B. Aug. 7, 1965, Joliet, IL
Illinois 6'7" 270 lbs.

1988	LARI	N	15	DE
1989			14	DE
1990			16	DE
1991			16	DE
1994			14	DE
5 yrs.	75 games			

Scott Davis

DAVIS, SCOTT
B. Jan. 29, 1970, Glenwood, IA
Iowa 6'3" 289 lbs.

1993	NYG	N	4	G
1994			15	G
2 yrs.	19 games			

Sonny Davis

DAVIS, ARNOLD ALLEN
B. Sep. 25, 1938
Baylor 6'2" 220 lbs.

1961	DAL	N	2	LB

Stan Davis

DAVIS, STANLEY WAYNE
B. Jul. 13, 1950, Memphis, TN
Memphis State 5'10" 180 lbs.

1973	PHI	N	8	WR

Stephen Davis

DAVIS, STEPHEN
B. Mar. 1, 1974, Spartanburg, SC
Auburn 6'0" 227 lbs.

1996	WAS	N	12	RB

Steve Davis

DAVIS, STEVEN TIMOTHY
B. Nov. 10, 1948, Lexington, VA
Delaware State 6'1" 216 lbs.

1972	PIT	N	11	RB
1973			14	RB
1974			14	RB
1975	NYJ	N	14	RB
1976			14	RB
5 yrs.	67 games			

Ted Davis

DAVIS, RICHARD KENNETH
B. Jul. 27, 1942, Memphis, TN
Georgia Tech 6'1" 230 lbs.

1964	BAL	N	14	LB
1965			14	LB
1966			10	LB
1967	NO	N	10	LB
1968			14	LB
1969			14	LB
1970	MIA	N	14	LB
7 yrs.	90 games			

Terrell Davis

DAVIS, TERRELL
B. Oct. 28, 1972, San Diego, CA
Long Beach State/Georgia 5'11" 200 lbs.

1995	DEN	N	14	RB
1996			16	RB
2 yrs.	30 games			

Tommy Davis

DAVIS, THOMAS RAY
B. Oct. 13, 1934, Shreveport, LA
D. Apr. 3, 1987, Millbrae, CA
Louisiana State 6'0" 215 lbs.

1959	SF	N	12	P, K
1960			12	P, K
1961			14	P, K
1962			14	P, K
1963			14	P, K
1964			14	P, K
1965			14	P, K
1966			14	P, K
1967			14	K
1968			9	K
1969			7	P, K
11 yrs.	138 games			

Tony Davis

DAVIS, MICHAEL E.
B. Jan. 21, 1953, Tecumseh, NE
Nebraska 5'10" 211 lbs.

1976	CIN	N	14	RB
1977			14	RB
1978			14	RB
1979	TB	N	16	RB
1980			15	RB
1981			16	RB
6 yrs.	89 games			

Travis Davis

DAVIS, TRAVIS
B. Jan. 10, 1973, Harbor City, CA
Notre Dame 6'0" 200 lbs.

1995	JAC	N	9	S
1996			16	S
2 yrs.	25 games			

Travis Davis

DAVIS, TRAVIS NEIL
B. May 10, 1966, Warren, OH
Michigan State 6'2" 279 lbs.

1990	NO	N	2	NT
1991	IND	N	16	DT
2 yrs.	18 games			

Ty Davis

DAVIS, TYRONE
B. Nov. 17, 1961, Athens, GA
Clemson 6'1" 190 lbs.

1985	NYG	N	7	CB, S

Tyree Davis

DAVIS, TYREE
B. Sep. 28, 1970, Altheimer, AR
Central Arkansas 5'9" 175 lbs.

1995	TB	N	1	WR

Tyrone Davis

DAVIS, TYRONE
B. Jun. 30, 1972, Halifax, VA
Virginia 6'4" 229 lbs.

1995	NYJ	N	4	WR
1996			2	WR
2 yrs.	6 games			

Van Davis

DAVIS, VAN ANDREW, JR.
B. 1922
D. Jul. 11, 1987
Georgia 6'2" 215 lbs.

1947	NY	AA	13	E
1948			13	E
1949	B, NY	AA	11	E
3 yrs.	37 games			

Vern Davis

DAVIS, VERNON
B. Nov. 2, 1949, Dowagiac, MI
Western Michigan 6'4" 208 lbs.

1971	PHI	N	3	DB

Wayne Davis

DAVIS, C. WAYNE
B. Mar. 10, 1964, Tuscaloosa, AL
Alabama 6'1" 213 lbs.

1987	STL	N	12	LB
1988	PHX	N	16	LB
2 yrs.	28 games			

Wayne Davis

DAVIS, WAYNE ELLIOT
B. Jul. 17, 1963, Cincinnati, OH
Indiana State 5'11" 175 lbs.

1985	SD		16	CB
1986			16	CB
1987	BUF	N	10	CB
1988			16	CB
1989			6	CB
1989	WAS	N	8	CB
1990			1	CB
6 yrs.	73 games			

Wendell Davis

DAVIS, WENDELL
B. Jun. 27, 1973, Wichita, KS
Oklahoma 5'10" 184 lbs.

1996	DAL	N	13	CB

Wendell Davis

DAVIS, WENDELL TYRONE
B. Jan. 3, 1966, Shreveport, LA
Louisiana State 5'11" 188 lbs.

1988	CHI	N	16	WR
1989			14	WR
1990			14	WR
1991			16	WR
1992			16	WR
1993			5	WR
6 yrs.	81 games			

Willie Davis

DAVIS, WILLIAM DELFORD
B. Jul. 24, 1934, Lisbon, LA
Grambling State 6'3" 243 lbs.

1958	CLE	N	12	E, T
1959			12	T
1960	GB	N	12	E
1961			14	DE
1962			14	DE
1963			14	DE
1964			14	DE
1965			14	DE
1966			14	DE
1967			14	DE
1968			14	DE
1969			14	DE
12 yrs.	162 games			

Willie Davis

DAVIS, WILLIE CLARK
B. Oct. 10, 1967, Little Rock, AR
Central Arkansas 6'0" 170 lbs.

1991	KC	N	1	WR
1992			16	WR
1993			16	WR
1994			14	WR
1995			16	WR
1996	HOU	N	16	WR
6 yrs.	79 games			

Jerone Davison

DAVISON, JERONE LAMAR

Jerone Davison continued

B. Sep. 16, 1970, Picayune, MS
Arizona State 6'1" 225 lbs.

1996	OAK	N	2	RB

Mike Davlin

DAVLIN, MICHAEL F.
B. 1928, Omaha, NE
Notre Dame/San Francisco 6'1" 230 lbs.

1955	WAS	N	9	T

Brian Dawkins

DAWKINS, BRIAN
B. Oct. 13, 1973, Jacksonville, FL
Clemson 5'11" 188 lbs.

1996	PHI	N	14	S

Dale Dawkins

DAWKINS, DALE
B. Oct. 30, 1966, Vero Beach, FL
Miami (Florida) 6'1" 190 lbs.

1990	NYJ	N	11	WR
1991			15	WR
1992			6	WR
1993			4	WR
4 yrs.	36 games			

Joe Dawkins

DAWKINS, JOSEPH, III
B. Jan. 27, 1948, Los Angeles, CA
Wisconsin 5'11" 221 lbs.

1970	HOU	N	14	RB
1971	DEN	N	8	RB
1972			14	RB
1973			14	RB
1974	NYG	N	14	RB
1975			14	RB
1976	HOU	N	14	RB
7 yrs.	92 games			

Julius Dawkins

DAWKINS, JULIUS
B. Jan. 4, 1961, Monessen, PA
Pittsburgh 6'1" 196 lbs.

1983	BUF	N	11	WR
1984			16	WR
2 yrs.	27 games			

Sean Dawkins

DAWKINS, SEAN RUSSELL
B. Feb. 3, 1971, Red Bank, NJ
California 6'4" 213 lbs.

1993	IND	N	16	WR
1994			16	WR
1995			16	WR
1996			15	WR
4 yrs.	63 games			

Tommy Dawkins

DAWKINS, TOMMY
B. May 8, 1965
Appalachian State 6'3" 260 lbs.

1987	PIT	N	2	DE

Fred Dawley

DAWLEY, FRED
B. 1921
Michigan 5'9" 190 lbs.

1944	DET	N	2	B

Lawrence Dawsey

DAWSEY, LAWRENCE
B. Nov. 16, 1967, Dothan, AL
Florida State 6'0" 195 lbs.

1991	TB	N	16	WR

Lawrence Dawsey continued

Year	Team		Games	Pos.
1992			15	WR
1993			4	WR
1994			10	WR
1995			12	WR
1996	NYG	N	16	WR

6 yrs. 73 games

Stacey Dawsey
DAWSEY, STACEY
B. Oct. 24, 1965, Bradenton, FL
Indiana 5'9" 154 lbs.

Year	Team		Games	Pos.
1987	NO	N	3	WR

Bill Dawson
DAWSON, WILLIAM
B. 1943
Florida State 6'3" 240 lbs.

Year	Team		Games	Pos.
1965	BOS	A	9	TE, DE

Dale Dawson
DAWSON, DALE
B. Nov. 2, 1964, West Palm Beach, FL
Eastern Kentucky 6'0" 213 lbs.

Year	Team		Games	Pos.
1987	MIN	N	3	K
1988	PHI	N	1	K
1988	GB	N	4	K

2 yrs. 8 games

Dermontti Dawson
DAWSON, DERMONTTI FARRA
B. Jul. 17, 1965, Lexington, KY
Kentucky 6'2" 271 lbs.

Year	Team		Games	Pos.
1988	PIT	N	8	C, G
1989			16	G, C
1990			16	C, G
1991			16	C
1992			16	C
1993			16	C
1994			16	C
1995			16	C
1996			16	C

9 yrs. 136 games

Doug Dawson
DAWSON, DOUGLAS ARLIN
B. Dec. 27, 1961, Houston, TX
Texas 6'3" 267 lbs.

Year	Team		Games	Pos.
1984	STL	N	15	G
1985			16	G
1986			1	G
1990	HOU	N	16	G, C
1991			14	G, C
1992			16	C, G
1993			16	G
1994	CLE	N	13	G

8 yrs. 107 games

Gib Dawson
DAWSON, GILBERT HENRY
B. Aug. 27, 1930, Bisbee, AZ
Texas 5'11" 180 lbs.

Year	Team		Games	Pos.
1953	GB	N	7	HB

Lake Dawson
DAWSON, LAKE
B. Jan. 2, 1972, Boston, MA
Notre Dame 6'1" 204 lbs.

Year	Team		Games	Pos.
1994	KC	N	12	WR
1995			16	WR
1996			4	WR

3 yrs. 32 games

Len Dawson
DAWSON, LEONARD RAY
B. Jun. 20, 1935, Alliance, OH

Len Dawson continued
Purdue 6'0" 190 lbs.

Year	Team		Games	Pos.
1957	PIT	N	3	QB
1958			4	QB
1959			12	QB
1960	CLE	N	2	QB
1961			6	QB
1962	DAL	A	14	QB
1963	KC	A	14	QB
1964			14	QB
1965			14	QB
1966			14	QB
1967			14	QB
1968			14	QB
1969			8	QB
1970	KC	N	13	QB
1971			14	QB
1972			14	QB
1973			9	QB
1974			14	QB
1975			12	QB

19 yrs. 209 games

Lin Dawson
DAWSON, JAMES LINWOOD
B. Jun. 24, 1959, Norfolk, VA
North Carolina State 6'3" 240 lbs.

Year	Team		Games	Pos.
1981	NE	N	15	TE
1982			8	TE
1983			13	TE
1984			16	TE
1985			16	TE
1987			12	TE
1988			6	TE
1989			16	TE
1990			3	TE

9 yrs. 105 games

Mike Dawson
DAWSON, MICHAEL D.
B. Oct. 16, 1953, Dorking, England
Arizona 6'3" 260 lbs.

Year	Team		Games	Pos.
1976	STL	N	13	DT
1977			14	DT
1978			16	DT
1979			16	DT
1980			4	DE
1981			16	DT
1982			9	DT
1983	DET	N	16	DT
1984	KC	N	9	NT

9 yrs. 113 games

Rhett Dawson
DAWSON, RHETT MOTTE
B. Dec. 22, 1948, Valdosta, GA
Florida State 6'1" 185 lbs.

Year	Team		Games	Pos.
1972	HOU	N	14	WR
1973	MIN	N	2	WR

2 yrs. 16 games

Al Day
DAY, ALBERT E.
B. 1938
Eastern Michigan 6'2" 216 lbs.

Year	Team		Games	Pos.
1960	DEN	A		LB

Eagle Day
DAY, HERMAN S.
B. Oct. 2, 1932, Columbia, MS
Mississippi 6'0" 183 lbs.

Year	Team		Games	Pos.
1959	WAS	N	4	QB
1960			12	QB, P

2 yrs. 16 games

Fred Day
DAY, FREDERIC SAMUEL
B. Jul. 4, 1896

Fred Day continued
Deceased
Ohio Wesleyan 6'2" 195 lbs.

Year	Team		Games	Pos.
1921	CIN	A	1	T

Tom Day
DAY, THOMAS FREDERICK
B. Aug. 20, 1935, Washington, DC
North Carolina A&T 6'2" 252 lbs.

Year	Team		Games	Pos.
1960	STL	N	10	T, G
1961	BUF	A	12	DT
1962			14	DT, G
1963			14	G
1964			14	DE
1965			14	DE
1966			14	DE
1967	SD	A	11	DE
1968	BUF	A	14	DE

9 yrs. 117 games

Harry Dayhoff
DAYHOFF, HARRY OSCAR
B. May 25, 1896, Gettysburg, PA
D. Feb. 17, 1963, Harrisburg, PA
Bucknell 5'8" 170 lbs.

Year	Team		Games	Pos.
1924	FRA	N	11	HB, FB, QB
1925	POT	N	1	HB, QB

2 yrs. 12 games

Tony Daykin
DAYKIN, ANTHONY ALBERT
B. May 13, 1955, Taipei, Taiwan
Georgia Tech 6'1" 215 lbs.

Year	Team		Games	Pos.
1977	DET	N	14	LB
1978			16	LB
1979	ATL	N	11	LB
1980			16	LB
1981			16	LB

5 yrs. 73 games

Rufus Deal
DEAL, RUFUS COPELAND (Gus)
B. Dec. 7, 1917, Moundsville, AL
Auburn 6'0" 205 lbs.

Year	Team		Games	Pos.
1942	WAS	N	5	B

Dean
DEAN
None

Year	Team		Games	Pos.
1926	CLE	A	1	T

Floyd Dean
DEAN, THOMAS FLOYD
B. Aug. 19, 1940
Florida 6'4" 245 lbs.

Year	Team		Games	Pos.
1964	SF	N	6	LB
1965			9	LB

2 yrs. 15 games

Fred Dean
DEAN, FREDERICK RUDOLPH
B. Feb. 24, 1952, Arcadia, LA
Louisiana Tech 6'3" 227 lbs.

Year	Team		Games	Pos.
1975	SD	N	14	DE
1976			14	DE
1977			11	DE
1978			15	DE
1979			13	DE
1980			14	DE
1981			3	DE
1981	SF	N	11	DE
1982			9	DE
1983			16	DE
1984			5	DE
1985			16	DE

11 yrs. 141 games

Fred Dean
DEAN, FREDERICK GREGORY
B. Mar. 30, 1955, Gainesville, FL
Texas Southern 6'3" 253 lbs.

Year	Team		Games	Pos.
1978	WAS	N	8	G
1979			15	G
1980			12	G
1982			5	G

4 yrs. 40 games

Hal Dean
DEAN, HAL S.
B. Oct. 30, 1922, Wooster, OH
Ohio State 6'0" 205 lbs.

Year	Team		Games	Pos.
1947	LA	N	12	G
1948			11	G
1949			12	G

3 yrs. 35 games

Jimmy Dean
DEAN, JIMMY
B. Jan. 8, 1955, Bryan, TX
Texas A&M 6'4" 252 lbs.

Year	Team		Games	Pos.
1978	HOU	N	3	DE

Kevin Dean
DEAN, KEVIN JAMES
B. Feb. 5, 1965, Newton, TX
Texas Christian 6'1" 235 lbs.

Year	Team		Games	Pos.
1987	SF	N	4	LB

Randy Dean
DEAN, RANDOLPH HUME
B. Jun. 10, 1955, Milwaukee, WI
Northwestern 6'3" 195 lbs.

Year	Team		Games	Pos.
1977	NYG	N	1	QB
1978			6	QB
1979			16	QB

3 yrs. 23 games

Ted Dean
DEAN, THEODORE CURTIS
B. Mar. 24, 1938
Wichita State 6'2" 211 lbs.

Year	Team		Games	Pos.
1960	PHI	N	12	HB, FB
1961			14	HB
1962			2	HB
1963			14	HB
1964	MIN	N	2	HB, FB

5 yrs. 44 games

Tom Dean
DEAN, THOMAS E.
B. 1924
Deceased
Southern Methodist 6'2" 248 lbs.

Year	Team		Games	Pos.
1946	BOS	N	9	T
1947			12	T

2 yrs. 21 games

Vernon Dean
DEAN, VERNON
B. May 5, 1959, Los Angeles, CA
U.S. International/San Diego State 5'11" 178 lbs.

Year	Team		Games	Pos.
1982	WAS	N	9	CB, S
1983			16	CB, S
1984			16	CB
1985			16	CB
1986			16	CB
1987			12	CB
1988	SEA	N	16	S

7 yrs. 101 games

Walter Dean
DEAN, WALTER KEVIN

Year	Team	Games	Pos.

Walter Dean *continued*

B. May 1, 1968, Ruston, LA
Grambling State 5'10" 216 lbs.

Year	Team		Games	Pos.
1991	GB	N	9	RB

Kiki DeAyala
DEAYALA, JULIAN LEWIS
B. Oct. 23, 1961, Miami, FL
Texas 6'1" 225 lbs.

1986	CIN	N	16	LB
1987			12	LB
2 yrs.		28 games		

Steve DeBerg
DEBERG, STEVEN L.
B. Jan. 19, 1954, Oakland, CA
San Jose State 6'3" 210 lbs.

1978	SF	N	12	QB
1979			16	QB
1980			11	QB
1981	DEN	N	14	QB
1982			9	QB
1983			10	QB
1984	TB	N	11	QB
1985			11	QB
1986			16	QB
1987			12	QB
1988	KC	N	13	QB
1989			12	QB
1990			16	QB
1991			16	QB
1992	TB	N	6	QB
1993			3	QB
1993	MIA	N	5	QB
16 yrs.		198 games		

Fred DeBernardi
DEBERNARDI, FRANK FREDERICK
B. Mar. 2, 1949, Saugus, CA
Texas-El Paso 6'4" 250 lbs.

| 1974 | KC | N | 7 | DE |

Case deBruijn
DEBRUIJN, CASE
B. Apr. 11, 1960, The Hague, Netherlands
Idaho State 6'1" 176 lbs.

| 1982 | KC | N | 1 | P |

Nick DeCarbo
DECARBO, NICHOLAS FRED
B. Jan. 29, 1906, Pennsylvania
D. Apr., 1964, Pennsylvania
Duquesne 5'9" 185 lbs.

| 1933 | PIT | N | 11 | G |

Art DeCarlo
DECARLO, ARTHUR ANTHONY, JR.
B. Mar. 23, 1931, Youngstown, OH
Georgia 6'2" 196 lbs.

1953	PIT	N	12	DB
1956	WAS	N	12	DB
1957			2	DB
1957	BAL	N	6	DB
1958			12	DB, OE
1959			8	DB, OE
1960			9	DB, OE
6 yrs.		61 games		

Frank DeClerk
DECLERK, FRANCIS P.
B. 1899
Deceased
St. Ambrose 5'9" 189 lbs.

| 1923 | RI | N | 6 | C |

Frank DeClerk *continued*

1924			8	C
1925			6	C
3 yrs.		20 games		

Bill deCorrevont
DECORREVONT, WILLIAM JOHN
B. Nov. 26, 1918, Chicago, IL
D. Sep. 6, 1995, Largo, FL
Northwestern 6'0" 186 lbs.

1945	WAS	N	10	HB, DB
1946	DET	N	9	HB, DB
1947	CHIC	N	12	HB, DB
1948	CHIB	N	10	HB, DB
1949			8	HB, DB
5 yrs.		49 games		

Bob Dee
DEE, ROBERT HENRY
B. Jan. 9, 1935, Quincy, MA
D. Apr. 18, 1979, Portsmouth, NH
Holy Cross 6'3" 248 lbs.

1957	WAS	N	11	DE
1958			11	DE
1960	BOS	A	14	DE
1961			14	DE
1962			14	DE
1963			14	DE
1964			14	DE
1965			14	DE
1966			14	DE
1967			14	DE
10 yrs.		134 games		

Donnie Dee
DEE, DONNIE, JR.
B. Mar. 17, 1965, Kansas City, MO
Tulsa 6'4" 247 lbs.

1988	IND	N	13	TE
1989			1	TE
1989	SEA	N	4	TE
2 yrs.		18 games		

Don Deeks
DEEKS, DONALD P.
B. Feb. 10, 1923, Portland, OR
Washington 6'4" 238 lbs.

1945	BOS	N	7	T
1946			8	T
1947			3	T
1947	WAS		3	T
1948	GB	N	8	G
4 yrs.		29 games		

Dick Deer Slayer
DEER SLAYER, DICK
None 190 lbs.

| 1922 | OOR | N | 2 | E |

Bob Dees
DEES, ROBERT
B. 1930
Southwest Missouri State 6'4" 245 lbs.

| 1952 | GB | N | 9 | T |

Derrick Deese
DEESE, DERRICK
B. May 17, 1970, Culver City, CA
Southern California 6'3" 270 lbs.

1994	SF	N	16	G
1995			2	G
1996			16	G
3 yrs.		34 games		

Nick DeFelice
DEFELICE, NICHOLAS FRANCIS
B. Feb. 4, 1940, Derby, CT
Southern Connecticut State 6'3" 250 lbs.

1965	NY	A	14	OT
1966	NY	A	3	OT
2 yrs.		17 games		

Lou DeFilippo
DEFILIPPO, LOUIS PHILLIP
B. Aug. 28, 1916, East Haven, CT
Fordham 6'1" 230 lbs.

1941	NYG	N	11	C
1945			10	C
1946			11	C
1947			4	C
4 yrs.		36 games		

Joe DeForest
DEFOREST, JOE
B. Apr. 17, 1965, Teaneck, NJ
Southwestern Louisiana 6'1" 240 lbs.

| 1987 | NO | N | 3 | LB |

Chris DeFrance
DEFRANCE, CHRIS ANTHONY
B. Sep. 13, 1956, Waldo, AR
Arizona State 6'1" 205 lbs.

| 1979 | WAS | N | 4 | WR |

Bob DeFruiter
DEFRUITER, ROBERT ALBERT
B. Jun. 3, 1918, Smithfield, NE
Nebraska 6'0" 190 lbs.

1945	WAS	N	3	HB
1946			7	HB
1947			1	HB
1947	DET	N	8	HB
1948	LA	N	3	HB
4 yrs.		22 games		

Dick Degen
DEGEN, RICHARD
B. Mar. 4, 1942, Jamestown, ND
Long Beach State 6'1" 223 lbs.

1965	SD	A	12	LB
1966			10	LB
2 yrs.		22 games		

Allen DeGraffenreid
DEGRAFFENREID, ALLEN
B. May 1, 1970, Cincinnati, OH
Ohio State 6'3" 200 lbs.

| 1993 | CIN | N | 2 | WR |

Tony DeGrate
DEGRATE, TONY
B. Apr. 25, 1962, Snyder, TX
Texas 6'4" 280 lbs.

| 1985 | GB | N | 1 | DE |

Walt DeGree
DEGREE, WALTER BERNARD (Cy)
B. Jul. 7, 1898, St. Cloud, MN
D. Nov., 1961, Detroit, MI
Notre Dame 6'1" 210 lbs.

| 1921 | DET | A | 6 | T, G |

Jack DeGrenier
DEGRENIER, JOHN
B. Feb. 25, 1951, Chicago, IL
Texas-Arlington 6'1" 225 lbs.

| 1974 | NO | N | 12 | RB |

Art Deibel
DEIBEL, ARTHUR F.
B. Apr. 3, 1896
D. Apr., 1984, Clinton, OH
Lafayette 6'3" 235 lbs.

| 1926 | CAN | N | 7 | T, G |

Charles DeJurnett
DEJURNETT, CHARLES RAY
B. Jun. 17, 1952, Picayune, MS
San Jose State 6'4" 256 lbs.

1976	SD	N	13	DT
1977			11	DT
1978			15	DT
1979			12	DT
1980			15	DT
1982	LARM	N	4	DT
1983			10	DT
1984			16	NT
1985			15	NT
1986			7	NT
10 yrs.		118 games		

Al Dekdebrun
DEKDEBRUN, ALLEN EDWARD
B. May 11, 1921, Buffalo, NY
Cornell 5'11" 182 lbs.

1946	BUF	AA	14	QB
1947	CHI	AA	12	QB
1948	NY	AA	4	HB
1948	BOS	N	2	HB
3 yrs.		32 games		

Paul Dekker
DEKKER, PAUL N. (Hands)
B. Feb. 24, 1931, Muskegon, MI
Michigan State 6'5" 220 lbs.

| 1953 | WAS | N | 11 | E |

Joe DeLamielleure
DELAMIELLEURE, JOSEPH MICHAEL
B. Mar. 16, 1951, Detroit, MI
Michigan State 6'3" 256 lbs.

1973	BUF	N	14	G
1974			14	G
1975			14	G
1976			14	G
1977			14	G
1978			16	G
1979			16	G
1980	CLE	N	16	G
1981			16	G
1982			9	G
1983			16	G
1984			16	G
1985	BUF	N	10	G
13 yrs.		185 games		

Eddie Delaney
DELANEY, EDWARD
Villanova

| 1921 | SYR | A | 3 | HB |

Jeff Delaney
DELANEY, JEFFREY JOHN
B. Dec. 28, 1956, Pittsburgh, PA
Pittsburgh 6'0" 195 lbs.

1980	LA	N	16	S
1981	DET	N	5	CB
1981	TB	N	2	S
1982	BAL	N	8	S
1983			11	S
4 yrs.		42 games		

Joe Delaney
DELANEY, JOE ALTON

Year	Team		Games	Pos.

Joe Delaney *continued*

B. Oct. 30, 1958, Henderson, TX
D. Jun. 29, 1983, Monroe, LA
Northwestern State (Louisiana) 5'10"
184 lbs.

1981	KC	N	15	RB
1982			8	RB
2 yrs.	23 games			

Darroll DeLaPorte

DELAPORTE, DARROLL
B. Oct. 30, 1903
D. Dec., 1980, Bartow, FL
None

| 1925 | MIL | N | 1 | FB |

Bob DeLauer

DELAUER, ROBERT
B. Aug. 30, 1920, San Francisco, CA
Southern California 6'1" 218 lbs.

1945	CLE	N	2	C, LB
1946	LA	N	11	C, LB
2 yrs.	13 games			

Burt Delavan

DELAVAN, BURT DARRELL
B. Dec. 2, 1929, Westwood, CA
Pacific 6'2" 236 lbs.

1955	CHIC	N	12	T
1956			2	T
2 yrs.	14 games			

Jack Del Bello

DEL BELLO, JOHN V.
B. Dec. 9, 1927, Philadelphia, PA
Miami (Florida) 6'1" 190 lbs.

| 1953 | BAL | N | 5 | QB |

Tom DeLeone

DELEONE, THOMAS DENNING
B. Aug. 13, 1950, Ravenna, OH
Ohio State 6'2" 249 lbs.

1972	CIN	N	13	C, G
1973			14	C
1974	CLE	N	12	C
1975			14	C
1976			14	C
1977			14	C
1978			16	C
1979			16	C
1980			16	C
1981			8	C
1982			9	C
1983			16	C
1984			15	C
13 yrs.	177 games			

Jim Del Gaizo

DEL GAIZO, JAMES ROBERT
B. May 31, 1947, Everett, MA
Syracuse/Tampa 6'1" 194 lbs.

1972	MIA	N	4	QB
1973	GB	N	8	QB
1974	NYG	N	4	QB
3 yrs.	16 games			

Al Del Greco

DEL GRECO, ALBERT LOUIS, JR.
B. Mar. 2, 1962, Providence, RI
Auburn 5'10" 191 lbs.

1984	GB	N	9	K
1985			16	K
1986			16	K
1987			5	K
1987	STL	N	3	K
1988	PHX	N	16	K

Al Del Greco *continued*

1989			16	K
1990			16	K
1991	HOU	N	7	K
1992			16	K
1993			16	K
1994			16	K
1995			16	K
1996			16	K
13 yrs.	184 games			

Steve DeLine

DELINE, STEVE BRAUN
B. Aug. 19, 1961, Denver, CO
Colorado State 5'11" 185 lbs.

1988	SD	N	5	K
1989	PHI	N	3	K
2 yrs.	8 games			

Jim DeLisle

DELISLE, JAMES
B. Jan. 20, 1949, Wausau, WI
Wisconsin 6'4" 254 lbs.

| 1971 | GB | N | 9 | DT |

Jeff Dellenbach

DELLENBACH, JEFFREY ALAN
B. Feb. 14, 1963, Wausau, WI
Wisconsin 6'4" 280 lbs.

1985	MIA	N	11	OT
1986			13	OT
1987			11	OT
1988			16	OT, C
1989			16	C, OT
1990			15	OT, C
1991			15	OT, C
1992			16	OT, C
1993			16	OT, C
1994			16	C
1995	NE	N	15	C
1996			2	C, OT
1996	GB	N	3	C
12 yrs.	165 games			

Spiro Dellerba

DELLERBA, SPIRO
B. Jan. 25, 1923, Ashtabula, OH
D. Aug., 1968
Ohio State 5'11" 200 lbs.

1947	CLE	AA	8	FB, LB
1948	BAL	AA	14	LB
1949			9	LB
3 yrs.	31 games			

Larry Dellinger

DELLINGER, LAWRENCE
B. 1892
Deceased
None 5'11" 204 lbs.

1920	DAY	A	4	G
1921			7	G
1922	DAY	N	3	G
1923			6	G
4 yrs.	20 games			

Johnny Dell Isola

DELL ISOLA, JOHN JOSEPH
B. Feb. 12, 1912, Everett, MA
D. Oct. 21, 1986, Arlington, MA
Fordham 5'11" 201 lbs.

1934	NYG	N	6	C
1935			8	C, G
1936			10	G, C
1937			9	G
1938			11	G
1939			11	G
1940			10	G
7 yrs.	65 games			

Ralph DeLoach

DELOACH, RALPH ALAN
B. Jan. 13, 1957, Sacramento, CA
California 6'5" 254 lbs.

| 1981 | NYJ | N | 1 | DE |

Greg DeLong

DELONG, GREG
B. Apr. 3, 1973, Orefield, PA
North Carolina 6'4" 245 lbs.

1995	MIN	N	2	TE
1996			16	TE
2 yrs.	18 games			

Keith DeLong

DELONG, KEITH ALLEN
B. Aug. 14, 1967, San Diego, CA
Tennessee 6'2" 245 lbs.

1989	SF	N	15	LB
1990			16	LB
1991			15	LB
1992			14	LB
1993			4	LB
5 yrs.	64 games			

Steve DeLong

DELONG, STEVEN CYRIL
B. Jul. 3, 1943, Chesapeake, VA
Tennessee 6'3" 251 lbs.

1965	SD	A	12	DE
1966			14	DE
1967			7	DT
1968			14	DT
1969			14	DE
1970	SD	N	14	DE
1971			14	DT
1972	CHI	N	14	DE
8 yrs.	103 games			

Jack Deloplaine

DELOPLAINE, JACK
B. Apr. 21, 1954, Pottstown, PA
Salem 5'10" 205 lbs.

1976	PIT	N	14	RB
1977			8	RB
1978	WAS	N	2	RB
1978	PIT	N	10	RB
1979	CHI	N		RB
1979	PIT	N	1	RB
4 yrs.	35 games			

Robert Delpino

DELPINO, ROBERT LEWIS
B. Nov. 2, 1965, Dodge City, KS
Missouri 6'0" 205 lbs.

1988	LARM	N	15	RB
1989			16	RB
1990			15	RB
1991			16	RB
1992			10	RB
1993	DEN	N	16	RB
6 yrs.	88 games			

Jack Del Rio

DEL RIO, JACK
B. Apr. 4, 1963, Castro Valley, CA
Southern California 6'4" 238 lbs.

1985	NO	N	16	LB
1986			16	LB
1987	KC	N	10	LB
1988			15	LB
1989	DAL	N	14	LB
1990			16	LB
1991			16	LB
1992	MIN	N	16	LB
1993			16	LB
1994			16	LB

Jack Del Rio *continued*

| 1995 | | | 9 | LB |
| 11 yrs. | 160 games | | | |

Sam DeLuca

DELUCA, SAMUEL FRANK
B. May 2, 1936, Brooklyn, NY
South Carolina 6'2" 247 lbs.

1960	LA	A	13	OT
1961	SD	A	14	OT
1963			14	G
1964	NY	A	11	G
1965			14	G
1966			14	G
6 yrs.	80 games			

Tony DeLuca

DELUCA, TONY LAWRENCE
B. Nov. 16, 1960, Greenwich, CT
RhoDeIsland 6'4" 250 lbs.

| 1984 | GB | N | 1 | NT |

Jerry DeLucca

DELUCCA, GERALD
B. Jul. 17, 1936, Riverside, IL
Tennessee/Middle Tennessee State 6'3"
249 lbs.

1959	PHI	N	12	OT
1960	BOS	A		OT
1961			14	OT
1962	BUF	A	14	OT
1963			2	OT
1963	BOS	A	3	DT
1964			2	DT
6 yrs.	47 games			

Al DeMao

DEMAO, ALBERT MARCELLUS
B. Feb. 29, 1920, New Kensington, PA
Duquesne 6'2" 214 lbs.

1945	WAS	N	5	C
1946			11	C
1947			12	C
1948			9	C
1949			12	C
1950			12	C
1951			12	C
1952			12	C
1953			12	C
9 yrs.	97 games			

Bob DeMarco

DEMARCO, ROBERT ALBERT
B. Sep. 16, 1938, Jersey City, NJ
Indiana/Dayton 6'3" 243 lbs.

1961	STL	N	4	G
1962			14	G
1963			14	C
1964			12	C
1965			14	C
1966			9	C
1967			14	C
1968			12	C
1969			14	C
1970	MIA	N	11	C
1971			14	C
1972	CLE	N	12	C
1973			13	C
1974			14	C
1975	LA	N	14	C
15 yrs.	185 games			

Brian DeMarco

DEMARCO, BRIAN
B. Apr. 9, 1972, Berea, OH
Michigan State 6'5" 314 lbs.

| 1995 | JAC | N | 16 | OT |

Year	Team		Games	Pos.

Brian DeMarco *continued*

Year	Team		Games	Pos.
1996			10	OT
2 yrs.	26 games			

Mario DeMarco

DEMARCO, MARIO
B. 1927, Boonton, NJ
Deceased
Miami (Florida) 5'11" 200 lbs.

1949	DET	N	12	G

John Demarie

DEMARIE, JOHN E.
B. Aug. 28, 1945, Lake Charles, LA
Louisiana State 6'3" 250 lbs.

1967	CLE	N	14	OT
1968			14	G
1969			14	G
1970			14	G
1971			13	G
1972			14	G
1973			14	G
1974			11	G
1975			14	C
1976	SEA	N	9	G
10 yrs.	131 games			

George Demas

DEMAS, GEORGE J.
B. Jan. 7, 1907
D. Nov., 1977
Washington & Jefferson 6'0" 194 lbs.

1932	SI	N	3	G, C
1934	BKN	N	1	G
2 yrs.	4 games			

Calvin Demery

DEMERY, CALVIN LOUIS
B. Aug. 7, 1950, Phoenix, AZ
Arizona State 6'0" 190 lbs.

1972	MIN	N	5	WR

George Demko

DEMKO, GEORGE
B. 1935
Appalachian State 6'3" 240 lbs.

1961	PIT	N	1	DE

Joe Demmy

DEMMY, JOSEPH
None 190 lbs.

1930	SI	N	4	T
1931			3	T
2 yrs.	7 games			

Bill Demory

DEMORY, JOHN W.
B. Dec. 1, 1950, Phoenix, AZ
Arizona 6'2" 195 lbs.

1973	NYJ	N	6	QB
1974			1	QB
2 yrs.	7 games			

Bob De Moss

DEMOSS, ROBERT ALONZO
B. Jan. 27, 1927, Dayton, KY
Purdue 6'2" 185 lbs.

1949	NYB	N	3	QB

Dempsey

DEMPSEY
None

1921	SYR	A	1	T

Frank Dempsey

DEMPSEY, JAMES FRANKLIN
B. May 27, 1925, Dothan, AL
Florida 6'3" 235 lbs.

1950	CHIB	N	6	T
1951			12	G
1952			10	G
1953			11	G
4 yrs.	39 games			

John Dempsey

DEMPSEY, JOHN
B. Mar. 12, 1912, Scranton, PA
D. Aug. 26, 1988, Saratoga, CA
Bucknell 6'2" 225 lbs.

1934	PHI	N	1	T
1934	PIT	N	1	T
1937	PHI	N	2	T
2 yrs.	4 games			

Tom Dempsey

DEMPSEY, THOMAS JOHN
B. Jan. 12, 1947, Milwaukee, WI
Palomar JC 6'1" 260 lbs.

1969	NO	N	14	K
1970			14	K
1971	PHI	N	5	K
1972			14	K
1973			14	K
1974			14	K
1975	LA	N	14	K
1976			14	K
1977	HOU	N	5	K
1978	BUF	N	14	K
1979			3	K
11 yrs.	125 games			

Fred Denfield

DENFIELD, D.N. (Gibby)
B. Oct., 1897, Duluth, MN
Deceased
Navy 6'0" 195 lbs.

1920	RI	A	3	G
1925	DUL	N	2	G, T
2 yrs.	5 games			

Vern Den Herder

DEN HERDER, VERN WAYNE
B. Nov. 28, 1948, Le Mars, IA
Central (Iowa) 6'6" 251 lbs.

1971	MIA	N	14	DE
1972			14	DE
1973			14	DE
1974			14	DE
1975			14	DE
1976			14	DE
1977			11	DE
1978			16	DE
1979			16	DE
1980			16	DE
1981			16	DE
1982			7	DE
12 yrs.	166 games			

Mark Dennard

DENNARD, MARK WESLEY
B. Nov. 2, 1955, Bay City, TX
Texas A&M 6'4" 260 lbs.

1979	MIA	N	16	C
1980			16	C
1981			11	C
1982			8	C
1983			8	C
1984	PHI	N	16	C
1985			16	C
7 yrs.	91 games			

Preston Dennard

DENNARD, PRESTON JACKSON
B. Nov. 28, 1955, Cordele, GA
New Mexico 6'1" 184 lbs.

1978	LA	N	11	WR
1979			15	WR
1980			16	WR
1981			15	WR
1982	LARM	N	9	WR
1983			14	WR
1984	BUF	N	16	WR
1985	GB	N	16	WR
8 yrs.	112 games			

Jerry Dennerlein

DENNERLEIN, GERALD
B. 1913, Ambridge, PA
St. Mary's (California) 6'2" 240 lbs.

1937	NYG	N	11	T
1940			11	T
2 yrs.	22 games			

Mike Dennery

DENNERY, MICHAEL KEVIN
B. Jun. 26, 1950, Philadelphia, PA
Southern Mississippi 6'0" 224 lbs.

1974	OAK	N	14	LB
1975			14	LB
1976	MIA	N	3	LB
3 yrs.	31 games			

Vince Dennery

DENNERY, VINCENT P., SR.
B. Nov. 17, 1916, Jersey City, NJ
D. Aug. 9, 1989, Philadelphia, PA
Fordham 5'11" 190 lbs.

1941	NYG	N	9	E

Austin Denney

DENNEY, AUSTIN C.
B. Jan. 2, 1944, Nashville, TN
Tennessee 6'2" 230 lbs.

1967	CHI	N	7	TE
1968			14	TE
1969			14	TE
1970	BUF	N	14	TE
4 yrs.	49 games			

Al Dennis

DENNIS, ALBERT RUDOLPH, III
B. Jun. 24, 1951, Independence, LA
Grambling State 6'4" 250 lbs.

1973	SD	N	7	G
1976	CLE	N	10	G
1977			14	G
3 yrs.	31 games			

Guy Dennis

DENNIS, GUY DURELL
B. Feb. 28, 1947, Walnut Hill, FL
Florida 6'2" 254 lbs.

1969	CIN	A	14	G
1970	CIN	N	14	G
1971			14	G
1972			13	G
1973	DET	N	10	G
1974			12	G
1975			12	G, C
7 yrs.	89 games			

Mark Dennis

DENNIS, MARK FRANCIS
B. Apr. 15, 1965, Junction City, KS
Illinois 6'6" 291 lbs.

1987	MIA	N	5	OT
1988			13	OT
1989			8	OT

Mark Dennis *continued*

1990			16	OT
1991			16	OT
1992			16	OT
1993			16	OT
1994	CIN	N	6	OT
1995	CAR	N	12	OT
1996			16	OT
10 yrs.	124 games			

Mike Dennis

DENNIS, MICHAEL D.
B. Jun. 6, 1958, Los Angeles, CA
Wyoming 5'10" 190 lbs.

1980	NYG	N	13	CB
1981			16	CB
1982			9	CB
1983			16	CB
1984	SD	N	2	CB, S
1984	NYJ	N	6	DB
5 yrs.	62 games			

Mike Dennis

DENNIS, WALTER MICHAEL
B. Jul. 22, 1944, Philadelphia, MS
Mississippi 6'1" 207 lbs.

1968	LA	N	14	RB
1969			1	RB
2 yrs.	15 games			

Doug Dennison

DENNISON, WILLIAM DOUGLAS
B. Dec. 18, 1951, Lancaster, PA
Kutztown State 6'2" 202 lbs.

1974	DAL	N	10	RB
1975			13	RB
1976			14	RB
1977			8	RB
1978			5	RB
5 yrs.	52 games			

Glenn Dennison

DENNISON, GLENN
B. Nov. 17, 1961, Beaver Falls, PA
Miami (Florida) 6'3" 225 lbs.

1984	NYJ	N	16	TE
1987	WAS	N	2	TE
2 yrs.	18 games			

Rick Dennison

DENNISON, RICK STEVEN
B. Jun. 22, 1958, Kalispell, MT
Colorado State 6'3" 220 lbs.

1982	DEN	N	9	LB
1983			16	LB
1984			16	LB
1985			15	LB
1986			16	LB
1987			12	LB
1988			16	LB
1989			15	LB
1990			13	LB
9 yrs.	128 games			

Earl Denny

DENNY, EARL LIVINGSTON
B. Jul. 21, 1945, El Paso, TX
Missouri 6'1" 200 lbs.

1967	MIN	N	13	RB
1968			14	RB
2 yrs.	27 games			

Al Denson

DENSON, ALFRED FREDDIE
B. Jan. 2, 1942, Jacksonville, FL

Year	Team	Games	Pos.

Al Denson continued
Florida A&M 6'2" 208 lbs.

Year	Team		Games	Pos.
1964	DEN	A	14	FL
1965			14	FL
1966			14	FL
1967			14	OE
1968			8	FL
1969			13	WR
1970	DEN	N	14	WR
1971	MIN	N	7	WR

8 yrs. 98 games

Keith Denson
DENSON, KEITH ARMANDO
B. Aug. 30, 1952, Camp Lejeune, NC
San Diego State 5'8" 185 lbs.

1976	NYJ	N	2	WR

Moses Denson
DENSON, MOSES
B. Jul. 6, 1944, Vredenburgh, AL
Maryland-Eastern Shore 6'1" 215 lbs.

1974	WAS	N	13	RB
1975			13	RB

2 yrs. 26 games

Burnell Dent
DENT, BURNELL JOSEPH
B. Mar. 16, 1963, New Orleans, LA
Tulane 6'1" 236 lbs.

1986	GB	N	16	LB
1987			9	LB
1988			10	LB
1989			16	LB
1990			15	LB
1991			14	LB
1992			15	LB

7 yrs. 95 games

Richard Dent
DENT, RICHARD LAMAR
(Sack-Man)
B. Dec. 13, 1960, Atlanta, GA
Tennessee State 6'5" 263 lbs.

1983	CHI	N	16	DE
1984			16	DE
1985			16	DE
1986			15	DE
1987			12	DE
1988			13	DE
1989			15	DE
1990			16	DE
1991			16	DE
1992			16	DE
1993			16	DE
1994	SF	N	2	DE
1995	CHI	N	3	DE, DT
1996	IND	N	16	DE

14 yrs. 188 games

Bob Denton
DENTON, ROBERT
B. Jul. 24, 1934, Fresno, CA
Pacific 6'4" 241 lbs.

1960	CLE	N	12	OT
1961	MIN	N	14	OT
1962			14	DE
1963			14	DE
1964			14	DE

5 yrs. 68 games

Winnie Denton
DENTON, WINFIELD
KIRKPATRICK
B. Oct. 28, 1896
D. Nov. 2, 1971
DePauw 6'1" 200 lbs.

1922	EVA	N	1	G

John Denvir
DENVIR, JOHN
B. 1938
Colorado 6'4" 245 lbs.

1962	DEN	A	11	G

Steve DeOssie
DEOSSIE, STEVEN LEONARD
B. Nov. 22, 1962, Tacoma, WA
Boston College 6'2" 249 lbs.

1984	DAL	N	16	LB
1985			16	LB
1986			16	LB
1987			11	LB
1988			16	LB
1989	NYG		9	LB
1990			16	LB
1991			16	LB
1992			12	LB
1993			8	LB
1993	NYJ		7	LB
1994	NE		16	LB
1995			16	LB

12 yrs. 175 games

Carmine DePascal
DEPASCAL, CARMINE
B. 1918, Pittsburgh, PA
Wichita State 6'0" 188 lbs.

1945	PIT	N	1	E

Tom DePaso
DEPASO, THOMAS J.
B. Feb. 22, 1956, White Plains, NY
Penn State 6'2" 223 lbs.

1978	CIN	N	12	RB

Henry DePaul
DEPAUL, HENRY
B. Apr. 12, 1917
D. Oct., 1985, Beaver Falls, PA
Duquesne 5'11" 225 lbs.

1945	PIT	N	4	G

Jack Depler
DEPLER, JOHN C. (Fat)
B. Jan. 6, 1899
D. Dec., 1970, Lewiston, ID
Illinois 5'10" 220 lbs.

1921	HAM	A	5	C
1929	ORA	N	1	T

2 yrs. 6 games

Jerry DePoyster
DEPOYSTER, JERRY
B. Jul. 6, 1946, Omaha, NE
Wyoming 6'1" 202 lbs.

1971	OAK	N	12	K
1972			14	K

2 yrs. 26 games

Lee DeRamus
DERAMUS, LEE
B. Aug. 24, 1972, Sicklerville, NJ
Wisconsin 6'0" 191 lbs.

1995	NO	N	8	WR
1996			15	WR

2 yrs. 23 games

Jimmy DeRatt
DERATT, JIM
B. Jan. 19, 1953, Wilson, NC
North Carolina 6'0" 203 lbs.

1975	NO	N	6	S

Dean Derby
DERBY, CLARENCE DEAN
B. Jul. 11, 1935, Leavenworth, WA
Washington 6'0" 187 lbs.

1957	PIT	N	8	HB, DB
1958			12	DB
1959			12	DB
1960			12	DB
1961	MIN	N	13	DB
1962			11	DB

6 yrs. 68 games

Glenn Derby
DERBY, GLENN E., JR.
B. Jun. 27, 1964, Oconomowoc, WI
Wisconsin 6'6" 290 lbs.

1989	NO	N	3	OT
1990			4	OT

2 yrs. 7 games

John Derby
DERBY, JOHN
B. Mar. 24, 1968, Oconomowoc, WI
Iowa 6'0" 232 lbs.

1992	DET	N	1	LB

Art Deremer
DEREMER, ARTHUR M.
B. Dec. 16, 1917, Pittsburgh, PA
Niagara 6'3" 208 lbs.

1942	BKN	N	6	C

Fred DeRiggi
DERIGGI, FRED JOHN
B. Jan. 15, 1967, Scranton, PA
Syracuse 6'2" 268 lbs.

1990	NE	N	2	NT

Al DeRogatis
DEROGATIS, ALBERT J.
B. 1927
D. Dec. 26, 1995, Neptune, NJ
Duke 6'4" 239 lbs.

1949	NYG	N	11	T
1950			12	T
1951			11	T
1952			12	T

4 yrs. 46 games

Brian DeRoo
DEROO, BRIAN CHARLES
B. Apr. 25, 1956, Redlands, CA
Redlands 6'3" 193 lbs.

1979	BAL	N	16	WR
1980			16	WR
1981			16	WR

3 yrs. 48 games

Dan DeRose
DEROSE, DANIEL
B. Jan. 25, 1962
Southern Colorado 6'0" 230 lbs.

1987	NYG	N	3	LB

Ben Derr
DERR, BENJAMIN H.
B. Jun. 25, 1892
D. Jul., 1977, Mesa, AZ
Pennsylvania 5'10" 180 lbs.

1920	CHIT	A	2	HB
1921	HAM	A	4	HB

2 yrs. 6 games

Dan DeSantis
DESANTIS, DANIEL J.

Dan DeSantis continued
B. Sep. 20, 1918, Niagara Falls, NY
Niagara 6'0" 180 lbs.

1941	PHI	N	10	HB

Dick Deschaine
DESCHAINE, RICHARD
B. Apr. 28, 1932, Menominee, WI
None 6'0" 206 lbs.

1955	GB	N	12	E
1956			12	E
1957			12	E
1958	CLE	N	12	E

4 yrs. 48 games

Chuck DeShane
DESHANE, CHARLES
FREDERICK
B. Dec. 10, 1918, Waukesha, WI
Alabama 6'1" 212 lbs.

1945	DET	N	9	HB, DB
1946			10	HB, DB
1947			11	G
1948			10	G, LB
1949			8	G, LB

5 yrs. 48 games

Paul Des Jardien
DES JARDIEN, PAUL RAYMOND
(Shorty)
B. Aug. 24, 1893, Coffeyville, KS
D. Mar. 7, 1956, Monrovia, CA
Chicago 6'4" 210 lbs.

1920	CHIT	A	7	C

Versil Deskin
DESKIN, VERSIL E.
B. Feb. 14, 1913, Avery, IA
D. Mar. 7, 1992, Ankeny, IA
Drake 6'0" 199 lbs.

1935	CHIC	N	1	E
1936			9	E
1937			11	E
1938			11	E
1939			9	E

5 yrs. 41 games

Don Deskins
DESKINS, DONALD
B. 1933
Michigan 6'3" 240 lbs.

1960	OAK	A		G

Darrell Dess
DESS, DARRELL CHARLES
B. Jul. 11, 1935, New Castle, PA
North Carolina State 6'0" 243 lbs.

1958	PIT	N	12	T
1959	NYG	N	12	G
1960			9	G
1961			14	G
1962			14	G
1963			14	G
1964			14	G
1965	WAS	N	13	G
1966			1	G
1966	NYG	N	11	G
1967			14	G
1968			13	G
1969			6	G

12 yrs. 147 games

Fred DeStefano
DESTEFANO, FREDERICK W.
B. 1900
Deceased

Year	Team		Games	Pos.

Fred DeStefano *continued*

Northwestern 195 lbs.

Year	Team		Games	Pos.
1924	CHIC	N	4	HB, FB
1925			2	FB

2 yrs.   6 games

Wayne DeSutter

DESUTTER, WAYNE
B. May 17, 1944, Atkinson, IL
Illinois/Western Illinois 6'4" 250 lbs.

1966	BUF	A	14	OT

Harold Deters

DETERS, HAROLD LEE
B. Jan. 16, 1944, Du Bois, PA
North Carolina State 6'0" 200 lbs.

1967	DAL	N	3	K

Ty Detmer

DETMER, TY HUBERT
B. Oct. 30, 1967, San Marcos, TX
Brigham Young 6'0" 183 lbs.

1993	GB	N	3	QB
1995			4	QB
1996	PHI	N	13	QB

3 yrs.   20 games

Chuck Detwiler

DETWILER, CHARLES MICHAEL
B. Mar. 6, 1947, Rome, NY
Utah State 6'0" 185 lbs.

1970	SD	N	11	DB
1971			1	S
1972			13	S
1973	STL	N	10	S

4 yrs.   35 games

John Detwiler

DETWILER, JOHN
B. Mar. 14, 1892
D. Feb. 6, 1988, Smith, KS
Kansas 5'8" 190 lbs.

1923	HAM	N	2	HB, FB
1924			1	QB

2 yrs.   3 games

Dennis DeVaughn

DEVAUGHN, DENNIS WAYNE
B. Oct. 28, 1960, Los Angeles, CA
Bishop 5'10" 175 lbs.

1982	PHI	N	4	S
1983			9	CB, S

2 yrs.   13 games

Rob DeVita

DEVITA, ROBERT
B. Nov. 29, 1965
Illinois Benedictine 6'2" 222 lbs.

1987	SEA	N	1	LB

Chuck DeVleigher

DEVLEIGHER, CHARLES
B. Jan. 2, 1947, Paterson, NJ
Memphis State 6'4" 265 lbs.

1969	BUF	A	4	DT

Chris Devlin

DEVLIN, CHRISTOPHER JAMES
B. Nov. 22, 1953, Pittsburgh, PA
Penn State 6'2" 226 lbs.

1975	CIN	N	14	LB
1976			9	LB
1978			1	LB
1978	CHI	N	6	LB

3 yrs.   30 games

Joe Devlin

DEVLIN, JOSEPH
B. Feb. 23, 1954, Phoenixville, PA
Iowa 6'5" 280 lbs.

1976	BUF	N	14	OT
1977			14	OT
1978			14	OT
1979			16	OT
1980			16	OT
1981			16	OT
1982			9	OT
1984			16	OT
1985			16	OT
1986			16	OT
1987			12	OT
1988			16	OT
1989			16	G

13 yrs.   191 games

Mark Devlin

DEVLIN, MARK (Spoke)
B. Dec. 5, 1894
D. Dec. 12, 1973, Lawrence, MA
Holy Cross 5'10" 173 lbs.

1920	CLE	A	3	QB
1921	NY	A	1	QB

2 yrs.   4 games

Mike Devlin

DEVLIN, MIKE
B. Nov. 16, 1969, Marlton, NJ
Iowa 6'1" 293 lbs.

1993	BUF	N	12	C
1994			16	C, G
1995			16	C, G
1996	ARI	N	11	C

4 yrs.   55 games

Jed DeVries

DEVRIES, JED
B. Jan. 6, 1971, Gden, UT
Utah State 6'6" 300 lbs.

1995	CLE	N	3	OT

Jim Dewar

DEWAR, JAMES A.
B. Jun. 17, 1922, Oak Park, IL
D. Jun. 30, 1989
Indiana 6'1" 190 lbs.

1947	CLE	AA	10	B
1948	BKN	AA	1	B

2 yrs.   11 games

Ebby DeWeese

DEWEESE, EVERETT
B. 1905
None 6'0" 188 lbs.

1927	DAY	N	6	G
1928			1	HB
1930	POR	N	11	G

3 yrs.   18 games

Billy Dewell

DEWELL, WILLIAM AUSTIN
B. Jan. 2, 1917, Concordia, KS
Southern Methodist 6'4" 208 lbs.

1940	CHIC	N	4	E
1945			9	E
1946			11	E
1947			11	E
1948			11	E
1949			12	E

6 yrs.   58 games

Herb DeWitz

DEWITZ, HERBERT A.
B. Jun. 9, 1900

Herb DeWitz *continued*

Nebraska 5'9" 175 lbs.

1924	KC	N	8	HB, QB
1927	CLE	N	13	HB, FB

2 yrs.   21 games

Rufe DeWitz

DEWITZ, RUFUS
B. Jun. 9, 1900
D. Mar., 1984, Roselle, IL
Nebraska 5'9" 170 lbs.

1926	KC	N	8	HB, FB

Willard Dewveall

DEWVEALL, WILLARD CHARLES (Duke)
B. Apr. 29, 1936, Springtown, TX
Southern Methodist 6'4" 224 lbs.

1959	CHIB	N	11	E
1960	CHI	N	12	E
1961	HOU	A	7	OE
1962			14	OE
1963			14	OE
1964			14	OE

6 yrs.   72 games

James Dexter

DEXTER, JAMES
B. Mar. 3, 1973, Springfield, VA
South Carolina 6'5" 300 lbs.

1996	ARI	N	5	OT

Alan Dial

DIAL, ALAN ROY
B. Feb. 2, 1965, Anniston, AL
UCLA 6'1" 188 lbs.

1989	PHI	N	1	S

Benjy Dial

DIAL, BENJAMIN F.
B. May 21, 1943, Memphis, TN
Eastern New Mexico 6'1" 185 lbs.

1967	PHI	N	1	QB

Buddy Dial

DIAL, GILBERT LEROY
B. Jan. 17, 1937, Ponca City, OK
Rice 6'1" 194 lbs.

1959	PIT	N	12	E
1960			12	E
1961			14	OE
1962			14	OE
1963			14	OE
1964	DAL	N	10	OE
1965			12	FL
1966			10	FL

8 yrs.   98 games

Bill Diamond

DIAMOND, WILLIAM
B. 1940
Miami (Florida) 6'0" 240 lbs.

1963	KC	A	5	G

Charlie Diamond

DIAMOND, CHARLES
B. 1936
Miami (Florida) 6'2" 249 lbs.

1960	DAL	A		OT
1961			14	OT
1962			14	OT
1963	KC	A	9	OT

4 yrs.   37 games

Rich Diana

DIANA, RICHARD
B. Sep. 6, 1960, Hamden, CT
Yale 5'9" 220 lbs.

1982	MIA	N	9	RB

Jorge Diaz

DIAZ, JORGE
B. Nov. 15, 1973, Houston, TX
Texas A&M-Kingsville 6'4" 295 lbs.

1996	TB	N	11	G

David Diaz-Infante

DIAZ-INFANTE, DAVID
B. Mar. 31, 1964, San Jose, CA
San Jose State 6'2" 272 lbs.

1987	SD	N	3	C, G
1996	DEN	N	9	G

2 yrs.   12 games

John Dibb

DIBB, JOHN
B. 1906
Army 6'0" 200 lbs.

1930	NEW	N	2	T

Dorne Dibble

DIBBLE, DORNE ALLEN
B. Apr. 26, 1929, Adrian, MI
Michigan State 6'2" 195 lbs.

1951	DET	N	12	E
1953			12	E
1954			12	E
1955			8	E
1956			12	E
1957			12	E

6 yrs.   68 games

Rick DiBernardo

DIBERNARDO, RICHARD ANTHONY
B. Jun. 12, 1964, Redondo Beach, CA
Notre Dame 6'3" 225 lbs.

1986	STL	N	16	LB
1987	LARM	N	3	LB

2 yrs.   19 games

Dicely

DICELY
None

1930	SI	N	1	T

Jim Dick

DICK, JAMES
B. Jun. 18, 1964, Illinois
North Dakota State 6'1" 230 lbs.

1987	MIN	N	3	LB

Dan Dickel

DICKEL, DANIEL LEE
B. Aug. 24, 1952, Fort Riley, KS
Iowa 6'3" 225 lbs.

1974	BAL	N	14	LB
1975			14	LB
1976			14	LB
1977			14	LB
1978	DET	N		LB

5 yrs.   56 games

Andy Dickerson

DICKERSON, ANDY
B. Mar. 10, 1963
California Lutheran 6'5" 260 lbs.

1987	LARI	N	1	G

Year	Team		Games	Pos.

Anthony Dickerson
DICKERSON, ANTHONY CHARLES
B. Jun. 9, 1957, Texas City, TX
Southern Methodist 6'2" 225 lbs.

Year	Team		Games	Pos.
1980	DAL	N	16	LB
1981			16	LB
1982			9	LB
1983			16	LB
1984			16	LB
1985	BUF	N	16	LB
6 yrs.	89 games			

Bryan Dickerson
DICKERSON, BRYAN
B. Mar. 22, 1971, Louisville, KY
Eastern Kentucky 6'1" 260 lbs.

Year	Team		Games	Pos.
1995	JAC	N	1	RB

Eric Dickerson
DICKERSON, ERIC DEMETRIC
B. Sep. 2, 1960, Sealy, TX
Southern Methodist 6'3" 220 lbs.

Year	Team		Games	Pos.
1983	LARM	N	16	RB
1984			16	RB
1985			14	RB
1986			16	RB
1987			3	RB
1987	IND	N	9	RB
1988			16	RB
1989			15	RB
1990			11	RB
1991			10	RB
1992	LARI	N	16	RB
1993	ATL	N	4	RB
11 yrs.	146 games			

Ron Dickerson
DICKERSON, RONALD LEE, JR.
B. Aug. 31, 1971, Denver, CO
Arkansas 6'0" 211 lbs.

Year	Team		Games	Pos.
1993	KC	N	6	WR
1994			9	WR
2 yrs.	15 games			

Charlie Dickey
DICKEY, CHARLES J.
B. Dec. 13, 1962, Ottumwa, IA
Arizona 6'3" 270 lbs.

Year	Team		Games	Pos.
1987	PIT	N	1	G

Curtis Dickey
DICKEY, CURTIS
B. Nov. 27, 1956, Madisonville, TX
Texas A&M 6'1" 213 lbs.

Year	Team		Games	Pos.
1980	BAL	N	15	RB
1981			15	RB
1982			8	RB
1983			16	RB
1984	IND	N	10	RB
1985			6	RB
1985	CLE	N	1	RB
1986			14	RB
7 yrs.	85 games			

Eldridge Dickey
DICKEY, ELDRIDGE RENO
B. Dec. 24, 1945, Houston, TX
Tennessee State 6'2" 198 lbs.

Year	Team		Games	Pos.
1968	OAK	A	11	QB, FL
1971	OAK	N	7	WR
2 yrs.	18 games			

Lynn Dickey
DICKEY, CLIFFORD LYNN
B. Oct. 19, 1949, Paola, KS

Lynn Dickey *continued*
Kansas State 6'4" 210 lbs.

Year	Team		Games	Pos.
1971	HOU	N	6	QB
1973			14	QB
1974			14	QB
1975			14	QB
1976	GB		10	QB
1977			9	QB
1979			5	QB
1980			16	QB
1981			13	QB
1982			9	QB
1983			14	QB
1984			15	QB
1985			12	QB
13 yrs.	153 games			

Wallace Dickey
DICKEY, WALLACE
B. Feb. 15, 1941, San Antonio, TX
Southwest Texas State 6'3" 260 lbs.

Year	Team		Games	Pos.
1968	DEN	A	10	OT
1969			12	OT
2 yrs.	22 games			

Bo Dickinson
DICKINSON, RICHARD
B. Jul. 18, 1935, Hattiesburg, MS
Southern Mississippi 6'2" 218 lbs.

Year	Team		Games	Pos.
1960	DAL	A		FB
1961			14	FB
1962	DEN	A	14	FB
1963			6	FB
1963	HOU	A	5	FB
1964	OAK	A	7	FB
5 yrs.	46 games			

Parnell Dickinson
DICKINSON, PARNELL
B. Mar. 14, 1953, Brighton, AL
Mississippi Valley State 6'2" 185 lbs.

Year	Team		Games	Pos.
1976	TB	N	8	QB
1977			8	QB
2 yrs.	16 games			

Tom Dickinson
DICKINSON, THOMAS P.
B. 1897
Deceased
Syracuse 5'8" 175 lbs.

Year	Team		Games	Pos.
1920	DET	A	1	E

Paul Dickson
DICKSON, PAUL SERAFIN
B. Feb. 26, 1937, Waco, TX
Baylor 6'5" 252 lbs.

Year	Team		Games	Pos.
1959	LA	N	10	OT
1960	DAL	N	8	OT
1961	MIN	N	7	OT, DT
1962			14	DT
1963			14	DT
1964			14	DT
1965			14	DT
1966			12	DT
1967			14	DT
1968			13	DT
1969			14	DT
1970			14	DT
1971	STL	N	5	DT
13 yrs.	152 games			

Chuck Dicus
DICUS, CHARLES WAYNE
B. Oct. 2, 1948, Odessa, TX
Arkansas 6'0" 174 lbs.

Year	Team		Games	Pos.
1971	SD	N	14	WR
1972			10	WR
2 yrs.	24 games			

Clint Didier
DIDIER, CLINT
B. Apr. 4, 1959, Connell, WA
Portland State 6'5" 240 lbs.

Year	Team		Games	Pos.
1982	WAS	N	8	TE
1983			16	TE
1984			11	TE
1985			16	TE
1986			14	TE
1987			9	TE
1988	GB	N	15	TE
1989			16	TE
8 yrs.	105 games			

Mark Didio
DIDIO, MARK
B. Feb. 17, 1969, Syracuse, NY
Connecticut 5'11" 181 lbs.

Year	Team		Games	Pos.
1992	PIT	N	2	WR

John Didion
DIDION, JOHN LAWRENCE
B. Oct. 24, 1947, Woodland, CA
Oregon State 6'4" 247 lbs.

Year	Team		Games	Pos.
1969	WAS	N	14	C
1971	NO	N	14	LB, C
1972			14	C
1973			14	C
1974			14	C
5 yrs.	70 games			

Charlie Diehl
DIEHL, CHARLES
B. 1906
Deceased
Idaho 6'0" 208 lbs.

Year	Team		Games	Pos.
1930	CHIC	N	5	G
1931			8	G
1934	C-S	N	1	T
3 yrs.	14 games			

Dave Diehl
DIEHL, DAVID DOUGLAS
B. Sep. 29, 1918, Dansville, MI
Michigan State 6'0" 195 lbs.

Year	Team		Games	Pos.
1939	DET	N	3	E
1940			10	E
1944			10	E
1945			3	E
4 yrs.	26 games			

John Diehl
DIEHL, JOHN
B. Jan. 27, 1936, Philadelphia, PA
Virginia 6'7" 276 lbs.

Year	Team		Games	Pos.
1961	BAL	N	3	DT
1962			14	DT
1963			14	DT
1964			14	DT
1965	OAK	A	8	DT
5 yrs.	53 games			

Wally Diehl
DIEHL, GLENN WALTER
B. 1904, Mount Carmel, PA
D. May 29, 1954, Somerton, PA
Bucknell 6'0" 204 lbs.

Year	Team		Games	Pos.
1928	FRA	N	14	FB, HB
1929			18	FB, HB
1930			5	FB, HB
3 yrs.	37 games			

Doug Dieken
DIEKEN, DOUG H.
B. Feb. 12, 1949, Streator, IL
Illinois 6'5" 250 lbs.

Year	Team		Games	Pos.
1971	CLE	N	14	OT

Doug Dieken *continued*

Year	Team		Games	Pos.
1972			14	OT
1973			14	OT
1974			14	OT
1975			14	OT
1976			14	OT
1977			14	OT
1978			16	OT
1979			16	OT
1980			16	OT
1981			16	OT
1982			9	OT
1983			16	OT
1984			16	OT
14 yrs.	203 games			

Dan Dierdorf
DIERDORF, DANIEL LEE
B. Jun. 29, 1949, Canton, OH
Michigan 6'3" 280 lbs.

Year	Team		Games	Pos.
1971	STL	N	12	OT
1972			14	G
1973			14	G, OT
1974			14	OT
1975			14	OT
1976			14	OT
1977			12	OT
1978			16	OT
1979			2	OT
1980			16	OT
1981			16	OT
1982			9	C
1983			7	C
13 yrs.	160 games			

Scott Dierking
DIERKING, SCOTT EDWARD
B. May 24, 1955, Great Lakes, IL
Purdue 5'10" 215 lbs.

Year	Team		Games	Pos.
1977	NYJ	N	14	RB
1978			15	RB
1979			16	RB
1980			16	RB
1981			16	RB
1982			9	RB
1983			16	RB
1984	TB	N	8	RB
8 yrs.	110 games			

Herb Dieter
DIETER, HERBERT
B. 1896
Deceased
Pennsylvania 6'1" 195 lbs.

Year	Team		Games	Pos.
1922	BUF	N	9	G, T

Chris Dieterich
DIETERICH, CHRISTIAN JEFFERY
B. Jul. 27, 1958, Freeport, NY
North Carolina State 6'3" 262 lbs.

Year	Team		Games	Pos.
1980	DET	N	8	G
1981			7	OT
1982			5	OT
1983			16	OT
1984			16	OT
1985			9	G
1986			3	G
7 yrs.	64 games			

John Diettrich
DIETTRICH, JOHN MICHAEL
B. May 9, 1963, Fort Wayne, IN
Ball State 6'2" 190 lbs.

Year	Team		Games	Pos.
1987	HOU	N	2	K

Dave DiFilippo
DIFILIPPO, DAVID E.

Year	Team		Games	Pos.

Dave DiFilippo continued
B. Oct. 9, 1916, Philadelphia, PA
D. Aug. 29, 1983, Wildwood, NJ
Villanova 5'10" 210 lbs.

| 1941 | PHI | N | 5 | G |

Shelton Diggs
DIGGS, SHELTON
B. Apr. 23, 1955, San Bernardino, CA
Southern California 6'1" 190 lbs.

| 1977 | NYJ | N | 7 | WR |

Curt DiGiacomo
DIGIACOMO, CURT JOSEPH
B. Oct. 24, 1963, San Diego, CA
Arizona 6'4" 275 lbs.

1986	SD	N	3	G
1988	KC	N	12	OL
2 yrs.	15 games			

Bernie Digris
DIGRIS, BERNARD S.
B. Jun. 9, 1919
D. Nov., 1978
Holy Cross 6'0" 212 lbs.

| 1943 | CHIB | N | 2 | T, G |

Trent Dilfer
DILFER, TRENT FARRIS
B. Mar. 13, 1972, Santa Cruz, CA
Fresno State 6'4" 230 lbs.

1994	TB	N	5	QB
1995			16	QB
1996			16	QB
3 yrs.	37 games			

Ken Dilger
DILGER, KEN
B. Feb. 2, 1971, Mariah Hill, IN
Illinois 6'5" 256 lbs.

1995	IND	N	16	TE
1996			16	TE
2 yrs.	32 games			

Scott Dill
DILL, GERALD SCOTT
B. Apr. 5, 1966, Birmingham, AL
Memphis State 6'5" 272 lbs.

1988	PHX	N	13	G
1989			16	OT
1990	TB	N	3	OT
1991			8	G
1992			4	OT
1993			16	OT
1994			16	OT, G
1995			12	OT
1996	MIN	N	9	OT
9 yrs.	97 games			

Ellis Dillahunt
DILLAHUNT, ELLIS ARTO, JR.
B. Nov. 25, 1964, New Bern, NC
East Carolina 5'11" 198 lbs.

| 1988 | CIN | N | 10 | S |

Stacey Dillard
DILLARD, STACEY BERTRAND
B. Sep. 17, 1968, Clarksville, TX
Oklahoma 6'5" 288 lbs.

1992	NYG	N	12	NT
1993			16	NT
1994			16	DT
1995			15	DT
4 yrs.	59 games			

Bobby Dillon
DILLON, BOBBY DAN
B. Feb. 23, 1930, Temple, TX
Texas 6'1" 182 lbs.

1952	GB	N	12	HB
1953			10	HB
1954			12	HB
1955			12	HB
1956			12	HB
1957			12	HB
1958			12	HB
1959			12	HB
8 yrs.	94 games			

Terry Dillon
DILLON, TERRANCE
B. 1941
D. May, 1964
Montana 6'0" 193 lbs.

| 1963 | MIN | N | 7 | DB |

Steve Dils
DILS, STEPHEN WHITFIELD
B. Dec. 8, 1955, Seattle, WA
Stanford 6'1" 191 lbs.

1979	MIN	N	1	QB
1980			16	QB
1981			2	QB
1982			9	QB
1983			16	QB
1984			3	QB
1984	LARM	N	7	QB
1985			15	QB
1986			15	QB
1987			15	QB
1988	ATL	N	7	QB
10 yrs.	106 games			

Bucky Dilts
DILTS, DOUGLAS RIGGS
B. Dec. 6, 1953, Corpus Christi, TX
Georgia 5'9" 185 lbs.

1977	DEN	N	14	P
1978			16	P
1979	BAL	N	16	P
3 yrs.	46 games			

Anthony Dilweg
DILWEG, ANTHONY HUME
B. Mar. 28, 1965, Washington, DC
Duke 6'3" 215 lbs.

1989	GB	N	1	QB
1990			9	QB
2 yrs.	10 games			

Lavern Dilweg
DILWEG, LAVERN RALPH (Lavie)
B. Jan. 11, 1903, Milwaukee, WI
D. Jan. 2, 1968, St. Petersburg, FL
Marquette 6'3" 200 lbs.

1926	MIL	N	9	E
1927	GB	N	10	E
1928			12	E
1929			13	E
1930			12	E
1931			14	E
1932			14	E
1933			10	E
1934			12	E
9 yrs.	106 games			

Babe Dimancheff
DIMANCHEFF, BORIS STEPHAN
B. Sep. 6, 1922, Indianapolis, IN
Butler/Purdue 5'11" 178 lbs.

1945	BOS	N	5	HB
1946			8	HB
1947	CHIC	N	12	HB

Babe Dimancheff continued
1948			12	HB
1949			10	HB
1950			6	HB
1952	CHIB	N	9	HB
7 yrs.	62 games			

Tony DiMidio
DIMIDIO, TONY JAMES
B. Aug. 20, 1942, Bryn Mawr, PA
West Chester State 6'3" 250 lbs.

1966	KC	A	14	OT
1967			12	OT
2 yrs.	26 games			

Tom Dimitroff
DIMITROFF, THOMAS
B. 1935
Miami (Ohio) 5'11" 200 lbs.

| 1960 | BOS | A | | QB |

Rich Dimler
DIMLER, RICHARD ALAN
B. Jul. 18, 1956, Bayonne, NJ
Southern California 6'6" 260 lbs.

1979	CLE	N	12	DT
1980	GB	N	3	DT
2 yrs.	15 games			

Don Dimmick
DIMMICK, DONALD
B. 1903
D. Jun., 1949
Hobart 5'8" 160 lbs.

| 1926 | BUF | N | 1 | HB |

Tom Dimmick
DIMMICK, THOMAS
B. May 1, 1931
Houston 6'6" 253 lbs.

1956	PHI	N	12	T
1960	DAL	A		C
2 yrs.	12 games			

Charles Dimry
DIMRY, CHARLES LOUIS, III
B. Jan. 31, 1966, San Diego, CA
Nevada-Las Vegas 6'0" 175 lbs.

1988	ATL	N	16	CB
1989			16	CB, S
1990			16	CB
1991	DEN	N	16	CB
1992			16	CB
1993			12	CB
1994	TB	N	16	CB
1995			16	CB
1996			16	CB
9 yrs.	140 games			

Mike Dingle
DINGLE, MIKE
B. Jan. 30, 1969, Moncks Corner, SC
South Carolina 6'2" 240 lbs.

| 1991 | CIN | N | 8 | RB |

Nate Dingle
DINGLE, NATE
B. Jul. 23, 1971, Wells, ME
Cincinnati 6'3" 254 lbs.

1995	PHI	N	6	LB
1996	JAC	N	2	LB
2 yrs.	8 games			

Tom Dinkel
DINKEL, THOMAS

Tom Dinkel continued
B. Jul. 25, 1956, Topeka, KS
Kansas 6'3" 241 lbs.

1978	CIN	N	16	LB
1979			16	LB
1980			16	LB
1981			16	LB
1982			9	LB
1983			16	LB
1985			13	LB
7 yrs.	102 games			

Howard Dinkins
DINKINS, HOWARD
B. Apr. 26, 1969, Jacksonville, FL
Florida State 6'1" 230 lbs.

| 1993 | ATL | N | 3 | LB |

Bob Dinsmore
DINSMORE, ROBERT
B. 1902
Princeton 5'8" 165 lbs.

| 1926 | PHI | A | 9 | QB, HB, FB |

Terry Dion
DION, TERRY MARK
B. Nov. 22, 1957, Shelton, WA
Oregon 6'6" 254 lbs.

| 1980 | SEA | N | 9 | DE |

Jerry Diorio
DIORIO, JERRY
B. Jan. 11, 1962
Michigan 6'3" 245 lbs.

| 1987 | DET | N | 2 | TE |

Ray DiPierro
DIPIERRO, RAMON F.
B. Aug. 22, 1926, Toledo, OH
Ohio State 5'11" 210 lbs.

1950	GB	N	12	G
1951			6	G
2 yrs.	18 games			

Johnnie Dirden
DIRDEN, JOHNNIE
B. Mar. 14, 1952, Houston, TX
Sam Houston State 6'0" 188 lbs.

1978	HOU	N	16	WR
1979	KC	N	4	WR
1981	PIT	N	6	WR
3 yrs.	26 games			

Fred DiRenzo
DIRENZO, FRED
B. Jan. 28, 1961
New Haven 5'11" 234 lbs.

| 1987 | NYG | N | 1 | RB |

Bob DiRico
DIRICO, ROBERT
B. Nov. 22, 1963
Kutztown State 5'10" 202 lbs.

| 1987 | NYG | N | 3 | RB |

Mike Dirks
DIRKS, MARION GEARHART, JR.
B. Aug. 28, 1946, Monticello, IA
Wyoming 6'2" 247 lbs.

1968	PHI	N	14	G
1969			12	DT
1970			12	DT
1971			5	DT
4 yrs.	43 games			

Year	Team		Games	Pos.

Tony Discenzo
DISCENZO, TONY
B. 1936
Michigan State 6'5" 240 lbs.

Year	Team		Games	Pos.
1960	**BUF**	**A**		OT
1960	**BOS**	**A**		OT

Leo Disend
DISEND, LEO (Moose)
B. Nov. 7, 1915, Roselle, NJ
D. May 13, 1985, Baldwin, NY
Albright 6'2" 224 lbs.

Year	Team		Games	Pos.
1938	**BKN**	**N**	11	T
1939			11	T
1940	**GB**	**N**	5	T, E
3 yrs.	27 games			

Cris Dishman
DISHMAN, CRIS EDWARD
B. Aug. 13, 1965, Louisville, KY
Purdue 6'0" 180 lbs.

Year	Team		Games	Pos.
1988	**HOU**	**N**	15	CB
1989			16	CB
1990			16	CB
1991			15	CB
1992			15	CB
1993			16	CB
1994			16	CB
1995			15	CB
1996			16	CB
9 yrs.	140 games			

Mike Ditka
DITKA, MICHAEL KELLER (Iron Mike)
B. Oct. 18, 1939, Carnegie, PA
Pittsburgh 6'3" 228 lbs.

Year	Team		Games	Pos.
1961	**CHI**	**N**	14	OE
1962			14	OE
1963			14	OE
1964			14	OE
1965			14	OE
1966			14	TE
1967	**PHI**	**N**	9	TE
1968			11	TE
1969	**DAL**	**N**	12	TE
1970			14	TE
1971			14	TE
1972			14	TE
12 yrs.	158 games			

John Dittrich
DITTRICH, JOHN
B. May 7, 1933, Sheboygan, WI
Wisconsin 6'1" 236 lbs.

Year	Team		Games	Pos.
1956	**CHIC**	**N**	12	G
1959	**GB**	**N**	12	G
1960	**OAK**	**A**		G
1961	**BUF**	**A**	12	G
4 yrs.	36 games			

Joe DiVito
DIVITO, JOSEPH
B. 1946
Boston College 6'2" 205 lbs.

Year	Team		Games	Pos.
1968	**DEN**	**A**	3	QB

Al Dixon
DIXON, ALBERT D.
B. Apr. 5, 1954, Drew, MS
Iowa State 6'5" 230 lbs.

Year	Team		Games	Pos.
1977	**NYG**	**N**	8	TE
1978			15	TE
1979			5	TE
1979	**KC**	**N**	3	TE
1980			12	TE
1981			16	TE
1982			8	TE

Al Dixon continued

Year	Team		Games	Pos.
1983	**PHI**	**N**	9	TE
1984	**SD**	**N**	1	TE
1984	**SF**	**N**	2	TE
8 yrs.	79 games			

Cal Dixon
DIXON, CALVERT RAY
B. Oct. 11, 1969, Fort Lauderdale, FL
Florida 6'4" 284 lbs.

Year	Team		Games	Pos.
1992	**NYJ**	**N**	11	C
1993			16	C
1994			15	C
1995			13	C, G
1996	**MIA**	**N**	11	C, G
5 yrs.	66 games			

David Dixon
DIXON, DAVID
B. Jan. 5, 1969, Auckland, New Zealand
Arizona State 6'5" 350 lbs.

Year	Team		Games	Pos.
1994	**MIN**	**N**	1	G
1995			15	G
1996			13	G
3 yrs.	29 games			

Dwayne Dixon
DIXON, DWAYNE K.
B. Aug. 2, 1962, Gainesville, FL
Florida 6'1" 205 lbs.

Year	Team		Games	Pos.
1984	**TB**	**N**	10	WR
1987			2	WR
2 yrs.	12 games			

Ernest Dixon
DIXON, ERNEST
B. Oct. 17, 1971, Fort Mill, SC
South Carolina 6'1" 250 lbs.

Year	Team		Games	Pos.
1994	**NO**	**N**	15	LB
1995			16	LB
1996			16	LB
3 yrs.	47 games			

Floyd Dixon
DIXON, FLOYD EUGENE
B. Apr. 9, 1964, Beaumont, TX
Stephen F. Austin 5'9" 170 lbs.

Year	Team		Games	Pos.
1986	**ATL**	**N**	16	WR
1987			12	WR
1988			14	WR
1989			16	WR
1990			16	WR
1991			11	WR
1992	**PHI**	**N**	7	WR
7 yrs.	92 games			

Gerald Dixon
DIXON, GERALD SCOTT
B. Jun. 20, 1969, Charlotte, NC
South Carolina 6'3" 252 lbs.

Year	Team		Games	Pos.
1993	**CLE**	**N**	11	LB
1994			16	LB
1995			16	LB
1996	**CIN**	**N**	16	LB
4 yrs.	59 games			

Hanford Dixon
DIXON, HANFORD
B. Dec. 25, 1958, Mobile, AL
Southern Mississippi 5'11" 186 lbs.

Year	Team		Games	Pos.
1981	**CLE**	**N**	16	CB
1982			9	CB
1983			16	CB
1984			16	CB
1985			16	CB
1986			16	CB

Hanford Dixon continued

Year	Team		Games	Pos.
1987			12	CB
1988			15	CB
1989			15	CB
9 yrs.	131 games			

Hewritt Dixon
DIXON, HEWRITT FREDERICK, JR. (Tank)
B. Jan. 8, 1940, Alachua, FL
Florida A&M 6'2" 223 lbs.

Year	Team		Games	Pos.
1963	**DEN**	**A**	5	FB
1964			14	HB, OE
1965			14	OE
1966	**OAK**	**A**	14	FB
1967			13	RB
1968			14	RB
1969			11	RB
1970	**OAK**	**N**	14	RB
8 yrs.	99 games			

James Dixon
DIXON, JAMES ANTHONY
B. Feb. 2, 1967, Vernon, TX
Houston 5'10" 181 lbs.

Year	Team		Games	Pos.
1989	**DAL**	**N**	16	WR
1990			15	WR
1991			7	WR
3 yrs.	38 games			

Joe Dixon
DIXON, WILLIE JOE, JR.
B. Jan. 8, 1964, Fort Smith, AR
Tulsa 6'3" 275 lbs.

Year	Team		Games	Pos.
1987	**HOU**	**N**	2	NT

Randy Dixon
DIXON, RANDY C.
B. Mar. 12, 1965, Clewiston, FL
Pittsburgh 6'3" 293 lbs.

Year	Team		Games	Pos.
1987	**IND**	**N**	3	OT
1988			16	OT
1989			16	G
1990			15	G
1991			12	G
1992			15	G
1993			15	G
1994			14	G
1995			12	G
9 yrs.	118 games			

Rich Dixon
DIXON, RICHARD MARVIN
B. Aug. 6, 1959, Roswell, MN
California 6'2" 235 lbs.

Year	Team		Games	Pos.
1983	**ATL**	**N**	14	LB

Rickey Dixon
DIXON, RICKEY
B. Dec. 26, 1966, Dallas, TX
Oklahoma 5'11" 181 lbs.

Year	Team		Games	Pos.
1988	**CIN**	**N**	15	CB
1989			16	CB
1990			13	S
1991			15	S
1992			14	S
1993	**LARI**	**N**	9	S
6 yrs.	82 games			

Ronnie Dixon
DIXON, RONNIE CHRISTOPHER
B. May 10, 1971, Clinton, NC
Cincinnati 6'2" 292 lbs.

Year	Team		Games	Pos.
1993	**NO**	**N**	2	NT
1995	**PHI**	**N**	16	DT
1996			16	DT
3 yrs.	34 games			

Titus Dixon
DIXON, TITUS L.
B. Jun. 15, 1966, Clewiston, FL
Troy State 5'6" 152 lbs.

Year	Team		Games	Pos.
1989	**NYJ**	**N**	3	WR
1989	**IND**	**N**	1	WR
1 yr.	4 games			

Zack Dixon
DIXON, ZACHARY
B. Mar. 5, 1956, Dorchester, MA
Temple 6'0" 201 lbs.

Year	Team		Games	Pos.
1979	**DEN**	**N**	5	RB
1979	**NYG**	**N**	3	RB
1980	**PHI**	**N**	5	RB
1980	**BAL**	**N**	1	RB
1981			16	RB
1982			9	RB
1983			2	RB
1983	**SEA**	**N**	13	RB
1984			13	RB
6 yrs.	67 games			

Dinger Doane
DOANE, ERLING JOSEPH
B. 1895, Natick, MA
D. Jun. 5, 1949
Tufts 5'10" 190 lbs.

Year	Team		Games	Pos.
1920	**CLE**	**A**	4	FB, T
1921	**NY**	**A**	1	HB
1922	**MIL**	**N**	9	FB, HB, E
1923			10	FB
1924			11	FB
1925	**DET**	**N**	11	FB
1926			12	FB, E
1927	**POT**	**N**	2	FB, G
1927	**PRO**	**N**	5	FB
8 yrs.	65 games			

Herbie Dobbins
DOBBINS, HERBERT
B. Jun. 22, 1951, Pomona, CA
San Diego State 6'4" 260 lbs.

Year	Team		Games	Pos.
1974	**PHI**	**N**	3	OT

Glenn Dobbs
DOBBS, GLENN, JR.
B. Jul. 12, 1922, McKinney, TX
Tulsa 6'4" 211 lbs.

Year	Team		Games	Pos.
1946	**BKN**	**AA**	12	QB, P
1947	**BKN**	**AA**	7	QB, P
1947	**LA**	**AA**	9	QB, P
1948	**LA**	**AA**	14	QB, P
1949			12	QB, P
4 yrs.	49 games			

Dick Dobeleit
DOBELEIT, RICHARD
B. Jul. 4, 1903, Dayton, OH
D. Mar., 1978, Highland Park, FL
Ohio State 5'4" 155 lbs.

Year	Team		Games	Pos.
1925	**DAY**	**N**	6	HB, QB
1926			6	HB, FB
2 yrs.	12 games			

Bob Dobelstein
DOBELSTEIN, ROBERT EDWARD
B. Oct. 17, 1922, Bridgeport, CT
Tennessee 5'11" 214 lbs.

Year	Team		Games	Pos.
1946	**NYG**	**N**	10	G
1947			12	G
1948			11	G
1949	**LA**	**AA**	8	G
4 yrs.	41 games			

Year	Team	Games	Pos.

Conrad Dobler
DOBLER, CONRAD FRANCIS
B. Oct. 1, 1950, Chicago, IL
Wyoming 6'3" 254 lbs.

Year	Team		Games	Pos.
1972	STL	N	12	G
1973			12	G
1974			14	G
1975			14	G
1976			14	G
1977			14	G
1978	NO	N	3	G
1979			16	G
1980	BUF	N	16	G
1981			14	G
10 yrs.	129 games			

E.A. Dobrey
DOBREY, E.A.
None 5'11" 175 lbs.

Year	Team		Games	Pos.
1928	FRA	N	1	E

Pete Dobrus
DOBRUS, PETER
B. 1917
Carnegie-Mellon 6'0" 215 lbs.

Year	Team		Games	Pos.
1941	BKN	N	1	T

John Dockery
DOCKERY, JOHN
B. Sep. 6, 1944, Brooklyn, NY
Harvard 6'0" 186 lbs.

Year	Team		Games	Pos.
1968	NY	A	3	CB
1969			14	CB
1970	NYJ	N	14	CB
1971			14	CB
1972	PIT	N	6	CB
1973			10	CB
6 yrs.	61 games			

Al Dodd
DODD, ALVIN ROY
B. Aug. 21, 1945, New Orleans, LA
D. Apr. 9, 1987, Opelika, AL
Northwestern State (Louisiana) 6'0" 180 lbs.

Year	Team		Games	Pos.
1967	CHI	N	6	DB
1969	NO	N	14	WR
1970			14	WR
1971			10	WR
1973	ATL	N	13	WR
1974			14	WR
6 yrs.	71 games			

Dedrick Dodge
DODGE, DEDRICK ALLEN
B. Jun. 14, 1967, Neptune, NJ
Florida State 6'2" 184 lbs.

Year	Team		Games	Pos.
1991	SEA	N	11	S
1992			14	S
1994	SF	N	15	S
1995			16	S
1996			16	S
5 yrs.	72 games			

Kirk Dodge
DODGE, KIRK JAMES
B. Jun. 4, 1962, Whittier, CA
Nevada-Las Vegas 6'0" 231 lbs.

Year	Team		Games	Pos.
1984	DET	N	11	LB
1986	HOU	N	9	LB
1987	DEN	N	3	LB
3 yrs.	23 games			

Dale Dodrill
DODRILL, DALE F.
B. Feb. 1, 1926, Stockton, KS

Dale Dodrill continued
Colorado State 6'1" 211 lbs.

Year	Team		Games	Pos.
1951	PIT	N	7	G
1952			12	G
1953			12	G
1954			12	G
1955			12	G
1956			12	G
1957			12	G
1958			12	G
1959			12	G
9 yrs.	103 games			

Les Dodson
DODSON, LESLIE
B. Apr. 18, 1916, Birmingham, AL
Mississippi 6'1" 180 lbs.

Year	Team		Games	Pos.
1941	PIT	N	2	B

John Doehring
DOEHRING, JOHN M. (Bull)
B. Nov. 6, 1909, Milwaukee, WI
D. Nov. 18, 1972, Milwaukee, WI
None 6'0" 216 lbs.

Year	Team		Games	Pos.
1932	CHIB	N	7	HB
1933			8	HB
1934			2	HB
1935	PIT	N	2	HB
1936	CHIB	N	6	HB
1937			3	HB
6 yrs.	28 games			

Sonny Doell
DOELL, WALT (Tex)
B. 1907
Texas 6'0" 200 lbs.

Year	Team		Games	Pos.
1933	CIN	N	1	T

Fred Doelling
DOELLING, FRED
B. 1939, Valparaiso, IN
Pennsylvania 5'10" 190 lbs.

Year	Team		Games	Pos.
1960	DAL	N	2	DB

Jerry Doerger
DOERGER, JEROME WILLIAM
B. Jul. 18, 1960, Cincinnati, OH
Wisconsin 6'5" 270 lbs.

Year	Team		Games	Pos.
1982	CHI	N	1	OT
1985	SD	N	8	OT, C
2 yrs.	9 games			

Chris Doering
DOERING, CHRIS
B. May 19, 1973, Gainesville, FL
Florida 6'3" 191 lbs.

Year	Team		Games	Pos.
1996	IND	N	1	WR

Kevin Dogins
DOGINS, KEVIN
B. Dec. 7, 1972, Eagle Lake, TX
Texas A&M-Kingsville 6'1" 290 lbs.

Year	Team		Games	Pos.
1996	TB	N	1	C

Bill Doherty
DOHERTY, WILLIAM
B. 1883
Deceased
None 5'11" 190 lbs.

Year	Team		Games	Pos.
1921	CIN	N	4	C

George Doherty
DOHERTY, GEORGE
B. Sep. 5, 1920, Camden, MS
D. Dec. 31, 1987, Natchitoches, LA

George Doherty continued
Louisiana Tech 6'1" 218 lbs.

Year	Team		Games	Pos.
1944	BKN	N	9	T
1945	BOS	N	9	T
1946	NY	AA	1	G
1946	BUF	AA	12	G
1947			11	G
4 yrs.	42 games			

Tom Dohring
DOHRING, THOMAS EDWARD
B. May 24, 1968, Detroit, MI
Michigan 6'6" 290 lbs.

Year	Team		Games	Pos.
1992	KC	N	3	OT

Steve Doig
DOIG, STEPHEN GUGEL
B. Mar. 28, 1960, Melrose, MA
New Hampshire 6'2" 240 lbs.

Year	Team		Games	Pos.
1982	DET	N	9	LB
1983			9	LB
1984			16	LB
1986	NE	N	5	LB
1987			1	LB
5 yrs.	40 games			

Phil Dokes
DOKES, PHILLIP D.
B. Sep. 7, 1955, North Little Rock, AR
D. Dec. 7, 1989, Jacksonville, AR
Oklahoma State 6'5" 257 lbs.

Year	Team		Games	Pos.
1977	BUF	N	12	DE, DT
1978			13	DE
2 yrs.	25 games			

Cliff Dolaway
DOLAWAY, CLIFFORD
B. Dec. 11, 1913
D. Dec., 1968
Carnegie-Mellon 6'0" 215 lbs.

Year	Team		Games	Pos.
1935	PIT	N	2	E

Jack Dolbin
DOLBIN, JOHN TICE
B. Oct. 12, 1948, Pottsville, PA
Wake Forest 5'10" 181 lbs.

Year	Team		Games	Pos.
1975	DEN	N	14	WR
1976			14	WR
1977			14	WR
1978			16	WR
1979			4	WR
5 yrs.	62 games			

Chris Doleman
DOLEMAN, CHRISTOPHER JOHN
B. Oct. 19, 1961, Indianapolis, IN
Pittsburgh 6'5" 260 lbs.

Year	Team		Games	Pos.
1985	MIN	N	16	LB
1986			16	LB
1987			12	DE
1988			16	DE
1989			16	DE
1990			16	DE
1991			16	DE
1992			16	DE
1993			16	DE
1994	ATL	N	14	DE
1995			16	DE
1996	SF	N	16	DE
12 yrs.	186 games			

Don Doll
DOLL, DONALD LEROY
B. Aug. 29, 1926, Los Angeles, CA
Southern California 5'10" 185 lbs.

Year	Team		Games	Pos.
1949	DET	N	12	HB

Don Doll continued

Year	Team		Games	Pos.
1950			11	HB
1951			12	HB
1952			12	HB
1953	WAS	N	12	HB
1954	LA	N	12	HB
6 yrs.	71 games			

Tony Dollinger
DOLLINGER, TONY
B. Oct. 18, 1962
Evangel 5'11" 205 lbs.

Year	Team		Games	Pos.
1987	DET	N	2	RB

Dick Dolly
DOLLY, JOHN RICHARD
B. Dec. 12, 1917, Onego, WV
D. May 30, 1959, North Augusta, SC
West Virginia 6'3" 211 lbs.

Year	Team		Games	Pos.
1941	PIT	N	8	E
1945			10	E
2 yrs.	18 games			

Paul Dombroski
DOMBROSKI, PAUL MATTHEW
B. Aug. 8, 1956, Sumter, SC
Hawaii/Linfield 6'0" 185 lbs.

Year	Team		Games	Pos.
1980	KC	N	16	S
1981			5	CB, S
1981	NE	N	6	CB
1982			9	CB
1983			7	CB, S
1984			14	CB, S
1985	TB	N	6	S
6 yrs.	63 games			

Jim Dombrowski
DOMBROWSKI, JAMES MATTHEW
B. Oct. 19, 1963, Williamsville, NY
Virginia 6'6" 295 lbs.

Year	Team		Games	Pos.
1986	NO	N	3	OT
1987			10	OT
1988			16	OT
1989			16	OT
1990			16	OT
1991			16	OT
1992			16	OT
1993			16	OT
1994			16	G
1995			16	G
1996			10	G
11 yrs.	151 games			

Joe Domnanovich
DOMNANOVICH, JOSEPH JOHN
B. Mar. 18, 1921, South Bend, IN
Alabama 6'1" 213 lbs.

Year	Team		Games	Pos.
1946	BOS	N	11	C
1947			8	C
1948			12	C
1949	NYB	N	12	C
1950	NYY	N	12	C
1951			12	C
6 yrs.	67 games			

Marty Domres
DOMRES, MARTIN FRANCIS
B. Apr. 17, 1947, Ithaca, NY
Columbia 6'4" 219 lbs.

Year	Team		Games	Pos.
1969	SD	A	10	QB
1970	SD	N	7	QB
1971			4	QB
1972	BAL	N	12	QB
1973			10	QB
1974			14	QB
1975			14	QB
1976	SF	N	5	QB

Year	Team		Games	Pos.

Marty Domres continued

Year	Team		Games	Pos.
1977	NYJ	N	12	QB
9 yrs.	88 games			

Tom Domres
DOMRES, THOMAS BRUCE
B. Oct. 19, 1946, Marshfield, WI
Wisconsin 6'3" 257 lbs.

1968	HOU	A	14	DE, DT
1969			14	DT
1970	HOU	N	14	DT
1971	DEN		5	DT
1972			11	DT
5 yrs.	58 games			

Donahue
DONAHUE
None

1926	COL	N	1	QB

Jack Donahue
DONAHUE, JOHN (Jiggs)
B. 1905
Boston College 6'2" 230 lbs.

1926	PRO	N	13	G, T

Mark Donahue
DONAHUE, MARK JOSEPH
B. Jan. 29, 1956, Evergreen Park, IL
Michigan 6'3" 256 lbs.

1978	CIN	N	15	G
1979			16	G
2 yrs.	31 games			

Mitch Donahue
DONAHUE, MITCHELL TODD
B. Feb. 4, 1968, Los Angeles, CA
Wyoming 6'2" 254 lbs.

1991	SF	N	13	LB
1992			2	LB
1993	DEN	N	13	LB
1994			4	DE, LB
4 yrs.	32 games			

Oscar Donahue
DONAHUE, OSCAR
B. 1938
San Jose State 6'3" 195 lbs.

1962	MIN	N	13	HB

Gene Donaldson
DONALDSON, EUGENE
B. Nov. 4, 1942, Birmingham, AL
Purdue 6'2" 225 lbs.

1967	BUF	N		RB

Gene Donaldson
DONALDSON, GENE
B. 1930
Kentucky 5'9" 215 lbs.

1953	CLE	N	11	G

Jeff Donaldson
DONALDSON, JEFF
B. Apr. 19, 1962, Fort Collins, CO
Colorado 6'0" 194 lbs.

1984	HOU	N	16	CB, S
1985			16	S
1986			16	S
1987			12	S
1988			16	S
1989			14	S
1990	KC	N	16	S
1991	ATL	N	16	S
1992			16	S

Jeff Donaldson continued

Year	Team		Games	Pos.
1993			13	S
10 yrs.	151 games			

John Donaldson
DONALDSON, JOHN C.
B. Aug. 22, 1925, Jesup, GA
Georgia 5'10" 180 lbs.

1949	LA	AA	1	B
1949	CHI	AA	7	B
1 yr.	8 games			

Ray Donaldson
DONALDSON, RAYMOND CANUTE
B. May 18, 1958, Rome, GA
Georgia 6'4" 275 lbs.

1980	BAL	N	16	C, G
1981			16	C
1982			9	C
1983			16	C
1984	IND	N	16	C
1985			16	C
1986			16	C
1987			12	C
1988			16	C
1989			16	C
1990			16	C
1991			3	C
1992			16	C
1993	SEA	N	16	C
1994			16	C
1995	DAL	N	12	C
1996			16	C
17 yrs.	244 games			

Waldo Don Carlos
DON CARLOS, WALDO EMERSON
B. Oct. 16, 1909, Greenfield, IA
Drake 6'2" 190 lbs.

1931	GB	N	12	C

Tom Donchez
DONCHEZ, THOMAS
B. Oct. 3, 1952, Bethlehem, PA
Penn State 6'2" 216 lbs.

1975	CHI	N	14	RB

Billy Donckers
DONCKERS, WILLIAM LEWIS
B. Jan. 8, 1951, Renton, WA
San Diego State 6'1" 206 lbs.

1976	STL	N	1	QB
1977			5	QB
2 yrs.	6 games			

Al Donelli
DONELLI, ALLAN A.
B. Dec. 22, 1917, Morgan, PA
Duquesne 5'7" 165 lbs.

1941	PIT	N	7	HB, DB
1942			4	HB, DB
1942	PHI	N	1	HB, DB
2 yrs.	12 games			

Jim Donlan
DONLAN, JAMES
B. 1900, Connecticut
Deceased
None

1926	HAR	N	1	G

Doug Donley
DONLEY, DOUGLAS MAX
B. Feb. 6, 1959, Cambridge, OH

Doug Donley continued

Year	Team		Games	Pos.
Ohio State 6'0" 178 lbs.

1981	DAL	N	11	WR
1982			6	WR
1983			11	WR
1984			15	WR
4 yrs.	43 games			

Roger Donnahoo
DONNAHOO, ROGER J.
B. 1938
Michigan State 6'0" 185 lbs.

1960	NY	A		DB

Kevin Donnalley
DONNALLEY, KEVIN
B. Jan. 17, 1958, Warren, OH
North Dakota State 5'11" 180 lbs.

1981	NE	N	1	DB

Kevin Donnalley
DONNALLEY, KEVIN THOMAS
B. Jun. 10, 1968, St. Louis, MO
Davidson/North Carolina 6'5" 299 lbs.

1991	HOU	N	16	OT
1992			16	OT
1993			16	OT
1994			13	G
1995			16	G
1996			16	G
6 yrs.	93 games			

Rick Donnalley
DONNALLEY, WILLIAM FREDERICK
B. Dec. 11, 1958, Wilmington, DE
North Carolina 6'2" 267 lbs.

1982	PIT	N	5	C, G
1983			16	C, G
1984	WAS	N	15	C, G
1985			13	C, G
1986	KC	N	16	C, G
1987			6	C
6 yrs.	71 games			

Ben Donnell
DONNELL, BEN CLAY
B. 1937
Vanderbilt 6'5" 248 lbs.

1960	LA	A		DE

George Donnelly
DONNELLY, GEORGE
B. Sep. 4, 1942, Chicago, IL
Illinois 6'3" 207 lbs.

1965	SF	N	14	DB
1966			7	DB
1967			12	DB
3 yrs.	33 games			

Rick Donnelly
DONNELLY, RICK
B. May 17, 1962, Miller Place, NY
Wyoming 6'0" 190 lbs.

1985	ATL	N	11	P
1986			16	P
1987			12	P
1988			16	P
1990	SEA	N	16	P
1991			3	P
6 yrs.	74 games			

Mark D'Onofrio
D'ONOFRIO, MARK EMIL
B. Mar. 17, 1969, Hoboken, NJ

Mark D'Onofrio continued

Year	Team		Games	Pos.
Penn State 6'2" 235 lbs.

1992	GB	N	2	LB

Mike Donohoe
DONOHOE, MICHAEL PIERCE
B. May 6, 1945, San Francisco, CA
San Francisco 6'3" 228 lbs.

1968	ATL	N	14	TE
1970			14	TE
1971			10	TE
1973	GB	N	13	TE
1974			14	TE
5 yrs.	65 games			

Bill Donohue
DONOHUE, WILLIAM W.
B. 1904
Carnegie-Mellon 5'9" 165 lbs.

1927	FRA	N	8	QB, HB

Leon Donohue
DONOHUE, LEON
B. Mar. 25, 1939, Star City, AR
San Jose State 6'4" 245 lbs.

1962	SF	N	14	OT
1963			14	OT
1964			14	G
1965	DAL	N	14	G
1966			14	G
1967			14	G
6 yrs.	84 games			

Art Donovan
DONOVAN, ARTHUR, JR. (Fatso)
B. Jun. 5, 1925, Bronx, NY
Boston College 6'2" 263 lbs.

1950	BAL	N	12	DT, OT
1951	NYY	N	12	DT
1952	DAL	N	7	DT
1953	BAL	N	12	DT
1954			11	DT
1955			12	DT
1956			11	DT
1957			12	DT
1958			12	DT
1959			12	DT
1960			12	DT
1961			14	DT
12 yrs.	139 games			

Pat Donovan
DONOVAN, PATRICK EMERY
B. Jul. 1, 1953, Helena, MT
Stanford 6'5" 257 lbs.

1975	DAL	N	13	OT
1976			14	OT
1977			14	OT
1978			16	OT
1979			16	OT
1980			16	OT
1981			16	OT
1982			9	OT
1983			15	OT
9 yrs.	129 games			

Tom Donovan
DONOVAN, THOMAS EDWARD
B. Jan. 13, 1957, Flushing, NY
Penn State 5'11" 179 lbs.

1980	NO	N	5	WR

Jack Doolan
DOOLAN, JOHN J.
B. May 16, 1919, Brooklyn, NY
Georgetown (DC) 6'1" 191 lbs.

1945	WAS	N	1	HB

Year	Team	Games	Pos.

Jack Doolan *continued*

Year	Team		Games	Pos.
1945	NYG	N	5	HB
1946			5	HB
1947	CHIC	N	12	E
1948			12	E
4 yrs.	35 games			

Jim Dooley
DOOLEY, JAMES WILLIAM
B. Feb. 8, 1930, Stoutsville, MO
Miami (Florida) 6'4" 198 lbs.

Year	Team		Games	Pos.
1952	CHIB	N	12	HB, DB
1953			12	OE
1954			12	OE
1956			3	OE
1957			12	OE
1959			12	FL
1960	CHI	N	11	OE
1961			3	OE
8 yrs.	77 games			

Johnny Dooley
DOOLEY, JOHN M.
B. Sep. 29, 1897
D. Oct. 31, 1991, Syracuse, NY
Syracuse/Bucknell 6'1" 225 lbs.

Year	Team		Games	Pos.
1921	SYR	A	3	T
1922	ROC	N	5	G, T
1924			5	T, G
1925			6	T
4 yrs.	19 games			

Dan Doornink
DOORNINK, DANIEL E.
B. Feb. 1, 1956, Yakima, WA
Washington State 6'3" 210 lbs.

Year	Team		Games	Pos.
1978	NYG	N	12	RB
1979	SEA	N	16	FB
1980			15	FB
1981			15	FB
1982			8	RB
1983			16	RB
1984			16	FB
1985			6	FB
8 yrs.	104 games			

Jim Doran
DORAN, JAMES ROBERT
B. Aug. 11, 1927, Paton, IA
D. Jun. 30, 1994
Iowa State 6'2" 201 lbs.

Year	Team		Games	Pos.
1951	DET	N	12	OE, DE
1952			11	OE, DE
1953			7	OE, DE
1954			7	OE, DE
1955			10	OE
1956			11	OE
1957			12	OE
1958			9	OE
1959			10	OE
1960	DAL	N	12	OE
1961			14	OE
11 yrs.	115 games			

Joe D'Orazio
D'ORAZIO, JOSEPH
B. Oct. 5, 1914
D. Sep., 1972
Ithaca 5'11" 220 lbs.

Year	Team		Games	Pos.
1944	DET	N	4	T

Art Dorfman
DORFMAN, ARTHUR
B. 1907
Boston University 5'10" 210 lbs.

Year	Team		Games	Pos.
1929	BUF	N	9	C, E

Torin Dorn
DORN, TORIN
B. Feb. 29, 1968, Greenwood, SC
North Carolina 6'0" 190 lbs.

Year	Team		Games	Pos.
1990	LARI	N	16	CB
1991			16	CB
1992			15	CB
1993			15	CB
1995	STL	N	12	CB
1996			10	CB
6 yrs.	84 games			

Thom Dornbrook
DORNBROOK, THOMAS JOHN
B. Dec. 1, 1956, Berea, OH
Kentucky 6'2" 240 lbs.

Year	Team		Games	Pos.
1979	PIT	N	16	G, C
1980	MIA	N	4	G, C
2 yrs.	20 games			

Keith Dorney
DORNEY, KEITH ROBERT
B. Dec. 3, 1957, Allentown, PA
Penn State 6'5" 265 lbs.

Year	Team		Games	Pos.
1979	DET	N	16	OT
1980			9	OT
1981			16	OT
1982			9	OT
1983			13	OT
1984			16	OT
1985			16	OT
1986			12	G, OT
1987			5	G, OT
9 yrs.	112 games			

Dale Dorning
DORNING, DALE
B. Feb. 7, 1962, Burien, WA
Oregon 6'5" 260 lbs.

Year	Team		Games	Pos.
1987	SEA	N	3	DE

Al Dorow
DOROW, ALBERT RICHARD
B. Nov. 15, 1929, Imlay City, MI
Michigan State 6'0" 193 lbs.

Year	Team		Games	Pos.
1954	WAS	N	11	QB
1955			8	QB
1956			12	QB
1957	PHI	N	6	QB
1960	NY	A	14	QB
1961			14	QB
1962	BUF	A	4	QB
7 yrs.	69 games			

Andy Dorris
DORRIS, ANDREW MICHAEL
B. Aug. 11, 1951, Bellaire, OH
New Mexico State 6'4" 238 lbs.

Year	Team		Games	Pos.
1973	STL	N	4	DE
1973	NO	N	1	DE
1974			14	DE
1975			13	DE
1976			14	DE
1977	SEA	N	4	DE
1977	HOU	N	5	DE
1978			16	DE
1979			16	DE
1980			16	DE
1981			15	DE
9 yrs.	118 games			

Anthony Dorsett
DORSETT, ANTHONY DREW, JR.
B. Sep. 14, 1973, Aliquippa, PA
Pittsburgh 5'11" 190 lbs.

Year	Team		Games	Pos.
1996	HOU	N	8	CB

Matthew Dorsett
DORSETT, MATTHEW HERBERT
B. Aug. 23, 1973, New Orleans, LA
Southern University 5'11" 187 lbs.

Year	Team		Games	Pos.
1995	GB	N	10	CB

Tony Dorsett
DORSETT, ANTHONY DREW, SR. (T.D.)
B. Apr. 7, 1954, Rochester, PA
Pittsburgh 5'11" 191 lbs.

Year	Team		Games	Pos.
1977	DAL	N	14	RB
1978			16	RB
1979			14	RB
1980			15	RB
1981			16	RB
1982			9	RB
1983			16	RB
1984			16	RB
1985			16	RB
1986			13	RB
1987			12	RB
1988	DEN	N	16	RB
12 yrs.	173 games			

Dean Dorsey
DORSEY, DEAN
B. Mar. 13, 1957, Toronto, Ont.
Toronto 5'11" 190 lbs.

Year	Team		Games	Pos.
1988	PHI	N	3	K
1988	GB	N	3	K
1 yr.	6 games			

Dick Dorsey
DORSEY, DICK
B. 1938
Southern California/Oklahoma 6'3" 200 lbs.

Year	Team		Games	Pos.
1962	OAK	A	11	OE

Eric Dorsey
DORSEY, ERIC HALL
B. Aug. 5, 1964, Washington, DC
Notre Dame 6'5" 280 lbs.

Year	Team		Games	Pos.
1986	NYG	N	16	DE
1987			12	DE
1988			16	DE
1989			2	DE
1990			16	DE
1991			11	DE
1992			16	DE
7 yrs.	89 games			

John Dorsey
DORSEY, JOHN MICHAEL
B. Aug. 31, 1960, Leonardtown, MD
Connecticut 6'3" 240 lbs.

Year	Team		Games	Pos.
1984	GB	N	16	LB
1985			16	LB
1986			16	LB
1987			12	LB
1988			16	LB
5 yrs.	76 games			

Larry Dorsey
DORSEY, LARRY DARNELL
B. Aug. 15, 1953, Corinth, MS
Tennessee State 6'1" 195 lbs.

Year	Team		Games	Pos.
1976	SD	N	13	WR
1977			13	WR
1978	KC	N	16	WR
3 yrs.	42 games			

Nate Dorsey
DORSEY, NATHANIEL EUGENE
B. Dec. 6, 1950, Tampa, FL

Nate Dorsey *continued*
Mississippi Valley State 6'4" 240 lbs.

Year	Team		Games	Pos.
1973	NE	N	2	DE

Noble Doss
DOSS, NOBLE W.
B. May 22, 1920, Temple, TX
Texas 6'0" 186 lbs.

Year	Team		Games	Pos.
1947	PHI	N	9	HB
1948			11	HB
1949	B-NY	AA	4	HB
3 yrs.	24 games			

Reggie Doss
DOSS, REGINALD LEE
B. Dec. 7, 1956, Mobile, AL
Hampton Institute 6'4" 267 lbs.

Year	Team		Games	Pos.
1978	LA	N	16	DE
1979			16	DE
1980			16	DE
1981			16	DE
1982	LARM	N	9	DE
1983			16	DE
1984			16	DE
1985			16	DE
1986			16	DE
1987			12	DE
10 yrs.	149 games			

Al Dotson
DOTSON, ALPHONSE ALAN
B. Feb. 25, 1943, Houston, TX
Grambling State 6'4" 258 lbs.

Year	Team		Games	Pos.
1965	KC	A	1	DT
1966	MIA	A	9	DT
1968	OAK	A	13	DT
1969			13	DT
1970	OAK	N	11	DT
5 yrs.	47 games			

Dewayne Dotson
DOTSON, JACK DEWAYNE
B. Jun. 10, 1971, Hendersonville, TN
Tennessee/Mississippi 6'1" 256 lbs.

Year	Team		Games	Pos.
1995	MIA	N	15	LB

Earl Dotson
DOTSON, EARL CHRISTOPHER
B. Dec. 17, 1970, Beaumont, TX
Texas A&I-Kingsville 6'4" 315 lbs.

Year	Team		Games	Pos.
1993	GB	N	13	OT
1994			4	OT
1995			16	OT
1996			16	OT
4 yrs.	49 games			

Santana Dotson
DOTSON, SANTANA
B. Dec. 19, 1969, New Orleans, LA
Baylor 6'5" 270 lbs.

Year	Team		Games	Pos.
1992	TB	N	16	DE
1993			16	DE
1994			16	DT, DE
1995			16	DT
1996	GB	N	16	DT
5 yrs.	80 games			

Kayo Dottley
DOTTLEY, JOHN
B. Aug. 25, 1928, McGehee, AR
Mississippi 6'1" 200 lbs.

Year	Team		Games	Pos.
1951	CHIB	N	12	FB
1952			5	FB
1953			10	FB
3 yrs.	27 games			

Year	Team	Games	Pos.

Dan Doubiago
DOUBIAGO, DANIEL CLARKE
B. Sep. 25, 1960, Mendocino, CA
Utah 6'5" 283 lbs.

Year	Team	Games	Pos.
1987	**KC** N	3	OT

Forrest Douds
DOUDS, FORREST M. (Jap)
B. Apr. 21, 1905
D. Aug. 16, 1979, Sewickley, PA
Washington & Jefferson 5'10" 216 lbs.

Year	Team	Games	Pos.
1930	**PRO** N	9	T
1930	**POR** N	3	T
1931		13	T
1932	**CHIC** N	9	T, E
1933	**PIT** N	7	T
1934		11	G, T
5 yrs.	52 games		

Bob Dougherty
DOUGHERTY, ROBERT
B. Apr. 20, 1932
Deceased
Cincinnati/Kentucky 6'0" 238 lbs.

Year	Team	Games	Pos.
1957	**LA** N	10	C, LB
1958	**PIT** N	12	LB
1960	**OAK** A		LB
1961		14	LB
1962		14	LB
1963		5	LB
6 yrs.	55 games		

Phil Dougherty
DOUGHERTY, PHILIP F.
B. Sep. 20, 1912, San Francisco, CA
Santa Clara 5'11" 185 lbs.

Year	Team	Games	Pos.
1938	**CHIC** N	10	C

Glenn Doughty
DOUGHTY, GLENN
B. Jan. 30, 1951, Detroit, MI
Michigan 6'1" 204 lbs.

Year	Team	Games	Pos.
1972	**BAL** N	5	WR
1973		14	WR
1974		13	WR
1975		14	WR
1976		14	WR
1977		13	WR
1978		15	WR
1979		15	WR
8 yrs.	103 games		

Ben Douglas
DOUGLAS, BENJAMIN
B. 1909
Grinnell 6'0" 185 lbs.

Year	Team	Games	Pos.
1933	**BKN** N	5	HB

Bob Douglas
DOUGLAS, ROBERT
B. 1915
Kansas State 6'0" 195 lbs.

Year	Team	Games	Pos.
1938	**PIT** N	1	FB, DB

David Douglas
DOUGLAS, DAVID GLENN
B. Mar. 20, 1963, Spring City, TN
Tennessee 6'4" 280 lbs.

Year	Team	Games	Pos.
1986	**CIN** N	14	OT
1987		12	OT
1988		14	OT
1989	**NE** N	5	OT
1990		11	G, C
5 yrs.	56 games		

Derrick Douglas
DOUGLAS, DERRICK DEWAYNE
B. Aug. 10, 1968, Shreveport, LA
Louisiana Tech 5'10" 222 lbs.

Year	Team	Games	Pos.
1991	**CLE** N	2	RB

Everett Douglas
DOUGLAS, EVERETT DEWAYNE
B. 1932
Florida 6'3" 240 lbs.

Year	Team	Games	Pos.
1953	**NYG** N	5	T

George Douglas
DOUGLAS, GEORGE
Marquette 200 lbs.

Year	Team	Games	Pos.
1926	**MIL** N	1	G

Hugh Douglas
DOUGLAS, HUGH
B. Aug. 23, 1971, Mansfield, OH
Central State (Ohio) 6'2" 265 lbs.

Year	Team	Games	Pos.
1995	**NYJ** N	15	DE
1996		10	DE
2 yrs.	25 games		

Jay Douglas
DOUGLAS, JAY
B. Sep. 1, 1950, Palco, KS
Memphis State 6'6" 251 lbs.

Year	Team	Games	Pos.
1973	**SD** N	14	C
1974		14	C
2 yrs.	28 games		

John Douglas
DOUGLAS, JOHN HENRY
B. Jan. 12, 1945, Fort Worth, TX
Texas Southern 6'1" 195 lbs.

Year	Team	Games	Pos.
1967	**NO** N	14	DB
1968		14	DB
1969	**HOU** A	8	CB
3 yrs.	36 games		

John Douglas
DOUGLAS, JOHN LOUIS
B. Sep. 6, 1945, Columbia, MO
Missouri 6'2" 227 lbs.

Year	Team	Games	Pos.
1970	**NYG** N	14	LB
1971		14	LB
1972		14	LB
1973		14	LB
4 yrs.	56 games		

Leland Douglas
DOUGLAS, LELAND
B. Sep. 23, 1963
Baylor 6'0" 179 lbs.

Year	Team	Games	Pos.
1987	**MIA** N	3	WR

Merrill Douglas
DOUGLAS, MERRILL GEORGE
B. Mar. 15, 1936, Salt Lake City, UT
Utah 6'0" 204 lbs.

Year	Team	Games	Pos.
1958	**CHIB** N	12	FB
1959		12	FB
1960	**CHI** N	12	FB
1961	**DAL** N	6	FB
1962	**PHI** N	13	FB
5 yrs.	55 games		

Omar Douglas
DOUGLAS, OMAR
B. Jun. 3, 1972, New Orleans, LA
Minnesota 5'10" 170 lbs.

Year	Team	Games	Pos.
1994	**NYG** N	7	WR
1995		8	WR

Omar Douglas *continued*

Year	Team	Games	Pos.
1996		4	WR
3 yrs.	19 games		

Otis Douglas
DOUGLAS, OTIS W., JR.
B. Jul. 25, 1911, Readsville, VA
D. Mar. 21, 1989, Kilmarnock, PA
William & Mary 6'1" 224 lbs.

Year	Team	Games	Pos.
1946	**PHI** N	11	T
1947		12	T
1948		5	T
1949		2	T
4 yrs.	30 games		

Bobby Douglass
DOUGLASS, ROBERT GILCHRIST
B. Jun. 22, 1947, Manhattan, KS
Kansas 6'3" 224 lbs.

Year	Team	Games	Pos.
1969	**CHI** N	9	QB
1970		3	QB
1971		12	QB
1972		14	QB
1973		13	QB
1974		7	QB
1975		1	QB
1975	**SD** N	3	QB
1975	**NO** N	1	QB
1976		11	QB
1977		4	QB
1978	**GB** N	12	QB
10 yrs.	90 games		

Freddie Douglass
DOUGLASS, FREDDIE
B. Mar. 28, 1954, McGehee, AR
Arkansas 5'9" 185 lbs.

Year	Team	Games	Pos.
1976	**TB** N	7	WR

Leo Douglass
DOUGLASS, LEO
B. Feb. 13, 1901
D. Apr., 1985, Wakefield, MA
Lehigh/Vermont 5'11" 190 lbs.

Year	Team	Games	Pos.
1926	**FRA** N	2	FB, HB
1926	**BKN** N	4	FB, HB
1 yr.	6 games		

Maurice Douglass
DOUGLASS, MAURICE GERRARD
B. Feb. 12, 1964, Muncie, IN
Kentucky 5'11" 200 lbs.

Year	Team	Games	Pos.
1986	**CHI** N	4	CB, S
1987		12	CB, S
1988		15	CB, S
1989		10	CB, S
1990		11	CB, S
1991		16	CB
1992		16	CB
1993		16	CB
1994		16	CB
1995	**NYG** N	8	S
1996		15	CB
11 yrs.	139 games		

Mike Douglass
DOUGLASS, MICHAEL REESE
B. Mar. 15, 1955, St. Louis, MO
Arizona State/San Diego State 6'0" 220 lbs.

Year	Team	Games	Pos.
1978	**GB** N	16	LB
1979		16	LB
1980		16	LB
1981		16	LB
1982		9	LB

Mike Douglass *continued*

Year	Team	Games	Pos.
1983		15	LB
1984		16	LB
1985		16	LB
1986	**SD** N	7	LB
9 yrs.	127 games		

Earl Douthitt
DOUTHITT, EARL
B. Sep. 8, 1952, Cleveland, OH
Iowa 6'2" 188 lbs.

Year	Team	Games	Pos.
1975	**CHI** N	9	S

Bob Dove
DOVE, ROBERT LEO PATRICK
B. Feb. 21, 1921, Youngstown, OH
Notre Dame 6'2" 222 lbs.

Year	Team	Games	Pos.
1946	**CHI** AA	14	E
1947		13	E
1948	**CHIC** N	12	E
1949		12	E
1950		12	E
1951		12	E
1952		10	E
1953		4	E
1953	**DET** N	4	E
1954		12	E
9 yrs.	105 games		

Eddie Dove
DOVE, EDWARD E.
B. Apr. 4, 1937, Hygiene, CO
Colorado 6'2" 181 lbs.

Year	Team	Games	Pos.
1959	**SF** N	12	DB
1960		12	DB
1961		14	DB
1962		14	DB
1963		2	DB
1963	**NYG** N	14	DB
5 yrs.	68 games		

Jerome Dove
DOVE, JEROME
B. Oct. 3, 1953, Newport News, VA
Colorado State 6'2" 190 lbs.

Year	Team	Games	Pos.
1977	**SD** N	14	CB
1978		14	CB
1979		16	CB
1980		16	CB
4 yrs.	60 games		

Wes Dove
DOVE, WESLEY WALTER
B. Feb. 9, 1964, Buffalo, NY
D. Mar. 4, 1989, Gaithersburg, MD
Syracuse 6'7" 270 lbs.

Year	Team	Games	Pos.
1987	**SEA** N	2	DE

Harley Dow
DOW, HARLEY
B. 1925
San Jose State 6'2" 220 lbs.

Year	Team	Games	Pos.
1950	**SF** N	12	G

Ken Dow
DOW, KENNETH WILLIAM
B. Nov. 18, 1918, Ephrata, WA
D. Dec. 1, 1988
Oregon State 5'10" 198 lbs.

Year	Team	Games	Pos.
1941	**WAS** N	2	B

Woody Dow
DOW, JESS ELWOOD (Rowdy, Cap)
B. Dec. 16, 1916, Littlefield, TX
West Texas State 6'0" 195 lbs.

Year	Team	Games	Pos.
1938	**PHI** N	10	HB, DB

Year	Team		Games	Pos.

Woody Dow continued

Year	Team		Games	Pos.
1939			9	FB, LB
2 yrs.	19 games			

Jerry Dowd
DOWD, GERALD
B. 1916
St. Mary's (California) 6'0" 210 lbs.
| 1939 | CLE | N | 8 | C, LB |

Harry Dowda
DOWDA, HARRY C.
B. Dec. 29, 1922, Atlanta, GA
Deceased
Wake Forest 6'2" 199 lbs.
1949	WAS	N	12	HB
1950			12	HB
1951			12	HB
1952			12	HB
1953			12	HB
1954	PHI	N	12	HB
1955			12	HB
7 yrs.	84 games			

Marcus Dowdell
DOWDELL, MARCUS
B. May 22, 1970, Birmingham, AL
Tennessee State 5'10" 179 lbs.
1992	NO	N	4	WR
1993			9	WR
1995	ARI	N	13	WR
1996			15	WR
4 yrs.	41 games			

Corey Dowden
DOWDEN, COREY
B. Oct. 18, 1968, New Orleans, LA
Tulane 5'11" 190 lbs.
1996	GB	N	9	CB
1996	BAL	N	3	CB
1 yr.	12 games			

Steve Dowden
DOWDEN, STEPHAN H.
B. Feb. 24, 1929, Odessa, TX
Baylor 6'2" 235 lbs.
| 1952 | GB | N | 12 | T |

Mike Dowdle
DOWDLE, DON MICHAEL
B. Dec. 6, 1937, Eliasville, TX
D. Dec. 5, 1993, Houston, TX
Texas 6'3" 226 lbs.
1960	DAL	N	2	LB
1961			14	LB
1962			14	LB
1963	SF	N	13	LB
1964			14	LB
1965			10	LB
1966			14	LB
7 yrs.	81 games			

Mule Dowell
DOWELL, GWYNN C.
B. Jun. 27, 1913, Ben Franklin, TX
Texas Tech 6'2" 206 lbs.
1935	CHIC	N	5	FB
1936			10	FB, HB, E
2 yrs.	15 games			

Boyd Dowler
DOWLER, BOYD HAMILTON
B. Oct. 18, 1937, Rock Springs, WY
Colorado 6'5" 224 lbs.
| 1959 | GB | N | 12 | OE |
| 1960 | | | 12 | OE |

Boyd Dowler continued

Year	Team		Games	Pos.
1961			14	OE
1962			14	OE
1963			14	OE
1964			14	OE
1965			14	OE
1966			14	OE
1967			14	OE
1968			14	OE
1969			14	WR
1971	WAS	N	12	WR
12 yrs.	162 games			

Tommy Dowler
DOWLER, THOMAS (Flash)
B. Jul. 3, 1908
D. Dec., 1986, Atlanta, GA
Colgate 5'8" 160 lbs.
| 1931 | BKN | N | 2 | B |

Brian Dowling
DOWLING, BRIAN JOHN (B.D.)
B. Apr. 1, 1947, Cleveland, OH
Yale 6'2" 207 lbs.
1972	NE	N	14	QB
1973			11	QB
1977	GB	N	5	QB
3 yrs.	30 games			

Pat Dowling
DOWLING, PATRICK J. (Smoke Screen)
B. Feb. 19, 1904
D. Nov. 24, 1974, Arcadia, CA
DePaul 185 lbs.
| 1929 | CHIC | N | 13 | E |

Sean Dowling
DOWLING, SEAN
B. Feb. 19, 1963, New York, NY
C.W. Post 6'4" 280 lbs.
| 1987 | BUF | N | 3 | OT |

Walt Downing
DOWNING, WALT
B. Jun. 11, 1956, Coatesville, PA
Michigan 6'3" 254 lbs.
1978	SF	N	16	G
1979			16	G
1980			14	C, G
1981			16	C, G
1982			9	C, G
1983			12	C, G
6 yrs.	83 games			

Gary Downs
DOWNS, GARY MCLINTON
B. Jun. 28, 1971, Columbus, GA
North Carolina State 6'0" 212 lbs.
1994	NYG	N	14	RB
1995	DEN	N	1	RB
1996	NYG	N	6	RB
3 yrs.	21 games			

Michael Downs
DOWNS, MICHAEL
B. Jun. 9, 1959, Dallas, TX
Rice 6'3" 200 lbs.
1981	DAL	N	16	S
1982			9	S
1983			16	S
1984			16	S
1985			16	S
1986			16	S
1987			12	S
1988			16	S
8 yrs.	117 games			

Xavier Downwind
DOWNWIND, XAVIER (Chief Red Fang)
B. Dec. 24, 1893
D. Jul., 1968, Redby, MN
Carlisle 6'0" 200 lbs.
| 1922 | OOR | N | 3 | T, E |

Perry Dowrick
DOWRICK, PERRY
B. Jul., 1894
Deceased
None 160 lbs.
| 1921 | WAS | A | 2 | HB, FB |

Dick Doyle
DOYLE, RICHARD A. (Skip)
B. 1931
Ohio State 6'0" 193 lbs.
1955	PIT	N	12	DB
1960	DEN	A		DB
2 yrs.	12 games			

Ed Doyle
DOYLE, EDWARD
B. 1903
Deceased
Canisius
| 1927 | BUF | N | 4 | C, T-G |

Eddie Doyle
DOYLE, EDWARD JAMES
B. Aug. 17, 1898, New York, NY
D. Nov. 8, 1942, Morocco
Army 5'9" 175 lbs.
1924	FRA	N	10	E
1925	POT	N	9	E
2 yrs.	19 games			

Ted Doyle
DOYLE, THEODORE DENNISON
B. Jan. 12, 1914, Curtis, NE
Nebraska 6'2" 224 lbs.
1938	PIT	N	8	T
1939			9	T, G
1940			8	T, G
1941			9	T
1942			10	T
1943	P, P	N	10	T
1944	C, P	N	9	T, B
1945	PIT	N	10	T
8 yrs.	73 games			

Cornelius Dozier
DOZIER, CORNELIUS
B. May 2, 1964, Dallas, TX
Southern Methodist 6'2" 190 lbs.
| 1987 | KC | N | 2 | S |

D.J. Dozier
DOZIER, WILLIAM HENRY, JR.
B. Sep. 21, 1965, Norfolk, VA
Penn State 6'0" 198 lbs.
1987	MIN	N	9	RB
1988			8	RB
1989			8	RB
1990			6	RB
1991	DET	N	6	RB
5 yrs.	37 games			

Oscar Dragon
DRAGON, OSCAR LEE
B. Mar. 2, 1950, Madera, CA
Arizona State 6'0" 214 lbs.
| 1972 | SD | N | 13 | RB |

Bill Drake
DRAKE, WILLIAM
B. May 22, 1950, Portland, OR
Oregon 6'1" 195 lbs.
1973	LA	N	4	S
1974			8	S
2 yrs.	12 games			

Jerry Drake
DRAKE, JERRY
B. Jul. 9, 1969, Kingston, NY
Hastings 6'4" 292 lbs.
1995	ARI	N	2	DT
1996			11	DE
2 yrs.	13 games			

Joe Drake
DRAKE, JOE LYNN
B. May 28, 1963, San Francisco, CA
Arizona 6'2" 290 lbs.
1985	PHI	N	16	NT
1987	SF	N	3	NT
2 yrs.	19 games			

Johnny Drake
DRAKE, JOHN W.
B. Mar. 27, 1916, Chicago, IL
D. Mar. 26, 1973, Detroit, MI
Purdue 6'1" 213 lbs.
1937	CLE	N	11	FB, HB
1938			11	FB, HB
1939			11	FB
1940			11	FB
1941			11	FB
5 yrs.	55 games			

Troy Drake
DRAKE, TROY
B. May 15, 1972, Rockford, IL
Indiana 6'6" 289 lbs.
1995	PHI	N	1	OT
1996			11	OT
2 yrs.	12 games			

Tyronne Drakeford
DRAKEFORD, TYRONNE JAMES
B. Jun. 21, 1971, Camden, SC
Virginia Tech 5'9" 185 lbs.
1994	SF	N	13	CB
1995			16	CB
1996			16	CB
3 yrs.	45 games			

Dwight Drane
DRANE, DWIGHT
B. May 6, 1962, Miami, FL
Oklahoma 6'1" 200 lbs.
1986	BUF	N	13	S
1987			11	S
1988			16	S
1989			16	S
1990			12	S
1991			14	S
6 yrs.	82 games			

Leo Draveling
DRAVELING, LEO F. (Firpo)
B. Jun. 23, 1907
D. Jul. 2, 1955
Michigan 6'2" 210 lbs.
| 1933 | CIN | N | 9 | T, E |

Clarence Drayer
DRAYER, CLARENCE T. (Shorty)
B. Aug. 29, 1901
D. Oct. 8, 1977, Indianapolis, IN

Year	Team	Games	Pos.

Clarence Drayer *continued*

Illinois 6'3" 235 lbs.

1925	DAY	N	4	T

Troy Drayton

DRAYTON, TROY ANTHONY

B. Jun. 29, 1970, Harrisburg, PA
Penn State 6'3" 255 lbs.

1993	LARM	N	16	TE
1994			16	TE
1995	STL	N	16	TE
1996			3	TE
1996	MIA	N	10	TE

4 yrs.   61 games

Chuck Drazenovich

DRAZENOVICH, CHARLES M.

B. Aug. 27, 1927, Jere, WV
Penn State 6'1" 225 lbs.

1950	WAS	N	12	FB
1951			9	FB
1952			12	FB
1953			8	FB
1954			12	FB
1955			12	FB
1956			12	FB
1957			12	FB
1958			12	FB
1959			12	FB

10 yrs.   113 games

Dave Drechsler

DRECHSLER, DAVE

B. Jul. 18, 1960, Cleveland, NC
North Carolina 6'3" 264 lbs.

1983	GB	N	16	G
1984			16	G

2 yrs.   32 games

Fred Dreher

DREHER, FERDINAND A.

B. 1913
Denver 6'3" 205 lbs.

1938	CHIB	N	3	E

Chris Dressel

DRESSEL, CHRIS

B. Feb. 7, 1961, Placentia, CA
Stanford 6'4" 239 lbs.

1983	HOU	N	16	TE
1984			16	TE
1985			16	TE
1986			16	TE
1987	SF	N	1	TE
1989	KC	N	7	TE
1989	NYJ	N	8	TE
1990			15	TE
1991			15	TE
1992	SF	N	1	TE

9 yrs.   111 games

Chuck Dressen

DRESSEN, CHARLES WALTER
(Dynamite)

B. Sep. 20, 1898, Decatur, IL
D. Aug. 10, 1966, Detroit, MI
None 5'6" 147 lbs.

1920	DEC	A	1	QB
1922	RAC	N	7	QB
1923			1	QB

3 yrs.   9 games

Doug Dressler

DRESSLER, DOUGLAS J.

B. Mar. 19, 1948, Sacramento, CA
Chico State 6'3" 225 lbs.

1970	CIN	N	14	RB

Doug Dressler *continued*

1971			14	RB
1972			14	RB
1974			13	RB
1975	NE	N	5	RB
1975	KC	N	8	RB

5 yrs.   68 games

Willie Drewrey

DREWREY, WILLIE

B. Apr. 28, 1963, Columbus, NJ
West Virginia 5'7" 164 lbs.

1985	HOU	N	14	WR
1986			15	WR
1987			12	WR
1988			14	WR
1989	TB	N	16	WR
1990			16	WR
1991			16	WR
1992			9	WR
1993	HOU	N	16	WR

9 yrs.   128 games

Ted Drews

DREWS, THEODORE W.

B. Dec. 15, 1902
D. Apr. 15, 1982
Princeton 6'0" 185 lbs.

1926	BKN	A	4	E
1926	BKN	N	3	E
1928	CHIB	N	7	E

2 yrs.   14 games

Wally Dreyer

DREYER, WALTER O.

B. Feb. 25, 1923, Milwaukee, WI
Michigan/Wisconsin 5'10" 170 lbs.

1949	CHIB	N	12	HB
1950	GB	N	12	HB

2 yrs.   24 games

Paddy Driscoll

DRISCOLL, JOHN LEO

B. Jan. 11, 1895, Evanston, IL
D. Jun. 29, 1968, Chicago, IL
Northwestern 5'8" 165 lbs.

1920	CHIC	A	6	QB, HB
1920	DEC	A	1	QB, HB
1921	CHIC	A	8	QB, HB
1922	CHIC	N	11	QB, HB
1923			10	QB, HB, FB
1924			10	QB, HB
1925			13	HB, QB
1926	CHIB	N	16	HB, FB
1927			12	HB, FB
1928			12	HB, QB
1929			14	HB, QB

10 yrs.   115 games

Joe Driskill

DRISKILL, JOSEPH

B. Aug. 10, 1957, Arcadia, LA
Northeast Louisiana 6'1" 195 lbs.

1960	STL	N	6	DB
1961			14	DB

2 yrs.   20 games

Stacey Driver

DRIVER, STACEY

B. Mar. 4, 1964
Clemson 5'7" 190 lbs.

1987	CLE	N	3	RB

Shane Dronett

DRONETT, SHANE

B. Jan. 12, 1971, Orange, TX

Shane Dronett *continued*

Texas 6'6" 275 lbs.

1992	DEN	N	16	DE, NT
1993			16	DE
1994			16	DE
1995			13	DE, DT
1996	ATL	N	5	DE
1996	DET	N	7	DE

5 yrs.   73 games

Jeff Drost

DROST, JEFF

B. Jan. 27, 1964
Iowa 6'5" 286 lbs.

1987	GB	N	2	NT

Tom Drouglas

DROUGLAS, THOMAS
CHRISTOPHER, JR.

B. Dec. 25, 1949, Portland, OR
Oregon 6'4" 258 lbs.

1972	BAL	N	14	OT
1973			13	OT
1974	DEN	N	4	OT
1974	KC	N	7	OT
1975	MIA	N	14	OT
1976			14	OT

5 yrs.   66 games

Darren Drozdov

DROZDOV, DARREN

B. Apr. 7, 1969, Mays Landing, NJ
Maryland 6'3" 280 lbs.

1993	DEN	N	6	NT

Al Drulis

DRULIS, ALBERT ANTHONY

B. Aug. 30, 1921, Girardville, PA
Temple 5'10" 193 lbs.

1945	CHIC	N	9	FB
1946			5	FB
1947	PIT	N	10	FB

3 yrs.   24 games

Chuck Drulis

DRULIS, CHARLES JOHN

B. Mar. 18, 1918, Girardville, PA
D. Aug. 23, 1972
Temple 5'10" 216 lbs.

1942	CHIB	N	11	G
1945			3	G
1946			11	G
1947			12	G
1948			12	G
1949			12	G
1950	GB	N	11	G

7 yrs.   72 games

Robert Drummond

DRUMMOND, ROBERT C.

B. Jun. 21, 1967, Apopka, FL
Syracuse 6'1" 205 lbs.

1989	PHI	N	16	RB
1990			4	RB
1991			16	RB

3 yrs.   36 games

Wop Drumstead

DRUMSTADT, WALTER

B. Sep., 1898
Deceased
None 185 lbs.

1925	HAM	N	1	G

Elbert Drungo

DRUNGO, ELBERT, JR. (Sunny)

Elbert Drungo *continued*

B. Apr. 30, 1943, Columbus, MS
Tennessee State 6'5" 260 lbs.

1969	HOU	A	14	OT
1970	HOU	N	14	OT
1971			11	G
1973			14	OT
1974			13	OT
1975			13	OT
1976			14	OT
1977			14	OT
1978	BUF	N	13	OT

9 yrs.   120 games

Hoot Drury

DRURY, LYLE THOMAS

B. Feb. 18, 1906
D. Aug. 26, 1989, Itasca, IL
St. Louis 6'4" 189 lbs.

1930	CHIB	N	12	E
1931			10	E

2 yrs.   22 games

Rick Druschel

DRUSCHEL, RICH

B. Jan. 15, 1952, Greensburg, PA
North Carolina State 6'2" 248 lbs.

1974	PIT	N	11	OT, G

John Druze

DRUZE, JOHN F.

B. 1914
Fordham 6'0" 195 lbs.

1938	BKN	N	10	E

Fred Dryer

DRYER, JOHN FREDERICK

B. Jun. 6, 1946, Hawthorne, CA
San Diego State 6'6" 238 lbs.

1969	NYG	N	14	DE
1970			14	DE
1971			14	DE
1972	LA	N	14	DE
1973			14	DE
1974			14	DE
1975			14	DE
1976			14	DE
1977			14	DE
1978			16	DE
1979			16	DE
1980			16	DE
1981			2	DE

13 yrs.   176 games

Ron Drzewiecki

DRZEWIECKI, RONALD

B. Jan. 25, 1923, Milwaukee, WI
Marquette 5'11" 185 lbs.

1955	CHIB	N	12	HB

George Duarte

DUARTE, GEORGE

B. Feb. 9, 1964
Northern Arizona 5'9" 178 lbs.

1987	CHI	N	3	CB, S

Elbert Dubenion

DUBENION, ELBERT (Golden
Wheels)

B. Feb. 16, 1935, Griffin, GA
Bluffton 6'0" 189 lbs.

1960	BUF	A	14	HB
1961			14	HB
1962			14	HB
1963			14	HB
1964			14	FL
1965			3	FL

Year	Team		Games	Pos.

Elbert Dubenion *continued*

Year	Team		Games	Pos.
1966			14	FL
1967			12	FL
1968			4	FL
9 yrs.	103 games			

Greg Dubinetz
DUBINETZ, GREGORY GEORGE
B. Apr. 15, 1954, Chicago, IL
Yale 6'4" 260 lbs.

| 1979 | WAS | N | 15 | G |

Tom Dublinski
DUBLINSKI, THOMAS EUGENE, JR.
B. Aug. 8, 1930, Hinsdale, IL
Utah 6'2" 197 lbs.

1952	DET	N	5	QB
1953			7	QB
1954			12	QB
1958	NYG	N	1	QB
1960	DEN	A		QB
5 yrs.	25 games			

Maury Dubofsky
DUBOFSKY, MAURICE (Mush)
B. 1909
D. Jan. 25, 1970
Georgetown (DC) 5'10" 210 lbs.

| 1932 | NYG | N | 5 | G |

Phil DuBois
DUBOIS, PHIL
B. Nov. 15, 1956, Rochester, MN
San Diego State 6'2" 220 lbs.

1979	WAS	N	15	TE
1980			2	TE
2 yrs.	17 games			

Demetrius DuBose
DUBOSE, ADOLPHUS DEMETRIUS
B. Mar. 23, 1971, Seattle, WA
Notre Dame 6'1" 240 lbs.

1993	TB	N	15	LB
1994			16	LB
1995			15	LB
1996			14	LB
4 yrs.	60 games			

Doug DuBose
DUBOSE, DOUG
B. Mar. 14, 1964, New London, CT
Nebraska 5'11" 190 lbs.

1987	SF	N	2	RB
1988			14	RB
2 yrs.	16 games			

Jimmy DuBose
DUBOSE, JIMMY DUWAYNE
B. Oct. 25, 1954, Enterprise, AL
Florida 5'11" 216 lbs.

1976	TB	N	13	RB
1977			13	RB
1978			6	RB
3 yrs.	32 games			

Walt Dubzinski
DUBZINSKI, WALTER
B. Oct. 26, 1919, Gardner, MA
Boston College 5'10" 205 lbs.

1943	NYG	N	5	C
1944	BOS	N	3	C
2 yrs.	8 games			

Mark Duckens
DUCKENS, MARK ANTHONY
B. Mar. 4, 1965, Wichita, KS
Wichita State/Arizona State 6'4" 270 lbs.

1989	NYG	N	15	DE
1990	DET	N	15	DE
1992	TB	N	5	DE, NT
3 yrs.	35 games			

Forey Duckett
DUCKETT, FOREY
B. Feb. 5, 1970, Pinole, CA
Nevada-Reno 6'3" 195 lbs.

1994	CIN	N	2	DB
1994	GB	N	3	DB
1994	SEA	N	2	DB
1 yr.	7 games			

Kenny Duckett
DUCKETT, KENNY WAYNE
B. Oct. 1, 1959, Winston-Salem, NC
Wake Forest 5'11" 187 lbs.

1982	NO	N	7	WR
1983			14	WR
1984			11	WR
1985			1	WR
1985	DAL	N	3	WR
4 yrs.	36 games			

Robert Ducksworth
DUCKSWORTH, ROBERT
B. Jan. 5, 1963, Biloxi, MS
Southern Mississippi 5'11" 200 lbs.

| 1986 | NYJ | N | 2 | CB |

Bobby Duckworth
DUCKWORTH, BOBBY RAY
B. Nov. 27, 1958, Crossett, AR
Arkansas 6'3" 197 lbs.

1982	SD	N	5	WR
1983			16	WR
1984			16	WR
1985	LARM	N	14	WR
1986			7	WR
1986	PHI	N	4	WR
5 yrs.	62 games			

Joe Duckworth
DUCKWORTH, JOSEPH W.
B. Jul. 3, 1921, Orange, NJ
Colgate 6'2" 220 lbs.

| 1947 | WAS | N | 12 | E |

Moon Ducote
DUCOTE, RICHARD (Duke)
B. Aug. 28, 1897
Deceased
Auburn 5'11" 190 lbs.

| 1920 | CLE | A | 1 | HB |

Mark Duda
DUDA, MARK DAVID
B. Feb. 4, 1961, Wilkes-Barre, PA
Maryland 6'3" 273 lbs.

1983	STL	N	14	DT
1984			8	DT
1985			16	DT
1986			14	DT
1987			3	NT
5 yrs.	55 games			

Joe Dudek
DUDEK, JOSEPH
B. Jan. 22, 1964

Joe Dudek *continued*
Plymouth State 6'0" 181 lbs.

| 1987 | DEN | N | 2 | RB |

Mitch Dudek
DUDEK, MITCHELL
B. 1944
Xavier (Ohio) 6'4" 245 lbs.

| 1966 | NY | A | 14 | OT |

Dick Duden
DUDEN, HENRY RICHARD, JR.
B. Nov. 29, 1924, Pottstown, PA
Navy 6'3" 212 lbs.

| 1949 | NYG | N | 12 | E |

Andy Dudish
DUDISH, ANDREW C.
B. Oct. 13, 1921, Breslau, PA
Georgia 5'11" 182 lbs.

1946	BUF	AA	11	HB
1947	BAL	AA	14	HB
1948	DET	N	4	HB
3 yrs.	29 games			

Bill Dudley
DUDLEY, WILLIAM MCGARVEY
(Bullet Bill)
B. Dec. 24, 1921, Bluefield, VA
Virginia 5'10" 175 lbs.

1942	PIT	N	11	HB
1945			4	HB
1946			11	HB
1947	DET	N	9	HB
1948			7	HB
1949			12	HB
1950	WAS	N	12	HB
1951			12	HB
1953			12	HB
9 yrs.	90 games			

Brian Dudley
DUDLEY, BRIAN CHRISTOPHER
B. Aug. 30, 1960, Los Angeles, CA
Bethune-Cookman 6'1" 180 lbs.

| 1987 | CLE | N | 3 | S |

Paul Dudley
DUDLEY, PAUL
B. Jan. 16, 1939
Arkansas 6'0" 185 lbs.

1962	NYG	N	11	HB
1963	PHI	N	9	HB
2 yrs.	20 games			

Rickey Dudley
DUDLEY, RICKEY
B. Jul. 15, 1972, Henderson, TX
Ohio State 6'6" 248 lbs.

| 1996 | OAK | N | 16 | TE |

Dave Duerson
DUERSON, DAVID RUSSELL
B. Nov. 28, 1960, Muncie, IN
Notre Dame 6'1" 203 lbs.

1983	CHI	N	16	CB
1984			16	S
1985			15	S
1986			16	S
1987			12	S
1988			15	S
1989			12	S
1990	NYG	N	16	S
1991	PHX	N	11	S
1992			15	S

Dave Duerson *continued*

| 1993 | | | 16 | S |
| 11 yrs. | 160 games | | | |

Don Dufek
DUFEK, DON P.
B. Apr. 28, 1954, Ann Arbor, MI
Michigan 6'0" 195 lbs.

1976	SEA	N	14	DB
1977			13	S
1979			13	S
1980			8	S
1981			15	S
1982			9	S
1983			14	S
1984			9	S
8 yrs.	95 games			

Joe Dufek
DUFEK, JOSEPH E.
B. Aug. 23, 1961, Ann Arbor, MI
Yale 6'4" 215 lbs.

1983	BUF	N	16	QB
1984			5	QB
2 yrs.	21 games			

Jamal Duff
DUFF, JAMAL EDWIN
B. Mar. 11, 1972, Columbus, OH
San Diego State 6'7" 259 lbs.

| 1995 | NYG | N | 15 | DE |

John Duff
DUFF, JOHN
B. Jul. 31, 1967, Columbus, OH
New Mexico 6'7" 250 lbs.

1993	LARI	N	1	TE
1994			4	DE, TE
2 yrs.	5 games			

Jim Dufft
DUFFT, JAMES (Big Jim)
B. Jun. 25, 1896
Deceased
Rutgers/Fordham 6'0" 250 lbs.

1921	ROC	A	1	G
1921	NY	A	1	T
1922	MIL	N	8	G
2 yrs.	10 games			

Pat Duffy
DUFFY, PATRICK
B. Dec. 6, 1906
Dayton 5'10" 185 lbs.

| 1929 | DAY | N | 5 | FB, HB, QB |

Roger Duffy
DUFFY, ROGER THOMAS
B. Jul. 16, 1967, Pittsburgh, PA
Penn State 6'3" 285 lbs.

1990	NYJ	N	16	C
1991			12	C
1992			16	C
1993			16	G, C
1994			16	G
1995			16	G
1996			16	G
7 yrs.	108 games			

Dukes Duford
DUFORD, WILFRED J.
B. 1898
D. May 8, 1981, Davenport, IA
Marquette 5'10" 180 lbs.

| 1924 | GB | N | 3 | FB, E, HB |

447

Year	Team	Games	Pos.

Dan Dufour
DUFOUR, DAN
B. Oct. 18, 1960, Lynn, MA
UCLA 6'5" 280 lbs.

Year	Team	Games	Pos.
1983	ATL N	16	G
1984		6	G
2 yrs.	22 games		

Paul DuFault
DUFAULT, PAUL
B. Feb. 15, 1964, Bridgeport, CT
New Hampshire 6'4" 255 lbs.

Year	Team	Games	Pos.
1987	LARI N	1	C

Bill Dugan
DUGAN, WILLIAM H.
B. Jun. 5, 1959, Hornell, NY
Penn State 6'4" 280 lbs.

Year	Team	Games	Pos.
1981	SEA N	16	G
1982		9	G
1983		15	G
1984	MIN N	1	G
1987	NYG N	3	G
5 yrs.	44 games		

Fred Dugan
DUGAN, FRED
B. May 12, 1934, Stamford, CT
Dayton 6'3" 197 lbs.

Year	Team	Games	Pos.
1958	SF	12	OE
1959		12	OE
1960	DAL N	12	OE
1961	WAS N	13	OE
1962		12	OE
1963		14	OE
6 yrs.	75 games		

Len Dugan
DUGAN, LEONARD
B. Sep. 26, 1911
D. Sep., 1981, Seattle, WA
Wichita State 6'0" 218 lbs.

Year	Team	Games	Pos.
1936	NYG N	3	C
1937	CHIC N	11	C
1938		8	C
1939		4	C
1939	PIT N	1	C
4 yrs.	27 games		

Eddie Duggan
DUGGAN, EDWARD D.
B. May 19, 1891, Indiana
D. Oct. 16, 1950, Houston, TX
Notre Dame 6'0" 205 lbs.

Year	Team	Games	Pos.
1921	RI A	2	FB

Gil Duggan
DUGGAN, GILFORD R. (Cactus Face)
B. Dec. 26, 1917, Benton, OK
D. Oct. 18, 1974, Harrah, OK
Oklahoma 6'3" 229 lbs.

Year	Team	Games	Pos.
1940	NYG N	9	T
1942	CHIC N	11	T
1943		10	T
1944	C-P N	10	T
1945	CHIC N	8	T
1946	LA AA	11	T
1947	BUF AA	12	T
7 yrs.	71 games		

Jack Dugger
DUGGER, JOHN R.
B. Jan. 13, 1923, Pittsburgh, PA
D. Feb. 23, 1988
Ohio State 6'3" 230 lbs.

Year	Team	Games	Pos.
1946	BUF AA	7	E, T

Jack Dugger *continued*

Year	Team	Games	Pos.
1947	DET N	12	T
1948		12	T
1949	CHIB N	6	E
4 yrs.	37 games		

George Duggins
DUGGINS, GEORGE HERBERT
B. Mar. 15, 1912
D. Jul. 20, 1988, Yelm, WA
Purdue 6'3" 200 lbs.

Year	Team	Games	Pos.
1934	CHIC N	11	E, T

Paul Duhart
DUHART, PAUL A.
B. Dec. 30, 1920, Montreal, Que.
Florida 6'0" 180 lbs.

Year	Team	Games	Pos.
1944	GB N	8	HB
1945	PIT N	2	HB
1945	BOS N	3	HB
2 yrs.	13 games		

A.J. Duhe
DUHE, ADAM JOSEPH, JR.
B. Nov. 27, 1955, New Orleans, LA
Louisiana State 6'4" 249 lbs.

Year	Team	Games	Pos.
1977	MIA N	14	DE
1978		13	DE
1979		13	DE
1980		16	DE
1981		16	DE, LB
1982		9	LB
1983		15	LB
1984		12	LB
8 yrs.	108 games		

Bobby Duhon
DUHON, ROBERT JOSEPH, JR.
B. Sep. 6, 1946, Abbeville, LA
Tulane 6'0" 194 lbs.

Year	Team	Games	Pos.
1968	NYG N	13	RB, DB
1970		14	RB
1971		13	RB
1972		4	RB
4 yrs.	44 games		

Steve Duich
DUICH, STEVEN
B. Feb. 28, 1946, Long Beach, CA
San Diego State 6'3" 248 lbs.

Year	Team	Games	Pos.
1968	ATL N	12	G
1969	WAS N	11	G
2 yrs.	23 games		

Paul Duke
DUKE, PAUL A.
B. 1926
Georgia Tech 6'1" 210 lbs.

Year	Team	Games	Pos.
1947	NY AA	10	C

Jamie Dukes
DUKES, JAMIE DONNELL
B. Jun. 14, 1964, Schenectady, NY
Florida State 6'1" 270 lbs.

Year	Team	Games	Pos.
1986	ATL N	14	G
1987		4	G
1988		12	G
1989		16	G
1990		16	G
1991		16	C
1992		16	C
1993		16	C
1994	GB N	6	C
1995	ARI N	9	C
10 yrs.	125 games		

Mike Dukes
DUKES, MICHAEL
B. 1936
Clemson 6'3" 231 lbs.

Year	Team	Games	Pos.
1960	HOU A		LB
1961		14	LB
1962		14	LB
1963		14	LB
1964	BOS A	14	LB
1965		11	LB
1965	NY	3	LB
6 yrs.	70 games		

Bill DuLac
DULAC, WILLIAM FRANK
B. Jan. 15, 1951, Detroit, MI
Eastern Michigan 6'4" 260 lbs.

Year	Team	Games	Pos.
1974	NE N	14	G
1975		13	G
2 yrs.	27 games		

Chris Duliban
DULIBAN, CHRIS E.
B. Jan. 9, 1963, Champaign, IL
Texas 6'2" 216 lbs.

Year	Team	Games	Pos.
1987	DAL	3	LB

Gary Dulin
DULIN, GARY
B. Jan. 20, 1957, Madisonville, KY
Ohio State 6'4" 275 lbs.

Year	Team	Games	Pos.
1986	STL N	3	DE
1987		3	DE
2 yrs.	6 games		

Mike Dumas
DUMAS, MICHAEL DION
B. Mar. 18, 1969, Grand Rapids, MI
Indiana 5'11" 178 lbs.

Year	Team	Games	Pos.
1991	HOU N	13	S
1992		16	S
1994	BUF N	14	S
1995	JAC N	14	S
4 yrs.	57 games		

Troy Dumas
DUMAS, TROY
B. Sep. 30, 1972, Riverside, CA
Nebraska 6'3" 238 lbs.

Year	Team	Games	Pos.
1996	KC N	5	LB

Jon Dumbauld
DUMBAULD, JONATHAN
B. Feb. 14, 1963, Anaheim, CA
Kentucky 6'4" 259 lbs.

Year	Team	Games	Pos.
1986	NO N	9	DE
1987	PHI N	6	DE
1988	NO N	1	DE
1988	PHI N	1	DE
3 yrs.	17 games		

Leon Dumbrowski
DUMBROWSKI, LEON
B. 1938
Delaware 6'0" 215 lbs.

Year	Team	Games	Pos.
1960	NY A		LB

Doug Dumler
DUMLER, DOUGLAS MARVIN
B. Dec. 15, 1950, Hoisington, KS
Nebraska 6'3" 243 lbs.

Year	Team	Games	Pos.
1973	NE N	14	C
1974		14	C
1975		14	C
1976	MIN N	14	C

Doug Dumler *continued*

Year	Team	Games	Pos.
1977		14	C
5 yrs.	70 games		

Billy DuMoe
DUMOE, WILLIAM G.
B. Mar. 14, 1898, Canosia Township, MN
D. May, 1983, Minneapolis, MN
None 5'10" 175 lbs.

Year	Team	Games	Pos.
1921	GB A	6	E

Joe DuMoe
DUMOE, JOSEPH T. (Stub)
B. Sep. 11, 1894, Duluth, MN
Deceased
Syracuse/Fordham/Lafayette 5'9" 178 lbs.

Year	Team	Games	Pos.
1921	ROC A	2	E

Jim Dumont
DUMONT, JAMES
B. Jul. 16, 1961, Bristol, CT
Rutgers 6'1" 224 lbs.

Year	Team	Games	Pos.
1984	CLE N	12	LB

Craig Dunaway
DUNAWAY, CRAIG CARTER
B. Mar. 27, 1961, Lake Charles, LA
Michigan 6'2" 233 lbs.

Year	Team	Games	Pos.
1983	PIT N	11	TE

Dave Dunaway
DUNAWAY, DAVID
B. Jan. 1, 1945, Philadelphia, PA
Duke 6'2" 205 lbs.

Year	Team	Games	Pos.
1968	GB N	2	WR
1968	ATL N	10	FL
1969	NYG N	3	WR
2 yrs.	15 games		

Jim Dunaway
DUNAWAY, JAMES KENNETH
B. Sep. 3, 1941, Columbia, MS
Mississippi 6'4" 278 lbs.

Year	Team	Games	Pos.
1963	BUF A	14	DT
1964		14	DT
1965		14	DT
1966		14	DT
1967		14	DT
1968		14	DT
1969		14	DT
1970	BUF N	14	DT
1971		14	DT
1972	MIA N	6	DT
10 yrs.	132 games		

Jubilee Dunbar
DUNBAR, ALLEN
B. May 17, 1949, New Orleans, LA
Southern University 6'0" 176 lbs.

Year	Team	Games	Pos.
1973	NO N	14	WR
1974	CLE N	5	WR
2 yrs.	19 games		

Karl Dunbar
DUNBAR, KARL
B. May 18, 1967, Opelousas, LA
Louisiana State 6'4" 275 lbs.

Year	Team	Games	Pos.
1993	NO N	13	DE
1994	ARI N	3	DE
1995		5	DT, DE
3 yrs.	21 games		

Year	Team	Games	Pos.

Vaughn Dunbar
DUNBAR, VAUGHN ALLEN
B. Sep. 4, 1968, Fort Wayne, IN
Indiana 5'10" 204 lbs.

Year	Team		Games	Pos.
1992	NO	N	16	RB
1994			8	RB
1995			1	RB
1995	JAC	N	14	RB
3 yrs.			39 games	

Brian Duncan
DUNCAN, JAMES BRIAN
B. Mar. 31, 1952, Olney, TX
Southern Methodist 6'0" 201 lbs.

Year	Team		Games	Pos.
1976	CLE	N	14	RB
1977			14	RB
1978	HOU	N	5	RB
3 yrs.			33 games	

Clyde Duncan
DUNCAN, CLYDE LOUIS
B. Feb. 5, 1961, Oxon Hill, MD
Tennessee 6'1" 202 lbs.

Year	Team		Games	Pos.
1984	STL	N	8	WR
1985			11	WR
2 yrs.			19 games	

Curtis Duncan
DUNCAN, CURTIS EVERETT
B. Jan. 26, 1965, Detroit, MI
Northwestern 5'11" 184 lbs.

Year	Team		Games	Pos.
1987	HOU	N	10	WR
1988			16	WR
1989			16	WR
1990			16	WR
1991			16	WR
1992			16	WR
1993			12	WR
7 yrs.			102 games	

Frank Duncan
DUNCAN, FRANK MILTON
B. Nov. 16, 1956, San Francisco, CA
San Francisco State 6'1" 188 lbs.

Year	Team		Games	Pos.
1979	SD	N	4	S
1980			15	S
1981			7	S
3 yrs.			26 games	

Jim Duncan
DUNCAN, JAMES
B. 1926
Deceased
Duke/Wake Forest 6'2" 205 lbs.

Year	Team		Games	Pos.
1950	NYG	N	8	E
1951			12	E
1952			12	E
1953			11	E
4 yrs.			43 games	

Jim Duncan
DUNCAN, JAMES
B. Aug. 3, 1946, Lancaster, SC
D. Oct. 20, 1972, Lancaster, SC
Maryland-Eastern Shore 6'2" 200 lbs.

Year	Team		Games	Pos.
1969	BAL	N	13	CB
1970			14	CB, S
1971			11	CB
3 yrs.			38 games	

Ken Duncan
DUNCAN, KENNETH
B. Feb. 18, 1946, Rock Island, IL
Tulsa 6'2" 210 lbs.

Year	Team		Games	Pos.
1971	GB	N	3	P

Maury Duncan
DUNCAN, MAURICE
B. Jul. 18, 1931
San Francisco State 6'1" 185 lbs.

Year	Team		Games	Pos.
1954	SF	N	6	QB
1955			6	QB
2 yrs.			12 games	

Randy Duncan
DUNCAN, RANDALL
B. 1937
Iowa 6'0" 185 lbs.

Year	Team		Games	Pos.
1961	DAL	A	14	QB

Rick Duncan
DUNCAN, RICK
B. Aug. 14, 1942, Mattoon, IL
Eastern Montana 6'0" 208 lbs.

Year	Team		Games	Pos.
1967	DEN	A	2	K
1968	PHI	N	1	P
1969	DET	N	1	P
3 yrs.			4 games	

Ron Duncan
DUNCAN, RONALD NEELY
B. Sep. 8, 1943, Lakeland, FL
Wittenberg 6'6" 255 lbs.

Year	Team		Games	Pos.
1967	CLE	N	3	TE

Speedy Duncan
DUNCAN, LESLIE HERBERT
B. Aug. 10, 1942, Tuscaloosa, AL
Jackson State 5'10" 177 lbs.

Year	Team		Games	Pos.
1964	SD	A	5	DB
1965			6	DB
1966			14	DB
1967			14	DB
1968			10	DB
1969			14	CB
1970	SD	N	6	CB
1971	WAS	N	14	CB
1972			7	CB
1973			14	S
1974			1	S
11 yrs.			105 games	

Bobby Duncom
DUNCOM, ROBERT ELDON
B. Aug. 14, 1944, Austin, TX
West Texas State 6'3" 250 lbs.

Year	Team		Games	Pos.
1968	STL	N	4	OT

Ken Dunek
DUNEK, KENNETH ROBERT
B. Jun. 20, 1957, Chicago, IL
Memphis State 6'6" 235 lbs.

Year	Team		Games	Pos.
1980	PHI	N	2	TE

Tony Dungy
DUNGY, ANTHONY KEVIN
B. Oct. 6, 1955, Jackson, MI
Minnesota 6'0" 189 lbs.

Year	Team		Games	Pos.
1977	PIT	N	14	QB, DB
1978			16	S
1979	SF	N	15	S
3 yrs.			45 games	

Tommy Duniven
DUNIVEN, TOM
B. May 20, 1954, Pampa, TX
Texas Tech 6'3" 210 lbs.

Year	Team		Games	Pos.
1977	HOU	N	1	QB

Bob Dunlap
DUNLAP, ROBERT L.

Bob Dunlap *continued*
B. Oct. 29, 1912, Haskell, OK
D. Jul. 30, 1966
Oklahoma 6'1" 191 lbs.

Year	Team		Games	Pos.
1935	CHIB	N	11	QB, DB
1936	NYG	N	5	DB
2 yrs.			16 games	

Lenny Dunlap
DUNLAP, LEONARD
B. Jun. 25, 1949, Monroe, LA
North Texas State 6'1" 197 lbs.

Year	Team		Games	Pos.
1971	BAL	N	4	DB
1972	SD	N	14	CB
1973			14	CB
1974			8	CB
1975	DET	N	6	CB
5 yrs.			46 games	

Bob Dunn
DUNN, ROBERT (Baron)
B. Jul. 1, 1905
D. Jan., 1984, Springfield, MA
New York University 6'1" 200 lbs.

Year	Team		Games	Pos.
1929	SI	N	7	C, T, G

Coye Dunn
DUNN, COYE
B. Mar. 7, 1916, Colorado
Southern California 6'0" 198 lbs.

Year	Team		Games	Pos.
1943	WAS	N	3	HB, DB

David Dunn
DUNN, DAVID
B. Jun. 10, 1972, San Diego, CA
Fresno State 6'3" 210 lbs.

Year	Team		Games	Pos.
1995	CIN	N	16	WR
1996			16	WR
2 yrs.			32 games	

Gary Dunn
DUNN, GARY EDWARD
B. Aug. 24, 1953, Coral Gables, FL
Miami (Florida) 6'3" 270 lbs.

Year	Team		Games	Pos.
1976	PIT	N	5	DT
1978			16	DT
1979			16	DT
1980			16	DT
1981			16	DT
1982			9	DT
1983			13	NT
1984			16	NT
1985			10	NT
1986			16	NT
1987			13	NT
11 yrs.			146 games	

Jason Dunn
DUNN, JASON
B. Nov. 15, 1973, Harrodsburg, KY
Eastern Kentucky 6'4" 257 lbs.

Year	Team		Games	Pos.
1996	PHI	N	16	TE

K.D. Dunn
DUNN, KELDRICK A.
B. Apr. 28, 1963, Fort Hood, TX
Clemson 6'3" 235 lbs.

Year	Team		Games	Pos.
1985	TB	N	7	TE
1986			7	TE
1987	WAS	N	3	TE
1988	NYJ	N	15	TE
1989	CIN	N	1	TE
5 yrs.			33 games	

Pat Dunn
DUNN, PAT

Pat Dunn *continued*
B. 1888
Deceased
Dickinson 182 lbs.

Year	Team		Games	Pos.
1920	DET	A	4	FB
1921			2	FB
2 yrs.			6 games	

Paul Dunn
DUNN, PAUL, JR.
B. Jul. 14, 1948, Little Rock, AR
San Francisco State/U.S. International 6'0" 210 lbs.

Year	Team		Games	Pos.
1970	CIN	N	5	WR

Perry Lee Dunn
DUNN, PERRY LEE
B. Jan. 20, 1941, Natchez, MS
Mississippi 6'2" 208 lbs.

Year	Team		Games	Pos.
1964	DAL	N	14	HB
1965			13	HB
1966	ATL	N	14	RB
1967			14	RB
1968			14	RB
1969	BAL	N	5	RB
6 yrs.			74 games	

Red Dunn
DUNN, JOSEPH ALOYSIUS
B. 1902
D. 1957
None 5'10" 175 lbs.

Year	Team		Games	Pos.
1924	MIL	N	13	QB
1925	CHIC	N	10	QB
1926			11	QB, HB
1927	GB	N	10	QB
1928			12	QB
1929			11	QB, HB
1930			13	QB
1931			12	QB
8 yrs.			92 games	

Roddy Dunn
DUNN, RODERICK
B. Oct., 1894, Duluth, MN
Deceased
Syracuse 5'10" 200 lbs.

Year	Team		Games	Pos.
1921	SYR	A	2	T, G
1923	DUL	N	2	T, G
2 yrs.			4 games	

Pat Dunnigan
DUNNIGAN, MERTON
B. Jan. 24, 1894
Deceased
Minnesota 5'10" 206 lbs.

Year	Team		Games	Pos.
1922	GB	N	2	E
1924	MIN	N	5	T
1925	MIL	N	6	T
1926			8	G
4 yrs.			21 games	

Pat Dunsmore
DUNSMORE, PATRICK NEIL
B. Oct. 2, 1959, Duluth, MN
Drake 6'3" 237 lbs.

Year	Team		Games	Pos.
1983	CHI	N	16	TE
1984			11	TE
2 yrs.			27 games	

Bill Dunstan
DUNSTAN, WILLIAM ELWYN
B. Jan. 3, 1949, Oakland, CA
Utah State 6'4" 250 lbs.

Year	Team		Games	Pos.
1973	PHI	N	14	DT
1974			14	DT
1975			14	DT

Year	Team	Games	Pos.

Bill Dunstan *continued*

1976		14	DT
1977	**BUF** N	14	DT
1979	**LA** N	10	DT
6 yrs.	80 games		

Elwyn Dunstan
DUNSTAN, W. ELWYN (Moose)
B. Feb. 4, 1915, San Francisco, CA
Portland 6'3" 238 lbs.

1938	**CHIC** N	5	T
1939		1	T
1939	**CLE** N	7	T
1940		10	T
1941		11	T
4 yrs.	34 games		

Reggie Dupard
DUPARD, JON REGINALD
B. Oct. 30, 1963, New Orleans, LA
Southern Methodist 5'11" 205 lbs.

1986	**NE** N	6	RB
1987		8	RB
1988		16	RB
1989		7	RB
1989	**WAS** N	7	RB
1990		7	RB
5 yrs.	51 games		

Mark Duper
DUPAS, MARK KIRBY (MARK SUPER)
B. Jan. 25, 1959, Pineville, LA
Northwestern State (Louisiana) 5'9" 187 lbs.

1982	**MIA** N	2	WR
1983		16	WR
1984		16	WR
1985		9	WR
1986		16	WR
1987		11	WR
1988		13	WR
1989		15	WR
1990		16	WR
1991		16	WR
1992		16	WR
11 yrs.	146 games		

Charlie Dupre
DUPRE, CHARLES LEROY
B. Nov. 11, 1933, Texas City, TX
Baylor 6'1" 195 lbs.

| 1960 | **NY** A | | DB |

L.G. Dupre
DUPRE, LOUIS GEORGE (Long Gone)
B. Sep. 10, 1932, New Orleans, LA
Baylor 5'11" 190 lbs.

1955	**BAL** N	11	HB
1956		11	HB
1957		12	HB
1958		10	HB
1959		4	HB
1960	**DAL** N	11	HB
1961		10	HB
7 yrs.	69 games		

Billy Joe Dupree
DUPREE, BILLY JOE
B. Mar. 7, 1950, Monroe, LA
Michigan State 6'4" 228 lbs.

1973	**DAL** N	14	TE
1974		14	TE
1975		14	TE
1976		14	TE
1977		14	TE
1978		16	TE

Billy Joe Dupree *continued*

1979		16	TE
1980		16	TE
1981		16	TE
1982		9	TE
1983		16	TE
11 yrs.	159 games		

Marcus Dupree
DUPREE, MARCUS L.
B. May 22, 1964, Philadelphia, MS
Oklahoma/Southern Mississippi* 6'3" 235 lbs.

1990	**LARM** N	7	RB
1991		8	RB
2 yrs.	15 games		

Myron Dupree
DUPREE, MYRON RAY
B. Oct. 15, 1961, New York, NY
North Carolina Central 5'11" 180 lbs.

| 1983 | **DEN** N | 16 | CB, S |

Pete Duranko
DURANKO, PETER NICHOLAS
B. Dec. 15, 1943, Johnstown, PA
Notre Dame 6'2" 249 lbs.

1967	**DEN** A	14	DE
1968		14	DE
1969		14	DE
1970	**DEN** N	14	DE
1972		14	DE
1973		14	DE
1974		14	DE
7 yrs.	98 games		

Don Durdan
DURDAN, DONALD E.
B. 1920
Deceased
Oregon State 5'9" 175 lbs.

1946	**SF** AA	12	HB
1947		1	HB
2 yrs.	13 games		

Clarence Duren
DUREN, CLARENCE EDWARD
B. Dec. 9, 1950, Compton, CA
California 6'1" 190 lbs.

1973	**STL** N	11	S
1974		14	S
1975		13	S
1976		13	S
1977	**SD** N	14	S
5 yrs.	65 games		

Steve Durham
DURHAM, STEVE ALLEN
B. Oct. 11, 1958, Greer, SC
Clemson 6'5" 256 lbs.

| 1982 | **BAL** N | 8 | DE |

Jack Durishan
DURISHAN, JOHN
B. Jul. 7, 1922
D. May 13, 1978
Pittsburgh 6'2" 230 lbs.

| 1947 | **NY** AA | 6 | G, T |

Charlie Durkee
DURKEE, CHARLES MICHAEL (Mickey)
B. Jun. 25, 1944, Tulsa, OK
Oklahoma State 5'11" 165 lbs.

| 1967 | **NO** N | 14 | K |
| 1968 | | 14 | K |

Charlie Durkee *continued*

1971		12	K
1972		6	K
4 yrs.	46 games		

John Durko
DURKO, JOHN
B. Jul. 23, 1919, Mahanoy City, PA
D. Jan. 1, 1963
Albright 6'4" 235 lbs.

1944	**PHI** N	5	E
1945	**CHIC** N	1	E
2 yrs.	6 games		

Sandy Durko
DURKO, SANDY VINCENT
B. Aug. 29, 1948, Los Angeles, CA
Southern California 6'1" 185 lbs.

1970	**CIN** N	1	CB
1971		14	S
1973	**NE** N	14	S
1974		14	S
4 yrs.	43 games		

Jeff Durkota
DURKOTA, JEFFREY
B. Dec. 20, 1923, Pittsburgh, PA
Penn State 6'0" 205 lbs.

| 1948 | **LA** AA | 12 | B |

Mike Durrette
DURRETTE, MICHAEL RAY
B. Aug. 11, 1957, Charlottesville, VA
West Virginia 6'4" 280 lbs.

1986	**SF** N	9	G
1987		3	G
2 yrs.	12 games		

Mark Dusbabek
DUSBABEK, MARK EDWARD
B. Jun. 23, 1964, Faribault, MN
Minnesota 6'3" 230 lbs.

1989	**MIN** N	16	LB
1990		14	LB
1991		1	LB
3 yrs.	31 games		

Brad Dusek
DUSEK, JOHN BRADLEY
B. Dec. 13, 1950, Temple, TX
Texas A&M 6'2" 217 lbs.

1974	**WAS** N	14	LB
1975		14	LB
1976		14	LB
1977		14	LB
1978		16	LB
1979		16	LB
1980		16	LB
1981		10	LB
8 yrs.	114 games		

Bill Dusenbery
DUSENBERY, BILL
B. Sep. 15, 1948, Washington, DC
Johnson C. Smith 6'2" 198 lbs.

| 1970 | **NO** N | 8 | WR |

Joe Dusossoit
DUSOSSOIT, FLORIMOND JOSEPH
B. Oct. 2, 1895
Deceased
Dartmouth 5'11" 185 lbs.

1921	**TON** A	1	E
1921	**NY** A	2	E
1 yr.	3 games		

Bill Dutton
DUTTON, WILLIAM
B. Dec. 9, 1920
Deceased
Pittsburgh 5'10" 180 lbs.

| 1946 | **PIT** N | 11 | HB |

John Dutton
DUTTON, JOHN OWEN
B. Feb. 6, 1951, Rapid City, SD
Nebraska 6'7" 270 lbs.

1974	**BAL** N	14	DE
1975		14	DE
1976		14	DE
1977		12	DE
1978		14	DE
1979	**DAL** N	8	DE
1980		16	DE
1981		16	DT
1982		9	DT
1983		16	DT
1984		16	DT
1985		16	DT
1986		16	DT
1987		4	DT
14 yrs.	185 games		

Earl Duvall
DUVALL, EARL (Mooney, Rowdy)
B. Jun. 20, 1899
D. Aug., 1966, Marble Cliff, OH
Ohio University 6'0" 225 lbs.

1924	**COL** N	8	G, C
1925		7	G, E
1926		4	T, G
3 yrs.	19 games		

Ben Dvorak
DVORAK, BENJAMIN ANTON
B. Jan. 20, 1895
D. May 7, 1974, Minneapolis, MN
Minnesota 5'10" 170 lbs.

| 1921 | **MIN** A | 4 | HB |

Rick Dvorak
DVORAK, RICHARD JOSEPH
B. Apr. 21, 1952, Spearville, KS
Wichita State 6'4" 240 lbs.

1974	**NYG** N	13	DE
1975		14	DE
1976		14	DE
1977		5	DE
1977	**MIA** N	1	DE
4 yrs.	47 games		

Dan Dworsky
DWORSKY, DANIEL L.
B. Oct. 4, 1927, Minneapolis, MN
Michigan 6'0" 211 lbs.

| 1949 | **LA** AA | 11 | B |

Bob Dwyer
DWYER, ROBERT
B. Aug. 30, 1905
D. Mar., 1974, Washington, DC
Georgetown (DC) 5'9" 160 lbs.

| 1929 | **ORA** N | 1 | HB |

Jack Dwyer
DWYER, JACK
B. Jan. 15, 1927, Los Angeles, CA
Loyola (California) 5'11" 175 lbs.

1951	**WAS** N	12	HB
1952	**LA** N	10	HB
1953		12	HB
1954		11	HB
4 yrs.	45 games		

Mike Dwyer

DWYER, MIKE
B. Jun. 13, 1963
Massachusetts 6'3" 280 lbs.

Year	Team		Games	Pos.
1987	DAL	N	3	DT

Mike Dyal

DYAL, MICHAEL EBEN
B. May 20, 1966, San Antonio, TX
Texas A&I-Kingsville 6'2" 240 lbs.

Year	Team		Games	Pos.
1989	LARI	N	16	TE
1990			3	TE
1992	KC	N	3	TE
1993			6	TE
1993	SD	N	4	TE
4 yrs.	32 games			

Ernest Dye

DYE, ERNEST THADDIUS
B. Jul. 15, 1971, Greenwood, SC
South Carolina 6'6" 325 lbs.

Year	Team		Games	Pos.
1993	PHX	N	7	OT
1994	ARI	N	16	G
1995			6	OT
1996			8	G
4 yrs.	37 games			

Les Dye

DYE, LESTER H.
B. Jul. 15, 1918, Forestville, NY
Syracuse 6'1" 181 lbs.

Year	Team		Games	Pos.
1944	WAS	N	9	E
1945			10	E
2 yrs.	19 games			

Henry Dyer

DYER, HENRY LOUIS
B. Jan. 28, 1945, Baton Rouge, LA
Grambling State 6'2" 230 lbs.

Year	Team		Games	Pos.
1966	LA	N	8	FB
1968			9	RB
1969	WAS	N	13	RB
1970			12	RB
4 yrs.	42 games			

Ken Dyer

DYER, KENNETH JAMES
B. Mar. 16, 1946, Ann Arbor, MI
Arizona State 6'3" 187 lbs.

Year	Team		Games	Pos.
1968	SD	A	14	OE, DB
1969	CIN	A	1	S
1970	CIN	N	12	S
1971			3	S
4 yrs.	30 games			

Donald Dykes

DYKES, DONALD R.
B. Aug. 24, 1955, Independence, MO
Southeastern Louisiana 5'11" 183 lbs.

Year	Team		Games	Pos.
1979	NYJ	N	16	CB
1980			16	CB
1981			14	CB
1982	SD	N	1	CB
4 yrs.	47 games			

Hart Lee Dykes

DYKES, HART LEE, JR.
B. Sep. 2, 1966, Bay City, TX
Oklahoma State 6'4" 218 lbs.

Year	Team		Games	Pos.
1989	NE	N	16	WR
1990			10	WR
2 yrs.	26 games			

Sean Dykes

DYKES, SEAN RENE
B. Aug. 8, 1964, New Orleans, LA

Sean Dykes *continued*

Bowling Green 5'10" 170 lbs.

Year	Team		Games	Pos.
1987	NYJ	N	6	CB

Chris Dyko

DYKO, CHRISTOPHER EDWARD
B. Mar. 16, 1966, Champaign, IL
Washington State 6'6" 295 lbs.

Year	Team		Games	Pos.
1989	CHI	N	8	OT

Dyner

DYNER
None

Year	Team		Games	Pos.
1929	DAY	N	1	E, T

Matt Dyson

DYSON, MATT
B. Aug. 1, 1972, La Plata, MD
Michigan 6'3" 265 lbs.

Year	Team		Games	Pos.
1995	OAK	N	4	DT

James Eaddy

EADDY, JAMES
B. May 31, 1963, Queens, NY
C.W. Post/New York Tech 6'2" 280 lbs.

Year	Team		Games	Pos.
1987	CIN	N	2	NT

Alex Eagle

EAGLE, ALEX F., JR.
B. Mar. 13, 1913, San Francisco, CA
Oregon 6'2" 220 lbs.

Year	Team		Games	Pos.
1935	BKN	N	10	T

Eagle Feather

Born BEAMUS PIERCE
None 6'0" 220 lbs.

Year	Team		Games	Pos.
1922	OOR	N	7	FB, T
1923			11	FB, HB
2 yrs.	18 games			

Larry Eaglin

EAGLIN, LAWRENCE
B. Aug. 27, 1948, Raywood, TX
Stephen F. Austin 6'3" 195 lbs.

Year	Team		Games	Pos.
1973	HOU	N	11	CB

Kay Eakin

EAKIN, OLIVER KAY, JR.
B. Aug. 3, 1917, Atkins, AR
Deceased
Arkansas 6'0" 180 lbs.

Year	Team		Games	Pos.
1940	NYG	N	7	HB
1941			11	HB
1946	MIA	AA	13	HB
3 yrs.	31 games			

Ralph Earhart

EARHART, RALPH GLOYD
B. Mar. 29, 1923, Milburn, OK
Texas Tech/Pittsburg State/Texas Tech 5'10" 165 lbs.

Year	Team		Games	Pos.
1948	GB	N	12	HB
1949			12	HB
2 yrs.	24 games			

Robin Earl

EARL, ROBIN DANIEL
B. Mar. 18, 1955, Boise, ID
Washington 6'5" 242 lbs.

Year	Team		Games	Pos.
1977	CHI	N	14	RB
1978			16	RB
1979			13	RB
1980			16	RB, TE
1981			16	TE

Robin Earl *continued*

Year	Team		Games	Pos.
1982			9	TE
6 yrs.	84 games			

Jim Earley

EARLEY, JAMES H.
B. Jan. 23, 1956, Dayton, OH
Michigan State 6'1" 230 lbs.

Year	Team		Games	Pos.
1978	NYJ	N	2	FB

Guy Early

EARLY, GUY BURDETTE
B. Oct., 1892
Deceased
Miami (Ohio) 6'3" 210 lbs.

Year	Team		Games	Pos.
1920	DAY	A	3	G
1921	CIN	A	1	G, FB
2 yrs.	4 games			

Quinn Early

EARLY, QUINN REMAR
B. Apr. 13, 1965, West Hempstead, NY
Iowa 6'0" 188 lbs.

Year	Team		Games	Pos.
1988	SD	N	16	WR
1989			6	WR
1990			14	WR
1991	NO	N	15	WR
1992			16	WR
1993			16	WR
1994			16	WR
1995			16	WR
1996	BUF	N	16	WR
9 yrs.	131 games			

Blaine Earon

EARON, BLAINE A.
B. 1929, Altoona, PA
Duke 6'1" 195 lbs.

Year	Team		Games	Pos.
1952	DET	N	12	E
1953			6	E
2 yrs.	18 games			

Jug Earps

EARPS, FRANCIS LOUIS
Played as Jug Earpe 1927-1932
B. Jul. 22, 1897, Monmouth, IL
D. Jan. 8, 1969, Green Bay, WI
Monmouth 6'0" 236 lbs.

Year	Team		Games	Pos.
1921	RI	A	6	C
1922	RI	N	2	C
1922	GB	N	6	T
1923			8	T, C
1924			11	C, T
1925			13	T, C
1925	FRA	N	1	T
1926	GB	N	12	C
1927			10	C
1927	NYY	N	3	T
1928	GB	N	13	C, T
1929			11	C
1930			13	C, T, E, G
1931			12	C, T, G
1932			8	T, G, C
12 yrs.	129 games			

Kenny Easley

EASLEY, KENNY
B. Jan. 15, 1959, Chesapeake, VA
UCLA 6'3" 206 lbs.

Year	Team		Games	Pos.
1981	SEA	N	14	S
1982			8	S
1983			16	S
1984			16	S
1985			13	S
1986			10	S
1987			12	S
7 yrs.	89 games			

Walt Easley

EASLEY, WALTER
B. Sep. 8, 1957, Charleston, WV
West Virginia 6'1" 226 lbs.

Year	Team		Games	Pos.
1981	SF	N	12	FB
1982			2	RB
2 yrs.	14 games			

Ricky Easmon

EASMON, WILLIE CHARLES
B. Jul. 3, 1963, Inverness, FL
Florida 5'10" 160 lbs.

Year	Team		Games	Pos.
1985	DAL	N	8	CB, S
1985	TB	N	6	CB
1986			9	CB
2 yrs.	23 games			

Bo Eason

EASON, BO
B. Mar. 10, 1961, Walnut Grove, CA
California-Davis 6'2" 200 lbs.

Year	Team		Games	Pos.
1984	HOU	N	10	S
1985			16	S
1986			9	S
1987			3	S
4 yrs.	38 games			

John Eason

EASON, JOHN
B. Jul. 30, 1945, Ocala, FL
Florida A&M 6'2" 220 lbs.

Year	Team		Games	Pos.
1968	OAK	A	3	OE

Roger Eason

EASON, ROGER
B. Jul. 31, 1918, Paul's Valley, OK
Oklahoma 6'2" 227 lbs.

Year	Team		Games	Pos.
1945	CLE	N	2	T
1946	LA	N	9	G
1947			11	G
1948			10	G
1949	GB	N	12	G
5 yrs.	44 games			

Tony Eason

EASON, CHARLES CARROLL, IV
B. Oct. 8, 1959, Blythe, CA
Illinois 6'4" 212 lbs.

Year	Team		Games	Pos.
1983	NE	N	16	QB
1984			16	QB
1985			16	QB
1986			15	QB
1987			4	QB
1988			2	QB
1989			3	QB
1989	NYJ	N	2	QB
1990			16	QB
8 yrs.	90 games			

Ron East

EAST, RONALD ALLAN
B. Aug. 26, 1943, Portland, OR
Montana State/Oregon State 6'4" 244 lbs.

Year	Team		Games	Pos.
1967	DAL	N	14	DT
1968			14	DT
1969			14	DT
1970			14	DT
1971	SD	N	14	DT
1972			12	DT
1973			13	DT
1975	CLE	N	14	DE
1976	ATL	N	14	DT
1977	SEA	N	14	DT
10 yrs.	137 games			

Year	Team		Games	Pos.

Ray Easterling
EASTERLING, CHARLES RAY
B. Sep. 3, 1949, Richmond, VA
Richmond 6'0" 192 lbs.

Year	Team		Games	Pos.
1972	ATL	N	8	S
1973			1	S
1974			14	S
1975			14	S
1976			14	S
1977			14	S
1978			2	S
1979			16	S
8 yrs.	83 games			

Irv Eatman
EATMAN, IRVIN HUMPHREY
B. Jan. 1, 1961, Birmingham, AL
UCLA 6'7" 293 lbs.

Year	Team		Games	Pos.
1986	KC	N	16	OT
1987			12	OT
1988			16	OT
1989			13	OT
1990			12	OT
1991	NYJ	N	16	OT
1992			12	OT
1993	LARM	N	16	OT
1994	ATL	N	4	OT
1995	HOU	N	16	OT
1996			16	OT
11 yrs.	149 games			

Chad Eaton
EATON, CHAD EVERETT
B. Apr. 4, 1972, Exeter, NH
Washington State 6'4" 292 lbs.

Year	Team		Games	Pos.
1996	NE	N	4	DT

Lou Eaton
EATON, LOUIS
B. 1915
California 6'2" 215 lbs.

Year	Team		Games	Pos.
1945	NYG	N	2	T

Scott Eaton
EATON, THOMAS SCOTT
B. Aug. 20, 1944, Salem, OR
Oregon State 6'3" 199 lbs.

Year	Team		Games	Pos.
1967	NYG	N	12	DB
1968			14	DB
1969			14	CB
1970			7	CB
1971			12	CB
5 yrs.	59 games			

Tracey Eaton
EATON, TRACEY BRUCE
B. Jul. 19, 1965, Medford, OR
Portland State 6'1" 195 lbs.

Year	Team		Games	Pos.
1989	HOU	N	16	S
1990	PHX	N	11	S
1991	ATL	N	16	S
1993			16	S
4 yrs.	59 games			

Vic Eaton
EATON, VICTOR ROE
B. 1933
Missouri 6'2" 200 lbs.

Year	Team		Games	Pos.
1955	PIT	N	12	QB

Harry Ebding
EBDING, HARRY JOSEPH (Irish)
B. Sep. 12, 1908, Walla Walla, WA
D. Sep. 11, 1980, Mecca, CA
St. Mary's (California) 5'11" 199 lbs.

Year	Team		Games	Pos.
1931	POR	N	14	E
1932			12	E

Harry Ebding continued

Year	Team		Games	Pos.
1933			11	E
1934	DET	N	12	E, HB
1935			11	E
1936			12	E
1937			10	E
7 yrs.	82 games			

Rick Eber
EBER, RICK L.
B. Apr. 17, 1945, Torrance, CA
Tulsa 6'0" 181 lbs.

Year	Team		Games	Pos.
1968	ATL	N	1	FL
1969	SD	A	5	WR
1970	SD	N	6	WR
3 yrs.	12 games			

Jess Eberdt
EBERDT, JESS
B. 1906
Alabama 6'2" 215 lbs.

Year	Team		Games	Pos.
1932	BKN	N	3	C

Hal Ebersole
EBERSOLE, HAROLD L.
B. Sep. 24, 1899
D. Sep., 1984, Atlanta, GA
Cornell 6'3" 190 lbs.

Year	Team		Games	Pos.
1923	CLE	N	2	G

John Ebersole
EBERSOLE, JOHN JOEL
B. Nov. 5, 1948, Altoona, PA
Penn State 6'3" 234 lbs.

Year	Team		Games	Pos.
1970	NYJ	N	14	DE
1971			14	DE
1972			14	LB
1973			13	LB
1974			14	LB
1975			13	LB
1976			13	LB
1977			13	LB
8 yrs.	108 games			

Beanie Eberts
EBERTS, BERNARD L.
B. May 21, 1901, Columbus, OH
D. Apr., 1983, Chevy Chase, MD
Catholic 5'11" 198 lbs.

Year	Team		Games	Pos.
1924	MIN	N	3	G, T

Ray Ebli
EBLI, RAYMOND HENRY (Lil' Abner)
B. Oct. 6, 1919, Ironwood, MI
Notre Dame 6'2" 210 lbs.

Year	Team		Games	Pos.
1942	CHIC	N	6	E
1946	BUF	AA	9	E
1947	CHI	AA	5	E
3 yrs.	20 games			

Byron Eby
EBY, BYRON
B. 1905
Ohio State 6'0" 185 lbs.

Year	Team		Games	Pos.
1930	POR	N	3	HB, QB

Scott Eccles
ECCLES, SCOTT
B. Jun. 28, 1963, New Orleans, LA
Eastern New Mexico 6'5" 245 lbs.

Year	Team		Games	Pos.
1987	HOU	N	1	TE

Donnie Echols
ECHOLS, DONALD WAYNE

Donnie Echols continued
B. Dec. 16, 1957, Dallas, TX
Oklahoma State 6'3" 240 lbs.

Year	Team		Games	Pos.
1987	CLE	N	3	TE

Fate Echols
ECHOLS, FATE L.
B. 1939, Union Springs, AL
Northwestern 6'1" 258 lbs.

Year	Team		Games	Pos.
1962	STL	N	5	OT
1963			3	DT
2 yrs.	8 games			

Terry Echols
ECHOLS, TERRY
B. Jan. 10, 1962, Mullens, WV
Marshall 6'0" 200 lbs.

Year	Team		Games	Pos.
1984	PIT	N	4	LB

Keith Eck
ECK, KEITH CURREN
B. Nov. 28, 1955, Newport News, VA
UCLA 6'5" 255 lbs.

Year	Team		Games	Pos.
1979	NYG	N	13	C

Ed Ecker
ECKER, ENRIQUE
B. Jan. 21, 1923, Cleveland, OH
D. Jan. 4, 1990, Los Angeles, CA
John Carroll 6'7" 276 lbs.

Year	Team		Games	Pos.
1947	CHIB	N	12	T
1948	CHI	AA	8	T
1950	GB	N	12	T
1951			7	T
1952	WAS	N	8	T
5 yrs.	47 games			

Ox Eckhardt
ECKHARDT, OSCAR GEORGE
B. Dec. 23, 1901, Yorktown, TX
D. Apr. 22, 1951, Yorktown, TX
Texas 6'1" 190 lbs.

Year	Team		Games	Pos.
1928	NYG	N	11	HB, FB, QB

Bob Eckl
ECKL, ROBERT
B. Nov. 20, 1917
D. Sep., 1961
Wisconsin 6'1" 233 lbs.

Year	Team		Games	Pos.
1945	CHIC	N	6	T

Brad Ecklund
ECKLUND, BRADFORD STERLING (Whitey)
B. May 9, 1922, Los Angeles, CA
Oregon 6'3" 215 lbs.

Year	Team		Games	Pos.
1949	B, NY	AA	12	C
1950	NYY	N	12	C
1951			12	C
1952	DAL	N	12	C
1953	BAL	N	12	C
5 yrs.	60 games			

Dolph Eckstein
ECKSTEIN, ADOLPH WILLIAM
B. May 7, 1902, Elizabeth, NJ
D. Jun. 28, 1963
Brown 5'10" 180 lbs.

Year	Team		Games	Pos.
1925	PRO	N	12	C
1926			13	C
2 yrs.	25 games			

Jerry Eckwood
ECKWOOD, JERRY L.
B. Dec. 26, 1954, Brinkley, AR

Jerry Eckwood continued
Arkansas 6'0" 198 lbs.

Year	Team		Games	Pos.
1979	TB	N	16	RB
1980			15	RB
1981			16	RB
3 yrs.	47 games			

Floyd Eddings
EDDINGS, FLOYD, JR.
B. Dec. 15,1958, Birmingham, AL
California 5'11" 177 lbs.

Year	Team		Games	Pos.
1982	NYG	N	4	WR
1983			9	WR
2 yrs.	13 games			

Nick Eddy
EDDY, NICHOLAS, M.
B. Aug. 23, 1944, Dunsmuir, CA
Notre Dame 6'1" 207 lbs.

Year	Team		Games	Pos.
1968	DET	N	5	RB
1969			11	RB
1970			11	RB
1972			2	RB
4 yrs.	29 games			

Brad Edelman
EDELMAN, BRAD M.
B. Sep. 3, 1960, Jacksonville, FL
Missouri 6'6" 265 lbs.

Year	Team		Games	Pos.
1982	NO	N	9	C
1983			16	G
1984			11	G
1985			8	G
1986			13	G
1987			11	G
1988			14	G
1989			8	G
8 yrs.	90 games			

Alex Edgar
EDGAR, ALEXANDER WILLIS
B. Sep. 17, 1898
D. Dec. 18, 1970, Butler, PA
Washington & Jefferson/Pittsburgh/Bucknell 6'2" 185 lbs.

Year	Team		Games	Pos.
1923	BUF	N	2	HB, FB
1923	AKR	N	3	G, T
1 yr.	5 games			

Shayne Edge
EDGE, RANDALL SHAYNE
B. Aug. 21, 1971, Lake City, FL
Florida 5'11" 174 lbs.

Year	Team		Games	Pos.
1996	PIT	N	4	P

Booker Edgerson
EDGERSON, BOOKER TYRONE
B. Jul. 5, 1939, Rock Island, IL
Western Illinois 5'10" 182 lbs.

Year	Team		Games	Pos.
1962	BUF	A	14	DB
1963			14	DB
1964			10	DB
1965			14	DB
1966			7	DB
1967			14	DB
1968			13	DB
1969			14	CB
1970	DEN	N	6	CB
9 yrs.	106 games			

Bob Edler
EDLER, ROBERT KARL (Deke)
B. Aug. 29, 1898
Deceased
Ohio Wesleyan 5'9" 170 lbs.

Year	Team		Games	Pos.
1923	CLE	N	4	HB

Bobby Joe Edmonds
EDMONDS, BOBBY JOE, JR.
B. Sep. 26, 1964, Nashville, TN
Arkansas 5'11" 186 lbs.

Year	Team		Games	Pos.
1986	SEA	N	15	RB
1987			11	RB
1988			16	RB
1989	LARI	N	7	RB
1995	TB	N	16	RB
5 yrs.	65 games			

Van Edmonson
EDMONSON, CHARLES VAN
(Gus)
B. Jun. 8, 1899
Deceased
Oklahoma 5'10" 210 lbs.

Year	Team		Games	Pos.
1926	BUF	N	5	C

Ferrell Edmunds
EDMUNDS, FERRELL, JR.
B. Apr. 16, 1965, South Boston, MA
Maryland 6'6" 248 lbs.

Year	Team		Games	Pos.
1988	MIA	N	16	TE
1989			16	TE
1990			16	TE
1991			8	TE
1992			10	TE
1993	SEA	N	16	TE
1994			7	TE
7 yrs.	89 games			

Randy Edmunds
EDMUNDS, GEORGE RANDALL
B. Jun. 24, 1946, Washington, GA
Georgia Tech 6'2" 223 lbs.

Year	Team		Games	Pos.
1968	MIA	A	14	LB
1969			14	LB
1971	NE	N	14	LB
1972	BAL	N	3	LB
4 yrs.	45 games			

Al Edwards
EDWARDS, AL
B. May 18, 1967, New Orleans, LA
Northwestern State (Louisiana) 5'8" 168 lbs.

Year	Team		Games	Pos.
1990	BUF	N	14	WR
1991			16	WR
1992			7	WR
3 yrs.	37 games			

Anthony Edwards
EDWARDS, ANTHONY
B. May 26, 1966, Casa Grande, AZ
New Mexico Highlands 5'11" 195 lbs.

Year	Team		Games	Pos.
1989	PHI	N	9	WR
1990			5	WR
1991	PHX	N	13	WR
1992			16	WR
1993			16	WR
1995	ARI	N	15	WR
1996			16	WR
7 yrs.	90 games			

Antonio Edwards
EDWARDS, ANTONIO
B. Mar. 10, 1970, Moultrie, GA
Valdosta State 6'3" 270 lbs.

Year	Team		Games	Pos.
1993	SEA	N	9	DE
1994			15	DE
1995			13	DE
1996			12	DE
4 yrs.	49 games			

Brad Edwards
EDWARDS, BRADFORD WAYNE

Brad Edwards continued
B. Feb. 22, 1966, Lumberton, NC
South Carolina 6'1" 200 lbs.

Year	Team		Games	Pos.
1988	MIN	N	16	S
1989			9	S
1990	WAS	N	16	S
1991			16	S
1992			16	S
1993			16	S
1994	ATL	N	4	S
1995			13	S
1996			16	S
9 yrs.	122 games			

Bud Edwards
EDWARDS, CHARLES H.
B. 1906
Deceased
Brown 5'11" 190 lbs.

Year	Team		Games	Pos.
1930	PRO	N	9	HB, FB
1931	CHIB	N	1	HB
1931	PRO	N	9	HB, FB, E
2 yrs.	19 games			

Cid Edwards
EDWARDS, CLEOPHUS
B. Sep. 10, 1943, Selma, AL
Tennessee State 6'2" 230 lbs.

Year	Team		Games	Pos.
1968	STL	N	14	RB
1969			14	RB
1970			11	RB
1971			12	RB
1972	SD	N	12	RB
1973			13	RB
1974			10	RB
1975	CHI	N	8	RB
8 yrs.	94 games			

Danny Edwards
EDWARDS, DANIEL MOODY
B. Jul. 18, 1926, Osage, TX
Georgia 6'1" 197 lbs.

Year	Team		Games	Pos.
1948	BKN	AA	11	E
1949	CHI	AA	12	E
1950	NYY	N	12	E
1951			10	E
1952	DAL	N	1	E
1953	BAL	N	12	E
1954			12	E
7 yrs.	70 games			

Dave Edwards
EDWARDS, DAVID LEE
B. Mar. 31, 1962, Senoia, GA
Illinois 6'0" 195 lbs.

Year	Team		Games	Pos.
1985	PIT	N	14	S
1986			16	S
1987			3	S
3 yrs.	33 games			

Dave Edwards
EDWARDS, DAVID MONROE
B. Dec. 14, 1939, Columbia, AL
Auburn 6'3" 224 lbs.

Year	Team		Games	Pos.
1963	DAL	N	14	LB
1964			14	LB
1965			14	LB
1966			14	LB
1967			14	LB
1968			14	LB
1969			14	LB
1970			13	LB
1971			14	LB
1972			14	LB
1973			14	LB
1974			14	LB
1975			14	LB
13 yrs.	181 games			

Dennis Edwards
EDWARDS, DENNIS RAY
B. Oct. 6, 1959, Stockton, CA
Southern California 6'4" 253 lbs.

Year	Team		Games	Pos.
1987	LARM	N	3	NT

Dixon Edwards
EDWARDS, DIXON VOLDEAN, III
B. Mar. 25, 1968, Cincinnati, OH
Michigan State 6'1" 224 lbs.

Year	Team		Games	Pos.
1991	DAL	N	12	LB
1992			16	LB
1993			16	LB
1994			16	LB
1995			15	LB
1996	MIN	N	14	LB
6 yrs.	89 games			

Donnie Edwards
EDWARDS, DONALD LEWIS
B. Apr. 6, 1973, San Diego, CA
UCLA 6'2" 225 lbs.

Year	Team		Games	Pos.
1996	KC	N	15	LB

Earl Edwards
EDWARDS, EARL
B. Mar. 17, 1946, Statesboro, GA
Wichita State 6'6" 261 lbs.

Year	Team		Games	Pos.
1969	SF	N	14	DT
1970			14	DE, DT
1971			14	DT
1972			13	DT
1973	BUF	N	14	DE
1974			14	DE
1975			14	DT
1976	CLE	N	14	DE, DT
1977			14	DE, DT
1978			16	DT
1979	GB	N	9	DT
11 yrs.	150 games			

Eddie Edwards
EDWARDS, EDDIE
B. Apr. 25, 1954, Sumter, SC
Miami (Florida) 6'5" 257 lbs.

Year	Team		Games	Pos.
1977	CIN	N	12	DT
1978			16	DT
1979			14	DT
1980			16	DT
1981			14	DE
1982			9	DE
1983			16	DE
1984			16	DE
1985			16	DE
1986			16	DE
1987			14	DE
1988			11	DE
12 yrs.	170 games			

Emmett Edwards
EDWARDS, EMMETT LEE
B. Jun. 6, 1952, Tulsa, OK
Kansas 6'1" 189 lbs.

Year	Team		Games	Pos.
1975	HOU	N	11	WR
1976			3	WR
1976	BUF	N	6	WR
2 yrs.	20 games			

Glen Edwards
EDWARDS, GLEN (Pine)
B. Jul. 31, 1947, St. Petersburg, FL
Florida A&M 6'0" 184 lbs.

Year	Team		Games	Pos.
1971	PIT	N	8	S
1972			12	S
1973			14	S
1974			14	S
1975			14	S
1976			14	S

Glen Edwards continued

Year	Team		Games	Pos.
1977			13	S
1978	SD	N	14	S
1979			15	S
1980			16	S
1981			8	S
11 yrs.	142 games			

Herman Edwards
EDWARDS, HERMAN LEE
B. Apr. 27, 1954, Fort Monmouth, NJ
California/San Diego State 6'0" 192 lbs.

Year	Team		Games	Pos.
1977	PHI	N	14	DB
1978			16	S
1979			16	S
1980			16	CB
1981			16	CB
1982			9	CB
1983			16	CB
1984			16	CB
1985			16	CB
1986	LATM	N	4	CB
1986	ATL	N	3	CB
10 yrs.	142 games			

Howard Edwards
EDWARDS, HOWARD (Cap, Horse)
B. May, 1888, South Bend, IN
D. 1944
Notre Dame 6'0" 207 lbs.

Year	Team		Games	Pos.
1920	CAN	A	5	G
1921			2	G
1922	TOL	N	9	G, T
1923	CLE	N	2	T, G
1924			7	T, G
5 yrs.	25 games			

Jimmy Edwards
EDWARDS, JIMMY LAROY
B. Sep. 19, 1952, Oklahoma City, OK
Oklahoma/Northeast Louisiana 5'9" 185 lbs.

Year	Team		Games	Pos.
1979	MIN	N	14	RB
1980			15	RB
2 yrs.	29 games			

Kelvin Edwards
EDWARDS, KELVIN
B. Jul. 19, 1964, Birmingham, AL
Liberty 6'2" 197 lbs.

Year	Team		Games	Pos.
1986	NO	N	14	WR
1987	DAL	N	13	WR
1988			8	WR
3 yrs.	35 games			

Lloyd Edwards
EDWARDS, LLOYD
B. Nov. 26, 1946, Long Beach, CA
San Diego State 6'3" 248 lbs.

Year	Team		Games	Pos.
1969	OAK	A	14	TE

Marshall Edwards
EDWARDS, MARSHALL
B. 1916
Wake Forest 6'1" 190 lbs.

Year	Team		Games	Pos.
1943	BKN	N	1	B

Monk Edwards
EDWARDS, WILLIAM BENNETT
B. Jul. 19, 1920, Ireland, TX
Baylor 6'3" 213 lbs.

Year	Team		Games	Pos.
1940	NYG	N	8	T
1941			11	G, T
1942			11	G
1946			10	G
4 yrs.	40 games			

Year	Team	Games	Pos.

Randy Edwards
EDWARDS, RICHARD RANDOLPH
B. Mar. 9, 1961, Marietta, GA
Alabama 6'4" 262 lbs.

Year	Team	Games	Pos.
1984	**SEA** N	13	DE
1985		16	DE
1986		16	DE
1987		7	DE
4 yrs.	52 games		

Ron Edwards
EDWARDS, RONALD EUGENE
B. Sep. 18, 1971, Myrtle Beach, SC
North Carolina A&T 6'5" 311 lbs.

Year	Team	Games	Pos.
1994	**CIN** N	1	OT

Stan Edwards
EDWARDS, STANLEY
B. May 20, 1960, Detroit, MI
Michigan 6'0" 210 lbs.

Year	Team	Games	Pos.
1982	**HOU** N	7	FB
1983		14	RB
1984		14	RB
1985		15	RB
1986		3	RB
1987	**DET** N	3	RB
6 yrs.	56 games		

Tim Edwards
EDWARDS, TIM
B. Aug. 29, 1968, Philadelphia, MS
Delta State 6'1" 270 lbs.

Year	Team	Games	Pos.
1992	**NE** N	14	DE

Tom Edwards
EDWARDS, THOMAS L.
B. Dec. 12, 1899, Central Lake, MI
D. Jan. 28, 1980, Central Lake, MI
Central Michigan/Michigan 5'11" 185 lbs.

Year	Team	Games	Pos.
1926	**DET** N	12	T, E

Turk Edwards
EDWARDS, ALBERT GLEN
B. Sep. 28, 1907, Clarkston, WA
D. Jan. 10, 1973, Seattle, WA
Washington State 6'2" 255 lbs.

Year	Team	Games	Pos.
1932	**BOS** N	7	T
1933		12	T
1934		12	T
1935		11	T
1936		12	T
1937	**WAS** N	11	T
1938		9	T
1939		11	T
1940		2	T
9 yrs.	87 games		

Vernon Edwards
EDWARDS, VERNON LAJVIN
B. Jun. 23, 1972, Houston, TX
Southern Methodist 6'4" 255 lbs.

Year	Team	Games	Pos.
1996	**SD** N	5	DE

Weldon Edwards
EDWARDS, WELDON (Scratch)
B. Apr. 15, 1924, Comanche, TX
Deceased
Texas Christian 6'0" 225 lbs.

Year	Team	Games	Pos.
1948	**WAS** N	5	T

Dick Egan
EGAN, DICK
DePaul 165 lbs.

Year	Team	Games	Pos.
1920	**CHIC** A	4	HB, FB

Year	Team	Games	Pos.

Dick Egan continued

Year	Team	Games	Pos.
1921		1	HB
1922	**CHIC** N	9	E
1923		4	E
1924	**KEN** N	2	E
5 yrs.	20 games		

Dick Egan
EGAN, JOHN RICHARD
B. Feb. 2, 1904
D. May, 1984, Germantown, OH
Wilmington 165 lbs.

Year	Team	Games	Pos.
1924	**DAY** N	3	G

Doug Eggers
EGGERS, DOUGLAS BOYD
B. Sep. 21, 1930, Wagner, SD
South Dakota State 6'0" 213 lbs.

Year	Team	Games	Pos.
1954	**BAL** N	11	LB
1955		12	LB
1956		12	LB
1957		11	LB
1958	**CHIC** N	8	LB
5 yrs.	54 games		

Ron Egloff
EGLOFF, RONALD
B. Oct. 3, 1955, Garden City, MI
Wisconsin 6'5" 231 lbs.

Year	Team	Games	Pos.
1977	**DEN** N	13	TE
1978		8	TE
1979		15	TE
1980		16	TE
1981		16	TE
1982		9	TE
1983		16	TE
1984	**SD** N	12	TE
8 yrs.	105 games		

Patrick Egu
EGU, OKECHUKWU PATRICK
B. Feb. 20, 1967, Owerri, Nigeria
Nevada-Reno 5'11" 205 lbs.

Year	Team	Games	Pos.
1989	**NE** N	7	RB

Chuck Ehin
EHIN, CHARLES KALEV
B. Jul. 1, 1961, Marysville, CA
Brigham Young 6'5" 256 lbs.

Year	Team	Games	Pos.
1983	**SD** N	9	DE
1984		16	DE
1985		16	DE
1986		12	NT
1987		12	NT
5 yrs.	65 games		

Tom Ehlers
EHLERS, TOM SLICK
B. Jul. 14, 1952, South Bend, IN
Kentucky 6'2" 218 lbs.

Year	Team	Games	Pos.
1975	**PHI** N	14	LB
1976		14	LB
1977		14	LB
1978	**BUF** N	8	LB
4 yrs.	50 games		

Clyde Ehrhardt
EHRHARDT, CLYDE W.
B. Jul. 4, 1921, Bardwell, KY
D. Feb. 4, 1963
Georgia 6'1" 232 lbs.

Year	Team	Games	Pos.
1946	**WAS** N	10	C
1948		12	C
1949		12	C
3 yrs.	34 games		

Year	Team	Games	Pos.

Joe Ehrmann
EHRMANN, JOSEPH CHARLES
B. Mar. 29, 1949, Buffalo, NY
Syracuse 6'3" 250 lbs.

Year	Team	Games	Pos.
1973	**BAL** N	12	DT
1974		14	DT
1975		14	DT
1976		9	DT
1977		14	DT
1978		16	DT
1979		16	DT
1980		16	DT
1981	**DET** N	4	DT
1982		9	DT
10 yrs.	122 games		

John Eibner
EIBNER, JOHN R.
B. Mar. 13, 1916, Elyria, OH
Deceased
Kentucky 6'2" 228 lbs.

Year	Team	Games	Pos.
1941	**PHI** N	11	T
1942		10	T
1946		9	T
3 yrs.	30 games		

Ray Eichenlaub
EICHENLAUB, RAYMOND J.
B. Dec. 26, 1891
D. Jul., 1969, Chicago, IL
Notre Dame 6'0" 225 lbs.

Year	Team	Games	Pos.
1925	**COL** N	4	FB, T

Ed Eiden
EIDEN, EDMUND
B. Nov. 16, 1921, Scranton, PA
Scranton 6'0" 205 lbs.

Year	Team	Games	Pos.
1944	**DET** N	1	C

Jim Eiden
EIDEN, HAROLD C.
B. Oct. 16, 1901
D. Apr. 18, 1990, Jensen Beach, FL
None

Year	Team	Games	Pos.
1926	**LOU** N	1	T

Jim Eidson
EIDSON, JAMES
B. May 10, 1954, Anderson, SC
Mississippi State 6'3" 264 lbs.

Year	Team	Games	Pos.
1976	**DAL** N	9	G

Jim Eifrid
EIFRID, JAMES JOHN
B. Oct. 22, 1938, Fort Wayne, IN
Colorado State 6'0" 240 lbs.

Year	Team	Games	Pos.
1961	**DEN** A	1	LB

Charley Eikenberg
EIKENBERG, CHARLES VIRGIL
B. Feb. 22, 1924, Old Gulf, TX
Rice 6'2" 205 lbs.

Year	Team	Games	Pos.
1948	**CHIC** N	9	QB

Pat Eilers
EILERS, PATRICK CHRISTOPHER
B. Sep. 3, 1966, St. Paul, MN
Notre Dame 5'11" 195 lbs.

Year	Team	Games	Pos.
1990	**MIN** N	8	S
1991		16	S
1992	**WAS** N	1	S
1993		11	S
1994		16	S
1995	**CHI** N	9	S
6 yrs.	61 games		

Year	Team	Games	Pos.

Mike Eischeid
EISCHEID, MICHAEL DUNCAN
B. Sep. 29, 1940, Orange City, IA
Upper Iowa 6'0" 190 lbs.

Year	Team	Games	Pos.
1966	**OAK** A	12	K, P
1967		14	P
1968		14	P
1969		14	P
1970	**OAK** N	14	P
1971		2	P
1972	**MIN** N	14	P
1973		14	P
1974		14	P
9 yrs.	112 games		

Larry Eisenhauer
EISENHAUER, LAWRENCE CONWAY
B. Feb. 22, 1940, Hicksville, NY
Boston College 6'5" 247 lbs.

Year	Team	Games	Pos.
1961	**BOS** A	14	DE
1962		14	DE
1963		14	DE
1964		14	DE
1965		14	DE
1966		9	DE
1967		8	DE
1968		8	DE
1969		14	DE
9 yrs.	115 games		

Stan Eisenhooth
EISENHOOTH, STANLEY EMERSON
B. Jul. 8, 1963, Harrisburg, PA
Towson State 6'5" 275 lbs.

Year	Team	Games	Pos.
1987	**SEA** N	1	C
1988		13	C, OT
1989	**IND** N	16	OT, G
3 yrs.	30 games		

Alfred Eissler
EISSLER, ALFRED
B. Nov., 1896
Deceased
None

Year	Team	Games	Pos.
1920	**CHIT** A	2	FB

Gus Ekberg
EKBERG, GUSTAVIUS
B. 1901, Minneapolis, MN
Deceased
West Virginia 5'9" 180 lbs.

Year	Team	Games	Pos.
1925	**CLE** N	1	FB

Andy Ekern
EKERN, ANDERSON ERIK
B. Jul. 26, 1961, Columbia, MO
Missouri 6'6" 265 lbs.

Year	Team	Games	Pos.
1984	**IND** N	2	OT

Carl Ekern
EKERN, CARL FREDERICK
B. May 27, 1954, Richland, VA
D. Aug. 1, 1990
San Jose State 6'3" 222 lbs.

Year	Team	Games	Pos.
1976	**LA** N	14	LB
1977		14	LB
1978		16	LB
1980		15	LB
1981		16	LB
1982	**LARM** N	3	LB
1983		16	LB
1984		16	LB
1985		16	LB
1986		13	LB
1987		11	LB

Year	Team	Games	Pos.

Carl Ekern continued

Year	Team	Games	Pos.
1988		16	LB
12 yrs.	166 games		

Cleveland Elam
ELAM, CLEVELAND
B. Apr. 5, 1952, Memphis, TN
Tennessee State 6'4" 252 lbs.

1975	SF	N	14	DE
1976			14	DE
1977			14	DT
1978			12	DT
1979	DET	N	8	DT
5 yrs.	62 games			

Jason Elam
ELAM, JASON
B. Mar. 8, 1970, Fort Walton Beach, FL
Hawaii 5'11" 192 lbs.

1993	DEN	N	16	K
1994			16	K
1995			16	K
1996			16	K
4 yrs.	64 games			

Onzy Elam
ELAM, ONZY
B. Dec. 1, 1964, Miami, FL
Tennessee State 6'2" 225 lbs.

1987	NYJ	N	5	LB
1988			4	LB
1989	DAL	N	1	LB
3 yrs.	10 games			

Donnie Elder
ELDER, DONALD EUGENE
B. Dec. 13, 1963, Chattanooga, TN
Memphis State 5'9" 175 lbs.

1985	NYJ	N	10	CB
1986	PIT	N	9	CB
1986	DET	N	3	CB
1988	TB	N	16	DB
1989			16	CB, S
1990	SD	N	12	CB
1991			16	CB
6 yrs.	82 games			

Mo Elewonibi
ELEWONIBI, MOHAMMED THOMAS DAVID
B. Dec. 16, 1965, Lagos, Nigeria
Brigham Young 6'4" 298 lbs.

1992	WAS	N	5	OT
1993			15	OT
1995	PHI	N	6	OT
3 yrs.	26 games			

Clifton Eley
ELEY, CLIFTON
B. Jun. 21, 1961, Clarksdale, MS
Mississippi State 6'5" 230 lbs.

1987	MIN	N	2	TE

Monroe Eley
ELEY, MONROE
B. Apr. 17, 1949, Rocky Mount, NC
Arizona State 6'2" 210 lbs.

1975	ATL	N	6	RB
1977			7	RB
2 yrs.	13 games			

Bruce Elia
ELIA, BRUCE LOUIS
B. Jan. 10, 1953, Hoboken, NJ

Bruce Elia continued
Ohio State 6'1" 220 lbs.

1975	MIA	N	14	LB
1976	SF	N	12	LB
1977			13	LB
1978			16	LB
4 yrs.	55 games			

Homer Elias
ELIAS, HOMER CARY
B. May 1, 1955, Fort Benning, GA
Tennessee State 6'3" 255 lbs.

1978	DET	N	16	G
1979			15	G
1980			14	G
1981			16	G
1982			9	G
1983			14	G
1984			12	G
7 yrs.	96 games			

Keith Elias
ELIAS, KEITH
B. Feb. 3, 1972, Lacey Township, NJ
Princeton 5'9" 191 lbs.

1994	NYG	N	2	RB
1995			15	RB
1996			9	RB
3 yrs.	26 games			

Don Eliason
ELIASON, DONALD CARLTON
B. Jul. 24, 1918, Owatonna, MN
Hamline 6'2" 215 lbs.

1942	BKN	N	5	E
1946	BOS	N	3	E
2 yrs.	8 games			

Jim Eliopulos
ELIOPULOS, JIM A.
B. Apr. 18, 1959, Dearborn, MI
Westminster/Wyoming 6'2" 229 lbs.

1983	STL	N	4	LB
1983	NYJ	N	8	LB
1984			11	LB
1985			8	LB
3 yrs.	31 games			

Chief Elkins
ELKINS, FAIT (Pete)
B. 1900
Deceased
Haskell/Nebraska 5'11" 190 lbs.

1928	FRA	N	10	HB, FB, QB, E
1929			7	HB, FB
1929	CHIC	N	2	HB
1933	CIN	N	1	HB
3 yrs.	20 games			

Ev Elkins
ELKINS, EVERETT LEE (Boots)
B. Nov. 17, 1917, Hamlin, WV
D. Jun., 1977, Hamlin, WV
Marshall 5'11" 190 lbs.

1940	CHIC	N	1	B

Larry Elkins
ELKINS, LAWRENCE CLAYTON (Elk)
B. Jul. 28, 1943, Brownwood, TX
Baylor 6'1" 193 lbs.

1966	HOU	A	14	SE
1967			4	FL
2 yrs.	18 games			

Mike Elkins
ELKINS, MICHAEL DAVID
B. Jul. 20, 1966, Greensboro, NC
Wake Forest 6'3" 225 lbs.

1989	KC	N	1	QB

Bill Elko
ELKO, WILLIAM
B. Dec. 28, 1959, New York, NY
Arizona State/Louisiana State 6'5" 277 lbs.

1983	SD	N	11	G
1984			15	G
1987	IND	N	3	NT
3 yrs.	29 games			

Henry Ellard
ELLARD, HENRY
B. Apr. 21, 1961, Fresno, CA
Fresno State 5'11" 175 lbs.

1983	LARM	N	12	WR
1984			16	WR
1985			16	WR
1986			9	WR
1987			12	WR
1988			16	WR
1989			14	WR
1990			15	WR
1991			16	WR
1992			16	WR
1993			16	WR
1994	WAS	N	16	WR
1995			15	WR
1996			16	WR
14 yrs.	205 games			

Jack Ellena
ELLENA, JOHN
B. Oct. 27, 1931
UCLA 6'1" 225 lbs.

1955	LA	N	12	G
1956			9	G
2 yrs.	21 games			

Bill Ellenbogen
ELLENBOGEN, WILLIAM A.
B. Dec. 8, 1950, Glen Cove, NY
Buffalo/Virginia Tech 6'5" 258 lbs.

1976	NYG	N	11	G
1977			12	G
2 yrs.	23 games			

Rich Ellender
ELLENDER, RICHARD
B. Jun. 9, 1957, Sulphur, LA
McNeese State 5'11" 171 lbs.

1979	HOU	N	13	RB

Gene Ellenson
ELLENSON, EUGENE
B. 1921
Georgia 6'1" 210 lbs.

1946	MIA	AA	13	T

Carl Eller
ELLER, CARL L. (Moose)
B. Feb. 25, 1942, Winston-Salem, NC
Minnesota 6'6" 252 lbs.

1964	MIN	N	14	DT, DE
1965			14	DE
1966			14	DE
1967			14	DE
1968			14	DE
1969			14	DE
1970			14	DE
1971			14	DE
1972			14	DE

Carl Eller continued

1973			14	DE
1974			14	DE
1975			14	DE
1976			13	DE
1977			14	DE
1978			14	DE
1979	SEA	N	16	DE
16 yrs.	225 games			

Don Ellersick
ELLERSICK, DONALD
B. May 7, 1938, Ione, WA
Washington State 6'1" 193 lbs.

1960	LA	N	12	HB

Gary Ellerson
ELLERSON, GARY
B. Jul. 17, 1963, Albany, GA
Wisconsin 5'11" 219 lbs.

1985	GB	N	15	RB
1986			16	RB
1987	DET	N	8	RB
3 yrs.	39 games			

Al Elliott
ELLIOTT, ALVAH CHARLES (Rowdy)
B. Oct. 13, 1894, Muscoda, WI
D. Dec. 18, 1975, Naperville, IL
Wisconsin 5'9" 175 lbs.

1922	RAC	N	11	HB
1923			10	HB, E
1924			7	HB
3 yrs.	28 games			

Carl Elliott
ELLIOTT, CARLTON B. (Stretch)
B. Nov. 12, 1927, Laurel, DE
Virginia 6'4" 220 lbs.

1951	GB	N	12	E
1952			12	E
1953			12	E
1954			12	E
4 yrs.	48 games			

Charlie Elliott
ELLIOTT, CHARLES J.
B. Dec. 30, 1921, Corvallis, OR
D. Sep., 1980, Oregon City, OR
Oregon 6'2" 240 lbs.

1947	NY	AA	10	T
1948	CHI	AA	1	T
1948	SF	AA	3	T
2 yrs.	14 games			

Doc Elliott
ELLIOTT, WALLACE
B. Apr. 6, 1900
D. Jan. 11, 1976, Fort Myers, FL
Lafayette 5'10" 209 lbs.

1922	CAN	N	7	FB
1923			9	FB
1924	CLE	N	7	FB, HB
1925			14	FB
1926	CLE	A	3	FB
1926	PHI	N	2	FB
1931	CLE	N	2	FB
6 yrs.	44 games			

Jim Elliott
ELLIOTT, JAMES
B. Aug. 18, 1944, Montgomery, AL
Presbyterian 5'11" 184 lbs.

1967	PIT	N	14	P

Year	Team		Games	Pos.

John Elliott
ELLIOTT, DARRELL JOHN
B. Oct. 26, 1944, Beaumont, TX
Texas 6'4" 244 lbs.

Year	Team		Games	Pos.
1967	NY	A	13	DE, DT
1968			14	DT
1969			14	DT
1970	NYJ	N	14	DT
1971			4	DT
1972			13	DT
1973			13	DT
7 yrs.	85 games			

Jumbo Elliott
ELLIOTT, JOHN S.
B. Apr. 1, 1965, Lake Ronkonkoma, NY
Michigan 6'7" 305 lbs.

Year	Team		Games	Pos.
1988	NYG	N	16	OT
1989			13	OT
1990			8	OT
1991			16	OT
1992			16	OT
1993			11	OT
1994			16	OT
1995			16	OT
1996	NYJ	N	14	OT
9 yrs.	126 games			

Lenvil Elliott
ELLIOTT, LENVIL OLON
B. Sep. 2, 1951, Lexington, MO
Northeast Missouri State 6'0" 207 lbs.

Year	Team		Games	Pos.
1973	CIN	N	6	RB
1974			10	RB
1975			14	RB
1976			12	RB
1977			14	RB
1978			10	RB
1979	SF	N	16	RB
1980			15	RB
1981			4	RB
9 yrs.	101 games			

Lin Elliott
ELLIOTT, LINDLEY FRANKLIN
B. Nov. 11, 1968, Euless, TX
Texas Tech 6'0" 182 lbs.

Year	Team		Games	Pos.
1992	DAL	N	16	K
1993			2	K
1994	KC	N	16	K
1995			16	K
4 yrs.	50 games			

Matt Elliott
ELLIOTT, MATT
B. Oct. 1, 1968, Carmel, IN
Michigan 6'1" 265 lbs.

Year	Team		Games	Pos.
1992	WAS	N	16	C
1995	CAR	N	15	G
1996			16	G
3 yrs.	47 games			

Ted Elliott
ELLIOTT, TED
B. Nov. 16, 1964
Mankato State 6'6" 275 lbs.

Year	Team		Games	Pos.
1987	NO	N	3	NT

Tony Elliott
ELLIOTT, ANTHONY ROBERT
B. Apr. 28, 1959, New York, NY
Wisconsin/North Texas State 6'2" 290 lbs.

Year	Team		Games	Pos.
1982	NO	N	9	DE
1983			12	NT
1984			4	NT
1985			16	NT

Tony Elliott continued

Year	Team		Games	Pos.
1986			15	NT
1987			14	NT
1988			14	NT
7 yrs.	84 games			

Tony Elliott
ELLIOTT, TONY
B. Jan. 10, 1964
Central Michigan 5'10" 195 lbs.

Year	Team		Games	Pos.
1987	GB	N	1	S

Allan Ellis
ELLIS, ALAN DELON
B. Aug. 19, 1951, Los Angeles, CA
UCLA 5'10" 179 lbs.

Year	Team		Games	Pos.
1973	CHI	N	14	DB
1974			14	CB
1975			14	CB
1976			14	CB
1977			14	CB
1979			8	CB
1980			16	CB
1981	SD	N	11	CB
8 yrs.	105 games			

Clarence Ellis
ELLIS, CLARENCE JOSEPH, JR.
B. Feb. 11, 1950, Grand Rapids, MI
Notre Dame 5'11" 191 lbs.

Year	Team		Games	Pos.
1972	ATL	N	13	S
1973			14	S
1974			14	S
3 yrs.	41 games			

Craig Ellis
ELLIS, CRAIG
B. Jan. 26, 1961, Los Angeles, CA
San Diego State 5'11" 180 lbs.

Year	Team		Games	Pos.
1986	MIA	N	9	RB
1987	LARI	N	3	RB
2 yrs.	12 games			

Drew Ellis
ELLIS, B. DREW
B. Dec. 27, 1914
D. May 18, 1988
Texas Christian 6'1" 215 lbs.

Year	Team		Games	Pos.
1938	PHI	N	11	T
1939			11	T
2 yrs.	22 games			

Gerry Ellis
ELLIS, GERRY LYNN
B. Nov. 12, 1957, Columbia, MO
Missouri 5'11" 230 lbs.

Year	Team		Games	Pos.
1980	GB	N	15	FB
1981			15	FB
1982			9	FB
1983			15	FB
1984			16	FB
1985			16	FB
1986			16	FB
7 yrs.	102 games			

Herb Ellis
ELLIS, HERBERT W.
B. Dec. 18, 1925, Vernon, TX
Texas A&M 6'2" 205 lbs.

Year	Team		Games	Pos.
1949	NYB	N	12	C

Jim Ellis
ELLIS, JAMES
B. Mar. 25, 1964
Boise State 6'3" 240 lbs.

Year	Team		Games	Pos.
1987	LARI	N	3	LB

John Ellis
ELLIS, JOHN T.
B. Dec. 21, 1919 Sherman, TX
Vanderbilt 5'10" 212 lbs.

Year	Team		Games	Pos.
1944	BKN	N	6	G

Ken Ellis
ELLIS, KENNETH A.
B. Sep. 27, 1947, Woodbine, GA
Southern University 5'10" 191 lbs.

Year	Team		Games	Pos.
1970	GB	N	14	DB
1971			14	CB
1972			14	CB
1973			14	CB
1974			14	CB
1975			14	CB
1976	HOU	N	1	CB
1976	MIA	N	12	CB
1977	CLE	N	9	CB
1979	DET	N	7	CB
1979	LA	N	3	CB
9 yrs.	116 games			

Kwame Ellis
ELLIS, KWAME
B. Feb. 27, 1974, Berkeley, CA
Stanford 5'10" 188 lbs.

Year	Team		Games	Pos.
1996	NYJ	N	8	CB

Larry Ellis
ELLIS, LAWRENCE R., JR.
B. May 27, 1922, York Village, ME
D. Aug. 24, 1988, Auburn, NY
Syracuse 6'1" 204 lbs.

Year	Team		Games	Pos.
1948	DET	N	4	QB

Ray Ellis
ELLIS, KERWIN RAY
B. Apr. 27, 1959, Canton, OH
Ohio State 6'1" 196 lbs.

Year	Team		Games	Pos.
1981	PHI	N	16	CB
1982			9	CB, S
1983			16	S
1984			16	S
1985			16	S
1986	CLE	N	15	S
1987			12	S
7 yrs.	100 games			

Roger Ellis
ELLIS, ROGER C.
B. 1939
Maine 6'3" 233 lbs.

Year	Team		Games	Pos.
1960	NY	A		LB
1961			14	C
1962			14	LB
1963			1	LB
4 yrs.	29 games			

Walt Ellis
ELLIS, WALTER J. (Speed)
B. Nov., 1898
Deceased
Detroit 5'11" 224 lbs.

Year	Team		Games	Pos.
1924	COL	N	8	T
1925			9	T
1925	DET	N	1	T
1926	CHIC	N	10	T, G
1927			8	T
4 yrs.	36 games			

Glenn Ellison
ELLISON, GLENN
B. Mar. 9, 1947, Jacksonville, FL
Arkansas 6'1" 215 lbs.

Year	Team		Games	Pos.
1971	OAK	N	1	RB

Jerry Ellison
ELLISON, JERRY
B. Dec. 20, 1971, Augusta, GA
Tennessee-Chattanooga 5'10" 194 lbs.

Year	Team		Games	Pos.
1995	TB	N	16	RB
1996			16	RB
2 yrs.	32 games			

Mark Ellison
ELLISON, MARK
B. Apr. 15, 1948, Pittsburgh, PA
Dayton 6'2" 250 lbs.

Year	Team		Games	Pos.
1972	NYG	N	14	G
1973			14	G
2 yrs.	28 games			

'Omar Ellison
ELLISON, 'OMAR
B. Oct. 8, 1971, Griffin, GA
Florida State 6'1" 200 lbs.

Year	Team		Games	Pos.
1995	SD	N	2	WR
1996			9	WR
2 yrs.	11 games			

Riki Ellison
GRAY, RIKI MORGAN
B. Aug. 15, 1960, Christchurch, New Zealand
Southern California 6'2" 225 lbs.

Year	Team		Games	Pos.
1983	SF	N	16	LB
1984			16	LB
1985			16	LB
1986			16	LB
1987			3	LB
1988			13	LB
1990	LARI	N	16	LB
1991			16	LB
1992			12	LB
9 yrs.	124 games			

Willie Ellison
ELLISON, WILLIAM HENRY
B. Nov. 1, 1945, Lockhart, TX
Texas Southern 6'1" 204 lbs.

Year	Team		Games	Pos.
1967	LA	N	14	RB
1968			14	RB
1969			14	RB
1970			14	RB
1971			14	RB
1972			12	RB
1973	KC	N	10	RB
1974			5	RB
8 yrs.	97 games			

Luther Elliss
ELLISS, LUTHER
B. Mar. 22, 1973, Mancos, CO
Utah 6'5" 291 lbs.

Year	Team		Games	Pos.
1995	DET	N	16	DE
1996			14	DT
2 yrs.	30 games			

Bud Ellor
ELLOR, ALBERT W.
B. 1906, Bloomfield, NJ
D. Feb. 11, 1932, Newark, NJ
Bucknell 6'2" 205 lbs.

Year	Team		Games	Pos.
1930	NEW	N	10	G, E

Swede Ellstrom
ELLSTROM, MARVIN L.
B. May 15, 1908, Moline, IL
Deceased
Oklahoma 6'1" 203 lbs.

Year	Team		Games	Pos.
1934	BOS	N	3	FB
1934	PHI	N	8	HB
1935	PIT	N	3	FB

Year	Team	Games	Pos.

Swede Ellstrom continued

1936	CHIC	N	1	FB

3 yrs. 15 games

Percy Ellsworth

ELLSWORTH, PERCY
B. Oct. 19, 1974, Drewryville, VA
Virginia 6'2" 199 lbs.

1996	NYG	N	14	S

Charley Ellzey

ELLZEY, CHARLES
B. Feb. 17, 1938, Meridian, MS
Southern Mississippi 6'3" 243 lbs.

1960	STL	N	9	C, LB
1961			5	C

2 yrs. 14 games

Hicham El-Mashtoub

EL-MASHTOUB, HICHAM
B. May 11, 1972, Lebanon
Arizona 6'2" 288 lbs.

1995	HOU	N	2	C, G
1996			1	C, G

2 yrs. 3 games

Dave Elmendorf

ELMENDORF, DAVID COLE
B. Jun. 20, 1949, San Antonio, TX
Texas A&M 6'1" 195 lbs.

1971	LA	N	14	S
1972			14	S
1973			14	S
1974			14	S
1975			14	S
1976			14	S
1977			14	S
1978			16	S
1979			16	S

9 yrs. 130 games

Doug Elmore

ELMORE, JAMES DOUGLAS
B. Dec. 15, 1939, Reform, AL
Mississippi 6'0" 188 lbs.

1962	WAS	N	14	HB

Shorty Elness

ELNESS, LELAND
B. May 10, 1906
D. Nov., 1965
Bradley 5'8" 166 lbs.

1929	CHIB	N	4	QB, HB

Jimbo Elrod

ELROD, JAMES WHITTINGTON
B. May 25, 1954, Memphis, TN
Oklahoma 6'0" 220 lbs.

1976	KC	N	6	LB
1977			14	LB
1978			16	LB

3 yrs. 36 games

Earl Elser

ELSER, EARL
B. Mar. 21, 1908
D. Aug., 1974, Gary, IN
Butler 6'1" 229 lbs.

1933	POR	N	4	T
1934	C-S	N	10	T

2 yrs. 14 games

Earl Elsey

ELSEY, EARL D.
B. 1919

Earl Elsey continued

Deceased
Loyola (California) 5'8" 175 lbs.

1946	LA	AA	13	HB

Neil Elshire

ELSHIRE, NEIL JAMES
B. Mar. 8, 1958, Salem, OR
Oregon 6'6" 260 lbs.

1981	MIN	N	4	DE
1982			5	DE
1983			16	DE
1984			12	DE
1985			16	DE
1986			10	DE

6 yrs. 63 games

Art Elston

ELSTON, ARTHUR W. (Dutch)
B. Oct. 19, 1918, Texhoma, TX
D. Sep. 10, 1989, San Francisco, CA
South Carolina 5'11" 191 lbs.

1942	CLE	N	11	LB
1946	SF	AA	13	C
1947			9	G, C
1948			12	G, C

4 yrs. 45 games

Leo Elter

ELTER, LEO WILLIAM
B. Oct. 21, 1929, Pittsburgh, PA
Duquesne/Villanova 5'10" 201 lbs.

1953	PIT	N	12	FB
1954			11	FB
1955	WAS	N	11	FB
1956			12	FB
1957			12	FB
1958	PIT	N	7	FB
1959			8	FB

7 yrs. 73 games

John Elway

ELWAY, JOHN ALBERT
B. Jun. 28, 1960, Port Angeles, WA
Stanford 6'3" 210 lbs.

1983	DEN	N	11	QB
1984			15	QB
1985			16	QB
1986			16	QB
1987			12	QB
1988			15	QB
1989			15	QB
1990			16	QB
1991			16	QB
1992			12	QB
1993			16	QB
1994			14	QB
1995			16	QB
1996			15	QB

14 yrs. 205 games

Jack Elwell

ELWELL, JOHN M.
B. 1940, Cleveland, OH
Purdue 6'3" 200 lbs.

1962	STL	N	13	OE, DB

Harold Ely

ELY, HAROLD
B. Dec. 26, 1909
D. Jul. 12, 1983, Jasper, AL
Iowa 6'2" 268 lbs.

1932	CHIB	N	5	T
1932	BKN	N	3	T, G
1933			10	T
1934			11	T

3 yrs. 29 games

Larry Ely

ELY, LAWRENCE ORLO, JR.
B. Dec. 19, 1947, Iowa City, IA
Iowa 6'1" 230 lbs.

1970	CIN	N	11	LB
1971			6	LB
1975	CHI	N	12	LB

3 yrs. 29 games

Paul Elzey

ELZEY, PAUL VINCENT
B. May 13, 1946, Toledo, OH
Toledo 6'3" 235 lbs.

1968	CIN	A	4	LB

Bert Emanuel

EMANUEL, BERT TYRONE
B. Oct. 27, 1970, Kansas City, MO
Rice 5'10" 171 lbs.

1994	ATL	N	16	WR
1995			16	WR
1996			14	WR

3 yrs. 46 games

Frank Emanuel

EMANUEL, THOMAS FRANK
B. Dec. 4, 1942, Clio, SC
Tennessee 6'3" 225 lbs.

1966	MIA	A	14	LB
1967			14	LB
1968			14	LB
1969			14	LB
1970	NO	N	3	LB

5 yrs. 59 games

John Embree

EMBREE, JOHN WILLIAM
B. Jul. 13, 1944, St. Louis, MO
Los Angeles State 6'4" 201 lbs.

1969	DEN	A	13	WR
1970	DEN	N	7	WR

2 yrs. 20 games

Jon Embree

EMBREE, JON W.
B. Oct. 15, 1965, Los Angeles, CA
Colorado 6'2" 230 lbs.

1987	LARM	N	1	TE
1988			12	TE

2 yrs. 13 games

Mel Embree

EMBREE, MELVIN
B. 1927
Pepperdine 6'3" 190 lbs.

1953	BAL	N	12	E
1954	CHIC	N	5	E

2 yrs. 17 games

Pete Emelianchik

EMELIANCHIK, PETER ADAM
B. Nov. 19, 1943, Brooklyn, NY
Emporia State/Richmond 6'2" 220 lbs.

1967	PHI	N	1	TE

Bob Emerick

EMERICK, ROBERT W.
B. Feb. 21, 1913, Stockton, CA
Miami (Ohio) 6'2" 225 lbs.

1934	DET	N	9	T, G
1937	CLE	N	11	G, T

2 yrs. 20 games

Ox Emerson

EMERSON, GEORGE CONNER

Ox Emerson continued

B. Dec. 18, 1907, Douglas, TX
Texas 5'11" 203 lbs.

1931	POR	N	14	G
1932			12	G
1933			11	G
1934	DET	N	13	G
1935			8	G
1936			10	G
1937			11	G
1938	BKN	N	11	G

8 yrs. 90 games

Vern Emerson

EMERSON, VERNON E.
B. Sep. 2, 1945, Anoka, MN
Minnesota-Duluth 6'5" 260 lbs.

1969	STL	N	5	OT
1970			14	OT
1971			4	OT

3 yrs. 23 games

Larry Emery

EMERY, LARRY G.
B. Jul. 13, 1964, Macon, GA
Wisconsin 5'9" 195 lbs.

1987	ATL	N	5	RB

Carlos Emmons

EMMONS, CARLOS
B. Sep. 3, 1973, Greenwood, MS
Arkansas State 6'4" 240 lbs.

1996	PIT	N	14	LB

Frank Emmons

EMMONS, FRANKLIN B.
B. 1918
Oregon 6'1" 213 lbs.

1940	PHI	N	11	FB, HB

Red Emslie

EMSLIE, GEORGE
B. Apr. 14, 1898
D. Nov., 1977, Bridgeport, CT
None

1923	ROC	N	1	G

Steve Emtman

EMTMAN, STEVEN CHARLES
B. Apr. 16, 1970, Spokane, WA
Washington 6'4" 290 lbs

1992	IND	N	9	DT
1993			5	DE
1994			4	DT, DE
1995	MIA	N	16	DT
1996			13	DT

5 yrs. 47 games

Dick Enderle

ENDERLE, RICHARD ALLYN
B. Nov. 6, 1947, Breckenridge, MN
Minnesota 6'1" 250 lbs.

1969	ATL	N	14	G
1970			12	G
1971			14	G
1972	NYG	N	14	G
1973			14	G
1974			14	G
1975			9	G
1976	SF	N	2	G
1976	GB	N	3	G

8 yrs. 96 games

Vic Endress

ENDRESS, VICTOR
B. May 25, 1903, Evansville, IN

Vic Endress *continued*

D. Aug. 29, 1970, Moline, IL
None

Year	Team		Games	Pos.
1922	EVA	N	1	FB

Al Endriss

ENDRISS, ALBERT
B. 1929
San Francisco State 6'2" 200 lbs.

Year	Team		Games	Pos.
1952	SF	N	2	E

Tiny Engebretsen

ENGEBRETSEN, PAUL J.
B. Jul. 27, 1910, Chariton, IA
D. Jul. 31, 1979, Chariton, IA
Northwestern 6'1" 238 lbs.

Year	Team		Games	Pos.
1932	CHIB	N	14	T
1933	PIT	N	9	T
1933	CHIC	N	2	G
1934	BKN	N	5	T
1934	GB	N	5	G, T
1935			9	G, T
1936			11	G
1937			7	G
1938			10	G
1939			10	G
1940			8	G
1941			1	G
10 yrs.	91 games			

Greg Engel

ENGEL, GREGORY ALLEN
B. Jan. 18, 1971, Davenport, IA
Illinois 6'3" 285 lbs.

Year	Team		Games	Pos.
1995	SD	N	10	C
1996			12	C
2 yrs.	22 games			

Steve Engel

ENGEL, STEVEN
B. Oct. 13, 1947, Englewood, CO
Colorado 6'1" 218 lbs.

Year	Team		Games	Pos.
1970	CLE	N	3	RB

Joe Engelhard

ENGELHARD, JOSEPH
B. Oct. 15, 1898
D. Jul. 4, 1981, Prospect, KY
Rose-Hulman Tech 185 lbs.

Year	Team		Games	Pos.
1921	LOU	A	1	HB
1922	LOU	N	1	HB
2 yrs.	2 games			

Wuert Engelmann

ENGELMANN, WUERT
B. Feb. 11, 1908, Miller, SD
D. Jan. 8, 1970, Green Bay, WI
South Dakota State 6'3" 191 lbs.

Year	Team		Games	Pos.
1930	GB	N	9	HB
1931			14	HB
1932			12	HB, FB
1933			9	HB, QB
4 yrs.	44 games			

Rick Engels

ENGELS, RICK B.
B. Aug. 18, 1954, Tulsa, OK
Tulsa 5'11" 177 lbs.

Year	Team		Games	Pos.
1976	SEA	N	14	P
1977			1	P
1977	PIT	N	1	P
2 yrs.	16 games			

Eric England

ENGLAND, ERIC JEVON
B. Mar. 25, 1971, Fort Wayne, IN

Eric England *continued*

Texas A&M 6'2" 283 lbs.

Year	Team		Games	Pos.
1994	ARI	N	10	DE, DT
1995			15	DE
1996			12	DE
3 yrs.	37 games			

Doug English

ENGLISH, LOWELL DOUGLAS
B. Aug. 25, 1953, Dallas, TX
Texas 6'5" 256 lbs.

Year	Team		Games	Pos.
1975	DET	N	14	DT
1976			7	DT
1977			14	DT
1978			14	DT
1979			16	DT
1981			16	DT
1982			9	DT
1983			15	DT
1984			16	DT
1985			10	DT
10 yrs.	131 games			

Keith English

ENGLISH, KEITH ALAN
B. Mar. 10, 1966, Denver, CO
Colorado 6'3" 220 lbs.

Year	Team		Games	Pos.
1990	LARM	N	16	P

Harry Englund

ENGLUND, HARRY C. (Skins)
B. Aug. 13, 1900, Rockford, IL
D. Mar. 16, 1988, Rockford, IL
None 5'11" 185 lbs.

Year	Team		Games	Pos.
1921	DEC	A	2	E
1922	CHIB	N	10	E
2 yrs.	12 games			

Bobby Engram

ENGRAM, BOBBY
B. Jan. 7, 1973, Camden, SC
Penn State 5'10" 187 lbs.

Year	Team		Games	Pos.
1996	CHI	N	16	WR

Art Engstrom

ENGSTROM, ARTHUR (George)
B. Jan. 1, 1897
D. Nov., 1970, Watertown, MN
Chicago/Kansas 5'9" 185 lbs.

Year	Team		Games	Pos.
1924	DUL	N	1	G, T

Steve Enich

ENICH, STEVE
B. 1923
Marquette 5'10" 212 lbs.

Year	Team		Games	Pos.
1945	CHIC	N	5	G

Hunter Enis

ENIS, HUNTER
B. Dec. 10, 1936, Fort Worth, TX
Texas Christian 6'2" 192 lbs.

Year	Team		Games	Pos.
1960	DAL	A		QB
1961	SD	A	13	QB
1962	DEN	A	4	QB
1962	OAK	A	7	QB
3 yrs.	24 games			

Fred Enke

ENKE, FREDERICK WILLIAM, JR.
B. Dec. 15, 1924, Louisville, KY
Arizona 6'1" 201 lbs.

Year	Team		Games	Pos.
1948	DET	N	12	QB
1949			12	QB
1950			12	QB
1951			12	QB

Fred Enke *continued*

Year	Team		Games	Pos.
1952	PHI	N	9	QB
1953	BAL	N	8	QB
6 yrs.	65 games			

Rex Enright

ENRIGHT, REX
B. 1900
D. Apr. 6, 1960, Columbia, SC
Notre Dame 5'10" 198 lbs.

Year	Team		Games	Pos.
1926	GB	N	10	FB
1927			9	FB, HB
2 yrs.	19 games			

Bill Enyart

ENYART, WILLIAM DONALD (Earthquake)
B. Apr. 28, 1947, Pawhuska, OK
Oregon State 6'4" 236 lbs.

Year	Team		Games	Pos.
1969	BUF	A	14	RB
1970	BUF	N	14	RB
1971	OAK	N	1	RB
3 yrs.	29 games			

Pat Epperson

EPPERSON, PATRICK
B. 1936
Adams State 6'3" 225 lbs.

Year	Team		Games	Pos.
1960	DEN	A		OE

Bobby Epps

EPPS, ROBERT H.
B. Mar. 25, 1932
Pittsburgh 5'9" 198 lbs.

Year	Team		Games	Pos.
1954	NYG	N	10	FB
1955			9	FB
1957			12	FB
3 yrs.	31 games			

Jack Epps

EPPS, JOHN
B. Mar. 20, 1963
Kansas State 6'0" 197 lbs.

Year	Team		Games	Pos.
1987	KC	N	3	S

Phillip Epps

EPPS, PHILLIP EARL
B. Nov. 11, 1959, Atlanta, GA
Texas Christian 5'10" 165 lbs.

Year	Team		Games	Pos.
1982	GB	N	9	WR
1983			16	WR
1984			16	WR
1985			16	WR
1986			12	WR
1987			10	WR
1988			6	WR
1989	NYJ	N	10	WR
8 yrs.	95 games			

Tory Epps

EPPS, TORY
B. May 28, 1967, Uniontown, PA
Memphis State 6'0" 277 lbs.

Year	Team		Games	Pos.
1990	ATL	N	16	NT
1991			16	NT
1992			16	NT
1993			2	NT
1993	CHI	N	3	DT
1994			5	DT
1995	NO	N	11	DT
6 yrs.	69 games			

Dick Erdlitz

ERDLITZ, RICHARD A.
B. Oct. 12, 1919, Milwaukee, WI

Dick Erdlitz *continued*

Northwestern 5'10" 181 lbs.

Year	Team		Games	Pos.
1942	PHI	N	11	HB, DB
1945			7	HB, DB
1946	MIA	AA	14	DB
3 yrs.	32 games			

Archie Erehart

EREHART, ARCHIBALD
B. Mar. 27, 1894
Deceased
Indiana 5'8" 165 lbs.

Year	Team		Games	Pos.
1920	MUN	A	1	HB

Rich Erenberg

ERENBERG, RICHARD MARK
B. Apr. 17, 1962, Chappaqua, NY
Colgate 5'10" 205 lbs.

Year	Team		Games	Pos.
1984	PIT	N	16	RB
1985			14	RB
1986			16	RB
3 yrs.	46 games			

Bernie Erickson

ERICKSON, JOHN BERNARD
B. Oct. 16, 1944, Clifton, TX
Abilene Christian 6'2" 239 lbs.

Year	Team		Games	Pos.
1967	SD	N	13	LB
1968			8	LB
1968	CIN	N	13	LB
2 yrs.	34 games			

Bill Erickson

ERICKSON, WILLIAM C.
B. 1922
Mississippi 6'2" 210 lbs.

Year	Team		Games	Pos.
1948	NYG	N	9	G
1949	B, NY	AA	6	G
2 yrs.	15 games			

Bud Erickson

ERICKSON, CARLETON
B. Jan. 10, 1916, Seattle, WA
D. Oct., 1969
Washington 6'1" 198 lbs.

Year	Team		Games	Pos.
1938	WAS	N	2	C
1939			1	C
2 yrs.	3 games			

Craig Erickson

ERICKSON, CRAIG NEIL
B. May 17, 1969, Boynton Beach, FL
Miami (Florida) 6'2" 200 lbs.

Year	Team		Games	Pos.
1992	TB	N	6	QB
1993			16	QB
1994			15	QB
1995	IND	N	6	QB
1996	MIA	N	8	QB
5 yrs.	51 games			

E. Erickson

ERICKSON, E.
None

Year	Team		Games	Pos.
1921	MIN	A	1	E

Hal Erickson

ERICKSON, HAROLD (Swede)
B. Mar. 10, 1899, Maynard, MN
D. Jan. 28, 1962
St. Olaf/Washington & Jefferson 5'9" 191 lbs.

Year	Team		Games	Pos.
1923	MIL	N	11	HB
1924			4	HB
1925	CHIC	N	14	HB
1926			11	HB
1927			8	HB, FB

Year	Team		Games	Pos.

Hal Erickson continued

Year	Team		Games	Pos.
1928			6	HB
1929	MIN	N	9	HB, FB
1930			4	HB, T
8 yrs.	67 games			

Harold Erickson
ERICKSON, HAROLD
B. Aug. 2, 1894
D. Jan. 28, 1963
None 195 lbs.

1921	MIN	A	4	T
1922	MIN	N	4	T
2 yrs.	8 games			

Mickey Erickson
ERICKSON, MILTON L.
B. May 16, 1905, Cambridge, MA
D. Jan. 26, 1984, Phoenix, AZ
Northwestern 6'2" 208 lbs.

1930	CHIC	N	11	C
1931			8	C, T
1932			1	C
1932	BOS	N	9	C
3 yrs.	29 games			

Walden Erickson
ERICKSON, WALDEN D.
B. Sep. 3, 1902
D. Dec., 1968, Chicago, IL
Washington 6'1" 205 lbs.

1926	LA	A	13	T
1927	POT	N	12	T, G
2 yrs.	25 games			

Tom Erlandson
ERLANDSON, THOMAS DEAN
B. Mar. 24, 1940, Seattle, WA
Washington State 6'3" 229 lbs.

1962	DEN	A	4	LB
1963			11	LB
1964			5	LB
1965			14	LB
1966	MIA	A	14	LB
1967			10	LB
1968	SD	A	10	LB
7 yrs.	68 games			

Tom Erlandson
ERLANDSON, TOM A.
B. Jun. 19, 1966, Denver, CO
Washington 6'1" 220 lbs.

1988	BUF	N	4	LB

Jack Ernst
ERNST, JOHN O.
B. Dec. 4, 1899
D. Mar., 1968, South Williamsport, PA
Lafayette 5'11" 178 lbs.

1925	POT	N	12	QB
1926			14	QB
1927			11	QB, HB
1928			10	QB
1928	NYY	N	1	HB
1929	BOS	N	7	QB
1930	FRA	N	8	HB, QB, FB
6 yrs.	63 games			

Mike Ernst
ERNST, MICHAEL
B. Oct. 12, 1950, Lynwood, CA
Fullerton State 6'1" 190 lbs.

1972	DEN	N	1	QB
1973	CIN	N	1	QB
2 yrs.	2 games			

Ricky Ervins
ERVINS, RICKY
B. Dec. 7, 1968, Fort Wayne, IN
Southern California 5'7" 200 lbs.

1991	WAS	N	15	RB
1992			16	RB
1993			15	RB
1994			16	RB
1995	SF	N	14	RB
5 yrs.	76 games			

Terry Erwin
ERWIN, TERRY L.
B. Aug. 30, 1946, Weymouth, MA
Boston College 6'0" 190 lbs.

1968	DEN	A	9	RB

Russell Erxleben
ERXLEBEN, RUSSELL ALLEN
B. Jan. 13, 1957, Seguin, TX
Texas 6'4" 219 lbs.

1979	NO	N	1	K, P
1980			16	K, P
1981			16	P
1982			9	P, K
1983			16	P
1987	DET	N	1	P
6 yrs.	59 games			

Herb Eschbach
ESCHBACH, HERBERT S.
B. 1907
Penn State 6'0" 190 lbs.

1930	PRO	N	7	C
1931			3	C
2 yrs.	10 games			

Len Eshmont
ESHMONT, LEONARD C.
B. Aug. 16, 1917, Mount Carmel, PA
D. May, 1957
Fordham 5'11" 179 lbs.

1941	NYG	N	9	HB, DB
1946	SF	AA	10	HB, DB
1947			13	HB, DB
1948			13	HB, DB
1949			12	HB, DB
5 yrs.	57 games			

Boomer Esiason
ESIASON, NORMAN JULIUS
B. Apr. 17, 1961, West Islip, NY
Maryland 6'4" 220 lbs.

1984	CIN	N	10	QB
1985			15	QB
1986			16	QB
1987			12	QB
1988			16	QB
1989			16	QB
1990			16	QB
1991			14	QB
1992			12	QB
1993	NYJ	N	16	QB
1994			15	QB
1995			12	QB
1996	ARI	N	10	QB
13 yrs.	180 games			

Al Espie
ESPIE, ALLEN D.
None

1923	LOU	N	1	T

Alex Espinoza
ESPINOZA, ALEX
B. May 31, 1964, Los Angeles, CA

Alex Espinoza continued
Fullerton State/Iowa State 6'1" 193 lbs.

1987	KC	N	1	QB

Mike Esposito
ESPOSITO, MICHAEL JOHN
B. Apr. 24, 1953, Everett, MA
Boston College 6'0" 183 lbs.

1976	ATL	N	10	RB
1977			14	RB
1978			16	RB
3 yrs.	40 games			

Clarence Esser
ESSER, CLARENCE JOSEPH
B. May 13, 1925, Madison, WI
Wisconsin 6'0" 190 lbs.

1947	CHIC	N	7	E

Ron Essink
ESSINK, RONALD ARDEN
B. Jul. 30, 1958, Zeeland, MI
Grand Valley State 6'6" 246 lbs.

1980	SEA	N	16	OT
1981			16	OT
1982			7	OT
1983			16	OT
1984			16	OT
1985			12	OT
6 yrs.	83 games			

Charlie Essman
ESSMAN, CHARLES P.
B. 1881
Deceased
Christian Brothers

1920	COL	A	1	G

Richard Estell
ESTELL, RICHARD
B. Oct. 13, 1963, Kansas City, KS
Kansas 6'2" 210 lbs.

1987	KC	N	2	WR

Mike Estep
ESTEP, MIKE
B. Dec. 29, 1963
Bowling Green 6'4" 270 lbs.

1987	BUF	N	2	G
1987	GB	N	1	G
1 yr.	30 games			

Don Estes
ESTES, DONALD
B. Oct. 14, 1943, Tomball, TX
Louisiana State 6'2" 250 lbs.

1966	SD	A	5	G

Larry Estes
ESTES, LAWRENCE G.
B. Dec. 9, 1946, Louisville, MS
Alcorn State 6'6" 255 lbs.

1970	NO	N	14	DE
1971			8	DE
1972	PHI	N	7	DE
1975	KC	N	4	DE, DT
1976			14	DE, DT
5 yrs.	47 games			

Sam Etcheverry
ETCHEVERRY, SAMUEL
B. May 20, 1930, Carlsbad, NM
Denver 5'11" 190 lbs.

1961	STL	N	14	QB

Sam Etcheverry continued

1962			14	QB
2 yrs.	28 games			

Carl Etelman
ETELMAN, CARL EDWARD
(Midget)
B. Apr. 2, 1900, Fairhaven, MA
Deceased
Boston University/Harvard/Tufts 5'8" 160 lbs.

1926	BOS	A	3	QB, HB
1926	PRO	N	1	HB
1 yr.	4 games			

Carlos Etheredge
ETHEREDGE, CARLOS SEBASTIAN
B. Aug. 10, 1970, Albuquerque, NM
Miami (Florida) 6'5" 259 lbs.

1994	IND	N	9	TE

Dave Etherly
ETHERLY, DAVID
B. Dec. 22, 1962
Portland State 6'1" 195 lbs.

1987	WAS	N	3	CB

Joe Ethridge
ETHRIDGE, JOE PAUL
B. Apr. 15, 1928, Conway, TX
Southern Methodist 6'0" 230 lbs.

1949	GB	N	12	T

Ray Ethridge
ETHRIDGE, RAYMOND, ARTHUR, JR.
B. Sep. 11, 1968, San Diego, CA
Pasadena CC 5'10" 180 lbs.

1996	BAL	N	14	WR

LeRoy Etienne
ETIENNE, LEROY JOSEPH
B. Jul. 25, 1966, Lafayette, LA
Nebraska 6'2" 245 lbs.

1990	SF	N	10	LB

Earl Ettenhaus
ETTENHAUS, EARL
B. 1902
Deceased
None

1921	ROC	A	2	G, T

Bob Etter
ETTER, ROBERT
B. Aug. 8, 1945, Chattanooga, TN
Georgia 5'11" 152 lbs.

1968	ATL	N	14	K
1969			14	K
2 yrs.	28 games			

Don Ettinger
ETTINGER, DONALD N. (Red)
B. 1921
D. Feb. 13, 1992, Cookeville, KS
Kansas 6'2" 213 lbs.

1948	NYG	N	10	G
1949			11	G
1950			12	G
3 yrs.	33 games			

Bobby Evans
EVANS, ROBERT D.

Year	Team	Games	Pos.

Bobby Evans continued

B. 1942
Texas A&M 6'3" 250 lbs.

| 1965 | HOU | A | 4 | DE |

Byron Evans

EVANS, BYRON NELSON
B. Feb. 23, 1962, Phoenix, AZ
Arizona 6'2" 225 lbs.

1987	PHI	N	12	LB
1988			16	LB
1989			16	LB
1990			16	LB
1991			16	LB
1992			16	LB
1993			11	LB
1994			10	LB
8 yrs.		113 games		

Charlie Evans

EVANS, CHARLES J.
B. Jan. 10, 1948, Gardena, CA
Utah/Southern California 6'1" 219 lbs.

1971	NYG	N	6	RB
1972			8	RB
1973			5	RB
1974	WAS	N	6	RB
4 yrs.		25 games		

Chuck Evans

EVANS, CHARLES
B. Apr. 16, 1967, Augusta, GA
Clark-Atlanta 6'1" 226 lbs.

1993	MIN	N	3	RB
1994			14	RB
1995			16	RB
1996			16	RB
4 yrs.		49 games		

Chuck Evans

EVANS, CHARLES ALLEN, III
B. Dec. 19, 1956, West Covina, CA
Stanford 6'3" 235 lbs.

1980	NO	N	10	LB
1981			16	LB
2 yrs.		26 games		

Dale Evans

EVANS, JAY DALE
B. 1939
Kansas State 6'3" 210 lbs.

| 1961 | DEN | A | 5 | HB |

David Evans

EVANS, DAVID WAYNE
B. May 1, 1959, Naples, TX
Central Arkansas 6'0" 178 lbs.

1986	MIN	N	16	CB
1987			3	CB
2 yrs.		19 games		

Dick Evans

EVANS, RICHARD JACOB
B. May 31, 1917, Chicago, IL
Iowa 6'3" 205 lbs.

1940	GB	N	7	E
1941	CHIC	N	11	E
1942			2	E
1943	GB	N	10	E
4 yrs.		30 games		

Donald Evans

EVANS, DONALD LEE
B. Mar. 14, 1964, Raleigh, NC
Winston-Salem State 6'2" 256 lbs.

| 1987 | LARM | N | 1 | DE |

Donald Evans continued

1988	PHI	N	5	DE
1990	PIT	N	16	DE
1991			16	DE
1992			16	DE
1993			16	DE
1994	NYJ	N	16	DE
1995			4	DE
8 yrs.		90 games		

Doug Evans

EVANS, DOUGLAS EDWARDS
B. May 13, 1970, Shreveport, LA
Louisiana Tech 6'1" 168 lbs.

1993	GB	N	16	CB, S
1994			16	CB
1995			16	CB
1996			16	CB
4 yrs.		64 games		

Earl Evans

EVANS, EARL (Buck)
B. 1900
D. Mar. 18, 1992
Marquette/Harvard 5'11" 204 lbs.

1925	CHIC	N	14	T
1926	CHIB	N	14	T, G
1927			10	T
1928			9	T, G
1929			6	G, T
5 yrs.		53 games		

Fred Evans

EVANS, FREDERICK O., JR. (Dippy)
B. May 23, 1921, Grand Rapids, MI
Notre Dame 5'11" 185 lbs.

1946	CLE	AA	6	HB, DB
1947	BUF	AA	4	HB, DB
1947	CHI	AA	9	HB, DB
1948			1	HB, DB
1948	CHIB	N	3	HB, DB
3 yrs.		23 games		

Greg Evans

EVANS, GREG
B. Jun. 28, 1971, Daingerfield, TX
Texas Christian 6'1" 205 lbs.

| 1995 | BUF | N | 16 | S |

Jack Evans

EVANS, JOHN ALEXANDER
B. Aug. 17, 1906, Colorado Springs, CO
D. Sep. 5, 1988, Claremont, CA
California 5'9" 175 lbs.

| 1929 | GB | N | 3 | QB |

James Evans

EVANS, JAMES MARCUS
B. Aug. 17, 1963, Prichard, AL
Southern University 6'0" 220 lbs.

| 1987 | KC | N | 2 | RB |

Jerry Evans

EVANS, GERALD KRISTIN
B. Sep. 28, 1968, Lorain, OH
Toledo 6'4" 250 lbs.

1993	DEN	N	14	TE
1994			16	TE
1995			13	TE
3 yrs.		43 games		

Jimmy Evans

EVANS, JAMES
B. Oct. 24, 1939

Jimmy Evans continued

Texas Western 6'1" 190 lbs.

1964	NY	A	12	FL
1965			9	FL
2 yrs.		21 games		

John Evans

EVANS, JOHN
B. Jun. 13, 1964
Stephen F. Austin 6'2" 243 lbs.

| 1987 | ATL | N | 1 | TE |

Johnny Evans

EVANS, JOHN ALBERT
B. Feb. 18, 1956, High Point, NC
North Carolina State 6'1" 175 lbs.

1978	CLE	N	16	P, QB
1979			16	P, QB
1980			16	P, PB
3 yrs.		48 games		

Jon Evans

EVANS, JON A.
B. 1936
Oklahoma State 6'4" 205 lbs.

| 1958 | PIT | N | 1 | E |

Josh Evans

EVANS, MIJOSHKI ANTWON
B. Sep. 6, 1972, Langdale, AL
Alabama-Birmingham 6'2" 283 lbs.

1995	HOU	N	7	DT
1996			9	DT
2 yrs.		16 games		

Larry Evans

EVANS, LAWRENCE EUGENE
B. Jul. 11, 1953, Biloxi, MS
Mississippi College 6'2" 217 lbs.

1976	DEN	N	14	LB
1977			14	LB
1978			16	LB
1979			16	LB
1980			16	LB
1981			16	LB
1982			9	LB
1983	SD		3	LB
8 yrs.		104 games		

Leomont Evans

EVANS, LEOMONT
B. Jul. 12, 1974, Abbeville, SC
Clemson 6'1" 200 lbs.

| 1996 | WAS | N | 11 | S |

Leon Evans

EVANS, LEON
B. Oct. 12, 1961, Silver Spring, MD
Miami (Florida) 6'5" 282 lbs.

1985	DET	N	8	DE
1986			16	DE
2 yrs.		24 games		

Lon Evans

EVANS, LON
B. Dec. 25, 1911, Fort Worth, TX
D. Dec. 11, 1992, Fort Worth, TX
Texas Christian 6'2" 223 lbs.

1933	GB	N	11	G
1934			13	T, G
1935			12	G
1936			11	G, T
1937			11	G
5 yrs.		58 games		

Mike Evans

EVANS, MICHAEL JAMES
B. Jun. 2, 1967, St. Croix, Virgin Islands
Michigan 6'3" 269 lbs.

| 1992 | KC | N | 12 | DT |

Mike Evans

EVANS, WILLIAM MICHAEL
B. Aug. 6, 1946, Philadelphia, PA
Boston College 6'5" 250 lbs.

1968	PHI	N	6	C
1969			13	C
1970			14	C
1971			14	C
1972			12	C
1973			14	C
6 yrs.		73 games		

Murray Evans

EVANS, MURRAY CHARLES
B. Jun. 23, 1919, Nashville, TX
Hardin-Simmons 6'1" 205 lbs.

1942	DET	N	10	QB
1943			9	QB
2 yrs.		19 games		

Myles Evans

EVANS, MYLES (Mike)
B. Dec. 3, 1901
D. Nov., 1982, Cleveland, OH
Ohio Wesleyan 185 lbs.

| 1926 | CLE | A | 5 | T |

Norm Evans

EVANS, NORMAN EARL
B. Sep. 28, 1942, Santa Fe, NM
Texas Christian 6'5" 248 lbs.

1965	HOU	A	14	OT
1966	MIA	A	14	OT
1967			14	OT
1968			13	OT
1969			12	OT
1970	MIA	N	14	OT
1971			14	OT
1972			14	OT
1973			14	OT
1974			14	OT
1975			14	OT
1976	SEA	N	10	OT
1977			13	OT
1978			13	OT
14 yrs.		187 games		

Ray Evans

EVANS, RAY R.
B. Sep. 22, 1922, Kansas City, KS
Kansas 6'1" 195 lbs.

| 1948 | PIT | N | 9 | HB |

Ray Evans

EVANS, RAYMOND (Sugar)
B. Jan. 10, 1924, Electra, TX
Texas Western 6'1" 225 lbs.

1949	SF	AA	10	T
1950	SF	N	12	G
2 yrs.		22 games		

Reggie Evans

EVANS, REGGIE
B. Jan. 5, 1959, Newport News, VA
Richmond 5'11" 201 lbs.

| 1983 | WAS | N | 16 | WR |

Russell Evans

EVANS, RUSSELL

Year	Team	Games	Pos.

Russell Evans *continued*
B. Feb. 3, 1965
Northeast Missouri State 5'8" 165 lbs.

Year	Team	Games	Pos.
1987	SEA	N	1	WR

Scott Evans
EVANS, SCOTT ALLEN
B. Mar. 2, 1968, Cincinnati, OH
Oklahoma 6'3" 261 lbs.

| 1991 | PHX | N | 1 | LB |

Vince Evans
EVANS, VINCENT TOBIAS
B. Jun. 14, 1955, Greensboro, NC
Southern California 6'2" 213 lbs.

1977	CHI	N	7	QB
1978			3	QB
1979			4	QB
1980			13	QB
1981			16	QB
1982			4	QB
1983			9	QB
1987	LARI	N	3	QB
1989			1	QB
1990			5	QB
1991			4	QB
1992			5	QB
1993			8	QB
1994			9	QB
1995	OAK	N	9	QB
15 yrs.		100 games	

Paul Evansen
EVANSEN, PAUL ARNOLD (Tiny)
B. May 10, 1922, San Francisco, CA
Oregon State 6'3" 240 lbs.

| 1948 | SF | AA | 1 | G |

Eric Everett
EVERETT, ERIC EUGENE
B. Jul. 13, 1966, Daingerfield, TX
Texas Tech 5'10" 161 lbs.

1988	PHI	N	16	CB
1989			15	CB
1990	TB	N	16	CB, S
1991	KC	N	11	CB
4 yrs.		58 games	

Jim Everett
EVERETT, JAMES SAMUEL, III
B. Jan. 3, 1963, Emporia, KS
Purdue 6'5" 212 lbs.

1986	LARM	N	6	QB
1987			11	QB
1988			16	QB
1989			16	QB
1990			16	QB
1991			16	QB
1992			16	QB
1993			10	QB
1994	NO	N	16	QB
1995			16	QB
1996			15	QB
11 yrs.		154 games	

Major Everett
EVERETT, MAJOR DONEL
B. Jan. 4, 1960, New Hebron, MS
Mississippi College 5'10" 218 lbs.

1983	PHI	N	16	RB
1984			16	FB
1985			15	FB
1986	CLE	N	9	RB
1987			4	RB
1987	ATL	N	7	RB
5 yrs.		67 games	

Thomas Everett
EVERETT, THOMAS GREGORY
B. Nov. 21, 1964, Daingerfield, TX
Baylor 5'9" 179 lbs.

1987	PIT	N	12	S
1988			14	S
1989			16	S
1990			15	S
1991			16	S
1992	DAL	N	11	S
1993			16	S
1994	TB	N	15	S
1995			13	S
9 yrs.		128 games	

Steve Everitt
EVERITT, STEVEN MICHAEL
B. Aug. 21, 1970, Miami, FL
Michigan 6'5" 292 lbs.

1993	CLE	N	16	C, G
1994			15	C
1995			15	C
1996	BAL	N	8	C
4 yrs.		54 games	

William Evers
EVERS, WILLIAM
B. Sep. 24, 1968, Cairo, GA
Florida A&M 5'10" 175 lbs.

1990	ATL	N	2	CB
1991			2	CB
2 yrs.		4 games	

Dick Evey
EVEY, RICHARD THEODORE
B. Feb. 13, 1941, State College, PA
Tennessee 6'2" 238 lbs.

1964	CHI	N	14	G
1965			14	DE
1966			14	DT
1967			12	DT
1968			14	DT
1969			14	DT
1970	LA	N	9	DT
1971	DET	N	11	DT
8 yrs.		102 games	

Nick Eyre
EYRE, NICK
B. Jun. 16, 1959, Las Vegas, NV
Brigham Young 6'5" 274 lbs.

| 1981 | HOU | N | 4 | OT |

Vilnis Ezerins
EZERINS, VILNIS
B. Apr. 22, 1944, Latvia
Wisconsin-Whitewater 6'1" 217 lbs.

| 1968 | LA | N | 14 | RB |

Blake Ezor
EZOR, BLAKE
B. Oct. 11, 1966, Las Vegas, NV
Michigan State 5'9" 183 lbs.

| 1990 | DEN | N | 9 | RB |

Nuu Faaola
FAAOLA, SINATAUSILINUU
B. Jan. 15, 1964, Honolulu, HI
Hawaii 5'11" 215 lbs.

1986	NYJ	N	12	RB
1987			12	RB
1988			16	RB
1989			2	RB
1989	MIA	N	10	RB
4 yrs.		52 games	

Rob Fada
FADA, ROBERT ALAN
B. May 7, 1961, Fairborn, OH
Pittsburgh 6'2" 258 lbs.

1983	CHI	N	12	G
1984			14	G
1985	KC	N	5	G
3 yrs.		31 games	

Julian Fagan
FAGAN, JULIAN WALTER, III
B. Feb. 21, 1948, Laurel, MS
Mississippi 6'3" 205 lbs.

1970	NO	N	14	P
1971			14	P
1972			14	P
1973	NYJ	N	14	P
4 yrs.		56 games	

Kevin Fagan
FAGAN, KEVIN
B. Apr. 25, 1963, Lake Worth, FL
Miami (Florida) 6'3" 260 lbs.

1987	SF	N	7	DE
1988			14	DE
1989			16	DE
1990			16	DE
1991			8	DE
1992			15	DE
1993			7	DE
7 yrs.		83 games	

Carl Fagiolo
FAGIOLO, CARL
B. Apr. 26, 1917
None 6'0" 200 lbs.

| 1944 | PHI | N | 1 | G |

John Fahay
FAHAY, JOHN (Big Jawn)
B. Jun. 16, 1902
D. Jan., 1980, Fort Lauderdale, FL
St. Thomas/Marquette 6'0" 189 lbs.

1925	MIL	N	1	G
1926	CHI	A	1	E
1926	RAC	N	2	E
1929	MIN	N	4	HB, E-G
3 yrs.		8 games	

Jim Fahnhorst
FAHNHORST, JAMES JOHN
B. Nov. 8, 1958, St. Cloud, MN
Minnesota 6'4" 230 lbs.

1984	SF	N	14	LB
1985			15	LB
1986			16	LB
1987			11	LB
1988			16	LB
1989			7	LB
1990			3	LB
7 yrs.		82 games	

Keith Fahnhorst
FAHNHORST, KEITH VICTOR
B. Feb. 6, 1952, St. Cloud, MN
Minnesota 6'6" 271 lbs.

1974	SF	N	14	OT
1975			14	OT
1976			13	OT
1977			14	OT
1978			15	OT
1979			16	OT
1980			16	OT
1981			16	OT
1982			9	OT
1983			16	OT
1984			15	OT
1985			16	OT

Keith Fahnhorst *continued*

1986			16	OT
1987			3	OT
14 yrs.		193 games	

Fred Failing
FAILING, FRED C.
B. Jun. 7, 1904, Caro, MI
D. Sep. 7, 1972, Green Bay, WI
Central Wisconsin State 5'11" 200 lbs.

| 1930 | CHIC | N | 1 | G |

Richard Fain
FAIN, RICHARD ALEXANDER
B. Feb. 29, 1968, North Fort Myers, FL
Florida 5'10" 183 lbs.

1991	CIN	N	6	CB
1991	PHX	N	6	CB
1992	CHI	N	16	CB
2 yrs.		28 games	

Bill Fairband
FAIRBAND, BILL
B. Jun. 11, 1941, Los Gatos, CA
Colorado 6'3" 228 lbs.

1967	OAK	A	7	LB
1968			2	LB
2 yrs.		9 games	

Don Fairbanks
FAIRBANKS, DON
B. Feb. 13, 1964, Lakewood, CO
Colorado 6'3" 253 lbs.

| 1987 | SEA | N | 3 | DE |

Greg Fairchild
FAIRCHILD, GREG
B. Mar. 10, 1954, St. Louis, MO
Tulsa 6'4" 257 lbs.

1976	CIN	N	12	G, OT
1977			13	G, OT
1978	CLE	N	3	G
3 yrs.		28 games	

Paul Fairchild
FAIRCHILD, PAUL JAY
B. Sep. 14, 1961, Carroll, IA
Kansas 6'4" 270 lbs.

1984	NE	N	7	G
1985			16	G
1986			15	G
1987			11	G
1988			16	G, C
1989			14	G, C
6 yrs.		79 games	

Art Faircloth
FAIRCLOTH, ARTHUR T.
B. 1920
North Carolina State/Guilford 6'0" 190 lbs.

| 1948 | NYG | N | 2 | HB |

Leonard Fairley
FAIRLEY, LEONARD
B. Jan. 2, 1951, Biloxi, MS
Alcorn State 5'11" 200 lbs.

| 1974 | HOU | N | 2 | CB |

Eric Fairs
FAIRS, ERIC JEROME
B. Feb. 17, 1964, Memphis, TN
Memphis State 6'3" 235 lbs.

| 1986 | HOU | N | 12 | LB |

Eric Fairs continued

Year	Team	Games	Pos.
1987		12	LB
1988		16	LB
1989		16	LB
1990		16	LB
1991		16	LB
6 yrs.		88 games	

Derrick Faison
FAISON, DERRICK
B. Aug. 24, 1967, Lake City, SC
Howard 6'4" 200 lbs.

Year	Team		Games	Pos.
1990	LARM	N	15	WR

Earl Faison
FAISON, WILLIAM EARL
B. Jan. 31, 1939, Newport News, VA
Indiana 6'5" 263 lbs.

Year	Team		Games	Pos.
1961	SD	A	14	DE
1962			8	DE
1963			14	DE
1964			14	DE
1965			14	DE
1966			3	DE
1966	MIA	A	6	DE
6 yrs.			73 games	

Nello Falaschi
FALASCHI, NELLO D. (Flash)
B. Mar. 19, 1914, Dos Palos, CA
D. Jul. 29, 1986, Oakland, CA
Santa Clara 6'0" 195 lbs.

Year	Team		Games	Pos.
1938	NYG	N	9	QB
1939			11	FB, HB
1940			11	FB, QB
1941			11	QB
4 yrs.			42 games	

Dick Falcon
FALCON, RAY C.
B. 1896, Illinois
Deceased
None

Year	Team		Games	Pos.
1920	CHIT	A	2	G, C

Guil Falcon
FALCON, GUILFORD W. (Hawk)
B. Dec. 16, 1892, Evanston, IN
D. Jul., 1982, Hallandale, FL
None 5'10" 220 lbs.

Year	Team		Games	Pos.
1920	CHIT	A	7	FB
1920	HAM	A	1	FB
1921			1	FB
1921	CAN	A	7	FB
1922	TOL	N	8	FB, HB
1923			2	FB
1924	HAM	N	5	FB
1925	AKR	N	8	FB, QB, G
1925	HAM	N	1	FB
1925	ROC	N	1	FB
6 yrs.			41 games	

Terry Falcon
FALCON, THEODORE LEE
B. Aug. 30, 1955, Culbertson, MT
Minot State/Montana 6'3" 260 lbs.

Year	Team		Games	Pos.
1978	NE	N	8	G
1979			10	G
1980	NYG	N	13	G
3 yrs.			31 games	

Tony Falkenstein
FALKENSTEIN, ANTHONY J.
B. Feb. 16, 1915, Pueblo, CO
St. Mary's (California) 5'10" 205 lbs.

Year	Team		Games	Pos.
1943	GB	N	10	FB
1944	BKN	N	6	FB, QB

Tony Falkenstein continued

Year	Team		Games	Pos.
1944	BOS	N	2	FB
2 yrs.			18 games	

Mickey Fallon
FALLON, MICHAEL W.
B. Apr. 15, 1898
D. Mar., 1972, Morris Heights
(Bronx), NY
Muhlenberg/Fordham 5'9" 170 lbs.

Year	Team		Games	Pos.
1922	MIL	N	7	G, E, QB

Mike Falls
FALLS, MICHAEL
B. Mar. 3, 1934, Bemidji, MN
Minnesota 6'1" 240 lbs.

Year	Team		Games	Pos.
1960	DAL	N	11	G
1961			14	G
2 yrs.			25 games	

Gary Famiglietti
FAMIGLIETTI, GARY J.
B. Nov. 28, 1913, Boston, MA
D. Jul. 12, 1986, Chicago, IL
Boston University 6'0" 225 lbs.

Year	Team		Games	Pos.
1938	CHIB		6	FB
1939			10	FB
1940			11	FB, HB
1941			7	HB, FB
1942			10	FB
1943			10	FB
1944			10	FB
1945			10	FB
1946	BOS	N	11	FB
9 yrs.			85 games	

Chad Fann
FANN, CHAD FITZGERALD
B. Jun. 7, 1970, Jacksonville, FL
Mississippi/Florida A&M 6'3" 250 lbs.

Year	Team		Games	Pos.
1993	PHX	N	1	TE
1994	ARI	N	16	TE
1995			16	TE
3 yrs.			33 games	

Mike Fanning
FANNING, MICHAEL LAVERN
B. Feb. 2, 1953, Mount Clemens, MI
Notre Dame 6'6" 256 lbs.

Year	Team		Games	Pos.
1975	LA	N	8	DE
1976			14	DE
1977			14	DT
1978			16	DT
1979			16	DT
1980			15	DT
1981			16	DT
1982	LARM	N	8	DT
1983	DET	N	14	DT
1984	SEA	N	16	NT
10 yrs.			137 games	

Stan Fanning
FANNING, STANLEY
B. Nov. 22, 1937, Peoria, IL
Idaho 6'6" 267 lbs.

Year	Team		Games	Pos.
1960	CHI	N	12	OT
1961			14	OT
1962			14	DT
1963	LA	N	10	DE
1964	HOU	A	5	DE
1964	DEN		7	DE
5 yrs.			62 games	

Ken Fantetti
FANTETTI, KEN MARK
B. Apr. 7, 1957, Toledo, OH

Ken Fantetti continued
Wyoming 6'2" 230 lbs.

Year	Team		Games	Pos.
1979	DET	N	16	LB
1980			16	LB
1981			16	LB
1982			9	LB
1983			16	LB
1984			14	LB
1985			8	LB
7 yrs.			95 games	

Ledio Fanucchi
FANUCCHI, LEDIO
B. Mar. 27, 1931, Fresno, CA
Fresno State 6'2" 225 lbs.

Year	Team		Games	Pos.
1954	CHIC	N	12	T

Mike Fanucci
FANUCCI, MICHAEL JOSEPH
B. Sep. 25, 1949, Scranton, PA
Arizona State 6'4" 236 lbs.

Year	Team		Games	Pos.
1972	WAS	N	14	DE
1973	HOU	N	13	DE
1974	GB	N	13	DE
3 yrs.			40 games	

Chris Farasopoulas
FARASOPOULAS, CHRIS V.
B. Jul. 20, 1949, Piraeus, Greece
Brigham Young 5'11" 190 lbs.

Year	Team		Games	Pos.
1971	NYJ	N	14	DB
1972			14	S
1973			9	S
1974	NO		6	S
4 yrs.			43 games	

Hap Farber
FARBER, LOUIS A.
B. Jul. 1, 1948, Norfolk, VA
Mississippi 6'1" 220 lbs.

Year	Team		Games	Pos.
1970	MIN	N	3	LB
1970	NO	N	5	LB
1 yr.			8 games	

Ralph Farina
FARINA, RALPH ROBERT (Nick)
B. Feb. 21, 1905, Steelton, PA
D. Sep. 22, 1984, Harrisburg, PA
Villanova 5'10" 195 lbs.

Year	Team		Games	Pos.
1927	POT	N	1	C

Andy Farkas
FARKAS, ANDREW G.
B. May 2, 1916, Clay Center, OH
Detroit 5'10" 192 lbs.

Year	Team		Games	Pos.
1938	WAS	N	9	FB, HB
1939			11	FB
1940			1	FB
1941			10	FB
1942			10	FB
1943			10	FB
1944			10	HB
1945	DET	N	8	FB
8 yrs.			69 games	

Dale Farley
FARLEY, DALE
B. May 27, 1949, Sparta, TN
West Virginia 6'4" 235 lbs.

Year	Team		Games	Pos.
1971	MIA	N	4	LB
1972	BUF	N	7	LB
1973			2	LB
3 yrs.			13 games	

Dick Farley
FARLEY, RICHARD

Dick Farley continued
B. May 30, 1946, Danvers, MA
Boston University 6'0" 185 lbs.

Year	Team		Games	Pos.
1968	SD	A	10	DB
1969			14	S
2 yrs.			24 games	

John Farley
FARLEY, JOHN HOWARD
B. Aug. 11, 1961, Stockton, CA
Sacramento State 5'10" 202 lbs.

Year	Team		Games	Pos.
1984	CIN	N	13	RB

Dick Farman
FARMAN, RICHARD
B. Jul. 26, 1916, Belmond, IA
Washington State 6'0" 219 lbs.

Year	Team		Games	Pos.
1939	WAS	N	10	G, T
1940			11	G
1941			11	G
1942			11	G
1943			6	G
5 yrs.			49 games	

Dave Farmer
FARMER, DAVID W.
B. May 20, 1954, Phoenix, AZ
Southern California 6'0" 205 lbs.

Year	Team		Games	Pos.
1978	TB	N	3	RB

George Farmer
FARMER, GEORGE, III
B. Dec. 5, 1958, Los Angeles, CA
Southern University 5'10" 175 lbs.

Year	Team		Games	Pos.
1982	LARM	N	8	WR
1983			16	WR
1984			14	WR
1987	MIA	N	1	WR
4 yrs.			39 games	

George Farmer
FARMER, GEORGE T.
B. Apr. 19, 1948, Chattanooga, TN
UCLA 6'4" 212 lbs.

Year	Team		Games	Pos.
1970	CHI	N	11	WR
1971			14	WR
1972			14	WR
1973			14	WR
1974			9	WR
1975			2	WR
1975	DET	N	6	WR
6 yrs.			70 games	

Karl Farmer
FARMER, KARL ANTHONY
B. Aug. 28, 1954, Oklahoma City, OK
Pittsburgh 5'11" 165 lbs.

Year	Team		Games	Pos.
1977	ATL	N	14	WR
1978	TB	N	2	WR
2 yrs.			16 games	

Lonnie Farmer
FARMER, LONNIE
B. 1941, Steubenville, OH
*Northwestern/Tennessee-Chattanooga
6'0" 220 lbs.*

Year	Team		Games	Pos.
1964	BOS	A	14	LB
1965			3	LB
1966			14	LB
3 yrs.			31 games	

Ray Farmer
FARMER, RAY
B. Jul. 1, 1972, White Plains, NY
Duke 6'3" 225 lbs.

Year	Team		Games	Pos.
1996	PHI	N	16	LB

Year	Team		Games	Pos.

Roger Farmer
FARMER, ROGER
B. Nov. 10, 1955, Barbados, WI
Baker 6'3" 195 lbs.

| 1979 | NYJ | N | 4 | WR |

Teddy Farmer
FARMER, TED
B. Sep. 8, 1953, St. Louis, MO
Oregon 5'11" 175 lbs.

| 1978 | STL | N | 2 | RB |

Tom Farmer
FARMER, THOMAS
B. Apr. 17, 1921, Cedar Rapids, IA
D. Jul. 1, 1980, Iowa City, IA
Iowa 5'11" 190 lbs.

1946	LA	N	8	HB
1947	WAS	N	10	HB
1948			9	HB
3 yrs.	27 games			

John Farquhar
FARQUHAR, JOHN
B. Mar. 22, 1972, Stanford, CA
Duke 6'6" 240 lbs.

1996	TB	N	1	TE
1996	PIT	N	4	TE
1 yr.	5 games			

D'Marco Farr
FARR, D'MARCO
B. Jun. 9, 1971, San Pablo, CA
Washington 6'1" 270 lbs.

1994	LARM	N	10	DT
1995	STL	N	16	DT
1996			16	DT
3 yrs.	42 games			

Mel Farr
FARR, MELVIN, SR.
B. Nov. 3, 1944, Beaumont, TX
UCLA 6'2" 208 lbs.

1967	DET	N	13	RB
1968			9	RB
1969			5	RB
1970			12	RB
1971			9	RB
1972			10	RB
1973			11	RB
7 yrs.	69 games			

Mel Farr
FARR, MELVIN, JR.
B. Aug. 12, 1966, Santa Monica, CA
UCLA 6'0" 223 lbs.

| 1989 | LARM | N | 1 | RB |

Mike Farr
FARR, MICHAEL ANTHONY
B. Aug. 8, 1967, Santa Monica, CA
UCLA 5'10" 192 lbs.

1990	DET	N	12	WR
1991			16	WR
1992			13	WR
3 yrs.	41 games			

Miller Farr
FARR, MILLER, JR.
B. Apr. 8, 1943, Beaumont, TX
Wichita State 6'1" 190 lbs.

1965	DEN	A	7	DB
1965	SD	A	3	DB
1966		A	14	DB
1967	HOU	A	14	DB

Miller Farr continued

1968			14	DB
1969			14	CB
1970	STL	N	14	CB
1971			14	CB
1972			13	CB
1973	DET	N	6	CB
9 yrs.	113 games			

Ken Farragut
FARRAGUT, KENNETH D.
B. Dec. 23, 1928, Ponchatoula, LA
Mississippi 6'4" 240 lbs.

1951	PHI	N	11	C
1952			12	C
1953			12	C
1954			8	C
4 yrs.	43 games			

Vinnie Farrar
FARRAR, VENICE
B. Dec. 22, 1910, Youngstown, OH
D. Jan. 1, 1973, Youngstown, OH
North Carolina State 5'10" 200 lbs.

| 1939 | PIT | N | 6 | G, B |

Scrapper Farrell
FARRELL, EDWARD F.
B. 1915
Deceased
Muhlenberg 5'9" 204 lbs.

1938	PIT	N	5	FB, HB
1938	BKN	N	7	FB
1939	BKN	N	2	FB
2 yrs.	14 games			

Sean Farrell
FARRELL, SEAN WARD
B. May 25, 1960, Southampton, NY
Penn State 6'3" 260 lbs.

1982	TB	N	9	G
1983			10	G
1984			15	G
1985			14	G
1986			16	G
1987	NE	N	14	G
1988			15	G
1989			14	G
1990	DEN	N	5	G
1991			5	G
1992	SEA	N	6	G
11 yrs.	123 games			

Paul Farren
FARREN, PAUL V.
B. Dec. 24, 1960, Weymouth, MA
Boston University 6'5" 280 lbs.

1983	CLE	N	16	OT
1984			15	OT
1985			13	OT
1986			16	OT
1987			12	OT, G
1988			15	OT, G
1989			16	OT, G
1990			16	OT, G
1991			13	OT, G
9 yrs.	132 games			

Curt Farrier
FARRIER, CURT
B. Jun. 25, 1941, Yakima, WA
Montana State 6'6" 253 lbs.

1963	KC	A	5	DT
1964			14	DT
1965			8	DT
3 yrs.	27 games			

Bo Farrington
FARRINGTON, JOHN
B. Jan. 18, 1936, Dewalt, TX
D. Jul. 26, 1964, Rensselaer, IN
Prairie View A&M 6'3" 217 lbs.

1960	CHI	N	6	OE
1961			11	OE
1962			14	OE
1963			14	OE
4 yrs.	45 games			

John Farris
FARRIS, JOHN
B. Nov. 2, 1940, Kansas City, MO
San Diego State 6'4" 245 lbs.

1965	SD	A	14	G
1966			14	G
2 yrs.	28 games			

Tom Farris
FARRIS, THOMAS GEORGE
B. Sep. 16, 1920, Casper, WY
Wisconsin 6'1" 185 lbs.

1946	CHIB	N	11	QB
1947			9	QB
1948	CHI	AA	13	QB
3 yrs.	33 games			

Shipley Farroh
FARROH, SHIPLEY (King Kong)
B. Aug. 13, 1915
D. Apr. 1973, Gary, IN
Iowa 5'11" 225 lbs.

| 1938 | PIT | N | 5 | FB, HB |

Brett Faryniarz
FARYNIARZ, BRETT ALLEN
B. Jul. 23, 1965, Carmichael, CA
San Diego State 6'3" 225 lbs.

1988	LARM	N	15	LB
1989			16	LB
1990			16	LB
1991			12	LB
1993	SF	N	2	LB
1994	HOU	N	16	LB
1995	CAR	N	15	LB
7 yrs.	92 games			

Chuck Faucette
FAUCETTE, CHARLES, JR.
B. Oct. 7, 1963, Levittown, PA
Maryland 6'3" 238 lbs.

1987	SD	N	2	LB
1988			8	LB
2 yrs.	10 games			

Marshall Faulk
FAULK, MARSHALL WILLIAM
B. Feb. 26, 1973, New Orleans, LA
San Diego State 5'10" 200 lbs.

1994	IND	N	16	RB
1995			16	RB
1996			13	RB
3 yrs.	45 games			

Mike Faulkerson
FAULKERSON, MICHAEL WAYNE
B. Sep. 9, 1970, Kingsport, TN
North Carolina 6'0" 237 lbs.

1995	CHI	N	5	RB
1996			16	RB
2 yrs.	21 games			

Chris Faulkner
FAULKNER, CHRISTOPHER

Chris Faulkner continued
ALAN
B. Apr. 13, 1960, Tipton, IN
Florida 6'4" 255 lbs.

1984	LARM	N	8	TE
1985	SD	N	9	TE
2 yrs.	17 games			

Jeff Faulkner
FAULKNER, JEFFREY
B. Apr. 4, 1964, St. Thomas, Virgin Islands
Southern University 6'3" 270 lbs.

1987	KC	N	3	NT
1990	IND	N	7	DE
1991	PHX	N	16	DE
1992			16	DE
1993	NO	N	1	DE
1993	WAS	N	5	DE
1996	NYJ	N	4	DT
6 yrs.	52 games			

Staley Faulkner
FAULKNER, STALEY
B. 1941
Texas 6'3" 245 lbs.

| 1964 | HOU | A | 1 | OT |

Wilson Faumina
FAUMINA, WILSON
B. Aug. 11, 1954, American Samoa
San Jose State 6'5" 275 lbs.

1977	ATL	N	14	DT
1978			16	DT
1979			14	DT
1980			14	DT
1981			16	DT
5 yrs.	74 games			

Ta'Ase Faumui
FAUMUI, TA'ASE
B. Mar. 19, 1971, Western Samoa
Hawaii 6'3" 278 lbs.

1994	PIT	N	5	DE
1995			2	DE
2 yrs.	7 games			

Christian Fauria
FAURIA, CHRISTIAN
B. Sep. 22, 1971, Harbor City, CA
Colorado 6'5" 245 lbs.

1995	SEA	N	14	TE
1996			10	TE
2 yrs.	24 games			

Ron Faurot
FAUROT, RON EDWARD
B. Jan. 27, 1962, Wichita, KS
Arkansas 6'7" 262 lbs.

1984	NYJ	N	15	DE, DT
1985			5	DE
2 yrs.	20 games			

Frank Fausch
FAUSCH, FRANKLIN L. (Whitey, Fox)
B. Jun. 13, 1895
Deceased
Kalamazoo 6'6" 250 lbs.

1921	EVA	N	4	FB
1922	EVA	N	3	HB, FB, T
2 yrs.	7 games			

Dick Faust
FAUST, RICHARD A.
B. 1903

Year	Team	Games	Pos.

Dick Faust continued

D. Apr. 15, 1955
Otterbein 6'1" 208 lbs.

Year	Team		Games	Pos.
1924	DAY	N	1	E, G
1928			7	T, E, G
1929			5	T

3 yrs.   13 games

George Faust

FAUST, GEORGE J.
B. Nov. 16, 1917
D. Jun., 1983, Chicago, IL
Minnesota 6'1" 205 lbs.

1939	CHIC	N	9	QB

Paul Faust

FAUST, PAUL T.
B. Jul. 23, 1943, Minneapolis, MN
Minnesota 6'0" 220 lbs.

1967	MIN	N	1	LB

Hal Faverty

FAVERTY, HAROLD
B. Sep. 26, 1927, Hammond, IN
Wisconsin 6'2" 220 lbs.

1952	GB		11	E

Brett Favre

FAVRE, BRETT LORENZO
B. Oct. 10, 1969, Pass Christian, MS
Southern Mississippi 6'2" 220 lbs.

1991	ATL	N	2	QB
1992	GB	N	15	QB
1993			16	QB
1994			16	QB
1995			16	QB
1996			16	QB

6 yrs.   81 games

Calvin Favron

FAVRON, CALVIN
B. Jul. 3, 1957, New Orleans, LA
Southeastern Louisiana 6'1" 225 lbs.

1979	STL	N	16	LB
1980			16	LB
1981			14	LB
1982			4	LB

4 yrs.   50 games

Jake Fawcett

FAWCETT, JACOB R.
B. May 29, 1919, Hillsboro, TX
Deceased
Southern Methodist 5'11" 223 lbs.

1942	CLE	N	9	T
1943	BKN	N	10	T
1944	CLE	N	10	T
1946	LA	N	4	T

4 yrs.   33 games

Jerry Fay

FAY, JEREMIAH L.
B. Jul. 18, 1897
D. Aug. 23, 1978, Manchester, CT
Grove City 6'4" 220 lbs.

1926	PHI	A	5	T, G, E

Doc Faye

FAYE, ALLEN
Marquette 175 lbs.

1922	GB	N	1	E

John Faylor

FAYLOR, JOHN
B. Feb. 10, 1963

John Faylor continued

Santa Clara 6'1" 197 lbs.

1987	SF	N	3	S

Ron Fazio

FAZIO, RON
B. Jun. 5, 1962, Meadowbrook, PA
Maryland 6'4" 242 lbs.

1987	PHI	N	1	TE

Ricky Feacher

FEACHER, IVY RICKY
B. Feb. 11, 1954, Crystal River, FL
Mississippi Valley State 5'10" 174 lbs.

1976	NE	N	3	WR
1976	CLE	N	10	WR
1977			14	WR
1978			16	WR
1979			16	WR
1980			16	WR
1981			16	WR
1982			9	WR
1983			9	WR
1984			16	WR

9 yrs.   125 games

Wiley Feagin

FEAGIN, WILEY
B. Aug. 28, 1937, Conroe, TX
Houston 6'2" 236 lbs.

1961	BAL	N	14	G
1962			14	G
1963	WAS	N	2	G

3 yrs.   30 games

Jeff Feagles

FEAGLES, JEFFREY ALLAN
B. Mar. 7, 1966, Scottsdale, AZ
Miami (Florida) 6'0" 198 lbs.

1988	NE	N	16	P
1989			16	P
1990	PHI	N	16	P
1991			16	P
1992			16	P
1993			16	P
1994	ARI	N	16	P
1995			16	P
1996			16	P

9 yrs.   144 games

Tom Feamster

FEAMSTER, THOMAS
B. 1931
Florida State 6'7" 260 lbs.

1956	BAL	N	12	T

Tom Fears

FEARS, THOMAS JESSE
B. Dec. 3, 1923, Los Angeles, CA
Santa Clara/UCLA 6'2" 213 lbs.

1948	LA	N	12	E
1949			12	E
1950			12	E
1951			7	E
1952			12	E
1953			8	E
1954			10	E
1955			12	E
1956			2	E

9 yrs.   87 games

Willie Fears

FEARS, WILLIE
B. Jun. 4, 1964, Chicago, IL
Northwestern State (Louisiana) 6'3" 278 lbs.

1987	CIN	N	3	DE

Willie Fears continued

1990	MIN	N	2	DE

2 yrs.   5 games

Grant Feasel

FEASEL, GRANT EARL
B. Jun. 28, 1960, Barstow, CA
Abilene Christian 6'8" 267 lbs.

1983	BAL	N	11	C
1984	IND	N	6	C
1984	MIN	N	9	C
1987	SEA	N	12	C
1988			16	C
1989			16	C
1990			16	C
1991			15	C
1992			16	C

8 yrs.   117 games

Greg Feasel

FEASEL, GREGORY DUANE
B. Nov. 7, 1959, Barstow, CA
Abilene Christian 6'7" 301 lbs.

1986	GB	N	15	OT
1987	SD	N	3	OT

2 yrs.   18 games

Bill Feaster

FEASTER, WILLIAM GEORGE
(Vin)
B. 1904
D. Dec. 12, 1950
Fordham 5'11" 205 lbs.

1929	ORA	N	12	T
1930	NEW	N	10	T, E

2 yrs.   22 games

Tiny Feather

FEATHER, ELVIN E. (Tiny)
B. 1903
Kansas State 6'0" 197 lbs.

1927	CLE	N	10	FB, HB
1928	DET	N	10	FB
1929	NYG	N	15	FB, HB
1930			15	FB, HB
1931	SI	N	11	HB, E-FB, QB
1931	NYG	N	2	FB
1932			9	HB, FB
1933			7	E, HB, FB
1934	C-S	N	5	HB

8 yrs.   84 games

Beattie Feathers

FEATHERS, WILLIAM BEATTIE
B. Aug. 4, 1908, Bristol, VA
D. Mar. 10, 1979, Winston-Salem, NC
Tennessee 5'10" 185 lbs.

1934	CHIB	N	11	HB
1935			8	HB
1936			12	HB
1937			11	HB
1938	BKN	N	7	HB
1939			4	HB
1940	GB	N	1	HB

7 yrs.   54 games

Creig Federico

FEDERICO, CREIG RONALD
B. May 7, 1963
Illinois State 6'2" 205 lbs.

1987	DET	N	3	S

John Federovich

FEDEROVICH, JOHN (Ace)
B. Jun. 26, 1917, Wyano, PA
Davis & Elkins 6'5" 261 lbs.

1941	CHIB	N	11	T

John Federovich continued

1946			3	T

2 yrs.   14 games

Joe Federspiel

FEDERSPIEL, JOSEPH MICHAEL
B. May 6, 1950, Louisville, KY
Kentucky 6'1" 230 lbs.

1972	NO	N	14	LB
1973			13	LB
1974			14	LB
1975			14	LB
1976			14	LB
1977			14	LB
1978			16	LB
1979			16	LB
1980			15	LB
1981	BAL	N	11	LB

10 yrs.   141 games

Walt Fedora

FEDORA, WALTER E. (Fuzzy)
B. Sep. 15, 1918, Decatur, IL
D. Sep., 1968
George Washington 5'11" 190 lbs.

1942	BKN	N	8	FB, DB

Gerry Feehery

FEEHERY, GERALD
B. Mar. 9, 1960, Philadelphia, PA
Syracuse 6'2" 268 lbs.

1983	PHI	N	2	C
1984			6	C, G
1985			15	C
1986			6	C
1987			12	C
1988	KC	N	6	C

6 yrs.   47 games

Al Feeney

FEENEY, ALBERT G.
B. Nov. 12, 1892, Indianapolis, IN
D. Nov. 12, 1950, Indianapolis, IN
Notre Dame 5'11" 185 lbs.

1920	CAN	A	8	C
1921			7	C

2 yrs.   15 games

Howard Feggins

FEGGINS, HOWARD
B. May 6, 1965, South Hills, VA
North Carolina 5'10" 190 lbs.

1989	NE	N	11	CB

Nick Feher

FEHER, NICHOLAS JOHN
B. 1925, Youngstown, OH
D. Dec. 28, 1992, Kingman, AZ
Georgia 6'0" 224 lbs.

1951	SF	N	12	G
1952			6	G
1953			10	G
1954			12	G
1955	PIT	N	2	G

5 yrs.   42 games

Bernie Feibish

FEIBISH, BERNARD
B. 1918
Deceased
New York University 6'2" 223 lbs.

1941	PHI	N	3	C

Andy Feichtinger

FEICHTINGER, ANDREW
B. Nov. 16, 1897

Year	Team	Games	Pos.

Andy Feichtinger *continued*
D. Dec., 1962
None 5'9" 170 lbs.

Year	Team		Games	Pos.
1920	DEC	A	1	E

Lou Feist
FEIST, LOUIS
B. 1903
D. Nov. 12, 1926
Columbia/Canisius 6'1" 200 lbs.

1924	BUF	N	10	T, E, G
1925			6	E
1926			5	E, HB
3 yrs.	21 games			

Gene Fekete
FEKETE, EUGENE
B. Aug. 31, 1922, Sugar Creek, OH
Ohio State 6'0" 195 lbs.

| 1946 | CLE | AA | 6 | FB |

John Fekete
FEKETE, JOHN
B. 1921
Ohio University 5'11" 200 lbs.

| 1946 | BUF | AA | 2 | HB |

Fred Felber
FELBER, FRED N. (Nip)
B. 1909
North Dakota 6'2" 190 lbs.

| 1932 | BOS | N | 10 | E |

Bill Feldhaus
FELDHAUS, WILLIAM B. (Butch)
B. Dec. 8, 1912
D. Jun. 2, 1974, Cincinnati, OH
Cincinnati 6'0" 226 lbs.

1937	DET	N	10	G, T
1938			11	G
1939			10	G, LB
1940			11	G, LB
4 yrs.	42 games			

Paul Feldhausen
FELDHAUSEN, PAUL ELVIE
B. Jun. 14, 1946, Madison, WI
Northland 6'6" 270 lbs.

| 1968 | BOS | A | 2 | OT |

Todd Feldman
FELDMAN, TODD
B. Aug. 7, 1962
Kent State 5'10" 184 lbs.

| 1987 | MIA | N | 1 | WR |

Gene Felker
FELKER, EUGENE
B. 1929
Wisconsin 6'1" 198 lbs.

| 1952 | DAL | N | 6 | E |

Happy Feller
FELLER, JAMES PATRICK
B. Jun. 13, 1949, Fredericksburg, TX
Texas 5'11" 185 lbs.

1971	PHI	N	9	K
1972	NO	N	6	K
1973			6	K
3 yrs.	21 games			

Mark Fellows
FELLOWS, CHARLES MARK
B. Feb. 22, 1963, Billings, MT

Mark Fellows *continued*
Montana State 6'1" 233 lbs.

1985	SD	N	2	LB
1986			1	LB
2 yrs.	3 games			

Ron Fellows
FELLOWS, RONALD LEE
B. Nov. 7, 1958, South Bend, IN
Missouri 6'0" 173 lbs.

1981	DAL	N	16	CB, S
1982			9	CB
1983			16	CB
1984			16	CB
1985			13	CB
1986			16	CB
1987	LARI	N	12	CB
1988			14	CB
8 yrs.	112 games			

Dick Felt
FELT, RICHARD
B. 1933
Brigham Young 6'0" 184 lbs.

1960	NY	A	14	DB
1961			14	DB
1962	BOS	A	14	DB
1963			14	DB
1964			9	DB
1965			1	DB
1966			14	DB
7 yrs.	80 games			

Eric Felton
FELTON, ERIC NORMAN
B. Oct. 8, 1955, Austin, TX
Texas Tech 6'0" 200 lbs.

1978	NO	N	16	CB
1979			13	CB
1980	NYG	N	6	DB
3 yrs.	35 games			

Joe Felton
FELTON, JOSEPH
B. Oct. 16, 1964
Albion 6'2" 266 lbs.

| 1987 | DET | N | 2 | G |

Ralph Felton
FELTON, RALPH D.
B. May 21, 1932, Midway, PA
Maryland 5'11" 210 lbs.

1954	WAS	N	12	FB, LB
1955			12	LB
1956			7	LB
1957			12	LB
1958			8	LB
1959			12	LB
1960			12	LB
1961	BUF	A	14	LB
1962			4	LB
9 yrs.	93 games			

Bobby Felts
FELTS, BOB
B. Jun. 26, 1942, Miami, FL
Florida A&M 6'2" 203 lbs.

1965	BAL	N	7	HB
1965	DET	N	7	HB
1966			10	RB
1967			14	RB
3 yrs.	38 games			

Tom Fena
FENA, THOMAS M.
B. Dec. 27, 1914
D. Sep. 7, 1985, Burlingame, CA

Tom Fena *continued*
Denver 5'11" 200 lbs.

| 1937 | DET | N | 2 | G |

Gary Fencik
FENCIK, JOHN GARY
B. Jun. 11, 1954, Chicago, IL
Yale 6'1" 196 lbs.

1976	CHI	N	13	S
1977			14	S
1978			16	S
1979			14	S
1980			15	S
1981			16	S
1982			9	S
1983			8	S
1984			16	S
1985			16	S
1986			16	S
1987			12	S
12 yrs.	165 games			

Dick Fencil
FENCIL, RICHARD J.
B. Feb. 24, 1910
D. Jun. 25, 1972, Chicago, IL
Northwestern 5'11" 160 lbs.

| 1933 | PHI | N | 5 | E |

Chuck Fenenbock
FENENBOCK, CHARLES B.
(Mighty Mouse)
B. Aug. 28, 1918, Oakland, CA
UCLA 5'9" 174 lbs.

1943	DET	N	9	HB
1945			10	HB
1946	LA	AA	13	HB
1947			14	HB
1948			1	HB
1948	CHI	AA	13	HB
5 yrs.	60 games			

Gill Fenerty
FENERTY, LAWRENCE GILL
B. Aug. 24, 1963, New Orleans, LA
Holy Cross 6'0" 205 lbs.

1990	NO	N	15	RB
1991			16	RB
2 yrs.	31 games			

Bob Fenimore
FENIMORE, ROBERT DALE
B. Oct. 6, 1925, Woodward, OK
Oklahoma State 6'1" 195 lbs.

| 1947 | CHIB | N | 10 | HB |

Carl Fennema
FENNEMA, CARL
B. Oct. 17, 1926, San Francisco, CA
Washington 6'2" 210 lbs.

1948	NYG	N	8	C
1949			3	C
2 yrs.	11 games			

Derrick Fenner
FENNER, DERRICK STEVEN
B. Apr. 6, 1967, Washington, DC
North Carolina 6'3" 229 lbs.

1989	SEA	N	5	RB
1990			16	RB
1991			11	RB
1992	CIN	N	16	RB
1993			15	RB
1994			16	RB
1995	OAK	N	16	RB
1996			16	RB
8 yrs.	111 games			

Lane Fenner
FENNER, LANE
B. Dec. 7, 1945, Evansville, IN
Florida State 6'5" 210 lbs.

| 1968 | SD | A | 11 | OE |

Lee Fenner
FENNER, LEONARD D.
B. Nov. 10, 1895
D. Apr., 1963
none 5'10" 171 lbs.

1920	DAY	A	7	E, HB
1921			7	E
1922	DAY	N	6	E
1923			5	E
1924			7	E
1925			8	E
1926			6	E
1927			7	E
1929			6	E
1930	POR	N	1	E
10 yrs.	60 games			

Rick Fenney
FENNEY, RICKY DALE
B. Dec. 7, 1964, Everett, WA
Washington 6'1" 240 lbs.

1987	MIN	N	11	RB
1988			13	RB
1989			16	RB
1990			12	RB
1991			11	RB
5 yrs.	63 games			

Duke Fergersen
FERGERSEN, DUKE
B. Apr. 21, 1954, Boise, ID
Washington State/San Diego State 6'1" 189 lbs.

1977	SEA	N	13	WR
1978			16	WR
1979			4	WR
1980	BUF	N	9	WR
4 yrs.	42 games			

Bill Ferguson
FERGUSON, WILLIAM MICHAEL
B. Jul. 7, 1951, El Cajon, CA
Washington/San Diego State 6'3" 225 lbs.

1973	NYJ	N	11	LB
1974			13	LB
2 yrs.	24 games			

Bob Ferguson
FERGUSON, ROBERT E.
B. Aug. 29, 1939
Ohio State 5'11" 220 lbs.

1962	PIT	N	13	FB
1963			5	FB
1963	MIN	N	7	FB
2 yrs.	25 games			

Charley Ferguson
FERGUSON, CHARLES EDWARD
B. Nov. 15, 1939, Dallas, TX
Tennessee State 6'5" 218 lbs.

1961	CLE	N	12	OE
1962	MIN	N	10	OE
1963	BUF	A	12	OE
1965			12	OE
1966			14	OE
1969			4	OE
6 yrs.	64 games			

Gene Ferguson
FERGUSON, GENE

Year	Team		Games	Pos.

Gene Ferguson continued

B. Jun. 5, 1948, Lynchburg, VA
Norfolk State 6'7" 302 lbs.

Year	Team		Games	Pos.
1969	SD	A	12	OT
1970	SD	N	14	OT
1971	HOU	N	14	OT
1972			1	OT
4 yrs.	41 games			

Howie Ferguson

FERGUSON, HOWARD, JR.
B. Aug. 5, 1930, New Iberia, LA
None 6'2" 214 lbs.

Year	Team		Games	Pos.
1953	GB	N	11	FB
1954			12	FB
1955			12	FB
1956			11	FB
1957			12	FB
1958			7	FB
1960	LA	A		FB
7 yrs.	65 games			

Jim Ferguson

FERGUSON, JAMES T.
B. Oct. 15, 1942, Oakland, CA
Southern California 6'4" 240 lbs.

Year	Team		Games	Pos.
1968	NO	N	4	LB
1969	ATL	N		C
1969	CHI	N	4	C
2 yrs.	8 games			

Joe Ferguson

FERGUSON, JOE CARLTON, JR.
B. Apr. 23, 1950, Alvin, TX
Arkansas 6'1" 190 lbs.

Year	Team		Games	Pos.
1973	BUF	N	14	QB
1974			14	QB
1975			14	QB
1976			7	QB
1977			14	QB
1978			16	QB
1979			16	QB
1980			16	QB
1981			16	QB
1982			9	QB
1983			16	QB
1984			12	QB
1985	DET	N	8	QB
1986			6	QB
1988	TB	N	2	QB
1989			5	QB
1990	IND	N	1	QB
17 yrs.	186 games			

Keith Ferguson

FERGUSON, KEITH TYRONE
B. Apr. 3, 1959, Miami, FL
Ohio State 6'5" 260 lbs.

Year	Team		Games	Pos.
1981	SD	N	16	DE
1982			9	DE
1983			16	DE
1984			16	DE
1985			10	DE
1985	DET	N	5	DE
1986			16	DE
1987			12	DE
1988			14	DE
1989			4	DE
1990			16	DE
10 yrs.	134 games			

Kevin Ferguson

FERGUSON, KEVIN
B. Apr. 12, 1965
Virginia 6'2" 223 lbs.

Year	Team		Games	Pos.
1987	SD	N	2	TE

Larry Ferguson

FERGUSON, LARRY
B. Mar. 19, 1940, Madison, IL
Iowa 5'10" 185 lbs.

Year	Team		Games	Pos.
1963	DET	N	7	HB

Tom Ferguson

FERGUSON, THOMAS C.
B. Sep. 24, 1893
D. Dec., 1979, Fort Lauderdale, CA
None

Year	Team		Games	Pos.
1921	LOU	A	2	T

Vagas Ferguson

FERGUSON, VASQUERO DIAZ
B. Mar. 6, 1957, Richmond, IN
Notre Dame 6'1" 194 lbs.

Year	Team		Games	Pos.
1980	NE	N	16	RB
1981			13	RB
1982			2	RB
1983	HOU	N	1	RB
1983	CLE	N	1	RB
4 yrs.	33 games			

Fritz Ferko

FERKO, JOHN
B. Jul. 6, 1912
D. Mar., 1984, Perth Amboy, NJ
West Chester State 6'1" 242 lbs.

Year	Team		Games	Pos.
1937	PHI	N	11	T
1938			2	T
2 yrs.	13 games			

Ron Fernandes

FERNANDES, RONALD MICHAEL
B. Sep. 11, 1951, Ypsilanti, MI
Eastern Michigan 6'4" 251 lbs.

Year	Team		Games	Pos.
1976	BAL	N	13	DE
1977			14	DE
1979			13	DE
3 yrs.	40 games			

Manny Fernandez

FERNANDEZ, MANUEL J.
B. Jul. 3, 1946, Oakland, CA
Utah 6'2" 250 lbs.

Year	Team		Games	Pos.
1968	MIA	A	13	DE
1969			14	DE
1970	MIA	N	13	DT
1971			14	DT
1972			14	DT
1973			13	DT
1974			12	DT
1975			10	DT
8 yrs.	103 games			

Mervyn Fernandez

FERNANDEZ, MERVYN (Swervin' Mervyn)
B. Dec. 29, 1959, Merced, CA
San Jose State 6'3" 200 lbs.

Year	Team		Games	Pos.
1987	LARI	N	7	WR
1988			16	WR
1989			16	WR
1990			16	WR
1991			16	WR
1992			15	WR
6 yrs.	86 games			

Vince Ferragamo

FERRAGAMO, VINCE
B. Apr. 24, 1954, Torrance, CA
California/Nebraska 6'3" 209 lbs.

Year	Team		Games	Pos.
1977	LA	N	3	QB
1978			9	QB

Vince Ferragamo continued

Year	Team		Games	Pos.
1979			8	QB
1980			16	QB
1982	LARM	N	7	QB
1983			16	QB
1984			3	QB
1985	BUF	N	10	QB
1986	GB	N	3	QB
9 yrs.	75 games			

Jack Ferrante

FERRANTE, JOHN A.
B. Mar. 9, 1916, Camden, NJ
None 6'1" 197 lbs.

Year	Team		Games	Pos.
1941	PHI	N	3	E
1944			10	E
1945			10	E
1946			11	E
1947			11	E
1948			12	E
1949			12	E
1950			12	E
8 yrs.	81 games			

Orlando Ferrante

FERRANTE, ORLANDO
B. 1933
Southern California 6'0" 230 lbs.

Year	Team		Games	Pos.
1960	LA	A		G
1961	SD	A	14	G
2 yrs.	14 games			

Ron Ferrari

FERRARI, RONALD LEE
B. Jul. 30, 1959, Springfield, IL
Illinois 6'0" 215 lbs.

Year	Team		Games	Pos.
1982	SF		9	LB
1983			16	LB
1984			11	LB
1985			16	LB
1986			16	LB
5 yrs.	68 games			

Bobby Ferrell

FERRELL, ROBERT STEVEN
B. Nov. 13, 1952, Los Angeles, CA
UCLA 6'0" 216 lbs.

Year	Team		Games	Pos.
1976	SF	N	10	RB
1977			14	RB
1978			16	RB
1979			16	RB
1980			12	RB
5 yrs.	68 games			

Earl Ferrell

FERRELL, EARL THOMAS
B. Mar. 27, 1958, Halifax, VA
East Tennessee State 6'0" 220 lbs.

Year	Team		Games	Pos.
1982	STL	N	9	RB
1983			16	RB
1984			16	RB
1985			11	RB
1986			16	RB
1987			11	FB
1988	PHX	N	16	RB
1989			15	RB
8 yrs.	110 games			

Neil Ferris

FERRIS, NEIL GEORGE
B. Oct. 31, 1927, Bell, CA
Deceased
Loyola (California) 5'11" 181 lbs.

Year	Team		Games	Pos.
1951	WAS	N	12	HB
1952			4	HB
1952	PHI	N	8	HB

Neil Ferris continued

Year	Team		Games	Pos.
1953	LA	N	5	HB
3 yrs.	29 games			

Lou Ferry

FERRY, LOUIS ANTHONY
B. Aug. 31, 1927, Big Springs, TX
Villanova 6'2" 244 lbs.

Year	Team		Games	Pos.
1949	GB	N	12	T
1951	CHIC	N	12	T
1952	PIT	N	12	T
1953			12	T
1954			11	T
1955			12	T
6 yrs.	71 games			

Paul Fersen

FERSEN, PAUL CLINTON
B. Feb. 16, 1950, Columbus, GA
Georgia 6'5" 260 lbs.

Year	Team		Games	Pos.
1973	NO	N	3	OT
1974			1	OT
2 yrs.	4 games			

Howard Fest

FEST, HOWARD ARTHUR
B. Apr. 11, 1946, San Antonio, TX
Texas 6'6" 263 lbs.

Year	Team		Games	Pos.
1968	CIN	A	14	OT
1969			14	OT
1970	CIN	N	14	OT
1971			14	OT
1972			14	OT, G
1973			14	OT, G
1974			14	OT, G
1975			14	G
1976	TB	N	14	G
9 yrs.	126 games			

Jim Fetherton

FETHERTON, JAMES
B. Jun. 2, 1945, Modesto, CA
California 6'2" 225 lbs.

Year	Team		Games	Pos.
1968	SD	A	13	LB
1969			14	LB
2 yrs.	27 games			

Gus Fetz

FETZ, GUSTAVE
B. 1899
Deceased
None 145 lbs.

Year	Team		Games	Pos.
1923	CHIB	N	8	HB, FB

Dan Ficca

FICCA, DANIEL
B. Feb. 7, 1939
Southern California 6'1" 244 lbs.

Year	Team		Games	Pos.
1962	OAK	A	14	G
1963	NY	A	14	G
1964			14	G
1965			14	G
1966			14	G
5 yrs.	70 games			

Leon Fichman

FICHMAN, LEON
B. Feb. 23, 1921, Los Angeles, CA
Alabama 6'1" 215 lbs.

Year	Team		Games	Pos.
1946	DET	N	11	T

Brad Fichtel

FICHTEL, BRAD ALAN
B. Mar. 10, 1970, Oswego, IL

Year	Team	Games	Pos.

Brad Fichtel continued
Eastern Illinois 6'2" 285 lbs.

| 1994 | **LARM** N | 3 | C |

Ross Fichtner
FICHTNER, ROSS WILLIAM
B. Oct. 26, 1938, McKeesport, PA
Purdue 6'0" 186 lbs.

1960	**CLE** N	12	DB
1961		13	DB
1962		14	DB
1963		13	DB
1964		8	DB
1965		14	DB
1966		14	DB
1967		14	DB
1968	**NO** N	4	DB

9 yrs. 106 games

Amod Field
FIELD, AMOD LLOYD
B. Oct. 11, 1967
Montclair State 5'11" 181 lbs.

| 1991 | **PHX** N | 2 | WR |

Doak Field
FIELD, RICHARD DOAK, JR.
B. Oct. 8, 1958, Burnet, TX
Baylor 6'2" 228 lbs.

| 1981 | **STL** N | 7 | LB |

Harry Field
FIELD, HARRY NUUANU
B. Aug. 18, 1911, Wailuku, HI
Deceased
Oregon State 6'1" 230 lbs.

1934	**CHIC** N	11	T
1935		10	T
1936		12	T

3 yrs. 33 games

Bill Fielder
FIELDER, WILLIAM F.
B. Nov. 9, 1914
D. Feb., 1976
Pennsylvania 5'9" 200 lbs.

| 1938 | **PHI** N | 1 | G |

Don Fielder
FIELDER, DON SINCLAIR
B. Oct. 20, 1959, Las Cruces, NM
Kentucky 6'3" 240 lbs.

| 1985 | **TB** N | 11 | DE |

Jay Fielder
FIELDER, JAY
B. Dec. 29, 1971, Oceanside, NY
Dartmouth 6'1" 215 lbs.

| 1994 | **PHI** N | 1 | QB |
| 1995 | | 1 | QB |

2 yrs. 2 games

Anthony Fieldings
FIELDINGS, ANTHONY
B. Jul. 7, 1971, Eustis, FL
Morningside 6'1" 237 lbs.

| 1995 | **DAL** N | 4 | LB |

Angelo Fields
FIELDS, ANGELO B.
B. Sep. 14, 1957, Washington, DC
Michigan State 6'6" 315 lbs.

| 1980 | **HOU** N | 16 | OT |
| 1981 | | 14 | OT |

2 yrs. 30 games

Anthony Fields
FIELDS, ANTHONY
B. Jan. 17, 1964
Eastern Michigan 6'1" 192 lbs.

| 1987 | **DET** N | 3 | CB |

Edgar Fields
FIELDS, EDGAR EUGENE
B. Mar. 10, 1954, Austin, TX
Texas A&M 6'2" 255 lbs.

1977	**ATL** N	14	DT, DE
1978		16	DT
1979		16	DT, DE
1980		14	DT
1981	**DET** N	2	DT

5 yrs. 62 games

Floyd Fields
FIELDS, FLOYD CORNELIUS
B. Jan. 7, 1969, South Holland, IL
Arizona State 6'0" 208 lbs.

1991	**SD** N	1	S
1992		16	S
1993		13	S

3 yrs. 30 games

George Fields
FIELDS, GEORGE
B. 1936
Bakersfield State 6'3" 245 lbs.

| 1960 | **OAK** A | | DE |
| 1961 | | 1 | DT |

2 yrs. 1 games

Greg Fields
FIELDS, GREGORY KEITH
B. Jan. 23, 1955, San Francisco, CA
Grambling State 6'6" 265 lbs.

| 1979 | **BAL** N | 16 | DE |
| 1980 | | 16 | DE |

2 yrs. 32 games

Jaime Fields
FIELDS, JAIME
B. Aug. 28, 1970, Compton, CA
Washington 5'11" 230 lbs.

| 1993 | **KC** N | 6 | LB |
| 1994 | | 10 | LB |

2 yrs. 16 games

Jeff Fields
FIELDS, JEFF
B. Jul. 3, 1967, Jackson, MS
Arkansas State 6'3" 320 lbs.

| 1995 | **CAR** N | 2 | NT |

Jerry Fields
FIELDS, JERRY E.
B. May 24, 1938, Ironton, OH
Ohio State 6'1" 222 lbs.

| 1961 | **NY** A | 5 | LB |
| 1962 | | 14 | LB |

2 yrs. 19 games

Jitter Fields
FIELDS, ALFRED
B. Aug. 16, 1962, Dallas, TX
Texas 5'8" 188 lbs.

1984	**NO** N	13	DB
1987	**IND** N	1	CB
1987	**KC** N	5	DB

2 yrs. 19 games

Joe Fields
FIELDS, JOSEPH CHARLES, JR.
B. Nov. 14, 1953, Woodbury, NJ
Rutgers-Camden/Widener 6'2" 250 lbs.*

1975	**NYJ** N	14	C, G
1976		14	C, G
1977		14	C
1978		16	C, G
1979		15	C, G
1980		13	C
1981		16	C
1982		9	C
1983		12	C
1984		16	C
1985		15	C
1986		9	C
1987		10	C, G
1988	**NYG** N	13	C

14 yrs. 186 games

Mark Fields
FIELDS, MARK LEE
B. Nov. 9, 1972, Los Angeles, CA
Washington State 6'2" 244 lbs.

| 1995 | **NO** N | 16 | LB |
| 1996 | | 16 | LB |

2 yrs. 32 games

Scott Fields
FIELDS, SCOTT
B. Apr. 22, 1973, Ontario, CA
Southern California 6'2" 220 lbs.

| 1996 | **ATL** N | 6 | LB |

Ralph Fife
FIFE, RALPH DONALD
B. Jan. 26, 1920, Pittsburgh, PA
Pittsburgh 6'0" 207 lbs.

1942	**CHIC** N	4	G
1945		1	
1946	**PIT** N	10	G

3 yrs. 15 games

Bill Fifer
FIFER, WILLIAM CHARLES
B. Oct. 26, 1955, Kerrville, TX
West Texas State 6'4" 250 lbs.

| 1978 | **DET** N | 6 | OT |
| 1978 | **NO** N | 4 | G |

1 yr. 10 games

Cedric Figaro
FIGARO, CEDRIC NOAH
B. Aug. 17, 1966, Lafayette, LA
Notre Dame 6'2" 255 lbs.

1988	**SD** N	6	LB
1989		16	LB
1990		16	LB
1991	**IND** N	1	LB
1991	**CLE** N	12	LB
1992		16	LB
1995	**STL** N	16	LB
1996		15	LB

7 yrs. 98 games

George Figner
FIGNER, GEORGE (Bunny)
B. Apr. 30, 1931, Dayton, OH
Colorado 6'0" 185 lbs.

| 1953 | **CHIB** N | 5 | DB |

Deon Figures
FIGURES, DEON JUNIEL
B. Jan. 10, 1970, Bellflower, CA
Colorado 6'0" 200 lbs.

| 1993 | **PIT** N | 15 | CB |

Deon Figures continued

1994		16	CB
1995		14	CB
1996		16	CB

4 yrs. 61 games

Dan Fike
FIKE, DAN CLEMENT, JR.
B. Jun. 16, 1961, Mobile, AL
Florida 6'7" 280 lbs.

1985	**CLE** N	13	G, OT
1986		16	G, OT
1987		12	G
1988		16	G
1989		13	G
1990		10	G
1991		16	G
1992		16	G
1993	**PIT** N	3	G, OT

9 yrs. 115 games

Jack Filak
FILAK, JOHN
B. 1904
Deceased
Penn State 6'0" 190 lbs.

1927	**FRA** N	11	T, G
1928		14	T, G-E
1929		14	T, G

3 yrs. 39 games

Frank Filchock
FILCHOCK, FRANK JOSEPH
(Frankie)
B. Oct. 18, 1916, Crucible, PA
D. Jun. 20, 1994, Crucible, PA
Indiana 5'11" 193 lbs.

1938	**PIT** N	6	HB, QB, DB
1938	**WAS** N	6	HB, QB, DB
1939		11	HB, QB, DB
1940		10	HB, QB, DB
1941		11	HB, QB, DB
1944		10	QB, HB, DB
1945		10	QB, HB, DB
1946	**NYG** N	11	QB
1950	**BAL** N	1	QB

8 yrs. 76 games

Jim Files
FILES, JAMES DALE
B. Jan. 16, 1948, Paris, AR
Oklahoma 6'4" 240 lbs.

1970	**NYG** N	14	LB
1971		14	LB
1972		14	LB
1973		14	LB

4 yrs. 56 games

Steve Filipowicz
FILIPOWICZ, STEPHEN CHARLES
B. Jun. 28, 1921, Donora, PA
D. Feb. 21, 1975, Wilkes-Barre, PA
Fordham 5'8" 200 lbs.

| 1945 | **NYG** N | 10 | FB, LB |
| 1946 | | 11 | FB, LB |

2 yrs. 21 games

Gene Filipski
FILIPSKI, EUGENE C.
B. Jun. 14, 1931, Sacramento, CA
Army/Villanova 5'11" 185 lbs.

| 1956 | **NYG** N | 12 | HB |
| 1957 | | 12 | HB |

2 yrs. 24 games

Year	Team		Games	Pos.

John Fina
FINA, JOHN JOSEPH
B. Mar. 11, 1969, Rochester, MN
Arizona 6'4" 282 lbs.

Year	Team		Games	Pos.
1992	BUF	N	16	G, OT
1993			16	OT, G
1994			12	OT
1995			16	OT
1996			15	OT
5 yrs.	75 games			

Bull Finch
FINCH, OLIN
B. 1893
D. 1956
Whittier 5'8" 180 lbs.

Year	Team		Games	Pos.
1926	LA	N	7	HB, FB

Karl Finch
FINCH, KARL
B. Jul. 7, 1939, Modesto, CA
Iowa/California Poly (Pomona) 6'3" 195 lbs.

Year	Team		Games	Pos.
1962	LA	N	7	OE

Steve Finch
FINCH, STEPHEN
B. Jan. 2, 1961, Great Lakes, IL
Elmhurst 6'0" 200 lbs.

Year	Team		Games	Pos.
1987	MIN	N	1	WR

Mike Fink
FINK, PAUL MICHAEL
B. Dec. 24, 1950, Kansas City, MO
Missouri 5'11" 180 lbs.

Year	Team		Games	Pos.
1973	NO	N	13	CB

Jim Finks
FINKS, JAMES EDWARD
B. Aug. 31, 1927, St. Louis, MO
D. May 8, 1994, New Orleans, LA
Tulsa 6'0" 175 lbs.

Year	Team		Games	Pos.
1949	PIT	N	11	HB, QB, DB
1950			9	HB, QB, DB
1951			12	HB, QB, DB
1952			12	QB
1953			12	QB
1954			12	QB
1955			12	QB
7 yrs.	80 games			

Jack Finlay
FINLAY, JOHN
B. Sep. 8, 1921, Los Angeles, CA
UCLA 6'1" 217 lbs.

Year	Team		Games	Pos.
1947	LA	N	12	G
1948			12	G
1949			12	G
1950			10	G
1951			9	G
5 yrs.	55 games			

Bernie Finn
FINN, BERNARD
B. Dec. 31, 1907
D. Sep. 24, 1993
Holy Cross 5'10" 180 lbs.

Year	Team		Games	Pos.
1930	NEW	N	9	QB, HB
1930	SI	N	5	QB, HB, FB
1932			1	QB
1932	CHIC	N	2	QB
2 yrs.	17 games			

Jack Finn
FINN, JOHN
B. 1899

Jack Finn continued
Deceased
Villanova 5'7" 172 lbs.

Year	Team		Games	Pos.
1924	FRA	N	9	HB, QB, FB

Jimmy Finnegan
FINNEGAN, JAMES P.
B. Jan. 20, 1901
D. Sep. 6, 1967, Missouri
St. Louis 5'8" 160 lbs.

Year	Team		Games	Pos.
1923	STL	N	2	E, QB

Garry Finneran
FINNERAN, GARRY
B. 1934
Southern California 6'3" 240 lbs.

Year	Team		Games	Pos.
1960	LA	A		DT
1961	OAK	A	13	DT
2 yrs.	13 games			

Roger Finnie
FINNIE, ROGER LEWIS
B. Nov. 6, 1945, Miami, FL
Florida A&M 6'3" 247 lbs.

Year	Team		Games	Pos.
1969	NY	A	14	OT
1970	NYJ	N	3	OT
1971			7	OT
1972			14	G
1973	STL	N	12	G
1974			14	G
1975			14	G, OT
1976			14	OT
1977			14	OT
1978			7	OT
1979	NO	N	8	OT
11 yrs.	121 games			

Tom Finnin
FINNIN, THOMAS R.
B. Sep. 27, 1927, Chicago, IL
Detroit 6'2" 262 lbs.

Year	Team		Games	Pos.
1953	BAL	N	11	T
1954			12	T
1955			11	T
1956			10	T
1957	CHIC		8	T
5 yrs.	52 games			

Russ Finsterwald
FINSTERWALD, RUSSELL WILLIAM (Wild Bill)
B. 1894
D. Oct. 18, 1962, Athens, OH
Ohio University/Syracuse 5'9" 165 lbs.

Year	Team		Games	Pos.
1920	DET	A	1	HB

Dave Finzer
FINZER, DAVID M.
B. Feb. 3, 1959, Chicago, IL
Illinois/DePauw 6'1" 195 lbs.

Year	Team		Games	Pos.
1984	CHI	N	16	P
1985	SEA	N	12	P
2 yrs.	28 games			

Al Fiorentino
FIORENTINO, ALBERT
B. Feb. 28, 1917, Watertown, NY
Boston College 5'7" 201 lbs.

Year	Team		Games	Pos.
1943	WAS	N	10	G
1944			10	G
1945	BOS	N	8	G
3 yrs.	28 games			

Bill Fischer
FISCHER, WILLIAM
B. Mar. 10, 1927, Chicago, IL

Bill Fischer continued
Notre Dame 6'2" 248 lbs.

Year	Team		Games	Pos.
1949	CHIC	N	12	T
1950			12	T
1951			12	T
1952			12	G
1953			11	G
5 yrs.	59 games			

Clarke Fischer
FISCHER, CLARKE JOHN
B. Mar. 30, 1900
D. Oct, 1979, Pana, IL
Marquette/Campion/Catholic 5'8" 165 lbs.

Year	Team		Games	Pos.
1926	MIL	N	2	HB

Clete Fischer
FISCHER, CLETUS
B. 1925
Nebraska 5'9" 170 lbs.

Year	Team		Games	Pos.
1949	NYG	N	11	HB, DB

Darrell Fischer
FISCHER, DARRELL C.
B. May, 1903
Deceased
Iowa 5'11" 190 lbs.

Year	Team		Games	Pos.
1925	BUF	N	5	HB, FB

Pat Fischer
FISCHER, PATRICK
B. Jan. 2, 1940, St. Edward, NE
Nebraska 5'10" 170 lbs.

Year	Team		Games	Pos.
1961	STL	N	12	DB
1962			12	DB
1963			14	DB
1964			14	DB
1965			14	DB
1966			7	DB
1967			14	DB
1968	WAS	N	14	DB
1969			14	CB
1970			14	CB
1971			14	CB
1972			14	CB
1973			14	CB
1974			14	CB
1975			11	CB
1976			14	CB
1977			3	CB
17 yrs.	213 games			

Joe Fishback
FISHBACK, JOE
B. Nov. 29, 1967, Knoxville, TN
Carson-Newman 5'11" 198 lbs.

Year	Team		Games	Pos.
1991	ATL	N	14	CB, S
1992	NYJ	N	5	S
1992	ATL	N	8	S
1993	DAL	N	6	S
1994			11	S
4 yrs.	44 games			

Dick Fishel
FISHEL, RICHARD W.
B. Sep. 19, 1909
D. Aug. 12, 1972
Syracuse 5'9" 190 lbs.

Year	Team		Games	Pos.
1933	BKN	N	8	FB, QB, HB

Bob Fisher
FISHER, ROBERT A.
B. Aug. 27, 1916, Los Angeles, CA
D. May 29, 1983, Laguna Beach, CA
Southern California 6'2" 220 lbs.

Year	Team		Games	Pos.
1940	WAS	N	6	T, G

Bob Fisher
FISHER, ROBERT LEE
B. Mar. 17, 1958, Pasadena, CA
Southern Methodist 6'3" 240 lbs.

Year	Team		Games	Pos.
1980	CHI	N	16	TE
1981			6	TE
2 yrs.	22 games			

Doug Fisher
FISHER, DOUGLAS
B. Mar. 8, 1947, Fresno, CA
San Diego State 6'1" 225 lbs.

Year	Team		Games	Pos.
1969	PIT	N	6	LB
1970			4	LB
2 yrs.	10 games			

Ed Fisher
FISHER, EDWIN LOUIS
B. May 31, 1949, Stockton, CA
Arizona State 6'3" 249 lbs.

Year	Team		Games	Pos.
1974	HOU	N	11	C
1975			14	C
1976			14	G
1977			14	G
1978			16	G, C
1979			16	G
1980			16	G
1981			16	G
1982			9	G
9 yrs.	126 games			

Eddie Fisher
FISHER, EDWARD
B. Jul. 18, 1901
D. Feb., 1984, Buffalo, NY
Columbia 5'11" 210 lbs.

Year	Team		Games	Pos.
1925	BUF	N	2	G

Ev Fisher
FISHER, EVERETT (King)
B. 1915
Deceased
Santa Clara 5'11" 205 lbs.

Year	Team		Games	Pos.
1938	CHIC	N	11	E, HB, LB
1939			11	HB, LB, E
1940	PIT	N	4	HB, LB
3 yrs.	26 games			

George Fisher
FISHER, GEORGE L.
B. Aug. 17, 1901
D. Oct. 30, 1968, Leesburg, IN
Indiana 6'0" 200 lbs.

Year	Team		Games	Pos.
1926	HAM	N	2	T

Jeff Fisher
FISHER, JEFFREY MICHAEL
B. Feb. 25, 1958, Culver City, CA
Southern California 5'11" 188 lbs.

Year	Team		Games	Pos.
1981	CHI	N	16	CB
1982			9	CB
1983			8	CB
1984			16	CB
4 yrs.	49 games			

Mike Fisher
FISHER, JAMES MICHAEL
B. Apr. 22, 1958, Gatesville, TX
Baylor 5'11" 172 lbs.

Year	Team		Games	Pos.
1981	STL	N	3	WR

Ray Fisher
FISHER, RAYMOND
B. 1934
Eastern Illinois 6'0" 230 lbs.

Year	Team		Games	Pos.
1959	PIT	N	12	T

Year	Team	Games	Pos.

Alex Fishman
FISHMAN, ALEXANDER
B. 1898
Deceased
None 5'11" 218 lbs.

Year	Team		Games	Pos.
1921	**EVA**	**A**	5	G, FB

Bill Fisk
FISK, WILLIAM G.
B. Nov. 6, 1916, Los Angeles, CA
Southern California 6'0" 199 lbs.

Year	Team		Games	Pos.
1940	**DET**	**N**	10	E
1941			11	E
1942			11	E
1943			10	E
1946	**SF**	**AA**	14	E
1947			14	E
1948	**LA**	**AA**	13	E

7 yrs. 83 games

Jason Fisk
FISK, JASON
B. Sep. 4, 1972, Davis, CA
Stanford 6'3" 286 lbs.

Year	Team		Games	Pos.
1995	**MIN**	**N**	8	DT
1996			16	DT

2 yrs. 24 games

Max Fiske
FISKE, MAX J. (Baxie)
B. Aug. 27, 1914
D. Mar. 15, 1973, Chicago, IL
DePaul 6'0" 199 lbs.

Year	Team		Games	Pos.
1936	**PIT**	**N**	11	QB, HB
1937			7	HB, QB
1938			9	HB, FB, E
1939			1	E, DB

4 yrs. 28 games

Galen Fiss
FISS, GALEN R.
B. Jul. 30, 1931, Johnson, KS
Kansas 6'0" 226 lbs.

Year	Team		Games	Pos.
1956	**CLE**	**N**	12	LB
1957			12	LB
1958			12	LB
1959			12	LB
1960			12	LB
1961			13	LB
1962			14	LB
1963			13	LB
1964			13	LB
1965			12	LB
1966			14	LB

11 yrs. 139 games

Fitzgerald
FITZGERALD
None 150 lbs.

Year	Team		Games	Pos.
1920	**DET**	**A**	4	E

Francis Fitzgerald
FITZGERALD, FRANCIS
B. May 20, 1896
D. Mar., 1976, Springfield, MA
Detroit 5'10" 180 lbs.

Year	Team		Games	Pos.
1923	**TOL**	**N**	7	QB

Freeman Fitzgerald
FITZGERALD, FREEMAN C.
B. 1892, Parkersville, OR
D. May 6, 1942, Milwaukee, WI
Notre Dame 6'0" 195 lbs.

Year	Team		Games	Pos.
1920	**RI**	**A**	7	C, G
1921			2	C

2 yrs. 9 games

Greg Fitzgerald
FITZGERALD, GREG
B. Jul. 3, 1963
Iowa 6'4" 265 lbs.

Year	Team		Games	Pos.
1987	**CHI**	**N**	3	DT

Jamie Fitzgerald
FITZGERALD, JAMIE
B. Apr. 30, 1965, Spokane, WA
Idaho State 6'0" 180 lbs.

Year	Team		Games	Pos.
1987	**MIN**	**N**	2	CB, S

Jim Fitzgerald
FITZGERALD, JAMES A.
B. 1903
St. John's (New York) 5'5" 150 lbs.

Year	Team		Games	Pos.
1926	**BKN**	**A**	2	QB

Jim Fitzgerald
FITZGERALD, JAMES P.
B. 1907
Holy Cross 5'11" 215 lbs.

Year	Team		Games	Pos.
1930	**SI**	**N**	11	C
1931			8	C

2 yrs. 19 games

John Fitzgerald
FITZGERALD, JOHN ROBERT
B. Apr. 16, 1948, Southbridge, MA
Boston College 6'5" 255 lbs.

Year	Team		Games	Pos.
1971	**DAL**	**N**	14	C
1972			14	C
1973			14	C
1974			13	C
1975			14	C
1976			14	C
1977			12	C
1978			14	C
1979			15	C
1980			14	C

10 yrs. 138 games

Kevin Fitzgerald
FITZGERALD, KEVIN
B. Jun. 30, 1964
Wisconsin-Eau Claire 6'3" 235 lbs.

Year	Team		Games	Pos.
1987	**GB**	**N**	1	TE

Mickey Fitzgerald
FITZGERALD, MARION MAXWELL, JR.
B. Apr. 10, 1958, Lynchburg, VA
Virginia Tech 6'2" 235 lbs.

Year	Team		Games	Pos.
1981	**ATL**	**N**	1	RB
1981	**PHI**	**N**	1	RB

1 yr. 2 games

Mike Fitzgerald
FITZGERALD, MICHAEL
B. May 4, 1941, Detroit, MI
Iowa State 5'10" 180 lbs.

Year	Team		Games	Pos.
1966	**MIN**	**N**	9	DB
1967	**ATL**	**N**	10	DB
1967	**MIN**	**N**	6	DB
1967	**NYG**	**N**	2	DB

2 yrs. 27 games

Paul Fitzgibbons
FITZGIBBONS, PAUL
B. 1903
Deceased
Creighton 5'8" 176 lbs.

Year	Team		Games	Pos.
1926	**DUL**	**N**	14	HB, FB, QB, E
1927	**FRA**	**N**	11	HB, QB, FB
1928	**CHIC**	**N**	6	HB, QB
1930	**GB**	**N**	9	HB, QB

Paul Fitzgibbons *continued*

Year	Team		Games	Pos.
1931			10	QB, HB
1932			4	QB, HB

6 yrs. 54 games

Steve Fitzhugh
FITZHUGH, STEVE
B. Jan. 28, 1963
Miami (Ohio) 5'11" 188 lbs.

Year	Team		Games	Pos.
1987	**DEN**	**N**	3	S

Bob Fitzke
FITZKE, PAUL FREDERICK HERMAN
B. Jul. 30, 1900, La Crosse, WI
D. Jun. 30, 1950, Sacramento, CA
Wyoming/Idaho 5'10" 195 lbs.

Year	Team		Games	Pos.
1925	**FRA**	**N**	16	HB, FB

Scott Fitzkee
FITZKEE, SCOTT AUSTIN
B. Aug. 4, 1957, York, PA
Penn State 6'0" 187 lbs.

Year	Team		Games	Pos.
1979	**PHI**	**N**	15	WR
1980			7	WR
1981	**SD**	**N**	5	WR
1982			9	WR

4 yrs. 36 games

James FitzPatrick
FITZPATRICK, JAMES
B. Feb. 1, 1964, Heidelberg, Germany
Southern California 6'8" 305 lbs.

Year	Team		Games	Pos.
1986	**SD**	**N**	4	OT
1987			10	OT
1988			11	OT
1989			13	OT
1990	**LARI**	**N**	11	OT
1991			16	OT

6 yrs. 65 games

Jack Flagerman
FLAGERMAN, JACK M.
B. Mar. 27, 1922, San Francisco, CA
St. Mary's (California) 6'0" 218 lbs.

Year	Team		Games	Pos.
1948	**LA**	**AA**	14	C

Terrence Flagler
FLAGLER, R. TERRENCE
B. Sep. 24, 1964, New York, NY
Clemson 6'0" 200 lbs.

Year	Team		Games	Pos.
1987	**SF**	**N**	3	RB
1988			3	RB
1989			15	RB
1990	**PHX**	**N**	13	RB
1991			7	RB

5 yrs. 41 games

Dick Flaherty
FLAHERTY, RICHARD (Red)
B. Aug. 8, 1900
D. Feb., 1984, Spokane, WA
Marquette 5'10" 200 lbs.

Year	Team		Games	Pos.
1926	**GB**	**N**	12	E

Harry Flaherty
FLAHERTY, HAROLD
B. Dec. 15, 1961
Holy Cross 6'1" 232 lbs.

Year	Team		Games	Pos.
1987	**DAL**	**N**	2	LB

Jim Flaherty
FLAHERTY, JAMES
B. Dec. 26, 1895
D. Jan., 1978, Winter Haven, FL

Jim Flaherty *continued*
Georgetown (DC) 204 lbs.

Year	Team		Games	Pos.
1923	**CHIB**	**N**	11	E, HB

Pat Flaherty
FLAHERTY, PATRICK
None

Year	Team		Games	Pos.
1926	**BKN**	**A**	1	HB

Ray Flaherty
FLAHERTY, RAYMOND PAUL
B. Sep. 1, 1904, Spokane, WA
D. Jul. 19, 1994, Coeur d'Alene, ID
Gonzaga 6'0" 190 lbs.

Year	Team		Games	Pos.
1926	**LA**	**A**	14	E
1927	**NYY**	**N**	13	E
1928	**NYG**	**N**	1	E
1928	**NYY**	**N**	11	E
1929	**NYG**	**N**	15	E
1931			13	E
1932			12	E
1933			11	E
1934			9	E
1935			2	E

9 yrs. 101 games

Tom Flaherty
FLAHERTY, TOM
B. Sep. 24, 1964
Northwestern 6'3" 223 lbs.

Year	Team		Games	Pos.
1987	**CIN**	**N**	3	LB

Dick Flanagan
FLANAGAN, RICHARD E.
B. Oct. 31, 1927, Sidney, OH
Ohio State 6'0" 216 lbs.

Year	Team		Games	Pos.
1948	**CHIB**	**N**	11	G
1949			12	G
1950	**DET**	**N**	7	G
1951			12	G
1952			12	G
1953	**PIT**	**N**	12	G
1954			5	G
1955			12	C

8 yrs. 83 games

Ed Flanagan
FLANAGAN, EDWARD JOSEPH
B. Feb. 23, 1944, Altoona, PA
Purdue 6'3" 246 lbs.

Year	Team		Games	Pos.
1965	**DET**	**N**	14	C
1966			14	C
1967			14	C
1968			14	C
1969			14	C
1970			14	C
1971			14	C
1972			14	C
1973			14	C
1974			13	C
1975	**SD**	**N**	14	C
1976			12	C

12 yrs. 165 games

Hoot Flanagan
FLANAGAN, WILLIAM HAROLD
B. Apr. 27, 1901, Buckhannon, WV
D. Feb. 3, 1976, Martinsburg, WV
West Virginia Wesleyan/Pittsburgh 6'0" 169 lbs.

Year	Team		Games	Pos.
1925	**POT**	**N**	10	HB, FB
1926			8	HB

2 yrs. 18 games

Latham Flanagan
FLANAGAN, LATHAM
B. Jan. 14, 1907, Buckhannon, WV

Latham Flanagan continued

D. May, 1981, Downtown, OR
Carnegie-Mellon 6'2" 185 lbs.

Year	Team	Games	Pos.
1931	CHIB N	2	E
1931	CHIC N	2	E
1 yr.	4 games		

Jim Flanigan

FLANIGAN, JAMES MICHAEL, SR.
B. Apr. 15, 1945, Pittsburgh, PA
Pittsburgh 6'3" 238 lbs.

Year	Team	Games	Pos.
1967	GB N	12	LB
1968		13	LB
1969		4	LB
1970		11	LB
1971	NO N	14	LB
5 yrs.	54 games		

Jim Flanigan

FLANIGAN, JAMES MICHAEL, JR.
B. Aug. 27, 1971, Green Bay, WI
Notre Dame 6'2" 280 lbs.

Year	Team	Games	Pos.
1994	CHI N	14	DT
1995		16	DT
1996		14	DT
3 yrs.	44 games		

John Flannery

FLANNERY, JOHN JOSEPH
B. Jan. 13, 1969, Pottsville, PA
Syracuse 6'3" 304 lbs.

Year	Team	Games	Pos.
1991	HOU N	16	C
1992		15	C, G
1994		16	C
1996	DAL N	1	G
4 yrs.	48 games		

Flannigan

FLANNIGAN
None

Year	Team	Games	Pos.
1924	ROC N	1	HB

Bill Flannigan

FLANNIGAN, WILLIAM
B. 1901
Deceased
None 210 lbs.

Year	Team	Games	Pos.
1926	LOU N	2	T

Paul Flatley

FLATLEY, PAUL RICHARD
B. Jan. 30, 1941, Richmond, IN
Northwestern 6'1" 187 lbs.

Year	Team	Games	Pos.
1963	MIN N	14	HB
1964		10	OE
1965		14	OE
1966		13	OE
1967		13	OE
1968	ATL N	14	OE
1969		14	WR
1970		14	WR
8 yrs.	106 games		

Willie Flattery

FLATTERY, WILSON I. (Pud)
B. 1902
Deceased
Wooster 6'0" 220 lbs.

Year	Team	Games	Pos.
1925	CAN N	6	G
1926		10	G, E
2 yrs.	16 games		

Jack Flavin

FLAVIN, JOHN
B. 1900

Jack Flavin continued

Deceased
Georgetown (DC) 5'11" 175 lbs.

Year	Team	Games	Pos.
1923	BUF N	1	FB
1924		2	FB
2 yrs.	3 games		

Bill Fleckenstein

FLECKENSTEIN, WILLIAM P.
B. Nov. 4, 1903
D. Jan., 1967
Carleton/Iowa 6'1" 208 lbs.

Year	Team	Games	Pos.
1925	CHIB N	15	G
1926		10	C, G, E
1927		10	G
1928		12	G, C
1929		15	G, E
1930		2	E
1930	POR N	10	E, G
1931	FRA N	6	G, E
1931	BKN N	2	C, G
7 yrs.	82 games		

Jack Fleischman

FLEISCHMAN, GOFRID J. (Butter)
B. Michigan
D. Apr. 27, 1988
Purdue 5'6" 184 lbs.

Year	Team	Games	Pos.
1925	DET N	9	G, C
1926		12	G
1927	PRO N	14	G, T
1928		11	G
1929		12	G
5 yrs.	58 games		

Bill Fleming

FLEMING, WILMER
B. Jun. 28, 1903
Deceased
Mount Union 5'11" 165 lbs.

Year	Team	Games	Pos.
1925	CAN N	1	HB

Cory Fleming

FLEMING, CORY LAMONT
B. Mar. 19, 1971, Nashville, TN
Tennessee 6'1" 207 lbs.

Year	Team	Games	Pos.
1994	DAL N	2	WR
1995		14	WR
2 yrs.	16 games		

Don Fleming

FLEMING, DONALD
B. Jun. 11, 1937, Bellaire, OH
D. Jun. 4, 1963, FL
Florida 6'0" 187 lbs.

Year	Team	Games	Pos.
1960	CLE N	12	DB
1961		14	DB
1962		12	DB
3 yrs.	38 games		

George Fleming

FLEMING, GEORGE
B. 1938
Washington 5'11" 188 lbs.

Year	Team	Games	Pos.
1961	OAK A	14	HB

Marv Fleming

FLEMING, MARVIN
B. Jan. 2, 1942, Longview, TX
Utah 6'4" 233 lbs.

Year	Team	Games	Pos.
1963	GB N	14	OE
1964		14	OE
1965		13	OE
1966		14	TE
1967		14	TE
1968		14	TE
1969		12	TE

Marv Fleming continued

Year	Team	Games	Pos.
1970	MIA N	14	TE
1971		14	TE
1972		14	TE
1973		11	TE
1974		14	TE
12 yrs.	162 games		

Mack Flenniken

FLENNIKEN, MAX
B. 1906
D. May 26, 1956
Geneva 6'1" 200 lbs.

Year	Team	Games	Pos.
1930	CHIC N	8	HB, FB
1931	NYG N	2	HB, FB
2 yrs.	10 games		

Andy Fletcher

FLETCHER, ANDY
Maryland

Year	Team	Games	Pos.
1921	TON A	1	HB

Billy Fletcher

FLETCHER, BILLY RAY
B. May 2, 1943, Memphis, TN
Memphis State 5'10" 190 lbs.

Year	Team	Games	Pos.
1966	DEN A	1	DB

Chris Fletcher

FLETCHER, CHRISTOPHER C.
B. Dec. 25, 1948, Morristown, NJ
Temple/U.S. International 5'11" 186 lbs.

Year	Team	Games	Pos.
1970	SD N	13	DB
1971		14	CB
1972		1	S
1973		9	S
1974		12	S
1975		14	S
1976		13	S
7 yrs.	76 games		

John Fletcher

FLETCHER, JOHN
B. Aug. 22, 1965, Uvalde, TX
Texas A&I-Kingsville 6'3" 293 lbs.

Year	Team	Games	Pos.
1987	CIN N	3	G

Ollie Fletcher

FLETCHER, OLIVER
B. 1924
Southern California 6'3" 210 lbs.

Year	Team	Games	Pos.
1949	LA AA	3	G
1950	BAL N	2	G, LB
2 yrs.	5 games		

Simon Fletcher

FLETCHER, SIMON RAYNARD
B. Feb. 18, 1962, Bay City, TX
Houston 6'5" 240 lbs.

Year	Team	Games	Pos.
1985	DEN N	16	NT
1986		16	DE
1987		12	DE
1988		16	LB, DE
1989		16	LB
1990		16	LB
1991		16	LB
1992		16	LB
1993		16	LB
1994		16	LB
1995		16	DE
11 yrs.	172 games		

Terrell Fletcher

FLETCHER, TERRELL
B. Sep. 14, 1973, St. Louis, MO

Terrell Fletcher continued

Wisconsin 5'8" 196 lbs.

Year	Team	Games	Pos.
1995	SD N	16	RB
1996		16	RB
2 yrs.	32 games		

Tom Flick

FLICK, TOM
B. Aug. 30, 1958, Patuxent River, MD
Washington 6'3" 190 lbs.

Year	Team	Games	Pos.
1981	WAS N	6	QB
1982	NE N	3	QB
1984	CLE N	1	QB
1986	SD N	11	QB
4 yrs.	21 games		

Paul Flinn

FLINN, PAUL A.
B. Sep. 11, 1895
Deceased
Minnesota 5'11" 180 lbs.

Year	Team	Games	Pos.
1922	MIN N	3	E
1923		8	E
2 yrs.	11 games		

George Flint

FLINT, GEORGE
B. Feb. 20, 1939, Erie, PA
Arizona State 6'4" 243 lbs.

Year	Team	Games	Pos.
1962	BUF A	14	OT
1963		9	G
1964		14	G
1965		14	G
1968		14	G
5 yrs.	65 games		

Judson Flint

FLINT, JUDSON
B. Jan. 26, 1957, Farrell, PA
California State (PA)/Memphis State 6'0" 201 lbs.

Year	Team	Games	Pos.
1980	CLE N	13	CB
1981		16	CB
1982		9	CB
1983	BUF N	1	S
4 yrs.	39 games		

Brian Flones

FLONES, BRIAN
B. Sep. 1, 1959, Mount Vernon, WA
Washington State 6'1" 228 lbs.

Year	Team	Games	Pos.
1981	SEA N	4	LB
1982		9	LB
2 yrs.	13 games		

Anthony Florence

FLORENCE, ANTHONY W.
B. Dec. 11, 1966, Delray Beach, FL
Bethune-Cookman 6'0" 185 lbs.

Year	Team	Games	Pos.
1991	CLE N	6	CB

Paul Florence

FLORENCE, PAUL ROBERT
B. Apr. 22, 1900, Chicago, IL
D. May 28, 1986, Gainesville, FL
Loyola (Illinois)/Georgetown 6'1" 178 lbs.

Year	Team	Games	Pos.
1920	CHIC A	6	E

Mike Flores

FLORES, MIKE
B. Dec. 1, 1966, Youngstown, OH
Louisville 6'3" 256 lbs.

Year	Team	Games	Pos.
1991	PHI N	4	DE
1992		15	DE
1993		16	DE

Year	Team	Games	Pos.

Mike Flores continued

Year	Team	Games	Pos.
1994		15	DE
1995	WAS N	10	DE
1995	SF N	1	DE
5 yrs.	61 games		

Tom Flores
FLORES, THOMAS RAYMOND
B. Mar. 21, 1937, Fresno, CA
Pacific 6'1" 194 lbs.

1960	OAK A	14	QB
1961		14	QB
1963		14	QB
1964		14	QB
1965		14	QB
1966		14	QB
1967	BUF A	13	QB
1968		1	QB
1969		2	QB
1969	KC A	11	QB
9 yrs.	111 games		

Jim Flower
FLOWER, JAMES T.
B. Oct. 17, 1895
D. May 6, 1965
Ohio State 6'1" 193 lbs.

1920	COL A	5	E
1921	AKR A	10	E, G, T
1922	AKR N	10	C, G
1923		7	T, E, C
1924		8	T, C
1925		1	T
6 yrs.	41 games		

Bernie Flowers
FLOWERS, BENJAMIN BERNARD
B. Feb. 14, 1930, Erie, PA
Purdue 6'2" 190 lbs.

1956	BAL	1	E

Bob Flowers
FLOWERS, ROBERT C.
B. Aug. 6, 1917, Big Springs, TX
Deceased
Texas Tech 6'1" 210 lbs.

1942	GB N	2	C
1943		10	C
1944		9	C
1945		10	C
1946		10	C
1947		12	C
1948		11	C
7 yrs.	64 games		

Charlie Flowers
FLOWERS, CHARLES
B. 1937
Mississippi 6'1" 215 lbs.

1960	LA A		FB
1961	SD A	14	FB
1962	NY A	4	FB
3 yrs.	18 games		

Dick Flowers
FLOWERS, RICHARD R.
B. Aug. 13, 1927, South Bend, IN
Northwestern 6'0" 190 lbs.

1953	BAL N	1	QB

Keith Flowers
FLOWERS, KEITH
B. 1931, Perryton, TX
Texas Christian 6'0" 211 lbs.

1952	DAL	6	C, G, FB

Kenny Flowers
FLOWERS, KENNETH C.
B. Mar. 14, 1964, Daytona Beach, FL
Clemson 6'0" 210 lbs.

1987	ATL N	8	RB
1989		16	RB
2 yrs.	24 games		

Larry Flowers
FLOWERS, LARRY DARNELL
B. Apr. 19, 1958, Temple, TX
Texas Tech 6'1" 195 lbs.

1981	NYG N	16	CB
1982		6	S
1983		14	S
1984		16	S
1985		9	S
1985	NYJ N	7	S
5 yrs.	68 games		

Lethon Flowers
FLOWERS, LETHON
B. Jan. 14, 1973, Columbia, SC
Georgia Tech 6'0" 202 lbs.

1995	PIT N	10	CB
1996		16	CB
2 yrs.	26 games		

Richmond Flowers
FLOWERS, RICHMOND MCDAVID, JR.
B. Jun. 13, 1947, Montgomery, AL
Tennessee 6'0" 181 lbs.

1969	DAL N	6	WR
1970		14	S
1971		5	S
1971	NYG N	8	S
1972		14	S
1973		8	S
5 yrs.	55 games		

Bobby Jack Floyd
FLOYD, BOBBY JACK
B. Dec. 8, 1929, Paris, TX
Texas Christian 6'0" 210 lbs.

1952	GB N	12	FB
1953	CHIB N	6	FB
2 yrs.	18 games		

Don Floyd
FLOYD, DONALD WAYNE
B. Jul. 10, 1938, Abilene, TX
Texas Christian 6'4" 242 lbs.

1960	HOU A	14	DE
1961		14	DE
1962		14	DE
1963		9	DE
1964		14	DE
1965		14	DE
1966		6	DE
1967		12	DE
8 yrs.	97 games		

Eric Floyd
FLOYD, ERIC CUNNINGHAM
B. Oct. 28, 1965, Rome, GA
Auburn 6'5" 305 lbs.

1990	SD N	16	OT
1991		2	OT
1992	PHI N	16	G, OT
1993		3	G
1995	ARI N	1	G
5 yrs.	38 games		

George Floyd
FLOYD, GEORGE, JR.
B. Dec. 21, 1960, Tampa, FL

George Floyd continued
Eastern Kentucky 5'11" 190 lbs.

1982	NYJ N	7	S
1984		8	S, CB
2 yrs.	15 games		

John Floyd
FLOYD, JOHN MANUEL
B. Sep. 10, 1956, Big Sandy, TX
Northeast Louisiana 6'1" 195 lbs.

1979	SD N	8	WR
1980		15	WR
1981	STL N	4	WR
3 yrs.	27 games		

Malcolm Floyd
Born MALCOLM SEABORN
B. Dec. 29, 1972, San Francisco, CA
Fresno State 6'0" 194 lbs.

1996	HOU N	16	WR

Owen Floyd
FLOYD, OWEN (Slivers)
B. Dec. 7, 1896
D. 1960
Rose-Hulman Tech 6'0" 195 lbs.

1920	MUN A	1	C
1921		2	C
2 yrs.	3 games		

Victor Floyd
FLOYD, VICTOR LEONARD
B. Jan. 24, 1966, Pensacola, FL
Florida State 6'1" 201 lbs.

1989	SD N	6	RB

William Floyd
FLOYD, WILLIAM ALI (Bar None)
B. Feb. 17, 1972, St. Petersburg, FL
Florida State 6'1" 242 lbs.

1994	SF N	16	RB
1995		8	RB
1996		10	FB
3 yrs.	34 games		

Darren Flutie
FLUTIE, DARREN PAUL
B. Nov. 18, 1966, Baltimore, MD
Boston College 5'10" 184 lbs.

1988	SD N	16	WR

Doug Flutie
FLUTIE, DOUG
B. Oct. 23, 1962, Manchester, MD
Boston College 5'9" 176 lbs.

1986	CHI N	4	QB
1987		1	QB
1987	NE N	1	QB
1988		11	QB
1989		5	QB
4 yrs.	22 games		

Don Flynn
FLYNN, DONALD
B. 1935
Houston 6'0" 205 lbs.

1960	DAL A		DB
1961		6	DB
1961	NY A	7	DB
2 yrs.	13 games		

Furlong Flynn
FLYNN, FURLONG H.
B. Dec. 27, 1901, Waterford, NY
D. Nov. 1, 1977, Vernon, CT

Furlong Flynn continued
Cornell 6'0" 210 lbs.

1926	HAR N	8	G, T

Tom Flynn
FLYNN, THOMAS JEFFERY
B. Mar. 24, 1962, Verona, PA
Pittsburgh 6'0" 195 lbs.

1984	GB N	15	S
1985		15	S
1986		7	S
1986	NYG N	2	S
1987		12	S
1988		16	S
5 yrs.	67 games		

Mark Flythe
FLYTHE, MARK
B. Oct. 4, 1968, Philadelphia, PA
Penn State 6'7" 290 lbs.

1993	NYG N	2	DE

Fred Foggie
FOGGIE, FREDERICK JEROME
B. Jun. 10, 1969, Waterloo, SC
Minnesota 6'0" 188 lbs.

1992	CLE N	2	CB, S
1994	PIT N	3	DB
2 yrs.	5 games		

Hank Foldberg
FOLDBERG, HENRY CHRISTIAN, JR.
B. Mar. 12, 1923, Dallas, TX
Army 6'1" 203 lbs.

1948	BKN AA	13	E
1949	CHI AA	12	E
2 yrs.	25 games		

Dave Foley
FOLEY, DAVID
B. Oct. 28, 1947, Cincinnati, OH
Ohio State 6'5" 252 lbs.

1970	NYJ N	14	OT
1971		14	OT
1972	BUF N	12	OT
1973		14	OT
1974		14	OT
1975		14	OT
1976		14	OT
1977		13	OT
8 yrs.	109 games		

Glenn Foley
FOLEY, GLENN EDWARD
B. Oct. 10, 1970, Cherry Hill, NJ
Boston College 6'2" 205 lbs.

1994	NYJ N	1	QB
1995		1	QB
1996		5	QB
3 yrs.	7 games		

Jim Foley
FOLEY, JAMES E. (Shrimp)
B. 1903
Deceased
Syracuse 5'8" 165 lbs.

1926	HAR N	9	HB, QB, FB

Steve Foley
FOLEY, STEPHEN JAMES
B. Nov. 11, 1953, New Orleans, LA
Tulane 6'3" 190 lbs.

1976	DEN N	14	S
1977		13	S
1978		16	S

Year	Team	Games	Pos.

Steve Foley *continued*

1979		16	CB
1980		16	CB
1981		16	CB
1982		1	S
1983		14	S
1984		16	S
1985		12	S
1986		16	S
11 yrs.	150 games		

Tim Foley
FOLEY, THOMAS DAVID
B. Jan. 22, 1948, Evanston, IL
Purdue 6'0" 194 lbs.

1970	MIA	N	14	DB
1971			14	CB
1972			14	CB
1973			11	CB
1974			13	CB
1975			14	CB
1976			2	CB
1977			14	CB, S
1978			16	S, CB
1979			15	S, CB
1980			7	S
11 yrs.	134 games		

Tim Foley
FOLEY, TIM J.
B. May 30, 1958, Cincinnati, OH
Notre Dame 6'6" 275 lbs.

| 1981 | BAL | N | 6 | OT |

Dick Folk
FOLK, RICHARD
B. Jul. 27, 1916
D. Jun., 1970, Bishopville, SC
Arkansas State/Illinois Wesleyan 6'0" 200 lbs.

| 1939 | BKN | N | 2 | B |

Lee Folkins
FOLKINS, LEE
B. Jul. 4, 1939, Wallace, ID
Washington 6'5" 219 lbs.

1961	GB	N	14	OE
1962	DAL	N	14	OE
1963			13	OE
1964			14	OE
1965	PIT	N	8	WR
5 yrs.	63 games		

Beryl Follet
FOLLET, BERYL
B. Apr. 26, 1903
D. May, 1982, Stony Brook, NY
New York University 5'9" 165 lbs.

1930	SI	N	10	QB, HB
1931			2	FB, HB
2 yrs.	12 games		

Brendan Folmar
FOLMAR, BRENDAN ARTHUR
B. Apr. 2, 1964, Birmingham, AL
California (Pennsylvania) 6'1" 200 lbs.

| 1987 | DET | N | 1 | QB |

Steve Folsom
FOLSOM, STEVEN MARK
B. Mar. 21, 1958, Los Angeles, CA
Long Beach State/Utah 6'4" 230 lbs.

1981	PHI	N	3	TE
1982	NYG	N	2	TE
1987	DAL	N	9	TE
1988			16	TE

Steve Folsom *continued*

1989		16	TE
1990		1	TE
6 yrs.	47 games		

James Folston
FOLSTON, JAMES EDWARD
B. Aug. 14, 1971, Cocoa, FL
Northeast Louisiana 6'3" 240 lbs.

1994	LARI	N	7	LB
1995	OAK	N	15	LB
1996			12	LB
3 yrs.	34 games		

Vern Foltz
FOLTZ, VERNON
B. Aug. 27, 1918, Clearfield, PA
St. Vincent's 6'1" 205 lbs.

1944	WAS	N	10	C
1945	PIT	N	4	C
2 yrs.	14 games		

Art Folz
FOLZ, ARTHUR
B. 1902
Deceased
Chicago 158 lbs.

1923	CHIC	N	3	QB, HB, FB
1924			9	HB, QB
1925			5	HB, QB, FB
3 yrs.	17 games		

Al Fontenot
FONTENOT, ALBERT PAUL
B. Sep. 17, 1970, Houston, TX
Baylor 6'4" 265 lbs.

1993	CHI	N	16	DE
1994			16	DT, DE
1995			13	DE
1996			16	DE
4 yrs.	61 games		

Herman Fontenot
FONTENOT, HERMAN J.
B. Sep. 12, 1963, St. Elizabeth, TX
Louisiana State 6'0" 206 lbs.

1985	CLE	N	9	RB
1986			16	RB
1987			12	RB
1988			16	RB
1989	GB	N	16	RB
1990			14	RB
6 yrs.	83 games		

Jerry Fontenot
FONTENOT, JERRY PAUL
B. Nov. 21, 1966, Lafayette, LA
Texas A&M 6'3" 278 lbs.

1989	CHI	N	16	G
1990			16	C, G
1991			16	G
1992			16	G
1993			16	G, C
1994			16	C
1995			16	C
1996			15	C
8 yrs.	127 games		

Wayne Fontes
FONTES, WAYNE HOWARD JOSEPH
B. Feb. 2, 1940, New Bedford, MA
Michigan State 6'0" 190 lbs.

| 1962 | NY | A | 9 | DB |

Chris Foote
FOOTE, CHRIS D.
B. Dec. 2, 1956, Louisville, KY
Southern California 6'4" 260 lbs.

1980	BAL	N	16	C
1981			16	C
1982	NYG	N	7	C
1983			11	C
1987	MIN	N	6	C
1988			16	C
1989			16	C
1990			16	C
8 yrs.	104 games		

Jim Foote
FOOTE, JAMES
B. Sep. 10, 1951, Carlisle, PA
Delaware Valley 6'2" 210 lbs.

| 1974 | HOU | N | 14 | QB |

Dan Footman
FOOTMAN, DAN ELLIS
B. Jan. 13, 1969, Tampa, FL
Florida State 6'5" 285 lbs.

1993	CLE	N	8	DE
1994			16	DE
1995			16	DT
1996	BAL	N	10	DT
4 yrs.	50 games		

Marlon Forbes
FORBES, MARLON
B. Dec. 25, 1971, Long Island, NY
Penn State 6'1" 205 lbs.

| 1996 | CHI | N | 15 | CB, S |

Adrian Ford
FORD, ADRIAN
B. Jan. 1, 1904
D. Jul., 1977, Youngstown, OH
Lafayette 5'10" 190 lbs.

1926	PHI	A	9	HB, E
1927	POT	N	3	E, G
1927	FRA	N	8	HB, QB, E
2 yrs.	20 games		

Bernard Ford
FORD, BERNARD
B. Feb. 27, 1966, Cordele, GA
Central Florida 5'9" 168 lbs.

1989	DAL	N	10	WR
1990	HOU	N	14	WR
2 yrs.	24 games		

Brad Ford
FORD, BRAD
B. Jan. 11, 1974, Alexander City, AL
Alabama 5'10" 170 lbs.

| 1996 | DET | N | 14 | CB |

Charlie Ford
FORD, CHARLES GLENN
B. Dec. 10, 1948, Beaumont, TX
Houston 6'3" 187 lbs.

1971	CHI	N	14	CB
1972			14	CB
1973			13	CB
1974	PHI	N	7	CB
1975	BUF	N	5	CB
1975	NYG	N	8	CB
5 yrs.	61 games		

Chris Ford
FORD, CHRISTOPHER DAVID
B. May 20, 1967, Houston, TX

Chris Ford *continued*
Lamar 6'1" 185 lbs.

| 1990 | TB | N | 1 | WR |

Cole Ford
FORD, COLE
B. Dec. 31, 1972, Tucson, AZ
Southern California 6'2" 195 lbs.

1995	OAK	N	5	K
1996			16	K
2 yrs.	21 games		

Darryl Ford
FORD, DARRYL
B. Jun. 22, 1966, Dallas, TX
New Mexico State 6'1" 225 lbs.

1992	PIT	N	8	LB
1992	DET	N	1	LB
1993			11	LB
1994	ATL	N	15	LB
3 yrs.	35 games		

Fred Ford
FORD, FRED
B. 1938
California Poly (Pomona) 5'8" 180 lbs.

| 1960 | BUF | A | | HB |
| 1960 | LA | A | | HB |

Garrett Ford
FORD, GARRETT, SR.
B. May 4, 1945, Washington, DC
West Virginia 6'2" 230 lbs.

| 1968 | DEN | A | 14 | RB |

Henry Ford
FORD, HENRY
B. Nov. 1, 1931, Homestead, PA
Pittsburgh 6'0" 180 lbs.

1955	CLE	N	2	HB
1956	PIT	N	12	HB
2 yrs.	14 games		

Henry Ford
FORD, HENRY
B. Oct. 30, 1971, Fort Worth, TX
Arkansas 6'3" 284 lbs.

1994	HOU	N	13	DE
1995			16	DE
1996			15	DE
3 yrs.	44 games		

Jim Ford
FORD, JAMES LEON
B. Sep. 11, 1949, Jacksonville, FL
Texas Southern 6'0" 203 lbs.

1971	NO	N	9	RB
1972			5	RB
2 yrs.	14 games		

John Ford
FORD, JOHN ALLEN
B. Jul. 31, 1966, Belle Glade, FL
Virginia 6'2" 204 lbs.

| 1989 | DET | N | 7 | WR |

Len Ford
FORD, LEONARD G.
B. Feb. 18, 1926, Washington, DC
D. Mar. 13, 1972, Detroit, MI
Morgan State/Michigan 6'4" 245 lbs.

1948	LA	AA	14	E
1949			12	E
1950	CLE	N	5	E
1951			12	E

Len Ford *continued*

Year	Team		Games	Pos.
1952			12	E
1953			12	E
1954			12	E
1955			12	E
1956			12	E
1957			11	E
1958	GB	N	11	E
11 yrs.	125 games			

Moses Ford
FORD, MOSES
B. Feb. 9, 1964, Dillon, SC
Fayetteville State 6'2" 220 lbs.

Year	Team		Games	Pos.
1987	PIT	N	1	WR

Salem Ford
FORD, SALEM H.
B. Feb. 14, 1896
D. Jun. 17, 1976, Louisville, KY
Louisville 5'7" 150 lbs.

Year	Team		Games	Pos.
1922	LOU	N	2	HB, QB

Brian Forde
FORDE, BRIAN
B. Nov. 1, 1963, Montreal, Que.
Washington State 6'2" 225 lbs.

Year	Team		Games	Pos.
1988	NO	N	16	LB
1989			16	LB
1990			16	LB
1991			16	LB
4 yrs.	64 games			

Jim Fordham
FORDHAM, JAMES ABNER
B. Dec. 6, 1916, Graymont, GA
D. Apr., 1969
Georgia 5'11" 215 lbs.

Year	Team		Games	Pos.
1944	CHIB	N	10	FB
1945			9	FB
2 yrs.	19 games			

Chuck Foreman
FOREMAN, WALTER EUGENE
B. Oct. 26, 1950, Frederick, MD
Miami (Florida) 6'2" 209 lbs.

Year	Team		Games	Pos.
1973	MIN	N	12	RB
1974			13	RB
1975			14	RB
1976			14	RB
1977			14	RB
1978			14	RB
1979			14	RB
1980	NE	N	16	RB
8 yrs.	111 games			

Bill Forester
FORESTER, GEORGE W.
B. Aug. 9, 1932, Dallas, TX
Southern Methodist 6'3" 237 lbs.

Year	Team		Games	Pos.
1953	GB	N	12	T, LB
1954			12	LB
1955			12	LB
1956			12	LB
1957			12	LB
1958			12	LB
1959			12	LB
1960			12	LB
1961			14	LB
1962			14	LB
1963			14	LB
11 yrs.	138 games			

Herschel Forester
FORESTER, HERSCHEL VINCENT
B. Apr. 14, 1931, Dallas, TX

Herschel Forester *continued*
Southern Methodist 6'0" 230 lbs.

Year	Team		Games	Pos.
1954	CLE	N	12	G
1955			12	G
1956			12	G
1957			12	G
4 yrs.	48 games			

Nick Forkovitch
FORKOVITCH, NICHOLAS J.
B. Mar. 1, 1920
William & Mary 5'11" 195 lbs.

Year	Team		Games	Pos.
1948	BKN	AA	9	B

Phil Forney
FORNEY, PHILLIP L.
B. Sep. 18, 1963, Rutherfordton, NC
East Tennessee State 6'2" 230 lbs.

Year	Team		Games	Pos.
1987	STL	N	3	LB

Ed Forrest
FORREST, EDWIN GEORGE
B. Jun. 12, 1921, San Francisco, CA
Santa Clara 5'11" 210 lbs.

Year	Team		Games	Pos.
1946	SF	AA	11	C, LB
1947			14	G, LB
2 yrs.	25 games			

Tom Forrest
FORREST, THOMAS WESLEY
B. Apr. 11, 1952, Washington, DC
Cincinnati 6'2" 255 lbs.

Year	Team		Games	Pos.
1974	CHI	N	8	G

Fred Forsberg
FORSBERG, FRED CARL
B. Jul. 4, 1944, Tacoma, WA
Washington 6'1" 233 lbs.

Year	Team		Games	Pos.
1968	DEN	A	13	LB
1970	DEN	N	14	LB
1971			14	LB
1972			9	LB
1973			3	LB
1973	BUF	N	7	LB
1974	SD	N	6	LB
6 yrs.	66 games			

Dutch Forst
FORST, ARTHUR H.
B. Feb. 17, 1891
D. Oct., 1963
Villanova 5'8" 195 lbs.

Year	Team		Games	Pos.
1926	PRO	N	2	FB

Aldo Forte
FORTE, HERMAN JOHN
B. Jan. 20, 1918, Chicago, IL
Montana 6'0" 213 lbs.

Year	Team		Games	Pos.
1939	CHIB	N	10	G, T
1940			10	G
1941			11	G
1946	DET	N	3	G
1946	CHIB	N	6	G
1947	GB	N	10	G
5 yrs.	50 games			

Bob Forte
FORTE, ROBERT D.
B. Jul. 15, 1922, Lake Village, AR
Deceased
Arkansas 6'0" 199 lbs.

Year	Team		Games	Pos.
1946	GB	N	9	HB
1947			12	HB
1948			12	HB
1949			12	HB
1950			12	HB

Bob Forte *continued*

Year	Team		Games	Pos.
1952			12	HB
1953			11	HB
7 yrs.	80 games			

Ike Forte
FORTE, DONALD R.
B. Mar. 8, 1954, Texarkana, AR
Arkansas 6'0" 203 lbs.

Year	Team		Games	Pos.
1976	NE	N	10	RB
1977			13	RB
1978	WAS	N	13	RB
1979			11	RB
1980			12	RB
1981	NYG	N	5	RB
6 yrs.	64 games			

Roman Fortin
FORTIN, ROMAN BRIAN
B. Feb. 26, 1967, Columbus, OH
Oregon/San Diego State 6'5" 290 lbs.

Year	Team		Games	Pos.
1991	DET	N	16	OT
1992	ATL	N	16	G
1993			16	G
1994			16	C
1995			16	C
1996			16	C
6 yrs.	96 games			

Danny Fortmann
FORTMANN, DANIEL JOHN
B. Apr. 11, 1916, Pearl River, NY
Colgate 6'0" 210 lbs.

Year	Team		Games	Pos.
1936	CHIB	N	12	G
1937			10	G
1938			11	G
1939			11	G
1940			10	G
1941			11	G
1942			11	G
1943			10	G
8 yrs.	86 games			

Joe Fortunato
FORTUNATO, JOSEPH FRANCIS
B. Mar. 28, 1931, Mingo Junction, OH
Virginia Military Institute/Mississippi State 6'0" 225 lbs.

Year	Team		Games	Pos.
1955	CHIB	N	12	LB
1956			12	LB
1957			12	FB, LB
1958			12	LB
1959			12	LB
1960	CHI	N	12	LB
1961			14	LB
1962			14	LB
1963			14	LB
1964			13	LB
1965			14	LB
1966			14	LB
12 yrs.	155 games			

Bill Fortune
FORTUNE, WILLIAM
B. Oct., 1897
Deceased
Michigan 218 lbs.

Year	Team		Games	Pos.
1924	HAM	N	4	G
1925			5	G, C
2 yrs.	9 games			

Elliott Fortune
FORTUNE, ELLIOTT DAVID
B. May 28, 1974, Roosevelt, NY
Georgia Tech 6'4" 275 lbs.

Year	Team		Games	Pos.
1996	BAL	N	14	DE

Hosea Fortune
FORTUNE, HOSEA
B. Mar. 4, 1959, New Orleans, LA
Rice 6'0" 176 lbs.

Year	Team		Games	Pos.
1983	SD	N	4	WR

John Foruria
FORURIA, JOHN G.
B. Nov. 26, 1944, Emmett, ID
Idaho 6'2" 205 lbs.

Year	Team		Games	Pos.
1967	PIT	N	8	DB
1968			6	LB
2 yrs.	14 games			

Bob Fosdick
FOSDICK, ROBERT E.
B. Nov., 1895
D. Jan. 30, 1990, Tucson, AZ
Iowa 5'10" 225 lbs.

Year	Team		Games	Pos.
1923	MIN	N	5	G

Barry Foster
FOSTER, BARRY
B. Dec. 8, 1968, Hurst, TX
Arkansas 5'10" 223 lbs.

Year	Team		Games	Pos.
1990	PIT	N	16	RB
1991			10	RB
1992			16	RB
1993			9	RB
1994			11	RB
5 yrs.	62 games			

Bob Foster
FOSTER, ROBINS J.
B. Oct., 1886
Deceased
None 188 lbs.

Year	Team		Games	Pos.
1922	RAC	N	9	HB, T, G
1923			9	T, HB, G, FB
1924	MIL	N	2	G
3 yrs.	20 games			

Derrick Foster
FOSTER, DERRICK
B. Oct. 12, 1963
William Paterson 5'11" 205 lbs.

Year	Team		Games	Pos.
1987	NYJ	N	3	RB

Eddie Foster
FOSTER, EDDIE
B. Jun. 5, 1954, Houston, TX
Houston 5'10" 185 lbs.

Year	Team		Games	Pos.
1977	HOU	N	14	WR

Fred Foster
FOSTER, FREDERICK F. (Fritz)
B. Feb. 11, 1899
D. Feb., 1976, Buffalo, NY
Syracuse 5'11" 185 lbs.

Year	Team		Games	Pos.
1923	BUF	N	1	FB
1923	ROC	N	1	FB
1924			4	HB, FB
2 yrs.	6 games			

Geno Foster
FOSTER, IRVING EUGENE
B. Mar. 20, 1942, Salem, NJ
Arizona State 5'11" 214 lbs.

Year	Team		Games	Pos.
1965	SD	A	14	HB
1966			14	HB
1967			10	RB
1968			10	RB
1969			13	RB
1970	SD	N	7	RB
6 yrs.	68 games			

Year	Team		Games	Pos.

Jerome Foster
FOSTER, JEROME
B. Jul. 25, 1960, Detroit, MI
Ohio State 6'2" 270 lbs.

Year	Team		Games	Pos.
1983	**HOU**	N	16	DE
1984			9	DE
1986	**MIA**	N	14	DE
1986	**NYJ**	N	1	DE
1987			4	DE

4 yrs.   44 games

Ralph Foster
FOSTER, RALPH ELSWORTH, JR.
B. Jun. 12, 1917, Perry, OK
Idaho/Oklahoma State 6'1" 230 lbs.

Year	Team		Games	Pos.
1945	**CHIC**	N	9	T
1946			10	T

2 yrs.   19 games

Ron Foster
FOSTER, RONALD CALVIN
B. Nov. 25, 1963, Los Angeles, CA
Northridge State 6'0" 200 lbs.

Year	Team		Games	Pos.
1987	**LARI**	N	3	S

Roy Foster
FOSTER, ROY ALLEN
B. May 24, 1960, Los Angeles, CA
Southern California 6'4" 275 lbs.

Year	Team		Games	Pos.
1982	**MIA**	N	9	G, OT
1983			16	G, OT
1984			16	G, OT
1985			16	G
1986			16	G
1987			12	G
1988			15	G
1989			16	G
1990			16	G
1991	**SF**	N	16	G
1992			16	G
1993			1	G

12 yrs.   165 games

Wally Foster
FOSTER, JAMES WALLACE
B. Oct. 29, 1902, Pittsburgh, PA
D. Aug. 31, 1978, Oakmont, PA
Bucknell 5'10" 165 lbs.

Year	Team		Games	Pos.
1925	**BUF**	N	9	QB

Will Foster
FOSTER, WILL HENRY
B. Oct. 2, 1948, Grady, FL
Eastern Michigan 6'2" 230 lbs.

Year	Team		Games	Pos.
1973	**NE**	N	10	LB
1974			12	LB

2 yrs.   22 games

Elbert Foules
FOULES, ELBERT
B. Jul. 4, 1961, Greenville, MS
Alcorn State 5'11" 185 lbs.

Year	Team		Games	Pos.
1983	**PHI**	N	16	CB, S
1984			16	CB
1985			16	CB
1986			16	CB
1987			9	CB

5 yrs.   73 games

Jamal Fountaine
FOUNTAINE, JAMAL
B. Jan. 29, 1971, San Francisco, CA
Washington 6'3" 240 lbs.

Year	Team		Games	Pos.
1995	**SF**	N	7	DE

John Fourcade
FOURCADE, JOHN CHARLES, JR.
B. Oct. 11, 1960, Gretna, LA
Mississippi 6'1" 208 lbs.

Year	Team		Games	Pos.
1987	**NO**	N	3	QB
1988			1	QB
1989			13	QB
1990			7	QB

4 yrs.   24 games

Keith Fourcade
FOURCADE, KEITH J.
B. Oct. 20, 1961, Marrero, LA
Mississippi 5'11" 225 lbs.

Year	Team		Games	Pos.
1987	**NO**	N	2	LB

Sid Fournet
FOURNET, SIDNEY
B. Aug. 27, 1932
Louisiana State 6'0" 235 lbs.

Year	Team		Games	Pos.
1955	**LA**	N	12	G
1956			12	G
1957	**PIT**	N	2	G
1960	**DAL**	A		G
1961			14	G
1962	**NY**	A	14	G
1963			14	G

7 yrs.   68 games

Dan Fouts
FOUTS, DANIEL FRANCIS
B. Jun. 10, 1951, San Francisco, CA
Oregon 6'3" 204 lbs.

Year	Team		Games	Pos.
1973	**SD**	N	10	QB
1974			11	QB
1975			10	QB
1976			14	QB
1977			4	QB
1978			15	QB
1979			16	QB
1980			16	QB
1981			16	QB
1982			9	QB
1983			10	QB
1984			13	QB
1985			14	QB
1986			12	QB
1987			11	QB

15 yrs.   181 games

Amos Fowler
FOWLER, AMOS EMANUEL
B. Feb. 11, 1956, Pensacola, FL
Southern Mississippi 6'3" 250 lbs.

Year	Team		Games	Pos.
1978	**DET**	N	16	G
1979			12	G
1980			13	C
1981			16	C
1982			9	C
1983			16	C
1984			15	C

7 yrs.   97 games

Aubrey Fowler
FOWLER, ROBERT A.
B. Jun. 12, 1920, Hamburg, AR
Arkansas 5'10" 160 lbs.

Year	Team		Games	Pos.
1948	**BAL**	AA	14	HB, DB

Bobby Fowler
FOWLER, BOBBY LANE
B. Sep. 11, 1960, Temple, TX
Texas-El Paso/Louisiana Tech 6'2" 230 lbs.

Year	Team		Games	Pos.
1985	**NO**	N	10	TE

Bobby Fowler
FOWLER, ROBERT
B. 1936
Martin JC 5'11" 212 lbs.

Year	Team		Games	Pos.
1962	**NY**	A	1	FB

Charlie Fowler
FOWLER, CHARLES CLARK
B. Nov. 10, 1944, Nashville, TN
Auburn/Houston 6'2" 260 lbs.

Year	Team		Games	Pos.
1967	**MIA**	A	6	G, OT
1968			14	G, OT

2 yrs.   20 games

Dan Fowler
FOWLER, DANIEL GABRIEL
B. Apr. 12, 1956, Euclid, OH
Kentucky 6'5" 260 lbs.

Year	Team		Games	Pos.
1979	**NYG**	N	1	G

Jerry Fowler
FOWLER, JERRY
B. 1940
Northwestern State (Louisiana) 6'3" 255 lbs.

Year	Team		Games	Pos.
1964	**HOU**	A	4	OT

Todd Fowler
FOWLER, STEVEN TODD
B. Jun. 9, 1962, Van, TX
Stephen F. Austin 6'3" 221 lbs.

Year	Team		Games	Pos.
1985	**DAL**	N	8	RB
1986			16	RB
1987			12	RB
1988			16	RB

4 yrs.   52 games

Wayne Fowler
FOWLER, WAYNE
B. Sep. 18, 1948, Glen Burnie, MD
Richmond 6'3" 260 lbs.

Year	Team		Games	Pos.
1970	**BUF**	N	10	OT

Willmer Fowler
FOWLER, WILLMER
B. Jun. 3, 1937, Andalusia, AL
Northwestern 5'11" 185 lbs.

Year	Team		Games	Pos.
1960	**BUF**	A		HB
1961			2	HB

2 yrs.   2 games

Dennis Fowlkes
FOWLKES, DENNIS JAMES
B. Mar. 11, 1961, Columbus, OH
West Virginia 6'2" 240 lbs.

Year	Team		Games	Pos.
1983	**MIN**	N	11	LB
1984			14	LB
1985			15	LB
1987	**MIA**	N	3	LB

4 yrs.   43 games

Chas Fox
FOX, CHARLES
B. Oct. 3, 1963, Lafayette, IN
Furman 5'11" 180 lbs.

Year	Team		Games	Pos.
1986	**STL**	N	4	WR

Mike Fox
FOX, MIKE
B. Aug. 5, 1967, Akron, OH
West Virginia 6'6" 275 lbs.

Year	Team		Games	Pos.
1990	**NYG**	N	16	DE
1991			15	DE
1992			16	DE

Mike Fox continued

Year	Team		Games	Pos.
1993			16	DE
1994			16	DE
1995	**CAR**	N	16	DE
1996			11	DE

7 yrs.   106 games

Sam Fox
FOX, SAMUEL S.
B. Jun. 19, 1920
D. Nov., 1987, Shelby, NC
Ohio State 6'2" 215 lbs.

Year	Team		Games	Pos.
1945	**NYG**	N	8	E

Scott Fox
FOX, SCOTT
B. Dec. 28, 1963
Austin Peay 6'2" 222 lbs.

Year	Team		Games	Pos.
1987	**HOU**	N	2	LB

Terry Fox
FOX, TERRENCE P.
B. Jul. 6, 1919, Newark, NJ
Miami (Florida) 6'1" 208 lbs.

Year	Team		Games	Pos.
1941	**PHI**	N	11	FB
1945			2	FB
1946	**MIA**	AA	8	FB

3 yrs.   21 games

Tim Fox
FOX, TIMOTHY RICHARD
B. Nov. 1, 1953, Canton, OH
Ohio State 5'11" 188 lbs.

Year	Team		Games	Pos.
1976	**NE**	N	13	S
1977			14	S
1978			16	S
1979			16	S
1980			16	S
1981			16	S
1982	**SD**	N	7	S
1983			12	S
1984			11	S
1985	**LARM**	N	6	S
1986			14	S

11 yrs.   141 games

Dion Foxx
FOXX, DION LAMONT
B. Jun. 11, 1971, Richmond, VA
James Madison 6'3" 249 lbs.

Year	Team		Games	Pos.
1994	**MIA**	N	16	LB
1995			2	LB
1995	**WAS**	N	2	LB

2 yrs.   20 games

Dick Frahm
FRAHM, HERALD SAMUEL
B. Apr. 6, 1906
D. Oct. 19, 1977, St. Louis, MO
Nebraska 5'10" 195 lbs.

Year	Team		Games	Pos.
1932	**SI**	N	9	HB, DB
1935	**PHI**	N	1	HB, DB
1935	**BOS**	N	1	HB, DB

2 yrs.   11 games

Todd Frain
FRAIN, TODD L.
B. Jan. 31, 1962, Council Bluffs, IA
Nebraska 6'3" 240 lbs.

Year	Team		Games	Pos.
1986	**WAS**	N	1	TE
1987	**NE**	N	3	TE

2 yrs.   4 games

Bill Fralic
FRALIC, WILLIAM P., JR.

Year	Team	Games	Pos.

Bill Fralic continued
B. Oct. 31, 1962, Penn Hills, PA
Pittsburgh 6'5" 280 lbs.

Year	Team		Games	Pos.
1985	ATL	N	15	OT
1986			16	G, OT
1987			12	OT, G
1988			14	OT, G
1989			15	G, OT
1990			16	G
1991			12	G
1992			16	G
1993	DET	N	16	G
9 yrs.			132 games	

Doug France
FRANCE, FREDERICK DOUGLAS, JR.
B. Apr. 26, 1953, Dayton, OH
Ohio State 6'5" 270 lbs.

Year	Team		Games	Pos.
1975	LA	N	14	OT
1976			14	OT
1977			13	OT
1978			16	OT
1979			16	OT
1980			16	OT
1981			8	OT
1983	HOU	N	13	OT
8 yrs.			110 games	

Pete Franceschi
FRANCESCHI, PETER L.
B. 1920
San Francisco 5'9" 170 lbs.

Year	Team		Games	Pos.
1946	SF	AA	9	HB

Jason Franci
FRANCI, JASON ARTHUR
B. Oct. 17, 1943, Gualala, CA
California-Santa Barbara 6'1" 210 lbs.

Year	Team		Games	Pos.
1966	DEN	A	10	OE

Dave Francis
FRANCIS, DAVID L.
B. Apr. 15, 1941, Columbus, OH
Ohio State 6'1" 210 lbs.

Year	Team		Games	Pos.
1963	WAS	N	8	FB

Gene Francis
FRANCIS, EUGENE A.
B. Jul. 1, 1903
D. Nov., 1968, Wickenburg, AZ
Chicago 5'10" 190 lbs.

Year	Team		Games	Pos.
1926	CHIC	N	10	FB, E

James Francis
FRANCIS, JAMES
B. Aug. 4, 1968, Houston, TX
Baylor 6'5" 252 lbs.

Year	Team		Games	Pos.
1990	CIN	N	16	LB
1991			16	LB
1992			14	LB
1993			14	LB
1994			16	LB
1995			11	LB
1996			16	LB
7 yrs.			103 games	

Jeff Francis
FRANCIS, JEFFREY LEE
B. Jul. 7, 1966, Park Ridge, IL
Tennessee 6'4" 225 lbs.

Year	Team		Games	Pos.
1990	CLE	N	1	QB
1992			2	QB
2 yrs.			3 games	

Joe Francis
FRANCIS, JOSEPH
B. Apr. 21, 1936, Honolulu, HI
Oregon State 6'1" 195 lbs.

Year	Team		Games	Pos.
1958	GB	N	12	QB
1959			12	QB
2 yrs.			24 games	

Jon Francis
FRANCIS, CHARLES NAEKAUNA
B. Jun. 21, 1964, Corvallis, OR
Colorado State/Boise State 5'11" 207 lbs.

Year	Team		Games	Pos.
1987	LARM	N	9	RB

Phil Francis
FRANCIS, PHILLIP K.
B. Jan. 10, 1957, Kewanee, IL
Stanford 6'1" 205 lbs.

Year	Team		Games	Pos.
1979	SF	N	16	RB
1980			5	RB
2 yrs.			21 games	

Ron Francis
FRANCIS, RONALD BERNARD
B. Apr. 7, 1964, La Marque, TX
Baylor 5'9" 199 lbs.

Year	Team		Games	Pos.
1987	DAL	N	11	CB
1988			13	CB
1989			15	CB
1990			15	CB
4 yrs.			54 games	

Russ Francis
FRANCIS, RUSSELL ROSS
B. Apr. 3, 1953, Seattle, WA
Oregon 6'6" 242 lbs.

Year	Team		Games	Pos.
1975	NE	N	14	TE
1976			13	TE
1977			10	TE
1978			15	TE
1979			12	TE
1980			15	TE
1982	SF	N	9	TE
1983			16	TE
1984			10	TE
1985			16	TE
1986			16	TE
1987			8	TE
1987	NE	N	1	TE
1988			12	TE
13 yrs.			167 games	

Sam Francis
FRANCIS, HARRISON
B. Oct. 26, 1913
Nebraska 6'0" 207 lbs.

Year	Team		Games	Pos.
1937	CHIB	N	8	FB, HB
1938			11	FB
1939	PIT	N	5	FB
1939	BKN	N	5	FB, HB
1940			11	FB, HB
4 yrs.			40 games	

Wallace Francis
FRANCIS, WALLACE DIRON
B. Nov. 7, 1951, Franklin, LA
Arkansas-Pine Bluff 5'11" 190 lbs.

Year	Team		Games	Pos.
1973	BUF	N	12	WR
1974			14	WR
1975	ATL	N	14	WR
1976			14	WR
1977			14	WR
1978			16	WR
1979			16	WR
1980			16	WR
1981			16	WR
9 yrs.			132 games	

George Franck
FRANCK, GEORGE H.
B. Sep. 23, 1918, Davenport, IA
Minnesota 6'0" 176 lbs.

Year	Team		Games	Pos.
1941	NYG	N	11	HB
1945			5	HB
1946			10	HB
1947			7	HB
4 yrs.			33 games	

Tom Franckhauser
FRANCKHAUSER, THOMAS ANTHONY
B. May 26, 1937, Steubenville, OH
D. Apr. 17, 1997, Houston, TX
Purdue 6'0" 195 lbs.

Year	Team		Games	Pos.
1959	LA	N	12	DB
1960	DAL	N	12	DB
1961			6	DB
1962	MIN	N	14	DB
1963			14	DB
5 yrs.			58 games	

Mike Franckowiak
FRANCKOWIAK, MICHAEL JEROME
B. Mar. 25, 1953, Grand Rapids, MI
Central Michigan 6'3" 221 lbs.

Year	Team		Games	Pos.
1975	DEN	N	14	RB
1976			14	RB
1977	BUF	N	13	RB
1978			16	RB
4 yrs.			57 games	

Brian Franco
FRANCO, BRIAN DAVID
B. Dec. 3, 1959, Annapolis, MD
Penn State 5'8" 165 lbs.

Year	Team		Games	Pos.
1987	CLE	N	2	K

Ed Franco
FRANCO, EDMUND J.
B. Apr. 24, 1915, New York, NY
D. Nov. 18, 1992, Bayonne, NJ
Fordham 5'8" 205 lbs.

Year	Team		Games	Pos.
1944	BOS	N	10	T

Bill Frank
FRANK, WILLIAM
B. Apr. 13, 1938, Denver, CO
Colorado 6'5" 255 lbs.

Year	Team		Games	Pos.
1964	DAL	N	4	OT

Donald Frank
FRANK, DONALD LEE
B. Oct. 24, 1965, Edgecombe County, NC
Winston-Salem State 6'0" 197 lbs.

Year	Team		Games	Pos.
1990	SD	N	16	CB, S
1991			16	CB
1992			16	CB
1993			16	CB
1994	LARI	N	16	CB
1995	MIN	N	12	CB
6 yrs.			92 games	

Joe Frank
FRANK, JOSEPH C.
B. Jul. 14, 1915, Bronx, NY
D. Aug., 1981, Flushing, NY
Georgetown (DC) 6'1" 217 lbs.

Year	Team		Games	Pos.
1941	PHI	N	10	T, G
1942			1	G
1943	P, P	N	4	G
3 yrs.			15 games	

John Frank
FRANK, JOHN E.
B. Apr. 17, 1962, Pittsburgh, PA
Ohio State 6'3" 225 lbs.

Year	Team		Games	Pos.
1984	SF	N	15	TE
1985			16	TE
1986			16	TE
1987			12	TE
1988			7	TE
5 yrs.			66 games	

Malcolm Frank
FRANK, MALCOLM
B. Dec. 5, 1968, Mamou, LA
Baylor 5'8" 182 lbs.

Year	Team		Games	Pos.
1992	SEA	N	15	CB

Paul Frank
FRANK, PAUL
B. May 8, 1907
D. Nov., 1970, Bridgeville, PA
Waynesburg 200 lbs.

Year	Team		Games	Pos.
1930	NEW	N	3	FB, HB

Ike Frankian
FRANKIAN, MALCOLM J.
B. Apr. 3, 1907, Worcester, MA
D. Apr. 14, 1963
St. Mary's (California) 5'11" 208 lbs.

Year	Team		Games	Pos.
1933	BOS	N	11	E
1934	NYG	N	13	E
1935			12	E
3 yrs.			36 games	

Andra Franklin
FRANKLIN, ANDRA BERNARD
B. Aug. 22, 1959, Anniston, AL
Nebraska 5'10" 225 lbs.

Year	Team		Games	Pos.
1981	MIA	N	16	FB
1982			9	RB
1983			15	RB
1984			2	FB
4 yrs.			42 games	

Arnold Franklin
FRANKLIN, ARNOLD LEE
B. Dec. 6, 1963, Cincinnati, OH
North Carolina 6'3" 246 lbs.

Year	Team		Games	Pos.
1987	NE	N	3	TE

Bobby Franklin
FRANKLIN, BOBBY RAY
B. Oct. 5, 1936, Clarksdale, MS
Mississippi 5'11" 182 lbs.

Year	Team		Games	Pos.
1960	CLE	N	12	DB
1961			14	DB
1962			9	DB
1963			14	DB
1964			14	DB
1965			14	DB
1966			9	DB
7 yrs.			86 games	

Byron Franklin
FRANKLIN, BYRON PAUL
B. Sep. 3, 1958, Florence, AL
Auburn 6'1" 179 lbs.

Year	Team		Games	Pos.
1981	BUF	N	13	WR
1983			15	WR
1984			16	WR
1985	SEA	N	13	WR
1986			14	WR
1987			6	WR
6 yrs.			77 games	

Year	Team		Games	Pos.

Cleveland Franklin
FRANKLIN, CLEVELAND
B. Apr. 24, 1955, Brenham, TX
Baylor 6'2" 216 lbs.

Year	Team		Games	Pos.
1977	PHI	N	14	RB
1978			16	RB
1980	BAL	N	13	RB
1981			9	RB
1982			9	RB
5 yrs.	61 games			

Dennis Franklin
FRANKLIN, DENNIS
B. Aug. 24, 1953, Massillon, OH
Michigan 6'1" 185 lbs.

Year	Team		Games	Pos.
1975	DET	N	4	WR
1976			5	WR
2 yrs.	9 games			

George Franklin
FRANKLIN, GEORGE
B. Jul. 5, 1954, Seguin, TX
Texas A&I-Kingsville 6'3" 226 lbs.

Year	Team		Games	Pos.
1978	ATL	N	15	RB

Jerrell Franklin
FRANKLIN, JERRELL LYNN
B. May 4, 1959, Houston, TX
Kansas State/Southern University 6'3" 287 lbs.

Year	Team		Games	Pos.
1987	HOU	N	3	OT

Jethro Franklin
FRANKLIN, JETHRO FITZGERALD
B. Oct. 25, 1965, St. Lazaire, France
Fresno State 6'1" 258 lbs.

Year	Team		Games	Pos.
1989	SEA	N	7	DE

Keith Franklin
FRANKLIN, KEITH
B. Mar. 4, 1970, Los Angeles, CA
South Carolina 6'2" 230 lbs.

Year	Team		Games	Pos.
1995	OAK	N	2	LB

Larry Franklin
FRANKLIN, LARRY DARNELL
B. Aug. 2, 1955, Memphis, TN
Jackson State 6'1" 185 lbs.

Year	Team		Games	Pos.
1978	TB	N	2	WR

Pat Franklin
FRANKLIN, PATRICK DIJON
B. Aug. 16, 1963, Bay City, TX
Houston/Southwest Texas State 6'1" 230 lbs.

Year	Team		Games	Pos.
1986	TB	N	8	RB
1987	CIN	N	2	RB
2 yrs.	10 games			

Paul Franklin
FRANKLIN, PAUL
B. Jan. 2, 1906
D. Aug., 1952
Franklin (Indiana) 6'2" 198 lbs.

Year	Team		Games	Pos.
1931	CHIB	N	12	FB, HB
1932			8	FB, E
1933			2	E, HB
3 yrs.	22 games			

Red Franklin
FRANKLIN, NORMAN C.
B. Dec. 13, 1911, Hope, RI
Deceased
Oregon State 5'10" 163 lbs.

Year	Team		Games	Pos.
1935	BKN	N	11	HB

Red Franklin *continued*

Year	Team		Games	Pos.
1936			1	HB
1937			1	HB
3 yrs.	13 games			

Tony Franklin
FRANKLIN, ANTHONY RAY
B. Nov. 18, 1956, Big Spring, TX
Texas A&M 5'8" 182 lbs.

Year	Team		Games	Pos.
1979	PHI	N	16	K
1980			16	K
1981			16	K
1982			9	K
1983			16	K
1984	NE	N	16	K
1985			16	K
1986			16	K
1987			14	K
1988	MIA	N	5	K
10 yrs.	140 games			

Willie Franklin
FRANKLIN, WILLIE
B. Oct. 9, 1949, San Diego, CA
Oklahoma 6'2" 195 lbs.

Year	Team		Games	Pos.
1972	BAL	N	4	WR

Ray Frankowski
FRANKOWSKI, RAYMOND W.
B. Sep. 14, 1917, Chicago, IL
Washington 5'11" 223 lbs.

Year	Team		Games	Pos.
1945	GB	N	2	G
1946	LA	AA	12	G
1947			14	G
1948			14	G
4 yrs.	42 games			

Dennis Franks
FRANKS, DENNIS
B. May 29, 1953, McKeesport, PA
Michigan 6'1" 241 lbs.

Year	Team		Games	Pos.
1976	PHI	N	14	C
1977			14	C
1978			16	C
1979	DET	N	13	C
4 yrs.	57 games			

Elvis Franks
FRANKS, ELVIS
B. Jul. 9, 1957, Doucette, TX
Morgan State 6'4" 260 lbs.

Year	Team		Games	Pos.
1980	CLE	N	16	DE
1981			16	DE
1982			9	DE
1983			16	DE
1984			16	DE
1985	LARI	N	3	DE
1986			4	DE
1986	NYJ	N	3	DE
7 yrs.	83 games			

Chief Franta
FRANTA, HERBERT
B. Mar. 10, 1905
Deceased
St. Thomas (Minnesota) 6'0" 220 lbs.

Year	Team		Games	Pos.
1929	MIN	N	10	T
1930			6	T
1930	GB	N	2	G
2 yrs.	18 games			

Jack Frantz
FRANTZ, JOHN EDWARD
B. Jul. 1, 1945, Kokomo, IN
California 6'3" 230 lbs.

Year	Team		Games	Pos.
1968	BUF	A	2	C

Nolan Franz
FRANZ, NOLAN CLARENCE
B. Sep. 11, 1959, New Orleans, LA
Tulane 6'2" 183 lbs.

Year	Team		Games	Pos.
1986	GB	N	1	WR

Tracy Franz
FRANZ, TRACY MARK
B. Mar. 26, 1960, Sacramento, CA
San Jose State 6'5" 280 lbs.

Year	Team		Games	Pos.
1987	SF		3	OT

Paul Frase
FRASE, PAUL MILES
B. May 6, 1965, Elmira, NY
Syracuse 6'5" 273 lbs.

Year	Team		Games	Pos.
1988	NYJ	N	16	DE
1989			16	DE
1991			16	DE, DT
1992			16	DE, DT
1993			16	DT, DE
1994			16	DT
1995	JAC	N	9	DE, DT
1996			14	DT
8 yrs.	119 games			

Jim Fraser
FRASER, JAMES G.
B. May 29, 1936, Philadelphia, PA
Wisconsin 6'3" 236 lbs.

Year	Team		Games	Pos.
1962	DEN	A	14	LB, P
1963			14	LB, P
1965	KC	A	14	LB, P
1966	BOS	A	14	LB, P
1968	NO	N	2	P
5 yrs.	58 games			

Al Frazier
FRAZIER, ADOLPHUS CORNELIUS
B. Mar. 28, 1935, Jacksonville, FL
Florida A&M 5'11" 180 lbs.

Year	Team		Games	Pos.
1961	DEN	A	14	HB
1962			14	HB
1963			3	FL
3 yrs.	31 games			

Charlie Frazier
FRAZIER, CHARLES DOUGLAS
B. Aug. 12, 1939, Houston, TX
Texas Southern* 6'0" 177 lbs.

Year	Team		Games	Pos.
1962	HOU	A	14	OE
1963			10	OE
1964			11	OE
1965			12	OE
1966			14	OE
1967			13	OE
1968			13	OE
1969	BOS	A	14	WR
1970	BOS	N	9	WR
9 yrs.	110 games			

Cliff Frazier
FRAZIER, CLIFF
B. Nov. 23, 1952, St. Louis, MO
UCLA 6'4" 265 lbs.

Year	Team		Games	Pos.
1977	KC	N	14	DT

Curt Frazier
FRAZIER, CURTIS
B. Mar. 11, 1945, Berkeley, CA
Fresno State 5'11" 183 lbs.

Year	Team		Games	Pos.
1968	CIN	A	14	DB

Derrick Frazier
FRAZIER, DERRICK
B. Apr. 29, 1970, Sugar Land, TX

Derrick Frazier *continued*
Texas A&M 5'10" 178 lbs.

Year	Team		Games	Pos.
1994	PHI	N	13	CB
1995			7	CB
1996	IND	N	5	CB
3 yrs.	25 games			

Frank Frazier
FRAZIER, FRANK
B. Jun. 15, 1960, Tampa, FL
Miami (Florida) 6'5" 290 lbs.

Year	Team		Games	Pos.
1987	WAS	N	3	G

Guy Frazier
FRAZIER, GUY SHELTON
B. Jul. 20, 1959, Detroit, MI
Wyoming 6'2" 217 lbs.

Year	Team		Games	Pos.
1981	CIN	N	16	LB
1982			9	LB
1983			10	LB
1984			16	LB
1985	BUF	N	16	LB
1986			7	LB
6 yrs.	74 games			

Leslie Frazier
FRAZIER, LESLIE ANTONIO
B. Apr. 3, 1959, Columbus, MS
Alcorn State 6'0" 189 lbs.

Year	Team		Games	Pos.
1981	CHI	N	12	DB
1982			9	CB, S
1983			16	CB
1984			11	CB
1985			16	CB
5 yrs.	64 games			

Paul Frazier
FRAZIER, DANIEL PAUL
B. Nov. 12, 1967, Beaumont, TX
Northwestern State (Louisiana) 5'8" 188 lbs.

Year	Team		Games	Pos.
1989	NO	N	15	RB

Randy Frazier
FRAZIER, RANDY
B. 1964
Morehead State 6'3" 235 lbs.

Year	Team		Games	Pos.
1987	KC	N	3	LB

Wayne Frazier
FRAZIER, WILLIAM WAYNE
B. Mar. 5, 1939, Evergreen, LA
Auburn 6'2" 243 lbs.

Year	Team		Games	Pos.
1962	SD	A	7	C, LB
1965	HOU	A	14	C
1966	KC	A	14	C
1967			7	C
1967	BUF	A	6	C
4 yrs.	48 games			

Willie Frazier
FRAZIER, WILLIE
B. Jun. 19, 1942, El Dorado, AR
Arkansas-Pine Bluff 6'4" 235 lbs.

Year	Team		Games	Pos.
1964	HOU	A	14	OE
1965			12	OE
1966	SD	A	14	OE
1967			14	TE
1968			9	TE
1969			11	TE
1970	SD	N	14	TE
1971	KC	N	8	TE
1972			14	TE
1975	HOU	N	5	TE
10 yrs.	115 games			

Year	Team	Games	Pos.

Andy Frederick
FREDERICK, ANDREW BRIAN
B. Jul. 25, 1954, Oak Park, IL
New Mexico 6'6" 265 lbs.

Year	Team		Games	Pos.
1977	DAL	N	14	OT
1978			16	OT
1979			16	OT
1980			16	OT
1981			16	OT
1982	CLE	N	7	OT
1983	CHI	N	16	OT
1984			16	OT
1985			16	OT
9 yrs.		133 games		

Mike Frederick
FREDERICK, THOMAS MICHAEL
B. Aug. 6, 1972, Abington, PA
Virginia 6'5" 280 lbs.

Year	Team		Games	Pos.
1995	CLE	N	16	DE
1996	BAL	N	16	DE
2 yrs.		32 games		

Rob Frederickson
FREDERICKSON, ROB
B. May 13, 1971, St. Joseph, MI
Michigan State 6'4" 235 lbs.

Year	Team		Games	Pos.
1994	LARI	N	16	LB
1995	OAK	N	16	LB
1996			10	LB
3 yrs.		42 games		

Tucker Frederickson
FREDERICKSON, IVAN CHARLES
B. Jan. 12, 1943, Fort Lauderdale, FL
Auburn 6'3" 233 lbs.

Year	Team		Games	Pos.
1965	NYG	N	13	RB
1967			10	RB
1968			14	RB
1969			5	RB
1970			14	RB
1971			10	RB
6 yrs.		66 games		

Solomon Freelon
FREELON, SOLOMON, JR.
B. Feb. 19, 1951, Monroe, LA
Grambling State 6'2" 250 lbs.

Year	Team		Games	Pos.
1972	HOU	N	14	G
1973			11	G
1974			14	G
3 yrs.		39 games		

Antonio Freeman
FREEMAN, ANTONIO MICHAEL
B. May 27, 1972, Baltimore, MD
Virginia Tech 6'0" 187 lbs.

Year	Team		Games	Pos.
1995	GB	N	11	WR
1996			12	WR
2 yrs.		23 games		

Bobby Freeman
FREEMAN, ROBERT CLAYTON
B. Oct. 19, 1932, Decatur, AL
Auburn 6'1" 202 lbs.

Year	Team		Games	Pos.
1957	CLE	N	9	DB
1958			12	HB, DB
1959	GB	N	12	DB
1960	PHI	N	12	DB
1961			14	DB
1962	WAS	N	14	DB
6 yrs.		73 games		

Jack Freeman
FREEMAN, JACK LENARD
B. 1922

Jack Freeman *continued*
Texas 6'0" 198 lbs.

Year	Team		Games	Pos.
1946	BKN	AA	12	G

Lorenzo Freeman
FREEMAN, LORENZO Z.
B. May 23, 1964, East Camden, NJ
Pittsburgh 6'5" 270 lbs.

Year	Team		Games	Pos.
1987	PIT	N	6	NT
1988			13	NT
1989			16	NT
1990			11	NT
1991	NYG	N	16	NT
5 yrs.		62 games		

Mike Freeman
FREEMAN, MIKE
B. Jul. 13, 1944, Los Angeles, CA
Fresno State 5'11" 187 lbs.

Year	Team		Games	Pos.
1968	ATL	N	9	DB
1969			14	CB
2 yrs.		23 games		

Mike Freeman
FREEMAN, MICHAEL JOSEPH
B. Oct. 13, 1961, Mount Holly, NJ
Arizona 6'3" 256 lbs.

Year	Team		Games	Pos.
1984	DEN	N	9	G
1986			4	G
1987			13	G
1988	LARI	N	2	C
4 yrs.		28 games		

Phil Freeman
FREEMAN, PHILLIP EMERY
B. Dec. 9, 1962, St. Paul, MN
Arizona 5'11" 185 lbs.

Year	Team		Games	Pos.
1985	TB	N	14	WR
1986			15	WR
1987			8	WR
3 yrs.		37 games		

Reggie Freeman
FREEMAN, REGGIE
B. May 8, 1970, Clewiston, FL
Florida State 6'1" 233 lbs.

Year	Team		Games	Pos.
1993	NO	N	10	LB

Russell Freeman
FREEMAN, RUSSELL WILLIAMS
B. Sep. 2, 1969, Homestead, PA
Georgia Tech 6'7" 290 lbs.

Year	Team		Games	Pos.
1992	DEN	N	16	G, OT
1993			14	OT
1994			13	OT
1995	OAK	N	15	OT
4 yrs.		58 games		

Steve Freeman
FREEMAN, STEVEN JAY
B. May 8, 1953, Lamesa, TX
Mississippi State 5'11" 185 lbs.

Year	Team		Games	Pos.
1975	BUF	N	14	S
1976			14	S
1977			14	S
1978			16	S
1979			16	S
1980			16	S
1981			16	S
1982			9	S
1983			16	S
1984			15	S
1985			16	S
1986			16	S
1987	MIN	N	12	S
13 yrs.		190 games		

Jess Freitas
FREITAS, JESSE
B. 1922
Santa Clara 5'10" 170 lbs.

Year	Team		Games	Pos.
1946	SF	AA	10	QB
1947			10	QB
1948	CHI	AA	10	QB
1949	BUF	AA	1	QB
4 yrs.		31 games		

Jesse Freitas
FREITAS, JESSE LEE
B. Sep. 19, 1951, San Mateo, CA
Stanford/San Diego State 6'1" 198 lbs.

Year	Team		Games	Pos.
1974	SD	N	5	QB
1975			8	QB
2 yrs.		13 games		

Rocky Freitas
FREITAS, ROCKNE CROWNINGBURG
B. Sep. 7, 1945, Kailua, HI
Oregon State 6'6" 271 lbs.

Year	Team		Games	Pos.
1968	DET	N	6	OT
1969			14	OT
1970			14	OT
1971			14	OT
1972			14	OT
1973			14	OT
1974			14	OT
1975			14	OT
1976			14	OT
1977			3	OT
1978	TB	N	13	OT
11 yrs.		134 games		

Barry French
FRENCH, BARRY A. (Bear)
B. Feb. 12, 1922, Chamberlain, SD
D. Mar. 16, 1990, Vero Beach, FL
Purdue 6'0" 225 lbs.

Year	Team		Games	Pos.
1947	BAL	AA	14	G
1949			11	G
1950	BAL	N	12	T
1951	DET	N	12	G
4 yrs.		49 games		

Ernest French
FRENCH, ERNEST CLAUZELL
B. Sep. 5, 1959, Tensaw, AL
Alabama A&M 5'11" 195 lbs.

Year	Team		Games	Pos.
1982	PIT	N	3	S

Walt French
FRENCH, WALTER EDWARD (Fritz)
B. Jul. 12, 1899, Moorestown, NJ
D. May 13, 1984, Mountain Home, AR
Rutgers/Army 5'7" 155 lbs.

Year	Team		Games	Pos.
1925	POT		9	HB, QB, FB

Gus Frerotte
FREROTTE, GUSTAVE JOSEPH
B. Jul. 31, 1971, Kittanning, PA
Tulsa 6'2" 221 lbs.

Year	Team		Games	Pos.
1994	WAS	N	5	QB
1995			16	QB
1996			16	QB
3 yrs.		37 games		

Mitch Frerotte
FREROTTE, PAUL MITCHEL
B. Mar. 30, 1965, Kittanning, PA
Penn State 6'3" 280 lbs.

Year	Team		Games	Pos.
1987	BUF	N	12	G
1990			16	G
1991			16	G

Mitch Frerotte *continued*

Year	Team		Games	Pos.
1992			14	G
4 yrs.		58 games		

Dick Frey
FREY, RICHARD H.
B. 1931
Texas A&M 6'2" 233 lbs.

Year	Team		Games	Pos.
1960	DAL	A		DE
1961	HOU	A	7	DE, G
2 yrs.		7 games		

Glenn Frey
FREY, GLENN (Wackie)
B. Mar. 6, 1912
D. Jan. 5, 1980, New Port Richey, FL
Temple 5'10" 193 lbs.

Year	Team		Games	Pos.
1936	PHI	N	11	QB, HB
1937			6	HB, QB
2 yrs.		17 games		

Ray Frick
FRICK, RAYMOND AUGUSTUS
B. Jan. 16, 1919, Bloomfield, NJ
Pennsylvania 6'1" 205 lbs.

Year	Team		Games	Pos.
1941	BKN	N	3	C

Larry Friday
FRIDAY, LARRY
B. Jan. 23, 1958, Jackson, MS
Alcorn State/Mississippi State 6'4" 215 lbs.

Year	Team		Games	Pos.
1987	BUF	N	1	S

Mike Friede
FRIEDE, MICHAEL GORDON
B. Sep. 22, 1957, Havre, MT
Indiana 6'3" 203 lbs.

Year	Team		Games	Pos.
1980	DET	N	4	WR
1980	NYG	N	7	WR
1981			16	WR
2 yrs.		27 games		

Bob Friedlund
FRIEDLUND, ROBERT M.
B. 1920
Michigan State 6'3" 210 lbs.

Year	Team		Games	Pos.
1946	PHI	N	2	E

Andy Friedman
FRIEDMAN, ANDY
None

Year	Team		Games	Pos.
1921	SYR	A	1	FB

Benny Friedman
FRIEDMAN, BENJAMIN
B. Mar. 18, 1905, Cleveland, OH
D. Nov. 23, 1982, New York, NY
Michigan 5'10" 183 lbs.

Year	Team		Games	Pos.
1927	CLE	N	13	QB, HB, FB
1928	DET	N	10	QB, HB
1929	NYG	N	15	QB, HB, FB
1930			15	QB
1931			8	QB, FB, HB
1932	BKN	N	11	QB, HB
1933			7	QB, HB
1934			1	QB, HB
8 yrs.		80 games		

Bob Friedman
FRIEDMAN, ROBERT (Buck)
B. Sep. 11, 1921, Allentown, PA
Deceased
Washington 6'2" 215 lbs.

Year	Team		Games	Pos.
1944	PHI	N	10	T

Year	Team	Games	Pos.

Jake Friedman
FRIEDMAN, JACOB
B. Feb. 21, 1896
D. Nov. 9, 1988, Florida
None

Year	Team		Games	Pos.
1926	HAR	N	4	E

Ben Friend
FRIEND, BENJAMIN
B. 1917
Louisiana State 6'5" 248 lbs.

1939	CLE	N	9	T

Mike Frier
FRIER, MIKE
B. Mar. 20, 1969, Jacksonville, NC
Appalachian State 6'5" 299 lbs.

1992	CIN	N	15	DE
1993		N	16	DE
1994			1	DT
1994	SEA	N	2	DT

3 yrs.   34 games

Sherwood Fries
FRIES, SHERWOOD M.
B. Nov. 14, 1920
D. Dec. 9, 1986, San Juan Capistrano, CA
Colorado State 6'1" 235 lbs.

1943	GB	N	5	G

John Friesz
FRIESZ, JOHN MELVIN
B. May 19, 1967, Missoula, MT
Idaho 6'4" 209 lbs.

1990	SD	N	1	QB
1991		N	16	QB
1993			12	QB
1994	WAS	N	15	QB
1995	SEA	N	6	QB
1996			8	QB

6 yrs.   58 games

David Frisch
FRISCH, DAVID JOSEPH
B. Jun. 22, 1970, Kirkwood, MO
Colorado State 6'7" 260 lbs.

1993	CIN	N	11	TE
1994		N	16	TE
1995	NE	N	2	TE
1996	MIN	N	10	TE

4 yrs.   39 games

Ernie Fritsch
FRITSCH, ERNEST
B. 1937
Detroit 6'0" 230 lbs.

1960	STL	N	1	C, LB

Louie Fritsch
FRITSCH, LOUIS E.
B. Oct., 1879, Evansville, IN
D. Jan. 20, 1958, Indianapolis, IN
Georgetown 240 lbs.

1921	EVA	A	1	G

Ted Fritsch
FRITSCH, THEODORE EDWARD, SR.
B. Oct. 31, 1920, Superior, WI
D. Oct. 4, 1979, Superior, WI
Wisconsin-Stevens Point 5'10" 210 lbs.

1942	GB	N	11	FB
1943			9	FB
1944			9	FB

Ted Fritsch continued

1945		10	FB
1946		11	FB
1947		12	FB
1948		12	FB
1949		12	FB
1950		12	FB

9 yrs.   98 games

Ted Fritsch
FRITSCH, THEODORE EDWARD, JR.
B. Aug. 26, 1950, Green Bay, WI
St. Norbert 6'2" 242 lbs.

1972	ATL	N	14	C
1973			14	C
1974			14	C
1976	WAS	N	14	C
1977			14	C
1978			16	C
1979			16	C, G

7 yrs.   102 games

Toni Fritsch
FRITSCH, ANTON
B. Jul. 10, 1945, Vienna, Austria
None 5'7" 188 lbs.

1971	DAL	N	2	K
1972			14	K
1973			13	K
1975			14	K
1976	SD	N	5	K
1977	HOU	N	8	K
1978			16	K
1979			16	K
1980			15	K
1981			16	K
1982	NO	N	5	K

11 yrs.   124 games

George Fritts
FRITTS, GEORGE H.
B. Dec. 30, 1919
D. Feb., 1987, Savannah, GA
Clemson 5'11" 205 lbs.

1945	PHI	N	10	T

Stan Fritts
FRITTS, STANLEY
B. Dec. 18, 1952, Oak Ridge, TN
North Carolina State 6'1" 215 lbs.

1975	CIN	N	13	RB
1976			13	RB

2 yrs.   26 games

Ralph Fritz
FRITZ, RALPH A.
B. Nov. 23, 1917, New Kensington, PA
Michigan 5'9" 202 lbs.

1941	PHI	N	10	G

Jim Fritzche
FRITZCHE, JAMES BRIAN
B. Oct. 11, 1960, Parma, OH
Purdue 6'8" 265 lbs.

1983	PHI	N	15	OT

William Frizzell
FRIZZELL, WILLIAM JASPER
B. Sep. 8, 1962, Greenville, NC
North Carolina Central 6'3" 198 lbs.

1984	DET	N	16	CB, S
1985			8	CB
1986	PHI	N	8	S
1987			12	S
1988			16	S
1989			16	S

William Frizzell continued

1990			16	CB, S
1991	TB	N	16	CB, S
1992	PHI	N	10	S
1993			16	S

10 yrs.   134 games

Len Frketich
FRKETICH, LEONARD LAWRENCE
B. Nov. 18, 1917, Monessen, PA
Penn State 6'1" 290 lbs.

1945	PIT	N	2	T

Bill Frohbose
FROHBOSE, WILLIAM
B. May 20, 1952, Washington, DC
Miami (Florida) 6'0" 185 lbs.

1974	DET	N	2	S

Andy Fronczek
FRONCZEK, ANDREW A.
B. Sep. 21, 1916, Harvey, IL
Richmond 6'0" 200 lbs.

1941	BKN	N	11	T

John Frongillo
FRONGILLO, JOHN R.
B. 1940
Baylor 6'3" 252 lbs.

1962	HOU	A	14	G
1963			3	C
1964			14	G
1965			9	G
1966			14	C

5 yrs.   54 games

Ken Frost
FROST, KENNETH
B. Nov. 17, 1938
Tennessee 6'4" 245 lbs.

1961	DAL	N	14	DT
1962			3	DT

2 yrs.   17 games

Jim Frugone
FRUGONE, JAMES (Babe)
B. Oct. 23, 1897
D. Jun., 1972, Brooklyn, NY
Syracuse 5'11" 150 lbs.

1925	NYG	N	3	HB, QB
1926	BKN	A	4	HB, FB

2 yrs.   7 games

Babe Frump
FRUMP, MILTON
B. Jul. 15, 1901
Ohio Wesleyan 6'0" 225 lbs.

1930	CHIB	N	9	G

Ed Frutig
FRUTIG, EDWARD C.
B. Aug. 19, 1920, River Rouge, MI
Michigan 6'1" 190 lbs.

1941	GB	N	8	E
1945			1	E
1945	DET		8	E
1946			7	E

3 yrs.   24 games

Bob Fry
FRY, ROBERT N.
B. Nov. 11, 1930, Cincinnati, OH
Kentucky 6'4" 235 lbs.

1953	LA	N	12	OT

Bob Fry continued

1956			12	OT
1957			12	OT
1958			12	OT
1959			12	OT
1960	DAL	N	12	OT
1961			14	OT
1962			14	OT
1963			14	OT
1964			12	OT

10 yrs.   126 games

Harry Fry
FRY, HARRY
B. Jan. 7, 1907
D. Dec., 1983, Matamoras, PA
Bucknell 6'3" 210 lbs.

1932	SI	N	3	E

Wes Fry
FRY, WESLEY L. (Cowboy)
B. Dec. 10, 1902
D. Nov. 11, 1970, La Mesa, CA
Iowa 5'10" 190 lbs.

1926	NY	A	10	FB, HB, QB
1927	NYY	N	15	FB, HB, QB

2 yrs.   25 games

Irving Fryar
FRYAR, IRVING DALE
B. Sep. 28, 1962, Mount Holly, NJ
Nebraska 6'0" 200 lbs.

1984	NE	N	14	WR
1985			16	WR
1986			14	WR
1987			12	WR
1988			15	WR
1989			11	WR
1990			16	WR
1991			16	WR
1992			16	WR
1993	MIA	N	16	WR
1994			16	WR
1995			16	WR
1996	PHI	N	16	WR

13 yrs.   193 games

David Frye
FRYE, DAVID
B. Jun. 21, 1961, Cincinnati, OH
Purdue 6'2" 223 lbs.

1983	ATL	N	16	LB
1984			16	LB
1985			14	LB
1986	MIA	N	9	LB
1987			12	LB
1988			8	LB
1989			11	LB

7 yrs.   86 games

Phil Frye
FRYE, PHIL
B. Dec. 20, 1958, Washington, DC
California Lutheran 5'11" 180 lbs.

1987	MIN	N	1	RB

Brian Fryer
FRYER, BRIAN
B. Jul. 16, 1953, Edmonton, Alb.
Alberta 6'1" 185 lbs.

1976	WAS	N	4	WR

Kenny Fryer
FRYER, KENNETH W.
B. Nov. 17, 1918, Cliftonville, WV
West Virginia 6'0" 200 lbs.

1944	BKN	N	3	HB

Year	Team		Games	Pos.

Dom Fucci
FUCCI, DOMINIC A.
B. Sep. 14, 1928
D. Jun. 23, 1987, Lexington, KY
Kentucky 5'11" 190 lbs.

| 1955 | DET | N | 12 | HB |

Jean Fugett
FUGETT, JEAN SCHLOSS, JR.
B. Dec. 16, 1951, Baltimore, MD
Amherst 6'3" 225 lbs.

1972	DAL		14	TE
1973			12	TE
1974			12	TE
1975			14	TE
1976	WAS	N	12	TE
1977			14	TE
1978			14	TE
1979			11	TE
8 yrs.			103 games	

Dick Fugler
FUGLER, RICHARD GUY
B. Jul. 19, 1931, Dallas, TX
Tulane 6'2" 238 lbs.

1952	PIT	N	10	T
1954	CHIC	N	12	T
2 yrs.			22 games	

Bill Fulcher
FULCHER, WILLIAM M.
B. 1934
Georgia Tech 6'0" 193 lbs.

1956	WAS	N	9	G
1957			2	G
1958			12	G
3 yrs.			23 games	

David Fulcher
FULCHER, DAVID DWAYNE
B. Sep. 28, 1964, Los Angeles, CA
Arizona State 6'3" 228 lbs.

1986	CIN	N	16	S
1987			11	S
1988			16	S
1989			16	S
1990			13	S
1991			16	S
1992			12	S
1993	LARI	N	3	S
8 yrs.			103 games	

Scott Fulhage
FULHAGE, SCOTT ALAN
B. Nov. 17, 1961, Beloit, KS
Kansas State 5'11" 291 lbs.

1987	CIN	N	11	P
1988			13	P
1989	ATL	N	16	P
1990			16	P
1991			16	P
1992			16	P
6 yrs.			88 games	

Charley Fuller
FULLER, CHARLES
B. 1939
San Francisco State 5'11" 176 lbs.

1961	OAK	A	14	HB
1962			3	HB
2 yrs.			17 games	

Corey Fuller
FULLER, COREY
B. May 11, 1971, Tallahassee, FL
Florida State 5'10" 197 lbs.

| 1995 | MIN | N | 16 | CB |

Corey Fuller *continued*

| 1996 | | | 16 | CB |
| 2 yrs. | | | 32 games | |

Eddie Fuller
FULLER, EDDIE JEROME
B. Jun. 22, 1968, Leesville, LA
Louisiana Tech 5'9" 201 lbs.

1991	BUF	N	5	RB
1992			14	RB
1993			7	RB
3 yrs.			26 games	

Frank Fuller
FULLER, FRANK
B. Aug. 5, 1929, Du Bois, PA
D. 1993
Kentucky 6'4" 244 lbs.

1953	LA	N	9	T
1955			12	T, G, E
1957			10	T
1958			12	T
1959	CHIC	N	10	T
1960	STL	N	7	T
1961			14	DT
1962			14	DT
1963	PHI	N	5	DT
9 yrs.			95 games	

James Fuller
FULLER, JAMES RAY
B. Aug. 5, 1969, Tacoma, WA
Portland State 6'0" 208 lbs.

1993	SD	N	10	S
1996	PHI	N	13	S
2 yrs.			23 games	

Jeff Fuller
FULLER, JEFFERY AVERY
B. Aug. 8, 1962, Dallas, TX
Texas A&M 6'2" 216 lbs.

1984	SF	N	13	S
1985			16	S
1986			6	S, LB
1987			14	S, LB
1988			16	S
1989			7	S
6 yrs.			72 games	

Joe Fuller
FULLER, JOE ROBERT
B. Sep. 25, 1964, Milligan, FL
Northern Iowa 5'11" 180 lbs.

1990	SD	N	4	CB
1991	GB	N	16	CB
2 yrs.			20 games	

Johnny Fuller
FULLER, JOHN CHARLES
B. Mar. 3, 1946, Beaumont, TX
Lamar 6'0" 182 lbs.

1968	SF	N	14	S
1969			7	S
1970			14	S
1971			14	S
1972			13	S
1973	NO	N	13	S
1974			12	S
1975			11	S
8 yrs.			98 games	

Larry Fuller
FULLER, LAWRENCE
B. Jan. 28, 1923, Faust, NY
None 5'10" 192 lbs.

| 1944 | WAS | N | 6 | FB |

Larry Fuller *continued*

1945			1	FB
1945	CHIC	N	1	FB
2 yrs.			8 games	

Mike Fuller
FULLER, MICHAEL DARWIN
B. Apr. 7, 1953, Jackson, MS
Auburn 5'9" 187 lbs.

1975	SD	N	14	DB
1976			14	S
1977			14	S
1978			16	S
1979			16	S
1980			16	S
1981	CIN	N	15	S
1982			9	S
8 yrs.			114 games	

Randy Fuller
FULLER, RANDY LAMAR
B. Jun. 2, 1970, Columbus, GA
Tennessee State 5'9" 173 lbs.

1994	DEN	N	10	CB
1995	PIT	N	13	CB
1996			13	CB
3 yrs.			36 games	

Steve Fuller
FULLER, STEPHEN RAY
B. Jan. 5, 1957, Enid, OK
Clemson 6'4" 195 lbs.

1979	KC	N	16	QB
1980			14	QB
1981			13	QB
1982			9	QB
1984	CHI	N	6	QB
1985			16	QB
1986			16	QB
7 yrs.			90 games	

William Fuller
FULLER, WILLIAM HENRY, JR.
B. Mar. 8, 1962, Norfolk, VA
North Carolina 6'3" 255 lbs.

1986	HOU	N	13	DE
1987			12	DE
1988			16	DE
1989			15	DE
1990			16	DE
1991			16	DE
1992			15	DE
1993			16	DE
1994	PHI	N	16	DE
1995			16	DE
1996			16	DE
11 yrs.			165 games	

Ed Fullerton
FULLERTON, EDWARD
B. Apr. 7, 1931
Maryland 5'10" 190 lbs.

| 1953 | PIT | N | 1 | DB |

Darrell Fullington
FULLINGTON, DARRELL
B. Apr. 17, 1964, New Smyrna Beach, FL
Miami (Florida) 6'1" 197 lbs.

1988	MIN	N	15	S
1989			16	S
1990			16	S
1991	NE	N	5	S
1991	TB	N	6	S
1992			16	S
5 yrs.			74 games	

Brent Fullwood
FULLWOOD, BRENT LANARD
B. Oct. 10, 1963, Kissimmee, FL
Auburn 5'11" 209 lbs.

1987	GB	N	11	RB
1988			14	RB
1989			15	RB
1990			5	RB
1990	CLE	N	1	RB
4 yrs.			46 games	

Danny Fulton
FULTON, DAN B.
B. Sep. 2, 1956, Memphis, TN
Nebraska/Nebraska-Omaha 6'2" 183 lbs.

1979	BUF	N	6	WR
1981	CLE	N	5	WR
1982			9	WR
3 yrs.			20 games	

Ed Fulton
FULTON, ED
B. Jan. 27, 1956, Abington, PA
Maryland 6'3" 250 lbs.

1978	LA	N	4	G
1979	BUF	N	5	G
2 yrs.			9 games	

Ken Fulton
FULTON, KEN
B. Jun., 1899, Muncie, IN
Deceased
None

| 1921 | MUN | A | 1 | G |

Ted Fulton
FULTON, THEODORE (Curly)
B. Nov. 5, 1905
Oglethorpe 6'0" 196 lbs.

1931	BKN	N	11	G, T
1932			1	G
2 yrs.			12 games	

Mike Fultz
FULTZ, MICHAEL DEAN
B. Jan. 28, 1954, Lincoln, NE
Nebraska 6'5" 278 lbs.

1977	NO	N	12	DT
1978			12	DT
1979			13	DT
1980			12	DT
1981	MIA	N	4	DT
1981	BAL	N	5	DT
5 yrs.			58 games	

Tom Funchess
FUNCHESS, TOMMIE (Moose)
B. Sep. 12, 1964, Crystal Springs, MS
Jackson State 6'5" 264 lbs.

1968	BOS	A	14	OT
1969			14	OT
1970	BOS	N	11	OT
1971	HOU	N	12	OT
1972			14	OT
1973			14	OT
1974	MIA	N	8	OT
7 yrs.			87 games	

John Fuqua
FUQUA, JOHN WILLIAM (Frenchy)
B. Sep. 12, 1946, Detroit, MI
Morgan State 5'11" 200 lbs.

1969	NYG	N	14	RB
1970	PIT	N	12	RB
1971			12	RB

Year	Team		Games	Pos.

John Fuqua continued

Year	Team		Games	Pos.
1972			13	RB
1973			11	RB
1974			9	RB
1975			14	RB
1976			14	RB
8 yrs.	101 games			

Ray Fuqua
FUQUA, RAYMOND
B. Mar. 21, 1912, Shreveport, LA
D. Oct., 1983, Ballinger, TX
Southern Methodist 6'0" 190 lbs.

1935	BKN	N	10	E
1936			12	E
2 yrs.	22 games			

Jim Furey
FUREY, JAMES A.
B. Sep. 22, 1933
Kansas State 6'0" 228 lbs.

| 1961 | NY | A | 9 | LB |

Tony Furjanic
FURJÁNIC, ANTHONY JOSEPH
B. Feb. 26, 1964, Chicago, IL
Notre Dame 6'1" 228 lbs.

1986	BUF	N	14	LB
1987			8	LB
1988	MIA	N	6	LB
3 yrs.	28 games			

Steve Furness
FURNESS, STEPHEN ROBERT
B. Dec. 5, 1950, Providence, RI
Rhode Island 6'4" 255 lbs.

1972	PIT	N	2	DT
1973			6	DT, DE
1974			14	DT, DE
1975			14	DT, DE
1976			9	DT, DE
1977			14	DT, DE
1978			10	DT, DE
1979			12	DT, DE
1980			16	DT, DE
1981	DET	N	9	DT
10 yrs.	106 games			

Will Furrer
FURRER, WILLIAM MASON
B. Feb. 5, 1968, Danville, PA
Virginia Tech 6'3" 208 lbs.

1992	CHI	N	2	QB
1994	DEN	N	1	QB
1995	HOU	N	7	QB
3 yrs.	10 games			

Tony Furst
FURST, ANTHONY RAYMOND
B. Apr. 26, 1918, Dayton, OH
Dayton 6'1" 217 lbs.

1940	DET	N	9	T
1941			10	T
1944			2	T
3 yrs.	21 games			

Chuck Fusina
FUSINA, CHARLES ANTHONY
B. May 31, 1957, Pittsburgh, PA
Penn State 6'1" 197 lbs.

1979	TB	N	1	QB
1980			2	QB
1981			4	QB
1986	GB	N	7	QB
4 yrs.	14 games			

Tommy Fussell
FUSSELL, THOMAS PAUL
B. May 25, 1945, Cleveland, OH
Louisiana State 6'3" 245 lbs.

| 1967 | BOS | A | 12 | DE |

Bobby Futrell
FUTRELL, BOBBY LEE
B. Aug. 4, 1962, Ahoskie, NC
D. May 31, 1992, Tampa, FL
Elizabeth City State 5'11" 190 lbs.

1986	TB	N	16	CB, S
1987			12	CB, S
1988			16	CB, S
1989			16	CB, S
1990			1	CB, S
5 yrs.	61 games			

Steve Gabbard
GABBARD, STEPHEN EDWARD
B. Jul. 19, 1966, Lexington, KY
Florida State 6'4" 297 lbs.

| 1991 | GB | N | 4 | OT |

John Gabler
GABLER, JOHN
B. Apr. 16, 1906
D. Mar., 1975, Dayton, OH
none

| 1925 | DAY | N | 1 | G |

Roman Gabriel
GABRIEL, ROMAN, JR. (Gabe)
B. Aug. 5, 1940, Wilmington, NC
North Carolina State 6'4" 225 lbs.

1962	LA	N	6	QB
1963			12	QB
1964			7	QB
1965			7	QB
1966			14	QB
1967			14	QB
1968			14	QB
1969			14	QB
1970			14	QB
1971			14	QB
1972			14	QB
1973	PHI	N	14	QB
1974			11	QB
1975			11	QB
1976			4	QB
1977			13	QB
16 yrs.	183 games			

Dennis Gadbois
GADBOIS, DENNIS RICHARD
B. Sep. 18, 1963, Biddeford, ME
Boston University 6'1" 183 lbs.

1987	NE	N	3	WR
1988			2	WR
2 yrs.	5 games			

Bob Gaddis
GADDIS, ROBERT
B. Jan. 20, 1952, Jackson, MS
Mississippi Valley State 5'11" 178 lbs.

| 1976 | BUF | N | 2 | WR |

Mike Gaechter
GAECHTER, MICHAEL THEODORE
B. Jan. 9, 1940, Santa Monica, CA
Oregon 6'0" 192 lbs.

1962	DAL	N	14	DB
1963			14	DB
1964			11	DB
1965			14	DB
1966			14	DB

Mike Gaechter continued

1967			14	DB
1968			14	DB
1969			13	DB
8 yrs.	108 games			

Derrick Gaffney
GAFFNEY, DERRICK TYRONE
B. May 24, 1955, Jacksonville, FL
Florida 6'1" 179 lbs.

1978	NYJ	N	16	WR
1979			16	WR
1980			13	WR
1981			16	WR
1982			9	WR
1983			16	WR
1984			12	WR
1987			2	WR
8 yrs.	100 games			

Jim Gaffney
GAFFNEY, JAMES T., JR.
B. Apr. 21, 1921, Cumberland, MD
Tennessee 6'1" 204 lbs.

1945	WAS	N	2	HB
1946			10	HB
2 yrs.	12 games			

Jeff Gaffney
GAFFNEY, JEFF
B. Oct. 22, 1964
Virginia 6'2" 195 lbs.

| 1987 | SD | N | 3 | K |

Monk Gafford
GAFFORD, ROY H.
B. Oct. 1, 1920
D. Feb. 19, 1987, Montgomery, AL
Auburn 5'11" 195 lbs.

1946	MIA	AA	12	HB
1946	BKN	AA	2	HB
1947			14	HB
1948			12	HB
3 yrs.	40 games			

Bobby Gage
GAGE, ROBERT, II
B. Dec. 16, 1927
Clemson 5'11" 175 lbs.

1949	PIT	N	12	HB
1950			10	HB
2 yrs.	22 games			

Steve Gage
GAGE, STEVE
B. May 10, 1964, Claremore, OK
Tulsa 6'3" 210 lbs.

1987	WAS	N	4	S
1988			16	S
2 yrs.	20 games			

Bob Gagliano
GAGLIANO, ROBERT FRANK
B. Sep. 5, 1958, Los Angeles, CA
U.S. International/Utah State 6'3" 195 lbs.

1982	KC	N	1	QB
1983			1	QB
1987	SF	N	3	QB
1988	IND	N	2	QB
1989	DET	N	11	QB
1990			9	QB
1991	SD	N	2	QB
1992			5	QB
8 yrs.	34 games			

Larry Gagner
GAGNER, LAWRENCE JOSEPH
B. Dec. 30, 1943, Cleveland, OH
Florida 6'3" 246 lbs.

1966	PIT	N	14	G
1967			14	G
1968			12	G
1969			14	G
1972	KC	N	6	G
5 yrs.	60 games			

Dave Gagnon
GAGNON, DAVID JOHN
B. Jan. 17, 1951, Garden City, MI
Ferris State 5'10" 210 lbs.

| 1974 | CHI | N | 13 | RB |

Roy Gagnon
GAGNON, ROY JOSEPH MAURICE (Rosy)
B. Jan. 6, 1913, Minneapolis, MN
Oregon 5'11" 210 lbs.

| 1935 | DET | N | 4 | G |

Bob Gain
GAIN, ROBERT
B. Jun. 21, 1929, Weirton, WV
Kentucky 6'3" 256 lbs.

1952	CLE	N	6	DT
1954			2	DT
1955			11	DT
1956			12	DT, DE, LB
1957			12	DT
1958			12	DT, DE
1959			12	DE
1960			12	DT
1961			14	DT
1962			14	DT
1963			14	DT
1964			4	DT
12 yrs.	125 games			

Derrick Gainer
GAINER, DERRICK LUTHER
B. Aug. 15, 1966, Plant City, FL
Florida A&M 5'11" 235 lbs.

1990	CLE	N	16	RB
1992	LARI	N	2	RB
1992	DAL	N	5	RB
1993			11	RB
3 yrs.	34 games			

Chris Gaines
GAINES, CHRISTOPHER RANDALL
B. Feb. 3, 1965, Nashville, TN
Vanderbilt 6'0" 238 lbs.

| 1988 | MIA | N | 4 | LB |

Clark Gaines
GAINES, CLARK
B. Feb. 1, 1954, Elberton, GA
Wake Forest 6'1" 210 lbs.

1976	NYJ	N	14	RB
1977			14	RB
1978			16	RB
1979			16	RB
1980			5	RB
1982	KC	N	9	RB
6 yrs.	74 games			

Greg Gaines
GAINES, GREGORY SCOTT
B. Oct. 16, 1958, Martinsdale, VA
Tennessee 6'3" 212 lbs.

| 1981 | SEA | N | 8 | LB |
| 1983 | | | 15 | LB |

Year	Team		Games	Pos.

Greg Gaines continued

Year	Team		Games	Pos.
1984			16	LB
1985			16	LB
1986			16	LB
1987			11	LB
1988			6	LB
7 yrs.	88 games			

Lawrence Gaines
GAINES, LAWRENCE
B. Dec. 15, 1953, Vernon, TX
Wyoming 6'1" 237 lbs.

Year	Team		Games	Pos.
1976	DET	N	14	RB
1978			13	RB
1979			16	RB
3 yrs.	43 games			

Sheldon Gaines
GAINES, SHELDON
B. Apr. 22, 1964, Los Angeles, CA
Long Beach State 5'9" 155 lbs.

Year	Team		Games	Pos.
1987	BUF	N	3	WR

Wendall Gaines
GAINES, WENDALL
B. Jan. 17, 1972, Vernon, TX
Oklahoma State 6'4" 293 lbs.

Year	Team		Games	Pos.
1995	ARI	N	16	TE

Wentford Gaines
GAINES, WENTFORD ELIJAH
B. Feb. 4, 1953, Anderson, SC
Tennessee Tech/Cincinnati 6'0" 185 lbs.

Year	Team		Games	Pos.
1978	PIT	N	1	CB
1978	CHI	N	11	CB
1979			16	CB
1980			8	CB
3 yrs.	36 games			

William Gaines
GAINES, WILLIAM ALBERT
B. Jun. 20, 1971, Jackson, MS
Florida 6'5" 300 lbs.

Year	Team		Games	Pos.
1994	MIA	N	8	DT
1995	WAS	N	15	DT
1996			16	DT
3 yrs.	39 games			

Charlie Gainor
GAINOR, CHARLES E.
B. 1916
North Dakota 6'3" 190 lbs.

Year	Team		Games	Pos.
1939	CHIC	N	1	E

George Gaiser
GAISER, GEORGE NOLAN
B. May 9, 1945, San Antonio, TX
Southern Methodist 6'4" 255 lbs.

Year	Team		Games	Pos.
1968	DEN	A	10	OT

Blane Gaison
GAISON, BLANE
B. May 13, 1958, Kaneohe, HI
Hawaii 6'0" 185 lbs.

Year	Team		Games	Pos.
1981	ATL	N	14	CB, S
1982			9	S
1983			16	S
1984			15	S
4 yrs.	54 games			

Bob Gaiters
GAITERS, ROBERT
B. Feb. 26, 1938, Zanesville, OH
New Mexico State 5'11" 210 lbs.

Year	Team		Games	Pos.
1961	NYG	N	14	HB

Bob Gaiters continued

Year	Team		Games	Pos.
1962			2	HB
1962	SF	N	11	HB
1963	DEN	A		HB
3 yrs.	27 games			

Bill Gaiver
GAIVER, WILLIAM EINAR
B. May 29, 1898
Georgia Tech 5'9" 190 lbs.

Year	Team		Games	Pos.
1922	HAM	N	4	HB
1923	RI	N	8	HB, FB
1924	RAC	N	10	HB, FB
1925	HAM	N	4	FB, HB
1926	CHI	A	1	HB
1926	LOU	N	2	HB
5 yrs.	29 games			

Hokie Gajan
GAJAN, HOWARD LEE, JR.
B. Sep. 6, 1959, Baton Rouge, LA
Louisiana State 5'11" 220 lbs.

Year	Team		Games	Pos.
1982	NO	N	9	FB
1983			16	FB
1984			14	FB
1985			8	FB
4 yrs.	47 games			

Stan Galazin
GALAZIN, STANLEY B.
B. Aug. 8, 1915
D. Jan. 3, 1989, Queens, NY
Villanova 6'3" 211 lbs.

Year	Team		Games	Pos.
1937	NYG	N	1	C
1938			5	C, G
1939			3	C
3 yrs.	9 games			

Scott Galbraith
GALBRAITH, ALAN SCOTT
B. Jan. 7, 1967, Sacramento, CA
Southern California 6'3" 260 lbs.

Year	Team		Games	Pos.
1990	CLE	N	16	TE
1991			16	TE
1992			14	TE
1993	DAL	N	7	TE
1994			15	TE
1995	WAS	N	16	TE
1996			16	TE
7 yrs.	100 games			

Harry Galbreath
GALBREATH, HARRY CURTIS
B. Jan. 1, 1965, Clarksville, TN
Tennessee 6'1" 275 lbs.

Year	Team		Games	Pos.
1988	MIA	N	16	G
1989			14	G, C
1990			16	G, C
1991			16	G
1992			16	G
1993	GB	N	16	G
1994			16	G
1995			16	G
1996	NYJ	N	15	G
9 yrs.	141 games			

Tony Galbreath
GALBREATH, ANTHONY DALE
B. Jan. 29, 1954, Fulton, MO
Missouri 6'0" 228 lbs.

Year	Team		Games	Pos.
1976	NO	N	14	RB
1977			14	RB
1978			16	RB
1979			15	FB
1980			16	FB
1981	MIN	N	14	RB
1982			8	RB
1983			13	RB

Tony Galbreath continued

Year	Team		Games	Pos.
1984	NYG	N	16	RB
1985			16	RB
1986			16	RB
1987			12	RB
12 yrs.	170 games			

Arnie Galiffa
GALIFFA, ARNOLD ANTHONY
B. Jan. 29, 1927, Donora, PA
D. Sep. 5, 1978, Glenview, IL
Army 6'2" 193 lbs.

Year	Team		Games	Pos.
1953	NYG	N	3	QB
1954	SF	N	4	QB
2 yrs.	7 games			

Ed Galigher
GALIGHER, EDWARD ALBERT
B. Oct. 15, 1950, Hayward, CA
UCLA 6'4" 253 lbs.

Year	Team		Games	Pos.
1972	NYJ	N	13	DE
1973			7	DE, DT
1974			13	DE
1975			13	DT
1976			14	DT
1977	SF	N	12	DT
1978			15	DT
7 yrs.	87 games			

Willie Galimore
GALIMORE, WILLIE LEE
(The Wisp)
B. Mar. 30, 1935, St. Augustine, FL
D. Jul. 26, 1964, Rensselaer, IN
Florida A&M 6'1" 187 lbs.

Year	Team		Games	Pos.
1957	CHIB	N	12	HB
1958			12	HB
1959			12	HB
1960	CHI	N	12	HB
1961			14	HB
1962			7	HB
1963			13	HB
7 yrs.	82 games			

Bernie Gallagher
GALLAGHER, BERNARD J.
B. Nov. 8, 1921, Philadelphia, PA
D. Nov. 17, 1988, East Lansdowne, PA
*Pennsylvania/Princeton/Pennsylvania
6'0" 234 lbs.*

Year	Team		Games	Pos.
1947	LA	AA	8	G

Dave Gallagher
GALLAGHER, DAVID DILLON
B. Jan. 2, 1952, Piqua, OH
Michigan 6'4" 256 lbs.

Year	Team		Games	Pos.
1974	CHI	N	14	DE, DT
1975	NYG	N	12	DE
1976			14	DE
1978	DET	N	1	DT
1979			10	DT
5 yrs.	51 games			

Ed Gallagher
GALLAGHER, J. EDWARD
B. Feb. 3, 1903
D. Oct., 1963
Washington & Jefferson 6'1" 205 lbs.

Year	Team		Games	Pos.
1928	NYY	N	11	T, G

Frank Gallagher
GALLAGHER, FRANK J.
B. Mar. 2, 1943, Chester, PA
North Carolina 6'2" 243 lbs.

Year	Team		Games	Pos.
1967	DET	N	13	G
1968			14	G
1969			14	G

Frank Gallagher continued

Year	Team		Games	Pos.
1970			14	G
1971			14	G
1972			14	G
1973	ATL	N	3	G
1973	MIN	N	4	G
7 yrs.	90 games			

Allen Gallaher
GALLAHER, ALLEN
B. Nov. 30, 1950, San Fernando, CA
Southern California 6'3" 255 lbs.

Year	Team		Games	Pos.
1974	NE	N	14	OT

Hugh Gallarneau
GALLARNEAU, HUGH H.
B. Apr. 2, 1917, Detroit, MI
Stanford 6'0" 190 lbs.

Year	Team		Games	Pos.
1941	CHIB	N	11	HB
1942			10	HB
1945			8	HB
1946			10	HB
1947			12	HB
5 yrs.	51 games			

Chan Gallegos
GALLEGOS, CHAN
B. 1940
San Jose State 5'9" 175 lbs.

Year	Team		Games	Pos.
1962	OAK	A	6	QB

Jim Gallery
GALLERY, JAMES PATRICK
B. Sep. 15, 1961, Redwood Falls, MN
Minnesota 6'1" 190 lbs.

Year	Team		Games	Pos.
1987	STL	N	13	K
1989	CIN	N	4	K
1990	MIN	N	2	K
3 yrs.	19 games			

Tony Gallovich
GALLOVICH, ANTHONY RICHARD
B. Oct. 10, 1917, Vandergrift, PA
Wake Forest 5'9" 170 lbs.

Year	Team		Games	Pos.
1941	CLE	N	4	HB, DB

David Galloway
GALLOWAY, DAVID LAWRENCE
B. Feb. 16, 1959, Tampa, FL
Florida 6'3" 279 lbs.

Year	Team		Games	Pos.
1982	STL	N	5	DT
1983			16	DT
1984			14	DT
1985			16	DT
1986			14	DT
1987			4	DE
1988	PHX	N	8	DE
1989			12	DE
1990	DEN	N	10	DE
9 yrs.	99 games			

Duane Galloway
GALLOWAY, DUANE KEITH
B. Nov. 7, 1961, Los Angeles, CA
Arizona State 5'8" 181 lbs.

Year	Team		Games	Pos.
1985	DET	N	2	CB
1986			16	CB, S
1987			10	CB, S
3 yrs.	28 games			

Joey Galloway
GALLOWAY, JOEY
B. Nov. 20, 1971, Bellaire, OH
Ohio State 5'11" 188 lbs.

Year	Team		Games	Pos.
1995	SEA	N	16	WR

481

Year	Team		Games	Pos.

Joey Galloway continued

Year	Team		Games	Pos.
1996			16	WR
2 yrs.	32 games			

John Galvin
GALVIN, JOHN BLAKE, JR.
B. Jul. 9, 1965, Lowell, MA
Boston College 6'3" 226 lbs.

1988	NYJ	N	2	LB
1990			16	LB
1991			9	LB
3 yrs.	27 games			

John Galvin
GALVIN, JOHN E.
B. Dec. 7, 1920, Chicago, IL
Purdue 5'10" 170 lbs.

| 1947 | BAL | AA | 13 | QB, P |

Scott Galyon
GALYON, SCOTT
B. Mar. 23, 1974, Seymour, TN
Tennessee 6'2" 237 lbs.

| 1996 | NYG | N | 16 | LB |

Vince Gamache
GAMACHE, VINCENT LUCKY
B. Nov. 18, 1961, Los Angeles, CA
Fullerton State 5'11" 186 lbs.

1986	SEA	N	16	P
1987	LARI	N	3	P
2 yrs.	19 games			

Lu Gambino
GAMBINO, LUCIEN ANTHONY
B. Sep. 21, 1963, Berwyn, IL
Indiana/Maryland 6'1" 205 lbs.

1948	BAL	AA	9	FB, LB
1949			10	FB
2 yrs.	19 games			

Kenny Gamble
GAMBLE, KENNETH P.
B. Mar. 8, 1965, Holyoke, MA
Colgate 5'10" 197 lbs.

1988	KC	N	16	RB
1989			2	RB
1990			1	RB
3 yrs.	19 games			

R.C. Gamble
GAMBLE, R.C.
B. Mar. 2, 1943, Chester, PA
South Carolina State 6'3" 220 lbs.

1968	BOS	A	14	RB
1969			13	RB
2 yrs.	27 games			

Chris Gambol
GAMBOL, CHRISTOPHER HUGHES
B. Sep. 14, 1964, Pittsburgh, PA
Iowa 6'6" 303 lbs.

1988	SD	N	11	OT
1988	IND	N	1	OT
1989	DET	N	6	OT
1990	NE	N	16	OT
3 yrs.	34 games			

Bob Gambold
GAMBOLD, ROBERT LEE
B. Feb. 5, 1929, Longview, WA
Washington State 6'4" 215 lbs.

| 1953 | PHI | N | 3 | QB |

Billy Gambrell
GAMBRELL, WILLIAM EDWARD
B. Sep. 18, 1941, Athens, GA
South Carolina 5'10" 175 lbs.

1963	STL	N	14	FL
1964			13	OE
1965			10	OE
1966			14	OE
1967			12	OE
1968	DET	N	14	OE
6 yrs.	77 games			

Kendall Gammon
GAMMON, KENDALL ROBERT
B. Oct. 28, 1968, Wichita, KS
Pittsburg State 6'4" 279 lbs.

1992	PIT	N	16	G
1993			16	C, G
1994			16	C
1995			16	C
1996	NO	N	16	C
5 yrs.	80 games			

Rusty Ganas
GANAS, RUSTY
B. Sep. 12, 1949, Waycross, GA
South Carolina 6'4" 257 lbs.

| 1971 | BAL | N | 1 | DT |

Sonny Gandee
GANDEE, SHERWIN K.
B. Feb. 27, 1929, Akron, OH
D. Oct., 1985, Cleveland, OH
Ohio State 6'1" 216 lbs.

1952	DAL	N	2	E
1952	DET	N	8	E
1953			8	E
1954			11	E
1955			12	E
1956			12	E
5 yrs.	53 games			

Wayne Gandy
GANDY, WAYNE LAMAR
B. Feb. 10, 1971, Haines City, FL
Auburn 6'4" 289 lbs.

1994	LARM	N	16	OT
1995	STL	N	16	OT
1996			16	OT
3 yrs.	48 games			

Mike Gann
GANN, MIKE ALAN
B. Oct. 19, 1963, Stillwater, OK
Notre Dame 6'5" 275 lbs.

1985	ATL	N	16	DE
1986			16	DE
1987			12	DE
1988			16	DE
1989			16	DE
1990			16	DE
1991			5	DE
1992			13	DE
1993			8	DE
9 yrs.	118 games			

Chris Gannon
GANNON, CHRISTOPHER STEPHEN
B. Jan. 20, 1966, Brandon, FL
Southwestern Louisiana 6'6" 263 lbs.

1989	SD	N	10	TE
1990	NE	N	6	DE
1991			8	DE
1992			12	DE
1993			4	DE
5 yrs.	40 games			

Rich Gannon
GANNON, RICHARD JOSEPH
B. Dec. 20, 1965, Philadelphia, PA
Delaware 6'3" 197 lbs.

1987	MIN	N	5	QB
1988			3	QB
1990			14	QB
1991			15	QB
1992			12	QB
1993	WAS	N	8	QB
1995	KC	N	2	QB
1996			4	QB
8 yrs.	63 games			

Al Gansberg
GANSBERG, ALFRED HENRY
B. Oct. 16, 1901, Lake Forest, IL
D. Aug. 24, 1976, Evanston, IL
Miami (Ohio) 5'11" 187 lbs.

| 1926 | LOU | N | 2 | E, T |

Brian Gant
GANT, BRIAN KEITH
B. Sep. 6, 1965, Gary, IN
Illinois State 6'0" 235 lbs.

| 1987 | TB | N | 11 | LB |

Earl Gant
GANT, EARL LEON
B. Jul. 6, 1957, Chicago, IL
Missouri 6'0" 207 lbs.

1979	KC	N	16	RB
1980			4	RB
2 yrs.	20 games			

Kenneth Gant
GANT, KENNETH DWAYNE
B. Apr. 18, 1967, Lakeland, FL
Albany State 5'11" 187 lbs.

1990	DAL	N	12	CB
1991			16	CB
1992			16	CB
1993			12	S
1994			16	S
1995	TB	N	16	S
1996			16	S
7 yrs.	104 games			

Reuben Gant
GANT, REUBEN CHARLES
B. Apr. 12, 1952, Tulsa, OK
Oklahoma State 6'4" 226 lbs.

1974	BUF	N	13	TE
1975			14	TE
1976			14	TE
1977			14	TE
1978			16	TE
1979			14	TE
1980			16	TE
7 yrs.	101 games			

Milt Gantenbein
GANTENBEIN, MILTON E.
B. May 31, 1909, New Albin, IA
D. Dec. 18, 1988, Carmichael, CA
Wisconsin 6'0" 199 lbs.

1931	GB	N	14	E
1932			9	E
1933			11	E
1934			10	E
1935			11	E
1936			9	E
1937			11	E
1938			11	E
1939			11	E
1940			5	E
10 yrs.	102 games			

Jerome Gantt
GANTT, JEROME FLOYD
B. Oct. 20, 1948, Greensboro, NC
North Carolina Central 6'4" 266 lbs.

| 1970 | BUF | N | 6 | OT |

Greg Gantt
GANTT, GREGORY
B. Oct. 30, 1951, Birmingham, AL
Alabama 5'11" 188 lbs.

1974	NYJ	N	14	P, K
1975			14	P
2 yrs.	28 games			

Bob Gaona
GAONA, ROBERT JOHN
B. Feb. 3, 1931
Wake Forest 6'3" 243 lbs.

1953	PIT	N	10	T
1954			12	T
1955			12	T
1956			12	T
1957	PHI	N	12	T
5 yrs.	58 games			

Mark Garalczyk
GARALCZYK, MARK PATRICK
B. Aug. 12, 1965, Roseville, MI
Western Michigan 6'5" 272 lbs.

1987	STL	N	11	DT
1988	PHX	N	6	DT
1988	NYJ	N	7	DE
2 yrs.	24 games			

Tony Garbarczyk
GARBARCZYK, ANTHONY
B. Jan. 29, 1964, Queens Village, NY
Wake Forest 6'4" 275 lbs.

| 1987 | NYJ | N | 2 | DE |

Bubba Garcia
GARCIA, JESSE CLARENCE
B. Oct. 18, 1957, New Braunfels, TX
Texas-El Paso 5'11" 185 lbs.

| 1980 | KC | N | 5 | WR |

Eddie Garcia
GARCIA, EDGAR I.
B. Apr. 15, 1960, New Orleans, LA
Southern Methodist 5'8" 178 lbs.

1983	GB	N	12	K
1984			7	K
2 yrs.	19 games			

Frank Garcia
GARCIA, FRANK
B. Jan. 28, 1972, Phoenix, AZ
Washington 6'1" 290 lbs.

1995	CAR	N	15	G, C
1996			14	G
2 yrs.	29 games			

Frank Garcia
GARCIA, FRANK BENITEZ
B. Jun. 5, 1957, Tucson, AZ
Arizona State/UNLV/Arizona 6'0" 210 lbs.

1981	SEA	N	1	P
1983	TB	N	16	P
1984			16	P
1985			16	P
1986			16	P
1987			12	P
6 yrs.	77 games			

Year	Team		Games	Pos.

Jim Garcia
GARCIA, JAMES RONALD
B. Mar. 7, 1944, Chicago, IL
Purdue 6'4" 248 lbs.

Year	Team		Games	Pos.
1965	CLE	N	12	DE
1966	NYG	N	10	DE
1967	NO	N	12	DE
1968	ATL	N	1	DT, DE
4 yrs.		35 games		

Teddy Garcia
GARCIA, ALFONSO TEDDY
B. Jun. 4, 1964, Caddo Parish, LA
Northeast Louisiana 5'10" 190 lbs.

Year	Team		Games	Pos.
1988	NE	N	16	K
1989	MIN	N	3	K
1990	HOU	N	9	K
3 yrs.		28 games		

Gus Gardella
GARDELLA, AUGUSTUS (Hope)
B. Jul. 22, 1895
D. Jun., 1985, Bridgeport, CT
None 190 lbs.

Year	Team		Games	Pos.
1922	GB	N	7	FB, HB

Frank Garden
GARDEN, FRANK
B. Jun. 3, 1898
D. Jun. 26, 1966, Santa Monica, CA
None 5'11" 188 lbs.

Year	Team		Games	Pos.
1920	RI	A	1	E

Daryl Gardener
GARDENER, DARYL
B. Feb. 25, 1973, Lawton, OK
Baylor 6'6" 320 lbs.

Year	Team		Games	Pos.
1996	MIA	N	16	DT

Ron Gardin
GARDIN, RONALD L.
B. Sep. 25, 1944, New Haven, CT
Arizona 5'11" 180 lbs.

Year	Team		Games	Pos.
1970	BAL	N	13	CB
1971			2	CB
1971	NE	N	8	WR, DB
2 yrs.		23 games		

Carwell Gardner
GARDNER, CARWELL ERNEST
B. Nov. 27, 1966, Louisville, KY
Louisville 6'2" 235 lbs.

Year	Team		Games	Pos.
1990	BUF	N	7	RB
1991			16	RB
1992			16	RB
1993			13	RB
1994			16	RB
1995			15	RB
1996	BAL	N	13	RB
7 yrs.		96 games		

Donnie Gardner
GARDNER, REDONDO LEE
B. Feb. 17, 1968, Louisville, KY
Kentucky 6'3" 260 lbs.

Year	Team		Games	Pos.
1991	MIA	N	10	DE

Ellis Gardner
GARDNER, ELLIS PENISTON
B. Sep. 16, 1961, Chattanooga, TN
Georgia Tech 6'5" 260 lbs.

Year	Team		Games	Pos.
1983	KC	N	8	OT
1984	IND	N	9	OT, G
2 yrs.		17 games		

George Gardner
GARDNER, GEORGE
None 170 lbs.

Year	Team		Games	Pos.
1923	CLE	N	2	E

Milt Gardner
GARDNER, MILTON L. (Moose)
B. Jul. 2, 1894, Ashland, WI
Deceased
Wisconsin 6'1" 220 lbs.

Year	Team		Games	Pos.
1920	DET	A	2	G
1921			7	G
1921	BUF	A	1	G
1922	GB	N	9	G, E
1923			9	G
1924			11	G
1925			13	G, T
1926			13	G
7 yrs.		65 games		

Moe Gardner
GARDNER, MORRIS
B. Aug. 10, 1968, Indianapolis, IN
Illinois 6'2" 258 lbs.

Year	Team		Games	Pos.
1991	ATL	N	16	NT
1992			16	NT
1993			16	NT
1994			16	DT
1995			16	DT
1996			10	DT
6 yrs.		90 games		

Chris Gardocki
GARDOCKI, CHRISTOPHER ALLEN
B. Feb. 7, 1970, Stone Mountain, GA
Clemson 6'1" 194 lbs.

Year	Team		Games	Pos.
1991	CHI	N	4	P
1992			16	P
1993			16	P
1994			16	P
1995	IND	N	16	P
1996			16	P
6 yrs.		84 games		

Chris Garlich
GARLICH, CHRISTOPHER J.
B. Jul. 17, 1957, St. Louis, MO
Missouri 6'1" 220 lbs.

Year	Team		Games	Pos.
1979	STL	N	9	LB

Tom Garlick
GARLICK, TOM
B. Sep. 22, 1971, Philadelphia, PA
Fordham 5'11" 180 lbs.

Year	Team		Games	Pos.
1994	PHI	N	1	WR

Don Garlin
GARLIN, DONALD ARTHUR
B. Nov. 10, 1926, Porterville, CA
Southern California 5'11" 188 lbs.

Year	Team		Games	Pos.
1949	SF	AA	11	HB
1950	SF	N	8	HB
2 yrs.		19 games		

John Garlington
GARLINGTON, JOHN
B. Jun. 5, 1946, Jonesboro, LA
Louisiana State 6'1" 222 lbs.

Year	Team		Games	Pos.
1968	CLE	N	13	LB
1969			14	LB
1970			11	LB
1971			14	LB
1972			14	LB
1973			14	LB
1974			14	LB

John Garlington *continued*

Year	Team		Games	Pos.
1975			7	LB
1976			14	LB
1977				LB
10 yrs.		115 games		

Bill Garnaas
GARNAAS, WILFORD B.
B. Oct. 8, 1921
Minnesota 5'11" 187 lbs.

Year	Team		Games	Pos.
1946	PIT	N	10	QB
1947			10	QB
2 yrs.		20 games		

Bob Garner
GARNER, ROBERT
B. 1923
None 6'0" 238 lbs.

Year	Team		Games	Pos.
1945	NYG	N	1	G

Bob Garner
GARNER, ROBERT
B. 1935
Fresno State 5'10" 185 lbs.

Year	Team		Games	Pos.
1960	LA	A		DB
1961	OAK	A	13	DB
1962			14	DB
3 yrs.		27 games		

Charlie Garner
GARNER, CHARLIE
B. Feb. 13, 1972, Falls Church, VA
Tennessee 5'9" 181 lbs.

Year	Team		Games	Pos.
1994	PHI	N	10	RB
1995			15	RB
1996			15	RB
3 yrs.		40 games		

Dwight Garner
GARNER, DWIGHT E.
B. Oct. 25, 1964, San Francisco, CA
California 5'8" 183 lbs.

Year	Team		Games	Pos.
1986	WAS	N	2	RB

Hal Garner
GARNER, HAL E., JR.
B. Jan. 18, 1962, New Iberia, LA
Utah State 6'4" 225 lbs.

Year	Team		Games	Pos.
1985	BUF	N	13	LB
1986			16	LB
1988			12	LB
1990			10	LB
1991			16	LB
5 yrs.		67 games		

Dave Garnett
GARNETT, DAVID EUGENE
B. Dec. 6, 1970, Pittsburgh, PA
Stanford 6'2" 219 lbs.

Year	Team		Games	Pos.
1993	MIN	N	16	LB
1994			9	LB
1995	DEN	N	3	LB
1996	MIN	N	12	LB
4 yrs.		40 games		

Scott Garnett
GARNETT, SCOTT AARON
B. Dec. 3, 1962, Harrisburg, PA
Washington 6'2" 271 lbs.

Year	Team		Games	Pos.
1984	DEN	N	16	NT
1985	SF	N	3	NT
1986	SD	N	5	NT
1987	BUF	N	3	DE, NT
3 yrs.		27 games		

Bill Garnjorst
GARNJORST, WILLIAM TECUMSEH SHERMAN (Sherm)
B. Dec., 1892
D. 1958
Columbia 5'10" 190 lbs.

Year	Team		Games	Pos.
1921	EVA	A	5	G, C

Al Garrett
GARRETT, ALFRED T. (Budge)
B. 1893
D. Jun. 7, 1950
Rutgers 5'11" 200 lbs.

Year	Team		Games	Pos.
1920	AKR	A	6	G, T, E
1922	MIL	N	6	E, G, FB
2 yrs.		12 games		

Alvin Garrett
GARRETT, ALVIN LYNN
B. Oct. 1, 1956, Mineral Wells, TX
Angelo State 5'7" 178 lbs.

Year	Team		Games	Pos.
1980	NYG	N	15	WR
1981			9	WR
1981	WAS	N	4	WR
1982			9	WR
1983			15	WR
1984			3	WR
5 yrs.		55 games		

Bill Garrett
GARRETT, WILLIAM D., JR. (Dub)
B. Aug. 12, 1926, Dundee, MS
Deceased
Mississippi State 6'1" 237 lbs.

Year	Team		Games	Pos.
1948	BAL	AA	14	G
1949			11	G
1950	CHIB	N	3	DT
3 yrs.		28 games		

Bobby Garrett
GARRETT, ROBERT D.
B. Aug. 16, 1932, Los Angeles, CA
D. Dec. 5, 1987, Westminster, CA
Stanford 6'1" 198 lbs.

Year	Team		Games	Pos.
1954	GB	N	9	QB

Carl Garrett
GARRETT, CARL L.
B. Aug. 31, 1947, Denton, TX
New Mexico Highlands 5'11" 209 lbs.

Year	Team		Games	Pos.
1969	BOS	A	14	RB
1970	BOS	N	13	RB
1971	NE	N	14	RB
1972			11	RB
1973	CHI	N	13	RB
1974			7	RB
1975	NYJ	N	13	RB
1976	OAK	N	12	RB
1977			14	RB
9 yrs.		111 games		

Curtis Garrett
GARRETT, CURTIS
B. Jun. 9, 1962
Illinois State 6'5" 203 lbs.

Year	Team		Games	Pos.
1987	NYG	N	3	DE

Drake Garrett
GARRETT, DRAKE F.
B. Mar. 19, 1946, Dayton, OH
Michigan State 5'9" 183 lbs.

Year	Team		Games	Pos.
1968	DEN	A	14	DB
1970	DEN	N	9	DB
2 yrs.		15 games		

Year	Team	Games	Pos.

Jason Garrett
GARRETT, JASON CALVIN
B. Mar. 28, 1966, Abington, PA
Princeton 6'2" 195 lbs.

Year	Team		Games	Pos.
1993	DAL	N	5	QB
1994			2	QB
1995			1	QB
1996			1	QB
4 yrs.			9 games	

J.D. Garrett
GARRETT, J.D.
B. Nov. 28, 1941, Natchitoches, LA
Grambling State 5'11" 195 lbs.

Year	Team		Games	Pos.
1964	BOS	A	14	HB
1965			12	HB
1966			14	HB
1967			10	RB
4 yrs.			50 games	

John Garrett
GARRETT, JOHN MORGAN
B. Mar. 2, 1965, Danville, PA
Columbia/Princeton 5'11" 180 lbs.

Year	Team		Games	Pos.
1989	CIN	N	1	WR

Len Garrett
GARRETT, LEONARD NEAL
B. Dec. 18, 1948, Silsbee, TX
New Mexico Highlands 6'3" 230 lbs.

Year	Team		Games	Pos.
1971	GB	N	14	TE
1972			14	TE
1973			2	TE
1973	NO	N	12	TE
1974			10	TE
1975			1	TE
1975	SF	N	2	TE
5 yrs.			55 games	

Mike Garrett
GARRETT, MICHAEL LOCKETT
B. Apr. 12, 1944, Los Angeles, CA
Southern California 5'9" 199 lbs.

Year	Team		Games	Pos.
1966	KC	A	14	RB
1967			14	RB
1968			13	RB
1969			14	RB
1970	SD	N	9	RB
1971			13	RB
1972			14	RB
1973			10	RB
8 yrs.			101 games	

Mike Garrett
GARRETT, MICHAEL STEVEN
B. Jun. 13, 1957, Atlanta, GA
Georgia 6'1" 184 lbs.

Year	Team		Games	Pos.
1981	BAL	N	16	P

Reggie Garrett
GARRETT, REGINALD
B. Nov. 22, 1951, Silsbee, TX
Eastern Michigan 6'1" 174 lbs.

Year	Team		Games	Pos.
1974	PIT	N	14	WR
1975			14	WR
2 yrs.			28 games	

Shane Garrett
GARRETT, MARCUS SHANE
B. Nov. 16, 1967, Lafayette, LA
Texas A&M 5'11" 185 lbs.

Year	Team		Games	Pos.
1991	CIN	N	4	WR

Thurman Garrett
GARRETT, THURMAN
B. 1924

Thurman Garrett continued
Oklahoma State 6'3" 268 lbs.

Year	Team		Games	Pos.
1947	CHIB	N	10	C
1948			10	C
2 yrs.			20 games	

Norberto Garrido
GARRIDO, NORBERTO
B. Oct. 4, 1972, La Puente, CA
Southern California 6'7" 313 lbs.

Year	Team		Games	Pos.
1996	CAR	N	10	OT

Gary Garrison
GARRISON, GARY LYNN (Ghost)
B. Jan. 21, 1944, Amarillo, TX
San Diego State 6'1" 194 lbs.

Year	Team		Games	Pos.
1966	SD	A	14	OE
1967			14	OE
1968			14	OE
1969			10	WR
1970	SD	N	14	WR
1971			14	WR
1972			14	WR
1973			7	WR
1974			14	WR
1975			14	WR
1976			2	WR
1977	HOU	N	2	WR
12 yrs.			133 games	

Walt Garrison
GARRISON, WALTER BENTON
B. Jul. 23, 1944, Denton, TX
Oklahoma State 6'0" 204 lbs.

Year	Team		Games	Pos.
1966	DAL	N	14	RB
1967			13	RB
1968			14	RB
1969			13	RB
1970			11	RB
1971			13	RB
1972			13	RB
1973			13	RB
1974			14	RB
9 yrs.			119 games	

Gregg Garrity
GARRITY, GREGG DAVID
B. Nov. 24, 1960, Pittsburgh, PA
Penn State 5'10" 170 lbs.

Year	Team		Games	Pos.
1983	PIT	N	15	WR
1984			6	WR
1984	PHI	N	4	WR
1985			12	WR
1986			12	WR
1987			12	WR
1988			9	WR
1989			9	WR
7 yrs.			79 games	

Larry Garron
GARRON, LAWRENCE, JR.
B. May 23, 1937, Marks, MS
Western Illinois 6'0" 199 lbs.

Year	Team		Games	Pos.
1960	BOS	A	4	HB
1961			14	HB
1962			11	HB, FB
1963			14	FB
1964			14	FB
1965			10	FB
1966			14	FB
1967			14	RB
1968			4	RB
9 yrs.			99 games	

Leon Garror
GARROR, LEON
B. May 2, 1948, Mobile, AL

Leon Garror continued
Alcorn State 6'0" 180 lbs.

Year	Team		Games	Pos.
1972	BUF	N	12	CB
1973			4	CB
2 yrs.			16 games	

Ben Garry
GARRY, BEN EARL
B. Feb. 11, 1956, Hazelhurst, MS
Southern Mississippi 6'0" 215 lbs.

Year	Team		Games	Pos.
1979	BAL	N	12	RB
1980			3	RB
2 yrs.			15 games	

Chris Gartner
GARTNER, SVEN CHRIS
B. Jul. 12, 1950, Gothenburg, Sweden
Indiana 6'0" 170 lbs.

Year	Team		Games	Pos.
1974	CLE	N	11	K

Art Garvey
GARVEY, ARTHUR A. (Hec)
B. Feb. 20, 1900, Holyoke, MA
D. Sep. 22, 1973, Chicago, IL
Notre Dame 6'1" 234 lbs.

Year	Team		Games	Pos.
1922	CHIB	N	12	E, T, G
1923			13	G, E
1925			1	G
1926	HAR	N	4	T, G
1926	BKN	A	2	T
1926	BKN	A	1	C
1926	NY	A	2	G
1927	NYG	N	8	G
1928			10	G, E
1929	PRO	N	9	G, T
1930	BKN	N	12	G
1931	SI	N	11	G, T
9 yrs.			85 games	

Frank Garvey
GARVEY, FRANCIS
B. Aug. 27, 1900
D. Sep., 1972, Worcester, MA
Holy Cross 6'1" 175 lbs.

Year	Team		Games	Pos.
1925	PRO	N	9	E
1926			10	E
2 yrs.			19 games	

Cleveland Gary
GARY, CLEVELAND EVERETTE
B. May 4, 1966, Stuart, FL
Miami (Florida) 6'0" 226 lbs.

Year	Team		Games	Pos.
1989	LARM	N	10	RB
1990			15	RB
1991			10	RB
1992			16	RB
1993			15	RB
1994	MIA	N	2	RB
6 yrs.			68 games	

Keith Gary
GARY, KEITH JERROLD
B. Sep. 14, 1959, Bethesda, MD
Oklahoma 6'3" 260 lbs.

Year	Team		Games	Pos.
1983	PIT	N	16	DE
1984			16	DE
1985			12	DE
1986			16	DE
1987			11	DE
1988			15	DE
6 yrs.			86 games	

Russell Gary
GARY, RUSSELL CRAIG
B. Jul. 31, 1959, Minneapolis, MN
Nebraska 5'11" 195 lbs.

Year	Team		Games	Pos.
1981	NO	N	14	CB, S

Russell Gary continued

Year	Team		Games	Pos.
1982			9	S
1983			14	S
1984			16	S
1985			6	S
1986			7	S
1986	PHI	N	6	S
1987			12	S
7 yrs.			84 games	

Dan Garza
GARZA, DANIEL ROBERT
B. 1924, Anderson, SC
Missouri State/Oregon 6'3" 203 lbs.

Year	Team		Games	Pos.
1949	B-NY	AA	12	E
1951	NYY	N	11	E
2 yrs.			23 games	

Mike Garzoni
GARZONI, MICHAEL JOHN
B. Aug. 19, 1923, Los Angeles, CA
Southern California 5'11" 218 lbs.

Year	Team		Games	Pos.
1947	WAS	N	10	G
1948	NYG	N	5	G
1948	NY	AA	2	G
2 yrs.			17 games	

Sam Gash
GASH, SAMUEL LEE
B. Mar. 7, 1969, Hendersonville, NC
Penn State 5'11" 224 lbs.

Year	Team		Games	Pos.
1992	NE	N	15	FB
1993			16	FB
1994			13	FB
1995			15	FB
1996			14	FB
5 yrs.			72 games	

Thane Gash
GASH, THANE ALVIN
B. Sep. 1, 1965, Hendersonville, NC
East Tennessee State 6'0" 200 lbs.

Year	Team		Games	Pos.
1988	CLE	N	16	S
1989			16	S
1990			16	S
1992	SF	N	16	S
4 yrs.			64 games	

Percell Gaskins
GASKINS, PERCELL
B. Apr. 25, 1972, Daytona Beach, FL
Northwestern Oklahoma State/Kansas State 6'0" 225 lbs.

Year	Team		Games	Pos.
1996	STL	N	15	LB

Joe Gasparella
GASPARELLA, JOSEPH RICHARD
B. Feb. 5, 1927, Apollo, PA
Notre Dame 6'4" 222 lbs.

Year	Team		Games	Pos.
1948	PIT	N	9	QB
1950			11	QB
1951			4	QB
1951	CHIC	N	2	QB
3 yrs.			26 games	

Ron Gassert
GASSERT, RON
B. Jul. 22, 1940, Mount Holly, NJ
Virginia 6'3" 250 lbs.

Year	Team		Games	Pos.
1962	GB	N	11	DT

Mark Gastineau
GASTINEAU, MARCUS D.
B. Nov. 20, 1956, Ardmore, OK

Year	Team		Games	Pos.

Mark Gastineau *continued*

Arizona State/East Central Oklahoma
6'5" 270 lbs.

Year	Team		Games	Pos.
1979	**NYJ**	**N**	16	DE, DT
1980			16	DE
1981			16	DE
1982			9	DE
1983			16	DE
1984			16	DE
1985			16	DE
1986			10	DE
1987			15	DE
1988			7	DE
10 yrs.	137 games			

Les Gatewood

GATEWOOD, LESTER B. (Buddy)
B. May 30, 1921, Dallas, TX
Baylor/Tulane 6'2" 198 lbs.

Year	Team		Games	Pos.
1946	**GB**	**N**	11	C
1947			12	C
2 yrs.	23 games			

Tom Gatewood

GATEWOOD, THOMAS, JR.
B. May 7, 1950, Baltimore, MD
Notre Dame 6'3" 215 lbs.

Year	Team		Games	Pos.
1972	**NYG**	**N**	10	WR, TE
1973			7	TE
2 yrs.	17 games			

Frank Gatski

GATSKI, FRANK (Gunner)
B. Mar. 12, 1922, Farmington, WV
Marshall/Auburn 6'3" 233 lbs.

Year	Team		Games	Pos.
1946	**CLE**	**AA**	10	C
1947			12	C
1948			14	C
1949			12	C
1950	**CLE**	**N**	12	C
1951			12	C
1952			12	C
1953			12	C
1954			12	C
1955			12	C
1956			12	C
1957	**DET**	**N**	12	C
12 yrs.	144 games			

Dennis Gaubatz

GAUBATZ, DENNIS E.
B. Feb. 11, 1940, Needville, TX
Louisiana State 6'2" 225 lbs.

Year	Team		Games	Pos.
1963	**DET**	**N**	14	LB
1964			14	LB
1965	**BAL**	**N**	14	LB
1966			13	LB
1967			14	LB
1968			14	LB
1969			12	LB
7 yrs.	95 games			

Bob Gaudio

GAUDIO, ANGELO ROBERT
B. Jul. 13, 1925, Ashtabula, OH
Ohio State 5'10" 219 lbs.

Year	Team		Games	Pos.
1947	**CLE**	**AA**	14	G
1948			13	G
1949			12	G
1951	**CLE**	**N**	12	G
4 yrs.	51 games			

Charlie Gauer

GAUER, CHARLES E., JR.
B. Sep. 24, 1919, Chicago, IL
D. Oct. 22, 1973, Philadelphia, PA
Colgate 6'2" 213 lbs.

Year	Team		Games	Pos.
1943	**P, P**	**N**	9	FB, E

Charlie Gauer *continued*

Year	Team		Games	Pos.
1944	**PHI**	**N**	8	E
1945			7	E
3 yrs.	24 games			

Frank Gaul

GAUL, FRANCIS EDWARD (Speed)
B. Aug. 8, 1926, Cleveland, OH
Notre Dame 6'0" 200 lbs.

Year	Team		Games	Pos.
1949	**NYB**	**N**	12	T

Hal Gaulke

GAULKE, HAROLD
B. Aug., 1894, Columbus, OH
Deceased
None 5'7" 175 lbs.

Year	Team		Games	Pos.
1920	**COL**	**A**	5	QB, FB
1921			4	QB, E
1922	**COL**	**N**	7	QB
3 yrs.	16 games			

Billy Gault

GAULT, WILLIAM
B. Dec. 19, 1936, Monroe, LA
Texas Christian 6'1" 185 lbs.

Year	Team		Games	Pos.
1961	**MIN**	**N**	4	DB

Don Gault

GAULT, DONALD J.
B. Aug. 30, 1946, Lynbrook, NY
Hofstra 6'2" 190 lbs.

Year	Team		Games	Pos.
1970	**CLE**	**N**	2	QB

Willie Gault

GAULT, WILLIE JAMES
B. Sep. 5, 1960, Griffin, GA
Tennessee 6'1" 183 lbs.

Year	Team		Games	Pos.
1983	**CHI**	**N**	16	WR
1984			16	WR
1985			16	WR
1986			16	WR
1987			12	WR
1988	**LARI**	**N**	15	WR
1989			16	WR
1990			16	WR
1991			16	WR
1992			16	WR
1993			15	WR
11 yrs.	170 games			

Steve Gaunty

GAUNTY, STEVE
B. May 3, 1957, Chicago, IL
Northern Colorado 5'10" 175 lbs.

Year	Team		Games	Pos.
1979	**KC**	**N**	9	WR

Art Gaustad

GAUSTAD, ARTHUR M. (Heavy)
B. 1889, Minnesota
Deceased
None 212 lbs.

Year	Team		Games	Pos.
1921	**MIN**	**A**	4	G
1922	**MIN**	**N**	4	G
1923			6	G
3 yrs.	14 games			

Prentice Gautt

GAUTT, PRENTICE
B. Feb. 8, 1938, Oklahoma City, OK
Oklahoma 6'0" 204 lbs.

Year	Team		Games	Pos.
1960	**CLE**	**N**	12	HB
1961	**STL**	**N**	13	HB
1962			14	HB
1963			1	HB
1964			14	FB

Prentice Gautt *continued*

Year	Team		Games	Pos.
1965			7	FB
1966			14	HB
1967			14	RB
8 yrs.	89 games			

Mike Gavigan

GAVIGAN, MICHAEL THOMAS
B. Apr., 1899
Deceased
St. Bonaventure 176 lbs.

Year	Team		Games	Pos.
1923	**ROC**	**N**	2	FB, HB

Chuck Gavin

GAVIN, CHARLES
B. Dec. 26, 1933, Lake, MS
Tennessee State 6'1" 243 lbs.

Year	Team		Games	Pos.
1960	**DEN**	**A**		DE
1961			8	DE
1962			14	DE
1963			14	DE
4 yrs.	36 games			

Pat Gavin

GAVIN, PATRICK J. (Buck)
B. Jun. 22, 1895
D. Apr., 1981, Daytona Beach, FL
Marquette 5'10" 179 lbs.

Year	Team		Games	Pos.
1920	**BUF**	**A**	5	HB, FB
1921	**DET**	**A**	3	FB
1921	**RI**	**A**	2	FB
1922	**RI**	**N**	7	FB
1922	**BUF**	**N**	3	FB, HB
1923	**GB**	**N**	9	FB
1924	**RI**	**N**	9	FB, HB
1925			5	FB
1926	**HAM**	**N**	2	FB, HB
7 yrs.	45 games			

Momcilo Gavric

GAVRIC, MOMCILO
B. Aug. 4, 1938, Senj, Yugoslavia
None 5'10" 167 lbs.

Year	Team		Games	Pos.
1969	**SF**	**N**	7	K

Billy Gay

GAY, WILLIAM THEODORE
B. Nov. 12, 1927, Chicago, IL
Notre Dame 5'11" 180 lbs.

Year	Team		Games	Pos.
1951	**CHIC**	**N**	3	DB
1952			2	DB
2 yrs.	5 games			

Blenda Gay

GAY, BLENDA
B. Nov. 22, 1950, Greenville, NC
D. Dec. 19, 1976, Blackwood, NJ
Fayetteville State 6'5" 254 lbs.

Year	Team		Games	Pos.
1974	**SD**	**N**	2	DE
1975	**PHI**	**N**	14	DE
1976			14	DE
3 yrs.	30 games			

Chet Gay

GAY, C.J.
B. Jan. 8, 1900, Moose Lake, MN
D. Mar. 12, 1978, Moose Lake, MN
Minnesota 6'0" 215 lbs.

Year	Team		Games	Pos.
1925	**BUF**	**N**	8	G, T
1926	**MIL**	**N**	6	T, G, C
2 yrs.	14 games			

Everett Gay

GAY, EVERETT CARLTON
B. Oct. 23, 1964, Houston, TX

Everett Gay *continued*

Texas 6'2" 209 lbs.

Year	Team		Games	Pos.
1988	**DAL**	**N**	16	WR
1989	**TB**	**N**	1	WR
2 yrs.	17 games			

Matt Gay

GAY, MATTHEW GILBERT
B. Apr. 3, 1970, Chicago, IL
Kansas 5'11" 180 lbs.

Year	Team		Games	Pos.
1994	**KC**	**N**	2	S

William Gay

GAY, WILLIAM H.
B. May 28, 1955, San Francisco, CA
Southern California 6'5" 250 lbs.

Year	Team		Games	Pos.
1978	**DET**	**N**	16	DE
1979			15	DE
1980			16	DE
1981			16	DE
1982			9	DT, DE
1983			15	DE, DT
1984			16	DE
1985			16	DE
1986			16	DE
1987			11	DE
1988	**MIN**	**N**	5	DE
11 yrs.	151 games			

Kent Gaydos

GAYDOS, KENT BRYAN
B. Sep. 8, 1949, South Bend, IN
Florida State 6'6" 228 lbs.

Year	Team		Games	Pos.
1975	**GB**	**N**	6	WR

Walt Gayer

GAYER, WALTER (Chuck)
B. Jul. 29, 1901
Deceased
St. Mary's (Minnesota)/Creighton 6'0" 205 lbs.

Year	Team		Games	Pos.
1926	**DUL**	**N**	8	T

Rashid Gayle

GAYLE, RASHID ALI
B. Apr. 16, 1974, New York, NY
Boise State 5'8" 174 lbs.

Year	Team		Games	Pos.
1996	**JAC**	**N**	2	CB

Shaun Gayle

GAYLE, SHAUN LANARD
B. Mar. 8, 1962, Newport News, VA
Ohio State 5'11" 193 lbs.

Year	Team		Games	Pos.
1984	**CHI**	**N**	15	CB, S
1985			16	CB
1986			16	CB
1987			8	CB
1988			4	CB
1989			14	S
1990			16	S
1991			12	S
1992			11	S
1993			16	S
1994			16	S
1995	**SD**	**N**	16	S
12 yrs.	160 games			

Doug Gaynor

GAYNOR, DOUG
B. Jul. 5, 1963, Fresno, CA
Long Beach State 6'2" 205 lbs.

Year	Team		Games	Pos.
1986	**CIN**	**N**	1	QB

Frank Gaziano

GAZIANO, FRANCIS J.
B. May 2, 1916, Realemonte, Italy

Year	Team	Games	Pos.

Frank Gaziano continued
Holy Cross 5'8" 218 lbs.

Year	Team	Games	Pos.
1944	BOS N	10	G

Ron Geater
GEATER, RON
B. Apr. 23, 1969, Marion, IA
Iowa 6'6" 270 lbs.

Year	Team	Games	Pos.
1992	DEN N	3	DE, NT

Jumpy Geathers
GEATHERS, JAMES
B. Jun. 26, 1960, Georgetown, SC
Wichita State 6'7" 290 lbs.

Year	Team	Games	Pos.
1984	NO N	16	NT
1985		16	DE
1986		16	DE
1987		1	DE
1988		16	DE
1989		15	DE
1990	WAS N	9	DE
1991		16	DT
1992		16	DT
1993	ATL N	14	DT
1994		16	DT
1995		16	DT
1996	DEN N	16	DT

13 yrs. 183 games

Lou Gebhard
GEBHARD, LOUIS
B. Sep. 15, 1902
Deceased
Lafayette 5'11" 175 lbs.

Year	Team	Games	Pos.
1926	PHI A	1	HB

Bob Geddes
GEDDES, ROBERT ERIC
B. Apr. 22, 1947, Seattle, WA
UCLA 6'2" 240 lbs.

Year	Team	Games	Pos.
1972	DEN N	14	LB
1973	NE N	2	LB
1974		9	LB
1975		13	LB

4 yrs. 38 games

Ken Geddes
GEDDES, KENNETH LEWIS
B. Sep. 27, 1947, Jacksonville, FL
Nebraska 6'3" 235 lbs.

Year	Team	Games	Pos.
1971	LA N	14	LB
1972		2	LB
1973		14	LB
1974		14	LB
1975		14	LB
1976	SEA N	11	LB
1977		14	LB
1978		12	LB

8 yrs. 95 games

Gene Gedman
GEDMAN, EUGENE WILLIAM
B. Jan. 9, 1932, Duquesne, PA
D. Aug. 19, 1974, Chicago, IL
Indiana 5'11" 195 lbs.

Year	Team	Games	Pos.
1953	DET N	12	HB
1956		12	HB
1957		10	HB
1958		11	HB

4 yrs. 45 games

Chris Gedney
GEDNEY, CHRISTOPHER JOSEPH
B. Aug. 9, 1970, Liverpool, NY
Syracuse 6'5" 262 lbs.

Year	Team	Games	Pos.
1993	CHI N	7	TE

Chris Gedney continued

Year	Team	Games	Pos.
1994		7	TE
1995		14	TE
1996		1	TE

4 yrs. 29 games

Mark Gehring
GEHRING, MARK
B. Apr. 16, 1964, Burien, WA
Eastern Washington 6'4" 235 lbs.

Year	Team	Games	Pos.
1987	HOU N	6	TE

Bruce Gehrke
GEHRKE, BRUCE R.
B. Sep. 12, 1924
D. Apr., 1976, Manhasset, NY
Columbia 6'2" 190 lbs.

Year	Team	Games	Pos.
1948	NYG N	8	E

Erwin Gehrke
GEHRKE, ERWIN L.
B. Apr. 25, 1898
D. Jun., 1966, Lancaster, OH
Harvard 6'1" 190 lbs.

Year	Team	Games	Pos.
1926	BOS A	6	HB, FB, QB

Fred Gehrke
GEHRKE, CLARENCE FRED
B. Apr. 24, 1918, Salt Lake City, UT
Utah 5'11" 189 lbs.

Year	Team	Games	Pos.
1940	CLE N	2	HB
1945		10	HB
1946	LA N	10	HB
1947		11	HB
1948		12	HB
1949		12	HB
1950	CHIC N	7	HB
1950	SF N	4	HB

7 yrs. 68 games

Jack Gehrke
GEHRKE, JACK F.
B. Jan. 14, 1946, Salt Lake City, UT
Utah 6'0" 178 lbs.

Year	Team	Games	Pos.
1968	KC A	2	WR
1969	CIN A	10	WR
1971	DEN N	14	WR

3 yrs. 26 games

Chris Geile
GEILE, CHRIS
B. Apr. 14, 1964
Eastern Illinois 6'4" 305 lbs.

Year	Team	Games	Pos.
1987	DET N	3	G

Chuck Gelatka
GELATKA, CHARLES
B. 1913
Mississippi State 6'1" 185 lbs.

Year	Team	Games	Pos.
1937	NYG N	4	E
1938		10	E
1939		10	E
1940		10	E

4 yrs. 34 games

Stan Gelbaugh
GELBAUGH, STANLEY MORRIS
B. Dec. 4, 1962, Carlisle, PA
Maryland 6'3" 207 lbs.

Year	Team	Games	Pos.
1989	BUF N	1	QB
1991	PHX N	6	QB
1992	SEA N	10	QB
1993		1	QB
1994		2	QB
1996		1	QB

6 yrs. 21 games

Pete Gent
GENT, GEORGE DAVIS
B. Aug. 23, 1942, Bangor, MI
Michigan State 6'4" 209 lbs.

Year	Team	Games	Pos.
1964	DAL N	7	OE
1965		10	OE
1966		14	FL
1967		7	FL
1968		10	FL

5 yrs. 48 games

Bryon Gentry
GENTRY, BYRON B. (Pills)
B. Oct. 20, 1913
D. Feb. 10, 1992, Paso Robles, CA
Southern California 5'11" 227 lbs.

Year	Team	Games	Pos.
1937	PIT N	3	G
1938		11	G
1939		11	G

3 yrs. 25 games

Curtis Gentry
GENTRY, CURTIS WILLIAM
B. Aug. 8, 1941, Waco, TX
Maryland-Eastern Shore 6'0" 186 lbs.

Year	Team	Games	Pos.
1966	CHI N	13	DB
1967		14	DB
1968		11	DB

3 yrs. 38 games

Dale Gentry
GENTRY, DALE LEE (Professor)
B. Jul. 2, 1919, Umapine, OR
D. Jan. 30, 1966
St. Mary's/Washington State 6'3" 223 lbs.

Year	Team	Games	Pos.
1946	LA AA	14	E
1947		14	E
1948		14	E

3 yrs. 42 games

Dennis Gentry
GENTRY, DENNIS LOUIS
B. Feb. 10, 1959, Lubbock, TX
Baylor 5'8" 181 lbs.

Year	Team	Games	Pos.
1982	CHI N	9	RB
1983		15	RB
1984		16	RB
1985		16	RB
1986		15	RB
1987		12	WR
1988		16	WR
1989		16	WR
1990		14	WR
1991		15	WR
1992		15	WR

11 yrs. 159 games

Lee Gentry
GENTRY, LEE
B. Dec. 1, 1918, Shawnee, OK
Tulsa 6'0" 198 lbs.

Year	Team	Games	Pos.
1941	WAS N	5	B

Weldon Gentry
GENTRY, WELDON C. (Cash, Spot)
B. Sep. 9, 1906
D. Mar. 19, 1990
Oklahoma 5'10" 195 lbs.

Year	Team	Games	Pos.
1930	PRO N	5	G
1931		7	G

2 yrs. 12 games

Bill George
GEORGE, WILLIAM J.
B. Oct. 27, 1929, Waynesburg, PA

Bill George continued
D. Sep. 30, 1982, Rockford, IL
Wake Forest 6'2" 237 lbs.

Year	Team	Games	Pos.
1952	CHIB N	12	T, G, LB
1953		12	G, LB
1954		12	G, LB
1955		12	LB
1956		12	LB
1957		12	LB
1958		12	LB
1959		12	LB
1960	CHI N	12	LB
1961		14	LB
1962		13	LB
1963		14	LB
1964		8	LB
1965		7	LB
1965	LA N	2	LB
1966		14	LB

15 yrs. 180 games

Carl George
GEORGE, CARL
B. Mar. 13, 1892, New York State
D. Oct., 1965, Ohio
Carroll (Wisconsin)/Loras 5'11" 170 lbs.

Year	Team	Games	Pos.
1922	RAC N	3	G, T

Ed George
GEORGE, EDWARD GARY
B. Aug. 10, 1946, Norfolk, VA
Wake Forest 6'4" 270 lbs.

Year	Team	Games	Pos.
1975	BAL N	12	OT
1976	PHI N	14	OT
1977		14	OT
1978			OT

4 yrs. 40 games

Eddie George
GEORGE, EDDIE
B. Sep. 24, 1973, Philadelphia, PA
Ohio State 6'3" 232 lbs.

Year	Team	Games	Pos.
1996	HOU N	15	RB

Jeff George
GEORGE, JEFFREY L.
B. Dec. 24, 1957, Atchison, KS
Illinois State 6'1" 185 lbs.

Year	Team	Games	Pos.
1987	TB N	2	CB

Jeff George
GEORGE, JEFFREY SCOTT
B. Dec. 8, 1967, Indianapolis, IN
Purdue/Illinois 6'4" 221 lbs.

Year	Team	Games	Pos.
1990	IND N	13	QB
1991		16	QB
1992		10	QB
1993		13	QB
1994	ATL N	16	QB
1995		16	QB
1996		3	QB

7 yrs. 87 games

Ray George
GEORGE, RAYMOND L.
B. Apr. 1, 1916
D. Nov. 1, 1985, Watsonville, CA
Southern California 6'0" 229 lbs.

Year	Team	Games	Pos.
1939	DET N	11	T
1940	PHI N	2	T

2 yrs. 13 games

Ron George
GEORGE, RON
B. Mar. 20, 1970, Heidelberg, Germany

Year	Team	Games	Pos.

Ron George continued
Air Force/Stanford 6'0" 225 lbs.

Year	Team		Games	Pos.
1993	ATL	N	12	LB
1994			16	LB
1995			16	LB
1996			16	LB

4 yrs.   60 games

Steve George
GEORGE, STEPHEN ELWOOD
B. Apr. 11, 1951, Sulphur Springs, TX
Houston 6'6" 265 lbs.

| 1974 | STL | N | 13 | DT |
| 1976 | ATL | N | 1 | DT |

2 yrs.   14 games

Tim George
GEORGE, TIMOTHY A.
B. Oct. 4, 1951, Alcoa, TN
Carson-Newman 6'5" 218 lbs.

| 1973 | CIN | N | 12 | WR |
| 1974 | CLE | N | 8 | WR |

2 yrs.   20 games

Art Georke
GEORKE, ARTHUR
B. 1895, New York State
Deceased
None 5'6" 165 lbs.

| 1921 | TON | A | 1 | E |

John Gerak
GERAK, JOHN MATTHEW
B. Jan. 6, 1970, Youngstown, OH
Penn State 6'3" 285 lbs.

1993	MIN	N	4	G
1994			13	G
1995			15	G
1996			14	G

4 yrs.   46 games

Patsy Gerardi
GERARDI, PASQUAL
B. Feb. 27, 1892, Washington, DC
D. Jun., 1973, Maryland
None 165 lbs.

| 1921 | WAS | A | 1 | E |

Ed Gerber
GERBER, ELWOOD (Woody)
B. Aug. 7, 1920, Kankakee, IL
Alabama 6'0" 223 lbs.

| 1941 | PHI | N | 5 | G |
| 1942 | | | 11 | G |

2 yrs.   16 games

Tom Geredine
GEREDINE, THOMAS ALLEN
B. Jun. 17, 1950, St. Louis, MO
Northeast Missouri State 6'2" 191 lbs.

1973	ATL	N	12	WR
1974			12	WR
1976	LA	N	10	WR

3 yrs.   34 games

Roy Gerela
GERELA, ROY
B. Apr. 2, 1948, Sarrail, Alb.
New Mexico State 5'10" 185 lbs.

1969	HOU	A	14	P, K
1970	HOU	N	14	K
1971	PIT	N	14	K
1972			14	K
1973			14	K
1974			14	K
1975			14	K

Roy Gerela continued

1976			14	K
1977			14	K
1978			16	K
1979	SD	N	3	K

11 yrs.   145 games

Chris Gerhard
GERHARD, CHRIS
B. Jul. 6, 1964
East Stroudsburg 5'10" 185 lbs.

| 1987 | PHI | N | 3 | S |

Tom Gerhart
GERHART, THOMAS EDWARD
B. Jun. 4, 1965, Lebanon, PA
*Salem (West Virginia)/Ohio University
6'1" 195 lbs.*

| 1992 | PHI | N | 1 | DB |

Joe Geri
GERI, JOSEPH STEVEN
B. Oct. 20, 1924, Phoenixville, PA
Georgia 5'10" 185 lbs.

1949	PIT	N	12	HB
1950			12	HB
1951			12	HB
1952	CHIC	N	12	HB

4 yrs.   48 games

Jimmy German
GERMAN, JAMES
B. Nov. 6, 1917, Louisville, KY
D. Aug., 1945
Centre 6'0" 180 lbs.

| 1939 | WAS | N | 8 | HB |
| 1940 | CHIC | N | 1 | HB |

2 yrs.   9 games

Willie Germany
GERMANY, WILLIE JAMES, JR.
B. May 9, 1949, Columbus, GA
Morgan State 6'0" 192 lbs.

1972	ATL	N	12	S
1973	DET	N	6	S
1975	HOU	N	14	S
1976	NE	N	10	S

4 yrs.   42 games

Carl Gersbach
GERSBACH, CARL
B. Jan. 8, 1947, Syracuse, NY
Duke/West Chester State 6'1" 230 lbs.

1970	PHI	N	6	LB
1971	MIN	N	13	LB
1972			14	LB
1973	SD	N	14	LB
1974			12	LB
1975	CHI	N	10	LB
1976	STL	N	7	LB

7 yrs.   76 games

Rick Gervais
GERVAIS, RICHARD P.
B. Nov. 4, 1959, Bend, OR
Stanford 5'11" 190 lbs.

1981	SF	N	8	CB, S
1982			9	S
1983			5	S

3 yrs.   22 games

John Gesek
GESEK, JOHN CHRISTIAN, JR.
B. Feb. 18, 1963, San Francisco, CA
Sacramento State 6'5" 275 lbs.

| 1987 | LARI | N | 3 | G |

John Gesek continued

1988			12	C, G
1989			16	G, C
1990	DAL	N	15	G
1991			16	G
1992			16	G
1993			14	G
1994	WAS	N	15	C
1995			16	C, G

9 yrs.   123 games

Gorham Getchell
GETCHELL, CHARLES GORHAM
B. Aug. 14, 1920, Abington, PA
D. Jul. 7, 1980, Manhattan Beach, CA
Temple 6'4" 225 lbs.

| 1947 | BAL | AA | 8 | E |

Charlie Getty
GETTY, CHARLES MATTHEW
B. Jul. 24, 1952, Pompton Lakes, NJ
Penn State 6'4" 263 lbs.

1974	KC	N	14	OT
1975			14	OT
1976			14	OT
1977			14	G
1978			16	G
1979			16	G, OT
1980			6	OT
1981			16	OT
1982			9	OT
1983	GB	N	16	OT

10 yrs.   135 games

Fred Getz
GETZ, FREDERICK
B. Mar. 16, 1909
D. Oct., 1971, Norfolk, VA
Tennessee-Chattanooga 6'1" 192 lbs.

| 1930 | BKN | N | 1 | E |

Lee Getz
GETZ, LEE
B. 1964
Rutgers 6'3" 250 lbs.

| 1987 | KC | N | 3 | G |

Bill Geyer
GEYER, WILLIAM
B. Oct. 3, 1919, Bloomfield, NJ
Colgate 5'10" 173 lbs.

1942	CHIB	N	5	HB
1943			3	HB
1946			1	HB

3 yrs.   9 games

Lou Ghecas
GHECAS, LOUIS
B. Jul. 14, 1918, Danbury, CT
Georgetown (DC) 5'9" 175 lbs.

| 1941 | PHI | N | 8 | HB |

Milt Ghee
GHEE, MILTON POMEROY
B. Nov. 17, 1891
D. Mar. 16, 1975, Corte Madera, CA
Dartmouth 5'7" 167 lbs.

| 1920 | CHIT | A | 7 | QB |
| 1921 | CLE | A | 4 | QB |

2 yrs.   11 games

Vern Ghersanich
GHERSANICH, VERNON GEORGE
Deceased
Auburn 5'11" 210 lbs.

| 1943 | CHIC | N | 4 | G |

Ralph Giacomarro
GIACOMARRO, RALPH
B. Jan. 17, 1961, Passaic, NJ
Penn State 6'1" 192 lbs.

1983	ATL	N	16	P
1984			16	P
1985			5	P
1987	DEN	N	3	P

4 yrs.   40 games

Louie Giammona
GIAMMONA, LOUIS JEAN
B. Mar. 3, 1953, St. Helena, CA
Utah State 5'9" 180 lbs.

1976	NYJ	N	14	RB
1978	PHI	N	7	RB
1979			15	RB
1980			16	RB
1981			8	RB
1982			9	RB

6 yrs.   69 games

Hal Giancanelli
GIANCANELLI, HAROLD ARTHUR (Skip)
B. May 21, 1929, Farr, CO
Loyola (California) 5'10" 177 lbs.

1953	PHI	N	12	HB
1954			10	HB
1955			12	HB
1956			7	HB

4 yrs.   41 games

Mario Giannelli
GIANNELLI, MARIO (YoYo)
B. Dec. 24, 1920, Everett, MA
Boston College 6'0" 265 lbs.

1948	PHI	N	12	G
1949			10	G
1950			12	G
1951			10	G

4 yrs.   44 games

Frank Giannetti
GIANNETTI, FRANK JOHN
B. Mar. 14, 1968, Toms River, NJ
Penn State 6'2" 267 lbs.

| 1991 | IND | N | 3 | LB |

Jack Giannoni
GIANNONI, JOHN MICHAEL
B. Aug. 27, 1914, Sacramento, CA
St. Mary's (California) 6'1" 210 lbs.

| 1938 | CLE | N | 3 | E |

Nick Giaquinto
GIAQUINTO, NICHOLAS ALBERT
B. Apr. 4, 1955, Bridgeport, CT
Bridgeport/Connecticut 5'11" 204 lbs.

1980	MIA	N	16	RB
1981			8	RB
1981	WAS	N	6	RB
1982			7	RB
1983			16	RB

4 yrs.   53 games

Jim Gibbons
GIBBONS, JAMES EDWIN
B. Sep. 26, 1936, Chicago, IL
Iowa 6'2" 220 lbs.

1958	DET	N	12	E
1959			12	E
1960			12	E
1961			14	OE
1962			14	OE
1963			14	OE

<del>

</del>

Year	Team		Games	Pos.

Jim Gibbons continued

Year	Team		Games	Pos.
1964			2	OE
1965			13	OE
1966			7	TE
1967			14	TE
1968			14	TE
11 yrs.	128 games			

Mike Gibbons
GIBBONS, MIKE L.
B. Jan. 23, 1951, Duncan, OK
Southwestern Oklahoma State 6'4" 262 lbs.

Year	Team		Games	Pos.
1976	NYG	N	11	OT
1977			5	OT
2 yrs.	16 games			

Donnie Gibbs
GIBBS, DONNIE
B. Dec. 31, 1945
Texas Christian 6'2" 205 lbs.

Year	Team		Games	Pos.
1974	NO	N	1	K

Pat Gibbs
GIBBS, PATRICK HENRY
B. Apr. 5, 1950, Marshall, TX
Lamar 5'10" 188 lbs.

Year	Team		Games	Pos.
1972	PHI	N	2	CB

Sonny Gibbs
GIBBS, GUY
B. 1941
Texas Christian 6'7" 230 lbs.

Year	Team		Games	Pos.
1964	DET	N	14	QB

Andy Gibler
GIBLER, JAMES ANDREW
B. Apr. 30, 1961, Independence, MO
Missouri 6'4" 234 lbs.

Year	Team		Games	Pos.
1983	CIN	N	2	TE

Robert Giblin
GIBLIN, ROBERT JAMES
B. Nov. 18, 1952, Omaha, NE
Houston 6'2" 208 lbs.

Year	Team		Games	Pos.
1975	NYG	N	12	DB
1977	STL	N	11	S
2 yrs.	23 games			

Abe Gibron
GIBRON, ABE
B. Sep. 22, 1925, Michigan City, IN
Valparaiso/Purdue 5'11" 243 lbs.

Year	Team		Games	Pos.
1949	BUF	AA	10	G
1950	CLE	N	12	G
1951			12	G
1952			12	G
1953			10	G
1954			12	G
1955			12	G
1956			7	G
1956	PHI	N	2	G
1957			12	G
1958	CHIB	N	12	G
1959			12	G
11 yrs.	125 games			

Alec Gibson
GIBSON, ALEC
B. Dec. 9, 1963
Illinois 6'4" 260 lbs.

Year	Team		Games	Pos.
1987	WAS	N	3	DT

Antonio Gibson
GIBSON, ANTONIO MAURICE

Antonio Gibson continued

B. Jul. 5, 1962, Jackson, MS
Cincinnati 6'3" 204 lbs.

Year	Team		Games	Pos.
1986	NO	N	16	S
1987			10	S
1988			10	S
1989			16	S
1992			6	S
5 yrs.	58 games			

Claude Gibson
GIBSON, CLAUDE (Hoot)
B. May 26, 1939, Spruce Pine, NC
North Carolina State 6'1" 191 lbs.

Year	Team		Games	Pos.
1961	SD	A	14	DB
1962			14	DB
1963	OAK	A	14	DB
1964			14	DB
1965			14	DB
5 yrs.	70 games			

Dennis Gibson
GIBSON, DENNIS MICHAEL
B. Feb. 8, 1964, Des Moines, IA
Iowa State 6'2" 240 lbs.

Year	Team		Games	Pos.
1987	DET	N	12	LB
1988			16	LB
1989			6	LB
1990			11	LB
1991			16	LB
1992			16	LB
1993			15	LB
1994	SD	N	16	LB
1995			13	LB
9 yrs.	121 games			

Denver Gibson
GIBSON, DENVER (Butch)
B. 1904, Middlebranch, OH
Deceased
Grove City 5'9" 204 lbs.

Year	Team		Games	Pos.
1930	NYG	N	13	G, T
1931			14	G
1932			11	G
1933			14	G
1934			13	G
5 yrs.	65 games			

Dick Gibson
GIBSON, RICHARD M.
B. Mar. 2, 1902
D. Feb., 1973, Melbourne, FL
Centre 6'0" 188 lbs.

Year	Team		Games	Pos.
1922	LOU	N	2	T
1923			3	T, G
2 yrs.	5 games			

Ernest Gibson
GIBSON, ERNEST GERARD
B. Oct. 3, 1961, Jacksonville, FL
Furman 5'10" 185 lbs.

Year	Team		Games	Pos.
1984	NE	N	15	CB, S
1985			9	CB
1986			15	CB
1987			12	CB
1988			16	CB
1989	MIA	N	5	CB
6 yrs.	72 games			

George Gibson
GIBSON, GEORGE F.
B. Oct. 2, 1905, Kendaia, NY
Minnesota 6'0" 208 lbs.

Year	Team		Games	Pos.
1930	MIN	N	9	G
1930	FRA	N	5	G
1 yr.	14 games			

Joe Gibson
GIBSON, WILLIAM JOSEPH
B. Jun. 28, 1919, Nocona, TX
Tulsa 6'3" 213 lbs.

Year	Team		Games	Pos.
1942	CLE	N	11	E
1943	WAS	N	5	E, B
1944	CLE	N	9	C, E
1946	BKN	AA	14	C
1947			14	C
5 yrs.	53 games			

Oliver Gibson
GIBSON, OLIVER DONNOVAN
B. Mar. 15, 1972, Chicago, IL
Notre Dame 6'2" 283 lbs.

Year	Team		Games	Pos.
1995	PIT	N	12	DT
1996			16	DT
2 yrs.	28 games			

Paul Gibson
GIBSON, PAUL
B. Jun. 20, 1948, Paris, AR
D. May 23, 1975, El Paso, TX
Texas-El Paso 6'2" 195 lbs.

Year	Team		Games	Pos.
1972	GB	N	1	S

Paul Gibson
GIBSON, PAUL EDWARD (Spider)
B. Oct. 28, 1917, Winston-Salem, NC
D. 1975
North Carolina State 6'2" 195 lbs.

Year	Team		Games	Pos.
1947	BUF	AA	14	E
1948			7	E
1949			9	E
3 yrs.	30 games			

Reuben Gibson
GIBSON, REUBEN
B. Jun. 16, 1955, Cedartown, GA
Memphis State 6'0" 196 lbs.

Year	Team		Games	Pos.
1977	BUF	N		RB

Tom Gibson
GIBSON, THOMAS ANTHONY
B. Dec. 20, 1963, San Fernando, CA
Northern Arizona 6'7" 257 lbs.

Year	Team		Games	Pos.
1989	CLE	N	16	NT, DE
1990			12	DE
1991	LARM	N	4	DE
3 yrs.	32 games			

Frank Giddens
GIDDENS, FRANK D.
B. Jan. 20, 1959, Lubbock, TX
New Mexico 6'7" 300 lbs.

Year	Team		Games	Pos.
1981	PHI	N	16	OT
1982			9	OT
2 yrs.	25 games			

Hershel Giddens
GIDDENS, HERSHEL O. (Wimpy)
B. Nov. 25, 1914, Ringgold, LA
Louisiana Tech 6'2" 220 lbs.

Year	Team		Games	Pos.
1938	PHI	N	8	T
1944	BOS	N	6	T, G
2 yrs.	14 games			

Jon Giesler
GIESLER, JON WILLIAM
B. Dec. 23, 1956, Toledo, OH
Michigan 6'5" 265 lbs.

Year	Team		Games	Pos.
1979	MIA	N	16	OT
1980			10	OT
1981			16	OT
1982			9	OT
1983			16	OT

Jon Giesler continued

Year	Team		Games	Pos.
1984			16	OT
1985			13	OT
1986			7	OT
1987			10	OT
1988			13	OT
10 yrs.	126 games			

Bob Gifford
GIFFORD, ROBERT
B. Nov. 11, 1918, Chicago, IL
D. Feb., 1987, Pleasure Beach, CT
Denver 6'0" 200 lbs.

Year	Team		Games	Pos.
1942	BKN	N	4	B

Frank Gifford
GIFFORD, FRANCIS NEWTON
(Golden Boy, Giffer)
B. Aug. 16, 1930, Bakersfield, CA
Southern California 6'1" 197 lbs.

Year	Team		Games	Pos.
1952	NYG	N	10	HB
1953			12	HB
1954			9	HB
1955			11	HB
1956			12	HB
1957			12	HB
1958			10	HB
1959			11	HB
1960			8	HB
1962			14	OE
1963			14	FL
1964			13	FL
12 yrs.	136 games			

Wayne Gift
GIFT, LELAND WAYNE
B. Oct. 21, 1915, Medina, OH
Purdue 5'8" 175 lbs.

Year	Team		Games	Pos.
1937	CLE	N	10	QB

Daren Gilbert
GILBERT, DAREN
B. Oct. 3, 1963, San Diego, CA
Fullerton State 6'6" 295 lbs.

Year	Team		Games	Pos.
1985	NO	N	16	OT
1986			9	OT
1987			6	OT
1988			11	OT
4 yrs.	42 games			

Freddie Gilbert
GILBERT, FREDDIE GENE
B. Apr. 8, 1962, Griffin, GA
Georgia 6'4" 275 lbs.

Year	Team		Games	Pos.
1986	DEN	N	15	DE
1987			7	DE
1988			13	DE
1989	PHX	N	2	DE
4 yrs.	37 games			

Gale Gilbert
GILBERT, GALE
B. Dec. 20, 1961, Red Bluff, CA
California 6'3" 206 lbs.

Year	Team		Games	Pos.
1985	SEA	N	9	QB
1986			16	QB
1990	BUF	N	1	QB
1993			1	QB
1994	SD	N	16	QB
1995			16	QB
6 yrs.	59 games			

Kline Gilbert
GILBERT, KLINE
B. Nov. 22, 1930, Hollandale, MS
D. Jun. 14, 1987, Jackson, MS

488

Kline Gilbert *continued*

Mississippi 6'2" 233 lbs.

Year	Team		Games	Pos.
1953	CHIB	N	12	T
1954			12	G
1955			12	T
1956			12	T
1957			12	T
5 yrs.	60 games			

Lewis Gilbert

GILBERT, LEWIS HOWE, JR.
B. May 24, 1956, Naples, FL
Florida 6'4" 225 lbs.

Year	Team		Games	Pos.
1978	ATL	N	4	TE
1980	PHI	N	3	TE
1980	SF	N	6	TE
1981	LA	N	6	TE
3 yrs.	19 games			

Sean Gilbert

GILBERT, SEAN
B. Apr. 10, 1970, Aliquippa, PA
Pittsburgh 6'4" 315 lbs.

Year	Team		Games	Pos.
1992	LARM	N	16	DT, DE
1993			16	DT
1994			14	DT
1995	STL	N	14	DE
1996	WAS	N	16	DE
5 yrs.	76 games			

Wally Gilbert

GILBERT, WALTER JOHN
B. Dec. 19, 1900, Oscoda, MI
D. Sep. 7, 1958, Duluth, MN
Valparaiso 6'1" 180 lbs.

Year	Team		Games	Pos.
1923	DUL	N	6	HB
1924			5	HB
1925			2	HB, FB
1926			2	HB
4 yrs.	15 games			

Tom Gilburg

GILBURG, THOMAS D.
B. Nov. 27, 1938, Bronxville, NY
Syracuse 6'5" 245 lbs.

Year	Team		Games	Pos.
1961	BAL	N	14	G, OT, P
1962			14	OT, P
1963			13	OT, P
1964			14	OT, P
1965			14	OT, P
5 yrs.	69 games			

Cookie Gilchrist

GILCHRIST, CARLTON CHESTER
B. May 25, 1935, Brackenridge, PA
none 6'3" 249 lbs.

Year	Team		Games	Pos.
1962	BUF	A	14	FB
1963			14	FB
1964			14	FB
1965	DEN	A	14	FB
1966	MIA	A	8	FB
1967	DEN	A	1	FB
6 yrs.	65 games			

George Gilchrist

GILCHRIST, GEORGE
B. Jan. 28, 1929, Memphis, TN
Tennessee State 6'0" 260 lbs.

Year	Team		Games	Pos.
1953	CHIC		11	T

Denny Gildea

GILDEA, DENNIS ANTHONY
B. Oct. 9, 1898, Roxbury, MA
D. Feb. 22, 1976, Lynn, MA
Holy Cross 5'9" 190 lbs.

Year	Team		Games	Pos.
1926	HAR	N	6	C, T, G

Johnny Gildea

GILDEA, JOHN T.
B. Mar. 9, 1910, Boston Run, PA
D. Nov., 1979, Tamaqua, PA
St. Bonaventure 6'2" 205 lbs.

Year	Team		Games	Pos.
1935	PIT	N	12	QB, HB
1936			12	QB, HB
1937			11	QB, HB
1938	NYG	N	9	HB, LB
4 yrs.	44 games			

Jason Gildon

GILDON, JASON LARUE
B. Jul. 31, 1972, Altus, OK
Oklahoma State 6'3" 237 lbs.

Year	Team		Games	Pos.
1994	PIT	N	16	LB
1995			16	LB
1996			14	LB
3 yrs.	46 games			

Jimmie Giles

GILES, JIMMIE, JR.
B. Nov. 8, 1954, Natchez, MS
Alcorn State 6'3" 238 lbs.

Year	Team		Games	Pos.
1977	HOU	N	14	TE
1978	TB	N	16	TE
1979			16	TE
1980			16	TE
1981			16	TE
1982			9	TE
1983			11	TE
1984			14	TE
1985			16	TE
1986			7	TE
1986	DET	N	9	TE
1987			4	TE
1987	PHI	N	8	TE
1988			16	TE
1989			16	TE
13 yrs.	188 games			

Owen Gill

GILL, OWEN
B. Feb. 19, 1962, London, England
Iowa 6'1" 230 lbs.

Year	Team		Games	Pos.
1985	IND	N	15	RB
1986			16	RB
1987	LARM	N	1	RB
3 yrs.	32 games			

Randy Gill

GILL, RANDY
B. Aug. 1, 1956, Los Angeles, CA
San Jose State 6'2" 230 lbs.

Year	Team		Games	Pos.
1978	STL	N	7	LB
1978	TB	N	1	LB
1 yr.	8 games			

Roger Gill

GILL, ROGER EWING
B. Oct. 14, 1940
Texas Tech 6'1" 200 lbs.

Year	Team		Games	Pos.
1964	PHI	N	12	HB
1965			13	TE
2 yrs.	25 games			

Sloko Gill

GILL, SLOKO
B. Mar. 8, 1918, Campbell, OH
Youngstown State 5'10" 185 lbs.

Year	Team		Games	Pos.
1942	DET	N	11	C

John Gillen

GILLEN, JOHN
B. Nov. 5, 1958, Arlington Heights, IL
Illinois 6'3" 227 lbs.

Year	Team		Games	Pos.
1981	STL	N	16	LB

John Gillen *continued*

Year	Team		Games	Pos.
1982			4	LB
1983	NE	N	8	LB
3 yrs.	28 games			

Fernandars Gillespie

GILLESPIE, FERNANDARS (Scoop)
B. Feb. 26, 1962, St. Louis, MO
William Jewell 5'10" 178 lbs.

Year	Team		Games	Pos.
1984	PIT	N	14	RB

Willie Gillespie

GILLESPIE, WILLIE E.
B. Oct. 24, 1961, Starkville, MS
Tennessee-Chattanooga 5'9" 170 lbs.

Year	Team		Games	Pos.
1986	TB	N	2	WR
1987	MIN	N	1	WR
2 yrs.	3 games			

Fred Gillett

GILLETT, FREDERICK
B. Dec. 16, 1936
Los Angeles State 6'3" 228 lbs.

Year	Team		Games	Pos.
1962	SD	A	6	HB
1964	OAK	A	3	HB
2 yrs.	9 games			

Jim Gillette

GILLETTE, JAMES T., JR.
B. Nov. 19, 1917, Courtland, VA
D. Jan. 9, 1990, Richmond, VA
Virginia 6'1" 185 lbs.

Year	Team		Games	Pos.
1940	CLE	N	4	HB
1944			7	HB
1945			10	HB
1946	BOS	N	11	HB
1947	GB	N	10	HB
1948	DET	N	10	HB
6 yrs.	52 games			

Walker Gillette

GILLETTE, WALKER ADAMS
B. Mar. 16, 1947, Norfolk, VA
Richmond 6'5" 200 lbs.

Year	Team		Games	Pos.
1970	SD	N	13	WR
1971			12	WR
1972	STL	N	14	WR
1973			14	WR
1974	NYG	N	11	WR
1975			14	WR
1976			13	WR
7 yrs.	91 games			

Joe Gilliam

GILLIAM, JOE W., JR.
B. Dec. 29, 1950, Charleston, WV
Tennessee State 6'2" 187 lbs.

Year	Team		Games	Pos.
1972	PIT	N	2	QB
1973			5	QB
1974			9	QB
1975			4	QB
4 yrs.	20 games			

John Gilliam

GILLIAM, JOHN RALLY
B. Aug. 1, 1945, Greenwood, SC
South Carolina State 6'1" 192 lbs.

Year	Team		Games	Pos.
1967	NO	N	13	RB
1968			14	WR
1969	STL	N	14	WR
1970			14	WR
1971			14	WR
1972	MIN	N	14	WR
1973			14	WR
1974			14	WR
1975			14	WR

John Gilliam *continued*

Year	Team		Games	Pos.
1976	ATL	N	14	WR
1977	CHI	N	2	WR
1977	NO	N	8	WR
11 yrs.	149 games			

Jon Gilliam

GILLIAM, JON R.
B. Oct. 22, 1938, Oklahoma City, OK
East Texas State 6'2" 238 lbs.

Year	Team		Games	Pos.
1961	DAL	A	14	C
1962			14	C
1963	KC	A	14	C
1964			14	C
1965			14	C
1966			1	C
1967			5	C
7 yrs.	76 games			

Fred Gillies

GILLIES, FREDERICK M. (Boo)
B. Dec. 9, 1895
D. May 8, 1974, Flossmoor, IL
Cornell 6'3" 215 lbs.

Year	Team		Games	Pos.
1920	CHIC	A	6	T
1921			8	T
1922	CHIC	N	11	T
1923			7	T
1924			10	T
1925			13	T
1926			7	T
1928			1	T
8 yrs.	63 games			

Gale Gillingham

GILLINGHAM, GALE HERBERT
B. Feb. 3, 1944, Madison, WI
Minnesota 6'3" 257 lbs.

Year	Team		Games	Pos.
1966	GB	N	14	G
1967			14	G
1968			14	G
1969			14	G
1970			14	G
1971			14	G
1972			2	G
1973			14	G
1974			14	G
1976			14	G
10 yrs.	128 games			

Don Gillis

GILLIS, DONALD
B. Mar. 31, 1935, Corpus Christi, TX
Rice 6'3" 245 lbs.

Year	Team		Games	Pos.
1958	CHIC	N	12	C
1959			12	C
1960	STL	N	12	C
1961			9	C
4 yrs.	45 games			

Joe Gillis

GILLIS, JOSEPH A.
B. Apr. 24, 1896
D. Dec., 1967, Detroit, MI
Detroit 5'8" 210 lbs.

Year	Team		Games	Pos.
1923	TOL	N	7	G, T

Hank Gillo

GILLO, HENRY CHARLES
B. Oct. 5, 1894, Milwaukee, WI
D. Sep. 6, 1948
Colgate 5'10" 193 lbs.

Year	Team		Games	Pos.
1920	HAM	A	3	FB
1921			1	FB
1922	RAC	N	11	FB
1923			10	FB
1924			10	FB
1925	MIL	N	2	FB

Year	Team	Games	Pos.

Hank Gillo *continued*

Year	Team	Games	Pos.
1926	RAC	N	3	FB

7 yrs.   40 games

Horace Gillom
GILLOM, HORACE A.
B. Mar. 3, 1921, Roanoke, AL
Ohio State*/Nevada-Reno 6'1" 221 lbs.

Year	Team	Games	Pos.
1947	CLE	AA	14	E
1948			13	E
1949			12	E
1950	CLE	N	12	E
1951			12	E
1952			12	E
1953			12	E
1954			12	E
1955			12	E
1956			5	E

10 yrs.   116 games

Bob Gillson
GILLSON, ROBERT WILLIAM
B. May 4, 1905, Binghamton, NY
Colgate 6'0" 208 lbs.

Year	Team	Games	Pos.
1930	BKN	N	11	G, T
1931			11	G

2 yrs.   22 games

Willie Gillus
GILLUS, WILLIE
B. Sep. 1, 1963, Emporia, VA
Norfolk State 6'4" 215 lbs.

Year	Team	Games	Pos.
1987	GB	N	1	QB

Harry Gilmer
GILMER, HARRY V., JR. (Hurlin' Harry)
B. Apr. 14, 1926, Birmingham, AL
Alabama 6'0" 169 lbs.

Year	Team	Games	Pos.
1948	WAS	N	1	QB
1949			12	QB
1950			10	QB
1951			10	QB
1952			12	HB, QB
1954			12	HB, QB
1955	DET	N	8	QB
1956			6	QB

8 yrs.   71 games

Jim Gilmore
GILMORE, JAMES THOMAS
B. Dec. 19, 1962, Philadelphia, PA
Villanova/Ohio State 6'5" 262 lbs.

Year	Team	Games	Pos.
1986	PHI	N	2	OT
1987	MIA	N	3	G

2 yrs.   5 games

Gilroy
GILROY
None

Year	Team	Games	Pos.
1930	NYG	N	1	G

Johnny Gilroy
GILROY, ROLAND JOHN
B. Nov., 1895, Massachusetts
Deceased
Georgetown (DC) 5'11" 175 lbs.

Year	Team	Games	Pos.
1920	CAN	A	4	QB, HB
1920	CLE	A	1	HB
1921	WAS	A	1	HB
1926	BOS	A	2	HB

3 yrs.   8 games

Ralph Gilroy
GILROY, RALPH CHARLES
B. 1900

Ralph Gilroy *continued*

Deceased
Princeton 5'9" 175 lbs.

Year	Team	Games	Pos.
1926	BOS	A	6	HB, FB, E

Hubie Ginn
GINN, HUBERT
B. Jan. 4, 1947, Savannah, GA
Florida A&M 5'11" 187 lbs.

Year	Team	Games	Pos.
1970	MIA	N	12	RB
1971			14	RB
1972			14	RB
1973			3	RB
1973	BAL	N	6	RB
1974	MIA	N	9	RB
1975			11	RB
1976	OAK	N	7	RB
1977			10	RB
1978			1	RB

9 yrs.   87 games

Tommie Ginn
GINN, TOMMIE WEBSTER
B. Jan. 25, 1958, Scotia, CA
Arkansas 6'3" 253 lbs.

Year	Team	Games	Pos.
1980	DET	N	14	G
1981			12	G

2 yrs.   26 games

Jerry Ginney
GINNEY, JERALD W.
B. Apr. 9, 1916
D. Oct. 22, 1984, San Jose, CA
Santa Clara 5'11" 217 lbs.

Year	Team	Games	Pos.
1940	PHI	N	1	G

Paul Gipson
GIPSON, PAUL
B. Mar. 21, 1946, Jacksonville, TX
Houston 6'0" 208 lbs.

Year	Team	Games	Pos.
1969	ATL	N	10	RB
1970			13	RB
1971	DET	N	5	RB
1973	NE	N	5	RB

4 yrs.   33 games

Tom Gipson
GIPSON, THOMAS ALLEN
B. Jul. 28, 1948, Refugio, TX
North Texas State 6'6" 290 lbs.

Year	Team	Games	Pos.
1971	OAK	N	4	DT

Earl Girard
GIRARD, EARL F. (Jug)
B. Jan. 25, 1927, Marinette, WI
Wisconsin 5'11" 176 lbs.

Year	Team	Games	Pos.
1948	GB	N	10	HB
1949			12	HB
1950			12	HB
1951			12	HB
1952	DET	N	11	HB
1953			11	HB
1954			12	HB, OE
1955			12	HB, OE
1956			10	HB, OE
1957	PIT	N	12	OE

10 yrs.   114 games

Mike Gisler
GISLER, MIKE
B. Aug. 26, 1969, Runge, TX
Houston 6'4" 300 lbs.

Year	Team	Games	Pos.
1993	NE	N	12	G, OT
1994			14	C, G
1995			16	C
1996			14	C

4 yrs.   56 games

Andy Gissinger
GISSINGER, ANDREW, III
B. Jul. 4, 1959, Barberton, OH
Syracuse 6'5" 279 lbs.

Year	Team	Games	Pos.
1982	SD	N	9	OT
1983			16	OT
1984			16	OT

3 yrs.   41 games

Patsy Giugliano
GIUGLIANO, PATSY
B. Dec. 11, 1900
D. Mar., 1976, Bancroft, KY
None 5'4" 140 lbs.

Year	Team	Games	Pos.
1923	LOU	N	1	QB

Ernest Givins
GIVINS, ERNEST P.
B. Sep. 3, 1964, St. Petersburg, FL
Louisville 5'9" 175 lbs.

Year	Team	Games	Pos.
1986	HOU	N	15	WR
1987			12	WR
1988			16	WR
1989			15	WR
1990			16	WR
1991			16	WR
1992			16	WR
1993			16	WR
1994			16	WR
1995	JAC	N	9	WR

10 yrs.   147 games

Scotty Glacken
GLACKEN, EDWARD SCOTT
B. Jul. 28, 1944, Washington, DC
Duke 6'0" 190 lbs.

Year	Team	Games	Pos.
1966	DEN	A	8	QB
1967			2	QB

2 yrs.   10 games

Chet Gladchuk
GLADCHUK, CHESTER S., SR.
B. Apr. 4, 1917, Bridgeport, CT
D. Sep. 4, 1967, Northampton, MA
Boston College 6'4" 248 lbs.

Year	Team	Games	Pos.
1941	NYG	N	7	T, C
1946			11	C
1947			10	C

3 yrs.   28 games

Mack Gladden
GLADDEN, JAMES MACK
B. May 22, 1912, Turney, MO
Missouri 6'2" 195 lbs.

Year	Team	Games	Pos.
1934	C, S		3	E

Bob Gladieux
GLADIEUX, ROBERT JOSEPH (Harpo)
B. Jan. 2, 1947, Louisville, OH
Notre Dame 5'11" 191 lbs.

Year	Team	Games	Pos.
1969	BOS	A	10	RB
1970	BOS	N	8	RB
1971	NE	N	14	RB

3 yrs.   32 games

Charles Gladman
GLADMAN, CHARLES
B. Feb. 2, 1966
Pittsburgh 5'11" 205 lbs.

Year	Team	Games	Pos.
1987	TB	N	2	RB

Tony Gladney
GLADNEY, ANTHONY
B. Jul. 20, 1964
Nevada-Las Vegas 6'3" 200 lbs.

Year	Team	Games	Pos.
1987	SF	N	2	WR

Joe Glamp
GLAMP, JOSEPH
B. May 13, 1921
D. Jan. 13, 1989, Greensburg, PA
Louisiana State 5'11" 185 lbs.

Year	Team	Games	Pos.
1947	PIT	N	12	HB
1948			12	HB

2 yrs.   24 games

Brian Glasgow
GLASGOW, BRIAN
B. Jun. 9, 1961, Burlington, IA
Northern Illinois 6'2" 230 lbs.

Year	Team	Games	Pos.
1987	CHI	N	3	TE

Nesby Glasgow
GLASGOW, NESBY LEE
B. Apr. 15, 1967, Los Angeles, CA
Washington 5'10" 186 lbs.

Year	Team	Games	Pos.
1979	BAL	N	16	CB, S
1980			16	CB
1981			14	S
1982			9	S
1983			16	S
1984	IND		16	S
1985			16	S
1986			14	S
1987			11	S
1988	SEA		16	S
1989			16	S
1990			16	S
1991			16	S
1992			13	S

14 yrs.   205 games

Bill Glass
GLASS, WILLIAM SHEPPARD
B. Aug. 16, 1935, Texarkana, TX
Baylor 6'5" 252 lbs.

Year	Team	Games	Pos.
1958	DET	N	12	OT, C
1959			12	DE
1960			12	DE
1961			14	DE
1962	CLE	N	14	DE
1963			14	DE
1964			14	DE
1965			14	DE
1966			14	DE
1967			14	DE
1968			9	DE

11 yrs.   143 games

Billy Glass
GLASS, WILLIAM PARKER
B. Dec. 21, 1957, Harlingen, TX
Baylor 6'4" 261 lbs.

Year	Team	Games	Pos.
1980	CIN	N	15	G

Chip Glass
GLASS, CHARLES
B. Jun. 25, 1947, Homestead, FL
Florida State 6'4" 236 lbs.

Year	Team	Games	Pos.
1969	CLE	N	14	TE
1970			14	TE
1971			14	TE
1972			14	TE
1973			12	TE
1974	NYG	N	13	TE

6 yrs.   81 games

Glenn Glass
GLASS, GLENN MURRAY
B. Feb. 16, 1940, Holopaw, FL
Tennessee 6'0" 197 lbs.

Year	Team	Games	Pos.
1962	PIT	N	7	DB
1963			14	DB
1964	PHI	N	13	DB

Year	Team	Games	Pos.

Glenn Glass *continued*

Year	Team	Games	Pos.
1965		12	FL
1966	ATL	N	3	FL
1966	DEN	A	6	FL
5 yrs.	55 games		

Leland Glass
GLASS, LELAND STROTHER
B. Nov. 5, 1950, Sacramento, CA
Oregon 6'0" 185 lbs.

1972	GB	N	14	WR
1973		12	WR
2 yrs.	26 games		

Bill Glassgow
GLASSGOW, WILLIS A.
B. Feb. 25, 1908
D. Mar., 1984, Wilson, NC
Iowa 5'10" 190 lbs.

1930	POR	N	12	HB, QB
1931	CHIC	N	9	HB
2 yrs.	21 games		

Tom Glassic
GLASSIC, THOMAS JOSEPH
B. Apr. 17, 1954, Elizabeth, NJ
Virginia 6'3" 258 lbs.

1976	DEN	N	14	G
1977		14	G
1978		11	G
1979		16	G
1980		13	G
1981		16	G
1982		9	G
1983		12	G
8 yrs.	105 games		

Frank Glassman
GLASSMAN, FRANK
B. Feb., 1910
Wilmington 6'0" 210 lbs.

| 1929 | BUF | N | 9 | G, T |

Morris Glassman
GLASSMAN, MORRIS
B. Feb. 19, 1900
D. Feb., 1980, Columbus, OH
None 5'10" 166 lbs.

1921	COL	A	9	E
1922	COL	N	6	E
2 yrs.	15 games		

Fred Glatz
GLATZ, FRED
B. 1934
Pittsburgh 6'1" 200 lbs.

| 1956 | PIT | N | 4 | E |

Charles Glaze
GLAZE, CHARLES
B. Sep. 12, 1965
South Carolina State 5'11" 200 lbs.

| 1987 | SEA | N | 3 | CB |

Bob Glazebrook
GLAZEBROOK, BOB
B. Mar. 7, 1956, Fresno, CA
Fresno State 6'1" 200 lbs.

1978	ATL	N	8	DB
1979		13	S, CB
1980		16	CB, S
1981		16	S
1982		9	S
1983		16	S
6 yrs.	78 games		

Year	Team	Games	Pos.

Aaron Glenn
GLENN, AARON DEVON
B. Jul. 16, 1972, Humble, TX
Texas A&M 5'9" 185 lbs.

1994	NYJ	N	16	CB
1995		16	CB
1996		16	CB
3 yrs.	48 games		

Bill Glenn
GLENN, WILLIAM
B. Mar. 15, 1918, St. Louis, MO
Eastern Illinois 6'0" 157 lbs.

| 1944 | CHIB | N | 3 | B |

Howard Glenn
GLENN, HOWARD
B. 1935, Vancouver, WA
D. Oct. 9, 1960
Linfield 6'0" 225 lbs.

| 1960 | NY | A | | G |

Kerry Glenn
GLENN, KERRY R.
B. Jan. 3, 1962, East St. Louis, IL
Minnesota 5'9" 175 lbs.

1985	NYJ	N	16	CB
1986		1	CB
1987		8	CB
1989		14	CB
1990	MIA	N	16	CB
1991		3	CB
1992		16	CB
7 yrs.	74 games		

Terry Glenn
GLENN, TERRY
B. Jul. 23, 1974, Columbus, OH
Ohio State 5'10" 184 lbs.

| 1996 | NE | N | 15 | WR |

Vencie Glenn
GLENN, VENCIE LEONARD
B. Oct. 26, 1964, Grambling, LA
Indiana State 6'0" 183 lbs.

1986	NE	N	4	S
1986	SD	N	12	S
1987		12	S
1988		16	S
1989		16	S
1990		14	S
1991	NO	N	16	S
1992	MIN	N	16	S
1993		16	S
1994		16	S
1995	NYG	N	15	S
10 yrs.	153 games		

George Glennie
GLENNIE, GEORGE
B. Mar. 31, 1902, Wisconsin
D. Jun., 1980, Andover, MA
Ripon 185 lbs.

| 1926 | RAC | N | 5 | E, G-T, FB |

Eddie Glick
GLICK, EDWARD I.
B. Apr. 23, 1900, Marinette, WI
D. Aug. 13, 1976, De Pere, WI
Lawrence/Marquette 5'8" 165 lbs.

| 1922 | GB | N | 6 | HB, QB, FB |

Fred Glick
GLICK, FREDERICK COUTURE
B. Feb. 25, 1937, Aurora, CO
Colorado State 6'1" 189 lbs.

| 1959 | CHIC | N | 1 | DB |

Year	Team	Games	Pos.

Fred Glick *continued*

Year	Team	Games	Pos.
1960	STL	N	4	DB
1961	HOU	A	12	DB
1962		14	DB
1963		14	DB
1964		14	DB
1965		14	DB
1966		10	DB
8 yrs.	83 games		

Gary Glick
GLICK, GARY G.
B. May 14, 1930, Grant, NE
Colorado State 6'2" 195 lbs.

1956	PIT	N	8	DB
1957		12	DB
1958		12	DB
1959		2	DB
1959	WAS	N	11	HB, DB
1960		11	DB
1961	BAL	N	14	DB
1963	SD	A	6	DB
7 yrs.	76 games		

Norm Glockson
GLOCKSON, NORMAN STANLEY
B. Jun. 15, 1894, Blue Island, IL
D. Aug. 5, 1955, Maywood, IL
None 6'0" 230 lbs.

| 1922 | RAC | N | 1 | G |

Fred Gloden
GLODEN, FREDERICK J., JR.
B. Dec. 21, 1918, Dubuque, IA
Tulane 5'10" 187 lbs.

1941	PHI	N	7	HB
1946	MIA	AA	7	HB
2 yrs.	14 games		

Clyde Glosson
GLOSSON, CLYDE
B. Jan. 22, 1947, San Antonio, TX
Texas-El Paso 5'11" 175 lbs.

| 1970 | BUF | | 11 | WR |

Andrew Glover
GLOVER, ANDREW LEE
B. Aug. 12, 1967, New Orleans, LA
Grambling State 6'6" 245 lbs.

1991	LARI	N	16	TE
1992		16	TE
1993		15	TE
1994		16	TE
1995	OAK	N	16	TE
1996		13	TE
6 yrs.	92 games		

Clyde Glover
GLOVER, CLYDE M.
B. Jul. 16, 1960, New Orleans, LA
Fresno State 6'6" 280 lbs.

| 1987 | SF | N | 13 | DE |

Kevin Glover
GLOVER, KEVIN BERNARD
B. Jun. 17, 1963, Washington, DC
Maryland 6'2" 267 lbs.

1985	DET	N	10	C, G
1986		4	C, G
1987		12	C, G
1988		16	C, G
1989		16	C, G
1990		16	C, G
1991		7	C
1992		16	C
1993		16	C

Year	Team	Games	Pos.

Kevin Glover *continued*

Year	Team	Games	Pos.
1994		16	C
1995		16	C
1996		16	C
12 yrs.	161 games		

La'Roi Glover
GLOVER, LA'ROI DAMON
B. Jul. 4, 1974, San Diego, CA
San Diego State 6'0" 281 lbs.

| 1996 | OAK | N | 2 | DT |

Rich Glover
GLOVER, RICHARD EDWARD
B. Feb. 6, 1950, Jersey City, NJ
Nebraska 6'1" 242 lbs.

1973	NYG	N	13	DT
1975	PHI	N	14	DT
2 yrs.	27 games		

Larry Glueck
GLUECK, LAWRENCE
B. Oct. 5, 1941, Norristown, PA
Villanova 6'0" 190 lbs.

1963	CHI	N	14	DB
1964		11	DB
1965		12	DB
3 yrs.	37 games		

Paul Goad
GOAD, PAUL
B. Sep. 7, 1934, Cincinnati, OH
D. Nov. 29, 1978, Little Rock, AR
Abilene Christian 6'0" 195 lbs.

| 1956 | SF | N | 4 | FB |

Tim Goad
GOAD, TIMOTHY RAY
B. Feb. 28, 1966, Claudville, VA
North Carolina 6'3" 280 lbs.

1988	NE	N	16	NT
1989		16	NT
1990		16	NT
1991		16	NT
1992		16	NT
1993		16	NT
1994		13	NT
1995	CLE	N	16	DT
1996	BAL	N	16	DT
9 yrs.	141 games		

Art Gob
GOB, ARTHUR J.
B. Nov. 7, 1937, Pittsburgh, PA
Pittsburgh 6'4" 230 lbs.

1959	WAS	N	11	DE
1960		1	DE
1960	LA	A		DE
2 yrs.	12 games		

Les Goble
GOBLE, LESTER BOIS
B. Jul. 23, 1932, Waverly, NY
Alfred 5'11" 158 lbs.

1954	CHIC	N	12	HB, DB
1955		9	HB, DB
2 yrs.	21 games		

Ed Goddard
GODDARD, EDWIN (Rip)
B. 1915
Washington State 5'10" 183 lbs.

1937	BKN	N	4	QB, HB, DB
1937	CLE	N	4	QB, HB, DB
1938		10	QB, HB, DB
2 yrs.	18 games		

Year	Team		Games	Pos.

Chris Godfrey
GODFREY, CHRISTOPHER JAMES
B. May 17, 1958, Detroit, MI
Michigan 6'3" 260 lbs.

Year	Team		Games	Pos.
1980	NYJ	N	6	DE, DT
1984	NYG	N	10	G
1985			16	G
1986			16	G
1987			8	G
1988	SEA	N	9	G
6 yrs.	65 games			

Herb Godfrey
GODFREY, HERBERT
B. Aug. 23, 1919, Port Angeles, WA
Washington State 6'1" 187 lbs.

Year	Team		Games	Pos.
1942	CLE	N	3	E

Randall Godfrey
GODFREY, RANDALL EURALENTRIS
B. Apr. 6, 1973, Valdosta, GA
Georgia 6'2" 237 lbs.

Year	Team		Games	Pos.
1996	DAL	N	16	LB

Bill Godwin
GODWIN, WILLIAM D.
B. Nov. 20, 1920
D. Jun., 1969, Augusta, GA
Georgia 6'3" 241 lbs.

Year	Team		Games	Pos.
1947	BOS	N	12	C
1948			12	C
2 yrs.	24 games			

Walt Godwin
GODWIN, WALTER
B. Sep. 29, 1899
D. Oct., 1954
Georgia Tech 5'7" 205 lbs.

Year	Team		Games	Pos.
1929	SI	N	8	G

Leo Goeas
GOEAS, LEO DOUGLAS
B. Aug. 15, 1966, Honolulu, HI
Hawaii 6'4" 289 lbs.

Year	Team		Games	Pos.
1990	SD	N	15	OT
1991			9	G, OT
1992			16	G, OT
1993	LARM	N	16	G, OT
1994			13	G
1995	STL	N	15	G, OT
1996			16	G
7 yrs.	100 games			

Brad Goebel
GOEBEL, BRAD ARLEN
B. Oct. 13, 1967, Cuero, TX
Baylor 6'3" 198 lbs.

Year	Team		Games	Pos.
1991	PHI	N	4	QB
1992	CLE	N	1	QB
1994			1	QB
3 yrs.	6 games			

Hank Goebel
GOEBEL, HANK
B. Nov. 1, 1964, Evergreen Park, IL
Fullerton State 6'7" 280 lbs.

Year	Team		Games	Pos.
1987	LARM	N	3	OT

Joe Goebel
GOEBEL, JOSEPH ROBERT
B. Dec. 12, 1963, Tulsa, OK
UCLA 6'5" 264 lbs.

Year	Team		Games	Pos.
1987	SD	N	2	C

Paul Goebel
GOEBEL, PAUL G.
B. May 28, 1901
D. Jan. 26, 1988, Grand Rapids, MI
Michigan 6'3" 200 lbs.

Year	Team		Games	Pos.
1923	COL	N	10	E
1924			8	E
1925			8	E
1925	CHIB	N	1	E
1926	NY	A	10	E
4 yrs.	37 games			

George Goeddeke
GOEDDEKE, GEORGE ALOYSIUS
B. Jul. 29, 1945, Detroit, MI
Notre Dame 6'3" 250 lbs.

Year	Team		Games	Pos.
1967	DEN	A	10	C
1968			14	G, C
1969			14	G
1970	DEN	N	14	G
1971			12	G
1972			2	G
6 yrs.	66 games			

Gus Goetz
GOETZ, ANGUS G.
B. Jul. 6, 1897
D. Jul. 24, 1977, Grosse Pointe, MI
Michigan 6'0" 190 lbs.

Year	Team		Games	Pos.
1922	BUF	N	7	E, T
1923	COL	N	2	T
1926	NY	A	5	T
3 yrs.	14 games			

Clark Goff
GOFF, CLARK
B. 1918
Florida 6'3" 235 lbs.

Year	Team		Games	Pos.
1940	PIT	N	11	T

Robert Goff
GOFF, ROBERT LAMAR (Pig)
B. Oct. 2, 1965, Rochester, NY
Auburn 6'3" 270 lbs.

Year	Team		Games	Pos.
1988	TB	N	16	DE
1989			12	DE
1990	NO	N	15	NT
1991			15	NT
1992			16	NT
1993			16	NT
1994			16	NT, DE
1995			11	NT
1996	MIN	N	4	DT
9 yrs.	121 games			

Willard Goff
GOFF, WILLARD E., JR.
B. Oct. 17, 1961, Lamar, CO
Illinois/West Texas State 6'4" 265 lbs.

Year	Team		Games	Pos.
1985	ATL	N	7	DT
1987	SD	N	1	DE
2 yrs.	8 games			

Derrel Gofourth
GOFOURTH, DERREL GLEN
B. Mar. 20, 1955, Little Parsons, KS
Oklahoma State 6'3" 260 lbs.

Year	Team		Games	Pos.
1977	GB	N	14	C
1978			16	C
1979			16	G
1980			16	G
1981			15	G
1982			9	G
1983	SD	N	15	G, C
1984			16	G, C
8 yrs.	117 games			

Kevin Gogan
GOGAN, KEVIN PATRICK
B. Nov. 2, 1964, San Francisco, CA
Washington 6'7" 310 lbs.

Year	Team		Games	Pos.
1987	DAL	N	11	OT
1988			15	OT
1989			13	OT
1990			16	OT
1991			16	OT
1992			16	G
1993			16	G, OT
1994	LARI	N	16	G
1995	OAK	N	16	G
1996			16	G
10 yrs.	151 games			

Keith Goganious
GOGANIOUS, KEITH LORENZO
B. Dec. 7, 1968, Virginia Beach, VA
Penn State 6'2" 237 lbs.

Year	Team		Games	Pos.
1992	BUF	N	13	LB
1993			16	LB
1994			16	LB
1995	JAC	N	16	LB
1996	BAL	N	13	LB
5 yrs.	74 games			

Charley Gogolak
GOGOLAK, CHARLES PAUL
B. Dec. 29, 1944, Rabahidveg, Hungary
Princeton 5'10" 168 lbs.

Year	Team		Games	Pos.
1966	WAS	N	14	K
1967			1	K
1968			14	K
1970	BOS	N	6	K
1971	NE	N	14	K
1972			6	K
6 yrs.	55 games			

Pete Gogolak
GOGOLAK, PETER KORNEL
B. Apr. 18, 1942, Budapest, Hungary
Cornell 6'2" 193 lbs.

Year	Team		Games	Pos.
1964	BUF	A	14	K
1965			14	K
1966	NYG	N	14	K
1967			9	K
1968			14	K
1969			14	K
1970			14	K
1971			14	K
1972			14	K
1973			14	K
1974			14	K
11 yrs.	149 games			

Dan Goich
GOICH, DANIEL JOHN
B. Apr. 30, 1944, Chicago, IL
California 6'4" 258 lbs.

Year	Team		Games	Pos.
1969	DET	N	14	DT
1970			14	DT
1971	NO	N	10	DT
1972	NYG	N	4	DT
1973			14	DT
5 yrs.	56 games			

Bill Goldberg
GOLDBERG, WILLIAM SCOTT
B. Dec. 27, 1966, Tulsa, OK
Georgia 6'2" 266 lbs.

Year	Team		Games	Pos.
1992	ATL	N	4	NT
1993			5	NT
1994			5	DT
3 yrs.	14 games			

Marshall Goldberg
GOLDBERG, MARSHALL (Biggie)

continued
B. Oct. 25, 1917, Elkins, WV
Pittsburgh 5'11" 190 lbs.

Year	Team		Games	Pos.
1939	CHIC	N	9	HB
1940			1	HB, FB
1941			11	HB, FB
1942			11	FB, HB
1943			1	HB
1946			10	HB
1947			12	HB
1948			11	HB
8 yrs.	66 games			

Tim Golden
GOLDEN, TIMOTHY GEORGE
B. Nov. 15, 1959, Pahokee, FL
Florida 6'2" 220 lbs.

Year	Team		Games	Pos.
1982	NE	N	9	LB
1983			16	LB
1984			15	LB
1985	PHI	N	2	LB
4 yrs.	42 games			

Buckets Goldenberg
GOLDENBERG, CHARLES R.
B. Apr. 14, 1911, Odessa, Ukraine
D. Apr. 16, 1986, Glendale, WI
Wisconsin 5'10" 220 lbs.

Year	Team		Games	Pos.
1933	GB		11	FB, DB
1934			10	FB, DB
1935			12	FB, DB
1936			7	G, FB, LB
1937			8	G, LB, FB
1938			11	G, LB
1939			9	G, LB
1940			11	G, LB
1941			8	G, LB
1942			11	G, LB
1943			10	G, LB
1944			8	G, LB
1945			4	G
13 yrs.	120 games			

Joe Golding
GOLDING, JOSEPH G., JR.
B. Feb. 26, 1921, Eufaula, OK
D. Dec. 26, 1971, OK
Oklahoma 6'0" 184 lbs.

Year	Team		Games	Pos.
1947	BOS	N	12	HB, DB
1948			12	HB, DB
1949	NYB	N	11	HB, DB
1950	NYY	N	12	DB
1951			11	DB
5 yrs.	58 games			

Sam Goldman
GOLDMAN, SAMUEL
B. Nov. 10, 1916, Cleveland, OH
D. Nov. 8, 1978, Pensacola, FL
Ohio State/Samford 6'3" 228 lbs.

Year	Team		Games	Pos.
1944	BOS	N	6	E
1946			11	E
1947			12	E
1948	CHIC	N	11	E
1949	DET	N	8	E
5 yrs.	48 games			

John Goldsberry
GOLDSBERRY, JOHN GARARD
B. Nov. 22, 1926, Indianapolis, IN
D. Jan., 1972
Indiana 6'2" 245 lbs.

Year	Team		Games	Pos.
1949	CHIC	N	10	T
1950			11	T
2 yrs.	21 games			

Earl Goldsmith
GOLDSMITH, ARTHUR EARL

Year	Team	Games	Pos.

Earl Goldsmith *continued*

(Goney)
B. Apr. 14, 1894, Evansville, IN
D. Jan., 1971, Crewe, VA
Indiana

Year	Team		Games	Pos.
1921	**EVA**	**A**	5	E
1922	**EVA**	**N**	1	E

2 yrs.   6 games

Wen Goldsmith

GOLDSMITH, WENDELL
B. Dec. 25, 1918
Emporia State 6'0" 202 lbs.

Year	Team		Games	Pos.
1940	**NYG**	**N**	1	C

Al Goldstein

GOLDSTEIN, ALAN
B. 1936
North Carolina 6'0" 204 lbs.

Year	Team		Games	Pos.
1960	**OAK**	**A**		OE

Izzy Goldstein

GOLDSTEIN, G. (Goldie)
B. 1903
Deceased
Florida 6'3" 210 lbs.

Year	Team		Games	Pos.
1926	**NEW**	**A**	4	G

Ralph Goldston

GOLDSTON, RALPH PETER, SR.
B. Feb. 25, 1929, Campbell, OH
Indiana/Youngstown State 5'11" 195 lbs.

Year	Team		Games	Pos.
1952	**PHI**	**N**	9	HB
1954			8	HB
1955			10	HB

3 yrs.   27 games

Archie Golembeski

GOLEMBESKI, ANTHONY
B. May 25, 1900
D. Mar. 9, 1976, Worcester, MA
Holy Cross 5'10" 182 lbs.

Year	Team		Games	Pos.
1925	**PRO**	**N**	11	E, G, QB
1926			8	E
1929			8	C, G, HB, T

3 yrs.   27 games

John Golemgeske

GOLEMGESKE, JOHN
B. 1915
Wisconsin 6'2" 225 lbs.

Year	Team		Games	Pos.
1937	**BKN**	**N**	10	T, G
1938			11	G, T
1939			11	T, G
1940			10	T

4 yrs.   42 games

Bob Golic

GOLIC, ROBERT PERRY
B. Oct. 26, 1957, Cleveland, OH
Notre Dame 6'2" 260 lbs.

Year	Team		Games	Pos.
1980	**NE**	**N**	16	LB
1981			16	LB
1982	**CLE**	**N**	6	NT
1983			16	NT
1984			15	NT
1985			16	NT
1986			16	NT
1987			12	NT
1988			16	NT
1989	**LARI**	**N**	16	DT
1990			16	DT
1991			16	DT
1992			9	DT

13 yrs.   186 games

Mike Golic

GOLIC, MIKE
B. Dec. 12, 1962, Willowick, OH
Notre Dame 6'5" 272 lbs.

Year	Team		Games	Pos.
1986	**HOU**	**N**	16	DT
1987			2	NT
1987	**PHI**	**N**	6	DE, DT
1988			12	DE, DT
1989			16	DT
1990			16	DT
1991			16	DT
1992			16	DT
1993	**MIA**	**N**	15	NT

8 yrs.   115 games

Rudy Gollomb

GOLLOMB, RUDOLPH P.
B. Oct. 6, 1910, Oshkosh, WI
D. Sep. 11, 1991, Oshkosh, WI
Carroll (Wisconsin) 5'11" 205 lbs.

Year	Team		Games	Pos.
1936	**PHI**	**N**	5	G, B

Gene Golsen

GOLSEN, EUGENE (Rip)
B. Jul. 6, 1902
Deceased
Georgetown (DC) 5'11" 209 lbs.

Year	Team		Games	Pos.
1926	**LOU**	**N**	3	FB, HB

Tom Golsen

GOLSEN, THOMAS
B. Jul. 6, 1902
D. Nov., 1986, Chicago, IL
Georgetown (DC) 5'11" 175 lbs.

Year	Team		Games	Pos.
1926	**LOU**	**N**	1	G

Jerry Golsteyn

GOLSTEYN, JERRY MARK
B. Aug. 6, 1954, West Allis, WI
Northern Illinois 6'4" 210 lbs.

Year	Team		Games	Pos.
1977	**NYG**	**N**	6	QB
1978			7	QB
1979	**DET**	**N**	1	QB
1979	**BAL**	**N**	1	QB
1982	**TB**	**N**	1	QB
1983			5	QB

5 yrs.   21 games

Rick Goltz

GOLTZ, RICARDO
B. Mar. 19, 1955, Vancouver, B.C.
Simon Fraser 6'4" 255 lbs.

Year	Team		Games	Pos.
1987	**LARI**	**N**	1	DE

Chris Golub

GOLUB, CHRISTOPHER
B. Dec. 2, 1954, Kansas City, MO
Kansas 6'2" 196 lbs.

Year	Team		Games	Pos.
1977	**KC**	**N**	1	S

Bill Gompers

GOMPERS, WILLIAM GEORGE
B. Mar. 20, 1928, Wheeling, WV
Notre Dame 6'1" 185 lbs.

Year	Team		Games	Pos.
1948	**BUF**	**AA**	14	HB, DB

George Gonda

GONDA, GEORGE
B. 1921
Duquesne 5'10" 175 lbs.

Year	Team		Games	Pos.
1942	**PIT**	**N**	5	HB, E

Goose Gonsoulin

GONSOULIN, AUSTIN WILLIAM

Goose Gonsoulin *continued*

B. Jun. 7, 1938, Port Arthur, TX
Baylor 6'3" 209 lbs.

Year	Team		Games	Pos.
1960	**DEN**	**A**	14	DB
1961			14	DB
1962			14	DB
1963			14	DB
1964			14	DB
1965			14	DB
1966			10	DB
1967	**SF**	**N**	14	DB

8 yrs.   108 games

Bob Gonya

GONYA, ROBERT J.
B. 1910
Northwestern 6'2" 208 lbs.

Year	Team		Games	Pos.
1933	**PHI**	**N**	2	T
1934			9	T, E

2 yrs.   11 games

John Gonzaga

GONZAGA, JOHN L.
B. Mar. 6, 1933, Martinez, CA
none 6'3" 247 lbs.

Year	Team		Games	Pos.
1956	**SF**	**N**	9	OT, G
1957			12	OT
1958			12	OT
1959			12	OT
1960	**DAL**	**N**	11	DE
1961	**DET**	**N**	13	DT
1962			14	DT
1963			14	G, OT
1964			14	G, OT
1965			14	G, OT
1966	**DEN**	**A**	11	G

11 yrs.   132 games

Leon Gonzalez

GONZALEZ, LEON EUGENE, III
B. Sep. 21, 1963, Jacksonville, FL
Bethune-Cookman 5'10" 162 lbs.

Year	Team		Games	Pos.
1985	**DAL**	**N**	11	WR
1987	**ATL**	**N**	2	WR

2 yrs.   13 games

Noe Gonzalez

GONZALEZ, NOE MIO
B. Feb. 5, 1951, Alice, TX
Southwest Texas State 6'0" 210 lbs.

Year	Team		Games	Pos.
1974	**NE**	**N**	2	RB

Jeff Gooch

GOOCH, JEFF
B. Oct. 31, 1974, Nashville, TN
Austin Peay 5'11" 218 lbs.

Year	Team		Games	Pos.
1996	**TB**	**N**	15	LB

Tom Good

GOOD, THOMAS
B. 1944
Marshall 6'0" 230 lbs.

Year	Team		Games	Pos.
1966	**SD**	**A**	2	LB

Royce Goodbread

GOODBREAD, ROYCE
B. 1908
Florida 5'11" 207 lbs.

Year	Team		Games	Pos.
1930	**FRA**	**N**	13	HB, FB
1930	**MIN**	**N**	1	HB, FB
1931	**PRO**	**N**	4	HB, FB

2 yrs.   18 games

Kelly Goodburn

GOODBURN, KELLY JOE
B. Apr. 14, 1962, Cherokee, IA

Kelly Goodburn *continued*

Iowa State/Emporia State 6'2" 195 lbs.

Year	Team		Games	Pos.
1987	**KC**	**N**	13	P
1988			16	P
1989			16	P
1990			3	P
1990	**WAS**	**N**	4	P
1991			16	P
1992			16	P
1993			1	P

7 yrs.   85 games

Chris Goode

GOODE, CHRIS K.
B. Sep. 17, 1963, Town Creek, AL
North Alabama/Alabama 6'0" 193 lbs.

Year	Team		Games	Pos.
1987	**IND**	**N**	8	DB
1988			13	CB, S
1989			15	CB
1990			16	CB
1991			15	CB, S
1992			15	CB, S
1993			14	CB, S

7 yrs.   96 games

Conrad Goode

GOODE, CONRAD LAWRENCE
B. Jan. 19, 1962, St. Louis, MO
Missouri 6'6" 285 lbs.

Year	Team		Games	Pos.
1984	**NYG**	**N**	8	OT
1985			16	OT
1987	**TB**	**N**	11	OT

3 yrs.   35 games

Don Goode

GOODE, DONALD RAY
B. Jun. 21, 1951, Houston, TX
Kansas 6'2" 230 lbs.

Year	Team		Games	Pos.
1974	**SD**	**N**	14	LB
1975			13	LB
1976			13	LB
1977			14	LB
1978			14	LB
1979			12	LB
1980	**CLE**	**N**	15	LB
1981			16	LB

8 yrs.   111 games

Irv Goode

GOODE, IRVIN LEE
B. Oct. 12, 1940, Newport, KY
Kentucky 6'5" 255 lbs.

Year	Team		Games	Pos.
1962	**STL**	**N**	14	C
1963			13	OT
1964			14	OT
1965			12	G
1966			11	G
1967			14	G, C
1968			14	G, C
1969			14	G, C
1970			14	G, C
1971			14	G
1973	**MIA**	**N**	14	G, C
1974			14	C, G

12 yrs.   162 games

John Goode

GOODE, JOHN TIMOTHY
B. Nov. 5, 1962, Cleveland Heights, OH
Youngstown State 6'2" 222 lbs.

Year	Team		Games	Pos.
1984	**STL**	**N**	16	TE
1985	**PHI**	**N**	14	TE

2 yrs.   30 games

Kerry Goode

GOODE, KERRY
B. Jul. 28, 1965, Town Creek, AL

493

Year Team	Games	Pos.

Kerry Goode *continued*
Alabama 5'11" 200 lbs.

Year	Team		Games	Pos.
1988	**TB**	N	14	RB
1989	**MIA**	N	1	RB

2 yrs. 15 games

Rob Goode
GOODE, ROBERT L.
B. Jun. 5, 1927, Roby, TX
Texas A&M 6'4" 222 lbs.

Year	Team		Games	Pos.
1949	**WAS**	N	12	HB
1950			12	FB
1951			12	FB
1954			12	FB
1955	**PHI**	N	8	HB
1955	**WAS**	N	3	FB

5 yrs. 59 games

Tom Goode
GOODE, THOMAS GUNN
B. Dec. 1, 1938, West Point, MS
Mississippi State 6'3" 244 lbs.

Year	Team		Games	Pos.
1962	**HOU**	A	14	LB
1963			14	LB
1964			14	C
1965			14	C
1966	**MIA**	A	14	C
1967			14	C
1968			14	C
1969			14	C
1970	**BAL**	N	1	C

9 yrs. 113 games

Daryl Goodlow
GOODLOW, DARYL
B. Nov. 2, 1960, Maplewood, MO
Oklahoma 6'2" 235 lbs.

Year	Team		Games	Pos.
1987	**LARI**	N	2	LB

Eugene Goodlow
GOODLOW, EUGENE
B. Dec. 19, 1958, St. Louis, MO
Kansas State 6'2" 190 lbs.

Year	Team		Games	Pos.
1983	**NO**	N	16	WR
1984			10	WR
1985			12	WR
1986			16	WR

4 yrs. 54 games

Aubrey Goodman
GOODMAN, AUBREY LOUIS
B. Feb. 18, 1904, Lott, TX
D. Mar. 7, 1922, Waco, TX
Baylor/Chicago 6'2" 225 lbs.

Year	Team		Games	Pos.
1926	**CHI**	A	13	T, E
1927	**CHIC**	N	1	T

2 yrs. 14 games

Brian Goodman
GOODMAN, BRIAN
B. Dec. 7, 1949, Los Angeles, CA
UCLA 6'2" 250 lbs.

Year	Team		Games	Pos.
1973	**HOU**	N	3	G
1974			14	G

2 yrs. 17 games

Don Goodman
GOODMAN, DON CHARLES
B. Apr. 23, 1959, Los Angeles, CA
Cincinnati 5'11" 214 lbs.

Year	Team		Games	Pos.
1987	**STL**	N	3	RB

Hank Goodman
GOODMAN, HENRY JOSEPH
B. Apr. 18, 1917, Bradford, PA

Hank Goodman *continued*
St. Bonaventure/George Washington/West Va. 6'3" 220 lbs.

Year	Team		Games	Pos.
1942	**DET**	N	11	T

Harvey Goodman
GOODMAN, HARVEY FRANKLIN
B. Sep. 16, 1952, Los Angeles, CA
Colorado 6'4" 260 lbs.

Year	Team		Games	Pos.
1976	**DEN**	N	14	G

John Goodman
GOODMAN, JOHN RICHARD
B. Nov. 12, 1958, Oklahoma City, OK
Oklahoma 6'6" 254 lbs.

Year	Team		Games	Pos.
1981	**PIT**	N	15	DE
1982			9	DE, DT
1983			13	DE
1984			14	DE
1985			12	DE

5 yrs. 63 games

Les Goodman
GOODMAN, LESLIE EDWARD, JR.
B. Sep. 1, 1950, Port Jefferson, NY
Yankton 5'11" 206 lbs.

Year	Team		Games	Pos.
1973	**GB**	N	6	RB
1974			13	RB

2 yrs. 19 games

Clyde Goodnight
GOODNIGHT, CLYDE DAVIS
B. Mar. 3, 1924, Holland, TX
Tulsa 6'1" 196 lbs.

Year	Team		Games	Pos.
1945	**GB**	N	10	E
1946			8	E
1947			11	E
1948			8	E
1949	**WAS**	N	10	E
1950			10	E

6 yrs. 57 games

Owen Goodnight
GOODNIGHT, OWEN
B. Aug. 27, 1917, Holland, TX
D. May, 1967
Hardin-Simmons 6'0" 195 lbs.

Year	Team		Games	Pos.
1941	**CLE**	N	9	HB, FB

Robert Goodridge
GOODRIDGE, ROBERT WAYNE
B. May 11, 1946, Cincinnati, OH
Vanderbilt 6'2" 202 lbs.

Year	Team		Games	Pos.
1968	**MIN**	N	11	OE

Charlie Goodrum
GOODRUM, CHARLES LEO
B. Jan. 11, 1950, Miami, FL
Florida A&M 6'3" 256 lbs.

Year	Team		Games	Pos.
1973	**MIN**	N	10	G
1974			12	OT, G
1975			14	OT, G
1976			14	OT
1977			14	OT
1978			16	OT
1979			15	OT
1980			15	OT

8 yrs. 110 games

John Goodson
GOODSON, JOHN WARREN
B. Mar. 18, 1960, Houston, TX
Texas 6'3" 204 lbs.

Year	Team		Games	Pos.
1982	**PIT**	N	9	P

Mark Goodspeed
GOODSPEED, MARK JUDSON
B. Dec. 1, 1956, Kansas City, KS
Nebraska 6'5" 270 lbs.

Year	Team		Games	Pos.
1980	**STL**	N	3	OT

Doug Goodwin
GOODWIN, DOUGLAS
B. Mar. 11, 1942, Charleston, SC
Maryland-Eastern Shore 6'2" 228 lbs.

Year	Team		Games	Pos.
1966	**BUF**	A	3	FB
1968	**ATL**	N	2	FB

2 yrs. 5 games

Earl Goodwin
GOODWIN, EARL
B. 1904
Deceased
West Texas State/Bucknell 6'1" 195 lbs.

Year	Team		Games	Pos.
1928	**POT**	N	7	E, T

Hunter Goodwin
GOODWIN, ROBERT HUNTER
B. Oct. 10, 1972, Bellville, TX
Texas A&M, Kingsville/Texas A&M 6'5" 277 lbs.

Year	Team		Games	Pos.
1996	**MIN**	N	9	TE

Merl Goodwin
GOODWIN, MERL
B. 1904
Deceased
West Texas State/Bucknell 6'1" 195 lbs.

Year	Team		Games	Pos.
1928	**POT**	N	3	QB, E, FB

Ronnie Goodwin
GOODWIN, RONALD RAY
B. Jan. 9, 1941, Phillips, TX
Baylor 6'0" 180 lbs.

Year	Team		Games	Pos.
1963	**PHI**	N	10	FL
1964			14	FL
1965			11	E, FL
1966			12	E, FL
1967			7	E, FL
1968			2	E, FL

6 yrs. 56 games

Tod Goodwin
GOODWIN, CHARLES R.
B. Dec. 5, 1911, Fairmont, WV
West Virginia 6'0" 184 lbs.

Year	Team		Games	Pos.
1935	**NYG**	N	11	E
1936			8	E

2 yrs. 19 games

Johnny Goodyear
GOODYEAR, JOHN
B. Jun. 10, 1920, La Grange, IL
Marquette 6'0" 190 lbs.

Year	Team		Games	Pos.
1942	**WAS**	N	3	B

Jim Goolsby
GOOLSBY, JAMES (Shag)
B. 1917
Mississippi State 6'2" 195 lbs.

Year	Team		Games	Pos.
1940	**CLE**	N	8	C

Tom Goosby
GOOSBY, THOMAS
B. May 24, 1941, Alliance, OH
Baldwin-Wallace 6'0" 235 lbs.

Year	Team		Games	Pos.
1963	**CLE**	N	1	LB
1966	**WAS**	N	14	G

2 yrs. 15 games

Ron Goovert
GOOVERT, RONALD EDWARD
B. Feb. 2, 1944, Detroit, MI
Michigan State 5'11" 225 lbs.

Year	Team		Games	Pos.
1967	**DET**	N	14	LB

Alex Gordon
GORDON, ALEX GRONCIER
B. Sep. 14, 1964, Jacksonville, FL
Cincinnati 6'5" 246 lbs.

Year	Team		Games	Pos.
1987	**NYJ**	N	12	LB
1988			13	LB
1989			16	LB
1990	**LARI**	N	10	LB
1991	**CIN**	N	14	LB
1992			15	LB
1993			16	LB

7 yrs. 96 games

Bobby Gordon
GORDON, ROBERT
B. Dec. 7, 1935, Pulaski, TN
D. Aug. 16, 1990, Strawberry Plains, TN
Tennessee 6'0" 195 lbs.

Year	Team		Games	Pos.
1958	**CHIC**	N	12	DB
1960	**HOU**	A	14	DB

2 yrs. 12 games

Cornell Gordon
GORDON, CORNELL KERMIT
B. Jan. 6, 1941, Norfolk, VA
North Carolina A&T 6'0" 187 lbs.

Year	Team		Games	Pos.
1965	**NY**	A	14	DB
1966			10	DB
1967			2	DB
1968			14	DB
1969			14	CB, S
1970	**DEN**	N	14	CB
1971			14	CB
1972			1	CB

8 yrs. 83 games

Darrien Gordon
GORDON, DARRIEN X. JAMAL
B. Nov. 14, 1970, Shawnee, OK
Stanford 5'11" 182 lbs.

Year	Team		Games	Pos.
1993	**SD**	N	16	CB
1994			16	CB
1996			16	CB

3 yrs. 48 games

Dick Gordon
GORDON, RICHARD FREDERICK
B. Jan. 1, 1944, Cincinnati, OH
Michigan State 5'11" 190 lbs.

Year	Team		Games	Pos.
1965	**CHI**	N	14	OE
1966			14	OE
1967			14	OE
1968			14	OE
1969			14	WR
1970			14	WR
1971			13	WR
1972	**LA**	N	4	WR
1973			5	WR
1973	**GB**	N	2	WR
1974	**SD**	N	7	WR

10 yrs. 115 games

Dwayne Gordon
GORDON, DWAYNE
B. Nov. 2, 1969, White Plains, NY
New Hampshire 6'1" 231 lbs.

Year	Team		Games	Pos.
1993	**ATL**	N	5	LB
1994			16	LB
1995	**SD**	N	15	LB
1996			13	LB

4 yrs. 49 games

Ira Gordon

GORDON, IRA C.
B. May 5, 1948, Kilbourne, LA
Kansas State 6'3" 270 lbs.

Year	Team		Games	Pos.
1970	SD	N	8	G
1971			14	G
1972			6	OT
1973			6	OT
1974			14	OT, G
1975			14	G
6 yrs.	62 games			

John Gordon

GORDON, JOHN
B. Aug. 29, 1948, Detroit, MI
New Mexico State/Hawaii 6'6" 260 lbs.

Year	Team		Games	Pos.
1972	DET	N	2	DT

Larry Gordon

GORDON, LAWRENCE WAYNE
B. Jul. 8, 1954, Monroe, LA
D. Jun. 25, 1983, Phoenix, AZ
Arizona State 6'4" 230 lbs.

Year	Team		Games	Pos.
1976	MIA	N	14	LB
1977			14	LB
1978			16	LB
1979			16	LB
1980			15	LB
1981			16	LB
1982			9	LB
7 yrs.	100 games			

Lou Gordon

GORDON, LOUIS JAMES
B. Jul. 15, 1908, Chicago, IL
D. Apr. 4, 1976, Chicago, IL
Illinois 6'5" 224 lbs.

Year	Team		Games	Pos.
1930	CHIC	N	9	T, G
1931			1	T
1931	BKN	N	5	T, E
1932	CHIC	N	7	T
1933			11	T
1934			11	T, E
1935			12	T, G
1936	GB	N	12	T
1937			10	T
1938	CHIB	N	2	T
9 yrs.	80 games			

Sonny Gordon

GORDON, DENMAN PRESTON
B. Jul. 30, 1965, Lynn, MA
Ohio State 5'11" 182 lbs.

Year	Team		Games	Pos.
1987	TB	N	7	S

Tim Gordon

GORDON, TIM CARVELLE
B. May 7, 1965, Ardmore, OK
Tulsa 6'0" 188 lbs.

Year	Team		Games	Pos.
1987	ATL	N	11	CB
1988			16	S
1989			14	S
1990			5	S
1991	NE	N	11	S
1992			10	S
6 yrs.	67 games			

John Gordy

GORDY, JOHN T.
B. Jul. 17, 1935, Nashville, TN
Tennessee 6'3" 248 lbs.

Year	Team		Games	Pos.
1957	DET	N	12	G
1959			12	G, T
1960			12	G
1961			14	G, OT
1962			14	OT, G
1963			14	G, OT
1964			14	G

John Gordy continued

Year	Team		Games	Pos.
1965			14	G
1966			14	G
1967			14	G
10 yrs.	134 games			

Gordon Gore

GORE, WILFRED GORDON
B. 1911
Southwestern Oklahoma State 6'0" 215 lbs.

Year	Team		Games	Pos.
1939	DET	N	7	HB

Stacy Gore

GORE, STACY
B. May 20, 1963
Arkansas State 6'0" 200 lbs.

Year	Team		Games	Pos.
1987	MIA	N	3	P

Chuck Gorecki

GORECKI, CHARLES
B. Apr. 7, 1964
Boston College 6'4" 237 lbs.

Year	Team		Games	Pos.
1987	PHI	N	3	LB

Alex Gorgal

GORGAL, ALEX
B. Jan. 16, 1900, Poland
D. Jun., 1986, Peru, IL
None 5'9" 180 lbs.

Year	Team		Games	Pos.
1923	RI	N	3	HB, FB

Ken Gorgal

GORGAL, KENNETH R.
B. Feb. 13, 1929, Peru, IL
Purdue 6'2" 200 lbs.

Year	Team		Games	Pos.
1950	CLE	N	12	DB
1953			12	DB
1954			11	DB
1955	CHIB	N	12	DB
1956			6	DB
1956	GB	N	5	DB
5 yrs.	58 games			

Pete Gorgone

GORGONE, PIETRO
B. May 8, 1920, Bruca, Italy
D. Dec. 1, 1992, Salisbury Township, PA
Muhlenberg 6'0" 220 lbs.

Year	Team		Games	Pos.
1946	NYG	N	9	QB

Walt Gorinski

GORINSKI, WALTER
B. Dec. 20, 1919
D. Jul., 1977, Bossier City, LA
Louisiana State 6'1" 207 lbs.

Year	Team		Games	Pos.
1946	PIT	N	6	FB

Doc Gorman

GORMAN, OTHO ADDISON
B. Jul. 24, 1893, Pawnee, IL
D. Sep. 22, 1938
St. Louis

Year	Team		Games	Pos.
1921	EVA	A	1	E
1922	EVA	N	1	T
2 yrs.	2 games			

Earl Gorman

GORMAN, EARL (Bud)
B. Jun. 27, 1896
D. Nov., 1962
None 225 lbs.

Year	Team		Games	Pos.
1922	RAC	N	11	G, T
1923			8	G

Earl Gorman continued

Year	Team		Games	Pos.
1924	KEN	N	3	G, T
3 yrs.	22 games			

Tom Gormley

GORMLEY, THOMAS F.
B. Mar. 25, 1889
D. Jan., 1947
Villanova/Ursinus/Catholic/Georgetown (DC) 5'11" 225 lbs.

Year	Team		Games	Pos.
1920	CLE	A	7	G
1921	NY	A	1	T
1921	WAS	A	3	G, T
2 yrs.	11 games			

Paul Gorrill

GORRILL, PAUL (Flop)
B. 1900
Deceased
Ohio State 5'11" 178 lbs.

Year	Team		Games	Pos.
1926	COL	N	6	E

Antonio Goss

GOSS, ANTONIO DERRELL
B. Aug. 11, 1966, Randleman, NC
North Carolina 6'4" 228 lbs.

Year	Team		Games	Pos.
1989	SF	N	8	LB
1991			14	LB
1992			16	LB
1993			14	LB
1994			16	LB
1995			16	LB
1996	STL	N	8	LB
7 yrs.	92 games			

Don Goss

GOSS, ROBERT D.
B. May 19, 1933, Dallas, TX
Southern Methodist 6'5" 260 lbs.

Year	Team		Games	Pos.
1956	CLE	N	6	T

Gene Gossage

GOSSAGE, EZRA EUGENE
B. Feb. 17, 1935
Northwestern 6'3" 239 lbs.

Year	Team		Games	Pos.
1960	PHI	N	12	E, T
1961			14	OT, G
1962			14	DE, G
3 yrs.	40 games			

Bruce Gossett

GOSSETT, DANIEL BRUCE
B. Nov. 9, 1941, Cecil, PA
Clarion/Duquesne/Richmond 6'2" 229 lbs.

Year	Team		Games	Pos.
1964	LA	N	14	K
1965			14	K
1966			14	K
1967			14	K
1968			14	K
1969			14	K
1970	SF	N	14	K
1971			14	K
1972			14	K
1973			14	K
1974			14	K
11 yrs.	154 games			

Jeff Gossett

GOSSETT, JEFFERY ALAN
B. Jan. 25, 1957, Charleston, IL
Eastern Illinois 6'2" 200 lbs.

Year	Team		Games	Pos.
1981	KC	N	7	P
1982			8	P
1983	CLE	N	16	P
1985			16	P
1986			16	P

Jeff Gossett continued

Year	Team		Games	Pos.
1987			5	P
1987	HOU	N	4	P
1988	LARI	N	16	P
1989			16	P
1990			16	P
1991			16	P
1992			16	P
1993			16	P
1994			16	P
1995	OAK	N	16	P
1996			12	P
15 yrs.	212 games			

Preston Gothard

GOTHARD, PRESTON
B. Feb. 23, 1962, Montgomery, AL
Alabama 6'4" 240 lbs.

Year	Team		Games	Pos.
1985	PIT	N	16	TE
1986			16	TE
1987			2	TE
1988			16	TE
4 yrs.	50 games			

Len Gotshalk

GOTSHALK, LEONARD WILLIAM
B. Oct. 21, 1949, Lakeport, CA
Humboldt State 6'4" 255 lbs.

Year	Team		Games	Pos.
1972	ATL	N	14	OT
1973			14	OT
1974			10	OT
1975			14	G
1976			14	G
5 yrs.	66 games			

Darren Gottschalk

GOTTSCHALK, DARREN
B. Dec. 1, 1964
California Lutheran 6'4" 225 lbs.

Year	Team		Games	Pos.
1987	NO	N	1	TE

Kurt Gouveia

GOUVEIA, KURT KEOLA
B. Sep. 14, 1964, Honolulu, HI
Brigham Young 6'1" 227 lbs.

Year	Team		Games	Pos.
1987	WAS	N	11	LB
1988			16	LB
1989			15	LB
1990			16	LB
1991			14	LB
1992			16	LB
1993			16	LB
1994			14	LB
1995	PHI	N	16	LB
1996	SD	N	16	LB
10 yrs.	150 games			

Paul Governali

GOVERNALI, PAUL V. (Pitchin' Paul)
B. Jan. 5, 1921, Bronx, NY
D. Feb. 15, 1978, San Diego, CA
Columbia 5'11" 193 lbs.

Year	Team		Games	Pos.
1946	BOS	N	11	QB
1947			4	QB
1947	NYG	N	8	QB
1948			9	QB
3 yrs.	32 games			

Cornell Gowdy

GOWDY, CORNELL ANTHONY
B. Oct. 2, 1963, Washington, DC
Morgan State 6'0" 192 lbs.

Year	Team		Games	Pos.
1986	DAL	N	3	DB
1987	PIT	N	13	DB
1988			16	S, CB
3 yrs.	32 games			

Year	Team		Games	Pos.

Casimir Gozdowski
GOZDOWSKI, KAZMIERA
(Hippo)
B. Mar. 4, 1897
D. Jul., 1976, Spring Lake, NJ
None

Year	Team		Games	Pos.
1922	**TOL**	N	4	G, C, FB

Ted Grabinski
GRABINSKI, THADDEUS
B. 1915
Duquesne 6'2" 207 lbs.

1939	**PIT**	N	10	C
1940			11	C
2 yrs.	21 games			

Gene Grabosky
GRABOSKY, H. EUGENE
B. 1937
Syracuse 6'5" 275 lbs.

| 1960 | **BUF** | A | 2 | DT |

Jim Grabowski
GRABOWSKI, JAMES S.
B. Sep. 9, 1944, Chicago, IL
Illinois 6'2" 221 lbs.

1966	**GB**	N	14	FB
1967			9	RB
1968			14	RB
1969			14	RB
1970			14	RB
1971	**CHI**	N	12	RB
6 yrs.	77 games			

Les Grace
GRACE, LESLIE (Red)
B. 1905
D. Aug., 1968
Temple 5'11" 200 lbs.

| 1930 | **NEW** | N | 1 | E |

Sam Graddy
GRADDY, SAMUEL LOUIS
B. Feb. 10, 1964, Gaffney, SC
Tennessee 5'10" 165 lbs.

1987	**DEN**	N	1	WR
1988			7	WR
1990	**LARI**	N	16	WR
1991			12	WR
1992			7	WR
5 yrs.	43 games			

Randy Gradishar
GRADISHAR, RANDY CHARLES
B. Mar. 3, 1952, Warren, OH
Ohio State 6'3" 231 lbs.

1974	**DEN**	N	14	LB
1975			14	LB
1976			14	LB
1977			14	LB
1978			16	LB
1979			16	LB
1980			16	LB
1981			16	LB
1982			9	LB
1983			16	LB
10 yrs.	145 games			

Garry Grady
GRADY, GARRY
B. Oct. 17, 1946, Northville, MI
Eastern Michigan 5'11" 180 lbs.

| 1969 | **MIA** | A | 3 | RB |

Dave Graf
GRAF, DAVID FRANCIS
B. Aug. 5, 1953, Dunkirk, NY
Penn State 6'2" 217 lbs.

1975	**CLE**	N	14	LB
1976			14	LB
1977			14	LB
1978			7	LB
1979			16	LB
1981	**WAS**	N	6	LB
6 yrs.	71 games			

Rick Graf
GRAF, RICHARD GLENN
B. Aug. 29, 1964, Iowa City, IA
Wisconsin 6'5" 239 lbs.

1987	**MIA**	N	12	LB
1988			16	LB
1989			4	LB
1990			8	LB
1991	**HOU**	N	12	LB
1992			16	LB
1993	**WAS**	N	5	LB
7 yrs.	73 games			

Neil Graff
GRAFF, NEIL HOWARD
B. Jan. 12, 1950, Sioux Falls, SD
Wisconsin 6'3" 202 lbs.

1974	**NE**	N	14	QB
1975			11	QB
1977	**PIT**	N	4	QB
3 yrs.	29 games			

Scott Gragg
GRAGG, SCOTT
B. Feb. 28, 1972, Altus, OK
Montana 6'8" 316 lbs.

1995	**NYG**	N	13	OT
1996			16	OT
2 yrs.	29 games			

Aaron Graham
GRAHAM, AARON
B. May 22, 1973, Las Vegas, NM
Nebraska 6'3" 295 lbs.

| 1996 | **ARI** | N | 16 | C |

Al Graham
GRAHAM, ALFRED (Pup)
B. Sep. 27, 1905
D. Oct., 1969, Dayton, OH
none 6'0" 211 lbs.

1925	**DAY**	N	8	G
1926			6	G
1927			8	G
1928			7	G
1929			5	G, T
1930	**PRO**	N	9	G
1930	**POR**	N	3	G
1931	**PRO**	N	11	G
1932	**CHIC**	N	8	G
1933			8	G
9 yrs.	73 games			

Art Graham
GRAHAM, ARTHUR WILLIAM, III
B. Mar. 6, 1941, Somerville, MA
Boston College 6'1" 205 lbs.

1963	**BOS**	A	14	OE
1964			14	OE
1965			10	OE
1966			14	OE
1967			12	OE
1968			11	OE
6 yrs.	75 games			

Bill Graham
GRAHAM, WILLIAM ROGER
B. Sep. 27, 1959, Silsbee, TX
Texas 5'11" 191 lbs.

1982	**DET**	N	7	S
1983			14	CB, S
1984			14	S
1985			16	S
1986			16	S
1987			2	S
6 yrs.	69 games			

Clarence Graham
GRAHAM, CLARENCE
None

| 1928 | **DAY** | N | 2 | FB, HB |

Dave Graham
GRAHAM, DAVID ELLIOT
B. Feb. 1, 1939, Bridgeport, CT
Virginia 6'3" 248 lbs.

1963	**PHI**	N	14	OT, G
1964			13	OT
1965			14	OT
1966			14	OT
1968			14	OT
1969			14	OT
6 yrs.	83 games			

David Graham
GRAHAM, DAVID JEROME
B. Apr. 6, 1959, Chicago, IL
Morehouse 6'6" 250 lbs.

1982	**SEA**	N	3	DE
1987			3	NT
2 yrs.	6 games			

Derrick Graham
GRAHAM, DETRICE ANDREW
B. Mar. 18, 1967, Groveland, FL
Appalachian State 6'4" 306 lbs.

1990	**KC**	N	6	OT
1991			16	OT
1992			2	OT
1993			11	OT
1994			16	OT
1995	**CAR**	N	11	OT
1996	**SEA**	N	16	OT
7 yrs.	78 games			

Don Graham
GRAHAM, DONALD JOHN
B. Jan. 31, 1964, Pittsburgh, PA
Penn State 6'2" 244 lbs.

1987	**TB**	N	2	LB
1988	**BUF**	N	8	LB
1989	**WAS**	N	1	LB
3 yrs.	11 games			

Fred Graham
GRAHAM, FREDERICK HARTLEY
B. Dec. 11, 1900, Morgantown, WV
D. Aug. 29, 1953, Fairmont, WV
Indiana State/West Virginia 6'0" 175 lbs.

1926	**FRA**	N	1	E
1926	**CHI**	A	5	E
1 yr.	6 games			

Hason Graham
GRAHAM, HASON AARON
B. Mar. 21, 1971, Decatur, GA
Georgia 5'10" 176 lbs.

1995	**NE**	N	10	WR
1996			9	WR
2 yrs.	19 games			

Jeff Graham
GRAHAM, JEFF TODD
B. Feb. 14, 1969, Dayton, OH
Ohio State 6'1" 195 lbs.

1991	**PIT**	N	13	WR
1992			14	WR
1993			15	WR
1994	**CHI**	N	16	WR
1995			16	WR
1996	**NYJ**	N	11	WR
6 yrs.	85 games			

Kenny Graham
GRAHAM, JAMES KENNY
B. Nov. 25, 1941, Texarkana, TX
Washington State 6'0" 201 lbs.

1964	**SD**	A	14	DB
1965			14	DB
1966			13	DB
1967			13	DB
1968			14	DB
1969			14	S
1970	**CIN**	N	5	S
1970	**PIT**	N	3	S
7 yrs.	90 games			

Kent Graham
GRAHAM, KENT DOUGLAS
B. Nov. 1, 1968, Winfield, IL
Notre Dame/Ohio State 6'5" 220 lbs.

1992	**NYG**	N	6	QB
1993			9	QB
1994			13	QB
1995	**DET**	N	2	QB
1996	**ARI**	N	10	QB
5 yrs.	40 games			

Les Graham
GRAHAM, LESTER JAMES
B. Jul. 1, 1916, Hominy, OK
Deceased
Tulsa 6'0" 215 lbs.

| 1938 | **DET** | N | 11 | G |

Lyle Graham
GRAHAM, SAMUEL LYLE, JR.
B. Oct. 28, 1915, Kenbridge, VA
Richmond 6'3" 210 lbs.

| 1941 | **PHI** | N | 11 | C |

Mike Graham
GRAHAM, MICHAEL N.
B. Apr. 3, 1925, Warren, OH
Cincinnati 6'0" 200 lbs.

| 1948 | **LA** | AA | 14 | B |

Milt Graham
GRAHAM, MILTON R.
B. 1935, Massachusetts
Colgate 6'6" 235 lbs.

1961	**BOS**	A	3	OT
1962			14	OT, DE
1963			11	DT
3 yrs.	28 games			

Otto Graham
GRAHAM, OTTO EVERETT, JR.
(Automatic Otto)
B. Dec. 6, 1921, Waukegan, IL
Northwestern 6'1" 196 lbs.

1946	**CLE**	AA	14	QB
1947			14	QB
1948			14	QB
1949			12	QB
1950	**CLE**	N	12	QB
1951			12	QB

Year	Team		Games	Pos.

Otto Graham *continued*

Year	Team		Games	Pos.
1952			12	QB
1953			12	QB
1954			12	QB
1955			12	QB
10 yrs.	126 games			

Roger Graham
GRAHAM, ROGER ALTON
B. Nov. 8, 1972, Bronx, NY
New Haven 5'11" 217 lbs.

1996	JAC	N	1	RB

Scottie Graham
GRAHAM, JAMES OTIS
B. Mar. 28, 1969, Long Beach, CA
Ohio State 5'9" 220 lbs.

1992	NYJ	N	2	RB
1993	MIN	N	7	RB
1994			16	RB
1995			16	RB
1996			11	RB
5 yrs.	52 games			

Tom Graham
GRAHAM, THOMAS
B. Aug. 14, 1909
D. Aug., 1961
Temple 6'3" 210 lbs.

1935	PHI	N	2	G

Tom Graham
GRAHAM, TOM LAWRENCE
B. Apr. 15, 1950, Los Angeles, CA
Oregon 6'2" 235 lbs.

1972	DEN	N	14	LB
1973			14	LB
1974			6	LB
1974	KC	N	8	LB
1975	SD	N	14	LB
1976			10	LB
1977			12	LB
1978	BUF	N	11	LB
7 yrs.	89 games			

Ed Grain
GRAIN, EDWIN E.
B. Feb. 25, 1922, Baltimore, MD
D. Oct. 6, 1984, Deerfield, IL
Pennsylvania 6'0" 230 lbs.

1947	NY	AA	2	G
1947	BAL	AA	10	G
1948			11	G
2 yrs.	23 games			

Ken Grandberry
GRANDBERRY, KENNETH JAMES
B. Jan. 25, 1952, Waco, TX
Washington State 6'0" 198 lbs.

1974	CHI	N	14	RB

John Granby
GRANBY, JOHN EDWARD, JR.
B. Nov. 11, 1968, Virginia Beach, VA
Virginia Tech 6'1" 198 lbs.

1992	DEN	N	4	WR

Sonny Grandelius
GRANDELIUS, EVERETT JOHN
B. Apr. 16, 1930, Muskegon, MI
Michigan State 6'0" 195 lbs.

1953	NYG	N	12	HB

Rufus Granderson
GRANDERSON, RUFUS
B. 1937
Prairie View A&M 6'5" 277 lbs.

1960	DAL	A		DT

George Grandinette
GRANDINETTE, GEORGE
B. 1917
Fordham 5'9" 215 lbs.

1943	BKN	N	9	G

Garland Grange
GRANGE, GARLAND A.
B. Dec. 2, 1906, Forksville, PA
D. May, 1981, Miami, FL
Illinois 6'0" 173 lbs.

1929	CHIB	N	14	E, HB
1930			12	E
1931			12	E
3 yrs.	38 games			

Red Grange
GRANGE, HAROLD EDWARD
(The Galloping Ghost/ The Wheaton Iceman)
B. Jun. 13, 1903, Wheaton, IL
D. Jan. 28, 1991, Lake Wales, FL
Illinois 5'11" 183 lbs.

1925	CHIB	N	7	HB
1926	NY	A	13	HB, QB
1927	NYY		13	QB, HB, FB
1929	CHIB	N	14	HB
1930			14	HB
1931			13	HB
1932			12	HB
1933			12	HB
1934			12	HB, QB
9 yrs.	110 games			

Charlie Granger
GRANGER, CHARLES
B. 1938, Lake Charles, LA
Southern University 6'2" 240 lbs.

1961	STL	N	6	OT

Hoyle Granger
GRANGER, HOYLE JOHN
B. Mar. 7, 1944, Oberlin, LA
Mississippi State 6'1" 225 lbs.

1966	HOU	A	11	FB
1967			14	RB
1968			13	RB
1969			13	RB
1970	HOU	N	5	RB
1971	NO	N	14	RB
1972	HOU	N	13	RB
7 yrs.	83 games			

Norm Granger
GRANGER, NORMAN LANCE
B. Sep. 14, 1961, Newark, NJ
Iowa 5'10" 225 lbs.

1984	DAL	N	15	RB
1987	ATL	N	3	RB
2 yrs.	18 games			

Dave Grannell
GRANNELL, DAVID MATTHEW
B. Oct. 4, 1962, Denver, CO
Arizona State 6'4" 230 lbs.

1974	SD	N	9	TE

Grant
GRANT

Grant continued
None

1925	MIL	N	1	FB

Aaron Grant
GRANT, AARON (Heavy)
B. Jul. 3, 1908
D. Sep., 1966
Tennessee-Chattanooga 6'2" 285 lbs.

1930	POR	N	1	C

African Grant
GRANT, AFRICAN NIGERIA
B. Aug. 2, 1965, New York, NY
Illinois 6'0" 200 lbs.

1990	MIA	N	4	S

Alan Grant
GRANT, ALAN
B. Oct. 1, 1966, Pasadena, CA
Stanford 5'10" 187 lbs.

1990	IND	N	16	CB, S
1991			16	CB, S
1992	SF	N	15	CB
1993			3	CB
1993	CIN	N	9	CB
1994	WAS	N	13	CB
5 yrs.	72 games			

Bob Grant
GRANT, ROBERT BERNARD
B. Oct. 14, 1946, Jacksonville, NC
Wake Forest 6'2" 225 lbs.

1968	BAL	N	7	LB
1969			14	LB
1970			14	LB
1971	WAS	N	6	LB
4 yrs.	41 games			

Bud Grant
GRANT, HAROLD PETER
B. May 20, 1927, Superior, WI
Minnesota 6'3" 199 lbs.

1951	PHI	N	12	E
1952			12	E
2 yrs.	24 games			

Darryl Grant
GRANT, DARRYL
B. Nov. 22, 1959, San Antonio, TX
Rice 6'1" 270 lbs.

1981	WAS	N	15	OG, OT, C
1982			9	DT
1983			16	DT
1984			15	DT
1985			8	DT
1986			16	DT
1987			12	DT
1988			16	DT
1989			16	DT
1990			16	DT
1991	TB	N	2	DT
11 yrs.	141 games			

David Grant
GRANT, DAVID
B. Sep. 17, 1965, Belleville, NJ
West Virginia 6'4" 277 lbs.

1988	CIN	N	16	NT
1989			16	NT
1990			16	NT
1991			13	NT
1992	TB	N	2	DE, NT
1993	GB	N	7	DE
6 yrs.	70 games			

Frank Grant
GRANT, FRANK
B. Feb. 15, 1950, Brooklyn, NY
Southern Colorado 5'11" 181 lbs.

1973	WAS	N	13	WR
1974			14	WR
1975			14	WR
1976			14	WR
1977			14	WR
1978			6	WR
1978	TB	N	10	WR
6 yrs.	85 games			

Hugh Grant
GRANT, HUGH E. (Ducky)
B. Dec. 24, 1902
D. Sep., 1985, Fountain Valley, CA
St. Mary's (California) 5'11" 175 lbs.

1928	CHIC	N	6	QB, HB

John Grant
GRANT, JOHN DAVID
B. Jun. 28, 1950, Boise, ID
Southern California 6'3" 241 lbs.

1973	DEN	N	13	DE
1974			13	DE
1975			14	DE
1976			13	DE
1977			14	DT
1978			16	DT
1979			16	DT
7 yrs.	99 games			

Len Grant
GRANT, LEONARD M. (Fish)
B. Jan. 17, 1906, Boston, MA
D. Aug. 7, 1938, Dedham, MA
New York University 6'3" 235 lbs.

1930	NYG	N	12	T, G
1931			10	T
1932			12	T
1933			13	T, G
1934			13	T
1935			12	T
1936			8	T
1937			8	T
8 yrs.	88 games			

Otis Grant
GRANT, OTIS
B. Aug. 13, 1961, Atlanta, GA
Michigan State 6'3" 197 lbs.

1983	LARM	N	16	WR
1984			14	WR
1987	PHI	N	3	WR
3 yrs.	33 games			

Reggie Grant
GRANT, REGINALD LEON
B. Sep. 2, 1955, Atlanta, GA
Oregon 5'9" 185 lbs.

1978	NYJ	N	14	CB

Ross Grant
GRANT, ROSS (Rosie)
B. Apr. 16, 1908
D. Apr., 1974, Cedar Lake, IN
New York University 5'10" 198 lbs.

1932	SI	N	11	G, C
1933	CIN	N	7	G
1934	C, S	N	1	G
3 yrs.	19 games			

Rupert Grant
GRANT, RUPERT
B. Nov. 5, 1973, Washington, DC

Year	Team	Games	Pos.

Rupert Grant *continued*
Howard 6'1" 233 lbs.

Year	Team	Games	Pos.
1995	NE **N**	7	RB

Steve Grant
GRANT, STEPHEN
B. Dec. 23, 1969, Miami, FL
West Virginia 6'0" 231 lbs.

Year	Team	Games	Pos.
1992	IND **N**	16	LB
1993		16	LB
1994		16	LB
1995		15	LB
1996		11	LB

5 yrs.   74 games

Wes Grant
GRANT, WESLEY LOUIS
B. Sep. 24, 1946, Los Angeles, CA
UCLA 6'3" 245 lbs.

Year	Team	Games	Pos.
1971	SD **N**	2	DE
1973	HOU **N**	3	DE

2 yrs.   5 games

Will Grant
GRANT, WILFRED L.
B. Mar. 7, 1954, Boston, MA
Kentucky 6'3" 260 lbs.

Year	Team	Games	Pos.
1978	BUF **N**	16	C
1979		16	C
1980		16	C
1981		16	C
1982		9	C
1983		16	C
1984		16	C
1985		16	C
1986	SEA **N**	7	C
1987	BUF **N**	1	C

10 yrs.   129 games

Larry Grantham
GRANTHAM, JAMES LARRY
B. Sep. 16, 1938, Crystal Springs, MS
Mississippi 6'0" 204 lbs.

Year	Team	Games	Pos.
1960	NY **A**	14	LB
1961		11	LB
1962		14	LB
1963		14	LB
1964		14	LB
1965		14	LB
1966		14	LB
1967		14	LB
1968		13	LB
1969		14	LB
1970	NYJ **N**	14	LB
1971		14	LB
1972		11	LB

13 yrs.   175 games

Paul Grasmanis
GRASMANIS, PAUL RYAN
B. Aug. 2, 1974, Grand Rapids, MI
Notre Dame 6'2" 295 lbs.

Year	Team	Games	Pos.
1996	CHI **N**	14	DT

Carl Grate
GRATE, CARL
B. 1920
Georgia 6'0" 215 lbs.

Year	Team	Games	Pos.
1945	NYG **N**	6	C

Willie Grate
GRATE, WILLIE
B. May 25, 1947, Georgetown, SC
South Carolina State 6'4" 225 lbs.

Year	Team	Games	Pos.
1969	BUF **A**	11	TE
1970	BUF **N**	14	TE

2 yrs.   25 games

Year	Team	Games	Pos.

Gordon Gravelle
GRAVELLE, GORDON CARR
B. Jun. 12, 1949, Oakland, CA
Brigham Young 6'5" 251 lbs.

Year	Team	Games	Pos.
1972	PIT **N**	14	OT
1973		6	OT
1974		14	OT
1975		14	OT
1976		6	OT
1977	NYG **N**	14	OT
1978		16	OT
1979		4	OT
1979	LA **N**	8	OT

8 yrs.   96 games

Marsharne Graves
GRAVES, MARSHARNE DEWAYNE
B. Jul. 8, 1962, Memphis, TN
Arizona 6'3" 272 lbs.

Year	Team	Games	Pos.
1984	DEN **N**	1	OT
1987	IND **N**	3	OT

2 yrs.   4 games

Ray Graves
GRAVES, SAMUEL RAY
B. Dec. 31, 1918, Rockwood, TN
Tennessee 6'1" 205 lbs.

Year	Team	Games	Pos.
1942	PHI **N**	11	C
1943	P, P **N**	10	C
1946	PHI **N**	7	C

3 yrs.   28 games

Rory Graves
GRAVES, RORY ANTHONY
B. Jul. 21, 1963, Atlanta, GA
Ohio State 6'6" 285 lbs.

Year	Team	Games	Pos.
1988	LARI **N**	16	OT
1989		15	OT
1990		15	OT
1991		3	OT

4 yrs.   49 games

Tom Graves
GRAVES, THOMAS EDWARD
B. Dec. 18, 1955, Norfolk, VA
Michigan State 6'3" 228 lbs.

Year	Team	Games	Pos.
1979	PIT **N**	11	LB

White Graves
GRAVES, WHITE SOLOMON, III
B. Mar. 20, 1942, Jackson, MS
Louisiana State 6'0" 185 lbs.

Year	Team	Games	Pos.
1965	BOS **A**	14	DB
1966		14	DB
1967		12	DB
1968	CIN **A**	2	DB

4 yrs.   42 games

Bill Gray
GRAY, WILLIAM R., JR.
B. Dec. 27, 1922, Portland, OR
Oregon State/Southern California/Oregon State 5'11" 210 lbs.

Year	Team	Games	Pos.
1947	WAS **N**	12	G
1948		12	G

2 yrs.   24 games

Carlton Gray
GRAY, CARLTON PATRICK
B. Jun. 26, 1971, Cincinnati, OH
UCLA 6'0" 191 lbs.

Year	Team	Games	Pos.
1993	SEA **N**	10	CB
1994		11	CB
1995		16	CB
1996		16	CB

4 yrs.   53 games

Year	Team	Games	Pos.

Cecil Gray
GRAY, CECIL TALIK
B. Feb. 16, 1968, Harlem, NY
North Carolina 6'4" 269 lbs.

Year	Team	Games	Pos.
1990	PHI **N**	12	G, DT
1991		2	G
1992	GB **N**	2	OT
1993	IND **N**	6	OT
1994		16	OT
1995	ARI **N**	7	OT

6 yrs.   45 games

Chris Gray
GRAY, CHRISTOPHER WILLIAM
B. Jun. 19, 1970, Birmingham, AL
Auburn 6'4" 286 lbs.

Year	Team	Games	Pos.
1993	MIA **N**	5	G, OT
1994		16	G, OT
1995		10	G
1996		11	G

4 yrs.   42 games

Dan Gray
GRAY, DANIEL THOMAS
B. Jan. 29, 1956, Phillipsburg, NJ
Rutgers 6'6" 240 lbs.

Year	Team	Games	Pos.
1978	DET **N**	14	DE

David Gray
GRAY, DAVID
B. Mar. 28, 1955, San Diego, CA
Oregon State/San Diego State 6'0" 190 lbs.

Year	Team	Games	Pos.
1979	NO **N**	16	CB

Derwin Gray
GRAY, DERWIN LAMONT
B. Apr. 9, 1971, San Antonio, TX
Brigham Young 5'10" 190 lbs.

Year	Team	Games	Pos.
1993	IND **N**	11	CB, S
1994		16	S
1995		16	S
1996		10	S

4 yrs.   53 games

Earnest Gray
GRAY, EARNEST
B. Mar. 2, 1957, Greenwood, MS
Memphis State 6'3" 195 lbs.

Year	Team	Games	Pos.
1979	NYG **N**	16	WR
1980		16	WR
1981		16	WR
1982		9	WR
1983		16	WR
1984		12	WR
1985	STL **N**	5	WR

7 yrs.   90 games

Hector Gray
GRAY, HECTOR BERNARD
B. Jan. 2, 1957, Miami, FL
Florida State 6'1" 197 lbs.

Year	Team	Games	Pos.
1981	DET **N**	16	CB
1982		8	CB
1983		1	CB

3 yrs.   25 games

Jack Gray
GRAY, JOHN (Dolly)
Princeton 160 lbs.

Year	Team	Games	Pos.
1923	STL **N**	3	E
1923	GB **N**	1	E

1 yr.   4 games

Jim Gray
GRAY, JAMES

Year	Team	Games	Pos.

Jim Gray *continued*
B. Aug. 23, 1941
Toledo 6'0" 181 lbs.

Year	Team	Games	Pos.
1966	NY **A**	6	DB
1967	PHI **N**	3	DB

2 yrs.   9 games

Jerry Gray
GRAY, JERRY
B. Dec. 16, 1962, Lubbock, TX
Texas 6'0" 185 lbs.

Year	Team	Games	Pos.
1985	LARM **N**	16	CB
1986		16	CB
1987		12	CB
1988		16	CB
1989		16	CB
1990		12	CB
1991		16	CB
1992	HOU **N**	16	CB
1993	TB **N**	14	CB

9 yrs.   134 games

Johnnie Gray
GRAY, JOHNNIE LEE
B. Dec. 18, 1953, Lake Charles, LA
Fullerton State 5'11" 185 lbs.

Year	Team	Games	Pos.
1975	GB **N**	14	DB
1976		14	CB, S
1977		14	S
1978		16	S
1979		16	S
1980		16	S
1981		9	S
1982		9	S
1983		16	S

9 yrs.   124 games

Ken Gray
GRAY, KENNETH DON
B. Mar. 10, 1936, San Saba, TX
Howard Payne 6'2" 245 lbs.

Year	Team	Games	Pos.
1958	CHIC **N**	10	G
1959		12	G
1960	STL **N**	10	G
1961		13	G
1962		14	G
1963		14	G
1964		14	G
1965		14	G
1966		11	G
1967		13	G
1968		14	G
1969		12	G
1970	HOU **N**	11	G

13 yrs.   162 games

Kevin Gray
GRAY, KEVIN
B. Sep. 11, 1957, Chicago, IL
Eastern Illinois 5'11" 179 lbs.

Year	Team	Games	Pos.
1982	NO **N**	8	CB, S

Leon Gray
GRAY, LEON
B. Nov. 15, 1951, Olive Branch, MS
Jackson State 6'3" 265 lbs.

Year	Team	Games	Pos.
1973	NE **N**	9	OT
1974		14	OT
1975		14	OT
1976		11	OT
1977		16	OT
1978		16	OT
1979	HOU **N**	16	OT
1980		14	OT
1981		16	OT
1982	NO **N**	7	OT
1983		11	OT

11 yrs.   142 games

Mel Gray
GRAY, MELVIN DEAN
B. Sep. 28, 1948, Fresno, CA
Missouri 5'9" 172 lbs.

Year	Team		Games	Pos.
1971	STL	N	14	WR
1972			7	WR
1973			12	WR
1974			14	WR
1975			14	WR
1976			11	WR
1977			14	WR
1978			13	WR
1979			13	WR
1980			16	WR
1981			12	WR
1982			5	WR

12 yrs.   145 games

Mel Gray
GRAY, MELVIN JUNIUS
B. Mar. 16, 1961, Williamsburg, PA
Purdue 5'9" 166 lbs.

Year	Team		Games	Pos.
1986	NO	N	16	RB
1987			12	RB
1988			14	RB
1989	DET	N	10	WR
1990			16	WR
1991			16	WR
1992			15	WR
1993			11	WR
1994			16	WR
1995	HOU	N	15	WR
1996			14	WR

11 yrs.   155 games

Moses Gray
GRAY, MOSES W.
B. 1938
Indiana 6'3" 260 lbs.

Year	Team		Games	Pos.
1961	NY	A	3	OT
1962			2	OT, DT

2 yrs.   5 games

Oscar Gray
GRAY, OSCAR
B. Aug. 7, 1972, Houston, TX
Arkansas 6'1" 255 lbs.

Year	Team		Games	Pos.
1996	SEA	N	9	FB

Paul Gray
GRAY, PAUL
B. Jun. 30, 1962, Gilbertsville, KY
Western Kentucky 6'2" 231 lbs.

Year	Team		Games	Pos.
1987	ATL	N	2	LB

Sam Gray
GRAY, SAMUEL
B. Jan. 1, 1919
D. Jun., 1979
Tulsa 6'0" 195 lbs.

Year	Team		Games	Pos.
1946	PIT	N	6	E
1947			10	E

2 yrs.   16 games

Tim Gray
GRAY, TIMOTHY
B. Nov. 11, 1952, Houston, TX
Texas A&M 6'1" 200 lbs.

Year	Team		Games	Pos.
1975	STL	N	14	CB
1976	KC		12	S
1977			10	S
1978			14	S
1979	SF	N	16	S

5 yrs.   66 games

Mike Graybill
GRAYBILL, MICHAEL ALTON

Mike Graybill *continued*
B. Oct. 14, 1966, Washington, DC
Boston University 6'7" 275 lbs.

Year	Team		Games	Pos.
1989	CLE	N	6	TE

Gray Horse
GRAY HORSE
None 5'8" 180 lbs.

Year	Team		Games	Pos.
1923	OOR	N	2	G, HB

Dave Grayson
GRAYSON, DAVID LEE, SR.
B. Jun. 6, 1939, San Diego, CA
Oregon 5'10" 184 lbs.

Year	Team		Games	Pos.
1961	DAL	A	13	DB
1962			14	DB
1963	KC	A	14	DB
1965	OAK	A	14	DB
1966			14	DB
1967			14	DB
1968			14	DB
1969			14	CB, S
1970	OAK	N	14	CB

9 yrs.   125 games

David Grayson
GRAYSON, DAVID LEE, JR.
B. Feb. 27, 1964, San Diego, CA
California Poly (Pomona)/Fresno State 6'2" 229 lbs.

Year	Team		Games	Pos.
1987	CLE	N	11	LB
1988			16	LB
1989			10	LB
1990			16	LB
1991	SD	N	1	LB

5 yrs.   54 games

Elvis Grbac
GRBAC, ELVIS
B. Aug. 13, 1970, Cleveland, OH
Michigan 6'5" 232 lbs.

Year	Team		Games	Pos.
1994	SF	N	12	QB
1995			16	QB
1996			15	QB

3 yrs.   43 games

Gary Greaves
GREAVES, GARY
B. 1936
Miami (Florida) 6'3" 235 lbs.

Year	Team		Games	Pos.
1960	HOU	A		OT

Dick Grecni
GRECNI, RICHARD
B. Mar. 27, 1938, Akron, OH
Ohio University 6'1" 230 lbs.

Year	Team		Games	Pos.
1961	MIN	N	12	LB

Don Greco
GRECO, DONALD
B. Apr. 1, 1959, St. Louis, MO
Western Illinois 6'3" 260 lbs.

Year	Team		Games	Pos.
1982	DET	N	9	G
1983			12	G
1984			16	G
1985			8	G

4 yrs.   45 games

Alex Green
GREEN, WILLIAM ALEX
B. Nov. 3, 1965
Indiana 6'1" 194 lbs.

Year	Team		Games	Pos.
1987	DAL	N	3	S

Allen Green
GREEN, ALLEN L.
B. 1938
Mississippi 6'2" 215 lbs.

Year	Team		Games	Pos.
1961	DAL	N	14	K

Art Green
GREEN, ARTHUR
B. Sep. 18, 1949, Atlanta, GA
Albany State 5'11" 198 lbs.

Year	Team		Games	Pos.
1972	NO	N	7	RB

Bobby Joe Green
GREEN, BOBBY JOE
B. May 7, 1936, Vernon, TX
Florida 5'11" 175 lbs.

Year	Team		Games	Pos.
1960	PIT	N	12	P
1961			14	P
1962	CHI		14	P
1963			14	P
1964			14	P
1965			14	P
1966			14	P
1967			14	P
1968			7	P
1969			14	P
1970			14	P
1971			14	P
1972			14	P
1973			14	P

14 yrs.   187 games

Boyce Green
GREEN, BOYCE K.
B. Jun. 24, 1960, Beaufort, SC
Carson-Newman 5'11" 215 lbs.

Year	Team		Games	Pos.
1983	CLE	N	13	RB
1984			16	RB
1985			13	RB
1986	KC	N	16	RB
1987	SEA	N	2	RB

5 yrs.   60 games

Bubba Green
GREEN, ANTHONY WAYNE
B. Sep. 30, 1957, Cape May, NJ
North Carolina State 6'4" 278 lbs.

Year	Team		Games	Pos.
1981	BAL	N	15	DT

Charlie Green
GREEN, CHARLES
B. Mar. 14, 1944, West Milton, OH
Wittenberg 6'0" 190 lbs.

Year	Team		Games	Pos.
1966	OAK	A	14	QB

Chris Green
GREEN, CHRIS ALLEN
B. Feb. 26, 1968, Lawrenceburg, IN
Illinois 5'11" 188 lbs.

Year	Team		Games	Pos.
1991	MIA	N	16	CB
1992			4	CB
1993			14	CB, S
1994			16	S
1995	BUF	N	16	S

5 yrs.   66 games

Cleveland Green
GREEN, CLEVELAND CARL
B. Sep. 11, 1957, Bolton, MS
Southern University 6'6" 264 lbs.

Year	Team		Games	Pos.
1979	MIA	N	16	OT
1980			12	OT
1981			6	OT
1982			3	OT
1983			16	OT
1984			16	OT

Cleveland Green *continued*

Year	Team		Games	Pos.
1985			12	OT
1986			11	OT

8 yrs.   92 games

Cornell Green
GREEN, CORNELL
B. Feb. 10, 1940, Oklahoma City, OK
Utah State 6'4" 211 lbs.

Year	Team		Games	Pos.
1962	DAL	N	14	DB
1963			14	DB
1964			14	DB
1965			14	DB
1966			14	DB
1967			14	DB
1968			14	DB
1969			14	CB
1970			14	CB
1971			14	S
1972			14	S
1973			14	S
1974			14	S

13 yrs.   182 games

Curtis Green
GREEN, CURTIS
B. Jun. 3, 1957, Quincy, FL
Alabama State 6'3" 260 lbs.

Year	Team		Games	Pos.
1981	DET	N	14	DT
1982			7	DE, DT
1983			16	DE, DT
1984			16	DE
1985			15	DT
1986			16	NT, DE
1987			12	DE, NT
1988			11	DE, NT
1989			16	DE, NT

9 yrs.   123 games

Darrell Green
GREEN, DARRELL
B. Feb. 15, 1960, Houston, TX
Texas A&I-Kingsville 5'8" 170 lbs.

Year	Team		Games	Pos.
1983	WAS	N	16	CB
1984			16	CB
1985			16	CB
1986			16	CB
1987			12	CB
1988			15	CB
1989			7	CB
1990			16	CB
1991			8	CB
1992			16	CB
1993			16	CB
1994			16	CB
1995			16	CB
1996			16	CB

14 yrs.   202 games

Dave Green
GREEN, DAVID ELLIOTT
B. Sep. 21, 1949, Mason City, IL
Ohio University 5'11" 206 lbs.

Year	Team		Games	Pos.
1973	HOU	N	4	P
1973	CIN	N	6	P
1974			14	P
1975			14	P
1976	TB	N	14	P
1977			14	P
1978			16	P

6 yrs.   82 games

David Green
GREEN, DAVID
B. Apr. 18, 1972, Mount Kisco, NY
Boston College 5'11" 193 lbs.

Year	Team		Games	Pos.
1995	NE	N	2	RB

Year	Team	Games	Pos.

David Green
GREEN, DAVID FENDELL
B. Sep. 7, 1953, Jacksonville, NC
Edinboro State 5'10" 200 lbs.

Year	Team		Games	Pos.
1982	CLE	N	9	RB

Donnie Green
GREEN, DONNIE GERALD
B. Jul. 12, 1948, Washington, DC
Purdue 6'7" 266 lbs.

Year	Team		Games	Pos.
1971	BUF	N	10	OT
1972			14	OT
1973			14	OT
1974			10	OT
1975			14	OT
1976			13	OT
1977	PHI	N	10	OT
1978	DET	N		OT

8 yrs. 85 games

Eric Green
GREEN, BERNARD ERIC
B. Jun. 22, 1967, Savannah, GA
Liberty 6'5" 274 lbs.

Year	Team		Games	Pos.
1990	PIT	N	13	TE
1991			11	TE
1992			7	TE
1993			16	TE
1994			15	TE
1995	MIA	N	14	TE
1996	BAL	N	6	TE

7 yrs. 82 games

Ernie Green
GREEN, ERNEST
B. Oct. 15, 1938, Columbus, GA
Louisville 6'2" 205 lbs.

Year	Team		Games	Pos.
1962	CLE	N	13	HB
1963			14	HB
1964			14	HB
1965			13	HB
1966			14	HB
1967			13	RB
1968			8	RB

7 yrs. 89 games

Gary Green
GREEN, GARY F.
B. Oct. 22, 1955, San Antonio, TX
Baylor 5'11" 187 lbs.

Year	Team		Games	Pos.
1977	KC	N	11	CB
1978			16	CB
1979			16	CB
1980			16	CB
1981			16	CB
1982			9	CB
1983			16	CB
1984	LARM	N	16	CB
1985			16	CB

9 yrs. 132 games

Gaston Green
GREEN, GASTON ALFRED, III
B. Aug. 1, 1966, Los Angeles, CA
UCLA 5'10" 189 lbs.

Year	Team		Games	Pos.
1988	LARM	N	10	RB
1989			6	RB
1990			15	RB
1991	DEN	N	13	RB
1992			14	RB

5 yrs. 58 games

Harold Green
GREEN, HAROLD
B. Jan. 29, 1968, Ladson, SC
South Carolina 6'2" 222 lbs.

Year	Team		Games	Pos.
1990	CIN	N	12	RB
1991			14	RB

Harold Green continued

Year	Team		Games	Pos.
1992			16	RB
1993			15	RB
1994			14	RB
1995			15	RB
1996	STL	N	16	RB

7 yrs. 102 games

Hugh Green
GREEN, HUGH DONELL
B. Jul. 29, 1959, Natchez, MS
Pittsburgh 6'2" 225 lbs.

Year	Team		Games	Pos.
1981	TB	N	16	LB
1982			9	LB
1983			16	LB
1984			8	LB
1985			5	LB
1985	MIA	N	11	LB
1986			3	LB
1987			9	LB
1988			16	LB
1989			16	LB
1990			16	LB
1991			11	LB

11 yrs. 136 games

Jacob Green
GREEN, JACOB CARL
B. Jan. 21, 1957, Pasadena, TX
Texas A&M 6'3" 250 lbs.

Year	Team		Games	Pos.
1980	SEA	N	14	DE
1981			16	DE
1982			9	DE
1983			16	DE
1984			16	DE
1985			16	DE
1986			16	DE
1987			12	DE
1988			16	DE
1989			15	DE
1990			16	DE
1991			16	DE
1992	SF	N	2	DE

13 yrs. 180 games

Jerry Green
GREEN, JEROME A.
B. 1937
Georgia Tech 6'0" 190 lbs.

Year	Team		Games	Pos.
1960	BOS	A		HB

Jessie Green
GREEN, JESSIE RAY
B. Feb. 21, 1954, Malakoff, TX
Tulsa 6'3" 191 lbs.

Year	Team		Games	Pos.
1979	SEA	N	12	WR
1980			11	WR

2 yrs. 23 games

Joe Green
GREEN, JOSEPH DAVID
B. Nov. 20, 1948, Aberdeen, MS
Bowling Green 5'11" 195 lbs.

Year	Team		Games	Pos.
1970	NYG	N	14	CB
1971			14	S

2 yrs. 28 games

Johnny Green
GREEN, JOHN
B. Oct. 12, 1937, West Point, MS
Tennessee-Chattanooga 6'3" 203 lbs.

Year	Team		Games	Pos.
1960	BUF	A		QB
1961			8	QB
1962	NY	A	11	QB
1963			1	QB

4 yrs. 20 games

Johnny Green
GREEN, JOHN
B. Oct. 14, 1921, Hastings, OK
Tulsa 6'1" 192 lbs.

Year	Team		Games	Pos.
1947	PHI	N	12	E
1948			12	E
1949			7	E
1950			12	E
1951			1	E

5 yrs. 44 games

Larry Green
GREEN, LAWRENCE
B. Jun. 3, 1894
D. Nov., 1976, Bradenton, FL
Georgetown (DC) 6'0" 180 lbs.

Year	Team		Games	Pos.
1920	CAN	A	3	E

Mark Green
GREEN, MARK ANTHONY
B. Mar. 22, 1967, Riverside, CA
Notre Dame 5'11" 184 lbs.

Year	Team		Games	Pos.
1989	CHI	N	10	RB
1990			12	RB
1991			16	RB
1992			15	RB

4 yrs. 53 games

Mike Green
GREEN, MICHAEL JAMES
B. Jun. 29, 1961, Port Arthur, TX
Oklahoma State 6'0" 226 lbs.

Year	Team		Games	Pos.
1983	SD	N	16	LB
1984			16	LB
1985			15	LB

3 yrs. 47 games

Paul Green
GREEN, PAUL EARL
B. Oct. 8, 1966, Coalinga, CA
Southern California 6'3" 230 lbs.

Year	Team		Games	Pos.
1992	SEA	N	4	TE
1993			15	TE
1994			16	TE
1996	NO	N	14	TE

4 yrs. 49 games

Robert Green
GREEN, ROBERT
B. Sep. 10, 1970, Washington, DC
William & Mary 5'8" 207 lbs.

Year	Team		Games	Pos.
1992	WAS	N	15	RB
1993	CHI	N	16	RB
1994			15	RB
1995			12	RB
1996			10	RB

5 yrs. 68 games

Rogerick Green
GREEN, ROGERICK
B. Dec. 14, 1969, San Antonio, TX
Kansas State 5'10" 180 lbs.

Year	Team		Games	Pos.
1992	TB	N	1	CB, S
1994			11	CB
1995	JAC	N	14	CB

3 yrs. 26 games

Ron Green
GREEN, RONALD M.
B. Nov. 27, 1943, Fargo, ND
North Dakota 6'1" 200 lbs.

Year	Team		Games	Pos.
1967	CLE	N	4	FL
1968			1	FL

2 yrs. 5 games

Roy Green
GREEN, ROY
B. Jun. 30, 1957, Magnolia, AR
Henderson State 6'0" 195 lbs.

Year	Team		Games	Pos.
1979	STL	N	16	CB, S
1980			15	S
1981			16	WR, DB
1982			9	WR
1983			16	WR
1984			16	WR
1985			13	WR
1986			11	WR
1987			12	WR
1988	PHX	N	12	WR
1989			12	WR
1990			16	WR
1991	PHI	N	13	WR
1992			9	WR

14 yrs. 190 games

Sammy Green
GREEN, SAMMY LEE
B. Oct. 12, 1954, Bradenton, FL
Florida 6'2" 230 lbs.

Year	Team		Games	Pos.
1976	SEA	N	14	LB
1977			14	LB
1978			16	LB
1979			16	LB
1980	HOU	N	2	LB

5 yrs. 62 games

Tim Green
GREEN, TIMOTHY JOHN
B. Dec. 16, 1963, Liverpool, NY
Syracuse 6'2" 249 lbs.

Year	Team		Games	Pos.
1986	ATL	N	11	LB
1987			9	LB
1988			10	LB
1989			16	LB
1990			16	LB
1991			16	LB
1992			12	DE
1993			9	DE

8 yrs. 99 games

Tony Green
GREEN, TONY EDWARD
B. Sep. 26, 1956, Rochester, NY
Florida 5'9" 185 lbs.

Year	Team		Games	Pos.
1978	WAS	N	16	RB
1979	NYG	N	4	RB
1979	SEA	N	11	RB

2 yrs. 31 games

Van Green
GREEN, VAN HAROLD
B. Apr. 21, 1951, Auburndale, FL
Shaw 6'1" 192 lbs.

Year	Team		Games	Pos.
1973	CLE	N	14	S, CB
1974			14	S
1975			14	S
1976			1	S
1976	BUF	N	5	S

4 yrs. 48 games

Vee Green
GREEN, VIVIAN J.
B. Oct. 9, 1900
D. May 13, 1967, Urbana, IL
Illinois 6'0" 195 lbs.

Year	Team		Games	Pos.
1926	LOU	N	2	T

Victor Green
GREEN, VICTOR BERNARD
B. Dec. 8, 1969, Americus, GA
Akron 5'9" 195 lbs.

Year	Team		Games	Pos.
1993	NYJ	N	11	CB
1994			16	CB, S

Year	Team	Games	Pos.

Victor Green *continued*

Year	Team	Games	Pos.
1995		16	S, CB
1996		16	CB

4 yrs.   59 games

Willie Green
GREEN, WILLIE AARON
B. Apr. 2, 1966, Athens, GA
Mississippi 6'2" 179 lbs.

1991	DET	N	16	WR
1992			15	WR
1993			16	WR
1994	TB	N	5	WR
1995	CAR	N	16	WR
1996			15	WR

6 yrs.   83 games

Woody Green
GREEN, WOODROW, JR.
B. Jul. 20, 1952, Warren, OH
Arizona State 6'1" 205 lbs.

1974	KC	N	10	RB
1975			12	RB
1976			6	RB

3 yrs.   28 games

Ben Greenberg
GREENBERG, BENJAMIN
B. 1907
Rutgers 5'9" 170 lbs.

1930	BKN	N	2	HB

A.J. Greene
GREENE, A.J.
B. 1966
Wake Forest 5'8" 167 lbs.

1991	NYG	N	2	CB

Al Greene
GREENE, AL
B. Mar. 1, 1900
D. Jan., 1977, Hallandale, FL
None 5'8" 160 lbs.

1922	MIL	N	2	HB

Andrew Greene
GREENE, ANDREW
B. Sep. 24, 1969, Kingston, Jamaica
Indiana 6'3" 304 lbs.

1995	MIA	N	6	G

Danny Greene
GREENE, THEODORE DANIEL, II
B. Dec. 26, 1961, Compton, CA
Washington 5'11" 190 lbs.

1985	SEA	N	4	WR

Doug Greene
GREENE, DOUGLAS P.
B. Feb. 10, 1956, Los Angeles, CA
Texas A&I-Kingsville 6'2" 205 lbs.

1978	STL	N	15	CB
1979	BUF	N	15	S
1980			8	S

3 yrs.   38 games

Ed Greene
GREENE, EDWARD (Babe)
B. Sep. 28, 1900
D. Sep., 1960
Loyola (Illinois) 5'11" 185 lbs.

1926	CHIC	N	9	G, T

Frank Greene
**GREENE, FRANK STOKES
(Toadie)**
B. Mar. 29, 1911, San Diego, CA
Deceased
Tulsa 5'11" 190 lbs.

1934	CHIC	N	11	QB, FB, HB

Joe Greene
**GREENE, CHARLES EDWARD
(Mean Joe)**
B. Sep. 24, 1946, Temple, TX
North Texas State 6'4" 269 lbs.

1969	PIT	N	14	DT
1970			14	DT
1971			14	DT
1972			14	DT
1973			14	DT
1974			14	DT
1975			10	DT
1976			14	DT
1977			13	DT
1978			16	DT
1979			15	DT
1980			15	DT
1981			14	DT

13 yrs.   181 games

John Greene
GREENE, JOHN JOSEPH
B. Apr. 1, 1920, Pittsburgh, PA
Michigan 6'0" 210 lbs.

1944	DET	N	8	G, B, E
1945			10	E
1946			11	E
1947			12	E
1948			12	E
1949			12	E
1950			12	E

7 yrs.   77 games

Ken Greene
GREENE, KEN
B. May 8, 1956, Lewiston, ID
Washington State 6'3" 203 lbs.

1978	STL	N	16	CB
1979			16	S
1980			12	S
1981			15	S
1982			8	S
1983	SD	N	16	S
1984			15	S

7 yrs.   98 games

Kevin Greene
GREENE, KEVIN DARWIN
B. Jul. 31, 1962, New York, NY
Auburn 6'3" 238 lbs.

1985	LARM	N	15	LB
1986			16	LB
1987			9	LB
1988			16	LB
1989			16	LB
1990			15	LB
1991			16	DE
1992			16	LB
1993	PIT	N	16	LB
1994			16	LB
1995			16	LB
1996	CAR	N	16	LB

12 yrs.   183 games

Marcellus Greene
GREENE, MARCELLUS L.
B. Dec. 12, 1957, Indianapolis, IN
Arizona 6'0" 185 lbs.

1984	MIN	N	14	CB

Nelson Greene
GREENE, NELSON
B. Mar. 21, 1924
D. May, 1983, Houston, TX
Tulsa 6'2" 235 lbs.

1948	NY	AA	14	T

Scott Greene
GREENE, SCOTT
B. Jun. 1, 1972, Honeoye, NY
Michigan State 5'11" 230 lbs.

1996	CAR	N	8	RB

Ted Greene
GREENE, THEODORE
B. Jan. 25, 1934
Tampa 6'1" 230 lbs.

1960	DAL	A		LB
1961			14	LB
1962			4	LB

3 yrs.   18 games

Tiger Greene
GREENE, GEORGE
B. Feb. 15, 1962, Hendersonville, NC
Western Carolina 6'0" 194 lbs.

1985	ATL	N	10	CB
1986	GB	N	13	DB
1987			11	DB
1988			16	CB, S
1989			16	CB, S
1990			16	S

6 yrs.   82 games

Tom Greene
GREENE, THOMAS
B. 1938
Holy Cross 6'1" 190 lbs.

1960	BOS	A		QB
1961	DAL	A	1	QB

2 yrs.   1 games

Tony Greene
GREENE, ANTHONY
B. Aug. 29, 1949, Bethesda, MD
Maryland 5'10" 171 lbs.

1971	BUF	N	14	CB
1972			14	CB
1973			14	CB
1974			12	CB
1975			14	S
1976			14	S
1977			14	S
1978			16	S
1979			16	S

9 yrs.   128 games

Tracy Greene
GREENE, TRACY LAMAR
B. Nov. 5, 1972, Monroe, LA
Grambling State 6'4" 276 lbs.

1994	KC	N	7	TE
1995	PIT	N	16	TE

2 yrs.   23 games

Norm Greeney
GREENEY, NORMAN J.
B. May 7, 1910
D. Oct., 1985, Kelleys Island, OH
Notre Dame 5'11" 212 lbs.

1933	GB	N	7	G
1934	PIT	N	11	G, T
1935			1	G

3 yrs.   19 games

Tom Greenfield
GREENFIELD, TOM GUY
B. Nov. 10, 1917, Glendale, AZ
Arizona 6'4" 213 lbs.

1939	GB	N	6	C
1940			9	C
1941			3	C

3 yrs.   18 games

Bobby Greenhalgh
GREENHALGH, ROBERT
B. 1924
San Francisco 6'1" 200 lbs.

1949	NYG	N	10	B

Harley Greenich
GREENICH, HARLEY (Duke)
B. Oct. 16, 1921
Mississippi 5'11" 185 lbs.

1944	CHIB	N	1	B

Fritz Greenlee
GREENLEE, WILLIAM F.
B. Nov. 5, 1943, Des Moines, IA
Air Force/Arizona State 6'2" 230 lbs.

1969	SF	N	4	LB

Donn Greenshields
GREENSHIELDS, DONN
B. 1905
Deceased
Penn State 6'1" 190 lbs.

1932	BKN	N	9	T
1933			2	T

2 yrs.   11 games

Carl Greenwood
GREENWOOD, CARLANDITT KEITH
B. Mar. 11, 1972, Fort Ord, CA
UCLA 5'11" 186 lbs.

1995	NYJ	N	10	CB
1996			14	CB

2 yrs.   24 games

David Greenwood
GREENWOOD, DAVID MARK
B. Mar. 25, 1960, Park Falls, WI
Wisconsin 6'3" 210 lbs.

1985	TB	N	16	S
1986	GB	N	9	S
1988	LARI	N	2	S

3 yrs.   27 games

Don Greenwood
GREENWOOD, DONALD
B. Feb. 18, 1921, Detroit, MI
D. Mar. 21, 1983, Princeville, IL
Missouri/Illinois 6'0" 195 lbs.

1945	CLE	N	9	FB
1946	CLE	AA	13	HB
1947			11	HB

3 yrs.   33 games

Glen Greenwood
GREENWOOD, GLEN
B. Feb. 4, 1896
D. Jul. 1, 1970, Los Angeles, CA
Iowa 5'10" 185 lbs.

1926	LOU	N	1	FB, E

L.C. Greenwood
GREENWOOD, L.C. HENDERSON
B. Sep. 8, 1946, Canton, MS

501

Year	Team		Games	Pos.

L.C. Greenwood *continued*
Arkansas-Pine Bluff 6'5" 246 lbs.

Year	Team		Games	Pos.
1970	**PIT**	**N**	12	DE
1971			14	DE
1972			13	DE
1973			14	DE
1974			14	DE
1975			14	DE
1976			13	DE
1977			9	DE
1978			14	DE
1979			12	DE
1980			15	DE
1981			14	DE
12 yrs.	158 games			

Al Greer
GREER, ALBERT
B. Apr. 15, 1940, Anniston, AL
Jackson State 6'4" 190 lbs.

1963	**DET**	**N**	1	OE

Charles Greer
GREER, CHARLES ANTHONY
B. Apr. 4, 1946, Atlanta, GA
Colorado 6'0" 205 lbs.

1968	**DEN**	**A**	14	DB
1969			12	CB
1970	**DEN**	**N**	14	S
1971			13	S
1972			14	S
1973			10	S
1974			12	S
7 yrs.	89 games			

Curtis Greer
GREER, CURTIS WILLIAM
B. Nov. 10, 1957, Detroit, MI
Michigan 6'4" 256 lbs.

1980	**STL**	**N**	11	DE
1981			16	DE
1982			9	DE
1983			16	DE
1984			16	DE
1985			16	DE
1987			10	DE
7 yrs.	94 games			

Jim Greer
GREER, JAMES
B. Jul. 7, 1931, Huntington, WV
Elizabeth City State 6'3" 215 lbs.

1960	**DEN**	**A**		OE

Terry Greer
GREER, TERRY LEE
B. Sep. 27, 1957, Memphis, TN
Alabama State 6'2" 197 lbs.

1986	**CLE**	**N**	11	WR
1987	**SF**	**N**	3	WR
1988			10	WR
1989			11	WR
1990	**DET**	**N**	15	WR
5 yrs.	50 games			

Ted Grefe
GREFE, THEODORE F.
B. Oct. 26, 1917
D. Oct. 27, 1989
Northwestern 6'0" 205 lbs.

1945	**DET**	**N**	2	E

Ed Gregg
GREGG, EDGAR
B. Aug., 1897, Louisville, KY
D. Nov. 9, 1961
Kentucky 5'7" 155 lbs.

1922	**LOU**	**N**	2	E

Forrest Gregg
GREGG, ALVIS FORREST
B. Oct. 18, 1933, Birthright, TX
Southern Methodist 6'4" 249 lbs.

1956	**GB**	**N**	11	C
1958			12	G
1959			12	T
1960			12	T
1961			14	OT
1962			14	OT
1963			14	OT
1964			14	OT
1965			13	OT
1966			14	G, OT
1967			14	OT, G
1968			14	OT
1969			14	OT
1970			14	OT
1971	**DAL**	**N**	6	OT, G
15 yrs.	192 games			

Bob Gregor
GREGOR, ROBERT LEE
B. Feb. 10, 1957, Riverside, CA
Washington State 6'2" 187 lbs.

1981	**SD**	**N**	14	CB
1982			4	S
1983			5	S
1984			7	S
4 yrs.	30 games			

Ben Gregory
GREGORY, BENJAMIN
B. Oct. 3, 1947, Uniontown, PA
Nebraska 6'3" 220 lbs.

1968	**BUF**	**A**	6	RB

Bill Gregory
GREGORY, WILLIAM PENN, JR.
B. Dec. 14, 1949, Galveston, TX
Wisconsin 6'5" 256 lbs.

1971	**DAL**	**N**	14	DT
1972			13	DT
1973			14	DT
1974			14	DT
1975			14	DT
1976			14	DT
1977			13	DT
1978	**SEA**	**N**	16	DE
1979			16	DE
1980			14	DE
10 yrs.	142 games			

Bruce Gregory
GREGORY, BRUCE R.
B. May 13, 1903, Ann Arbor, MI
D. Dec., 1960
Michigan 5'10" 170 lbs.

1926	**DET**	**N**	12	HB, QB

Frank Gregory
GREGORY, FRANK GILBERT (Gil)
B. Jan. 18, 1898
D. Nov. 11, 1980, Hamburg, NY
Williams 5'11" 165 lbs.

1923	**BUF**	**N**	1	FB
1924			3	HB, FB
2 yrs.	4 games			

Garland Gregory
GREGORY, GARLAND D.
B. Mar. 8, 1919, Columbia, LA
Louisiana Tech 5'11" 185 lbs.

1946	**SF**	**AA**	13	G
1947			14	G
2 yrs.	27 games			

Glynn Gregory
GREGORY, GLYNN S.
B. Jul. 6, 1939, Paris, TX
Southern Methodist 6'2" 200 lbs.

1961	**DAL**	**N**	14	OE
1962			6	OE
2 yrs.	20 games			

Jack Gregory
GREGORY, JACK, SR.
B. Feb. 14, 1916, Okolona, MS
Tennessee-Chattanooga 6'2" 210 lbs.

1941	**CLE**	**N**	7	G

Jack Gregory
GREGORY, JACK, JR.
B. Oct. 3, 1944, Okolona, MS
Tennessee-Chattanooga/Delta State 6'6" 251 lbs.

1967	**CLE**	**N**	14	DE
1968			14	DE
1969			14	DE
1970			14	DE
1971			14	DE
1972	**NYG**	**N**	14	DE
1973			13	DE
1974			14	DE
1975			14	DE
1976			11	DE
1977			14	DE
1978			16	DE
1979	**CLE**	**N**	16	DE
13 yrs.	182 games			

Ken Gregory
GREGORY, KENNETH
B. Feb. 1, 1937
Whittier 6'0" 190 lbs.

1961	**BAL**	**N**	14	OE
1962	**PHI**	**N**	2	OE
1963	**NY**	**A**	14	OE
3 yrs.	30 games			

Mike Gregory
GREGORY, MICHAEL
B. Jul. 30, 1905
Denison 5'11" 215 lbs.

1931	**CLE**	**N**	7	G

Ted Gregory
GREGORY, THEODORE ANTHONY
B. Feb. 11, 1965, Queens, NY
Syracuse 6'2" 270 lbs.

1988	**NO**	**N**	3	NT

Hank Gremminger
GREMMINGER, CHARLES HENRY
B. Sep. 1, 1934, Windthorst, TX
Baylor 6'1" 201 lbs.

1956	**GB**	**N**	12	DB
1957			12	DB
1958			12	DB
1959			12	DB
1960			12	DB
1961			14	DB
1962			14	DB
1963			13	DB
1964			13	DB
1965			8	DB
1966	**LA**	**N**	8	DB
11 yrs.	131 games			

Bob Gresham
GRESHAM, ROBERT CLARK
B. Jul. 9, 1948, Porter, AL
West Virginia 5'11" 196 lbs.

1971	**NO**	**N**	13	RB

Bob Gresham *continued*

Year	Team		Games	Pos.
1972			14	RB
1973	**HOU**	**N**	13	RB
1974			14	RB
1975	**NYJ**	**N**	10	RB
1976			11	RB
6 yrs.	75 games			

Visco Grgich
GRGICH, VISCO G.
B. Jan. 19, 1923
Santa Clara (Freshmen) 5'11" 217 lbs.

1946	**SF**	**AA**	12	G
1947			14	T
1948			14	T
1949			12	G
1950	**SF**	**N**	12	G
1951			12	G
1952			2	G
7 yrs.	78 games			

Billy Gribben
GRIBBEN, WILLIAM J.
B. Oct. 24, 1901
D. Jun., 1971, Canada
Case Western Reserve 160 lbs.

1926	**CLE**	**A**	3	HB, FB

Marrio Grier
GRIER, MARRIO
B. Dec. 5, 1971, Charlotte, NC
Clemson/Tennessee-Chattanooga 6'0" 238 lbs.

1996	**NE**	**N**	16	RB

Roosevelt Grier
GRIER, ROOSEVELT (Rosey)
B. Jul. 14, 1932, Cuthbert, GA
Penn State 6'5" 284 lbs.

1955	**NYG**	**N**	12	T
1956			12	T
1958			10	T
1959			12	T
1960			12	T
1961			14	DT
1962			14	DT
1963	**LA**	**N**	14	DT
1964			14	DT
1965			14	DT
1966			14	DT
11 yrs.	142 games			

Bob Griese
GRIESE, ROBERT ALLEN
B. Feb. 3, 1945, Evansville IN
Purdue 6'1" 190 lbs.

1967	**MIA**	**A**	12	QB
1968			13	QB
1969			9	QB
1970	**MIA**	**N**	14	QB
1971			14	QB
1972			6	QB
1973			13	QB
1974			13	QB
1975			10	QB
1976			13	QB
1977			14	QB
1978			11	QB
1979			14	QB
1980			5	QB
14 yrs.	161 games			

Hal Griffen
GRIFFEN, HAROLD W. (Tubby)
B. Mar., 1902
Deceased
Iowa 6'1" 247 lbs.

1926	**NY**	**A**	13	C

Year	Team		Games	Pos.

Bob Gresham continued

Year	Team		Games	Pos.
1928	GB	N	5	C
1930	POR	N	2	T
1932			2	C, T
4 yrs.	22 games			

Archie Griffin
GRIFFIN, ARCHIE MASON
B. Aug. 21, 1954, Columbus, OH
Ohio State 5'9" 188 lbs.

1976	CIN	N	14	RB
1977			12	RB
1978			16	RB
1979			16	RB
1980			15	RB
1981			16	RB
1982			9	RB
7 yrs.	98 games			

Bob Griffin
GRIFFIN, ROBERT
B. Feb. 12, 1929, Fort Worth, TX
Arkansas 6'3" 235 lbs.

1953	LA	N	2	C, LB
1954			12	LB
1955			12	C, LB
1956			6	LB
1957			12	C, LB
5 yrs.	44 games			

Bobby Griffin
GRIFFIN, ROBERT JOEL (Spider)
B. 1928
Baylor 6'0" 180 lbs.

1951	NYY	N	12	DB

Courtney Griffin
GRIFFIN, COURTNEY
B. Dec. 19, 1966, Madera, CA
Fresno State 5'10" 180 lbs.

1993	LARM	N	7	CB

Don Griffin
GRIFFIN, DONALD D.
B. Oct. 15, 1922, Benton Harbor, MI
Illinois 5'11" 195 lbs.

1946	CHI	AA	13	HB

Don Griffin
GRIFFIN, DONALD FREDERICK
B. Mar. 17, 1964, Pelham, CA
Middle Tennessee State 6'0" 176 lbs.

1986	SF	N	16	CB
1987			12	CB
1988			10	CB
1989			16	CB
1990			16	CB
1991			16	CB
1992			16	CB
1993			12	CB
1994	CLE	N	15	CB
1995			16	CB
1996	PHI	N	16	CB
11 yrs.	161 games			

James Griffin
GRIFFIN, JAMES VICTOR
B. Sep. 7, 1961, Camilla, GA
Middle Tennessee State 6'2" 197 lbs.

1983	CIN	N	16	S
1984			16	S
1985			16	S
1986	DET	N	16	S
1987			12	S
1988			16	S
1989			16	S
7 yrs.	108 games			

Jeff Griffin
GRIFFIN, JEFFERY E.
B. Jul. 19, 1958, Carson, CA
Utah 6'0" 185 lbs.

1981	STL	N	16	CB, S
1982			9	CB
1983			3	CB
1984			8	CB
1985			12	CB
1987	PHI	N	2	S
6 yrs.	50 games			

Jim Griffin
GRIFFIN, JAMES BAUMAN
B. Feb. 8, 1942, Lake Charles, LA
Grambling State 6'3" 258 lbs.

1966	SD	A	14	DE
1967			14	DE
1968	CIN	A	14	DE
3 yrs.	42 games			

John Griffin
GRIFFIN, JOHN WATSON
B. Nov. 2, 1940, Nashville, TN
Memphis 6'1" 190 lbs.

1963	LA	N	10	DB
1964	DEN	A	7	DB
1965			14	DB
1966			4	DB
4 yrs.	35 games			

Keith Griffin
GRIFFIN, KEITH
B. Oct. 26, 1961, Columbus, OH
Miami (Florida) 5'8" 185 lbs.

1984	WAS	N	16	RB
1985			16	RB
1986			16	RB
1987			9	RB
1988			8	RB
5 yrs.	65 games			

Larry Griffin
GRIFFIN, LARRY ANTHONY
B. Jan. 11, 1962, Chesapeake, VA
North Carolina 6'1" 197 lbs.

1986	HOU	N	3	S
1987	PIT	N	7	S, CB
1988			15	S, CB
1989			16	S
1990			16	S
1991			6	S
1992			14	S
1993			12	S
8 yrs.	89 games			

Leonard Griffin
GRIFFIN, LEONARD JAMES, JR.
B. Sep. 22, 1962, Lake Providence, LA
Grambling State 6'4" 252 lbs.

1986	KC	N	9	DE
1987			12	DE
1988			15	DE
1989			16	DE
1990			16	DE
1991			16	DE
1992			15	DE
1993			4	DE
8 yrs.	103 games			

Ray Griffin
GRIFFIN, RAYMOND
B. Jun. 29, 1956, Columbus, OH
Ohio State 5'10" 185 lbs.

1978	CIN	N	15	CB
1979			12	CB
1980			16	CB
1981			8	CB

Ray Griffin continued

Year	Team		Games	Pos.
1982			9	CB
1983			16	CB
1984			12	CB
7 yrs.	88 games			

Steve Griffin
GRIFFIN, STEVE B.
B. Dec. 17, 1963, Charlotte, NC
Clemson 5'10" 185 lbs.

1987	ATL	N	3	WR

Steve Griffin
GRIFFIN, STEPHEN
B. Aug. 14, 1964
Tennessee State 5'10" 205 lbs.

1987	KC	N	1	RB

Steve Griffin
GRIFFIN, STEVEN LEROY
B. Dec. 24, 1964, Miami, FL
Purdue 5'11" 188 lbs.

1987	ATL	N	2	WR

Wade Griffin
GRIFFIN, WADE HAMPTON, JR.
B. Aug. 7, 1954, Winona, MS
Mississippi 6'5" 260 lbs.

1977	BAL	N	14	OT
1978			16	OT
1979			16	OT
1980			16	OT
1981			15	OT
5 yrs.	77 games			

Glynn Griffing
GRIFFING, GLYNN
B. Dec. 1, 1940, Bentonia, MS
Mississippi 6'1" 200 lbs.

1963	NYG	N	13	QB

Forrest Griffith
GRIFFITH, FORREST
B. 1929
Kansas 5'11" 190 lbs.

1950	NYG	N	6	HB
1951			10	HB
2 yrs.	16 games			

Homer Griffith
GRIFFITH, HOMER OLIVER, JR.
B. Jul. 24, 1912, Los Angeles, CA
D. Jan. 31, 1990, Tarzana, CA
Southern California 5'11" 165 lbs.

1934	CHIC	N	8	HB, DB

Howard Griffith
GRIFFITH, HOWARD THOMAS
B. Nov. 17, 1967, Chicago, IL
Illinois 6'0" 226 lbs.

1993	LARM	N	15	RB
1994			16	RB
1995	CAR	N	15	RB
1996			16	RB
4 yrs.	62 games			

Rich Griffith
GRIFFITH, RICHARD POPE
B. Jul. 31, 1969, Tucson, AZ
Arizona 6'5" 256 lbs.

1993	NE	N	3	TE
1995	JAC	N	16	TE
1996			16	TE
3 yrs.	35 games			

Robert Griffith
GRIFFITH, ROBERT OTIS
B. Nov. 30, 1970, Lanham, MD
San Diego State 5'11" 200 lbs.

1994	MIN	N	15	S
1995			16	S
1996			14	S
3 yrs.	45 games			

Russell Griffith
GRIFFITH, RUSSELL
B. 1965
Weber State 5'11" 175 lbs.

1987	SEA	N	2	P

Paul Griffiths
GRIFFITHS, PAUL
B. Jan. 9, 1898
D. Feb., 1977, Finleyville, PA
Penn State 5'8" 190 lbs.

1921	CAN	A	1	G

Johnny Grigas
GRIGAS, JOHN J.
B. Aug. 19, 1920, Chelsea, MA
Holy Cross 6'0" 204 lbs.

1943	CHIC	N	10	FB, HB
1944	C-P	N	9	FB
1945	BOS	N	10	FB
1946			11	FB
1947			9	FB
5 yrs.	49 games			

Forrest Grigg
GRIGG, FORREST P., JR. (Chubby)
B. Jan. 10, 1926, El Dorado, AR
D. Oct. 10, 1983, Ore City, TX
Tulsa 6'2" 294 lbs.

1946	BUF	AA	8	T
1947	CHI	AA	13	T
1948	CLE	AA	14	T
1949			12	T
1950	CLE	N	11	T
1951			11	T
1952	DAL	N	12	T, G, C
7 yrs.	81 games			

Tex Grigg
GRIGG, CECIL (Ranger)
B. Feb. 15, 1891, Nashville, TN
D. Sep. 5, 1968, Houston, TX
Austin 5'11" 189 lbs.

1920	CAN	A	7	QB
1921			7	HB, QB
1922	CAN	N	4	HB, FB
1923			12	HB, E
1924	ROC	N	1	HB
1925			7	QB, FB
1926	NYG	N	13	QB, HB, FB
1927	FRA	N	1	QB
8 yrs.	52 games			

Anthony Griggs
GRIGGS, ANTHONY
B. Feb. 12, 1960, Lawton, OK
Villanova/Ohio State 6'3" 230 lbs.

1982	PHI	N	9	LB
1983			16	LB
1984			16	LB
1985			16	LB
1986	CLE	N	16	LB
1987			12	LB
1988			5	LB
7 yrs.	90 games			

Billy Griggs
GRIGGS, WILLIAM EDWARD, III
B. Aug. 4, 1962, Camden, NJ

Year	Team	Games	Pos.

Billy Griggs *continued*

Virginia 6'3" 230 lbs.

Year	Team		Games	Pos.
1985	NYJ	N	16	TE
1986			16	TE
1987			12	TE
1988			15	TE
1989			5	TE

5 yrs.   64 games

David Griggs

GRIGGS, DAVID WESLEY

B. Feb. 5, 1967, Camden, NJ
D. Jun., 1995, Davie, FL
Virginia 6'3" 245 lbs.

1989	MIA	N	5	LB
1990			16	LB
1991			16	LB
1992			16	LB
1993			9	LB
1994	SD	N	16	LB

6 yrs.   78 games

Hal Griggs

GRIGGS, HALDANE

B. 1901, Indianapolis, IN
Deceased
Butler 5'10" 170 lbs.

1926	AKR	N	5	HB

Perry Griggs

GRIGGS, PERRY

B. Aug. 17, 1957, Lafayette, AL
Troy State 5'10" 182 lbs.

1977	BAL	N	1	WR

Frank Grigonis

GRIGONIS, FRANK JOHN

B. Oct. 10, 1918, Calumet City, IL
Tennessee-Chattanooga 5'10" 182 lbs.

1942	DET	N	10	FB

Ryan Grigson

GRIGSON, RYAN R.

B. Feb. 23, 1972
Purdue 6'6" 290 lbs.

1995	DET	N	1	G

Bob Grim

GRIM, ROBERT LEE

B. May 8, 1945, Oakland, CA
Oregon State 6'0" 196 lbs.

1967	MIN	N	13	DB, FL
1968			1	WR
1969			14	WR
1970			14	WR
1971			14	WR
1972	NYG	N	13	WR
1973			14	WR
1974			14	WR
1975	CHI	N	14	WR
1976	MIN	N	8	WR
1977			14	WR

11 yrs.   133 games

Billy Joe Grimes

GRIMES, WILLIAM JOSEPH

B. Jul. 27, 1927, County Line, OK
Oklahoma State 6'1" 195 lbs.

1949	LA	AA	12	B
1950	GB	N	12	HB
1951			12	HB
1952			12	HB

4 yrs.   48 games

George Grimes

GRIMES, GEORGE

George Grimes *continued*

B. 1922
Virginia 5'11" 190 lbs.

1948	DET	N	9	HB

Phil Grimes

GRIMES, PHILIP

B. Feb. 26, 1965, Montgomery, AL
Central Missouri State 6'4" 230 lbs.

1987	LARI	N	2	DE

Randy Grimes

GRIMES, RANDALL COLLINS

B. Jul. 20, 1960, Tyler, TX
Baylor 6'4" 270 lbs.

1983	TB	N	15	OT, G
1984			10	G, C
1985			16	C, G
1986			16	C
1987			12	C
1988			16	C
1989			16	C
1990			16	C
1992			2	C

9 yrs.   119 games

Dan Grimm

GRIMM, DANIEL JAY

B. Feb. 7, 1941, Perry, IA
Colorado 6'3" 244 lbs.

1963	GB	N	14	G
1964			14	G
1965			14	G
1966	ATL	N	14	G
1967			2	G
1968			14	G
1969	BAL	N	2	G

7 yrs.   74 games

Russ Grimm

GRIMM, RUSS

B. May 2, 1959, Scottdale, PA
Pittsburgh 6'3" 270 lbs.

1981	WAS	N	14	G, C
1982			9	G
1983			16	G
1984			16	G
1985			16	G
1986			15	G
1987			6	G
1988			5	G
1989			12	G
1990			15	G
1991			16	G

11 yrs.   140 games

Ed Grimsley

GRIMSLEY, EDWARD PAUL

B. Mar. 22, 1963, Canton, OH
Akron 6'0" 237 lbs.

1987	IND	N	5	LB

John Grimsley

GRIMSLEY, JOHN GLENN

B. Feb. 25, 1962, Canton, OH
Kentucky 6'2" 236 lbs.

1984	HOU	N	16	LB
1985			15	LB
1986			16	LB
1987			12	LB
1988			16	LB
1989			16	LB
1990			15	LB
1992	MIA	N	14	LB
1993			13	LB

9 yrs.   133 games

Clif Groce

GROCE, CLIFTON ALLEN

B. Jul. 30, 1972, College Station, TX
Texas A&M 5'11" 244 lbs.

1995	IND	N	1	RB
1996			15	RB

2 yrs.   16 games

Ron Groce

GROCE, RONALD

B. Jul. 1, 1954, Minneapolis, MN
Macalester 6'2" 210 lbs.

1976	MIN	N	4	RB

Steve Grogan

GROGAN, STEVEN JAMES

B. Jul. 24, 1953, San Antonio, TX
Kansas State 6'4" 210 lbs.

1975	NE	N	13	QB
1976			14	QB
1977			14	QB
1978			16	QB
1979			16	QB
1980			12	QB
1981			8	QB
1982			6	QB
1983			12	QB
1984			3	QB
1985			7	QB
1986			4	QB
1987			7	QB
1988			6	QB
1989			7	QB
1990			4	QB

16 yrs.   149 games

Bill Groman

GROMAN, WILLIAM

B. 1936
Heidelberg 6'0" 195 lbs.

1960	HOU	A	14	OE
1961			14	OE
1962			14	OE
1963	DEN	A	14	OE
1964	BUF	A	5	OE
1965			5	OE

6 yrs.   66 games

Jerry Groom

GROOM, JEROME PAUL

B. Aug. 15, 1929, Des Moines, IA
Notre Dame 6'3" 236 lbs.

1951	CHIC	N	12	LB
1952			12	DT, C
1953			12	DT
1954			11	DT
1955			11	DT

5 yrs.   58 games

Mel Groomes

GROOMES, MELVIN H.

B. 1927, Trenton, NJ
Indiana 6'0" 178 lbs.

1948	DET	N	6	HB
1949			3	HB

2 yrs.   9 games

Elois Grooms

GROOMS, ELOIS

B. May 20, 1953, Tompkinsville, KY
Tennessee Tech 6'4" 249 lbs.

1975	NO	N	10	DE
1976			11	DE
1977			14	DE
1978			16	DE
1979			16	DE
1980			16	DE
1981			16	DE
1982	STL	N	9	DE

Elois Grooms *continued*

1983			11	DE
1984			11	DT
1985			5	DT
1987	PHI	N	3	DE, DT

12 yrs.   138 games

Earl Gros

GROS, EARL ROY

B. Aug. 29, 1940, Lafourche Parish, LA
Louisiana State 6'3" 224 lbs.

1962	GB	N	14	FB
1963			14	FB
1964	PHI	N	13	FB
1965			14	FB
1966			14	FB
1967	PIT	N	12	RB
1968			13	RB
1969			14	RB
1970	NO	N	1	RB

9 yrs.   109 games

Al Gross

GROSS, ALFRED E., JR.

B. Jan. 4, 1961, Stockton, CA
Arizona 6'3" 195 lbs.

1983	CLE	N	16	S
1984			16	S
1985			16	S
1986			4	S
1987			6	S

5 yrs.   58 games

Andy Gross

GROSS, ANDY

B. Oct. 13, 1945, Berkam, Austria
Auburn 6'0" 230 lbs.

1967	NYG	N	14	G
1968			14	G

2 yrs.   28 games

George Gross

GROSS, GEORGE

B. Jan. 26, 1941, Weilou, Romania
Auburn 6'3" 260 lbs.

1963	SD	A	14	DT
1964			14	DT
1965			14	DT
1966			14	DT
1967			14	DT

5 yrs.   70 games

Lee Gross

GROSS, LEE MONROE, III

B. Jul. 29, 1953, Montgomery, AL
Auburn 6'3" 237 lbs.

1975	NO	N	9	C, G
1976			14	C
1977			9	C
1979	BAL	N	16	C

4 yrs.   48 games

Lee Grosscup

GROSSCUP, CLYDE LEE EDWARD

B. Dec. 27, 1936, Santa Monica, CA
Utah 6'1" 186 lbs.

1960	NYG	N	4	QB
1961			4	QB
1962	NY	A	8	QB

3 yrs.   16 games

Burt Grossman

GROSSMAN, BURT

B. Apr. 10, 1967, Philadelphia, PA
Pittsburgh 6'6" 267 lbs.

1989	SD	N	16	DE

Year	Team		Games	Pos.

Burt Grossman *continued*

Year	Team		Games	Pos.
1990			15	DE
1991			16	DE
1992			15	DE
1993			10	DE
1994	PHI	N	13	DE
6 yrs.	85 games			

Jack Grossman
GROSSMAN, JOHN
B. 1910
Rutgers 6'1" 193 lbs.

1932	BKN	N	12	HB, QB
1934			11	HB, QB
1935			12	HB, QB
3 yrs.	35 games			

Randy Grossman
GROSSMAN, CURT RANDY
B. Sep. 20, 1952, Philadelphia, PA
Temple 6'1" 218 lbs.

1974	PIT	N	14	TE
1975			14	TE
1976			14	TE
1977			13	TE
1978			16	TE
1979			16	TE
1980			15	TE
1981			16	TE
8 yrs.	118 games			

Rex Grossman
GROSSMAN, REX D.
B. Feb. 5, 1924, Huntington, IN
D. Jun., 1980
Indiana 6'1" 215 lbs.

1948	BAL	AA	14	FB, LB, K
1949			11	FB, LB, K
1950	BAL	N	8	FB, LB, K
1950	DET	N	4	FB, LB, K
3 yrs.	37 games			

George Grosvenor
GROSVENOR, GEORGE A.
B. Aug. 4, 1911, Jefferson, OK
Colorado 6'0" 174 lbs.

1935	CHIB	N	11	HB
1936			1	HB
1936	CHIC	N	9	HB, QB
1937			11	HB
3 yrs.	32 games			

Jeff Groth
GROTH, JEFFREY EUGENE
B. Jul. 2, 1957, Mankato, MN
Bowling Green 5'10" 178 lbs.

1979	MIA	N	4	WR
1979	HOU	N	6	WR
1980			16	WR
1981	NO	N	15	WR
1982			9	WR
1983			16	WR
1984			16	WR
1985			12	WR
7 yrs.	94 games			

Bob Grottkau
GROTTKAU, ROBERT F.
B. Mar. 22, 1937, Oakland, CA
Oregon 6'4" 228 lbs.

1959	DET	N	12	G
1960			5	G
1961	DAL	N	13	G
3 yrs.	30 games			

Roger Grove
GROVE, ROGER R. (Roy)

Roger Grove *continued*
B. Jun. 19, 1908
D. Dec., 1986, Hemet, CA
Michigan State 6'0" 182 lbs.

1931	GB	N	14	QB
1932			11	QB, FB
1933			13	QB, HB
1934			11	HB, QB
1935			3	QB, HB
5 yrs.	52 games			

George Groves
GROVES, GEORGE NOAH
B. Jun. 10, 1921, Hammond, IN
Marquette 5'11" 195 lbs.

1947	BUF	AA	7	G
1948	BAL	AA	2	G
2 yrs.	9 games			

Monty Grow
GROW, MONTY ROY
B. Sep. 4, 1971, Inverness, FL
Florida 6'3" 214 lbs.

1994	KC	N	15	S
1995	JAC	N	4	S
2 yrs.	19 games			

Lou Groza
GROZA, LOUIS ROY (The Toe)
B. Jan. 25, 1924, Martins Ferry, OH
Ohio State (Freshmen) 6'3" 240 lbs.

1946	CLE	AA	14	T, K
1947			12	T, K
1948			12	T, K
1949			12	T, K
1950	CLE	N	10	T, K
1951			12	T, K
1952			12	T, K
1953			12	T, K
1954			12	T, K
1955			12	T, K
1956			12	T, K
1957			12	T, K
1958			12	T, K
1959			12	T, K
1961			14	OT, K
1962			14	OT, K
1963			14	K
1964			14	K
1965			14	K
1966			14	K
1967			14	K
21 yrs.	268 games			

Charlie Grube
GRUBE, CHARLES
B. Jun. 11, 1904
D. Jan., 1976, Hollywood, FL
Michigan 5'10" 175 lbs.

1926	DET	N	2	E

Frank Grube
GRUBE, FRANKLIN THOMAS
B. Jan. 7, 1905, Easton, PA
D. Jul. 2, 1945, New York, NY
Lafayette 5'9" 180 lbs.

1928	NYY	N	11	E

Bob Gruber
GRUBER, ROBERT LEON, JR.
B. Jun. 7, 1958, Del Rio, TX
Pittsburgh 6'5" 265 lbs.

1986	CLE	N	5	OT
1987	GB	N	1	OT
2 yrs.	6 games			

Herb Gruber
GRUBER, HERBERT C.
B. Dec. 22, 1901
D. Feb. 1, 1979, Beechwood Village, KY
Kentucky 5'9" 155 lbs.

1921	LOU	A	2	E
1922	LOU	N	3	E
1923			2	E
3 yrs.	7 games			

Paul Gruber
GRUBER, PAUL BLAKE
B. Feb. 24, 1965, Madison, WI
Wisconsin 6'5" 290 lbs.

1988	TB	N	16	OT
1989			16	OT
1990			16	OT
1991			16	OT
1992			16	OT
1993			10	OT
1994			16	OT
1995			16	OT
1996			13	OT
9 yrs.	135 games			

Sam Gruneisen
GRUNEISEN, SAMUEL KENNETH
B. Jan. 16, 1941, Louisville, KY
Villanova 6'1" 248 lbs.

1962	SD	A	9	G, LB
1963			7	G, LB
1964			11	G
1965			14	G
1966			14	G
1967			14	C
1968			14	C
1969			14	C
1970	SD	N	14	C
1971			2	C
1972			7	C
1973	HOU	N	9	C
12 yrs.	129 games			

Tim Grunhard
GRUNHARD, TIMOTHY GERARD
B. May 17, 1968, Chicago, IL
Notre Dame 6'2" 301 lbs.

1990	KC	N	14	C, G
1991			16	C
1992			12	C
1993			16	C
1994			16	C
1995			16	C
1996			16	C
7 yrs.	106 games			

Bob Grupp
GRUPP, ROBERT WILLIAM
B. May 8, 1955, Philadelphia, PA
Duke 5'11" 193 lbs.

1979	KC	N	16	P
1980			16	P
1981			9	P
3 yrs.	41 games			

Mike Gruttadauria
GRUTTADAURIA, MICHAEL JASON
B. Dec. 6, 1972, Fort Lauderdale, FL
Central Florida 6'4" 290 lbs.

1996	STL	N	8	C

Al Grygo
GRYGO, ALBERT
B. Aug. 14, 1918, Erie, PA

Al Grygo *continued*
D. Sep., 1971, Chapin, SC
South Carolina 5'10" 173 lbs.

1944	CHIB	N	9	HB
1945			10	HB
2 yrs.	19 games			

Darrell Grymes
GRYMES, DARRELL
B. 1962
Central State (Ohio) 6'2" 183 lbs.

1987	DET	N	2	WR

Albert Guarnieri
GUARNIERI, ALBERT (Chick)
B. Jul. 1, 1899
Deceased
Niagara/Canisius 5'10" 175 lbs.

1924	BUF	N	11	E
1925	CAN	N	1	E
2 yrs.	12 games			

Pat Gucciardo
GUCCIARDO, PATRICK
B. 1944
Kent State 5'11" 185 lbs.

1966	NY	A	1	DB

Pete Gudauskas
GUDAUSKAS, PETER
B. Oct. 19, 1916, Georgetown, IL
Murray State 6'2" 219 lbs.

1940	CLE	N	1	G
1943	CHIB	N	5	G
1944			9	G
1945			8	G
4 yrs.	23 games			

Len Gudd
GUDD, LEONARD
B. 1911
Temple 6'3" 212 lbs.

1934	PHI	N	1	E

Bob Gude
GUDE, BOB
B. 1922
Vanderbilt 6'1" 225 lbs.

1946	PHI	N	2	C

Scotty Gudmundson
GUDMUNDSON, WAYNE SCOTT
B. Apr. 3, 1921, Ogden, UT
George Washington 5'10" 178 lbs.

1944	BOS	N	7	QB, DB
1945			10	QB, DB
2 yrs.	17 games			

Mike Guendling
GUENDLING, MICHAEL ANTHONY
B. Jun. 18, 1962, Chicago, IL
Northwestern 6'3" 238 lbs.

1985	SD	N	9	LB

Jim Gueno
GUENO, JAMES ANDRE
B. Jan. 15, 1954, Crowley, LA
Tulane 6'2" 220 lbs.

1976	GB	N	14	LB
1977			14	LB
1978			15	LB
1979			16	LB
1980			16	LB
5 yrs.	75 games			

Year	Team		Games	Pos.

Dick Guesman
GUESMAN, RICHARD EUGENE
B. Jan. 22, 1938, Brownsville, PA
West Virginia 6'4" 255 lbs.

Year	Team		Games	Pos.
1960	NY	A		DT
1961			14	DT
1962			7	DT
1963			14	DT
4 yrs.	35 games			

Terry Guess
GUESS, TERRY
B. Sep. 22, 1974, Orangeburg, SC
Gardner-Webb 6'0" 200 lbs.

Year	Team		Games	Pos.
1996	NO	N	3	WR

Roy Guffey
GUFFEY, ROY C.
B. 1902, Columbus Grove, OH
D. Mar. 25, 1994, Dallas, TX
Oklahoma 6'0" 194 lbs.

Year	Team		Games	Pos.
1926	BUF	N	9	E, T

Neal Guggemos
GUGGEMOS, NEAL E.
B. Jun. 14, 1964, Winsted, MN
St. Thomas/Minnesota 6'0" 187 lbs.

Year	Team		Games	Pos.
1986	MIN	N	4	CB
1987			12	S
1988	NYG	N	11	S
3 yrs.	27 games			

Ralph Guglielmi
GUGLIELMI, RALPH VINCENT
B. Jun. 26, 1934, Columbus, OH
Notre Dame 6'1" 195 lbs.

Year	Team		Games	Pos.
1955	WAS		9	QB
1958			8	QB
1959			9	QB
1960			11	QB
1961	STL	N	9	QB
1962	NYG	N	14	QB
1963			2	QB
1963	PHI	N	5	QB
7 yrs.	67 games			

Kevin Guidry
GUIDRY, KEVIN DALE
B. May 16, 1964, Lake Charles, LA
Louisiana State 6'0" 176 lbs.

Year	Team		Games	Pos.
1988	DEN	N	14	CB
1989	PHX	N	3	CB
2 yrs.	17 games			

Paul Guidry
GUIDRY, PAUL MICHAEL
B. Jan. 14, 1944, Breaux Bridge, LA
Louisiana State/McNeese State 6'3" 229 lbs.

Year	Team		Games	Pos.
1966	BUF	A	14	LB
1967			14	LB
1968			14	LB
1969			8	LB
1970	BUF	N	14	LB
1971			14	LB
1972			14	LB
1973	HOU	N	14	LB
8 yrs.	106 games			

Rusty Guilbeau
GUILBEAU, DAVID RUSTON
B. Nov. 20, 1958, Opalousas, LA
McNeese State 6'4" 240 lbs.

Year	Team		Games	Pos.
1982	NYJ	N	4	DE
1983			16	DE
1984			16	LB
1985			14	LB

Rusty Guilbeau *continued*

Year	Team		Games	Pos.
1986			6	LB
1987	CLE	N	1	LB
6 yrs.	57 games			

John Guillory
GUILLORY, JOHN L.
B. Jul. 28, 1945, Berkeley, CA
Stanford 5'10" 190 lbs.

Year	Team		Games	Pos.
1969	CIN	A	11	CB, S
1970	CIN	N	7	CB
2 yrs.	18 games			

Tony Guillory
GUILLORY, ANTHONY
B. Nov. 20, 1942, Opelousas, LA
Nebraska/Lamar 6'4" 232 lbs.

Year	Team		Games	Pos.
1965	LA		14	LB
1967			14	LB
1968			13	LB
1969	PHI	N	12	LB
4 yrs.	53 games			

Mike Gulian
GULIAN, MILANESE J. (Doggy)
B. Jul. 29, 1900
D. Jan., 1970, Boston, MA
Brown 6'0" 205 lbs.

Year	Team		Games	Pos.
1923	BUF	N	11	T
1924	FRA	N	13	T, C
1925	PRO	N	8	T
1926			13	T
1927			2	T
5 yrs.	47 games			

Eric Guliford
GULIFORD, ERIC ANDRE
B. Oct. 25, 1969, Kansas City, KS
Arizona State 5'8" 165 lbs.

Year	Team		Games	Pos.
1993	MIN	N	10	WR
1994			7	WR
1995	CAR	N	14	WR
3 yrs.	31 games			

David Gulledge
GULLEDGE, DAVID
B. Oct. 26, 1967, Pell City, AL
Jacksonville State 6'1" 203 lbs.

Year	Team		Games	Pos.
1992	WAS	N	4	S

Don Gulseth
GULSETH, DONALD M.
B. 1942
North Dakota 6'1" 240 lbs.

Year	Team		Games	Pos.
1966	DEN	A	5	LB

George Gulyanics
GULYANICS, GEORGE (Little Bronko)
B. Jun. 11, 1921, Mishawaka, IN
D. Jan. 19, 1990, Mishawaka, IN
Alabama 6'0" 198 lbs.

Year	Team		Games	Pos.
1947	CHIB	N	12	HB
1948			12	HB
1949			11	HB
1950			12	HB
1951			12	HB
1952			2	HB
6 yrs.	61 games			

Mike Guman
GUMAN, MICHAEL DONALD
B. Apr. 21, 1958, Allentown, PA
Penn State 6'2" 210 lbs.

Year	Team		Games	Pos.
1980	LA	N	16	RB
1981			16	RB

Mike Guman *continued*

Year	Team		Games	Pos.
1982	LARM	N	9	RB
1983			16	RB
1984			16	RB
1985			8	RB
1986			12	RB
1987			12	RB
1988			1	RB
9 yrs.	106 games			

Andy Gump
GUMP, ANDREW
Rose-Hulman Tech 203 lbs.

Year	Team		Games	Pos.
1922	COL	N	3	G, T

Bob Gunderman
GUNDERMAN, ROBERT E.
B. Oct. 18, 1934
Virginia 6'2" 195 lbs.

Year	Team		Games	Pos.
1957	PIT	N	1	E

Harry Gunderson
GUNDERSON, ARTHUR HARRY (Battling)
B. Nov. 9, 1887
D. Nov., 1975, Everett, MA
Iowa 6'2" 203 lbs.

Year	Team		Games	Pos.
1920	RI	A	3	C
1921	MIN	A	4	C
2 yrs.	7 games			

Jimmy Gunn
GUNN, JAMES
B. Nov. 27, 1948, Augusta, AR
Southern California 6'1" 220 lbs.

Year	Team		Games	Pos.
1970	CHI	N	14	LB
1971			14	LB
1972			14	LB
1973			3	LB
1974			14	LB
1975			4	LB
1975	NYG	N	14	LB
1976	TB	N	14	LB
7 yrs.	91 games			

Lance Gunn
GUNN, LANCE CAMERON
B. Jan. 9, 1970, Whiteman AFB, MO
Texas 6'3" 222 lbs.

Year	Team		Games	Pos.
1993	CIN	N	8	S

Mark Gunn
GUNN, MARK
B. Jul. 24, 1968, Cleveland, OH
Pittsburgh 6'5" 288 lbs.

Year	Team		Games	Pos.
1991	NYJ	N	15	DT
1992			16	DE
1993				DT, DE
1994			3	DT
1995	PHI	N	12	DE, DT
1996			3	DT
1996	NYJ	N	8	DE
6 yrs.	69 games			

Riley Gunnels
GUNNELS, JOHN RILEY
B. Aug. 24, 1937, Atlanta, GA
Georgia 6'3" 250 lbs.

Year	Team		Games	Pos.
1960	PHI	N	12	DT
1961			14	DT
1962			14	DT
1963			9	DT
1964			14	DT
1965	PIT	N	14	DT
1966			14	DT
7 yrs.	91 games			

Harry Gunner
GUNNER, HARRY JAMES
B. Nov. 25, 1944, Port Arthur, TX
Oregon State 6'6" 250 lbs.

Year	Team		Games	Pos.
1968	CIN	A	14	DE
1969			14	DE
1970	CHI	N	14	DE
3 yrs.	42 games			

Michael Gunter
GUNTER, MICHAEL WAYNE
B. Feb. 18, 1961, Gladewater, TX
Tulsa 5'11" 210 lbs.

Year	Team		Games	Pos.
1984	KC	N	4	RB

Al Gursky
GURSKY, ALBERT
B. Nov. 23, 1940, West Reading, PA
Penn State 6'1" 210 lbs.

Year	Team		Games	Pos.
1963	NYG	N	2	DB

Mike Gussie
GUSSIE, MICHAEL
B. Sep. 13, 1917, Everettstown, PA
D. Feb. 24, 1977, Alexandria, VA
West Virginia 6'0" 204 lbs.

Year	Team		Games	Pos.
1940	BKN	N	8	G

Ed Gustafson
GUSTAFSON, EDSEL WARREN
B. Apr. 4, 1922, Moline, IL
George Washington/Dartmouth 6'3" 205 lbs.

Year	Team		Games	Pos.
1947	BKN	AA	13	C
1948			14	C
2 yrs.	27 games			

Jim Gustafson
GUSTAFSON, JAMES JOEL
B. Mar. 16, 1961, Minneapolis, MN
St. Thomas 6'1" 181 lbs.

Year	Team		Games	Pos.
1986	MIN	N	14	WR
1987			12	WR
1988			16	WR
1989			16	WR
4 yrs.	58 games			

Grant Guthrie
GUTHRIE, GRANT M.
B. Feb. 9, 1948, Waynesboro, PA
Florida State 6'0" 210 lbs.

Year	Team		Games	Pos.
1970	BUF	N	14	K
1971			6	K
2 yrs.	20 games			

Keith Guthrie
GUTHRIE, KEITH EDWIN
B. Aug. 17, 1962, Tyler, TX
Texas A&M 6'4" 264 lbs.

Year	Team		Games	Pos.
1984	SD	N	11	NT

Al Gutknecht
GUTKNECHT, ALBERT RUDOLPH
B. Jun. 11, 1917, Arnold, PA
Niagara 6'0" 205 lbs.

Year	Team		Games	Pos.
1943	BKN	N	2	G
1944	CLE	N	3	E
2 yrs.	5 games			

Ace Gutowsky
GUTOWSKY, LEROY E.
B. Aug. 2, 1909, Komolty, Russia
D. Dec., 1976, Oklahoma City, OK
Oklahoma City 5'11" 201 lbs.

Year	Team		Games	Pos.
1932	POR	N	10	FB, LB

Ace Gutowsky *continued*

Year	Team		Games	Pos.
1933			10	FB, LB
1934	DET	N	13	FB, LB
1935			12	FB, LB
1936			12	FB, LB
1937			11	FB, LB
1938			11	FB, LB
1939	BKN	N	9	FB, LB

8 yrs.   88 games

Bill Gutteron

GUTTERON, WILLIAM A. (Little Bill)
B. Nov. 26, 1899
D. May, 1987, Cross Plains, WI
Nevada-Reno 155 lbs.

Year	Team		Games	Pos.
1926	LA	N	2	QB

Buzz Guy

GUY, MELWOOD
B. Mar. 20, 1936, New Castle, PA
Duke 6'3" 248 lbs.

Year	Team		Games	Pos.
1958	NYG	N	10	G
1959			12	G
1960	DAL	N	12	G
1961	HOU	A	1	G
1961	DEN	A	9	G

4 yrs.   44 games

Charlie Guy

GUY, CHARLES H. (Boots)
B. Dec. 5, 1896
D. Apr. 9, 1974, Tampa, FL
Washington & Jefferson 6'0" 170 lbs.

Year	Team		Games	Pos.
1920	DET	A	4	G, C
1921			7	C
1921	BUF	A	5	C
1922	BUF	N	10	C
1923	CLE	N	7	C
1925	DAY	N	5	G, C

5 yrs.   38 games

Louis Guy

GUY, LOUIS B.
B. May 26, 1941, McComb, MS
Mississippi 6'0" 188 lbs.

Year	Team		Games	Pos.
1963	NYG	N	5	DB, HB
1964	OAK	A	6	DB

2 yrs.   11 games

Ray Guy

GUY, WILLIAM RAY
B. Dec. 22, 1949, Swainsboro, GA
Southern Mississippi 6'3" 200 lbs.

Year	Team		Games	Pos.
1973	OAK	N	14	P
1974			14	P
1975			14	P
1976			14	P
1977			14	P
1978			16	P
1979			16	P
1980			16	P
1981			16	P
1982	LARI	N	9	P
1983			16	P
1984			16	P
1985			16	P
1986			16	P

14 yrs.   207 games

Joe Guyon

GUYON, JOSEPH NAPOLEON (Indian Joe)
B. Nov. 26, 1892, Mahnomen, MN
D. Nov. 27, 1971, Louisville, KY
Carlisle/Georgia Tech 5'10" 195 lbs.

Year	Team		Games	Pos.
1920	CAN	A	8	HB, QB
1921	CLE	A	6	HB

Joe Guyon *continued*

Year	Team		Games	Pos.
1921	WAS	A	1	HB
1921	CLE	A	2	HB
1922	OOR	N	9	HB, QB
1923			4	HB
1924	RI	N	3	HB, E, QB
1925	KC	N	1	HB, E
1927	NYG	N	7	HB, QB, T

7 yrs.   41 games

Myron Guyton

GUYTON, MYRON MYNARD
B. Aug. 26, 1967, Metcalf, GA
Eastern Kentucky 6'1" 205 lbs.

Year	Team		Games	Pos.
1989	NYG	N	16	CB, S
1990			16	S
1991			16	S
1992			4	S
1993			16	S
1994	NE	N	16	S
1995			14	S

7 yrs.   98 games

John Guzik

GUZIK, JOHN
B. Jul. 12, 1936, Lawrence, PA
Pittsburgh 6'3" 231 lbs.

Year	Team		Games	Pos.
1959	LA	N	12	LB
1960			12	G
1961	HOU	A	3	LB

3 yrs.   27 games

John Guzik

GUZIK, JOHN
B. Sep. 25, 1962
Ohio University 6'4" 270 lbs.

Year	Team		Games	Pos.
1987	NE	N	3	NT

Ross Gwinn

GWINN, CHARLES ROSS
B. Jul. 25, 1944, Deport, TX
Northwestern State (Louisiana) 6'3" 273 lbs.

Year	Team		Games	Pos.
1968	NO	N	2	G

Milo Gwosden

GWOSDEN, MILO
B. 1899
D. 1959
Pittsburgh 6'0" 185 lbs.

Year	Team		Games	Pos.
1925	BUF	N	6	E, HB

Bob Haak

HAAK, ROBERT A. (Spanky)
B. 1916
D. Nov. 1, 1992
Indiana 6'1" 245 lbs.

Year	Team		Games	Pos.
1939	BKN	N	10	G, T

Bob Haas

HAAS, ROBERT J.
B. May 25, 1906
D. Sep., 1979, Huntsville, OH
None

Year	Team		Games	Pos.
1929	DAY	N	4	HB

Bruno Haas

HAAS, BRUNO PHILIP
B. May 5, 1891, Worcester, MA
D. Jun. 5, 1952, Sarasota, FL
Worcester Tech 5'10" 180 lbs.

Year	Team		Games	Pos.
1921	CLE	A	8	HB
1921	AKR	A	1	HB
1922	DAY	N	1	G

2 yrs.   10 games

Ira Haaven

HAAVEN, IRA (Ike)
B. Jun. 6, 1894
D. Jun., 1971, Minneapolis, MN
Hamline 6'2" 192 lbs.

Year	Team		Games	Pos.
1923	DUL	N	3	E, G

Brian Habib

HABIB, BRIAN RICHARD
B. Dec. 2, 1964, Ellensburg, WA
Washington 6'7" 293 lbs.

Year	Team		Games	Pos.
1989	MIN	N	16	OT
1990			16	OT
1991			16	OT
1992			16	G
1993	DEN	N	16	G
1994			16	G
1995			16	G
1996			16	G

8 yrs.   128 games

Bill Hachten

HACHTEN, WILLIAM A.
B. 1925
Stanford 6'0" 210 lbs.

Year	Team		Games	Pos.
1947	NYG	N	8	G

Dale Hackbart

HACKBART, DALE LEONARD (Hackie)
B. Jul. 21, 1938, Madison, WI
Wisconsin 6'3" 210 lbs.

Year	Team		Games	Pos.
1960	GB	N	12	DB
1961	WAS	N	12	DB
1962			14	DB
1963			14	DB
1966	MIN	N	14	DB
1967			13	DB
1968			14	DB
1969			12	S
1970			14	DB
1971	STL	N	14	S
1972			14	S
1973	DEN	N	3	DB

12 yrs.   150 games

Johnny Hackenbruck

HACKENBRUCK, JOHN
B. 1915
D. Oct. 26, 1988, Corvallis, OR
Oregon State 6'2" 215 lbs.

Year	Team		Games	Pos.
1940	DET	N	7	T

Dino Hackett

HACKETT, BARRY DEAN
B. Jun. 28, 1964, Greensboro, NC
Appalachian State 6'3" 225 lbs.

Year	Team		Games	Pos.
1986	KC	N	16	LB
1987			11	LB
1988			13	LB
1989			13	LB
1990			16	LB
1991			16	LB
1993	SEA	N	3	LB

7 yrs.   88 games

Joey Hackett

HACKETT, JOSEPH GLENN
B. Sep. 29, 1958, Greensboro, NC
Elon 6'5" 267 lbs.

Year	Team		Games	Pos.
1986	DEN	N	16	TE
1987	GB	N	11	TE
1988			9	TE

3 yrs.   36 games

Elmer Hackney

HACKNEY, ELMER LOYD (One-

Elmer Hackney *continued*

Man Gang)
B. Jul. 8, 1916, Oberlin, KS
D. May, 1969, Manhattan, KS
Kansas State 6'2" 202 lbs.

Year	Team		Games	Pos.
1940	PHI	N	8	FB, LB
1941	PIT	N	9	FB, LB
1942	DET	N	8	FB, LB
1943			9	FB, LB
1944			9	FB, LB
1945			8	FB, LB
1946			6	LB

7 yrs.   57 games

Gary Hadd

HADD, GARY ALLAN
B. Oct. 19, 1965, St. Paul, MN
Minnesota 6'4" 270 lbs.

Year	Team		Games	Pos.
1988	DET	N	5	DT
1989	PHX	N	10	DT

2 yrs.   15 games

Michael Haddix

HADDIX, MICHAEL
B. Dec. 27, 1961, Tippah County, MS
Mississippi State 6'2" 226 lbs.

Year	Team		Games	Pos.
1983	PHI	N	14	RB
1984			14	FB
1985			16	FB
1986			16	FB
1987			12	FB
1988			16	RB
1989	GB	N	16	RB
1990			16	RB

8 yrs.   120 games

Wayne Haddix

HADDIX, WAYNE
B. Jul. 23, 1965, Bolivar, TN
Liberty 6'1" 203 lbs.

Year	Team		Games	Pos.
1987	NYG	N	5	CB
1988			7	CB
1990	TB	N	16	CB
1991			6	CB, S
1991	CIN	N	7	CB

4 yrs.   41 games

Al Haddon

HADDON, ALDOUS B.
B. Nov. 8, 1899
D. Feb. 26, 1969, Toledo, OH
Washington & Jefferson 5'8" 186 lbs.

Year	Team		Games	Pos.
1925	DET	N	12	HB, FB
1926			12	HB
1927	PRO	N	10	HB, FB, QB
1928	CHIB	N	1	HB
1928	PRO	N	9	FB, HB, G
1929			10	FB, E-T, HB
1930			9	FB, HB

6 yrs.   63 games

Jack Haden

HADEN, JOHN
B. 1915
Deceased
Arkansas 6'4" 232 lbs.

Year	Team		Games	Pos.
1936	NYG	N	9	T
1937			11	T
1938			11	T

3 yrs.   31 games

Nick Haden

HADEN, NICHOLAS SCOTT
B. Nov. 7, 1962, Pittsburgh, PA
Penn State 6'2" 270 lbs.

Year	Team		Games	Pos.
1986	PHI	N	8	G, C

Pat Haden

HADEN, PATRICK CAPPER
B. Jan. 23, 1953, Westbury, NY
Southern California 5'11" 183 lbs.

Year	Team		Games	Pos.
1976	LA	N	10	QB
1977			12	QB
1978			16	QB
1979			10	QB
1980			4	QB
1981			13	QB
6 yrs.	65 games			

John Hadl

HADL, JOHN WILLARD
B. Feb. 15, 1940, Lawrence, KS
Kansas 6'2" 213 lbs.

Year	Team		Games	Pos.
1962	SD	A	14	QB
1963			14	QB
1964			14	QB
1965			14	QB
1966			14	QB
1967			14	QB
1968			14	QB
1969			14	QB
1970	SD	N	14	QB
1971			14	QB
1972			14	QB
1973	LA	N	14	QB
1974			6	QB
1974	GB	N	7	QB
1975			14	QB
1976	HOU	N	14	QB
1977			14	QB
16 yrs.	223 games			

Dave Hadley

HADLEY, DAVID
B. Oct. 8, 1948, Amory, MA
Alcorn State 5'9" 189 lbs.

Year	Team		Games	Pos.
1970	KC	N	14	CB
1971			14	CB
2 yrs.	28 games			

Ron Hadley

HADLEY, RONALD ARTHUR
B. Nov. 9, 1963, Caldwell, ID
Washington 6'2" 240 lbs.

Year	Team		Games	Pos.
1987	SF	N	3	LB
1988			3	LB
2 yrs.	6 games			

James Hadnot

HADNOT, JAMES WELDON
B. Jul. 11, 1957, Jasper, TX
Texas Tech 6'2" 244 lbs.

Year	Team		Games	Pos.
1980	KC	N	13	RB
1981			16	RB
1982			9	RB
1983			5	RB
4 yrs.	43 games			

Bernie Hafen

HAFEN, BANARD ERVIN
B. 1923, Santa Clara, UT
Utah 6'2" 196 lbs.

Year	Team		Games	Pos.
1949	DET	N	12	E
1950			12	E
2 yrs.	24 games			

Mike Haffner

HAFFNER, MICHAEL ARTHUR
B. Jul. 7, 1942, Waterloo, IA
UCLA 6'2" 205 lbs.

Year	Team		Games	Pos.
1968	DEN	A	14	OE
1969			9	WR
1970	DEN	N	11	WR
1971	CIN	N	3	WR
4 yrs.	37 games			

Roger Hagberg

HAGBERG, ROGER W.
B. Feb. 28, 1939, Winnebago, MN
Minnesota 6'2" 216 lbs.

Year	Team		Games	Pos.
1965	OAK	A	14	FB
1966			14	FB
1967			12	FB
1968			14	FB
1969			14	TE
5 yrs.	68 games			

Rudy Hagberg

HAGBERG, RUDOLPH E. (Swede)
B. Jun. 18, 1907, Charleroi, PA
D. Nov. 25, 1960, Steubenville, OH
West Virginia 6'4" 219 lbs.

Year	Team		Games	Pos.
1929	BUF	N	9	HB, E, C, FB
1930	BKN	N	12	C, T, FB, QB
2 yrs.	21 games			

Fred Hageman

HAGEMAN, FRED JOHN
B. Jun. 30, 1937, Bunkie, LA
Arkansas/Kansas 6'4" 243 lbs.

Year	Team		Games	Pos.
1961	WAS	N	13	C
1962			14	C
1963			14	C
1964			14	C
4 yrs.	55 games			

Halvor Hagen

HAGEN, HALVOR REINI
B. Feb. 4, 1947, Oslo, Norway
Weber State 6'5" 252 lbs.

Year	Team		Games	Pos.
1969	DAL		12	OT, DE
1970			6	OT, DE
1971	NE	N	14	G
1972			14	G
1973	BUF	N	5	OT
1974			8	OT
1975			13	OT
7 yrs.	72 games			

Mike Hagen

HAGEN, MIKE
B. Nov. 30, 1959, Auburn, WA
Montana 6'0" 240 lbs.

Year	Team		Games	Pos.
1987	SEA	N	2	RB

Vern Hagenbuckle

HAGENBUCKLE, VERNON
B. 1901
Dartmouth 5'8" 185 lbs.

Year	Team		Games	Pos.
1926	BOS	A	1	G
1926	PRO	N	2	E
1 yr.	3 games			

Britt Hager

HAGER, HARLEY BRITT
B. Feb. 20, 1966, Odessa, TX
Texas 6'1" 223 lbs.

Year	Team		Games	Pos.
1989	PHI	N	16	LB
1990			16	LB
1991			16	LB
1992			10	LB
1993			16	LB
1994			16	LB
1995	DEN	N	16	LB
1996			2	LB
8 yrs.	108 games			

Jack Hagerty

HAGERTY, JOHN L. (Black Bear)
B. Jul. 3, 1903
D. Mar. 23, 1982, Washington, DC
Georgetown (DC) 5'9" 164 lbs.

Year	Team		Games	Pos.
1926	NYG	N	9	HB, QB

Jack Hagerty continued

Year	Team		Games	Pos.
1927			12	QB, HB, FB
1928			11	QB, HB, FB
1929			14	QB, HB
1930			12	QB, HB
1932			4	QB, HB
6 yrs.	62 games			

Loris Hagerty

HAGERTY, LORIS (Horse)
B. 1905
Iowa 5'10" 185 lbs.

Year	Team		Games	Pos.
1930	BKN	N	7	HB, FB

John Haggerty

HAGGERTY, JOHN (Doc)
B. May 9, 1895, Ohio
D. Jul., 1964
Tufts 205 lbs.

Year	Team		Games	Pos.
1920	CLE	A	4	G
1920	CAN	A	1	G
1921	NY	A	1	G
2 yrs.	6 games			

Mike Haggerty

HAGGERTY, MIKE K.
B. Oct. 14, 1945, Royal Oak, MI
Miami (Florida) 6'4" 239 lbs.

Year	Team		Games	Pos.
1967	PIT		14	OT
1968			1	OT
1969			14	OT
1970			14	OT
1971	NE	N	13	OT
1973	DET	N	4	OT
6 yrs.	60 games			

Steve Haggerty

HAGGERTY, STEVEN
B. May 17, 1953, Denver, CO
Nevada-Las Vegas 5'10" 175 lbs.

Year	Team		Games	Pos.
1975	DEN	N	1	DB

Odell Haggins

HAGGINS, ODELL
B. Feb. 27, 1967, Lakeland, FL
Florida State 6'2" 278 lbs.

Year	Team		Games	Pos.
1991	BUF	N	5	NT

Isaac Hagins

HAGINS, ISAAC
B. Mar. 2, 1954, Shreveport, LA
Southern University 5'9" 180 lbs.

Year	Team		Games	Pos.
1977	TB	N	13	WR
1978			4	WR
1979			16	WR
1980			16	WR
4 yrs.	49 games			

Scott Hagler

HAGLER, SCOTT
B. Jul. 19, 1964
South Carolina 5'8" 160 lbs.

Year	Team		Games	Pos.
1987	SEA	N	2	K

Rickey Hagood

HAGOOD, RICKEY GABRIEL
B. Apr. 24, 1961, Easley, SC
South Carolina 6'2" 286 lbs.

Year	Team		Games	Pos.
1984	SD	N	2	NT

John Hagy

HAGY, JOHN KEVIN
B. Dec. 9, 1965, Okinawa, Japan
Texas 5'11" 190 lbs.

Year	Team		Games	Pos.
1988	BUF	N	3	S

John Hagy continued

Year	Team		Games	Pos.
1989			9	S
1990			16	S
3 yrs.	28 games			

Ray Hahn

HAHN, RAYMOND D.
B. Nov. 19, 1897
D. Nov. 8, 1989, McPherson, KS
Kansas State 5'10" 190 lbs.

Year	Team		Games	Pos.
1926	HAM	N	4	E

Mike Haight

HAIGHT, MICHAEL
B. Oct. 6, 1962, Manchester, IA
Iowa 6'4" 270 lbs.

Year	Team		Games	Pos.
1986	NYJ	N	2	OT, G
1987			6	G, OT
1988			14	G, OT
1989			13	G, OT
1990			14	G
1991			7	G
1992	WAS	N	7	OT
1992	DET	N	2	G
7 yrs.	65 games			

Mac Haik

HAIK, JOSEPH MICHEL
B. Jan. 19, 1946, Meridian, MS
Mississippi 6'1" 196 lbs.

Year	Team		Games	Pos.
1968	HOU	A	14	OE
1969			13	WR
1970	HOU	N	13	WR
1971			4	WR
4 yrs.	44 games			

By Haines

HAINES, BYRON
B. 1914
Washington 5'11" 185 lbs.

Year	Team		Games	Pos.
1937	PIT	N	6	HB

Harry Haines

HAINES, HARRY J. (Hoot, Red)
B. Jun. 13, 1907
D. Dec., 1964
Colgate 6'0" 205 lbs.

Year	Team		Games	Pos.
1930	BKN	N	8	T, G
1931			8	T, G, E
1931	SI	N	2	G, T
2 yrs.	18 games			

Hinkey Haines

HAINES, HENRY LUTHER
B. Dec. 23, 1898, Red Lion, PA
D. Jan. 9, 1979, Sharon Hills, PA
Lebanon Valley/Penn State 5'10" 168 lbs.

Year	Team		Games	Pos.
1925	NYG	N	11	HB, FB, QB
1926			13	HB, QB
1927			13	QB, HB, FB
1928			8	QB, HB
1929	SI	N	4	QB, HB
1931			2	QB, HB
6 yrs.	51 games			

John Haines

HAINES, JOHN YANCY
B. Dec. 16, 1961, Fort Worth, TX
Texas 6'7" 286 lbs.

Year	Team		Games	Pos.
1984	MIN	N	8	NT
1986	IND	N	11	DT, DE
2 yrs.	19 games			

Kris Haines

HAINES, DAVID KRIS

Year	Team		Games	Pos.

Kris Haines *continued*

B. Jul. 23, 1957, Akron, OH
Notre Dame 5'11" 181 lbs.

Year	Team		Games	Pos.
1979	WAS	N	1	WR
1979	CHI	N	2	WR
1980			16	WR
1981			1	WR
1987	BUF	N	1	WR

4 yrs. 21 games

Carl Hairston

HAIRSTON, CARL BLAKE
B. Dec. 15, 1952, Martinsville, VA
Maryland-Eastern Shore 6'4" 260 lbs.

Year	Team		Games	Pos.
1976	PHI	N	14	DE
1977			14	DE
1978			16	DE
1979			15	DE
1980			16	DE
1981			16	DE
1982			9	DE
1983			16	DE
1984	CLE	N	16	DE
1985			16	DE
1986			16	DE
1987			14	DE
1988			14	DE, LB
1989			16	DT
1990	PHX	N	16	DT

15 yrs. 224 games

Russell Hairston

HAIRSTON, RUSSELL
B. Feb. 10, 1964
Kentucky 6'3" 208 lbs.

Year	Team		Games	Pos.
1987	PIT	N	3	WR

Stacey Hairston

HAIRSTON, STACEY
B. Aug. 16, 1967, Columbus, OH
Ohio Northern 5'9" 180 lbs.

Year	Team		Games	Pos.
1993	CLE	N	16	CB
1994			15	CB

2 yrs. 31 games

Chuck Hajek

HAJEK, CHARLES JOSEPH
B. Nov. 11, 1910, Chicago, IL
D. Feb. 21, 1979, Centerport, NY
Northwestern 6'1" 210 lbs.

Year	Team		Games	Pos.
1934	PHI	N	11	C, G

Ali Haji-Sheikh

HAJI-SHEIKH, ALI
B. Jan. 11, 1961, Ann Arbor, MI
Michigan 6'0" 172 lbs.

Year	Team		Games	Pos.
1983	NYG	N	16	K
1984			16	K
1985			2	K
1986	ATL	N	6	K
1987	WAS	N	11	K

5 yrs. 51 games

Mike Halapin

HALAPIN, MIKE
B. Jul. 1, 1973, Apollo, PA
Pittsburgh 6'4" 294 lbs.

Year	Team		Games	Pos.
1996	HOU	N	8	DT

George Halas

HALAS, GEORGE STANLEY (Papa Bear)
B. Feb. 2, 1895, Chicago, IL
D. Oct. 31, 1983, Chicago, IL
Illinois 6'0" 182 lbs.

Year	Team		Games	Pos.
1920	DEC	A	8	E
1921			11	E

George Halas *continued*

Year	Team		Games	Pos.
1922	CHIB	N	12	E
1923			13	E
1924			11	E
1925			14	E
1926			16	E
1927			10	E
1928			4	E

9 yrs. 99 games

Chris Hale

HALE, CHRIS
B. Jan. 4, 1966, Monrovia, CA
Nebraska/Southern California 5'7" 163 lbs.

Year	Team		Games	Pos.
1989	BUF	N	16	CB
1990			8	CB
1991			5	CB
1992			14	CB

4 yrs. 43 games

Dave Hale

HALE, DAVID ROBERT
B. Jun. 21, 1947, McCook, NE
Ottawa (Kansas) 6'7" 251 lbs.

Year	Team		Games	Pos.
1969	CHI	N	3	DE
1970			14	DT
1971			12	DT
1973			1	DT

4 yrs. 30 games

Art Haley

HALEY, ARTHUR
B. 1895, Beaver Falls, PA
D. Feb. 14, 1946, Zanesville, OH
Akron 5'8" 165 lbs.

Year	Team		Games	Pos.
1921	DAY	A	2	HB
1923	AKR	N	3	HB

2 yrs. 5 games

Charles Haley

HALEY, CHARLES LEWIS
B. Jan. 6, 1964, Gladys, VA
James Madison 6'5" 230 lbs.

Year	Team		Games	Pos.
1986	SF	N	16	LB
1987			12	DE, LB
1988			16	DE, LB
1989			16	LB, DE
1990			16	LB, DE
1991			14	LB, DE
1992	DAL	N	15	DE
1993			14	DE
1994			16	DE
1995			13	DE
1996			8	DE

11 yrs. 156 games

Darryl Haley

HALEY, DARRYL
B. Feb. 16, 1961, Los Angeles, CA
Utah 6'5" 270 lbs.

Year	Team		Games	Pos.
1982	NE	N	9	OT
1983			16	OT
1984			16	OT
1986			16	OT
1987	CLE	N	9	OT, G
1988	GB	N	13	OT

6 yrs. 79 games

Dick Haley

HALEY, G. RICHARD, JR.
B. Oct. 2, 1937, Midway, PA
Pittsburgh 5'10" 193 lbs.

Year	Team		Games	Pos.
1959	WAS	N	12	HB, DB, OE
1960			10	HB
1961	MIN	N	13	DB
1961	PIT	N	12	DB
1962			14	DB

Dick Haley *continued*

Year	Team		Games	Pos.
1963			14	DB
1964			13	DB

6 yrs. 75 games

Ronnie Haliburton

HALIBURTON, RONNIE MAURICE
B. Apr. 14, 1968, New Orleans, LA
Louisiana State 6'4" 230 lbs.

Year	Team		Games	Pos.
1990	DEN	N	9	LB
1991			8	LB

2 yrs. 17 games

Eddie Halicki

HALICKI, EDWARD H.
B. Dec. 23, 1905
D. Apr., 1986, Ashley, PA
Bucknell 5'9" 185 lbs.

Year	Team		Games	Pos.
1929	FRA	N	15	HB, FB
1930			13	HB, FB, QB
1930	MIN	N	1	HB, FB

2 yrs. 29 games

Al Hall

HALL, ALVIN
B. Aug. 12, 1934, Fayette, MS
none 6'0" 195 lbs.

Year	Team		Games	Pos.
1961	LA	N	9	DB
1962			14	DB
1963			3	DB
1963	PIT	N	3	DB

3 yrs. 29 games

Alvin Hall

HALL, ALVIN EUGENE
B. Aug. 12, 1958, Dayton, OH
Miami (Ohio) 5'10" 193 lbs.

Year	Team		Games	Pos.
1981	DET	N	16	CB
1982			9	CB
1983			16	CB, S
1984			16	S
1985			16	S
1987			3	S

6 yrs. 76 games

Charlie Hall

HALL, CHARLES LESLIE
B. Dec. 2, 1948, Yoakum, TX
Houston 6'3" 228 lbs.

Year	Team		Games	Pos.
1971	CLE	N	14	LB
1972			14	LB
1973			14	DB
1974			14	LB
1975			14	LB
1976			14	LB
1977			14	LB
1978			16	LB
1979			16	LB
1980			16	LB

10 yrs. 146 games

Charlie Hall

HALL, CHARLES VAL, JR.
B. Mar. 31, 1949, Philadelphia, PA
Pittsburgh 6'1" 193 lbs.

Year	Team		Games	Pos.
1971	GB	N	14	CB
1972			14	CB
1973			13	CB
1974			13	CB
1975			14	CB
1976			14	CB

6 yrs. 82 games

Chris Hall

HALL, CHARLES CHRISTOPHER
B. Apr. 25, 1970, Fort Dix, NJ

Chris Hall *continued*

East Carolina 6'2" 184 lbs.

Year	Team		Games	Pos.
1993	DAL	N	1	S

Courtney Hall

HALL, COURTNEY CAESAR
B. Aug. 26, 1968, Los Angeles, CA
Rice 6'2" 277 lbs.

Year	Team		Games	Pos.
1989	SD	N	16	C
1990			16	C
1991			16	G, C
1992			16	C, G
1993			16	C, G
1994			15	C
1995			16	C
1996			7	C

8 yrs. 118 games

Dana Hall

HALL, DANA ERIC
B. Jul. 8, 1969, Bellflower, CA
Washington 6'2" 206 lbs.

Year	Team		Games	Pos.
1992	SF	N	15	S
1993			13	S
1994			16	S
1995	CLE	N	15	S
1996	JAC	N	16	S

5 yrs. 75 games

Darryl Hall

HALL, DARRYL
B. Oct. 23, 1959, Greensboro, NC
San Diego State 5'11" 180 lbs.

Year	Team		Games	Pos.
1987	LARM	N	1	CB, S

Darryl Hall

HALL, DARRYL
B. Aug. 1, 1966, Oscoda, MI
Washington 6'2" 210 lbs.

Year	Team		Games	Pos.
1993	DEN	N	16	S
1994			16	S
1995	SF	N	12	CB, S

3 yrs. 44 games

Delton Hall

HALL, DELTON DWAYNE
B. Jan. 16, 1965, Greensboro, NC
Clemson 6'1" 205 lbs.

Year	Team		Games	Pos.
1987	PIT	N	12	CB
1988			16	CB
1989			16	CB, S
1990			12	CB
1991			6	CB
1992	SD	N	16	S

6 yrs. 76 games

Dick Hall

HALL, RICHARD L.
B. Jun. 6, 1903
D. Sep. 6, 1971, Homewood, IL
Butler/Illinois 6'2" 220 lbs.

Year	Team		Games	Pos.
1926	NY	A	15	T
1927	NYY	N	15	T, G

2 yrs. 30 games

Dino Hall

HALL, DONALD RICHARD
B. Dec. 6, 1955, Atlantic City, NJ
Glassboro State 5'7" 165 lbs.

Year	Team		Games	Pos.
1979	CLE	N	11	RB
1980			16	RB
1981			12	RB
1982			9	RB
1983			16	RB

5 yrs. 64 games

Year	Team	Games	Pos.

Forrest Hall
HALL, FORREST J.
B. Oct. 29, 1921, Oil City, PA
Duquesne/San Francisco 5'8" 155 lbs.

Year	Team		Games	Pos.
1948	**SF**	**AA**	14	B

Galen Hall
HALL, GALEN
B. Aug. 14, 1940, Altoona, PA
Penn State 5'10" 200 lbs.

Year	Team		Games	Pos.
1962	**WAS**	**N**	3	QB
1963	**NY**	**A**	13	QB
2 yrs.	16 games			

Harold Hall
HALL, HAROLD
B. Sep. 27, 1913
D. Jun., 1981, Fairport, NY
Springfield 6'2" 210 lbs.

Year	Team		Games	Pos.
1942	**NYG**	**N**	1	C

Harry Hall
HALL, HARRY A. (Swede)
B. Oct. 5, 1902
Deceased
Chicago/Illinois 5'11" 170 lbs.

Year	Team		Games	Pos.
1926	**CHI**	**N**	2	QB, HB

Irv Hall
HALL, IRVING A., JR.
B. Nov. 23, 1913, Raynham, MA
Deceased
Brown 6'0" 210 lbs.

Year	Team		Games	Pos.
1942	**PHI**	**N**	7	FB

James Hall
HALL, JAMES
B. Jan. 27, 1963, Natchez, MS
Northwestern State (Louisiana) 6'1" 252 lbs.

Year	Team		Games	Pos.
1987	**ATL**	**N**	3	LB

John Hall
HALL, JOHN
B. Jun. 30, 1933
Iowa 6'1" 220 lbs.

Year	Team		Games	Pos.
1955	**NYG**	**N**	2	E

Johnny Hall
HALL, JOHN ROBERT
B. Dec. 14, 1916, Kaufman, TX
Texas Christian 6'0" 196 lbs.

Year	Team		Games	Pos.
1940	**CHIC**	**N**	11	HB, FB
1941			11	HB
1942	**DET**	**N**	7	HB
1943	**CHIC**	**N**	7	HB
4 yrs.	36 games			

Ken Hall
HALL, KENNETH
B. Dec. 13, 1935, Sugar Land, TX
Texas A&M 6'1" 205 lbs.

Year	Team		Games	Pos.
1959	**CHIC**	**N**	12	HB
1960	**HOU**	**A**		HB
1961			3	HB
1961	**STL**	**N**	8	HB
3 yrs.	23 games			

Lemanski Hall
HALL, LEMANSKI
B. Nov. 24, 1970, Valley, AL
Alabama 6'0" 229 lbs.

Year	Team		Games	Pos.
1994	**HOU**	**N**	1	LB
1995			12	LB
1996			3	LB
3 yrs.	16 games			

Mark Hall
HALL, MARK JAMES
B. Aug. 21, 1965, Morgan City, LA
Southwestern Louisiana 6'4" 285 lbs.

Year	Team		Games	Pos.
1989	**GB**	**N**	7	DE
1990			3	DE
2 yrs.	10 games			

Parker Hall
HALL, LINUS PARKER (Bullet)
B. Dec. 10, 1916, Tunica, MS
Mississippi 6'0" 198 lbs.

Year	Team		Games	Pos.
1939	**CLE**	**N**	11	QB, DB
1940			11	QB, DB
1941			10	QB, DB
1942			10	QB, DB
1946	**SF**	**AA**	11	QB, DB
5 yrs.	53 games			

Pete Hall
HALL, PETER
B. Feb. 28, 1939
Marquette 6'2" 200 lbs.

Year	Team		Games	Pos.
1961	**NYG**	**N**	12	QB

Randy Hall
HALL, RANDY LEE
B. Feb. 8, 1952, East Wenatchee, WA
Idaho 6'3" 190 lbs.

Year	Team		Games	Pos.
1974	**BAL**	**N**	14	S
1976			13	S
2 yrs.	27 games			

Ray Hall
HALL, HAYWARD RAY
B. Mar. 2, 1971, Seattle, WA
Washington State 6'4" 294 lbs.

Year	Team		Games	Pos.
1995	**JAC**	**N**	12	DT

Rhett Hall
HALL, RHETT FLOYD
B. Dec. 5, 1968, San Jose, CA
California 6'2" 264 lbs.

Year	Team		Games	Pos.
1991	**TB**	**N**	16	DE, DT
1992			4	DE, DT
1993			1	DE, NT
1994	**SF**	**N**	12	DT
1995	**PHI**	**N**	3	DT
1996			16	DT
6 yrs.	52 games			

Ron Hall
HALL, RONALD A.
B. Mar. 15, 1964, Fort Huachuca, AZ
California Poly (Pomona)/Hawaii 6'4" 238 lbs.

Year	Team		Games	Pos.
1987	**TB**	**N**	10	TE
1988			15	TE
1989			16	TE
1990			16	TE
1991			15	TE
1992			12	TE
1993			16	TE
1994	**DET**	**N**	12	TE
1995			6	TE
9 yrs.	118 games			

Ronnie Hall
HALL, RONALD GENE
B. Apr. 30, 1937, Goreville, IL
Missouri Valley 6'0" 190 lbs.

Year	Team		Games	Pos.
1959	**PIT**	**N**	2	DB
1961	**BOS**	**A**	9	DB
1962			14	DB
1963			14	DB
1964			14	DB
1965			14	DB

Ronnie Hall continued

Year	Team	Games	Pos.
1966		14	DB
1967		9	DB
8 yrs.	90 games		

Steven Hall
HALL, STEVEN LAMONT
B. Apr. 15, 1973, Fort Wayne, IN
Kentucky 6'0" 209 lbs.

Year	Team		Games	Pos.
1996	**MIN**	**N**	1	CB
1996	**IND**	**N**	2	S
1 yr.	3 games			

Tim Hall
HALL, TIM
B. Feb. 15, 1974, Kansas City, MO
Robert Morris 6'0" 217 lbs.

Year	Team		Games	Pos.
1996	**OAK**	**N**	2	RB

Tom Hall
HALL, THOMAS FRANCIS
B. Apr. 3, 1940, Wilmington, DE
Minnesota 6'1" 195 lbs.

Year	Team		Games	Pos.
1962	**DET**	**N**	13	OE, DB
1963			14	OE, DB
1964	**MIN**	**N**	14	FL
1965			14	FL
1966			14	FL, OE
1967	**NO**	**N**	10	FL
1967	**MIN**	**N**	1	FL
1968			13	FL
1969			3	WR
8 yrs.	96 games			

Travis Hall
HALL, TRAVIS
B. Aug. 3, 1972, Kenai, AK
Brigham Young 6'5" 278 lbs.

Year	Team		Games	Pos.
1995	**ATL**	**N**	1	DE
1996			14	DT
2 yrs.	15 games			

Willie Hall
HALL, WILLIE CHARLES
B. Sep. 29, 1949, Montrose, GA
Southern California 6'2" 223 lbs.

Year	Team		Games	Pos.
1972	**NO**	**N**	14	LB
1973			7	LB
1975	**OAK**	**N**	7	LB
1976			14	LB
1977			14	LB
1978			11	LB
6 yrs.	67 games			

Windlan Hall
HALL, WINDLAN EDSEL
B. Mar. 11, 1950, Los Angeles, CA
Arizona State 5'11" 176 lbs.

Year	Team		Games	Pos.
1972	**SF**	**N**	14	DB
1973			14	CB
1974			13	S
1975			13	S
1976	**MIN**	**N**	14	S
1977			5	S
1977	**WAS**	**N**	8	S
6 yrs.	81 games			

Death Halladay
HALLADAY, ROBERT THAYER
B. Oct. 29, 1900
D. Nov. 12, 1988, Burr Ridge, IL
Chicago 6'0" 175 lbs.

Year	Team		Games	Pos.
1923	**RAC**	**N**	7	E
1924			10	E
2 yrs.	17 games			

Neil Halleck
HALLECK, NEIL
None

Year	Team		Games	Pos.
1924	**COL**	**N**	5	HB

Paul Halleck
HALLECK, PAUL
B. Jul. 11, 1913
D. Mar., 1974
Ohio University 6'0" 195 lbs.

Year	Team		Games	Pos.
1937	**CLE**	**N**	11	E

Alan Haller
HALLER, ALAN
B. Aug. 9, 1970, Lansing, MI
Michigan State 5'11" 185 lbs.

Year	Team		Games	Pos.
1992	**PIT**	**N**	3	CB
1992	**CLE**	**N**	14	DB
1993	**PIT**	**N**	4	CB
1995	**CAR**	**N**	2	CB
3 yrs.	23 games			

Jack Halliday
HALLIDAY, JACK P.
B. 1928
Southern Methodist 6'3" 238 lbs.

Year	Team		Games	Pos.
1951	**LA**	**N**	11	T

Ty Hallock
HALLOCK, TY EDWARD
B. Apr. 30, 1971, Greenville, MI
Michigan State 6'3" 249 lbs.

Year	Team		Games	Pos.
1993	**DET**	**N**	16	TE
1994			15	TE
1996	**JAC**	**N**	7	TE
3 yrs.	38 games			

Clarence Halloran
HALLORAN, CLARENCE (Dimp)
B. May 27, 1896, Framingham, MA
D. Nov., 1970, Framingham, MA
Boston College/Fordham 5'8" 175 lbs.

Year	Team		Games	Pos.
1921	**SYR**	**A**		QB, FB
1926	**HAR**	**N**	2	QB, FB
2 yrs.	3 games			

Shawn Halloran
HALLORAN, SHAWN
B. Apr. 23, 1964
Boston College 6'4" 217 lbs.

Year	Team		Games	Pos.
1987	**STL**	**N**	3	QB

Stone Hallquist
HALLQUIST, STONE
B. Apr. 8, 1902, Stockholm, Sweden
D. Jun., 1981, Sun City, AZ
Middlebury 5'9" 168 lbs.

Year	Team		Games	Pos.
1926	**MIL**	**N**	9	QB, HB, FB

Ron Hallstrom
HALLSTROM, RONALD DAVID
B. Jun. 11, 1959, Holden, MA
Iowa 6'6" 290 lbs.

Year	Team		Games	Pos.
1982	**GB**	**N**	7	G
1983			16	G
1984			16	OT
1985			16	OT
1986			16	G
1987			12	G
1988			16	G
1989			16	G
1990			16	G
1991			16	G
1992			16	G
1993	**PHI**	**N**	12	G
12 yrs.	175 games			

Year	Team	Games	Pos.

Bob Halperin
HALPERIN, ROBERT (Buck)
B. 1911
Deceased
None 5'11" 200 lbs.

| 1932 | BKN | N | 2 | HB, QB |

Willie Halpern
HALPERN, ROBERT WILLIAM
B. 1906
CCNY 5'11" 220 lbs.

| 1930 | SI | N | 3 | G, T |

Bernie Halstrom
HALSTROM, BERNARD C.
(Swede)
B. Apr. 18, 1895
Deceased
Illinois 5'9" 160 lbs.

1920	CHIC	A	6	HB, FB
1921			5	HB
2 yrs.		11 games		

Jim Haluska
HALUSKA, JAMES
B. Oct. 9, 1932, Racine, WI
Wisconsin 6'0" 190 lbs.

| 1956 | CHIB | N | 5 | QB |

Bill Halverson
HALVERSON, WILLIAM
B. Aug. 2, 1918, Spokane, WA
Oregon State 6'3" 242 lbs.

| 1942 | PHI | N | 9 | T |

Dean Halverson
HALVERSON, DEAN
B. Aug. 24, 1946, Olympia, WA
Washington 6'2" 221 lbs.

1968	LA	N	1	LB
1970	ATL	N	7	LB
1971	LA	N	12	LB
1972			14	LB
1973	PHI		5	LB
1974			13	LB
1975			14	LB
7 yrs.		66 games		

Jack Ham
HAM, JACK RAPHAEL
B. Dec. 23, 1948, Johnstown, PA
Penn State 6'3" 224 lbs.

1971	PIT	N	14	LB
1972			14	LB
1973			13	LB
1974			14	LB
1975			14	LB
1976			14	LB
1977			14	LB
1978			14	LB
1979			15	LB
1980			16	LB
1981			12	LB
1982			8	LB
12 yrs.		162 games		

Johnny Haman
HAMAN, JOHN A.
B. Aug. 18, 1918, Naperville, IL
Deceased
Northwestern 6'1" 212 lbs.

1940	CLE	N	11	C, G
1941			10	C
2 yrs.		21 games		

Steve Hamas
HAMAS, STEVEN
B. Jan. 9, 1907
D. Nov., 1974, Levittown, NY
Penn State 6'0" 195 lbs.

| 1929 | ORA | N | 12 | FB, HB |

Ernie Hambacher
HAMBACHER, ERNEST A.
B. Dec. 12, 1906
Bucknell 5'8" 170 lbs.

| 1929 | ORA | N | 3 | QB, HB, FB, G |

Mike Hamby
HAMBY, MIKE
B. Nov. 2, 1962, Salt Lake City, UT
Utah State 6'4" 270 lbs.

| 1986 | BUF | N | 16 | NT |

Dean Hamel
HAMEL, DEAN
B. Jul. 7, 1961, Detroit, MI
Tulsa 6'3" 275 lbs.

1985	WAS	N	16	DT
1986			16	DT
1987			12	DT
1988			16	DT
1989	DAL	N	16	DT
1990			12	DT
6 yrs.		88 games		

Tex Hamer
HAMER, ERNEST
B. Oct. 4, 1901
D. May 11, 1981, Dallas, TX
Pennsylvania 6'1" 191 lbs.

1924	FRA	N	14	FB
1925			19	FB, HB, QB
1926			17	HB, FB
1927			4	HB, FB, QB
4 yrs.		54 games		

Andy Hamilton
HAMILTON, LADELLE
ANDREW, JR.
B. Apr. 8, 1950, Ruston, LA
Louisiana State 6'3" 190 lbs.

1973	KC	N	5	WR
1974			10	WR
1975	NO	N	9	WR
3 yrs.		24 games		

Bobby Hamilton
HAMILTON, BOBBY
B. Jan. 7, 1971, Columbia, MS
Southern Mississippi 6'5" 280 lbs.

| 1996 | NYJ | N | 15 | DE |

Conrad Hamilton
HAMILTON, CONRAD
B. Nov. 5, 1974, Alamogordo, NM
Eastern New Mexico 5'10" 195 lbs.

| 1996 | NYG | N | 15 | CB |

Darrell Hamilton
HAMILTON, DARRELL
FRANKLIN
B. May 11, 1965, Washington, DC
North Carolina 6'5" 288 lbs.

1990	DEN	N	15	OT
1991			6	OT
2 yrs.		21 games		

Harry Hamilton
HAMILTON, HARRY E.

Harry Hamilton *continued*
B. Nov. 29, 1962, Jamaica, NY
Penn State 6'0" 193 lbs.

1984	NYJ	N	8	S
1985			11	S
1986			15	S
1987			12	S
1988	TB	N	16	DB
1989			13	CB, S
1990			16	S
1991			7	S
8 yrs.		98 games		

Keith Hamilton
HAMILTON, KEITH LAMARR
B. May 25, 1971, Paterson, NJ
Pittsburgh 6'6" 280 lbs.

1992	NYG	N	16	DE
1993			16	DE
1994			15	DE
1995			14	DE
1996			14	DE
5 yrs.		75 games		

Ray Hamilton
HAMILTON, RAYMOND (Bones)
B. Jun. 6, 1916, Sheridan, AR
Arkansas 6'4" 212 lbs.

1938	CLE	N	8	E
1939	DET	N	8	E
1944	CLE	N	7	E
1945			9	E
1946	LA	N	11	E
1947			12	E
6 yrs.		55 games		

Ray Hamilton
HAMILTON, RAYMOND LEE
(Sugar Bear)
B. Jan. 20, 1951, Omaha, NE
Oklahoma 6'1" 244 lbs.

1973	NE	N	14	DE
1974			14	DE
1975			14	DT
1976			14	DT
1977			14	NT
1978			16	NT
1979			16	NT
1980			15	NT
1981			15	NT
9 yrs.		132 games		

Rick Hamilton
HAMILTON, RICK
B. Apr. 19, 1970, Inverness, FL
Central Florida 6'2" 241 lbs.

1993	WAS	N	16	LB
1994			1	LB
1994	KC	N	2	LB
1996	NYJ	N	15	LB
3 yrs.		34 games		

Ruffin Hamilton
HAMILTON, RUFFIN
B. Mar. 2, 1971, Detroit, MI
Tulane 6'1" 230 lbs.

| 1994 | GB | N | 5 | LB |

Skip Hamilton
HAMILTON, LENWOOD
B. May 14, 1959, Philadelphia, PA
North Carolina State/Southern University 6'2" 265 lbs.

| 1987 | PHI | N | 1 | DT |

Steve Hamilton
HAMILTON, STEVEN

Steve Hamilton *continued*
B. Sep. 28, 1961, Niagara Falls, NY
East Carolina 6'4" 255 lbs.

1985	WAS	N	7	DE
1986			12	DE
1987			12	DE, DT
1988			15	DE, DT
4 yrs.		46 games		

Wes Hamilton
HAMILTON, WESLEY DEAN
B. Apr. 24, 1953, Texas City, TX
Tulsa 6'3" 257 lbs.

1976	MIN	N	13	G
1977			14	G
1978			16	G
1979			16	G
1980			13	G
1981			16	G
1982			9	G
1983			15	G
1984			4	G
9 yrs.		116 games		

Gene Hamlin
HAMLIN, EUGENE ROBERT
B. Jul. 26, 1946, Detroit, MI
Western Michigan 6'3" 245 lbs.

1970	WAS	N	3	C
1971	CHI	N	7	C
1972	DET	N	5	C
3 yrs.		15 games		

Bob Hamm
HAMM, BOB
B. Apr. 24, 1959, Kansas City, MO
Nevada-Reno 6'4" 263 lbs.

1983	HOU	N	16	DE
1984			12	DE
1985	KC	N	14	DE
1987	IND	N	3	DE
4 yrs.		45 games		

Mal Hammack
HAMMACK, MALCOLM EUGENE
B. Jun. 19, 1933, Roscoe, TX
Florida 6'2" 205 lbs.

1955	CHIC	N	9	FB
1957			12	FB
1958			10	FB
1959			12	FB
1960	STL	N	9	FB
1961			7	FB
1962			14	FB
1963			13	FB, OE
1964			14	OE, LB
1965			14	TE
1966			14	TE
11 yrs.		128 games		

Mike Hammerstein
HAMMERSTEIN, MICHAEL
SCOTT
B. Mar. 3, 1963, Kokomo, IN
Michigan 6'4" 270 lbs.

1986	CIN	N	15	DE
1987			11	DE
1989			15	DE
1990			16	DE
4 yrs.		57 games		

Jim Hammill
HAMMILL, JAMES (Ching)
B. 1902
D. Nov. 25, 1925, Bridgeport, CT
Connecticut/Georgetown/Villanova 5'7" 158 lbs.

| 1925 | PRO | N | 1 | QB |

Year	Team	Games	Pos.

Bobby Hammond
HAMMOND, ROBERT
B. Feb. 20, 1952, Orangeburg, SC
Morgan State 5'10" 171 lbs.

Year	Team		Games	Pos.
1976	NYG	N	2	RB
1977			14	RB
1978			14	RB
1979			4	RB
1979	WAS	N	5	RB
4 yrs.	39 games			

Gary Hammond
HAMMOND, GARY ALLEN
B. Jul. 31, 1949, Port Arthur, TX
Southern Methodist 5'11" 184 lbs.

Year	Team		Games	Pos.
1973	STL	N	9	WR
1974			12	WR
1975			14	WR
1976			14	WR
4 yrs.	49 games			

Henry Hammond
HAMMOND, HENRY
B. Jul. 13, 1913
Rhodes 5'11" 190 lbs.

Year	Team		Games	Pos.
1937	CHIB	N	7	E

Kim Hammond
HAMMOND, KIM CRANE
B. Oct. 12, 1944, Miami, FL
Florida State 6'1" 192 lbs.

Year	Team		Games	Pos.
1968	MIA	A	3	QB
1969	BOS	A	2	QB
2 yrs.	5 games			

Steve Hammond
HAMMOND, STEVEN REED
B. Feb. 5, 1960, Hartford, CT
Wake Forest 6'4" 225 lbs.

Year	Team		Games	Pos.
1988	NYJ	N	2	LB

Wayne Hammond
HAMMOND, WAYNE
B. Jan. 30, 1953, Minneapolis, MN
Montana State 6'5" 255 lbs.

Year	Team		Games	Pos.
1976	DEN	N	5	DT

Shelly Hammonds
HAMMONDS, SHELTON CORNELIUS
B. Feb. 13, 1971, Barnwell, SC
Penn State 5'10" 187 lbs.

Year	Team		Games	Pos.
1995	MIN	N	2	CB, S

Alonzo Hampton
HAMPTON, ALONZO
B. Jan. 19, 1967, Butler, AL
Pittsburgh 5'10" 191 lbs.

Year	Team		Games	Pos.
1990	MIN	N	10	CB
1991	TB	N	15	CB, S
2 yrs.	25 games			

Dan Hampton
HAMPTON, DANIEL OLIVER
B. Sep. 19, 1957, Oklahoma City, OK
Arkansas 6'5" 257 lbs.

Year	Team		Games	Pos.
1979	CHI	N	16	DT
1980			16	DE, DT
1981			16	DT, DE
1982			9	DE, DT
1983			11	DT
1984			15	DT
1985			16	DT
1986			16	DT
1987			8	DE

Dan Hampton continued

Year	Team	Games	Pos.
1988		16	DE
1989		4	DE
1990		14	DT, DE
12 yrs.	157 games		

Dave Hampton
HAMPTON, DAVID
B. May 7, 1947, Akron, OH
Wyoming 6'0" 207 lbs.

Year	Team		Games	Pos.
1969	GB	N	14	RB
1970			6	RB
1971			6	RB
1972	ATL	N	13	RB
1973			9	RB
1974			14	RB
1975			14	RB
1976			2	RB
1976	PHI	N	8	RB
8 yrs.	86 games			

Kwante Hampton
HAMPTON, KWANTE
B. Dec. 11, 1963
Long Beach State 6'1" 182 lbs.

Year	Team		Games	Pos.
1987	ATL	N	1	WR

Lorenzo Hampton
HAMPTON, LORENZO TIMOTHY
B. Mar. 12, 1962, Lake Wales, FL
Florida 6'0" 212 lbs.

Year	Team		Games	Pos.
1985	MIA	N	16	RB
1986			16	RB
1987			12	RB
1988			16	RB
1989			10	RB
5 yrs.	70 games			

Rodney Hampton
HAMPTON, RODNEY CRAIG
B. Apr. 3, 1969, Houston, TX
Georgia 5'11" 215 lbs.

Year	Team		Games	Pos.
1990	NYG	N	15	RB
1991			14	RB
1992			16	RB
1993			12	RB
1994			14	RB
1995			16	RB
1996			15	RB
7 yrs.	102 games			

James Hamrick
HAMRICK, JAMES
B. 1963
Rice 5'11" 177 lbs.

Year	Team		Games	Pos.
1987	KC	N	3	K

Chris Hanburger
HANBURGER, CHRISTIAN, JR.
B. Aug. 13, 1941, Fort Bragg, NC
North Carolina 6'2" 218 lbs.

Year	Team		Games	Pos.
1965	WAS	N	14	LB
1966			13	LB
1967			13	LB
1968			14	LB
1969			14	LB
1970			14	LB
1971			14	LB
1972			14	LB
1973			14	LB
1974			14	LB
1975			14	LB
1976			14	LB
1977			5	LB
1978			16	LB
14 yrs.	187 games			

Anthony Hancock
HANCOCK, ANTHONY DUANE
B. Jun. 10, 1960, Cleveland, OH
Tennessee 6'0" 200 lbs.

Year	Team		Games	Pos.
1982	KC	N	9	WR
1983			16	WR
1984			14	WR
1985			16	WR
1986			4	WR
5 yrs.	59 games			

Kevin Hancock
HANCOCK, KEVIN DREW
B. Jan. 6, 1962, Longview, TX
Baylor 6'2" 225 lbs.

Year	Team		Games	Pos.
1987	IND	N	1	LB

Mike Hancock
HANCOCK, CARL MICHAEL
B. Feb. 25, 1950, Woodlake, CA
Idaho State 6'4" 220 lbs.

Year	Team		Games	Pos.
1973	WAS	N	10	TE
1974			10	TE
2 yrs.	20 games			

Jon Hand
HAND, JON THOMAS
B. Nov. 13, 1962, Sylacauga, AL
Alabama 6'6" 280 lbs.

Year	Team		Games	Pos.
1986	IND	N	15	NT
1987			12	DE
1988			15	DE
1989			16	DE
1990			12	DE
1991			16	DE
1992			15	DE
1993			15	DE
1994			5	DE
9 yrs.	121 games			

Larry Hand
HAND, LARRY THOMAS
B. Jul. 10, 1940, Paterson, NJ
Appalachian State 6'5" 247 lbs.

Year	Team		Games	Pos.
1965	DET	N	14	DE
1966			14	DE
1967			14	DE
1968			1	DE
1969			14	DE
1970			14	DE
1971			14	DE
1972			14	DE
1973			14	DE
1974			13	DE
1975			14	DE
1976			10	DT
1977			14	DT
13 yrs.	164 games			

Norman Hand
HAND, NORMAN
B. Sep. 4, 1972, Walterboro, SC
Mississippi 6'3" 329 lbs.

Year	Team		Games	Pos.
1996	MIA	N	9	DT

Phil Handler
HANDLER, PHILIP JACOB
(Motsy)
B. Jul. 21, 1908, Fort Worth, TX
D. Dec. 8, 1968, Skokie, IL
Texas Christian 6'0" 212 lbs.

Year	Team		Games	Pos.
1930	CHIC	N	6	G
1931			7	G
1932			9	G
1933			8	G
1934			8	G
1935			10	G

Phil Handler continued

Year	Team	Games	Pos.
1936		2	G
7 yrs.	50 games		

Dick Handley
HANDLEY, RICHARD
B. May 22, 1922, Tulare, CA
Fresno State 6'1" 215 lbs.

Year	Team		Games	Pos.
1947	BAL	AA	14	C

Carl Hanke
HANKE, CARL C.
B. Dec. 31, 1897
D. May, 1964, Chicago, IL
Minnesota 6'0" 190 lbs.

Year	Team		Games	Pos.
1921	HAM	A	4	E
1922	HAM	N	1	E
1922	CHIB	N	2	E
1923	HAM	N	7	E
1924	CHIC	N	8	E
4 yrs.	22 games			

Ray Hanken
HANKEN, RAYMOND G.
B. Dec. 3, 1911
D. Nov., 1980, Vienna, VA
George Washington 5'11" 190 lbs.

Year	Team		Games	Pos.
1937	NYG	N	11	E
1938			10	E
2 yrs.	21 games			

Ben Hanks
HANKS, BEN
B. Jul. 31, 1972, Miami, FL
Florida 6'2" 223 lbs.

Year	Team		Games	Pos.
1996	MIN	N	12	LB

Merton Hanks
HANKS, MERTON EDWARD
B. Mar. 12, 1968, Dallas, TX
Iowa 6'2" 185 lbs.

Year	Team		Games	Pos.
1991	SF	N	13	CB
1992			16	CB
1993			16	CB
1994			16	S, CB
1995			16	S
1996			16	S
6 yrs.	93 games			

Bo Hanley
HANLEY, G.
B. Dec. 14, 1887
D. Sep., 1980, Milwaukee, WI
Marquette 5'7" 150 lbs.

Year	Team		Games	Pos.
1920	DET	A	3	HB

Bob Hanlon
HANLON, ROBERT SELDON
B. Aug. 24, 1924, Springfield, OH
Notre Dame/Loras 6'1" 195 lbs.

Year	Team		Games	Pos.
1948	CHIC	N	10	HB
1949	PIT	N	12	HB
2 yrs.	22 games			

Jim Hanna
HANNA, JIM
B. Aug. 10, 1971, West Palm Beach, FL
Louisville 6'4" 255 lbs.

Year	Team		Games	Pos.
1994	NO	N	7	NT, DE

Zip Hanna
HANNA, ELZAPHAN
B. Dec. 1, 1916, Chester, SC
South Carolina 5'10" 218 lbs.

Year	Team		Games	Pos.
1945	WAS	N	9	G

Charley Hannah
HANNAH, CHARLES ALVIN
B. Jul. 26, 1955, Albertville, AL
Alabama 6'6" 260 lbs.

Year	Team		Games	Pos.
1977	TB	N	9	DE
1978			16	DE
1979			14	OT
1980			16	OT
1981			16	OT
1982			7	OT
1983	LARI	N	16	G
1984			15	G
1985			15	G
1986			12	G
1987			5	G
1988			8	G
12 yrs.	149 games			

Herb Hannah
HANNAH, HERBERT
Alabama 6'3" 220 lbs.

Year	Team		Games	Pos.
1951	NYG	N	12	T

John Hannah
HANNAH, JOHN ALLEN (Hog, Ham Hocks)
B. Apr. 4, 1951, Canton, GA
Alabama 6'3" 265 lbs.

Year	Team		Games	Pos.
1973	NE	N	13	G
1974			14	G
1975			14	G
1976			14	G
1977			11	G
1978			16	G
1979			16	G
1980			16	G
1981			16	G
1982			8	G
1983			16	G
1984			15	G
1985			14	G
13 yrs.	183 games			

Travis Hannah
HANNAH, TRAVIS LAMONT
B. Jan. 31, 1970, Los Angeles, CA
Southern California 5'7" 161 lbs.

Year	Team		Games	Pos.
1993	HOU	N	12	WR
1994			8	WR
1995			16	WR
3 yrs.	36 games			

Chuck Hanneman
HANNEMAN, CHARLES B.
B. Sep. 16, 1914, Flint, MI
Deceased
Eastern Michigan 6'0" 209 lbs.

Year	Team		Games	Pos.
1937	DET	N	10	E
1938			10	E
1939			10	E
1940			9	E
1941			6	E
1941	CLE	N	1	E
5 yrs.	46 games			

Cliff Hanneman
HANNEMAN, CLIFFORD
B. Oct. 21, 1964
Fresno State 6'2" 235 lbs.

Year	Team		Games	Pos.
1987	CLE	N	3	LB

Craig Hanneman
HANNEMAN, CRAIG
B. Jul. 1, 1949, Salem, OR
Oregon State 6'3" 243 lbs.

Year	Team		Games	Pos.
1972	PIT	N	13	DT
1973			14	DE

Craig Hanneman *continued*

Year	Team		Games	Pos.
1974	NE	N	14	DE
1975			11	DE
4 yrs.	52 games			

Dave Hanner
HANNER, JOEL DAVID (Hawg)
B. May 22, 1930, Parkin, AR
Arkansas 6'2" 257 lbs.

Year	Team		Games	Pos.
1952	GB	N	12	DT
1953			12	DT
1954			12	DT
1955			12	DT
1956			12	DT
1957			12	DT
1958			12	DT
1959			12	DT
1960			12	DT
1961			13	DT
1962			14	DT
1963			14	DT
1964			11	DT
13 yrs.	160 games			

Tom Hannon
HANNON, THOMAS
B. Mar. 5, 1955, Massillon, OH
Michigan State 5'11" 192 lbs.

Year	Team		Games	Pos.
1977	MIN	N	12	S
1978			16	S
1979			16	S
1980			16	S
1981			16	S
1982			9	S
1983			16	S
1984			16	S
8 yrs.	117 games			

Jim Hannula
HANNULA, JAMES
B. Jul. 2, 1959, Elgin, IL
Northern Illinois 6'6" 264 lbs.

Year	Team		Games	Pos.
1983	CIN	N	15	OT

Frank Hanny
HANNY, FRANK (Duke)
B. Dec. 10, 1897
Deceased
Indiana 6'0" 199 lbs.

Year	Team		Games	Pos.
1923	CHIB	N	12	E
1924			11	E
1925			17	E
1926			16	E, FB, HB
1927			14	E
1928	PRO	N	11	E
1929			10	E, T, G
1930	GB	N	2	T
1930	POR	N	4	T, G
8 yrs.	97 games			

Matt Hanousek
HANOUSEK, MATTHEW JOSEPH
B. Aug. 16, 1963, St. Paul, MN
Drake/Utah State 6'4" 265 lbs.

Year	Team		Games	Pos.
1987	SEA	N	3	G

Terry Hanratty
HANRATTY, TERRENCE HUGH
B. Jan. 19, 1948, Butler, PA
Notre Dame 6'1" 206 lbs.

Year	Team		Games	Pos.
1969	PIT	N	8	QB
1970			13	QB
1971			6	QB
1972			7	QB
1973			9	QB
1974			3	QB
1975			1	QB

Terry Hanratty *continued*

Year	Team		Games	Pos.
1976	TB	N	3	QB
8 yrs.	50 games			

Ralph Hanricus
HANRICUS, RALPH
B. 1896, New York State
Deceased
St. Mary's (Maryland) 6'0" 175 lbs.

Year	Team		Games	Pos.
1922	ROC	N	2	HB

Brian Hansen
HANSEN, BRIAN
B. Oct. 26, 1960, Hawarden, IA
Sioux Falls 6'3" 207 lbs.

Year	Team		Games	Pos.
1984	NO	N	16	P
1985			16	P
1986			16	P
1987			12	P
1988			16	P
1990	NE	N	16	P
1991	CLE	N	16	P
1992			16	P
1993			16	P
1994	NYJ	N	16	P
1995			16	P
1996			16	P
12 yrs.	188 games			

Bruce Hansen
HANSEN, BRUCE B.
B. Sep. 18, 1961, American Fork, UT
Brigham Young 6'1" 225 lbs.

Year	Team		Games	Pos.
1987	NE	N	6	RB

Cliff Hansen
HANSEN, CLIFFORD
B. Oct. 15, 1909
D. Feb., 1980, Hamlin, IA
Luther 6'1" 190 lbs.

Year	Team		Games	Pos.
1933	CHIC	N	4	HB, QB

Dale Hansen
HANSEN, WARREN DALE
B. Jan. 27, 1921, Detroit, MI
D. May 6, 1978, Birmingham, MI
Michigan State 6'3" 223 lbs.

Year	Team		Games	Pos.
1944	DET	N	1	DE, T
1948			12	T
2 yrs.	13 games			

Don Hansen
HANSEN, DONALD RAY
B. Aug. 20, 1944, Warrick County, IN
Illinois 6'3" 227 lbs.

Year	Team		Games	Pos.
1966	MIN	N	13	LB
1967			12	LB
1969	ATL	N	11	LB
1970			14	LB
1971			14	LB
1972			14	LB
1973			14	LB
1974			14	LB
1975			14	LB
1976	SEA	N	2	LB
1976	GB	N	12	LB
1977			13	LB
11 yrs.	147 games			

Hal Hansen
HANSEN, HARLAN C. (King Hal)
B. Sep. 3, 1892
D. Sep., 1977, Des Moines, IA
Minnesota 5'10" 200 lbs.

Year	Team		Games	Pos.
1923	GB	N	1	HB
1926	NEW	A	3	FB, E, HB
2 yrs.	4 games			

Phil Hansen
HANSEN, PHIL
B. May 20, 1968, Ellendale, ND
North Dakota State 6'5" 272 lbs.

Year	Team		Games	Pos.
1991	BUF	N	14	DE
1992			16	DE
1993			11	DE
1994			16	DE
1995			16	DE
1996			16	DE
6 yrs.	89 games			

Ron Hansen
HANSEN, RONALD M.
B. Feb. 10, 1932, Northfield, MN
Minnesota 6'0" 220 lbs.

Year	Team		Games	Pos.
1954	WAS	N	12	G

Roscoe Hansen
HANSEN, ROSCOE HAROLD
B. Sep. 24, 1929, New York, NY
North Carolina 6'3" 215 lbs.

Year	Team		Games	Pos.
1951	PHI	N	9	T

Wayne Hansen
HANSEN, GEORGE WAYNE (Tex)
B. Oct. 6, 1928, Monahans, TX
D. Aug. 24, 1987, El Paso, TX
Texas Western 6'2" 231 lbs.

Year	Team		Games	Pos.
1950	CHIB	N	11	G
1951			12	G
1952			10	C, G
1953			12	C, G, OT, LB
1954			12	C, G, OT, LB
1955			12	OT, C, LB
1956			12	LB
1957			12	LB
1958			5	LB
1960	DAL	N	12	LB
10 yrs.	110 games			

Dick Hanson
HANSON, RICHARD
B. Dec. 25, 1949, Hillsboro, ND
North Dakota State 6'6" 280 lbs.

Year	Team		Games	Pos.
1971	NYG	N	3	DT

Hal Hanson
HANSON, HAROLD D.
B. Nov. 18, 1895, South Dakota
D. Oct., 1973, Bradenton, FL
South Dakota 6'1" 190 lbs.

Year	Team		Games	Pos.
1921	RI	A	3	G, T
1923	MIN	N	1	C
2 yrs.	4 games			

Hal Hanson
HANSON, HAROLD W.
B. 1906
D. Sep. 29, 1977, Mora, MN
Minnesota 6'1" 195 lbs.

Year	Team		Games	Pos.
1928	FRA	N	16	G
1929			18	G, T
1930			15	G, T, E
1930	MIN	N	1	G
3 yrs.	50 games			

Homer Hanson
HANSON, HOMER P.
B. Jul. 25, 1910
D. Oct. 5, 1989, Marysville, KS
Kansas State 6'0" 217 lbs.

Year	Team		Games	Pos.
1934	C, S	N	2	G
1935	CHIC	N	1	G
1936			1	T
3 yrs.	4 games			

Year	Team	Games	Pos.

Jason Hanson
HANSON, JASON DOUGLAS
B. Jun. 17, 1970, Spokane, WA
Washington State 5'11" 183 lbs.

Year	Team		Games	Pos.
1992	**DET**	N	16	K
1993			16	K
1994			16	K
1995			16	K
1996			16	K
5 yrs.	80 games			

Mark Hanson
HANSON, MARK
B. 1965
Mankato State 6'2" 260 lbs.

Year	Team		Games	Pos.
1987	**MIN**	N	1	G

Ray Hanson
HANSON, RAYMOND
B. Jul. 16, 1893
D. Sep., 1968, Minerva, OH
Ohio State/Ohio Wesleyan 5'9" 185 lbs.

Year	Team		Games	Pos.
1923	**COL**	N	2	G, C

Steve Hanson
HANSON, STEVEN H.
B. Apr. 27, 1902, Racine, WI
D. Aug., 1981, Racine, WI
Carthage 6'2" 192 lbs.

Year	Team		Games	Pos.
1926	**LOU**	N	1	E

Tom Hanson
HANSON, THOMAS TUCKER
(Swede)
B. Nov. 10, 1908, Navesink, NJ
D. Aug. 5, 1970, Philadelphia, PA
Temple 6'1" 192 lbs.

Year	Team		Games	Pos.
1931	**BKN**	N	11	HB, FB
1932	**SI**	N	3	HB
1933	**PHI**	N	9	FB, HB
1934			11	HB, FB
1935			11	HB
1936			11	HB
1937			2	FB, HB
1938	**PIT**	N	5	FB, HB
8 yrs.	63 games			

Bob Hantla
HANTLA, ROBERT DEAN
B. Oct. 3, 1931, St. John, KS
Kansas 6'1" 220 lbs.

Year	Team		Games	Pos.
1954	**SF**	N	9	G
1955			10	G
2 yrs.	19 games			

Chet Hanulak
HANULAK, CHESTER EDWARD
(The Jet)
B. Mar. 28, 1923, Hackensack, NJ
Maryland 5'10" 185 lbs.

Year	Team		Games	Pos.
1954	**CLE**	N	12	HB
1957			12	HB
2 yrs.	24 games			

Merle Hapes
HAPES, MERLE
B. May 9, 1919, Garden Grove, CA
D. Jul. 18, 1994, Biloxi, MS
Mississippi 5'10" 190 lbs.

Year	Team		Games	Pos.
1942	**NYG**	N	11	HB
1946			10	FB
2 yrs.	21 games			

Jim Harbaugh
HARBAUGH, JAMES JOSEPH
B. Dec. 23, 1964, Toledo, OH

Jim Harbaugh continued
Michigan 6'3" 202 lbs.

Year	Team		Games	Pos.
1987	**CHI**	N	6	QB
1988			10	QB
1989			12	QB
1990			14	QB
1991			16	QB
1992			16	QB
1993			15	QB
1994	**IND**	N	12	QB
1995			15	QB
1996			14	QB
10 yrs.	130 games			

Dave Harbour
HARBOUR, DAVID LYNN
B. Oct. 23, 1965, Boston, MA
Illinois 6'4" 265 lbs.

Year	Team		Games	Pos.
1988	**WAS**	N	15	C
1989			16	C
2 yrs.	31 games			

James Harbour
HARBOUR, JAMES EDWARD
B. Nov. 10, 1962, Meridian, MS
Mississippi 6'1" 192 lbs.

Year	Team		Games	Pos.
1986	**IND**	N	9	WR

Milton Hardaway
HARDAWAY, MILTON BUDDY, JR.
B. Dec. 12, 1954, Seguin, TX
Oklahoma State 6'9" 309 lbs.

Year	Team		Games	Pos.
1978	**SD**	N	12	OT

Billy Hardee
HARDEE, ABRAHAM WILLIAM
B. Aug. 12, 1954, Lakeland, FL
Virginia Tech 6'0" 185 lbs.

Year	Team		Games	Pos.
1977	**NYJ**	N	14	CB

Buddy Hardeman
HARDEMAN, WILLIE RILEY
B. Oct. 21, 1954, Auburn, NY
Iowa State 6'0" 196 lbs.

Year	Team		Games	Pos.
1979	**WAS**	N	10	RB
1980			15	RB
2 yrs.	25 games			

Don Hardeman
HARDEMAN, DONALD RAY
B. Aug. 13, 1952, Waco, TX
Texas A&I-Kingsville 6'2" 235 lbs.

Year	Team		Games	Pos.
1975	**HOU**	N	13	RB
1976			13	RB
1977			12	RB
1978	**BAL**	N	13	RB
1979			12	RB
5 yrs.	63 games			

Bobby Harden
HARDEN, BOBBY LEE
B. Feb. 8, 1967, Pahokee, FL
Miami (Florida) 6'0" 192 lbs.

Year	Team		Games	Pos.
1990	**MIA**	N	1	S
1991			16	S
1992			4	S
1993			8	S
4 yrs.	29 games			

Derrick Harden
HARDEN, DERRICK
B. Apr. 21, 1964, Milwaukee, WI
Eastern New Mexico 6'1" 175 lbs.

Year	Team		Games	Pos.
1987	**GB**	N	3	WR

Lee Harden
HARDEN, LEON
B. Aug. 17, 1947, Kansas City, MO
Texas-El Paso 5'11" 195 lbs.

Year	Team		Games	Pos.
1970	**GB**	N	8	S

Mike Harden
HARDEN, MICHAEL
B. Feb. 16, 1959, Memphis, TN
Michigan 6'1" 192 lbs.

Year	Team		Games	Pos.
1980	**DEN**	N	16	S
1981			16	S
1982			5	S
1983			15	S
1984			16	S
1985			16	CB
1986			16	CB
1987			12	CB
1988			16	CB, S
1989	**LARI**	N	15	S
1990			15	S
11 yrs.	158 games			

Pat Harder
HARDER, MARLIN M.
B. May 6, 1922, Milwaukee, WI
D. Sep. 7, 1992, Waukesha, WI
Wisconsin 5'11" 203 lbs.

Year	Team		Games	Pos.
1946	**CHIC**	N	11	FB
1947			12	FB
1948			12	FB
1949			11	FB
1950			12	FB
1951	**DET**	N	12	FB
1952			11	FB
1953			5	FB
8 yrs.	86 games			

Steve Hardin
HARDIN, STEVEN JOHN
B. Dec. 30, 1971, Bellevue, WA
Oregon 6'7" 334 lbs.

Year	Team		Games	Pos.
1996	**IND**	N	1	OT

Greg Harding
HARDING, GREG
B. Jul. 31, 1960, New Orleans, LA
Nicholls State 6'2" 202 lbs.

Year	Team		Games	Pos.
1984	**NO**	N	3	S
1987	**PHI**	N	1	CB, S
2 yrs.	4 games			

Roger Harding
HARDING, ROGER
B. Jun. 11, 1923, Oakland, CA
California 6'2" 211 lbs.

Year	Team		Games	Pos.
1945	**CLE**	N	6	C
1946	**LA**	N	10	C
1947	**PHI**	N	6	C
1948	**DET**	N	11	C
1949	**NYB**	N	3	C
5 yrs.	36 games			

Dee Hardison
HARDISON, WILLIAM DAVID
B. May 2, 1956, Jacksonville, NC
North Carolina 6'4" 280 lbs.

Year	Team		Games	Pos.
1978	**BUF**	N	16	DT
1979			16	DT
1980			16	NT
1982	**NYG**	N	5	DE
1983			16	DE
1984			15	DE
1985			13	DE
1986	**SD**	N	15	DE
1987			3	DE
1988	**KC**	N	7	DE
10 yrs.	122 games			

Cedric Hardman
HARDMAN, CEDRICK WARD
B. Oct. 4, 1948, Houston, TX
North Texas State 6'3" 250 lbs.

Year	Team		Games	Pos.
1970	**SF**	N	14	DE, DT
1971			14	DE
1972			14	DE
1973			14	DE
1974			14	DE
1975			11	DE
1976			14	DE
1977			16	DE
1978			14	DE
1979			16	DE
1980	**OAK**	N	16	DE
1981			16	DE
12 yrs.	171 games			

Adrian Hardy
HARDY, ADRIAN PAUL
B. Aug. 16, 1970, New Orleans, LA
Northwestern State (Louisiana) 5'11" 194 lbs.

Year	Team		Games	Pos.
1993	**SF**	N	10	CB
1994			2	CB
1994	**CIN**	N	14	S
1995			10	CB
3 yrs.	36 games			

Andre Hardy
HARDY, ANDRE
B. Nov. 28, 1961, San Diego, CA
Weber State/St. Mary's (California) 6'1" 233 lbs.

Year	Team		Games	Pos.
1984	**PHI**	N	6	RB
1985	**SEA**	N	3	RB
1987	**SF**	N	1	RB
3 yrs.	10 games			

Bruce Hardy
HARDY, BRUCE
B. Jun. 1, 1956, Murray, UT
Arizona State 6'5" 232 lbs.

Year	Team		Games	Pos.
1978	**MIA**	N	16	TE
1979			16	TE
1980			16	TE
1981			16	TE
1982			9	TE
1983			15	TE
1984			16	TE
1985			16	TE
1986			16	TE
1987			12	TE
1988			2	TE
1989			1	TE
12 yrs.	151 games			

Carroll Hardy
HARDY, CARROLL WILLIAM
B. Mar. 18, 1933, Sturgis, SD
Colorado 6'0" 185 lbs.

Year	Team		Games	Pos.
1955	**SF**	N	8	HB

Charley Hardy
HARDY, CHARLES
B. 1934
San Jose State 6'0" 184 lbs.

Year	Team		Games	Pos.
1960	**OAK**	A		OE
1961			14	OE
1962			5	OE
3 yrs.	19 games			

Cliff Hardy
HARDY, CLIFTON
B. Jan. 28, 1947, Fairfield, CA
Michigan State 6'0" 187 lbs.

Year	Team		Games	Pos.
1971	**CHI**	N	1	DB

Year	Team		Games	Pos.

Darryl Hardy
HARDY, DARRYL GERROD
B. Nov. 22, 1968, Cincinnati, OH
Tennessee 6'2" 220 lbs.

1995	ARI	N	4	LB
1995	DAL	N	4	LB
1 yr.	8 games			

David Hardy
HARDY, DAVID
B. Jul. 7, 1959, Fort Worth, TX
Texas A&M 5'7" 180 lbs.

| 1987 | LARI | N | 2 | K |

Dick Hardy
HARDY, RICHARD
B. Sep. 1, 1904
D. Feb., 1970, York Center, ME
Boston College 5'10" 220 lbs.

| 1926 | RAC | N | 5 | T, G |

Edgar Hardy
HARDY, EDGAR C.
B. Mar. 11, 1951, Magee, MS
Jackson State 6'4" 242 lbs.

| 1973 | SF | N | 3 | G |

Isham Hardy
HARDY, ISHAM
B. Mar. 28, 1899
D. Jan. 23, 1983, Hampton, VA
William & Mary

1923	AKR	N	1	G
1926			2	HB, FB, G
2 yrs.	3 games			

Jim Hardy
HARDY, JAMES FRED
B. Apr. 24, 1923, Los Angeles, CA
Southern California 6'0" 180 lbs.

1946	LA	N	9	QB
1947			9	QB
1948			12	QB
1949	CHIC	N	12	QB
1950			12	QB
1951			7	QB
1952	DET	N	9	QB
7 yrs.	70 games			

John Hardy
HARDY, JOHN LOUIS, JR.
B. Jun. 11, 1968, Pasadena, CA
California 5'10" 166 lbs.

| 1991 | CHI | N | 4 | CB |

Kevin Hardy
HARDY, KEVIN
B. Jul. 28, 1945, Oakland, CA
Notre Dame 6'5" 271 lbs.

1968	SF	N	12	DE
1970	GB	N	14	DT
1971	SD	N	13	DT
1972			6	DT
4 yrs.	45 games			

Kevin Hardy
HARDY, KEVIN
B. Jul. 24, 1973, Evansville, IN
Illinois 6'4" 245 lbs.

| 1996 | JAC | N | 16 | LB |

Larry Hardy
HARDY, LARRY
B. Jul. 9, 1956, Mendenhall, MS
Jackson State 6'3" 240 lbs.

| 1978 | NO | N | 16 | TE |

Larry Hardy *continued*

1979			16	TE
1980			16	TE
1981			16	TE
1982			9	TE
1983			6	TE
1984			6	TE
1985			16	TE
8 yrs.	101 games			

Robert Hardy
HARDY, ROBERT EMMITT
B. Jul. 3, 1956, Tulsa, OK
Jackson State 6'2" 250 lbs.

1979	SEA	N	16	DT
1980			16	DT
1981			14	DT
1982			8	DT
4 yrs.	54 games			

Robert Hardy
HARDY, ROBERT KENNETH
B. Sep. 1, 1967, Gaffney, SC
Carson-Newman 5'10" 210 lbs.

| 1991 | TB | N | 16 | RB |

Cecil Hare
HARE, CECIL J.
B. Mar. 21, 1919, Glenbush, Sask.
D. Apr. 14, 1963
Gonzaga 5'11" 195 lbs.

1941	WAS	N	11	HB, LB
1942			10	HB, LB
1945			9	HB, DB
1946	NYG	N	8	HB, DB
4 yrs.	38 games			

Eddie Hare
HARE, EDWARD EVERETT
B. May 30, 1957, Ulysses, KS
Tulsa 6'4" 209 lbs.

| 1979 | NE | N | 16 | P |

Ray Hare
HARE, RAYMOND L.
B. Nov. 21, 1917, North Battleford, Sask.
D. Sep. 2, 1975, Chewelah, WA
Gonzaga 6'1" 204 lbs.

1940	WAS	N	5	HB, DB
1941			10	HB, DB
1942			10	HB, DB
1943			9	HB, DB
1944	BKN	N	10	HB, DB
1946	NY	AA	4	HB, DB
6 yrs.	48 games			

Tony Hargain
HARGAIN, ANTHONY MICHAEL
B. Dec. 26, 1967, Palo Alto, CA
Oregon 6'0" 194 lbs.

| 1992 | KC | N | 12 | WR |

Edd Hargett
HARGETT, EDWARD EUGENE
B. Jun. 26, 1947, Marietta, TX
Texas A&M 5'11" 187 lbs.

1969	NO	N	6	QB
1970			10	QB
1971			14	QB
1972			14	QB
1973	HOU	N	5	QB
5 yrs.	49 games			

Jimmy Hargrove
HARGROVE, JAMES

Jimmy Hargrove *continued*
B. Nov. 13, 1957, Newton Grove, NC
Wake Forest 6'2" 228 lbs.

1981	CIN	N	15	FB
1987	GB	N	2	FB
2 yrs.	17 games			

Jimmy Hargrove
HARGROVE, JAMES L.
B. Feb. 21, 1945, Temple, TX
Howard Payne 6'3" 229 lbs.

1967	MIN	N	14	LB
1969			6	LB
1970			12	LB
1971	STL	N	14	LB
1972			10	LB
5 yrs.	56 games			

Marvin Hargrove
HARGROVE, MARVIN
B. 1968
Richmond 5'10" 178 lbs.

| 1990 | PHI | N | 7 | WR |

Lance Harkey
HARKEY, LANCE
B. Oct. 30, 1965
Illinois 5'10" 180 lbs.

| 1987 | LARI | N | 2 | CB, S |

Lem Harkey
HARKEY, LEMUEL
B. 1934
Emporia State 6'1" 205 lbs.

| 1955 | SF | N | 1 | FB |

Steve Harkey
HARKEY, STEPHEN DOUGLAS
B. Aug. 3, 1949, Atlanta, GA
Georgia Tech 6'0" 215 lbs.

1971	NYJ	N	14	RB
1972			11	RB
2 yrs.	25 games			

Jim Harlan
HARLAN, JAMES THOMAS
B. Jun. 14, 1954, Shreveport, LA
Howard Payne 6'4" 250 lbs.

| 1978 | WAS | N | 14 | OT, C |

Chic Harley
HARLEY, CHARLES WESLEY
B. Sep. 15, 1895, Chicago, IL
D. Apr. 21, 1974, Danville, IL
Ohio State 5'8" 165 lbs.

| 1921 | DEC | A | 9 | HB |

Pat Harlow
HARLOW, PATRICK CHRISTOPHER
B. Mar. 16, 1969, Norco, CA
Southern California 6'6" 290 lbs.

1991	NE	N	16	OT
1992			16	OT
1993			16	OT
1994			16	OT
1995			10	OT
1996	OAK	N	10	OT
6 yrs.	84 games			

Andy Harmon
HARMON, ANDREW PHILLIP
B. Apr. 6, 1969, Centerville, OH
Kent State 6'4" 265 lbs.

| 1991 | PHI | N | 16 | DE |

Andy Harmon *continued*

1992			16	DE
1993			16	DT
1994			16	DT
1995			15	DT
1996			2	DT
6 yrs.	81 games			

Clarence Harmon
HARMON, CLARENCE, JR.
B. Nov. 30, 1955, Kosciusko, MS
Mississippi State 5'11" 202 lbs.

1977	WAS	N	12	RB
1978			16	RB
1979			16	RB
1980			15	RB
1981			5	RB
1982			9	RB
6 yrs.	73 games			

Derrick Harmon
HARMON, DERRICK TODD
B. Apr. 26, 1963, New York, NY
Cornell 5'10" 202 lbs.

1984	SF	N	16	RB
1985			15	RB
1986			8	RB
3 yrs.	39 games			

Ed Harmon
HARMON, EDWARD
B. Dec. 16, 1946, North Tonawanda, NY
Louisville 6'4" 230 lbs.

| 1969 | CIN | A | 11 | LB |

Ham Harmon
HARMON, HAMILTON
B. 1914
Tulsa 6'0" 220 lbs.

| 1937 | CHIC | N | 6 | C |

Kevin Harmon
HARMON, KEVIN ANTHONY
B. Oct. 26, 1966, Queens, NY
Iowa 6'0" 190 lbs.

1988	SEA	N	5	RB
1989			4	RB
2 yrs.	9 games			

Mike Harmon
HARMON, MICHAEL
B. Jul. 24, 1961, Kosciusko, MS
Mississippi 6'0" 185 lbs.

| 1983 | NYJ | N | 9 | WR |

Ronnie Harmon
HARMON, RONNIE KEITH
B. May 7, 1964, Queens, NY
Iowa 5'11" 192 lbs.

1986	BUF	N	14	RB
1987			12	RB
1988			16	RB
1989			15	RB
1990	SD	N	16	RB
1991			16	RB
1992			16	RB
1993			16	RB
1994			16	RB
1995			16	RB
1996	HOU	N	16	RB
11 yrs.	169 games			

Tom Harmon
HARMON, THOMAS ROCKWELL
B. Jul. 1, 1945, Omaha, NE

Year	Team		Games	Pos.

Tom Harmon continued

Gustavus Adolphus 6'4" 238 lbs.

Year	Team		Games	Pos.
1967	ATL	N	10	OT

Tommy Harmon

HARMON, THOMAS DUDLEY (Ol' 98)
B. Sep. 28, 1919, Gary, IN
D. Mar. 15, 1990, Los Angeles, CA
Michigan 6'1" 199 lbs.

Year	Team		Games	Pos.
1946	LA	N	10	HB
1947			12	HB
2 yrs.		22 games		

Art Harms

HARMS, ARTHUR GUSTAV
B. Jun. 25, 1902
D. Jul., 1986, North Providence, RI
Vermont 6'1" 200 lbs.

Year	Team		Games	Pos.
1925	FRA	N	8	T
1926	NYG	N	6	T, E, G
1927			1	T
3 yrs.		15 games		

Jim Harness

HARNESS, JAMES
B. Apr. 6, 1934
Mississippi State 5'11" 180 lbs.

Year	Team		Games	Pos.
1956	BAL	N	1	HB

George Harold

HAROLD, GEORGE ALTON
B. Apr. 13, 1942, Augusta, GA
Allen 6'3" 198 lbs.

Year	Team		Games	Pos.
1966	BAL	N	12	DB
1967			2	DB
1968	WAS	N	8	DB
3 yrs.		22 games		

Alvin Harper

HARPER, ALVIN CRAIG
B. Jul. 6, 1967, Lake Wells, FL
Tennessee 6'3" 203 lbs.

Year	Team		Games	Pos.
1991	DAL	N	15	WR
1992			16	WR
1993			16	WR
1994			16	WR
1995	TB	N	13	WR
1996			12	WR
6 yrs.		88 games		

Bruce Harper

HARPER, BRUCE S.
B. Jun. 20, 1955, Englewood, NJ
Kutztown State 5'8" 176 lbs.

Year	Team		Games	Pos.
1977	NYJ	N	14	RB
1978			16	RB
1979			16	RB
1980			16	RB
1981			16	RB
1982			9	RB
1983			9	RB
1984			4	RB
8 yrs.		99 games		

Charlie Harper

HARPER, CHARLES LYNWOOD
B. Aug. 14, 1944, Haskell, OK
Oklahoma State 6'2" 250 lbs.

Year	Team		Games	Pos.
1966	NYG	N	14	G
1967			14	G
1968			14	G
1969			14	OT, G
1970			14	G, OT
1971			14	G, OT
1972			1	G
7 yrs.		85 games		

Darrell Harper

HARPER, DARRELL
B. 1938
Michigan 6'1" 195 lbs.

Year	Team		Games	Pos.
1960	BUF	A		HB

Dave Harper

HARPER, DAVID DOUGLAS
B. May 5, 1966, Eureka, CA
Humboldt State 6'1" 220 lbs.

Year	Team		Games	Pos.
1990	DAL	N	6	LB

Dwayne Harper

HARPER, DWAYNE ANTHONY
B. Mar. 29, 1966, Orangeburg, SC
South Carolina State 5'11" 165 lbs.

Year	Team		Games	Pos.
1988	SEA	N	16	CB
1989			16	CB
1990			16	CB
1991			16	CB
1992			16	CB
1993			14	CB
1994	SD	N	16	CB
1995			16	CB
1996			6	CB
9 yrs.		132 games		

Jack Harper

HARPER, JACK RIDLEY
B. Oct. 8, 1944, Lakeland, FL
Florida 5'11" 190 lbs.

Year	Team		Games	Pos.
1967	MIA	A	9	RB
1968			5	RB
2 yrs.		14 games		

John Harper

HARPER, JOHN
B. Jun. 12, 1960, Memphis, TN
Southern Illinois 6'3" 230 lbs.

Year	Team		Games	Pos.
1983	ATL	N	13	LB

LaSalle Harper

HARPER, LASALLE
B. May 16, 1967, Galveston, TX
Arkansas 6'1" 235 lbs.

Year	Team		Games	Pos.
1989	NYG	N	1	LB
1989	CHI	N	3	LB
1 yr.		4 games		

Mark Harper

HARPER, MARK
B. Nov. 5, 1961, Memphis, TN
Alcorn State 5'9" 174 lbs.

Year	Team		Games	Pos.
1986	CLE	N	16	CB
1987			12	CB
1988			13	CB
1989			16	CB
1990			5	CB
5 yrs.		62 games		

Maurice Harper

HARPER, MAURICE (Moose)
B. May 14, 1914, Bandera, TX
Deceased
Austin 6'4" 227 lbs.

Year	Team		Games	Pos.
1937	PHI	N	8	C
1938			11	C
1939			11	C
1940			9	C
1941	PIT	N	1	C
5 yrs.		40 games		

Michael Harper

HARPER, MICHAEL
B. May 11, 1961, Kansas City, MO
Southern California 5'10" 180 lbs.

Year	Team		Games	Pos.
1986	NYJ	N	16	WR

Michael Harper continued

Year	Team		Games	Pos.
1987			3	WR
1988			10	WR
1989			6	WR
4 yrs.		35 games		

Roger Harper

HARPER, ROGER
B. Oct. 26, 1970, Columbus, OH
Ohio State 6'2" 223 lbs.

Year	Team		Games	Pos.
1993	ATL	N	16	S
1994			10	S
1995			16	S
1996	DAL	N	16	S
4 yrs.		58 games		

Roland Harper

HARPER, ROLAND
B. Feb. 28, 1953, Seguin, TX
Louisiana Tech 6'0" 208 lbs.

Year	Team		Games	Pos.
1975	CHI	N	13	RB
1976			14	RB
1977			11	RB
1978			16	RB
1980			12	RB
1981			15	RB
1982			8	RB
7 yrs.		89 games		

Shawn Harper

HARPER, SHAWN
B. Jul. 9, 1968, Columbus, OH
Indiana 6'4" 290 lbs.

Year	Team		Games	Pos.
1995	IND	N	8	OT

Willie Harper

HARPER, WILLIE MILES
B. Jul. 30, 1950, Toledo, OH
Nebraska 6'2" 213 lbs.

Year	Team		Games	Pos.
1973	SF	N	14	LB
1974			14	LB
1975			13	LB
1976			14	LB
1977			12	LB
1979			16	LB
1980			14	LB
1981			16	LB
1982			5	LB
1983			16	LB
10 yrs.		134 games		

Dennis Harrah

HARRAH, DENNIS WAYNE (Herk)
B. Mar. 9, 1953, Charleston, WV
Miami (Florida) 6'5" 260 lbs.

Year	Team		Games	Pos.
1975	LA	N	14	G
1976			14	G
1977			8	G
1978			15	G
1979			13	G
1980			15	G
1981			15	G
1982	LARM	N	9	G
1983			15	G
1984			16	G
1985			10	G
1986			16	G
1987			8	G
13 yrs.		168 games		

Charley Harraway

HARRAWAY, CHARLES EDWARD, JR.
B. Sep. 21, 1944, Oklahoma City, OK
San Jose State 6'2" 221 lbs.

Year	Team		Games	Pos.
1966	CLE	N	14	FB
1967			14	RB

Charley Harraway contin-

Year	Team		Games	Pos.
1968			13	RB
1969	WAS	N	14	RB
1970			13	RB
1971			14	RB
1972			14	RB
1973			14	RB
8 yrs.		110 games		

Gary Harrell

HARRELL, GARY
B. Jan. 23, 1972, Miami, FL
Howard 5'7" 170 lbs.

Year	Team		Games	Pos.
1995	NYG	N	4	WR

James Harrell

HARRELL, JAMES CLARENCE, JR.
B. Jul. 19, 1957, Tampa, FL
Florida 6'1" 230 lbs.

Year	Team		Games	Pos.
1979	DET	N	9	LB
1980			5	LB
1981			16	LB
1982			9	LB
1983			16	LB
1985			7	LB
1986			16	LB
1987	KC	N	11	LB
8 yrs.		89 games		

Ricky Harrell

HARRELL, RICK
B. Aug. 8, 1951, Morristown, NJ
Clemson 6'3" 238 lbs.

Year	Team		Games	Pos.
1973	NYJ	N	4	G

Sam Harrell

HARRELL, SAMUEL DELMAR, JR.
B. Feb. 7, 1957, Ahoskie, NC
East Carolina 6'2" 213 lbs.

Year	Team		Games	Pos.
1981	MIN	N	4	RB
1982			1	RB
1987			1	RB
3 yrs.		6 games		

Willard Harrell

HARRELL, WILLARD RACE
B. Sep. 16, 1952, Stockton, CA
Pacific 5'9" 182 lbs.

Year	Team		Games	Pos.
1975	GB	N	14	RB
1976			13	RB
1977			13	RB
1978	STL	N	13	RB
1979			14	RB
1980			16	RB
1981			16	RB
1982			7	RB
1983			14	RB
1984			16	RB
10 yrs.		136 games		

John Harrington

HARRINGTON, JOHN PATRICK
B. Apr. 15, 1921, Reedsburg, WI
D. Jan. 8, 1992, Green Bay, WI
Marquette 6'3" 198 lbs.

Year	Team		Games	Pos.
1946	CLE	AA	12	E
1947	CHI	AA	13	E
2 yrs.		25 games		

LaRue Harrington

HARRINGTON, LARUE HENRY
B. Jun. 28, 1957, Norfolk, VA
Norfolk State 6'0" 210 lbs.

Year	Team		Games	Pos.
1980	SD	N	4	QB

Year	Team		Games	Pos.

Perry Harrington
HARRINGTON, PERRY DONELL
B. May 13, 1958, Bentonia, MS
Jackson State 5'11" 210 lbs.

Year	Team		Games	Pos.
1980	**PHI**	**N**	14	FB
1981			4	FB
1982			9	RB
1983			15	RB
1984	**STL**	**N**	6	RB
1985			11	RB

6 yrs.   59 games

Al Harris
HARRIS, ALFRED CARL
B. Dec. 31, 1956, Bangor, ME
Arizona State 6'5" 260 lbs.

Year	Team		Games	Pos.
1979	**CHI**	**N**	4	DE
1980			16	DE
1981			16	DE
1982			8	DE
1983			12	LB
1984			16	LB
1986			16	LB
1987			12	DE
1988			16	DE
1989	**PHI**	**N**	16	LB
1990			16	LB

11 yrs.   148 games

Ames Harris
HARRIS, AMES EDWIN (Mike)
B. 1921
Mississippi State 6'0" 210 lbs.

Year	Team		Games	Pos.
1947	**BKN**	**AA**	14	G
1948			14	G

2 yrs.   28 games

Anthony Harris
HARRIS, ANTHONY JERROD
B. Jan. 25, 1973, Fort Pierce, FL
Auburn 6'1" 224 lbs.

Year	Team		Games	Pos.
1996	**MIA**	**N**	7	LB

Archie Harris
HARRIS, ARCHIE
B. Nov. 17, 1964, Orange, NJ
William & Mary 6'5" 260 lbs.

Year	Team		Games	Pos.
1987	**DEN**	**N**	3	G, OT

Bernardo Harris
HARRIS, BERNARDO JAMAINE
B. Oct. 15, 1971, Chapel Hill, NC
North Carolina 6'2" 243 lbs.

Year	Team		Games	Pos.
1995	**GB**	**N**	11	LB
1996			16	LB

2 yrs.   27 games

Bill Harris
HARRIS, WILLIAM
B. 1914
Hardin-Simmons 6'2" 196 lbs.

Year	Team		Games	Pos.
1937	**PIT**	**N**	1	E

Bill Harris
HARRIS, WILLIAM ANDREWS, JR.
B. Jan. 17, 1946, Galveston, TX
Colorado 6'0" 198 lbs.

Year	Team		Games	Pos.
1968	**ATL**	**N**	6	RB
1969	**MIN**	**N**	13	RB
1971	**NO**	**N**	2	RB

3 yrs.   21 games

Bo Harris
HARRIS, CLINTON LEE
B. Jan. 16, 1953, Leesville, PA

Bo Harris *continued*
Louisiana State 6'3" 235 lbs.

Year	Team		Games	Pos.
1975	**CIN**	**N**	12	LB
1976			14	LB
1977			14	LB
1978			8	LB
1979			15	LB
1980			15	LB
1981			16	LB
1982			9	LB

8 yrs.   103 games

Bob Harris
HARRIS, BOB
B. Nov. 11, 1960, Everett, WA
Auburn 6'3" 202 lbs.

Year	Team		Games	Pos.
1983	**STL**	**N**	8	LB
1984			16	LB
1985			10	LB
1987	**KC**	**N**	3	LB

4 yrs.   37 games

Charles Harris
HARRIS, CHARLES
B. Oct. 7, 1961
West Virginia 6'3" 255 lbs.

Year	Team		Games	Pos.
1987	**CHI**	**N**	3	OT, G

Cliff Harris
HARRIS, CLIFFORD ALLEN
B. Nov. 12, 1948, Fayetteville, AR
Ouachita Baptist 6'0" 188 lbs.

Year	Team		Games	Pos.
1970	**DAL**	**N**	11	S
1971			14	S
1972			14	S
1973			14	S
1974			14	S
1975			14	S
1976			14	S
1977			14	S
1978			16	S
1979			16	S

10 yrs.   141 games

Corey Harris
HARRIS, COREY LAMONT
B. Oct. 25, 1969, Indianapolis, IN
Vanderbilt 5'11" 195 lbs.

Year	Team		Games	Pos.
1992	**HOU**	**N**	5	DB
1992	**GB**	**N**	5	DB
1993			11	CB, S
1994			16	CB, S
1995	**SEA**	**N**	16	CB
1996			16	CB

5 yrs.   69 games

Darryl Harris
HARRIS, DARRYL LYNN
B. Feb. 20, 1966, Jackson, MS
Arizona State 5'10" 178 lbs.

Year	Team		Games	Pos.
1988	**MIN**	**N**	14	RB

Derrick Harris
HARRIS, DERRICK
B. Sep. 18, 1972, Willowridge, TX
Miami (Florida) 6'0" 253 lbs.

Year	Team		Games	Pos.
1996	**STL**	**N**	11	RB

Dick Harris
HARRIS, RICHARD
B. Jul. 24, 1937, Denver, CO
Ouachita Baptist 6'0" 185 lbs.

Year	Team		Games	Pos.
1960	**LA**	**A**		DB
1961	**SD**	**A**	14	DB
1962			14	DB
1963			14	DB
1964			6	DB

Dick Harris *continued*

Year	Team		Games	Pos.
1965			14	DB

6 yrs.   62 games

Donnie Harris
HARRIS, DON
B. Feb. 8, 1954, Elizabeth, NJ
Northland (Wisconsin)/Rutgers 6'2" 185 lbs.

Year	Team		Games	Pos.
1978	**WAS**	**N**	16	CB
1979			16	S
1980	**NYG**	**N**	11	S

3 yrs.   43 games

Dud Harris
HARRIS, DUDLEY
B. Oct. 24, 1903
Ohio State/Marietta 6'2" 240 lbs.

Year	Team		Games	Pos.
1930	**POR**	**N**	13	T, E

Duriel Harris
HARRIS, DURIEL LADON, JR.
B. Nov. 27, 1954, Port Arthur, TX
New Mexico State 5'11" 178 lbs.

Year	Team		Games	Pos.
1976	**MIA**	**N**	12	WR
1977			14	WR
1978			16	WR
1979			15	WR
1980			12	WR
1981			15	WR
1982			9	WR
1983			12	WR
1984	**CLE**	**N**	11	WR
1984	**DAL**	**N**	5	WR
1985	**MIA**	**N**	6	WR

10 yrs.   127 games

Elmore Harris
HARRIS, ELMORE THOMAS (Pepper)
B. Jun. 3, 1922, Huntsville, AL
D. Dec. 8, 1968
Morgan State 5'11" 175 lbs.

Year	Team		Games	Pos.
1947	**BKN**	**AA**	10	HB

Elroy Harris
HARRIS, ELROY
B. Aug. 18, 1966, Orlando, FL
Eastern Kentucky 5'9" 218 lbs.

Year	Team		Games	Pos.
1989	**SEA**	**N**	14	RB

Eric Harris
HARRIS, ERIC WAYNE
B. Aug. 11, 1955, Memphis, TN
Memphis State 6'3" 191 lbs.

Year	Team		Games	Pos.
1980	**KC**	**N**	15	CB
1981			16	CB
1982			8	CB
1983	**LARM**	**N**	16	CB
1984			7	CB
1985			9	CB

6 yrs.   71 games

Franco Harris
HARRIS, FRANCO
B. Mar. 7, 1950, Fort Dix, NJ
Penn State 6'2" 227 lbs.

Year	Team		Games	Pos.
1972	**PIT**	**N**	14	RB
1973			12	RB
1974			12	RB
1975			14	RB
1976			14	RB
1977			14	RB
1978			16	RB
1979			15	RB
1980			13	RB
1981			16	RB

Franco Harris *continued*

Year	Team		Games	Pos.
1982			9	RB
1983			16	RB
1984	**SEA**	**N**	8	FB

13 yrs.   173 games

Frank Harris
HARRIS, FRANK
B. Jul. 1, 1964
North Carolina State 6'1" 196 lbs.

Year	Team		Games	Pos.
1987	**CHI**	**N**	3	RB

George Harris
HARRIS, GEORGE (Fatty)
B. Mar. 8, 1884
D. Oct., 1963
None

Year	Team		Games	Pos.
1921	**LOU**	**A**	2	T

Hank Harris
HARRIS, HENRY FRANKLIN
B. Feb. 26, 1923, Camden, AL
Texas 6'0" 265 lbs.

Year	Team		Games	Pos.
1947	**WAS**	**N**	10	G
1948			2	G, T

2 yrs.   12 games

Harry Harris
HARRIS, HARRY FRANK
B. Sep. 10, 1895
D. Mar., 1969, Martins Ferry, OH
West Virginia Wesleyan/West Virginia 5'9" 175 lbs.

Year	Team		Games	Pos.
1920	**AKR**	**A**	9	QB

Herbert Harris
HARRIS, HERBERT H.
B. May 4, 1961, Houston, TX
Lamar 6'1" 206 lbs.

Year	Team		Games	Pos.
1986	**NO**	**N**	7	WR
1987			2	WR

2 yrs.   9 games

Ike Harris
HARRIS, ISIAH, JR.
B. Nov. 27, 1952, West Memphis, AR
Iowa State 6'3" 207 lbs.

Year	Team		Games	Pos.
1975	**STL**	**N**	14	WR
1976			14	WR
1977			14	WR
1978	**NO**	**N**	15	WR
1979			14	WR
1980			16	WR
1981			3	WR

7 yrs.   90 games

Jack Harris
HARRIS, WELTON JOHN
B. Aug. 29, 1902
D. Dec., 1973, Indianapolis, IN
Wisconsin 5'11" 190 lbs.

Year	Team		Games	Pos.
1925	**GB**	**N**	10	FB, HB, E, G
1926			9	E, HB

2 yrs.   19 games

Jackie Harris
HARRIS, JACKIE BERNARD
B. Jan. 4, 1968, Pine Bluff, AR
Northeast Louisiana 6'3" 240 lbs.

Year	Team		Games	Pos.
1990	**GB**	**N**	16	TE
1991			16	TE
1992			16	TE
1993			12	TE
1994	**TB**	**N**	9	TE
1995			16	TE
1996			13	TE

7 yrs.   98 games

Year	Team		Games	Pos.

James Harris
HARRIS, JAMES EDWARD
B. May 3, 1968, East St. Louis, IL
Temple 6'4" 270 lbs.

Year	Team		Games	Pos.
1993	MIN	N	6	DE
1994			16	DE
1995			12	DE
1996	STL	N	15	DE
4 yrs.	49 games			

James Harris
HARRIS, JAMES LARNELL (Shack)
B. Jul. 20, 1947, Monroe, LA
Grambling State 6'3" 215 lbs.

Year	Team		Games	Pos.
1969	BUF	A	4	QB
1970	BUF		7	QB
1971			7	QB
1973	LA		7	QB
1974			11	QB
1975			13	QB
1976			7	QB
1977	SD	N	9	QB
1978			9	QB
1979			8	QB
10 yrs.	82 games			

Jim Harris
HARRIS, JAMES, JR.
B. Feb. 24, 1943, Lake Charles, LA
Utah State 6'4" 275 lbs.

Year	Team		Games	Pos.
1965	NY	A	14	DT
1966			14	DT
1967			14	DT
3 yrs.	42 games			

Jimmy Harris
HARRIS, JAMES
B. Sep. 18, 1946, Brownwood, TX
Howard Payne 5'11" 173 lbs.

Year	Team		Games	Pos.
1970	WAS	N	3	CB

Jimmy Harris
HARRIS, JAMES BEDFORD
B. Nov. 12, 1934, Terrell, TX
Oklahoma 6'1" 178 lbs.

Year	Team		Games	Pos.
1957	PHI	N	12	DB
1958	LA	N	12	DB
1960	DAL	A		DB
1961	DAL	N	11	DB
4 yrs.	35 games			

Joe Harris
HARRIS, JOSEPH ALEXANDER
B. Dec. 6, 1962, Fayetteville, NC
Georgia Tech 6'1" 225 lbs.

Year	Team		Games	Pos.
1977	WAS	N	11	LB
1978	SF	N	16	LB
1979	MIN	N	2	LB
1979	LA	N	13	LB
1980			16	LB
1981			16	LB
1982	BAL	N	9	LB
6 yrs.	83 games			

John Harris
HARRIS, JOHN
B. 1935
Santa Monica CC 6'1" 195 lbs.

Year	Team		Games	Pos.
1960	OAK	A		DB
1961			14	DB
2 yrs.	14 games			

John Harris
HARRIS, JOHN EDWARD
B. Jun. 13, 1956, Fort Benning, GA
Arizona State 6'2" 200 lbs.

Year	Team		Games	Pos.
1978	SEA	N	16	S

John Harris continued

Year	Team		Games	Pos.
1979			14	S
1980			16	S
1981			16	S
1982			9	S
1983			16	S
1984			16	S
1985			16	S
1986	MIN	N	16	S
1987			12	S
1988			13	S
11 yrs.	160 games			

John Harris
HARRIS, JOHN T. (Soldier)
B. 1898, Connecticut
Deceased
None 196 lbs.

Year	Team		Games	Pos.
1926	HAR	N	2	FB

Ken Harris
HARRIS, KENNETH M. (Bunk)
B. Jun., 1894
Deceased
Syracuse/Columbia 6'0" 190 lbs.

Year	Team		Games	Pos.
1923	DUL	N	6	FB

Larry Harris
HARRIS, LARRY E.
B. Aug. 4, 1954, Sherman, TX
Oklahoma State 6'3" 274 lbs.

Year	Team		Games	Pos.
1978	HOU	N		G

Leonard Harris
HARRIS, LEONARD MILTON
B. Nov. 27, 1960, McKinney, TX
Austin/Texas Tech 5'8" 155 lbs.

Year	Team		Games	Pos.
1986	TB	N	6	WR
1987	HOU	N	3	WR
1988			16	WR
1989			11	WR
1990			14	WR
1991			9	WR
1992			14	WR
1993			4	WR
1994	ATL	N	10	WR
9 yrs.	87 games			

Leotis Harris
HARRIS, LEOTIS
B. Jun. 28, 1955, Little Rock, AR
Arkansas 6'1" 269 lbs.

Year	Team		Games	Pos.
1978	GB	N	13	G
1979			15	G
1980			16	G
1981			16	G
1982			9	G
1983			6	G
6 yrs.	75 games			

Leroy Harris
HARRIS, LEROY
B. Jul. 3, 1954, Savannah, GA
Arkansas State 5'9" 225 lbs.

Year	Team		Games	Pos.
1977	MIA	N	11	RB
1978			15	RB
1979	PHI	N	15	FB
1980			15	FB
1982			7	RB
5 yrs.	63 games			

Louis Harris
HARRIS, LOUIS
B. Mar. 25, 1946, Washington, DC
Kent State 6'0" 180 lbs.

Year	Team		Games	Pos.
1968	PIT	N	14	DB

Mark Harris
HARRIS, MARK
B. Apr. 28, 1970, Clovis, NM
Stanford 6'3" 195 lbs.

Year	Team		Games	Pos.
1996	SF	N	1	WR

Marshall Harris
HARRIS, MARSHALL KURT
B. Dec. 6, 1955, San Antonio, TX
Texas Christian 6'6" 261 lbs.

Year	Team		Games	Pos.
1980	CLE	N	16	DE
1981			15	DE
1982			9	DE
1983	NE	N	6	DE
4 yrs.	46 games			

Marv Harris
HARRIS, MARVIN K.
B. Jul. 8, 1942, Coos Bay, OR
Stanford 6'1" 225 lbs.

Year	Team		Games	Pos.
1964	LA	N	14	G

Michael Harris
HARRIS, ANTHONY MICHAEL
B. Aug. 30, 1966, Shreveport, LA
Grambling State 6'4" 306 lbs.

Year	Team		Games	Pos.
1989	KC	N	3	C, G

M.L. Harris
HARRIS, MICHAEL LEE
B. Jan. 16, 1954, Columbus, OH
Tampa/Kansas State 6'5" 238 lbs.

Year	Team		Games	Pos.
1980	CIN	N	12	TE
1981			15	TE
1982			9	TE
1983			12	TE
1984			16	TE
1985			10	TE
6 yrs.	74 games			

Odie Harris
HARRIS, ODIE LAZAR, JR.
B. Apr. 1, 1966, Bryan, TX
Sam Houston State 6'0" 190 lbs.

Year	Team		Games	Pos.
1988	TB	N	16	DB
1989			16	CB, S
1990			16	S
1991	CLE	N	16	DB
1992			4	CB, S
1992	PHX	N	8	S
1993			16	S
1994	ARI	N	13	S
1995	HOU	N	16	CB, S
8 yrs.	121 games			

Paul Harris
HARRIS, PAUL
B. Dec. 19, 1954, Mobile, AL
Alabama 6'3" 220 lbs.

Year	Team		Games	Pos.
1977	TB	N	14	LB
1978	MIN	N	1	LB
1978	TB	N	5	LB
2 yrs.	20 games			

Phil Harris
HARRIS, PHILIP LEON
B. Sep. 13, 1944, Jackson Hole, WY
Texas 6'0" 195 lbs.

Year	Team		Games	Pos.
1966	NYG	N	14	DB

Raymont Harris
HARRIS, RAYMONT LESHAWN
B. Dec. 23, 1970, Lorain, OH
Ohio State 6'1" 225 lbs.

Year	Team		Games	Pos.
1994	CHI	N	16	RB
1995			2	RB

Raymont Harris continued

Year	Team		Games	Pos.
1996			12	RB
3 yrs.	30 games			

Richard Harris
HARRIS, RICHARD DREW
B. Jan. 21, 1948, Shreveport, LA
Grambling State 6'4" 258 lbs.

Year	Team		Games	Pos.
1971	PHI	N	14	DE
1972			14	DE
1973			11	DE
1974	CHI	N	10	DE
1975			12	DE
1976	SEA	N	11	DT
1977			14	DT
7 yrs.	86 games			

Rickie Harris
HARRIS, RICKIE CALVIN
B. May 15, 1943, St. Louis, MO
Arizona 6'0" 182 lbs.

Year	Team		Games	Pos.
1965	WAS	N	14	DB
1966			13	DB
1967			14	DB
1968			14	DB
1969			14	S
1970			14	S
1971	NE	N	14	S
1972			14	S
8 yrs.	111 games			

Robert Harris
HARRIS, ROBERT LEE
B. Jun. 13, 1969, Riviera Beach, FL
Southern University 6'4" 287 lbs.

Year	Team		Games	Pos.
1992	MIN	N	7	DT
1993			16	DE
1994			11	DE
1995	NYG	N	15	DE
1996			16	DE
5 yrs.	65 games			

Rod Harris
HARRIS, RODERICK WORLD
B. Nov. 14, 1966, Dallas, TX
Texas A&M 5'10" 183 lbs.

Year	Team		Games	Pos.
1989	NO	N	11	WR
1990	DAL	N	7	WR
1990	PHI	N	4	WR
1991			16	WR
3 yrs.	38 games			

Ronnie Harris
HARRIS, RONNIE JAMES
B. Jun. 4, 1970, Granada Hills, CA
Oregon 5'10" 170 lbs.

Year	Team		Games	Pos.
1993	NE	N	5	WR
1994			1	WR
1994	SEA	N	1	WR
1995			13	WR
1996			15	WR
4 yrs.	35 games			

Roy Harris
HARRIS, ROY ELLIOTT
B. Mar. 26, 1961, Winter Garden, FL
Florida 6'2" 266 lbs.

Year	Team		Games	Pos.
1984	ATL	N	15	DE
1985			5	DT
1987	TB	N	3	DE
3 yrs.	23 games			

Rudy Harris
HARRIS, ONZELL ANDRE
B. Sep. 18, 1971, Brockton, MA
Clemson 6'1" 255 lbs.

Year	Team		Games	Pos.
1993	TB	N	10	RB

Year	Team	Games	Pos.

Rudy Harris *continued*

Year	Team	Games	Pos.
1994		8	RB
2 yrs.	18 games		

Sean Harris

HARRIS, SEAN EUGENE
B. Feb. 25, 1972, Tucson, AZ
Arizona 6'3" 244 lbs.

1995	CHI N	11	LB
1996		15	LB
2 yrs.	26 games		

Steve Harris

HARRIS, STEVEN
B. Dec. 12, 1962, Chicago, IL
Northern Iowa 5'11" 194 lbs.

1987	MIN N	2	RB

Tim Harris

HARRIS, TIM ALLEN
B. Jun. 15, 1961, Compton, CA
Washington State 5'9" 206 lbs.

1983	PIT N	14	RB

Tim Harris

HARRIS, TIMOTHY DAVID
B. Sep. 10, 1964, Birmingham, AL
Memphis State 6'5" 235 lbs.

1986	GB N	16	LB
1987		12	LB
1988		16	LB
1989		16	LB
1990		16	LB
1991	SF N	11	LB
1992		16	DE
1993	PHI N	4	DE
1994	SF N	5	DE, LB
1995		10	DE
10 yrs.	122 games		

Tony Harris

HARRIS, TONY
B. Apr. 20, 1948, Cleveland, OH
Toledo 6'2" 189 lbs.

1971	SF N	4	RB

Walt Harris

HARRIS, WALTER L.
B. Apr. 1, 1964
Stanford 6'1" 195 lbs.

1987	SD N	3	S

Walt Harris

HARRIS, WALTER LEE
B. Aug. 10, 1974, La Grange, GA
Mississippi State 5'11" 188 lbs.

1996	CHI N	15	CB

Wendell Harris

HARRIS, WENDELL
B. Oct. 2, 1940, Baton Rouge, LA
Louisiana State 5'11" 188 lbs.

1962	BAL N	14	DB
1963		14	DB
1964		14	DB
1965		14	DB
1966	NYG N	13	DB
1967		13	DB
6 yrs.	82 games		

William Harris

HARRIS, WILLIAM MILTON, JR.
B. Feb. 10, 1965, Houston, TX
Texas/Bishop 6'4" 243 lbs.

1987	STL N	10	TE

William Harris *continued*

1989	TB N	16	TE
1990	GB N	4	TE
3 yrs.	30 games		

Anthony Harrison

HARRISON, ANTHONY
B. Sep. 26, 1965
Georgia Tech 6'1" 195 lbs.

1987	GB N	3	S

Bob Harrison

HARRISON, ROBERT
B. Nov. 15, 1938
Ohio University 5'11" 187 lbs.

1961	BAL N	14	DB

Bob Harrison

HARRISON, ROBERT LUCIUS, JR.
B. Aug. 8, 1937, Stamford, TX
Oklahoma 6'2" 233 lbs.

1959	SF N	12	LB
1960		12	LB
1961		14	LB
1962	PHI N	13	LB
1963		9	LB
1964	PIT N	11	LB
1965	SF N	7	LB
1966		14	LB
1967		14	LB
9 yrs.	106 games		

Chris Harrison

HARRISON, CHRISTOPHER ALLEN
B. Feb. 25, 1972, Washington, DC
Virginia 6'3" 290 lbs.

1996	DET N	2	G

Dennis Harrison

HARRISON, DENNIS
B. Jul. 31, 1956, Cleveland, OH
Vanderbilt 6'8" 280 lbs.

1978	PHI N	16	DE
1979		12	DE
1980		15	DE
1981		13	DE
1982		9	DE
1983		16	DE
1984		16	DE
1985	LARM N	12	DE
1986	SF N	5	DE
1986	ATL N	11	TE
1987		11	DE
10 yrs.	136 games		

Dick Harrison

HARRISON, RICHARD
B. Apr. 13, 1916, Buffalo, NY
D. May, 1981, Boston, MA
Boston College 6'0" 195 lbs.

1944	BOS N	4	E

Dwight Harrison

HARRISON, DWIGHT WEBSTER
B. Oct. 12, 1948, Beaumont, TX
Texas A&I-Kingsville 6'1" 183 lbs.

1971	DEN N	10	WR
1972		2	WR
1972	BUF N	5	WR
1973		14	DB
1974		13	CB
1975		13	CB
1976		12	CB
1977		12	CB
1978	BAL N	15	CB

Dwight Harrison *continued*

1979		7	CB
1980	OAK N	2	CB
10 yrs.	105 games		

Ed Harrison

HARRISON, EDWARD
B. Oct. 3, 1902
D. May, 1981, Bronxville, NY
Boston College 6'0" 178 lbs.

1926	BKN A	4	E
1926	BKN N	3	E
1 yr.	7 games		

Glynn Harrison

HARRISON, GLYNN
B. May 25, 1954, Atlanta, GA
Georgia 5'11" 190 lbs.

1976	KC N	8	RB

Gran Harrison

HARRISON, GRANVILLE PEARL
B. Jul. 1, 1917, Ashland, MS
Mississippi State 6'3" 211 lbs.

1942	DET N	4	E

James Harrison

HARRISON, JAMES H.
B. Sep. 10, 1948, San Antonio, TX
Missouri 6'4" 236 lbs.

1971	CHI N	2	RB
1972		14	RB
1973		13	RB
1974		14	RB
4 yrs.	43 games		

Kenny Harrison

HARRISON, KENNETH WAYNE
B. Dec. 12, 1953, Beaumont, TX
Southern Methodist 6'0" 176 lbs.

1976	SF N	11	WR
1977		14	WR
1978		8	WR
1980	WAS N	9	WR
4 yrs.	42 games		

Martin Harrison

HARRISON, MARTIN ALLEN
B. Sep. 20, 1967, Livermore, CA
Washington 6'5" 240 lbs.

1990	SF N	2	LB, DE
1992		16	LB
1993		11	DE
1994	MIN N	13	DE
1995		11	DE
1996		16	DE
6 yrs.	69 games		

Marvin Harrison

HARRISON, MARVIN DANIEL
B. Aug. 25, 1972, Philadelphia, PA
Syracuse 6'0" 188 lbs.

1996	IND N	16	WR

Max Harrison

HARRISON, MAX LAMAR
B. 1916
Auburn 6'1" 208 lbs.

1940	NYG N	8	E

Nolan Harrison

HARRISON, NOLAN
B. Jan. 25, 1969, Chicago, IL
Indiana 6'5" 285 lbs.

1991	LARI N	14	DT

Nolan Harrison *continued*

1992		14	DT
1993		16	DT
1994		16	DE, DT
1995	OAK N	7	DE, DT
1996	CHI N	14	DT
6 yrs.	81 games		

Pat Harrison

HARRISON, PATRICK
B. 1914
Samford 6'2" 215 lbs.

1937	BKN N	3	T

Reggie Harrison

HARRISON, REGINALD
B. Jan. 9, 1951, Somerville, NJ
Cincinnati 5'11" 218 lbs.

1974	STL N	1	RB
1974	PIT N	4	RB
1975		14	RB
1976		12	RB
1977		14	RB
4 yrs.	45 games		

Rob Harrison

HARRISON, ROBERT
B. Aug. 31, 1963, Fortuna, CA
San Diego State/Sacramento State 6'2" 220 lbs.

1987	LARI N	2	CB, S

Rodney Harrison

HARRISON, RODNEY SCOTT
B. Dec. 15, 1972, Markham, IL
Western Illinois 6'0" 201 lbs.

1994	SD N	15	S
1995		11	S
1996		16	S
3 yrs.	42 games		

Todd Harrison

HARRISON, TODD
B. Mar. 20, 1969, Gainesville, FL
North Carolina State 6'4" 260 lbs.

1992	TB N	1	TE

Vic Harrison

HARRISON, VICTOR MACK
B. Feb. 9, 1961, Henderson, NC
North Carolina 5'9" 184 lbs.

1987	NO N	3	WR

Carl Harry

HARRY, CARL
B. Oct. 26, 1967, Fountain Valley, CA
Utah 5'9" 168 lbs.

1989	WAS N	1	WR
1992		1	WR
2 yrs.	2 games		

Emile Harry

HARRY, EMILE MICHAEL
B. Apr. 5, 1963, Los Angeles, CA
Stanford 5'11" 175 lbs.

1986	KC N	12	WR
1988		16	WR
1989		16	WR
1990		16	WR
1991		12	WR
1992		7	WR
1992	LARM N	4	WR
6 yrs.	83 games		

Year	Team	Games	Pos.

Ben Hart
HART, BENJAMIN
B. Aug. 19, 1945, Oklahoma City, OK
Oklahoma 6'2" 205 lbs.

Year	Team		Games	Pos.
1967	NO	N	1	DB

Dick Hart
HART, RICHARD KAY
B. Mar. 14, 1943, Morrisville, PA
none 6'2" 250 lbs.

Year	Team		Games	Pos.
1967	PHI	N	14	G
1968			14	G
1969			14	G
1970			14	G
4 yrs.	56 games			

Douglas Hart
HART, DOUGLAS WAYNE
B. Jun. 6, 1939, Handley, TX
Texas-Arlington 6'0" 190 lbs.

Year	Team		Games	Pos.
1964	GB	N	14	DB
1965			14	DB
1966			14	DB
1967			14	DB
1968			14	DB
1969			14	S
1970			14	S
1971			14	DB
8 yrs.	112 games			

Harold Hart
HART, HAROLD JEROME
B. Jul. 13, 1952, Lake City, FL
Texas Southern 6'0" 207 lbs.

Year	Team		Games	Pos.
1974	OAK	N	13	RB
1975			9	RB
1977	NYG	N	1	RB
1978	OAK	N	7	RB
4 yrs.	30 games			

Jeff Hart
HART, JEFFERY ALLEN
B. Sep. 10, 1953, Portland, OR
Oregon State 6'5" 263 lbs.

Year	Team		Games	Pos.
1975	SF	N	14	OT
1976	NO	N	14	OT
1979	BAL	N	16	OT
1980			16	OT
1981			16	OT
1982			9	OT
1983			14	OT
7 yrs.	99 games			

Jim Hart
HART, JAMES WARREN
B. Apr. 29, 1944, Evanston, IL
Southern Illinois 6'2" 205 lbs.

Year	Team		Games	Pos.
1966	STL	N	1	QB
1967			14	QB
1968			13	QB
1969			9	QB
1970			14	QB
1971			11	QB
1972			6	QB
1973			12	QB
1974			14	QB
1975			14	QB
1976			14	QB
1977			14	QB
1978			15	QB
1979			14	QB
1980			15	QB
1981			10	QB
1982			4	QB
1983			5	QB
1984	WAS	N	2	QB
19 yrs.	201 games			

Leo Hart
HART, LEO
B. Mar. 3, 1949, Kinston, NC
Duke 6'4" 203 lbs.

Year	Team		Games	Pos.
1971	ATL	N	1	QB
1972	BUF	N	2	QB
2 yrs.	3 games			

Leon Hart
HART, LEON JOSEPH
B. Nov. 2, 1928, Turtle Creek, PA
Notre Dame 6'5" 257 lbs.

Year	Team		Games	Pos.
1950	DET	N	12	OE
1951			12	OE
1952			11	OE
1953			12	OE
1954			12	OE
1955			11	OE, FB
1956			11	OE, FB
1957			11	FB, OE
8 yrs.	92 games			

Les Hart
HART, J. LESLIE
B. 1908
Colgate 5'11" 180 lbs.

Year	Team		Games	Pos.
1931	SI	N	5	QB, HB

Pete Hart
HART, PETE
B. 1938
Hardin-Simmons 5'9" 190 lbs.

Year	Team		Games	Pos.
1960	NY	A		FB

Roy Hart
HART, ROY, JR.
B. Jul. 10, 1965, Tifton, GA
South Carolina 6'1" 280 lbs.

Year	Team		Games	Pos.
1989	SEA	N	16	NT
1991	LARI	N	1	DT
2 yrs.	17 games			

Tommy Hart
HART, TOMMY LEE
B. Nov. 7, 1944, Macon, GA
Morris Brown 6'3" 244 lbs.

Year	Team		Games	Pos.
1968	SF	N	5	LB
1969			14	DE
1970			14	DE
1971			14	DE
1972			14	DE
1973			14	DE
1974			14	DE
1975			14	DE
1976			14	DE
1977			14	DE
1978	CHI	N	16	DE
1979			15	DE
1980	NO	N	15	DE
13 yrs.	177 games			

Mike Hartenstine
HARTENSTINE, MICHAEL ALBERT
B. Jul. 27, 1953, Bethlehem, PA
Penn State 6'3" 254 lbs.

Year	Team		Games	Pos.
1975	CHI	N	14	DE
1976			14	DE
1977			14	DE
1978			16	DE
1979			16	DE
1980			16	DE
1981			16	DE
1982			9	DE
1983			16	DE
1984			16	DE
1985			16	DE
1986			16	DE

Mike Hartenstine continued

Year	Team		Games	Pos.
1987	MIN	N	5	DE
12 yrs.	168 games			

Jeff Hartings
HARTINGS, JEFFREY ALLEN
B. Sep. 7, 1972, Henry, OH
Penn State 6'3" 283 lbs.

Year	Team		Games	Pos.
1996	DET	N	11	G

Greg Hartle
HARTLE, GREGORY ALAN
B. Feb. 14, 1951, Savannah, GA
Newberry 6'2" 225 lbs.

Year	Team		Games	Pos.
1974	STL	N	14	LB
1975			13	LB
1976			1	LB
3 yrs.	28 games			

Frank Hartley
HARTLEY, FRANK
B. Dec. 15, 1967, Chicago, IL
Illinois 6'2" 268 lbs.

Year	Team		Games	Pos.
1994	CLE	N	10	TE
1995			15	TE
1996	BAL	N	8	TE
3 yrs.	33 games			

Howard Hartley
HARTLEY, HOWARD PAUL
B. Sep. 26, 1924, Ravenswood, WV
Duke 6'0" 185 lbs.

Year	Team		Games	Pos.
1948	WAS	N	12	HB
1949	PIT	N	12	HB
1950			12	HB
1951			12	HB
1952			9	HB
5 yrs.	57 games			

Ken Hartley
HARTLEY, KENNETH P.
B. Apr. 28, 1957, Bermuda, CO
Catawba 6'2" 200 lbs.

Year	Team		Games	Pos.
1981	NE	N	2	P

Bill Hartman
HARTMAN, WILLIAM C., JR.
B. Mar. 17, 1915, Thomaston, GA
Georgia 6'0" 190 lbs.

Year	Team		Games	Pos.
1938	WAS	N	10	HB, FB

Fred Hartman
HARTMAN, FREDERICK
B. 1920
Deceased
Rice 6'1" 229 lbs.

Year	Team		Games	Pos.
1947	CHIB	N	11	T
1948	PHI	N	12	T
2 yrs.	23 games			

Jim Hartman
HARTMAN, JAMES
B. 1913
Colorado State 6'2" 205 lbs.

Year	Team		Games	Pos.
1936	BKN	N	3	E

Perry Hartnett
HARTNETT, PERRY EDMUND
B. Apr. 28, 1960, Galveston, TX
Southern Methodist 6'5" 275 lbs.

Year	Team		Games	Pos.
1982	CHI	N	9	G
1983			2	G
1987	GB	N	1	G
3 yrs.	12 games			

George Hartong
HARTONG, GEORGE HOWARD
B. Jul. 18, 1896
D. Aug., 1973, Burr Ridge, IL
Chicago 6'0" 210 lbs.

Year	Team		Games	Pos.
1921	HAM	A	3	G
1923	RAC	N	8	G
1924	CHIC	N	10	G, T, C
3 yrs.	21 games			

Larry Hartshorn
HARTSHORN, LARRY L.
B. 1933
Kansas State 6'0" 225 lbs.

Year	Team		Games	Pos.
1955	CHIC	N	2	G

Carter Hartwig
HARTWIG, CARTER
B. Feb. 27, 1956, Culver City, CA
Southern California 6'0" 198 lbs.

Year	Team		Games	Pos.
1979	HOU	N	16	CB, S
1980			15	CB
1981			16	CB
1982			9	CB, S
1983			16	CB, S
1984			14	S
6 yrs.	86 games			

Keith Hartwig
HARTWIG, MALCOLM KEITH
B. Dec. 10, 1953, Corona Del Mar, CA
Arizona 6'0" 186 lbs.

Year	Team		Games	Pos.
1977	GB	N	7	WR

John Harty
HARTY, JOHN DANIEL
B. Dec. 17, 1958, Sioux City, IA
Iowa 6'4" 263 lbs.

Year	Team		Games	Pos.
1981	SF	N	14	DT
1982			9	NT
1983			5	DT
1985			7	NT
1986			7	DE
5 yrs.	42 games			

Howard Hartzog
HARTZOG, HOWARD G. (Bug)
B. Apr. 11, 1901
D. May, 1968, Port Lavaca, TX
Baylor 5'11" 195 lbs.

Year	Team		Games	Pos.
1926	RI	A	9	G, T
1928	NYG	N	13	G, T, C, E
2 yrs.	22 games			

Claude Harvey
HARVEY, CLAUDE
B. Mar. 27, 1948, Willis, TX
Prairie View A&M 6'4" 225 lbs.

Year	Team		Games	Pos.
1970	HOU	N	5	LB

Frank Harvey
HARVEY, FRANK
B. Jan. 19, 1971, Dawson, GA
Georgia 6'0" 245 lbs.

Year	Team		Games	Pos.
1994	ARI	N	2	RB

George Harvey
HARVEY, GEORGE EVERETT
B. Aug. 18, 1945, Topeka, KS
Kansas 6'4" 245 lbs.

Year	Team		Games	Pos.
1967	NO	N	6	G

James Harvey
HARVEY, JAMES M.

Year	Team	Games	Pos.

James Harvey continued
B. Nov. 27, 1965, New Orleans, LA
Jackson State 6'3" 265 lbs.

Year	Team		Games	Pos.
1987	KC	N	3	G
1988			1	G

2 yrs.   4 games

Jim Harvey
HARVEY, JAMES BRITTON, JR.
B. Aug. 20, 1943, Jackson, MS
Mississippi 6'5" 247 lbs.

1966	OAK	A	14	OT
1967			10	OT
1968			14	G
1969			14	G, OT
1970	OAK	N	14	G
1971			12	G

6 yrs.   78 games

John Harvey
HARVEY, JOHN LEWIS
B. Dec. 28, 1966, New York, NY
Texas-El Paso 5'11" 185 lbs.

| 1990 | TB | N | 16 | RB |

Ken Harvey
HARVEY, KENNETH RAY
B. May 6, 1965, Austin, TX
California 6'2" 225 lbs.

1988	PHX	N	16	LB
1989			16	LB
1990			16	LB
1991			16	LB
1992			10	LB
1993			16	LB
1994	WAS	N	16	LB
1995			16	LB
1996			16	LB

9 yrs.   138 games

Marvin Harvey
HARVEY, MARVIN D.
B. Oct. 17, 1959, Donalsonville, GA
Southern Mississippi 6'3" 220 lbs.

| 1981 | KC | N | 7 | TE |

Maurice Harvey
HARVEY, MAURICE
B. Jan. 14, 1956, Cincinnati, OH
Ball State 5'10" 190 lbs.

1978	DEN	N	16	DB
1980			15	CB, S
1981	GB	N	16	S
1982			9	S
1983			4	S
1983	DET	N	9	S
1984	TB	N	15	S
1987	DET	N	2	CB

7 yrs.   86 games

Norm Harvey
HARVEY, NORMAN
B. Aug. 27, 1896
D. Feb., 1963
Detroit 6'0" 196 lbs.

1925	BUF	N	5	T
1926	DET	N	8	T
1927	BUF	N	5	T
1927	NYY	N	9	T
1928	PRO	N	8	E
1929			8	T, C, E, G

5 yrs.   43 games

Richard Harvey
HARVEY, RICHARD
B. Oct. 22, 1945, Gulfport, MS

Richard Harvey continued
Jackson State 6'2" 190 lbs.

| 1970 | PHI | N | 4 | CB |
| 1971 | NO | N | 3 | CB |

2 yrs.   7 games

Richard Harvey
HARVEY, RICHARD CLEMONT
B. Sep. 11, 1966, Pascagoula, MS
Tulane 6'1" 227 lbs.

1990	NE	N	16	LB
1991			1	LB
1992	BUF	N	12	LB
1993			15	LB
1994	DEN	N	16	LB
1995	NO	N	16	LB
1996			14	LB

7 yrs.   90 games

Stacey Harvey
HARVEY, STACEY
B. Mar. 8, 1965, Pasadena, CA
Arizona State 6'4" 245 lbs.

| 1989 | KC | N | 9 | LB |

Waddey Harvey
HARVEY, JAMES WALLACE
B. Mar. 26, 1947, Richmond, VA
Virginia Tech 6'4" 276 lbs.

| 1969 | BUF | A | 13 | DT |
| 1970 | BUF | N | 14 | DT |

2 yrs.   27 games

Allen Harvin
HARVIN, ALLEN NATHANIEL
B. Mar. 18, 1959, Philadelphia, PA
Cincinnati 5'9" 200 lbs.

| 1987 | WAS | N | 1 | RB |

John Hasbrouck
HASBROUCK, JOHN (Ziggy)
B. Jan. 20, 1895
D. May 18, 1945
Rutgers 6'0" 190 lbs.

| 1921 | ROC | A | 1 | FB |
| 1921 | RI | A | 1 | HB |

1 yr.   2 games

Carlton Haselrig
HASELRIG, CARLTON LEE
B. Jan. 22, 1966, Johnstown, PA
Pittsburgh-Johnstown* 6'1" 293 lbs.

1990	PIT	N	16	G
1991			16	G
1992			16	G
1993			9	G
1995	NYJ	N	11	G

5 yrs.   68 games

George Hasenohrl
HASENOHRL, GEORGE
B. Mar. 10, 1951, Cleveland, OH
Ohio State 6'1" 260 lbs.

| 1974 | NYG | N | 5 | DT |

Clint Haslerig
HASLERIG, CLINTON EDWARD
B. Apr. 9, 1952, Cincinnati, OH
Michigan 6'0" 191 lbs.

1974	CHI	N	3	WR
1974	BUF	N	9	RB
1975			3	RB
1975	MIN	N	7	WR
1976	NYJ	N	5	WR, RB

3 yrs.   27 games

Jim Haslett
HASLETT, JAMES DONALD
B. Dec. 9, 1955, Pittsburgh, PA
Indiana (Pennsylvania) 6'3" 234 lbs.

1979	BUF	N	16	LB
1980			16	LB
1981			16	LB
1982			6	LB
1983			5	LB
1984			15	LB
1985			16	LB
1987	NYJ	N	3	LB

8 yrs.   93 games

Wilbert Haslip
HASLIP, WILBERT
B. Dec. 8, 1956, El Centro, CA
Hawaii 5'11" 212 lbs.

| 1979 | KC | N | 5 | RB |

Harald Hasselbach
HASSELBACH, HARALD
B. Sep. 22, 1967, Amsterdam, Holland
Washington 6'6" 280 lbs.

1994	DEN	N	16	DE, DT
1995			16	DE
1996			16	DE

3 yrs.   48 games

Don Hasselbeck
HASSELBECK, DONALD WILLIAM
B. Apr. 1, 1955, Cincinnati, OH
Colorado 6'7" 244 lbs.

1977	NE	N	14	TE
1978			16	TE
1979			16	TE
1980			16	TE
1981			14	TE
1982			9	TE
1983			1	TE
1983	LARI	N	14	TE
1984	MIN	N	16	TE
1985	NYG	N	7	TE

9 yrs.   123 games

Andre Hastings
HASTINGS, ANDRE ORLANDO
B. Nov. 7, 1970, Macon, GA
Georgia 6'0" 188 lbs.

1993	PIT	N	6	WR
1994			16	WR
1995			16	WR
1996			16	WR

4 yrs.   54 games

Charlie Hastings
HASTINGS, CHARLES E. (Sandy)
B. Aug., 1895, Allegheny, PA
Deceased
Pittsburgh 5'8" 178 lbs.

| 1920 | CLE | A | 3 | HB, FB |

George Hastings
HASTINGS, GEORGE
B. Sep. 23, 1905
D. Aug., 1981, Boston, MA
Ohio University 6'2" 190 lbs.

| 1930 | POR | N | 1 | T |
| 1931 | | | 1 | T |

2 yrs.   2 games

James Hasty
HASTY, JAMES EDWARD

James Hasty continued
B. May 23, 1965, Seattle, WA
Central Washington/Washington State 6'0" 200 lbs.

1988	NYJ	N	15	CB
1989			16	CB
1990	NYJ	N	16	CB
1991			16	CB
1992			16	CB
1993			16	CB
1994			16	CB
1995	KC	N	16	CB
1996			15	CB

9 yrs.   142 games

Dale Hatcher
HATCHER, ROGER DALE
B. Apr. 5, 1963, Cheraw, SC
Clemson 6'2" 200 lbs.

1985	LARM	N	16	P
1986			16	P
1987			15	P
1988			7	P
1989			16	P
1991			13	P
1993	MIA	N	16	P

7 yrs.   99 games

Ron Hatcher
HATCHER, RONALD A.
B. Jul. 3, 1939, Pittsburgh, PA
Michigan State 5'11" 215 lbs.

| 1962 | WAS | N | 3 | FB |

Derrick Hatchett
HATCHETT, DERRICK K.
B. Aug. 14, 1958, Bryan, TX
Texas 5'11" 183 lbs.

1980	BAL	N	16	CB
1981			16	CB
1982			9	CB
1983			7	CB
1983	HOU	N	1	CB

4 yrs.   49 games

Russ Hathaway
HATHAWAY, RUSSELL G.
B. Jan. 14, 1896, Terre Haute, IN
D. Aug. 19, 1988, Clay City, IN
Indiana 5'11" 231 lbs.

1920	MUN	A	1	G
1920	DAY	A	2	T
1921			8	T, G
1922	DAY	N	8	T
1922	CAN	N	2	T
1923	DAY	N	8	T
1924			8	T, G
1925	POT	N	12	T
1926			10	T, G
1927	BUF	N	3	T, G

8 yrs.   62 games

Steve Hathaway
HATHAWAY, STEVEN FRANCIS
B. Apr. 26, 1962, Beaver, PA
West Virginia 6'4" 238 lbs.

| 1984 | IND | N | 6 | DE |

Dave Hathcock
HATHCOCK, DAVID GARY
B. Jul. 20, 1943, Memphis, TN
Memphis State 6'0" 193 lbs.

| 1966 | GB | N | 14 | DB |
| 1967 | NYG | N | 6 | DB |

2 yrs.   20 games

Year	Team	Games	Pos.

John Hatley
HATLEY, JOHNNY RAY
B. Mar. 16, 1930, Lometa, TX
Baylor/Sul Ross 6'3" 249 lbs.

Year	Team	Games	Pos.
1953	CHIB	N	10	G
1954	CHIC	N	12	G
1955			12	G
1960	DEN	A		DT
4 yrs.		34 games	

Tim Hauck
HAUCK, TIMOTHY CHARLES
B. Dec. 20, 1966, Butte, MT
Pacific (Oregon)/Montana 5'11" 183 lbs.

Year	Team	Games	Pos.
1990	NE	N	10	S
1991	GB	N	16	S
1992			16	S
1993			13	S
1994			13	S
1995	DEN	N	16	S
1996			16	S
7 yrs.		100 games	

Art Hauser
HAUSER, ARTHUR
B. Jun. 19, 1920, Cincinnati, OH
Xavier (Ohio) 6'0" 237 lbs.

Year	Team	Games	Pos.
1954	LA	N	12	G
1955			12	T
1956			12	T
1957			12	T
1959	CHIC	N	2	G
1959	NYG	N	4	T
1960	BOS	A		DT
1961	DEN	A	14	DT
7 yrs.		68 games	

Earl Hauser
HAUSER, WILLIAM EARL
B. Dec., 1897
Deceased
Miami (Ohio) 6'1" 191 lbs.

Year	Team	Games	Pos.
1920	DAY	A	5	T, E
1921	CIN	A	4	E
2 yrs.		9 games	

Ken Hauser
HAUSER, KENNETH (One Round, Truck)
B. 1899
Deceased
None 6'1" 224 lbs.

Year	Team	Games	Pos.
1927	BUF	N	2	FB
1930	NEW	N	2	FB
2 yrs.		4 games	

Len Hauss
HAUSS, LEONARD MOORE
B. Jul. 11, 1942, Jesup, GA
Georgia 6'2" 234 lbs.

Year	Team	Games	Pos.
1964	WAS	N	14	C
1965			14	C
1966			14	C
1967			14	C
1968			14	C
1969			14	C
1970			14	C
1971			14	C
1972			14	C
1973			14	C
1974			14	C
1975			14	C
1976			14	C
1977			14	C
14 yrs.		196 games	

Charlie Havens
HAVENS, CHARLES
B. Jul. 12, 1906
D. Mar., 1981, Macclenny, FL
Western Maryland 5'10" 205 lbs.

Year	Team	Games	Pos.
1930	FRA	N	13	C

Dave Haverdick
HAVERDICK, DAVID GEORGE
B. Jan. 19, 1948, Canton, OH
Morehead State 6'4" 245 lbs.

Year	Team	Games	Pos.
1970	DET	N	8	DE

Kevin Haverdink
HAVERDINK, KEVIN DEAN
B. Oct. 20, 1965, Holland, MI
Western Michigan 6'5" 285 lbs.

Year	Team	Games	Pos.
1989	NO	N	16	OT
1990			15	OT
1991			10	OT
3 yrs.		41 games	

Dennis Havig
HAVIG, DENNIS EUGENE
B. May 6, 1949, Powell, WY
Colorado 6'2" 253 lbs.

Year	Team	Games	Pos.
1972	ATL	N	14	G
1973			14	G
1974			14	G
1975			14	G
1976	HOU	N	14	G
1977	GB	N	9	G
6 yrs.		79 games	

Sam Havrilak
HAVRILAK, SAMUEL CHARLES
B. Dec. 13, 1947, Monessen, PA
Bucknell 6'2" 195 lbs.

Year	Team	Games	Pos.
1969	BAL	N	14	RB
1970			13	RB
1971			14	WR
1972			14	WR
1973			14	WR
1974	NO	N	6	WR
6 yrs.		75 games	

Alex Hawkins
HAWKINS, CHILTON ALEXANDER (The Hawk)
B. Jul. 2, 1937, Welch, WV
South Carolina 6'1" 188 lbs.

Year	Team	Games	Pos.
1959	BAL	N	11	HB
1960			12	HB
1961			11	HB
1962			13	HB
1963			14	HB
1964			14	OE, HB
1965			14	OE
1966	ATL	N	12	FL
1967			3	OE, FL
1967	BAL	N	14	OE
1968			10	OE, FL
10 yrs.		128 games	

Andy Hawkins
HAWKINS, ANTHONY JAMES
B. Mar. 31, 1958, Bay City, TX
Texas A&I-Kingsville 6'2" 225 lbs.

Year	Team	Games	Pos.
1980	TB	N	16	LB
1981			16	LB
1982			9	LB
1983			6	LB
1986	SD	N	10	LB
1987			2	LB
1988	KC	N	7	LB
7 yrs.		66 games	

Ben Hawkins
HAWKINS, BENJAMIN CHARLES
B. Mar. 22, 1944, Newark, NJ
Arizona State 6'0" 180 lbs.

Year	Team	Games	Pos.
1966	PHI	N	14	FL
1967			14	FL, OE
1968			14	FL, OE
1969			14	WR
1970			14	WR
1971			14	WR
1972			14	WR
1973			4	WR
1974	CLE	N	2	WR
9 yrs.		104 games	

Bill Hawkins
HAWKINS, BILL
B. May 9, 1966, Miami, FL
Miami (Florida) 6'6" 268 lbs.

Year	Team	Games	Pos.
1989	LARM	N	13	DT
1990			15	DT
1991			6	DT
1992			8	DE
4 yrs.		42 games	

Clarence Hawkins
HAWKINS, CLARENCE L.
B. Jul. 15, 1956, Newport News, VA
Florida A&M 6'0" 205 lbs.

Year	Team	Games	Pos.
1979	OAK	N	7	RB

Courtney Hawkins
HAWKINS, COURTNEY TYRONE, JR.
B. Dec. 12, 1969, Flint, MI
Michigan State 5'9" 180 lbs.

Year	Team	Games	Pos.
1992	TB	N	16	WR
1993			16	WR
1994			13	WR
1995			16	WR
1996			16	WR
5 yrs.		77 games	

Frank Hawkins
HAWKINS, FRANK
B. Jul. 3, 1959, Las Vegas, NV
Nevada-Reno 5'9" 210 lbs.

Year	Team	Games	Pos.
1981	OAK	N	13	RB
1982	LARI	N	9	RB
1983			16	RB
1984			16	RB
1985			16	RB
1986			16	RB
6 yrs.		86 games	

Garland Hawkins
HAWKINS, GARLAND ANTHONY
B. Feb. 19, 1970, Washington, DC
Syracuse 6'3" 253 lbs.

Year	Team	Games	Pos.
1995	CHI	N	1	DE

Mike Hawkins
HAWKINS, MICHAEL DOUGLAS
B. Nov. 29, 1955, Bay City, TX
Texas A&I-Kingsville 6'3" 240 lbs.

Year	Team	Games	Pos.
1978	NE	N	12	LB
1979			16	LB
1980			16	LB
1981			8	LB
1982	LARI	N	3	LB
5 yrs.		55 games	

Nate Hawkins
HAWKINS, NATHANIEL ALFRED
B. Feb. 8, 1950, Houston, TX

Nate Hawkins continued
Nevada-Las Vegas 6'1" 190 lbs.

Year	Team	Games	Pos.
1975	HOU	N	11	WR

Rip Hawkins
HAWKINS, ROSS COOPER
B. Apr. 21, 1939, Winchester, TN
North Carolina 6'3" 231 lbs.

Year	Team	Games	Pos.
1961	MIN	N	14	LB
1962			14	LB
1963			14	LB
1964			14	LB
1965			14	LB
5 yrs.		70 games	

Steve Hawkins
HAWKINS, STEVE
B. Mar. 16, 1971, Detroit, MI
Western Michigan 6'5" 207 lbs.

Year	Team	Games	Pos.
1994	NE	N	7	WR

Wayne Hawkins
HAWKINS, WAYNE ALLEN
B. Jun. 17, 1938, Fort Peck, MT
Pacific 6'0" 239 lbs.

Year	Team	Games	Pos.
1960	OAK	A	14	G
1961			14	G
1962			14	G
1963			14	G
1964			14	G
1965			14	G
1966			14	G
1967			14	G
1968			10	G
1969			14	G
10 yrs.		136 games	

Steve Haworth
HAWORTH, STEVE
B. Sep. 16, 1961, Manila, Philippines
Oklahoma 5'11" 190 lbs.

Year	Team	Games	Pos.
1983	ATL	N	11	CB
1984			5	CB
2 yrs.		16 games	

Kurt Haws
HAWS, KURT
B. Sep. 25, 1969, Mesa, AZ
Utah 6'5" 248 lbs.

Year	Team	Games	Pos.
1994	WAS	N	6	TE

Les Haws
HAWS, HARVEY LESTER
B. 1900
D. Jan. 20, 1966
Dartmouth 5'8" 165 lbs.

Year	Team	Games	Pos.
1924	FRA	N	13	QB
1925			13	QB, HB, FB
2 yrs.		26 games	

Ed Hawthorne
HAWTHORNE, ED
B. Jul. 30, 1970, St. Louis, MO
Minnesota 6'1" 305 lbs.

Year	Team	Games	Pos.
1995	MIA	N	1	WR

Greg Hawthorne
HAWTHORNE, GREGORY DALE
B. Sep. 5, 1956, Fort Worth, TX
Baylor 6'2" 230 lbs.

Year	Team	Games	Pos.
1979	PIT	N	15	RB
1980			15	RB
1981			10	RB
1982			9	RB
1983			10	RB

Year	Team	Games	Pos.

Greg Hawthorne *continued*

Year	Team	Games	Pos.
1984	**NE** N	14	WR
1985		15	WR, RB
1986		14	TE
1987	**IND** N	3	TE
9 yrs.	105 games		

Ken Haycraft
HAYCRAFT, KENNETH C.
B. Feb. 16, 1907, Bemidji, MN
Minnesota 6'0" 178 lbs.

1929	**MIN** N	9	E
1930		5	E
2 yrs.	14 games		

Aaron Hayden
HAYDEN, AARON CHAUTEZZ
B. Apr. 13, 1973, Detroit, MI
Tennessee 6'0" 218 lbs.

1995	**SD** N	7	RB
1996		11	RB
2 yrs.	18 games		

Ken Hayden
HAYDEN, KENNETH
B. Oct. 21, 1919, Hamburg, AR
Arkansas 6'0" 205 lbs.

1942	**PHI** N	9	C, G
1943	**WAS** N	7	C
2 yrs.	16 games		

Leo Hayden
HAYDEN, LEOPHUS, JR.
B. Jun. 2, 1948, Louisville, KY
Ohio State 6'0" 211 lbs.

1971	**MIN** N	7	RB
1972	**STL** N	4	RB
1973		2	RB
3 yrs.	13 games		

Henry Hayduk
HAYDUK, HENRY HAROLD
(Duke)
B. Sep. 26, 1913
D. Jun., 1969
Washington State 6'0" 200 lbs.

1935	**BKN** N	1	G
1935	**PIT** N	8	G
1 yr.	9 games		

Hayes
HAYES
None

| 1924 | **ROC** N | 1 | G |

Billie Hayes
HAYES, BILLIE
B. Jun. 22, 1947, Riverside, CA
San Diego State 6'1" 175 lbs.

| 1972 | **NO** N | 14 | CB |

Bob Hayes
HAYES, ROBERT LEE (Bullet Bob)
B. Dec. 20, 1942, Jacksonville, FL
Florida A&M 6'0" 187 lbs.

1965	**DAL** N	13	FL
1966		14	OE
1967		13	OE
1968		14	OE
1969		10	WR
1970		13	WR
1971		14	WR
1972		12	WR
1973		13	WR
1974		12	WR
10 yrs.	128 games		

Brandon Hayes
HAYES, WILLIAM BRANDON
B. Mar. 11, 1973, Muncie, IN
Central State (Ohio) 6'4" 308 lbs.

| 1996 | **CAR** N | 6 | G |

Chris Hayes
HAYES, CHRIS
B. May 7, 1972, San Bernardino, CA
Washington State 5'11" 191 lbs.

| 1996 | **GB** N | 2 | S |

Dave Hayes
HAYES, DAVID (Butts)
B. 1897
Deceased
Notre Dame 5'8" 165 lbs.

1921	**RI** A	2	E
1921	**GB** A	6	E
1922	**GB** N	7	E
2 yrs.	15 games		

Ed Hayes
HAYES, EDWARD ROGERS
B. Aug. 14, 1947, Jacksonville, FL
Morgan State 6'1" 185 lbs.

| 1970 | **PHI** N | 4 | S |

Eric Hayes
HAYES, ERIC
B. Nov. 12, 1967, Tampa, FL
Florida State 6'3" 292 lbs.

1990	**SEA** N	16	NT
1991		5	DT
1992	**LARM** N	1	DT
1993	**TB** N	2	DE, NT
4 yrs.	24 games		

Gary Hayes
HAYES, GARY L.
B. Aug. 19, 1957, Tucson, AZ
Fresno State 5'10" 180 lbs.

1984	**GB** N	16	CB, S
1985		16	CB
1986		10	CB, S
3 yrs.	42 games		

Jarius Hayes
HAYES, JARIUS
B. Mar. 27, 1973, Sheffield, AL
North Alabama 6'3" 255 lbs.

| 1996 | **ARI** N | 4 | TE |

Jeff Hayes
HAYES, JEFFREY
B. Aug. 19, 1959, Elkin, NC
North Carolina 5'11" 175 lbs.

1982	**WAS** N	9	P
1983		16	P
1984		16	P
1985		4	P
1986	**CIN** N	16	P
1987	**MIA** N	2	P
6 yrs.	63 games		

Jim Hayes
HAYES, JAMES WILLIAM
B. Nov. 26, 1940, Meridian, MS
Jackson State 6'4" 263 lbs.

1965	**HOU** A	14	DT
1966		14	DT
2 yrs.	28 games		

Joe Hayes
HAYES, JOSEPH
B. Sep. 15, 1960, Dallas, TX
Texas A&I-Kingsville 5'9" 185 lbs.

| 1984 | **PHI** N | 12 | WR |

Jonathan Hayes
HAYES, JONATHAN MICHAEL
B. Aug. 11, 1962, South Fayette, PA
Iowa 6'5" 240 lbs.

1985	**KC** N	16	TE
1986		16	TE
1987		12	TE
1988		16	TE
1989		16	TE
1990		12	TE
1991		16	TE
1992		16	TE
1993		16	TE
1994	**PIT** N	16	TE
1995		16	TE
1996		16	TE
12 yrs.	184 games		

Larry Hayes
HAYES, LARRY GENE
B. Jul. 21, 1935, Nashville, TN
Vanderbilt 6'3" 230 lbs.

1961	**NYG** N	14	LB
1962	**LA** N	9	C, LB
1963		9	C
3 yrs.	32 games		

Lester Hayes
HAYES, LESTER (The Molester)
B. Jan. 22, 1955, Houston, TX
Texas A&M 6'0" 200 lbs.

1977	**OAK** N	14	CB
1978		16	CB
1979		16	CB
1980		16	CB
1981		16	CB
1982	**LARI** N	9	CB
1983		16	CB
1984		16	CB
1985		16	CB
1986		14	CB
10 yrs.	149 games		

Luther Hayes
HAYES, LUTHER
B. 1939, San Diego, CA
Southern California 6'4" 200 lbs.

| 1961 | **SD** A | 14 | OE |

Melvin Hayes
HAYES, MELVIN ANTHONY
B. Apr. 28, 1973, New Orleans, LA
Mississippi State 6'6" 329 lbs.

1995	**NYJ** N	3	OT
1996		2	OT
2 yrs.	5 games		

Mercury Hayes
HAYES, MERCURY
B. Jan. 1, 1973, Houston, TX
Michigan 5'11" 195 lbs.

| 1996 | **NO** N | 7 | WR |

Norb Hayes
HAYES, NORBERT P. (Bud)
B. Nov. 21, 1896, Kaukauna, WI
Deceased
Marquette 5'11" 175 lbs.

1922	**RAC** N	11	E, FB
1923	**GB** N	6	E
2 yrs.	17 games		

Ray Hayes
HAYES, RAYMOND
B. Feb. 25, 1935, Pawhuska, OK
*Maryland State/Central Oklahoma 6'3"
235 lbs.*

| 1961 | **MIN** N | 13 | FB |

Ray Hayes
HAYES, RAYMOND ROY
B. Sep. 5, 1946, Hazel Park, MI
Toledo 6'5" 248 lbs.

| 1968 | **NY** A | 6 | DT |

Rudy Hayes
HAYES, RUDY
B. Jan. 12, 1935
Clemson 6'0" 217 lbs.

1959	**PIT** N	12	LB
1960		12	LB
1962		4	LB
3 yrs.	28 games		

Tom Hayes
HAYES, THOMAS, JR.
B. Apr. 18, 1946, Riverside, CA
San Diego State 6'1" 197 lbs.

1971	**ATL** N	14	CB, S
1972		14	CB
1973		14	CB
1974		13	CB
1975		14	CB
1976	**SD** N	9	CB
6 yrs.	78 games		

Wendell Hayes
HAYES, WENDELL
B. Aug. 5, 1940, Dallas, TX
Humboldt State 6'2" 215 lbs.

1963	**DAL** N	1	HB
1965	**DEN** A	14	HB
1966		11	HB
1967		14	RB
1968	**KC** A	11	RB
1969		14	RB
1970	**KC** N	14	RB
1971		14	RB
1972		13	RB
1973		13	RB
1974		14	RB
11 yrs.	133 games		

Bill Hayhoe
HAYHOE, WILLIAM, II
B. Sep. 6, 1946, Los Angeles, CA
Southern California 6'8" 258 lbs.

1969	**GB** N	14	OT
1970		14	OT
1971		14	OT
1972		14	OT
1973		6	OT
5 yrs.	62 games		

Conway Hayman
HAYMAN, CONWAY
B. Jan. 9, 1949, Newark, DE
Delaware 6'3" 264 lbs.

1975	**HOU** N	14	G
1976		14	G
1977		13	G
1978		16	OT, G
1979		16	OT, G
1980		5	OT
6 yrs.	78 games		

Gary Hayman
HAYMAN, GARY

Gary Hayman continued

B. Sep. 8, 1951, Newark, DE
Penn State 6'1" 200 lbs.

Year	Team		Games	Pos.
1975	BUF	N	14	RB

Alvin Haymond

HAYMOND, ALVIN HENRY
B. Aug. 31, 1942, New Orleans, LA
Southern University 6'0" 193 lbs.

Year	Team		Games	Pos.
1964	BAL	N	9	DB
1965			14	DB
1966			14	DB
1967			8	DB
1968	PHI	N	11	DB
1969	LA	N	14	S
1970			14	S, CB
1971			10	S, CB
1972	WAS	N	4	S, CB
1973	HOU	N	6	S

10 yrs. 104 games

Abner Haynes

HAYNES, ABNER
B. Sep. 19, 1937, Denton, TX
North Texas State 6'0" 188 lbs.

Year	Team		Games	Pos.
1960	DAL	A	14	HB
1961			14	HB
1962			14	HB
1963	KC	A	14	HB
1965	DEN	A	14	HB
1966			14	HB
1967	MIA	A	11	RB
1967	NY	A	14	RB

7 yrs. 109 games

Hall Haynes

HAYNES, HALL
B. Oct. 3, 1928, Duncan, OK
Deceased
Santa Clara 6'0" 187 lbs.

Year	Team		Games	Pos.
1950	WAS	N	12	HB
1953			8	HB
1954	LA	N	11	HB
1955			7	HB

4 yrs. 38 games

James Haynes

HAYNES, JAMES
B. Aug. 9, 1960, Tallulah, LA
Mississippi Valley State 6'2" 232 lbs.

Year	Team		Games	Pos.
1984	NO	N	10	LB
1985			16	LB
1986			16	LB
1987			12	LB
1988			4	LB
1989			3	LB

6 yrs. 61 games

Joe Haynes

HAYNES, JOSEPH
B. Mar. 26, 1921, Barnsdall, OK
Tulsa 6'3" 225 lbs.

Year	Team		Games	Pos.
1947	BUF	AA	9	C, G

Louis Haynes

HAYNES, LOUIS JULES
B. Jan. 17, 1960, New Orleans, LA
Bishop/North Texas State 6'0" 227 lbs.

Year	Team		Games	Pos.
1982	KC	N	6	LB
1983			5	LB

2 yrs. 11 games

Mark Haynes

HAYNES, MARK
B. Nov. 6, 1958, Kansas City, KS
Colorado 5'11" 190 lbs.

Year	Team		Games	Pos.
1980	NYG	N	15	CB

Mark Haynes continued

Year	Team		Games	Pos.
1981			16	CB
1982			9	CB
1983			15	CB
1984			15	CB
1985			5	CB
1986	DEN	N	11	CB
1987			12	CB
1988			15	CB
1989			14	CB

10 yrs. 127 games

Michael Haynes

HAYNES, MICHAEL DAVID
B. Dec. 24, 1965, New Orleans, LA
Northern Arizona 6'0" 180 lbs.

Year	Team		Games	Pos.
1988	ATL	N	15	WR
1989			13	WR
1990			13	WR
1991			16	WR
1992			14	WR
1993			16	WR
1994	NO	N	16	WR
1995			16	WR
1996			16	WR

9 yrs. 135 games

Mike Haynes

HAYNES, MICHAEL JAMES
B. Jul. 1, 1953, Denison, TX
Arizona State 6'2" 190 lbs.

Year	Team		Games	Pos.
1976	NE	N	14	CB
1977			14	CB
1978			16	CB
1979			16	CB
1980			13	CB
1981			16	CB
1982			9	CB
1983	LARI	N	5	CB
1984			16	CB
1985			16	CB
1986			13	CB
1987			8	CB
1988			16	CB
1989			13	CB

14 yrs. 185 games

Reggie Haynes

HAYNES, REGINALD EUGENE
B. Sep. 15, 1954, Denison, TX
Nevada-Las Vegas 6'2" 229 lbs.

Year	Team		Games	Pos.
1978	WAS	N	14	TE

Tommy Haynes

HAYNES, THOMAS W., JR.
B. Feb. 6, 1963, Chicago, IL
Southern California 6'0" 190 lbs.

Year	Team		Games	Pos.
1987	DAL	N	3	S

George Hays

HAYS, GEORGE
B. Aug. 29, 1924
D. 1988
St. Bonaventure 6'2" 211 lbs.

Year	Team		Games	Pos.
1950	PIT	N	12	E
1951			12	E
1952			11	E
1953	GB	N	9	E

4 yrs. 44 games

Harold Hays

HAYS, LEO HAROLD
B. Aug. 24, 1939, Gulfport, MS
Southern Mississippi 6'3" 227 lbs.

Year	Team		Games	Pos.
1963	DAL	N	14	LB
1964			14	LB
1965			14	LB
1966			14	LB

Harold Hays continued

Year	Team		Games	Pos.
1967			14	LB
1968	SF	N	14	LB
1969			12	LB

7 yrs. 96 games

Alfred Haywood

HAYWOOD, ALFRED
B. Aug. 6, 1948, Jacksonville, FL
Bethune-Cookman 5'11" 215 lbs.

Year	Team		Games	Pos.
1975	DEN	N	2	RB

Tracy Hayworth

HAYWORTH, TRACY KEITH
B. Dec. 18, 1967, Winchester, TN
Tennessee 6'3" 257 lbs.

Year	Team		Games	Pos.
1990	DET	N	16	LB
1991			16	LB
1992			4	LB
1993			11	LB
1994			9	LB
1995			16	LB

6 yrs. 72 games

Bob Hazelhurst

HAZELHURST, ROBERT GERALD
B. Jul. 21, 1924, Denver, CO
D. Nov. 11, 1988, Denver, CO
Denver 6'0" 188 lbs.

Year	Team		Games	Pos.
1948	BOS	N	12	HB, DB

Matt Hazeltine

HAZELTINE, MATTHEW EMORY, JR.
B. Aug. 2, 1933, San Francisco, CA
D. Jan. 13, 1987, San Francisco, CA
California 6'1" 220 lbs.

Year	Team		Games	Pos.
1955	SF	N	12	LB
1956			12	LB
1957			12	LB
1958			12	LB
1959			12	LB
1960			12	LB
1961			14	LB
1962			14	LB
1963			13	LB
1964			14	LB
1965			8	LB
1966			14	LB
1967			13	LB
1968			14	LB
1970	NYG	N	14	LB

15 yrs. 190 games

Major Hazelton

HAZELTON, MAJOR
B. Sep. 9, 1944, Bartow, FL
Florida A&M 6'1" 185 lbs.

Year	Team		Games	Pos.
1968	CHI	N	14	DB
1969			9	CB
1970	NO	N	3	CB

3 yrs. 26 games

Ted Hazelwood

HAZELWOOD, THEODORE E.
B. Apr. 25, 1924, Silverwood, IN
North Carolina 6'1" 235 lbs.

Year	Team		Games	Pos.
1949	CHI	AA	9	T
1953	WAS	N	6	T

2 yrs. 15 games

Andy Headen

HEADEN, ANDREW ROOSEVELT
B. Jul. 8, 1960, Asheboro, NC
Clemson 6'5" 240 lbs.

Year	Team		Games	Pos.
1983	NYG	N	16	LB
1984			11	LB

Andy Headen continued

Year	Team		Games	Pos.
1985			16	LB
1986			15	LB
1987			12	LB
1988			4	LB

6 yrs. 74 games

Sherrill Headrick

HEADRICK, SHERRILL DARLON
B. Mar. 13, 1937, Waco, TX
Texas Christian 6'2" 223 lbs.

Year	Team		Games	Pos.
1960	DAL	A	14	LB
1961			14	LB
1962			14	LB
1963	KC	A	14	LB
1964			14	LB
1965			14	LB
1966			14	LB
1967			11	LB
1968	CIN	A	8	LB

9 yrs. 117 games

Ed Healey

HEALEY, EDWARD FRANCIS, JR.
B. Dec. 28, 1894, Indian Orchard, MA
D. Dec. 10, 1978, Durham, NC
Dartmouth 6'1" 207 lbs.

Year	Team		Games	Pos.
1920	RI	A	6	G, T
1921			7	T, G, E
1922	RI	N	7	T
1922	CHIB	N	3	G, T
1923			12	T, G
1924			11	T
1925			15	T
1926			15	T, E
1927			11	T

8 yrs. 87 games

Chip Healy

HEALY, WILLIAM RAYMOND, JR.
B. Aug. 16, 1947, Atlanta, GA
Vanderbilt 6'3" 233 lbs.

Year	Team		Games	Pos.
1969	STL	N	14	LB
1970			14	LB

2 yrs. 28 games

Don Healy

HEALY, MICHAEL DONALD
B. Aug. 28, 1936, Rome, NY
Maryland 6'3" 259 lbs.

Year	Team		Games	Pos.
1958	CHIB	N	12	G
1959			12	G
1960	DAL	N	12	DT
1961			14	DT
1962	BUF	A	1	DT

5 yrs. 51 games

Joe Heap

HEAP, JOSEPH LAWRENCE
B. Oct. 26, 1931, New Orleans, LA
Notre Dame 5'11" 185 lbs.

Year	Team		Games	Pos.
1955	NYG	N	12	HB

Walt Heap

HEAP, WALTER RICHMOND, JR.
B. Sep. 18, 1921, Taylor, TX
D. May 20, 1989
Texas 6'1" 210 lbs.

Year	Team		Games	Pos.
1947	LA	AA	13	HB, DB
1948			14	HB, DB

2 yrs. 27 games

Herman Heard

HEARD, HERMAN WILLIE, JR.
B. Nov. 24, 1961, Denver, CO
Fort Lewis/Southern Colorado 5'10" 190 lbs.

Year	Team		Games	Pos.
1984	KC	N	16	RB

Year	Team	Games	Pos.

Herman Heard continued

Year	Team		Games	Pos.
1985			16	RB
1986			15	RB
1987			12	RB
1988			12	RB
1989			16	RB
6 yrs.		87 games		

Les Hearden
HEARDEN, LEONARD
B. Apr. 24, 1902
D. Dec. 25, 1978, Green Bay, WI
Marquette/St. Ambrose 5'8" 175 lbs.

1924	GB	N	2	HB

Tom Hearden
HEARDEN, THOMAS F. (Red)
B. Sep. 8, 1904, Green Bay, WI
D. Dec. 27, 1964
Notre Dame 6'5" 178 lbs.

1927	GB	N	4	HB
1928			3	HB
1929	CHIB	N	1	HB
3 yrs.		8 games		

Garrison Hearst
HEARST, GERALD GARRISON
B. Jan. 4, 1971, Lincolnton, GA
Georgia 5'11" 215 lbs.

1993	PHX	N	6	RB
1994	ARI	N	9	RB
1995			16	RB
1996	CIN	N	16	RB
4 yrs.		47 games		

Don Heater
HEATER, DONALD PERRY
B. Jun. 22, 1950, Helena, MT
Montana State 6'2" 205 lbs.

1972	STL	N	2	RB

Larry Heater
HEATER, LARRY
B. Jan. 9, 1958, Cincinnati, OH
Arizona 5'11" 205 lbs.

1980	NYG	N	14	RB
1982			9	RB
1983			6	RB
3 yrs.		29 games		

Red Heater
HEATER, WILLIAM A.
B. 1919
Syracuse 6'2" 220 lbs.

1940	BKN	N	8	T

Clayton Heath
HEATH, CLAYTON
B. Feb. 15, 1951, Chester County, SC
Wake Forest 5'11" 195 lbs.

1976	BUF	N	2	RB
1976	MIA	N	6	RB
1 yr.		8 games		

JoJo Heath
HEATH, JOSEPH LEROY
B. Mar. 9, 1957, Monessen, PA
Pittsburgh 5'10" 182 lbs.

1980	CIN	N	10	CB
1981	PHI	N	15	CB
1987	NYJ	N	2	CB, S
3 yrs.		27 games		

Leon Heath
HEATH, HERMAN LEON (Mule Train)

Leon Heath continued
B. Oct. 27, 1928, Hollis, OK
Oklahoma 6'1" 203 lbs.

1951	WAS	N	11	FB
1952			10	FB
1953			9	FB
3 yrs.		30 games		

Stan Heath
HEATH, STANLEY R.
B. Mar. 5, 1927, Toledo, OH
Wisconsin/Nevada-Reno 6'1" 190 lbs.

1949	GB	N	12	QB

Bobby Hebert
HEBERT, BOBBY JOSEPH, JR.
B. Aug. 19, 1960, Baton Rouge, LA
Northwestern State (Louisiana) 6'4" 215 lbs.

1985	NO	N	6	QB
1986			5	QB
1987			12	QB
1988			16	QB
1989			14	QB
1991			9	QB
1992			16	QB
1993	ATL	N	14	QB
1994			10	QB
1995			4	QB
1996			14	QB
11 yrs.		120 games		

Bud Hebert
HEBERT, DARRYL
B. Oct. 12, 1956, Beaumont, TX
Oklahoma 6'0" 190 lbs.

1980	NYG	N	10	S

Ken Hebert
HEBERT, KENNETH
B. Sep. 9, 1944, San Bernardino, CA
Houston 6'0" 200 lbs.

1968	PIT	N	3	OE

Vaughn Hebron
HEBRON, VAUGHN
B. Oct. 7, 1970, Baltimore, MD
Virginia Tech 5'8" 196 lbs.

1993	PHI	N	16	RB
1994			16	RB
1996	DEN	N	16	RB
3 yrs.		48 games		

George Hecht
HECHT, GEORGE (Al)
B. 1922
Alabama 6'0" 235 lbs.

1947	CHI	AA	10	G

Andy Heck
HECK, ANDREW ROBERT
B. Jan., 1967, Fargo, ND
Notre Dame 6'6" 296 lbs.

1989	SEA	N	16	OT
1990			16	OT
1991			16	OT
1992			13	OT
1993			16	OT
1994	CHI	N	14	OT
1995			16	OT
1996			16	OT
8 yrs.		123 games		

Bob Heck
HECK, ROBERT ELGIN
B. Jun. 17, 1925, South Bend, IN

Bob Heck continued
Purdue 6'3" 207 lbs.

1949	CHI	AA	4	E

Ralph Heck
HECK, RALPH ADAM
B. Nov. 6, 1941, Pittsburgh, PA
Colorado 6'2" 228 lbs.

1963	PHI	N	14	LB
1964			14	LB
1965			12	LB
1966	ATL	N	14	LB
1967			14	LB
1968			13	LB
1969	NYG	N	14	LB
1970			14	LB
1971			11	LB
9 yrs.		120 games		

Steve Heckard
HECKARD, ROBERT STEPHEN
B. Apr. 12, 1943, Winston-Salem, NC
Southern California/Davidson 6'1" 195 lbs.

1965	LA	N	13	OE
1966			12	OE
2 yrs.		25 games		

Norb Hecker
HECKER, NORBERT EARL
B. May 26, 1927, Berea, OH
Baldwin-Wallace 6'2" 193 lbs.

1951	LA	N	10	E, DB
1952			10	E, DB
1953			12	E, DB
1955	WAS	N	12	DB
1956			12	DB
1957			8	DB
6 yrs.		64 games		

Johnny Hector
HECTOR, JOHNNY LYNDELL
B. Nov. 26, 1960, Lafayette, LA
Texas A&M 5'11" 200 lbs.

1983	NYJ	N	10	RB
1984			13	RB
1985			14	RB
1986			13	RB
1987			11	RB
1988			16	RB
1989			15	RB
1990			15	RB
1991			14	RB
1992			5	RB
10 yrs.		126 games		

Willie Hector
HECTOR, WILLIE
B. Dec. 23, 1939, New Iberia, LA
Pacific 6'2" 220 lbs.

1961	LA	N	12	G

Randy Hedberg
HEDBERG, RANDY R.
B. Dec. 27, 1954, Parshall, ND
Minot State 6'3" 200 lbs.

1977	TB	N	7	QB

Pat Heenan
HEENAN, PATRICK DENNIS
B. Mar. 1, 1938, Detroit, MI
Notre Dame 6'1" 190 lbs.

1960	WAS	N	11	HB

Gene Heeter
HEETER, EUGENE

Gene Heeter continued
B. Apr. 19, 1941
West Virginia 6'4" 235 lbs.

1963	NY	A	9	OE
1964			14	OE
1965			2	OE
3 yrs.		25 games		

Dave Heffernan
HEFFERNAN, DAVID
B. Oct. 28, 1962, Boston, MA
Miami (Florida) 6'4" 255 lbs.

1987	TB	N	2	OT

Victor Heflin
HEFLIN, VICTOR
B. Jul. 7, 1960, Springfield, MA
Delaware State 6'0" 184 lbs.

1983	STL	N	8	CB
1984			16	CB
2 yrs.		24 games		

Vince Heflin
HEFLIN, VINCENT GEORGE
B. Jul. 7, 1959, Dayton, OH
Central State (Ohio) 6'0" 185 lbs.

1982	MIA	N	6	WR
1983			14	WR
1984			16	WR
1985			5	WR
1986	TB	N	6	WR
5 yrs.		47 games		

Larry Hefner
HEFNER, LARRY DOUGLAS
B. Aug. 2, 1949, Charlotte, NC
Clemson 6'2" 226 lbs.

1972	GB	N	2	LB
1973			14	LB
1974			14	LB
1975			4	LB
4 yrs.		34 games		

George Hegamin
HEGAMIN, GEORGE RUSSELL
B. Feb. 14, 1973, Camden, NJ
North Carolina State 6'7" 355 lbs.

1994	DAL	N	1	OT
1996			16	OT
2 yrs.		17 games		

Bill Hegarty
HEGARTY, WILLIAM
B. Oct. 13, 1927, Medford, MS
Georgia/Villanova 6'4" 240 lbs.

1953	PIT	N	1	T
1953	WAS	N	2	E, T
1 yr.		3 games		

Mike Hegman
HEGMAN, MICHAEL WILLIAM
B. Jan. 17, 1953, Memphis, TN
Alabama A&M/Tennessee State 6'1" 226 lbs.

1976	DAL	N	14	LB
1977			14	LB
1978			16	LB
1979			16	LB
1980			16	LB
1981			11	LB
1982			9	LB
1983			16	LB
1984			16	LB
1985			16	LB
1986			16	LB
1987			10	LB
12 yrs.		170 games		

Year	Team		Games	Pos.

Jim Heidel
HEIDEL, JAMES BYRNES
B. Dec. 1, 1943, Yazoo City, MS
Mississippi 6'1" 185 lbs.

Year	Team		Games	Pos.
1966	STL	N	14	DB
1967	NO	N	14	DB
2 yrs.	28 games			

Ralph Heikkenen
HEIKKENEN, RALPH I.
B. 1917
D. Jan. 11, 1990, Pontiac, MI
Michigan 5'10" 180 lbs.

Year	Team		Games	Pos.
1939	BKN	N	3	G

Charlie Heileman
HEILEMAN, CHARLES
B. Jan. 25, 1915
D. Feb. 23, 1966
Iowa State 6'2" 197 lbs.

Year	Team		Games	Pos.
1939	CHIB	N	2	E

Steve Heimkreiter
HEIMKREITER, STEVE
B. Jun. 9, 1957, Cincinnati, OH
Notre Dame 6'2" 226 lbs.

Year	Team		Games	Pos.
1980	BAL	N	15	LB

Johnny Heimsch
HEIMSCH, JOHN
B. 1902
Marquette 5'10" 175 lbs.

Year	Team		Games	Pos.
1926	MIL	N	9	HB, FB

Lakei Heimuli
HEIMULI, LAKEI
B. Jun. 24, 1965, Vavau, Tonga Islands
Brigham Young 5'11" 192 lbs.

Year	Team		Games	Pos.
1987	CHI	N	3	RB

Bob Hein
HEIN, ROBERT
B. 1921
Kent State 6'3" 220 lbs.

Year	Team		Games	Pos.
1947	BKN	AA	5	E

Mel Hein
HEIN, MELVIN JOHN
(Old Indestructible)
B. Aug. 22, 1909, Redding, CA
D. Feb. 1, 1992, San Clemente, CA
Washington State 6'2" 225 lbs.

Year	Team		Games	Pos.
1931	NYG	N	12	C
1932			12	C
1933			11	C, LB
1934			13	C, LB
1935			12	C, LB
1936			11	C, LB
1937			11	C, LB
1938			11	C, LB
1939			11	C, LB
1940			11	C, LB
1941			11	C, LB
1942			11	C, LB
1943			10	C, LB
1944			10	C, LB
1945			10	C, LB
15 yrs.	167 games			

Ken Heineman
HEINEMAN, KENNETH R.
B. Jan. 13, 1918, El Paso, TX
Texas Western 5'9" 168 lbs.

Year	Team		Games	Pos.
1940	CLE	N	3	HB
1943	BKN	N	8	HB
2 yrs.	11 games			

Fred Heinisch
HEINISCH, FREDERICK (Fritz)
B. Jun. 22, 1900
D. Dec., 1983, Racine, WI
None 5'10" 173 lbs.

Year	Team		Games	Pos.
1922	RAC	N	5	E
1923			5	E, HB
1924	KEN	N	3	E
1926	RAC	N	2	FB, E
1926	DUL	N	2	HB
4 yrs.	17 games			

Don Heinrich
HEINRICH, DONALD
B. Sep. 19, 1930, Chicago, IL
D. Feb. 29, 1992, Saratoga, CA
Washington 6'0" 182 lbs.

Year	Team		Games	Pos.
1954	NYG	N	2	QB
1955			10	QB
1956			12	QB
1957			4	QB
1958			7	QB
1959			8	QB
1960	DAL	N	12	QB
1962	OAK	A	1	QB
8 yrs.	56 games			

Bob Heinz
HEINZ, ROBERT KENNETH
B. Jul. 25, 1947, Milwaukee, WI
Pacific 6'6" 268 lbs.

Year	Team		Games	Pos.
1969	MIA	A	14	DT
1970	MIA		14	DT
1971			14	DT
1972			11	DT
1973			14	DT
1974			14	DT
1976			14	DT
1977			14	DT
1978	WAS	N	2	DT
9 yrs.	111 games			

George Hekkers
HEKKERS, GEORGE
B. Feb. 18, 1923, Milwaukee, WI
Wisconsin 6'4" 229 lbs.

Year	Team		Games	Pos.
1946	MIA	AA	8	T
1947	BAL	AA	3	T
1947	DET		6	T
1948			12	T
1949			12	T
4 yrs.	41 games			

Paul Held
HELD, PAUL E.
B. 1928
San Diego State 6'2" 195 lbs.

Year	Team		Games	Pos.
1954	PIT	N	8	QB
1955	GB	N	5	QB
2 yrs.	13 games			

Carl Heldt
HELDT, CARL DEIDERICH
B. Mar. 20, 1913, Evansville, IN
D. Jul. 20, 1983, Kerrville, TX
Purdue 6'2" 206 lbs.

Year	Team		Games	Pos.
1935	BKN	N	7	T
1936			12	T, G
2 yrs.	19 games			

John Heldt
HELDT, JOHN
B. Dec. 2, 1899
D. Oct., 1975, Mallard, IA
Iowa 5'9" 208 lbs.

Year	Team		Games	Pos.
1923	COL	N	1	C
1926			6	G
2 yrs.	7 games			

Ron Heller
HELLER, RONALD JEFFERY
B. Sep. 18, 1963, Grass Valley, CA
Oregon State 6'3" 235 lbs.

Year	Team		Games	Pos.
1987	SF	N	13	TE
1988			16	TE
1989	ATL	N	15	TE
1990	SEA	N	16	TE
1992			16	TE
5 yrs.	76 games			

Ron Heller
HELLER, RONALD RAMON
B. Aug. 25, 1962, East Meadow, NY
Penn State 6'6" 280 lbs.

Year	Team		Games	Pos.
1984	TB	N	14	OT
1985			16	OT
1986			16	OT
1987			12	OT
1988	PHI	N	15	OT
1989			16	OT
1990			16	OT
1991			16	OT
1992			12	OT
1993	MIA	N	16	OT
1994			16	OT
1995			7	OT
12 yrs.	172 games			

Warren Heller
HELLER, WARREN (Fats)
B. Nov. 24, 1910, Pittsburgh, PA
D. Oct. 29, 1982, Oakmont, PA
Pittsburgh 5'11" 195 lbs.

Year	Team		Games	Pos.
1934	PIT	N	12	HB
1935			12	HB
1936			12	HB
3 yrs.	36 games			

Dale Hellestrae
HELLESTRAE, DALE ROBERT
B. Jul. 11, 1962, Phoenix, AZ
Southern Methodist 6'5" 275 lbs.

Year	Team		Games	Pos.
1985	BUF	N	4	OT
1986			8	OT
1988			16	OT
1990	DAL	N	16	C, G
1991			16	C, G
1992			16	C, G
1993			16	C, G
1994			16	C, G
1995			16	C, G
1996			16	C
10 yrs.	140 games			

Jerry Helluin
HELLUIN, FRANCIS JEROME
B. Aug. 8, 1929, Donaldsonville, LA
Tulane 6'2" 272 lbs.

Year	Team		Games	Pos.
1952	CLE	N	12	DT
1953			6	DT
1954	GB	N	12	DT
1955			12	DT
1956			12	DT
1957			12	DT
1960	HOU	A		DT
7 yrs.	66 games			

Jack Helms
HELMS, JOHN A.
B. 1921
Georgia Tech 6'4" 215 lbs.

Year	Team		Games	Pos.
1946	DET	N	7	E

Barry Helton
HELTON, BARRY BRET
B. Jan. 2, 1965, Colorado Springs, CO

Barry Helton continued
Colorado 6'3" 205 lbs.

Year	Team		Games	Pos.
1988	SF	N	15	P
1989			16	P
1990			16	P
1991	LARM	N	3	P
4 yrs.	50 games			

Darius Helton
HELTON, DARIUS
B. Oct. 2, 1954, Charlotte, NC
North Carolina Central 6'2" 260 lbs.

Year	Team		Games	Pos.
1977	KC	N	6	G

Chuck Helvie
HELVIE, CHARLES (Chunk)
B. Oct. 8, 1891, Indiana
D. May, 1964
None 5'8" 181 lbs.

Year	Team		Games	Pos.
1920	MUN	A	1	E
1920	DAY	A	3	E, T
1921	MUN	A	2	E
2 yrs.	6 games			

John Helwig
HELWIG, JOHN F.
B. Dec. 5, 1927, Los Angeles, CA
D. Dec. 2, 1994, Pontiac, MI
Notre Dame 6'2" 208 lbs.

Year	Team		Games	Pos.
1953	CHIB	N	12	G
1954			12	G
1955			12	E
1956			6	E
4 yrs.	42 games			

Bill Hempel
HEMPEL, WILLIAM
B. Feb. 10, 1920, Lincoln, NE
Carroll (Wisconsin) 6'0" 235 lbs.

Year	Team		Games	Pos.
1942	CHIB	N	8	T

Darryl Hemphill
HEMPHILL, DARRYL ANTHONY
B. Mar. 29, 1960, San Antonio, TX
West Texas State 6'0" 195 lbs.

Year	Team		Games	Pos.
1982	BAL	N	3	S

Hessley Hempstead
HEMPSTEAD, HESSLEY
B. Jan. 29, 1972, Upland, CA
Kansas 6'1" 295 lbs.

Year	Team		Games	Pos.
1995	DET	N	3	G, C
1996			13	G
2 yrs.	16 games			

Andy Hendel
HENDEL, ANDREW CAREY
B. Mar. 4, 1961, Rochester, NY
North Carolina State 6'1" 230 lbs.

Year	Team		Games	Pos.
1986	MIA	N	16	LB

Larry Hendershot
HENDERSHOT, LARRY LELAND
B. Jan. 15, 1944, Indianapolis, IN
Arizona State 6'3" 240 lbs.

Year	Team		Games	Pos.
1967	WAS	N	4	LB

Herb Henderson
HENDERSON, HERBERT RAYMOND (Buzz)
B. Jun. 21, 1899
Ohio State 5'11" 170 lbs.

Year	Team		Games	Pos.
1921	EVA		4	HB

Jerome Henderson
HENDERSON, JEROME VIRGIL
B. Aug. 8, 1969, Statesville, NC
Clemson 5'10" 189 lbs.

Year	Team		Games	Pos.
1991	NE	N	16	CB
1992			16	CB
1993			1	CB
1993	BUF	N	2	CB
1994			12	CB
1995	PHI	N	15	CB
1996	NE	N	7	CB
6 yrs.	69 games			

John Henderson
HENDERSON, JOHN WILLIAM
B. Mar. 21, 1943, Dayton, OH
Michigan 6'3" 191 lbs.

Year	Team		Games	Pos.
1965	DET	N	12	OE
1966			13	OE
1967			14	OE, FL
1968	MIN	N	7	FL, OE
1969			14	WR
1970			14	WR
1971			7	WR
1972			12	WR
8 yrs.	93 games			

Jon Henderson
HENDERSON, JON ELLIOTT
B. Dec. 17, 1944, Pittsburgh, PA
Colorado State 6'0" 198 lbs.

Year	Team		Games	Pos.
1968	PIT	N	14	DB, WR
1969			9	WR
1970	WAS	N	14	WR
3 yrs.	37 games			

Keith Henderson
HENDERSON, KEITH PERNELL
B. Aug. 4, 1966, Carterville, GA
Georgia 6'1" 220 lbs.

Year	Team		Games	Pos.
1989	SF	N	6	RB
1990			2	RB
1991			14	RB
1992			2	RB
1992	MIN	N	13	RB
4 yrs.	37 games			

Othello Henderson
HENDERSON, OTHELLO
B. Aug. 23, 1972, Oakland, CA
UCLA 6'0" 192 lbs.

Year	Team		Games	Pos.
1993	NO	N	5	S
1994			16	S
2 yrs.	21 games			

Reuben Henderson
HENDERSON, REUBEN STANLEY
B. Oct. 3, 1958, Santa Monica, CA
Oklahoma State/San Diego State 6'1" 200 lbs.

Year	Team		Games	Pos.
1981	CHI	N	16	CB
1982			5	CB
1983	SD	N	14	CB
1984			12	CB
4 yrs.	47 games			

Thomas Henderson
HENDERSON, THOMAS EDWARD (Hollywood)
B. Mar. 1, 1953, Austin, TX
Langston 6'2" 221 lbs.

Year	Team		Games	Pos.
1975	DAL	N	13	LB
1976			14	LB
1977			14	LB
1978			15	LB
1979			11	LB
1980	SF	N	1	LB

Thomas Henderson cont.

Year	Team		Games	Pos.
1980	HOU	N	7	LB
6 yrs.	75 games			

Wilbur Henderson
HENDERSON, WILBUR W.
B. 1898
Deceased
None 195 lbs.

Year	Team		Games	Pos.
1920	HAM	A	1	FB

William Henderson
HENDERSON, WILLIAM TERRELLE
B. Feb. 19, 1971, Chester, VA
North Carolina 6'1" 248 lbs.

Year	Team		Games	Pos.
1995	GB	N	15	RB
1996			16	RB
2 yrs.	31 games			

Wyatt Henderson
HENDERSON, WYATT MONROE
B. Nov. 10, 1956, Bakersfield, CA
Fresno State 5'10" 180 lbs.

Year	Team		Games	Pos.
1981	SD	N	15	WR

Wymon Henderson
HENDERSON, WYMON
B. Dec. 15, 1961, North Miami Beach, FL
Nevada-Las Vegas 5'10" 186 lbs.

Year	Team		Games	Pos.
1987	MIN	N	12	DB
1988			16	CB, S
1989	DEN	N	16	CB
1990			15	CB
1991			16	CB
1992			15	CB
1993	LARM	N	9	CB
1994			14	CB, S
8 yrs.	113 games			

Zac Henderson
HENDERSON, ZAC RYALL
B. Oct. 14, 1955, Jena, LA
Oklahoma 6'1" 190 lbs.

Year	Team		Games	Pos.
1980	PHI	N	12	S

Dick Hendley
HENDLEY, RICHARD
B. Aug. 6, 1926
Clemson 6'0" 198 lbs.

Year	Team		Games	Pos.
1951	PIT	N	7	HB

David Hendley
HENDLEY, DAVID
B. Jun. 29, 1964
Southern Connecticut State 6'0" 188 lbs.

Year	Team		Games	Pos.
1987	NE	N	2	CB

Jim Hendley
HENDLEY, JAMES
B. Oct. 25, 1964
Florida State 6'3" 257 lbs.

Year	Team		Games	Pos.
1987	ATL	N	3	C

Bob Hendren
HENDREN, ROBERT G.
B. Aug. 10, 1923, Burlington Junction, MO
Southern California 6'8" 244 lbs.

Year	Team		Games	Pos.
1949	WAS	N	12	T
1950			12	T
1951			12	E, T
3 yrs.	36 games			

Jerry Hendren
HENDREN, JERRY WAYNE
B. Nov. 4, 1947, Spokane, WA
Idaho 6'2" 187 lbs.

Year	Team		Games	Pos.
1970	DEN	N	10	WR

John Hendren
HENDREN, JOHN D.
B. Apr. 25, 1897
D. Jun., 1964
Bucknell 5'9" 175 lbs.

Year	Team		Games	Pos.
1920	CAN	A	1	HB
1921	CLE	A	4	FB, HB, QB
2 yrs.	5 games			

Dutch Hendrian
HENDRIAN, OSCAR G.
B. 1897
Deceased
DePauw/Detroit/Pittsburgh/Princeton* 5'9" 182 lbs.*

Year	Team		Games	Pos.
1923	AKR	N	5	QB
1923	CAN	N	4	HB, FB
1924	GB	N	11	FB, HB, QB
1925	RI	N	1	HB
1925	NYG	N	11	QB, HB
3 yrs.	32 games			

Ted Hendricks
HENDRICKS, THEODORE PAUL (The Mad Stork)
B. Nov. 1, 1947, Guatemala City, Guatemala
Miami (Florida) 6'7" 230 lbs.

Year	Team		Games	Pos.
1969	BAL	N	14	LB
1970			14	LB
1971			14	LB
1972			14	LB
1973			14	LB
1974	GB	N	14	LB
1975	OAK	N	14	LB
1976			14	LB
1977			14	LB
1978			16	LB
1979			16	LB
1980			16	LB
1981			16	LB
1982	LARI	N	9	LB
1983			16	LB
15 yrs.	215 games			

Steve Hendrickson
HENDRICKSON, STEVEN DANIEL
B. Aug. 30, 1966, Richmond, VA
California 6'0" 251 lbs.

Year	Team		Games	Pos.
1989	SF	N	11	LB
1989	DAL	N	4	LB
1990	SD	N	14	LB
1991			15	LB
1992			16	LB
1993			16	LB
1994			16	LB
1995	PHI	N	3	LB
1995	HOU	N	5	LB
7 yrs.	100 games			

David Hendrix
HENDRIX, DAVID TYRONE
B. May 29, 1972, Jesup, GA
Georgia Tech 6'1" 213 lbs.

Year	Team		Games	Pos.
1995	SD	N	5	S
1996			14	S
2 yrs.	19 games			

Manny Hendrix
HENDRIX, MANUEL
B. Oct. 20, 1964, Phoenix, AZ

Manny Hendrix continued
Utah 5'10" 178 lbs.

Year	Team		Games	Pos.
1986	DAL	N	13	DB
1987			12	DB
1988			16	CB, S
1989			16	CB
1990			16	CB
1991			16	CB
6 yrs.	89 games			

Tim Hendrix
HENDRIX, TIM
B. Sep. 14, 1965, De Soto, TX
Tennessee 6'5" 241 lbs.

Year	Team		Games	Pos.
1987	DAL	N	3	TE

John Hendy
HENDY, JOHN HERALD
B. Oct. 9, 1962, Guatemala City, Guatemala
Long Beach State 5'11" 199 lbs.

Year	Team		Games	Pos.
1985	SD	N	16	CB

Brian Henesey
HENESEY, BRIAN
B. Dec. 10, 1969, Villanova, PA
Bucknell 5'10" 215 lbs.

Year	Team		Games	Pos.
1994	ARI	N	3	RB

Brad Henke
HENKE, BRAD WILLIAM
B. Apr. 10, 1966, Columbus, NE
Iowa State/Arizona 6'3" 275 lbs.

Year	Team		Games	Pos.
1989	DEN	N	2	DE

Ed Henke
HENKE, EDGAR E.
B. Dec. 13, 1927, Ontario, CA
Southern California 6'3" 227 lbs.

Year	Team		Games	Pos.
1949	LA	AA	11	G, T
1951	SF	N	12	DE
1952			12	DE
1956			12	DE, T
1957			12	DE
1958			12	DE
1959			12	DE
1960			8	DE
1961	STL	N	14	DE
1962			8	DE
1963			10	DE
11 yrs.	123 games			

Karl Henke
HENKE, KARL ALFRED
B. Mar. 8, 1945, Ventura, CA
Tulsa 6'4" 245 lbs.

Year	Team		Games	Pos.
1968	NY	A	6	DE
1969	BOS	A	10	DE
2 yrs.	16 games			

Carey Henley
HENLEY, CAREY
B. 1939
Tennessee-Chattanooga 5'10" 200 lbs.

Year	Team		Games	Pos.
1962	BUF	A	1	HB

Darryl Henley
HENLEY, DARRYL KEITH
B. Oct. 30, 1966, Los Angeles, CA
UCLA 5'9" 170 lbs.

Year	Team		Games	Pos.
1989	LARM	N	15	CB
1990			9	CB
1991			16	CB
1992			16	CB
1993			5	CB
1994			15	CB
6 yrs.	76 games			

Year	Team	Games	Pos.

Thomas Henley
HENLEY, THOMAS H., III
B. Jul. 28, 1965, Hillsboro, TX
Stanford 5'11" 185 lbs.

Year	Team		Games	Pos.
1987	SF	N	1	WR

Tom Hennessey
HENNESSEY, THOMAS EDWARD
B. Feb. 15, 1942, Boston, MA
Holy Cross 6'0" 183 lbs.

Year	Team		Games	Pos.
1965	BOS	A	14	DB
1966			14	DB
2 yrs.		28 games		

Jerry Hennessy
HENNESSY, JERRY J.
B. Feb. 22, 1926, Los Angeles, CA
Santa Clara 6'2" 219 lbs.

Year	Team		Games	Pos.
1950	CHIC	N	9	E
1951			12	E
1952	WAS	N	10	E
1953			8	E
4 yrs.		39 games		

John Hennessy
HENNESSY, JOHN W.
B. Mar. 12, 1955, Chicago, IL
Michigan 6'3" 243 lbs.

Year	Team		Games	Pos.
1977	NYJ	N	14	DE
1978			16	DE
1979			16	LB, DE
3 yrs.		46 games		

Charley Hennigan
HENNIGAN, CHARLES TAYLOR
B. Mar. 19, 1935, Bienville, LA
*Louisiana State/Northwestern State
(Louisiana) 6'0" 187 lbs.*

Year	Team		Games	Pos.
1960	HOU	A	14	OE
1961			14	OE
1962			14	OE
1963			14	OE
1964			14	FL
1965			14	FL
1966			14	FL
7 yrs.		98 games		

Mike Hennigan
HENNIGAN, THOMAS MICHAEL
B. Oct. 24, 1951, Davenport, IA
Tennessee Tech 6'2" 217 lbs.

Year	Team		Games	Pos.
1973	DET	N	8	LB
1974			14	LB
1975			4	LB
1976	NYJ	N	12	LB
1977			14	LB
1978			12	LB
6 yrs.		64 games		

Dan Henning
HENNING, DANIEL ERNEST
B. Jun. 21, 1942, Bronx, NY
William & Mary 6'0" 195 lbs.

Year	Team		Games	Pos.
1966	SD	A	1	QB

Chad Hennings
HENNINGS, CHAD WILLIAM
B. Oct. 20, 1965, Elberon, IA
Air Force 6'6" 277 lbs.

Year	Team		Games	Pos.
1992	DAL	N	8	DE
1993			13	DE, DT
1994			16	DT
1995			16	DT
1996			15	DT
5 yrs.		68 games		

Bernard Henry
HENRY, BERNARD
B. Apr. 9, 1960, Los Angeles, CA
Arizona State 6'1" 180 lbs.

Year	Team		Games	Pos.
1982	BAL	N	6	WR
1983			15	WR
1984	IND	N	14	WR
1985			1	WR
1987	LARM	N	3	WR
5 yrs.		39 games		

Charles Henry
HENRY, CHARLES W.
B. Apr. 18, 1964, St. Petersburg, FL
Miami (Florida) 6'4" 230 lbs.

Year	Team		Games	Pos.
1991	MIA	N	6	TE

Fritz Henry
HENRY, FRED
B. Nov. 30, 1895
D. Jan., 1974, Columbus, OH
None 190 lbs.

Year	Team		Games	Pos.
1925	AKR		N	1	G

Kevin Henry
HENRY, KEVIN LERELL
B. Oct. 23, 1968, Mound Bayou, MS
Mississippi State 6'4" 275 lbs.

Year	Team		Games	Pos.
1993	PIT	N	12	DE
1994			16	DE
1995			13	DE
1996			12	DE
4 yrs.		53 games		

Maurice Henry
HENRY, MAURICE EUGENE
B. Mar. 12, 1967, Starkville, MS
Kansas State 5'11" 220 lbs.

Year	Team		Games	Pos.
1990	PHI	N	7	LB

Mike Henry
HENRY, MICHAEL D.
B. Aug. 15, 1936, Los Angeles, CA
Southern California 6'2" 220 lbs.

Year	Team		Games	Pos.
1959	PIT	N	12	LB
1960			12	LB
1961			10	LB
1962	LA	N	14	LB
1963			14	LB
1964			14	LB
6 yrs.		76 games		

Pete Henry
HENRY, WILBUR FRANCIS (Fats)
B. Oct. 31, 1897, Mansfield, OH
D. Feb. 7, 1952, Washington, PA
Washington & Jefferson 5'11" 245 lbs.

Year	Team		Games	Pos.
1920	CAN	A	8	T
1921			10	T
1922	CAN	N	11	T
1923			12	T
1925			6	T
1926			13	T, G
1927	NYG	N	4	T
1927	POT	N	8	T
1928			7	T, E
8 yrs.		79 games		

Steve Henry
HENRY, STEVEN A.
B. Mar. 5, 1957, Kansas City, KS
Emporia State 6'2" 190 lbs.

Year	Team		Games	Pos.
1979	STL	N	8	CB
1980	NYG	N	5	S
1981	BAL	N	2	CB
3 yrs.		15 games		

Urban Henry
HENRY, URBAN A.
B. Jun. 7, 1935, Berwick, LA
Georgia Tech 6'4" 265 lbs.

Year	Team		Games	Pos.
1961	LA	N	14	DT
1963	GB	N	14	DE, DT
1964	PIT	N	10	DT
3 yrs.		38 games		

Wally Henry
HENRY, WALLACE
B. Oct. 30, 1954, San Diego, CA
UCLA 5'8" 174 lbs.

Year	Team		Games	Pos.
1977	PHI	N	10	WR
1978			16	WR
1979			12	WR
1980			7	WR
1981			16	WR
1982			8	WR
6 yrs.		69 games		

Wilbur Henry
HENRY, WILBUR A.
Stanford

Year	Team		Games	Pos.
1930	SI	N	1	G

Dick Hensley
HENSLEY, RICHARD
B. Sep. 8, 1927, Williamson, WV
Kentucky 6'4" 213 lbs.

Year	Team		Games	Pos.
1949	NYG	N	11	E
1952	PIT	N	11	E
1953	CHIB	N	11	E
3 yrs.		33 games		

Gary Henson
HENSON, GARY OWEN
B. Sep. 8, 1940
Colorado 6'3" 200 lbs.

Year	Team		Games	Pos.
1963	PHI	N	11	OE

Harold Henson
HENSON, HAROLD (Champ)
B. Jun. 1, 1953, Columbus, OH
Ohio State 6'3" 240 lbs.

Year	Team		Games	Pos.
1975	CIN	N	6	RB

Ken Henson
HENSON, KENNETH
B. 1943
Texas Christian 6'6" 260 lbs.

Year	Team		Games	Pos.
1965	PIT	N	4	C

Luther Henson
HENSON, LUTHER
B. Mar. 25, 1959, Sandusky, OH
Ohio State 6'0" 275 lbs.

Year	Team		Games	Pos.
1982	NE	N	8	NT, DE
1983			4	NT
1984			9	NT
3 yrs.		21 games		

Anthony Henton
HENTON, OSCAR ANTHONY
B. Jul. 27, 1963, Bessemer, AL
Troy State 6'1" 218 lbs.

Year	Team		Games	Pos.
1986	PIT	N	16	LB
1988			16	LB
2 yrs.		32 games		

Craig Hentrich
HENTRICH, CRAIG ANTHONY
B. May 18, 1971, Alton, IL
Notre Dame 6'3" 200 lbs.

Year	Team		Games	Pos.
1994	GB	N	16	P

Craig Hentrich continued

Year	Team	Games	Pos.
1995		16	P
1996		16	P
3 yrs.	48 games		

Lonnie Hepburn
HEPBURN, LONNIE LORENZO
B. May 12, 1949, Miami, FL
Texas Southern 5'11" 182 lbs.

Year	Team		Games	Pos.
1971	BAL	N	3	CB
1972			14	CB
1974	DEN	N	14	S
3 yrs.		31 games		

Arnie Herber
**HERBER, ARNOLD CHARLES
(Flash)**
B. Apr. 2, 1910, Green Bay, WI
D. Oct. 14, 1969, Green Bay, WI
Wisconsin/Regis 5'11" 203 lbs.

Year	Team		Games	Pos.
1930	GB	N	10	QB, DB
1931			3	QB, DB
1932			14	QB, DB
1933			11	QB, DB
1934			12	QB, DB
1935			11	QB, DB
1936			12	QB, DB
1937			9	QB, DB
1938			8	QB, DB
1939			9	QB, DB
1940			10	QB, DB
1944	NYG	N	9	QB
1945			10	QB
13 yrs.		128 games		

Bill Herchman
HERCHMAN, WILLIAM
B. Mar. 10, 1933, Vernon, TX
Texas Tech 6'2" 246 lbs.

Year	Team		Games	Pos.
1956	SF	N	12	DT
1957			12	DT
1958			12	DT
1959			12	DT
1961	DAL	N	14	DT
1962	HOU	A	12	DT
6 yrs.		74 games		

Joe Hergert
HERGERT, JOSEPH
B. Jun. 7, 1936, Bunnell, FL
Florida 6'1" 216 lbs.

Year	Team		Games	Pos.
1960	BUF	A		LB
1961			9	LB
2 yrs.		9 games		

Matt Herkenhoff
**HERKENHOFF, MATTHEW
BERNARD**
B. Apr. 12, 1951, Melrose, MN
Minnesota 6'4" 280 lbs.

Year	Team		Games	Pos.
1976	KC	N	14	OT
1977			14	OT
1978			16	OT
1979			5	OT
1980			14	OT
1981			16	OT
1982			9	OT
1983			12	OT
1984			15	OT
1985			10	OT
10 yrs.		125 games		

Alan Herline
HERLINE, ALAN JOSEPH
B. Sep. 16, 1964
Vanderbilt 6'0" 168 lbs.

Year	Team		Games	Pos.
1987	NE	N	3	P

Year	Team	Games	Pos.

Chuck Herman
HERMAN, CHARLES
B. Oct. 7, 1958, North Little Rock, AR
Arkansas 6'3" 250 lbs.

Year	Team	Games	Pos.
1980	ATL	N	2	G

Dave Herman
HERMAN, DAVID JON
B. Sep. 3, 1941, Bryan, OH
Michigan State 6'2" 255 lbs.

Year	Team	Games	Pos.
1964	NY	A	5	G
1965		14	G
1966		14	G
1967		14	G
1968		14	G
1969		12	G
1970	NYJ	N	14	G
1971		14	G
1972		13	G
1973		14	G

10 yrs. 128 games

Ed Herman
HERMAN, EDWARD (Red)
B. Jan. 22, 1902
D. May, 1979, Evanston, IL
Northwestern 5'10" 175 lbs.

Year	Team	Games	Pos.
1925	RI	N	1	E

Dick Hermann
HERMANN, RICHARD
B. Jul. 11, 1942, Marianna, FL
Florida State 6'2" 215 lbs.

Year	Team	Games	Pos.
1965	OAK	A	14	LB

Johnny Hermann
HERMANN, JOHN W.
B. Oct. 17, 1933, San Fernando, CA
UCLA 6'1" 180 lbs.

Year	Team	Games	Pos.
1956	NYG	N	2	HB
1956	BAL	N	7	HB

1 yr. 9 games

Terry Hermeling
HERMELING, TERRY ALLEN
B. Apr. 25, 1946, Santa Maria, CA
Nevada-Reno 6'5" 255 lbs.

Year	Team	Games	Pos.
1970	WAS	N	5	OT
1971		8	OT
1972		14	OT
1973		13	OT
1975		9	OT
1976		12	OT
1977		13	G
1978		16	OT
1979		16	OT
1980		14	OT

10 yrs. 120 games

Joe Hernandez
HERNANDEZ, JOSEPH M.
B. Feb. 2, 1940, Bakersfield, CA
Arizona 6'2" 180 lbs.

Year	Team	Games	Pos.
1964	WAS	N	14	FL

Matt Hernandez
HERNANDEZ, MATTHEW
B. Oct. 16, 1961, Detroit, MI
Purdue 6'6" 260 lbs.

Year	Team	Games	Pos.
1983	SEA	N	8	OT
1984	MIN	N	13	OT

2 yrs. 21 games

Scott Hernandez
HERNANDEZ, SCOTT
B. Oct. 17, 1959, Kenmore, NY

Scott Hernandez continued
Kent State 6'0" 250 lbs.

Year	Team	Games	Pos.
1987	BUF	N	2	NT

Don Herndon
HERNDON, DONALD
B. Jun. 4, 1936
Tampa 6'0" 195 lbs.

Year	Team	Games	Pos.
1960	NY	A		HB

Ken Herock
HEROCK, KENNETH BARRY
B. Jul. 16, 1941, Munhall, PA
West Virginia 6'2" 230 lbs.

Year	Team	Games	Pos.
1963	OAK	A	14	OE
1964		14	OE
1965		14	OE
1967		12	OE
1968	CIN	A	13	TE
1969	BOS	A	6	TE

6 yrs. 73 games

Fred Heron
HERON, FRED ROGER
B. Oct. 6, 1944, Stockton, CA
San Jose State 6'4" 255 lbs.

Year	Team	Games	Pos.
1966	STL	N	11	DT, DE
1967		12	DT, DE
1968		14	DT, DE
1969		13	DT
1970		14	DT
1971		9	DT
1972		6	DT

7 yrs. 79 games

Brian Herosian
HEROSIAN, BRIAN BERGE
B. Sep. 14, 1950, Worcester, MA
Connecticut 6'3" 200 lbs.

Year	Team	Games	Pos.
1973	BAL	N	12	S

Efren Herrera
HERRERA, EFREN
B. Jul. 30, 1951, Guadalajara, Mexico
UCLA 5'9" 189 lbs.

Year	Team	Games	Pos.
1974	DAL	N	11	K
1976		14	K
1977		14	K
1978	SEA	N	16	K
1979		16	K
1980		16	K
1981		12	K
1982	BUF	N	7	K

8 yrs. 106 games

Houston Herrin
HERRIN, HOUSTON (Hoot)
B. 1904
Deceased
St. Mary's 5'10" 190 lbs.

Year	Team	Games	Pos.
1931	CLE	N	1	C, G

George Herring
HERRING, GEORGE
B. Jun. 18, 1934, Gadsden, AL
Southern Mississippi 6'2" 200 lbs.

Year	Team	Games	Pos.
1960	DEN	A		QB
1961		14	QB

2 yrs. 14 games

Hal Herring
HERRING, HAL M.
B. Feb. 24, 1924, Lanett, AL
Auburn 6'1" 211 lbs.

Year	Team	Games	Pos.
1949	BUF	AA	12	C
1950	CLE	N	12	C

Hal Herring continued

Year	Team	Games	Pos.
1951		10	C
1952		12	C

4 yrs. 46 games

Don Herrmann
HERRMANN, DONALD BRUCE
B. Jun. 5, 1947, Newark, NJ
Waynesburg State 6'2" 199 lbs.

Year	Team	Games	Pos.
1969	NYG	N	12	WR
1970		13	WR
1971		9	WR
1972		14	WR
1973		14	WR
1974		8	WR
1975	NO	N	3	WR
1976		14	WR
1977		13	WR

9 yrs. 100 games

Mark Herrmann
HERRMANN, MARK DONALD
B. Jan. 8, 1959, Cincinnati, OH
Purdue 6'4" 199 lbs.

Year	Team	Games	Pos.
1982	DEN	N	2	QB
1983	BAL	N	2	QB
1984	IND	N	3	QB
1985	SD	N	9	QB
1986		6	QB
1987		3	QB
1988	LARM	N	6	QB
1989		3	QB
1990	IND	N	3	QB
1991		2	QB
1992		1	QB

11 yrs. 40 games

Jeff Herrod
HERROD, JEFF SYLVESTER
B. Jul. 29, 1966, Birmingham, AL
Mississippi 6'0" 243 lbs.

Year	Team	Games	Pos.
1988	IND	N	16	LB
1989		15	LB
1990		13	LB
1991		14	LB
1992		16	LB
1993		14	LB
1994		15	LB
1995		16	LB
1996		14	LB

9 yrs. 133 games

Bruce Herron
HERRON, BRUCE WAYNE
B. Apr. 14, 1954, Victoria, TX
New Mexico 6'2" 220 lbs.

Year	Team	Games	Pos.
1978	CHI	N	15	LB
1979		15	LB
1980		16	LB
1981		16	LB
1982		9	LB

5 yrs. 71 games

Mack Herron
HERRON, MACK W.
B. Jul. 24, 1948, Biloxi, MS
Kansas State 5'5" 174 lbs.

Year	Team	Games	Pos.
1973	NE	N	14	RB
1974		14	RB
1975		9	RB
1975	ATL	N	4	RB

3 yrs. 41 games

Pat Herron
HERRON, JAMES PATRICK
B. Aug. 12, 1894
D. Dec. 21, 1967, Monongahela, PA
Pittsburgh 5'10" 170 lbs.

Year	Team	Games	Pos.
1920	CLE	A	1	E

Kirk Hershey
HERSHEY, KIRK
B. Jul. 7, 1918
D. 1979, North Palm Beach, FL
Carroll (Wisconsin)/Cornell 6'2" 215 lbs.

Year	Team	Games	Pos.
1941	CLE	N	2	E
1941	PHI	N	6	E

1 yr. 8 games

Rob Hertel
HERTEL, ROBERT ALDEN
B. Feb. 21, 1955, Montebello, CA
Southern California 6'2" 195 lbs.

Year	Team	Games	Pos.
1978	CIN	N	3	QB

Craig Hertwig
HERTWIG, JOHN CRAIG
B. Jan. 15, 1952, Columbus, GA
Georgia 6'8" 270 lbs.

Year	Team	Games	Pos.
1975	DET	N	9	OT
1976		14	OT
1977		14	OT

3 yrs. 37 games

Frank Hertz
HERTZ, FRANK
B. Nov. 6, 1902
D. Jul. 20, 1963
Carroll (Wisconsin) 5'10" 185 lbs.

Year	Team	Games	Pos.
1926	MIL	N	7	E

Wally Hess
HESS, WALTER
B. Oct. 28, 1894
D. Aug., 1963
Indiana 5'9" 177 lbs.

Year	Team	Games	Pos.
1920	HAM	A	1	QB
1921		4	QB, HB
1922	HAM	N	6	QB, HB
1923		7	QB, HB
1924		5	QB
1925		4	FB, HB, QB

6 yrs. 27 games

Jessie Hester
HESTER, JESSIE LEE
B. Jan. 21, 1963, Belle Glade, FL
Florida State 5'11" 170 lbs.

Year	Team	Games	Pos.
1985	LARI	N	16	WR
1986		13	WR
1987		10	WR
1988	ATL	N	16	WR
1990	IND	N	16	WR
1991		16	WR
1992		16	WR
1993		16	WR
1994	LARM	N	16	WR
1995	STL	N	12	WR

10 yrs. 147 games

Jim Hester
HESTER, JAMES CONWAY
B. Dec. 13, 1944, Rock Island, IL
North Dakota 6'4" 238 lbs.

Year	Team	Games	Pos.
1967	NO	N	5	TE
1968		14	TE
1969		10	TE
1970	CHI	N	5	TE

4 yrs. 34 games

Ray Hester
HESTER, RAY
B. Mar. 31, 1949, New Orleans, LA
Tulane 6'2" 215 lbs.

Year	Team	Games	Pos.
1971	NO	N	14	LB
1972		7	LB
1973		6	LB

3 yrs. 27 games

Year	Team	Games	Pos.

Ron Hester
HESTER, RONALD
B. May 26, 1959, Atlanta, GA
Florida State 6'2" 222 lbs.

1982	MIA	N	9	LB

Chris Hetherington
HETHERINGTON, CHRISTOPHER RAYMOND
B. Nov. 27, 1972, North Branford, CT
Yale 6'2" 233 lbs.

1996	IND	N	6	RB

Dave Hettema
HETTEMA, DAVID
B. Nov. 7, 1942, Pasadena, CA
New Mexico 6'4" 249 lbs.

1967	SF	N	7	OT
1970	ATL	N	6	OT
2 yrs.		13 games		

Bill Hewitt
HEWITT, WILLIAM ERNEST
B. Oct. 8, 1909, Bay City, MI
D. Jan. 14, 1947, Philadelphia, PA
Michigan 5'9" 190 lbs.

1932	CHIB	N	12	E
1933			13	E
1934			13	E
1935			12	E
1936			12	E
1937	PHI	N	11	E
1938			11	E
1939			10	E
1943	P, P	N	6	E
9 yrs.		100 games		

Bob Hewko
HEWKO, ROBERT TODD
B. Jun. 8, 1960, Abington, PA
Florida 6'3" 195 lbs.

1983	TB	N	2	QB

Craig Heyward
HEYWARD, CRAIG W. (Iron Head)
B. Sep. 26, 1966, Passaic, NJ
Pittsburgh 5'11" 251 lbs.

1988	NO	N	11	RB
1989			16	RB
1990			16	RB
1991			7	RB
1992			16	RB
1993	CHI	N	16	RB
1994	ATL	N	16	RB
1995			16	RB
1996			15	RB
9 yrs.		129 games		

Ralph Heywood
HEYWOOD, RALPH H.
B. Sep. 11, 1921, Los Angeles, CA
Southern California 6'2" 203 lbs.

1946	CHI	AA	14	E
1947	DET	N	12	E
1948	BOS	N	8	E
1949	NYB	N	12	E
4 yrs.		46 games		

Jesse Hibbs
HIBBS, JESSE J.
B. Jan. 11, 1906
D. Feb. 4, 1985, Castellammare, CA
Southern California 6'0" 195 lbs.

1931	CHIB	N	9	T

Mike Hibler
HIBLER, MICHAEL KEITH
B. Jan. 29, 1946, Mountain View, CA
Stanford 6'1" 235 lbs.

1968	CIN	A	11	LB

Gene Hickerson
HICKERSON, ROBERT EUGENE
B. Feb. 15, 1936, Trenton, TN
Mississippi 6'3" 248 lbs.

1958	CLE	N	12	G
1959			12	G
1960			12	G
1962			12	G
1963			14	G
1964			14	G
1965			14	G
1966			14	G
1967			14	G
1968			14	G
1969			14	G
1970			14	G
1971			14	G
1972			14	G
1973			14	G
15 yrs.		202 games		

Bo Hickey
HICKEY, THOMAS
B. Oct. 7, 1945, Stamford, CT
Maryland 5'11" 225 lbs.

1967	DEN	A	12	RB

Red Hickey
HICKEY, HOWARD W.
B. Feb. 14, 1917, Clarksville, AR
Arkansas 6'2" 204 lbs.

1941	PIT	N	1	E
1941	CLE	N	10	E
1945			8	E
1946	LA	N	8	E
1947			11	E
1948			12	E
5 yrs.		50 games		

Ray Hickl
HICKL, RAYMOND
B. Dec. 24, 1946, Rattan, TX
Texas A&I-Kingsville 6'2" 215 lbs.

1969	NYG	N	9	LB
1970			1	LB
2 yrs.		10 games		

Dallas Hickman
HICKMAN, DALLAS MARK
B. Feb. 16, 1952, Martinez, CA
California 6'6" 238 lbs.

1976	WAS	N	14	DE
1977			14	DE
1978			16	LB, DE
1979			16	LB, DE
1980			16	LB, DE
1981	BAL	N	5	DE
1981	WAS	N	5	LB, DE
6 yrs.		86 games		

Donnie Hickman
HICKMAN, DONNIE J.
B. Jun. 11, 1955, Flagstaff, AZ
Southern California 6'2" 260 lbs.

1978	WAS	N	3	G
1978	DET	N	7	G
1 yr.		10 games		

Herman Hickman
HICKMAN, HERMAN MICHAEL, JR.

Herman Hickman cont.
B. Oct. 1, 1911, Johnson City, TN
D. Apr. 25, 1958, Washington, DC
Tennessee 5'10" 246 lbs.

1932	BKN	N	3	G
1933			10	G
1934			11	G
3 yrs.		24 games		

Kevin Hickman
HICKMAN, KEVIN
B. Aug. 20, 1971, Cherry Hill, NJ
Navy 6'4" 258 lbs.

1995	DET	N	7	TE

Larry Hickman
HICKMAN, LAWRENCE
B. Oct. 16, 1935, Spring Hill, TX
Baylor 6'2" 227 lbs.

1959	CHIC	N	12	FB
1960	GB	N	12	FB
2 yrs.		24 games		

Bryan Hicks
HICKS, MARK BRYAN
B. Jan. 24, 1957, Lake Charles, LA
McNeese State 6'0" 192 lbs.

1980	CIN	N	16	CB, S
1981			16	S
1982			7	S
3 yrs.		39 games		

Cliff Hicks
HICKS, CLIFFORD WENDELL, JR.
B. Aug. 18, 1964, San Diego, CA
Oregon 5'10" 188 lbs.

1987	LARM	N	11	CB
1988			7	CB
1989			15	CB
1990			1	CB
1990	BUF	N	4	CB
1991			16	CB
1992			12	CB
1993	NYJ	N	10	CB
1994			16	CB
1995	DEN	N	6	CB
9 yrs.		98 games		

Dwight Hicks
HICKS, DWIGHT
B. Apr. 5, 1956, Mount Holly, NJ
Michigan 6'1" 192 lbs.

1979	SF	N	8	S
1980			16	S
1981			16	S
1982			9	S
1983			15	S
1984			16	S
1985			16	S
1986	IND	N	9	S
8 yrs.		105 games		

Eddie Hicks
HICKS, EDDIE JAMES
B. Jul. 26, 1955, Henderson, NC
East Carolina 6'2" 210 lbs.

1979	NYG	N	14	RB
1980			3	RB
2 yrs.		17 games		

Ivan Hicks
HICKS, IVAN L.
B. Jun. 30, 1963
Michigan 6'2" 185 lbs.

1987	DET	N	1	CB, S

John Hicks
HICKS, JOHN CHARLES, JR.
B. Mar. 21, 1951, Cleveland, OH
Ohio State 6'2" 258 lbs.

1974	NYG	N	14	G
1975			14	G
1976			14	G
1977			14	G
4 yrs.		56 games		

Mark Hicks
HICKS, MARK
B. Nov. 7, 1960, Los Angeles, CA
Arizona State 6'2" 225 lbs.

1983	SEA	N	8	LB
1987	DET	N	1	LB
2 yrs.		9 games		

Max Hicks
HICKS, MAX
B. 1894
Deceased
Geneva 175 lbs.

1921	HAM	A	1	E

Michael Hicks
HICKS, MICHAEL
B. Feb. 1, 1973, Barnesville, GA
South Carolina State 6'0" 190 lbs.

1996	CHI	N	4	RB

Richard Hicks
HICKS, RICHARD W. (R.W.)
B. Jan. 4, 1951, Cleveland, OH
Humboldt State 6'4" 250 lbs.

1975	DET	N	11	C

Sylvester Hicks
HICKS, SYLVESTER
B. Apr. 2, 1955, Jackson, TN
Tennessee State 6'4" 251 lbs.

1978	KC	N	16	DE
1979			16	DE
1980			10	DE
1981			2	DE
4 yrs.		44 games		

Tom Hicks
HICKS, THOMAS LOGAN
B. Dec. 18, 1952, Chicago, IL
Illinois 6'4" 233 lbs.

1976	CHI	N	14	LB
1977			12	LB
1978			9	LB
1979			15	LB
1980			14	LB
5 yrs.		64 games		

Victor Hicks
HICKS, VICTOR LONELL
B. Jan. 19, 1957, Lubbock, TX
Oklahoma 6'3" 250 lbs.

1980	LA	N	16	TE

W.K. Hicks
HICKS, WILMER KENZIE
B. Jul. 14, 1942, Texarkana, TX
Texas Southern 6'1" 191 lbs.

1964	HOU	A	14	DB
1965			14	DB
1966			14	DB
1967			14	DB
1968			14	DB
1969			14	S
1970	NYJ	N	14	CB, S
1971			13	S

Year	Team		Games	Pos.

W.K. Hicks continued

Year	Team		Games	Pos.
1972			14	S
9 yrs.	125 games			

Ed Hiemstra
HIEMSTRA, EDWARD
B. Mar. 18, 1920, Columbus, MO
Sterling 6'0" 200 lbs.

Year	Team		Games	Pos.
1942	NYG	N	11	G, C

Alex Higdon
HIGDON, ALEX
B. Sep. 9, 1966, Cincinnati, OH
Ohio State 6'5" 247 lbs.

Year	Team		Games	Pos.
1988	ATL	N	3	TE

Austin Higgins
HIGGINS, AUSTIN
B. Nov. 29, 1897
D. Mar., 1976, Kingsley, KY
None

Year	Team		Games	Pos.
1921	LOU	A	2	C
1922	LOU	N	4	C
1923			1	E
3 yrs.	7 games			

Bob Higgins
HIGGINS, ROBERT ARLINGTON
B. Dec. 24, 1893, Corning, NY
D. Jun. 6, 1969, Bellefonte, PA
Penn State 5'10" 195 lbs.

Year	Team		Games	Pos.
1920	CAN	A	3	E
1921			8	E
2 yrs.	11 games			

Jim Higgins
HIGGINS, JAMES
B. Jan. 20, 1942, Cincinnati, OH
Xavier (Ohio) 6'1" 250 lbs.

Year	Team		Games	Pos.
1966	MIA	A	7	G, OT

John Higgins
HIGGINS, JOHN
B. Jan. 10, 1920, Maypearl, TX
Trinity (Texas) 6'1" 200 lbs.

Year	Team		Games	Pos.
1941	CHIC	N	5	G

Luke Higgins
HIGGINS, LUKE MARTIN
B. May 3, 1921, Edgewater, NJ
D. Oct. 11, 1991
Notre Dame 6'0" 210 lbs.

Year	Team		Games	Pos.
1947	BAL	AA	11	G

Tom Higgins
HIGGINS, THOMAS
B. Feb. 26, 1930, Newark, NJ
North Carolina 6'2" 230 lbs.

Year	Team		Games	Pos.
1953	CHIC	N	12	T
1954	PHI		5	T
1955			12	T
3 yrs.	29 games			

Tom Higgins
HIGGINS, THOMAS
B. Jul. 13, 1954, Newark, NJ
North Carolina State 6'1" 235 lbs.

Year	Team		Games	Pos.
1979	BUF	N	16	LB

Mark Higgs
HIGGS, MARK DEYON
B. Apr. 11, 1966, Chicago, IL
Kentucky 5'7" 196 lbs.

Year	Team		Games	Pos.
1988	DAL	N	5	RB

Mark Higgs continued

Year	Team		Games	Pos.
1989	PHI	N	16	RB
1990	MIA	N	12	RB
1991			14	RB
1992			16	RB
1993			16	RB
1994			5	RB
1994	ARI	N	6	RB
1995			3	RB
8 yrs.	93 games			

Alonzo Highsmith
HIGHSMITH, ALONZO WALTER
B. Feb. 26, 1965, Bartow, FL
Miami (Florida) 6'1" 235 lbs.

Year	Team		Games	Pos.
1987	HOU	N	8	RB
1988			16	RB
1989			16	RB
1990	DAL	N	7	RB
1991			2	RB
1991	TB	N	9	RB
1992			5	RB
6 yrs.	63 games			

Don Highsmith
HIGHSMITH, DONALD CORNELIUS
B. Mar. 12, 1948, New Brunswick, NJ
Michigan State 6'0" 200 lbs.

Year	Team		Games	Pos.
1970	OAK	N	14	RB
1971			14	RB
1972			8	RB
1973	GB	N	7	RB
4 yrs.	43 games			

Wally Highsmith
HIGHSMITH, WALTER (Buzz)
B. Aug. 27, 1943, Tampa, FL
Florida A&M 6'4" 238 lbs.

Year	Team		Games	Pos.
1968	DEN	A	14	G
1969			9	G
1972	HOU	N	9	C, OT
3 yrs.	32 games			

Ben Hightower
HIGHTOWER, JOHN BENJAMIN
B. Dec. 5, 1918, Beaumont, TX
Sam Houston State 6'2" 184 lbs.

Year	Team		Games	Pos.
1942	CLE	N	10	E
1943	DET	N	9	E
2 yrs.	19 games			

Jay Hilgenberg
HILGENBERG, JAY WALTER
B. Mar. 21, 1959, Iowa City, IA
Iowa 6'3" 256 lbs.

Year	Team		Games	Pos.
1981	CHI	N	16	C
1982			9	C
1983			16	C
1984			16	C
1985			16	C
1986			16	C
1987			12	C
1988			16	C
1989			16	C
1990			14	C
1991			16	C
1992	CLE	N	16	C
1993	NO	N	9	C
13 yrs.	188 games			

Joel Hilgenberg
HILGENBERG, JOEL
B. Jul. 10, 1962, Iowa City, IA
Iowa 6'3" 251 lbs.

Year	Team		Games	Pos.
1984	NO	N	10	C
1985			15	C, G
1986			16	C, G

Joel Hilgenberg continued

Year	Team		Games	Pos.
1987			12	C, G
1988			16	C, G
1989			16	C, G
1990			16	C, G
1991			16	C, G
1992			16	C, G
1993			9	C, G
10 yrs.	142 games			

Wally Hilgenberg
HILGENBERG, WALTER
B. Sep. 19, 1942, Marshalltown, IA
Iowa 6'3" 230 lbs.

Year	Team		Games	Pos.
1964	DET	N	14	G, LB
1965			13	LB
1966			14	LB
1968	MIN	N	14	LB
1969			14	LB
1970			14	LB
1971			14	LB
1972			14	LB
1973			13	LB
1974			13	LB
1975			14	LB
1976			14	LB
1977			11	LB
1978			15	LB
1979			8	LB
1980			7	LB
16 yrs.	206 games			

Rusty Hilger
HILGER, RUSSELL TODD
B. May 9, 1962, Oklahoma City, OK
Oklahoma State 6'4" 205 lbs.

Year	Team		Games	Pos.
1985	LARI	N	4	QB
1986			2	QB
1987			5	QB
1988	DET	N	11	QB
1991	IND	N	1	QB
5 yrs.	23 games			

Barry Hill
HILL, BARRY
B. Jan. 26, 1953, Eglin AFB, FL
Iowa State 6'3" 185 lbs.

Year	Team		Games	Pos.
1975	MIA	N	14	S
1976			6	S
2 yrs.	20 games			

Bill Hill
HILL, WILLIAM
B. Apr. 21, 1959, Neptune, NJ
Rutgers 5'9" 172 lbs.

Year	Team		Games	Pos.
1987	DAL	N	3	CB

Bob Hill
HILL, ROBERT (WAR HORSE)
B. 1891
Deceased
Carlisle 5'11" 190 lbs.

Year	Team		Games	Pos.
1922	OOR	N	6	G

Bruce Hill
HILL, BRUCE EDWARD
B. Feb. 29, 1964, Fort Dix, NJ
Arizona State 6'0" 175 lbs.

Year	Team		Games	Pos.
1987	TB	N	8	WR
1988			14	WR
1989			16	WR
1990			13	WR
1991			6	WR
5 yrs.	57 games			

Calvin Hill
HILL, CALVIN

Calvin Hill continued
B. Jan. 2, 1947, Baltimore, MD
Yale 6'3" 228 lbs.

Year	Team		Games	Pos.
1969	DAL	N	13	RB
1970			12	RB
1971			8	RB
1972			14	RB
1973			14	RB
1974			12	RB
1976	WAS	N	14	RB
1977			14	RB
1978	CLE	N	12	RB
1979			14	RB
1980			15	RB
1981			14	RB
12 yrs.	156 games			

Charlie Hill
HILL, CHARLES (Chub)
B. 1901
D. Jun. 6, 1944, France
Baker 6'0" 180 lbs.

Year	Team		Games	Pos.
1924	KC	N	6	FB, HB
1925			8	HB, FB, T
1926			10	HB, E
3 yrs.	24 games			

Chuck Hill
HILL, CHARLES K.
B. May 26, 1904
D. Jan., 1986, Saratoga, CA
Iowa State 5'8" 190 lbs.

Year	Team		Games	Pos.
1925	RI	N	1	HB
1926	RI	A	8	FB, E
2 yrs.	9 games			

Dave Hill
HILL, DAVID HARRIS
B. Feb. 1, 1941, Lanett, AL
Auburn 6'5" 259 lbs.

Year	Team		Games	Pos.
1963	KC	A	11	OT
1964			14	OT
1965			14	OT
1966			14	OT
1967			14	OT
1968			14	OT
1969			14	OT
1970	KC	N	14	OT
1971			14	OT
1972			13	OT
1973			8	OT
1974			5	OT
12 yrs.	149 games			

David Hill
HILL, DAVID
B. Jan. 1, 1954, San Antonio, TX
Texas A&I-Kingsville 6'2" 240 lbs.

Year	Team		Games	Pos.
1976	DET	N	14	TE
1977			14	TE
1978			16	TE
1979			16	TE
1980			16	TE
1981			15	TE
1982			9	TE
1983	LARM	N	16	TE
1984			16	TE
1985			16	TE
1986			16	TE
1987			12	TE
12 yrs.	176 games			

Derek Hill
HILL, DEREK KEITH
B. Nov. 4, 1967, Detroit, MI
Arizona 6'1" 193 lbs.

Year	Team		Games	Pos.
1989	PIT	N	16	WR
1990			16	WR
2 yrs.	32 games			

Year	Team		Games	Pos.

Don Hill
HILL, DONALD K.
B. Sep. 18, 1904
D. Feb., 1967
Stanford 5'10" 175 lbs.

Year	Team		Games	Pos.
1929	**GB**	N	3	HB
1929	**CHIC**	N	9	HB, C, QB
1 yr.		12 games		

Drew Hill
HILL, ANDREW
B. Oct. 5, 1956, Newnan, GA
Georgia Tech 5'9" 168 lbs.

Year	Team		Games	Pos.
1979	**LA**	N	16	WR
1980			16	WR
1981			16	WR
1982	**LARM**	N	9	WR
1984			16	WR
1985	**HOU**	N	16	WR
1986			16	WR
1987			12	WR
1988			16	WR
1989			14	WR
1990			16	WR
1991			16	WR
1992	**ATL**	N	16	WR
1993			16	WR
14 yrs.		211 games		

Eddie Hill
HILL, EDDIE WAYNE
B. May 13, 1957, Nashville, TN
Memphis State 6'2" 201 lbs.

Year	Team		Games	Pos.
1979	**LA**	N	16	RB
1980			7	RB
1981	**MIA**	N	11	RB
1982			9	RB
1983			16	RB
1984			16	RB
6 yrs.		75 games		

Eric Hill
HILL, ERIC D.
B. Nov. 14, 1966, Galveston, TX
Louisiana State 6'1" 253 lbs.

Year	Team		Games	Pos.
1989	**PHX**	N	15	LB
1990			16	LB
1991			16	LB
1992			16	LB
1993			13	LB
1994	**ARI**	N	16	LB
1995			15	LB
1996			16	LB
8 yrs.		123 games		

Fred Hill
HILL, FREDERICK GORDON
B. Aug. 13, 1942, Los Angeles, CA
Southern California 6'2" 215 lbs.

Year	Team		Games	Pos.
1965	**PHI**	N	12	OE
1966			14	OE
1967			14	OE
1968			14	OE
1969			8	TE
1970			14	TE
1971			7	TE
7 yrs.		83 games		

Gary Hill
HILL, GARY
B. 1944
Southern California 6'0" 200 lbs.

Year	Team		Games	Pos.
1965	**MIN**	N	8	DB

Greg Hill
HILL, GREGORY LAMONTE'
B. Feb. 23, 1972, Dallas, TX
Texas A&M 5'11" 207 lbs.

Year	Team		Games	Pos.
1994	**KC**	N	16	RB

Greg Hill continued

Year	Team		Games	Pos.
1995			16	RB
1996			15	RB
3 yrs.		47 games		

Greg Hill
HILL, GREGORY M.
B. Feb. 12, 1961, Orange, TX
Oklahoma State 6'1" 199 lbs.

Year	Team		Games	Pos.
1983	**HOU**	N	14	CB
1984	**KC**	N	15	CB
1985			16	CB
1986			13	CB
1987	**LARI**	N	2	CB
1987	**KC**	N	4	CB
1988			15	CB
6 yrs.		79 games		

Harlon Hill
HILL, HARLON JUNIUS
B. May 4, 1932, Killen, AL
North Alabama 6'3" 199 lbs.

Year	Team		Games	Pos.
1954	**CHIB**	N	12	OE
1955			12	OE
1956			12	OE
1957			8	OE
1958			8	OE
1959			11	OE
1960	**CHI**	N	12	OE
1961			14	DB, OE
1962	**PIT**	N	7	OE
1962	**DET**	N	14	OE
9 yrs.		110 games		

Harold Hill
HILL, HAROLD
B. 1916
Samford 6'0" 200 lbs.

Year	Team		Games	Pos.
1938	**BKN**	N	8	G, E
1939			9	E
1940			9	E
3 yrs.		26 games		

Harry Hill
**HILL, HARRY FRANKLIN
(Cowboy)**
B. Mar. 30, 1899
D. Feb. 3, 1966
Oklahoma 5'8" 176 lbs.

Year	Team		Games	Pos.
1923	**TOL**	N	8	HB, FB
1924	**KC**	N	5	HB, FB
1925			8	HB, FB
1925	**NYG**	N	1	HB, FB
1926			8	FB, HB, QB
4 yrs.		30 games		

Ike Hill
HILL, IKE
B. Apr. 15, 1947, Winston-Salem, NC
Catawba 5'10" 180 lbs.

Year	Team		Games	Pos.
1970	**BUF**	N	6	CB
1971			14	CB, WR
1973	**CHI**	N	14	WR
1974			13	WR
1976	**MIA**	N	2	CB
5 yrs.		63 games		

Irv Hill
HILL, IRVING
B. Oct. 9, 1908
D. Mar., 1984, Carle Place, NY
Trinity (Texas) 6'1" 207 lbs.

Year	Team		Games	Pos.
1931	**CHIC**	N	8	FB
1932			7	FB
2 yrs.		15 games		

Jack Hill
HILL, JACK
B. 1933
Utah State 6'1" 15 lbs.

Year	Team		Games	Pos.
1961	**DEN**	A	14	HB

J.D. Hill
HILL, J.D.
B. Oct. 30, 1948, Stockton, CA
Arizona State 6'1" 190 lbs.

Year	Team		Games	Pos.
1971	**BUF**	N	5	WR
1972			14	WR
1973			14	WR
1974			14	WR
1975			14	WR
1976	**DET**	N	1	WR
1977			11	WR
7 yrs.		73 games		

Jeff Hill
HILL, JEFF
B. Sep. 24, 1972, Mount Healthy, OH
Purdue 5'11" 178 lbs.

Year	Team		Games	Pos.
1994	**CIN**	N	1	WR
1995			16	WR
1996			9	WR
3 yrs.		26 games		

Jerry Hill
HILL, GERALD ALLEN
B. Oct. 12, 1939, Torrington, WY
Wyoming 5'11" 212 lbs.

Year	Team		Games	Pos.
1961	**BAL**	N	1	HB, FB
1963			14	HB
1964			13	FB
1965			14	FB
1966			11	FB
1967			14	RB
1968			9	RB
1969			14	RB
1970			11	RB
9 yrs.		101 games		

Jim Hill
HILL, JAMES WEBSTER
B. Oct. 21, 1946, San Antonio, TX
Texas A&I-Kingsville 6'2" 192 lbs.

Year	Team		Games	Pos.
1969	**SD**	A	14	S
1970	**SD**	N	14	S
1971			14	S
1972	**GB**	N	14	S
1973			13	S
1974			14	S
1975	**CLE**	N	11	DB
7 yrs.		94 games		

Jimmy Hill
HILL, JAMES
B. Jun. 27, 1928, Dallas, TX
Sam Houston State 6'2" 192 lbs.

Year	Team		Games	Pos.
1955	**CHIC**	N	9	DB
1956			12	DB
1957			10	DB
1959			12	DB
1960	**STL**	N	12	DB
1961			13	DB
1962			14	DB
1963			12	DB
1964			9	DB
1965	**DET**	N	4	DB
1966	**KC**	A	3	DB
11 yrs.		110 games		

Jimmy Hill
HILL, JAMES CLIFFORD
B. Jun. 7, 1928, Knoxville, TN
Tennessee 6'0" 188 lbs.

Year	Team		Games	Pos.
1951	**DET**	N	12	HB

Jimmy Hill continued

Year	Team		Games	Pos.
1952			9	HB
1955	**PIT**	N	12	HB
3 yrs.		33 games		

John Hill
HILL, JOHN STARK (Otto)
B. Apr. 16, 1950, East Orange, NJ
Lehigh 6'2" 246 lbs.

Year	Team		Games	Pos.
1972	**NYG**	N	14	C, OT
1973			12	OT
1974			12	OT
1975	**NO**	N	14	OT
1976			14	C
1977			14	C
1978			16	C
1979			16	C
1980			15	C
1981			13	C
1982			9	C
1983			16	C
1984			11	C
1985	**SF**	N	2	C
14 yrs.		178 games		

Kenny Hill
HILL, KENNETH W.
B. Jul. 25, 1958, Oak Grove, LA
Yale 6'0" 195 lbs.

Year	Team		Games	Pos.
1981	**OAK**	N	9	S
1982	**LARI**	N	9	S
1983			16	S
1984	**NYG**	N	12	S
1985			12	S
1986			12	S
1987			12	S
1988			16	S
1989	**KC**	N	8	S
9 yrs.		110 games		

Kent Hill
HILL, KENT ANGELO
B. Mar. 7, 1957, Americus, GA
Georgia Tech 6'5" 260 lbs.

Year	Team		Games	Pos.
1979	**LA**	N	16	G
1980			16	G
1981			16	G, OT
1982	**LARM**	N	9	G
1983			16	G
1984			16	G
1985			16	G
1986			2	G
1986	**HOU**	N	13	G
1987			12	G
9 yrs.		132 games		

Kid Hill
HILL, JOHN A. (Bozo)
B. May 6, 1904
D. Dec., 1973, Scottsdale, AZ
Amherst 5'11" 185 lbs.

Year	Team		Games	Pos.
1926	**NYG**	N	1	HB

King Hill
HILL, STUART KING
B. Nov. 8, 1936, Hamilton, TX
Rice 6'3" 212 lbs.

Year	Team		Games	Pos.
1958	**CHIC**	N	7	QB
1959			11	QB, P
1960	**STL**	N	12	QB, P
1961	**PHI**	N	14	QB, P
1962			14	QB, P
1963			14	QB, P
1964			8	QB, P
1965			8	QB, P
1966			10	QB, P
1967			1	QB
1968			3	QB
1968	**MIN**	N	11	QB, P

Year	Team		Games	Pos.

King Hill *continued*

Year	Team		Games	Pos.
1969	STL	N	14	QB, P

12 yrs.   127 games

Lonzell Hill
HILL, LONZELL RAMON (Mo)
B. Sep. 25, 1965, Stockton, CA
Washington 5'11" 189 lbs.

1987	NO	N	10	WR
1988			16	WR
1989			16	WR
1990			13	WR

4 yrs.   55 games

Mack Lee Hill
HILL, MACK LEE
B. Aug. 17, 1940
D. Dec. 14, 1965
Southern University 5'11" 225 lbs.

1964	KC	A	14	FB
1965			13	FB

2 yrs.   27 games

Nate Hill
HILL, NATHANIEL
B. Feb. 21, 1966, La Grange, GA
Auburn 6'4" 273 lbs.

1988	GB	N	3	DE
1988	MIA	N	1	DE

1 yr.   4 games

Ralph Hill
HILL, RALPH EDWARD
B. Nov. 10, 1949, Chicago, IL
Florida A&M 6'1" 245 lbs.

1976	NYG	N	14	C
1977			12	C

2 yrs.   26 games

Randal Hill
HILL, RANDAL THRILL
B. Sep. 21, 1969, Miami, FL
Miami (Florida) 5'10" 177 lbs.

1991	MIA	N	1	WR
1991	PHX	N	15	WR
1992			16	WR
1993			16	WR
1994	ARI	N	14	WR
1995	MIA	N	12	WR
1996			14	WR

6 yrs.   88 games

Rod Hill
HILL, RODRICK
B. Mar. 14, 1959, Detroit, MI
Kentucky State 6'0" 186 lbs.

1982	DAL		9	CB
1983			14	CB
1984	BUF	N	2	CB
1985			10	CB
1986			6	CB
1986	DET	N	3	CB
1987	LARI	N	4	CB

6 yrs.   48 games

Sean Hill
HILL, SEAN TERRELL
B. Aug. 14, 1971, Dowagiac, MI
Montana State 5'10" 175 lbs.

1994	MIA	N	16	CB
1995			16	CB
1996			12	CB

3 yrs.   44 games

Tony Hill
HILL, ANTONIO LAVOSIA

Tony Hill *continued*

(Thrill)
B. Oct. 23, 1968, Augusta, GA
Tennessee-Chattanooga 6'6" 248 lbs.

1991	DAL	N	8	DE
1992			5	DE

2 yrs.   13 games

Tony Hill
HILL, LEROY ANTHONY, JR.
B. Jun. 23, 1956, San Diego, CA
Stanford 6'2" 203 lbs.

1977	DAL	N	14	WR
1978			16	WR
1979			16	WR
1980			16	WR
1981			16	WR
1982			9	WR
1983			16	WR
1984			11	WR
1985			15	WR
1986			16	WR

10 yrs.   141 games

Travis Hill
HILL, TRAVIS LAVELL
B. Oct. 3, 1969, Texas City, TX
Nebraska 6'1" 240 lbs.

1994	CLE	N	14	LB
1995	CAR	N	3	LB
1995	CLE	N	4	LB

2 yrs.   21 games

Will Hill
HILL, WILL J.
B. Mar. 5, 1963, Vero Beach, FL
Bishop 6'0" 200 lbs.

1988	CLE	N	16	CB, S

Winston Hill
HILL, WINSTON CORDELL
B. Oct. 23, 1941, Seguin, TX
Texas Southern 6'4" 278 lbs.

1963	NY	A	13	OT
1964			14	OT
1965			14	OT
1966			14	OT
1967			14	OT
1968			14	OT
1969			14	OT
1970	NYJ	N	14	OT
1971			14	OT
1972			14	OT
1973			14	OT
1974			14	OT
1975			14	OT
1976			14	OT
1977	LA	N	3	OT

15 yrs.   198 games

Ira Hillary
HILLARY, IRA MCDONALD
B. Nov. 13, 1962, Edgefield, SC
South Carolina 5'11" 190 lbs.

1987	CIN	N	11	WR
1988			16	WR
1989			16	WR
1990	MIN	N	3	WR

4 yrs.   46 games

Jerry Hillebrand
HILLEBRAND, GERALD JOHN
B. Mar. 28, 1940, Davenport, IA
Colorado 6'3" 240 lbs.

1963	NYG	N	14	LB
1964			11	LB
1965			13	LB
1966			11	LB

Jerry Hillebrand *continued*

1967	STL	N	14	LB
1968	PIT	N	14	LB
1970			12	LB

7 yrs.   89 games

Billy Hillenbrand
HILLENBRAND, WILLIAM FRANK
B. Mar. 29, 1922, Armstrong, IN
D. Jul. 14, 1994, Indianapolis, IN
Indiana 6'0" 188 lbs.

1946	CHI	AA	14	HB, DB
1947	BAL	AA	13	HB, DB
1948			14	HB, DB

3 yrs.   41 games

Andy Hillhouse
HILLHOUSE, ANDREW FITCH
B. Sep. 15, 1896, Willimantic, CT
D. Mar. 6, 1979, Boynton Beach, FL
Brown 6'2" 190 lbs.

1921	BUF	A	1	HB

Dalton Hilliard
HILLIARD, DALTON
B. Jan. 21, 1964, Patterson, LA
Louisiana State 5'8" 204 lbs.

1986	NO	N	16	RB
1987			12	RB
1988			16	RB
1989			16	RB
1990			6	RB
1991			10	RB
1992			16	RB
1993			16	RB

8 yrs.   108 games

Randy Hilliard
HILLIARD, RANDY
B. Jun. 2, 1967, Metairie, LA
Northwestern State (Louisiana) 5'11" 160 lbs.

1990	CLE	N	15	CB
1991			14	CB
1992			16	CB
1993			12	CB
1994	DEN	N	15	CB
1995			12	CB
1996			13	CB

7 yrs.   97 games

Bill Hillman
HILLMAN, WILLIAM
B. 1920, Erie, PA
Deceased
Tennessee 5'11" 200 lbs.

1947	DET	N	2	B

Keno Hills
HILLS, KENO
B. Jun. 13, 1973, Tampa, FL
Kent State/Southwestern Louisiana 6'6" 320 lbs.

1996	NO	N	1	OT

Hal Hilpert
HILPERT, HAROLD
B. 1908
Oklahoma City 5'9" 188 lbs.

1930	NYG	N	9	E
1933	CIN	N	1	E

2 yrs.   10 games

Carl Hilton
HILTON, CARL PATRICK

Carl Hilton *continued*

B. Feb. 28, 1964, Galveston, TX
Houston 6'3" 232 lbs.

1986	MIN	N	16	TE
1987			11	TE
1988			8	TE
1989			1	TE

4 yrs.   36 games

John Hilton
HILTON, JOHN JUSTIN
B. Mar. 12, 1942, Albany, NY
Richmond 6'5" 222 lbs.

1965	PIT	N	14	OE
1966			14	OE
1967			13	TE
1968			14	TE
1969			12	TE
1970	GB	N	14	TE
1971	MIN	N	7	TE
1972	DET	N	5	TE
1973			14	TE

9 yrs.   107 games

Roy Hilton
HILTON, ROY LEE
B. Mar. 23, 1943, Georgetown, MS
Jackson State 6'6" 240 lbs.

1965	BAL	N	14	DE
1966			14	DE
1967			14	DE
1968			14	DE
1969			14	DE
1970			14	DE
1971			14	DE
1972			14	DE
1973			13	DE
1974	NYG	N	14	DE
1975	ATL	N	12	DE

11 yrs.   151 games

Scott Hilton
HILTON, SCOTT
B. May 28, 1954, Harrisburg, PA
Salem 6'4" 228 lbs.*

1979	SF	N	7	LB
1980			13	LB

2 yrs.   20 games

Dick Himes
HIMES, RICHARD DEAN
B. May 25, 1946, Canton, OH
Ohio State 6'4" 251 lbs.

1968	GB	N	14	OT
1969			14	OT
1970			14	OT
1971			14	OT
1972			14	OT
1973			14	OT
1974			14	OT
1975			14	OT
1976			14	OT
1977			14	OT

10 yrs.   140 games

Hubert Hinchman
HINCHMAN, HUBERT (Curly)
B. Nov. 12, 1907
D. Jan., 1968, Anderson, IN
Butler 5'10" 190 lbs.

1933	CHIC	N	9	FB
1934			8	HB
1934	DET	N	3	HB, FB

2 yrs.   20 games

Stan Hindman
HINDMAN, STANLEY CHATHAM
B. Mar. 1, 1944, Houlton, ME

Year	Team		Games	Pos.

Stan Hindman continued
Mississippi 6'3" 236 lbs.

Year	Team		Games	Pos.
1966	SF	N	14	DE
1967			13	DE
1968			14	DE
1969			10	DE
1970			6	DE
1971			9	DE, DT
1974			8	DT
7 yrs.	74 games			

Andre Hines
HINES, ANDRE PIERRE
B. Feb. 28, 1958, Oakland, CA
Stanford 6'6" 275 lbs.

1980	SEA	N	9	OT

Glen Ray Hines
HINES, GLEN RAY
B. Oct. 26, 1943, El Dorado, AR
Arkansas 6'5" 264 lbs.

1966	HOU	A	14	OT
1967			14	OT
1968			14	OT
1969			14	OT
1970	HOU	N	14	OT
1971	NO	N	14	OT
1972			14	OT
1973	PIT		14	OT
8 yrs.	112 games			

Jimmy Hines
HINES, JIMMY
B. Sep. 10, 1946, Dumas, AR
Texas Southern 6'0" 175 lbs.

1969	MIA	A	10	E
1970	KC	N	1	WR
2 yrs.	11 games			

Bryan Hinkle
HINKLE, BRYAN ERIC
B. Jun. 4, 1959, Long Beach, CA
Oregon 6'1" 218 lbs.

1982	PIT	N	9	LB
1983			16	LB
1984			15	LB
1985			14	LB
1986			16	LB
1987			12	LB
1988			13	LB
1989			13	LB
1990			14	LB
1991			14	LB
1992			13	LB
1993			12	LB
12 yrs.	163 games			

Clarke Hinkle
HINKLE, WILLIAM CLARKE
B. Apr. 10, 1909, Toronto, OH
D. Nov. 9, 1988, Toronto, OH
Bucknell 5'11" 202 lbs.

1932	GB	N	13	FB
1933			13	FB
1934			9	FB
1935			12	FB
1936			11	FB
1937			11	FB
1938			11	FB
1939			11	FB
1940			10	FB
1941			11	FB
10 yrs.	113 games			

George Hinkle
HINKLE, GEORGE ALLEN, JR.
B. Mar. 17, 1965, St. Louis, MO

Clarke Hinkle continued
Arizona 6'5" 267 lbs.

1988	SD	N	3	DE, NT
1989			14	DE
1990			16	DE
1991			13	DE
1992	MIN	N	9	DT
1993	CIN	N	13	DE
6 yrs.	68 games			

Jack Hinkle
HINKLE, JOHN
B. Oct. 31, 1917, Milton, PA
Syracuse 6'0" 195 lbs.

1940	NYG	N	3	HB
1943	P, P	N	10	HB
1944	PHI	N	10	HB
1945			3	HB
1946			10	HB
1947			3	HB
6 yrs.	39 games			

Mike Hinnant
HINNANT, MICHAEL WESLEY
B. Sep. 8, 1966, Washington, DC
Temple 6'3" 258 lbs.

1988	PIT	N	16	TE
1989			5	TE
1992	DET	N	15	TE
3 yrs.	36 games			

Hal Hinte
HINTE, HAROLD
B. Jan. 25, 1920, Pittsburgh, PA
Pittsburgh 6'1" 195 lbs.

1942	GB	N	1	E
1942	PIT	N	3	E
1 yr.	4 games			

Chris Hinton
HINTON, CHRISTOPHER JERROD
B. Jul. 31, 1961, Chicago, IL
Northwestern 6'4" 288 lbs.

1983	BAL	N	16	G
1984	IND	N	6	G
1985			16	G
1986			16	G
1987			12	G
1988			14	G
1989			14	OT
1990	ATL		15	OT
1991			16	OT
1992			16	OT
1993			16	OT
1994	MIN	N	16	OT
1995			4	G
13 yrs.	177 games			

Chuck Hinton
HINTON, CHARLES DUDLEY
B. Aug. 11, 1939, Raleigh, NC
North Carolina Central 6'5" 257 lbs.

1964	PIT	N	14	DT
1965			14	DT
1966			14	DT
1968			14	DT
1969			14	DT
1970			14	DT
1971			4	DT
1971	NYJ	N	8	DT
1972	BAL	N	14	DT
8 yrs.	110 games			

Chuck Hinton
HINTON, CHARLES RICHARD
B. Dec. 6, 1942, Wilkinson, MS

Chuck Hinton continued
Mississippi 6'2" 235 lbs.

1968	NYG	N	14	C
1969			8	C
2 yrs.	22 games			

Eddie Hinton
HINTON, EDDIE GERALD
B. Jun. 26, 1947, Lawton, OK
Oklahoma 6'0" 200 lbs.

1969	BAL	N	12	WR
1970			13	WR
1971			14	WR
1972			8	WR
1973	HOU	N	11	WR
1974	NE	N	9	WR
6 yrs.	67 games			

J.W. Hinton
HINTON, J.W. (Grassy)
B. 1907
D. Dec. 10, 1944
Texas Christian 6'0" 185 lbs.

1932	SI		11	QB

Marcus Hinton
HINTON, MARCUS
B. Dec. 27, 1971, Wiggins, MS
Alcorn State 6'4" 260 lbs.

1996	OAK	N	2	TE

Mike Hintz
HINTZ, MICHAEL
B. Aug. 8, 1965
Wisconsin-Platteville 6'1" 190 lbs.

1987	CHI	N	3	CB, S

Sam Hipa
HIPA, SAM
B. Oct. 12, 1900, Hawaii
D. Oct., 1961
Dayton 5'11" 165 lbs.

1927	DAY	N	1	E
1928			5	E
2 yrs.	6 games			

I.M. Hipp
HIPP, ISIAH MOSES WALTER
B. Feb. 15, 1956, Chapin, SC
Nebraska 5'10" 200 lbs.

1980	OAK	N	1	RB

Eric Hipple
HIPPLE, ERIC ELLSWORTH
B. Sep. 16, 1957, Lubbock, TX
Utah State 6'2" 198 lbs.

1980	DET	N	15	QB
1981			16	QB
1982			9	QB
1983			16	QB
1984			8	QB
1985			16	QB
1986			16	QB
1988			5	QB
1989			1	QB
9 yrs.	102 games			

Claude Hipps
HIPPS, CLAUDE
B. Apr. 23, 1927
Georgia 6'1" 189 lbs.

1952	PIT	N	12	HB
1953			5	HB
2 yrs.	17 games			

Doug Hire
HIRE, DOUGLAS
B. Apr. 22, 1965
Linfield 6'2" 245 lbs.

1987	SEA	N	3	C

Ed Hirsch
HIRSCH, EDWARD NORMAN (Buckets)
B. Mar. 26, 1921, Clarence, NY
Northwestern 5'10" 207 lbs.

1947	BUF	AA	14	B
1948			13	B
1949			6	B
3 yrs.	33 games			

Elroy Hirsch
HIRSCH, ELROY LEON (Crazy Legs)
B. Jun. 17, 1924, Wausau, WI
Wisconsin/Michigan 6'2" 190 lbs.

1946	CHI	AA	14	HB
1947			5	HB
1948			5	HB
1949	LA	N	12	HB
1950			12	HB
1951			12	E, HB
1952			10	E, HB
1953			12	E, HB
1954			12	E, HB
1955			9	HB, E
1956			12	E
1957			12	E
12 yrs.	127 games			

Steve Hirsch
HIRSCH, STEVE
B. May 18, 1962
Northern Illinois 6'0" 195 lbs.

1987	DET	N	3	CB

Bill Hitchcock
HITCHCOCK, BILL
B. Aug. 26, 1965, Kirkland, Que.
Purdue 6'6" 291 lbs.

1991	SEA	N	16	OT
1992			16	OT
1993			14	G
1994			5	G
4 yrs.	51 games			

Jimmy Hitchcock
HITCHCOCK, JIMMY DAVIS, JR.
B. Nov. 9, 1971, Concord, NC
North Carolina 5'10" 188 lbs.

1995	NE	N	8	CB
1996			13	CB
2 yrs.	21 games			

Ray Hitchcock
HITCHCOCK, RAEBERN B.
B. Jun. 20, 1965, St. Paul, MN
Minnesota 6'2" 289 lbs.

1987	WAS	N	5	C

Joel Hitt
HITT, JOEL R.
B. Dec. 30, 1916
Mississippi College 6'1" 180 lbs.

1939	CLE	N	3	E

Billy Hix
HIX, WILLIAM
B. Jan. 18, 1929, Batesville, AR
Arkansas 6'2" 215 lbs.

1950	PHI	N	11	E

Year	Team		Games	Pos.

Terry Hoage
HOAGE, TERRELL LEE
B. Apr. 11, 1962, Ames, IA
Georgia 6'3" 198 lbs.

Year	Team		Games	Pos.
1984	NO	N	14	S
1985			16	S
1986	PHI	N	16	S
1987			11	S
1988			16	S
1989			6	S
1990			16	S
1991	WAS	N	6	S
1993	SF	N	4	S
1993	HOU	N	3	S
1994	ARI	N	16	S
1995			13	S
1996			5	S
12 yrs.	142 games			

Fred Hoaglin
HOAGLIN, GEORGE FREDERICK, JR.
B. Jan. 28, 1944, Alliance, OH
Pittsburgh 6'4" 246 lbs.

Year	Team		Games	Pos.
1966	CLE	N	6	C
1967			14	C
1968			14	C
1969			14	C
1970			14	C
1971			11	C
1972			14	C
1973	BAL	N	14	C
1974	HOU	N	14	C
1975			14	C
1976	SEA	N	13	C
11 yrs.	142 games			

Joe Hoague
HOAGUE, JOSEPH D.
B. Feb. 8, 1918, Brookline, MA
D. Jan. 4, 1991, Lakeville, MA
Colgate 6'2" 203 lbs.

Year	Team		Games	Pos.
1941	PIT	N	10	FB
1942			10	FB
1946	BOS	N	7	FB
3 yrs.	27 games			

Dick Hoak
HOAK, RICHARD JOHN
B. Dec. 8, 1939, Jeannette, PA
Penn State 5'11" 191 lbs.

Year	Team		Games	Pos.
1961	PIT	N	14	HB
1962			14	HB
1963			12	HB
1964			14	HB
1965			14	HB
1966			13	HB
1967			14	RB
1968			14	RB
1969			14	RB
1970			12	RB
10 yrs.	135 games			

Leroy Hoard
HOARD, LEROY
B. May 5, 1968, New Orleans, LA
Michigan 5'11" 230 lbs.

Year	Team		Games	Pos.
1990	CLE	N	14	RB
1991			16	RB
1992			16	RB
1993			16	RB
1994			16	RB
1995			12	RB
1996	BAL	N	2	RB
1996	CAR	N	3	RB
1996	MIN	N	6	RB
7 yrs.	101 games			

Mike Hoban
HOBAN, MICHAEL A.
B. Jan. 9, 1952, Chicago, IL
Michigan 6'2" 235 lbs.

Year	Team		Games	Pos.
1974	CHI	N	1	G

Jim Hobbins
HOBBINS, JAMES R.
B. Jun. 3, 1965
Minnesota 6'6" 275 lbs.

Year	Team		Games	Pos.
1987	GB	N	3	G

Billy Hobbs
HOBBS, WILLIAM
B. Sep. 18, 1946, Mount Pleasant, TX
Texas A&M 6'0" 218 lbs.

Year	Team		Games	Pos.
1969	PHI	N	14	LB
1970			12	LB
1971			1	LB
1972	NO	N	6	LB
4 yrs.	33 games			

Daryl Hobbs
HOBBS, DARYL RAY
B. May 23, 1968, Victoria, TX
Pacific 6'2" 180 lbs.

Year	Team		Games	Pos.
1993	LARI	N	3	WR
1994			10	WR
1995	OAK	N	16	WR
1996			16	WR
4 yrs.	45 games			

Homer Hobbs
HOBBS, HOMER BROWN (Dick)
B. Feb. 13, 1923, Lexington, SC
Georgia 5'11" 210 lbs.

Year	Team		Games	Pos.
1949	SF	AA	12	G
1950	SF	N	10	G
2 yrs.	22 games			

Stephen Hobbs
HOBBS, STEVIE
B. Nov. 14, 1965, Mendenhall, MS
North Alabama 5'11" 195 lbs.

Year	Team		Games	Pos.
1990	WAS	N	7	WR
1991			16	WR
1992			2	WR
3 yrs.	25 games			

Marion Hobby
HOBBY, MARION EUGENE, JR.
B. Nov. 7, 1966, Birmingham, AL
Tennessee 6'4" 277 lbs.

Year	Team		Games	Pos.
1990	NE	N	16	DE
1991			15	DE
1992			11	DE
3 yrs.	42 games			

Billy Joe Hobert
HOBERT, BILLY JOE
B. Jan. 8, 1971, Puyallup, WA
Washington 6'3" 225 lbs.

Year	Team		Games	Pos.
1995	OAK	N	4	QB
1996			8	QB
2 yrs.	12 games			

Liffort Hobley
HOBLEY, LIFFORT W.
B. May 12, 1962, Shreveport, LA
Louisiana State 6'0" 207 lbs.

Year	Team		Games	Pos.
1985	STL	N	5	S
1987	MIA	N	14	S
1988			16	S
1989			16	S
1990			14	S
1992			15	S

Liffort Hobley continued

Year	Team		Games	Pos.
1993			4	S
7 yrs.	84 games			

Fred Hobscheid
HOBSCHEID, FRED J.
B. Apr. 20, 1904
D. Apr., 1967
Chicago 5'11" 202 lbs.

Year	Team		Games	Pos.
1926	RAC	N	5	T, G

Ben Hobson
HOBSON, BENJAMIN
B. Jul. 25, 1902
D. Jul., 1975, Leawood, KS
None 5'10" 190 lbs.

Year	Team		Games	Pos.
1926	BUF	N	10	FB, HB
1927			5	QB, HB
2 yrs.	15 games			

John Hock
HOCK, JOHN JOSEPH
B. Mar. 7, 1928, Pittsburgh, PA
Santa Clara 6'2" 230 lbs.

Year	Team		Games	Pos.
1950	CHIC	N	12	T
1953	LA	N	9	G
1955			12	G
1956			12	G
1957			12	G
5 yrs.	57 games			

Merwin Hodel
HODEL, MERWIN
B. May 27, 1931
Colorado 6'2" 205 lbs.

Year	Team		Games	Pos.
1953	NYG	N	2	FB

Floyd Hodge
HODGE, FLOYD
B. Jul. 18, 1959, Compton, CA
Utah 6'0" 195 lbs.

Year	Team		Games	Pos.
1982	ATL	N	9	WR
1983			12	WR
1984			12	WR
3 yrs.	33 games			

Milford Hodge
HODGE, MILFORD
B. Mar. 11, 1961, Los Angeles, CA
Washington State 6'3" 285 lbs.

Year	Team		Games	Pos.
1986	NO	N	1	DE
1986	NE	N	6	DE
1987			12	DE
1988			15	NT
1989			16	NT
4 yrs.	50 games			

Eric Hodges
HODGES, ERIC
B. Jun. 3, 1964
Florida 6'1" 189 lbs.

Year	Team		Games	Pos.
1987	KC	N	1	WR

Herman Hodges
HODGES, HERMAN (Country)
B. Nov. 22, 1914, Ozark, AL
Samford 6'1" 198 lbs.

Year	Team		Games	Pos.
1939	BKN	N	9	E
1940			9	E
1941			11	E
1942			10	E
4 yrs.	39 games			

Norm Hodgins
HODGINS, NORMAN FRANCIS, JR.

Norm Hodgins continued
B. Mar. 1, 1952, New Orleans, LA
Louisiana State 6'1" 190 lbs.

Year	Team		Games	Pos.
1974	CHI	N	14	S

Pat Hodgson
HODGSON, PATRICK
B. Jan. 30, 1944, Columbus, GA
Georgia 6'2" 190 lbs.

Year	Team		Games	Pos.
1966	WAS	N	10	OE

Tommy Hodson
HODSON, THOMAS PAUL
B. Jan. 28, 1967, Mathews, LA
Louisiana State 6'3" 195 lbs.

Year	Team		Games	Pos.
1990	NE	N	7	QB
1991			16	QB
1992			9	QB
1995	NO	N	4	QB
4 yrs.	36 games			

Bob Hoel
HOEL, ROBERT MALCOLM
B. Jun. 5, 1913, Alden, MN
Pittsburgh 6'0" 208 lbs.

Year	Team		Games	Pos.
1935	PIT	N	12	G
1937	CHIC	N	1	G
1938			5	G
3 yrs.	18 games			

Dick Hoerner
HOERNER, LESTER J.
B. Jul. 22, 1922, Dubuque, IA
Iowa 6'4" 219 lbs.

Year	Team		Games	Pos.
1947	LA	N	4	FB
1948			12	FB
1949			12	FB
1950			12	HB
1951			12	HB
1952	DAL	N	11	FB, HB
6 yrs.	63 games			

Bob Hoernschemeyer
HOERNSCHEMEYER, ROBERT JAMES (Hunchy)
B. Sep. 24, 1925, Cincinnati, OH
D. Jun. 17, 1980, Detroit, MI
Indiana 5'11" 194 lbs.

Year	Team		Games	Pos.
1946	CHI	AA	14	QB
1947			2	QB
1947	BKN	AA	12	QB
1948			14	QB
1949	CHI	AA	12	QB
1950	DET	N	10	HB
1951			11	HB
1952			10	HB
1953			12	HB
1954			11	HB
1955			5	HB
10 yrs.	113 games			

George Hoey
HOEY, GEORGE WILLIAM
B. Nov. 14, 1946, Gaffney, SC
Michigan 5'10" 174 lbs.

Year	Team		Games	Pos.
1971	STL	N	6	CB
1972	NE	N	14	CB
1973			14	CB
1974	SD	N	13	CB
1975	DEN	N	1	DB
1975	NYJ	N	5	DB
5 yrs.	53 games			

Paul Hofer
HOFER, PAUL DAVID
B. May 13, 1952, Memphis, TN

Year	Team		Games	Pos.

Paul Hofer *continued*
Mississippi 6'0" 194 lbs.

Year	Team		Games	Pos.
1976	SF	N	14	RB
1977			14	RB
1978			16	RB
1979			15	RB
1980			6	RB
1981			12	RB
6 yrs.	77 games			

Bill Hoffman
HOFFMAN, WILLIAM J.
B. Mar. 31, 1902
D. Dec., 1981, Brooksville, PA
Lehigh 5'10" 235 lbs.

1924	FRA	N	1	G
1925			19	G
1926			16	G, T, E
3 yrs.	36 games			

Bob Hoffman
HOFFMAN, WAYNE ROBERT
B. Dec. 13, 1917, Star City, WV
Southern California 6'1" 208 lbs.

1940	WAS	N	8	HB, LB
1941			3	HB, LB
1946	LA	N	10	FB, LB
1947			10	FB, LB
1948			11	FB, LB
1949	LA	AA	12	FB, LB
6 yrs.	54 games			

Dalton Hoffman
HOFFMAN, DALTON J.
B. 1942
Baylor 6'0" 207 lbs.

1964	HOU	A	5	FB
1965			4	FB
2 yrs.	9 games			

Gary Hoffman
HOFFMAN, GARY E.
B. Sep. 28, 1961, Sacramento, CA
Santa Clara 6'7" 282 lbs.

1984	GB	N	1	OT, G
1987	SF	N	3	OT
2 yrs.	4 games			

Jack Hoffman
HOFFMAN, JACK H.
B. Dec. 8, 1925, Little Rock, AR
Xavier (Ohio) 6'5" 234 lbs.

1952	CHIB	N	12	E
1955			12	E
1956			12	E
1957			12	E
1958			7	E
5 yrs.	55 games			

Jake Hoffman
HOFFMAN, JACOB H.
B. Jul. 21, 1895, New York State
D. Feb., 1977, Jordan, NY
None 5'8" 170 lbs.

| 1925 | ROC | N | 3 | FB |

John Hoffman
HOFFMAN, JOHN (Big John)
B. Dec. 8, 1925, Little Rock, AR
D. Apr., 1987, Little Rock, AR
Arkansas 6'2" 215 lbs.

1949	CHIB	N	12	FB, LB
1950			12	FB, LB
1951			12	E, LB
1952			4	E, LB
1953			12	FB, LB
1954			12	OE, DB

John Hoffman *continued*

1955			12	FB, DB
1956			11	FB, DB
8 yrs.	87 games			

John Hoffman
HOFFMAN, JOHN FREDERICK
B. Aug. 2, 1943, Santa Monica, CA
Hawaii 6'7" 264 lbs.

1969	WAS	N	13	DE
1970			14	DE
1971	CHI	N	1	DE
1972	STL	N	2	DE
1972	DEN	N	2	DE
4 yrs.	32 games			

Dave Hoffmann
HOFFMANN, DAVID PAUL
B. Jul. 24, 1970, San Luis Obispo, CA
Washington 6'2" 233 lbs.

| 1993 | PIT | N | 1 | LB |

Darrell Hogan
HOGAN, DARRELL
B. Jul. 2, 1926, San Antonio, TX
Baylor/Trinity (Texas) 5'10" 210 lbs.

1949	PIT	N	12	G
1950			12	G
1951			12	G
1952			12	G
1953			12	G
5 yrs.	60 games			

Marc Hogan
HOGAN, MARC
B. Apr. 21, 1962
Baruch-CUNY 6'0" 180 lbs.

| 1987 | NYJ | N | 3 | CB |

Mike Hogan
HOGAN, MICHAEL L.
B. Nov. 1, 1954, Rome, GA
Tennessee-Chattanooga 6'2" 213 lbs.

1976	PHI	N	8	RB
1977			12	RB
1978			14	RB
1979	SF	N	2	RB
1980	NYG	N	6	RB
1980	PHI	N	13	FB
5 yrs.	55 games			

Paul Hogan
HOGAN, PAUL
B. Sep. 5, 1898
D. Aug., 1976, Las Vegas, NV
*Notre Dame/Niagara/Wash. &
Jefferson/Detroit 5'8" 170 lbs.*

1924	AKR	N	6	HB, E, QB
1925	CAN	N	6	QB, HB, FB
1926	NYG	N	11	HB, FB, QB
1926	FRA	N	3	HB, QB
3 yrs.	26 games			

Tom Hogan
HOGAN, THOMAS
B. Apr. 26, 1898
D. Jan., 1978, Boston, MA
Detroit/Fordham 6'2" 193 lbs.

1925	DET	N	11	T, G, E
1926	CHIC	N	1	G
2 yrs.	12 games			

Merril Hoge
HOGE, MERRIL D.
B. Jan. 26, 1965, Pocatello, ID
Idaho State 6'2" 212 lbs.

| 1987 | PIT | N | 13 | RB |

Merril Hoge *continued*

1988			16	RB
1989			16	RB
1990			16	RB
1991			16	RB
1992			16	RB
1993			16	RB
1994	CHI	N	5	RB
8 yrs.	114 games			

Gary Hogeboom
HOGEBOOM, GARY KEITH
B. Aug. 21, 1958, Grand Rapids, MI
Central Michigan 6'4" 207 lbs.

1980	DAL	N	2	QB
1981			1	QB
1982			4	QB
1983			6	QB
1984			16	QB
1985			16	QB
1986	IND	N	5	QB
1987			6	QB
1988			9	QB
1989	PHX	N	14	QB
10 yrs.	79 games			

D.D. Hoggard
HOGGARD, WILLIAM BENJAMIN
B. May 7, 1961, Windsor, NC
North Carolina State 6'0" 188 lbs.

1985	CLE	N	2	CB
1986			16	CB
1987			1	CB
3 yrs.	19 games			

Doug Hogland
HOGLAND, M. DOUGLAS
B. May 8, 1931, Farmington, NM
Oregon State 6'3" 239 lbs.

1953	SF	N	12	G, T
1954			12	G, T
1955			12	G
1956	CHIC	N	12	G
1957			12	G
1958			2	G
1958	DET	N	12	G
6 yrs.	74 games			

Frank Hogue
HOGUE, FRANCIS E.
B. Jan. 19, 1899
D. Jan., 1967, Cleveland, OH
None

| 1924 | AKR | N | 3 | QB, HB |

Murrell Hogue
HOGUE, MURRELL
B. 1904
Deceased
Centenary 6'1" 208 lbs.

1928	NYY	N	10	G, T
1929	CHIC	N	10	T, G, E
1930	MIN	N	1	T
3 yrs.	21 games			

Mike Hohensee
HOHENSEE, MICHAEL LOUIS
B. Feb. 22, 1961, Inglewood, CA
Minnesota 6'0" 205 lbs.

| 1987 | CHI | N | 3 | QB |

Jon Hohman
HOHMAN, JON CARL
B. Oct. 23, 1942, Antigo, WI
Wisconsin 6'1" 243 lbs.

1965	DEN	A	10	G
1966			14	G
2 yrs.	24 games			

Bob Hohn
HOHN, ROBERT
B. Jun. 4, 1941, Beatrice, NE
Nebraska 6'0" 187 lbs.

1965	PIT	N	10	DB
1966			4	DB
1967			13	DB
1968			8	DB
1969			11	CB
5 yrs.	46 games			

Al Hoisington
HOISINGTON, ALLAN
B. 1935
Pasadena CC 6'3" 200 lbs.

| 1960 | OAK | A | | OE |
| 1960 | BUF | A | | OE |

Jon Hoke
HOKE, JONATHAN DAVID
B. Jan. 24, 1957, Hamilton, OH
Ball State 5'11" 175 lbs.

| 1980 | CHI | N | 11 | CB |

Steve Hokuf
HOKUF, STEPHEN MELVIN
B. Sep. 26, 1910, Wilber, NE
Nebraska 6'0" 199 lbs.

1933	BOS	N	11	E, QB
1934			10	Q, E
1935			7	QB, FB, E
3 yrs.	28 games			

Holbert
HOLBERT
None

| 1923 | HAM | N | 1 | E |

Bill Holcomb
HOLCOMB, WILLIAM (Tex)
B. Apr. 9, 1913
D. Jan., 1978, Odessa, TX
Texas Tech 6'2" 235 lbs.

1937	PIT	N	7	T
1937	PHI	N	1	T
1 yr.	8 games			

Kelly Holcomb
HOLCOMB, KELLY
B. Jul. 9, 1973
Middle Tennessee State 6'2" 219 lbs.

| 1996 | IND | N | 1 | QB |

Mike Hold
HOLD, JAMES MICHEL, JR.
B. Mar. 16, 1963, Phoenix, AZ
South Carolina 6'0" 190 lbs.

| 1987 | TB | N | | QB |

Sam Holden
HOLDEN, SAMUEL LEE, JR.
B. Feb. 24, 1957, Magnolia, MS
*Southern Illinois/Grambling State 6'3"
258 lbs.*

| 1971 | NO | N | 9 | OT |

Steve Holden
HOLDEN, STEVE ANTHONY
B. Aug. 2, 1951, Los Angeles, CA
Arizona State 6'0" 195 lbs.

1973	CLE	N	11	WR
1974			10	WR
1975			13	WR
1976			14	WR
1977	CIN	N	6	WR
5 yrs.	54 games			

Year	Team	Games	Pos.

Lew Holder
HOLDER, LEWIS G.
B. Oct., 1923, Dallas, TX
Texas 6'0" 191 lbs.

Year	Team	Games	Pos.
1949	**LA** AA	12	E

Babe Hole
HOLE, BABE
None

Year	Team	Games	Pos.
1921	**MUN** A	2	G

Ernie Hole
HOLE, ERNEST (Sarp)
B. 1896
Deceased
None

Year	Team	Games	Pos.
1920	**MUN** A	1	G

Mick Hole
HOLE, MICKEY
B. Feb., 1892
Deceased
None 5'9" 180 lbs.

Year	Team	Games	Pos.
1920	**MUN** A	1	HB
1921		2	HB, FB
2 yrs.	3 games		

John Holecek
HOLECEK, JOHN
B. May 7, 1972, Steger, IL
Illinois 6'2" 238 lbs.

Year	Team	Games	Pos.
1995	**BUF** N	1	LB

Jimmy Holifield
HOLIFIELD, JAMES
B. Jan. 18, 1946, Bessemer, AL
Jackson State 6'3" 195 lbs.

Year	Team	Games	Pos.
1968	**NYG** N	14	DB
1969		14	CB
2 yrs.	28 games		

John Holifield
HOLIFIELD, JOHNATHAN MARK
B. Jul. 14, 1964, Wayne, MI
West Virginia 6'0" 202 lbs.

Year	Team	Games	Pos.
1989	**CIN** N	3	RB

Bobby Holladay
HOLLADAY, ROBERT
B. Mar. 13, 1932, Shreveport, LA
Tulsa 5'11" 175 lbs.

Year	Team	Games	Pos.
1956	**SF** N	7	HB
1957		7	HB
2 yrs.	14 games		

Darius Holland
HOLLAND, DARIUS
B. Nov. 10, 1973, Petersburg, VA
Colorado 6'4" 305 lbs.

Year	Team	Games	Pos.
1995	**GB** N	14	DT
1996		16	DT
2 yrs.	30 games		

Jamie Holland
HOLLAND, JAMIE LORENZA
B. Feb. 1, 1964, Raleigh, NC
Ohio State 6'2" 186 lbs.

Year	Team	Games	Pos.
1987	**SD** N	12	WR
1988		16	WR
1989		16	WR
1990	**LARI** N	16	WR
1991		16	WR
1992	**CLE** N	4	WR
6 yrs.	80 games		

John Holland
HOLLAND, JOHN CALVIN
B. Feb. 28, 1952, Beckley, WV
Tennessee State 6'0" 190 lbs.

Year	Team	Games	Pos.
1974	**MIN** N	11	WR
1975	**BUF** N	12	WR
1976		13	WR
1977		3	WR
4 yrs.	39 games		

Johnny Holland
HOLLAND, JOHNNY RAY
B. Mar. 11, 1965, Beckley, TX
Texas A&M 6'2" 221 lbs.

Year	Team	Games	Pos.
1987	**GB** N	12	LB
1988		13	LB
1989		16	LB
1990		16	LB
1991		16	LB
1992		14	LB
1993		16	LB
7 yrs.	103 games		

Vernon Holland
HOLLAND, VERNON EDWARD
B. Jun. 28, 1948, San Antonio, TX
Tennessee State 6'5" 268 lbs.

Year	Team	Games	Pos.
1971	**CIN** N	14	OT
1972		14	OT
1973		14	OT
1974		2	OT
1975		14	OT
1976		14	OT
1977		14	OT
1978		16	OT
1979		16	OT
1980	**DET** N	2	OT
1980	**NYG** N	12	OT
10 yrs.	132 games		

John Hollar
HOLLAR, JOHN HENRY
B. Aug. 7, 1902, Boone, NC
Appalachian State 6'0" 223 lbs.

Year	Team	Games	Pos.
1922	**TOL** N	1	QB
1948	**WAS** N	9	FB
1949		2	FB
1949	**DET** N	6	FB
3 yrs.	18 games		

Donald Hollas
HOLLAS, DONALD WAYNE
B. Nov. 27, 1967, Kingsville, TX
Rice 6'3" 215 lbs.

Year	Team	Games	Pos.
1991	**CIN** N	8	QB
1992		10	QB
1994		2	QB
3 yrs.	20 games		

Hugo Hollas
HOLLAS, HUGO ANDREW
B. Nov. 30, 1945, Schulenburg, TX
Rice 6'1" 190 lbs.

Year	Team	Games	Pos.
1970	**NO** N	10	S
1971		14	S
1972		14	S
1974	**SF** N	7	S
4 yrs.	45 games		

Eric Holle
HOLLE, ERIC W.
B. Sep. 5, 1960, Houston, TX
Texas 6'5" 260 lbs.

Year	Team	Games	Pos.
1984	**KC** N	16	DE
1985		16	DE, NT
1986		16	DE, NT
1987		8	DE, NT
4 yrs.	56 games		

Ed Holler
HOLLER, ED
B. Jan. 23, 1940
South Carolina 6'2" 233 lbs.

Year	Team	Games	Pos.
1963	**GB** N	2	LB
1964	**PIT** N	13	LB
2 yrs.	15 games		

Tommy Holleran
HOLLERAN, THOMAS V. (Speed)
B. Dec. 18, 1896
D. Nov., 1972, Pittsburgh, PA
Pittsburgh 5'7" 170 lbs.

Year	Team	Games	Pos.
1923	**BUF** N	5	HB

Ken Holley
HOLLEY, KENNETH J.
B. 1920
Holy Cross 5'10" 185 lbs.

Year	Team	Games	Pos.
1946	**MIA** AA	5	QB

Corey Holliday
HOLLIDAY, COREY LAMONT
B. Jan. 31, 1971, Richmond, VA
North Carolina 6'2" 208 lbs.

Year	Team	Games	Pos.
1995	**PIT** N	3	WR
1996		12	WR
2 yrs.	15 games		

Marcus Holliday
HOLLIDAY, MARCUS
B. Jul. 16, 1973, Memphis, TN
Memphis 5'11" 222 lbs.

Year	Team	Games	Pos.
1996	**STL** N	1	FB

Ron Holliday
HOLLIDAY, RON
B. Feb. 12, 1948, West Chester, PA
Pittsburgh 5'9" 168 lbs.

Year	Team	Games	Pos.
1973	**SD** N	11	WR

Doug Hollie
HOLLIE, DOUGLAS
B. Dec. 15, 1960, Detroit, MI
Southern Methodist 6'4" 265 lbs.

Year	Team	Games	Pos.
1987	**SEA** N	2	DE
1988		3	DE
2 yrs.	5 games		

Dwight Hollier
HOLLIER, DWIGHT LEON
B. Apr. 21, 1969, Hampton, VA
North Carolina 6'2" 242 lbs.

Year	Team	Games	Pos.
1992	**MIA** N	16	LB
1993		16	LB
1994		10	LB
1995		16	LB
1996		16	LB
5 yrs.	74 games		

Joe Hollingsworth
HOLLINGSWORTH, JOSEPH
B. Jun. 20, 1925
D. 1975
Eastern Kentucky 6'0" 200 lbs.

Year	Team	Games	Pos.
1949	**PIT** N	11	FB
1950		10	FB
1951		10	FB
3 yrs.	31 games		

Shawn Hollingsworth
HOLLINGSWORTH, SHAWN
B. Dec. 4, 1961, Brownwood, TX
New Mexico/Angelo State 6'2" 260 lbs.

Year	Team	Games	Pos.
1983	**DEN** N	5	OT

Lamont Hollinquest
HOLLINQUEST, LAMONT
B. Oct. 24, 1970, Lynwood, CA
Southern California 6'3" 245 lbs.

Year	Team	Games	Pos.
1993	**WAS** N	16	LB
1994		14	LB
1996	**GB** N	16	LB
3 yrs.	46 games		

David Hollis
HOLLIS, DAVID LANIER
B. Jul. 4, 1965, Harbor City, CA
Nevada-Las Vegas 5'11" 175 lbs.

Year	Team	Games	Pos.
1987	**SEA** N	11	CB
1988	**KC** N	2	CB, S
1988	**SEA** N	6	CB
1989		10	S
3 yrs.	29 games		

Mike Hollis
HOLLIS, MICHAEL SHANE
B. May 22, 1972, Kellogg, ID
Idaho 5'7" 180 lbs.

Year	Team	Games	Pos.
1995	**JAC** N	16	K
1996		16	K
2 yrs.	32 games		

Gus Holloman
HOLLOMAN, GUS MARTIN
B. Oct. 23, 1945, Beaumont, TX
Houston 6'3" 195 lbs.

Year	Team	Games	Pos.
1968	**DEN** A	13	DB
1969		14	S
1970	**NYJ** N	14	S
1971		11	S
1972		14	S
5 yrs.	66 games		

Brian Holloway
HOLLOWAY, BRIAN DOUGLASS
B. Jul. 25, 1959, Omaha, NE
Stanford 6'7" 280 lbs.

Year	Team	Games	Pos.
1981	**NE** N	16	OT
1982		9	OT
1983		16	OT
1984		16	OT
1985		16	OT
1986		15	OT
1987	**LARI** N	12	OT
1988		2	G, OT
8 yrs.	102 games		

Cornell Holloway
HOLLOWAY, CORNELL DUANE
B. Jan. 30, 1966, Alliance, OH
Pittsburgh 5'11" 182 lbs.

Year	Team	Games	Pos.
1990	**IND** N	15	CB, S
1991		10	CB, S
1992		7	CB, S
3 yrs.	32 games		

Derek Holloway
HOLLOWAY, DEREK LANCE
B. Jan. 17, 1961, Riverside, NJ
Arkansas 5'7" 166 lbs.

Year	Team	Games	Pos.
1986	**WAS** N	9	WR
1987	**TB** N	1	WR
2 yrs.	10 games		

Glen Holloway
HOLLOWAY, GLEN L.
B. Jan. 22, 1948, Corpus Christi, TX
North Texas State 6'3" 249 lbs.

Year	Team	Games	Pos.
1970	**CHI** N	14	G
1971		14	G
1972		14	G
1973		14	G

Year	Team	Games	Pos.

Glen Holloway continued

Year	Team	Games	Pos.
1974	CLE N	14	G
5 yrs.	70 games		

Johnny Holloway
HOLLOWAY, JOHNNY OWEN
B. Nov. 8, 1963, Galveston, TX
Northwestern/Kansas 5'11" 182 lbs.

Year	Team	Games	Pos.
1986	DAL N	16	CB
1987	STL N	3	CB
2 yrs.	19 games		

Randy Holloway
HOLLOWAY, RANDY
B. Aug. 26, 1955, Sharon, PA
Pittsburgh 6'5" 246 lbs.

Year	Team	Games	Pos.
1978	MIN N	16	DE
1979		16	DE
1980		16	DE
1981		16	DE
1982		9	DE
1983		16	DE
1984		8	DE
1984	STL N	6	DE
7 yrs.	103 games		

Stan Holloway
HOLLOWAY, STAN
B. Sep. 28, 1957, San Francisco, CA
California 6'2" 218 lbs.

Year	Team	Games	Pos.
1980	NO N	11	LB

Steve Holloway
HOLLOWAY, STEVE
B. Aug. 23, 1964, Montgomery, AL
Tennessee State 6'3" 235 lbs.

Year	Team	Games	Pos.
1987	TB N	6	TE

Tony Holloway
HOLLOWAY, ANTHONY LAMBERT
B. Apr. 21, 1964, Puerto Rico
Nebraska 6'2" 222 lbs.

Year	Team	Games	Pos.
1987	KC N	1	DE

Bob Holly
HOLLY, ROBERT C.
B. Jun. 1, 1960, Clifton, NJ
Princeton 6'2" 205 lbs.

Year	Team	Games	Pos.
1983	WAS N	5	QB
1985	ATL N	4	QB
2 yrs.	9 games		

Bernie Holm
HOLM, BERNARD (Tony)
B. May 22, 1908
D. Jul. 15, 1978, Waukegan, IL
Alabama 6'1" 214 lbs.

Year	Team	Games	Pos.
1930	PRO N	3	HB, FB
1931	POR N	14	FB, HB
1932	CHIC N	8	FB
1933	PIT N	9	FB
4 yrs.	34 games		

John Holman
HOLMAN, JOHN
B. 1902, New Orleans, LA
Deceased
None

Year	Team	Games	Pos.
1928	NYG N	1	T

Rodney Holman
HOLMAN, RODNEY A.
B. Apr. 20, 1960, Ypsilanti, MI
Tulane 6'3" 238 lbs.

Year	Team	Games	Pos.
1982	CIN N	9	TE

Year	Team	Games	Pos.

Rodney Holman continued

Year	Team	Games	Pos.
1983		16	TE
1984		16	TE
1985		16	TE
1986		16	TE
1987		12	TE
1988		16	TE
1989		16	TE
1990		16	TE
1991		16	TE
1992		13	TE
1993	DET N	16	TE
1994		15	TE
1995		16	TE
14 yrs.	209 games		

Scott Holman
HOLMAN, SCOTT HUNTINGTON
B. Sep. 27, 1962, Portland, OR
Oregon 6'2" 195 lbs.

Year	Team	Games	Pos.
1986	STL N	3	WR
1987	NYJ N	3	WR
2 yrs.	6 games		

Walter Holman
HOLMAN, WALTER REE
B. Apr. 6, 1959, Vaiden, MS
West Virginia State 5'10" 208 lbs.

Year	Team	Games	Pos.
1987	WAS N	3	RB

Willie Holman
HOLMAN, WILLIE JOSEPH
B. Feb. 27, 1945, St. Mathews, SC
South Carolina State 6'4" 250 lbs.

Year	Team	Games	Pos.
1968	CHI N	14	DE
1969		14	DE
1970		14	DE
1971		14	DE
1972		4	DE
1973		6	DE
1973	WAS N	11	DE
6 yrs.	77 games		

Rob Holmberg
HOLMBERG, ROBERT ANTHONY
B. May 6, 1971, Mt. Pleasant, PA
Penn State 6'3" 225 lbs.

Year	Team	Games	Pos.
1994	LARI N	16	LB
1995	OAK N	16	LB
1996		13	LB
3 yrs.	45 games		

Walt Holmer
HOLMER, WALTER R.
B. Dec. 5, 1902
D. Aug. 28, 1976, Cashmere, WA
Northwestern 6'0" 185 lbs.

Year	Team	Games	Pos.
1929	CHIB N	15	FB
1930		11	HB, FB
1931	CHIC N	8	HB
1932		10	HB
1933	BOS N	5	FB, HB
1933	PIT N	4	HB
5 yrs.	53 games		

Bruce Holmes
HOLMES, BRUCE
B. Oct. 24, 1965, El Paso, TX
Minnesota 6'2" 237 lbs.

Year	Team	Games	Pos.
1987	KC N	3	LB
1993	MIN N	1	LB
2 yrs.	4 games		

Clayton Holmes
HOLMES, CLAYTON ANTWAN

Year	Team	Games	Pos.

Clayton Holmes continued

B. Aug. 23, 1969, Florence, SC
Carson-Newman 5'10" 181 lbs.

Year	Team	Games	Pos.
1992	DAL N	15	CB
1994		15	CB
1995		8	CB
3 yrs.	38 games		

Darick Holmes
HOLMES, DARICK
B. Jul. 1, 1971, Pasadena, CA
Portland State 6'0" 226 lbs.

Year	Team	Games	Pos.
1995	BUF N	16	RB
1996		16	RB
2 yrs.	32 games		

Darryl Holmes
HOLMES, DARRYL DEWAYNE
B. Sep. 6, 1964, Birmingham, AL
Fort Valley State 6'2" 190 lbs.

Year	Team	Games	Pos.
1987	NE N	15	S
1988		16	S
1989		13	S
3 yrs.	44 games		

Don Holmes
HOLMES, DON IRA
B. Apr. 1, 1961, Miami, FL
Colorado/Mesa (Colorado) 5'10" 180 lbs.

Year	Team	Games	Pos.
1986	STL N	12	WR
1987		11	WR
1988	PHX N	16	WR
1989		15	WR
1990		6	WR
5 yrs.	60 games		

Earl Holmes
HOLMES, EARL
B. Apr. 28, 1973, Tallahassee, FL
Florida A&M 6'1" 238 lbs.

Year	Team	Games	Pos.
1996	PIT N	3	LB

Ernie Holmes
HOLMES, EARNEST LEE (Fats)
B. Jul. 11, 1948, Jamestown, TX
Texas Southern 6'3" 260 lbs.

Year	Team	Games	Pos.
1972	PIT N	14	DT
1973		14	DT
1974		13	DT
1975		13	DT
1976		14	DT
1977		13	DT
1978	NE N	3	NT
7 yrs.	84 games		

Jack Holmes
HOLMES, JACK
B. Jun. 20, 1953, Rolling Fork, MS
Texas Southern 5'11" 210 lbs.

Year	Team	Games	Pos.
1978	NO N	11	RB
1979		16	RB
1980		16	RB
1981		16	RB
1982		5	RB
5 yrs.	64 games		

Jerry Holmes
HOLMES, JERRY
B. Dec. 22, 1957, Hampton, VA
West Virginia 6'2" 175 lbs.

Year	Team	Games	Pos.
1980	NYJ N	12	DB
1981		16	CB, S
1982		9	CB, S
1983		16	CB
1986		15	CB
1987		8	CB
1988	DET N	16	CB

Year	Team	Games	Pos.

Jerry Holmes continued

Year	Team	Games	Pos.
1989		16	CB
1990	GB N	16	CB
1991		13	CB
10 yrs.	137 games		

John Holmes
HOLMES, JOHN L.
B. 1944
Florida A&M 6'2" 248 lbs.

Year	Team	Games	Pos.
1966	MIA A	3	DE

Lester Holmes
HOLMES, LESTER
B. Sep. 27, 1969, Tylertown, MS
Jackson State 6'3" 301 lbs.

Year	Team	Games	Pos.
1993	PHI N	12	G
1994		16	G
1995		2	OT
1996		16	OT
4 yrs.	46 games		

Mel Holmes
HOLMES, MELVIN
B. Jan. 22, 1950, Miami, FL
North Carolina A&T 6'3" 250 lbs.

Year	Team	Games	Pos.
1971	PIT N	14	OT
1972		14	OT
1973		3	G, OT
3 yrs.	31 games		

Mike Holmes
HOLMES, MICHAEL RAPHAEL
B. Nov. 18, 1950, Galveston, TX
Texas Southern 6'2" 195 lbs.

Year	Team	Games	Pos.
1974	SF N	3	S, CB
1975		14	CB, S
1976	BUF N	1	DB
1976	MIA N	3	WR
3 yrs.	31 games		

Pat Holmes
HOLMES, JAMES PATRICK
B. Aug. 3, 1940, Durant, OK
Texas Tech 6'5" 254 lbs.

Year	Team	Games	Pos.
1966	HOU A	14	DT
1967		14	DT
1968		13	DE
1969		14	DE
1970	HOU N	14	DE
1971		14	DE
1972		14	DE
1973	KC N	10	DE
8 yrs.	107 games		

Robert Holmes
HOLMES, ROBERT (Tank)
B. Oct. 5, 1945, Huntsville, TX
Southern University 5'9" 220 lbs.

Year	Team	Games	Pos.
1968	KC A	14	RB
1969		14	RB
1970	KC N	14	RB
1971	HOU N	8	RB
1972		6	RB
1973	SD N	13	RB
1975	HOU N	14	RB
7 yrs.	83 games		

Ron Holmes
HOLMES, RONALD
B. Aug. 26, 1963, Fort Benning, GA
Washington 6'4" 255 lbs.

Year	Team	Games	Pos.
1985	TB N	16	DE
1986		14	DE
1987		10	DE
1988		10	DE
1989	DEN N	15	DE

Year	Team	Games	Pos.

Ron Holmes *continued*

Year	Team		Games	Pos.
1990			14	DE
1991			15	DE
7 yrs.	94 games			

Rudy Holmes
HOLMES, RUDELL LERON
B. Jul. 19, 1952, Oakland, CA
Drake 5'10" 178 lbs.

1974	ATL	N	8	CB

Tom Holmoe
HOLMOE, TOM
B. Mar. 7, 1960, Los Angeles, CA
Brigham Young 6'2" 190 lbs.

1983	SF	N	16	CB, S
1984			16	CB, S
1986			16	S
1987			11	S
1988			16	S
1989			7	S
6 yrs.	82 games			

Pete Holohan
HOLOHAN, PETER JOSEPH
B. Jul. 25, 1959, Albany, NY
Notre Dame 6'4" 232 lbs.

1981	SD	N	7	TE
1982			9	TE
1983			16	TE
1984			15	TE
1985			15	TE
1986			16	TE
1987			12	TE
1988	LARM	N	16	TE
1989			16	TE
1990			16	TE
1991	KC	N	16	TE
1992	CLE	N	4	TE
12 yrs.	158 games			

Mike Holovak
HOLOVAK, MICHAEL JOSEPH
B. Sep. 19, 1919, Lansford, PA
Boston College 6'1" 213 lbs.

1946	LA	N	11	FB
1947	CHIB	N	12	FB
1948			11	FB
3 yrs.	34 games			

Bernard Holsey
HOSLEY, BERNARD
B. Dec. 10, 1973, Cave Springs, GA
Duke 6'2" 284 lbs.

1996	NYG	N	16	DT

Mike Holston
HOLSTON, MICHAEL
B. Jan. 8, 1958, Seat Pleasant, MD
Morgan State 6'3" 184 lbs.

1981	HOU	N	16	WR
1982			9	WR
1983			16	WR
1984			16	WR
1985			3	WR
1985	KC	N	4	WR
5 yrs.	64 games			

Harry Holt
HOLT, HARRY THOMPSON, III
B. Dec. 29, 1957, Harlingen, TX
Arizona 6'4" 240 lbs.

1983	CLE	N	15	TE
1984			12	TE
1985			11	TE
1986			14	TE
1987	SD	N	3	TE
5 yrs.	55 games			

Issiac Holt
HOLT, ISSIAC, III
B. Oct. 4, 1962, Birmingham, AL
Alcorn State 6'1" 200 lbs.

1985	MIN	N	15	CB
1986			16	CB
1987			9	CB
1988			13	CB
1989			5	CB
1989	DAL	N	9	CB
1990			15	CB
1991			15	CB
1992			16	CB
8 yrs.	113 games			

John Holt
HOLT, JOHN STEPHANIE
B. May 14, 1959, Lawton, OK
West Texas State 5'11" 180 lbs.

1981	TB	N	16	CB, S
1982			9	CB
1983			16	CB, S
1984			15	CB
1985			16	CB
1986	IND	N	16	CB
1987			12	CB
1988			9	CB
8 yrs.	109 games			

Pierce Holt
HOLT, PIERCE
B. Jan. 1, 1962, Marlin, TX
Angelo State 6'4" 280 lbs.

1988	SF	N	9	DE, NT
1989			16	NT
1990			16	DE
1991			13	DE
1992			16	DE
1993	ATL	N	16	DE
1994			12	DT
1995			11	DT
8 yrs.	109 games			

Robert Holt
HOLT, ROBERT JAMES (Radar)
B. Oct. 4, 1959, Denison, TX
Baylor 6'1" 182 lbs.

1982	BUF	N	7	WR

Glenn Holtzman
HOLTZMAN, GLENN
B. Oct. 9, 1930, Shreveport, LA
D. May 6, 1980, Reno, NV
North Texas State 6'3" 250 lbs.

1955	LA	N	12	OT
1956			12	OT
1957			12	OT, DE
1958			12	DE
4 yrs.	48 games			

E.J. Holub
HOLUB, EMIL JOE
B. Jan. 5, 1938, Lubbock, TX
Texas Tech 6'4" 231 lbs.

1961	DAL	A	14	LB
1962			14	C, LB
1963	KC	A	14	C, LB
1964			9	LB
1965			14	LB
1966			14	LB
1967			6	LB, C
1968			14	C
1969			14	C
1970	KC	N	14	C
10 yrs.	127 games			

Gordy Holz
HOLZ, GORDON FRANCIS

Gordy Holz *continued*
B. May 14, 1933, St. Paul, MN
Minnesota 6'4" 264 lbs.

1960	DEN	A		OT
1961			14	DT
1962			14	DT
1963			14	DT
1964	NY	A	14	DT
5 yrs.	56 games			

Tom Holzer
HOLZER, THOMAS ROBERT
B. Aug. 2, 1945, Indianapolis, IN
Louisville 6'4" 250 lbs.

1967	SF	N	14	DE

Dennis Homan
HOMAN, DENNIS
B. Jan. 9, 1946, Muscle Shoals, AL
Alabama 6'1" 180 lbs.

1968	DAL	N	10	OE
1969			11	WR
1970			10	WR
1971	KC	N	8	WR
1972			7	WR
5 yrs.	46 games			

Henry Homan
HOMAN, HENRY (Two-Bits, Babe)
B. 1902
Deceased
Lebanon Valley 5'5" 145 lbs.

1925	FRA	N	16	QB
1926			6	QB
1927			16	HB, QB, FB
1928			11	QB, HB
1929			17	QB, FB
1930			13	QB
6 yrs.	79 games			

Tom Homco
HOMCO, THOMAS ROSS
B. Jan. 8, 1970, Hammond, IN
Northwestern 6'0" 245 lbs.

1993	LARM	N	16	LB
1994			15	LB
1995	STL	N	11	LB
1996			3	LB
4 yrs.	45 games			

Charlie Honaker
HONAKER, FRANK CHARLES
B. Oct. 11, 1899
D. Apr. 21, 1974, Huntington, WV
Ohio State 5'11" 185 lbs.

1924	CLE	N	6	E, HB

Todd Hons
HONS, TODD
B. Sep. 5, 1961
Arizona State 6'1" 195 lbs.

1987	DET	N	3	QB

Estus Hood
HOOD, ESTUS, III
B. Nov. 14, 1955, Hattiesburg, MS
Illinois State 5'11" 180 lbs.

1978	GB	N	16	CB
1979			16	CB
1980			15	CB
1981			16	CB
1982			9	CB
1983			16	CB, S
1984			16	CB, S
7 yrs.	104 games			

Frank Hood
HOOD, FRANKLIN
B. Oct. 5, 1908
D. Sep., 1973, Bonneau, SC
Pittsburgh 6'0" 235 lbs.

1933	PIT	N	3	HB, DB

Winford Hood
HOOD, WINFORD DEWAYNE
B. Mar. 29, 1962, Atlanta, GA
Georgia 6'3" 262 lbs.

1984	DEN	N	16	G
1985			16	OT
1986			9	OT
1987			3	G
1988			3	G
5 yrs.	47 games			

Fair Hooker
HOOKER, FAIR, JR.
B. May 22, 1947, Los Angeles, CA
Arizona State 6'1" 198 lbs.

1969	CLE	N	13	WR
1970			13	WR
1971			14	WR
1972			14	WR
1973			13	WR
1974			7	WR
6 yrs.	74 games			

Alvin Hooks
HOOKS, ALVIN LEE
B. May 7, 1957, Los Angeles, CA
Northridge State 5'11" 170 lbs.

1981	PHI	N	3	WR

Jim Hooks
HOOKS, JAMES EARL
B. Oct. 23, 1950, Oklahoma City, OK
Central Oklahoma 5'11" 225 lbs.

1973	DET	N	11	RB
1974			8	RB
1975			12	RB
1976			1	RB
4 yrs.	32 games			

Roland Hooks
HOOKS, ROLAND
B. Jan. 2, 1953, Brooklyn, NY
North Carolina State 6'0" 196 lbs.

1976	BUF	N	14	RB
1977			14	RB
1978			16	RB
1979			16	RB
1980			16	RB
1981			16	RB
1982			6	RB
7 yrs.	98 games			

Hooley
HOOLEY
None

1924	MIN	N	3	E, G

Harry Hooligan
HOOLIGAN, HARRY
B. 1938
Bishop 6'2" 225 lbs.

1965	HOU	A	1	FB

Trell Hooper
HOOPER, JOHN LUTRELL
B. Dec. 22, 1961
Memphis State 5'11" 182 lbs.

1987	MIA	N	3	CB

Year	Team		Games	Pos.

Mitch Hoopes
HOOPES, MITCHELL KENT
B. Jul. 8, 1953, Bisbee, AZ
Arizona 6'1" 207 lbs.

Year	Team		Games	Pos.
1975	DAL	N	14	P
1976	SD		9	P
1976	HOU	N	1	P
1977	DET	N	1	P
3 yrs.	25 games			

Houston Hoover
HOOVER, HOUSTON ROOSEVELT
B. Jun. 2, 1965, Yazoo City, MS
Jackson State 6'2" 285 lbs.

Year	Team		Games	Pos.
1988	ATL	N	15	OT
1989			16	OT
1990			16	OT, G
1991			16	G
1992			16	G
1993	CLE	N	16	G
1994	MIA	N	3	G
7 yrs.	98 games			

Mel Hoover
HOOVER, MELVIN CHARLES
B. Sep. 21, 1959, Charlotte, NC
Arizona State 6'0" 185 lbs.

Year	Team		Games	Pos.
1982	PHI	N	7	WR
1983			11	WR
1984			12	WR
1987	DET	N	2	WR
4 yrs.	32 games			

Charles Hope
HOPE, CHARLES
B. Mar. 12, 1970, Wilmington, DE
Central State (Ohio) 6'3" 303 lbs.

Year	Team		Games	Pos.
1994	GB	N	6	G

Neil Hope
HOPE, NEIL
B. Mar. 22, 1963, Memphis, TN
Southern California 6'2" 235 lbs.

Year	Team		Games	Pos.
1987	LARM	N	3	LB

Andy Hopkins
HOPKINS, ANDREW
B. Oct. 19, 1949, Crockett, TX
Stephen F. Austin 5'10" 187 lbs.

Year	Team		Games	Pos.
1971	HOU	N	2	RB

Brad Hopkins
HOPKINS, BRAD
B. Sep. 5, 1970, Columbia, SC
Illinois 6'3" 306 lbs.

Year	Team		Games	Pos.
1993	HOU	N	16	OT
1994			16	OT
1995			16	OT
1996			16	OT
4 yrs.	64 games			

Jerry Hopkins
HOPKINS, JERRY WAYNE
B. Jan. 24, 1941, Chalk Bluff, TX
Texas A&M 6'2" 236 lbs.

Year	Team		Games	Pos.
1963	DEN	A	7	LB
1964			14	LB
1965			14	LB
1966			14	LB
1967	MIA	A	13	LB
1968	OAK	A	5	LB
6 yrs.	67 games			

Roy Hopkins
HOPKINS, ROY LEE
B. Feb. 18, 1945, Gilmer, TX
Texas Southern 6'1" 233 lbs.

Year	Team		Games	Pos.
1967	HOU	A	14	RB
1968			14	RB
1969			14	RB
1970	HOU	N	12	RB
4 yrs.	54 games			

Ted Hopkins
HOPKINS, EDWARD
B. Dec. 5, 1890
D. Mar., 1973, Hills and Dales, OH
None 5'9" 180 lbs.

Year	Team		Games	Pos.
1921	COL	A	3	E, T
1922	COL	N	4	E, G-T
2 yrs.	7 games			

Thomas Hopkins
HOPKINS, THOMAS
B. Jan. 13, 1960, Butler, AL
Alabama A&M 6'6" 260 lbs.

Year	Team		Games	Pos.
1983	CLE	N	2	OT

Wes Hopkins
HOPKINS, WES
B. Sep. 26, 1961, Birmingham, AL
Southern Methodist 6'1" 210 lbs.

Year	Team		Games	Pos.
1983	PHI	N	14	S
1984			16	S
1985			15	S
1986			4	S
1988			16	S
1989			16	S
1990			15	S
1991			16	S
1992			10	S
1993			15	S
10 yrs.	137 games			

Harry Hopp
HOPP, HARRY
B. Dec. 13, 1918, Hastings, NE
D. Dec. 22, 1964, Hastings, NE
Nebraska 6'0" 209 lbs.

Year	Team		Games	Pos.
1941	DET	N	10	FB, LB
1942			10	FB, LB
1943			10	FB, LB
1946	BUF	AA	10	QB, FB, LB
1946	MIA	AA	3	FB, LB
1947	LA	AA	9	FB, LB
5 yrs.	52 games			

Darrel Hopper
HOPPER, DARREL
B. Mar. 14, 1964, Los Angeles, CA
Southern California 6'1" 196 lbs.

Year	Team		Games	Pos.
1987	SD	N	4	CB, S

Doug Hoppock
HOPPOCK, DOUGLAS GENE
B. Jan. 3, 1960, Wichita, KS
Kansas State 6'4" 280 lbs.

Year	Team		Games	Pos.
1987	KC	N	3	OT

Al Hoptowit
HOPTOWIT, ALBERT WILLIAM
B. Sep. 7, 1915, Yakima, WA
Washington State 6'1" 217 lbs.

Year	Team		Games	Pos.
1942	CHIB	N	11	T
1943			10	T
1944			9	T
1945			10	T
4 yrs.	40 games			

Mike Horan
HORAN, MICHAEL WILLIAM
B. Feb. 1, 1959, Orange, TX
Long Beach State 5'11" 190 lbs.

Year	Team		Games	Pos.
1984	PHI	N	16	P
1985			16	P
1986	DEN	N	4	P
1987			12	P
1988			16	P
1989			16	P
1990			15	P
1991			16	P
1992			8	P
1993	NYG	N	8	P
1994			16	P
1995			16	P
1996			16	P
13 yrs.	175 games			

Roy Hord
HORD, AMBROSE ROY, JR.
B. Dec. 25, 1934, Charlotte, NC
Duke 6'4" 244 lbs.

Year	Team		Games	Pos.
1960	LA	N	12	G
1961			14	G
1962			4	G
1962	PHI	N	10	G
1963	NY	A	13	G
4 yrs.	53 games			

Alvin Horn
HORN, ALVIN RAMONE, JR.
B. Mar. 7, 1965
Nevada-Las Vegas 5'11" 185 lbs.

Year	Team		Games	Pos.
1987	CLE	N	3	S

Bob Horn
HORN, ROBERT ALLEN
B. Feb. 6, 1954, Salem, OR
Oregon State 6'3" 233 lbs.

Year	Team		Games	Pos.
1976	SD	N	14	LB
1977			14	LB
1978			16	LB
1979			16	LB
1980			16	LB
1981			16	LB
1982	SF	N	9	LB
1983			8	LB
8 yrs.	109 games			

Dick Horn
HORN, RICHARD H.
B. 1930
Stanford 6'1" 195 lbs.

Year	Team		Games	Pos.
1958	BAL	N	5	QB

Don Horn
HORN, DONALD GLENN
B. Mar. 9, 1945, South Gate, CA
Washington State/San Diego State 6'2" 195 lbs.

Year	Team		Games	Pos.
1967	GB	N	3	QB
1968			1	QB
1969			9	QB
1970			7	QB
1971	DEN	N	9	QB
1972			2	QB
1973	CLE	N	14	QB
7 yrs.	45 games			

Joe Horn
HORN, JOE
B. Jan. 16, 1972, Tupelo, MS
Itawamba JC 6'1" 195 lbs.

Year	Team		Games	Pos.
1996	KC	N	10	WR

Marty Horn
HORN, MARTIN
B. Mar. 27, 1963
Lehigh 6'2" 206 lbs.

Year	Team		Games	Pos.
1987	PHI	N	1	QB

Rod Horn
HORN, ROD LEE
B. Nov. 23, 1956, Fresno, CA
Nebraska 6'4" 268 lbs.

Year	Team		Games	Pos.
1980	CIN	N	7	DT
1981			16	NT
2 yrs.	23 games			

Jay Hornbeak
HORNBEAK, JAY W.
B. 1912
Washington 5'11" 185 lbs.

Year	Team		Games	Pos.
1935	BKN	N	5	QB

Dick Horne
HORNE, RICHARD COURTLAND
B. 1918
Oregon 6'2" 214 lbs.

Year	Team		Games	Pos.
1941	NYG	N	2	E
1946	MIA	AA	10	E
1947	SF	AA	10	E
3 yrs.	22 games			

Greg Horne
HORNE, GREG
B. Nov. 22, 1964, Russellville, AR
Arkansas 6'0" 188 lbs.

Year	Team		Games	Pos.
1987	CIN	N	4	P
1987	STL	N	5	P
1988	PHX	N	16	P
2 yrs.	25 games			

Sam Horner
HORNER, SAMUEL WATSON, III
B. Mar. 4, 1938, Fort Sill, OK
Virginia Military Institute 6'0" 197 lbs.

Year	Team		Games	Pos.
1960	WAS	N	10	HB, DB
1961			14	HB, DB
1962	NYG	N	9	DB
3 yrs.	33 games			

Bill Hornick
HORNICK, WILLIAM M.
B. 1919
Tulane 6'1" 207 lbs.

Year	Team		Games	Pos.
1947	PIT	N	4	T

Clarence Horning
HORNING, CLARENCE E. (Steamer)
B. Nov. 15, 1892, Caledonia, NY
D. Jan. 24, 1982, Southfield, MI
Colgate 6'0" 198 lbs.

Year	Team		Games	Pos.
1920	DET	A	4	T
1921			7	T
1921	BUF	A	2	T
1922	TOL	N	9	T
1923			8	T
4 yrs.	30 games			

Ronnie Hornsby
HORNSBY, RONALD JOSEPH
B. Aug. 16, 1949, Baton Rouge, LA
Southeastern Louisiana 6'3" 231 lbs.

Year	Team		Games	Pos.
1971	NYG	N	14	LB
1972			13	LB
1973			13	LB
1974			9	LB
4 yrs.	49 games			

Year	Team		Games	Pos.

Paul Hornung
HORNUNG, PAUL VERNON
(Golden Boy)
B. Dec. 23, 1935, Louisville, KY
Notre Dame 6'2" 215 lbs.

Year	Team		Games	Pos.
1957	**GB**	N	12	HB, K
1958			12	HB, K
1959			12	HB, K
1960			12	HB, K
1961			12	HB, K
1962			9	HB, K
1964			14	HB, K
1965			12	HB, K
1966			9	HB
9 yrs.	104 games			

Bill Horrell
HORRELL, WILLIAM G.
B. Mar. 15, 1930, New Kensington, PA
Michigan State 5'11" 222 lbs.

Year	Team		Games	Pos.
1952	**PHI**	N	4	G

Roy Horstmann
HORSTMANN, ROY J.
B. 1911
Purdue 6'0" 188 lbs.

Year	Team		Games	Pos.
1933	**BOS**	N	8	FB, HB
1934	**CHIC**	N	9	FB
2 yrs.	17 games			

Bob Horton
HORTON, ROBERT
B. 1943
Boston University 6'2" 230 lbs.

Year	Team		Games	Pos.
1964	**SD**	A	10	LB
1965			12	LB
2 yrs.	22 games			

Ethan Horton
HORTON, ETHAN SHANE
B. Dec. 19, 1962, Kannapolis, NC
North Carolina 6'3" 228 lbs.

Year	Team		Games	Pos.
1985	**KC**	N	6	RB
1987	**LARI**	N	4	RB
1989			16	TE
1990			16	TE
1991			16	TE
1992			16	TE
1993			16	TE
1994	**WAS**	N	16	TE
8 yrs.	116 games			

Greg Horton
HORTON, GREGORY KEITH
B. Jan. 1, 1951, San Bernardino, CA
Colorado 6'4" 246 lbs.

Year	Team		Games	Pos.
1976	**LA**	N	14	G
1977			14	G
1978			2	G
1978	**TB**	N	14	G
1979			16	G
1980	**LA**	N	3	G, C
5 yrs.	63 games			

Larry Horton
HORTON, LAWRENCE
B. Apr. 29, 1949, Gary, IN
Iowa 6'2" 248 lbs.

Year	Team		Games	Pos.
1972	**CHI**	N	10	DE

Les Horton
HORTON, LES
Rutgers

Year	Team		Games	Pos.
1930	**NEW**	N	1	FB

Ray Horton
HORTON, RAYMOND ANTHONY
B. Apr. 12, 1960, Tacoma, WA
Washington 5'11" 190 lbs.

Year	Team		Games	Pos.
1983	**CIN**	N	16	CB
1984			15	CB
1985			16	CB
1986			16	CB
1987			12	CB
1988			13	CB
1989	**DAL**	N	16	S
1990			14	S
1991			16	S
1992			12	S
10 yrs.	146 games			

Les Horvath
HORVATH, LESLIE
B. Sep. 12, 1921, South Bend, IN
Ohio State 5'10" 173 lbs.

Year	Team		Games	Pos.
1947	**LA**	N	10	HB
1948			12	HB
1949	**CLE**	AA	12	HB
3 yrs.	34 games			

Arnie Horween
HOROWITZ, ARNOLD (PLAYED AS MCMAHON)
B. Jul. 7, 1898, Chicago, IL
D. Aug. 5, 1985, Chicago, IL
Harvard 5'11" 206 lbs.

Year	Team		Games	Pos.
1921	**CHIC**	A	2	HB
1922	**CHIC**	N	11	HB
1923			10	HB, T, FB
1924			8	HB
4 yrs.	31 games			

Ralph Horween
HOROWITZ, RALPH (PLAYED AS MCMAHON)
B. Aug. 3, 1896, Chicago, IL
D. May 26, 1997, Charlottesville, VA
Harvard 5'10" 206 lbs.

Year	Team		Games	Pos.
1921	**CHIC**	A	3	QB
1922	**CHIC**	N	8	FB, HB, QB
1923			9	HB, T, QB
3 yrs.	20 games			

Bob Hoskins
HOSKINS, ROBERT JUAN
B. Sep. 16, 1945, Highland, IL
Wichita State 6'2" 246 lbs.

Year	Team		Games	Pos.
1970	**SF**	N	14	G
1971			7	G
1972			14	DT
1973			14	DT
1974			14	DT
1975			14	DT
6 yrs.	77 games			

Derrick Hoskins
HOSKINS, DERRICK
B. Nov. 4, 1970, Meridian, MS
Southern Mississippi 6'2" 200 lbs.

Year	Team		Games	Pos.
1992	**LARI**	N	16	S
1993			16	S
1994			15	S
1995	**OAK**	N	13	S
1996	**NO**	N	1	S
5 yrs.	61 games			

Clarence Hosmer
HOSMER, CLARENCE
B. Jul. 28, 1891
D. Nov., 1968, Buffalo, NY
None 5'10" 205 lbs.

Year	Team		Games	Pos.
1921	**TON**	N	1	G

Clark Hoss
HOSS, CLARK
B. Feb. 19, 1949, Portland, OR
Oregon State 6'8" 235 lbs.

Year	Team		Games	Pos.
1972	**PHI**	N	4	TE

Jeff Hostetler
HOSTETLER, JEFF W. (Hoss)
B. Apr. 22, 1961, Hollsopple, PA
West Virginia 6'3" 212 lbs.

Year	Team		Games	Pos.
1985	**NYG**	N	5	QB
1986			13	QB
1988			16	QB
1989			16	QB
1990			16	QB
1991			12	QB
1992			13	QB
1993	**LARI**	N	15	QB
1994			16	QB
1995	**OAK**	N	11	QB
1996			13	QB
11 yrs.	146 games			

Babe Houck
HOUCK, ORLAN G.
B. Aug. 20, 1897
D. Jul., 1983, Athens, OH
None 6'0" 275 lbs.

Year	Team		Games	Pos.
1920	**COL**	A	1	G
1921			7	G
2 yrs.	8 games			

Jim Hough
HOUGH, JAMES HUSEN
B. Aug. 4, 1956, Lynwood, CA
Utah State 6'2" 268 lbs.

Year	Team		Games	Pos.
1978	**MIN**	N	15	C
1979			16	C
1980			10	C
1981			16	C
1982			9	C
1983			16	G
1984			9	G
1985			4	G
1986			16	G
9 yrs.	111 games			

Jerry Houghton
HOUGHTON, JERALD
B. Apr. 18, 1926, Yakima, WA
Washington State 6'2" 226 lbs.

Year	Team		Games	Pos.
1950	**WAS**	N	12	T

Bill Houle
HOULE, WILFRID
B. Mar. 3, 1901
D. Aug., 1964
St. Thomas (Minnesota) 5'8" 165 lbs.

Year	Team		Games	Pos.
1924	**MIN**	N	6	QB

Kevin House
HOUSE, KEVIN NATHANIEL
B. Dec. 20, 1957, St. Louis, MO
Southern Illinois 6'1" 175 lbs.

Year	Team		Games	Pos.
1980	**TB**	N	14	WR
1981			16	WR
1982			9	WR
1983			16	WR
1984			16	WR
1985			16	WR
1986			7	WR
1986	**LARM**	N	8	WR
1987			12	WR
8 yrs.	114 games			

Bill Houser
HOUSER, WILLIAM A.
B. 1899
None

Year	Team		Games	Pos.
1921	**LOU**	A	1	G

John Houser
HOUSER, JOHN
B. Jun. 21, 1935, Nashville, TN
Redlands 6'3" 239 lbs.

Year	Team		Games	Pos.
1957	**LA**	N	12	G
1958			12	G
1959			12	G
1960	**DAL**	N	11	C
1961			14	G
1963	**STL**	N	7	G
6 yrs.	68 games			

Walter Housman
HOUSMAN, WALTER
B. Oct. 13, 1962
Upsala 6'5" 285 lbs.

Year	Team		Games	Pos.
1987	**NO**	N	3	OT, G

Bill Houston
HOUSTON, WILLIAM
B. Aug. 22, 1951, Oxford, MS
Jackson State 6'3" 208 lbs.

Year	Team		Games	Pos.
1974	**DAL**	N	14	WR

Bobby Houston
HOUSTON, BOBBY
B. Oct. 26, 1967, Washington, DC
North Carolina State 6'2" 236 lbs.

Year	Team		Games	Pos.
1990	**GB**	N	1	LB
1991	**NYJ**	N	14	LB
1992			16	LB
1993			16	LB
1994			16	LB
1995			16	LB
1996			15	LB
7 yrs.	94 games			

Jim Houston
HOUSTON, JAMES EDWARD, SR.
B. Nov. 3, 1937, Massillon, OH
Ohio State 6'2" 239 lbs.

Year	Team		Games	Pos.
1960	**CLE**	N	12	DE
1961			14	DE
1962			14	DE
1963			14	LB
1964			14	LB
1965			12	LB
1966			14	LB
1967			13	LB
1968			14	LB
1969			4	LB
1970			14	LB
1971			14	LB
1972			14	LB
13 yrs.	167 games			

Ken Houston
HOUSTON, KENNETH RAY
B. Nov. 12, 1944, Lufkin, TX
Prairie View A&M 6'3" 196 lbs.

Year	Team		Games	Pos.
1967	**HOU**	A	14	DB
1968			9	DB
1969			14	S
1970	**HOU**	N	14	S
1971			14	S
1972			14	S
1973	**WAS**	N	14	S
1974			14	S
1975			14	S
1976			14	S
1977			14	S

| Year | Team | Games | Pos. | | Year | Team | Games | Pos. | | Year | Team | Games | Pos. | | Year | Team | Games | Pos. |

Ken Houston *continued*

Year	Team	Games	Pos.
1978		16	S
1979		13	S
1980		13	S
14 yrs.	191 games		

Lin Houston
HOUSTON, LINDELL LEE
B. Jan. 11, 1921, Carbondale, IL
Ohio State 6'0" 213 lbs.

Year	Team		Games	Pos.
1946	CLE	AA	12	G
1947			14	G
1948			13	G
1949			12	G
1950	CLE	N	12	G
1951			11	G
1952			11	G
1953			12	G
8 yrs.	97 games			

Rich Houston
HOUSTON, RICHARD CHARLES
B. Nov. 16, 1945, Texarkana, TX
East Texas State 6'2" 196 lbs.

Year	Team		Games	Pos.
1969	NYG	N	6	WR
1970			13	WR
1971			13	WR
1972			14	WR
1973			14	WR
5 yrs.	60 games			

Wally Houston
HOUSTON, L. WALTER
B. 1933, Wolf Lake, IL
Purdue 6'0" 217 lbs.

Year	Team		Games	Pos.
1955	WAS	N	10	G

Don Hover
HOVER, DON R.
B. Dec. 13, 1954, Seattle, WA
Washington State 6'2" 225 lbs.

Year	Team		Games	Pos.
1978	WAS	N	16	LB
1979			16	LB
2 yrs.	32 games			

John Hovious
HOVIOUS, JOHN A. (Junie)
B. 1919
Mississippi 5'8" 180 lbs.

Year	Team		Games	Pos.
1945	NYG	N	6	HB

Anthony Howard
HOWARD, ANTHONY
B. Jul. 16, 1960
Tennessee 6'3" 267 lbs.

Year	Team		Games	Pos.
1987	NYG	N	3	G

Billy Howard
HOWARD, BILLY
B. Aug. 17, 1950, Clarksdale, MS
Alcorn State 6'4" 252 lbs.

Year	Team		Games	Pos.
1974	DET	N	12	DT
1975			13	DT, DE
1976			13	DE
3 yrs.	38 games			

Bob Howard
HOWARD, ROBERT (Dorsey)
B. Dec. 25, 1900
D. Mar., 1979, Denham, IA
Marietta 6'0" 225 lbs.

Year	Team		Games	Pos.
1925	KC	N	8	G
1926			7	G
1927	CLE	N	12	G
1928	DET	N	8	G

Bob Howard *continued*

Year	Team		Games	Pos.
1929	NYG	N	12	G, T
1930			15	G, T
6 yrs.	62 games			

Bobby Howard
HOWARD, ROBERT
B. Jun. 1, 1964, Pittsburgh, PA
Indiana 6'0" 210 lbs.

Year	Team		Games	Pos.
1986	TB	N	7	RB
1987			12	RB
1988			3	RB
3 yrs.	22 games			

Bobby Howard
HOWARD, ROBERT LEE
B. Nov. 24, 1944, Tallulah, LA
San Diego State 6'1" 181 lbs.

Year	Team		Games	Pos.
1967	SD	A	14	DB
1968			14	DB
1969			14	CB
1970	SD	N	14	CB
1971			14	CB
1972			5	CB
1973			13	CB
1974			14	CB
1975	NE	N	14	CB
1976			14	CB
1977			14	CB
1978	PHI	N	10	CB
1979			16	CB
13 yrs.	170 games			

Bryan Howard
HOWARD, BRYAN EDWARD
B. Mar. 6, 1959, New Orleans, LA
Tennessee State 6'1" 200 lbs.

Year	Team		Games	Pos.
1982	MIN	N	2	S

Carl Howard
HOWARD, CARL DELANO, JR.
B. Sep. 20, 1961, Newark, NJ
Rutgers 6'2" 190 lbs.

Year	Team		Games	Pos.
1984	DAL	N	10	CB
1985	TB	N	4	CB
1985	NYJ	N	3	CB
1986			14	CB
1987			12	CB, S
1988			16	CB, S
1989			15	CB, S
1990			1	CB
7 yrs.	75 games			

Dana Howard
HOWARD, DANA
B. Feb. 25, 1972, East St. Louis, IL
Illinois 6'0" 238 lbs.

Year	Team		Games	Pos.
1995	STL	N	16	LB
1996	CHI	N	3	LB
2 yrs.	19 games			

David Howard
HOWARD, DAVID
B. Dec. 8, 1961, Enterprise, AL
Oregon State/Long Beach State 6'2" 232 lbs.

Year	Team		Games	Pos.
1985	MIN	N	16	LB
1986			14	LB
1987			10	LB
1988			16	LB
1989			5	LB
1989	DAL	N	11	LB
1990			16	LB
1991	NE	N	16	LB
1992			16	LB
8 yrs.	120 games			

Desmond Howard
HOWARD, DESMOND KEVIN
B. May 15, 1970, Cleveland, OH
Michigan 5'9" 182 lbs.

Year	Team		Games	Pos.
1992	WAS	N	16	WR
1993			16	WR
1994			16	WR
1995	JAC	N	13	WR
1996	GB	N	16	WR
5 yrs.	77 games			

Erik Howard
HOWARD, ERIK
B. Nov. 12, 1964, Pittsfield, MA
Washington State 6'4" 268 lbs.

Year	Team		Games	Pos.
1986	NYG	N	8	NT
1987			12	NT
1988			16	NT
1989			16	NT
1990			16	NT
1991			6	NT
1992			16	NT
1993			16	NT
1994			16	DT
1995	NYJ	N	16	DE, DT
1996			1	DT
11 yrs.	139 games			

Gene Howard
HOWARD, EUGENE
B. Dec. 22, 1946, Little Rock, AR
Langston 6'0" 190 lbs.

Year	Team		Games	Pos.
1968	NO	N	14	DB
1969			14	CB
1970			8	CB
1971	LA	N	14	CB
1972			13	CB
5 yrs.	63 games			

Harry Howard
HOWARD, HARRY
B. Oct. 7, 1949, Cincinnati, OH
Ohio State 6'0" 189 lbs.

Year	Team		Games	Pos.
1976	NYJ	N	1	S

Leroy Howard
HOWARD, LEROY
B. Jun. 16, 1949, Port Arthur, TX
Bishop 5'11" 175 lbs.

Year	Team		Games	Pos.
1971	HOU	N	7	DB

Joey Howard
HOWARD, JOSEPH EISSIX
B. Sep. 14, 1965, Springfield, OH
Tennessee 6'6" 305 lbs.

Year	Team		Games	Pos.
1989	SD	N	9	OT

Lynn Howard
HOWARD, LYNN W. (Tubby)
B. Jul. 10, 1894
D. May, 1969, Prescott, AZ
Ripon/Wisconsin/Indiana 5'10" 210 lbs.

Year	Team		Games	Pos.
1921	GB	A	4	FB, HB
1922	GB	N	8	E
2 yrs.	12 games			

Paul Howard
HOWARD, PAUL EUGENE
B. Sep. 12, 1950, San Jose, CA
Brigham Young 6'3" 260 lbs.

Year	Team		Games	Pos.
1973	DEN	N	14	G
1974			14	G
1975			14	G
1976			14	G
1977			14	G
1978			13	G
1979			14	G
1980			14	G
1981			16	G

Paul Howard *continued*

Year	Team		Games	Pos.
1982			9	G
1983			16	G
1984			16	G
1985			16	G
1986			15	G
13 yrs.	187 games			

Percy Howard
HOWARD, PERCY LENARD
B. Jan. 21, 1952, Savannah, GA
Austin Peay 6'4" 210 lbs.*

Year	Team		Games	Pos.
1975	DAL	N	8	WR

Red Howard
HOWARD, ALBERT FRANKLIN
B. Nov. 23, 1900
D. May 29, 1973, Essex Fells, NJ
New Hampshire/Princeton 5'11" 192 lbs.

Year	Team		Games	Pos.
1926	BKN	A	4	G
1926	BKN	N	3	G
1927	NYG	N	2	G, T
2 yrs.	9 games			

Ron Howard
HOWARD, RONALD FORD
B. Mar. 3, 1951, Oakland, CA
Seattle 6'4" 229 lbs.*

Year	Team		Games	Pos.
1974	DAL	N	12	TE
1975			10	TE
1976	SEA	N	14	TE
1977			12	TE
1978			16	TE
1979	BUF	N	1	TE
6 yrs.	65 games			

Sherman Howard
HOWARD, SHERMAN JOHN
B. Nov. 28, 1924, New Orleans, LA
Iowa/Nevada-Reno 5'11" 193 lbs.

Year	Team		Games	Pos.
1949	B, NY	AA	12	HB
1950	NYY	N	12	HB
1951			12	HB
1952	CLE	N	5	HB
1953			12	HB, DB
5 yrs.	53 games			

Thomas Howard
HOWARD, JAMES THOMAS
B. Aug. 18, 1954, Lubbock, TX
Texas Tech 6'2" 215 lbs.

Year	Team		Games	Pos.
1977	KC	N	13	LB
1978			16	LB
1979			16	LB
1980			16	LB
1981			9	LB
1982			9	LB
1983			16	LB
1984	STL	N	15	LB
1985			3	LB
9 yrs.	113 games			

Todd Howard
HOWARD, WALTER LEE
B. Feb. 18, 1965, Bryan, TX
Texas A&M 6'2" 235 lbs.

Year	Team		Games	Pos.
1987	KC	N	12	LB
1988			7	LB
2 yrs.	19 games			

William Howard
HOWARD, WILLIAM DOTSON
B. Jun. 2, 1964, Lima, OH
Tennessee 6'0" 240 lbs.

Year	Team		Games	Pos.
1988	TB	N	15	RB
1989			16	RB
2 yrs.	31 games			

Year	Team	Games	Pos.

Garry Howe
HOWE, GARRY WILLIAM
B. Jun. 20, 1968, Spencer, IA
Drake/Colorado 6'1" 298 lbs.

Year	Team		Games	Pos.
1992	PIT	N	11	NT
1993	CIN	N	1	NT
1994	IND	N	1	NT

3 yrs.   13 games

Glen Howe
HOWE, BOBBY GLEN
B. Oct. 18, 1961, New Albany, MS
Southern Mississippi 6'7" 298 lbs.

Year	Team		Games	Pos.
1985	PIT	N	2	OT
1985	ATL	N	5	OT
1986			7	OT

2 yrs.   14 games

Bill Howell
HOWELL, WILFRED DANIEL
B. Apr. 21, 1904
D. Aug., 1981, Washington, DC
Catholic 5'11" 175 lbs.

Year	Team		Games	Pos.
1929	BOS	N	5	E

Clarence Howell
HOWELL, JOHN C. (Cotton)
B. 1927
Texas A&M 6'1" 188 lbs.

Year	Team		Games	Pos.
1948	SF	AA	12	E

Delles Howell
HOWELL, DELLES
B. Aug. 22, 1948, Vallejo, CA
Grambling State 6'3" 199 lbs.

Year	Team		Games	Pos.
1970	NO	N	12	CB
1971			14	CB
1972			10	CB
1973	NYJ	N	14	CB
1974			10	CB
1975			10	CB

6 yrs.   70 games

Dixie Howell
HOWELL, MILLARD FILLMORE
B. Nov. 24, 1912, Hartford, AL
D. Mar. 2, 1971, Hollywood, CA
Alabama 5'11" 175 lbs.

Year	Team		Games	Pos.
1937	WAS	N	5	HB

Earl Howell
HOWELL, EARL OTTO (Dixie)
B. Aug. 28, 1924, Talladega, AL
Mississippi/Muhlenberg/Mississippi 5'10" 189 lbs.

Year	Team		Games	Pos.
1949	LA	AA	12	HB

Foster Howell
HOWELL, FOSTER (Dick)
B. Feb., 1911
Texas Christian 6'3" 215 lbs.

Year	Team		Games	Pos.
1934	C, S	N	6	T

John Howell
HOWELL, JOHN
B. 1915
Nebraska 5'10" 185 lbs.

Year	Team		Games	Pos.
1938	GB	N	6	HB, LB

Jim Lee Howell
HOWELL, JAMES LEE
B. Sep. 27, 1914, Lonoke, AR
D. Jan. 4, 1995, Lonoke, AR
Arkansas 6'6" 210 lbs.

Year	Team		Games	Pos.
1937	NYG	N	8	E

Jim Lee Howell *continued*

Year	Team	Games	Pos.
1938		10	E
1939		7	E
1940		11	E
1941		11	E
1942		10	E
1946		11	E
1947		6	E

8 yrs.   74 games

Lane Howell
HOWELL, AUTREY LANE
B. Jul. 28, 1941, Monroe, LA
Grambling State 6'5" 264 lbs.

Year	Team		Games	Pos.
1963	NYG	N	14	DT, OT
1964			14	OT
1965	PHI	N	14	OT
1966			10	OT
1967			11	OT
1968			14	OT
1969			14	OT

7 yrs.   91 games

Mike Howell
HOWELL, MICHAEL LIONEL
B. Jul. 5, 1943, West Monroe, LA
Grambling State 6'1" 189 lbs.

Year	Team		Games	Pos.
1965	CLE	N	14	DB
1966			14	DB
1967			14	DB
1968			14	DB
1969			4	S
1970			14	S
1971			14	S

7 yrs.   88 games

Pat Howell
HOWELL, PAT GERARD
B. Mar. 12, 1957, Fresno, CA
Southern California 6'5" 262 lbs.

Year	Team		Games	Pos.
1979	ATL	N	15	G
1980			5	G
1981			16	G
1982			9	G
1983			2	G
1983	HOU	N	7	G
1984			11	G
1985			2	G

7 yrs.   67 games

Steve Howell
HOWELL, STEPHEN GLEN
B. Dec. 20, 1956, Corsicana, TX
Baylor 6'2" 227 lbs.

Year	Team		Games	Pos.
1979	MIA	N	16	FB
1980			16	FB
1981			10	FB

3 yrs.   42 games

Karl Hower
HOWER, KARL
B. 1902
Deceased
None

Year	Team		Games	Pos.
1921	LOU	A	1	FB

Bobby Howfield
HOWFIELD, BOBBY
B. Dec. 3, 1936, Bushey, England
None 5'9" 180 lbs.

Year	Team		Games	Pos.
1968	DEN	A	12	K
1969			14	K
1970	DEN	N	14	K
1971	NYJ	N	14	K
1972			14	K
1973			14	K
1974			7	K

7 yrs.   89 games

Ian Howfield
HOWFIELD, IAN MICHAEL
B. Jun. 4, 1966, Watford, England
Tennessee 6'2" 196 lbs.

Year	Team		Games	Pos.
1991	HOU	N	9	K

Chuck Howley
HOWLEY, CHARLES LOUIS
B. Jun. 28, 1936, Wheeling, WV
West Virginia 6'3" 228 lbs.

Year	Team		Games	Pos.
1958	CHIB	N	12	LB
1959			3	LB
1961	DAL	N	13	LB
1962			14	LB
1963			14	LB
1964			12	LB
1965			14	LB
1966			14	LB
1967			14	LB
1968			14	LB
1969			14	LB
1970			14	LB
1971			14	LB
1972			13	LB
1973			1	LB

15 yrs.   180 games

Billy Howton
HOWTON, WILLIAM
B. Jul. 5, 1930, Middlefield, TX
Rice 6'2" 191 lbs.

Year	Team		Games	Pos.
1952	GB	N	12	OE
1953			8	OE
1954			12	OE
1955			12	OE
1956			12	OE
1957			12	OE
1958			12	OE
1959	CLE	N	12	OE
1960	DAL	N	11	OE
1961			14	OE
1962			14	OE
1963			11	OE

12 yrs.   142 games

Lynn Hoyem
HOYEM, LYNN DOUGLAS
B. Jun. 27, 1939, Fargo, ND
Long Beach State 6'4" 244 lbs.

Year	Team		Games	Pos.
1962	DAL	N	14	C
1963			14	C, G
1964	PHI	N	14	C, G
1965			14	G, C
1966			14	G, C
1967			14	G, C

6 yrs.   84 games

Steve Hoyem
HOYEM, STEVE
B. Nov. 12, 1970, Boise, ID
Stanford 6'7" 287 lbs.

Year	Team		Games	Pos.
1994	BUF	N	5	OT

Bobby Hoying
HOYING, BOBBY
B. Sep. 20, 1972, St. Henry, OH
Ohio State 6'3" 221 lbs.

Year	Team		Games	Pos.
1996	PHI	N	2	QB

Frank Hrabetin
HRABETIN, FRANK GEORGE
B. Sep. 14, 1915, Los Angeles, CA
Loyola (California) 6'4" 233 lbs.

Year	Team		Games	Pos.
1942	PHI	N	7	T
1946	BKN	AA	8	T
1946	MIA	AA	2	T

2 yrs.   17 games

Gary Hrivnak
HRIVNAK, GARY ANDREW
B. Mar. 3, 1951, Johnstown, PA
Purdue 6'5" 252 lbs.

Year	Team		Games	Pos.
1973	CHI	N	13	DE
1974			14	DE
1975			14	DE

3 yrs.   41 games

John Huard
HUARD, JOHN ROLAND
B. Mar. 9, 1944, Waterville, ME
Maine 6'0" 220 lbs.

Year	Team		Games	Pos.
1967	DEN	A	14	LB
1968			14	LB
1969			14	LB
1971	NO	N	1	LB

4 yrs.   43 games

John Huarte
HUARTE, JOHN GREGORY
B. Apr. 6, 1944, Anaheim, CA
Notre Dame 6'0" 188 lbs.

Year	Team		Games	Pos.
1966	BOS	A	14	QB
1967			4	QB
1968	PHI	N	2	QB
1969	KC	A	3	QB
1970	KC	N	1	QB
1971			1	QB
1972	CHI	N	2	QB

7 yrs.   27 games

Mike Hubach
HUBACH, MICHAEL ANDREW
B. Jan. 26, 1958, Cleveland, OH
Kansas 5'10" 185 lbs.

Year	Team		Games	Pos.
1980	NE	N	16	P
1981			5	P

2 yrs.   21 games

Cal Hubbard
HUBBARD, ROBERT CAL
(Big Cal)
B. Oct. 11, 1900, Keytesville, MO
D. Oct. 16, 1977, St. Petersburg, FL
Centenary/Geneva 6'2" 253 lbs.

Year	Team		Games	Pos.
1927	NYG	N	10	E, C
1928			13	E, C
1929	GB	N	12	T, E
1930			14	T, E
1931			12	T, E, G
1932			13	T
1933			13	T
1935			12	T, E
1936	PIT	N	1	G
1936	NYG	N	6	T

9 yrs.   106 games

Dave Hubbard
HUBBARD, DAVE
B. Sep. 29, 1955, Napa, CA
Brigham Young 6'7" 270 lbs.

Year	Team		Games	Pos.
1977	NO	N	5	OT

Marv Hubbard
HUBBARD, MARVIN RONALD
B. May 7, 1946, Salamanca, NY
Colgate 6'1" 224 lbs.

Year	Team		Games	Pos.
1969	OAK	A	14	RB
1970	OAK	N	14	RB
1971			14	RB
1972			14	RB
1973			14	RB
1974			14	RB
1975			7	RB
1977	DET	N	13	RB

8 yrs.   104 games

Wes Hubbard
HUBBARD, WESLEY (Bud)
B. Jan. 8, 1911
D. Jun., 1981, San Jose, CA
San Jose State 6'0" 190 lbs.

Year	Team		Games	Pos.
1935	**BKN**	**N**	10	E

Frank Hubbell
HUBBELL, FRANKLIN S. (Bud)
B. Jan. 19, 1922, Bridgeport, CT
Tennessee 6'2" 222 lbs.

Year	Team		Games	Pos.
1947	**LA**	**N**	12	E
1948			12	E
1949			12	E
3 yrs.	36 games			

Brad Hubbert
HUBBERT, BRADLEY
B. Jun. 5, 1941, Boligee, Al
Arizona 6'1" 230 lbs.

Year	Team		Games	Pos.
1967	**SD**	**A**	14	RB
1968			2	RB
1969			14	RB
1970	**SD**	**N**	8	RB
4 yrs.	38 games			

Pooley Hubert
HUBERT, ALLISON THOMAS S. (Papa)
B. Apr. 6, 1901, Meridian, MS
D. Feb. 26, 1978, Waynesboro, GA
Alabama 5'11" 187 lbs.

Year	Team		Games	Pos.
1926	**NY**	**A**	14	FB, HB, QB

Gene Hubka
HUBKA, EUGENE LEWIS
B. May 18, 1924, Perth Amboy, NJ
Bucknell 5'10" 175 lbs.

Year	Team		Games	Pos.
1947	**PIT**	**N**	1	HB

Harlan Huckleby
HUCKLEBY, HARLAN CHARLES
B. Dec. 30, 1957, Detroit, MI
Michigan 6'1" 200 lbs.

Year	Team		Games	Pos.
1980	**GB**	**N**	16	RB
1981			16	RB
1982			9	RB
1983			16	RB
1984			16	RB
1985			11	RB
6 yrs.	84 games			

Jim Huddleston
HUDDLESTON, JAMES W.
B. Sep. 22, 1962, San Pedro, CA
Virginia 6'4" 270 lbs.

Year	Team		Games	Pos.
1987	**TB**	**N**	1	G

John Huddleston
HUDDLESTON, JOHN C.
B. Apr. 10, 1954, Los Angeles, CA
Utah 6'3" 230 lbs.

Year	Team		Games	Pos.
1978	**OAK**	**N**	11	LB
1979			16	LB
2 yrs.	27 games			

Floyd Hudlow
HUDLOW, FLOYD LEROY
B. Nov. 9, 1943, Phoenix, AZ
Arizona 5'11" 192 lbs.

Year	Team		Games	Pos.
1965	**BUF**	**A**	6	FL
1967	**ATL**	**N**	10	FL, DB
1968			7	DB
3 yrs.	23 games			

Mike Hudock
HUDOCK, MICHAEL EDWARD
B. Sep. 29, 1934, Pittston, PA
Miami (Florida) 6'1" 245 lbs.

Year	Team		Games	Pos.
1960	**NY**	**A**	14	C
1961			11	C
1962			14	C
1963			14	C
1964			11	C
1965			14	C
1966	**MIA**	**A**	14	C
1967	**KC**	**A**	4	C
8 yrs.	96 games			

Billy Hudson
HUDSON, WILLIAM ALEX
B. 1936, Lamar, SC
Clemson 6'4" 267 lbs.

Year	Team		Games	Pos.
1961	**SD**	**A**	14	DT
1962			14	DT
1963	**BOS**	**A**	4	DT
3 yrs.	32 games			

Bob Hudson
HUDSON, ROBERT
B. Apr. 5, 1930, Lamar, SC
Clemson 6'4" 225 lbs.

Year	Team		Games	Pos.
1951	**NYG**	**N**	11	OE
1952			12	OE
1953	**PHI**	**N**	12	DB
1954			12	DB
1955			12	LB, DB
1957			12	LB, DB
1958			11	LB, DB
1959	**WAS**	**N**	3	LB, DB
1960	**DAL**	**A**		LB
1960	**DEN**	**A**		LB
1961			14	LB
10 yrs.	99 games			

Bob Hudson
HUDSON, ROBERT
B. Mar. 21, 1948, Hominy, OK
Northeastern Oklahoma 5'11" 207 lbs.

Year	Team		Games	Pos.
1972	**GB**	**N**	12	RB
1973	**OAK**	**N**	14	RB
1974			14	RB
3 yrs.	40 games			

Chris Hudson
HUDSON, CHRIS
B. Oct. 6, 1971, Houston, TX
Colorado 5'9" 195 lbs.

Year	Team		Games	Pos.
1995	**JAC**	**N**	1	S
1996			16	S
2 yrs.	17 games			

Craig Hudson
HUDSON, CRAIG
B. May 7, 1967
Wisconsin 6'3" 245 lbs.

Year	Team		Games	Pos.
1990	**GB**	**N**	9	TE

Dick Hudson
HUDSON, RICHARD (Super Six)
None 182 lbs.

Year	Team		Games	Pos.
1923	**MIN**	**N**	3	FB, HB
1925	**HAM**	**N**	2	HB, FB
1926			3	HB, FB
3 yrs.	8 games			

Dick Hudson
HUDSON, RICHARD SMITH
B. Jul. 30, 1940, Memphis, TN
Memphis State 6'4" 266 lbs.

Year	Team		Games	Pos.
1962	**SD**	**A**	14	G, OT
1963	**BUF**	**A**	2	OT, G

Dick Hudson continued

Year	Team		Games	Pos.
1964			14	G
1965			14	OT
1966			14	OT
1967			8	OT
6 yrs.	66 games			

Doug Hudson
HUDSON, DOUG BENJAMIN
B. Sep. 11, 1964, Memphis, TN
Nicholls State 6'2" 201 lbs.

Year	Team		Games	Pos.
1987	**KC**	**N**	1	QB

Gordon Hudson
HUDSON, GORDON
B. Jun. 22, 1962, Kennewick, WA
Brigham Young 6'4" 241 lbs.

Year	Team		Games	Pos.
1986	**SEA**	**N**	16	TE

Jim Hudson
HUDSON, JAMES CLARK
B. Mar. 31, 1943, Steubenville, OH
Texas 6'2" 210 lbs.

Year	Team		Games	Pos.
1965	**NY**	**A**	2	DB, HB
1966			14	DB
1967			13	DB
1968			14	DB
1969			4	S
1970	**NYJ**	**N**	7	S
6 yrs.	54 games			

John Hudson
HUDSON, JOHN LEWIS
B. Jan. 29, 1968, Memphis, TN
Auburn 6'2" 275 lbs.

Year	Team		Games	Pos.
1991	**PHI**	**N**	16	G, C
1992			3	G, C
1993			16	G, C
1994			16	G, C
1995			16	C, G
1996	**NYJ**	**N**	16	G
6 yrs.	83 games			

Johnnie Hudson
HUDSON, JOHN RANDOLPH
B. Oct. 7, 1898, Shelby, NC
Deceased
North Carolina State 5'9" 170 lbs.

Year	Team		Games	Pos.
1921	**WAS**	**A**	3	HB

Mike Hudson
HUDSON, MICHAEL
B. Dec. 25, 1963
Oklahoma State 6'0" 202 lbs.

Year	Team		Games	Pos.
1987	**SD**	**N**	3	S

Nat Hudson
HUDSON, NATHANIEL LAMAR
B. Oct. 11, 1957, Rome, GA
Georgia 6'3" 270 lbs.

Year	Team		Games	Pos.
1981	**NO**	**N**	16	G
1982			4	G
1982	**BAL**	**N**	2	G
2 yrs.	22 games			

Jack Hueller
HUELLER, JOHN
B. 1896, Wisconsin
Deceased
None 5'10" 200 lbs.

Year	Team		Games	Pos.
1922	**RAC**	**N**	7	G, HB
1923			7	G
1924			2	G
3 yrs.	16 games			

Carlos Huerta
HUERTA, CARLOS ANTONIO
B. Jun. 29, 1969, Miami, FL
Miami (Florida) 5'7" 185 lbs.

Year	Team		Games	Pos.
1996	**CHI**	**N**	3	K
1996	**STL**	**N**	1	K
1 yr.	4 games			

Gene Huey
HUEY, EUGENE
B. Jul. 20, 1947, Uniontown, PA
Wyoming 5'11" 190 lbs.

Year	Team		Games	Pos.
1969	**SD**	**A**	4	S

Alan Huff
HUFF, ALAN
B. Oct. 20, 1963, East Liverpool, OH
Marshall 6'4" 265 lbs.

Year	Team		Games	Pos.
1987	**PIT**	**N**	2	NT

Charles Huff
HUFF, CHARLES
B. Feb. 24, 1963, Statesboro, GA
Presbyterian 5'11" 195 lbs.

Year	Team		Games	Pos.
1987	**ATL**	**N**	3	CB

Gary Huff
HUFF, GARY EARL
B. Apr. 27, 1951, Natchez, MS
Florida State 6'1" 197 lbs.

Year	Team		Games	Pos.
1973	**CHI**	**N**	8	QB
1974			13	QB
1975			14	QB
1976			8	QB
1977	**TB**	**N**	8	QB
1978			6	QB
6 yrs.	57 games			

Ken Huff
HUFF, KENNETH WAYNE
B. Feb. 21, 1953, Hutchinson, KS
North Carolina 6'4" 252 lbs.

Year	Team		Games	Pos.
1975	**BAL**	**N**	9	G
1976			8	G
1977			14	G
1978			16	G
1979			14	G
1980			16	G
1981			16	G
1982			9	G
1983	**WAS**	**N**	13	G
1984			15	G
1985			16	G
11 yrs.	146 games			

Marty Huff
HUFF, RALPH MARTIN
B. Dec. 19, 1948, Houston, TX
Michigan 6'2" 234 lbs.

Year	Team		Games	Pos.
1972	**SF**	**N**	3	LB

Sam Huff
HUFF, ROBERT LEE
B. Oct. 4, 1935, Morgantown, WV
West Virginia 6'1" 230 lbs.

Year	Team		Games	Pos.
1956	**NYG**	**N**	12	LB
1957			12	LB
1958			12	LB
1959			12	LB
1960			12	LB
1961			14	LB
1962			14	LB
1963			14	LB
1964	**WAS**	**N**	14	LB
1965			14	LB
1966			14	LB

Year	Team		Games	Pos.

Sam Huff *continued*

Year	Team		Games	Pos.
1967			10	LB
1969			14	LB
13 yrs.	168 games			

Ken Huffine
HUFFINE, KENNETH W.
B. Dec. 22, 1897
D. Sep. 26, 1977, Bradenton, FL
Purdue 6'3" 208 lbs.

1920	MUN	A	1	FB
1921	DEC	A	10	FB
1922	DAY	N	8	FB, HB
1923			8	FB
1924			7	HB, FB
1925			8	FB, T, G
6 yrs.	42 games			

Darvell Huffman
HUFFMAN, DARVELL DENARIO
B. May 5, 1967, Boston, MA
Boston University 5'8" 158 lbs.

| 1991 | IND | N | 3 | WR |

Dave Huffman
HUFFMAN, DAVID LAMBERT
B. Apr. 4, 1957, Canton, OH
Notre Dame 6'6" 280 lbs.

1979	MIN	N	13	C
1980			16	C
1981			13	C
1982			9	C
1983			15	C, G
1985			15	G
1986			16	G
1987			12	G
1988			2	G
1989			16	G
1990			1	G
11 yrs.	128 games			

Dick Huffman
HUFFMAN, RICHARD
B. Mar. 27, 1923, Charleston, WV
D. Sep. 13, 1992
Tennessee 6'2" 255 lbs.

1947	LA	N	11	T
1948			12	T
1949			12	T
1950			12	T
4 yrs.	47 games			

Frank Huffman
HUFFMAN, FRANK
B. May 22, 1915, Pittsburgh, PA
D. Sep., 1980, Fayetteville, WV
Marshall 6'2" 207 lbs.

1939	CHIC	N	10	T, G, E
1940			9	G, E
1941			9	G
3 yrs.	28 games			

Iolas Huffman
HUFFMAN, IOLAS M.
B. Feb. 4, 1898
D. Nov. 12, 1989, Cleveland, OH
Ohio State 5'11" 228 lbs.

1923	CLE	N	7	T, G
1924	BUF	N	6	T, G
2 yrs.	13 games			

Tim Huffman
HUFFMAN, TIMOTHY PATRICK
B. Aug. 31, 1959, Canton, OH
Notre Dame 6'5" 277 lbs.

| 1981 | GB | N | 4 | OT, G |
| 1982 | | | 9 | G |

Tim Huffman *continued*

Year	Team		Games	Pos.
1983			15	G
1984			16	G
1985			2	OT
5 yrs.	46 games			

Vern Huffman
HUFFMAN, VERNON R.
B. Nov. 18, 1914
D. Mar., 1995, Bloomington, IN
Indiana 6'2" 215 lbs.

1937	DET	N	10	QB, DB
1938			11	QB, DB
2 yrs.	21 games			

Guy Hufford
HUFFORD, DARRELL GUY
B. Jan. 18, 1901
D. Jun., 1984, Camarillo, CA
California 5'11" 185 lbs.

| 1926 | LA | N | 10 | E |

John Hufnagel
HUFNAGEL, JOHN COLEMAN
B. Sep. 13, 1951, Pittsburgh, PA
Penn State 6'1" 194 lbs.

1974	DEN	N	4	QB
1975			5	QB
2 yrs.	9 games			

Harry Hugasian
HUGASIAN, HARRY
B. Mar. 5, 1931, Pasadena, CA
Stanford 6'1" 192 lbs.

1955	BAL	N	2	HB
1955	CHIB	N	4	HB
1 yr.	6 games			

Roy Huggins
HUGGINS, ROY
B. Oct. 6, 1918, Nashville, TN
Vanderbilt 5'11" 195 lbs.

| 1944 | CLE | N | 6 | FB |

Bernie Hughes
HUGHES, BERNARD B.
(Honolulu)
B. Jan. 9, 1910, Dorris, CA
D. Dec. 26, 1967, Medford, OR
Oregon 6'1" 192 lbs.

1934	CHIC	N	10	C, G
1935			10	C
1936			12	C
3 yrs.	32 games			

Bill Hughes
HUGHES, WILLIAM (Hoss)
B. Apr. 11, 1915, Van Alstyne, TX
D. Jul. 6, 1978, Tampa, FL
Texas 6'1" 226 lbs.

1937	PHI	N	11	G
1938			11	G
1939			11	G
1940			7	G
1941	CHIB	N	6	C, LB
5 yrs.	46 games			

Bob Hughes
HUGHES, ROBERT
B. Nov. 17, 1944, Columbus, MS
Jackson State 6'4" 253 lbs.

1967	ATL	N	2	DE
1969			14	DE
2 yrs.	16 games			

Chuck Hughes
HUGHES, CHARLES FREDERICK
B. Mar. 24, 1943, Philadelphia, PA
D. Oct. 24, 1971, Detroit, MI
Texas Western 5'11" 173 lbs.

1967	PHI	N	9	FL
1968			7	FL
1969			7	WR
1970	DET	N	13	WR
4 yrs.	36 games			

Danan Hughes
HUGHES, ROBERT DANAN
B. Dec. 11, 1970, Bayonne, NJ
Iowa 6'1" 201 lbs.

1993	KC	N	6	WR
1994			16	WR
1995			16	WR
1996			15	WR
4 yrs.	53 games			

David Hughes
HUGHES, DAVID A.
B. Jun. 1, 1959, Honolulu, HI
Boise State 6'0" 220 lbs.

1981	SEA	N	16	FB
1982			9	RB
1983			16	RB
1984			16	FB
1985			12	FB
1986	PIT	N	5	RB
6 yrs.	74 games			

Dennis Hughes
HUGHES, DENNIS
B. Feb. 22, 1948, Seneca, SC
Georgia 6'1" 220 lbs.

1970	PIT	N	11	TE
1971	HOU	N	7	TE
2 yrs.	18 games			

Denny Hughes
HUGHES, DENNIS (Dinty)
B. 1900
George Washington 5'11" 185 lbs.

| 1925 | POT | N | 7 | C |

Dick Hughes
HUGHES, RICHARD
B. 1932, Buffalo, NY
Tulsa 5'9" 185 lbs.

| 1957 | PIT | N | 1 | HB |

Ed Hughes
HUGHES, EDWARD D.
B. Oct. 23, 1927, Buffalo, NY
North Carolina State/Tulsa 6'1" 184 lbs.

1954	LA	N	11	HB
1955			12	HB
1956	NYG	N	12	HB
1957			8	HB
1958			10	HB
5 yrs.	53 games			

Ernie Hughes
HUGHES, ERNIE
B. Jan. 24, 1955, Boise, ID
Notre Dame 6'3" 260 lbs.

1978	SF	N	15	G
1980			3	G
1981	NYG	N	10	G
1982			5	C
1983			12	C
5 yrs.	45 games			

George Hughes
HUGHES, GEORGE SAMUEL
B. Aug. 19, 1925, Norfolk, VA
William & Mary 6'1" 225 lbs.

1950	PIT	N	12	G
1951			12	G
1952			12	G
1953			12	G
1954			12	G
5 yrs.	60 games			

Hank Hughes
HUGHES, HENRY (Honolulu)
B. 1907
Deceased
Oregon State 5'10" 195 lbs.

| 1932 | BOS | N | 10 | HB, QB, FB |

Pat Hughes
HUGHES, WILLIAM PATRICK
B. Jun. 2, 1947, Everett, MA
Boston University 6'2" 231 lbs.

1970	NYG	N	14	C
1971			14	LB
1972			14	LB
1973			11	LB
1974			14	LB
1975			14	LB
1976			14	LB
1977	NO	N	14	LB
1978			16	LB
1979			16	LB
10 yrs.	141 games			

Randy Hughes
HUGHES, JAMES RANDELL
B. Apr. 3, 1953, Oklahoma City, OK
Oklahoma 6'4" 207 lbs.

1975	DAL	N	14	DB
1976			14	S
1977			13	S
1978			16	S
1979			15	S
1980			5	S
6 yrs.	77 games			

Tyrone Hughes
HUGHES, TYRONE CHRISTOPHER
B. Jan. 14, 1970, New Orleans, LA
Nebraska 5'9" 175 lbs.

1993	NO	N	16	CB
1994			15	CB
1995			16	CB
1996			16	CB
4 yrs.	63 games			

Van Hughes
HUGHES, CURTIS VAN
B. Nov. 14, 1960, Waco, TX
Texas Tech/Southwest Texas State 6'3" 280 lbs.

1986	STL	N	7	DE
1987	SEA	N	1	DE
2 yrs.	8 games			

Tommy Hughitt
HUGHITT, ERNEST THOMAS (Tiny)
B. Dec. 27, 1892, Genoa, B.C.
Deceased
Michigan 5'8" 159 lbs.

1920	BUF	A	6	QB
1921			12	QB, HB
1922	BUF	N	12	QB
1923			12	QB, HB
1924			11	QB, HB, E, FB
5 yrs.	51 games			

Year	Team	Games	Pos.

George Hughley
HUGHLEY, GEORGE
B. Jun. 26, 1939, Los Angeles, CA
Central Oklahoma 6'2" 223 lbs.

Year	Team	Games	Pos.
1965	WAS	N	14	HB

Joe Hugret
HUGRET, JOSEPH J. (Sugar)
B. Apr. 11, 1909
D. Sep., 1977, Minot, ND
New York University 6'2" 195 lbs.

| 1934 | BKN | N | 1 | E |

Bill Hull
HULL, WILLIAM
B. 1941
Wake Forest 6'6" 245 lbs.

| 1962 | DAL | A | 14 | DE |

Kent Hull
HULL, JAMES KENT
B. Jan. 13, 1961, Pontotoc, MS
Mississippi State 6'4" 262 lbs.

1986	BUF	N	16	C
1987		12	C
1988		16	C
1989		16	C
1990		16	C
1991		16	C
1992		16	C
1993		14	C
1994		16	C
1995		16	C
1996		16	C
11 yrs.	170 games		

Mike Hull
HULL, MICHAEL BRUCE
B. Jan. 2, 1945, La Crescenta, CA
Southern California 6'3" 220 lbs.

1968	CHI	N	14	TE, RB
1969		10	RB
1970		13	RB
1971	WAS	N	11	RB
1972		14	RB
1973		13	RB
1974		14	RB
7 yrs.	89 games		

Tom Hull
HULL, THOMAS MICHAEL
B. Jun. 30, 1952, Cumberland, MD
Penn State 6'3" 230 lbs.

1974	SF	N	13	LB
1975	GB	N	13	LB
2 yrs.	26 games		

Vivian Hultman
HULTMAN, VIVIAN J.
B. Jan. 26, 1903
D. 1988, Seminole, FL
Michigan State 5'8" 178 lbs.

1925	DET	N	11	E
1926		9	E, G
1927	POT	N	9	E
3 yrs.	29 games		

Don Hultz
HULTZ, WILLIAM DONALD
B. Dec. 16, 1940, Moss Point, MS
Southern Mississippi 6'3" 238 lbs.

1963	MIN	N	14	DE
1964	PHI	N	12	DE
1965		14	DE
1966		13	DE
1967		13	DE
1968		10	DE
1969		14	DE

Don Hultz continued

1970		11	DE
1971		14	DT
1972		14	DT
1973		12	DT
1974	CHI	N	8	DT
12 yrs.	149 games		

George Hultz
HULTZ, GEORGE
B. 1939, Moss Point, MS
Southern Mississippi 6'4" 250 lbs.

| 1962 | STL | N | 13 | OT |

Dick Humbert
HUMBERT, RICHARD
B. Dec. 31, 1918, Reading, PA
Richmond 6'1" 179 lbs.

1941	PHI	N	11	E
1945		4	E
1946		11	E
1947		11	E
1948		12	E
1949		11	E
6 yrs.	60 games		

Weldon Humble
HUMBLE, WELDON G.
B. Apr. 24, 1921, San Antonio, TX
Rice/Southwestern Louisiana/Rice 6'1" 221 lbs.

1947	CLE	AA	12	G
1948		13	G
1949		10	G
1950	CLE	N	12	G
1952	DAL	N	11	G
5 yrs.	58 games		

Mike Humiston
HUMISTON, MICHAEL
B. Jan. 8, 1959, Oceanside, CA
Weber State 6'3" 238 lbs.

1981	BUF	N	16	LB
1982	BAL	N	7	LB
1984	IND	N	16	LB
1987	SD	N	7	LB
4 yrs.	46 games		

David Humm
HUMM, DAVID HENRY
B. Apr. 2, 1952, Las Vegas, NV
Nebraska 6'2" 187 lbs.

1975	OAK	N	7	QB
1976		14	QB
1977		14	QB
1978		16	QB
1979		16	QB
1980	BUF	N	16	QB
1981	BAL	N	1	QB
1982		2	QB
1983	LARI	N	6	QB
1984		3	QB
10 yrs.	95 games		

Arnie Hummel
HUMMEL, ANTHUS
B. Oct. 25, 1897
D. Aug., 1970, Davenport, IA
Lombard 195 lbs.

1926	KC	N	5	FB, HB
1927	CHIC	N	9	G
2 yrs.	14 games		

Swede Hummel
HUMMEL, ARTHUR
B. May 30, 1902
D. Oct., 1964

Swede Hummel continued

None 195 lbs.

| 1926 | PRO | N | 3 | HB |

Charlie Hummell
HUMMELL, CHARLES E. (Mickey)
B. Mar., 1898, Newark, NJ
Deceased
Lafayette 5'10"

| 1926 | BKN | A | 3 | T |

John Hummon
HUMMON, JOHN MACK (Mack, Mousie)
B. Jul. 4, 1901, Leipsic, OH
D. Feb. 27, 1992, Oakwood, OH
Wittenberg 5'11" 180 lbs.

1926	DAY	N	4	E
1928		4	E
2 yrs.	8 games		

Bobby Humphery
HUMPHERY, ROBERT CHARLES
B. Aug. 23, 1961, Lubbock, TX
New Mexico State 5'10" 180 lbs.

1984	NYJ	N	16	WR
1985		12	WR
1986		16	CB
1987		12	CB
1988		16	CB
1989		16	CB
1990	LARM	N	16	CB
7 yrs.	104 games		

Bobby Humphrey
HUMPHREY, BOBBY
B. Oct. 11, 1966, Birmingham, AL
Alabama 6'1" 201 lbs.

1989	DEN	N	16	RB
1990		15	RB
1991		4	RB
1992	MIA	N	16	RB
4 yrs.	51 games		

Buddy Humphrey
HUMPHREY, LOYIE NAWLIN
B. Sep. 29, 1935, Kilgore, TX
D. Apr. 21, 1988, Kilgore, TX
Baylor 6'1" 198 lbs.

1959	LA	N	2	QB
1960		4	QB
1961	DAL	N	2	QB
1963	STL	N	4	QB
1964		1	QB
1965		7	QB
1966	HOU	A	6	QB
7 yrs.	26 games		

Claude Humphrey
HUMPHREY, CLAUDE B.
B. Jun. 29, 1944, Memphis, TN
Tennessee State 6'5" 258 lbs.

1968	ATL	N	14	DE
1969		14	DE
1970		12	DE
1971		14	DE
1972		14	DE
1973		14	DE
1974		14	DE
1976		13	DE
1977		14	DE
1978		4	DE
1979	PHI	N	16	DE
1980		16	DE
1981		12	DE
13 yrs.	171 games		

Donnie Humphrey
HUMPHREY, DONNIE RAY
B. Apr. 20, 1961, Huntsville, AL
Auburn 6'3" 290 lbs.

1984	GB	N	16	DE
1985		16	DE
1986		16	DE
3 yrs.	48 games		

Paul Humphrey
HUMPHREY, PAUL EUGENE
B. Jul. 18, 1917, Terre Haute, IN
Purdue 6'0" 195 lbs.

| 1939 | BKN | N | 11 | C, G |

Ronald Humphrey
HUMPHREY, RONALD LYNN
B. Mar. 3, 1969, Garland, TX
Mississippi Valley State 5'10" 201 lbs.

1994	IND	N	15	RB
1995		11	RB
2 yrs.	26 games		

Tom Humphrey
HUMPHREY, TOM
B. Dec. 16, 1962
Iowa 6'3" 280 lbs.

| 1987 | NYJ | N | 3 | G |

Tommy Humphrey
HUMPHREY, THOMAS
B. Mar. 24, 1950, Comanche, TX
Abilene Christian 6'6" 260 lbs.

| 1974 | KC | N | 5 | C |

Bob Humphreys
HUMPHREYS, ROBERT
B. Mar. 30, 1940, Los Angeles, CA
Wichita State 6'1" 240 lbs.

1967	DEN	A	8	K
1968		2	K
2 yrs.	10 games		

Leonard Humphries
HUMPHRIES, LEONARD DESHAWN
B. Jun. 19, 1970, Akron, OH
Penn State 5'9" 180 lbs.

| 1994 | IND | N | 13 | CB, S |

Stan Humphries
HUMPHRIES, STAN
B. Apr. 14, 1965, Shreveport, LA
Louisiana State/Northeast Louisiana 6'2" 223 lbs.

1989	WAS	N	2	QB
1990		7	QB
1992	SD	N	16	QB
1993		12	QB
1994		15	QB
1995		15	QB
1996		13	QB
7 yrs.	80 games		

Stefan Humphries
HUMPHRIES, STEFAN GOVAN
B. Jan. 20, 1962, Fort Lauderdale, FL
Michigan 6'3" 268 lbs.

1984	CHI	N	10	G
1985		11	G
1986		4	G
1987	DEN	N	7	G
1988		1	G
5 yrs.	33 games		

Year	Team		Games	Pos.

James Hundon
HUNDON, JAMES
B. Apr. 9, 1971, Daly City, CA
Portland State 6'1" 195 lbs.

Year	Team		Games	Pos.
1996	CIN	N	5	WR

Charlie Huneke
HUNEKE, CHARLES F.
B. Jan. 1, 1921, Lincoln, IL
Deceased
St. Mary's (Texas)/St. Benedict's (Kansas)
6'3" 225 lbs.

Year	Team		Games	Pos.
1946	CHI	AA	14	T
1947			1	T
1947	BKN	AA	12	T
1948			2	T
3 yrs.	29 games			

Lamonte Hunley
HUNLEY, KENNETH LAMONTE
B. Jan. 31, 1963, Richmond, VA
Arizona 6'2" 241 lbs.

Year	Team		Games	Pos.
1985	IND	N	16	LB
1986			6	LB
2 yrs.	22 games			

Ricky Hunley
HUNLEY, RICKY CARDELL
B. Nov. 11, 1961, Petersburg, VA
Arizona 6'2" 238 lbs.

Year	Team		Games	Pos.
1984	DEN	N	8	LB
1985			16	LB
1986			16	LB
1987			12	LB
1988	PHX	N	16	LB
1989	LARI	N	12	LB
1990			11	LB
7 yrs.	91 games			

Chuck Hunsinger
HUNSINGER, CHARLES
B. Jul. 25, 1925, Harrisburg, IL
Florida 6'0" 188 lbs.

Year	Team		Games	Pos.
1950	CHIB	N	10	HB
1951			12	HB
1952			12	HB
3 yrs.	34 games			

Ed Hunsinger
HUNSINGER, EDWARD
B. 1900
D. Aug. 24, 1960
Notre Dame 5'11" 175 lbs.

Year	Team		Games	Pos.
1926	BKN	A	4	E

Ben Hunt
HUNT, BEN
B. Sep. 16, 1900
D. Jun., 1981, Scottsboro, AL
Alabama 5'9" 185 lbs.

Year	Team		Games	Pos.
1923	TOL	N	3	T

Bob Hunt
HUNT, BOB
B. Sep. 3, 1951, Toledo, OH
Heidelberg 6'1" 210 lbs.

Year	Team		Games	Pos.
1974	CLE	N	2	RB

Bobby Hunt
HUNT, ROBERT KENNETH
B. Aug. 15, 1940, Lanett, AL
Auburn 6'1" 188 lbs.

Year	Team		Games	Pos.
1962	DAL	A	14	DB
1963	KC	A	14	DB
1964			14	DB
1965			14	DB

Bobby Hunt continued

Year	Team		Games	Pos.
1966			14	DB
1967			14	DB
1968	CIN	A	14	DB
1969			14	DB
8 yrs.	112 games			

Byron Hunt
HUNT, BYRON RAY
B. Dec. 17, 1958, Longview, TX
Southern Methodist 6'5" 240 lbs.

Year	Team		Games	Pos.
1981	NYG	N	16	LB
1982			9	LB
1983			16	LB
1984			13	LB
1985			16	LB
1986			16	LB
1987			12	LB
1988			2	LB
8 yrs.	100 games			

Calvin Hunt
HUNT, CALVIN CORNELIUS
B. Dec. 31, 1947, Oceanside, CA
Baylor 6'3" 244 lbs.

Year	Team		Games	Pos.
1970	PHI	N	7	C
1972	HOU	N	10	C
1973			4	C
3 yrs.	21 games			

Charlie Hunt
HUNT, CHARLES EDWARD
B. Feb. 1, 1951, St. Augustine, FL
Florida State 6'2" 215 lbs.

Year	Team		Games	Pos.
1973	SF	N	8	LB
1976	TB	N	5	LB
2 yrs.	13 games			

Daryl Hunt
HUNT, DARYL LYNN
B. Nov. 3, 1956, Odessa, TX
Oklahoma 6'3" 230 lbs.

Year	Team		Games	Pos.
1979	HOU	N	16	LB
1980			16	LB
1981			16	LB
1982			9	LB
1983			16	LB
1984			5	LB
6 yrs.	78 games			

Ervin Hunt
HUNT, ERVIN
B. Jul. 1, 1947, Sacramento, CA
Fresno State 6'2" 190 lbs.

Year	Team		Games	Pos.
1970	GB	N	7	CB

Gary Hunt
HUNT, GARY
B. Oct. 28, 1963
Memphis State 5'11" 175 lbs.

Year	Team		Games	Pos.
1987	CIN	N	3	CB

George Hunt
HUNT, GEORGE ARTHUR
B. Aug. 3, 1949, Marietta, OK
Tennessee 6'1" 215 lbs.

Year	Team		Games	Pos.
1973	BAL	N	14	K
1975	NYG	N	14	K, P
2 yrs.	28 games			

Jackie Hunt
HUNT, JOHN JACK
B. 1919
D. Jun., 1991
Marshall 6'0" 192 lbs.

Year	Team		Games	Pos.
1945	CHIB	N	4	HB

Jim Hunt
HUNT, JAMES LEE (Earthquake)
B. Oct. 5, 1938, Atlanta, TX
Prairie View A&M 5'11" 249 lbs.

Year	Team		Games	Pos.
1960	BOS	A	7	DT
1961			14	DT
1962			9	DE
1963			14	DE
1964			14	DE, DT
1965			14	DE
1966			14	DE, DT
1967			14	DT
1968			14	DT
1969			14	DT
1970	BOS	N	14	DT
11 yrs.	142 games			

John Hunt
HUNT, JOHN STEPHEN
B. Nov. 6, 1962, Orlando, FL
Florida 6'4" 254 lbs.

Year	Team		Games	Pos.
1984	DAL	N	2	OT, G
1987	TB	N	1	G
2 yrs.	3 games			

Kevin Hunt
HUNT, RICHARD KEVIN
B. Nov. 29, 1948, Burlington, VT
Doane 6'5" 260 lbs.

Year	Team		Games	Pos.
1972	GB	N	3	OT
1973	NE	N	1	OT
1973	HOU	N	4	OT
1974			13	OT
1975			13	OT
1976			13	OT
1977			14	OT
1978	NO	N	10	OT
7 yrs.	71 games			

Mike Hunt
HUNT, MICHAEL ANTHONY
B. Oct. 6, 1956, Madison, MN
Minnesota 6'2" 240 lbs.

Year	Team		Games	Pos.
1978	GB	N	16	LB
1979			3	LB
1980			3	LB
3 yrs.	22 games			

Ron Hunt
HUNT, RON MICHELE
B. Jan. 27, 1955, Los Angeles, CA
Oregon 6'6" 261 lbs.

Year	Team		Games	Pos.
1976	CIN	N	12	OT
1977			13	OT
1978			3	OT
3 yrs.	28 games			

Sam Hunt
HUNT, SAMUEL KAY
B. Aug. 6, 1951, Longview, TX
Stephen F. Austin 6'1" 248 lbs.

Year	Team		Games	Pos.
1974	NE	N	14	LB
1975			13	LB
1976			14	LB
1977			13	LB
1978			15	LB
1979			15	LB
6 yrs.	84 games			

Al Hunter
HUNTER, ALFONSE
B. Feb. 21, 1955, Greenville, NC
Notre Dame 5'11" 195 lbs.

Year	Team		Games	Pos.
1977	SEA	N	12	RB
1978			16	RB
1979			15	RB
1980			9	RB
4 yrs.	52 games			

Art Hunter
HUNTER, ARTHUR
B. Apr. 24, 1933, Fairport Harbor, OH
Notre Dame 6'4" 243 lbs.

Year	Team		Games	Pos.
1954	GB	N	12	T
1956	CLE	N	8	C, T
1957			12	C
1958			12	C
1959			12	C
1960	LA	N	12	C
1961			14	C
1962			2	C
1963			12	C
1964			11	C
1965	PIT	N	9	C
11 yrs.	116 games			

Daniel Hunter
HUNTER, DANIEL LEWIS
B. Sep. 1, 1962, Arkadelphia, PA
Henderson State 5'11" 175 lbs.

Year	Team		Games	Pos.
1985	DEN	N	16	CB
1986			10	S
1986	SD	N	5	CB
1987			12	CB
3 yrs.	43 games			

Earnest Hunter
HUNTER, EARNEST
B. Dec. 21, 1970, Longview, TX
Southeast Oklahoma State 5'8" 201 lbs.

Year	Team		Games	Pos.
1995	CLE	N	10	RB
1996	BAL	N	6	RB
1996	NO	N	6	RB
2 yrs.	21 games			

Eddie Hunter
HUNTER, EDWARD LEE
B. Jan. 20, 1965, Reno, NV
Virginia Tech 5'11" 205 lbs.

Year	Team		Games	Pos.
1987	NYJ	N	3	RB
1987	TB	N	3	RB
1 yr.	6 games			

George Hunter
HUNTER, GEORGE WILLIAM (Bill)
B. Nov. 5, 1942, Camden, NJ
Syracuse 6'1" 183 lbs.

Year	Team		Games	Pos.
1965	WAS	N	12	FL, DB
1966	MIA	A	4	RB
2 yrs.	16 games			

Herman Hunter
HUNTER, HERMAN
B. Feb. 14, 1961, Columbus, GA
Tennessee State 6'1" 193 lbs.

Year	Team		Games	Pos.
1985	PHI	N	16	RB
1986	DET	N	16	RB
1987	HOU	N	3	RB
3 yrs.	35 games			

Ivy Joe Hunter
HUNTER, IVY JOE
B. Nov. 16, 1966, Gainesville, FL
Kentucky 6'0" 237 lbs.

Year	Team		Games	Pos.
1989	IND	N	16	RB
1990			16	RB
1991	NE	N	13	RB
3 yrs.	45 games			

James Hunter
HUNTER, JAMES
B. Mar. 8, 1954, Silsbee, TX
Grambling State 6'3" 195 lbs.

Year	Team		Games	Pos.
1976	DET	N	13	DB
1977			14	S

Year	Team	Games	Pos.

James Hunter continued

Year	Team	Games	Pos.
1978		9	CB
1979		15	CB
1980		16	S
1981		12	S
1982		7	CB
7 yrs.	86 games		

James Hunter
HUNTER, JAMES DALE
B. Sep. 13, 1957, Oklahoma City, OK
Southern California 6'5" 251 lbs.

Year	Team	Games	Pos.
1982	BAL N	9	DE

Jeff Hunter
HUNTER, JEFFREY ORLANDO
B. Apr. 12, 1966, Hampton, VA
Albany State 6'2" 285 lbs.

Year	Team	Games	Pos.
1990	BUF N	3	DE
1990	DET N	6	DE
1991		16	DE
1992		4	DE
1992	MIA N	7	DE
1993		5	DE
1994	TB N	1	DE
5 yrs.	42 games		

John Hunter
HUNTER, JOHN ROSEL
B. Aug. 16, 1965, Roseburg, OR
Brigham Young 6'8" 296 lbs.

Year	Team	Games	Pos.
1989	ATL N	4	OT
1990		15	OT
1991		2	OT
1992	SEA N	5	G
4 yrs.	26 games		

Merle Hunter
HUNTER, MERLE
B. Apr. 28, 1906, Indiana
D. Jul., 1982, Ossian, IN
Ashland 185 lbs.

Year	Team	Games	Pos.
1925	HAM N	3	G, T
1926		1	T
2 yrs.	4 games		

Monty Hunter
HUNTER, MONTY
B. Jan. 21, 1959, Dover, OH
Salem (West Virginia) 6'0" 202 lbs.

Year	Team	Games	Pos.
1982	DAL N	9	S
1983	STL N	5	CB, S
2 yrs.	14 games		

Patrick Hunter
HUNTER, PATRICK EDWARD
B. Oct. 24, 1964, San Francisco, CA
Nevada-Reno 5'11" 185 lbs.

Year	Team	Games	Pos.
1986	SEA N	16	CB
1987		11	CB
1988		12	CB
1989		16	CB
1990		16	CB
1991		15	CB
1992		16	CB
1993	DET N	15	DB
1994	SEA N	5	CB
1995	ARI N	5	CB
10 yrs.	127 games		

Ramey Hunter
HUNTER, RAYMOND Q.
B. Aug. 26, 1910, Huntington, WV
D. Jan. 17, 1992, Livingston, MT
Marshall 178 lbs.

Year	Team	Games	Pos.
1933	POR N	2	E

Scott Hunter
HUNTER, JAMES SCOTT
B. Nov. 19, 1947, Mobile, AL
Alabama 6'2" 205 lbs.

Year	Team	Games	Pos.
1971	GB N	14	QB
1972		14	QB
1973		8	QB
1974	BUF N	1	QB
1976	ATL N	8	QB
1977		7	QB
1979	DET N	13	QB
7 yrs.	65 games		

Stan Hunter
HUNTER, STAN
B. Nov. 29, 1963
Bowling Green 6'2" 184 lbs.

Year	Team	Games	Pos.
1987	NYJ N	3	WR

Tony Hunter
HUNTER, TONY F.
B. Feb. 24, 1963, Memphis, TN
Minnesota 5'9" 215 lbs.

Year	Team	Games	Pos.
1987	GB N	1	RB

Tony Hunter
HUNTER, TONY WAYNE
B. May 22, 1960, Cincinnati, OH
Notre Dame 6'4" 237 lbs.

Year	Team	Games	Pos.
1983	BUF N	13	TE
1984		11	TE
1985	LARM N	16	TE
1986		7	TE
4 yrs.	47 games		

Torey Hunter
HUNTER, TOREY HAYWARD
B. Feb. 10, 1972, Tacoma, WA
Washington State 5'9" 176 lbs.

Year	Team	Games	Pos.
1995	HOU N	11	CB

Greg Huntington
HUNTINGTON, GREGORY GERARD
B. Sep. 22, 1970, Mountain Brook, AL
Penn State 6'3" 287 lbs.

Year	Team	Games	Pos.
1993	WAS N	9	C
1995	JAC N	4	G
1996		2	C, G
3 yrs.	15 games		

Richard Huntley
HUNTLEY, RICHARD
B. Sep. 18, 1972, Monroe, NC
Winston-Salem State 5'11" 224 lbs.

Year	Team	Games	Pos.
1996	ATL N	1	RB

Tom Hupke
HUPKE, THOMAS GEORGE
B. Dec. 29, 1910, East Chicago, IN
D. Sep., 1959
Alabama 5'10" 192 lbs.

Year	Team	Games	Pos.
1934	DET N	8	G, T
1935		9	G, T
1936		6	G
1937		11	G
1938	CLE N	9	G
1939		7	G
6 yrs.	50 games		

Jeff Hurd
HURD, JEFFERY TONJA
B. May 25, 1964, Monroe, LA
Kansas State 6'2" 245 lbs.

Year	Team	Games	Pos.
1987	DAL N	5	LB

John Hurlburt
HURLBURT, JOHN B.
B. May 10, 1899
D. Jul., 1980, Portland, OR
Chicago 6'0" 175 lbs.

Year	Team	Games	Pos.
1924	CHIC N	9	HB, FB
1925		5	HB, FB
2 yrs.	14 games		

Bill Hurley
HURLEY, WILLIAM JOHN, JR.
B. May 16, 1957, Kenmore, NY
Syracuse 5'11" 195 lbs.

Year	Team	Games	Pos.
1982	NO N	9	CB, S
1983		4	S
1983	BUF N	10	S
2 yrs.	23 games		

George Hurley
HURLEY, GEORGE
B. Oct. 19, 1909
D. Dec. 17, 1989, Twain Harte, CA
Washington State 6'0" 200 lbs.

Year	Team	Games	Pos.
1932	BOS N	10	G
1933		10	G
2 yrs.	20 games		

John Hurley
HURLEY, JOHN
B. Dec. 6, 1906
D. May, 1983, Johnson City, OR
Washington State 6'3" 192 lbs.

Year	Team	Games	Pos.
1931	CLE N	10	E

Bill Hurst
HURST, WILLIAM (Pep)
B. Jun. 23, 1903, Rock Island, IL
D. Nov., 1966
None 6'1" 202 lbs.

Year	Team	Games	Pos.
1924	KEN N	5	T

Maurice Hurst
HURST, MAURICE ROY
B. Sep. 17, 1967, New Orleans, LA
Southern University 5'10" 185 lbs.

Year	Team	Games	Pos.
1989	NE N	16	CB
1990		16	CB
1991		15	CB
1992		16	CB
1993		16	CB
1994		16	CB
1995		10	CB
7 yrs.	105 games		

Chuck Hurston
HURSTON, CHARLES FREDERICK
B. Nov. 9, 1942, Columbus, GA
Auburn 6'6" 237 lbs.

Year	Team	Games	Pos.
1965	KC A	14	DE
1966		14	DE
1967		14	LB
1968		14	LB
1969		14	LB
1970	KC N	14	LB
1971	BUF N	9	LB
7 yrs.	93 games		

Eric Hurt
HURT, ERIC
B. Jun. 11, 1957
San Jose State 5'11" 171 lbs.

Year	Team	Games	Pos.
1980	DAL N	4	CB

Hurtjun
HURTJUN

Hurtjun continued

None

Year	Team	Games	Pos.
1923	ROC N	1	HB

Ed Husmann
HUSMANN, EDWARD E.
B. Aug. 6, 1931, Schuyler, NE
Nebraska 6'0" 235 lbs.

Year	Team	Games	Pos.
1953	CHIC N	12	G
1956		12	G
1957		12	G
1958		4	E, G
1959		12	DT
1960	DAL N	12	DT
1961	HOU A	14	DT
1962		14	DT
1963		14	DT
1964		14	DT
1965		14	DT
11 yrs.	134 games		

Al Hust
HUST, ALBERT
B. Apr. 9, 1921, Czechoslovakia
D. Apr., 1984, Knoxville, TN
Tennessee 6'1" 220 lbs.

Year	Team	Games	Pos.
1946	CHIC N	10	E

Michael Husted
HUSTED, MICHAEL JAMES
B. Jun. 16, 1970, El Paso, TX
Virginia 6'0" 190 lbs.

Year	Team	Games	Pos.
1993	TB N	16	K
1994		16	K
1995		16	K
1996		16	K
4 yrs.	64 games		

Ken Hutcherson
HUTCHERSON, KEN
B. Jul. 14, 1952, Anniston, AL
Livingston State 6'1" 219 lbs.

Year	Team	Games	Pos.
1974	DAL N	14	LB
1975	SD N	8	LB
2 yrs.	22 games		

Paul Hutchins
HUTCHINS, PAUL ANDRE
B. Feb. 11, 1970, Chicago, IL
Western Michigan 6'5" 335 lbs.

Year	Team	Games	Pos.
1993	GB N	1	OT
1994		16	OT
2 yrs.	17 games		

Bill Hutchinson
HUTCHINSON, WILLIAM DAVID
B. 1916, New York, NY
Dartmouth 5'9" 180 lbs.

Year	Team	Games	Pos.
1942	NYG N	3	B

Ralph Hutchinson
HUTCHINSON, RALPH
B. 1925
Tennessee-Chattanooga 6'2" 230 lbs.

Year	Team	Games	Pos.
1949	NYG N	10	T

Scott Hutchinson
HUTCHINSON, SCOTT RAWLS
B. May 27, 1956, Winter Park, FL
Florida 6'4" 248 lbs.

Year	Team	Games	Pos.
1978	BUF N	16	DE
1979		16	DE
1980		16	DE
1981	TB N	16	DE
1983	BUF N	5	DE
5 yrs.	69 games		

Year	Team	Games	Pos.

Tom Hutchinson
HUTCHINSON, THOMAS
B. Jun. 15, 1941, Stanford, KY
Kentucky 6'1" 190 lbs.

Year	Team		Games	Pos.
1963	CLE	N	14	OE
1964			14	OE
1965			14	OE
1966	ATL	N	5	OE

4 yrs.   47 games

Anthony Hutchison
HUTCHISON, ANTHONY LARUE
B. Feb. 4, 1961, Houston, TX
Texas Tech 5'10" 186 lbs.

Year	Team		Games	Pos.
1983	CHI	N	16	RB
1984			12	RB
1985	BUF	N	5	RB

3 yrs.   33 games

Chuck Hutchison
HUTCHISON, CHARLES ARTHUR
B. Nov. 17, 1948, Canton, OH
Ohio State 6'3" 242 lbs.

Year	Team		Games	Pos.
1970	STL	N	7	G
1971			13	G
1972			4	G
1973	CLE	N	2	G
1974			7	G
1975			14	G

6 yrs.   47 games

Elvin Hutchison
HUTCHISON, ELVIN CLARENCE (The Red Oak Express)
B. Oct. 14, 1912, Guthrie Center, IA
Whittier 5'11" 195 lbs.

Year	Team		Games	Pos.
1939	DET	N	2	HB

Gerry Huth
HUTH, GERALD BERNARD
B. Jul. 23, 1933, Floyds Knobs, IN
Wake Forest 6'0" 226 lbs.

Year	Team		Games	Pos.
1956	NYG	N	11	G
1959	PHI	N	10	G
1960			12	G
1961	MIN	N	14	G
1962			14	G
1963			13	G

6 yrs.   74 games

Bruce Huther
HUTHER, BRUCE ALBERT
B. Jul. 23, 1954, Paterson, NJ
New Hampshire 6'1" 221 lbs.

Year	Team		Games	Pos.
1977	DAL	N	14	LB
1978			16	LB
1979			16	LB
1980			15	LB
1981	CLE	N	16	LB
1982	CHI	N	4	LB
1983	DAL	N	11	LB

7 yrs.   92 games

Brian Hutson
HUTSON, BRIAN S.
B. Feb. 20, 1965, Jackson, MS
Mississippi State 6'1" 198 lbs.

Year	Team		Games	Pos.
1990	NE	N	2	S

Don Hutson
HUTSON, DONALD MONTGOMERY (The Alabama Antelope)
B. Jan. 31, 1913, Pine Bluff, AR

Year	Team	Games	Pos.

Don Hutson *continued*
D. Jun. 26, 1997, Rancho Mirage, CA
Alabama 6'1" 183 lbs.

Year	Team		Games	Pos.
1935	GB	N	10	E
1936			12	E
1937			11	E
1938			10	E, K
1939			10	E, K
1940			11	E, K
1941			11	E, K
1942			11	E, K
1943			10	E, K
1944			10	E, K
1945			10	E, K

11 yrs.   116 games

Merle Hutson
HUTSON, MERLE
B. Aug. 27, 1908
Heidelberg 6'0" 210 lbs.

Year	Team		Games	Pos.
1931	CLE	N	10	G, T

Jack Hutton
HUTTON, LEON JOHN H. (Diz)
B. Aug. 12, 1906, Arkansas
D. Jan. 2, 1969
Purdue 6'1" 192 lbs.

Year	Team		Games	Pos.
1930	FRA	N	3	E, HB

Tom Hutton
HUTTON, TOM
B. Jul. 8, 1972, Memphis, TN
Tennessee 6'1" 193 lbs.

Year	Team		Games	Pos.
1995	PHI	N	16	P
1996			16	P

2 yrs.   32 games

Ken Huxhold
HUXHOLD, KENNETH WAYNE
B. Aug. 10, 1929, Kenosha, WI
Wisconsin 6'1" 226 lbs.

Year	Team		Games	Pos.
1954	PHI	N	11	G
1955			12	G
1956			12	G
1957			12	G
1958			12	G

5 yrs.   59 games

John Huzvar
HUZVAR, JOHN
B. Aug. 6, 1929, Carlisle, PA
North Carolina State/Pittsburgh 6'4" 247 lbs.

Year	Team		Games	Pos.
1952	PHI	N	12	FB
1953	BAL	N	12	FB
1954			8	FB

3 yrs.   32 games

Freddie Hyatt
HYATT, FREDDIE PHILLIP
B. Jun. 28, 1946, Roanoke, AL
Auburn 6'3" 203 lbs.

Year	Team		Games	Pos.
1968	STL	N	1	WR
1969			6	WR
1970			9	WR
1971			14	WR
1972			12	WR
1973	NO	N	1	WR
1973	WAS	N	2	WR

6 yrs.   45 games

Steve Hyche
HYCHE, STEVE JAY
B. Jun. 12, 1963, Jasper, AL
Livingston 6'3" 241 lbs.

Year	Team		Games	Pos.
1989	CHI	N	6	LB

Year	Team	Games	Pos.

Steve Hyche *continued*

Year	Team		Games	Pos.
1991	PHX	N	16	LB
1992			16	LB
1993			2	LB

4 yrs.   40 games

Glenn Hyde
HYDE, GLENN THATCHER
B. Mar. 14, 1951, Boston, MA
Pittsburgh 6'3" 255 lbs.

Year	Team		Games	Pos.
1976	DEN	N	11	OT
1977			14	OT
1978			15	OT
1979			16	OT
1980			16	OT
1981			16	OT
1982	BAL	N	5	OT
1985	DEN	N	11	G, C
1986	SEA	N	3	C
1987	KC	N	7	C

10 yrs.   114 games

Bob Hyland
HYLAND, ROBERT JOSEPH
B. Jul. 21, 1945, White Plains, NY
Boston College 6'5" 253 lbs.

Year	Team		Games	Pos.
1967	GB	N	14	C, G
1968			14	C, G
1969			14	C, G
1970	CHI	N	14	C
1971	NYG	N	14	C
1972			10	G
1973			14	C
1974			11	C
1975			14	C
1976	GB	N	14	C
1977	NE	N		C

11 yrs.   133 games

Paul Hynes
HYNES, PAUL
B. 1940
Louisiana Tech 6'1" 210 lbs.

Year	Team		Games	Pos.
1961	DAL	A	1	DB
1961	NY	A	6	DB
1962			13	DB

2 yrs.   20 games

Henry Hynoski
HYNOSKI, HENRY
B. May 30, 1953, Mount Carmel, PA
Temple 6'0" 210 lbs.

Year	Team		Games	Pos.
1975	CLE	N	14	RB

Cosmo Iacavazzi
IACAVAZZI, COSMO J.
B. Aug. 18, 1943
Princeton 5'11" 200 lbs.

Year	Team		Games	Pos.
1965	NY	A	10	HB

Mike Iaquaniello
IAQUANIELLO, MICHAEL
B. Feb. 13, 1968, Detroit, MI
Michigan State 6'3" 208 lbs.

Year	Team		Games	Pos.
1991	MIA	N	15	S

Mekeli Ieremia
IEREMIA, MEKELI TOLUFALE
B. Mar. 4, 1954, Niosafutu, American Samoa
Brigham Young 6'2" 244 lbs.

Year	Team		Games	Pos.
1978	BUF	N	2	DT

Israel Ifeanyi
IFEANYI, ISRAEL

Year	Team	Games	Pos.

Israel Ifeanyi *continued*
B. Nov. 21, 1970, Lagos, Nigeria
Southern California 6'3" 246 lbs.

Year	Team		Games	Pos.
1996	SF	N	3	DE

Floyd Iglehart
IGLEHART, FLOYD, JR.
B. Jan. 25, 1934
D. Sep. 5, 1987, Dallas, TX
Wiley 6'4" 197 lbs.

Year	Team		Games	Pos.
1958	LA	N	1	HB

Donald Igwebuike
IGWEBUIKE, DONALD AMECHI
B. Dec. 27, 1960, Anambra, Nigeria
Clemson 5'9" 185 lbs.

Year	Team		Games	Pos.
1985	TB	N	16	K
1986			16	K
1987			12	K
1988			12	K
1989			16	K
1990	MIN	N	8	K

6 yrs.   80 games

Hank Ilesic
ILESIC, HANK
B. Sep. 7, 1959, Edmonton, Alb.
none 6'1" 210 lbs.

Year	Team		Games	Pos.
1989	SD	N	14	P

Ray Ilg
ILG, RAYMOND A.
B. Nov. 25, 1945, Wellesley, MA
Colgate 6'1" 220 lbs.

Year	Team		Games	Pos.
1967	BOS	A	14	LB
1968				LB

2 yrs.   28 games

Mark Ilgenfritz
ILGENFRITZ, MARK M.
B. Aug. 9, 1952, Honolulu, HI
Vanderbilt 6'4" 250 lbs.

Year	Team		Games	Pos.
1974	CLE	N	14	DE

Tunch Ilkin
ILKIN, TUNCH ALI
B. Sep. 23, 1957, Istanbul, Turkey
Indiana State 6'3" 265 lbs.

Year	Team		Games	Pos.
1980	PIT	N	10	OT, G
1981			16	OT, G
1982			8	OT
1983			11	OT
1984			16	OT
1985			16	OT
1986			15	OT
1987			11	OT
1988			16	OT
1989			16	OT
1990			13	OT
1991			16	OT
1992			12	OT
1993	GB	N	1	OT

14 yrs.   177 games

Ted Illman
ILLMAN, TED
B. Nov. 27, 1902
Deceased
Montana 6'0" 190 lbs.

Year	Team		Games	Pos.
1926	LA	A	10	HB, FB
1928	CHIC	N	4	FB

2 yrs.   14 games

Roy Ilowit
ILOWIT, ROY

Year	Team	Games	Pos.

Roy Ilowit continued

B. Apr. 3, 1917, New York, NY
D. Jan. 3, 1990, Long Beach, NY
CCNY 6'2" 220 lbs.

Year	Team	Games	Pos.
1937	**BKN** N	4	T

Ken Iman

IMAN, KENNETH CHARLES
B. Feb. 8, 1939, St. Louis, MO
Southeast Missouri State 6'1" 236 lbs.

Year	Team	Games	Pos.
1960	**GB** N	12	C
1961		14	C
1962		14	C
1963		14	C
1965	**LA**	14	C
1966		14	C
1967		14	C
1968		14	C
1969		14	C
1970		14	C
1971		14	C
1972		14	C
1973		14	C
1974		14	C

14 yrs.   194 games

Martin Imhof

IMHOF, MARTIN CARL
B. Oct. 9, 1949, Seattle, WA
San Diego State 6'6" 256 lbs.

Year	Team	Games	Pos.
1972	**STL** N	13	DE
1974	**WAS** N	14	DE
1975	**NE** N	5	DE
1976	**DEN** N	1	DE

4 yrs.   33 games

Tut Imlay

IMLAY, TALMA W.
B. Mar. 20, 1902
D. Mar. 20, 1976, Del Monte Forest, CA
California 5'8" 165 lbs.

Year	Team	Games	Pos.
1926	**LA** N	10	QB, HB
1927	**NYG** N	7	QB, HB, FB

2 yrs.   17 games

Bob Ingalls

INGALLS, ROBERT D.
B. Feb. 23, 1919, Marblehead, MA
D. Apr. 8, 1970, Willimantic, CT
Michigan 6'3" 200 lbs.

Year	Team	Games	Pos.
1942	**GB** N	10	C

Mark Ingle

INGLE, MARK B.
B. 1889
Deceased
None

Year	Team	Games	Pos.
1921	**EVA** A	1	G

Tim Inglis

INGLIS, TIMOTHY JAMES
B. Mar. 10, 1964, Toledo, OH
Toledo 6'3" 232 lbs.

Year	Team	Games	Pos.
1987	**CIN**	8	LB
1988		4	LB

2 yrs.   12 games

Brian Ingram

INGRAM, BRIAN DEWAYNE
B. Oct. 31, 1959, Memphis, TN
Tennessee 6'4" 230 lbs.

Year	Team	Games	Pos.
1982	**NE** N	8	LB
1983		4	LB
1984		12	LB
1985		15	LB
1987	**SD** N	1	LB

5 yrs.   40 games

Byron Ingram

INGRAM, BYRON KIMBLE
B. Nov. 17, 1964, Lexington, KY
Eastern Kentucky 6'2" 295 lbs.

Year	Team	Games	Pos.
1987	**KC** N	1	C, G
1988		12	G

2 yrs.   13 games

Darryl Ingram

INGRAM, DARRYL
B. May 2, 1966, Lubbock, TX
California 6'2" 240 lbs.

Year	Team	Games	Pos.
1989	**MIN** N	16	TE
1991	**CLE** N	2	TE
1992	**GB** N	16	TE
1993		2	TE

4 yrs.   36 games

Kevin Ingram

INGRAM, KEVIN
B. Apr. 26, 1962
East Carolina 6'0" 178 lbs.

Year	Team	Games	Pos.
1987	**NO** N	2	QB

Mark Ingram

INGRAM, MARK J.
B. Aug. 23, 1965, Rock Island, IL
Michigan State 5'10" 188 lbs.

Year	Team	Games	Pos.
1987	**NYG** N	9	WR
1988		7	WR
1989		16	WR
1990		16	WR
1991		16	WR
1992		12	WR
1993	**MIA** N	16	WR
1994		15	WR
1995	**GB** N	16	WR
1996	**PHI** N	5	WR

10 yrs.   128 games

Stephen Ingram

INGRAM, STEPHEN
B. May 8, 1971, Seat Pleasant, MD
Maryland 6'4" 311 lbs.

Year	Team	Games	Pos.
1995	**TB** N	2	OT, G

Burt Ingwersen

INGWERSEN, BURTON A.
B. Aug. 29, 1898
D. Jul. 17, 1969, Champaign, IL
Illinois 5'11" 180 lbs.

Year	Team	Games	Pos.
1920	**DEC** A	8	T

Jerry Inman

INMAN, JERRY FRANKLIN
B. Feb. 14, 1940, Manhattan, KS
Oregon 6'3" 255 lbs.

Year	Team	Games	Pos.
1966	**DEN** A	7	DT
1967		14	DT
1968		7	DT
1969		14	DT
1970	**DEN** N	11	DT
1971		14	DT
1973		8	DT

7 yrs.   75 games

Earl Inmon

INMON, EARL
B. Mar. 21, 1954, Umatilla, FL
Bethune-Cookman 6'1" 215 lbs.

Year	Team	Games	Pos.
1978	**TB** N	2	LB

Dou Innocent

INNOCENT, DOU
B. Jul. 9, 1972, Pompano Beach, FL
Mississippi 5'11" 212 lbs.

Year	Team	Games	Pos.
1996	**SEA** N	4	RB

Marne Intrieri

INTRIERI, MARINO
B. 1908
Loyola (Maryland) 5'8" 250 lbs.

Year	Team	Games	Pos.
1932	**SI** N	10	C, G
1933	**BOS** N	3	C, T, E
1934		6	G, T

3 yrs.   19 games

Tony Ippolito

IPPOLITO, ANTHONY
B. Sep. 19, 1917, Chicago, IL
D. Nov. 12, 1951
Purdue 5'10" 220 lbs.

Year	Team	Games	Pos.
1943	**CHIB** N	9	G

Darwin Ireland

IRELAND, DARWIN
B. May 26, 1971, Pine Bluff, AR
Arkansas 5'11" 240 lbs.

Year	Team	Games	Pos.
1994	**CHI** N	2	LB
1995		1	LB

2 yrs.   3 games

Einar Irgens

IRGENS, EINAR
B. Jun., 1883
Deceased
None 5'8" 175 lbs.

Year	Team	Games	Pos.
1921	**MIN** A	2	HB, QB
1922	**MIN** N	3	QB, HB
1923		5	QB, HB

3 yrs.   10 games

Gerald Irons

IRONS, GERALD DWAYNE
B. May 2, 1947, Gary, IN
Maryland-Eastern Shore 6'2" 231 lbs.

Year	Team	Games	Pos.
1970	**OAK** N	14	LB
1971		7	LB
1972		14	LB
1973		14	LB
1974		14	LB
1975		14	LB
1976	**CLE** N	14	LB
1977		14	LB
1978		14	LB
1979		16	LB

10 yrs.   135 games

Barlow Irvin

IRVIN, BARLOW (Bones)
B. Dec. 31, 1903
D. Nov., 1985, Bryan, TX
Texas A&M 5'10" 225 lbs.

Year	Team	Games	Pos.
1926	**BUF** N	10	G
1927		5	T

2 yrs.   15 games

Darrell Irvin

IRVIN, DARRELL BRUCE
B. Jan. 21, 1957, Pawhuska, OK
Oklahoma 6'4" 255 lbs.

Year	Team	Games	Pos.
1980	**BUF** N	7	DE
1981		13	DE
1982		9	DE
1983	**SEA** N	16	DE

4 yrs.   45 games

Ken Irvin

IRVIN, KEN
B. Jul. 11, 1972, Lindale, GA
Memphis 5'10" 182 lbs.

Year	Team	Games	Pos.
1995	**BUF** N	16	CB
1996		16	CB

2 yrs.   32 games

LeRoy Irvin

IRVIN, LEROY, JR.
B. Sep. 15, 1957, Fort Dix, NJ
Kansas 5'11" 184 lbs.

Year	Team	Games	Pos.
1980	**LA** N	16	CB
1981		16	CB
1982	**LARM** N	9	CB
1983		15	CB
1984		16	CB
1985		16	CB
1986		16	CB
1987		10	CB
1988		16	CB
1989		13	CB
1990	**DET** N	16	CB

11 yrs.   159 games

Mark Irvin

IRVIN, MARK
B. Oct. 12, 1964
Bethune-Cookman 5'10" 190 lbs.

Year	Team	Games	Pos.
1987	**MIA** N	3	S

Michael Irvin

IRVIN, MICHAEL JEROME
B. Mar. 5, 1966, Fort Lauderdale, FL
Miami (Florida) 6'2" 202 lbs.

Year	Team	Games	Pos.
1988	**DAL** N	14	WR
1989		6	WR
1990		12	WR
1991		16	WR
1992		16	WR
1993		16	WR
1994		16	WR
1995		16	WR
1996		11	WR

9 yrs.   123 games

Tex Irvin

IRVIN, CECIL P.
B. Oct. 9, 1906, De Leon, TX
D. Feb., 1978, De Leon, TX
Davis & Elkins 6'0" 225 lbs.

Year	Team	Games	Pos.
1931	**PRO** N	11	T, FB
1932	**NYG** N	11	T
1933		12	T
1934		13	T
1935		12	T, G

5 yrs.   59 games

Willie Irvin

IRVIN, WILLIE
B. Jan. 3, 1930, St. Augustine, FL
Florida A&M 6'3" 203 lbs.

Year	Team	Games	Pos.
1953	**PHI** N	3	E

Terry Irving

IRVING, TERRY DUANE
B. Jul. 3, 1971, Galveston, TX
McNeese State 6'0" 224 lbs.

Year	Team	Games	Pos.
1994	**ARI** N	16	LB
1995		16	LB
1996		16	LB

3 yrs.   48 games

Don Irwin

IRWIN, DONALD (Bull)
B. Jul. 22, 1913, New York, NY
D. Jun. 8, 1983, Detroit, MI
Colgate 6'1" 196 lbs.

Year	Team	Games	Pos.
1936	**BOS** N	1	FB
1937	**WAS** N	10	FB
1938		10	FB, HB
1939		7	HB

4 yrs.   28 games

Dutch Irwin

IRWIN, HARRY S.

Year	Team		Games	Pos.

Dutch Irwin *continued*
B. Aug., 1899, New York State
Deceased
Mercer 5'7" 170 lbs.

Year	Team		Games	Pos.
1920	ROC	A	1	HB

Jim Irwin
IRWIN, JAMES
B. Mar. 9, 1897
D. Dec., 1965
None 5'7" 165 lbs.

Year	Team		Games	Pos.
1921	LOU	A	1	FB
1922	LOU	N	1	FB
2 yrs.	2 games			

Tim Irwin
IRWIN, TIMOTHY EDWARD
B. Dec. 13, 1958, Knoxville, TN
Tennessee 6'7" 285 lbs.

Year	Team		Games	Pos.
1981	MIN	N	7	OT
1982			9	OT
1983			16	OT
1984			16	OT
1985			16	OT
1986			16	OT
1987			12	OT
1988			16	OT
1989			16	OT
1990			16	OT
1991			16	OT
1992			16	OT
1993			16	OT
1994	TB	N	8	OT
1994	MIA	N	5	OT
14 yrs.	201 games			

Ted Isaacson
ISAACSON, THEODORE F.
B. Mar. 2, 1912, Seattle, WA
Deceased
Washington 6'4" 272 lbs.

Year	Team		Games	Pos.
1934	CHIC	N	10	T, G
1935			12	T
2 yrs.	22 games			

Wilmer Isabel
ISABEL, WILMER E.
B. Oct. 1, 1899, Columbus, OH
D. Sep., 1975, Bexley, OH
Ohio State 6'0" 175 lbs.

Year	Team		Games	Pos.
1923	COL	N	10	HB
1924			7	HB
2 yrs.	17 games			

Sale Isaia
ISAIA, SALE, JR.
B. Jun. 13, 1972, Honolulu, HI
UCLA 6'5" 315 lbs.

Year	Team		Games	Pos.
1996	BAL	N	9	G

Cecil Isbell
ISBELL, CECIL F.
B. Jul. 11, 1915, Iola, TX
D. Jun. 23, 1985, Hammond, IN
Purdue 6'1" 190 lbs.

Year	Team		Games	Pos.
1938	GB	N	11	HB
1939			11	HB
1940			10	HB
1941			11	HB
1942			11	HB
5 yrs.	54 games			

Joe Bob Isbell
ISBELL, JOE BOB
B. Jul. 7, 1940, Gorman, TX
Houston 6'1" 238 lbs.

Year	Team		Games	Pos.
1962	DAL	N	9	G
1963			8	G

Joe Bob Isbell *continued*

Year	Team		Games	Pos.
1964			14	G
1966	CLE	N	14	G
4 yrs.	45 games			

John Isenbarger
ISENBARGER, JOHN PHILLIPS
B. Dec. 5, 1947, Muncie, IN
Indiana 6'3" 203 lbs.

Year	Team		Games	Pos.
1970	SF	N	13	RB
1971			14	RB
1972			14	RB
1973			14	WR
4 yrs.	55 games			

Qadry Ismail
ISMAIL, QADRY RAHMADAN
B. Nov. 8, 1970, Newark, NJ
Syracuse 6'0" 192 lbs.

Year	Team		Games	Pos.
1993	MIN	N	15	WR
1994			16	WR
1995			16	WR
1996			16	WR
4 yrs.	63 games			

Raghib Ismail
ISMAIL, RAGHIB RAMADIAN
(Rocket)
B. Nov. 18, 1969, Elizabeth, NJ
Notre Dame 5'10" 180 lbs.

Year	Team		Games	Pos.
1993	LARI	N	13	WR
1994			16	WR
1995	OAK	N	16	WR
1996	CAR	N	13	WR
4 yrs.	58 games			

Ray Isom
ISOM, RAYMOND CLINTON
B. Dec. 27, 1965, Harrisburg, PA
Penn State 5'9" 190 lbs.

Year	Team		Games	Pos.
1987	TB	N	6	S
1988			2	CB, S
2 yrs.	8 games			

Rickey Isom
ISOM, RICKEY LAMARR
B. Nov. 30, 1963, Harrisburg, PA
North Carolina State 6'0" 224 lbs.

Year	Team		Games	Pos.
1987	MIA	N	3	FB

Steve Israel
ISRAEL, STEVEN DOUGLAS
B. Mar. 16, 1969, Lawnside, NJ
Pittsburgh 5'10" 186 lbs.

Year	Team		Games	Pos.
1992	LARM	N	16	CB
1993			16	CB
1994			10	CB
1995	SF	N	8	CB
1996			14	CB
5 yrs.	64 games			

Ralph Isselhardt
ISSELHARDT, RALPH L.
B. Jan. 13, 1910, Hillsboro, IL
D. Oct., 1972, East Grand Rapids, MI
Franklin (Ohio) 6'1" 205 lbs.

Year	Team		Games	Pos.
1937	DET	N	1	G
1937	CLE	N	8	G
1 yr.	9 games			

Jack Itzel
ITZEL, JOHN F.
B. Nov. 12, 1924
D. Dec., 1966
Pittsburgh/Georgetown 6'0" 190 lbs.

Year	Team		Games	Pos.
1945	PIT	N	10	FB

Duke Iverson
IVERSON, CHRIS ARNOLD
B. Feb. 26, 1920, Petaluma, CA
Oregon 6'2" 200 lbs.

Year	Team		Games	Pos.
1947	NYG	N	8	LB
1948	NY	AA	10	HB, DB
1949	B, NY	AA	12	HB, DB
1950	NYY	N	7	DB
1951			9	DB
5 yrs.	46 games			

Eddie Lee Ivery
IVERY, EDDIE LEE
B. Jul. 30, 1957, McDuffie County, GA
Georgia Tech 6'1" 208 lbs.

Year	Team		Games	Pos.
1979	GB	N	1	RB
1980			16	RB
1981			1	RB
1982			9	RB
1983			8	RB
1984			10	RB
1985			15	RB
1986			12	RB
8 yrs.	72 games			

John Ivlow
IVLOW, JOHN DAVID
B. Jan. 26, 1970, Joliet, IL
Northwestern/Colorado State 5'11" 226 lbs.

Year	Team		Games	Pos.
1993	CHI	N	2	RB

Horace Ivory
IVORY, HORACE ORLANDO
B. Aug. 8, 1954, Fort Worth, TX
Oklahoma 6'0" 198 lbs.

Year	Team		Games	Pos.
1977	NE	N	5	RB
1978			15	RB
1979			10	RB
1980			14	RB
1981			1	RB
1981	SEA	N	6	RB
1982			6	RB
6 yrs.	57 games			

Pop Ivy
IVY, LEE FRANK
B. Jan. 25, 1916, Skiatook, OK
Oklahoma 6'3" 208 lbs.

Year	Team		Games	Pos.
1940	PIT	N	4	E
1940	CHIC	N	5	E
1941			10	E
1942			11	E
1945			3	E
1946			11	E
1947			12	E
6 yrs.	56 games			

Mark Iwanowski
IWANOWSKI, MARK D.
B. Sep. 8, 1955, Hazleton, PA
Pennsylvania 6'4" 230 lbs.

Year	Team		Games	Pos.
1978	NYJ	N	5	TE

George Izo
IZO, GEORGE
B. Sep. 20, 1937, Barberton, OH
Notre Dame 6'3" 218 lbs.

Year	Team		Games	Pos.
1960	STL	N	2	QB
1961	WAS	N	5	QB
1962			1	QB
1963			5	QB
1964			3	QB
1965	DET	N	6	QB
1966	PIT	N	4	QB
7 yrs.	26 games			

Larry Izzo
IZZO, LAWRENCE ALEXANDER
B. Sep. 26, 1974, Fort Belvoir, VA
Rice 5'10" 220 lbs.

Year	Team		Games	Pos.
1996	MIA	N	16	LB

Eric Jack
JACK, ERIC DEMOND
B. Apr. 19, 1972, Dallas, TX
New Mexico 5'10" 177 lbs.

Year	Team		Games	Pos.
1994	ATL	N	16	CB

Chris Jacke
JACKE, CHRISTOPHER LEE
B. Mar. 12, 1966, Richmond, VA
Texas-El Paso 6'0" 197 lbs.

Year	Team		Games	Pos.
1989	GB	N	16	K
1990			16	K
1991			16	K
1992			16	K
1993			16	K
1994			16	K
1995			14	K
1996			16	K
8 yrs.	126 games			

Al Jackson
JACKSON, AL
B. Sep. 7, 1971, Pensacola, FL
Georgia 6'0" 182 lbs.

Year	Team		Games	Pos.
1994	PHI	N	11	CB

Alfred Jackson
JACKSON, ALFRED
B. Aug. 3, 1955, Cameron, TX
Texas 5'11" 176 lbs.

Year	Team		Games	Pos.
1978	ATL	N	15	WR
1979			12	WR
1980			16	WR
1981			16	WR
1982			9	WR
1983			4	WR
1984			16	WR
7 yrs.	88 games			

Alfred Jackson
JACKSON, ALFRED MELVIN, JR.
B. Jul. 10, 1967, Tulare, CA
San Diego State 6'0" 179 lbs.

Year	Team		Games	Pos.
1989	LARM	N	7	CB, S
1990			5	CB
1991	CLE	N	6	CB
1992			4	CB
1995	MIN	N	8	CB
1996			14	CB
6 yrs.	44 games			

Andrew Jackson
JACKSON, ANDREW LEON
B. May 6, 1964, Los Angeles, CA
Southern California/Iowa State 5'10" 190 lbs.

Year	Team		Games	Pos.
1987	HOU	N	7	RB

Bernard Jackson
JACKSON, BERNARD FRANK
B. Sep. 24, 1950, Washington, DC
D. May 26, 1997, Lompoc, CA
Washington State 6'0" 178 lbs.

Year	Team		Games	Pos.
1972	CIN	N	14	DB
1973			14	CB
1974			14	CB
1975			14	S, CB
1976			12	S
1977	DEN	N	14	S
1978			16	S, CB
1979			12	S
1980			4	CB

551

Year	Team	Games	Pos.

Bernard Jackson continued

Year	Team		Games	Pos.
1980	SD	N	4	S
9 yrs.	118 games			

Bill Jackson
JACKSON, WILLIAM STEVEN
B. Jul. 1, 1960, Winston-Salem, NC
North Carolina 6'1" 202 lbs.

1982	CLE	N	9	CB, S

Billy Jackson
JACKSON, BILLY THURMAN
B. Sep. 13, 1959, Phenix City, AL
Alabama 5'10" 223 lbs.

1981	KC	N	16	RB
1982			9	RB
1983			16	RB
1984			16	RB
4 yrs.	57 games			

Bo Jackson
JACKSON, VINCENT EDWARD
B. Nov. 30, 1962, Bessemer, AL
Auburn 6'1" 230 lbs.

1987	LARI	N	7	RB
1988			10	RB
1989			11	RB
1990			10	RB
4 yrs.	38 games			

Bob Jackson
JACKSON, ROBERT (Stonewall)
B. 1925
North Carolina A&T 5'11" 210 lbs.

1950	NYG	N	12	FB
1951			12	FB
2 yrs.	24 games			

Bob Jackson
JACKSON, ROBERT
B. Mar. 16, 1940, Shreveport, LA
New Mexico State 6'3" 232 lbs.

1962	SD	A	14	FB
1963			12	FB
1964	HOU	A	6	FB
1964	OAK		8	FB
1965	HOU	A	10	FB
4 yrs.	50 games			

Bob Jackson
JACKSON, ROBERT E.
B. Apr. 1, 1953, Charlotte, NC
Duke 6'5" 253 lbs.

1975	CLE	N	14	OT
1976			14	G
1977			14	G
1978			16	G
1979			16	G
1980			14	G
1981			16	G
1982			9	G
1983			16	G
1984			16	G
1985			15	G
11 yrs.	160 games			

Bobby Jackson
JACKSON, ROBERT
B. Jan. 10, 1936, Mobile, AL
Alabama 6'1" 190 lbs.

1960	PHI	N	12	DB
1961	CHI	N	9	DB
2 yrs.	21 games			

Bobby Jackson
JACKSON, ROBERT CHARLES

Bobby Jackson continued
B. Dec. 23, 1956, Albany, GA
Florida State 5'10" 180 lbs.

1978	NYJ	N	16	CB
1979			16	CB
1980			15	CB
1981			9	CB
1982			9	CB
1983			15	CB
1984			3	CB
1985			12	CB
8 yrs.	95 games			

Calvin Jackson
JACKSON, CALVIN BERNARD
B. Oct. 28, 1972, Miami, FL
Auburn 5'10" 179 lbs.

1994	MIA	N	2	CB
1995			9	CB
1996			16	CB
3 yrs.	27 games			

Cedric Jackson
JACKSON, CEDRIC ANTHONY
B. Jan. 13, 1968, Texarkana, TX
Texas Christian 5'11" 229 lbs.

1991	DET	N	8	RB

Charles Jackson
JACKSON, CHARLES
B. Mar. 12, 1963
Texas Tech 6'4" 210 lbs.

1987	WAS	N	1	S

Charles Jackson
JACKSON, CHARLES MELVIN
B. Mar. 22, 1965, Los Angeles, CA
Washington 6'2" 226 lbs.

1978	KC	N	16	LB
1979			12	LB
1980			16	LB
1981			14	LB
1982			9	LB
1983			15	LB
1984			4	LB
1985	NYJ	N	16	LB
1986			15	LB
9 yrs.	117 games			

Charlie Jackson
JACKSON, CHARLES
B. Mar. 3, 1936, Paris, TX
Southern Methodist 5'11" 180 lbs.

1958	CHIC	N	10	DB
1960	DAL	A		DB
2 yrs.	10 games			

Cleveland Jackson
JACKSON, CLEVELAND LEE
B. Oct. 1, 1956, Crossett, AR
Michigan State/Nevada-Las Vegas 6'4" 230 lbs.

1979	NYG	N	2	TE

Colville Jackson
JACKSON, COLVILLE C. (Red)
B. Apr. 15, 1897
D. Nov., 1963, Mississippi
Chicago 6'0" 200 lbs.

1921	HAM	A	2	T

David Jackson
JACKSON, DAVID
B. Jan. 2, 1965
Southeast Missouri State 5'8" 170 lbs.

1987	TB	N	1	WR

Don Jackson
JACKSON, DONALD FLETCHER
B. 1914
D. 1946
North Carolina 5'11" 184 lbs.

1936	PHI	N	9	HB

Earnest Jackson
JACKSON, EARNEST
B. Dec. 18, 1959, Needville, TX
Texas A&M 5'9" 208 lbs.

1983	SD	N	12	RB
1984			16	RB
1985	PHI	N	16	RB
1986	PIT	N	13	RB
1987			12	RB
1988			12	RB
6 yrs.	81 games			

Enis Jackson
JACKSON, ENIS
B. May 16, 1963, Helena, AR
Memphis State 5'9" 180 lbs.

1987	CLE	N	1	CB, S

Ernie Jackson
JACKSON, EARNEST
B. Apr. 11, 1950, Hopkins, SC
Duke 5'10" 175 lbs.

1972	NO	N	9	CB
1973			14	CB
1974			13	CB
1975			10	CB
1976			10	CB
1977			11	CB
1978	ATL	N	16	CB
1979	DET	N	2	CB
8 yrs.	88 games			

Frank Jackson
JACKSON, FRANK HARDIN
B. Apr. 14, 1939, Levelland, TX
Southern Methodist 6'1" 187 lbs.

1961	DAL	A	14	HB
1962			14	HB
1963	KC	A	14	HB
1964			14	FL
1965			14	FL
1966	MIA	A	10	FL
1967			10	FL
7 yrs.	90 games			

Gerald Jackson
JACKSON, GERALD
B. Mar. 5, 1956, Moss Point, MS
Mississippi State 6'1" 195 lbs.

1979	KC	N	16	S

Greg Jackson
JACKSON, GREGORY ALLEN
B. Aug. 20, 1966, Hialeah, FL
Louisiana State 6'1" 200 lbs.

1989	NYG	N	16	S
1990			14	S
1991			13	S
1992			16	S
1993			16	S
1994	PHI	N	16	S
1995			16	S
1996	NO	N	16	S
8 yrs.	123 games			

Harold Jackson
JACKSON, HAROLD
B. Jan. 6, 1946, Hattiesburg, MS
Jackson State 5'10" 175 lbs.

1968	LA	N	2	WR

Harold Jackson continued

1969	PHI	N	14	WR
1970			14	WR
1971			14	WR
1972			14	WR
1973	LA	N	14	WR
1974			14	WR
1975			14	WR
1976			14	WR
1977			14	WR
1978	NE	N	16	WR
1979			16	WR
1980			16	WR
1981			16	WR
1982	MIN	N	1	WR
1983	SEA	N	15	WR
16 yrs.	208 games			

Honor Jackson
JACKSON, HONOR W.
B. Nov. 21, 1948, Mill Valley, CA
Pacific 6'1" 195 lbs.

1972	NE	N	14	DB
1973			7	S
1973	NYG	N	2	CB
1974			12	CB
3 yrs.	35 games			

Jack Jackson
JACKSON, ELLIOT CORNELIUS, JR.
B. Nov. 11, 1972, Moss Point, MS
Florida 5'8" 174 lbs.

1996	CHI	N	12	WR

Jazz Jackson
JACKSON, CLARENCE
B. Mar. 5, 1952, Knoxville, TN
Western Kentucky 5'8" 169 lbs.

1974	NYJ	N	13	RB
1975			13	RB
1976			7	RB
3 yrs.	33 games			

Jeff Jackson
JACKSON, JEFFERY PAUL
B. Oct. 9, 1961, Shreveport, LA
Auburn 6'1" 232 lbs.

1984	ATL	N	16	LB
1985			11	LB
1987	SD	N	11	LB
1988			14	LB
4 yrs.	52 games			

Jim Jackson
JACKSON, JAMES GEORGE
B. Apr. 19, 1944, Alton, IL
Western Illinois 6'0" 187 lbs.

1966	SF	N	10	HB
1967			3	DB
2 yrs.	13 games			

Joe Jackson
JACKSON, JOE
B. Oct. 15, 1962
San Francisco State 6'1" 225 lbs.

1987	SEA	N	3	LB

Joey Jackson
JACKSON, JOE
B. May 7, 1949, Cincinnati, OH
New Mexico State 6'4" 263 lbs.

1972	NYJ	N	14	DE
1973			3	DE, DT
1977	MIN	N	3	DT
3 yrs.	20 games			

John Jackson
JACKSON, JOHN
B. Jan. 4, 1965, Camp Kwe, Okinawa, Japan
Eastern Kentucky 6'6" 282 lbs.

Year	Team		Games	Pos.
1988	PIT	N	16	OT
1989			14	OT
1990			16	OT
1991			16	OT
1992			16	OT
1993			16	OT
1994			16	OT
1995			11	OT
1996			16	OT
9 yrs.	137 games			

John Jackson
JACKSON, JOHN
B. Jan. 2, 1967, Brooklyn, NY
Southern California 5'10" 175 lbs.

Year	Team		Games	Pos.
1990	PHX	N	9	WR
1991			16	WR
1992			6	WR
1996	CHI	N	5	WR
4 yrs.	36 games			

Johnnie Jackson
JACKSON, JOHNNIE BOBBY
B. Jan. 11, 1967, Harlingen, TX
Houston 6'1" 204 lbs.

Year	Team		Games	Pos.
1989	SF	N	16	S
1990			16	S
1991			16	S
1992			5	S
1992	GB	N	1	S
4 yrs.	54 games			

Johnny Jackson
JACKSON, JOHNNY
B. Jul. 1, 1953, Lima, OH
Tennessee State/Southern University 6'2" 250 lbs.

Year	Team		Games	Pos.
1977	PHI	N	2	DE

Keith Jackson
JACKSON, KEITH JEROME
B. Apr. 19, 1965, Little Rock, AR
Oklahoma 6'2" 250 lbs.

Year	Team		Games	Pos.
1988	PHI	N	16	TE
1989			14	TE
1990			14	TE
1991			16	TE
1992	MIA	N	13	TE
1993			16	TE
1994			16	TE
1995	GB	N	9	TE
1996			16	TE
9 yrs.	129 games			

Ken Jackson
JACKSON, KENNETH G.
B. Apr. 26, 1929, Austin, TX
Texas 6'2" 236 lbs.

Year	Team		Games	Pos.
1952	DAL	N	11	T
1953	BAL	N	12	T
1954			12	T
1955			8	T
1956			9	T
1957			12	G, T
6 yrs.	64 games			

Kenny Jackson
JACKSON, KENNY
B. Feb. 15, 1962, Neptune, NJ
Penn State 6'0" 180 lbs.

Year	Team		Games	Pos.
1984	PHI	N	11	WR
1985			16	WR

Kenny Jackson continued

Year	Team		Games	Pos.
1986			16	WR
1987			12	WR
1988			7	WR
1989	HOU	N	10	WR
1990	PHI	N	14	WR
1991			16	WR
8 yrs.	102 games			

Kirby Jackson
JACKSON, KIRBY
B. Feb. 2, 1965, Sturgis, MS
Mississippi State 5'10" 180 lbs.

Year	Team		Games	Pos.
1987	LARM	N	5	CB
1988	BUF	N	8	CB
1989			14	CB
1990			12	CB
1991			16	CB
1992			15	CB
6 yrs.	70 games			

Larron Jackson
JACKSON, LARRON DEONNE
(Hungry Jack)
B. Aug. 26, 1949, St. Louis, MO
Missouri 6'3" 265 lbs.

Year	Team		Games	Pos.
1971	DEN	N	14	G
1972			14	G
1973			13	G
1974			13	G
1975	ATL	N	14	G
1976			14	G
6 yrs.	82 games			

Lawrence Jackson
JACKSON, LAWRENCE
B. Aug. 10, 1964
Presbyterian 6'1" 275 lbs.

Year	Team		Games	Pos.
1987	ATL	N	3	G

Leonard Jackson
JACKSON, LEONARD
B. Oct. 5, 1964, Pine Bluff, AR
Oklahoma State 6'0" 240 lbs.

Year	Team		Games	Pos.
1987	CHI	N	1	DE
1987	LARI	N	1	LB
1 yr.	2 games			

Leroy Jackson
JACKSON, LEROY
B. Dec. 8, 1939, Chicago Heights, IL
Western Illinois 6'0" 190 lbs.

Year	Team		Games	Pos.
1962	WAS	N	10	HB
1963			5	HB
2 yrs.	15 games			

Louis Jackson
JACKSON, LOUIS BERNARD
B. Jan. 27, 1958, Fresno, CA
California Poly (San Luis Obispo) 5'11" 195 lbs.

Year	Team		Games	Pos.
1981	NYG	N	11	RB

Marcus Jackson
JACKSON, MARCUS
B. Jun. 8, 1957, Lima, OH
Purdue 6'5" 260 lbs.

Year	Team		Games	Pos.
1987	IND	N	1	NT

Mark Jackson
JACKSON, MARK ANTHONY
B. Jul. 23, 1963, Chicago, IL
Purdue 5'9" 174 lbs.

Year	Team		Games	Pos.
1986	DEN	N	16	WR

Mark Jackson continued

Year	Team		Games	Pos.
1987			12	WR
1988			12	WR
1989			16	WR
1990			16	WR
1991			12	WR
1992			16	WR
1993	NYG	N	16	WR
1994			2	WR
1994	IND	N	12	WR
9 yrs.	130 games			

Mark Jackson
JACKSON, MARK DEVALON
B. Mar. 16, 1962, Amarillo, TX
Abilene Christian 5'9" 180 lbs.

Year	Team		Games	Pos.
1987	STL	N	11	CB

Mel Jackson
JACKSON, MELVIN, JR.
B. May 5, 1954, Los Angeles, CA
Southern California 6'1" 267 lbs.

Year	Team		Games	Pos.
1976	GB	N	13	G
1977			14	G
1978			16	G
1979			16	G
1980			6	G
5 yrs.	65 games			

Michael Jackson
JACKSON, MICHAEL ANTHONY
B. Jul. 15, 1957, Pasco, WA
Washington 6'1" 226 lbs.

Year	Team		Games	Pos.
1979	SEA	N	15	LB
1980			15	LB
1981			16	LB
1982			8	LB
1983			11	LB
1984			8	LB
1985			16	LB
1986			16	LB
8 yrs.	105 games			

Michael Jackson
JACKSON, MICHAEL DWAYNE
B. Apr. 12, 1969, Tangipahoa, LA
Southern Mississippi 6'4" 195 lbs.

Year	Team		Games	Pos.
1991	CLE	N	16	WR
1992			16	WR
1993			15	WR
1994			9	WR
1995			13	WR
1996	BAL	N	16	WR
6 yrs.	85 games			

Monte Jackson
JACKSON, MONTE CARL
B. Jul. 14, 1953, Sherman, TX
San Diego State 5'11" 192 lbs.

Year	Team		Games	Pos.
1975	LA	N	14	CB
1976			14	CB
1977			14	CB
1978	OAK	N	16	CB
1979			8	CB
1980			16	CB
1981			16	CB
1982	LARI	N	9	CB
1983	LARM	N	6	CB
9 yrs.	113 games			

Noah Jackson
JACKSON, NOAH DALE
B. Apr. 14, 1951, Jacksonville Beach, FL
Tampa 6'2" 268 lbs.

Year	Team		Games	Pos.
1975	CHI	N	14	G
1976			12	G

Noah Jackson continued

Year	Team		Games	Pos.
1977			14	G
1978			16	G
1979			15	G
1980			16	G
1981			16	G
1982			9	G
1983			13	G
1984	TB	N	6	G
10 yrs.	131 games			

Perry Jackson
SHOCKLEY, ARNOLD
B. 1905
Southwestern Oklahoma State 6'1" 202 lbs.

Year	Team		Games	Pos.
1928	PRO	N	10	T
1929			7	T, E, HB
1930			9	T
3 yrs.	26 games			

Pete Jackson
JACKSON, PETE
B. Aug. 13, 1904
D. Mar., 1967
Missouri 5'10" 200 lbs.

Year	Team		Games	Pos.
1928	DET	N	6	FB, HB

Randy Jackson
JACKSON, RANDALL
B. Nov. 13, 1948, Atlanta, GA
Wichita State 6'0" 220 lbs.

Year	Team		Games	Pos.
1972	BUF	N	5	RB
1973	SF	N	2	RB
1974	PHI	N	14	RB
3 yrs.	21 games			

Randy Jackson
JACKSON, RANDY
B. Mar. 6, 1944, Lake City, FL
Florida 6'5" 247 lbs.

Year	Team		Games	Pos.
1967	CHI	N	14	OT
1968			14	OT
1969			10	OT
1970			14	OT
1971			14	OT
1972			14	OT
1973			14	OT
1974			14	OT
8 yrs.	108 games			

Ray Jackson
JACKSON, RAYMOND DEWAYNE
B. Feb. 17, 1973, Denver, CO
Colorado State 5'10" 189 lbs.

Year	Team		Games	Pos.
1996	BUF	N	12	CB

Red Jackson
JACKSON, RED
None

Year	Team		Games	Pos.
1926	LOU	N	2	HB, C

Richard Jackson
JACKSON, RICHARD SAMUEL
(Tombstone)
B. Jul. 22, 1941, New Orleans, LA
Southern University 6'2" 252 lbs.

Year	Team		Games	Pos.
1966	OAK	A	5	LB
1967	DEN	A	14	DE
1968			14	DE
1969			14	DE
1970	DEN	N	14	DE
1971			7	DE
1972			4	DE
1972	CLE	N	10	DE
7 yrs.	82 games			

Year	Team	Games	Pos.

Rickey Jackson
JACKSON, RICKEY ANDERSON
B. Mar. 20, 1958, Pahokee, FL
Pittsburgh 6'2" 240 lbs.

Year	Team		Games	Pos.
1981	NO	N	16	LB
1982			9	LB
1983			16	LB
1984			16	LB
1985			16	LB
1986			16	LB
1987			12	LB
1988			16	LB
1989			14	LB
1990			16	LB
1991			16	LB
1992			16	LB
1993			16	LB
1994	SF	N	16	LB
1995			16	LB
15 yrs.			227 games	

Robert Jackson
JACKSON, ROBERT LEE
B. Aug. 7, 1954, Houston, TX
Texas A&M 6'1" 230 lbs.

Year	Team		Games	Pos.
1978	CLE	N	14	LB
1979			16	LB
1980			14	LB
1981			14	LB
1982	ATL	N	4	LB
5 yrs.			62 games	

Robert Jackson
JACKSON, ROBERT MICHAEL
B. Oct. 10, 1958, Grand Rapids, MI
Central Michigan 5'10" 186 lbs.

Year	Team		Games	Pos.
1982	CIN	N	9	S
1983			16	S
1984			16	S
1985			16	S
1986			7	S
1987			12	S
1989			14	S
7 yrs.			90 games	

Roger Jackson
JACKSON, ROGER
B. Feb. 28, 1959, Macon, GA
Bethune-Cookman 6'0" 186 lbs.

Year	Team		Games	Pos.
1982	DEN	N	9	DB
1983			16	CB, S
1984			16	S
1985			9	S
1987			3	S
5 yrs.			53 games	

Roland Jackson
JACKSON, ROLAND
B. 1940
Rice 6'0" 210 lbs.

Year	Team		Games	Pos.
1962	STL	N	5	FB

Rusty Jackson
JACKSON, DALTON SHERMAN
B. Nov. 17, 1950, Tuscaloosa, AL
Louisiana State 6'2" 193 lbs.

Year	Team		Games	Pos.
1976	LA	N	14	P
1978	BUF	N	16	P
1979			16	P
3 yrs.			46 games	

Stephen Jackson
JACKSON, STEPHEN FRANKLIN
B. Dec. 8, 1942, McKinney, TX
Texas-Arlington 6'1" 225 lbs.

Year	Team		Games	Pos.
1966	WAS	N	14	LB
1967			11	LB
2 yrs.			25 games	

Steve Jackson
JACKSON, STEVE LORAN
B. Apr. 6, 1955, Chatom, AL
Louisiana State 6'1" 192 lbs.

Year	Team		Games	Pos.
1977	OAK	N	6	S

Steve Jackson
JACKSON, STEVEN WAYNE
B. Apr. 8, 1969, Houston, TX
Purdue 5'8" 185 lbs.

Year	Team		Games	Pos.
1991	HOU	N	15	CB
1992			16	CB
1993			16	CB
1994			12	CB
1995			10	CB
1996			16	CB
6 yrs.			85 games	

Terry Jackson
JACKSON, TERENCE LEON
B. Dec. 9, 1955, Sherman, TX
San Diego State 5'11" 197 lbs.

Year	Team		Games	Pos.
1978	NYG	N	15	CB
1979			16	CB
1980			8	CB
1981			16	CB
1982			8	CB
1983			12	CB
1984	SEA	N	16	CB
1985			16	CB
8 yrs.			107 games	

Tim Jackson
JACKSON, TIM
B. Nov. 7, 1965, Dallas, TX
Nebraska 5'11" 192 lbs.

Year	Team		Games	Pos.
1989	DAL	N	1	CB, S

T.J. Jackson
JACKSON, TRENTON J.
B. Feb. 28, 1944, Rochester, NY
Illinois 6'0" 180 lbs.

Year	Team		Games	Pos.
1966	PHI	N	3	FL
1967	WAS	N	3	DB, FL
2 yrs.			6 games	

Tom Jackson
JACKSON, THOMAS
B. Apr. 4, 1951, Cleveland, OH
Louisville 5'11" 220 lbs.

Year	Team		Games	Pos.
1973	DEN	N	8	LB
1974			13	LB
1975			14	LB
1976			14	LB
1977			13	LB
1978			13	LB
1979			16	LB
1980			16	LB
1981			16	LB
1982			9	LB
1983			12	LB
1984			16	LB
1985			12	LB
1986			16	LB
14 yrs.			188 games	

Tyoka Jackson
JACKSON, TYOKA
B. Nov. 22, 1971, Forestville, MD
Penn State 6'1" 266 lbs.

Year	Team		Games	Pos.
1994	MIA	N	1	DE
1996	TB	N	13	DE
2 yrs.			14 games	

Vestee Jackson
JACKSON, VESTEE, II
B. Aug. 14, 1963, Fresno, CA

Vestee Jackson *continued*
Washington 6'0" 186 lbs.

Year	Team		Games	Pos.
1986	CHI	N	16	CB
1987			12	CB
1988			16	CB
1989			16	CB
1990			16	CB
1991	MIA	N	16	CB
1992			11	CB
1993			16	CB
8 yrs.			119 games	

Victor Jackson
JACKSON, VICTOR ALAN
B. Aug. 6, 1959, Princess Anne, MD
Bowie State 6'2" 205 lbs.

Year	Team		Games	Pos.
1986	IND	N	2	CB, S
1987	LARI	N	2	S
2 yrs.			4 games	

Wilbur Jackson
JACKSON, WILBUR
B. Nov. 19, 1951, Ozark, AL
Alabama 6'1" 217 lbs.

Year	Team		Games	Pos.
1974	SF	N	14	RB
1975			14	RB
1976			14	RB
1977			16	RB
1979			16	RB
1980	WAS	N	16	RB
1981			6	RB
1982			1	RB
8 yrs.			95 games	

Willie Jackson
JACKSON, WILLIE BERNARD
B. Aug. 16, 1971, Gainesville, FL
Florida 6'1" 205 lbs.

Year	Team		Games	Pos.
1994	DAL	N	1	WR
1995	JAC	N	14	WR
1996			16	WR
3 yrs.			31 games	

Frank Jackunas
JACKUNAS, FRANK
B. 1941
Detroit 6'3" 225 lbs.

Year	Team		Games	Pos.
1962	BUF	A	3	C

Jacobs
JACOBS
None

Year	Team		Games	Pos.
1920	DET	A	1	HB

Allen Jacobs
JACOBS, ALLEN WINNITT
B. May 19, 1941, Los Angeles, CA
Utah 6'1" 215 lbs.

Year	Team		Games	Pos.
1965	GB	N	14	RB
1966	NYG	N	14	RB
1967			6	RB
3 yrs.			34 games	

Cam Jacobs
JACOBS, THOMAS CAMERON
B. Mar. 10, 1962, Oklahoma City, OK
Kentucky 6'2" 230 lbs.

Year	Team		Games	Pos.
1987	TB	N	3	LB

Dave Jacobs
JACOBS, DAVID J.
B. Jul. 15, 1957, Scranton, PA
Syracuse 5'7" 153 lbs.

Year	Team		Games	Pos.
1979	NYJ	N	4	K
1981	CLE	N	5	K
1987	PHI	N	3	K, P
3 yrs.			12 games	

Harry Jacobs
JACOBS, HARRY EDWARD
B. Feb. 4, 1937, Canton, IL
Bradley 6'2" 228 lbs.

Year	Team		Games	Pos.
1960	BOS	A	14	DE
1961			9	LB
1962			14	LB
1963	BUF	A	14	LB
1964			14	LB
1965			14	LB
1966			14	LB
1967			7	LB
1968			14	LB
1969			14	LB
1970	NO	N	6	LB
11 yrs.			134 games	

Jack Jacobs
JACOBS, JACK (Indian Jack)
B. Aug. 7, 1919, Holdenville, OK
D. Jan. 12, 1974, Greensboro, NC
Oklahoma 6'1" 186 lbs.

Year	Team		Games	Pos.
1942	CLE	N	8	QB, DB
1945			2	QB, DB
1946	WAS	N	9	QB, DB
1947	GB	N	12	QB, DB
1948			12	QB, DB
1949			12	QB, DB
6 yrs.			55 games	

Marv Jacobs
JACOBS, MARVIN ELZIE
B. 1925
Central Washington State 6'2" 235 lbs.

Year	Team		Games	Pos.
1948	CHIC	N	5	T

Proverb Jacobs
JACOBS, PROVERB
B. May 25, 1935, Marksville, LA
California 6'4" 258 lbs.

Year	Team		Games	Pos.
1958	PHI	N	12	OT
1960	NYG	N	8	DT
1961	NY	A	10	DT
1962			4	DT
1963	OAK	A	14	OT
1964			6	OT
6 yrs.			54 games	

Ray Jacobs
JACOBS, HERSHELL RAY
B. Nov. 21, 1939, Corsicana, TX
Howard Payne 6'3" 276 lbs.

Year	Team		Games	Pos.
1963	DEN	A	7	DE
1964			14	DT
1965			14	DT
1966			11	DT
1967	MIA	A	14	DT
1968			11	DT
1969	BOS	A	8	DT, DE
7 yrs.			79 games	

Ray Jacobs
JACOBS, RAY ANTHONY
B. Aug. 18, 1972, Hampstead, NC
North Carolina 6'2" 244 lbs.

Year	Team		Games	Pos.
1994	DEN	N	16	LB
1995			15	LB
2 yrs.			31 games	

Tim Jacobs
JACOBS, TIM
B. Apr. 5, 1970, Washington, DC
Delaware 5'10" 185 lbs.

Year	Team		Games	Pos.
1993	CLE	N	2	CB
1994			10	CB
1995			14	CB
1996	MIA	N	12	CB
4 yrs.			38 games	

Year	Team	Games	Pos.

Jack Jacobson
JACOBSON, JACK C.
B. 1941
Oklahoma State 6'2" 200 lbs.

Year	Team		Games	Pos.
1965	SD	A	3	DB

Larry Jacobson
JACOBSON, LARRY
B. Dec. 10, 1949, Sioux Falls, SD
Nebraska 6'6" 260 lbs.

Year	Team		Games	Pos.
1972	NYG	N	14	DE, DT
1973			9	DT
1974			11	DT

3 yrs. 34 games

Steve Jacobson
JACOBSON, STEVE
B. Nov. 18, 1962
Abilene Christian 6'3" 255 lbs.

Year	Team		Games	Pos.
1987	MIA	N	3	G

Joe Jacoby
JACOBY, JOE
B. Jul. 6, 1959, Louisville, KY
Louisville 6'7" 300 lbs.

Year	Team		Games	Pos.
1981	WAS	N	14	OT
1982			9	OT
1983			16	OT
1984			16	OT
1985			11	OT
1986			16	OT
1987			12	OT
1988			16	OT
1989			10	OT
1990			16	OT
1991			16	G, OT
1992			13	OT, G
1993			5	G, OT

13 yrs. 170 games

Jim Jacquith
JACQUITH, JAMES M.
B. Apr., 1899, Council Grove, KS
Emporia State 5'9" 175 lbs.

Year	Team		Games	Pos.
1926	KC	N	1	QB

Harry Jacunski
JACUNSKI, HARRY A.
B. Oct. 20, 1915, New Britain, CT
Fordham 6'2" 200 lbs.

Year	Team		Games	Pos.
1939	GB	N	10	E
1940			10	E
1941			10	E
1942			5	E
1943			10	E
1944			9	E

6 yrs. 54 games

Jeff Jaeger
JAEGER, JEFF TODD
B. Nov. 26, 1964, Tacoma, WA
Washington 5'11" 189 lbs.

Year	Team		Games	Pos.
1987	CLE	N	10	K
1989	LARI	N	16	K
1990			16	K
1991			16	K
1992			16	K
1993			16	K
1994			16	K
1995	OAK	N	11	K
1996	CHI	N	13	K

9 yrs. 130 games

Johnny Jaffurs
JAFFURS, JOHN
B. Apr. 15, 1923, Wilkinsburg, PA
Penn State 5'10" 200 lbs.

Year	Team		Games	Pos.
1946	WAS	N	8	G

Harry Jagade
JAGADE, HARRY CHARLES
(Chick)
B. Dec. 9, 1926, Chicago, IL
D. Nov. 24, 1968, Washington Island, WA
Indiana 6'0" 213 lbs.

Year	Team		Games	Pos.
1949	BAL	AA	10	FB
1951	CLE	N	11	FB
1952			12	FB
1953			12	FB
1954	CHIB	N	11	FB
1955			12	FB

6 yrs. 68 games

Harry Jagielski
JAGIELSKI, HARRY A.
B. Dec. 25, 1931, Pittsburgh, PA
D. Oct. 9, 1993, Chicago, IL
Indiana 6'0" 257 lbs.

Year	Team		Games	Pos.
1956	CHIC	N	4	T
1956	WAS	N	5	T
1960	BOS	A		DT
1961			5	DT
1961	OAK	A	8	DT

3 yrs. 22 games

Van Jakes
JAKES, VAN
B. May 10, 1961, Phenix City, AL
Kent State 5'11" 185 lbs.

Year	Team		Games	Pos.
1983	KC	N	14	CB
1984			8	CB
1986	NO		12	DB
1987			12	DB
1988			16	CB
1989	GB	N	16	CB, S

6 yrs. 78 games

George Jakowenko
JAKOWENKO, GEORGE
B. Jun. 26, 1948, Charleroi, Belgium
Syracuse 5'9" 175 lbs.

Year	Team		Games	Pos.
1974	OAK	N	6	K
1976	BUF	N	11	K

2 yrs. 17 games

Charlie Jamerson
JAMERSON, CHARLES DEWEY
(Lefty)
B. Enfield., IL
D. Aug. 4, 1980, Mocksville, NC
Arkansas 6'1" 195 lbs.

Year	Team		Games	Pos.
1926	HAR	N	2	E

Angelo James
JAMES, ANGELO
B. Jun. 13, 1962
Sacramento State 6'0" 180 lbs.

Year	Team		Games	Pos.
1987	PHI	N	3	CB

Arrike James
JAMES, ARRIKE
B. Dec. 31, 1964, Dumas, AR
Delta State 6'4" 238 lbs.

Year	Team		Games	Pos.
1987	HOU	N	3	TE

Claudis James
JAMES, CLAUDIS RAY
B. Nov. 7, 1943, Columbia, MS
Jackson State 6'2" 190 lbs.

Year	Team		Games	Pos.
1967	GB	N	1	RB
1968			14	RB, FL

2 yrs. 15 games

Craig James
JAMES, JESSE CRAIG
B. Jan. 2, 1961, Jacksonville, TX
Southern Methodist 6'0" 215 lbs.

Year	Team		Games	Pos.
1984	NE	N	15	RB
1985			16	RB
1986			13	RB
1987			2	RB
1988			6	RB

5 yrs. 52 games

Dan James
JAMES, DANIEL ANTHONY
B. Aug. 10, 1937, Cincinnati, OH
Ohio State 6'4" 262 lbs.

Year	Team		Games	Pos.
1960	PIT	N	12	C, OT
1961			14	OT
1962			14	OT
1963			14	OT
1964			14	OT
1965			13	OT
1966			10	OT
1967	CHI		2	OT

8 yrs. 93 games

Dick James
JAMES, RICHARD ALWIN
B. May 22, 1934, Grants Pass, OR
Oregon 5'9" 179 lbs.

Year	Team		Games	Pos.
1956	WAS	N	7	HB
1957			11	HB
1958			12	HB
1959			12	HB
1960			12	HB
1961			14	HB
1962			14	HB
1963			14	HB
1964	NYG	N	14	HB
1965	MIN	N	4	HB

10 yrs. 114 games

Garry James
JAMES, GARRY MALCOLM
B. Sep. 4, 1963, Marrero, LA
Louisiana State 5'10" 214 lbs.

Year	Team		Games	Pos.
1986	DET	N	16	RB
1987			8	RB
1988			16	RB

3 yrs. 40 games

Jesse James
JAMES, JESSE
B. Sep. 16, 1971, Mobile, AL
Mississippi State 6'4" 318 lbs.

Year	Team		Games	Pos.
1995	STL	N	2	OT, G
1996			1	G

2 yrs. 3 games

John James
JAMES, JOHN WILBUR, JR.
B. Jan. 21, 1949, Panama City, FL
Florida 6'3" 199 lbs.

Year	Team		Games	Pos.
1972	ATL	N	14	P
1973			14	P
1974			14	P
1975			14	P
1976			14	P
1977			14	P
1978			16	P
1979			16	P
1980			16	P
1981			16	P
1982	DET	N	2	P
1982	HOU	N	5	P
1983			16	P
1984			16	P

13 yrs. 187 games

June James
JAMES, JUNE, IV
B. Dec. 2, 1962, Jennings, LA
Texas 6'1" 218 lbs.

Year	Team		Games	Pos.
1985	DET	N	16	LB
1987	IND	N	11	LB

2 yrs. 27 games

Lionel James
JAMES, LIONEL (The Little Train)
B. May 25, 1962, Albany, GA
Auburn 5'6" 171 lbs.

Year	Team		Games	Pos.
1984	SD	N	16	RB
1985			16	RB
1986			7	RB
1987			12	RB, WR
1988			16	WR, RB

5 yrs. 67 games

Lynn James
JAMES, LYNN
B. Jan. 25, 1965, Navasota, TX
Arizona State 6'0" 191 lbs.

Year	Team		Games	Pos.
1990	CIN	N	11	WR
1991			11	WR
1991	CLE		10	WR

2 yrs. 31 games

Nate James
JAMES, NATHANIEL
B. Feb. 20, 1944, Bartow, FL
Florida A&M 6'1" 195 lbs.

Year	Team		Games	Pos.
1968	CLE	N	12	DB

Phillip James
JAMES, PHILLIP
B. Dec. 3, 1964
Southern University 6'2" 265 lbs.

Year	Team		Games	Pos.
1987	NO	N	3	C

Robert James
JAMES, ROBERT DEMATRICE
B. Jul. 7, 1947, Murfreesboro, TN
Fisk 6'1" 182 lbs.

Year	Team		Games	Pos.
1969	BUF	A	13	CB
1970	BUF	N	14	CB
1971			14	CB
1972			14	CB
1973			13	CB
1974			14	CB

6 yrs. 82 games

Roland James
JAMES, ROLAND ORLANDO
B. Feb. 18, 1958, Xenia, OH
Tennessee 6'2" 190 lbs.

Year	Team		Games	Pos.
1980	NE	N	16	CB
1981			16	CB, S
1982			7	CB, S
1983			16	S
1984			15	S
1985			16	S
1986			15	S
1987			9	S
1988			15	S
1989			14	S
1990			6	S

11 yrs. 145 games

Ron James
JAMES, RON (Po)
B. Mar. 19, 1949, New Brighton, PA
New Mexico State 6'1" 202 lbs.

Year	Team		Games	Pos.
1972	PHI	N	14	RB
1973			10	RB
1974			11	RB
1975			14	RB

4 yrs. 49 games

Year	Team	Games	Pos.

Ted James
JAMES, THEODORE LAWRENCE
B. Aug. 8, 1906, Wymore, NE
Nebraska 6'2" 190 lbs.

Year	Team		Games	Pos.
1929	**FRA**	**N**	10	G, C

Tommy James
JAMES, THOMAS L., JR. (Red)
B. Sep. 16, 1923, Canton, OH
Ohio State 5'10" 184 lbs.

Year	Team		Games	Pos.
1948	**CLE**	**AA**	14	HB, DB
1949			12	HB, DB
1950	**CLE**	**N**	12	HB, DB
1951			12	HB, DB
1952			12	HB, DB
1953			12	HB, DB
1954			12	HB, DB
1955			8	HB, DB
1956	**BAL**	**N**	2	HB, DB
9 yrs.	96 games			

Tory James
JAMES, TORY
B. May 18, 1973, New Orleans, LA
Louisiana State 6'1" 188 lbs.

Year	Team		Games	Pos.
1996	**DEN**	**N**	16	CB

Larry Jameson
JAMESON, GEORGE LARRY
B. Feb. 1, 1953, Washington, DC
Indiana 6'7" 270 lbs.

Year	Team		Games	Pos.
1976	**TB**	**N**	1	DT

Bob Jamieson
JAMIESON, ROBERT J.
B. Feb. 3, 1902
D. Jun., 1982, Palmerton, PA
Franklin & Marshall 6'0" 195 lbs.

Year	Team		Games	Pos.
1924	**FRA**	**N**	3	C

Dick Jamieson
JAMIESON, RICHARD
B. Nov. 13, 1937, Streator, IL
Bradley 6'1" 191 lbs.

Year	Team		Games	Pos.
1960	**NY**	**A**		QB
1961			3	QB
2 yrs.	3 games			

Al Jamison
JAMISON, ALFRED G.
Colgate 6'5" 245 lbs.

Year	Team		Games	Pos.
1960	**HOU**	**A**		OT
1961			14	OT
1962			14	OT
3 yrs.	28 games			

George Jamison
JAMISON, GEORGE R.
B. Sep. 30, 1962, Bridgeton, NJ
Cincinnati 6'1" 226 lbs.

Year	Team		Games	Pos.
1987	**DET**	**N**	12	LB
1988			16	LB
1989			11	LB
1990			14	LB
1991			16	LB
1992			16	LB
1993			16	LB
1994	**KC**	**N**	13	LB
1995			14	LB
1996			5	LB
10 yrs.	133 games			

John Janata
JANATA, JOHN MICHAEL
B. Apr. 10, 1961, Chicago, IL
Illinois 6'7" 255 lbs.

Year	Team		Games	Pos.
1983	**CHI**	**N**	15	OT

Bobby Jancik
JANCIK, ROBERT LEE, JR.
B. Feb. 9, 1940, Houston, TX
Lamar 5'11" 178 lbs.

Year	Team		Games	Pos.
1962	**HOU**	**A**	14	DB
1963			14	DB
1964			14	DB
1965			14	DB
1966			14	DB
1967			12	DB
6 yrs.	82 games			

Clarence Janecek
JANECEK, CLARENCE ROBERT
B. Apr. 1, 1911, Chicago, IL
D. Jan. 16, 1990
Purdue 6'0" 200 lbs.

Year	Team		Games	Pos.
1933	**PIT**	**N**	11	G

Charlie Janerette
JANERETTE, CHARLES F., JR.
B. Dec. 1, 1938, Philadelphia, PA
Deceased
Penn State 6'3" 253 lbs.

Year	Team		Games	Pos.
1960	**LA**	**N**	12	G
1961	**NYG**	**N**	14	OT
1962			12	DT
1963	**NY**	**A**	14	DT
1964	**DEN**	**A**	14	DT
1965			14	DT
6 yrs.	80 games			

Ernie Janet
JANET, ERNIE J.
B. Jul. 22, 1949, Renton, WV
Washington 6'4" 253 lbs.

Year	Team		Games	Pos.
1972	**CHI**	**N**	3	G
1973			12	G
1974			14	G
1975	**GB**	**N**	1	G
1975	**PHI**	**N**	1	G
4 yrs.	31 games			

Len Janiak
JANIAK, LEONARD
B. Oct. 29, 1915, Cleveland, OH
D. May, 1980, Cleveland, OH
Ohio University 6'1" 203 lbs.

Year	Team		Games	Pos.
1939	**BKN**	**N**	10	HB, FB
1940	**CLE**	**N**	11	FB
1941			10	FB
1942			10	FB
4 yrs.	41 games			

Tommy Janik
JANIK, THOMAS ALVIN
B. Sep. 6, 1940, Poth, TX
Texas A&M/Texas A&I-Kingsville 6'3" 198 lbs.

Year	Team		Games	Pos.
1963	**DEN**	**A**	14	DB
1964			9	DB, P
1965	**BUF**	**A**	10	DB
1966			14	DB
1967			14	DB
1968			11	DB
1969	**BOS**	**A**	14	S, P
1970	**BOS**	**N**	14	S, P
1971	**NE**	**N**	14	P, S
9 yrs.	114 games			

Keever Jankovich
JANKOVICH, KEEVER
B. Jan. 6, 1928, Wilmington, NC
D. Feb., 1979
Pacific 6'0" 215 lbs.

Year	Team		Games	Pos.
1952	**DAL**	**N**	11	LB
1953	**CHIC**	**N**	2	DE
2 yrs.	13 games			

Bruce Jankowski
JANKOWSKI, BRUCE D.
B. Aug. 12, 1949, Paterson, NJ
Ohio State 5'11" 185 lbs.

Year	Team		Games	Pos.
1971	**KC**	**N**	5	WR
1972			4	WR
2 yrs.	9 games			

Ed Jankowski
JANKOWSKI, EDWARD
B. Jun. 23, 1913, Milwaukee, WI
Deceased
Wisconsin 5'9" 201 lbs.

Year	Team		Games	Pos.
1937	**GB**	**N**	11	FB
1938			11	FB
1939			10	FB
1940			7	FB
1941			11	FB
5 yrs.	50 games			

Vic Janowicz
JANOWICZ, VICTOR FELIX (Crash)
B. Feb. 26, 1930, Elyria, OH
D. Feb. 27, 1996, Columbus, OH
Ohio State 5'9" 187 lbs.

Year	Team		Games	Pos.
1954	**WAS**	**N**	10	HB
1955			12	HB
2 yrs.	22 games			

Val Jansante
JANSANTE, VALERIO R.
B. Sep. 27, 1920, La Belle, PA
Duquesne/Villanova 6'1" 190 lbs.

Year	Team		Games	Pos.
1946	**PIT**	**N**	11	E
1947			12	E
1948			12	E
1949			12	E
1950			12	E
1951			6	E
1951	**GB**	**N**	3	E
6 yrs.	68 games			

Lou Jansing
JANSING, LOUIS
B. Sep. 17, 1890
D. Aug., 1968, Willey, IA
None

Year	Team		Games	Pos.
1922	**LOU**	**N**	3	FB, HB, E

Mike January
JANUARY, MIKE
B. Jun. 30, 1964
Texas 6'1" 234 lbs.

Year	Team		Games	Pos.
1987	**CHI**	**N**	3	LB

Paul Jappe
JAPPE, PAUL E.
B. Jan. 16, 1898
D. Apr. 1, 1989, Daytona Beach, FL
Syracuse 6'1" 195 lbs.

Year	Team		Games	Pos.
1925	**NYG**	**N**	11	E
1926	**BKN**	**N**	11	T, E
1927	**NYG**	**N**	13	E, G
1928			11	G, E, T
4 yrs.	46 games			

Jon Jaqua
JAQUA, JON
B. Sep. 10, 1948, Eugene, OR
Lewis & Clark 6'0" 190 lbs.

Year	Team		Games	Pos.
1970	**WAS**	**N**	14	CB
1971			14	S
1972			8	S
3 yrs.	36 games			

Pete Jaquess
JAQUESS, LINDEL GLENN
B. Dec. 25, 1940, Earth, TX
Eastern New Mexico 6'0" 182 lbs.

Year	Team		Games	Pos.
1964	**HOU**	**A**	14	DB
1965			14	DB
1966	**MIA**	**A**	14	DB
1967			7	DB
1967	**DEN**	**A**	10	DB
1968			13	DB
1969			7	CB
1970	**DEN**	**N**	13	CB
7 yrs.	92 games			

Mike Jarmoluk
JARMOLUK, MICHAEL, JR.
B. Oct. 22, 1922, Philadelphia, PA
Temple 6'5" 252 lbs.

Year	Team		Games	Pos.
1946	**CHIB**	**N**	10	T
1947			12	E, T
1948	**BOS**	**N**	12	T
1949	**NYB**	**N**	2	T
1949	**PHI**	**N**	9	T
1950			12	T
1951			12	T
1952			12	T
1953			12	T
1954			12	T
1955			12	T
10 yrs.	117 games			

Ilia Jarostchuk
JAROSTCHUK, ILIA
B. Aug. 1, 1964, Utica, NY
New Hampshire 6'3" 231 lbs.

Year	Team		Games	Pos.
1987	**STL**	**N**	12	LB
1988	**MIA**	**N**	6	LB
1989	**PHX**	**N**	16	LB
1990	**NE**	**N**	12	LB
4 yrs.	46 games			

Toimi Jarvi
JARVI, TOIMI
B. Feb. 29, 1920, De Kalb, IL
D. Nov., 1977, Chicago, IL
Northern Illinois 6'0" 200 lbs.

Year	Team		Games	Pos.
1944	**PHI**	**N**	3	B
1945	**PIT**	**N**	1	HB
2 yrs.	4 games			

Bruce Jarvis
JARVIS, J. BRUCE
B. Nov. 3, 1948, Seattle, WA
Washington 6'7" 248 lbs.

Year	Team		Games	Pos.
1971	**BUF**	**N**	14	C
1972			1	C
1973			8	C
1974			1	C
4 yrs.	24 games			

Curt Jarvis
JARVIS, CURTIS, JR.
B. Jan. 28, 1965, Birmingham, AL
Alabama 6'2" 266 lbs.

Year	Team		Games	Pos.
1987	**TB**	**N**	2	DL
1988			15	NT, DE
1989			14	NT
1990			7	NT
4 yrs.	38 games			

Ralph Jarvis
JARVIS, RALPH A.
B. Jun. 1, 1965, Philadelphia, PA
Temple 6'4" 255 lbs.

Year	Team		Games	Pos.
1990	**IND**	**N**	8	DE

Year	Team	Games	Pos.

Ray Jarvis
JARVIS, LEON RAEMINTON
B. Feb. 2, 1949, Chesapeake, VA
Norfolk State 6'1" 192 lbs.

Year	Team		Games	Pos.
1971	ATL	N	3	WR
1972			4	WR
1973	BUF	N	12	WR
1974	DET	N	13	WR
1975			14	WR
1976			14	WR
1977			14	WR
1978			2	WR
1979	NE	N	7	WR
9 yrs.	83 games			

Vince Jasper
JASPER, VINCENT
B. Nov. 30, 1964, Hawarden, IA
Iowa State 6'4" 270 lbs.

Year	Team		Games	Pos.
1987	NYJ	N	3	G

Floyd Jaszewski
JASZEWSKI, FLOYD ROMAN
B. 1927, Minneapolis, MN
Minnesota 6'4" 230 lbs.

Year	Team		Games	Pos.
1950	DET	N	12	T
1951			12	T
2 yrs.	24 games			

Dick Jauron
JAURON, RICHARD MANUEL
B. Oct. 7, 1950, Swampscott, MA
Yale 6'0" 189 lbs.

Year	Team		Games	Pos.
1973	DET	N	14	S
1974			14	S
1975			10	S
1976			6	S
1977			14	S
1978	CIN	N	16	S
1979			16	S
1980			10	S
8 yrs.	100 games			

Heinie Jawish
JAWISH, SHAUKEY HENRY (Hy)
B. Jan. 4, 1900
D. Jan., 1976, Asia
George Washington/Georgetown (DC)
5'8" 210 lbs.

Year	Team		Games	Pos.
1926	POT	N	8	T, G

Matt Jaworski
JAWORSKI, MATTHEW JOSEPH
B. Oct. 23, 1967, Blasdell, NY
Colgate 6'1" 226 lbs.

Year	Team		Games	Pos.
1991	IND	N	8	LB

Ron Jaworski
JAWORSKI, RONALD VINCENT
(The Polish Rifle, Jaws)
B. Mar. 23, 1951, Lackawanna, NY
Youngstown State 6'2" 198 lbs.

Year	Team		Games	Pos.
1974	LA	N	5	QB
1975			14	QB
1976			5	QB
1977	PHI	N	14	QB
1978			16	QB
1979			16	QB
1980			16	QB
1981			16	QB
1982			9	QB
1983			16	QB
1984			13	QB
1985			16	QB
1986			10	QB
1988	MIA	N	16	QB
1989	KC	N	6	QB
15 yrs.	188 games			

Garth Jax
JAX, JAMES GARTH
B. Sep. 16, 1963, Houston, TX
Florida State 6'2" 225 lbs.

Year	Team		Games	Pos.
1986	DAL	N	16	LB
1987			3	LB
1988			16	LB
1989	PHX	N	16	LB
1990			16	LB
1991			12	LB
1992			16	LB
1993			16	LB
1994	ARI	N	16	LB
1995			16	LB
10 yrs.	143 games			

Craig Jay
JAY, CRAIG
B. Feb. 5, 1963
Mount Senario 6'4" 257 lbs.

Year	Team		Games	Pos.
1987	GB	N	3	TE

Dave Jaynes
JAYNES, DAVID
B. Dec. 12, 1952, Kansas City, KS
Kansas 6'2" 210 lbs.

Year	Team		Games	Pos.
1974	KC	N	1	QB

Garland Jean Batiste
JEAN BATISTE, GARLAND
B. Apr. 2, 1965
Louisiana State 6'0" 208 lbs.

Year	Team		Games	Pos.
1987	NO	N	3	RB

Ralph Jecha
JECHA, RALPH LEROY
B. Dec. 1, 1931, Summit, IL
Northwestern 6'2" 235 lbs.

Year	Team		Games	Pos.
1955	CHIB	N	12	G
1956	PIT	N	7	G
2 yrs.	19 games			

Jim Jeffcoat
JEFFCOAT, JAMES WILSON, JR.
B. Apr. 1, 1961, Long Branch, NJ
Arizona State 6'5" 260 lbs.

Year	Team		Games	Pos.
1983	DAL	N	16	DE
1984			16	DE
1985			16	DE
1986			16	DE
1987			12	DE
1988			16	DE
1989			16	DE
1990			16	DE
1991			16	DE
1992			16	DE
1993			16	DE
1994			16	DE
1995	BUF	N	16	DE, NT
1996			16	DT
14 yrs.	220 games			

Ed Jeffers
JEFFERS, W. EDWARD
B. 1923
Oklahoma State 6'3" 215 lbs.

Year	Team		Games	Pos.
1947	BKN	AA	14	G

Patrick Jeffers
JEFFERS, PATRICK CHRISTOPHER
B. Feb. 2, 1973, Fort Campbell, KY
Virginia 6'3" 217 lbs.

Year	Team		Games	Pos.
1996	DEN	N	4	WR

Ben Jefferson
JEFFERSON, BEN
B. Jan. 15, 1966, New Rochelle, NY
Maryland 6'9" 330 lbs.

Year	Team		Games	Pos.
1990	CLE	N	4	OT

Billy Jefferson
JEFFERSON, WILLIAM C.
B. May 17, 1918, Pheba, MS
D. Mar., 1974
Mississippi State 6'2" 208 lbs.

Year	Team		Games	Pos.
1941	DET	N	11	HB
1942	PHI	N	3	B
1942	BKN	N	3	B
2 yrs.	17 games			

Charles Jefferson
JEFFERSON, CHARLES RAY
B. May 5, 1957, New Orleans, LA
McNeese State 6'0" 178 lbs.

Year	Team		Games	Pos.
1979	HOU	N	5	CB

Greg Jefferson
JEFFERSON, GREG
B. Aug. 31, 1971, Orlando, FL
Central Florida 6'3" 257 lbs.

Year	Team		Games	Pos.
1995	PHI	N	3	DE
1996			11	DE
2 yrs.	14 games			

James Jefferson
JEFFERSON, JAMES ANDREW, III
B. Nov. 18, 1963, Portsmouth, VA
Texas A&I-Kingsville 6'1" 199 lbs.

Year	Team		Games	Pos.
1989	SEA	N	16	CB
1990			15	CB
1991			16	CB
1992			1	CB
1993			10	CB
5 yrs.	58 games			

John Jefferson
JEFFERSON, JOHN LARRY (J.J.)
B. Feb. 3, 1956, Dallas, TX
Arizona State 6'1" 200 lbs.

Year	Team		Games	Pos.
1978	SD	N	14	WR
1979			15	WR
1980			16	WR
1981	GB	N	13	WR
1982			8	WR
1983			16	WR
1984			13	WR
1985	CLE	N	7	WR
8 yrs.	102 games			

Kevin Jefferson
JEFFERSON, KEVIN
B. Jan. 14, 1974, Greensburg, PA
Lehigh 6'2" 232 lbs.

Year	Team		Games	Pos.
1994	CIN	N	6	LB
1995			16	LB
2 yrs.	22 games			

Norm Jefferson
JEFFERSON, NORMAN, JR.
B. Aug. 7, 1964, Marrero, LA
Louisiana State 5'10" 183 lbs.

Year	Team		Games	Pos.
1987	GB	N	12	DB
1988			2	CB, S
2 yrs.	14 games			

Roy Jefferson
JEFFERSON, ROY LEE
B. Nov. 9, 1943, Texarkana, TX
Utah 6'2" 194 lbs.

Year	Team		Games	Pos.
1965	PIT	N	10	HB, OE
1966			14	OE

Roy Jefferson continued

Year	Team		Games	Pos.
1967			13	FL
1968			14	FL
1969			14	WR
1970	BAL	N	14	WR
1971	WAS	N	14	WR
1972			14	WR
1973			14	WR
1974			14	WR
1975			13	WR
1976			14	WR
12 yrs.	162 games			

Shawn Jefferson
JEFFERSON, VANCHI LASHAWN
B. Feb. 22, 1969, Jacksonville, FL
Central Florida 5'11" 172 lbs.

Year	Team		Games	Pos.
1991	SD	N	16	WR
1992			16	WR
1993			16	WR
1994			16	WR
1995			16	WR
1996	NE	N	15	WR
6 yrs.	95 games			

Thad Jefferson
JEFFERSON, THADIUS
B. Mar. 11, 1964
Hawaii 5'11" 225 lbs.

Year	Team		Games	Pos.
1987	HOU	N	3	LB

Tony Jeffery
JEFFERY, TONY LORENZO
B. Jul. 8, 1964, Gladewater, TX
Texas Christian 5'11" 208 lbs.

Year	Team		Games	Pos.
1988	PHX	N	3	RB

Haywood Jeffires
JEFFIRES, HAYWOOD FRANKLIN
B. Dec. 12, 1964, Greensboro, NC
North Carolina State 6'2" 198 lbs.

Year	Team		Games	Pos.
1987	HOU	N	9	WR
1988			2	WR
1989			16	WR
1990			16	WR
1991			16	WR
1992			16	WR
1993			16	WR
1994			16	WR
1995			16	WR
1996	NO	N	9	WR
10 yrs.	132 games			

Neal Jeffrey
JEFFREY, JAMES NEAL, JR.
B. Jul. 23, 1953, Fort Worth, TX
Baylor 6'1" 180 lbs.

Year	Team		Games	Pos.
1976	SD	N	5	QB

Bob Jeffries
JEFFRIES, ROBERT J.
B. Aug. 19, 1919, Kansas City, MO
Missouri 6'2" 206 lbs.

Year	Team		Games	Pos.
1942	BKN	N	5	G

Curtis Jeffries
JEFFRIES, CURTIS
B. Oct. 26, 1964
Louisville 6'4" 236 lbs.

Year	Team		Games	Pos.
1987	CIN	N	3	TE

Dameian Jeffries
JEFFRIES, DAMEIAN
B. May 7, 1973, Sylacauga, AL
Alabama 6'4" 277 lbs.

Year	Team		Games	Pos.
1995	NO	N	3	DE

Year	Team	Games	Pos.

Eric Jeffries
JEFFRIES, ERIC
B. Jul. 25, 1964, Springfield, MO
Texas 5'10" 161 lbs.

Year	Team	Games	Pos.
1987	CHI N	3	DB

Greg Jeffries
JEFFRIES, GREG LEMONT
B. Oct. 16, 1971, High Point, NC
Virginia 5'9" 184 lbs.

Year	Team	Games	Pos.
1993	DET N	7	CB
1994		16	CB
1995		14	CB
1996		16	CB
4 yrs.	53 games		

Jon Jelacic
JELACIC, JON F.
B. Dec. 19, 1936, Brainerd, MN
D. Sep. 17, 1993, St. Paul, MN
Minnesota 6'3" 250 lbs.

Year	Team	Games	Pos.
1958	NYG N	9	G
1961	OAK A	4	DE
1962		14	DE
1963		14	DE
1964		3	DE
5 yrs.	44 games		

Tom Jelesky
JELESKY, THOMAS JOHN
B. Oct. 4, 1960, Merrillville, IN
Purdue 6'6" 275 lbs.

Year	Team	Games	Pos.
1985	PHI N	16	OT
1986		9	OT
2 yrs.	25 games		

Tom Jelley
JELLEY, THOMAS J.
B. Nov. 20, 1926
Miami (Florida) 6'5" 225 lbs.

Year	Team	Games	Pos.
1951	PIT N	5	E

Dietrich Jells
JELLS, DIETRICH
B. Apr. 11, 1972, Erie, PA
Pittsburgh 5'10" 186 lbs.

Year	Team	Games	Pos.
1996	NE N	7	WR

Jimmy Jemail
JEMAIL, MANUEL JAMES
B. Sep. 12, 1893
D. Jul., 1978, New York, NY
Brown 5'6" 165 lbs.

Year	Team	Games	Pos.
1921	NY A	1	QB

Bob Jencks
JENCKS, ROBERT
B. Jul. 15, 1941, Columbus, OH
Miami (Ohio) 6'5" 227 lbs.

Year	Team	Games	Pos.
1963	CHI N	14	OE
1964		14	OE, K
1965	WAS N	14	OE, K
3 yrs.	42 games		

Ray Jenison
JENISON, RAYMOND
B. Jan. 3, 1910
South Dakota State 6'3" 198 lbs.

Year	Team	Games	Pos.
1931	GB N	2	T

Noel Jenke
JENKE, NOEL CHARLES
B. Dec. 17, 1946, Owatonna, MN
Minnesota 6'2" 221 lbs.

Year	Team	Games	Pos.
1971	MIN N	4	LB
1972	ATL N	1	LB

Noel Jenke continued

Year	Team	Games	Pos.
1973	GB N	2	LB
1974		8	LB
4 yrs.	25 games		

A.J. Jenkins
JENKINS, A.J.
B. Apr. 12, 1966, Havelock, NC
Fullerton State 6'2" 237 lbs.

Year	Team	Games	Pos.
1989	PIT N	16	DE
1990		5	LB, DE
2 yrs.	21 games		

Al Jenkins
JENKINS, ALFRED JOSEPH
B. Jul. 15, 1946, New Orleans, LA
Southern Illinois/Tulsa 6'2" 250 lbs.

Year	Team	Games	Pos.
1969	CLE N	8	G
1970		5	OT
1972	MIA N	14	OT
1973	HOU N	13	G
4 yrs.	40 games		

Alfred Jenkins
JENKINS, ALFRED DONELL
B. Jan. 25, 1952, Hogansville, GA
Morris Brown 5'10" 170 lbs.

Year	Team	Games	Pos.
1975	ATL N	14	WR
1976		14	WR
1977		14	WR
1978		1	WR
1979		16	WR
1980		16	WR
1981		16	WR
1982		9	WR
1983		11	WR
9 yrs.	111 games		

Carlos Jenkins
JENKINS, CARLOS EDWARD
B. Jul. 12, 1968, Palm Beach, FL
Michigan State 6'3" 222 lbs.

Year	Team	Games	Pos.
1991	MIN N	3	LB
1992		16	LB
1993		16	LB
1994		16	LB
1995	STL N	16	LB
1996		13	LB
6 yrs.	80 games		

Deron Jenkins
JENKINS, DERON CHARLES
B. Nov. 14, 1973, St. Louis, MO
Tennessee 5'11" 177 lbs.

Year	Team	Games	Pos.
1996	BAL N	15	CB

Eddie Jenkins
JENKINS, EDDIE JAY
B. Aug. 31, 1950, Jacksonville, FL
Holy Cross 6'2" 210 lbs.

Year	Team	Games	Pos.
1972	MIA N	3	RB
1974	NYG N	4	RB
1974	BUF N	5	RB
1974	NE N	3	RB
2 yrs.	15 games		

Fletcher Jenkins
JENKINS, FLETCHER
B. Nov. 4, 1959, Tacoma, WA
Washington 6'2" 258 lbs.

Year	Team	Games	Pos.
1982	BAL N	9	DT

Izel Jenkins
JENKINS, IZEL, JR.
B. May 27, 1964, Wilson, NC
North Carolina State 5'10" 191 lbs.

Year	Team	Games	Pos.
1988	PHI N	16	CB

Izel Jenkins continued

Year	Team	Games	Pos.
1989		16	CB
1990		15	CB
1991		14	CB
1992	MIN N	15	CB, S
1993	MIN N	4	CB
1993	NYG N	5	CB
6 yrs.	85 games		

Jack Jenkins
JENKINS, JACQUE S.
B. May 6, 1921, Texarkana, TX
Deceased
Vanderbilt 6'1" 206 lbs.

Year	Team	Games	Pos.
1943	WAS N	2	B
1946		8	FB
1947		12	FB
3 yrs.	22 games		

James Jenkins
JENKINS, JAMES
B. Aug. 17, 1967, Staten Island, NY
Rutgers 6'2" 238 lbs.

Year	Team	Games	Pos.
1991	WAS N	4	TE
1992		5	TE
1993		15	TE
1994		16	TE
1995		16	TE
1996		16	TE
6 yrs.	72 games		

Jon Jenkins
JENKINS, JONATHAN R.
B. Jun. 17, 1926, Frostburg, MO
Dartmouth 6'2" 225 lbs.

Year	Team	Games	Pos.
1949	BAL AA	11	T
1950	BAL N	3	T
1950	NYY N	1	T
2 yrs.	15 games		

Ken Jenkins
JENKINS, KENNETH WALTON
B. May 8, 1959, Washington, DC
Bucknell 5'8" 184 lbs.

Year	Team	Games	Pos.
1983	DET N	12	RB
1984		14	RB
1985	WAS N	13	RB
1986		12	RB
4 yrs.	51 games		

Keyvan Jenkins
JENKINS, KEYVAN
B. Jan. 6, 1961, Stockton, CA
Nevada-Las Vegas 5'10" 190 lbs.

Year	Team	Games	Pos.
1987	SD N	3	RB
1988	KC N	2	RB
2 yrs.	5 games		

Leon Jenkins
JENKINS, LEON (Sonny)
B. Aug. 18, 1950, Columbus, OH
West Virginia 5'11" 165 lbs.

Year	Team	Games	Pos.
1972	DET N	4	DB

Melvin Jenkins
JENKINS, MELVIN
B. Mar. 16, 1962, Jackson, MS
Cincinnati 5'10" 170 lbs.

Year	Team	Games	Pos.
1987	SEA N	12	DB
1988		16	CB
1989		16	CB
1990		16	CB
1991	DET N	16	CB
1992		16	CB
1993	ATL N	14	CB
1993	DET N	1	CB
7 yrs.	107 games		

Robert Jenkins
BORN ROBERT LLOYD COX
PLAYED AS ROBERT COX
1987–1990
B. Dec. 30, 1963, San Francisco, CA
UCLA 6'5" 258 lbs.

Year	Team	Games	Pos.
1987	LARM N	10	OT
1988		16	OT
1989		16	OT
1990		11	OT
1991		12	OT
1992		9	OT
1993		8	OT
1994	LARI N	10	OT
1995	OAK N	15	OT
1996		10	OT
10 yrs.	117 games		

Trezelle Jenkins
JENKINS, TREZELLE
B. Mar. 13, 1973, Chicago, IL
Michigan 6'7" 323 lbs.

Year	Team	Games	Pos.
1995	KC N	1	OT
1996		6	OT
2 yrs.	7 games		

Walt Jenkins
JENKINS, WALTER B.
B. 1931
Wayne State 6'1" 223 lbs.

Year	Team	Games	Pos.
1955	DET N	2	E, T

Dave Jennings
JENNINGS, DAVID TUTHILL
B. Jun. 8, 1952, New York, NY
St. Lawrence 6'4" 200 lbs.

Year	Team	Games	Pos.
1974	NYG N	14	P
1975		14	P
1976		14	P
1977		14	P
1978		16	P
1979		16	P
1980		16	P
1981		16	P
1982		9	P
1983		16	P
1984		16	P
1985	NYJ N	16	P
1986		16	P
1987		12	P
14 yrs.	205 games		

Jack Jennings
JENNINGS, JOHN WELDON
B. Feb. 23, 1926, Columbus, OH
D. Jun. 11, 1993, Rocky River, OH
Ohio State 6'4" 245 lbs.

Year	Team	Games	Pos.
1950	CHIC N	11	T
1951		11	T
1952		7	T
1953		12	T
1954		12	T
1955		12	T
1956		12	T
1957		12	T
8 yrs.	89 games		

Jim Jennings
JENNINGS, JAMES BENTON
B. Nov. 14, 1933, Crystal Springs, MO
Missouri 6'3" 195 lbs.

Year	Team	Games	Pos.
1955	GB N	6	E

Keith Jennings
JENNINGS, KEITH O'NEAL
B. May 19, 1966, Summerville, SC
Clemson 6'4" 251 lbs.

Year	Team	Games	Pos.
1989	DAL N	10	TE

Year	Team		Games	Pos.

Keith Jennings continued

1991	CHI	N	10	TE
1992			16	TE
1993			13	TE
1994			9	TE
1995			16	TE
1996			6	TE
7 yrs.	80 games			

Lou Jennings
JENNINGS, LEWIS BLUE SUN
B. Mar. 5, 1904
D. Nov., 1983, Dripping Springs, TX
Haskell/Centenary 6'3" 230 lbs.

1929	PRO	N	2	C
1930	POR	N	9	E
2 yrs.	11 games			

Ricky Jennings
JENNINGS, RICHARD
B. Apr. 17, 1953, Houston, TX
Maryland 5'9" 180 lbs.

1976	OAK	N	11	RB
1977	SF	N	3	WR
1977	OAK	N	2	WR
2 yrs.	16 games			

Stanford Jennings
JENNINGS, STANFORD JAMISON
B. Mar. 12, 1962, Summerville, SC
Furman 6'1" 205 lbs.

1984	CIN	N	15	RB
1985			16	RB
1986			16	RB
1987			12	RB
1988			16	RB
1989			16	RB
1990			16	RB
1991	NO	N	5	RB
1992	TB	N	11	RB
9 yrs.	123 games			

Bob Jensen
JENSEN, ROBERT P.
B. Dec. 29, 1925, Chicago, IL
D. Dec., 1984, Sioux Falls, SD
Iowa State 6'2" 218 lbs.

1948	CHI	AA	14	E
1949			11	E
1950	BAL		9	E
3 yrs.	34 games			

Derrick Jensen
JENSEN, DERRICK
B. Apr. 27, 1956, Waukegan, IL
Texas-Arlington 6'1" 220 lbs.

1979	OAK	N	16	RB
1980			16	RB
1981			16	RB
1982	LARI	N	9	RB
1983			16	RB
1984			16	TE, RB
1985			16	TE, RB
1986			1	RB
8 yrs.	106 games			

Greg Jensen
JENSEN, GREG
None

| 1987 | GB | N | 1 | G |

Jim Jensen
JENSEN, JAMES CHRISTOPHER
B. Nov. 14, 1958, Abington, PA
Boston University 6'4" 215 lbs.

| 1981 | MIA | N | 16 | QB |

Jim Jensen continued

1982			6	QB
1983			16	QB
1984			16	WR
1985			16	WR
1986			16	WR
1987			12	WR, QB
1988			16	WR, RB
1989			16	WR, RB
1990			15	WR, RB
1991			16	WR
1992			3	WR
12 yrs.	164 games			

Jim Jensen
JENSEN, JAMES DOUGLAS
B. Nov. 28, 1953, Waterloo, IA
Iowa 6'3" 232 lbs.

1976	DAL	N	14	RB
1977	DEN	N	11	RB
1979			16	RB
1980			14	RB
1981	GB	N	15	RB
1982			8	RB
6 yrs.	78 games			

Leo Jensvold
JENSVOLD, LEO
B. Mar. 29, 1908
D. May, 1966
Iowa 5'8" 173 lbs.

1931	CHIB	N	1	HB
1931	CLE	N	7	HB
1 yr.	8 games			

Luther Jeralds
JERALDS, LUTHER
B. 1938
North Carolina Central 6'3" 235 lbs.

| 1961 | DAL | A | 9 | DE |

Jim Jerome
JEROME, JAMES L.
B. Feb. 8, 1954, Watertown, NY
Syracuse 6'4" 225 lbs.

| 1977 | NYJ | N | | LB |

Mark Jerue
JERUE, MARK DARRELL
B. Jan. 15, 1960, Seattle, WA
Washington 6'3" 229 lbs.

1983	LARM	N	16	LB
1984			16	LB
1985			16	LB
1986			16	LB
1987			4	LB
1988			12	LB
1989			6	LB
7 yrs.	86 games			

Travis Jervey
JERVEY, TRAVIS RICHARD
B. May 5, 1972, Columbia, SC
The Citadel 5'11" 225 lbs.

1995	GB	N	16	RB
1996			16	RB
2 yrs.	32 games			

Ernie Jessen
JESSEN, ERNEST R.
B. May 1, 1905
D. Sep., 1987, Cedar Rapids, IA
Iowa 6'1" 250 lbs.

| 1931 | CLE | N | 8 | T |

Ron Jessie
JESSIE, RON RAY
B. Feb. 4, 1948, Yuma, AZ
Kansas 6'0" 183 lbs.

1971	DET	N	14	WR
1972			14	WR
1973			14	WR
1974			12	WR
1975	LA	N	14	WR
1976			14	WR
1977			3	WR
1978			16	WR
1979			6	WR
1980	BUF	N	16	WR
1981			15	WR
11 yrs.	138 games			

Tim Jessie
JESSIE, TIMOTHY LAWAYNE
B. Mar. 1, 1963, Opp, AL
Auburn 5'11" 190 lbs.

| 1987 | WAS | N | 3 | RB |

Billy Jessup
JESSUP, BILL
B. Mar. 17, 1929, Wray, CO
Southern California 6'1" 195 lbs.

1951	SF	N	10	E
1952			4	E
1954			12	E, HB
1956			3	E, HB
1957			12	E, HB
1958			12	E, HB
1960	DEN	A		OE
7 yrs.	53 games			

Bob Jeter
JETER, ROBERT DELAFAYETTE, JR.
B. May 9, 1937, Union, SC
Iowa 6'1" 203 lbs.

1963	GB	N	13	HB
1964			13	FL
1965			13	OE, FL
1966			14	DB
1967			14	DB
1968			12	DB
1969			14	CB
1970			14	CB
1971	CHI	N	9	CB
1972			10	CB
1973			13	CB
11 yrs.	139 games			

Gary Jeter
JETER, GARY MICHAEL
B. Jan. 24, 1955, Weirton, WV
Southern California 6'4" 258 lbs.

1977	NYG	N	14	DT
1978			13	DT
1979			16	DT
1980			16	DE
1981			12	DE
1982			4	DE
1983	LARM	N	16	DE
1984			5	DE
1985			16	DE
1986			15	DE
1987			12	DE
1988			15	DE
1989	NE	N	14	DE
13 yrs.	168 games			

Gene Jeter
JETER, EUGENE
B. Feb. 9, 1942, Montgomery, AL
Arkansas-Pine Bluff 6'3" 230 lbs.

| 1965 | DEN | A | 14 | LB |
| 1966 | | | 14 | LB |

Gene Jeter continued

| 1967 | | | 2 | LB |
| 3 yrs. | 30 games | | | |

Perry Jeter
JETER, PERRY
B. May 17, 1931, Brevard, NC
California Poly (Pomona) 5'7" 178 lbs.

1956	CHIB	N	7	HB
1957			9	HB
2 yrs.	16 games			

Tommy Jeter
JETER, TOMMY
B. Sep. 20, 1969, Nacogdoches, TX
Texas 6'5" 282 lbs.

1992	PHI	N	15	DT
1993			7	DT
1994			14	DT
1996	CAR	N	1	DT
4 yrs.	37 games			

Tony Jeter
JETER, ANTHONY
B. Sep. 8, 1944, Steubenville, OH
Nebraska 6'3" 222 lbs.

1966	PIT	N	9	TE
1968			2	TE
2 yrs.	11 games			

Cliff Jetmore
JETMORE, CLIFFORD
B. May 14, 1895, Indiana
None

| 1923 | TOL | N | 1 | HB |

James Jett
JETT, JAMES
B. Dec. 28, 1970, Charlestown, WV
West Virginia 5'10" 165 lbs.

1993	LARI	N	16	WR
1994			16	WR
1995	OAK	N	16	WR
1996			16	WR
4 yrs.	64 games			

John Jett
JETT, JOHN
B. Jan. 15, 1917, Kane, PA
D. Aug. 3, 1975
Wake Forest 6'7" 225 lbs.

| 1941 | DET | N | 5 | E |

John Jett
JETT, JOHN
B. Nov. 11, 1968, Richmond, VA
East Carolina 6'0" 184 lbs.

1993	DAL	N	16	P
1994			16	P
1995			16	P
1996			16	P
4 yrs.	64 games			

Paul Jetton
JETTON, PAUL RAY
B. Oct. 6, 1964, Houston, TX
Texas 6'4" 292 lbs.

1989	CIN	N	5	G
1990			15	G
1991			8	C
1992	NO	N	2	C, G
4 yrs.	30 games			

Bob Jewett
JEWETT, ROBERT G.

Year	Team	Games	Pos.

Bob Jewett continued
B. Nov. 14, 1934, Mason, MI
Michigan State 6'2" 198 lbs.

Year	Team		Games	Pos.
1958	CHIB	N	12	E

Dan Jiggetts
JIGGETTS, DANIEL MARCELLUS
B. Mar. 10, 1954, Brooklyn, NY
Harvard 6'5" 270 lbs.

1976	CHI	N	14	OT
1977			12	OT
1978			16	OT
1979			16	OT
1980			15	OT
1981			16	OT
1982			9	OT

7 yrs.   98 games

Dan Jilek
JILEK, DAN
B. Dec. 3, 1953, Cedar Rapids, IA
Michigan 6'2" 220 lbs.

1976	BUF	N	14	LB
1977			14	LB
1978			15	LB
1979			15	LB

4 yrs.   58 games

Dwayne Jiles
JILES, DWAYNE
B. Nov. 23, 1961, Linden, TX
Texas Tech 6'4" 242 lbs.

1985	PHI	N	10	LB
1986			16	LB
1987			9	LB
1988			16	LB
1989			1	LB
1989	NYG	N	9	LB

5 yrs.   61 games

A.J. Jimerson
JIMERSON, A.J.
B. May 12, 1968, Erie, PA
Norfolk State 6'3" 233 lbs.

| 1990 | LARI | N | 4 | LB |
| 1991 | | | 13 | LB |

2 yrs.   17 games

Steve Joachim
JOACHIM, STEVEN
B. Mar. 27, 1952, Newtown Square, PA
Penn State/Temple 6'3" 215 lbs.

| 1976 | NYJ | N | 1 | QB |

Bill Jobko
JOBKO, WILLIAM KERMIT
B. Oct. 7, 1935, Martins Ferry, OH
Ohio State 6'2" 224 lbs.

1958	LA	N	9	LB
1959			12	LB
1960			12	LB
1961			11	LB
1962			13	LB
1963	MIN	N	9	LB
1964			14	LB
1965			14	LB
1966	ATL	N	14	LB

9 yrs.   107 games

Art Jocher
JOCHER, ARTHUR HAMBLE
B. Oct. 19, 1915, Philadelphia, PA
Manhattan 6'1" 205 lbs.

| 1940 | BKN | N | 10 | G |
| 1942 | | | 11 | G |

2 yrs.   21 games

Jim Jodat
JODAT, JAMES STEVEN
B. Mar. 3, 1954, Milwaukee, WI
Carthage 5'11" 211 lbs.

1977	LA	N	14	RB
1978			16	RB
1979			7	FB
1980	SEA	N	16	FB
1981			12	FB
1982	SD	N	7	RB
1983			15	RB

7 yrs.   87 games

Billy Joe
JOE, WILLIAM
B. Oct. 14, 1940, Aynor, SC
Villanova 6'2" 243 lbs.

1963	DEN	A	14	HB, FB
1965	BUF	A	14	FB
1966	MIA	A	14	FB
1967	NY	A	11	RB
1968			10	RB
1969			1	RB

6 yrs.   64 games

Larry Joe
JOE, LAWRENCE
B. Jul. 6, 1923, New Derry, PA
Penn State 5'9" 190 lbs.

| 1949 | BUF | AA | 1 | B |

Greg Joelson
JOELSON, GREG
B. Aug. 22, 1966, Roseburg, OR
Willamette/Arizona State 6'3" 270 lbs.

| 1991 | SF | N | 4 | DE |

Herb Joesting
JOESTING, HERBERT W. (The Owatonna Thunderbolt)
B. Apr. 17, 1905, Little Falls, MN
D. Oct. 2, 1963, Shoreview, MN
Minnesota 6'2" 194 lbs.

1929	MIN	N	10	FB, HB
1930			6	FB
1930	FRA	N	1	FB
1930	MIN	N	1	FB
1930	FRA	N	2	FB
1930	MIN	N	1	FB
1930	MIN	N	2	FB
1930	MIN	N	1	FB
1931	FRA	N	8	FB, HB
1931	CHIB	N	6	FB
1932			3	FB

4 yrs.   41 games

Ove Johansson
JOHANSSON, OVE
B. Mar. 31, 1948, Gothenburg, Sweden
Davis & Elkins/Abilene Christian 5'10" 175 lbs.

| 1977 | PHI | N | 2 | K |

Freeman Johns
JOHNS, FREEMAN, III
B. Dec. 20, 1953, Waco, TX
Southern Methodist 6'1" 175 lbs.

| 1977 | LA | N | 5 | WR |

Jim Johns
JOHNS, JAMES EDWARD
B. Feb. 22, 1900
D. Dec., 1984, Marble Cliff, OH
Michigan State/Michigan 6'0" 175 lbs.

| 1923 | CLE | N | 4 | G |
| 1924 | MIN | N | 2 | G |

2 yrs.   6 games

Paul Johns
JOHNS, PAUL V.
B. Nov. 14, 1958, Waco, TX
Tulsa 5'11" 170 lbs.

1981	SEA	N	16	WR
1982			9	WR
1983			11	WR
1984			4	WR

4 yrs.   40 games

Pete Johns
JOHNS, PETER MURRAY
B. Aug. 14, 1945, Cleveland, OH
Tulane 6'3" 189 lbs.

| 1967 | HOU | A | 13 | DB |
| 1968 | | | 13 | DB |

2 yrs.   26 games

A.J. Johnson
JOHNSON, ANTHONY SEAN
B. Jun. 22, 1967, Lompoc, CA
Southwest Texas State 5'8" 176 lbs.

1989	WAS	N	16	CB
1990			5	CB
1991			11	CB
1992			14	CB
1993			13	CB
1994			12	CB
1995	SD	N	1	CB

7 yrs.   72 games

Al Johnson
JOHNSON, ALBERT ALPHONSO, JR.
B. Jun. 17, 1950, Baltimore, MD
Cincinnati 6'0" 200 lbs.

1972	HOU	N	14	RB
1973			5	RB
1974			14	RB
1976			14	RB
1977			14	RB
1978			7	S

6 yrs.   68 games

Al Johnson
JOHNSON, ALVIN
B. Aug. 15, 1922, Munday, TX
Hardin-Simmons 6'0" 175 lbs.

| 1948 | PHI | N | 5 | QB |

Alex Johnson
JOHNSON, ALEX DEXTER
B. Aug. 18, 1968, Miami, FL
Miami (Florida) 5'9" 167 lbs.

| 1991 | HOU | N | 5 | WR |

Alonzo Johnson
JOHNSON, ALONZO
B. Apr. 4, 1963, Panama City, FL
Florida 6'3" 222 lbs.

| 1986 | PHI | N | 15 | LB |
| 1987 | | | 3 | LB |

2 yrs.   18 games

Andy Johnson
JOHNSON, ANDERSON SIDNEY
B. Oct. 18, 1952, Athens, GA
Georgia 6'0" 204 lbs.

1974	NE	N	14	RB
1975			14	RB
1976			14	RB
1978			15	RB
1979			5	RB
1980			16	RB
1981			16	RB

7 yrs.   94 games

Anthony Johnson
JOHNSON, ANTHONY SCOTT
B. Oct. 25, 1967, Indianapolis, IN
Notre Dame 6'0" 222 lbs.

1990	IND	N	16	RB
1991			9	RB
1992			15	RB
1993			13	RB
1994	NYJ	N	15	RB
1995	CHI	N	8	RB
1995	CAR	N	7	RB
1996			16	RB

7 yrs.   99 games

Art Johnson
JOHNSON, ARTHUR
B. Jan. 14, 1896
D. Apr., 1972, Duluth, MN
Fordham 5'11" 189 lbs.

1923	DUL	N	7	T
1924			6	T, G
1925			3	T
1926			11	T

4 yrs.   27 games

Barry Johnson
JOHNSON, BARRY
B. Feb. 1, 1968, Baltimore, MD
Maryland 6'2" 197 lbs.

| 1991 | DEN | N | 4 | WR |

Benny Johnson
JOHNSON, BENNY L.
B. Jun. 29, 1949, Fort Valley, GA
Johnson C. Smith 5'11" 178 lbs.

1970	HOU	N	14	CB
1971			10	CB
1972			14	CB
1973			13	CB
1976	NO	N	9	CB

5 yrs.   60 games

Bert Johnson
JOHNSON, ALBERT EDWARD
B. Feb. 18, 1912, Ashland, KY
D. Aug. 13, 1993, Lexington, KY
Kentucky 6'0" 212 lbs.

1937	BKN	N	10	HB, FB
1938	CHIB	N	9	FB
1939			1	FB
1939	CHIC	N	9	FB, HB
1940			10	QB
1941			11	QB, HB
1942	PHI	N	9	HB

6 yrs.   59 games

Bill Johnson
JOHNSON, WILLIAM
B. Jul. 9, 1944, Tuscaloosa, AL
Livingston 6'4" 208 lbs.

| 1970 | NYG | N | 11 | P |

Bill Johnson
JOHNSON, WILLIAM E.
B. Oct. 4, 1916, Larrabee, IA
Minnesota 6'1" 196 lbs.

| 1941 | GB | N | 3 | G, T, E |

Bill Johnson
JOHNSON, WILLIAM EDWARD
B. Dec. 9, 1968, Chicago, IL
Michigan State 6'4" 305 lbs.

1992	CLE	N	16	DE, DT
1993			10	DE, DT
1994			14	DT
1995	PIT	N	9	DT
1996			15	DT

5 yrs.   64 games

Year	Team		Games	Pos.

Bill Johnson
JOHNSON, WILLIAM LEVI, SR.
(Tiger)
B. Jul. 14, 1926, Tyler, TX
Texas A&M/Tyler JC 6'3" 228 lbs.

Year	Team		Games	Pos.
1948	SF	AA	5	C
1949			12	C
1950	SF	N	12	C
1951			12	C
1952			11	C
1953			12	C
1954			12	C
1955			12	C
1956			7	C

9 yrs.   95 games

Bill Johnson
JOHNSON, WILLIAM ORVILLE
(Bull)
B. Feb. 1, 1921
D. Apr. 8, 1978, Dallas, TX
Southern Methodist/North Carolina 6'0" 210 lbs.

Year	Team		Games	Pos.
1947	CHIB	N	6	G

Bill Johnson
JOHNSON, WILLIAM THOMAS
B. Oct. 31, 1960, Poughkeepsie, NY
Arkansas State 6'2" 230 lbs.

Year	Team		Games	Pos.
1985	CIN	N	13	RB
1986			14	RB
1987			11	RB

3 yrs.   38 games

Billy Johnson
JOHNSON, WILLIAM
B. Feb. 19, 1943, Stanton, NE
Nebraska 5'11" 178 lbs.

Year	Team		Games	Pos.
1966	BOS	A	12	DB
1967			6	DB
1968			14	DB

3 yrs.   32 games

Billy Johnson
JOHNSON, WILLIAM ARTHUR
(White Shoes)
B. Jan. 27, 1952, Boothwyn, PA
Widener 5'9" 170 lbs.

Year	Team		Games	Pos.
1974	HOU	N	14	WR
1975			14	WR
1976			14	WR
1977			14	WR
1978			5	WR
1979			2	WR
1980			16	WR
1982	ATL		9	WR
1983			16	WR
1984			6	WR
1985			16	WR
1986			4	WR
1987			12	WR
1988	WAS	N	1	WR

14 yrs.   143 games

Bob Johnson
JOHNSON, ROBERT (Spider)
B. 1907
Tennessee-Chattanooga 6'4" 205 lbs.

Year	Team		Games	Pos.
1930	POR	N	2	T

Bob Johnson
JOHNSON, ROBERT DOUGLAS
B. Aug. 19, 1946, Cleveland, TN
Tennessee 6'5" 257 lbs.

Year	Team		Games	Pos.
1968	CIN	A	14	C
1969			14	C
1970	CIN	N	14	C

Bob Johnson continued

Year	Team		Games	Pos.
1971			14	C
1972			14	C
1973			14	C
1974			10	C
1975			14	C
1976			14	C
1977			14	C
1978			13	C
1979			5	C

12 yrs.   154 games

Bobby Johnson
JOHNSON, BOBBY CHARLES
B. Sep. 1, 1960, La Grange, TX
Texas 6'0" 190 lbs.

Year	Team		Games	Pos.
1983	NO	N	16	DB
1984			16	CB, S
1985	STL	N	11	S
1986			3	S
1986	NO	N	8	DB

4 yrs.   54 games

Bobby Lee Johnson
JOHNSON, BOBBY LEE
B. Dec. 14, 1961, East St. Louis, IL
Kansas 5'11" 171 lbs.

Year	Team		Games	Pos.
1984	NYG	N	16	WR
1985			16	WR
1986			16	WR

3 yrs.   48 games

Brad Johnson
JOHNSON, JAMES BRADLEY
B. Sep. 13, 1968, Marietta, GA
Florida State 6'5" 221 lbs.

Year	Team		Games	Pos.
1994	MIN	N	4	QB
1995			5	QB
1996			12	QB

3 yrs.   21 games

Brent Johnson
JOHNSON, BRENT
B. May 16, 1963
Tennessee-Chattanooga 6'2" 255 lbs.

Year	Team		Games	Pos.
1987	CHI	N	3	C, G

Butch Johnson
JOHNSON, MICHAEL MCCOLLY
B. May 28, 1954, Los Angeles, CA
California-Riverside 6'1" 191 lbs.

Year	Team		Games	Pos.
1976	DAL	N	14	WR
1977			14	WR
1978			16	WR
1979			11	WR
1980			16	WR
1981			16	WR
1982			9	WR
1983			16	WR
1984	DEN	N	16	WR
1985			16	WR

10 yrs.   144 games

Byron Johnson
JOHNSON, BYRON
B. Oct. 21, 1962
Baylor 6'1" 220 lbs.

Year	Team		Games	Pos.
1987	HOU	N	3	LB

Carl Johnson
JOHNSON, CARL KNUD
B. Dec. 26, 1949, Phoenix, AZ
Nebraska 6'3" 248 lbs.

Year	Team		Games	Pos.
1972	NO	N	14	OT
1973			14	OT

2 yrs.   28 games

Carroll Johnson
JOHNSON, CARROLL W.
B. Feb. 10, 1894
D. Apr., 1974, Batavia, IL
Northwestern 5'10" 175 lbs.

Year	Team		Games	Pos.
1920	HAM	A	3	E

Cecil Johnson
JOHNSON, CECIL ELLORD
B. Aug. 19, 1955, Miami, FL
Pittsburgh 6'2" 230 lbs.

Year	Team		Games	Pos.
1977	TB	N	13	LB
1978			13	LB
1979			15	LB
1980			16	LB
1981			16	LB
1982			9	LB
1983			5	LB
1984			8	LB
1985			16	LB

9 yrs.   111 games

Cecil Johnson
JOHNSON, CECIL O.
B. Sep. 3, 1921, Franklin, TX
D. Mar., 1961
East Texas State 5'11" 197 lbs.

Year	Team		Games	Pos.
1943	BKN	N	9	HB
1944			6	HB

2 yrs.   15 games

Charles Johnson
JOHNSON, CHARLES
B. May 8, 1956, Mansfield, LA
Grambling State 5'10" 180 lbs.

Year	Team		Games	Pos.
1979	SF	N	4	CB
1980			16	CB
1981	STL	N	5	CB

3 yrs.   25 games

Charles Johnson
JOHNSON, CHARLES
B. Jun. 29, 1957, Baltimore, MD
Maryland 6'1" 262 lbs.

Year	Team		Games	Pos.
1979	GB	N	16	DT
1980			15	DT
1983			15	NT

3 yrs.   46 games

Charles Johnson
JOHNSON, CHARLES EVERETT
B. Jan. 3, 1972, San Bernardino, CA
Colorado 6'0" 189 lbs.

Year	Team		Games	Pos.
1994	PIT	N	16	WR
1995			14	WR
1996			16	WR

3 yrs.   46 games

Charley Johnson
JOHNSON, CHARLES LANE
B. Nov. 22, 1938, Big Spring, TX
New Mexico State 6'0" 191 lbs.

Year	Team		Games	Pos.
1961	STL	N	4	QB
1962			11	QB
1963			14	QB
1964			14	QB
1965			11	QB
1966			9	QB
1967			5	QB
1968			7	QB
1969			14	QB
1970	HOU	N	11	QB
1971			14	QB
1972	DEN	N	12	QB
1973			14	QB
1974			14	QB
1975			14	QB

15 yrs.   168 games

Charlie Johnson
JOHNSON, CHARLES
B. Jan. 17, 1952, West Columbia, TX
Colorado 6'3" 262 lbs.

Year	Team		Games	Pos.
1977	PHI	N	12	DT
1978			16	MG
1979			16	MG
1980			16	DT
1981			16	MG
1982	MIN	N	9	DT
1983			16	NT
1984			16	NT

8 yrs.   117 games

Charlie Johnson
JOHNSON, CHARLIE WILBUR
B. Sep. 29, 1944, Columbus, GA
Louisville 6'2" 265 lbs.

Year	Team		Games	Pos.
1966	SF	N	13	DT
1967			14	DT
1968			2	DT

3 yrs.   29 games

Chris Johnson
JOHNSON, CHRISTOPHER T'MAUL
B. Aug. 7, 1971, Dallas, TX
San Diego State 6'0" 205 lbs.

Year	Team		Games	Pos.
1996	MIN	N	5	S

Chris Johnson
JOHNSON, CHRIS
B. Dec. 3, 1960
Millersville State 6'4" 225 lbs.

Year	Team		Games	Pos.
1987	PHI	N	2	CB, S

Chuck Johnson
JOHNSON, CHARLES RAY
B. May 22, 1969, Freeport, TX
Texas 6'5" 275 lbs.

Year	Team		Games	Pos.
1992	DEN	N	16	G, OT

Chuckie Johnson
JOHNSON, CHARLES LEWIS
B. Mar. 5, 1969, Fayetteville, NC
Auburn 6'4" 310 lbs.

Year	Team		Games	Pos.
1993	PHX	N	5	DT

Clyde Johnson
JOHNSON, CLYDE ELMER
B. Aug. 22, 1917, Ashland, KY
Kentucky 6'6" 269 lbs.

Year	Team		Games	Pos.
1946	LA	N	11	T
1947			12	T
1948	LA	AA	9	T

3 yrs.   32 games

Cornelius Johnson
JOHNSON, CORNELIUS O.
B. Jun. 12, 1943, Richmond, VA
Virginia Union 6'2" 245 lbs.

Year	Team		Games	Pos.
1968	BAL	N	14	G
1969			14	G
1970			7	G
1971			13	G
1972			12	G

6 yrs.   74 games

Curley Johnson
JOHNSON, JOHN CURLEY
B. Jul. 2, 1935, Anna, TX
Houston 6'0" 215 lbs.

Year	Team		Games	Pos.
1960	DAL	A	14	HB, P
1961	NY	A	14	OE, P
1962			14	HB, P

Year	Team		Games	Pos.

Curley Johnson *continued*

Year	Team		Games	Pos.
1963			14	HB, P
1964			14	HB, P
1965			14	HB, P
1966			14	P, TE
1967			14	P, TE
1968			14	P, TE
1969	NYG	N		P

10 yrs. 124 games

Curtis Johnson
JOHNSON, CURTIS WISE
B. Jun. 22, 1948, Toledo, OH
Toledo 6'2" 196 lbs.

Year	Team		Games	Pos.
1970	MIA	N	14	DB
1971			14	CB
1972			14	CB
1973			14	CB
1974			13	CB
1975			14	CB
1976			13	CB
1977			14	CB
1978			15	CB

9 yrs. 125 games

Damian Johnson
JOHNSON, DAMIAN C.
B. Dec. 18, 1962, Great Bend, KS
Kansas State 6'5" 290 lbs.

Year	Team		Games	Pos.
1986	NYG	N	16	OT
1987			12	OT
1988			6	OT
1989			4	G
1990	NE	N	16	OT

5 yrs. 54 games

Damone Johnson
JOHNSON, DAMONE
B. Mar. 2, 1962, Los Angeles, CA
California Poly (San Luis Obispo) 6'4" 230 lbs.

Year	Team		Games	Pos.
1986	LARM	N	5	TE
1988			16	TE
1989			16	TE
1990			13	TE
1991			16	TE
1992			16	TE

6 yrs. 82 games

Dan Johnson
JOHNSON, DANIEL JEROME
B. May 17, 1960, Minneapolis, MN
Iowa State 6'3" 240 lbs.

Year	Team		Games	Pos.
1983	MIA	N	16	TE
1984			16	TE
1985			12	TE
1986			15	TE
1987			7	TE

5 yrs. 66 games

Danny Johnson
JOHNSON, DANNY
B. May 7, 1955, Normandy, TN
Tennessee State 6'1" 216 lbs.

Year	Team		Games	Pos.
1978	GB	N		LB

Darrius Johnson
JOHNSON, DARRIUS
B. Sep. 17, 1972, Terrell, TX
Oklahoma 5'9" 175 lbs.

Year	Team		Games	Pos.
1996	DEN	N	13	CB

Daryl Johnson
JOHNSON, DARYL EVANS
B. Aug. 11, 1946, Richmond, VA
Morgan State 5'11" 190 lbs.

Year	Team		Games	Pos.
1968	BOS	A	14	DB

Daryl Johnson *continued*

Year	Team		Games	Pos.
1969			14	DB
1970	BOS	N	14	CB

3 yrs. 42 games

David Johnson
JOHNSON, DAVID
B. Jun. 8, 1963
Alabama 6'4" 295 lbs.

Year	Team		Games	Pos.
1987	TB	N	1	OT

Demetrious Johnson
JOHNSON, DEMETRIOUS
B. Jul. 21, 1961, St. Louis, MO
Missouri 5'11" 190 lbs.

Year	Team		Games	Pos.
1983	DET	N	14	CB, S
1984			16	CB, S
1985			16	S
1986			16	S
1987	MIA	N	3	S

5 yrs. 65 games

Dennis Johnson
JOHNSON, DENNIS CRAIG
B. Jun. 19, 1958, Flint, MI
Southern California 6'3" 230 lbs.

Year	Team		Games	Pos.
1980	MIN	N	12	LB
1981			16	LB
1982			9	LB
1983			16	LB
1984			16	LB
1985			8	LB
1985	TB		8	LB

6 yrs. 85 games

Dennis Johnson
JOHNSON, DENNIS D.
B. Feb. 26, 1956, Weir, MS
Mississippi State 6'3" 220 lbs.

Year	Team		Games	Pos.
1978	BUF	N	16	RB
1979			3	FB
1980	NYG	N	3	TE

3 yrs. 22 games

Dennis Johnson
JOHNSON, DENNIS LEROY
B. Oct. 22, 1951, Passaic, NJ
Delaware 6'4" 261 lbs.

Year	Team		Games	Pos.
1974	WAS	N	13	DT
1975			14	DT
1976			13	DT
1977			11	DE
1978	BUF	N	14	DT

5 yrs. 65 games

Dick Johnson
JOHNSON, RICHARD J.
B. 1940
Minnesota 6'4" 220 lbs.

Year	Team		Games	Pos.
1963	KC	A	5	OE

D.J. Johnson
JOHNSON, DAVID ALLEN
B. Jul. 14, 1966, Louisville, KY
Kentucky 6'0" 185 lbs.

Year	Team		Games	Pos.
1989	PIT	N	16	CB
1990			16	CB
1991			16	CB
1992			15	CB
1993			16	CB
1994	ATL	N	16	CB
1995			13	CB
1996			2	CB
1996	ARI	N	8	CB

8 yrs. 118 games

Don Johnson
JOHNSON, DONALD
B. Sep. 14, 1920, Chicago, IL
Northwestern 6'0" 205 lbs.

Year	Team		Games	Pos.
1942	CLE	N	1	C

Don Johnson
JOHNSON, DONALD
B. Oct. 31, 1931, Bakersfield, CA
California 6'0" 187 lbs.

Year	Team		Games	Pos.
1953	PHI	N	12	HB
1954			6	HB
1955			2	HB

3 yrs. 20 games

Donnell Johnson
JOHNSON, DONNELL
B. Dec. 24, 1969, Miami, FL
Johnson C. Smith 6'7" 310 lbs.

Year	Team		Games	Pos.
1993	CIN	N	7	DE

Earl Johnson
JOHNSON, EARL, JR.
B. Oct. 20, 1963, Daytona Beach, FL
South Carolina 6'0" 190 lbs.

Year	Team		Games	Pos.
1985	NO	N	2	CB
1987	DEN	N	3	S

2 yrs. 5 games

Eddie Johnson
JOHNSON, EDDIE
B. Feb. 3, 1959, Albany, GA
Louisville 6'1" 220 lbs.

Year	Team		Games	Pos.
1981	CLE	N	16	LB
1982			9	LB
1983			16	LB
1984			16	LB
1985			16	LB
1986			16	LB
1987			12	LB
1988			15	LB
1989			16	LB
1990			16	LB

10 yrs. 148 games

Ellis Johnson
JOHNSON, ELLIS
B. Oct. 30, 1973, Wildwood, FL
Florida 6'2" 298 lbs.

Year	Team		Games	Pos.
1995	IND	N	16	DT, DE
1996			12	DT

2 yrs. 28 games

Ellis Johnson
JOHNSON, ELLIS EDWARD
B. Jul. 9, 1943, Baton Rouge, LA
Southeastern Louisiana 6'2" 190 lbs.

Year	Team		Games	Pos.
1965	BOS	A	14	HB, DB
1966			14	OE

2 yrs. 28 games

Eric Johnson
JOHNSON, ERIC
B. Jul. 23, 1952, Ephrata, WA
Washington State 6'1" 192 lbs.

Year	Team		Games	Pos.
1977	PHI	N	14	DB
1978			16	S
1979	SF	N	8	S

3 yrs. 38 games

Essex Johnson
JOHNSON, ESSEX L.
B. Oct. 15, 1946, Shreveport, LA
Grambling State 5'9" 197 lbs.

Year	Team		Games	Pos.
1968	CIN	A	14	RB
1969			12	RB
1970	CIN	N	13	RB

Essex Johnson *continued*

Year	Team		Games	Pos.
1971			14	RB
1972			14	RB
1973			14	RB
1974			5	RB
1975			12	RB
1976	TB	N	14	RB

9 yrs. 112 games

Ezra Johnson
JOHNSON, EZRA RAY
B. Oct. 2, 1955, Shreveport, LA
Morris Brown 6'4" 260 lbs.

Year	Team		Games	Pos.
1977	GB	N	14	DE
1978			16	DE
1979			11	DE
1980			15	DE
1981			16	DE
1982			9	DE
1983			16	DE
1984			13	DE
1985			16	DE
1986			16	DE
1987			6	DE
1988	IND	N	10	DE
1989			16	DE
1990	HOU	N	16	DE
1991			2	DE

15 yrs. 192 games

Farnham Johnson
JOHNSON, FARNHAM JAMES (Gunner)
B. Jun. 23, 1924, St. Paul, MN
Wisconsin/Michigan 6'0" 210 lbs.

Year	Team		Games	Pos.
1948	CHI	AA	8	E

Filmel Johnson
JOHNSON, FILMEL
B. Dec. 24, 1970, Detroit, MI
Illinois 5'10" 187 lbs.

Year	Team		Games	Pos.
1995	BUF	N	2	CB

Flip Johnson
JOHNSON, FULTON
B. Jul. 13, 1963, Cheek, TX
McNeese State 5'10" 185 lbs.

Year	Team		Games	Pos.
1988	BUF	N	11	WR
1989			16	WR

2 yrs. 27 games

Frank Johnson
JOHNSON, FRANK (Pike)
B. Sep. 30, 1896
D. Apr., 1963, Massachusetts
Washington & Lee 5'11" 185 lbs.

Year	Team		Games	Pos.
1920	AKR	A	9	T
1921			12	T, G

2 yrs. 21 games

Gary Johnson
JOHNSON, GARY LYNN (Big Hands)
B. Aug. 31, 1962, Shreveport, LA
Grambling State 6'2" 260 lbs.

Year	Team		Games	Pos.
1975	SD	N	14	DE
1976			14	DT
1977			14	DT
1978			15	DT
1979			16	DT
1980			16	DT
1981			16	DT
1982			9	DT
1983			16	DT
1984			4	NT
1984	SF	N	12	NT
1985			11	NT

11 yrs. 157 games

Gene Johnson
JOHNSON, EUGENE
B. Sep. 18, 1935, Charleston, WV
Cincinnati 6'0" 187 lbs.

Year	Team		Games	Pos.
1959	PHI	N	12	B
1960			11	B
1961	NYG	N	7	DB
3 yrs.	30 games			

Gil Johnson
JOHNSON, GILBERT
B. Dec. 4, 1923, Tyler, TX
Southern Methodist 5'11" 195 lbs.

Year	Team		Games	Pos.
1949	B, NY	AA	9	B

Gilvanni Johnson
JOHNSON, GILVANNI
B. Sep. 12, 1963
Michigan 6'1" 195 lbs.

Year	Team		Games	Pos.
1987	DET	N	3	WR

Glenn Johnson
JOHNSON, GLENN M.
B. 1922, Mesa, AZ
Arizona State 6'4" 263 lbs.

Year	Team		Games	Pos.
1948	NY	AA	9	T
1949	GB	N	8	T
2 yrs.	17 games			

Greg Johnson
JOHNSON, GREG
B. Dec. 3, 1953, Leesburg, FL
Florida State 6'4" 240 lbs.

Year	Team		Games	Pos.
1977	BAL	N	2	DT
1977	TB	N	3	DE
1 yr.	5 games			

Greg Johnson
JOHNSON, GREGORY KENT
B. Dec. 19, 1964, Oklahoma City, OK
Oklahoma 6'4" 295 lbs.

Year	Team		Games	Pos.
1988	MIA	N	2	TE

Greggory Johnson
JOHNSON, GREGGORY DA-MARR
B. Oct. 20, 1958, Houston, TX
Oklahoma State 6'1" 188 lbs.

Year	Team		Games	Pos.
1981	SEA	N	16	S
1982			9	CB
1983			16	CB
1986			15	S
1987	STL	N	8	DB
5 yrs.	64 games			

Harvey Johnson
JOHNSON, HARVEY P. (Stud)
B. Jun. 22, 1919, Bridgeton, NJ
D. Aug. 8, 1983, Orchard Park, NY
William & Mary 5'11" 212 lbs.

Year	Team		Games	Pos.
1946	NY	AA	13	FB
1947			14	B
1948			14	B
1949	B, NY	AA	12	G
1951	NYY	N	12	B
5 yrs.	65 games			

Henry Johnson
JOHNSON, HENRY WILLIAM, III
B. Mar. 20, 1958, Wrens, GA
Georgia Tech 6'1" 235 lbs.

Year	Team		Games	Pos.
1980	MIN	N	16	LB
1981			16	LB
1982			9	LB
1983			5	LB
4 yrs.	46 games			

Herb Johnson
JOHNSON, HERBERT L.
B. 1929
Army/Washington 5'10" 172 lbs.

Year	Team		Games	Pos.
1954	NYG	N	11	HB

Herbert Johnson
JOHNSON, HERBERT
B. Oct. 13, 1963, Fulton, MO
Missouri 5'11" 182 lbs.

Year	Team		Games	Pos.
1987	CHI	N	3	WR

Holbert Johnson
JOHNSON, HOLBERT
B. Jul. 14, 1960
New Mexico State 5'9" 180 lbs.

Year	Team		Games	Pos.
1987	LARM	N	12	TE

Howard Johnson
JOHNSON, HOWARD W. (Smiley)
B. Sep. 22, 1916, Nashville, TN
D. Feb. 26, 1945, Iwo Jima
Georgia 5'9" 198 lbs.

Year	Team		Games	Pos.
1940	GB	N	11	G
1941			11	G
2 yrs.	22 games			

Jack Johnson
JOHNSON, JOHN C.
B. Dec. 11, 1933, Pittsburgh, PA
Miami (Florida) 6'3" 198 lbs.

Year	Team		Games	Pos.
1957	CHIB	N	11	HB
1958			12	HB
1959			6	HB
1960	BUF	A		DB
1961			3	DB
1961	DAL	A	1	DB
5 yrs.	33 games			

Jack Johnson
JOHNSON, JOHN DENVIL
B. Nov. 28, 1909, Grantsville, UT
D. Oct. 27, 1978, Tooele, UT
Utah 6'4" 216 lbs.

Year	Team		Games	Pos.
1934	DET	N	13	T
1935			10	T
1936			11	T
1937			11	T
1938			10	T
1939			10	T
1940			11	T
7 yrs.	76 games			

James Johnson
JOHNSON, JAMES EARL
B. Nov. 30, 1945, Charleston, SC
South Carolina State 6'1" 190 lbs.

Year	Team		Games	Pos.
1969	CIN	A	11	DB

James Johnson
JOHNSON, JAMES L.
B. Jun. 21, 1962, Los Angeles, CA
San Diego State 6'2" 236 lbs.

Year	Team		Games	Pos.
1986	DET	N	11	LB
1987	SF	N	1	LB
1987	SD	N	1	LB
2 yrs.	13 games			

Jason Johnson
JOHNSON, JASON MANSFIELD
B. Nov. 8, 1965, Gary, IN
Illinois State 5'10" 178 lbs.

Year	Team		Games	Pos.
1988	DEN	N	8	WR
1989	PIT	N	14	WR
2 yrs.	22 games			

Jay Johnson
JOHNSON, OLIVER M.
B. Oct. 8, 1945, East Orange, NJ
East Texas State 6'3" 230 lbs.

Year	Team		Games	Pos.
1969	PHI	N	3	LB
1970			5	LB
2 yrs.	8 games			

Jerry Johnson
JOHNSON, JERRY
B. 1895
Deceased
Morningside 6'0" 195 lbs.

Year	Team		Games	Pos.
1921	RI	A	1	HB
1922	RI	N	5	HB
1922	RAC	N	3	HB
2 yrs.	9 games			

Jesse Johnson
JOHNSON, JESSE
B. Aug. 23, 1957, Fort Collins, CO
Colorado 6'3" 185 lbs.

Year	Team		Games	Pos.
1980	NYJ	N	16	CB, S
1981			16	CB, S
1982			9	S, CB
1983			4	S
4 yrs.	45 games			

Jimmie Johnson
JOHNSON, JIMMIE
B. Oct. 6, 1966, Augusta, GA
Howard 6'2" 246 lbs.

Year	Team		Games	Pos.
1989	WAS	N	16	TE
1990			16	TE
1991			6	TE
1992	DET	N	16	TE
1993			6	TE
1994	KC	N	7	TE
1995	PHI	N	16	TE
1996			16	TE
8 yrs.	99 games			

Jimmy Johnson
JOHNSON, JAMES EARL
B. Mar. 31, 1938, Dallas, TX
UCLA 6'2" 188 lbs.

Year	Team		Games	Pos.
1961	SF	N	12	DB
1962			12	FL
1963			13	FL, DB
1964			14	DB
1965			14	DB
1966			14	DB
1967			11	DB
1968			13	DB
1969			14	CB
1970			14	CB
1971			14	CB
1972			14	CB
1973			13	CB
1974			12	CB
1975			14	CB
1976			14	CB
16 yrs.	212 games			

Joe Johnson
BORN JOSEPH PERNELL HOWARD
B. Dec. 21, 1962, Washington, DC
Notre Dame 5'8" 170 lbs.

Year	Team		Games	Pos.
1989	WAS	N	15	WR
1990			15	WR
1991			2	WR
1992	MIN	N	15	WR
4 yrs.	47 games			

Joe Johnson
JOHNSON, JOE
B. Jul. 11, 1972, St. Louis, MO

Joe Johnson *continued*
Louisville 6'4" 280 lbs.

Year	Team		Games	Pos.
1994	NO	N	15	DE
1995			14	DE, DT
1996			13	DE
3 yrs.	42 games			

Joe Johnson
JOHNSON, JOE C.
B. 1925
Mississippi 6'2" 195 lbs.

Year	Team		Games	Pos.
1948	NYG	N	11	HB

Joe Johnson
JOHNSON, JOSEPH F.
B. Nov. 3, 1929, New Haven, CT
Boston College 6'0" 185 lbs.

Year	Team		Games	Pos.
1954	GB	N	12	HB
1955			12	HB
1956			11	HB
1957			12	HB
1958			6	HB
1960	BOS	A		OE
1961			6	OE
7 yrs.	59 games			

John Johnson
JOHNSON, JOHN HOWARD
B. Jul. 5, 1941, Gary, IN
Indiana 6'5" 260 lbs.

Year	Team		Games	Pos.
1963	CHI	N	12	OT
1964			14	DT
1965			14	DT
1966			13	DT
1967			14	DT
1968			14	DT
1969	NYG	N	5	DT
7 yrs.	86 games			

John Johnson
JOHNSON, JOHN VERNARD
B. May 8, 1968, La Grange, GA
Clemson 6'3" 230 lbs.

Year	Team		Games	Pos.
1991	SF	N	9	LB
1992			16	LB
1993			15	LB
1994	CIN	N	5	LB
1995	NO	N	1	LB
5 yrs.	46 games			

John Henry Johnson
JOHNSON, JOHN HENRY
B. Nov. 24, 1929, Pittsburgh, CA
St. Mary's (California)/Arizona State 6'2" 210 lbs.

Year	Team		Games	Pos.
1954	SF	N	12	HB
1955			7	HB
1956			5	HB
1957	DET	N	12	FB
1958			9	FB
1959			10	FB
1960	PIT	N	12	FB
1961			14	FB
1962			12	FB
1963			14	FB
1964			1	FB
1965			1	FB
1966	HOU	A	14	FB
13 yrs.	136 games			

Johnnie Johnson
JOHNSON, JOHNNIE, JR.
B. Oct. 8, 1956, La Grange, TX
Texas 6'1" 185 lbs.

Year	Team		Games	Pos.
1980	LA	N	16	S
1981			16	S
1982	LARM	N	9	S
1983			15	S

Year	Team		Games	Pos.

Johnnie Johnson continued

Year	Team		Games	Pos.
1984			9	S
1985			16	S
1986			16	S
1987			7	S
1988			16	S
1989	SEA	N	3	S
10 yrs.	124 games			

Johnny Johnson

JOHNSON, JOHNNY
B. Jun. 11, 1968, Santa Clara, CA
San Jose State 6'2" 218 lbs.

1990	PHX	N	14	RB
1991			15	RB
1992			12	RB
1993	NYJ	N	15	RB
1994			16	RB
5 yrs.	72 games			

Kelley Johnson

JOHNSON, KELLEY ANTONIO
B. Jun. 3, 1962, Carlsbad, NM
Colorado 5'8" 168 lbs.

1987	IND	N	3	WR

Ken Johnson

JOHNSON, KENNETH EUGENE
B. Mar. 25, 1955, Nashville, TN
Knoxville 6'5" 253 lbs.

1979	BUF	N	3	DT
1980			16	DE
1981			16	DE
1982			6	DE
1983			16	DE
1984			16	DE
1987	KC	N	3	DE
7 yrs.	76 games			

Ken Johnson

JOHNSON, KENNETH LEE
B. Sep. 14, 1966, Thomaston, GA
Florida A&M 6'2" 197 lbs.

1989	MIN	N	1	S
1990			4	S
1990	NYJ	N	4	S
2 yrs.	9 games			

Ken Johnson

JOHNSON, RALPH KENNETH
B. Feb. 12, 1947, Anderson, IN
Indiana 6'5" 261 lbs.*

1971	CIN	N	10	DE
1972			11	DT
1973			9	DT
1974			13	DT
1975			14	DT
1976			13	DT
1977			10	DE
7 yrs.	80 games			

Kenny Johnson

JOHNSON, KENNETH
B. Nov. 27, 1956, Miami, FL
Miami (Florida) 6'2" 220 lbs.

1979	NYG	N	9	RB

Kenny Johnson

JOHNSON, KENNETH
B. Dec. 28, 1963, Weir, MS
Mississippi State 6'0" 185 lbs.

1987	GB	N	12	CB

Kenny Johnson

JOHNSON, KENNETH RAY
B. Jan. 7, 1958, Columbia, MS

Kenny Johnson continued

Mississippi State 5'11" 175 lbs.

1980	ATL	N	16	S
1981			16	S
1982			9	CB
1983			16	CB
1984			16	CB
1985			5	S
1986			7	S
1986	HOU	N	1	S
1987			12	S
1988			13	S
1989			16	S
10 yrs.	127 games			

Kermit Johnson

JOHNSON, KERMIT DEKOVEN
B. Feb. 22, 1952, Los Angeles, CA
UCLA 6'0" 201 lbs.

1975	SF	N	11	RB
1976			11	RB
2 yrs.	22 games			

Keshon Johnson

JOHNSON, KESHON LORENZO
B. Jul. 17, 1970, Fresno, CA
Arizona 5'10" 179 lbs.

1993	CHI	N	15	CB
1994			6	CB
1994	GB	N	7	CB
1995	CHI	N	12	CB
3 yrs.	40 games			

Kevin Johnson

JOHNSON, KEVIN
B. Oct. 30, 1970, Los Angeles, CA
Texas Southern 6'1" 310 lbs.

1995	PHI	N	11	DT
1996			12	DT
2 yrs.	23 games			

Keyshawn Johnson

JOHNSON, KEYSHAWN
B. Jul. 22, 1972, Los Angeles, CA
Southern California 6'3" 215 lbs.

1996	NYJ	N	14	WR

Knute Johnson

JOHNSON, KNUTE
B. Feb. 16, 1900
D. Aug., 1984, Bellerose, NY
Muhlenberg 6'1" 185 lbs.

1926	PHI	A	2	E

Larry Johnson

JOHNSON, LAWRENCE (Chief)
B. Mar. 28, 1909, Odanah, WI
Haskell 6'3" 223 lbs.

1933	BOS	N	9	C, G
1934			12	E, C
1935			2	C, HB
1936	NYG	N	5	C
1937			8	C
1938			10	C
1939			4	C
1944	WAS	N	5	C, G
8 yrs.	55 games			

Lawrence Johnson

JOHNSON, LAWRENCE WENDELL
B. Sep. 11, 1957, Gary, IN
Wisconsin 5'11" 204 lbs.

1979	CLE	N	16	CB
1980			2	CB
1981			16	CB
1982			8	CB

Lawrence Johnson continued

1983			16	CB
1984			6	CB
1984	BUF	N	10	CB
1985			16	CB
1987			6	S
8 yrs.	96 games			

Lee Johnson

JOHNSON, LEE
B. Nov. 27, 1961, Dallas, TX
Brigham Young 6'1" 199 lbs.

1985	HOU	N	16	P
1986			16	P
1987			9	P
1987	CLE	N	3	P
1988			3	P
1988	CIN	N	12	P, K
1989			16	P
1990			16	P
1991			16	P, K
1992			16	P
1993			16	P
1994			16	P
1995			16	P
1996			16	P
12 yrs.	187 games			

Len Johnson

JOHNSON, LEONARD
B. Nov. 5, 1902
D. Apr., 1975, New York, NY
Syracuse

1926	COL	N	1	HB

Len Johnson

JOHNSON, LEONARD
B. Jan. 26, 1946, Worthington, MN
St. Cloud State 6'2" 250 lbs.

1970	NYG	N	2	G

Leo Johnson

JOHNSON, LEO DANIEL
B. Oct. 1, 1944, Houston, TX
Tennessee State 6'1" 204 lbs.

1969	SF	N	14	WR
1970			7	WR
2 yrs.	21 games			

Leon Johnson

JOHNSON, W.B.
B. Sep. 30, 1906
D. Sep., 1978, Florence, NJ
Columbia 5'11" 185 lbs.

1929	ORA	N	5	E, G

LeShon Johnson

JOHNSON, LESHON EUGENE
B. Jan. 15, 1971, Tulsa, OK
Northern Illinois 5'11" 203 lbs.

1994	GB	N	12	RB
1995			2	RB
1995	ARI	N	4	RB
1996			15	RB
3 yrs.	33 games			

Levi Johnson

JOHNSON, LEVI
B. Oct. 30, 1950, Corpus Christi, TX
Texas A&I-Kingsville 6'3" 196 lbs.

1973	DET	N	14	DB
1974			14	CB
1975			14	CB
1976			14	CB
1977			3	CB
5 yrs.	59 games			

Lonnie Johnson

JOHNSON, LONNIE
B. Feb. 14, 1971, Miami, FL
Florida State 6'3" 235 lbs.

1994	BUF	N	10	TE
1995			16	TE
1996			16	TE
3 yrs.	42 games			

Lorne Johnson

JOHNSON, LORNE
B. 1910
Temple 6'2" 195 lbs.

1934	PHI	N	1	FB

Mario Johnson

JOHNSON, MARIO CHAVEZ
B. Jan. 30, 1970, St. Louis, MO
Missouri 6'3" 292 lbs.

1992	NYJ	N	14	DT
1993	NE	N	6	NT
2 yrs.	20 games			

Mark Johnson

JOHNSON, MARK
B. Mar. 20, 1964, Houston, TX
Western Kentucky 6'1" 194 lbs.

1987	CIN	N	3	S

Mark Johnson

**JOHNSON, MARK STEVEN
(Country)**
B. Aug. 14, 1953, Moline, IL
Missouri 6'2" 239 lbs.

1975	BUF	N	11	DE
1976			13	LB
1977	CLE	N	7	LB
3 yrs.	31 games			

Marshall Johnson

JOHNSON, MARSHALL DONELL
B. Nov. 1, 1952, Jacksonville, TX
Houston 6'1" 192 lbs.

1975	BAL	N	14	RB
1977			3	WR
1978			15	WR
3 yrs.	32 games			

Marv Johnson

JOHNSON, MARVIN
B. Apr. 13, 1927, San Francisco, CA
Deceased
San Jose State 5'11" 183 lbs.

1951	LA	N	9	HB
1952	GB	N	5	HB
1953			7	HB
3 yrs.	21 games			

Maurice Johnson

JOHNSON, MAURICE EDWARD
B. Jan. 9, 1967, Washington, DC
Temple 6'2" 243 lbs.

1991	PHI	N	12	TE
1992			11	TE
1993			16	TE
1994			16	TE
4 yrs.	55 games			

Melvin Johnson

JOHNSON, MELVIN CARLTON, III
B. Apr. 15, 1972, Cincinnati, OH
Kentucky 6'0" 195 lbs.

1995	TB	N	11	S
1996			16	S
2 yrs.	27 games			

Mike Johnson
JOHNSON, MICHAEL
B. Nov. 26, 1962, Southport, NC
Virginia Tech 6'1" 228 lbs.

Year	Team		Games	Pos.
1986	CLE	N	16	LB
1987			11	LB
1988			16	LB
1989			16	LB
1990			16	LB
1991			5	LB
1992			16	LB
1993			16	LB
1994	DET	N	16	LB
1995			16	LB
10 yrs.	144 games			

Mike Johnson
JOHNSON, MICHAEL ALAN
B. Oct. 7, 1943, Denver, CO
Kansas 5'10" 185 lbs.

Year	Team		Games	Pos.
1966	DAL	N	14	DB
1967			14	DB
1968			14	DB
1969			12	CB
4 yrs.	54 games			

Mike Johnson
JOHNSON, MIKE
B. Apr. 24, 1962, Chicago, IL
Illinois 6'5" 225 lbs.

Year	Team		Games	Pos.
1984	HOU	N	16	DE

Mitch Johnson
JOHNSON, MITCHELL ALLEN
B. Mar. 1, 1942, Chicago, IL
Los Angeles State/UCLA 6'4" 249 lbs.

Year	Team		Games	Pos.
1965	DAL	N	12	OT
1966	WAS	N	14	OT
1967			14	OT
1969	LA	N	14	OT
1970			14	OT
1971	CLE	N	11	OT
6 yrs.	79 games			

M.L. Johnson
JOHNSON, MICHAEL LAMAR
B. Jan. 24, 1964, New York, NY
Hawaii 6'3" 225 lbs.

Year	Team		Games	Pos.
1987	SEA	N	8	LB
1988			16	LB
1989			12	LB
3 yrs.	36 games			

Monte Johnson
JOHNSON, MONTE CHARLES
B. Oct. 26, 1951, Denver, CO
Nebraska 6'4" 239 lbs.

Year	Team		Games	Pos.
1973	OAK	N	13	LB
1974			14	LB
1975			14	LB
1976			14	LB
1977			14	LB
1978			14	LB
1979			16	LB
7 yrs.	99 games			

Nate Johnson
JOHNSON, NATHANIEL
B. May 12, 1957, St. Petersburg, FL
Hillsdale 5'11" 192 lbs.

Year	Team		Games	Pos.
1980	NYG	N	16	WR

Nate Johnson
JOHNSON, NATHANIEL ELIJAH
B. Jun. 18, 1920, Benton, IL
Illinois 6'3" 244 lbs.

Year	Team		Games	Pos.
1946	NY	AA	14	T

Nate Johnson continued

Year	Team		Games	Pos.
1947			14	T
1948	CHI	AA	14	T
1949			12	T
1950	NYY	N	11	T
5 yrs.	65 games			

Nate Johnson
JOHNSON, NATHANIEL JAMES
B. Oct. 25, 1963
Texas Southern 6'2" 224 lbs.

Year	Team		Games	Pos.
1987	NO	N	1	RB

Norm Johnson
JOHNSON, NORM
B. May 31, 1960, Inglewood, CA
UCLA 6'2" 198 lbs.

Year	Team		Games	Pos.
1982	SEA	N	9	K
1983			16	K
1984			16	K
1985			16	K
1986			16	K
1987			13	K
1988			16	K
1989			16	K
1990			16	K
1991	ATL	N	14	K
1992			16	K
1993			15	K
1994			16	K
1995	PIT	N	16	K
1996			16	K
15 yrs.	227 games			

Oscar Johnson
JOHNSON, OSCAR GOTTHARD
B. 1901, Lynn, MA
Deceased
Vermont 5'10" 200 lbs.

Year	Team		Games	Pos.
1924	CHIB	N	1	FB
1926	BOS	A	6	FB, HB
2 yrs.	7 games			

Pat Johnson
JOHNSON, JOHN PATRICK
B. Jun. 10, 1972, Mineral Point, MO
Purdue 6'1" 204 lbs.

Year	Team		Games	Pos.
1995	MIA	N	14	S

Pepper Johnson
JOHNSON, THOMAS
B. Jun. 29, 1964, Detroit, MI
Ohio State 6'3" 248 lbs.

Year	Team		Games	Pos.
1986	NYG	N	16	LB
1987			12	LB
1988			16	LB
1989			14	LB
1990			16	LB
1991			16	LB
1992			16	LB
1993	CLE	N	16	LB
1994			16	LB
1995			16	LB
1996	DET	N	15	LB
11 yrs.	169 games			

Pete Johnson
JOHNSON, PETE
B. Mar. 2, 1954, Peach County, GA
Ohio State 6'0" 247 lbs.

Year	Team		Games	Pos.
1977	CIN	N	14	RB
1978			16	RB
1979			16	RB
1980			12	FB
1981			16	RB
1982			9	RB
1983			11	RB
1984	SD	N	3	RB

Pete Johnson continued

Year	Team		Games	Pos.
1984	MIA	N	13	RB
8 yrs.	110 games			

Pete Johnson
JOHNSON, PETER
B. Aug. 9, 1937, Roanoke, VA
Virginia Military Institute 6'2" 200 lbs.

Year	Team		Games	Pos.
1959	CHIB	N	7	HB

Preston Johnson
JOHNSON, PRESTON
B. 1945
Florida A&M 6'2" 230 lbs.

Year	Team		Games	Pos.
1968	BOS	A	3	RB

Randy Johnson
JOHNSON, RANDOLPH KLAUS
B. Jun. 17, 1944, San Antonio, TX
Texas A&I-Kingsville 6'3" 202 lbs.

Year	Team		Games	Pos.
1966	ATL	N	14	QB
1967			14	QB
1968			8	QB
1969			6	QB
1970			4	QB
1971	NYG	N	5	QB
1972			4	QB
1973			9	QB
1975	WAS	N	8	QB
1976	GB	N	3	QB
10 yrs.	75 games			

Randy Johnson
JOHNSON, ROBERT RANDALL
B. Jan. 2, 1953, Floyd County, GA
Georgia 6'2" 255 lbs.

Year	Team		Games	Pos.
1977	TB	N	12	G
1978			10	G
2 yrs.	22 games			

Ray Johnson
JOHNSON, RAYMOND
B. 1914
Denver 6'1" 195 lbs.

Year	Team		Games	Pos.
1937	CLE	N	2	HB
1938			1	B
1938	CHIB	N	1	B
2 yrs.	4 games			

Raylee Johnson
JOHNSON, RAYLEE TERRELL
B. Jun. 1, 1970, Fordyce, AR
Arkansas 6'3" 245 lbs.

Year	Team		Games	Pos.
1993	SD	N	9	DE
1994			15	DE
1995			16	DE
1996			14	DE
4 yrs.	54 games			

Reggie Johnson
JOHNSON, REGGIE
B. Jan. 27, 1968, Pensacola, FL
Florida State 6'2" 256 lbs.

Year	Team		Games	Pos.
1991	DEN	N	16	TE
1992			15	TE
1993			13	TE
1994	GB	N	9	TE
1995	PHI	N	9	TE
1996	KC	N	11	TE
6 yrs.	73 games			

Richard Johnson
JOHNSON, RICHARD
B. Sep. 16, 1963, Harvey, IL
Wisconsin 6'1" 190 lbs.

Year	Team		Games	Pos.
1985	HOU	N	16	CB

Richard Johnson continued

Year	Team		Games	Pos.
1986			16	CB
1987			5	CB
1988			16	CB
1989			14	CB
1990			16	CB
1991			14	CB
1992			1	CB
8 yrs.	98 games			

Richard Johnson
JOHNSON, RICHARD L.
B. May 13, 1947, Canton, IL
Illinois 6'1" 210 lbs.

Year	Team		Games	Pos.
1969	HOU	A	14	RB

Richard Johnson
JOHNSON, RICHARD LAVON
B. Oct. 19, 1961, Los Angeles, CA
Colorado 5'7" 178 lbs.

Year	Team		Games	Pos.
1987	WAS	N	1	WR
1989	DET	N	16	WR
1990			16	WR
3 yrs.	33 games			

Rick Johnson
JOHNSON, RICK
B. Dec. 12, 1963
Grand Valley State 6'6" 255 lbs.

Year	Team		Games	Pos.
1987	DET	N	1	OT

Rob Johnson
JOHNSON, ROB
B. Mar. 18, 1973, Newport Beach, CA
Southern California 6'3" 220 lbs.

Year	Team		Games	Pos.
1995	JAC	N	1	QB
1996			2	QB
2 yrs.	3 games			

Ron Johnson
JOHNSON, RON
B. Jun. 8, 1956, Detroit, MI
Eastern Michigan 5'10" 200 lbs.

Year	Team		Games	Pos.
1978	PIT	N	16	CB
1979			11	CB
1980			16	CB
1981			12	CB
1982			9	CB, S
1983			12	S
1984			15	S
7 yrs.	91 games			

Ron Johnson
JOHNSON, RONALD
B. Sep. 21, 1958, Monterey, CA
Long Beach State 6'3" 186 lbs.

Year	Team		Games	Pos.
1985	PHI	N	8	WR
1986			12	WR
1987			3	WR
1988			10	WR
1989			14	WR
5 yrs.	47 games			

Ron Johnson
JOHNSON, RONALD ADOLPHUS
B. Oct. 17, 1947, Detroit, MI
Michigan 6'1" 205 lbs.

Year	Team		Games	Pos.
1969	CLE	N	14	RB
1970	NYG	N	14	RB
1971			2	RB
1972			14	RB
1973			12	RB
1974			7	RB
1975			14	RB
7 yrs.	77 games			

Rudy Johnson
JOHNSON, RUDOLPH
B. Aug. 12, 1941, Houston, TX
Nebraska 5'11" 190 lbs.

Year	Team		Games	Pos.
1964	SF	N	5	HB
1965			14	HB
1966	ATL	N	1	RB

3 yrs. 20 games

Sam Johnson
JOHNSON, SAMUEL
B. Sep. 7, 1964, East Los Angeles, CA
Prairie View A&M 5'11" 180 lbs.

Year	Team		Games	Pos.
1987	LARM	N	3	WR

Sammy Johnson
JOHNSON, SAMUEL LEE
B. Sep. 22, 1952, Burlington, NC
North Carolina 6'0" 224 lbs.

Year	Team		Games	Pos.
1974	SF	N	14	RB
1975			14	RB
1976			6	RB
1976	MIN	N	8	RB
1977			14	RB
1978			3	RB
1979	GB	N	3	RB

6 yrs. 62 games

Sidney Johnson
JOHNSON, SIDNEY
B. Mar. 7, 1965, Los Angeles, CA
California 5'9" 175 lbs.

Year	Team		Games	Pos.
1988	KC	N	13	CB
1990	WAS	N	10	CB
1991			15	CB
1992			8	CB

4 yrs. 46 games

Stan Johnson
JOHNSON, GEORGE STANLEY
B. Jun. 18, 1955, Sandusky, OH
Tennessee State 6'4" 275 lbs.

Year	Team		Games	Pos.
1978	KC	N	10	DT

Steve Johnson
JOHNSON, STEVEN EMIL
B. Jun. 22, 1965, Huntsville, AL
Virginia Tech 6'6" 245 lbs.

Year	Team		Games	Pos.
1988	NE	N	14	TE

Ted Johnson
JOHNSON, TED
B. Dec. 4, 1972, Alameda, CA
Colorado 6'3" 240 lbs.

Year	Team		Games	Pos.
1995	NE	N	12	LB
1996			16	LB

2 yrs. 28 games

Tim Johnson
JOHNSON, TIMOTHY
B. Jan. 29, 1965, Sarasota, FL
Penn State 6'3" 260 lbs.

Year	Team		Games	Pos.
1987	PIT	N	12	DL
1988			15	DE, NT
1989			14	DE, NT
1990	WAS	N	16	DT
1991			16	DT
1992			16	DT
1993			15	DT
1994			14	DT
1995			14	DT, DE
1996	CIN	N	14	DT

10 yrs. 146 games

Tom Johnson
JOHNSON, THOMAS

Tom Johnson continued

B. Jan. 19, 1931, Chicago, IL
Michigan 6'2" 230 lbs.

Year	Team		Games	Pos.
1952	GB	N	8	T

Tommy Johnson
JOHNSON, TOMMY POSTELL
B. Dec. 5, 1971, Rome, GA
Alabama 5'10" 180 lbs.

Year	Team		Games	Pos.
1995	JAC	N	1	CB

Tony Johnson
JOHNSON, TONY
B. Feb. 5, 1972, Como, MS
Alabama 6'5" 256 lbs.

Year	Team		Games	Pos.
1996	NO	N	8	TE

Tracy Johnson
JOHNSON, TRACY ILLYA
B. Nov. 29, 1966, Concord, NC
Clemson 6'0" 232 lbs.

Year	Team		Games	Pos.
1989	HOU	N	15	RB
1990	ATL	N	16	RB
1991			16	RB
1992	SEA	N	16	RB
1993			16	RB
1994			16	RB
1995			15	RB
1996	TB	N	10	FB

8 yrs. 120 games

Tré Johnson
JOHNSON, EDWARD STANTON, III
B. Aug. 30, 1971, Manhattan, NY
Temple 6'2" 315 lbs.

Year	Team		Games	Pos.
1994	WAS	N	14	OT
1995			10	G
1996			15	OT

3 yrs. 39 games

Troy Johnson
JOHNSON, TROY ANTWAIN
B. Nov. 10, 1964, Houston, TX
Oklahoma 6'2" 236 lbs.

Year	Team		Games	Pos.
1988	CHI	N	16	LB
1989			7	LB
1990	NYJ	N	16	LB
1991			16	LB
1992	DET	N	9	LB

5 yrs. 64 games

Troy Johnson
JOHNSON, TROY DWAN
B. Oct. 20, 1962, Houma, LA
Southeastern Louisiana/Southern University 6'1" 175 lbs.

Year	Team		Games	Pos.
1986	STL	N	13	WR
1987			14	WR
1988	PIT	N	14	WR
1989	DET	N	9	WR

4 yrs. 50 games

Trumaine Johnson
JOHNSON, TRUMAINE
B. Nov. 16, 1960, Bogalusa, LA
Grambling State 6'2" 192 lbs.

Year	Team		Games	Pos.
1985	SD	N	11	WR
1986			16	WR
1987	BUF	N	12	WR
1988			16	WR

4 yrs. 55 games

Tyrone Johnson
JOHNSON, TYRONE

Tyrone Johnson continued

B. Sep. 4, 1971, Aurora, CO
Western State (Colorado) 5'11" 171 lbs.

Year	Team		Games	Pos.
1994	NO	N	1	WR

Undra Johnson
JOHNSON, UNDRA JEROME
B. Jan. 8, 1966, Valdosta, GA
West Virginia 5'9" 199 lbs.

Year	Team		Games	Pos.
1989	NO	N	5	RB
1989	ATL	N	1	RB

1 yr. 6 games

Vance Johnson
JOHNSON, VANCE EDWARD
B. Mar. 13, 1963, Trenton, NJ
Arizona 5'11" 174 lbs.

Year	Team		Games	Pos.
1985	DEN	N	16	WR
1986			12	WR
1987			11	WR
1988			16	WR
1989			16	WR
1990			16	WR
1991			10	WR
1992			11	WR
1993			10	WR
1995			10	WR

10 yrs. 128 games

Vaughan Johnson
JOHNSON, VAUGHAN MONROE
B. Mar. 24, 1962, Morehead City, NC
North Carolina State 6'3" 235 lbs.

Year	Team		Games	Pos.
1986	NO	N	16	LB
1987			12	LB
1988			16	LB
1989			16	LB
1990			16	LB
1991			13	LB
1992			16	LB
1993			15	LB
1994	PHI	N	4	LB

9 yrs. 124 games

Walter Johnson
JOHNSON, WALTER
B. Nov. 13, 1942, Cincinnati, OH
Los Angeles State/New Mexico State 6'3" 268 lbs.

Year	Team		Games	Pos.
1965	CLE	N	14	DT
1966			14	DT
1967			14	DT
1968			14	DT
1969			14	DT
1970			14	DT
1971			14	DT
1972			14	DT
1973			14	DT
1974			14	DT
1975			14	DT
1976			14	DT
1977	CIN	N		DT

13 yrs. 168 games

Walter Johnson
JOHNSON, WALTER
B. Sep. 13, 1965
Pittsburgh 6'1" 250 lbs.

Year	Team		Games	Pos.
1987	DAL	N	1	DT, DE

Walter Johnson
JOHNSON, WALTER CLARKE
B. Nov. 25, 1943, Atlanta, GA
Tuskegee Institute 6'4" 225 lbs.

Year	Team		Games	Pos.
1967	SF	N	1	LB

Walter Johnson
JOHNSON, WALTER ULYSSES
B. Nov. 13, 1963, Monroe, LA
Louisiana Tech 6'0" 241 lbs.

Year	Team		Games	Pos.
1987	HOU	N	10	LB
1988			16	LB
1989	NO	N	15	LB

3 yrs. 41 games

Will Johnson
JOHNSON, WILLIAM ALEXANDER
B. Dec. 4, 1964, Monroe, LA
Northeast Louisiana 6'4" 245 lbs.

Year	Team		Games	Pos.
1987	CHI	N	11	LB

Luke Johnsos
JOHNSOS, LUKE A.
B. Dec. 6, 1905, Chicago, IL
D. Dec. 10, 1984, Evanston, IL
Northwestern 6'2" 195 lbs.

Year	Team		Games	Pos.
1929	CHIB	N	15	E
1930			13	E
1931			13	E
1932			13	E
1933			6	E
1934			13	E
1935			12	E
1936			11	E

8 yrs. 96 games

Art Johnston
JOHNSTON, ARTHUR (Swede)
B. 1910
Lawrence 5'10" 186 lbs.

Year	Team		Games	Pos.
1931	GB	N	2	FB

Brian Johnston
JOHNSTON, BRIAN
B. Nov. 26, 1962, Highland, MD
North Carolina 6'3" 275 lbs.

Year	Team		Games	Pos.
1986	NYG	N	4	C
1987			5	C

2 yrs. 9 games

Charlie Johnston
JOHNSTON, CHARLES F.
B. Sep. 13, 1900
D. Apr., 1986, Hartford, CT
Stanford 6'0" 190 lbs.

Year	Team		Games	Pos.
1926	LA	A	7	T, G

Chet Johnston
JOHNSTON, CHESTER ARTHUR (Swede)
B. Mar. 7, 1910, Appleton, WI
Marquette/Elmhurst 5'10" 197 lbs.

Year	Team		Games	Pos.
1934	GB	N	1	FB
1934	C, S	N	3	FB, HB
1935	GB	N	10	FB
1936			7	FB
1937			1	FB
1938			2	B, G
1939	PIT	N	8	FB
1940			10	FB

7 yrs. 42 games

Daryl Johnston
JOHNSTON, DARYL PETER (Moose)
B. Feb. 10, 1966, Youngstown, NY
Syracuse 6'2" 234 lbs.

Year	Team		Games	Pos.
1989	DAL	N	16	RB
1990			16	RB
1991			16	RB
1992			16	RB
1993			16	RB

Year	Team	Games	Pos.

Daryl Johnston *continued*

1994		16	RB
1995		16	RB
1996		16	RB
8 yrs.		128 games	

Jimmy Johnston
JOHNSTON, JAMES EVERETT
B. Apr. 16, 1917, Parma, ID
D. Nov. 27, 1973, Caldwell, ID
Washington 6'1" 193 lbs.

1939	WAS	N	11	HB
1940			11	FB
1940	CHIC	N	1	B
1946			6	HB
3 yrs.		29 games		

Mark Johnston
JOHNSTON, MARK R.
B. 1938
Northwestern 6'0" 201 lbs.

1960	HOU	A		DB
1961			14	DB
1962			14	DB
1963			14	DB
1964	OAK	A	1	DB
1964	NY	A	8	DB
5 yrs.		51 games		

Preston Johnston
JOHNSTON, LUTHER P.
B. 1921
Southern Methodist 6'0" 205 lbs.

1946	MIA	AA	3	FB
1946	BUF	AA	8	FB
1 yr.		11 games		

Rex Johnston
JOHNSTON, REX DAVID
B. Nov. 8, 1937, Colton, CA
Southern California 6'1" 195 lbs.

| 1960 | PIT | N | 12 | HB |

Lance Johnstone
JOHNSTONE, LANCE
B. Jun. 11, 1973, Philadelphia, PA
Temple 6'3" 233 lbs.

| 1996 | OAK | N | 16 | DE |

Charlie Joiner
JOINER, CHARLES, JR.
B. Oct. 14, 1947, Many, LA
Grambling State 5'11" 184 lbs.

1969	HOU	A	7	WR
1970	HOU	N	9	WR
1971			14	WR
1972			6	WR
1972	CIN		6	WR
1973			5	WR
1974			14	WR
1975			14	WR
1976	SD	N	14	WR
1977			14	WR
1978			16	WR
1979			16	WR
1980			16	WR
1981			16	WR
1982			9	WR
1983			12	WR
1984			16	WR
1985			16	WR
1986			15	WR
18 yrs.		235 games		

Tim Joiner
JOINER, TIMOTHY LANE
B. Jan. 17, 1961, Monrovia, CA

Tim Joiner *continued*

Louisiana Tech 6'4" 235 lbs.

1983	HOU	N	15	LB
1984			11	LB
1987	DEN	N	3	LB
3 yrs.		29 games		

Vernon Joines
JOINES, VERNON WILLIS
B. Jun. 20, 1965, Charlotte, NC
Maryland 6'2" 200 lbs.

1989	CLE	N	4	WR
1990			16	WR
2 yrs.		20 games		

Evan Jolitz
JOLITZ, EVAN C.
B. Jul. 26, 1951, St. Mary's, OH
Xavier/Cincinnati 6'2" 225 lbs.

| 1974 | CIN | N | 12 | LB |

Al Jolley
JOLLEY, ALVIN JAY (Rocky)
B. Sep. 29, 1899, Onaga, KS
D. Aug. 26, 1948, Marietta, OH
Marietta/Tulsa/Kansas State 6'2" 220 lbs.

1922	AKR	N	10	T
1923	DAY	N	1	G
1923	OOR	N	3	T
1929	BUF	N	7	T, E
1930	BKN	N	8	T
1931	CLE	N	6	T
5 yrs.		35 games		

Gordon Jolley
JOLLEY, GORDON HAROLD
B. May 22, 1949, Provo, UT
Utah 6'5" 244 lbs.

1972	DET	N	5	OT
1973			14	OT
1974			11	OT
1975			2	G
1976	SEA	N	14	OT, G
1977			13	OT
6 yrs.		59 games		

Lewis Jolley
JOLLEY, LEWIS
B. Nov. 15, 1949, Bostic, NC
North Carolina 6'0" 210 lbs.

1972	HOU	N	7	RB
1973			10	RB
2 yrs.		17 games		

Ken Jolly
JOLLY, KENNETH CLAY
B. Feb. 28, 1962, Dallas, TX
Mid-America Nazarene 6'2" 220 lbs.

1984	KC		16	LB
1985			16	LB
2 yrs.		32 games		

Mike Jolly
JOLLY, MICHAEL ANTHONY JOSEPH
B. Mar. 19, 1958, Detroit, MI
Michigan 6'3" 185 lbs.

1980	GB	N	16	S
1982			7	S
1983			12	S
3 yrs.		35 games		

Don Jonas
JONAS, DON
B. Dec. 3, 1938, Scranton, PA

Don Jonas *continued*

Penn State 5'11" 195 lbs.

| 1962 | PHI | N | 1 | B |

Marv Jonas
JONAS, MARVIN FREDERICK
B. Apr. 25, 1909
D. Jan., 1987, Burbank, CA
Utah 5'11" 186 lbs.

| 1931 | BKN | N | 2 | G |

Charlie Jonasen
JONASEN, CHARLES
B. Dec. 20, 1890
D. Mar. 9, 1989, Minneapolis, MN
None

| 1921 | MIN | A | 1 | E |

Eric Jonassen
JONASSEN, ERIC GUSTAV
B. Aug. 16, 1968, Baltimore, MD
Penn State/Bloomsburg 6'5" 310 lbs.

1993	SD	N	16	OT
1994			16	OT
2 yrs.		32 games		

Aaron Jones
JONES, AARON DELMAS, II
B. Dec. 18, 1966, Orlando, FL
Eastern Kentucky 6'5" 251 lbs.

1988	PIT	N	15	DE
1989			16	DE, LB
1990			7	DE
1991			16	DE
1992			14	DE
1993	NE	N	11	DE, DT
1994			16	DE
1995			10	DE
1996	MIA	N	8	DE
9 yrs.		113 games		

A.J. Jones
JONES, ANTHONY LEVINE (Jam)
B. May 30, 1959, Youngstown, OH
Texas 6'1" 210 lbs.

1982	LARM	N	6	RB
1983			9	RB
1984			13	RB
1985			1	RB
1985	DET	N	8	RB
4 yrs.		37 games		

Andre Jones
JONES, ANDRE
B. May 15, 1969, Washington, DC
Notre Dame 6'2" 245 lbs.

| 1992 | DET | N | 9 | LB |

Anthony Jones
JONES, ANTHONY
B. May 16, 1960, Baltimore, MD
Maryland-Eastern Shore/Wichita State 6'3" 248 lbs.

1984	WAS	N	16	TE
1985			16	TE
1986			15	TE
1987			2	TE
1988			8	TE
1988	SD	N	4	TE
5 yrs.		61 games		

Arrington Jones
JONES, ARRINGTON, III
B. Feb. 10, 1959, Richmond, VA
Winston-Salem State 6'0" 225 lbs.

| 1981 | SF | N | 1 | RB |

Art Jones
JONES, ARTHUR EDWARD JONES, JR.
B. Jul. 13, 1919, Farmville, PA
Richmond 6'2" 192 lbs.

1941	PIT	N	11	HB
1945			7	HB
2 yrs.		18 games		

Ben Jones
JONES, BEN
B. 1900
Deceased
Grove City 5'11" 202 lbs.

1923	CAN	N	12	FB, HB
1924	CLE	N	8	FB, HB
1925	CAN	N	6	HB, FB
1925	FRA	N	4	FB, HB
1926			14	QB, FB, HB
1927	CHIC	N	9	QB, HB, FB
1928			5	FB, HB
6 yrs.		58 games		

Bert Jones
JONES, BERTRAM HAYS
B. Sep. 7, 1951, Ruston, LA
Louisiana State 6'3" 210 lbs.

1973	BAL	N	8	QB
1974			11	QB
1975			14	QB
1976			14	QB
1977			14	QB
1978			3	QB
1979			15	QB
1980			15	QB
1981			15	QB
1982	LARM	N	4	QB
10 yrs.		102 games		

Bill Jones
JONES, WILLIAM
B. Sep. 10, 1966, Abilene, TX
Southwest Texas State 5'11" 228 lbs.

1990	KC	N	16	RB
1991			15	RB
1992			7	RB
3 yrs.		38 games		

Billy Jones
JONES, WILLIAM H.
B. 1920
Morris Harvey/West Virginia Wesleyan 6'0" 220 lbs.

| 1947 | BKN | AA | 7 | G |

Bob Jones
JONES, BOB
B. Feb. 10, 1951, Boardman, FL
Virginia Union 6'1" 194 lbs.

1973	CIN	N	9	DB
1974			14	S
1975	ATL	N	14	DB
1976			14	CB, S
4 yrs.		51 games		

Bob Jones
JONES, ROBERT DEAN
B. Aug. 25, 1945, Warren, OH
San Diego State 6'1" 194 lbs.

1967	CHI	N	14	FL
1968			1	OE
2 yrs.		15 games		

Bob Jones
JONES, ROBERT J.
B. 1912
Indiana 6'2" 215 lbs.

| 1934 | GB | N | 13 | G |

Year	Team		Games	Pos.

Bobby Jones
JONES, ROBERT E.
B. Jul. 12, 1955, Sharon, PA
Youngstown State/Millikin 5'11" 180 lbs.

Year	Team		Games	Pos.
1978	NYJ	N	16	WR
1979			10	WR
1980			15	WR
1981			16	WR
1982			9	WR
1983	CLE	N	15	WR

6 yrs.   81 games

Boyd Jones
JONES, BOYD
B. May 30, 1961, Galveston, TX
Texas Southern 6'3" 265 lbs.

1984	GB	N	2	OT

Brent Jones
JONES, BRENT MICHAEL
B. Feb. 13, 1963, Santa Clara, CA
Santa Clara 6'4" 230 lbs.

1987	SF	N	4	TE
1988			11	TE
1989			16	TE
1990			16	TE
1991			10	TE
1992			15	TE
1993			16	TE
1994			15	TE
1995			16	TE
1996			11	TE

10 yrs.   130 games

Brian Jones
JONES, BRIAN KEITH
B. Jan. 22, 1968, Iowa City, IA
UCLA/Texas 6'1" 240 lbs.

1991	IND	N	11	LB
1995	NO	N	16	LB
1996			16	LB

3 yrs.   43 games

Bruce Jones
JONES, BRUCE
B. Apr. 19, 1905
D. Aug., 1978, Escondido, CA
Alabama 6'1" 219 lbs.

1927	GB	N	9	G, T
1928			13	G
1930	NEW	N	2	G, E
1932	BKN	N	12	G, E
1933			7	G
1934			10	G, T

6 yrs.   53 games

Bruce Jones
JONES, BRUCE WAYNE
B. Dec. 26, 1962, Courtland, AL
North Alabama 6'1" 197 lbs.

1987	PIT	N	2	CB, S

Bryant Jones
JONES, BRYANT LYDELL
B. Dec. 5, 1963
Toledo 5'11" 186 lbs.

1987	IND	N	3	CB

Calvin Jones
JONES, CALVIN
B. Jan. 26, 1951, San Francisco, CA
Washington 5'7" 170 lbs.

1973	DEN	N	14	DB
1974			14	DB
1975			8	CB
1976			10	CB

4 yrs.   46 games

Calvin Jones
JONES, CALVIN
B. Nov. 27, 1970, Omaha, NE
Nebraska 5'11" 212 lbs.

1994	LARI	N	7	RB
1995	OAK	N	9	RB
1996	GB	N	1	RB

3 yrs.   17 games

Cedric Jones
JONES, CEDRIC
B. Apr. 30, 1974, Houston, TX
Oklahoma 6'4" 275 lbs.

1996	NYG	N	16	DE

Cedric Jones
JONES, CEDRIC DECORRUS
B. Jun. 1, 1960, Norfolk, VA
Duke 6'1" 184 lbs.

1982	NE	N	2	WR
1983			15	WR
1984			14	WR
1985			16	WR
1986			16	WR
1987			12	WR
1988			16	WR
1989			15	WR
1990			14	WR

9 yrs.   120 games

Charlie Jones
JONES, CHARLES
B. 1929, Summers, AR
George Washington 6'1" 202 lbs.

1955	WAS	N	10	E

Charlie Jones
JONES, CHARLIE
B. Dec. 1, 1972, Hanford, CA
Fresno State 5'8" 175 lbs.

1996	SD	N	14	WR

Chris T. Jones
JONES, CHRIS TODD
B. Aug. 7, 1971, West Palm Beach, FL
Miami (Florida) 6'3" 209 lbs.

1995	PHI	N	13	WR
1996			16	WR

2 yrs.   29 games

Clarence Jones
JONES, CLARENCE
B. May 6, 1968, Brooklyn, NY
Maryland 6'6" 280 lbs.

1991	NYG	N	3	OT
1992			3	OT
1993			4	OT
1994	LARM	N	16	OT
1995	STL	N	13	OT
1996	NO	N	16	OT

6 yrs.   55 games

Clint Jones
JONES, CLINTON
B. May 24, 1945, Cleveland, OH
Michigan State 6'0" 206 lbs.

1967	MIN	N	14	RB
1968			12	RB
1969			14	RB
1970			14	RB
1971			14	RB
1972			7	RB
1973	SD	N	12	RB

7 yrs.   87 games

Cody Jones
JONES, CODY C.
B. May 3, 1951, San Francisco, CA
San Jose State 6'5" 241 lbs.

1974	LA	N	12	DE, DT
1975			14	DT
1976			14	DT
1977			14	DT, DE
1978			16	DT, DE
1980			15	DT
1981			16	DT
1982	LARM	N	9	DT

8 yrs.   110 games

Curt Jones
JONES, CURTIS
B. Dec. 20, 1943, Stanton, TN
Missouri 6'2" 245 lbs.

1968	SD	A	1	G

Dale Jones
JONES, DALE
B. Mar. 8, 1963
Tennessee 6'1" 234 lbs.

1987	DAL	N	3	LB

Dan Jones
JONES, DAN
B. Jul. 22, 1970, Malden, MA
Maine 6'7" 294 lbs.

1993	CIN	N	15	OT
1994			14	OT
1995			5	OT, G

3 yrs.   34 games

Dante Jones
JONES, DANTE DELANEO
B. Mar. 23, 1965, Dallas, TX
Oklahoma 6'1" 236 lbs.

1988	CHI	N	15	LB
1989			10	LB
1990			2	LB
1991			16	LB
1992			13	LB
1993			16	LB
1994			15	LB
1995	DEN	N	5	LB

8 yrs.   92 games

Daryll Jones
JONES, DARYLL KEITH
B. Mar. 23, 1962, Columbia, GA
Georgia 6'0" 190 lbs.

1984	GB	N	16	S
1985			8	S
1987	DEN	N	1	S

3 yrs.   25 games

Dave Jones
JONES, DAVID R.
B. Aug. 10, 1947, Goodland, KS
Kansas State 6'2" 185 lbs.

1969	CLE	N	13	WR
1970			14	WR
1971			14	WR

3 yrs.   41 games

David Jones
JONES, DAVID DENNISON
B. Nov. 9, 1968, East Orange, NJ
Delaware State 6'2" 220 lbs.

1992	LARI	N	16	TE

David Jones
JONES, DAVID J.
B. Oct. 25, 1961, Taipei, Taiwan

David Jones continued
Texas 6'3" 266 lbs.

1984	DET	N	10	C
1985			9	C
1987	DEN	N	3	G
1987	WAS	N	5	C

3 yrs.   27 games

Deacon Jones
JONES, DAVID (The Secretary of Defense)
B. Dec. 9, 1938, Eatonville, FL
South Carolina State 6'5" 254 lbs.

1961	LA	N	14	DE
1962			13	DE
1963			14	DE
1964			14	DE
1965			14	DE
1966			14	DE
1967			14	DE
1968			14	DE
1969			14	DE
1970			14	DE
1971			11	DE
1972	SD	N	14	DE
1973			12	DE
1974	WAS	N	14	DE

14 yrs.   190 games

Don Jones
JONES, DONALD RAY
B. Mar. 26, 1969, Lynchburg, VA
Washington 6'0" 231 lbs.

1992	NYJ	N	2	LB
1993			6	LB

2 yrs.   8 games

Donta Jones
JONES, MARKEYSIA DONTA
B. Aug. 27, 1972, Washington, DC
Nebraska 6'2" 226 lbs.

1995	PIT	N	16	LB
1996			15	LB

2 yrs.   31 games

Doug Jones
JONES, DOUGLAS CHARLES
B. May 31, 1950, San Diego, CA
Arizona State/Cal. State-Northridge 6'2" 204 lbs.

1973	KC	N	4	DB
1974			14	DB
1976	BUF	N	14	CB, S
1977			14	S
1978			12	S
1979	DET	N	10	CB

6 yrs.   68 games

Drew Jones
JONES, ANDREW
B. Oct. 23, 1952, Jackson, MS
Washington State 6'2" 216 lbs.

1975	NO	N	13	RB
1976			2	RB

2 yrs.   15 games

Dub Jones
JONES, WILLIAM AUGUSTUS
B. Dec. 29, 1924, Arcadia, LA
Tulane/Louisiana State 6'4" 202 lbs.

1946	MIA	AA	9	HB
1946	BKN	AA	2	HB
1947			8	B
1948	CLE	AA	12	B
1949			11	B
1950	CLE	N	12	HB
1951			12	HB
1952			12	HB

Year	Team		Games	Pos.

Dub Jones *continued*

Year	Team		Games	Pos.
1953			12	HB
1954			12	HB
1955			12	HB
10 yrs.	114 games			

Earl Jones
JONES, DARREL EARL
B. Jul. 19, 1957, Tuscaloosa, AL
Norfolk State 6'0" 178 lbs.

1980	ATL	N	16	CB
1981			16	CB
1982			9	CB
1983			16	CB
4 yrs.	57 games			

Ed Jones
JONES, EDWARD (Too Small)
B. Jun. 29, 1952, Long Branch, NJ
Rutgers 6'0" 185 lbs.

| 1975 | BUF | N | 12 | S |

Ed Jones
JONES, EDWARD LEE (Too Tall)
B. Feb. 23, 1951, Jackson, TN
Tennessee State 6'9" 270 lbs.

1974	DAL	N	14	DE, DT
1975			14	DE
1976			14	DE
1977			14	DE
1978			16	DE
1980			16	DE
1981			16	DE
1982			9	DE
1983			16	DE
1984			16	DE
1985			16	DE
1986			16	DE
1987			15	DE
1988			16	DE
1989			16	DE
15 yrs.	224 games			

Edgar Jones
JONES, EDGAR F. (Special Delivery)
B. May 6, 1920, Scranton, PA
Pittsburg 5'10" 193 lbs.

1945	CHIB	N	1	HB
1946	CLE	AA	14	HB
1947			9	B
1948			13	B
1949			7	B
5 yrs.	44 games			

E.J. Jones
JONES, EARNEST
B. Feb. 1, 1962, Chicago, IL
Kansas 5'11" 212 lbs.

1985	KC	N	5	RB
1987	DAL	N	3	RB
2 yrs.	8 games			

Ellis Jones
JONES, ELLIS NATHANIEL
B. Mar. 16, 1921, Abilene, TX
Tulsa 6'0" 190 lbs.

| 1945 | BOS | N | 8 | G |

Elmer Jones
JONES, ELMER JOHN
B. 1920, Buffalo, NY
Deceased
Wake Forest 6'0" 224 lbs.

1946	BUF	AA	12	G
1947	DET	N	10	G
1948			9	G
3 yrs.	31 games			

Ernie Jones
JONES, ERNEST
B. Jan. 3, 1953, Boca Raton, FL
Miami (Florida) 6'3" 180 lbs.

1976	SEA	N	9	CB
1977	NYG	N	14	S
1978			16	S
1979			5	S
4 yrs.	44 games			

Ernie Jones
JONES, ERNEST LEE
B. Dec. 15, 1964, Elkhart, IN
Indiana 5'11" 186 lbs.

1988	PHX	N	16	WR
1989			15	WR
1990			15	WR
1991			16	WR
1992			11	WR
1993	LARM	N	10	WR
6 yrs.	83 games			

Ernie Jones
JONES, ERNEST LEE
B. Apr. 1, 1971, Utica, NY
Oregon 6'2" 270 lbs.

1995	NO	N	1	DE
1996	DEN	N	6	DT
2 yrs.	7 games			

Ezell Jones
JONES, EZELL
B. Jul. 11, 1947, Collierville, TN
Minnesota 6'4" 255 lbs.

1969	BOS	A	14	OT
1970	BOS	N	4	OT
2 yrs.	18 games			

Fred Jones
JONES, FRED
B. 1965
Florida State 6'3" 240 lbs.

| 1987 | KC | N | 2 | CB |

Fred Jones
JONES, FREDERICK CORNELIUS
B. Mar. 6, 1967, Atlanta, GA
Grambling State 5'9" 175 lbs.

1990	KC	N	6	WR
1991			11	WR
1992			14	WR
1993			10	WR
4 yrs.	41 games			

Gary Jones
JONES, GARY DEWAYNE
B. Nov. 30, 1967, San Augustine, TX
Texas A&M 6'1" 203 lbs.

1990	PIT	N	16	CB
1991			9	S
1993			13	S
1994			14	S
1995	NYJ	N	11	S
1996			15	S
6 yrs.	78 games			

Gene Jones
JONES, EUGENE
B. Oct. 18, 1936, Woodson, TX
Rice 6'0" 200 lbs.

| 1961 | HOU | A | 1 | LB |

Gordon Jones
JONES, GORDON
B. Jul. 25, 1957, Buffalo, NY
Pittsburg 6'0" 190 lbs.

| 1979 | TB | N | 12 | WR |

Gordon Jones *continued*

1980			16	WR
1981			13	WR
1982			9	WR
1983	LARM	N	11	WR
5 yrs.	61 games			

Greg Jones
JONES, GREGORY MARTIN
B. Feb. 2, 1948, San Francisco, CA
UCLA 6'1" 200 lbs.

1970	BUF	N	10	RB
1971			14	RB
2 yrs.	24 games			

Harris Jones
JONES, HARRIS
B. Oct. 3, 1945, Lake City, SC
Johnson C. Smith 6'4" 241 lbs.

1971	SD	N	11	G
1973	HOU	N	5	G
1974			11	G
3 yrs.	27 games			

Harry Jones
JONES, HARRY
B. Jul. 25, 1945, Huntington, WV
Arkansas 6'2" 205 lbs.

1967	PHI	N	11	RB
1968			4	RB
1969			12	RB
1970			2	RB
4 yrs.	29 games			

Hassan Jones
JONES, HASSAN AMEER
B. Jul. 2, 1964, Clearwater, FL
Florida State 6'0" 195 lbs.

1986	MIN	N	16	WR
1987			12	WR
1988			16	WR
1989			16	WR
1990			15	WR
1991			16	WR
1992			9	WR
1993	KC	N	8	WR
8 yrs.	108 games			

Harvey Jones
JONES, HARVEY M.
B. Apr. 15, 1921, Beaumont, TX
Baylor 6'0" 175 lbs.

1944	CLE	N	9	FB, QB, HB
1945			9	HB
2 yrs.	18 games			

Henry Jones
JONES, HENRY
B. Dec. 29, 1967, St. Louis, MO
Illinois 5'11" 197 lbs.

1991	BUF	N	15	S
1992			16	S
1993			16	S
1994			16	S
1995			13	S
1996			5	S
6 yrs.	81 games			

Henry Jones
JONES, HENRY D.
B. Feb. 24, 1946, Baton Rouge, LA
Grambling State 6'2" 235 lbs.

| 1969 | DEN | A | 2 | RB |

Homer Jones
JONES, HOMER CARROLL

Homer Jones *continued*

B. Feb. 18, 1941, Pittsburg, TX
Texas Southern 6'2" 211 lbs.

1964	NYG	N	3	HB
1965			14	FL
1966			14	FL
1967			14	OE
1968			14	OE
1969			14	WR
1970	CLE	N	14	WR
7 yrs.	87 games			

Horace Jones
JONES, HORACE ARTHUR
B. Jul. 31, 1949, Pensacola, FL
Louisville 6'3" 251 lbs.

1971	OAK	N	14	DE
1972			14	DE
1973			14	DE
1974			14	DE
1975			14	DE
1977	SEA	N	1	DE
6 yrs.	71 games			

James Jones
JONES, JAMES
B. Oct. 24, 1964
North Carolina A&T 6'5" 250 lbs.

| 1987 | NYG | N | 3 | C |

James Jones
JONES, JAMES, JR.
B. Dec. 6, 1958, Vicksburg, MS
Mississippi State 5'10" 201 lbs.

1980	DAL	N	16	RB
1981			16	RB
1982			5	RB
1984			9	RB
1985			16	RB
5 yrs.	62 games			

James Jones
JONES, JAMES ALFIE
B. Feb. 6, 1969, Davenport, IA
Northern Iowa 6'2" 292 lbs.

1991	CLE	N	16	DL
1992			16	DE, DT
1993			16	DT
1994			16	DT
1995	DEN	N	16	DT
1996	BAL	N	16	DT
6 yrs.	96 games			

James Jones
JONES, JAMES ROOSEVELT
B. Mar. 21, 1961, Pompano Beach, FL
Florida 6'2" 229 lbs.

1983	DET	N	14	RB
1984			16	FB
1985			14	FB
1986			16	RB
1987			11	FB
1988			14	RB
1989	SEA	N	2	RB
1990			16	RB
1991			16	RB
1992			16	RB
10 yrs.	135 games			

Jeff Jones
JONES, JEFF RAYMOND
B. May 30, 1972, Killeen, TX
Texas A&M 6'6" 310 lbs.

1995	DET	N	2	OT
1996			7	OT
2 yrs.	9 games			

Year	Team	Games	Pos.

Jerry Jones
JONES, GERALD
B. 1894
Deceased
Notre Dame 6'1" 205 lbs.

Year	Team		Games	Pos.
1920	DEC	A	8	G
1922	RI	N	5	G
1923	TOL	N	8	G, T
1924	CLE	N	5	G

4 yrs.   26 games

Jerry Jones
JONES, JERRY
B. Feb. 14, 1944, Dayton, OH
Bowling Green 6'3" 269 lbs.

Year	Team		Games	Pos.
1966	ATL	N	7	DT
1967	NO	N	9	OT
1968			14	OT
1969			14	OT

4 yrs.   44 games

Jim Jones
JONES, JAMES
B. 1936
Washington 6'1" 204 lbs.

Year	Team		Games	Pos.
1958	LA	N	12	HB
1961	OAK	A	1	FB

2 yrs.   13 games

Jim Jones
JONES, JAMES ALEXANDER (Casey)
B. Dec. 15, 1920, Florence, AL
D. Dec., 1979, Sneedville, TN
Union (Tennessee) 6'0" 180 lbs.

Year	Team		Games	Pos.
1946	DET	N	1	B

Jimmie Jones
JONES, JIMMIE
B. Jan. 17, 1947, Columbia, SC
Wichita State 6'3" 215 lbs.

Year	Team		Games	Pos.
1969	NY	A	14	LB
1970	NYJ	N	3	DE
1971	WAS	N	14	DE
1972			3	DE
1973			6	DE

5 yrs.   40 games

Jimmie Jones
JONES, JIMMIE SIMS
B. Jan. 9, 1966, Lakeland, FL
Miami (Florida) 6'4" 278 lbs.

Year	Team		Games	Pos.
1990	DAL	N	16	DT
1991			16	DT
1992			16	DE, DT
1993			15	DT
1994	LARM	N	14	DT
1995	STL	N	16	NT
1996			14	DT

7 yrs.   107 games

Jimmie Lee Jones
JONES, JIMMIE LEE
B. Jun. 14, 1950, Los Angeles, CA
UCLA 5'10" 205 lbs.

Year	Team		Games	Pos.
1974	DET	N	14	RB

Jimmy Jones
JONES, JAMES CLYDE
B. Mar. 3, 1941, Henderson, NC
Wisconsin 6'2" 189 lbs.

Year	Team		Games	Pos.
1965	CHI	N	13	OE
1966			14	OE
1967			14	OE
1968	DEN	A	13	WR

4 yrs.   54 games

J.J. Jones
JONES, JOHN J.
B. Apr. 16, 1952
Fisk 6'1" 180 lbs.

Year	Team		Games	Pos.
1975	NYJ	N	7	QB

Jock Jones
JONES, JOCK STACEY
B. Mar. 13, 1968, Ashland, VA
Virginia Tech 6'2" 235 lbs.

Year	Team		Games	Pos.
1990	CLE	N	11	LB
1991			9	LB
1991	PHX	N	5	LB
1992			14	LB
1993			7	LB

4 yrs.   46 games

Joe Jones
JONES, JOE
B. Jun. 26, 1962, Windber, PA
Virginia Tech 6'5" 255 lbs.

Year	Team		Games	Pos.
1987	IND	N	3	TE

Joe Jones
JONES, JOE WILLIE (Turkey)
B. Jan. 7, 1948, Dallas, TX
Tennessee State 6'6" 249 lbs.

Year	Team		Games	Pos.
1970	CLE	N	14	DE
1971			14	DE
1973			14	DE
1974	PHI	N	14	DE
1975			7	DE
1975	CLE	N	7	DE
1976			14	DE
1977			14	DE
1978			14	DE
1979	WAS	N	16	DE
1980			7	DE

10 yrs.   135 games

Joey Jones
JONES, JOSEPH RUSSELL
B. Oct. 29, 1962, Mobile, AL
Alabama 5'8" 165 lbs.

Year	Team		Games	Pos.
1986	ATL	N	11	WR

Johnny Jones
JONES, JOHNNY (Lam)
B. Apr. 4, 1958, Lawton, OK
Texas 5'11" 190 lbs.

Year	Team		Games	Pos.
1980	NYJ	N	16	WR
1981			15	WR
1982			8	WR
1983			14	WR
1984			8	WR

5 yrs.   61 games

June Jones
JONES, JUNE SHELDON, III
B. Feb. 19, 1953, Portland, OR
Oregon/Hawaii/Portland State 6'4" 200 lbs.

Year	Team		Games	Pos.
1977	ATL	N	1	QB
1978			7	QB
1979			5	QB
1981			4	QB

4 yrs.   17 games

Keith Jones
JONES, KEITH
B. Feb. 5, 1966, Omaha, NE
Nebraska 5'10" 182 lbs.

Year	Team		Games	Pos.
1989	CLE	N	16	RB

Keith Jones
JONES, KEITH

Keith Jones *continued*
B. Mar. 20, 1966, Rock Hill, MO
Illinois 6'1" 210 lbs.

Year	Team		Games	Pos.
1989	ATL	N	14	RB
1990			15	RB
1991			5	WR
1992			16	RB

4 yrs.   50 games

Ken Jones
JONES, KENNETH EUGENE
B. Dec. 1, 1962, St. Louis, MO
Arkansas State 6'5" 270 lbs.

Year	Team		Games	Pos.
1976	BUF	N	12	DE
1977			14	G, OT
1978			16	OT
1979			16	OT
1980			16	OT
1981			15	OT
1982			9	OT
1983			16	OT
1984			16	OT
1985			16	OT
1986			12	OT
1987	NYJ	N	3	OT

12 yrs.   161 games

Ken Jones
JONES, KENNETH H.
B. Sep. 2, 1897
D. Jan., 1983, Solsville, NY
Franklin & Marshall 6'3" 185 lbs.

Year	Team		Games	Pos.
1924	BUF	N	5	HB, E

Kim Jones
JONES, KIM RICHARD
B. Jan. 19, 1952, Waterloo, IA
Colorado State 6'4" 238 lbs.

Year	Team		Games	Pos.
1976	NO	N	11	RB
1977			14	RB
1978			16	RB
1979			2	FB

4 yrs.   43 games

LaCurtis Jones
JONES, LACURTIS
B. Jun. 23, 1972, Waco, TX
Baylor 6'0" 200 lbs.

Year	Team		Games	Pos.
1996	TB	N	10	LB

Larry Jones
JONES, LAWRENCE ALLEN
B. Mar. 4, 1951, Lemoore, CA
Northeast Missouri State 5'10" 170 lbs.

Year	Team		Games	Pos.
1974	WAS	N	13	CB
1975			14	CB
1976			1	CB
1977			14	WR
1978	SF	N	9	WR

5 yrs.   51 games

Lenoy Jones
JONES, LENOY
B. Sep. 25, 1974, Groesbeck, TX
Texas Christian 6'1" 232 lbs.

Year	Team		Games	Pos.
1996	HOU	N	11	LB

Leonard Jones
JONES, LEONARD DEWAYNE
B. Oct. 28, 1964, St. Louis, MO
Texas Tech 6'0" 187 lbs.

Year	Team		Games	Pos.
1987	DEN	N	2	S

Leroy Jones
JONES, LEROY

Leroy Jones *continued*
B. Sep. 29, 1950, Greenwood, NJ
Norfolk State 6'8" 261 lbs.

Year	Team		Games	Pos.
1976	SD	N	14	DE
1977			14	DE
1978			16	DE
1979			16	DE
1980			15	DE
1981			16	DE
1982			8	DE
1983			12	DE

8 yrs.   111 games

Lew Jones
JONES, LEWIS
B. Nov. 3, 1911
D. Sep., 1970
Weatherford JC 6'0" 215 lbs.

Year	Team		Games	Pos.
1943	BKN	N	10	G

Lyndell Jones
JONES, ANTHONY LYNDELL
B. Mar. 18, 1959, Seattle, WA
Hawaii 5'9" 175 lbs.

Year	Team		Games	Pos.
1987	ATL	N	3	CB

Marcus Jones
JONES, MARCUS
B. Aug. 15, 1973, Jacksonville, FL
North Carolina 6'6" 280 lbs.

Year	Team		Games	Pos.
1996	TB	N	16	DT

Marlon Jones
JONES, MARLON
B. Jul. 1, 1964, Baltimore, MD
Central State (Ohio) 6'4" 260 lbs.

Year	Team		Games	Pos.
1987	CLE	N	1	RB
1988			16	DE
1989			12	DE

3 yrs.   29 games

Marshall Jones
JONES, MARSHALL D. (Deacon)
B. Dec. 10, 1894
Deceased
North Dakota 5'11" 165 lbs.

Year	Team		Games	Pos.
1920	HAM	A	1	HB
1920	DET	A	1	HB
1921	AKR	A	7	HB, FB

2 yrs.   9 games

Marvin Jones
JONES, MARVIN MAURICE
B. Jun. 28, 1972, Miami, FL
Florida State 6'2" 240 lbs.

Year	Team		Games	Pos.
1993	NYJ	N	9	LB
1994			15	LB
1995			10	LB
1996			12	LB

4 yrs.   46 games

Melvin Jones
JONES, MELVIN
B. Sep. 27, 1955, Houston, TX
Houston 6'2" 260 lbs.

Year	Team		Games	Pos.
1981	WAS	N	11	G

Mike Jones
JONES, MICHAEL
B. Aug. 14, 1964, New York, NY
SUNY-Brockport 6'4" 224 lbs.

Year	Team		Games	Pos.
1987	BUF	N	1	LB

Mike Jones
JONES, MICHAEL ANTHONY

Year	Team		Games	Pos.

Mike Jones *continued*

B. Apr. 14, 1960, Chattanooga, TN
Tennessee State 5'11" 180 lbs.

Year	Team		Games	Pos.
1983	MIN	N	16	WR
1984			16	WR
1985			16	WR
1986	NO	N	16	WR
1987			12	WR
1989			3	WR
6 yrs.		79 games		

Mike Jones

JONES, MICHAEL ANTHONY
B. Apr. 15, 1969, Kansas City, MO
Missouri 6'1" 228 lbs.

Year	Team		Games	Pos.
1991	LARI	N	16	LB
1992			16	LB
1993			16	LB
1994			16	LB
1995	OAK	N	16	LB
1996			15	LB
6 yrs.		95 games		

Mike Jones

JONES, MICHAEL DAVID
B. Aug. 25, 1969, Columbia, SC
North Carolina State 6'4" 288 lbs.

Year	Team		Games	Pos.
1991	PHX	N	16	DL
1992			15	DE, DT
1993			16	DE, DT
1994	NE	N	16	DE
1995			13	DE, NT
1996			16	DE
6 yrs.		92 games		

Mike Jones

JONES, MICHAEL LENERE
B. Nov. 10, 1966, Bridgeport, CT
Texas A&M 6'3" 255 lbs.

Year	Team		Games	Pos.
1990	MIN	N	11	TE
1991			16	TE
1992	SEA	N	4	TE
3 yrs.		31 games		

Mike Jones

JONES, MIKE
B. Jul. 12, 1954, Chicago, IL
Alcorn State 6'2" 214 lbs.

Year	Team		Games	Pos.
1977	SEA	N	12	LB

Quintin Jones

JONES, QUINTIN MAURICE
B. Jul. 28, 1966, Miami, FL
Pittsburgh 5'11" 193 lbs.

Year	Team		Games	Pos.
1988	HOU	N	4	CB
1990			1	S
2 yrs.		5 games		

Ralph Jones

JONES, RALPH
None

Year	Team		Games	Pos.
1921	HAM	A	1	HB

Ralph Jones

JONES, RALPH CARROLL
B. Feb. 15, 1922, Florence, AL
Union (Tennessee)/Alabama 6'3" 200 lbs.

Year	Team		Games	Pos.
1946	DET	N	11	E
1947	BAL	AA	6	E
2 yrs.		17 games		

Ray Jones

JONES, RAYMOND
B. Dec. 24, 1947, Lufkin, TX
Southern University 6'0" 187 lbs.

Year	Team		Games	Pos.
1970	PHI	N	12	DB

Ray Jones *continued*

Year	Team		Games	Pos.
1971			2	DB
1972	SD	N	14	CB
3 yrs.		28 games		

Reggie Jones

JONES, REGGIE
B. May 5, 1971, Kansas City, MO
Louisiana State 6'0" 175 lbs.*

Year	Team		Games	Pos.
1995	CAR	N	1	WR

Reggie Jones

JONES, REGINALD MOORE
B. Jan. 11, 1969, Memphis, TN
Memphis State 6'1" 202 lbs.

Year	Team		Games	Pos.
1991	NO	N	13	CB
1992			15	CB
1993			12	CB
1994			1	CB
4 yrs.		41 games		

Reno Jones

JONES, RENO V.
B. Feb. 20, 1897
D. Jan. 7, 1989, Wyckoff, NJ
Cornell 6'0" 195 lbs.

Year	Team		Games	Pos.
1922	TOL	N	3	G

Richard Jones

JONES, RICHARD
B. Aug. 4, 1973, Waco, TX
Texas A&M-Kingsville 5'9" 174 lbs.

Year	Team		Games	Pos.
1996	IND	N	3	S

Ricky Jones

JONES, BRODERICK
B. Mar. 9, 1955, Birmingham, AL
Tuskegee Institute 6'2" 215 lbs.

Year	Team		Games	Pos.
1977	CLE	N	3	S
1978			15	DB
1979			16	S
1980	BAL	N	12	LB
1981			16	LB
1982			9	LB
1983			16	LB
7 yrs.		87 games		

Robbie Jones

JONES, ROBERT WASHINGTON
B. Dec. 25, 1959, Demopolis, AL
Alabama 6'2" 230 lbs.

Year	Team		Games	Pos.
1984	NYG	N	16	LB
1985			16	LB
1986			16	LB
1987			12	LB
4 yrs.		60 games		

Robert Jones

JONES, ROBERT LEE
B. Sep. 27, 1969, Blackstone, VA
East Carolina 6'2" 238 lbs.

Year	Team		Games	Pos.
1992	DAL	N	15	LB
1993			13	LB
1994			16	LB
1995			12	LB
1996	STL	N	16	LB
5 yrs.		72 games		

Rod Jones

JONES, ROD
B. Jan. 11, 1974, Detroit, MI
Kansas 6'4" 315 lbs.

Year	Team		Games	Pos.
1996	CIN	N	3	G

Rod Jones

JONES, RODERICK EARL
B. Mar. 3, 1964, Richmond, CA
Washington 6'4" 242 lbs.

Year	Team		Games	Pos.
1987	KC	N	3	TE
1988			2	TE
1989	SEA	N	4	TE
3 yrs.		9 games		

Rod Jones

JONES, RODERICK WAYNE
B. Mar. 31, 1964, Dallas, TX
Southern Methodist 6'0" 175 lbs.

Year	Team		Games	Pos.
1986	TB	N	16	CB, S
1987			11	DB
1988			14	CB
1989			16	CB, S
1990	CIN	N	16	CB
1991			4	CB
1992			16	CB
1993			16	CB
1994			16	CB
1995			13	CB
1996			8	CB
11 yrs.		146 games		

Roger Jones

JONES, ROGER CARVER
B. Apr. 22, 1969, Cleveland, OH
Tennessee State 5'9" 175 lbs.

Year	Team		Games	Pos.
1991	TB	N	6	CB
1992			9	CB
1993			16	CB
1994	CIN	N	16	CB
1995			16	CB
1996			14	CB
6 yrs.		77 games		

Ron Jones

JONES, RONALD
B. Jul. 17, 1947, Dallas, TX
Texas-El Paso 6'3" 220 lbs.

Year	Team		Games	Pos.
1969	GB	N	6	TE

Rondell Jones

JONES, RONDELL TONY
B. May 7, 1971, Sunderland, MA
North Carolina 6'2" 210 lbs.

Year	Team		Games	Pos.
1993	DEN	N	16	S
1994			16	S
1995			14	S
1996			16	S
4 yrs.		62 games		

Rulon Jones

JONES, RULON KENT
B. Mar. 25, 1958, Salt Lake City, UT
Utah State 6'6" 260 lbs.

Year	Team		Games	Pos.
1980	DEN	N	16	DE
1981			16	DE
1982			9	DE
1983			12	DE
1984			16	DE
1985			16	DE
1986			16	DE
1987			12	DE
1988			16	DE
9 yrs.		129 games		

Scott Jones

JONES, ROBERT SCOTT
B. Mar. 20, 1966, Portland, OR
Washington 6'5" 281 lbs.

Year	Team		Games	Pos.
1989	CIN	N	15	OT
1990	NYJ	N	3	OT
1991	GB	N	2	OT
1991	CIN	N	2	OT
3 yrs.		22 games		

Sean Jones

JONES, DWIGHT SEAN
B. Dec. 19, 1962, Kingston, Jamaica
Northeastern 6'7" 275 lbs.

Year	Team		Games	Pos.
1984	LARI	N	16	DE
1985			15	DE
1986			16	DE
1987			12	DE
1988	HOU	N	16	DE
1989			16	DE
1990			16	DE
1991			16	DE
1992			15	DE
1993			16	DE
1994	GB	N	16	DE
1995			16	DE
1996			15	DE
13 yrs.		201 games		

Selwyn Jones

JONES, SELWYN ALDRIDGE
B. May 13, 1970, Houston, TX
Colorado State 6'0" 185 lbs.

Year	Team		Games	Pos.
1993	CLE	N	11	CB
1994	NO	N	5	CB
1995	SEA	N	15	CB
1996			16	CB
4 yrs.		47 games		

Shawn Jones

JONES, ANDREW SHAWN
B. Jun. 16, 1970, Thomasville, GA
Georgia Tech 6'1" 200 lbs.

Year	Team		Games	Pos.
1993	MIN	N	1	S

Spike Jones

JONES, JOHN AMOS
B. Jul. 9, 1947, Louisville, GA
Middle Georgia/Georgia 6'2" 191 lbs.*

Year	Team		Games	Pos.
1970	HOU	N	14	P
1971	BUF	N	13	P
1972			14	P
1973			14	P
1974			8	P
1975	PHI	N	12	P
1976			14	P
1977			14	P
8 yrs.		103 games		

Stan Jones

JONES, STANLEY PAUL
B. Nov. 24, 1931, Altoona, PA
Maryland 6'1" 252 lbs.

Year	Team		Games	Pos.
1954	CHIB	N	12	T
1955			12	G
1956			11	C
1957			12	G
1958			12	T
1959			12	G
1960	CHI	N	12	G
1961			14	G
1962			14	G
1963			13	G
1964			14	DT
1965			6	DT
1966	WAS	N	13	DT
13 yrs.		157 games		

Steve Jones

JONES, STEVE HUNTER
B. Mar. 6, 1951, Sanford, NC
Duke 6'0" 199 lbs.

Year	Team		Games	Pos.
1973	BUF	N	11	RB
1974			4	RB
1974	STL	N	7	RB
1975			13	RB
1976			13	RB
1977			14	RB
1978			16	RB
6 yrs.		78 games		

Year	Team	Games	Pos.

Terry Jones
JONES, TERRY WAYNE
B. Nov. 8, 1956, Sandersville, GA
Alabama 6'2" 259 lbs.

Year	Team		Games	Pos.
1978	**GB**	N	16	DT
1979			12	DT
1980			15	DT
1981			16	DT
1982			9	NT
1983			1	NT
1984			16	DT

7 yrs. 85 games

Thurman Jones
JONES, THURMAN L. (Tugboat)
B. Apr. 6, 1918, Wilson, OK
D. Nov. 16, 1988, Tidwell, TX
Abilene Christian 5'10" 198 lbs.

Year	Team		Games	Pos.
1941	**BKN**	N	1	B
1942			5	B, G

2 yrs. 6 games

Todd Jones
JONES, TODD
B. Jul. 3, 1967, Hope, AR
Arkansas/Henderson State 6'3" 295 lbs.

Year	Team		Games	Pos.
1993	**NE**	N	4	C

Tom Jones
JONES, THOMAS
B. Jun. 22, 1931
D. Aug. 28, 1978, Port Chevron, Canada
Miami (Ohio) 6'6" 300 lbs.

Year	Team		Games	Pos.
1955	**CLE**	N	2	T

Tom Jones
JONES, THOMAS CLINTON (Potsy)
B. Oct. 15, 1909, Llewellyn, PA
D. Jul. 3, 1990, Lucama, NC
Bucknell 5'11" 216 lbs.

Year	Team		Games	Pos.
1930	**FRA**	N	12	G
1930	**MIN**	N	1	G
1930	**FRA**	N	2	G
1930	**MIN**	N	1	G
1931	**FRA**	N	8	G, T
1932	**NYG**	N	10	G
1933			6	G
1934			12	G
1935			9	G
1936			10	G
1938	**GB**	N	8	G

8 yrs. 79 games

Tony Jones
JONES, ANTHONY BERNARD
B. Dec. 30, 1965, Grapeland, TX
Texas 5'7" 145 lbs.

Year	Team		Games	Pos.
1990	**HOU**	N	15	WR
1991			16	WR
1992	**ATL**	N	10	WR
1993	**HOU**	N	2	WR

4 yrs. 43 games

Tony Jones
JONES, TONY
B. Feb. 16, 1971, Tampa, FL
Syracuse 6'4" 200 lbs.

Year	Team		Games	Pos.
1995	**ARI**	N	2	S

Tony Jones
JONES, TONY EDWARD
B. May 24, 1966, Royston, GA
Western Carolina 6'5" 280 lbs.

Year	Team		Games	Pos.
1988	**CLE**	N	4	OT
1989			9	OT

Tony Jones continued

Year	Team		Games	Pos.
1990			16	OT
1991			16	OT
1992			16	OT
1993			16	OT
1994			16	OT
1995			16	OT
1996	**BAL**	N	15	OT

9 yrs. 124 games

Tyrone Jones
JONES, TYRONE
B. Aug. 3, 1961, St. Mary's, GA
Southern University 6'0" 220 lbs.

Year	Team		Games	Pos.
1988	**PHX**	N	1	LB

Tyrone Jones
JONES, TYRONE
B. Nov. 9, 1966, Ruston, LA
Arkansas State 6'4" 223 lbs.

Year	Team		Games	Pos.
1989	**PHI**	N	3	S

Victor Jones
JONES, VICTOR PERNELL
B. Oct. 19, 1966, Rockville, MD
Virginia Tech 6'2" 250 lbs.

Year	Team		Games	Pos.
1988	**TB**	N	8	LB
1989	**DET**	N	11	LB
1990			16	LB
1991			10	LB
1992			16	LB
1993			16	LB
1994			16	LB

7 yrs. 93 games

Victor Jones
JONES, VICTOR TYRONE
B. Dec. 5, 1967, Zachary, LA
Louisiana State 5'8" 214 lbs.

Year	Team		Games	Pos.
1990	**HOU**	N	10	RB
1991			14	RB
1992	**DEN**	N	16	RB
1993	**PIT**	N	16	RB
1994			10	RB
1994	**KC**	N	1	RB

5 yrs. 67 games

Wayne Jones
JONES, WAYNE WALTER
B. May 10, 1960, Grand Island, NE
Utah 6'4" 270 lbs.

Year	Team		Games	Pos.
1987	**MIN**	N	6	G

Willie Jones
JONES, WILLIE
B. 1940
Purdue 5'11" 208 lbs.

Year	Team		Games	Pos.
1962	**BUF**	A	10	FB

Willie Jones
JONES, WILLIE LEE
B. May 28, 1942, Moro, AR
Kansas State 6'2" 260 lbs.

Year	Team		Games	Pos.
1967	**HOU**	A	6	DE
1968	**CIN**	A	1	DE
1970	**CIN**	N	10	DT
1971			5	DT

4 yrs. 22 games

Willie Jones
JONES, WILLIE LORENZO
B. Nov. 22, 1957, Dublin, GA
Florida State 6'4" 244 lbs.

Year	Team		Games	Pos.
1979	**OAK**	N	16	DE
1980			16	DE
1981			8	DE

3 yrs. 40 games

Andrew Jordan
JORDAN, ANDREW
B. Jun. 21, 1972, Charlotte, NC
Western Carolina 6'4" 268 lbs.

Year	Team		Games	Pos.
1994	**MIN**	N	16	TE
1995			13	TE
1996			13	TE

3 yrs. 42 games

Brian Jordan
JORDAN, BRIAN O'NEIL
B. Mar. 29, 1967, Baltimore, MD
Richmond 5'11" 202 lbs.

Year	Team		Games	Pos.
1989	**ATL**	N	4	S
1990			16	S
1991			16	S

3 yrs. 36 games

Buford Jordan
JORDAN, PAUL BUFORD
B. Jun. 26, 1962, Lafayette, IN
McNeese State 6'0" 223 lbs.

Year	Team		Games	Pos.
1986	**NO**	N	16	RB
1987			12	FB
1988			14	RB
1989			11	RB
1990			6	RB
1991			14	RB
1992			2	RB

7 yrs. 75 games

Charles Jordan
JORDAN, CHARLES
B. Oct. 9, 1969, Los Angeles, CA
Long Beach CC 5'10" 170 lbs.

Year	Team		Games	Pos.
1994	**GB**	N	10	WR
1995			6	WR
1996	**MIA**	N	6	WR

3 yrs. 22 games

Curtis Jordan
JORDAN, CURTIS WAYNE
B. Jan. 25, 1954, Lubbock, TX
Texas Tech 6'2" 200 lbs.

Year	Team		Games	Pos.
1976	**TB**	N	11	DB
1977			12	S
1978			16	CB, S
1979			16	CB, S
1980			16	S, CB
1981	**WAS**	N	2	DB
1982			9	CB, S
1983			15	CB, S
1984			16	S
1985			16	S
1986			16	S

11 yrs. 145 games

Darin Jordan
JORDAN, DARIN GODFREY
B. Dec. 4, 1964, Boston, MA
Northeastern 6'1" 235 lbs.

Year	Team		Games	Pos.
1988	**PIT**	N	15	LB
1991	**SF**	N	15	LB
1992			15	LB
1993			14	LB

4 yrs. 59 games

David Jordan
JORDAN, DAVID TURNER
B. Jul. 14, 1962, Birmingham, AL
Auburn 6'6" 276 lbs.

Year	Team		Games	Pos.
1984	**NYG**	N	14	G
1985			16	G
1987	**TB**	N	3	G

3 yrs. 33 games

Donald Jordan
JORDAN, DONALD RAY
B. Feb. 9, 1962, Houston, TX
Houston 6'0" 210 lbs.

Year	Team		Games	Pos.
1984	**CHI**	N	13	FB

Frank Jordan
JORDAN, FRANK D.
B. Jul. 10, 1898, Jefferson County, WI
D. Dec., 1976, Elkhorn, WI
None 168 lbs.

Year	Team		Games	Pos.
1920	**RI**	A	1	HB

Henry Jordan
JORDAN, HENRY WENDELL
B. Jan. 26, 1935, Emporia, VA
D. Feb. 21, 1977, Milwaukee, WI
Virginia 6'3" 249 lbs.

Year	Team		Games	Pos.
1957	**CLE**	N	12	T
1958			12	T
1959	**GB**	N	12	T
1960			12	T
1961			14	DT
1962			14	DT
1963			14	DT
1964			12	DT, DE
1965			14	DT
1966			14	DT
1967			14	DT
1968			14	DT
1969			5	DT

13 yrs. 163 games

Jeff Jordan
JORDAN, JEFF FLYNN
B. Nov. 23, 1943, San Antonio, TX
Tulsa 6'4" 190 lbs.

Year	Team		Games	Pos.
1965	**MIN**	N	12	DB
1966			14	DB
1967			11	DB

3 yrs. 37 games

Jeff Jordan
JORDAN, JEFFREY LINCOLN
B. Jul. 12, 1943, St. Louis, MO
Washington 6'1" 215 lbs.

Year	Team		Games	Pos.
1970	**LA**	N	9	RB
1971	**WAS**	N	1	RB

2 yrs. 10 games

Jimmy Jordan
JORDAN, JIM
B. Aug. 11, 1944
Florida 6'1" 200 lbs.

Year	Team		Games	Pos.
1967	**NO**	N	1	RB

Ken Jordan
JORDAN, KENNETH
B. Apr. 29, 1964
Tuskegee Institute 6'2" 235 lbs.

Year	Team		Games	Pos.
1987	**GB**	N	3	LB

Larry Jordan
JORDAN, LAWRENCE
B. 1939
Youngstown State 6'6" 230 lbs.

Year	Team		Games	Pos.
1962	**DEN**	A	2	DE
1964			8	LB

2 yrs. 10 games

Lee Roy Jordan
JORDAN, LEE ROY
B. Apr. 27, 1941, Excel, AL
Alabama 6'2" 219 lbs.

Year	Team		Games	Pos.
1963	**DAL**	N	7	LB
1964			12	LB

Year	Team	Games	Pos.

Lee Roy Jordan *continued*

1965		13	LB
1966		14	LB
1967		14	LB
1968		14	LB
1969		14	LB
1970		14	LB
1971		14	LB
1972		14	LB
1973		14	LB
1974		14	LB
1975		14	LB
1976		14	LB

14 yrs. 186 games

Randy Jordan
JORDAN, RANDY LOMENT
B. Jun. 6, 1970, Henderson, NC
North Carolina 5'10" 205 lbs.

1993	LARI	N	10	RB
1995	JAC	N	12	RB
1996			15	RB

3 yrs. 37 games

Shelby Jordan
JORDAN, SHELBY LEWIS
B. Jan. 23, 1952, East St. Louis, IL
Washington (Missouri) 6'7" 270 lbs.

1975	NE	N	14	OT
1977			10	OT
1978			16	OT
1979			14	OT
1980			16	OT
1981			16	OT
1982			9	OT
1983	LARI	N	13	OT
1984			11	OT
1985			16	OT
1986			16	OT

11 yrs. 151 games

Steve Jordan
JORDAN, STEVE
B. Mar. 30, 1963
Southern California 5'10" 205 lbs.

| 1987 | IND | N | 3 | K |

Steve Jordan
JORDAN, STEVEN RUSSELL
B. Jan. 10, 1961, Phoenix, AZ
Brown 6'4" 238 lbs.

1982	MIN	N	9	TE
1983			13	TE
1984			14	TE
1985			16	TE
1986			16	TE
1987			12	TE
1988			16	TE
1989			16	TE
1990			16	TE
1991			16	TE
1992			14	TE
1993			14	TE
1994			4	TE

13 yrs. 176 games

Tim Jordan
JORDAN, TIMOTHY
B. Apr. 26, 1964, Madison, WI
Wisconsin 6'3" 221 lbs.

1987	NE	N	5	LB
1988			16	LB
1989			9	LB

3 yrs. 30 games

Tony Jordan
JORDAN, ANTHONY T.
B. May 8, 1965, Rochester, NY

Tony Jordan *continued*
Kansas State 6'2" 220 lbs.

| 1988 | PHX | N | 9 | RB |
| 1989 | | | 13 | RB |

2 yrs. 22 games

Tim Jorden
JORDEN, TIMOTHY ROBERT
B. Oct. 30, 1966, Lakewood, OH
Indiana 6'2" 235 lbs.

1990	PHX	N	16	RB
1991			16	TE
1992	PIT	N	15	TE
1993			16	TE

4 yrs. 63 games

Carl Jorgensen
JORGENSEN, CARL W. (Bud)
B. Feb. 5, 1911
D. Jul., 1984, Arcadia, CA
St. Mary's (California) 6'0" 205 lbs.

| 1934 | GB | N | 9 | T, G |
| 1935 | PHI | N | 11 | T |

2 yrs. 20 games

Wagner Jorgensen
JORGENSEN, WAGNER
B. Jul. 31, 1913
D. Jul., 1977, San Mateo, CA
St. Mary's (California) 6'2" 215 lbs.

| 1936 | BKN | N | 8 | C |
| 1937 | | | 10 | C |

2 yrs. 18 games

Dwayne Joseph
JOSEPH, DWAYNE LEONARD
B. Jun. 2, 1972, Miami, FL
Syracuse 5'9" 188 lbs.

| 1995 | CHI | N | 16 | CB |

James Joseph
JOSEPH, JAMES
B. Oct. 28, 1967, Phenix City, AL
Auburn 6'0" 222 lbs.

1991	PHI	N	16	RB
1992			16	RB
1993			16	RB
1994			14	RB
1995	CIN	N	16	RB

5 yrs. 78 games

Red Joseph
JOSEPH, CHALMERS (Red)
B. 1903
Miami (Ohio)/Ohio State 6'3" 187 lbs.

| 1927 | DAY | N | 8 | E |
| 1930 | POR | N | 12 | E |

2 yrs. 20 games

Vance Joseph
JOSEPH, VANCE
B. Sep. 20, 1972, Marrero, LA
Colorado 6'0" 202 lbs.

| 1995 | NYJ | N | 13 | CB |
| 1996 | IND | N | 4 | CB |

2 yrs. 17 games

Zern Joseph
JOSEPH, ZERN C. (Zip)
B. May, 1903
D. Nov., 1977
Miami (Ohio) 6'2" 170 lbs.

| 1925 | DAY | N | 4 | C, G, T |
| 1927 | | | 5 | E, C |

2 yrs. 9 games

Les Josephson
JOSEPHSON, LESTER ANDREW (Whitey)
B. Jul. 29, 1942, Minneota, MN
Augustana (South Dakota) 6'0" 209 lbs.

1964	LA	N	14	FB
1965			13	FB
1966			14	HB
1967			14	RB
1969			14	RB
1970			12	RB
1971			13	RB
1972			8	RB
1973			14	RB
1974			12	RB

10 yrs. 128 games

Bob Joswick
JOSWICK, ROBERT
B. Jan. 12, 1946, Uniontown, PA
Tulsa 6'5" 250 lbs.

| 1968 | MIA | A | 1 | DT, DE |
| 1969 | | | 8 | DE |

2 yrs. 9 games

Yonel Jourdain
JOURDAIN, YONEL
B. Apr. 20, 1971, Brooklyn, NY
Southern Illinois 5'11" 204 lbs.

| 1994 | BUF | N | 9 | RB |
| 1995 | | | 8 | RB |

2 yrs. 17 games

Bill Joyce
JOYCE, WILLIAM
B. Apr. 10, 1897
D. Jun., 1983, Providence, RI
Holy Cross 5'8" 180 lbs.

| 1920 | DET | A | 2 | QB, HB |

Don Joyce
JOYCE, DONALD GILBERT
B. Oct. 8, 1929, Steubenville, OH
Tulane 6'3" 253 lbs.

1951	CHIC	N	12	T
1952			12	T
1953			10	T
1954	BAL	N	12	E
1955			11	E
1956			12	E
1957			12	E
1958			12	E
1959			11	E
1960			11	E, T
1961	MIN	N	14	DE
1962	DEN	A	6	DE

12 yrs. 135 games

Matt Joyce
JOYCE, MATT
B. Mar. 30, 1972, St. Petersburg, FL
Richmond 6'7" 283 lbs.

| 1995 | SEA | N | 16 | G |
| 1996 | ARI | N | 2 | OT |

2 yrs. 18 games

Terry Joyce
JOYCE, TERRY PATRICK
B. Jul. 18, 1954, Kirksville, MO
Wichita State/Missouri Southern State 6'6" 229 lbs.

| 1976 | STL | N | 14 | P |
| 1977 | | | 4 | P, TE |

2 yrs. 18 games

Larry Joyner
JOYNER, LARRY

Larry Joyner *continued*
B. 1964
6'0" 207 lbs.

| 1987 | HOU | N | 1 | S |

L.C. Joyner
JOYNER, L.C. (Jet)
B. 1935
East Contra Costa JC 6'1" 197 lbs.

| 1960 | OAK | A | | HB |

Seth Joyner
JOYNER, SETH
B. Nov. 18, 1964, Spring Valley, NY
Texas-El Paso 6'2" 241 lbs.

1986	PHI	N	14	LB
1987			12	LB
1988			16	LB
1989			14	LB
1990			16	LB
1991			16	LB
1992			16	LB
1993			16	LB
1994	ARI	N	16	LB
1995			16	LB
1996			16	LB

11 yrs. 168 games

Willie Joyner
JOYNER, WILLIE
B. Apr. 2, 1962, Brooklyn, NY
Maryland 5'10" 200 lbs.

| 1984 | HOU | N | 10 | RB |

Brian Jozwiak
JOZWIAK, BRIAN JOSEPH
B. Jun. 20, 1963, Baltimore, MD
West Virginia 6'5" 308 lbs.

1986	KC	N	15	OT
1987			10	OT
1988			3	G

3 yrs. 28 games

Saxon Judd
JUDD, SAXON T.
B. Nov. 29, 1921
Tulsa 6'1" 190 lbs.

1946	BKN	AA	13	E
1947			14	E
1948			14	E

3 yrs. 41 games

Ed Judie
JUDIE, EDWARD CHARLIE
B. Jul. 6, 1959, Tyler, TX
Northern Arizona 6'2" 231 lbs.

1982	SF	N	7	LB
1983			4	LB
1983	TB	N	11	LB
1984	MIA	N	2	LB

3 yrs. 24 games

William Judson
JUDSON, WILLIAM THADIUS
B. Mar. 26, 1959, Detroit, MI
South Carolina State 6'2" 190 lbs.

1982	MIA	N	9	CB
1983			16	CB
1984			16	CB
1985			16	CB
1986			12	CB
1987			16	CB
1988			16	CB
1989			14	CB

8 yrs. 115 games

Year	Team		Games	Pos.

Dave Juenger
JUENGER, DAVID WILLIAM
B. Feb. 4, 1951, Chillicothe, OH
Ohio University 6'1" 195 lbs.

| 1973 | CHI | N | 1 | WR |

Fred Julian
JULIAN, FREDERICK
B. 1938
Michigan 5'9" 185 lbs.

| 1960 | NY | A | | DB |

Kevin Juma
JUMA, KEVIN
B. Jul. 30, 1962
Idaho 6'2" 195 lbs.

| 1987 | SEA | N | 3 | WR |

Harold Jungmichel
JUNGMICHEL, HAROLD NEVE
B. Oct. 18, 1919
D. Aug., 1982, Austin, TX
Texas 5'9" 200 lbs.

| 1946 | MIA | AA | 14 | G |

E.J. Junior
JUNIOR, ESTER JAMES, III
B. Dec. 8, 1959, Salisbury, NC
Alabama 6'3" 235 lbs.

1981	STL	N	16	LB
1982			9	LB
1983			12	LB
1984			16	LB
1985			16	LB
1986			13	LB
1987			13	LB
1988	PHX	N	16	LB
1989	MIA	N	16	LB
1990			16	LB
1991			16	LB
1992	TB	N	2	LB
1992	SEA	N	5	LB
1993			4	LB
13 yrs.		170 games		

Steve Junker
JUNKER, STEVEN
B. May 22, 1935, Cincinnati, OH
Xavier (Ohio) 6'3" 217 lbs.

1957	DET	N	12	E
1959			6	E
1960			12	E
1961	WAS	N	11	OE
1962			14	OE
5 yrs.		55 games		

Mike Junkin
JUNKIN, MICHAEL WAYNE
B. Nov. 21, 1964, North Little Rock, AR
Duke 6'3" 242 lbs.

1987	CLE	N	4	LB
1988			11	LB
1989	KC	N	5	LB
3 yrs.		20 games		

Trey Junkin
JUNKIN, ABNER KIRK
B. Jan. 23, 1961, Conway, AR
Louisiana Tech 6'2" 221 lbs.

1983	BUF	N	16	LB
1984			2	LB
1984	WAS	N	12	LB
1985	LARI	N	16	LB
1986			3	TE
1987			12	TE
1988			16	TE
1989			16	TE

Trey Junkin *continued*

1990	SEA	N	12	TE
1991			16	TE
1992			16	TE
1993			16	TE
1994			16	TE
1995			16	TE
1996	OAK	N	6	TE
1996	ARI	N	10	TE
14 yrs.		201 games		

Sonny Jurgensen
JURGENSEN, CHRISTIAN ADOLPH, III
B. Aug. 23, 1934, Wilmington, NC
Duke 5'11" 202 lbs.

1957	PHI	N	10	QB
1958			12	QB
1959			12	B
1960			12	B
1961			14	QB
1962			14	QB
1963			9	QB
1964	WAS	N	14	QB
1965			13	QB
1966			14	QB
1967			14	QB
1968			12	QB
1969			13	QB
1970			14	QB
1971			5	QB
1972			7	QB
1973			14	QB
1974			14	QB
18 yrs.		217 games		

Mike Jurich
JURICH, MICHAEL
B. Jan. 7, 1919, Ruth, NV
Denver 6'1" 230 lbs.

1941	BKN	N	4	T
1942			11	T
2 yrs.		15 games		

Tom Jurich
JURICH, TOM M.
B. Jul. 26, 1956, Alhambra, CA
Northern Arizona 5'10" 185 lbs.

| 1978 | NO | N | 1 | K |

Jim Juriga
JURIGA, JAMES ALLEN
B. Sep. 12, 1965, Fort Wayne, IN
Illinois 6'6" 269 lbs.

1988	DEN	N	16	G, OT
1989			16	G, OT
1990			12	G, OT
3 yrs.		44 games		

Walt Jurkiewicz
JURKIEWICZ, WALTER STEPHEN
B. Feb. 16, 1919, Scott Haven, PA
Indiana 6'1" 220 lbs.

| 1946 | DET | N | 11 | C |

John Jurkovic
JURKOVIC, JOHN IVAN
B. Aug. 18, 1967, Friedrischafen, Germany
Eastern Illinois 6'2" 297 lbs.

1991	GB	N	5	NT
1992			16	NT
1993			16	NT
1994			16	NT
1995			16	NT
1996	JAC	N	16	NT
6 yrs.		85 games		

Bob Jury
JURY, ROBERT VINCENT
B. Oct. 5, 1955, Los Angeles, CA
Pittsburgh 6'1" 188 lbs.

| 1978 | SF | N | 15 | S |

Rube Juster
JUSTER, RUBIN J.
B. Sep. 9, 1923
D. Jan., 1985, Chicago, IL
Minnesota 6'2" 230 lbs.

| 1946 | BOS | N | 4 | T |

Charlie Justice
JUSTICE, CHARLES (Choo-Choo)
B. May 18, 1924, Asheville, NC
North Carolina 5'10" 176 lbs.

1950	WAS	N	8	HB
1952			8	HB
1953			12	HB
1954			12	HB
4 yrs.		40 games		

Ed Justice
JUSTICE, EDWARD S. (Chug)
B. Nov. 19, 1912, Posh Falls, ID
D. Oct. 26, 1991, Anacortes, WA
Gonzaga 6'1" 200 lbs.

1936	BOS	N	11	HB, FB
1937	WAS	N	10	HB
1938			11	HB
1939			8	FB, HB
1940			7	HB
1941			7	HB, E
1942			9	HB
7 yrs.		63 games		

Kerry Justin
JUSTIN, KERRY AUGUST
B. May 3, 1955, New Orleans, LA
Oregon State 5'11" 175 lbs.

1978	SEA	N	16	CB
1979			14	CB
1980			11	CB
1981			15	CB
1982			9	CB
1983			16	CB
1986			16	CB
1987			7	CB
8 yrs.		104 games		

Paul Justin
JUSTIN, PAUL DONALD
B. May 19, 1968, Schaumburg, IL
Arizona State 6'4" 202 lbs.

1995	IND	N	3	QB
1996			8	QB
2 yrs.		11 games		

Sid Justin
JUSTIN, SIDNEY ARTHUR
B. Aug. 14, 1954, New Orleans, LA
Long Beach State 5'10" 170 lbs.

1979	LA	N	13	CB
1982	BAL	N	5	CB
2 yrs.		18 games		

Steve Juzwik
JUZWIK, STEPHEN ROBERT
B. Jun. 18, 1918, Gary, IN
D. Jun. 6, 1964
Notre Dame 5'8" 186 lbs.

1942	WAS	N	2	HB
1946	BUF	AA	13	HB
1947			10	B
1948	CHI	AA	4	B
4 yrs.		29 games		

Vyto Kab
KAB, VYTO
B. Dec. 23, 1959, Albany, GA
Penn State 6'5" 250 lbs.

1982	PHI	N	9	TE
1983			14	TE
1984			16	TE
1985			1	TE
1985	NYG	N	11	TE
1987	DET	N	7	TE
5 yrs.		58 games		

Mike Kabealo
KABEALO, MICHAEL
B. Sep. 30, 1915, Youngstown, OH
Deceased
Ohio State 5'8" 185 lbs.

| 1944 | CLE | N | 10 | HB |

John Kacherski
KACHERSKI, JOHN RICHARD
B. Jun. 27, 1967, Oceanside, NY
Ohio State 6'3" 240 lbs.

| 1992 | DEN | N | 7 | LB |

Jeff Kacmarek
KACMAREK, JEFF
B. Apr. 12, 1963
Western Michigan 6'2" 240 lbs.

| 1987 | DET | N | 3 | NT |

Mike Kaczmarek
KACZMAREKI, MICHAEL LOUIS
B. Oct. 31, 1951, Gary, IN
Southern Illinois 6'4" 235 lbs.

| 1973 | BAL | N | 14 | DE |

Max Kadesky
KADESKY, MAX
B. Feb. 8, 1901
D. Aug. 14, 1970, Dubuque, IA
Iowa 5'11" 170 lbs.

| 1923 | RI | N | 8 | E |

Mike Kadish
KADISH, MICHAEL S.
B. May 27, 1950, Grand Rapids, MI
Notre Dame 6'5" 270 lbs.

1973	BUF	N	12	DT
1974			14	DT
1975			14	OT
1976			14	DT
1977			14	DT
1978			11	DT
1979			16	DT
1980			16	DT
1981			16	NT
9 yrs.		127 games		

Ron Kadziel
KADZIEL, RONALD DENNIS
B. Feb. 27, 1949, Pomona, CA
Stanford 6'4" 230 lbs.

| 1972 | NE | N | 14 | LB |

Mort Kaer
KAER, MORTON ARMOUR (Devil May)
B. Sep. 7, 1902, Omaha, NE
D. Jan. 12, 1992, Los Angeles, CA
Southern California 5'11" 167 lbs.

| 1931 | FRA | N | 8 | QB, HB |

Kurt Kafentzis
KAFENTZIS, KURT

Kurt Kafentzis *continued*

B. Dec. 31, 1962, Richland, WA
Hawaii 6'2" 190 lbs.

Year	Team		Games	Pos.
1987	HOU	N	2	S

Mark Kafentzis

KAFENTZIS, MARK KEVIN
B. Jun. 30, 1958, Richland, WA
Hawaii 5'10" 185 lbs.

Year	Team		Games	Pos.
1982	CLE	N	9	S
1983	BAL	N	15	S
1984	IND	N	16	S
3 yrs.			40 games	

Cy Kahl

KAHL, CYRUS P.
B. Nov. 29, 1904
D. Jul., 1971, Portsmouth, OH
North Dakota 6'1" 195 lbs.

Year	Team		Games	Pos.
1930	POR	N	9	QB, HB, FB
1931			1	B
2 yrs.			10 games	

Bob Kahler

KAHLER, ROBERT W.
B. Feb. 13, 1917, Grand Island, NE
Nebraska 6'3" 201 lbs.

Year	Team		Games	Pos.
1942	GB	N	6	B
1943			6	B
1944			6	B
3 yrs.			18 games	

Royal Kahler

KAHLER, ROYAL JAMES
B. Mar. 22, 1918, Grand Island, NE
Nebraska 6'2" 226 lbs.

Year	Team		Games	Pos.
1941	PIT	N	8	T
1942	GB	N	8	T
2 yrs.			16 games	

Eddie Kahn

KAHN, EDWIN BERNARD
B. Nov. 9, 1911, Roxbury, MA
D. Feb. 17, 1945
North Carolina 5'9" 194 lbs.

Year	Team		Games	Pos.
1935	BOS	N	9	G
1936			7	G
1937	WAS	N	10	G
3 yrs.			26 games	

Karl Kaimer

KAIMER, KARL J.
B. 1939
Boston University 6'3" 230 lbs.

Year	Team		Games	Pos.
1962	NY	A	8	OE

John Kaiser

KAISER, JOHN FREDERICK
B. Jun. 6, 1962, Oconomowoc, WI
Arizona 6'3" 230 lbs.

Year	Team		Games	Pos.
1984	SEA	N	16	LB
1985			16	LB
1986			16	LB
1987	BUF	N	12	LB
4 yrs.			60 games	

George Kakasic

KAKASIC, GEORGE
B. 1912
Duquesne 5'10" 200 lbs.

Year	Team		Games	Pos.
1936	PIT	N	12	G, T
1937			11	G
1938			4	G
1939			11	G
4 yrs.			38 games	

Ike Kakela

KAKELA, WAYNE
B. Jul. 16, 1905
D. Oct., 1981, Rolla, ND
Minnesota 6'2" 220 lbs.

Year	Team		Games	Pos.
1930	MIN	N	2	C, G

Jim Kalafat

KALAFAT, JAMES
B. Feb. 21, 1962, Great Falls, MT
Montana State 6'0" 235 lbs.

Year	Team		Games	Pos.
1987	LARM	N	1	LB

Dave Kalina

KALINA, DAVID
B. Sep. 2, 1947, Ponca City, OK
Miami (Florida) 6'3" 205 lbs.

Year	Team		Games	Pos.
1970	PIT	N	2	WR

Todd Kalis

KALIS, TODD ALEXANDER
B. May 10, 1965, Stillwater, MN
Arizona State 6'5" 284 lbs.

Year	Team		Games	Pos.
1988	MIN	N	14	G
1989			16	G
1990			15	G
1991			16	G
1993			16	G
1994	PIT	N	11	G
1995	CIN	N	16	G
7 yrs.			104 games	

Ed Kallina

KALLINA, EDWARD
B. 1901
Southwest Texas State 6'0" 205 lbs.

Year	Team		Games	Pos.
1928	CHIB	N	4	T, G

Tommy Kalmanir

KALMANIR, THOMAS (Cricket)
B. Mar. 31, 1926, Jerome, PA
Pittsburgh/Nevada-Reno 5'8" 171 lbs.

Year	Team		Games	Pos.
1949	LA	N	12	HB
1950			10	HB
1951			12	HB
1953	BAL	N	9	HB
4 yrs.			43 games	

Bob Kalsu

KALSU, ROBERT
B. Apr. 13, 1945, Oklahoma City, OK
Oklahoma 6'3" 235 lbs.

Year	Team		Games	Pos.
1968	BUF	A		G

John Kamana

KAMANA, JOHN MAIA, III
B. Dec. 3, 1961, Honolulu, HI
Southern California 6'0" 230 lbs.

Year	Team		Games	Pos.
1984	LARM	N	3	RB
1987	ATL	N	2	RB
2 yrs.			5 games	

Lew Kamanu

KAMANU, LEW
B. Apr. 9, 1944, Honolulu, HI
Weber State 6'4" 245 lbs.

Year	Team		Games	Pos.
1967	DET	N	9	DE
1968			4	DE
2 yrs.			13 games	

Larry Kaminski

KAMINSKI, LARRY MICHAEL
B. Jan. 6, 1945, Cleveland, OH
Purdue 6'2" 244 lbs.

Year	Team		Games	Pos.
1966	DEN	A	14	C

Larry Kaminski *continued*

Year	Team		Games	Pos.
1967			14	C
1968			14	C
1969			14	C
1970	DEN	N	14	C
1971			3	C
1972			11	C
1973			12	C
8 yrs.			96 games	

Carl Kammerer

KAMMERER, CARLTON CORDELL
B. Mar. 20, 1937, Stockton, CA
San Francisco State/Pacific 6'3" 240 lbs.

Year	Team		Games	Pos.
1961	SF	N	14	LB
1962			14	LB
1963	WAS	N	14	LB
1964			14	LB
1965			14	DE
1966			14	DE
1967			11	DE
1968			14	DE
1969			14	DE
9 yrs.			123 games	

Jim Kamp

KAMP, JAMES
B. 1909
Oklahoma City 6'0" 210 lbs.

Year	Team		Games	Pos.
1932	SI	N	9	T, G
1933	BOS	N	9	G
2 yrs.			18 games	

Bob Kampa

KAMPA, ROBERT EUGENE
B. Apr. 26, 1951, San Francisco, CA
California 6'4" 249 lbs.

Year	Team		Games	Pos.
1973	BUF	N	7	DE
1974			3	DE
1974	DEN	N	4	DT
2 yrs.			14 games	

Carl Kane

KANE, CARL
B. Jan. 24, 1913
D. Sep., 1983, Vero Beach, FL
St. Louis 5'11" 195 lbs.

Year	Team		Games	Pos.
1936	PHI	N	1	B

George Kane

KANE, GEORGE
B. Jul. 13, 1891, New York State
D. Aug., 1969, Bradenton, FL
Fordham 5'9" 195 lbs.

Year	Team		Games	Pos.
1921	NY	A	1	G

Herb Kane

KANE, HERBERT RUSSELL
B. Dec. 24, 1920, Carroll, IA
D. Apr. 19, 1995, Nevada
East Central State (Oklahoma) 6'1" 218 lbs.

Year	Team		Games	Pos.
1944	NYG	N	7	T
1945			2	T
2 yrs.			9 games	

Rick Kane

KANE, RICHARD JAMES
B. Nov. 12, 1954, Lincoln, NE
Oregon/San Jose State 6'0" 200 lbs.

Year	Team		Games	Pos.
1977	DET	N	14	RB
1978			15	RB
1979			16	RB
1980			16	RB
1981			16	RB
1982			6	RB

Rick Kane *continued*

Year	Team		Games	Pos.
1983			14	RB
1984	WAS	N	12	RB
1985	DET	N	16	RB
9 yrs.			125 games	

Tommy Kane

KANE, THOMAS HENRY
B. Jan. 14, 1964, Montreal, Que.
Syracuse 5'11" 180 lbs.

Year	Team		Games	Pos.
1988	SEA	N	9	WR
1989			5	WR
1990			16	WR
1991			16	WR
1992			11	WR
5 yrs.			57 games	

Danny Kanell

KANELL, DANNY
B. Nov. 21, 1973, Fort Lauderdale, FL
Florida State 6'3" 222 lbs.

Year	Team		Games	Pos.
1996	NYG	N	4	QB

Jim Kanicki

KANICKI, JAMES H.
B. Dec. 17, 1941, Bay City, MI
Michigan State 6'4" 270 lbs.

Year	Team		Games	Pos.
1963	CLE	N	13	DT
1964			14	DT
1965			14	DT
1966			14	DT
1967			14	DT
1968			13	DT
1969			6	DT
1970	NYG	N	14	DT
1971			14	DT
9 yrs.			116 games	

Joe Kantor

KANTOR, JOSEPH
B. 1943
Notre Dame 6'1" 217 lbs.

Year	Team		Games	Pos.
1966	WAS	N	4	RB

Al Kanya

KANYA, ALBERT J.
B. Mar. 7, 1908
D. Oct., 1985, Flushing, NY
Syracuse 6'0" 200 lbs.

Year	Team		Games	Pos.
1931	SI	N	11	T, E
1932			12	T, E
2 yrs.			23 games	

John Kapele

KAPELE, JOHN
B. Oct. 19, 1937, Hawaii
Brigham Young 6'0" 240 lbs.

Year	Team		Games	Pos.
1960	PIT	N	12	T
1961			14	DE
1962			6	DE
1962	PHI	N	6	DT
3 yrs.			38 games	

Bernie Kapitansky

KAPITANSKY, BERNARD
B. Jan. 1, 1921, Brooklyn, NY
Long Island 6'1" 212 lbs.

Year	Team		Games	Pos.
1942	BKN	N	7	G

Ave Kaplan

KAPLAN, AVOLD R.
B. Nov. 15, 1899
D. Dec. 28, 1989, Birmingham, AL
Hamline 5'9" 165 lbs.

Year	Team		Games	Pos.
1923	MIN	N	8	QB, HB
1926	RI	A	9	HB, QB
2 yrs.			17 games	

Year	Team	Games	Pos.

Bernard Kaplan
KAPLAN, BERNARD
B. May 7, 1913, Philadelphia, PA
D. Oct., 1982, Bronx, NY
Western Maryland 6'0" 208 lbs.

Year	Team	Games	Pos.
1935	NYG	N	12	G
1936			7	G
1942	PHI	N	3	G
3 yrs.	22 games		

Ken Kaplan
KAPLAN, KENNETH SCOTT
B. Jan. 12, 1960, Boston, MA
New Hampshire 6'4" 275 lbs.

1984	TB	N	16	OT
1985			16	OT
1987	NO	N	3	OT
3 yrs.	35 games		

Sam Kaplan
KAPLAN, SAMUEL
B. Jan., 1899, Washington, DC
Deceased
Lehigh 166 lbs.

| 1921 | WAS | A | 2 | E |

Carl Kaplanoff
KAPLANOFF, CARL G.
B. 1917
Ohio State 6'0" 235 lbs.

| 1939 | BKN | N | 11 | T, G |

Al Kaporch
KAPORCH, ALBERT JOHN
B. Oct. 6, 1913, Jenkins Township, PA
Deceased
St. Bonaventure 5'10" 215 lbs.

1943	DET	N	10	T
1944			10	T
1945			2	T
3 yrs.	22 games		

Joe Kapp
KAPP, JOE
B. Mar. 19, 1939, Santa Fe, NM
California 6'2" 214 lbs.

1967	MIN	N	13	QB
1968			14	QB
1969			13	QB
1970	BOS	N	11	QB
4 yrs.	51 games		

Alex Kapter
KAPTER, ALEXANDER J.
B. Mar. 26, 1922, Waukegan, IL
Northwestern 6'0" 205 lbs.

| 1946 | CLE | AA | 6 | G |

George Karamatic
KARAMATIC, GEORGE
(Automatic)
B. 1917, Seattle, WA
Gonzaga 5'8" 187 lbs.

| 1938 | WAS | N | 9 | HB, FB |

Emil Karas
KARAS, EMIL
B. Dec. 13, 1933, Pittsburgh, PA
D. Nov. 25, 1974, San Diego, CA
Dayton 6'3" 230 lbs.

1959	WAS	N	11	E
1960	LA	A		LB
1961	SD	A	14	LB
1962			14	LB
1963			14	LB

Emil Karas continued

1964			4	LB
1966			2	LB
7 yrs.	59 games		

Bob Karch
KARCH, ROBERT H.
B. Jul. 4, 1894, Columbus, OH
Deceased
Ohio State 6'1" 220 lbs.

1922	COL	N	4	T
1923	LOU	N	2	T
2 yrs.	6 games		

Jim Karcher
KARCHER, JAMES N.
B. May 2, 1914, Forest, OH
Ohio State 6'0" 205 lbs.

1936	BOS	N	9	G
1937	WAS	N	11	G
1938			10	G
1939			11	G
4 yrs.	41 games		

Ken Karcher
KARCHER, KENNETH PAUL
B. Jul. 1, 1963, Pittsburgh, PA
Notre Dame/Tulane 6'3" 205 lbs.

1987	DEN	N	3	QB
1988			1	QB
2 yrs.	4 games		

John Karcis
KARCIS, JOHN (Bull)
B. Dec. 3, 1908, Monaca, PA
D. Sep. 4, 1973, Pittsburgh, PA
Carnegie-Mellon 5'9" 223 lbs.

1932	BKN	N	11	FB, G
1933			10	FB, HB
1934			9	FB
1935			11	FB
1936	PIT		12	FB
1937			10	FB
1938			3	FB
1938	NYG		8	FB
1939			10	B
1943			8	B
9 yrs.	92 games		

Carl Karilivacz
KARILIVACZ, CARL E. (Kava)
B. Nov. 20, 1930, Glen Cove, NY
D. Aug. 30, 1969, Glen Cove, NY
Syracuse 6'0" 188 lbs.

1953	DET	N	12	DB
1955			12	DB
1956			11	DB
1957			12	DB
1958	NYG	N	12	DB
1959	LA	N	6	DB
1960			9	DB
7 yrs.	74 games		

Rich Karlis
KARLIS, RICHARD JOHN
B. May 23, 1959, Salem, OH
Cincinnati 6'0" 180 lbs.

1982	DEN	N	9	K
1983			16	K
1984			16	K
1985			16	K
1986			16	K
1987			12	K
1988			16	K
1989	MIN	N	13	K
1990	DET	N	6	K
9 yrs.	120 games		

Mike Karmazin
KARMAZIN, MICHAEL L.
B. 1919
Duke 5'11" 210 lbs.

| 1946 | NY | AA | 10 | G |

Abe Karnofsky
KARNOFSKY, ABRAHAM (Sonny)
B. Sep. 22, 1922, California
Arizona (Freshmen) 5'10" 175 lbs.

1945	PHI	N	8	HB
1946	BOS	N	11	HB
2 yrs.	19 games		

Keith Karpinski
KARPINSKI, KEITH CARL
B. Oct. 12, 1966, Southfield, MI
Penn State 6'3" 225 lbs.

| 1989 | DET | N | 16 | LB |

Ed Karpowich
KARPOWICH, EDWARD
B. Sep. 28, 1912, Duquesne, PA
Catholic 6'4" 223 lbs.

1936	PIT	N	11	T, B, G
1937			10	T
1938			8	T, E
1939			6	T
1940			1	T
5 yrs.	36 games		

Bill Karr
KARR, WILLIAM MORRISON
B. Mar. 29, 1911, Ripley, WV
D. Oct. 29, 1979, Clendenin, WV
West Virginia 6'1" 190 lbs.

1933	CHIB	N	12	E
1934			12	E
1935			10	E
1936			8	E
1937			10	E
1938			9	E
6 yrs.	61 games		

Alex Karras
KARRAS, ALEX GEORGE
B. Jul. 15, 1935, Gary, IN
Iowa 6'2" 248 lbs.

1958	DET	N	12	T
1959			12	T
1960			12	T
1961			14	DT
1962			14	DT
1964			14	DT
1965			14	DT
1966			14	DT
1967			14	DT
1968			14	DT
1969			14	DT
1970			13	DT
12 yrs.	161 games		

Johnny Karras
KARRAS, JOHN
B. Jan. 29, 1928, Chicago, IL
Illinois 5'11" 187 lbs.

| 1952 | CHIC | N | 6 | B |

Lou Karras
KARRAS, LOUIS G.
B. Sep. 19, 1927, Gary, IN
Purdue 6'4" 241 lbs.

1950	WAS	N	11	T
1951			12	T
2 yrs.	23 games		

Ted Karras
KARRAS, TED
B. 1965
Northwestern 6'2" 265 lbs.

| 1987 | WAS | N | 1 | DT |

Ted Karras
KARRAS, THEODORE GEORGE
B. Jan. 31, 1934, Gary, IN
Indiana 6'1" 240 lbs.

1958	PIT	N	12	T
1959			12	T
1960	CHI	N	12	G
1961			14	G
1962			14	G
1963			14	G
1964			14	G
1965	DET	N	12	G
1966	LA	N	4	G
9 yrs.	108 games		

John Karrs
KARRS, JOHN B.
B. Sep. 19, 1915, Pittsburgh, PA
Duquesne 6'1" 210 lbs.

| 1944 | CLE | N | 10 | QB |

George Karstens
KARSTENS, GEORGE J.
B. 1924
Indiana 6'4" 205 lbs.

| 1949 | DET | N | 2 | C |

Keith Kartz
KARTZ, KEITH LEONARD
B. May 5, 1963, Las Vegas, NV
California 6'4" 270 lbs.

1987	DEN	N	12	OT
1988			13	OT
1989			16	G, OT
1990			16	C
1991			16	C
1992			15	C
1993			12	C
7 yrs.	100 games		

Mike Kasap
KASAP, MICHAEL
B. Nov. 20, 1922, Glesby, IL
Illinois/Purdue/Illinois 6'2" 255 lbs.

| 1947 | BAL | AA | 12 | T |

John Kasay
KASAY, JOHN DAVID
B. Oct. 27, 1969, Athens, GA
Georgia 5'10" 189 lbs.

1991	SEA	N	16	K
1992			16	K
1993			16	K
1994			16	K
1995	CAR	N	16	K
1996			16	K
6 yrs.	96 games		

Tony Kaska
KASKA, ANTHONY
B. 1911
Illinois Wesleyan 5'11" 193 lbs.

1935	DET	N	1	FB
1936	BKN	N	12	B
1937			10	HB
1938			11	HB
4 yrs.	34 games		

Ed Kasky
KASKY, EDWARD T.

Year	Team	Games	Pos.

Ed Kasky *continued*
B. Jun. 22, 1919, Brooklyn, NY
Villanova 6'1" 220 lbs.

1942	PHI	N	9	T

Dick Kasparek
KASPAREK, DICK
B. Feb. 6, 1943, St. Peter, MN
Iowa State 6'3" 225 lbs.

1966	STL	N	4	C
1967			2	C
1968			14	C
3 yrs.	20 games			

Tom Kasper
KASPER, THOMAS C. (Cy)
B. 1897
Deceased
Notre Dame 5'10" 170 lbs.

1923	ROC	N	1	HB

Chuck Kassel
KASSEL, CHARLES E.
B. Nov. 20, 1903
D. Nov., 1977, Elgin, IL
Illinois 6'1" 191 lbs.

1927	CHIB	N	1	E
1927	FRA		10	E
1928			14	E
1929	CHIC	N	13	E
1930			13	E
1931			9	E
1932			10	E
1933			8	E
7 yrs.	78 games			

Karl Kassulke
KASSULKE, KARL OTTO
B. Mar. 20, 1941, Milwaukee, WI
Marquette/Drake 6'0" 194 lbs.

1963	MIN	N	14	DB
1964			14	DB
1965			14	DB
1966			14	DB
1967			14	DB
1968			14	DB
1969			13	S
1970			14	S
1971			12	DB
1972			8	S
10 yrs.	131 games			

Leo Katalinas
KATALINAS, LEO
B. Feb. 4, 1915
D. Jul., 1977, Teaneck, NJ
Catholic 6'2" 240 lbs.

1938	GB	N	8	T, G

Jim Katcavage
KATCAVAGE, JAMES R. (Kat)
B. Oct. 28, 1934, Wilkes-Barre, PA
D. Feb. 22, 1995, Maple Glen, PA
Dayton 6'3" 237 lbs.

1956	NYG	N	12	DE
1957			10	DE
1958			11	DE
1959			12	DE
1960			8	DE
1961			14	DE
1962			14	DE
1963			14	DE
1964			14	DE
1965			14	DE
1966			14	DE
1967			14	DE
1968			14	DE
13 yrs.	165 games			

Joe Katcik
KATCIK, JOE
B. 1934
Notre Dame 6'9" 290 lbs.

1960	NY	A		DT

Mike Katolin
KATOLIN, MICHAEL ROSS
B. Jan. 30, 1958, Pasadena, CA
San Jose State 6'3" 255 lbs.

1987	CLE	N	3	C

Mike Katrishen
KATRISHEN, MICHAEL
B. May 7, 1923, Hazleton, PA
Deceased
Southern Mississippi 6'1" 214 lbs.

1948	WAS	N	12	G
1949			11	G
2 yrs.	23 games			

Eric Kattus
KATTUS, JOHN ERIC
B. Mar. 4, 1963, Cincinnati, OH
Michigan 6'5" 235 lbs.

1986	CIN	N	16	TE
1987			11	TE
1988			4	TE
1989			16	TE
1990			16	TE
1991			16	TE
1992	NYJ	N	4	TE
7 yrs.	83 games			

Kani Kauahi
KAUAHI, DANIEL KANI
B. Sep. 6, 1959, Kekaha, HI
Arizona State/Hawaii 6'2" 260 lbs.

1982	SEA	N	2	G
1983			10	C
1984			16	C
1985			16	C
1986			16	C
1988	GB	N	16	C
1989	PHX	N	16	C
1990			15	C
1991			16	C
1992	KC	N	16	C
1993	PHX	N	1	C
11 yrs.	140 games			

John Kauffman
KAUFFMAN, JOHN R.
B. Nov. 27, 1905, Ohio
D. Oct., 1982, Morrison, CO
None

1929	DAY	N	1	T, G

Kaufman
KAUFMAN
None

1925	FRA	N	1	T

Mel Kaufman
KAUFMAN, MEL
B. Feb. 24, 1958, Los Angeles, CA
California Poly (San Luis Obispo) 6'2" 218 lbs.

1981	WAS	N	11	LB
1982			9	LB
1983			16	LB
1984			15	LB
1985			15	LB
1986			2	LB
1987			12	LB
1988			11	LB
8 yrs.	91 games			

Napoleon Kaufman
KAUFMAN, NAPOLEON
B. Jun. 7, 1973, Kansas City, MO
Washington 5'9" 185 lbs.

1995	OAK	N	16	RB
1996			16	RB
2 yrs.	32 games			

Steve Kaufusi
KAUFUSI, STEVE
B. Oct. 17, 1963, Nukualofa, Tonga Islands
Brigham Young 6'4" 274 lbs.

1989	PHI	N	16	DE
1990			16	DE, DT
2 yrs.	32 games			

Thom Kaumeyer
KAUMEYER, THOM
B. Mar. 17, 1967, La Jolla, CA
Oregon 5'11" 187 lbs.

1989	SEA	N	1	CB, S
1990			13	S
2 yrs.	14 games			

Jerry Kauric
KAURIC, JERRY
B. Jun. 28, 1963, Windsor, Ont.
none 6'0" 210 lbs.

1990	CLE	N	14	K

Ken Kavanaugh
KAVANAUGH, KENNETH W., SR.
B. Nov. 23, 1916, Little Rock, AR
Louisiana State 6'3" 207 lbs.

1940	CHIB	N	11	E
1941			11	E
1945			10	E
1946			10	E
1947			12	E
1948			12	E
1949			12	E
1950			12	E
8 yrs.	90 games			

George Kavel
KAVEL, GEORGE
B. 1910
Carnegie-Mellon 5'11" 170 lbs.

1934	PIT	N	1	HB
1934	PHI	N	1	HB
1 yr.	2 games			

Eddie Kaw
KAW, EDGAR LAWRENCE
B. Jan. 18, 1897, Houston, TX
D. Dec. 13, 1971, Walnut Creek, CA
Cornell 5'11" 185 lbs.

1924	BUF	N	11	HB

Eddie Kawal
KAWAL, EDWARD JOSEPH
B. Oct. 13, 1909, Cicero, IL
D. Sep., 1960
Illinois/Widener 6'2" 200 lbs.

1931	CHIB	N	1	C
1934			13	C
1935			12	C, G
1936			10	C
1937	WAS	N	9	C
5 yrs.	45 games			

Bill Kay
KAY, WILLIAM HENRY
B. Jan. 10, 1960, Detroit, MI
Purdue 6'1" 190 lbs.

1981	HOU	N	16	CB, S

Bill Kay *continued*

1982			9	CB, S
1983			16	CB
1984	STL	N	10	S
1984	SD	N	5	CB
4 yrs.	56 games			

Clarence Kay
KAY, CLARENCE HUBERT
B. Jul. 30, 1961, Seneca, SC
Georgia 6'2" 237 lbs.

1984	DEN	N	16	TE
1985			16	TE
1986			13	TE
1987			12	TE
1988			14	TE
1989			16	TE
1990			16	TE
1991			16	TE
1992			16	TE
9 yrs.	135 games			

Rick Kay
KAY, RICHARD FLOYD
B. Nov. 10, 1949, Henderson, NV
Colorado 6'4" 235 lbs.

1973	LA	N	14	LB
1975			14	LB
1976			3	LB
1977			5	LB
1977	ATL	N	7	LB
4 yrs.	43 games			

Duce Keahey
KEAHEY, EULIS
B. Jul. 24, 1917, Meriden, CT
George Washington 6'2" 215 lbs.

1942	NYG	N	2	T
1942	BKN	N	1	T
1 yr.	3 games			

Jim Keane
KEANE, JAMES P., JR.
B. Jan. 11, 1924, Bellaire, OH
Iowa/Northwestern 6'4" 217 lbs.

1946	CHIB	N	10	E
1947			12	E
1948			11	E
1949			12	E
1950			12	E
1951			12	E
1952	GB	N	11	E
7 yrs.	80 games			

Tom Keane
KEANE, THOMAS LAWRENCE
B. Sep. 7, 1926, Bellaire, OH
Ohio State/West Virginia 6'1" 192 lbs.

1948	LA	N	11	HB
1949			10	E
1950			9	E
1951			10	E, HB
1952	DAL	N	12	QB, HB, E
1953	BAL	N	12	HB
1954			12	HB
1955	CHIC	N	11	HB
8 yrs.	87 games			

Frank Kearney
KEARNEY, FRANCIS
B. Dec. 27, 1903
D. Jun., 1971, New Rochelle, NY
Cornell 5'11" 190 lbs.

1926	NY	A	13	T

Jim Kearney
KEARNEY, JAMES LEE

Year Team		Games	Pos.

Jim Kearney *continued*

B. Jan. 21, 1943, Wharton, TX
Prairie View A&M 6'2" 204 lbs.

Year	Team		Games	Pos.
1965	DET	N	7	DB
1966			6	DB
1967	KC	A	3	DB
1968			14	DB
1969			14	S
1970	KC	N	14	S
1971			14	S
1972			14	S
1973			14	S
1974			14	S
1975			14	S
1976	NO	N	14	S

12 yrs. 142 games

Tim Kearney

KEARNEY, TIMOTHY EDWARD
B. Oct. 5, 1950, Kingsford, MI
Northern Michigan 6'2" 225 lbs.

Year	Team		Games	Pos.
1972	CIN	N	1	LB
1973			14	LB
1974			12	LB
1975	KC	N	14	LB
1976	STL	N	12	LB
1977			14	LB
1978			15	LB
1979			5	LB
1980			13	LB
1981			6	LB

10 yrs. 106 games

Tom Kearns

KEARNS, THOMAS NORMAN
B. Nov. 26, 1920, Bedford, MA
Miami (Florida) 6'4" 247 lbs.

Year	Team		Games	Pos.
1945	NYG	N	3	T
1946	CHIC	N	9	T

2 yrs. 12 games

Tim Kearse

KEARSE, TIM ALLYNN
B. Oct. 24, 1959, York, PA
San Jose State 5'10" 182 lbs.

Year	Team		Games	Pos.
1987	IND	N	3	WR

Bill Keating

KEATING, WILLIAM FRANCIS
B. Nov. 22, 1944, Chicago, IL
Michigan 6'2" 236 lbs.

Year	Team		Games	Pos.
1966	DEN	A	14	DT
1967			6	DT
1967	MIA	A	2	DT

2 yrs. 22 games

Chris Keating

KEATING, CHRISTOPHER PAUL
B. Oct. 12, 1957, Boston, MA
Maine 6'2" 223 lbs.

Year	Team		Games	Pos.
1979	BUF	N	16	LB
1980			15	LB
1981			2	LB
1982			9	LB
1983			16	LB
1984			16	LB
1985	WAS	N	10	LB

7 yrs. 84 games

Tom Keating

KEATING, THOMAS ARTHUR
B. Sep. 2, 1942, Chicago, IL
Michigan 6'3" 246 lbs.

Year	Team		Games	Pos.
1964	BUF	A	3	DT
1965			6	DT
1966	OAK	A	14	DT
1967			14	DT
1969			14	DT

Tom Keating *continued*

Year	Team		Games	Pos.
1970	OAK	N	13	DT
1971			7	DT
1972			8	DT
1973	PIT	N	12	DT
1974	KC	N	14	DT
1975			9	DT

11 yrs. 114 games

Stan Keck

KECK, JAMES STANTON
B. Sep. 11, 1897, Greensburg, PA
D. Jan. 20, 1951, Pittsburgh, PA
Princeton 5'11" 205 lbs.

Year	Team		Games	Pos.
1923	CLE	N	2	G, T

Val Keckin

KECKIN, VALDEMAR
B. Feb. 12, 1938, Los Angeles, CA
Southern Mississippi 6'4" 215 lbs.

Year	Team		Games	Pos.
1962	SD	A	6	QB

Dan Kecman

KECMAN, DAN
B. Jun. 10, 1948, Pittsburgh, PA
Maryland 6'2" 230 lbs.

Year	Team		Games	Pos.
1970	BOS	N	1	LB

Jerry Keeble

KEEBLE, JERRY A.
B. Aug. 19, 1963
Minnesota 6'3" 230 lbs.

Year	Team		Games	Pos.
1987	SF	N	3	LB

Joe Keeble

KEEBLE, JOSEPH
B. Aug. 29, 1909
D. Apr., 1984, Atascadero, CA
UCLA 6'0" 190 lbs.

Year	Team		Games	Pos.
1937	CLE	N	7	HB, FB

Emmett Keefe

KEEFE, EMMETT JERRY
B. Apr. 28, 1893
D. Sep. 11, 1965
Notre Dame 5'10" 195 lbs.

Year	Team		Games	Pos.
1920	CHIT	A	7	G
1921	RI	A	7	G
1922	RI	N	5	G
1922	MIL	N	2	G, T

3 yrs. 21 games

Jack Keefer

KEEFER, JACKSON MILLIMAN
B. May 1, 1900
D. Aug. 3, 1966, Dayton, OH
Michigan/Brown 5'9" 172 lbs.

Year	Team		Games	Pos.
1926	PRO	N	10	HB, FB
1928	DAY	N	3	HB, FB

2 yrs. 13 games

Mark Keel

KEEL, MARK ANTHONY
B. Oct. 1, 1961, Fort Worth, TX
Arizona 6'4" 228 lbs.

Year	Team		Games	Pos.
1987	SEA	N	3	TE
1987	KC	N	7	TE

1 yr. 10 games

Ray Keeling

KEELING, RAYMOND GRIGSBY
(King Kong)
B. Aug. 24, 1915, Dallas, TX
Texas 6'3" 259 lbs.

Year	Team		Games	Pos.
1938	PHI	N	9	T

Ray Keeling *continued*

Year	Team		Games	Pos.
1939			9	T, G

2 yrs. 18 games

Rex Keeling

KEELING, REX
B. 1944
Samford 6'3" 220 lbs.

Year	Team		Games	Pos.
1968	CIN	A	1	DB, K

Allen Keen

KEEN, DELBERT ALLEN (Rabbit)
B. 1915
Arkansas 5'9" 170 lbs.

Year	Team		Games	Pos.
1937	PHI	N	8	B
1938			2	B

2 yrs. 10 games

Eddie Keenan

KEENAN, EDWARD
B. Oct. 30, 1895
D. Jan., 1984, Waterbury, CT
Washington (Missouri) 6'4" 320 lbs.

Year	Team		Games	Pos.
1926	HAR	N	10	G

Jack Keenan

KEENAN, JOHN
B. Jun. 8, 1919, Greensboro, NC
South Carolina 5'10" 214 lbs.

Year	Team		Games	Pos.
1944	WAS	N	9	T, C
1945			3	G

2 yrs. 12 games

Bob Keene

KEENE, ROBERT
B. Aug. 26, 1919, Detroit, MI
Detroit 5'11" 191 lbs.

Year	Team		Games	Pos.
1943	DET	N	6	QB
1944			10	HB
1945			1	HB

3 yrs. 17 games

Brad Keeney

KEENEY, BRAD O'HARA
B. Nov. 20, 1973, Augusta, GA
The Citadel 6'3" 294 lbs.

Year	Team		Games	Pos.
1996	NYJ	N	1	DT

Durwood Keeton

KEETON, DURWOOD LEE
B. Aug. 14, 1952, Bonham, TX
Oklahoma 5'10" 180 lbs.

Year	Team		Games	Pos.
1975	NE	N	12	S

Carl Keever

KEEVER, CARL
B. Aug. 17, 1961
Boise State 6'2" 236 lbs.

Year	Team		Games	Pos.
1987	SF	N	3	LB

Scott Kehoe

KEHOE, SCOTT ANTON
B. Sep. 20, 1964, Oak Lawn, IL
Illinois 6'4" 282 lbs.

Year	Team		Games	Pos.
1987	MIA	N	3	OT

Rich Kehr

KEHR, KARL RICHARD
B. Jun. 18, 1959, Phoenixville, PA
Carthage 6'3" 285 lbs.

Year	Team		Games	Pos.
1987	WAS	N	5	G

Mike Keim

KEIM, MIKE
B. Nov. 12, 1965, Anaheim, CA
Brigham Young 6'7" 293 lbs.

Year	Team		Games	Pos.
1991	NO	N	1	OT
1992	SEA	N	1	OT
1993			3	OT
1994			15	OT
1995			6	OT

5 yrs. 26 games

Craig Keith

KEITH, CRAIG CARLTON
B. Apr. 27, 1971, Raleigh, NC
Lenoir-Rhyne 6'3" 262 lbs.

Year	Team		Games	Pos.
1993	PIT	N	1	TE
1994			16	TE
1995	JAC	N	11	TE

3 yrs. 28 games

Gary Keithley

KEITHLEY, GARY TOM
B. Jan. 11, 1951, Alvin, TX
Texas/Texas-El Paso 6'3" 210 lbs.

Year	Team		Games	Pos.
1973	STL	N	14	QB

Jim Kekeris

KEKERIS, JAMES J.
B. Oct. 17, 1923, St. Louis, MO
Missouri 6'1" 266 lbs.

Year	Team		Games	Pos.
1947	PHI	N	10	T
1948	GB	N	5	T

2 yrs. 15 games

Louie Kelcher

KELCHER, LOUIE JAMES
B. Aug. 23, 1953, Beaumont, TX
Southern Methodist 6'5" 290 lbs.

Year	Team		Games	Pos.
1975	SD	N	13	DT
1976			14	DT
1977			12	DT
1978			15	DT
1979			1	DT
1980			15	DT
1981			14	DT
1982			8	DT
1983			8	DT
1984	SF	N	16	NT

10 yrs. 116 games

Paul Kell

KELL, PAUL ERNEST
B. Jul. 8, 1915
D. May, 1977, Chippewa Falls, WI
Notre Dame 6'2" 217 lbs.

Year	Team		Games	Pos.
1939	GB	N	8	T
1940			11	T

2 yrs. 19 games

Bill Kellagher

KELLAGHER, WILLIAM M.
(Spinner)
B. Aug. 13, 1920, Locust Gap, PA
Fordham 5'11" 205 lbs.

Year	Team		Games	Pos.
1946	CHI	AA	12	FB
1947			14	B
1948			12	B

3 yrs. 38 games

Bill Kellar

KELLAR, WILLIAM ELDEN
B. Feb. 8, 1956, Longview, WA
Stanford 5'11" 187 lbs.

Year	Team		Games	Pos.
1978	KC	N	5	WR

Mark Kellar
KELLAR, MARK PETER
B. Jul. 17, 1952, Chicago, IL
Northern Illinois 6'0" 225 lbs.

Year	Team		Games	Pos.
1976	MIN	N	6	RB
1977			14	RB
1978			16	RB
3 yrs.	36 games			

Scott Kellar
KELLAR, SCOTT JEFFREY
B. Dec. 31, 1963, Elgin, IL
Northern Illinois 6'3" 278 lbs.

Year	Team		Games	Pos.
1986	IND	N	14	DE
1987			3	NT
2 yrs.	17 games			

Kenny Keller
KELLER, KENNETH RAY
B. Sep. 12, 1934, Salinas, PA
North Carolina 5'11" 185 lbs.

Year	Team		Games	Pos.
1956	PHI	N	11	HB
1957			12	HB
2 yrs.	23 games			

Larry Keller
KELLER, LARRY RAY
B. Oct. 2, 1953, San Benito, TX
Houston 6'2" 223 lbs.

Year	Team		Games	Pos.
1976	NYJ	N	14	LB
1977			14	LB
1978			16	LB
3 yrs.	44 games			

Mike Keller
KELLER, MICHAEL
B. Dec. 13, 1949, Chicago, IL
Michigan 6'4" 220 lbs.

Year	Team		Games	Pos.
1972	DAL	N	5	LB

Ernie Kellerman
KELLERMAN, ERNIE JAMES
B. Dec. 17, 1943, Cleveland, OH
Miami (Ohio) 6'0" 184 lbs.

Year	Team		Games	Pos.
1966	CLE	N	14	DB
1967			14	DB
1968			14	DB
1969			11	S
1970			14	S
1971			14	S
1972	CIN	N	4	S
1973	BUF	N	10	S
8 yrs.	95 games			

Doug Kellermeyer
KELLERMEYER, DOUGLAS ARTHUR
B. Jun. 1, 1961, Bucyrus, OH
Brigham Young 6'3" 275 lbs.

Year	Team		Games	Pos.
1987	HOU	N	3	OT

Billy Kelley
KELLEY, BILLY R.
B. Aug. 23, 1926, Boston, TX
Texas Tech 6'2" 195 lbs.

Year	Team		Games	Pos.
1949	GB	N	12	E

Bob Kelley
KELLEY, ROBERT
B. May 8, 1930, Hereford, TX
West Texas State 6'2" 232 lbs.

Year	Team		Games	Pos.
1955	PHI	N	12	C
1956			12	C
2 yrs.	24 games			

Brian Kelley
KELLEY, BRIAN LEE
B. Sep. 1, 1951, Dallas, TX
California Lutheran 6'3" 222 lbs.

Year	Team		Games	Pos.
1973	NYG	N	14	LB
1974			13	LB
1975			14	LB
1976			14	LB
1977			13	LB
1978			16	LB
1979			16	LB
1980			2	LB
1981			16	LB
1982			9	LB
1983			16	LB
11 yrs.	143 games			

Chris Kelley
KELLEY, CHRIS
B. Nov. 13, 1964, Lorain, OH
Akron 6'4" 239 lbs.

Year	Team		Games	Pos.
1987	CLE	N	2	TE

Doc Kelley
KELLEY, ALBERT J.
B. Mar. 1, 1902
Deceased
Northwestern 5'10" 170 lbs.

Year	Team		Games	Pos.
1924	DUL	N	5	HB
1925			3	HB
1926			6	HB, QB
3 yrs.	14 games			

Ed Kelley
KELLEY, EDWARD ALLEN
B. Feb. 18, 1924, Sugar Land, TX
Texas 6'4" 230 lbs.

Year	Team		Games	Pos.
1949	LA	AA	12	T

Ed Kelley
KELLEY, EDWARD C., JR.
B. 1935
Texas 6'2" 195 lbs.

Year	Team		Games	Pos.
1961	DAL	A	13	DB
1962			1	DB
2 yrs.	14 games			

Frank Kelley
KELLEY, FRANK
B. Oct., 1903
Deceased
South Dakota State 5'10" 165 lbs.

Year	Team		Games	Pos.
1927	CLE	N	8	HB

Gordon Kelley
KELLEY, GORDON
B. Jun. 11, 1938, Atlanta, GA
Georgia 6'3" 230 lbs.

Year	Team		Games	Pos.
1960	SF	N	12	LB
1961			14	LB
1962	WAS	N	11	LB
1963			14	LB
4 yrs.	51 games			

Ike Kelley
KELLEY, DWIGHT ALLEN
B. Jul. 14, 1944, Ludington, MI
Ohio State 5'11" 224 lbs.

Year	Team		Games	Pos.
1966	PHI	N	14	LB
1967			14	LB
1969			14	LB
1970			11	LB
1971			14	LB
5 yrs.	67 games			

Les Kelley
KELLEY, LESLIE HOWARD
B. Dec. 9, 1944, Decatur, AL
Alabama 6'3" 233 lbs.

Year	Team		Games	Pos.
1967	NO	N	4	LB
1968			14	LB
1969			14	LB
3 yrs.	32 games			

Mike Kelley
KELLEY, MICHAEL DENNIS
B. Dec. 31, 1959, Sonora, CA
Georgia Tech 6'3" 195 lbs.

Year	Team		Games	Pos.
1987	SD	N	3	QB

Mike Kelley
KELLEY, MIKE
B. Aug. 27, 1962, Westfield, MA
Notre Dame 6'5" 266 lbs.

Year	Team		Games	Pos.
1985	HOU	N	16	C, G
1987			1	G
2 yrs.	17 games			

Kevin Kellin
KELLIN, KEVIN ROBERT
B. Nov. 16, 1959, Hampton, IA
Minnesota 6'6" 265 lbs.

Year	Team		Games	Pos.
1986	TB	N	9	DE
1987			7	DE
1988			4	DE
3 yrs.	20 games			

John Kellison
KELLISON, JOHN SNOWDEN (Honest)
B. Nov. 3, 1886, Buckeye, WV
D. May 7, 1971, Marlinton, WV
West Virginia Wesleyan 6'1" 210 lbs.

Year	Team		Games	Pos.
1920	CAN	A	3	G
1921			3	G
1922	TOL	N	1	T
3 yrs.	7 games			

Kellogg
KELLOGG
None

Year	Team		Games	Pos.
1921	MUN	A	1	HB

Bill Kellogg
KELLOGG, WILLIAM J.
B. Mar. 3, 1897
D. Nov., 1969, Syracuse, NY
Syracuse 5'10" 178 lbs.

Year	Team		Games	Pos.
1924	FRA	N	4	HB, FB
1925	ROC	N	5	HB, FB
2 yrs.	9 games			

Bobby Kellogg
KELLOGG, ROBERT F.
B. Aug. 4, 1917
D. May 9, 1985, Columbus, MS
Tulane 5'10" 175 lbs.

Year	Team		Games	Pos.
1940	CHIC	N	3	B

Clarence Kellogg
KELLOGG, CLARENCE
B. 1912
D. Sep. 3, 1988, Denver, CO
St. Mary's (California) 5'10" 205 lbs.

Year	Team		Games	Pos.
1936	CHIC	N	12	FB

Mike Kellogg
KELLOGG, MICHAEL KARL
B. Oct. 28, 1943, Long Beach, CA
Santa Clara 6'0" 220 lbs.

Year	Team		Games	Pos.
1966	DEN	A	8	FB

Mike Kellogg continued

Year	Team		Games	Pos.
1967			2	RB
2 yrs.	10 games			

Marv Kellum
KELLUM, MARVIN LEE
B. Jun. 23, 1952, Topeka, KS
Wichita State 6'2" 225 lbs.

Year	Team		Games	Pos.
1974	PIT	N	14	LB
1975			14	LB
1976			14	LB
1977	STL	N	14	LB
4 yrs.	56 games			

Bill Kelly
KELLY, WILLIAM (Wild Bill)
B. Jun. 24, 1905, Denver, CO
D. Nov. 14, 1931, New York, NY
Montana 5'10" 184 lbs.

Year	Team		Games	Pos.
1927	NYY	N	12	QB, FB, HB
1928			12	HB, QB
1929	FRA	N	17	QB, HB
1930	BKN	N	12	HB, QB
4 yrs.	53 games			

Bob Kelly
KELLY, ROBERT
B. Aug. 8, 1941, Carlsbad, NM
New Mexico State 6'3" 261 lbs.

Year	Team		Games	Pos.
1961	HOU	A	14	OT
1962			6	DT
1963			11	OT
1964			1	OT
1967	KC	A	3	OT
1968	CIN	A	4	OT
6 yrs.	39 games			

Bob Kelly
KELLY, ROBERT JOSEPH
B. Jun. 6, 1925, Chicago, IL
Notre Dame/Navy 5'10" 192 lbs.

Year	Team		Games	Pos.
1947	LA	AA	12	B
1948			4	B
1949	BAL	AA	10	B
3 yrs.	26 games			

Clancy Kelly
KELLY, CLARENCE A. (Tex)
B. Oct. 29, 1898, Colorado
D. Feb., 1978, Shawnee, OK
None 6'3" 220 lbs.

Year	Team		Games	Pos.
1922	TOL	N	6	G, T, E
1923	BUF	N	2	G, T
1925	ROC	N	6	T, C
1926	BUF	N	1	G
1929	ORA	N	1	T
5 yrs.	16 games			

Ellison Kelly
KELLY, ELLISON L.
B. May 17, 1936, Lake City, FL
Michigan State 6'1" 235 lbs.

Year	Team		Games	Pos.
1959	NYG	N	12	G

Elmo Kelly
KELLY, ELMO
B. Feb. 10, 1917, Tipton, OK
Wichita State 6'1" 210 lbs.

Year	Team		Games	Pos.
1944	CHIB	N	5	E

Jim Kelly
KELLY, JAMES
B. Aug. 7, 1951, Columbia, TN
Tennessee State 6'4" 210 lbs.

Year	Team		Games	Pos.
1974	CHI	N	14	TE

Year Team	Games	Pos.

Jim Kelly
KELLY, JAMES EDWARD
B. Feb. 14, 1960, Pittsburgh, PA
Miami (Florida) 6'3" 215 lbs.

Year	Team		Games	Pos.
1986	BUF	N	16	QB
1987			12	QB
1988			16	QB
1989			13	QB
1990			14	QB
1991			15	QB
1992			16	QB
1993			16	QB
1994			14	QB
1995			15	QB
1996			13	QB

11 yrs. 160 games

Jim Kelly
KELLY, JAMES HARRY
B. Apr. 23, 1942, McKeesport, PA
Notre Dame 6'3" 225 lbs.

Year	Team		Games	Pos.
1964	PIT	N	6	OE
1965	PHI	N	1	OE
1967			12	TE

3 yrs. 19 games

Jimmy Kelly
KELLY, JAMES J., JR.
B. 1890, Michigan
Deceased
St. Louis/Detroit 5'9" 160 lbs.

Year	Team		Games	Pos.
1920	DET	A	3	HB

Joe Kelly
KELLY, JOSEPH WINSTON
B. Dec. 11, 1964, Sun Valley, CA
Washington 6'2" 227 lbs.

Year	Team		Games	Pos.
1986	CIN	N	16	LB
1987			10	LB
1988			16	LB
1989			16	LB
1990	NYJ	N	12	LB
1991			16	LB
1992			9	LB
1993	LARI	N	16	LB
1994	LARM	N	16	LB
1995	GB	N	13	LB
1996	PHI	N	16	LB

11 yrs. 156 games

John Kelly
KELLY, JOHN D.
B. Mar. 31, 1944, Fort Lauderdale, FL
Florida A&M 6'3" 257 lbs.

Year	Team		Games	Pos.
1966	WAS	N	2	C
1967			14	OT

2 yrs. 16 games

John Kelly
KELLY, JOHN SIMMS (Shipwreck)
B. Jul. 8, 1910
Deceased
Kentucky 6'2" 190 lbs.

Year	Team		Games	Pos.
1932	NYG	N	5	HB
1933	BKN	N	10	HB, QB
1934			9	QB, HB
1937			1	HB

4 yrs. 25 games

Leroy Kelly
KELLY, LEROY
B. May 20, 1942, Philadelphia, PA
Morgan State 6'0" 199 lbs.

Year	Team		Games	Pos.
1964	CLE	N	14	HB
1965			13	HB
1966			14	RB
1967			14	RB
1968			14	RB

Leroy Kelly continued

Year	Games	Pos.
1969	13	RB
1970	13	RB
1971	14	RB
1972	14	RB
1973	13	RB

10 yrs. 136 games

Mike Kelly
KELLY, MICHAEL GREY
B. Jan. 14, 1948, Davidson, NC
Davidson 6'4" 217 lbs.

Year	Team		Games	Pos.
1970	CIN	N	12	TE, WR
1971			14	TE
1972			13	TE
1973	NO	N	1	TE

4 yrs. 40 games

Pat Kelly
KELLY, PATRICK JOSEPH
B. Oct. 29, 1965, Rochester, NY
Syracuse 6'6" 252 lbs.

Year	Team		Games	Pos.
1988	DEN	N	16	TE
1989			16	TE
1990	NYJ	N	1	TE
1991			8	TE

4 yrs. 41 games

Todd Kelly
KELLY, TODD ERIC
B. Nov. 27, 1970, Hampton, VA
Tennessee 6'2" 259 lbs.

Year	Team		Games	Pos.
1993	SF	N	14	LB
1994			11	DE
1995	CIN	N	16	DE
1996			3	DE
1996	ATL	N	2	DE

4 yrs. 46 games

Larry Kelm
KELM, LARRY DEAN
B. Nov. 29, 1964, Corpus Christi, TX
Texas A&M 6'4" 226 lbs.

Year	Team		Games	Pos.
1987	LARM	N	12	LB
1988			16	LB
1989			7	LB
1990			11	LB
1991			16	LB
1992			16	LB
1993	SF	N	10	LB

7 yrs. 88 games

Matt Kelsch
KELSCH, MATTHEW L.
B. Oct. 11, 1906
D. Jan., 1976, Brooklyn, NY
Iowa 5'11" 190 lbs.

Year	Team		Games	Pos.
1930	BKN	N	2	E

Mose Kelsch
KELSCH, CHRISTIAN
B. 1896
D. Jul., 1935, Pittsburgh, PA
None 5'10" 223 lbs.

Year	Team		Games	Pos.
1933	PIT	N	8	FB, HB
1934			8	FB

2 yrs. 16 games

Mark Kelso
KELSO, MARK ALAN
B. Jul. 23, 1963, Pittsburgh, PA
William & Mary 5'11" 177 lbs.

Year	Team		Games	Pos.
1986	BUF	N	3	S
1987			12	S
1988			16	S
1989			16	S
1990			6	S

Mark Kelso continued

Year	Games	Pos.
1991	16	S
1992	16	S
1993	14	S

8 yrs. 99 games

Bobby Kemp
KEMP, BOBBY
B. May 29, 1959, Oakland, CA
Fullerton State 6'0" 191 lbs.

Year	Team		Games	Pos.
1981	CIN	N	16	CB, S
1982			9	S
1983			16	S
1984			10	S
1985			16	S
1986			16	S
1987	TB	N	12	S

7 yrs. 95 games

Jack Kemp
KEMP, JOHN FRENCH
B. Jul. 13, 1935, Los Angeles, CA
Occidental 6'1" 201 lbs.

Year	Team		Games	Pos.
1957	PIT	N	4	QB
1960	LA	A	13	QB
1961	SD	A	14	QB
1962			2	QB
1963	BUF	A	14	QB
1964			14	QB
1965			14	QB
1966			14	QB
1967			14	QB
1969			14	QB

10 yrs. 117 games

Jeff Kemp
KEMP, JEFFREY ALLAN
B. Jul. 11, 1959, Santa Ana, CA
Dartmouth 6'0" 201 lbs.

Year	Team		Games	Pos.
1981	LA	N	1	QB
1983	LARM	N	4	QB
1984			14	QB
1985			5	QB
1986	SF	N	10	QB
1987	SEA	N	13	QB
1988			11	QB
1989			9	QB
1990			15	QB
1991			7	QB
1991	PHI	N	9	QB

10 yrs. 98 games

Perry Kemp
KEMP, PERRY COMMODORE
B. Dec. 31, 1961, Canonsburg, PA
California (Pennsylvania) 5'11" 170 lbs.

Year	Team		Games	Pos.
1987	CLE	N	3	WR
1988	GB	N	16	WR
1989			14	WR
1990			16	WR
1991			16	WR

5 yrs. 65 games

Ray Kemp
KEMP, RAYMOND HOWARD
B. Apr. 4, 1907, Cecil, PA
Duquesne 6'1" 215 lbs.

Year	Team		Games	Pos.
1933	PIT	N	4	T

Florian Kempf
KEMPF, FLORIAN GERARD
B. May 25, 1956, Philadelphia, PA
Pennsylvania 5'9" 170 lbs.

Year	Team		Games	Pos.
1982	HOU	N	9	K
1983			16	K
1984			9	K
1987	NO	N	1	K

4 yrs. 35 games

Charles Kempinska
KEMPINSKA, CHARLES C. (Butch)
B. 1939
Mississippi 6'0" 235 lbs.

Year	Team		Games	Pos.
1960	LA	A		G

Herb Kempton
KEMPTON, HERBERT MAYBERRY (Fido)
B. Dec. 8, 1892, Malden, MA
D. Sep. 23, 1970, Ocala, FL
Yale 5'8" 155 lbs.

Year	Team		Games	Pos.
1921	CAN	A	7	QB

Chuck Kendall
KENDALL, CHARLES
B. 1935
UCLA 6'2" 185 lbs.

Year	Team		Games	Pos.
1960	HOU	A		DB

Pete Kendall
KENDALL, PETER MARCUS
B. Jul. 9, 1973, Weymouth, MA
Boston College 6'5" 292 lbs.

Year	Team		Games	Pos.
1996	SEA	N	12	G

Jim Kendrick
KENDRICK, JAMES M.
B. Aug. 22, 1893
Texas A&M 6'0" 197 lbs.

Year	Team		Games	Pos.
1922	CAN	N	4	E
1922	TOL	N	2	E
1923	LOU	N	3	E, HB, T, G
1924	CHIB	N	9	HB
1925	RI	N	1	E
1925	HAM	N	2	QB
1925	BUF	N	7	HB
1925	ROC	N	1	C
1926	BUF	N	10	QB
1927	NYG	N	8	E, G

6 yrs. 47 games

Vince Kendrick
KENDRICK, VINCENT
B. Mar. 18, 1952, Miami, FL
Florida 6'0" 231 lbs.

Year	Team		Games	Pos.
1974	ATL	N	14	RB
1976	TB	N	1	RB

2 yrs. 15 games

John Kenerson
KENERSON, JOHN
B. Mar. 18, 1938, Chicago, IL
Kentucky State 6'3" 255 lbs.

Year	Team		Games	Pos.
1960	LA	N	7	T
1962	PIT	N	1	DT
1962	NY	A	8	DE

2 yrs. 16 games

Mike Kenn
KENN, MICHAEL LEE
B. Feb. 9, 1956, Evanston, IL
Michigan 6'7" 275 lbs.

Year	Team		Games	Pos.
1978	ATL	N	16	OT
1979			16	OT
1980			16	OT
1981			9	OT
1982			9	OT
1983			16	OT
1984			14	OT
1985			11	OT
1986			16	OT
1987			12	OT
1988			16	OT
1989			15	OT
1990			16	OT

Year	Team	Games	Pos.

Mike Kenn *continued*

Year	Team		Games	Pos.
1991			16	OT
1992			16	OT
1993			16	OT
1994			15	OT
17 yrs.	252 games			

Derek Kennard
KENNARD, DEREK
B. Sep. 9, 1962, Stockton, CA
Nevada-Reno 6'3" 285 lbs.

1986	STL	N	15	G
1987			12	G
1988	PHX	N	16	C
1989			14	C, G
1990			16	C, G
1991	NO	N	3	G
1992			16	G
1993			16	G
1994	DAL		16	G
1995			8	C, G
1996			1	G
11 yrs.	133 games			

George Kennard
KENNARD, GEORGE
B. 1929
Kansas 6'0" 210 lbs.

1952	NYG	N	12	G
1953			12	G
1954			12	G
1955			12	G
4 yrs.	48 games			

Ken Kennard
KENNARD, KENNETH
B. Oct. 4, 1954, Fort Worth, TX
Angelo State 6'2" 252 lbs.

1977	HOU	N	14	MG
1978			16	MG
1979			16	MG
1980			16	NT
1981			16	DT
1982			9	NT
6 yrs.	87 games			

George Kenneally
KENNEALLY, GEORGE V., SR.
B. Apr. 12, 1902, South Boston, MA
D. Sep. 3, 1968, Dorchester, MA
St. Bonaventure 6'0" 190 lbs.

1926	POT	N	11	E, HB
1927			13	E
1928			9	E
1929	BOS	N	8	E
1930	CHIC	N	11	E
1932	BOS	N	10	E
1933	PHI	N	8	E
1934			11	E
1935			8	E, QB
9 yrs.	89 games			

Allan Kennedy
KENNEDY, ALLAN STEPHEN
B. Jan. 18, 1958, Vancouver, B.C.
Washington State 6'7" 268 lbs.

1981	SF	N	3	OT
1983			16	OT
1984			15	OT
3 yrs.	34 games			

Bill Kennedy
KENNEDY, WILLIAM JAMES
B. Mar. 13, 1919, Lee, MA
Michigan State 5'11" 200 lbs.

1942	DET	N	11	G
1947	BOS	N	12	G
2 yrs.	23 games			

Bob Kennedy
KENNEDY, ROBERT H.
B. 1921
Washington State 5'11" 195 lbs.

1946	NY	AA	13	FB
1947			14	B
1948			14	B
1949	B-NY	AA	12	B
1950	NYY	N	5	B
5 yrs.	58 games			

Bob Kennedy
KENNEDY, ROBERT M.
B. Sep. 16, 1928, Weehawken, NJ
North Carolina 6'0" 178 lbs.

1949	LA	AA	10	B

Cortez Kennedy
KENNEDY, CORTEZ
B. Aug. 23, 1968, Osceola, AR
Miami (Florida) 6'3" 293 lbs.

1990	SEA	N	16	NT
1991			16	DT
1992			16	DT
1993			16	DT
1994			16	DT
1995			16	DT
1996			16	DT
7 yrs.	112 games			

Jimmie Kennedy
KENNEDY, JAMES DALE
B. Jul. 30, 1952, Laurel, MS
Hiram/Colorado State 6'5" 231 lbs.

1975	BAL	N	14	TE
1976			14	TE
1977			9	TE
3 yrs.	37 games			

Jimmy Kennedy
KENNEDY, JAMES DAVID
B. Feb. 16, 1901
D. Aug. 4, 1968
Boston College/Holy Cross 5'9" 160 lbs.

1925	BUF	N	1	FB

Lincoln Kennedy
KENNEDY, TAMERLANE LINCOLN
B. Feb. 12, 1971, York, PA
Washington 6'6" 335 lbs.

1993	ATL	N	16	OT, G
1994			16	G, OT
1995			16	G, OT
1996	OAK	N	16	OT
4 yrs.	64 games			

Mike Kennedy
KENNEDY, MICHAEL SCOTT
B. Feb. 26, 1959, Toledo, OH
Toledo 6'0" 195 lbs.

1983	BUF	N	12	S
1984	HOU	N	11	S
2 yrs.	23 games			

Sam Kennedy
KENNEDY, SAMUEL EDWARD
B. Jul. 10, 1964, San Mateo, CA
San Jose State 6'3" 235 lbs.

1988	SF	N	16	LB

Tom Kennedy
KENNEDY, THOMAS
B. Jun. 4, 1920, Pittsfield, MA
Wayne State 6'0" 218 lbs.

1944	DET	N	1	T

Tom Kennedy
KENNEDY, THOMAS PATRICK
B. Nov. 27, 1940, Maywood, CA
Los Angeles State 6'1" 200 lbs.

1966	NYG	N	6	QB

Bill Kenney
KENNEY, WILLIAM PATRICK
B. Jan. 20, 1955, San Francisco, CA
Arizona State/Northern Colorado 6'4" 217 lbs.

1980	KC	N	3	QB
1981			13	QB
1982			7	QB
1983			16	QB
1984			9	QB
1985			16	QB
1986			15	QB
1987			11	QB
1988			16	QB
9 yrs.	106 games			

Steve Kenney
KENNEY, STEVEN FAUCETTE
B. Dec. 26, 1955, Wilmington, NC
Clemson 6'4" 262 lbs.

1980	PHI	N	15	OT
1981			13	OT
1982			9	G
1983			16	G
1984			11	G
1985			16	G
1986	DET	N	9	G
7 yrs.	89 games			

Eddie Kennison
KENNISON, EDDIE JOSEPH, III
B. Jan. 20, 1973, Lake Charles, LA
Louisiana State 6'0" 191 lbs.

1996	STL	N	15	WR

Greg Kent
KENT, EDWARD GREG
B. Jul. 18, 1944, Elkhorn, WI
Wisconsin/Utah 6'6" 270 lbs.

1966	OAK	A	7	DE
1968	DET	N	5	OT
2 yrs.	12 games			

Bill Kenyon
KENYON, WILLIAM CURTIS
B. Dec. 5, 1898, Manchester, NH
Deceased
Georgetown (DC) 5'9" 180 lbs.

1925	NYG	N	1	QB

Crawford Ker
KER, CRAWFORD FRANCIS
B. May 5, 1962, Philadelphia, PA
Florida 6'3" 285 lbs.

1985	DAL	N	5	G
1986			16	G
1987			12	G
1988			16	G
1989			16	G
1990			14	G
1991	DEN	N	12	G
7 yrs.	91 games			

Nick Kerasiotis
KERASIOTIS, NICHOLAS PETER
B. Jul. 4, 1918, Chicago, IL
St. Ambrose 5'11" 195 lbs.

1942	CHIB	N	9	G
1945			1	G
2 yrs.	10 games			

Randy Kerbow
KERBOW, RANDALL
B. 1941
Rice 6'1" 190 lbs.

1963	HOU	A	8	FL

Bob Kercher
KERCHER, ROBERT FRED
B. Jan. 14, 1919, Evansville, IN
Georgetown 6'2" 196 lbs.

1944	GB	N	1	E

Dick Kercher
KERCHER, RICHARD S.
B. 1932
Tulsa 6'2" 205 lbs.

1954	DET	N	7	HB

Ralph Kercheval
KERCHEVAL, RALPH
B. Dec. 1, 1911, Lexington, KY
Kentucky 6'1" 190 lbs.

1934	BKN	N	11	HB
1935			12	QB, HB
1936			12	HB
1937			8	HB, QB
1938			11	HB
1939			9	HB
1940			10	B
7 yrs.	74 games			

Gary Kerkorian
KERKORIAN, GARY R.
B. Jan. 14, 1930
Stanford 5'11" 185 lbs.

1952	PIT	N	10	QB
1954	BAL	N	9	QB
1955			4	QB
1956			3	QB
4 yrs.	26 games			

Bill Kern
KERN, WILLIAM F.
B. Sep. 3, 1906
D. Apr. 8, 1985, Pittsburgh, PA
Pittsburgh 6'0" 187 lbs.

1929	GB	N	11	T
1930			6	T, E
2 yrs.	17 games			

Don Kern
KERN, DON EMIT, III
B. Aug. 25, 1962, Los Gatos, CA
Arizona State 6'4" 235 lbs.

1984	CIN	N	16	TE
1985			8	TE
1986	BUF	N	1	TE
3 yrs.	25 games			

Rex Kern
KERN, REX WILLIAM
B. May 28, 1949, Lancaster, OH
Ohio State 5'11" 190 lbs.

1971	BAL	N	14	DB
1972			5	CB
1973			14	CB
1974	BUF	N	8	CB, S
4 yrs.	41 games			

Marlon Kerner
KERNER, MARLON
B. Mar. 18, 1973, Columbus, OH
Ohio State 5'10" 187 lbs.

1995	BUF	N	14	CB
1996			15	CB
2 yrs.	29 games			

Year	Team		Games	Pos.

John Kerns

KERNS, JOHN E. (Moose)
B. Jun. 17, 1923, Ashtabula, OH
Deceased
Ohio U./Duke/North Carolina/Ohio U.
6'3" 243 lbs.

Year	Team		Games	Pos.
1947	**BUF**	**AA**	14	T
1948			14	T
1949			12	T
3 yrs.	40 games			

Graham Kernwein

KERNWEIN, GRAHAM A.
B. Oct. 23, 1904
D. Jan., 1983, Rockford, IL
Chicago 5'11" 175 lbs.

Year	Team		Games	Pos.
1926	**RAC**	**N**	4	HB

Bill Kerr

KERR, WILLIAM H.
B. 1916
Notre Dame 6'0" 220 lbs.

Year	Team		Games	Pos.
1946	**LA**	**AA**	11	E

George Kerr

KERR, GEORGE (Doc)
B. Aug. 28, 1893
D. Oct., 1977, Frazeysburg, OH
Catholic 6'1" 211 lbs.

Year	Team		Games	Pos.
1920	**CLE**	**A**	1	T
1921	**NY**	**A**	1	G
1926	**NEW**	**A**	1	G
3 yrs.	3 games			

Jim Kerr

KERR, JAMES N.
B. Jul. 23, 1939, Colver, PA
Penn State 6'0" 195 lbs.

Year	Team		Games	Pos.
1961	**WAS**	**N**	13	DB
1962			11	DB
2 yrs.	24 games			

Mike Kerrigan

KERRIGAN, MICHAEL JOSEPH
B. Apr. 27, 1960, Chicago, IL
Northwestern 6'3" 205 lbs.

Year	Team		Games	Pos.
1983	**NE**	**N**	1	QB
1984			1	QB
2 yrs.	2 games			

Tom Kerrigan

KERRIGAN, THOMAS
B. Jul. 7, 1906
D. Jul., 1979, Stamford, CT
Columbia 6'2" 200 lbs.

Year	Team		Games	Pos.
1929	**ORA**	**N**	1	G
1930	**NEW**	**N**	3	G
2 yrs.	4 games			

Merritt Kersey

KERSEY, MERRITT WARREN
B. Feb. 22, 1950, Alexandria, VA
West Chester State 6'1" 205 lbs.

Year	Team		Games	Pos.
1974	**PHI**	**N**	14	P
1975			2	P
2 yrs.	16 games			

George Kershaw

KERSHAW, GEORGE A.
B. 1927
Colgate 6'4" 210 lbs.

Year	Team		Games	Pos.
1949	**NYG**	**N**	9	E

Wally Kersten

KERSTEN, WALLACE TODD

Wally Kersten continued

B. Dec. 8, 1959, Minneapolis, MN
Minnesota 6'5" 270 lbs.

Year	Team		Games	Pos.
1982	**LARM**	**N**	3	OT

Bob Keseday

KESEDAY, BOB
B. Jan. 9, 1965
Texas-El Paso 6'4" 225 lbs.

Year	Team		Games	Pos.
1987	**STL**	**N**	3	TE

Alex Ketzko

KETZKO, ALEXANDER G.
B. 1918
D. Dec. 23, 1944, France
Michigan State 5'11" 215 lbs.

Year	Team		Games	Pos.
1943	**DET**		9	T

Ken Keuper

KEUPER, KENNETH E. (Red)
B. Nov. 14, 1918, Waukesha, WI
Georgia 6'0" 207 lbs.

Year	Team		Games	Pos.
1945	**GB**	**N**	9	FB
1946			10	HB
1947			12	HB
1948	**NYG**	**N**	7	HB
4 yrs.	38 games			

Allan Key

KEY, ALLAN WADE
B. Oct. 14, 1946, San Antonio, TX
Texas/Southwest Texas State 6'4" 245 lbs.

Year	Team		Games	Pos.
1970	**PHI**	**N**	14	OT
1971			14	OT
1972			13	OT
1973			12	OT
1974			14	G
1975			2	G
1976			13	G
1977			14	G
1978			13	G
1979			12	G
10 yrs.	121 games			

David Key

KEY, DAVID RUSSELL
B. Mar. 27, 1968, Columbus, OH
Michigan 5'10" 190 lbs.

Year	Team		Games	Pos.
1991	**NE**	**N**	3	CB

Bob Keyes

KEYES, ROBERT
B. 1936
San Diego State 5'10" 183 lbs.

Year	Team		Games	Pos.
1960	**OAK**	**A**		HB

Jimmy Keyes

KEYES, JIMMY ELTON
B. Jun. 16, 1944, Laurel, MS
Mississippi 6'2" 225 lbs.

Year	Team		Games	Pos.
1968	**MIA**	**A**	12	LB, K
1969			5	LB, K
2 yrs.	17 games			

Leroy Keyes

KEYES, LEROY
B. Feb. 18, 1947, Newport News, VA
Purdue 6'3" 208 lbs.

Year	Team		Games	Pos.
1969	**PHI**	**N**	14	RB
1970			3	RB
1971			14	RB
1972			14	S
1973	**KC**	**N**	3	S
5 yrs.	48 games			

Marcus Keyes

KEYES, WILLIS MARCUS
B. Oct. 20, 1973, Taylorsville, MS
North Alabama 6'3" 310 lbs.

Year	Team		Games	Pos.
1996	**CHI**	**N**	2	DT

Brady Keys

KEYS, BRADY, JR.
B. May 19, 1936, Austin, TX
Colorado State 6'0" 189 lbs.

Year	Team		Games	Pos.
1961	**PIT**		12	DB
1962			14	DB
1963			11	DB
1964			14	DB
1965			14	DB
1966			14	DB
1967			6	DB
1967	**MIN**	**N**	14	DB
1968	**STL**	**N**	7	CB
8 yrs.	106 games			

Howard Keys

KEYS, HOWARD N. (Sonny)
B. Jan. 24, 1935, Orlando, OK
Oklahoma State 6'3" 239 lbs.

Year	Team		Games	Pos.
1960	**PHI**	**N**	12	C, T
1961			14	C
1962			13	C
1963			2	C, G, OT
4 yrs.	41 games			

Tyrone Keys

KEYS, TYRONE P.
B. Oct. 24, 1960, Jackson, MS
Mississippi State 6'7" 260 lbs.

Year	Team		Games	Pos.
1983	**CHI**	**N**	14	DE
1984			14	DE
1985			16	DE
1986	**TB**		14	DE
1987			3	DE
1988	**SD**	**N**	13	DE
6 yrs.	74 games			

Jon Keyworth

KEYWORTH, JONATHAN KIMBALL
B. Dec. 15, 1950, San Diego, CA
Colorado 6'3" 231 lbs.

Year	Team		Games	Pos.
1974	**DEN**	**N**	14	RB
1975			14	RB
1976			14	RB
1977			11	RB
1978			16	RB
1979			16	RB
1980			10	RB
7 yrs.	95 games			

Bob Khayat

KHAYAT, ROBERT CONRAD
B. Apr. 18, 1938, Moss Point, MS
Mississippi 6'2" 230 lbs.

Year	Team		Games	Pos.
1960	**WAS**	**N**	12	C, G, K
1962			14	G, K
1963			14	K
3 yrs.	40 games			

Eddie Khayat

KHAYAT, EDWARD MICHAEL
B. Sep. 14, 1935, Moss Point, MS
Millsaps/Tulane 6'3" 240 lbs.

Year	Team		Games	Pos.
1957	**WAS**	**N**	12	T
1958	**PHI**	**N**	5	T
1959			9	E
1960			12	T
1961			14	DT
1962	**WAS**	**N**	14	DT

Eddie Khayat continued

Year	Team		Games	Pos.
1963			10	DT
1964	**PHI**	**N**	13	DE
1965			14	DT
1966	**BOS**	**A**	14	DT
10 yrs.	117 games			

Bill Kibler

KIBLER, WILLIAM
B. Apr., 1896
Deceased
None

Year	Team		Games	Pos.
1922	**BUF**	**N**	2	HB, QB

Walt Kichefski

KICHEFSKI, WALTER RAYMOND
B. Jun. 17, 1916, Rhinelander, WI
D. Jan. 9, 1992, Miami, FL
Miami (Florida) 6'1" 212 lbs.

Year	Team		Games	Pos.
1940	**PIT**		11	E
1941			11	E
1942			11	E
1944	**C, P**	**N**	10	E, G
4 yrs.	43 games			

Billy Kidd

KIDD, WILLIAM WAYNE, JR.
B. Nov. 28, 1959, Dallas, TX
Houston 6'3" 270 lbs.

Year	Team		Games	Pos.
1987	**HOU**		7	C

Carl Kidd

KIDD, CARL
B. Jun. 14, 1973, Pine Bluff, AR
Arkansas 6'1" 205 lbs.

Year	Team		Games	Pos.
1995	**OAK**	**N**	13	CB
1996			16	CB
2 yrs.	29 games			

John Kidd

KIDD, MAX JOHN
B. Aug. 22, 1961, Springfield, IL
Northwestern 6'3" 208 lbs.

Year	Team		Games	Pos.
1984	**BUF**	**N**	16	P
1985			16	P
1986			16	P
1987			12	P
1988			16	P
1989			16	P
1990	**SD**	**N**	16	P
1991			16	P
1992			16	P
1993			14	P
1994			2	P
1994	**MIA**	**N**	4	P
1995			16	P
1996			16	P
13 yrs.	192 games			

Keith Kidd

KIDD, KEITH DARRYL
B. Sep. 10, 1962, Crossett, AR
Arkansas 6'1" 195 lbs.

Year	Team		Games	Pos.
1987	**MIN**	**N**	1	WR

Blair Kiel

KIEL, BLAIR ARMSTRONG
B. Nov. 29, 1961, Columbus, IN
Notre Dame 6'0" 200 lbs.

Year	Team		Games	Pos.
1984	**TB**	**N**	10	QB
1986	**IND**	**N**	3	QB
1987			4	QB
1988	**GB**	**N**	1	QB
1990			3	QB
1991			4	QB
6 yrs.	25 games			

Year	Team		Games	Pos.

Max Kielbasa
KIELBASA, MAXIMILIAN
B. Aug. 23, 1921
D. Jan., 1980, Pittsburgh, PA
Duquesne 6'1" 185 lbs.

Year	Team		Games	Pos.
1946	PIT	N	2	HB

Walt Kiesling
KIESLING, WALTER ANDREW
B. Mar. 27, 1903, St. Paul, MN
D. Mar. 2, 1962, Pittsburgh, PA
St. Thomas (Minnesota) 6'2" 249 lbs.

Year	Team		Games	Pos.
1926	DUL	N	14	T, G
1927			6	G, T
1928	POT	N	10	G
1929	CHIC	N	12	G
1930			11	G
1931			9	G
1932			10	G
1933			8	G
1934	CHIB	N	13	G, T
1935	GB	N	9	G
1936			8	G
1937	PIT	N	7	G, T
1938			5	G, T
13 yrs.	122 games			

Jeff Kiewel
KIEWEL, JEFFREY CLAYTON
B. Sep. 27, 1960, Tucson, AZ
Arizona 6'4" 270 lbs.

Year	Team		Games	Pos.
1985	ATL	N	16	G
1987			12	G
2 yrs.	28 games			

George Kiick
KIICK, GEORGE HERMAN
B. Sep. 5, 1917, Hanover, PA
Bucknell 6'0" 198 lbs.

Year	Team		Games	Pos.
1940	PIT	N	11	FB
1945			6	HB
2 yrs.	17 games			

Jim Kiick
KIICK, JAMES FORREST
B. Aug. 9, 1946, Lincoln Park, NJ
Wyoming 5'11" 215 lbs.

Year	Team		Games	Pos.
1968	MIA	A	14	RB
1969			14	RB
1970	MIA	N	14	RB
1971			13	RB
1972			14	RB
1973			14	RB
1974			14	RB
1976	DEN	N	14	RB
1977			3	RB
1977	WAS	N	1	RB
9 yrs.	115 games			

Wally Kilbourne
KILBOURNE, WARREN (Cleats)
B. 1916
Deceased
Minnesota 6'3" 240 lbs.

Year	Team		Games	Pos.
1939	GB	N	3	T

Bob Kilcullen
KILCULLEN, ROBERT BRIAN
B. May 13, 1936, St. Louis, MO
Texas Tech 6'3" 245 lbs.

Year	Team		Games	Pos.
1958	CHIB	N	12	T
1960	CHI	N	4	T
1961			14	DE
1962			14	DE
1963			14	DT
1964			13	DE
1965			8	DE
1966			14	DE
8 yrs.	93 games			

Howard Kiley
KILEY, HOWARD
B. Aug., 1896, Michigan
None 5'8" 208 lbs.

Year	Team		Games	Pos.
1923	DUL	N	7	T
1924			6	T
1925			2	T
1926	CHIC	N	7	G, T
4 yrs.	22 games			

Rodger Kiley
KILEY, RODGER JOSEPH
B. Oct. 23, 1900, Chicago, IL
D. Sep. 9, 1974, River Forest, IL
Notre Dame 6'0" 180 lbs.

Year	Team		Games	Pos.
1923	CHIC	N	11	E

Jon Kilgore
KILGORE, JON
B. Dec. 3, 1943, Fort Jackson, SC
Auburn 6'1" 203 lbs.

Year	Team		Games	Pos.
1965	LA	N	5	P
1966			14	P
1967			14	P
1969	SF	N	7	P
4 yrs.	40 games			

Terry Killens
KILLENS, TERRY DELEON
B. Mar. 24, 1974, Cincinnati, OH
Penn State 6'1" 232 lbs.

Year	Team		Games	Pos.
1996	HOU	N	14	LB

Charlie Killett
KILLETT, CHARLES
B. Nov. 8, 1940, Helena, AR
Mississippi/Memphis State 6'1" 205 lbs.

Year	Team		Games	Pos.
1963	NYG	N	13	HB

Gene Killian
KILLIAN, EUGENE
B. Sep. 22, 1952, Tampa, FL
Tennessee 6'4" 250 lbs.

Year	Team		Games	Pos.
1974	DAL	N	7	G, OT

Lyons Killiher
KILLIHER, LYONS
B. 1903
None

Year	Team		Games	Pos.
1928	CHIC	N	1	G

Glenn Killinger
KILLINGER, WILLIAM GLENN
B. Sep. 13, 1898, Harrisburg, PA
D. Jul. 25, 1988, Stanton, DE
Penn State 5'9" 162 lbs.

Year	Team		Games	Pos.
1921	CAN	A	1	HB
1926	NYG	N	1	HB
1926	PHI	A	1	HB
2 yrs.	3 games			

Pat Killorin
KILLORIN, PATRICK MICHAEL
B. Jun. 11, 1944, Watertown, NY
Syracuse 6'2" 220 lbs.

Year	Team		Games	Pos.
1966	PIT	N	5	C

Billy Kilmer
KILMER, WILLIAM ORLAND, JR.
B. Sep. 5, 1939, Topeka, KS
UCLA 6'0" 201 lbs.

Year	Team		Games	Pos.
1961	SF	N	11	QB
1962			12	QB
1964			10	HB, QB
1966			6	QB
1967	NO	N	10	QB

Billy Kilmer continued

Year	Team		Games	Pos.
1968			12	QB
1969			14	QB
1970			13	QB
1971	WAS	N	14	QB
1972			12	QB
1973			10	QB
1974			11	QB
1975			12	QB
1976			10	QB
1977			8	QB
1978			5	QB
16 yrs.	170 games			

Frank Kilroy
KILROY, FRANCIS JOSEPH
(Bucko)
B. May 30, 1921, Philadelphia, PA
Temple 6'2" 243 lbs.

Year	Team		Games	Pos.
1943	P-P	N	10	T
1944	PHI	N	10	T
1945			9	T
1946			9	T
1947			12	G
1948			12	G
1949			12	G
1950			12	G, T
1951			12	T
1952			12	G
1953			12	G
1954			12	G
1955			1	G
13 yrs.	135 games			

David Kilson
KILSON, DAVID WAYNE
B. Aug. 11, 1960, San Francisco, CA
Nevada-Reno 6'1" 200 lbs.

Year	Team		Games	Pos.
1983	BUF	N	16	CB, S

Bobby Kimball
KIMBALL, ROBERT LUND
B. Mar. 12, 1957, Camarillo, CA
Oklahoma 6'1" 190 lbs.

Year	Team		Games	Pos.
1979	GB	N	7	WR
1980			1	WR
2 yrs.	8 games			

Bruce Kimball
KIMBALL, BRUCE MICHAEL
B. Aug. 19, 1959, Beverly, MA
Massachusetts 6'2" 260 lbs.

Year	Team		Games	Pos.
1982	NYG	N	1	G
1983	WAS	N	16	G
1984			8	G
3 yrs.	25 games			

Bill Kimber
KIMBER, WILLIAM
B. 1936
Florida State 6'2" 192 lbs.

Year	Team		Games	Pos.
1959	NYG	N	1	E
1960			3	E
1961	BOS	A	4	OE
3 yrs.	8 games			

Frank Kimble
KIMBLE, FRANK
B. Nov. 9, 1917, Williamson, WV
West Virginia 6'5" 205 lbs.

Year	Team		Games	Pos.
1945	PIT	N	9	E

Garry Kimble
KIMBLE, GARRY
B. Apr. 5, 1963, Missouri City, TX
Sam Houston State 5'11" 184 lbs.

Year	Team		Games	Pos.
1987	WAS	N	3	CB

Elbert Kimbrough
KIMBROUGH, ELBERT LEON
B. Mar. 24, 1938, Galesburg, IL
Northwestern 5'11" 193 lbs.

Year	Team		Games	Pos.
1961	LA	N	5	DB
1962	SF	N	14	DB
1963			14	DB
1964			14	DB
1965			14	DB
1966			14	DB
1968	NO	N	10	DB
7 yrs.	85 games			

John Kimbrough
KIMBROUGH, JOHN
B. Aug. 12, 1954, Mount Vernon, AL
St. Cloud State 5'10" 165 lbs.

Year	Team		Games	Pos.
1977	BUF	N	14	WR

John Kimbrough
KIMBROUGH, JOHN A. (Jarrin' John)
B. Jun. 14, 1918, Haskell, TX
Texas A&M 6'2" 210 lbs.

Year	Team		Games	Pos.
1946	LA	AA	14	FB
1947			14	B
1948			10	B
3 yrs.	38 games			

Tony Kimbrough
KIMBROUGH, TONY
B. Sep. 17, 1970, Weir, MS
Jackson State 6'2" 192 lbs.

Year	Team		Games	Pos.
1993	DEN	N	15	WR
1994			12	WR
2 yrs.	27 games			

Jamie Kimmel
KIMMEL, JAMES L.
B. Mar. 28, 1962, Johnson City, NY
Syracuse 6'3" 235 lbs.

Year	Team		Games	Pos.
1986	LARI	N	16	LB
1987			15	LB
2 yrs.	31 games			

J.D. Kimmel
KIMMEL, JOHN D.
B. Sep. 30, 1929, Omaha, TX
Army/Houston 6'4" 248 lbs.

Year	Team		Games	Pos.
1955	WAS	N	12	T
1956			12	T
1958	GB	N	12	T
3 yrs.	36 games			

Jerry Kimmel
KIMMEL, JERRY M.
B. Jul. 18, 1963, Johnson City, NY
Syracuse 6'2" 240 lbs.

Year	Team		Games	Pos.
1987	NYG	N	2	LB

Jon Kimmel
KIMMEL, JON JOSEPH
B. Jul. 21, 1960, Binghamton, NY
Colgate 6'4" 240 lbs.

Year	Team		Games	Pos.
1985	PHI	N	4	LB
1987	WAS	N	1	LB
2 yrs.	5 games			

Billy Kinard
KINARD, WILLIAM RUSSELL
B. Dec. 16, 1933, Jackson, MS
Mississippi 6'0" 189 lbs.

Year	Team		Games	Pos.
1956	CLE	N	7	HB
1957	GB	N	12	HB
1958			12	HB
1960	BUF	A		DB
4 yrs.	31 games			

Frank Kinard
KINARD, FRANK MANNING, SR.
(Bruiser)
B. Oct. 23, 1914, Pelahatchie, MS
D. Sep. 7, 1985, Jackson, MS
Mississippi 6'1" 216 lbs.

Year	Team		Games	Pos.
1938	BKN	N	11	T
1939			11	T
1940			9	T
1941			11	T
1942			11	T
1943			10	T, FB
1944			10	T
1946	NY	AA	14	T
1947			14	T
9 yrs.	101 games			

George Kinard
KINARD, GEORGE T.
B. Oct. 9, 1916, Crystal Springs, MS
Mississippi 6'1" 202 lbs.

Year	Team		Games	Pos.
1941	BKN	N	11	G
1942			7	G
1946	NY	AA	11	G
3 yrs.	29 games			

Terry Kinard
KINARD, ALFRED TERANCE
B. Nov. 24, 1959, Bitburg, Germany
Clemson 6'1" 200 lbs.

Year	Team		Games	Pos.
1983	NYG	N	16	S
1984			15	S
1985			16	S
1986			14	S
1987			12	S
1988			16	S
1989			16	S
1990	HOU	N	16	S
8 yrs.	121 games			

Jim Kincaid
KINCAID, JAMES (Blackie)
B. 1931
South Carolina 5'11" 180 lbs.

Year	Team		Games	Pos.
1954	WAS	N	2	HB

Brian Kinchen
KINCHEN, BRIAN DOUGLAS
B. Aug. 6, 1965, Baton Rouge, LA
Louisiana State 6'2" 238 lbs.

Year	Team		Games	Pos.
1988	MIA	N	16	TE
1989			16	TE
1990			4	TE
1991	CLE	N	14	TE
1992			16	TE
1993			16	TE
1994			16	TE
1995			13	TE
1996	BAL	N	16	TE
9 yrs.	127 games			

Todd Kinchen
KINCHEN, TODD
WHITTINGTON
B. Jan. 7, 1969, Baton Rouge, LA
Louisiana State 6'0" 187 lbs.

Year	Team		Games	Pos.
1992	LARM	N	14	WR
1993			6	WR
1994			13	WR
1995	STL	N	16	WR
1996	DEN	N	7	WR
5 yrs.	56 games			

George Kinderdine
KINDERDINE, GEORGE (Hobby)
B. Aug. 13, 1891
D. Jun., 1967, Miamisburg, OH
none 5'11" 181 lbs.

Year	Team		Games	Pos.
1920	DAY	N	8	C

George Kinderdine *cont.*

Year	Team		Games	Pos.
1921			9	C
1922	DAY	N	8	C
1923			8	C
1924			8	C, G
1925			8	C, HB
1926			6	C
1927			8	C
1928			7	C
1929			6	C, G
10 yrs.	76 games			

Harry Kinderdine
KINDERDINE, HARRY R. (Shine)
B. Sep., 1893
D. Feb. 17, 1947
none 6'0" 195 lbs.

Year	Team		Games	Pos.
1924	DAY	N	1	G

Walt Kinderdine
KINDERDINE, WALTER (Babe)
B. Aug., 1899
Deceased
None

Year	Team		Games	Pos.
1923	DAY	N	4	FB, HB
1924			4	HB
1925			2	HB, FB
3 yrs.	10 games			

Keith Kinderman
KINDERMAN, KEITH
B. Apr. 16, 1940, Chicago, IL
Iowa/Florida State 6'0" 213 lbs.

Year	Team		Games	Pos.
1963	SD	A	3	DB
1964			8	FB, DB
1965	HOU	A	4	FB
3 yrs.	15 games			

Howard Kindig
KINDIG, HOWARD WAYNE, JR.
B. Jun. 22, 1941, Mexico, MO
*Los Angeles State/Louisiana State 6'6"
260 lbs.*

Year	Team		Games	Pos.
1965	SD	A	14	FB
1966			14	DE
1967			7	DE
1967	BUF	A	5	DE
1968			14	DE
1969			12	DE, C
1970	BUF	N	10	OT
1971			14	OT, C
1972	MIA	N	14	C
1974	NYJ	N	8	C
9 yrs.	112 games			

Greg Kindle
KINDLE, GREGORY LAMARR
B. Sep. 16, 1950, Houston, TX
Tennessee State 6'4" 265 lbs.

Year	Team		Games	Pos.
1974	STL	N	10	OT
1975			14	OT
1976	ATL	N	10	G
1977			1	G
4 yrs.	35 games			

Bill Kindricks
KINDRICKS, WILLIAM ALFRED
B. Jul. 24, 1946, Opelika, AL
Alabama A&M 6'3" 268 lbs.

Year	Team		Games	Pos.
1968	CIN	A	9	DT

Don Kindt
KINDT, DONALD J., JR.
B. Mar. 9, 1961, Milwaukee, WI
Wisconsin-La Crosse 6'6" 242 lbs.

Year	Team		Games	Pos.
1987	CHI	N	3	TE

Don Kindt
KINDT, DONALD J., SR.
B. Jul. 2, 1925, Milwaukee, WI
Wisconsin 6'1" 207 lbs.

Year	Team		Games	Pos.
1947	CHIB	N	12	HB
1948			12	FB
1949			12	HB
1950			12	FB
1951			12	HB
1952			12	HB
1953			12	HB
1954			12	HB
1955			12	HB
9 yrs.	108 games			

George Kinek
KINEK, GEORGE
B. 1929
D. Jan. 21, 1995 Salisbury, Township,
PA
Tulane 6'2" 190 lbs.

Year	Team		Games	Pos.
1954	CHIC	N	12	B

Mike Kinek
KINEK, MICHAEL
B. 1917
Michigan State 6'1" 200 lbs.

Year	Team		Games	Pos.
1940	CLE	N	2	E

Steve Kiner
KINER, STEVEN ALBERT
B. Jun. 12, 1947, Sandstone, MN
Tennessee 6'0" 221 lbs.

Year	Team		Games	Pos.
1970	DAL	N	14	LB
1971	NE	N	14	LB
1973			14	LB
1974	HOU	N	14	LB
1975			14	LB
1976			14	LB
1977			14	LB
1978			16	LB
8 yrs.	114 games			

Andy King
KING, ANDREW V. (Rip)
B. 1897
D. Mar. 4, 1950, Reno, NV
West Virginia 6'1" 202 lbs.

Year	Team		Games	Pos.
1920	AKR	A	9	FB
1921			12	FB, HB, QB
1922	AKR	N	6	FB
1923	CHIC	N	11	HB, FB
1924			2	HB
1925	HAM	N	2	HB, QB, FB
6 yrs.	42 games			

Angelo King
KING, ANGELO TYRONE
B. Feb. 10, 1958, Columbia, SC
South Carolina State 6'1" 222 lbs.

Year	Team		Games	Pos.
1981	DAL	N	15	LB
1982			9	LB
1983			16	LB
1984	DET	N	16	LB
1985			16	LB
1986			11	LB
1987			1	LB
7 yrs.	84 games			

Bruce King
KING, BRUCE ERIC
B. Jan. 7, 1963, Clarksville, IN
Purdue 6'1" 219 lbs.

Year	Team		Games	Pos.
1985	KC	N	16	RB
1986			4	RB
1986	BUF	N	5	FB
1987			3	RB
3 yrs.	28 games			

Charley King
KING, CHARLES RONNIE
B. Jan. 7, 1943, Canton, OH
Purdue 6'0" 185 lbs.

Year	Team		Games	Pos.
1966	BUF	A	14	DB
1967			14	DB
1968	CIN	A	14	DB
1969			9	CB
4 yrs.	51 games			

Claude King
KING, CLAUDE
B. 1939
Houston 5'11" 190 lbs.

Year	Team		Games	Pos.
1961	HOU	A	11	HB
1962	BOS	A	14	HB
2 yrs.	25 games			

David King
KING, DAVID JOEL
B. May 19, 1963, Mobile, AL
Auburn 5'9" 175 lbs.

Year	Team		Games	Pos.
1985	SD	N	1	CB
1987	GB	N	3	CB, S
2 yrs.	4 games			

Dick King
KING, RICHARD STEWART C.
B. May 23, 1893
D. Nov., 1961
Harvard 5'8" 175 lbs.

Year	Team		Games	Pos.
1921	HAM	N	5	FB, HB
1922	MIL	N	4	HB
1922	ROC	N	3	HB, FB
1923	STL	N	6	FB, HB
3 yrs.	18 games			

Don King
KING, DONALD
B. Mar. 11, 1929, McBee, SC
Kentucky 6'3" 260 lbs.

Year	Team		Games	Pos.
1954	CLE	N	8	T
1956	PHI	N	3	T
1956	GB	N	6	T
1960	DEN	A		OT
3 yrs.	17 games			

Ed King
KING, ED E'DAINIA
B. Dec. 3, 1969, Fort Benning, GA
Auburn 6'4" 303 lbs.

Year	Team		Games	Pos.
1991	CLE	N	16	G
1992			16	G
1993			6	OT, G
1995	NO	N	1	G
1996			16	G
5 yrs.	55 games			

Eddie King
KING, EDWARD JOSEPH
B. May 11, 1925, Chestnut Hill, PA
Boston College 6'0" 217 lbs.

Year	Team		Games	Pos.
1948	BUF	AA	14	E
1949			5	G
1950	BAL	N	12	G, C
3 yrs.	31 games			

Emanuel King
KING, EMANUEL
B. Aug. 15, 1963, Leroy, AL
Alabama 6'4" 251 lbs.

Year	Team		Games	Pos.
1985	CIN	N	16	LB
1986			16	LB
1987			12	LB
1988			7	LB
1989	LARI	N	16	LB
5 yrs.	67 games			

Year	Team		Games	Pos.

Emmett King
KING, EMMETT
B. 1933
None 5'9" 195 lbs.

Year	Team		Games	Pos.
1954	CHIC	N	12	B

Fay King
KING, HENRY LAFAYETTE
(Dolly)
B. Mar. 7, 1922, Dothan, AL
D. Jul., 1969, Albany, GA
Georgia 6'3" 195 lbs.

Year	Team		Games	Pos.
1946	BUF	AA	14	E
1947			14	E
1948	CHI	AA	14	E
1949			8	E
4 yrs.	50 games			

Fred King
KING, FRED J.
B. Jun. 3, 1913
D. Mar., 1987, Reading, MA
Hobart 6'2" 205 lbs.

Year	Team		Games	Pos.
1937	BKN	N	1	HB

Gordon King
KING, GORDON DAVID
B. Feb. 3, 1956, Madison, WI
Stanford 6'6" 270 lbs.

Year	Team		Games	Pos.
1978	NYG	N	11	OT
1979			7	OT
1980			12	OT
1981			16	OT
1982			9	OT
1983			14	OT
1985			15	OT
1986	NYJ	N	11	OT, G
1987			2	OT
9 yrs.	97 games			

Gus King
KING, P.A.
B. Sep. 28, 1896
D. Nov., 1979, Mont Belvieu, TX
Centre 6'0" 180 lbs.

Year	Team		Games	Pos.
1922	TOL	N	3	E, HB

Henry King
KING, HENRY
B. Jan. 25, 1945, San Francisco, CA
Utah State 6'4" 205 lbs.

Year	Team		Games	Pos.
1967	NY	A	13	DB

Horace King
KING, HORACE EDWARD
B. Mar. 5, 1953, Athens, GA
Georgia 5'10" 209 lbs.

Year	Team		Games	Pos.
1975	DET	N	14	RB
1976			7	RB
1977			14	RB
1978			15	RB
1979			16	RB
1980			16	RB
1981			16	RB
1982			9	FB
1983			16	RB
9 yrs.	123 games			

Jerome King
KING, JEROME MANUAL
B. Jan. 4, 1955, Jersey City, NJ
Purdue 5'10" 173 lbs.

Year	Team		Games	Pos.
1979	ATL	N	1	CB
1980			2	CB
1980	NYG	N	1	DB
2 yrs.	4 games			

Joe King
KING, JOE
B. May 7, 1968, Dallas, TX
Oklahoma State 6'2" 212 lbs.

Year	Team		Games	Pos.
1991	CIN	N	6	CB, S
1991	CLE	N	7	CB, S
1992	TB	N	14	CB
1993			15	S
1995	OAK	N	16	S
4 yrs.	58 games			

Ken King
KING, KENNETH
B. Aug. 21, 1901
D. Dec., 1973, Midland, MI
Kentucky 5'10" 175 lbs.

Year	Team		Games	Pos.
1926	NEW	A	3	E

Kenny King
KING, KENNETH L.
B. Mar. 7, 1957, Clarendon, TX
Oklahoma 5'11" 205 lbs.

Year	Team		Games	Pos.
1979	HOU	N	12	RB
1980	OAK	N	15	RB
1981			14	RB
1982	LARI	N	9	RB
1983			15	RB
1984			16	RB
1985			16	RB
7 yrs.	97 games			

Linden King
KING, LINDEN KEITH
B. Jul. 28, 1955, Memphis, TN
Colorado State 6'4" 245 lbs.

Year	Team		Games	Pos.
1978	SD	N	14	S
1979			16	LB
1980			5	LB
1981			16	LB
1982			9	LB
1983			16	LB
1984			16	LB
1985			16	LB
1986	LARI	N	16	RB
1987			12	LB
1988			14	LB
1989			14	LB
12 yrs.	164 games			

Phil King
KING, PHILLIP EDGAR
B. Jun. 22, 1936, Nashville, TN
D. Jan. 18, 1973, Memphis, TN
Vanderbilt 6'4" 223 lbs.

Year	Team		Games	Pos.
1958	NYG	N	12	HB
1959			12	HB
1960			10	HB
1961			5	HB, FB
1962			14	HB
1963			14	HB
1964	PIT		8	HB
1965	MIN	N	14	HB
1966			14	HB
9 yrs.	103 games			

Ralph King
KING, RALPH W.
B. Nov. 2, 1901
D. Feb., 1978, Fairhope, AL
Chicago 6'0" 250 lbs.

Year	Team		Games	Pos.
1924	RAC	N	8	G
1925	CHIB	N	1	C
2 yrs.	9 games			

Shawn King
KING, SHAWN
B. Jun. 24, 1972, West Monroe, LA

Shawn King *continued*
*Louisiana State/Northeast Louisiana 6'3"
279 lbs.*

Year	Team		Games	Pos.
1995	CAR	N	13	DE
1996			16	DE
2 yrs.	29 games			

Steve King
KING, GEORGE STEPHEN
B. Jun. 10, 1951, McAlester, OK
Tulsa 6'4" 232 lbs.

Year	Team		Games	Pos.
1973	NE	N	7	LB
1974			14	LB
1975			14	LB
1976			11	LB
1977			14	LB
1978			16	LB
1979			16	LB
1980			16	LB
1981			16	LB
9 yrs.	124 games			

Tim King
KING, TIMOTHY
B. Mar. 7, 1960, New York, NY
Delaware State 6'2" 190 lbs.

Year	Team		Games	Pos.
1987	TB	N	3	CB

Tony King
KING, ANTHONY
B. May 6, 1944, Alliance, OH
Findlay 6'1" 194 lbs.

Year	Team		Games	Pos.
1967	BUF	A	7	FL

Ellsworth Kingery
KINGERY, ELLSWORTH
B. 1929
Tulane 5'11" 180 lbs.

Year	Team		Games	Pos.
1954	CHIC	N	9	B

Wayne Kingery
KINGERY, B. WAYNE
B. Jun. 5, 1927, Lake Charles, LA
*Louisiana State/McNeese State 5'11"
175 lbs.*

Year	Team		Games	Pos.
1949	BAL	AA	9	B

Rick Kingrea
KINGREA, RICHARD OWEN
B. Jul. 18, 1949, Pearisburg, VA
Tulane 6'1" 228 lbs.

Year	Team		Games	Pos.
1971	CLE	N	14	LB
1972			7	LB
1973	BUF	N	4	LB
1973	NO	N	9	LB
1974			14	LB
1975			14	LB
1976			14	LB
1977			14	LB
1978			1	LB
8 yrs.	91 games			

Doug Kingsriter
KINGSRITER, DOUGLAS JAMES
B. Jan. 29, 1950, Little Falls, MN
Minnesota 6'2" 222 lbs.

Year	Team		Games	Pos.
1973	MIN	N	11	TE
1974			14	TE
1975			3	TE
3 yrs.	28 games			

Reggie Kinlaw
KINLAW, REGGIE
B. Jan. 9, 1957, Miami, FL
Oklahoma 6'2" 245 lbs.

Year	Team		Games	Pos.
1979	OAK	N	16	DT

Reggie Kinlaw *continued*

Year	Team		Games	Pos.
1980			14	DT
1981			1	NT
1982	LARI	N	9	NT
1983			16	NT
1984			13	NT
1985	SEA	N	16	NT
1986			14	NT
8 yrs.	99 games			

Larry Kinnebrew
KINNEBREW, LARRY D.
B. Jun. 11, 1960, Rome, GA
Tennessee State 6'1" 258 lbs.

Year	Team		Games	Pos.
1983	CIN	N	16	RB
1984			16	RB
1985			12	RB
1986			16	RB
1987			11	RB
1989	BUF	N	15	RB
1990			2	RB
7 yrs.	88 games			

George Kinney
KINNEY, GEORGE
B. 1944
Wiley 6'4" 250 lbs.

Year	Team		Games	Pos.
1965	HOU	A	1	DE

Jeff Kinney
KINNEY, JEFF BRUCE
B. Nov. 1, 1949, Oxford, NE
Nebraska 6'2" 215 lbs.

Year	Team		Games	Pos.
1972	KC	N	9	RB
1973			14	RB
1974			13	RB
1975			13	RB
1976			1	RB
1976	BUF	N	12	RB
5 yrs.	62 games			

Steve Kinney
KINNEY, STEVE ARTHUR
B. Jun. 27, 1949, San Jose, CA
Utah State 6'5" 257 lbs.

Year	Team		Games	Pos.
1973	CHI	N	2	OT
1974			10	OT
2 yrs.	12 games			

Vince Kinney
KINNEY, VINCENT MARC
B. Mar. 7, 1956, Baltimore, MD
Maryland 6'2" 190 lbs.

Year	Team		Games	Pos.
1978	DEN	N	8	WR
1979			15	WR
2 yrs.	23 games			

Carl Kinscherf
KINSCHERF, CARL R.
B. Oct. 20, 1919, Brooklyn, NY
Colgate 6'1" 188 lbs.

Year	Team		Games	Pos.
1943	NYG	N	8	FB
1944			5	B
2 yrs.	13 games			

Matt Kinzer
KINZER, MATTHEW ROY
B. Jun. 17, 1963, Indianapolis, IN
Purdue 6'2" 225 lbs.

Year	Team		Games	Pos.
1987	DET	N	1	P

Kippley
KIPPLEY
None

Year	Team		Games	Pos.
1921	SYR	A	1	C

Jack Kirby
KIRBY, JACK
B. Sep. 21, 1923, Los Angeles, CA
Southern California 5'11" 185 lbs.

Year	Team		Games	Pos.
1949	GB	N	6	HB

John Kirby
KIRBY, JOHN PATRICK
B. May 30, 1942, David City, NE
Nebraska 6'3" 229 lbs.

Year	Team		Games	Pos.
1964	MIN	N	14	LB
1965			14	LB
1966			10	LB
1967			14	LB
1968			14	LB
1969			2	LB
1969	NYG	N	10	LB
1970			14	LB
7 yrs.	92 games			

Terry Kirby
KIRBY, TERRY GAYLE
B. Jan. 20, 1970, Hampton, VA
Virginia 6'1" 221 lbs.

Year	Team		Games	Pos.
1993	MIA	N	16	RB
1994			4	RB
1995			16	RB
1996	SF	N	14	RB
4 yrs.	50 games			

Kelly Kirchbaum
KIRCHBAUM, KELLY
B. Jun. 14, 1957, Fort Knox, KY
Kentucky 6'2" 240 lbs.

Year	Team		Games	Pos.
1980	KC	N	1	C
1987	PHI	N	3	LB
2 yrs.	4 games			

Bill Kirchiro
KIRCHIRO, WILLIAM
B. Jun. 29, 1940
Maryland 6'1" 235 lbs.

Year	Team		Games	Pos.
1962	BAL	N	8	G

Mark Kirchner
KIRCHNER, MARK STEVEN
B. Oct. 19, 1960, Pasadena, TX
Baylor 6'3" 265 lbs.

Year	Team		Games	Pos.
1983	PIT	N	3	OT
1983	KC	N	5	OL
1984	IND	N	11	OT
1986			13	OT
3 yrs.	32 games			

Ernie Kirk
KIRK, ERNEST
B. Apr. 14, 1952, Marlin, TX
Howard Payne 6'2" 265 lbs.

Year	Team		Games	Pos.
1977	HOU	N	14	DE

George Kirk
KIRK, GEORGE A.
B. Jul. 4, 1899, Tennessee
D. Mar., 1974, Petersburg, TX
Baylor 6'0" 205 lbs.

Year	Team		Games	Pos.
1926	BUF	N	7	C

Ken Kirk
KIRK, KEN H.
B. Feb. 26, 1938, Tupelo, MS
Mississippi 6'2" 229 lbs.

Year	Team		Games	Pos.
1960	CHI	N	12	C
1961			10	C
1962	PIT	N	14	LB
1963	LA	N	8	C
4 yrs.	44 games			

Randy Kirk
KIRK, RANDALL SCOTT
B. Dec. 27, 1964, San Jose, CA
San Diego State 6'2" 235 lbs.

Year	Team		Games	Pos.
1987	SD	N	13	LB
1988			16	LB
1989	PHX	N	6	LB
1990	WAS	N	1	LB
1991	CLE	N	2	LB
1991	SD	N	5	LB
1992	CIN	N	15	LB
1993			16	LB
1994	ARI	N	16	LB
1995			16	LB
1996	SF	N	16	LB
10 yrs.	122 games			

Heinie Kirkgard
KIRKGARD, HENRY
B. Sep. 2, 1898
D. Feb., 1967, Dallas, TX
None 165 lbs.

Year	Team		Games	Pos.
1923	TOL	N	5	HB

Bo Kirkland
KIRKLAND, BO
B. Jun. 22, 1911, Columbus, GA
D. Dec., 1981, Lakeland, FL
Alabama 6'0" 215 lbs.

Year	Team		Games	Pos.
1935	BKN	N	11	G
1936			12	G
2 yrs.	23 games			

Levon Kirkland
KIRKLAND, LORENZO LEVON
B. Feb. 17, 1969, Lamar, SC
Clemson 6'0" 247 lbs.

Year	Team		Games	Pos.
1992	PIT	N	16	LB
1993			16	LB
1994			16	LB
1995			16	LB
1996			16	LB
5 yrs.	80 games			

Mike Kirkland
KIRKLAND, MICHAEL
B. Jun. 29, 1954, Pasadena, TX
Arkansas 6'1" 195 lbs.

Year	Team		Games	Pos.
1978	BAL	N	16	QB

Frank Kirkleski
KIRKLESKI, FRANK W.
B. May 19, 1904
D. May, 1980, Chatham, NJ
Lafayette 5'10" 179 lbs.

Year	Team		Games	Pos.
1927	POT	N	12	HB, QB
1929	ORA	N	12	HB, QB
1930	NEW	N	12	QB, HB, FB
1931	BKN	N	3	HB, QB
4 yrs.	39 games			

Roger Kirkman
KIRKMAN, ROGER R. (Red)
B. Oct. 17, 1905, Woodland, WV
D. Nov., 1973, Columbus, OH
Case Western Reserve/Washington & Jefferson 6'1" 195 lbs.

Year	Team		Games	Pos.
1933	PHI	N	9	QB, HB
1934			11	HB
1935			1	QB
3 yrs.	21 games			

Jon Kirksey
KIRKSEY, JON
B. Feb. 21, 1970, Greenville, SC
Sacramento State 6'4" 350 lbs.

Year	Team		Games	Pos.
1996	STL	N	11	DT

Roy Kirksey
KIRKSEY, ROY LEWIS
B. Sep. 18, 1947, Greenville, SC
Maryland-Eastern Shore 6'1" 235 lbs.

Year	Team		Games	Pos.
1971	NYJ	N	4	G
1972			10	G
1973	PHI	N	7	G
1974			14	G
4 yrs.	35 games			

William Kirksey
KIRKSEY, WILLIAM
B. Jan. 29, 1966, Birmingham, AL
Southern Mississippi 6'2" 221 lbs.

Year	Team		Games	Pos.
1990	MIN	N	9	LB

Gary Kirner
KIRNER, GARY BURGESS
B. Jun. 22, 1942, Los Angeles, CA
Southern California 6'3" 238 lbs.

Year	Team		Games	Pos.
1964	SD	A	14	OT
1965			14	OT
1966			14	OE
1967			14	OT
1968			14	OT
1969			7	G
6 yrs.	77 games			

Lou Kirouac
KIROUAC, LOU
B. May 17, 1940, Manchester, NH
Boston College 6'3" 238 lbs.

Year	Team		Games	Pos.
1963	NYG	N	14	OE
1964	BAL	N	14	OT
1966	ATL	N	14	G
3 yrs.	42 games			

Paul Kiser
KISER, PAUL DAVID
B. Nov. 19, 1963, Valdese, NC
Wake Forest 6'4" 270 lbs.

Year	Team		Games	Pos.
1987	DET	N	1	G

Ben Kish
KISH, BENJAMIN E.
B. Mar. 31, 1917, Tonawanda, NY
D. Feb. 24, 1989, Philadelphia, PA
Pittsburgh 6'0" 207 lbs.

Year	Team		Games	Pos.
1940	BKN	N	11	QB
1941			7	B
1943	P, P	N	10	FB
1944	PHI	N	10	FB, HB
1945			9	FB
1946			10	FB
1947			12	FB
1948			9	FB
1949			7	FB
9 yrs.	85 games			

George Kisiday
KISIDAY, GEORGE JOHN
B. Apr. 16, 1923, Ambridge, PA
D. Nov. 9, 1970
Duquesne/Columbia 6'1" 220 lbs.

Year	Team		Games	Pos.
1948	BUF	AA	14	E

Adolph Kissell
KISSELL, ADOLPH J.
B. Sep. 11, 1920, Nashua, NH
D. Aug. 7, 1983, Wareham, MA
Boston College 5'11" 190 lbs.

Year	Team		Games	Pos.
1942	CHIB	N	4	HB

Ed Kissell
KISSELL, EDWARD JOHN JULIUS

Ed Kissell continued
B. Sep. 29, 1929, Nashua, NH
Wake Forest 6'1" 193 lbs.

Year	Team		Games	Pos.
1952	PIT	N	6	QB
1954			7	QB
2 yrs.	13 games			

John Kissell
KISSELL, JOHN JAY
B. May 14, 1923, Nashua, NH
D. Apr. 9, 1992, Nashua, NH
Boston College 6'3" 245 lbs.

Year	Team		Games	Pos.
1948	BUF	AA	14	T
1949			12	T
1950	CLE	N	12	T
1951			12	T
1952			12	T
1954			12	T
1955			12	T
1956			12	T
8 yrs.	98 games			

Vito Kissell
KISSELL, VITO JOSEPH
B. Jun. 13, 1927, Nashua, NH
Holy Cross 5'10" 205 lbs.

Year	Team		Games	Pos.
1949	BUF	AA	9	B
1950	BAL	N	11	FB
2 yrs.	20 games			

Syd Kitson
KITSON, SYD
B. Sep. 27, 1958, Orange, NJ
Wake Forest 6'4" 252 lbs.

Year	Team		Games	Pos.
1980	GB	N	14	G
1981			11	G
1983			14	G
1984			8	G
1984	DAL	N	1	G
4 yrs.	48 games			

Paul Kitteredge
KITTEREDGE, PAUL
B. 1904, Clinton, MA
Holy Cross 5'10" 170 lbs.

Year	Team		Games	Pos.
1929	BOS	N	7	HB, QB

John Kitzmiller
KITZMILLER, JOHN W. (Dutch)
B. Nov. 25, 1904, Harrisburg, PA
D. Apr. 2, 1986, Dallas, OR
Army/Oregon 5'11" 170 lbs.

Year	Team		Games	Pos.
1931	NYG	N	12	HB, FB, QB

Lee Kizzire
KIZZIRE, LEE
B. 1914
D. Dec. 5, 1943
Wyoming 6'0" 200 lbs.

Year	Team		Games	Pos.
1937	DET	N	7	HB, QB, FB

Earl Klapstein
KLAPSTEIN, EARL
B. 1922
Pacific 6'0" 220 lbs.

Year	Team		Games	Pos.
1946	PIT	N	9	T

John Klasnic
KLASNIC, JOHN
B. Feb. 23, 1927, McKeesport, PA
none 6'0" 185 lbs.

Year	Team		Games	Pos.
1948	BKN	AA	1	B

Fee Klaus
KLAUS, FERYL

Year	Team	Games	Pos.

Fee Klaus continued

B. Sep. 26, 1902, Green Bay, WI
D. Feb., 1951
None 5'9" 190 lbs.

Year	Team		Games	Pos.
1921	GB	A	4	C, HB

Dick Klawitter

KLAWITTER, DOMINIC
B. Sep. 29, 1930, Chicago, IL
South Dakota State 6'7" 270 lbs.

Year	Team		Games	Pos.
1956	CHIB	N	5	C

Joe Klecko

KLECKO, JOSEPH EDWARD
B. Oct. 15, 1953, Chester, PA
Temple 6'3" 263 lbs.

Year	Team		Games	Pos.
1977	NYJ	N	13	DT
1978			16	DT
1979			16	DE
1980			15	DE, DT
1981			16	DE
1982			2	DE
1983			16	DE
1984			12	DT, DE
1985			16	DT, DE
1986			11	DT, DE
1987			7	NT
1988	IND	N	5	NT
12 yrs.			155 games	

Bob Klein

KLEIN, ROBERT OWEN
B. Jul. 27, 1947, South Gate, CA
Southern California 6'5" 237 lbs.

Year	Team		Games	Pos.
1969	LA	N	14	TE
1970			7	TE
1971			14	TE
1972			14	TE
1973			14	TE
1974			14	TE
1975			14	TE
1976			14	TE
1977	SD	N	12	TE
1978			16	TE
1979			15	TE
11 yrs.			148 games	

Dick Klein

KLEIN, RICHARD
B. Feb. 11, 1934, Pana, IL
Georgia/Iowa 6'4" 254 lbs.

Year	Team		Games	Pos.
1958	CHIB	N	12	T
1959			12	T
1960	DAL	N	7	OT
1961	BOS	A	10	OT
1962			4	OT
1963	OAK	A	14	OT
1964			14	OT
7 yrs.			73 games	

Perry Klein

KLEIN, PERRY SANDOR
B. Mar. 25, 1971, Santa Monica, CA
California/C.W. Post 6'2" 214 lbs.

Year	Team		Games	Pos.
1994	ATL	N	2	QB

Quentin Klenk

KLENK, QUENTIN E.
B. Feb. 13, 1919, Long Beach, CA
D. Jan. 4, 1979, San Mateo, CA
Southern California 6'2" 225 lbs.

Year	Team		Games	Pos.
1946	BUF	AA	3	T
1946	CHI	AA	7	T
1 yr.			10 games	

Rocky Klever

KLEVER, VICTOR K.

Rocky Klever continued

B. Jul. 10, 1959, Portland, OR
Montana 6'3" 228 lbs.

Year	Team		Games	Pos.
1983	NYJ	N	5	RB
1984			16	RB
1985			16	TE
1986			16	TE
1987			12	TE
5 yrs.			65 games	

Ed Klewicki

KLEWICKI, EDWARD LEONARD
B. May 4, 1911, Pittsburgh, PA
Michigan State 5'10" 209 lbs.

Year	Team		Games	Pos.
1935	DET	N	11	E, HB
1936			11	E
1937			11	E
1938			10	E
4 yrs.			43 games	

Roger Kliebhan

KLIEBHAN, ROGER
None

Year	Team		Games	Pos.
1921	GB	A	1	QB

Tony Klimek

KLIMEK, ANTHONY FRANCIS
B. Nov. 24, 1925, Chicago, IL
Illinois 5'11" 200 lbs.

Year	Team		Games	Pos.
1951	CHIC	N	12	E
1952			12	G
2 yrs.			24 games	

Alan Kline

KLINE, ALAN
B. May 25, 1971, Tiffin, OH
Ohio State 6'5" 277 lbs.

Year	Team		Games	Pos.
1995	NO	N	3	OT

Harry Kline

KLINE, HARRY S. (Jiggs)
B. Oct. 22, 1913, Elmdale, KS
Emporia State 6'1" 196 lbs.

Year	Team		Games	Pos.
1939	NYG	N	9	E
1940			6	E
1942			10	E
3 yrs.			25 games	

Chuck Klingbeil

KLINGBEIL, CHUCK
B. Nov. 2, 1965, Houghton, MI
Northern Michigan 6'1" 263 lbs.

Year	Team		Games	Pos.
1991	MIA	N	15	NT
1992			15	NT
1993			16	NT
1994			16	NT
1995			16	NT
5 yrs.			78 games	

John Klingel

KLINGEL, JOHN
B. Dec. 21, 1963, Marion, OH
Eastern Kentucky 6'3" 267 lbs.

Year	Team		Games	Pos.
1987	PHI	N	5	DE
1988			16	DE
2 yrs.			21 games	

David Klingler

KLINGLER, DAVID
B. Feb. 17, 1969, Stratford, TX
Houston 6'2" 205 lbs.

Year	Team		Games	Pos.
1992	CIN	N	4	QB
1993			14	QB
1994			10	QB
1995			3	QB
1996	OAK	N	1	QB
5 yrs.			32 games	

Harry Kloppenburg

KLOPPENBURG, HARRY
B. 1907
Fordham 6'1" 210 lbs.

Year	Team		Games	Pos.
1930	SI	N	8	E, G
1931	BKN	N	1	E
1933			1	E
1934			6	E, T
4 yrs.			16 games	

Don Klosterman

KLOSTERMAN, DONALD CLEMENT (Duke)
B. Jan. 18, 1930, Le Mars, IA
Loyola (California) 5'10" 180 lbs.

Year	Team		Games	Pos.
1952	LA	N	3	QB

Bruce Klostermann

KLOSTERMANN, BRUCE DONALD
B. Apr. 17, 1963, Dubuque, IA
Iowa/South Dakota State 6'4" 225 lbs.

Year	Team		Games	Pos.
1987	DEN	N	9	LB
1988			12	LB
1989			16	LB
1990	LARM	N	5	LB
4 yrs.			42 games	

Mike Klotovich

KLOTOVICH, MICHAEL
B. 1917
St. Mary's (California) 5'10" 180 lbs.

Year	Team		Games	Pos.
1945	NYG	N	6	HB

Jack Klotz

KLOTZ, JOHN
B. 1934
Widener 6'5" 256 lbs.

Year	Team		Games	Pos.
1960	NY	A		OT
1961			14	OT
1962	SD	A	3	OT
1962	NY	A	3	OT
1963			13	OT
1964	HOU	A	8	OT
5 yrs.			41 games	

Al Klug

KLUG, ALFRED W.
B. Dec. 19, 1920, Milwaukee, WI
Marquette 6'1" 215 lbs.

Year	Team		Games	Pos.
1946	BUF	AA	12	G
1947	BAL	AA	11	T
1948			13	G
3 yrs.			36 games	

Dave Klug

KLUG, DAVID JOHN
B. May 17, 1958, Litchfield, MN
Concordia 6'4" 230 lbs.

Year	Team		Games	Pos.
1981	KC	N	15	LB
1982			9	LB
1983			1	LB
3 yrs.			25 games	

John Klumb

KLUMB, JOHN JAMES
B. Jan. 22, 1916, Aurora, NE
Washington State 6'3" 200 lbs.

Year	Team		Games	Pos.
1939	CHIC	N	3	E
1940			6	E
1940	PIT	N	4	E
2 yrs.			13 games	

Nick Klutka

KLUTKA, NICHOLAS
B. 1921

Nick Klutka continued

Florida 5'11" 200 lbs.

Year	Team		Games	Pos.
1946	BUF	AA	11	E

Pete Kmetovic

KMETOVIC, PETER G.
B. 1920
Deceased
Stanford 5'9" 175 lbs.

Year	Team		Games	Pos.
1946	PHI	N	5	HB
1947	DET	N	11	HB
2 yrs.			16 games	

Shiner Knab

KNAB, STANLEY
B. Mar. 25, 1894
D. Nov., 1974, Groveland, FL
None 6'1" 190 lbs.

Year	Team		Games	Pos.
1921	CIN	A	4	HB, FB, QB

Glenn Knack

KNACK, GLENN
B. Mar. 29, 1901
D. Sep., 1983, Niagara Falls, NY
None

Year	Team		Games	Pos.
1922	BUF	N	1	G
1924			1	T
2 yrs.			2 games	

Gary Knafelc

KNAFELC, GARY
B. Jan. 2, 1932, Pueblo, CO
Colorado 6'4" 217 lbs.

Year	Team		Games	Pos.
1954	CHIC	N	1	E
1954	GB	N	8	E
1955			12	E
1956			12	E
1957			3	E
1958			6	E
1959			12	E
1960			12	E
1961			13	OE
1962			11	OE
1963	SF	N	10	OE
10 yrs.			100 games	

Greg Knafelc

KNAFELC, GREGORY KURT
B. Feb. 20, 1959, Green Bay, WI
Notre Dame 6'4" 220 lbs.

Year	Team		Games	Pos.
1983	NO	N	6	QB

Ken Knapczyk

KNAPCZYK, KEN
B. Apr. 21, 1963
Northern Iowa 5'11" 190 lbs.

Year	Team		Games	Pos.
1987	CHI	N	3	WR

Lindsay Knapp

KNAPP, LINDSAY HAINES
B. Feb. 25, 1970, Arlington Heights, IL
Notre Dame 6'6" 280 lbs.

Year	Team		Games	Pos.
1994	KC	N	1	G
1996	GB	N	9	G
2 yrs.			10 games	

Jack Knapper

KNAPPER, FREEMAN
B. Jan. 12, 1910
D. Apr., 1953
Ottawa (Kansas) 6'3" 190 lbs.

Year	Team		Games	Pos.
1934	PHI	N	2	FB

Jeff Knapple

KNAPPLE, JEFF SCOTT

Year	Team	Games	Pos.

Jeff Knapple *continued*

B. Aug. 27, 1956, Wertzburg, Germany
UCLA/Colorado/Northern Colorado 6'2"
200 lbs.

1980	**DEN** N	2	QB

Bill Knecht

KNECHT, WILLIAM
B. Jul., 1899
Deceased
Xavier (Ohio) 6'1" 200 lbs.

1925	**DAY** N	4	T, FB

Gayle Knief

KNIEF, GAYLE
B. Dec. 28, 1946, Denison, IA
Morningside 6'3" 205 lbs.

1970	**BOS** N	3	WR

Charlie Knight

KNIGHT, CHARLES
B. Oct. 1, 1899
D. Feb., 1979, Miami, FL
Northwestern 6'2" 200 lbs.

1920	**CHIC** A	2	C
1921		4	C, T
2 yrs.	6 games		

Curt Knight

KNIGHT, LUTHER CURTIS, JR.
B. Apr. 14, 1943, Gulfport, MS
Coast Guard 6'1" 190 lbs.

1969	**WAS** N	14	K
1970		14	K
1971		14	K
1972		14	K
1973		14	K
5 yrs.	70 games		

David Knight

KNIGHT, DAVID RANDLE
B. Feb. 1, 1951, Trieste, Italy
William & Mary 6'1" 177 lbs.

1973	**NYJ** N	14	WR
1974		14	WR
1975		6	WR
1976		14	WR
1977		10	WR
5 yrs.	58 games		

George Knight

KNIGHT, GEORGE F.
B. 1898
Deceased
Loyola (Illinois) 199 lbs.

1920	**CHIC** A	1	T

Leander Knight

KNIGHT, LEANDER, JR.
B. Feb. 16, 1963, East Orange, NJ
Montclair State 6'1" 193 lbs.

1987	**ATL** N	1	CB, S
1988		2	CB
1989	**NYJ** N	13	CB, S
1990	**HOU** N	16	CB, S
4 yrs.	32 games		

Marion Knight

KNIGHT, MARION
B. Apr. 19, 1965
Nevada-Las Vegas 6'2" 265 lbs.

1987	**LARM** N	2	NT

Pat Knight

KNIGHT, JON P.

Pat Knight *continued*

B. 1929
Southern Methodist 6'2" 207 lbs.

1952	**NYG** N	2	FB
1954		10	E
1955		8	E
3 yrs.	20 games		

Shawn Knight

KNIGHT, SHAWN MATT
B. Jun. 4, 1964, Provo, UT
Brigham Young 6'6" 288 lbs.

1987	**NO** N	10	DE
1988	**DEN** N	14	DL
1989	**PHX** N	7	DT
3 yrs.	31 games		

Steve Knight

KNIGHT, STEVEN PAUL
B. Mar. 13, 1962, Abingdon, VA
Tennessee 6'4" 298 lbs.

1987	**IND** N	3	G

Kurt Knoff

KNOFF, KURT
B. Apr. 6, 1954, East Grand Forks, MN
Kansas 6'2" 191 lbs.

1977	**HOU** N	3	S
1978		16	S
1979	**MIN** N	10	S
1980		16	S
1981		16	S
1982		9	S
6 yrs.	70 games		

Johnny Knolla

KNOLLA, JOHN
B. Mar. 19, 1919, Chicago, IL
Creighton 5'10" 180 lbs.

1942	**CHIC** N	11	HB
1945		7	HB
2 yrs.	18 games		

Oscar Knop

KNOP, ROBERT OSCAR
B. 1895
D. Nov. 5, 1952
Illinois 6'0" 191 lbs.

1920	**CHIT** A	7	E
1921	**HAM** A	4	HB, E
1922	**HAM** N	4	HB, FB
1923		4	FB
1923	**CHIB** N	9	FB
1924		11	FB
1925		17	FB, E
1926		14	FB, HB
1927		10	FB, E
8 yrs.	80 games		

Larry Knorr

KNORR, LAWRENCE FRANK
B. Apr. 22, 1917, New York, NY
Alabama/Dayton 6'2" 194 lbs.

1942	**DET** N	8	E
1945		2	E
2 yrs.	10 games		

Knowland

KNOWLAND
None

1921	**SYR** A	1	FB

Bill Knox

KNOX, WILLIAM
B. Jun. 19, 1951, Elba, AL
Purdue 5'9" 192 lbs.

1974	**CHI** N	14	DB

Bill Knox *continued*

1975		14	CB
1976		14	CB
3 yrs.	42 games		

Charlie Knox

KNOX, CHARLES
St. Edmond's 5'11" 185 lbs.

1937	**PHI** N	1	B

Daryl Knox

KNOX, DARYL A.
B. Sep. 3, 1962
Nevada-Las Vegas 6'3" 220 lbs.

1987	**PIT** N	3	LB

Kevin Knox

KNOX, KEVIN DEVON
B. Jan. 30, 1971, Niceville, FL
Florida State 6'3" 194 lbs.

1994	**ARI** N	2	WR

Mike Knox

KNOX, MIKE
B. Nov. 21, 1962
Nebraska 6'2" 240 lbs.

1987	**DEN** N	3	LB

Ronnie Knox

KNOX, RONALD
B. Feb. 14, 1935, Chicago, IL
California/UCLA 6'1" 198 lbs.

1957	**CHIB** N	1	QB

Sam Knox

KNOX, FRANK SAMUEL (Dutch)
B. Mar. 29, 1910, Concord, NH
D. May, 1981, Bradenton, FL
New Hampshire/Illinois 6'0" 213 lbs.

1934	**DET** N	11	T, G
1935		9	G
1936		11	G, B
3 yrs.	31 games		

Gene Knutson

KNUTSON, EUGENE PETER
B. Nov. 10, 1932, Beloit, WI
Michigan 6'2" 218 lbs.

1954	**GB** N	12	E
1956		6	E
2 yrs.	18 games		

Steve Knutson

KNUTSON, STEVEN CRAIG
B. Oct. 5, 1951, Bagley, MN
Southern California 6'3" 254 lbs.

1976	**GB** N	12	OT
1977		14	OT
1978	**SF** N	15	G
3 yrs.	41 games		

Matt Koart

KOART, MATT
B. Sep. 28, 1963
Southern California 6'5" 258 lbs.

1986	**GB** N	6	DE

Stephen Kobolinski

KOBOLINSKI, STEPHEN
B. 1904
Deceased
Boston College 5'8" 170 lbs.

1926	**BKN** N	1	C

Mickey Kobrosky

KOBROSKY, M.L.
B. 1915
Trinity (Connecticut) 6'0" 187 lbs.

1937	**NYG** N	7	B

George Koch

KOCH, GEORGE T.
B. Jul. 2, 1919, Temple, TX
D. Sep., 1966
Baylor/St. Mary's (Texas) 6'0" 200 lbs.

1945	**CLE** N	5	HB
1947	**BUF** AA	13	B
2 yrs.	18 games		

Greg Koch

KOCH, GREGORY MICHAEL
B. Jun. 14, 1955, Bethesda, MD
Arkansas 6'4" 265 lbs.

1977	**GB** N	14	G, OT
1978		16	OT
1979		16	OT
1980		16	OT
1981		16	OT
1982		9	OT
1983		15	OT
1984		15	OT
1985		16	OT
1986	**MIA** N	16	OT
1987		1	OT
1987	**MIN** N	9	OT
11 yrs.	159 games		

Markus Koch

KOCH, MARKUS
B. Feb. 13, 1963, Niedermarsberg,
Germany
Boise State 6'5" 275 lbs.

1986	**WAS** N	16	DE, DT
1987		12	DE
1988		11	DE
1989		10	DE
1990		13	DE
1991		6	DE
6 yrs.	68 games		

Pete Koch

KOCH, PETER ALAN
B. Jan. 23, 1962, Nassau County, NY
Maryland 6'6" 270 lbs.

1984	**CIN** N	16	NT
1985	**KC** N	16	DE
1986		16	DE
1987		6	DE
1989	**LARI** N	4	DE
5 yrs.	58 games		

Polly Koch

KOCH, WALTER
B. Jan. 27, 1895
D. Jun., 1976, Hartford, WI
Wisconsin 5'11" 181 lbs.

1920	**RI** A	3	T, G

Mike Kochel

KOCHEL, MICHAEL J.
B. 1917
D. Aug. 18, 1994, Bellevue, NE
Fordham 5'11" 195 lbs.

1939	**CHIC** N	8	G

Roger Kochman

KOCHMAN, ROGER
B. 1942
Penn State 6'2" 205 lbs.

1963	**BUF** A	5	HB

Dave Kocourek
KOCOUREK, DAVID ALLEN
B. Aug. 20, 1937, Chicago, IL
Wisconsin 6'5" 237 lbs.

Year	Team		Games	Pos.
1960	LA	A	14	OE
1961	SD	A	14	OE
1962			14	OE
1963			14	OE
1964			14	OE
1965			14	OE
1966	MIA	A	14	TE
1967	OAK	A	14	TE
1968			7	TE
9 yrs.	119 games			

Joe Kodba
KODBA, JOSEPH S.
B. Feb. 27, 1922, Yugoslavia
Purdue 5'11" 190 lbs.

Year	Team		Games	Pos.
1947	BAL	AA	13	C

Vic Koegel
KOEGEL, VICTOR
B. Nov. 2, 1952, Cincinnati, OH
Ohio State 6'0" 215 lbs.

Year	Team		Games	Pos.
1974	CIN	N	6	LB

Warren Koegel
KOEGEL, WARREN DEWITT
B. Nov. 1, 1949, Mineola, NY
Penn State 6'3" 253 lbs.

Year	Team		Games	Pos.
1971	OAK	N	1	C
1973	STL	N	3	OT
1974	NYJ	N	2	C
3 yrs.	6 games			

Bob Koehler
KOEHLER, ROBERT A.C.
B. Apr. 7, 1894
Deceased
Northwestern 5'11" 185 lbs.

Year	Team		Games	Pos.
1920	DEC	A	7	FB
1921	CHIC	A	8	FB
1922	CHIC	N	10	FB
1923			10	FB, HB
1924			10	FB
1925			13	FB
1926			10	FB
7 yrs.	68 games			

Art Koeninger
KOENINGER, ARTHUR
B. Nov. 1, 1906
D. Dec. 1990, Chattanooga, TN
Tennessee-Chattanooga 6'1" 202 lbs.

Year	Team		Games	Pos.
1931	FRA	N	1	T
1932	SI		7	C
1933	PHI	N	1	C
3 yrs.	9 games			

Rich Koeper
KOEPER, RICHARD
B. Jul. 23, 1943
Oregon State 6'4" 245 lbs.

Year	Team		Games	Pos.
1966	ATL	N	3	OT

Matt Kofler
KOFLER, MATTHEW JOSEPH
B. Aug. 30, 1959, Longview, WA
San Diego State 6'3" 192 lbs.

Year	Team		Games	Pos.
1982	BUF	N	4	QB
1983			16	QB
1984			16	QB
1985	IND	N	5	QB
4 yrs.	41 games			

Dutch Kohl
KOHL, GEORGE H.
B. Sep., 1893
Deceased
None 185 lbs.

Year	Team		Games	Pos.
1920	HAM	A	2	E
1922	HAM	N	4	E
2 yrs.	6 games			

Joe Kohlbrand
KOHLBRAND, JOE
B. Mar. 18, 1963, Merritt Island, FL
Miami (Florida) 6'4" 242 lbs.

Year	Team		Games	Pos.
1985	NO	N	12	DE
1986			16	LB
1987			12	LB
1988			16	LB
1989			16	LB
5 yrs.	72 games			

Bob Kohrs
KOHRS, ROBERT HENRY
B. Nov. 8, 1958, Phoenix, AZ
Arizona State 6'3" 240 lbs.

Year	Team		Games	Pos.
1981	PIT	N	16	LB
1982			9	DE
1983			9	LB, DE
1984			10	LB
1985			11	LB
5 yrs.	55 games			

Mike Koken
KOKEN, MICHAEL R.
B. 1910
Deceased
Notre Dame 5'11" 180 lbs.

Year	Team		Games	Pos.
1933	CHIC	N	9	QB, HB

Jon Kolb
KOLB, JON PAUL
B. Aug. 30, 1947, Ponca City, OK
Oklahoma State 6'2" 256 lbs.

Year	Team		Games	Pos.
1969	PIT	N	14	C
1970			14	C
1971			14	OT, C
1972			14	OT
1973			14	OT
1974			14	OT
1975			14	OT
1976			13	OT
1977			16	OT
1978			14	OT
1979			7	OT
1980			15	OT
1981			15	OT
13 yrs.	177 games			

Elmer Kolberg
KOLBERG, ELMER
B. Jan. 21, 1916, Orange, CA
Oregon State 6'4" 199 lbs.

Year	Team		Games	Pos.
1939	PHI	N	8	E
1940			10	HB
1941	PIT	N	5	E, B
3 yrs.	23 games			

Mike Kolen
KOLEN, MIKE
B. Jan. 31, 1948, Birmingham, AL
Auburn 6'2" 220 lbs.

Year	Team		Games	Pos.
1970	MIA	N	14	LB
1971			14	LB
1972			13	LB
1973			14	LB
1974			14	LB
1975			9	LB
1977			6	LB
7 yrs.	84 games			

Bob Kolesar
KOLESAR, ROBERT C.
B. Apr. 5, 1921, Cleveland, OH
Michigan 5'10" 200 lbs.

Year	Team		Games	Pos.
1946	CLE	AA	2	G

Larry Kolic
KOLIC, LAWRENCE VINCENT
B. Aug. 31, 1963, Cleveland, OH
Ohio State 6'1" 242 lbs.

Year	Team		Games	Pos.
1986	MIA	N	2	LB
1987			7	LB
1988			7	LB
3 yrs.	16 games			

Bill Kollar
KOLLAR, WILLIAM WALLACE
B. Nov. 12, 1952, Warren, OH
Montana State 6'4" 253 lbs.

Year	Team		Games	Pos.
1974	CIN	N	14	DT
1975			14	DT
1976			9	DT
1977	TB	N	14	DT
1978			16	DT
1979			15	DE, DT
1980			15	DE, DT
1981			12	DE, NT
8 yrs.	109 games			

Louie Kolls
KOLLS, LOUIS
B. Dec. 15, 1892, Chattanooga, TN
D. Feb., 1941
St. Ambrose 6'1" 205 lbs.

Year	Team		Games	Pos.
1920	CHIC	A	1	C
1920	HAM	A	2	C, E
1922	RI	N	5	C
1923			6	C, G
1924			9	C, E
1925			11	C, E
1926	RI	A	3	C
1927	NYY	N	2	C
7 yrs.	39 games			

Ed Kolman
KOLMAN, EDWARD V. (Big Ed)
B. Oct. 21, 1917, New York, NY
D. Jul. 31, 1985, New Hyde Park, NY
Temple 6'2" 232 lbs.

Year	Team		Games	Pos.
1940	CHIB	N	10	T
1941			11	T
1942			11	T
1946			10	T
1947			12	T
1949	NYG	N	11	T

6 yrs. 65 games

Chris Kolodziejski
KOLODZIEJSKI, CHRISTOPHER JAMES
B. Jan. 5, 1961, Augsburg, Germany
Wyoming 6'3" 231 lbs.

Year	Team		Games	Pos.
1984	PIT	N	7	TE

Bill Koman
KOMAN, WILLIAM
B. Sep. 16, 1934, Ambridge, PA
North Carolina 6'2" 229 lbs.

Year	Team		Games	Pos.
1956	BAL	N	12	LB
1957	PHI	N	11	LB
1958			12	LB
1959	CHIC	N	11	LB
1960	STL	N	12	LB
1961			14	LB

Bill Koman continued

Year	Team		Games	Pos.
1962			14	LB
1963			14	LB
1964			14	LB
1965			14	LB
1966			14	LB
1967			14	LB
12 yrs.	156 games			

Jeff Komlo
KOMLO, WILLIAM JEFFREY
B. Jul. 30, 1956, Cheverly, MD
Delaware 6'2" 202 lbs.

Year	Team		Games	Pos.
1979	DET	N	16	QB
1980			4	QB
1981			3	QB
1983	TB	N	2	QB
4 yrs.	25 games			

John Kompara
KOMPARA, JOHN
B. Apr. 12, 1936
South Carolina 6'2" 245 lbs.

Year	Team		Games	Pos.
1960	LA	A		DT

Mark Koncar
KONCAR, MARK (Claw)
B. May 5, 1953, Murray, UT
Colorado 6'5" 269 lbs.

Year	Team		Games	Pos.
1976	GB	N	14	OT
1977			13	OT
1979			12	OT
1980			1	OT
1981			14	OT
1982	HOU	N	5	OT
6 yrs.	59 games			

John Kondria
KONDRIA, JOHN
B. 1920
St. Vincent 6'0" 185 lbs.

Year	Team		Games	Pos.
1945	PIT	N	1	T

Mark Konecny
KONECNY, MARK WILLIAM
B. Apr. 2, 1963, Chicago, IL
Alma 5'11" 197 lbs.

Year	Team		Games	Pos.
1987	MIA	N	3	RB
1988	PHI	N	16	RB
2 yrs.	19 games			

Floyd Konetsky
KONETSKY, FLOYD W.
B. May 21, 1920, Marianna, PA
Deceased
Florida 6'0" 197 lbs.

Year	Team		Games	Pos.
1944	CLE	N	9	E
1945			10	E
1947	BAL	AA	6	E
3 yrs.	25 games			

John Koniszewski
KONISZEWSKI, JOHN EDWARD (Jock)
B. Aug. 29, 1921, Dickson City, PA
George Washington 6'3" 243 lbs.

Year	Team		Games	Pos.
1945	WAS	N	8	T
1946			9	T
1948			12	T
3 yrs.	29 games			

Ed Konopasek
KONOPASEK, EDWARD STEVEN
B. Apr. 12, 1964, Gary, IN
Ball State 6'6" 289 lbs.

Year	Team		Games	Pos.
1987	GB	N	3	OT

Year	Team	Games	Pos.

Bob Konovsky
KONOVSKY, ROBERT E.
B. Aug. 19, 1934, Chicago, IL
D. Mar. 6, 1982, Chicago, IL
Wisconsin 6'2" 246 lbs.

Year	Team		Games	Pos.
1956	**CHIC**	N	12	G
1957			12	G
1958			12	G
1961	**DEN**	A	13	DE
4 yrs.	49 games			

Kenny Konz
KONZ, KENNETH
B. Sep. 25, 1928, Weimar, TX
Louisiana State 5'10" 184 lbs.

Year	Team		Games	Pos.
1953	**CLE**	N	12	HB
1954			12	HB
1955			12	HB
1956			12	HB
1957			12	HB
1958			12	HB
1959			12	HB
7 yrs.	84 games			

George Koonce
KOONCE, GEORGE EARL, JR.
B. Oct. 15, 1968, New Bern, NC
Chowan/East Carolina 6'1" 238 lbs.

Year	Team		Games	Pos.
1992	**GB**	N	16	LB
1993			15	LB
1994			16	LB
1995			16	LB
1996			16	LB
5 yrs.	79 games			

Joe Koons
KOONS, JOSEPH L.
B. Jan. 12, 1915, Wilkes-Barre, PA
D. Oct. 20, 1993, Shelby, MI
Long Island 6'1" 190 lbs.

Year	Team		Games	Pos.
1941	**BKN**	N	6	C, G

Ed Koontz
KOONTZ, ED
B. Jun. 11, 1946, Littletown, PA
Catawba 6'2" 230 lbs.

Year	Team		Games	Pos.
1968	**BOS**	A	6	LB

Joe Koontz
KOONTZ, JOSEPH
B. Aug. 13, 1945, Visalia, CA
San Francisco State 6'1" 192 lbs.

Year	Team		Games	Pos.
1968	**NYG**	N	14	C

Dave Kopay
KOPAY, DAVID MARQUETTE
B. Jun. 28, 1942, Chicago, IL
Washington 6'2" 220 lbs.

Year	Team		Games	Pos.
1964	**SF**	N	14	HB
1965			12	HB
1966			14	HB
1967			7	RB
1968	**DET**	N	13	RB
1969	**WAS**	N	13	RB
1970			14	RB
1971	**NO**	N	10	RB
1972	**GB**	N	14	RB
9 yrs.	111 games			

Joe Kopcha
KOPCHA, JOSEPH EDWARD
B. Dec. 23, 1905, Whiting, IN
D. Jul. 29, 1986, Hobart, IN
Tennessee-Chattanooga 6'0" 221 lbs.

Year	Team		Games	Pos.
1929	**CHIB**	N	11	G, T
1932			11	G
1933			13	G

Joe Kopcha continued

Year	Team		Games	Pos.
1934			11	G, T
1935			12	G
1936	**DET**	N	12	G
6 yrs.	70 games			

Joe Koplow
KOPLOW, JACOB
B. Jun. 7, 1901
D. Sep., 1986, Boston, MA
Boston University 6'3" 235 lbs.

Year	Team		Games	Pos.
1926	**PRO**	N	1	T

Jeff Kopp
KOPP, JEFF
B. Jul. 8, 1971, Danville, CA
Southern California 6'3" 234 lbs.

Year	Team		Games	Pos.
1995	**MIA**	N	16	LB
1996	**JAC**	N	12	LB
2 yrs.	28 games			

Walt Koppisch
KOPPISCH, WALTER FREDERIC
B. 1902
D. Nov. 5, 1953
Columbia 5'10" 180 lbs.

Year	Team		Games	Pos.
1925	**BUF**	N	6	HB, FB
1926	**NYG**	N	8	HB, FB, QB
2 yrs.	14 games			

Mark Korff
KORFF, MARK
B. Apr. 5, 1963, Canoga Park. CA
Florida 6'1" 230 lbs.

Year	Team		Games	Pos.
1987	**SF**	N	2	LB

Ed Korisky
KORISKY, EDWARD A.
B. Aug. 23, 1918, Hartford, CT
D. Jul. 13, 1992, Hartford, CT
Villanova 6'1" 210 lbs.

Year	Team		Games	Pos.
1944	**BOS**	N	9	C

R.J. Kors
KORS, RICHARD
B. Jun. 27, 1966, Santa Monica, CA
Southern California/Long Beach State 6'0" 195 lbs.

Year	Team		Games	Pos.
1991	**NYJ**	N	16	S
1992			14	CB, S
1993	**CIN**	N	7	CB, S
3 yrs.	37 games			

Ken Kortas
KORTAS, KENNETH CONRAD
B. May 17, 1942, Chicago, IL
Louisville 6'2" 282 lbs.

Year	Team		Games	Pos.
1964	**STL**	N	14	DT
1965	**PIT**	N	14	DT
1966			14	DT
1967			14	DT
1968			14	DT
1969	**CHI**	N	3	DT
6 yrs.	73 games			

Steve Korte
KORTE, STEVE
B. Jan. 15, 1960, Denver, CO
Arkansas 6'2" 260 lbs.

Year	Team		Games	Pos.
1983	**NO**	N	16	G
1984			15	G
1985			12	C
1986			16	C
1987			3	C
1988			16	C

Steve Korte continued

Year	Team		Games	Pos.
1989			5	C
7 yrs.	83 games			

Kelvin Korver
KORVER, KELVIN MITCHELL
B. Feb. 21, 1949, Dallas, TX
Texas A&M/Northwestern (Iowa) 6'6" 267 lbs.

Year	Team		Games	Pos.
1973	**OAK**	N	14	DT
1974			9	DT
1975			1	DT
3 yrs.	24 games			

Bernie Kosar
KOSAR, BERNIE
B. Nov. 25, 1963, Boardman, OH
Miami (Florida) 6'5" 210 lbs.

Year	Team		Games	Pos.
1985	**CLE**	N	12	QB
1986			16	QB
1987			12	QB
1988			9	QB
1989			16	QB
1990			13	QB
1991			16	QB
1992			7	QB
1993			2	QB
1993	**DAL**	N	4	QB
1994	**MIA**	N	2	QB
1995			9	QB
1996			3	QB
12 yrs.	126 games			

Stan Kosel
KOSEL, STANLEY
B. Aug. 17, 1916
D. May, 1982, Carteret, NJ
Albright 5'11" 190 lbs.

Year	Team		Games	Pos.
1938	**BKN**	N	8	FB
1939			5	HB, E
2 yrs.	13 games			

Terry Kosens
KOSENS, TERRENCE
B. Oct. 3, 1941, Brooklyn, NY
Hofstra 6'3" 195 lbs.

Year	Team		Games	Pos.
1963	**MIN**	N	8	DB

Frank Kosikowski
KOSIKOWSKI, FRANK LEON
B. Jul. 23, 1926, Cudahy, WI
Marquette/Notre Dame 6'1" 200 lbs.

Year	Team		Games	Pos.
1948	**CLE**	AA	12	E

Gary Kosins
KOSINS, GARY JAMES
B. Jan. 21, 1949, Warsaw, IN
Dayton 6'1" 216 lbs.

Year	Team		Games	Pos.
1972	**CHI**	N	14	RB
1973			12	RB
1974			14	RB
3 yrs.	40 games			

Stan Koslowski
KOSLOWSKI, STANLEY J.
B. 1925
D. Aug. 23, 1972, Littleton, MA
Holy Cross 6'1" 200 lbs.

Year	Team		Games	Pos.
1946	**MIA**	AA	5	FB

Stein Koss
KOSS, STEIN JEFFREY
B. Aug. 21, 1963
Arizona State 6'2" 225 lbs.

Year	Team		Games	Pos.
1987	**KC**	N	2	TE

Ron Kostelnik
KOSTELNIK, RONALD MICHAEL
B. Jan. 14, 1940, Colver, PA
D. Jan. 30, 1993, Scott County, KY
Cincinnati 6'4" 260 lbs.

Year	Team		Games	Pos.
1961	**GB**	N	14	DT
1962			14	DT
1963			13	DT
1964			14	DT
1965			14	DT
1966			14	DT
1967			14	DT
1968			13	DT
1969	**BAL**	N	10	DT
9 yrs.	120 games			

Mike Kostiuk
KOSTIUK, MICHAEL A.
B. Aug. 1, 1919, Krydor, Sask.
Detroit Tech 6'0" 212 lbs.

Year	Team		Games	Pos.
1941	**CLE**	N	1	G
1945	**DET**	N	6	T
2 yrs.	7 games			

Stan Kostka
KOSTKA, STANISLAUS CLARENCE
B. Jul. 8, 1913, St. Paul, MN
Oregon/Minnesota 5'11" 215 lbs.

Year	Team		Games	Pos.
1935	**BKN**	N	10	FB

Joe Kostos
KOSTOS, JOSEPH
B. Mar. 9, 1896
D. Apr., 1976, Philadelphia, PA
Bucknell 5'9" 165 lbs.

Year	Team		Games	Pos.
1926	**PHI**	A	3	E

Marty Kostos
KOSTOS, MARTIN
B. Nov. 11, 1901
D. Sep., 1961
Schuylkill 5'11" 185 lbs.

Year	Team		Games	Pos.
1929	**FRA**	N	6	E, HB

Tony Kostos
KOSTOS, ANTHONY JOSEPH
B. Jun. 12, 1905
D. Nov. 16, 1984, New Brunswick, NJ
Bucknell 5'11" 191 lbs.

Year	Team		Games	Pos.
1927	**FRA**	N	7	E, T
1928			16	E, CG
1929			19	E, G
1930			13	E, G-C
1930	**MIN**	N	1	E
1930	**FRA**	N	2	E
1930	**MIN**	N	1	T
1931	**FRA**	N	5	E
5 yrs.	64 games			

Eddie Kotal
KOTAL, EDWARD L. (The Lawrence Flash)
B. Sep. 1, 1902
D. Jan. 27, 1973, North Hollywood, CA
Illinois/Lawrence 5'8" 170 lbs.

Year	Team		Games	Pos.
1925	**GB**	N	5	HB, E, QB, FB
1926			11	HB, QB
1927			8	HB
1928			12	HB
1929			10	HB
5 yrs.	46 games			

Doug Kotar
KOTAR, DOUGLAS ALLAN
B. Jun. 11, 1951, Canonsburg, PA

Year	Team	Games	Pos.

Doug Kotar continued

Kentucky 5'11" 205 lbs.

Year	Team		Games	Pos.
1974	NYG	N	12	RB
1975			14	RB
1976			14	RB
1977			12	RB
1978			15	RB
1979			16	RB
1981			7	RB

7 yrs.   90 games

Rich Kotite

KOTITE, RICHARD EDWARD
B. Oct. 13, 1942, Brooklyn, NY
Wagner 6'3" 233 lbs.

Year	Team		Games	Pos.
1967	NYG	N	4	OE
1968	PIT	N	12	OE
1969	NYG	N	3	TE
1971			14	TE
1972			2	TE

5 yrs.   35 games

Marty Kottler

KOTTLER, MARTIN A. (Butch)
B. 1910
Deceased
Centre 5'9" 180 lbs.

Year	Team		Games	Pos.
1933	PIT	N	3	FB, QB

Ed Kovac

KOVAC, EDWARD
B. Apr. 22, 1938, McKeesport, PA
Cincinnati 6'0" 199 lbs.

Year	Team		Games	Pos.
1960	BAL	N	12	HB
1962	NY	A	3	HB, DB

2 yrs.   15 games

Jim Kovach

KOVACH, JIM
B. May 1, 1956, Parma Heights, OH
Kentucky 6'2" 225 lbs.

Year	Team		Games	Pos.
1979	NO	N	16	LB
1980			11	LB
1981			15	LB
1982			8	LB
1983			16	LB
1984			15	LB
1985			2	LB
1985	SF	N	4	LB

7 yrs.   87 games

Bill Kovacsy

KOVACSY, WILLIAM
B. Feb. 15, 1901
D. May, 1980, Hammond, IN
Illinois

Year	Team		Games	Pos.
1923	HAM	N	3	G

Mike Kovaleski

KOVALESKI, MICHAEL
B. Jul. 3, 1965
Notre Dame 6'2" 225 lbs.

Year	Team		Games	Pos.
1987	CLE	N	1	LB

Johnny Kovatch

KOVATCH, JOHN GEORGE
B. Jul. 21, 1920, South Bend, IN
Deceased
Notre Dame 6'3" 197 lbs.

Year	Team		Games	Pos.
1942	WAS	N	8	E
1946			10	E
1947	GB	N	3	E

3 yrs.   21 games

Johnny Kovatch

KOVATCH, JOHN P.

Johnny Kovatch continued

B. Jun. 6, 1912, South Bend, IN
Northwestern 5'11" 172 lbs.

Year	Team		Games	Pos.
1938	CLE	N	5	E

Walt Kowalczyk

KOWALCZYK, WALTER J.
B. Apr. 17, 1935, Rochester, MI
Michigan State 6'0" 208 lbs.

Year	Team		Games	Pos.
1958	PHI	N	12	FB
1959			12	FB
1960	DAL	N	12	FB
1961	OAK	A	4	FB

4 yrs.   40 games

Bob Kowalkowski

KOWALKOWSKI, ROBERT
B. Nov. 5, 1943, Drexel Hill, PA
Virginia 6'3" 243 lbs.

Year	Team		Games	Pos.
1966	DET	N	14	G
1967			14	G
1968			14	G
1969			2	G
1970			10	G
1971			14	G
1972			14	G
1973			14	G
1974			14	G
1975			14	G
1976			14	G
1977	GB	N	9	G

12 yrs.   147 games

Scott Kowalkowski

KOWALKOWSKI, SCOTT THOMAS
B. Aug. 23, 1968, Royal Oak, MI
Notre Dame 6'2" 228 lbs.

Year	Team		Games	Pos.
1991	PHI	N	16	LB
1992			16	LB
1994	DET	N	16	LB
1995			16	LB
1996			16	LB

5 yrs.   80 games

Adolph Kowalski

KOWALSKI, ADOLPH
B. 1921
Tulsa 6'3" 205 lbs.

Year	Team		Games	Pos.
1947	BKN	AA	10	B

Andy Kowalski

KOWALSKI, ANDREW
B. Jun. 3, 1920, Gloucester, NJ
Mississippi State 6'1" 199 lbs.

Year	Team		Games	Pos.
1943	BKN	N	8	E
1944			10	E
1945	BOS	N	3	E

3 yrs.   21 games

Gary Kowalski

KOWALSKI, GARY STUART
B. Jul. 2, 1960, New Haven, CT
Boston College 6'6" 280 lbs.

Year	Team		Games	Pos.
1983	LARM	N	16	OT
1985	SD	N	13	OT
1986			16	OT
1987			12	G, OT
1988			2	G, OT

5 yrs.   59 games

Nick Kowgios

KOWGIOS, NICHOLAS
B. Nov. 19, 1962, Yonkers, NY
Lafayette 6'0" 216 lbs.

Year	Team		Games	Pos.
1987	DET	N	3	RB

Ernie Koy

KOY, ERNEST MELVIN
B. Oct. 22, 1942, Bellville, TX
Texas 6'2" 228 lbs.

Year	Team		Games	Pos.
1965	NYG	N	13	HB, P
1966			13	HB, P
1967			14	RB, P
1968			13	RB, P
1969			14	RB, P
1970			12	RB, P

6 yrs.   79 games

Ted Koy

KOY, JAMES THEO
B. Sep. 15, 1947, Bellville, TX
Texas 6'1" 211 lbs.

Year	Team		Games	Pos.
1970	OAK	N	14	TE
1971	BUF	N	14	TE
1972			14	TE
1973			13	TE
1974			12	TE

5 yrs.   67 games

Scott Kozak

KOZAK, SCOTT ALLEN
B. Nov. 28, 1965, Hillsboro, OR
Oregon 6'3" 225 lbs.

Year	Team		Games	Pos.
1989	HOU	N	16	LB
1990			16	LB
1991			16	LB
1992			16	LB
1993			16	LB

5 yrs.   80 games

Chet Kozel

KOZEL, CHESTER R.
B. Nov. 15, 1919, Kenosha, WI
Deceased
Mississippi 6'2" 211 lbs.

Year	Team		Games	Pos.
1947	BUF	AA	12	T
1948			8	
1948	CHI	AA	5	G

2 yrs.   19 games

Bruce Kozerski

KOZERSKI, BRUCE
B. Apr. 2, 1962, Plains, PA
Holy Cross 6'4" 275 lbs.

Year	Team		Games	Pos.
1984	CIN	N	16	OT, C
1985			14	C
1986			16	C
1987			8	C
1988			16	G
1989			15	C, G
1990			16	C
1991			16	C
1992			16	C
1993			15	G
1994			16	OT, G
1995			8	G

12 yrs.   172 games

Mike Koziak

KOZIAK, MICHAEL
B. 1893
Deceased
None 5'9" 185 lbs.

Year	Team		Games	Pos.
1925	DUL	N	1	G

Bill Kozlek

KOZLEK, BILL
B. 1900
Deceased
None

Year	Team		Games	Pos.
1926	BKN	A	2	T

Brian Kozlowski

KOZLOWSKI, BRIAN SCOTT
B. Oct. 4, 1970, Rochester, NY
Connecticut 6'3" 250 lbs.

Year	Team		Games	Pos.
1994	NYG	N	16	TE
1995			16	TE
1996			5	TE

3 yrs.   37 games

Glen Kozlowski

KOZLOWSKI, GLEN ALLEN
B. Dec. 31, 1962, Honolulu, HI
Brigham Young 6'1" 190 lbs.

Year	Team		Games	Pos.
1987	CHI	N	3	WR
1988			16	WR
1989			15	WR
1990			12	WR
1991			16	WR
1992			4	WR

6 yrs.   66 games

Mike Kozlowski

KOZLOWSKI, MICHAEL JOHN
B. Feb. 24, 1956, Newark, NJ
Colorado 6'0" 198 lbs.

Year	Team		Games	Pos.
1979	MIA	N	16	S
1981			14	S
1982			9	S
1983			16	S
1984			16	S
1985			5	S
1986			15	S

7 yrs.   91 games

Joe Kozlowsky

KOZLOWSKY, JOSEPH
B. Aug. 9, 1901
D. Dec., 1970, Boston, MA
Boston College 5'10" 201 lbs.

Year	Team		Games	Pos.
1925	PRO	N	11	T
1926			10	T, E
1927			12	T, G
1929	BOS	N	8	T
1930	PRO	N	7	T, G

5 yrs.   48 games

Dave Kraayeveid

KRAAYEVEID, DAVID RAY
B. Oct. 26, 1955, Elkhorn, WI
Wisconsin-Whitewater/Milton 6'5" 255 lbs.

Year	Team		Games	Pos.
1978	SEA	N	12	DE, DT

George Kracum

KRACUM, GEORGE
B. Jan. 24, 1918, Trescow, PA
D. Jun., 1981, Minneapolis, MN
Pittsburgh 6'1" 212 lbs.

Year	Team		Games	Pos.
1941	BKN	N	11	B

Ollie Kraehe

KRAEHE, OLIVER R.
B. Aug. 22, 1898, St. Louis, MO
D. Nov. 2, 1969, St. Louis, MO
Washington (Missouri) 5'10" 180 lbs.

Year	Team		Games	Pos.
1922	RI	N	1	C
1923	STL	N	7	G, E

2 yrs.   8 games

Eldred Kraemer

KRAEMER, ELDRED J.
B. 1930
D. Sep. 16, 1992, Pittsburgh, PA
Pittsburgh 6'2" 225 lbs.

Year	Team		Games	Pos.
1955	SF	N	9	G

Year	Team	Games	Pos.

Ren Kraft
KRAFT, REYNOLD R. (Dolly)
B. Mar. 29, 1895
D. Nov. 7, 1951
Illinois 5'11" 170 lbs.

Year	Team	Games	Pos.
1922	MIN	N	2	E

Rudy Kraft
KRAFT, RUDOLPH G.
B. Oct. 21, 1896
D. Nov., 1978, Sloan, NY
Penn State 5'10" 190 lbs.

| 1921 | TON | A | 2 | G, C |

Greg Kragen
KRAGEN, GREG JOHN
B. Mar. 4, 1962, Chicago, IL
Utah State 6'3" 245 lbs.

1985	DEN	N	16	NT
1986			16	NT
1987			12	NT
1988			16	NT
1989			14	NT
1990			16	NT
1991			16	NT
1992			16	NT
1993			14	NT
1994	KC	N	16	DT
1995	CAR	N	16	NT
1996			16	NT

12 yrs.   184 games

Jimmy Krahl
KRAHL, JAMES KENNETH
B. Nov. 19, 1955, Houston, TX
Texas Tech 6'5" 252 lbs.

1978	NYG	N	16	DT
1979	BAL	N	1	DT
1980			2	DT
1980	SF	N	2	DT

3 yrs.   21 games

Merv Krakau
KRAKAU, MERVIN FLOYD
B. May 16, 1951, Jefferson, IA
Iowa State 6'2" 237 lbs.

1973	BUF	N	14	LB
1974			12	LB
1975			14	LB
1976			14	LB
1977			14	LB
1978			5	LB
1978	NE	N	1	LB

6 yrs.   74 games

Joe Kraker
KRAKER, JOSEPH
B. 1896
Deceased
None 6'1" 170 lbs.

| 1924 | RI | N | 5 | G |

Joe Krakoski
KRAKOSKI, JOE ANDREW
B. Dec. 18, 1937, Danville, IL
Illinois 6'2" 196 lbs.

1961	WAS	N	11	DB
1963	OAK	A	14	DB
1964			14	DB
1965			12	DB
1966			12	DB

5 yrs.   63 games

Joe Krakoski
KRAKOSKI, JOSEPH JOSHUA
B. Nov. 11, 1962, Aurora, IL
Washington 6'1" 224 lbs.

| 1986 | WAS | N | 8 | LB |

Jerry Krall
KRALL, GERALD S.
B. Apr. 19, 1927, Toledo, OH
Ohio State 5'10" 185 lbs.

| 1950 | DET | N | 7 | HB |

Erik Kramer
KRAMER, ERIK
B. Nov. 6, 1964, Encino, CA
North Carolina State 6'0" 192 lbs.

1987	ATL	N	3	QB
1991	DET	N	13	QB
1992			7	QB
1993			5	QB
1994	CHI	N	6	QB
1995			16	QB
1996			4	QB

7 yrs.   54 games

Fritz Kramer
KRAMER, FREDERICK
B. 1903
Washington State 6'0" 230 lbs.

| 1927 | NYY | N | 11 | G, C |

George Kramer
KRAMER, GEORGE
B. Jun. 2, 1894, Illinois
D. Sep., 1974, Chicago, IL
None 6'2" 240 lbs.

1921	MIN	N	3	G
1922	MIN	N	3	G
1923			7	T, G, HB
1924			6	G, T, HB

4 yrs.   19 games

Jack Kramer
KRAMER, JOHN
B. 1923
Marquette 6'0" 220 lbs.

| 1946 | BUF | AA | 13 | T |

Jerry Kramer
KRAMER, GERALD LOUIS
B. Jan. 23, 1936, Jordan, MT
Idaho 6'3" 246 lbs.

1958	GB	N	12	G
1959			12	G
1960			12	G
1961			7	G
1962			14	G, K
1963			14	G, K
1964			2	G
1965			14	G
1966			14	G
1967			14	G
1968			14	G, K

11 yrs.   129 games

Kent Kramer
KRAMER, KENT DEVLIN
B. Jul. 21, 1944, Los Angeles, CA
Minnesota 6'5" 234 lbs.

1966	SF	N	14	TE
1967	NO	N	10	TE
1969	MIN	N	13	TE
1970			11	TE
1971	PHI	N	10	TE
1972			14	TE
1973			12	TE

7 yrs.   84 games

Kyle Kramer
KRAMER, KYLE MEVOY
B. Jan. 12, 1967, Kansas City, MO
Bowling Green 6'3" 190 lbs.

| 1989 | CLE | N | 14 | S |

Ron Kramer
KRAMER, RONALD JOHN
B. Jun. 24, 1935, Girard, KS
Michigan 6'3" 234 lbs.

1957	GB	N	9	E
1959			12	E
1960			12	E
1961			14	OE
1962			14	OE
1963			12	OE
1964			14	OE
1965	DET	N	14	OE
1966			14	TE
1967			12	TE

10 yrs.   127 games

Tommy Kramer
KRAMER, THOMAS FRANCIS
B. Mar. 7, 1955, San Antonio, TX
Rice 6'2" 205 lbs.

1977	MIN	N	6	QB
1978			4	QB
1979			16	QB
1980			15	QB
1981			14	QB
1982			9	QB
1983			3	QB
1984			9	QB
1985			15	QB
1986			13	QB
1987			6	QB
1988			10	QB
1989			8	QB
1990	NO	N	1	QB

14 yrs.   129 games

Bob Kratch
KRATCH, BOB
B. Jan. 6, 1966, Brooklyn, NY
Iowa 6'3" 288 lbs.

1989	NYG	N	4	G
1990			14	G
1991			15	G
1992			16	G
1993			16	G
1994	NE	N	16	G
1995			16	G
1996			8	G

8 yrs.   105 games

Dan Kratzer
KRATZER, DANIEL LEON
B. Jul. 7, 1949, Kearney, MO
Missouri Valley 6'3" 194 lbs.

| 1973 | KC | N | 1 | WR |

Frank Kraus
KRAUS, FRANCIS L. (Babe)
B. Sep. 2, 1899
D. Sep., 1966, Geneva, NY
Colgate/Hobart 6'2" 220 lbs.

| 1924 | BUF | N | 6 | T, G |

Bill Krause
KRAUSE, WILLIAM
B. 1915
Baldwin-Wallace 6'0" 210 lbs.

| 1938 | CLE | N | 1 | G |

Larry Krause
KRAUSE, LARRY J.
B. Apr. 22, 1948, Stanley, WI
St. Norbert 6'0" 208 lbs.

1970	GB	N	14	RB
1971			9	RB
1973			14	RB
1974			14	RB

4 yrs.   51 games

Max Krause
KRAUSE, MAX JOSEPH (Bananas)
B. Apr. 5, 1909, Spokane, WA
D. Jul., 1984, Spokane, WA
Gonzaga 5'10" 202 lbs.

1933	NYG	N	5	FB
1934			12	FB
1935			6	FB
1936			9	FB
1937	WAS	N	9	FB
1938			4	FB, HB
1939			2	HB
1940			9	HB

8 yrs.   56 games

Paul Krause
KRAUSE, PAUL JAMES
B. Feb. 19, 1942, Flint, MI
Iowa 6'3" 199 lbs.

1964	WAS	N	14	OE, DB
1965			14	DB
1966			13	DB
1967			13	DB
1968	MIN	N	14	DB
1969			14	S
1970			14	S
1971			14	S
1972			14	S
1973			11	S
1974			14	S
1975			14	S
1976			14	S
1977			16	S
1978			16	S
1979			16	S
1980			16	S

17 yrs.   239 games

Red Krause
KRAUSE, HENRY, JR.
B. Aug. 28, 1913, St. Louis, MO
D. Feb. 20, 1987, Beltsville, MD
St. Louis 6'1" 212 lbs.

1936	BKN	N	11	C
1937			5	C
1937	WAS	N	3	C
1938			9	C

3 yrs.   28 games

Barry Krauss
KRAUSS, RICHARD BARRY
B. Mar. 17, 1957, Pompano Beach, FL
Alabama 6'3" 239 lbs.

1979	BAL	N	15	LB
1980			16	LB
1981			9	LB
1982			9	LB
1983			16	LB
1984	IND	N	16	LB
1985			16	LB
1986			4	LB
1987			12	LB
1988			16	LB
1989	MIA	N	16	LB

11 yrs.   152 games

Rich Kraynak
KRAYNAK, RICH
B. Jan. 20, 1961, Phoenixville, PA
Pittsburgh 6'1" 226 lbs.

1983	PHI	N	16	LB
1984			14	LB
1985			16	LB
1986			6	LB
1987	ATL	N	9	LB

5 yrs.   61 games

John Kreamcheck
KREAMCHECK, JOHN

Year	Team		Games	Pos.

John Kreamcheck *continued*
B. Jan. 7, 1927, Vestaburg, PA
William & Mary 6'5" 255 lbs.

Year	Team		Games	Pos.
1953	CHIB	N	12	T
1954			12	T
1955			12	T

3 yrs.   36 games

Ed Kregenow
KREGENOW, EDWIN L.
B. Feb. 12, 1900
Deceased
Akron 5'8" 170 lbs.

1926	CLE	A	5	E

Steve Kreider
KREIDER, STEVE KENNETH
B. May 12, 1958, Reading, PA
Lehigh 6'3" 192 lbs.

1979	CIN	N	15	WR
1980			16	WR
1981			16	WR
1982			9	WR
1983			16	WR
1984			16	WR
1985			16	WR
1986			10	WR

8 yrs.   114 games

Earl Kreiger
KREIGER, EARL (Irish)
B. Aug. 31, 1896
Ohio University 5'11" 185 lbs.

1921	DET	A	4	HB
1922	COL	N	8	T

2 yrs.   12 games

Walt Kreinheder
KREINHEDER, WALTER
B. 1900
Michigan 6'2" 208 lbs.

1922	AKR	N	5	C, QB
1923	STL	N	6	C
1925	CLE	N	5	C, T

3 yrs.   16 games

Rich Kreitling
KREITLING, RICHARD ALLEN
B. Mar. 13, 1936, Chicago, IL
Auburn/Illinois 6'2" 208 lbs.

1959	CLE		12	E
1960			12	E
1961			13	OE
1962			14	OE
1963			14	OE
1964	CHI	N	14	OE

6 yrs.   79 games

Joe Krejci
KREJCI, JOE ALBERT
B. Mar. 16, 1906, Plattsmouth, NE
Peru State 6'0" 190 lbs.

1934	CHIC	N	1	E

Ken Kremer
KREMER, JAMES KENDALL
B. Jul. 16, 1957, Hammond, IN
Ball State 6'4" 250 lbs.

1979	KC	N	16	DE
1980			14	NT
1981			16	DE, NT
1982			9	NT
1983			16	NT
1984			16	NT

6 yrs.   87 games

Karl Kremser
KREMSER, KARL FRIEDRICH
B. Aug. 3, 1945, Salzwedel, Germany
Army/Tennessee 6'0" 178 lbs.

1969	MIA	A	14	K
1970	MIA	N	1	K

2 yrs.   15 games

Mitch Krenk
KRENK, MITCH
B. Nov. 19, 1959, Crete, NE
Nebraska 6'4" 225 lbs.

1984	CHI	N	8	TE

Ty Krentler
KRENTLER, WALTER A.
B. Apr. 25, 1895, Detroit, MI
D. Nov., 1971, Southfield, MI
Detroit 160 lbs.

1920	DET	A	2	FB

Keith Krepfle
KREPFLE, KEITH ROBERT
B. Feb. 4, 1952, Dubuque, IA
Iowa State 6'3" 226 lbs.

1975	PHI	N	14	TE
1976			13	TE
1977			14	TE
1978			10	TE
1979			16	TE
1980			13	TE
1981			16	TE
1982	ATL	N	4	TE

8 yrs.   100 games

Mark Krerowicz
KREROWICZ, MARK
B. Mar. 1, 1963, Toledo, OH
Ohio State 6'4" 282 lbs.

1987	CLE	N	3	G

Joe Kresky
KRESKY, JOSEPH LAWRENCE (Mink)
B. Apr. 27, 1906, Marinette, WI
D. Dec. 24, 1988, Naples, FL
Wisconsin 6'0" 215 lbs.

1932	BOS		8	G, T
1933	PHI	N	9	G, E
1934			11	G
1935			9	T, G
1935	PIT		1	G

4 yrs.   38 games

Al Kreuz
KREUZ, ALBERT F.
B. Aug. 21, 1898
D. Aug., 1975, Menominee, WI
Western Michigan/Pennsylvania 5'9" 190 lbs.

1926	PHI	A	10	FB

Al Krevis
KREVIS, AL
B. Jul. 9, 1952, Lake Hiawatha, NJ
Boston College 6'5" 263 lbs.

1975	CIN	N	3	OT, G
1976	NYJ	N	10	OT

2 yrs.   13 games

Dave Krieg
KRIEG, DAVID M.
B. Oct. 20, 1958, Iola, WI
Milton 6'1" 192 lbs.

1980	SEA	N	1	QB
1981			7	QB

Dave Krieg *continued*

Year	Team		Games	Pos.
1982			3	QB
1983			9	QB
1984			16	QB
1985			16	QB
1986			15	QB
1987			12	QB
1988			9	QB
1989			15	QB
1990			16	QB
1991			10	QB
1992	KC	N	16	QB
1993			12	QB
1994	DET	N	14	QB
1995	ARI	N	16	QB
1996	CHI	N	13	QB

17 yrs.   200 games

Jim Krieg
KRIEG, JAMES LEO
B. May 29, 1949, Buffalo, NY
Washington 5'9" 172 lbs.

1972	DEN	N	6	WR

Bob Krieger
KRIEGER, ROBERT E.
B. May 2, 1918, Minneapolis, MN
D. Oct. 17, 1980, Minneapolis, MN
Dartmouth 6'1" 190 lbs.

1941	PHI	N	11	E
1946			7	E

2 yrs.   18 games

Emmett Kriel
KRIEL, EMMETT (Sally)
B. May 2, 1916
D. Nov., 1984, Houston, TX
Baylor 6'2" 200 lbs.

1939	PHI	N	1	G

Doug Kriewald
KRIEWALD, DOUGLAS CLARK
B. Aug. 30, 1945, Seguin, TX
West Texas State 6'4" 245 lbs.

1967	CHI	N	2	G
1968			13	G

2 yrs.   15 games

John Krimm
KRIMM, JOHN JOSEPH, JR.
B. May 30, 1960, Philadelphia, PA
Notre Dame 6'1" 190 lbs.

1982	NO	N	9	S

Fran Kring
KRING, FRANK
B. 1919
Texas Christian 6'0" 190 lbs.

1945	DET	N	4	FB

Krink
KRINK
None

1927	CLE	N	1	C

Billy Krisher
KRISHER, WILLIAM
B. Sep. 18, 1935, Perry, OK
Oklahoma 6'1" 233 lbs.

1958	PIT	N	8	G
1960	DAL	A		G
1961			14	G

3 yrs.   22 games

Howie Kriss
KRISS, HOWARD E. (The Buckeye Bullet)
B. Jun., 1907
D. Jun. 13, 1992, El Paso, TX
Ohio State 5'9" 175 lbs.

1931	CLE	N	2	HB

Frank Kristufek
KRISTUFEK, FRANK CHARLES
B. Dec. 12, 1915, Pittsburgh, PA
Pittsburgh 6'0" 209 lbs.

1940	BKN	N	11	T
1941			11	T

2 yrs.   22 games

Joe Krivonak
KRIVONAK, JOSEPH
B. 1918
South Carolina 6'2" 230 lbs.

1946	MIA	AA	4	G

Leo Kriz
KRIZ, LEO J. (Tiny)
B. 1903
Iowa/George Washington 6'1" 205 lbs.

1926	NY	A	8	G, T

Joe Krol
KROL, JOSEPH (Whitey)
B. Apr. 23, 1918
D. Aug., 1975, Detroit, MI
Western Ontario 6'1" 210 lbs.

1945	DET	N	2	HB

Alex Kroll
KROLL, ALEXANDER
B. 1938
Rutgers 6'3" 230 lbs.

1962	NY	A	14	OT, C

Bob Kroll
KROLL, ROBERT LEE
B. Jun. 9, 1950, Green Bay, WI
Northern Michigan 6'1" 195 lbs.

1972	GB	N	5	DB

Gary Kroner
KRONER, GARY LEE
B. Nov. 6, 1940, Green Bay, WI
Wisconsin 6'1" 200 lbs.

1965	DEN	A	14	DB, K
1966			14	DB, K
1967			3	K

3 yrs.   31 games

Kropp
KROPP
None

1920	HAM	A	1	E

Ray Krouse
KROUSE, RAYMOND
B. Apr. 21, 1927
D. Apr. 7, 1966
Maryland 6'3" 263 lbs.

1951	NYG	N	12	T
1952			12	T
1953			10	T
1954			12	T
1955			12	T
1956	DET	N	12	T
1957			12	T
1958	BAL	N	12	T
1959			12	T

Year	Team		Games	Pos.

Ray Krouse *continued*

Year	Team		Games	Pos.
1960	WAS	N	12	T
10 yrs.	118 games			

Mike Kruczek

KRUCZEK, MICHAEL
B. Mar. 15, 1953, Washington, DC
Boston College 6'1" 202 lbs.

Year	Team		Games	Pos.
1976	PIT	N	10	QB
1977			2	QB
1978			9	QB
1979			8	QB
1980	WAS	N	7	QB
5 yrs.	36 games			

Al Krueger

KRUEGER, ALVIN JOHN
B. Apr. 3, 1919, Orange, CA
Southern California 6'1" 188 lbs.

Year	Team		Games	Pos.
1941	WAS	N	8	B
1942			11	E
1946	LA	AA	10	E
3 yrs.	29 games			

Charlie Krueger

KRUEGER, CHARLES ANDREW
B. Jan. 28, 1937, Caldwell, TX
Texas A&M 6'4" 256 lbs.

Year	Team		Games	Pos.
1959	SF	N	12	DE
1960			12	DE
1961			14	DE
1962			14	DE
1963			7	DT
1964			14	DT
1965			14	DT
1966			14	DT
1967			13	DT
1968			14	DT
1969			14	DT
1970			14	DT
1971			14	DT
1972			14	DT
1973			14	DT
15 yrs.	198 games			

Jimmy Krueger

KRUEGER, JAMES
B. Aug. 18, 1901
Drake 5'10" 180 lbs.

Year	Team		Games	Pos.
1924	KC	N	5	T

Rolf Krueger

KRUEGER, ROLF FRANK
B. Dec. 8, 1946, Caldwell, TX
Texas A&M 6'4" 251 lbs.

Year	Team		Games	Pos.
1969	STL	N	14	DE, DT
1970			14	DE
1971			14	DE, DT
1972	SF	N	4	DE, DT
1973			14	DE, DT
1974			9	DT
6 yrs.	69 games			

Todd Krumm

KRUMM, TODD ALAN
B. Dec. 18, 1965, Royal Oak, MI
Michigan State 6'0" 189 lbs.

Year	Team		Games	Pos.
1988	CHI	N	15	S

Tim Krumrie

KRUMRIE, TIMOTHY A.
B. May 20, 1960, Eau Claire, WI
Wisconsin 6'2" 262 lbs.

Year	Team		Games	Pos.
1983	CIN	N	16	NT
1984			16	NT
1985			16	NT
1986			16	NT

Tim Krumrie *continued*

Year	Team		Games	Pos.
1987			12	NT
1988			16	NT
1989			16	NT
1990			16	NT
1991			16	NT
1992			16	NT
1993			16	NT
1994			16	DT
12 yrs.	188 games			

Joe Krupa

KRUPA, JOSEPH S.
B. Jul. 6, 1933, Chicago, IL
Purdue 6'2" 232 lbs.

Year	Team		Games	Pos.
1956	PIT	N	12	T
1957			12	T
1958			12	T
1959			9	T
1960			12	T
1961			14	DT
1962			14	DT
1963			14	DT
1964			11	DT
9 yrs.	110 games			

Bob Kruse

KRUSE, ROBERT
B. Feb. 8, 1942, Franklin Park, IL
Colorado State/Wayne State (Nebraska) 6'2" 250 lbs.

Year	Team		Games	Pos.
1967	OAK	A	13	G
1968			12	G
1969	BUF	A	3	DT
3 yrs.	28 games			

Larry Krutko

KRUTKO, LAWRENCE LEROY
B. Jun. 27, 1935, Carmichael, PA
West Virginia 6'0" 220 lbs.

Year	Team		Games	Pos.
1958	PIT	N	6	FB
1959			12	FB
1960			7	FB
3 yrs.	25 games			

Jerry Krysl

KRYSL, JERRY
B. Jan. 26, 1905
Kansas State 5'11" 200 lbs.

Year	Team		Games	Pos.
1927	CLE	N	7	T

Johnny Ksionzyk

KSIONZYK, JOHN L.
B. Jan. 28, 1919, Binghamton, NY
St. Bonaventure 5'10" 190 lbs.

Year	Team		Games	Pos.
1947	LA	N	3	QB

Ray Kubala

KUBALA, RAYMOND GEORGE
B. Oct. 26, 1942, West, TX
Texas A&M 6'4" 245 lbs.

Year	Team		Games	Pos.
1964	DEN	A	8	C
1965			14	C
1966			14	C
1967			5	C
1967	KC	A	5	C
4 yrs.	46 games			

Bob Kuberski

KUBERSKI, ROBERT KENNETH, JR.
B. Apr. 5, 1971, Chester, PA
Navy 6'4" 300 lbs.

Year	Team		Games	Pos.
1995	GB	N	9	NT
1996			1	NT
2 yrs.	10 games			

Gary Kubiak

KUBIAK, GARY WAYNE
B. Aug. 15, 1961, Houston, TX
Texas A&M 6'0" 192 lbs.

Year	Team		Games	Pos.
1983	DEN	N	4	QB
1984			7	QB
1985			16	QB
1986			16	QB
1987			12	QB
1988			16	QB
1989			16	QB
1990			16	QB
1991			16	QB
9 yrs.	119 games			

Larry Kubin

KUBIN, LARRY
B. Feb. 26, 1959, Union, NJ
Penn State 6'2" 236 lbs.

Year	Team		Games	Pos.
1982	WAS	N	9	LB
1983			12	LB
1984			16	LB
1985	BUF	N	2	LB
1985	TB	N	4	LB
4 yrs.	43 games			

Ted Kucharski

KUCHARSKI, THEODORE M.
B. 1908
Holy Cross 6'1" 185 lbs.

Year	Team		Games	Pos.
1930	PRO	N	7	E

Frank Kuchta

KUCHTA, FRANK
B. Sep. 18, 1936, Cleveland, OH
Notre Dame 6'2" 225 lbs.

Year	Team		Games	Pos.
1958	WAS	N	2	C
1959			12	C
1960	DEN	A		C
3 yrs.	14 games			

Paul Kuczo

KUCZO, PAUL, SR.
B. Feb. 4, 1903
D. Dec., 1970, Stamford, CT
Virginia 5'9" 165 lbs.

Year	Team		Games	Pos.
1929	SI	N	3	QB, FB, HB

Bernie Kuczynski

KUCZYNSKI, BERNARD CARL
B. Jan. 8, 1920, Philadelphia, PA
Pennsylvania 6'0" 196 lbs.

Year	Team		Games	Pos.
1943	DET	N	2	E
1946	PHI	N	3	E
2 yrs.	5 games			

Bob Kuechenberg

KUECHENBERG, ROBERT JOHN
B. Oct. 14, 1947, Gary, IN
Notre Dame 6'3" 253 lbs.

Year	Team		Games	Pos.
1970	MIA	N	14	G
1971			14	G
1972			14	G
1973			13	G
1974			14	G
1975			14	OT, G
1976			10	G
1977			14	G
1978			16	G, OT
1979			16	G, OT
1980			16	G, OT
1981			16	G, OT
1982			9	G
1983			16	G
14 yrs.	196 games			

Rudy Kuechenberg

KUECHENBERG, RUDOLPH BERNARD
B. Feb. 7, 1943, Hobart, IN
Indiana 6'2" 215 lbs.

Year	Team		Games	Pos.
1967	CHI	N	14	LB
1968			14	LB
1969			14	LB
1970	CLE	N	3	LB
1970	GB	N	6	LB
1971	ATL	N	3	LB
5 yrs.	54 games			

Ryan Kuehl

KUEHL, RYAN PHILIP
B. Jan. 18, 1972, Washington, DC
Virginia 6'4" 276 lbs.

Year	Team		Games	Pos.
1996	WAS	N	2	DT

Waddy Kuehl

KUEHL, WALTER (Babe)
B. Feb., 1892
Deceased
Dubuque 5'9" 165 lbs.

Year	Team		Games	Pos.
1920	RI	A	7	HB, QB
1921	DET	A	6	HB, FB
1921	BUF	A	2	HB
1922	BUF	A	10	HB, E
1923	RI	N	8	HB
1924	DAY	N	3	HB
5 yrs.	36 games			

Art Kuehn

KUEHN, ARTHUR BERT
B. Feb. 12, 1953, Victoria, B.C.
San Jose State/UCLA 6'3" 258 lbs.

Year	Team		Games	Pos.
1976	SEA	N	14	C
1977			14	C
1978			16	C
1979			16	C
1980			16	C
1981			16	C
1982			6	C
1983	NE	N	2	C
8 yrs.	100 games			

Oscar Kuehner

KUEHNER, OSCAR
B. 1895
Deceased
None 6'0" 200 lbs.

Year	Team		Games	Pos.
1920	COL	A	5	T
1921			7	T, G, E
2 yrs.	12 games			

Ray Kuffel

KUFFEL, RAYMOND F.
B. Dec. 9, 1921, Milwaukee, WI
D. Dec., 1974
Marquette/Notre Dame 6'3" 213 lbs.

Year	Team		Games	Pos.
1947	BUF	AA	7	E
1948	CHI	AA	14	E
1949			2	E
3 yrs.	23 games			

Pete Kugler

KUGLER, PETE DAVID
B. Aug. 9, 1959, Philadelphia, PA
Penn State 6'4" 255 lbs.

Year	Team		Games	Pos.
1981	SF	N	13	DT
1982			7	NT
1983			16	NT
1986			3	NT
1987			11	NT, DE
1988			6	NT, DE
1989			14	DE
1990			10	NT
8 yrs.	80 games			

Year	Team	Games	Pos.

Joe Kuharich
KUHARICH, JOSEPH LAWRENCE
B. Apr. 14, 1917, South Bend, IN
D. Jan. 25, 1981, Philadelphia, PA
Notre Dame 5'11" 195 lbs.

Year	Team		Games	Pos.
1940	CHIC	N	11	G
1941			10	G
1945			6	G
3 yrs.	27 games			

George Kuhrt
KUHRT, GEORGE
B. Jul., 1896
Deceased
None 5'11" 185 lbs.

Year	Team		Games	Pos.
1921	TON	A	2	T

Stan Kuick
KUICK, STANLEY
B. Apr. 24, 1904
D. Aug., 1977, Orlando, FL
Beloit 5'10" 192 lbs.

Year	Team		Games	Pos.
1926	MIL	N	9	G

Joe Kulbacki
KULBACKI, JOSEPH
B. 1938
Purdue 6'0" 185 lbs.

Year	Team		Games	Pos.
1960	BUF	A		HB

Vic Kulbitski
KULBITSKI, VICTOR JOHN
B. Jun. 15, 1921, Virginia, MN
Minnesota/Notre Dame 5'11" 205 lbs.

Year	Team		Games	Pos.
1946	BUF	AA	13	FB
1947			13	B
1948			14	B
3 yrs.	40 games			

Mike Kullman
KULLMAN, MICHAEL
B. Jan. 22, 1962, Frankfurt, Germany
Kutztown State 6'1" 185 lbs.

Year	Team		Games	Pos.
1987	PHI	N	3	S

Eric Kumerow
KUMEROW, ERIC PALMER
B. Apr. 17, 1965, Chicago, IL
Ohio State 6'7" 260 lbs.

Year	Team		Games	Pos.
1988	MIA	N	14	DE
1989			12	DE
1990			10	DE
3 yrs.	36 games			

George Kunz
KUNZ, GEORGE JAMES
B. Jul. 5 1947, Fort Sheridan, IL
Notre Dame 6'5" 260 lbs.

Year	Team		Games	Pos.
1969	ATL	N	14	OT
1970			9	OT
1971			14	OT
1972			14	OT
1973			14	OT
1974			14	OT
1975	BAL	N	12	OT
1976			14	OT
1977			14	OT
1978			1	OT
1980			9	OT
11 yrs.	129 games			

Lee Kunz
KUNZ, LEE ROY
B. Apr. 21, 1957, Golden, CO
Nebraska 6'2" 224 lbs.

Year	Team		Games	Pos.
1979	CHI	N	16	LB

Lee Kunz continued

Year	Team	Games	Pos.
1980		16	LB
1981		16	LB
3 yrs.	48 games		

Terry Kunz
KUNZ, TERRENCE
B. Oct. 26, 1952, Denver, CO
Colorado 6'1" 215 lbs.

Year	Team		Games	Pos.
1976	OAK	N	7	RB

Irv Kupcinet
KUPCINET, IRVING
B. Jul. 31, 1912, Chicago, IL
Northwestern/North Dakota 6'1" 190 lbs.

Year	Team		Games	Pos.
1935	PHI	N	2	QB, HB

Craig Kupp
KUPP, CRAIG MARION
B. Apr. 14, 1967, Sunnyside, WA
Montana Tech/Pacific Lutheran 6'4" 215 lbs.

Year	Team		Games	Pos.
1991	PHX	N	1	QB

Jake Kupp
KUPP, JACOB RALPH
B. Mar. 12, 1941, Pasadena, CA
Washington 6'3" 240 lbs.

Year	Team		Games	Pos.
1964	DAL	N	14	G
1965			14	G
1966	WAS	N	14	G
1967	ATL	N	6	G
1967	NO	N	11	G
1968			14	G
1969			14	G
1970			14	G
1971			14	G
1972			3	G
1973			14	G
1974			14	G
1975			14	G
12 yrs.	160 games			

Ralph Kurek
KUREK, RALPH EAMER
B. Feb. 23, 1943, Milwaukee, WI
Wisconsin 6'2" 210 lbs.

Year	Team		Games	Pos.
1965	CHI	N	14	FB
1966			14	FB
1967			14	RB
1968			14	RB
1969			14	RB
1970			11	RB
6 yrs.	81 games			

Jamie Kurisko
KURISKO, JAMIE
B. Dec. 22, 1963
Southern Connecticut State 6'4" 236 lbs.

Year	Team		Games	Pos.
1987	NYJ	N	3	TE

Howie Kurnick
KURNICK, HOWARD RAYMOND
B. May 13, 1957, Cleveland, OH
Cincinnati 6'2" 219 lbs.

Year	Team		Games	Pos.
1979	CIN	N	15	LB

Roy Kurrasch
KURRASCH, ROY (Crash)
B. Oct. 8, 1922, Toledo, OH
UCLA 6'2" 195 lbs.

Year	Team		Games	Pos.
1947	NY	AA	10	E
1948	PIT	N	9	E
2 yrs.	19 games			

Joe Kurth
KURTH, JOSEPH J.
B. May 12, 1911
D. Aug., 1982, Ridgefield, WA
Notre Dame 6'1" 202 lbs.

Year	Team		Games	Pos.
1933	GB	N	12	T
1934			7	T
2 yrs.	19 games			

Rod Kush
KUSH, ROD RANDLE
B. Dec. 29, 1956, Omaha, NE
Nebraska-Omaha 6'0" 188 lbs.

Year	Team		Games	Pos.
1980	BUF	N	5	S
1981			16	S
1982			9	S
1983			4	S
1984			16	S
1985	HOU	N	16	S
6 yrs.	66 games			

Johnny Kusko
KUSKO, JOHN
B. 1914
Deceased
Temple 5'11" 194 lbs.

Year	Team		Games	Pos.
1936	PHI	N	12	FB, HB
1937			10	HB, QB, FB
2 yrs.	22 games			

Lou Kusserow
KUSSEROW, LOUIS JOSEPH
B. Sep. 6, 1927, Braddock, PA
Columbia 6'1" 200 lbs.

Year	Team		Games	Pos.
1949	B-NY	AA	11	B
1950	NYY	N	11	B
2 yrs.	22 games			

Rudy Kutler
KUTLER, RUDOLPH J.
B. Nov. 14, 1901
D. Mar., 1974, Brecksville, OH
Ohio State 5'9" 190 lbs.

Year	Team		Games	Pos.
1925	CLE	N	1	G

Mal Kutner
KUTNER, MALCOLM JAMES
B. Mar. 27, 1921, Dallas, TX
Texas 6'2" 197 lbs.

Year	Team		Games	Pos.
1946	CHIC	N	11	E
1947			12	E
1948			12	E
1949			12	E
1950			9	E
5 yrs.	56 games			

Bill Kuusisto
KUUSISTO, WILLIAM
B. Apr. 26, 1918, Herman, MI
D. May 28, 1973, Paynesville, MN
Wisconsin/Minnesota 6'0" 228 lbs.

Year	Team		Games	Pos.
1941	GB	N	11	G
1942			10	G
1943			9	G
1944			10	G, T
1945			10	G
1946			4	G
6 yrs.	54 games			

Fulton Kuykendall
KUYKENDALL, FULTON GERALD (Captain Crazy)
B. Jun. 10, 1953, Coronado, CA
UCLA 6'5" 225 lbs.

Year	Team		Games	Pos.
1975	ATL	N	14	LB
1976			7	LB
1977			5	LB

Fulton Kuykendall contin-

Year	Team		Games	Pos.
1978			16	LB
1979			16	LB
1980			10	LB
1981			16	LB
1982			9	LB
1983			14	LB
1984			16	LB
1985	SF	N	1	LB
11 yrs.	124 games			

Bob Kuziel
KUZIEL, ROBERT CHARLES
B. Jul. 24, 1950, New Haven, CT
Pittsburgh 6'5" 255 lbs.

Year	Team		Games	Pos.
1972	NO	N	1	C
1975	WAS	N	14	C
1976			14	C
1977			14	C
1978			16	C, OT
1979			16	C
1980			15	C
7 yrs.	90 games			

John Kuzman
KUZMAN, JOHN N.
B. Jun. 29, 1915, Coaldale, PA
Fordham 6'1" 232 lbs.

Year	Team		Games	Pos.
1941	CHIC	N	4	T
1946	SF	AA	11	T
1947	CHI	AA	13	T
3 yrs.	28 games			

Zvonimir Kvaternik
KVATERNIK, ZVONIMIR
B. Oct. 18, 1911, Kansas City, KS
Kansas 5'11" 210 lbs.

Year	Team		Games	Pos.
1934	PIT	N	1	G

Ted Kwalick
KWALICK, THADDEUS JOHN
B. Apr. 15, 1947, McKees Rocks, PA
Penn State 6'4" 226 lbs.

Year	Team		Games	Pos.
1969	SF	N	13	TE
1970			14	TE
1971			14	TE
1972			14	TE
1973			14	TE
1974			14	TE
1975	OAK	N	6	TE
1976			7	TE
1977			12	TE
9 yrs.	108 games			

Aaron Kyle
KYLE, AARON DOUGLAS
B. Apr. 6, 1954, Detroit, MI
Wyoming 5'11" 185 lbs.

Year	Team		Games	Pos.
1976	DAL	N	14	CB, S
1977			14	CB
1978			16	CB
1979			16	CB
1980	DEN	N	10	CB
1981			13	CB
1982			9	CB
7 yrs.	92 games			

Jason Kyle
KYLE, JASON
B. May 12, 1972, Mesa, AZ
Arizona State 6'3" 240 lbs.

Year	Team		Games	Pos.
1995	SEA	N	16	LB
1996			16	LB
2 yrs.	32 games			

John Kyle
KYLE, JOHN W.

Year	Team	Games	Pos.

John Kyle *continued*

B. Sep. 12, 1898
D. May, 1974, Valparaiso, IN
Indiana 5'9" 190 lbs.

Year	Team		Games	Pos.
1923	CLE	N	7	FB, T

Rip Kyle

KYLE, JAMES W.
B. Aug. 15, 1901
D. Feb. 10, 1967, Palo Alto, CA
Gettysburg 6'0" 240 lbs.

1925	CAN	N	4	T, G
1926			11	C, T
2 yrs.		15 games		

Troy Kyles

KYLES, TROY THOMAS
B. Aug. 13, 1968, Lorain, OH
Howard 6'0" 180 lbs.

1990	NYG	N	9	WR

Jeff Kysar

KYSAR, JEFFREY JOHN CHARLES
B. Jun. 14, 1972, Norman, OK
Arizona State 6'7" 320 lbs.

1995	OAK	N	2	OT

Galen Laack

LAACK, GALEN
B. Apr. 3, 1932
D. Jan. 1, 1959
Pacific 6'0" 230 lbs.

1958	PHI	N	8	G

Eric Laakso

LAAKSO, ERIC HENRY
B. Nov. 29, 1956, New York, NY
Tulane 6'4" 265 lbs.

1978	MIA	N	16	OT
1979			10	OT, G
1980			16	OT, G
1981			16	OT, G
1982			9	OT
1983			15	OT
1984			4	OT
7 yrs.		86 games		

Paul Laaveg

LAAVEG, PAUL MARTIN
B. Oct. 1, 1948, Sioux Falls, SD
Iowa 6'4" 247 lbs.

1970	WAS	N	11	OT
1971			14	G
1972			14	G
1973			14	G
1974			14	G
1975			5	G
6 yrs.		72 games		

Sandy LaBeaux

LABEAUX, SANDY, JR.
B. Aug. 22, 1961, San Antonio, TX
Hayward State 6'3" 210 lbs.

1983	TB	N	3	CB, S

Tony LaBissoniere

LABISSONIERE, HORACE
B. Sep. 13, 1896
D. Jan., 1972, St. Paul, MN
St. Thomas (Minnesota)/Michigan

1922	HAM	N	2	C, G

Matt LaBounty

LABOUNTY, MATTHEW JAMES

Matt LaBounty *continued*

B. Jan. 3, 1969, San Francisco, CA
Oregon 6'4" 254 lbs.

1993	SF	N	6	DE
1995	GB	N	14	DE
1996	SEA	N	3	DE
3 yrs.		23 games		

Bob Lacey

LACEY, ROBERT
B. Mar. 30, 1942, Port Chester, NY
North Carolina 6'3" 205 lbs.

1964	MIN	N	1	OE
1965	NYG	N	1	OE
2 yrs.		2 games		

Steve Lach

LACH, STEPHEN JOHN
B. Aug. 6, 1920, Altoona, PA
D. Jul. 12, 1961, Altoona, PA
Duke 6'2" 207 lbs.

1942	CHIC	N	9	HB
1946	PIT	N	11	FB
1947			12	FB
3 yrs.		32 games		

Sean LaChapelle

LACHAPELLE, SEAN PAUL
B. Jul. 29, 1970, Sacramento, CA
UCLA 6'3" 205 lbs.

1993	LARM	N	10	WR
1996	KC	N	12	WR
2 yrs.		22 games		

Jim Lachey

LACHEY, JAMES MICHAEL
B. Jun. 4, 1963, St. Henry, OH
Ohio State 6'7" 289 lbs.

1985	SD	N	16	OT
1986			16	OT
1987			12	OT
1988	LARI	N	1	OT
1988	WAS	N	15	OT
1989			14	OT
1990			16	OT
1991			15	OT
1992			10	OT
1994			13	OT
1995			3	OT
10 yrs.		131 games		

Corbin Lacina

LACINA, CORBIN
B. Nov. 2, 1970, Woodbury, MN
Augustana (South Dakota) 6'4" 300 lbs.

1994	BUF	N	11	G, OT
1995			16	G
1996			12	G
3 yrs.		39 games		

Rick Lackman

LACKMAN, RICHARD H.
B. Sep. 19, 1911, Philadelphia, PA
None 5'11" 186 lbs.

1933	PHI	N	3	HB, FB
1934			9	HB
1935			11	HB, QB
3 yrs.		23 games		

Dave LaCrosse

LACROSSE, DAVID JOSEPH
B. Dec. 22, 1955, Philadelphia, PA
Wake Forest 6'3" 210 lbs.

1977	PIT	N	14	LB

Ken Lacy

LACY, KENNETH WAYNE
B. Nov. 1, 1960, Waco, TX
Tulsa 6'0" 222 lbs.

1984	KC	N	15	RB
1985			2	RB
1987			3	RB
3 yrs.		20 games		

Ernie Ladd

LADD, ERNEST
B. Nov. 28, 1938, Rayville, LA
Grambling State 6'9" 302 lbs.

1961	SD	A	14	DT
1962			14	DT
1963			14	DT
1964			14	DT
1965			14	DT
1966	HOU	A	14	DT
1967			4	DT
1967	KC		14	DT
1968			14	DT
8 yrs.		116 games		

Jim Ladd

LADD, JAMES
B. Jul. 29, 1932, Put-in-Bay, OH
Deceased
Bowling Green 6'4" 205 lbs.

1954	CHIC	N	9	E

Doc Ladorum

LADORUM, DOC
None

1921	MUN	A	1	FB

Wally Ladrow

LADROW, WALTER
B. Oct. 16, 1895
D. Jul., 1974, Green Bay, WI
None 5'9" 180 lbs.

1921	GB	A	1	HB

Tiny Ladson

LADSON, GLESSIE MERRITT
B. Dec. 17, 1895
D. Nov., 1978, Hanover, IN
None 254 lbs.

1922	EVA	N	3	G

Pete Ladygo

LADYGO, PETER GLENN
B. Jun. 23, 1928, West Brownsville, PA
Maryland 6'2" 218 lbs.

1952	PIT	N	12	G
1954			12	G
2 yrs.		24 games		

Dave Lafary

LAFARY, DAVID WALTER
B. Jan. 13, 1955, Cincinnati, OH
Purdue 6'7" 280 lbs.

1977	NO	N	10	OT
1978			15	OT
1979			16	G
1980			15	G, OT
1981			16	OT
1982			9	OT
1983			16	OT
1984			1	OT
1985			11	OT
9 yrs.		109 games		

Bill LaFitte

LAFITTE, WILLIAM S. (Foots)
B. Jan. 23, 1926, Stonewall, LA

Bill LaFitte *continued*

Ouachita Baptist 6'1" 170 lbs.

1944	BKN	N	3	E

Greg LaFleur

LAFLEUR, GREGORY LOUIS
B. Sep. 16, 1958, Lafayette, LA
Louisiana State 6'4" 237 lbs.

1981	STL	N	16	TE
1982			9	TE
1983			16	TE
1984			16	TE
1985			16	TE
1986			4	TE
1986	IND	N	9	TE
6 yrs.		86 games		

Joe LaFleur

LAFLEUR, JOSEPH M. (Frenchy)
B. Mar. 3, 1896
D. Oct., 1973, LaCrosse, WI
St. Norbert 6'0" 223 lbs.

1922	CHIB	N	10	G, FB
1923			10	G, FB, C
1924			7	G, C
3 yrs.		27 games		

Jeff Lageman

LAGEMAN, JEFFREY DAVID
B. Jul. 18, 1967, Fairfax, VA
Virginia 6'5" 264 lbs.

1989	NYJ	N	16	LB
1990			16	LB
1991			16	DE
1992			2	DE
1993			16	DE
1994			16	DE
1995	JAC	N	11	DE
1996			12	DE
8 yrs.		105 games		

Chet Lagod

LAGOD, CHESTER
B. Jan. 8, 1928, Fairpoint, OH
Tennessee-Chattanooga 6'2" 220 lbs.

1953	NYG	N	7	G

Morris LaGrand

LAGRAND, MORRIS
B. Feb. 3, 1953, Tampa, FL
Tampa 6'1" 220 lbs.

1975	KC	N	11	RB
1975	NO	N	2	RB

Hal Lahar

LAHAR, HAROLD W. (Toad)
B. Jul. 14, 1919, Durant, OK
Oklahoma 6'0" 221 lbs.

1941	CHIB	N	7	G, T
1946	BUF	AA	12	G
1947			14	G
1948			13	G
4 yrs.		46 games		

Thomas Lahey

LAHEY, THOMAS PATRICK (Pat)
B. Oct. 21, 1919, Dunbridge, OH
John Carroll 6'2" 218 lbs.

1946	CHI	AA	13	E
1947			13	E
2 yrs.		26 games		

Mike LaHood

LAHOOD, MIKE
B. Dec. 11, 1944, Peoria, IL

Year	Team		Games	Pos.

Mike LaHood continued
Wyoming 6'3" 250 lbs.

Year	Team		Games	Pos.
1969	LA	N	14	G
1970	STL	N	14	G
1971	LA	N	9	G
1972			14	G
4 yrs.	51 games			

Warren Lahr
LAHR, WARREN E.
B. Sep. 5, 1923, Mount Zion, PA
D. Jan. 19, 1969, Cleveland, OH
Case Western Reserve 5'11" 189 lbs.

Year	Team		Games	Pos.
1949	CLE	AA	11	HB
1950	CLE	N	12	HB
1951			12	HB
1952			12	HB
1953			12	HB
1954			12	HB
1955			12	HB
1956			12	HB
1957			11	HB
1958			7	HB
1959			12	HB
11 yrs.	125 games			

Scott Laidlaw
LAIDLAW, ROBERT SCOTT
B. Feb. 17, 1953, Hawthorne, CA
Stanford 6'0" 205 lbs.

Year	Team		Games	Pos.
1975	DAL	N	8	RB
1976			13	RB
1977			14	RB
1978			16	RB
1979			16	RB
1980	NYG	N	7	RB
6 yrs.	74 games			

Aaron Laing
LAING, AARON MATTHEW
B. Jul. 19, 1971, Houston, TX
New Mexico State 6'3" 264 lbs.

Year	Team		Games	Pos.
1994	SD	N	5	TE
1996	STL	N	12	TE
2 yrs.	17 games			

Porter Lainhart
LAINHART, PORTER
B. 1908
Washington State 6'0" 180 lbs.

Year	Team		Games	Pos.
1933	PHI	N	1	QB

Bruce Laird
LAIRD, BRUCE ALLAN
B. May 23, 1950, Lowell, MA
American International 6'0" 193 lbs.

Year	Team		Games	Pos.
1972	BAL	N	14	S
1973			12	CB, S
1974			14	DB
1975			14	S
1976			14	S
1977			14	S
1978			14	S
1979			15	S
1980			15	S
1981			15	S
1982	SD	N	9	S
1983			14	S
12 yrs.	164 games			

Jim Laird
LAIRD, JAMES T.
B. Sep. 10, 1897
D. Aug. 16, 1970, Lebanon, CT
Colgate 6'0" 194 lbs.

Year	Team		Games	Pos.
1920	ROC	A	1	HB
1920	BUF	A	1	HB
1921			1	FB

Jim Laird continued

Year	Team		Games	Pos.
1921	ROC	A	6	FB, HB
1921	CAN	A	1	FB
1922	BUF	N	10	FB
1925	PRO	N	11	FB, G
1926			9	FB
1927			14	G
1928			8	G
1931	SI	N	8	G, T
8 yrs.	70 games			

Bill Lajousky
LAJOUSKY, WILLIAM
B. Apr. 18, 1913, Lithuania
D. Jan., 1973, South China, ME
Catholic 5'11" 200 lbs.

Year	Team		Games	Pos.
1936	PIT	N	10	G

Carnell Lake
LAKE, CARNELL AUGUSTINO
B. Jul. 15, 1967, Salt Lake City, UT
UCLA 6'1" 205 lbs.

Year	Team		Games	Pos.
1989	PIT	N	15	S
1990			16	S
1991			16	S
1992			16	S
1993			14	S
1994			16	S
1995			16	CB, S
1996			13	CB
8 yrs.	122 games			

Roland Lakes
LAKES, ROLAND HAYES
B. Dec. 25, 1939, Vicksburg, MS
Wichita State 6'4" 267 lbs.

Year	Team		Games	Pos.
1961	SF	N	14	C, DT
1962			14	OT, DE
1963			14	OT
1964			14	DT
1965			14	DT
1966			14	DT
1967			14	DT
1968			14	DT
1969			14	DT
1970			14	DT
1971	NYG	N	14	DT
11 yrs.	154 games			

Bob Lally
LALLY, ROBERT
B. Feb. 12, 1952, Hoboken, NJ
Cornell 6'2" 230 lbs.

Year	Team		Games	Pos.
1976	GB	N	2	LB

Roger LaLonde
LALONDE, ROGER
B. Jan. 6, 1942, Antwerp, NY
Muskingum 6'3" 255 lbs.

Year	Team		Games	Pos.
1964	DET	N	14	DT
1965	NYG	N	11	DT
2 yrs.	25 games			

Peter Lamana
LAMANA, PETER CHARLES
B. May 15, 1921, Bristol, CT
Boston University 5'11" 210 lbs.

Year	Team		Games	Pos.
1946	CHI	AA	10	FB
1947			12	C
1948			13	C
3 yrs.	35 games			

Kevin Lamar
LAMAR, KEVIN T.
B. Nov. 29, 1961
Stanford 6'4" 260 lbs.

Year	Team		Games	Pos.
1987	BUF	N	1	G

Joe Lamas
LAMAS, JOSEPH
B. Jan. 10, 1916, Havana, Cuba
Mount St. Mary's 5'10" 216 lbs.

Year	Team		Games	Pos.
1942	PIT	N	9	G

Brad Lamb
LAMB, BRAD
B. Oct. 7, 1967, Springboro, OH
Anderson 5'10" 171 lbs.

Year	Team		Games	Pos.
1992	BUF	N	7	WR
1993			1	WR
2 yrs.	8 games			

Mack Lamb
LAMB, MACK EDWARD
B. May 9, 1944, Miami, FL
Tennessee State 6'1" 188 lbs.

Year	Team		Games	Pos.
1967	MIA	A	2	DB
1968			13	DB
2 yrs.	15 games			

Roddy Lamb
LAMB, ROY
B. Aug. 19, 1899
Deceased
Lombard 5'6" 160 lbs.

Year	Team		Games	Pos.
1925	RI	N	9	HB, QB, FB
1926	CHIC	N	10	HB
1927			9	HB, QB, FB
1933			4	QB, HB
4 yrs.	32 games			

Ron Lamb
LAMB, RONALD
B. Feb. 3, 1944, New London, CT
South Carolina 6'2" 227 lbs.

Year	Team		Games	Pos.
1968	DEN	A	3	RB
1968	CIN	A	9	RB
1969			14	RB
1970	CIN	N	14	RB
1971			12	RB
1972	ATL	N	7	RB
5 yrs.	59 games			

Walt Lamb
LAMB, WALTER G.
B. 1921, Ardmore, OK
D. Jan. 4, 1991
Oklahoma 6'1" 195 lbs.

Year	Team		Games	Pos.
1946	CHIB	N	8	E

Curly Lambeau
LAMBEAU, EARL LOUIS
B. Apr. 9, 1898, Green Bay, WI
D. Jun. 1, 1965, Sturgeon Bay, WI
Wisconsin/Notre Dame 5'10" 187 lbs.

Year	Team		Games	Pos.
1921	GB	A	6	QB, FB
1922	GB	N	8	HB, FB
1923			10	HB, FB
1924			11	HB, FB
1925			9	HB, QB, FB
1926			12	HB, QB, E
1927			10	HB, FB
1928			8	FB, QB, E, HB
1929			1	HB
9 yrs.	75 games			

Dion Lambert
LAMBERT, DION ADRIAN
B. Feb. 12, 1969, Lakeview Terrace, CA
UCLA 6'0" 185 lbs.

Year	Team		Games	Pos.
1992	NE	N	16	CB
1993			14	CB
1994	SEA	N	1	S
3 yrs.	31 games			

Frank Lambert
LAMBERT, FRANKLIN TALLEY
B. Apr. 17, 1943, Hattiesburg, MS
Mississippi 6'3" 200 lbs.

Year	Team		Games	Pos.
1965	PIT	N	14	P
1966			14	P
2 yrs.	28 games			

Gordon Lambert
LAMBERT, GORDON
B. Jul. 5, 1945, Leckie, WV
West Virginia/Tennessee-Martin 6'5" 245 lbs.

Year	Team		Games	Pos.
1968	DEN	A	10	LB
1969			4	LB
2 yrs.	14 games			

Jack Lambert
LAMBERT, JOHN HAROLD
B. Jul. 8, 1952, Mantua, OH
Kent State 6'4" 219 lbs.

Year	Team		Games	Pos.
1974	PIT	N	14	LB
1975			14	LB
1976			14	LB
1977			11	LB
1978			16	LB
1979			16	LB
1980			14	LB
1981			16	LB
1982			8	LB
1983			15	LB
1984			8	LB
11 yrs.	146 games			

Pat Lamberti
LAMBERTI, PATRICK
B. 1938
Richmond 6'2" 225 lbs.

Year	Team		Games	Pos.
1961	NY	A	5	LB
1961	DEN	A	7	LB
1 yr.	12 games			

Mike Lambrecht
LAMBRECHT, MICHAEL JAMES
B. May 2, 1963, Watertown, MN
St. Cloud State 6'1" 271 lbs.

Year	Team		Games	Pos.
1987	MIA		5	NT
1988			8	NT
1989			6	NT
3 yrs.	19 games			

Lamer
LAMER
None

Year	Team		Games	Pos.
1925	KC	N	2	G, C

Buck Lamme
LAMME, EMERALD FORD
B. Jul. 2, 1905
D. Sep., 1954
Ohio Wesleyan 6'2" 180 lbs.

Year	Team		Games	Pos.
1931	CLE	N	1	E

Pete Lammons
LAMMONS, PETER SPENCER, JR.
B. Oct. 20, 1943, Crockett, TX
Texas 6'3" 229 lbs.

Year	Team		Games	Pos.
1966	NY	A	14	TE, LB
1967			14	TE
1968			13	TE
1969			14	TE
1970	NYJ	N	14	TE
1971			14	TE
6 yrs.	83 games			

597

Daryle Lamonica

LAMONICA, DARYLE PAT (Mad Bomber)
B. Jul. 17, 1941, Fresno, CA
Notre Dame 6'2" 215 lbs.

Year	Team		Games	Pos.
1963	**BUF**	A	14	QB
1964			14	QB
1965			14	QB
1966			14	QB
1967	**OAK**	A	14	QB
1968			13	QB
1969			14	QB
1970	**OAK**	N	14	QB
1971			14	QB
1972			14	QB
1973			8	QB
1974			3	QB
12 yrs.		150 games		

Chuck Lamson

LAMSON, CHARLES WATT
B. Mar. 14, 1939, Webster City, IA
Iowa State/Wyoming 6'0" 189 lbs.

Year	Team		Games	Pos.
1962	**MIN**	N	14	DB
1963			12	DB
1965	**LA**	N	13	DB
1966			14	DB
1967			14	DB
5 yrs.		67 games		

Dan Land

LAND, DAN
B. Jul. 3, 1965, Donalsonville, GA
Albany State (Georgia) 6'0" 190 lbs.

Year	Team		Games	Pos.
1987	**TB**	N	3	RB
1989	**LARI**	N	10	CB
1990			16	CB
1991			16	S
1992			16	CB
1993			15	CB
1994			16	S, CB
1995	**OAK**	N	15	S
1996			16	S
9 yrs.		123 games		

Fred Land

LAND, FRED N.
B. 1925
Louisiana State 6'1" 220 lbs.

Year	Team		Games	Pos.
1948	**SF**	AA	2	T, G

Mel Land

LAND, MELVIN
B. Nov. 30, 1955, Youngstown, OH
Michigan State 6'3" 243 lbs.

Year	Team		Games	Pos.
1979	**MIA**	N	16	LB
1980	**SF**	N	3	DE
2 yrs.		19 games		

Lowell Lander

LANDER, LOWELL
B. 1933
Westminster (Pennsylvania) 6'0" 195 lbs.

Year	Team		Games	Pos.
1958	**CHIC**	N	1	HB

Walt Landers

LANDERS, WALTER JAMES
B. Jul. 4, 1953, Lanett, AL
Clark 6'0" 214 lbs.

Year	Team		Games	Pos.
1978	**GB**	N	4	FB
1979			9	FB
2 yrs.		13 games		

Sean Landeta

LANDETA, SEAN EDWARD
B. Jan. 6, 1962, Baltimore, MD
Towson State 6'0" 200 lbs.

Year	Team		Games	Pos.
1985	**NYG**	N	16	P

Sean Landeta continued

Year	Team		Games	Pos.
1986			16	P
1987			12	P
1988			1	P
1989			16	P
1990			16	P
1991			15	P
1992			11	P
1993			8	P
1993	**LARM**	N	8	P
1994			16	P
1995	**STL**	N	16	P
1996			16	P
12 yrs.		167 games		

Jim Landrigan

LANDRIGAN, JAMES M.
B. May 31, 1923, Everett, MA
D. Jun., 1974, Wakefield, MA
Holy Cross/Dartmouth 6'4" 235 lbs.

Year	Team		Games	Pos.
1947	**BAL**	AA	5	T

Mike Landrum

LANDRUM, MICHAEL GEDDIE
B. Nov. 6, 1961, Laurel, MS
Southern Mississippi 6'2" 231 lbs.

Year	Team		Games	Pos.
1984	**ATL**	N	15	TE

Greg Landry

LANDRY, GREGORY PAUL
B. Dec. 18, 1946, Nashua, NH
Massachusetts 6'4" 207 lbs.

Year	Team		Games	Pos.
1968	**DET**	N	5	QB
1969			10	QB
1970			12	QB
1971			14	QB
1972			14	QB
1973			7	QB
1974			5	QB
1975			6	QB
1976			14	QB
1977			11	QB
1978			5	QB
1979	**BAL**	N	16	QB
1980			16	QB
1981			11	QB
1984	**CHI**	N	2	QB
15 yrs.		148 games		

Tom Landry

LANDRY, THOMAS WADE
B. Sep. 11, 1924, Mission, TX
Texas 6'1" 195 lbs.

Year	Team		Games	Pos.
1949	**B, NY**	AA	12	HB
1950	**NYG**	N	12	HB
1951			10	HB
1952			12	HB
1953			10	HB
1954			12	HB
1955			12	HB
7 yrs.		80 games		

Mort Landsberg

LANDSBERG, MORTIMER W., JR.
B. Jul. 25, 1918, New York, NY
D. Dec., 1970
Cornell 5'11" 180 lbs.

Year	Team		Games	Pos.
1941	**PHI**	N	11	HB
1947	**LA**	AA	6	HB
2 yrs.		17 games		

Bob Landsee

LANDSEE, BOB
B. Mar. 21, 1964, Iron Mountain, MI
Wisconsin 6'4" 273 lbs.

Year	Team		Games	Pos.
1986	**PHI**	N	7	C, G
1987			3	G, C
2 yrs.		10 games		

Bobby Lane

LANE, BOBBY A.
B. Oct. 30, 1939, Wagoner, OK
Baylor 6'2" 222 lbs.

Year	Team		Games	Pos.
1963	**SD**	A	7	LB
1964			1	LB
2 yrs.		8 games		

Clayton Lane

LANE, CLAYTON HAROLD
B. Nov. 23, 1922, Worcester, MA
New Hampshire 6'0" 215 lbs.

Year	Team		Games	Pos.
1948	**NY**	AA	1	T

Eric Lane

LANE, ERIC
B. Jan. 6, 1959, Oakland, CA
Brigham Young 6'0" 200 lbs.

Year	Team		Games	Pos.
1981	**SEA**	N	14	RB
1982			9	RB
1983			16	RB
1984			15	RB
1985			16	RB
1986			15	RB
1987			12	RB
7 yrs.		97 games		

Frank Lane

LANE, FRANCIS OSCAR (Oxie)
B. Oct. 18, 1902
D. May 5, 1973, Lewistown, PA
Marquette 6'4" 222 lbs.

Year	Team		Games	Pos.
1926	**MIL**	N	9	T

Garcia Lane

LANE, GARCIA R.
B. Dec. 31, 1961, Youngstown, OH
Ohio State 5'9" 180 lbs.

Year	Team		Games	Pos.
1985	**KC**	N	16	CB, S
1987			1	CB
2 yrs.		17 games		

Gary Lane

LANE, GARY OWEN
B. Dec. 21, 1942, Alton, IL
Missouri 6'1" 210 lbs.

Year	Team		Games	Pos.
1966	**CLE**	N	8	QB
1967			3	QB
1968	**NYG**	N	7	QB
3 yrs.		18 games		

Les Lane

LANE, LESLIE
B. 1916
South Dakota 6'3" 193 lbs.

Year	Team		Games	Pos.
1939	**BKN**	N	2	G

Lew Lane

LANE, LINDLEY
B. Jan. 28, 1898
D. Aug., 1963
St. Mary's (Kansas)

Year	Team		Games	Pos.
1924	**KC**	N	5	HB, QB, FB

MacArthur Lane

LANE, MACARTHUR
B. Mar. 16, 1942, Oakland, CA
Utah State 6'0" 220 lbs.

Year	Team		Games	Pos.
1968	**STL**	N	14	RB
1969			9	RB
1970			14	RB
1971			13	RB
1972	**GB**	N	14	RB
1973			13	RB
1974			14	RB
1975	**KC**	N	9	RB
1976			14	RB
1977			3	RB

MacArthur Lane continued

Year	Team		Games	Pos.
1978			16	RB
11 yrs.		133 games		

Max Lane

LANE, MAX AARON
B. Feb. 22, 1971, Norborne, MO
Navy 6'6" 307 lbs.

Year	Team		Games	Pos.
1994	**NE**	N	14	OT
1995			16	OT
1996			16	OT
3 yrs.		46 games		

Night Train Lane

LANE, RICHARD (Dick)
B. Apr. 16, 1928, Austin, TX
Scottsbluff JC 6'1" 194 lbs.

Year	Team		Games	Pos.
1952	**LA**	N	12	E, DB
1953			11	E, DB
1954	**CHIC**	N	12	E, DB
1955			12	E, DB
1956			12	E, DB
1957			8	DB
1958			12	DB
1959			12	DB
1960	**DET**	N	12	DB
1961			14	DB
1962			14	DB
1963			12	DB
1964			7	DB
1965			7	DB
14 yrs.		157 games		

Skip Lane

LANE, PAUL JOHN, JR.
B. Jan. 30, 1960, Norwalk, CT
Mississippi 6'1" 208 lbs.

Year	Team		Games	Pos.
1984	**NYJ**	N	3	CB, S
1984	**KC**	N	1	DB
1987	**WAS**	N	3	S
2 yrs.		7 games		

Chick Lang

LANG, JAMES H. (Tex)
B. Oct. 7, 1900
D. Oct. 25, 1976, Mount Aukum, CA
None

Year	Team		Games	Pos.
1927	**DUL**	N	2	G

David Lang

LANG, DAVID
B. Mar. 28, 1968, San Bernardino, CA
Northern Arizona 5'11" 201 lbs.

Year	Team		Games	Pos.
1991	**LARM**	N	16	RB
1992			11	RB
1993			6	RB
1994			13	RB
1995	**DAL**	N	16	RB
5 yrs.		62 games		

Gene Lang

LANG, GENE ERIC
B. Mar. 15, 1962, Pass Christian, MS
Louisiana State 5'10" 196 lbs.

Year	Team		Games	Pos.
1984	**DEN**	N	16	RB
1985			12	RB
1986			15	RB
1987			12	RB
1988	**ATL**	N	16	RB
1989			15	RB
1990			3	RB
7 yrs.		89 games		

Izzy Lang

LANG, ISRAEL ALVIN
B. Feb. 2, 1942, Tampa, FL
Tennessee State 6'1" 231 lbs.

Year	Team		Games	Pos.
1964	**PHI**	N	12	HB

Year	Team		Games	Pos.

Izzy Lang *continued*

1965			14	FB
1966			14	FB
1967			14	RB
1968			11	RB
1969	LA	N	14	RB
6 yrs.		79 games		

Le-Lo Lang
LANG, LE-LO
B. Jan. 23, 1967, Los Angeles, CA
Washington 5'11" 185 lbs.

1990	DEN	N	6	CB, S
1991			16	CB, S
1992			16	CB, S
1993			16	CB
4 yrs.		54 games		

Bob Langas
LANGAS, ROBERT
B. Jan. 22, 1930
Wayne State 6'4" 230 lbs.

| 1954 | BAL | N | 8 | E |

Bill Lange
LANGE, WILLIAM HENRY
B. Jan. 12, 1928, Delphos, OH
Dayton 6'1" 239 lbs.

1951	LA	N	12	G
1952			10	G
1953	BAL	N	10	G
1954	CHIC	N	10	G
1955			12	G
5 yrs.		56 games		

Jim Lange
LANGE, JAMES (Cowboy)
Montana 195 lbs.

| 1929 | CHIC | N | 3 | E, G |

Jim Langer
LANGER, JAMES JOHN
B. May 16, 1948, Little Falls, MN
South Dakota State 6'2" 251 lbs.

1970	MIA	N	6	G
1971			14	G
1972			14	G
1973			14	G
1974			14	G
1975			14	C
1976			14	C
1977			14	C
1978			16	C
1979			9	C
1980	MIN	N	13	C
1981			9	C
12 yrs.		151 games		

Jevon Langford
LANGFORD, JEVON
B. Feb. 16, 1974, Washington, DC
Oklahoma State 6'3" 275 lbs.

| 1996 | CIN | N | 12 | DE |

Antonio Langham
LANGHAM, COLLIE ANTONIO
B. Jul. 31, 1972, Town Creek, AL
Alabama 6'0" 180 lbs.

1994	CLE	N	16	CB
1995			16	CB
1996	BAL	N	15	CB
3 yrs.		47 games		

Irv Langhoff
LANGHOFF, IRVING
B. Aug., 1897

Irv Langhoff *continued*
D. Jan., 1952
Marquette 5'8" 158 lbs.

1922	RAC	N	11	HB, QB
1923			4	HB
2 yrs.		15 games		

Reggie Langhorne
LANGHORNE, REGINALD DEVAN
B. Apr. 7, 1963, Suffolk, VA
Elizabeth City State 6'2" 195 lbs.

1985	CLE	N	16	WR
1986			16	WR
1987			12	WR
1988			16	WR
1989			16	WR
1990			12	WR
1991			14	WR
1992	IND	N	16	WR
1993			16	WR
9 yrs.		134 games		

Charlie Lanham
LANHAM, CHARLES
B. Dec., 1894
Deceased
None 170 lbs.

| 1923 | LOU | N | 1 | T |

Ken Lanier
LANIER, KENNETH WAYNE
B. Jul. 8, 1959, Columbus, OH
Florida State 6'3" 269 lbs.

1981	DEN	N	8	OT
1982			9	OT
1983			16	OT
1984			16	OT
1985			16	OT
1986			16	OT
1987			12	OT
1988			16	OT
1989			16	OT
1990			16	OT
1991			16	OT
1992			16	OT
1993	LARI	N	2	OT
1994	DEN	N	5	OT
14 yrs.		180 games		

Willie Lanier
LANIER, WILLIE EDWARD
B. Aug. 21, 1945, Clover, VA
Morgan State 6'1" 245 lbs.

1967	KC	A	10	LB
1968			14	LB
1969			14	LB
1970	KC	N	14	LB
1971			14	LB
1972			13	LB
1973			14	LB
1974			14	LB
1975			14	LB
1976			14	LB
1977			14	LB
11 yrs.		149 games		

Jim Lankas
LANKAS, JAMES
B. Aug. 26, 1918, Atwood, KS
D. Aug., 1978, Thayer, KS
St. Mary's 6'2" 220 lbs.

1942	PHI	N	2	B
1943	GB	N	3	B
2 yrs.		5 games		

Paul Lankford
LANKFORD, PAUL JAY

Paul Lankford *continued*
B. Jun. 15, 1958, New York, NY
Penn State 6'2" 184 lbs.

1982	MIA	N	7	CB
1983			16	CB
1984			16	CB
1985			16	CB
1986			12	CB
1987			12	CB
1988			13	CB
1989			16	CB
1990			7	CB
1991			15	CB
10 yrs.		130 games		

Dan Lanphear
LANPHEAR, DANIEL
B. 1938
Wisconsin 6'2" 225 lbs.

1960	HOU	A		DE
1962			2	DE
2 yrs.		2 games		

Grenny Lansdell
LANSDELL, GRENVILLE A., JR.
B. Jul. 16, 1918
D. May 14, 1984, Newport Beach, CA
Southern California 6'0" 190 lbs.

| 1940 | NYG | N | 2 | HB |

Buck Lansford
LANSFORD, ALEX JOHN
B. Nov. 4, 1933, Catarina, TX
Texas 6'2" 232 lbs.

1955	PHI	N	12	G, T
1956			12	T
1957			10	T
1958	LA	N	12	G
1959			4	G
1960			11	G
6 yrs.		61 games		

Jim Lansford
LANSFORD, JAMES A.
B. 1930
D. Jan. 17, 1989
Texas 6'3" 235 lbs.

| 1952 | DAL | N | 12 | T |

Mike Lansford
LANSFORD, MICHAEL JOHN
B. Jul. 20, 1958, Monterey Park, CA
Washington 6'0" 183 lbs.

1982	LARM	N	9	K
1983			4	K
1984			16	K
1985			16	K
1986			16	K
1987			15	K
1988			16	K
1989			16	K
1990			16	K
9 yrs.		124 games		

Monty Lantz
LANTZ, MONTGOMERY S.
B. Nov. 24, 1903
D. Nov. 2, 1969, Pittsburgh, PA
Grove City 5'11" 185 lbs.

| 1933 | PIT | N | 10 | C |

Ralph Lanum
LANUM, RALPH L. (Jake)
B. Sep. 13, 1896
D. Mar. 19, 1968, Homewood, IL
Illinois/Millikin 6'0" 190 lbs.

| 1920 | DEC | A | 7 | HB, FB |

Ralph Lanum *continued*

1921			6	HB
1922	CHIB	N	12	HB, FB
1923			11	HB
1924			6	FB, HB
5 yrs.		42 games		

Chuck Lanza
LANZA, CHARLES LOUIS
B. Sep. 20, 1964, Coraopolis, PA
Notre Dame 6'2" 263 lbs.

1988	PIT	N	16	C
1989			11	C
2 yrs.		27 games		

Bill Lapham
LAPHAM, WILLIAM
B. Feb. 2, 1934, Des Moines, IA
Drake/Iowa 6'3" 250 lbs.

1960	PHI	N	12	C
1961	MIN	N	14	C
2 yrs.		26 games		

Dave Lapham
LAPHAM, DAVID ALLEN
B. Jun. 24, 1952, Melrose, MA
Syracuse 6'4" 259 lbs.

1974	CIN	N	14	OT
1975			13	OT
1976			14	OT
1977			13	G
1978			16	G
1979			16	G
1980			16	G
1981			13	G
1982			9	G
1983			16	C
10 yrs.		140 games		

Myron Lapka
LAPKA, MYRON LYNN
B. May 10, 1956, Van Nuys, CA
Southern California 6'4" 255 lbs.

1980	NYG	N	10	DT
1982	LARM	N	2	DT
1983			4	NT
3 yrs.		16 games		

Ted Lapka
LAPKA, THEODORE A.
B. Apr. 20, 1920, Hawthorne, IL
DePaul/St. Ambrose 6'1" 193 lbs.

1943	WAS	N	8	E
1944			5	E
1946			7	E
3 yrs.		20 games		

Ron LaPointe
LAPOINTE, RONALD
B. Feb. 28, 1957, Framingham, MA
Penn State 6'2" 235 lbs.

| 1980 | BAL | N | 2 | TE |

Phil LaPorta
LAPORTA, PHILIP
B. May 4, 1952, Valley Stream, NY
Penn State 6'4" 256 lbs.

1974	NO	N	6	OT
1975			14	OT
2 yrs.		20 games		

Benny LaPresta
LAPRESTA, BENJAMIN
B. Jan. 22, 1909
D. Aug. 11, 1975, St. Louis, MO
St. Louis 5'9" 185 lbs.

| 1933 | BOS | N | 8 | QB, HB |

Benny LaPresta *continued*

Year	Team	Games	Pos.
1934	C-S N	1	HB
2 yrs.	9 games		

Bob Laraba
LARABA, ROBERT
B. May 30, 1933, Niagara Falls, NY
Texas Western 6'3" 195 lbs.

Year	Team	Games	Pos.
1960	LA A		QB, LB
1961	SD A	14	HB, LB
2 yrs.	14 games		

Jack Laraway
LARAWAY, JOHN
B. 1936
Purdue 6'1" 218 lbs.

Year	Team	Games	Pos.
1960	BUF A		LB
1961	HOU A	10	LB
2 yrs.	10 games		

Larden
LARDEN
None

Year	Team	Games	Pos.
1925	CLE N	5	E, G

Steve Largent
LARGENT, STEVE M.
B. Sep. 28, 1954, Tulsa, OK
Tulsa 5'11" 184 lbs.

Year	Team	Games	Pos.
1976	SEA N	14	WR
1977		14	WR
1978		16	WR
1979		15	WR
1980		16	WR
1981		16	WR
1982		8	WR
1983		15	WR
1984		16	WR
1985		16	WR
1986		16	WR
1987		13	WR
1988		15	WR
1989		10	WR
14 yrs.	200 games		

Eric Larkin
LARKIN, ERIC
B. May 14, 1962
Miami (Florida) 6'4" 265 lbs.

Year	Team	Games	Pos.
1987	HOU N	1	DE

Gordon Laro
LARO, GORDON EDWARD
B. Apr. 17, 1972, Lynn, MA
Michigan/Boston College 6'3" 257 lbs.

Year	Team	Games	Pos.
1995	JAC N	2	TE

Paul LaRosa
LAROSA, PAUL
B. 1893
Deceased
None 174 lbs.

Year	Team	Games	Pos.
1920	CHIC A	6	E
1921		2	E
2 yrs.	8 games		

Danny LaRose
LAROSE, MARVIN DANIEL
B. Feb. 8, 1939, Crystal City, MO
Missouri 6'5" 250 lbs.

Year	Team	Games	Pos.
1961	DET N	14	DE, OT
1962		14	OT
1963		9	OT
1964	PIT N	12	DE
1965	SF N	5	DE
1966	DEN A	11	DE
6 yrs.	65 games		

Carl Larpenter
LARPENTER, CARL JAMES
B. Jul. 1, 1936, Port Arthur, TX
Texas 6'4" 237 lbs.

Year	Team	Games	Pos.
1960	DEN A		G
1961		14	G
1962	DAL A	2	G, OT
3 yrs.	16 games		

Jack Larscheid
LARSCHEID, JOHN
B. 1934
Pacific 5'6" 162 lbs.

Year	Team	Games	Pos.
1960	OAK A	14	HB
1961		2	HB
2 yrs.	16 games		

Gary Larsen
LARSEN, GARY LEE
B. Mar. 13, 1940, Fargo, ND
Concordia (Minnesota) 6'5" 256 lbs.

Year	Team	Games	Pos.
1964	LA N	14	DE
1965	MIN N	12	DT
1966		14	DT
1967		14	DT
1968		14	DT
1969		14	DT
1970		14	DT
1971		14	DT
1972		14	DT
1973		14	DT
1974		11	DT
11 yrs.	149 games		

Bill Larson
LARSON, WILLIAM
B. 1939
Illinois Wesleyan 5'10" 190 lbs.

Year	Team	Games	Pos.
1960	BOS A		FB

Bill Larson
LARSON, WILLIAM HARRY
B. Oct. 7, 1953, Greenfield, IA
Colorado State 6'4" 224 lbs.

Year	Team	Games	Pos.
1975	SF N	14	TE
1977	DET N	12	TE
1978	PHI N	5	TE
1980	DEN N	2	TE
1980	GB N	9	TE
4 yrs.	42 games		

Fred Larson
LARSON, FREDERIC A. (Ojay)
B. Oct. 15, 1897, Calumet, MI
D. May, 1977, Mequon, WI
Notre Dame 6'1" 199 lbs.

Year	Team	Games	Pos.
1922	CHIB N	10	C
1924	MIL N	10	C
1925	GB N	13	C
1926	CHI A	14	C
1929	CHIB N	1	C
1929	CHIC N	10	C, G
5 yrs.	56 games		

Greg Larson
LARSON, GREGORY KENNETH
B. Nov. 15, 1939, Minneapolis, MN
Minnesota 6'2" 249 lbs.

Year	Team	Games	Pos.
1961	NYG N	14	C
1962		14	OT, C
1963		14	C, G
1964		13	C
1965		12	C
1966		14	C
1967		14	C
1968		14	C
1969		14	C
1970		14	C

Greg Larson *continued*

Year	Team	Games	Pos.
1971		14	C
1972		14	C
1973		14	C
13 yrs.	179 games		

Kurt Larson
LARSON, KURT ARVIN
B. Feb. 25, 1966, Waukesha, WI
Michigan State 6'4" 236 lbs.

Year	Team	Games	Pos.
1989	IND N	13	LB
1990		16	LB
1991	GB N	13	LB
3 yrs.	42 games		

Louie Larson
LARSON, LOUIS
B. Jan. 5, 1898
D. May, 1982, Benbrook, TX
None 168 lbs.

Year	Team	Games	Pos.
1926	DUL N	7	QB, E, G, FB
1929	CHIC N	3	FB, HB
2 yrs.	10 games		

Lynn Larson
LARSON, LYNDON A.
B. Mar. 9, 1948, Phoenix, AZ
Kansas State 6'4" 254 lbs.

Year	Team	Games	Pos.
1971	BAL N	1	OT

Paul Larson
LARSON, PAUL L. (Pitchin' Paul)
B. Mar. 19, 1932, Turlock, CA
California 5'11" 183 lbs.

Year	Team	Games	Pos.
1957	CHIC N	5	QB
1960	OAK A		QB
2 yrs.	5 games		

Pete Larson
LARSON, PETER
B. May 30, 1944, Wilmington, DE
Cornell 6'1" 200 lbs.

Year	Team	Games	Pos.
1967	WAS N	8	RB
1968		14	RB
2 yrs.	22 games		

Swede Larson
LARSON, LOU
None

Year	Team	Games	Pos.
1923	HAM N	3	HB, QB

Yale Lary
LARY, ROBERT YALE, JR.
B. Nov. 24, 1930, Fort Worth, TX
Texas A&M 6'0" 187 lbs.

Year	Team	Games	Pos.
1952	DET N	12	DB, P
1953		11	DB, P
1956		12	DB, P
1957		12	DB, P
1958		12	DB, P
1959		10	DB, P
1960		12	DB, P
1961		14	DB, P
1962		14	DB, P
1963		10	DB, P
1964		14	DB, P
11 yrs.	133 games		

Johnny Lascari
LASCARI, JOHN
B. Mar. 5, 1918, Lodi, NJ
D. Jul., 1971
Georgetown (DC) 6'2" 210 lbs.

Year	Team	Games	Pos.
1942	NYG N	10	E

Jim Lash
LASH, JAMES VERLE
B. Nov. 12, 1951, Akron, OH
Northwestern 6'2" 200 lbs.

Year	Team	Games	Pos.
1973	MIN N	9	WR
1974		14	WR
1975		14	WR
1976		5	WR
1976	SF	8	WR
1977		10	WR
5 yrs.	60 games		

Tim Lashar
LASHAR, TIM
B. Sep. 5, 1964
Oklahoma 5'9" 160 lbs.

Year	Team	Games	Pos.
1987	CHI N	3	K

Greg Lasker
LASKER, GREG
B. Sep. 28, 1964, St. Louis, MO
Arkansas 6'0" 200 lbs.

Year	Team	Games	Pos.
1986	NYG N	16	S
1987		11	S
1988		4	S
1988	CHI N	1	S
1988	PHX N	1	CB, S
3 yrs.	33 games		

Bill Laskey
LASKEY, WILLIAM GRANT
B. Feb. 10, 1943, Ann Arbor, MI
Michigan 6'2" 237 lbs.

Year	Team	Games	Pos.
1965	BUF A	14	LB
1966	OAK A	14	LB
1967		13	LB
1969		12	LB
1970	OAK N	14	LB
1971	BAL N	13	LB
1972		14	LB
1973	DEN N	11	LB
1974		14	LB
9 yrs.	119 games		

Frank Lasky
LASKY, FRANCIS JOSEPH
B. Oct. 10, 1941, New York, NY
Florida 6'2" 265 lbs.

Year	Team	Games	Pos.
1964	NYG N	4	OT
1965		14	OT
2 yrs.	18 games		

Jim Laslavic
LASLAVIC, JAMES EDWARD
B. Oct. 24, 1951, Etna, PA
Penn State 6'2" 237 lbs.

Year	Team	Games	Pos.
1973	DET N	14	LB
1974		14	LB
1975		14	LB
1976		12	LB
1977		14	LB
1978	SD N	16	LB
1980		16	LB
1981		16	LB
1982	GB N	6	LB
9 yrs.	122 games		

Lou Lassahn
LASSAHN, LOUIS
B. 1913
Western Maryland 6'0" 205 lbs.

Year	Team	Games	Pos.
1938	PIT N	2	E

Dick Lasse
LASSE, RICHARD STEPHEN
B. Nov. 13, 1935, Quincy, MA
Syracuse 6'2" 222 lbs.

Year	Team	Games	Pos.
1958	PIT N	12	E, LB

Dick Lasse continued

Year	Team		Games	Pos.
1959			12	LB
1960	WAS	N	12	LB
1961			14	LB
1962	NYG	N	4	LB
5 yrs.	54 games			

Derrick Lassic

LASSIC, DERRICK OWENS
B. Jan. 26, 1970, Haverstraw, NY
Alabama 5'10" 188 lbs.

Year	Team		Games	Pos.
1993	DAL	N	10	RB

Ike Lassiter

LASSITER, ISAAC THOMAS
B. Nov. 15, 1940, Wilson, NC
St. Augustine's 6'5" 270 lbs.

Year	Team		Games	Pos.
1962	DEN	A	14	DT
1963			7	DE, E
1964			2	DE
1965	OAK	A	14	DE
1966			14	DE
1967			14	DE
1968			14	DE
1969			14	DE
1970	BOS	N	5	DE
1971	NE	N	14	DE
10 yrs.	112 games			

Kwamie Lassiter

LASSITER, KWAMIE
B. Dec. 3, 1969, Newport News, VA
Kansas 5'11" 180 lbs.

Year	Team		Games	Pos.
1995	ARI	N	5	CB, S
1996			14	S
2 yrs.	19 games			

Art Laster

LASTER, ARTHUR L.
B. Mar. 2, 1948, Gary, IN
Maryland-Eastern Shore 6'4" 280 lbs.

Year	Team		Games	Pos.
1970	BUF	N	14	OT

Don Laster

LASTER, ANTHONY DONALD
B. Dec. 13 1958, Albany, GA
Tennessee State 6'5" 285 lbs.

Year	Team		Games	Pos.
1982	WAS	N	8	OT
1984	DET	N	14	OT
2 yrs.	22 games			

Greg Lathan

LATHAN, GREGORY
B. Sep. 2, 1964, San Diego, CA
Cincinnati 6'1" 195 lbs.

Year	Team		Games	Pos.
1987	LARI	N	3	WR

Lamar Lathon

LATHON, LAMAR LAVANTHA
B. Dec. 23, 1967, Wharton, TX
Houston 6'3" 249 lbs.

Year	Team		Games	Pos.
1990	HOU	N	11	LB
1991			16	LB
1992			11	LB
1993			13	LB
1994			16	LB
1995	CAR	N	15	LB
1996			16	LB
7 yrs.	98 games			

Kit Lathrop

LATHROP, KIT DOUGLAS
B. Aug. 10, 1956, San Jose, CA
Arizona State 6'5" 260 lbs.

Year	Team		Games	Pos.
1979	DEN	N	9	DT

Kit Lathrop continued

Year	Team		Games	Pos.
1979	GB	N	2	DT
1980			15	DT
1986	KC	N	16	DE
1987	WAS	N	1	DT
4 yrs.	43 games			

Al Latimer

LATIMER, ALBERT
B. Oct. 14, 1957, Winter Park, FL
Clemson 5'11" 172 lbs.

Year	Team		Games	Pos.
1979	PHI	N	13	CB
1982	DET	N	4	CB
1983			8	CB, S
1984			15	CB
4 yrs.	40 games			

Don Latimer

LATIMER, DON B.
B. Mar. 1, 1955, Fort Pierce, FL
Miami (Florida) 6'3" 259 lbs.

Year	Team		Games	Pos.
1978	DEN	N	14	DT
1979			15	DT
1980			14	DT
1981			16	NT
1982			9	NT
1983			12	NT
6 yrs.	80 games			

Jerry Latin

LATIN, JERRY LOUIS
B. Aug. 25, 1953, Rockford, IL
Northern Illinois 5'10" 188 lbs.

Year	Team		Games	Pos.
1975	STL	N	10	RB
1976			11	RB
1977			14	RB
1978			2	RB
1978	LA	N	14	RB
4 yrs.	51 games			

Tony Latone

LATONE, ANTHONY (Tony the Terrible)
B. Apr. 18, 1897, Spring Valley, IL
D. Nov. 24, 1975, Detroit, MI
None 5'11" 195 lbs.

Year	Team		Games	Pos.
1925	POT	N	12	HB, FB
1926			11	HB, FB
1927			12	HB, FB
1928			10	HB, FB
1929	BOS	N	8	HB, FB
1930	PRO	N	11	FB, HB, QB
6 yrs.	64 games			

Chuck Latourette

LATOURETTE, CHARLES PIERRE
B. Jul. 21, 1945, San Antonio, TX
Rice 6'0" 190 lbs.

Year	Team		Games	Pos.
1967	STL	N	14	DB, P
1968			14	DB, P
1970			14	P, S
1971			13	P, S
4 yrs.	55 games			

Greg Latta

LATTA, GREGORY EDWIN
B. Oct. 13, 1952, Newark, NJ
D. Sep. 28, 1994
Morgan State 6'3" 227 lbs.

Year	Team		Games	Pos.
1975	CHI	N	14	TE
1976			14	TE
1977			14	TE
1978			16	TE
1979			15	TE
5 yrs.	73 games			

Brian Lattimore

LATTIMORE, BRIAN KEITH
B. Oct. 29, 1966, St. Petersburg, FL
Southeast Missouri State 6'1" 202 lbs.

Year	Team		Games	Pos.
1991	IND	N	3	RB

Johnny Lattner

LATTNER, JOHN JOSEPH
B. Oct. 24, 1932, Chicago, IL
Notre Dame 6'1" 195 lbs.

Year	Team		Games	Pos.
1954	PIT	N	12	HB

Paul Latzke

LATZKE, PAUL LEWIS
B. Mar. 22, 1942, Hollywood, CA
Pacific 6'4" 242 lbs.

Year	Team		Games	Pos.
1966	SD		2	C
1967			13	C
1968			7	C
3 yrs.	22 games			

Al Lauer

LAUER, ALFRED
B. Jun., 1899
D. Jul. 9, 1950, Evansville, IN
None 5'6" 165 lbs.

Year	Team		Games	Pos.
1922	EVA	N	1	QB

Hal Lauer

LAUER, HAROLD S. (Dutch)
B. Jan., 1896
D. Aug. 9, 1978, Southfield, MI
Detroit 5'10" 185 lbs.

Year	Team		Games	Pos.
1922	RI	N	7	HB
1922	GB	N	2	QB, HB
1923	TOL	N	7	HB, FB, QB
1925	DET	N	11	HB, E
1926			10	E, HB
4 yrs.	37 games			

Larry Lauer

LAUER, LAWRENCE GENE
B. Aug. 27, 1929, Winnetka, IL
D. Jan. 3, 1992
Alabama 6'3" 235 lbs.

Year	Team		Games	Pos.
1956	GB	N	6	C
1957			12	C
2 yrs.	18 games			

Babe Laufenberg

LAUFENBERG, BRANDON HUGH
B. Dec. 5, 1959, Burbank, CA
Stanford/Missouri 6'3" 214 lbs.

Year	Team		Games	Pos.
1986	NO	N	1	QB
1988	SD	N	8	QB
1989	DAL	N	3	QB
1990			4	QB
4 yrs.	16 games			

Laughing Gas

LAUGHING GAS
None

Year	Team		Games	Pos.
1922	OOR	N	1	HB

Henry Laughlin

LAUGHLIN, HENRY (Bud)
B. 1931
Kansas 6'1" 200 lbs.

Year	Team		Games	Pos.
1955	SF	N	8	FB

Jim Laughlin

LAUGHLIN, JAMES DAVID
B. Jul. 5, 1958, Euclid, OH
Ohio State 6'1" 222 lbs.

Year	Team		Games	Pos.
1980	ATL	N	16	LB

Jim Laughlin continued

Year	Team		Games	Pos.
1981			14	LB
1982			9	LB
1983	GB	N	15	LB
1984	LARM	N	3	LB
1985			10	LB
1986			16	LB
1987	ATL	N	5	LB
8 yrs.	88 games			

Jim Laughton

LAUGHTON, JAMES EDWARD
B. Jan. 18, 1960, Salinas, CA
San Diego State 6'5" 225 lbs.

Year	Team		Games	Pos.
1986	SEA	N	6	TE

Hank Lauricella

LAURICELLA, FRANCIS E.
B. Oct. 19, 1930, Harahan, LA
Tennessee 5'11" 175 lbs.

Year	Team		Games	Pos.
1952	DAL	N	10	HB

Frank Laurinaitis

LAURINAITIS, FRANCIS T. (Fritz)
B. Dec. 20, 1922, New Philadelphia, PA
Richmond 5'10" 200 lbs.

Year	Team		Games	Pos.
1947	BKN	AA	8	B

Lindy Lauro

LAURO, LINDARO
B. 1924
Pittsburgh 5'10" 195 lbs.

Year	Team		Games	Pos.
1951	CHIC	N	1	B

Ted Laux

LAUX, THEODORE
B. Mar. 1, 1918, Swedesboro, NJ
St. Joseph (Pennsylvania) 5'10" 185 lbs.

Year	Team		Games	Pos.
1943	P, P	N	4	B
1944	PHI	N	1	B
2 yrs.	5 games			

Al Lavan

LAVAN, ALTON
B. Sep. 13, 1946, Pierce, FL
Colorado State 6'1" 194 lbs.

Year	Team		Games	Pos.
1969	ATL	N	11	CB
1970			13	CB, S
2 yrs.	24 games			

Dante Lavelli

LAVELLI, DANTE BERT JOSEPH (Gluefingers)
B. Feb. 23, 1923, Hudson, OH
Ohio State 6'0" 191 lbs.

Year	Team		Games	Pos.
1946	CLE	AA	14	E
1947			13	E
1948			8	E
1949			9	E
1950	CLE	N	12	E
1951			12	E
1952			8	E
1953			12	E
1954			12	E
1955			12	E
1956			11	E
11 yrs.	123 games			

Joe Lavender

LAVENDER, JOE (Big Bird)
B. Feb. 10, 1949, Rayville, LA
San Diego State 6'4" 190 lbs.

Year	Team		Games	Pos.
1973	PHI	N	13	CB

Year	Team		Games	Pos.

Joe Lavender _continued_

1974			14	CB
1975			13	CB
1976	**WAS**	N	14	CB
1977			14	CB
1978			16	CB
1979			16	CB
1980			16	CB
1981			16	CB
1982			7	CB

10 yrs. 139 games

Robert Lavette
LAVETTE, ROBERT L.
B. Sep. 8, 1963, Cartersville, GA
Georgia Tech 5'11" 190 lbs.

1985	**DAL**	N	12	RB
1986			16	RB
1987			4	RB
1987	**PHI**	N	1	RB

3 yrs. 33 games

Paul Lavine
LAVINE, PAUL
B. May 1, 1962
Utah State 6'2" 207 lbs.

| 1987 | **SEA** | N | 3 | LB |

Dennis Law
LAW, RAYMOND DENNIS
B. Apr. 4, 1955, Commerce, GA
East Tennessee State 6'1" 179 lbs.

| 1978 | **CIN** | N | 14 | WR |

Hubbard Law
LAW, HUBBARD PAUL (Red)
B. Jan. 27, 1921, Houston, TX
Sam Houston State 6'1" 210 lbs.

| 1942 | **PIT** | N | 10 | G |
| 1945 | | | 6 | G |

2 yrs. 16 games

John Law
LAW, JOHN
B. Sep. 22, 1907
D. May, 1981, Green Island, NY
Notre Dame 5'9" 180 lbs.

| 1930 | **NEW** | N | 1 | T |

Ty Law
LAW, TY
B. Feb. 10, 1974, Aliquippa, PA
Michigan 5'11" 196 lbs.

| 1995 | **NE** | N | 14 | CB |
| 1996 | | | 13 | CB |

2 yrs. 27 games

Al Lawler
LAWLER, ALLEN
B. 1924
Texas 5'10" 175 lbs.

| 1948 | **CHIB** | N | 7 | HB |

Burton Lawless
LAWLESS, RICHARD BURTON
B. Nov. 1, 1953, Dothan, AL
Florida 6'4" 252 lbs.

1975	**DAL**	N	14	G
1976			14	G
1977			14	G
1978			16	G
1979			15	G
1980	**DET**	N	9	G

6 yrs. 82 games

Year	Team		Games	Pos.

Amos Lawrence
LAWRENCE, AMOS, JR. (Famous Amos)
B. Jan. 9, 1958, Norfolk, VA
North Carolina 5'11" 181 lbs.

| 1981 | **SF** | N | 13 | RB |
| 1982 | | | 8 | RB |

2 yrs. 21 games

Ben Lawrence
LAWRENCE, BEN
B. Sep. 19, 1961, Sparta, WI
Indiana (Pennsylvania) 6'1" 325 lbs.

| 1987 | **PIT** | N | 1 | G |

Don Lawrence
LAWRENCE, DONALD
B. Jun. 4, 1937, Cleveland, OH
Notre Dame 6'1" 245 lbs.

1959	**WAS**	N	12	T, G
1960			12	T
1961			11	OT

3 yrs. 35 games

Ed Lawrence
LAWRENCE, EDWARD JAMES
B. 1905
D. Nov. 21, 1961, Moapa, NV
Brown 5'8" 170 lbs.

| 1929 | **BOS** | N | 6 | FB, HB |
| 1930 | **SI** | N | 3 | E, FB |

2 yrs. 9 games

Henry Lawrence
LAWRENCE, HENRY
B. Sep. 26, 1951, Danville, PA
Florida A&M 6'4" 270 lbs.

1974	**OAK**	N	14	OT
1975			14	OT
1976			8	OT
1977			14	OT
1978			16	OT
1979			16	OT
1980			16	OT
1981			16	OT
1982	**LARI**	N	9	OT
1983			16	OT
1984			16	OT
1985			16	OT
1986			16	OT

13 yrs. 187 games

Jimmy Lawrence
LAWRENCE, JAMES BOYDSTON
B. Mar. 15, 1914, Dawson, TX
Deceased
Texas Christian 5'11" 190 lbs.

1936	**CHIC**	N	7	HB
1937			11	HB
1938			11	HB
1939			1	HB
1939	**GB**	N	3	HB

4 yrs. 33 games

Kent Lawrence
LAWRENCE, KENT
B. Jun. 3, 1946, Anderson, SC
Georgia 5'11" 175 lbs.

| 1969 | **PHI** | N | 9 | WR |
| 1970 | **ATL** | N | 1 | WR |

2 yrs. 10 games

Larry Lawrence
LAWRENCE, LARRY ROBERT
B. Apr. 11, 1949, Mount Pleasant, IA
Iowa/Miami (Florida)/Calgary 6'1" 208 lbs.

| 1974 | **OAK** | N | 7 | QB |

Year	Team		Games	Pos.

Larry Lawrence _continued_

| 1975 | | | 1 | QB |
| 1976 | **TB** | N | 1 | QB |

3 yrs. 9 games

Reggie Lawrence
LAWRENCE, REGGIE
B. Sep. 4, 1969, Camden, NJ
North Carolina A&T 6'0" 178 lbs.

| 1993 | **PHI** | N | | WR |

Rolland Lawrence
LAWRENCE, ROLLAND DERENFRO
B. Mar. 24, 1951, Franklin, PA
Tabor 5'10" 179 lbs.

1973	**ATL**	N	14	CB
1974			14	CB
1975			14	CB
1976			14	CB
1977			14	CB
1978			16	CB
1979			16	CB
1980			16	CB

8 yrs. 118 games

Joe Laws
LAWS, JOSEPH R.
B. Jun. 16, 1911, Colfax, IA
D. Aug. 24, 1979, Green Bay, WI
Iowa 5'9" 186 lbs.

1934	**GB**	N	13	HB, QB
1935			12	HB, QB
1936			11	HB
1937			1	HB, FB, QB
1938			10	HB
1939			9	HB
1940			3	HB
1941			10	HB
1942			10	HB
1943			10	HB
1944			10	HB
1945			10	HB

12 yrs. 109 games

Al Lawson
LAWSON, ALPHONZO
B. Jun. 6, 1941
Delaware State 5'11" 190 lbs.

| 1964 | **NY** | A | 1 | FL |

Jamie Lawson
LAWSON, JAMIE LEE
B. Oct. 2, 1965, New Orleans, LA
Nicholls State 5'10" 240 lbs.

1989	**TB**	N	5	RB
1990			6	RB
1990	**NE**	N	1	RB

2 yrs. 12 games

Jerry Lawson
LAWSON, JEROME
B. Sep. 30, 1945, Oklahoma City, OK
Utah 5'11" 192 lbs.

| 1968 | **BUF** | A | 1 | DB |

Jim Lawson
LAWSON, JAMES WILMER
B. Mar. 11, 1902, Long Beach, CA
D. Jan. 3, 1989, Carmel-by-the-Sea, CA
Stanford 5'11" 190 lbs.

| 1926 | **LA** | A | 10 | E |
| 1927 | **NYY** | N | 10 | E, T |

2 yrs. 20 games

Year	Team		Games	Pos.

Odell Lawson
LAWSON, ODELL
B. Dec. 30, 1947, Ponca City, OK
Langston 6'2" 212 lbs.

1970	**BOS**	N	14	RB
1971	**NE**	N	2	RB
1973	**NO**	N	12	RB
1974			9	RB

4 yrs. 37 games

Roger Lawson
LAWSON, ROGER ALAN
B. Sep. 29, 1949, Detroit, MI
Western Michigan 6'2" 215 lbs.

| 1972 | **CHI** | N | 12 | RB |
| 1973 | | | 10 | RB |

2 yrs. 22 games

Steve Lawson
LAWSON, STEPHEN WENDELL
B. Jan. 4, 1949, Athens, GA
Kansas 6'3" 264 lbs.

1971	**CIN**	N	7	G
1972			2	G
1973	**MIN**	N	2	G
1974			12	G
1975			11	G
1976	**SF**	N	14	G
1977			14	G

7 yrs. 62 games

Russ Lay
LAY, RUSSELL M.
B. 1911
Michigan State 5'11" 198 lbs.

| 1934 | **DET** | N | 1 | G |
| 1934 | **C, S** | N | 3 | G |

1 yr. 4 games

Bob Layden
LAYDEN, ROBERT
B. 1920
Southwestern (Kansas) 6'2" 215 lbs.

| 1943 | **DET** | N | 4 | E, T |

Elmer Layden
LAYDEN, ELMER F.
B. May 4, 1903, Davenport, IA
D. Jun. 30, 1973, Chicago, IL
Notre Dame 5'11" 180 lbs.

| 1926 | **RI** | A | 1 | FB |
| 1926 | **BKN** | A | 1 | FB |

1 yr. 2 games

Pete Layden
LAYDEN, JOHN PETER, JR.
B. Dec. 30, 1919, Dallas, TX
D. Jul. 18, 1982, Edna, TX
Texas 5'11" 192 lbs.

1948	**NY**	AA	9	B
1949	**B-NY**	AA	12	B
1950	**NYY**	N	10	B

3 yrs. 31 games

Jason Layman
LAYMAN, JASON TODD
B. Jul. 29, 1973, Sevierville TN
Tennessee 6'5" 306 lbs.

| 1996 | **HOU** | N | 16 | OT |

Bobby Layne
LAYNE, ROBERT LAWRENCE (Blond Bomber)
B. Dec. 19, 1926, Lubbock, TX
D. Dec. 1, 1986, Lubbock, TX
Texas 6'1" 201 lbs.

| 1948 | **CHIB** | N | 11 | QB |

Year	Team	Games	Pos.

Bobby Layne continued

Year	Team		Games	Pos.
1949	NYB	N	12	QB
1950	DET	N	12	QB
1951			12	QB
1952			12	QB
1953			12	QB
1954			12	QB
1955			12	QB
1956			12	QB
1957			11	QB
1958	PIT	N	10	QB
1959			12	QB
1960			12	QB
1961			8	QB
1962			13	QB
15 yrs.	173 games			

Johnnie Layport

LAYPORT, JOHN E.
B. Mar. 19, 1901
D. Nov., 1986, Hendersonville, NC
Wooster 5'9" 170 lbs.

Year	Team		Games	Pos.
1924	COL	N	5	G, C
1925	DAY	N	4	G
1926			3	T
3 yrs.	12 games			

Bill Lazetich

LAZETICH, WILLIAM V.
B. Oct. 16, 1916, Anaconda, MT
Montana 6'0" 198 lbs.

Year	Team		Games	Pos.
1939	CLE	N	5	HB
1942			9	HB
2 yrs.	14 games			

Milan Lazetich

LAZETICH, MILAN (Mike, Sheriff)
B. Aug. 27, 1921, Anaconda, MT
D. Jul. 9, 1969
Montana/Michigan 6'1" 211 lbs.

Year	Team		Games	Pos.
1945	CLE	N	10	G
1946	LA	N	10	G
1947			11	G
1948			12	G
1949			7	G
1950			9	G
6 yrs.	59 games			

Pete Lazetich

LAZETICH, PETER GARY
B. Feb. 4, 1950, Billings, MT
Stanford 6'3" 241 lbs.

Year	Team		Games	Pos.
1972	SD	N	14	DE
1973			12	LB
1974			9	DE
1976	PHI	N	10	DT
1977			14	MG
5 yrs.	59 games			

Paul Lea

LEA, PAUL
B. Feb. 10, 1929, New Orleans, LA
Tulane 6'2" 240 lbs.

Year	Team		Games	Pos.
1951	PIT	N	9	T

Bill Leach

LEACH, WILLIAM
B. Jul. 2, 1964
North Carolina State 6'5" 280 lbs.

Year	Team		Games	Pos.
1987	NO	N	3	LB

Scott Leach

LEACH, SCOTT
B. Sep. 18, 1963, Bridgeport, CT
Ohio State 6'2" 221 lbs.

Year	Team		Games	Pos.
1987	NO	N	1	G, OT

Gar Leaf

LEAF, GARFIELD (Sock)
B. May 26, 1902
D. Mar. 20, 1990
Lake Forest/Syracuse 6'1" 195 lbs.

Year	Team		Games	Pos.
1926	LOU	N	3	T

Bernie Leahy

LEAHY, BERNARD P.
B. Aug. 15, 1908
D. Mar. 12, 1978, Walnut Creek, CA
Notre Dame 5'11" 185 lbs.

Year	Team		Games	Pos.
1932	CHIB	N	1	HB

Gerry Leahy

LEAHY, GERALD LEO
B. Oct. 19, 1934, Bay City, MI
Colorado 6'2" 220 lbs.

Year	Team		Games	Pos.
1957	PIT	N	1	T

Pat Leahy

LEAHY, PATRICK JOSEPH
B. Mar. 19, 1951, St. Louis, MO
St. Louis* 6'0" 196 lbs.

Year	Team		Games	Pos.
1974	NYJ	N	6	K
1975			14	K
1976			14	K
1977			14	K
1978			16	K
1979			6	K
1980			16	K
1981			16	K
1982			9	K
1983			16	K
1984			16	K
1985			16	K
1986			16	K
1987			12	K
1988			16	K
1989			16	K
1990			16	K
1991			15	K
18 yrs.	250 games			

Robert Leahy

LEAHY, ROBERT
B. Sep. 5, 1947, Lindenhurst, NY
Emporia State 6'2" 205 lbs.

Year	Team		Games	Pos.
1971	PIT	N	1	QB

Roosevelt Leaks

LEAKS, ROOSEVELT, JR.
B. Jan. 31, 1953, Beaumont, TX
Texas 5'10" 224 lbs.

Year	Team		Games	Pos.
1975	BAL	N	11	RB
1976			13	RB
1977			11	RB
1978			12	FB
1979			7	FB
1980	BUF	N	16	RB
1981			16	RB
1982			9	RB
1983			12	RB
9 yrs.	107 games			

Wes Leaper

LEAPER, WESLEY
B. 1896
Deceased
Wisconsin 5'11" 175 lbs.

Year	Team		Games	Pos.
1923	GB	N	2	E

Les Lear

LEAR, LESLIE
B. Aug. 22, 1918, Grafton, ND
D. Jan. 5, 1979, Hollywood, FL
Manitoba 5'11" 225 lbs.

Year	Team		Games	Pos.
1944	CLE	N	8	G

Les Lear continued

Year	Team		Games	Pos.
1945			9	G
1946	LA	N	1	G
3 yrs.	18 games			

Tom Leary

LEARY, THOMAS
B. Nov. 1, 1902
D. Jan., 1969, Philadelphia, PA
Fordham 5'11" 180 lbs.

Year	Team		Games	Pos.
1927	FRA	N	1	E
1929	SI	N	10	E
1930	NEW	N	6	E
1931	FRA	N	7	E
4 yrs.	24 games			

Wesley Leasy

LEASY, WESLEY
B. Sep. 7, 1971, Vicksburg, MS
Mississippi State 6'2" 234 lbs.

Year	Team		Games	Pos.
1995	ARI	N	12	LB
1996			16	LB
2 yrs.	28 games			

Paul Leatherman

LEATHERMAN, PAUL
B. 1897
Deceased
Chicago 5'9" 200 lbs.

Year	Team		Games	Pos.
1922	HAM	N	4	G, C

Milt Leathers

LEATHERS, MILTON, JR. (Red)
B. 1909
Georgia 5'11" 198 lbs.

Year	Team		Games	Pos.
1933	PHI	N	4	G

Allan Leavitt

LEAVITT, ALLAN JAMES
B. Oct. 22, 1955, St. Petersburg, FL
Georgia 5'11" 176 lbs.

Year	Team		Games	Pos.
1977	TB	N	8	K

Frank Leavitt

LEAVITT, FRANCIS (Soldier)
B. 1893
Deceased
None 240 lbs.

Year	Team		Games	Pos.
1921	NY	A	2	G

Eddie LeBaron

**LEBARON, EDWARD WAYNE, JR.
(The Little General)**
B. Jan. 7, 1930, San Rafael, CA
Pacific 5'9" 166 lbs.

Year	Team		Games	Pos.
1952	WAS	N	12	QB
1953			12	QB
1955			12	QB
1956			10	QB
1957			12	QB
1958			12	QB
1959			12	QB
1960	DAL	N	11	QB
1961			14	QB
1962			14	QB
1963			13	QB
11 yrs.	134 games			

Dick LeBeau

LEBEAU, CHARLES RICHARD
B. Sep. 9, 1937, London, OH
Ohio State 6'1" 185 lbs.

Year	Team		Games	Pos.
1959	DET	N	6	DB
1960			12	DB
1961			14	DB
1962			14	DB

Dick LeBeau continued

Year	Team		Games	Pos.
1963			14	DB
1964			14	DB
1965			14	DB
1966			14	DB
1967			14	DB
1968			14	DB
1969			14	CB
1970			14	CB
1971			13	CB
1972			14	CB
14 yrs.	185 games			

Harper LeBel

LEBEL, BRIAN HARPER
B. Jul. 14, 1963, Granada Hills, CA
Colorado State 6'4" 251 lbs.

Year	Team		Games	Pos.
1989	SEA	N	16	TE
1990	PHI	N	16	TE
1991	ATL	N	3	TE
1992			16	TE
1993			16	TE
1994			16	TE
1995			16	TE
1996			16	TE
8 yrs.	115 games			

Howard Lebengood

LEBENGOOD, HOWARD (Fungy)
B. Apr. 23, 1902, Pottsville, PA
D. Jan., 1980, Lakeland, FL
Villanova 5'11" 175 lbs.

Year	Team		Games	Pos.
1925	POT	N	5	HB

Bob Leberman

LEBERMAN, ROBERT W.
B. 1932
Syracuse 6'1" 180 lbs.

Year	Team		Games	Pos.
1954	BAL	N	12	HB

Bob LeBlanc

LEBLANC, ROBERT
B. Nov. 5, 1962, Panama City, FL
Elon 6'4" 243 lbs.

Year	Team		Games	Pos.
1987	BUF	N	3	LB

Mike LeBlanc

LEBLANC, MICHAEL
B. May 5, 1962
Stephen F. Austin 5'11" 195 lbs.

Year	Team		Games	Pos.
1987	NE	N	4	RB

Ed Lechner

LECHNER, EDGAR H.
B. Dec. 14, 1919, Fessenden, ND
Minnesota 6'1" 200 lbs.

Year	Team		Games	Pos.
1942	NYG	N	4	G

Roy Lechthaler

LECHTHALER, ROY
B. Apr. 1, 1908
D. Dec., 1980, Mechanicsburg, PA
Lebanon Valley 5'10" 198 lbs.

Year	Team		Games	Pos.
1933	PHI	N	4	G

Bill Leckonby

**LECKONBY, WILLIAM BADER
(Wild Bill)**
B. Sep. 16, 1917, Greenville, OH
St. Lawrence 6'0" 185 lbs.

Year	Team		Games	Pos.
1939	BKN	N	5	HB
1940			8	HB
1941			10	HB
3 yrs.	23 games			

Year	Team	Games	Pos.

Jim LeClair
LECLAIR, JAMES
B. Mar. 23, 1944, Mount Vernon, NY
C.W. Post 6'1" 208 lbs.

Year	Team		Games	Pos.
1967	DEN	A	6	QB
1968			3	QB

2 yrs.   9 games

Jim LeClair
LECLAIR, JAMES MICHAEL
B. Oct. 30, 1950, South St. Paul, MN
North Dakota 6'3" 234 lbs.

Year	Team		Games	Pos.
1972	CIN	N	14	LB
1973			10	LB
1974			8	LB
1975			14	LB
1976			14	LB
1977			14	LB
1978			16	LB
1979			16	LB
1980			16	LB
1981			14	LB
1982			8	LB
1983			14	LB

12 yrs.   158 games

Roger LeClerc
LECLERC, ROGER
B. Oct. 1, 1936, Springfield, MA
Trinity (Connecticut) 6'3" 236 lbs.

Year	Team		Games	Pos.
1960	CHI	N	12	C, LB
1961			14	C, K
1962			14	LB, K
1963			14	LB, K
1964			14	LB, K
1965			14	LB, K
1966			14	C, K
1967	DEN	A	8	C, K

8 yrs.   104 games

Terry LeCount
LECOUNT, TERRY
B. Jul. 9, 1956, Jacksonville, FL
Florida 5'10" 176 lbs.

Year	Team		Games	Pos.
1978	SF	N	3	WR
1979			2	WR
1979	MIN	N	12	WR
1980			16	WR
1981			16	WR
1982			9	WR
1983			11	WR
1984			2	WR
1987			1	WR

8 yrs.   72 games

Jim Lecture
LECTURE, JAMES WAYNE, SR.
B. Oct. 29, 1924, Chicago, IL
Washington (Missouri)/Northwestern 5'10" 220 lbs.

Year	Team		Games	Pos.
1946	BUF	AA	1	G

Homer Ledbetter
LEDBETTER, HOMER (Doc)
B. 1908
Deceased
Arkansas 5'10" 190 lbs.

Year	Team		Games	Pos.
1932	SI	N	6	FB, HB
1932	CHIC	N	2	FB
1933			7	FB, HB

2 yrs.   15 games

Monte Ledbetter
LEDBETTER, MONTE RICHARDS
B. Aug. 13, 1943, Roanoke, LA
Northwestern State (Louisiana) 6'2" 185 lbs.

Year	Team		Games	Pos.
1967	HOU	A	5	OE

Monte Ledbetter *continued*

Year	Team		Games	Pos.
1967	BUF	A	10	FL
1968			7	FL
1969			8	WR
1969	ATL	N	2	WR

3 yrs.   32 games

Toy Ledbetter
LEDBETTER, TOY W.
B. Oct. 20, 1927, Morris, OK
Oklahoma State 5'10" 198 lbs.

Year	Team		Games	Pos.
1950	PHI	N	10	HB
1953			10	HB
1954			12	HB
1955			8	HB

4 yrs.   40 games

Hal Ledyard
LEDYARD, HAROLD
B. 1931, Montgomery, AL
D. Apr. 21, 1973, Big Sur, CA
Tennessee-Chattanooga 6'0" 185 lbs.

Year	Team		Games	Pos.
1953	SF	N	10	QB

Amp Lee
LEE, ANTHONIA WAYNE
B. Oct. 1, 1971, Chipley, FL
Florida State 5'11" 200 lbs.

Year	Team		Games	Pos.
1992	SF	N	16	RB
1993			15	RB
1994	MIN	N	13	RB
1995			16	RB
1996			16	RB

5 yrs.   76 games

Bernie Lee
LEE, BERNARD
B. 1914
Villanova 5'11" 190 lbs.

Year	Team		Games	Pos.
1938	PIT	N	3	QB

Bill Lee
LEE, WILLIAM E.
B. Aug. 19, 1911, Eutaw, AL
Alabama 6'2" 231 lbs.

Year	Team		Games	Pos.
1935	BKN	N	12	T
1936			11	T
1937			5	T
1937	GB	N	4	T
1938			11	T
1939			11	T
1940			11	T
1941			10	T
1942			1	T
1946			4	T

9 yrs.   81 games

Bivian Lee
LEE, BIVIAN LEWIS, JR.
B. Aug. 3, 1948, Austin, TX
Prairie View A&M 6'3" 200 lbs.

Year	Team		Games	Pos.
1971	NO	N	14	CB
1972			13	CB
1973			14	CB
1974			13	CB
1975			11	CB

5 yrs.   65 games

Bob Lee
LEE, ROBERT
B. 1936
Missouri 6'1" 245 lbs.

Year	Team		Games	Pos.
1960	BOS	A		G

Bob Lee
LEE, ROBERT MELVILLE (General)

Bob Lee *continued*
B. Aug. 7, 1946, Columbus, OH
Arizona State/Pacific 6'2" 195 lbs.

Year	Team		Games	Pos.
1969	MIN	N	14	QB, P
1970			6	QB
1971			14	QB, P
1972			2	QB
1973	ATL	N	12	QB
1974			9	QB
1975	MIN	N	4	QB
1976			4	QB
1977			5	QB
1978			3	QB
1979	LA	N	3	QB
1980			1	QB

12 yrs.   77 games

Bobby Lee
LEE, BOBBY D.
B. Aug. 25, 1945, Montgomery, AL
Minnesota 6'3" 200 lbs.

Year	Team		Games	Pos.
1968	STL	N	2	FL
1969	ATL	N	4	WR

2 yrs.   6 games

Byron Lee
LEE, BYRON
B. Sep. 8, 1964, Columbus, OH
Ohio State 6'2" 230 lbs.

Year	Team		Games	Pos.
1986	PHI	N	3	LB
1987			3	LB

2 yrs.   6 games

Carl Lee
LEE, CARL, III
B. Apr. 6, 1961, South Charleston, WV
Marshall 5'11" 187 lbs.

Year	Team		Games	Pos.
1983	MIN	N	16	CB, S
1984			16	CB, S
1985			15	CB, S
1986			16	CB, S
1987			12	CB
1988			16	CB
1989			16	CB
1990			16	CB
1991			14	CB
1992			16	CB
1993			16	CB
1994	NO	N	13	CB

12 yrs.   182 games

Danzell Lee
LEE, DANZELL IVAN
B. Mar. 16, 1963, Corsicana, TX
Lamar 6'2" 232 lbs.

Year	Team		Games	Pos.
1987	PIT	N	13	TE
1988	ATL	N	5	TE

2 yrs.   18 games

David Lee
LEE, DAVID ALLEN
B. Nov. 8, 1943, Shreveport, LA
Louisiana Tech 6'4" 223 lbs.

Year	Team		Games	Pos.
1966	BAL	N	14	P
1967			13	P
1968			14	P
1969			14	P
1970			14	P
1971			14	P
1972			14	P
1973			14	P
1974			14	P
1975			14	P
1976			14	P
1977			14	P
1978			16	P

13 yrs.   183 games

Dwight Lee
LEE, DWIGHT L.
B. Sep. 3, 1945, Mount Clemens, MI
Michigan State 6'2" 198 lbs.

Year	Team		Games	Pos.
1968	SF	N	2	RB
1968	ATL	N	13	RB

1 yr.   15 games

Gary Lee
LEE, GARY DEWAYNE
B. Feb. 12, 1965, Albany, GA
Georgia Tech 6'1" 202 lbs.

Year	Team		Games	Pos.
1987	DET	N	12	WR
1988			14	WR

2 yrs.   26 games

Gene Lee
LEE, EUGENE O.
B. 1922
Florida 6'3" 226 lbs.

Year	Team		Games	Pos.
1946	BOS	N	11	C

Greg Lee
LEE, GREGORY LAMONT
B. Jan. 15, 1965, Pine Bluff, AR
Arkansas State 6'1" 207 lbs.

Year	Team		Games	Pos.
1988	PIT	N	16	TE

Herman Lee
LEE, WILLIE HERMAN
B. Aug. 29, 1931, Phenix City, AL
Florida A&M 6'4" 244 lbs.

Year	Team		Games	Pos.
1957	PIT	N	8	G
1958	CHIB	N	12	T
1959			12	T
1960	CHI	N	12	T
1961			14	OT
1962			14	OT
1963			14	OT
1964			14	OT
1965			14	OT
1966			13	OT

10 yrs.   127 games

Hilary Lee
LEE, HILARY (Biff)
B. 1908
Oklahoma 6'0" 226 lbs.

Year	Team		Games	Pos.
1931	POR	N	1	G
1931	CLE	N	7	G, C
1933	CIN	N	8	G
1934	C, S		8	G

3 yrs.   24 games

Jack Lee
LEE, JOHN (Whitey)
B. 1917
Carnegie-Mellon 5'10" 205 lbs.

Year	Team		Games	Pos.
1939	PIT	N	5	B

Jacky Lee
LEE, JACK ROSS
B. Jul. 11, 1939, Minneapolis, MN
Cincinnati 6'1" 186 lbs.

Year	Team		Games	Pos.
1960	HOU	A	14	QB
1961			14	QB
1962			14	QB
1963			14	QB
1964	DEN	A	14	QB
1965			4	QB
1966	HOU	A	8	QB
1967			4	QB
1967	KC	A	9	QB
1968			6	QB
1969			3	QB

10 yrs.   104 games

Year	Team	Games	Pos.

Jeff Lee
LEE, JEFF
B. May 23, 1955, Racine, WI
Nebraska 6'2" 195 lbs.

Year	Team	Games	Pos.
1980	STL	N	4	WR

John Lee
LEE, JOHN DANA
B. Feb. 17, 1953, Fort Monmouth, NJ
Nebraska 6'2" 235 lbs.

Year	Team	Games	Pos.
1976	SD	N	14	DT
1977			12	DE
1978			1	DE
1979			10	DE
1980			11	DE
1981	NE	N	4	DE
6 yrs.	52 games		

John Lee
LEE, JOHN MIN
B. May 19, 1964, Seoul, South Korea
UCLA 5'11" 182 lbs.

Year	Team	Games	Pos.
1986	STL	N	11	K

Keith Lee
LEE, KEITH LAMAR
B. Dec. 22, 1957, San Antonio, TX
Colorado State 5'11" 193 lbs.

Year	Team	Games	Pos.
1981	NE	N	15	DB
1982			9	CB, S
1983			15	CB, S
1984			15	CB, S
1985	IND	N	14	DB
5 yrs.	68 games		

Ken Lee
LEE, KENNETH ALAN
B. Sep. 3, 1948, Honolulu, HI
Washington 6'4" 231 lbs.

Year	Team	Games	Pos.
1971	DET	N	1	LB
1972	BUF	N	12	LB
2 yrs.	13 games		

Kevin Lee
LEE, KEVIN
B. Jan. 1, 1971, Mobile, AL
Alabama 6'1" 194 lbs.

Year	Team	Games	Pos.
1995	NE	N	7	WR
1996	SF	N	2	WR
2 yrs.	9 games		

Larry Lee
LEE, LARRY DWAYNE
B. Sep. 10, 1959, Dayton, OH
UCLA 6'2" 265 lbs.

Year	Team	Games	Pos.
1981	DET	N	16	G
1982			9	G, C
1983			16	G, C
1984			15	G, C
1985			6	G, C
1985	MIA	N	5	G, C
1986			16	G, C
1987	DEN	N	9	G, C
1988			4	C, G
8 yrs.	96 games		

Mark Lee
LEE, MARK ANTHONY
B. Mar. 20, 1958, Hanford, CA
Washington 5'11" 187 lbs.

Year	Team	Games	Pos.
1980	GB	N	15	CB, S
1981			16	CB
1982			9	CB
1983			16	CB
1984			16	CB
1985			14	CB
1986			16	CB, S

Mark Lee *continued*

Year	Team	Games	Pos.
1987			12	CB, S
1988			15	CB, S
1989			12	CB, S
1990			16	CB
1991	SF	N	5	CB
1991	NO	N	3	CB
12 yrs.	165 games		

Mike Lee
LEE, MICHAEL
B. Aug. 31, 1951, San Diego, CA
Nevada-Las Vegas 6'0" 232 lbs.

Year	Team	Games	Pos.
1974	SD	N	7	LB

Monte Lee
LEE, MONTE VERN
B. Jul. 11, 1938, Ballinger, TX
Texas 6'4" 221 lbs.

Year	Team	Games	Pos.
1961	STL	N	12	LB
1963	DET	N	8	LB
1964			14	LB
1965	BAL	N	5	LB
4 yrs.	39 games		

Oudious Lee
LEE, OUDIOUS
B. Jun. 14, 1956, Omaha, NE
Nebraska 6'1" 253 lbs.

Year	Team	Games	Pos.
1980	STL	N	1	DE, DT

Ron Lee
LEE, RONNELL
B. Sep. 17, 1953, Bellaire, OH
West Virginia 6'4" 226 lbs.

Year	Team	Games	Pos.
1976	BAL	N	14	RB
1977			13	RB
1978			15	FB
3 yrs.	42 games		

Ronnie Lee
LEE, RONALD VAN
B. Dec. 24, 1956, Pine Bluff, AR
Baylor 6'4" 255 lbs.

Year	Team	Games	Pos.
1979	MIA	N	16	TE
1980			16	TE
1981			16	TE
1982			9	TE
1983	ATL	N	12	G
1984	MIA	N	16	G
1985			15	G
1986			10	G
1987			9	G, C
1988			15	OT
1989			15	OT
1990	SEA	N	15	OT
1991			10	OT
1992			9	OT
14 yrs.	184 games		

Shawn Lee
LEE, SHAWN SWABODA
B. Oct. 24, 1966, Brooklyn, NY
North Alabama 6'2" 290 lbs.

Year	Team	Games	Pos.
1988	TB	N	15	NT
1989			15	NT
1990	MIA	N	13	NT
1991			3	NT
1992	SD	N	9	DT
1993			16	DT
1994			15	DT
1995			16	DT
1996			15	DT
9 yrs.	117 games		

Willie Lee
LEE, WILLIE

Willie Lee *continued*
B. Jul. 13, 1950, Daytona Beach, FL
Bethune-Cookman 6'5" 249 lbs.

Year	Team	Games	Pos.
1976	KC	N	14	DT
1977			14	DT
2 yrs.	28 games		

Zeph Lee
LEE, ZEPHRINI
B. Jun. 17, 1963, San Francisco, CA
Southern California 6'2" 212 lbs.

Year	Team	Games	Pos.
1987	DEN	N	1	RB
1987	LARI	N	2	RB
1988			8	DB
1989			13	S
3 yrs.	24 games		

Tuffy Leemans
LEEMANS, ALPHONSE EMIL
B. Nov. 12, 1912, Superior, WI
D. Jan. 19, 1979, Hillsboro Beach, FL
Oregon/George Washington 6'0" 195 lbs.

Year	Team	Games	Pos.
1936	NYG	N	12	HB, QB
1937			9	QB, HB
1938			10	HB
1939			10	QB
1940			9	FB
1941			11	FB
1942			8	FB
1943			9	FB
8 yrs.	78 games		

Max Leetzow
LEETZOW, MAX ARTHUR
B. Sep. 17, 1943, Lodi, CA
Idaho 6'4" 240 lbs.

Year	Team	Games	Pos.
1965	DEN	A	14	DT
1966			14	DT
2 yrs.	28 games		

Dick Leeuwenburg
LEEUWENBURG, RICHARD P.
B. Mar. 26, 1942, Salt Lake City, UT
Stanford 6'5" 242 lbs.

Year	Team	Games	Pos.
1965	CHI	N	9	OT

Jay Leeuwenburg
LEEUWENBURG, JAY ROBERT
B. Jun. 18, 1969, St. Louis, MO
Colorado 6'2" 290 lbs.

Year	Team	Games	Pos.
1992	CHI	N	12	C
1993			16	C
1994			16	G
1995			16	G
1996	IND	N	15	G
5 yrs.	75 games		

Billy Lefear
LEFEAR, BILLY RAY
B. Feb. 12, 1950, Magnolia, AR
Henderson State 5'11" 197 lbs.

Year	Team	Games	Pos.
1972	CLE	N	9	RB
1973			13	RB
1974			11	RB
1975			10	WR
4 yrs.	43 games		

Gil LeFebvre
LEFEBVRE, GILBERT (Frenchy)
B. Mar. 10, 1910, Douglas, AZ
D. May 7, 1987, Bellflower, CA
none 5'6" 155 lbs.

Year	Team	Games	Pos.
1933	CIN	N	10	HB
1934	C, S	N	3	HB
1935	DET	N	1	HB
3 yrs.	14 games		

Clyde LeForce
LEFORCE, CLYDE
B. Jun. 4, 1923, Pawnee, OK
Tulsa 5'11" 176 lbs.

Year	Team	Games	Pos.
1947	DET	N	9	QB
1948			12	QB
1949			11	QB
3 yrs.	32 games		

Dick Leftridge
LEFTRIDGE, RICHARD
B. Apr. 14, 1944
West Virginia 6'2" 240 lbs.

Year	Team	Games	Pos.
1966	PIT	N	4	FB

Burnie Legette
LEGETTE, BURNIE A.
B. Dec. 5, 1970, Colorado Springs, CO
Michigan 6'0" 243 lbs.

Year	Team	Games	Pos.
1993	NE	N	7	RB
1994			3	RB
2 yrs.	10 games		

Tyrone Legette
LEGETTE, TYRONE
B. Feb. 15, 1970, Columbia, SC
Nebraska 5'9" 177 lbs.

Year	Team	Games	Pos.
1992	NO	N	8	CB
1993			14	CB
1994			15	CB
1995			16	CB
1996	TB	N	15	CB
5 yrs.	68 games		

Brad Leggett
LEGGETT, BRAD
B. Jan. 16, 1966, Vicksburg, MS
Southern California 6'4" 270 lbs.

Year	Team	Games	Pos.
1991	NO	N	4	C

Dave Leggett
LEGGETT, WILLIAM DAVID
B. Dec. 16, 1932, Lake Village, AR
Ohio State 6'2" 198 lbs.

Year	Team	Games	Pos.
1955	CHIC	N	4	QB

Earl Leggett
LEGGETT, EARL FRANKLIN
B. Mar. 5, 1933, Jacksonville, FL
Louisiana State 6'3" 264 lbs.

Year	Team	Games	Pos.
1957	CHIB	N	12	T
1958			12	T
1959			12	E, T
1960	CHI	N	12	T
1962			14	DE
1963			12	DT
1964			14	DT
1965			14	DT
1966	LA	N	10	DT
1967	NO	N	5	DT
1968			14	DT
11 yrs.	131 games		

Scott Leggett
LEGGETT, SCOTT
B. Sep. 2, 1962
Oklahoma/Central Oklahoma 6'3" 285 lbs.

Year	Team	Games	Pos.
1987	PHI	N	2	G

Chris Lehrer
LEHRER, CHRISTOPHER
B. 1894
Deceased
None 185 lbs.

Year	Team	Games	Pos.
1921	SYR	A	2	HB

Year	Team		Games	Pos.

Chris Lehrer *continued*

Year	Team		Games	Pos.
1922	ROC	N	1	FB
2 yrs.	3 games			

Jake Leicht
LEICHT, JACOB
B. Oct. 1, 1920, Jamestown, ND
Deceased
Oregon 5'9" 170 lbs.

1948	BAL	AA	14	B
1949			12	B
2 yrs.	26 games			

Jeff Leiding
LEIDING, JEFFREY JAMES
B. Oct. 28, 1961, Kansas City, MO
Texas 6'3" 232 lbs.

1986	IND	N	12	LB
1987			9	LB
2 yrs.	21 games			

Charlie Leigh
LEIGH, CHARLES IRVING
B. Oct. 29, 1945, Halifax, VA
none 5'11" 203 lbs.

1968	CLE	N	14	RB
1969			13	RB
1971	MIA	N	14	RB
1972			14	RB
1973			14	RB
1974			1	RB
1974	GB	N	12	RB
6 yrs.	82 games			

Joe Leighty
LEIGHTY, ORLAND (Dutch)
B. 1896
Deceased
Georgetown (DC) 5'11" 168 lbs.

| 1921 | WAS | A | 3 | HB |

Tony Leiker
LEIKER, TONY W.
B. Sep. 26, 1964
Stanford 6'5" 250 lbs.

| 1987 | GB | N | 1 | DE |

Rube Leisk
LEISK, WARDELL
B. 1914
Louisiana State 6'0" 195 lbs.

| 1937 | BKN | N | 11 | G, T |

Al Leith
LEITH, ALFRED
B. Mar. 14, 1903
D. Apr. 12, 1969, Media, PA
Pennsylvania 5'9" 175 lbs.

| 1926 | BKN | N | 7 | HB, QB |

Walt LeJeune
LEJEUNE, WALTER
B. 1900
Deceased
Missouri/Bethany (Kansas) 6'0" 231 lbs.

1922	AKR	N	9	G, FB, HB, T
1923			7	G, C
1924	MIL	N	10	G
1925	GB	N	10	G, T
1925	FRA	N	3	T
1926	GB	N	10	C, T, G
1927	POT	N	2	T
6 yrs.	51 games			

Frank LeMaster
LEMASTER, FRANK PRESTON
B. Mar. 12, 1952, Lexington, KY
Kentucky 6'2" 232 lbs.

1974	PHI	N	14	LB
1975			14	LB
1976			14	LB
1977			14	LB
1978			16	LB
1979			16	LB
1980			16	LB
1981			16	LB
1982			9	LB
9 yrs.	129 games			

Ray Lemek
LEMEK, RAYMOND EDWARD
B. Jun. 28, 1934, Sioux City, IA
Notre Dame 6'0" 238 lbs.

1957	WAS	N	12	T
1958			12	T
1959			11	T
1960			12	T
1961			14	OT
1962	PIT	N	14	G
1963			14	G
1964			14	G
1965			14	G
9 yrs.	117 games			

Bruce Lemmerman
LEMMERMAN, BRUCE
B. Oct. 4, 1945, Los Angeles, CA
Cal. State Northridge 6'1" 196 lbs.

1968	ATL	N	4	QB
1969			7	QB
2 yrs.	11 games			

Jim LeMoine
LEMOINE, JAMES DOUGLAS
B. Apr. 29, 1945, Alameda, CA
Utah State 6'2" 245 lbs.

1967	BUF	A	8	OT
1968	HOU	A	14	G
1969			14	G
3 yrs.	36 games			

Cliff Lemon
LEMON, CLIFFORD W.
B. 1902
Deceased
Centre 5'9" 190 lbs.

| 1926 | CHIB | N | 2 | E |

Mike Lemon
LEMON, MICHAEL DONALD
B. Feb. 26, 1951, Topeka, KS
Kansas 6'2" 218 lbs.

1975	NO	N	2	LB
1975	DEN	N	1	LB
1976	TB	N	5	LB
1977			14	LB
3 yrs.	22 games			

George Lenc
LENC, GEORGE (Chilly)
B. 1918
Augustana (Illinois) 6'3" 204 lbs.

| 1939 | BKN | N | 2 | E |

Bill Lenkaitis
LENKAITIS, WILLIAM EDWARD
B. Jun. 30, 1946, Cleveland, OH
Penn State 6'3" 255 lbs.

1968	SD	A	6	C
1969			14	C
1970	SD	N	9	G, C

Bill Lenkaitis *continued*

Year	Team		Games	Pos.
1971	NE	N	14	G
1972			14	G
1973			12	G
1974			14	G
1975			11	C
1976			14	C
1977			14	C
1978			16	C
1979			16	C
1980			16	C
1981			12	C
14 yrs.	182 games			

Reid Lennan
LENNAN, BURGESS REID
B. Aug. 17, 1922, Baltimore, MD
Maryland 6'0" 232 lbs.

1945	WAS	N	10	G
1947	LA	AA	7	G
2 yrs.	17 games			

Greg Lens
LENS, GREGORY JOSEPH
B. Mar. 11, 1945, Marshall, MN
Trinity (Texas) 6'5" 260 lbs.

1970	ATL	N	14	DT
1971			7	DT
2 yrs.	21 games			

Vince Lensing
LENSING, VINCENT
B. 1901, Evansville, IN
D. Aug. 26, 1951, Evansville, IN
None 6'0" 200 lbs.

| 1921 | EVA | A | 4 | G, T |

Jack Lentz
LENTZ, HENRY EDGAR, JR.
B. Feb. 22, 1945, Baltimore, MD
Holy Cross 6'0" 195 lbs.

1967	DEN	A	14	DB
1968			12	DB
2 yrs.	26 games			

Lawren Lentz
LENTZ, LAWREN (Pesky)
B. Oct., 1896
D. May 30, 1966
Wittenberg 5'10" 175 lbs.

| 1920 | DAY | A | 2 | HB, FB |

Bobby Leo
LEO, ROBERT SAMUEL
B. Jan. 19, 1945, Everett, MA
Harvard 5'10" 180 lbs.

1967	BOS	A	2	RB
1968			1	RB
2 yrs.	3 games			

Chuck Leo
LEO, CHARLES J.
B. Aug. 29, 1934, Niagara Falls, NY
Indiana 6'0" 238 lbs.

1960	BOS	A		G
1961			14	G
1962			7	G
1963	BUF	A	4	G
4 yrs.	25 games			

Jim Leo
LEO, JAMES
B. Jun. 18, 1937
Cincinnati 6'1" 222 lbs.

1960	NYG	N	12	LB
1962	MIN	N	14	DE
2 yrs.	26 games			

Tony Leon
LEON, ANTHONY DAVID
B. Feb. 18, 1917, Follansbee, WV
Alabama 5'9" 203 lbs.

1943	WAS	N	9	G
1944	BKN	N	10	G
1945	BOS	N	10	G
1946			10	G
4 yrs.	39 games			

Bill Leonard
LEONARD, WILLIAM, JR.
B. Apr. 27, 1927, Youngstown, OH
Notre Dame 6'2" 200 lbs.

| 1949 | BAL | AA | 11 | E |

Cecil Leonard
LEONARD, CECIL
B. Jul. 20, 1946, Sylacauga, AL
Tuskegee Institute 5'11" 165 lbs.

1969	NY	A	8	CB
1970	NYJ	N	5	CB
2 yrs.	13 games			

Jim Leonard
LEONARD, JAMES
B. Oct. 19, 1957, Santa Cruz, CA
Santa Clara 6'3" 260 lbs.

1980	TB	N	16	C
1981			16	C
1982			9	C, G
1983			15	C, G
1985	SF	N	9	C
1985	SD	N	7	C
1986			15	C
6 yrs.	87 games			

Jim Leonard
LEONARD, JAMES M.
B. Jan. 2, 1899
D. Feb. 2, 1979, Naples, FL
Colgate 6'0" 205 lbs.

| 1923 | ROC | N | 2 | T |

Jim Leonard
LEONARD, JAMES R., SR. (Big Jim)
B. Feb. 14, 1910, Philadelphia, PA
D. Nov. 28, 1993, Woodbury, NJ
Notre Dame 6'0" 202 lbs.

1934	PHI	N	9	QB, HB, FB
1935			11	FB
1936			10	QB, HB
1937			2	HB
4 yrs.	32 games			

John Leonard
LEONARD, JOHN E.
B. 1896
Deceased
Indiana 6'2" 200 lbs.

1922	CHIC	N	5	T
1923			6	T
2 yrs.	11 games			

Tony Leonard
LEONARD, ANTHONY
B. Feb. 28, 1953, Richmond, VA
Virginia Union 5'11" 169 lbs.

1976	SF	N	14	CB, S
1977			13	CB
1978			13	CB
1978	DET	N	3	CB
1979			1	CB
4 yrs.	44 games			

Bob Leonetti
LEONETTI, ROBERT P.
B. Jan. 1, 1923
Deceased
Wake Forest 6'0" 230 lbs.

Year	Team		Games	Pos.
1948	BUF	AA	2	G
1948	BKN	AA	9	G
1 yr.	11 games			

Bobby Leopold
LEOPOLD, LEROY J.
B. Oct. 18, 1957, Port Arthur, TX
Notre Dame 6'1" 220 lbs.

Year	Team		Games	Pos.
1980	SF	N	16	LB
1981			16	LB
1982			6	LB
1983			16	LB
1986	GB	N	12	LB
5 yrs.	66 games			

Barney Lepper
LEPPER, BERNARD
B. Sep., 1895
Deceased
None 5'10" 185 lbs.

Year	Team		Games	Pos.
1920	BUF	A	1	T

Jimmy Lesane
LESANE, JAMES E.
B. Mar. 8, 1931, Raleigh, NC
Virginia 5'10" 176 lbs.

Year	Team		Games	Pos.
1952	CHIB	N	10	HB
1954			3	HB
1954	BAL	N	10	HB
2 yrs.	23 games			

Darrell Lester
LESTER, DARRELL G.
B. Apr. 29, 1914
D. Jul. 30, 1993, Fort Worth, TX
Texas Christian 6'3" 220 lbs.

Year	Team		Games	Pos.
1937	GB	N	8	C
1938			10	C, G
2 yrs.	18 games			

Darrell Lester
LESTER, MARCUS DARRELL
B. Nov. 6, 1940, Lake Charles, LA
Louisiana State/McNeese State 6'2" 223 lbs.

Year	Team		Games	Pos.
1964	MIN	N	6	FB
1965	DEN	A	12	FB
1966			11	FB
3 yrs.	29 games			

Harold Lester
LESTER, HAROLD (Pinky)
B. Mar. 13, 1900, New London, CT
D. Jan. 1, 1972, Providence, RI
None 5'6" 160 lbs.

Year	Team		Games	Pos.
1926	PRO	N	8	E, T

Keith Lester
LESTER, KEITH
B. 1962
Murray State 6'5" 235 lbs.

Year	Team		Games	Pos.
1987	IND	N	1	TE

Tim Lester
LESTER, TIM LEE
B. Jun. 15, 1968, Miami, FL
Eastern Kentucky 5'9" 215 lbs.

Year	Team		Games	Pos.
1992	LARM	N	1	RB
1993			16	RB
1994			14	RB
1995	PIT		6	RB

Tim Lester continued

Year	Team		Games	Pos.
1996			16	RB
5 yrs.	61 games			

Russ Letlow
LETLOW, WILLARD RUSSELL
B. Oct. 5, 1913, Dinuba, CA
Deceased
San Francisco 6'0" 214 lbs.

Year	Team		Games	Pos.
1936	GB	N	9	G
1937			11	G
1938			11	G
1939			10	G
1940			11	G
1941			4	G
1942			11	G, T
1946			5	G
8 yrs.	72 games			

Cotton Letner
LETNER, ROBERT
B. 1939
Tennessee 6'1" 215 lbs.

Year	Team		Games	Pos.
1961	BUF	A	5	LB

John Letsinger
LETSINGER, JOHN
B. 1911
Purdue 5'10" 190 lbs.

Year	Team		Games	Pos.
1933	PIT	N	1	G

Leon Lett
LETT, LEON
B. Oct. 12, 1968, Mobile, AL
Emporia State 6'6" 290 lbs.

Year	Team		Games	Pos.
1991	DAL		5	DL
1992			16	DE, DT
1993			11	DE, DT
1994			16	DT
1995			12	DT, DE
1996			13	DT
6 yrs.	73 games			

Steve Levanitis
LEVANITIS, STEVEN J.
B. Mar. 26, 1920, Cambridge, MA
Boston College 6'1" 220 lbs.

Year	Team		Games	Pos.
1942	PHI	N	5	T

Lou Levanti
LEVANTI, LOUIS
B. Apr. 4, 1925
Illinois 6'1" 215 lbs.

Year	Team		Games	Pos.
1952	PIT	N	8	C

Jack LeVeck
LEVECK, JACK C.
B. Feb. 3, 1950, Columbus, OH
Ohio University 6'0" 224 lbs.

Year	Team		Games	Pos.
1973	STL	N	11	LB
1974			13	LB
1975	CLE	N	7	LB
3 yrs.	31 games			

Dave Levenick
LEVENICK, DAVID JOHN
B. May 28, 1959, Milwaukee, WI
Wisconsin 6'3" 220 lbs.

Year	Team		Games	Pos.
1983	ATL	N	16	LB
1984			8	LB
2 yrs.	24 games			

Dorsey Levens
LEVENS, HEBERT DORSEY
B. May 21, 1970, Syracuse, NY

Dorsey Levens continued
Georgia Tech 6'1" 229 lbs.

Year	Team		Games	Pos.
1994	GB	N	14	RB
1995			15	RB
1996			16	RB
3 yrs.	45 games			

Mike Levenseller
LEVENSELLER, MICHAEL THOMAS
B. Feb. 21, 1956, Bremerton, WA
Washington State 6'1" 181 lbs.

Year	Team		Games	Pos.
1978	BUF	N	2	WR
1978	TB	N	2	WR
1979	CIN	N	12	WR
1980			8	WR
3 yrs.	24 games			

Jim Levey
LEVEY, JAMES JULIUS
B. Sep. 13, 1906, Pittsburgh, PA
D. Mar. 14, 1970, Dallas, TX
None 5'10" 163 lbs.

Year	Team		Games	Pos.
1934	PIT	N	1	HB
1935			8	HB
1936			4	HB
3 yrs.	13 games			

Jerry LeVias
LEVIAS, JERRY
B. Sep. 5, 1946, Beaumont, TX
Southern Methodist 5'10" 177 lbs.

Year	Team		Games	Pos.
1969	HOU	A	14	WR
1970	HOU	N	14	WR
1971	SD	N	14	WR
1972			1	WR
1973			14	WR
1974			13	WR
6 yrs.	70 games			

Chuck Levy
LEVY, CHARLES
B. Jan. 7, 1972, Torrance, CA
Arizona 6'0" 197 lbs.

Year	Team		Games	Pos.
1994	ARI	N	11	RB

Harvey Levy
LEVY, HARVEY S.
B. Jun. 8, 1902
D. Sep. 29, 1986, North Olmstead, OH
Syracuse 5'10" 212 lbs.

Year	Team		Games	Pos.
1928	NYY	N	12	T, G

Len Levy
LEVY, LEONARD BERNARD (Butch)
B. Feb. 19, 1921, Minneapolis, MN
Minnesota 6'0" 256 lbs.

Year	Team		Games	Pos.
1945	CLE	N	7	T
1946	LA	N	10	G
1947	LA	AA	11	G
1948			14	G
4 yrs.	42 games			

Verne Lewellen
LEWELLEN, VERNE C.
B. Sep. 29, 1901, Lincoln, NE
D. Apr. 16, 1980, Rockville, MD
Nebraska 6'1" 182 lbs.

Year	Team		Games	Pos.
1924	GB	N	9	HB
1925			10	HB, QB
1926			12	HB
1927			10	HB
1927	NYY	N	4	HB
1928	GB	N	13	HB, QB, FB
1929			13	HB, QB
1930			14	HB, QB

Verne Lewellen continued

Year	Team		Games	Pos.
1931			7	HB
1932			14	HB, QB, FB
9 yrs.	106 games			

Albert Lewis
LEWIS, ALBERT RAY
B. Oct. 6, 1960, Mansfield, LA
Grambling State 6'2" 192 lbs.

Year	Team		Games	Pos.
1983	KC	N	16	CB
1984			15	CB
1985			16	CB
1986			15	CB
1987			12	CB
1988			14	CB
1989			16	CB
1990			15	CB
1991			8	CB
1992			9	CB
1993			14	CB
1994	LARI	N	14	CB
1995	OAK	N	16	CB
1996			16	CB
14 yrs.	196 games			

Art Lewis
LEWIS, ARTHUR E.
B. Mar. 1, 1901, Indiana
D. Oct., 1972, Cincinnati, OH
None

Year	Team		Games	Pos.
1921	CIN	A	3	T

Art Lewis
LEWIS, ARTHUR E. (Pappy)
B. Feb. 8, 1911, Middleport, OH
D. Jun. 13, 1962
Ohio University 6'3" 226 lbs.

Year	Team		Games	Pos.
1936	NYG	N	12	T, G
1938	CLE	N	8	G
1939			7	G, T
3 yrs.	27 games			

Bill Lewis
LEWIS, WILLIAM GLENN
B. Jul. 12, 1963, Sioux City, IA
Nebraska 6'7" 275 lbs.

Year	Team		Games	Pos.
1986	LARI	N	4	C
1987			8	C
1988			14	G, C
1990	PHX	N	16	C
1991			16	C
1992			6	C
1993	NE	N	7	C
7 yrs.	71 games			

Bill Lewis
LEWIS, WILTON
Texas Christian 5'11" 186 lbs.

Year	Team		Games	Pos.
1934	C, S	N	2	HB, QB

Charles Lewis
LEWIS, MAC CHARLES
B. Aug. 28, 1937, Pittsburgh, PA
Iowa 6'6" 290 lbs.

Year	Team		Games	Pos.
1959	CHIC	N	8	T, C

Cliff Lewis
LEWIS, CLIFF
B. Nov. 9, 1959, Benton, AL
Southern Mississippi 6'1" 226 lbs.

Year	Team		Games	Pos.
1981	GB	N	16	LB
1982			9	LB
1983			16	LB
1984			16	LB
4 yrs.	57 games			

Year	Team		Games	Pos.

Cliff Lewis
LEWIS, CLIFFORD A.
B. Mar. 22, 1923, Cleveland, OH
Duke 5'11" 167 lbs.

Year	Team		Games	Pos.
1946	CLE	AA	10	QB, DB
1947			13	QB, DB
1948			14	QB, DB
1949			11	QB, DB
1950	CLE	N	11	QB, DB
1951			12	QB, DB
6 yrs.	71 games			

Danny Lewis
LEWIS, DANIEL
B. Feb. 14, 1936, Freehold, NJ
Wisconsin 6'1" 199 lbs.

Year	Team		Games	Pos.
1958	DET	N	11	HB
1959			11	HB
1960			12	HB
1961			13	HB
1962			12	HB
1963			14	HB
1964			11	HB
1965	WAS	N	13	RB
1966	NYG	N	13	RB
9 yrs.	110 games			

Darren Lewis
LEWIS, DARREN
B. Nov. 7, 1968, Dallas, TX
Texas A&M 5'10" 230 lbs.

Year	Team		Games	Pos.
1991	CHI	N	15	RB
1992			16	RB
1993			2	RB
3 yrs.	33 games			

Darryl Lewis
LEWIS, DARRYL
B. Apr. 16, 1961, Mount Pleasant, TX
Texas-Arlington 6'5" 227 lbs.

Year	Team		Games	Pos.
1984	CLE	N	2	TE

Darryll Lewis
LEWIS, DARRYLL LAMONT
B. Dec. 16, 1968, Bellflower, CA
Arizona 5'9" 188 lbs.

Year	Team		Games	Pos.
1991	HOU	N	16	CB
1992			13	CB
1993			4	CB
1994			16	CB
1995			16	CB
1996			16	CB
6 yrs.	81 games			

Dave Lewis
LEWIS, DAVID RAY
B. Oct. 16, 1945, Clovis, CA
Stanford 6'2" 216 lbs.

Year	Team		Games	Pos.
1970	CIN	N	14	P, QB
1971			14	P, QB
1972			14	P
1973			14	P
4 yrs.	56 games			

Dave Lewis
LEWIS, DAVID RODNEY
B. Oct. 15, 1954, San Diego, CA
Southern California 6'4" 238 lbs.

Year	Team		Games	Pos.
1977	TB	N	14	LB
1978			16	LB
1979			16	LB
1980			16	LB
1981			13	LB
1982	SD	N	9	LB
1983	LARM	N	13	LB
7 yrs.	97 games			

David Lewis
LEWIS, DAVID WAYNE
B. Jun. 8, 1961, Portland, OR
California 6'2" 235 lbs.

Year	Team		Games	Pos.
1984	DET	N	16	TE
1985			15	TE
1986			11	TE
1987	MIA	N	5	TE
4 yrs.	47 games			

D.D. Lewis
LEWIS, DWIGHT DOUGLAS
B. Oct. 16, 1945, Knoxville, TN
Mississippi State 6'2" 218 lbs.

Year	Team		Games	Pos.
1968	DAL	N	14	LB
1970			12	LB
1971			14	LB
1972			12	LB
1973			14	LB
1974			14	LB
1975			14	LB
1976			14	LB
1977			13	LB
1978			16	LB
1979			16	LB
1980			16	LB
1981			16	LB
13 yrs.	185 games			

Eddie Lewis
LEWIS, EDWARD
B. Dec. 15, 1953, Mobile, AL
Kansas 6'0" 175 lbs.

Year	Team		Games	Pos.
1976	SF	N	14	CB
1977			14	CB, S
1978			16	CB, S
1979			7	CB
1979	DET	N	8	CB
1980			14	CB
5 yrs.	73 games			

Ernie Lewis
LEWIS, ERNEST CLAYTON
B. Nov. 20, 1923, Boonville, MO
Colorado 6'1" 211 lbs.

Year	Team		Games	Pos.
1946	CHI	AA	12	FB
1947			14	FB
1948			14	FB
1949			6	FB
4 yrs.	46 games			

Frank Lewis
LEWIS, FRANK DOUGLAS
B. Jul. 4, 1947, Houma, LA
Grambling State 6'1" 196 lbs.

Year	Team		Games	Pos.
1971	PIT	N	9	WR
1972			13	WR
1973			9	WR
1974			12	WR
1975			10	WR
1976			12	WR
1977			10	WR
1978	BUF	N	15	WR
1979			15	WR
1980			15	WR
1981			16	WR
1982			8	WR
1983			11	WR
13 yrs.	155 games			

Franklin Lewis
LEWIS, FRANKLIN
B. Aug. 2, 1902
D. Jan., 1974, Tampa, FL

Year	Team		Games	Pos.
1931	CLE	N	1	HB

Garry Lewis
LEWIS, GARRY

Garry Lewis continued
B. Aug. 25, 1967, New Orleans, LA
Alcorn State 5'11" 185 lbs.

Year	Team		Games	Pos.
1990	LARI	N	12	CB
1991			16	CB
1992	TB	N	16	CB
1993	KC	N	1	CB
4 yrs.	45 games			

Gary Lewis
LEWIS, GARY
B. Jan. 14, 1961, Oklahoma City, OK
Oklahoma State 6'3" 260 lbs.

Year	Team		Games	Pos.
1983	NO	N	6	NT

Gary Lewis
LEWIS, GARY ROGERS
B. Feb. 22, 1942, New Orleans, LA
D. Dec. 12, 1986, Seattle, WA
Washington State/Arizona State 6'3" 228 lbs.

Year	Team		Games	Pos.
1964	SF	N	8	FB
1965			14	FB
1966			14	FB
1967			13	RB
1968			14	RB
1969			9	RB
1970	NO	N	1	RB
7 yrs.	73 games			

Gary Lewis
LEWIS, GARY WAYNE
B. Dec. 30, 1958, Mount Pleasant, TX
Texas-Arlington 6'5" 234 lbs.

Year	Team		Games	Pos.
1981	GB	N	16	TE
1982			9	TE
1983			16	TE
1984			3	TE
4 yrs.	44 games			

Greg Lewis
LEWIS, GREGORY ALAN
B. Aug. 10, 1969, Port St. Joe, FL
Washington 5'10" 214 lbs.

Year	Team		Games	Pos.
1991	DEN	N	16	RB
1992			16	RB
2 yrs.	32 games			

H. Lewis
LEWIS, H.
B. 1896
Deceased
None 5'8" 175 lbs.

Year	Team		Games	Pos.
1921	LOU	A	1	G

Hal Lewis
LEWIS, HAROLD
B. Sep. 22, 1936, Houston, TX
Houston 6'0" 200 lbs.

Year	Team		Games	Pos.
1959	BAL	N	12	HB
1960	BUF	A		HB
1962	OAK	A	11	HB
3 yrs.	23 games			

Hal Lewis
LEWIS, HAROLD
B. 1943
Arizona State 6'2" 188 lbs.

Year	Team		Games	Pos.
1968	DEN	A	1	DB

Jeff Lewis
LEWIS, JEFF SCOTT
B. Apr. 17, 1973, Columbus, OH
Northern Arizona 6'1" 217 lbs.

Year	Team		Games	Pos.
1996	DEN	N	2	QB

Jermaine Lewis
LEWIS, JERMAINE
B. Oct. 16, 1974, Lanham, MD
Maryland 5'7" 172 lbs.

Year	Team		Games	Pos.
1996	BAL	N	16	WR

Jess Lewis
LEWIS, JESS
B. Jul. 28, 1947, Aumsville, OR
Oregon State 6'1" 230 lbs.

Year	Team		Games	Pos.
1970	HOU	N	9	LB

Joe Lewis
LEWIS, JOSEPH
B. Jan. 23, 1936, Los Angeles, CA
Compton JC 6'2" 256 lbs.

Year	Team		Games	Pos.
1958	PIT	N	12	T
1959			5	T
1960			12	T
1961	BAL	N	11	DT
1962	PHI	N	13	DT
5 yrs.	53 games			

John Lewis
LEWIS, JOHN
B. Mar. 8, 1962, Levittown, PA
Pittsburgh 5'10" 175 lbs.

Year	Team		Games	Pos.
1987	BUF	N	3	CB

Kenny Lewis
LEWIS, KENNETH
B. Oct. 2, 1957, Danville, VA
Virginia Tech 6'0" 190 lbs.

Year	Team		Games	Pos.
1980	NYJ	N	7	RB
1981			5	RB
1983			7	RB
3 yrs.	19 games			

Kevin Lewis
LEWIS, KEVIN
B. Nov. 14, 1966, New Orleans, LA
Northwestern State (Louisiana) 5'11" 173 lbs.

Year	Team		Games	Pos.
1990	SF	N	10	CB
1991			16	CB
2 yrs.	26 games			

Leo Lewis
LEWIS, LEO E., III (Little Leo)
B. Sep. 17, 1956, Columbia, MO
Missouri 5'8" 170 lbs.

Year	Team		Games	Pos.
1981	MIN	N	4	WR
1982			9	WR
1983			14	WR
1984			16	WR
1985			10	WR
1986			16	WR
1987			12	WR
1988			16	WR
1989			16	WR
1990	CLE	N	3	WR
1990	MIN	N	11	WR
1991			16	WR
11 yrs.	143 games			

Mark Lewis
LEWIS, MARK JOSEPH
B. May 5, 1961, Houston, TX
Texas A&M 6'2" 218 lbs.

Year	Team		Games	Pos.
1985	GB	N	1	TE
1986			16	TE
1987			1	TE
1987	DET	N	9	TE
1988			3	TE
4 yrs.	30 games			

Year	Team	Games	Pos.

Marvin Lewis
LEWIS, MARVIN VICTOR
B. Jan. 15, 1960, Texarkana, TX
Tulane 6'3" 225 lbs.

Year	Team		Games	Pos.
1982	NO	N	1	RB

Mike Lewis
LEWIS, MICHAEL HENRY
B. Jul. 14, 1949, Houston, TX
Arkansas-Pine Bluff 6'3" 255 lbs.

Year	Team		Games	Pos.
1971	ATL	N	9	DE
1972			14	DE
1973			14	DT
1974			14	DT
1975			14	DT
1976			12	DT
1977			14	DT
1978			16	DT
1979			13	DT
1980	GB	N	10	DT
10 yrs.		130 games		

Mo Lewis
LEWIS, MORRIS C.
B. Oct. 21, 1969, Atlanta, GA
Georgia 6'3" 248 lbs.

Year	Team		Games	Pos.
1991	NYJ	N	16	LB
1992			16	LB
1993			16	LB
1994			16	LB
1995			16	LB
1996			9	LB
6 yrs.		89 games		

Nate Lewis
LEWIS, NATE
B. Oct. 19, 1966, Moultrie, GA
Oregon Tech 5'11" 189 lbs.

Year	Team		Games	Pos.
1990	SD	N	12	WR
1991			16	WR
1992			15	WR
1993			16	WR
1994	CHI	N	13	WR
1995			11	WR
6 yrs.		82 games		

Ray Lewis
LEWIS, RAY ANTHONY
B. May 15, 1975, Lakeland, FL
Miami (Florida) 6'1" 235 lbs.

Year	Team		Games	Pos.
1996	BAL	N	14	LB

Reggie Lewis
LEWIS, REGINALD ANTHONY
B. Jan. 20, 1954, New Orleans, LA
Oregon/San Diego State 6'2" 260 lbs.

Year	Team		Games	Pos.
1982	NO	N	9	DE
1983			12	DE
1984			13	NT
3 yrs.		34 games		

Reggie Lewis
LEWIS, REGINALD PAUL
B. May 6, 1956, Port Arthur, TX
North Texas State 6'3" 258 lbs.

Year	Team		Games	Pos.
1979	TB	N	12	DE
1980			10	DE
2 yrs.		22 games		

Rich Lewis
LEWIS, RICHARD
B. Jun. 8, 1950, Portland, OR
Portland State 6'3" 217 lbs.

Year	Team		Games	Pos.
1972	HOU	N	10	LB
1973	BUF	N	10	LB
1974			6	LB
1974	NYJ	N	2	LB

Rich Lewis continued

Year	Team		Games	Pos.
1975			11	LB
4 yrs.		39 games		

Rod Lewis
LEWIS, RODERICK ALBERT
B. Jun. 9, 1971, Washington, DC
Arizona 6'5" 254 lbs.

Year	Team		Games	Pos.
1994	HOU	N	4	TE
1995			15	TE
1996			16	TE
3 yrs.		35 games		

Rodney Lewis
LEWIS, RODNEY EARL
B. Apr. 2, 1959, Minneapolis, MN
Nebraska 5'11" 190 lbs.

Year	Team		Games	Pos.
1982	NO	N	9	CB
1983			2	CB
1984			16	CB
3 yrs.		27 games		

Ron Lewis
LEWIS, RON
B. Nov. 17, 1972, Los Angeles, CA
Washington State 6'3" 299 lbs.

Year	Team		Games	Pos.
1995	WAS	N	4	G

Ron Lewis
LEWIS, RONALD ALEXANDER
B. Mar. 25, 1968, Jacksonville, FL
Florida State 5'11" 173 lbs.

Year	Team		Games	Pos.
1990	SF	N	8	WR
1992			5	WR
1992	GB	N	6	WR
1993			9	WR
1994			6	WR
4 yrs.		34 games		

Sherman Lewis
LEWIS, SHERMAN PAUL
B. Jun. 29, 1942, Louisville, KY
Michigan State 5'10" 180 lbs.

Year	Team		Games	Pos.
1966	NY	A	5	DB
1967			5	DB
2 yrs.		10 games		

Sid Lewis
LEWIS, SIDNEY
B. May 30, 1964, Canton, OH
Penn State 5'11" 180 lbs.

Year	Team		Games	Pos.
1987	NYJ	N	2	OT, G

Stan Lewis
LEWIS, STANLEY
B. Sep. 11, 1953, Chicago, IL
Wayne State (Nebraska) 6'4" 240 lbs.

Year	Team		Games	Pos.
1975	CLE	N	6	DE

Tahaun Lewis
LEWIS, TAHAUN
B. Sep. 29, 1968, Los Angeles, CA
Nebraska 5'10" 175 lbs.

Year	Team		Games	Pos.
1992	KC	N	9	CB

Terry Lewis
LEWIS, TERRENCE L.
B. Dec. 9, 1962, Detroit, MI
Michigan State 5'11" 193 lbs.

Year	Team		Games	Pos.
1985	SD	N	10	CB

Thomas Lewis
LEWIS, THOMAS
B. Jan. 10, 1972, Akron, OH

Thomas Lewis continued
Indiana 6'1" 185 lbs.

Year	Team		Games	Pos.
1994	NYG	N	10	WR
1995			8	WR
1996			13	WR
3 yrs.		31 games		

Tim Lewis
LEWIS, TIMOTHY JAY
B. Dec. 18, 1961, Quakertown, PA
Pittsburgh 5'11" 191 lbs.

Year	Team		Games	Pos.
1983	GB	N	16	CB, S
1984			16	CB, S
1985			16	CB
1986			3	CB, S
4 yrs.		51 games		

Tiny Lewis
LEWIS, LOREN LELAND
B. Oct. 19, 1906
Deceased
Northwestern 6'2" 210 lbs.

Year	Team		Games	Pos.
1930	POR		12	FB, QB, HB

Vernon Lewis
LEWIS, VERNON
B. Oct. 27, 1970, Houston, TX
Pittsburgh 5'10" 192 lbs.

Year	Team		Games	Pos.
1993	NE	N	10	CB, S
1994			11	CB
1995			16	CB
1996			7	CB
4 yrs.		44 games		

Will Lewis
LEWIS, WILL L.
B. Jan. 16, 1958, Quakertown, PA
Millersville State 5'9" 185 lbs.

Year	Team		Games	Pos.
1980	SEA	N	16	CB
1981			10	CB
2 yrs.		26 games		

Woodley Lewis
LEWIS, WOODLEY, JR.
B. Jun. 14, 1925, Los Angeles, CA
Oregon 6'0" 193 lbs.

Year	Team		Games	Pos.
1950	LA	N	12	DB
1951			12	DB
1952			12	DB, HB
1953			12	DB, HB
1954			12	DB, HB, E
1955			12	OE
1956	CHIC	N	12	DB
1957			12	OE
1958			12	OE
1959			12	OE
1960	DAL		6	OE
11 yrs.		126 games		

John Leypoldt
LEYPOLDT, JOHN HOWARD
B. Mar. 31, 1946, Washington, DC
Northern Virginia CC 6'2" 229 lbs.

Year	Team		Games	Pos.
1971	BUF	N	8	K
1972			14	K
1973			14	K
1974			14	K
1975			14	K
1976			1	K
1976	SEA	N	11	K
1977			13	K
1978	NO	N	2	K
8 yrs.		91 games		

Dennis Lick
LICK, DENNIS ALLEN
B. Apr. 26, 1954, Chicago, IL

Dennis Lick continued
Wisconsin 6'3" 267 lbs.

Year	Team		Games	Pos.
1976	CHI	N	14	OT
1977			14	OT
1978			16	OT
1979			16	OT
1980			16	OT
1981			3	OT
6 yrs.		79 games		

Carl Lidberg
LIDBERG, CARL L. (Cully, Swede)
B. Aug. 25, 1900
D. Jun. 26, 1987, Minneapolis, MN
Hamline/Minnesota 5'10" 191 lbs.

Year	Team		Games	Pos.
1926	GB	N	10	FB
1929			9	FB
1930			5	FB
3 yrs.		24 games		

Dave Liddick
LIDDICK, DAVID L.
B. Dec. 10, 1935, Harrisburg, PA
George Washington 6'2" 240 lbs.

Year	Team		Games	Pos.
1957	PIT	N	4	T

Frank Liebel
LIEBEL, FRANK E.
B. Nov. 19, 1919, Erie, PA
Norwich 6'1" 211 lbs.

Year	Team		Games	Pos.
1942	NYG	N	7	E
1943			10	E
1944			10	E
1945			11	E
1946			11	E
1947			11	E
1948	CHIC	N	5	E
7 yrs.		64 games		

Todd Liebenstein
LIEBENSTEIN, TODD
B. Jan. 9, 1960, Las Vegas, NV
Nevada-Las Vegas 6'6" 245 lbs.

Year	Team		Games	Pos.
1982	WAS	N	9	DE
1983			15	DE
1984			1	DE
1985			4	DE
4 yrs.		29 games		

Don Lieberum
LIEBERUM, DONALD
B. Jul. 3, 1918, Pittsburgh, PA
D. Nov., 1982, Fort Wayne, IN
Manchester (Indiana) 6'0" 175 lbs.

Year	Team		Games	Pos.
1942	NYG	N	11	B

Bob Liggett
LIGGETT, ROBERT
B. Dec. 8, 1946, Aliquippa, PA
Nebraska 6'2" 255 lbs.

Year	Team		Games	Pos.
1970	KC	N	14	DT

Alva Liles
LILES, ALVA EDISON
B. Mar. 6, 1956, Oklahoma City, OK
Boise State 6'3" 255 lbs.

Year	Team		Games	Pos.
1980	OAK	N	2	G
1980	DET	N	1	DT

Elvin Liles
LILES, ELVIN MERLE (Sonny)
B. Aug. 9, 1919, Marlow, OK
Oklahoma State 5'9" 188 lbs.

Year	Team		Games	Pos.
1943	DET	N	4	G
1944			9	G
1945				G

Year	Team	Games	Pos.

Elvin Liles *continued*

Year	Team	Games	Pos.
1945	**CLE** N	8	G
3 yrs.	22 games		

George Lilja
LILJA, GEORGE VINCENT
B. Mar. 3, 1958, Evergreen Park, IL
Michigan 6'4" 260 lbs.

1982	**LARM** N	9	C
1983	**NYJ** N	1	C
1984		3	C
1984	**CLE** N	4	OT
1985		16	OT
1986		16	G, C
1987	**DAL** N	5	C
6 yrs.	54 games		

Joe Lillard
LILLARD, JOSEPH
B. 1906
Oregon 6'0" 185 lbs.

1932	**CHIC** N	7	HB
1933		11	HB
2 yrs.	18 games		

Bob Lilly
LILLY, ROBERT LEWIS (Tiger)
B. Jul. 26, 1939, Olney, TX
Texas Christian 6'4" 256 lbs.

1961	**DAL** N	14	DE
1962		14	DE
1963		14	DE
1964		14	DE, DT
1965		14	DT
1966		14	DT
1967		14	DT
1968		14	DT
1969		14	DT
1970		14	DT
1971		14	DT
1972		14	DT
1973		14	DT
1974		14	DT
14 yrs.	196 games		

Kevin Lilly
LILLY, KEVIN PASCHAL
B. May 14, 1963, Tulsa, OK
Tulsa 6'4" 265 lbs.

1988	**SF** N	9	NT
1989	**DAL** N	1	NT
1989	**SF** N	1	NT
2 yrs.	11 games		

Sammy Lilly
LILLY, SAMUEL JULIUS, IV
B. Feb. 12, 1965, Anchorage, AK
Georgia Tech 5'9" 178 lbs.

1989	**PHI** N	15	CB, S
1990		8	CB
1990	**SD** N	2	CB
1991	**LARM** N	16	CB, S
1992		12	CB
4 yrs.	53 games		

Tony Lilly
LILLY, ROBERT ANTHONEY
B. Feb. 16, 1962, Alexandria, VA
Notre Dame 6'0" 199 lbs.

1984	**DEN** N	13	S
1985		16	S
1986		16	S
1987		13	S
4 yrs.	58 games		

Verl Lillywhite
LILLYWHITE, VERL THOMAS

Verl Lillywhite *continued*
B. Dec. 5, 1926
Southern California 5'10" 185 lbs.

1948	**SF** AA	14	B
1949		12	B
1950	**SF** N	9	FB
1951		12	HB
4 yrs.	47 games		

Garrett Limbrick
LIMBRICK, GARRETT, IV
B. Nov. 16, 1965, Houston, TX
Oklahoma State 6'2" 240 lbs.

1990	**MIA** N	7	RB

Dave Lince
LINCE, DAVID LEROY (Butch)
B. May 17, 1944, Fargo, ND
North Dakota 6'6" 258 lbs.

1966	**PHI** N	4	TE
1967		14	TE
2 yrs.	18 games		

Jeremy Lincoln
LINCOLN, JEREMY ARLO
B. Apr. 7, 1969, Toledo, OH
Tennessee 5'10" 180 lbs.

1993	**CHI** N	16	CB
1994		15	CB
1995		16	CB
1996	**STL** N	13	CB
4 yrs.	60 games		

Keith Lincoln
LINCOLN, KEITH PAYSON
B. May 8, 1939, Reading, MI
Washington State 6'2" 212 lbs.

1961	**SD** A	14	HB
1962		14	DB
1963		14	HB
1964		14	FB
1965		10	FB
1966		14	FB
1967	**BUF** A	14	RB
1968		4	RB
1968	**SD** A	5	RB
8 yrs.	103 games		

Mike Lind
LIND, MIKE HARRY
B. Feb. 22, 1940, Chicago, IL
Notre Dame 6'2" 220 lbs.

1963	**SF** N	11	FB
1964		13	FB
1965	**PIT** N	14	FB
1966		6	FB
4 yrs.	44 games		

Virgil Lindahl
LINDAHL, VIRGIL YOUNGQUIST
B. Mar. 14, 1919, Tilden, NE
Wayne State (Nebraska)/Kentucky 6'1" 197 lbs.

1945	**NYG** N	2	G

Errol Linden
LINDEN, ERROL JOSEPH
B. Oct. 21, 1937, New Orleans, LA
Houston 6'5" 258 lbs.

1961	**CLE** N	10	OT
1962	**MIN** N	12	OT
1963		14	OT
1964		14	OT
1965		14	OT
1966	**ATL** N	14	OT
1967		14	OT

Errol Linden *continued*

1968		14	OT
1969	**NO** N	14	OT
1970		14	OT
10 yrs.	134 games		

Luther Lindon
LINDON, LUTHER W. (Luke)
B. Jun. 23, 1917, Salyersville, KY
Deceased
Kentucky 5'10" 243 lbs.

1944	**DET** N	10	T
1945		4	T
2 yrs.	14 games		

Allen Lindow
LINDOW, ALLEN L.
B. 1919
Deceased
Washington (Missouri) 6'0" 165 lbs.

1945	**CHIC** N	1	B

Paul Lindquist
LINDQUIST, PAUL
B. 1938
New Hampshire 6'3" 265 lbs.

1961	**BOS** A	2	DT

Everett Lindsay
LINDSAY, EVERETT ERIC
B. Sep. 18, 1970, Burlington, IA
Mississippi 6'4" 290 lbs.

1993	**MIN** N	12	G
1995		16	G
2 yrs.	28 games		

Hub Lindsay
LINDSAY, HUBERT
B. 1945
Wyoming 5'11" 196 lbs.

1968	**DEN** A	3	RB

Dale Lindsey
LINDSEY, PHILIP DALE
B. Jan. 18, 1943, Bedford, IN
Kentucky/Western Kentucky 6'3" 224 lbs.

1965	**CLE** N	14	LB
1966		13	LB
1967		14	LB
1968		12	LB
1969		14	LB
1970		14	LB
1971		11	LB
1972		11	LB
1973	**NO** N	5	LB
1973	**CLE** N	8	LB
9 yrs.	116 games		

Jim Lindsey
LINDSEY, JAMES EDGAR
B. Nov. 24, 1944, Caldwell, AR
Arkansas 6'2" 206 lbs.

1966	**MIN** N	14	HB
1967		9	RB
1968		14	RB
1969		10	RB
1970		11	RB
1971		14	RB
6 yrs.	72 games		

Menz Lindsey
LINDSEY, ELLIS MENZIES (Flash)
B. 1898, Boonville, IN
D. Sep. 20, 1961, Evansville, IN
Wabash 5'6" 130 lbs.

1921	**EVA** A	5	QB

Vic Lindskog
LINDSKOG, VICTOR J.
B. Dec. 3, 1915, Roundup, MT
Stanford 6'1" 203 lbs.

1944	**PHI** N	7	C, LB
1945		10	C, LB
1946		11	C, LB
1947		10	C, LB
1948		12	C, LB
1949		5	C
1950		12	C
1951		11	C
8 yrs.	78 games		

Chris Lindstrom
LINDSTROM, CHRISTOPHER ANDREW
B. Aug. 3, 1960, Weymouth, MA
Boston University 6'7" 260 lbs.

1983	**CIN** N	1	NT
1985	**TB** N	13	DE
1987	**KC** N	3	DE
3 yrs.	17 games		

Dave Lindstrom
LINDSTROM, DAVID ALAN
B. Nov. 16, 1954, Cambridge, MA
Boston University 6'6" 250 lbs.

1978	**KC** N	16	DE
1979		13	DE
1980		16	DE
1981		16	DE
1982		9	DE
1983		16	DE
1984		16	DE
1985		16	DE
8 yrs.	118 games		

Bill Line
LINE, BILLY BOYD, JR.
B. Aug. 11, 1948, San Angelo, TX
Air Force/Southern Methodist 6'7" 260 lbs.

1972	**CHI** N	13	DT

Bob Lingenfelter
LINGENFELTER, ROBERT
B. Sep. 1, 1954, Norfolk, NE
Nebraska 6'7" 277 lbs.

1977	**CLE** N	14	OT
1978	**MIN** N	5	OT
2 yrs.	19 games		

Goran Lingmerth
LINGMERTH, GORAN (Swede)
B. Nov. 11, 1964, Sweden
Northern Arizona 5'8" 160 lbs.

1987	**CLE** N	1	K

Adam Lingner
LINGNER, ADAM JAMES
B. Nov. 2, 1960, Indianapolis, IN
Illinois 6'4" 260 lbs.

1983	**KC** N	16	C
1984		16	C, G
1985		16	C, G
1986		12	C, G
1987	**BUF** N	12	C
1988	**KC** N	16	C
1989	**BUF** N	16	C
1990		16	C
1991		16	C
1992		16	C
1993		16	C
1994		16	C
1995		16	C
13 yrs.	200 games		

Year	Team	Games	Pos.

Chim Lingrel
LINGREL, CHIM (TOMAHAWK)
B. 1895
Deceased
Carlisle 6'2" 200 lbs.

Year	Team	Games	Pos.
1923	**OOR** N	6	HB, FB

Toni Linhart
LINHART, ANTON HANSJORG
B. Jul. 24, 1942, Donawitz, Austria
Austrian Technical* 6'0" 178 lbs.

Year	Team	Games	Pos.
1972	**NO** N	2	K
1974	**BAL** N	14	K
1975		14	K
1976		14	K
1977		14	K
1978		16	K
1979		3	K
1979	**NYJ** N	5	K
7 yrs.	82 games		

Ray Lininger
LININGER, RAYMOND JACK
B. Jun. 17, 1927, Van Wert, OH
Ohio State 5'11" 217 lbs.

Year	Team	Games	Pos.
1950	**DET** N	12	C
1951		12	C
2 yrs.	24 games		

Jack Linn
LINN, JACK LAROY, JR.
B. Jun. 10, 1967, Sewickley, PA
West Virginia 6'5" 290 lbs.

Year	Team	Games	Pos.
1991	**IND** N	1	OT
1992	**DET** N	4	OT
1993		3	OT
1993	**CIN** N	3	G
3 yrs.	11 games		

Frank Linnan
LINNAN, FRANCIS
B. 1899
Deceased
Marquette 6'2" 198 lbs.

Year	Team	Games	Pos.
1922	**RAC** N	3	T, G
1926		2	T, G
2 yrs.	5 games		

Aubrey Linne
LINNE, AUBREY, JR.
B. Apr. 19, 1939
Texas Christian 6'7" 235 lbs.

Year	Team	Games	Pos.
1961	**BAL** N	1	OE

Larry Linne
LINNE, LARRY
B. Jul. 20, 1962
Texas-El Paso 6'1" 185 lbs.

Year	Team	Games	Pos.
1987	**NE** N	3	WR

Chris Linnin
LINNIN, CHRIS
B. May 4, 1957, Pasadena, CA
Washington 6'4" 255 lbs.

Year	Team	Games	Pos.
1980	**NYG** N	10	DT

Joe Lintzenich
LINTZENICH, JOSEPH F.
B. Mar. 26, 1908
D. Jun. 23, 1985, St. Louis, MO
St. Louis 5'11" 187 lbs.

Year	Team	Games	Pos.
1930	**CHIB** N	13	HB, FB
1931		11	HB
2 yrs.	24 games		

Augie Lio
LIO, AGOSTINO SALVATORE
B. Apr. 30, 1918, East Boston, MA
D. Sep. 3, 1989, Clifton, NJ
Georgetown (DC) 6'0" 234 lbs.

Year	Team	Games	Pos.
1941	**DET** N	10	G
1942		11	G
1943		10	G, T
1944	**BOS** N	10	G
1945		10	G
1946	**PHI** N	11	G
1947	**BAL** AA	10	G
7 yrs.	72 games		

James Lipinski
LIPINSKI, JAMES J. (J.J.)
B. 1927
Fairmont State 6'4" 238 lbs.

Year	Team	Games	Pos.
1950	**CHIC** N	1	T

Ronnie Lippett
LIPPETT, RONNIE LEON
B. Dec. 10, 1960, Melbourne, FL
Miami (Florida) 5'11" 180 lbs.

Year	Team	Games	Pos.
1983	**NE** N	16	CB
1984		16	CB
1985		16	CB
1986		15	CB
1987		12	CB
1988		15	CB
1990		16	CB
1991		16	CB
8 yrs.	122 games		

Louis Lipps
LIPPS, LOUIS ADAM (Hot)
B. Aug. 9, 1962, New Orleans, LA
Southern Mississippi 5'10" 185 lbs.

Year	Team	Games	Pos.
1984	**PIT** N	14	WR
1985		16	WR
1986		13	WR
1987		4	WR
1988		16	WR
1989		16	WR
1990		14	WR
1991		15	WR
1992	**NO** N	2	WR
9 yrs.	110 games		

Big Daddy Lipscomb
LIPSCOMB, EUGENE
B. Aug. 9, 1931, Detroit, MI
D. May 10, 1963, Baltimore, MD
None 6'6" 284 lbs.

Year	Team	Games	Pos.
1953	**LA** N	2	DE
1954		11	DT
1955		12	DT
1956	**BAL** N	11	DT
1957		12	DT
1958		12	DT
1959		12	DT
1960		12	DT
1961	**PIT** N	14	DT
1962		14	DT
10 yrs.	112 games		

Paul Lipscomb
LIPSCOMB, PAUL F.
B. Jan. 13, 1923, Benton, IL
D. Aug. 20, 1964
Tennessee 6'5" 246 lbs.

Year	Team	Games	Pos.
1945	**GB** N	10	T
1946		11	T
1947		12	T
1948		12	T
1949		12	T
1950	**WAS** N	12	T
1951		12	T
1952		12	T

Paul Lipscomb continued

Year	Team	Games	Pos.
1953		12	T
1954		1	T
1954	**CHIB** N	12	T
10 yrs.	118 games		

John Lipski
LIPSKI, JOHN (Bull)
B. 1909
Temple 5'11" 200 lbs.

Year	Team	Games	Pos.
1933	**PHI** N	8	C
1934		11	C
2 yrs.	19 games		

Don Lisbon
LISBON, DONALD
B. Jan. 15, 1941
Bowling Green 6'0" 194 lbs.

Year	Team	Games	Pos.
1963	**SF** N	14	HB, DB
1964		6	HB
2 yrs.	20 games		

Rusty Lisch
LISCH, RUSSELL JOHN
B. Dec. 21, 1956, Belleville, IL
Notre Dame 6'4" 215 lbs.

Year	Team	Games	Pos.
1980	**STL** N	2	QB
1981		9	QB
1982		8	QB
1983		4	QB
1984	**CHI** N	7	QB
5 yrs.	30 games		

Tony Liscio
LISCIO, ANTHONY FRED
B. Jul. 2, 1940, Pittsburgh, PA
Tulsa 6'5" 251 lbs.

Year	Team	Games	Pos.
1963	**DAL** N	7	OT
1964		10	OT
1966		14	OT
1967		14	G, OT
1968		14	OT
1969		14	OT
1970		11	OT
1971		5	OT
8 yrs.	89 games		

Pete Liske
LISKE, PETER A.
B. May 24, 1942, Plainfield, NJ
Penn State 6'2" 199 lbs.

Year	Team	Games	Pos.
1964	**NY** A	4	QB, DB
1969	**DEN** A	7	QB
1970	**DEN** A	7	QB
1971	**PHI** N	14	QB
1972		14	QB
5 yrs.	46 games		

Paul Liston
LISTON, EDWARD PAUL
B. Jul. 31, 1903, Pennsylvania
D. May, 1979, Boston, MA
Georgetown (DC) 5'11" 185 lbs.

Year	Team	Games	Pos.
1930	**NEW** N	1	G

Ed Listopad
LISTOPAD, ED
B. Aug. 28, 1929, Baltimore, MD
Wake Forest 6'2" 230 lbs.

Year	Team	Games	Pos.
1952	**CHIC** N	4	G

Greg Liter
LITER, GREG
B. Dec. 31, 1963
Iowa State 6'6" 275 lbs.

Year	Team	Games	Pos.
1987	**SF** N	1	DE

Greg Liter continued

Year	Team	Games	Pos.
1987	**PHI** N	1	DE
1 yr.	2 games		

Red Litkus
LITKUS, BERNARD HOWARD
B. 1896
Deceased
None 187 lbs.

Year	Team	Games	Pos.
1921	**WAS** A	3	T, E

David Little
LITTLE, DAVID GENE
B. Apr. 18, 1961, Selma, CA
Middle Tennessee State 6'2" 236 lbs.

Year	Team	Games	Pos.
1984	**KC** N	10	TE
1985	**PHI** N	15	TE
1986		16	TE
1987		12	TE
1988		10	TE
1989		15	TE
1990	**PHX** N	11	TE
1991	**DET** N	2	TE
8 yrs.	91 games		

David Little
LITTLE, DAVID LAMAR
B. Jan. 3, 1959, Miami, FL
Florida 6'1" 230 lbs.

Year	Team	Games	Pos.
1981	**PIT** N	16	LB
1982		9	LB
1983		16	LB
1984		16	LB
1985		16	LB
1986		16	LB
1987		12	LB
1988		16	LB
1989		16	LB
1990		16	LB
1991		14	LB
1992		16	LB
12 yrs.	179 games		

Everett Little
LITTLE, EVERETT
B. Jun. 12, 1954, Lufkin, TX
Houston 6'4" 265 lbs.

Year	Team	Games	Pos.
1976	**TB** N	10	G, OT

Floyd Little
LITTLE, FLOYD DOUGLAS
B. Jul. 4, 1942, New Haven, CT
Syracuse 5'10" 196 lbs.

Year	Team	Games	Pos.
1967	**DEN** A	13	RB
1968		11	RB
1969		9	RB
1970	**DEN** N	14	RB
1971		14	RB
1972		14	RB
1973		14	RB
1974		14	RB
1975		14	RB
9 yrs.	117 games		

George Little
LITTLE, GEORGE WILLARD
B. Jun. 27, 1963, Duquesne, PA
Iowa 6'4" 278 lbs.

Year	Team	Games	Pos.
1985	**MIA** N	14	NT
1986		16	NT
1987		9	DE
3 yrs.	39 games		

Jack Little
LITTLE, JACK H.
B. 1931
Texas A&M 6'4" 235 lbs.

Year	Team	Games	Pos.
1953	**BAL** N	9	T

Year	Team		Games	Pos.

Jack Little continued

Year	Team		Games	Pos.
1954			11	T
2 yrs.	20 games			

John Little
LITTLE, JOHN D., JR.
B. May 3, 1947, Tallulah, LA
Oklahoma State 6'3" 241 lbs.

Year	Team		Games	Pos.
1970	NYJ	N	14	LB
1971			14	DT, DE
1972			14	DT, DE
1973			14	DT
1974			14	DE
1975	HOU	N	14	DE, DT
1976			14	DT
1977	BUF	N	12	DT
8 yrs.	110 games			

Larry Little
LITTLE, LARRY CHATMAN
B. Nov. 2, 1945, Groveland, GA
Bethune-Cookman 6'1" 266 lbs.

Year	Team		Games	Pos.
1967	SD	A	10	G
1968			14	DT, G
1969	MIA	A	12	G
1970	MIA	N	14	G, OT
1971			14	G
1972			14	G
1973			13	G
1974			14	G
1975			14	G
1976			14	G
1977			14	G
1978			16	G, OT
1979			15	G, OT
1980			5	OT
14 yrs.	183 games			

Lou Little
PICCOLO, LUIGI
B. Dec. 6, 1893, Boston, MA
D. May 29, 1979, Delray Beach, FL
Vermont/Pennsylvania 6'0" 205 lbs.

Year	Team		Games	Pos.
1920	BUF	A	6	T
1921			7	T
2 yrs.	13 games			

Steve Little
LITTLE, STEVE
B. Feb. 19, 1956, Springfield, IL
Arkansas 6'0" 180 lbs.

Year	Team		Games	Pos.
1978	STL	N	11	K, P
1979			16	P, K
1980			6	P, K
3 yrs.	33 games			

Carl Littlefield
LITTLEFIELD, CARL (Moon Eyes)
B. 1916
Washington State 6'0" 200 lbs.

Year	Team		Games	Pos.
1938	CLE	N	9	FB, HB
1939	PIT	N	10	FB
1940			1	B
3 yrs.	20 games			

Joe Little Twig
JOHNSON, JOSEPH
B. 1893
D. 1937
Carlisle 5'11" 183 lbs.

Year	Team		Games	Pos.
1922	OOR	N	2	T, E
1923			11	E, T
1924	RI	N	7	E, T
1925			10	E
1926	CAN	N	6	E
1926	AKR	N	1	E
5 yrs.	37 games			

Harry Livers
LIVERS, HAROLD (Mickey)
B. Nov. 30, 1895
D. Sep., 1977, Hampton, VA
Georgetown (DC) 5'10" 180 lbs.

Year	Team		Games	Pos.
1921	WAS	A	1	FB

Virgil Livers
LIVERS, VIRGIL CHESTER, JR.
B. Mar. 26, 1952, Bardstown, KY
Western Kentucky 5'9" 178 lbs.

Year	Team		Games	Pos.
1975	CHI	N	14	DB
1976			14	CB
1977			14	CB
1978			13	CB
1979			13	CB
5 yrs.	68 games			

Andy Livingston
LIVINGSTON, ANDREW LEON
B. Oct. 21, 1944, Eufaula, OK
Phoenix JC 6'0" 234 lbs.

Year	Team		Games	Pos.
1964	CHI	N	2	HB
1965			14	HB
1967			12	RB
1968			4	RB
1969	NO	N	14	RB
1970			1	RB
6 yrs.	47 games			

Bruce Livingston
LIVINGSTON, BRUCE
B. Aug. 7, 1963
Arkansas Tech 5'10" 169 lbs.

Year	Team		Games	Pos.
1987	DAL	N	3	CB, S

Cliff Livingston
LIVINGSTON, CLIFFORD LYMAN
B. Jul. 2, 1930, Compton, CA
UCLA 6'3" 212 lbs.

Year	Team		Games	Pos.
1954	NYG	N	12	E
1955			4	E
1956			12	E
1957			10	E
1958			12	E
1959			12	LB
1960			11	LB
1961			12	LB
1962	MIN	N	12	LB
1963	LA	N	14	LB
1964			14	LB
1965			10	LB
12 yrs.	135 games			

Dale Livingston
LIVINGSTON, DALE ROGER
B. Mar. 12, 1945, Plymouth, MI
Eastern Michigan/Western Michigan 6'0" 210 lbs.

Year	Team		Games	Pos.
1968	CIN	A	12	K, P
1969			12	K, P
1970	GB	N	14	K, P
3 yrs.	38 games			

Howie Livingston
LIVINGSTON, HOWARD
B. May 15, 1922, Los Angeles, CA
D. Jul. 16, 1994
Fullerton JC 6'1" 183 lbs.

Year	Team		Games	Pos.
1944	NYG	N	9	HB
1945			10	FB
1946			10	HB
1947			10	HB
1948	WAS	N	7	HB
1949			12	HB
1950			4	HB
1950	SF		7	HB

Howie Livingston continued

Year	Team		Games	Pos.
1953	CHIB	N	2	HB
8 yrs.	71 games			

Mike Livingston
LIVINGSTON, MICHAEL PAUL
B. Nov. 14, 1945, Dallas, TX
Southern Methodist 6'3" 211 lbs.

Year	Team		Games	Pos.
1968	KC	A	2	QB
1969			14	QB
1970	KC	N	2	QB
1971			3	QB
1972			5	QB
1973			8	QB
1974			9	QB
1975			7	QB
1976			14	QB
1977			13	QB
1978			14	QB
1979			5	QB
12 yrs.	95 games			

Ted Livingston
LIVINGSTON, THEODORE ALFRED
B. Feb. 18, 1913, Geneseo, KS
D. Jun., 1984, Cleveland, OH
Kansas State/Indiana 6'3" 219 lbs.

Year	Team		Games	Pos.
1937	CLE	N	11	T
1938			9	T
1939			11	G, T
1940			9	G
4 yrs.	40 games			

Walt Livingston
LIVINGSTON, WALTER
B. 1935, Newberry, SC
Heidelberg 6'0" 185 lbs.

Year	Team		Games	Pos.
1960	BOS	A		HB

Warren Livingston
LIVINGSTON, WARREN
B. Jul. 5, 1938, Eufaula, OK
Arizona 5'10" 185 lbs.

Year	Team		Games	Pos.
1961	DAL	N	8	DB
1962			3	DB
1963			14	S
1964			14	DB
1965			14	DB
1966			14	DB
6 yrs.	67 games			

Bob Livingstone
LIVINGSTONE, ROBERT E.
B. May 11, 1922, Hammond, IN
Notre Dame 6'0" 173 lbs.

Year	Team		Games	Pos.
1948	CHI	AA	13	HB, DB
1949			6	HB, DB
1949	BUF	AA	5	HB, DB
1950	BAL	N	11	HB, DB
3 yrs.	35 games			

Dan Lloyd
LLOYD, DANIEL B.
B. Nov. 9, 1953, Heber, UT
Washington 6'2" 225 lbs.

Year	Team		Games	Pos.
1976	NYG	N	14	LB
1977			14	LB
1978			16	LB
1979			13	LB
4 yrs.	57 games			

Dave Lloyd
LLOYD, DAVID ALLEN
B. Nov. 9, 1936, Sapulpa, OK
Georgia 6'3" 247 lbs.

Year	Team		Games	Pos.
1959	CLE	N	12	C

Dave Lloyd continued

Year	Team		Games	Pos.
1960			12	C
1961			14	C
1962	DET	N	14	C, LB
1963	PHI	N	14	LB
1964			11	LB
1965			13	LB
1966			14	LB
1967			14	LB
1968			13	LB
1969			14	LB
1970			12	LB
12 yrs.	157 games			

Doug Lloyd
LLOYD, DOUGLAS G.
B. Aug. 31, 1965, Beaver Dam, WI
North Dakota State 6'1" 220 lbs.

Year	Team		Games	Pos.
1991	LARI	N	1	RB

Greg Lloyd
LLOYD, GREGORY LENARD
B. May 26, 1965, Miami, FL
Fort Valley State 6'2" 234 lbs.

Year	Team		Games	Pos.
1988	PIT	N	9	LB
1989			16	LB
1990			15	LB
1991			16	LB
1992			16	LB
1993			15	LB
1994			15	LB
1995			16	LB
1996			1	LB
9 yrs.	119 games			

Jeff Lloyd
LLOYD, JEFFERY JOHN
B. Mar. 14, 1954, St. Mary's, PA
West Texas State 6'6" 255 lbs.

Year	Team		Games	Pos.
1976	BUF	N	9	DT
1978	KC	N	16	DE
2 yrs.	25 games			

Bill Lobenstein
LOBENSTEIN, BILL
B. May 11, 1961
Wisconsin-Whitewater 6'3" 261 lbs.

Year	Team		Games	Pos.
1987	DEN	N	3	DE, NT

Greg Loberg
LOBERG, GREG
B. Dec. 7, 1961, San Rafael, CA
California 6'4" 264 lbs.

Year	Team		Games	Pos.
1987	NO	N	3	G

Charles Lockett
LOCKETT, CHARLES EDWARD
B. Oct. 1, 1965, Los Angeles, CA
Long Beach State 6'0" 179 lbs.

Year	Team		Games	Pos.
1987	PIT	N	11	WR
1988			16	WR
2 yrs.	27 games			

Dannie Lockett
LOCKETT, DANNIE KEY
B. Jul. 11, 1964, Fort Valley, GA
Arizona 6'2" 228 lbs.

Year	Team		Games	Pos.
1987	DET	N	13	LB
1988			16	LB
2 yrs.	29 games			

Frank Lockett
LOCKETT, FRANK ARTHUR
B. Jun. 1, 1957, Independence, LA
Nebraska 5'11" 192 lbs.

Year	Team		Games	Pos.
1985	MIA	N	3	WR

Year	Team		Games	Pos.

J.W. Lockett
LOCKETT, J.W.
B. Mar. 23, 1937, Bardwell, TX
Central Oklahoma 6'2" 229 lbs.

Year	Team		Games	Pos.
1961	**DAL**	N	14	FB
1962			14	FB
1963	**BAL**	N	12	FB
1964	**WAS**	N	14	FB
4 yrs.	54 games			

Wade Lockett
LOCKETT, WADE
B. Feb. 13, 1964, Alabama
Fullerton State 6'1" 190 lbs.

Year	Team		Games	Pos.
1987	**LARI**	N	2	WR

Eugene Lockhart
LOCKHART, EUGENE, JR.
B. Mar. 8, 1961, Crockett, TX
Houston 6'2" 235 lbs.

Year	Team		Games	Pos.
1984	**DAL**	N	15	LB
1985			16	LB
1986			16	LB
1987			9	LB
1988			16	LB
1989			16	LB
1990			16	LB
1991	**NE**	N	16	LB
1992			16	LB
9 yrs.	136 games			

Spider Lockhart
LOCKHART, CARL FORD
B. Apr. 6, 1943, Dallas, TX
North Texas State 6'2" 176 lbs.

Year	Team		Games	Pos.
1965	**NYG**	N	14	DB, P
1966			14	DB, P
1967			12	DB
1968			14	DB, P
1969			11	S
1970			14	S
1971			13	S
1972			13	S
1973			14	S
1974			14	S
1975			12	S
11 yrs.	145 games			

Billy Locklin
LOCKLIN, BILLY RAY
B. Aug. 9, 1937
New Mexico State 6'2" 225 lbs.

Year	Team		Games	Pos.
1960	**OAK**	A		LB

Kerry Locklin
LOCKLIN, KERRY BARTH
B. Sep. 9, 1959, Las Cruces, NM
New Mexico State 6'3" 217 lbs.

Year	Team		Games	Pos.
1982	**LARM**	N	6	TE
1987	**DEN**	N	3	TE
2 yrs.	9 games			

Scott Lockwood
LOCKWOOD, SCOTT NELSON
B. Mar. 23, 1968, Los Angeles, CA
Southern California 5'10" 196 lbs.

Year	Team		Games	Pos.
1992	**NE**	N	4	RB
1993			2	RB
2 yrs.	6 games			

Mike Lodish
LODISH, MICHAEL TIMOTHY
B. Aug. 11, 1967, Detroit, MI
UCLA 6'3" 269 lbs.

Year	Team		Games	Pos.
1990	**BUF**	N	12	NT
1991			16	NT
1992			16	NT
1993			15	NT

Mike Lodish continued

Year	Team		Games	Pos.
1994			16	NT
1995	**DEN**	N	16	DT
1996			16	NT
7 yrs.	107 games			

Dick Loepfe
LOEPFE, RICHARD
B. Jan. 1, 1922, Milwaukee, WI
Wisconsin 6'2" 230 lbs.

Year	Team		Games	Pos.
1948	**CHIC**	N	7	T
1949			6	T
2 yrs.	13 games			

Chuck Loewen
LOEWEN, CHARLES DUANE
B. Jan. 23, 1957, Mountain Lake, MN
South Dakota State 6'3" 259 lbs.

Year	Team		Games	Pos.
1980	**SD**	N	16	G, OT
1981			9	G, OT
1982			9	G, OT
1984			13	G, OT
4 yrs.	47 games			

James Lofton
LOFTON, JAMES DAVID
B. Jul. 5, 1956, Fort Ord, CA
Stanford 6'3" 195 lbs.

Year	Team		Games	Pos.
1978	**GB**	N	16	WR
1979			16	WR
1980			16	WR
1981			16	WR
1982			9	WR
1983			16	WR
1984			16	WR
1985			16	WR
1986			15	WR
1987	**LARI**	N	12	WR
1988			16	WR
1989	**BUF**	N	12	WR
1990			16	WR
1991			15	WR
1992			16	WR
1993	**LARM**	N	1	WR
1993	**PHI**		9	WR
16 yrs.	233 games			

Oscar Lofton
LOFTON, OSCAR
B. 1938
Southeastern Louisiana 6'6" 218 lbs.

Year	Team		Games	Pos.
1960	**BOS**	A		OE

Steve Lofton
LOFTON, STEVEN LYNN
B. Nov. 26, 1968, Jacksonville, FL
Texas A&M 5'9" 180 lbs.

Year	Team		Games	Pos.
1991	**PHX**	N	11	CB
1992			4	CB
1993			13	CB
1995	**CAR**	N	9	CB
1996			11	CB
5 yrs.	48 games			

Andy Logan
WYHOWANEC, ANDREW
B. Feb. 17, 1918, Connorville, OH
Case Western Reserve 6'0" 222 lbs.

Year	Team		Games	Pos.
1941	**DET**	N	7	T, C

Chuck Logan
LOGAN, CHARLES RUSSELL
B. Apr. 10, 1943, Chicago, IL
Northwestern 6'4" 215 lbs.

Year	Team		Games	Pos.
1964	**PIT**	N	14	OE
1965	**STL**	N	4	OE
1967			14	OE

Chuck Logan continued

Year	Team		Games	Pos.
1968			14	OE
4 yrs.	46 games			

Dave Logan
LOGAN, DAVID
B. Feb. 2, 1954, Fargo, ND
Colorado 6'4" 221 lbs.

Year	Team		Games	Pos.
1976	**CLE**	N	14	WR
1977			14	WR
1978			16	WR
1979			16	WR
1980			16	WR
1981			14	WR
1982			9	WR
1983			16	WR
1984	**DEN**	N	4	WR
9 yrs.	119 games			

Dave Logan
LOGAN, DAVID
B. Oct. 25, 1956, Pittsburgh, PA
Pittsburgh 6'2" 250 lbs.

Year	Team		Games	Pos.
1979	**TB**	N	5	DT
1980			16	DT, DE
1981			16	NT
1982			9	NT
1983			16	NT
1984			16	NT
1985			16	NT
1986			16	NT
1987	**GB**	N	2	NT
9 yrs.	112 games			

Dick Logan
LOGAN, RICHARD L.
B. May 4, 1930, Mansfield, OH
Ohio State 6'2" 238 lbs.

Year	Team		Games	Pos.
1952	**GB**	N	7	T
1953			12	G
2 yrs.	19 games			

Ernie Logan
LOGAN, ERNEST EDWARD
B. May 18, 1968, Fort Bragg, NC
East Carolina 6'3" 276 lbs.

Year	Team		Games	Pos.
1991	**CLE**	N	15	DL
1992			16	DE, DT
1993	**ATL**	N	8	DE
1995	**JAC**	N	15	DE
1996			4	DE
5 yrs.	58 games			

James Logan
LOGAN, JAMES
B. Dec. 6, 1972, Opp, AL
Memphis 6'2" 210 lbs.

Year	Team		Games	Pos.
1995	**HOU**	N	3	LB
1995	**CIN**	N	1	LB
1995	**SEA**	N	6	LB
1996			6	LB
2 yrs.	16 games			

Jerry Logan
LOGAN, JERRY DON
B. Aug. 27, 1941, Graham, TX
West Texas State 6'1" 188 lbs.

Year	Team		Games	Pos.
1963	**BAL**	N	14	DB
1964			14	DB
1965			14	DB
1966			14	DB
1967			14	DB
1968			14	DB
1969			14	S
1970			14	S
1971			14	S
1972			14	S
10 yrs.	140 games			

Jim Logan
LOGAN, JAMES ZIMMERMAN
B. Dec. 22, 1916, Richmond, IN
Indiana 5'11" 190 lbs.

Year	Team		Games	Pos.
1943	**CHIB**	N	9	G

Marc Logan
LOGAN, MARC ANTHONY
B. May 9, 1965, Lexington, KY
Kentucky 5'11" 204 lbs.

Year	Team		Games	Pos.
1987	**CIN**	N	3	RB
1988			9	RB
1989	**MIA**	N	11	RB
1990			16	RB
1991			16	RB
1992	**SF**	N	16	RB
1993			14	RB
1994			10	RB
1995	**WAS**	N	16	RB
1996			14	RB
10 yrs.	125 games			

Obert Logan
LOGAN, OBERT CLARK
B. Dec. 6, 1941, Yoakum, TX
Trinity (Texas) 5'10" 180 lbs.

Year	Team		Games	Pos.
1965	**DAL**	N	14	DB
1966			14	DB
1967	**NO**	N	14	DB
3 yrs.	42 games			

Randy Logan
LOGAN, RANDOLPH
B. May 1, 1951, Detroit, MI
Michigan 6'1" 195 lbs.

Year	Team		Games	Pos.
1973	**PHI**	N	14	S
1974			14	S
1975			14	S
1976			14	S
1977			14	S
1978			16	S
1979			16	S
1980			16	S
1981			16	S
1982			9	S
1983			16	S
11 yrs.	159 games			

Bob Logel
LOGEL, ROBERT JAMES
B. Jul. 29, 1928, East Aurora, NY
None 6'3" 210 lbs.

Year	Team		Games	Pos.
1949	**BUF**	AA	1	E

John Lohmeyer
LOHMEYER, JOHN CARL
B. Jan. 15, 1951, Emporia, KS
Emporia State 6'4" 229 lbs.

Year	Team		Games	Pos.
1973	**KC**	N	7	DE
1975			7	DE
1976			13	DE
1977			14	DE
4 yrs.	41 games			

Chip Lohmiller
LOHMILLER, JOHN M.
B. Jul. 16, 1966, Woodbury, MN
Minnesota 6'3" 213 lbs.

Year	Team		Games	Pos.
1988	**WAS**	N	16	K
1989			16	K
1990			16	K
1991			16	K
1992			16	K
1993			16	K
1994			16	K
1995	**NO**	N	8	K
1996	**STL**	N	15	K
9 yrs.	135 games			

Joe Lokanc
LOKANC, JOSEPH A.
B. Mar. 11, 1917, East Chicago, IN
Northwestern 5'11" 205 lbs.

Year	Team		Games	Pos.
1941	CHIC	N	9	G

George Lollar
LOLLAR, GEORGE (Slick)
B. 1906
Samford 5'11" 200 lbs.

Year	Team		Games	Pos.
1928	GB	N	3	FB, HB

Al Lolotai
LOLOTAI, ALBERT
B. Jun. 22, 1920, Laie, HI
D. Sep., 1990, Pago Pago, American Samoa
Weber State 6'0" 224 lbs.

Year	Team		Games	Pos.
1945	WAS	N	10	T
1946	LA	AA	14	G
1947			13	G
1948			14	G
1949			8	G
5 yrs.	59 games			

Tony Lomack
LOMACK, TONY J.
B. Apr. 27, 1968, Tallahassee, FL
Florida 5'8" 180 lbs.

Year	Team		Games	Pos.
1990	LARM	N	3	WR
1991	PHX	N	1	WR
2 yrs.	4 games			

John Lomakoski
LOMAKOSKI, JOHN
B. Nov. 11, 1940
Western Michigan 6'4" 250 lbs.

Year	Team		Games	Pos.
1962	DET	N	3	OT

Mark Lomas
LOMAS, MARK ARNOLD
B. Jun. 8, 1948, Los Angeles, CA
Northern Arizona 6'4" 241 lbs.

Year	Team		Games	Pos.
1970	NYJ	N	14	DE
1971			14	DT, DE
1972			14	DE
1973			14	DE, DT
1974			11	DE
5 yrs.	67 games			

Tom Lomasney
LOMASNEY, THOMAS
B. May 11, 1906
D. Dec., 1976, Salem, MA
Villanova 6'0" 180 lbs.

Year	Team		Games	Pos.
1929	SI		3	E

Neil Lomax
LOMAX, NEIL VINCENT
B. Feb. 17, 1959, Portland, OR
Portland State 6'3" 215 lbs.

Year	Team		Games	Pos.
1981	STL	N	14	QB
1982			9	QB
1983			13	QB
1984			16	QB
1985			16	QB
1986			14	QB
1987			12	QB
1988	PHX	N	14	QB
8 yrs.	108 games			

Antonio London
LONDON, ANTONIO MONTE
B. Apr. 14, 1971, Tullahoma, TN
Alabama 6'2" 234 lbs.

Year	Team		Games	Pos.
1993	DET	N	14	LB

Antonio London continued

Year	Team		Games	Pos.
1994			16	LB
1995			15	LB
1996			14	LB
4 yrs.	59 games			

Mike London
LONDON, MICHAEL
B. Dec. 31, 1944, Madison, WI
Wisconsin 6'2" 230 lbs.

Year	Team		Games	Pos.
1966	SD	A	3	LB

Tommy London
LONDON, TOM
B. Jun. 15, 1954, Shelby, NC
North Carolina State 6'1" 197 lbs.

Year	Team		Games	Pos.
1978	CLE	N	15	S

Keith Loneker
LONEKER, KEITH JOSEPH
B. Jun. 21, 1971, Roselle Park, NJ
Kansas 6'3" 330 lbs.

Year	Team		Games	Pos.
1993	LARM	N	4	G
1994			2	G
1995	STL	N	13	G
3 yrs.	19 games			

Frank Lone Star
LONE STAR, FRANK
B. Jan. 27, 1887
D. Sep., 1984, Pittsburgh, PA
Carlisle 5'11" 200 lbs.

Year	Team		Games	Pos.
1920	COL	A	3	G, T

Ted Lone Wolf
LONE WOLF, TED
None 6'2" 212 lbs.

Year	Team		Games	Pos.
1922	OOR	N	5	G, T, C, HB
1923			4	G
2 yrs.	9 games			

Bill Long
LONG, WILLIAM
B. Sep. 11, 1926
Oklahoma State 6'1" 200 lbs.

Year	Team		Games	Pos.
1949	PIT	N	10	E

Bob Long
LONG, ROBERT
B. Feb. 24, 1934, Anaheim, CA
UCLA 6'3" 232 lbs.

Year	Team		Games	Pos.
1955	DET	N	10	E
1956			12	E
1957			12	LB
1958			12	LB
1959			12	LB
1960	LA	N	9	LB
1961			13	LB
1962	DAL	N	7	LB
8 yrs.	87 games			

Bob Long
LONG, ROBERT ALBERT
B. 1922
Tennessee 5'10" 190 lbs.

Year	Team		Games	Pos.
1947	BOS	N	2	HB

Bob Long
LONG, ROBERT ANDREW
B. Jun. 16, 1942, McKeesport, PA
Wichita State 6'3" 199 lbs.

Year	Team		Games	Pos.
1964	GB	N	7	FL
1965			13	FL

Bob Long continued

Year	Team		Games	Pos.
1966			5	FL
1967			10	FL
1968	ATL	N	9	FL
1969	WAS	N	14	WR
1970	LA	N	2	WR
7 yrs.	60 games			

Carson Long
LONG, CARSON GERALD
B. Dec. 16, 1954, Pottsville, PA
Pittsburgh 5'10" 210 lbs.

Year	Team		Games	Pos.
1977	BUF	N	9	K

Charley Long
LONG, CHARLES B.
B. Apr. 6, 1938, De Kalb County, AL
Tennessee-Chattanooga 6'3" 247 lbs.

Year	Team		Games	Pos.
1961	BOS	A	14	OT
1962			14	OT
1963			14	OT
1964			14	G
1965			14	G
1966			14	G
1967			14	G
1968			13	G
1969			13	G
9 yrs.	124 games			

Chuck Long
LONG, CHARLES FRANKLIN, II
B. Feb. 18, 1963, Norman, OK
Iowa 6'4" 211 lbs.

Year	Team		Games	Pos.
1986	DET	N	3	QB
1987			12	QB
1988			7	QB
1989			1	QB
1990	LARM	N	4	QB
5 yrs.	27 games			

Cutter Long
LONG, BUFORD
B. 1932
Florida 6'1" 193 lbs.

Year	Team		Games	Pos.
1953	NYG	N	10	HB
1954			12	HB
1955			4	HB
3 yrs.	26 games			

Darren Long
LONG, DARREN M.
B. Jul. 12, 1959, Exeter, CA
Long Beach State 6'3" 240 lbs.

Year	Team		Games	Pos.
1986	LARM	N	4	TE

Dave Long
LONG, DAVID FRANK
B. Sep. 6, 1944, Jefferson, IA
Iowa 6'4" 241 lbs.

Year	Team		Games	Pos.
1966	STL	N	14	DE
1967			14	DE, DT
1968			14	DE, DT
1969	NO	N	14	DE
1970			12	DE
1971			14	DT
1972			14	DT
7 yrs.	96 games			

Doug Long
LONG, DOUG
B. May 24, 1955, Spokane, WA
Whitworth 6'0" 189 lbs.

Year	Team		Games	Pos.
1977	SEA	N	1	DB
1978			15	S
2 yrs.	16 games			

Harvey Long
LONG, HARVEY
B. Sep. 20, 1904
D. Mar., 1985, Cadillac, MI
Detroit 6'0" 195 lbs.

Year	Team		Games	Pos.
1929	CHIB	N	4	T, G
1930	FRA	N	1	T
2 yrs.	5 games			

Howie Long
LONG, HOWARD M.
B. Jan. 6, 1960, Somerville, MA
Villanova 6'5" 270 lbs.

Year	Team		Games	Pos.
1981	OAK	N	16	DT
1982	LARI	N	9	DE
1983			16	DE
1984			16	DE
1985			16	DE
1986			13	DE
1987			14	DE
1988			7	DE
1989			14	DE
1990			12	DE
1991			14	DE
1992			16	DE
1993			16	DE
13 yrs.	179 games			

Johnny Long
LONG, JOHN ANTON
B. Dec. 13, 1914, South Orange, NJ
D. Feb. 3, 1975
Colgate 6'0" 185 lbs.

Year	Team		Games	Pos.
1944	CHIB	N	8	QB, HB
1945			3	QB
2 yrs.	11 games			

Ken Long
LONG, KENNETH DONALD
B. Jul. 24, 1953, Pittsburgh, PA
Purdue 6'3" 265 lbs.

Year	Team		Games	Pos.
1976	DET	N	13	G

Kevin Long
LONG, KEVIN FERNANDO
B. Jan. 20, 1955, Clinton, SC
South Carolina 6'1" 212 lbs.

Year	Team		Games	Pos.
1977	NYJ	N	14	RB
1978			16	RB
1979			12	FB
1980			15	RB
1981			16	FB
5 yrs.	73 games			

Louie Long
LONG, LOUIS
B. 1909
Southern Methodist 6'0" 185 lbs.

Year	Team		Games	Pos.
1931	POR	N	13	E

Matt Long
LONG, MATTHEW SCOTT
B. Mar. 16, 1961, Glendale, CA
San Diego State 6'3" 270 lbs.

Year	Team		Games	Pos.
1987	PHI	N	3	C

Mel Long
LONG, MEL
B. Nov. 22, 1946, Toledo, OH
Toledo 6'0" 228 lbs.

Year	Team		Games	Pos.
1972	CLE	N	14	LB
1973			14	LB
1974			14	LB
3 yrs.	42 games			

Year	Team	Games	Pos.

Mike Long
LONG, MICHAEL
B. 1939
Brandeis 6'0" 188 lbs.

| 1960 | BOS | A | OE |

Terry Long
LONG, TERRY LUTHER
B. Jul. 21, 1959, Columbia, SC
East Carolina 5'11" 270 lbs.

1984	PIT	N	12	G
1985			15	G
1986			16	G
1987			13	G
1988			12	G
1989			13	G
1990			16	G
1991			8	G

8 yrs.   105 games

Tim Long
LONG, TIM
B. Apr. 20, 1963, Cleveland, TN
Memphis State 6'6" 295 lbs.

| 1987 | SF | N | 2 | C |

Tom Long
LONG, THOMAS N.
B. Aug. 7, 1899
D. Jul., 1969, Columbus, OH
Ohio State 6'0" 205 lbs.

| 1925 | COL | | 5 | G, QB |

Ken Longenecker
LONGENECKER, KENNETH
B. 1938
Lebanon Valley 6'4" 285 lbs.

| 1960 | PIT | N | 4 | T |

Clint Longley
LONGLEY, HOWARD CLINTON, JR. (Mad Bomber)
B. Jul. 28, 1952, Wichita Falls, TX
Abilene Christian 6'1" 194 lbs.

1974	DAL	N	2	QB
1975			4	QB
1976	SD	N	3	QB

3 yrs.   9 games

Sam Longmire
LONGMIRE, SAMUEL ROBERT
B. Jan. 3, 1943, Birmingham, AL
Purdue 6'3" 195 lbs.

| 1967 | KC | A | 3 | DB |
| 1968 | | | 2 | DB |

2 yrs.   5 games

Tom Longo
LONGO, THOMAS VICTOR
B. Feb. 21, 1944, Lyndhurst, NJ
Notre Dame 6'1" 199 lbs.

1969	NYG	N	13	CB
1970			14	S
1971	STL	N	2	S

3 yrs.   29 games

Roy Longstreet
LONGSTREET, ROY (Shorty)
B. 1901
Iowa State 5'11" 185 lbs.

| 1926 | RAC | N | 1 | C |

Long Time Sleep
Born NICHOLAS LASSIEX
B. 1897

Long Time Sleep continued
Deceased
Carlisle/Haskell 5'10" 205 lbs.

| 1922 | OOR | N | 9 | T, E, G |
| 1923 | | | 11 | C, G, T |

2 yrs.   20 games

Paul Longua
LONGUA, PAUL
B. Apr. 17, 1903
D. Jun., 1983, Allentown, NJ
Villanova 5'10" 175 lbs.

| 1929 | ORA | N | 11 | E |
| 1930 | NEW | N | 6 | E |

2 yrs.   17 games

Dean Look
LOOK, DEAN ZACHARY
B. Jul. 23, 1937, Lansing, MI
Michigan State 5'11" 185 lbs.

| 1962 | NY | A | 1 | QB |

Jack Lookabaugh
LOOKABAUGH, JOHN
B. Sep. 13, 1922, Ridgeley, WV
D. May 16, 1993, Millville, NJ
Maryland 6'4" 216 lbs.

| 1946 | WAS | N | 3 | E |
| 1947 | | | 6 | E |

2 yrs.   9 games

Ace Loomis
LOOMIS, ACE
B. 1928
Wisconsin-LaCrosse 6'1" 190 lbs.

1951	GB	N	12	HB
1952			11	HB
1953			10	HB

3 yrs.   33 games

Don Looney
LOONEY, JOE DONALD
B. Sep. 2, 1917, Sulphur Springs, TX
Deceased
Texas Christian 6'2" 182 lbs.

1940	PHI	N	11	E
1941	PIT	N	9	E, B
1942			4	E

3 yrs.   24 games

Jim Looney
LOONEY, JAMES
B. Aug. 18, 1957, Bastrop, LA
Purdue 6'0" 225 lbs.

| 1981 | SF | N | 1 | LB |

Joe Don Looney
LOONEY, JOE DON
B. Oct. 10, 1943, San Angelo, TX
D. Sep. 24, 1988, Nine Point Mesa, TX
Texas/Texas Christian/Oklahoma 6'1" 230 lbs.

1964	BAL	N	13	FB
1965	DET	N	9	FB
1966			3	HB
1966	WAS		13	RB
1967			4	RB
1969	NO	N	3	RB

5 yrs.   45 games

Bill Lopasky
LOPASKY, WILLIAM
B. 1937
West Virginia 6'2" 235 lbs.

| 1961 | SF | N | 10 | LB |

Karl Lorch
LORCH, KARL P., JR.
B. Jun. 14, 1950, Honolulu, HI
Southern California 6'3" 258 lbs.

1976	WAS	N	13	DE
1977			14	DE
1978			16	DE
1979			15	DE
1980			16	DE
1981			16	DE

6 yrs.   90 games

Jack Lord
LORD, JOHN W.
B. 1904
D. Mar. 11, 1958
Rutgers 6'0" 195 lbs.

| 1929 | SI | N | 4 | G, E |

Tony Lorick
LORICK, WILLIAM ANTHONY
B. May 25, 1941, Los Angeles, CA
Arizona State 6'1" 214 lbs.

1964	BAL	N	14	HB
1965			14	FB
1966			14	FB
1967			14	RB
1968	NO	N	13	RB
1969			14	RB

6 yrs.   83 games

Jack Losch
LOSCH, JOHN
B. Aug. 13, 1934, New York, NY
Miami (Florida) 6'1" 205 lbs.

| 1956 | GB | N | 12 | HB |

Ed Lothamer
LOTHAMER, EDWARD DEWEY
B. May 20, 1942, Detroit, MI
Michigan State 6'5" 261 lbs.

1964	KC	A	11	DE
1965			14	DE
1966			9	DE
1967			13	DT
1968			14	DT, G
1969			13	DT
1971	KC	N	14	DT
1972			2	DT

8 yrs.   90 games

Billy Lothridge
LOTHRIDGE, WILLIAM LAMAR
B. Jan. 1, 1942, Cleveland, GA
Deceased
Georgia Tech 6'1" 194 lbs.

1964	DAL	N	14	QB, P
1965	LA	N	9	P
1966	ATL	N	14	P
1967			14	P
1968			14	P
1969			14	P, S
1970			14	P, S
1971			9	P
1972	MIA	N	2	P

9 yrs.   104 games

Billy Lott
LOTT, BILLY REX
B. Nov. 8, 1934, Sumrall, MS
Mississippi 6'0" 203 lbs.

1958	NYG	N	12	HB
1960	OAK	A	14	FB
1961	BOS	A	14	FB
1962			7	FB
1963			14	FB

5 yrs.   61 games

John Lott
LOTT, JOHN
B. Nov. 13, 1905
D. Jan., 1970, Kaywood Gardens, MD
None

| 1929 | ORA | N | 2 | T |
| 1930 | BKN | N | 2 | T |

2 yrs.   4 games

John Lott
LOTT, JOHN
B. May 9, 1964
North Texas State 6'2" 260 lbs.

| 1987 | PIT | N | 1 | C |

Ronnie Lott
LOTT, RONALD MANDEL
B. May 8, 1959, Albuquerque, NM
Southern California 6'0" 200 lbs.

1981	SF	N	16	CB, S
1982			9	CB
1983			15	CB
1984			12	S, CB
1985			16	S, CB
1986			14	S, CB
1987			12	S
1988			13	S
1989			11	S
1990			11	S
1991	LARI	N	16	S
1992			16	S
1993	NYJ	N	16	S
1994			15	S

14 yrs.   192 games

Thomas Lott
LOTT, THOMAS WILLIE, JR.
B. Aug. 1, 1957, San Antonio, TX
Oklahoma 5'11" 205 lbs.

| 1979 | STL | N | 10 | RB |

Ron Lou
LOU, RONALD W.
B. Jul. 24, 1951, Los Angeles, CA
Arizona State 6'2" 240 lbs.

1973	HOU	N	9	C
1975	PHI	N	14	C
1976	HOU	N	14	C

3 yrs.   37 games

Fletcher Louallen
LOUALLEN, FLETCHER ALLISON
B. Sep. 12, 1962, Jefferson, SC
Livingston 6'0" 195 lbs.

| 1987 | MIN | N | 3 | S |

Corey Louchiey
LOUCHIEY, COREY
B. Oct. 10, 1971, Greenville, SC
Tennessee/South Carolina 6'7" 305 lbs.*

| 1995 | BUF | N | 13 | OT |
| 1996 | | | 15 | OT |

2 yrs.   28 games

Ed Loucks
LOUCKS, EDWIN E.
B. Sep. 15, 1895
D. Sep. 14, 1959
Washington & Jefferson 5'9" 170 lbs.

| 1925 | CLE | N | 1 | E |

Rommie Loudd
LOUDD, ROMMIE
B. Jun. 8, 1933, Madisonville, TX
UCLA 6'3" 227 lbs.

| 1960 | LA | A | | LB |

Year	Team		Games	Pos.

Rommie Loudd continued

Year	Team		Games	Pos.
1961	BOS	A	13	LB
1962			14	LB
3 yrs.	27 games			

Tom Louderback
LOUDERBACK, THOMAS
B. Mar. 5, 1933, Petaluma, CA
San Jose State 6'2" 235 lbs.

1958	PHI	N	12	LB
1959			12	LB
1960	OAK	A	12	LB
1961			14	LB
1962	BUF	A	2	LB
5 yrs.	40 games			

Angelo Loukas
LOUKAS, ANGELO G.
B. Feb. 25, 1947, Corinth, Greece
Northwestern 6'3" 250 lbs.

1969	BUF	A	13	G
1970	BOS	N	2	OL
2 yrs.	15 games			

Duval Love
LOVE, DUVAL LEE
B. Jun. 24, 1963, Los Angeles, CA
UCLA 6'3" 275 lbs.

1985	LARM	N	6	G
1986			16	G
1987			10	G
1988			15	G
1989			15	G
1990			16	G
1991			16	G
1992	PIT	N	16	G, OT
1993			16	G
1994			16	G
1995	ARI	N	16	G
1996			9	G
12 yrs.	167 games			

John Love
LOVE, JOHN LOUIS
B. Feb. 24, 1944, Linden, TX
North Texas State 5'11" 185 lbs.

1967	WAS	N	13	FL
1972	LA	N	5	WR
2 yrs.	18 games			

Randy Love
LOVE, RANDY
B. Sep. 30, 1956, Garland, TX
Houston 6'1" 205 lbs.

1979	STL	N	4	RB
1980			16	RB
1981			16	RB
1982			9	RB
1983			16	RB
1984			16	FB
1985			12	RB
7 yrs.	89 games			

Sean Love
LOVE, SEAN FITZGERALD
B. Sep. 6, 1968, Tamaqua, PA
Penn State 6'3" 290 lbs.

1993	TB	N	2	G
1994			6	G
1995	CAR	N	11	G
3 yrs.	19 games			

Terry Love
LOVE, TERRY LEE
B. Aug. 25, 1958, Forest City, AR
Murray State 6'2" 205 lbs.

1987	MIN	N	1	CB, S

Walter Love
LOVE, WALTER JAMES
B. Jun. 4, 1950, Cleveland, OH
Westminster (Utah) 5'9" 180 lbs.

1973	NYG	N	12	WR

Calvin Loveall
LOVEALL, CALVIN E.
B. Jul. 23, 1962, Kennewick, WA
Idaho 5'9" 180 lbs.

1988	HOU	N	3	CB
1988	KC	N	4	DB
1988	ATL	N	4	CB, S

Edwin Lovelady
LOVELADY, EDWIN
B. Apr. 23, 1963
Memphis State 5'9" 180 lbs.

1987	NYG	N	3	WR

John LoVetere
LOVOTERE, JOHN
B. May 31, 1936, Boston, MA
Compton JC* 6'4" 280 lbs.

1959	LA	N	12	T
1960			12	T
1961			13	DT
1962			14	DT
1963	NYG	N	14	DT
1964			4	DT
1965			4	DT
7 yrs.	73 games			

Derek Loville
LOVILLE, DEREK KEVIN
B. Jul. 4, 1968, San Francisco, CA
Oregon 5'9" 196 lbs.

1990	SEA	N	11	RB
1991			16	RB
1994	SF	N	14	RB
1995			16	RB
1996			12	RB
5 yrs.	69 games			

Fritz Lovin
LOVIN, FRED
B. Jun. 11, 1894
D. Oct., 1975, Baxter, MN
None 182 lbs.

1929	MIN	N	7	G

Warren Loving
LOVING, WARREN
B. Nov. 12, 1961, Jersey City, NJ
William Penn 6'1" 230 lbs.

1987	BUF	N	2	RB

Frank LoVuolo
LOVUOLO, FRANK
B. 1924
St. Bonaventure 6'2" 210 lbs.

1949	NYG	N	11	E

Kirk Lowdermilk
LOWDERMILK, ROBERT KIRK
B. Apr. 10, 1963, Canton, OH
Ohio State 6'3" 269 lbs.

1985	MIN	N	16	C
1986			11	C
1987			12	C
1988			12	C
1989			16	C
1990			15	C
1991			16	C
1992			16	C
1993	IND	N	16	C

Kirk Lowdermilk continued

1994			16	C
1995			16	C
1996			16	C
12 yrs.	178 games			

Gary Lowe
LOWE, GARY R.
B. May 4, 1934, Trenton, MI
Michigan State 5'11" 196 lbs.

1956	WAS	N	11	HB
1957			1	B
1957	DET	N	7	HB
1958			12	HB
1959			12	HB
1960			11	HB
1961			14	DB
1962			13	DB
1963			3	DB
1964			13	DB
9 yrs.	97 games			

George Lowe
LOWE, GEORGE H. (Bull)
B. Jun. 21, 1895, Arlington, MA
Deceased
Lafayette/Fordham 5'11" 180 lbs.

1920	CAN	A	6	E
1921	CLE	A	7	T
1925	PRO	N	2	E
1925	FRA	N	8	E, T
1926	BOS	N	6	E
1926	FRA	N	2	E
1927	PRO	N	11	E
5 yrs.	42 games			

Lloyd Lowe
LOWE, LLOYD
B. Dec. 18, 1928, Prairie Hill, TX
North Texas State 5'10" 155 lbs.

1953	CHIB	N	7	HB

Paul Lowe
LOWE, PAUL EDWARD
B. Sep. 27, 1936, Homer, LA
Oregon State 6'0" 200 lbs.

1960	LA	A	14	HB
1961	SD	A	14	HB
1963			14	HB
1964			14	HB
1965			14	HB
1966			14	HB
1967			7	RB
1968			1	RB
1968	KC	N	2	RB
1969			7	RB
9 yrs.	101 games			

Bull Lowe
LOWE, R.V.
B. 1899
Deceased
Dubuque 180 lbs.

1923	RI	N	5	HB, FB, E

Woodrow Lowe
LOWE, WOODROW
B. Jun. 9, 1954, Columbus, GA
Alabama 6'0" 227 lbs.

1976	SD	N	14	LB
1977			14	LB
1978			16	LB
1979			16	LB
1980			16	LB
1981			16	LB
1982			9	LB
1983			16	LB
1984			15	LB

Woodrow Lowe continued

1985			16	LB
1986			16	LB
11 yrs.	164 games			

Darby Lowery
LOWERY, DARBY
B. 1892
Deceased
None 6'0" 213 lbs.

1920	ROC	A	1	E
1921			5	E
1922	ROC	N	5	G, T, E
1923			4	T, G
1924			7	G
1925			7	G
6 yrs.	29 games			

Michael Lowery
LOWERY, MICHAEL
B. Feb. 14, 1974, McComb, TX
Mississippi 6'0" 224 lbs.

1996	CHI	N	16	LB

Nick Lowery
LOWERY, DOMINIC GERALD
B. May 27, 1956, Munich, Germany
Dartmouth 6'4" 190 lbs.

1978	NE	N	2	K
1980	KC	N	16	K
1981			16	K
1982			9	K
1983			16	K
1984			16	K
1985			16	K
1986			16	K
1987			12	K
1988			16	K
1989			16	K
1990			16	K
1991			16	K
1992			16	K
1993			16	K
1994	NYJ	N	16	K
1995			14	K
1996			16	K
18 yrs.	260 games			

Orlando Lowry
LOWRY, ORLANDO DEWEY
B. Aug. 14, 1961, Cleveland, OH
Ohio State 6'4" 237 lbs.

1985	IND	N	16	LB
1986			16	LB
1987			8	LB
1988			16	LB
1989			9	LB
1989	NE	N	2	LB
5 yrs.	67 games			

Quentin Lowry
LOWRY, QUENTIN IVORY
B. Nov. 11, 1957, Cleveland, OH
Youngstown State 6'3" 235 lbs.

1981	WAS	N	9	LB
1982			9	LB
1983			3	LB
1983	TB	N	6	LB
3 yrs.	27 games			

Russ Lowther
LOWTHER, JACK RUSSELL
B. Dec. 27, 1922, Detroit, MI
D. Sep., 1952
Detroit 5'8" 165 lbs.

1944	DET	N	7	HB
1945	PIT	N	2	HB
2 yrs.	9 games			

Year	Team		Games	Pos.

Alex Loyd
LOYD, EDGAR ALEX
B. Aug. 7, 1927, Stigler, OK
D. May, 1976, Dallas, TX
Oklahoma State 6'4" 198 lbs.

Year	Team		Games	Pos.
1950	SF	N	12	E

Mike Loyd
LOYD, MIKE
B. May 6, 1956, Joplin, MO
Kansas/Tulsa/Missouri Southern State 6'2" 216 lbs.

| 1980 | STL | N | 5 | QB |

Steve Lubischer
LUBISCHER, STEVE
B. Jun. 29, 1962, Long Branch, NJ
Boston College 6'3" 240 lbs.

| 1987 | MIA | N | 1 | LB |

Milo Lubratovich
LUBRATOVICH, MILO M.
B. Apr. 19, 1909, Indiana Harbor, IN
Wisconsin 6'2" 230 lbs.

1931	BKN	N	14	T, G
1932			12	T
1933			10	T
1934			10	T, C
1935			7	T
5 yrs.	53 games			

Dick Lucas
LUCAS, RICHARD
B. Jan. 9, 1934, Boston, MA
Boston College 6'2" 213 lbs.

1958	PIT	N	4	E
1960	PHI	N	12	E
1961			14	OE
1962			9	OE
1963			3	OE
5 yrs.	42 games			

Jeff Lucas
LUCAS, JEFFREY ALAN
B. May 30, 1964, Hackensack, NJ
West Virginia 6'7" 288 lbs.

| 1987 | PIT | N | 3 | OT |

Ray Lucas
LUCAS, RAY
B. Aug. 6, 1972, Harrison, NJ
Rutgers 6'2" 201 lbs.

| 1996 | NE | N | 2 | WR |

Richie Lucas
LUCAS, RICHARD
B. Apr. 15, 1938, Glassport, PA
Penn State 6'0" 190 lbs.

1960	BUF	A		QB
1961			8	QB, DB
2 yrs.	8 games			

Tim Lucas
LUCAS, TIMOTHY BRIAN
B. Apr. 3, 1961, Stockton, CA
California 6'3" 230 lbs.

1987	DEN	N	11	LB
1988			16	LB
1989			16	LB
1990			11	LB
1991			5	LB
1992			9	LB
1993			7	LB
7 yrs.	75 games			

Mike Lucci
LUCCI, MICHAEL GENE
B. Dec. 29, 1939, Ambridge, PA
Pittsburgh/Tennessee 6'2" 230 lbs.

1962	CLE	N	13	LB
1963			10	LB
1964			14	LB
1965	DET	N	11	LB
1966			13	LB
1967			14	LB
1968			12	LB
1969			14	LB
1970			14	LB
1971			14	LB
1972			14	LB
1973			11	LB
12 yrs.	154 games			

Derrel Luce
LUCE, DERREL JOE
B. Sep. 29, 1952, Lake Jackson, TX
Baylor 6'3" 226 lbs.

1975	BAL	N	14	LB
1976			14	LB
1977			12	LB
1978			16	LB
1979	MIN	N	16	LB
1980			4	LB
1980	DET	N	9	LB
6 yrs.	85 games			

Lew Luce
LUCE, LLEWELLYN ATTSETT, JR.
B. Apr. 3, 1938, Washington, DC
Penn State 6'0" 187 lbs.

| 1961 | WAS | N | | HB |

Johnny Lucente
LUCENTE, JOHN
B. 1922, Clarksburg, WV
West Virginia 5'9" 200 lbs.

| 1945 | PIT | N | 10 | FB |

Oliver Luck
LUCK, OLIVER
B. Apr. 5, 1960, Cleveland, OH
West Virginia 6'2" 196 lbs.

1983	HOU	N	7	QB
1984			4	QB
1985			5	QB
1986			4	QB
4 yrs.	20 games			

Terry Luck
LUCK, TERRY
B. Dec. 14, 1952, Fayetteville, NC
Nebraska 6'3" 205 lbs.

| 1977 | CLE | N | 4 | QB |

Mick Luckhurst
LUCKHURST, MICHAEL CHRISTOPHER WILBERT
B. Mar. 31, 1958, Redbourne, England
St. Cloud State/California 6'1" 180 lbs.

1981	ATL	N	16	K
1982			9	K
1983			16	K
1984			16	K
1985			16	K
1986			10	K
1987			12	K
7 yrs.	95 games			

Sid Luckman
LUCKMAN, SIDNEY
B. Nov. 21, 1916, Brooklyn, NY

Sid Luckman *continued*
Columbia 6'0" 197 lbs.

1939	CHIB	N	11	HB, QB
1940			11	QB
1941			11	QB
1942			11	QB
1943			10	QB
1944			7	QB
1945			10	QB
1946			11	QB
1947			12	QB
1948			12	QB
1949			11	QB
1950			11	QB
12 yrs.	128 games			

Bill Lucky
LUCKY, WILLIAM H., JR.
B. Aug. 24, 1931, Temple, TX
Baylor 6'3" 250 lbs.

| 1955 | GB | N | 12 | T |

Bill Lueck
LUECK, WILLIAM M.
B. Apr. 7, 1946, Buckeye, AZ
Arizona 6'3" 239 lbs.

1968	GB	N	11	G
1969			14	G
1970			14	G
1971			14	G
1972			14	G
1973			14	G
1974			9	G
1975	PHI	N	11	G
8 yrs.	101 games			

Don Luft
LUFT, DON R.
B. Feb. 14, 1930, Fisk, WI
Indiana 6'5" 220 lbs.

| 1954 | PHI | N | 12 | E |

Nolan Luhn
LUHN, NOLAN HARRY
B. Jul. 27, 1921, Kenney, TX
Tulsa 6'3" 200 lbs.

1945	GB	N	9	E
1946			11	E
1947			12	E
1948			12	E
1949			12	E
5 yrs.	56 games			

Johnny Lujack
LUJACK, JOHN C., JR.
B. Jan. 4, 1925, Connellsville, PA
Notre Dame 6'0" 186 lbs.

1948	CHIB	N	9	QB
1949			12	QB
1950			12	QB
1951			12	QB
4 yrs.	45 games			

Steve Luke
LUKE, STEVEN N.
B. Sep. 4, 1953, Massillon, OH
Ohio State 6'2" 205 lbs.

1975	GB	N	14	S
1976			13	CB, S
1977			14	S
1978			16	S
1979			16	S
1980			16	S
6 yrs.	89 games			

Tommy Luke
LUKE, TOMMY J.

Tommy Luke *continued*
B. Jan. 26, 1944, Louisville, MS
Mississippi 6'0" 190 lbs.

| 1968 | DEN | A | 7 | DB |

Tom Luken
LUKEN, THOMAS JAMES
B. Jun. 15, 1950, Cincinnati, OH
Purdue 6'3" 253 lbs.

1972	PHI	N	12	G
1973			3	G
1974			13	G
1975			5	G
1977			14	G
1978			16	G
6 yrs.	63 games			

Jim Lukens
LUKENS, JAMES WILLIE, JR.
B. Sep. 6, 1924, Swarthmore, PA
Washington & Lee 6'4" 205 lbs.

| 1949 | BUF | AA | 11 | E |

Jack Lummus
LUMMUS, JOHN
B. Oct. 22, 1917, Ennis, TX
D. Mar. 8, 1945, Iwo Jima
Baylor 6'3" 194 lbs.

| 1941 | NYG | N | 10 | E |

Joey Lumpkin
LUMPKIN, JOEY LYNN
B. Feb. 19, 1960, Ardmore, OK
Arizona State 6'2" 230 lbs.

1982	BUF	N	6	LB
1983			14	LB
2 yrs.	20 games			

Ron Lumpkin
LUMPKIN, RON
B. Jun. 22, 1951, Los Angeles, CA
Arizona State 6'2" 200 lbs.

| 1973 | NYG | N | 1 | S |

Roy Lumpkin
LUMPKIN, ROY (Father)
B. 1908, Dallas, TX
Deceased
Georgia Tech 6'2" 211 lbs.

1930	POR		14	FB, QB, HB
1931			14	HB, FB
1932			12	HB, FB
1933			11	HB, FB
1934	DET	N	13	HB
1935	BKN	N	12	HB, QB
1936			12	QB
1937			5	HB
8 yrs.	93 games			

Sean Lumpkin
LUMPKIN, SEAN FRANKLIN
B. Jan. 4, 1970, Golden Valley, MN
Minnesota 6'0" 206 lbs.

1992	NO	N	16	S
1993			12	S
1994			16	S
1995			16	S
1996			7	S
5 yrs.	67 games			

Bobby Luna
LUNA, ROBERT KENDAL
B. Mar. 25, 1933, Lewisburg, TN
Alabama 5'11" 187 lbs.

1955	SF	N	12	HB
1959	PIT	N	12	HB
2 yrs.	24 games			

Year	Team		Games	Pos.

Dave Lunceford
LUNCEFORD, DAVID G.
B. May 6, 1934, Canton, TX
Baylor 6'4" 240 lbs.

1957	CHIC	N	12	T

Bill Lund
LUND, WILLIAM HAROLD
B. Oct. 27, 1924, Akron, OH
Case Western Reserve 5'10" 180 lbs.

1946	CLE	AA	10	HB
1947			8	B
2 yrs.	18 games			

Ken Lunday
LUNDAY, KENNETH (Kayo)
B. Aug. 13, 1913, Cleora, OK
Arkansas 6'3" 217 lbs.

1937	NYG	N	10	G
1938			11	G
1939			11	C, G
1940			10	C
1941			11	G, C
1946			7	G
1947			6	G
7 yrs.	66 games			

Bob Lundell
LUNDELL, WILBUR HARVEY
(Gloom)
B. Jun. 21, 1907
Deceased
Gustavus Adolphus 6'4" 215 lbs.

1929	MIN	N	10	E, FB
1930			4	E
1930	SI	N	6	E
2 yrs.	20 games			

Dennis Lundy
LUNDY, DENNIS LEONARD
B. Jul. 6, 1972, Tampa, FL
Northwestern 5'9" 190 lbs.

1995	HOU	N	7	RB
1995	CHI	N	2	RB
1 yr.	9 games			

Lamar Lundy
LUNDY, LAMAR
B. Apr. 17, 1935, Richmond, IN
Purdue 6'7" 245 lbs.

1957	LA	N	12	DE
1958			12	DE
1959			12	DE
1960			12	DE
1961			14	DE
1962			14	DE
1963			14	DT
1964			13	DE
1965			12	DE
1966			14	DE
1967			14	DE
1968			5	DE
1969			4	DE
13 yrs.	152 games			

Charlie Lungren
LUNGREN, CHARLES HOWARD,
JR. (Babe)
B. Jun. 23, 1894
D. Mar. 21, 1972, Milwaukee, WI
Swarthmore 5'8" 158 lbs.

1923	RI	N	4	HB, QB, E

Mel Lunsford
LUNSFORD, MELVIN T.
B. Jun. 13, 1950, Cincinnati, OH
Central State (Ohio) 6'3" 256 lbs.

1973	NE	N	4	DT

Year	Team		Games	Pos.

Mel Lunsford continued

1974			14	DT
1975			4	DE
1976			14	DE
1977			13	DE
1978			16	DE
1979			16	DE
1980			12	DE
8 yrs.	93 games			

Jerry Lunz
LUNZ, GERALD A.
B. Mar. 13, 1903
D. Jan. 11, 1974, Milwaukee, WI
Marquette 6'3" 210 lbs.

1925	CHIC	N	14	G
1926			12	G
1930	FRA	N	1	T
3 yrs.	27 games			

LaDue Lurth
LURTH, LADUE
B. 1905
Gustavus Adolphus 5'8" 160 lbs.

1929	MIN	N	1	HB

Bob Lurtsema
LURTSEMA, ROBERT ROSS
B. Mar. 29, 1942, Grand Rapids, MI
Michigan Tech/Western Michigan 6'6"
250 lbs.

1967	NYG	N	14	DT
1968			14	DT
1969			13	DT
1970			14	DT
1971			7	DT
1972	MIN	N	14	DE
1973			14	DE
1974			14	DE, DT
1975			14	DE, DT
1976			1	DE
1976	SEA	N	13	DE
1977			14	DE
11 yrs.	146 games			

Vaughn Lusby
LUSBY, ALAWANDRA VAUGHN
B. Aug. 23, 1956, Fort Polk, LA
Arkansas 5'10" 180 lbs.

1979	CIN	N	16	CB
1980	CHI	N	2	CB
2 yrs.	18 games			

Jim Luscinski
LUSCINSKI, JAMES V.
B. Dec. 16, 1958, Arlington, MA
Norwich 6'5" 275 lbs.

1982	NYJ	N	6	OT, G

Mike Lush
LUSH, MICHAEL STEPHEN
B. Apr. 18, 1958, Allentown, PA
East Stroudsburg State 6'2" 195 lbs.

1986	IND	N	4	S
1986	MIN	N	6	S
1987	ATL	N	3	S
2 yrs.	13 games			

Henry Lusk
LUSK, HENRY
B. May 8, 1972, Seaside, CA
Utah 6'1" 240 lbs.

1996	NO	N	16	TE

Herb Lusk
LUSK, HERBERT

Year	Team		Games	Pos.

Herb Lusk continued
B. Feb. 19, 1953, Memphis, TN
Long Beach State 6'0" 190 lbs.

1976	PHI	N	14	RB
1977			11	RB
1978			3	RB
3 yrs.	28 games			

Booth Lusteg
LUSTEG, WALLACE BOOTH
B. May 8, 1941, New Haven, CT
Connecticut 5'11" 190 lbs.

1966	BUF	A	14	K
1967	MIA	A	8	K
1968	PIT	N	13	K
1969	GB	N	4	K
4 yrs.	39 games			

Ed Luther
LUTHER, EDWARD AUGUSTINE
B. Jan. 2, 1957, Gardena, CA
San Jose State 6'3" 200 lbs.

1980	SD	N	6	QB
1981			16	QB
1982			9	QB
1983			16	QB
1984			15	QB
5 yrs.	62 games			

Dave Lutz
LUTZ, DAVID GRAHAM
B. Dec. 30, 1959, Monroe, NC
Georgia Tech 6'5" 280 lbs.

1983	KC	N	16	OT
1984			7	OT
1985			16	OT
1986			9	OT
1987			12	OT
1988			15	OT
1989			16	OT
1990			16	G, OT
1991			16	G
1992			16	G
1993	DET	N	16	G, OT
1994			16	G
1995			16	G
13 yrs.	187 games			

Allen Lyday
LYDAY, ALLEN
B. Sep. 16, 1960, Wichita, KS
Texas Southern/Nebraska 5'10" 196 lbs.

1984	HOU	N	4	S
1985			13	CB, S
1986			12	S
1987			7	S
4 yrs.	36 games			

Todd Lyght
LYGHT, TODD WILLIAM
B. Feb. 9, 1969, Kwajalein, Marshall
Isl.
Notre Dame 6'0" 186 lbs.

1991	LARM	N	12	CB
1992			12	CB
1993			9	CB
1994			16	CB
1995	STL	N	16	CB
1996			16	CB
6 yrs.	81 games			

Dewey Lyle
LYLE, DEWITT W.
B. Mar. 23, 1891
D. Nov. 27, 1980, Paso Robles, CA
Minnesota 5'11" 196 lbs.

1920	RI	A	6	T, G
1921			7	G

Year	Team		Games	Pos.

Dewey Lyle continued

1922	RI	N	6	G, E, T
1922	GB		2	G
1923			9	E, G, T
4 yrs.	30 games			

Garry Lyle
LYLE, GARRY
B. Oct. 20, 1945, Martinsville, WV
George Washington 6'2" 197 lbs.

1968	CHI	N	12	RB
1969			13	RB
1970			14	S
1971			14	S
1972			3	S
1973			14	S
1974			14	S
7 yrs.	84 games			

Keith Lyle
LYLE, KEITH ALLEN
B. Apr. 17, 1972, Washington, DC
Virginia 6'2" 200 lbs.

1994	LARM	N	16	S
1995	STL	N	16	S
1996			16	S
3 yrs.	48 games			

Rick Lyle
LYLE, RICK JAMES EARL
B. Feb. 26, 1971, Monroe, LA
Missouri 6'5" 275 lbs.

1994	CLE	N	3	DE
1996	BAL	N	11	DE
2 yrs.	14 games			

Lenny Lyles
LYLES, LEONARD EVERETT
B. Jan. 26, 1936, Nashville, TN
Louisville 6'2" 202 lbs.

1958	BAL	N	12	DB
1959	SF	N	12	DB
1960			12	DB
1961	BAL	N	14	DB
1962			6	DB
1963			14	DB
1964			14	DB
1965			11	DB
1966			14	DB
1967			12	DB
1968			14	DB
1969			14	DB
12 yrs.	149 games			

Lester Lyles
LYLES, LESTER EVERETT
B. Dec. 27, 1962, Washington, DC
Virginia 6'3" 218 lbs.

1985	NYJ	N	6	S
1986			16	S, LB
1987			4	S
1988	PHX	N	6	S
1989	SD	N	16	S
1990			15	S
6 yrs.	63 games			

Robert Lyles
LYLES, ROBERT
B. Mar. 21, 1961, Los Angeles, CA
Texas Christian 6'1" 225 lbs.

1984	HOU	N	6	LB
1985			16	LB
1986			16	LB
1987			12	LB
1988			16	LB
1989			13	LB
1990			3	LB
1990	ATL	N	11	LB

Robert Lyles continued

Year	Team		Games	Pos.
1991			16	LB
8 yrs.	109 games			

Dell Lyman
LYMAN, DELBERT M.
B. Jul. 9, 1918, Aberdeen, WA
D. Dec. 19, 1986, Ojai, CA
UCLA 6'3" 223 lbs.

Year	Team		Games	Pos.
1941	GB	N	5	T
1941	CLE	N	4	T
1944			1	T
2 yrs.	10 games			

Jeff Lyman
LYMAN, JEFFREY
B. Aug. 21, 1950, Salt Lake City, UT
Brigham Young 6'2" 230 lbs.

Year	Team		Games	Pos.
1972	STL	N	2	LB
1972	BUF	N	1	LB
1 yr.	3 games			

Link Lyman
LYMAN, WILLIAM ROY
B. Nov. 30, 1898, Table Rock, NE
D. Dec. 28, 1972, Baker, CA
Nebraska 6'2" 233 lbs.

Year	Team		Games	Pos.
1922	CAN	N	12	T
1923			12	T
1924	CLE	N	9	T
1925	CAN	N	7	T
1925	FRA	N	4	T
1926	CHIB	N	15	T
1927			14	T
1928			13	T
1930			11	T
1931			10	T, G
1933			13	T
1934			12	T
11 yrs.	132 games			

Carl Lynch
LYNCH, CARL
B. 1893
Deceased
Ohio Wesleyan

Year	Team		Games	Pos.
1921	CIN	A	2	G

Dick Lynch
LYNCH, RICHARD
B. Apr. 29, 1936, Oceanside, NY
Notre Dame 6'1" 202 lbs.

Year	Team		Games	Pos.
1958	WAS	N	12	DB
1959	NYG	N	12	DB
1960			12	DB
1961			14	DB
1962			14	DB
1963			14	DB
1964			10	DB
1965			14	DB
1966			8	DB
9 yrs.	110 games			

Eddie Lynch
LYNCH, EDWARD J. (Ace)
B. Oct. 4, 1896
D. Aug. 24, 1967, Dearborn, MI
Catholic 6'0" 191 lbs.

Year	Team		Games	Pos.
1925	ROC	N	6	E
1926	DET	N	12	E
1926	HAR	N	1	E
1927	PRO	N	12	E
1929	ORA	N	4	T
4 yrs.	35 games			

Eric Lynch
LYNCH, ERIC

Eric Lynch continued
B. May 16, 1970, Woodhaven, MI
Grand Valley State 5'10" 224 lbs.

Year	Team		Games	Pos.
1992	DET	N	4	RB
1993			4	RB
1994			12	RB
1995			5	RB
1996			16	RB
5 yrs.	41 games			

Fran Lynch
LYNCH, FRANCIS XAVIER
B. Dec. 3, 1945, Bridgeport, MA
Hofstra 6'1" 203 lbs.

Year	Team		Games	Pos.
1967	DEN	A	6	RB
1968			9	RB
1969			11	RB
1970	DEN	N	14	RB
1971			10	RB
1972			14	RB
1973			9	RB
1974			12	RB
1975			14	RB
9 yrs.	99 games			

Jim Lynch
LYNCH, JAMES ROBERT
B. Aug. 28, 1945, Lima, OH
Notre Dame 6'1" 232 lbs.

Year	Team		Games	Pos.
1967	KC	A	14	LB
1968			14	LB
1969			14	LB
1970	KC	N	14	LB
1971			14	LB
1972			14	LB
1973			14	LB
1974			14	LB
1975			14	LB
1976			14	LB
1977			11	LB
11 yrs.	151 games			

John Lynch
LYNCH, JOHN TERRENCE
B. Sep. 25, 1971, Hinsdale, IL
Stanford 6'2" 220 lbs.

Year	Team		Games	Pos.
1993	TB	N	15	S
1994			16	S
1995			9	S
1996			16	S
4 yrs.	56 games			

Lorenzo Lynch
LYNCH, LORENZO
B. Apr. 6, 1963, Oakland, CA
Sacramento State 5'9" 197 lbs.

Year	Team		Games	Pos.
1987	CHI	N	3	DB
1988			9	CB, S
1989			16	CB, S
1990	PHX	N	16	CB
1991			16	CB
1992			16	CB
1993			16	CB
1994	ARI	N	15	S, CB
1995			12	S
1996	OAK	N	16	S
10 yrs.	135 games			

Lynn Lynch
LYNCH, LYNN
B. Aug. 10, 1929, Indianapolis, IN
Illinois 6'2" 225 lbs.

Year	Team		Games	Pos.
1951	CHIC	N	3	G

Paul Lynch
LYNCH, E. PAUL (Deacon)
B. 1901
D. Sep. 25, 1961

Paul Lynch continued
Ohio Northern 6'1" 190 lbs.

Year	Team		Games	Pos.
1925	COL	N	7	HB, QB

Tom Lynch
LYNCH, THOMAS FRANK
B. May 24, 1955, Chicago, IL
Boston College 6'5" 260 lbs.

Year	Team		Games	Pos.
1977	SEA	N	14	G
1978			16	G
1979			15	G
1980			16	G
1981	BUF	N	4	G
1982			8	G
1983			15	G
1984			16	G
8 yrs.	104 games			

Anthony Lynn
LYNN, ANTHONY RAY
B. Dec. 21, 1968, McKinney, TX
Texas Tech 6'3" 230 lbs.

Year	Team		Games	Pos.
1993	DEN	N	13	RB
1995	SF	N	6	RB
1996			16	RB
3 yrs.	35 games			

Johnny Lynn
LYNN, JOHNNY ROSS
B. Dec. 19, 1956, Los Angeles, CA
UCLA 6'0" 196 lbs.

Year	Team		Games	Pos.
1979	NYJ	N	16	CB
1981			13	CB
1982			8	CB
1983			16	CB
1984			14	CB, S
1985			14	CB, S
1986			16	CB
7 yrs.	97 games			

George Lyon
LYON, GEORGE C. (Babe)
B. Mar. 30, 1907
D. Dec., 1970, Manhattan, KS
Kansas State 6'2" 235 lbs.

Year	Team		Games	Pos.
1929	NYG	N	1	T
1930	POR	N	10	T, E
1931	CHIB	N	1	T
1931	CLE	N	7	T, G
1932	BKN	N	10	T
1934	C, S	N	3	T
5 yrs.	32 games			

Dicky Lyons
LYONS, RICHARD
B. Aug. 11, 1947, Louisville, KY
Kentucky 6'0" 190 lbs.

Year	Team		Games	Pos.
1970	NO	N	4	S

John Lyons
LYONS, JOHN
B. 1912
Tulsa 6'1" 185 lbs.

Year	Team		Games	Pos.
1933	BKN	N	2	E

Lamar Lyons
LYONS, LAMAR
B. Mar. 25, 1973, Los Angeles, CA
Washington 6'3" 210 lbs.

Year	Team		Games	Pos.
1996	OAK	N	6	S

Marty Lyons
LYONS, MARTIN A.
B. Jan. 13, 1957, Takoma Park, MD
Alabama 6'5" 265 lbs.

Year	Team		Games	Pos.
1979	NYJ	N	16	DE, DT

Marty Lyons continued

Year	Team		Games	Pos.
1980			16	DT, DE
1981			12	DT
1982			7	DT
1983			16	DT
1984			13	DT
1985			16	DE, DT
1986			12	DE, DT
1987			13	DE, DT
1988			16	DE, DT
1989			10	DE, DT
11 yrs.	147 games			

Mitch Lyons
LYONS, MITCHELL WARREN
B. May 13, 1970, Grand Rapids, MI
Michigan State 6'4" 255 lbs.

Year	Team		Games	Pos.
1993	ATL	N	16	TE
1994			7	TE
1995			13	TE
1996			14	TE
4 yrs.	50 games			

Robert Lyons
LYONS, ROBERT LOUIS
B. May 16, 1966, Wheeling, WV
Akron 6'1" 195 lbs.

Year	Team		Games	Pos.
1989	CLE	N	9	S

Tommy Lyons
LYONS, TOMMY
B. Aug. 7, 1948, Atlanta, GA
Georgia 6'2" 229 lbs.

Year	Team		Games	Pos.
1971	DEN	N	11	C
1972			11	G
1973			14	G
1974			14	G
1975			10	G
1976			14	G
6 yrs.	74 games			

Rob Lytle
LYTLE, ROBERT WILLIAM
B. Nov. 12, 1954, Fremont, OH
Michigan 6'1" 196 lbs.

Year	Team		Games	Pos.
1977	DEN	N	14	RB
1978			13	RB
1979			15	RB
1980			16	RB
1981			16	RB
1982			9	RB
1983			4	RB
7 yrs.	87 games			

Herb Maack
MAACK, HERBERT W.
B. 1917
Columbia 6'2" 210 lbs.

Year	Team		Games	Pos.
1946	BKN	AA	7	T

J.D. Maarleveld
MAARLEVELD, JOHN DAVID
B. Oct. 24, 1961, Jersey City, NJ
Notre Dame/Maryland 6'6" 300 lbs.

Year	Team		Games	Pos.
1986	TB	N	14	OT
1987			11	OT
2 yrs.	25 games			

Bill Maas
MAAS, WILLIAM THOMAS
B. Mar. 2, 1962, Newtown Square, PA
Pittsburgh 6'5" 270 lbs.

Year	Team		Games	Pos.
1984	KC	N	14	NT
1985			16	NT
1986			16	NT, DE
1987			11	NT
1988			8	NT

Year	Team		Games	Pos.

Bill Maas *continued*

Year	Team		Games	Pos.
1989			10	NT
1990			16	NT, DE
1991			16	DE
1992			9	DE
1993	**GB**	**N**	14	NT

10 yrs. 130 games

Ron Mabra
MABRA, RONALD EDWIN
B. Jun. 4, 1951, Talladega, AL
Howard 5'10" 166 lbs.

1975	**ATL**	**N**	8	DB
1976			8	CB, S
1977	**NYJ**	**N**	3	CB

3 yrs. 19 games

Ken MacAfee
MACAFEE, KENNETH ADAMS, SR.
B. Aug. 3, 1929, North Easton, MA
Alabama 6'2" 212 lbs.

1954	**NYG**	**N**	11	E
1955			8	E
1956			12	E
1957			11	E
1958			10	E
1959	**PHI**	**N**	4	E
1959	**WAS**	**N**	7	E

6 yrs. 63 games

Ken MacAfee
MACAFEE, KENNETH ADAMS, II
B. Jan. 9, 1956, Portland, OR
Notre Dame 6'5" 248 lbs.

1978	**SF**	**N**	13	TE
1979			16	TE

2 yrs. 29 games

John Macaulay
MACAULAY, JOHN DUNN
B. Apr. 27, 1959, San Diego, CA
Stanford 6'3" 254 lbs.

1984	**SF**	**N**	3	C

Max MacCullom
MACCULLOM, MAXWELL S. (Red)
B. 1900
D. Sep. 25, 1943
Centre 5'11" 165 lbs.

1922	**LOU**	**N**	1	E

Allen MacDonald
MACDONALD, ALLEN J.
B. Mar., 1896, Duluth, MN
Deceased
None 5'10" 169 lbs.

1923	**DUL**	**N**	1	HB
1924			6	HB, FB

2 yrs. 7 games

Buck MacDonald
MACDONALD, GEORGE R.
B. May 5, 1894
D. Mar., 1985, Hialeah, FL
Lehigh 5'10" 180 lbs.

1921	**TON**	**A**	2	G
1921	**NY**	**A**	1	G, C

1 yr. 3 games

Danny MacDonald
MACDONALD, DANTE
B. Sep. 2, 1963
Idaho State 6'2" 230 lbs.

1987	**DEN**		3	LB

Mark MacDonald
MACDONALD, MARK GOODWIN
B. Apr. 30, 1961, West Roxbury, MA
Boston College 6'4" 267 lbs.

1985	**MIN**	**N**	16	G
1986			10	G
1987			12	G
1988			5	G
1988	**PHX**	**N**	1	OT, G

4 yrs. 44 games

Jay MacDowell
MACDOWELL, JAY
B. Sep. 14, 1919, Oak Park, IL
D. Jun. 15, 1992, Springfield, DE
Washington 6'2" 217 lbs.

1946	**PHI**	**N**	6	E
1947			12	T
1948			12	T
1949			8	T
1950			12	T
1951			12	T

6 yrs. 62 games

Mel Maceau
MACEAU, MELVIN A.
B. Dec. 25, 1921, Milwaukee, WI
D. Dec., 1981
Marquette 6'0" 203 lbs.

1946	**CLE**	**AA**	12	C
1947			14	C
1948			11	C

3 yrs. 37 games

Don Macek
MACEK, DONALD MATTHEW
B. Jul. 21, 1964, Manchester, NH
Boston College 6'2" 265 lbs.

1976	**SD**	**N**	14	G
1977			14	G
1978			14	G
1979			10	G, C
1980			16	G, C
1981			15	C, G
1982			9	C
1983			11	C, G
1984			13	C
1985			15	C
1986			13	C
1987			11	C
1988			5	C
1989			2	C

14 yrs. 162 games

John Macerelli
MACERELLI, JOHN
B. Nov. 2, 1930, Muse, PA
D. Oct., 1984, Canonsburg, PA
St. Vincent 6'2" 230 lbs.

1956	**CLE**	**N**	12	T, G

Mike Machurek
MACHUREK, MICHAEL BRUCE
B. Jul. 22, 1960, Las Vegas, NV
Idaho State 6'1" 205 lbs.

1984	**DET**	**N**	4	QB

Art Macioszczyk
MACIOSZCZYK, ARTHUR (Choo-Choo)
B. Oct. 19, 1920, Hamtramck, MI
D. May 6, 1982, Hamtramck, MI
Western Michigan 5'9" 208 lbs.

1944	**PHI**	**N**	10	FB
1947			11	FB
1948	**WAS**	**N**	1	FB

3 yrs. 22 games

Bill Mack
MACK, WILLIAM RICHARD (Red)
B. Jun. 19, 1937, Oconto, WI
Notre Dame 5'10" 185 lbs.

1961	**PIT**	**N**	11	HB
1962			14	OE, HB
1963			14	OE
1964	**PHI**	**N**	8	FL
1965	**PIT**	**N**	2	FL
1966	**ATL**	**N**	1	WR
1966	**GB**	**N**	9	FL

6 yrs. 59 games

Cedric Mack
MACK, CEDRIC MANUEL
B. Sep. 14, 1960, Freeport, TX
Baylor 6'0" 194 lbs.

1983	**STL**	**N**	16	CB
1984			12	CB
1985			16	WR, CB
1986			15	CB
1987			10	CB
1988	**PHX**	**N**	16	CB
1989			16	CB
1990			16	CB
1991	**SD**	**N**	7	CB
1992	**KC**	**N**	1	CB
1992	**NO**	**N**	14	CB
1993			1	CB

11 yrs. 140 games

Kevin Mack
MACK, KEVIN
B. Aug. 9, 1962, Kings Mountain, NC
Clemson 6'0" 224 lbs.

1985	**CLE**	**N**	16	RB
1986			12	RB
1987			12	FB
1988			11	RB
1989			4	RB
1990			14	RB
1991			14	RB
1992			12	RB
1993			4	RB

9 yrs. 99 games

Kim Mack
MACK, KIM
B. 1962
Florida State 6'0" 190 lbs.

1987	**SEA**	**N**	1	S

Milton Mack
MACK, MILTON JEROME
B. Sep. 20, 1963, Jackson, MS
Alcorn State 5'11" 182 lbs.

1987	**NO**	**N**	13	CB
1988			14	CB
1989			16	CB
1990			16	CB
1992	**TB**	**N**	16	CB
1993			12	CB
1994	**DET**	**N**	16	CB

7 yrs. 119 games

Rico Mack
MACK, RICO RODRIGUS
B. Feb. 22, 1971, Winder, GA
Appalachian State 6'4" 239 lbs.

1993	**PIT**	**N**	8	LB

Terence Mack
MACK, TERENCE
B. Sep. 9, 1964, Winnsboro, SC
Clemson 6'3" 240 lbs.

1987	**STL**	**N**	5	LB

Tom Mack
MACK, THOMAS LEE
B. Nov. 1, 1943, Cleveland, OH
Michigan 6'3" 249 lbs.

1966	**LA**	**N**	14	G
1967			14	G
1968			14	G
1969			14	G
1970			14	G
1971			14	G
1972			14	G
1973			14	G
1974			14	G
1975			14	G
1976			14	G
1977			14	G
1978			16	G

13 yrs. 184 games

Earsell Mackbee
MACKBEE, JAMES EARSELL
B. Jan. 15, 1941, Brookhaven, MS
Utah State 6'1" 195 lbs.

1965	**MIN**	**N**	10	DB
1966			14	DB
1967			14	DB
1968			14	DB
1969			14	CB

5 yrs. 66 games

Jack Mackenroth
MACKENROTH, JACK W.
B. 1916
North Dakota 6'2" 215 lbs.

1938	**DET**	**N**	2	C

Roy Mackert
MACKERT, CHARLES LEROY
B. Feb. 2, 1894, Sunbury, PA
Lebanon Valley/Maryland 6'2" 200 lbs.

1925	**ROC**	**N**	2	C, T

Dee Mackey
MACKEY, DEE
B. Oct. 16, 1934
East Texas State 6'5" 232 lbs.

1960	**SF**	**N**	12	E
1961	**BAL**	**N**	14	OE
1962			14	OE
1963	**NY**	**A**	14	OE
1964			14	OE
1965			10	OE

6 yrs. 78 games

John Mackey
MACKEY, JOHN
B. Sep. 24, 1941, New York, NY
Syracuse 6'3" 222 lbs.

1963	**BAL**	**N**	14	OE
1964			14	OE
1965			14	OE
1966			14	TE
1967			14	TE
1968			14	TE
1969			14	TE
1970			14	TE
1971			14	TE
1972	**SD**	**N**	13	TE

10 yrs. 139 games

Kyle Mackey
MACKEY, KYLE ERICKSON
B. Mar. 2, 1962, Gladewater, TX
East Texas State 6'3" 219 lbs.

1987	**MIA**	**N**	3	QB
1989	**NYJ**	**N**	4	QB

2 yrs. 7 games

Year	Team	Games	Pos.

Doug Mackie
MACKIE, DOUGLAS BRIAN
B. Feb. 18, 1957, Saugus, MA
Ohio State 6'4" 280 lbs.

Year	Team	Games	Pos.
1987	ATL	N	3	OT

Jacque MacKinnon
MACKINNON, JACQUE HAROLD
B. Nov. 10, 1938, Dover, NJ
D. Mar., 1975, San Diego, CA
Colgate 6'4" 245 lbs.

Year	Team		Games	Pos.
1961	SD	A	9	G, OE
1962			14	FB
1963			14	FB
1964			14	OE
1965			14	OE
1966			14	OE
1967			14	TE
1968			14	OE
1969			7	TE
1970	OAK	N	4	TE

10 yrs. 118 games

John Mackorell
MACKORELL, JOHN
B. Nov. 3, 1912
D. Apr., 1980, Morganton, NC
Davidson 5'10" 178 lbs.

Year	Team		Games	Pos.
1935	NYG	N	1	HB

Bill Mackrides
MACKRIDES, WILLIAM
B. Jul. 8, 1925, Philadelphia, PA
Nevada-Reno 5'11" 182 lbs.

Year	Team		Games	Pos.
1947	PHI	N	8	QB
1948			10	QB
1949			7	QB
1950			8	QB
1951			6	QB
1953	PIT	N	10	QB
1953	NYG	N	2	QB

6 yrs. 51 games

Bob MacLeod
MACLEOD, ROBERT F.
B. Oct. 15, 1917, Glen Ellyn, IL
Dartmouth 6'0" 190 lbs.

Year	Team		Games	Pos.
1939	CHIB	N	9	HB

Tom MacLeod
MACLEOD, THOMAS WILLIAM
B. Jan. 10, 1951, Proctor, MN
Minnesota 6'3" 225 lbs.

Year	Team		Games	Pos.
1973	GB	N	11	LB
1974	BAL	N	14	LB
1975			14	LB
1977			14	LB
1978			12	LB

5 yrs. 65 games

Stu MacMillan
MACMILLAN, STUART
B. Feb. 13, 1908
North Dakota 5'9" 175 lbs.

Year	Team		Games	Pos.
1931	CLE	N	2	G, C

Jim MacMurdo
MACMURDO, JAMES E. (Big Jim)
B. Sep. 2, 1909, Ellwood City, PA
D. Aug., 1981, Lansdowne, PA
Pittsburgh 6'1" 209 lbs.

Year	Team		Games	Pos.
1932	BOS	N	10	T, G
1933			10	G
1934	PHI	N	11	T
1935			3	T

Jim MacMurdo continued

Year	Team	Games	Pos.
1936		9	T
1937		2	T

6 yrs. 45 games

Ray MacMurray
MACMURRAY, RAYMOND
B. Jul. 3, 1889
D. Feb., 1966, Huntington, IN
None

Year	Team		Games	Pos.
1921	MUN	A	1	G

Eddie Macon
MACON, EDWIN
B. Mar. 7, 1927, Shafter, CA
Pacific 6'0" 177 lbs.

Year	Team		Games	Pos.
1952	CHIB	N	11	HB
1953			12	HB
1960	OAK	A		DB

3 yrs. 23 games

Waddy MacPhee
MACPHEE, WALTER SCOTT
B. Dec. 23, 1899, Brooklyn, NY
D. Jan. 20, 1980, Charlotte, NC
Brooklyn College/Princeton 5'8" 160 lbs.

Year	Team		Games	Pos.
1926	PRO	N	9	HB, FB

Kile MacWherter
MACWHERTER, KILE
B. Jul. 19, 1892
D. Dec., 1977, Garden City, CO
Millikin/Bethany (West Virginia) 5'9" 210 lbs.

Year	Team		Games	Pos.
1920	DEC	A	1	FB

Jack Maczuzak
MACZUZAK, JOHN
B. Apr. 4, 1941
Pittsburgh 6'5" 250 lbs.

Year	Team		Games	Pos.
1964	KC	A	1	OT

Elmer Madar
MADAR, ELMER F.
B. 1921, Sykesville, PA
Michigan 5'11" 185 lbs.

Year	Team		Games	Pos.
1947	BAL	AA	9	E

Elmer Madarik
MADARIK, ELMER LAURENCE (Tippy)
B. Jul. 15, 1922, Joliet, IL
D. Mar. 3, 1974
Detroit 5'11" 200 lbs.

Year	Team		Games	Pos.
1945	DET	N	1	HB
1946			10	HB
1947			8	HB
1948	WAS	N	1	HB

4 yrs. 20 games

Lloyd Madden
MADDEN, LLOYD
B. Aug. 27, 1918, Lewis, KS
Colorado Mines 6'1" 195 lbs.

Year	Team		Games	Pos.
1940	CHIC	N	9	HB

Bob Maddock
MADDOCK, ROBERT CHARLES
B. Aug. 6, 1920, Santa Ana, CA
Notre Dame 6'0" 200 lbs.

Year	Team		Games	Pos.
1942	CHIC	N	2	G
1946			7	G

2 yrs. 9 games

Bob Maddox
MADDOX, ROBERT EARL
B. May 2, 1949, Frederick, MD
Frostburg State 6'5" 237 lbs.

Year	Team		Games	Pos.
1974	CIN	N	14	DE
1975	KC	N	6	DL
1976			8	DT, DE

3 yrs. 28 games

Buster Maddox
MADDOX, GEORGE W.
B. Nov. 4, 1911, Greenville, TX
D. Mar. 14, 1956
Kansas State 6'3" 240 lbs.

Year	Team		Games	Pos.
1935	GB	N	1	T

Mark Maddox
MADDOX, MARK ANTHONY
B. Mar. 23, 1968, Milwaukee, WI
Northern Michigan 6'1" 233 lbs.

Year	Team		Games	Pos.
1992	BUF	N	15	LB
1993			11	LB
1994			15	LB
1995			4	LB
1996			14	LB

5 yrs. 59 games

Tommy Maddox
MADDOX, THOMAS ALFRED
B. Sep. 2, 1971, Shreveport, LA
UCLA 6'4" 200 lbs.

Year	Team		Games	Pos.
1992	DEN	N	13	QB
1993			16	QB
1994	LARM	N	5	QB
1995	NYG	N	16	QB

4 yrs. 50 games

George Maderos
MADEROS, GEORGE
B. Nov. 3, 1933, Chico, CA
Chico State 6'1" 187 lbs.

Year	Team		Games	Pos.
1955	SF	N	7	HB
1956			7	HB

2 yrs. 14 games

John Madigan
MADIGAN, JOHN
B. Mar. 12, 1899
D. Jan., 1976, St. Paul, MN
St. Mary's (Minnesota)/St. Thomas 6'0" 185 lbs.

Year	Team		Games	Pos.
1922	MIN	N	2	C
1923	DUL	N	7	T
1924	MIN	N	6	C

3 yrs. 15 games

Lynn Madsen
MADSEN, LYNN T.
B. Aug. 8, 1960, Blair, NE
Washington 6'4" 260 lbs.

Year	Team		Games	Pos.
1986	HOU	N	15	DE

Chet Maeda
MAEDA, CHESTER
B. 1919
Colorado State 5'10" 187 lbs.

Year	Team		Games	Pos.
1945	CHIC	N	1	HB

Al Maeder
MAEDER, ALBERT R.
B. Jan. 25, 1906
D. Aug., 1984, Eden Prairie, MN
Minnesota 5'9" 185 lbs.

Year	Team		Games	Pos.
1929	MIN	N	7	T

Mike Magac
MAGAC, MICHAEL STEPHEN
B. May 25, 1938, East St. Louis, IL
Missouri 6'3" 240 lbs.

Year	Team		Games	Pos.
1960	SF	N	12	G
1961			6	G
1962			14	G
1963			10	G
1964			14	G
1965	PIT	N	8	G
1966			14	G

7 yrs. 78 games

George Mageda
MAGEDA, GEORGE
Illinois Tech 180 lbs.

Year	Team		Games	Pos.
1926	HAM	N	3	HB, QB

Calvin Magee
MAGEE, CALVIN
B. Apr. 23, 1963, New Orleans, LA
Southern University 6'3" 240 lbs.

Year	Team		Games	Pos.
1985	TB	N	16	TE
1986			16	TE
1987			11	TE
1988			13	TE

4 yrs. 56 games

Jim Magee
MAGEE, JAMES J.
B. Nov. 27, 1920, Philadelphia, PA
D. Mar., 1970
Villanova 6'1" 202 lbs.

Year	Team		Games	Pos.
1944	BOS	N	9	C
1945			9	C
1946			11	C

3 yrs. 29 games

John Magee
MAGEE, JOHN WESLEY, JR.
B. Jul. 21, 1923, Robstown, TX
D. Nov. 22, 1991, Kaplan, LA
Rice 5'10" 220 lbs.

Year	Team		Games	Pos.
1948	PHI	N	12	G
1949			12	G
1950			12	G
1951			12	G
1952			12	G
1953			12	G
1954			12	G
1955			7	G

8 yrs. 91 games

Archie Maggiolo
MAGGIOLO, ACHILLE FRED (Chick)
B. May 27, 1922, Mishawaka, IN
Indiana/Notre Dame/Illinois 5'11" 178 lbs.

Year	Team		Games	Pos.
1948	BUF	AA	7	B
1949	DET	N	12	HB
1950	BAL	N	7	HB

3 yrs. 26 games

Don Maggs
MAGGS, DONALD JAMES
B. Nov. 1, 1961, Youngstown, OH
Tulane 6'5" 287 lbs.

Year	Team		Games	Pos.
1986	HOU	N	14	OT, G
1988			16	OT, G
1989			16	OT, G
1990			16	OT, G
1991			16	OT, G
1992			16	OT
1993	DEN	N	7	OT
1994			11	OT, C

8 yrs. 112 games

Year	Team	Games	Pos.

Al Maginnes
MAGINNES, ALBERT BRISTOL
B. Apr. 5, 1897, Boston, MA
D. Jan., 1966
Lehigh 6'1" 188 lbs.

1921	NY	A	2	G, T

Dave Maginnes
MAGINNES, WILLIAM DAVID
B. Nov. 29, 1894, Dorchester, MA
D. Jul. 26, 1981, Exeter, NH
Lehigh 5'10" 165 lbs.

1921	NY	A	2	HB

Joe Magliolo
MAGLIOLO, JOSEPH, JR.
B. 1922
Texas 6'0" 210 lbs.

1948	NY	AA	13	B

Al Maglisceau
MAGLISCEAU, ALBERT
B. May 21, 1904
D. Nov., 1985, Ruskin, FL
Geneva 6'1" 210 lbs.

1929	FRA	N	5	T, G

Dante Magnani
MAGNANI, DANTE A.
B. Mar. 17, 1918, Vallejo, CA
D. Dec. 22, 1985, Vallejo, CA
St. Mary's (California) 5'10" 182 lbs.

1940	CLE	N	11	HB
1941			9	HB
1942			11	HB, FB
1943	CHIB	N	11	HB
1946			10	HB
1947	LA	N	12	HB
1948			8	HB
1949	CHIB	N	6	HB
1950	DET	N	7	HB
9 yrs.	85 games			

Jimmy Magner
MAGNER, JAMES EDWARD
B. Jul. 22, 1903
D. Sep. 20, 1977, Philadelphia, PA
Widener/North Carolina 6'0" 165 lbs.

1931	FRA	N	2	QB, HB

Glenn Magnuson
MAGNUSON, GLENN (Ole)
B. Jul. 30, 1899
Northwestern 5'11" 225 lbs.

1925	HAM	N	1	G

Paul Maguire
MAGUIRE, PAUL LEO
B. Aug. 22, 1938, Youngstown, OH
The Citadel 6'0" 224 lbs.

1960	LA	A	11	DE, P
1961	SD	A	14	LB, P
1962			14	LB, P
1963			14	LB, P
1964	BUF	A	14	LB, P
1965			14	LB, P
1966			14	LB, P
1967			14	LB, P
1968			14	LB, P
1969			14	LB, P
1970	BUF	N	14	P
11 yrs.	151 games			

George Magulick
MAGULICK, GEORGE
B. Jan. 10, 1919, Spangler, PA

George Magulick *continued*
Deceased
St. Francis (Pennsylvania) 5'9" 150 lbs.

1944	C, P	N	9	HB

Drew Mahalic
MAHALIC, DREW A.
B. May 22, 1953, Albany, NY
Notre Dame 6'4" 226 lbs.

1975	SD	N	13	LB
1976	PHI	N	13	LB
1977			14	LB
1978			9	LB
4 yrs.	49 games			

Bob Mahan
MAHAN, ROBERT
B. Feb. 6, 1904
Washington (Missouri) 5'9" 178 lbs.

1929	BUF	N	8	FB, HB
1930	BKN	N	11	E, HB, FB
2 yrs.	19 games			

Walter Mahan
MAHAN, WALTER EVERETT (Red)
B. Jun. 23, 1902, Follansbee, WV
D. May 10, 1990, Wheeling, WV
West Virginia 5'10" 212 lbs.

1926	FRA	N	1	G
1926	CHI	A	10	G
1 yr.	11 games			

Bernie Maher
MAHER, BERNIE (Birdie)
B. 1891
Deceased
Detroit 5'8" 180 lbs.

1920	DET	A	2	E

Bruce Maher
MAHER, BRUCE DAVID
B. Jul. 25, 1937, Detroit, MI
Detroit 5'11" 190 lbs.

1960	DET	N	12	DB
1961			12	DB
1962			14	DB
1963			14	DB
1964			14	DB
1965			14	DB
1966			14	DB
1967			14	DB
1968	NYG	N	14	DB
1969			14	S
10 yrs.	136 games			

Frank Maher
MAHER, FRANCIS
B. May 8, 1918, Detroit, MI
Deceased
Toledo 6'1" 195 lbs.

1941	PIT	N	2	B
1941	CLE	N	2	B
1 yr.	4 games			

Eric Mahlum
MAHLUM, ERIC
B. Dec. 6, 1970, San Diego, CA
California 6'4" 284 lbs.

1994	IND	N	16	G
1995			7	G
1996			13	G
3 yrs.	36 games			

Frank Mahoney
MAHONEY, FRANK JOHN (Ike)

Frank Mahoney *continued*
B. Oct. 25, 1901
D. May, 1963
Creighton 5'9" 173 lbs.

1925	CHIC	N	7	QB, HB
1926			11	QB, E, HB
1927			9	HB, QB, FB
1928			5	HB, E
1931			1	B
5 yrs.	33 games			

John Mahoney
MAHONEY, JOHN (Buck)
B. Oct. 16, 1899
D. Sep., 1980, Clarence, NY
Canisius 6'0" 183 lbs.

1923	BUF	N	7	HB, FB, E

Rog Mahoney
MAHONEY, ROGER
B. Jul. 19, 1906
D. Mar., 1981, Radnor, PA
Penn State 6'0" 205 lbs.

1928	FRA	N	14	C, G, E
1929			17	C, T, E
1930			9	C, G, T, E
1930	MIN	N	1	G
3 yrs.	41 games			

Al Mahrt
MAHRT, ALPHONSE H.
B. Oct. 11, 1893, Dayton, OH
D. Jun. 24, 1970, Chillicothe, OH
Dayton 5'11" 168 lbs.

1920	DAY	A	8	QB
1921			7	QB, HB
1922	DAY	N	8	QB
3 yrs.	23 games			

Armin Mahrt
MAHRT, ARMIN RICHARD
B. Nov., 1897, Dayton, OH
Dayton/West Virginia 5'11" 175 lbs.

1924	DAY	N	7	HB
1925			8	HB
1925	POT	N	2	HB
1926	DAY	N	4	HB, E
3 yrs.	21 games			

Johnny Mahrt
MAHRT, C. JOHN
B. Dec. 22, 1899
D. Aug., 1967, Dayton, OH
Dayton 5'9" 180 lbs.

1925	DAY	N	1	E

Lou Mahrt
MAHRT, LOUIS R.
B. Jul. 30, 1904
D. Aug., 1962, Dayton, OH
Dayton 5'11" 178 lbs.

1926	DAY	N	6	QB
1927			2	QB
2 yrs.	8 games			

Steve Maidlow
MAIDLOW, STEVEN KENNETH
B. Jun. 6, 1960, Lansing, MI
Michigan State 6'2" 236 lbs.

1983	CIN	N	16	LB
1984			16	LB
1985	BUF	N	16	LB
1987			2	LB
4 yrs.	50 games			

Ralph Mailliard
MAILLIARD, RALPH J.
B. Oct. 10, 1905
D. May 9, 1990, Omaha, NE
Creighton 6'2" 190 lbs.

1929	CHIB	N	4	T, G

Gil Mains
MAINS, GILBERT L.
B. Dec. 17, 1929, Mount Carmel, IL
Murray State 6'2" 243 lbs.

1954	DET	N	12	T
1955			12	T
1956			8	T
1957			12	T
1958			11	T
1959			12	T
1960			12	T
1961			3	DT
8 yrs.	82 games			

Jack Maitland
MAITLAND, JOHN FREDERICK
B. Feb. 2, 1948, Pittsburgh, PA
Williams 6'1" 210 lbs.

1970	BAL	N	14	RB
1971	NE	N	14	RB
2 yrs.	28 games			

Don Majkowski
MAJKOWSKI, DONALD VINCENT (Magic Man)
B. Feb. 25, 1964, Buffalo, NY
Virginia 6'2" 197 lbs.

1987	GB	N	7	QB
1988			13	QB
1989			16	QB
1990			9	QB
1991			9	QB
1992			14	QB
1993	IND	N	3	QB
1994			9	QB
1995	DET	N	8	QB
1996			5	QB
10 yrs.	93 games			

Bill Majors
MAJORS, WILLIAM
B. Nov. 7, 1938, Lynchburg, TN
Tennessee 6'0" 175 lbs.

1961	BUF	A	1	DB

Bobby Majors
MAJORS, BOBBY
B. Jul. 7, 1949, Lynchburg, TN
Tennessee 6'1" 193 lbs.

1972	CLE	N	8	S

Siupeli Malamala
MALAMALA, SIUPELI
B. Jan. 15, 1969, Tofoa, Tonga Islands
Washington 6'5" 310 lbs.

1992	NYJ	N	9	OT
1993			15	OT
1994			12	OT
1995			6	OT, G
1996			4	OT
5 yrs.	46 games			

Rydell Malancon
MALANCON, RYDELL J.
B. Jan. 10, 1962, New Orleans, LA
Louisiana State 6'1" 227 lbs.

1984	ATL	N	7	LB
1987	GB	N	3	LB
2 yrs.	10 games			

Year	Team	Games	Pos.

Harry Malcolm
MALCOLM, HARRY
B. Nov. 25, 1905
D. Sep., 1987, Wayne, PA
Washington & Jefferson 6'0" 195 lbs.

Year	Team		Games	Pos.
1929	FRA	N	14	T, G

Howie Maley
MALEY, HOWARD E. (Red)
B. 1922
Southern Methodist 5'11" 187 lbs.

1946	BOS	N	11	HB
1947			12	HB
2 yrs.		23 games		

Bill Malinchak
MALINCHAK, WILLIAM JOHN
B. Apr. 2, 1944, Charleroi, PA
Indiana 6'1" 198 lbs.

1966	DET	N	14	OE
1967			14	OE
1968			14	OE
1969			6	WR
1970	WAS	N	9	WR
1971			13	WR
1972			6	WR
1973			14	WR
1974			14	WR
1976			3	WR
10 yrs.		107 games		

Gene Malinowski
MALINOWSKI, EUGENE P.
B. 1925, Detroit, MI
D. Nov. 24, 1993
Detroit 6'1" 210 lbs.

| 1948 | BOS | N | 12 | B |

Joe Malkovich
MALKOVICH, JOSEPH N. (Hunk)
B. Jan. 17, 1912, Calumet, MI
D. Feb. 17, 1981, Camarillo, CA
Duquesne 6'3" 205 lbs.

| 1935 | PIT | N | 3 | C |

Fran Mallick
MALLICK, FRANCIS
B. Feb. 25, 1941
none 6'3" 245 lbs.

| 1965 | PIT | N | 6 | DE, OT |

Irvin Mallory
MALLORY, IRVIN
B. Feb. 1, 1949, Glen Allen, VA
Virginia Union 6'1" 196 lbs.

| 1971 | NE | N | 2 | DB |

John Mallory
MALLORY, JOHN
B. Jul. 24, 1946, Summit, NJ
West Virginia 6'0" 188 lbs.

1968	PHI	N	14	DB
1969	ATL	N	13	S
1970			14	DB
1971			14	CB, S
4 yrs.		55 games		

Larry Mallory
MALLORY, LARRY MONTEL
B. Jul. 21, 1952, Memphis, TN
Tennessee State 5'11" 185 lbs.

1976	NYG	N	14	DB
1977			14	S
1978			16	S
3 yrs.		44 games		

Rick Mallory
MALLORY, RICK LEROY
B. Oct. 21, 1960, Seattle, WA
Washington 6'2" 265 lbs.

1985	TB	N	13	G
1986			16	G
1987			12	G
1988			16	G
4 yrs.		57 games		

Ray Mallouf
MALLOUF, RAYMOND LUCIAN
B. Jul. 11, 1918, Sayre, OK
Southern Methodist 5'11" 180 lbs.

1941	CHIC	N	8	HB, FB
1946			5	QB
1947			11	QB
1948			12	QB
1949	NYG	N	11	QB
5 yrs.		47 games		

Les Malloy
MALLOY, LESLIE A.
B. 1909
Deceased
Loyola (Illinois) 6'0" 200 lbs.

1931	CHIC	N	7	QB, HB
1932			8	QB, HB
1933			10	QB, HB
3 yrs.		25 games		

Art Malone
MALONE, ARTHUR LEE
B. Mar. 20, 1948, Tyler, TX
Arizona State 5'11" 213 lbs.

1970	ATL	N	14	RB
1971			13	RB
1972			14	RB
1973			9	RB
1974			13	RB
1975	PHI	N	13	RB
1976			3	RB
7 yrs.		79 games		

Benny Malone
MALONE, BENNY
B. Feb. 3, 1952, Tyler, TX
Arizona State 5'10" 193 lbs.

1974	MIA	N	13	RB
1975			10	RB
1976			14	RB
1977			14	RB
1978			6	RB
1978	WAS	N	9	RB
1979			16	RB
6 yrs.		82 games		

Charley Malone
MALONE, CHARLES C.
B. Jun. 18, 1910, Hillsboro, TX
D. May, 1992, Lake San Marcos, CA
Texas A&M 6'4" 206 lbs.

1934	BOS	N	12	E
1935			11	E
1936			12	E
1937	WAS	N	11	E
1938			11	E
1939			11	E
1940			11	E
1942			5	E
8 yrs.		84 games		

Darrell Malone
MALONE, DARRELL KENYATTA
B. Nov. 23, 1967, Mobile, AL
Jacksonville State 5'10" 177 lbs.

| 1992 | KC | N | 4 | CB |
| 1992 | MIA | N | 4 | CB |

Darrell Malone continued

1993			16	CB
1994			6	CB
3 yrs.		30 games		

Grover Malone
MALONE, JOHN GROVER (Molly)
B. Nov. 13, 1895
D. Nov., 1985, Milwaukee, WI
Notre Dame 5'8" 175 lbs.

1920	CHIT	A	6	HB
1921	RI	A	2	HB
1921	GB	A	6	HB
1923	AKR	N	2	E
3 yrs.		16 games		

Mark Malone
MALONE, MARK M.
B. Nov. 22, 1958, El Cajon, CA
Arizona State 6'4" 220 lbs.

1980	PIT	N	1	QB
1981			8	QB
1983			2	QB
1984			13	QB
1985			10	QB
1986			14	QB
1987			12	QB
1988	SD	N	12	QB
1989	NYJ	N	1	QB
9 yrs.		73 games		

Ralph Malone
MALONE, RALPH DEVAUGHN
B. Jan. 12, 1964, Huntsville, AL
Georgia Tech 6'5" 225 lbs.

| 1986 | CLE | N | 16 | DE |

Van Malone
MALONE, VAN BUREN
B. Jul. 1, 1970, Houston, TX
Texas 5'11" 186 lbs.

1994	DET	N	16	S
1995			16	S
1996			15	S
3 yrs.		47 games		

Norm Maloney
MALONEY, NORMAN EDWARD
B. Apr. 21, 1923, Chicago, IL
Purdue 6'1" 190 lbs.

1948	SF	AA	14	E
1949			12	E
2 yrs.		26 games		

Red Maloney
MALONEY, GERALD S.
B. Sep. 5, 1901
D. May, 1976, Boston, MA
Dartmouth 5'11" 180 lbs.

1925	PRO	N	12	E
1926	NY	A	14	E, G, HB
1927	NYY	N	12	E
1929	BOS	N	8	E
4 yrs.		46 games		

Mike Mamula
MAMULA, MICHAEL BRIAN
B. Aug. 14, 1973, Lackawanna, NY
Boston College 6'4" 248 lbs.

1995	PHI	N	14	DE
1996			16	DE
2 yrs.		30 games		

Massimo Manca
MANCA, MASSIMO
B. Sep. 9, 1964, Sassari, Italy

Massimo Manca continued
Penn State 5'10" 211 lbs.

| 1987 | CIN | N | 3 | K |

Vaughn Mancha
MANCHA, VAUGHN HALL
B. Oct. 7, 1921
Alabama 6'1" 230 lbs.

| 1948 | BOS | N | 12 | C |

Tony Mandarich
MANDARICH, TONY JOSEPH
B. Sep. 23, 1966, Oakville, Ont.
Michigan State 6'5" 304 lbs.

1989	GB	N	14	OT
1990			16	OT
1991			15	OT
1996	IND	N	15	OT
4 yrs.		60 games		

Mike Mandarino
MANDARINO, MICHAEL P.
B. Mar. 16, 1921, Philadelphia, PA
D. Dec. 7, 1985, Media, PA
LaSalle 5'11" 240 lbs.

1944	PHI	N	8	T, G, C
1945			5	C
2 yrs.		13 games		

Dave Manders
MANDERS, DAVID F.
B. Feb. 20, 1941, Milwaukee, WI
Michigan State 6'2" 247 lbs.

1964	DAL	N	14	C
1965			14	C
1966			14	C
1968			14	C
1969			14	C
1970			14	C
1971			14	C
1972			14	C
1973			13	C
1974			14	C
10 yrs.		139 games		

Jack Manders
MANDERS, JOHN ALBERT (Automatic)
B. Jan. 13, 1909, Milbank, SD
D. Jan. 28, 1977, Chicago, IL
Minnesota 6'0" 203 lbs.

1933	CHIB	N	13	FB, HB
1934			13	FB, HB
1935			12	FB
1936			12	FB
1937			11	HB
1938			11	HB
1939			11	HB
1940			10	HB
8 yrs.		93 games		

Pug Manders
MANDERS, CLARENCE E.
B. May 5, 1913, Milbank, SD
D. Jan., 1985, Des Moines, IA
Drake 6'0" 202 lbs.

1939	BKN	N	11	FB, HB
1940			11	FB
1941			11	FB
1942			11	FB
1943			10	FB
1944			10	FB
1945	BOS	N	10	FB
1946	NY	AA	13	FB
1947	BUF	AA	3	B
9 yrs.		90 games		

Year	Team	Games	Pos.

Chris Mandeville
MANDEVILLE, CHRIS SCOTT
B. Feb. 1, 1965, Santa Barbara, CA
California-Davis 6'1" 213 lbs.

Year	Team		Games	Pos.
1987	GB	N	4	S
1989	WAS	N	1	S

2 yrs.   5 games

Jim Mandich
MANDICH, JAMES MICHAEL
B. Jul. 30, 1948, Cleveland, OH
Michigan 6'3" 222 lbs.

Year	Team		Games	Pos.
1970	MIA	N	14	TE
1971			11	TE
1972			14	TE
1973			14	TE
1974			14	TE
1975			14	TE
1976			14	TE
1977			14	TE
1978	PIT	N	10	TE

9 yrs.   119 games

Pete Mandley
MANDLEY, WILLIAM H.
B. Jul. 29, 1961, Mesa, AZ
Northern Arizona 5'10" 191 lbs.

Year	Team		Games	Pos.
1984	DET	N	15	WR
1985			16	WR
1986			16	WR
1987			12	WR
1988			15	WR
1989	KC	N	13	WR
1990			5	WR

7 yrs.   92 games

Dom Manella
MANELLA, DOMINICK
B. Aug. 15, 1892
D. Apr., 1981, Old Forge, PA
None 5'9" 205 lbs.

Year	Team		Games	Pos.
1926	NEW	A	3	G

James Maness
MANESS, JAMES
B. May 1, 1963, Decatur, TX
Texas Christian 6'1" 174 lbs.

Year	Team		Games	Pos.
1985	CHI	N	8	WR

Tony Manfreda
MANFREDA, ANTHONY A.
B. Feb. 19, 1904
D. Oct. 9, 1988, Brooksville, FL
Holy Cross 5'8" 172 lbs.

Year	Team		Games	Pos.
1930	NEW	N	1	HB

Mark Manges
MANGES, MARK ROY
B. Jan. 10, 1956, Cumberland, MD
Maryland 6'2" 210 lbs.

Year	Team		Games	Pos.
1978	STL	N	1	QB

Dino Mangiero
MANGIERO, DINO M.
B. Dec. 29, 1958, New York, NY
Rutgers 6'2" 265 lbs.

Year	Team		Games	Pos.
1980	KC	N	16	NT
1981			9	NT
1982			6	NT
1983			16	NT, DE
1984	SEA	N	15	NT
1987	NE	N	2	NT

6 yrs.   64 games

John Mangum
MANGUM, JOHN WAYNE, SR.

John Mangum continued
B. Sep. 30, 1942, Magee, MS
Southern Mississippi 6'3" 273 lbs.

Year	Team		Games	Pos.
1966	BOS	A	14	DT
1967			14	DT

2 yrs.   28 games

John Mangum
MANGUM, JOHN WAYNE, JR.
B. Mar. 16, 1967, Magee, MS
Alabama 5'10" 176 lbs.

Year	Team		Games	Pos.
1990	CHI	N	16	CB, S
1991			16	CB
1992			5	CB
1993			12	CB
1994			16	S
1995			11	S
1996			16	S

7 yrs.   92 games

Pete Mangum
MANGUM, ERNEST G.
B. Jan. 17, 1932
Mississippi 6'0" 219 lbs.

Year	Team		Games	Pos.
1954	NYG	N	2	FB
1960	DEN	A		LB

2 yrs.   2 games

Joe Maniaci
MANIACI, JOSEPH VINCENT
B. Jan. 23, 1914, New York, NY
Fordham 6'1" 212 lbs.

Year	Team		Games	Pos.
1936	BKN	N	11	HB
1937			11	HB, FB
1938			2	HB
1938	CHIB	N	9	HB
1939			8	FB
1940			11	FB, HB
1941			6	B

6 yrs.   58 games

Jason Maniecki
MANIECKI, JASON
B. Aug. 15, 1972, Wisconsin Dells, WI
Wisconsin 6'4" 295 lbs.

Year	Team		Games	Pos.
1996	TB	N	5	DT

Jimmy Manion
MANION, JAMES (Skipper)
B. Sep. 20, 1904
D. Jul., 1978, Pipestone, MN
*St. Mary's (Minn.)/St. Thomas (Minn.)
5'10" 178 lbs.*

Year	Team		Games	Pos.
1926	DUL	N	10	G
1927			6	G

2 yrs.   16 games

Carl Mankat
MANKAT, CARL
B. Jan. 13, 1904
D. Nov., 1963
Colgate 6'3" 208 lbs.

Year	Team		Games	Pos.
1928	DAY	N	6	E, T, G
1929			6	T, G

2 yrs.   12 games

Jim Mankins
MANKINS, JAMES FRANK
B. Jun. 23, 1944, Chino, CA
Oklahoma/Florida State 6'1" 235 lbs.

Year	Team		Games	Pos.
1967	ATL	N	11	RB

Dexter Manley
MANLEY, DEXTER
B. Feb. 2, 1959, Houston, TX

Dexter Manley continued
Oklahoma State 6'3" 256 lbs.

Year	Team		Games	Pos.
1981	WAS	N	16	DE
1982			9	DE
1983			16	DE
1984			15	DE
1985			16	DE
1986			16	DE
1987			11	DE
1988			16	DE
1989			10	DE
1990	PHX	N	4	DE
1991	TB	N	14	DE

11 yrs.   143 games

Jack Manley
MANLEY, JACK
B. 1929
Mississippi State 6'3" 215 lbs.

Year	Team		Games	Pos.
1953	SF	N	12	C

Willie Manley
MANLEY, WILLIAM LEON
B. May 20, 1926, Hollis, OK
Oklahoma 6'2" 218 lbs.

Year	Team		Games	Pos.
1950	GB	N	12	G, T
1951			12	T

2 yrs.   24 games

Bob Mann
MANN, ROBERT
B. Apr. 8, 1924, New Bern, NC
Michigan 5'11" 172 lbs.

Year	Team		Games	Pos.
1948	DET	N	12	E
1949			12	E
1950	GB	N	3	E
1951			11	E
1952			12	E
1953			10	E

6 yrs.   60 games

Charles Mann
MANN, CHARLES
B. Apr. 12, 1961, Sacramento, CA
Nevada-Reno 6'6" 270 lbs.

Year	Team		Games	Pos.
1983	WAS	N	16	DE
1984			16	DE
1985			16	DE
1986			15	DE
1987			12	DE
1988			14	DE
1989			16	DE
1990			15	DE
1991			15	DE
1992			16	DE
1993			12	DE
1994	SF	N	12	DE

12 yrs.   177 games

Dave Mann
MANN, DAVID CARL (Super)
B. Jun. 2, 1932, Berkeley, CA
Oregon State 6'1" 190 lbs.

Year	Team		Games	Pos.
1955	CHIC	N	12	HB
1956			12	HB
1957			12	HB

3 yrs.   36 games

Errol Mann
MANN, ERROL DENIS
B. Jun. 27, 1941, Breckenridge, MN
North Dakota 6'0" 202 lbs.

Year	Team		Games	Pos.
1968	GB	N	2	K
1969	DET	N	14	K
1970			14	K
1971			14	K
1972			14	K
1973			8	K

Errol Mann continued

Year	Team		Games	Pos.
1974			14	K
1975			14	K
1976			6	K
1976	OAK	N	7	K
1977			14	K
1978			16	K

11 yrs.   137 games

Aaron Manning
MANNING, AARON
B. Aug. 26, 1961
Iowa State 5'10" 178 lbs.

Year	Team		Games	Pos.
1987	CIN	N	3	CB

Archie Manning
MANNING, ELISHA ARCHIE, III
B. May 19, 1949, Cleveland, MS
Mississippi 6'3" 205 lbs.

Year	Team		Games	Pos.
1971	NO	N	14	QB
1972			14	QB
1973			13	QB
1974			11	QB
1975			13	QB
1977			10	QB
1978			16	QB
1979			16	QB
1980			16	QB
1981			12	QB
1982			1	QB
1982	HOU		3	QB
1983			3	QB
1983	MIN	N	2	QB
1984			6	QB

13 yrs.   153 games

Joe Manning
MANNING, JAMES JOSEPH
B. Nov. 20, 1900
D. Aug. 5, 1973, Springfield, MA
Fordham 5'11" 195 lbs.

Year	Team		Games	Pos.
1926	PRO	N	1	HB
1926	HAR	N	7	HB

1 yr.   8 games

Pete Manning
MANNING, PETER
B. Aug. 11, 1937, Hudson, MA
Wake Forest 6'3" 208 lbs.

Year	Team		Games	Pos.
1960	CHI	N	6	E
1961			3	DB

2 yrs.   9 games

Roosevelt Manning
MANNING, ROOSEVELT, JR.
B. May 31, 1950, Wichita Falls, TX
Northeastern Oklahoma 6'5" 257 lbs.

Year	Team		Games	Pos.
1972	ATL	N	3	DT
1973			1	DT
1974			8	DT
1975			2	DT
1975	PHI	N	10	DT

4 yrs.   24 games

Wade Manning
MANNING, WADE RONALD ARTHUR
B. July 25, 1955, Readville, PA
Ohio State 5'11" 190 lbs.*

Year	Team		Games	Pos.
1979	DAL	N	9	DB
1981	DEN	N	16	WR
1982			9	WR

3 yrs.   34 games

Tim Manoa
MANOA, TIM
B. Sep. 9, 1964, Tonga Islands

Year	Team	Games	Pos.

Tim Manoa continued
Penn State 6'1" 227 lbs.

Year	Team		Games	Pos.
1987	CLE	N	12	RB
1988			16	RB
1989			16	RB
1991	IND	N	9	RB
4 yrs.	53 games			

Brison Manor
MANOR, BRISON, JR.
B. Aug. 10, 1952, Bridgeton, NJ
Arkansas 6'4" 248 lbs.

Year	Team		Games	Pos.
1977	DEN	N	13	DE
1978			14	DE
1979			16	DE
1980			16	DE
1981			16	DE
1982			9	DE
1983			16	DE
1984			4	DE
1984	TB		6	DE
8 yrs.	110 games			

Sam Manos
MANOS, SAM
B. Oct. 2, 1963
Marshall 6'3" 265 lbs.

Year	Team		Games	Pos.
1987	CIN	N	3	C

Don Manoukian
MANOUKIAN, DONALD J.
B. 1935
Stanford 5'9" 242 lbs.

Year	Team		Games	Pos.
1960	OAK	A		G

Jerry Mansfield
MANSFIELD, GERALD
B. 1894, Iowa
D. Oct. 27, 1960
None 5'8" 160 lbs.

Year	Team		Games	Pos.
1920	RI	A	6	FB, E, HB
1921			1	FB
2 yrs.	7 games			

Ray Mansfield
MANSFIELD, JAMES RAY (The Old Ranger)
B. Jan. 21, 1941, Bakersfield, CA
Deceased
Washington 6'3" 252 lbs.

Year	Team		Games	Pos.
1963	PHI	N	14	DE, DT
1964	PIT	N	14	DT
1965			14	DT
1966			14	DT
1967			14	C
1968			14	C
1969			14	C
1970			14	C
1971			14	C
1972			14	C
1973			14	C
1974			14	C
1975			14	C
1976			14	C
14 yrs.	196 games			

Von Mansfield
MANSFIELD, EDWARD VON
B. Jul. 12, 1960, Anderson, IN
Wisconsin 5'11" 185 lbs.

Year	Team		Games	Pos.
1982	PHI	N	7	DB
1987	GB	N	3	CB, S
2 yrs.	10 games			

Ed Manske
MANSKE, EDGAR (Eggs)
B. Jul. 4, 1913, Nekoosa, WI

Ed Manske continued
Northwestern 6'0" 185 lbs.

Year	Team		Games	Pos.
1935	PHI	N	10	E
1936			12	E
1937	CHIB	N	11	E
1938			6	E, B
1938	PIT	N	7	E
1939	CHIB	N	11	E, G
1940			9	E
6 yrs.	66 games			

Joe Mantell
MANTELL, JOSEPH

Year	Team		Games	Pos.
1924	COL	N	1	G

Tillie Manton
MANTON, TALDON
B. Aug. 24, 1910, Ryan, OK
D. Feb., 1991
Louisiana State/Texas Christian 5'11" 188 lbs.

Year	Team		Games	Pos.
1936	NYG	N	12	FB
1937			10	FB
1938			1	B
1938	WAS	N	7	QB, FB
1943	BKN	N	10	QB
4 yrs.	40 games			

Dan Manucci
MANUCCI, DANIEL JOSEPH
B. Sep. 3, 1957, Erie, PA
Kansas State 6'2" 194 lbs.

Year	Team		Games	Pos.
1979	BUF	N	14	QB
1980			2	QB
1987			3	QB
3 yrs.	19 games			

Lionel Manuel
MANUEL, LIONEL, JR.
B. Apr. 13, 1962, Rancho Cucamonga, CA
Pacific 5'11" 180 lbs.

Year	Team		Games	Pos.
1984	NYG	N	16	WR
1985			12	WR
1986			4	WR
1987			12	WR
1988			16	WR
1989			16	WR
1990			14	WR
7 yrs.	90 games			

Sean Manuel
MANUEL, SEAN
B. Dec. 1, 1973, Los Gatos, NM
New Mexico State 6'2" 245 lbs.

Year	Team		Games	Pos.
1996	SF	N	11	TE

Frank Manumaleuga
MANUMALEUGA, TOTO'A FRANK
B. May 9, 1956, Laie, Samoa
UCLA/San Jose State 6'2" 245 lbs.

Year	Team		Games	Pos.
1979	KC	N	15	LB
1980			16	LB
1981			5	LB
3 yrs.	36 games			

Greg Manusky
MANUSKY, GREGORY
B. Aug. 12, 1966, Wilkes-Barre, PA
Colgate 6'1" 240 lbs.

Year	Team		Games	Pos.
1988	WAS	N	7	LB
1989			16	LB
1990			16	LB
1991	MIN	N	16	LB
1992			11	LB
1993			16	LB

Greg Manusky continued

Year	Team		Games	Pos.
1994	KC	N	16	LB
1995			16	LB
1996			16	LB
9 yrs.	130 games			

Bap Manzini
MANZINI, BAPTISTE JOHN
B. Aug. 27, 1920, Dunlevy, PA
St. Vincent 5'11" 195 lbs.

Year	Team		Games	Pos.
1944	PHI	N	9	C
1945			9	C
1948			3	C
3 yrs.	21 games			

Joe Manzo
MANZO, JOSEPH M.
B. Feb. 3, 1919, Medford, MA
Boston College 6'1" 220 lbs.

Year	Team		Games	Pos.
1945	DET	N	3	T

Howie Maple
MAPLE, HOWARD ALBERT
B. Jul. 20, 1903, Adrian, MO
D. Nov. 9, 1970, Portland, OR
Oregon State 5'7" 175 lbs.

Year	Team		Games	Pos.
1930	CHIC	N	7	HB, QB

Bobby Maples
MAPLES, BOBBY RAY
B. Dec. 28, 1942, Mount Vernon, TX
Baylor 6'3" 247 lbs.

Year	Team		Games	Pos.
1965	HOU	A	14	LB
1966			13	LB
1967			14	LB
1968			14	C
1969			14	C
1970	HOU	N	14	C
1971	PIT	N	3	C
1972	DEN	N	12	C
1973			14	C
1974			14	C
1975			14	C
1976			14	C
1977			14	C
1978				C
14 yrs.	168 games			

Jimmy Maples
MAPLES, JAMES (Butch)
B. Jan. 28, 1941
Baylor 6'4" 225 lbs.

Year	Team		Games	Pos.
1963	BAL	N	5	LB

Tal Maples
MAPLES, TALMADGE R. (Sheriff)
B. 1911
D. Apr. 19, 1975, Pompano Beach, FL
Tennessee 6'0" 195 lbs.

Year	Team		Games	Pos.
1934	C, S	N	4	C

Gary Marangi
MARANGI, GARY ANGELO
B. Jul. 29, 1952, Rockville Centre, NY
Boston College 6'1" 201 lbs.

Year	Team		Games	Pos.
1974	BUF	N	3	QB
1975			5	QB
1976			11	QB
3 yrs.	19 games			

Joe Maras
MARAS, JOSEPH T.
B. 1916
Duquesne 6'1" 203 lbs.

Year	Team		Games	Pos.
1938	PIT	N	5	C
1939			10	C

Joe Maras continued

Year	Team		Games	Pos.
1940			2	C
3 yrs.	16 games			

Gino Marchetti
MARCHETTI, GINO
B. Jan. 2, 1927, Smithers, WV
San Francisco 6'4" 244 lbs.

Year	Team		Games	Pos.
1952	DAL	N	12	DE, DT
1953	BAL	N	11	DT
1954			10	DE
1955			8	DE
1956			12	DE
1957			12	DE
1958			12	DE
1959			12	DE
1960			12	DE
1961			14	DE
1962			14	DE
1963			14	DE
1964			14	DE
1966			4	DE
14 yrs.	161 games			

Basilio Marchi
MARCHI, BASILIO
B. Jul. 14, 1909, Middleport, OH
New York University 6'2" 220 lbs.

Year	Team		Games	Pos.
1934	PIT	N	5	G
1942	PHI	N	7	C, G
2 yrs.	12 games			

Ted Marchibroda
MARCHIBRODA, THEODORE JOSEPH
B. Mar. 15, 1931, Franklin, PA
Detroit/St. Bonaventure 5'10" 178 lbs.

Year	Team		Games	Pos.
1953	PIT	N	4	QB
1955			10	QB
1956			12	QB
1957	CHIC	N	7	QB
4 yrs.	33 games			

Ken Marchiol
MARCHIOL, KENNETH
B. Aug. 27, 1965
Mesa (Arizona) 6'2" 248 lbs.

Year	Team		Games	Pos.
1987	NO	N	3	LB

Frank Marchlewski
MARCHLEWSKI, FRANK CHARLES
B. Oct. 14, 1943, New Kensington, PA
Minnesota 6'2" 237 lbs.

Year	Team		Games	Pos.
1965	LA	N	14	C
1966	ATL	N	14	C
1967			14	C
1968			1	C
1968	LA	N	14	C
1969			5	C
1970	BUF	N	14	C
6 yrs.	76 games			

Ron Marciniak
MARCINIAK, RONALD J.
B. 1932
Kansas State 6'1" 218 lbs.

Year	Team		Games	Pos.
1955	WAS	N	12	G

Chester Marcol
MARCOL, CZESLAW BOLESLAW
B. Oct. 24, 1949, Opole, Poland
Hillsdale 6'0" 190 lbs.

Year	Team		Games	Pos.
1972	GB	N	14	K
1973			14	K
1974			14	K
1975			5	K

Year	Team	Games	Pos.

Chester Marcol continued

Year	Team		Games	Pos.
1976			14	K
1977			14	K
1978			16	K
1979			10	K
1980			5	K
1980	HOU	N	1	K
9 yrs.	107 games			

Hugo Marcolini
MARCOLINI, HUGO FRANCIS
B. Apr. 7, 1923, Brooklyn, NY
D. Oct., 1973
St. Bonaventure 6'0" 203 lbs.

1948	BKN	AA	10	B

Joe Marconi
MARCONI, JOSEPH
B. Feb. 6, 1934, Fredericktown, PA
D. Aug. 22, 1992, Chicago, IL
West Virginia 6'2" 225 lbs.

1956	LA	N	12	FB
1957			10	FB
1958			12	FB
1959			12	FB
1960			12	FB
1961			13	FB
1962	CHI	N	13	FB
1963			14	FB
1964			13	FB
1965			14	FB
1966			10	FB
11 yrs.	135 games			

Ed Marcontell
MARCONTELL, EDMON DWIGHT
B. Jul. 10, 1945, Liberty, TX
Lamar 6'0" 220 lbs.

1967	STL	N	2	G
1967	HOU	A	2	G
1 yr.	4 games			

Pete Marcus
MARCUS, PETER
B. Dec. 17, 1918, Rillton, PA
Kentucky 6'2" 200 lbs.

1944	WAS	N	3	E

Greg Marderian
MARDERIAN, GREGORY
B. Jan. 15, 1952, Burbank, CA
Southern California 6'4" 250 lbs.

1976	ATL	N	1	DT

Andy Marefos
MAREFOS, ANDREW G. (Anvil Andy)
B. Jul. 16, 1917, San Francisco, CA
Deceased
St. Mary's (California) 6'0" 223 lbs.

1941	NYG	N	10	B
1942			11	FB
1946	LA	AA	13	FB
3 yrs.	34 games			

Jodie Marek
MAREK, JODIE
B. Mar. 7, 1916, Temple, TX
Texas Tech 5'11" 182 lbs.

1943	BKN	N	7	FB

Ray Marelli
MARELLI, RAY
B. Jan. 23, 1901
D. Dec., 1976, Rockford, IL

Ray Marelli continued
Notre Dame 5'10" 190 lbs.

1928	CHIC	N	2	G

Bob Margarita
MARGARITA, HENRY ROBERT
B. Nov. 3, 1920, Boston, MA
Brown 5'11" 178 lbs.

1944	CHIB	N	10	HB
1945			10	HB
1946			1	B
3 yrs.	21 games			

Ken Margerum
MARGERUM, KENNETH
B. Oct. 5, 1958, Fountain Valley, CA
Stanford 6'0" 180 lbs.

1981	CHI	N	16	WR
1982			9	WR
1983			15	WR
1985			16	WR
1986			1	WR
1986	SF	N	5	WR
1987			2	WR
6 yrs.	64 games			

Joe Margucci
MARGUCCI, JOSEPH AMERICUS
B. Sep. 5, 1921, Brooklyn, NY
Deceased
Southern California 5'10" 182 lbs.

1947	DET	N	11	QB
1948			11	HB
2 yrs.	22 games			

Joe Marhefka
MARHEFKA, JOSEPH
B. Feb. 16, 1902
Penn State/Lafayette 5'6" 160 lbs.

1926	PHI	A	2	HB

Ed Marinaro
MARINARO, EDWARD FRANCIS
B. Mar. 31, 1950, New York, NY
Cornell 6'2" 212 lbs.

1972	MIN	N	10	RB
1973			13	RB
1974			14	RB
1975			14	RB
1976	NYJ	N	6	RB
1977	SEA	N	1	FB
6 yrs.	58 games			

Dan Marino
MARINO, DANIEL CONSTANTINE, JR.
B. Sep. 15, 1961, Pittsburgh, PA
Pittsburgh 6'4" 216 lbs.

1983	MIA	N	11	QB
1984			16	QB
1985			16	QB
1986			16	QB
1987			12	QB
1988			16	QB
1989			16	QB
1990			16	QB
1991			16	QB
1992			16	QB
1993			5	QB
1994			16	QB
1995			14	QB
1996			13	QB
14 yrs.	199 games			

Vic Marino
MARINO, VICTOR IRVING
B. Oct. 2, 1918, Columbus, OH

Vic Marino continued
Ohio State 5'8" 205 lbs.

1947	BAL	AA	13	G

Marv Marinovich
MARINOVICH, MARVIN
B. Aug. 6, 1939, Watsonville, CA
Southern California 6'3" 260 lbs.

1965	OAK	A	1	G

Todd Marinovich
MARINOVICH, TODD MARVIN
B. Jul. 4, 1969, San Leandro, CA
Southern California 6'4" 215 lbs.

1991	LARI	N	1	QB
1992			7	QB
2 yrs.	8 games			

Brock Marion
MARION, BROCK ELLIOT
B. Jun. 11, 1970, Bakersfield, CA
Nevada-Reno 5'11" 189 lbs.

1993	DAL	N	15	CB
1994			14	S
1995			16	S
1996			10	S
4 yrs.	55 games			

Frank Marion
MARION, FRANK N., II
B. Mar. 16, 1951, Mount Brook, FL
Florida A&M 6'3" 238 lbs.

1977	NYG	N	3	LB
1978			16	LB
1979			16	LB
1980			11	LB
1981			16	LB
1982			9	LB
1983			10	LB
7 yrs.	81 games			

Fred Marion
MARION, FRED D.
B. Jan. 2, 1959, Gainesville, FL
Miami (Florida) 6'2" 192 lbs.

1982	NE	N	9	S
1983			16	CB, S
1984			16	S
1985			16	S
1986			16	S
1987			12	S
1988			16	S
1989			16	S
1990			16	S
1991			11	S
10 yrs.	144 games			

Jerry Marion
MARION, JERRY
B. Aug. 7, 1944, Bakersfield, CA
Wyoming 5'10" 175 lbs.

1967	PIT	N	6	DB, FL

Phil Marion
MARION, PHILLIP E. (Dutch)
B. Jun. 18, 1902
D. Jul. 23, 1985, Dearborn, MI
Washington & Jefferson/Michigan 5'9" 180 lbs.

1925	DET	N	10	FB
1926			12	FB
2 yrs.	22 games			

Greg Mark
MARK, GREG
B. Jul. 7, 1967, Pennsauken, NJ

Greg Mark continued
Miami (Florida) 6'3" 252 lbs.

1990	MIA	N	4	DE
1990	PHI	N	2	DE
1 yr.	6 games			

Cliff Marker
MARKER, CLIFFORD
B. Jun. 13, 1903
D. Jul., 1972, Tacoma, WA
Washington State 5'10" 190 lbs.

1926	CAN	N	13	E, HB, FB
1927	NYG	N	2	E
1927	FRA	N	2	E
2 yrs.	17 games			

Harry Marker
MARKER, HARRY J.
B. Sep. 17, 1910, Ligonier, PA
D. Mar. 19, 1989, Satellite Beach, FL
West Virginia 5'6" 155 lbs.

1934	PIT	N	1	HB

Dale Markham
MARKHAM, DALE JON
B. Jul. 24, 1957, Whitewater, WI
North Dakota 6'8" 280 lbs.

1980	NYG	N	1	DE
1981	STL	N	2	OT
2 yrs.	3 games			

Jeff Markland
MARKLAND, JEFFREY STUART
B. Nov. 16, 1965, Los Angeles, CA
Illinois 6'3" 245 lbs.

1988	PIT	N	1	TE

Steve Marko
MARKO, STEPHEN
B. May 26, 1924, Philadelphia, PA
D. May, 1985, Cherry Hill, NJ
none 6'0" 200 lbs.

1944	BKN	N	2	HB

Vic Markov
MARKOV, VICTOR
B. Dec. 18, 1916
Washington 6'0" 215 lbs.

1938	CLE	N	10	T

Mark Markovich
MARKOVICH, MARK JAMES
B. Nov. 7, 1952, Latrobe, PA
Penn State 6'5" 256 lbs.

1974	SD	N	9	G
1975			14	C
1976	DET	N	14	C
1977			4	C
4 yrs.	41 games			

Larry Marks
MARKS, LAWRENCE E.
B. Dec. 20, 1902
D. Jan., 1974, Kalamazoo, MI
Indiana 5'11" 185 lbs.

1926	NY	A	14	HB, FB, QB, E
1927	NYY	N	13	HB, FB, QB
1928	GB	N	11	HB, FB, QB
3 yrs.	38 games			

Lou Marks
MARKS, LOU
B. Jan. 30, 1915
D. Jan. 18, 1992, West Haverstraw, NY
North Carolina State 6'0" 196 lbs.

1938	BKN	N	11	C

Year	Team	Games	Pos.

Lou Marks *continued*

Year	Team	Games	Pos.
1939		11	C
1940		11	C
1945	**BOS** N	6	E
4 yrs.	39 games		

Sal Marone

MARONE, SALVATORE J.
B. Aug. 10, 1917
D. Jan. 12, 1975, Walden, NY
Manhattan 5'10" 195 lbs.

1943	**NYG** N	8	G

Duke Maronic

MARONIC, DUSAN
B. Jul. 13, 1921, Steelton, PA
Deceased
None 5'9" 209 lbs.

1944	**PHI** N	10	G, T
1945		8	G
1946		11	G
1947		4	G
1948		12	G
1949		11	G
1950		12	G
1951	**NYG** N	10	G
8 yrs.	78 games		

Steve Maronic

MARONIC, STEVE JESSE
B. May 30, 1917
D. May, 1980, Durham, NC
North Carolina 6'0" 225 lbs.

1939	**DET** N	10	T
1940		5	T
2 yrs.	15 games		

Lou Marotti

MAROTTI, LOUIS J.
B. Mar. 28, 1918, Chisholm, MN
Toledo 5'10" 210 lbs.

1943	**CHIC** N	8	G
1944	**C-P** N	7	G
1945	**CHIC** N	1	G
3 yrs.	16 games		

John Marquart

MARQUART, JOHN (Rube)
B. Mar. 17, 1888
D. Aug., 1973
Illinois

1921	**CHIC** A	2	E

Bob Marques

MARQUES, ROBERT
B. 1937
Boston University 6'0" 220 lbs.

1960	**NY** A		LB

Marran

MARRAN
None

1926	**BUF** N	3	E, HB

Doug Marrone

MARRONE, DOUGLAS CHARLES
B. Jul. 25, 1964, Bronx, NY
Syracuse 6'5" 269 lbs.

1987	**MIA** N	4	OT, G
1989	**NO** N	3	G
2 yrs.	7 games		

Vince Marrow

MARROW, VINCENT CHARLES
B. Aug. 17, 1968, Youngstown, OH

Vince Marrow *continued*

Youngstown State/Toledo 6'3" 251 lbs.

1994	**BUF** N	9	TE

Jim Marsalis

MARSALIS, JAMES
B. Oct. 10, 1945, Pascagoula, MS
Tennessee State 5'11" 193 lbs.

1969	**KC** A	14	CB
1970	**KC** N	14	CB
1971		14	CB
1972		14	CB
1973		10	CB
1974		2	CB
1975		10	CB
1977	**NO** N	12	S
8 yrs.	90 games		

Aaron Marsh

MARSH, AARON
B. Jul. 27, 1945, Dayton, OH
Eastern Kentucky 6'0" 190 lbs.

1968	**BOS** A	14	OE
1969		14	WR
2 yrs.	28 games		

Amos Marsh

MARSH, AMOS, JR.
B. May 7, 1939, Williams, AZ
Oregon State 6'0" 218 lbs.

1961	**DAL** N	14	FB
1962		14	FB
1963		14	FB
1964		12	HB
1965	**DET** N	13	HB
1966		14	HB
1967		14	RB
7 yrs.	95 games		

Curt Marsh

MARSH, CURT
B. Aug. 25, 1959, Tacoma, WA
Washington 6'5" 275 lbs.

1981	**OAK** N	11	OT
1982	**LARI** N	9	G
1984		16	G
1985		7	G
1986		2	G
5 yrs.	45 games		

Curtis Marsh

MARSH, CURTIS JOSEPH
B. Nov. 24, 1970, Simi Valley, CA
Utah 6'1" 212 lbs.

1995	**JAC** N	9	WR
1996		1	WR
2 yrs.	10 games		

Doug Marsh

MARSH, DOUG
B. Jun. 18, 1958, Akron, OH
Michigan 6'3" 238 lbs.

1980	**STL** N	16	TE
1981		4	TE
1982		8	TE
1983		16	TE
1984		16	TE
1985		16	TE
1986		16	TE
7 yrs.	92 games		

Frank Marsh

MARSH, FRANK
B. Jan. 1, 1941
Oregon State 6'2" 205 lbs.

1967	**SD** A	1	DB

Al Marshall

MARSHALL, ALBERT COLVIN
B. Jan. 7, 1951, Santa Cruz, CA
Boise State 6'2" 190 lbs.

1974	**NE** N	4	WR

Anthony Marshall

MARSHALL, ANTHONY DEWAYNE
B. Sep. 16, 1970, Mobile, AL
Louisiana State 6'1" 203 lbs.

1994	**CHI** N	3	S
1995		16	S, CB
1996		13	S
3 yrs.	32 games		

Arthur Marshall

MARSHALL, ARTHUR JAMES
B. Apr. 29, 1969, Fort Gordon, GA
Georgia 5'11" 174 lbs.

1992	**DEN** N	16	WR
1993		16	WR
1994	**NYG** N	16	WR
1995		15	WR
1996		5	WR
5 yrs.	68 games		

Bobby Marshall

MARSHALL, ROBERT W. (Rube)
B. Mar. 12, 1880, Milwaukee, WI
Minnesota 6'2" 190 lbs.

1920	**RI** A	7	E
1925	**DUL** N	2	E
2 yrs.	9 games		

Charles Marshall

MARSHALL, CHARLES (Tank)
B. Jan. 6, 1955, Dallas, TX
Texas A&M 6'4" 245 lbs.

1977	**NYJ** N	5	DE

Charley Marshall

MARSHALL, CHARLES
B. Oct. 17, 1906
D. Nov., 1986, Staten Island, NY
New York University 6'0" 193 lbs.

1931	**SI** N	8	E, T
1932		6	E, G
2 yrs.	14 games		

Chuck Marshall

MARSHALL, CHARLES EDWARD
B. Feb. 13, 1939, Hickory, MS
Oregon State 6'0" 180 lbs.

1962	**DEN** A	5	DB

David Marshall

MARSHALL, DAVID MARK
B. Jan. 31, 1961, Cleveland, OH
Eastern Michigan 6'3" 220 lbs.

1984	**CLE** N	16	LB
1987	**MIA** N	2	LB
2 yrs.	18 games		

Ed Marshall

MARSHALL, EDWARD L.
B. Sep. 23, 1947, Corpus Christi, TX
Cameron State 6'5" 199 lbs.

1971	**CIN** N	13	WR
1976	**NYJ** N	1	WR
1976	**NYG** N	6	WR
1977		14	WR
3 yrs.	34 games		

Greg Marshall

MARSHALL, GREGORY EDWARD
B. Sep. 9, 1956, Beverly, MA
Oregon State 6'3" 257 lbs.

1978	**BAL** N	2	DT

Henry Marshall

MARSHALL, HENRY H.
B. Aug. 9, 1954, Broxton, GA
Missouri 6'2" 212 lbs.

1976	**KC** N	14	WR
1977		14	WR
1978		16	WR
1979		16	WR
1980		16	WR
1981		12	WR
1982		9	WR
1983		13	WR
1984		16	WR
1985		11	WR
1986		16	WR
1987		12	WR
12 yrs.	165 games		

James Marshall

MARSHALL, JAMES
B. Sep. 8, 1952, Magnolia, MS
Jackson State 6'0" 187 lbs.

1980	**NO** N	16	CB

Jim Marshall

MARSHALL, JAMES LAWRENCE
B. Dec. 30, 1937, Danville, KY
Ohio State 6'3" 239 lbs.

1960	**CLE** N	12	DE
1961	**MIN** N	14	DE
1962		14	DE
1963		14	DE
1964		14	DE
1965		14	DE
1966		14	DE
1967		14	DE
1968		14	DE
1969		14	DE
1970		14	DE
1971		14	DE
1972		14	DE
1973		14	DE
1974		14	DE
1975		14	DE
1976		14	DE
1977		14	DE
1978		16	DE
1979		16	DE
20 yrs.	282 games		

Larry Marshall

MARSHALL, LAWRENCE EUGENE
B. Mar. 2, 1950, Levittown, PA
Maryland 5'10" 195 lbs.

1972	**KC** N	11	DB
1973		10	CB
1974	**MIN** N	5	DB
1974	**PHI** N	8	S
1975		10	S
1976		12	DB
1977		14	DB
1978	**KC** N	2	RB
1978	**LA** N	3	RB
7 yrs.	75 games		

Leonard Marshall

MARSHALL, LEONARD ALLEN
B. Oct. 22, 1961, Franklin, LA
Louisiana State 6'3" 285 lbs.

1983	**NYG** N	14	DE
1984		16	DE
1985		16	DE

Year	Team	Games	Pos.

Leonard Marshall *continued*

Year	Team		Games	Pos.
1986			16	DE
1987			10	DE
1988			15	DE
1989			16	DE
1990			16	DE
1991			16	DE
1992			14	DE
1993	NYJ	N	12	DT
1994	WAS	N	16	DE, DT

12 yrs. 177 games

Marvin Marshall
MARSHALL, MARVIN
B. Jun. 21, 1972, Aschaffenburg, Germany
South Carolina State 5'10" 162 lbs.

1996	TB	N	5	WR

Phil Marshall
MARSHALL, A. PHILIP
B. Mar. 28, 1895
D. Aug. 9, 1962
Carnegie-Mellon 5'8" 165 lbs.

1920	CLE	A	1	E

Randy Marshall
MARSHALL, RANDALL DONN
B. Dec. 14, 1946, Oregon City, OR
Linfield 6'5" 237 lbs.

1970	ATL	N	9	DE
1971			6	DE

2 yrs. 15 games

Rich Marshall
MARSHALL, RICHARD ARLEN (Bud)
B. Sep. 12, 1941, Carthage, TX
Baylor/Stephen F. Austin 6'5" 271 lbs.

1965	GB	N	14	DT
1966	WAS	N	6	DT
1966	ATL	N	12	DT
1967	HOU	A	11	DT
1968			11	DT

4 yrs. 54 games

Warren Marshall
MARSHALL, WARREN KEITH
B. Jul. 24, 1964, High Point, NC
James Madison 6'0" 216 lbs.

1987	DEN	N	1	RB

Whit Marshall
MARSHALL, THOMAS WHITFIELD
B. Jan. 6, 1973, Atlanta, GA
Georgia 6'2" 247 lbs.

1996	PHI	N	1	LB

Wilber Marshall
MARSHALL, WILBER BUDDYHIA
B. Apr. 18, 1962, Titusville, FL
Florida 6'1" 228 lbs.

1984	CHI	N	15	LB
1985			16	LB
1986			16	LB
1987			12	LB
1988	WAS	N	16	LB
1989			16	LB
1990			16	LB
1991			16	LB
1992			16	LB
1993	HOU	N	10	LB
1994	ARI	N	15	LB
1995	NYJ	N	15	LB

12 yrs. 179 games

Ralph Marston
MARSTON, RALPH F. (Red)
B. Feb. 16, 1907, Massachusetts
D. Dec., 1967
Boston University 5'9" 170 lbs.

1929	BOS	N	1	QB

Herm Martell
MARTELL, HERMAN
B. Dec. 8, 1900
D. Oct. 27, 1957
None 5'8" 155 lbs.

1921	GB	A	1	E

Paul Martha
MARTHA, JOHN PAUL
B. Jun. 22, 1942, Pittsburgh, PA
Pittsburgh 6'0" 186 lbs.

1964	PIT	N	14	FL, HB
1965			12	OE, FL
1966			12	FL, HB
1967			14	DB
1968			9	DB
1969			14	S
1970	DEN	N	13	CB

7 yrs. 88 games

Aaron Martin
MARTIN, AARON BEAMON
B. Feb. 10, 1942, New Bern, NC
North Carolina Central 6'0" 187 lbs.

1964	LA	N	14	DB
1965			4	DB
1966	PHI	N	14	DB
1967			14	DB
1968	WAS	N	14	DB

5 yrs. 60 games

Abe Martin
MARTIN, GLENN
B. Apr. 12, 1910
D. Sep., 1979, Havana, IL
Southern Illinois 6'0" 185 lbs.

1932	CHIC	N	9	HB, FB, QB

Amos Martin
MARTIN, ANTHONY IRL
B. Jan. 30, 1949, Indianapolis, IN
Louisville 6'3" 228 lbs.

1972	MIN	N	5	LB
1973			14	LB
1974			14	LB
1975			5	LB
1976			14	LB
1977	SEA	N	2	LB

6 yrs. 54 games

Billy Martin
MARTIN, JAKE WILLIAM, SR.
B. Oct. 27, 1942, Gainesville, GA
Georgia Tech 6'4" 238 lbs.

1964	CHI	N	14	OE
1965			14	OE
1966	ATL	N	14	TE
1967			14	TE
1968	MIN	N	14	TE

5 yrs. 70 games

Billy Martin
MARTIN, WILLIAM V.
B. Jun. 6, 1938, Chicago, IL
Minnesota 5'11" 196 lbs.

1962	CHI	N	14	HB
1963			4	HB
1964			14	HB

3 yrs. 32 games

Blanche Martin
MARTIN, BLANCHE
B. 1937
Michigan State 6'0" 195 lbs.

1960	NY	A		FB
1960	LA	A		FB

Bob Martin
MARTIN, ROBERT
Colgate

1921	SYR	A	2	G

Bob Martin
MARTIN, ROBERT
B. Nov. 14, 1953, David City, NE
Nebraska 6'1" 219 lbs.

1976	NYJ	N	13	LB
1977			5	LB
1978			16	LB
1979			3	LB
1979	SF	N	13	LB

4 yrs. 50 games

Caleb Martin
MARTIN, CALEB
B. 1923
D. Sep. 10, 1994, Winnsboro, LA
Louisiana Tech 6'4" 245 lbs.

1947	CHIC		10	T

Charles Martin
MARTIN, CHARLES M.
B. Aug. 31, 1959, Canton, GA
Livingston 6'4" 280 lbs.

1984	GB	N	16	DE
1985			16	DE
1986			14	DE
1987			2	DE
1987	HOU	N	12	NT
1988	ATL	N	16	NT

5 yrs. 76 games

Chris Martin
MARTIN, CHRISTOPHER
B. Dec. 19, 1960, Huntsville, AL
Auburn 6'2" 234 lbs.

1983	NO	N	15	LB
1984	MIN	N	16	LB
1985			12	LB
1986			16	LB
1987			12	LB
1988			9	LB
1988	KC	N	6	LB
1989			16	LB
1990			16	LB
1991			16	LB
1992			14	LB
1993	LARM	N	16	LB
1994			14	LB

12 yrs. 178 games

Chris Martin
MARTIN, CHRIS
B. Sep. 1, 1974, Tampa, FL
Northwestern 5'9" 181 lbs.

1996	CHI	N	1	QB

Curtis Martin
MARTIN, CURTIS
B. May 1, 1973, Pittsburgh, PA
Pittsburgh 5'11" 203 lbs.

1995	NE	N	16	RB
1996			16	RB

2 yrs. 32 games

D'Artagnan Martin
MARTIN, D'ARTAGNAN ATHOS (Dee)
B. Mar. 28, 1949, New Orleans, LA
Kentucky State 6'1" 190 lbs.

1971	NO	N	14	CB

Dave Martin
MARTIN, DAVID
B. Oct. 23, 1946, Kansas City, KS
Notre Dame 6'0" 220 lbs.

1968	KC	A	2	LB
1969	CHI	N	8	LB

2 yrs. 10 games

David Martin
MARTIN, DAVID EARL
B. Mar. 15, 1959, Philadelphia, PA
Villanova 5'9" 187 lbs.

1986	SD	N	4	CB
1987	BUF	N	3	CB

2 yrs. 7 games

Derrick Martin
MARTIN, DERRICK ROY
B. May 31, 1957, Los Angeles, CA
Arizona State/San Jose State 6'0" 185 lbs.

1987	SF	N	3	CB

Don Martin
MARTIN, DONALD JOE
B. Sep. 17, 1949, Carrollton, ME
Yale 5'11" 186 lbs.

1973	NE	N	14	CB
1975	KC	N	14	DB
1976	TB	N	1	DB

3 yrs. 29 games

Doug Martin
MARTIN, DOUG
B. May 22, 1957, Fairfield, CA
Washington 6'3" 258 lbs.

1980	MIN	N	11	DT
1981			16	DE
1982			9	DE
1983			16	DE
1984			13	DE
1985			16	DE
1986			15	DE
1987			12	DE
1988			11	DE
1989			7	DE

10 yrs. 126 games

Emanuel Martin
MARTIN, EMANUEL
B. Jul. 31, 1969, Miami, FL
Alabama State 5'11" 184 lbs.

1993	HOU	N	1	CB
1996	BUF	N	16	CB

2 yrs. 17 games

Emerson Martin
MARTIN, EMERSON FLOYD
B. May 6, 1970, Elizabethtown, NC
Catawba/Hampton 6'2" 297 lbs.

1995	CAR	N	2	G

Eric Martin
MARTIN, ERIC W.
B. Nov. 8, 1961, Van Vleck, TX
Louisiana State 6'1" 205 lbs.

1985	NO	N	16	WR

Year	Team		Games	Pos.

Eric Martin *continued*

Year	Team		Games	Pos.
1986			16	WR
1987			15	WR
1988			16	WR
1989			16	WR
1990			16	WR
1991			16	WR
1992			16	WR
1993			16	WR
1994	KC	N	10	WR

10 yrs. 153 games

Frank Martin

MARTIN, FRANK HAYES
B. Jun. 13, 1919, Calera, AL
D. Nov., 1981, Birmingham, AL
Alabama 5'10" 177 lbs.

Year	Team		Games	Pos.
1943	BKN	N	10	HB
1944			6	HB
1945	BOS	N	6	HB
1945	NYG	N	3	HB

3 yrs. 25 games

George Martin

MARTIN, GEORGE DWIGHT
B. Feb. 16, 1953, Greenville, SC
Oregon 6'4" 255 lbs.

Year	Team		Games	Pos.
1975	NYG	N	14	DE
1976			14	DE
1977			10	DE
1978			16	DE
1979			16	DE
1980			16	DE
1981			16	DE
1982			9	DE
1983			14	DE
1984			16	DE
1985			16	DE
1986			16	DE
1987			12	DE
1988			16	DE

14 yrs. 201 games

Harvey Martin

MARTIN, HARVEY BANKS
B. Nov. 16, 1950, Dallas, TX
East Texas State 6'5" 260 lbs.

Year	Team		Games	Pos.
1973	DAL	N	14	DE
1974			14	DE
1975			13	DE
1976			14	DE
1977			14	DE
1978			16	DE
1979			16	DE
1980			16	DE
1981			16	DE
1982			9	DE
1983			16	DE

11 yrs. 158 games

Hersh Martin

MARTIN, HERSCHEL (Jack, Buzz-Saw)
B. Nov. 17, 1905
D. Oct., 1975, Medford Lakes, NJ
None 5'11" 180 lbs.

Year	Team		Games	Pos.
1929	SI	N	8	HB, QB, FB
1930	NEW	N	4	HB, FB

2 yrs. 12 games

Ike Martin

MARTIN, ISAAC ROY
B. Jul. 15, 1887
D. Jul. 20, 1979, Aurora, OH
William Jewell 5'11" 190 lbs.

Year	Team		Games	Pos.
1920	CAN	A	5	HB, FB

Jack Martin

MARTIN, JACK T.
B. Apr. 10, 1922, Flint, MI
Princeton/Navy 6'3" 238 lbs.

Year	Team		Games	Pos.
1947	LA	N	11	C
1948			12	C
1949			12	C

3 yrs. 35 games

Jamie Martin

MARTIN, JAMIE BLANE
B. Feb. 8, 1970, Orange, CA
Weber State 6'2" 215 lbs.

Year	Team		Games	Pos.
1996	STL	N	7	QB

Jim Martin

MARTIN, JAMES RICHARD
B. Apr. 28, 1924, Cleveland, OH
Notre Dame 6'2" 227 lbs.

Year	Team		Games	Pos.
1950	CLE	N	12	DE, OT
1951	DET	N	12	DE, OT
1952			12	G, LB
1953			8	G, LB, K
1954			12	G, LB, K
1955			9	LB, K
1956			12	LB, K
1957			12	LB, K
1958			12	LB, K
1959			12	LB, K
1960			12	LB, K
1961				LB, K
1963	BAL	N	14	K
1964	WAS	N	14	K

14 yrs. 153 games

Joe Martin

MARTIN, JOSEPH
B. Feb. 5, 1895, Tennessee
D. May, 1965, Louisville, KY

Year	Team		Games	Pos.
1921	LOU	A	1	HB

John Martin

MARTIN, JOHN JAY
B. Jan. 8, 1918, Nashville, AR
Deceased
Oklahoma 6'1" 195 lbs.

Year	Team		Games	Pos.
1941	CHIC	N	9	HB
1942			11	HB
1943			10	HB, E, FB
1944	C, P	N	1	HB
1944	BOS	N	7	HB, FB
1945			3	HB

5 yrs. 41 games

Kelvin Martin

MARTIN, KELVIN BRIAN
B. May 14, 1965, San Diego, CA
Boston College 5'9" 163 lbs.

Year	Team		Games	Pos.
1987	DAL	N	7	WR
1988			16	WR
1989			11	WR
1990			16	WR
1991			16	WR
1992			16	WR
1993	SEA	N	16	WR
1994			16	WR
1995	PHI	N	9	WR
1996	DAL	N	16	WR

10 yrs. 139 games

Larry Martin

MARTIN, LAWRENCE
B. 1942
San Diego State 6'2" 270 lbs.

Year	Team		Games	Pos.
1966	SD	A	1	DT

Mike Martin

MARTIN, MICHAEL
B. Nov. 18, 1960, Washington, DC
Illinois 5'10" 186 lbs.

Year	Team		Games	Pos.
1983	CIN	N	10	WR
1984			15	WR
1985			16	WR
1986			7	WR
1987			12	WR
1988			4	WR
1989			12	WR

7 yrs. 76 games

Robbie Martin

MARTIN, ROBBIE L.
B. Dec. 3, 1958, Los Angeles, CA
California (San Luis Obispo) 5'8" 187 lbs.

Year	Team		Games	Pos.
1981	DET	N	16	WR
1982			9	WR
1983			10	WR
1984			14	WR
1985	IND	N	16	WR
1986			7	WR

6 yrs. 72 games

Rod Martin

MARTIN, RODERICK D.
B. Apr. 7, 1954, Welch, WV
Southern California 6'2" 220 lbs.

Year	Team		Games	Pos.
1977	OAK	N	1	LB
1978			15	LB
1979			16	LB
1980			16	LB
1981			16	LB
1982	LARI	N	9	LB
1983			16	LB
1984			16	LB
1985			16	LB
1986			16	LB
1987			12	LB
1988			16	LB

12 yrs. 165 games

Saladin Martin

MARTIN, SALADIN
B. Jan. 17, 1956, San Diego, CA
San Diego State 6'0" 180 lbs.

Year	Team		Games	Pos.
1980	NYJ	N	3	CB
1981	SF	N	15	CB

2 yrs. 18 games

Sammy Martin

MARTIN, SAMMY
B. Aug. 21, 1965, Gretna, LA
Louisiana State 5'11" 175 lbs.

Year	Team		Games	Pos.
1988	NE	N	16	WR
1989			10	WR
1990			10	WR
1991			4	WR
1991	IND	N	8	WR

4 yrs. 48 games

Steve Martin

MARTIN, STEVE ALBERT
B. May 31, 1974, St. Paul, MN
Missouri 6'4" 292 lbs.

Year	Team		Games	Pos.
1996	IND	N	14	DT

Steve Martin

MARTIN, STEVEN
B. Dec. 24, 1964
Jackson State 6'3" 260 lbs.

Year	Team		Games	Pos.
1987	WAS	N	3	DE

Tony Martin

MARTIN, TONY DERRICK
B. Sep. 5, 1965, Miami, FL
Bishop/Mesa State 6'0" 180 lbs.

Year	Team		Games	Pos.
1990	MIA	N	16	WR
1991			16	WR
1992			16	WR
1993			12	WR
1994	SD	N	16	WR
1995			16	WR
1996			16	WR

7 yrs. 108 games

Tracy Martin

MARTIN, TRACY A.
B. Dec. 4, 1964, Minneapolis, MN
North Dakota 6'3" 205 lbs.

Year	Team		Games	Pos.
1987	NYJ	N	12	WR

Vern Martin

MARTIN, VERNON
B. May 2, 1920, Amarillo, TX
Texas 5'10" 195 lbs.

Year	Team		Games	Pos.
1942	PIT	N	11	QB

Wayne Martin

MARTIN, GERALD WAYNE
B. Oct. 26, 1965, Forrest City, AR
Arkansas 6'5" 275 lbs.

Year	Team		Games	Pos.
1989	NO	N	16	DE
1990			11	DE
1991			16	DE
1992			16	DE
1993			16	DE
1994			16	DE
1995			16	DT
1996			16	DT

8 yrs. 123 games

Roy Martineau

MARTINEAU, ROY
B. 1900
Buffalo/Syracuse 6'0" 210 lbs.

Year	Team		Games	Pos.
1923	BUF	N	6	G, FB, T, HB
1924	ROC	N	5	G, C, T
1925			7	G

3 yrs. 18 games

John Martinelli

MARTINELLI, PATSY JOHN (Pat)
B. 1920
Scranton 6'0" 227 lbs.

Year	Team		Games	Pos.
1946	BUF	AA	3	C

Rich Martini

MARTINI, RICHARD WILLIAM
B. Nov. 19, 1955, Berkeley, CA
California-Davis 6'2" 185 lbs.

Year	Team		Games	Pos.
1979	OAK	N	16	WR
1980			16	WR
1981	NO	N	12	WR

3 yrs. 44 games

John Martinkovic

MARTINKOVIC, JOHN GEORGE
B. Feb. 4, 1927, Hamilton, OH
Xavier (Ohio) 6'3" 241 lbs.

Year	Team		Games	Pos.
1951	GB	N	12	E
1952			12	E
1953			12	E
1954			12	E
1955			12	E
1956			12	E
1957	NYG	N	12	E

7 yrs. 84 games

629

Year	Team		Games	Pos.

Phil Martinovich
MARTINOVICH, PHILIP JOSEPH
(Iron Mike)
B. Feb. 9, 1915
D. Sep. 22, 1964, Sacramento County, CA
Pacific 5'10" 220 lbs.

Year	Team		Games	Pos.
1939	DET	N	4	G
1940	CHIB	N	2	G, E
1946	BKN	AA	10	G
1947			14	G
4 yrs.	30 games			

Lonnie Marts
MARTS, LONNIE
B. Nov. 10, 1968, New Orleans, LA
Tulane 6'1" 239 lbs.

Year	Team		Games	Pos.
1991	KC	N	16	LB
1992			15	LB
1993			16	LB
1994	TB	N	16	LB
1995			15	LB
1996			16	LB
6 yrs.	94 games			

Tommy Marvaso
MARVASO, TOMMY
B. Oct. 2, 1953, Washington, DC
Cincinnati 6'1" 191 lbs.

Year	Team		Games	Pos.
1976	NYJ	N	12	DB
1977				S, CB
2 yrs.	12 games			

Eugene Marve
MARVE, EUGENE RAYMOND
B. Aug. 14, 1960, Flint, MI
Saginaw Valley State 6'2" 237 lbs.

Year	Team		Games	Pos.
1982	BUF	N	9	LB
1983			16	LB
1984			16	LB
1985			14	LB
1986			16	LB
1987			5	LB
1988	TB	N	16	LB
1989			16	LB
1990			16	LB
1991			16	LB
1992	SD	N	16	LB
11 yrs.	156 games			

Mickey Marvin
MARVIN, MICKEY
B. Oct. 5, 1955, Hendersonville, NC
Tennessee 6'4" 265 lbs.

Year	Team		Games	Pos.
1977	OAK	N	8	OT
1978			14	G
1979			2	G
1980			16	G
1981			16	G
1982	LARI	N	9	G
1983			14	G
1984			9	G
1985			15	G
1986			16	G
1987			1	G
11 yrs.	120 games			

Greg Marx
MARX, GREGORY ALLAN
B. Jul. 18, 1950, Detroit, MI
Notre Dame 6'4" 260 lbs.

Year	Team		Games	Pos.
1973	ATL	N	14	DT

Russell Maryland
MARYLAND, RUSSELL
B. Mar. 22, 1969, Chicago, IL
Miami (Florida) 6'1" 277 lbs.

Year	Team		Games	Pos.
1991	DAL	N	16	DT

Russell Maryland continued

Year	Team		Games	Pos.
1992			14	DT
1993			16	DT
1994			16	DT
1995			13	DT
1996	OAK	N	16	DT
6 yrs.	91 games			

Len Masini
MASINI, LEONARD LEROY
B. Oct. 6, 1922, Firebaugh, CA
Fresno State 6'0" 225 lbs.

Year	Team		Games	Pos.
1947	SF	AA	11	B
1948			2	B
1948	LA	AA	11	B
2 yrs.	24 games			

John Maskas
MASKAS, JOHN L.D.
B. Aug. 15, 1920, Chios, Greece
Virginia Tech 5'11" 212 lbs.

Year	Team		Games	Pos.
1947	BUF	AA	7	G
1949			11	T
2 yrs.	18 games			

Matt Maslowski
MASLOWSKI, MATT
B. Sep. 10, 1949, Chicago, IL
San Diego 6'3" 210 lbs.

Year	Team		Games	Pos.
1971	LA	N	14	WR
1972	CHI	N	1	WR
2 yrs.	15 games			

Dave Mason
MASON, DAVID CLAYTON
B. Nov. 2, 1949, Menominee, MI
Nebraska 6'0" 198 lbs.

Year	Team		Games	Pos.
1973	NE	N	8	S
1974	GB	N	12	DB
2 yrs.	20 games			

Eddie Mason
MASON, EDDIE LEE
B. Jan. 9, 1972, Siler City, NC
North Carolina 6'0" 230 lbs.

Year	Team		Games	Pos.
1995	NYJ	N	15	LB

Joel Mason
MASON, JOEL GREGORY
B. Mar. 12, 1912, Stambaugh, MI
Western Michigan 6'0" 199 lbs.

Year	Team		Games	Pos.
1939	CHIC	N	9	E, B
1942	GB	N	10	E
1943			10	E
1944			10	E
1945			10	E
5 yrs.	49 games			

Larry Mason
MASON, LARRY DARNELL
B. Mar. 21, 1961, Birmingham, AL
Southern Mississippi/Troy State 5'11" 205 lbs.

Year	Team		Games	Pos.
1987	CLE	N	3	RB
1988	GB	N	15	RB
2 yrs.	18 games			

Lindsey Mason
MASON, LINDSEY MICHAEL
B. Aug. 1, 1955, Baltimore, MD
Kansas 6'5" 265 lbs.

Year	Team		Games	Pos.
1978	OAK	N	16	OT
1980			16	OT
1981			11	OT
1982	SF	N	9	OT
1983	BAL	N	5	OT
5 yrs.	57 games			

Sam Mason
MASON, SAMUEL ANTHONY
B. Jul. 21, 1899, Hampton, VA
D. Mar. 7, 1971, Richmond, VA
Virginia Military Institute 5'8" 175 lbs.

Year	Team		Games	Pos.
1922	MIN	N	2	FB
1925	MIL	N	5	FB, QB
2 yrs.	7 games			

Tommy Mason
MASON, THOMAS CYRIL
B. Jul. 8, 1939, Lake Charles, LA
Tulane 6'0" 195 lbs.

Year	Team		Games	Pos.
1961	MIN	N	13	HB
1962			14	HB
1963			13	HB
1964			13	HB
1965			10	HB
1966			7	HB
1967	LA	N	13	RB, FL
1968			12	RB
1969			12	RB
1970			6	RB
1971	WAS	N	10	RB
11 yrs.	123 games			

Wayne Mass
MASS, WAYNE
B. Mar. 11, 1946, Portales, NM
Clemson 6'4" 243 lbs.

Year	Team		Games	Pos.
1968	CHI	N	14	OT
1969			11	OT
1970			14	OT
1971	MIA	N	11	OT
1972	PHI	N	3	G
5 yrs.	53 games			

Carlton Massey
MASSEY, CARLTON
B. Jan. 17, 1930, Nevada, TX
D. May 22, 1989, Dilley, TX
Texas 6'2" 221 lbs.

Year	Team		Games	Pos.
1954	CLE	N	11	E
1955			12	E
1956			12	E
1957	GB	N	12	E
1958			2	E
5 yrs.	49 games			

Jim Massey
MASSEY, JAMES
B. May 24, 1948, Rockaway, OR
Linfield 5'11" 198 lbs.

Year	Team		Games	Pos.
1974	NE	N	3	CB
1975			14	CB
2 yrs.	17 games			

Robert Massey
MASSEY, ROBERT LEE
B. Feb. 17, 1967, Rock Hill, SC
North Carolina Central 5'10" 189 lbs.

Year	Team		Games	Pos.
1989	NO	N	16	CB
1990			16	CB
1991	PHX	N	12	CB
1992			15	CB
1993			10	CB
1994	DET	N	16	CB
1995			16	CB, S
1996	JAC	N	16	CB
8 yrs.	117 games			

Rick Massie
MASSIE, RICHARD RAY
B. Jan. 16, 1960, Paris, KY
Kentucky 6'1" 190 lbs.

Year	Team		Games	Pos.
1987	DEN	N	9	WR
1988			4	WR
2 yrs.	13 games			

Billy Masters
MASTERS, WILLIAM JOEL
B. Mar. 15, 1944, Grayson, LA
Louisiana State 6'5" 236 lbs.

Year	Team		Games	Pos.
1967	BUF	A	14	TE
1968			14	TE
1969			14	TE
1970	DEN	N	14	TE
1971			14	TE
1972			14	TE
1973			11	TE
1974			13	TE
1975	KC	N	14	TE
1976			10	TE
10 yrs.	132 games			

Bob Masters
MASTERS, GEORGE ROBERT
(Chief)
B. Jun. 26, 1911, Comanche, TX
D. Feb. 9, 1987
Baylor 5'11" 200 lbs.

Year	Team		Games	Pos.
1937	PHI	N	8	HB
1938			1	HB
1939	PIT	N	4	HB
1942	PHI	N	4	HB
1943	P-P	N	3	HB
1943	CHIB	N	2	HB
1944			9	FB, HB
6 yrs.	31 games			

Norm Masters
MASTERS, NORMAN DONALD
B. Sep. 19, 1933, Detroit, MI
Michigan State 6'2" 249 lbs.

Year	Team		Games	Pos.
1957	GB	N	12	T
1958			12	T
1959			12	T
1960			12	T
1961			14	OT
1962			14	OT
1963			14	OT
1964			14	OT
8 yrs.	104 games			

Walt Masters
MASTERS, WALTER THOMAS
B. Mar. 28, 1907, Pen Argyl, PA
D. Jul. 10, 1992, Ottawa, Ont.
Pennsylvania 5'10" 192 lbs.

Year	Team		Games	Pos.
1936	PHI	N	2	HB
1943	CHIC	N	7	HB
1944	C-P	N	2	HB
3 yrs.	11 games			

Bernie Masterson
MASTERSON, BERNARD EDWARD (Bat)
B. Aug. 10, 1911, Shenandoah, IA
D. May 16, 1963
Nebraska 6'3" 195 lbs.

Year	Team		Games	Pos.
1934	CHIB	N	8	QB
1935			12	QB
1936			12	QB
1937			10	QB
1938			10	QB, HB
1939			10	QB
1940			7	QB
7 yrs.	70 games			

Bob Masterson
MASTERSON, ROBERT P.
B. Jan. 5, 1915, North Branch, NJ
D. Jul. 1, 1994
Miami (Florida) 6'1" 213 lbs.

Year	Team		Games	Pos.
1938	WAS	N	11	E
1939			10	E
1940			11	E
1941			11	E

Year	Team		Games	Pos.

Bob Masterson *continued*

Year	Team		Games	Pos.
1942			11	E
1943			9	E
1944	BKN	N	10	E
1945	BOS	N	10	E
1946	NY	AA	14	E
9 yrs.	97 games			

Forrest Masterson
MASTERSON, FORREST (Matt)
B. Apr. 2, 1922
Iowa 6'3" 246 lbs.

1945	CHIB	N	6	C

Le'Shai Maston
MASTON, LE'SHAI EDWOIN
B. Oct. 7, 1970, Dallas, TX
Baylor 6'1" 215 lbs.

1993	HOU	N	10	RB
1994			7	RB
1995	JAC	N	16	RB
1996			15	RB
4 yrs.	48 games			

John Mastrangelo
MASTRANGELO, JOHN B.
B. Mar. 10, 1926
D. Oct. 2, 1987, Vandergrift, PA
Notre Dame 6'1" 228 lbs.

1947	PIT	N	11	G
1948			12	T
1949	B-NY	AA	12	G
1950	NYG	N	9	G
4 yrs.	44 games			

Gus Mastrogany
MASTROGANY, AUGUST N.
B. Oct. 25, 1907
D. May 12, 1992, Northbrook, IL
Iowa 6'0" 180 lbs.

1931	CHIB	N	1	E

Stan Mataele
MATAELE, STANLEY
B. Jun. 24, 1963, Tonga Islands
Arizona 6'2" 278 lbs.

1987	GB	N	2	LB

Bill Matan
MATAN, WILLIAM D.
B. Jul. 22, 1944, St. Louis, MO
Kansas State 6'4" 240 lbs.

1966	NYG	N	3	DE

Chris Matau
MATAU, CHRISTOPHER
B. Jan. 22, 1964
Brigham Young 6'3" 310 lbs.

1987	LARM	N	3	G

Ed Matesic
MATESIC, EDWARD
B. 1911
Pittsburgh 6'1" 198 lbs.

1934	PHI	N	11	HB
1935			11	HB
1936	PIT	N	12	HB
3 yrs.	34 games			

Joe Matesic
MATESIC, JOSEPH
B. 1928
Arizona State 6'4" 250 lbs.

1954	PIT	N	1	T

Bob Matheson
MATHESON, ROBERT EDWARD
B. Nov. 25, 1944, Boone, NC
D. Sep. 5, 1994, Durham, NC
Duke 6'4" 238 lbs.

1967	CLE	N	14	LB
1968			14	LB
1969			14	LB
1970			13	LB
1971	MIA	N	14	LB
1972			14	LB
1973			14	LB
1974			14	LB
1975			14	LB
1976			13	LB
1977			14	LB
1978			12	LB
1979			16	LB
13 yrs.	180 games			

Jack Matheson
MATHESON, JOHN K.
B. Jun. 9, 1920, Detroit, MI
Western Michigan 6'2" 221 lbs.

1943	DET	N	9	E
1944			10	E
1945			9	E
1946			11	E
1947	CHIB	N	3	E
5 yrs.	42 games			

Riley Matheson
MATHESON, RILEY
B. Dec. 6, 1914, Sharon, TX
D. Jun., 1987, Paraguay
Texas Western 6'2" 207 lbs.

1939	CLE	N	2	G
1940			11	G
1941			11	G
1942			10	G
1943	DET	N	10	G
1944	CLE	N	9	G
1945			10	G
1946	LA	N	11	G
1947			11	G
1948	SF	AA	14	G
10 yrs.	99 games			

Barney Mathews
MATHEWS, FRANK E.
B. Jul. 1, 1903, St. Louis, MO
D. Apr., 1970, St. Louis, MO
Northwestern 5'8" 186 lbs.

1926	RAC	N	5	E

Jason Mathews
MATHEWS, JASON
B. Feb. 9, 1971, Orange, TX
Texas A&M 6'5" 284 lbs.

1994	IND	N	10	OT
1995			16	OT
1996			16	OT
3 yrs.	42 games			

Ned Mathews
MATHEWS, NED A.
B. Aug. 11, 1918, Provo, UT
UCLA 5'10" 187 lbs.

1941	DET	N	8	HB
1942			9	HB
1943			10	HB
1945	BOS	N	9	HB
1946	CHI	AA	8	HB
1946	SF	AA	6	HB
1947			12	HB
6 yrs.	62 games			

Neil Mathews
MATHEWS, NELSON

Neil Mathews *continued*
B. Sep. 13, 1893
D. Jul. 17, 1965
Pennsylvania 6'0" 191 lbs.

1920	CHIT	A	6	T

Ray Mathews
MATHEWS, RAYMOND DYRAL
B. Feb. 26, 1929, Dayton, PA
Clemson 6'0" 185 lbs.

1951	PIT	N	12	HB
1952			12	HB
1953			12	HB
1954			12	HB
1955			12	HB
1956			12	E
1957			12	E
1958			12	E, HB
1959			12	E
1960	DAL	N	6	FL
10 yrs.	114 games			

Bill Mathis
MATHIS, WILLIAM HART
B. Dec. 10, 1938, Rocky Mount, NC
Clemson 6'1" 219 lbs.

1960	NY	A	14	FB
1961			14	FB
1962			11	FB
1963			14	FB
1964			14	HB
1965			14	HB
1966			14	HB
1967			14	RB
1968			14	RB
1969			14	RB
10 yrs.	137 games			

Dedric Mathis
MATHIS, DEDRIC
B. Sep. 26, 1973, Cuero, TX
Houston 5'10" 196 lbs.

1996	IND	N	16	CB

Mark Mathis
MATHIS, MARK
B. Aug. 23, 1965, Mount Clemens, MI
Liberty 5'9" 178 lbs.

1987	STL	N	2	CB

Reggie Mathis
MATHIS, REGINALD LEVI
B. Mar. 18, 1956, Chattanooga, TN
Oklahoma 6'2" 220 lbs.

1979	NO	N	16	LB
1980			16	LB
2 yrs.	32 games			

Terance Mathis
MATHIS, TERANCE
B. Jun. 7, 1967, Detroit, MI
New Mexico 5'10" 170 lbs.

1990	NYJ	N	16	WR
1991			16	WR
1992			10	WR
1993			16	WR
1994	ATL	N	16	WR
1995			14	WR
1996			16	WR
7 yrs.	104 games			

Bruce Mathison
MATHISON, BRUCE MARTIN
B. Apr. 25, 1959, Superior, WI
Nebraska 6'3" 205 lbs.

1983	SD	N	1	QB
1984			2	QB

Bruce Mathison *continued*

1985	BUF	N	10	QB
1986	SD	N	2	QB
1987	SEA	N	3	QB
5 yrs.	18 games			

Charlie Mathys
MATHYS, CHARLES P.
B. Jun. 20, 1897, Green Bay, WI
D. Jan. 18, 1983, Green Bay, WI
Ripon/Indiana 5'7" 165 lbs.

1921	HAM	A	5	QB, HB
1922	GB	N	10	QB
1923			10	QB
1924			11	QB
1925			12	QB
1926			4	QB
6 yrs.	52 games			

Trevor Matich
MATICH, TREVOR ANTHONY
B. Oct. 9, 1961, Sacramento, CA
Brigham Young 6'4" 277 lbs.

1985	NE	N	1	C
1986			11	C
1987			6	C
1988			11	C
1989	DET	N	11	C
1990	NYJ	N	16	C, G, OT
1991			15	C, G, OT, TE
1992	IND	N	16	G, OT
1993			16	C
1994	WAS	N	16	C
1995			16	C
1996			16	C
12 yrs.	148 games			

John Matisi
MATISI, JOHN BERNARD
B. Nov. 2, 1920, New York, NY
Duquesne 6'2" 218 lbs.

1943	BKN	N	4	T, G, C
1946	BUF	AA	12	T
2 yrs.	16 games			

Tony Matisi
MATISI, ANTHONY FRANCIS
B. Aug. 23, 1914, New York, NY
D. Aug. 26, 1969, Endicott, NY
Pittsburgh 6'2" 230 lbs.

1938	DET	N	5	T

John Matlock
MATLOCK, JOHN JAMES
B. Oct. 19, 1944, Louisville, KY
Miami (Florida) 6'4" 250 lbs.

1967	NY	A	10	C
1968	CIN	A	12	C
1970	ATL	N	14	C
1971			13	C
1972	BUF	N	11	C
5 yrs.	60 games			

Ollie Matson
MATSON, OLLIE GENOA
B. May 1, 1930, Trinity, TX
San Francisco 6'2" 220 lbs.

1952	CHIC	N	11	FB
1954			12	FB
1955			12	HB
1956			12	HB
1957			12	HB
1958			12	HB
1959	LA	N	12	FB
1960			12	FB
1961			14	FB
1962			13	FB
1963	DET	N	8	FB

Ollie Matson continued

Year	Team		Games	Pos.
1964	PHI	N	12	HB
1965			14	HB
1966			14	HB
14 yrs.	170 games			

Pat Matson
MATSON, PATRICK WILLIAM
B. Jul. 22, 1944, Laramie, WY
Oregon 6'1" 246 lbs.

Year	Team		Games	Pos.
1966	DEN	A	14	G
1967			14	G
1968	CIN	A	14	G
1969			6	G
1970	CIN	N	13	G
1971			14	G
1972			14	G
1973			14	G
1974			14	G
1975	GB	N	14	G
10 yrs.	131 games			

Archie Matsos
MATSOS, EMIL GEORGE
B. Nov. 22, 1934, Detroit, MI
Michigan State 6'0" 215 lbs.

Year	Team		Games	Pos.
1960	BUF	A	14	LB
1961			14	LB
1962			14	LB
1963	OAK	A	14	LB
1964			14	LB
1965			12	LB
1966	DEN	A	9	LB
1966	SD	A	5	LB
7 yrs.	96 games			

Art Matsu
MATSU, ICHYA
B. Apr. 30, 1904, Glasgow, Scotland
D. May 28, 1987, Prescott, AZ
William & Mary 5'7" 168 lbs.

Year	Team		Games	Pos.
1928	DAY	N	6	QB, HB

Tom Matte
MATTE, THOMAS ROLAND
B. Jun. 14, 1939, Pittsburgh, PA
Ohio State 6'0" 207 lbs.

Year	Team		Games	Pos.
1961	BAL	N	8	HB
1962			14	HB
1963			14	HB
1964			14	HB
1965			14	HB, QB
1966			14	RB
1967			14	RB
1968			14	RB
1969			14	RB
1970			2	RB
1971			14	RB
1980	NYG	N	15	RB
1981			5	RB
1981	MIA	N	3	RB
13 yrs.	159 games			

Frank Matteo
MATTEO, FRANCIS PASQUALE
(Patty)
B. Apr. 2, 1896
D. Dec. 19, 1983, Oneida Castle, NY
Syracuse 5'11" 195 lbs.

Year	Team		Games	Pos.
1921	SYR	A	3	T, G
1922	ROC	N	3	T
1923			4	T, G
1924			5	T, G
1925			4	T
5 yrs.	19 games			

Joey Mattern
MATTERN, JOSEPH

Joey Mattern continued
B. Sep. 9, 1892
Deceased
Miami (Ohio)/Minnesota 155 lbs.

Year	Team		Games	Pos.
1920	CLE	A	1	HB
1922	MIN	N	1	HB
2 yrs.	2 games			

Ron Mattes
MATTES, RONALD ANTHONY
B. Aug. 8, 1963, Shenandoah, PA
Virginia 6'6" 304 lbs.

Year	Team		Games	Pos.
1986	SEA	N	16	OT
1987			12	OT
1988			16	OT
1989			16	OT
1990			16	OT
1991	CHI	N	15	OT
1992	IND	N	5	OT
7 yrs.	96 games			

Al Matthews
MATTHEWS, ALVIN LEON
B. Nov. 7, 1947, Austin, TX
Texas A&I, Kingsville 5'11" 190 lbs.

Year	Team		Games	Pos.
1970	GB	N	14	CB
1971			14	DB
1972			14	CB
1973			14	S
1974			14	S
1975			14	S
1976	SEA	N	14	S
1977	SF	N	1	DB
8 yrs.	99 games			

Allama Matthews
MATTHEWS, ALLAMA UZAIR
B. Aug. 24, 1961, Jacksonville, FL
Vanderbilt 6'3" 230 lbs.

Year	Team		Games	Pos.
1983	ATL	N	16	TE
1984			6	TE
1985			15	TE
3 yrs.	37 games			

Aubrey Matthews
MATTHEWS, AUBREY DERRON
B. Sep. 15, 1962, Pascagoula, MS
Delta State 5'7" 165 lbs.

Year	Team		Games	Pos.
1986	ATL	N	4	WR
1987			12	WR
1988			4	WR
1988	GB	N	7	WR
1989			13	WR
1990	DET	N	12	WR
1991			1	WR
1992			13	WR
1993			14	WR
1994			14	WR
1995			12	WR
1996			16	WR
11 yrs.	122 games			

Bill Matthews
MATTHEWS, WILLIAM MARVIN
B. Mar. 12, 1956, Santa Monica, CA
South Dakota State 6'2" 235 lbs.

Year	Team		Games	Pos.
1979	NE	N	16	LB
1980			16	LB
1981			16	LB
3 yrs.	48 games			

Bo Matthews
MATTHEWS, WILLIAM PIERCE
B. Nov. 15, 1951, Huntsville, AL
Colorado 6'4" 227 lbs.

Year	Team		Games	Pos.
1974	SD	N	14	RB
1975			14	RB
1976			12	RB

Bo Matthews continued

Year	Team		Games	Pos.
1977			12	RB
1978			11	RB
1979			16	FB
6 yrs.	79 games			

Bruce Matthews
MATTHEWS, BRUCE
B. Aug. 8, 1961, Arcadia, CA
Southern California 6'4" 288 lbs.

Year	Team		Games	Pos.
1983	HOU	N	16	OT
1984			16	G, OT
1985			16	OT
1986			16	OT
1987			8	OT
1988			16	OT, G
1989			16	G
1990			16	G
1991			16	G, C
1992			16	C, G
1993			16	C, G
1994			16	C, OT
1995			16	G
1996			16	G
14 yrs.	216 games			

Clay Matthews
MATTHEWS, WILLIAM CLAY, SR.
B. Aug. 1, 1928
Georgia Tech 6'3" 219 lbs.

Year	Team		Games	Pos.
1950	SF	N	12	E
1953			9	E
1954			12	E
1955			12	E
4 yrs.	45 games			

Clay Matthews
MATTHEWS, WILLIAM CLAY, JR.
B. Mar. 15, 1956, Palo Alto, CA
Southern California 6'2" 238 lbs.

Year	Team		Games	Pos.
1978	CLE	N	15	LB
1979			16	LB
1980			14	LB
1981			16	LB
1982			2	LB
1983			16	LB
1984			14	LB
1985			16	LB
1986			16	LB
1987			12	LB
1988			16	LB
1989			16	LB
1990			15	LB
1991			16	LB
1992			16	LB
1993			16	LB
1994	ATL	N	15	LB
1995			16	LB
1996			15	LB
19 yrs.	278 games			

Henry Matthews
MATTHEWS, HENRY
B. Mar. 17, 1949, Akron, OH
Michigan State 6'2" 203 lbs.

Year	Team		Games	Pos.
1972	NE	N	3	RB
1973	NO	N	6	RB
1973	ATL	N	3	RB
2 yrs.	12 games			

Ira Matthews
MATTHEWS, IRA RICHARD, III
B. Aug. 23, 1957, Rockford, IL
Wisconsin 5'8" 175 lbs.

Year	Team		Games	Pos.
1979	OAK	N	16	RB
1980			16	RB, WR
1981			5	WR
3 yrs.	37 games			

Shane Matthews
MATTHEWS, MICHAEL SHANE
B. Jun. 1, 1970, Pascagoula, MS
Florida 6'3" 197 lbs.

Year	Team		Games	Pos.
1996	CHI	N	2	QB

Wes Matthews
MATTHEWS, WESLEY
B. 1944
Northeastern Oklahoma 5'10" 180 lbs.

Year	Team		Games	Pos.
1966	MIA	A	4	FL

Frank Mattiace
MATTIACE, FRANK LOUIS
B. Jan. 29, 1961, Paterson, NJ
Holy Cross 6'1" 264 lbs.

Year	Team		Games	Pos.
1987	IND	N	3	NT

Jack Mattiford
MATTIFORD, JACK BLAKER
B. Jun. 24, 1916, Peora, WV
Deceased
Marshall 5'10" 216 lbs.

Year	Team		Games	Pos.
1941	DET	N	10	G

Fran Mattingly
MATTINGLY, FRANCIS EDWARD
(Sax)
B. 1920
Texas A&I, Kingsville 5'11" 215 lbs.

Year	Team		Games	Pos.
1947	CHI	AA	1	G

Frank Mattioli
MATTIOLI, FRANCIS
B. 1923
Pittsburgh 6'0" 210 lbs.

Year	Team		Games	Pos.
1946	PIT	N	11	G

Harry Mattos
MATTOS, HARRY (The Toe, The Horse)
B. Apr. 7, 1911, Oakland, CA
D. Feb. 5, 1992, San Jose, CA
St. Mary's (Oakland) 6'0" 198 lbs.

Year	Team		Games	Pos.
1936	GB	N	2	HB
1937	CLE	N	6	HB
2 yrs.	8 games			

Jack Mattox
MATTOX, JACK V.
B. Aug. 3, 1938, Fresno, CA
Fresno State 6'4" 240 lbs.

Year	Team		Games	Pos.
1961	DEN	A	8	DT

Marv Mattox
MATTOX, MARVIN BRUCE
(Monk)
B. Feb. 11, 1900, Leesville, VA
Deceased
Washington & Lee 5'9" 190 lbs.

Year	Team		Games	Pos.
1923	MIL	N	5	HB, F, G

Riley Mattson
MATTSON, RILEY
B. Dec. 18, 1938, Portland, OR
Oregon 6'4" 252 lbs.

Year	Team		Games	Pos.
1961	WAS	N	14	OT
1962			14	OT
1963			14	OT
1964			14	OT
1966	CHI	N	12	OT
5 yrs.	68 games			

John Matuszak

MATUSZAK, JOHN DANIEL
(Tooz)
B. Oct. 25, 1950, Milwaukee, WI
D. Jun. 17, 1989, Los Angeles, CA
Missouri/Tampa 6'8" 278 lbs.

Year	Team		Games	Pos.
1973	HOU	N	14	DT
1974	KC	N	8	DE
1975			14	DE
1976	OAK	N	13	DE
1977			14	DE
1978			16	DE
1979			12	DE
1980			16	DE
1981			16	DE
9 yrs.		123 games		

Marv Matuszak

MATUSZAK, MARVIN
B. Sep. 12, 1931, South Bend, IN
Tulsa 6'3" 232 lbs.

Year	Team		Games	Pos.
1953	PIT	N	12	G
1955			4	G
1956			9	G
1957	SF	N	12	LB
1959	BAL	N	11	LB
1960			12	LB
1961			14	LB
1962	BUF	A	14	LB
1963			14	LB
1964	DEN	A	14	LB
10 yrs.		116 games		

Al Matuza

MATUZA, ALBERT C.
B. Sep. 11, 1918, Shenandoah, PA
Georgetown (DC) 6'2" 200 lbs.

Year	Team		Games	Pos.
1941	CHIB	N	10	C, E
1942			11	C
1943			10	C
3 yrs.		31 games		

Carl Mauck

MAUCK, CARL FREY
B. Jul. 7, 1947, McLeansboro, IL
Southern Illinois 6'3" 245 lbs.

Year	Team		Games	Pos.
1969	BAL	N	4	LB
1970	MIA	N	3	C
1971	SD	N	13	C
1972			14	C
1973			14	C
1974			14	C
1975	HOU	N	14	C
1976			14	C
1977			14	C
1978			16	C
1979			16	C
1980			16	C
1981			14	C
13 yrs.		166 games		

Tuffy Maul

MAUL, ELMO A.
B. Jun. 20, 1902
D. Mar. 16, 1974, Fresno, CA
St. Mary's (California) 5'11" 200 lbs.

Year	Team		Games	Pos.
1926	LA	N	10	FB

Stan Mauldin

MAULDIN, STANLEY HUBERT
B. Dec. 27, 1920, Amarillo, TX
D. Sep. 24, 1948, Chicago, IL
Texas 6'2" 225 lbs.

Year	Team		Games	Pos.
1946	CHIC	N	6	T
1947			12	T
1948			1	T
3 yrs.		19 games		

Chris Maumalanga

MAUMALANGA, CHRIS
B. Dec. 15, 1971, Redwood City, CA
Kansas 6'2" 288 lbs.

Year	Team		Games	Pos.
1994	NYG	N	7	DT
1995	ARI	N	9	DT
1996			1	DT
3 yrs.		17 games		

Adrian Maurer

MAURER, ADRIAN HAROLD
(Sparky, Red)
B. 1903
Piedmont (Georgia)/Oglethorpe 5'8" 185 lbs.

Year	Team		Games	Pos.
1926	NEW	A	3	HB

Andy Maurer

MAURER, ANDREW LEE
B. Sep. 30, 1948, Silverton, OR
Oregon 6'3" 265 lbs.

Year	Team		Games	Pos.
1970	ATL	N	14	G
1971			14	G
1972			14	G
1973			14	G
1974	NO	N	5	G
1974	MIN	N	8	G
1975			14	G
1976	SF	N	13	G
1977	DEN	N	13	OT
8 yrs.		109 games		

Rich Mauti

MAUTI, RICHARD DOMINIC
B. May 25, 1954, Hollis Place, LA
Penn State 6'0" 190 lbs.

Year	Team		Games	Pos.
1977	NO	N	14	WR
1978			16	WR
1979			15	WR
1980			9	WR
1982			9	WR
1983			16	WR
1984	WAS	N	16	WR
7 yrs.		95 games		

Menil Mavraides

MAVRAIDES, MENIL (Minnie)
B. Nov. 17, 1931, Lowell, MA
Notre Dame 6'1" 235 lbs.

Year	Team		Games	Pos.
1954	PHI	N	12	G
1957			12	G
2 yrs.		24 games		

Kevin Mawae

MAWAE, KEVIN JAMES
B. Jan. 23, 1971, Leesville, LA
Louisiana State 6'4" 286 lbs.

Year	Team		Games	Pos.
1994	SEA	N	14	G, C
1995			16	C
1996			16	G
3 yrs.		46 games		

Curtis Maxey

MAXEY, CURTIS
B. Jan. 28, 1965, Indianapolis, IN
Grambling State 6'3" 298 lbs.

Year	Team		Games	Pos.
1988	CIN	N	3	NT
1989	ATL	N	2	NT
2 yrs.		5 games		

Brett Maxie

MAXIE, BRETT DERRELL
B. Jan. 13, 1962, Dallas, TX
Texas Southern 6'2" 193 lbs.

Year	Team		Games	Pos.
1985	NO	N	16	DB
1986			15	CB, S
1987			12	DB
1988			16	S

Brett Maxie continued

Year	Team		Games	Pos.
1989			16	S
1990			16	S
1991			16	S
1992			10	S
1993			1	S
1994	ATL	N	4	S
1995	CAR	N	16	S
1996			13	S
12 yrs.		151 games		

Alvin Maxson

MAXSON, ALVIN EARL
B. Nov. 12, 1951, Beaumont, TX
Southern Methodist 5'11" 203 lbs.

Year	Team		Games	Pos.
1974	NO	N	14	RB
1975			13	RB
1976			14	RB
1977	PIT	N	7	RB
1978			5	RB
1978	TB	N	1	RB
1978	HOU	N	1	RB
1978	NYG	N	1	RB
5 yrs.		56 games		

Bruce Maxwell

MAXWELL, BRUCE
B. Mar. 23, 1947, Crossett, AR
Arkansas 6'1" 220 lbs.

Year	Team		Games	Pos.
1970	DET	N	11	RB

Joey Maxwell

MAXWELL, JOSEPH
B. Nov. 5, 1904
D. Feb., 1983, Ardsley, PA
Notre Dame 6'2" 197 lbs.

Year	Team		Games	Pos.
1927	FRA	N	18	C, E
1928			8	C
1929			11	E, C
3 yrs.		37 games		

Tommy Maxwell

MAXWELL, THOMAS MARSHALL
B. May 5, 1947, Houston, TX
Texas A&M 6'2" 195 lbs.

Year	Team		Games	Pos.
1969	BAL	N	13	CB
1970			14	CB
1971	OAK	N	13	CB
1972			7	CB
1973			8	S
1974	HOU	N	12	S
6 yrs.		67 games		

Vernon Maxwell

MAXWELL, VERNON LEROY
B. Oct. 25, 1961, Birmingham, AL
Arizona State 6'2" 233 lbs.

Year	Team		Games	Pos.
1983	BAL	N	16	LB
1984	IND	N	16	LB
1985	DET	N	9	LB
1986			15	LB
1987			12	LB
1989	SEA	N	9	LB
6 yrs.		77 games		

Art May

MAY, ARTHUR LEE
B. Nov. 16, 1948, Bessemer, AL
Tuskegee Institute 6'3" 245 lbs.

Year	Team		Games	Pos.
1971	NE	N	11	DE

Bill May

MAY, WILLIAM
B. 1914
Louisiana State 5'11" 188 lbs.

Year	Team		Games	Pos.
1937	CHIC	N	9	HB, QB

Bill May continued

Year	Team		Games	Pos.
1938			2	QB
2 yrs.		11 games		

Chad May

MAY, CHAD
B. Sep. 28, 1971, West Covina, CA
Fullerton State/Kansas State 6'1" 219 lbs.

Year	Team		Games	Pos.
1996	ARI	N	2	QB

Dean May

MAY, DEAN CURTIS
B. May 26, 1962, Orlando, FL
Louisville 6'5" 220 lbs.

Year	Team		Games	Pos.
1984	PHI	N	2	QB
1987	DEN	N	3	QB
2 yrs.		5 games		

Deems May

MAY, BERT DEEMS, JR.
B. Mar. 6, 1969, Lexington, NC
North Carolina 6'4" 250 lbs.

Year	Team		Games	Pos.
1992	SD	N	16	TE
1993			15	TE
1994			5	TE
1995			5	TE
1996			16	TE
5 yrs.		57 games		

Jack May

MAY, JACK
B. Apr. 16, 1915
D. Nov., 1969
Centenary 5'10" 210 lbs.

Year	Team		Games	Pos.
1938	CLE	N	8	C, E

Marc May

MAY, MARC
B. Jan. 1, 1958, Chicago, IL
Purdue 6'4" 230 lbs.

Year	Team		Games	Pos.
1987	MIN	N	3	TE

Mark May

MAY, MARK
B. Nov. 2, 1959, Oneonta, NY
Pittsburgh 6'6" 295 lbs.

Year	Team		Games	Pos.
1981	WAS	N	16	OT
1982			8	OT
1983			15	G
1984			16	OT
1985			16	OT
1986			16	OT
1987			10	OT
1988			16	OT
1989			9	G, OT
1991	SD	N	9	G
1992	PHX	N	16	G, OT
1993			11	G
12 yrs.		158 games		

Ray May

MAY, RAY
B. Jun. 4, 1945, Los Angeles, CA
Southern California 6'1" 230 lbs.

Year	Team		Games	Pos.
1967	PIT	N	14	LB
1968			12	LB
1969			14	LB
1970	BAL	N	14	LB
1971			13	LB
1972			3	LB
1973	DEN	N	11	CB
1974			14	LB
1975			8	LB
9 yrs.		117 games		

Year	Team		Games	Pos.

Sheriden May
MAY, SHERIDEN
B. Aug. 10, 1973, Tacoma, WA
Idaho 6'0" 215 lbs.

Year	Team		Games	Pos.
1995	**NYJ**	N	5	RB
1996			8	FB
2 yrs.	13 games			

Walt May
MAY, WALTER O. (Red)
B. Feb. 27, 1897, IL
D. 1933
None 6'1" 205 lbs.

1920	**DEC**	A	1	G

Doug Mayberry
MAYBERRY, DOUGLAS
B. Mar. 23, 1937, Arbuckle, CA
California/Utah State 6'1" 223 lbs.

1961	**MIN**	N	4	FB
1962			13	FB
1963	**OAK**	A	2	FB
3 yrs.	19 games			

James Mayberry
MAYBERRY, JAMES LOYD
B. Nov. 5, 1957, Amarillo, TX
Colorado 5'11" 210 lbs.

1979	**ATL**	N	16	RB
1980			16	RB
1981			16	RB
3 yrs.	48 games			

Jermane Mayberry
MAYBERRY, JERMANE
B. Aug. 29, 1973, Floresville, TX
Texas A&M, Kingsville 6'4" 325 lbs.

1996	**PHI**	N	3	G

Tony Mayberry
MAYBERRY, EINO ANTHONY
B. Dec. 8, 1967, Wurzburg, Germany
Wake Forest 6'4" 287 lbs.

1990	**TB**	N	16	C
1991			16	C
1992			16	C
1993			16	C
1994			16	C
1995			16	C
1996			16	C
7 yrs.	112 games			

Emil Mayer
MAYER, EMIL (Puss)
B. Jul. 3, 1903, East Liverpool, OH
Bethany (West Virginia)/Catholic 6'0" 190 lbs.

1927	**POT**	N	1	E
1930	**POR**	N	8	E
2 yrs.	9 games			

Frank Mayer
MAYER, FRANK
B. Jun. 18, 1902
Deceased
Iowa State/Notre Dame 5'11" 215 lbs.

1927	**GB**	N	10	G, T

Ben Mayes
MAYES, BENJAMIN
B. Mar. 16, 1945, St. Petersburg, FL
Drake 6'5" 265 lbs.

1969	**HOU**	A	5	DE

Derrick Mayes
MAYES, DERRICK
B. Jan. 28, 1974, Indianapolis, IN
Notre Dame 6'0" 201 lbs.

1996	**GB**	N	7	WR

Mike Mayes
MAYES, MICHAEL O.
B. Aug. 17, 1966, De Ridder, LA
Louisiana State 5'10" 182 lbs.

1989	**NO**	N	2	CB
1990	**NYJ**	N	16	CB
1991	**MIN**	N	9	CB
3 yrs.	27 games			

Rueben Mayes
MAYES, RUEBEN
B. Jun. 6, 1963, North Battleford, Sask.
Washington State 5'11" 200 lbs.

1986	**NO**	N	16	RB
1987			12	RB
1988			16	RB
1990			15	RB
1992	**SEA**	N	16	RB
1993			1	RB
6 yrs.	76 games			

Rufus Mayes
MAYES, RUFUS LEE
B. Dec. 5, 1947, Memphis, TN
Ohio State 6'5" 259 lbs.

1969	**CHI**	N	13	OT
1970	**CIN**	N	14	OT
1971			14	OT
1972			6	OT
1973			13	OT
1974			14	OT
1975			14	OT
1976			14	OT
1977			12	OT
1978			8	OT
1979	**PHI**	N	16	OT
11 yrs.	138 games			

Tony Mayes
MAYES, ANTHONY CURTIS
B. Mar. 19, 1964, Tazewell, TN
Kentucky 6'0" 200 lbs.

1987	**STL**	N	3	S

Corey Mayfield
MAYFIELD, ARTHUR COREY
B. Feb. 25, 1970, Tyler, TX
Oklahoma 6'3" 280 lbs.

1992	**TB**	N	11	DL
1995	**JAC**	N	16	DT
2 yrs.	27 games			

Lindy Mayhew
MAYHEW, HAYDEN L. (Tex)
B. Aug. 24, 1907
D. Feb. 21, 1990, Lilburn, GA
Texas Western 6'1" 223 lbs.

1936	**PIT**	N	12	G, T
1937			10	G, T
1938			6	G
3 yrs.	28 games			

Martin Mayhew
MAYHEW, MARTIN
B. Oct. 8, 1965, Daytona Beach, FL
Florida State 5'8" 172 lbs.

1989	**WAS**	N	16	CB
1990			16	CB
1991			16	CB
1992			10	CB
1993	**TB**	N	15	CB

Martin Mayhew continued

1994			16	CB
1995			13	CB
1996			16	CB
8 yrs.	118 games			

Gene Mayl
MAYL, EUGENE A.
B. Oct. 23, 1901
D. Jul. 12, 1986, Dayton, OH
Dayton/Notre Dame 6'2" 198 lbs.

1925	**DAY**	N	8	E
1926			4	E
2 yrs.	12 games			

Don Maynard
MAYNARD, DONALD
B. Jan. 25, 1937, Crosbyton, TX
Rice/Texas Western 6'0" 180 lbs.

1958	**NYG**	N	12	HB
1960	**NY**	A	13	OE
1961			14	FL
1962			14	FL
1963			12	FL
1964			14	FL
1965			14	FL
1966			14	FL
1967			14	FL
1968			13	FL
1969			10	WR
1970	**NYJ**	N	10	WR
1971			14	WR
1972			14	WR
1973	**STL**	N	2	WR
15 yrs.	184 games			

Les Maynard
MAYNARD, LESTER
B. 1911
Coast Guard/Rider 6'3" 210 lbs.

1932	**SI**	N	7	E

Lew Mayne
MAYNE, LEWIS ELWOOD
B. Mar. 21, 1920, Cuero, TX
Texas 6'1" 190 lbs.

1946	**BKN**	AA	13	HB
1947	**CLE**	AA	13	HB
1948	**BAL**	AA	8	HB
3 yrs.	34 games			

Ron Mayo
MAYO, RONALD
B. Oct. 11, 1950, Washington, DC
Morgan State 6'3" 223 lbs.

1973	**HOU**	N	13	TE
1974	**BAL**	N	9	TE
2 yrs.	22 games			

Mike Mayock
MAYOCK, MICHAEL FRANCIS, JR.
B. Aug. 14, 1958, Philadelphia, PA
Boston College 6'2" 198 lbs.

1982	**NYG**	N	3	S
1983			6	S
2 yrs.	9 games			

Alvoid Mays
MAYS, ALVOID
B. Jul. 10, 1966, Palmetto, FL
West Virginia 5'9" 180 lbs.

1990	**WAS**	N	15	CB
1991			13	CB
1992			16	CB
1993			15	CB

Alvoid Mays continued

1994			2	CB
1995	**PIT**	N	13	CB
6 yrs.	74 games			

Damon Mays
MAYS, DAMON
B. May 20, 1968, Phoenix, AZ
Missouri 5'9" 170 lbs.

1992	**HOU**	N	1	WR
1993			1	WR
2 yrs.	2 games			

Dave Mays
MAYS, DAVID
B. Jun. 20, 1949, Pine Bluff, AR
Texas Southern 6'1" 204 lbs.

1976	**CLE**	N	4	K, QB
1977			7	QB
1978	**BUF**	N	1	QB
3 yrs.	12 games			

Jerry Mays
MAYS, GERALD AVERY
B. Nov. 24, 1939, Dallas, TX
D. Jul. 17, 1994, Lake Lewisville, TX
Southern Methodist 6'4" 250 lbs.

1961	**DAL**	A	14	DT
1962			14	DE, OT
1963	**KC**	A	14	DE, OT
1964			14	DE
1965			14	DT
1966			14	DT
1967			14	DE
1968			14	DE
1969			14	DE
1970	**KC**	N	14	DE
10 yrs.	140 games			

Jerry Mays
MAYS, JERRY DEWAYNE
B. Dec. 8, 1967, Augusta, GA
Georgia Tech 5'7" 176 lbs.

1990	**SD**	N	2	RB

Stafford Mays
MAYS, STAFFORD EARL
B. Mar. 13, 1958, Lawrence, KS
Washington 6'2" 251 lbs.

1980	**STL**	N	16	DT
1981			16	DE
1982			8	DE
1983			16	DE
1984			16	DE
1985			16	DE
1986			16	DE
1987	**MIN**	N	12	DE
1988			3	DT
9 yrs.	119 games			

Frank Maznicki
MAZNICKI, FRANCIS STANLEY
B. Jul. 19, 1920, West Warwick, RI
Boston College 5'9" 181 lbs.

1942	**CHIB**	N	11	HB
1946			9	HB
1947	**BOS**	N	12	HB
3 yrs.	32 games			

Fred Mazurek
MAZUREK, FREDERICK HENRY
B. Mar. 21, 1943, Uniontown, PA
Catholic/Pittsburgh 5'11" 192 lbs.

1965	**WAS**	N	1	HB
1966			12	FL, DB
2 yrs.	13 games			

Year	Team		Games	Pos.

Vince Mazza

MAZZA, VINCENT L.
B. Mar. 25, 1925, Niagara Falls, NY
D. Dec. 5, 1993, Winona, Ont.
none 6'1" 216 lbs.

Year	Team		Games	Pos.
1945	DET	N	5	E
1946			1	E
1947	BUF	AA	13	E
1948			14	E
1949			12	E

5 yrs. 45 games

Gino Mazzanti

MAZZANTI, GINO
B. 1929, Lake Village, AR
Arkansas 5'11" 190 lbs.

1950	BAL	N	5	HB

Jerry Mazzanti

MAZZANTI, JERRY EDWARD
B. Jul. 13, 1940, Lake Village, AR
Arkansas 6'3" 240 lbs.

1963	PHI	N	5	DE
1966	DET	N	13	DE
1967	PIT	N	12	DE

3 yrs. 30 games

Tim Mazzetti

MAZZETTI, TIMOTHY ALAN
B. Feb. 1, 1956, Old Greenwich, CT
Pennsylvania 6'1" 175 lbs.

1978	ATL	N	10	K
1979			16	K
1980			16	K

3 yrs. 42 games

Bob McAdams

MCADAMS, ROBERT
B. Nov. 1, 1939, Durham, NC
North Carolina Central 6'3" 250 lbs.

1963	NY	A	12	DT
1964			14	DT

2 yrs. 26 games

Carl McAdams

MCADAMS, CARL LEE
B. Apr. 26, 1944, Dumas, TX
Oklahoma 6'3" 240 lbs.

1967	NY	A	8	LB
1968			14	LB
1969			4	DT, DE

3 yrs. 26 games

Dean McAdams

MCADAMS, DEAN
B. Oct. 13, 1917, Caldwell, ID
Washington 6'1" 193 lbs.

1941	BKN	N	11	HB
1942			11	HB
1943			7	HB

3 yrs. 29 games

Derrick McAdoo

MCADOO, DERRICK MARK
B. Apr. 2, 1965, Pensacola, FL
Baylor 5'10" 198 lbs.

1987	STL	N	15	RB
1988	TB	N	5	RB
1988	PHX	N	1	RB

2 yrs. 21 games

Fred McAfee

MCAFEE, FRED LEE
B. Jun. 20, 1968, Philadelphia, MS
Mississippi College 5'10" 193 lbs.

1991	NO	N	9	RB

Fred McAfee continued

1992			14	RB
1993			15	RB
1994	ARI	N	7	RB
1994	PIT	N	6	RB
1995			16	RB
1996			14	RB

6 yrs. 81 games

George McAfee

MCAFEE, GEORGE (One Play)
B. Mar. 13, 1918, Ironton, OH
Duke 6'0" 178 lbs.

1940	CHIB	N	10	HB
1941			11	HB
1945			3	HB
1946			4	HB
1947			12	HB
1948			12	HB
1949			12	HB
1950			12	HB

8 yrs. 76 games

Wes McAfee

MCAFEE, WESLEY TAYLOR
B. Oct. 20, 1919, Ironton, OH
D. Jan., 1984, Myrtle Beach, SC
Duke 5'11" 175 lbs.

1941	PHI	N	8	HB

Ed McAleney

MCALENEY, EDWARD P.
B. Sep. 21, 1953, Portland, ME
Massachusetts 6'2" 235 lbs.

1976	TB	N	2	DE

James McAlister

MCALISTER, JAMES EDWARD
B. Sep. 5, 1951, Little Rock, AR
UCLA 6'1" 205 lbs.

1975	PHI	N	14	RB
1976			13	RB
1978	NE	N	16	RB

3 yrs. 43 games

Ken McAlister

MCALISTER, KEN H.
B. Apr. 15, 1960, Oakland, CA
San Francisco 6'5" 220 lbs.*

1982	SEA	N	9	LB
1983			2	S
1983	SF	N	4	LB
1984	KC	N	15	LB
1986			3	LB
1987			1	LB

5 yrs. 34 games

Jack McArthur

MCARTHUR, JACKSON
B. 1904
St. Mary's (California) 5'11" 211 lbs.

1926	LA	N	10	C
1927	BUF	N	5	C
1927	NYY	N	7	C
1928			13	C
1929	ORA	N	9	G, C
1930	NEW	N	1	G
1930	PRO	N	3	C
1930	FRA	N	2	T
1930	BKN	N	5	C, T, G
1931	PRO	N	7	T, G, E, C

6 yrs. 62 games

Kevin McArthur

MCARTHUR, KEVIN LEE
B. May 11, 1963, Cameron, CA

Kevin McArthur continued

Lamar 6'2" 244 lbs.

1986	NYJ	N	8	LB
1987			12	LB
1988			16	LB
1989			9	LB

4 yrs. 45 games

Jack McAuliffe

MCAULIFFE, JOHN
B. May 23, 1901
D. Nov., 1971, Butte, MT
Beloit 5'7" 155 lbs.

1926	GB	N	8	HB, FB

Mike McBath

MCBATH, MICHAEL
B. May 29, 1946, Woodbury, NJ
Penn State 6'4" 248 lbs.

1968	BUF	A	9	OT
1969			14	OT, DE
1970	BUF	N	14	DE
1971			13	DE
1972			2	DT

5 yrs. 52 games

Adrian McBride

MCBRIDE, ADRIAN
B. Mar. 23, 1963
Tennessee/Missouri 6'0" 195 lbs.

1987	STL	N	3	WR

Charlie McBride

MCBRIDE, CHARLES
B. Jul. 6, 1914
D. Apr., 1972
Washington State 5'10" 185 lbs.

1936	CHIC	N	1	B

Jack McBride

MCBRIDE, JOHN F.
B. 1902
D. Oct., 1966
Syracuse 5'11" 185 lbs.

1925	NYG	N	12	FB, HB
1926			12	FB, HB
1927			12	FB, HB
1928			9	FB, HB
1929	PRO	N	12	FB, HB
1930	BKN	N	11	FB, HB
1931			13	FB, QB
1932			2	FB, HB
1932	NYG	N	6	FB, HB
1933			11	HB, FB
1934			2	QB, HB

10 yrs. 102 games

Norm McBride

MCBRIDE, NORMAN
B. Feb. 21, 1947, Los Angeles, CA
Utah 6'3" 240 lbs.

1969	MIA	A	14	LB
1970	MIA	N	2	DE

2 yrs. 16 games

Oscar McBride

MCBRIDE, OSCAR
B. Jul. 23, 1972, Gainesville, FL
Notre Dame 6'5" 266 lbs.

1995	ARI	N	16	TE
1996			2	TE

2 yrs. 18 games

Ron McBride

MCBRIDE, RON

Ron McBride continued

B. Oct. 12, 1948, Fulton, MO
Missouri 6'0" 200 lbs.

1973	GB	N	1	RB

Gerald McBurrows

MCBURROWS, GERALD
B. Oct. 7, 1973, Detroit, MI
Kansas 5'11" 188 lbs.

1995	STL	N	14	S
1996			16	S

2 yrs. 30 games

Jerry McCabe

MCCABE, JEROME FRANCIS
B. Jan. 25, 1965, Detroit, MI
Holy Cross 6'1" 225 lbs.

1987	NE	N	3	LB
1988	KC	N	3	LB

2 yrs. 6 games

Richie McCabe

MCCABE, RICHARD PAUL
B. Mar. 12, 1934, Pittsburgh, PA
D. Jan. 4, 1983, Denver, CO
Pittsburgh 6'1" 185 lbs.

1955	PIT	N	12	HB
1957			2	HB
1958			5	HB
1959	WAS	N	10	HB
1960	BUF	A		DB
1961			9	DB

6 yrs. 38 games

Don McCafferty

MCCAFFERTY, DONALD WILLIAM
B. Mar. 12, 1921, Cleveland, OH
D. Jul. 28, 1974
Ohio State 6'4" 220 lbs.

1946	NYG	N	9	E

Art McCaffray

MCCAFFRAY, ARTHUR J.
B. Dec. 26, 1921
Pacific 5'11" 190 lbs.

1946	PIT	N	11	T

Bob McCaffrey

MCCAFFREY, ROBERT A.
B. Apr. 16, 1952, Bakersfield, CA
Southern California 6'2" 245 lbs.

1975	GB	N	14	C

Ed McCaffrey

MCCAFFREY, EDWARD T.
B. Aug. 17, 1968, Allentown, PA
Stanford 6'5" 215 lbs.

1991	NYG	N	16	WR
1992			16	WR
1993			16	WR
1994	SF	N	16	WR
1995	DEN	N	16	WR
1996			15	WR

6 yrs. 95 games

Mike McCaffrey

MCCAFFREY, MICHAEL
B. Apr. 11, 1946, Bakersfield, CA
California 6'3" 235 lbs.

1970	BUF	N	11	LB

Bob McCain

MCCAIN, ROBERT

Year	Team	Games	Pos.

Bob McCain *continued*
B. 1922
Mississippi 5'11" 195 lbs.

Year	Team		Games	Pos.
1946	BKN	AA	11	E

Bob McCall
MCCALL, ROBERT HENRY
B. Apr. 26, 1950, Sarasota, FL
Arizona 6'0" 205 lbs.

Year	Team		Games	Pos.
1973	NE	N	8	RB

Don McCall
MCCALL, DONALD CHARLES
B. Sep. 21, 1944, Birmingham, AL
Southern California 5'11" 195 lbs.

Year	Team		Games	Pos.
1967	NO	N	14	RB
1968			13	RB
1969	PIT	N	13	RB
1970	NO	N	2	RB
4 yrs.	42 games			

Joe McCall
MCCALL, JOSEPH SHEPARD
B. Feb. 17, 1962, Miami, FL
Pittsburgh 6'0" 200 lbs.

Year	Team		Games	Pos.
1984	LARI	N	3	RB

Reese McCall
MCCALL, REESE, II
B. Jun. 16, 1956, Bessemer, AL
Auburn 6'6" 240 lbs.

Year	Team		Games	Pos.
1978	BAL	N	16	TE
1979			14	TE
1980			16	TE
1981			16	TE
1982			7	TE
1983	DET		16	TE
1984			16	TE
1985			16	TE
8 yrs.	117 games			

Ron McCall
MCCALL, RONALD
B. Jul. 11, 1944, San Bernardino, CA
Weber State 6'2" 245 lbs.

Year	Team		Games	Pos.
1967	SD	A	2	LB
1968			3	LB
2 yrs.	5 games			

Fred McCallister
MCCALLISTER, FREDERICK M.
B. Feb. 17, 1962, Melbourne, FL
Florida 6'1" 250 lbs.

Year	Team		Games	Pos.
1987	TB	N	3	LB

Napoleon McCallum
MCCALLUM, NAPOLEON ARDEL
B. Oct. 6, 1963, Milford, OH
Navy 6'2" 215 lbs.

Year	Team		Games	Pos.
1986	LARI	N	15	RB
1990			16	RB
1991			16	RB
1992			13	RB
1993			13	RB
1994			1	RB
6 yrs.	74 games			

John McCambridge
MCCAMBRIDGE, JOHN R.
B. Aug. 30, 1944, Omaha, NE
Northwestern 6'4" 245 lbs.

Year	Team		Games	Pos.
1967	DET	N	6	DE

Ernie McCann
MCCANN, ERNEST H.
B. Aug. 5, 1902
D. Nov. 25, 1971, Acton, CA
Penn State 6'0" 175 lbs.

Year	Team		Games	Pos.
1926	HAR	N	9	T, E, G

Jim McCann
MCCANN, JAMES
B. Mar. 29, 1949, Phoenix, AZ
Arizona State 6'2" 265 lbs.

Year	Team		Games	Pos.
1971	SF	N	13	P
1972			13	P
1973	NYG	N	2	P
1975	KC	N	3	P
4 yrs.	31 games			

Tim McCann
MCCANN, TIMOTHY J.
B. May 15, 1947, Milwaukee, WI
Princeton 6'5" 265 lbs.

Year	Team		Games	Pos.
1969	NYG	N	1	DT

Keith McCants
MCCANTS, ALVIN KEITH
B. Apr. 19, 1968, Mobile, AL
Alabama 6'3" 260 lbs.

Year	Team		Games	Pos.
1990	TB	N	15	LB
1991			16	LB
1992			16	DE
1993	HOU		13	DE
1994			4	DE
1994	ARI		8	DE
1995			16	DE, DT
6 yrs.	88 games			

Keenan McCardell
MCCARDELL, KEENAN WAYNE
B. Jan. 6, 1970, Houston, TX
Nevada-Las Vegas 6'1" 185 lbs.

Year	Team		Games	Pos.
1992	CLE	N	2	WR
1993			6	WR
1994			14	WR
1995			16	WR
1996	JAC	N	16	WR
5 yrs.	54 games			

Larry McCarren
MCCARREN, LAURENCE ANTHONY
B. Nov. 9, 1951, Park Forest, IL
Illinois 6'3" 246 lbs.

Year	Team		Games	Pos.
1973	GB	N	5	C
1974			14	C
1975			14	C
1976			14	C
1977			14	C
1978			16	C
1979			16	C
1980			16	C
1981			16	C
1982			9	C
1983			16	C
1984			12	C
12 yrs.	162 games			

Brendan McCarthy
MCCARTHY, BRENDAN
B. Aug. 6, 1945, Washington, DC
Boston College 6'3" 220 lbs.

Year	Team		Games	Pos.
1968	ATL	N	7	RB
1968	DEN	A	7	RB
1969			1	RB
2 yrs.	15 games			

Don McCarthy
MCCARTHY, DONALD

Don McCarthy *continued*
B. 1897
Deceased
Lehigh 5'10" 175 lbs.

Year	Team		Games	Pos.
1921	WAS	A	3	E

Jack McCarthy
MCCARTHY, JACK
California 186 lbs.

Year	Team		Games	Pos.
1927	DUL	N	8	T

Jim McCarthy
MCCARTHY, JAMES P.
B. Nov. 28, 1921, Lockport, IL
Illinois 6'1" 205 lbs.

Year	Team		Games	Pos.
1946	BKN	AA	14	E
1947			14	E
1948	CHI	AA	14	E
1949			12	E
4 yrs.	54 games			

John McCarthy
MCCARTHY, JOHN P.
B. Aug. 9, 1916, Philadelphia, PA
St. Francis (Pennsylvania) 5'8" 160 lbs.

Year	Team		Games	Pos.
1944	C-P	N	7	QB

Shawn McCarthy
MCCARTHY, SHAWN MICHAEL
B. Feb. 22, 1968, Fremont, OH
Purdue 6'6" 227 lbs.

Year	Team		Games	Pos.
1991	NE	N	13	P
1992			16	P
2 yrs.	29 games			

Vince McCarthy
MCCARTHY, VINCENT J.
B. Nov. 3, 1899, Illinois
D. Nov., 1968, Fort Lauderdale, FL
St. Viator 5'10" 155 lbs.

Year	Team		Games	Pos.
1924	RI	N	2	QB, HB
1925			4	HB
1926	RI	A	6	HB, FB, QB
3 yrs.	12 games			

Pete McCartney
MCCARTNEY, PETE
B. Jun. 15, 1962
Louisville 6'6" 260 lbs.

Year	Team		Games	Pos.
1987	NYJ	N	3	G

Ronnie McCartney
MCCARTNEY, RON
B. Jul. 29, 1954, Charleston, WV
Tennessee 6'1" 220 lbs.

Year	Team		Games	Pos.
1977	ATL	N	14	LB
1978			15	LB
1979			16	LB
3 yrs.	45 games			

Mickey McCarty
MCCARTY, MICKEY
B. Nov. 15, 1946, Jonesboro, AR
Texas Christian 6'5" 255 lbs.

Year	Team		Games	Pos.
1969	KC	A	3	TE

Don McCauley
MCCAULEY, DONALD FREDERICK, JR.
B. May 12, 1949, Worcester, MA
North Carolina 6'1" 211 lbs.

Year	Team		Games	Pos.
1971	BAL	N	13	RB
1972			14	RB
1973			13	RB
1974			13	RB

Don McCauley *continued*

Year	Team	Games	Pos.
1975		14	RB
1976		13	RB
1977		14	RB
1978		15	RB
1979		15	RB
1980		16	RB
1981		16	RB
11 yrs.	156 games		

Thomas McCauley
MCCAULEY, THOMAS MICHAEL
B. May 3, 1947, Superior, WI
Wisconsin 6'3" 190 lbs.

Year	Team		Games	Pos.
1969	ATL	N	14	WR
1970			14	WR
1971			4	WR
3 yrs.	32 games			

Leo McCausland
MCCAUSLAND, LEO J.
B. Jun. 14, 1895
D. Sep., 1968, Akron, OH
Detroit 6'0" 197 lbs.

Year	Team		Games	Pos.
1922	AKR	N	4	G, E, C, T

Bill McCaw
MCCAW, WILLIAM GLASS (Bud)
B. Feb. 6, 1898
D. Apr. 19, 1942, Bloomington, IN
Indiana 6'2" 192 lbs.

Year	Team		Games	Pos.
1923	RAC	N	3	G, E
1926	LOU	N	4	G
2 yrs.	7 games			

Bob McChesney
MCCHESNEY, ROBERT
B. Jul. 12, 1912, Los Angeles, CA
D. Sep., 1986, Silver City, NM
UCLA 6'2" 195 lbs.

Year	Team		Games	Pos.
1936	BOS	N	8	E
1937	WAS	N	10	E
1938			10	E
1939			8	E
1940			11	E
1941			11	E
1942			10	E
7 yrs.	68 games			

Bob McChesney
MCCHESNEY, ROBERT EUGENE
B. Oct. 27, 1926, Van Nuys, CA
Hardin-Simmons 6'2" 190 lbs.

Year	Team		Games	Pos.
1950	NYG	N	12	E
1951			12	E
1952			12	E
3 yrs.	36 games			

Cliff McClain
MCCLAIN, CLIFFORD
B. Dec. 29, 1947, Orlando, FL
South Carolina State 6'0" 217 lbs.

Year	Team		Games	Pos.
1970	NYJ	N	10	RB
1971			11	RB
1972			13	RB
1973			12	RB
4 yrs.	46 games			

Clint McClain
MCCLAIN, CLINTON (Red)
B. Jun. 18, 1918, Lufkin, TX
D. Dec 11, 1994, Dallas, TX
Southern Methodist 5'9" 182 lbs.

Year	Team		Games	Pos.
1941	NYG	N	6	B

Year	Team		Games	Pos.

Dewey McClain
MCCLAIN, DEWEY LOREN
B. Apr. 25, 1954, Okmulgee, OK
East Central (Oklahoma) 6'3" 236 lbs.

Year	Team		Games	Pos.
1976	ATL	N	14	LB
1977			13	LB
1978			16	LB
1979			15	LB
1980			15	LB
5 yrs.	73 games			

Joe McClain
MCCLAIN, JOSEPH
B. Apr. 5, 1905
D. Apr., 1967, Mount Carmel, PA
St. John's (New York)/Canisius 6'0" 200 lbs.

Year	Team		Games	Pos.
1928	NYY	N	6	G, T

Jack McClairen
MCCLAIREN, JOHN (Goose)
B. Jan. 21, 1931, Panama City, FL
Bethune-Cookman 6'4" 213 lbs.

Year	Team		Games	Pos.
1955	PIT	N	12	E
1956			7	E
1957			12	E
1958			12	E
1959			1	E
1960			1	E
6 yrs.	45 games			

Brent McClanahan
MCCLANAHAN, BRENT ANTHONY
B. Sep. 21, 1950, Bakersfield, CA
Arizona State 5'10" 202 lbs.

Year	Team		Games	Pos.
1973	MIN	N	13	RB
1974			14	RB
1975			12	RB
1976			13	RB
1977			14	RB
1978			12	RB
1979			16	RB
7 yrs.	94 games			

Randy McClanahan
MCCLANAHAN, RANDALL DUANE
B. Dec. 12, 1954, Lincoln, NE
Southwestern Louisiana 6'5" 225 lbs.

Year	Team		Games	Pos.
1977	OAK	N	14	LB
1978	BUF	N	16	LB
1980	OAK	N	14	LB
1981			16	LB
1982	LARI	N	1	LB
5 yrs.	61 games			

Billy McClard
MCCLARD, BILL
B. Oct. 15, 1950, Purcell, OK
Arkansas 5'10" 202 lbs.

Year	Team		Games	Pos.
1972	SD	N	9	K
1973	NO	N	8	K
1974			14	K
1975			3	K
4 yrs.	34 games			

Mike McClellan
MCCLELLAN, WILLIAM MICHAEL
B. Oct. 10, 1939
Oklahoma 6'1" 185 lbs.

Year	Team		Games	Pos.
1962	PHI	N	14	DB
1963			9	DB
2 yrs.	23 games			

Skip McClendon
MCCLENDON, KENNETH CHRISTOPHER
B. Apr. 9, 1964, Detroit, MI
Northwestern/Arizona State 6'6" 282 lbs.

Year	Team		Games	Pos.
1987	CIN	N	12	DE
1988			16	DE
1989			16	DE
1990			15	DE
1991			5	DE
1991	SD	N	2	DE
1992	MIN	N	3	DE
1992	IND	N	7	DL
1993			16	DE, DT
7 yrs.	92 games			

Willie McClendon
MCCLENDON, WILLIE EDWARD
B. Sep. 13, 1957, Brunswick, GA
Georgia 6'1" 205 lbs.

Year	Team		Games	Pos.
1979	CHI	N	16	RB
1980			16	RB
1981			16	RB
1982			9	RB
4 yrs.	57 games			

J.J. McCleskey
MCCLESKEY, TOMMY JOE
B. Apr. 10, 1970, Knoxville, TN
Tennessee 5'7" 177 lbs.

Year	Team		Games	Pos.
1994	NO	N	13	S
1995			14	S, CB
1996			5	DB
1996	ARI	N	5	CB
3 yrs.	37 games			

Curtis McClinton
MCCLINTON, CURTIS REALIOUS, JR.
B. Jun. 25, 1939, Muskogee, OK
Kansas 6'3" 230 lbs.

Year	Team		Games	Pos.
1962	DAL	A	14	FB
1963	KC	A	14	FB
1964			14	FB
1965			14	FB
1966			14	FB
1967			14	RB
1968			9	RB
1969			14	TE
8 yrs.	107 games			

Mike McCloskey
MCCLOSKEY, MIKE J.
B. Feb. 2, 1961, Philadelphia, PA
Penn State 6'5" 246 lbs.

Year	Team		Games	Pos.
1983	HOU	N	15	TE
1984			16	TE
1985			16	TE
1987	PHI	N	1	TE
4 yrs.	48 games			

Dave McCloughan
MCCLOUGHAN, DAVID KENT
B. Nov. 20, 1966, San Leandro, CA
Colorado 6'1" 180 lbs.

Year	Team		Games	Pos.
1991	IND	N	15	CB
1992	GB	N	5	CB
1993	SEA	N	15	S
1994			13	S
4 yrs.	48 games			

Kent McCloughan
MCCLOUGHAN, KENT AUBURN
B. Feb. 12, 1940, Scottsbluff, NE
Nebraska 6'1" 190 lbs.

Year	Team		Games	Pos.
1965	OAK	A	14	DB
1966			14	DB

Kent McCloughan continued

Year	Team		Games	Pos.
1967			14	DB
1968			8	DB
1969			4	CB
1970	OAK	N	13	CB
6 yrs.	67 games			

Willie McClung
MCCLUNG, WILLIAM ALBERT
B. May 9, 1930, Marion, AR
Florida A&M 6'2" 250 lbs.

Year	Team		Games	Pos.
1955	PIT	N	12	T
1956			12	T
1957			12	T
1958	CLE	N	12	T
1959			12	T
1960	DET	N	11	T
1961			3	OT
7 yrs.	74 games			

Bob McClure
MCCLURE, ROBERT D. (Buster)
B. Jul. 8, 1924, Dardanelle, AR
Drake/Nevada-Reno 6'1" 224 lbs.

Year	Team		Games	Pos.
1947	BOS	N	10	G
1948			12	G
2 yrs.	22 games			

Brian McClure
MCCLURE, BRIAN
B. Dec. 28, 1963, Ravenna, OH
Bowling Green 6'6" 222 lbs.

Year	Team		Games	Pos.
1987	BUF	N	1	QB

Wayne McClure
MCCLURE, WAYNE L.
B. Jul. 2, 1946, Hattiesburg, MS
Mississippi 6'1" 225 lbs.

Year	Team		Games	Pos.
1970	CIN	N	14	LB

David McCluskey
MCCLUSKEY, DAVID
B. Nov. 5, 1963
Georgia 6'1" 227 lbs.

Year	Team		Games	Pos.
1987	CIN	N	3	RB

Bill McColl
MCCOLL, WILLIAM FRAZER
B. Apr. 2, 1930, San Diego, CA
Stanford 6'4" 230 lbs.

Year	Team		Games	Pos.
1952	CHIB	N	12	E
1953			12	E
1954			12	E
1955			12	E
1956			12	E
1957			12	E
1958			12	E
1959			12	E
8 yrs.	96 games			

Milt McColl
MCCOLL, MILTON B.
B. Aug. 28, 1959, Oak Park, IL
Stanford 6'6" 230 lbs.

Year	Team		Games	Pos.
1981	SF	N	16	LB
1982			9	LB
1983			12	LB
1984			16	LB
1985			16	LB
1986			16	LB
1987			12	LB
1988	LARI	N	15	LB
8 yrs.	112 games			

Andy McCollum
MCCOLLUM, ANDREW JON

Andy McCollum continued
B. Jun. 6, 1970, Akron, OH
Toledo 6'5" 270 lbs.

Year	Team		Games	Pos.
1995	NO	N	11	G, C
1996			16	G
2 yrs.	27 games			

Harley McCollum
MCCOLLUM, HARLEY R.
B. 1918
Tulane 6'4" 245 lbs.

Year	Team		Games	Pos.
1946	NY	AA	10	T
1947	CHI	AA	13	T
2 yrs.	23 games			

Jim McCollum
MCCOLLUM, JAMES (Bubba)
B. Sep. 13, 1952, Louisville, KY
Kentucky 6'0" 250 lbs.

Year	Team		Games	Pos.
1974	HOU	N	11	LB

Don McComb
MCCOMB, DONALD
B. 1935
Villanova 6'4" 240 lbs.

Year	Team		Games	Pos.
1960	BOS	A		DE

Nat McCombs
MCCOMBS, NATHANIEL (SPEICHA)
B. Dec. 18, 1904, Oklahoma
D. Jul., 1965
Haskell 5'11" 226 lbs.

Year	Team		Games	Pos.
1926	AKR	N	8	G, C, E

Phil McConkey
MCCONKEY, PHILIP JOSEPH
B. Feb. 24, 1957, Buffalo, NY
Navy 5'10" 170 lbs.

Year	Team		Games	Pos.
1984	NYG	N	13	WR
1985			16	WR
1986	GB	N	4	WR
1986	NYG	N	12	WR
1987			12	WR
1988			16	WR
1989	PHX	N	6	WR
1989	SD	N	5	WR
6 yrs.	84 games			

Brian McConnell
MCCONNELL, BRIAN T.
B. Jan. 21, 1950, Passaic, NJ
Michigan State 6'4" 207 lbs.

Year	Team		Games	Pos.
1973	BUF	N	1	LB
1973	HOU	N	7	LB
1 yr.	8 games			

Dewey McConnell
MCCONNELL, DEWEY
B. 1929
Wyoming 6'0" 190 lbs.

Year	Team		Games	Pos.
1954	PIT	N	9	HB, E

Frank McConnell
MCCONNELL, FRANK
B. Aug. 23, 1900
D. Nov., 1985, Loveland, OH
Georgia Tech 6'0" 195 lbs.

Year	Team		Games	Pos.
1927	BUF	N	5	G

Darris McCord
MCCORD, DARRIS PAUL
B. Jan. 4, 1933, Franklin, TN
Tennessee 6'4" 250 lbs.

Year	Team		Games	Pos.
1955	DET	N	12	T

Year	Team		Games	Pos.

Darris McCord *continued*

Year	Team		Games	Pos.
1956			12	T
1957			12	T
1958			12	T
1959			12	T
1960			12	E
1961			14	DE
1962			14	DE
1963			13	DE
1964			14	DE
1965			14	DE
1966			13	DE
1967			14	DE

13 yrs. 168 games

Dave McCormack
MCCORMACK, DAVID OLIVER
B. Jul. 10, 1943, Winnsboro, LA
Louisiana State 6'6" 250 lbs.

Year	Team		Games	Pos.
1966	SF	N	14	OT
1967	NO	N	2	OT
1968			1	OT

3 yrs. 17 games

Hurvin McCormack
MCCORMACK, HURVIN
B. Apr. 6, 1972, Brooklyn, NY
Indiana 6'5" 271 lbs.

Year	Team		Games	Pos.
1994	DAL	N	3	DT
1995			14	DT, DE
1996			16	DT

3 yrs. 33 games

Mike McCormack
MCCORMACK, MICHAEL JOSEPH, JR.
B. Jun. 21, 1930, Chicago, IL
Kansas 6'4" 246 lbs.

Year	Team		Games	Pos.
1951	NYY	N	12	T
1954	CLE	N	12	T
1955			12	T
1956			12	T
1957			12	T
1958			9	T
1959			10	T
1960			12	T
1961			14	OT
1962			14	OT

10 yrs. 119 games

Elmer McCormick
MCCORMICK, ELMER (Moose)
B. Feb. 22, 1899, Holyoke, MA
D. Jul., 1966, Marion Center, PA
Detroit/Canisius 5'7" 220 lbs.

Year	Team		Games	Pos.
1923	BUF	N	8	G, T, HB, C
1924			3	C
1925			7	G, C, T
1925	FRA	N	8	G, C, T
1926	HAR	N	2	G, C

4 yrs. 28 games

Felix McCormick
MCCORMICK, FELIX G.
B. May 21, 1905
D. Mar., 1971, Glen Ridge, NJ
Bucknell 5'7" 185 lbs.

Year	Team		Games	Pos.
1929	ORA	N	10	HB, FB, G
1930	NEW	N	2	HB

2 yrs. 12 games

Frank McCormick
MCCORMICK, FRANK G.
B. Nov. 5, 1894
D. Mar., 1976, Fullerton, CA
South Dakota 5'11" 190 lbs.

Year	Team		Games	Pos.
1920	AKR	A	9	HB
1921			3	HB, E

Frank McCormick *cont.*

Year	Team		Games	Pos.
1921	CIN	A	1	FB

2 yrs. 13 games

John McCormick
MCCORMICK, JOHN JOSEPH, JR.
B. May 26, 1937, Boston, MA
Massachusetts 6'1" 201 lbs.

Year	Team		Games	Pos.
1962	MIN	N	13	QB
1963	DEN	A	9	QB
1965			14	QB
1966			14	QB
1968			1	QB

5 yrs. 51 games

Len McCormick
MCCORMICK, LEONARD G. (Tuffy)
B. Oct. 28, 1922, Eldorado, TX
Southwestern (Texas)/Baylor 6'3" 232 lbs.

Year	Team		Games	Pos.
1948	BAL	AA	11	C

Tom McCormick
MCCORMICK, THOMAS
B. 1930, Waco, TX
Pacific 5'11" 185 lbs.

Year	Team		Games	Pos.
1953	LA	N	11	HB
1954			9	HB
1955			6	HB
1956	SF	N	5	HB

4 yrs. 31 games

Walt McCormick
MCCORMICK, WALTER KENDELL
B. 1927
Washington/Southern California 6'1" 215 lbs.

Year	Team		Games	Pos.
1948	SF	AA	9	C

Kez McCorvey
MCCORVEY, KEZ
B. Jan. 23, 1972, Gautier, MS
Florida State 6'0" 180 lbs.

Year	Team		Games	Pos.
1995	DET	N	2	WR
1996			1	WR

2 yrs. 3 games

Joel McCoy
MCCOY, JOEL LAWSON, JR.
B. Aug. 22, 1920, Birmingham, AL
Alabama 5'10" 170 lbs.

Year	Team		Games	Pos.
1946	DET	N	10	HB

Larry McCoy
MCCOY, LARRY
B. Aug. 12, 1961, Madisonville, TX
Lamar 6'2" 245 lbs.

Year	Team		Games	Pos.
1984	LARI	N	4	LB
1987	NO	N	3	LB

2 yrs. 7 games

Lloyd McCoy
MCCOY, LLOYD
B. 1942
San Diego State 6'1" 245 lbs.

Year	Team		Games	Pos.
1964	SD	A	1	G

Mike McCoy
MCCOY, MICHAEL CHARLES (M.C.)
B. Aug. 16, 1953, West Memphis, AR
Colorado 5'11" 183 lbs.

Year	Team		Games	Pos.
1976	GB	N	14	DB

Mike McCoy *continued*

Year	Team		Games	Pos.
1977			14	CB
1978			16	CB
1979			16	S
1980			16	S
1981			16	CB
1982			9	CB
1983			9	CB, S

8 yrs. 110 games

Mike McCoy
MCCOY, MICHAEL PATRICK
B. Sep. 6, 1948, Erie, PA
Notre Dame 6'5" 278 lbs.

Year	Team		Games	Pos.
1970	GB	N	14	DT
1971			14	DT
1972			12	DT
1973			14	DT
1974			14	DT
1975			14	DT
1976			14	DT
1977	OAK	N	14	DT
1978			15	DT
1979	NYG	N	3	DT
1980			2	DT
1980	DET	N	4	DT

11 yrs. 134 games

Tony McCoy
MCCOY, ANTHONY BERNARD
B. Jun. 10, 1969, Orlando, FL
Florida 6'0" 279 lbs.

Year	Team		Games	Pos.
1992	IND	N	16	NT
1993			6	NT
1994			15	DT
1995			16	DT
1996			15	DT

5 yrs. 68 games

Fred McCrary
MCCRARY, FRED
B. Sep. 19, 1972, Naples, FL
Mississippi State 6'0" 210 lbs.

Year	Team		Games	Pos.
1995	PHI	N	13	RB

Greg McCrary
MCCRARY, GREGORY ALONZA
B. Mar. 24, 1952, Griffin, GA
Clark 6'3" 233 lbs.

Year	Team		Games	Pos.
1975	ATL	N	13	TE
1977			13	TE
1978	WAS	N	5	TE
1978	SD	N	8	TE
1979			14	TE
1980			16	TE
1981	WAS	N	5	TE

6 yrs. 74 games

Hurdis McCrary
MCCRAY, HURDIS W.
B. Jun. 9, 1904
Deceased
Georgia 6'0" 207 lbs.

Year	Team		Games	Pos.
1929	GB	N	13	HB, FB, QB
1930			14	FB, HB
1931			12	FB
1932			11	FB, HB
1933			2	FB

5 yrs. 52 games

Michael McCrary
MCCRARY, MICHAEL
B. Jul. 7, 1970, Vienna, VA
Wake Forest 6'4" 250 lbs.

Year	Team		Games	Pos.
1993	SEA	N	15	DE
1994			16	DE
1995			11	DE
1996			16	DE

4 yrs. 58 games

Bruce McCray
MCCRAY, BRUCE
B. Oct. 27, 1963
Western Illinois 5'9" 181 lbs.

Year	Team		Games	Pos.
1987	CHI	N	3	CB, S

Prentice McCray
MCCRAY, PRENTICE, JR.
B. Mar. 1, 1951, Los Angeles, CA
Arizona State 6'1" 188 lbs.

Year	Team		Games	Pos.
1974	NE	N	14	CB
1975			14	CB
1976			14	S
1977			14	S
1978			8	S
1979			14	S
1980			3	S
1980	DET	N	7	S

7 yrs. 88 games

Willie McCray
MCCRAY, WILLIE LEE, JR.
B. Jul. 17, 1953, Fort Lee, VA
Alabama/Troy State 6'5" 234 lbs.

Year	Team		Games	Pos.
1978	SF	N	16	DE

Bob McCreary
MCCREARY, ROBERT
B. 1939
Wake Forest 6'5" 256 lbs.

Year	Team		Games	Pos.
1961	DAL	N	9	OT

Loaird McCreary
MCCREARY, LOAIRD ARTHUR
B. Mar. 15, 1953, Crawfordville, GA
Tennessee State 6'5" 227 lbs.

Year	Team		Games	Pos.
1976	MIA	N	14	TE
1977			14	TE
1978			16	TE
1979	NYG	N	11	TE

4 yrs. 55 games

Ed McCrillis
MCCRILLIS, EDGAR VINCENT FRED
B. Sep. 7, 1904, New York, NY
D. Sep. 1, 1940, Warwick, RI
Brown 6'0" 205 lbs.

Year	Team		Games	Pos.
1926	PRO	N	2	G
1929	BOS	N	7	G

2 yrs. 9 games

John McCrumbly
MCCRUMBLY, JOHN
B. Jul. 28, 1952, Dallas, TX
Texas A&M 6'1" 245 lbs.

Year	Team		Games	Pos.
1975	BUF	N	13	LB

Dale McCullers
MCCULLERS, DALE GREEN
B. Oct. 11, 1947, Lake City, FL
Florida State 6'1" 215 lbs.

Year	Team		Games	Pos.
1969	MIA	A	14	LB

Earl McCullouch
MCCULLOUCH, EARL R.
B. Jan. 10, 1946, Clarksville, TX
Southern California 5'11" 175 lbs.

Year	Team		Games	Pos.
1968	DET	N	14	FL
1969			14	WR
1970			10	WR
1971			13	WR
1972			10	WR
1973			11	WR
1974	NO	N	3	WR

7 yrs. 75 games

Year	Team		Games	Pos.

Bob McCullough
MCCULLOUGH, ROBERT VERNON
B. Nov. 18, 1940, Helena, MT
Colorado 6'5" 244 lbs.

Year	Team		Games	Pos.
1962	DEN	A	14	G
1963			14	G
1964			14	G
1965			14	G
4 yrs.	56 games			

Hal McCullough
MCCULLOUGH, HAROLD F.
B. Apr. 4, 1918, New York, NY
D. Feb. 13, 1991, Doylestown, PA
Cornell 5'11" 170 lbs.

Year	Team		Games	Pos.
1942	BKN	N	9	B

Hugh McCullough
MCCULLOUGH, HUGH W.
B. May 18, 1916, Anadarko, OK
Oklahoma 6'0" 185 lbs.

Year	Team		Games	Pos.
1939	PIT	N	10	HB
1940	CHIC	N	11	HB, FB
1941			7	HB
1943	P, P	N	1	B
1945	BOS	N	7	HB
5 yrs.	36 games			

Richard McCullough
MCCULLOUGH, RICHARD CHARLES
B. Jul. 22, 1965, Loris, SC
Clemson 6'5" 270 lbs.

Year	Team		Games	Pos.
1989	DEN	N	10	DE
1990			6	DE
2 yrs.	16 games			

Sam McCullum
MCCULLUM, SAMUEL CHARLES
B. Nov. 30, 1952, McComb, MS
Montana State 6'2" 200 lbs.

Year	Team		Games	Pos.
1974	MIN	N	12	WR
1975			9	WR
1976	SEA	N	14	WR
1977			13	WR
1978			16	WR
1979			16	WR
1980			16	WR
1981			16	WR
1982	MIN	N	6	WR
1983			10	WR
10 yrs.	128 games			

Dave McCurry
MCCURRY, DAVID GENE
B. Feb. 23, 1951, Grinnell, IA
Iowa State 6'1" 187 lbs.

Year	Team		Games	Pos.
1974	NE	N	2	S

Mike McCurry
MCCURRY, MICHAEL L.
B. Mar. 26, 1963, Indianapolis, IN
Indiana 6'3" 258 lbs.

Year	Team		Games	Pos.
1987	MIN	N	3	G

Jim McCusker
MCCUSKER, JAMES B.
B. May 19, 1936, Jamestown, NY
Pittsburgh 6'2" 246 lbs.

Year	Team		Games	Pos.
1958	CHIC	N	11	T
1959	PHI	N	12	T
1960			12	T
1961			13	OT
1962			14	OT
1963	CLE	N	7	OT
1964	NY	A	14	OT
7 yrs.	83 games			

Lawrence McCutcheon
MCCUTCHEON, LAWRENCE
B. Jun. 2, 1950, Plainview, TX
Colorado State 6'1" 205 lbs.

Year	Team		Games	Pos.
1972	LA	N	3	RB
1973			12	RB
1974			14	RB
1975			13	RB
1976			14	RB
1977			14	RB
1978			8	RB
1979			11	RB
1980	DEN	N	6	RB
1980	SEA	N	8	RB
1981	BUF	N	6	RB
10 yrs.	109 games			

Karl McDade
MCDADE, WILLIAM
B. Nov. 3, 1914
D. Mar., 1973, Chester, PA
Portland 6'3" 195 lbs.

Year	Team		Games	Pos.
1938	PIT	N	6	C

Ed McDaniel
MCDANIEL, ED
B. Feb. 23, 1969, Batesburg, SC
Clemson 5'11" 232 lbs.

Year	Team		Games	Pos.
1992	MIN	N	8	LB
1993			7	LB
1994			16	LB
1995			16	LB
4 yrs.	47 games			

Emmanuel McDaniel
MCDANIEL, EMMANUEL
B. Jul. 27, 1972, Griffin, GA
East Carolina 5'9" 182 lbs.

Year	Team		Games	Pos.
1996	CAR	N	2	CB

Johnny McDaniel
MCDANIEL, JOHNNY
B. Sep. 23, 1951, Birmingham, AL
Lincoln (Missouri) 6'1" 196 lbs.

Year	Team		Games	Pos.
1974	CIN	N	14	WR
1975			14	WR
1976			14	WR
1977			14	WR
1978	WAS	N	15	WR
1979			15	WR
1980			10	WR
7 yrs.	96 games			

LeCharls McDaniel
MCDANIEL, LECHARLS
B. Oct. 15, 1958, Fort Bragg, NC
California Poly (San Luis Obispo) 5'11" 183 lbs.

Year	Team		Games	Pos.
1981	WAS	N	6	CB
1982			9	CB
1983	NYG	N	9	CB
3 yrs.	24 games			

Orlando McDaniel
MCDANIEL, ORLANDO KEITH
B. Dec. 1, 1960, Shreveport, LA
Louisiana State 6'0" 180 lbs.

Year	Team		Games	Pos.
1982	DEN	N	3	WR

Randall McDaniel
MCDANIEL, RANDALL CORNELL
B. Dec. 19, 1964, Phoenix, AZ
Arizona State 6'3" 274 lbs.

Year	Team		Games	Pos.
1988	MIN	N	16	G
1989			14	G
1990			16	G

Randall McDaniel cont.

Year	Team		Games	Pos.
1991			16	G
1992			16	G
1993			16	G
1994			16	G
1995			16	G
1996			16	G
9 yrs.	142 games			

Terry McDaniel
MCDANIEL, TERENCE LEE
B. Feb. 8, 1965, Saginaw, MI
Tennessee 5'10" 177 lbs.

Year	Team		Games	Pos.
1988	LARI	N	2	CB
1989			16	CB
1990			16	CB
1991			16	CB
1992			16	CB
1993			16	CB
1994			16	CB
1995	OAK	N	16	CB
1996			16	CB
9 yrs.	130 games			

Wahoo McDaniel
MCDANIEL, EDWARD
B. Jun. 19, 1938, Burnice, LA
Oklahoma 6'0" 235 lbs.

Year	Team		Games	Pos.
1960	HOU	A	14	G
1961	DEN	A	14	LB
1962			14	LB
1963			14	LB
1964	NY	A	12	LB
1965			14	LB
1966	MIA	A	12	LB
1967			14	LB
1968			4	LB
9 yrs.	112 games			

Dave McDaniels
MCDANIELS, DAVID
B. Apr. 9, 1945, Miami, FL
Mississippi Valley State 6'4" 200 lbs.

Year	Team		Games	Pos.
1968	DAL	N	4	OE

Pellom McDaniels
MCDANIELS, PELLOM
B. Feb. 21, 1968, San Jose, CA
Oregon State 6'3" 278 lbs.

Year	Team		Games	Pos.
1993	KC	N	10	DE
1994			12	DE
1995			16	DE
1996			9	DE
4 yrs.	47 games			

McDermott
MCDERMOTT
None

Year	Team		Games	Pos.
1926	CHI	A	1	G

Gary McDermott
MCDERMOTT, GARY
B. Jun. 9, 1946, Longview, TX
Tulsa 6'1" 211 lbs.

Year	Team		Games	Pos.
1968	BUF	N	14	RB
1969	ATL	N	4	RB
2 yrs.	18 games			

Lloyd McDermott
MCDERMOTT, LLOYD IVAN
B. Dec. 20, 1925, Covington, KY
Deceased
Kentucky 6'2" 240 lbs.

Year	Team		Games	Pos.
1950	CHIC	N	11	T
1951			12	T
2 yrs.	23 games			

Mardye McDole
MCDOLE, MARDYE
B. May 1, 1959, Pensacola, FL
Mississippi State 5'11" 195 lbs.

Year	Team		Games	Pos.
1981	MIN	N	9	WR
1982			2	WR
1983			15	WR
3 yrs.	26 games			

Ron McDole
MCDOLE, RONALD OWEN (The Dancing Bear)
B. Sep. 9, 1939, Chester, OH
Nebraska 6'3" 266 lbs.

Year	Team		Games	Pos.
1961	STL	N	13	DT
1962	HOU	A	4	DE
1963	BUF	A	12	DE
1964			14	DE
1965			14	DE
1966			14	DE
1967			13	DE
1968			14	DE
1969			14	DE
1970	BUF	N	14	DE
1971	WAS	N	14	DE
1972			14	DE
1973			14	DE
1974			14	DE
1975			14	DE
1976			14	DE
1977			14	DE
1978			16	DE
18 yrs.	240 games			

McDonald
MCDONALD

Year	Team		Games	Pos.
1926	DET	N	1	HB

McDonald
MCDONALD
None 165 lbs.

Year	Team		Games	Pos.
1925	HAM	N	3	G, E

Cy McDonald
MCDONALD, CYRIL
B. Dec. 17, 1896
D. Jan., 1968, New York, NY
None 6'1" 197 lbs.

Year	Team		Games	Pos.
1921	WAS	A	4	G

Devon McDonald
MCDONALD, DEVON LINTON
B. Nov. 8, 1969, Kingston, Jamaica
Notre Dame 6'4" 240 lbs.

Year	Team		Games	Pos.
1993	IND	N	16	LB
1994			16	LB
1995			15	LB
1996	ARI	N	16	LB
4 yrs.	63 games			

Don McDonald
MCDONALD, DONALD
B. 1937
Houston 5'11" 186 lbs.

Year	Team		Games	Pos.
1961	BUF	A	11	DB

Don McDonald
MCDONALD, DONALD G. (Flip)
B. Feb. 12, 1921, Webb City, MO
D. Jun., 1980, Syracuse, KS
Oklahoma 6'2" 200 lbs.

Year	Team		Games	Pos.
1944	BKN	N	2	E
1944	PHI	N	5	E
1945			9	E
1946			1	E
1948	NY	AA	2	E
4 yrs.	19 games			

Year	Team	Games	Pos.

Dwight McDonald
MCDONALD, DWIGHT VINSON
B. May 24, 1951, Nixon, TX
U.S. International/San Diego State 6'2" 187 lbs.

Year	Team		Games	Pos.
1975	**SD**	N	14	WR
1976			12	WR
1977			11	WR
1978			12	WR
4 yrs.	49 games			

Ed McDonald
MCDONALD, EDWARD (Jim)
B. Feb. 27, 1911
D. Feb., 1980, Homestead, PA
Duquesne 6'0" 195 lbs.

Year	Team		Games	Pos.
1936	**PIT**	N	4	HB

James McDonald
MCDONALD, JAMES
B. Mar. 29, 1961, Long Beach, CA
Southern California 6'5" 235 lbs.

Year	Team		Games	Pos.
1983	**LARM**	N	16	TE
1984			16	TE
1985	**DET**	N	6	TE
1985	**LARM**	N	9	TE
1987			5	TE
4 yrs.	52 games			

Jim McDonald
MCDONALD, JAMES ALLEN
B. Jun. 9, 1915, Springfield, OH
Ohio State 6'1" 193 lbs.

Year	Team		Games	Pos.
1938	**DET**	N	11	HB, FB
1939			9	HB, FB
2 yrs.	20 games			

John McDonald
MCDONALD, JOHN
B. Mar. 20, 1900
Lawrence 6'0" 195 lbs.

Year	Team		Games	Pos.
1921	**EVA**	A	1	T
1926	**LOU**		2	G
2 yrs.	3 games			

Keith McDonald
MCDONALD, KEITH
B. Nov. 7, 1963
San Jose State 5'9" 170 lbs.

Year	Team		Games	Pos.
1987	**HOU**	N	3	WR
1989	**DET**	N	6	WR
2 yrs.	9 games			

Les McDonald
MCDONALD, LESTER B.
B. Sep. 29, 1914
D. Jul. 26, 1971, Grand Island, NE
Nebraska 6'4" 200 lbs.

Year	Team		Games	Pos.
1937	**CHIB**		8	E
1938			9	E
1939			11	E
1940	**PHI**	N	9	E
1940	**DET**	N	1	E
4 yrs.	38 games			

Mike McDonald
MCDONALD, MIKE
B. Jun. 20, 1953, St. Augustine, FL
Catawba 6'2" 215 lbs.

Year	Team		Games	Pos.
1976	**STL**	N	4	LB

Mike McDonald
MCDONALD, MIKE
B. Jun. 22, 1958, North Hollywood, CA
Southern California 6'1" 238 lbs.

Year	Team		Games	Pos.
1984	**LARM**	N	16	LB

Mike McDonald continued

Year	Team		Games	Pos.
1986			13	LB
1987			10	LB
1988			16	LB
1989			16	LB
1990			16	LB
1991			16	LB
1992	**DET**	N	1	LB
8 yrs.	104 games			

Quintus McDonald
MCDONALD, QUINTUS ALONZO
B. Dec. 14, 1966, Rockingham, NC
Penn State 6'3" 259 lbs.

Year	Team		Games	Pos.
1989	**IND**	N	15	LB
1990			9	LB
1991			16	LB
3 yrs.	40 games			

Paul McDonald
MCDONALD, PAUL
B. Feb. 23, 1958, Montebello, CA
Southern California 6'2" 185 lbs.

Year	Team		Games	Pos.
1980	**CLE**	N	15	QB
1981			12	QB
1982			9	QB
1983			16	QB
1984			16	QB
1985			16	QB
1986	**DAL**	N	1	QB
7 yrs.	85 games			

Ray McDonald
MCDONALD, RAY
B. May 7, 1944, McKinney, TX
D. May, 1993
Idaho 6'4" 248 lbs.

Year	Team		Games	Pos.
1967	**WAS**	N	12	RB
1968			1	RB
2 yrs.	13 games			

Ricardo McDonald
MCDONALD, RICARDO MILTON
B. Nov. 8, 1969, Kingston, Jamaica
Pittsburgh 6'2" 235 lbs.

Year	Team		Games	Pos.
1992	**CIN**	N	16	LB
1993			14	LB
1994			13	LB
1995			16	LB
1996			16	LB
5 yrs.	75 games			

Tim McDonald
MCDONALD, TIM
B. Jan. 6, 1965, Fresno, CA
Southern California 6'2" 210 lbs.

Year	Team		Games	Pos.
1987	**STL**	N	3	S
1988	**PHX**	N	16	S
1989			16	CB, S
1990			16	CB, S
1991			13	S
1992			16	S
1993	**SF**	N	16	S
1994			16	S
1995			16	S
1996			16	S
10 yrs.	144 games			

Tommy McDonald
MCDONALD, THOMAS FRANKLIN
B. Jul. 26, 1934, Roy, NM
Oklahoma 5'9" 176 lbs.

Year	Team		Games	Pos.
1957	**PHI**	N	12	FL
1958			10	FL
1959			12	FL
1960			12	FL

Tommy McDonald cont.

Year	Team		Games	Pos.
1961			14	FL
1962			14	FL
1963			14	FL
1964	**DAL**	N	14	FL
1965	**LA**	N	14	FL
1966			13	FL
1967	**ATL**	N	14	FL
1968	**CLE**	N	9	FL
12 yrs.	152 games			

Walt McDonald
MCDONALD, WALTER
B. Oct. 22, 1911, Worland, WY
Utah 5'10" 210 lbs.

Year	Team		Games	Pos.
1935	**BKN**	N	11	C

Walt McDonald
MCDONALD, WALTER VINCENT
B. Nov. 5, 1920, Lowellville, OH
Tulane 6'1" 210 lbs.

Year	Team		Games	Pos.
1946	**MIA**	AA	4	B
1946	**BKN**	AA	9	B
1947			12	B
1948			12	B
1949	**CHI**	AA	9	B
4 yrs.	46 games			

Mickey McDonnell
MCDONNELL, JOHN
B. 1904
None 5'8" 159 lbs.

Year	Team		Games	Pos.
1925	**DUL**	N	3	HB
1925	**CHIC**	N	1	HB
1926			11	HB, QB
1927			8	HB
1928			6	HB, QB
1929			13	HB, QB
1930			7	HB, QB
1931	**FRA**	N	2	HB, QB
7 yrs.	51 games			

Bob McDonough
MCDONOUGH, BOB
B. Mar. 7, 1963
California (Pennsylvania) 6'1" 170 lbs.

Year	Team		Games	Pos.
1987	**DET**	N	3	CB, S

Bob McDonough
MCDONOUGH, ROBERT WALTER
B. May 31, 1919, Orange, NJ
Duke 5'11" 205 lbs.

Year	Team		Games	Pos.
1946	**PHI**	N	10	G

Coley McDonough
MCDONOUGH, COLEMAN R.
B. Oct. 10, 1914, North Braddock, PA
D. Jul., 1965
North Carolina State/Dayton 6'1" 189 lbs.

Year	Team		Games	Pos.
1939	**CHIC**	N	3	HB
1939	**PIT**	N	7	HB
1940			4	HB
1941			6	HB
1944	**C-P**	N	2	HB
4 yrs.	22 games			

Paul McDonough
MCDONOUGH, PAUL ROY
B. Dec. 14, 1916, Salt Lake City, UT
D. Aug. 11, 1960, Salt Lake City, UT
Utah 6'4" 222 lbs.

Year	Team		Games	Pos.
1938	**PIT**	N	7	E
1939	**CLE**	N	9	E
1940			11	E, HB
1941			10	E
4 yrs.	37 games			

Bob McDougal
MCDOUGAL, ROBERT J.
B. Mar. 29, 1921, Oconto, WI
Miami (Florida) 6'2" 205 lbs.

Year	Team		Games	Pos.
1947	**GB**	N	1	FB

Gerry McDougall
MCDOUGALL, GERRY
B. Mar. 21, 1935, Long Beach, CA
UCLA 6'2" 225 lbs.

Year	Team		Games	Pos.
1962	**SD**	A	4	FB
1963			14	FB
1964			7	FB
3 yrs.	25 games			

Doug McDougald
MCDOUGALD, DOUGLAS E.
B. Feb. 6, 1957, Fayetteville, NC
Virginia Tech 6'5" 271 lbs.

Year	Team		Games	Pos.
1980	**NE**	N	8	DE

Anthony McDowell
MCDOWELL, ANTHONY LEGUINN
B. Nov. 12, 1968, Killeen, TX
Texas Tech 5'11" 230 lbs.

Year	Team		Games	Pos.
1992	**TB**	N	12	RB
1993			4	RB
1994			14	RB
3 yrs.	30 games			

Bubba McDowell
MCDOWELL, LEONARD
B. Nov. 4, 1966, Fort Gaines, GA
Miami (Florida) 6'1" 196 lbs.

Year	Team		Games	Pos.
1989	**HOU**	N	16	S
1990			15	S
1991			16	S
1992			16	S
1993			14	S
1994			9	S
1995	**CAR**	N	16	S
7 yrs.	102 games			

John McDowell
MCDOWELL, JOHN
B. 1943
St. John's (Minnesota) 6'3" 260 lbs.

Year	Team		Games	Pos.
1964	**GB**	N	12	OT
1965	**NYG**	N	14	OT
1966	**STL**	N	1	OT
3 yrs.	27 games			

George McDuffie
MCDUFFIE, GEORGE
B. Jan. 20, 1963
Findlay 6'6" 270 lbs.

Year	Team		Games	Pos.
1987	**DET**	N	3	DE

O.J. McDuffie
MCDUFFIE, OTIS JAMES
B. Dec. 2, 1969, Marion, OH
Penn State 5'10" 191 lbs.

Year	Team		Games	Pos.
1993	**MIA**	N	16	WR
1994			15	WR
1995			16	WR
1996			16	WR
4 yrs.	63 games			

Hugh McElhenny
MCELHENNY, HUGH EDWARD (The King)
B. Dec. 31, 1928, Los Angeles, CA
Washington 6'1" 197 lbs.

Year	Team		Games	Pos.
1952	**SF**	N	12	HB
1953			12	HB

Year	Team	Games	Pos.

Hugh McElhenny *continued*

Year	Team	Games	Pos.
1954		6	HB
1955		12	HB
1956		12	HB
1957		12	HB
1958		12	HB
1959		10	HB
1960		9	HB
1961	MIN N	13	HB
1962		11	FB
1963	NYG N	14	HB
1964	DET N	8	HB

13 yrs. 143 games

Bucky McElroy
MCELROY, WILLIAM
B. 1929
Southern Mississippi 5'11" 195 lbs.

1954	CHIB N		HB

Leeland McElroy
MCELROY, LEELAND
B. Jun. 25, 1974, Beaumont, TX
Texas A&M 5'9" 198 lbs.

1996	ARI N	16	RB

Ray McElroy
MCELROY, RAY
B. Jul. 31, 1972, Bellwood, IL
Eastern Illinois 5'11" 195 lbs.

| 1995 | IND N | 16 | CB |
| 1996 | | 16 | CB |

2 yrs. 32 games

Reggie McElroy
MCELROY, REGINALD LEE
B. Mar. 4, 1960, Beaumont, TX
West Texas State 6'6" 281 lbs.

1983	NYJ N	16	OT
1984		16	OT
1985		13	OT
1986		8	OT
1987		8	OT
1988		16	OT
1989		15	OT
1991	LARI N	16	OT
1992		10	OT
1993	KC N	8	OT, G
1994	MIN N	10	OT
1995	DEN N	16	OT
1996		7	OT

13 yrs. 159 games

Vann McElroy
MCELROY, VANN WILLIAM
B. Jan. 13, 1960, Birmingham, AL
Baylor 6'2" 193 lbs.

1982	LARI N	7	S
1983		16	S
1984		16	S
1985		12	S
1986		16	S
1987		12	S
1988		12	S
1989		7	S
1990		3	S
1990	SEA N	10	S

9 yrs. 111 games

Bill McElwain
MCELWAIN, WILLIAM T.
B. May 14, 1903
Northwestern 5'10" 170 lbs.

| 1924 | CHIC N | 3 | HB |
| 1926 | | 8 | HB, FB, QB |

2 yrs. 11 games

Doug McEnulty
MCENULTY, DOUGLAS
B. Jan. 16, 1922, Tonganoxie, KS
Wichita State 6'3" 221 lbs.

| 1943 | CHIB N | 9 | FB |
| 1944 | | 10 | HB |

2 yrs. 19 games

Ed McEvoy
MCEVOY, EDWARD
B. Nov. 6, 1903
D. Aug., 1976, Houston, TX
Spring Hill 5'11" 190 lbs.

1926	HAR N	6	HB, QB

Craig McEwen
MCEWEN, CRAIG
B. Dec. 16, 1965, Northport, NY
Utah 6'1" 222 lbs.

1987	WAS N	4	TE
1988		14	TE
1989	SD N	4	TE
1990		16	TE
1991		16	TE

5 yrs. 54 games

Banks McFadden
MCFADDEN, JAMES BANKS
B. Feb. 7, 1917, Fort Lawn, SC
Clemson 6'2" 180 lbs.

1940	BKN N	11	HB

Marv McFadden
MCFADDEN, MARVIN G.
B. Jan. 18, 1930
Michigan State 6'0" 223 lbs.

| 1953 | PIT N | 12 | G |
| 1956 | | 12 | G |

2 yrs. 24 games

Paul McFadden
MCFADDEN, PAUL
B. Sep. 24, 1961, Cleveland, OH
Youngstown State 5'11" 163 lbs.

1984	PHI N	16	K
1985		16	K
1986		16	K
1987		12	K
1988	NYG N	12	K
1989	ATL N	9	K

6 yrs. 81 games

Thad McFadden
MCFADDEN, THAD DWAYNE
B. Aug. 14, 1962, Flint, MI
Wisconsin 6'2" 200 lbs.

1987	BUF N	3	WR

Bud McFadin
MCFADIN, LEWIS P.
B. Aug. 28, 1928, Rankin, TX
Texas 6'3" 260 lbs.

1952	LA N	1	G
1953		7	G
1954		12	G, T
1955		12	T
1956		12	T
1960	DEN A		DT
1961		14	DT
1962		14	DT
1963		14	DT
1964	HOU A	14	DT
1965		12	DT

11 yrs. 112 games

Jim McFarland
MCFARLAND, JAMES DARRELL
B. Oct. 4, 1947, North Platte, NE
Nebraska 6'5" 225 lbs.

1970	STL N	9	TE
1971		14	TE
1972		10	TE
1973		14	TE
1974		14	TE
1975	MIA N	6	TE

6 yrs. 67 games

Kay McFarland
MCFARLAND, RUSSELL KAY
B. Apr. 10, 1938, Quincy, IL
Colorado State 6'2" 182 lbs.

1962	SF N	6	FL
1963		12	FL
1964		12	FL
1965		12	OE
1966		12	OE
1968		9	FL

6 yrs. 63 games

Nyle McFarlane
MCFARLANE, NYLE
B. 1936
Brigham Young 6'2" 205 lbs.

1960	OAK A		HB

Barney McGarry
MCGARRY, BERNARD DUANE
B. Dec. 24, 1917, Park City, UT
Utah 6'1" 203 lbs.

1939	CLE N	10	G, T
1940		11	G
1941		11	G
1942		5	G

4 yrs. 37 games

John McGarry
MCGARRY, JOHN
B. Nov. 24, 1963
St. Joseph's 6'5" 288 lbs.

1987	GB N	2	G

Walt McGaw
MCGAW, RAYMOND P.
B. Dec. 27, 1899
D. Oct. 8, 1979, Trego, WI
Beloit 195 lbs.

1926	GB N	1	G

Clarence McGeary
MCGEARY, CLARENCE V. (Clink)
B. Aug. 8, 1926, St. Paul, MN
North Dakota State 6'5" 250 lbs.

1950	GB N	12	T

Ben McGee
MCGEE, BENJAMIN, JR.
B. Jan. 26, 1939, Starkville, MS
Jackson State 6'2" 255 lbs.

1964	PIT N	14	DT
1965		13	DE
1966		14	DE
1967		9	DE
1968		14	DE
1969		14	DE
1970		14	DE
1971		13	DE
1972		14	DT

9 yrs. 119 games

Buford McGee
MCGEE, BUFORD LAMAR

Buford McGee *continued*
B. Apr. 16, 1960, Durant, MI
Mississippi 6'0" 205 lbs.

1984	SD N	16	RB
1985		11	RB
1986		9	RB
1987	LARM N	3	RB
1988		16	RB
1989		16	RB
1990		16	RB
1991		16	RB
1992	GB N	4	RB

9 yrs. 107 games

Carl McGee
MCGEE, CARL DEMETRIUS
B. Jul. 15, 1956, Cincinnati, OH
Duke 6'3" 228 lbs.

1980	SD N	6	LB

Ed McGee
MCGEE, EDWARD D.
B. Feb. 26, 1916, Fort Edward, NY
Temple 6'1" 224 lbs.

1940	NYG N	3	G
1944	BOS N	10	T
1945		8	T
1946		11	T

4 yrs. 32 games

George McGee
MCGEE, GEORGE
B. 1936
Southern University 6'2" 259 lbs.

1960	BOS A		OT

Harry McGee
MCGEE, HARRY L.
B. Apr. 27, 1905
D. Oct., 1983, Florida
Kansas State 6'1" 198 lbs.

1927	CLE N	2	G
1929	SI N	8	C
1930	NEW N	1	C, T
1932	SI N	1	G

4 yrs. 12 games

Max McGee
MCGEE, WILLIAM MAX
B. Jul. 16, 1932, Sexton City, TX
Tulane 6'3" 210 lbs.

1954	GB N	12	OE
1957		12	OE
1958		12	OE
1959		12	OE
1960		12	OE
1961		13	OE
1962		14	OE
1963		14	OE
1964		13	OE
1965		12	OE
1966		12	OE
1967		10	OE

12 yrs. 148 games

Mike McGee
MCGEE, MICHAEL
B. Dec. 1, 1938, Washington, DC
Duke 6'1" 230 lbs.

1960	STL N	11	G
1961		13	G
1962		13	G

3 yrs. 37 games

Sylvester McGee
MCGEE, SYLVESTER (Molly)
B. Aug. 26, 1952, Haverstraw, NY

Sylvester McGee continued

Rhode Island 5'10" 184 lbs.

Year	Team		Games	Pos.
1974	ATL	N	10	RB

Tim McGee

MCGEE, TIMOTHY DWAYNE HATCHETT
B. Aug. 7, 1964, Cleveland, OH
Tennessee 5'10" 176 lbs.

Year	Team		Games	Pos.
1986	CIN	N	16	WR
1987			11	WR
1988			16	WR
1989			16	WR
1990			16	WR
1991			16	WR
1992			16	WR
1993	WAS	N	13	WR
1994	CIN	N	15	WR

9 yrs. 135 games

Tony McGee

MCGEE, ANTHONY EUGENE
B. Jan. 18, 1949, Battle Creek, MI
Wyoming/Bishop 6'4" 248 lbs.

Year	Team		Games	Pos.
1971	CHI	N	14	DE
1972			16	DE
1973			14	DE
1974	NE	N	14	DE
1975			13	DE
1976			14	DE
1977			14	DE
1978			16	DE
1979			16	DE
1980			16	DE
1981			16	DE
1982	WAS	N	9	DE
1983			16	DE
1984			16	DE

14 yrs. 202 games

Tony McGee

MCGEE, TONY L.
B. Apr. 21, 1971, Terre Haute, IN
Michigan 6'3" 246 lbs.

Year	Team		Games	Pos.
1993	CIN	N	15	TE
1994			16	TE
1995			16	TE
1996			16	TE

4 yrs. 63 games

Willie McGee

MCGEE, WILLIE
B. May 14, 1950, New Orleans, LA
Alcorn State 5'11" 179 lbs.

Year	Team		Games	Pos.
1973	SD	N	11	CB
1974	LA	N	14	WR
1975			14	WR
1976	SF	N	6	WR
1977			7	WR
1978	DET	N	4	WR

6 yrs. 56 games

John McGeever

MCGEEVER, JOHN
B. Feb. 14, 1939, Bogalusa, LA
Auburn 6'1" 195 lbs.

Year	Team		Games	Pos.
1962	DEN	A	14	DB
1963			13	DB
1964			14	DB
1965			14	DB
1966	MIA	A	12	DB

5 yrs. 67 games

Rich McGeorge

MCGEORGE, RICHARD EUGENE
B. Sep. 14, 1948, Roanoke, VA
Elon 6'4" 232 lbs.

Year	Team		Games	Pos.
1970	GB	N	14	TE

Rich McGeorge continued

Year	Team		Games	Pos.
1971			14	TE
1972			2	TE
1973			14	TE
1974			14	TE
1975			14	TE
1976			14	TE
1977			14	TE
1978			16	TE

9 yrs. 116 games

Kanavis McGhee

MCGHEE, KANAVIS
B. Oct. 4, 1968, Houston, TX
Colorado 6'4" 257 lbs.

Year	Team		Games	Pos.
1991	NYG	N	16	LB
1992			14	LB
1993			10	LB
1994	CIN	N	2	DE
1995	HOU	N	9	DE

5 yrs. 51 games

Charlie McGibbony

MCGIBBONY, CHARLES WILLIAM (Dub)
B. Oct. 23, 1915, Pine Bluff, AR
Alabama/Central Arkansas 5'10" 160 lbs.

Year	Team		Games	Pos.
1944	BKN	N	7	HB

Firpo McGilbra

MCGILBRA, L. VANCE
B. 1906
Haskell 6'1" 210 lbs.

Year	Team		Games	Pos.
1926	BUF	N	4	T, G

Eddie McGill

MCGILL, EDWARD HOYT
B. Jul. 5, 1960, Asheville, NC
Western Carolina 6'6" 225 lbs.

Year	Team		Games	Pos.
1982	STL	N	9	TE
1983			2	TE

2 yrs. 11 games

George McGill

MCGILL, GEORGE (Mickey)
B. Sep. 17, 1897
D. Jan., 1966
Marquette 5'10" 180 lbs.

Year	Team		Games	Pos.
1922	RAC	N	3	G

Karmeeleyah McGill

MCGILL, KARMEELEYAH
B. Jan. 11, 1971, Clearwater, FL
Notre Dame 6'3" 224 lbs.

Year	Team		Games	Pos.
1993	CIN	N	4	LB

Lenny McGill

MCGILL, CHARLES LEONARD
B. May 31, 1971, Long Beach, CA
Arizona State 6'1" 194 lbs.

Year	Team		Games	Pos.
1994	GB	N	6	CB
1995			15	CB
1996	ATL	N	16	CB

3 yrs. 37 games

Mike McGill

MCGILL, MICHAEL RAY
B. Nov. 21, 1946, Hammond, IN
Notre Dame 6'2" 236 lbs.

Year	Team		Games	Pos.
1968	MIN	N	14	LB
1969			10	LB
1970			14	LB
1971	STL	N	11	LB
1972			4	LB

5 yrs. 53 games

Ralph McGill

MCGILL, RALPH LOUIS
B. Apr. 28, 1950, Thomasville, GA
Tulsa 5'11" 181 lbs.

Year	Team		Games	Pos.
1972	SF	N	11	DB
1973			14	CB
1974			13	CB
1975			9	CB, S
1976			10	CB, S
1977			13	S
1978	NO	N	16	S
1979			13	S

8 yrs. 99 games

Willie McGinest

MCGINEST, WILLIE
B. Dec. 11, 1971, Long Beach, CA
Southern California 6'5" 252 lbs.

Year	Team		Games	Pos.
1994	NE	N	16	LB
1995			16	LB
1996			16	DE

3 yrs. 48 games

Ed McGinley

MCGINLEY, EDWARD FRANCIS, JR.
B. Aug. 9, 1899
D. Apr. 16, 1985, Sea Girt, NJ
Pennsylvania 5'11" 185 lbs.

Year	Team		Games	Pos.
1925	NYG	N	2	T

Larry McGinnis

MCGINNIS, JAMES LAWRENCE
B. Nov. 23, 1897
D. Nov., 1964
Marquette 6'1" 210 lbs.

Year	Team		Games	Pos.
1923	MIL	N	8	G, E
1924			12	G, C

2 yrs. 20 games

Len McGirl

MCGIRL, LEONARD E.
B. 1909
Deceased
Missouri 6'2" 206 lbs.

Year	Team		Games	Pos.
1934	C-S	N	3	G

Ed McGlasson

MCGLASSON, EDWARD TANDY
B. Jul. 11, 1956, Annapolis, MD
Youngstown State 6'4" 248 lbs.

Year	Team		Games	Pos.
1979	NYJ	N	7	C
1980	LA	N	1	C
1981	NYG	N	16	C

3 yrs. 24 games

Chester McGlockton

MCGLOCKTON, CHESTER
B. Sep. 16, 1969, Whiteville, NC
Clemson 6'4" 320 lbs.

Year	Team		Games	Pos.
1992	LARI	N	10	DE
1993			16	DT
1994			16	DT, DE
1995	OAK	N	16	DT
1996			16	DT

5 yrs. 74 games

Joe McGlone

MCGLONE, JOSEPH C.
B. Sep., 1896, Natick, MA
D. 1963
Harvard 5'7" 150 lbs.

Year	Team		Games	Pos.
1926	PRO	N	1	QB
1926	BOS	A	5	QB

1 yr. 6 games

Hugh McGoldrick

MCGOLDRICK, HUGH
B. Nov. 22, 1900
D. Oct., 1965, Cotuit, MA
Lehigh 5'10" 180 lbs.

Year	Team		Games	Pos.
1925	PRO	N	1	T, E

Bruce McGonnigal

MCGONNIGAL, JOSEPH BRUCE
B. May 1, 1968, Cambridge, MA
Virginia 6'4" 230 lbs.

Year	Team		Games	Pos.
1991	CLE	N	2	TE

Rob McGovern

MCGOVERN, ROBERT PATRICK
B. Oct. 1, 1966, Teaneck, NJ
Holy Cross 6'2" 223 lbs.

Year	Team		Games	Pos.
1989	KC	N	16	LB
1990			11	LB
1991	PIT	N	15	LB
1992	NE	N	4	LB

4 yrs. 46 games

Reggie McGowan

MCGOWAN, REGGIE
B. Sep. 25, 1964
Abilene Christian 5'8" 165 lbs.

Year	Team		Games	Pos.
1987	NYG	N	3	WR

Joe McGrail

MCGRAIL, JOE J.
B. Jun. 6, 1964, Philadelphia, PA
Delaware 6'3" 280 lbs.

Year	Team		Games	Pos.
1987	BUF	N	2	NT

Brian McGrath

MCGRATH, BRIAN
B. Mar. 18, 1901
D. Jan., 1985, Bronx, NY
None 245 lbs.

Year	Team		Games	Pos.
1922	LOU	N	1	G

Dick McGrath

MCGRATH, RICHARD
B. Oct. 20, 1897
D. Aug., 1975, Bayside, NH
Holy Cross 5'10" 190 lbs.

Year	Team		Games	Pos.
1926	BKN	N	10	T, C

Frank McGrath

MCGRATH, FRANK
B. 1904
Georgetown (DC) 5'11" 192 lbs.

Year	Team		Games	Pos.
1927	FRA	N	11	E, T
1928	NYY	N	11	E

2 yrs. 22 games

Mark McGrath

MCGRATH, MARK ALLEN
B. Dec. 17, 1957, San Diego, CA
Montana State 5'11" 175 lbs.

Year	Team		Games	Pos.
1981	SEA	N	6	WR
1983	WAS	N	2	WR
1984			13	WR
1985			5	WR

4 yrs. 26 games

Mike McGraw

MCGRAW, MICHAEL SHANE
B. Dec. 27, 1953, Denver, CO
Wyoming 6'2" 225 lbs.

Year	Team		Games	Pos.
1976	STL	N	4	LB

Thurman McGraw

MCGRAW, THURMAN FAY (Fum)

Year	Team	Games	Pos.

Thurman McGraw cont.
B. Jul. 17, 1927, Garden City, KS
Colorado State 6'5" 235 lbs.

Year	Team	Games	Pos.
1950	DET N	12	T
1951		8	T
1952		12	T
1953		11	T
1954		6	T

5 yrs. 49 games

Keli McGregor
MCGREGOR, KELI SCOTT
B. Jan. 23, 1963, Primghar, IA
Colorado State 6'6" 250 lbs.

| 1985 | DEN N | 2 | TE |
| 1985 | IND N | 6 | TE |

1 yr. 8 games

Dan McGrew
MCGREW, DANIEL
B. 1937
Purdue 6'2" 250 lbs.

| 1960 | BUF A | | C |

Larry McGrew
MCGREW, LAWRENCE
B. Jul. 23, 1957, Berkeley, CA
Southern California 6'5" 233 lbs.

1980	NE N	11	LB
1982		8	LB
1983		16	LB
1984		16	LB
1985		13	LB
1986		14	LB
1987		12	LB
1988		16	LB
1989		16	LB
1990	NYG N	11	LB

10 yrs. 133 games

Sly McGrew
MCGREW, SYLVESTER
B. Feb. 27, 1960, New Orleans, LA
Tulane 6'4" 257 lbs.

| 1987 | GB N | 3 | DE |

Curtis McGriff
MCGRIFF, CURTIS
B. May 17, 1958, Donalsonville, GA
Alabama 6'5" 275 lbs.

1980	NYG N	13	DT
1981		14	DT
1982		9	DE
1983		8	DE
1984		16	DE
1985		16	DE
1987	WAS N	1	DT

7 yrs. 77 games

Lee McGriff
MCGRIFF, LEE COLSON
B. Oct. 3, 1953, Gainesville, FL
Florida 5'9" 163 lbs.

| 1976 | TB N | 6 | WR |

Tyrone McGriff
MCGRIFF, TYRONE KEITH
B. Jan. 13, 1958, Vero Beach, FL
Florida A&M 6'0" 270 lbs.

1980	PIT N	16	G
1981		12	G
1982		8	C

3 yrs. 36 games

Lamar McGriggs
MCGRIGGS, LAMAR
B. May 9, 1968, Chicago, IL

Year	Team	Games	Pos.

Lamar McGriggs continued
*Oklahoma State/Western Illinois 6'3"
210 lbs.*

1991	NYG N	16	DB
1992		16	CB, S
1993	MIN N	9	S
1994		16	S

4 yrs. 57 games

Mike McGruder
MCGRUDER, MICHAEL J.P.
B. May 4, 1964, Cleveland Heights,
OH
Kent State 5'11" 186 lbs.

1989	GB N	2	CB, S
1990	MIA N	1	CB
1991		16	CB
1992	SF N	9	CB
1993		16	CB
1994	TB N	15	CB
1995		16	CB
1996	NE N	14	CB

8 yrs. 89 games

Gene McGuire
MCGUIRE, WALTER EUGENE
B. Jul. 17, 1970, Fort Dix, NJ
Notre Dame 6'2" 285 lbs.

| 1993 | CHI N | 9 | C |
| 1996 | GB N | 8 | C |

2 yrs. 17 games

Monte McGuire
MCGUIRE, MONTE
B. May 7, 1964
Texas Tech 6'4" 202 lbs.

| 1987 | DEN N | 2 | QB |

Warren McGuirk
MCGUIRK, WARREN P.
B. Jan. 2, 1906
D. Feb. 19, 1981, Boston, MA
Boston College 5'11" 200 lbs.

| 1929 | PRO N | 12 | T |
| 1930 | | 11 | T |

2 yrs. 23 games

Dan McGwire
MCGWIRE, DANIEL SCOTT
B. Dec. 18, 1967, Pomona, CA
Iowa/San Diego State 6'8" 243 lbs.

1991	SEA N	1	QB
1992		2	QB
1993		2	QB
1994		7	QB
1995	MIA N	1	QB

5 yrs. 13 games

Joe McHale
MCHALE, JOSEPH T.
B. Sep. 26, 1963, Clifton, NJ
Delaware 6'2" 227 lbs.

| 1987 | NE N | 3 | LB |

Tom McHale
MCHALE, THOMAS
B. Feb. 25, 1963, Gaithersburg, MD
Cornell 6'4" 282 lbs.

1987	TB N	3	DE
1988		10	DE
1989		15	G
1990		7	G
1991		15	G
1992		9	G
1993	PHI N	8	G
1994		13	OT
1995	MIA N	7	G, OT

9 yrs. 87 games

Year	Team	Games	Pos.

Lamar McHan
MCHAN, CLARENCE LAMAR
B. Dec. 16, 1932, Lake Village, AR
Arkansas 6'1" 210 lbs.

1954	CHIC N	12	QB
1955		12	QB
1956		12	QB
1957		12	QB
1958		12	QB
1959	GB N	12	QB
1960		12	QB
1961	BAL N	7	QB
1962		10	QB
1963		1	QB
1963	SF N	12	QB

10 yrs. 114 games

Pat McHugh
MCHUGH, WILLIAM PATRICK
B. Dec. 21, 1919, Selma, AL
Georgia Tech 5'11" 185 lbs.

1947	PHI N	9	HB
1948		10	HB
1949		12	HB
1950		12	HB
1951		3	HB

5 yrs. 46 games

Dan McIlhany
MCILHANY, JOE DANIEL
B. Jan. 12, 1943, Brownwood, TX
Texas A&M 6'1" 195 lbs.

| 1965 | LA N | 10 | DB |

Don McIlhenny
MCILHENNY, DONALD
BROOKES
B. Nov. 22, 1934, Nashville, TN
Southern Methodist 6'0" 197 lbs.

1956	DET N	9	HB
1957	GB N	12	HB
1958		12	HB
1959		12	HB
1960	DAL N	11	HB
1961	SF N	8	HB

6 yrs. 64 games

Wally McIllwain
MCILLWAIN, WALLACE W.
B. Jan. 20, 1903
D. Jun., 1963
Illinois 5'9" 169 lbs.

| 1926 | RAC N | 5 | HB |

Pat McInally
MCINALLY, PAT
B. May 7, 1953, Villa Park, CA
Harvard 6'6" 210 lbs.

1976	CIN N	14	P, WR
1977		14	P, WR
1978		16	P, WR
1979		16	P, WR
1980		16	P, WR
1981		16	P, WR
1982		9	P, WR
1983		16	P
1984		16	P
1985		16	P

10 yrs. 149 games

George McIndoe
MCINDOE, GEORGE R. (Mac)
B. Dec. 6, 1896
D. Jan., 1958
None

| 1921 | MUN A | 2 | E |

Year	Team	Games	Pos.

Nick McInerney
MCINERNEY, NICHOLAS (Bull)
B. 1896
Deceased
None 6'2" 201 lbs.

1920	CHIC A	5	FB, HB
1921		5	T
1922	CHIC N	11	C, T
1923		11	C
1924		9	C, T
1925		9	E, C, G, T
1926		11	E, C, FB, T
1927		7	G

8 yrs. 68 games

Sean McInerney
MCINERNEY, SEAN
B. Dec. 27, 1960
Frostburg State 6'3" 255 lbs.

| 1987 | CHI N | 3 | DT |

Hugh McInnis
MCINNIS, HUGH
B. Sep. 18, 1938, Mobile, AL
Southern Mississippi 6'3" 219 lbs.

1960	STL N	12	OE
1961		3	OE
1962		9	OE
1964	DET N	14	OE

4 yrs. 38 games

Ira McIntosh
MCINTOSH, IRA DANIEL (Al,
Chick)
B. Apr. 12, 1903
Deceased
Rhode Island 5'9" 180 lbs.

| 1925 | PRO N | 9 | HB |
| 1926 | | 2 | HB |

2 yrs. 11 games

Joe McIntosh
MCINTOSH, JOE
B. Dec. 9, 1962, Lexington, NC
North Carolina State 5'10" 192 lbs.

| 1987 | ATL N | 2 | RB |

Toddrick McIntosh
MCINTOSH, TODDRICK
B. Jan. 22, 1972, Tallahassee, FL
Florida State 6'3" 277 lbs.

| 1994 | TB N | 4 | DT |
| 1995 | | 11 | DT, DE |

2 yrs. 15 games

Guy McIntyre
MCINTYRE, GUY MAURICE
B. Feb. 17, 1961, Thomasville, GA
Georgia 6'3" 268 lbs.

1984	SF N	16	G
1985		15	G
1986		16	G
1987		3	G
1988		16	G
1989		16	G
1990		16	G
1991		16	G
1992		16	G
1993		16	G
1994	GB N	10	G
1995	PHI N	16	G
1996		15	G

13 yrs. 187 games

Jeff McIntyre
MCINTYRE, JEFF
B. Sep. 20, 1955, Beaumont, TX
Arizona State 6'3" 232 lbs.

| 1979 | SF N | 14 | LB |

Year	Team		Games	Pos.

Jeff McIntyre continued

Year	Team		Games	Pos.
1980	STL	N	10	LB
2 yrs.	24 games			

Secedrick McIntyre

MCINTYRE, SECEDRICK
B. Jun. 2, 1954, Montgomery, AL
Auburn 5'10" 190 lbs.

Year	Team		Games	Pos.
1977	ATL	N	6	RB

Everett McIver

MCIVER, EVERETT
B. Aug. 5, 1970, Fayetteville, NC
Elizabeth City State 6'6" 315 lbs.

Year	Team		Games	Pos.
1994	NYJ	N	4	OT, G
1995			14	G, OT
1996	MIA	N	7	G, OT
3 yrs.	25 games			

Rick McIvor

MCIVOR, RICK E.
B. Sep. 26, 1960, Fort Davis, TX
Texas 6'4" 210 lbs.

Year	Team		Games	Pos.
1984	STL	N	4	QB
1985			2	QB
2 yrs.	6 games			

Paul McJulien

MCJULIEN, PAUL DORIEN
B. Feb. 24, 1965, Chicago, IL
Jackson State 5'10" 190 lbs.

Year	Team		Games	Pos.
1991	GB	N	16	P
1992			9	P
1993	LARM	N	5	P
3 yrs.	30 games			

Bill McKalip

MCKALIP, WILLIAM WARD (Wild Bill)
B. Jun. 5, 1907, Pittsburgh, PA
D. Jul. 11, 1993, Corvallis, OR
Oregon State 6'1" 195 lbs.

Year	Team		Games	Pos.
1931	POR	N	14	E
1932			12	E
1934	DET	N	13	E
1936			10	E, HB
4 yrs.	49 games			

Bob McKay

MCKAY, ROBERT CHARLES
B. Dec. 27, 1947, Seminole, TX
Texas 6'5" 262 lbs.

Year	Team		Games	Pos.
1970	CLE	N	8	OT
1971			14	OT
1972			10	OT
1973			14	OT
1974			14	OT
1975			7	OT
1976	NE	N	14	G, OT
1977			12	OT
1978			13	OT
9 yrs.	106 games			

John McKay

MCKAY, JOHN KENNETH (J.K.)
B. Mar. 28, 1953, Eugene, OR
Southern California 5'11" 182 lbs.

Year	Team		Games	Pos.
1976	TB	N	14	WR
1977			14	WR
1978			15	WR
3 yrs.	43 games			

Roy McKay

MCKAY, ROY DALE (Tex)
B. Feb. 2, 1920, Mason City, TX
D. May, 1969

Year	Team		Games	Pos.

Roy McKay continued

Texas 6'0" 193 lbs.

Year	Team		Games	Pos.
1944	GB	N	3	HB
1945			10	HB
1946			11	FB
1947			11	HB
4 yrs.	35 games			

Paul McKee

MCKEE, PAUL MELVIN (Beaver)
B. Apr. 26, 1923, Beaver Falls, PA
Syracuse 6'3" 217 lbs.

Year	Team		Games	Pos.
1947	WAS	N	11	E
1948			12	E
2 yrs.	23 games			

James McKeehan

MCKEEHAN, JAMES BELL
B. Aug. 9, 1973, Houston, TX
Texas A&M 6'3" 251 lbs.

Year	Team		Games	Pos.
1996	HOU	N	14	TE

Marlin McKeever

MCKEEVER, MARLIN THOMAS
B. Jan. 1, 1940, Cheyenne, WY
Southern California 6'1" 233 lbs.

Year	Team		Games	Pos.
1961	LA	N	3	LB
1962			14	LB
1963			13	OE
1964			14	OE
1965			12	OE
1966			11	TE
1967	MIN	N	14	TE
1968	WAS	N	14	LB
1969			12	LB
1970			14	LB
1971	LA	N	14	LB
1972			14	LB
1973	PHI	N	13	LB
13 yrs.	162 games			

Vito McKeever

MCKEEVER, JUAN DEVITO
B. Oct. 8, 1961, Inverness, FL
Florida 6'0" 180 lbs.

Year	Team		Games	Pos.
1986	TB	N	16	DB
1987			1	CB
2 yrs.	17 games			

Keith McKeller

MCKELLER, KEITH
B. Jul. 9, 1964, Fairfield, AL
Jacksonville State 6'6" 240 lbs.

Year	Team		Games	Pos.
1987	BUF	N	1	TE
1988			12	TE
1989			16	TE
1990			16	TE
1991			16	TE
1992			11	TE
1993			8	TE
7 yrs.	80 games			

Keith McKenzie

MCKENZIE, KEITH
B. Oct. 17, 1973, Detroit, MI
Ball State 6'2" 242 lbs.

Year	Team		Games	Pos.
1996	GB	N	10	LB

Raleigh McKenzie

MCKENZIE, RALEIGH
B. Feb. 8, 1963, Knoxville, TN
Tennessee 6'2" 273 lbs.

Year	Team		Games	Pos.
1985	WAS	N	6	G
1986			15	G
1987			12	G
1988			16	G
1989			15	C, G
1990			16	C, G

Year	Team		Games	Pos.

Raleigh McKenzie continued

Year	Team		Games	Pos.
1991			16	C, G
1992			16	C, G
1993			16	C, G
1994			16	G, C
1995	PHI	N	16	C
1996			16	C
12 yrs.	176 games			

Reggie McKenzie

MCKENZIE, REGINALD
B. Jul. 27, 1950, Detroit, MI
Michigan 6'5" 252 lbs.

Year	Team		Games	Pos.
1972	BUF	N	14	G
1973			14	G
1974			14	G
1975			14	G
1976			14	G
1977			14	G
1978			16	G
1979			16	G
1980			16	G
1981			6	G
1982			9	G
1983	SEA	N	14	G
1984			10	G
13 yrs.	171 games			

Reggie McKenzie

MCKENZIE, REGINALD
B. Feb. 8, 1963, Knoxville, TN
Tennessee 6'1" 239 lbs.

Year	Team		Games	Pos.
1985	LARI	N	16	LB
1986			16	LB
1987			10	LB
1988			16	LB
1992	SF	N	2	G, OT
5 yrs.	60 games			

Rich McKenzie

MCKENZIE, RICHARD ANTHONY
B. Apr. 15, 1971, Fort Lauderdale, FL
Penn State 6'2" 258 lbs.

Year	Team		Games	Pos.
1995	CLE	N	8	DE

Mike McKibben

MCKIBBEN, MICHAEL WAYNE
B. Sep. 3, 1956, Mount Carmel, IL
Kent State 6'3" 228 lbs.

Year	Team		Games	Pos.
1979	NYJ	N	16	LB
1980			9	LB
2 yrs.	25 games			

Bill McKinley

MCKINLEY, WILLIAM J.
B. Jan. 14, 1949, Vincennes, IN
Arizona 6'1" 240 lbs.

Year	Team		Games	Pos.
1971	BUF	N	7	DE, LB

Phil McKinnely

MCKINNELY, PHILIP BYRON
B. Jul. 8, 1954, Oakland, CA
UCLA 6'4" 248 lbs.

Year	Team		Games	Pos.
1976	ATL	N	12	OT
1977			14	OT
1978			14	OT
1979			15	OT
1980			7	OT
1981	LA	N	7	OT
1982	CHI	N	8	OT
7 yrs.	77 games			

Bill McKinney

MCKINNEY, WILLIAM
B. Jul. 14, 1945, Borger, TX
West Texas State 6'1" 226 lbs.

Year	Team		Games	Pos.
1972	CHI	N	8	LB

Year	Team		Games	Pos.

Odis McKinney

MCKINNEY, ODIS, JR.
B. May 19, 1957, Detroit, MI
Colorado 6'2" 190 lbs.

Year	Team		Games	Pos.
1978	NYG	N	14	CB
1979			15	CB
1980	OAK	N	16	CB
1981			16	CB
1982	LARI	N	9	S
1983			16	S
1984			16	S
1985	KC	N	5	S
1985	LARI	N	10	S
1986			2	S
9 yrs.	119 games			

Royce McKinney

MCKINNEY, ROYCE
B. Nov. 3, 1953, River Rouge, MI
Kentucky State 6'1" 190 lbs.

Year	Team		Games	Pos.
1975	BUF	N	9	DB

Zion McKinney

MCKINNEY, ZION
B. Feb. 10, 1958, Pickens, SC
South Carolina 6'0" 200 lbs.

Year	Team		Games	Pos.
1980	WAS	N	10	WR

Hugh McKinnis

MCKINNIS, HUGH LEE, JR.
B. Jun. 9, 1948, Sharon, PA
Arizona State 6'0" 220 lbs.

Year	Team		Games	Pos.
1973	CLE	N	14	RB
1974			13	RB
1975			14	RB
1976	SEA	N	11	RB
4 yrs.	52 games			

Dennis McKinnon

MCKINNON, DENNIS LEWIS
B. Aug. 22, 1961, Quitman, GA
Florida State 6'1" 182 lbs.

Year	Team		Games	Pos.
1983	CHI	N	16	WR
1984			12	WR
1985			14	WR
1987			12	WR
1988			15	WR
1989			16	WR
1990	DAL	N	9	WR
7 yrs.	94 games			

Don McKinnon

MCKINNON, DONALD
B. 1942
Dartmouth 6'3" 233 lbs.

Year	Team		Games	Pos.
1963	BOS	A	14	LB
1964			3	LB
2 yrs.	17 games			

Roland McKinnon

MCKINNON, ROLAND
B. Sep. 20, 1973, Fort Rucker, AL
North Alabama 5'11" 230 lbs.

Year	Team		Games	Pos.
1996	ARI	N	16	LB

Dick McKissack

MCKISSACK, JAMES R.
B. 1926
Southern Methodist 6'2" 208 lbs.

Year	Team		Games	Pos.
1952	DAL	N	1	FB

Dennis McKnight

MCKNIGHT, DENNIS N.
B. Sep. 12, 1959, Dallas, TX
Drake 6'3" 271 lbs.

Year	Team		Games	Pos.
1982	SD	N	7	C, G

Year	Team		Games	Pos.

Dennis McKnight *continued*

Year	Team		Games	Pos.
1983			16	C, G
1984			16	C, G
1985			16	C, G
1986			16	C, G
1987			12	C, G
1988			16	C, G
1990	DET	N	14	C, G
1991	PHI	N	16	C, G
1992	DET	N	12	G
10 yrs.	141 games			

James McKnight
MCKNIGHT, JAMES
B. Jun. 17, 1972, Orlando, FL
Liberty 6'0" 181 lbs.

Year	Team		Games	Pos.
1994	SEA	N	2	WR
1995			16	WR
1996			16	WR
3 yrs.	34 games			

Ted McKnight
MCKNIGHT, THEODORE ROBERT
B. Feb. 26, 1954, Duluth, MN
Minnesota-Duluth 6'1" 209 lbs.

Year	Team		Games	Pos.
1977	KC	N	13	RB
1978			16	RB
1979			15	RB
1980			16	RB
1981			5	RB
1982	BUF	N	3	RB
6 yrs.	68 games			

Billy McKoy
MCKOY, WILLIAM EDMOND
B. Jul. 17, 1948, Winston-Salem, NC
Purdue 6'3" 233 lbs.

Year	Team		Games	Pos.
1970	DEN	N	2	LB
1971			14	LB
1972			14	LB
1974	SF	N	14	LB
4 yrs.	44 games			

Tim McKyer
MCKYER, TIM B.
B. Sep. 5, 1963, Orlando, FL
Texas-Arlington 6'0" 174 lbs.

Year	Team		Games	Pos.
1986	SF	N	16	CB
1987			12	CB
1988			16	CB
1989			7	CB
1990	MIA	N	16	CB
1991	ATL	N	16	CB
1992			16	CB
1993	DET	N	15	CB
1994	PIT	N	16	CB
1995	CAR	N	16	CB
1996	ATL	N	8	CB
11 yrs.	154 games			

Kevin McLain
MCLAIN, KEVIN
B. Sep. 15, 1954, Tulsa, OK
Colorado State 6'2" 230 lbs.

Year	Team		Games	Pos.
1976	LA	N	14	LB
1977			8	LB
1978			16	LB
1979			10	LB
4 yrs.	48 games			

Mayes McLain
MCLAIN, MAYES W. (Chief)
B. Apr. 16, 1905
D. Mar. 11, 1983, Marietta, GA
Haskell/Iowa 6'3" 225 lbs.

Year	Team		Games	Pos.
1930	POR	N	13	FB, HB, QB
1931			1	FB

Mayes McLain *continued*

Year	Team		Games	Pos.
1931	SI	N	8	HB, FB
2 yrs.	22 games			

Charlie McLaughlin
MCLAUGHLIN, CHARLES
B. Mar. 11, 1910
D. Feb., 1983, Pamplin, VA
Wichita State 6'0" 183 lbs.

Year	Team		Games	Pos.
1934	C-S	N	1	HB

Joe McLaughlin
MCLAUGHLIN, JOSEPH
B. Jul. 1, 1957, Stoneham, MA
Massachusetts 6'1" 235 lbs.

Year	Team		Games	Pos.
1979	GB	N	3	LB
1980	NYG	N	8	LB
1981			16	LB
1982			8	LB
1983			7	LB
1984			16	LB
6 yrs.	58 games			

Lee McLaughlin
MCLAUGHLIN, LEE M.
B. Feb. 28, 1917, Brownsburg, VA
D. Aug. 13, 1968
Virginia 6'1" 226 lbs.

Year	Team		Games	Pos.
1941	GB	N	10	G

Leon McLaughlin
MCLAUGHLIN, LEON C.
B. May 30, 1925, San Diego, CA
UCLA 6'2" 228 lbs.

Year	Team		Games	Pos.
1951	LA	N	12	C
1952			12	C
1953			12	C
1954			12	C
1955			12	C
5 yrs.	60 games			

Steve McLaughlin
MCLAUGHLIN, STEVEN JOHN
B. Oct. 2, 1971, Tucson, AZ
Arizona 6'0" 167 lbs.

Year	Team		Games	Pos.
1995	STL	N	8	K

Tom McLaughlin
MCLAUGHLIN, THOMAS
B. Jan. 22, 1889
D. Jun., 1964
Notre Dame 5'10" 185 lbs.

Year	Team		Games	Pos.
1921	TON	A	2	HB, FB

John McLaughry
MCLAUGHRY, JOHN JACKSON
B. Apr. 8, 1917, New Wilmington, PA
Brown 6'1" 205 lbs.

Year	Team		Games	Pos.
1940	NYG	N	9	B

Ray McLean
MCLEAN, RAYMOND (Toody)
B. Sep. 13, 1897
D. Oct., 1967, Detroit, MI
None 5'7" 155 lbs.

Year	Team		Games	Pos.
1921	GB	A	3	FB, HB

Ray McLean
MCLEAN, RAYMOND (Scooter)
B. Dec. 6, 1915, Lowell, MA
D. Mar. 4, 1964, Ann Arbor, MI
St. Anselm's 5'10" 167 lbs.

Year	Team		Games	Pos.
1940	CHIB	N	10	HB
1941			10	HB
1942			11	HB

Ray McLean *continued*

Year	Team		Games	Pos.
1943			10	HB
1944			9	HB
1945			5	HB
1946			8	HB
1947			12	HB
8 yrs.	75 games			

Ron McLean
MCLEAN, RONALD
B. Mar. 16, 1963, Everett, WA
Fullerton State 6'3" 267 lbs.

Year	Team		Games	Pos.
1987	DEN	N	3	DE, NT
1988	KC	N	6	DE, NT
2 yrs.	9 games			

Scott McLean
MCLEAN, ROBERT SCOTT
B. Dec. 16, 1960, Clermont, FL
Florida State 6'4" 233 lbs.

Year	Team		Games	Pos.
1983	DAL	N	4	LB

Chris McLemore
MCLEMORE, CHRIS
B. Dec. 31, 1963, Las Vegas, NV
Colorado/Arizona 6'2" 232 lbs.

Year	Team		Games	Pos.
1987	IND	N	2	RB
1987	LARI	N	3	RB
1988			7	RB
2 yrs.	12 games			

Dana McLemore
MCLEMORE, DANA
B. Jul. 1, 1960, Los Angeles, CA
Hawaii 5'10" 183 lbs.

Year	Team		Games	Pos.
1982	SF	N	8	S
1983			14	CB
1984			16	CB
1985			16	CB
1986			3	CB
1986	NO	N	3	DB
1987	SF	N	12	CB
6 yrs.	72 games			

Emmett McLemore
MCLEMORE, EMMETT (RED FOX)
B. Sep. 12, 1899, Oklahoma
D. May, 1973, Stilwell, OK
Haskell/Pittsburg State 5'7" 163 lbs.

Year	Team		Games	Pos.
1923	OOR	N	9	QB
1924	KC	N	4	QB, E
2 yrs.	13 games			

Tom McLemore
MCLEMORE, THOMAS
B. Mar. 14, 1970, Shreveport, LA
Southern University 6'5" 245 lbs.

Year	Team		Games	Pos.
1992	DET	N	11	TE
1993	CLE	N	4	TE
1994			2	TE
1995	IND	N	1	TE
4 yrs.	18 games			

Bob McLeod
MCLEOD, ROBERT
B. Nov. 10, 1938
Abilene Christian 6'5" 231 lbs.

Year	Team		Games	Pos.
1961	HOU	A	14	OE
1962			14	OE
1963			14	OE
1964			14	OE
1965			14	OE
1966			14	OE
6 yrs.	84 games			

Mike McLeod
MCLEOD, MICHAEL JAMES
B. May 4, 1958, Bozeman, MT
Minnesota 6'0" 180 lbs.

Year	Team		Games	Pos.
1984	GB	N	11	S
1985			8	S
2 yrs.	19 games			

Russ McLeod
MCLEOD, RUSSELL F.
B. Jul. 29, 1906
D. Apr. 4, 1977, Los Angeles, CA
St. Louis 6'0" 190 lbs.

Year	Team		Games	Pos.
1934	C-S	N	3	C

Harold McLinton
MCLINTON, HAROLD LUCIOUS
B. Jul. 1, 1947, Fort Valley, GA
D. Oct. 31, 1980, Washington, DC
Southern University 6'2" 235 lbs.

Year	Team		Games	Pos.
1969	WAS	N	7	LB
1970			14	LB
1971			14	LB
1972			13	LB
1973			8	LB
1974			13	LB
1975			14	LB
1976			14	LB
1977			14	LB
1978			16	LB
10 yrs.	127 games			

Art McMahon
MCMAHON, ARTHUR JOHN
B. Feb. 24, 1946, Newark, NJ
North Carolina State 5'11" 188 lbs.

Year	Team		Games	Pos.
1968	BOS	A	12	DB
1969			10	S
1970	BOS	N	7	S
1972	NE	N	14	S
4 yrs.	43 games			

Byron McMahon
MCMAHON, BYRON
None

Year	Team		Games	Pos.
1923	CHIC	N	6	HB, T

Harry McMahon
MCMAHON, HARRY (Shorty)
B. Oct. 25, 1898
D. Jan. 12, 1984, Southbridge, MA
Holy Cross 5'7" 150 lbs.

Year	Team		Games	Pos.
1926	HAR	N	2	HB

Jim McMahon
MCMAHON, JAMES ROBERT
B. Aug. 21, 1959, Jersey City, NJ
Brigham Young 6'1" 191 lbs.

Year	Team		Games	Pos.
1982	CHI	N	8	QB
1983			14	QB
1984			9	QB
1985			13	QB
1986			6	QB
1987			7	QB
1988			9	QB
1989	SD	N	12	QB
1990	PHI	N	5	QB
1991			12	QB
1992			4	QB
1993	MIN	N	12	QB
1994	ARI	N	3	QB
1995	GB	N	1	QB
1996			5	QB
15 yrs.	120 games			

Tommy McMahon
MCMAHON, THOMAS F. (Gig)

Year	Team		Games	Pos.

Tommy McMahon *continued*
B. May 19, 1891
D. Nov., 1962
Denison 5'11" 200 lbs.

Year	Team		Games	Pos.
1921	CIN	A	3	FB, HB

John McMakin
MCMAKIN, JOHN GARVIN
B. Sep. 24, 1950, Spartanburg, SC
Clemson 6'3" 229 lbs.

1972	PIT	N	14	TE
1973			14	TE
1974			8	TE
1975	DET	N	11	TE
1976	SEA	N	13	TE
5 yrs.		60 games		

Art McManus
MCMANUS, ARTHUR
B. Sep. 4, 1903
D. Dec., 1975, Hollywood, FL
Boston College 6'0" 190 lbs.

1926	NEW	A	1	G
1926	BOS	A	2	G
1 yr.		3 games		

Tom McManus
MCMANUS, THOMAS EDWARD
B. Jul. 30, 1970, Buffalo Grove, IL
Boston College 6'2" 252 lbs.

1995	JAC	N	13	LB
1996			16	LB
2 yrs.		29 games		

Herb McMath
MCMATH, HERBERT
B. Sep. 6, 1954, Coahoma, MS
Morningside 6'4" 248 lbs.

1976	OAK	N	14	LB
1977	GB	N	9	DT
2 yrs.		23 games		

John McMichael
MCMICHAEL, JOHN
B. Dec. 14, 1917, Cordova, AL
D. Dec. 25, 1991, Birmingham, AL
Birmingham-Southern 5'11" 190 lbs.

1944	BKN	N	1	B

Steve McMichael
MCMICHAEL, STEVE DOUGLAS
(Mongo)
B. Oct. 17, 1957, Houston, TX
Texas 6'2" 263 lbs.

1980	NE	N	6	NT
1981	CHI	N	10	DT
1982			9	DE, DT
1983			16	DT
1984			16	DT
1985			16	DT
1986			16	DT
1987			12	DT
1988			16	DT
1989			16	DT
1990			15	DT
1991			16	DT
1992			16	DT
1993			16	DT
1994	GB	N	16	DT
15 yrs.		212 games		

Eddie McMillan
MCMILLAN, EDWARD ALEXANDER
B. Nov. 25, 1951, Tampa, FL
Florida State 6'0" 189 lbs.

1973	LA	N	14	CB
1974			14	CB

Eddie McMillan *continued*

1975			14	CB
1976	SEA	N	14	DB
1977			14	CB
1978	BUF	N	14	CB
6 yrs.		84 games		

Erik McMillan
MCMILLAN, ERIK CHARLES
B. May 3, 1965, St. Louis, MO
Missouri 6'2" 197 lbs.

1988	NYJ	N	13	S
1989			16	S
1990			16	S
1991			16	S
1992			16	CB, S
1993	PHI	N	6	S
1993	CLE	N	3	S
1993	KC	N	1	S
6 yrs.		87 games		

Ernie McMillan
MCMILLAN, ERNEST CHARLES
B. Feb. 21, 1938, Chicago Heights, IL
Illinois 6'6" 258 lbs.

1961	STL	N	6	OT
1962			14	OT
1963			14	OT
1964			14	OT
1965			14	OT
1966			14	OT
1967			14	OT
1968			14	OT
1969			14	OT
1970			14	OT
1971			14	OT
1972			14	OT
1973			7	OT
1974			11	OT
1975	GB	N	13	OT
15 yrs.		191 games		

Randy McMillan
MCMILLAN, LEWIS LORANDO
B. Dec. 17, 1958, Havre de Grace, MD
Pittsburgh 6'0" 216 lbs.

1981	BAL	N	16	FB
1982			9	RB
1983			16	RB
1984	IND	N	16	FB
1985			14	FB
1986			16	RB
6 yrs.		87 games		

Dan McMillen
MCMILLEN, DAN
B. Feb. 23, 1964, Weisbaden, Germany
Colorado 6'5" 240 lbs.

1987	PHI	N	1	DE
1987	LARI	N	1	LB
1 yr.		2 games		

Jim McMillen
MCMILLEN, JAMES W.
B. Oct. 22, 1902
D. Jan. 28, 1984, Antioch, IL
Illinois 6'1" 215 lbs.

1924	CHIB	N	11	G
1925			15	G
1926			16	G
1927			14	G
1928			13	G, T
5 yrs.		69 games		

Audrey McMillian
MCMILLIAN, AUDREY GLENN
B. Aug. 13, 1963, Carthage, TX
Houston 6'0" 190 lbs.

1985	HOU	N	16	DB

Audrey McMillian *cont.*

1986			16	S, CB
1987			12	CB
1989	MIN	N	16	CB
1990			15	CB
1991			16	CB
1992			16	CB
1993			16	CB
8 yrs.		123 games		

Henry McMillian
MCMILLIAN, HENRY JAMES
B. Oct. 17, 1971, Folkston, GA
Florida 6'3" 275 lbs.

1995	SEA	N	1	DT
1996			2	DT
2 yrs.		3 games		

Mark McMillian
MCMILLIAN, MARK
B. Apr. 29, 1970, Los Angeles, CA
Alabama 5'7" 162 lbs.

1992	PHI	N	16	CB, S
1993			16	CB
1994			16	CB
1995			16	CB
1996	NO	N	16	CB
5 yrs.		80 games		

Bo McMillin
MCMILLIN, ALVIN NUGENT
B. Jan. 12, 1895, Prairie Hill, TX
D. Mar. 31, 1952, Bloomington, IN
Centre 5'9" 155 lbs.

1922	MIL	N	2	HB
1923	CLE	N	1	HB
1923	MIL	N	3	HB
2 yrs.		6 games		

Jim McMillin
MCMILLIN, JAMES
B. Sep. 18, 1939, Pleasant Hill, CA
Colorado State 5'11" 190 lbs.

1961	DEN	A	14	DB
1962			14	DB
1963	OAK	A	14	DB
1964			1	DB
1964	DEN	A	7	DB
1965			12	DB
5 yrs.		62 games		

John McMullan
MCMULLAN, JOHN
B. Jun. 28, 1935
Notre Dame 6'0" 244 lbs.

1960	NY	A	1	G
1961			14	G
2 yrs.		14 games		

John McMullan
MCMULLAN, JOHN
B. Jun. 4, 1903, Illinois
D. Apr., 1971, Buffalo, NY
Notre Dame 6'2" 250 lbs.

1926	CHI	A	14	T

Danny McMullen
MCMULLEN, DANIEL E. (Wild Man)
B. May 8, 1906, Belleville, KS
D. Aug. 22, 1983, St. Francis, KS
Nebraska 5'8" 231 lbs.

1929	NYG	N	12	G, T
1930	CHIB	N	10	G
1931			11	G, T
1932	POR	N	1	G
4 yrs.		34 games		

Chuck McMurty
MCMURTY, CHARLES
B. Feb. 15, 1937, Chandler, OK
Whittier 6'0" 286 lbs.

1960	BUF	A		DT
1961			14	DT
1962	OAK	A	11	DT
1963			14	DT
4 yrs.		39 games		

Greg McMurtry
MCMURTY, GREGORY WENDELL
B. Oct. 15, 1967, Brockton, MA
Michigan 6'2" 207 lbs.

1990	NE	N	13	WR
1991			15	WR
1992			16	WR
1993			14	WR
1994	CHI	N	8	WR
5 yrs.		66 games		

Dexter McNabb
MCNABB, DEXTER EUGENE
B. Jul. 9, 1969, De Funiak Springs, FL
Florida 6'2" 245 lbs.

1992	GB	N	16	RB
1993			16	RB
1995	PHI	N	1	RB
3 yrs.		33 games		

Steve McNair
MCNAIR, STEVE
B. Feb. 14, 1973, Mount Olive, MS
Alcorn State 6'2" 224 lbs.

1995	HOU	N	6	QB
1996			10	QB
2 yrs.		16 games		

Todd McNair
MCNAIR, TODD DARREN
B. Oct. 7, 1965, Camden, NJ
Temple 6'1" 185 lbs.

1989	KC	N	14	RB
1990			15	RB
1991			14	RB
1992			16	RB
1993			15	RB
1994	HOU	N	16	RB
1995			15	RB
1996	KC	N	16	RB
8 yrs.		121 games		

Frank McNally
MCNALLY, FRANK J.
B. Mar. 19, 1907, Nevada
D. Feb. 5, 1993, Delray Beach, FL
St. Mary's (California) 6'1" 203 lbs.

1931	CHIC	N	8	C
1932			7	C
1933			11	C, T
1934			10	C
4 yrs.		36 games		

Bob McNamara
MCNAMARA, JOHN ROBERT
B. 1932, Hastings, MN
Minnesota 6'0" 189 lbs.

1960	DEN	A		DB
1961			14	DB
2 yrs.		14 games		

Ed McNamara
MCNAMARA, EDWARD
Holy Cross 6'2" 225 lbs.

1945	PIT	N	1	T

Year	Team	Games	Pos.

Tom McNamara
MCNAMARA, THOMAS
B. Aug. 31, 1897
D. Mar., 1966, Ludlow Center, MA
Tufts/Detroit 5'10" 210 lbs.

Year	Team		Games	Pos.
1923	TOL	N	8	G, FB
1925	DET	N	12	G
1926			11	G
3 yrs.	31 games			

Sean McNanie
MCNANIE, SEAN
B. Sep. 9, 1961, Mundelein, IL
Arizona State/San Diego State 6'5" 265 lbs.

Year	Team		Games	Pos.
1984	BUF	N	15	DE
1985			16	DE
1986			16	DE
1987			12	DE
1988	PHX	N	12	DE
1990	IND	N	1	DE
6 yrs.	72 games			

Don McNeal
MCNEAL, DONALD
B. May 6, 1958, Atmore, AL
Alabama 5'11" 192 lbs.

Year	Team		Games	Pos.
1980	MIA	N	13	CB
1981			12	CB
1982			9	CB
1984			11	CB
1985			10	CB
1986			15	CB
1987			12	CB
1988			16	CB
1989			12	CB
9 yrs.	110 games			

Travis McNeal
MCNEAL, TRAVIS
B. Jan. 10, 1967, Birmingham, AL
Tennessee-Chattanooga 6'3" 248 lbs.

Year	Team		Games	Pos.
1989	SEA	N	16	TE
1990			16	TE
1991			16	TE
1992	LARM	N	12	TE
1993			16	TE
5 yrs.	76 games			

Charlie McNeil
MCNEIL, CHARLES
B. Aug. 8, 1936, Caldwell, TX
D. Jan. 1994, Houston, TX
Compton JC 5'11" 179 lbs.

Year	Team		Games	Pos.
1960	LA	A		DB
1961	SD	A	14	DB
1962			4	DB
1963			10	DB
1964			6	DB
5 yrs.	34 games			

Clifton McNeil
MCNEIL, CLIFTON ANTHONY
B. May 25, 1940, Mobile, AL
Grambling State 6'2" 186 lbs.

Year	Team		Games	Pos.
1964	CLE	N	14	FL
1965			13	FL
1966			14	FL
1967			2	FL
1968	SF	N	14	FL
1969			11	WR
1970	NYG	N	14	WR
1971			6	WR
1971	WAS	N	8	WR
1972			7	WR
1973	HOU	N	3	WR
10 yrs.	106 games			

Emanuel McNeil
MCNEIL, EMANUEL
B. Jun. 9, 1967, Richmond, VA
Tennessee-Martin 6'3" 285 lbs.

Year	Team		Games	Pos.
1989	NE	N	1	NT
1990	NYJ	N	2	NT
2 yrs.	3 games			

Frank McNeil
MCNEIL, FRANCIS
B. Dec. 23, 1909
D. Oct., 1971
Washington & Jefferson 6'0" 185 lbs.

Year	Team		Games	Pos.
1932	BKN	N	6	E

Fred McNeil
MCNEIL, FREDERICK ARNOLD
B. May 6, 1952, Durham, NC
UCLA 6'2" 229 lbs.

Year	Team		Games	Pos.
1974	MIN	N	14	LB
1975			14	LB
1976			13	LB
1977			14	LB
1978			14	LB
1979			16	LB
1980			16	LB
1981			16	LB
1982			9	LB
1983			16	LB
1984			13	LB
1985			10	LB
12 yrs.	165 games			

Freeman McNeil
MCNEIL, FREEMAN
B. Apr. 22, 1959, Jackson, MS
UCLA 5'11" 214 lbs.

Year	Team		Games	Pos.
1981	NYJ	N	11	RB
1982			9	RB
1983			9	RB
1984			12	RB
1985			14	RB
1986			12	RB
1987			9	RB
1988			16	RB
1989			11	RB
1990			16	RB
1991			13	RB
1992			12	RB
12 yrs.	144 games			

Gerald McNeil
MCNEIL, GERALD LYNN (Ice Cube)
B. Mar. 27, 1962, Frankfurt, Germany
Baylor 5'7" 145 lbs.

Year	Team		Games	Pos.
1986	CLE	N	16	WR
1987			12	WR
1988			16	WR
1989			16	WR
1990	HOU	N	16	WR
5 yrs.	76 games			

Pat McNeil
MCNEIL, PATRICK
B. Feb. 28, 1954, Pittsburgh, PA
Baylor 5'9" 208 lbs.

Year	Team		Games	Pos.
1976	KC	N	12	RB
1977			1	RB
2 yrs.	13 games			

Ryan McNeil
MCNEIL, RYAN DARRELL
B. Oct. 4, 1970, Fort Pierce, FL
Miami (Florida) 6'0" 175 lbs.

Year	Team		Games	Pos.
1993	DET	N	16	CB
1994			14	CB
1995			16	CB
1996			16	CB
4 yrs.	62 games			

Rod McNeill
MCNEILL, RODNEY CARLYLE
B. Mar. 26, 1951, Durham, NC
Southern California 6'2" 218 lbs.

Year	Team		Games	Pos.
1974	NO	N	11	RB
1975			14	RB
1976			2	RB
1976	TB	N	11	RB
3 yrs.	38 games			

Tom McNeill
MCNEILL, THOMAS GEORGE
B. Aug. 12, 1942, Rockford, IL
Stephen F. Austin 6'1" 195 lbs.

Year	Team		Games	Pos.
1967	NO	N	14	P
1968			10	P
1969			2	P
1970	MIN	N	14	P
1971	PHI	N	14	P
1972			2	P
1973			10	P
7 yrs.	66 games			

Bill McNellis
MCNELLIS, WILLIAM
B. 1903, Duluth, MN
D. 1942
St. Mary's (Minnesota) 5'11" 177 lbs.

Year	Team		Games	Pos.
1927	DUL	N	3	QB, FB

Bruce McNorton
MCNORTON, BRUCE EDWARD
B. Feb. 28, 1959, Daytona Beach, FL
Georgetown (Kentucky) 5'11" 175 lbs.

Year	Team		Games	Pos.
1982	DET	N	4	CB
1983			16	CB, S
1984			16	CB
1985			16	S, CB
1986			16	CB
1987			12	CB
1988			16	CB
1989			8	CB
1990			12	CB
9 yrs.	116 games			

Paul McNulty
MCNULTY, PAUL D.
B. Aug. 9, 1902
D. Sep. 27, 1985, Chicago, IL
Notre Dame 6'0" 175 lbs.

Year	Team		Games	Pos.
1924	CHIC	N	9	E
1925			1	E
2 yrs.	10 games			

Bill McPeak
MCPEAK, WILLIAM PATRICK
B. Jul. 24, 1926, New Castle, PA
D. May 7, 1991, Foxboro, MA
Pittsburgh 6'1" 208 lbs.

Year	Team		Games	Pos.
1949	PIT	N	12	E
1950			11	E
1951			12	E
1952			12	E
1953			12	E
1954			12	E
1955			10	E
1956			12	E
1957			12	E
9 yrs.	105 games			

Buck McPhail
MCPHAIL, COLEMAN
B. Dec. 25, 1929, Oklahoma City, OK
Oklahoma 6'1" 195 lbs.

Year	Team		Games	Pos.
1953	BAL	N	12	FB

Hal McPhail
MCPHAIL, HAROLD T. (Bumper)

Hal McPhail continued
B. Oct. 26, 1912
D. Aug., 1977, Newport, KY
Army/Xavier (Ohio) 6'1" 230 lbs.

Year	Team		Games	Pos.
1934	BOS	N	11	FB
1935			7	FB, HB
2 yrs.	18 games			

Jerris McPhail
MCPHAIL, JERRIS
B. Jun. 26, 1972, Clinton, NC
Mount Olive/East Carolina 5'11" 201 lbs.*

Year	Team		Games	Pos.
1996	MIA	N	9	RB

Frank McPhee
MCPHEE, FRANK M.
B. Mar. 19, 1931, Youngstown, OH
Princeton 6'3" 195 lbs.

Year	Team		Games	Pos.
1955	CHIC	N	2	E

Forrest McPherson
MCPHERSON, FORREST W. (Aimie)
B. Oct. 22, 1911, Fairbury, NE
D. Oct., 1989, Onalaska, WA
Nebraska 5'11" 233 lbs.

Year	Team		Games	Pos.
1935	CHIB	N	1	G
1935	PHI	N	7	C, G
1936			12	G
1937			3	G
1943	GB	N	5	C, T
1944			6	C, T
1945			5	T
6 yrs.	39 games			

Miles McPherson
MCPHERSON, MILES GREGORY
B. Mar. 30, 1960, Queens, NY
New Haven 5'11" 186 lbs.

Year	Team		Games	Pos.
1982	SD	N	6	S
1983			11	S
1984			9	CB
1985			9	CB, S
4 yrs.	35 games			

Johnny McQuade
MCQUADE, JOHN DOYLE
B. Jun. 4, 1895
D. Dec., 1980, Bradford Woods, PA
Georgetown (DC) 5'10" 176 lbs.

Year	Team		Games	Pos.
1922	CAN	N	4	HB, QB

Dan McQuaid
MCQUAID, DAN
B. Oct. 4, 1960, Cortland, CA
Nevada-Las Vegas 6'7" 278 lbs.

Year	Team		Games	Pos.
1985	WAS	N	16	OT
1986			13	OT
1987			1	OT
1988	MIN	N	3	OT
1988	IND	N		OT, G
4 yrs.	34 games			

Ed McQuarters
MCQUARTERS, EDDIE LEE
B. Apr. 16, 1943, Tulsa, OK
Oklahoma 6'1" 250 lbs.

Year	Team		Games	Pos.
1965	STL	N	1	G

Jack McQuary
MCQUARY, JOHN E.
B. Jun. 20, 1920
D. Dec. 20, 1986, Pebble Beach, CA
California 6'1" 208 lbs.

Year	Team		Games	Pos.
1946	LA	AA	1	HB

Year	Team	Games	Pos.

Leon McQuay
MCQUAY, LEON
B. Mar. 19, 1950, Tampa, FL
Tampa 5'9" 197 lbs.

Year	Team		Games	Pos.
1974	NYG	N	13	RB
1975	NE	N	13	RB
1976	NO	N	4	RB
3 yrs.	30 games			

Kim McQuilken
MCQUILKEN, KIM EVAN
B. Feb. 26, 1951, Allentown, PA
Lehigh 6'2" 203 lbs.

Year	Team		Games	Pos.
1974	ATL	N	5	QB
1975			3	QB
1976			8	QB
1977			7	QB
1979	WAS	N	3	QB
5 yrs.	26 games			

Bennie McRae
MCRAE, BENJAMIN PRINCE
B. Dec. 8, 1939, Pinehurst, NC
Michigan 6'1" 180 lbs.

Year	Team		Games	Pos.
1962	CHI	N	14	DB
1963			14	DB
1964			14	DB
1965			14	DB
1966			14	DB
1967			14	DB
1968			14	DB
1969			14	CB, S
1970			13	CB
1971	NYG	N	8	CB
10 yrs.	133 games			

Charles McRae
MCRAE, CHARLES EDWARD
B. Sep. 16, 1968, Clinton, TN
Tennessee 6'7" 295 lbs.

Year	Team		Games	Pos.
1991	TB	N	16	OT
1992			16	OT
1993			13	OT
1994			15	G, OT
1995			11	G, OT
1996	OAK	N	12	OT
6 yrs.	83 games			

Ed McRae
MCRAE, EDWARD
B. Jan. 12, 1902
Washington 5'7" 186 lbs.

Year	Team		Games	Pos.
1926	LA	A	7	G

Frank McRae
MCRAE, FRANKLIN
B. Mar. 18, 1944, Memphis, TN
Tennessee State 6'7" 270 lbs.

Year	Team		Games	Pos.
1967	CHI	N	5	DT

Jerrold McRae
MCRAE, JERROLD ELISHA
B. Apr. 9, 1955, Laurel, MS
Tennessee State 6'0" 194 lbs.

Year	Team		Games	Pos.
1978	KC	N	3	WR
1979	PHI	N	5	WR
2 yrs.	8 games			

Stan McRae
MCRAE, STAN
B. 1915
Minnesota 5'11" 190 lbs.

Year	Team		Games	Pos.
1946	WAS	N	9	HB

Bill McRaven
MCRAVEN, WILLIAM (Bullet Bill)

Bill McRaven *continued*
B. 1918
Murray State 5'11" 170 lbs.

Year	Team		Games	Pos.
1939	CLE	N	8	HB

Bob McRoberts
MCROBERTS, ROBERT
B. Apr. 28, 1924, Eau Galle, WI
Wisconsin-Stout 5'11" 190 lbs.

Year	Team		Games	Pos.
1944	BOS	N	1	B

Wade McRoberts
MCROBERTS, WADE
B. Jan. 7, 1901
D. Nov., 1941
Westminster (Pennsylvania) 6'0" 210 lbs.

Year	Team		Games	Pos.
1925	CAN	N	4	C
1926			9	C, E, G
2 yrs.	13 games			

Charles McShane
MCSHANE, CHARLES
B. Jan. 4, 1954, Long Beach, CA
California Lutheran 6'3" 230 lbs.

Year	Team		Games	Pos.
1977	SEA	N	14	LB
1978			14	LB
1979			1	LB
3 yrs.	29 games			

Joe McShea
MCSHEA, JOSEPH MAURICE
B. Dec. 13, 1899
D. Dec., 1985, Rochester, NY
Rochester 5'8" 170 lbs.

Year	Team		Games	Pos.
1923	ROC	N	1	G

Chuck McSwain
MCSWAIN, ANTHONY
B. Feb. 21, 1961, Rutherford, NJ
Clemson 6'0" 191 lbs.

Year	Team		Games	Pos.
1983	DAL	N	1	RB
1984			15	RB
1987	NE	N	3	RB
3 yrs.	19 games			

Rod McSwain
MCSWAIN, RODNEY
B. Jan. 28, 1962, Caroleen, NC
Clemson 6'1" 198 lbs.

Year	Team		Games	Pos.
1984	NE	N	15	CB
1985			16	CB
1986			9	CB
1987			12	CB
1988			16	CB
1989			9	CB
1990			13	CB
7 yrs.	90 games			

Warren McVea
MCVEA, WARREN DOUGLAS
B. Jul. 30, 1946, San Antonio, TX
Houston 5'10" 182 lbs.

Year	Team		Games	Pos.
1968	CIN	A	12	FL
1969	KC	A	12	RB
1970	KC	N	12	RB
1971			12	RB
1973			7	RB
5 yrs.	55 games			

John McVeigh
MCVEIGH, JOHN
B. Oct. 19, 1962
Kentucky/Miami (Florida) 6'1" 226 lbs.

Year	Team		Games	Pos.
1987	SEA	N	3	LB

Bill McWatters
MCWATTERS, WILLIAM
B. 1943
North Texas State 6'0" 225 lbs.

Year	Team		Games	Pos.
1964	MIN	N	11	FB

Bill McWilliams
MCWILLIAMS, WILLIAM HENRY
B. Nov. 28, 1910, Dubuque, IA
Iowa 6'1" 205 lbs.

Year	Team		Games	Pos.
1934	DET	N	5	HB

Johnny McWilliams
MCWILLIAMS, JOHNNY
B. Dec. 14, 1972, Ontario, CA
Southern California 6'4" 261 lbs.

Year	Team		Games	Pos.
1996	ARI	N	12	TE

Tom McWilliams
MCWILLIAMS, THOMAS EDWARD (Shorty)
B. May 12, 1926, Newton, MS
Mississippi State/Army/Mississippi State 5'11" 183 lbs.

Year	Team		Games	Pos.
1949	LA	AA	12	HB
1950	PIT	N	10	HB
2 yrs.	22 games			

Jack Mead
MEAD, JOHN M.
B. Apr. 18, 1921, Appleton, WI
Wisconsin 6'3" 213 lbs.

Year	Team		Games	Pos.
1946	NYG	N	10	E
1947			10	E
2 yrs.	20 games			

Jim Meade
MEADE, JAMES
B. Feb. 28, 1917, Philadelphia, PA
D. Aug., 1977, Peachtree City, GA
Maryland 6'1" 197 lbs.

Year	Team		Games	Pos.
1939	WAS	N	8	HB
1940			10	HB
2 yrs.	18 games			

Mike Meade
MEADE, MICHAEL LEE
B. Feb. 12, 1960, Dover, DE
Penn State 5'11" 228 lbs.

Year	Team		Games	Pos.
1982	GB	N	2	FB
1983			16	RB
1984	DET	N	15	FB
1985			16	FB
4 yrs.	49 games			

Eddie Meador
MEADOR, EDWARD DOYLE
B. Aug. 10, 1937, Dallas, TX
Arkansas Tech 5'11" 193 lbs.

Year	Team		Games	Pos.
1959	LA	N	12	DB
1960			12	DB
1961			14	DB
1962			14	DB
1963			14	DB
1964			14	DB
1965			14	DB
1966			14	DB
1967			14	DB
1968			14	DB
1969			14	S
1970			13	S
12 yrs.	163 games			

Ralph Meadow
MEADOW, RALPH
None 6'2" 195 lbs.

Year	Team		Games	Pos.
1920	CAN	A	1	E

Darryl Meadows
MEADOWS, DARRYL SCOTT
B. Feb. 15, 1961, Cincinnati, OH
Toledo 6'1" 199 lbs.

Year	Team		Games	Pos.
1983	HOU	N	16	S
1984			14	S
2 yrs.	30 games			

Ed Meadows
MEADOWS, EDWARD A. (Country)
B. Feb. 19, 1932, Oxford, NC
D. Oct. 22, 1974, Morehead City, NC
Duke 6'2" 221 lbs.

Year	Team		Games	Pos.
1954	CHIB	N	12	E
1955	PIT	N	12	E
1956	CHIB	N	12	E
1957			12	E
1958	PHI	N	12	E
1959	WAS	N	5	E
6 yrs.	65 games			

Johnny Meads
MEADS, JOHNNY
B. Jun. 25, 1961, Labadieville, LA
Nicholls State 6'2" 231 lbs.

Year	Team		Games	Pos.
1984	HOU	N	16	LB
1985			5	LB
1986			16	LB
1987			12	LB
1988			16	LB
1989			16	LB
1990			16	LB
1991			4	LB
1992	WAS	N	2	LB
9 yrs.	119 games			

Jack Meagher
MEAGHER, JOHN J.
B. Oct. 1, 1896, Chicago, IL
D. Nov. 7, 1968, San Francisco, CA
Notre Dame 5'10" 178 lbs.

Year	Team		Games	Pos.
1920	CHIT	A	4	E

Tim Meamber
MEAMBER, TIMOTHY FREDERICK
B. Oct. 29, 1962, Yreka, CA
Washington 6'3" 228 lbs.

Year	Team		Games	Pos.
1985	MIN	N	4	LB

Dave Means
MEANS, DAVID MITCHELL
B. Jan. 23, 1952, Hopkinsville, KY
Southeast Missouri State 6'4" 235 lbs.

Year	Team		Games	Pos.
1974	BUF	N	9	LB

Natrone Means
MEANS, NATRONE JERMAINE (Bomb)
B. Apr. 26, 1972, Harrisburg, NC
North Carolina 5'10" 245 lbs.

Year	Team		Games	Pos.
1993	SD	N	16	RB
1994			16	RB
1995			10	RB
1996	JAC	N	14	RB
4 yrs.	56 games			

Curt Mecham
MECHAM, CURTIS
B. Mar. 2, 1920, Bakersfield, CA
Oregon 6'0" 180 lbs.

Year	Team		Games	Pos.
1942	BKN	N	6	B

Year	Team	Games	Pos.

Karl Mecklenburg
MECKLENBURG, KARL BERNARD
B. Sep. 1, 1960, Seattle, WA
Augustana (South Dakota)/Minnesota 6'3" 236 lbs.

Year	Team	Games	Pos.
1983	**DEN** N	16	NT, DE
1984		16	LB
1985		16	DE, LB
1986		16	LB
1987		12	DE, LB
1988		9	LB, DE
1989		15	LB
1990		16	LB
1991		16	LB
1992		16	LB
1993		16	LB
1994		16	LB
12 yrs.	180 games		

Dan Medlin
MEDLIN, DANIEL ELLIS
B. Oct. 12, 1949, High Point, NC
North Carolina State 6'3" 254 lbs.

Year	Team	Games	Pos.
1974	**OAK** N	6	G
1975		14	G
1976		13	G
1977	**TB** N	14	G
1978		14	G
1979	**OAK** N	15	G
6 yrs.	76 games		

Ron Medved
MEDVED, RONALD GEORGE
B. May 27, 1944, Tacoma, WA
Washington 6'1" 205 lbs.

Year	Team	Games	Pos.
1966	**PHI** N	14	DB
1967		8	DB
1968		14	DB
1969		3	S
1970		12	S
5 yrs.	51 games		

Greg Meehan
MEEHAN, GREG
B. Apr. 27, 1963
Bowling Green 6'0" 191 lbs.

Year	Team	Games	Pos.
1987	**CIN** N	3	WR

Herb Meeker
MEEKER, HERBERT (Butch, Shorty)
B. Jul. 14, 1904
D. Apr., 1980, Brandon, FL
Washington State 5'3" 143 lbs.

Year	Team	Games	Pos.
1930	**PRO** N	11	QB, HB, FB
1931		9	QB, HB
2 yrs.	20 games		

Bob Meeks
MEEKS, ROBERT EARL, JR.
B. May 28, 1969, Andalusia, AL
Auburn 6'2" 279 lbs.

Year	Team	Games	Pos.
1993	**DEN** N	8	C

Bryant Meeks
MEEKS, BRYANT ADAMS, JR. (Meatball)
B. Jan. 16, 1926, Jacksonville, FL
Georgia/South Carolina 6'2" 193 lbs.

Year	Team	Games	Pos.
1947	**PIT** N	8	C
1948		10	C
2 yrs.	18 games		

Eddie Meeks
MEEKS, JOHN EDWARD
B. Sep. 30, 1897, Louisville, KY

Eddie Meeks *continued*
D. Oct., 1963
Louisville 155 lbs.

Year	Team	Games	Pos.
1922	**LOU** N	1	HB

Ward Meese
MEESE, WARD
B. 1902
Deceased
Wabash 5'10" 175 lbs.

Year	Team	Games	Pos.
1922	**MIL** N	2	E
1923	**STL** N	5	E
1924	**HAM** N	1	E
1925		1	E
4 yrs.	9 games		

Dave Meggett
MEGGETT, DAVID LEE
B. Apr. 30, 1966, Charleston, SC
Morgan State/Towson State 5'7" 180 lbs.

Year	Team	Games	Pos.
1989	**NYG** N	16	RB
1990		16	RB
1991		16	RB
1992		16	RB
1993		16	RB
1994		16	RB
1995	**NE** N	16	RB
1996		16	RB
8 yrs.	128 games		

Dave Meggyesy
MEGGYESY, DAVID MICHAEL
B. Nov. 1, 1941, Cleveland, OH
Syracuse 6'1" 221 lbs.

Year	Team	Games	Pos.
1963	**STL** N	6	LB
1964		14	LB
1965		14	LB
1966		14	LB
1967		14	LB
1968		12	LB
1969		8	LB
7 yrs.	82 games		

Charlie Mehelich
MEHELICH, CHARLES J.
B. Aug. 3, 1922
D. Dec. 2, 1984, Willow Grove, PA
Duquesne 6'1" 199 lbs.

Year	Team	Games	Pos.
1946	**PIT** N	10	E
1947		11	E
1948		12	E
1949		9	E
1950		12	E
1951		5	E
6 yrs.	59 games		

Tom Mehelich
MEHELICH, THOMAS TONY
B. Aug. 4, 1906, Grand Rapids, MN
D. May 20, 1972, Coleraine, MN
St. Mary's (Minnesota) 5'11" 195 lbs.

Year	Team	Games	Pos.
1929	**MIN** N	7	G, HB

Lance Mehl
MEHL, LANCE ALAN
B. Feb. 14, 1958, Bellaire, OH
Penn State 6'3" 235 lbs.

Year	Team	Games	Pos.
1980	**NYJ** N	14	LB
1981		15	LB
1982		9	LB
1983		16	LB
1984		16	LB
1985		16	LB
1986		8	LB
1987		3	LB
8 yrs.	97 games		

Harry Mehre
MEHRE, HARRY JAMES (Red)
B. Sep. 18, 1901, Lincoln, IN
D. Sep. 26, 1978, Atlanta, GA
Notre Dame 6'1" 190 lbs.

Year	Team	Games	Pos.
1922	**MIN** N	2	C
1923		9	C
2 yrs.	11 games		

Pete Mehringer
MEHRINGER, PETER JOSEPH (Champ)
B. Jul. 15, 1910, Jetmore, KS
D. Aug., 1987, Pullman, WA
Kansas 6'2" 206 lbs.

Year	Team	Games	Pos.
1934	**CHIC** N	7	T, G
1935		8	G, T
1936		4	T, HB
3 yrs.	19 games		

Steve Meilinger
MEILINGER, STEVE
B. Dec. 12, 1930, Bethlehem, PA
Kentucky 6'2" 227 lbs.

Year	Team	Games	Pos.
1956	**WAS** N	12	E
1957		12	E
1958	**GB** N	12	E
1960		12	E
4 yrs.	48 games		

Dale Meinert
MEINERT, DALE H.
B. Dec. 18, 1933, Lone Wolf, OK
Oklahoma State 6'2" 220 lbs.

Year	Team	Games	Pos.
1958	**CHIC** N	12	G
1959		12	G
1960	**STL** N	12	LB
1961		14	LB
1962		5	LB
1963		14	LB
1964		14	LB
1965		14	LB
1966		14	LB
1967		14	LB
10 yrs.	125 games		

George Meinhardt
MEINHARDT, GEORGE
B. Nov. 24, 1897
D. Apr., 1971, St. Louis, MO
St. Louis 5'9" 200 lbs.

Year	Team	Games	Pos.
1923	**STL** N	6	G, C

Darrell Meisenheimer
MEISENHEIMER, DARRELL
B. 1927
Oklahoma State 5'10" 195 lbs.

Year	Team	Games	Pos.
1951	**NYY** N	9	B

Bill Meisner
MEISNER, WILLIAM L.
B. Feb. 19, 1893
D. Feb., 1968, North Tonawanda, NY
Syracuse 5'11" 185 lbs.

Year	Team	Games	Pos.
1921	**TON** A	1	HB

Greg Meisner
MEISNER, GREGORY PAUL
B. Apr. 23, 1959, New Kensington, PA
Pittsburgh 6'3" 257 lbs.

Year	Team	Games	Pos.
1981	**LA** N	9	DT
1982	**LARM** N	6	DE
1983		16	DE
1984		16	NT
1985		14	NT
1986		15	NT
1987		15	NT

Greg Meisner *continued*

Year	Team	Games	Pos.
1988		12	NT
1989	**KC** N	12	NT
1990		16	DE, NT
1991	**NYG** N	4	NT
11 yrs.	135 games		

Ed Meixler
MEIXLER, EDWARD
B. 1943
Boston University 6'3" 245 lbs.

Year	Team	Games	Pos.
1965	**BOS** A	4	LB

Jon Melander
MELANDER, JON JAMES
B. Dec. 27, 1966, Fridley, MN
Minnesota 6'7" 280 lbs.

Year	Team	Games	Pos.
1991	**NE** N	10	G
1992	**CIN** N	15	OT
1993	**DEN** N	14	G
1994		15	G
4 yrs.	54 games		

Mike Melinkovich
MELINKOVICH, MICHAEL JOSEPH
B. Jan. 7, 1942, Tonasket, WA
Grays Harbor JC 6'4" 243 lbs.

Year	Team	Games	Pos.
1965	**STL** N	14	DE
1966		10	DE
1967	**DET** N	7	DE
3 yrs.	31 games		

Jim Melka
MELKA, JAMES
B. Jan. 15, 1962, West Allis, WI
Wisconsin 6'1" 235 lbs.

Year	Team	Games	Pos.
1987	**GB** N	1	LB

John Mellekas
MELLEKAS, JOHN STAVROS
B. Jun. 14, 1933, Newport, RI
Arizona 6'3" 255 lbs.

Year	Team	Games	Pos.
1956	**CHIB** N	12	T
1958		12	C
1959		12	C
1960	**CHI** N	12	C
1961		14	OT
1962	**SF** N	11	C
1963	**PHI** N	11	DT
7 yrs.	84 games		

Jim Mello
MELLO, JAMES ANTHONY
B. Nov. 8, 1920, Warwick, RI
Notre Dame 5'10" 190 lbs.

Year	Team	Games	Pos.
1947	**BOS** N	9	FB
1948	**LA** N	3	FB
1948	**LA** AA	6	HB
1949	**DET** N	10	HB
3 yrs.	28 games		

John Mellus
MELLUS, JOHN G.
B. Jun. 16, 1917, Plymouth, PA
Villanova 6'0" 214 lbs.

Year	Team	Games	Pos.
1938	**NYG** N	9	T
1939		11	T
1940		8	T
1941		11	T
1946	**SF** AA	14	T
1947	**BAL** AA	14	T
1948		14	T
1949		12	T
8 yrs.	93 games		

Year	Team	Games	Pos.

Andy Melontree
MELONTREE, ANDREW RICHARD, JR.
B. Dec. 1, 1957, Tyler, TX
Baylor 6'4" 228 lbs.

1980	**CIN** **N**	16	LB

Dan Melville
MELVILLE, DANIEL
B. Mar. 4, 1946, San Diego, CA
California 6'0" 185 lbs.

1979	**SF** **N**	16	P

Melvin
MELVIN
None 6'1" 185 lbs.

1921	**CIN** **A**	2	E

Dale Memmelaar
MEMMELAAR, DALE EDWARD
B. Jan. 15, 1938, Goshen, NY
Wyoming 6'2" 247 lbs.

1959	**CHIC** **N**	12	G
1960	**STL** **N**	12	T
1961		8	OT
1962	**DAL** **N**	14	OT
1963		14	OT
1964	**CLE** **N**	14	G
1965		14	G
1966	**BAL** **N**	12	G
1967		7	G
9 yrs.	107 games		

Don Menasco
MENASCO, DON DEAN
B. Oct. 8, 1930, Tynan, TX
Texas 6'0" 185 lbs.

1952	**NYG** **N**	12	HB
1953		8	HB
1954	**WAS** **N**	6	HB
3 yrs.	26 games		

John Mendenhall
MENDENHALL, JOHN RUFUS
B. Dec. 3, 1948, Cullen, LA
Grambling State 6'1" 255 lbs.

1972	**NYG** **N**	14	DE
1973		8	DT
1974		13	DT
1975		9	DT
1976		14	DT
1977		14	DT
1978		16	DT
1979		13	DT
1980	**DET** **N**	15	DT
9 yrs.	116 games		

Ken Mendenhall
MENDENHALL, KEN ERNEST
B. Aug. 11, 1948, Enid, OK
Oklahoma 6'3" 242 lbs.

1971	**BAL** **N**	14	C
1972		12	C
1973		13	C
1974		14	C
1975		14	C
1976		14	C
1977		14	C
1978		14	C
1979		16	C
1980		16	C
10 yrs.	143 games		

Mat Mendenhall
MENDENHALL, MAT
B. May 14, 1954, Salt Lake City, UT
Brigham Young 6'6" 253 lbs.

1981	**WAS** **N**	14	DE

Mat Mendenhall continued

1982		9	DE
2 yrs.	23 games		

Terry Mendenhall
MENDENHALL, TERRY
B. Apr. 16, 1949, Los Angeles, CA
San Diego State 6'1" 210 lbs.

1971	**OAK** **N**	14	LB
1972		3	LB
2 yrs.	17 games		

Mario Mendez
MENDEZ, MARIO
B. 1942
San Diego State 5'11" 200 lbs.

1964	**SD** **A**	1	HB

Ruben Mendoza
MENDOZA, RUBEN EDWARD
B. May 10, 1964, Crystal City, TX
Yankton/Wayne State (Nebraska) 6'4" 290 lbs.

1986	**GB** **N**	6	G

Hartwell Menefee
MENEFEE, HARTWELL
B. Jan. 1, 1943, Fort Worth, TX
New Mexico State 6'1" 198 lbs.

1966	**NYG** **N**	7	FL

Vic Menefee
MENEFEE, VICTOR (Bud)
B. 1899
Deceased
Morningside 6'0" 185 lbs.

1921	**RI** **A**	2	E

Chuck Mercein
MERCEIN, CHARLES S.
B. Apr. 9, 1943, Milwaukee, WI
Yale 6'3" 227 lbs.

1965	**NYG** **N**	13	FB
1966		13	FB, K
1967		1	RB
1967	**GB** **N**	7	RB, K
1968		11	RB, K
1969	**WAS** **N**	5	RB
1970	**NYJ** **N**	9	RB
6 yrs.	59 games		

Ken Mercer
MERCER, KENNETH E.
B. Jun. 9, 1903
D. Feb., 1970, Asbury, IA
Simpson 5'11" 183 lbs.

1927	**FRA** **N**	17	HB, QB, FB
1928		14	QB, HB, FB
1929		12	HB, FB
3 yrs.	43 games		

Mike Mercer
MERCER, MICHAEL
B. Nov. 21, 1935, Algona, IA
Minn./Florida St./Hardin-Simmons/N. Arizona 6'0" 208 lbs.

1961	**MIN** **N**	14	P, K
1962		4	P, K
1963	**OAK** **A**	14	K, P
1964		14	K, P
1965		14	K, P
1966		2	K
1966	**KC** **A**	10	K, P
1967	**BUF** **A**	14	K
1968		3	K
1968	**GB** **N**	6	K

Mike Mercer continued

1969		10	K
1970	**SD** **N**	14	K, P
10 yrs.	119 games		

Don Meredith
MEREDITH, JOSEPH DON (Dandy Don)
B. Apr. 10, 1938, Mount Vernon, TX
Southern Methodist 6'2" 202 lbs.

1960	**DAL** **N**	6	QB
1961		8	QB
1962		13	QB
1963		13	QB
1964		12	QB
1965		14	QB
1966		13	QB
1967		11	QB
1968		13	QB
9 yrs.	104 games		

Dudley Meredith
MEREDITH, CECIL DUDLEY
B. Jan. 16, 1935, Smithwick, TX
Florida/Midwestern/Lamar 6'4" 280 lbs.

1963	**HOU** **A**	14	DT
1964	**BUF** **A**	11	DT
1965		14	DT
1966		14	DT
1967		14	DT
1968		4	DT
1968	**HOU** **A**	10	DT
6 yrs.	81 games		

Russ Meredith
MEREDITH, RUSSELL DELMAR
B. Jun. 27, 1897, Fairmont, WV
D. May 22, 1989, Fairmont, WV
West Virginia 5'11" 200 lbs.

1925	**CLE** **N**	9	T, G

Mike Mergen
MERGEN, MICHAEL
B. 1929
San Francisco 6'5" 245 lbs.

1952	**CHIC** **N**	9	T

Art Mergenthal
MERGENTHAL, ARTHUR
B. Mar. 22, 1921, Bellevue, KY
Xavier/Bowling Green/Notre Dame 5'11" 215 lbs.

1945	**CLE** **N**	10	G
1946	**LA** **N**	9	G
2 yrs.	19 games		

Lou Merillat
MERILLAT, LOUIS ALFRED, JR.
B. Jun. 9, 1892, Chicago, IL
D. Apr. 26, 1948, Chicago, IL
Illinois Tech/Army 5'9" 165 lbs.

1925	**CAN** **N**	6	E

Monte Merkel
MERKEL, MONTE
B. Nov. 6, 1916
D. Jun., 1981, Missoula, MT
Kansas 5'10" 215 lbs.

1943	**CHIB** **N**	1	G

Guido Merkens
MERKENS, GUIDO A.
B. Aug. 14, 1955, San Antonio, TX
Sam Houston State 6'1" 200 lbs.

1978	**HOU** **N**	12	WR, S
1979		16	WR, S

Guido Merkens continued

1980		3	WR
1980	**NO** **N**	1	DB
1981		16	CB, S
1982		9	WR
1983		16	QB
1984		16	QB
1985		16	QB, WR
1987	**PHI** **N**	3	QB
9 yrs.	108 games		

Ed Merkle
MERKLE, EDWARD L.
B. Jul. 3, 1917, Windsor, MO
Oklahoma State 5'10" 215 lbs.

1944	**WAS** **N**	10	G

Al Merkovsky
MERKOVSKY, ALBERT J.
B. Apr. 13, 1917, North Braddock, PA
D. Jun. 28, 1982, Long Beach, CA
Pittsburgh 6'1" 223 lbs.

1944	**C, P** **N**	7	T, G
1945	**PIT** **N**	10	T
1946		4	T
3 yrs.	21 games		

Ed Merlin
MERLIN, EDWARD
B. 1916
Vanderbilt 5'10" 210 lbs.

1938	**BKN** **N**	11	G
1939		5	G
2 yrs.	16 games		

Jim Merlo
MERLO, JAMES LOUIS
B. Oct. 3, 1951, Sanger, CA
Stanford 6'1" 221 lbs.

1973	**NO** **N**	14	LB
1974		14	LB
1976		14	LB
1977		14	LB
1978		16	LB
1979		16	LB
6 yrs.	88 games		

Casey Merrill
MERRILL, RICHARD CASEY
B. Jul. 16, 1957, Oakland, CA
California-Davis 6'4" 255 lbs.

1979	**GB** **N**	11	DE
1980		16	DE
1981		16	DE
1982		9	DE
1983		5	DE
1983	**NYG** **N**	10	DE
1984		16	DE
1985		11	DE
1986	**NO** **N**	1	DE
8 yrs.	95 games		

Mark Merrill
MERRILL, MARK CHRISTOPHER
B. May 5, 1945, St. Paul, MN
Minnesota 6'4" 238 lbs.

1978	**NYJ** **N**	16	LB
1979		6	LB
1979	**CHI** **N**	9	LB
1981	**DEN** **N**	15	LB
1982		2	LB
1982	**GB** **N**	4	LB
1983	**BUF** **N**	12	LB
1984		2	LB
1984	**LARI** **N**	3	LB
6 yrs.	69 games		

650

Year	Team		Games	Pos.

Walt Merrill
MERRILL, WALTER O.
B. Aug. 7, 1917, Andalusia, AL
Deceased
Alabama 6'2" 217 lbs.

Year	Team		Games	Pos.
1940	BKN	N	11	T, E
1941			6	T
1942			11	T
3 yrs.	28 games			

Sam Merriman
MERRIMAN, SAM
B. May 5, 1961, Tucson, AZ
Idaho 6'3" 230 lbs.

Year	Team		Games	Pos.
1983	SEA	N	16	LB
1984			16	LB
1985			14	LB
1986			16	LB
1987			9	LB
5 yrs.	71 games			

David Merritt
MERRITT, DAVID LEE
B. Sep. 8, 1971, Raleigh, NC
North Carolina State 6'1" 237 lbs.

Year	Team		Games	Pos.
1993	MIA	N	4	LB
1993	PHX	N	3	LB
1994	ARI	N	16	LB
1995			15	LB
3 yrs.	38 games			

Jim Merritts
MERRITTS, JAMES
B. Mar. 22, 1961, Roaring Springs, PA
Connecticut/West Virginia 6'3" 255 lbs.

Year	Team		Games	Pos.
1987	IND	N	1	NT

Mike Merriweather
MERRIWEATHER, MICHAEL LAMAR
B. Nov. 26, 1960, St. Albans, NY
Pacific 6'2" 219 lbs.

Year	Team		Games	Pos.
1982	PIT	N	9	LB
1983			16	LB
1984			16	LB
1985			16	LB
1986			16	LB
1987			12	LB
1989	MIN	N	16	LB
1990			16	LB
1991			16	LB
1992			16	LB
1993	NYJ	N	1	LB
11 yrs.	150 games			

Jeff Merrow
MERROW, JEFFREY COLIN
B. Jul. 12, 1953, Akron, OH
West Virginia 6'4" 245 lbs.

Year	Team		Games	Pos.
1975	ATL	N	12	DT
1976			14	DE
1977			14	DE
1978			14	DE
1979			3	DE
1980			16	DE
1981			11	DE
1982			8	DE
1983			16	DE
9 yrs.	108 games			

Scott Mersereau
MERSEREAU, SCOTT ROBERT
B. Apr. 8, 1965, Riverhead, NY
Southern Connecticut State 6'3" 275 lbs.

Year	Team		Games	Pos.
1987	NYJ	N	13	DE
1988			16	DE
1989			16	DT, DE
1990			16	DT, DE

Scott Mersereau *continued*

Year	Team		Games	Pos.
1991			13	DT
1992			15	DT
1993			13	DT
7 yrs.	102 games			

Jerry Mertens
MERTENS, JERRY
B. Jan. 5, 1936, Racine, WI
Drake 6'0" 184 lbs.

Year	Team		Games	Pos.
1958	SF	N	12	DB
1959			12	DB
1960			12	DB
1961			14	DB
1962			14	DB
1964			14	DB
1965			13	DB
7 yrs.	91 games			

Jim Mertens
MERTENS, JAMES
B. May 25, 1947, Cumberland, MD
Fairmont State 6'2" 235 lbs.

Year	Team		Games	Pos.
1969	MIA	A	14	TE

Bus Mertes
MERTES, BERNARD JAMES
B. Oct. 6, 1923, Chicago, IL
Iowa 6'0" 201 lbs.

Year	Team		Games	Pos.
1945	CHIC	N	8	HB
1946	LA	AA	9	HB
1947	BAL	AA	14	HB
1948			13	HB
1949			2	HB
1949	NYG	N	8	HB
5 yrs.	54 games			

Curt Merz
MERZ, CURTIS CARL
B. Apr. 17, 1938, Newark, NJ
Iowa 6'4" 257 lbs.

Year	Team		Games	Pos.
1962	DAL	A	14	G
1963	KC	A	14	G
1964			14	G, DE
1965			14	G
1966			14	G
1967			8	G
1968			14	G
7 yrs.	92 games			

Dick Mesak
MESAK, RICHARD
B. 1920
St. Mary's (California) 6'2" 225 lbs.

Year	Team		Games	Pos.
1945	DET	N	6	T

Mark Meseroll
MESEROLL, MARK
B. Jul. 22, 1955, Piscataway, NJ
Florida 6'5" 270 lbs.

Year	Team		Games	Pos.
1978	NO	N	16	OT

Bruce Mesner
MESNER, BRUCE M.
B. Mar. 21, 1964, New York, NY
Maryland 6'5" 280 lbs.

Year	Team		Games	Pos.
1987	BUF	N	11	NT

Dale Messer
MESSER, LYNDY DALE
B. Aug. 6, 1937, Lemoore, CA
Fresno State 5'10" 175 lbs.

Year	Team		Games	Pos.
1961	SF	N	4	HB
1962			13	HB, DB
1963			14	HB
1964			6	HB

Dale Messer *continued*

Year	Team		Games	Pos.
1965			9	FL
5 yrs.	46 games			

Mark Messner
MESSNER, MARK W.
B. Dec. 29, 1965, Riverview, MI
Michigan 6'2" 256 lbs.

Year	Team		Games	Pos.
1989	LARM	N	4	LB

Max Messner
MESSNER, MAX C.
B. Oct. 13, 1938, Ashland, OH
Deceased
Cincinnati 6'3" 225 lbs.

Year	Team		Games	Pos.
1960	DET	N	1	LB
1961			14	LB
1962			14	LB
1963			14	LB
1964	NYG	N	6	LB
1964	PIT	N	13	LB
1965			14	LB
6 yrs.	76 games			

Frank Mestnik
MESTNIK, FRANK
B. Feb. 23, 1938, Cleveland, OH
Marquette 6'2" 200 lbs.

Year	Team		Games	Pos.
1960	STL	N	9	FB
1961			13	FB
1963	GB	N	11	FB
3 yrs.	33 games			

Bo Metcalf
METCALF, ISAAC SCOTT
B. Apr. 18, 1961, Waco, TX
Baylor 6'2" 193 lbs.

Year	Team		Games	Pos.
1984	IND	N	2	CB, S

Eric Metcalf
METCALF, ERIC QUINN
B. Jan. 23, 1968, Seattle, WA
Texas 5'10" 187 lbs.

Year	Team		Games	Pos.
1989	CLE	N	16	RB
1990			16	RB
1991			8	RB
1992			16	RB
1993			16	RB
1994			16	RB
1995	ATL	N	16	WR
1996			16	WR
8 yrs.	120 games			

Terry Metcalf
METCALF, TERRANCE RANDOLPH
B. Sep. 24, 1951, Seattle, WA
Long Beach State 5'10" 185 lbs.

Year	Team		Games	Pos.
1973	STL	N	12	RB
1974			14	RB
1975			13	RB
1976			12	RB
1977			14	RB
1981	WAS	N	16	RB
6 yrs.	81 games			

Russ Method
METHOD, RUSSELL (Cuss)
B. Jun. 27, 1897
D. Sep. 17, 1971, Two Feathers, MN
None 5'10" 192 lbs.

Year	Team		Games	Pos.
1923	DUL	N	7	HB
1924			5	HB
1925			3	QB, HB, FB
1926			12	QB, HB, E
1927			7	QB, HB, G

Russ Method *continued*

Year	Team		Games	Pos.
1929	CHIC	N	9	HB, QB, FB
6 yrs.	43 games			

Pete Metzelaars
METZELAARS, PETER HENRY
B. May 24, 1960, Three Rivers, MI
Wabash 6'7" 245 lbs.

Year	Team		Games	Pos.
1982	SEA	N	9	TE
1983			16	TE
1984			9	TE
1985	BUF	N	16	TE
1986			16	TE
1987			12	TE
1988			16	TE
1989			16	TE
1990			16	TE
1991			16	TE
1992			16	TE
1993			16	TE
1994			16	TE
1995	CAR	N	14	TE
1996	DET	N	15	TE
15 yrs.	219 games			

Ed Metzger
METZGER, ED
None

Year	Team		Games	Pos.
1926	LOU	N	3	FB, QB

Kevin Meutch
MEUTCH, KEVIN
B. May 4, 1964
Southwest Texas State 6'5" 270 lbs.

Year	Team		Games	Pos.
1987	NYG	N	3	OT

Dennis Meyer
MEYER, DENNIS
B. Apr. 8, 1950, Jefferson City, MO
Arkansas State 5'11" 186 lbs.

Year	Team		Games	Pos.
1973	PIT	N	11	DB

Eddie Meyer
MEYER, EDWARD
B. 1937
West Texas A&M 6'2" 240 lbs.

Year	Team		Games	Pos.
1960	BUF	A		OT

Ernie Meyer
MEYER, ERNIE (Puss, Egg)
B. Jul. 3, 1903
D. Jan. 23, 1971, Malinta, OH
Geneva 6'2" 200 lbs.

Year	Team		Games	Pos.
1930	POR	N	8	G

Fred Meyer
MEYER, FREDERICK D.
B. Sep. 29, 1919, Mount Sterling, IL
Stanford 6'2" 193 lbs.

Year	Team		Games	Pos.
1942	PHI	N	11	E
1945			8	E
2 yrs.	19 games			

Gil Meyer
MEYER, GILBERT
B. Nov. 25, 1920, Baltimore, MD
Wake Forest 6'2" 200 lbs.

Year	Team		Games	Pos.
1947	BAL	AA	13	E

Jim Meyer
MEYER, JAMES DAVID
B. Jun. 9, 1963, Glenview, IL
Illinois State 6'5" 290 lbs.

Year	Team		Games	Pos.
1987	GB	N	2	OT

Year	Team	Games	Pos.

John Meyer
MEYER, JOHN
B. Feb. 20, 1942, Chicago, IL
Notre Dame 6'1" 225 lbs.

Year	Team		Games	Pos.
1966	HOU	A	14	LB

Ron Meyer
MEYER, RONALD ALLEN
B. Aug. 27, 1944, Austin, MN
South Dakota State 6'4" 205 lbs.

1966	PIT	N	4	QB

Bob Meyers
MEYERS, ROBERT E., JR.
B. 1930
Stanford 6'2" 184 lbs.

1952	SF	N	1	FB

Jerry Meyers
MEYERS JERRY EDWARD
B. Feb. 21, 1954, Chicago, IL
Northern Illinois 6'4" 249 lbs.

1976	CHI	N	12	DT
1977			13	DE
1978			16	DE
1979			6	DE
1980	KC	N	2	DT
5 yrs.	49 games			

John Meyers
MEYERS, JOHN DOUGLAS
B. Jan. 16, 1940, Forest City, IA
Washington 6'6" 272 lbs.

1962	DAL	N	14	DT
1963			14	DT
1964	PHI	N	14	DT
1965			14	DT
1966			14	DT
1967			14	DT
6 yrs.	84 games			

Klinks Meyers
MEYERS, STANTON
B. Oct., 1893
None 165 lbs.

1920	HAM	A	2	HB, QB

Paul Meyers
MEYERS, PAUL (Chief)
B. Dec. 3, 1894
D. Oct., 1970, Akron, OH
Wisconsin-Milwaukee 5'11" 170 lbs.

1921	NY	A	1	E
1923	RAC	N	8	E
2 yrs.	9 games			

Wayne Meylan
MEYLAN, WAYNE A.
B. Mar. 2, 1946, Bay Citym, MI
Nebraska 6'1" 237 lbs.

1968	CLE	N	14	LB
1969			14	LB
1970	MIN	N	2	LB
3 yrs.	30 games			

Larry Mialik
MIALIK. LAWRENCE
B. May 15, 1950, Passaic, NJ
Wisconsin 6'2" 226 lbs.

1972	ATL	N	14	TE
1973			14	TE
1974			14	TE
1976	SD	N	7	TE
4 yrs.	49 games			

Rich Miano
MIANO, RICHARD JAMES
B. Sep. 3, 1962, Newton, MA
Hawaii 6'0" 200 lbs.

1985	NYJ	N	16	S
1986			14	S
1987			12	S
1988			16	S
1989			2	S
1991	PHI	N	16	DB
1992			16	CB, S
1993			16	S
1994			16	S
1995	ATL	N	11	S
10 yrs.	135 games			

Phil Micech
MICECH, PHIL
B. 1961
Wisconsin-Platteville 6'5" 265 lbs.

1987	MIN	N	3	DE

Bill Michael
MICHAEL, PAUL WILLIAM
B. 1934
Ohio State 6'2" 240 lbs.

1957	PIT	N	3	G

Rich Michael
MICHAEL, RICH
B. 1939
Ohio State 6'3" 230 lbs.

1960	HOU	A	10	OT
1961			14	OT
1962			14	OT
1963			14	OT
1965	HOU	A	14	OT
1966			14	OT
6 yrs.	80 games			

Al Michaels
MICHAELS, ALTON C. (Bud)
B. 1900
Deceased
Heidelberg/Ohio State 6'0" 190 lbs.

1923	AKR	N	6	FB, HB
1924			6	HB, FB
1925	CLE	N	14	HB
1926	CLE	A	5	HB, FB
4 yrs.	31 games			

Eddie Michaels
MIKOLAJEWSKI, EDWARD J. (Whitey)
B. Jun. 11, 1914, Wilmington, DE
D. Jan. 21, 1976, Wilmington, DE
Villanova 5'11" 205 lbs.

1936	CHIB	N	12	G
1937	WAS	N	11	G
1943	P, P	N	10	G
1944	PHI	N	10	G
1945			9	G
1946			10	G
6 yrs.	62 games			

Lou Michaels
MICHAELS, LOUIS ANDREW
B. Sep. 28, 1936, Swoyersville, PA
Kentucky 6'2" 243 lbs.

1958	LA	N	12	E
1959			12	T
1960			11	E
1961	PIT	N	14	DE
1962			14	DE, K
1963			14	DE
1964	BAL	N	14	DE
1965			14	DE, K
1966			14	DE, K

Lou Michaels continued

1967			14	DE, K
1968			14	DE, K
1969			14	DE, K
1971	GB	N	10	K
13 yrs.	171 games			

Walt Michaels
MICHAELS, WALTER
B. Oct. 16, 1929, Swoyersville, PA
Washington & Lee 6'0" 231 lbs.

1951	GB	N	12	LB
1952	CLE	N	11	LB
1953			12	LB
1954			12	LB
1955			12	LB
1956			12	LB
1957			12	LB
1958			12	LB
1959			12	LB
1960			11	LB
1961				LB
1963	NY	A	1	LB
12 yrs.	119 games			

Art Michalik
MICHALIK, ARTHUR
B. 1930
St. Ambrose 6'2" 229 lbs.

1953	SF	N	12	G
1954			2	G
1955	PIT	N	12	G
1956			12	G
4 yrs.	38 games			

Mike Michalske
MICHALSKE, AUGUST M. (Iron Mike)
B. Apr. 24, 1902, Cleveland, OH
D. Oct. 26, 1983, Green Bay, WI
Penn State 6'0" 210 lbs.

1926	NY	A	12	G, T
1927	NYY	N	13	G, QB, FB
1928			13	G, T
1929	GB	N	13	G
1930			14	G, T, C
1931			12	G
1932			12	G
1933			13	G, T
1934			13	G
1935			10	G
1937			7	G
11 yrs.	132 games			

Mike Michel
MICHEL, MICHAEL WALTER
B. Aug. 4, 1954, Ventura, CA
Stanford 5'10" 177 lbs.

1977	MIA	N	13	P, K
1978	PHI	N	10	P, K
2 yrs.	23 games			

Tom Michel
MICHEL, THOMAS
B. 1941
East Carolina 6'0" 210 lbs.

1964	MIN	N	11	HB

John Michels
MICHELS, JOHN
B. Mar. 19, 1973, La Jolla, CA
Southern California 6'7" 290 lbs.

1996	GB	N	15	OT

John Michels
MICHELS, JOHN JOSEPH
B. Feb. 15, 1931, Philadelphia, PA

John Michels continued
Tennessee 5'11" 200 lbs.

1953	PHI	N	11	G

Bobby Micho
MICHO, ROBERT ANTHONY
B. Mar. 7, 1962, Omaha, NE
Texas 6'3" 240 lbs.

1984	SD	N	6	TE
1986	DEN	N	5	TE
1987			15	TE
3 yrs.	26 games			

Mike Micka
MICKA, MICHAEL
B. Jun. 18, 1921, Clairton, PA
D. Jan. 4, 1988, Gaithersburg, MD
Colgate 6'0" 188 lbs.

1944	WAS	N	10	FB, HB
1945			6	FB
1945	BOS	N	3	FB
1946			11	HB
1947			12	HB
1948			12	HB
5 yrs.	54 games			

Jeff Mickel
MICKEL, ARTHUR JEFFERY
B. Aug. 4, 1966, Limestone, ME
Eastern Washington 6'6" 300 lbs.

1990	LARM	N	1	G

Darren Mickell
MICKELL, DARREN
B. Aug. 3, 1970, Miami, FL
Florida 6'4" 274 lbs.

1992	KC	N	1	DE
1993			16	DE
1994			16	DE, DT
1995			12	DE
1996	NO	N	12	DE
5 yrs.	57 games			

Arnold Mickens
MICKENS, ARNOLD
B. Oct. 12, 1972, Indianapolis, IN
Indiana/Butler 5'11" 217 lbs.

1996	IND	N	3	RB

Ray Mickens
MICKENS, RAY
B. Jan. 4, 1973, Frankfurt, Germany
Texas A&M 5'8" 178 lbs.

1996	NYJ	N	15	CB

Terry Mickens
MICKENS, TERRY KAJUAN
B. Feb. 21, 1971, Tallahassee, FL
Florida A&M 6'0" 203 lbs.

1994	GB	N	12	WR
1995			16	WR
1996			8	WR
3 yrs.	36 games			

Joey Mickey
MICKEY, JOEY
B. Nov. 29, 1970, Oklahoma City, OK
Oklahoma 6'5" 274 lbs.

1993	DAL	N	5	TE

Joe Mickles
MICKLES, JOE
B. Dec. 25, 1965, Birmingham, AL
Mississippi 5'10" 221 lbs.

1989	WAS	N	9	RB

Year	Team		Games	Pos.

Joe Mickles continued

Year	Team		Games	Pos.
1990	SD	N	1	RB
2 yrs.	10 games			

Dave Middendorf

MIDDENDORF, DAVID WARREN
B. Nov. 23, 1945, Seattle, WA
Washington State 6'3" 260 lbs.

1968	CIN	A	14	G
1969			12	G
1970	NYJ	N	8	G
3 yrs.	34 games			

Oren Middlebrook

MIDDLEBROOK, OREN JAMES
B. Jan. 23, 1953, Aberdeen, MS
Arkansas State 6'2" 185 lbs.

| 1978 | PHI | N | 16 | WR |

Dave Middleton

MIDDLETON, DAVID HINTON
B. Nov. 23, 1933, Birmingham, AL
Auburn 6'1" 194 lbs.

1955	DET	N	12	HB
1956			12	E
1957			8	E
1958			12	E
1959			12	E
1960			7	E
1961	MIN	N	12	OE
7 yrs.	75 games			

Frank Middleton

MIDDLETON, FRANKLIN
B. Oct. 28, 1960, Savannah, GA
Florida A&M 5'11" 205 lbs.

1984	IND	N	16	RB
1985			6	RB
1987	SD	N	3	RB
3 yrs.	25 games			

Kelvin Middleton

MIDDLETON, KELVIN BERNARD
B. Sep. 8, 1961, Macon, GA
Wichita State 6'0" 186 lbs.

| 1987 | PIT | N | 2 | S |

Rick Middleton

MIDDLETON, RICHARD RAY
B. Nov. 28, 1951, Columbus, OH
Ohio State 6'2" 229 lbs.

1974	NO	N	14	LB
1975			14	LB
1976	SD	N	10	LB
1977			14	LB
1978			12	LB
5 yrs.	64 games			

Ron Middleton

MIDDLETON, RONALD ALLEN
B. Jul. 17, 1965, Atmore, AL
Auburn 6'2" 262 lbs.

1986	ATL	N	16	TE
1987			12	TE
1988	WAS	N	2	TE
1989	CLE	N	9	TE
1990	WAS	N	16	TE
1991			12	TE
1992			16	TE
1993			16	TE
1994	LARM	N	16	TE
1995	SD	N	3	TE
10 yrs.	118 games			

Terdell Middleton

MIDDLETON, TERDELL
B. Apr. 8, 1955, Memphis, TN
Memphis State 6'0" 195 lbs.

1977	GB	N	14	RB
1978			16	RB
1979			14	RB
1980			13	RB
1981			12	RB
1982	TB	N	2	RB
1983			7	RB
7 yrs.	78 games			

Lou Midler

MIDLER, LOUIS T.
B. Jul. 21, 1915
D. Aug. 29, 1992, Minnesota
Minnesota 6'1" 223 lbs.

1939	PIT	N	11	T, G
1940	GB	N	7	G, T
2 yrs.	18 games			

Saul Mielziner

MIELZINER, SAUL
B. Jun. 1, 1905
D. Oct., 1985, Levittown, PA
Carnegie-Mellon 6'1" 245 lbs.

1929	NYG	N	13	G, T
1930			15	G, C, T, HB
1931	BKN	N	8	C, G
1932			11	C
1933			6	T
1934			5	T, G
6 yrs.	58 games			

Ed Mieszkowski

MIESZKOWSKI, EDWARD T.
B. 1925
Notre Dame 6'2" 220 lbs.

1946	BKN	AA	13	T
1947			10	T
2 yrs.	23 games			

Paul Migliazzo

MIGLIAZZO, PAUL SALVATORE
B. Mar. 11, 1964, Kansas City, MO
Oklahoma 6'1" 228 lbs.

| 1987 | CHI | N | 3 | LB |

Lou Mihajlovich

MIHAJLOVICH, LOUIS
B. Feb. 19, 1925, Detroit, MI
Indiana 5'11" 175 lbs.

| 1948 | LA | AA | 9 | E |

Joe Mihal

MIHAL, JOSEPH
B. Apr. 2, 1916, Homestead, PA
D. Sep., 1979, Dallas, TX
Purdue 6'3" 234 lbs.

1940	CHIB	N	11	T
1941			6	T
1946	LA	AA	12	T
1947	CHI	AA	1	T
4 yrs.	30 games			

Bob Mike

MIKE, ROBERT MELVIN (Big Bob)
B. Oct. 29, 1923
Florida A&M/UCLA 6'1" 220 lbs.

1948	SF	AA	14	T
1949			12	T
2 yrs.	26 games			

Nick Mike-Mayer

MIKE-MAYER, NICHOLAS
B. Mar. 1, 1950, Bologna, Italy
Temple 5'8" 186 lbs.

1973	ATL	N	14	K
1974			14	K
1975			14	K
1976			14	K
1977			7	K
1977	PHI	N	3	K
1978			12	K
1979	BUF	N	16	K
1980			16	K
1981			16	K
1982			2	K
10 yrs.	128 games			

Steve Mike-Mayer

MIKE-MAYER, ISTVAN
B. Sep. 8, 1947, Budapest, Hungary
Maryland 6'0" 180 lbs.

1975	SF	N	14	K
1976			14	K
1977	DET	N	14	K
1978	NO	N	9	K
1979	BAL	N	13	K
1980			16	K
6 yrs.	80 games			

Russ Mikeska

MIKESKA, RUSSELL E.
B. Sep. 10, 1955, Temple, TX
Texas A&M 6'3" 225 lbs.

1979	ATL	N	16	TE
1980			16	TE
1981			16	TE
1982			5	TE
4 yrs.	53 games			

Andy Miketa

MIKETA, ANDREW
B. 1931
North Carolina 6'2" 210 lbs.

1954	DET	N	12	C
1955			12	C
2 yrs.	24 games			

Bill Miklich

MIKLICH, WILLIAM
B. 1921
Idaho 6'0" 208 lbs.

1947	NYG	N	7	G, LB
1948			4	G, LB
1948	DET	N	7	G, LB
2 yrs.	18 games			

Pete Mikolajewski

MIKOLAJEWSKI, PETE
B. 1943
Kent State 6'1" 210 lbs.

| 1969 | SD | A | 1 | QB |

Ron Mikolajczyk

MIKOLAJCZYK, RONALD
B. Mar. 2, 1950, Passaic, NJ
Marshall/Tampa 6'3" 275 lbs.

1976	NYG	N	9	OT
1977			13	OT
1978			8	OT
1979			1	OT
4 yrs.	31 games			

Doug Mikolas

MIKOLAS, DOUG ADOLPH
B. Jun. 7, 1961, Manteca, CA
Oregon Tech/Portland State 6'1" 270 lbs.

| 1987 | SF | N | 8 | NT |

Doug Mikolas continued

1988			1	NT
1988	HOU	N	1	NT
2 yrs.	10 games			

Tom Mikula

MIKULA, THOMAS MICHAEL
B. Sep. 26, 1926, Johnstown, PA
William & Mary 5'10" 200 lbs.

| 1948 | BKN | AA | 1 | B |

Mike Mikulak

MIKULAK, MICHAEL N. (Iron Mike)
B. Dec. 2, 1912, Minneapolis, MN
Oregon 6'1" 210 lbs.

1934	CHIC	N	10	FB, HB
1935			12	FB
1936			12	QB, HB, FB
3 yrs.	34 games			

Barnes Milam

MILAM, BARNES T.
B. Jan. 4, 1906
D. Dec. 18, 1979, Austin, TX
Austin 190 lbs.

| 1934 | PHI | N | 2 | G, T |

Joe Milam

MILAM, JOSEPH
B. Jan. 26, 1899
D. Aug., 1977, Stone Mountain, GA
Phillips 5'11" 180 lbs.

| 1925 | KC | N | 6 | G, E, T |

Don Milano

MILANO, DONALD LEE
B. Jan. 12, 1949, Glendale, CA
California Poly (San Luis Obispo) 6'3" 196 lbs.

| 1975 | GB | N | 14 | QB |

Arch Milano

MILANO, ARCH
B. 1919
St. Francis (Pennsylvania) 6'0" 197 lbs.

| 1945 | DET | N | 1 | E |

Scott Milanovich

MILANOVICH, SCOTT
B. Jan. 29, 1973, Butler, PA
Maryland 6'3" 227 lbs.

| 1996 | TB | N | 1 | QB |

Darryl Milburn

MILBURN, DARRYL WAYNE
B. Oct. 25, 1968, Baton Rouge, LA
Grambling State 6'3" 260 lbs.

| 1991 | DET | N | 2 | DE |

Glyn Milburn

MILBURN, GLYN
B. Feb. 19, 1971, Santa Monica, CA
Oklahoma/Stanford 5'8" 177 lbs.

1993	DEN	N	16	RB
1994			16	RB
1995			16	RB
1996	DET	N	16	RB
4 yrs.	64 games			

Jack Mildren

MILDREN, LARRY JACK, JR.
B. Oct. 10, 1949, Kingsville, TX
Oklahoma 6'1" 200 lbs.

| 1972 | BAL | N | 14 | S |

Year	Team		Games	Pos.

Jack Mildren *continued*

1973			14	S
1974	**NE**	**N**	14	S
3 yrs.	42 games			

Eddie Miles
MILES, EDDIE
B. Sep. 13, 1968, Miami, FL
Minnesota 6'1" 233 lbs.

1990	**PIT**	**N**	1	LB

Leo Miles
MILES, LEO
B. 1931
Virginia State 6'0" 200 lbs.

1953	**NYG**	**N**	3	HB

Mark Miles
MILES, MARK R. (Buck)
B. Apr. 22, 1889
D. Jan., 1964
Washington & Lee 6'2" 195 lbs.

1920	**AKR**	**A**	1	HB

Ostell Miles
MILES, OSTELL SHAWN
B. Aug. 6, 1971, Denver, CO
Houston 6'0" 236 lbs.

1992	**CIN**	**N**	11	RB
1993			15	RB
2 yrs.	26 games			

Joe Milinichick
MILINICHICK, JOSEPH MICHAEL
B. Mar. 30, 1963, Allentown, PA
North Carolina State 6'5" 284 lbs.

1987	**DET**	**N**	11	OL
1988			15	G, OT
1989			15	G, OT
1990	**LARM**	**N**	8	G
1991			5	G
1992			16	G
1993	**SD**	**N**	10	G
1994			16	G
8 yrs.	96 games			

Jack Milks
MILKS, JOHN
B. 1943
San Diego State 6'0" 222 lbs.

1966	**SD**	**A**	3	LB

Bryan Millard
MILLARD, BRYAN
B. Dec. 2, 1960, Sioux City, IA
Texas 6'5" 283 lbs.

1984	**SEA**	**N**	14	OT
1985			16	OT
1986			16	G
1987			12	G
1988			15	G
1989			16	G
1990			16	G
1991			16	G
8 yrs.	121 games			

Keith Millard
MILLARD, KEITH
B. Mar. 18, 1962, Pleasanton, CA
Washington State 6'5" 262 lbs.

1985	**MIN**	**N**	16	DE
1986			15	DE
1987			9	DT
1988			15	DT
1989			15	DT

Keith Millard *continued*

1990			4	DT
1992	**SEA**	**N**	2	DT
1992	**GB**	**N**	2	DE
1993	**PHI**	**N**	14	DT
8 yrs.	92 games			

Hugh Millen
MILLEN, HUGH
B. Nov. 22, 1963, Des Moines, IA
Washington 6'5" 216 lbs.

1987	**LARM**	**N**	1	QB
1988	**ATL**	**N**	3	QB
1989			5	QB
1990			3	QB
1991	**NE**	**N**	13	QB
1992			7	QB
1994	**DEN**	**N**	6	QB
1995			3	QB
8 yrs.	41 games			

Matt Millen
MILLEN, MATT G.
B. Mar. 12, 1958, Hokendauqua, PA
Penn State 6'2" 250 lbs.

1980	**OAK**	**N**	16	LB
1981			16	LB
1982	**LARI**		9	LB
1983			16	LB
1984			16	LB
1985			16	LB
1986			16	LB
1987			12	LB
1988			16	LB
1989	**SF**	**N**	15	LB
1990			16	LB
1991	**WAS**	**N**	16	LB
12 yrs.	180 games			

Al Miller
MILLER, ALFRED HENRY (Truck)
B. Mar. 17, 1904
Harvard 5'11" 210 lbs.

1929	**BOS**	**N**	7	HB, QB, FB

Alan Miller
MILLER, ALAN
B. Jun. 19, 1937, Waltham, MA
Boston College 6'0" 202 lbs.

1960	**BOS**	**A**		FB
1961	**OAK**	**A**	14	FB
1962			14	FB
1963			14	FB
1965			14	FB
5 yrs.	56 games			

Allen Miller
MILLER, ALLEN
B. Apr. 18, 1940, Fostoria, OH
Ohio University 6'0" 224 lbs.

1962	**WAS**	**N**	14	C, LB
1963			11	LB
2 yrs.	25 games			

Anthony Miller
MILLER, LAWRENCE ANTHONY
B. Apr. 15, 1965, Los Angeles, CA
San Diego State/Tennessee 5'11" 185 lbs.

1988	**SD**	**N**	16	WR
1989			16	WR
1990			16	WR
1991			13	WR
1992			16	WR
1993			16	WR
1994	**DEN**	**N**	16	WR
1995			14	WR
1996			16	WR
9 yrs.	139 games			

Bill Miller
MILLER, WILLIAM
B. 1938, West Virginia
New Mexico Highlands 6'4" 270 lbs.

1962	**HOU**	**A**	4	DT

Bill Miller
MILLER, WILLIAM JOSEPH
B. Apr. 17, 1940, McKeesport, PA
Miami (Florida) 6'0" 192 lbs.

1962	**DAL**	**A**	14	OE
1963	**BUF**	**A**	14	OE
1964	**OAK**	**A**	12	OE
1966			5	OE
1967			12	OE
1968			10	OE
6 yrs.	67 games			

Bing Miller
MILLER, JAMES
B. Dec. 6, 1903, Syracuse, NY
D. Oct. 12, 1964
New York University 6'1" 188 lbs.

1929	**SI**		10	T
1930			9	T
1931			9	T, G
3 yrs.	28 games			

Blake Miller
MILLER, BLAKE
B. Aug. 23, 1968, Alexandria, LA
Louisiana State 6'1" 282 lbs.

1992	**DET**	**N**	14	C

Blake Miller
MILLER, W. BLAKE (Dutch)
B. May 3, 1889
D. Jan. 9, 1987, Michigan
Michigan State 5'10" 170 lbs.

1921	**DET**	**A**	3	HB, E

Bob Miller
MILLER, ROBERT M.
B. Dec. 11, 1929, Norwalk, CT
Virginia 6'3" 242 lbs.

1952	**DET**	**N**	11	T
1953			11	T
1954			12	T
1955			12	T
1956			12	T
1957			12	T
1958			10	T
7 yrs.	80 games			

Brett Miller
MILLER, BRETT
B. Oct. 2, 1958, Lynwood, CA
Iowa 6'7" 293 lbs.

1983	**ATL**	**N**	16	OT
1984			15	OT
1985			12	OT
1986			8	OT
1987			2	OT
1988			15	OT
1989	**SD**	**N**	15	OT
1990	**NYJ**	**N**	16	OT
1991			15	OT
9 yrs.	114 games			

Bronzell Miller
MILLER, BRONZELL LAJAMES
B. Oct. 2, 1971, Federal Way, WA
Utah 6'4" 245 lbs.

1995	**JAC**	**N**	3	DE

Calvin Miller
MILLER, CALVIN
B. Aug. 11, 1953, Gulfport, MS
Oklahoma State 6'2" 260 lbs.

1979	**NYG**	**N**	11	DT
1980	**ATL**	**N**	2	DT
2 yrs.	13 games			

Candy Miller
MILLER, RAY F.
B. Feb. 28, 1898
D. Nov. 3, 1986, Central City, KY
Purdue 6'3" 215 lbs.

1922	**CAN**	**N**	3	FB, HB
1922	**RAC**	**N**	8	T, E
1923			6	E, T
2 yrs.	17 games			

Chris Miller
MILLER, CHRISTOPHER JAMES
B. Aug. 9, 1965, Pomona, CA
Oregon 6'2" 200 lbs.

1987	**ATL**	**N**	3	QB
1988			13	QB
1989			15	QB
1990			12	QB
1991			15	QB
1992			8	QB
1993			3	QB
1994	**LARM**	**N**	13	QB
1995	**STL**	**N**	13	QB
9 yrs.	95 games			

Chuckie Miller
MILLER, CHARLES ELLIOT
B. May 9, 1965, Anniston, AL
UCLA 5'10" 180 lbs.

1988	**IND**	**N**	3	CB

Clark Miller
MILLER, FRANK CLARK
B. Aug. 11, 1938, Oakland, CA
Utah State 6'5" 246 lbs.

1962	**SF**	**N**	10	DE
1963			14	DE
1964			14	DE
1965			14	DE
1966			14	DE
1967			13	DE
1968			10	DE
1969	**WAS**	**N**	2	DE
1970	**LA**	**N**	6	DL
9 yrs.	97 games			

Clay Miller
MILLER, CLAY
B. Aug. 27, 1963, Columbus, OH
Michigan 6'4" 275 lbs.

1987	**HOU**	**N**	3	OT

Cleo Miller
MILLER, CLEOPHUS, JR.
B. Sep. 5, 1951, Gould, AR
Arkansas-Pine Bluff 5'11" 207 lbs.

1974	**KC**	**N**	14	RB
1975			6	RB
1975	**CLE**	**N**	5	RB
1976			12	RB
1977			14	RB
1978			15	FB
1979			16	FB
1980			16	FB
1981			12	FB
1982			5	RB
9 yrs.	115 games			

Year	Team	Games	Pos.

Corey Miller
MILLER, COREY
B. Oct. 25, 1968, Pageland, SC
South Carolina 6'2" 255 lbs.

Year	Team		Games	Pos.
1991	**NYG**	**N**	16	LB
1992			16	LB
1993			16	LB
1994			15	LB
1995			14	LB
1996			14	LB
6 yrs.		91 games		

Dan Miller
MILLER, DANIEL SCOTT
B. Dec. 30, 1960, West Palm Beach, FL
Miami (Florida) 5'10" 172 lbs.

Year	Team		Games	Pos.
1982	**WAS**	**N**	1	K
1982	**NE**	**N**	2	K
1982	**BAL**	**N**	3	K

Darrin Miller
MILLER, DARRIN JAMES
B. Mar. 24, 1965, Flemington, NJ
Tennessee 6'1" 227 lbs.

Year	Team		Games	Pos.
1988	**SEA**	**N**	16	LB
1989			16	LB
2 yrs.		32 games		

Don Miller
MILLER, DONALD C.
B. Mar. 2, 1902, Defiance, OH
D. Jul. 28, 1979, Cleveland, OH
Notre Dame 5'11" 170 lbs.

Year	Team		Games	Pos.
1925	**PRO**	**N**	1	HB

Don Miller
MILLER, JACK DONALD
B. May 24, 1932, Houston, TX
Southern Methodist 6'2" 195 lbs.

Year	Team		Games	Pos.
1954	**PHI**	**N**	2	HB

Donald Miller
MILLER, DONALD
B. Apr. 6, 1964, Chicago, IL
Utah State/Idaho State 6'2" 223 lbs.

Year	Team		Games	Pos.
1990	**SEA**	**N**	7	LB

Doug Miller
MILLER, DOUG ALAN
B. Oct. 29, 1969, Cheyenne, WY
South Dakota State 6'3" 232 lbs.

Year	Team		Games	Pos.
1993	**SD**	**N**	8	LB
1994			15	LB
2 yrs.		23 games		

Dub Miller
MILLER, W. MILFORD
B. Sep. 28, 1911, Litchfield, NE
D. Apr., 1981, Chadron, NE
Chadron State 6'0" 218 lbs.

Year	Team		Games	Pos.
1935	**CHIB**	**N**	10	T, G
1936	**CHIC**	**N**	3	T
1937			8	T
3 yrs.		21 games		

Dutch Miller
MILLER, J. ROBERT
B. Feb. 23, 1906
D. Jul. 6, 1987
Wittenberg 5'11" 212 lbs.

Year	Team		Games	Pos.
1931	**POR**	**N**	1	C

Eddie Miller
MILLER, EDDIE
B. Jun. 20, 1969, Tumison, GA

Eddie Miller *continued*
South Carolina 6'0" 185 lbs.

Year	Team		Games	Pos.
1992	**IND**	**N**	14	WR
1993			1	WR
2 yrs.		15 games		

Eddie Miller
MILLER, EDWARD
B. 1917
New Mexico State 5'10" 165 lbs.

Year	Team		Games	Pos.
1939	**NYG**	**N**	8	B
1940			8	B
2 yrs.		16 games		

Fred Miller
MILLER, FRED
B. Feb. 6, 1973, Aldine, TX
Baylor 6'7" 305 lbs.

Year	Team		Games	Pos.
1996	**STL**	**N**	14	OT

Fred Miller
MILLER, FRED DAVID
B. Aug. 8, 1940, Homer, LA
Louisiana State 6'3" 248 lbs.

Year	Team		Games	Pos.
1963	**BAL**	**N**	13	DT
1964			14	DT
1965			12	DT
1966			14	DT
1967			14	DT
1968			14	DT
1969			14	DT
1970			12	DT
1971			14	DT
1972			12	DT
10 yrs.		133 games		

Fred Miller
MILLER, FREDERICK
B. 1931
Pacific 6'3" 225 lbs.

Year	Team		Games	Pos.
1955	**WAS**	**N**	12	T

Hal Miller
MILLER, HAROLD
B. 1930
Georgia Tech 6'4" 230 lbs.

Year	Team		Games	Pos.
1953	**SF**	**N**	12	T

Heinie Miller
MILLER, HENRY J.
B. 1894
D. Jun. 25, 1958
Pennsylvania 5'10" 185 lbs.

Year	Team		Games	Pos.
1920	**BUF**	**A**	6	E
1921			7	E
1925	**MIL**	**N**	1	G
3 yrs.		14 games		

Jamir Miller
MILLER, JAMIR MALIK
B. Nov. 19, 1973, Philadelphia, PA
UCLA 6'4" 242 lbs.

Year	Team		Games	Pos.
1994	**ARI**	**N**	16	LB
1995			11	LB
1996			16	LB
3 yrs.		43 games		

Jim Miller
MILLER, JAMES
B. 1907
West Virginia Wesleyan 195 lbs.

Year	Team		Games	Pos.
1930	**BKN**	**N**	3	QB, HB, FB

Jim Miller
MILLER, JAMES G.

Jim Miller *continued*
B. Jul. 5, 1957, Ripley, MS
Mississippi 5'11" 184 lbs.

Year	Team		Games	Pos.
1980	**SF**	**N**	16	P
1981			16	P
1982			9	P
1983	**DAL**	**N**	2	P
1984			1	P
1987	**NYG**	**N**	1	P
6 yrs.		45 games		

Jim Miller
MILLER, JAMES ROBERT
B. Jul. 24, 1949, Iowa City, IA
Iowa 6'3" 240 lbs.

Year	Team		Games	Pos.
1971	**ATL**	**N**	14	G
1972			2	G
1974			14	G
3 yrs.		30 games		

Jim Miller
MILLER, JIM
B. Feb. 9, 1971, Grosse Pointe, MI
Michigan State 6'2" 226 lbs.

Year	Team		Games	Pos.
1994	**PIT**	**N**	1	QB
1995			4	QB
1996			2	QB
3 yrs.		7 games		

John Miller
MILLER, JOHN FRANK
B. Sep. 22, 1960, Oberlin, OH
Mississippi State 6'2" 218 lbs.

Year	Team		Games	Pos.
1987	**GB**	**N**	1	LB

John Miller
MILLER, JOHN M.
B. Mar. 31, 1893
D. Mar., 1968, Bryan, OH
Notre Dame 6'0" 180 lbs.

Year	Team		Games	Pos.
1921	**DAY**	**A**	1	FB

John Miller
MILLER, JOHN THOMAS
B. Jul. 22, 1966, Detroit, MI
Michigan State 6'1" 195 lbs.

Year	Team		Games	Pos.
1989	**DET**	**N**	9	S
1990			4	S
2 yrs.		13 games		

Johnny Miller
MILLER, JOHN
B. Feb. 1, 1934, Lowell, MA
Boston College 6'5" 253 lbs.

Year	Team		Games	Pos.
1956	**WAS**	**N**	12	T
1958			12	T
1959			12	T
1960	**GB**	**N**	5	T
4 yrs.		41 games		

Johnny Miller
MILLER, JOHNNY
B. Feb. 3, 1954, Ellerbee, NC
Livingstone 6'1" 247 lbs.

Year	Team		Games	Pos.
1977	**SF**	**N**	6	G

Josh Miller
MILLER, JOSH
B. Jul. 14, 1970, East Brunswick, NJ
Arizona 6'3" 215 lbs.

Year	Team		Games	Pos.
1996	**PIT**	**N**	12	P

Junior Miller
MILLER, JUNIOR
B. Nov. 26, 1957, Midland, TX

Junior Miller *continued*
Nebraska 6'4" 239 lbs.

Year	Team		Games	Pos.
1980	**ATL**	**N**	16	TE
1981			16	TE
1982			9	TE
1983			15	TE
1984	**NO**	**N**	15	TE
5 yrs.		71 games		

Kevin Miller
MILLER, KEVIN VON
B. Mar. 21, 1955, Wheeling, WV
Louisville 5'10" 181 lbs.

Year	Team		Games	Pos.
1978	**MIN**	**N**	16	WR
1979			3	WR
1980			4	WR
3 yrs.		23 games		

Larry Miller
MILLER, LARRY
B. Feb. 8, 1962, Chicago, IL
Northern Iowa 6'4" 220 lbs.

Year	Team		Games	Pos.
1987	**MIN**	**N**	2	LB

Les Miller
MILLER, LES P.
B. Mar. 1, 1965, Arkansas City, KS
Kansas State/Fort Hays State 6'7" 290 lbs.

Year	Team		Games	Pos.
1987	**SD**	**N**	9	DE
1988			13	DE
1989			14	DE
1990			14	DT
1991	**NO**	**N**	16	NT
1992			16	DE
1993			13	DE
1994			8	DE
1994	**SD**	**N**	4	DT
1996	**CAR**	**N**	15	DE
9 yrs.		122 games		

Mark Miller
MILLER, MARK
B. Nov. 6, 1962, Grand Junction, CO
Mesa (Colorado) 6'2" 210 lbs.

Year	Team		Games	Pos.
1987	**BUF**	**N**	1	QB

Mark Miller
MILLER, MARK GEORGE
B. Aug. 13, 1956, Canton, OH
Bowling Green 6'2" 176 lbs.

Year	Team		Games	Pos.
1978	**CLE**	**N**	8	QB
1979			2	QB
2 yrs.		10 games		

Matt Miller
MILLER, MATT
B. Jul. 6, 1956, Durango, CO
None 6'6" 270 lbs.

Year	Team		Games	Pos.
1979	**CLE**	**N**	16	OT
1981			16	OT, G
1982			9	OT
3 yrs.		41 Games		

Mike Miller
MILLER, MICHAEL
B. Dec. 29, 1959, Flint, MI
Tennessee 5'11" 182 lbs.

Year	Team		Games	Pos.
1983	**NYG**	**N**	13	WR
1985	**NO**	**N**	3	WR
2 yrs.		16 games		

Nick Miller
MILLER, NICHOLAS GALEN
B. Oct. 26, 1963, Brunswick, ME
Arkansas 6'2" 238 lbs.

Year	Team		Games	Pos.
1987	**CLE**	**N**	9	LB

Year	Team	Games	Pos.

Ookie Miller

MILLER, CHARLES LEWIS
B. Nov. 11, 1909, Marion, IN
Purdue 6'0" 209 lbs.

Year	Team		Games	Pos.
1932	CHIB	N	12	C
1933			13	C
1934			11	C
1935			11	C
1936			11	C
1937	CLE	N	11	G, C
1938	GB	N	11	C
2 yrs.			80 games	

Pat Miller

MILLER, LEON PATRICK
B. Jun. 24, 1964, Panama, FL
Florida 6'1" 220 lbs.

Year	Team		Games	Pos.
1987	SD	N	1	DB
1988			8	DB
2 yrs.			9 games	

Paul Miller

MILLER, PAUL
B. Nov. 8, 1930
Louisiana State 6'2" 226 lbs.

Year	Team		Games	Pos.
1954	LA	N	12	C, DE
1955			12	DE
1956			12	DE
1957			12	DE
1960	DAL	A		DE
1961			14	DE
1962	SD	A	2	DE
7 yrs.			64 games	

Paul Miller

MILLER, PAUL W.
B. Oct. 30, 1913
D. Jan. 19, 1989, Buffalo Gap, SD
South Dakota State 5'11" 180 lbs.

Year	Team		Games	Pos.
1936	GB	N	12	HB, QB
1937			10	HB, E
1938			10	HB
3 yrs.			32 games	

Primo Miller

MILLER, RALPH
B. Apr. 9, 1916
D. Oct., 1979, Krum, TX
Rice 6'2" 220 lbs.

Year	Team		Games	Pos.
1937	CLE	N	11	T
1938			7	T
2 yrs.			18 games	

Ralph Miller

MILLER, RALPH
B. Aug. 13, 1948, Hartford, AL
Alabama State/California Lutheran 6'3" 260 lbs.

Year	Team		Games	Pos.
1972	HOU	N	6	G
1973			1	G
2 yrs.			7 games	

Robert Miller

MILLER, ROBERT LAVERNE
B. Jan. 9, 1953, Houston, TX
Kansas 5'11" 204 lbs.

Year	Team		Games	Pos.
1975	MIN	N	14	RB
1976			14	RB
1977			14	RB
1978			15	RB
1979			16	RB
1980			16	RB
6 yrs.			89 games	

Ron Miller

MILLER, RONALD RUDOLPH
B. Aug. 19, 1939, Lyons, IL

Ron Miller *continued*

Wisconsin 6'0" 190 lbs.

Year	Team		Games	Pos.
1962	LA	N	6	QB

Ron Miller

MILLER, RONALD W.
B. Apr. 17, 1933
Southern California 6'4" 200 lbs.

Year	Team		Games	Pos.
1956	LA	N	7	E

Scott Miller

MILLER, SCOTT PATRICK
B. Oct. 20, 1968, Phoenix, AZ
UCLA 5'10" 179 lbs.

Year	Team		Games	Pos.
1991	MIA	N	16	WR
1992			15	WR
1993			3	WR
1994			9	WR
1996			12	WR
5 yrs.			55 games	

Shawn Miller

MILLER, SHAWN
B. Mar. 14, 1961, Gden, UT
Utah State 6'4" 255 lbs.

Year	Team		Games	Pos.
1984	LARM	N	8	NT
1985			16	NT
1986			16	NT
1987			6	NT
1988			16	NT
1989			16	DT
6 yrs.			78 games	

Solomon Miller

MILLER, SOLOMON
B. Dec. 6, 1964, Los Angeles, CA
Utah State 6'1" 185 lbs.

Year	Team		Games	Pos.
1986	NYG	N	16	WR
1987	TB	N	8	WR
2 yrs.			24 games	

Terry Miller

MILLER, ROBERT TERRY
B. Apr. 11, 1946, Mattoon, IL
Illinois 6'2" 224 lbs.

Year	Team		Games	Pos.
1970	DET	N	1	LB
1971	STL	N	9	LB
1972			12	LB
1973			14	LB
1974			5	LB
5 yrs.			41 games	

Terry Miller

MILLER, TERRY
B. Jan. 7, 1956, Columbus, GA
Oklahoma State 5'10" 196 lbs.

Year	Team		Games	Pos.
1978	BUF	N	16	RB
1979			16	RB
1980			16	RB
1981	SEA	N	1	RB
4 yrs.			49 games	

Tom Miller

MILLER, THOMAS M.
B. May 22, 1918, Milton, PA
Hampden-Sydney 6'2" 202 lbs.

Year	Team		Games	Pos.
1943	P-P	N	10	E
1944	PHI	N	9	E
1945	WAS	N	9	E
1946	GB	N	2	E
4 yrs.			30 games	

Verne Miller

MILLER, VERNE
B. May 11, 1908
D. Oct., 1982, Milltown, WI

Verne Miller *continued*

St. Mary's (Minnesota) 5'8" 152 lbs.

Year	Team		Games	Pos.
1930	MIN	N	5	HB

Willie Miller

MILLER, WILLIE T.
B. Apr. 26, 1947, Birmingham, AL
Colorado State 5'9" 172 lbs.

Year	Team		Games	Pos.
1975	CLE	N	14	WR
1976			6	WR
1978	LA	N	16	WR
1979			3	WR
1980			16	WR
1981			13	WR
1982	LARM	N	9	WR
7 yrs.			77 games	

Al Milling

MILLING, ALBERT
B. 1920
Richmond 5'9" 170 lbs.

Year	Team		Games	Pos.
1942	PHI	N	1	G

James Milling

MILLING, JAMES THOMAS, JR.
B. Feb. 14, 1965, Winnsboro, NC
Maryland 5'9" 156 lbs.

Year	Team		Games	Pos.
1988	ATL	N	6	WR
1990			7	WR
1992			5	WR
3 yrs.			18 games	

Ted Million

MILLION, TED
B. 1963
Duke 6'4" 260 lbs.

Year	Team		Games	Pos.
1987	MIN	N	1	G

Bob Millman

MILLMAN, ROBERT
B. May 17, 1903
D. Mar., 1963
Lafayette 5'11" 178 lbs.

Year	Team		Games	Pos.
1925	POT	N	2	HB
1926			6	HB
1927			3	HB
3 yrs.			11 games	

Wayne Millner

MILLNER, WAYNE VERNAL
B. Jan. 31, 1913, Roxbury, MA
D. Nov. 19, 1976, Falls Church, VA
Notre Dame 6'1" 189 lbs.

Year	Team		Games	Pos.
1936	BOS	N	12	E
1937	WAS	N	11	E
1938			11	E
1939			11	E
1940			10	E
1941			11	E
1945			10	E
7 yrs.			76 games	

Lawyer Milloy

MILLOY, LAWYER
B. Nov. 11, 1973, St. Louis, MO
Washington 6'0" 208 lbs.

Year	Team		Games	Pos.
1996	NE	N	16	S

Dick Mills

MILLS, RICHARD
B. Mar. 6, 1939
Pittsburgh 6'3" 240 lbs.

Year	Team		Games	Pos.
1961	DET	N	14	OT
1962			8	G
2 yrs.			22 games	

Ernie Mills

MILLS, ERNEST LEE
B. Oct. 28, 1968, Dunnellon, FL
Florida 5'11" 178 lbs.

Year	Team		Games	Pos.
1991	PIT	N	16	WR
1992			16	WR
1993			14	WR
1994			15	WR
1995			16	WR
1996			9	WR
6 yrs.			86 games	

Jeff Mills

MILLS, JEFF JONATHAN
B. Oct. 8, 1968, Montclair, NJ
Nebraska 6'3" 244 lbs.

Year	Team		Games	Pos.
1990	SD	N	5	LB
1990	DEN	N	2	LB
1991			12	LB
1992			14	LB
1993			13	LB
4 yrs.			46 games	

Jim Mills

MILLS, JAMES
B. Sep. 23, 1961, Vancouver, B.C.
Hawaii 6'9" 281 lbs.

Year	Team		Games	Pos.
1983	BAL	N	7	OT
1984	IND	N	14	OT
2 yrs.			21 games	

Jim Mills

MILLS, JIM
B. Mar. 30, 1973, Marysville, WA
Idaho 6'4" 290 lbs.

Year	Team		Games	Pos.
1996	SD	N	1	OT

Joe Mills

MILLS, JOSEPH
B. Sep. 3, 1897
D. May, 1967, Sebring, OH
Carnegie-Mellon 6'3" 212 lbs.

Year	Team		Games	Pos.
1922	AKR	N	7	HB
1923			6	C, T
1925			5	C, G
1926			5	C, G, QB
4 yrs.			23 games	

John Henry Mills

MILLS, JOHN HENRY
B. Oct. 31, 1969, Jacksonville, FL
Wake Forest 6'0" 222 lbs.

Year	Team		Games	Pos.
1993	HOU	N	16	LB
1994			16	LB
1995			16	LB
1996			16	LB
4 yrs.			64 games	

Lamar Mills

MILLS, LAMAR
B. Jan. 26, 1971, Detroit, MI
Indiana 6'5" 270 lbs.

Year	Team		Games	Pos.
1994	WAS	N	13	DE, DT

Sam Mills

MILLS, SAMUEL DAVIS, JR.
B. Jun. 3, 1959, Neptune, NJ
Montclair State 5'9" 225 lbs.

Year	Team		Games	Pos.
1986	NO	N	16	LB
1987			12	LB
1988			16	LB
1989			16	LB
1990			16	LB
1991			16	LB
1992			16	LB
1993			9	LB
1994			16	LB

Year	Team	Games	Pos.

Sam Mills *continued*

Year	Team		Games	Pos.
1995	CAR	N	16	LB
1996			16	LB
11 yrs.	165 games			

Stan Mills
MILLS, STANLEY A. (Tommy)
B. Dec. 3, 1893
D. Jun., 1973, Andalusia, PA
Penn State 5'9" 180 lbs.

1922	GB	N	8	FB, HB
1923			9	HB, FB
1924	AKR	N	6	E
3 yrs.	23 games			

Sullivan Mills
MILLS, SULLIVAN (Pete)
B. 1943
Wichita State 5'11" 180 lbs.

1965	BUF	A	2	OE
1966			1	OE
2 yrs.	3 games			

Brian Milne
MILNE, BRIAN FITZSIMONS
B. Jan. 7, 1973, Waterford, PA
Penn State 6'3" 254 lbs.

| 1996 | CIN | N | 6 | RB |

Billy Milner
MILNER, BILLY
B. Jun. 21, 1972, Atlanta, GA
Houston 6'5" 293 lbs.

1995	MIA	N	16	OT
1996			4	OT
1996	STL	N	9	OT
2 yrs.	29 games			

Charles Milner
MILNER, CHARLES EDGAR (Bill)
B. Mar. 7, 1919, Waynesville, NC
South Carolina/Duke 6'1" 217 lbs.

1947	CHIB	N	12	G
1948			12	G
1949			12	E
1950	NYG	N	12	G
4 yrs.	48 games			

Ray Milo
MILO, RAYMOND
B. Feb. 19, 1954, Conroe, TX
New Mexico State 5'11" 178 lbs.

| 1978 | KC | N | 2 | S |

Rich Milot
MILOT, RICHARD
B. May 28, 1957, Coraopolis, PA
Penn State 6'4" 236 lbs.

1979	WAS	N	14	LB
1980			16	LB
1981			11	LB
1982			9	LB
1983			16	LB
1984			14	LB
1985			16	LB
1986			16	LB
1987			9	LB
9 yrs.	121 games			

Century Milstead
MILSTEAD, CENTURY ALLEN (Wally)
B. Jan. 1, 1900, Rock Island, IL
D. Jun. 6, 1963, Pleasantville, NY
Wabash/Yale 6'1" 213 lbs.

| 1925 | NYG | N | 12 | T |

Century Milstead *continued*

1926	PHI	A	9	T
1927	NYG	N	7	T
1928			11	T
4 yrs.	39 games			

Charley Milstead
MILSTEAD, CHARLES F.
B. 1938
Texas A&M 6'2" 190 lbs.

1960	HOU	A		QB
1961			8	DB
2 yrs.	8 games			

Rod Milstead
MILSTEAD, RODERICK LEON, JR.
B. Nov. 10, 1969, Washington, DC
Delaware State 6'2" 293 lbs.

1994	SF	N	6	G
1995			16	G
1996			11	G
3 yrs.	33 games			

Eldridge Milton
MILTON, ELDRIDGE
B. Feb. 1, 1962
Clemson 6'1" 235 lbs.

| 1987 | CHI | N | 3 | LB |

Eugene Milton
MILTON, EUGENE
B. Sep. 28, 1944, Ocala, FL
Florida A&M 5'10" 170 lbs.

1968	MIA	A	13	WR
1969			14	WR
2 yrs.	27 games			

Jack Milton
MILTON, JACK
None 168 lbs.

| 1923 | RAC | N | 2 | HB, G |

Johnny Milton
MILTON, JOHN (Jack)
B. 1899
Deceased
Southern California 175 lbs.

1923	STL	N	5	E
1924	KC	N	8	E, HB, QB
2 yrs.	13 games			

Chris Mims
MIMS, CHRISTOPHER EDDIE
B. Sep. 29, 1970, Los Angeles, CA
Tennessee 6'5" 280 lbs.

1992	SD	N	16	DE
1993			16	DE
1994			16	DE
1995			15	DE
1996			15	DE
5 yrs.	78 games			

David Mims
MIMS, DAVID JAMES
B. Jul. 7, 1970, Daingerfield, TX
Baylor 5'8" 191 lbs.

1993	ATL	N	15	WR
1994			3	WR
2 yrs.	18 games			

Hank Minarik
MINARIK, HENRY J.
B. Sep. 1, 1927
Michigan State 6'2" 200 lbs.

| 1951 | PIT | N | 11 | E |

Charles Mincy
MINCY, CHARLES ANTHONY
B. Dec. 16, 1969, Los Angeles, CA
Washington 5'11" 197 lbs.

1992	KC	N	16	S
1993			16	S
1994			16	S
1995	MIN	N	16	S
1996	TB	N	2	S
5 yrs.	66 games			

Tom Miner
MINER, THOMAS E.
B. 1932
D. Jan. 1, 1988, Tucson, AZ
Tulsa 6'4" 235 lbs.

| 1958 | PIT | N | 12 | E |

Gene Mingo
MINGO, EUGENE
B. Sep. 22, 1938, Akron, OH
none 6'1" 199 lbs.

1960	DEN	A	14	HB, P
1961			10	HB, P
1962			14	HB, P
1963			14	HB, P
1964			7	HB, K
1964	OAK	A	7	HB
1965			14	HB, K
1966	MIA	A	14	HB, K
1967			6	K
1967	WAS	N	6	K
1969	PIT	N	14	K
1970			10	K
10 yrs.	130 games			

Paul Minick
MINICK, PAUL D.
B. Dec., 1899
D. Feb. 3, 1976
Iowa 6'0" 197 lbs.

1926	NY	A	12	G
1927	BUF	N	5	G
1928	GB	N	11	G, E
1929			6	
4 yrs.	34 games			

Kevin Miniefield
MINIEFIELD, KEVIN LAMAR
B. Mar. 2, 1970, Phoenix, AZ
Arizona State 5'9" 178 lbs.

1993	CHI	N	8	CB
1994			12	S
1995			15	CB
3 yrs.	35 games			

Frank Minini
MININI, FRANK
B. Jan. 10, 1927, Paso Robles, CA
San Jose State 6'1" 209 lbs.

1947	CHIB	N	12	HB
1948			12	HB
1949	PIT	N	12	HB
3 yrs.	36 games			

Tony Minisi
MINISI, ANTHONY S. (Skippy)
B. 1927
Deceased
Pennsylvania/Navy/Pennsylvania 5'11" 190 lbs.

| 1948 | NYG | N | 12 | HB |

Randy Minniear
MINNIEAR, RANDOLPH
B. Dec. 27, 1943, Indianapolis, IN
Purdue 6'0" 205 lbs.

| 1967 | NYG | N | 6 | RB |

Randy Minniear *continued*

1968			2	RB
1969			11	RB
1970	CLE	N	8	RB
4 yrs.	27 games			

Frank Minnifield
MINNIFIELD, FRANK LYDALE
B. Jan. 1, 1960, Lexington, KY
Louisville 5'9" 182 lbs.

1984	CLE	N	15	CB
1985			16	CB
1986			15	CB
1987			12	CB
1988			15	CB
1989			16	CB
1990			9	CB
1991			14	CB
1992			10	CB
1996	CHI	N	13	CB
10 yrs.	135 games			

Claudie Minor
MINOR, CLAUDIE DEE, JR.
B. Apr. 21, 1951, Pomona, CA
San Diego State 6'4" 279 lbs.

1974	DEN	N	14	OT
1975			14	OT
1976			14	OT
1977			14	OT
1978			16	OT
1979			16	OT
1980			15	OT
1981			13	OT
1982			9	OT
9 yrs.	125 games			

Lincoln Minor
MINOR, LINCOLN
B. Jan. 22, 1950, New Orleans, LA
New Mexico State 6'2" 210 lbs.

| 1973 | NO | N | 9 | RB |

Vic Minor
MINOR, VICTOR WAYNE
B. Nov. 28, 1958, Shreveport, LA
Northeast Louisiana 6'0" 198 lbs.

1980	SEA	N	16	S
1981			4	S
2 yrs.	20 games			

Barry Minter
MINTER, BARRY ANTOINE
B. Jan. 28, 1970, Mount Pleasant, TX
Tulsa 6'2" 242 lbs.

1993	CHI	N	2	LB
1994			13	LB
1995			16	LB
1996			16	LB
4 yrs.	47 games			

Cedric Minter
MINTER, CEDRIC ALWYN
B. Nov. 13, 1958, Charleston, SC
Boise State 5'10" 200 lbs.

1984	NYJ	N	8	RB
1985			3	RB
2 yrs.	11 games			

Mike Minter
MINTER, MICHAEL JEROME
B. Aug. 13, 1965, Mount Pleasant, TX
North Texas State 6'3" 275 lbs.

| 1987 | PIT | N | 3 | NT |

Year	Team		Games	Pos.

Tommy Minter
MINTER, TOMMY E.
B. 1940
Baylor 5'10" 178 lbs.

1962	DEN	A	7	DB
1962	BUF	A	5	DB

1 yr.   12 games

Jack Mintun
MINTUN, JOHN F.
B. Jul. 12, 1894
D. Feb. 25, 1976, Decatur, IL
None 5'9" 191 lbs.

1920	DEC	A	1	C
1921			3	C
1922	RAC	N	7	C
1923			10	C
1924			10	C
1925	KC	N	8	C
1926	RAC	N	2	C

7 yrs.   41 games

Ed Mioduszewski
MIODUSZEWSKI, EDWARD
B. 1930
William & Mary 5'10" 185 lbs.

1953	BAL	N	12	HB

Frank Miotke
MIOTKE, FRANK
B. Dec. 22, 1965, Dearborn, MI
Grand Valley State 6'0" 175 lbs.

1991	HOU	N	8	WR

George Mira
MIRA, GEORGE, SR.
B. Jan. 11, 1942, Key West, FL
Miami (Florida) 5'11" 190 lbs.

1964	SF	N	7	QB
1965			10	QB
1966			14	QB
1967			3	QB
1968			13	QB
1969	PHI	N	7	QB
1971	MIA	N	6	QB

7 yrs.   60 games

Dean Miraldi
MIRALDI, DEAN MARTIN
B. Apr. 8, 1958, Culver City, CA
Utah 6'5" 270 lbs.

1982	PHI	N	1	G
1983			13	G
1984			16	OT, G
1985	DEN	N	10	OT
1987	LARI	N	10	G

5 yrs.   50 games

Rick Mirer
MIRER, RICK
B. Mar. 3, 1970, Goshen, IN
Notre Dame 6'2" 216 lbs.

1993	SEA	N	16	QB
1994			13	QB
1995			15	QB
1996			11	QB

4 yrs.   55 games

Rex Mirich
MIRICH, REX
B. Mar. 11, 1942, Florence, AZ
Arizona State 6'4" 251 lbs.

1964	OAK	A	14	DT
1965			14	DT
1966			14	DT
1967	DEN	A	13	DE
1968			14	DE

Rex Mirich *continued*

1969			7	DT
1970	BOS	N	7	DT

7 yrs.   83 games

Bob Mischak
MISCHAK, ROBERT MICHAEL
B. Oct. 25, 1932, Newark, NJ
Army 6'0" 237 lbs.

1958	NYG	N	12	G
1960	NY	A		G
1961			14	G
1962			14	G
1963	OAK	A	14	OE, G
1964			13	OE, G
1965			8	G

7 yrs.   75 games

Dave Mishel
MISHEL, DAVID F.
B. Jul. 6, 1905, Lynn, MA
D. Mar. 12, 1974, Newton, MA
Brown 5'9" 179 lbs.

1927	PRO	N	4	HB, QB
1931	CLE	N	5	QB, HB

2 yrs.   9 games

John Misko
MISKO, JOHN C.
B. Oct. 1, 1954, Highland Park, MI
Oregon State 6'5" 207 lbs.

1982	LARM	N	9	P
1983			16	P
1984			16	P
1987	DET	N	1	P

4 yrs.   42 games

John Mistler
MISTLER, JOHN ANDREW
B. Oct. 28, 1958, Columbia, MO
Arizona State 6'2" 186 lbs.

1981	NYG	N	16	WR
1982			9	WR
1983			16	WR
1984			3	WR
1984	BUF	N	1	WR

4 yrs.   45 games

Gene Mitcham
MITCHAM, EUGENE
B. May 18, 1932
Arizona State 6'2" 206 lbs.

1958	PHI	N	2	E

Aaron Mitchell
MITCHELL, AARON TEMPLETON, JR.
B. Dec. 15, 1956, Los Angeles, CA
Morris Brown/Nevada-Las Vegas 6'1" 196 lbs.

1979	DAL	N	16	CB
1980			15	CB
1981	TB	N	14	S

3 yrs.   45 games

Al Mitchell
MITCHELL, ALBERT (Tally)
B. Aug. 30, 1897
D. May, 1967, Livonia, NY
Thiel 6'1" 180 lbs.

1924	BUF	N	6	T, C, E, G

Alvin Mitchell
MITCHELL, ALVIN EUGENE
B. Oct. 18, 1943, Philadelphia, PA
Morgan State 6'3" 195 lbs.

1968	CLE	N	12	DB

Alvin Mitchell *continued*

1969			14	CB
1970	DEN	N	2	WR, DB

3 yrs.   28 games

Alvin Mitchell
MITCHELL, ALVIN JEROME
B. Aug. 20, 1964, Venice, FL
Auburn 6'0" 235 lbs.

1989	TB	N	5	RB

Bob Mitchell
MITCHELL, ROBERT S.
B. Jan. 27, 1921, Turlock, CA
Stanford 5'11" 195 lbs.

1946	LA	AA	11	B
1947			12	B
1948			13	B

3 yrs.   36 games

Bobby Mitchell
MITCHELL, ROBERT CORNELIUS
B. Jun. 6, 1935, Hot Springs, AR
Illinois 6'0" 192 lbs.

1958	CLE	N	12	HB
1959			12	HB
1960			12	HB
1961			14	HB
1962	WAS	N	14	HB
1963			14	HB
1964			14	FL
1965			14	FL
1966			14	FL
1967			14	FL
1968			14	FL

11 yrs.   148 games

Brian Mitchell
MITCHELL, BRIAN KEITH
B. Aug. 18, 1968, Fort Polk, LA
Southwestern Louisiana 5'10" 199 lbs.

1990	WAS	N	15	RB
1991			16	RB
1992			16	RB
1993			16	RB
1994			16	RB
1995			16	RB
1996			16	RB

7 yrs.   111 games

Brian Mitchell
MITCHELL, BRIAN KEITH
B. Dec. 13, 1968, Indianapolis, IN
Brigham Young 5'9" 164 lbs.

1991	ATL	N	15	CB, S
1992			16	CB
1993			5	CB

3 yrs.   36 games

Charlie Mitchell
MITCHELL, CHARLES E., JR.
B. Dec. 28, 1920, Oilton, OK
Southeast Missouri State/Tulsa 6'0" 188 lbs.

1945	CHIB	N	8	HB
1946	GB	N	2	HB

2 yrs.   10 games

Charlie Mitchell
MITCHELL, CHARLES HOWARD
B. May 25, 1940, McNary, AZ
Washington 5'11" 185 lbs.

1963	DEN	A	14	HB
1964			14	HB
1965			1	HB
1966			13	HB

Charlie Mitchell *continued*

1967			14	RB
1968	BUF	A	3	RB

6 yrs.   59 games

Dale Mitchell
MITCHELL, DALE
B. Sep. 1, 1953, Oceanside, CA
Southern California 6'3" 224 lbs.

1976	SF	N	13	LB

Derrell Mitchell
MITCHELL, DERRELL LAVOICE
B. Sep. 16, 1971, Miami, FL
Texas Tech 5'9" 190 lbs.

1994	NO	N	14	WR

Devon Mitchell
MITCHELL, DEVON D.
B. Dec. 30, 1962, Kingston, Jamaica
Iowa 6'1" 194 lbs.

1986	DET	N	16	S
1988			10	S

2 yrs.   26 games

Ed Mitchell
MITCHELL, EDWARD LEVINE
B. Sep. 5, 1942, Galveston, TX
Southern University 6'2" 275 lbs.

1965	SD	A	3	G
1966			14	G
1967			4	G
1967	HOU	A	4	G

3 yrs.   25 games

Fondren Mitchell
MITCHELL, FONDREN L.
B. 1921
Florida 6'0" 185 lbs.

1946	MIA	AA	7	HB

Gran Mitchell
MITCHELL, GRANVILLE MYRICK (Buster)
B. Feb. 16, 1906, Irene, TX
Deceased
Davis & Elkins 6'0" 205 lbs.

1931	POR	N	13	E
1932			10	E, T, G
1933			11	T, E
1934	DET	N	13	E
1935			3	E
1935	NYG	N	2	E
1936			8	E
1937	BKN	N	11	E, T

7 yrs.   71 games

Hal Mitchell
MITCHELL, HAROLD
B. 1932
UCLA 6'1" 225 lbs.

1952	NYG	N	11	T, G

Jim Mitchell
MITCHELL, JAMES HALCOT
B. Sep. 15, 1948, Danville, VA
Virginia State 6'3" 247 lbs.

1970	DET	N	14	DE
1971			13	DE
1972			14	DE
1973			9	DE
1974			14	DE
1975			14	DT, DE
1976			14	DE
1977			8	DE

8 yrs.   100 games

Year	Team		Games	Pos.

Jim Mitchell
MITCHELL, JAMES ROBERT
B. Oct. 19, 1947, Shelbyville, TN
Prairie View A&M 6'2" 234 lbs.

Year	Team		Games	Pos.
1969	ATL	N	14	TE
1970			14	TE
1971			13	TE
1972			14	TE
1973			14	TE
1974			14	TE
1975			14	TE
1976			14	TE
1977			12	TE
1978			16	TE
1979			16	TE
11 yrs.	155 games			

Johnny Mitchell
MITCHELL, JOHNNY
B. Jan. 20, 1971, Chicago, IL
Nebraska 6'3" 249 lbs.

Year	Team		Games	Pos.
1992	NYJ	N	11	TE
1993			14	TE
1994			16	TE
1995			12	TE
1996	DAL	N	4	TE
5 yrs.	57 games			

Ken Mitchell
MITCHELL, KENNETH WAYNE
B. Nov. 14, 1948, Denio, NV
Nevada-Las Vegas 6'1" 224 lbs.

Year	Team		Games	Pos.
1973	ATL	N	14	LB
1974			14	LB
2 yrs.	28 games			

Kevin Mitchell
MITCHELL, KEVIN DANYELLE
B. Jan. 1, 1971, Harrisburg, PA
Syracuse 6'1" 260 lbs.

Year	Team		Games	Pos.
1994	SF	N	16	LB
1995			15	LB
1996			12	LB
3 yrs.	43 games			

Leonard Mitchell
MITCHELL, LEONARD BOYD
B. Oct. 12, 1958, Houston, TX
Houston 6'7" 290 lbs.

Year	Team		Games	Pos.
1981	PHI	N	16	DE
1982			9	DE
1983			10	DE
1984			16	DE
1985			16	OT
1986			10	OT
1987	ATL	N	12	OT
7 yrs.	89 games			

Leroy Mitchell
MITCHELL, LEROY
B. Sep. 22, 1944, Wharton, TX
Texas Southern 6'2" 192 lbs.

Year	Team		Games	Pos.
1967	BOS	A	14	DB
1968			14	DB
1970	HOU	N	14	CB
1971	DEN	N	14	CB
1972			14	CB
1973			12	CB
6 yrs.	82 games			

Lydell Mitchell
MITCHELL, LYDELL DOUGLAS
(Worm)
B. May 30, 1949, Salem, NJ
Penn State 5'11" 199 lbs.

Year	Team		Games	Pos.
1972	BAL	N	11	RB
1973			14	RB
1974			14	RB

Lydell Mitchell *continued*

Year	Team		Games	Pos.
1975			14	RB
1976			14	RB
1977			14	RB
1978	SD	N	16	RB
1979			12	RB
1980	LA	N	2	RB
9 yrs.	111 games			

Mack Mitchell
MITCHELL, MACK HENRY
B. Aug. 16, 1952, Diboll, TX
Houston 6'7" 246 lbs.

Year	Team		Games	Pos.
1975	CLE	N	14	DE
1976			14	DE
1977			14	DE
1978			14	DE
1979	CIN	N	13	DT
5 yrs.	69 games			

Martin Mitchell
MITCHELL, MARTIN
B. Jan. 10, 1954, Lake Charles, LA
Tulane 6'1" 180 lbs.

Year	Team		Games	Pos.
1977	PHI	N	14	DB

Melvin Mitchell
MITCHELL, MELVIN
B. Feb. 21, 1953, Dallas, TX
Tennessee State 6'3" 260 lbs.

Year	Team		Games	Pos.
1976	MIA	N	12	G
1977			3	G
1977	DET	N	9	C, G
1978	MIA	N	4	G
1980	MIN	N	6	G
4 yrs.	34 games			

Mike Mitchell
MITCHELL, MICHAEL G.
B. Oct. 18, 1961, Waco, TX
Howard Payne 5'10" 180 lbs.

Year	Team		Games	Pos.
1987	WAS	N	3	CB
1989	NYJ	N	5	CB
2 yrs.	8 games			

Paul Mitchell
MITCHELL, PAUL ANTHONY
B. Aug. 10, 1922, Minneapolis, MN
Minnesota 6'3" 235 lbs.

Year	Team		Games	Pos.
1946	LA	AA	10	T
1947			11	T
1948			4	T
1948	NY	AA	8	T
1949	B-NY	AA	12	T
1950	NYY	N	12	T
1951			12	T
6 yrs.	69 games			

Pete Mitchell
MITCHELL, PETER CLARK
B. Oct. 9, 1971, Bloomfield Hills, MI
Boston College 6'2" 243 lbs.

Year	Team		Games	Pos.
1995	JAC	N	16	TE
1996			16	TE
2 yrs.	32 games			

Randall Mitchell
MITCHELL, RANDALL
B. Sep. 19, 1963
Tennessee-Chattanooga 6'1" 275 lbs.

Year	Team		Games	Pos.
1987	PHI	N	3	NT

Roland Mitchell
MITCHELL, ROLAND EARL
B. May 15, 1964, Columbus, TX
Texas Tech 5'11" 180 lbs.

Year	Team		Games	Pos.
1987	BUF	N	11	CB

Roland Mitchell *continued*

Year	Team		Games	Pos.
1988			3	CB
1988	PHX	N	11	CB
1989			3	CB
1990	ATL	N	13	CB
1991	GB	N	16	CB
1992			15	CB, S
1993			16	CB
1994			1	CB
8 yrs.	89 games			

Russ Mitchell
MITCHELL, RUSSELL B.
B. Dec. 28, 1960
Mississippi 6'5" 288 lbs.

Year	Team		Games	Pos.
1987	NYG	N	3	C

Scott Mitchell
MITCHELL, SCOTT
B. Jan. 2, 1968, Salt Lake City, UT
Utah 6'6" 236 lbs.

Year	Team		Games	Pos.
1991	MIA	N	2	QB
1992			16	QB
1993			13	QB
1994	DET	N	9	QB
1995			16	QB
1996			14	QB
6 yrs.	70 games			

Shannon Mitchell
MITCHELL, SHANNON LAMONT
B. Mar. 28, 1972, Alcoa, TN
Georgia 6'2" 245 lbs.

Year	Team		Games	Pos.
1994	SD	N	16	TE
1995			15	TE
1996			16	TE
3 yrs.	47 games			

Stan Mitchell
MITCHELL, STANTON EARL
B. Aug. 17, 1944, Wayne, MI
Tennessee 6'2" 220 lbs.

Year	Team		Games	Pos.
1966	MIA	A	2	OE
1967			14	RB
1968			9	RB
1969			3	RB
1970	MIA	N	14	RB
5 yrs.	42 games			

Stump Mitchell
MITCHELL, LYVONIA ALBERT
B. Mar. 15, 1959, St. Mary's, GA
The Citadel 5'9" 188 lbs.

Year	Team		Games	Pos.
1981	STL	N	16	RB
1982			9	RB
1983			15	RB
1984			16	RB
1985			16	RB
1986			15	RB
1987			12	HB
1988	PHX	N	14	RB
1989			3	RB
9 yrs.	116 games			

Ted Mitchell
MITCHELL, F.B.
B. Aug. 4, 1905
D. May 12, 1967
Bucknell 5'10" 195 lbs.

Year	Team		Games	Pos.
1929	ORA	N	12	C
1930	NEW	N	10	C
2 yrs.	22 games			

Tom Mitchell
MITCHELL, THOMAS GORDON
B. Aug. 22, 1944, Newport, RI

Tom Mitchell *continued*
Bucknell 6'2" 219 lbs.

Year	Team		Games	Pos.
1966	OAK	A	14	OE
1968	BAL	N	14	OE
1969			8	TE
1970			14	TE
1971			14	TE
1972			14	TE
1973			13	TE
1974	SF	N	14	TE
1975			13	TE
1976			14	TE
1977			13	TE
11 yrs.	145 games			

Willie Mitchell
MITCHELL, WILLIAM ANDERSON
B. Aug. 28, 1940, San Antonio, TX
Tennessee State 6'1" 185 lbs.

Year	Team		Games	Pos.
1964	KC	A	9	DB
1965			14	DB
1966			14	DB
1967			9	DB
1968			13	DB
1969			14	CB
1970	KC	N	14	CB
1971	HOU	N	14	CB, S
8 yrs.	101 games			

Bob Mitinger
MITINGER, ROBERT
B. Feb. 13, 1940, Greensburg, PA
Penn State 6'2" 232 lbs.

Year	Team		Games	Pos.
1962	SD	A	14	LB
1963			14	LB
1964*			9	LB
1966			2	LB
1968			3	LB
5 yrs.	42 games			

Alonzo Mitz
MITZ, ALONZO LOQWONE
B. Jun. 5, 1963, Henderson, NC
Florida 6'3" 274 lbs.

Year	Team		Games	Pos.
1986	SEA	N	6	NT
1987			6	DE
1988			16	DE
1989			12	DE
1991	CIN	N	15	DE
1992			16	DE
6 yrs.	71 games			

Bryant Mix
MIX, BRYANT
B. Jul. 28, 1972, Water Valley, MS
Alcorn State 6'3" 301 lbs.

Year	Team		Games	Pos.
1996	HOU	N	6	DE

Ron Mix
MIX, RONALD JACK
B. Mar. 10, 1938, Los Angeles, CA
Southern California 6'4" 249 lbs.

Year	Team		Games	Pos.
1960	LA	A	14	OT
1961	SD	A	10	OT
1962			14	OT
1963			14	G, OT
1964			14	OT
1965			14	OT
1966			14	OT
1967			14	OT
1968			14	OT
1969			8	OT
1971	OAK	N	12	OT
11 yrs.	142 games			

Billy Mixon
MIXON, BILLY RAYMOND

659

Year	Team		Games	Pos.

Billy Mixon *continued*
B. May 24, 1929, Tifton, GA
Georgia 5'11" 191 lbs.

Year	Team		Games	Pos.
1953	SF	N	10	HB
1954			12	HB
2 yrs.	22 games			

Warner Mizell
MIZELL, LAWRENCE WARNER
B. Oct. 8, 1907
D. May, 1971, Newport News, VA
Georgia Tech 5'10" 188 lbs.

1931	BKN	N	4	HB, FB
1931	FRA	N	3	HB, FB
1 yr.	7 games			

Kelly Moan
MOAN, EMMETT (Auto)
B. 1913, Long Beach, CA
D. Aug. 3, 1954, Wheeling, WV
West Virginia 6'0" 193 lbs.

| 1939 | CLE | N | 2 | HB |

John Mobley
MOBLEY, JOHN
B. Oct. 10, 1973, Chester, PA
Kutztown State 6'1" 230 lbs.

| 1996 | DEN | N | 16 | LB |

Orson Mobley
MOBLEY, ORSON ODELL
B. Mar. 4, 1963, Brooksville, FL
Florida State/Salem (West Virginia) 6'5" 256 lbs.

1986	DEN	N	14	TE
1987			10	TE
1988			16	TE
1989			12	TE
1990			9	TE
5 yrs.	61 games			

Rudy Mobley
MOBLEY, RUDOLPH HAMILTON (Little Doc)
B. Dec. 8, 1921, Paducah, TX
Hardin-Simmons 5'7" 155 lbs.

| 1947 | BAL | AA | 14 | B |

Stacey Mobley
MOBLEY, STACEY LANCE
B. Sep. 15, 1965, Daytona Beach, FL
Jackson State 5'8" 168 lbs.

1987	LARM	N	3	WR
1989	DET	N	10	WR
2 yrs.	13 games			

Mike Mock
MOCK, MICHAEL EARL
B. Feb. 25, 1955, Trondheim, Norway
Texas Tech 6'1" 225 lbs.

| 1978 | NYJ | N | 15 | LB, P |

Charlie Mockmore
MOCKMORE, CHARLES A.
B. Nov., 1891
Deceased
Iowa 5'11" 181 lbs.

| 1920 | RI | A | 5 | G |

Jeff Modesitt
MODESITT, JEFF A.
B. Jan. 1, 1964
Delaware 6'5" 245 lbs.

| 1987 | TB | N | 1 | TE |

Dick Modzelewski
MODZELEWSKI, RICHARD BLAIR (Little Mo)
B. Jan. 16, 1931, West Natrona, PA
Maryland 6'0" 258 lbs.

Year	Team		Games	Pos.
1953	WAS	N	12	DT
1954			12	DT
1955	PIT	N	12	DT
1956	NYG	N	12	DT
1957			12	DT
1958			12	DT
1959			12	DT
1960			12	DT
1961			14	DT
1962			14	DT
1963			14	DT
1964	CLE	N	14	DT
1965			14	DT
1966			14	DT
14 yrs.	180 games			

Ed Modzelewski
MODZELEWSKI, EDWARD WALTER (Big Mo)
B. Jan. 13, 1929, West Natrona, PA
Maryland 6'0" 217 lbs.

1952	PIT	N	10	FB
1955	CLE	N	12	FB
1956			8	FB
1957			12	FB
1958			12	FB
1959			12	FB
6 yrs.	66 games			

Hal Moe
MOE, HAROLD W.
B. Mar. 28, 1910, Spokane, WA
Oregon State 5'10" 182 lbs.

| 1933 | CHIC | N | 10 | HB |

Eddie Moegel
MOEGEL, EDGAR L.
B. 1897
Deceased
Detroit 5'9" 186 lbs.

| 1921 | DET | A | 5 | HB |

Dicky Moegle
MOEGLE, RICHARD LEE
B. Sep. 14, 1934, Taylor, TX
Rice 6'0" 190 lbs.

1955	SF	N	11	HB, DB
1956			12	HB, DB
1957			12	HB, DB
1958			4	HB
1959			8	HB
1960	PIT	N	12	DB
1961	DAL	N	14	S
7 yrs.	73 games			

Tim Moffett
MOFFETT, TIMOTHY
B. Feb. 8, 1962, Laurel, MS
Mississippi 6'2" 180 lbs.

1985	LARI	N	13	WR
1986			16	WR
1987	SD	N	2	WR
3 yrs.	31 games			

Mike Moffitt
MOFFITT, MICHAEL JEROME
B. Jul. 28, 1963, Los Angeles, CA
Fresno State 6'4" 211 lbs.

| 1986 | GB | N | 4 | TE |

Johnny Mohardt
MOHARDT, JOHN HENRY

Johnny Mohardt *continued*
B. Jan. 21, 1898, Pittsburgh, PA
D. Nov. 24, 1961, La Jolla, CA
Notre Dame 5'10" 167 lbs.

Year	Team		Games	Pos.
1922	CHIC	N	10	HB, FB
1923			10	HB, FB
1924	RAC	N	8	HB, QB
1925	CHIB	N	14	HB, QB
1926	CHI	A	12	HB
5 yrs.	54 games			

Chris Mohr
MOHR, CHRISTOPHER GARRETT
B. May 11, 1966, Atlanta, GA
Alabama 6'4" 220 lbs.

1989	TB	N	16	P
1991	BUF	N	16	P
1992			15	P
1993			16	P
1994			16	P
1995			16	P
1996			16	P
7 yrs.	111 games			

John Mohring
MOHRING, JOHN DENNIS
B. Nov. 14, 1956, Glen Cove, NY
C.W. Post 6'3" 240 lbs.

1980	DET	N	1	LB
1980	CLE	N	14	LB
1 yr.	15 games			

Louie Mohs
MOHS, LOUIS M. (Big)
B. Jan., 1896
D. Aug., 1967
St. Thomas (Minnesota) 6'3" 220 lbs.

1923	MIN	N	9	E
1924			5	E, T
2 yrs.	14 games			

Dick Moje
MOJE, RICHARD
B. 1927
Loyola (California) 6'2" 210 lbs.

| 1951 | GB | N | 2 | E |

Ralf Mojsiejenko
MOJSIEJENKO, RALF
B. Jan. 28, 1963, Salzgitter Lebenstadt, Germany
Michigan State 6'3" 209 lbs.

1985	SD	N	16	P
1986			16	P
1987			12	P
1988			16	P
1989	WAS	N	16	P
1990			12	P
1991	SF	N	5	P
7 yrs.	93 games			

Alex Molden
MOLDEN, ALEX
B. Aug. 4, 1973, Detroit, MI
Oregon 5'10" 190 lbs.

| 1996 | NO | N | 14 | CB |

Frank Molden
MOLDEN, WILLIAM FRANCIS
B. Jul. 28, 1942, Town, MS
Jackson State 6'5" 282 lbs.

1965	LA	N	11	DT
1968	PHI	N	13	DT
1969	NYG	N	7	DT
3 yrs.	31 games			

Fred Molden
MOLDEN, FRED
B. Aug. 12, 1963, Singing River, MS
Southern Mississippi/Jackson State 6'2" 272 lbs.

Year	Team		Games	Pos.
1987	MIN	N	2	DT

Bo Molenda
MOLENDA, JOHN J.
B. Feb. 20, 1905, Glesby, IL
D. Jul. 20, 1986, Banning, CA
Michigan 5'10" 210 lbs.

1927	NYY	N	10	FB, HB
1928			7	FB
1928	GB	N	4	FB
1929			12	FB, HB
1930			13	FB
1931			12	FB
1932			2	FB
1932	NYG	N	10	HB, FB
1933			12	FB, HB
1934			13	FB
1935			12	FB, HB
9 yrs.	107 games			

Keith Molesworth
MOLESWORTH, KEITH FRANK
B. Oct. 20, 1905, Washington, IA
D. Mar. 12, 1966
Monmouth (Illinois) 5'9" 167 lbs.

1931	CHIB	N	11	HB
1932			14	QB
1933			13	QB, HB
1934			12	HB, QB
1935			11	HB
1936			10	HB
1937			9	QB, HB
7 yrs.	80 games			

Lou Molinet
MOLINET, IGNACIO S.
B. Nov. 30, 1904, Chappara, Cuba
D. Aug., 1977, Palm Beach Gardens, FL
Cornell 5'11" 195 lbs.

| 1927 | FRA | N | 9 | FB, QB, HB |

Bob Momsen
MOMSEN, ROBERT EDWARD
B. May 28, 1929, Toledo, OH
Ohio State 6'3" 225 lbs.

1951	DET	N	12	G
1952	SF	N	10	G
2 yrs.	22 games			

Tony Momsen
MOMSEN, ANTON
B. Jan. 29, 1928
D. Mar. 6, 1994, Columbus, OH
Michigan 6'1" 215 lbs.

1951	PIT	N	11	C
1952	WAS	N	1	C
2 yrs.	12 games			

Jim Monachino
MONACHINO, JAMES
B. 1929
California 5'10" 187 lbs.

1951	SF	N	8	HB
1953			5	FB
1955	WAS	N	7	HB
3 yrs.	20 games			

Ray Monaco
MONACO, RAYMOND W.
B. Feb. 10, 1918, Providence, RI
Holy Cross 5'10" 212 lbs.

| 1944 | WAS | N | 4 | G |

Year	Team	Games	Pos.

Ray Monaco continued

Year	Team		Games	Pos.
1945	CLE	N	1	G

2 yrs. 5 games

Rob Monaco
MONACO, ROBIN GABRIEL
B. Sep. 5, 1961, Hamden, CT
Vanderbilt 6'3" 283 lbs.

| 1985 | STL | N | 6 | OT |

Ronnie Monaco
MONACO, RON CARL
B. May 3, 1963, New Haven, CT
San Diego State/Vanderbilt/South Carolina 6'1" 225 lbs.

| 1986 | STL | N | 15 | C |
| 1987 | GB | N | 2 | LB |

2 yrs. 17 games

Regis Monahan
MONAHAN, JOHN REGIS (Monty)
B. Nov. 15, 1908, Pittsburgh, PA
D. Apr. 23, 1979, Detroit, MI
Ohio State 5'10" 216 lbs.

1935	DET	N	12	G
1936			10	G, T
1937			11	G
1938			9	G
1939	CHIC	N	2	G

5 yrs. 44 games

Wonder Monds
MONDS, WONDERFUL, JR.
B. May 3, 1952, Fort Pierce, FL
Nebraska 6'3" 215 lbs.

| 1978 | SF | N | 16 | S |

Avery Monfort
MONFORT, WILLIAM AVERY
B. Dec. 19, 1918, Copan, OK
New Mexico 5'10" 178 lbs.

| 1941 | CHIC | N | 2 | HB |

Matt Monger
MONGER, MATTHEW L.
B. Nov. 15, 1961, Denver, CO
Oklahoma State 6'1" 238 lbs.

1985	NYJ	N	15	LB
1986			16	LB
1987			12	LB
1989	BUF	N	9	LB
1990			4	LB

5 yrs. 56 games

Art Monk
MONK, J. ARTHUR
B. Dec. 5, 1957, White Plains, NY
Syracuse 6'3" 210 lbs.

1980	WAS	N	16	WR
1981			16	WR
1982			9	WR
1983			12	WR
1984			16	WR
1985			15	WR
1986			16	WR
1987			9	WR
1988			16	WR
1989			16	WR
1990			16	WR
1991			16	WR
1992			16	WR
1993			16	WR
1994	NYJ	N	16	WR
1995	PHI	N	3	WR

16 yrs. 224 games

Bob Monnett
MONNETT, ROBERT C.
B. Feb. 27, 1910, Bucyrus, OH
D. Aug., 1978, Galion, OH
Michigan State 5'9" 182 lbs.

1933	GB	N	10	HB
1934			11	HB
1935			11	HB, QB
1936			11	HB, QB
1937			10	HB, QB
1938			8	HB

6 yrs. 61 games

Carl Monroe
MONROE, CARL
B. Feb. 20, 1960, Pittsburgh, PA
D. 1989
Utah 5'8" 166 lbs.

1983	SF	N	5	RB
1984			16	RB
1985			14	RB
1986			5	RB, WR
1987			3	WR

5 yrs. 43 games

Henry Monroe
MONROE, HENRY EVANS
B. Dec. 30, 1956, Mobile, AL
Mississippi State 5'11" 180 lbs.

| 1979 | PHI | N | 3 | CB |

Tommy Mont
MONT, THOMAS ALLISON, JR.
B. Jun. 20, 1922, Mount Savage, MD
Maryland 6'0" 194 lbs.

1947	WAS	N	4	HB
1948			11	QB
1949			12	QB

3 yrs. 27 games

Dave Montagne
MONTAGNE, DAVID ANDREW
B. Apr. 18, 1964, Berkeley, CA
Oregon State 6'2" 184 lbs.

| 1987 | KC | N | 3 | WR |

Mel Montalbo
MONTALBO, MELVIN
B. 1939
Utah State 6'1" 190 lbs.

| 1962 | OAK | A | 2 | DB |

Joe Montana
MONTANA, JOSEPH C.
B. Jun. 11, 1956, Monongahela, PA
Notre Dame 6'2" 197 lbs.

1979	SF	N	16	QB
1980			15	QB
1981			16	QB
1982			9	QB
1983			16	QB
1984			16	QB
1985			15	QB
1986			8	QB
1987			13	QB
1988			14	QB
1989			13	QB
1990			15	QB
1992			1	QB
1993	KC	N	11	QB
1994			14	QB

15 yrs. 192 games

Alton Montgomery
MONTGOMERY, ALTON
B. Jun. 16, 1968, Griffin, GA
Houston 6'0" 195 lbs.

| 1990 | DEN | N | 15 | CB, S |

Alton Montgomery cont.

1991			16	CB, S
1992			12	S
1993	ATL	N	8	S
1994			4	S
1995			15	S

6 yrs. 70 games

Bill Montgomery
MONTGOMERY, WILLIAM
B. May, 1909
St. Louis 5'9" 200 lbs.

| 1934 | C-S | N | 3 | G |

Bill Montgomery
MONTGOMERY, WILLIAM
B. 1923
Louisiana State 6'0" 205 lbs.

| 1946 | CHIC | N | 1 | B |

Blanchard Montgomery
MONTGOMERY, BLANCHARD, III
B. Feb. 17, 1961, Los Angeles, CA
UCLA 6'2" 236 lbs.

| 1983 | SF | N | 11 | LB |
| 1984 | | | 16 | LB |

2 yrs. 27 games

Cleo Montgomery
MONTGOMERY, CLEOTHA
B. Jul. 1, 1956, Greenville, MS
Abilene Christian 5'8" 183 lbs.

1980	CIN	N	14	WR
1981	CLE	N	4	WR
1981	OAK	N	1	RB
1982	LARI	N	9	RB
1983			14	RB
1984			16	WR
1985			4	WR

6 yrs. 62 games

Cliff Montgomery
MONTGOMERY, CLIFFORD EARL
B. Sep. 17, 1910, Natrona Heights, PA
Columbia 5'9" 165 lbs.

| 1934 | BKN | N | 11 | QB |

Glenn Montgomery
MONTGOMERY, GLENN STEVEN
B. Mar. 31, 1967, New Orleans, LA
Houston 6'0" 276 lbs.

1989	HOU	N	15	NT
1990			15	NT
1991			16	DT
1992			16	DT
1993			16	DT
1994			14	DT
1995			15	DT
1996	SEA	N	7	DT

8 yrs. 114 games

Greg Montgomery
MONTGOMERY, GREGORY HUGH, JR.
B. Oct. 29, 1964, Morristown, NJ
Penn State/Michigan State 6'3" 213 lbs.

1988	HOU	N	16	P
1989			16	P
1990			16	P
1991			15	P
1992			16	P
1993			15	P
1994	DET	N	16	P
1996	BAL	N	16	P

8 yrs. 126 games

Jim Montgomery
MONTGOMERY, JAMES BROWN, JR.
B. Mar. 18, 1922, Breckenridge, TX
D. Aug. 14, 1992, Dallas, TX
Texas A&M 6'4" 235 lbs.

| 1946 | DET | N | 11 | T |

Marv Montgomery
MONTGOMERY, MARVIN
B. Feb. 8, 1948, Torrance, CA
Southern California 6'6" 255 lbs.

1971	DEN	N	12	OT
1972			12	OT
1973			10	OT
1974			3	OT
1975			14	OT
1976			3	OT
1976	NO	N	9	OT
1977			14	OT
1978	ATL	N	1	OT

8 yrs. 78 games

Mike Montgomery
MONTGOMERY, JAMES MICHAEL
B. Jul. 10, 1949, Wichita Falls, TX
Kansas State 6'2" 208 lbs.

1971	SD	N	11	RB
1972	DAL	N	12	RB
1973			9	WR
1974	HOU	N	5	WR

4 yrs. 37 games

Randy Montgomery
MONTGOMERY, RANDY
B. Aug. 12, 1947, Houston, TX
Weber State 5'11" 183 lbs.

1971	DEN	N	3	CB
1972			14	CB
1973			9	CB
1974	CHI	N	14	CB

4 yrs. 40 games

Ross Montgomery
MONTGOMERY, ROSS ELLIOTT
B. Dec. 10, 1946, Detroit, MI
Texas Christian 6'3" 220 lbs.

| 1969 | CHI | N | 12 | RB |
| 1970 | | | 14 | RB |

2 yrs. 26 games

Sully Montgomery
MONTGOMERY, J.R.
B. 1901
Deceased
Centre 6'3" 213 lbs.

| 1923 | CHIC | N | 11 | T |
| 1927 | FRA | N | 4 | T |

2 yrs. 15 games

Tyrone Montgomery
MONTGOMERY, TYRONE
B. Aug. 3, 1970, Greenville, MS
Mississippi 6'0" 190 lbs.

| 1993 | LARI | N | 12 | RB |
| 1994 | | | 6 | RB |

2 yrs. 18 games

Wilbert Montgomery
MONTGOMERY, WILBERT
B. Sep. 16, 1954, Greenville, MS
Abilene Christian 5'10" 195 lbs.

1977	PHI	N	14	RB
1978			14	RB
1979			16	RB
1980			12	RB

Year	Team		Games	Pos.

Wilbert Montgomery *cont.*

Year	Team		Games	Pos.
1981			15	RB
1982			8	RB
1983			5	RB
1984			16	RB
1985	DET	N	7	RB
9 yrs.	107 games			

Mike Montler
MONTLER, MICHAEL R.
B. Jan. 11, 1954, Columbus, OH
Colorado 6'4" 256 lbs.

1969	BOS	A	14	G
1970	BOS	N	11	G, C
1971	NE	N	14	G, C
1972			14	OT
1973	BUF	N	10	G, OT
1974			14	C, OT
1975			14	C
1976			14	C
1977	DEN	N	14	C
1978	DET	N		C
10 yrs.	119 games			

Sankar Montoute
MONTOUTE, SANKAR
B. Feb. 2, 1961, Trinidad
Wisconsin/St. Leo 6'3" 230 lbs.*

| 1987 | TB | N | 3 | LB |

Max Montoya
MONTOYA, MAX, JR.
B. May 12, 1956, Montebello, CA
UCLA 6'5" 282 lbs.

1979	CIN	N	11	OT
1980			16	OT
1981			16	OT
1982			9	G
1983			16	G
1984			16	G
1985			16	G
1986			16	G
1987			10	G
1988			16	G
1989			16	G
1990	LARI	N	16	G
1991			11	G
1992			10	G
1993			16	G
1994			13	G
16 yrs.	223 games			

Mark Montreuil
MONTREUIL, MARK ALLEN
B. Dec. 29, 1971, Montreal, Que.
Concordia (Canada) 6'2" 200 lbs.

1995	SD	N	16	CB
1996			13	CB
2 yrs.	29 games			

Keith Moody
MOODY, KEITH M.
B. Jun. 13, 1955, Salisbury, NC
Syracuse 5'10" 171 lbs.

1976	BUF	N	14	DB
1977			14	CB
1978			14	CB
1979			16	CB
1980	OAK	N	5	CB
5 yrs.	63 games			

Mike Moody
MOODY, MIKE
B. May 9, 1969, San Francisco, CA
Southern California 6'7" 305 lbs.

| 1994 | SEA | N | 1 | OT |

Wilkie Moody
MOODY, WILKIE O.
B. May 12, 1897
D. Feb., 1976, Granville OH
Denison 5'7" 179 lbs.

1920	COL	A	4	HB, FB
1921	DAY	A	1	HB
1924	COL	N	3	HB, T, FB, G
1925			2	HB, FB
4 yrs.	10 games			

Doug Mooers
MOOERS, DOUGLAS
B. Mar. 11, 1947, Seattle, WA
Whittier 6'6" 265 lbs.

1971	NO	N	4	DT
1972			14	DT
2 yrs.	18 games			

Aaron Moog
MOOG, AARON
B. Feb. 3, 1962, Loma Linda, CA
Nevada-Las Vegas 6'4" 260 lbs.

| 1987 | CLE | N | 3 | DE |

Warren Moon
MOON, HAROLD WARREN
B. Nov. 18, 1956, Los Angeles, CA
Washington 6'3" 210 lbs.

1984	HOU	N	16	QB
1985			14	QB
1986			15	QB
1987			12	QB
1988			11	QB
1989			15	QB
1990			15	QB
1991			16	QB
1992			11	QB
1993			15	QB
1994	MIN	N	15	QB
1995			16	QB
1996			8	QB
13 yrs.	180 games			

Ed Mooney
MOONEY, EDWARD JOHN
B. Feb. 26, 1945, Brooklyn, NY
Texas Tech 6'2" 231 lbs.

1968	DET	N	14	LB
1969			14	LB
1970			14	LB
1971			14	LB
1973	BAL	N	13	LB
5 yrs.	69 games			

George Mooney
MOONEY, GEORGE W. (Gyp)
B. Feb. 22, 1896
D. Feb. 10, 1985, Glendale, CA
None 5'8" 163 lbs.

1922	MIL	N	4	QB, HB
1923			6	E, HB, FB
1924			3	FB, E, HB
3 yrs.	13 games			

Jim Mooney
MOONEY, JAMES L.
B. Sep. 16, 1907, Chicago, IL
D. Aug. 12, 1944, France
Georgetown (DC) 5'11" 200 lbs.

1930	NEW	N	12	T, G, FB, E
1930	BKN	N	3	T, QB
1931			13	T, G
1933	CIN	N	7	E
1934	C, S	N	8	E
1935	CHIC	N	5	E
5 yrs.	48 games			

Mike Mooney
MOONEY, MICHAEL PAUL
B. May 31, 1969, Baltimore, MD
Georgia Tech 6'6" 320 lbs.

| 1993 | SD | N | 1 | OT |

Tipp Mooney
MOONEY, BOW TIPP
B. Apr. 19, 1919, Shamrock, TX
Abilene Christian 6'0" 187 lbs.

1944	CHIB	N	6	HB
1945			7	HB
2 yrs.	13 games			

Tim Mooney
MOONEY, TIMOTHY
B. Jan. 25, 1962
Anderson/Western Kentucky 6'2" 265 lbs.

| 1987 | PHI | N | 2 | DE |

Buddy Moor
MOOR, MORRIS HOWARD
B. Dec. 1, 1958, Greenville, MS
Eastern Kentucky 6'5" 250 lbs.

| 1987 | ATL | N | 3 | DE |

Moore
MOORE
None

| 1921 | CLE | A | 1 | T |

Al Moore
MOORE, ALBERT B.
B. Apr. 17, 1908
D. Mar. 23, 1991
Northwestern 5'9" 170 lbs.

| 1932 | CHIB | N | 2 | HB, QB |

Al Moore
MOORE, ALLEN A.
B. 1914
Texas A&M 6'2" 218 lbs.

| 1939 | GB | N | 4 | E |

Alex Moore
MOORE, ALEXANDER
B. 1946
Norfolk State 6'0" 195 lbs.

| 1968 | DEN | A | 3 | DB |

Alvin Moore
MOORE, ALVIN
B. May 3, 1959, Randolph, AZ
Arizona State 6'0" 194 lbs.

1983	BAL	N	15	RB
1984	IND	N	13	RB
1985	DET	N	16	RB
1986			13	RB
1987	SEA	N	1	RB
5 yrs.	58 games			

Arthur Moore
MOORE, ARTHUR CLARK
B. Apr. 4, 1951, Daingerfield, TX
Tulsa 6'5" 255 lbs.

1973	NE	N	13	DT
1974			11	DT
1976			4	DT
1977				NT
4 yrs.	28 games			

Bill Moore
MOORE, WILLIAM

Bill Moore *continued*
B. 1906
Loyola (Louisiana) 5'11" 185 lbs.

1932	CHIC	N	4	HB
1933	PIT	N	5	HB
2 yrs.	9 games			

Bill Moore
MOORE, WILLIAM (Red)
B. 1923
Penn State 5'11" 218 lbs.

1947	PIT	N	12	G
1948			12	G
1949			12	G
3 yrs.	36 games			

Bill Moore
MOORE, WILLIAM J.
B. Feb. 4, 1912
Deceased
North Carolina 6'1" 195 lbs.

| 1939 | DET | N | 9 | E |

Blake Moore
MOORE, E. BLAKE
B. May 18, 1958, Durham, NC
Wooster 6'5" 264 lbs.

1980	CIN	N	16	C
1981			14	C
1982			4	C
1983			16	C
1984	GB	N	11	C, G
1985			16	C, G
6 yrs.	77 games			

Bob Moore
MOORE, ROBERT RORY
B. Feb. 12, 1949, Baltimore, MD
Stanford 6'3" 222 lbs.

1971	OAK	N	14	TE
1972			14	TE
1973			14	TE
1974			14	TE
1975			14	TE
1976	TB	N	11	TE
1977			3	TE
1978	DEN	N	8	TE
8 yrs.	92 games			

Booker Moore
MOORE, BOOKER THOMAS
B. Jun. 23, 1959, Flint, MI
Penn State 5'11" 224 lbs.

1982	BUF	N	5	FB
1983			15	RB
1984			15	FB
1985			16	FB
4 yrs.	51 games			

Brandon Moore
MOORE, BRANDON CHRISTOPHER
B. Jun. 21, 1970, Ardmore, PA
Duke 6'6" 290 lbs.

1993	NE	N	16	OT
1994			4	OT
1995			6	OT
3 yrs.	26 games			

Brent Moore
MOORE, BRENT ALLEN
B. Jan. 9, 1963, Novato, CA
Southern California 6'5" 242 lbs.

| 1987 | GB | N | 4 | LB |

Charlie Moore
MOORE, CHARLES
B. Jan. 3, 1940, Marianna, AR
Arkansas 6'5" 200 lbs.

Year	Team		Games	Pos.
1962	WAS	N	14	DE

Cliff Moore
MOORE, CLIFFORD
Penn State 6'1" 202 lbs.

Year	Team		Games	Pos.
1934	C-S	N	1	T

Dana Moore
MOORE, DANA
B. Sep. 7, 1961, Baton Rouge, LA
Mississippi State 5'10" 180 lbs.

Year	Team		Games	Pos.
1987	NYG	N	2	P

Darryl Moore
MOORE, DARRYL
B. Jan. 27, 1969, Minden, LA
Texas-El Paso 6'2" 292 lbs.

Year	Team		Games	Pos.
1993	WAS	N	12	G

Dave Moore
MOORE, DAVID EDWARD
B. Nov. 11, 1969, Morristown, NJ
Pittsburgh 6'2" 245 lbs.

Year	Team		Games	Pos.
1992	MIA	N	1	TE
1992	TB	N	4	TE
1993			15	TE
1994			15	TE
1995			16	TE
1996			16	TE
5 yrs.		67 games		

Dean Moore
MOORE, DEAN IRVIN
B. Jan. 26, 1955, Birmingham, AL
Iowa 6'2" 210 lbs.

Year	Team		Games	Pos.
1978	SF	N	16	LB

Denis Moore
MOORE, JAMES DENIS, III
B. Jul. 18, 1944, Berkeley, CA
D. May 27, 1995, Spokane, WA
Southern California 6'5" 247 lbs.

Year	Team		Games	Pos.
1967	DET	N	5	DT
1968			12	DT
1969			14	DT
1970	PHI	N	2	DT
4 yrs.		33 games		

Derland Moore
MOORE, DERLAND PAUL
B. Oct. 7, 1951, Malden, MO
Oklahoma 6'4" 265 lbs.

Year	Team		Games	Pos.
1973	NO	N	13	DT
1974			14	DT
1975			14	DT
1976			14	DT
1977			10	DT
1978			15	DT
1979			15	DT
1980			16	DT
1981			16	DT
1982			9	NT
1983			16	NT
1984			12	NT
1985			6	NT
1986	NYJ	N	1	DT
14 yrs.		171 games		

Derrick Moore
MOORE, DERRICK
B. Oct. 13, 1967, Albany, GA

Derrick Moore *continued*
Troy State/Northeastern Oklahoma State
6'1" 227 lbs.

Year	Team		Games	Pos.
1993	DET	N	13	RB
1994			16	RB
1995	CAR	N	13	RB
3 yrs.		42 games		

Dinty Moore
MOORE, WALTER
B. 1904
Lafayette 5'8" 160 lbs.

Year	Team		Games	Pos.
1927	POT	N	7	HB, QB

Eric Moore
MOORE, ERIC
B. Jan. 21, 1965, Berkeley, MO
Indiana 6'5" 293 lbs.

Year	Team		Games	Pos.
1988	NYG	N	11	OT
1989			16	OT
1990			15	OT
1991			16	OT
1992			10	OT
1993			7	OT
1994	CIN	N	6	OT
1995	CLE	N	1	OT
1995	MIA	N	2	OT
8 yrs.		84 games		

Fred Moore
MOORE, FREDERICK
B. Dec. 18, 1939, Sulligent, AL
Oklahoma/Memphis State 6'4" 260 lbs.

Year	Team		Games	Pos.
1964	SD	A	4	DT
1965			12	DT
1966			13	DT
3 yrs.		29 games		

Gene Moore
MOORE, EUGENE
B. 1913
Colorado 6'3" 205 lbs.

Year	Team		Games	Pos.
1938	BKN	N	7	C

Gene Moore
MOORE, EUGENE
B. May 12, 1947, San Diego, CA
Occidental 6'0" 208 lbs.

Year	Team		Games	Pos.
1969	SF	N	5	RB

Greg Moore
MOORE, GREG
B. Mar. 20, 1965
Tennessee-Chattanooga 6'1" 240 lbs.

Year	Team		Games	Pos.
1987	NE	N	3	LB

Henry Moore
MOORE, HENRY
B. 1934
Arkansas 6'1" 195 lbs.

Year	Team		Games	Pos.
1956	NYG	N	5	HB
1957	BAL	N	11	HB
2 yrs.		16 games		

Herman Moore
MOORE, HERMAN JOSEPH
B. Oct. 20, 1969, Danville, VA
Virginia 6'3" 208 lbs.

Year	Team		Games	Pos.
1991	DET	N	13	WR
1992			12	WR
1993			15	WR
1994			16	WR
1995			16	WR
1996			16	WR
6 yrs.		88 games		

Jeff Moore
MOORE, JEFFERY D.
B. Aug. 20, 1956, Kosciusko, MS
Jackson State 6'0" 195 lbs.

Year	Team		Games	Pos.
1979	SEA	N	16	RB
1980			14	RB
1981			2	RB
1982	SF	N	9	RB
1983			15	RB
1984	WAS	N	7	RB
6 yrs.		63 games		

Jeff Moore
MOORE, JEFFREY BERNARD
B. Mar. 2, 1957, Memphis, TN
Tennessee 6'1" 194 lbs.

Year	Team		Games	Pos.
1980	LA	N	14	WR
1981			10	WR
2 yrs.		24 games		

Jerald Moore
MOORE, JERALD
B. Nov. 20, 1974, Houston, TX
Oklahoma 5'9" 233 lbs.

Year	Team		Games	Pos.
1996	STL	N	11	RB

Jerry Moore
MOORE, JERRY P.
B. Mar. 16, 1949, Belleville, KY
Arkansas 6'3" 208 lbs.

Year	Team		Games	Pos.
1971	CHI	N	11	DB
1972			13	S
1973	NO	N	10	S
1974			9	S
4 yrs.		43 games		

Jimmy Moore
MOORE, JIMMY LEE, JR.
B. Jan. 28, 1957, Pittsburgh, PA
Ohio State 6'5" 268 lbs.

Year	Team		Games	Pos.
1981	BAL	N	4	G

Joe Moore
MOORE, JOSEPH LEE, JR.
B. Jun. 29, 1949, St. Louis, MO
Missouri 6'1" 205 lbs.

Year	Team		Games	Pos.
1971	CHI	N	9	RB
1973			14	RB
2 yrs.		23 games		

Ken Moore
MOORE, KENNETH
B. Jun. 15, 1916
D. Jan., 1981, Moundsville, WV
West Virginia Wesleyan 6'0" 212 lbs.

Year	Team		Games	Pos.
1940	NYG	N	8	G

Ken Moore
MOORE, KENNETH
B. Jul. 25, 1954, Merigold, MS
Northern Illinois 6'4" 232 lbs.

Year	Team		Games	Pos.
1978	ATL	N	6	TE

Lenny Moore
MOORE, LEONARD EDWARD
(Spats)
B. Nov. 25, 1933, Reading, PA
Penn State 6'1" 191 lbs.

Year	Team		Games	Pos.
1956	BAL	N	12	HB
1957			12	HB
1958			12	HB
1959			12	HB
1960			12	HB
1961			13	HB
1962			10	HB
1963			7	HB

Lenny Moore *continued*

Year	Team		Games	Pos.
1964			14	HB
1965			12	HB
1966			13	HB
1967			14	HB
12 yrs.		143 games		

Leonard Moore
MOORE, LEONARD
B. Jan. 27, 1963, Cartersville, GA
Jackson State 6'0" 222 lbs.

Year	Team		Games	Pos.
1987	MIN	N	1	RB

Leroy Moore
MOORE, LEROY FRANKLIN
(Sweet Pea)
B. Sep. 16, 1936, Pontiac, MI
Fort Valley State 6'0" 231 lbs.

Year	Team		Games	Pos.
1960	BUF	A		DE
1961	BOS	A	14	DE
1962			5	DE
1962	BUF	A	6	DE
1963			2	DE
1964	DEN	A	12	DE
1965			14	DE
6 yrs.		53 games		

Mack Moore
MOORE, MACK
B. Mar. 4, 1959, Monroe, LA
Texas A&M 6'4" 258 lbs.

Year	Team		Games	Pos.
1985	MIA	N	16	DE
1986			7	DE
1986	SD	N	3	DE
2 yrs.		26 games		

Malcolm Moore
MOORE, MALCOLM G.
B. Jun. 24, 1961, San Fernando, CA
Southern California 6'3" 240 lbs.

Year	Team		Games	Pos.
1987	LARM	N	3	TE

Manfred Moore
MOORE, MANFRED
B. Dec. 22, 1950, Martinez, CA
Southern California 6'0" 197 lbs.

Year	Team		Games	Pos.
1974	SF	N	14	RB
1975			14	RB
1976	TB	N	12	RB
1976	OAK	N	1	RB
1977	MIN	N	12	RB
4 yrs.		53 games		

Mark Moore
MOORE, MARK QUENTIN
B. Sep. 3, 1964, Nacogdoches, TX
Oklahoma State 6'0" 194 lbs.

Year	Team		Games	Pos.
1987	SEA	N	5	S

Marty Moore
MOORE, MARTIN NEFF
B. Mar. 19, 1971, Phoenix, AZ
Kentucky 6'0" 242 lbs.

Year	Team		Games	Pos.
1994	NE	N	16	LB
1995			16	LB
1996			16	LB
3 yrs.		48 games		

Maulty Moore
MOORE, MAULTY
B. Aug. 12, 1946, Milligan, FL
Bethune-Cookman 6'5" 265 lbs.

Year	Team		Games	Pos.
1972	MIA	N	14	DT
1973			12	DT
1974			14	DT
1975	CIN	N	13	DT

Year	Team	Games	Pos.

Maulty Moore *continued*

1976	TB	N	5	DT

5 yrs. 58 games

McNeil Moore

MOORE, McNEIL
B. Jun. 26, 1933, Center, TX
Rice/Sam Houston State 6'0" 185 lbs.

1954	CHIB	N	12	HB
1956			11	HB
1957			12	HB

3 yrs. 35 games

Nat Moore

MOORE, NATHANIEL
B. Sep. 19, 1951, Tallahassee, FL
Tennessee-Martin/Florida 5'9" 188 lbs.

1974	MIA	N	13	WR
1975			14	WR
1976			9	WR
1977			14	WR
1978			16	WR
1979			16	WR
1980			16	WR
1981			13	WR
1982			9	WR
1983			16	WR
1984			16	WR
1985			15	WR
1986			16	WR

13 yrs. 183 games

Paul Moore

MOORE, PAUL NEELY (June)
B. Jan. 23, 1918, York, SC
D. May, 1975
Presbyterian 5'9" 208 lbs.

1940	DET	N	7	HB
1941			7	QB, C

2 yrs. 14 games

Randy Moore

MOORE, RANDY
B. Apr. 5, 1954, Johnstown, PA
Arizona State 6'2" 241 lbs.

1976	DEN	N	8	DT

Reynaud Moore

MOORE, REYNAUD
B. Oct. 17, 1949, Los Angeles, CA
UCLA 6'2" 190 lbs.

1971	NO	N	14	S

Rich Moore

MOORE, RICHARD CLIFTON
B. Apr. 26, 1947, Cleveland, OH
Villanova 6'6" 285 lbs.

1969	GB	N	14	DT
1970			6	DT

2 yrs. 20 games

Ricky Moore

MOORE, RICKY
B. Apr. 7, 1963, Huntsville, AL
Alabama 5'11" 234 lbs.

1986	BUF	N	11	FB
1987	HOU	N	3	RB
1988	PHX	N	8	RB

3 yrs. 22 games

Rob Moore

MOORE, ROBERT S.
B. Sep. 27, 1968, New York, NY
Syracuse 6'3" 205 lbs.

1990	NYJ	N	15	WR
1991			16	WR

Rob Moore *continued*

1992			16	WR
1993			13	WR
1994			16	WR
1995	ARI	N	15	WR
1996			16	WR

7 yrs. 107 games

Robert Moore

MOORE, ROBERT ANTHONY
B. Aug. 15, 1964, Shreveport, LA
Northwestern State (Louisiana) 5'11" 190 lbs.

1986	ATL	N	16	S
1987			12	S
1988			16	S
1989			16	S

4 yrs. 60 games

Rocco Moore

MOORE, ROCCO RAY
B. Mar. 31, 1955, Charlotte, MI
Western Michigan 6'5" 276 lbs.

1980	CHI	N	7	G

Ron Moore

MOORE, RONALD
B. Nov. 26, 1970, Spencer, OK
Pittsburg State 5'10" 220 lbs.

1993	PHX	N	16	RB
1994	ARI	N	16	RB
1995	NYJ	N	15	RB
1996			16	RB

4 yrs. 63 games

Shawn Moore

MOORE, SHAWN LEVIQUE
B. Apr. 4, 1968, Martinsville, VA
Virginia 6'2" 214 lbs.

1992	DEN	N	3	QB

Steve Moore

MOORE, STEPHEN ELLIOTT
B. Oct. 1, 1960, Memphis, TN
Tennessee State 6'4" 295 lbs.

1983	NE	N	4	OT
1984			16	OT
1985			16	OT
1986			11	G, OT
1987			5	OT

5 yrs. 52 games

Stevon Moore

MOORE, STEVON NATHANIEL
B. Feb. 9, 1967, Wiggins, MS
Mississippi 5'11" 204 lbs.

1990	MIA	N	7	CB
1992	CLE	N	14	S
1993			16	S
1994			16	S
1995			16	S
1996	BAL	N	16	S

6 yrs. 85 games

Tom Moore

MOORE, THOMAS MARSHALL
B. Jul. 17, 1938, Goodlettsville, TN
Vanderbilt 6'2" 213 lbs.

1960	GB	N	12	HB
1961			13	HB
1962			14	HB
1963			12	HB
1964			14	HB
1965			13	HB
1966	LA	N	14	HB
1967	ATL	N	10	HB

8 yrs. 102 games

Wayne Moore

MOORE, SOLOMON WAYNE, SR.
B. Aug. 17, 1945, Beaumont, TX
Lamar* 6'6" 265 lbs.

1970	MIA	N	14	OT
1971			4	OT
1972			9	OT
1973			13	OT
1974			3	OT
1975			14	OT
1976			14	OT
1977			14	OT
1978			16	OT

9 yrs. 101 games

Wilbur Moore

MOORE, WILBUR JOHN (Little Indian)
B. Apr. 22, 1916, Austin, MN
D. Aug. 9, 1965
Minnesota 5'11" 187 lbs.

1939	WAS	N	10	FB
1940			10	HB
1941			6	HB
1942			11	HB, FB
1943			9	HB
1944			10	HB
1945			7	HB
1946			11	HB

8 yrs. 74 games

Will Moore

MOORE, WILL
B. Feb. 21, 1970, Dallas, TX
Texas Southern 6'2" 180 lbs.

1995	NE	N	14	WR
1996			14	WR

2 yrs. 28 games

Zeke Moore

MOORE, EZEKIEL, JR.
B. Dec. 2, 1943, Tuskegee, AL
Lincoln (Missouri) 6'2" 195 lbs.

1967	HOU	A	14	DB
1968			14	DB
1969			13	CB
1970	HOU	N	14	CB
1971			13	CB
1972			8	CB
1973			13	CB
1974			14	CB
1975			14	CB
1976			14	CB
1977			14	CB

11 yrs. 145 games

Emery Moorehead

MOOREHEAD, EMERY MATTHEW
B. Mar. 22, 1954, Evanston, IL
Colorado 6'2" 220 lbs.

1977	NYG	N	13	WR
1978			10	WR
1979			13	WR
1980	DEN	N	16	WR
1981	CHI	N	10	WR
1982			9	WR
1983			16	TE
1984			16	TE
1985			15	TE
1986			16	TE
1987			12	TE
1988			13	TE

12 yrs. 159 games

John Mooring

MOORING, JOHN
B. May 8, 1947, Falfurrias, TX
Tampa 6'6" 255 lbs.

1971	NYJ	N	14	OT

John Mooring *continued*

1972			14	G, OT
1973			14	OT, C
1974	NO	N	11	OT

4 yrs. 53 games

Mo Moorman

MOORMAN, MAURICE, JR.
B. Jul. 24, 1925, Louisville, KY
Kentucky/Texas A&M 6'5" 232 lbs.

1968	KC	A	13	G
1969			11	G
1970	KC	N	14	G
1971			9	G
1972			13	G
1973			13	G

6 yrs. 73 games

Jim Mooty

MOOTY, JAMES
B. 1938
Arkansas 5'11" 177 lbs.

1960	DAL	N	7	DB

Tim Morabito

MORABITO, TIMOTHY ROBERT
B. Oct. 12, 1973, Garnerville, NY
Boston College 6'3" 288 lbs.

1996	CIN	N	6	DT

Gonzalo Morales

MORALES, GONZALO
B. Jun. 10, 1922, San Francisco, CA
St. Mary's (California) 6'0" 188 lbs.

1947	PIT	N	8	HB
1948			10	HB

2 yrs. 18 games

Moran

MORAN
None 165 lbs.

1923	STL	N	2	FB, QB

Eric Moran

MORAN, ERIC
B. Jun. 10, 1960, Spokane, WA
Washington 6'5" 294 lbs.

1984	HOU	N	8	OT
1985			15	OT
1986			14	OT

3 yrs. 37 games

Fran Moran

MORAN, FRANCIS DALE (Hap)
B. Jul. 31, 1901, Belle Plaine, IA
D. Dec. 30, 1994, New Milford, CT
Grinnell/Carnegie-Mellon 6'1" 190 lbs.

1926	FRA	N	12	HB, QB
1927			6	HB, FB
1927	CHIC	N	5	HB, FB
1928	POT	N	10	HB, FB
1928	NYG	N	1	FB
1929			13	HB, FB
1930			16	HB, E, FB
1931			14	HB, QB
1932			11	QB, HB
1933			8	HB, FB

8 yrs. 96 games

Frank Moran

MORAN, FRANK C.
B. Mar. 18, 1887
D. Dec. 14, 1967, Hollywood, CA
None 6'4" 285 lbs.

1920	HAM	A	2	C
1920	AKR	A	1	T

1 yr. 3 games

Year	Team	Games	Pos.

Jim Moran
MORAN, JAMES PATRICK
B. Sep. 27, 1912, South Boston, MA
D. Aug., 1983, Natick, MA
Holy Cross 6'1" 208 lbs.

Year	Team	Games	Pos.
1935	**BOS** N	11	G
1936		4	G

2 yrs.   15 games

Jim Moran
MORAN, JAMES HARRY
B. May 4, 1942, Spokane, WA
Idaho 6'5" 260 lbs.

Year	Team	Games	Pos.
1964	**NYG** N	8	DT
1966		10	DT
1967		10	DT

3 yrs.   28 games

Rich Moran
MORAN, RICHARD JAMES
B. Mar. 19, 1962, Boise, ID
San Diego State 6'3" 276 lbs.

Year	Team	Games	Pos.
1985	**GB** N	16	OT, G
1986		5	C, G
1987		12	C, G
1988		16	C, G
1989		16	C, G
1990		16	G
1991		16	G
1992		8	G
1993		3	G

9 yrs.   108 games

Sean Moran
MORAN, SEAN FARRELL
B. Jun. 5, 1973, Denver, CO
Colorado State 6'3" 255 lbs.

Year	Team	Games	Pos.
1996	**BUF** N	16	DE

Tom Moran
MORAN, THOMAS
B. 1898
Deceased
Centre 5'8" 160 lbs.

Year	Team	Games	Pos.
1925	**NYG** N	1	QB

Doug Moreau
MOREAU, DOUGLAS PAUL
B. Feb. 15, 1945, Thibodaux, LA
Louisiana State 6'2" 207 lbs.

Year	Team	Games	Pos.
1966	**MIA** A	3	OE
1967		14	TE
1968		11	TE, K
1969		5	TE

4 yrs.   33 games

Joe Moreino
MOREINO, JOE P., JR.
B. Apr. 4, 1955, Providence, RI
Idaho State 6'6" 246 lbs.

Year	Team	Games	Pos.
1978	**NYJ** N	1	DL

Fran Morelli
MORELLI, FRANCIS P.
B. 1939
Colgate 6'2" 258 lbs.

Year	Team	Games	Pos.
1962	**NY** A	12	OT

John Morelli
MORELLI, JOHN
B. Jun. 11, 1923, Revere, MA
Georgetown 5'10" 191 lbs.

Year	Team	Games	Pos.
1944	**BOS** N	10	G
1945		9	G

2 yrs.   19 games

Tim Moresco
MORESCO, TIMOTHY JOHN
B. Oct. 3, 1954, Ithaca, NY
Syracuse 5'11" 178 lbs.

Year	Team	Games	Pos.
1977	**GB** N	14	DB
1978	**NYJ** N	11	S
1979		16	S
1980		11	S

4 yrs.   52 games

Arnold Morgado
MORGADO, ARNOLD T., JR.
B. Mar. 27, 1952, Honolulu, HI
Michigan State/Hawaii 6'0" 209 lbs.

Year	Team	Games	Pos.
1977	**KC** N	14	RB
1978		16	RB
1979		11	RB
1980		11	RB

4 yrs.   52 games

Anthony Morgan
MORGAN, ANTHONY EUGENE
B. Nov. 15, 1967, Cleveland, OH
Tennessee 6'1" 195 lbs.

Year	Team	Games	Pos.
1991	**CHI** N	14	WR
1992		12	WR
1993		1	WR
1993	**GB** N	2	WR
1994		16	WR
1995		16	WR
1996		3	WR

6 yrs.   64 games

Bill Morgan
MORGAN, WILLIAM
B. May 8, 1910, Portland, OR
D. Jul. 10, 1985, Canby, OR
Oregon 6'2" 232 lbs.

Year	Team	Games	Pos.
1933	**NYG** N	12	T
1934		13	T
1935		12	T
1936		10	T

4 yrs.   47 games

Bob Morgan
MORGAN, ROBERT
B. Jun. 28, 1930, Freeport, PA
Maryland 6'0" 235 lbs.

Year	Team	Games	Pos.
1954	**WAS** N	10	T

Bobby Morgan
MORGAN, ROBERT B.
B. Aug. 7, 1940, Warnego, KS
New Mexico 6'0" 205 lbs.

Year	Team	Games	Pos.
1967	**PIT** N	5	DB

Boyd Morgan
MORGAN, BOYD F. (Red)
B. Oct. 24, 1915, Comanche, OK
D. Jun. 8, 1988, Los Angeles, CA
Southern California 6'0" 198 lbs.

Year	Team	Games	Pos.
1939	**WAS** N	5	HB
1940		6	HB

2 yrs.   11 games

Dan Morgan
MORGAN, DANIEL SCOTT
B. Feb. 2, 1964, Wheeling, WV
Penn State 6'6" 285 lbs.

Year	Team	Games	Pos.
1987	**NYG** N	2	G

Dennis Morgan
MORGAN, DENNIS
B. Jun. 26, 1952, White Plains, NY
Western Illinois 5'11" 198 lbs.

Year	Team	Games	Pos.
1974	**DAL** N	13	RB

Dennis Morgan continued

Year	Team	Games	Pos.
1975	**PHI** N	4	RB

2 yrs.   17 games

Joe Morgan
MORGAN, JOSEPH
B. Oct. 23, 1928
Southern Mississippi 6'1" 245 lbs.

Year	Team	Games	Pos.
1949	**SF** AA	8	T

Karl Morgan
MORGAN, MICHAEL KARL
B. Feb. 23, 1961, Houma, LA
UCLA 6'1" 255 lbs.

Year	Team	Games	Pos.
1984	**TB** N	13	NT
1985		16	NT
1986		12	NT
1986	**HOU** N	1	NT

3 yrs.   42 games

Melvin Morgan
MORGAN, MELVIN
B. Mar. 31, 1953, Gulfport, MS
Mississippi Valley State 6'0" 183 lbs.

Year	Team	Games	Pos.
1976	**CIN** N	14	DB
1977		12	CB, S
1978		15	CB
1979	**SF** N	8	CB
1980		6	CB

5 yrs.   55 games

Michael Morgan
MORGAN, MICHAEL LEE
B. Jan. 19, 1956, Tallassee, AL
Wisconsin 5'11" 218 lbs.

Year	Team	Games	Pos.
1978	**CHI** N	5	RB

Mike Morgan
MORGAN, MICHAEL LEE
B. Jan. 31, 1942, Shreveport, LA
Deceased
Louisiana State 6'4" 241 lbs.

Year	Team	Games	Pos.
1964	**PHI** N	14	LB
1965		14	LB
1966		9	LB
1967		13	LB
1968	**WAS** N	14	LB
1969	**NO** N	14	LB
1970		9	LB

7 yrs.   87 games

Stanley Morgan
MORGAN, STANLEY DOUGLAS
(Stanley Steamer)
B. Feb. 17, 1955, Easley, NC
Tennessee 5'11" 180 lbs.

Year	Team	Games	Pos.
1977	**NE** N	14	WR
1978		16	WR
1979		16	WR
1980		16	WR
1981		13	WR
1982		9	WR
1983		16	WR
1984		16	WR
1985		15	WR
1986		16	WR
1987		9	WR
1988		16	WR
1989		10	WR
1990	**IND** N	16	WR

14 yrs.   195 games

Larry Moriarty
MORIARTY, LARRY
B. Apr. 24, 1958, Santa Barbara, CA
Notre Dame 6'1" 240 lbs.

Year	Team	Games	Pos.
1983	**HOU** N	16	RB

Larry Moriarty continued

Year	Team	Games	Pos.
1984		14	RB
1985		15	RB
1986		5	RB
1986	**KC** N	10	RB
1987		12	RB
1988		9	RB

6 yrs.   81 games

Pat Moriarty
MORIARTY, PATRICK JOHN
B. May 19, 1955, Cleveland, OH
Georgia Tech 6'0" 195 lbs.

Year	Team	Games	Pos.
1979	**CLE** N	16	RB

Tom Moriarty
MORIARTY, THOMAS, JR.
B. Apr. 7, 1953, Lima, OH
Bowling Green 6'0" 183 lbs.

Year	Team	Games	Pos.
1977	**ATL** N	14	S
1978		14	S
1979		16	S
1980	**PIT** N	4	S
1981	**ATL** N	9	S

5 yrs.   57 games

Milt Morin
MORIN, MILTON DENIS
B. Oct. 15, 1942, Leominster, MA
Massachusetts 6'4" 243 lbs.

Year	Team	Games	Pos.
1966	**CLE** N	11	TE
1967		6	TE
1968		14	TE
1969		14	TE
1970		14	TE
1971		14	TE
1972		14	TE
1973		14	TE
1974		14	TE
1975		14	TE

10 yrs.   129 games

Brett Moritz
MORITZ, BRETT I.
B. Jul. 15, 1955, Lincoln, NE
Army/Nebraska 6'5" 250 lbs.

Year	Team	Games	Pos.
1978	**TB** N	6	G

Sam Morley
MORLEY, SAMUEL ROBERTSON
B. May 12, 1932, Pasadena, CA
Stanford 6'2" 192 lbs.

Year	Team	Games	Pos.
1954	**WAS** N	1	E

Jack Morlock
MORLOCK, JOHN
B. Apr. 7, 1916
D. Jan., 1976
Marshall 5'9" 165 lbs.

Year	Team	Games	Pos.
1940	**DET** N	2	B

Mike Moroski
MOROSKI, MICHAEL HENRY
B. Sep. 4, 1957, Bakersfield, CA
California-Davis 6'4" 200 lbs.

Year	Team	Games	Pos.
1979	**ATL** N	2	QB
1980		3	QB
1981		3	QB
1982		9	QB
1983		16	QB
1984		16	QB
1985	**HOU** N	4	QB
1986	**SF** N	15	QB

8 yrs.   68 games

Earl Morrall
MORRALL, EARL EDWIN (Old Bones)
B. May 17, 1934, Muskegon, MI
Michigan State 6'1" 205 lbs.

Year	Team		Games	Pos.
1956	SF	N	12	QB
1957	PIT	N	12	QB
1958			2	QB
1958	DET	N	9	QB
1959			12	QB
1960			12	QB
1961			13	QB
1962			14	QB
1963			14	QB
1964			6	QB
1965	NYG	N	14	QB
1966			7	QB
1967			8	QB
1968	BAL	N	14	QB
1969			9	QB
1970			14	QB
1971			14	QB
1972	MIA	N	14	QB
1973			14	QB
1974			14	QB
1975			13	QB
1976			14	QB
21 yrs.		255 games		

Kyle Morrell
MORRELL, KYLE DOUGLAS
B. Oct. 9, 1963, Scottsdale, AZ
Brigham Young 6'1" 189 lbs.

Year	Team		Games	Pos.
1986	MIN	N	5	S

Bam Morris
MORRIS, BYRON
B. Jan. 13, 1972, Cooper, TX
Texas Tech 6'0" 235 lbs.

Year	Team		Games	Pos.
1994	PIT	N	15	RB
1995			13	RB
1996	BAL	N	11	RB
3 yrs.		39 games		

Bob Morris
MORRIS, ROBERT
B. Jul. 23, 1904
D. Jul., 1970, Cortland, NY
Cornell 5'10" 200 lbs.

Year	Team		Games	Pos.
1926	BKN	N	5	G

Bobby Morris
MORRIS, ROBERT
B. 1924
Southern California 5'11" 180 lbs.

Year	Team		Games	Pos.
1947	NYG	N	1	B

Chris Morris
MORRIS, CHRISTOPHER S.
B. Oct. 7, 1949, Indianapolis, IN
Indiana 6'3" 250 lbs.

Year	Team		Games	Pos.
1972	CLE	N	14	OT
1973			2	OT
2 yrs.		16 games		

Dennit Morris
MORRIS, DENNIT E.
B. 1936, Hanna, OK
Oklahoma 6'1" 228 lbs.

Year	Team		Games	Pos.
1958	SF	N	12	LB
1960	HOU	A		LB
1961			14	LB
3 yrs.		26 games		

Donnie Joe Morris
MORRIS, DONNIE JOE
B. Feb. 16, 1950, Amarillo, TX

Donnie Joe Morris cont.
North Texas State 5'11" 195 lbs.

Year	Team		Games	Pos.
1974	KC	N	3	OT

Dwaine Morris
MORRIS, DWAINE
B. Aug. 24, 1963, Independence, LA
Southwestern Louisiana 6'2" 260 lbs.

Year	Team		Games	Pos.
1985	PHI	N	1	NT
1987	ATL	N	3	DE
2 yrs.		4 games		

Frank Morris
MORRIS, FRANCIS M.
B. May 25, 1918, Newton, MA
D. Oct. 16, 1988, North Kensington, RI
Boston University 6'2" 214 lbs.

Year	Team		Games	Pos.
1942	CHIB	N	7	FB

George Morris
MORRIS, GEORGE
B. Feb. 24, 1919, East Palestine, OH
Baldwin-Wallace 5'11" 188 lbs.

Year	Team		Games	Pos.
1941	CLE	N	10	HB
1942			9	HB, QB
2 yrs.		19 games		

George Morris
MORRIS, GEORGE
B. 1931, Vicksburg, MS
Georgia Tech 6'2" 220 lbs.

Year	Team		Games	Pos.
1956	SF	N	8	C

Glenn Morris
MORRIS, GLENN E. (Tarzan)
B. Jun. 18, 1912, St. Louis, MO
D. Jan. 31, 1974, San Mateo, CA
Colorado State 6'0" 200 lbs.

Year	Team		Games	Pos.
1940	DET	N	4	E

Jack Morris
MORRIS, JOHN
B. Nov. 1, 1931, White City, KS
Oregon 6'0" 189 lbs.

Year	Team		Games	Pos.
1958	LA	N	12	DB
1959			12	DB
1960			3	DB
1960	PIT	N	4	DB
1961	MIN	N	14	DB
4 yrs.		45 games		

Jamie Morris
MORRIS, JAMES W.
B. Jun. 6, 1965, Southern Pines, NC
Michigan 5'7" 188 lbs.

Year	Team		Games	Pos.
1988	WAS	N	16	RB
1989			13	RB
1990	NE	N	5	RB
3 yrs.		34 games		

Jim Bob Morris
MORRIS, JAMES ROBERT
B. May 17, 1961, Burbank, CA
Kansas State 6'3" 211 lbs.

Year	Team		Games	Pos.
1987	GB	N	11	DB

Joe Morris
MORRIS, JOSEPH E.
B. Sep. 15, 1960, Fort Bragg, NC
Syracuse 5'7" 195 lbs.

Year	Team		Games	Pos.
1982	NYG	N	5	RB
1983			15	RB
1984			16	RB
1985			16	RB

Joe Morris continued

Year	Team		Games	Pos.
1986			15	RB
1987			11	RB
1988			16	RB
1991	CLE	N	16	RB
8 yrs.		110 games		

Johnny Morris
MORRIS, JOHN EDWARD
B. Sep. 26, 1936, Long Beach, CA
California-Santa Barbara 5'10" 180 lbs.

Year	Team		Games	Pos.
1958	CHIB	N	12	HB
1959			12	HB
1960	CHI		12	HB
1961			14	HB
1962			14	HB
1963			13	HB
1964			14	FL
1965			14	FL
1966			2	FL
1967			14	FL
10 yrs.		121 games		

Jon Morris
MORRIS, JON NICHOLSON
B. Apr. 5, 1942, Washington, DC
Holy Cross 6'4" 247 lbs.

Year	Team		Games	Pos.
1964	BOS	A	14	C
1965			14	C
1966			14	C
1967			14	C
1968			14	C
1969			14	C
1970	BOS		14	C
1971	NE	N	14	C
1972			14	C
1973			2	C
1974			14	C
1975	DET		14	C
1976			14	C
1977			14	C
1978	CHI	N		C
15 yrs.		184 games		

Larry Morris
MORRIS, LARRY
B. Feb. 27, 1962
Syracuse 5'7" 207 lbs.

Year	Team		Games	Pos.
1987	GB		2	RB

Larry Morris
MORRIS, LARRY C.
B. Dec. 10, 1933, Decatur, GA
Georgia Tech 6'2" 226 lbs.

Year	Team		Games	Pos.
1955	LA	N	12	C
1956			7	C
1957			6	C, LB
1959	CHIB	N	12	LB
1960	CHI		14	LB
1961			14	LB
1962			14	LB
1963			14	LB
1964			10	LB
1965			14	LB
1966	ATL	N	12	LB
11 yrs.		125 games		

Lee Morris
MORRIS, LEE A., JR.
B. Jul. 14, 1964, Oklahoma City, OK
Oklahoma 5'11" 180 lbs.

Year	Team		Games	Pos.
1987	GB	N	5	WR

Max Morris
MORRIS, GLEN MAX
B. Mar. 14, 1925
Illinois/Northwestern 6'2" 200 lbs.

Year	Team		Games	Pos.
1946	CHI	AA	11	E

Max Morris continued

Year	Team		Games	Pos.
1947			14	E
1948	BKN	AA	13	E
3 yrs.		38 games		

Mercury Morris
MORRIS, EUGENE
B. Jan. 5, 1947, Pittsburgh, PA
West Texas State 5'10" 190 lbs.

Year	Team		Games	Pos.
1969	MIA	A	14	RB
1970	MIA	N	12	RB
1971			14	RB
1972			14	RB
1973			13	RB
1974			5	RB
1975			14	RB
1976	SD	N	13	RB
8 yrs.		99 games		

Mike Morris
MORRIS, MICHAEL STEPHEN
B. Feb. 22, 1961, Centerville, IA
Northeast Missouri State 6'5" 278 lbs.

Year	Team		Games	Pos.
1987	STL	N	14	G
1989	KC		5	G, C
1989	NE	N	11	C
1990	SEA	N	4	G, C
1990	CLE	N	10	C
1991	MIN	N	16	C
1992			16	C
1993			16	C
1994			16	C
1995			16	C
1996			16	C
9 yrs.		140 games		

Randall Morris
MORRIS, RANDALL
B. Apr. 22, 1961, Anniston, AL
Tennessee 6'0" 195 lbs.

Year	Team		Games	Pos.
1984	SEA	N	10	RB
1985			16	RB
1986			16	RB
1987			10	RB
1988			10	RB
1988	DET	N	3	RB
5 yrs.		65 games		

Raymond Morris
MORRIS, RAYMOND
B. Jun. 8, 1961, Crane, TX
Texas-El Paso 5'10" 222 lbs.

Year	Team		Games	Pos.
1987	CHI	N	3	LB

Reilly Morris
MORRIS, REILLY
B. 1938
Florida A&M 6'2" 230 lbs.

Year	Team		Games	Pos.
1960	OAK	A		LB
1961			14	LB
1962			4	DE
3 yrs.		18 games		

Ron Morris
MORRIS, RONALD WAYNE
B. Nov. 14, 1964, Cooper, TX
Southern Methodist 6'1" 187 lbs.

Year	Team		Games	Pos.
1987	CHI	N	12	WR
1988			16	WR
1989			16	WR
1990			16	WR
1991			3	WR
1992			4	WR
6 yrs.		67 games		

Tom Morris
MORRIS, THOMAS LEWIS

Tom Morris *continued*

B. Apr. 2, 1960, Anniston, AL
Michigan State 5'11" 175 lbs.

Year	Team	Lg	Games	Pos.
1982	TB	N	8	S
1983			12	CB, S
2 yrs.			20 games	

Victor Morris

MORRIS, VICTOR
B. Jan. 25, 1964, Boynton Beach, FL
Miami (Florida) 6'1" 243 lbs.

Year	Team	Lg	Games	Pos.
1987	MIA	N	3	LB

Wayne Morris

MORRIS, WAYNE LEE
B. May 3, 1954, Dallas, TX
Southern Methodist 6'0" 207 lbs.

Year	Team	Lg	Games	Pos.
1976	STL	N	14	RB
1977			12	RB
1978			13	RB
1979			15	RB
1980			16	RB
1981			16	RB
1982			9	RB
1983			15	RB
1984	SD	N	10	RB
9 yrs.			120 games	

Charlie Morrison

MORRISON, CHARLES
B. Jun. 15, 1900
D. Mar., 1978, Buffalo, NY
None 185 lbs.

Year	Team	Lg	Games	Pos.
1926	BOS	A	5	E, G

Darryl Morrison

MORRISON, DARRYL LAMON
B. May 19, 1971, Phoenix, AZ
Arizona 5'11" 185 lbs.

Year	Team	Lg	Games	Pos.
1993	WAS	N	4	S
1994			16	S
1995			16	S
1996			12	S
4 yrs.			48 games	

Dennis Morrison

MORRISON, DENNIS C.
B. May 18, 1951, Pico Rivera, CA
Kansas State 6'3" 211 lbs.

Year	Team	Lg	Games	Pos.
1974	SF	N	7	QB

Doc Morrison

MORRISON, MAYNARD D.
B. 1909
Michigan 5'11" 210 lbs.

Year	Team	Lg	Games	Pos.
1933	BKN	N	10	C
1934			11	C
2 yrs.			21 games	

Don Morrison

MORRISON, DON ALAN
B. Dec. 16, 1949, Fort Worth, TX
Texas-Arlington 6'5" 255 lbs.

Year	Team	Lg	Games	Pos.
1971	NO	N	14	OT
1972			14	OT
1973			14	OT
1974			11	OT
1975			13	OT
1976			14	OT
1977			14	OT
1978	BAL	N	14	OT
1979	DET	N	15	OT, G
9 yrs.			123 games	

Duke Morrison

MORRISON, JESSE B.

Duke Morrison *continued*

B. Feb. 14, 1897
D. Feb. 23, 1981, Mill Valley, CA
California 6'0" 175 lbs.

Year	Team	Lg	Games	Pos.
1926	LA	A	8	FB, HB

Fred Morrison

MORRISON, FRED LEW (Curly)
B. Oct. 7, 1926, Columbus, OH
Ohio State 6'2" 215 lbs.

Year	Team	Lg	Games	Pos.
1950	CHIB	N	12	FB
1951			12	FB
1952			12	FB
1953			12	FB
1954	CLE	N	12	FB
1955			12	FB
1956			12	HB
7 yrs.			84 games	

Joe Morrison

MORRISON, JOSEPH R.
B. Aug. 21, 1937, Lima, OH
D. Feb. 5, 1989, Columbia, SC
Cincinnati 6'1" 210 lbs.

Year	Team	Lg	Games	Pos.
1959	NYG	N	12	HB
1960			12	HB
1961			13	HB
1962			14	HB, DB
1963			14	HB, DB
1964			14	FL, HB
1965			13	FL
1966			14	FL
1967			13	FL
1968			14	WR
1969			14	WR
1970			10	RB
1971			13	RB
1972			14	WR
14 yrs.			184 games	

Pat Morrison

MORRISON, PAT
B. Mar. 21, 1965
Southern Connecticut State 6'2" 194 lbs.

Year	Team	Lg	Games	Pos.
1987	NYG	N	1	S

Ram Morrison

MORRISON, CLARENCE E.
B. Sep. 8, 1899
Oklahoma 5'11" 180 lbs.

Year	Team	Lg	Games	Pos.
1926	LA	A	12	HB, FB, T

Reece Morrison

MORRISON, REECE EARSAL
B. Oct. 21, 1945, Tulsa, OK
Southwest Texas State 6'0" 206 lbs.

Year	Team	Lg	Games	Pos.
1968	CLE	N	14	RB
1969			14	RB
1970			14	RB
1971			9	RB
1972			4	RB
1972	CIN		6	RB
1973			3	RB
6 yrs.			64 games	

Steve Morrison

MORRISON, STEVE
B. Dec. 28, 1971, Birmingham, MI
Michigan 6'3" 238 lbs.

Year	Team	Lg	Games	Pos.
1995	IND	N	10	LB
1996			16	LB
2 yrs.			26 games	

Tim Morrison

MORRISON, TIMOTHY
B. Apr. 3, 1963, Raeford, NC
North Carolina 6'1" 195 lbs.

Year	Team	Lg	Games	Pos.
1986	WAS	N	16	S

Tim Morrison *continued*

Year	Team	Lg	Games	Pos.
1987			7	CB
2 yrs.			23 games	

Guy Morriss

MORRISS, GUY WALKER
B. May 13, 1951, Colorado City, TX
Texas Christian 6'4" 254 lbs.

Year	Team	Lg	Games	Pos.
1973	PHI	N	14	C
1974			14	C
1975			14	C
1976			14	C
1977			13	C
1978			16	C
1979			16	C
1980			16	C
1981			16	C
1982			9	C
1983			16	C
1984	NE	N	16	C
1985			16	C
1986			16	C, G
1987			11	C, G
15 yrs.			217 games	

Frank Morrissey

MORRISSEY, FRANK J.
B. Mar. 11, 1899
D. Nov. 19, 1968, Wynnewood, PA
Boston College 6'1" 203 lbs.

Year	Team	Lg	Games	Pos.
1921	TON	A	1	T
1921	ROC	A	6	G, T
1922	BUF	N	10	T
1923			12	G, T, E
1924			2	T
1924	MIL	N	2	G, C
4 yrs.			33 games	

Jim Morrissey

MORRISSEY, JAMES M.
B. Dec. 24, 1962, Flint, MI
Michigan State 6'3" 223 lbs.

Year	Team	Lg	Games	Pos.
1985	CHI	N	15	LB
1986			16	LB
1987			10	LB
1988			11	LB
1989			6	LB
1990			16	LB
1991			16	LB
1992			16	LB
1993			2	LB
1993	GB	N	6	LB
9 yrs.			114 games	

Bob Morrow

MORROW, ROBERT
B. May 5, 1918, Madison, WI
Illinois Wesleyan 6'0" 222 lbs.

Year	Team	Lg	Games	Pos.
1941	CHIC	N	6	FB
1942			10	FB
1943			7	QB, FB
1946	NY	AA	13	QB
4 yrs.			39 games	

Harold Morrow

MORROW, HAROLD
B. Feb. 24, 1973, Maplesville, AL
Auburn 5'11" 210 lbs.

Year	Team	Lg	Games	Pos.
1996	MIN	N	8	RB

Jim Morrow

MORROW, JAMES
B. Jan. 27, 1896
D. Sep., 1970, Cleveland, OH
Pittsburgh 5'10" 170 lbs.

Year	Team	Lg	Games	Pos.
1921	CAN	A	5	HB, FB, QB
1922	BUF	N	1	HB
2 yrs.			6 games	

John Morrow

MORROW, JOHN
B. Feb. 21, 1916, Nebraska
D. Jan., 1977
Kearney State 5'11" 230 lbs.

Year	Team	Lg	Games	Pos.
1937	CHIC	N	11	G
1938			5	T, G
2 yrs.			16 games	

John Morrow

MORROW, JOHN MELVILLE, JR.
B. Apr. 27, 1933, Port Huron, MI
Michigan 6'3" 244 lbs.

Year	Team	Lg	Games	Pos.
1956	LA	N	12	G
1958			12	C
1959			11	C
1960	CLE	N	12	C
1961			14	C
1962			14	C
1963			14	C
1964			14	C
1965			14	C
1966			8	C
10 yrs.			125 games	

Russ Morrow

MORROW, RUSSELL
B. 1924
Tennessee 6'7" 205 lbs.

Year	Team	Lg	Games	Pos.
1946	BKN	AA	9	C
1947			1	C
2 yrs.			10 games	

Tommy Morrow

MORROW, THOMAS
B. Jun. 3, 1938, Georgiana, AL
Southern Mississippi 5'11" 185 lbs.

Year	Team	Lg	Games	Pos.
1962	OAK	A	14	DB
1963			14	DB
1964			14	DB
3 yrs.			42 games	

Bobby Morse

MORSE, ROBERT W.
B. Oct. 3, 1965, Muskegon, MI
Michigan State 5'10" 207 lbs.

Year	Team	Lg	Games	Pos.
1987	PHI	N	11	RB
1989	NO	N	11	RB
1990			10	RB
1991			6	RB
4 yrs.			38 games	

Max Morse

MORSE, MAX (Hap)
B. 1899
Deceased
None 198 lbs.

Year	Team	Lg	Games	Pos.
1923	DUL	N	1	G

Ray Morse

MORSE, RAYMOND JOSEPH (Butch)
B. Dec. 5, 1911, Cleveland, OH
D. May 22, 1995, Corvallis, OR
Oregon 6'1" 199 lbs.

Year	Team	Lg	Games	Pos.
1935	DET	N	12	E, T
1936			12	E
1937			10	E
1938			8	E
1940			2	E
5 yrs.			44 games	

Steve Morse

MORSE, STEVEN BRYAN
B. May 28, 1963, Mobile, AL
Virginia 5'11" 214 lbs.

Year	Team	Lg	Games	Pos.
1985	PIT	N	16	RB

Year	Team		Games	Pos.

Emmett Mortell
MORTELL, EMMETT FRANCIS
B. Apr. 8, 1916, Appleton, WI
Wisconsin 6'1" 181 lbs.

Year	Team		Games	Pos.
1937	PHI	N	11	HB, QB
1938			11	HB
1939			8	QB

3 yrs. 30 games

Craig Morton
MORTON, LARRY CRAIG
B. Feb. 5, 1943, Flint, MI
California 6'4" 213 lbs.

Year	Team		Games	Pos.
1965	DAL	N	4	QB
1966			6	QB
1967			10	QB
1968			13	QB
1969			13	QB
1970			12	QB
1971			10	QB
1972			14	QB
1973			14	QB
1974			6	QB
1974	NYG	N	8	QB
1975			14	QB
1976			12	QB
1977	DEN	N	14	QB
1978			14	QB
1979			14	QB
1980			12	QB
1981			15	QB
1982			3	QB

18 yrs. 208 games

Dave Morton
MORTON, DAVID BYRON
B. May 13, 1955, Fresno, CA
UCLA 6'2" 224 lbs.

Year	Team		Games	Pos.
1979	SF	N	3	LB

Greg Morton
MORTON, GREG
B. Oct. 8, 1953, Akron, OH
Michigan 6'1" 230 lbs.

Year	Team		Games	Pos.
1977	BUF	N	9	LB

Jack Morton
MORTON, JOHN J.
B. Jul. 22, 1922, East St. Louis, IL
D. Dec., 1983, Manteno, IL
Missouri/Purdue 6'0" 197 lbs.

Year	Team		Games	Pos.
1945	CHIB	N	8	E
1946	LA	AA	12	E
1947	BUF	AA	2	E

3 yrs. 22 games

John Morton
MORTON, JOHN
B. 1929
Texas Christian 6'2" 220 lbs.

Year	Team		Games	Pos.
1953	SF	N	10	FB

Johnnie Morton
MORTON, JOHNNIE JAMES
B. Oct. 7, 1971, Inglewood, CA
Southern California 5'9" 190 lbs.

Year	Team		Games	Pos.
1994	DET	N	14	WR
1995			16	WR
1996			16	WR

3 yrs. 46 games

Michael Morton
MORTON, MICHAEL DA'MOND
B. Feb. 6, 1960, Birmingham, AL
Nevada-Las Vegas 5'8" 180 lbs.

Year	Team		Games	Pos.
1982	TB	N	9	RB
1983			16	RB

Johnnie Morton continued

Year	Team		Games	Pos.
1984			16	RB
1985	WAS	N	1	RB
1987	SEA	N	2	RB

5 yrs. 44 games

Mike Morton
MORTON, MICHAEL ANTHONY, JR.
B. Mar. 28, 1972, Kannapolis, NC
North Carolina 6'4" 235 lbs.

Year	Team		Games	Pos.
1995	OAK	N	12	LB
1996			16	LB

2 yrs. 28 games

Frank Morze
MORZE, FRANK
B. Mar. 21, 1933, Gardner, MA
Boston College 6'4" 272 lbs.

Year	Team		Games	Pos.
1957	SF	N	12	C
1958			4	C
1959			12	C
1960			12	C
1961			14	C
1962	CLE	N	2	C
1963			14	C
1964	SF	N	14	C

8 yrs. 84 games

Jim Moscrip
MOSCRIP, JAMES HENDERSON (Monk)
B. Sep. 17, 1913, Adena, OH
D. Oct. 11, 1980, Atherton, CA
Stanford 6'0" 195 lbs.

Year	Team		Games	Pos.
1938	DET	N	11	E
1939			11	E

2 yrs. 22 games

Don Mosebar
MOSEBAR, DONALD HOWARD
B. Sep. 11, 1961, Yakima, WA
Southern California 6'6" 288 lbs.

Year	Team		Games	Pos.
1983	LARI	N	14	OT
1984			10	OT
1985			16	G
1986			16	G
1987			12	C
1988			13	C
1989			12	C
1990			16	C
1991			16	C
1992			16	C
1993			16	C
1994			16	C

12 yrs. 173 games

Mark Moseley
MOSELEY, MARK DEWAYNE
B. Mar. 12, 1948, Lanesville, TX
Texas A&M/Stephen F. Austin 6'0" 200 lbs.

Year	Team		Games	Pos.
1970	PHI	N	14	K
1971	HOU	N	12	K
1972			1	K
1974	WAS	N	13	K
1975			14	K
1976			14	K
1977			16	K
1978			16	K
1979			16	K
1980			16	K
1981			9	K
1982			9	K
1983			16	K
1984			16	K
1985			16	K
1986			6	K

Mark Moseley continued

Year	Team		Games	Pos.
1986	CLE	N	4	K

16 yrs. 213 games

Dom Moselle
MOSELLE, DOM ANGELO
B. Jun. 3, 1925, Hurley, WI
Wisconsin-Superior 6'0" 192 lbs.

Year	Team		Games	Pos.
1950	CLE	N	11	HB
1951	GB	N	12	HB
1952			8	HB
1954	PHI	N	12	HB

4 yrs. 43 games

Bob Moser
MOSER, ROBERT
B. Dec. 26, 1928, Modesto, CA
Pacific 6'3" 238 lbs.

Year	Team		Games	Pos.
1951	CHIB	N	12	C
1952			12	C
1953			6	C

3 yrs. 30 games

Rick Moser
MOSER, RICHARD AVERY
B. Dec. 18, 1956, White Plains, NY
Rhode Island 6'0" 210 lbs.

Year	Team		Games	Pos.
1978	PIT	N	15	RB
1979			16	RB
1980	MIA	N	4	RB
1981	KC	N	1	RB
1981	PIT	N	6	RB
1982			6	RB
1982	TB	N	1	RB

5 yrs. 49 games

Ted Moser
MOSER, THEODORE (Doc)
B. Jun. 14, 1897
D. Aug., 1986, Dayton, OH
None 5'9" 195 lbs.

Year	Team		Games	Pos.
1921	LOU	A	1	T

Don Moses
MOSES, DONALD
B. 1907
Southern California 5'11" 185 lbs.

Year	Team		Games	Pos.
1933	CIN	N	3	B

Haven Moses
MOSES, HAVEN CHRISTOPHER
B. Jul. 27, 1946, Los Angeles, CA
San Diego State 6'3" 204 lbs.

Year	Team		Games	Pos.
1968	BUF	A	14	FL
1969			14	WR
1970	BUF	N	14	WR
1971			12	WR
1972			5	WR
1972	DEN	N	8	WR
1973			14	WR
1974			13	WR
1975			14	WR
1976			14	WR
1977			16	WR
1978			16	WR
1979			15	WR
1980			16	WR
1981			16	WR

14 yrs. 199 games

Clure Mosher
MOSHER, CLURE H.
B. Jan. 11, 1920, Fort Worth, TX
D. Jul. 23, 1966, New York, NY
Louisville 6'1" 215 lbs.

Year	Team		Games	Pos.
1942	PIT	N	3	C

John Mosier
MOSIER, JOHN PAUL
B. Mar. 1, 1948, Wichita State, TX
Kansas 6'3" 220 lbs.

Year	Team		Games	Pos.
1971	DEN	N	11	TE
1972	BAL	N	14	TE
1973	NE	N	3	TE

3 yrs. 28 games

Anthony Mosley
MOSLEY, ANTHONY
B. Jun. 17, 1965, Selma, CA
Fresno State 5'9" 204 lbs.

Year	Team		Games	Pos.
1987	CHI	N		RB

Henry Mosley
MOSLEY, HENRY
B. Feb. 10, 1931, Chattanooga, TN
Morris Brown 6'2" 210 lbs.

Year	Team		Games	Pos.
1955	CHIB	N	1	HB

Mike Mosley
MOSLEY, MICHAEL GENE
B. Jun. 30, 1958, Hillsboro, TX
Texas A&M 6'2" 192 lbs.

Year	Team		Games	Pos.
1982	BUF	N	9	WR
1983			7	WR
1984			4	WR

3 yrs. 20 games

Norm Mosley
MOSLEY, NORMAN S. (Monk)
B. 1922
Alabama 5'9" 185 lbs.

Year	Team		Games	Pos.
1948	PIT	N	3	HB

Russ Mosley
MOSLEY, RUSSELL C.
B. Jul. 22, 1918, Puxico, MO
Alabama 5'10" 170 lbs.

Year	Team		Games	Pos.
1945	GB	N	6	HB
1946			2	HB

2 yrs. 8 games

Wayne Mosley
MOSLEY, WAYNE
B. Oct. 6, 1952, Decatur, AL
Alabama A&M 6'0" 190 lbs.

Year	Team		Games	Pos.
1974	BUF	N	2	RB

Brent Moss
MOSS, BRENT
B. Jan. 30, 1972, Racine, WI
Wisconsin 5'8" 211 lbs.

Year	Team		Games	Pos.
1995	STL	N	4	RB

Eddie Moss
MOSS, EDDIE B.
B. Sep. 27, 1918, Dell, AR
Southeast Missouri State 6'0" 215 lbs.

Year	Team		Games	Pos.
1973	STL	N	5	RB
1974			11	RB
1975			8	RB
1976			2	RB
1977	WAS	N	9	RB

5 yrs. 35 games

Gary Moss
MOSS, GARY
B. Jul. 18, 1964
Georgia 5'10" 192 lbs.

Year	Team		Games	Pos.
1987	ATL	N	3	S

Year	Team	Games	Pos.

Joe Moss
MOSS, JOSEPH
B. Apr. 9, 1930, Elkins, WV
Maryland 6'1" 221 lbs.

Year	Team		Games	Pos.
1952	**WAS**	N	12	T

Martin Moss
MOSS, MARTIN
B. Dec. 16, 1958, San Diego, CA
UCLA 6'4" 252 lbs.

1982	**DET**	N	5	DT
1983			15	DT
1984			16	DT
1985			6	DE

4 yrs.   42 games

Paul Moss
MOSS, PAUL
B. May 7, 1909
D. Jun., 1954
Purdue 6'2" 200 lbs.

1933	**PIT**	N	10	E
1934	**C-S**	N	3	E

2 yrs.   13 games

Perry Moss
MOSS, PERRY L.
B. Aug. 4, 1926, Tulsa, OK
Tulsa/Illinois 5'10" 170 lbs.

1948	**GB**	N	6	QB

Roland Moss
MOSS, ROLAND
B. Sep. 20, 1946, St. Matthews, SC
Toledo 6'3" 215 lbs.

1969	**BAL**	N	6	RB
1970	**SD**	N	2	RB
1970	**BUF**	N	4	RB, TE
1971	**NE**	N	14	TE

3 yrs.   26 games

Winston Moss
MOSS, WINSTON N.
B. Dec. 24, 1965, Miami, FL
Miami (Florida) 6'3" 236 lbs.

1987	**TB**	N	12	LB
1988			16	LB
1989			16	LB
1990			16	LB
1991	**LARI**	N	16	LB
1992			15	LB
1993			16	LB
1994			16	LB
1995	**SEA**	N	16	LB
1996			16	LB

10 yrs.   155 games

Zefross Moss
MOSS, ZEFROSS
B. Aug. 17, 1966, Holt, AL
Alabama State 6'6" 333 lbs.

1989	**IND**	N	16	OT
1990			16	OT
1991			11	OT
1992			13	OT
1993			16	OT
1994			11	OT
1995	**DET**	N	15	OT
1996			15	OT

8 yrs.   113 games

Rich Mostardi
MOSTARDI, RICH
B. Jul. 1, 1938, Bryn Mawr, PA
Morris Harvey/Kent State 5'11" 188 lbs.

1960	**CLE**	N	10	DB
1961	**MIN**	N	11	DB

Rich Mostardi continued

1962	**OAK**	A	5	DB

3 yrs.   26 games

Kelley Mote
MOTE, KELLEY H.
B. Apr. 27, 1923, Hapeville, GA
South Carolina/Duke 6'2" 189 lbs.

1947	**DET**	N	12	E
1948			12	E
1949			12	E
1950	**NYG**	N	9	E
1951			12	E
1952			12	E

6 yrs.   69 games

Bobby Moten
MOTEN, BOBBY EARL
B. Jan. 29, 1943, Clarksville, TX
Bishop 6'4" 212 lbs.

1968	**DEN**	A	3	WR

Eric Moten
MOTEN, ERIC DEAN
B. Apr. 11, 1968, Cleveland, OH
Michigan State 6'2" 306 lbs.

1991	**SD**	N	16	G
1992			16	G
1993			4	G
1995			16	G
1996			15	G

5 yrs.   67 games

Gary Moten
MOTEN, GARY KIM
B. Apr. 3, 1961, Galveston, TX
Southern Methodist 6'1" 210 lbs.

1983	**SF**	N	6	LB
1987	**KC**	N	1	LB

2 yrs.   7 games

Bob Motl
MOTL, ROBERT JOSEPH
B. 1920, Chicago, IL
Northwestern 6'3" 196 lbs.

1946	**CHI**	AA	14	E

Marion Motley
MOTLEY, MARION
B. Jun. 5, 1920, Leesburg, GA
South Carolina State/Nevada-Reno 6'1" 232 lbs.

1946	**CLE**	AA	13	FB
1947			14	FB
1948			14	FB
1949			11	FB
1950	**CLE**	N	12	FB
1951			11	FB
1952			12	FB
1953			12	FB
1955	**PIT**	N	7	FB

9 yrs.   106 games

Joe Mott
MOTT, JOSEPH CHRISTOPHER
B. Oct. 9, 1965, Endicott, NY
Iowa 6'4" 253 lbs.

1989	**NYJ**	N	16	LB
1990			16	LB
1993	**GB**	N	2	LB

3 yrs.   34 games

Norm Mott
MOTT, NORMAN (Buster)
B. 1909
Deceased

Norm Mott continued
Georgia 5'8" 193 lbs.

1933	**GB**	N	3	HB, FB
1934	**C-S**	N	1	B
1934	**PIT**	N	1	HB

2 yrs.   5 games

Steve Mott
MOTT, WALTER STEPHEN, III
B. Mar. 24, 1961, New Orleans, LA
Alabama 6'3" 265 lbs.

1983	**DET**	N	13	C
1984			6	C
1985			16	C
1986			14	C
1987			11	C
1988			16	C

6 yrs.   76 games

Eric Moulds
MOULDS, ERIC SHANNON
B. Jul. 17, 1973, Lucedale, MS
Mississippi State 6'0" 204 lbs.

1996	**BUF**	N	16	WR

Zeke Mowatt
MOWATT, ZEKE
B. Mar. 5, 1961, Wauchula, FL
Florida State 6'3" 239 lbs.

1983	**NYG**	N	16	TE
1984			16	TE
1986			16	TE
1987			12	TE
1988			16	TE
1989			16	TE
1990	**NE**	N	10	TE
1991	**NYG**	N	16	TE

8 yrs.   118 games

Alex Moyer
MOYER, ALEX, III
B. Oct. 25, 1963, Detroit, MI
Northwestern 6'1" 221 lbs.

1985	**MIA**	N	10	LB
1986			3	LB

2 yrs.   13 games

Ken Moyer
MOYER, KENNETH WAYNE
B. Nov. 19, 1966, Canoga Park, CA
Toledo 6'6" 294 lbs.

1989	**CIN**	N	8	OT
1990			16	OT
1991			15	OT
1993			16	OT
1994			16	G, C

5 yrs.   71 games

Paul Moyer
MOYER, PAUL STEWART
B. Jul. 26, 1961, Villa Park, CA
Arizona State 6'1" 200 lbs.

1983	**SEA**	N	16	S
1984			16	S
1985			11	S
1986			16	S
1987			12	S
1988			16	S
1989			11	S

7 yrs.   98 games

Dick Moynihan
MOYNIHAN, RICHARD A.
B. 1903, Haverhill, MA
Villanova 5'8" 160 lbs.

1927	**FRA**	N	9	QB, HB, FB

Tim Moynihan
MOYNIHAN, TIMOTHY A.
B. Apr. 23, 1907
D. Dec., 1970, Marlborough, MA
Notre Dame 6'1" 204 lbs.

1932	**CHIC**	N	10	C
1933			7	C

2 yrs.   17 games

Mark Mraz
MRAZ, MARK DAVID
B. Feb. 9, 1965, Glendale, CA
Utah State 6'4" 258 lbs.

1987	**ATL**	N	11	DE
1989	**LARI**	N	11	DE

2 yrs.   22 games

George Mrkonic
MRKONIC, GEORGE
B. Dec. 7, 1929, McKeesport, PA
Kansas 6'2" 225 lbs.

1953	**PHI**	N	10	T

Bob Mrosko
MROSKO, ROBERT ALLEN
B. Nov. 13, 1965, Cleveland, OH
Penn State 6'6" 265 lbs.

1989	**HOU**	N	15	TE
1990	**NYG**	N	16	TE
1991	**IND**	N	11	TE

3 yrs.   42 games

Rudy Mucha
MUCHA, RUDOLPH J.
B. Jul. 22, 1918, Chicago, IL
D. Sep. 7, 1982, Dolton, IL
Washington 6'1" 236 lbs.

1941	**CLE**	N	10	G
1945			3	G
1945	**CHIB**	N	4	G
1946			11	G, C

3 yrs.   28 games

Jerry Muckensturm
MUCKENSTURM, JERRY RAY
B. Oct. 13, 1953, Belleville, IL
Arkansas State 6'4" 223 lbs.

1976	**CHI**	N	13	LB
1977			14	LB
1978			16	LB
1979			16	LB
1980			15	LB
1982			6	LB
1983			1	LB

7 yrs.   81 games

Larry Mucker
MUCKER, LARRY DONELL
B. Aug. 15, 1954, Fresno, CA
Arizona State 5'11" 191 lbs.

1977	**TB**	N	14	WR
1978			16	WR
1979			16	WR
1980			7	WR

4 yrs.   53 games

Howard Mudd
MUDD, HOWARD EDWARD
B. Feb. 10, 1942, Midland, MI
Michigan State/Hillsdale 6'3" 251 lbs.

1964	**SF**	N	14	G
1965			14	G
1966			14	G
1967			14	G
1968			14	G
1969	**CHI**	N	13	G
1970			10	G

7 yrs.   93 games

Year	Team	Games	Pos.

Frank Muehlheuser
MUEHLHEUSER, FRANK PAUL
(Moose)
B. Jul. 2, 1926, Irvington, NJ
Colgate 6'2" 218 lbs.

Year	Team		Games	Pos.
1948	BOS	N	12	B
1949	NYB	N	8	B
2 yrs.	20 games			

Ed Muelhaupt
MUELHAUPT, EDWARD
B. Dec. 11, 1935, Canton, OH
Iowa State 6'3" 230 lbs.

Year	Team		Games	Pos.
1960	BUF	A		G
1961			14	G
2 yrs.	14 games			

Jamie Mueller
MUELLER, JAMIE F.
B. Oct. 4, 1964, Cleveland, OH
Benedictine (Kansas) 6'1" 225 lbs.

Year	Team		Games	Pos.
1987	BUF	N	12	RB
1988			15	RB
1989			14	RB
1990			16	RB
4 yrs.	57 games			

Vance Mueller
MUELLER, VANCE ALAN
B. May 5, 1964, Tucson, AZ
Occidental 6'0" 211 lbs.

Year	Team		Games	Pos.
1986	LARI	N	15	RB
1987			12	RB
1988			14	RB
1989			16	RB
1990			16	RB
5 yrs.	73 games			

Bill Muellner
MUELLNER, WILLIAM
B. 1915
DePaul 5'11" 175 lbs.

Year	Team		Games	Pos.
1937	CHIC	N	1	E

Garvin Mugg
MUGG, GARVIN BRAY
B. Feb. 19, 1920, Weston, TX
D. Oct. 27, 1990, Tallapoosa, GA
North Texas State 6'1" 215 lbs.

Year	Team		Games	Pos.
1945	DET	N	3	T

Joe Muha
MUHA, JOSEPH
B. Apr. 28, 1921, Central City, PA
D. Apr. 1, 1993, Hemet, CA
Virginia Military Institute 6'1" 205 lbs.

Year	Team		Games	Pos.
1946	PHI	N	10	FB
1947			12	FB
1948			11	FB
1949			12	FB
1950			11	FB
5 yrs.	56 games			

Calvin Muhammad
RAINEY, CALVIN VINCENT
B. Dec. 10, 1958, Jacksonville, FL
Texas Southern 5'11" 190 lbs.

Year	Team		Games	Pos.
1982	LARI	N	7	WR
1983			15	WR
1984	WAS	N	10	WR
1985			12	WR
1987	SD	N	2	WR
5 yrs.	46 games			

Mushin Muhammad
MUHAMMAD, MUSHIN

Mushin Muhammad *cont.*
B. May 5, 1973, Lansing, MI
Michigan State 6'2" 217 lbs.

Year	Team		Games	Pos.
1996	CAR	N	9	WR

Horst Muhlmann
MUHLMANN, HORST HERBERT ERICH
B. Jan. 2, 1940, Dortmund, Germany
none 6'1" 215 lbs.

Year	Team		Games	Pos.
1969	CIN	A	14	K, P
1970	CIN	A	14	K
1971			14	K
1972			14	K
1973			14	K
1974			14	K
1975	PHI	N	14	K
1976			14	K
1977			9	K
9 yrs.	121 games			

Stan Muirhead
MUIRHEAD, STANLEY N.
B. 1901
Deceased
Michigan 6'0" 180 lbs.

Year	Team		Games	Pos.
1924	CLE	N	3	T
1924	DAY	N	3	T, G
1 yr.	6 games			

Mike Mularkey
MULARKEY, MICHAEL RENE
B. Nov. 19, 1961, Miami, FL
Florida 6'4" 240 lbs.

Year	Team		Games	Pos.
1983	MIN	N	3	TE
1984			16	TE
1985			15	TE
1986			16	TE
1987			9	TE
1988			16	TE
1989	PIT	N	14	TE
1990			16	TE
1991			9	TE
9 yrs.	114 games			

Joe Mulbarger
MULBARGER, JOSEPH G. (Dutch, Tiny)
B. 1897, Ohio
Deceased
None 5'9" 221 lbs.

Year	Team		Games	Pos.
1920	COL	A	4	T
1921			8	T
1922	COL	N	8	T
1923			10	T
1924			8	G, T
1925			9	G
1926			7	G
7 yrs.	54 games			

Herb Mul-Key
MUL-KEY, HERBERT FELTON
B. Nov. 15, 1949, Atlanta, GA
None 6'0" 190 lbs.

Year	Team		Games	Pos.
1972	WAS	N	2	RB
1973			14	RB
1974			5	RB
3 yrs.	21 games			

Tom Mullady
MULLADY, THOMAS FRANCIS
B. Jan. 30, 1957, Dayton, OH
Southwestern (Memphis) 6'3" 232 lbs.

Year	Team		Games	Pos.
1979	NYG	N	2	TE
1980			16	TE
1981			16	TE
1982			9	TE
1983			16	TE

Tom Mullady *continued*

Year	Team		Games	Pos.
1984			16	TE
6 yrs.	75 games			

Mark Mullaney
MULLANEY, MARK ALAN
B. Apr. 30, 1953, Denver, CO
Colorado State 6'6" 246 lbs.

Year	Team		Games	Pos.
1975	MIN	N	14	DE
1976			12	DE
1977			14	DE
1978			15	DE
1979			16	DE
1980			16	DE
1981			15	DE
1982			9	DE
1983			7	DE
1984			7	DE
1985			15	DE
1986			11	DE
12 yrs.	151 games			

Chief Mullen
MULLEN, SAMUEL
B. Jan. 9, 1894, Lawton, OK
D. May, 1976, Lawton, OK
Haskell 165 lbs.

Year	Team		Games	Pos.
1921	EVA	A	2	HB

Davlin Mullen
MULLEN, DAVLIN
B. Feb. 17, 1960, McKeesport, PA
Western Kentucky 6'1" 177 lbs.

Year	Team		Games	Pos.
1983	NYJ	N	11	CB
1984			15	CB
1985			11	CB
1986			5	CB
4 yrs.	42 games			

Gary Mullen
MULLEN, GARY
B. Feb. 1, 1963, McKeesport, PA
West Virginia 5'11" 174 lbs.

Year	Team		Games	Pos.
1987	CHI	N	3	WR

Roderick Mullen
MULLEN, RODERICK
B. Dec. 5, 1972, Baton Rouge, LA
Grambling State 6'1" 204 lbs.

Year	Team		Games	Pos.
1995	GB	N	8	CB
1996			16	S
2 yrs.	24 games			

Tom Mullen
MULLEN, THOMAS PATRICK
B. Nov. 30, 1951, Kirkwood, MO
Southwest Missouri State 6'3" 248 lbs.

Year	Team		Games	Pos.
1974	NYG	N	11	G, OT
1975			12	G
1976			12	OT
1977			8	OT
1978	STL	N	7	G
5 yrs.	50 games			

Verne Mullen
MULLEN, VERNE E. (Moon)
B. Feb. 27, 1900
D. Sep. 14, 1980, Taft, CA
Illinois 6'0" 186 lbs.

Year	Team		Games	Pos.
1923	CAN	N	5	E
1924	CHIB	N	11	E
1925			15	E
1926			15	E, HB, T
1927	CHIC	N	1	E
1927	POT	N	8	E
5 yrs.	55 games			

Carl Mulleneaux
MULLENEAUX, CARL K. (Moose)
B. Apr. 1, 1917, Phoenix, AZ
D. Jan. 23, 1995, California
Utah State 6'3" 209 lbs.

Year	Team		Games	Pos.
1938	GB	N	9	E
1939			10	E
1940			10	E
1941			10	E
1945			5	E
1946			1	E
6 yrs.	45 games			

Lee Mulleneaux
MULLENEAUX, CECIL LEE
(Brute)
B. Apr. 1, 1908
D. Nov. 14, 1985, Whittier, CA
Northern Arizona 6'2" 221 lbs.

Year	Team		Games	Pos.
1932	NYG	N	6	FB
1933	CIN	N	8	HB, QB, FB
1934	C-S	N	10	C, FB
1935	PIT	N	6	C
1936			12	C
1938	CHIC	N	4	C
1938	GB	N	5	C
6 yrs.	51 games			

Brick Muller
MULLER, HAROLD POWERS
B. Jun. 12, 1901, Dunsmuir, CA
D. May 17, 1962, Berkeley, CA
California 6'3" 195 lbs.

Year	Team		Games	Pos.
1926	LA	N	10	E

George Mulligan
MULLIGAN, GEORGE E.
B. Jun. 7, 1914, Waterbury, CT
Deceased
Catholic 6'1" 198 lbs.

Year	Team		Games	Pos.
1936	PHI	N	9	E, FB

Wayne Mulligan
MULLIGAN, WAYNE EUGENE
B. May 5, 1947, Baltimore, MD
Clemson 6'2" 246 lbs.

Year	Team		Games	Pos.
1969	STL	N	14	C
1970			14	C
1971			7	C
1972			12	C
1973			13	C
1974	NYJ	N	13	C
1975			14	C
7 yrs.	87 games			

Don Mullins
MULLINS, DON RAY
B. 1939
Houston 6'1" 195 lbs.

Year	Team		Games	Pos.
1961	CHI	N	4	DB
1962			9	DB
2 yrs.	13 games			

Eric Mullins
MULLINS, ERIC D.
B. Jul. 30, 1962, Houston, TX
Stanford 5'11" 181 lbs.

Year	Team		Games	Pos.
1984	HOU	N	13	WR

Gerry Mullins
MULLINS, GERALD BLAINE
(Moon)
B. Aug. 14, 1949, Fullerton, CA
Southern California 6'3" 242 lbs.

Year	Team		Games	Pos.
1971	PIT	N	14	G
1972			14	G
1973			13	OT, G

Year	Team		Games	Pos.

Gerry Mullins *continued*
1974			12	G, OT
1975			14	G, OT
1976			14	G, OT
1977			12	G, OT
1978			16	G
1979			15	G

9 yrs. 124 games

Noah Mullins
MULLINS, NOAH (Moon)
B. May 23, 1920, Midway, KY
Kentucky 5'11" 182 lbs.
1946	CHIB	N	9	HB, FB
1947			12	HB
1948			12	HB
1949	NYG	N	11	HB

4 yrs. 44 games

Jerry Mulready
MULREADY, GERALD
B. 1922
Deceased
Minnesota/North Dakota State 6'1" 205 lbs.
| 1947 | CHI | AA | 9 | E |

Vince Mulvey
MULVEY, VINCENT
B. Oct. 6, 1891
D. Feb. 25, 1988
Syracuse 155 lbs.
| 1923 | BUF | N | 4 | FB, HB, T |

Tony Mumford
MUMFORD, TONY V.
B. Jun. 14, 1963, Philadelphia, PA
Penn State 6'0" 215 lbs.
| 1985 | STL | N | 2 | RB |

Jock Mumgavin
MUMGAVIN, JAMES F.
B. Sep., 1893
Deceased
Wisconsin-Whitewater/Wisconsin 5'10" 170 lbs.
| 1920 | CHIT | A | 2 | E |

Nick Mumley
MUMLEY, NICHOLAS
B. Jan. 26, 1937
Purdue 6'6" 252 lbs.
1960	NY	A		OT, DE
1961			14	DE
1962			14	DE

3 yrs. 28 games

Lloyd Mumphord
MUMPHORD, LLOYD N.
B. Dec. 20, 1946, Los Angeles, CA
Texas Southern 5'11" 179 lbs.
1969	MIA	A	12	CB
1970	MIA	N	14	S
1971			14	CB
1972			14	CB
1973			11	CB
1974			13	CB
1975	BAL	N	14	CB
1976			13	CB
1977			2	CB
1978			16	CB

10 yrs. 123 games

Lloyd Mumphrey
MUMPHREY, LLOYD ELLIS
B. Feb. 14, 1961, Memphis, TN

Lloyd Mumphrey *continued*
Mississippi Valley State 6'3" 260 lbs.
| 1987 | KC | N | 3 | NT |

Mike Munchak
MUNCHAK, MIKE
B. Mar. 5, 1960, Scranton, PA
Penn State 6'3" 281 lbs.
1982	HOU	N	4	G
1983			16	G
1984			16	G
1985			16	G
1986			6	G
1987			12	G
1988			16	G
1989			16	G
1990			16	G
1991			13	G
1992			15	G
1993			13	G

12 yrs. 159 games

Chuck Muncie
MUNCIE, HARRY VANCE
B. Mar. 17, 1953, Uniontown, PA
California 6'2" 227 lbs.
1976	NO	N	12	RB
1977			14	RB
1978			13	RB
1979			16	RB
1980			4	RB
1980	SD	N	11	RB
1981			15	RB
1982			9	RB
1983			15	RB
1984			1	RB

9 yrs. 110 games

George Munday
MUNDAY, GEORGE (Sunny)
B. Jun. 13, 1907
D. Oct., 1975, Miami, FL
Emporia State 6'2" 213 lbs.
1931	CLE	N	1	G
1931	NYG	N	2	T
1932			3	T
1933	CIN	N	10	T
1934	C-S	N	10	T, G

4 yrs. 26 games

Fred Mundee
MUNDEE, FREDERICK WILLIAM
B. May 20, 1913, Youngstown, OH
D. Jan. 15, 1990, Chicago, IL
Notre Dame 6'1" 220 lbs.
1943	CHIB	N	6	C
1944			9	C, G
1945			6	C

3 yrs. 21 games

Marc Munford
MUNFORD, MARC CHRISTOPHER
B. Feb. 14, 1965, Lincoln, NE
Nebraska 6'2" 231 lbs.
1987	DEN	N	12	LB
1988			7	LB
1989			16	LB
1990			13	LB

4 yrs. 48 games

Munger
MUNGER
None
| 1924 | CHIC | N | 1 | T |

Lyle Munn
MUNN, LYLE (Doc)
B. Apr. 13, 1902
D. Jan., 1984, Topeka, KS
Kansas State 6'0" 186 lbs.
1925	KC	N	7	E
1926			11	E
1927	CLE	N	10	E
1928	DET	N	10	E, HB, FB, G
1929	NYG	N	15	E

5 yrs. 53 games

George Munns
MUNNS, GEORGE (Yats)
B. Jun., 1898, Oxford, OH
Miami (Ohio) 5'9" 165 lbs.
| 1921 | CIN | A | 4 | QB, HB |

Anthony Munoz
MUNOZ, MICHAEL ANTHONY
B. Aug. 19, 1958, Ontario, CA
Southern California 6'6" 278 lbs.
1980	CIN	N	16	OT
1981			16	OT
1982			9	OT
1983			16	OT
1984			16	OT
1985			16	OT
1986			16	OT
1987			11	OT
1988			16	OT
1989			16	OT
1990			16	OT
1991			13	OT
1992			7	OT

13 yrs. 184 games

Nelson Munsey
MUNSEY, NELSON EMORY
B. Jul. 2, 1948, Uniontown, PA
Wyoming 6'1" 188 lbs.
1972	BAL	N	9	CB
1973			14	CB, S
1974			14	CB
1975			14	CB
1976			8	CB
1977			13	CB

6 yrs. 72 games

Bill Munson
MUNSON, WILLIAM ALAN
B. Aug. 11, 1941, Sacramento, CA
Utah State 6'2" 203 lbs.
1964	LA	N	11	QB
1965			10	QB
1966			5	QB
1967			5	QB
1968	DET	N	12	QB
1969			8	QB
1970			8	QB
1971			4	QB
1972			2	QB
1973			10	QB
1974			11	QB
1975			5	QB
1976	SEA	N	5	QB
1977	SD	N	4	QB
1978	BUF	N	4	QB
1979			3	QB

16 yrs. 107 games

Art Murakowski
MURAKOWSKI, ARTHUR R.
B. May 15, 1925, East Chicago, IN
D. Sep. 13, 1985
Northwestern 6'0" 195 lbs.
| 1951 | DET | N | 12 | FB |

Ed Muransky
MURANSKY, EDWARD WILLIAM
B. Jan. 20, 1960, Youngstown, OH
Michigan 6'7" 280 lbs.
1982	LARI	N	5	OT
1983			16	OT
1984			3	OT

3 yrs. 24 games

Lee Murchison
MURCHISON, OLA LEE
B. 1938
Pacific 6'3" 205 lbs.
| 1961 | DAL | N | 14 | OE |

Guy Murdock
MURDOCK, GUY BOYD
B. Jun. 27, 1950, Chicago, IL
Michigan 6'2" 245 lbs.
| 1972 | HOU | N | 14 | C |

Jesse Murdock
MURDOCK, JESSE
B. 1939
California Western 6'2" 203 lbs.
| 1963 | OAK | A | 1 | HB |
| 1963 | BUF | A | 6 | FB |

1 yr. 7 games

Les Murdock
MURDOCK, LES
B. Jun. 30, 1942, Hollywood, FL
Florida State 6'3" 245 lbs.
| 1967 | NYG | N | 4 | K |

Dick Murley
MURLEY, RICHARD
B. Aug. 1, 1933
Purdue 6'0" 247 lbs.
| 1956 | PIT | N | 2 | T |
| 1956 | PHI | N | 5 | T |

1 yr. 7 games

Bill Murphy
MURPHY, BILL, JR.
B. 1947
Cornell 6'1" 185 lbs.
| 1968 | BOS | A | 6 | OE |

Bill Murphy
MURPHY, WILLIAM
B. 1904
Boston University 5'11" 200 lbs.
| 1926 | BOS | A | 4 | E, G |

Bill Murphy
MURPHY, WILLIAM
B. Apr. 7, 1914, Owensboro, KY
Washington (Missouri) 6'0" 203 lbs.
| 1940 | CHIC | N | 8 | G |
| 1941 | | | 5 | G |

2 yrs. 13 games

Dennis Murphy
MURPHY, DENNIS
B. Mar. 9, 1943, Cairo, GA
Florida 6'1" 250 lbs.
| 1965 | CHI | N | 2 | DT |

Fred Murphy
MURPHY, FRED J.
B. Feb. 20, 1938, Atlanta, GA
Georgia Tech 6'3" 205 lbs.
| 1960 | CLE | N | 9 | E |

Year	Team	Games	Pos.

George Murphy
MURPHY, GEORGE
B. May 10, 1927, Santa Monica, CA
D. Aug. 25, 1987, Chula Vista, CA
Southern California 6'0" 200 lbs.

Year	Team		Games	Pos.
1949	LA	AA	11	B

Ham Murphy
MURPHY, HARVEY A.
B. Jan. 17, 1917
D. Jan., 1981, Upper Sandusky, OH
Mississippi 5'10" 194 lbs.

Year	Team		Games	Pos.
1940	CLE	N	2	E

James Murphy
MURPHY, JAMES J.
B. Oct. 10, 1959, De Land, FL
Utah State 5'10" 177 lbs.

Year	Team		Games	Pos.
1981	KC	N	10	WR

Jim Murphy
MURPHY, JAMES (Irish)
B. Nov. 3, 1904
St. Thomas (Minnesota) 6'0" 184 lbs.

Year	Team		Games	Pos.
1926	RAC	N	5	E, C, HB
1926	DUL	N	3	C, FB
1928	CHIC	N	1	HB
2 yrs.		9 games		

Joe Murphy
MURPHY, JOSEPH THOMAS
(Cuddy)
B. May 15, 1897, Concord, NH
D. May 21, 1940
Harvard/Dartmouth 5'9" 215 lbs.

Year	Team		Games	Pos.
1921	CLE	A	5	G

Kevin Murphy
MURPHY, KEVIN DION
B. Sep. 8, 1963, Plano, TX
Oklahoma 6'2" 233 lbs.

Year	Team		Games	Pos.
1986	TB	N	16	LB
1987			9	LB
1988			16	LB
1989			16	LB
1990			15	LB
1991			16	LB
1992	SD	N	14	LB
1993	SEA	N	14	LB
8 yrs.		116 games		

Mark Murphy
MURPHY, MARK HODGE
B. Jul. 13, 1955, Fulton, NY
Colgate 6'4" 210 lbs.

Year	Team		Games	Pos.
1977	WAS	N	14	S
1978			16	S
1979			16	S
1980			16	S
1981			16	S
1982			9	S
1983			15	S
1984			7	S
8 yrs.		109 games		

Mark Murphy
MURPHY, MARK STEVEN
B. Apr. 22, 1958, Canton, OH
West Liberty State 6'2" 200 lbs.

Year	Team		Games	Pos.
1980	GB	N	1	S
1981			16	S
1982			9	S
1983			16	S
1984			16	S
1985			14	S
1987			12	S

Mark Murphy continued

Year	Team	Games	Pos.
1988		14	S
1989		16	S
1990		16	S
1991		16	S
11 yrs.		146 games	

Mike Murphy
MURPHY, MICHAEL WILLIAM
B. Jan. 14, 1957, St. Louis, MO
Southwest Missouri State 6'2" 222 lbs.

Year	Team		Games	Pos.
1979	HOU	N	3	LB

Phil Murphy
MURPHY, PHILIP JOHN
B. Sep. 26, 1957, New London, CT
South Carolina State 6'5" 290 lbs.

Year	Team		Games	Pos.
1980	LA	N	16	DT
1981			16	DT
2 yrs.		32 games		

Tom Murphy
MURPHY, THOMAS
B. Jan. 22, 1900
D. Dec., 1986, Tacoma, WA
Wisconsin-Superior 5'8" 165 lbs.

Year	Team		Games	Pos.
1926	MIL	N	8	HB

Tom Murphy
MURPHY, THOMAS B.
B. Dec. 7, 1906, Jonesboro, AR
D. Oct., 1981, Houston, TX
Arkansas 5'11" 170 lbs.

Year	Team		Games	Pos.
1934	CHIC	N	5	QB

Tommy Murphy
MURPHY, THOMAS F.
B. 1903
St. Mary's (Kansas) 187 lbs.

Year	Team		Games	Pos.
1926	KC	N	1	E
1926	COL	N	6	QB, HB, FB
1 yr.		7 games		

Bill Murrah
MURRAH, WILLIAM E. (Cap)
B. Sep. 5, 1900
Texas A&M 5'10" 215 lbs.

Year	Team		Games	Pos.
1922	CAN	N	6	C
1923	STL	N	7	G, C
2 yrs.		13 games		

Calvin Murray
MURRAY, LEON CALVIN
B. Oct. 18, 1958, Middle Township, NJ
Ohio State 5'11" 188 lbs.

Year	Team		Games	Pos.
1981	PHI	N	7	RB
1982			1	RB
2 yrs.		8 games		

Dan Murray
MURRAY, DANIEL FRANCIS
B. Oct. 20, 1966, Teaneck, NJ
East Stroudsburg 6'1" 240 lbs.

Year	Team		Games	Pos.
1989	IND	N	2	LB

Earl Murray
MURRAY, EARL W.
B. Jul. 16, 1926, Dayton, KY
Deceased
Purdue 6'2" 240 lbs.

Year	Team		Games	Pos.
1950	BAL	N	12	G, T
1951	NYG	N	12	G
2 yrs.		24 games		

Eddie Murray
MURRAY, EDWARD PETER
(Money)
B. Aug. 29, 1956, Halifax, N.S.
Tulane 5'10" 173 lbs.

Year	Team		Games	Pos.
1980	DET	N	16	K
1981			16	K
1982			7	K
1983			16	K
1984			16	K
1985			16	K
1986			16	K, P
1987			12	K, P
1988			16	K
1989			16	K
1990			11	K
1991			16	K
1992	KC	N	1	K
1992	TB	N	7	K
1993	DAL	N	14	K
1994	PHI	N	16	K
1995	WAS	N	16	K
16 yrs.		228 games		

Franny Murray
MURRAY, FRANK
B. Dec. 11, 1915
D. Dec., 1968
Pennsylvania 6'0" 200 lbs.

Year	Team		Games	Pos.
1939	PHI	N	11	HB, FB
1940			11	HB
2 yrs.		22 games		

Jab Murray
MURRAY, RICHARD
B. Oct. 28, 1892
Deceased
Marquette 6'0" 215 lbs.

Year	Team		Games	Pos.
1921	GB	A	6	C, T
1922	GB	N	3	T, E
1922	RAC	N	8	G, C
1923	GB	N	9	E, T, G
1924			5	E
4 yrs.		31 games		

Jack Murray
MURRAY, JOHN
B. Feb. 19, 1904
D. Jul., 1969, Minneapolis, MN
St. Thomas (Minnesota) 6'1" 210 lbs.

Year	Team		Games	Pos.
1926	DUL	N	7	E, G

Joe Murray
MURRAY, JOE
B. Nov. 7, 1960, Los Angeles, CA
Southern California 6'4" 265 lbs.

Year	Team		Games	Pos.
1987	LARM	N	3	G, OT

Johnny Murray
MURRAY, JOHN A.
B. Mar. 7, 1905
D. Jun., 1977, Albany, GA
Georgia Tech 6'0" 180 lbs.

Year	Team		Games	Pos.
1926	NEW	A	3	C

Mark Murray
MURRAY, MARK ALLAN
B. Oct. 15, 1967, Orlando, FL
Florida 6'2" 240 lbs.

Year	Team		Games	Pos.
1991	DEN	N	6	LB

Walter Murray
MURRAY, WALTER C.
B. Dec. 13, 1962, Berkeley, CA
Hawaii 6'4" 200 lbs.

Year	Team		Games	Pos.
1986	IND	N	5	WR
1987			14	WR
2 yrs.		19 games		

Adrian Murrell
MURRELL, ADRIAN BRYAN
B. Oct. 16, 1970, Lafayette, LA
West Virginia 5'11" 205 lbs.

Year	Team		Games	Pos.
1993	NYJ	N	16	RB
1994			10	RB
1995			15	RB
1996			16	RB
5 yrs.		69 games		

Bill Murrell
MURRELL, WILLIAM ELLIS
B. Jun. 14, 1956, Walnut Grove, CA
Winston-Salem State 6'3" 220 lbs.

Year	Team		Games	Pos.
1979	STL	N	12	TE

Don Murry
MURRY, DONALD
B. 1900
D. Jul., 1951
Wisconsin 6'2" 191 lbs.

Year	Team		Games	Pos.
1922	RAC	N	3	T
1924			10	T
1925	CHIB	N	15	T
1926			15	T, E, HB
1927			11	E, T
1928			12	T, E
1929			13	T, G
1930			10	T
1931			13	T, G
1932			5	T
10 yrs.		107 games		

George Murtagh
MURTAGH, GEORGE (Mickey)
B. 1904
D. 1993
Georgetown (DC) 6'1" 189 lbs.

Year	Team		Games	Pos.
1926	NYG	N	11	C, E
1927			13	C, G
1928			10	C, G
1929			13	C, HB
1930			11	C, E, HB
1931			7	C
1932			5	C
7 yrs.		70 games		

Greg Murtha
MURTHA, GREGORY THOMAS
B. Apr. 23, 1957, Minneapolis, MN
Minnesota 6'6" 268 lbs.

Year	Team		Games	Pos.
1982	BAL	N	5	OT

Ted Murtha
MURTHA, TED
B. 1901
None

Year	Team		Games	Pos.
1921	COL	A	2	FB, G

Bill Musgrave
MUSGRAVE, WILLIAM SCOTT
B. Nov. 11, 1967, Grand Junction, CO
Oregon 6'2" 196 lbs.

Year	Team		Games	Pos.
1991	SF	N	1	QB
1993			1	QB
1994			1	QB
1995	DEN	N	4	QB
1996			6	QB
5 yrs.		13 games		

Spain Musgrove
MUSGROVE, SPAIN
B. Jul. 30, 1945, Kansas City, MO
Utah State 6'4" 275 lbs.

Year	Team		Games	Pos.
1967	WAS	N	6	DT
1968			14	DT

Year	Team		Games	Pos.

Spain Musgrove *continued*

Year	Team		Games	Pos.
1969			10	DE, DT
1970	HOU	N	7	DE, DT
4 yrs.	37 games			

Jim Musick
MUSICK, JAMES A. (Sweet)
B. May 5, 1910, Santa Ana, CA
D. Dec. 14, 1992, Santa Ana, CA
Southern California 5'11" 205 lbs.

1932	BOS	N	10	FB
1933			12	FB
1935			5	FB
1936			5	FB
4 yrs.	32 games			

Neal Musser
MUSSER, JAMES NEAL
B. Mar. 20, 1957, Elon, NC
North Carolina State 6'2" 218 lbs.

1981	ATL	N	7	LB
1982			8	LB
2 yrs.	15 games			

George Musso
MUSSO, GEORGE FRANCIS (Moose)
B. Apr. 8, 1910, Collinsville, IL
Millikin 6'2" 262 lbs.

1933	CHIB	N	12	T
1934			12	T
1935			12	T
1936			12	T
1937			11	G
1938			11	G
1939			11	G
1940			6	G
1941			11	G
1942			11	G
1943			10	G, T
1944			10	G
12 yrs.	129 games			

Johnny Musso
MUSSO, JOHN, JR. (The Italian Stallion)
B. Mar. 6, 1950, Birmingham, AL
Alabama 5'11" 201 lbs.

1975	CHI	N	2	RB
1976			14	RB
1977			14	RB
3 yrs.	30 games			

Brad Muster
MUSTER, BRAD WILLIAM
B. Apr. 11, 1965, Novato, CA
Stanford 6'3" 231 lbs.

1988	CHI	N	16	RB
1989			16	RB
1990			16	RB
1991			11	RB
1992			16	RB
1993	NO	N	13	RB
1994			7	RB
7 yrs.	95 games			

Najee Mustafaa
Born REGINALD BERNARD RUTLAND, Played as REGGIE RUTLAND 1987-91
B. Jun. 20, 1964, East Point, GA
Georgia Tech 6'1" 194 lbs.

1987	MIN	N	7	S
1988			16	S
1989			16	S
1990			16	S
1991			13	CB
1993	CLE	N	14	CB

Najee Mustafaa *continued*

Year	Team		Games	Pos.
1995	OAK	N	15	CB
7 yrs.	97 games			

Chet Mutryn
MUTRYN, CHESTER A.
B. Mar. 12, 1921, Cleveland, OH
D. Mar. 24, 1995, Cleveland, OH
Xavier (Ohio) 5'9" 179 lbs.

1946	BUF	AA	14	HB
1947			14	HB
1948			14	HB
1949			11	HB
1950	BAL	N	12	HB
5 yrs.	65 games			

Jim Mutscheller
MUTSCHELLER, JAMES FRANCIS
B. Mar. 31, 1930, Beaver Falls, PA
Notre Dame 6'1" 213 lbs.

1954	BAL	N	12	E
1955			12	E
1956			12	E
1957			12	E
1958			12	E
1959			12	E
1960			11	E
1961			14	OE
8 yrs.	97 games			

Steve Myer
MYER, STEVE PAUL
B. Jul. 17, 1954, Covina, CA
New Mexico 6'2" 191 lbs.

1977	SEA	N	7	QB
1978			4	QB
1979			1	QB
3 yrs.	12 games			

Bob Myers
MYERS, ROBERT C.
B. Jan. 31, 1933
Ohio State 6'0" 260 lbs.

| 1955 | BAL | N | 1 | T |

Brad Myers
MYERS, BRADFORD J.
B. Feb. 14, 1929
Bucknell 6'1" 197 lbs.

1953	LA	N	12	HB
1956			5	FB
1958	PHI	N	9	HB
3 yrs.	26 games			

Chip Myers
MYERS, PHIL LEON
B. Jul. 9, 1945, Panama City, FL
Northwestern State (Oklahoma) 6'4" 203 lbs.

1967	SF	N	12	FL
1969	CIN	A	14	WR
1970	CIN	N	14	WR
1971			10	WR
1972			14	WR
1973			5	WR
1974			14	WR
1975			13	WR
1976			13	WR
9 yrs.	109 games			

Cy Myers
MYERS, CYRIL E. (Truck)
B. Apr. 16, 1897
D. Jul. 19, 1969, Leesburg, FL
Ohio State 6'0" 177 lbs.

| 1922 | TOL | N | 8 | E |

Cy Myers *continued*

Year	Team		Games	Pos.
1923	CLE	N	5	E
1925			2	T
3 yrs.	15 games			

Dave Myers
MYERS, DAVID
B. Nov. 11, 1906
D. Mar., 1972, New York, NY
New York University 5'11" 183 lbs.

1930	SI	N	6	G, HB
1931	BKN	N	7	G, HB
2 yrs.	13 games			

Denny Myers
MYERS, DENNIS E.
B. Jan. 3, 1907
D. Jul., 1984, Topeka, KS
Iowa 6'1" 206 lbs.

| 1931 | CHIB | N | 2 | G |

Frank Myers
MYERS, FRANK
B. Jan. 4, 1956, San Bernardino, CA
Texas A&M 6'5" 255 lbs.

1978	MIN	N	12	OT
1979			14	OT
2 yrs.	26 games			

Greg Myers
MYERS, GREGORY JAY
B. Sep. 30, 1972, Tampa, FL
Colorado State 6'1" 197 lbs.

| 1996 | CIN | N | 14 | S |

Jack Myers
MYERS, JOHN (Moose)
B. Oct. 8, 1924, St. Louis, MO
UCLA 6'2" 200 lbs.

1948	PHI	N	12	FB
1949			12	FB
1950			12	FB
1952	LA	N	12	FB
4 yrs.	48 games			

Tom Myers
MYERS, THOMAS W.
B. Aug. 13, 1943, Piqua, OH
Northwestern 6'0" 188 lbs.

1965	DET	N	1	QB
1966			1	QB
2 yrs.	2 games			

Tommy Myers
MYERS, THOMAS
B. 1901
D. Jul. 1, 1944
Fordham 5'8" 170 lbs.

1925	NYG	N	2	HB
1926	BKN	N	2	HB
2 yrs.	4 games			

Tommy Myers
MYERS, THOMAS PATRICK
B. Oct. 24, 1950, Cohoes, NY
Syracuse 5'11" 181 lbs.

1972	NO	N	13	S
1973			13	S
1974			12	S
1975			9	S
1976			14	S
1977			12	S
1978			16	S
1979			15	S
1980			16	S
1981			16	S
10 yrs.	136 games			

Wilbur Myers
MYERS, WILBUR LEE
B. Aug. 17, 1961, Bassfield, MS
Delta State 5'11" 195 lbs.

| 1983 | DEN | N | 16 | S |

Steve Myhra
MYHRA, STEVEN M.
B. Apr. 2, 1934, Wahpeton, ND
D. Aug. 4, 1994, Detroit Lakes, MN
Minnesota/North Dakota 6'1" 237 lbs.

1957	BAL	N	12	G, K
1958			12	G, K
1959			12	G, LB, K
1960			12	G, K
1961			14	G, K
5 yrs.	62 games			

Godfrey Myles
MYLES, GODFREY CLARENCE
B. Sep. 22, 1968, Miami, FL
Florida 6'1" 241 lbs.

1991	DAL	N	3	LB
1992			16	LB
1993			10	LB
1994			15	LB
1995			16	LB
1996			16	LB
6 yrs.	76 games			

Henry Myles
MYLES, HENRY
B. Sep. 1, 1903
Hampden-Sydney 6'0" 190 lbs.

1929	BUF	N	5	T, G, E
1930	NEW	N	1	E
2 yrs.	6 games			

Jesse Myles
MYLES, JESSE JAMES
B. Sep. 28, 1960, New Orleans, LA
Louisiana State 5'10" 210 lbs.

1983	DEN	N	16	RB
1984			7	RB
2 yrs.	23 games			

Chip Myrtle
MYRTLE, CHARLES
B. Feb. 6, 1945, Hyattsville, MD
Maryland 6'4" 224 lbs.

1967	DEN	A	14	LB
1968			13	LB
1969			12	LB
1970	DEN	N	14	LB
1971			14	LB
1972			14	LB
1974	SD	N	8	LB
7 yrs.	89 games			

Tom Myslinski
MYSLINSKI, THOMAS JOSEPH
B. Dec. 7, 1968, Rome, NY
Tennessee 6'2" 291 lbs.

1992	WAS	N	1	G
1993	BUF	N	1	G
1993	CHI	N	1	G
1994			4	G
1995	JAC	N	9	G
1996	PIT	N	8	G
5 yrs.	24 games			

Roland Nabors
NABORS, ROLAND (Rafe)
B. 1924
Texas Tech 6'2" 200 lbs.

| 1948 | NY | AA | 10 | C |

Year	Team		Games	Pos.

Andy Nacrelli

NACRELLI, ANDREW
B. Aug. 15, 1933, Chester, PA
D. Sep. 14, 1991, Lake Oswego, OR
Fordham 6'1" 190 lbs.

Year	Team		Games	Pos.
1958	PHI	N	2	E

Peaches Nadolney

NADOLNEY, ROMANUS
B. May 23, 1899
D. Feb., 1963
Notre Dame 5'11" 211 lbs.

Year	Team		Games	Pos.
1922	GB	N	8	G, T
1923	MIL	N	3	G, C
1924			2	G
1925			6	G
4 yrs.	19 games			

Dana Nafziger

NAFZIGER, DANA A.
B. Oct. 26, 1953, Woodstock, IL
California Poly (San Luis Obispo) 6'1" 221 lbs.

Year	Team		Games	Pos.
1977	TB	N	14	TE
1978			14	LB
1979			16	LB
1981			16	LB
1982			8	LB
5 yrs.	68 games			

Ray Nagel

NAGEL, RAYMOND ROBERT
B. May 18, 1927, Los Angeles, CA
UCLA 5'11" 177 lbs.

Year	Team		Games	Pos.
1953	CHIC	N	4	B

Ross Nagel

NAGEL, ROSS OTTO
B. Jun. 12, 1923, St. Louis, MO
Maplewood CC/St. Louis 6'4" 234 lbs.

Year	Team		Games	Pos.
1942	CHIC	N	1	T
1951	NYY	N	9	T
2 yrs.	10 games			

Browning Nagle

NAGLE, BROWNING
B. Apr. 29, 1968, Philadelphia, PA
West Virginia/Louisville 6'3" 225 lbs.

Year	Team		Games	Pos.
1991	NYJ	N	1	QB
1992			14	QB
1993			3	QB
1994	IND	N	1	QB
1995	ATL	N	1	QB
1996			5	QB
6 yrs.	25 games			

Johnny Nagle

NAGLE, JOHN
B. Aug. 4, 1893
D. Nov., 1974, Reading, PA
None 5'9" 175 lbs.

Year	Team		Games	Pos.
1921	NY	A	1	E

Gern Nagler

NAGLER, GERN
B. Feb. 22, 1932, Yuba City, CA
Santa Clara 6'2" 190 lbs.

Year	Team		Games	Pos.
1953	CHIC	N	11	E
1955			11	E
1956			8	E
1957			12	E
1958			12	E
1959	PIT	N	12	E
1960	CLE	N	12	E
1961			13	OE
8 yrs.	91 games			

Bronko Nagurski

NAGURSKI, BRONISLAW
B. Nov. 3, 1908, Rainy River, Ont.
D. Jan. 7, 1990, International Falls, MN
Minnesota 6'2" 226 lbs.

Year	Team		Games	Pos.
1930	CHIB	N	11	FB, T
1931			10	FB
1932			14	FB
1933			13	FB
1934			13	FB, HB
1935			5	FB
1936			11	FB
1937			10	FB
1943			8	T, FB
9 yrs.	95 games			

John Naioti

NAIOTI, JOHN F.
B. Nov. 6, 1921, Fulton, NY
D. Sep. 5, 1990
St. Francis (Pennsylvania) 5'10" 180 lbs.

Year	Team		Games	Pos.
1942	PIT	N	2	HB
1945			6	HB
2 yrs.	8 games			

Harvey Nairn

NAIRN, HARVEY
B. Apr. 17, 1945, Miami, FL
Southern University 6'1" 178 lbs.

Year	Team		Games	Pos.
1968	NY	A		WR

Rob Nairne

NAIRNE, ROBERT C.
B. Mar. 24, 1954, Redding, CA
Oregon State 6'4" 221 lbs.

Year	Team		Games	Pos.
1977	DEN	N	13	LB
1978			16	LB
1979			10	LB
1980			16	LB
1981	NO	N	16	LB
1982			9	LB
1983			16	LB
7 yrs.	96 games			

Pete Najarian

NAJARIAN, PETER MICHAEL
B. Dec. 22, 1963, San Francisco, CA
Minnesota 6'2" 233 lbs.

Year	Team		Games	Pos.
1987	MIN	N	5	LB
1988	TB	N	1	LB
1989			12	LB
3 yrs.	18 games			

Tom Nalen

NALEN, THOMAS ANDREW
B. May 13, 1971, Foxboro, MA
Boston College 6'2" 280 lbs.

Year	Team		Games	Pos.
1994	DEN	N	8	C, G
1995			15	C
1996			16	C
3 yrs.	39 games			

Joe Namath

NAMATH, JOSEPH WILLIAM
(Broadway Joe)
B. May 31, 1943, Beaver Falls, PA
Alabama 6'2" 198 lbs.

Year	Team		Games	Pos.
1965	NY	A	14	QB
1966			14	QB
1967			14	QB
1968			14	QB
1969			14	QB
1970	NYJ	N	5	QB
1971			4	QB
1972			13	QB

Joe Namath continued

Year	Team		Games	Pos.
1973			6	QB
1974			14	QB
1975			14	QB
1976			11	QB
1977	LA	N	6	QB
13 yrs.	143 games			

Jim Nance

NANCE, JAMES SOLOMON (Bo)
B. Dec. 30, 1942, Indiana, PA
D. Jun. 16, 1992, Quincy, MA
Syracuse 6'1" 241 lbs.

Year	Team		Games	Pos.
1965	BOS	A	14	FB
1966			14	FB
1967			14	RB
1968			12	RB
1969			14	RB
1970	BOS	N	13	RB
1971	NE	N	13	RB
1973	NYJ	N	7	RB
8 yrs.	101 games			

Walter Napier

NAPIER, WALTER (Buffalo)
B. 1936
Paul Quinn 6'4" 275 lbs.

Year	Team		Games	Pos.
1960	DAL	A		DT
1961			6	DT
2 yrs.	6 games			

Bob Naponic

NAPONIC, ROBERT
B. Mar. 9, 1947, Greensburg, PA
Illinois 6'0" 190 lbs.

Year	Team		Games	Pos.
1970	HOU	N	2	QB

Eric Naposki

NAPOSKI, ERIC ANDREW
B. Dec. 20, 1966, Manhattan, NY
Connecticut 6'2" 230 lbs.

Year	Team		Games	Pos.
1988	NE	N	3	LB
1989			1	LB
1989	IND	N	1	LB
2 yrs.	5 games			

Nick Nardacci

NARDACCI, NICHOLAS JAMES
B. 1903, Youngstown, OH
D. Aug. 30, 1961, Youngstown, OH
West Virginia 5'8" 160 lbs.

Year	Team		Games	Pos.
1925	CLE	N	2	HB, QB

Dick Nardi

NARDI, RICHARD L.
B. Sep. 25, 1915
D. Dec., 1972
Ohio State 5'10" 200 lbs.

Year	Team		Games	Pos.
1938	DET	N	8	HB
1939	PIT	N	3	HB
1939	BKN	N	2	HB
2 yrs.	13 games			

Bob Nash

NASH, ROBERT A. (Nasty)
B. Dec. 16, 1892
D. Feb. 1, 1977, Winsted, CT
Cornell/Rutgers 6'1" 205 lbs.

Year	Team		Games	Pos.
1920	AKR	A	7	E
1921	BUF	A	11	T, E
1922	BUF		2	E
1923			7	T, E
1924	ROC	N	2	T
1925	NYG	N	3	E
6 yrs.	32 games			

Joe Nash

NASH, JOSEPH ANDREW
B. Oct. 11, 1960, Boston, MA
Boston College 6'2" 255 lbs.

Year	Team		Games	Pos.
1982	SEA	N	7	DT
1983			16	DT
1984			16	NT
1985			16	NT
1986			16	NT
1987			12	NT
1988			16	NT
1989			16	NT
1990			16	NT
1991			16	DT
1992			16	DT
1993			16	DT
1994			16	DT
1995			16	DT
1996			8	DT
15 yrs.	219 games			

Kenny Nash

NASH, KENNY
B. Oct. 28, 1963, Hollywood, CA
San Jose State 6'2" 193 lbs.

Year	Team		Games	Pos.
1987	KC	N	1	WR

Tom Nash

NASH, THOMAS A., JR.
B. Nov. 22, 1905
D. Aug. 24, 1972, Washington, GA
Georgia 6'3" 208 lbs.

Year	Team		Games	Pos.
1928	GB	N	8	E
1929			10	E
1930			12	E
1931			13	E
1932			10	E
1933	BKN	N	9	E
1934			3	E
7 yrs.	65 games			

Ed Nason

NASON, EDWARD
B. Apr. 8, 1899
D. Mar., 1977, Wichita, KS
None 5'8" 165 lbs.

Year	Team		Games	Pos.
1922	OOR	N	1	HB
1923			1	T
2 yrs.	2 games			

Tony Nathan

NATHAN, TONY CURTIS
B. Dec. 14, 1956, Birmingham, AL
Alabama 6'0" 206 lbs.

Year	Team		Games	Pos.
1979	MIA	N	16	RB
1980			16	RB
1981			13	RB
1982			8	RB
1983			16	RB
1984			16	RB
1985			16	RB
1986			16	RB
1987			6	RB
9 yrs.	123 games			

Andy Natowich

NATOWICH, ANDREW
B. Dec. 11, 1918, Derby, CT
Holy Cross 5'10" 175 lbs.

Year	Team		Games	Pos.
1944	WAS	N		B

Ricky Nattiel

NATTIEL, RICKY RENNARD
B. Jan. 25, 1966, Gainesville, FL
Florida 5'9" 180 lbs.

Year	Team		Games	Pos.
1987	DEN	N	12	WR
1988			15	WR
1989			8	WR

Ricky Nattiel continued

Year	Team	Games	Pos.
1990		15	WR
1991		16	WR
1992		4	WR
6 yrs.	70 games		

Fred Naumetz
NAUMETZ, FREDERICK
B. Mar. 28, 1922, Newburyport, MA
Boston College 6'1" 222 lbs.

Year	Team	Games	Pos.
1946	LA	N 11	C
1947		12	C
1948		11	C
1949		12	C
1950		12	C
5 yrs.	58 games		

Paul Naumoff
NAUMOFF, PAUL PETE (Butch)
B. Jul. 3, 1945, Columbus, OH
Tennessee 6'1" 216 lbs.

Year	Team	Games	Pos.
1967	DET	N 14	LB
1968		14	LB
1969		14	LB
1970		14	LB
1971		14	LB
1972		14	LB
1973		14	LB
1974		14	LB
1975		14	LB
1976		14	LB
1977		13	LB
1978		15	LB
12 yrs.	168 games		

Johnny Naumu
NAUMU, JOHN
B. Sep. 30, 1919, Honolulu, HI
D. Sep., 1982
Hawaii/Southern California 5'8" 175 lbs.

Year	Team	Games	Pos.
1948	LA	AA 9	B

Stevan Nave
NAVE, STEVAN
B. Aug. 29, 1963, Nowata, OK
Kansas 6'2" 250 lbs.

Year	Team	Games	Pos.
1987	CLE	N 2	LB

Clem Neacy
NEACY, CLEMENT F.
B. Jul. 19, 1898
D. Mar. 19, 1968, Palos Verdes Estates, CA
Wisconsin-Milwaukee/Colgate 6'3" 206 lbs.

Year	Team	Games	Pos.
1924	MIL	N 13	E
1925		6	E
1926		9	E
1927	CHIB	N 2	E
1927	DUL	N 5	E, T
1928	CHIC	N 6	E, C
5 yrs.	41 games		

Dan Neal
NEAL, THOMAS DANIEL
B. Aug. 30, 1949, Corbin, KY
Kentucky 6'4" 252 lbs.

Year	Team	Games	Pos.
1973	BAL	N 5	C
1974		14	C
1975	CHI	N 6	C
1976		14	C
1977		14	C, G
1978		16	C, G
1979		16	C, G
1980		16	C
1981		16	C
1982		9	C

Dan Neal continued

Year	Team	Games	Pos.
1983		8	C
11 yrs.	134 games		

Ed Neal
NEAL, WILLIAM EDWARD
B. Dec. 31, 1918, Wichita Falls, TX
D. Dec., 1984, Euless, TX
Tulane/Louisiana State 6'4" 285 lbs.

Year	Team	Games	Pos.
1945	GB	N 9	T
1946		10	G
1947		12	G
1948		12	G
1949		12	C
1950		12	C
1951	CHIB	N 4	C
7 yrs.	71 games		

Frankie Neal
NEAL, FRANKIE LEON
B. Oct. 1, 1965, Sebring, FL
Florida/Fort Hays State 6'1" 202 lbs.

Year	Team	Games	Pos.
1987	GB	N 12	WR

Lorenzo Neal
NEAL, LORENZO LAVON
B. Dec. 27, 1970, Hanford, CA
Fresno State 5'10" 228 lbs.

Year	Team	Games	Pos.
1993	NO	N 2	RB
1994		16	RB
1995		16	RB
1996		16	RB
4 yrs.	50 games		

Louis Neal
NEAL, LOUIS CHARLES
B. Jan. 10, 1951, San Francisco, CA
Prairie View A&M 6'4" 215 lbs.

Year	Team	Games	Pos.
1973	ATL	N 5	WR
1974		10	WR
2 yrs.	15 games		

Randy Neal
NEAL, RANDY PETER
B. Dec. 29, 1972, Hackensack, NJ
Virginia 6'3" 236 lbs.

Year	Team	Games	Pos.
1995	CIN	N 3	LB
1996		1	LB
2 yrs.	4 games		

Ray Neal
NEAL, RAYMOND ROBERT
B. Nov. 1, 1897
D. Nov. 25, 1977, Greencastle, IN
Wabash/Washington & Jefferson 5'9" 205 lbs.

Year	Team	Games	Pos.
1922	AKR	N 10	G, T
1924	HAM	N 5	T, G
1925		5	T
1926		3	G, T
4 yrs.	23 games		

Richard Neal
NEAL, RICHARD
B. Sep. 2, 1947, Minden, LA
Southern University 6'3" 258 lbs.

Year	Team	Games	Pos.
1969	NO	N 14	DE
1970		12	DE
1971		14	DE
1972		14	DE
1973	NYJ	N 14	DT, DE
1974		9	DE, DT
1975		13	DE, DT
1977		14	DE
1978	NO	N	DE
10 yrs.	118 games		

Speedy Neal
NEAL, ROBERT
B. Aug. 26, 1962, Key West, FL
Miami (Florida) 6'2" 254 lbs.

Year	Team	Games	Pos.
1984	BUF	N 12	FB

Mike Nease
NEASE, MICHAEL
B. Oct. 30, 1961, Parrottsville, TN
Tennessee-Chattanooga 6'3" 272 lbs.

Year	Team	Games	Pos.
1987	PHI	N 2	G

Tommy Neck
NECK, THOMAS
B. Jan. 10, 1939, Marksville, LA
Louisiana State 5'11" 190 lbs.

Year	Team	Games	Pos.
1962	CHI	N 2	DB

Derrick Ned
NED, DERRICK
B. Jan. 5, 1969, Eunice, LA
Grambling State 6'1" 210 lbs.

Year	Team	Games	Pos.
1993	NO	N 14	RB
1994		16	RB
1995		12	RB
3 yrs.	42 games		

Joe Nedney
NEDNEY, JOSEPH THOMAS
B. Mar. 22, 1973, San Jose, CA
San Jose State 6'4" 205 lbs.

Year	Team	Games	Pos.
1996	MIA	N 16	K

Bobby Neely
NEELY, ROBERT LEE
B. Mar. 22, 1974, Atlanta, GA
Virginia 6'3" 255 lbs.

Year	Team	Games	Pos.
1996	CHI	N 11	TE

Ralph Neely
NEELY, RALPH EUGENE
B. Sep. 12, 1943, Little Rock, AR
Oklahoma 6'5" 261 lbs.

Year	Team	Games	Pos.
1965	DAL	N 14	OT
1966		14	OT
1967		14	OT
1968		14	OT
1969		12	OT
1970		14	G, OT
1971		7	OT
1972		13	OT
1973		14	OT
1974		14	OT
1975		14	OT
1976		14	OT
1977		14	OT
13 yrs.	172 games		

Bobby Neff
NEFF, ROBERT MILAM
B. Mar. 5, 1944, Hearne, TX
Stephen F. Austin 6'0" 182 lbs.

Year	Team	Games	Pos.
1966	MIA	A 14	DB
1967		14	DB
1968		5	DB
3 yrs.	33 games		

Fred Negus
NEGUS, FREDERICK
B. Nov. 7, 1923, Martins Ferry, OH
Wisconsin/Michigan/Wisconsin 6'1" 208 lbs.

Year	Team	Games	Pos.
1947	CHI	AA 12	C
1948		14	C
1949		12	C

Fred Negus continued

Year	Team	Games	Pos.
1950	CHIB	N 11	C
4 yrs.	49 games		

Renaldo Nehemiah
NEHEMIAH, RENALDO (Skeets)
B. Mar. 24, 1959, Newark, NJ
Maryland 6'1" 177 lbs.*

Year	Team	Games	Pos.
1982	SF	N 8	WR
1983		16	WR
1984		16	WR
3 yrs.	40 games		

John Neidert
NEIDERT, JOHN THOMAS
B. Jun. 18, 1946, Akron, OH
Louisville 6'2" 230 lbs.

Year	Team	Games	Pos.
1968	CIN	A 8	LB
1968	NY	A 13	LB
1969		14	LB
1970	CHI	N 3	LB
3 yrs.	38 games		

Billy Neighbors
NEIGHBORS, WILLIAM WESLEY
B. Feb. 4, 1940, Tuscaloosa, AL
Alabama 5'11" 244 lbs.

Year	Team	Games	Pos.
1962	BOS	A 14	G
1963		14	G
1964		14	G
1965		14	G
1966	MIA	A 14	G
1967		14	G
1968		14	G
1969		14	G
8 yrs.	112 games		

Kenny Neil
NEIL, KENNY
B. Jan. 8, 1959, Cincinnati, OH
Iowa State 6'4" 249 lbs.

Year	Team	Games	Pos.
1981	NYJ	N 16	DE, DT
1982		9	DE, DT
1983		16	DE
1987	HOU	N 1	DE
4 yrs.	42 games		

Bill Neill
NEILL, WILLIAM
B. Mar. 15, 1959, Norristown, PA
Pittsburgh 6'4" 252 lbs.

Year	Team	Games	Pos.
1981	NYG	N 16	DT
1982		7	NT
1983		1	NT
1984	GB	N 16	NT
4 yrs.	40 games		

Jim Neill
NEILL, JAMES
B. 1915
Texas Tech 6'1" 185 lbs.

Year	Team	Games	Pos.
1937	NYG	N 3	HB
1939	CHIC	N 1	HB
2 yrs.	4 games		

Steve Neils
NEILS, STEVEN LYNN
B. May 2, 1951, St. Peter, MN
Minnesota 6'2" 217 lbs.

Year	Team	Games	Pos.
1974	STL	N 14	LB
1975		14	LB
1976		7	LB
1977		14	LB
1978		16	LB
1979		9	LB
1980		14	LB
7 yrs.	88 games		

Mike Nelms
NELMS, MICHAEL
B. Apr. 8, 1955, Fort Worth, TX
Sam Houston State/Baylor 6'1" 185 lbs.

Year	Team		Games	Pos.
1980	WAS	N	16	S
1981			16	S
1982			9	S
1983			12	S
1984			16	S
5 yrs.		69 games		

Bill Nelsen
NELSEN, WILLIAM KEITH
B. Jan. 29, 1941, Los Angeles, CA
Southern California 6'0" 195 lbs.

Year	Team		Games	Pos.
1963	PIT	N	2	QB
1964			5	QB
1965			12	QB
1966			5	QB
1967			8	QB
1968	CLE	N	14	QB
1969			14	QB
1970			12	QB
1971			14	QB
1972			4	QB
10 yrs.		90 games		

Nelson
NELSON
None

Year	Team		Games	Pos.
1921	SYR	A	1	G

Nelson
NELSON
None

Year	Team		Games	Pos.
1926	PHI	A	1	G

Al Nelson
NELSON, ALBERT
B. Oct. 27, 1943, Cincinnati, OH
Cincinnati 5'11" 185 lbs.

Year	Team		Games	Pos.
1965	PHI	N	14	DB
1966			13	DB
1967			1	DB
1968			14	DB
1969			14	DB
1970			12	CB
1971			14	CB
1972			14	CB
1973			8	CB
9 yrs.		104 games		

Andy Nelson
NELSON, ANDREW VAUGHAN
B. May 27, 1933, Athens, GA
Memphis State 6'1" 180 lbs.

Year	Team		Games	Pos.
1957	BAL	N	12	DB
1958			12	DB
1959			12	DB
1960			12	DB
1961			14	DB
1962			14	DB
1963			13	DB
1964	NYG	N	14	DB
8 yrs.		103 games		

Benny Nelson
NELSON, BENJAMIN
B. 1942
Alabama 6'0" 185 lbs.

Year	Team		Games	Pos.
1964	HOU	A		DB

Bill Nelson
NELSON, WILLIAM HOWARD
B. Mar. 9, 1948, Berkeley, CA
Oregon State 6'7" 270 lbs.

Year	Team		Games	Pos.
1971	LA	N	6	DT

Bill Nelson *continued*

Year	Team		Games	Pos.
1972			7	DT
1973			13	DT
1974			14	DT
1975			8	DT
5 yrs.		48 games		

Bob Nelson
NELSON, ROBERT COLE
B. Jan. 30, 1920, Emberson, TX
D. Nov. 3, 1986, Granbury, TX
Baylor 6'1" 214 lbs.

Year	Team		Games	Pos.
1941	DET	N	9	C, T
1945			9	C
1946	LA	AA	10	C
1947			14	C
1948			14	C
1949			12	C
1950	BAL	N	3	C
7 yrs.		71 games		

Bob Nelson
NELSON, ROBERT LEE
B. Jun. 30, 1953, Stillwater, MN
Nebraska 6'4" 231 lbs.

Year	Team		Games	Pos.
1976	BUF	N	14	LB
1977			11	LB
1979	SF	N	1	LB
1980	OAK	N	9	LB
1982	LARI	N	9	LB
1983			16	LB
1984			12	LB
7 yrs.		72 games		

Bob Nelson
NELSON, ROBERT WILLIAM
B. Mar. 3, 1959, Baltimore, MD
Miami (Florida) 6'3" 265 lbs.

Year	Team		Games	Pos.
1986	TB	N	16	NT
1988	GB	N	14	NT
1989			16	NT
1990			14	NT
4 yrs.		60 games		

Chuck Nelson
NELSON, CHARLES LAVERNE
B. Feb. 23, 1960, Seattle, WA
Washington 5'11" 175 lbs.

Year	Team		Games	Pos.
1983	LARM	N	12	K
1984	BUF	N	7	K
1986	MIN	N	16	K
1987			12	K
1988			16	K
5 yrs.		63 games		

Darrell Nelson
NELSON, DARRELL
B. Oct. 27, 1961, Memphis, TN
Memphis State 6'2" 235 lbs.

Year	Team		Games	Pos.
1984	PIT	N	11	TE
1985			5	TE
2 yrs.		16 games		

Darrin Nelson
NELSON, DARRIN MILO
B. Jan. 2, 1959, Sacramento, CA
Stanford 5'9" 188 lbs.

Year	Team		Games	Pos.
1982	MIN	N	7	RB
1983			15	RB
1984			15	RB
1985			16	RB
1986			16	RB
1987			10	RB
1988			13	RB
1989			5	RB
1989	SD	N		RB
1990			14	RB
1991	MIN	N	16	RB

Darrin Nelson *continued*

Year	Team		Games	Pos.
1992			16	RB
11 yrs.		153 games		

David Nelson
NELSON, DAVID
B. Nov. 23, 1963, Miami, FL
Heidelberg 6'2" 230 lbs.

Year	Team		Games	Pos.
1984	MIN	N	2	RB

Dennis Nelson
NELSON, DENNIS RAY
B. Feb. 2, 1946, Kewanee, IL
Illinois State 6'5" 260 lbs.

Year	Team		Games	Pos.
1970	BAL	N	6	OT
1971			14	OT
1972			13	OT
1973			14	OT
1974			14	OT
1976	PHI	N	14	OT
1977			2	OT
7 yrs.		77 games		

Derrie Nelson
NELSON, DERALD LAWRENCE
B. Feb. 8, 1958, York, NE
Nebraska 6'2" 237 lbs.

Year	Team		Games	Pos.
1983	SD	N	15	LB
1984			6	LB
1985			16	LB
1986			11	LB
4 yrs.		48 games		

Don Nelson
NELSON, DONALD FRITZ
B. May 12, 1915, Moline, IL
Iowa 5'9" 205 lbs.

Year	Team		Games	Pos.
1937	BKN	N	11	G

Don Nelson
NELSON, DONALD RUSSELL
B. Feb. 10, 1903
D. Oct. 26, 1980, Larkspur, CA
Ohio Wesleyan 6'1" 210 lbs.

Year	Team		Games	Pos.
1926	HAM	N	2	C
1926	CAN	N	6	T
1 yr.		8 games		

Edmund Nelson
NELSON, EDMUND CLAU-VON
B. Apr. 30, 1960, Live Oak, FL
Auburn 6'3" 270 lbs.

Year	Team		Games	Pos.
1982	PIT	N	7	DT
1983			16	NT, DE
1984			16	NT, DE
1985			6	NT, DE
1986			16	DE, DT
1987			10	NT, DE
1988	NE	N	12	DE
7 yrs.		83 games		

Ev Nelson
NELSON, EVERT F. (Packie)
B. Feb. 18, 1907
D. Dec. 1, 1992, Gaithersburg, MD
Illinois 5'11" 205 lbs.

Year	Team		Games	Pos.
1929	CHIB	N	7	T

Frank Nelson
NELSON, DEWEY FRANK
B. May 28, 1923, Salt Lake City, UT
Utah 5'9" 167 lbs.

Year	Team		Games	Pos.
1948	BOS	N	12	B
1949	NYB	N	4	B
2 yrs.		16 games		

Herb Nelson
NELSON, HERBERT
B. Apr. 25, 1921, Hartford, CT
Pennsylvania 6'4" 219 lbs.

Year	Team		Games	Pos.
1946	BUF	AA	14	E
1947	BKN	AA	14	E
1948			4	T
3 yrs.		30 games		

Jimmy Nelson
NELSON, JAMES G.
B. 1919
Alabama 5'11" 180 lbs.

Year	Team		Games	Pos.
1946	MIA	AA	14	HB

Karl Nelson
NELSON, KARL
B. Jun. 14, 1960, De Kalb, IL
Iowa State 6'6" 285 lbs.

Year	Team		Games	Pos.
1984	NYG	N	16	OT
1985			16	OT
1986			16	OT
1988			9	OT
4 yrs.		57 games		

Lee Nelson
NELSON, LEE MARTIN
B. Jan. 30, 1954, Kissimmee, FL
Florida State 5'10" 185 lbs.

Year	Team		Games	Pos.
1976	STL	N	9	S
1977			10	CB
1978			16	CB
1979			16	CB
1980			16	CB
1981			15	CB
1982			8	S
1983			16	S
1984			16	S
1985			13	S
10 yrs.		135 games		

Mark Nelson
NELSON, MARK
B. Jun. 22, 1964
Iowa State/Bowling Green 6'4" 270 lbs.*

Year	Team		Games	Pos.
1987	KC	N	1	OT

Ralph Nelson
NELSON, RALPH
B. Jan. 23, 1954, Los Angeles, CA
none 6'2" 195 lbs.

Year	Team		Games	Pos.
1975	WAS	N	14	RB
1976	SEA	N	8	RB
2 yrs.		22 games		

Shane Nelson
NELSON, CURTIS SHANE
B. May 25, 1955, Mathis, TX
Baylor 6'1" 230 lbs.

Year	Team		Games	Pos.
1977	BUF	N	14	LB
1978			16	LB
1979			16	LB
1980			16	LB
1981			10	LB
1982			1	LB
6 yrs.		73 games		

Steve Nelson
NELSON, STEVEN LEE
B. Apr. 26, 1951, Farmington, MN
North Dakota State 6'2" 230 lbs.

Year	Team		Games	Pos.
1974	NE	N	14	LB
1975			14	LB
1976			10	LB
1977			13	LB
1978			14	LB
1979			15	LB

Steve Nelson continued

Year	Team		Games	Pos.
1980			16	LB
1981			12	LB
1982			9	LB
1983			8	LB
1984			16	LB
1985			15	LB
1986			10	LB
1987			11	LB

14 yrs. 177 games

Teddy Nelson
NELSON, THEODORE R., JR.
B. Jan. 1, 1965
Nevada-Las Vegas 5'10" 203 lbs.

Year	Team		Games	Pos.
1987	KC	N	3	S

Terry Nelson
NELSON, TERRY LOUIS
B. May 20, 1951, Arkadelphia, AR
Arkansas-Pine Bluff 6'2" 233 lbs.

Year	Team		Games	Pos.
1973	LA	N	1	TE
1974			10	TE
1975			14	TE
1976			14	TE
1977			14	TE
1978			13	TE
1979			16	TE
1980			4	TE

8 yrs. 86 games

Andy Nemecek
NEMECEK, ANDREW J.
B. May 6, 1896
D. May, 1984, Cleveland, OH
Ohio State 6'4" 210 lbs.

Year	Team		Games	Pos.
1923	COL	N	10	G, T, C
1924			8	C, G
1925			6	FB, G

3 yrs. 24 games

Jerry Nemecek
NEMECEK, JERALD
B. Jan. 1, 1907
D. May, 1987, Pittsford, NY
New York University 6'0" 185 lbs.

Year	Team		Games	Pos.
1931	BKN	N	9	E

Steve Nemeth
NEMETH, STEPHEN JOSEPH
B. Dec. 10, 1922, South Bend, IN
Notre Dame 5'10" 174 lbs.

Year	Team		Games	Pos.
1945	CLE	N	9	QB
1946	CHI	AA	13	QB
1947	BAL	AA	4	QB

3 yrs. 26 games

Ted Nemzek
NEMZEK, THEODORE C.
B. 1904, Minnesota
Moorhead State (Minnesota) 205 lbs.

Year	Team		Games	Pos.
1930	MIN	N	4	T

Carl Nery
NERY, CARL N.
B. Jun. 17, 1917, Lawrenceville, PA
Duquesne 6'0" 214 lbs.

Year	Team		Games	Pos.
1940	PIT	N	11	G
1941			10	G

2 yrs. 21 games

Ron Nery
NERY, RONALD D.
B. Dec. 30, 1935, New Kensington, PA
Kansas State 6'6" 236 lbs.

Year	Team		Games	Pos.
1960	LA	A		DE

Ron Nery continued

Year	Team		Games	Pos.
1961	SD	A	14	DE
1962			14	DE
1963	DEN	A	4	DE

4 yrs. 32 games

Dick Nesbitt
NESBITT, RICHARD
B. 1908
D. Sep. 8, 1953
Drake 6'0" 204 lbs.

Year	Team		Games	Pos.
1930	CHIB	N	8	FB, HB
1931			13	HB, FB
1932			14	HB
1933			4	HB
1933	CHIC	N	6	FB, HB
1934	BKN	N	9	FB

5 yrs. 54 games

Val Ness
NESS, VAL
None

Year	Team		Games	Pos.
1922	MIN	N	1	G

Al Nesser
NESSER, ALFRED (Nappy, Whitey)
B. Jun. 6, 1893, Columbus, OH
D. Mar. 11, 1967, Akron, OH
None 6'0" 195 lbs.

Year	Team		Games	Pos.
1920	AKR	A	9	E
1921			12	G, E
1922	AKR	N	9	G, E
1923			7	E, G
1924			6	G, E
1925			6	G
1925	CLE	N	7	G, E
1926	AKR	N	3	G
1926	CLE	A	4	G, E
1926	NYG	N	4	G, C
1927			13	G, T, C
1928			4	G, C
1931	CLE	N	9	E, T, G

10 yrs. 93 games

Charlie Nesser
NESSER, CHARLES
B. 1900
Deceased
None 6'2" 182 lbs.

Year	Team		Games	Pos.
1921	COL	A	9	HB, T, QB

Frank Nesser
NESSER, FRANK
B. Jun. 3, 1889, Columbus, OH
D. Jan. 1, 1953, Columbus, OH
None 6'1" 245 lbs.

Year	Team		Games	Pos.
1920	COL	A	5	FB, T
1921			9	FB, G, HB
1922	COL	N	8	G, FB
1925			6	FB, G
1926			6	T, G, HB, FB

5 yrs. 34 games

Fred Nesser
NESSER, FRED
B. Sep. 10, 1887, Columbus, OH
D. Jul. 2, 1967
None 6'3" 228 lbs.

Year	Team		Games	Pos.
1921	COL	A	8	T, E, HB, FB

John Nesser
NESSER, JOHN (The Wolf)
B. Apr. 25, 1876
Deceased
None 5'8" 195 lbs.

Year	Team		Games	Pos.
1921	COL	A	2	G, HB

Phil Nesser
NESSER, PHILIP
B. Dec. 10, 1880
Deceased
None 6'0" 225 lbs.

Year	Team		Games	Pos.
1920	COL	A	1	G
1921			5	G, T, HB

2 yrs. 6 games

Ted Nesser
NESSER, THEODORE, JR.
B. Apr. 5, 1883
Deceased
None 5'7" 230 lbs.

Year	Team		Games	Pos.
1920	COL	A	3	G, T, HB
1921			9	C

2 yrs. 12 games

Bill Netherton
NETHERTON, WILLIAM JACKSON
B. Mar. 2, 1898, Worthington, KY
D. Aug. 10, 1984, Louisville, KY
None

Year	Team		Games	Pos.
1921	LOU	A	1	E
1922	LOU	N	2	E

2 yrs. 3 games

Doug Nettles
NETTLES, GORDON DOUGLAS
B. Aug. 13, 1951, Panama City, FL
Vanderbilt 6'0" 179 lbs.

Year	Team		Games	Pos.
1974	BAL	N	13	CB
1975			13	CB
1977			14	CB
1978			16	CB
1979			15	CB
1980	NYG	N	2	CB

6 yrs. 73 games

Jim Nettles
NETTLES, JAMES A.
B. Feb. 15, 1942, Muncie, IN
Wisconsin 5'9" 177 lbs.

Year	Team		Games	Pos.
1965	PHI	N	14	DB
1966			14	DB
1967			12	DB
1968			14	CB
1969	LA	N	13	CB
1970			14	CB
1971			14	CB
1972			14	CB

8 yrs. 109 games

Keith Neubert
NEUBERT, KEITH ROBERT
B. Sep. 13, 1964, Fort Atkinson, WI
Nebraska 6'5" 250 lbs.

Year	Team		Games	Pos.
1988	NYJ	N	1	TE
1989			16	TE

2 yrs. 17 games

Rick Neuheisel
NEUHEISEL, RICHARD GERALD, JR.
B. Feb. 7, 1961, Madison, WI
UCLA 6'1" 190 lbs.

Year	Team		Games	Pos.
1987	SD	N	3	QB

Quentin Neujahr
NEUJAHR, QUENTIN
B. Jan. 30, 1971, Seward, NE
Kansas State 6'4" 285 lbs.

Year	Team		Games	Pos.
1996	BAL	N	5	C

Bob Neuman
NEUMAN, ROBERT JOHN
B. Jan. 18, 1912, Mendota, IL
D. Jan., 1984
Illinois Wesleyan 6'0" 198 lbs.

Year	Team		Games	Pos.
1934	CHIC	N	5	E
1935			11	E
1936			8	E

3 yrs. 24 games

Tom Neumann
NEUMANN, THOMAS
B. 1941
Wisconsin/Northern Michigan 5'11" 205 lbs.

Year	Team		Games	Pos.
1963	BOS	A	10	HB

Ernie Nevers
NEVERS, ERNEST ALONZO
B. Jun. 11, 1903, Willow River, MN
D. May 3, 1976, San Rafael, CA
Stanford 6'0" 204 lbs.

Year	Team		Games	Pos.
1926	DUL	N	13	FB
1927			9	FB
1929	CHIC	N	11	FB
1930			11	FB, HB
1931			9	FB, HB

5 yrs. 53 games

Elijah Nevett
NEVETT, ELIJAH
B. Apr. 28, 1944, Bessemer, AL
Clark (Georgia) 6'0" 185 lbs.

Year	Team		Games	Pos.
1967	NO	N	2	FL
1968			10	CB
1969			14	CB
1970			12	CB

4 yrs. 38 games

Tom Neville
NEVILLE, THOMAS LEE
B. Sep. 4, 1961, Great Falls, MT
Weber State/Fresno State 6'5" 306 lbs.

Year	Team		Games	Pos.
1986	GB	N	16	OT, G
1987			12	OT, G
1988			2	OT, G
1991	SF	N	12	G
1992	GB	N	8	G

5 yrs. 50 games

Tom Neville
NEVILLE, THOMAS OLIVER, JR.
B. Aug. 12, 1943, Montgomery, AL
Mississippi State 6'4" 252 lbs.

Year	Team		Games	Pos.
1965	BOS	A	14	OT
1966			14	OT
1967			14	OT
1968			14	OT
1969			14	OT
1970	BOS	N	13	OT
1971	NE	N	14	OT
1972			13	OT
1973			8	OT
1974			14	OT
1976			14	OT
1977			14	OT
1978	DEN	N	6	OT
1979	NYG	N	14	OT

14 yrs. 180 games

Steve Newall
NEWALL, STEPHEN EUGENE
B. Dec. 27, 1944, Springfield, IL
Long Beach State 6'1" 185 lbs.

Year	Team		Games	Pos.
1967	SD	A	7	OE

Year	Team	Games	Pos.

Bill Newashe
NEWASHE, WILLIAM (Chief)
B. 1890
Deceased
Carlisle 5'11" 200 lbs.

Year	Team		Games	Pos.
1923	OOR	N	5	T

Tom Newberry
NEWBERRY, TOM G.
B. Dec. 20, 1962, Onalaska, WI
Wisconsin-La Crosse 6'2" 279 lbs.

Year	Team		Games	Pos.
1986	LARM	N	16	G
1987			12	G
1988			16	G
1990			15	G
1991			16	C, G
1992			16	C, G
1993			9	G
1994			15	G, C
1995	PIT	N	16	G
9 yrs.	131 games			

Rick Newbill
NEWBILL, RICHARD ARTHUR
B. Feb. 8, 1968, Camden, NJ
Miami (Florida) 6'1" 240 lbs.

Year	Team		Games	Pos.
1990	MIN	N	2	LB
1990	SEA	N	1	LB
1991			1	LB
1992			7	LB
3 yrs.	11 games			

Robert Newhouse
NEWHOUSE, ROBERT FULTON
B. Jan. 9, 1950, Longview, TX
Houston 5'10" 210 lbs.

Year	Team		Games	Pos.
1972	DAL	N	14	RB
1973			14	RB
1974			14	RB
1975			14	RB
1976			14	RB
1977			14	RB
1978			13	RB
1979			14	RB
1980			16	RB
1981			16	FB
1982			9	RB
1983			16	RB
12 yrs.	168 games			

Bob Newland
NEWLAND, ROBERT VAUGHN
B. Oct. 27, 1948, Medford, OR
Oregon 6'2" 190 lbs.

Year	Team		Games	Pos.
1971	NO	N	14	WR
1972			14	WR
1973			14	WR
1974			14	WR
4 yrs.	56 games			

Howard Newland
NEWLAND, HOWARD
B. Mar., 1892
Deceased
None

Year	Team		Games	Pos.
1921	LOU	A	2	E

Anthony Newman
NEWMAN, ANTHONY Q.
B. Nov. 21, 1965, Bellingham, WA
Oregon 6'0" 199 lbs.

Year	Team		Games	Pos.
1988	LARM	N	16	S, CB
1989			15	CB
1990			16	S
1991			16	S
1992			16	S
1993			16	S
1994			16	S

Year	Team		Games	Pos.

Anthony Newman continued

Year	Team		Games	Pos.
1995	NO	N	13	S, CB
1996			16	S
9 yrs.	140 games			

Ed Newman
NEWMAN, EDWARD KENNETH
B. Jun. 4, 1951, Woodbury, NY
Florida Atlantic*/Duke 6'2" 255 lbs.

Year	Team		Games	Pos.
1973	MIA	N	11	G
1974			14	G
1975			14	G
1976			14	G
1977			14	G
1978			12	G
1979			16	G, OT
1980			16	G
1981			16	G
1982			8	G
1983			16	G
1984			16	G
12 yrs.	167 games			

Harry Newman
NEWMAN, HARRY
B. Jan. 24, 1897
D. Dec., 1973, Beachwood, OH
None 5'6" 150 lbs.

Year	Team		Games	Pos.
1924	AKR	N	6	G, T

Harry Newman
NEWMAN, HARRY L., SR.
B. Sep. 5, 1909, Detroit, MI
Michigan 5'8" 179 lbs.

Year	Team		Games	Pos.
1933	NYG	N	14	QB
1934			10	QB
1935			7	QB
3 yrs.	31 games			

Olin Newman
NEWMAN, OLIN B. (Obie)
B. 1900
D. Jun. 4, 1949
Carnegie-Mellon 6'2" 203 lbs.

Year	Team		Games	Pos.
1925	AKR	N	8	E
1926			7	HB, QB
1926	HAM	N	1	FB
2 yrs.	16 games			

Pat Newman
NEWMAN, EDWARD PATRICK
B. Sep. 10, 1968, Memphis, TN
Utah State 5'11" 189 lbs.

Year	Team		Games	Pos.
1991	NO	N	7	WR
1992			10	WR
1993			16	WR
1994	CLE	N	2	WR
4 yrs.	35 games			

Tim Newman
NEWMAN, TIM
B. Jun. 11, 1964, Charlotte, NC
Johnson C. Smith 6'0" 220 lbs.

Year	Team		Games	Pos.
1987	NYJ	N	1	RB

Don Newmeyer
NEWMEYER, DONALD
B. 1902
Deceased
California 6'2" 205 lbs.

Year	Team		Games	Pos.
1926	LA	N	10	T

Tony Newsom
NEWSOM, ANTHONY
B. Jul. 20, 1965, Jacksonville, FL
Stephen F. Austin 5'8" 175 lbs.

Year	Team		Games	Pos.
1987	HOU	N	5	CB

Year	Team		Games	Pos.

Billy Newsome
NEWSOME, WILLIAM RAY
B. Mar. 2, 1948, Jacksonville, TX
Grambling State 6'4" 251 lbs.

Year	Team		Games	Pos.
1970	BAL	N	14	DE
1971			14	DE
1972			14	DE
1973	NO	N	14	DE
1974			13	DE
1975	NYJ	N	14	DE
1976			2	DE
1977	CHI	N	14	DE
8 yrs.	99 games			

Craig Newsome
NEWSOME, CRAIG
B. Aug. 10, 1971, San Bernardino, CA
Arizona State 5'11" 188 lbs.

Year	Team		Games	Pos.
1995	GB	N	16	CB
1996			16	CB
2 yrs.	32 games			

Harry Newsome
NEWSOME, HARRY KENT, JR.
B. Jan. 25, 1963, Cheraw, SC
Wake Forest 6'0" 186 lbs.

Year	Team		Games	Pos.
1985	PIT	N	16	P
1986			16	P
1987			12	P
1988			16	P
1989			16	P
1990	MIN	N	16	P
1991			16	P
1992			16	P
1993			16	P
9 yrs.	140 games			

Ozzie Newsome
NEWSOME, OZZIE
B. Mar. 16, 1956, Muscle Shoals, AL
Alabama 6'2" 232 lbs.

Year	Team		Games	Pos.
1978	CLE	N	16	TE
1979			16	TE
1980			16	TE
1981			16	TE
1982			9	TE
1983			16	TE
1984			16	TE
1985			16	TE
1986			16	TE
1987			13	TE
1988			16	TE
1989			16	TE
1990			16	TE
13 yrs.	198 games			

Timmy Newsome
NEWSOME, TIMOTHY ARTHUR
B. May 17, 1958, Ahoskie, NC
Winston-Salem State 6'1" 235 lbs.

Year	Team		Games	Pos.
1980	DAL	N	16	FB
1981			15	FB
1982			9	RB
1983			16	RB
1984			15	RB
1985			14	RB
1986			16	RB
1987			11	FB
1988			9	RB
9 yrs.	121 games			

Vince Newsome
NEWSOME, VINCENT KARL
B. Jan. 22, 1961, Braintree, MA
Washington 6'1" 179 lbs.

Year	Team		Games	Pos.
1983	LARM	N	16	S
1984			16	S
1985			16	S
1986			16	S

Year	Team		Games	Pos.

Vince Newsome continued

Year	Team		Games	Pos.
1987			8	S
1988			6	S
1989			16	S
1990			16	S
1991	CLE	N	15	S
1992			16	S
10 yrs.	141 games			

Ark Newton
NEWTON, R.D.
B. 1902
Deceased
Florida 185 lbs.

Year	Team		Games	Pos.
1926	NEW	A	2	HB

Bob Newton
NEWTON, ROBERT LEE
B. Aug. 16, 1959, Cerritos, CA
Nebraska 6'4" 257 lbs.

Year	Team		Games	Pos.
1971	CHI	N	12	OT, G
1972			14	G
1973			13	G
1974			14	G
1975			6	G
1976	SEA	N	12	G
1977			13	G
1978			16	G
1979			11	G
1980			16	G
1981			15	G
11 yrs.	142 games			

Chuck Newton
NEWTON, CHARLES
B. May 28, 1917
D. Jun. 27, 1991, Myrtle Point, OR
Washington 6'0" 205 lbs.

Year	Team		Games	Pos.
1939	PHI	N	9	HB, FB
1940			3	HB
2 yrs.	12 games			

Nate Newton
NEWTON, NATHANIEL, JR.
B. Dec. 20, 1961, Orlando, FL
Florida A&M 6'3" 317 lbs.

Year	Team		Games	Pos.
1986	DAL	N	11	G
1987			11	G
1988			15	G
1989			16	G
1990			16	G
1991			14	G
1992			15	G
1993			16	G
1994			16	G
1995			16	G
1996			16	G
11 yrs.	162 games			

Tim Newton
NEWTON, TIMOTHY REGINALD
B. Mar. 23, 1963, Orlando, FL
Florida 6'0" 292 lbs.

Year	Team		Games	Pos.
1985	MIN	N	16	NT
1986			14	NT
1987			9	DT
1988			14	DT
1989			9	DT
1990	TB	N	14	NT
1991			16	NT
1993	KC	N	16	DT
8 yrs.	108 games			

Tom Newton
NEWTON, THOMAS RICHARD
B. Mar. 8, 1954, Carmel, CA
California 6'0" 210 lbs.

Year	Team		Games	Pos.
1977	NYJ	N	14	RB

Year	Team		Games	Pos.

Tom Newton *continued*

1978			16	RB
1979			16	FB
1980			16	FB
1981			16	FB
1982			9	RB
6 yrs.	87 games			

Armand Niccolai
NICCOLAI, ARMAND
B. Nov. 8, 1911, Dunlevy, PA
D. Dec. 2, 1988, Pittsburgh, PA
Duquesne 6'2" 226 lbs.

1934	PIT	N	12	T
1935			12	T, E
1936			11	T
1937			11	T
1938			11	T
1939			11	T, G
1940			11	T
1941			8	T
1942			11	T, B
9 yrs.	98 games			

Al Nichelini
NICHELINI, ALLEN JAMES
B. Nov. 23, 1909, St. Helena, CA
D. Jan. 3, 1992, Fresno, CA
St. Mary's (California) 6'2" 207 lbs.

1935	CHIC	N	11	HB
1936			11	HB
2 yrs.	22 games			

Calvin Nicholas
NICHOLAS, CALVIN LEWIS
B. Jun. 11, 1964, Baton Rouge, LA
Grambling State 6'4" 208 lbs.

| 1988 | SF | N | 7 | WR |

Bob Nicholes
NICHOLES, ROBERT
B. Jul. 9, 1899
D. Jul., 1971, Easley, SC
Oglethorpe 5'10" 205 lbs.

| 1926 | BKN | A | 1 | T |

Al Nichols
NICHOLS, ALLEN
B. Oct. 28, 1916
D. Jun., 1981
Temple 5'10" 205 lbs.

| 1945 | PIT | N | 1 | FB |

Bob Nichols
NICHOLS, ROBERT GORDON, JR.
B. Jul. 18, 1943, Los Angeles, CA
Stanford 6'3" 250 lbs.

1965	PIT	N	14	OT
1966	LA	N	13	OT
1967			14	OT
3 yrs.	41 games			

Bobby Nichols
NICHOLS, BOB
B. 1944
Boston University 6'2" 220 lbs.

1967	BOS	A	9	TE
1968			6	TE
2 yrs.	15 games			

Gerald Nichols
NICHOLS, GERALD W.
B. Feb. 10, 1964, St. Louis, MO
Florida State 6'2" 261 lbs.

| 1987 | NYJ | N | 13 | NT |

Gerald Nichols *continued*

1988			16	DT
1989			16	DT, DE
1990			15	DT, DE
1991	TB	N	16	DE, DT
1993	PHI	N	7	DT
1993	WAS	N	2	DT
6 yrs.	85 games			

Ham Nichols
NICHOLS, HAMILTON JAMES, JR.
B. Oct. 18, 1924, Houston, TX
Rice 5'11" 209 lbs.

1947	CHIC	N	11	G
1948			12	G
1949			11	G
1951	GB	N	9	C
4 yrs.	43 games			

John Nichols
NICHOLS, JOHN H.
B. Jul. 30, 1904
D. Jun., 1978, Cleveland, OH
Ohio State 6'0" 200 lbs.

| 1926 | CAN | N | 13 | G, T |

Mark Nichols
NICHOLS, MARK R.
B. Oct. 23, 1956, Columbus, OH
Colorado State 6'3" 225 lbs.

| 1978 | SF | N | 15 | LB |

Mark Nichols
NICHOLS, MARK STEPHEN
B. Oct. 29, 1959, Bakersfield, CA
San Jose State 6'2" 210 lbs.

1981	DET	N	12	WR
1982			7	WR
1983			16	WR
1984			15	WR
1985			14	WR
1987			12	WR
6 yrs.	76 games			

Mike Nichols
NICHOLS, MIKE
B. Jul. 29, 1938, College Heights, AR
Arkansas-Pine Bluff 6'3" 225 lbs.

1960	DEN	A		C
1961			14	C
2 yrs.	14 games			

Ralph Nichols
NICHOLS, RALPH E.
B. Aug. 2, 1899
Kansas State 5'9" 190 lbs.

| 1926 | HAR | N | 10 | T, G |

Ricky Nichols
NICHOLS, RICKY ANTONIO
B. Jul. 27, 1962, Norfolk, VA
East Carolina 5'10" 176 lbs.

| 1985 | IND | N | 3 | WR |

Robbie Nichols
NICHOLS, ROBBIE
B. Nov. 17, 1946, Cleveland, OH
Tulsa 6'3" 220 lbs.

1970	BAL	N	14	LB
1971			4	LB
2 yrs.	18 games			

Sid Nichols
NICHOLS, SIDNEY W.

Sid Nichols *continued*
B. Apr. 15, 1895
D. Mar. 23, 1971, Paso Robles, CA
Illinois 5'7" 177 lbs.

1920	RI	A	6	QB, HB
1921			6	QB, HB
2 yrs.	12 games			

Calvin Nicholson
NICHOLSON, CALVIN T.
B. Jul. 9, 1967, Los Angeles, CA
Oregon State 5'9" 183 lbs.

1989	NO	N	1	CB
1991			8	CB
2 yrs.	9 games			

Frank Nicholson
NICHOLSON, FRANK
B. Mar. 6, 1961
Delaware State 6'2" 205 lbs.

| 1987 | NYG | N | 3 | LB |

Jim Nicholson
NICHOLSON, JAMES BURTON, JR.
B. Feb. 28, 1949, Honolulu, HI
Michigan State 6'6" 269 lbs.

1974	KC	N	13	OT
1975			12	OT
1976			14	OT
1977			12	OT
1978			6	OT
1979			15	OT
6 yrs.	72 games			

Elbie Nickel
NICKEL, ELBERT EVERETT
B. Dec. 28, 1922, Fullerton, KY
Cincinnati 6'1" 196 lbs.

1947	PIT	N	11	E
1948			12	E
1949			12	E
1950			12	E
1951			12	E
1952			12	E
1953			12	E
1954			12	E
1955			12	E
1956			12	E
1957			12	E
11 yrs.	131 games			

Hardy Nickerson
NICKERSON, HARDY OTTO
B. Sep. 1, 1965, Los Angeles, CA
California 6'2" 224 lbs.

1987	PIT	N	12	LB
1988			15	LB
1989			10	LB
1990			16	LB
1991			16	LB
1992			15	LB
1993	TB	N	16	LB
1994			14	LB
1995			16	LB
1996			16	LB
10 yrs.	146 games			

Ed Nickla
NICKLA, EDWARD
B. Aug. 11, 1933, New York, NY
Tennessee/Maryland 6'3" 240 lbs.

| 1959 | CHIB | N | 12 | T |

Pete Nicklas
NICKLAS, PETER L.
B. 1940

Pete Nicklas *continued*
Baylor 6'4" 240 lbs.

| 1962 | OAK | A | 14 | OT |

George Nicksich
NICKSICH, GEORGE
B. May 5, 1928
D. Jan., 1985
St. Bonaventure 6'0" 225 lbs.

| 1950 | PIT | N | 12 | G |

Scott Nicolas
NICOLAS, SCOTT STEPHEN
B. Aug. 7, 1960, Wichita Falls, TX
Miami (Florida) 6'3" 226 lbs.

1982	CLE	N	9	LB
1983			16	LB
1984			16	LB
1985			16	LB
1986			16	LB
1987	MIA	N	12	LB
6 yrs.	85 games			

Bruno Niedziela
NIEDZIELA, BRUNO
B. Apr. 12, 1923, Chicago, IL
Iowa 6'2" 225 lbs.

| 1947 | CHI | AA | 12 | T |

Frank Niehaus
NIEHAUS, FRANCIS W. (Fanny)
B. Mar. 16, 1902
D. Mar., 1985, Wadsworth, OH
Washington & Jefferson 6'0" 170 lbs.

1925	AKR	N	7	HB
1926	POT	N	4	HB
2 yrs.	11 games			

Ralph Niehaus
NIEHAUS, RALPH (Biff)
B. 1916
Dayton 6'4" 220 lbs.

| 1939 | CLE | N | 5 | T |

Steve Niehaus
NIEHAUS, STEVE
B. Sep. 25, 1954, Cincinnati, OH
Notre Dame 6'4" 263 lbs.

1976	SEA	N	14	DT
1977			8	DT
1978			14	DT
1979	MIN	N	3	DT
4 yrs.	39 games			

Rob Niehoff
NIEHOFF, ROB
B. May 9, 1964
Cincinnati 6'2" 205 lbs.

| 1987 | CIN | N | 3 | S |

Gifford Nielsen
NIELSEN, GIFFORD
B. Oct. 25, 1954, Provo, UT
Brigham Young 6'4" 205 lbs.

1978	HOU	N	2	QB
1979			16	QB
1980			15	QB
1981			4	QB
1982			9	QB
1983			7	QB
6 yrs.	53 games			

Nielson
NIELSON
None

| 1924 | ROC | N | 1 | HB |

Year	Team	Games	Pos.

Hans Nielson
NIELSON, HANS J.
B. Nov. 18, 1952, Vejle, Denmark
Michigan State 5'11" 165 lbs.

1981	CHI	N	3	K

Walt Nielson
NIELSON, WALTER RING
B. 1917
Arizona 6'3" 220 lbs.

1940	NYG	N	8	HB

Wally Niemann
NIEMANN, WALTER A.
B. Apr. 21, 1894
D. Dec., 1967, Powers, MI
Michigan 5'11" 180 lbs.

1922	GB	N	8	C
1923			9	C
1924			5	C

3 yrs.   22 games

Laurie Niemi
NIEMI, LAURIE JACK (Finn)
B. Mar. 19, 1925, Red Lodge, MT
D. Feb. 19, 1968, Spokane, WA
Washington State 6'1" 251 lbs.

1949	WAS	N	12	T
1950			8	T
1951			12	T
1952			12	T
1953			12	T

5 yrs.   56 games

John Nies
NIES, JOHN RICHARD
B. Feb. 13, 1964, Jersey City, NJ
Arizona 6'2" 199 lbs.

1990	BUF	N	4	P, K

Nick Nighswander
NIGHSWANDER, NICK
B. Nov. 3, 1952
Morehead State 6'0" 232 lbs.

1974	BUF	N	7	C

John Niland
NILAND, JOHN HUGH
B. Feb. 29, 1944, Quincy, MA
Iowa 6'4" 247 lbs.

1966	DAL	N	13	G
1967			14	G
1968			14	G
1969			14	G
1970			14	G
1971			14	G
1972			14	G
1973			13	G
1974			14	G
1975	PHI	N	14	G

10 yrs.   138 games

Jerry Niles
NILES, GERALD M.
B. 1920
Deceased
Iowa 6'1" 195 lbs.

1947	NYG	N	4	HB

Reed Nilsen
NILSEN, REED ELFIN
B. Jan. 31, 1921, Provo, UT
Brigham Young 6'0" 230 lbs.

1947	DET	N	2	C

Year	Team	Games	Pos.

Jim Ninowski
NINOWSKI, JAMES
B. Mar. 26, 1936, Detroit, MI
Michigan State 6'1" 206 lbs.

1958	CLE	N	4	QB
1959			2	QB
1960	DET	N	11	QB
1961			13	QB
1962	CLE	N	7	QB
1963			4	QB
1964			3	QB
1965			6	QB
1966			14	QB
1967	WAS	N	14	QB
1968			7	QB
1969	NO	N	4	QB

12 yrs.   89 games

Maury Nipp
NIPP, MAURICE
B. Mar. 31, 1930, Yankton, SD
Loyola (California) 6'0" 219 lbs.

1952	PHI	N	10	G
1953			12	G
1956			3	G

3 yrs.   25 games

Dave Nisbit
NISBIT, DAVID M.
B. Aug. 29, 1910
D. Dec., 1976, Seattle, WA
Washington 6'1" 180 lbs.

1933	CHIC	N	7	E

Jack Nisby
NISBY, JOHN
B. Sep. 9, 1936, San Francisco, CA
Pacific (Oregon) 6'1" 235 lbs.

1957	PIT	N	11	G
1958			12	G
1959			12	G
1960			12	G
1961			13	G
1962	WAS	N	14	G
1963			14	G
1964			14	G

8 yrs.   102 games

Ray Nitschke
NITSCHKE, RAYMOND ERNEST
B. Dec. 29, 1936, Elmwood Park, IL
Illinois 6'3" 235 lbs.

1958	GB	N	12	LB
1959			12	LB
1960			12	LB
1961			12	LB
1962			14	LB
1963			12	LB
1964			14	LB
1965			12	LB
1966			14	LB
1967			14	LB
1968			14	LB
1969			14	LB
1970			14	LB
1971			14	LB
1972			11	LB

15 yrs.   195 games

Bjorn Nittmo
NITTMO, BJORN ARNE
B. Jul. 26, 1966, Lund, Sweden
Appalachian State 5'11" 185 lbs.

1989	NYG	N	6	K

Doyle Nix
NIX, DOYLE E.
B. May 30, 1933, Dallas, TX

Year	Team	Games	Pos.

Doyle Nix continued
Southern Methodist 6'1" 191 lbs.

1955	GB	N	12	DB
1958	WAS	N	11	DB
1959			8	DB
1960	LA	A		DB
1961	DAL	A	11	DB

5 yrs.   42 games

Emery Nix
NIX, KENNETH EMERY
B. Dec. 1, 1919, Chillicothe, TX
Texas Christian 5'11" 180 lbs.

1943	NYG	N	10	HB
1946			4	HB

2 yrs.   14 games

George Nix
NIX, GEORGE (Chief)
B. Mar. 18, 1895, Alaska
D. Oct. 10, 1978, Tacoma, WA
Haskell 5'11" 195 lbs.

1926	BUF	N	2	G

Jack Nix
NIX, JACK
B. 1928
Southern California 6'2" 200 lbs.

1950	SF	N	9	E

Kent Nix
NIX, KENT
B. Mar. 12, 1944, Corpus Christi, TX
Texas Christian 6'1" 195 lbs.

1967	PIT	N	12	QB
1968			8	QB
1969			4	QB
1970	CHI	N	1	QB
1971			8	QB
1972	HOU	N	12	QB

6 yrs.   45 games

Roosevelt Nix
NIX, ROOSEVELT
B. Apr. 17, 1967, Toledo, OH
Central State (Ohio) 6'6" 292 lbs.

1992	CIN	N	6	DE
1993			10	DE
1994	MIN	N	2	DE

3 yrs.   18 games

Fred Nixon
NIXON, FREDERICK LENAR
B. Sep. 22, 1958, Camilla, GA
Oklahoma 5'11" 191 lbs.

1980	GB	N	15	WR
1981			8	WR

2 yrs.   23 games

Jeff Nixon
NIXON, JEFFRY ALLEN
B. Oct. 13, 1956, Fursten Feldbruck,
Germany
Richmond 6'3" 190 lbs.

1979	BUF	N	16	S
1980			7	S
1981			13	S
1982			7	S

4 yrs.   43 games

Mike Nixon
NICKSICK, MICHAEL REGIS
B. Nov. 12, 1911, Masontown, PA
Pittsburgh 5'11" 181 lbs.

1935	PIT	N	3	HB
1942	BKN	N	3	HB

2 yrs.   6 games

Year	Team	Games	Pos.

Tory Nixon
NIXON, TORRAN BLAKE
B. Feb. 24, 1962, Eugene, OR
San Diego State 5'11" 186 lbs.

1985	SF	N	16	CB
1986			16	CB
1987			12	CB
1988			6	CB

4 yrs.   50 games

Bob Niziolek
NIZIOLEK, ROBERT CRAIG
B. Jun. 30, 1958, Chicago, IL
Colorado 6'4" 220 lbs.

1981	DET	N	4	TE

Leo Nobile
NOBILE, LEO A.
B. Sep. 22, 1922, Ambridge, PA
Penn State 5'10" 213 lbs.

1947	WAS	N	9	G
1948	PIT	N	12	G
1949			12	G

3 yrs.   33 games

Tommy Nobis
NOBIS, THOMAS HENRY, JR.
B. Sep. 20, 1943, San Antonio, TX
Texas 6'2" 237 lbs.

1966	ATL	N	14	LB
1967			14	LB
1968			14	LB
1969			5	LB
1970			14	LB
1971			4	LB
1972			14	LB
1973			14	LB
1974			14	LB
1975			13	LB
1976			13	LB

11 yrs.   133 games

Brian Noble
NOBLE, BRIAN DAVID
B. Sep. 6, 1962, Anaheim, CA
Arizona State 6'3" 250 lbs.

1985	GB	N	16	LB
1986			16	LB
1987			12	LB
1988			16	LB
1989			16	LB
1990			14	LB
1991			16	LB
1992			13	LB
1993			2	LB

9 yrs.   117 games

Dave Noble
NOBLE, DAVID GORDON (Big Moose)
B. Jul. 29, 1900
D. Jan. 24, 1983, Omaha, NE
Nebraska 6'2" 195 lbs.

1924	CLE	N	9	HB, FB
1925			13	HB
1926	CLE	A	5	HB, FB

3 yrs.   27 games

Dick Noble
NOBLE, RICHARD B.
B. Dec. 4, 1902
D. May 14, 1973, Milford, CT
Trinity (Connecticut) 5'11" 178 lbs.

1926	HAR	N	1	G

Don Noble
NOBLE, DON

Year	Team	Games	Pos.

Don Noble continued
B. Oct. 11, 1965
California 6'2" 253 lbs.

Year	Team		Games	Pos.
1987	LARM	N	2	TE

James Noble
NOBLE, JAMES
B. Aug. 14, 1963, Jacksonville, TX
Stephen F. Austin 6'0" 193 lbs.

1986	WAS	N	6	WR
1987	IND	N	3	WR
2 yrs.	9 games			

Jim Noble
NOBLE, JAMES E.
B. Oct. 10, 1901
D. Sep., 1959
Syracuse 6'1" 190 lbs.

| 1925 | BUF | N | 9 | E |

Mike Noble
NOBLE, MICHAEL F.
B. Oct. 31, 1963
Stanford 6'4" 220 lbs.

| 1987 | LARI | N | 1 | LB |

John Nocera
NOCERA, JOHN STANLEY
B. May 4, 1934, Youngstown, OH
D. May 17, 1981, Youngstown, OH
Iowa 6'1" 220 lbs.

1959	PHI	N	12	LB
1960			10	LB
1961			14	LB
1962			14	LB
1963	DEN	A	9	LB
5 yrs.	59 games			

George Nock
NOCK, GEORGE VERDELL
B. Mar. 4, 1946, Baltimore, MD
Morgan State 5'10" 200 lbs.

1969	NY	A	2	RB
1970	NYJ		14	RB
1971			14	RB
1972	WAS	N	7	RB
4 yrs.	37 games			

Terry Nofsinger
NOFSINGER, WILLIAM
B. Jul. 13, 1938, Salt Lake City, UT
Utah 6'4" 209 lbs.

1961	PIT	N	5	QB
1962			1	QB
1963			2	QB
1964			1	QB
1965	STL	N	1	QB
1966			7	QB
1967	ATL	N	7	QB
7 yrs.	24 games			

Al Noga
NOGA, ALAPATI
B. Sep. 16, 1965, American Samoa
Hawaii 6'1" 261 lbs.

1988	MIN	N	9	NT
1989			16	DT
1990			16	DE
1991			16	DE
1992			16	DE
1993	WAS	N	16	DE
1994	IND	N	4	DE
7 yrs.	93 games			

Niko Noga
NOGA, FALANIKO

Niko Noga continued
B. Mar. 2, 1962, American Samoa
Hawaii 6'1" 230 lbs.

Year	Team		Games	Pos.
1984	STL	N	16	LB
1985			16	LB
1986			16	LB
1987			12	LB
1988	PHX	N	16	LB
1989	DET	N	14	LB
1990			16	LB
1991			16	LB
8 yrs.	122 games			

Pete Noga
NOGA, PETELO
B. Jun. 24, 1964
Hawaii 6'0" 212 lbs.

| 1987 | STL | N | 3 | LB |

Dick Nolan
NOLAN, RICHARD CHARLES
B. Mar. 26, 1932, Pittsburgh, PA
Maryland 6'1" 185 lbs.

1954	NYG	N	12	DB
1955			10	DB
1956			11	DB
1957			11	DB
1958	CHIC	N	12	DB
1959	NYG	N	12	DB
1960			10	DB
1961			9	DB
1962	DAL	N	11	DB
9 yrs.	99 games			

Earl Nolan
NOLAN, MICHAEL EARLE
B. Mar. 8, 1914
D. Mar. 23, 1981, Long Beach, CA
Arizona 6'1" 205 lbs.

1937	CHIC	N	8	T
1938			4	T
2 yrs.	12 games			

Jack Nolan
NOLAN, JOHN E.
B. Jul. 10, 1900
D. Oct. 21, 1971, San Diego, CA
Santa Clara 5'10" 185 lbs.

| 1926 | LA | N | 10 | G |

John Nolan
NOLAN, JOHN JOSEPH, JR. (Big John)
B. Feb. 26, 1926, Glens Falls, NY
Holy Cross/Penn State 6'2" 232 lbs.

1948	BOS	N	12	T
1949	NYB	N	12	T
1950	NYY	N	12	T
3 yrs.	36 games			

Don Nolander
NOLANDER, DONALD A.
B. Sep. 21, 1921, Minneapolis, MN
Minnesota 6'1" 210 lbs.

| 1946 | LA | AA | 11 | C |

Chuck Noll
NOLL, CHARLES HENRY
B. Jan. 5, 1932, Cleveland, OH
Dayton 6'1" 218 lbs.

1953	CLE	N	12	G
1954			12	G
1955			12	G
1956			12	G
1957			5	G
1958			12	G
1959			12	G
7 yrs.	77 games			

Ray Nolting
NOLTING, RAYMOND A.
B. Nov. 8, 1913, Cincinnati, OH
Cincinnati 5'11" 186 lbs.

Year	Team		Games	Pos.
1936	CHIB	N	10	HB
1937			11	HB
1938			11	HB
1939			11	HB
1940			11	HB
1941			9	HB
1942			11	HB
1943			7	HB
8 yrs.	81 games			

Leo Nomellini
NOMELLINI, LEO JOE (The Lion)
B. Aug. 13, 1926, Lucca, Italy
Minnesota 6'3" 259 lbs.

1950	SF	N	12	T
1951			12	T
1952			12	T
1953			12	T
1954			12	T
1955			12	T
1956			12	T
1957			12	T
1958			12	T
1959			12	T
1960			12	T
1961			14	DT
1962			14	DT
1963			14	DT
14 yrs.	174 games			

Tom Nomina
NOMINA, THOMAS JOHN
B. Dec. 27, 1941, Delphos, OH
Miami (Ohio) 6'5" 257 lbs.

1963	DEN	A	14	OT
1964			11	G
1965			12	G
1966	MIA	A	11	DT
1967			5	DT
1968			14	DT
6 yrs.	67 games			

Ike Nonnemaker
NONENMACHER, CLARENCE
B. 1901, Ohio
Deceased
None 5'8" 172 lbs.

| 1926 | COL | N | 6 | E, QB, HB |

Danny Noonan
NOONAN, DANIEL NICHOLAS
B. Jul. 14, 1965, Lincoln, NE
Nebraska 6'4" 270 lbs.

1987	DAL	N	11	DT
1988			16	DT
1989			7	DT
1990			16	DT
1991			15	DT, DE
1992	GB	N	6	NT
6 yrs.	73 games			

Jerry Noonan
NOONAN, GERALD
B. Oct. 13, 1898
D. Nov., 1967, San Francisco, CA
Fordham 6'1" 189 lbs.

1921	ROC	A	6	QB, HB, E
1921	NY	A	1	QB
1924	ROC	N	5	HB, FB, QB
2 yrs.	12 games			

Karl Noonan
NOONAN, KARL PAUL

Karl Noonan continued
B. Feb. 17, 1944, Dubuque, IA
Iowa 6'3" 193 lbs.

Year	Team		Games	Pos.
1966	MIA	A	14	FL, SE
1967			14	OE
1968			14	OE
1969			14	WR
1970	MIA	N	14	WR
1971			14	WR
6 yrs.	84 games			

John Noppenberg
NOPPENBERG, JOHN
B. Sep. 8, 1917, Wallace, MI
Miami (Florida) 6'0" 196 lbs.

1940	PIT	N	9	E, DB
1941			4	HB, DB
1941	DET	N	3	HB, DB
2 yrs.	16 games			

John Norbeck
NORBECK, JOHN W.
B. Jul. 25, 1898, Minneapolis, MN
D. Oct. 23, 1984, Santa Ana, CA
None 165 lbs.

| 1921 | MIN | A | | G, QB |

Hank Norberg
NORBERG, HENRY F., JR.
B. 1919
Stanford 6'2" 225 lbs.

1946	SF	AA	14	E
1947			11	E
1948	CHIB	N	10	E
3 yrs.	35 games			

John Norby
NORBY, JOHN
B. 1911, Rupert, ID
Idaho 6'0" 195 lbs.

1934	NYG	N	3	HB
1934	PHI	N	2	HB
1934	C-S	N	2	HB
1935	BKN	N	7	HB, FB
2 yrs.	14 games			

Keith Nord
NORD, KEITH
B. Mar. 13, 1957, Minneapolis, MN
St. Cloud State 6'0" 196 lbs.

1979	MIN	N	16	S
1980			16	S
1981			16	S
1982			9	S
1983			3	S
1985			16	S
6 yrs.	76 games			

Fred Nordgren
NORDGREN, FRED MARVIN
B. Dec. 11, 1959, Hillsboro, OR
Portland State 6'4" 240 lbs.

| 1987 | TB | N | 3 | NT |

Mark Nordquist
NORDQUIST, MARK ALLAN
B. Nov. 3, 1945, Long Beach, CA
Pacific 6'4" 245 lbs.

1968	PHI	N	14	OT
1969			14	OT
1970			14	C, G
1971			14	C
1972			14	G
1973			14	G
1974			12	G
1975	CHI	N	14	G

Year	Team	Games	Pos.

Mark Nordquist *continued*

Year	Team	Games	Pos.
1976		1	G
9 yrs.	111 games		

Harry Nordstrom
NORDSTROM, HARRY W. (Swede, Tiny)
B. Oct. 11, 1896
D. Feb. 13, 1963
Trinity (Connecticut) 6'2" 238 lbs.

Year	Team	Games	Pos.
1925	NYG	N	3	G, T
1926	BKN	N	3	G, T
2 yrs.	6 games		

Al Norgard
NORGARD, ALVAR A.
B. Nov. 3, 1907, Fort Bragg, CA
D. Nov. 20, 1975, Aptos, CA
Stanford 6'1" 194 lbs.

Year	Team	Games	Pos.
1934	GB	N	11	E

Erik Norgard
NORGARD, ERIK CHRISTIAN
B. Nov. 4, 1965, Bellevue, WA
Colorado 6'1" 278 lbs.

Year	Team	Games	Pos.
1990	HOU	N	16	C, G
1992		15	C, G
1993		16	C, G
1994		16	G, C
1995		12	G, C
1996		13	G
6 yrs.	88 games		

Reino Nori
NORI, REINO O.
B. Feb. 26, 1913, De Kalb, IL
D. Oct. 8, 1988, De Kalb, IL
Northern Illinois 5'8" 167 lbs.

Year	Team	Games	Pos.
1937	BKN	N	6	QB
1938	CHIB	N	1	QB
2 yrs.	7 games		

Ben Norman
NORMAN, BEN L.
B. Dec. 16, 1955, Elkin, NC
Colorado State 6'0" 212 lbs.

Year	Team	Games	Pos.
1980	DEN	N	3	RB

Bob Norman
NORMAN, ROBERT
B. Apr. 23, 1919
D. Apr., 1982, Marion, IL
None 6'1" 185 lbs.

Year	Team	Games	Pos.
1945	CHIC	N	1	C

Chris Norman
NORMAN, CHRIS COOPER
B. May 25, 1962, Albany, GA
South Carolina 6'2" 198 lbs.

Year	Team	Games	Pos.
1984	DEN	N	16	P
1985		16	P
1986		6	P
3 yrs.	38 games		

Dick Norman
NORMAN, RICHARD M.
B. Sep. 14, 1938, Downey, CA
Stanford 6'3" 210 lbs.

Year	Team	Games	Pos.
1961	CHI	N	3	QB

Jim Norman
NORMAN, JAMES
B. 1934
none 6'2" 248 lbs.

Year	Team	Games	Pos.
1955	WAS	N	7	T

Joe Norman
NORMAN, JOSEPH D.
B. Oct. 15, 1956, Millersburg, OH
Indiana 6'1" 220 lbs.

Year	Team	Games	Pos.
1979	SEA	N	15	LB
1980		16	LB
1981		8	LB
1983		11	LB
4 yrs.	50 games		

Pettis Norman
NORMAN, PETTIS BURCH
B. Jan. 1, 1940, Lincolnton, GA
Johnson C. Smith 6'3" 220 lbs.

Year	Team	Games	Pos.
1962	DAL	N	14	OE
1963		14	OE
1964		14	OE
1965		14	OE
1966		14	TE
1967		14	TE
1968		13	TE
1969		10	TE
1970		14	TE
1971	SD	N	14	TE
1972		13	TE
1973		14	TE
12 yrs.	162 games		

Tim Norman
NORMAN, TIMOTHY SCOTT
B. Jul. 10, 1959, Winfield, IL
Illinois 6'6" 273 lbs.

Year	Team	Games	Pos.
1983	CHI	N	1	G

Tony Norman
NORMAN, ANTHONY
B. Jan. 27, 1955, Atlanta, GA
Iowa State 6'5" 270 lbs.

Year	Team	Games	Pos.
1987	MIN	N	2	DE

Will Norman
NORMAN, WILLARD (Toad)
B. Sep. 22, 1903
D. Jul., 1964
Washington & Jefferson 6'0" 175 lbs.

Year	Team	Games	Pos.
1928	POT		9	HB, FB

David Norrie
NORRIE, DAVID DOHERTY
B. Nov. 30, 1963, Boston, MA
UCLA 6'4" 220 lbs.

Year	Team	Games	Pos.
1987	NYJ	N	2	QB

Hal Norris
NORRIS, HAROLD
B. Nov. 4, 1931, Baton Rouge, LA
California 5'11" 194 lbs.

Year	Team	Games	Pos.
1955	WAS	N	12	HB
1956		1	HB
2 yrs.	13 games		

Jack Norris
NORRIS, JOHN
B. Aug. 16, 1907
D. Nov., 1979, Newburg, MD
Western Maryland/Maryland 6'3" 185 lbs.

Year	Team	Games	Pos.
1932	SI	N	1	E

Jerome Norris
NORRIS, JEROME
B. Jan. 31, 1964
Furman 6'0" 187 lbs.

Year	Team	Games	Pos.
1987	ATL	N	3	S

Jim Norris
NORRIS, JAMES
B. 1940
Houston 6'4" 235 lbs.

Year	Team	Games	Pos.
1962	OAK	A	7	OT
1963		14	DT
1964		1	DT
3 yrs.	22 games		

Jimmy Norris
NORRIS, JIMMY
B. Aug. 12, 1965
Upsala 5'11" 188 lbs.

Year	Team	Games	Pos.
1987	NYG	N	3	CB

Jon Norris
NORRIS, JONATHAN
B. Nov. 1, 1962, Wales
American International 6'3" 260 lbs.

Year	Team	Games	Pos.
1987	CHI	N	3	DE

Ulysses Norris
NORRIS, ULYSSES, JR.
B. Jan. 15, 1957, Monticello, GA
Georgia 6'4" 230 lbs.

Year	Team	Games	Pos.
1979	DET	N	16	TE
1980		16	TE
1981		12	TE
1982		9	TE
1983		15	TE
1984	BUF	N	14	TE
1985		2	TE
7 yrs.	84 games		

Mike Norseth
NORSETH, MICHAEL ADAM
B. Aug. 22, 1964, Hollywood, CA
Kansas 6'2" 200 lbs.

Year	Team	Games	Pos.
1988	CIN	N	1	QB

Jim North
NORTH, JAMES
B. Aug. 11, 1919, Tukwila, WA
Central Washington 6'3" 235 lbs.

Year	Team	Games	Pos.
1944	WAS	N	7	T

John North
NORTH, JOHN PUCKETT
B. Jun. 17, 1921, Old Hickory, TN
Vanderbilt 6'2" 179 lbs.

Year	Team	Games	Pos.
1948	BAL	AA	14	E
1949		11	E
1950	BAL	N	5	E
3 yrs.	30 games		

Gabe Northern
NORTHERN, GABRIEL O'KARA
B. Jun. 8, 1974, Baton Rouge, LA
Louisiana State 6'2" 240 lbs.

Year	Team	Games	Pos.
1996	BUF	N	16	DE

Don Norton
NORTON, DONALD
B. Mar. 13, 1938, Iowa City, IA
Iowa 6'1" 190 lbs.

Year	Team	Games	Pos.
1960	LA	A	14	OE
1961	SD	A	14	OE
1962		14	OE
1963		7	OE
1964		14	OE
1965		14	OE
1966		14	OE
7 yrs.	91 games		

Jerry Norton
NORTON, JERRY R.
B. May 16, 1930, Dallas, TX
Southern Methodist 5'11" 195 lbs.

Year	Team	Games	Pos.
1954	PHI	N	12	HB, DB
1955		12	HB, DB
1956		6	DB
1957		12	HB, DB, P
1958		9	DB
1959	CHIC	N	12	HB, DB, P
1960	STL	N	12	HB, DB, P
1961		14	DB, P
1962	DAL	N	14	DB
1963	GB	N	14	DB, P
1964		14	DB, P
11 yrs.	131 games		

Jim Norton
NORTON, JAMES A.
B. Nov. 18, 1942, Wilmington, NC
Washington 6'4" 254 lbs.

Year	Team	Games	Pos.
1965	SF	N	14	OT
1966		14	DE, DT
1967	ATL	N	14	DE, DT
1968		7	DT
1968	PHI	N	13	DT
1969	WAS	N	5	DT
1970	NYG	N	4	DT
6 yrs.	71 games		

Jim Norton
NORTON, JAMES CHARLES
B. Oct. 20, 1938, Glendale, CA
Idaho 6'3" 187 lbs.

Year	Team	Games	Pos.
1960	HOU	A	14	DB
1961		14	DB, P
1962		14	DB, P
1963		14	DB, P
1964		14	DB, P
1965		14	DB, P
1966		14	DB, P
1967		14	DB, P
1968		14	DB, P
9 yrs.	126 games		

Ken Norton
NORTON, KENNETH HOWARD, JR.
B. Sep. 29, 1966, Jacksonville, IL
UCLA 6'2" 236 lbs.

Year	Team	Games	Pos.
1988	DAL	N	3	LB
1989		13	LB
1990		15	LB
1991		16	LB
1992		16	LB
1993		16	LB
1994	SF	N	16	LB
1995		16	LB
1996		16	LB
9 yrs.	127 games		

Marty Norton
NORTON, MARTIN
B. 1903
Deceased
None 5'6" 175 lbs.

Year	Team	Games	Pos.
1922	MIN	N	3	HB
1924		6	HB
1925	GB	N	10	HB
1926	RI	A	4	HB
4 yrs.	23 games		

Ray Norton
NORTON, RAYMOND
B. Sep. 22, 1937
San Jose State 6'2" 184 lbs.

Year	Team	Games	Pos.
1960	SF	N	3	HB
1961		6	HB
2 yrs.	9 games		

Year	Team	Games	Pos.

Raymond Norton
NORTON, RAYMOND (Nick)
B. 1900, New York State
Deceased
None

1925	**CLE** N	1	HB

Rick Norton
NORTON, RICHARD E.
B. Nov. 16, 1943, Louisville, KY
Kentucky 6'1" 192 lbs.

1966	**MIA** A	7	QB
1967		14	QB
1968		3	QB
1969		8	QB
1970	**GB** N	3	QB
5 yrs.	35 games		

Jay Norvell
NORVELL, MERRITT JAY
B. Mar. 28, 1963, Madison, WI
Iowa 6'2" 232 lbs.

1987	**CHI** N	6	LB

Ralph Norwood
NORWOOD, RALPH E.
B. Jan. 23, 1966, New Orleans, LA
D. Nov. 24, 1989
Louisiana State 6'7" 285 lbs.

1989	**ATL** N	11	OT

Scott Norwood
NORWOOD, SCOTT ALLAN
B. Jul. 17, 1960, Alexandria, VA
James Madison 6'0" 207 lbs.

1985	**BUF** N	16	K
1986		16	K
1987		12	K
1988		16	K
1989		16	K
1990		16	K
1991		16	K
7 yrs.	108 games		

John Nosich
NOSICH, JOHN
B. Oct. 12, 1915
D. Jul., 1985, McKeesport, PA
Duquesne 6'3" 230 lbs.

1938	**PIT** N	2	T

Doug Nott
NOTT, DOUGLAS, SR.
B. Jun. 14, 1911, Pontiac, MI
D. May 25, 1991, Walled Lake, MI
Detroit 6'0" 195 lbs.

1935	**DET** N	4	HB, QB, FB
1935	**BOS** N	4	QB, HB
1 yr.	8 games		

Mike Nott
NOTT, WESLEY MICHAEL
B. May 19, 1952, Sebastopol, CA
Santa Clara 6'3" 203 lbs.

1976	**KC** N	1	QB

Dexter Nottage
NOTTAGE, DEXTER
B. Nov. 14, 1970, Miami, FL
Florida A&M 6'4" 273 lbs.

1994	**WAS** N	15	DE
1995		16	DE, DT
1996		16	DE
3 yrs.	47 games		

Don Nottingham
NOTTINGHAM, DONALD RAY (The Human Bowling Ball)
B. Jun. 28, 1949, Widen, WV
Kent State 5'10" 210 lbs.

1971	**BAL** N	14	RB
1972		14	RB
1973		3	RB
1973	**MIA** N	11	RB
1974		14	RB
1975		14	RB
1976		14	RB
1977		14	RB
7 yrs.	98 games		

Jay Novacek
NOVACEK, JAY MCKINLEY
B. Oct. 24, 1962, Martin, SD
Wyoming 6'4" 217 lbs.

1985	**STL** N	16	WR
1986		8	TE
1987		7	TE
1988	**PHX** N	16	TE
1989		16	TE
1990	**DAL** N	16	TE
1991		16	TE
1992		16	TE
1993		16	TE
1994		16	TE
1995		15	TE
11 yrs.	158 games		

Eddie Novak
NOVAK, EDWARD (Five Yards)
B. Aug. 3, 1897
D. Jul., 1984, Webster, MN
None 5'10" 175 lbs.

1920	**RI** A	6	HB, FB
1921		7	HB
1922	**MIN** N	1	HB
1924		5	HB, QB
1925	**RI** N	11	HB, FB
1926	**RI** N	9	FB, HB, QB
6 yrs.	39 games		

Jack Novak
NOVAK, CLARENCE JOHN
B. Jun. 6, 1953, Kewaunee, WI
Wisconsin 6'4" 241 lbs.

1975	**CIN** N	14	TE
1976	**TB** N	13	TE
1977		14	TE
3 yrs.	41 games		

Jeff Novak
NOVAK, JEFF LADD
B. Jul. 27, 1967, Cook County, IL
Southwest Texas State 6'5" 295 lbs.

1994	**MIA** N	7	G
1995	**JAC** N	16	G, OT
1996		6	G
3 yrs.	29 games		

Ken Novak
NOVAK, KENNETH
B. Jul. 3, 1954, Willowick, OH
Purdue 6'7" 268 lbs.

1976	**BAL** N	11	DT
1977		12	DT
2 yrs.	23 games		

Craig Novitsky
NOVITSKY, CRAIG AARON
B. May 12, 1971, Washington, DC
UCLA 6'5" 295 lbs.

1994	**NO** N	9	C
1995		16	OT, C
1996		16	OT
3 yrs.	41 games		

Brent Novoselsky
NOVOSELSKY, BRENT HOWARD
B. Jan. 8, 1966, Skokie, IL
Pennsylvania 6'3" 232 lbs.

1988	**CHI** N	8	TE
1989	**MIN** N	15	TE
1990		16	TE
1991		16	TE
1992		16	TE
1993		15	TE
1994		12	TE
7 yrs.	98 games		

Ray Novotny
NOVOTNY, RAYMOND
B. Oct. 12, 1907
Ashland 5'10" 165 lbs.

1930	**POR** N	10	HB, FB, QB
1931	**CLE** N	10	HB, QB
1932	**BKN** N	9	QB, HB
3 yrs.	29 games		

Joe Novsek
NOVSEK, JOSEPH
B. 1940
Tulsa 6'4" 237 lbs.

1962	**OAK** A	14	DE

Gary Nowak
NOWAK, GARY WILLIAM
B. Dec. 8, 1948, Detroit, MI
Michigan State 6'4" 247 lbs.

1971	**SD** N	6	TE

Walt Nowak
NOWAK, WALTER
B. Sep. 14, 1920, Camden, NJ
Villanova 5'11" 185 lbs.

1944	**PHI** N	1	E

Bob Nowaskey
NOWASKEY, ROBERT J.
B. Feb. 3, 1918, Everett, IA
D. Mar. 21, 1971, Arlington Heights, IL
George Washington 6'0" 205 lbs.

1940	**CHIB** N	10	E
1941		11	E
1942		11	E
1946	**LA** AA	14	E
1947		14	E
1948		1	E
1948	**BAL** AA	13	E
1949		12	E
1950	**BAL** N	8	E
8 yrs.	94 games		

Tom Nowatzke
NOWATZKE, THOMAS MATTHEW
B. Sep. 30, 1942, La Porte, IN
Indiana 6'3" 229 lbs.

1965	**DET** N	14	FB
1966		14	FB
1967		14	RB
1968		14	RB
1969		9	RB
1970	**BAL** N	11	RB
1971		14	RB
1972		6	RB
8 yrs.	96 games		

Len Noyes
NOYES, LEONARD
B. Jul. 12, 1914
D. Dec., 1985, Winston-Salem, NC
Montana 6'0" 214 lbs.

1938	**BKN** N	5	G

Clem Nugent
NUGENT, CLEMENT
B. Nov., 1899
Deceased
Iowa 5'9" 155 lbs.

1924	**ROC** N	1	HB

Dan Nugent
NUGENT, DANIEL LAWRENCE
B. Aug. 22, 1953, Mount Clemens, MI
Auburn 6'3" 250 lbs.

1976	**WAS** N	14	G
1977		14	G
1978		16	G
1980		14	G
4 yrs.	58 games		

Phil Nugent
NUGENT, PHIL H.
B. Aug. 16, 1939, Lafayette, LA
Tulane 6'2" 195 lbs.

1961	**DEN** A	12	DB

Terry Nugent
NUGENT, TERENCE JOHN
B. Dec. 5, 1961, Merced, CA
Colorado State 6'4" 218 lbs.

1987	**IND** N	1	QB

Julian Nunamaker
NUNAMAKER, JULIAN
B. Feb. 13, 1946, Charleston, SC
Tennessee-Martin 6'3" 251 lbs.

1969	**BUF** A	10	DE
1970	**BUF** N	8	DE
2 yrs.	18 games		

Frank Nunley
NUNLEY, FRANK H. (Fudge Hammer)
B. Oct. 1, 1945, Lexington, AL
Michigan 6'2" 230 lbs.

1967	**SF** N	14	LB
1968		14	LB
1969		14	LB
1970		14	LB
1971		14	LB
1972		13	LB
1973		14	LB
1974		13	LB
1975		14	LB
1976		13	LB
10 yrs.	137 games		

Jeremy Nunley
NUNLEY, JODY JEREMY
B. Sep. 19, 1971, Winchester, TN
Alabama 6'5" 278 lbs.

1994	**HOU** N	12	DE

Freddie Joe Nunn
NUNN, FREDDIE JOE
B. Apr. 9, 1962, Noxubee County, MS
Mississippi 6'4" 255 lbs.

1985	**STL** N	16	LB
1986		16	LB
1987		12	LB
1988	**PHX** N	16	DE
1989		12	DE
1990		16	LB
1991		16	LB
1992		11	LB
1993		16	LB
1994	**IND** N	11	DE, DT
1995		10	DE
1996		5	DE
12 yrs.	157 games		

Year	Team	Games	Pos.

Bob Nunnery
NUNNERY, ROBERT BROCK
B. Dec. 28, 1933
Louisiana State 6'4" 275 lbs.

Year	Team	Games	Pos.
1960	**DAL**	**A**	OT

Bob Nussbaumer
NUSSBAUMER, ROBERT JOHN
B. Apr. 23, 1924, Oak Park, IL
Michigan 5'11" 172 lbs.

Year	Team	Games	Pos.
1946	**GB**	**N**	10	HB
1947	**WAS**	**N**	12	HB
1948			10	HB
1949	**CHIC**	**N**	12	HB
1950			2	HB
5 yrs.	46 games		

Doug Nussmeier
NUSSMEIER, DOUG KEITH
B. Dec. 11, 1970, Portland, OR
Idaho 6'3" 211 lbs.

Year	Team	Games	Pos.
1996	**NO**	**N**	3	QB

Tom Nutten
NUTTEN, TOM
B. Jun. 8, 1971, Magog, Que.
Western Michigan 6'4" 276 lbs.

Year	Team	Games	Pos.
1995	**BUF**	**N**	1	G

Buzz Nutter
NUTTER, MADISON MONROE
B. Feb. 16, 1931, Summersville, WV
Virginia Tech 6'4" 230 lbs.

Year	Team	Games	Pos.
1954	**BAL**	**N**	12	C
1955			8	C
1956			12	C
1957			12	C
1958			12	C
1959			12	C
1960			12	C
1961	**PIT**	**N**	14	C
1962			14	C
1963			14	C
1964			14	C
1965	**BAL**	**N**	13	C
12 yrs.	149 games		

Ed Nutting
NUTTING, JOHN EDWARD, JR.
B. Feb. 8, 1939, Washington, DC
Georgia Tech 6'4" 246 lbs.

Year	Team	Games	Pos.
1961	**CLE**	**N**	4	OT
1963	**DAL**	**N**	14	OT
2 yrs.	18 games		

Jerry Nuzum
NUZUM, JERRY HANSON
B. Sep. 8, 1923, Clovis, NM
New Mexico State 6'1" 199 lbs.

Year	Team	Games	Pos.
1948	**PIT**	**N**	10	HB
1949			12	HB
1950			12	HB
1951			11	HB
4 yrs.	45 games		

Rick Nuzum
NUZUM, FREDERICK MERRIL
B. Jun. 30, 1952, Charleston, WV
Kentucky 6'4" 238 lbs.

Year	Team	Games	Pos.
1977	**LA**	**N**	14	C
1978	**GB**	**N**	16	C
2 yrs.	30 games		

Chip Nuzzo
NUZZO, ANTHONY C.

Chip Nuzzo continued
B. Jul. 26, 1965, Olean, NY
Princeton 5'11" 190 lbs.

Year	Team	Games	Pos.
1987	**BUF**	**N**	3	S

Mally Nydahl
NYDAHL, MALVIN J.
B. Nov. 24, 1906, Minneapolis, MN
D. May, 1979, Sun City, AZ
Minnesota 5'11" 163 lbs.

Year	Team	Games	Pos.
1929	**MIN**	**N**	9	QB, HB
1930			9	HB
1930	**FRA**	**N**	4	QB
1931			4	HB, QB
3 yrs.	26 games		

Blaine Nye
NYE, BLAINE F.
B. Mar. 29, 1946, Gden, UT
Stanford 6'4" 252 lbs.

Year	Team	Games	Pos.
1968	**DAL**	**N**	13	OT
1969			14	OT
1970			14	G
1971			14	G
1972			14	G
1973			14	G
1974			14	G
1975			14	G
1976			14	G
9 yrs.	125 games		

Dick Nyers
NYERS, RICHARD
B. Oct. 8, 1934, Indianapolis, IN
Indiana Central 5'11" 177 lbs.

Year	Team	Games	Pos.
1956	**BAL**	**N**	5	HB
1957			7	HB
2 yrs.	12 games		

Bernie Nygren
NYGREN, BERNARD CLIFFORD
(Bud)
B. Nov. 14, 1918, Minneapolis, MN
D. Dec. 26, 1984, San Jose, CA
San Jose State 5'9" 193 lbs.

Year	Team	Games	Pos.
1946	**LA**	**AA**	14	HB
1947	**BKN**	**AA**	1	HB
2 yrs.	15 games		

Lee Nystrom
NYSTROM, LEE ALLEN
B. Oct. 30, 1951, Worthington, MN
Macalester 6'5" 260 lbs.

Year	Team	Games	Pos.
1974	**GB**	**N**	13	OT

Vic Nyvall
NYVALL, VICTOR
B. 1948
Northwestern State (Louisiana) 5'10" 185 lbs.

Year	Team	Games	Pos.
1970	**NO**	**N**	13	RB

Don Oakes
OAKES, DONALD SHERMAN
B. Jul. 22, 1938, Roanoke, VA
Virginia Tech 6'3" 253 lbs.

Year	Team	Games	Pos.
1961	**PHI**	**N**	14	OT, DT
1962			8	DT
1963	**BOS**	**A**	14	OT
1964			14	OT
1965			14	OT
1966			14	OT
1967			14	OT
1968			13	OT
8 yrs.	105 games		

Charley Oakley
OAKLEY, CHARLES
B. 1931
Louisiana State 5'10" 170 lbs.

Year	Team	Games	Pos.
1954	**CHIC**	**N**	1	B

Ben Oas
OAS, BENJAMIN
B. 1906
St. Mary's (Minnesota) 195 lbs.

Year	Team	Games	Pos.
1929	**MIN**	**N**	7	C, HB, FB, G

Bart Oates
OATES, BART STEVEN
B. Dec. 16, 1958, Mesa, AZ
Brigham Young 6'3" 265 lbs.

Year	Team	Games	Pos.
1985	**NYG**	**N**	16	C
1986			16	C
1987			12	C
1988			16	C
1989			16	C
1990			16	C
1991			16	C
1992			16	C
1993			16	C
1994	**SF**	**N**	16	C
1995			16	C
11 yrs.	172 games		

Brad Oates
OATES, ROBERT BRAD
B. Sep. 30, 1953, Mesa, AZ
Brigham Young 6'6" 274 lbs.

Year	Team	Games	Pos.
1976	**STL**	**N**	14	OT
1977			10	OT
1978	**DET**	**N**	16	OT
1979	**STL**	**N**	11	OT
1980			10	OT
1980	**KC**	**N**	1	OT
1981	**CIN**	**N**	5	OT
6 yrs.	67 games		

Victor Oatis
OATIS, VICTOR HUGO
B. Jan. 6, 1959, Monroe, LA
Northwestern State (Louisiana) 6'0" 177 lbs.

Year	Team	Games	Pos.
1983	**BAL**	**N**	9	WR

Carleton Oats
OATS, CARLETON
B. Apr. 24, 1942, Tampa, FL
Florida A&M 6'2" 252 lbs.

Year	Team	Games	Pos.
1965	**OAK**	**A**	14	DE
1966			14	DE
1967			9	DE
1968			14	DE
1969			13	DE
1970	**OAK**	**N**	13	DT
1971			12	DT
1972			14	DT
1973	**GB**	**N**	8	DT
9 yrs.	111 games		

Ronnie O'Bard
O'BARD, RONNIE ALEXANDER
B. Jun. 11, 1958, San Diego, CA
Idaho/Brigham Young 5'9" 190 lbs.

Year	Team	Games	Pos.
1985	**SD**	**N**	16	CB

Vic Obeck
OBECK, VICTOR F.
B. 1918
Springfield 6'0" 225 lbs.

Year	Team	Games	Pos.
1945	**CHIC**	**N**	10	G
1946	**BKN**	**AA**	12	G
2 yrs.	22 games		

Dunc Obee
OBEE, DUNCAN FRANCIS
B. Jul. 9, 1918, Battle Creek, MI
Dayton 5'11" 200 lbs.

Year	Team	Games	Pos.
1941	**DET**	**N**	3	C

Terry Obee
OBEE, TERRY
B. Jun. 15, 1968, Vallejo, CA
Oregon 5'10" 190 lbs.

Year	Team	Games	Pos.
1991	**MIN**	**N**	1	WR
1993	**CHI**	**N**	16	WR
2 yrs.	17 games		

Roman Oben
OBEN, ROMAN
B. Oct. 9, 1972, Cameroon
Louisville 6'4" 297 lbs.

Year	Team	Games	Pos.
1996	**NYG**	**N**	2	OT

Ray Oberbroekling
OBERBROEKLING, RAYMOND
B. 1899
Deceased
Loras 5'8" 198 lbs.

Year	Team	Games	Pos.
1924	**KEN**	**N**	2	T

Tom Oberg
OBERG, THOMAS H.
B. Aug. 7, 1945, Portland, OR
Oregon State/Portland State 6'0" 185 lbs.

Year	Team	Games	Pos.
1968	**DEN**	**A**	9	DB

Herman O'Berry
O'BERRY, HERMAN LEE
B. Jul. 11, 1971, Sacramento, CA
Oregon 5'9" 185 lbs.

Year	Team	Games	Pos.
1996	**STL**	**N**	9	CB

Harry O'Boyle
O'BOYLE, HARRY
B. 1905
D. May 5, 1994, Wheeling, IL
Notre Dame 5'9" 178 lbs.

Year	Team	Games	Pos.
1928	**GB**	**N**	11	FB
1932			11	QB
1933	**PHI**	**N**	2	QB
3 yrs.	24 games		

Ed O'Bradovich
O'BRADOVICH, EDWARD
B. May 21, 1940, Melrose Park, IL
Illinois 6'3" 255 lbs.

Year	Team	Games	Pos.
1962	**CHI**	**N**	14	DE
1963			6	DE
1964			7	DE
1965			13	DE
1966			14	DE
1967			14	DE
1968			14	DE
1969			14	DE
1970			14	DE
1971			14	DE
10 yrs.	124 games		

Jim Obradovich
OBRADOVICH, JAMES ROBERT
B. Apr. 2, 1953, Los Angeles, CA
Southern California 6'2" 228 lbs.

Year	Team	Games	Pos.
1975	**NYG**	**N**	14	TE
1976	**SF**	**N**	14	TE
1977			12	TE
1978	**TB**	**N**	16	TE
1979			16	TE
1980			16	TE

Year	Team	Games	Pos.

Jim Obradovich continued

Year	Team	Games	Pos.
1981		16	TE
1982		9	TE
1983		16	TE
9 yrs.	129 games		

Bill O'Brien
O'BRIEN, WILLIAM G.
B. 1924, Detroit, MI
None 6'0" 180 lbs.

1947	DET	N	9	HB, C

Con O'Brien
O'BRIEN, CORNELIUS
B. 1898
Deceased
Boston College 6'2" 195 lbs.

1921	NY	A	1	T

Dave O'Brien
O'BRIEN, DAVID HYDE
B. Jun. 13, 1941, Cambridge, MA
Boston College 6'3" 244 lbs.

1963	MIN	N	14	G, OT
1964			14	G
1965	NYG	N	10	OT
1966	STL	N	14	OL
1967			8	G, OT
5 yrs.	60 games			

Davey O'Brien
O'BRIEN, ROBERT DAVID
B. 1917
D. Nov. 18, 1977
Texas Christian 5'7" 151 lbs.

1939	PHI	N	11	QB
1940			11	QB
2 yrs.	22 games			

Fran O'Brien
O'BRIEN, FRANCIS JOSEPH
B. Apr. 17, 1936, Springfield, MA
Michigan State 6'1" 253 lbs.

1959	CLE	N	12	T
1960	WAS	N	12	G
1961			14	G
1962			14	OT
1963			13	OT
1964			14	OT
1965			14	OT
1966			2	OT
1966	PIT	N	13	OT
1967			4	OT
1968			14	OT
10 yrs.	126 games			

Gail O'Brien
O'BRIEN, GAIL JOSEPH (Obie)
B. Nov. 14, 1911, Cheyenne, WY
Nebraska 6'1" 219 lbs.

1934	BOS	N	10	T
1935			11	T
1936			11	T, G
3 yrs.	32 games			

Jack O'Brien
O'BRIEN, J.J.
B. 1899
Deceased
Minnesota 5'10" 170 lbs.

1929	MIN	N	1	QB

Jack O'Brien
O'BRIEN, JOHN
B. Oct. 21, 1932
Florida 6'2" 213 lbs.

1954	PIT	N	7	E

Jack O'Brien continued

1955			12	E
1956			12	E
3 yrs.	31 games			

Jim O'Brien
O'BRIEN, JAMES EUGENE
B. Feb. 2, 1947, El Paso, TX
Cincinnati 6'0" 195 lbs.

1970	BAL	N	14	K, WR
1971			14	K, WR
1972			14	K, WR
1973	DET	N	10	WR, K
4 yrs.	52 games			

Ken O'Brien
O'BRIEN, KENNETH JOHN, JR.
B. Nov. 27, 1960, Long Island, NY
Sacramento State/California-Davis 6'4" 210 lbs.

1984	NYJ	N	10	QB
1985			16	QB
1986			15	QB
1987			12	QB
1988			14	QB
1989			15	QB
1990			16	QB
1991			16	QB
1992			10	QB
1993	PHI	N	5	QB
10 yrs.	129 games			

Mike O'Brien
O'BRIEN, MICHAEL PATRICK
B. Apr. 25, 1956, Kirkland, WA
California 6'1" 195 lbs.

1979	SEA	N	3	DB

Tom O'Brien
O'BRIEN, THOMAS
B. 1905
Boston College 5'9" 210 lbs.

1926	BOS	A	3	T

Mike Obrovac
OBROVAC, MICHAEL LOUIS
B. Oct. 11, 1955, Canton, OH
Bowling Green 6'6" 275 lbs.

1981	CIN	N	6	OT
1982			9	OT
1983			10	OT
3 yrs.	25 games			

Henry Obst
OBST, HENRY
B. 1908
Syracuse 5'11" 192 lbs.

1931	SI	N	2	G
1933	PHI	N	1	G
2 yrs.	3 games			

John O'Callaghan
O'CALLAGHAN, JOHN
B. May 15, 1964
San Diego State 6'4" 245 lbs.

1987	SEA	N	1	TE

Grattan O'Connell
O'CONNELL, GRATTAN
B. 1902
Boston College 5'11" 185 lbs.

1926	HAR	N	10	E
1927	PRO	N	2	E
2 yrs.	12 games			

Milt O'Connell
O'CONNELL, MILTON
B. 1901
Lafayette 6'0" 175 lbs.

1924	FRA	N	12	E
1925			2	E
2 yrs.	14 games			

Tommy O'Connell
O'CONNELL, THOMAS BERNARD
B. Sep. 26, 1930, Chicago, IL
Illinois 5'11" 187 lbs.

1953	CHIB	N	12	QB
1956	CLE	N	7	QB
1957			11	QB
1960	BUF	A		QB
1961			1	QB
5 yrs.	31 games			

Bill O'Connor
O'CONNOR, WILLIAM FRANCIS (Zeke, Buck)
B. Aug. 24, 1923, Tulsa, OK
D. Sep. 13, 1990, Oklahoma City, OK
None 6'4" 220 lbs.

1948	BUF	AA	14	E
1949	CLE	AA	9	E
1951	NYY	N	12	E
3 yrs.	35 games			

Bob O'Connor
O'CONNOR, ROBERT C.
B. Jan. 27, 1910, Elmira, NY
Stanford 6'1" 220 lbs.

1935	GB	N	8	G

Dan O'Connor
O'CONNOR, DANIEL
B. 1894
Deceased
Georgetown (DC) 6'2" 210 lbs.

1920	CAN	A	6	G
1921	CLE	A	7	T, G
2 yrs.	13 games			

Frank O'Connor
O'CONNOR, FRANCIS
B. 1900
Deceased
Holy Cross 6'0" 210 lbs.

1926	HAR	N	2	T

Paul O'Connor
O'CONNOR, PAUL
B. Nov. 7, 1962
Miami (Florida) 6'3" 270 lbs.

1987	TB	N	2	G

Red O'Connor
O'CONNOR, RED
DePaul 5'8" 170 lbs.

1920	CHIC	A	3	E
1921			5	E
1922	CHIC	N	5	E
1924			3	E
4 yrs.	16 games			

Tom O'Connor
O'CONNOR, TOM
B. Nov. 8, 1963
South Carolina 6'1" 190 lbs.

1987	NYJ	N	3	P

Don Odegard
ODEGARD, DONALD BOYD
B. Nov. 22, 1966, Seattle, WA
Oregon State/Nevada-Las Vegas 6'0" 180 lbs.

1990	NYJ	N	14	CB
1991			16	CB
2 yrs.	30 games			

Stu O'Dell
O'DELL, STEWART HARRY
B. Nov. 27, 1951, Linton, IN
Indiana 6'1" 220 lbs.

1974	WAS	N	8	LB
1976			14	LB
1977			3	LB
1978	BAL	N	14	LB
4 yrs.	39 games			

Curly Oden
ODEN, O.G. (Swede)
B. 1898
Deceased
Brown 5'6" 162 lbs.

1925	PRO	N	8	QB
1926			13	QB, HB
1927			13	QB, HB
1928			11	QB, HB
1930			9	QB, HB
1931			11	QB, HB
1932	BOS	N	1	QB
7 yrs.	66 games			

Derrick Oden
ODEN, DERRICK
B. Sep. 29, 1970, Los Angeles, CA
Alabama 5'11" 230 lbs.

1993	PHI	N	12	LB
1994			11	LB
1995			12	LB
3 yrs.	35 games			

McDonald Oden
ODEN, MCDONALD
B. Mar. 28, 1958, Franklin, TN
Tennessee State 6'4" 228 lbs.

1980	CLE	N	16	TE
1981			16	TE
1982			9	TE
3 yrs.	41 games			

Phil Odle
ODLE, PHILLIP MORRIS
B. Nov. 23, 1942, Elgin, IL
Brigham Young 5'11" 191 lbs.

1968	DET	N	14	OE
1969			13	WR
1970			4	WR
3 yrs.	31 games			

Cliff Odom
ODOM, CLIFTON LOUIS
B. Aug. 15, 1958, Beaumont, TX
Texas-Arlington 6'2" 241 lbs.

1980	CLE	N	8	LB
1982	BAL	N	8	LB
1983			15	LB
1984	IND	N	16	LB
1985			16	LB
1986			16	LB
1987			12	LB
1988			13	LB
1989			16	LB
1990	MIA	N	16	LB
1991			14	LB
1992			3	LB
1993			14	LB
13 yrs.	167 games			

Year	Team	Games	Pos.

Henry Odom
ODOM, HENRY C.
B. Feb. 12, 1959, Bamberg, SC
South Carolina State 5'10" 200 lbs.

Year	Team	Games	Pos.
1983	**PIT** N	16	RB

Jason Odom
ODOM, JASON BRIAN
B. Mar. 31, 1974, Bartow, FL
Florida 6'4" 290 lbs.

| 1996 | **TB** N | 12 | OT |

Ricky Odom
ODOM, RICKY L.
B. Sep. 16, 1956, Jonesboro, LA
Southern California 6'0" 183 lbs.

1978	**KC** N	8	CB
1978	**SF** N	3	CB
1979	**LA** N	3	CB
2 yrs.	14 games		

Sammy Odom
ODOM, SAMMY JOE
B. 1942
Northwestern State (Louisiana) 6'2" 235 lbs.

| 1964 | **HOU** A | 14 | DT |

Steve Odom
ODOM, STEPHEN TALMAGE
B. Sep. 5, 1952, Oakland, CA
Utah 5'8" 173 lbs.

1974	**GB** N	14	WR
1975		14	WR
1976		12	WR
1977		14	WR
1978		12	WR
1979		9	WR
1979	**NYG** N	6	WR
6 yrs.	81 games		

Nate Odomes
ODOMES, NATHANIEL BERNARD
B. Aug. 25, 1965, Columbus, GA
Wisconsin 5'9" 188 lbs.

1987	**BUF** N	12	CB
1988		16	CB
1989		16	CB
1990		16	CB
1991		16	CB
1992		16	CB
1993		16	CB
1996	**ATL** N	7	CB
8 yrs.	115 games		

Riley Odoms
ODOMS, RILEY MACKEY
B. Mar. 1, 1950, Luling, TX
Houston 6'4" 230 lbs.

1972	**DEN** N	14	TE
1973		14	TE
1974		14	TE
1975		14	TE
1976		14	TE
1977		14	TE
1978		16	TE
1979		13	TE
1980		15	TE
1981		15	TE
1982		8	TE
1983		2	TE
12 yrs.	153 games		

Pat O'Donahue
O'DONAHUE, PATRICK
B. 1930

Pat O'Donahue *continued*
Wisconsin 6'1" 208 lbs.

Year	Team	Games	Pos.
1952	**SF** N	8	E
1955	**GB** N	12	E
2 yrs.	20 games		

Dicky O'Donnell
O'DONNELL, RICHARD
B. 1899
Deceased
None 6'0" 190 lbs.

1923	**DUL** N	7	E
1924	**GB** N	9	E
1925		12	E
1926		11	E
1927		9	E
1928		13	E
1929		11	E, T
1930		10	E
1931	**BKN** N	11	E, HB
9 yrs.	93 games		

Joe O'Donnell
O'DONNELL, JOSEPH RAYMOND
B. Aug. 31, 1941, Ann Arbor, MI
Michigan 6'2" 253 lbs.

1964	**BUF** A	14	G
1965		14	OT
1966		14	OT
1967		14	G
1969		14	G
1970	**BUF** N	14	G
1971		7	G
7 yrs.	91 games		

Neil O'Donnell
O'DONNELL, NEIL KENNEDY
B. Jul. 3, 1966, Morristown, NJ
Maryland 6'3" 221 lbs.

1991	**PIT** N	12	QB
1992		12	QB
1993		16	QB
1994		14	QB
1995		12	QB
1996	**NYJ** N	6	QB
6 yrs.	72 games		

Neil O'Donoghue
O'DONOGHUE, CORNELIUS JOSEPH
B. Jun. 18, 1953, Dublin, Ireland
Auburn 6'6" 207 lbs.

1977	**BUF** N	5	K
1978	**TB** N	15	K
1979		16	K
1980	**STL** N	10	K
1981		16	K
1982		8	K
1983		16	K
1984		16	K
1985		8	K
9 yrs.	110 games		

Urban Odson
ODSON, URBAN L.
B. Nov. 17, 1918, Clark, SD
D. Jun., 1986, Rapid City, SD
Minnesota 6'3" 251 lbs.

1946	**GB** N	6	T
1947		11	T
1948		12	T
1949		10	T
4 yrs.	39 games		

Matt O'Dwyer
O'DWYER, MATTHEW PHILLIP
B. Sep. 1, 1972, Lincolnshire, Il

Matt O'Dwyer *continued*
Northwestern 6'5" 308 lbs.

Year	Team	Games	Pos.
1995	**NYJ** N	12	G
1996		16	G
2 yrs.	28 games		

Vern Oech
OECH, VERNON M.
B. May 31, 1913, Beach, ND
Minnesota 6'1" 207 lbs.

| 1936 | **CHIB** N | 8 | G |

Johnny Oehler
OEHLER, JOHN (Cap)
B. 1911, Jackson Heights, NY
Purdue 6'0" 204 lbs.

1933	**PIT** N	11	C
1934		12	C
1935	**BKN** N	12	C
1936		4	C
4 yrs.	39 games		

Arnie Oehlrich
OEHLRICH, ARNOLD
B. 1906
Nebraska 5'11" 190 lbs.

1928	**FRA** N	16	HB
1929		17	HB, FB, QB
2 yrs.	33 games		

John Oelerich
OELERICH, JOHN
B. 1917
St. Ambrose 6'0" 192 lbs.

1938	**PIT** N	3	QB
1938	**CHIB** N	2	HB
1 yr.	5 games		

John Offerdahl
OFFERDAHL, JOHN ARNOLD
B. Aug. 17, 1964, Wisconsin Rapids, WI
Western Michigan 6'2" 232 lbs.

1986	**MIA** N	15	LB
1987		9	LB
1988		16	LB
1989		10	LB
1990		16	LB
1991		6	LB
1992		8	LB
1993		9	LB
8 yrs.	89 games		

Tony Office
OFFICE, ANTHONY
B. Feb. 24, 1960, Tifton, GA
Illinois State 6'2" 250 lbs.

| 1987 | **DET** N | 3 | LB |

Dave Ogas
OGAS, DAVID
B. Jun. 23, 1946, Silver City, NM
San Diego State 6'3" 240 lbs.

1968	**OAK** A	6	LB
1969	**BUF** A	14	LB
2 yrs.	20 games		

Jonathan Ogden
OGDEN, JONATHAN PHILLIP
B. Jul. 31, 1974, Washington, DC
UCLA 6'8" 318 lbs.

| 1996 | **BAL** N | 16 | G |

Ray Ogden
OGDEN, RAYMOND DOUGLAS

Ray Ogden *continued*
B. Sep. 2, 1942, Jesup, GA
Alabama 6'5" 225 lbs.

Year	Team	Games	Pos.
1965	**STL** N	3	FL
1966		14	OE
1967	**NO** N	2	SE
1967	**ATL** N	13	TE
1968		14	TE
1969	**CHI** N	11	TE
1970		9	WR, TE
1971		6	WR, TE
7 yrs.	72 games		

Rick Ogle
OGLE, RICHARD
B. Jan. 14, 1949, Bozeman, MT
Colorado 6'3" 230 lbs.

1971	**STL** N	6	LB
1972	**DET** N	4	LB
2 yrs.	10 games		

Alfred Oglesby
OGLESBY, ALFRED LEE
B. Jan. 27, 1967, Weimar, TX
Houston 6'3" 278 lbs.

1990	**MIA** N	13	NT
1991		12	NT
1992		6	NT
1992	**GB** N	7	NT
1994	**NYJ** N	15	DT, DE
1995	**CIN** N	7	DT
5 yrs.	60 games		

Paul Oglesby
OGLESBY, PAUL
B. 1940
UCLA 6'4" 235 lbs.

| 1960 | **OAK** A | | DT |

Craig Ogletree
OGLETREE, CRAIG ALGERNON
B. Apr. 2, 1968, Barnesville, GA
Auburn 6'2" 236 lbs.

| 1990 | **CIN** N | 11 | LB |

Pat Ogrin
OGRIN, PATRICK JOHN
B. Feb. 10, 1958, Butte, MT
Wyoming 6'5" 265 lbs.

1981	**WAS** N	5	DE
1982		3	DT
2 yrs.	8 games		

Ross O'Hanley
O'HANLEY, ROSS
B. 1939
Boston College 6'0" 183 lbs.

1960	**BOS** A		DB
1961		7	DB
1962		14	DB
1963		14	DB
1964		14	DB
1965		14	DB
6 yrs.	63 games		

Ed O'Hearn
O'HEARN, EDMUND
B. 1899
Deceased
Lehigh

| 1921 | **NY** A | 2 | T |

Jack O'Hearn
O'HEARN, J.E.
B. 1893
Deceased

Year	Team	Games	Pos.

Jack O'Hearn continued
Cornell 5'10" 180 lbs.

Year	Team		Games	Pos.
1920	CLE	A	4	G, T
1921	BUF	A	2	HB, E

2 yrs. 6 games

Earl Ohlgren
OHLGREN, EARL A.
B. Feb. 21, 1918, Cokato, MN
Minnesota 6'2" 210 lbs.

1942	GB	N	3	E

Ohmer
OHMER
None

1921	CIN	A	1	HB

Steve Okoniewski
OKONIEWSKI, JOHN STEPHEN
B. Aug. 22, 1949, Bremerton, WA
Montana 6'3" 257 lbs.

1972	BUF	N	10	DT
1973			5	DT
1974	GB	N	14	DT
1975			14	DT
1976	STL	N	8	DT

5 yrs. 51 games

Christian Okoye
OKOYE, CHRISTIAN EMEKA
(The Nigerian Nightmare)
B. Aug. 16, 1961, Enugu, Nigeria
Azusa Pacific 6'1" 253 lbs.

1987	KC	N	12	RB
1988			9	RB
1989			15	RB
1990			14	RB
1991			14	RB
1992			15	RB

6 yrs. 79 games

Cliff Olander
OLANDER, CLIFFORD VALMORE
B. Apr. 15, 1955, Hartford, CT
New Mexico State 6'5" 191 lbs.

1977	SD	N	5	P, QB
1978			9	QB, P
1979			4	QB

3 yrs. 18 games

Bob Olderman
OLDERMAN, ROBERT BRUCE
B. Jun. 5, 1962, Brookville, PA
D. Oct. 1993
Virginia 6'5" 202 lbs.

1985	KC	N	16	G

Doug Oldershaw
OLDERSHAW, DOUGLAS
B. Jul. 6, 1915, Bakersfield, CA
California-Santa Barbara 6'0" 195 lbs.

1939	NYG	N	10	G
1940			11	G
1941			10	G, E

3 yrs. 31 games

Chris Oldham
OLDHAM, CHRISTOPHER MARTIN
B. Oct. 26, 1968, Sacramento, CA
Oregon 5'9" 183 lbs.

1990	DET	N	16	CB
1991	BUF	N	2	CB, S
1991	PHX	N	2	CB, S
1992			1	CB

Chris Oldham continued

1993			16	CB
1994	ARI	N	11	CB
1995	PIT	N	15	CB
1996			16	CB

7 yrs. 79 games

Jim Oldham
OLDHAM, JAMES R. (Red)
B. 1905
Deceased
Arizona 5'10" 183 lbs.

1926	RAC	N	4	E, QB, HB, FB

Ray Oldham
OLDHAM, DONNIE RAY
B. Feb. 23, 1951, Gallatin, TN
Middle Tennessee State 6'0" 193 lbs.

1973	BAL	N	11	DB
1974			14	S
1975			14	S
1976			14	S, CB
1977			14	CB, S
1978			2	CB, S
1978	PIT	N	4	S
1979	NYG	N	15	S
1980	DET	N	16	S
1981			16	S
1982			5	S

10 yrs. 125 games

Bill Olds
OLDS, WILLIAM HENRY
B. Feb. 21, 1951, Kansas City, KS
Nebraska 6'1" 224 lbs.

1973	BAL	N	13	RB
1974			13	RB
1975			14	RB
1976	SEA	N	1	FB
1976	PHI	N	11	RB

4 yrs. 52 games

John Olenchalk
OLENCHALK, JOHN HUNT
B. Nov. 27, 1955, Stockton, CA
Stanford 6'0" 228 lbs.

1981	KC	N	1	LB
1982			9	C

2 yrs. 10 games

Stan Oleniczak
OLENICZAK, STANLEY (Oleo)
B. 1912
Pittsburgh 6'0" 220 lbs.

1935	PIT	N	12	T

Mitch Olenski
OLENSKI, MITCHELL J.
B. 1920, Benton, IL
Alabama 6'3" 222 lbs.

1946	MIA	AA	14	T
1947	DET	N	12	T

2 yrs. 26 games

Dave Olerich
OLERICH, DAVID BYRON
B. Nov. 14, 1944, Elmhurst, IL
San Francisco 6'1" 221 lbs.

1967	SF	N	6	TE
1968			14	TE
1969	STL	N	14	LB
1970			11	LB
1971	HOU	N	14	LB
1972	SF	N	12	LB
1973			14	LB

7 yrs. 85 games

Aaron Oliker
OLIKER, AARON EARL
B. 1904
West Virginia 170 lbs.

1926	POT	N	1	E

Elmer Oliphant
OLIPHANT, ELMER QUILLEN
B. Jul. 9, 1892, Bloomfield, IN
D. Jul. 3, 1975, New Canaan, CT
Purdue/Army 5'7" 175 lbs.

1920	ROC	A	1	FB
1921	BUF	A	10	HB

2 yrs. 11 games

Mike Oliphant
OLIPHANT, MICHAEL NATHANIEL
B. May 19, 1963, Jacksonville, FL
Puget Sound 5'10" 183 lbs.

1988	WAS	N	8	RB
1989	CLE	N	14	RB
1991			4	RB

3 yrs. 26 games

Bobby Olive
OLIVE, BOBBY LEE, JR.
B. Apr. 22, 1969, Paris, TN
Ohio State 6'0" 167 lbs.

1995	IND	N	1	WR
1996			1	WR

2 yrs. 2 games

Bill Oliver
OLIVER, WILLIAM SETH
(Country)
B. Feb. 16, 1902
D. May 1, 1932
Alabama 5'11" 180 lbs.

1926	NY	A	11	G, E
1927	NYY	N	13	G

2 yrs. 24 games

Bob Oliver
OLIVER, ROBERT
B. Jun. 17, 1947, Olney, TX
Abilene Christian 6'3" 240 lbs.

1969	CLE	N	8	DE

Chip Oliver
OLIVER, RALPH
B. Apr. 24, 1946, Winona, MS
Southern California 6'2" 220 lbs.

1968	OAK	A	14	LB
1969			14	LB

2 yrs. 28 games

Clancy Oliver
OLIVER, CLARENCE
B. Nov. 17, 1947, Bakersfield, CA
San Diego State 6'1" 180 lbs.

1969	PIT	N	9	DB
1970			14	CB
1973	STL	N	2	S

3 yrs. 25 games

Darryl Oliver
OLIVER, DARRYL
B. Jul. 13, 1964
Miami (Florida) 5'10" 194 lbs.

1987	ATL	N	2	RB

Frank Oliver
OLIVER, FRANK
B. Mar. 3, 1952, Wetumpka, AL

Frank Oliver continued
Kentucky State 6'0" 194 lbs.

1975	BUF	N	14	DB
1976	TB	N	4	DB

2 yrs. 18 games

Greg Oliver
OLIVER, GREG CURTIS
B. Jan. 15, 1949, San Antonio, TX
Trinity (Texas) 6'0" 192 lbs.

1973	PHI	N	11	RB
1974			14	RB

2 yrs. 25 games

Hubie Oliver
OLIVER, HUBERT
B. Nov. 12, 1957, Elyria, OH
Arizona 5'10" 230 lbs.

1981	PHI	N	13	FB
1983			16	RB
1984			16	FB
1985			1	RB
1986	IND	N	4	RB
1986	HOU	N	2	RB

5 yrs. 52 games

Jack Oliver
OLIVER, JOHN
B. Feb. 3, 1962, Washington, DC
Memphis State 6'3" 281 lbs.

1987	CHI	N	3	OT

Jeff Oliver
OLIVER, JEFFREY PETER
B. Jul. 28, 1965, Delhi, NY
Boston College 6'4" 292 lbs.

1989	NYJ	N	1	G

Louis Oliver
OLIVER, LOUIS
B. Mar. 9, 1966, Belle Glade, FL
Florida 6'2" 226 lbs.

1989	MIA	N	15	S
1990			16	S
1991			16	S
1992			16	S
1993			11	S
1994	CIN	N	12	S
1995	MIA	N	15	S
1996			16	S

8 yrs. 117 games

Maurice Oliver
OLIVER, MAURICE
B. Jun. 14, 1967, Birmingham, AL
Southern Mississippi 6'3" 235 lbs.

1991	TB	N	3	LB

Muhammad Oliver
OLIVER, MUHAMMAD RAMADAN
B. Mar. 12, 1969, Brooklyn, NY
Oregon 5'11" 170 lbs.

1992	DEN	N	3	CB, S
1993	KC	N	2	CB, S
1993	GB	N	2	CB
1994	MIA	N	13	CB
1995	WAS	N	1	CB

4 yrs. 21 games

Vince Oliver
OLIVER, VINCENT J.
B. 1919
Indiana 5'11" 180 lbs.

1945	CHIC	N	3	QB

Year	Team		Games	Pos.

Winslow Oliver
OLIVER, WINSLOW PAUL
B. Mar. 3, 1973, Houston, TX
New Mexico 5'7" 180 lbs.

Year	Team		Games	Pos.
1996	CAR	N	16	RB

Neal Olkewicz
OLKEWICZ, NEAL
B. Jan. 30, 1957, Phoenixville, PA
Maryland 6'0" 230 lbs.

Year	Team		Games	Pos.
1979	WAS	N	16	LB
1980			12	LB
1981			14	LB
1982			9	LB
1983			16	LB
1984			16	LB
1985			16	LB
1986			16	LB
1987			10	LB
1988			16	LB
1989			9	LB
11 yrs.	150 games			

John Olmstead
OLMSTEAD, JOHN
B. 1895
Deceased
Purdue 170 lbs.

Year	Team		Games	Pos.
1922	LOU	N	3	G
1923			3	G
2 yrs.	6 games			

Jerry Olsavsky
OLSAVSKY, JEROME DONALD
B. Mar. 29, 1967, Youngstown, OH
Pittsburgh 6'1" 222 lbs.

Year	Team		Games	Pos.
1989	PIT	N	16	LB
1990			15	LB
1991			16	LB
1992			7	LB
1993			7	LB
1994			1	LB
1995			15	LB
1996			15	LB
8 yrs.	92 games			

Merlin Olsen
OLSEN, MERLIN JAY
B. Sep. 15, 1940, Logan, UT
Utah State 6'5" 270 lbs.

Year	Team		Games	Pos.
1962	LA	N	12	DT
1963			14	DT
1964			14	DT
1965			14	DT
1966			14	DT
1967			14	DT
1968			14	DT
1969			14	DT
1970			14	DT
1971			14	DT
1972			14	DT
1973			14	DT
1974			14	DT
1975			14	DT
1976			14	DT
15 yrs.	208 games			

Norm Olsen
OLSEN, NORMAN E.
B. Dec. 1, 1921, New York, NY
Alabama 6'2" 220 lbs.

Year	Team		Games	Pos.
1944	CLE	N	9	T

Orrin Olsen
OLSEN, ORRIN JAMES
B. Jul. 7, 1963, Logan, UT
Brigham Young 6'1" 245 lbs.

Year	Team		Games	Pos.
1976	KC	N	14	C

Phil Olsen
OLSEN, PHILLIP VERNOR
B. Apr. 26, 1948, Logan, UT
Utah State 6'5" 263 lbs.

Year	Team		Games	Pos.
1971	LA	N	10	DT
1972			14	DT
1973			14	DT
1974			14	DT
1975	DEN	N	14	OT, DT
1976			14	C, DT
6 yrs.	80 games			

Ralph Olsen
OLSEN, RALPH KENNETH
B. Apr. 10, 1924, Salt Lake City, UT
D. Nov. 28, 1994, Fruit Heights, UT
Utah 6'4" 220 lbs.

Year	Team		Games	Pos.
1949	GB	N	12	E

Carl Olson
OLSON, CARL
B. Jan. 16, 1917, San Francisco, CA
UCLA 6'2" 206 lbs.

Year	Team		Games	Pos.
1942	CHIC	N	2	T

Forrest Olson
OLSON, FORREST (Tiny)
B. 1903
Deceased
Iowa 6'0" 205 lbs.

Year	Team		Games	Pos.
1927	NYY	N	2	G

Glenn Olson
OLSON, GLENN
B. 1916
Iowa 6'0" 195 lbs.

Year	Team		Games	Pos.
1940	CLE	N	1	B

Harold Olson
OLSON, HAROLD VINCENT
B. Jan. 19, 1938, Asheville, NC
Clemson 6'3" 259 lbs.

Year	Team		Games	Pos.
1960	BUF	A		OT
1961			14	OT
1962			14	OT
1963	DEN		14	OT
1964			14	OT
5 yrs.	56 games			

Swede Olson
OLSON, VINCENT
None

Year	Team		Games	Pos.
1926	BKN	A	2	G

Larry Olsonoski
OLSONOSKI, LAWRENCE R.
B. Sep. 10, 1925, Lancaster, MN
Minnesota 6'2" 214 lbs.

Year	Team		Games	Pos.
1948	GB	N	12	G
1949	NYB	N	8	G
2 yrs.	20 games			

Lance Olssen
OLSSEN, LANCE EVERETT
B. Apr. 17, 1947, Boston, MA
Purdue 6'5" 262 lbs.

Year	Team		Games	Pos.
1968	SF	N	7	OT, DT
1969			2	OT
2 yrs.	9 games			

Les Olsson
OLSSON, CARL LESTER (Swede)
B. Aug. 18, 1909, Akron, OH
Mercer 6'0" 232 lbs.

Year	Team		Games	Pos.
1934	BOS	N	12	G

Les Olsson continued

Year	Team		Games	Pos.
1935			11	T
1936			12	G
1937	WAS	N	11	G, T
1938			11	G
5 yrs.	57 games			

Al Olszewski
OLSZEWSKI, ALBERT
B. 1921
Penn State/Pittsburgh 6'2" 185 lbs.

Year	Team		Games	Pos.
1945	PIT	N	1	E

Johnny Olszewski
OLSZEWSKI, JOHN PETER
(Johnny O)
B. Dec. 21, 1930, Washington, DC
Deceased
California 5'11" 200 lbs.

Year	Team		Games	Pos.
1953	CHIC	N	12	FB
1954			11	FB
1955			11	FB
1956			11	FB
1957			11	FB
1958	WAS	N	10	FB
1959			10	FB
1960			11	FB
1961	DET	N	14	FB
1962	DEN	A	12	FB
10 yrs.	113 games			

Russ Oltz
OLTZ, RUSSELL (Fat)
B. Mar. 19, 1899
D. Jun. 2, 1956
Illinois 6'0" 213 lbs.

Year	Team		Games	Pos.
1920	HAM	A	2	G
1921			5	G
1923	HAM	N	7	C, FB, T
1924			5	T, C, G
1925			5	C, G
5 yrs.	24 games			

James O'Mahoney
O'MAHONEY, JAMES JOHN
B. Mar. 29, 1941, Pittsburgh, PA
Miami (Florida) 6'1" 231 lbs.

Year	Team		Games	Pos.
1965	NY	A	14	LB
1966			12	LB
2 yrs.	26 games			

Jim O'Malley
O'MALLEY, JAMES
B. Jul. 24, 1951, Youngstown, OH
Notre Dame 6'1" 230 lbs.

Year	Team		Games	Pos.
1973	DEN	N	12	LB
1974			14	LB
1975			14	LB
3 yrs.	40 games			

Joe O'Malley
O'MALLEY, JOSEPH
B. 1933
Georgia 6'2" 218 lbs.

Year	Team		Games	Pos.
1955	PIT	N	10	E
1956			12	E
2 yrs.	22 games			

Tom O'Malley
O'MALLEY, THOMAS
B. 1924
Cincinnati 5'11" 185 lbs.

Year	Team		Games	Pos.
1950	GB	N	1	QB

Omensky
OMENSKY

Omensky continued
None

Year	Team		Games	Pos.
1926	LOU	N	1	G

Brian O'Neal
O'NEAL, BRIAN
B. Feb. 25, 1970, Cincinnati, OH
Penn State 6'0" 233 lbs.

Year	Team		Games	Pos.
1994	PHI	N	14	RB
1995	SF	N	3	RB
2 yrs.	17 games			

Calvin O'Neal
O'NEAL, CALVIN
B. Oct. 6, 1954, Osceola, AR
Michigan 6'1" 235 lbs.

Year	Team		Games	Pos.
1978	BAL	N	15	LB

Jim O'Neal
O'NEAL, J.C. (Chief)
B. 1924
Texas Christian 6'1" 230 lbs.

Year	Team		Games	Pos.
1946	CHI	AA	12	G
1947			12	G
2 yrs.	24 games			

Ken O'Neal
O'NEAL, KENNETH ADRIAN
B. Jun. 21, 1962, San Francisco, CA
Idaho State 6'3" 240 lbs.

Year	Team		Games	Pos.
1987	NO	N	3	TE

Leslie O'Neal
O'NEAL, LESLIE CORNELIUS
B. May 7, 1964, Pulaski County, AR
Oklahoma State 6'4" 255 lbs.

Year	Team		Games	Pos.
1986	SD	N	13	DE
1988			9	DE
1989			16	DE
1990			16	LB
1991			16	LB
1992			15	DE
1993			16	DE
1994			16	DE
1995			16	DE
1996	STL	N	16	DE
10 yrs.	149 games			

Robert O'Neal
O'NEAL, ROBERT OLIVER
B. Feb. 1, 1971, Atlanta, GA
Clemson 6'1" 194 lbs.

Year	Team		Games	Pos.
1994	IND	N	2	CB

Steve O'Neal
O'NEAL, STEVE
B. Feb. 4, 1946, Hearne, TX
Texas A&M 6'3" 185 lbs.

Year	Team		Games	Pos.
1969	NY	A	14	P
1970	NYJ	N	14	P, WR
1971			14	P, WR
1972			14	P
1973	NO	N	14	P
5 yrs.	70 games			

Bob O'Neil
O'NEIL, ROBERT
B. 1933
Duquesne/Notre Dame 6'1" 229 lbs.

Year	Team		Games	Pos.
1956	PIT	N	12	G
1957			12	G
1961	NY	A	14	G
3 yrs.	38 games			

Year	Team		Games	Pos.

Chuck O'Neil
O'NEIL, CHARLES
B. 1899
Deceased
Phillips 5'10" 180 lbs.

Year	Team		Games	Pos.
1921	EVA	A	5	E, HB
1922	EVA	N	1	HB
1922	TOL	N	1	FB
1923			2	E, T
3 yrs.	9 games			

Ed O'Neil
O'NEIL, EDWARD WILLIAM
B. Sep. 8, 1952, Warren, PA
Penn State 6'3" 236 lbs.

Year	Team		Games	Pos.
1974	DET	N	14	LB
1975			14	LB
1976			14	LB
1977			14	LB
1978			16	LB
1979			16	LB
1980	GB	N	12	LB
7 yrs.	100 games			

Bill O'Neill
O'NEILL, WILLIAM J., JR. (Speedy, Sidecar)
B. 1910
Detroit 6'0" 185 lbs.

Year	Team		Games	Pos.
1935	DET	N	1	HB
1937	CLE	N	1	HB
2 yrs.	2 games			

Pat O'Neill
O'NEILL, PATRICK JAMES
B. Feb. 9, 1971, Scott AFB, IL
Syracuse 6'1" 195 lbs.

Year	Team		Games	Pos.
1994	NE	N	16	P
1995			8	P
1995	CHI	N	1	P
2 yrs.	25 games			

Red O'Neill
O'NEILL, MARTIN L.
B. 1902
Deceased
Connecticut 5'10" 190 lbs.

Year	Team		Games	Pos.
1926	HAR	N	9	C

Tip O'Neill
O'NEILL, GERALD R.
B. 1898
Deceased
St. Norbert/Detroit 5'10" 170 lbs.

Year	Team		Games	Pos.
1922	DAY	N	4	HB, FB

Wally O'Neill
O'NEILL, WALTER
B. 1901
Deceased
Wisconsin-Superior 6'0" 195 lbs.

Year	Team		Games	Pos.
1925	DUL	N	3	E, G, T

Larry Onesti
ONESTI, LAWRENCE J.
B. 1939
Northwestern 6'0" 200 lbs.

Year	Team		Games	Pos.
1962	HOU	A	4	DB
1963			14	LB
1964			6	LB
1965			14	LB
4 yrs.	38 games			

Dennis Onkontz
ONKONTZ, DENNIS HENRY
B. Feb. 6, 1948, North Hampton, GA

Dennis Onkontz *continued*
Penn State 6'1" 220 lbs.

Year	Team		Games	Pos.
1970	NYJ	N	9	LB, S

Bob Ontko
ONTKO, BOB
B. Mar. 21, 1964, Swoyersville, PA
Penn State 6'3" 237 lbs.

Year	Team		Games	Pos.
1987	IND	N	3	LB

Dave Opfar
OPFAR, DAVID LOUIS
B. Jan. 16, 1960, McKeesport, PA
Penn State 6'4" 270 lbs.

Year	Team		Games	Pos.
1987	PIT	N	3	NT

Edward Opolewski
OPOLEWSKI, EDWARD L., JR.
B. Nov. 11, 1919, Detroit, MI
D. Mar. 4, 1993, Novi, MI
Eastern Michigan 6'3" 230 lbs.

Year	Team		Games	Pos.
1943	DET	N	2	T
1944			10	T
2 yrs.	12 games			

Jim Opperman
OPPERMAN, JAMES
B. Dec. 18, 1953, Waterbury, CT
Colorado State 6'3" 220 lbs.

Year	Team		Games	Pos.
1975	PHI	N	10	LB

Johnny O'Quinn
O'QUINN, JOHN (Red)
B. Sep. 7, 1925, Asheboro, NC
Wake Forest 6'2" 195 lbs.

Year	Team		Games	Pos.
1950	CHIB	N	12	E
1951			2	E
1951	PHI	N	5	E
2 yrs.	19 games			

Joe Orduna
ORDUNA, JOSEPH MANUEL
B. Nov. 6, 1948, Omaha, NE
Nebraska 6'0" 195 lbs.

Year	Team		Games	Pos.
1972	NYG	N	11	RB
1973			14	RB
1974	BAL	N	14	DB
3 yrs.	39 games			

O'Reilly
O'REILLY,

Year	Team		Games	Pos.
1924	RAC		1	G

Frank Ori
ORI, FRANK
B. Mar. 20, 1964, Highland Park, IL
Northern Iowa 6'2" 255 lbs.

Year	Team		Games	Pos.
1987	MIN	N	3	G

Mike Oriard
ORIARD, MICHAEL VINCENT
B. May 26, 1948, Spokane, WA
Notre Dame 6'4" 223 lbs.

Year	Team		Games	Pos.
1970	KC	N	1	C
1971			14	C
1972			14	C
1973			13	C
4 yrs.	42 games			

Bob Oristaglio
ORISTAGLIO, ROBERT P.
B. Apr. 6, 1924, Philadelphia, PA
D. Feb. 14, 1995, York, PA
Pennsylvania 6'2" 214 lbs.

Year	Team		Games	Pos.
1949	BUF	AA	12	E

Bob Oristaglio *continued*

Year	Team		Games	Pos.
1950	BAL	N	12	E
1951	CLE	N	12	E
1952	PHI	N	4	E
4 yrs.	40 games			

Bo Orlando
ORLANDO, JOSEPH JOHN
B. Apr. 3, 1966, Berwick, PA
West Virginia 5'10" 180 lbs.

Year	Team		Games	Pos.
1990	HOU	N	16	S
1991			16	S
1992			6	S
1993			16	S
1994			16	S
1995	SD	N	16	S
1996	CIN	N	16	S
7 yrs.	102 games			

Dan Orlich
ORLICH, DANIEL E.
B. Dec. 21, 1924, Chisholm, MN
Nevada-Reno 6'5" 215 lbs.

Year	Team		Games	Pos.
1949	GB	N	12	E
1951			12	E
2 yrs.	24 games			

Elliott Ormsbee
ORMSBEE, EZRA ELLIOTT (Buzz)
B. Sep. 19, 1921, Hamilton, IL
Bradley 5'11" 185 lbs.

Year	Team		Games	Pos.
1946	PHI	N	4	HB

Fred Orns
ORNS, FRED
B. May 26, 1962
Chapman 6'2" 230 lbs.

Year	Team		Games	Pos.
1987	SEA	N	2	LB

Tom Orosz
OROSZ, THOMAS
B. Sep. 26, 1959, Painesville, OH
Ohio State 6'1" 204 lbs.

Year	Team		Games	Pos.
1981	MIA	N	16	P
1982			9	P
1983	SF	N	16	P
1984			2	P
4 yrs.	43 games			

Charlie O'Rourke
O'ROURKE, CHARLES C.
B. May 10, 1919, Montreal, Quebec
Boston College 5'11" 175 lbs.

Year	Team		Games	Pos.
1942	CHIB	N	11	QB
1946	LA	AA	14	QB
1947			14	QB
1948	BAL	AA	14	QB
1949			5	QB
5 yrs.	58 games			

Jimmy Orr
ORR, JAMES EDWARD, JR.
B. Oct. 24, 1935, Seneca, SC
Georgia 5'11" 185 lbs.

Year	Team		Games	Pos.
1958	PIT	N	12	E
1959			12	E
1960			12	E
1961	BAL	N	13	OE
1962			14	OE
1963			12	FL
1964			14	FL
1965			14	FL
1966			13	FL
1967			5	FL
1968			13	FL

Jimmy Orr *continued*

Year	Team		Games	Pos.
1969			7	WR
1970			9	WR
13 yrs.	150 games			

Terry Orr
ORR, TERRY
B. Sep. 27, 1961, Savannah, GA
Texas 6'3" 227 lbs.

Year	Team		Games	Pos.
1986	WAS	N	16	TE
1987			10	TE
1988			16	TE
1989			16	TE
1990			5	TE
1990	SD	N	9	TE
1991	WAS	N	16	TE
1992			16	TE
1993			4	TE
8 yrs.	108 games			

Ralph Ortega
ORTEGA, RALPH
B. Jul. 6, 1953, Havana, Cuba
Florida 6'2" 200 lbs.

Year	Team		Games	Pos.
1975	ATL	N	14	LB
1976			14	LB
1977			14	LB
1978			15	LB
1979	MIA	N	8	LB
1980			16	LB
6 yrs.	81 games			

Keith Ortego
ORTEGO, BRYANT KEITH
B. Aug. 30, 1963, Eunice, LA
McNeese State 6'0" 180 lbs.

Year	Team		Games	Pos.
1985	CHI	N	7	WR
1986			16	WR
1987			8	WR
3 yrs.	31 games			

Henry Orth
ORTH, HENRY
B. 1899
Deceased
Miami (Ohio) 6'0" 180 lbs.

Year	Team		Games	Pos.
1921	CIN	A	1	G

Chuck Ortmann
ORTMANN, CHARLES
B. Jun. 1, 1929
Michigan 6'1" 190 lbs.

Year	Team		Games	Pos.
1951	PIT	N	12	QB
1952	DAL	N	3	QB
2 yrs.	15 games			

Greg Orton
ORTON, GREG
B. Aug. 9, 1962
Nebraska 6'1" 265 lbs.

Year	Team		Games	Pos.
1987	DET	N	3	G

Herb Orvis
ORVIS, HERBERT VAUGHN
B. Oct. 17, 1946, Petoskey, MI
Colorado 6'5" 248 lbs.

Year	Team		Games	Pos.
1972	DET	N	14	DE
1973			14	DE
1974			14	DT
1975			14	DT
1976			2	DT
1977			14	DT
1978	BAL	N	2	DT
1979			16	DT
1980			16	DT
1981			16	DT
10 yrs.	122 games			

Year	Team		Games	Pos.

Ossie Orwoll
ORWOLL, OSWALD CHRISTIAN
B. Nov. 17, 1900, Portland, OR
D. May 8, 1967, Decorah, IA
Luther 6'0" 165 lbs.

| 1926 | MIL | N | 3 | HB |

Dave Osborn
OSBORN, DAVID VANCE
B. Mar. 18, 1943, Everett, WA
North Dakota 6'0" 206 lbs.

1965	MIN	N	14	HB
1966			14	HB
1967			14	RB
1968			4	RB
1969			14	RB
1970			14	RB
1971			11	RB
1972			14	RB
1973			11	RB
1974			12	RB
1975			14	RB
1976	GB	N	6	RB
12 yrs.	142 games			

Duke Osborn
OSBORN, ROBERT
B. 1897
Deceased
Penn State 5'10" 188 lbs.

1921	CAN	A	10	G, T
1922	CAN		12	C, G
1923			10	G
1924	CLE	N	9	C
1925	POT	N	11	G
1926			14	G
1927			8	G, C
1928			8	G, C, T
8 yrs.	82 games			

Mike Osborn
OSBORN, MICHAEL JOSEPH
B. Nov. 19, 1955, San Antonio, TX
Kansas State 6'5" 235 lbs.

| 1978 | PHI | N | 16 | LB |

Chuck Osborne
OSBORN, CHARLES WAYNE
B. Nov. 2, 1973, Los Angeles, CA
Arizona 6'2" 281 lbs.

| 1996 | STL | N | 15 | DT |

Clancy Osborne
OSBORNE, CLARENCE
B. Dec. 23, 1934, Lubbock, TX
Arizona State 6'3" 218 lbs.

1959	SF	N	8	LB
1960			8	LB
1961	MIN	N	14	LB
1962			14	LB
1963	OAK	A	14	LB
1964			14	LB
6 yrs.	72 games			

Eldonta Osborne
OSBORNE, ELDONTA R.
B. Aug. 12, 1967
Louisiana Tech 6'0" 226 lbs.

| 1990 | PHX | N | 12 | LB |

Jim Osborne
OSBORNE, JAMES HENRY (Jaws)
B. Sep. 7, 1949, Sylvania, GA
Southern University 6'3" 249 lbs.

1972	CHI	N	14	DT
1973			14	DT
1974			14	DT

Jim Osborne continued

1975			12	DT
1976			14	DT
1977			13	DT
1978			15	DT
1979			16	DT
1980			16	DT
1981			16	DT
1982			9	DT
1983			16	DT
1984			16	DT
13 yrs.	185 games			

Richard Osborne
OSBORNE, RICHARD
B. Oct. 31, 1953, Wichita, KS
Texas A&M 6'3" 230 lbs.

1976	NYJ	N	9	TE
1976	PHI	N	4	TE
1977			14	TE
1978			16	TE
1979	STL	N	7	TE
4 yrs.	50 games			

Tom Osborne
OSBORNE, THOMAS WILLIAM
B. Feb. 23, 1937, Hastings, NE
Hastings 6'3" 190 lbs.

1960	WAS	N	10	E
1961			14	FL
2 yrs.	24 games			

Vince Osby
OSBY, VINCENT LEE
B. Jul. 8, 1961, Los Angeles, CA
Illinois 5'11" 220 lbs.

1984	SD	N	16	LB
1985			7	LB
2 yrs.	23 games			

Terry O'Shea
O'SHEA, TERENCE WILLIAM
B. Dec. 3, 1966, Pittsburgh, PA
Indiana (Pennsylvania) 6'4" 236 lbs.

1989	PIT	N	16	TE
1990			16	TE
2 yrs.	32 games			

Willie Oshodin
OSHODIN, WILLIAM EHIZELA
B. Sep. 16, 1969, Benin City, Nigeria
Villanova 6'4" 265 lbs.

1993	DEN	N	15	DE
1994			13	DE
1995			2	DE
3 yrs.	30 games			

Sandy Osiecki
OSIECKI, STANLEY EUGENE
B. May 18, 1960, Ansonia, CT
Arizona State 6'5" 202 lbs.

| 1984 | KC | N | 4 | QB |

Willie Osley
OSLEY, WILLIE
B. Apr. 10, 1951, Detroit, MI
Illinois 6'0" 195 lbs.

1974	NE	N	10	CB
1974	KC	N	3	CB
1 yr.	13 games			

Bill Osmanski
OSMANSKI, WILLIAM THOMAS
B. Dec. 29, 1915, Providence, RI
Holy Cross 5'11" 197 lbs.

| 1939 | CHIB | N | 10 | FB |

Bill Osmanski continued

1940			8	FB
1941			10	FB
1942			1	FB
1943			4	FB
1946			11	FB
1947			4	FB
7 yrs.	48 games			

Joe Osmanski
OSMANSKI, JOSEPH
B. Dec. 26, 1919, Providence, RI
Deceased
Holy Cross 6'2" 218 lbs.

1946	CHIB	N	9	FB
1947			12	FB
1948			12	FB
1949			2	FB
1949	NYB	N	8	FB
4 yrs.	43 games			

Ted Ossowski
OSSOWSKI, THEODORE
B. 1922
Deceased
Oregon State/Southern California/Oregon State 6'0" 218 lbs.

| 1947 | NY | AA | 3 | T |

Dwayne O'Steen
O'STEEN, DWAYNE PHILIP
B. Dec. 20, 1954, Los Angeles, CA
California/San Jose State 6'1" 193 lbs.

1978	LA	N	13	CB
1979			16	CB
1980	OAK		15	CB
1981			16	CB
1982	BAL	N	3	CB
1983	TB	N	3	CB
1983	GB	N	7	CB
1984			4	CB, S
7 yrs.	77 games			

Jimmy Ostendarp
OSTENDARP, JAMES E.
B. 1925
Bucknell 5'8" 178 lbs.

1950	NYG	N	7	B
1951			2	B
2 yrs.	9 games			

Jerry Ostroski
OSTROSKI, JERRY
B. Jul. 12, 1970, Collegeville, PA
Tulsa 6'4" 310 lbs.

1994	BUF	N	4	G
1995			16	G
1996			16	G
3 yrs.	36 games			

Chet Ostrowski
OSTROWSKI, CHESTER CASMIR
B. Apr. 8, 1930, Chicago, IL
Notre Dame 6'1" 232 lbs.

1954	WAS	N	12	E
1955			11	E
1956			12	E
1957			12	E
1958			12	E, T
1959			9	E
6 yrs.	68 games			

Paul Oswald
OSWALD, PAUL EUGENE
B. Apr. 9, 1964, Topeka, KS
Kansas 6'3" 273 lbs.

| 1987 | PIT | N | 2 | C |

Paul Oswald continued

1988	DAL	N	1	C
1988	ATL	N	3	G
2 yrs.	6 games			

Jim Otis
OTIS, JAMES LLOYD
B. Apr. 29, 1948, Celina, OH
Ohio State 6'0" 223 lbs.

1970	NO	N	13	RB
1971	KC	N	13	RB
1972			10	RB
1973	STL	N	10	RB
1974			14	RB
1975			14	RB
1976			14	RB
1977			13	RB
1978			15	RB
9 yrs.	116 games			

Bill O'Toole
O'TOOLE, WILLIAM
B. 1900
Deceased
None

| 1924 | DUL | N | 1 | G |

Lowell Otte
OTTE, M. LOWELL
B. 1904
Iowa 6'2" 180 lbs.

1926	NY	A	8	E, G, T
1927	BUF	N	5	E
2 yrs.	13 games			

Dick Ottele
OTTELE, RICHARD
B. Dec. 8, 1926, Yuma, CO
Washington 6'3" 210 lbs.

| 1948 | LA | AA | 8 | B |

John Otterbacher
OTTERBACHER, JOHN
B. 1901
Deceased
Ohio State 190 lbs.

| 1926 | CLE | A | 2 | G |

Brad Ottis
OTTIS, BRAD ALLEN
B. Aug. 2, 1972, Wahoo, NE
Wayne State (Nebraska) 6'4" 271 lbs.

1994	LARM	N	13	DE, DT
1995	STL	N	12	DE, DT
1996	ARI	N	11	DT
3 yrs.	36 games			

Al Otto
OTTO, ALVIN (Bo)
None 182 lbs.

1922	LOU		4	T, G
1923			3	C
2 yrs.	7 games			

Bob Otto
OTTO, ROBERT
B. Dec. 16, 1962, Sacramento, CA
Idaho State 6'6" 251 lbs.

1986	DAL	N	4	DE
1987	HOU	N	3	DE
2 yrs.	7 games			

Gus Otto
OTTO, AUGUST JOSEPH
B. Dec. 8, 1943, St. Louis, MO

Year	Team		Games	Pos.

Gus Otto continued

Missouri 6'2" 220 lbs.

Year	Team		Games	Pos.
1965	OAK	A	14	LB
1966			14	LB
1967			14	LB
1968			13	LB
1969			14	LB
1970	OAK	N	14	LB
1971			9	LB
1972			11	LB
8 yrs.		103 games		

Jim Otto

OTTO, JAMES EDWIN (Double O)
B. Jan. 5, 1938, Wausau, WI
Miami (Florida) 6'2" 244 lbs.

Year	Team		Games	Pos.
1960	OAK	A	14	C
1961			14	C
1962			14	C
1963			14	C
1964			14	C
1965			14	C
1966			14	C
1967			14	C
1968			14	C
1969			14	C
1970	OAK	N	14	C
1971			14	C
1972			14	C
1973			14	C
1974			14	C
15 yrs.		210 games		

Louis Oubre

OUBRE, LOUIS BYRON, III
B. May 15, 1958, New Orleans, LA
Oklahoma 6'4" 262 lbs.

Year	Team		Games	Pos.
1982	NO	N	9	G
1983			16	G
1984			12	G
1987	MIA	N	3	G
4 yrs.		40 games		

Greg Ours

OURS, GREG
B. Oct. 29, 1963
Muskingum 6'5" 279 lbs.

Year	Team		Games	Pos.
1987	MIA	N	3	C

John Outlaw

OUTLAW, JOHN
B. Jan. 8, 1945, Clarksdale, MS
Jackson State 5'10" 160 lbs.

Year	Team		Games	Pos.
1969	BOS	A	9	DB
1970	BOS	N	5	CB
1971	NE	N	14	DB
1972			6	CB
1973	PHI	N	7	CB
1974			14	CB
1975			14	CB
1976			13	CB
1977			14	CB
1978				CB
10 yrs.		96 games		

Bill Overmyer

OVERMYER, WILLIAM LEE
B. Jun. 16, 1949, Fremont, OH
Ashland 6'3" 220 lbs.

Year	Team		Games	Pos.
1972	PHI	N	6	LB

David Overstreet

OVERSTREET, DAVID
B. Sep. 28, 1958, Big Sandy, TX
D. Jun. 24, 1984, Winona, TX
Oklahoma 5'11" 208 lbs.

Year	Team		Games	Pos.
1983	MIA	N	14	RB

Don Overton

OVERTON, DONALD EUGENE
B. Sep. 24, 1967, Columbus, OH
Fairmont State 6'0" 221 lbs.

Year	Team		Games	Pos.
1990	NE	N	7	RB
1991	DET	N	16	RB
1992			1	RB
3 yrs.		24 games		

Jerry Overton

OVERTON, JERRY L.
B. Jan. 24, 1941
Utah 6'2" 190 lbs.

Year	Team		Games	Pos.
1963	DAL	N	10	S

Al Owen

OWEN, ALTON (Blondie)
B. Feb. 16, 1913, Glen Ridge, NJ
St. Lawrence/Mercer 6'0" 194 lbs.

Year	Team		Games	Pos.
1939	NYG	N	6	HB
1940			4	HB
1942			7	HB
3 yrs.		17 games		

Bill Owen

OWEN, WILLIAM C. (Red)
B. Sep. 29, 1903, Aline, OK
Oklahoma State 6'0" 211 lbs.

Year	Team		Games	Pos.
1927	CLE	N	13	T, G
1928	DET	N	10	T, G
1929	NYG	N	15	T, G, E
1930			16	T, G
1931			14	T
1932			11	T
1933				T, G
1934			12	T
1935			11	G, T
1936			11	T, G
10 yrs.		113 games		

Steve Owen

OWEN, STEPHEN JOSEPH (Stout Steve)
B. Apr. 21, 1898, Cleo Springs, OK
D. May 17, 1964, New York, NY
Phillips 5'10" 235 lbs.

Year	Team		Games	Pos.
1924	KC	N	9	G, T
1925			8	T
1925	CLE	N	1	T
1927	NYG	N	13	T, G
1928			12	T, G
1929			15	T, G, C
1930			17	T, G
1931			7	T
1933				G
8 yrs.		82 games		

Tom Owen

OWEN, WILLIS THOMAS
B. Sep. 1, 1952, Shreveport, LA
Wichita State 6'1" 195 lbs.

Year	Team		Games	Pos.
1974	SF	N	10	QB
1975			4	QB
1976	NE	N	2	QB
1978			2	QB
1979			6	QB
1981			2	QB
6 yrs.		26 games		

Artie Owens

OWENS, ARTHUR GENE
B. Jan. 14, 1953, Montgomery, AL
West Virginia 5'10" 176 lbs.

Year	Team		Games	Pos.
1976	SD	N	14	WR
1977			11	WR
1978			13	WR
1979			16	RB
1980	BUF	N	4	WR

Artie Owens continued

Year	Team		Games	Pos.
1980	NO	N	3	WR
5 yrs.		61 games		

Billy Owens

OWENS, BILLY JOE, JR.
B. Dec. 2, 1965, Syracuse, NY
Pittsburgh 6'1" 207 lbs.

Year	Team		Games	Pos.
1988	DAL	N	16	CB, S

Brick Owens

OWENS, RALPH (Rip)
B. 1893
Deceased
Lawrence 5'10" 210 lbs.

Year	Team		Games	Pos.
1922	GB	N	3	G

Brig Owens

OWENS, BRIGMAN
B. Feb. 16, 1943, Linden, TX
Cincinnati 5'11" 190 lbs.

Year	Team		Games	Pos.
1966	WAS	N	14	DB
1967			14	DB
1968			14	DB
1969			14	S
1970			14	S
1971			14	S
1972			14	S
1973			14	S
1974			14	S
1975			14	S
1976			14	S
1977				S
12 yrs.		154 games		

Burgess Owens

OWENS, CLARENCE BURGESS, JR.
B. Aug. 2, 1951, Columbus, OH
Miami (Florida) 6'2" 199 lbs.

Year	Team		Games	Pos.
1973	NYJ	N	14	CB, S
1974			14	S
1975			11	S
1976			14	S
1977			14	S
1978			14	S
1979			16	S
1980	OAK	N	16	S
1981			16	S
1982	LARI	N	8	S
10 yrs.		137 games		

Dan Owens

OWENS, DANIEL WILLIAM
B. Mar. 16, 1967, Whittier, CA
Southern California 6'3" 277 lbs.

Year	Team		Games	Pos.
1990	DET	N	16	DE
1991			16	DE
1992			16	DE
1993			15	DE
1994			16	DE
1995			16	DE, DT
1996	ATL	N	16	NT
7 yrs.		111 games		

Darrick Owens

OWENS, DARRICK ALFRED
B. Nov. 5, 1970, Boynton Beach, FL
Mississippi 6'2" 195 lbs.

Year	Team		Games	Pos.
1992	PIT	N	3	WR

Dennis Owens

OWENS, DENNIS RAY
B. Feb. 24, 1960, Clinton, NC
North Carolina State 6'1" 256 lbs.

Year	Team		Games	Pos.
1982	NE	N	9	NT
1983			16	NT

Dennis Owens continued

Year	Team		Games	Pos.
1984			16	NT
1985			14	NT
1986			14	NT
5 yrs.		69 games		

Don Owens

OWENS, DONALD FRED
B. Apr. 3, 1932, St. Louis, MO
Southern Mississippi 6'5" 255 lbs.

Year	Team		Games	Pos.
1957	WAS	N	10	T
1958	PHI	N	12	T
1959			12	T
1960			3	T
1960	STL	N	9	T
1961			14	DT
1962			14	DT
1963			13	DT
7 yrs.		87 games		

Ike Owens

OWENS, ISAIAH H.
B. Jan. 8, 1921, Columbus, GA
Illinois 6'1" 190 lbs.

Year	Team		Games	Pos.
1948	CHI	AA	8	E

James Owens

OWENS, JAMES E.
B. Jul. 5, 1955, Sacramento, CA
UCLA 5'11" 188 lbs.

Year	Team		Games	Pos.
1979	SF	N	16	WR
1980			14	WR, RB
1981	TB	N	16	RB
1982			8	RB
1983			12	RB
1984			4	RB
6 yrs.		70 games		

Jim Owens

OWENS, JAMES DONALD
B. Mar. 6, 1927, Oklahoma City, OK
Oklahoma 6'3" 205 lbs.

Year	Team		Games	Pos.
1950	BAL	N	8	E

Joe Owens

OWENS, JOE
B. Nov. 8, 1946, Columbia, MS
Alcorn State 6'2" 244 lbs.

Year	Team		Games	Pos.
1970	SD	N	14	DE
1971	NO	N	14	DE
1972			14	DE
1973			14	DE
1974			14	DE
1975			14	DE
1976	HOU	N	3	DE
7 yrs.		87 games		

Luke Owens

OWENS, LUKE
B. Oct. 19, 1933, Cleveland, OH
Kent State 6'2" 254 lbs.

Year	Team		Games	Pos.
1957	BAL	N	11	T
1958	CHIC	N	11	T
1959			12	T
1960	STL	N	12	E
1961			14	DE
1962			14	DE
1963			13	DE
1964			14	DT
1965			13	DT
9 yrs.		114 games		

Marv Owens

OWENS, MARVIN DUANE
B. Jun. 16, 1950, Orange, CA
San Diego State 5'11" 205 lbs.

Year	Team		Games	Pos.
1973	STL	N	8	WR

Year	Team		Games	Pos.

Marv Owens continued

Year	Team		Games	Pos.
1974	NYJ	N	2	WR
2 yrs.	10 games			

Mel Owens
OWENS, MEL TYRAE
B. Dec. 7, 1958, Detroit, MI
Michigan 6'2" 225 lbs.

Year	Team		Games	Pos.
1981	LA	N	16	LB
1982	LARM	N	7	LB
1983			16	LB
1984			16	LB
1985			16	LB
1986			16	LB
1987			12	LB
1988			7	LB
1989			16	LB
9 yrs.	122 games			

Morris Owens
OWENS, MORRIS LAMAR
B. Feb. 14, 1953, Oakland, CA
Arizona State 6'0" 192 lbs.

Year	Team		Games	Pos.
1975	MIA	N	2	WR
1976			2	WR
1976	TB	N	12	WR
1977			14	WR
1978			16	WR
1979			16	WR
5 yrs.	62 games			

Pete Owens
OWENS, PETE
B. 1917
Texas Tech 5'11" 205 lbs.

Year	Team		Games	Pos.
1943	BKN	N	5	G

R. C. Owens
OWENS, R. C. (Alley Oop)
College of Idaho 6'3" 197 lbs.

Year	Team		Games	Pos.
1957	SF	N	12	FL
1958			12	FL
1959			12	FL
1960			11	FL
1961			14	FL
1962	BAL	N	14	FL
1963			3	FL
1964	NYG	N	11	FL
8 yrs.	89 games			

Rich Owens
OWENS, RICH
B. May 22, 1972, Philadelphia, PA
Lehigh 6'6" 263 lbs.

Year	Team		Games	Pos.
1995	WAS	N	10	DE
1996			16	DE
2 yrs.	26 games			

Steve Owens
OWENS, STEVE EVERETT
B. Dec. 9, 1947, Gore, OK
Oklahoma 6'2" 217 lbs.

Year	Team		Games	Pos.
1970	DET	N	6	RB
1971			14	RB
1972			10	RB
1973			12	RB
1974			11	RB
5 yrs.	53 games			

Terrell Owens
OWENS, TERRELL
B. Dec. 7, 1973, Alexander City, AL
Tennessee-Chattanooga 6'2" 213 lbs.

Year	Team		Games	Pos.
1996	SF	N	16	WR

Terry Owens
OWENS, TERRY WOODROW (Gomer)
B. Jul. 5, 1944, Jasper, AL
Jacksonville State 6'6" 263 lbs.

Year	Team		Games	Pos.
1966	SD	A	14	OT
1967			14	OT
1968			14	OT
1969			14	OT
1970	SD	N	14	OT
1971			14	OT
1972			14	OT
1973			14	OT
1974			14	OT
1975			7	OT
10 yrs.	133 games			

Tinker Owens
OWENS, CHARLES W.
B. Oct. 3, 1954, Miami, OK
Oklahoma 5'11" 170 lbs.

Year	Team		Games	Pos.
1976	NO	N	14	WR
1978			14	WR
1979			13	WR
1980			7	WR
4 yrs.	48 games			

Mike Ozdowski
OZDOWSKI, MICHAEL THOMAS
B. Sep. 24, 1955, Cleveland, OH
Virginia 6'5" 242 lbs.

Year	Team		Games	Pos.
1978	BAL	N	16	DE
1979			11	DE
1980			15	DE
1981			12	DE
4 yrs.	54 games			

Jim Pace
PACE, JAMES E.
B. Jan. 1, 1936, Little Rock, AR
D. Mar. 4, 1983, Culver City, CA
Michigan 6'0" 195 lbs.

Year	Team		Games	Pos.
1958	SF	N	12	HB

Dave Pacella
PACELLA, DAVID WADE
B. Feb. 7, 1960, Sewickley, PA
Maryland 6'3" 266 lbs.

Year	Team		Games	Pos.
1984	PHI	N	16	OT, G

Vince Pacewicz
PACEWICZ, VINCENT C.
B. May 28, 1920
D. Apr. 1, 1990, North Hollywood, CA
Loyola (California)/San Francisco 6'1" 205 lbs.

Year	Team		Games	Pos.
1947	WAS	N	2	FB

Chris Pacheco
PACHECO, CHRIS
B. Jan. 22, 1964
Fresno State 6'0" 250 lbs.

Year	Team		Games	Pos.
1987	LARM	N	3	NT

Walter Packer
PACKER, WALTER
B. Nov. 7, 1955, Leakesville, MS
Mississippi State 5'10" 174 lbs.

Year	Team		Games	Pos.
1977	SEA	N	10	CB
1977	TB	N	1	CB
1 yr.	11 games			

Bob Padan
PADAN, ROBERT
B. Aug., 1893
Deceased

Bob Padan continued
Ohio State/Otterbein 165 lbs.

Year	Team		Games	Pos.
1922	LOU	N	3	HB

Gary Padjen
PADJEN, GARY A.
B. Jul. 2, 1958, Salt Lake City, UT
Arizona State 6'2" 246 lbs.

Year	Team		Games	Pos.
1982	BAL	N	8	LB
1983			16	LB
1984	IND	N	16	LB
1987			1	LB
4 yrs.	41 games			

Max Padlow
PADLOW, MAX
B. Aug. 15, 1912, Russia
D. Aug. 8, 1971, Dayton, OH
Ohio State 6'1" 199 lbs.

Year	Team		Games	Pos.
1935	PHI	N	4	E
1936			1	E
2 yrs.	5 games			

Bob Paffrath
PAFFRATH, ROBERT WILLIAM
B. Jul. 3, 1918, Mankato, MN
Minnesota 5'8" 190 lbs.

Year	Team		Games	Pos.
1946	BKN	AA	5	HB
1946	MIA	AA	6	HB
1 yr.	11 games			

Fred Pagac
PAGAC, FRED
B. Apr. 26, 1952, Brownsville, PA
Ohio State 6'0" 220 lbs.

Year	Team		Games	Pos.
1974	CHI	N	14	TE
1976	TB	N	14	TE, LB
2 yrs.	28 games			

Alan Page
PAGE, ALAN CEDRIC
B. Aug. 7, 1945, Canton, OH
Notre Dame 6'5" 244 lbs.

Year	Team		Games	Pos.
1967	MIN	N	14	DE
1968			14	DT
1969			14	DT
1970			14	DT
1971			14	DT
1972			14	DT
1973			14	DT
1974			14	DT
1975			14	DT
1976			14	DT
1977			14	DT
1978			6	DT
1978	CHI	N	10	DT
1979			16	DT
1980			16	DT
1981			16	DT
15 yrs.	218 games			

Paul Page
PAGE, PAUL EUGENE
B. Sep. 16, 1927, Eldorado, TX
Southern Methodist 6'0" 180 lbs.

Year	Team		Games	Pos.
1949	BAL	AA	8	B

Mike Pagel
PAGEL, MICHAEL JONATHAN
B. Sep. 13, 1960, Douglas, AZ
Arizona State 6'2" 206 lbs.

Year	Team		Games	Pos.
1982	BAL	N	9	QB
1983			15	QB
1984	IND	N	11	QB
1985			16	QB
1986	CLE	N	1	QB
1987			4	QB

Mike Pagel continued

Year	Team		Games	Pos.
1988			5	QB
1989			16	QB
1990			16	QB
1991	LARM	N	16	QB
1992			16	QB
1993			7	QB
12 yrs.	132 games			

Joe Pagliei
PAGLIEI, JOSEPH ANTHONY
B. Apr. 12, 1934
Clemson 6'0" 220 lbs.

Year	Team		Games	Pos.
1959	PHI	N	7	FB
1960	NY	A		FB
2 yrs.	7 games			

Louie Pahl
PAHL, LOUIS
B. 1897
Deceased
None 5'8" 185 lbs.

Year	Team		Games	Pos.
1923	MIN	N	8	HB, FB
1924			3	FB, HB
2 yrs.	11 games			

Jeff Pahukoa
PAHUKOA, JEFF KALANI
B. Feb. 9, 1969, Vancouver, WA
Washington 6'2" 268 lbs.

Year	Team		Games	Pos.
1991	LARM	N	7	G, OT
1992			16	G, OT
1993			16	G, OT
1995	ATL	N	6	G
1996			14	G
5 yrs.	59 games			

Shane Pahukoa
PAHUKOA, SHANE
B. Nov. 25, 1970, Vancouver, WA
Washington 6'2" 202 lbs.

Year	Team		Games	Pos.
1995	NO	N	15	S

Lee Paige
PAIGE, LEE
B. Oct. 16, 1960
Florida State 6'0" 197 lbs.

Year	Team		Games	Pos.
1987	TB	N	3	CB

Stephone Paige
PAIGE, STEPHONE
B. Oct. 15, 1961, Long Beach, CA
Fresno State 6'2" 184 lbs.

Year	Team		Games	Pos.
1983	KC	N	16	WR
1984			16	WR
1985			16	WR
1986			16	WR
1987			12	WR
1988			16	WR
1989			14	WR
1990			16	WR
1991			3	WR
9 yrs.	125 games			

Tony Paige
PAIGE, ANTHONY R.
B. Oct. 14, 1962, Washington, DC
Virginia Tech 5'10" 225 lbs.

Year	Team		Games	Pos.
1984	NYJ	N	16	FB
1985			16	FB
1986			16	RB
1987	DET	N	5	RB
1988			16	RB
1989			16	RB
1990	MIA	N	13	RB
1991			16	RB
1992			16	RB
9 yrs.	130 games			

Year	Team	Games	Pos.

Homer Paine
PAINE, HOMER
B. Sep. 20, 1923, Hennessey, OK
Tulsa/Oklahoma 6'0" 235 lbs.

Year	Team		Games	Pos.
1949	CHI	AA	12	T

Jeff Paine
PAINE, JEFFREY FRANKLIN
B. Aug. 19, 1961, Garland, TX
Texas A&M 6'2" 224 lbs.

Year	Team		Games	Pos.
1984	KC	N	14	LB
1985			12	LB
1986	WAS	N	2	LB
1987	STL	N	1	LB

4 yrs. 29 games

Mike Painepinto
PAINEPINTO, MIKE
B. Nov. 17, 1965
Canisius 5'11" 202 lbs.

Year	Team		Games	Pos.
1987	BUF	N	1	RB

Carl Painter
PAINTER, CARL DREW
B. May 10, 1964, Norfolk, VA
Hampton Institute 5'9" 185 lbs.

Year	Team		Games	Pos.
1988	DET	N	12	RB
1989			15	RB

2 yrs. 27 games

Lou Palatella
PALATELLA, LOUIS
B. 1933, Vandergrift, PA
Pittsburgh 6'2" 230 lbs.

Year	Team		Games	Pos.
1955	SF	N	12	G
1956			12	G
1957			12	G
1958			12	G

4 yrs. 48 games

Lou Palazzi
PALAZZI, LOUIS J.
B. Jun. 25, 1921, Groton, CT
Penn State 6'0" 198 lbs.

Year	Team		Games	Pos.
1946	NYG	N	5	C
1947			11	C

2 yrs. 16 games

Lonnie Palelei
PALELEI, SIULAGI JACK
B. Oct. 15, 1970, Nu'uuli, American Samoa
Purdue/Nevada-Las Vegas 6'3" 311 lbs.

Year	Team		Games	Pos.
1993	PIT	N	3	G
1995			1	G

2 yrs. 4 games

Jim Palermo
PALERMO, JAMES V.
B. Mar. 31, 1902
D. Oct., 1983
Missouri 5'9" 180 lbs.

Year	Team		Games	Pos.
1926	KC	N	1	G

Al Palewicz
PALEWICZ, ALBERT PAUL
B. Mar. 23, 1950, Fort Worth, TX
Miami (Florida) 6'1" 215 lbs.

Year	Team		Games	Pos.
1973	KC		14	LB
1974			13	LB
1975			9	LB
1977	NYJ	N	14	LB

4 yrs. 50 games

Mike Palm
PALM, MYRON
B. Nov. 24, 1899
D. Apr. 8, 1974, Washington, DC
Penn State 5'10" 170 lbs.

Year	Team		Games	Pos.
1925	NYG	N	1	QB
1926			1	QB
1933	CIN	N	6	HB, QB

3 yrs. 8 games

Chuck Palmer
PALMER, CHARLES W.
B. Feb. 15, 1901
D. Feb., 1974, Littleton, CO
Northwestern 5'10" 185 lbs.

Year	Team		Games	Pos.
1924	RAC	N	3	HB
1926	LOU	N	4	QB

2 yrs. 7 games

David Palmer
PALMER, DAVID
B. Nov. 19, 1972, Birmingham, AL
Alabama 5'8" 167 lbs.

Year	Team		Games	Pos.
1994	MIN	N	13	RB
1995			14	RB
1996			11	RB

3 yrs. 38 games

Derrell Palmer
PALMER, DERRELL F.
B. Aug. 27, 1922, Breckenridge, TN
Texas Christian 6'2" 240 lbs.

Year	Team		Games	Pos.
1946	NY	AA	13	T
1947			14	T
1948			14	T
1949	CLE	AA	11	T
1950	CLE	N	12	T
1951			10	T
1952			11	T
1953			11	T

8 yrs. 96 games

Dick Palmer
PALMER, RICHARD HARRY
B. Apr. 9, 1947, Lexington, KY
Kentucky 6'2" 229 lbs.

Year	Team		Games	Pos.
1970	MIA	N	9	LB
1972	BUF	N	4	LB
1972	NO	N	6	LB
1973			10	LB
1974	ATL	N	14	LB

4 yrs. 43 games

Emile Palmer
PALMER, EMILE
B. Apr. 5, 1973, Cheverly, MD
Syracuse 6'3" 320 lbs.

Year	Team		Games	Pos.
1996	NO	N	1	DT

Gery Palmer
PALMER, GERY
B. Dec. 25, 1970, Weimar, TX
Kansas 6'4" 255 lbs.

Year	Team		Games	Pos.
1975	KC		3	G

Les Palmer
PALMER, LESLIE (Footsie)
B. 1924
North Carolina State 6'0" 180 lbs.

Year	Team		Games	Pos.
1948	PHI	N	5	HB

Mike Palmer
PALMER, MAJOR
B. Feb. 2, 1890, Wisconsin
D. Mar., 1972, Ceylon, MN
None 5'10" 190 lbs.

Year	Team		Games	Pos.
1921	MIN	A	4	T

Paul Palmer
**PALMER, PAUL WOODROW
(Boo Boo)**
B. Oct. 14, 1964, Bethesda, MD
Temple 5'9" 182 lbs.

Year	Team		Games	Pos.
1987	KC	N	12	RB
1988			15	RB
1989	DET	N	5	RB
1989	DAL	N	9	RB

3 yrs. 41 games

Scott Palmer
PALMER, DERRELL SCOTT
B. Sep. 15, 1947, Cleburne, TX
Texas 6'3" 243 lbs.

Year	Team		Games	Pos.
1971	NYJ	N	2	DT
1972	STL	N	5	DT

2 yrs. 7 games

Sterling Palmer
PALMER, STERLING
B. Feb. 4, 1971, Fort Lauderdale, FL
Florida State 6'5" 256 lbs.

Year	Team		Games	Pos.
1993	WAS	N	14	DE
1994			16	DE
1995			13	DE
1996			6	DE

4 yrs. 49 games

Tom Palmer
PALMER, THOMAS
B. Aug. 12, 1929
D. Feb., 1980, Kingsport, TN
Wake Forest 6'2" 240 lbs.

Year	Team		Games	Pos.
1953	PIT	N	11	T
1954			7	T

2 yrs. 18 games

John Paluck
PALUCK, JOHN J.
B. May 23, 1935, Swoyersville, PA
Pittsburgh 6'2" 241 lbs.

Year	Team		Games	Pos.
1956	WAS	N	11	E, T
1959			12	E
1960			12	E
1961			13	DE
1962			14	DE
1963			14	DE
1964			14	DE
1965			14	DE

8 yrs. 104 games

Sam Palumbo
PALUMBO, SAMUEL
B. Jun. 7, 1932, Cleveland, OH
Notre Dame 6'2" 226 lbs.

Year	Team		Games	Pos.
1955	CLE	N	8	C
1956			12	C
1957	GB	N	9	C

3 yrs. 29 games

Tony Panaccion
PANACCION, VICTOR ANTHONY (Toots)
B. 1908
D. Mar. 26, 1986, Bryn Mawr, PA
Penn State 6'1" 212 lbs.

Year	Team		Games	Pos.
1930	FRA	N	5	T

Don Panciera
PANCIERA, DONALD MATTHEW
B. Jun. 23, 1927, Westerly, RI
Boston College/San Francisco 6'1" 192 lbs.

Year	Team		Games	Pos.
1949	B-NY	AA	12	HB
1950	DET	N	4	HB

Don Panciera continued

Year	Team		Games	Pos.
1952	CHIC	N	8	HB

3 yrs. 24 games

Chris Pane
PANE, CHRIS ALBERT
B. May 19, 1953, Berkeley, CA
New Mexico/Chico State 5'11" 184 lbs.

Year	Team		Games	Pos.
1976	DEN	N	4	S
1977			11	S
1978			5	S
1979			16	CB

4 yrs. 36 games

John Panelli
PANELLI, JOHN ROCCO (Pep)
B. May 7, 1926, Morristown, NJ
Notre Dame 5'11" 200 lbs.

Year	Team		Games	Pos.
1949	DET	N	11	FB
1950			8	FB
1951	CHIC	N	12	FB
1952			12	FB
1953			11	LB

5 yrs. 54 games

Ken Panfil
PANFIL, KENNETH CHARLES
B. Sep. 16, 1930, Chicago, IL
Purdue 6'6" 262 lbs.

Year	Team		Games	Pos.
1956	LA	N	6	T
1957			12	T
1958			12	T
1959	CHIC	N	12	T
1960	STL	N	12	T
1961			3	OT
1962			1	OT

7 yrs. 58 games

Hal Pangle
PANGLE, HAROLD JAMES
B. May 4, 1912, Huntington Beach, CA
D. Jan. 1, 1968, Los Angeles County, CA
Oregon State 5'10" 200 lbs.

Year	Team		Games	Pos.
1935	CHIC	N	8	FB, HB, QB
1936			12	QB, HB
1937			11	FB
1938			4	QB, HB

4 yrs. 35 games

Irv Pankey
PANKEY, IRVIN LEE
B. Feb. 15, 1958, Aberdeen, MD
Penn State 6'4" 277 lbs.

Year	Team		Games	Pos.
1980	LA	N	16	OT
1981			13	OT
1982	LARM	N	9	OT
1984			16	OT
1985			16	OT
1986			16	OT
1987			12	OT
1988			16	OT
1989			14	OT
1990			16	OT
1991	IND	N	3	OT
1992			3	OT

12 yrs. 150 games

Ernie Pannell
PANNELL, ERNEST W.
B. Feb. 2, 1917, Austin, TX
Texas A&M 6'2" 220 lbs.

Year	Team		Games	Pos.
1941	GB	N	10	T
1942			5	T
1945			7	T

3 yrs. 22 games

693

Year	Team		Games	Pos.

Joe Panos
PANOS, JOE
B. Jan. 24, 1971, Brookfield, WI
Wisconsin 6'2" 296 lbs.

Year	Team		Games	Pos.
1994	PHI	N	16	G, C
1995			9	G
1996			16	G

3 yrs. 41 games

Ben Paolucci
PAOLUCCI, BENJAMIN J.
B. Mar. 5, 1937
Wayne State 6'2" 240 lbs.

1959	DET	N	4	T

Nick Papac
PAPAC, NICHOLAS
B. 1935
Fresno State 5'11" 190 lbs.

1961	OAK	A	14	QB

George Papach
PAPACH, GEORGE
B. Apr. 27, 1925
Purdue 6'2" 208 lbs.

1948	PIT	N	10	FB
1949			12	FB

2 yrs. 22 games

Vince Papale
PAPALE, VINCENT FRANCIS
B. Feb. 9, 1946, Chester, PA
St. Joseph's (Pennsylvania) 6'2" 195 lbs.

1976	PHI	N	14	WR
1977			14	WR
1978			13	WR

3 yrs. 41 games

Oran Pape
PAPE, ORAN H. (Nanny)
B. 1904, Waupeton, IA
D. Mar. 30, 1936, Muscatine, IA
Iowa 5'11" 180 lbs.

1930	MIN	N	6	HB
1930	GB	N	2	HB, QB
1931	PRO	N	11	HB, QB
1932	BOS	N	5	QB, FB, HB
1932	SI	N	2	HB

3 yrs. 26 games

Johnny Papit
PAPIT, JOHN
B. 1928
Virginia 6'0" 190 lbs.

1951	WAS	N	11	HB
1952			8	HB
1953			3	HB

3 yrs. 22 games

Joe Pappio
PAPPIO, JOSEPH
B. 1904
Haskell 6'0" 183 lbs.

1923	OOR	N	1	E
1930	CHIC	N	3	G, FB

2 yrs. 4 games

Jack Pardee
PARDEE, JOHN PERRY
B. Apr. 19, 1936, Exira, IA
Texas A&M 6'2" 224 lbs.

1957	LA	N	12	LB
1958			12	LB
1959			12	LB
1960			8	LB
1961			13	LB
1962			14	LB

Jack Pardee continued

1963			14	LB
1964			14	LB
1966			14	LB
1967			14	LB
1968			14	LB
1969			14	LB
1970			14	LB
1971	WAS	N	14	LB
1972			13	LB

15 yrs. 196 games

Paul Pardonner
PARDONNER, J. PAUL (Pudge)
B. Apr. 29, 1910, Ingomar, OH
D. Feb. 14, 1989, Columbus, OH
Purdue 5'8" 170 lbs.

1934	CHIC	N	6	QB
1935			10	QB

2 yrs. 16 games

Curt Pardridge
PARDRIDGE, CURTIS LYNN
B. Mar. 13, 1964, De Kalb, IL
Northern Illinois 5'10" 175 lbs.

1987	SEA	N	3	WR

Bob Paremore
PAREMORE, ROBERT C.
B. 1940, Tallahassee, FL
Florida A&M 5'11" 190 lbs.

1963	STL	N	14	HB
1964			4	HB

2 yrs. 18 games

Babe Parilli
PARILLI, VITO
B. May 7, 1929, Rochester, PA
Kentucky 6'1" 190 lbs.

1952	GB	N	12	QB
1953			12	QB
1956	CLE	N	5	QB
1957	GB	N	12	QB
1958			12	QB
1960	OAK	A	14	QB
1961	BOS	A	14	QB
1962			10	QB
1963			14	QB
1964			14	QB
1965			14	QB
1966			14	QB
1967			14	QB
1968	NY	A	14	QB
1969			14	QB

15 yrs. 189 games

Bubba Paris
PARIS, WILLIAM
B. Oct. 6, 1960, Louisville, KY
Michigan 6'6" 300 lbs.

1983	SF	N	16	OT
1984			16	OT
1985			16	OT
1986			10	OT
1987			11	OT
1988			16	OT
1989			16	OT
1990			16	OT
1991	IND	N	13	OT

9 yrs. 130 games

Don Parish
PARISH, DON E.
B. Jan. 4, 1948, Paso Robles, CA
Stanford 6'1" 220 lbs.

1970	STL	N	14	LB
1971			1	LB
1971	LA	N	1	LB

Don Parish continued

1972	STL	N	1	LB
1972	DEN	N	1	LB

3 yrs. 18 games

Ernie Park
PARK, ERNEST C.
B. Oct. 22, 1940, San Angelo, CA
McMurry 6'3" 247 lbs.

1963	SD	A	7	OT
1964			14	OT
1965			14	OT
1966	MIA	A	14	G
1967	DEN	A	14	G
1969	CIN	A	8	OT

6 yrs. 71 games

Kaulana Park
PARK, KAULANA H.
B. 1962
Stanford 6'2" 230 lbs.

1987	NYG	N	2	RB

Ace Parker
PARKER, CLARENCE MCKAY
B. May 17, 1912, Portsmouth, VA
Duke 6'0" 178 lbs.

1937	BKN	N	4	QB
1938			11	QB
1939			11	QB
1940			11	HB
1941			9	HB
1945	BOS	N	8	HB
1946	NY	AA	12	HB

7 yrs. 66 games

Andy Parker
PARKER, ANDY
B. Sep. 8, 1961, Redlands, CA
Utah 6'5" 244 lbs.

1984	LARI	N	9	TE
1985			16	TE
1986			13	TE
1987			12	TE
1988			16	TE
1989	SD	N	10	TE
1990	LARI	N	5	TE

7 yrs. 81 games

Anthony Parker
PARKER, WILL ANTHONY
B. Feb. 11, 1966, Sylacauga, AL
Arizona State 5'10" 181 lbs.

1989	IND	N	1	CB, S
1991	KC	N	2	CB, S
1992	MIN	N	16	CB
1993			14	CB
1994			15	CB
1995	STL	N	16	CB
1996			14	CB

7 yrs. 78 games

Artimus Parker
PARKER, ARTIMUS L. (T-Bone)
B. Jan. 16, 1952, Winston-Salem, NC
Southern California 6'3" 208 lbs.

1974	PHI	N	14	S
1975			14	S
1976			14	S
1977	NYJ	N	11	S

4 yrs. 53 games

Buddy Parker
PARKER, RAYMOND KLEIN
B. Dec. 16, 1913, Slaton, TX
D. Mar. 22, 1982, Kaufman, TX
North Texas/Centenary 6'0" 193 lbs.

1935	DET	N	12	FB, HB

Buddy Parker continued

1936			10	HB
1937	CHIC	N	10	FB
1938			10	FB
1939			8	E, FB
1940			10	FB
1941			11	FB
1942			10	FB
1943			4	FB

9 yrs. 85 games

Carl Parker
PARKER, CARL WAYNE
B. Feb. 5, 1965, Columbus, GA
Vanderbilt 6'2" 201 lbs.

1988	CIN	N	3	WR
1989			3	WR

2 yrs. 6 games

Charlie Parker
PARKER, CHARLIE RUFFING
B. Jun. 19, 1941, Greenville, MS
Southern Mississippi 6'1" 245 lbs.

1965	DEN	A	14	G

Daren Parker
PARKER, DAREN
B. 1969
South Carolina 6'0" 185 lbs.

1992	DEN	N	3	P

Dave Parker
PARKER, DAVID
B. Jan. 30, 1918, Novice, TX
D. Dec., 1991
Hardin-Simmons 6'3" 200 lbs.

1941	BKN	N	6	E

Don Parker
PARKER, DONALD MARTIN
B. Aug. 9, 1944, Honolulu, HI
Virginia 6'3" 235 lbs.

1967	SF	N	12	G

Ervin Parker
PARKER, ERVIN
B. Aug. 20, 1958, Georgetown, SC
South Carolina State 6'5" 236 lbs.

1980	BUF	N	16	LB
1981			16	LB
1982			9	LB
1983			16	LB

4 yrs. 57 games

Frank Parker
PARKER, BILLY FRANK
B. Oct. 16, 1939, Broken Bow, OK
Oklahoma State 6'5" 263 lbs.

1962	CLE	N	14	DT
1963			14	DT
1964			8	DT
1966			12	DT
1967			12	DT
1968	PIT	N	10	DT

6 yrs. 70 games

Freddie Parker
PARKER, FREDDIE
B. Jul. 6, 1962
Mississippi Valley State 5'10" 215 lbs.

1987	GB	N	1	RB

Glenn Parker
PARKER, GLENN ANDREW
B. Apr. 22, 1966, Westminster, CA

694

Year	Team	Games	Pos.

Glenn Parker continued
Arizona 6'5" 303 lbs.

Year	Team		Games	Pos.
1990	BUF	N	16	OT
1991			16	G
1992			13	G, OT
1993			16	G, OT
1994			16	OT, G
1995			13	OT
1996			14	OT
7 yrs.	104 games			

Howie Parker
PARKER, HOWARD I.
B. 1926
Southern Methodist 6'2" 220 lbs.

1948	NY	AA	3	B

Jeff Parker
PARKER, JEFFREY
B. Jul. 16, 1969, Daytona Beach, FL
Bethune-Cookman 5'10" 185 lbs.

1992	TB	N	3	WR

Jerry Parker
PARKER, JERRY
B. Sep. 13, 1964
Central State (Ohio) 6'0" 227 lbs.

1987	CLE	N	2	LB

Jim Parker
PARKER, JAMES THOMAS
B. Apr. 3, 1934, Macon, GA
Ohio State 6'3" 273 lbs.

1957	BAL	N	12	OT
1958			12	OT
1959			12	OT
1960			12	OT
1961			14	OT
1962			14	OT
1963			14	OT, G
1964			14	G
1965			14	G
1966			14	G
1967			3	OT
11 yrs.	135 games			

Joe Parker
PARKER, JOE JACKSON
B. Jul. 11, 1923, Wichita Falls, TX
Texas 6'1" 220 lbs.

1946	CHIC	N	8	E
1947			12	E
2 yrs.	20 games			

Joel Parker
PARKER, JOSEPH LEE
B. May 23, 1952, Louisville, KY
Florida 6'5" 213 lbs.

1974	NO	N	14	WR
1975			7	WR
1977			1	WR
3 yrs.	22 games			

Ken Parker
PARKER, KENNETH
B. Jul. 22, 1946, Paterson, NJ
Fordham 6'1" 190 lbs.

1970	NYG	N	14	S

Kerry Parker
PARKER, KERRY
B. Oct. 3, 1955, New Orleans, LA
Grambling State 6'1" 200 lbs.

1984	KC	N	15	CB
1987	BUF	N	2	CB
2 yrs.	17 games			

Orlando Parker
PARKER, ORLANDO LATEEF
B. Mar. 7, 1972, Montgomery, AL
Troy State 5'11" 190 lbs.

1994	NYJ	N	2	WR

Robert Parker
PARKER, ROBERT LEWIS
B. Jan. 7, 1963, Alexander City, AL
Brigham Young 6'1" 201 lbs.

1987	KC	N	3	RB

Rodney Parker
PARKER, RODNEY
B. Jul. 18, 1954, Mobile, AL
Tennessee State 6'1" 190 lbs.

1980	PHI	N	8	WR
1981			11	WR
2 yrs.	19 games			

Steve Parker
PARKER, STEVEN
B. Dec. 8, 1956, Spokane, WA
Washington/Idaho 6'6" 265 lbs.

1980	NO	N	4	DT

Steve Parker
PARKER, STEVEN R.
B. Sep. 21, 1959, Evanston, IL
Tennessee State 6'4" 250 lbs.

1983	BAL	N	16	DE
1984	IND	N	9	DE
2 yrs.	25 games			

Vaughn Parker
PARKER, VAUGHN ANTOINE
B. Jun. 5, 1971, Buffalo, NY
UCLA 6'3" 296 lbs.

1994	SD	N	6	OT, G
1995			14	OT, G
1996			16	OT
3 yrs.	36 games			

Willie Parker
PARKER, WILLIAM NOLAN
B. Dec. 28, 1948, Baytown, TX
North Texas State 6'3" 245 lbs.

1973	BUF	N	14	C, G
1974			14	C, G
1975			14	C, G
1976			2	G
1977			14	G
1978			16	C
1979			16	C
1980	DET	N	4	C
8 yrs.	94 games			

Willie Parker
PARKER, WILLIE DAVID
B. Mar. 12, 1945, Bastrop, LA
Arkansas-Pine Bluff 6'2" 266 lbs.

1967	HOU	A	14	DT
1968			14	DT
1969			12	DT
1970	HOU	N	14	DT
4 yrs.	54 games			

Dave Parkin
PARKIN, DAVID RODNEY
B. Jan. 7, 1956, Salt Lake City, UT
Utah State 6'0" 190 lbs.

1979	DET	N	9	S

Tom Parkinson
PARKINSON, THOMAS (Doc, Pug)

Tom Parkinson continued
B. Mar. 16, 1907
D. Dec. 28, 1976, California, PA
Pittsburgh 6'1" 195 lbs.

1931	SI	N	11	FB, HB

Billy Parks
PARKS, WILLIAM JAMES
B. Jan. 1, 1948, Santa Monica, CA
Long Beach State 6'1" 187 lbs.

1971	SD	N	10	WR
1972	DAL	N	12	WR
1973	HOU	N	14	WR
1974			14	WR
1975			10	WR
5 yrs.	60 games			

Dave Parks
PARKS, DAVID WAYNE
B. Dec. 25, 1941, Muenster, TX
Texas Tech 6'2" 202 lbs.

1964	SF	N	14	OE, FL
1965			14	OE
1966			13	OE
1967			9	OE
1968	NO	N	10	OE
1969			14	WR
1970			13	TE, WR
1971			14	TE
1972			12	TE
1973	HOU	N	5	TE
10 yrs.	118 games			

Ed Parks
PARKS, EDWARD HARRY (Mickey)
B. Feb. 26, 1917, Shawnee, OK
D. Jun., 1987, Dallas, TX
Oklahoma State 6'0" 225 lbs.

1938	WAS	N	8	C
1939			10	C
1940			6	C, G
1946	CHI	AA	13	C
4 yrs.	37 games			

Jeff Parks
PARKS, JEFFREY DUPREE
B. Sep. 14, 1964, Columbia, SC
Auburn 6'4" 238 lbs.

1986	HOU	N	5	TE
1987			7	TE
1988	TB	N	3	TE
3 yrs.	15 games			

Limbo Parks
PARKS, LIMBO
B. Mar. 21, 1965
Arkansas 6'3" 265 lbs.

1987	SF	N	3	OT

Rickey Parks
PARKS, RICKEY
B. 1964
Arkansas-Pine Bluff 6'1" 179 lbs.

1987	MIN	N	2	WR

Chet Parlavecchio
PARLAVECCHIO, CHET
B. Feb. 14, 1960, Newark, NJ
Penn State 6'2" 225 lbs.

1983	GB	N	3	LB
1983	STL	N	9	LB
1 yr.	12 games			

Bernie Parmalee
PARMALEE, BERNIE
B. Sep. 16, 1967, Jersey City, NJ

Bernie Parmalee continued
Ball State 5'11" 190 lbs.

1992	MIA	N	10	RB
1993			16	RB
1994			15	RB
1995			16	RB
1996			16	RB
5 yrs.	73 games			

Jim Parmer
PARMER, JAMES RICHARD
B. Apr. 15, 1927, Dallas, TX
Oklahoma State 6'0" 193 lbs.

1948	PHI	N	11	HB
1949			12	HB
1950			10	HB
1951			11	FB
1952			6	FB
1953			12	FB
1954			10	FB
1955			12	HB
1956			4	HB
9 yrs.	88 games			

Babe Parnell
PARNELL, FREDERICK
B. 1902
Deceased
Colgate/Allegheny 6'3" 205 lbs.

1925	NYG	N	11	T
1926			2	T
1927			1	G
3 yrs.	14 games			

John Parrella
PARRELLA, JOHN LORIN
B. Nov. 22, 1969, Topeka, KS
Nebraska 6'3" 296 lbs.

1993	BUF	N	10	DE, NT
1994	SD	N	13	DT, DE
1995			16	DT
1996			16	DT
4 yrs.	55 games			

Bill Parriott
PARRIOTT, WILLIAM WRIGHT
B. Apr. 11, 1911, Newburg, WV
D. Jan. 24, 1984, Morgantown, WV
West Virginia 5'10" 165 lbs.

1934	C-S	N	1	B

Gary Parris
PARRIS, GARY T.
B. Jun. 13, 1950, East St. Louis, IL
Florida State 6'2" 226 lbs.

1973	SD	N	9	TE
1974			14	TE
1975	CLE	N	14	TE
1976			14	TE
1977			14	TE
1978			16	TE
1979	STL	N	9	TE
1980			1	TE
8 yrs.	91 games			

Bernie Parrish
PARRISH, BERNARD PAUL
B. Apr. 29, 1936, Long Beach, CA
Florida 5'11" 194 lbs.

1959	CLE	N	12	DB
1960			12	DB
1961			14	DB
1962			13	DB
1963			14	DB
1964			14	DB
1965			14	DB
1966			1	DB
1966	HOU	A	11	DB
8 yrs.	105 games			

Year	Team		Games	Pos.

Don Parrish
PARRISH, DONALD
B. Apr. 6, 1955, Tallahassee, FL
Pittsburgh 6'2" 257 lbs.

Year	Team		Games	Pos.
1978	KC	N	15	DL
1979			16	NT, DE
1980			16	NT
1981			16	NT
1982			8	NT

5 yrs. 71 games

James Parrish
PARRISH, JAMES HERBERT
B. May 19, 1968, Baltimore, MD
Temple 6'6" 315 lbs.

Year	Team		Games	Pos.
1993	SF	N	1	OT
1993	DAL	N	1	OT
1995	PIT	N	16	OT
1996	NYJ	N	1	OT

3 yrs. 19 games

Lemar Parrish
PARRISH, LEMAR
B. Dec. 13, 1947, West Palm Beach, FL
Lincoln (Missouri) 5'11" 181 lbs.

Year	Team		Games	Pos.
1970	CIN	N	14	S
1971			14	CB
1972			14	CB
1973			14	CB
1974			13	CB
1975			11	CB
1976			14	CB
1977			11	CB
1978	WAS	N	11	CB
1979			16	CB
1980			15	CB
1981			12	CB
1982	BUF	N	7	CB

13 yrs. 166 games

Rick Parros
PARROS, RICK U.
B. Jun. 14, 1958, Brooklyn, NY
Utah State 5'11" 200 lbs.

Year	Team		Games	Pos.
1981	DEN	N	16	RB
1982			9	RB
1983			6	RB
1984			15	RB
1985	SEA	N	4	RB
1987			1	RB

6 yrs. 51 games

Owen Parry
PARRY, OWEN L. (Ox)
B. Nov. 17, 1914
D. Mar., 1976
Baylor 6'4" 230 lbs.

Year	Team		Games	Pos.
1937	NYG	N	11	T
1938			10	T
1939	NYG	N	11	T

3 yrs. 32 games

Ara Parseghian
PARSEGHIAN, ARA RAOUL
B. May 21, 1923, Akron, OH
Miami (Ohio) 5'10" 194 lbs.

Year	Team		Games	Pos.
1948	CLE	AA	12	B
1949			2	B

2 yrs. 14 games

Cliff Parsley
PARSLEY, CLIFFORD D.
B. Dec. 26, 1954, Kansas City, MO
Oklahoma State 6'1" 211 lbs.

Year	Team		Games	Pos.
1977	HOU	N	14	P
1978			16	P
1979			16	P

Cliff Parsley continued

Year	Team		Games	Pos.
1980			16	P
1981			16	P
1982			4	P

6 yrs. 82 games

Ray Parson
PARSON, RAY A.
B. May 30, 1947, Uniontown, PA
Minnesota 6'4" 250 lbs.

Year	Team		Games	Pos.
1971	DET	N	14	OT

Bob Parsons
PARSONS, ROBERT HERBER
B. Jun. 29, 1950, Bethlehem, PA
Penn State 6'5" 232 lbs.

Year	Team		Games	Pos.
1972	CHI	N	13	TE
1973			14	TE, P
1974			14	TE, P
1975			14	TE, P
1976			14	TE, P
1977			14	TE, P
1978			16	TE, P
1979			16	TE, P
1980			16	TE, P
1981			16	TE, P
1982			9	P
1983			14	P

12 yrs. 170 games

Earle Parsons
PARSONS, EARLE O.
B. 1920
Southern California 6'0" 180 lbs.

Year	Team		Games	Pos.
1946	SF	AA	10	HB
1947			11	HB

2 yrs. 21 games

Lloyd Parsons
PARSONS, LLOYD MARION
B. Jun. 10, 1918, Minneapolis, MN
D. Nov., 1986, Minneapolis, MN
Minnesota/Gustavus Adolphus 5'11" 197 lbs.

Year	Team		Games	Pos.
1941	DET	N	7	B

Dennis Partee
PARTEE, DENNIS F.
B. Sep. 1, 1946, Cameron, TX
Southern Methodist 6'2" 218 lbs.

Year	Team		Games	Pos.
1968	SD	A	14	P, K
1969			14	P, K
1970	SD	N	13	P
1971			14	P, K
1972			14	P, K
1973			14	P, K
1974			14	P, K
1975			14	P

8 yrs. 111 games

Ty Parten
PARTEN, TY DANILE
B. Oct. 13, 1969, Washington, DC
Arizona 6'4" 272 lbs.

Year	Team		Games	Pos.
1993	CIN	N	11	NT
1994			14	DE
1995			1	DE

3 yrs. 26 games

Lou Partlow
PARTLOW, LOUIS J.
B. Oct. 9, 1892
D. Apr. 14, 1981, Burbank, CA
none 6'1" 185 lbs.

Year	Team		Games	Pos.
1920	DAY	A	8	FB
1921			6	FB, HB

Lou Partlow continued

Year	Team		Games	Pos.
1922	DAY	N	6	HB, FB
1923			7	HB
1923	CLE	N	1	FB, HB
1923	DAY	N	1	HB
1924			8	FB, HB, QB
1925			2	FB
1926			4	HB, FB
1927			5	HB
1929			1	FB

9 yrs. 49 games

Rick Partridge
PARTRIDGE, RICHARD BLAKE
B. Aug. 26, 1957, Orange, CA
Utah 6'1" 175 lbs.

Year	Team		Games	Pos.
1979	NO	N	13	P
1980	SD	N	16	P
1987	BUF	N	3	P

3 yrs. 32 games

Bill Paschal
PASCHAL, WILLIAM A.
B. May 28, 1921, Atlanta, GA
Georgia Tech 6'0" 201 lbs.

Year	Team		Games	Pos.
1943	NYG	N	7	FB
1944			10	FB, HB
1945			4	FB
1946			10	FB
1947	BOS	N	8	FB
1948			12	B

6 yrs. 51 games

Doug Paschal
PASCHAL, DOUGLAS CLYDE
B. Mar. 5, 1958, Greenville, NC
North Carolina 6'2" 219 lbs.

Year	Team		Games	Pos.
1980	MIN	N	16	RB

Gordon Paschka
PASCHKA, GORDON
B. 1920, Chaska, MN
Deceased
Minnesota 6'0" 213 lbs.

Year	Team		Games	Pos.
1943	P-P	N	9	G, HB
1947	NYG	N	6	FB

2 yrs. 15 games

Bill Pashe
PASHE, WILLIAM
B. Aug. 5, 1940, New York, NY
George Washington 5'11" 185 lbs.

Year	Team		Games	Pos.
1964	NY	A	4	DB

Keith Paskett
PASKETT, KEITH PAXTON
B. Dec. 7, 1964, Nashville, TN
Western Kentucky 5'11" 180 lbs.

Year	Team		Games	Pos.
1987	GB	N	12	WR

George Paskvan
PASKVAN, GEORGE O.
B. Apr. 28, 1918, La Grange, IL
Wisconsin 6'0" 190 lbs.

Year	Team		Games	Pos.
1941	GB	N	7	FB

Joe Pasqua
PASQUA, JOSEPH BERNARD
B. Jul. 31, 1917, Dallas, TX
Southern Methodist 6'1" 226 lbs.

Year	Team		Games	Pos.
1942	CLE	N	11	T
1943	WAS	N	9	T
1946	LA	N	4	T

3 yrs. 24 games

Ron Pasquale
PASQUALE, RON R.
B. Feb. 28, 1964
Akron 6'2" 266 lbs.

Year	Team		Games	Pos.
1987	STL	N	1	G

Ralph Pasquariello
PASQUARIELLO, RALPH ANGELO
B. May 30, 1926, Brighton, MA
Villanova 6'2" 237 lbs.

Year	Team		Games	Pos.
1950	LA	N	9	HB
1951	CHIC	N	10	HB
1952			12	HB

3 yrs. 31 games

Tony Pasquesi
PASQUESI, ANTHONY LEONARD
B. Jun. 13, 1933, Chicago, IL
Notre Dame 6'4" 245 lbs.

Year	Team		Games	Pos.
1955	CHIC	N	5	T
1956			11	T
1957			11	T

3 yrs. 27 games

Bill Passuello
PASSUELLO, WILLIAM
B. Dec. 23, 1897
D. Jan., 1965
None 6'2" 230 lbs.

Year	Team		Games	Pos.
1923	COL	N	2	T, G

Frank Pastin
PASTIN, FRANK
B. Dec. 16, 1920, Pittsburgh, PA
Waynesburg 5'10" 197 lbs.

Year	Team		Games	Pos.
1942	PIT	N	1	G

Dan Pastorini
PASTORINI, DANTE ANTHONY, JR.
B. May 26, 1949, Sonora, CA
Santa Clara 6'3" 208 lbs.

Year	Team		Games	Pos.
1971	HOU	N	14	QB, P
1972			14	QB, P
1973			14	QB, P
1974			11	QB
1975			14	QB, P
1976			13	QB, P
1977			14	QB, P
1978			16	QB, P
1979			15	QB, P
1980	OAK	N	5	QB, P
1981	LA	N	7	QB, P
1983	PHI	N	3	QB

12 yrs. 140 games

Alan Pastrana
PASTRANA, CHARLES ALAN
B. Nov. 20, 1944, Annapolis, MD
Maryland 6'1" 190 lbs.

Year	Team		Games	Pos.
1969	DEN	A	2	QB
1970	DEN	N	5	QB

2 yrs. 7 games

Mike Patanelli
PATANELLI, MICHAEL JOSEPH
B. Aug. 12, 1922, Elkhart, IN
Manchester/Bowling Green/Ball State 6'2" 215 lbs.

Year	Team		Games	Pos.
1947	BKN	AA	2	E

Loyd Pate
PATE, LOYD
B. Mar. 11, 1946, Columbus, OH

Year	Team	Games	Pos.

Loyd Pate *continued*
Cincinnati 6'1" 205 lbs.

1970	**BUF** N	4	RB

Rupert Pate
PATE, RUPERT GEORGE
B. Sep. 6, 1917, Goldsboro, NC
Wake Forest 6'1" 205 lbs.

1940	**CHIC** N	2	G
1942	**PHI** N	8	G
2 yrs.	10 games		

Dennis Patera
PATERA, DENNIS ALLEN
B. Oct. 17, 1945, Portland, OR
Brigham Young 6'0" 225 lbs.

1968	**SF** N	5	K

Jack Patera
PATERA, JOHN ARLEN
B. Aug. 1, 1933, Bismarck, ND
Oregon 6'1" 234 lbs.

1955	**BAL** N	7	G, LB
1956		12	LB
1957		12	LB
1958	**CHIC** N	9	MG
1959		12	LB
1960	**DAL** N	3	LB
6 yrs.	55 games		

Angelo Paternoster
PATERNOSTER, ANGELO
B. Feb. 20, 1919, Passaic, NJ
Georgetown (DC) 5'11" 195 lbs.

1943	**WAS** N	1	G

Greg Paterra
PATERRA, GREG RICHARD
B. May 11, 1967, McKeesport, PA
Slippery Rock 5'11" 211 lbs.

1989	**ATL** N	10	RB

Herb Paterra
PATERRA, HERBERT E.
B. Nov. 8, 1940, Glassport, PA
Michigan State 6'1" 222 lbs.

1963	**BUF** A	10	LB

Frank Patrick
PATRICK, FRANK
B. 1916, East Chicago, IN
Pittsburgh 5'11" 190 lbs.

1938	**CHIC** N	8	QB, FB
1939		8	FB, HB, QB
2 yrs.	16 games		

Frank Patrick
PATRICK, FRANK
B. Mar. 11, 1947, Derry, PA
Nebraska 6'7" 225 lbs.

1970	**GB** N	14	QB
1971		14	QB
1972		2	QB
3 yrs.	30 games		

John Patrick
PATRICK, JOHN RAYMOND
B. Jan. 16, 1918, Central City, PA
Penn State 6'0" 202 lbs.

1941	**PIT** N	11	QB, FB
1945		3	FB
1946		4	QB
3 yrs.	18 games		

Garin Patrick
PATRICK, GARIN
B. Aug. 31, 1971, Canton, OH
Louisville 6'3" 265 lbs.

1995	**IND** N	5	C

Mike Patrick
PATRICK, CHARLES MICHAEL
B. Sep. 6, 1952, Austin, TX
Mississippi State 6'0" 209 lbs.

1975	**NE** N	14	P
1976		14	P
1977		14	P
1978		1	P
4 yrs.	43 games		

Wayne Patrick
PATRICK, WAYNE ALLEN
B. Sep. 1, 1946, Gainesville, FL
Louisville 6'2" 241 lbs.

1968	**BUF** A	3	RB
1969		14	RB
1970	**BUF** N	9	RB
1971		14	RB
1972		13	RB
5 yrs.	53 games		

Maury Patt
PATT, MAURICE H. (Babe)
B. Jan. 31, 1915, Altoona, PA
D. Apr., 1961
Carnegie-Mellon 6'2" 205 lbs.

1938	**DET** N	10	E
1939	**CLE** N	10	E
1940		10	E
1941		11	E
1942		6	E
5 yrs.	47 games		

Joel Patten
PATTEN, JOEL
B. Feb. 7, 1958, Augsburg, Germany
Duke 6'7" 289 lbs.

1980	**CLE** N	6	OT
1987	**IND** N	12	OT
1988		16	OT
1989	**SD** N	14	OT
1990		8	OT
1991	**LARI** N	1	OT
6 yrs.	57 games		

Steve Patten
PATTEN, STEVE
Boston College

1926	**BOS** A	5	G

Patterson
PATTERSON
None

1921	**CLE** A	2	QB, G

Billy Patterson
PATTERSON, J.W., JR.
B. Aug. 28, 1918
Baylor 5'10" 167 lbs.

1939	**CHIB** N	8	HB
1940	**PIT** N	11	HB
2 yrs.	19 games		

Clete Patterson
PATTERSON, CLETE
Ohio University 5'10" 205 lbs.

1924	**KEN** N	3	G

Craig Patterson
PATTERSON, CRAIG A.
B. Jul. 18, 1964, Santa Cruz, CA
Brigham Young 6'5" 314 lbs.

1991	**PHX** N	16	NT

Don Patterson
PATTERSON, DONALD RAY
B. Oct. 31, 1957, Gray, GA
Georgia Tech 5'11" 175 lbs.

1979	**DET** N	2	CB
1980	**NYG** N	3	CB
2 yrs.	5 games		

Elvis Patterson
PATTERSON, ELVIS VERNELL
(Toast)
B. Oct. 21, 1960, Bryan, TX
Kansas 5'11" 193 lbs.

1984	**NYG** N	15	CB
1985		16	CB
1986		15	CB
1987		1	CB
1987	**SD** N	13	CB
1988		14	CB
1989		16	CB
1990	**LARI** N	16	CB
1991		16	CB
1992		15	CB
1993		3	S
1993	**DAL** N	11	CB, S
10 yrs.	151 games		

Gordon Patterson
PATTERSON, GORDON
B. 1900, Vermont
Deceased
None 165 lbs.

1921	**WAS** A	3	E

Paul Patterson
PATTERSON, PAUL L.
B. Feb. 16, 1929
D. Jun. 11, 1982, Chicago, IL
Illinois 5'9" 185 lbs.

1949	**CHI** AA	12	B

Reno Patterson
PATTERSON, RENO
B. Apr. 22, 1961, Chicago, IL
Bethune-Cookman 6'3" 275 lbs.

1987	**SF** N	1	NT

Shawn Patterson
PATTERSON, KEVIN SHAWN
B. Jun. 13, 1964, Tempe, AZ
Arizona State 6'5" 265 lbs.

1988	**GB** N	15	NT, DE
1989		6	NT, DE
1990		11	DE
1991		11	DE
1993		5	DE
5 yrs.	48 games		

Darrell Pattillo
PATTILLO, DARRELL LESTER
B. Sep. 28, 1960, Los Angeles, CA
San Diego State/Long Beach State 5'10"
194 lbs.*

1983	**SD** N	1	CB

Mark Pattison
PATTISON, MARK LESTER
B. Dec. 13, 1961, Seattle, WA
Washington 6'2" 190 lbs.

1986	**LARM** N	1	WR

Mark Pattison *continued*

1986	**LARI** N	2	WR
1987	**NO** N	9	WR
1988		6	WR
3 yrs.	18 games		

Bob Patton
PATTON, ROBERT
B. 1928
Clemson 6'0" 226 lbs.

1952	**NYG** N	12	G

Bob Patton
PATTON, ROBERT
B. Oct. 21, 1954, Camp Lejeune, NC
Delaware 6'1" 245 lbs.

1976	**BUF** N	12	C

Cliff Patton
PATTON, JOHN CLIFTON
B. Jul. 29, 1924, Clyde, TX
Texas Christian 6'2" 243 lbs.

1946	**PHI** N	4	G
1947		12	G
1948		12	G
1949		12	G
1950		12	G
1951	**CHIC** N	12	G
6 yrs.	64 games		

James Patton
PATTON, JAMES
B. Jan. 7, 1970, Houston, TX
Texas 6'3" 287 lbs.

1993	**BUF** N	2	DE, NT
1994		11	NT, DE
2 yrs.	13 games		

Jerry Patton
PATTON, JERRY
B. Mar. 27, 1946, Saginaw, MI
Nebraska 6'3" 261 lbs.

1971	**MIN** N	3	DT
1972	**BUF** N	14	DT
1973		14	DT
1974	**PHI** N	14	DT
1975	**NE** N	3	DE
5 yrs.	48 games		

Jimmy Patton
PATTON, JAMES RUSSELL, JR.
B. Sep. 29, 1933, Greenville, MS
D. Dec. 22, 1972, Villa Rica, GA
Mississippi 6'0" 183 lbs.

1955	**NYG** N	11	DB
1956		12	DB
1957		12	DB
1958		12	DB
1959		11	DB
1960		12	DB
1961		14	DB
1962		14	DB
1963		14	DB
1964		14	DB
1965		14	DB
1966		13	DB
12 yrs.	153 games		

Joe Patton
PATTON, JOE
B. Jan. 5, 1972, Birmingham, AL
Alabama A&M 6'5" 288 lbs.

1994	**WAS** N	4	G
1995		16	OT, G
1996		16	OT
3 yrs.	36 games		

Year	Team	Games	Pos.

Marvcus Patton
PATTON, MARVCUS RAYMOND
B. May 1, 1967, Los Angeles, CA
UCLA 6'2" 224 lbs.

Year	Team		Games	Pos.
1990	**BUF**	**N**	16	LB
1991			16	LB
1992			16	LB
1993			16	LB
1994			16	LB
1995	**WAS**	**N**	16	LB
1996			16	LB
7 yrs.	112 games			

Ricky Patton
PATTON, RICKY RICCARDO
B. Apr. 6, 1954, Flint, MI
Ferris State/Jackson State 5'11" 190 lbs.

Year	Team		Games	Pos.
1978	**ATL**	**N**	16	RB
1979			4	RB
1979	**GB**	**N**	6	RB
1980	**SF**	**N**	9	RB
1981			16	RB
1982			1	RB
5 yrs.	52 games			

Walt Patulski
PATULSKI, WALTER GEORGE
B. Feb. 3, 1950, Fulton, NY
Notre Dame 6'6" 260 lbs.

Year	Team		Games	Pos.
1972	**BUF**	**N**	14	DE
1973			14	DE
1974			14	DE
1975			14	DE
1977	**STL**	**N**	14	DE
5 yrs.	70 games			

Don Paul
PAUL, DONALD
B. Mar. 18, 1925, Fresno, CA
UCLA 6'1" 228 lbs.

Year	Team		Games	Pos.
1948	**LA**	**N**	11	C, LB
1949			12	LB
1950			10	C, LB
1951			12	LB
1952			12	C, LB
1953			10	LB
1954			12	C, LB
1955			8	LB
8 yrs.	87 games			

Don Paul
PAUL, DONALD RAY
B. Jul. 23, 1926, Tacoma, WA
Washington State 6'0" 187 lbs.

Year	Team		Games	Pos.
1950	**CHIC**	**N**	12	HB, DB
1951			12	HB, DB
1952			4	HB, DB
1953			12	HB, DB
1954	**CLE**	**N**	12	DB
1955			11	DB
1956			12	DB
1957			12	DB
1958			12	DB
9 yrs.	99 games			

Harold Paul
PAUL, HAROLD
B. Nov. 8, 1949, Galveston, TX
Oklahoma 6'5" 245 lbs.

Year	Team		Games	Pos.
1974	**SD**	**N**	1	OT

Markus Paul
PAUL, MARKUS DWAYNE
B. Apr. 1, 1966, Orlando, FL
Syracuse 6'2" 199 lbs.

Year	Team		Games	Pos.
1989	**CHI**	**N**	16	S
1990			16	S
1991			14	S

Markus Paul continued

Year	Team		Games	Pos.
1992			16	S
1993			8	S
1993	**TB**	**N**	1	S
5 yrs.	71 games			

Tito Paul
PAUL, TITO
B. May 24, 1972, Kissimmee, FL
Ohio State 6'0" 195 lbs.

Year	Team		Games	Pos.
1995	**ARI**	**N**	15	CB
1996			16	CB
2 yrs.	31 games			

Whitney Paul
PAUL, WHITNEY
B. Oct. 8, 1955, Galveston, TX
Colorado 6'4" 220 lbs.

Year	Team		Games	Pos.
1976	**KC**	**N**	14	DE
1977			14	DE
1978			16	LB, DE
1979			15	LB
1980			12	LB
1981			15	LB
1982	**NO**	**N**	9	LB
1983			16	LB
1984			16	LB
1985			14	LB
1986	**KC**	**N**	13	LB
11 yrs.	154 games			

Tony Paulekas
PAULEKAS, ANTHONY
B. Aug. 9, 1912, Cherry Valley, PA
Washington & Jefferson 5'10" 210 lbs.

Year	Team		Games	Pos.
1936	**GB**	**N**	8	G, C

Frank Pauley
PAULEY, FRANK (Heavy)
B. Jan. 24, 1904
D. Jun. 10, 1968
Washington & Jefferson 6'1" 270 lbs.

Year	Team		Games	Pos.
1930	**CHIB**	**N**	6	T

Dainard Paulson
PAULSON, DAINARD
B. May 15, 1937
Oregon State 5'11" 190 lbs.

Year	Team		Games	Pos.
1961	**NY**	**A**	14	DB
1962			14	DB
1963			14	DB
1964			14	DB
1965			14	DB
1966			14	DB
6 yrs.	84 games			

Bryce Paup
PAUP, BRYCE ERIC
B. Feb. 29, 1968, Scranton, IA
Northern Iowa 6'5" 245 lbs.

Year	Team		Games	Pos.
1990	**GB**	**N**	5	LB
1991			12	LB
1992			16	LB
1993			15	LB
1994			16	LB
1995	**BUF**	**N**	15	LB
1996			12	LB
7 yrs.	91 games			

Ted Pavelec
PAVELEC, THEODORE CHARLES
B. Nov. 4, 1918, Kalamazoo, MI
None 6'0" 218 lbs.

Year	Team		Games	Pos.
1941	**DET**	**N**	10	T
1942			10	G

Ted Pavelec continued

Year	Team		Games	Pos.
1943			5	T
3 yrs.	25 games			

Stan Pavkov
PAVKOV, STONKO
B. 1915
Idaho 6'0" 212 lbs.

Year	Team		Games	Pos.
1939	**PIT**	**N**	2	G
1940			9	G
2 yrs.	11 games			

Charlie Pavlich
PAVLICH, CHARLES J.
B. 1921
none 6'2" 210 lbs.

Year	Team		Games	Pos.
1946	**SF**	**AA**	10	G

Ralph Paxton
PITTMAN, RALPH D. (Bullet)
B. Dec. 23, 1901
D. Jul., 1977, Washington, DC
Baylor 5'10" 200 lbs.

Year	Team		Games	Pos.
1926	**BUF**	**N**	3	HB, FB

Ken Payne
PAYNE, KENNETH EUGENE, JR.
B. Oct. 6, 1950, Oklahoma City, OK
Langston 6'1" 185 lbs.

Year	Team		Games	Pos.
1974	**GB**	**N**	12	WR
1975			14	WR
1976			14	WR
1977			4	WR
1978	**PHI**	**N**	16	WR
5 yrs.	60 games			

Russell Payne
PAYNE, RUSSELL
B. Mar. 21, 1965
Appalachian State 6'1" 240 lbs.

Year	Team		Games	Pos.
1987	**DEN**	**N**	1	TE

Eddie Payton
PAYTON, EDWARD (Sweet Pea)
B. Aug. 3, 1951, Columbia, MS
Jackson State 5'8" 176 lbs.

Year	Team		Games	Pos.
1977	**CLE**	**N**	2	RB
1977	**DET**		8	RB
1978	**KC**	**N**	14	RB
1980	**MIN**	**N**	16	RB
1981			16	RB
1982			9	RB
5 yrs.	65 games			

Sean Payton
PAYTON, SEAN
B. Dec. 29, 1963
Eastern Illinois 5'11" 200 lbs.

Year	Team		Games	Pos.
1987	**CHI**	**N**	3	QB

Walter Payton
PAYTON, WALTER JERRY
(Sweetness)
B. Jul. 25, 1954, Columbia, MS
Jackson State 5'10" 203 lbs.

Year	Team		Games	Pos.
1975	**CHI**	**N**	13	RB
1976			14	RB
1977			14	RB
1978			16	RB
1979			16	RB
1980			16	RB
1981			16	RB
1982			9	RB
1983			16	RB
1984			16	RB
1985			16	RB

Walter Payton continued

Year	Team		Games	Pos.
1986			16	RB
1987			12	RB
13 yrs.	190 games			

Dwight Peabody
PEABODY, DWIGHT V.
B. Jan. 26, 1894
D. Jan. 3, 1972, Venice, FL
Ohio State 5'11" 170 lbs.

Year	Team		Games	Pos.
1922	**TOL**	**N**	7	E, QB

Larry Peace
PEACE, LAWRENCE
B. Feb. 13, 1917, Bradford, PA
Pittsburgh 5'11" 185 lbs.

Year	Team		Games	Pos.
1941	**BKN**	**N**	7	B

Elvis Peacock
PEACOCK, ELVIS ZARING
B. Nov. 7, 1956, Miami, FL
Oklahoma 6'1" 212 lbs.

Year	Team		Games	Pos.
1979	**LA**	**N**	11	RB
1980			13	RB
1981	**CIN**	**N**	3	RB
3 yrs.	27 games			

Johnny Peacock
PEACOCK, JOHNNY BYRON
B. Mar. 2, 1947, Austin, TX
Houston 6'2" 203 lbs.

Year	Team		Games	Pos.
1969	**HOU**	**A**	14	S
1970	**HOU**	**N**	14	S
2 yrs.	28 games			

Clarence Peaks
PEAKS, CLARENCE EARL
B. Sep. 23, 1925, Flint, MI
Michigan State 6'1" 218 lbs.

Year	Team		Games	Pos.
1957	**PHI**	**N**	12	FB
1958			11	FB
1959			12	FB
1960			7	FB
1961			13	FB
1962			14	FB
1963			14	FB
1964	**PIT**	**N**	12	FB
1965			10	FB
9 yrs.	105 games			

Dave Pear
PEAR, DAVID LOUIS
B. Jun. 1, 1953, Vancouver, WA
Washington 6'2" 248 lbs.

Year	Team		Games	Pos.
1975	**BAL**	**N**	13	DT
1976	**TB**	**N**	13	DT
1977			14	DT
1978			16	NT
1979	**OAK**	**N**	16	DT
1980			8	DT
6 yrs.	80 games			

Harley Pearce
PEARCE, HARLEY C.
B. Mar. 24, 1901
D. May 13, 1979, Columbus, OH
Ohio Wesleyan 5'10" 180 lbs.

Year	Team		Games	Pos.
1926	**COL**	**N**	6	E, HB, G

Walt Pearce
PEARCE, WALTER J. (Pard)
B. Oct. 23, 1896
D. May 24, 1974, Johnston, RI
Pennsylvania 5'5" 150 lbs.

Year	Team		Games	Pos.
1920	**DEC**	**A**	8	QB

Year	Team		Games	Pos.

Walt Pearce continued

Year	Team		Games	Pos.
1921			10	QB
1922	CHIB	N	8	QB, HB
1924	KEN	N	2	QB, HB
1925	PRO	N	8	QB
5 yrs.		36 games		

Jim Pearcy
PEARCY, JAMES WHEELER
B. Jul. 26, 1920, Harrisville, WA
Marshall 5'11" 210 lbs.

1946	CHI	AA	13	G
1947			14	G
1948			14	G
1949			8	G
4 yrs.		49 games		

Irving Pearlman
PEARLMAN, IRVING RALPH (Red)
B. Jul. 31, 1898, Pittsburgh, PA
D. Nov., 1985, Hollywood, FL
Pittsburgh 6'0" 195 lbs.

1920	CLE	A	7	T, G
1921			8	G, T
1924	ROC	N	2	G, T
3 yrs.		17 games		

Aaron Pearson
PEARSON, AARON DANTIANTO
B. Aug. 22, 1964, Gadsden, AL
Mississippi State 6'0" 236 lbs.

1986	KC	N	15	LB
1987			12	LB
1988			16	LB
3 yrs.		43 games		

Barry Pearson
PEARSON, BARRY L.
B. Feb. 2, 1950, Geneseo, IL
Northwestern 5'11" 185 lbs.

1973	PIT	N	14	WR
1974	KC	N	14	WR
1975			14	WR
1976			8	WR
4 yrs.		50 games		

Bert Pearson
PEARSON, MADISON B.
B. Mar. 22, 1905, Manhattan, KS
Deceased
Kansas State 6'0" 206 lbs.

1929	CHIB	N	11	C
1930			13	C, G
1931			13	C
1932			7	C, G, T
1933			5	C, G
1934			4	G, C
1935	CHIC	N	10	C
1936			7	C, G
8 yrs.		70 games		

Dennis Pearson
PEARSON, DENNIS MACK
B. Feb. 9, 1955, Gordo, AL
San Diego State 5'11" 177 lbs.

1978	ATL	N	13	WR
1979			16	WR
2 yrs.		29 games		

Drew Pearson
PEARSON, DREW
B. Jan. 12, 1951, South River, NJ
Tulsa 6'0" 182 lbs.

1973	DAL	N	14	WR
1974			14	WR

Drew Pearson continued

Year	Team		Games	Pos.
1975			14	WR
1976			14	WR
1977			14	WR
1978			16	WR
1979			15	WR
1980			16	WR
1981			16	WR
1982			9	WR
1983			14	WR
11 yrs.		156 games		

Dud Pearson
PEARSON, DUDLEY
B. Feb. 8, 1896, Outagamie County, WI
D. Sep., 1982, Milwaukee, WI
Notre Dame 5'9" 165 lbs.

1922	RAC	N	5	QB

J.C. Pearson
PEARSON, JAYICE
B. Aug. 17, 1963, Japan
California Poly (Pomona)/Washington 5'11" 187 lbs.

1986	KC	N	8	CB, S
1987			12	CB
1989			16	CB
1990			16	CB
1991			14	CB
1992			7	CB, S
1993	MIN	N	13	CB
7 yrs.		86 games		

Lindy Pearson
PEARSON, LINDELL EUGENE
B. Mar. 6, 1929, Oklahoma City, OK
Oklahoma 6'0" 198 lbs.

1950	DET	N	11	HB
1951			12	HB
1952			3	HB
1952	GB	N	2	HB
3 yrs.		28 games		

Preston Pearson
PEARSON, PRESTON JAMES
B. Jan. 17, 1945, Freeport, IL
Illinois 6'1" 200 lbs.*

1967	BAL	N	7	DB
1968			14	RB
1969			14	RB
1970	PIT	N	14	RB
1971			14	RB
1972			11	RB
1973			14	RB
1974			9	RB
1975	DAL	N	14	RB
1976			10	RB
1977			14	RB
1978			16	RB
1979			14	RB
1980			11	RB
14 yrs.		176 games		

Willie Pearson
PEARSON, WILLIE, JR.
B. May 9, 1947, Bennettsville, SC
North Carolina A&T 6'0" 190 lbs.

1969	MIA	A	4	CB, S

Brent Pease
PEASE, BRENT RICHARD
B. Oct. 8, 1964, Moscow, ID
Montana 6'2" 200 lbs.

1987	HOU	N	6	QB
1988			13	QB
2 yrs.		19 games		

George Pease
PEASE, GEORGE
B. Jun. 18, 1903
D. Oct. 23, 1984, Dallas, TX
Columbia 5'8" 185 lbs.

1926	NY	A	14	QB, HB
1929	ORA	N	10	QB, HB
2 yrs.		24 games		

Todd Peat
PEAT, MARION TODD
B. May 20, 1964, Champaign, IL
Northern Illinois 6'2" 300 lbs.

1987	STL	N	12	G
1988	PHX	N	15	G
1989			4	G
1990	LARI	N	16	OT
1992			16	G
1993			16	G
6 yrs.		79 games		

Jack Peavey
PEAVEY, JACK
B. Jun. 6, 1963
Troy State 6'2" 260 lbs.

1987	DEN	N	3	C

Francis Peay
PEAY, FRANCIS
B. May 23, 1944, Pittsburgh, PA
Missouri 6'5" 250 lbs.

1966	NYG	N	9	OT
1967			13	OT
1968	GB	N	14	OT
1969			14	OT
1970			14	OT
1971			14	OT
1972			14	OT
1973	KC	N	9	OT
1974			10	OT
9 yrs.		111 games		

Win Pedersen
PEDERSEN, WINFIELD C.
B. Jun. 8, 1915, Chicago, IL
D. Jan. 17, 1983, Hopkins, MN
Minnesota 6'3" 225 lbs.

1941	NYG	N	10	T
1945			4	T
1946	BOS	N	10	T
3 yrs.		24 games		

Doug Pederson
PEDERSON, DOUG
B. Jan. 31, 1968, Bellingham, WA
Northeast Louisiana 6'3" 209 lbs.

1993	MIA	N	2	QB
1996	GB	N	1	QB
2 yrs.		8 games		

Jim Pederson
PEDERSON, WINFIELD JAMES
B. Oct. 19, 1907
D. Aug., 1978, Pawtucket, RI
Augsburg 5'9" 186 lbs.

1930	MIN	N	7	QB
1930	FRA	N	4	HB
1931			8	HB, QB
1932	CHIB	N	1	HB
3 yrs.		20 games		

Danny Peebles
PEEBLES, DANIEL PERCY, III
B. Apr. 30, 1966, Raleigh, NC
North Carolina State 5'11" 180 lbs.

1989	TB	N	13	WR
1990			10	WR

Danny Peebles continued

Year	Team		Games	Pos.
1991	CLE	N	7	WR
3 yrs.		30 games		

Jim Peebles
PEEBLES, JAMES MCADEN (Mac)
B. Aug. 27, 1920, Culleoka, TN
Vanderbilt 6'4" 231 lbs.

1946	WAS	N	11	E
1947			12	E
1948			11	E
1949			11	E
1951			12	E
5 yrs.		57 games		

Gordon Peery
PEERY, GORDON G. (Skeet)
B. 1904
Oklahoma State 5'10" 155 lbs.

1927	CLE	N	4	QB, HB, T

Rodney Peete
PEETE, RODNEY
B. Mar. 16, 1966, Mesa, AZ
Southern California 6'0" 193 lbs.

1989	DET	N	8	QB
1990			11	QB
1991			8	QB
1992			10	QB
1993			10	QB
1994	DAL	N	7	QB
1995	PHI	N	15	QB
1996			5	QB
8 yrs.		74 games		

Brian Peets
PEETS, BRIAN CANVIN
B. Jul. 15, 1956, Stockton, CA
Pacific 6'4" 225 lbs.

1978	SEA	N	7	TE
1979			16	TE
1981	SF	N	5	TE
3 yrs.		28 games		

Erric Pegram
PEGRAM, ERRIC DEMONT
B. Jan. 7, 1969, Dallas, TX
North Texas State 5'9" 188 lbs.

1991	ATL	N	16	RB
1992			16	RB
1993			16	RB
1994			13	RB
1995	PIT	N	15	RB
1996			12	RB
6 yrs.		88 games		

Willis Peguese
PEGUESE, WILLIS
B. Dec. 18, 1966, Miami, FL
Miami (Florida) 6'4" 269 lbs.

1990	HOU	N	2	DE
1991			7	DE
1992			1	DE
1992	IND	N	12	DE
1993			13	DE
4 yrs.		35 games		

Dan Peiffer
PEIFFER, DANIEL WILLIAM
B. Mar. 29, 1951, Sigourney, IA
Southeast Missouri State 6'3" 252 lbs.

1975	CHI	N	11	C
1976			4	C
1977			14	C
1980	WAS	N	8	C
4 yrs.		37 games		

Doug Pelfrey
PELFREY, THOMAS DOUGLAS
B. Sep. 25, 1970, Fort Thomas, KY
Kentucky 5'11" 185 lbs.

Year	Team		Games	Pos.
1993	CIN	N	15	K
1994			16	K
1995			16	K
1996			16	K
4 yrs.	63 games			

Ray Pelfrey
PELFREY, RAYMOND HARRISON
B. Jan. 11, 1928, Sardinia, OH
*Auburn/Eastern Kentucky State 6'0"
190 lbs.*

Year	Team		Games	Pos.
1951	GB	N	12	E
1952			1	E
1952	CHIC	N	2	E
1952	DAL	N	6	E
1953	NYG	N	12	E
3 yrs.	33 games			

Bob Pellegrini
PELLEGRINI, ROBERT
B. Nov. 13, 1934, Willamsport, PA
Maryland 6'2" 233 lbs.

Year	Team		Games	Pos.
1956	PHI	N	12	G, LB
1958			12	LB
1959			12	LB
1960			9	LB
1961			14	LB
1962	WAS	N	9	LB
1963			14	LB
1964			12	LB
1965			13	LB
9 yrs.	107 games			

Joe Pellegrini
PELLEGRINI, JOE
B. Apr. 8, 1957, Boston, MA
Harvard 6'4" 265 lbs.

Year	Team		Games	Pos.
1982	NYJ	N	9	C
1983			16	C, G
1984	ATL	N	15	OL
1985			5	G, C
1986			8	G, C
5 yrs.	53 games			

Joe Pellegrini
PELLEGRINI, JOE, JR.
B. Aug. 9, 1956, Aberdeen, WA
Idaho 6'2" 268 lbs.

Year	Team		Games	Pos.
1978	NYJ	N	9	DT
1979			4	DT
2 yrs.	13 games			

Bill Pellington
PELLINGTON, WILLIAM
B. Sep. 25, 1929, Paterson, NJ
D. Apr. 25, 1994, Baltimore, MD
Rutgers 6'2" 234 lbs.

Year	Team		Games	Pos.
1953	BAL	N	12	LB
1954			12	LB
1955			12	LB
1956			12	LB
1957			1	LB
1958			12	LB
1959			12	LB
1960			12	LB
1961			14	LB
1962			14	LB
1963			14	LB
1964			14	LB
12 yrs.	141 games			

Scott Pelluer
PELLUER, SCOTT JOHN
B. Apr. 26, 1959, Yakima, WA

Scott Pelluer continued
Washington State 6'2" 220 lbs.

Year	Team		Games	Pos.
1981	NO	N	16	LB
1982			6	LB
1983			16	LB
1984			16	LB
1985			11	LB
5 yrs.	65 games			

Steve Pelluer
PELLUER, STEVEN CARL
B. Jul. 29, 1962, Yakima, WA
Washington 6'4" 209 lbs.

Year	Team		Games	Pos.
1984	DAL	N	1	QB
1985			2	QB
1986			16	QB
1987			12	QB
1988			16	QB
1989	KC	N	5	QB
1990			13	QB
7 yrs.	65 games			

Bubba Pena
PENA, ROBERT B.
B. Aug. 8, 1949, Falmouth, MA
Massachusetts 6'2" 250 lbs.

Year	Team		Games	Pos.
1972	CLE	N	7	G

Jairo Penaranda
PENARANDA, JAIRO A.
B. Jun. 15, 1958, Barranquilla,
Colombia
UCLA 6'0" 217 lbs.

Year	Team		Games	Pos.
1981	LA	N	16	FB
1985	PHI	N	4	RB
2 yrs.	20 games			

Bob Penchion
PENCHION, ROBERT EARL
B. Aug. 11, 1949, Town Creek, AL
Alcorn State 6'5" 256 lbs.

Year	Team		Games	Pos.
1972	BUF	N	12	G
1973			5	G, OT
1974	SF	N	7	G
1975			9	G
1976	SEA	N	14	G
5 yrs.	47 games			

Chris Penn
**PENN, CHRISTOPHER
ANTHONY**
B. Apr. 20, 1971, Lenapah, OK
Tulsa 6'0" 198 lbs.

Year	Team		Games	Pos.
1994	KC	N	8	WR
1995			2	WR
1996			16	WR
3 yrs.	26 games			

Jesse Penn
PENN, JESSE ANDREW, II
B. Sep. 6, 1962, Martinsville, VA
Virginia Tech 6'3" 218 lbs.

Year	Team		Games	Pos.
1985	DAL	N	16	LB
1986			15	LB
1987			11	LB
3 yrs.	42 games			

Leon Pennington
PENNINGTON, LEON
B. Dec. 25, 1963
Florida 6'1" 225 lbs.

Year	Team		Games	Pos.
1987	TB	N	3	LB

Tom Pennington
PENNINGTON, DURWARD, JR.
B. 1940

Tom Pennington continued
Georgia 6'2" 210 lbs.

Year	Team		Games	Pos.
1962	DAL	A	3	K

Jay Pennison
PENNISON, JAY LESLIE
B. Sep. 9, 1961, Houma, LA
Nicholls State 6'1" 276 lbs.

Year	Team		Games	Pos.
1986	HOU	N	16	C
1987			12	C
1988			16	C
1989			12	C
1990			15	C
5 yrs.	71 games			

Carlos Pennywell
PENNYWELL, CARLOS JEROME
B. Mar. 18, 1956, Crowley, LA
Grambling State 6'2" 180 lbs.

Year	Team		Games	Pos.
1978	NE	N	16	WR
1979			6	WR
1980			11	WR
1981			5	WR
4 yrs.	38 games			

Robert Pennywell
PENNYWELL, ROBERT
B. Nov. 6, 1954, Shreveport, LA
Grambling State 6'1" 222 lbs.

Year	Team		Games	Pos.
1977	ATL	N	14	LB
1978			15	LB
1979			16	LB
1980			16	LB
4 yrs.	61 games			

Craig Penrose
PENROSE, CRAIG R.
B. Jul. 25, 1953, Woodland, CA
Colorado/San Diego State 6'3" 211 lbs.

Year	Team		Games	Pos.
1976	DEN	N	4	QB
1977			8	QB
1978			4	QB
1979			2	QB
4 yrs.	18 games			

Leon Pense
PENSE, LEON
B. 1922
Arkansas 6'0" 170 lbs.

Year	Team		Games	Pos.
1945	PIT	N	10	C

John Pentecost
PENTECOST, JOHN MATHEW
B. Dec. 23, 1943, Lawndale, CA
UCLA 6'2" 250 lbs.

Year	Team		Games	Pos.
1967	MIN	N	4	G

George Peoples
PEOPLES, GEORGE EVANS
B. Aug. 25, 1960, Tampa, FL
Auburn 6'0" 211 lbs.

Year	Team		Games	Pos.
1982	DAL	N	8	FB
1983	NE	N	16	RB
1984	TB	N	6	RB
1985			2	RB
4 yrs.	32 games			

Woody Peoples
PEOPLES, WOODROW
B. Aug. 16, 1943, Birmingham, AL
Grambling State 6'2" 251 lbs.

Year	Team		Games	Pos.
1968	SF	N	13	G
1969			14	G
1970			14	G
1971			14	G
1972			14	G

Woody Peoples continued

Year	Team		Games	Pos.
1973			14	G
1974			10	G
1975			14	G
1977			14	G
1978	PHI	N	15	G
1979			16	G
1980			16	G
12 yrs.	168 games			

Gene Pepper
PEPPER, EUGENE F.
B. Sep. 22, 1927, Overland, MO
Missouri 6'2" 239 lbs.

Year	Team		Games	Pos.
1950	WAS	N	12	G
1951			11	G, T
1952			12	G
1953			6	G
4 yrs.	41 games			

Frank Perantoni
PERANTONI, FRANCIS J.
B. Sep. 13, 1923
D. Sep. 11, 1991, Somerville, NJ
Princeton 6'0" 220 lbs.

Year	Team		Games	Pos.
1948	NY	AA	14	C
1949	B-NY	AA	12	C
2 yrs.	26 games			

Mac Percival
PERCIVAL, MAC
B. Feb. 26, 1940, Lubbock, TX
Texas Tech 6'4" 219 lbs.

Year	Team		Games	Pos.
1967	CHI	N	14	K
1968			14	K
1969			14	K
1970			14	K
1971			14	K
1972			14	K
1973			4	K
1974	DAL	N	3	K
8 yrs.	91 games			

Willard Perdue
**PERDUE, CHARLES WILLARD
(Bolo)**
B. 1917
D. Mar. 31, 1988
Duke/Arkansas 5'10" 206 lbs.

Year	Team		Games	Pos.
1940	NYG	N	10	E
1946	BKN	AA	10	E
2 yrs.	20 games			

Pete Perez
PEREZ, PETER J.
B. 1924
Illinois 5'9" 220 lbs.

Year	Team		Games	Pos.
1945	CHIB	N	3	G

John Pergine
PERGINE, JOHN SAMUEL
B. Sep. 13, 1946, Norristown, PA
Notre Dame 6'1" 225 lbs.

Year	Team		Games	Pos.
1969	LA	N	14	LB
1970			12	LB
1971			12	LB
1972			12	LB
1973	WAS	N	14	LB
1974			12	LB
1975			14	LB
7 yrs.	90 games			

Bob Perina
PERINA, ROBERT IAN
B. Jan. 16, 1921, Irvington, NJ
D. Aug. 2, 1991, Madison, WI
Princeton 6'1" 205 lbs.

Year	Team		Games	Pos.
1946	NY	AA	13	HB

Year	Team		Games	Pos.

Bob Perina continued

Year	Team		Games	Pos.
1947	BKN	AA	14	HB
1948	CHI	AA	13	HB
1950	BAL	N	3	HB
4 yrs.	43 games			

Pete Perini

PERINI, EVO PETE
B. Feb. 10, 1928, Washington, NJ
Ohio State 6'0" 225 lbs.

1954	CHIB	N	12	FB
1955	CLE	N	6	FB
2 yrs.	18 games			

Art Perkins

PERKINS, ARTHUR
B. May 1, 1940, Fort Worth, TX
North Texas State 6'0" 233 lbs.

1962	LA	N	13	FB
1963			13	FB
2 yrs.	26 games			

Bill Perkins

PERKINS, WILLIAM
B. 1940
Iowa 6'2" 225 lbs.

1963	NY	A	4	HB

Bruce Perkins

PERKINS, BRUCE KERRY
B. Aug. 14, 1967, Waterloo, IA
Arizona State 6'2" 230 lbs.

1990	TB	N	16	RB
1991	IND	N	14	RB
2 yrs.	30 games			

Don Perkins

PERKINS, DONALD ANTHONY
B. Mar. 4, 1938, Waterloo, IA
New Mexico 5'10" 200 lbs.

1961	DAL	N	14	HB
1962			14	HB
1963			11	HB
1964			13	FB
1965			13	FB
1966			14	FB
1967			14	RB
1968			14	RB
8 yrs.	107 games			

Don Perkins

PERKINS, DONALD E.
B. Sep. 18, 1917, Dodgeville, WI
Wisconsin-Platteville 6'0" 196 lbs.

1943	GB	N	1	FB
1944			10	FB
1945			7	FB
1945	CHIB	N	2	FB
1946			10	FB
4 yrs.	30 games			

Horace Perkins

PERKINS, HORACE A.
B. Mar. 15, 1954, El Campo, TX
Colorado 5'11" 180 lbs.

1979	KC	N	16	CB

Jim Perkins

PERKINS, JAMES WILLIAM
B. Jun. 16, 1939, Loyalton, CA
Colorado 6'5" 250 lbs.

1962	DEN	A	14	OT
1963			14	OT
1964			14	OT
3 yrs.	42 games			

Johnny Perkins

PERKINS, JOHN EUGENE
B. Apr. 21, 1953, Franklin, TX
Abilene Christian 6'2" 205 lbs.

1977	NYG	N	13	WR
1978			14	WR
1979			13	WR
1980			6	WR
1981			16	WR
1982			8	WR
1983			1	WR
7 yrs.	71 games			

Ray Perkins

PERKINS, RAYOTIS
B. Sep. 25, 1965
Virginia 6'5" 242 lbs.

1987	DAL	N	2	DE

Ray Perkins

PERKINS, WALTER RAY
B. Dec. 6, 1941, Mount Olive, MS
Alabama 6'0" 183 lbs.

1967	BAL	N	8	OE, FL
1968			14	OE
1969			11	WR
1970			11	WR
1971			14	WR
5 yrs.	58 games			

Willis Perkins

PERKINS, WILLIS
B. 1937
Texas Southern 6'0" 250 lbs.

1961	HOU	A	1	G
1961	BOS	A	1	G
1963	HOU	A	3	DE
2 yrs.	5 games			

John Perko

PERKO, JOHN F.
B. Apr. 8, 1918
D. Jun., 1984, Ely, MN
Minnesota/Notre Dame 6'1" 225 lbs.

1946	BUF	AA	14	G

John Perko

PERKO, JOHN J.
B. Aug. 14, 1916, Chisholm, MN
Duquesne 6'1" 207 lbs.

1937	PIT	N	10	G, C
1938			10	G
1939			8	G
1940			11	G
1944	C-P	N	10	G
1945	PIT	N	10	G
1946			9	G
1947			7	G
8 yrs.	75 games			

Mike Perko

PERKO, MICHAEL JOHN
B. Mar. 30, 1957, Seattle, WA
Gonzaga/Utah State 6'4" 235 lbs.

1982	ATL	N	9	NT

Tom Perko

PERKO, TOM
B. Jun. 17, 1954, Steubenville, OH
Pittsburgh 6'3" 233 lbs.

1976	GB	N	14	LB

Phil Perlo

PERLO, PHILLIP DONALD
B. Dec. 6, 1935, Washington, DC
Maryland 6'0" 220 lbs.

1960	HOU	A		LB

Petey Perot

PEROT, EDWARD JOSEPH
B. Apr. 18, 1957, Natchitoches, LA
Northwestern State (Louisiana) 6'2" 261 lbs.

1979	PHI	N	14	G
1980			16	G
1981			16	G
1982			9	G
1984			12	G
1985	NO	N	7	G
6 yrs.	74 games			

George Perpich

PERPICH, GEORGE RUDOLPH
B. Jun. 22, 1920, Croatia
D. May 26, 1993, Hibbing, MN
Georgetown (DC) 6'2" 233 lbs.

1946	BKN	AA	13	T
1947	BAL	AA	14	T
2 yrs.	27 games			

Pete Perreault

PERREAULT, PETER WAYNE
B. Mar. 1, 1939, Shrewsbury, MA
Boston University 6'3" 246 lbs.

1963	NY	A	3	G
1964			14	G
1965			3	G
1966			6	G
1967			9	G
1968	CIN	A	14	G
1969	NY	A	14	G
1970	NYJ	N	14	G
1971	MIN	N	10	G
9 yrs.	87 games			

Ralph Perretta

PERRETTA, RALPH JOSEPH
B. Jan. 30, 1953, Rockville Centre, NY
Purdue 6'2" 251 lbs.

1975	SD	N	3	G
1976			13	G
1977			14	G
1978			15	C
1979			16	G
1980			5	C
1980	NYG	N	6	C
6 yrs.	72 games			

Mike Perrie

PERRIE, MICHAEL (Iron Mike)
B. 1917
St. Mary's (California) 5'11" 197 lbs.

1939	CLE	N	2	QB

Brett Perriman

PERRIMAN, BRETT
B. Oct. 10, 1965, Miami, FL
Miami (Florida) 5'9" 175 lbs.

1988	NO	N	16	WR
1989			14	WR
1990			16	WR
1991	DET	N	15	WR
1992			16	WR
1993			15	WR
1994			16	WR
1995			16	WR
1996			16	WR
9 yrs.	140 games			

Benny Perrin

PERRIN, JESSE BENNETT
B. Oct. 20, 1959, Orange County, CA
Alabama 6'2" 178 lbs.

1982	STL	N	9	CB, S
1983			16	S
1984			16	S

Benny Perrin continued

Year	Team		Games	Pos.
1985			7	S
4 yrs.	48 games			

Jack Perrin

PERRIN, JOHN STEPHENSON
B. Feb. 4, 1898, Escanaba, MI
D. Jun. 24, 1969, Detroit, MI
Michigan 5'9" 160 lbs.

1926	HAR	N	6	QB, FB

Lonnie Perrin

PERRIN, LONNIE
B. Feb. 3, 1952, Norfolk, VA
Illinois 6'1" 222 lbs.

1976	DEN	N	14	RB
1977			14	RB
1978			16	RB
1979	WAS	N	5	RB
1979	CHI	N	9	RB
4 yrs.	58 games			

Mike Perrino

PERRINO, MICHAEL
B. Mar. 2, 1964, Chicago, IL
Notre Dame 6'5" 285 lbs.

1987	PHI	N	3	OT

Mike Perrotti

PERROTTI, MICHAEL A.
B. Jun. 12, 1923, Cleveland, OH
D. Nov., 1974
Ohio State/Cincinnati 6'3" 243 lbs.

1948	LA	AA	14	T
1949			12	T
2 yrs.	26 games			

Claude Perry

PERRY, CLAUDE
B. Oct. 31, 1901
D. Jul., 1975, Goodsprings, AL
Alabama 6'1" 210 lbs.

1927	GB	N	8	T, E
1928			13	T
1929			10	T, G
1930			9	T, G
1931			5	T
1931	BKN	N	4	T, E
1932	GB	N	11	T
1933			10	T, G
1934			12	T, G
1935			6	T
9 yrs.	88 games			

Darren Perry

PERRY, DARREN
B. Dec. 29, 1968, Chesapeake, VA
Penn State 5'10" 194 lbs.

1992	PIT	N	16	S
1993			16	S
1994			16	S
1995			16	S
1996			16	S
5 yrs.	80 games			

Gerald Perry

PERRY, GERALD
B. Nov. 12, 1964, Columbia, SC
Southern University 6'6" 305 lbs.

1988	DEN	N	16	OT
1989			16	OT
1990			11	OT
1991	LARM	N	11	OT
1992			16	OT
1993	LARI	N	15	OT
1994			12	OT
1995	OAK	N	3	OT
8 yrs.	100 games			

701

Year	Team		Games	Pos.

Jerry Perry

PERRY, GERALD E.
B. Jul. 17, 1930, Ballston Spa, NY
California 6'4" 237 lbs.

Year	Team		Games	Pos.
1954	DET	N	11	DT
1956			12	DT
1957			12	DT
1958			12	DT, K
1959			10	DT, K
1960	STL	N	12	DE, K
1961			13	OT, K
1962			14	OT, K

8 yrs.　96 games

Joe Perry

PERRY, FLETCHER JOSEPH
(The Jet)
B. Jan. 22, 1927, Stevens, AR
Compton JC 6'0" 203 lbs.

Year	Team		Games	Pos.
1948	SF	AA	14	FB
1949			11	FB
1950	SF	N	12	FB
1951			11	FB
1952			12	FB
1953			12	FB
1954			12	FB
1955			11	FB
1956			12	FB
1957			8	FB
1958			12	FB
1959			10	FB
1960			8	FB
1961	BAL	N	13	FB
1962			11	FB
1963	SF	N	9	FB

16 yrs.　178 games

Leon Perry

PERRY, LEON, JR.
B. Aug. 14, 1957, Gloster, MS
Mississippi 5'11" 225 lbs.

Year	Team		Games	Pos.
1980	NYG	N	10	FB
1981			16	FB
1982			5	RB

3 yrs.　31 games

Lowell Perry

PERRY, LOWELL
B. 1932
Michigan 6'0" 195 lbs.

Year	Team		Games	Pos.
1956	PIT	N	6	E

Mario Perry

PERRY, MARIO
B. Dec. 20, 1963, Chicago, IL
Mississippi 6'6" 240 lbs.

Year	Team		Games	Pos.
1987	LARI	N	3	TE

Marlo Perry

PERRY, MALCOLM MARLO
B. Aug. 25, 1972, Forest, MS
Jackson State 6'4" 250 lbs.

Year	Team		Games	Pos.
1994	BUF	N	2	LB
1995			16	LB
1996			13	LB

3 yrs.　31 games

Michael Dean Perry

PERRY, MICHAEL DEAN
B. Aug. 27, 1965, Aiken, SC
Clemson 6'1" 285 lbs.

Year	Team		Games	Pos.
1988	CLE	N	16	DE, NT
1989			16	DE
1990			16	DE
1991			16	DT
1992			14	DT
1993			16	DT
1994			15	DT

Michael Dean Perry cont.

Year	Team		Games	Pos.
1995	DEN	N	14	DT
1996			15	DT

9 yrs.　138 games

Rod Perry

PERRY, RODNEY CORNELL
B. Sep. 11, 1953, Fresno, CA
Colorado 5'9" 180 lbs.

Year	Team		Games	Pos.
1975	LA	N	9	CB
1976			14	CB
1977			5	CB
1978			16	CB
1979			9	CB
1980			16	CB
1981			16	CB
1982	LARM	N	9	CB
1983	CLE	N	16	CB
1984			8	CB

10 yrs.　118 games

Scott Perry

PERRY, SCOTT ENDECOTT
B. Mar. 11, 1954, Pleasanton, CA
Williams 6'0" 182 lbs.

Year	Team		Games	Pos.
1976	CIN	N	12	DB
1977			9	CB
1978			13	CB
1979			14	S
1980	SF	N	11	S
1980	SD	N	4	CB

5 yrs.　63 games

Todd Perry

PERRY, TODD JOSEPH
B. Nov. 28, 1970, Elizabethtown, KY
Kentucky 6'5" 298 lbs.

Year	Team		Games	Pos.
1993	CHI	N	13	G
1994			14	G
1995			15	G
1996			16	G

4 yrs.　58 games

Vernon Perry

PERRY, VERNON, JR. (June Bug)
B. Sep. 22, 1953, Jackson, MS
Jackson State 6'2" 211 lbs.

Year	Team		Games	Pos.
1979	HOU	N	15	CB, S
1980			16	S
1981			16	S
1982			7	S
1983	NO	N	12	S

5 yrs.　66 games

Victor Perry

PERRY, VICTOR A.
B. Feb. 26, 1964
Georgia 6'5" 278 lbs.

Year	Team		Games	Pos.
1987	STL	N	1	DT

William Perry

PERRY, WILLIAM (The Refrigerator)
B. Dec. 16, 1962, Aiken, SC
Clemson 6'2" 326 lbs.

Year	Team		Games	Pos.
1985	CHI	N	16	DT, RB
1986			16	DT, RB
1987			12	DT, RB
1988			3	DT
1989			13	DT
1990			16	DT
1991			16	DT
1992			15	DT
1993			7	DT
1993	PHI	N	8	DT
1994			16	DT

10 yrs.　138 games

Bob Perryman

PERRYMAN, ROBERT L.
B. Oct. 16, 1964, Raleigh, NC
Michigan 6'1" 233 lbs.

Year	Team		Games	Pos.
1987	NE	N	9	RB
1988			16	RB
1989			16	RB
1990			8	RB
1991	DEN	N	15	RB
1992			4	RB

6 yrs.　68 games

Dean Perryman

PERRYMAN, DEAN
B. Nov. 19, 1964
Washington 6'3" 260 lbs.

Year	Team		Games	Pos.
1987	SEA	N	1	C

Jim Perryman

PERRYMAN, JAMES T.
B. Dec. 23, 1960, Oakland, CA
Millikin 6'0" 175 lbs.

Year	Team		Games	Pos.
1985	BUF	N	11	S
1987	IND	N	14	S

2 yrs.　25 games

Ara Person

PERSON, ARA
B. Sep. 23, 1948, Baltimore, MD
Morgan State 6'2" 220 lbs.

Year	Team		Games	Pos.
1972	STL	N	4	TE

Dick Pesonen

PESONEN, RICHARD
B. Jun. 10, 1938, Grand Rapids, MN
Minnesota/Minnesota-Duluth 6'0" 190 lbs.

Year	Team		Games	Pos.
1960	GB	N	12	DB
1961	MIN	N	11	DB
1962	NYG	N	13	DB
1963			14	DB
1964			5	DB

5 yrs.　55 games

Louie Pessolano

PESSOLANO, LOUIS C.
B. Nov. 7, 1906
D. Nov., 1974, Staten Island, NY
Villanova 6'0" 215 lbs.

Year	Team		Games	Pos.
1929	SI	N	2	T, G

Wally Pesuit

PESUIT, WALTER GEORGE
B. Mar. 4, 1954, Steubenville, OH
Kentucky 6'4" 252 lbs.

Year	Team		Games	Pos.
1976	ATL	N	1	OT
1977	MIA	N	14	OT
1978			16	G, OT
1979	DET	N	16	G, C
1980			1	C

5 yrs.　48 games

John Petchel

PETCHEL, JOHN
B. May 27, 1919, Freeland, PA
D. Jan., 1988, Industry, PA
Duquesne 5'11" 185 lbs.

Year	Team		Games	Pos.
1942	CLE	N	7	QB
1944			10	QB
1945	PIT	N	9	QB

3 yrs.　26 games

Boni Petcoff

PETCOFF, BONI
B. Feb. 1, 1900
D. Aug. 5, 1965

Boni Petcoff continued

Ohio State 5'10" 230 lbs.

Year	Team		Games	Pos.
1924	COL	N	8	T
1925			9	T
1926			3	T

3 yrs.　20 games

Lawrence Pete

PETE, LAWRENCE
B. Jan. 18, 1966, Wichita, KS
Nebraska 6'0" 285 lbs.

Year	Team		Games	Pos.
1989	DET	N	16	NT
1990			6	NT
1991			14	NT
1992			13	NT
1993			12	NT

5 yrs.　61 games

Anton Peters

PETERS, ANTON B., JR.
B. Feb. 3, 1941, Fort Myers, FL
Florida 6'3" 250 lbs.

Year	Team		Games	Pos.
1963	DEN	A	10	DT

Floyd Peters

PETERS, FLOYD CHARLES
B. May 21, 1936, Council Bluffs, IA
San Francisco State 6'4" 254 lbs.

Year	Team		Games	Pos.
1959	CLE	N	12	DT
1960			12	DT
1961			13	DT
1962			14	DT
1963	DET	N	14	DT
1964	PHI	N	14	DT
1965			9	DT
1966			14	DT
1967			14	DT
1968			5	DT
1969			14	DT

11 yrs.　135 games

Frank Peters

PETERS, FRANK
B. Jul. 17, 1947, Lockbourne, OH
Ohio University 6'4" 250 lbs.

Year	Team		Games	Pos.
1969	CIN	A	3	OT

Frosty Peters

PETERS, FORREST I.
B. Apr. 22, 1904
D. Apr. 17, 1980, Decatur, IL
Montana State/Illinois 5'10" 183 lbs.

Year	Team		Games	Pos.
1930	PRO	N	9	HB, QB, T
1930	POR	N	3	HB, QB, FB
1931	BKN	N	9	QB, HB, FB
1932	CHIC	N	1	QB

3 yrs.　22 games

Tony Peters

PETERS, ANTHONY LAMONT
B. Apr. 28, 1953, Oklahoma City, OK
Oklahoma 6'1" 183 lbs.

Year	Team		Games	Pos.
1975	CLE	N	14	CB
1976			14	CB
1977			14	CB
1978			16	S
1979	WAS	N	16	S
1980			16	S
1981			16	S
1982			9	S
1984			8	S

9 yrs.　123 games

Volney Peters

PETERS, VOLNEY MONROE
B. Jan. 1, 1928, El Cajon, CA
Southern California 6'4" 237 lbs.

Year	Team		Games	Pos.
1952	CHIC	N	12	T

Year	Team		Games	Pos.

Volney Peters continued

Year	Team		Games	Pos.
1953			12	T
1954	WAS	N	8	T
1955			12	T
1956			12	T
1957			12	T
1958	PHI	N	10	T
1960	LA	A		DT
1961	OAK	A	12	DT
9 yrs.	90 games			

Ken Petersen
PETERSEN, THOMAS K.
B. Mar. 26, 1939, Logan, UT
Utah 6'2" 235 lbs.

Year	Team		Games	Pos.
1961	MIN	N	12	G

Kurt Petersen
PETERSEN, KURT DAVID
B. Jun. 17, 1957, St. Louis, MO
Missouri 6'4" 270 lbs.

Year	Team		Games	Pos.
1980	DAL	N	16	OT, G
1981			16	G
1982			9	G
1983			14	G
1984			13	G
1985			16	G
6 yrs.	84 games			

Ted Petersen
PETERSEN, THEODORE HANS, III
B. Feb. 7, 1955, Kankakee, IL
Eastern Illinois 6'5" 248 lbs.

Year	Team		Games	Pos.
1977	PIT	N	14	C
1978			15	C, OT
1979			16	C, OT
1980			16	C, OT
1981			2	C, OT
1982			7	OT
1983			13	OT
1984	CLE	N	4	OT
1984	IND	N	5	OT
1987	PIT	N	2	G
9 yrs.	94 games			

Brett Petersmark
PETERSMARK, BRETT
B. Mar. 5, 1964
Eastern Michigan 6'3" 280 lbs.

Year	Team		Games	Pos.
1987	HOU	N	3	G

Andrew Peterson
PETERSON, ANDREW
B. Jun. 11, 1972, Greenock, Scotland
Washington 6'5" 310 lbs.

Year	Team		Games	Pos.
1995	CAR	N	4	G

Bill Peterson
PETERSON, WILLIAM WALLACE
B. Jun. 6, 1945, San Jose, CA
San Jose State 6'3" 228 lbs.

Year	Team		Games	Pos.
1968	CIN	A	7	TE
1969	CIN	N	14	LB
1970	CIN	N	14	LB
1971			14	LB
1972			14	LB
1975	KC	N	14	LB
6 yrs.	77 games			

Cal Peterson
PETERSON, CALVIN ELSTON
B. Oct. 6, 1952, Los Angeles, CA
UCLA 6'3" 219 lbs.

Year	Team		Games	Pos.
1974	DAL	N	14	LB
1975			14	LB
1976	TB	N	5	LB

Cal Peterson continued

Year	Team		Games	Pos.
1979	KC	N	16	LB
1980			16	LB
1981			11	LB
1982	LARI	N	4	LB
7 yrs.	80 games			

Carl Peterson
PETERSON, CARL J. (Swede)
B. 1900
Nebraska 5'11" 175 lbs.

Year	Team		Games	Pos.
1924	KC	N	9	C

Jerry Peterson
PETERSON, GERALD RAY
B. Oct. 8, 1934, El Campo, TX
Texas 6'3" 290 lbs.

Year	Team		Games	Pos.
1956	BAL	N	1	T

Jim Peterson
PETERSON, JAMES
B. Jan. 20, 1950, San Diego, CA
San Diego State 6'5" 235 lbs.

Year	Team		Games	Pos.
1974	LA	N	14	LB
1975			14	LB
1976	TB	N	3	LB
3 yrs.	31 games			

Joe Peterson
PETERSON, JOE
B. Aug. 15, 1964
Nevada-Reno 5'10" 185 lbs.

Year	Team		Games	Pos.
1987	NE	N	3	CB

Ken Peterson
PETERSON, KENNETH (Ike)
B. 1912
Gonzaga 5'8" 185 lbs.

Year	Team		Games	Pos.
1935	CHIC	N	12	HB
1936	DET	N	11	HB, QB
2 yrs.	23 games			

Les Peterson
PETERSON, LESTER (Tex)
B. 1910
D. Mar., 1993
Texas 6'3" 206 lbs.

Year	Team		Games	Pos.
1931	POR	N	9	E, T, C
1932	GB	N	7	E
1932	SI	N	4	E
1933	BKN	N	9	E
1934	GB	N	11	E
4 yrs.	40 games			

Nelson Peterson
PETERSON, NELSON (Banty)
B. Sep. 22, 1913, Weston, WV
D. Dec. 4, 1990
West Virginia Wesleyan 5'8" 179 lbs.

Year	Team		Games	Pos.
1937	WAS	N	2	HB
1938	CLE	N	7	HB
2 yrs.	9 games			

Phil Peterson
PETERSON, PHILIP
B. Mar. 29, 1906
D. Mar., 1981, St. Croix Falls, WI
Wisconsin 5'11" 195 lbs.

Year	Team		Games	Pos.
1934	BKN	N	3	E

Ray Peterson
PETERSON, RAYMOND
B. Jan. 18, 1916
D. Jul., 1977, Seattle, WA
San Francisco 6'0" 190 lbs.

Year	Team		Games	Pos.
1937	GB	N	2	B

Russ Peterson
PETERSON, RUSSELL
B. 1909
Montana 6'3" 216 lbs.

Year	Team		Games	Pos.
1932	BOS	N	5	T, G

Todd Peterson
PETERSON, JOSEPH TODD
B. Feb. 4, 1970, Valdosta, GA
Navy/Georgia 5'10" 176 lbs.

Year	Team		Games	Pos.
1994	ARI	N	2	K
1995	SEA	N	16	K
1996			16	K
3 yrs.	34 games			

Tony Peterson
PETERSON, ANTHONY WAYNE
B. Jan. 23, 1972, Cleveland, OH
Notre Dame 6'0" 225 lbs.

Year	Team		Games	Pos.
1994	SF	N	14	LB
1995			15	LB
1996			13	LB
3 yrs.	42 games			

Johnny Petitbon
PETITBON, JOHN
B. Jun. 4, 1931, New Orleans, LA
Notre Dame 5'11" 186 lbs.

Year	Team		Games	Pos.
1952	DAL	N	11	HB
1955	CLE	N	12	HB
1956			12	HB
1957	GB	N	12	HB
4 yrs.	47 games			

Richie Petitbon
PETITBON, RICHARD ALVIN
B. Apr. 18, 1938, New Orleans, LA
Tulane 6'3" 206 lbs.

Year	Team		Games	Pos.
1959	CHIB	N	12	DB
1960	CHI	N	12	DB
1961			14	DB
1962			14	DB
1963			14	DB
1964			14	DB
1965			14	DB
1966			14	DB
1967			14	DB
1968			14	DB
1969	LA	N	12	S
1970			14	S
1971	WAS	N	14	S
1972			3	S
14 yrs.	179 games			

Joe Petree
PETREE, JOE
B. 1893
Deceased
Northeast Missouri State

Year	Team		Games	Pos.
1920	CLE	A	2	HB, FB

Bob Petrella
PETRELLA, ROBERT (Pete)
B. Nov. 7, 1944, Philadelphia, PA
Tennessee 6'0" 186 lbs.

Year	Team		Games	Pos.
1966	MIA	A	3	DB
1967			9	DB
1968			9	DB
1969			14	S
1970	MIA	N	14	CB, S
1971			12	S
6 yrs.	61 games			

John Petrella
PETRELLA, JOHN (Pepper)
B. 1920
Deceased

John Petrella continued
Penn State 5'7" 160 lbs.

Year	Team		Games	Pos.
1945	PIT	N	3	HB

Bob Petrich
PETRICH, ROBERT
B. Mar. 15, 1941, Long Beach, CA
West Texas State 6'4" 253 lbs.

Year	Team		Games	Pos.
1963	SD	A	14	DE
1964			14	DE
1965			14	DE
1966			14	DE
1967	BUF	A	6	DE
5 yrs.	62 games			

Elmer Petrie
PETRIE, ELMER
None

Year	Team		Games	Pos.
1922	TOL	N	5	HB, FB

Bill Petrilas
PETRILAS, WILLIAM
B. Sep. 28, 1915, New Haven, CT
D. Nov., 1976, New Haven, CT
none 6'1" 195 lbs.

Year	Team		Games	Pos.
1944	NYG	N	10	HB, DB
1945			5	DB
2 yrs.	15 games			

Steve Petro
PETRO, STEPHEN (Rock)
B. Oct. 21, 1914, Johnstown, PA
D. Aug. 15, 1994, Pittsburgh, PA
Pittsburgh 5'10" 195 lbs.

Year	Team		Games	Pos.
1940	BKN	N	11	G
1941			6	G
2 yrs.	17 games			

George Petrovich
PETROVICH, GEORGE JOHN, JR.
B. Mar. 22, 1926, Palestine, TX
Texas 6'2" 225 lbs.

Year	Team		Games	Pos.
1949	CHIC	N	12	T
1950			12	G
2 yrs.	24 games			

Stan Petry
PETRY, STANLEY EDWARD
B. Aug. 14, 1966, Alvin, TX
Texas Christian 5'11" 175 lbs.

Year	Team		Games	Pos.
1989	KC	N	16	CB
1990			16	CB
1991			2	CB
1991	NO	N	2	CB
3 yrs.	36 games			

Phil Pettey
PETTEY, PHIL
B. Apr. 17, 1962
Missouri 6'4" 274 lbs.

Year	Team		Games	Pos.
1987	WAS	N	3	G

Neal Petties
PETTIES, CORNELIUS
B. Sep. 16, 1940, San Diego, CA
San Diego State 6'2" 198 lbs.

Year	Team		Games	Pos.
1964	BAL	N	14	FL
1965			14	OE
1966			10	OE
3 yrs.	38 games			

Gary Pettigrew
PETTIGREW, GARY LOUIS
B. Oct. 10, 1944, Vancouver, B.C.
Stanford 6'4" 252 lbs.

Year	Team		Games	Pos.
1966	PHI	N	14	DE

Year	Team	Games	Pos.

Gary Pettigrew continued

1967		13	DE
1968		14	DE
1969		7	DE
1970		14	DT
1971		13	DT
1972		13	DT
1973		14	DT
1974		4	DT
1974	NYG N	5	DT

9 yrs. 111 games

Duane Pettit

PETTIT, DUANE EDWARD
B. Nov. 2, 1964, Long Beach, CA
San Diego State 6'4" 265 lbs.

| 1987 | SD N | 3 | DE |

John Petty

PETTY, JOHN
B. Oct. 3, 1919, Lebanon, PA
D. Apr. 6, 1979, Wilmington, OH
Purdue 6'1" 225 lbs.

| 1942 | CHIB N | 9 | FB |

Ross Petty

PETTY, MANLEY ROSS
B. Sep. 11, 1892
D. Mar. 13, 1966, Brookfield, WI
Illinois 180 lbs.

| 1920 | DEC A | 5 | G |

Barry Pettyjohn

PETTYJOHN, BARRY G.
B. Mar. 29, 1964, Cincinnati, OH
Pittsburgh 6'5" 285 lbs.

| 1987 | HOU N | 2 | OT |

David Petway

PETWAY, DAVID
B. Oct. 17, 1955, Chicago, IL
Northern Illinois 6'1" 207 lbs.

| 1981 | GB N | 5 | S |

Bob Peviani

PEVIANI, ROBERT
B. 1932
Southern California 6'1" 210 lbs.

| 1953 | NYG N | 10 | G |

Leo Peyton

PEYTON, LEO
None 5'11" 190 lbs.

| 1923 | ROC N | 1 | FB |
| 1924 | | 4 | HB, FB |

2 yrs. 5 games

Bob Pfohl

PFOHL, ROBERT S. (Stormy)
B. May 21, 1926, Vincennes, IN
*U.S. Merchant Marine Academy-Kings
Point/Purdue 6'0" 200 lbs.*

| 1948 | BAL AA | 14 | B |
| 1949 | | 12 | B |

2 yrs. 26 games

Art Pharmer

PHARMER, C. ARTHUR
B. Jul. 21, 1908
D. Feb., 1970
Minnesota 5'10" 186 lbs.

1930	MIN N	8	HB
1930	FRA N	5	HB
1931		2	FB, HB

2 yrs. 15 games

Tommy Pharr

PHARR, TOMMY
B. Jul. 31, 1947, Canton, GA
Mississippi State 5'10" 187 lbs.

| 1970 | BUF N | 10 | S |

Bob Phelan

PHELAN, ROBERT
B. Jun. 20, 1898
D. Aug., 1973, Fort Madison, IA
Notre Dame 5'11" 185 lbs.

1922	TOL N	8	HB, FB
1923	RI N	8	FB, HB
1924		6	HB, FB

3 yrs. 22 games

Don Phelps

PHELPS, DONALD (Dopey)
B. Jan. 7, 1924, Richmond, KY
D. Jun. 11, 1982, Frankfort, KY
Kentucky 5'11" 185 lbs.

1950	CLE N	12	HB
1951		4	HB
1952		1	HB

3 yrs. 17 games

Roman Phifer

PHIFER, ROMAN ZUBINSKY
B. Mar. 5, 1968, Plattsburgh, NY
UCLA 6'2" 230 lbs.

1991	LARM N	12	LB
1992		16	LB
1993		16	LB
1994		16	LB
1995	STL N	16	LB
1996		15	LB

6 yrs. 91 games

Gerry Philbin

PHILBIN, GERALD JOHN
B. Jul. 31, 1941, Pawtucket, RI
Buffalo 6'2" 245 lbs.

1964	NY A	6	DE
1965		14	DE
1966		14	DE
1967		14	DE
1968		14	DE
1969		13	DE
1970	NYJ N	11	DE
1971		10	DE
1972		14	DE
1973	PHI N	13	DE

10 yrs. 123 games

Todd Philcox

PHILCOX, TODD STUART
B. Sep. 25, 1966, Norwalk, CT
Syracuse 6'4" 217 lbs.

1990	CIN N	1	QB
1991	CLE N	4	QB
1992		2	QB
1993		5	QB

4 yrs. 12 games

Ed Philion

PHILION, ED
B. Mar. 27, 1970, Windsor, Ont.
Ferris State 6'2" 273 lbs.

| 1994 | BUF N | 4 | DT |
| 1995 | | 2 | DT |

2 yrs. 6 games

Anthony Phillips

PHILLIPS, ANTHONY DWAYNE
B. Oct. 5, 1970, Galveston, TX
Texas A&M, Kingsville 6'0" 217 lbs.

| 1994 | ATL N | 5 | CB |

Anthony Phillips continued

| 1995 | | 6 | CB |
| 1996 | | 6 | CB |

3 yrs. 17 games

Bobby Phillips

PHILLIPS, BOBBY
B. Dec. 8, 1969, Richmond, VA
Virginia Union 5'9" 194 lbs.

| 1995 | MIN N | 8 | RB |

Charles Phillips

PHILLIPS, CHARLES W.
B. Dec. 22, 1952, Greenville, MS
Southern California 6'2" 215 lbs.

1975	OAK N	14	DB
1976		14	S
1977		7	S
1978		16	S
1979		16	S

5 yrs. 67 games

Ewell Phillips

PHILLIPS, EWELL (Cap)
B. Apr. 20, 1910, Comanche, OK
Oklahoma Baptist 5'11" 210 lbs.

| 1936 | NYG N | 12 | G |

George Phillips

PHILLIPS, GEORGE C.
B. 1921
UCLA 6'3" 215 lbs.

| 1945 | CLE N | 1 | QB |

Irvin Phillips

PHILLIPS, IRVIN JEROME
B. Jan. 23, 1960, Leesburg, FL
Arkansas Tech 6'1" 192 lbs.

| 1981 | SD N | 15 | CB |
| 1983 | LARI N | 5 | CB |

2 yrs. 20 games

Jason Phillips

PHILLIPS, JASON HOWELL
B. Oct. 11, 1966, Crowley, LA
Houston 5'7" 168 lbs.

1989	DET N	16	WR
1990		13	WR
1991	ATL N	11	WR
1992		12	WR
1993		6	WR

5 yrs. 58 games

Jess Phillips

PHILLIPS, JESS W., JR.
B. Feb. 28, 1947, Beaumont, TX
Michigan State 6'1" 208 lbs.

1968	CIN A	14	DB
1969		14	RB
1970	CIN N	14	RB
1971		14	RB
1972		13	RB
1973	NO N	14	RB
1974		14	RB
1975	OAK N	14	RB
1976	NE N	13	RB
1977		14	RB

10 yrs. 138 games

Jim Phillips

PHILLIPS, JAMES JACKSON (Red)
B. Feb. 5, 1936, Alexander City, AL
Auburn 6'1" 197 lbs.

| 1958 | LA N | 12 | E |

Jim Phillips continued

1959		9	E
1960		12	E
1961		14	OE
1962		14	OE
1963		14	OE
1964		7	FL
1965	MIN N	12	FL
1966		12	FL
1967		13	FL

10 yrs. 119 games

Joe Phillips

PHILLIPS, JOE
B. Apr. 12, 1963, Franklin, KY
Kentucky 5'9" 188 lbs.

| 1985 | WAS N | 4 | WR |
| 1987 | | 2 | WR |

2 yrs. 6 games

Joe Phillips

PHILLIPS, JOSEPH GORDON
B. Jul. 15, 1963, Portland, OR
*Oregon State/Southern Methodist 6'5"
285 lbs.*

1986	MIN N	16	NT
1987	SD N	13	DE
1988		16	DE
1989		16	DE
1990		3	NT
1991		16	NT
1992	KC N	12	DT
1993		16	DT
1994		16	DT
1995		16	DT
1996		16	DT

11 yrs. 156 games

Kim Phillips

PHILLIPS, KIM DARNELL
B. Oct. 28, 1966, New Boston, TX
North Texas State 5'9" 188 lbs.

| 1989 | NO N | 5 | CB |
| 1990 | BUF N | 1 | DB |

2 yrs. 6 games

Kirk Phillips

PHILLIPS, KIRK DOUGLAS
B. Jul. 31, 1960, Poteau, OK
Tulsa 6'1" 195 lbs.

| 1984 | DAL N | 8 | WR |

Lawrence Phillips

PHILLIPS, LAWRENCE
B. May 12, 1975, Little Rock, AR
Nebraska 6'0" 229 lbs.

| 1996 | STL N | 15 | RB |

Loyd Phillips

PHILLIPS, LOYD
B. May 2, 1945, Fort Worth, TX
Arkansas 6'3" 237 lbs.

1967	CHI N	7	DE
1968		13	DE
1969		12	DE, LB

3 yrs. 32 games

Mel Phillips

PHILLIPS, MELVIN, JR.
B. Jan. 6, 1942, Shelby, NC
North Carolina A&T 6'0" 191 lbs.

1966	SF N	11	DB
1967		14	DB
1968		13	DB
1969		11	S, CB

Year	Team		Games	Pos.

Mel Phillips continued

Year	Team		Games	Pos.
1970			14	CB, S
1971			13	S
1972			14	S
1973			14	S
1974			6	S
1975			9	S
1976			14	S
1977			14	S
12 yrs.	147 games			

Mike Phillips
PHILLIPS, MICHAEL
B. Nov. 22, 1921, Clifton Heights, PA
Western Maryland 6'0" 208 lbs.

Year	Team		Games	Pos.
1947	BAL	AA	12	C

Ray Phillips
PHILLIPS, RAY
B. Mar. 18, 1954, Milwaukee, WI
Nebraska 6'4" 224 lbs.

Year	Team		Games	Pos.
1977	CIN	N	14	LB
1978			2	LB
1978	PHI	N	10	LB
1979			11	LB
1980			16	LB
1981			16	LB
5 yrs.	69 games			

Ray Phillips
PHILLIPS, RAYMOND THOMAS, JR.
B. Jul. 24, 1964, Mooresville, NC
North Carolina State 6'3" 245 lbs.

Year	Team		Games	Pos.
1986	ATL	N	1	LB
1987	PHI	N	3	DE, LB
2 yrs.	4 games			

Reggie Phillips
PHILLIPS, REGINALD
B. Dec. 29, 1960, Houston, TX
Southern Methodist 5'10" 170 lbs.

Year	Team		Games	Pos.
1985	CHI	N	16	CB, S
1986			16	CB, S
1987			12	CB
1988	PHX	N	16	CB
4 yrs.	60 games			

Rod Phillips
PHILLIPS, RODNEY AUGUSTUS
B. Dec. 23, 1952, Meridian, MS
Cincinnati/Jackson State 6'0" 220 lbs.

Year	Team		Games	Pos.
1975	LA	N	14	RB
1976			14	RB
1977			14	RB
1978			15	RB
1979	STL	N	11	RB
1980			16	RB
6 yrs.	84 games			

Dean Phillpott
PHILLPOTT, DEAN
B. Nov. 11, 1935, Mena, AR
Fresno State 6'0" 200 lbs.

Year	Team		Games	Pos.
1958	CHIC	N	9	FB

Ed Philpott
PHILPOTT, EDWARD
B. Sep. 14, 1945, Wichita, KS
Miami (Ohio) 6'3" 240 lbs.

Year	Team		Games	Pos.
1967	BOS	A	13	LB
1968			14	LB
1969			14	LB
1970	BOS	N	14	LB
1971	NE		13	LB
5 yrs.	68 games			

Charles Philyaw
PHILYAW, CHARLES HENRY (King Kong)
B. Feb. 25, 1954, Shreveport, LA
Texas Southern 6'9" 276 lbs.

Year	Team		Games	Pos.
1976	OAK	N	14	DE
1977			3	DE
1978			15	DE
1979			12	DE
4 yrs.	44 games			

Dino Philyaw
PHILYAW, DELVIC DINO
B. Oct. 30, 1970, Kenansville, NC
Oregon 5'10" 192 lbs.

Year	Team		Games	Pos.
1995	CAR	N	1	RB
1996			9	RB
2 yrs.	10 games			

Mike Phipps
PHIPPS, MICHAEL ELSTON
B. Nov. 19, 1947, Shelbyville, IN
Purdue 6'3" 208 lbs.

Year	Team		Games	Pos.
1970	CLE	N	14	QB
1971			14	QB
1972			14	QB
1973			14	QB
1974			14	QB
1975			14	QB
1976			4	QB
1977	CHI	N	3	QB
1978			6	QB
1979			12	QB
1980			7	QB
1981			3	QB
12 yrs.	119 games			

Alex Piasecky
PIASECKY, ALEXANDER
B. Feb. 1, 1917, Greensburg, PA
D. Sep. 16, 1992, Orange City, FL
Duke 6'2" 197 lbs.

Year	Team		Games	Pos.
1943	WAS	N	9	E
1944			10	E
1945			9	E
3 yrs.	28 games			

Bob Picard
PICARD, ROBERT
B. Nov. 24, 1949, Omak, WA
Eastern Washington 6'1" 196 lbs.

Year	Team		Games	Pos.
1973	PHI	N	14	WR
1974			14	WR
1975			14	WR
1976			4	WR
1976	DET	N	8	WR
4 yrs.	54 games			

Bill Piccolo
PICCOLO, WILLIAM J.
B. May 1, 1920, Buffalo, NY
Canisius 5'11" 185 lbs.

Year	Team		Games	Pos.
1943	NYG	N	9	C
1944			6	C
1945			4	C
3 yrs.	19 games			

Brian Piccolo
PICCOLO, LOUIS BRIAN (Pic)
B. Oct. 21, 1943, Pittsfield, MA
D. Jun. 16, 1970, New York, NY
Wake Forest 6'0" 205 lbs.

Year	Team		Games	Pos.
1966	CHI	N	14	HB
1967			14	RB
1968			14	RB
1969			9	RB
4 yrs.	51 games			

Lou Piccone
PICCONE, LOUIS JAMES
B. Jul. 17, 1949, Vineland, NJ
West Liberty State 5'9" 177 lbs.

Year	Team		Games	Pos.
1974	NYJ	N	14	WR
1975			13	WR
1976			14	WR
1977	BUF	N	14	WR
1978			16	WR
1979			16	WR
1980			9	WR
1981			14	WR
1982			8	WR
9 yrs.	118 games			

Bob Pickard
PICKARD, BOB
B. Sep. 3, 1952, Canton, OH
Xavier (Ohio) 6'0" 190 lbs.

Year	Team		Games	Pos.
1974	DET	N	14	WR

Bill Pickel
PICKEL, WILLIAM
B. Nov. 5, 1959, Queens, NY
Rutgers 6'5" 263 lbs.

Year	Team		Games	Pos.
1983	LARI	N	16	NT
1984			16	NT
1985			16	NT
1986			15	DT
1987			12	DT
1988			16	DT
1989			16	DT
1990			14	DT
1991	NYJ	N	15	DT
1992			11	DT
1993			16	DT
1994			11	DT
12 yrs.	174 games			

Bob Pickens
PICKENS, ROBERT JAMES
B. Feb. 2, 1943, Chicago, IL
Wisconsin/Nebraska 6'4" 258 lbs.

Year	Team		Games	Pos.
1967	CHI	N	12	OT
1968			4	OT
1969			3	OT
3 yrs.	19 games			

Bruce Pickens
PICKENS, BRUCE EVON
B. May 9, 1968, Kansas City, MO
Nebraska 5'11" 190 lbs.

Year	Team		Games	Pos.
1991	ATL	N	7	CB
1992			16	CB
1993			4	CB
1993	GB	N	2	CB
1993	KC	N	3	CB
1995	OAK	N	16	CB
4 yrs.	48 games			

Carl Pickens
PICKENS, CARL MCNALLY
B. Mar. 23, 1970, Murphy, NC
Tennessee 6'2" 206 lbs.

Year	Team		Games	Pos.
1992	CIN	N	16	WR
1993			13	WR
1994			15	WR
1995			16	WR
1996			16	WR
5 yrs.	76 games			

Lyle Pickens
PICKENS, LYLE
B. Sep. 5, 1964, New Orleans, LA
Colorado 5'10" 175 lbs.

Year	Team		Games	Pos.
1987	DEN	N	1	CB

Clay Pickering
PICKERING, CLAY FLOYD
B. Jun. 2, 1961, Jacksonville, FL
Maine 6'5" 215 lbs.

Year	Team		Games	Pos.
1984	CIN	N	3	WR
1985			1	WR
1986	CHI	N	4	WR
1987	NE	N	1	WR
4 yrs.	9 games			

Tim Pidgeon
PIDGEON, TIMOTHY CHARLES
B. Sep. 20, 1964, Oneonta, NY
Syracuse 6'0" 233 lbs.

Year	Team		Games	Pos.
1987	MIA	N	3	LB

Mike Piel
PIEL, MIKE LLOYD
B. Sep. 21, 1965, Carmel, CA
Illinois 6'4" 268 lbs.

Year	Team		Games	Pos.
1989	LARM	N	13	DE
1990			16	DT
1991			6	DT
1992			15	DT
4 yrs.	50 games			

Milt Piepul
PIEPUL, MILTON JOHN
B. Sep. 14, 1918, Springfield, MA
D. Mar. 19, 1994, Northampton, MA
Notre Dame 6'1" 215 lbs.

Year	Team		Games	Pos.
1941	DET	N	11	FB

Aaron Pierce
PIERCE, AARON
B. Sep. 6, 1969, Seattle, WA
Washington 6'5" 246 lbs.

Year	Team		Games	Pos.
1992	NYG	N	1	TE
1993			13	TE
1994			16	TE
1995			16	TE
1996			10	TE
5 yrs.	56 games			

Danny Pierce
PIERCE, JOHN DANIEL
B. Jan. 17, 1948, Laurel, MS
Memphis State 6'3" 215 lbs.

Year	Team		Games	Pos.
1970	WAS	N	2	RB

Dick Pierce
PIERCE, RICHARD
B. Mar. 1, 1896
D. Sep., 1966, Detroit, MI
Michigan 186 lbs.

Year	Team		Games	Pos.
1920	CHIT	A		G, T

Don Pierce
PIERCE, DONALD H.
B. Feb. 7, 1919, Topeka, KS
D. Jan. 2, 1965
Kansas 6'1" 186 lbs.

Year	Team		Games	Pos.
1942	BKN	N	3	C
1943	CHIC	N	1	C
2 yrs.	4 games			

Steve Pierce
PIERCE, STEPHEN
B. Dec. 12, 1963
Illinois 5'10" 190 lbs.

Year	Team		Games	Pos.
1987	CLE	N	2	WR

Damon Pieri
PIERI, MARK DAMON
B. Sep. 25, 1970, Phoenix, AZ

Year	Team	Games	Pos.

Damon Pieri *continued*
San Diego State 6'0" 186 lbs.

Year	Team		Games	Pos.
1993	NYJ	N	5	S
1996	CAR	N	16	S
2 yrs.	21 games			

Al Pierotti
PIEROTTI, ALBERT FELIX
B. Oct. 24, 1895, Boston, MA
D. Feb. 12, 1964, Everett, MA
Washington & Lee 5'10" 199 lbs.

Year	Team		Games	Pos.
1920	AKR	A	1	C
1920	CLE	A	4	C
1921	NY	A	2	C
1922	MIL	N	9	C
1923			3	C
1924			3	G, T
1926	BOS	A	5	C
1927	PRO	N	14	C, G, T
1929	BOS	N	7	C
8 yrs.	48 games			

Joe Pierre
PIERRE, JOSEPH
B. 1921
Pittsburgh 6'0" 185 lbs.

Year	Team		Games	Pos.
1945	PIT	N	10	E

Pete Pierson
PIERSON, PETER SAMUEL
B. Feb. 4, 1971, Portland, OR
Washington 6'5" 287 lbs.

Year	Team		Games	Pos.
1994	TB	N	1	OT
1995			11	OT
1996			10	OT
3 yrs.	22 games			

Reggie Pierson
PIERSON, REGGIE LEE
B. Dec. 13, 1952, Compton, CA
Oklahoma State 5'11" 185 lbs.

Year	Team		Games	Pos.
1976	DET	N	4	DB
1976	TB	N	5	CB
1 yr.	9 games			

Nick Pietrosante
PIETROSANTE, NICHOLAS VINCENT
B. Sep. 10, 1937, Ansonia, CT
D. Feb. 6, 1988, Royal Oak, MI
Notre Dame 6'2" 225 lbs.

Year	Team		Games	Pos.
1959	DET	N	10	FB
1960			12	FB
1961			14	FB
1962			13	FB
1963			12	FB
1964			14	FB
1965			14	FB
1966	CLE	N	13	RB
1967			14	RB
9 yrs.	116 games			

Jim Pietrzak
PIETRZAK, JAMES MICHAEL
B. Feb. 21, 1953, Hamtramck, MI
Eastern Michigan 6'5" 260 lbs.

Year	Team		Games	Pos.
1974	NYG	N	14	DT
1975			14	DT
1977			14	DT
1978			16	OT, C
1979			3	OT, C
1979	NO	N	8	C, DT
1980			15	C
1981			16	C
1982			9	C
1983			16	C
1984			10	C
1987	KC	N	2	C
11 yrs.	137 games			

Bob Pifferini
PIFFERINI, ROBERT M., SR.
B. Oct. 1, 1922, Oakdale, CA
San Jose State 6'0" 210 lbs.

Year	Team		Games	Pos.
1949	DET	N	12	C

Bob Pifferini
PIFFERINI, ROBERT M., JR.
B. Jun. 27, 1950, San Jose, CA
UCLA 6'2" 226 lbs.

Year	Team		Games	Pos.
1972	CHI	N	14	LB
1973			12	LB
1974			12	LB
1975			14	LB
1977	LA	N	5	LB
5 yrs.	57 games			

Bert Piggott
PIGGOTT, BERT COLEY
B. Mar. 5, 1921, Hinsdale, IL
Illinois 6'2" 195 lbs.

Year	Team		Games	Pos.
1947	LA	AA	13	B

Carl Pignatelli
PIGNATELLI, CARLO
B. Nov. 26, 1907
D. Jun. 14, 1964
Iowa 6'0" 210 lbs.

Year	Team		Games	Pos.
1931	CLE	N	7	HB, FB

Pete Pihos
PIHOS, PETER LOUIS (Big Dog)
B. Oct. 22, 1923, Orlando, FL
Indiana 6'1" 211 lbs.

Year	Team		Games	Pos.
1947	PHI	N	12	E
1948			12	E
1949			11	E
1950			12	E
1951			12	E
1952			12	E
1953			12	E
1954			12	E
1955			12	E
9 yrs.	107 games			

Chris Pike
PIKE, CHRIS HOLTZ
B. Jan. 13, 1964, Washington, DC
North Carolina/Tulsa 6'8" 290 lbs.

Year	Team		Games	Pos.
1989	CLE	N	12	NT, DE
1990			12	DT
1991	LARM	N	8	DT
3 yrs.	32 games			

Mark Pike
PIKE, MARK HAROLD
B. Dec. 27, 1963, Elizabethtown, KY
Georgia Tech 6'4" 268 lbs.

Year	Team		Games	Pos.
1987	BUF	N	3	LB
1988			16	DE
1989			16	DE
1990			16	DE
1991			16	DE
1992			16	DE
1993			14	DE
1994			16	DE
1995			16	DE
1996			16	DE
10 yrs.	145 games			

Joe Pilconis
PILCONIS, JOSEPH GEORGE
B. Oct. 9, 1911, Shenandoah, PA
D. Jun. 29, 1993, New Ringgold, PA
Temple 6'1" 189 lbs.

Year	Team		Games	Pos.
1934	PHI	N	10	E

Joe Pilconis *continued*

Year	Team		Games	Pos.
1936			12	E
1937			11	E
3 yrs.	33 games			

Evan Pilgrim
PILGRIM, EVAN
B. Aug. 14, 1972, Pittsburg, CA
Brigham Young 6'4" 304 lbs.

Year	Team		Games	Pos.
1996	CHI	N	4	G

Roger Pillath
PILLATH, ROGER ALLEN
B. Dec. 21, 1941, Marinette, WI
Wisconsin 6'4" 249 lbs.

Year	Team		Games	Pos.
1965	LA	N	14	OT
1966	PIT	N	6	OT
2 yrs.	20 games			

Lawrence Pillers
PILLERS, LAWRENCE D.
B. Nov. 4, 1952, Hazlehurst, MS
Alcorn State 6'3" 257 lbs.

Year	Team		Games	Pos.
1976	NYJ	N	14	DE
1977			13	DE
1978			16	DE
1979			16	DE
1980			3	DE
1980	SF	N	13	DE
1981			14	DE
1982			9	DE
1983			16	DT, DE
1984			16	DT, DE
1985	ATL	N	9	DE
10 yrs.	139 games			

Brian Pillman
PILLMAN, BRIAN
B. May 22, 1962, Cincinnati, OH
Miami (Ohio) 5'10" 228 lbs.

Year	Team		Games	Pos.
1984	CIN	N	6	LB

Frank Pillow
PILLOW, WILLIAM FRANK, JR.
B. Mar. 11, 1965, Nashville, TN
Tennessee State 5'10" 170 lbs.

Year	Team		Games	Pos.
1988	TB	N	15	WR
1989			3	WR
1990			16	WR
3 yrs.	34 games			

Erny Pinckert
PINCKERT, ERNY
B. May 1, 1907, Medford, OR
D. Aug. 30, 1977, Los Angeles, CA
Southern California 6'0" 197 lbs.

Year	Team		Games	Pos.
1932	BOS	N	9	HB, QB
1933			12	HB
1934			12	HB, QB
1935			11	HB, QB
1936			12	HB, QB
1937	WAS	N	11	HB, FB
1938			9	HB
1939			10	QB
1940			11	QB
9 yrs.	97 games			

Stan Pincura
PINCURA, STANLEY
B. May 2, 1913, Lorain, OH
D. Feb., 1979, Lorain, OH
Ohio State 5'11" 175 lbs.

Year	Team		Games	Pos.
1937	CLE	N	11	QB
1938			10	QB
2 yrs.	21 games			

Cyril Pinder
PINDER, CYRIL CALVIN
B. Nov. 13, 1946, Fort Lauderdale, FL
Illinois 6'2" 218 lbs.

Year	Team		Games	Pos.
1968	PHI	N	14	RB
1969			14	RB
1970			14	RB
1971	CHI	N	12	RB
1972			13	RB
1973	DAL	N	5	RB
6 yrs.	72 games			

Ed Pine
PINE, EDWARD
B. 1940, Reno, NV
Utah 6'4" 233 lbs.

Year	Team		Games	Pos.
1962	SF	N	14	LB
1963			14	LB
1964			14	LB
1965	PIT	N	8	LB
4 yrs.	50 games			

Johnny Pingel
PINGEL, JOHN SPENCER
B. Nov. 6, 1916, Mount Clemens, MI
Michigan State 6'0" 180 lbs.

Year	Team		Games	Pos.
1939	DET	N	9	QB, HB

Allen Pinkett
PINKETT, ALLEN JEROME
B. Jan. 25, 1964, Washington, DC
Notre Dame 5'9" 189 lbs.

Year	Team		Games	Pos.
1986	HOU	N	16	RB
1987			8	RB
1988			16	RB
1989			16	RB
1990			15	RB
1991			16	RB
6 yrs.	87 games			

Lovell Pinkney
PINKNEY, LOVELL
B. Aug. 18, 1972, Washington, DC
Texas 6'4" 248 lbs.

Year	Team		Games	Pos.
1995	STL	N	8	WR

Reggie Pinkney
PINKNEY, REGGIE
B. May 27, 1955, St. Louis, MO
East Carolina 5'11" 188 lbs.

Year	Team		Games	Pos.
1977	DET	N	11	DB
1978			13	S
1979	BAL	N	16	CB, S
1980			16	S
1981			16	S
5 yrs.	72 games			

Ray Pinney
PINNEY, RAYMON EARL, JR.
B. Jun. 29, 1954, Seattle, WA
Washington 6'4" 260 lbs.

Year	Team		Games	Pos.
1976	PIT	N	14	C, OT
1977			14	C, OT
1978			13	OT, C
1980			16	OT, C
1981			16	G, OT, C
1982			9	OT
1985			15	OL
1986			16	OT, C
1987			12	OT
9 yrs.	125 games			

Scott Piper
PIPER, SCOTT
B. Jun. 18, 1954, Philadelphia, PA
Colorado 6'1" 179 lbs.

Year	Team		Games	Pos.
1976	ATL	N	13	WR

Year	Team		Games	Pos.

Joyce Pipkin
PIPKIN, JOYCE CLARENCE
B. Jan. 9, 1924, Lono, AR
Arkansas 6'1" 204 lbs.

Year	Team		Games	Pos.
1948	NYG	N	11	E
1949	LA	AA	8	B
2 yrs.		19 games		

Woody Pippens
PIPPENS, WOODY
B. Feb. 7, 1963, Cleveland, OH
Thiel 5'11" 225 lbs.

1987	KC	N	2	RB

Hank Piro
PIRO, HENRY W.
B. Dec. 20, 1917, Brooklyn, NY
Syracuse 6'0" 186 lbs.

1941	PHI	N	10	E

Rocco Pirro
PIRRO, ROCCO (Rock)
B. Jun. 30, 1916, Syracuse, NY
D. Jan. 26, 1995, Solvay, NV
Catholic 6'0" 226 lbs.

1940	PIT	N	9	HB, DB
1941			10	LB
1946	BUF	AA	13	G
1947			13	G
1948			14	G
1949			11	G
6 yrs.		70 games		

Joe Pisarcik
PISARCIK, JOSEPH ANTHONY
B. Jul. 2, 1952, Kingston, PA
New Mexico State 6'4" 220 lbs.

1977	NYG	N	13	QB
1978			15	QB
1979			4	QB
1980	PHI	N	9	QB
1981			7	QB
1982			1	QB
1983			5	QB
1984			7	QB
8 yrs.		61 games		

Steve Pisarkiewicz
PISARKIEWICZ, STEPHEN JOHN
B. Nov. 10, 1953, Florissant, MO
Missouri 6'2" 205 lbs.

1978	STL	N	3	QB
1979			6	QB
1980	GB	N	1	QB
3 yrs.		10 games		

Roman Piskor
PISKOR, ROMAN J.
B. Aug. 9, 1917, North Tonawanda, NY
D. Aug., 1981, North Tonawanda, NY
Niagara 6'0" 245 lbs.

1946	NY	AA	12	T
1947	CLE	AA	10	T
1948	CHI	AA	12	T
3 yrs.		34 games		

Charles Pitcock
PITCOCK, CHARLES CLAYTON
B. Feb. 20, 1958, Homestead, FL
Tulane 6'4" 272 lbs.

1985	NO	N	1	G
1987	TB	N	2	C
2 yrs.		3 games		

Charlie Pittman
PITTMAN, CHARLES VERNON
B. Jan. 22, 1948, Baltimore, MD
Penn State 6'1" 200 lbs.

1970	STL	N	8	RB
1971	BAL	N	10	RB
2 yrs.		18 games		

Danny Pittman
PITTMAN, DANNY RAY
B. Apr. 3, 1958, Memphis, TN
Wyoming 6'2" 205 lbs.

1980	NYG	N	11	WR
1981			8	WR
1982			8	WR
1983			8	WR
1983	STL	N	4	WR
1984			10	WR
5 yrs.		49 games		

Kavika Pittman
PITTMAN, KAVIKA
B. Oct. 9, 1974, Leesville, LA
McNeese State 6'5" 263 lbs.

1996	DAL	N	15	DE

Mel Pittman
PITTMAN, MELVIN O. (Swede)
B. Feb. 23, 1908, Abilene, TX
Hardin-Simmons 6'0" 215 lbs.

1935	PIT	N	2	C

Ed Pitts
PITTS, EDWIN C. (Alabama)
B. 1910, Opelika, AL
D. Jun. 6, 1941, Valdese, NC
none 5'10" 185 lbs.

1935	PHI	N	3	HB

Elijah Pitts
PITTS, ELIJAH EUGENE
B. Feb. 3, 1938, Mayflower, AR
Philander Smith 6'1" 204 lbs.

1961	GB	N	14	HB
1962			14	HB
1963			14	HB
1964			14	HB
1965			14	HB
1966			14	HB
1967			8	RB
1968			14	RB
1969			14	RB
1970	NO	N	6	RB
1970	LA	N	2	RB
1971	GB	N	6	RB
11 yrs.		134 games		

Frank Pitts
PITTS, FRANK
B. Nov. 12, 1943, Atlanta, GA
Southern University 6'2" 198 lbs.

1965	KC	A	7	FL
1966			14	FL
1967			14	OE
1968			13	OE
1969			14	WR
1970	KC	N	12	WR
1971	CLE	N	13	WR
1972			14	WR
1973			13	WR
1974	OAK	N	12	WR
10 yrs.		126 games		

Hugh Pitts
PITTS, HUGH
B. Apr. 8, 1934
Texas Christian 6'2" 223 lbs.

1956	LA	N	9	C, LB

Hugh Pitts continued

1960	HOU	A		LB
2 yrs.		9 games		

John Pitts
PITTS, JOHN MARTIN
B. Feb. 28, 1945, Birmingham, AL
Arizona State 6'4" 218 lbs.

1967	BUF	A	14	DB
1968			14	DB
1969			14	S
1970	BUF	N	14	S
1971			14	S
1972			14	S
1973			3	S
1973	DEN	N	7	S
1974			14	S
1975			1	DB
1975	CLE	N	6	S
9 yrs.		115 games		

Mike Pitts
PITTS, MIKE
B. Sep. 25, 1960, Baltimore, MD
Alabama 6'5" 276 lbs.

1983	ATL	N	16	DE
1984			14	DE
1985			16	DT
1986			16	DT
1987	PHI	N	12	DT
1988			16	DT
1989			16	DT
1990			4	DT
1991			16	DT
1992			11	DT
1993	NE	N	16	DT
1994			16	DE
12 yrs.		169 games		

Ron Pitts
PITTS, RONALD DWAYNE
B. Oct. 14, 1962, Detroit, MI
UCLA 5'10" 175 lbs.

1986	BUF	N	10	S
1987			12	CB, S
1988	GB	N	14	CB, S
1989			14	CB, S
1990			16	CB
5 yrs.		66 games		

Joe Pivarnik
PIVARNIK, JOSEPH J. (Butch)
B. Feb. 18, 1912
D. Jan., 1976, Middletown, CT
Notre Dame 5'9" 217 lbs.

1936	PHI	N	6	G

Dave Pivec
PIVEC, DAVE JOHN
B. Sep. 25, 1943, Baltimore, MD
Notre Dame 6'3" 240 lbs.

1966	LA	N	3	TE
1967			14	TE
1968			14	TE
1969	DEN	A	14	TE
4 yrs.		45 games		

Joe Planansky
PLANANSKY, JOE
B. Oct. 21, 1971, Hemingford, NE
Chadron State 6'4" 250 lbs.

1995	MIA	N	2	TE

Doug Plank
PLANK, DOUGLAS WALTER
B. Mar. 4, 1953, Greensburg, PA
Ohio State 6'0" 200 lbs.

1975	CHI	N		DB

Doug Plank continued

1976			14	S
1977			11	S
1978			14	S
1979			16	S
1980			15	S
1981			16	S
1982			1	S
8 yrs.		101 games		

Earl Plank
PLANK, EARL
B. Jul. 28, 1905
D. Sep., 1952
None 174 lbs.

1926	COL	N	1	E
1930	BKN	N	8	E
2 yrs.		9 games		

Tony Plansky
PLANSKY, ANTHONY J.
B. Jun. 20, 1900
D. Feb. 10, 1979, Massachusetts
Georgetown (DC) 6'2" 209 lbs.

1928	NYG	N	5	HB, FB
1929			11	HB, FB
1932	BOS	N	1	HB
3 yrs.		17 games		

Ron Plantz
PLANTZ, RON
B. Jul. 27, 1964
Notre Dame 6'4" 272 lbs.

1987	IND	N	3	C, G

Jerry Planutis
PLANUTIS, GERALD R.
B. 1930
Michigan State 5'9" 175 lbs.

1956	WAS	N	3	HB

Dick Plasman
PLASMAN, HERBERT G.
B. Apr. 6, 1914, Metcalf, AZ
D. Jun. 20, 1981, Naples, FL
Vanderbilt 6'3" 218 lbs.

1937	CHIB	N	10	E
1938			8	E
1939			11	E
1940			11	E
1941			10	E
1944			2	E
1946	CHIC	N	3	E
1947			4	T, E
8 yrs.		59 games		

George Platukas
PLATUKAS, GEORGE P.
B. Mar. 15, 1915, West Hazleton, PA
D. May 17, 1973, Hazleton, PA
Duquesne 6'0" 196 lbs.

1938	PIT	N	4	E
1939			11	E
1940			11	E
1941			11	E
1942	CLE	N	9	E
5 yrs.		46 games		

Anthony Pleasant
PLEASANT, ANTHONY DEVON
B. Jan. 27, 1967, Century, FL
Tennessee State 6'5" 265 lbs.

1990	CLE	N	16	DE
1991			16	DE
1992			16	DE

Year	Team		Games	Pos.

Anthony Pleasant *continued*

Year	Team		Games	Pos.
1993			16	DE
1994			14	DE
1995			16	DE
1996	BAL	N	12	DE
7 yrs.	106 games			

Marquis Pleasant
PLEASANT, MARQUIS
B. Jun. 28, 1965
Southern Methodist 6'2" 172 lbs.

1987	CIN	N	3	WR

Mike Pleasant
PLEASANT, MICHAEL RICARDO
B. Aug. 16, 1958, Muskogee, OK
Oklahoma 6'1" 195 lbs.

1984	LARM	N	5	RB

Reggie Pleasant
PLEASANT, REGINALD LECARNO
B. May 2, 1962, Sumter, SC
Clemson 5'10" 175 lbs.

1985	ATL	N	3	CB

Joe Pliska
PLISKA, JOSEPH
B. Oct. 17, 1890, Chicago, IL
Deceased
Notre Dame 5'10" 180 lbs.

1920	HAM	A	1	HB
1921			1	HB
2 yrs.	2 games			

Kurt Ploeger
PLOEGER, KURT ALAN
B. Dec. 1, 1962, Iowa Falls, IA
Gustavus Adolphus 6'5" 259 lbs.

1986	DAL	N	3	DE
1986	GB	N	1	DE
1987	MIN	N	1	DT
2 yrs.	5 games			

Milt Plum
PLUM, MILTON ROSS
B. Jan. 20, 1935, Westville, NJ
Penn State 6'1" 205 lbs.

1957	CLE	N	9	QB
1958			12	QB
1959			12	QB
1960			12	QB
1961			14	QB
1962	DET	N	14	QB
1963			10	QB
1964			12	QB
1965			14	QB
1966			6	QB
1967			9	QB
1968	LA	N	4	QB
1969	NYG	N	1	QB
13 yrs.	129 games			

Bruce Plummer
PLUMMER, BRUCE ELLIOTT
B. Sep. 1, 1964, Bogalusa, LA
Mississippi State 6'1" 199 lbs.

1987	DEN	N	11	CB
1988			8	CB
1988	MIA	N	3	CB, S
1989	IND	N	16	S
1990	DEN	N	7	S
1990	SF	N	1	CB
1991	PHI	N	6	S
5 yrs.	52 games			

Gary Plummer
PLUMMER, GARY LEE
B. Jan. 26, 1960, Fremont, CA
California 6'2" 241 lbs.

1986	SD	N	15	LB
1987			8	LB
1988			16	LB
1989			16	LB
1990			16	LB
1991			16	LB
1992			16	LB
1993			16	LB
1994	SF	N	16	LB
1995			16	LB
1996			13	LB
11 yrs.	164 games			

Tony Plummer
PLUMMER, TONY LAMONT
B. Jan. 21, 1947, Dallas, TX
Pacific 5'11" 189 lbs.

1970	STL	N	1	S
1971	ATL	N	7	S
1972			14	S
1973			14	S
1974	LA	N	5	S
5 yrs.	41 games			

Dave Plump
PLUMP, DAVID
B. Dec. 13, 1942, Vicksburg, MS
Fresno State 6'1" 195 lbs.

1966	SD	A	14	DB

Ted Plumridge
PLUMRIDGE, THEODORE E.
B. 1902
D. 1962
Colgate/St. John's (New York) 6'2" 205 lbs.

1926	BKN	N	1	C
1926	BKN	N	2	C
1 yr.	3 games			

Art Plunkett
PLUNKETT, ARTHUR SCOTT
B. Mar. 8, 1959, Chicago, IL
Nevada-Las Vegas 6'7" 262 lbs.

1981	STL	N	8	OT
1982			9	OT
1983			16	OT
1984			16	OT
1985	NE	N	15	OT
1987			7	OT
6 yrs.	71 games			

Jim Plunkett
PLUNKETT, JAMES WILLIAM, JR.
B. Dec. 5, 1947, San Jose, CA
Stanford 6'2" 220 lbs.

1971	NE	N	14	QB
1972			14	QB
1973			14	QB
1974			14	QB
1975			5	QB
1976	SF	N	12	QB
1977			14	QB
1979	OAK	N	4	QB
1980			13	QB
1981			9	QB
1982	LARI	N	9	QB
1983			14	QB
1984			8	QB
1985			3	QB
1986			10	QB
15 yrs.	157 games			

Sherman Plunkett
PLUNKETT, SHERMAN EUGENE (Tank)
B. Apr. 7, 1934, Oklahoma City, OK
D. Nov. 18, 1989, Baltimore, MD
Maryland-Eastern Shore 6'4" 290 lbs.

1958	BAL	N	12	T
1959			12	T
1960			12	T
1961	SD	A	12	OT
1962			14	OT
1963	NY	A	14	OT
1964			14	OT
1965			14	OT
1966			14	OT
1967			14	OT
10 yrs.	132 games			

Warren Plunkett
PLUNKETT, WARREN FRANCIS
B. Aug. 4, 1920, St. Paul, MN
Minnesota 6'0" 200 lbs.

1942	CLE	N	10	QB, HB

Bobby Ply
PLY, ROBERT VERNON
B. Aug. 13, 1940, Mission, TX
Baylor 6'1" 190 lbs.

1962	DAL	A	14	DB
1963	KC	A	14	DB
1964			14	DB
1965			14	DB
1966			14	DB
1967			3	DB
1967	BUF	A	3	DB
1967	DEN	A	4	DB
6 yrs.	80 games			

Ray Poage
POAGE, RAYMOND COY, JR.
B. Nov. 14, 1940, Plainview, TX
Texas 6'4" 208 lbs.

1963	MIN	N	7	FL
1964	PHI	N	14	FL
1965			13	OE
1967	NO	N	12	OE
1968			10	OE
1969			14	TE
1970			12	WR, TE
1971	ATL	N	4	TE
8 yrs.	86 games			

Paul Podmajersky
PODMAJERSKY, PAUL, JR.
B. Nov. 17, 1916
D. Oct. 12, 1993, Roseburg, OR
Wyoming/Illinois 5'11" 220 lbs.

1944	CHIB	N	1	G

Ed Podolak
PODOLAK, EDWARD JOSEPH
B. Sep. 1, 1947, Atlantic, IA
Iowa 6'1" 204 lbs.

1969	KC	A	6	RB
1970	KC	N	14	RB
1971			13	RB
1972			13	RB
1973			14	RB
1974			9	RB
1975			14	RB
1976			10	RB
1977			13	RB
9 yrs.	106 games			

Jim Podoley
PODOLEY, JAMES
B. Sep. 16, 1933, Mount Morris, MI
Central Michigan 6'2" 200 lbs.

1957	WAS	N	12	HB

Jim Podoley *continued*

1958			10	HB
1959			11	HB
1960			10	HB
4 yrs.	43 games			

Billy Poe
POE, BILLY GENE, II
B. Apr. 26, 1964, Ironton, KY
Morehead State 6'3" 280 lbs.

1987	CIN	N	3	G

Johnnie Poe
POE, JOHNNIE EDWARD
B. Aug. 29, 1959, St. Louis, MO
Missouri 6'1" 192 lbs.

1981	NO	N	15	CB, S
1982			9	CB
1983			16	CB
1984			16	CB
1985			16	CB
1986			16	CB
1987			12	CB
7 yrs.	100 games			

John Pohlman
POHLMAN, JOHN THEODORE
B. Sep. 18, 1902, New Haven, CT
D. May 8, 1957, Milford, CT
Brown 5'9" 178 lbs.

1925	PRO	N	2	FB, HB

Dick Poillon
POILLON, RICHARD CHARLES
B. Aug. 13, 1920, Astoria, NY
D. Nov. 14, 1994
Canisius 6'0" 193 lbs.

1942	WAS	N	7	HB
1946			5	HB
1947			12	HB
1949			12	HB
4 yrs.	36 games			

Lance Poimboeuf
POIMBOEUF, LANCE
B. Oct. 11, 1940
Southwestern Louisiana 6'3" 225 lbs.

1963	DAL	N	1	K

John Pointer
POINTER, JOHN LESLIE
B. Jan. 16, 1958, Columbia, TN
Vanderbilt 6'2" 225 lbs.

1987	GB	N	3	LB

Frank Pokorney
POKORNEY, FRANK EDWARD
B. May 13, 1963, Uniontown, PA
Youngstown State 6'0" 198 lbs.

1985	PIT	N	4	WR

John Polanski
POLANSKI, JOHN B.
B. Sep. 6, 1918, Buffalo, NY
Deceased
Wake Forest 6'2" 211 lbs.

1942	DET	N	3	FB
1946	LA	AA	13	FB
2 yrs.	16 games			

John Polisky
POLISKY, JOHN (Bull)
B. Jan. 15, 1901
D. Apr., 1978, Wellesville, OH
St. Edward's/Notre Dame 6'0" 225 lbs.

1929	CHIB	N	9	G, T

Year	Team	Games	Pos.

Frank Pollack
POLLACK, FRANK STEVEN
B. Nov. 5, 1967, Camp Springs, MD
Northern Arizona 6'4" 281 lbs.

Year	Team	Games	Pos.
1990	**SF** **N**	15	OT
1991		15	OT
1994		12	OT
1995		15	OT
1996		16	OT

5 yrs. 73 games

Al Pollard
POLLARD, ALFRED LEE
B. Sep. 7, 1928, Glendale, CA
Loyola (California)/Army 6'0" 196 lbs.

Year	Team	Games	Pos.
1951	**PHI** **N**	6	HB
1952		12	HB
1953		12	FB

3 yrs. 30 games

Bob Pollard
POLLARD, ROBERT LEE
B. Dec. 30, 1948, Beaumont, TX
Texas Southern/Weber State 6'3" 248 lbs.

Year	Team	Games	Pos.
1971	**NO** **N**	14	DE
1972		14	DT
1973		14	DT
1974		14	DT
1975		14	DE, DT
1976		8	DT
1977		14	DE
1978	**STL** **N**	15	DE
1979		16	DE
1980		16	DE
1981		15	DE

11 yrs. 154 games

Darryl Pollard
POLLARD, CEDRIC DARRYL
B. May 11, 1965, Ellsworth, ME
Weber State 5'11" 187 lbs.

Year	Team	Games	Pos.
1987	**SF** **N**	3	CB
1988		14	CB
1989		16	CB
1990		16	CB
1992	**TB** **N**	16	CB

5 yrs. 65 games

Frank Pollard
POLLARD, FRANK
B. Jun. 15, 1957, Clifton, TX
Baylor 5'10" 220 lbs.

Year	Team	Games	Pos.
1980	**PIT** **N**	16	RB
1981		14	RB
1982		9	RB
1983		16	RB
1984		15	RB
1985		16	RB
1986		3	RB
1987		12	RB
1988		10	RB

9 yrs. 111 games

Fritz Pollard
POLLARD, FREDERICK DOUGLASS
B. Jan. 27, 1894, Chicago, IL
D. May 11, 1986, Silver Spring, MD
Bates/Brown 5'7" 149 lbs.

Year	Team	Games	Pos.
1920	**AKR** **A**	9	HB
1921		12	HB
1922	**MIL** **N**	7	HB, FB
1923	**HAM** **N**	2	HB
1925	**PRO** **N**	4	HB
1925	**HAM** **N**	1	HB
1925	**AKR** **N**	8	HB, QB, FB
1926		4	HB, QB

6 yrs. 47 games

Marcus Pollard
POLLARD, MARCUS
B. Feb. 8, 1972, Lanett, AL
Bradley* 6'4" 248 lbs.

Year	Team	Games	Pos.
1995	**IND** **N**	8	TE
1996		16	TE

2 yrs. 24 games

Trent Pollard
POLLARD, TRENT DESHAWN
B. Nov. 20, 1972, Seattle, WA
Eastern Washington 6'4" 325 lbs.

Year	Team	Games	Pos.
1994	**CIN** **N**	9	OT
1995		8	G
1996		1	G

3 yrs. 18 games

Tom Polley
POLLEY, TOM
B. Feb. 17, 1962, Minneapolis, MN
Nevada-Las Vegas 6'3" 235 lbs.

Year	Team	Games	Pos.
1985	**PHI** **N**	2	LB
1987	**CLE** **N**	2	LB

2 yrs. 4 games

Red Pollock
POLLOCK, WILLIAM HENRY
B. Dec. 5, 1911, Philadelphia, PA
D. Aug. 7, 1993, Freeport, NY
Widener 6'2" 194 lbs.

Year	Team	Games	Pos.
1935	**CHIB** **N**	10	HB, FB
1936		6	E

2 yrs. 16 games

Sheldon Pollock
POLLOCK, SHELDON
B. Nov. 2, 1904
D. Jul., 1956
Lafayette 6'0" 200 lbs.

Year	Team	Games	Pos.
1926	**BKN** **A**	3	C

Gordon Polofsky
POLOFSKY, GORDON
B. Oct. 10, 1931, Providence, RI
Tennessee 6'1" 219 lbs.

Year	Team	Games	Pos.
1952	**CHIC** **N**	10	G
1953		4	G
1954		10	G

3 yrs. 24 games

Larry Polowski
POLOWSKI, LARRY ROBERT
B. Sep. 15, 1957, Three Rivers, MI
Boise State 6'3" 235 lbs.

Year	Team	Games	Pos.
1979	**SEA** **N**	14	LB

Fran Polsfoot
POLSFOOT, FRANCIS CHARLES
B. Apr. 19, 1927, Montesano, WA
D. Apr. 5, 1985, Denver, CO
Washington State 6'3" 203 lbs.

Year	Team	Games	Pos.
1950	**CHIC** **N**	12	E
1951		12	E
1952		2	E
1953	**WAS** **N**	10	E

4 yrs. 36 games

Randy Poltl
POLTL, RANDALL PATRICK
B. Mar. 26, 1952, Long Beach, CA
Stanford 6'3" 190 lbs.

Year	Team	Games	Pos.
1974	**MIN** **N**	5	DB
1975	**DEN** **N**	13	S
1976		12	S
1977		14	S

4 yrs. 44 games

Dave Ponder
PONDER, DAVID
B. Jun. 27, 1962, Cairo, GA
Florida State 6'3" 250 lbs.

Year	Team	Games	Pos.
1985	**DAL** **N**	4	DT

David Pool
POOL, DAVID ALLEN
B. Dec. 20, 1966, Cincinnati, OH
Tennessee/Carson-Newman 5'9" 186 lbs.

Year	Team	Games	Pos.
1990	**BUF** **N**	9	CB
1991	**NE** **N**	15	CB
1992		16	CB
1993	**BUF** **N**	2	CB
1994	**MIA** **N**	1	CB

5 yrs. 43 games

Hamp Pool
POOL, J. HAMPTON
B. Mar. 11, 1915, San Miguel, CA
California/Stanford 6'3" 221 lbs.

Year	Team	Games	Pos.
1940	**CHIB** **N**	8	E
1941		8	E
1942		11	E
1943		10	E
1946	**MIA** **AA**	4	E

5 yrs. 41 games

Barney Poole
POOLE, GEORGE BARNEY
B. Oct. 29, 1923, Gloster, MS
Mississippi/N. Carolina/Army/Mississippi 6'2" 231 lbs.

Year	Team	Games	Pos.
1949	**B-NY** **AA**	11	E
1950	**NYY** **N**	12	E
1951		11	E
1952	**DAL** **N**	12	E, G
1953	**BAL** **N**	12	E
1954	**NYG** **N**	11	E

6 yrs. 69 games

Bob Poole
POOLE, BOB EDWARD
B. Oct. 5, 1941, Paducah, KY
Clemson 6'4" 216 lbs.

Year	Team	Games	Pos.
1964	**SF** **N**	13	OE
1965		9	OE
1966	**HOU** **A**	14	TE
1967		14	TE

4 yrs. 50 games

Jim Poole
POOLE, JAMES EUGENE, SR.
B. Sep. 9, 1915, Gloster, MS
D. Nov. 16, 1994, Oxford, MS
Mississippi 6'3" 218 lbs.

Year	Team	Games	Pos.
1937	**NYG** **N**	11	E
1938		11	E
1939		11	E
1940		11	E
1941		11	E
1945	**CHIC** **N**	9	E
1945	**NYG** **N**	3	E
1946		11	E

7 yrs. 78 games

Ken Poole
POOLE, KENNETH DAWAYNE
B. Oct. 20, 1958, Hermitage, AR
Northeast Louisiana 6'3" 251 lbs.

Year	Team	Games	Pos.
1981	**MIA** **N**	16	DE

Larry Poole
POOLE, LAWRENCE
B. Jul. 31, 1952, Akron, OH
Kent State 6'0" 195 lbs.

Year	Team	Games	Pos.
1975	**CLE** **N**	3	RB

Larry Poole continued

Year	Team	Games	Pos.
1976		13	RB
1977		13	RB
1978	**HOU** **N**	9	RB

4 yrs. 38 games

Nathan Poole
POOLE, NATHAN
B. Dec. 17, 1956, Alexander City, AL
Louisville 5'9" 210 lbs.

Year	Team	Games	Pos.
1979	**CIN** **N**	16	RB
1980		16	RB
1982	**DEN** **N**	9	RB
1983		16	RB
1985		3	RB
1987		2	RB

6 yrs. 62 games

Ollie Poole
POOLE, OLIVER LAMAR
B. Apr. 18, 1922, Gloster, MS
North Carolina/Mississippi 6'3" 220 lbs.

Year	Team	Games	Pos.
1947	**NY** **AA**	5	E
1948	**BAL** **AA**	9	E
1949	**DET** **N**	8	E

3 yrs. 22 games

Ray Poole
POOLE, RAY SMITH, SR.
B. Apr. 15, 1921, Gloster, MS
Mississippi/North Carolina/Mississippi 6'2" 215 lbs.

Year	Team	Games	Pos.
1947	**NYG** **N**	12	E
1948		12	E
1949		12	E
1950		12	E
1951		11	E
1952		12	E

6 yrs. 71 games

Shelley Poole
POOLE, SHELLEY O'NEAL
B. Dec. 3, 1964
Temple 5'7" 219 lbs.

Year	Team	Games	Pos.
1987	**ATL** **N**	1	RB

Steve Poole
POOLE, STEVEN
B. Aug. 25, 1952, Fort Oglethorpe, GA
Tennessee 6'1" 232 lbs.

Year	Team	Games	Pos.
1976	**NYJ** **N**	9	LB

Tyrone Poole
POOLE, TYRONE
B. Feb. 3, 1972, La Grange, GA
Fort Valley State 5'8" 185 lbs.

Year	Team	Games	Pos.
1995	**CAR** **N**	16	CB
1996		15	CB

2 yrs. 31 games

Eli Popa
POPA, ELI CHARLES
B. Nov. 4, 1930, Massillon, OH
Illinois 5'10" 202 lbs.

Year	Team	Games	Pos.
1952	**CHIC** **N**	5	B

Bucky Pope
POPE, FRANK BUCKLEY, III
B. Mar. 23, 1941, Pittsburgh, PA
Duke/Catawba 6'5" 199 lbs.

Year	Team	Games	Pos.
1964	**LA** **N**	14	OE
1966		3	OE
1967		13	OE
1968	**GB** **N**	3	OE

4 yrs. 33 games

Year	Team		Games	Pos.

Kenith Pope
POPE, KENITH
B. Dec. 28, 1951, Galveston, TX
Oklahoma 5'11" 200 lbs.

Year	Team		Games	Pos.
1974	**NE**	N	4	CB

Lew Pope
POPE, LEWIS LAWRENCE
(Chicken)
B. 1908
D. Feb. 5, 1964
Purdue 6'0" 196 lbs.

Year	Team		Games	Pos.
1931	**PRO**	N	8	HB, QB
1933	**CIN**	N	10	HB, FB
1934	**C-S**	N	8	HB, QB
3 yrs.	26 games			

Marquez Pope
POPE, MARQUEZ PHILLIPS
B. Oct. 29, 1970, Nashville, TN
Fresno State 5'10" 188 lbs.

Year	Team		Games	Pos.
1992	**SD**	N	7	CB
1993			16	CB
1994	**LARM**	N	16	S
1995	**SF**	N	16	CB
1996			16	S
5 yrs.	71 games			

Spencer Pope
POPE, SPENCER G.
B. Mar. 9, 1893
D. Sep. 9, 1976, Mechanicsburg, PA
Indiana 5'10" 170 lbs.

Year	Team		Games	Pos.
1920	**MUN**	A	1	E

Johnny Popovich
POPOVICH, JOHN
B. 1918
St. Vincent 5'8" 160 lbs.

Year	Team		Games	Pos.
1944	**C-P**	N	5	FB
1945	**PIT**	N	1	HB
2 yrs.	6 games			

Milt Popovich
POPOVICH, MILTON JOHN
B. Dec. 25, 1916, Butte, MT
Montana 5'11" 196 lbs.

Year	Team		Games	Pos.
1938	**CHIC**	N	6	HB
1939			10	HB
1940			10	FB
1941			7	G, FB
1942			10	G, E
5 yrs.	43 games			

Ted Popson
POPSON, TED
B. Sep. 10, 1966, Granada Hills, CA
Portland State 6'4" 250 lbs.

Year	Team		Games	Pos.
1994	**SF**	N	16	TE
1995			12	TE
1996			15	TE
3 yrs.	43 games			

Robert Porcher
PORCHER, ROBERT
B. Jul. 30, 1969, Wando, SC
Tennessee State/South Carolina State 6'3" 283 lbs.

Year	Team		Games	Pos.
1992	**DET**	N	16	DE
1993			16	DE
1994			15	DE
1995			16	DT
1996			16	DT
5 yrs.	79 games			

Tom Porell
PORELL, THOMAS
B. Sep. 23, 1964
Boston College 6'3" 275 lbs.

Year	Team		Games	Pos.
1987	**NE**	N	1	NT

Chris Port
PORT, CHRISTOPHER CHARLES
B. Nov. 2, 1967, Wanaque, NJ
Duke 6'5" 290 lbs.

Year	Team		Games	Pos.
1991	**NO**	N	14	G
1992			16	G
1993			15	G, OT
1994			16	G
1995			8	G, OT
5 yrs.	69 games			

Kerry Porter
PORTER, KERRY
B. Sep. 23, 1964, Vicenza, Italy
Washington State 6'1" 215 lbs.

Year	Team		Games	Pos.
1987	**BUF**	N	6	RB
1989	**LARI**	N	16	RB
1990	**DEN**	N	13	RB
3 yrs.	35 games			

Kevin Porter
PORTER, KEVIN JAMES
B. Apr. 11, 1966, Bronx, NY
Auburn 5'10" 215 lbs.

Year	Team		Games	Pos.
1988	**KC**	N	15	CB, S
1989			16	CB, S
1990			16	S
1991			16	S
1992			13	S
1992	**NYJ**	N	2	S
5 yrs.	78 games			

Lewis Porter
PORTER, LEWIS
B. Mar. 7, 1947, Clarksdale, MS
Southern University 5'11" 178 lbs.

Year	Team		Games	Pos.
1970	**KC**	N	6	WR

Rob Porter
PORTER, ROBERT BRYANT
B. May 9, 1962, Mahwah, NJ
Holy Cross 6'2" 210 lbs.

Year	Team		Games	Pos.
1987	**NYG**	N	3	S

Ricky Porter
PORTER, RICHARD ANTHONY
B. Jan. 14, 1960, Sylacauga, AL
Slippery Rock State 5'10" 195 lbs.

Year	Team		Games	Pos.
1982	**DET**	N	1	RB
1983	**BAL**	N	14	RB
1987	**BUF**	N	9	RB
3 yrs.	24 games			

Ron Porter
PORTER, RONALD DEAN
B. Jul. 27, 1945, Columbus, GA
Idaho 6'3" 232 lbs.

Year	Team		Games	Pos.
1967	**BAL**	N	14	LB
1968			14	LB
1969			3	LB
1969	**PHI**	N	12	LB
1970			14	LB
1971			14	LB
1972			14	LB
1973	**MIN**	N	13	LB
7 yrs.	96 games			

Rufus Porter
PORTER, RUFUS
B. May 18, 1965, Amite, LA

Rufus Porter continued
Southern University 6'1" 217 lbs.

Year	Team		Games	Pos.
1988	**SEA**	N	16	LB
1989			16	LB
1990			12	LB
1991			15	LB
1992			16	LB
1993			7	LB
1994			15	LB
1995	**NO**	N	14	LB
1996			13	LB
9 yrs.	124 games			

Tracy Porter
PORTER, TRACY RANDOLPH
B. Jun. 1, 1959, Baton Rouge, LA
Louisiana State 6'2" 220 lbs.

Year	Team		Games	Pos.
1981	**DET**	N	12	WR
1982			8	WR
1983	**BAL**	N	16	WR
1984	**IND**	N	16	WR
4 yrs.	52 games			

Willie Porter
PORTER, WILLIE CHURCH
B. Mar. 25, 1946, Victoria, TX
Texas Southern 5'11" 195 lbs.

Year	Team		Games	Pos.
1968	**BOS**	A	13	DB, OE

Garry Porterfield
PORTERFIELD, GARRY
B. Aug. 4, 1943, Pawnee, OK
Tulsa 6'3" 223 lbs.

Year	Team		Games	Pos.
1965	**DAL**	N	2	DE

David Posey
POSEY, DAVID E.
B. Apr. 1, 1956, Painesville, OH
Florida 5'10" 167 lbs.

Year	Team		Games	Pos.
1978	**NE**	N	11	K

Bob Post
POST, ROBERT
B. Jan. 12, 1944, Twin Falls, ID
U.S. Merchant Marine Academy-King's Point 6'1" 195 lbs.

Year	Team		Games	Pos.
1967	**NYG**	N	5	QB

Dickie Post
POST, RICHARD M.
B. Sep. 27, 1945, San Pedro, CA
Houston 5'9" 190 lbs.

Year	Team		Games	Pos.
1967	**SD**	A	13	RB
1968			13	RB
1969			14	RB
1970	**SD**	N	9	RB
1971	**PIT**	N	8	RB
1971	**DEN**	N	6	RB
1971	**HOU**	N	7	RB
5 yrs.	70 games			

Al Postus
POSTUS, ALBERT M.
B. Sep. 21, 1920, Philadelphia, PA
Villanova 5'10" 180 lbs.

Year	Team		Games	Pos.
1945	**PIT**	N	2	HB

Phil Poth
POTH, PHILIP
B. 1911
Gonzaga 5'11" 195 lbs.

Year	Team		Games	Pos.
1934	**PHI**	N	1	G

Johnny Poto
POTO, JOHN P.

Johnny Poto continued
B. Apr. 10, 1926, Boston, MA
D. Nov., 1965
none 5'10" 194 lbs.

Year	Team		Games	Pos.
1947	**BOS**	N	6	HB
1948			12	HB
2 yrs.	18 games			

Earl Potteiger
POTTEIGER, WILLIAM EARL
B. Jan. 11, 1891
D. Aug., 1962
Ursinus 5'7" 170 lbs.

Year	Team		Games	Pos.
1920	**BUF**	A	2	HB
1921	**CHIC**	A	1	HB
1922	**MIL**	N	2	HB, FB
1924	**KEN**	N	3	HB, QB, E
1925	**NYG**	N	2	QB, HB
1926			1	E
1927			2	FB, T
1928			8	HB, E
8 yrs.	21 games			

Kevin Potter
POTTER, KEVIN CRAIG
B. Dec. 19, 1959, St. Louis, MO
Missouri 5'10" 188 lbs.

Year	Team		Games	Pos.
1983	**HOU**	N	1	S
1983	**CHI**	N	4	S
1984			1	S
2 yrs.	6 games			

Steve Potter
POTTER, STEPHEN JOHN
B. Nov. 6, 1957, Bradford, PA
Virginia 6'3" 235 lbs.

Year	Team		Games	Pos.
1981	**MIA**	N	16	LB
1982			9	LB
1983	**KC**	N	16	LB
1984	**BUF**	N	10	LB
4 yrs.	51 games			

Myron Pottios
POTTIOS, MYRON JOSEPH
(Mike)
B. Jan. 18, 1939, Van Voorhis, PA
Notre Dame 6'2" 236 lbs.

Year	Team		Games	Pos.
1961	**PIT**	N	14	LB
1963			14	LB
1964			7	LB
1965			6	LB
1966	**LA**	N	12	LB
1967			11	LB
1968			14	LB
1969			5	LB
1970			14	LB
1971	**WAS**	N	14	LB
1972			12	LB
1973			6	LB
12 yrs.	129 games			

Bill Potts
POTTS, WILLIAM
B. 1910
Villanova 6'2" 215 lbs.

Year	Team		Games	Pos.
1934	**PIT**	N	1	HB

Bob Potts
POTTS, R.C. (Daddy)
B. Aug. 16, 1898
D. Aug., 1981, Columbia, SC
Clemson 6'1" 235 lbs.

Year	Team		Games	Pos.
1926	**FRA**	N	15	T, G

Charlie Potts
POTTS, CHARLES
B. Apr. 29, 1949, Chicago, IL

Year	Team		Games	Pos.

Charlie Potts *continued*
Purdue 6'3" 210 lbs.

Year	Team		Games	Pos.
1972	DET	N	10	DB

Roosevelt Potts
POTTS, ROOSEVELT BERNARD
B. Jan. 8, 1971, Rayville, LA
Northeast Louisiana 6'0" 258 lbs.

1993	IND	N	16	RB
1994			16	RB
1995			15	RB

3 yrs. 47 games

Ernie Pough
POUGH, ERNEST LEON
B. May 17, 1952, Jacksonville, FL
Texas Southern 6'1" 174 lbs.

1976	PIT	N	14	WR
1977			14	WR
1978	NYG	N	12	WR

3 yrs. 40 games

Darryl Pounds
POUNDS, DARRYL
B. Jul. 21, 1972, Fort Worth, TX
Nicholls State 5'10" 177 lbs.

| 1995 | WAS | N | 9 | CB |
| 1996 | | | 12 | CB |

2 yrs. 21 games

Shar Pourdanesh
POURDANESH, SHAR
B. Jul. 19, 1970, Iran
Nevada 6'6" 313 lbs.

| 1996 | WAS | N | 16 | OT |

Karl Powe
POWE, KARL ALANZO
B. Jan. 17, 1962, Mobile, AL
Alabama State 6'2" 176 lbs.

| 1985 | DAL | N | 15 | WR |
| 1986 | | | 1 | WR |

2 yrs. 16 games

Keith Powe
POWE, KEITH
B. Jun. 5, 1969, Biloxi, MS
Texas-El Paso 6'4" 265 lbs.

| 1994 | TB | N | 5 | DE |
| 1995 | | | 3 | DE |

2 yrs. 8 games

Alvin Powell
POWELL, ALVIN ROBERT, II
B. Nov. 19, 1959, Panama City, Panama
Winston-Salem State 6'5" 294 lbs.

1987	SEA	N	12	OT
1988			6	G
1989	MIA	N	2	G

3 yrs. 20 games

Andre Powell
POWELL, ANDRE MAURICE
B. Jun. 5, 1969, York, PA
Penn State 6'1" 226 lbs.

| 1993 | NYG | N | 15 | LB |
| 1994 | | | 1 | LB |

2 yrs. 16 games

Art Powell
POWELL, ARTHUR L.
B. Feb. 25, 1937, Dallas, TX
San Jose State 6'3" 211 lbs.

| 1959 | PHI | N | 12 | DB |

Year	Team		Games	Pos.

Art Powell *continued*

1960	NY	A	14	OE
1961			14	OE
1962			14	OE
1963	OAK	A	14	OE
1964			14	OE
1965			14	OE
1966			14	OE
1967	BUF	A	6	OE
1968	MIN	N	1	WR

10 yrs. 117 games

Charley Powell
POWELL, CHARLES
B. 1932
none 6'2" 226 lbs.

1952	SF	N	7	E
1953			12	E
1955			10	E
1956			12	E
1957			12	LB, E
1960	OAK	A		
1961			14	DE

7 yrs. 67 games

Craig Powell
POWELL, CRAIG
B. Nov. 13, 1971, Youngstown, OH
Ohio State 6'4" 230 lbs.

| 1995 | CLE | N | 3 | LB |
| 1996 | BAL | N | 9 | LB |

2 yrs. 12 games

Darnell Powell
POWELL, DARNELL
B. May 31, 1954, Atlanta, GA
Tennessee-Chattanooga 5'11" 199 lbs.

| 1976 | BUF | N | 11 | RB |
| 1978 | NYJ | N | 14 | RB |

2 yrs. 25 games

Dick Powell
POWELL, RICHARD (Tiny)
B. May 21, 1904
D. Apr., 1986, Martinsville, VA
Davis & Elkins 6'2" 215 lbs.

| 1932 | NYG | N | 2 | E |
| 1933 | CIN | N | 3 | E |

2 yrs. 5 games

Jeff Powell
POWELL, JEFF
B. May 27, 1963, Nashville, TN
William & Mary/Tennessee 5'10" 185 lbs.*

| 1987 | SD | N | 1 | RB |

Jesse Powell
POWELL, JESSE
B. Apr. 14, 1947, Matador, TX
West Texas State 6'1" 214 lbs.

1969	MIA	A	14	LB
1970	MIA	N	11	LB
1971			14	LB
1972			14	LB
1973			3	LB

5 yrs. 56 games

Marvin Powell
POWELL, MARVIN (Boomer)
B. Aug. 30, 1955, Fort Bragg, NC
Southern California 6'5" 270 lbs.

1977	NYJ	N	11	OT
1978			14	OT
1979			16	OT
1980			15	OT
1981			14	OT

Year	Team		Games	Pos.

Marvin Powell *continued*

1982			8	OT
1983			16	OT
1984			16	OT
1985			14	OT
1986	TB	N	3	OT
1987			6	OT

11 yrs. 133 games

Preston Powell
POWELL, PRESTON
B. Sep. 23, 1936, Winnfield, LA
Grambling State 6'2" 225 lbs.

| 1961 | CLE | N | 12 | HB |

Roger Powell
POWELL, ROGER
B. Aug. 17, 1894
D. Jan. 28, 1988, Waco, TX
Texas A&M 180 lbs.

| 1926 | BUF | N | 1 | FB |

Stan Powell
POWELL, STANCIL (WRINKLE MEAT) (Possum)
B. 1890
Deceased
Carlisle 5'11" 185 lbs.

| 1923 | OOR | N | 8 | G, C |

Steve Powell
POWELL, STEVEN ORVILLE
B. Jan. 2, 1956, St. Louis, MO
Northeast Missouri State 5'11" 186 lbs.

| 1978 | BUF | N | 10 | RB |
| 1979 | | | 15 | RB |

2 yrs. 25 games

Tim Powell
POWELL, TIM A.
B. Sep. 2, 1942
Northwestern 6'4" 248 lbs.

| 1965 | LA | N | 8 | DE |
| 1966 | PIT | N | 4 | TE, LB |

2 yrs. 12 games

Clyde Powers
POWERS, CLYDE JOSEPH
B. Aug. 19, 1951, Pascagoula, MS
Oklahoma 6'1" 195 lbs.

1974	NYG	N	14	DB
1975			14	S
1976			14	S
1977			14	S
1978	KC	N	1	S

5 yrs. 57 games

Jim Powers
POWERS, JAMES
B. 1928
Southern California 6'0" 185 lbs.

1950	SF	N	10	QB
1951			12	QB
1952			12	QB
1953			10	QB

4 yrs. 44 games

John Powers
POWERS, JOHN
B. Jun. 15, 1940
Notre Dame 6'2" 211 lbs.

1962	PIT	N	14	OE
1963			14	OE
1964			14	OE
1965			6	OE
1966	MIN	N	5	TE

5 yrs. 53 games

Year	Team		Games	Pos.

Ricky Powers
POWERS, RICKY
B. Nov. 30, 1970, Akron, OH
Michigan 6'0" 213 lbs.

| 1995 | CLE | N | 2 | RB |

Sammy Powers
POWERS, SAMMY
B. 1901
Deceased
None 5'10" 179 lbs.

| 1921 | GB | A | 4 | G, T |

Warren Powers
POWERS, WARREN
B. Feb. 4, 1965, Baltimore, MD
Maryland 6'6" 287 lbs.

1989	DEN	N	15	DE
1990			16	DE
1991			13	DE
1992	LARM	N	7	DE

4 yrs. 51 games

Warren Powers
POWERS, WARREN ANTHONY
B. Feb. 19, 1941, Kansas City, MO
Nebraska 6'0" 188 lbs.

1963	OAK	A	5	DB
1964			1	DB
1965			12	DB
1966			14	DB
1967			14	DB
1968			8	DB

6 yrs. 54 games

Phil Pozderac
POZDERAC, PHILIP
B. Dec. 19, 1959, Cleveland, OH
Notre Dame 6'9" 230 lbs.

1982	DAL	N	7	OT
1983			16	OT
1984			15	OT
1985			14	OT
1986			16	OT
1987			2	OT

6 yrs. 70 games

Dean Prater
PRATER, TROY DEAN
B. Sep. 29, 1958, Altus, OK
D. Mar. 14, 1996, Horseheads, NY
Oklahoma State 6'5" 225 lbs.

1982	KC	N	2	DE
1983			16	DE
1984	BUF	N	13	DE
1985			16	DE
1986			16	DE
1987			10	DE
1988			4	DE

7 yrs. 77 games

Dale Prather
PRATHER, DALE
B. Sep. 19, 1910
D. Sep., 1973
George Washington 6'2" 190 lbs.

| 1938 | CLE | N | 5 | E |

Guy Prather
PRATHER, GUY TYRONE
B. Mar. 28, 1958, Gaithersburg, MD
Grambling State 6'2" 230 lbs.

1981	GB	N	16	LB
1982			9	LB
1983			16	LB
1984			16	LB
1985			16	LB

5 yrs. 73 games

Year	Team	Games	Pos.

Bob Pratt

PRATT, ROBERT HENRY, JR.
B. May 25, 1951, Richmond, VA
North Carolina 6'4" 248 lbs.

Year	Team		Games	Pos.
1974	**BAL**	N	13	G
1975			14	G
1976			14	G
1977			14	G
1978			16	G
1979			16	G
1980			16	G
1981			15	G
1982	**SEA**	N	9	G
1983			15	G
1984			16	G
1985			12	G
12 yrs.	170 games			

John Prchlik

PRCHLIK, JOHN GEORGE
B. Jul. 20, 1925, Cleveland, OH
Yale 6'4" 234 lbs.

Year	Team		Games	Pos.
1949	**DET**	N	12	T
1950			12	T
1951			12	T
1952			12	T
1953			11	T
5 yrs.	59 games			

George Preas

PREAS, GEORGE
B. Jun. 25, 1933, Richmond, VA
Virginia Tech 6'2" 244 lbs.

Year	Team		Games	Pos.
1955	**BAL**	N	8	T
1956			12	T
1957			10	T
1958			12	T
1959			12	T
1960			12	T
1961			14	OT
1962			14	OT
1963			14	OT
1964			14	OT
1965			14	OT
11 yrs.	136 games			

Gene Prebola

PREBOLA, EUGENE NICHOLAS
B. Jun. 30, 1938, Bronx, NY
Boston University 6'3" 220 lbs.

Year	Team		Games	Pos.
1960	**OAK**	A		OE
1961	**DEN**	A	14	OE
1962			14	OE
1963			14	OE
4 yrs.	42 games			

Steve Preece

PREECE, STEVEN PACKER
B. Feb. 15, 1947, Boise, ID
Oregon State 6'1" 195 lbs.

Year	Team		Games	Pos.
1969	**NO**	N	14	S
1970	**PHI**	N	14	S
1971			7	S
1972			1	S
1972	**DEN**	N	13	S
1973	**LA**	N	14	S
1974			14	S
1975			14	S
1976			14	S
1977	**SEA**	N	14	S
9 yrs.	119 games			

Merv Pregulman

PREGULMAN, MERVIN
B. Oct. 10, 1922, Lansing, MI
Michigan 6'3" 215 lbs.

Year	Team		Games	Pos.
1946	**GB**	N	11	G, LB
1947	**DET**	N	12	C, LB

Merv Pregulman continued

Year	Team		Games	Pos.
1948			12	C, LB
1949	**NYB**	N	12	C
4 yrs.	47 games			

Leo Prendergast

PRENDERGAST, LEO
B. Aug. 13, 1901
D. Jun., 1969, Hallandale, FL
Lafayette 5'8" 170 lbs.

Year	Team		Games	Pos.
1926	**BKN**	A	3	T, C

Hal Prescott

PRESCOTT, HAROLD D. (Ace)
B. Oct. 28, 1920, Abilene, TX
Hardin-Simmons 6'2" 199 lbs.

Year	Team		Games	Pos.
1946	**GB**	N	2	E
1947	**PHI**	N	11	E
1948			11	E
1949	**NYB**	N	5	E
1949	**PHI**	N	3	E
4 yrs.	32 games			

Andre President

PRESIDENT, ANDRE
B. Jun. 16, 1971, Fort Worth, TX
Angelo State 6'3" 255 lbs.

Year	Team		Games	Pos.
1995	**NE**	N	1	TE
1995	**CHI**	N	2	TE
1 yr.	3 games			

Glenn Presnell

PRESNELL, GLENN EMERY
B. Jul. 28, 1905, Gilead, NE
Nebraska 5'10" 195 lbs.

Year	Team		Games	Pos.
1931	**POR**	N	14	QB, HB, FB
1932			11	HB, QB
1933			11	QB
1934	**DET**	N	13	QB, HB
1935			10	QB, HB
1936			12	QB
6 yrs.	71 games			

Leo Pressley

PRESSLEY, LEO
B. Mar. 16, 1923, El Campo, TX
D. Sep., 1975
Oklahoma 6'2" 230 lbs.

Year	Team		Games	Pos.
1945	**WAS**	N	8	C

Jim Prestel

PRESTEL, JAMES
B. Jun. 28, 1937, Indianapolis, IN
Idaho 6'5" 264 lbs.

Year	Team		Games	Pos.
1960	**CLE**	N	6	T
1961	**MIN**	N	14	DT
1962			14	DT
1963			14	DT
1964			14	DT
1965			14	DT
1966	**NYG**	N	13	DT
1967	**WAS**	N	8	DT
8 yrs.	97 games			

Dave Preston

PRESTON, RICHARD DAVID
B. May 29, 1955, Dayton, OH
Bowling Green 5'11" 195 lbs.

Year	Team		Games	Pos.
1978	**DEN**	N	16	RB
1979			10	RB
1980			12	RB
1981			16	RB
1982			8	RB
1983			14	RB
6 yrs.	76 games			

John Preston

PRESTON, JOHN STANLEY
B. Aug. 28, 1962, Dallas, TX
Texas Christian/Central Oklahoma 6'0" 207 lbs.

Year	Team		Games	Pos.
1987	**STL**	N	5	S

Pat Preston

PRESTON, PADDISON WADE
B. Jun. 15, 1921, Kernersville, NC
Wake Forest 6'2" 216 lbs.

Year	Team		Games	Pos.
1946	**CHIB**	N	10	G
1947			3	G
1948			12	G
1949			12	G
4 yrs.	37 games			

Ray Preston

PRESTON, RAYMOND NEWTON, JR.
B. Jan. 25, 1954, Lawrence, MA
Syracuse 6'0" 218 lbs.

Year	Team		Games	Pos.
1976	**SD**	N	14	LB
1977			11	LB
1978			16	LB
1979			16	LB
1980			14	LB
1981			16	LB
1982			9	LB
1983			16	LB
1984			10	LB
9 yrs.	122 games			

Roell Preston

PRESTON, ROELL
B. Jun. 23, 1972, Miami, FL
Mississippi 5'10" 187 lbs.

Year	Team		Games	Pos.
1995	**ATL**	N	14	WR
1996			15	WR
2 yrs.	29 games			

Luke Prestridge

PRESTRIDGE, LUKE EARL
B. Sep. 17, 1956, Houston, TX
Baylor 6'4" 235 lbs.

Year	Team		Games	Pos.
1979	**DEN**	N	16	P
1980			16	P
1981			16	P
1982			9	P
1983			16	P
1984	**NE**	N	9	P
6 yrs.	82 games			

Felton Prewitt

PREWITT, FELTON WINTERS
B. May 17, 1924, Corsicana, TX
Tulsa 5'11" 207 lbs.

Year	Team		Games	Pos.
1946	**BUF**	AA	14	C
1947			13	C
1948			7	C
1949	**BAL**	AA	12	C
4 yrs.	46 games			

Bill Priatko

PRIATKO, WILLIAM
B. Oct. 16, 1933, North Braddock, PA
Pittsburgh 6'2" 220 lbs.

Year	Team		Games	Pos.
1957	**PIT**	N	2	LB

Art Price

PRICE, ARTHUR
B. May 17, 1962, Newport News, VA
Wisconsin 6'3" 227 lbs.

Year	Team		Games	Pos.
1987	**ATL**	N	3	LB

Charley Price

PRICE, CHARLES WALEMON (Cotton)
B. May 31, 1919, Bridgeport, TX
Texas A&M 6'1" 183 lbs.

Year	Team		Games	Pos.
1940	**DET**	N	9	QB
1941			10	HB, QB
1945			8	HB
1946	**MIA**	AA	7	QB
4 yrs.	34 games			

Daryl Price

PRICE, DARYL
B. Oct. 23, 1972, Galveston, TX
Colorado 6'4" 274 lbs.

Year	Team		Games	Pos.
1996	**SF**	N	13	DE

Dennis Price

PRICE, DENNIS SEAN
B. Jun. 14, 1965, Los Angeles, CA
UCLA 6'1" 175 lbs.

Year	Team		Games	Pos.
1988	**LARI**	N	12	CB
1989			5	CB
1992	**NYJ**	N	14	CB
3 yrs.	31 games			

Derek Price

PRICE, DEREK
B. Aug. 12, 1972, Tempe, AZ
Iowa 6'3" 240 lbs.

Year	Team		Games	Pos.
1996	**DET**	N	13	TE

Eddie Price

PRICE, EDWARD J., JR.
B. Sep. 2, 1925, New Orleans, LA
D. Jul. 21, 1979, New Orleans, LA
Tulane 5'11" 190 lbs.

Year	Team		Games	Pos.
1950	**NYG**	N	10	FB
1951			12	FB
1952			11	FB
1953			12	FB
1954			12	FB
1955			6	FB
6 yrs.	63 games			

Elex Price

PRICE, ELEX DRUMMOND
B. Aug. 11, 1950, Yazoo City, MS
Alcorn State 6'3" 262 lbs.

Year	Team		Games	Pos.
1973	**NO**	N	14	DT
1974			14	DT
1975			14	DT
1976			11	DT
1977			14	DT
1978			16	DT
1979			6	DT
1980			14	DT
8 yrs.	103 games			

Ernie Price

PRICE, ERNEST
B. Sep. 20, 1950, Corpus Christi, TX
Texas A&I, Kingsville 6'4" 248 lbs.

Year	Team		Games	Pos.
1973	**DET**	N	12	DT
1974			11	DT
1975			13	DE
1976			14	DE
1977			12	DE
1978			3	DE
1978	**SEA**	N	12	DE
1979			4	DE
7 yrs.	81 games			

Jim Price

PRICE, JAMES
B. Oct. 2, 1966, Englewood, NJ
Stanford 6'4" 247 lbs.

Year	Team		Games	Pos.
1991	**LARM**	N	12	TE

Year	Team	Games	Pos.

Jim Price *continued*

1992		15	TE
1993	DAL	N	3	TE
1995	STL	N	13	TE
4 yrs.	43 games		

Jim Price
PRICE, JAMES BLUFORD
B. Sep. 17, 1940, Nettleton, MS
Auburn 6'2" 228 lbs.

1963	NY	A	14	LB
1964	DEN	A	6	LB
2 yrs.	20 games		

Kenny Price
PRICE, KEN
B. Apr. 7, 1950, Houston, TX
Iowa 6'1" 220 lbs.

| 1971 | NE | N | 1 | LB |

Mitchell Price
PRICE, MITCHELL
B. May 10, 1967, Jacksonville, FL
Southern Methodist/Tulane 5'9" 181 lbs.

1990	CIN	N	16	CB
1991		13	CB
1992		4	CB
1992	PHX	N	2	CB, S
1993	CIN	N	1	CB
1993	LARM	N	5	CB
4 yrs.	41 games		

Rod Price
PRICE, ROD
B. Jan. 25, 1963
Azusa Pacific 6'1" 275 lbs.

| 1987 | SD | N | 3 | LB |

Sam Price
PRICE, SAMUEL LEE
B. Oct. 1, 1943, Margaret, AL
Illinois 5'11" 215 lbs.

1966	MIA	A	14	FB, HB
1967		9	RB
1968		13	RB
3 yrs.	36 games		

Shawn Price
PRICE, SHAWN STERLING
B. Mar. 28, 1970, Jacksonville, FL
Pacific 6'5" 260 lbs.

1993	TB	N	9	DE
1994		8	DE
1995	CAR	N	16	DE
1996	BUF	N	15	DE
4 yrs.	48 games		

Terry Price
PRICE, TERRENCE TODD
B. Apr. 5, 1968, Atlanta, GA
Texas A&M 6'4" 272 lbs.

| 1990 | CHI | N | 2 | DT |

Billy Pricer
PRICER, BILLY C.
B. Sep. 3, 1934, Margaret, AL
Oklahoma 5'10" 208 lbs.

1957	BAL	N	12	FB
1958		12	FB
1959		12	FB
1960		12	FB
1961	DAL	A	6	FB
5 yrs.	54 games		

Danny Pride
PRIDE, DANIEL
B. Jun. 7, 1942, Ironton, OH
Tennessee State/Jackson State 6'3" 225 lbs.

1968	CHI	N	3	LB
1969		3	LB
2 yrs.	6 games		

Tom Pridemore
PRIDEMORE, LARRY THOMAS, JR.
B. Apr. 29, 1956, Oak Hill, WV
West Virginia 5'11" 186 lbs.

1978	ATL	N	16	S
1979		16	S
1980		16	S
1981		16	S
1982		9	S
1983		16	S
1984		16	S
1985		16	S
8 yrs.	121 games		

Bob Priestley
PRIESTLEY, ROBERT BAGLEY
B. Jan. 5, 1912, Everett, MA
Brown 5'11" 192 lbs.

| 1942 | PHI | N | 11 | E |

Frank Primeau
PRIMEAU, FRANCIS E.
B. Feb., 1895
Deceased
None 5'11" 170 lbs.

| 1921 | TON | A | 2 | QB, E |

Greg Primus
PRIMUS, GREG
B. Oct. 20, 1970, Denver, CO
Colorado State 5'11" 190 lbs.

1994	CHI	N	3	WR
1995		4	WR
2 yrs.	7 games		

James Primus
PRIMUS, JAMES DEWITT
B. May 18, 1964, Yuma, AZ
UCLA 5'11" 196 lbs.

1988	ATL	N	16	RB
1989		5	RB
2 yrs.	21 games		

Dom Principe
PRINCIPE, DOMINIC ALFRED
B. Feb. 9, 1917, Brockton, MA
Fordham 6'0" 205 lbs.

1940	NYG	N	6	HB
1941		9	HB
1942		11	HB
1946	BKN	AA	10	FB
4 yrs.	36 games		

Mike Prindle
PRINDLE, MIKE
B. Nov. 12, 1963
Western Michigan 5'9" 160 lbs.

| 1987 | DET | N | 3 | K |

Alan Pringle
PRINGLE, ALAN
B. Jan. 20, 1952, Caracas, Venezuela
Rice 6'0" 195 lbs.

| 1975 | DET | N | 1 | K |

Mike Pringle
PRINGLE, MICHAEL A.
B. Oct. 1, 1967, Los Angeles, CA
Washington State/Fullerton State 5'8" 186 lbs.

| 1990 | ATL | N | 3 | RB |

Bob Print
PRINT, ROBERT THOMAS
B. Jan. 16, 1944, Cleveland, OH
Dayton 6'0" 220 lbs.

1967	SD	A	7	LB
1968		8	LB
2 yrs.	15 games		

Anthony Prior
PRIOR, ANTHONY
B. Mar. 27, 1970, Mira Loma, CA
Washington State 5'11" 185 lbs.

1993	NYJ	N	16	CB, S
1994		13	CB
1995		11	CB
1996	MIN	N	3	CB
4 yrs.	43 games		

Mike Prior
PRIOR, MICHAEL ROBERT
B. Nov. 14, 1963, Chicago Heights, IL
Illinois State 6'0" 202 lbs.

1985	TB	N	16	S
1987	IND	N	12	S
1988		16	CB, S
1989		16	CB, S
1990		16	S
1991		9	S
1992		16	S
1993	GB	N	16	S
1994		16	S
1995		16	S
1996		16	S
11 yrs.	165 games		

Errol Prisby
PRISBY, ERROL
B. Jan. 24, 1943, Kent, OH
Cincinnati 5'10" 184 lbs.

| 1967 | DEN | A | 5 | DB |

Nick Prisco
PRISCO, NICHOLAS A.
B. Jan. 12, 1909
D. Jun. 12, 1981, Metuchen, NJ
Rutgers 5'8" 193 lbs.

| 1933 | PHI | N | 2 | HB |

Bill Pritchard
PRITCHARD, WILLIAM
B. Dec. 23, 1901
D. Apr., 1978, Buffalo, NY
Penn State 5'10" 185 lbs.

1927	PRO	N	12	FB, HB
1928	NYY	N	13	FB, HB
2 yrs.	25 games		

Bosh Pritchard
PRITCHARD, ABISHA COLLINS
B. Sep. 10, 1919, Windsor, NC
Deceased
Virginia Military Institute 5'11" 164 lbs.

1942	CLE	N	1	HB
1942	PHI	N	6	HB
1946		11	HB
1947		11	HB
1948		12	HB
1949		8	HB
1951		6	HB

Bosh Pritchard *continued*

| 1951 | NYG | N | 5 | HB |
| 6 yrs. | 60 games | | |

Mike Pritchard
PRITCHARD, MICHAEL ROBERT
B. Oct. 26, 1969, Shaw AFB, SC
Colorado 5'11" 180 lbs.

1991	ATL	N	16	WR
1992		16	WR
1993		15	WR
1994	DEN	N	3	WR
1995		15	WR
1996	SEA	N	15	WR
6 yrs.	81 games		

Ron Pritchard
PRITCHARD, RONALD DAVID
B. Apr. 2, 1947, Chicago, IL
Arizona State 6'1" 231 lbs.

1969	HOU	A	14	LB
1970	HOU	N	14	LB
1971		14	LB
1972		6	LB
1972	CIN	N	7	LB
1973		10	LB
1974		14	LB
1975		14	LB
1976		6	LB
1977		6	LB
9 yrs.	105 games		

Billy Pritchett
PRITCHETT, BILLY RAY
B. Feb. 22, 1951, Mart, TX
West Texas State 6'3" 231 lbs.

1975	CLE	N	14	RB
1976	ATL	N	6	RB
1977		9	RB
3 yrs.	29 games		

Kelvin Pritchett
PRITCHETT, KELVIN BRATODD
B. Oct. 24, 1969, Atlanta, GA
Mississippi 6'2" 281 lbs.

1991	DET	N	16	DE
1992		16	DE
1993		16	DE
1994		16	DE
1995	JAC	N	16	DT
1996		13	DT
6 yrs.	93 games		

Stanley Pritchett
PRITCHETT, STANLEY
B. Dec. 12, 1973, Atlanta, GA
South Carolina 6'1" 232 lbs.

| 1996 | MIA | N | 16 | RB |

Wes Pritchett
PRITCHETT, WESLEY ANDREW
B. Jul. 7, 1966, Atlanta, GA
Notre Dame 6'2" 234 lbs.

| 1991 | ATL | N | 3 | LB |

Steve Pritko
PRITKO, STEPHEN
B. Dec. 25, 1920, Northampton, PA
Villanova 6'2" 209 lbs.

1943	NYG	N	9	E
1944	CLE	N	10	E
1945		10	E
1946	LA	N	11	E
1947		11	E
1948	BOS	N	12	E
1949	NYB	N	2	E

Year	Team	Games	Pos.

Steve Pritko *continued*

Year	Team		Games	Pos.
1949	GB	N	8	E
1950			12	E

8 yrs. 85 games

Bryan Proby
PROBY, BRYAN CRAIG
B. Nov. 30, 1971, Compton, CA
Arizona State 6'5" 283 lbs.

1995	KC	N	3	DE

Ray Prochaska
PROCHASKA, RAYMOND
B. Aug. 9, 1919, Ulysses, NE
Nebraska 6'3" 205 lbs.

1941	CLE	N	9	E

Dewey Proctor
PROCTOR, DEWEY
B. Jul. 1, 1921, Lake View, SC
Furman 5'11" 215 lbs.

1946	NY	AA	4	FB
1947			11	B
1948	CHI	AA	9	B
1949	B-NY	AA	1	B

4 yrs. 25 games

Rex Proctor
PROCTOR, REX
B. Dec. 1, 1929, Sour Lake, TX
D. Nov., 1980, Millsap, TX
Rice 5'10" 180 lbs.

1953	CHIB	N	3	HB

Ricky Proehl
PROEHL, RICHARD SCOTT
B. Mar. 7, 1968, Belle Mead, NJ
Wake Forest 5'10" 185 lbs.

1990	PHX	N	16	WR
1991			16	WR
1992			16	WR
1993			16	WR
1994	ARI	N	16	WR
1995	SEA	N	8	WR
1996			16	WR

7 yrs. 104 games

Eugene Profit
PROFIT, EUGENE ANTHONY
B. Nov. 11, 1964, Baton Rouge, LA
Yale 5'10" 175 lbs.

1986	NE	N	4	CB
1987			7	CB
1988			1	CB

3 yrs. 12 games

Joe Profit
PROFIT, JOSEPH
B. Aug. 13, 1949, Lake Providence, LA
Northeast Louisiana 6'0" 210 lbs.

1971	ATL	N	4	RB
1972			8	RB
1973			5	RB
1973	NO	N	8	RB

3 yrs. 25 games

Eddie Prokop
PROKOP, EDWARD S.
B. Feb. 11, 1922, Cleveland, OH
D. May, 1955
Georgia Tech 5'11" 200 lbs.

1946	NY	AA	12	FB
1947			13	B
1948	CHI	AA	9	B
1949	B-NY	AA	6	B

4 yrs. 40 games

Joe Prokop
PROKOP, JOE
B. Jul. 7, 1960, St. Paul, MN
California Poly (Pomona) 6'3" 227 lbs.

1985	GB	N	9	P
1987	SD	N	3	P
1988	NYJ	N	16	P
1989			16	P
1990			16	P
1991	SF	N	11	P
1992	MIA	N	7	P
1992	NYG	N	1	P

7 yrs. 79 games

Joe Prokop
PROKOP, JOSEPH MICHAEL
B. Jan. 9, 1921, Cleveland, OH
Notre Dame/Bradley 6'2" 170 lbs.

1948	CHI	AA	2	B

Vin Promuto
PROMUTO, VINCENT LOUIS
B. Jun. 8, 1938, New York, NY
Holy Cross 6'1" 244 lbs.

1960	WAS	N	12	G
1961			14	G
1962			14	G
1963			14	G
1964			13	G
1965			14	G
1966			14	G
1967			14	G
1968			4	G
1969			14	G
1970			2	G

11 yrs. 129 games

Jack Protz
PROTZ, JOHN MICHAEL
B. Apr. 14, 1948, Jersey City, NJ
North Carolina/Syracuse 6'1" 218 lbs.

1970	SD	N	14	LB

Bob Prout
PROUT, BOB
B. May 11, 1951, Chicago, IL
Knox 6'1" 187 lbs.

1974	OAK	N	2	S
1975	NYJ	N	7	S

2 yrs. 9 games

Andrew Provence
PROVENCE, ANDREW
B. Mar. 8, 1961, Savannah, GA
South Carolina 6'3" 286 lbs.

1983	ATL	N	16	NT
1984			16	DT
1985			16	DE
1986			16	DE
1987			5	DE

5 yrs. 69 games

Ken Provincial
PROVINCIAL, J. KENNETH
B. 1907
Georgetown (DC) 6'2" 190 lbs.

1930	FRA	N	1	E

Fred Provo
PROVO, FREDERICK LEWIS
B. Apr. 17, 1922, Seattle, WA
Washington 5'9" 185 lbs.

1948	GB	N	9	HB

Ted Provost
PROVOST, TED R.

Ted Provost *continued*
B. Jul. 26, 1948, Navarre, OH
Ohio State 6'2" 195 lbs.

1970	MIN	N	7	CB
1971	STL	N	2	S

2 yrs. 9 games

Remi Prudhomme
PRUDHOMME, JOSEPH REMI
B. Apr. 24, 1942, Opelousas, LA
D. Dec. 6, 1990, New Orleans, LA
Louisiana State 6'4" 251 lbs.

1966	BUF	A	14	G
1967			10	G
1968	KC	N	14	DE, DT
1969			14	C
1971	NO	N	14	C, G
1972			5	C
1972	BUF	N	8	C

6 yrs. 79 games

Perry Pruett
PRUETT, PERRY
B. Mar. 7, 1949, Dallas, TX
North Texas State 6'1" 190 lbs.

1971	NE	N	11	CB

Greg Pruitt
PRUITT, GREGORY DONALD
B. Aug. 18, 1951, Houston, TX
Oklahoma 5'10" 190 lbs.

1973	CLE	N	13	RB
1974			14	RB
1975			14	RB
1976			14	RB
1977			14	RB
1978			12	RB
1979			6	RB
1980			16	RB
1981			15	RB
1982	LARI	N	9	RB
1983			16	RB
1984			15	RB

12 yrs. 158 games

James Pruitt
PRUITT, JAMES BOUBIAS
B. Jan. 29, 1964, Los Angeles, CA
Fullerton State 6'3" 199 lbs.

1986	MIA	N	16	WR
1987			12	WR
1988			11	WR
1988	IND	N	1	WR
1989			16	WR
1990	MIA	N	6	WR
1991			5	WR

6 yrs. 67 games

Mickey Pruitt
PRUITT, MICKEY AARON
B. Jan. 10, 1965, Bamberg, SC
Colorado 6'1" 206 lbs.

1988	CHI	N	14	LB
1989			14	LB
1990			16	LB
1991	DAL	N	12	LB
1992			6	LB

5 yrs. 62 games

Mike Pruitt
PRUITT, MICHAEL
B. Apr. 3, 1954, Chicago, IL
Purdue 6'0" 225 lbs.

1976	CLE	N	13	RB
1977			13	RB
1978			16	RB
1979			16	FB
1980			16	FB

Mike Pruitt *continued*

1981			16	FB
1982			9	RB
1983			15	RB
1984			10	RB
1985	BUF	N	4	RB
1985	KC	N	9	RB
1986			15	RB

11 yrs. 152 games

Barry Pryor
PRYOR, BARRY L.
B. Mar. 4, 1946, Pittsburgh, PA
Boston University 6'1" 215 lbs.

1969	MIA	A	14	RB
1970	MIA	N	2	RB

2 yrs. 16 games

Jim Psaltis
PSALTIS, DAVID JAMES
B. Dec. 14, 1927, Chicago, IL
Southern California 6'1" 190 lbs.

1953	CHIC	N	12	HB
1954	GB	N	11	HB
1955	CHIC	N	12	HB

3 yrs. 35 games

Bob Ptacek
PTACEK, ROBERT
B. 1937
Michigan 6'1" 205 lbs.

1959	CLE	N	12	QB

Benny Pucci
PUCCI, BENITO M.
B. Jan. 26, 1925, St. Louis, MO
None 6'4" 255 lbs.

1946	BUF	AA	12	T
1947	CHI	AA	13	T
1948	CLE	AA	12	T

3 yrs. 37 games

Hal Puddy
PUDDY, HAROLD MARVIN
B. Aug. 18, 1924
D. Jan., 1975
Oregon State 6'3" 220 lbs.

1948	SF	AA	4	T

Chet Pudloski
PUDLOSKI, CHESTER E.
B. Aug. 3, 1915, Wilkes-Barre, PA
Villanova 6'1" 210 lbs.

1944	CLE	N	10	T

Garry Puetz
PUETZ, GARRY SPENCER
B. Mar. 14, 1952, Elmhurst, IL
Valparaiso 6'3" 263 lbs.

1973	NYJ	N	7	OT
1974			14	G, OT
1975			14	G
1976			14	G
1977			14	G, OT
1978			6	OT
1978	TB	N	10	G, OT
1979	PHI	N	2	OT
1979	NE	N	5	OT
1980			16	OT
1981			15	OT
1982	WAS	N	2	OT

10 yrs. 119 games

Howie Pugh
PUGH, HOWIE
None

1922	MIL	N	1	T

Year	Team	Games	Pos.

Jethro Pugh
PUGH, JETHRO, JR.
B. Jul. 3, 1944, Windsor, NC
Elizabeth City State 6'6" 256 lbs.

Year	Team		Games	Pos.
1965	**DAL**	N	12	DE
1966			14	DE
1967			14	DT
1968			13	DT
1969			12	DT
1970			14	DT
1971			12	DT
1972			14	DT
1973			13	DT
1974			14	DT
1975			13	DT
1976			13	DT
1977			12	DT
1978			13	DT

14 yrs.   183 games

Marion Pugh
PUGH, MARION C.
B. Sep. 6, 1919, Fort Worth, TX
D. Nov. 20, 1976, College Station, TX
Texas A&M 6'1" 187 lbs.

Year	Team		Games	Pos.
1941	**NYG**	N	5	HB
1945			5	HB
1946	**MIA**	AA	14	QB

3 yrs.   24 games

Craig Puki
PUKI, CRAIG ALAN
B. Jan. 18, 1957, Deadwood, SD
Tennessee 6'1" 231 lbs.

Year	Team		Games	Pos.
1980	**SF**	N	16	LB
1981			16	LB
1982	**STL**	N	7	LB

3 yrs.   39 games

Don Pumphrey
PUMPHREY, DONALD (Bingo)
B. Nov. 22, 1963
Valdosta State 6'4" 275 lbs.

Year	Team		Games	Pos.
1987	**TB**	N	3	OT

Andy Puplis
PUPLIS, ANDREW JOSEPH
B. Feb. 1, 1915
D. Jan. 25, 1990, Maywood, IL
Notre Dame 5'9" 180 lbs.

Year	Team		Games	Pos.
1943	**CHIC**	N	8	B

Alfred Pupunu
PUPUNU, ALFRED SIONE
B. Oct. 17, 1969, Tonga Islands
Weber State 6'5" 240 lbs.

Year	Team		Games	Pos.
1992	**SD**	N	15	TE
1993			16	TE
1994			13	TE
1995			15	TE
1996			9	TE

5 yrs.   68 games

Cal Purdin
PURDIN, CALVIN O'NEIL
B. Feb. 2, 1921
D. Dec., 1982, Augusta, KS
Tulsa 6'2" 188 lbs.

Year	Team		Games	Pos.
1943	**CHIC**	N	4	HB
1946	**BKN**	AA	6	HB
1946	**MIA**	AA	2	HB

2 yrs.   12 games

Mike Purdy
PURDY, CLAIR J., JR.
B. 1895, Auburn, NY
D. Jan. 10, 1950, Auburn, NY

Mike Purdy *continued*
Brown 5'10" 179 lbs.

Year	Team		Games	Pos.
1920	**ROC**	A	1	HB
1921	**SYR**	A	1	QB
1921	**NY**	A	1	FB
1922	**MIL**	N	9	QB, HB, G, FB

3 yrs.   12 games

Pid Purdy
PURDY, EVERETT VIRGIL
B. Jun. 15, 1904, Beatrice, NE
D. Jan. 16, 1951, Beatrice, NE
Beloit 5'6" 145 lbs.

Year	Team		Games	Pos.
1926	**GB**	N	11	QB, HB
1927			6	QB, HB

2 yrs.   17 games

Dave Pureifory
PUREIFORY, DAVID LEE
B. Jul. 12, 1949, Pensacola, FL
Eastern Michigan 6'1" 256 lbs.

Year	Team		Games	Pos.
1972	**GB**	N	14	DE
1973			13	DE
1974			13	DE
1975			14	DE
1976			14	DE
1977			12	DT
1978	**CIN**	N	7	DE
1978	**DET**	N	8	DE
1979			15	DE
1980			16	DE
1981			15	DE
1982			9	DE

11 yrs.   150 games

Dave Purling
PURLING, DAVE
B. Jun. 26, 1962
Southern California 6'5" 240 lbs.

Year	Team		Games	Pos.
1987	**LARM**	N	1	NT

Frank Purnell
PURNELL, FRANKLIN
B. Apr. 5, 1933, Sweatman, MS
Alcorn State 5'11" 230 lbs.

Year	Team		Games	Pos.
1957	**GB**	N	9	FB

Jim Purnell
PURNELL, JAMES FRED
B. Dec. 12, 1941, La Porte, IN
Wisconsin 6'2" 229 lbs.

Year	Team		Games	Pos.
1964	**CHI**	N	6	LB
1965			12	LB
1966			14	LB
1967			14	LB
1968			14	LB
1969	**LA**	N	14	LB
1970			14	LB
1971			14	LB
1972			14	LB

9 yrs.   116 games

Lovett Purnell
PURNELL, LOVETT
B. Apr. 7, 1972, Seaford, DE
West Virginia 6'2" 250 lbs.

Year	Team		Games	Pos.
1996	**NE**	N	2	TE

Vic Purvis
PURVIS, JAMES VICTOR
B. Nov. 17, 1943, Brandon, MS
Southern Mississippi 5'11" 200 lbs.

Year	Team		Games	Pos.
1966	**BOS**	A	14	DB
1967			2	DB

2 yrs.   16 games

Duane Putnam
PUTNAM, DUANE
B. Sep. 5, 1928, Pollock, SD
Pacific 6'0" 228 lbs.

Year	Team		Games	Pos.
1952	**LA**	N	6	G
1953			9	G
1954			11	G
1955			12	G
1956			12	G
1957			12	G
1958			12	G
1959			10	G
1960	**DAL**	N	12	G
1961	**CLE**	N	14	G
1962	**LA**	N	11	G

11 yrs.   121 games

Earl Putnam
PUTNAM, EARL ROBERT
B. Jan. 10, 1932, Cincinnati, OH
Arizona State 6'6" 308 lbs.

Year	Team		Games	Pos.
1957	**CHIC**	N	11	C

Fred Putzier
PUTZIER, FRED
B. Jun. 11, 1899
D. Sep., 1986, Prescott, WI
St. Olaf 5'9" 174 lbs.

Year	Team		Games	Pos.
1924	**MIN**	N	2	E

Rollin Putzier
PUTZIER, ROLLIN W.
B. Dec. 10, 1965, Coeur d'Alene, ID
Oregon 6'4" 280 lbs.

Year	Team		Games	Pos.
1988	**PIT**	N	5	NT
1989	**SF**	N	11	NT

2 yrs.   16 games

Dave Puzzuoli
PUZZUOLI, PHILLIP DAVID
B. Jan. 12, 1961, Greenwich, CT
Pittsburgh 6'3" 260 lbs.

Year	Team		Games	Pos.
1983	**CLE**	N	16	NT
1984			16	NT
1985			16	NT
1986			16	NT
1987			12	NT

5 yrs.   76 games

Jack Pyburn
PYBURN, JACK HARRIS
B. Dec. 28, 1944, Shreveport, LA
Texas A&M 6'6" 245 lbs.

Year	Team		Games	Pos.
1967	**MIA**	A	10	OT
1968			13	OT

2 yrs.   23 games

Johnny Pyeatt
PYEATT, JOHN
B. Sep. 16, 1934
none 6'3" 204 lbs.

Year	Team		Games	Pos.
1960	**DEN**	A		DB
1961			3	DB

2 yrs.   3 games

Mike Pyle
PYLE, MICHAEL JOHNSON
B. Jul. 18, 1939, Keokuk, IA
Yale 6'3" 247 lbs.

Year	Team		Games	Pos.
1961	**CHI**	N	14	C
1962			14	C
1963			14	C
1964			11	C
1965			13	C
1966			13	C
1967			14	C
1968			14	C

Mike Pyle *continued*

Year	Team		Games	Pos.
1969			14	C

9 yrs.   121 games

Palmer Pyle
PYLE, WILLIAM PALMER
B. Jun. 6, 1937, Keokuk, IA
Michigan State 6'2" 248 lbs.

Year	Team		Games	Pos.
1960	**BAL**	N	11	G
1961			14	G
1962			6	G
1963			7	G
1964	**MIN**	N	10	G
1966	**OAK**	A	13	G

6 yrs.   61 games

Dave Pyles
PYLES, ROBERT DAVID
B. Sep. 3, 1960, Portsmouth, OH
Miami (Ohio) 6'5" 275 lbs.

Year	Team		Games	Pos.
1987	**LARI**	N	2	OT

Bob Pylman
PYLMAN, ROBERT
B. Oct. 30, 1913
D. Apr., 1971
South Dakota State 6'4" 214 lbs.

Year	Team		Games	Pos.
1938	**PHI**	N	9	T
1939			10	T

2 yrs.   19 games

George Pyne
PYNE, GEORGE, JR.
B. Oct. 17, 1909
D. Jun., 1974
Holy Cross 5'11" 218 lbs.

Year	Team		Games	Pos.
1931	**PRO**	N	2	

George Pyne
PYNE, GEORGE, III
B. 1943, Milford, MA
Olivet 6'4" 285 lbs.

Year	Team		Games	Pos.
1965	**BOS**	A	14	DT

Jim Pyne
PYNE, JIM
B. Nov. 23, 1971, Milford, MA
Virginia Tech 6'2" 282 lbs.

Year	Team		Games	Pos.
1995	**TB**	N	15	G, C
1996			12	G

2 yrs.   27 games

Jerry Quaerna
QUAERNA, JEROLD O.
B. Oct. 9, 1963
Michigan 6'6" 275 lbs.

Year	Team		Games	Pos.
1987	**DET**	N	3	OT

Red Quam
QUAM, ARTHUR CHARLES
B. Jul. 10, 1896
D. May, 1973, Nashwauk, MN
None 165 lbs.

Year	Team		Games	Pos.
1926	**DUL**		1	QB

Bernard Quarles
QUARLES, BERNARD
B. Jan. 4, 1960, Los Angeles, CA
UCLA/Hawaii 6'2" 215 lbs.

Year	Team		Games	Pos.
1987	**LARM**	N	1	QB

Johnny Quast
QUAST, JOHN HENRY
B. Apr. 4, 1900

Johnny Quast *continued*
D. Aug. 9, 1966, Louisville KY
Purdue 5'10" 165 lbs.

Year	Team		Games	Pos.
1923	LOU	N	1	E

Jess Quatse
QUATSE, JESS
B. Apr. 4, 1908
D. Dec. 27, 1977, Lakeland, FL
Pittsburgh 5'11" 226 lbs.

Year	Team		Games	Pos.
1933	GB	N	7	T
1933	PIT	N	1	T
1934			12	T
1935	NYG	N	10	T
3 yrs.	30 games			

Frank Quayle
QUAYLE, FRANK JOSEPH, III
B. Jan. 15, 1947, Brooklyn, NY
Virginia 5'10" 195 lbs.

Year	Team		Games	Pos.
1969	DEN	A	11	RB

Jeff Queen
QUEEN, JEFFREY RICHARD (Fox)
B. Aug. 15, 1946, Boston, MA
Morgan State 6'1" 221 lbs.

Year	Team		Games	Pos.
1969	SD	A	14	TE
1970	SD	N	14	TE
1971			14	RB
1972	OAK	N	14	RB
1973			9	RB, TE
1974	HOU	N	11	TE
6 yrs.	76 games			

Jeff Query
QUERY, JEFF LEE
B. Mar. 7, 1967, Decatur, IL
Millikin 6'0" 165 lbs.

Year	Team		Games	Pos.
1989	GB	N	16	WR
1990			16	WR
1991			16	WR
1992	CIN	N	10	WR
1993			16	WR
1994			10	WR
1995			1	WR
1995	WAS	N	1	WR
7 yrs.	86 games			

Greg Quick
QUICK, GREGORY
B. Apr. 26, 1964
Catawba 6'4" 280 lbs.

Year	Team		Games	Pos.
1987	ATL	N	1	G, OT

Jerry Quick
QUICK, JERRY DEAN
B. Dec. 30, 1963, Anthony, KS
Wichita State 6'5" 273 lbs.

Year	Team		Games	Pos.
1987	PIT	N	1	OT, G

Mike Quick
QUICK, MICHAEL ANTHONY
B. May 14, 1959, Hamlet, NC
North Carolina State 6'2" 190 lbs.

Year	Team		Games	Pos.
1982	PHI	N	9	WR
1983			16	WR
1984			14	WR
1985			16	WR
1986			16	WR
1987			12	WR
1988			8	WR
1989			6	WR
1990			4	WR
9 yrs.	101 games			

Red Quigley
QUIGLEY, GERALD
B. Dec. 18, 1895
D. Sep. 26, 1966, Rochester, NY
None 5'9" 155 lbs.

Year	Team		Games	Pos.
1920	ROC	A	1	QB

Fred Quillan
QUILLAN, FRED
B. Jan. 27, 1956, Portland, OR
Oregon 6'5" 264 lbs.

Year	Team		Games	Pos.
1978	SF	N	14	C
1979			16	C
1980			16	C
1981			16	C
1982			9	C
1983			14	C
1984			16	C
1985			15	C
1986			16	C
1987			11	C
10 yrs.	143 games			

Frank Quillen
QUILLEN, FRANK HARRIS
B. Dec. 18, 1921, Ridley Park, PA
D. Sep. 21, 1990
Pennsylvania 6'5" 225 lbs.

Year	Team		Games	Pos.
1946	CHI	AA	14	E
1947			6	E
2 yrs.	20 games			

Charley Quilter
QUILTER, CHARLES REW
B. May 8, 1926, Shreveport, LA
Tyler JC 6'1" 240 lbs.

Year	Team		Games	Pos.
1949	SF	AA	12	T
1950	SF	N	8	T
2 yrs.	20 games			

Bill Quinlan
QUINLAN, WILLIAM D.
B. Jun. 19, 1932, Lawrence, MA
Michigan State 6'3" 248 lbs.

Year	Team		Games	Pos.
1957	CLE	N	12	E
1958			10	E
1959	GB	N	12	E
1960			12	E
1961			14	DE
1962			14	DE
1963	PHI	N	10	DE
1964	DET	N	12	DE
1965	WAS	N	14	DE
9 yrs.	110 games			

Skeets Quinlan
QUINLAN, VOLNEY
B. Jun. 22, 1928
Texas Christian/San Diego State 5'11" 173 lbs.

Year	Team		Games	Pos.
1952	LA	N	12	HB
1953			12	HB
1954			11	HB
1955			6	HB
4 yrs.	41 games			

Ivan Quinn
QUINN, IVAN
B. May 26, 1899, Nebraska
D. Aug., 1969, Waukesha, WI
Carroll (Wisconsin)

Year	Team		Games	Pos.
1924	KC		1	G

Kelly Quinn
QUINN, KELLY B.
B. Aug. 20, 1963, Thomastown, GA
Michigan State 6'1" 220 lbs.

Year	Team		Games	Pos.
1987	MIN	N	3	LB

Paddy Quinn
QUINN, PATRICK GEORGE
B. Feb. 5, 1890
D. Feb., 1963
None 5'7" 160 lbs.

Year	Team		Games	Pos.
1920	RI	A	1	HB

Steve Quinn
QUINN, STEPHEN TIMOTHY
B. Feb. 11, 1946, Pittsburg, KS
Notre Dame 6'1" 225 lbs.

Year	Team		Games	Pos.
1968	HOU	A	9	C

Ed Quirk
QUIRK, EDWARD G.
B. Feb. 27, 1925, St. Louis, MO
Deceased
Missouri 6'1" 231 lbs.

Year	Team		Games	Pos.
1948	WAS	N	12	FB, LB
1949			8	FB, B
1950			12	C, LB
1951			6	LB
4 yrs.	38 games			

Marc Raab
RAAB, MARC
B. Jan. 26, 1969, San Diego, CA
Southern California 6'3" 265 lbs.

Year	Team		Games	Pos.
1993	WAS	N	2	C

Bob Raba
RABA, ROBERT
B. Apr. 23, 1955, Washington, DC
Maryland 6'1" 224 lbs.

Year	Team		Games	Pos.
1977	NYJ	N	14	TE
1978			4	TE
1979			8	TE
1980	BAL	N	3	TE
1981	WAS	N	8	TE
5 yrs.	37 games			

Warren Rabb
RABB, S. WARREN
B. Dec. 12, 1937, Baton Rouge, LA
Louisiana State 6'1" 202 lbs.

Year	Team		Games	Pos.
1960	DET	N	7	QB
1961	BUF	A	9	QB
1962			14	QB
3 yrs.	30 games			

Mike Rabold
RABOLD, MICHAEL JOHN
B. Mar. 12, 1937, Chicago, IL
D. Oct. 13, 1970, Greenwood, IN
Indiana 6'2" 239 lbs.

Year	Team		Games	Pos.
1959	DET	N	12	G
1960	STL	N	12	G
1961	MIN	N	14	G
1962			14	G
1964	CHI	N	14	G
1965			14	G
1966			14	G
1967			11	G
8 yrs.	105 games			

Buster Raborn
RABORN, CARROLL M.
B. Mar. 28, 1913
D. Dec. 21, 1991, Fortuna, CA
Southern Methodist 6'0" 198 lbs.

Year	Team		Games	Pos.
1936	PIT	N	12	C
1937			11	C, E
2 yrs.	23 games			

Frank Racis
RACIS, FRANK (Hercules)

Frank Racis *continued*
B. Nov. 9, 1899, Shenandoah, PA
D. Aug. 20, 1982, Shenandoah, PA
None 6'0" 200 lbs.

Year	Team		Games	Pos.
1925	POT	N	12	G
1926			14	T
1927			13	G, T
1928			10	T
1928	NYY	N	1	T
1929	BOS	N	7	G
1930	PRO	N	11	G
1931	FRA	N	8	T
7 yrs.	76 games			

David Rackley
RACKLEY, DAVID
B. Feb. 2, 1961, Miami, FL
Texas Southern 5'9" 170 lbs.

Year	Team		Games	Pos.
1985	NO	N	7	CB

George Radachowsky
RADACHOWSKY, GEORGE JOSEPH, JR.
B. Sep. 7, 1962, Danbury, CT
Boston College 5'11" 186 lbs.

Year	Team		Games	Pos.
1984	IND	N	16	DB
1985			3	CB, S
1987	NYJ	N	8	S
1988			9	S
1989			16	S
5 yrs.	52 games			

John Rade
RADE, JOHN
B. Aug. 31, 1960, Ceres, CA
Boise State 6'1" 232 lbs.

Year	Team		Games	Pos.
1983	ATL	N	5	LB
1984			7	LB
1985			16	LB
1986			15	LB
1987			11	LB
1988			15	LB
1989			15	LB
1990			16	LB
1991			11	LB
9 yrs.	111 games			

Keith Radecic
RADECIC, KEITH
B. Dec. 24, 1963
Penn State 6'1" 260 lbs.

Year	Team		Games	Pos.
1987	STL	N	3	C

Scott Radecic
RADECIC, J. SCOTT
B. Jun. 14, 1962, Pittsburgh, PA
Penn State 6'3" 241 lbs.

Year	Team		Games	Pos.
1984	KC	N	16	LB
1985			16	LB
1986			16	LB
1987	BUF	N	12	LB
1988			16	LB
1989			16	LB
1990	IND	N	15	LB
1991			14	LB
1992			16	LB
1993			16	LB
1994			16	LB
1995			13	LB
12 yrs.	182 games			

Bill Rademacher
RADEMACHER, WILLIAM
B. May 13, 1942, Menominee, MI
Northern Michigan 6'1" 190 lbs.

Year	Team		Games	Pos.
1964	NY	A	6	DB, FL
1965			4	DB
1966			4	OE

Year	Team	Games	Pos.

Bill Rademacher continued

Year	Team		Games	Pos.
1967			3	OE
1968			14	WR
1969	BOS	A	13	WR
1970	BOS	N	14	WR
7 yrs.	58 games			

Bruce Radford

RADFORD, BRUCE
B. Oct. 5, 1955, Pineville, LA
Grambling State 6'5" 257 lbs.

1979	DEN	N	16	DE
1980	TB	N	12	DE
1981	STL	N	9	DE
3 yrs.	37 games			

Ken Radick

RADICK, KENNETH (Fat)
B. Jun. 17, 1907
D. Aug., 1987, Oshkosh, WI
Indiana/Marquette 6'0" 210 lbs.

1930	GB	N	7	T, E
1931			1	E
1931	BKN	N	2	G, T, E
2 yrs.	10 games			

Wayne Radloff

RADLOFF, WAYNE R.
B. May 17, 1961, London, England
Georgia 6'5" 274 lbs.

1985	ATL	N	16	OL
1986			16	C, G
1987			12	C, G
1988			10	C
1989			11	G
5 yrs.	65 games			

Alex Rado

RADO, ALEXANDER (Pug)
B. Jul. 19, 1911, Dayton, OH
Deceased
West Virginia Tech 6'1" 200 lbs.

1934	PIT	N	8	HB

George Rado

RADO, GEORGE (Mousie)
B. Oct. 24, 1912, Youngstown, OH
D. Apr. 30, 1992, New Cumberland, WV
Duquesne 5'9" 194 lbs.

1935	PIT	N	12	G
1936			12	G, T
1937			1	
1937	PHI	N	9	G
1938			10	G, E
4 yrs.	44 games			

George Radosevich

RADOSEVICH, GEORGE
B. Jan. 25, 1928, Pittsburgh, PA
Pittsburgh 6'2" 238 lbs.

1954	BAL	N	10	C
1955			12	T
1956			8	T
3 yrs.	30 games			

Bill Radovich

RADOVICH, WILLIAM A.
B. Jun. 24, 1915, Chicago, IL
Southern California 5'10" 238 lbs.

1938	DET	N	10	G
1939			11	G
1940			10	G
1941			11	G
1945			9	G
1946	LA	AA	14	G

Bill Radovich continued

1947			14	G
7 yrs.	79 games			

Vic Radzevich

RADZEVICH, VICTOR
B. Jun. 8, 1903
D. Jun., 1974, Torrington, CT
Connecticut 5'10" 165 lbs.

1926	HAR	N	8	HB, FB, QB, G

Mike Rae

RAE, MICHAEL JOHN
B. Jul. 26, 1951, Long Beach, CA
Southern California 6'0" 193 lbs.

1976	OAK	N	7	QB
1977			10	QB
1978	TB	N	6	QB
1979			5	QB
4 yrs.	28 games			

Bill Raffel

RAFFEL, WILLIAM
B. Aug. 26, 1907
D. Jul. 24, 1982, Wynnewood, PA
Pennsylvania 5'11" 195 lbs.

1932	BKN	N	4	E

Tom Rafferty

RAFFERTY, THOMAS MICHAEL
B. Aug. 2, 1954, Syracuse, NY
Penn State 6'3" 256 lbs.

1976	DAL	N	13	G
1977			14	G, C
1978			16	G, C
1979			16	G
1980			16	G
1981			16	G
1982			9	G
1983			16	C, G
1984			16	C
1985			16	C
1986			16	C
1987			12	C
1988			15	C
1989			12	C
14 yrs.	203 games			

Vince Rafferty

RAFFERTY, VINCE
B. Aug. 6, 1961
Colorado 6'4" 285 lbs.

1987	GB	N	3	C

Billy Rafter

RAFTER, WILLIAM JOHN
B. Oct. 7, 1895, Troy, NY
D. Jun., 1966, Syracuse, NY
Syracuse 5'6" 155 lbs.

1921	ROC	A	1	HB
1921	SYR	A	3	QB, HB
1924	ROC	N	1	HB
2 yrs.	5 games			

Phil Ragazzo

RAGAZZO, PHILIP
B. Jun. 24, 1915, Niles, OH
Case Western Reserve 6'0" 216 lbs.

1938	CLE	N	9	G
1939			10	G
1940			1	G
1940	PHI	N	6	T
1941			10	T
1945	NYG	N	5	T
1946			11	T
1947			9	T
7 yrs.	61 games			

Floyd Raglin

RAGLIN, FLOYD
B. Oct. 2, 1961, Alton, IL
Nevada-Las Vegas/Southern University 5'9" 180 lbs.

1987	MIA	N	2	CB

George Ragsdale

RAGSDALE, GEORGE
B. Dec. 4, 1952, DinwiDDie, VA
North Carolina A&T 5'11" 185 lbs.

1977	TB	N	9	RB, WR
1978			15	RB
1979			15	RB
3 yrs.	39 games			

Pat Ragusa

RAGUSA, PAT
B. Mar. 17, 1963
St. John's (New York) 5'8" 180 lbs.

1987	NYJ	N	3	K

Steve Raible

RAIBLE, STEVEN CARL
B. Jun. 2, 1954, Louisville, KY
Georgia Tech 6'2" 195 lbs.

1976	SEA	N	13	WR
1977			14	WR
1978			16	WR
1979			16	WR
1980			16	WR
1981			9	WR
6 yrs.	84 games			

Dave Raimey

RAIMEY, DAVID
B. Nov. 18, 1940, Dayton, OH
Michigan 5'10" 195 lbs.

1964	CLE	N	5	DB

Ben Raimondi

RAIMONDI, BENJAMIN L.
B. Jan. 23, 1925, Brooklyn, NY
Indiana 5'10" 175 lbs.

1947	NY	AA	7	B

Mike Raines

RAINES, VAUGHN MICHAEL
B. Feb. 14, 1953, Montgomery, AL
Alabama 6'5" 255 lbs.

1974	SF	N	2	DT

Dan Rains

RAINS, DANIEL PAUL
B. Apr. 26, 1955, Rochester, PA
Cincinnati 6'1" 222 lbs.

1982	CHI	N	1	LB
1983			15	LB
1984			16	LB
1986			9	LB
4 yrs.	41 games			

Pete Rajkovich

RAJKOVICH, W. PETER
B. Jan. 17, 1911
D. Nov., 1979, Caro, MI
Detroit 5'10" 190 lbs.

1934	PIT	N	3	FB

Larry Rakestraw

RAKESTRAW, LARRY CLYDE
B. Apr. 22, 1942, Atlanta, GA
Georgia 6'2" 195 lbs.

1966	CHI	N	1	QB
1967			5	QB

Larry Rakestraw continued

1968			7	QB
3 yrs.	13 games			

Gregg Rakoczy

RAKOCZY, GREGG ADAM
B. May 18, 1965, Medford Lakes, NJ
Miami (Florida) 6'6" 286 lbs.

1987	CLE	N	12	OT
1988			16	OT
1989			16	C
1990			16	C
1991	NE	N	5	OL
1992			16	G, OT
6 yrs.	81 games			

Dan Ralph

RALPH, DANIEL ROY
B. Mar. 9, 1961, Denver, CO
Colorado/Oregon 6'5" 268 lbs.

1984	STL	N	6	DT

Jim Ramey

RAMEY, JAMES
B. Mar. 9, 1957, Louisville, KY
Kentucky 6'4" 247 lbs.

1979	STL	N	7	DE
1987	TB	N	3	DE
2 yrs.	10 games			

Joe Ramona

RAMONA, JOSEPH
B. 1931
Santa Clara 6'1" 210 lbs.

1953	NYG	N	8	G

Chuck Ramsey

RAMSEY, LOWELL WALLACE, JR.
B. Feb. 24, 1952, Rock Hill, SC
Wake Forest 6'2" 191 lbs.

1977	NYJ	N	12	P
1978			16	P
1979			16	P
1980			16	P
1981			16	P
1982			9	P
1983			16	P
1984			16	P
8 yrs.	117 games			

Derrick Ramsey

RAMSEY, DERRICK KENT
B. Dec. 23, 1956, Hastings, FL
Kentucky 6'5" 230 lbs.

1978	OAK	N	16	TE
1979			16	TE
1980			16	TE
1981			16	TE
1982	LARI	N	9	TE
1983			2	TE
1983	NE	N	14	TE
1984			16	TE
1985			16	TE
1987	DET	N	1	TE
9 yrs.	122 games			

Frank Ramsey

RAMSEY, FRANK
B. May 16, 1916
D. Jan., 1985, Corvallis, OR
Oregon State 6'1" 240 lbs.

1945	CHIB	N	9	T

Garrard Ramsey

RAMSEY, GARRARD S. (Buster)
B. Mar. 16, 1920, Townsend, TN

Year	Team		Games	Pos.

Garrard Ramsey *continued*
William & Mary 6'1" 219 lbs.

Year	Team		Games	Pos.
1946	CHIC	N	11	G
1947			8	G
1948			12	G
1949			12	G
1950			12	G
1951			2	G
6 yrs.	57 games			

Greg Ramsey
RAMSEY, GREG
B. Dec. 19, 1963, San Francisco, CA
Fresno State 6'3" 244 lbs.

1987	SEA	N	2	DE

Herschel Ramsey
RAMSEY, HERSCHEL (Red)
B. Apr. 9, 1911
D. Apr., 1984, Kemp, TX
Texas Tech 6'0" 196 lbs.

1938	PHI	N	10	E
1939			11	E
1940			11	E
1945			2	E
4 yrs.	34 games			

Knox Ramsey
RAMSEY, KNOX WAGNER
B. Feb. 13, 1926, Speed, IN
William & Mary 6'1" 216 lbs.

1948	LA	AA	13	G
1949			12	G
1950	CHIC	N	12	G, T
1951			10	G
1952	PHI	N	3	T
1952	WAS	N	7	G
1953			11	G
6 yrs.	68 games			

Nate Ramsey
RAMSEY, NATHAN LEE
B. Jul. 12, 1941, Neptune, NJ
Indiana 6'1" 200 lbs.

1963	PHI	N	14	DB
1964			13	DB
1965			14	DB
1966			12	DB
1967			14	DB
1968			14	DB
1969			14	S
1970			11	CB
1971			14	S
1972			14	CB
1973	NO	N	4	CB
11 yrs.	138 games			

Ray Ramsey
RAMSEY, RAYMOND LEROY
B. Jul. 18, 1921, Springfield, IL
Bradley 6'2" 166 lbs.

1947	CHI	AA	14	B
1948	BKN	AA	11	B
1949	CHI	AA	12	B
1950	CHIC	N	5	HB
1951			10	E
1952			12	E
1953			12	E
7 yrs.	76 games			

Steve Ramsey
RAMSEY, STEPHEN WAYNE
B. Apr. 22, 1948, Dallas, TX
North Texas State 6'2" 210 lbs.

1970	NO	N	1	QB
1971	DEN	N	9	QB
1972			9	QB
1973			9	QB

Steve Ramsey *continued*

Year	Team		Games	Pos.
1974			7	QB
1975			11	QB
1976			12	QB
7 yrs.	58 games			

Tom Ramsey
RAMSEY, THOMAS LLOYD
B. Jul. 9, 1961, Encino, CA
UCLA 6'1" 189 lbs.

1986	NE	N	5	QB
1987			9	QB
1988			7	QB
1989	IND	N	7	QB
4 yrs.	28 games			

Eason Ramson
RAMSON, EASON LLOYD
B. Apr. 30, 1956, Sacramento, CA
Washington State 6'2" 235 lbs.

1978	STL	N	15	TE
1979	SF	N	2	TE
1980			16	TE
1981			11	TE
1982			9	TE
1983			16	TE
1985	BUF	N	16	TE
7 yrs.	85 games			

Dennis Randall
RANDALL, DENNIS ALLEN
B. Jul. 7, 1945, Tulsa, OK
Oklahoma State 6'6" 243 lbs.

1967	NY	A	8	DE
1968	CIN	A	13	DE
2 yrs.	21 games			

Tom Randall
RANDALL, THOMAS GENE
B. Aug. 3, 1956, Mason City, IA
Iowa State 6'5" 245 lbs.

1978	DAL	N	11	G
1979	HOU	N	13	G
2 yrs.	24 games			

Proc Randels
RANDELS, HORACE
B. Aug. 5, 1900
Kansas State 6'0" 180 lbs.

1926	KC	N	11	E
1927	CLE	N	5	E
1928	DET	N	10	E
3 yrs.	26 games			

Ervin Randle
RANDLE, ERVIN
B. Oct. 12, 1962, Hearne, TX
Baylor 6'1" 250 lbs.

1985	TB	N	16	LB
1986			16	LB
1987			12	LB
1988			9	LB
1989			16	LB
1990			16	LB
1991	KC	N	12	LB
1992			13	LB
8 yrs.	110 games			

John Randle
RANDLE, JOHN
B. Dec. 12, 1967, Hearne, TX
Texas A&I, Kingsville 6'1" 266 lbs.

1990	MIN	N	16	DE
1991			16	DE
1992			16	DT
1993			16	DT
1994			16	DT
1995			16	DT

John Randle *continued*

Year	Team		Games	Pos.
1996			16	DT
7 yrs.	112 games			

Sonny Randle
RANDLE, ULMO SHANNON, JR.
B. Jan. 6, 1936, Fork Union, VA
Virginia 6'2" 189 lbs.

1959	CHIC	N	8	E
1960	STL	N	12	E
1961			14	OE
1962			14	OE
1963			14	OE
1964			7	OE
1965			14	OE
1966			14	OE
1967	SF	N	14	OE
1968			3	OE
1968	DAL	N	9	OE
10 yrs.	123 games			

Tate Randle
RANDLE, ERNEST TATE
B. Aug. 15, 1959, Fredericksburg, TX
Texas Tech 6'0" 209 lbs.

1982	HOU	N	7	CB
1983			2	CB
1983	BAL	N	10	CB
1984	IND	N	16	CB
1985			16	CB
1986			15	S
1987	MIA	N	3	S
6 yrs.	69 games			

Al Randolph
RANDOLPH, ALVIN CHESTER
B. Jul. 8, 1944, East St. Louis, IL
Iowa 6'2" 199 lbs.

1966	SF	N	13	DB
1967			14	DB
1968			14	DB
1969			14	S
1970			14	S
1971	GB	N	14	S
1972	DET	N	6	S
1973	MIN	N	11	S
1974	BUF	N	3	S
1974	SF	N	6	S
9 yrs.	109 games			

Clare Randolph
RANDOLPH, CLARE LORING
B. May 2, 1907, Chicago, IL
D. Dec. 24, 1972, Glendale, CA
Indiana 6'2" 204 lbs.

1930	CHIC	N	7	C, G
1931	POR	N	14	C
1932			11	C
1933			10	C
1934	DET	N	13	C
1935			12	C
1936			10	C
7 yrs.	77 games			

Harry Randolph
RANDOLPH, HARRY F.
B. 1900, Dickerson Run, PA
D. Dec. 3, 1957, Harrison, NJ
Bethany (West Virginia) 5'11" 195 lbs.

1923	COL	N	2	HB

Terry Randolph
RANDOLPH, TERRY ALLEN
B. Jul. 17, 1955, Brooklyn, NY
American International 6'0" 184 lbs.

1977	GB	N	14	DB
1978			14	CB
2 yrs.	28 games			

Thomas Randolph
RANDOLPH, THOMAS
B. Oct. 5, 1970, Norfolk, VA
Kansas State 5'9" 176 lbs.

1994	NYG	N	16	CB
1995			16	CB
1996			16	CB
3 yrs.	48 games			

Walt Rankin
RANKIN, WALTER V. (Bull)
B. Jan. 28, 1919, Liberty, OK
D. Nov. 7, 1993, Coahoma, TX
Texas Tech 5'11" 197 lbs.

1943	CHIC	N	10	QB
1944	C-P	N	10	QB
1945	CHIC	N	6	FB
1946			11	FB
1947			12	FB
5 yrs.	49 games			

Keith Ranspot
RANSPOT, KEITH E.
B. Dec. 11, 1914, Millsap, TX
Southern Methodist 6'3" 205 lbs.

1940	CHIC	N	1	E
1942	DET	N	1	E
1942	GB	N	4	E
1943	BKN	N	9	E
1944	BOS	N	10	E
1945			9	E
5 yrs.	34 games			

John Rapacz
RAPACZ, JOHN J.
B. Apr. 23, 1925, Rosedale, OH
D. Jan. 2, 1991, Midwest City, OK
Western Michigan/Oklahoma 6'4" 252 lbs.

1948	CHI	AA	10	C
1949			12	C
1950	NYG	N	10	C
1951			12	C
1952			6	C
1953			12	C
1954			12	C
7 yrs.	74 games			

Bob Rapp
RAPP, JOSEPH ROBERT (Goldie)
B. Feb. 18, 1898
D. Feb., 1968, Columbus, OH
None 5'8" 159 lbs.

1922	COL	N	7	HB, T
1923			10	HB
1924			8	HB, QB
1925			9	QB, HB
1926			6	HB, QB, FB
1929	BUF	N	3	HB
6 yrs.	43 games			

Herb Rapp
RAPP, HERBERT L. (Hub)
B. Jul. 21, 1905
D. Jul., 1983, Los Altos Hills, CA
Xavier (Ohio) 6'0" 195 lbs.

1930	SI	N	6	C, G
1931			11	C
2 yrs.	17 games			

Manny Rapp
RAPP, MANUEL
B. Sep. 17, 1913, Pevely, MO
Deceased
St. Louis 6'0" 215 lbs.

1934	C-S	N	3	HB, FB

Year	Team		Games	Pos.

Walter Rasby
RASBY, WALTER
B. Sep. 7, 1972, Washington, DC
Wake Forest 6'3" 247 lbs.

Year	Team		Games	Pos.
1994	PIT	N	2	TE
1995	CAR	N	9	TE
1996			15	TE

3 yrs. 26 games

Amby Rascher
RASCHER, AMBROSE H.
B. Nov. 3, 1908
D. Mar. 6, 1988
Indiana 6'2" 210 lbs.

Year	Team		Games	Pos.
1932	POR	N	8	G, T

Lou Rash
RASH, LOUIS
B. Jun. 5, 1960, Cleveland, MS
Mississippi Valley State 5'9" 170 lbs.

Year	Team		Games	Pos.
1984	PHI	N	4	CB, S
1987	GB	N	3	CB, S

2 yrs. 7 games

Ahmad Rashad
Born BOBBY MOORE, Played as MOORE 1972
B. Nov. 19, 1949, Portland, OR
Oregon 6'2" 202 lbs.

Year	Team		Games	Pos.
1972	STL	N	14	WR
1973			13	WR
1974	BUF	N	14	WR
1976	MIN	N	13	WR
1977			14	WR
1978			16	WR
1979			16	WR
1980			16	WR
1981			16	WR
1982			7	WR

10 yrs. 139 games

Kenyon Rasheed
RASHEED, KENYON
B. Aug. 23, 1970, Kansas City, MO
Oklahoma 5'10" 245 lbs.

Year	Team		Games	Pos.
1993	NYG	N	5	RB
1994			16	RB
1995	NYJ	N	3	RB

3 yrs. 24 games

Leo Raskowski
RASKOWSKI, LEO THOMAS (Fat)
B. Mar. 28, 1906, Cleveland, OH
Ohio State 6'3" 219 lbs.

Year	Team		Games	Pos.
1932	SI	N	9	T
1933	BKN	N	3	T
1933	PIT	N	3	T
1935	PHI	N	2	T

3 yrs. 17 games

Rocky Rasley
RASLEY, ROCKY
B. Apr. 27, 1947, Bakersfield, CA
Oregon State 6'3" 252 lbs.

Year	Team		Games	Pos.
1969	DET	N	12	G
1970			8	G
1972			14	G
1973			14	G
1974	NO	N	14	G
1975	KC	N	11	G
1976	SF	N	1	G

7 yrs. 74 games

Randy Rasmussen
RASMUSSEN, RANDALL LEE
B. May 10, 1945, St. Paul, NE
Kearney State 6'2" 256 lbs.

Year	Team		Games	Pos.
1967	NY	A	14	G

Randy Rasmussen continued

Year	Team		Games	Pos.
1968			14	G
1969			13	G
1970	NYJ	N	13	G
1971			14	G
1972			14	G
1973			14	G
1974			14	G
1975			14	G
1976			14	G
1977			14	G
1978			16	G
1979			16	G
1980			8	G
1981			15	G

15 yrs. 207 games

Randy Rasmussen
RASMUSSEN, RANDY ROBERT
B. Sep. 27, 1960, Minneapolis, MN
Minnesota 6'2" 253 lbs.

Year	Team		Games	Pos.
1984	PIT	N	16	C, G
1985			11	C, G
1986			4	G, C
1987	MIN	N	5	OL
1988			7	C, G
1989			7	C, G

6 yrs. 50 games

Wayne Rasmussen
RASMUSSEN, WAYNE FLOYD (Twiggy)
B. Jun. 7, 1942, Chicago, IL
South Dakota State 6'2" 179 lbs.

Year	Team		Games	Pos.
1964	DET	N	11	DB
1965			14	DB
1966			14	DB
1967			10	DB
1968			14	DB
1969			14	S
1970			14	S
1971			14	S
1972			7	DB

9 yrs. 112 games

Nick Rassas
RASSAS, NICHOLAS CHARLES
B. Jan. 13, 1944, Baltimore, MD
Notre Dame 6'0" 190 lbs.

Year	Team		Games	Pos.
1966	ATL	N	8	DB
1967			6	DB
1968			14	DB

3 yrs. 28 games

Ed Rate
RATE, EDWIN S. (Speedy)
B. May 27, 1899
Deceased
Purdue 5'9" 165 lbs.

Year	Team		Games	Pos.
1923	MIL	N	1	HB

Roy Ratekin
RATEKIN, ROY
B. 1899
Deceased
Colorado State 5'10" 180 lbs.

Year	Team		Games	Pos.
1921	AKR	A	2	E

Bo Rather
RATHER, DAVID ELMER
B. Oct. 7, 1950, Sandusky, OH
Michigan 6'1" 185 lbs.

Year	Team		Games	Pos.
1973	MIA	N	6	WR
1974	CHI	N	13	WR
1975			14	WR
1976			9	WR
1977			13	WR
1978			6	WR

Bo Rather continued

Year	Team		Games	Pos.
1978	MIA	N	3	WR

6 yrs. 64 games

Tom Rathman
RATHMAN, THOMAS DEAN
B. Oct. 7, 1962, Grand Island, NE
Nebraska 6'1" 232 lbs.

Year	Team		Games	Pos.
1986	SF	N	16	FB
1987			12	FB
1988			16	FB
1989			16	FB
1990			16	FB
1991			16	FB
1992			15	FB
1993			8	FB
1994	LARI	N	16	FB

9 yrs. 131 games

Joe Ratica
RATICA, JOSEPH
B. 1917
D. Oct. 21, 1942
St. Vincent 6'0" 205 lbs.

Year	Team		Games	Pos.
1939	BKN	N	7	C, G

Brian Ratigan
RATIGAN, BRIAN LEE
B. Dec. 27, 1970, Council Bluffs, IA
Notre Dame 6'4" 241 lbs.

Year	Team		Games	Pos.
1994	IND	N	14	LB

Ray Ratkowski
RATKOWSKI, RAYMOND
B. 1940
Notre Dame 6'0" 195 lbs.

Year	Team		Games	Pos.
1961	BOS	A	1	HB

Don Ratliff
RATLIFF, DONALD EUGENE
B. Jul. 17, 1950, Baltimore, MD
Maryland 6'5" 250 lbs.

Year	Team		Games	Pos.
1975	PHI	N	6	DE

Ratterman
RATTERMAN
None

Year	Team		Games	Pos.
1934	C-S	N	1	HB

George Ratterman
RATTERMAN, GEORGE WILLIAM
B. Nov. 12, 1926, Cincinnati, OH
Notre Dame 6'1" 192 lbs.

Year	Team		Games	Pos.
1947	BUF	AA	14	QB
1948			14	QB
1949			11	QB
1950	NYY	N	12	QB
1951			6	QB
1952	CLE	N	6	QB
1953			9	QB
1954			6	QB
1955			10	QB
1956			4	QB

10 yrs. 92 games

Dick Rauch
RAUCH, RICHARD
B. Jul. 15, 1893
D. Oct., 1970, Harrisburg, PA
Penn State 5'9" 178 lbs.

Year	Team		Games	Pos.
1925	POT	N	6	G
1928	NYY	N	2	C, G
1929	BOS	N	1	G

3 yrs. 9 games

John Rauch
RAUCH, JOHN
B. Aug. 20, 1927, Philadelphia, PA
Georgia 6'0" 197 lbs.

Year	Team		Games	Pos.
1949	NYB	N	9	QB, DB
1950	NYY	N	8	B, QB
1951			6	QB
1951	PHI	N	4	QB

3 yrs. 27 games

Bob Ravensburg
RAVENSBURG, ROBERT ALEXANDER
B. Oct. 20, 1925, Bellevue, TX
Indiana 6'0" 190 lbs.

Year	Team		Games	Pos.
1948	CHIC	N	11	E
1949			12	E

2 yrs. 23 games

Eric Ravotti
RAVOTTI, ERIC ALLEN
B. Mar. 16, 1971, Freeport, PA
Penn State 6'3" 254 lbs.

Year	Team		Games	Pos.
1994	PIT	N	2	LB
1995			6	LB
1996			15	LB

3 yrs. 23 games

Bob Rawlings
RAWLINGS, ROBERT
None

Year	Team		Games	Pos.
1922	BUF	N	6	FB, HB

Art Ray
RAY, ARTHUR
B. 1903
Deceased
Holy Cross 6'0" 185 lbs.

Year	Team		Games	Pos.
1926	BOS	A	3	G

Baby Ray
RAY, BUFORD G.
B. Sep. 30, 1914, Una, TN
D. Jan. 21, 1986, Nashville, TN
Vanderbilt 6'6" 249 lbs.

Year	Team		Games	Pos.
1938	GB	N	11	T
1939			11	T
1940			11	T
1941			11	T
1942			11	T
1943			8	T
1944			10	T
1945			10	T
1946			11	T
1947			11	T
1948			12	T

11 yrs. 117 games

Darrol Ray
RAY, DARROL ANTHONY
B. Jun. 25, 1958, San Francisco, CA
Oklahoma 6'1" 200 lbs.

Year	Team		Games	Pos.
1980	NYJ	N	16	S
1981			16	S
1982			9	S
1983			16	S
1984			15	S

5 yrs. 72 games

David Ray
RAY, DAVID EUGENE, JR.
B. Sep. 19, 1944, Phenix City, AL
Alabama 6'0" 195 lbs.

Year	Team		Games	Pos.
1969	LA	N	1	WR, K
1970			14	K, WR
1971			14	K, WR
1972			14	K, WR

719

Year	Team	Games	Pos.

David Ray continued

1973		14	K, WR
1974		13	K, WR
6 yrs.	70 games		

Eddie Ray
RAY, EDWARD B., JR.
B. Apr. 5, 1947, Vicksburg, MS
Louisiana State 6'1" 237 lbs.

1970	BOS	N	5	RB
1971	SD	N	4	RB
1972	ATL	N	7	RB
1973		14	RB
1974		11	RB
1976	BUF	N	7	RB
6 yrs.	48 games		

John Ray
RAY, JOHN WILLIAM
B. Apr. 26, 1969, Charleston, WV
West Virginia 6'8" 350 lbs.

| 1993 | IND | N | 2 | OT |

Ricky Ray
RAY, RICKY LEE
B. May 30, 1957, Waynesboro, VA
Norfolk State 5'11" 180 lbs.

1979	NO	N	6	CB
1980		13	CB
1981		4	CB
1981	MIA	N	8	CB
3 yrs.	31 games		

Terry Ray
RAY, TERRY
B. Oct. 12, 1969, Belgium
Oklahoma 6'1" 187 lbs.

1992	ATL	N	10	S
1993	NE	N	15	S
1994		16	S
1995		16	S
1996		16	S
5 yrs.	73 games		

Tom Rayam
RAYAM, THOMAS
B. Jan. 3, 1968, Orlando, FL
Alabama 6'6" 297 lbs.

1992	CIN	N	10	OT
1993		10	G
2 yrs.	20 games		

Israel Rayborn
RAYBORN, ISRAEL
B. Feb. 5, 1973, Lee, AL
North Alabama 6'6" 293 lbs.

| 1996 | PIT | N | 2 | DE |

Van Rayburn
RAYBURN, VIRGIL H.
B. Aug. 4, 1910
D. Jun. 15, 1991, Osceola, AR
Tennessee 6'1" 180 lbs.

| 1933 | BKN | N | 9 | E |

Jimmy Raye
RAYE, JAMES A.
B. Mar. 26, 1946, Fayetteville, NC
Michigan State 6'0" 185 lbs.

| 1969 | PHI | N | 2 | CB |

Jimmy Raye
RAYE, JAMES ARTHUR
B. Nov. 24, 1968, Fayetteville, NC
San Diego State 5'9" 165 lbs.

| 1991 | LARM | N | 2 | WR |

Fred Rayhle
RAYHLE, FRED
B. Apr. 9, 1954, Covington, KY
Tennessee-Chattanooga 6'5" 216 lbs.

| 1977 | SEA | N | 2 | TE |

Cory Raymer
RAYMER, CORY
B. Mar. 3, 1973, Fond du Lac, WI
Wisconsin 6'2" 293 lbs.

1995	WAS	N	3	C
1996		6	C
2 yrs.	9 games		

Corey Raymond
RAYMOND, COREY
B. Sep. 28, 1969, New Iberia, LA
Louisiana State 5'11" 180 lbs.

1992	NYG	N	1	CB
1993		16	S
1994		16	CB
1995	DET	N	16	CB
1996		13	CB
5 yrs.	62 games		

Rick Razzano
RAZZANO, RICK ANTHONY
B. Nov. 15, 1955, New Castle, PA
Virginia Tech 5'11" 227 lbs.

1980	CIN	N	14	LB
1981		16	LB
1982		9	LB
1983		16	LB
1984		10	LB
5 yrs.	65 games		

Kevin Reach
REACH, KEVIN
B. Oct. 24, 1963
Utah 6'3" 270 lbs.

| 1987 | SF | N | 3 | G |

Russ Reader
READER, RUSSELL B.
B. 1920
Michigan State 6'0" 185 lbs.

| 1947 | CHIB | N | 2 | HB |

Ike Readon
READON, ISAAC
B. May 16, 1963, Miami, FL
Hampton Institute 6'0" 273 lbs.

| 1987 | MIA | N | 3 | NT |

Ed Reagan
REAGAN, EDWARD
B. Jul. 23, 1905
D. Aug., 1980
None

| 1926 | BKN | N | 1 | T |

Frank Reagan
REAGAN, FRANCIS XAVIER
B. Jul. 28, 1919, Philadelphia, PA
D. Nov. 20, 1972, Philadelphia, PA
Pennsylvania 5'11" 182 lbs.

1941	NYG	N	5	FB, DB
1946		6	FB, DB
1947		10	QB, DB
1948		11	DB
1949	PHI	N	12	DB
1950		12	HB, DB
1951		12	DB
7 yrs.	68 games		

Chuck Ream
REAM, CHARLES DANIEL
B. Dec. 12, 1913, Youngstown, OH
Ohio State 6'2" 225 lbs.

| 1938 | CLE | N | 9 | T, E |

Tommy Reamon
REAMON, THOMAS WAVERLY
B. Mar. 12, 1952, Virgilina, VA
Missouri 5'10" 192 lbs.

| 1976 | KC | N | 11 | RB |

Kerry Reardon
REARDON, KERRY EDWARD
B. May 6, 1949, Kansas City, MO
Iowa 5'11" 180 lbs.

1971	KC	N	6	CB
1972		7	CB
1973		12	CB
1974		11	DB
1975		9	S
1976		14	S, CB
6 yrs.	59 games		

Gary Reasons
REASONS, GARY PHILLIP
B. Feb. 18, 1962, Crowley, TX
Northwestern State (Louisiana) 6'4" 234 lbs.

1984	NYG	N	16	LB
1985		16	LB
1986		16	LB
1987		10	LB
1988		16	LB
1989		16	LB
1990		16	LB
1991		16	LB
1992	CIN	N	12	LB
9 yrs.	134 games		

John Reaves
REAVES, THOMAS JOHNSON
B. Mar. 2, 1950, Anniston, AL
Florida 6'3" 209 lbs.

1972	PHI	N	11	QB
1973		1	QB
1974		4	QB
1975	CIN	N	7	QB
1976		3	QB
1977		9	QB
1978		9	QB
1981	HOU	N	5	QB
1987	TB	N	2	QB
9 yrs.	51 games		

Ken Reaves
REAVES, KENNETH MILTON
B. Oct. 29, 1944, Braddock, PA
Norfolk State 6'3" 206 lbs.

1966	ATL	N	14	DB
1967		14	DB
1968		14	DB
1969		14	CB
1970		14	CB
1971		14	CB
1972		14	CB
1973		14	CB
1974	NO	N	5	S
1974	STL	N	6	S
1975		14	S
1976		14	S
1977		14	S
12 yrs.	165 games		

Willard Reaves
REAVES, WILLARD
B. Aug. 17, 1959, Flagstaff, AZ
Northern Arizona 5'11" 200 lbs.

| 1989 | WAS | N | 1 | RB |

Willard Reaves continued

| 1989 | MIA | N | 2 | RB |
| 1 yr. | 3 games | | |

Dave Reavis
REAVIS, DAVID CRAIG
B. Jun. 19, 1950, Nashville, TN
Arkansas 6'5" 260 lbs.

1974	PIT	N	14	OT
1975		10	OT
1976	TB	N	2	OT
1977		14	OT
1978		16	OT, G
1979		16	OT
1980		16	OT
1981		12	OT
1982		7	OT
1983		15	OT
10 yrs.	122 games		

Rusty Rebowe
REBOWE, RUSTY
B. Jan. 17, 1956, Destrehan, LA
Nicholls State 5'10" 213 lbs.

| 1978 | NO | N | | LB |

Paul Rebseaman
REBSEAMAN, PAUL
B. 1905
Centenary 6'0" 188 lbs.

| 1927 | POT | N | 4 | C, G |

Dave Recher
RECHER, DAVID E.
B. Dec. 30, 1942, Chicago, IL
Iowa 6'1" 244 lbs.

1965	PHI	N	14	C
1966		10	C
1967		14	C
1968		8	C
4 yrs.	46 games		

Bert Rechichar
RECHICHAR, ALBERT DANIEL
B. Jul. 16, 1930, Belle Vernon, PA
Tennessee 6'1" 209 lbs.

1952	CLE	N	12	DB
1953	BAL	N	11	DB, K
1954		12	DB, K
1955		12	DB, K
1956		10	DB, K, P
1957		12	DB, K
1958		12	E, LB, K
1959		10	E, LB
1960	PIT	N	6	DB, K
1961	NY	A	2	DB
10 yrs.	99 games		

Ray Reckmark
RECKMARK, RAYMOND
B. Aug. 26, 1914
D. May 1, 1982, Emmaus, PA
Syracuse 6'0" 200 lbs.

1937	BKN	N	1	HB
1937	DET	N	1	HB
1 yr.	2 games		

Ron Rector
RECTOR, RONALD
B. May 29, 1944, Akron, OH
D. Jun. 29, 1968, Columbus, OH
Northwestern 6'0" 200 lbs.

1966	WAS	N	6	RB
1966	ATL	N	10	RB
1967		10	RB
2 yrs.	26 games		

720

Year	Team	Games	Pos.

Glen Redd
REDD, GLEN HERRSCHER
B. Jun. 17, 1958, Gden, UT
Brigham Young 6'1" 230 lbs.

Year	Team		Games	Pos.
1981	NO	N	16	LB
1983			16	LB
1984			16	LB
1985			16	LB
1986			4	LB
1986	IND	N	8	LB

5 yrs. 76 games

Barry Redden
REDDEN, BARRY
B. Jul. 21, 1960, Sarasota, FL
Richmond 5'10" 210 lbs.

Year	Team		Games	Pos.
1982	LARM	N	9	FB
1983			15	FB
1984			14	FB
1985			14	FB
1986			15	FB
1987	SD	N	12	FB
1988			8	FB
1989	CLE	N	16	FB
1990			5	FB

9 yrs. 108 games

Reggie Redding
REDDING, REGGIE
B. Sep. 22, 1968, Cincinnati, OH
Fullerton State 6'3" 298 lbs.

Year	Team		Games	Pos.
1991	ATL	N	13	OT
1992	NE	N	14	G

2 yrs. 27 games

Sheepy Redeen
REDEEN, ELMER
B. Feb., 1891
Deceased
None 185 lbs.

Year	Team		Games	Pos.
1921	MIN	A	4	E

Red Fang
RED FANG,
None

Year	Team		Games	Pos.
1922	OOR	N	2	C
1923			1	G

2 yrs. 3 games

Cornelius Redick
REDICK, CORNELIUS
B. Jan. 7, 1964, Los Angeles, CA
Fullerton State 185 lbs.

Year	Team		Games	Pos.
1987	GB	N	1	WR

Ruel Redinger
REDINGER, OTIS RUEL
B. Dec. 31, 1896
D. Sep. 26, 1969, Bay Village, OH
Penn State/Colgate 5'10" 185 lbs.

Year	Team		Games	Pos.
1925	CAN	N	6	HB

Gus Redman
REDMAN, AUGUSTUS
B. Dec., 1896, Massachusetts
Deceased
None 5'11" 170 lbs.

Year	Team		Games	Pos.
1921	MUN	A	2	HB, QB
1921	DAY	A	4	HB
1922	DAY	N	4	HB, FB
1924			6	QB

3 yrs. 16 games

Rick Redman
REDMAN, RICK C.
B. Mar. 7, 1943, Portland, OR

Rick Redman continued
Washington 5'11" 225 lbs.

Year	Team		Games	Pos.
1965	SD	A	10	LB
1966			14	LB
1967			14	LB
1968			1	LB
1969			14	LB
1970	SD	N	9	LB
1971			12	LB
1972			10	LB
1973			11	LB

9 yrs. 95 games

Anthony Redmond
REDMOND, KENDRICK ANTHONY
B. Apr. 9, 1971, Brewton, AL
Auburn 6'4" 308 lbs.

Year	Team		Games	Pos.
1994	ARI	N	6	G
1995			13	G, OT
1996			16	G

3 yrs. 35 games

Rudy Redmond
REDMOND, RUDY CRUZETTE
B. Aug. 25, 1947, Spokane, WA
Pacific 6'0" 190 lbs.

Year	Team		Games	Pos.
1969	ATL	N	14	CB
1970			14	CB
1971			8	CB
1972	DET	N	14	CB

4 yrs. 50 games

Tom Redmond
REDMOND, THOMAS BENJAMIN, JR.
B. Sep. 21, 1937, Atlanta, GA
Vanderbilt 6'5" 243 lbs.

Year	Team		Games	Pos.
1960	STL	N	12	DT
1961			10	G
1962			14	G
1963			9	DE
1964			14	DE
1965			1	DE

6 yrs. 60 games

Jarvis Redwine
REDWINE, JARVIS JOHN
B. May 16, 1957, Los Angeles, CA
Oregon State/Nebraska 5'10" 198 lbs.

Year	Team		Games	Pos.
1981	MIN	N	3	RB
1982			7	RB
1983			16	RB

3 yrs. 26 games

Lucian Reeberg
REEBERG, LUCIAN
B. Feb. 21, 1942, Bronx, NY
D. Jan. 31, 1964
Hampton Institute 6'4" 308 lbs.

Year	Team		Games	Pos.
1963	DET	N	14	OT

Beasley Reece
REECE, BEASLEY
B. Mar. 18, 1954, Waco, TX
North Texas State 6'1" 192 lbs.

Year	Team		Games	Pos.
1976	DAL	N	10	CB, S
1977	NYG	N	10	CB
1978			8	CB
1979			16	S
1980			16	S
1981			16	S
1982			9	S
1983			7	S
1983	TB	N	9	S
1984			16	S

9 yrs. 117 games

Danny Reece
REECE, DANIEL L.
B. Jan. 28, 1955, Wilmington, CA
Southern California 5'11" 190 lbs.

Year	Team		Games	Pos.
1976	TB	N	11	CB
1977			14	CB
1978			15	CB, S
1979			16	CB, S
1980			16	CB

5 yrs. 72 games

Don Reece
REECE, DONALD M. (Bull)
B. 1920
Missouri 6'1" 230 lbs.

Year	Team		Games	Pos.
1946	MIA	AA	13	T

Geoff Reece
REECE, GEOFFREY ROBERT
B. May 16, 1952, Everett, WA
Washington State 6'4" 247 lbs.

Year	Team		Games	Pos.
1976	LA	N	14	C
1977	SEA	N	3	C

2 yrs. 17 games

John Reece
REECE, JOHN
B. Jan. 24, 1971, Crowell, TX
Nebraska 6'0" 203 lbs.

Year	Team		Games	Pos.
1995	STL	N	5	CB

Alvin Reed
REED, ALVIN D.
B. Aug. 1, 1944, Kilgore, TX
Prairie View A&M 6'5" 232 lbs.

Year	Team		Games	Pos.
1967	HOU	A	14	TE
1968			14	TE
1969			14	TE
1970	HOU	N	13	TE
1971			14	TE
1972			14	TE
1973	WAS	N	5	TE
1974			14	TE
1975			14	TE

9 yrs. 116 games

Andre Reed
REED, ANDRE DARNELL
B. Jan. 29, 1964, Allentown, PA
Kutztown State 6'0" 188 lbs.

Year	Team		Games	Pos.
1985	BUF	N	16	WR
1986			15	WR
1987			12	WR
1988			15	WR
1989			16	WR
1990			16	WR
1991			16	WR
1992			15	WR
1993			16	WR
1994			16	WR
1995			6	WR
1996			16	WR

12 yrs. 175 games

Ben Reed
REED, H. BENTON
B. May 7, 1963, Baton Rouge, LA
Mississippi 6'5" 265 lbs.

Year	Team		Games	Pos.
1987	NE	N	3	DE

Bob Reed
REED, ROBERT
B. Nov. 14, 1939, New Orleans, LA
Pacific 5'11" 187 lbs.

Year	Team		Games	Pos.
1962	MIN	N	6	HB
1963			10	HB

2 yrs. 16 games

Bob Reed
REED, ROBERT, SR.
B. Feb. 23, 1943, Bonham, TX
Tennessee State 6'1" 250 lbs.

Year	Team		Games	Pos.
1965	WAS	N	8	G

Carl Reed
REED, CARL
None 208 lbs.

Year	Team		Games	Pos.
1921	AKR	A	1	G

Dick Reed
REED, RICHARD
B. Dec. 14, 1900
D. Oct., 1968, Eugene, OR
Oregon 6'0" 180 lbs.

Year	Team		Games	Pos.
1926	LA	A	9	E, T

Doug Reed
REED, DOUGLAS
B. Jul. 16, 1960, San Diego, CA
San Diego State 6'3" 254 lbs.

Year	Team		Games	Pos.
1984	LARM	N	9	DE
1985			16	DE
1986			16	DE
1987			12	DE
1988			16	DE
1989			11	DE
1990			16	DE

7 yrs. 96 games

Frank Reed
REED, FRANK
B. May 13, 1954, Seattle, WA
Washington 5'11" 193 lbs.

Year	Team		Games	Pos.
1976	ATL	N	14	DB
1977			14	CB
1978			16	CB
1979			11	CB
1980			16	CB

5 yrs. 71 games

Henry Reed
REED, HENRY ELAX, JR.
B. Jan. 15, 1948, Detroit, MI
Weber State 6'3" 230 lbs.

Year	Team		Games	Pos.
1971	NYG	N	14	DE
1972			14	DE
1973			10	DE
1974			13	LB

4 yrs. 51 games

Jake Reed
REED, JAKE
B. Sep. 28, 1967, Covington, GA
Grambling State 6'3" 216 lbs.

Year	Team		Games	Pos.
1991	MIN	N	1	WR
1992			16	WR
1993			10	WR
1994			16	WR
1995			16	WR
1996			16	WR

6 yrs. 75 games

James Reed
REED, JAMES
B. Oct. 10, 1955, Corpus Christi, TX
California 6'2" 230 lbs.

Year	Team		Games	Pos.
1977	PHI	N	4	LB

Joe Reed
REED, JOSEPH BUTLER
B. Jan. 8, 1948, Newport, RI
Baylor/Mississippi State 6'1" 194 lbs.

Year	Team		Games	Pos.
1972	SF	N	9	QB
1973				QB

Year	Team		Games	Pos.

Joe Reed *continued*

Year	Team		Games	Pos.
1974			6	QB
1975	DET	N	10	QB
1976			13	QB
1977			3	QB
1978			1	QB
1979			2	QB
8 yrs.	50 games			

J.T. Reed
REED, JOSEPH T. (Rock)
B. 1915
Louisiana State 5'8" 173 lbs.

1937	CHIC	N	8	HB
1939			4	HB
2 yrs.	12 games			

Leo Reed
REED, LEO
B. 1940
Colorado State 6'4" 240 lbs.

1961	HOU	A	5	G
1961	DEN	A	4	OT
1 yr.	9 games			

Mark Reed
REED, MARK
B. Feb. 21, 1959, Moorhead, MN
Moorhead State 6'3" 200 lbs.

| 1983 | BAL | N | 1 | QB |

Max Reed
REED, J. MAXWELL
B. 1902
Deceased
Bucknell 5'8" 185 lbs.

1925	BUF	N	9	C, G
1926	FRA	N	13	C
1927			11	C, E
1928	NYG	N	3	G, C
1929	BUF	N	1	T
5 yrs.	37 games			

Mike Reed
REED, MICHAEL JEROME
B. Aug. 16, 1972, Wilmington, DE
Boston College 5'9" 177 lbs.

1995	CAR	N	1	DB
1996			2	DB
2 yrs.	3 games			

Oscar Reed
REED, OSCAR LEE
B. Mar. 24, 1944, Jonestown, MS
Colorado State 5'11" 222 lbs.

1968	MIN	N	7	RB
1969			14	RB
1970			12	RB
1971			13	RB
1972			14	RB
1973			12	RB
1974			7	RB
1975	ATL	N	7	RB
8 yrs.	86 games			

Smith Reed
REED, SMITH
B. Jun. 25, 1942, Vicksburg, MS
Alcorn State 6'0" 215 lbs.

1965	NYG	N	10	HB
1966			1	HB
2 yrs.	11 games			

Taft Reed
REED, TAFT
B. Jun. 12, 1942, Hattiesburg, MS

Taft Reed *continued*
Jackson State 6'2" 200 lbs.

| 1967 | PHI | N | 6 | DB |

Tony Reed
REED, TONY WAYNE
B. Mar. 30, 1955, San Francisco, CA
Colorado 5'11" 197 lbs.

1977	KC	N	14	RB
1978			16	RB
1979			11	RB
1980			15	RB
1981	DEN	N	15	RB
1982	LARI	N	9	RB
6 yrs.	80 games			

Dan Reeder
REEDER, DANIEL ROBERT
B. Mar. 18, 1961, Shamokin, PA
Boston College/Delaware 5'11" 235 lbs.

1986	PIT	N	11	RB
1987			2	RB
2 yrs.	13 games			

Archie Reese
REESE, ARCHIE RONALD BERNARD
B. Feb. 4, 1956, Mayesville, SC
Clemson 6'3" 270 lbs.

1978	SF	N	16	DE
1979			16	DE
1980			16	DT
1981			16	DT
1983	LARI	N	10	NT
5 yrs.	74 games			

Booker Reese
REESE, BOOKER TED
B. Sep. 20, 1959, Jacksonville, FL
Bethune-Cookman 6'6" 260 lbs.

1982	TB	N	7	DE
1983			16	DE
1984			1	DE
1984	LARM	N	9	DE
1985			2	DE
4 yrs.	35 games			

Dave Reese
REESE, DAVID E.
B. Nov. 19, 1892, Massillon, OH
D. Jun. 29, 1978, Dayton, OH
Denison 6'0" 176 lbs.

1920	DAY	A	8	E
1921			9	E
1922	DAY	N	8	E
1923			8	E
4 yrs.	33 games			

Don Reese
REESE, DONALD FRANCIS
B. Sep. 4, 1951, Mobile, AL
Jackson State 6'6" 254 lbs.

1974	MIA	N	13	DE, DT
1975			14	DE, DT
1976			14	DT, DE
1978	NO	N	14	DE
1979			16	DE
1980			12	DE
1981	SD	N	5	DE
7 yrs.	88 games			

Guy Reese
REESE, GUY P.
B. Sep. 22, 1939, Dallas, TX
Southern Methodist 6'5" 255 lbs.

| 1962 | DAL | N | 14 | DT |
| 1963 | | | 14 | DT |

Guy Reese *continued*

1964	BAL	N	14	DT
1965			13	DT
1966	ATL	N	2	DT
5 yrs.	57 games			

Hank Reese
REESE, HENRY L.
B. Oct. 24, 1909, Scranton, PA
D. Aug. 3, 1975
Temple 5'11" 214 lbs.

1933	NYG	N	11	C, G
1934			13	G
1935	PHI	N	11	C
1936			10	C
1937			11	C
1938			11	C
1939			5	C, G
7 yrs.	72 games			

Jerry Reese
REESE, JERRY
B. Jan. 7, 1955, New Orleans, LA
Oklahoma 6'3" 192 lbs.

1979	KC	N	7	S
1980			14	S
2 yrs.	21 games			

Jerry Reese
REESE, JERRY
B. Jul. 11, 1964, Hopkinsville, KY
Kentucky 6'2" 267 lbs.

| 1988 | PIT | N | 15 | NT, DE |

Ken Reese
REESE, KENNETH E.
B. 1922
Deceased
Alabama 5'11" 175 lbs.

| 1947 | DET | N | 5 | B |

Lloyd Reese
REESE, LLOYD M. (Bronko)
B. 1922
Deceased
Tennessee 6'2" 240 lbs.

| 1946 | CHIB | N | 3 | B |

Steve Reese
REESE, STEPHEN
B. Jan. 7, 1952, Columbus, GA
Louisville 6'2" 229 lbs.

1974	NYJ	N	12	LB
1975			12	LB
1976	TB	N	13	LB
3 yrs.	37 games			

Lew Reeve
REEVE, LEWIS
B. Oct. 16, 1890
D. May 14, 1960
Iowa State 5'10" 193 lbs.

| 1920 | CHIT | A | 3 | T |

Bryan Reeves
REEVES, BRYAN
B. Jul. 10, 1970, Los Angeles, CA
Arizona State/Nevada-Reno 5'11" 185 lbs.*

1994	ARI	N	14	WR
1995			7	WR
2 yrs.	21 games			

Carl Reeves
REEVES, CARL

Carl Reeves *continued*
B. Dec. 17, 1971, Durham, NC
North Carolina State 6'4" 265 lbs.

| 1996 | CHI | N | 5 | DE |

Dan Reeves
REEVES, DANIEL EDWARD
B. Jan. 19, 1944, Rome, GA
South Carolina 6'1" 201 lbs.

1965	DAL	N	13	HB
1966			14	HB
1967			14	RB
1968			4	RB
1969			13	RB
1970			14	RB
1971			14	RB
1972			14	RB
8 yrs.	100 games			

Ken Reeves
REEVES, KEN
B. Oct. 4, 1961, Pittsburg, TX
Texas A&M 6'5" 272 lbs.

1985	PHI	N	15	OT, G
1986			15	OT, G
1987			10	OT, G
1988			15	OT, G
1989			14	OT, G
1990	CLE	N	16	OT
6 yrs.	85 games			

Marion Reeves
REEVES, MARION
B. Feb. 23, 1952, Lexington, SC
Clemson 6'1" 195 lbs.

| 1974 | PHI | N | 14 | CB |

Roy Reeves
REEVES, ROY
B. Feb. 8, 1946, Americus, GA
South Carolina 5'11" 182 lbs.

| 1969 | BUF | A | 2 | WR |

Walter Reeves
REEVES, WALTER JAMES
B. Dec. 15, 1965, Eufaula, AL
Auburn 6'4" 255 lbs.

1989	PHX	N	16	TE
1990			16	TE
1991			16	TE
1992			16	TE
1993			16	TE
1994	CLE	N	5	TE
1995			5	TE
1996	SD	N	9	TE
8 yrs.	98 games			

Jim Regan
REGAN, JAMES
Still 172 lbs.

| 1925 | COL | N | 3 | QB, FB |

Shawn Regent
REGENT, SHAWN
B. Apr. 14, 1963
Boston College 6'5" 280 lbs.

| 1987 | LARI | N | 3 | C |

John Reger
REGER, JOHN GEORGE
B. Sep. 11, 1931, Wheeling, WV
Pittsburgh 6'0" 225 lbs.

1955	PIT	N	12	G, LB
1956			12	LB
1957			13	LB
1958			12	LB

Year	Team	Games	Pos.

John Reger *continued*

Year	Team		Games	Pos.
1959			12	LB
1960			12	LB
1961			14	LB
1962			9	LB
1963			9	LB
1964	WAS	N	14	LB
1965			12	LB
1966			14	LB
12 yrs.	145 games			

Tom Regner
REGNER, THOMAS E.
B. Apr. 19, 1944, Kenosha, WI
Notre Dame 6'1" 255 lbs.

1967	HOU	A	14	G
1968			14	G
1969			14	G
1970	HOU	N	3	G
1971			8	G
1972			14	G
6 yrs.	67 games			

Pete Regnier
REGNIER, PETER M. (Doc)
B. Sep., 1896, Minnesota
Deceased
Minnesota 170 lbs.

1921	MIN	A	4	HB
1922	GB	N	5	HB
2 yrs.	9 games			

Moses Regular
REGULAR, MOSES
B. Oct. 30, 1971, Kissimmee, FL
Missouri Valley 6'3" 255 lbs.

1996	NYG	N	3	LB

Steve Rehage
REHAGE, STEPHEN
B. Nov. 6, 1963, New Orleans, LA
Louisiana State 6'1" 190 lbs.

1987	NYG	N	3	S

Tom Rehder
REHDER, THOMAS BERNARD, II
B. Jan. 27, 1965, Sacramento, CA
Notre Dame 6'7" 282 lbs.

1988	NE	N	16	OT
1989			16	OT
1990	NYG	N	8	OT, G
3 yrs.	40 games			

Milt Rehnquist
REHNQUIST, MILTON
B. 1897
Deceased
Bethany (Kansas) 6'0" 229 lbs.

1924	KC	N	2	C, G
1925			6	G
1925	CLE	N	3	G
1926	KC	N	9	G, T
1927	CLE	N	13	G, C
1928	PRO	N	11	G, C
1929			7	C
1930			10	G
1931			2	G
1931	NYG	N	8	G
1932	BOS	N	1	G
9 yrs.	72 games			

Frank Reich
REICH, FRANK MICHAEL
B. Dec. 4, 1961, Freeport, NY
Maryland 6'3" 209 lbs.

1985	BUF	N	1	QB

Frank Reich *continued*

Year	Team		Games	Pos.
1986			3	QB
1988			3	QB
1989			7	QB
1990			16	QB
1991			16	QB
1992			16	QB
1993			15	QB
1994			16	QB
1995	CAR	N	3	QB
1996	NYJ	N	11	QB
11 yrs.	107 games			

Bill Reichardt
REICHARDT, WILLIAM JOHN
B. Jun. 24, 1930, Iowa City, IA
Iowa 5'11" 210 lbs.

1952	GB	N	12	FB

Lou Reichel
REICHEL, LOUIS
B. 1902
Deceased
Butler 5'11" 180 lbs.

1926	COL	N	7	C

Mike Reichenbach
REICHENBACH, MIKE
B. Sep. 14, 1961, Fort Meade, MD
East Stroudsburg 6'2" 236 lbs.

1984	PHI	N	12	LB
1985			16	LB
1986			16	LB
1987			11	LB
1988			16	LB
1989			16	LB
1990	MIA	N	16	LB
1991			16	LB
8 yrs.	119 games			

Dick Reichle
REICHLE, RICHARD WENDELL
B. Nov. 23, 1896, Lincoln, IL
D. Jun. 13, 1967, St. Louis, MO
Illinois 6'0" 175 lbs.

1923	MIL	N	6	E

Chuck Reichow
REICHOW, CHARLES
B. Mar. 19, 1901
D. Mar. 29, 1993, Peoria, AZ
St. Thomas (Minnesota) 5'9" 183 lbs.

1925	MIL	N	2	FB, QB
1926	RAC	N	5	FB, HB
2 yrs.	7 games			

Jerry Reichow
REICHOW, GARET NEAL
B. May 19, 1934, Decorah, IA
Iowa 6'2" 217 lbs.

1956	DET	N	8	QB
1957			12	E, QB
1959			9	QB, E
1960	PHI	N	12	E, B
1961	MIN	N	14	HB, OE
1962			12	OE
1963			14	OE
1964			14	OE
8 yrs.	95 games			

Alan Reid
REID, ALAN DEWITT
B. Sep. 6, 1960, Wurzburg, Germany
Texas Christian/Minnesota 5'8" 197 lbs.

1987	PHI	N	1	RB

Andy Reid
REID, ANDREW
B. Feb. 26, 1954, Hamilton, OH
Georgia 6'0" 195 lbs.

1976	BUF	N	1	RB

Bill Reid
REID, WILLIAM JOHN
B. May 2, 1952, Long Beach, CA
Stanford 6'1" 242 lbs.

1975	SF	N	13	C

Floyd Reid
REID, FLOYD (Breezy)
B. Sep. 4, 1925, Hamilton, OH
D. May 15, 1994, Cincinnati, OH
Georgia 5'10" 187 lbs.

1950	GB	N	11	HB
1951			12	HB
1952			12	HB
1953			12	HB
1954			12	HB
1955			12	HB
1956			7	HB
7 yrs.	78 games			

Jim Reid
REID, JAMES JARRETT
B. Feb. 13, 1971, Newport News, VA
Virginia 6'6" 306 lbs.

1995	HOU	N	6	OT

Joe Reid
REID, JOSEPH
B. 1930
Louisiana State 6'3" 225 lbs.

1951	LA	N	11	C
1952	DAL	N	11	C, G
2 yrs.	22 games			

Michael Reid
REID, MICHAEL EDWARD
B. Jun. 25, 1964, Albany, GA
Wisconsin 6'7" 228 lbs.

1987	ATL	N	11	LB
1988			16	LB
1989			16	LB
1990			6	LB
1991			3	LB
1992			16	LB
6 yrs.	68 games			

Mike Reid
REID, MICHAEL BARRY
B. May 24, 1947, Altoona, PA
Penn State 6'3" 255 lbs.

1970	CIN	N	9	DT
1971			14	DT
1972			14	DT
1973			13	DT
1974			14	DT
5 yrs.	64 games			

Mike Reid
REID, MIKE
B. Nov. 24, 1970, Spartanburg, SC
North Carolina State 6'1" 218 lbs.

1993	PHI	N	9	S
1994			3	S
2 yrs.	12 games			

Bob Reifsnyder
REIFSNYDER, ROBERT H.
B. Jun. 18, 1937
Navy 6'2" 255 lbs.

1960	NY	A		DE

Bob Reifsnyder *continued*

Year	Team		Games	Pos.
1961			2	DE
2 yrs.	2 games			

George Reihner
REIHNER, GEORGE
B. Apr. 27, 1955, Pittsburgh, PA
Penn State 6'4" 263 lbs.

1977	HOU	N	13	G
1978			9	G
1979			2	G
1982			3	G
4 yrs.	27 games			

Dameon Reilly
REILLY, DAMEON
B. May 10, 1963
Rhode Island 5'11" 180 lbs.

1987	MIA	N	3	WR

Jim Reilly
REILLY, JAMES C.
B. Feb. 8, 1948, Yonkers, NY
Notre Dame 6'2" 250 lbs.

1970	BUF	N	13	G
1971			14	G
2 yrs.	27 games			

Kevin Reilly
REILLY, KEVIN PATRICK
B. Apr. 10, 1951, Wilmington, DE
Villanova 6'2" 220 lbs.

1973	PHI	N	7	LB
1974			14	LB
1975	NE	N	4	LB
3 yrs.	25 games			

Mike Reilly
REILLY, CHARLES MICHAEL
B. Mar. 27, 1942, Dubuque, IA
Iowa 6'2" 230 lbs.

1964	CHI	N	8	LB
1965			14	LB
1966			14	LB
1967			14	LB
1968			14	LB
1969	MIN	N	10	LB
6 yrs.	74 games			

Mike Reilly
REILLY, MICHAEL DENNIS
B. Feb. 14, 1959, Miami, FL
Oklahoma 6'4" 219 lbs.

1982	LARM	N	9	LB

Bruce Reimers
REIMERS, BRUCE MICHAEL
B. Sep. 18, 1960, Algona, IA
Iowa State 6'7" 285 lbs.

1984	CIN	N	15	OT, G
1985			14	OT
1986			16	OT
1987			10	OT
1988			16	OT
1989			15	OT
1990			12	OT
1991			10	G
1992	TB	N	16	G
1993			11	G
10 yrs.	135 games			

Mike Reinfeldt
REINFELDT, MICHAEL RAY
B. May 6, 1953, Baraboo, WI
Wisconsin-Milwaukee 6'2" 192 lbs.

1976	OAK	N	2	S

Year	Team		Games	Pos.

Mike Reinfeldt continued

Year	Team		Games	Pos.
1976	HOU	N	11	S
1977			14	S
1978			16	S
1979			16	S
1980			16	S
1981			16	S
1982			9	S
1983			4	S
8 yrs.	104 games			

Billy Reinhard
REINHARD, CARL WILLIAM
B. May 17, 1922, Los Angeles, CA
California 5'10" 168 lbs.

1947	LA	AA	8	B
1948			14	B
2 yrs.	22 games			

Bob Reinhard
REINHARD, ROBERT RICHARD
B. Oct. 17, 1920, Hollywood, CA
California 6'4" 234 lbs.

1946	LA	AA	14	T
1947			14	T, B
1948			14	T, B
1949			12	T
1950	LA	N	12	T
5 yrs.	66 games			

Earl Reiser
REISER, EARL
B. 1899
Deceased
None 160 lbs.

1923	LOU	N	2	HB

Bill Reissig
REISSIG, WILLIAM
B. 1915
Fort Hays State 6'0" 195 lbs.

1938	BKN	N	11	HB
1939			4	E
2 yrs.	15 games			

Albie Reisz
REISZ, ALBERT G.
B. Nov. 29, 1917, Lorain, OH
D. May 1, 1985, New Orleans, LA
Southeastern Louisiana 5'10" 174 lbs.

1944	CLE	N	10	HB
1945			10	QB
1946	LA	N	2	B
1947	BUF	AA	13	B
4 yrs.	35 games			

Peck Reiter
REITER, HERBERT G.
B. Feb. 15, 1899, Dayton, OH
D. May 15, 1968, Sherman Oaks, CA
Miami (Ohio)/Marietta 5'9" 170 lbs.

1926	DAY	N	6	G
1927			2	G
2 yrs.	8 games			

Johnny Rembert
REMBERT, JOHNNY
B. Jan. 19, 1961, Hollandale, MS
Clemson 6'3" 234 lbs.

1983	NE	N	15	LB
1984			7	LB
1985			16	LB
1986			16	LB
1987			11	LB
1988			16	LB
1989			16	LB
1990			5	LB

Johnny Rembert continued

1991			12	LB
1992			12	LB
10 yrs.	126 games			

Reggie Rembert
REMBERT, REGGIE
B. Dec. 25, 1966, Okeechobee, FL
West Virginia 6'5" 200 lbs.

1991	CIN	N	16	WR
1992			9	WR
1993			3	WR
3 yrs.	28 games			

Bill Remington
REMINGTON, JOSEPH WILLIAM
B. 1921
Washington State 6'1" 185 lbs.

1946	SF	AA	9	C

Dennis Remmert
REMMERT, DENNIS
B. 1939
Iowa State 6'3" 215 lbs.

1960	BUF			LB

Roger Remo
REMO, ROGER
B. Aug. 7, 1964
Syracuse 6'3" 237 lbs.

1987	IND	N	3	LB

Dan Remsberg
REMSBERG, DANIEL LLOYD
B. Apr. 7, 1962, Temple, TX
Abilene Christian 6'6" 275 lbs.

1986	DEN	N	16	G, OT
1987			5	OT
2 yrs.	21 games			

Dean Renfro
RENFRO, WELDON EUGENE
B. Jun. 15, 1932, Whitesboro, TX
North Texas State 5'11" 180 lbs.

1955	BAL	N	7	HB

Dick Renfro
RENFRO, GOLIE RICHARD
B. Jan. 25, 1919, Fort Worth, TX
Washington State 5'10" 200 lbs.

1946	SF	AA	3	FB

Leonard Renfro
RENFRO, LEONARD
B. Jun. 29, 1970, Detroit, MI
Colorado 6'2" 291 lbs.

1993	PHI	N	14	DT
1994			9	DT
2 yrs.	23 games			

Mel Renfro
RENFRO, MELVIN LACY
B. Dec. 30, 1941, Houston, TX
Oregon 6'0" 191 lbs.

1964	DAL	N	14	DB
1965			14	DB
1966			11	DB, HB
1967			9	DB
1968			14	DB
1969			14	CB, S
1970			14	CB, S
1971			14	CB
1972			14	CB
1973			14	CB
1974			11	CB

Mel Renfro continued

1975			11	CB
1976			9	CB
1977			11	CB
14 yrs.	174 games			

Mike Renfro
RENFRO, MICHAEL ROY
B. Jun. 19, 1955, Fort Worth, TX
Texas Christian 6'0" 186 lbs.

1978	HOU	N	14	WR
1979			15	WR
1980			16	WR
1981			12	WR
1982			9	WR
1983			9	WR
1984	DAL		16	WR
1985			16	WR
1986			12	WR
1987			14	WR
10 yrs.	133 games			

Ray Renfro
RENFRO, RAY AUSTIN
B. Nov. 7, 1929, Whitesboro, TX
D. Aug. 4, 1997, Fort Worth, TX
North Texas State 6'1" 190 lbs.

1952	CLE	N	11	HB
1953			12	HB
1954			7	HB
1955			12	HB
1956			12	HB
1957			12	HB
1958			12	HB
1959			12	HB
1960			12	HB
1961			14	HB
1962			14	HB
1963				HB
12 yrs.	130 games			

Will Renfro
RENFRO, WILLIAM ELLIS
B. Mar. 15, 1932, Memphis, TN
Memphis State 6'5" 233 lbs.

1957	WAS	N	11	T
1958			12	T
1959			11	G, T
1960	PIT	N	12	DT, DE
1961	PHI	N	14	DE
5 yrs.	60 games			

Mike Rengel
RENGEL, MICHAEL JAMES
B. Dec. 1, 1946, Minneapolis, MN
Air Force/Minnesota/Hawaii 6'5" 260 lbs.

1969	NO	N	5	OT

Neil Rengel
RENGEL, NEIL
B. Apr. 9, 1906
St. Cloud/Minnesota/Davis & Elkins 5'9" 205 lbs.

1930	FRA	N	13	FB, HB, E

Bobby Renn
RENN, ROBERT
B. May 25, 1934, Henderson, NC
Florida State 6'0" 180 lbs.

1961	NY	N	12	HB

Terry Rennaker
RENNAKER, TERRY LEWIS
B. May 1, 1958, Newport, RI
Stanford 6'6" 225 lbs.

1980	SEA	N	15	LB

Bill Renner
RENNER, WILLIAM ARTHUR, JR.
B. May 23, 1959, Quantico, VA
Virginia Tech 6'0" 198 lbs.

1986	GB	N	3	P
1987			3	P
2 yrs.	6 games			

Jess Reno
RENO, JESS H.
B. Sep., 1890
Deceased
None 5'9" 160 lbs.

1920	MUN	A	1	E
1922	EVA	N	2	E
2 yrs.	3 games			

Caesar Rentie
RENTIE, CAESAR HARRIS
B. Nov. 10, 1964, Hartshorne, OK
Oklahoma 6'3" 291 lbs.

1988	CHI	N	5	OT

Pug Rentner
RENTNER, ERNEST J.
B. Sep. 18, 1910, Joliet, IL
D. Aug. 24, 1978, Glencoe, IL
Northwestern 6'1" 187 lbs.

1934	BOS	N	10	HB
1935			11	HB, QB
1936			12	HB, FB, QB
1937	CHIB		10	HB, FB
4 yrs.	43 games			

Larry Rentz
RENTZ, RALPH LAWRENCE
B. Aug. 1, 1947, Miami, FL
Florida 6'1" 170 lbs.

1969	SD	A	2	RB

Lance Rentzel
RENTZEL, THOMAS LANCE
B. Oct. 14, 1943, Flushing, NY
Oklahoma 6'2" 203 lbs.

1965	MIN	N	11	HB
1966			9	HB, FL
1967	DAL		14	FL, OE
1968			14	FL, OE
1969			14	WR
1970			11	WR
1971	LA	N	14	WR
1972			14	WR
1974			14	WR
9 yrs.	115 games			

Jay Repko
REPKO, JAY KEVIN
B. Jun. 12, 1958, Pottstown, PA
Pennsylvania/Ursinus 6'3" 240 lbs.

1987	PHI	N	3	TE

Joe Repko
REPKO, JOSEPH
B. Mar. 15, 1921, Lansford, PA
Seton Hall/Boston College 6'0" 236 lbs.

1946	PIT	N	9	T
1947			8	T
1948	LA	N	12	T
1949			8	T
4 yrs.	37 games			

Mike Reppond
REPPOND, MICHAEL GENE
B. Nov. 24, 1951, San Diego, CA
Arkansas 6'0" 180 lbs.

1973	CHI	N	3	WR

Year	Team	Games	Pos.

Glenn Ressler
RESSLER, GLENN EMANUEL
B. May 21, 1943, Danville, PA
Penn State 6'3" 247 lbs.

Year	Team		Games	Pos.
1965	**BAL**	N	12	G, C
1966			13	C, OT
1967			14	G
1968			14	G
1969			8	G
1970			13	G
1971			14	G
1972			9	G
1973			14	G
1974				G
10 yrs.	111 games			

Joe Restic
RESTIC, JOSEPH WILLIAM, SR.
B. Jul. 21, 1927, Hastings, PA
Villanova 6'2" 180 lbs.

Year	Team		Games	Pos.
1952	**PHI**	N	3	E

Pete Retzlaff
RETZLAFF, PALMER EDWARD
(The Baron)
B. Aug. 21, 1932, Ellendale, ND
Ellendale State/South Dakota State 6'1" 211 lbs.

Year	Team		Games	Pos.
1956	**PHI**	N	10	FL
1957			12	FL
1958			12	FL
1959			10	FL
1960			12	FL
1961			14	OE
1962			8	OE
1963			14	OE
1964			12	OE
1965			14	OE
1966			14	TE
11 yrs.	132 games			

Vic Reuter
REUTER, VICTOR
B. 1908
Lafayette 6'0" 215 lbs.

Year	Team		Games	Pos.
1932	**SI**	N	1	C

Randy Reutershan
REUTERSHAN, RANDY
B. Jun. 30, 1955, New York, NY
Pittsburgh 5'10" 182 lbs.

Year	Team		Games	Pos.
1978	**PIT**	N	11	WR, CB

Ray Reutt
REUTT, RAYMOND
B. 1917
Virginia Military Institute 6'0" 195 lbs.

Year	Team		Games	Pos.
1943	**P-P**	N	1	E

Fuad Reveiz
REVEIZ, FUAD
B. Feb. 24, 1963, Bogota, Colombia
Tennessee 5'11" 220 lbs.

Year	Team		Games	Pos.
1985	**MIA**	N	16	K
1986			16	K
1987			11	K
1988			11	K
1990	**SD**	N	4	K
1990	**MIN**	N	9	K
1991			16	K
1992			16	K
1993			16	K
1994			16	K
1995			16	K
10 yrs.	147 games			

Freeman Rexer
REXER, FREEMAN
B. Jun. 18, 1918, Houston, TX
Tulane 6'1" 211 lbs.

Year	Team		Games	Pos.
1943	**CHIC**	N	10	E
1944	**BOS**	N	1	E
1944	**DET**	N	6	E
1945	**CHIC**	N	1	E
3 yrs.	18 games			

Al Reynolds
REYNOLDS, ALLAN F.
B. Feb. 15, 1938, Winchester, KS
Tarkio 6'3" 238 lbs.

Year	Team		Games	Pos.
1960	**DAL**	A	14	G
1961			14	G
1962			14	G
1963	**KC**	A	9	G
1964			13	G
1965			14	G
1966			14	G
1967			14	G
8 yrs.	106 games			

Bill Reynolds
REYNOLDS, WILLIAM
B. Oct. 10, 1918, Chicago, IL
Mississippi 5'8" 183 lbs.

Year	Team		Games	Pos.
1944	**BKN**	N	4	HB
1945	**CHIC**	N	9	HB
2 yrs.	13 games			

Billy Reynolds
REYNOLDS, WILLIAM DEAN
B. Jul. 20, 1932, St. Mary's, VA
Pittsburgh 5'10" 195 lbs.

Year	Team		Games	Pos.
1953	**CLE**	N	12	HB
1954			12	HB
1957			12	HB
1958	**PIT**	N	12	HB
1960	**OAK**	A		HB
5 yrs.	48 games			

Bob Reynolds
REYNOLDS, ROBERT LOUIS
B. Jan. 22, 1939, Nashville, TN
D. Oct. 10, 1996, Naperville, IL
Bowling Green 6'6" 264 lbs.

Year	Team		Games	Pos.
1963	**STL**	N	14	OT
1964			10	OT
1965			14	OT
1966			14	OT
1967			13	OT
1968			14	OT
1969			14	OT
1970			14	OT
1971			14	OT
1972	**NE**	N	12	OT
1973			8	OT
1973	**STL**	N	1	OT
11 yrs.	142 games			

Bob Reynolds
REYNOLDS, ROBERT O'DELL
B. Mar. 30, 1914, Norris, OK
D. Feb. 9, 1994, San Rafael, CA
Stanford 6'4" 221 lbs.

Year	Team		Games	Pos.
1937	**DET**	N	9	T
1938			11	T
2 yrs.	20 games			

Chuck Reynolds
REYNOLDS, CHARLES R.
B. Oct. 5, 1946, Fort Worth, TX
Texas Christian/Tulsa 6'2" 240 lbs.

Year	Team		Games	Pos.
1969	**CLE**	N	11	C
1970			14	
2 yrs.	25 games			

Ed Reynolds
REYNOLDS, EDWARD RANNELL
B. Sep. 23, 1961, Stuttgart, Germany
Virginia 6'5" 238 lbs.

Year	Team		Games	Pos.
1983	**NE**	N	12	LB
1984			16	LB
1985			12	LB
1986			16	LB
1987			12	LB
1988			14	LB
1989			16	LB
1990			12	LB
1991			9	LB
1992	**NYG**	N	16	LB
10 yrs.	135 games			

Homer Reynolds
REYNOLDS, HOMER
B. Nov. 20, 1910
D. Jul., 1981, Dallas, TX
Tulsa 5'10" 190 lbs.

Year	Team		Games	Pos.
1934	**C-S**	N	3	G

Jack Reynolds
REYNOLDS, JOHN SUMNER
(Hacksaw)
B. Nov. 22, 1947, Cincinnati, OH
Tennessee 6'1" 232 lbs.

Year	Team		Games	Pos.
1970	**LA**	N	14	LB
1971			4	LB
1972			14	LB
1973			14	LB
1974			14	LB
1975			14	LB
1976			14	LB
1977			9	LB
1978			16	LB
1979			16	LB
1980			16	LB
1981	**SF**	N	16	LB
1982			9	LB
1983			13	LB
1984			15	LB
15 yrs.	198 games			

Jerry Reynolds
REYNOLDS, JERRY BRADFORD
B. Apr. 2, 1970, Fort Thomas, KY
Nevada-Las Vegas 6'6" 315 lbs.

Year	Team		Games	Pos.
1994	**DAL**	N	1	OT
1996	**NYG**	N	8	OT
2 yrs.	9 games			

Jim Reynolds
REYNOLDS, JAMES G.
B. 1920
Auburn 6'1" 190 lbs.

Year	Team		Games	Pos.
1946	**MIA**	AA	7	FB

Jim Reynolds
REYNOLDS, JAMES STEPHEN
B. Aug. 21, 1922, Bethany, OK
Deceased
Oklahoma State 6'0" 193 lbs.

Year	Team		Games	Pos.
1946	**PIT**	N	2	HB

John Reynolds
REYNOLDS, JOHN D. (Tex)
B. 1914
Deceased
Baylor 5'10" 185 lbs.

Year	Team		Games	Pos.
1937	**CHIC**	N	5	C

M.C. Reynolds
REYNOLDS, MACK CHARLES
(Chief)
B. Feb. 11, 1935, Mansfield, LA

M.C. Reynolds *continued*
D. Sep. 8, 1991, Shreveport, LA
Louisiana State 6'0" 193 lbs.

Year	Team		Games	Pos.
1958	**CHIC**	N	11	QB
1959			7	QB
1960	**WAS**	N	8	QB
1961	**BUF**	A	12	QB
1962	**OAK**	A	1	QB
5 yrs.	39 games			

Owen Reynolds
REYNOLDS, OWEN GASTON
B. Jan. 12, 1900, Douglasville, GA
D. Mar. 11, 1984, Ann Arbor, MI
Georgia 6'3" 212 lbs.

Year	Team		Games	Pos.
1925	**NYG**	N	9	E, FB
1926	**BKN**	N	9	E, FB
2 yrs.	18 games			

Quentin Reynolds
REYNOLDS, QUENTIN JAMES
(Red)
B. Apr. 11, 1902, Brooklyn, NY
D. Mar. 17, 1965
Brown 6'1" 205 lbs.

Year	Team		Games	Pos.
1926	**BKN**	N	4	G, T

Ricky Reynolds
REYNOLDS, DERRICK SCOTT
B. Jan. 19, 1965, Sacramento, CA
Washington State 5'11" 182 lbs.

Year	Team		Games	Pos.
1987	**TB**	N	12	CB
1988			16	CB
1989			16	CB, S
1990			15	CB, S
1991			16	CB
1992			16	CB
1993			14	CB
1994	**NE**	N	15	CB
1995			16	CB
1996			12	CB
10 yrs.	148 games			

Tom Reynolds
REYNOLDS, RAOUL THOMAS, JR.
B. Apr. 11, 1949, Pasadena, CA
San Diego State 6'3" 200 lbs.

Year	Team		Games	Pos.
1972	**NE**	N	14	WR
1973	**CHI**	N	9	WR
2 yrs.	23 games			

Floyd Rhea
RHEA, FLOYD MACK (Scrap Iron)
B. Sep. 21, 1920, Rhea, AR
Oregon 6'0" 218 lbs.

Year	Team		Games	Pos.
1943	**CHIC**	N	1	G
1944	**BKN**	N	8	G
1945	**BOS**	N	8	G
3 yrs.	17 games			

Hughie Rhea
RHEA, HUGH
B. 1910
D. Oct. 18, 1973
Nebraska 6'3" 225 lbs.

Year	Team		Games	Pos.
1933	**BKN**	N	2	G

Steve Rhem
RHEM, STEVE
B. Nov. 9, 1971, Ocala, FL
Minnesota 6'2" 212 lbs.

Year	Team		Games	Pos.
1994	**NO**	N	7	WR
1995			5	WR
2 yrs.	12 games			

Year	Team	Games	Pos.

Elmer Rhenstrom
RHENSTROM, ELMER GUSTAF (Swede)
B. Aug. 18, 1895
D. Dec. 27, 1967, Ontario, CA
Beloit 5'10" 185 lbs.

Year	Team		Games	Pos.
1922	RAC	N	5	E

Errict Rhett
RHETT, ERRICT UNDRA
B. Dec. 11, 1970, Pembroke Pines, FL
Florida 5'11" 210 lbs.

Year	Team		Games	Pos.
1994	TB	N	16	RB
1995			16	RB
1996			9	RB
3 yrs.	41 games			

Jay Rhodemyre
RHODEMYRE, JAY E.
B. Dec. 16, 1922, Ashland, KY
D. Sep., 1968
Kentucky 6'1" 210 lbs.

Year	Team		Games	Pos.
1948	GB	N	9	C
1949			12	C
1951			12	C
1952			12	C
4 yrs.	45 games			

Bruce Rhodes
RHODES, BRUCE
B. Apr. 17, 1952, San Francisco, CA
San Francisco State 6'0" 189 lbs.

Year	Team		Games	Pos.
1976	SF	N	14	S
1978	DET	N	15	S
2 yrs.	29 games			

Danny Rhodes
RHODES, DANNY BOYIET
B. Mar. 18, 1951, Lake Jackson, TX
Arkansas 6'2" 220 lbs.

Year	Team		Games	Pos.
1974	BAL	N	14	LB

Don Rhodes
RHODES, DONALD N.
B. Jul. 9, 1909
D. Oct., 1968
Washington & Jefferson 6'2" 225 lbs.

Year	Team		Games	Pos.
1933	PIT	N	7	T

Ray Rhodes
RHODES, RAYMOND EARL
B. Oct. 20, 1950, Mexia, TX
Texas Christian/Tulsa 5'11" 185 lbs.

Year	Team		Games	Pos.
1974	NYG	N	14	WR
1975			14	WR
1976			13	WR
1977			14	CB
1978			13	CB
1979			15	CB
1980	SF	N	14	CB
7 yrs.	97 games			

Jerry Rhome
RHOME, GERALD BYRON
B. Mar. 6, 1942, Dallas, TX
Southern Methodist/Tulsa 6'0" 186 lbs.

Year	Team		Games	Pos.
1965	DAL	N	11	QB
1966			7	QB
1967			14	QB
1969	CLE	N	14	QB
1970	HOU	N	13	QB
1971	LA	N	14	QB
6 yrs.	73 games			

Earnie Rhone
RHONE, EARNEST CALVIN

Earnie Rhone continued
B. Aug. 20, 1953, Ashdown, AR
Henderson State 6'2" 218 lbs.

Year	Team		Games	Pos.
1975	MIA	N	14	LB
1977			4	LB
1978			16	LB
1979			16	LB
1980			14	LB
1981			16	LB
1982			9	LB
1983			12	LB
1984			15	LB
9 yrs.	116 games			

Buster Rhymes
RHYMES, GEORGE
B. Jan. 27, 1962, Miami, FL
Oklahoma 6'2" 218 lbs.

Year	Team		Games	Pos.
1985	MIN	N	15	WR
1986			5	WR
2 yrs.	20 games			

Frank Ribar
RIBAR, FRANK A.
B. Jan. 15, 1917, Wickhaven, PA
D. Oct., 1976
Duke 6'1" 190 lbs.

Year	Team		Games	Pos.
1943	WAS	N	3	G

Dave Ribble
RIBBLE, LORAN THOMAS (Tex, Babe)
B. Mar. 28, 1907, Brownwood, TX
D. 1944
Hardin-Simmons 6'1" 216 lbs.

Year	Team		Games	Pos.
1932	POR	N	1	T
1933	CHIC	N	1	G
1934	PIT	N	10	G
1935			3	G
4 yrs.	15 games			

Paul Riblett
RIBLETT, PAUL G.
B. May 23, 1908, Youngwood, PA
D. Mar. 1, 1976, Cherry Hill, NJ
Pennsylvania 5'10" 184 lbs.

Year	Team		Games	Pos.
1932	BKN	N	10	E
1933			10	E
1934			11	E
1935			12	E
1936			12	E
5 yrs.	55 games			

Benny Ricardo
RICARDO, BENITO CONCEPCION
B. Jan. 4, 1954, Asuncion, Paraguay
San Diego State 5'10" 172 lbs.

Year	Team		Games	Pos.
1976	BUF	N	2	K
1976	DET	N	8	K
1978			16	K
1979			16	K
1980	NO	N	14	K
1981			16	K
1983	MIN	N	16	K
1984	SD	N	2	K
7 yrs.	90 games			

Jim Ricca
RICCA, JAMES EMANUEL
B. Oct. 8, 1927, Rockville Centre, NY
Georgetown 6'4" 270 lbs.

Year	Team		Games	Pos.
1951	WAS	N	11	C
1952			12	T
1953			12	T
1954			12	T
1955	DET	N	6	G
1955	PHI	N	6	T

Jim Ricca continued

Year	Team		Games	Pos.
1956			1	T
6 yrs.	60 games			

Rice
RICE
None

Year	Team		Games	Pos.
1921	HAM	A	1	HB

Allen Rice
RICE, ALLEN TROY
B. Apr. 5, 1962, Houston, TX
Baylor 5'10" 203 lbs.

Year	Team		Games	Pos.
1984	MIN	N	14	RB
1985			14	RB
1986			14	RB
1987			12	RB
1988			16	RB
1989			4	RB
1990			15	RB
1991	GB	N	6	RB
8 yrs.	95 games			

Andy Rice
RICE, ANDREW
B. Sep. 6, 1941, Hallettsville, TX
Texas Southern 6'3" 268 lbs.

Year	Team		Games	Pos.
1966	KC	A	14	DT
1967			4	DT
1967	HOU	A	14	DT
1968	CIN	A	14	DT
1969			14	DT
1970	SD	N	9	DT
1971			13	DT
1972	CHI		14	DT
1973			14	DT
8 yrs.	110 games			

Bill Rice
RICE, WILLIAM
None 165 lbs.

Year	Team		Games	Pos.
1929	NYG	N	2	C

Daniel Rice
RICE, DANIEL
B. Nov. 9, 1963, Boston, MA
Michigan 6'1" 241 lbs.

Year	Team		Games	Pos.
1987	CIN	N	3	RB

Floyd Rice
RICE, FLOYD ELLIOTT
B. Aug. 31, 1949, Natchez, MS
Alcorn State 6'3" 224 lbs.

Year	Team		Games	Pos.
1971	HOU	N	14	TE
1972			14	LB
1973			7	LB
1973	SD	N	5	LB
1974			12	LB
1975			14	LB
1976	OAK	N	10	LB
1977			13	LB
1978	NO	N	15	LB
8 yrs.	104 games			

George Rice
RICE, GEORGE GAYLEN
B. Jun. 10, 1944, Liberty, MO
Louisiana State 6'3" 262 lbs.

Year	Team		Games	Pos.
1966	HOU	A	5	DT
1967			14	DT
1968			11	DT
1969			8	DT
4 yrs.	38 games			

Harold Rice
RICE, HAROLD

Harold Rice continued
B. Jun. 23, 1945, Nashville, TN
Tennessee State 6'2" 230 lbs.

Year	Team		Games	Pos.
1971	OAK	N	12	DE

Jerry Rice
RICE, JERRY LEE
B. Oct. 13, 1962, Starkville, MS
Mississippi Valley State 6'2" 200 lbs.

Year	Team		Games	Pos.
1985	SF	N	16	WR
1986			16	WR
1987			12	WR
1988			16	WR
1989			16	WR
1990			16	WR
1991			16	WR
1992			16	WR
1993			16	WR
1994			16	WR
1995			16	WR
1996			16	WR
12 yrs.	188 games			

Ken Rice
RICE, KENNETH EARL
B. Sep. 14, 1939, Bainbridge, GA
Auburn 6'2" 243 lbs.

Year	Team		Games	Pos.
1961	BUF	A	14	OT
1963			14	G
1964	OAK	A	14	G, OT
1965			14	G
1966	MIA	A	14	G
1967			9	G
6 yrs.	79 games			

Orian Rice
RICE, ORIAN (Bill)
B. 1904
Syracuse/Muhlenberg 6'0" 195 lbs.

Year	Team		Games	Pos.
1926	NEW	A	3	C, G

Rodney Rice
RICE, RODNEY DONADRAIN
B. Jun. 18, 1966, Albany, GA
Brigham Young 5'8" 180 lbs.

Year	Team		Games	Pos.
1989	NE	N	10	CB
1990	TB	N	16	CB, S
2 yrs.	26 games			

Ron Rice
RICE, RONALD WILSON
B. Nov. 9, 1972, Detroit, MI
Eastern Michigan 6'1" 206 lbs.

Year	Team		Games	Pos.
1996	DET	N	13	S

Simeon Rice
RICE, SIMEON
B. Feb. 24, 1974, Chicago, IL
Illinois 6'5" 265 lbs.

Year	Team		Games	Pos.
1996	ARI	N	16	DE

Herb Rich
RICH, HERBERT RICHARD
B. Oct. 7, 1928, Newark, NJ
Vanderbilt 5'11" 181 lbs.

Year	Team		Games	Pos.
1950	BAL	N	12	HB
1951	LA	N	7	HB
1952			12	HB
1953			7	HB
1954	NYG	N	11	HB
1955			11	HB
1956			5	HB
7 yrs.	65 games			

Randy Rich
RICH, RANDY

Year	Team	Games	Pos.

Randy Rich continued

B. Dec. 28, 1953, Bakersfield, CA
New Mexico 5'10" 178 lbs.

Year	Team		Games	Pos.
1977	DET	N	2	DB
1978	OAK	N	2	DB
1978	CLE	N	9	CB
1979			16	CB

3 yrs. 29 games

Gary Richard

RICHARD, GARY ROSS
B. Oct. 9, 1965, Denver, CO
Pittsburgh 5'9" 171 lbs.

1988	GB	N	10	CB

Stanley Richard

RICHARD, STANLEY PALMER
B. Oct. 21, 1967, Mineola, TX
Texas 6'2" 197 lbs.

1991	SD	N	15	S
1992			14	S
1993			16	S
1994			16	S
1995	WAS	N	16	S
1996			16	S

6 yrs. 93 games

Bobby Richards

RICHARDS, ROBERT GRIFFIN
B. Oct. 2, 1938, Columbus, MS
Louisiana State 6'2" 241 lbs.

1962	PHI	N	14	DT
1963			14	DE
1964			14	DE
1965			14	DE
1966	ATL	N	14	DE
1967			14	DE

6 yrs. 84 games

Curvin Richards

RICHARDS, CURVIN STEPHEN
(Swervin' Curvin)
B. Dec. 26, 1968, Port of Spain,
Trinidad
Pittsburgh 5'9" 195 lbs.

1991	DAL	N	2	RB
1992			9	RB
1993	DET	N	1	RB

3 yrs. 12 games

Dave Richards

RICHARDS, DAVID REED
B. Apr. 11, 1966, Staten Island, NY
Southern Methodist/UCLA 6'5" 310 lbs.

1988	SD	N	16	OT
1989			16	OT
1990			16	G, OT
1991			16	G, OT
1992			16	G
1993	DET	N	15	G
1994	ATL	N	15	G
1995			14	OT, G
1996			6	OT
1996	NE	N	6	OT

9 yrs. 136 games

Dick Richards

RICHARDS, RICHARD
B. Nov. 7, 1907
Kentucky 6'0" 194 lbs.

1933	BKN	N	8	HB, FB, QB

Elvin Richards

RICHARDS, ELVIN (Kink)
B. Dec. 27, 1910, Garden Grove, IA
D. Jul., 1976, Oakland, CA
Simpson 5'11" 195 lbs.

1933	NYG	N	9	HB, QB, FB

Elvin Richards continued

1934			12	HB
1935			12	HB, QB
1936			11	QB, HB
1937			11	QB, HB
1938			9	B
1939			9	HB

7 yrs. 73 games

Golden Richards

RICHARDS, JOHN GOLDEN
B. Dec. 31, 1951, Salt Lake City, UT
Brigham Young/Hawaii 6'0" 181 lbs.

1973	DAL	N	12	WR
1974			14	WR
1975			14	WR
1976			11	WR
1977			14	WR
1978			1	WR
1978	CHI	N	15	WR
1979			5	WR

7 yrs. 86 games

Howard Richards

RICHARDS, HOWARD GLENN,
JR.
B. Aug. 7, 1959, St. Louis, MO
Missouri 6'6" 268 lbs.

1981	DAL	N	16	OT, G
1982			8	OT
1983			16	G, OT
1984			11	G
1985			7	OT
1986			9	G, OT
1987	SEA	N	2	OT

7 yrs. 69 games

Jim Richards

RICHARDS, JAMES
B. Oct. 28, 1946, Charlotte, NC
Virginia Tech 6'1" 180 lbs.

1968	NY	A	13	DB, FL
1969			14	CB, S

2 yrs. 27 games

Perry Richards

RICHARDS, PERRY
B. Jan. 14, 1934, Detroit, MI
Detroit 6'2" 205 lbs.

1957	PIT	N	7	E
1958	DET	N	3	E
1959	CHIC	N	4	E
1960	STL	N	8	E
1961	BUF	A	11	OE
1962	NY	A	14	OE

6 yrs. 47 games

Pete Richards

RICHARDS, PETER
B. 1905
Swarthmore 5'10" 190 lbs.

1927	FRA	N	2	C

Ray Richards

RICHARDS, RAYMOND W.
B. Jul. 16, 1906, Liberty, NE
D. Sep. 18, 1974, La Harba, CA
Nebraska 6'1" 230 lbs.

1930	FRA	N	13	T, E
1933	CHIB	N	12	T, G
1934	DET	N	6	T, G
1935	CHIB	N	12	G, T
1936			1	G

5 yrs. 44 games

Ted Richards

RICHARDS, EDWARD J.

Ted Richards continued

B. Nov. 7, 1901, IL
D. Dec. 1, 1978, Stanwood, WA
Illinois 5'9" 174 lbs.

1929	CHIB	N	1	E

Al Richardson

RICHARDSON, ALVIN
B. Feb. 1, 1935
Grambling State 6'3" 250 lbs.

1960	BOS	A		DE

Al Richardson

RICHARDSON, ALPETTE
B. Sep. 23, 1957, Abbeville, AL
Georgia Tech 6'2" 218 lbs.

1980	ATL	N	16	LB
1981			16	LB
1982			8	LB
1983			5	LB
1984			16	LB
1985			16	LB

6 yrs. 77 games

Bob Richardson

RICHARDSON, ROBERT
GEORGE (Red)
B. Feb. 24, 1944, Minneapolis, MN
UCLA 6'1" 180 lbs.

1966	DEN	A	9	DB

Bucky Richardson

RICHARDSON, JOHN POWELL
B. Feb. 7, 1969, Baton Rouge, LA
Texas A&M 6'1" 221 lbs.

1992	HOU	N	7	QB
1993			2	QB
1994			7	QB

3 yrs. 16 games

Charlie Richardson

RICHARDSON, CHARLES
B. Dec. 23, 1907, IL
D. Mar., 1977, Chicago, IL
None 143 lbs.

1925	MIL	N	1	HB

C.J. Richardson

RICHARDSON, CARL RAY, JR.
B. Jun. 10, 1972, Dallas, TX
Miami (Florida) 5'10" 209 lbs.

1995	ARI	N	1	S

Darryl Richardson

RICHARDSON, DARRYL
B. Mar. 27, 1964
Northern Illinois 5'9" 178 lbs.

1987	CIN	N	3	G

Eric Richardson

RICHARDSON, ERIC
B. Apr. 18, 1962, San Francisco, CA
San Jose State 6'1" 185 lbs.

1985	BUF	N	16	WR
1986			14	WR

2 yrs. 30 games

Ernie Richardson

RICHARDSON, ERNEST
B. Jul. 17, 1950, Greenville, MS
Jackson State 6'5" 220 lbs.

1974	CLE	N	2	S

Gloster Richardson

RICHARDSON, GLOSTER VAN
B. Jul. 18, 1943, Greenville, MS
Jackson State 6'0" 200 lbs.

1967	KC	A	13	FL
1968			13	FL
1969			14	WR
1970	KC	N	12	WR
1971	DAL	N	11	WR
1972	CLE	N	7	WR
1973			14	WR
1974			9	WR

8 yrs. 93 games

Grady Richardson

RICHARDSON, GRADY GENE
B. Apr. 2, 1952, Houston, TX
Fullerton State 6'4" 225 lbs.

1979	WAS	N	3	TE
1980			1	TE

2 yrs. 4 games

Greg Richardson

RICHARDSON, GREGORY
LAMAR
B. Oct. 6, 1964, Mobile, AL
Alabama 5'7" 172 lbs.

1987	MIN	N	2	WR
1988	TB	N	2	WR

2 yrs. 4 games

Huey Richardson

RICHARDSON, HUEY
B. Feb. 2, 1968, Atlanta, GA
Florida 6'4" 263 lbs.

1991	PIT	N	5	LB
1992	WAS	N	4	LB
1992	NYJ	N	7	LB, DT

2 yrs. 16 games

Jeff Richardson

RICHARDSON, JEFFREY
B. Sep. 1, 1944, Johnstown, PA
Michigan State 6'3" 253 lbs.

1967	NY	A	11	DE, G
1968			14	G
1969	MIA	A	3	DT

3 yrs. 28 games

Jerry Richardson

RICHARDSON, GERALD
B. Jul. 11, 1936, Fayetteville, NC
Wofford 6'3" 195 lbs.

1959	BAL	N	11	E
1960			11	E, HB

2 yrs. 22 games

Jerry Richardson

RICHARDSON, JERRY
B. Nov. 13, 1941, Los Angeles, CA
West Texas State 6'3" 190 lbs.

1964	LA	N	14	DB
1965			14	DB
1966	ATL	N	14	DB
1967			13	DB

4 yrs. 55 games

Jesse Richardson

RICHARDSON, JESSE
B. Aug. 18, 1930, Philadelphia, PA
D. Jun. 17, 1975, Philadelphia, PA
Alabama 6'2" 261 lbs.

1953	PHI	N	12	G
1954			12	T
1955			12	T
1956			11	T
1958			12	T

727

Year	Team		Games	Pos.

Jesse Richardson *continued*

Year	Team		Games	Pos.
1959			12	T
1960			12	T
1961			14	DT
1962	**BOS**	**A**	14	DT
1963			14	DT
1964			14	DT
11 yrs.	139 games			

John Richardson
RICHARDSON, JOHN EDWARD
B. May 25, 1945, Minneapolis, MN
UCLA 6'2" 254 lbs.

1967	**MIA**	**A**	14	DT
1968			11	DT
1969			14	DT
1970	**MIA**	**N**	14	DT
1971			10	DT
1972	**STL**	**N**	11	DT
1973			14	DT
7 yrs.	88 games			

Mike Richardson
RICHARDSON, MICHAEL CALVIN
B. May 23, 1961, Compton, CA
Arizona State 6'0" 188 lbs.

1983	**CHI**	**N**	16	CB
1984			15	CB
1985			14	CB
1986			16	CB
1987			11	CB
1988			16	CB
1989	**SF**	**N**	3	CB
7 yrs.	91 games			

Mike Richardson
RICHARDSON, MICHAEL WAYNE
B. Dec. 8, 1946, Fort Worth, TX
Southern Methodist 5'11" 193 lbs.

1969	**HOU**	**A**	14	RB
1970	**HOU**	**N**	14	RB
1971			7	RB
3 yrs.	35 games			

Paul Richardson
RICHARDSON, PAUL
B. Feb. 25, 1969, Chicago, IL
UCLA 6'3" 204 lbs.

1993	**PHI**	**N**	1	WR

Pete Richardson
RICHARDSON, PETE
B. Oct. 17, 1946, Youngstown, OH
Dayton 6'1" 197 lbs.

1969	**BUF**	**A**	14	S
1970	**BUF**	**N**	12	S
1971			13	S
3 yrs.	39 games			

Reggie Richardson
RICHARDSON, REGGIE
B. Apr. 13, 1963
Utah 6'0" 180 lbs.

1987	**LARM**	**N**	3	S

Terry Richardson
RICHARDSON, TERRY
B. Oct. 8, 1971, Ft. Lauderdale, FL
Syracuse 6'0" 204 lbs.

1996	**PIT**	**N**	1	RB

Thomas Richardson
RICHARDSON, THOMAS
B. Oct. 15, 1944, Greenville, MS

Thomas Richardson *cont.*

Jackson State 6'2" 195 lbs.

1969	**BOS**	**A**	14	WR
1970	**BOS**	**N**	1	WR
2 yrs.	15 games			

Tony Richardson
RICHARDSON, ANTONIO
B. Dec. 17, 1971, Frankfurt, Germany
Auburn 6'1" 224 lbs.

1995	**KC**	**N**	14	RB
1996			13	FB
2 yrs.	27 games			

Willie Richardson
RICHARDSON, WILLIE LOUIS
B. Nov. 17, 1939, Clarksdale, MS
Jackson State 6'2" 198 lbs.

1963	**BAL**	**N**	13	OE
1964			11	FL
1965			9	FL
1966			13	FL
1967			14	FL
1968			14	FL
1969			14	WR
1970	**MIA**	**N**	14	WR
8 yrs.	102 games			

Doss Richerson
RICHERSON, DOSS
B. May 24, 1901
D. Aug., 1974, Kansas City, MO
Missouri 6'1" 225 lbs.

1926	**CHI**	**A**	7	G, E, T

Ray Richeson
RICHESON, THOMAS RAY
B. Sep. 27, 1923, Russellville, AL
Alabama 6'0" 235 lbs.

1949	**CHI**	**AA**	12	G

Mike Richey
RICHEY, JAMES MICHAEL
B. Jan. 30, 1947, Washington, DC
North Carolina 6'5" 257 lbs.

1969	**BUF**	**A**	14	OT
1970	**NO**	**N**	5	OT
2 yrs.	19 games			

Harry Richman
RICHMAN, HARRY E.
B. Jan. 9, 1907
D. May, 1967, Champaign, IL
Illinois 5'11" 186 lbs.

1929	**CHIB**	**N**	1	G

Rodney Richmond
RICHMOND, RODNEY (Rock)
B. Jan. 7, 1958, Los Angeles, CA
Oregon 5'10" 180 lbs.

1987	**PIT**	**N**	2	CB

Frank Richter
RICHTER, FRANK
B. Dec. 24, 1944, Toccoa, GA
Georgia 6'3" 230 lbs.

1967	**DEN**	**A**	9	LB
1968			11	LB
1969			14	LB
3 yrs.	34 games			

Les Richter
RICHTER, LESLIE ALAN
B. Oct. 26, 1930, Fresno, CA
California 6'3" 238 lbs.

1954	**LA**	**N**	12	LB

Les Richter *continued*

Year	Team		Games	Pos.
1955			12	LB
1956			12	LB
1957			12	LB
1958			12	LB
1959			12	LB
1960			12	LB
1961			14	LB
1962			14	LB
9 yrs.	112 games			

Pat Richter
RICHTER, HUGH VERNON
B. Sep. 9, 1941, Madison, WI
Wisconsin 6'5" 230 lbs.

1963	**WAS**	**N**	14	OE, P
1964			14	OE, P
1965			11	OE, P
1966			14	OE, P
1967			14	TE, P
1968			14	TE
1969			11	TE
1970			11	TE
8 yrs.	103 games			

Paul Rickards
RICKARDS, PAUL
B. Jun. 30, 1926, Wheeling, WV
Pittsburgh 6'1" 190 lbs.

1948	**LA**	**N**	3	QB

Tom Ricketts
RICKETTS, THOMAS GORDON, JR.
B. Nov. 21, 1965, Pittsburgh, PA
Pittsburgh 6'5" 294 lbs.

1989	**PIT**	**N**	12	OT
1990			16	OT
1991			14	OT
1992	**IND**	**N**	8	G
1993	**KC**	**N**	3	G
5 yrs.	53 games			

Harold Ricks
RICKS, HAROLD (Charlie)
B. Dec. 26, 1952
Tennessee-Chattanooga 5'10" 200 lbs.

1987	**TB**	**N**		RB

Lawrence Ricks
RICKS, LAWRENCE TALLMADGE
B. Jun. 4, 1961, Barberton, OH
Michigan 5'9" 194 lbs.

1983	**KC**	**N**	12	RB
1984			5	RB
2 yrs.	17 games			

Ted Riddell
RIDDELL, TED E. (Speed)
B. Jun. 17, 1896
D. Dec., 1968, Scottsbluff, NE
Nebraska 5'10" 185 lbs.

1920	**RI**	**A**	1	E

Louis Riddick
RIDDICK, LOUIS ANGELO
B. Mar. 15, 1969, Quakertown, PA
Pittsburgh 6'2" 216 lbs.

1992	**ATL**	**N**	16	S
1993	**CLE**	**N**	15	S
1994			16	S
1995			16	S
1996	**ATL**	**N**	16	S
5 yrs.	79 games			

Ray Riddick
RIDDICK, RAYMOND E.
B. Oct. 17, 1917, Lowell, MA
D. Jul. 14, 1976, Hampton, NH
Fordham 6'1" 211 lbs.

1940	**GB**	**N**	10	E
1941			11	E
1942			2	E
1946			2	E
4 yrs.	25 games			

Robb Riddick
RIDDICK, ROBERT LEE
B. Apr. 26, 1957, Quakertown, PA
Millersville State 6'0" 195 lbs.

1981	**BUF**	**N**	10	RB
1983			16	RB
1984			16	RB
1986			15	RB
1987			6	RB
1988			15	RB
6 yrs.	78 games			

Houston Ridge
RIDGE, HOUSTON ROBERT, JR.
B. Jul. 18, 1944, Madera, CA
San Diego State 6'4" 239 lbs.

1966	**SD**	**A**	11	DE
1967			4	DT
1968			14	DT
1969			5	DT
4 yrs.	44 games			

Elston Ridgle
RIDGLE, ELSTON ALBERT
B. Aug. 24, 1963, Los Angeles, CA
Northern Arizona/Nevada-Reno 6'6" 265 lbs.

1987	**SF**	**N**	3	DE
1989	**BUF**	**N**	1	DE
1990	**PHX**	**N**	10	DE
1992	**CIN**	**N**	7	DE
4 yrs.	21 games			

Colin Ridgway
RIDGWAY, COLIN
B. Feb. 19, 1939, Melbourne, Australia
D. May 13, 1993, University Park, TX
Lamar 6'5" 211 lbs.*

1965	**DAL**	**N**	3	P

Preston Ridlehuber
RIDLEHUBER, HOWARD PRESTON
B. Nov. 2, 1943, Greenwood, SC
Georgia 6'2" 215 lbs.

1966	**ATL**	**N**	3	RB
1968	**OAK**	**A**	10	RB
1969	**BUF**	**A**	9	RB
3 yrs.	22 games			

Don Ridler
RIDLER, DON G.
B. 1907
Michigan State 6'0" 210 lbs.

1931	**CLE**	**N**	1	T

Jimmy Ridlon
RIDLON, JAMES A.
B. Jul. 11, 1934, Nanuet, NY
Syracuse 6'1" 181 lbs.

1957	**SF**	**N**	12	DB
1958			12	DB
1959			12	DB
1960			12	DB
1961			11	DB
1962			9	DB

Year	Team	Games	Pos.

Jimmy Ridlon *continued*

Year	Team		Games	Pos.
1963	DAL	N	7	DB
1964			14	DB

8 yrs.   89 games

Chris Riehm
RIEHM, CHRISTOPHER ALAN
B. Apr. 14, 1961, Columbus, OH
Ohio State 6'6" 275 lbs.

1986	LARI	N	12	G
1987			1	G
1988			8	G

3 yrs.   21 games

John Rienstra
RIENSTRA, JOHN WILLIAM
B. Mar. 22, 1963, Grand Rapids, MI
Temple 6'5" 271 lbs.

1986	PIT	N	4	G
1987			12	G
1988			5	G
1989			15	G
1990			6	G
1991	CLE	N	16	G
1992			7	G

7 yrs.   65 games

Doug Riesenberg
RIESENBERG, DOUG
B. Jul. 22, 1965, Moscow, ID
California 6'5" 275 lbs.

1987	NYG	N	8	OT
1988			16	OT
1989			16	OT
1990			16	OT
1991			15	OT
1992			16	OT
1993			16	OT
1994			16	OT
1995			16	OT
1996	TB		10	OT

10 yrs.   145 games

Bill Rieth
RIETH, WILLIAM JOHN
B. Jun. 20, 1916, Cleveland, OH
Carnegie-Mellon 5'11" 203 lbs.

1941	CLE	N	8	C
1942			10	C, G
1944			8	G, C
1945			1	C

4 yrs.   27 games

Charley Rieves
RIEVES, CHARLES
B. 1940
Houston 5'11" 217 lbs.

1962	OAK	A	14	LB
1963			9	LB
1964	HOU	A	8	LB
1965			7	LB

4 yrs.   38 games

Dick Rifenburg
RIFENBURG, RICHARD G.
B. 1927
D. Dec. 5, 1994, Cheektowaga, NY
Michigan 6'3" 195 lbs.

1950	DET	N	12	E

Chuck Riffle
RIFFLE, CHARLES FRANCIS
B. Jan. 6, 1918, Dillonvale, OH
Notre Dame 6'0" 212 lbs.

1944	CLE	N	8	G
1946	NY	AA	14	G
1947			14	G

Chuck Riffle *continued*

Year	Team		Games	Pos.
1948			14	G

4 yrs.   50 games

Dick Riffle
RIFFLE, F. RICHARD
B. Feb. 2, 1915, Wellsboro, PA
D. Apr., 1981, Wellsboro, PA
Albright 6'1" 200 lbs.

1938	PHI	N	11	HB
1939			10	QB, HB
1940			11	FB, HB
1941	PIT	N	10	HB, FB
1942			11	FB

5 yrs.   53 games

Charles Riggins
RIGGINS, CHARLES LA CARDA
B. Nov. 9, 1959, Sanford, FL
Bethune-Cookman 6'5" 295 lbs.

1987	TB	N	3	DE

John Riggins
RIGGINS, JOHN (Diesel, Riggo)
B. Aug. 4, 1949, Centralia, KS
Kansas 6'2" 235 lbs.

1971	NYJ	N	14	RB
1972			12	RB
1973			11	RB
1974			10	RB
1975			14	RB
1976	WAS	N	14	RB
1977			5	RB
1978			15	RB
1979			16	FB
1981			15	RB
1982			8	RB
1983			15	RB
1984			14	RB
1985			12	RB

14 yrs.   175 games

Bob Riggle
RIGGLE, ROBERT D.
B. Feb. 5, 1944, Washington, PA
Penn State 6'1" 200 lbs.

1966	ATL	N	14	DB
1967			11	DB

2 yrs.   25 games

Gerald Riggs
RIGGS, GERALD ANTONIO
B. Nov. 6, 1960, Tullos, LA
Arizona State 6'1" 231 lbs.

1982	ATL	N	9	RB
1983			16	RB
1984			15	RB
1985			16	RB
1986			16	RB
1987			12	RB
1988			9	RB
1989	WAS	N	12	RB
1990			10	RB
1991			16	RB

10 yrs.   131 games

Jim Riggs
RIGGS, JIM THOMAS
B. Sep. 29, 1963, Fort Knox, KY
Clemson 6'5" 245 lbs.

1987	CIN	N	9	TE
1988			16	TE
1989			10	TE
1990			16	TE
1991			16	TE
1992			12	TE
1993	WAS	N	3	TE

7 yrs.   82 games

Thron Riggs
RIGGS, THRON
B. Apr. 25, 1921, Buckley, WA
Harvard/Washington 6'1" 225 lbs.*

1944	BOS	N	10	T

Joe Righetti
RIGHETTI, JOSEPH
B. Dec. 31, 1947, Fredericktown, PA
Waynesburg 6'3" 253 lbs.

1969	CLE	N	14	DT
1970			9	DT

2 yrs.   23 games

Avon Riley
RILEY, AVON
B. Feb. 10, 1958, Savannah, GA
UCLA 6'3" 240 lbs.

1981	HOU	N	16	LB
1982			9	LB
1983			16	LB
1984			15	LB
1985			16	LB
1986			16	LB
1987	PIT	N	3	LB

7 yrs.   91 games

Bob Riley
RILEY, ROBERT HENRY, III
B. Jun. 23, 1964, Pittsburgh, PA
Indiana 6'5" 276 lbs.

1987	CIN	N	3	OT

Butch Riley
RILEY, THOMAS
B. Mar. 13, 1947, Ingleside, TX
Texas A&I, Kingsville 6'2" 220 lbs.

1969	BAL	N	11	LB

Eric Riley
RILEY, ERIC
B. Oct. 10, 1964
Eastern Washington 6'3" 230 lbs.

1987	NYJ	N	2	TE

Eugene Riley
RILEY, M. EUGENE
B. Oct. 9, 1966, Cincinnati, OH
Ball State 6'2" 236 lbs.

1990	IND	N	1	TE
1991	DET	N	5	TE

2 yrs.   6 games

Jack Riley
RILEY, JOHN H.
B. Jun. 13, 1909
D. Mar. 2, 1993, Kenilworth, IL
Northwestern 6'2" 230 lbs.

1933	BOS	N	12	T

Jim Riley
RILEY, JAMES GLEN
B. Jul. 6, 1945, Galveston, TX
Oklahoma 6'4" 252 lbs.

1967	MIA	A	14	DE
1968			13	DE
1969			14	DE
1970	MIA	N	11	DE
1971			13	DE

5 yrs.   65 games

Ken Riley
RILEY, KENNETH JEROME
(Rattler)
B. Aug. 6, 1947, Bartow, FL

Ken Riley *continued*
Florida A&M 6'0" 183 lbs.

1969	CIN	A	14	CB
1970	CIN	N	14	CB
1971			13	CB
1972			12	CB
1973			14	CB
1974			14	CB
1975			14	CB
1976			14	CB
1977			14	CB
1978			16	CB
1979			13	CB
1980			16	CB
1981			16	CB
1982			9	CB
1983			14	CB

15 yrs.   207 games

Larry Riley
RILEY, LARRY
B. Nov. 21, 1954, Eustis, FL
Salem 5'10" 192 lbs.

1977	DEN	N	5	CB
1978	NYJ	N	4	CB

2 yrs.   9 games

Lee Riley
RILEY, LEON FRANCIS
B. Aug. 24, 1932, Schenectady, NY
Detroit 6'1" 192 lbs.

1955	DET	N	12	DB
1956	PHI	N	9	DB
1958			12	DB
1959			12	DB
1960	NYG	N	12	DB
1961	NY	A	12	DB
1962			14	DB

7 yrs.   83 games

Pat Riley
RILEY, PATRICK
B. Mar. 8, 1972, Marrero, LA
Miami (Florida) 6'5" 285 lbs.

1995	CHI	N	1	DE

Phillip Riley
RILEY, PHILLIP
B. Sep. 24, 1972, Orlando, FL
Florida State 5'11" 189 lbs.

1996	NYJ	N	1	WR

Preston Riley
RILEY, PRESTON TROY
B. Oct. 30, 1947, Vicksburg, MS
Memphis State 6'0" 180 lbs.

1970	SF	N	14	WR
1971			14	WR
1972			14	WR
1973	NO	N	1	WR

4 yrs.   43 games

Steve Riley
RILEY, STEVE BRUCE
B. Nov. 23, 1952, Chula Vista, CA
Southern California 6'6" 258 lbs.

1974	MIN	N	2	OT
1975			14	OT
1976			14	OT
1977			14	OT
1978			5	OT
1979			16	OT
1980			16	OT
1981			16	OT
1982			9	OT
1983			16	OT
1984			16	OT

11 yrs.   138 games

Year	Team	Games	Pos.

Dave Rimington
RIMINGTON, DAVE BRIAN
B. May 22, 1960, Omaha, NE
Nebraska 6'3" 288 lbs.

Year	Team		Games	Pos.
1983	CIN	N	12	C
1984			16	C
1985			16	C
1986			12	C
1987			8	C
1988	PHI	N	16	C
1989			6	C

7 yrs.   86 games

Stuart Rindy
RINDY, STUART
B. May 22, 1964
Wisconsin-Whitewater 6'5" 266 lbs.

Year	Team		Games	Pos.
1987	CHI	N	2	G, OT

Bill Ring
RING, BILL
B. Dec. 13, 1956, Des Moines, IA
Brigham Young 5'10" 205 lbs.

Year	Team		Games	Pos.
1981	SF	N	12	RB
1982			8	RB
1983			16	RB
1984			16	RB
1985			10	RB
1986			7	RB

6 yrs.   69 games

Jim Ringo
RINGO, JAMES STEPHEN
B. Nov. 21, 1932, Orange, NJ
Syracuse 6'1" 232 lbs.

Year	Team		Games	Pos.
1953	GB	N	5	C
1954			12	C
1955			12	C
1956			12	C
1957			12	C
1958			12	C
1959			12	C
1960			12	C
1961			14	C
1962			14	C
1963			14	C
1964	PHI	N	14	C
1965			14	C
1966			14	C
1967			14	C

15 yrs.   187 games

Carroll Ringwalt
RINGWALT, CARROLL WALTER
B. Dec. 15, 1907
D. Jun. 26, 1990, Indianapolis, IN
Indiana 6'0" 210 lbs.

Year	Team		Games	Pos.
1930	POR	N	3	G
1931	FRA	N	7	C, G

2 yrs.   10 games

Al Riopel
RIOPEL, A.D. (Hop)
B. Oct. 11, 1900
D. Sep., 1966, Worcester, MA
Holy Cross 5'8" 165 lbs.

Year	Team		Games	Pos.
1925	PRO	N	4	HB

Mike Riordan
**RIORDAN, CHARLES MICHAEL
(Iron Mike)**
B. Dec. 8, 1905
D. May, 1976, Trenton, NJ
New York University 5'11" 195 lbs.

Year	Team		Games	Pos.
1929	SI	N	8	E, HB, FB

Tim Riordan
RIORDAN, TIM P.
B. Jul. 15, 1960, New London, CT
Temple 6'1" 185 lbs.

Year	Team		Games	Pos.
1987	NO	N	1	QB

Alan Risher
RISHER, ALAN DAVID
B. May 6, 1961, New Orleans, LA
Louisiana State 6'2" 190 lbs.

Year	Team		Games	Pos.
1985	TB	N	16	QB
1987	GB	N	3	QB

2 yrs.   19 games

Cody Risien
RISIEN, CODY LEWIS
B. Mar. 22, 1957, Bryan, TX
Texas A&M 6'7" 269 lbs.

Year	Team		Games	Pos.
1979	CLE	N	15	OT
1980			16	OT
1981			16	OT
1982			9	OT
1983			16	OT
1985			12	OT
1986			16	OT
1987			13	OT
1988			16	OT
1989			16	OT

10 yrs.   145 games

Ed Risk
RISK, EDWARD
B. Apr. 5, 1908
D. Jan., 1969, Green Cove Springs, FL
Purdue 5'11" 180 lbs.

Year	Team		Games	Pos.
1932	CHIC	N	2	B

Elliot Risley
RISLEY, ELLIOT C.
B. Jan. 24, 1896
Deceased
Indiana 6'1" 205 lbs.

Year	Team		Games	Pos.
1921	HAM	A	5	T, E
1922	HAM	N	2	T
1923			2	T

3 yrs.   9 games

Andre Rison
RISON, ANDRE PREVIN
B. Mar. 18, 1967, Flint, MI
Michigan State 5'10" 185 lbs.

Year	Team		Games	Pos.
1989	IND	N	16	WR
1990	ATL	N	16	WR
1991			16	WR
1992			15	WR
1993			16	WR
1994			15	WR
1995	CLE	N	16	WR
1996	JAC	N	10	WR
1996	GB	N	5	WR

8 yrs.   125 games

Ray Rissmiller
**RISSMILLER, RAYMOND
HAROLD**
B. Jul. 22, 1942, Easton, PA
Georgia 6'4" 250 lbs.

Year	Team		Games	Pos.
1966	PHI	N	1	OT
1967	NO	N	11	OT
1968	BUF	A	4	OT

3 yrs.   16 games

Ray Risvold
RISVOLD, RAYMOND
B. Mar. 27, 1902, Illinois
D. Oct., 1984, Orlando, FL
None 170 lbs.

Year	Team		Games	Pos.
1927	CHIC	N	7	HB, FB, QB

Ray Risvold continued

Year	Team		Games	Pos.
1928			3	QB, HB

2 yrs.   10 games

Jim Ritcher
RITCHER, JAMES ALEXANDER
B. May 21, 1958, Berea, OH
North Carolina State 6'3" 265 lbs.

Year	Team		Games	Pos.
1980	BUF	N	14	C
1981			14	C
1982			9	C, G
1983			16	C, G
1984			14	G
1985			16	G
1986			16	G
1987			12	G
1988			16	G
1989			16	G
1990			16	G
1991			16	G
1992			16	G
1993			12	G
1994	ATL	N	2	G
1995			12	G

16 yrs.   217 games

Del Ritchhart
RITCHHART, DELBERT B.
B. 1911
D. Mar., 1981, Denver, CO
Colorado 6'0" 195 lbs.

Year	Team		Games	Pos.
1936	DET	N	11	C
1937			10	C

2 yrs.   21 games

Gabriel Rivera
RIVERA, GABRIEL
B. Apr. 7, 1961, Crystal City, TX
Texas Tech 6'2" 293 lbs.

Year	Team		Games	Pos.
1983	PIT	N	6	DT

Hank Rivera
RIVERA, HENRY
B. 1940
Oregon State 5'11" 180 lbs.

Year	Team		Games	Pos.
1962	OAK	A	9	DB
1963	BUF	A	3	DB

2 yrs.   12 games

Ron Rivera
RIVERA, RONALD EUGENE
B. Jan. 7, 1962, Fort Ord, CA
California 6'3" 239 lbs.

Year	Team		Games	Pos.
1984	CHI	N	15	LB
1985			16	LB
1986			16	LB
1987			12	LB
1988			16	LB
1989			16	LB
1990			14	LB
1991			16	LB
1992			16	LB

9 yrs.   137 games

Steve Rivera
RIVERA, STEVE JOSE
B. Aug. 5, 1954, Pensacola, FL
California 5'11" 184 lbs.

Year	Team		Games	Pos.
1976	SF	N	11	WR
1977			1	WR
1977	CHI	N	3	WR

2 yrs.   15 games

Garland Rivers
RIVERS, GARLAND A.
B. Nov. 3, 1964
Michigan 6'1" 181 lbs.

Year	Team		Games	Pos.
1987	CHI	N	2	CB, S

Jamie Rivers
RIVERS, JAMES ALBERT
B. Sep. 22, 1945, Youngstown, OH
Bowling Green 6'2" 238 lbs.

Year	Team		Games	Pos.
1968	STL	N	9	LB
1969			10	LB
1970			14	LB
1971			12	LB
1972			2	LB
1973			10	LB
1974	NYJ	N	13	LB
1975			6	LB

8 yrs.   76 games

Nate Rivers
RIVERS, NATE
B. Aug. 31, 1955, Wadmalaw Island, SC
South Carolina State 6'3" 215 lbs.

Year	Team		Games	Pos.
1980	NYG	N	2	RB

Reggie Rivers
RIVERS, REGGIE
B. Feb. 22, 1968, Dayton, OH
Southwest Texas State 6'1" 215 lbs.

Year	Team		Games	Pos.
1991	DEN	N	16	RB
1992			16	RB
1993			16	RB
1994			16	RB
1995			16	RB
1996			16	RB

6 yrs.   96 games

Ron Rivers
RIVERS, RONALD LEROY
B. Nov. 13, 1971, Elizabeth, NJ
Fresno State 5'8" 205 lbs.

Year	Team		Games	Pos.
1995	DET	N	16	RB
1996			15	RB

2 yrs.   31 games

Bob Rives
RIVES, ROBERT
B. Nov. 12, 1903
Vanderbilt 6'1" 200 lbs.

Year	Team		Games	Pos.
1926	NEW	N	4	T, E

Don Rives
RIVES, DONALD EARL
B. Aug. 30, 1951, Wheeler, TX
Texas Tech 6'2" 225 lbs.

Year	Team		Games	Pos.
1973	CHI	N	14	LB
1974			14	LB
1975			2	LB
1976			14	LB
1977			14	LB
1978			16	LB

6 yrs.   74 games

Jack Rizzo
RIZZO, JACK
B. Jun. 15, 1949, Westville, NH
Lehigh 5'10" 195 lbs.

Year	Team		Games	Pos.
1973	NYG	N	6	RB

Joe Rizzo
RIZZO, JOSEPH VINCENT
B. Dec. 17, 1950, New York, NY
U.S. Merchant Marine Academy-Kings Point 6'1" 220 lbs.

Year	Team		Games	Pos.
1974	DEN	N	11	LB
1975			14	LB
1976			12	LB
1977			13	LB
1978			14	LB
1979			13	LB
1980			4	LB

7 yrs.   81 games

Year	Team	Games	Pos.

John Roach
ROACH, JOHN G.
B. Mar. 26, 1933, Dallas, TX
Southern Methodist 6'4" 197 lbs.

Year	Team		Games	Pos.
1956	CHIC	N	8	QB, DB
1959			12	QB, DB
1960	STL	N	12	QB
1961	GB	N	7	QB
1962			8	QB
1963			8	QB
1964	DAL	N	9	QB
7 yrs.	64 games			

Rollin Roach
ROACH, ROLLIN
B. Dec. 20, 1902
Texas Christian

Year	Team		Games	Pos.
1927	CHIC	N	1	HB

Travis Roach
ROACH, TRAVIS
B. Mar. 18, 1950, Hamilton, TX
Texas 6'2" 260 lbs.

Year	Team		Games	Pos.
1974	NYJ	N	14	G

Carl Roaches
ROACHES, CARL
B. Oct. 2, 1953, Houston, TX
Texas A&M 5'8" 165 lbs.

Year	Team		Games	Pos.
1980	HOU	N	16	WR
1981			16	WR
1982			9	WR
1983			16	WR
1984			16	WR
1985	NO	N	3	WR
6 yrs.	76 games			

Willie Roaf
ROAF, WILLIAM LAYTON
B. Apr. 18, 1970, Pine Bluff, AR
Louisiana Tech 6'4" 299 lbs.

Year	Team		Games	Pos.
1993	NO	N	16	OT
1994			16	OT
1995			16	OT
1996			13	OT
4 yrs.	61 games			

Michael Roan
ROAN, MICHAEL
B. Aug. 29, 1972, Iowa City, IA
Wisconsin 6'3" 251 lbs.

Year	Team		Games	Pos.
1995	HOU	N	5	TE
1996			15	TE
2 yrs.	20 games			

Oscar Roan
ROAN, OSCAR BENNIE, III
B. Oct. 17, 1951, Dallas, TX
UCLA/Southern Methodist 6'6" 214 lbs.

Year	Team		Games	Pos.
1975	CLE	N	14	TE
1976			11	TE
1977			10	TE
1978			14	TE
4 yrs.	49 games			

Harry Robb
ROBB, HARRY D.
B. May 11, 1897
D. Dec., 1971, Greenville, PA
Penn State/Columbia 5'10" 185 lbs.

Year	Team		Games	Pos.
1921	CAN	A	5	QB, HB
1922	CAN	N	10	HB, QB
1923			11	QB, HB
1925			8	QB, HB
1926			13	QB, HB, FB
5 yrs.	47 games			

Joe Robb
ROBB, ALVIS JOE
B. Mar. 15, 1937, Lufkin, TX
D. Apr. 18, 1987, Houston, TX
Texas Christian 6'3" 238 lbs.

Year	Team		Games	Pos.
1959	PHI	N	12	DE
1960			12	DE
1961	STL	N	12	DE
1962			14	DE
1963			14	DE
1964			11	DE
1965			14	DE
1966			14	DE
1967			11	DE
1968	DET	N	9	DE
1969			14	DE
1970			6	DE
1971			14	DE
13 yrs.	157 games			

Stan Robb
ROBB, STANLEY
B. 1902
Centre 6'0" 185 lbs.

Year	Team		Games	Pos.
1926	CAN	N	3	E

Austin Robbins
ROBBINS, AUSTIN DION
B. Mar. 1, 1971, Washington, DC
North Carolina 6'6" 295 lbs.

Year	Team		Games	Pos.
1994	LARI	N	3	DE
1995	OAK	N	16	DT, DE
1996	NO	N	15	DT
3 yrs.	34 games			

Barret Robbins
ROBBINS, BARRET
B. Aug. 26, 1973, Houston, TX
Texas Christian 6'3" 205 lbs.

Year	Team		Games	Pos.
1995	OAK	N	16	C
1996			14	C
2 yrs.	30 games			

Jack Robbins
ROBBINS, JACK
B. Jan. 23, 1916, Little Rock, AR
D. Jan., 1983, Lafayette, LA
Arkansas 6'2" 183 lbs.

Year	Team		Games	Pos.
1938	CHIC	N	8	HB
1939			7	HB
2 yrs.	15 games			

Kevin Robbins
ROBBINS, KEVIN AVERY
B. Dec. 12, 1967, Washington, DC
Wichita State/Michigan State 6'6" 287 lbs.

Year	Team		Games	Pos.
1989	CLE	N	1	OT
1990			6	G, OT
1993	LARM	N	1	OT
3 yrs.	8 games			

Randy Robbins
ROBBINS, RANDY
B. Sep. 14, 1962, Casa Grande, AZ
Arizona 6'2" 189 lbs.

Year	Team		Games	Pos.
1984	DEN	N	16	CB
1985			10	CB
1986			16	S
1987			10	S
1988			16	S
1989			16	S
1990			16	S
1991			16	S
1992	NE	N	15	S
9 yrs.	131 games			

Tootie Robbins
ROBBINS, JAMES ELBERT
B. Jun. 2, 1958, Windsor, NC
East Carolina 6'5" 303 lbs.

Year	Team		Games	Pos.
1982	STL	N	9	OT
1983			13	OT
1984			16	OT
1985			12	OT
1986			12	OT
1987			14	OT
1988	PHX	N	15	OT
1989			9	OT
1990			16	OT
1991			16	OT
1992	GB	N	15	OT
1993			12	OT
12 yrs.	159 games			

Bo Roberson
ROBERSON, IRVIN
B. Jul. 23, 1935, Blakely, GA
Cornell 6'1" 192 lbs.

Year	Team		Games	Pos.
1961	SD	A	14	HB
1962	OAK	A	14	HB
1963			14	HB
1964			14	FL
1965			6	OE
1965	BUF	A	8	FL
1966	MIA	A	11	FL
6 yrs.	81 games			

James Roberson
ROBERSON, JAMES
B. May 3, 1971, Lake Wales, FL
Florida State 6'3" 275 lbs.

Year	Team		Games	Pos.
1996	HOU	N	15	DE

Lake Roberson
ROBERSON, J. LAKE, JR.
B. Aug. 5, 1918
D. Dec., 1984, Lyon, MS
Mississippi 6'1" 210 lbs.

Year	Team		Games	Pos.
1945	DET	N	4	E

Vern Roberson
ROBERSON, VERNON
B. Aug. 3, 1952, Natchitoches, LA
Grambling State 6'1" 195 lbs.

Year	Team		Games	Pos.
1977	MIA	N	4	S
1978	SF	N	16	S
2 yrs.	20 games			

Alfredo Roberts
ROBERTS, ALFREDO
B. Mar. 17, 1965, Fort Lauderdale, FL
Miami (Florida) 6'3" 250 lbs.

Year	Team		Games	Pos.
1988	KC	N	16	TE
1989			16	TE
1990			16	TE
1991	DAL	N	16	TE
1992			16	TE
5 yrs.	80 games			

Archie Roberts
ROBERTS, ARTHUR
B. Nov. 4, 1942, Holyoke, MA
Columbia/Case Western Reserve 6'1" 193 lbs.

Year	Team		Games	Pos.
1967	MIA	A	1	FL

Bill Roberts
ROBERTS, WILLIAM
B. Sep. 11, 1929, Dubuque, IA
Dartmouth 6'0" 200 lbs.

Year	Team		Games	Pos.
1956	GB	N	4	HB

Bill Roberts
ROBERTS, WILLIAM HAROLD
B. Aug. 5, 1962, Miami, FL
Ohio State 6'5" 280 lbs.

Year	Team		Games	Pos.
1984	NYG	N	11	OT
1986			16	OT
1987			12	OT
1988			16	OT
1989			16	OT
1990			16	OT
1991			16	OT
1992			16	OT
1993			16	G
1994			16	G, OT
1995	NE	N	16	G
1996			16	G
12 yrs.	183 games			

Cliff Roberts
ROBERTS, CLIFFORD
B. 1935
Illinois 6'3" 260 lbs.

Year	Team		Games	Pos.
1961	OAK	A	10	OT

C.R. Roberts
ROBERTS, CORNELIUS R.
B. Feb. 24, 1936, Los Angeles, CA
Southern California 6'3" 202 lbs.

Year	Team		Games	Pos.
1959	SF	N	1	FB
1960			12	FB
1961			12	FB
1962			2	FB
4 yrs.	27 games			

Fred Roberts
ROBERTS, FRED E.
B. 1907
Iowa 6'1" 200 lbs.

Year	Team		Games	Pos.
1930	POR	N	12	G, E
1931			12	G
1932			1	G
3 yrs.	25 games			

Gary Roberts
ROBERTS, GARY
B. Nov. 30, 1946, Parkersburg, WV
Purdue 6'2" 242 lbs.

Year	Team		Games	Pos.
1970	ATL	N	11	G

Gene Roberts
ROBERTS, EUGENE
B. 1926
Kansas/Tennessee-Chattanooga 5'11" 188 lbs.

Year	Team		Games	Pos.
1947	NYG	N	9	FB
1948			11	FB
1949			12	FB
1950			12	FB
4 yrs.	44 games			

George Roberts
ROBERTS, GEORGE WILLIAM
B. Jun. 10, 1955, Lynchburg, VA
Virginia Tech 6'0" 178 lbs.

Year	Team		Games	Pos.
1978	MIA	N	16	P
1979			16	P
1980			16	P
1981	SD	N	16	P
1982	ATL	N	3	P
5 yrs.	67 games			

Greg Roberts
ROBERTS, GREGORY LAFAYETTE
B. Nov. 29, 1956, Nacogdoches, TX
Oklahoma 6'3" 262 lbs.

Year	Team		Games	Pos.
1979	TB	N	16	G

731

Year	Team	Games	Pos.

Greg Roberts continued

Year	Team		Games	Pos.
1980			6	G
1981			16	G
1982			7	G

4 yrs. 45 games

Guy Roberts
ROBERTS, GUY M. (Zeke)
B. May 10, 1900, Schaller, IA
D. Jun. 8, 1993, Los Altos, CA
Iowa State 5'8" 175 lbs.

1926	CLE	A	4	HB, QB, FB
1926	CAN	N	3	HB
1927	POT	N	7	HB, QB, FB

2 yrs. 14 games

Guy Roberts
ROBERTS, GUY MICHAEL (Link)
B. Jun. 12, 1950, North Babylon, NY
Maryland 6'1" 218 lbs.

1972	HOU	N	7	CB
1973			14	LB
1974			14	LB
1975			14	LB
1976	ATL	N	14	LB
1977	MIA	N	14	S

6 yrs. 77 games

Hal Roberts
ROBERTS, HAROLD LYNN
B. Aug. 25, 1952, Dallas, TX
Houston 6'1" 180 lbs.

1974	STL	N	14	P

Jack Roberts
ROBERTS, JACK (Ripper)
B. 1909
Georgia 6'0" 210 lbs.

1932	BOS	N	2	QB
1932	SI	N	3	FB, HB
1933	PHI	N	9	HB
1934			1	HB
1934	PIT	N	0	HB, QB, FB

3 yrs. 15 games

Jim Roberts
ROBERTS, JAMES B. (Red)
B. 1900, Somerset, KY
D. Jun. 27, 1945, Middlesboro, KY
Centre 6'2" 235 lbs.

1922	TOL	N	2	HB, T
1923	AKR	N	1	E
1926	CLE	A	5	T

3 yrs. 8 games

Larry Roberts
ROBERTS, LARRY
B. Jun. 2, 1963, Dothan, AL
Alabama 6'3" 264 lbs.

1986	SF	N	16	DE
1987			11	DE
1988			16	DE
1989			15	DE
1990			6	DE
1991			16	DE
1992			3	DE
1993			6	DE

8 yrs. 89 games

Mace Roberts
ROBERTS, MASON W.
B. Jun. 25, 1896, Illinois
D. Jan., 1971, Hammond, IN
None 6'0" 185 lbs.

1920	HAM	A	2	E
1921			1	E
1922	HAM	N	2	T, G

Mace Roberts continued

Year	Team		Games	Pos.
1924			3	E, G

4 yrs. 8 games

Ray Roberts
ROBERTS, RICHARD RAY
B. Jun. 3, 1969, Asheville, NC
Virginia 6'6" 304 lbs.

1992	SEA	N	16	OT
1993			16	OT
1994			14	OT
1995			11	OT
1996	DET	N	16	OT

5 yrs. 73 games

Tim Roberts
ROBERTS, TIM
B. Apr. 14, 1969, Atlanta, GA
Southern Mississippi 6'6" 309 lbs.

1992	HOU	N	6	DT
1993			6	DT
1994			13	DT
1995	NE	N	13	DE

4 yrs. 38 games

Tom Roberts
ROBERTS, THOMAS A.
B. Apr. 1, 1916, New Troy, MI
D. Apr. 8, 1990, Chicago, IL
DePaul 6'1" 215 lbs.

1943	NYG	N	8	T, G
1944	CHIB	N	7	T, G
1945			9	T

3 yrs. 24 games

Walt Roberts
ROBERTS, WALTER (The Flea)
B. Feb. 15, 1942, Texarkana, TX
San Jose State 5'10" 167 lbs.

1964	CLE	N	14	FL
1965			14	FL
1966			14	OE
1967	NO	N	13	FL
1969	WAS	N	14	WR
1970			14	WR

6 yrs. 83 games

Wesley Roberts
ROBERTS, WESLEY LEE
B. Aug. 1, 1957, Dodge City, KS
Texas Christian 6'6" 253 lbs.

1980	NYJ	N	5	DE

Willie Roberts
ROBERTS, WILLIE
B. Jun. 28, 1948, Colquitt, GA
Houston 6'1" 190 lbs.

1973	CHI	N	4	CB

Wooky Roberts
ROBERTS, WOLCOTT A.
B. Sep. 1, 1897
D. Aug. 27, 1951
Colgate/Navy 5'7" 160 lbs.

1922	CAN	N	11	QB, HB
1923			8	QB
1924	CLE	N	9	QB
1925				QB
1926	FRA	N	7	QB, HB, FB

5 yrs. 37 games

Bob Robertson
ROBERTSON, JOHN ROBERT
B. Dec. 24, 1946, Pittsfield, IL
Illinois 6'4" 246 lbs.

1968	HOU	A	14	C

Bobbie Robertson
ROBERTSON, ROBERT JAMES
B. Jun. 18, 1917, Pine Ridge, SD
St. Mary's/Southern California 5'11" 185 lbs.

1942	BKN	N	11	HB

Harry Robertson
ROBERTSON, HAROLD J.
B. Mar. 4, 1896, Chambly, Ont.
Deceased
Syracuse 5'10" 185 lbs.

1922	ROC	N	1	T

Isiah Robertson
ROBERTSON, ISIAH (Butch)
B. Aug. 17, 1949, New Orleans, LA
Southern University 6'3" 225 lbs.

1971	LA	N	14	LB
1972			14	LB
1973			14	LB
1974			14	LB
1975			14	LB
1976			14	LB
1977			14	LB
1978			13	LB
1979	BUF	N	16	LB
1980			16	LB
1981			16	LB
1982			9	LB

12 yrs. 168 games

Jimmy Robertson
ROBERTSON, JAMES A.
B. Mar. 8, 1901
D. Dec., 1974, Cuyahoga Falls, OH
Carnegie-Mellon 5'8" 160 lbs.

1924	AKR	N	7	HB, QB, FB
1925			8	QB

2 yrs. 15 games

Marcus Robertson
ROBERTSON, MARCUS AARON
B. Oct. 2, 1969, Pasadena, CA
Iowa State 5'11" 197 lbs.

1991	HOU	N	16	CB
1992			16	CB, S
1993			13	S, CB
1994			16	S
1995			2	S
1996			16	S

6 yrs. 79 games

Tom Robertson
ROBERTSON, THOMAS B.
B. Jul. 25, 1917, Lawton, OK
Louisiana State/Tulsa 6'0" 199 lbs.

1941	BKN	N	11	C, G
1942			9	C
1946	NY	AA	14	C

3 yrs. 34 games

Paul Robeson
ROBESON, PAUL LEROY
B. Apr. 9, 1898, Princeton, NJ
D. Jan. 23, 1976, Philadelphia, PA
Rutgers 6'3" 219 lbs.

1921	AKR	A	9	E, T, G
1922	MIL	N	7	E, QB

2 yrs. 16 games

Bill Robinson
ROBINSON, WILLIAM
B. Sep. 29, 1929
Lincoln (Pennsylvania) 6'0" 195 lbs.

1952	GB	N	2	HB

Billy Robinson
ROBINSON, JOHN WILLIAM
B. Feb. 13, 1963
Arizona State 6'1" 200 lbs.

1987	CLE	N	3	S, CB

Bo Robinson
ROBINSON, MELVIN DELL
B. May 27, 1956, La Mesa, TX
West Texas State 6'2" 230 lbs.

1979	DET	N	14	FB
1980			14	RB
1981	ATL	N	15	RB
1982			9	RB
1983			12	RB
1984	NE	N	16	RB

6 yrs. 80 games

Charley Robinson
ROBINSON, CHARLES
B. May 30, 1927, Lester Manor, VA
Morgan State 6'0" 240 lbs.

1954	BAL	N		G

Craig Robinson
ROBINSON, JOE CRAIG
B. Dec. 23, 1948, Austin, TX
Houston 6'4" 250 lbs.

1972	NO	N	8	OT
1973			11	OT

2 yrs. 19 games

Dave Robinson
ROBINSON, RICHARD DAVID
B. May 3, 1941, Mount Holly, NJ
Penn State 6'3" 243 lbs.

1963	GB	N	14	LB
1964			11	LB
1965			14	LB
1966			14	LB
1967			14	LB
1968			14	LB
1969			14	LB
1970			4	LB
1971			4	LB
1972			14	LB
1973	WAS	N	14	LB
1974			14	LB

12 yrs. 145 games

DeJuan Robinson
ROBINSON, DEJUAN
B. Jun. 3, 1965, Selma, AL
Northern Arizona 5'10" 185 lbs.

1987	CLE	N	3	CB

Don Robinson
ROBINSON, DON
B. Feb. 5, 1965
Baylor 6'5" 280 lbs.

1987	ATL	N	2	OT, G

Ed Robinson
ROBINSON, ED
B. Dec. 7, 1970, De Funiak Springs, FL
Florida 6'0" 228 lbs.

1994	PIT	N	16	LB

Eddie Robinson
ROBINSON, EDDIE JOSEPH
B. Apr. 13, 1970, New Orleans, LA
Alabama State 6'1" 242 lbs.

1992	HOU	N	9	LB
1993			16	LB
1994			15	LB
1995			16	LB

Year	Team	Games	Pos.

Eddie Robinson continued
| 1996 | JAC N | 16 | LB |
| 5 yrs. | 72 games | | |

Eddie Robinson
ROBINSON, ELDRED
B. Aug. 26, 1904
D. Sep., 1986, Hoagland, IN
None 190 lbs.
1923	HAM N	3	HB, FB
1924		4	HB
1925		5	HB, QB
1926		1	HB
1926	LOU N	4	HB
4 yrs.	17 games		

Eugene Robinson
ROBINSON, EUGENE K.
B. May 28, 1963, Hartford, CT
Colgate 6'0" 186 lbs.
1985	SEA N	16	CB
1986		16	S
1987		12	S
1988		16	S
1989		16	S
1990		16	S
1991		16	S
1992		16	S
1993		16	S
1994		14	S
1995		16	S
1996	GB N	16	S
12 yrs.	186 games		

Frank Robinson
ROBINSON, FRANK LAWSON
B. Jan. 11, 1969, Newark, NJ
Boise State 5'11" 174 lbs.
1992	CIN N	3	LB
1992	DEN N	12	CB
1993		16	CB
2 yrs.	31 games		

Fred Robinson
ROBINSON, FRED LEE
B. Oct. 22, 1961, Miami, FL
Miami (Florida) 6'5" 240 lbs.
1984	SD N	16	DE
1985		16	DE
1986		10	LB
1986	MIA N	4	LB
3 yrs.	46 games		

Fred Robinson
ROBINSON, FREDERICK
B. Sep. 2, 1930, West Haven, CT
Washington 6'1" 242 lbs.
| 1957 | CLE N | 12 | G |

Freddie Robinson
ROBINSON, FREDDIE
B. Feb. 1, 1964, Mobile, AL
Alabama 6'1" 191 lbs.
1987	IND N	9	DB
1988		13	CB, S
2 yrs.	22 games		

Gerald Robinson
ROBINSON, GERALD
B. May 4, 1963, Tuskegee, AL
Auburn 6'3" 260 lbs.
1986	MIN N	12	DE
1987		4	DE
1989	SD N	2	DE
1990		10	DE
1991	LARM N	15	DE
1992		16	DE

Gerald Robinson continued
1993		16	DE
1994		13	DE
8 yrs.	88 games		

Gil Robinson
ROBINSON, GILMER G.
B. Apr. 18, 1910, Spencer, NC
D. Jul. 11, 1985, Hemet, CA
Catawba
| 1933 | PIT N | 1 | E |

Glenn Robinson
ROBINSON, GLENN WILLIAM
B. Oct. 20, 1951, Killeen, TX
Oklahoma State 6'6" 242 lbs.
1975	BAL N	11	DE
1976	TB N	14	DE
1977		14	DE
3 yrs.	39 games		

Greg Robinson
ROBINSON, GREG
B. Aug. 7, 1969, Grenada, MS
Northeast Louisiana 5'10" 200 lbs.
1993	LARI N	12	RB
1995	STL N	6	RB
1996		11	RB
3 yrs.	29 games		

Greg Robinson
ROBINSON, GREGORY LOUIS
B. Dec. 25, 1962, Sacramento, CA
Nevada-Reno/Sacramento State 6'5" 285 lbs.
1986	TB N	3	OT
1987	NE N	3	OT
2 yrs.	6 games		

Gregg Robinson
ROBINSON, GREGG ALAN
B. Aug. 16, 1956, Palmer, MS
Dartmouth 6'6" 255 lbs.
| 1978 | NYJ N | 16 | DT |

Jack Robinson
ROBINSON, JOHN
B. 1912, Miami, NM
Northeast Missouri State 6'3" 220 lbs.
1935	BKN N	8	T
1936		4	T
1936	CHIC N	8	T
1937		11	T
1938	PIT N	2	T
1938	CLE N	6	T, G
4 yrs.	39 games		

Jacque Robinson
ROBINSON, JACQUE
B. Mar. 5, 1963, Oakland, CA
Washington 5'11" 215 lbs.
| 1987 | PHI N | 3 | RB |

Jeff Robinson
ROBINSON, JEFF
B. Feb. 20, 1970, Kennewick, WA
Idaho 6'4" 265 lbs.
1993	DEN N	16	DE
1994		16	DE
1995		16	DE
1996		16	DE
4 yrs.	64 games		

Jeroy Robinson
ROBINSON, JEROY

Jeroy Robinson continued
B. Jun. 14, 1968, Houston, TX
Texas A&M 6'1" 241 lbs.
| 1990 | PHX N | 3 | LB |

Jerry Robinson
ROBINSON, JERRY
B. Mar. 9, 1939, Jonesboro, LA
Grambling State 5'11" 195 lbs.
1962	SD A	14	OE
1963		14	OE
1964		14	OE
1965	NY A	4	OE
4 yrs.	46 games		

Jerry Robinson
ROBINSON, JERRY DEWAYNE
B. Dec. 18, 1956, San Francisco, CA
UCLA 6'2" 220 lbs.
1979	PHI N	16	LB
1980		16	LB
1981		15	LB
1982		9	LB
1983		16	LB
1984		15	LB
1985	LARI N	11	LB
1986		16	LB
1987		12	LB
1988		15	LB
1989		11	LB
1990		16	LB
1991		16	LB
13 yrs.	184 games		

Jimmy Robinson
ROBINSON, JAMES PETER
B. Jan. 3, 1953, Atlanta, GA
Georgia Tech 5'9" 170 lbs.
1976	NYG N	12	WR
1977		14	WR
1978		16	WR
1979		11	WR
1980	SF N	5	WR
5 yrs.	58 games		

Johnnie Robinson
ROBINSON, JOHNNIE
B. Nov. 6, 1944, Mobile, AL
Tennessee State 6'3" 205 lbs.
| 1966 | DET N | 14 | OE |

Johnny Robinson
ROBINSON, JOHNNY DEAN
B. Feb. 14, 1959, Jonesboro, LA
Louisiana Tech 6'2" 260 lbs.
1981	OAK N	16	DT
1982	LARI N	7	NT
1983		4	NT
3 yrs.	27 games		

Johnny Robinson
ROBINSON, JOHNNY NOLAN
B. Sep. 9, 1938, Delhi, LA
Louisiana State 6'0" 200 lbs.
1960	DAL A	14	HB
1961		14	HB
1962		14	DB
1963	KC A	14	DB
1964		10	DB
1965		14	DB
1966		14	DB
1967		14	DB
1968		14	DB
1969		14	S
1970	KC N	14	S
1971		14	S
12 yrs.	164 games		

Junior Robinson
ROBINSON, DAVID LEE, JR.
B. Feb. 3, 1968, High Point, NC
East Carolina 5'9" 181 lbs.
1990	NE N	16	CB
1992	DET N	10	CB
2 yrs.	26 games		

Karl Robinson
ROBINSON, KARL E.
B. 1903
Pennsylvania 5'10" 180 lbs.
| 1926 | PHI A | 10 | C |

Larry Robinson
ROBINSON, LARRY
B. Apr. 6, 1951, Appomattox, VA
Tennessee 6'4" 210 lbs.*
| 1973 | DAL N | 4 | DB |

Larry Robinson
ROBINSON, LARRY WAYNE
B. Apr. 30, 1962, Natchitoches, LA
Northwestern State (Louisiana) 5'9" 194 lbs.
| 1987 | NYJ N | 3 | CB |

Lybrant Robinson
ROBINSON, LYBRANT
B. Aug. 31, 1964, Salisbury, MD
Delaware State 6'4" 250 lbs.
| 1989 | WAS N | 5 | DE |

Mark Robinson
ROBINSON, MARK LEON
B. Sep. 13, 1962, Washington, DC
Penn State 5'11" 204 lbs.
1984	KC N	16	S
1985		11	S
1986		9	S
1987		12	S
1988	TB N	9	DB
1989		15	CB, S
1990		16	S
7 yrs.	88 games		

Matt Robinson
ROBINSON, MATTHEW GILLETTE
B. Jun. 28, 1955, Farmington, MI
Georgia 6'2" 196 lbs.
1977	NYJ N	4	QB
1978		16	QB
1979		16	QB
1980	DEN N	14	QB
1981	BUF N	15	QB
1982		5	QB
6 yrs.	70 games		

Michael Robinson
ROBINSON, MICHAEL F.
B. Jun. 24, 1973, Richmond, VA
Hampton 6'1" 192 lbs.
| 1996 | GB N | 6 | CB |

Mike Robinson
ROBINSON, MICHAEL
B. Aug. 19, 1956, Cleveland, OH
Oklahoma State/Arizona 6'4" 270 lbs.
1981	CLE N	10	DE
1982		8	DE
2 yrs.	18 games		

Patrick Robinson
ROBINSON, PATRICK LAVEL

733

Year	Team		Games	Pos.

Patrick Robinson *continued*
B. Oct. 3, 1969, Memphis, TN
Tennessee State 5'8" 176 lbs.

Year	Team		Games	Pos.
1993	CIN	N	15	WR
1994	ARI	N	15	WR

2 yrs. 30 games

Paul Robinson
ROBINSON, PAUL HARVEY
(Cactus Comet)
B. Dec. 19, 1944, Tucson, AZ
Arizona 6'0" 199 lbs.

Year	Team		Games	Pos.
1968	CIN	A	14	HB
1969			14	RB
1970	CIN	N	14	RB
1971			14	RB
1972			4	RB
1972	HOU	N	8	RB
1973			11	RB

6 yrs. 79 games

Rafael Robinson
ROBINSON, EUGENE RAFAEL
B. Jun. 19, 1969, Marshall, TX
Wisconsin 5'11" 200 lbs.

Year	Team		Games	Pos.
1992	SEA	N	6	S
1993			16	S
1994			16	S
1995			13	S
1996	HOU	N	16	S

5 yrs. 67 games

Rex Robinson
ROBINSON, NOBLE REXFORD
B. Mar. 17, 1959, Marietta, GA
Georgia 5'11" 205 lbs.

Year	Team		Games	Pos.
1982	NE	N	3	K

Shelton Robinson
ROBINSON, SHELTON
B. Sep. 14, 1960, Goldsboro, NC
North Carolina 6'2" 233 lbs.

Year	Team		Games	Pos.
1982	SEA	N	9	LB
1983			16	LB
1984			16	LB
1985			15	LB
1986	DET	N	16	LB
1987			12	LB
1988			12	LB

7 yrs. 96 games

Stacy Robinson
ROBINSON, STACY
B. Feb. 19, 1962, St. Paul, MN
Prairie View A&M/North Dakota State 5'11" 186 lbs.

Year	Team		Games	Pos.
1985	NYG	N	4	WR
1986			12	WR
1987			5	WR
1988			11	WR
1989			6	WR
1990			5	WR

6 yrs. 43 games

Tony Robinson
ROBINSON, TONY
B. Jan. 22, 1964
Tennessee 6'3" 200 lbs.

Year	Team		Games	Pos.
1987	WAS	N	1	QB

Virgil Robinson
ROBINSON, VIRGIL, JR.
B. Nov. 2, 1947, Inverness, MS
Grambling State 5'11" 195 lbs.

Year	Team		Games	Pos.
1971	NO	N	11	RB
1972			3	RB

2 yrs. 14 games

Wayne Robinson
ROBINSON, WAYNE L.
B. Jan. 14, 1930, Minneapolis, MN
Minnesota 6'2" 225 lbs.

Year	Team		Games	Pos.
1952	PHI	N	12	C
1953			11	C
1954			12	C, LB
1955			12	LB
1956			11	LB

5 yrs. 58 games

Terry Robiskie
ROBISKIE, TERRY JOSEPH
B. Nov. 12, 1954, New Orleans, LA
Louisiana State 6'1" 210 lbs.

Year	Team		Games	Pos.
1977	OAK	N	14	RB
1978			7	RB
1979			3	RB
1980	MIA	N	8	FB
1981			1	RB

5 yrs. 33 games

Burle Robison
ROBISON, BURLE HOOVER
(Buke)
B. Feb. 18, 1910, Provo, UT
D. Dec. 8, 1962, Reno, NV
Brigham Young 6'4" 197 lbs.

Year	Team		Games	Pos.
1935	PHI	N	7	E, C

George Robison
ROBISON, GEORGE
B. 1930
Virginia Military Institute 6'2" 215 lbs.

Year	Team		Games	Pos.
1952	DAL	N	3	G

Tommy Robison
ROBISON, TOMMY L.
B. Nov. 17, 1961, Merkle, TX
Texas A&M 6'4" 290 lbs.

Year	Team		Games	Pos.
1987	GB	N	3	OT
1989	ATL	N	9	G

2 yrs. 12 games

Hal Robl
ROBL, HAROLD
B. 1918
Wisconsin-Oshkosh 6'0" 227 lbs.

Year	Team		Games	Pos.
1945	CHIC	N	2	FB

Ed Robnett
ROBNETT, WILLIAM EDWARD
B. 1920
D. Sep. 20, 1990
Texas A&M/Texas Tech 5'8" 205 lbs.

Year	Team		Games	Pos.
1947	SF	AA	4	B

Marshall Robnett
ROBNETT, MARSHALL FOCH
B. Mar. 8, 1919, Klondike, TX
D. Nov. 28, 1967, Dallas, TX
East Texas State/Texas A&M 6'0" 205 lbs.

Year	Team		Games	Pos.
1943	CHIC	N	9	G
1944	C-P	N	8	C, G
1945	CHIC	N	5	C

3 yrs. 22 games

Frank Robotti
ROBOTTI, FRANK
B. 1940
Boston College 6'0" 220 lbs.

Year	Team		Games	Pos.
1961	BOS	A	12	LB

Andy Robustelli
ROBUSTELLI, ANDREW RICHARD
B. Dec. 6, 1925, Stamford, CT
Arnold 6'1" 230 lbs.

Year	Team		Games	Pos.
1951	LA	N	11	E
1952			11	E
1953			12	E
1954			12	E
1955			12	E
1956	NYG	N	12	E
1957			12	E
1958			12	E
1959			12	E
1960			12	E
1961			14	DE
1962			14	DE
1963			14	DE
1964			14	DE

14 yrs. 174 games

Doug Roby
ROBY, DOUGLAS F.
B. 1898
Deceased
Phillips/Michigan 5'10" 160 lbs.

Year	Team		Games	Pos.
1923	CLE	N	7	HB

Reggie Roby
ROBY, REGINALD HENRY
B. Jul. 30, 1961, Waterloo, IA
Iowa 6'2" 243 lbs.

Year	Team		Games	Pos.
1983	MIA	N	16	P
1984			16	P
1985			15	P
1986			10	P
1987			15	P
1988			16	P
1989			16	P
1990			16	P
1991			16	P
1992			9	P
1993	WAS	N	15	P
1994			16	P
1995	TB	N	16	P
1996	HOU	N	16	P

14 yrs. 208 games

Alden Roche
ROCHE, ALDEN STEPHEN, JR.
B. Apr. 9, 1945, New Orleans, LA
Southern University 6'4" 255 lbs.

Year	Team		Games	Pos.
1970	DEN	N	14	DE
1971	GB	N	14	DE
1972			14	DE
1973			13	DE
1974			14	DE
1975			14	DE
1976			14	DE
1977	SEA	N	13	DE
1978			8	DE

9 yrs. 118 games

Brian Roche
ROCHE, BRIAN
B. May 5, 1973, Downey, CA
Cal Poly (San Luis Obispo)*/San Jose State 6'4" 255 lbs.

Year	Team		Games	Pos.
1996	SD	N	13	TE

Paul Rochester
ROCHESTER, PAUL GORDON
B. Jul. 15, 1938, Lansing, MI
Michigan State 6'2" 254 lbs.

Year	Team		Games	Pos.
1960	DAL	A	8	DT
1961			14	DT
1962			13	DT
1963	KC	A	9	DT
1964	NY	A	14	DT

Paul Rochester *continued*

Year	Team		Games	Pos.
1965			13	DT
1966			12	DT
1967			14	DT
1968			14	DT
1969			13	DT

10 yrs. 124 games

Walter Rock
ROCK, WALTER WARFIELD
B. Nov. 4, 1941, Cleveland, OH
Maryland 6'5" 252 lbs.

Year	Team		Games	Pos.
1963	SF	N	7	DT
1964			14	OT
1965			14	OT
1966			14	OT
1967			14	OT
1968	WAS	N	14	OT
1969			12	OT
1970			13	OT
1971			14	OT
1972			14	OT
1973			7	OT

11 yrs. 137 games

Lyle Rockenbach
ROCKENBACH, LYLE
B. Mar. 1, 1915, Prairie View, IL
Michigan State 5'9" 192 lbs.

Year	Team		Games	Pos.
1943	DET	N	8	G

David Rocker
ROCKER, DAVID DEAUNDRA
B. Mar. 12, 1969, Atlanta, GA
Auburn 6'4" 267 lbs.

Year	Team		Games	Pos.
1991	LARM	N	6	DT
1992			3	DT
1993			14	DT
1994			12	DT

4 yrs. 35 games

Tracy Rocker
ROCKER, TRACY QUINTON
B. Apr. 9, 1966, Atlanta, GA
Auburn 6'3" 288 lbs.

Year	Team		Games	Pos.
1989	WAS	N	16	DT
1990			8	DT

2 yrs. 24 games

Jim Rockford
ROCKFORD, JAMES KYLE
B. Sep. 5, 1961, Bloomington, IL
Oklahoma 5'10" 180 lbs.

Year	Team		Games	Pos.
1985	SD	N	1	CB, S

Chris Rockins
ROCKINS, CHRIS
B. May 18, 1962, Sherman, TX
Oklahoma State 6'0" 195 lbs.

Year	Team		Games	Pos.
1984	CLE	N	16	S
1985			16	S
1986			16	S
1987			12	S

4 yrs. 60 games

Hank Rockwell
ROCKWELL, HENRY ALBERT
B. Feb. 10, 1917, Whittier, CA
Arizona State 6'4" 231 lbs.

Year	Team		Games	Pos.
1940	CLE	N	11	G
1941			9	G
1942			7	C, E, T
1946	LA	AA	13	C
1948			13	G

5 yrs. 53 games

Mike Rodak
RODAK, MICHAEL
B. Feb. 11, 1917, Orient, PA
D. Dec., 1980, Weirton, WV
Case Western Reserve 5'10" 196 lbs.

Year	Team		Games	Pos.
1939	CLE	N	6	E, HB
1940			1	E, HB
1942	PIT	N	5	E, G
3 yrs.	12 games			

Jeff Rodenberger
RODENBERGER, JEFFREY LEE
B. Nov. 3, 1959, Quakertown, PA
Maryland 6'3" 235 lbs.

Year	Team		Games	Pos.
1987	NO	N	3	RB

Mark Rodenhauser
RODENHAUSER, MARK
B. Jun. 1, 1961, Addison, IL
Illinois State 6'5" 267 lbs.

Year	Team		Games	Pos.
1987	CHI	N	9	C
1989	MIN	N	16	C
1990	SD	N	16	C
1991			10	C
1992	CHI	N	13	C
1993	DET	N	16	C
1994			16	C
1995	CAR	N	16	C
1996			16	C
9 yrs.	128 games			

Mirro Roder
RODER, MIRRO
B. Jan. 22, 1944, Olomouc, Czechoslovakia
none 6'1" 221 lbs.

Year	Team		Games	Pos.
1973	CHI	N	13	K
1974			14	K
1976	TB	N	2	K
3 yrs.	29 games			

Ben Roderick
RODERICK, BENJAMIN A.
B. May 11, 1899
Deceased
Wooster/Boston College/Columbia 5'9" 175 lbs.

Year	Team		Games	Pos.
1923	CAN	N	4	HB
1923	BUF	N	4	HB
1926	CAN	N	11	HB, FB, QB
1927	BUF	N	3	HB
3 yrs.	22 games			

John Roderick
RODERICK, JOHN WILLIAM
B. Aug. 21, 1944, Fort Worth, TX
Southern Methodist 6'1" 180 lbs.

Year	Team		Games	Pos.
1966	MIA	A	6	FL, SE
1967			1	FL
1968	OAK	A	11	WR
3 yrs.	18 games			

Del Rodgers
RODGERS, RODERICK DEL
B. Jun. 22, 1960, Tacoma, WA
Utah 5'11" 197 lbs.

Year	Team		Games	Pos.
1982	GB	N	9	RB
1984			14	RB
1987	SF	N	7	RB
1988			1	RB
4 yrs.	31 games			

Hosea Rodgers
RODGERS, HOSEA W.
B. Dec. 25, 1921, Brewton, AL
Alabama/North Carolina 6'1" 192 lbs.

Year	Team		Games	Pos.
1949	LA	AA	12	B

John Rodgers
RODGERS, JOHN DARREN
B. Feb. 7, 1960, Omaha, TX
Louisiana Tech 6'2" 220 lbs.

Year	Team		Games	Pos.
1982	PIT	N	7	TE
1983			15	TE
1984			6	TE
3 yrs.	28 games			

Johnny Rodgers
RODGERS, JOHN STEVE
B. Jul. 5, 1951, Omaha, NE
Nebraska 5'10" 180 lbs.

Year	Team		Games	Pos.
1977	SD	N	11	WR
1978			6	RB, WR
2 yrs.	17 games			

Tom Rodgers
RODGERS, THOMAS EDWARD
B. 1923
Bucknell 6'0" 248 lbs.

Year	Team		Games	Pos.
1947	BOS	N	9	T

Tyrone Rodgers
RODGERS, TYRONE
B. Apr. 27, 1969, Longview, TX
Oklahoma/Washington 6'3" 266 lbs.

Year	Team		Games	Pos.
1992	SEA	N	16	DT
1993			16	DT
1994			5	DT
3 yrs.	37 games			

Willie Rodgers
RODGERS, WILLIE DANIEL, JR.
B. Feb. 8, 1949, Suffolk, VA
Kentucky State 6'0" 210 lbs.

Year	Team		Games	Pos.
1972	HOU		14	RB
1974			14	RB
1975			14	RB
3 yrs.	42 games			

Jess Rodriguez
RODRIGUEZ, JESS
B. Aug. 7, 1901, Aviles, Spain
D. Oct. 12, 1983, Clarksburg, WV
Salem 5'7" 160 lbs.

Year	Team		Games	Pos.
1929	BUF	N	5	HB, T, FB

Kelly Rodriguez
RODRIGUEZ, KELLY
B. Aug. 9, 1906, Aviles, Spain
West Virginia Wesleyan 5'10" 180 lbs.

Year	Team		Games	Pos.
1930	FRA	N	13	HB, FB
1930	MIN	N	2	QB
1 yr.	15 games			

Mike Rodriguez
RODRIGUEZ, MIKE
B. Dec. 5, 1961
Alabama 6'1" 275 lbs.

Year	Team		Games	Pos.
1987	LARI	N	1	DT

Ruben Rodriguez
RODRIGUEZ, RUBEN ANGEL
B. Mar. 3, 1965, Visalia, CA
Arizona 6'2" 209 lbs.

Year	Team		Games	Pos.
1987	SEA	N	12	P
1988			16	P
1989			16	P
1992	DEN	N	5	P
1992	NYG	N	4	P
4 yrs.	53 games			

Bill Roe
ROE, WILLIAM OLIVER, JR.

Bill Roe continued
B. Feb. 6, 1958, South Bend, IN
Colorado 6'3" 230 lbs.

Year	Team		Games	Pos.
1980	DAL	N	16	LB
1987	NO	N	3	LB
2 yrs.	19 games			

James Roe
ROE, JAMES
B. Aug. 23, 1973, Richmond, VA
Norfolk State 6'1" 187 lbs.

Year	Team		Games	Pos.
1996	BAL	N	1	WR

Herb Roedel
ROEDEL, HERBERT
B. 1939
Marquette 6'3" 230 lbs.

Year	Team		Games	Pos.
1961	OAK	A	14	G

Jon Roehlk
ROEHLK, JON
B. Jun. 25, 1961, Davenport, IA
Iowa 6'2" 251 lbs.

Year	Team		Games	Pos.
1987	CHI	N	3	G

Bill Roehnelt
ROEHNELT, WILLIAM EDWARD
B. Jun. 4, 1936, Peoria, IL
D. Jul. 19, 1968
Bradley 6'1" 227 lbs.

Year	Team		Games	Pos.
1958	CHIB	N	12	LB
1959			12	LB
1960	WAS	N	12	LB
1961	DEN	A	4	LB
1962			14	LB
5 yrs.	54 games			

Johnny Roepke
ROEPKE, JOHN P.
B. Dec. 28, 1905
D. Feb., 1962
Penn State 5'11" 175 lbs.

Year	Team		Games	Pos.
1928	FRA	N	10	HB, FB, QB

Fritz Roessler
ROESSLER, FREDERICK
B. Jul. 20, 1898, Wisconsin
D. Aug., 1967, Bradenton, FL
Marquette 6'1" 189 lbs.

Year	Team		Games	Pos.
1922	RAC	N	11	E
1923			7	E, G, HB
1924			2	E
1925	MIL	N	6	E
4 yrs.	26 games			

Bill Roffler
ROFFLER, WILLIAM H. (Bud)
B. Sep. 16, 1930, Pine City, WA
Washington State 6'1" 200 lbs.

Year	Team		Games	Pos.
1954	PHI	N	3	HB

John Rogalla
ROGALLA, JOHN FRANCIS
B. May 31, 1917, Duryea, PA
Scranton 6'0" 215 lbs.

Year	Team		Games	Pos.
1945	PHI	N	8	FB

Dan Rogas
ROGAS, DANIEL WILLIAM
B. Aug. 9, 1926, Port Arthur, TX
Tulane 6'1" 228 lbs.

Year	Team		Games	Pos.
1951	DET	N	12	T
1952	PHI	N	10	G
2 yrs.	22 games			

Fran Rogel
ROGEL, FRANCIS STEPHEN
B. Dec. 12, 1927
Penn State 5'11" 203 lbs.

Year	Team		Games	Pos.
1950	PIT	N	12	FB
1951			12	FB
1952			12	FB
1953			12	FB
1954			12	FB
1955			12	FB
1956			12	FB
1957			12	FB
8 yrs.	96 games			

Bill Rogers
ROGERS, WILLIAM C.
B. Jun. 24, 1913, Westborough, MA
D. Apr., 1977, Northborough, MA
Villanova 5'11" 243 lbs.

Year	Team		Games	Pos.
1938	DET	N	8	T
1939			9	T
1940			7	G, T
1944			2	T, G
4 yrs.	26 games			

Charley Rogers
ROGERS, CHARLES S.
B. 1904
D. Jun. 26, 1986
Pennsylvania 5'10" 167 lbs.

Year	Team		Games	Pos.
1927	FRA	N	18	HB, QB, FB
1928			13	HB, FB, QB
1929			7	HB, E, FB
3 yrs.	38 games			

Cullen Rogers
ROGERS, CULLEN JAMES
B. May 29, 1921, Mart, TX
Texas A&M 5'10" 178 lbs.

Year	Team		Games	Pos.
1946	PIT	N	5	HB

Don Rogers
ROGERS, DONALD
B. Dec. 4, 1936, East Orange, NJ
South Carolina 6'2" 245 lbs.

Year	Team		Games	Pos.
1960	LA	A		C
1961	SD	A	14	C
1962			12	C
1963			14	C, G
1964			14	C
5 yrs.	54 games			

Don Rogers
ROGERS, DONALD LAVERT
B. Sep. 17, 1962, Texarkana, AR
D. 1986
UCLA 6'1" 206 lbs.

Year	Team		Games	Pos.
1984	CLE	N	15	S
1985			16	S
2 yrs.	31 games			

Doug Rogers
ROGERS, DOUGLAS KEITH
B. Sep. 23, 1960, Chico, CA
Stanford 6'5" 275 lbs.

Year	Team		Games	Pos.
1982	ATL	N	9	DE
1983			2	DE
1983	NE	N	10	DE
1984			12	DE
1986	SF	N	8	DE
4 yrs.	41 games			

George Rogers
ROGERS, GEORGE WASHINGTON, JR.
B. Dec. 8, 1958, Duluth, GA
South Carolina 6'2" 229 lbs.

Year	Team		Games	Pos.
1981	NO	N	16	RB

Year	Team		Games	Pos.

George Rogers continued

1982			6	RB
1983			13	RB
1984			16	RB
1985	WAS	N	15	RB
1986			15	RB
1987			11	RB
7 yrs.	92 games			

Glenn Rogers
ROGERS, GLENN, JR.
B. Jun. 8, 1969, Memphis, TN
Memphis State 6'0" 185 lbs.

| 1991 | TB | N | 5 | CB, S |

Glynn Rogers
ROGERS, GLYNN
B. 1915
Texas Christian 5'10" 220 lbs.

| 1939 | CHIC | N | 1 | G |

Jimmy Rogers
ROGERS, JAMES LEE
B. Jun. 29, 1955, Forrest City, AR
Oklahoma 5'10" 190 lbs.

1980	NO	N	16	RB
1981			15	RB
1982			9	RB
1983			16	RB
1984			16	RB
5 yrs.	72 games			

John Rogers
ROGERS, JOHN B. (Bee)
B. Jan. 18, 1910
D. Oct., 1968
Notre Dame 5'8" 208 lbs.

1933	CIN	N	10	C
1934	C-S	N	5	C
2 yrs.	15 games			

Lamar Rogers
ROGERS, LAMAR
B. Nov. 5, 1967, Opp, AL
Auburn 6'4" 292 lbs.

1991	CIN	N	11	DE
1992			15	DE
2 yrs.	26 games			

Mel Rogers
ROGERS, MELVIN NATHANIEL
B. Apr. 23, 1947, St. Petersburg, FL
Florida A&M 6'2" 231 lbs.

1971	SD	N	13	LB
1973			10	LB
1974			3	LB
1976	LA	N	11	LB
1977	CHI	N	5	LB
5 yrs.	42 games			

Reggie Rogers
ROGERS, REGINALD O'KEITH
B. Jan. 21, 1964, Sacramento, CA
Washington 6'6" 278 lbs.

1987	DET	N	6	DE
1988			5	DE
1991	BUF	N	2	DE
1992	TB	N	2	DE
4 yrs.	15 games			

Sam Rogers
ROGERS, SAMMY LEE
B. May 30, 1970, Pontiac, MI
Colorado 6'3" 245 lbs.

| 1994 | BUF | N | 14 | LB |
| 1995 | | | 16 | LB |

Sam Rogers continued

| 1996 | | | 14 | LB |
| 3 yrs. | 44 games | | | |

Stan Rogers
ROGERS, STAN
B. Mar. 10, 1952, Peckville, PA
Maryland 6'4" 255 lbs.

| 1975 | DEN | N | 14 | OT |

Steve Rogers
ROGERS, STEVE
B. Aug. 26, 1953, Jonesboro, LA
Louisiana State 6'2" 203 lbs.

1975	NO	N	13	RB
1976	NYJ	N	1	RB
2 yrs.	14 games			

Steve Rogers
ROGERS, STEVEN C.
B. Jan. 9, 1959, Escondido, CA
Oregon State/Brigham Young 6'5" 260 lbs.

| 1987 | KC | N | 3 | OT |

Tracy Rogers
ROGERS, TRACY DARIN
B. Aug. 13, 1967, Taft, CA
Fresno State 6'2" 241 lbs.

1990	KC		10	LB
1991			10	LB
1992			8	LB
1993			14	LB
1994			14	LB
1995			16	LB
1996			3	LB
7 yrs.	75 games			

Walt Rogers
ROGERS, WALTER
B. Apr. 18, 1893
D. Sep., 1964
Christian Brothers/Ohio University 5'9" 215 lbs.

1921	COL	A	1	HB
1922	COL		3	FB, G
2 yrs.	4 games			

George Rogge
ROGGE, GEORGE
B. May 9, 1906
D. Sep., 1980, Panama City, FL
Iowa 6'0" 186 lbs.

1931	CHIC	N	6	E
1932			9	E
1933			6	E
1934	C-S	N	3	E
4 yrs.	24 games			

Tom Roggeman
ROGGEMAN, THOMAS JOHN
B. Sep. 5, 1931, Mishawaka, IN
Purdue 6'0" 235 lbs.

1956	CHIB	N	12	G
1957			12	G
2 yrs.	24 games			

Len Rohde
ROHDE, LEONARD EMIL
B. Apr. 16, 1938, Palatine, IL
Utah State 6'4" 246 lbs.

1960	SF	N	12	OT
1961			14	OT
1962			14	OT
1963			14	OT
1964			14	OT

Len Rohde continued

1965			14	OT
1966			14	OT
1967			14	OT
1968			14	OT
1969			14	OT
1970			14	OT
1971			14	OT
1972			14	OT
1973			14	OT
1974			14	OT
15 yrs.	208 games			

George Rohleder
ROHLEDER, GEORGE R.
B. Oct. 3, 1898, Ohio
D. Feb. 17, 1958
Wittenberg 5'11" 215 lbs.

1925	COL	N	9	G, HB, FB, T
1926	AKR	N	6	T, G, C
2 yrs.	15 games			

Ray Rohrabaugh
ROHRABAUGH, RAYMOND (Red)
B. Sep. 6, 1900
D. Feb., 1986, Frankfort, IN
Franklin 5'11" 190 lbs.

| 1926 | RI | A | 7 | HB, QB |

Jeff Rohrer
ROHRER, JEFFREY CHARLES
B. Dec. 25, 1958, Inglewood, CA
Yale 6'3" 225 lbs.

1982	DAL	N	8	LB
1983			16	LB
1984			16	LB
1985			15	LB
1986			16	LB
1987			12	LB
6 yrs.	83 games			

Herm Rohrig
ROHRIG, HERMAN FRANCIS (Stumpy)
B. Mar. 19, 1918, Mason City, IA
Nebraska 5'8" 190 lbs.

1941	GB	N	9	HB
1946			8	HB
1947			7	HB
3 yrs.	24 games			

John Rokisky
ROKISKY, JOHN S. (Rock)
B. Nov. 30, 1922, Clarksburg, WV
Duquesne 6'2" 202 lbs.

1946	CLE	AA	5	E
1947	CHI	AA	14	E
1948	NY	AA	6	E
3 yrs.	25 games			

Benji Roland
ROLAND, MITCHELL BENJAMIN
B. Apr. 4, 1967, Eastman, GA
Auburn 6'3" 260 lbs.

| 1990 | TB | N | 3 | DE |

Johnny Roland
ROLAND, JOHNNY EARL
B. May 21, 1943, Corpus Christi, TX
Missouri 6'2" 213 lbs.

1966	STL	N	14	HB
1967			13	RB
1968			14	RB
1969			14	RB
1970			14	RB
1971			14	RB

Johnny Roland continued

1972			14	RB
1973	NYG	N	7	RB
8 yrs.	104 games			

Butch Rolle
ROLLE, DONALD DEMETRIUS
B. Aug. 19, 1964, Miami, FL
Michigan State 6'3" 242 lbs.

1986	BUF		16	TE
1987			12	TE
1988			16	TE
1989			16	TE
1990			16	TE
1991			16	TE
1992	PHX	N	16	TE
1993			16	TE
8 yrs.	124 games			

Dave Rolle
ROLLE, DAVID
B. 1938
Oklahoma 6'0" 215 lbs.

| 1960 | DEN | A | 14 | FB |

Dave Roller
ROLLER, DAVID EUELL
B. Oct. 28, 1949, Dayton, TN
Kentucky 6'2" 270 lbs.

1971	NYG	N	14	DT
1975	GB	N	6	DT
1976			14	DT
1977			13	DT
1978			16	DT
1979	MIN	N	15	DT
1980			15	DT
7 yrs.	93 games			

Henry Rolling
ROLLING, HENRY LEE
B. Sep. 8, 1965, Fort Eustis, VA
Nevada-Reno 6'2" 232 lbs.

1988	TB	N	15	LB
1989			6	LB
1990	SD	N	16	LB
1991			15	LB
1992			15	LB
1993	LARM	N	12	LB
1994			9	LB
7 yrs.	88 games			

George Roman
ROMAN, GEORGE, JR.
B. Feb. 20, 1926, Rankin, PA
Case Western Reserve 6'4" 242 lbs.

1948	BOS	N	12	T
1949	NYB	N	8	T
1950	NYG	N	6	T
3 yrs.	26 games			

John Roman
ROMAN, JOHN GEORGE
B. Aug. 31, 1952, Ventnor City, NJ
Idaho State 6'4" 253 lbs.

1976	NYJ	N	11	OL
1977			9	G, OT
1978			16	OT, G
1979			16	OT
1980			16	OT
1981			16	OT
1982			9	OT
7 yrs.	93 games			

Nick Roman
ROMAN, NICHOLAS GEORGE
B. Sep. 23, 1947, Canton, OH
Ohio State 6'3" 235 lbs.

| 1970 | CIN | N | 3 | DE |

Nick Roman *continued*

Year	Team		Games	Pos.
1971			12	DE
1972	CLE	N	10	DE
1973			14	DE
1974			12	DE
5 yrs.	51 games			

Steve Romanik
ROMANIK, STEPHEN
B. May 27, 1924, Millville, NJ
Villanova 6'1" 190 lbs.

Year	Team		Games	Pos.
1950	CHIB	N	1	QB
1951			12	QB
1952			10	QB
1953			1	QB
1953	CHIC	N	6	QB
1954			6	QB
5 yrs.	36 games			

Jim Romaniszyn
ROMANISZYN, JAMES CHRISTOPHER
B. Sep. 17, 1951, Titusville, PA
Edinboro State 6'2" 219 lbs.

Year	Team		Games	Pos.
1973	CLE	N	14	LB
1974			12	LB
1976	NE	N	11	LB
3 yrs.	37 games			

Jim Romano
ROMANO, JAMES JOHN
B. Mar. 4, 1960, Glen Cove, NY
Penn State 6'3" 260 lbs.

Year	Team		Games	Pos.
1982	LARI	N	5	C
1983			1	C
1984			6	C
1984	HOU	N	8	C
1985			16	C
1986			9	C
5 yrs.	45 games			

Bill Romanowski
ROMANOWSKI, WILLIAM THOMAS
B. Apr. 2, 1966, Vernon, CT
Boston College 6'4" 235 lbs.

Year	Team		Games	Pos.
1988	SF	N	16	LB
1989			16	LB
1990			16	LB
1991			16	LB
1992			16	LB
1993			16	LB
1994	PHI	N	16	LB
1995			16	LB
1996	DEN	N	16	LB
9 yrs.	144 games			

Dave Romasko
ROMASKO, DAVE
B. Nov. 3, 1963, Pocatello, ID
Idaho/Carroll (Wisconsin) 6'3" 241 lbs.

Year	Team		Games	Pos.
1987	CIN	N	3	TE

Rudy Romboli
ROMBOLI, RUDOLPH
B. May 1, 1923, Everett, MA
D. Jan. 3, 1980, Boston, MA
None 5'10" 213 lbs.

Year	Team		Games	Pos.
1946	BOS	N	3	FB
1947			12	FB
1948			12	FB
3 yrs.	27 games			

Stan Rome
ROME, STANFORD B.
B. Jun. 4, 1956, Valdosta, GA
Clemson 6'3" 209 lbs.

Year	Team		Games	Pos.
1979	KC	N	9	WR

Stan Rome *continued*

Year	Team		Games	Pos.
1980			10	WR
1981			16	WR
1982			7	WR
4 yrs.	42 games			

Tag Rome
ROME, ANTHONY NICHOLAS
B. Aug. 13, 1961, Donaldsonville, LA
Northeast Louisiana 5'9" 175 lbs.

Year	Team		Games	Pos.
1987	SD	N	3	WR

Tony Romeo
ROMEO, ANTHONY LAMAR
B. Mar. 7, 1938, St. Petersburg, FL
Deceased
Florida State 6'2" 225 lbs.

Year	Team		Games	Pos.
1961	DAL	A	14	OE
1962	BOS		14	OE
1963			14	OE
1964			14	OE
1965			14	OE
1966			14	TE
1967			5	TE
7 yrs.	89 games			

Rich Romer
ROMER, RICH
B. Feb. 27, 1966, East Greenbush, NY
Union (New York) 6'3" 222 lbs.

Year	Team		Games	Pos.
1988	CIN	N	4	LB
1989			5	LB
2 yrs.	9 games			

Ray Romero
ROMERO, RAY R.
B. Dec. 1, 1927, Wichita, KS
Kansas State 5'11" 213 lbs.

Year	Team		Games	Pos.
1951	PHI	N	7	G

Charles Romes
ROMES, CHARLES MICHAEL
B. Dec. 16, 1954, Verdun, France
North Carolina Central 6'1" 190 lbs.

Year	Team		Games	Pos.
1977	BUF	N	14	DB
1978			16	S
1979			16	CB
1980			16	CB
1981			16	CB
1982			9	CB
1983			16	CB
1984			16	CB
1985			16	CB
1986			16	CB
1987	SD	N	5	CB
11 yrs.	156 games			

Dick Romey
ROMEY, RICHARD E.
B. Mar. 12, 1905
D. Jul. 16, 1980, Mason City, IA
Iowa 6'1" 186 lbs.

Year	Team		Games	Pos.
1926	CHI	A	14	E

Al Romine
ROMINE, ALTON
B. Mar. 10, 1932, Florence, AL
North Alabama 6'2" 191 lbs.

Year	Team		Games	Pos.
1955	GB	N	4	HB
1958			12	HB
1960	DEN	A		HB
1961	BOS	A	1	DB
4 yrs.	17 games			

Milt Romney
ROMNEY, MILTON ADDAS

Milt Romney *continued*
B. Jun. 20, 1899, Salt Lake City, UT
D. Nov. 10, 1975, North Little Rock, AR
Utah/Chicago 5'8" 166 lbs.

Year	Team		Games	Pos.
1923	RAC	N	8	HB, T, QB
1924			10	QB, FB
1925	CHIB	N	14	HB, QB, FB
1926			16	QB, HB
1927			14	QB, HB
1928			11	QB
6 yrs.	73 games			

Gene Ronzani
RONZANI, EUGENE
B. Mar. 28, 1909, Iron Mountain, MI
D. Sep. 12, 1975, Lac du Flambeau, WI
Marquette 5'9" 200 lbs.

Year	Team		Games	Pos.
1933	CHIB	N	10	HB, FB
1934			12	HB
1935			11	HB, FB
1936			10	HB
1937			11	QB, HB
1938			7	QB, HB
1944			8	QB
1945			7	QB
8 yrs.	76 games			

Bill Rooney
ROONEY, WILLIAM
B. Jul. 16, 1896, Canada
D. Mar., 1966, Bronx, NY
none 6'2" 194 lbs.

Year	Team		Games	Pos.
1923	DUL	N	5	HB, FB
1924			6	FB
1925			2	FB
1925	NYG	N	7	HB, FB
1926	BKN	N	6	HB, QB, C
1927	DUL	N	9	C, G
1929	CHIC	N	5	C
6 yrs.	40 games			

Cobb Rooney
ROONEY, HARRY COBB
B. Mar. 23, 1900, Virginia, MN
D. May 14, 1973, Bremerton, WA
none 6'0" 185 lbs.

Year	Team		Games	Pos.
1924	DUL	N	6	QB
1925			3	QB, E
1926			14	HB, QB
1927			8	HB, QB
1928	NYY	N	3	QB, FB, HB
1929	CHIC	N	11	HB, QB
1930			10	HB, QB
7 yrs.	55 games			

Joe Rooney
ROONEY, JOSEPH P.
B. Aug. 28, 1898, Canada
D. Mar., 1979
None 6'0" 177 lbs.

Year	Team		Games	Pos.
1923	DUL	N	7	E
1924			6	E
1925	RI	N	10	E
1926	DUL	N	12	E
1927			9	E, T
1928	POT	N	10	E, QB
6 yrs.	54 games			

Mark Roopenian
ROOPENIAN, MARK
B. Jul. 10, 1958, Medford, MA
Boston College 6'5" 254 lbs.

Year	Team		Games	Pos.
1982	BUF	N	9	NT
1983			3	NT
2 yrs.	12 games			

Jim Root
ROOT, JAMES FREDERICK
B. Aug. 17, 1931, Toledo, OH
Miami (Ohio) 6'1" 185 lbs.

Year	Team		Games	Pos.
1953	CHIC	N	11	QB
1956			9	QB
2 yrs.	20 games			

John Roper
ROPER, JOHN ALFRED
B. Oct. 4, 1965, Houston, TX
Texas A&M 6'1" 232 lbs.

Year	Team		Games	Pos.
1989	CHI	N	16	LB
1990			14	LB
1991			16	LB
1992			16	LB
1993	DAL	N	3	LB
1993	PHI	N	3	LB
5 yrs.	68 games			

Durwood Roquemore
ROQUEMORE, DURWOOD CLINTON
B. Jan. 19, 1960, Dallas, TX
Texas A&I, Kingsville 6'1" 180 lbs.

Year	Team		Games	Pos.
1982	KC	N	9	S
1983			15	S
1987	BUF	N	5	S
3 yrs.	29 games			

Jim Rorison
RORISON, JAMES (Red)
B. Jul. 23, 1916
D. Oct., 1980
Southern California 6'3" 250 lbs.

Year	Team		Games	Pos.
1938	PIT	N	5	T

Spencer Rork
RORK, SPENCER J.
B. 1896
Deceased

Year	Team		Games	Pos.
1922	EVA	N	2	QB, HB

Dan Rosado
ROSADO, DANIEL PETER
B. Jul. 6, 1959, Lawton, OK
Northern Illinois 6'3" 280 lbs.

Year	Team		Games	Pos.
1987	SD	N	4	G, OT
1988			12	G, OT
2 yrs.	16 games			

Sal Rosato
ROSATO, SALVATORE
B. Jun. 16, 1918, Williamsport, PA
D. Jan., 1959
Villanova 6'1" 228 lbs.

Year	Team		Games	Pos.
1945	WAS	N	7	FB
1946			10	FB
1947			11	FB
3 yrs.	28 games			

Rosey Rosatti
ROSATTI, ROMAN F.
B. Sep. 12, 1895
D. Jul. 9, 1975, Norway, MI
Northern Michigan/Michigan 6'0" 211 lbs.

Year	Team		Games	Pos.
1923	CLE	N	7	T
1924	GB	N	11	T
1926			10	T
1927			6	T
1928	NYG	N	11	T, G
5 yrs.	45 games			

Harrison Rosdahl
ROSDAHL, HARRISON LYNN

Year	Team		Games	Pos.

Harrison Rosdahl *continued*
(Hatch)
B. Aug. 21, 1941, Hackensack, NJ
Penn State 6'5" 250 lbs.

Year	Team		Games	Pos.
1964	BUF	A	4	DE
1964	KC	A	7	DT
1965			14	DT
1966			5	G
3 yrs.	30 games			

Al Rose
ROSE, ALFRED (Big Un)
B. Jan. 26, 1907, Temple, TX
D. 1988
Texas 6'3" 201 lbs.

Year	Team		Games	Pos.
1930	PRO	N	11	E
1931			11	E
1932	GB	N	11	E
1933			10	E
1934			10	E
1935			11	E
1936			2	E
7 yrs.	66 games			

Barry Rose
ROSE, BARRY ALLAN
B. Jul. 28, 1968, Hudson, WI
Wisconsin-Stevens Point 6'0" 185 lbs.

Year	Team		Games	Pos.
1993	DEN	N	3	WR

Carlton Rose
ROSE, CARLTON
B. Feb. 8, 1962, Pompano Beach, FL
Michigan 6'2" 220 lbs.

Year	Team		Games	Pos.
1987	WAS	N	2	LB

Donovan Rose
ROSE, DONOVAN
B. Mar. 9, 1957, Norfolk, VA
Hampton Institute 6'1" 190 lbs.

Year	Team		Games	Pos.
1980	KC	N	7	CB, S
1987	MIA		12	S
2 yrs.	19 games			

Gene Rose
ROSE, EUGENE HARRY
B. Jul. 11, 1904, Racine, WI
D. Feb. 1 1979, Torrance, CA
Wisconsin 5'8" 172 lbs.

Year	Team		Games	Pos.
1929	CHIC	N	13	HB, QB, FB
1930			10	HB, FB, QB
1931			7	HB, FB
1932			1	QB
4 yrs.	31 games			

George Rose
ROSE, GEORGE LEE
B. Jan. 1, 1942, Brunswick, GA
Auburn 5'11" 190 lbs.

Year	Team		Games	Pos.
1964	MIN	N	14	DB
1965			10	DB
1966			10	DB
1967	NO	N	14	DB
4 yrs.	48 games			

Joe Rose
ROSE, JOSEPH HAROLD
B. Jun. 24, 1957, Marysville, CA
California 6'3" 228 lbs.

Year	Team		Games	Pos.
1980	MIA	N	16	TE
1981			16	TE
1982			9	TE
1983			16	TE
1984			9	TE
1985			16	TE

Year	Team		Games	Pos.

Joe Rose *continued*

Year	Team		Games	Pos.
1986			12	TE
1987	LARM	N	1	TE
8 yrs.	95 games			

Ken Rose
ROSE, KENNY FRANK
B. Jun. 9, 1962, Sacramento, CA
Nevada-Las Vegas 6'1" 215 lbs.

Year	Team		Games	Pos.
1987	NYJ	N	10	LB
1988			12	LB
1989			15	LB
1990	CLE	N	7	LB
1990	PHI	N	8	LB
1991			16	LB
1992			16	LB
1993			5	LB
1994			16	LB
8 yrs.	105 games			

Roy Rose
ROSE, ROY EUGENE
B. Aug. 15, 1911, Cincinnati, OH
D. Jan., 1986, Memphis, TN
Tennessee 6'1" 185 lbs.

Year	Team		Games	Pos.
1936	NYG	N	7	E

Tam Rose
ROSE, WALTER S.
B. Jun. 20, 1889
D. Dec., 1965
Syracuse 5'11" 170 lbs.

Year	Team		Games	Pos.
1921	TON	A	1	HB

Tubby Rosecrans
ROSECRANS, TUBBY
Union

Year	Team		Games	Pos.
1921	SYR	A	1	FB

Rocky Rosema
ROSEMA, ROGER WILLIAM
B. Feb. 5, 1946, Grand Rapids, MI
Michigan 6'2" 228 lbs.

Year	Team		Games	Pos.
1968	STL	N	12	LB
1969			14	LB
1970			4	LB
1971			2	LB
4 yrs.	32 games			

Stan Rosen
ROSEN, STANLEY (Tex)
B. Mar. 28, 1906
D. Jul. 23, 1984, Claremont, NH
Rutgers 5'6" 155 lbs.

Year	Team		Games	Pos.
1929	BUF	N	8	QB, HB, FB

Timm Rosenbach
ROSENBACH, TIMM
B. Oct. 27, 1966, Everett, WA
Washington State 6'2" 210 lbs.

Year	Team		Games	Pos.
1989	PHX	N	2	QB
1990			16	QB
1992			8	QB
3 yrs.	26 games			

Tubby Rosenberger
ROSENBERGER, OTTO LEE
B. Nov. 6, 1896, Evansville, IN
D. Jan. 15, 1954
Wisconsin

Year	Team		Games	Pos.
1921	EVA	A	2	T

Erik Rosenmeier
ROSENMEIER, ERIK M.
B. May 26, 1965, Clark, NJ

Year	Team		Games	Pos.

Erik Rosenmeier *continued*
Colgate 6'4" 240 lbs.

Year	Team		Games	Pos.
1987	BUF	N	1	C

Ted Rosequist
ROSEQUIST, THEODORE ANTHONY
B. Apr. 17, 1908, Emlenton, PA
D. Nov. 29, 1988, West Palm Beach, FL
Ohio State 6'4" 222 lbs.

Year	Team		Games	Pos.
1934	CHIB	N	11	T, E, G
1935			11	T, E
1936			4	E
1937	CLE	N	7	T, E
4 yrs.	33 games			

Ken Roskie
ROSKIE, KENNETH
B. Nov. 29, 1920, Rockford, IL
D. Aug., 1986, Redmond, WA
South Carolina 6'1" 225 lbs.

Year	Team		Games	Pos.
1946	SF	AA	8	FB
1948	GB	N	6	FB
1948	DET	N	7	FB
2 yrs.	21 games			

Ted Rosnagle
ROSNAGLE, TED
B. Sep. 29, 1961, Pasadena, CA
Portland State 6'3" 202 lbs.

Year	Team		Games	Pos.
1985	MIN	N	6	CB, S
1987			3	S
2 yrs.	9 games			

Alvin Ross
ROSS, ALVIN
B. May 3, 1963, Chicago, IL
Oklahoma/Central Oklahoma 5'11" 235 lbs.

Year	Team		Games	Pos.
1987	PHI	N	2	RB

Dan Ross
ROSS, DANIEL RICHARD
B. Feb. 9, 1957, Malden, MA
Northeastern 6'4" 240 lbs.

Year	Team		Games	Pos.
1979	CIN	N	16	TE
1980			16	TE
1981			16	TE
1982			9	TE
1983			16	TE
1985			6	TE
1985	SEA	N	10	TE
1986	GB	N	15	TE
7 yrs.	104 games			

Dave Ross
ROSS, DAVE
B. Feb. 1, 1938
Los Angeles State 6'3" 210 lbs.

Year	Team		Games	Pos.
1960	NY	A		OE

Dominique Ross
ROSS, DOMINIQUE
B. Jan. 12, 1972, Jacksonville, FL
Valdosta State 6'0" 203 lbs.

Year	Team		Games	Pos.
1995	DAL	N	1	RB
1996			2	RB
2 yrs.	3 games			

Jermaine Ross
ROSS, JERMAINE LEWIS
B. Apr. 27, 1971, Jeffersonville, IN
Purdue 5'11" 192 lbs.

Year	Team		Games	Pos.
1994	LARM	N	4	WR
1996	STL	N	15	WR
2 yrs.	19 games			

Year	Team		Games	Pos.

Kevin Ross
ROSS, KEVIN LESLEY
B. Jan. 16, 1962, Camden, NJ
Temple 5'9" 182 lbs.

Year	Team		Games	Pos.
1984	KC	N	16	CB
1985			16	CB
1986			16	CB
1987			12	CB
1988			15	CB
1989			15	CB
1990			16	CB
1991			14	CB
1992			16	CB
1993			15	CB
1994	ATL	N	16	S
1995			15	S
1996	SD	N	16	S
13 yrs.	199 games			

Louis Ross
ROSS, LOUIS EDWARD
B. Aug. 31, 1947, Orlando, FL
South Carolina State 6'6" 248 lbs.

Year	Team		Games	Pos.
1971	BUF	N	5	DE
1972			14	DE
1975	KC	N	1	DT
3 yrs.	20 games			

Oliver Ross
ROSS, OLIVER
B. Sep. 18, 1950, Gainesville, FL
Alabama A&M 6'0" 210 lbs.

Year	Team		Games	Pos.
1973	DEN	N	4	RB
1974			7	RB
1975			14	RB
1976	SEA	N	10	RB
4 yrs.	35 games			

Scott Ross
ROSS, SCOTT
B. Dec. 7, 1968, El Toro, CA
Southern California 6'1" 235 lbs.

Year	Team		Games	Pos.
1991	NO	N	4	LB

Tom Ross
ROSS, TOM
B. Dec. 27, 1958
Bowling Green 6'5" 255 lbs.

Year	Team		Games	Pos.
1987	DET	N	3	LB

Willie Ross
ROSS, WILLIAM
B. Jun. 6, 1941, Helena, AR
Nebraska 5'10" 200 lbs.

Year	Team		Games	Pos.
1964	BUF	A	12	HB

George Rosso
ROSSO, GEORGE A.
B. Jan. 15, 1930, Pittsburgh, PA
Ohio State 5'11" 177 lbs.

Year	Team		Games	Pos.
1954	WAS	N	12	HB

Tim Rossovich
ROSSOVICH, TIMOTHY JOHN
B. Mar. 14, 1946, Palo Alto, CA
Southern California 6'4" 245 lbs.

Year	Team		Games	Pos.
1968	PHI	N	14	DE
1969			14	DE
1970			14	DE
1971			13	LB
1972	SD	N	6	LB
1973			13	LB
1976	HOU	N	14	LB
7 yrs.	88 games			

Year	Team	Games	Pos.

Ernie Rosteck
ROSTECK, ERNEST
B. May 12, 1922, Detroit, MI
D. Mar., 1986, Waterloo, IA
None 6'1" 218 lbs.

1943	DET	N	1	C
1944			8	C
2 yrs.		9 games		

Pete Rostosky
ROSTOSKY, PETER JOSEPH
B. Jul. 29, 1961, Monongahela, PA
Connecticut 6'4" 265 lbs.

1984	PIT	N	8	OT
1985			16	OT
1986			11	OT
3 yrs.		35 games		

Kyle Rote
ROTE, WILLIAM KYLE, SR.
B. Oct. 27, 1927, San Antonio, TX
Southern Methodist 6'0" 199 lbs.

1951	NYG	N	5	HB
1952			12	HB
1953			9	HB
1954			11	HB
1955			12	HB
1956			12	E
1957			7	E
1958			12	E
1959			10	E
1960			11	E
1961			14	OE
11 yrs.		115 games		

Tobin Rote
ROTE, TOBIN CORNELIUS
B. Jan. 18, 1928, San Antonio, TX
Rice 6'3" 211 lbs.

1950	GB	N	12	QB
1951			12	QB
1952			12	QB
1953			12	QB
1954			12	QB
1955			12	QB
1956			12	QB
1957	DET	N	12	QB
1958			12	QB
1959			10	QB
1963	SD	A	14	QB
1964			14	QB
1966	DEN	A	3	QB
13 yrs.		149 games		

Pete Roth
ROTH, PETE
B. Jan. 12, 1962
Northern Illinois 5'11" 210 lbs.

1987	MIA	N	3	RB

Tim Rother
ROTHER, TIM
B. Sep. 28, 1965, St. Paul, NE
Nebraska 6'7" 285 lbs.

1989	LARI	N	16	OT
1990			4	OT
2 yrs.		20 games		

Cliff Rothrock
ROTHROCK, CLIFFORD
B. 1922
North Dakota State 5'10" 198 lbs.

1947	CHI	AA	2	C

Doug Rothschild
ROTHSCHILD, DOUG
B. Apr. 27, 1965

Doug Rothschild *continued*
Wheaton 6'2" 231 lbs.

1987	CHI	N	3	LB

Fred Rothwell
ROTHWELL, D. FRED
B. Oct. 18, 1952, Lafayette, IN
Kansas State 6'3" 240 lbs.

1974	DET	N	14	C

Herb Roton
ROTON, HERBERT CARL
(Bummie)
B. Aug. 28, 1913, Montgomery, AL
Auburn 6'2" 210 lbs.

1937	PHI	N	8	E, T

George Roudebush
ROUDEBUSH, GEORGE MILTON
B. Jan. 25, 1894, Newtonville, OH
D. Mar. 1, 1992, Chardon, OH
Denison 5'10" 180 lbs.

1920	DAY	A	8	HB
1921			8	FB, HB
2 yrs.		16 games		

Tom Rouen
ROUEN, TOM
B. Jun. 9, 1968, Hinsdale, IL
Colorado State/Colorado 6'3" 215 lbs.

1993	DEN	N	16	P
1994			16	P
1995			16	P
1996			16	P
4 yrs.		64 games		

Ray Roundtree
ROUNDTREE, RAYMOND ANTHONY
B. Apr. 19, 1966, Aiken, SC
Penn State 6'0" 180 lbs.

1988	DET	N	4	WR

Jim Rourke
ROURKE, JAMES PETER
B. Feb. 10, 1957, Weymouth, MA
Boston College 6'5" 265 lbs.

1980	KC	N	15	G
1981			12	G
1982			9	G, OT
1983			11	OT, G
1984			13	OT, G
1985	NO	N	13	OT
1986	KC	N	4	OT
7 yrs.		77 games		

Tubby Rousch
ROUSCH, FRANK
B. 1896
Deceased
Toledo 170 lbs.

1922	TOL	N	4	HB, FB, T

Curtis Rouse
ROUSE, CURTIS LAMAR
B. Jul. 13, 1960, Augusta, GA
Tennessee-Chattanooga 6'3" 310 lbs.

1982	MIN	N	5	G
1983			16	G
1984			16	G
1985			16	G
1986			5	G
1987	SD	N	10	G, OT
6 yrs.		68 games		

James Rouse
ROUSE, JAMES DAVID
B. Dec. 18, 1966, Little Rock, AR
Arkansas 6'0" 220 lbs.

1990	CHI	N	16	RB
1991			14	RB
2 yrs.		30 games		

Stillman Rouse
ROUSE, STILLMAN I.
B. Sep. 22, 1917, St. Louis, MO
Missouri 6'2" 205 lbs.

1940	DET	N	10	E

Wardell Rouse
ROUSE, WARDELL
B. Jun. 9, 1972, Clewiston, FL
Clemson 6'2" 231 lbs.

1995	TB	N	16	LB

Lee Rouson
ROUSON, LEE
B. Oct. 18, 1962, Elizabeth City, NC
Colorado 6'1" 220 lbs.

1985	NYG	N	2	RB
1986			14	RB
1987			12	RB
1988			16	RB
1989			16	RB
1990			16	RB
1991	CLE	N	16	RB
7 yrs.		92 games		

Tom Roussel
ROUSSEL, THOMAS JAMES
B. Jan. 20, 1945, Thibodaux, LA
Southern Mississippi 6'3" 235 lbs.

1968	WAS	N	14	LB
1969			14	LB
1970			14	LB
1971	NO	N	7	LB
1972			14	LB
1973	PHI	N	3	LB
6 yrs.		66 games		

Mike Roussos
ROUSSOS, MICHAEL
B. Feb. 8, 1926, New Castle, PA
D. Apr., 1987, New Castle, PA
Pittsburgh 6'3" 238 lbs.

1948	WAS	N	12	T
1949			6	T
1949	DET	N	7	T
2 yrs.		25 games		

John Roveto
ROVETO, JOHN CHARLES
B. Feb. 20, 1958, Fort Lauderdale, FL
Southwestern Louisiana 5'11" 175 lbs.

1981	CHI	N	11	K
1982			7	K
2 yrs.		18 games		

Tony Rovinski
ROVINSKI, ANTHONY
B. 1909
Holy Cross 5'9" 195 lbs.

1933	NYG	N	1	E

Ev Rowan
ROWAN, EVERETT L.
B. 1903
D. Nov., 1956
Ohio State 6'1" 187 lbs.

1930	BKN	N	2	FB, HB
1932			10	E

Ev Rowan *continued*

1933	PHI	N	4	E, G
3 yrs.		16 games		

John Rowan
ROWAN, JOHN
B. Jun. 3, 1896
D. Apr., 1967, Belpre, OH
None 165 lbs.

1923	LOU	N	3	HB, QB

Larry Rowden
ROWDEN, L.D.
B. Mar. 17, 1949, Pampa, TX
Houston 6'2" 220 lbs.

1971	CHI	N	14	LB
1972			12	LB
2 yrs.		26 games		

Bob Rowe
ROWE, ROBERT
B. 1911
Colgate 6'0" 198 lbs.

1934	DET	N	11	HB, FB, QB
1935	PHI	N	4	FB, HB
2 yrs.		15 games		

Bob Rowe
ROWE, ROBERT BUELL
B. May 23, 1945, Flint, MI
Western Michigan 6'4" 258 lbs.

1967	STL	N	11	DE
1968			14	DE
1969			13	DT
1970			14	DT
1971			14	DT
1972			14	DT
1973			14	DT
1974			14	DT
1975			14	DT
9 yrs.		122 games		

Dave Rowe
ROWE, DAVID HOMEYER
B. Jun. 20, 1945, Neptune, NJ
Penn State 6'6" 273 lbs.

1967	NO	N	14	DT
1968			14	DT
1969			14	DT
1970			14	DT
1971	NE	N	14	DT
1972			14	DT
1973			14	DT
1974	SD	N	14	DT
1975			1	DT
1975	OAK	N	10	DT
1976			14	DT
1977			14	DT
1978			1	DT
1978	BAL	N	13	DT
12 yrs.		165 games		

Harmon Rowe
ROWE, HARMON B.
B. 1922
Baylor/San Francisco 6'0" 182 lbs.

1947	NY	AA	10	HB
1948			11	HB
1949	B-NY	AA	9	HB
1950	NYG	N	7	HB
1951			8	HB
1952			12	HB
6 yrs.		57 games		

Patrick Rowe
ROWE, PATRICK DONALD EDWARD

Year	Team	Games	Pos.

Patrick Rowe continued
B. Feb. 17, 1969, San Diego, CA
San Diego State 6'1" 195 lbs.

Year	Team		Games	Pos.
1993	CLE	N	5	WR

Ray Rowe
ROWE, RAYMOND HENRY
B. Jul. 28, 1969, Rota, Spain
San Diego State 6'2" 256 lbs.

1992	WAS	N	3	TE
1993			1	TE
2 yrs.			4 games	

Eugene Rowell
ROWELL, EUGENE
B. Jun. 12, 1968, New York, NY
Southern Mississippi 6'1" 180 lbs.

1990	CLE	N	3	WR

Gene Rowell
ROWELL, EUGENE
B. Feb. 15, 1958, San Diego, CA
Dubuque 6'3" 265 lbs.

1987	CHI	N	1	DT

Brad Rowland
ROWLAND, BRADLEY
B. Jul. 14, 1929, Hamlin, TX
McMurry 6'1" 190 lbs.

1951	CHIB	N	12	HB

Justin Rowland
ROWLAND, JUSTIN
B. May 10, 1937, Hamlin, TX
Texas Christian 6'2" 189 lbs.

1960	CHI		6	DB
1961	MIN	N	5	DB
1962	DEN	A	10	DB
3 yrs.			21 games	

Bob Rowley
ROWLEY, ELDWOOD R.
B. 1942
Virginia 6'2" 225 lbs.

1963	PIT	N	3	LB
1964	NY	A	6	LB
2 yrs.			9 games	

John Rowser
ROWSER, JOHN FELIX
B. Apr. 24, 1944, Birmingham, AL
Michigan 6'1" 185 lbs.

1967	GB	N	14	DB
1968			14	DB
1969			14	CB
1970	PIT	N	7	CB
1971			12	CB
1972			14	CB
1973			14	CB
1974	DEN	N	11	CB
1975			13	CB
1976			14	CB
10 yrs.			127 games	

Elmer Roy
ROY, ELMER T. (Spin)
B. 1895
Deceased
None 6'0" 175 lbs.

1921	TON	A	1	E
1921	ROC	A	2	E
1922	ROC		4	E
1923			4	E
1924			7	E
1925			2	E
1927	BUF	N	2	E
6 yrs.			22 games	

Frank Roy
ROY, FRANK EDWARD
B. Jun. 19, 1942, Montgomery, WV
Utah 6'2" 230 lbs.

1966	STL	N	11	G

Andre Royal
ROYAL, ANDRE
B. Dec. 1, 1972, Northport, AL
Alabama 6'2" 220 lbs.

1995	CAR	N	12	LB
1996			16	LB
2 yrs.			28 games	

Rickey Royal
ROYAL, RICKEY
B. Jul. 26, 1966, Gainesville, TX
Sam Houston State 5'9" 187 lbs.

1990	ATL	N	1	CB

Mark Royals
ROYALS, MARK ALAN
B. Jun. 22, 1964, Hampton, VA
Appalachian State 6'5" 216 lbs.

1987	STL	N	1	P
1987	PHI	N	1	P
1990	TB	N	16	P
1991			16	P
1992	PIT	N	16	P
1993			16	P
1994			16	P
1995	DET	N	16	P
1996			16	P
8 yrs.			114 games	

Orpheus Roye
ROYE, ORPHEUS
B. Jan. 21, 1974, Miami, FL
Florida State 6'3" 295 lbs.

1996	PIT	N	13	DE

Mazio Royster
ROYSTER, MAZIO DENMAR VESEY
B. Aug. 3, 1970, Pomona, CA
Southern California 6'1" 205 lbs.

1992	TB	N	5	RB
1993			14	RB
1994			14	RB
3 yrs.			33 games	

Ed Royston
ROYSTON, EDWIN F.
B. Sep. 19, 1923, Baltimore, MD
Wake Forest 6'1" 220 lbs.

1948	NYG	N	10	G
1949			11	G
2 yrs.			21 games	

Aubrey Rozelle
ROZELLE, AUBREY
B. Nov. 2, 1933, Clarksdale, MS
Delta State 6'2" 215 lbs.

1957	PIT	N	7	LB

Bob Rozier
ROZIER, ROBERT EARNEST
B. Jul. 28, 1955, Anchorage, AK
California 6'3" 240 lbs.

1979	STL	N	6	DE

Mike Rozier
ROZIER, MIKE
B. Mar. 1, 1961, Camden, NJ
Nebraska 5'10" 209 lbs.

1985	HOU	N	14	RB

Mike Rozier continued

1986			13	RB
1987			11	RB
1988			15	RB
1989			12	RB
1990			3	RB
1990	ATL	N	13	RB
1991			11	RB
7 yrs.			92 games	

Dave Rozumek
ROZUMEK, DAVID JOHN
B. Apr. 25, 1954, Lawrence, MA
New Hampshire 6'1" 215 lbs.

1976	KC	N	8	LB
1977			14	LB
1978			16	LB
1979			7	LB
4 yrs.			45 games	

Ed Rubbert
RUBBERT, ED
B. May 28, 1965
Louisville 6'5" 225 lbs.

1987	WAS	N	3	QB

Larry Rubens
RUBENS, LARRY DEAN
B. Jan. 25, 1959, Spokane, WA
Montana State 6'2" 262 lbs.

1982	GB	N	9	C
1983			16	C
1986	CHI	N	16	C
3 yrs.			41 games	

Rob Rubick
RUBICK, ROBIN JAMES
B. Sep. 27, 1960, Newberry, MI
Grand Valley State 6'3" 234 lbs.

1982	DET	N	7	TE
1983			16	TE
1984			16	TE
1985			9	TE
1986			16	TE
1987			9	TE
1988			15	TE
7 yrs.			88 games	

Tony Rubino
RUBINO, ANTHONY EUGENE
B. Jun. 30, 1921, Elizabeth, PA
D. Nov. 30, 1983, Elizabeth, PA
Wake Forest 5'10" 208 lbs.

1943	DET	N	10	G
1946			11	G
2 yrs.			21 games	

Karl Rubke
RUBKE, KARL JOHN
B. Dec. 6, 1935, Los Angeles, CA
Southern California 6'4" 240 lbs.

1957	SF	N	12	C, LB
1958			12	C, LB
1959			12	C, LB
1960			12	C
1961	MIN	N	13	LB
1962	SF	N	14	LB
1963			14	LB
1964			14	DE
1965			14	DE
1966	ATL	N	14	DE
1967			8	DT
1968	OAK	A	4	DT
12 yrs.			143 games	

T.J. Rubley
RUBLEY, THERON JOSEPH

T.J. Rubley continued
B. Nov. 29, 1968, Davenport, IA
Tulsa 6'3" 205 lbs.

1993	LARM	N	9	QB
1995	GB	N	1	QB
2 yrs.			10 games	

Martin Ruby
RUBY, MARTIN OWEN
B. Jun. 9, 1922, Lubbock, TX
Texas A&M 6'4" 249 lbs.

1946	BKN	AA	14	T
1947			14	T
1948			14	T
1949	B-NY	AA	11	T
1950	NYY	N	12	T
5 yrs.			65 games	

Todd Rucci
RUCCI, TODD
B. Jul. 14, 1970, Upper Darby, PA
Penn State 6'5" 291 lbs.

1993	NE	N	2	G
1994			13	G
1995			6	G
1996			16	G
4 yrs.			37 games	

Eddie Rucinski
RUCINSKI, EDWARD A.
B. Jul. 12, 1916, East Chicago, IN
Indiana 6'2" 197 lbs.

1941	BKN	N	11	E
1942			11	E
1943	CHIC	N	10	E
1944	C-P	N	10	E, HB
1945	CHIC	N	8	E
1946			10	E
6 yrs.			60 games	

Leo Rucka
RUCKA, LEO
B. 1932, Wooster, TX
Rice 6'3" 212 lbs.

1956	SF	N	4	C, LB

Conrad Rucker
RUCKER, CONRAD ROBERT
B. Nov. 15, 1954, Cincinnati, OH
Southern University 6'3" 255 lbs.

1978	HOU	N	13	TE
1979			16	TE
1980	TB	N	2	TE
1980	LA	N	2	TE
3 yrs.			33 games	

Keith Rucker
RUCKER, KEITH
B. Nov. 20, 1968, University Park, IL
Eastern Michigan/Ohio Wesleyan 6'3" 325 lbs.

1992	PHX	N	14	NT
1993			16	DT
1994	CIN	N	16	DT
1995			15	DT
4 yrs.			61 games	

Reggie Rucker
RUCKER, REGINALD JOSEPH
B. Sep. 21, 1947, Washington, DC
Boston University 6'2" 190 lbs.

1970	DAL	N	7	WR
1971			2	WR
1971	NYG	N	4	WR
1971	NE	N	5	WR
1972			14	WR
1973			14	WR

Year	Team	Games	Pos.

Reggie Rucker continued

Year	Team		Games	Pos.
1974			10	WR
1975	CLE	N	14	WR
1976			14	WR
1977			14	WR
1978			16	WR
1979			16	WR
1980			16	WR
1981			14	WR
12 yrs.	160 games			

Tim Ruddy
RUDDY, TIMOTHY DANIEL
B. Apr. 27, 1972, Scranton, PA
Notre Dame 6'3" 282 lbs.

1994	MIA	N	16	C
1995			16	C
1996			16	C
3 yrs.	48 games			

Jack Rudnay
RUDNAY, JOHN CARL
B. Nov. 20, 1947, Cleveland, OH
Northwestern 6'3" 240 lbs.

1970	KC	N	14	C
1971			13	C
1972			14	C
1973			14	C
1974			14	C
1975			14	C
1976			14	C
1977			14	C
1978			16	C
1979			16	C
1980			12	C
1981			16	C
1982			7	C
13 yrs.	178 games			

Tim Rudnick
RUDNICK, TIMOTHY JOHN
B. Mar. 6, 1952, Chicago, IL
Notre Dame 5'10" 185 lbs.

| 1974 | BAL | N | 14 | CB |

Ben Rudolph
RUDOLPH, BEN
B. Aug. 29, 1957, Evergreen, AL
Long Beach State 6'5" 271 lbs.

1981	NYJ	N	15	DT, DE
1982			9	DT, DE
1983			16	DT, DE
1984			16	DT, DE
1985			16	DE
1986			16	DE
6 yrs.	88 games			

Coleman Rudolph
RUDOLPH, COLEMAN HARRIS
B. Oct. 22, 1970, Valdosta, GA
Georgia Tech 6'4" 270 lbs.

1993	NYJ	N	4	DE, DT
1994	NYG	N	12	DE
1995			16	DE
1996			16	DE
4 yrs.	48 games			

Council Rudolph
RUDOLPH, COUNCIL, JR.
B. Jan. 18, 1950, Anniston, AL
Kentucky State 6'3" 255 lbs.

1972	HOU	N	14	DE
1973	STL	N	5	DE
1974			14	DE
1975			13	DE
1976	TB	N	13	DE
1977			14	DE
6 yrs.	73 games			

Jack Rudolph
RUDOLPH, JOHN LAWRENCE
B. Mar. 21, 1938, St. Louis, MO
Georgia Tech 6'3" 228 lbs.

1960	BOS	A	14	LB
1962			14	LB
1963			14	LB
1964			14	LB
1965			14	LB
1966	MIA	A	11	LB
6 yrs.	81 games			

Joe Rudolph
RUDOLPH, JOE
B. Jul. 21, 1972, Belle Vernon, PA
Wisconsin 6'1" 282 lbs.

| 1995 | PHI | N | 4 | G |

Martin Rudolph
RUDOLPH, MARTIN JEROME
B. Oct. 19, 1964
Arizona 5'10" 183 lbs.

| 1987 | DEN | N | 3 | CB |

Paul Rudzinski
RUDZINSKI, PAUL GERARD
B. Jul. 28, 1956, Detroit, MI
Michigan State 6'1" 220 lbs.

1978	GB	N	16	LB
1979			11	LB
1980			6	LB
3 yrs.	33 games			

Mike Ruether
RUETHER, MIKE ALAN
B. Sep. 20, 1962, Inglewood, CA
Texas 6'4" 279 lbs.

1986	STL	N	10	C
1987			12	C
1988	DEN	N	14	C
1989			3	C
1990	ATL	N	16	C
1991			16	C
1992			16	C
1993			16	C
8 yrs.	103 games			

Ken Ruettgers
RUETTGERS, KENNETH F.
B. Aug. 20, 1962, Bakersfield, CA
Southern California 6'5" 283 lbs.

1985	GB	N	16	OT
1986			16	OT
1987			12	OT
1988			15	OT
1989			16	OT
1990			11	OT
1991			4	OT
1992			16	OT
1993			16	OT
1994			16	OT
1995			15	OT
1996			4	OT
12 yrs.	157 games			

Howie Ruetz
RUETZ, HOWARD PETER
B. Aug. 18, 1927, Racine, WI
Loras 6'3" 257 lbs.

1951	GB	N	12	T
1952			3	T
1953			5	T
3 yrs.	20 games			

Joe Ruetz
RUETZ, JOSEPH HUBERT
B. Oct. 21, 1916, Racine, WI

Joe Ruetz continued

Notre Dame 6'0" 200 lbs.

1946	CHI	AA	13	G
1948			13	G
2 yrs.	26 games			

Guy Ruff
RUFF, GUY M.
B. Aug. 18, 1960, Ravenna, OH
Syracuse 6'1" 215 lbs.

| 1982 | PIT | N | 2 | LB |

Emmett Ruh
RUH, EMMETT
B. Aug. 29, 1893
D. Sep., 1979, Pompano Beach, FL
Davis & Elkins 5'8" 168 lbs.

1921	COL	A	7	HB, E
1922	COL		6	HB
2 yrs.	13 games			

Homer Ruh
RUH, HOMER
B. Sep. 19, 1895
D. Oct. 4, 1971, Madison, WI
none 5'9" 178 lbs.

1920	COL	A	5	E
1921			7	E
1922	COL	N	7	E
1923			8	E, HB, FB
1924			7	E
1925			8	E, HB
6 yrs.	42 games			

Justin Rukas
RUKAS, JUSTIN
B. 1910
Louisiana State 6'0" 205 lbs.

| 1936 | BKN | N | 12 | G |

Gordon Rule
RULE, GORDON
B. Mar. 1, 1946, Chandler, AZ
Dartmouth 6'2" 180 lbs.

1968	GB	N	1	DB
1969			14	S
2 yrs.	15 games			

Max Runager
RUNAGER, MAX CULP
B. Mar. 24, 1956, Greenwood, SC
South Carolina 6'1" 189 lbs.

1979	PHI	N	16	P
1980			16	P
1981			15	P
1982			9	P
1983			12	P
1984	SF	N	14	P
1985			16	P
1986			16	P
1987			12	P
1988			1	P
1988	CLE	N	13	P
1989	PHI	N	4	P
11 yrs.	144 games			

Elmer Rundquist
RUNDQUIST, ELMER T. (Swede)
B. Nov. 22, 1894
D. Feb. 7, 1958
Illinois 6'1" 200 lbs.

| 1922 | CHIC | N | 10 | T |

Harry Rundquist
RUNDQUIST, HARRY (Porky)
B. 1896

Harry Rundquist continued

Deceased
None 5'11" 220 lbs.

| 1926 | DUL | N | 4 | G, C |

Gil Runkel
RUNKEL, GILBERT A.
B. Jun. 2, 1891, Michigan
D. Oct., 1976, Michigan
None 210 lbs.

| 1920 | DET | A | 4 | C |

Tommy Runnels
RUNNELS, MELVIN THOMAS
B. Jan. 28, 1934, Fort Worth, TX
North Texas State 5'10" 187 lbs.

1956	WAS	N	11	HB
1957			10	HB
2 yrs.	21 games			

Running Deer
NASON, ED
Haskell

1922	OOR	N	4	HB, FB, E
1923			3	E
2 yrs.	7 games			

Jon Runyan
RUNYAN, JON
B. Nov. 27, 1973, Flint, MI
Michigan 6'7" 308 lbs.

| 1996 | HOU | N | 10 | OT |

Ernie Ruple
RUPLE, COY ERNEST
B. Oct. 27, 1945, Conway, AR
Arkansas 6'4" 256 lbs.

| 1968 | PIT | N | 14 | OT |

Nelson Rupp
RUPP, NELSON G. (Wocky)
B. Jun. 15, 1891
Deceased
Denison 5'10" 180 lbs.

| 1921 | DAY | A | 4 | HB, FB |

Bob Rush
RUSH, ROBERT JEFFREY
B. Feb. 27, 1955, Santa Monica, CA
Memphis State 6'5" 268 lbs.

1977	SD	N	14	C
1979			16	C
1980			15	C
1981			16	C
1982			9	C, OT
1983	KC	N	15	C
1984			16	C
1985			16	C
8 yrs.	117 games			

Clive Rush
RUSH, CLIVE H.
B. Feb. 14, 1931, De Graff, OH
D. Aug. 22, 1980, London, OH
Miami (Ohio) 6'2" 197 lbs.

| 1953 | GB | N | 11 | E |

Jerry Rush
RUSH, GERALD MITCHELL
B. Aug. 7, 1942, Pontiac, MI
Michigan State 6'4" 264 lbs.

1965	DET	N	11	DT
1966			11	DT
1967			14	DT
1968			14	DT

Year	Team		Games	Pos.

Jerry Rush *continued*

1969			11	DT
1970			14	DT
1971			14	DT
7 yrs.	89 games			

Tyrone Rush
RUSH, TYRONE
B. Feb. 5, 1971, Philadelphia, MS
North Alabama 5'11" 196 lbs.

| 1994 | WAS | N | 5 | RB |

Marion Rushing
RUSHING, MARION GLEN
B. Sep. 3, 1936, Pinckneyville, IL
Southern Illinois 6'2" 223 lbs.

1959	CHIC	N	12	LB
1962	STL	N	13	LB
1963			14	LB
1964			12	LB
1965			14	LB
1966	ATL	N	14	LB
1967			14	LB
1968			7	LB
1968	HOU	A	5	LB
8 yrs.	105 games			

Mike Rusinek
RUSINEK, MIKE
B. May 1, 1963, Scottsdale, AZ
California 6'3" 250 lbs.

| 1987 | CLE | N | 3 | NT |

Reggie Rusk
RUSK, REGGIE
B. Oct. 19, 1972, Galveston, TX
Kentucky 5'10" 182 lbs.

| 1996 | TB | N | 1 | CB |

Roy Ruskusky
RUSKUSKY, ROY J.
B. 1921
St. Mary's (California) 6'3" 200 lbs.

| 1947 | NY | AA | 11 | E |

Carl Russ
RUSS, JAMES CARLTON
B. Feb. 16, 1953, Muskegon, MI
Michigan 6'2" 227 lbs.

1975	ATL	N	14	LB
1976	NYJ	N	3	LB
1977			3	LB
3 yrs.	20 games			

Pat Russ
RUSS, PATRICK
B. Jan. 8, 1940, Cincinnati, OH
Purdue 6'4" 255 lbs.

| 1963 | MIN | N | 14 | DT |

Al Russas
RUSSAS, ALBERT
B. 1924
Tennessee 6'2" 210 lbs.

| 1949 | DET | N | 9 | T, E |

Andy Russell
RUSSELL, CHARLES ANDREW
B. Oct. 29, 1941, Detroit, MI
Missouri 6'3" 221 lbs.

1963	PIT	N	14	LB
1966			14	LB
1967			14	LB
1968			14	LB
1969			14	LB

Andy Russell *continued*

1970			14	LB
1971			14	LB
1972			14	LB
1973			14	LB
1974			14	LB
1975			14	LB
1976			14	LB
12 yrs.	168 games			

Benny Russell
RUSSELL, BENJAMIN
B. May 12, 1944, Brewton, AL
Louisville 6'1" 190 lbs.

| 1968 | BUF | A | 1 | QB |

Bo Russell
RUSSELL, TORRANCE A., JR.
B. Jan. 23, 1916, Birmingham, AL
Auburn 6'1" 233 lbs.

1939	WAS	N	11	T
1940			11	T
2 yrs.	22 games			

Booker Russell
RUSSELL, BOOKER TAYLOR
B. Feb. 28, 1956, Belton, TX
Southwest Texas State 6'2" 233 lbs.

1978	OAK	N	16	RB
1979			16	RB
1980	SD	N	16	RB
1981	PHI	N	12	RB
4 yrs.	60 games			

Damien Russell
RUSSELL, DAMIEN EDUARDO
B. Aug. 20, 1970, New York, NY
Virginia Tech 6'1" 204 lbs.

| 1993 | SF | N | 16 | S |

Darryl Russell
RUSSELL, DARRYL
B. Dec. 14, 1964, Chicago Heights, IL
Appalachian State 6'0" 190 lbs.

| 1987 | DEN | N | 3 | CB, S |

Derek Russell
RUSSELL, DEREK DWAYNE
B. Jun. 22, 1969, Little Rock, AR
Arkansas 6'0" 179 lbs.

1991	DEN	N	13	WR
1992			12	WR
1993			13	WR
1994			12	WR
1995	HOU	N	11	WR
1996			16	WR
6 yrs.	77 games			

Doug Russell
RUSSELL, DOUGAL
B. Jun. 11, 1911, Bulger, PA
Muskingum/Kansas State 6'0" 187 lbs.

1934	CHIC	N	11	HB
1935			11	HB
1936			2	HB
1937			11	HB
1938			8	HB
1939			1	HB
1939	CLE	N	7	HB
6 yrs.	51 games			

Fay Russell
RUSSELL, FAYETTE H. (Reb)
B. 1906
D. Mar. 16, 1978, Coffeyville, KS
Northwestern 6'1" 195 lbs.

| 1933 | NYG | N | 3 | FB |

Fay Russell *continued*

| 1933 | PHI | N | 7 | HB, FB |
| 1 yr. | 10 games | | | |

Jack Russell
RUSSELL, JACK M.
B. Aug. 29, 1921, Nemo, TX
Baylor 6'1" 215 lbs.

1946	NY	AA	14	E
1947			14	E
1948			14	E
1949	B-NY	AA	12	E
1950	NYY	N	11	E
5 yrs.	65 games			

Jim Russell
RUSSELL, JAMES L.
B. Aug. 18, 1911
D. Jan. 21, 1990, Butler, PA
Temple 5'11" 210 lbs.

1936	PHI	N	11	G
1937			3	G
2 yrs.	14 games			

Ken Russell
RUSSELL, KENNETH E.
B. Nov. 2, 1935, Fostoria, OH
Bowling Green 6'3" 252 lbs.

1957	DET	N	10	T
1958			12	T
1959			4	T
3 yrs.	26 games			

Leonard Russell
RUSSELL, LEONARD JAMES
B. Nov. 17, 1969, Long Beach, CA
Arizona State 6'2" 235 lbs.

1991	NE	N	16	RB
1992			11	RB
1993			16	RB
1994	DEN	N	14	RB
1995	STL	N	13	RB
1996	SD	N	15	RB
6 yrs.	85 games			

Reggie Russell
RUSSELL, REGINALD
None 190 lbs.

| 1928 | CHIB | N | 1 | E |

Rusty Russell
RUSSELL, RUSTY
B. Aug. 16, 1963, Orangeburg, SC
South Carolina 6'5" 295 lbs.

| 1984 | PHI | N | 1 | OT |

Wade Russell
RUSSELL, WADE
B. Aug. 16, 1963
Taylor 6'4" 250 lbs.

| 1987 | CIN | N | 3 | OT |

Reggie Rust
RUST, REGINALD
B. 1909
Oregon State 6'2" 210 lbs.

| 1932 | BOS | N | 5 | QB, FB, HB |

Joe Rutgens
RUTGENS, JOSEPH CASIMERE
B. Jan. 26, 1939, Cedar Point, IL
Illinois 6'2" 258 lbs.

1961	WAS	N	14	DT
1962			14	DT
1963			14	DT

Joe Rutgens *continued*

1964			13	DT
1965			14	DT
1966			5	DT
1967			12	DT
1968			12	DT
1969			9	DT
9 yrs.	109 games			

Mike Ruth
RUTH, MICHAEL JOSEPH
B. Jun. 25, 1964, Norristown, PA
Boston College 6'1" 266 lbs.

1986	NE	N	6	NT
1987			2	NT
2 yrs.	8 games			

Ralph Ruthstrom
RUTHSTROM, RALPH RIDGE
B. Jul. 12, 1921, Houston, TX
D. Mar. 19, 1962
Sam Houston State/Southern Methodist 6'5" 212 lbs.

1945	CLE	N	6	FB
1946	LA	N	6	FB
1949	BAL	AA	4	FB
3 yrs.	16 games			

Charlie Rutkowski
RUTKOWSKI, CHARLES
B. 1938
Ripon 6'3" 248 lbs.

| 1960 | BUF | A | | DE |

Ed Rutkowski
RUTKOWSKI, EDWARD JOHN ANTHONY
B. Mar. 21, 1941, Kingston, PA
Notre Dame 6'1" 204 lbs.

1963	BUF	A	14	HB
1964			14	FL
1965			14	FL
1966			14	FL
1967			14	FL
1968			13	FL
6 yrs.	83 games			

Craig Rutledge
RUTLEDGE, CRAIG ALAN
B. Jan. 30, 1964, Upland, CA
UCLA 6'0" 190 lbs.

| 1987 | LARM | N | 3 | S |

Jeff Rutledge
RUTLEDGE, JEFFREY RONALD
B. Jan. 22, 1957, Birmingham, AL
Alabama 6'1" 196 lbs.

1979	LA	N	3	QB
1980			1	QB
1981			4	QB
1983	NYG	N	4	QB
1984			16	QB
1985			16	QB
1986			13	QB
1987			1	QB
1988			1	QB
1989			1	QB
1990	WAS	N	10	QB
1991			16	QB
12 yrs.	101 games			

Tom Ruud
RUUD, THOMAS ROBERT
B. Jul. 26, 1953, Olivia, MN
Nebraska 6'2" 225 lbs.

| 1975 | BUF | N | 14 | LB |
| 1976 | | | 14 | LB |

Year	Team	Games	Pos.

Tom Ruud continued

Year	Team	Games	Pos.
1977		8	LB
1978	CIN N	7	LB
1979		16	LB
5 yrs.	59 games		

Roger Ruzek
RUZEK, ROGER BRIAN
B. Dec. 17, 1960, San Francisco, CA
Weber State 6'1" 195 lbs.

1987	DAL N	12	K
1988		14	K
1989		9	K
1989	PHI N	5	K
1990		16	K
1991		16	K
1992		16	K
1993		5	K
7 yrs.	93 games		

Steve Ruzich
RUZICH, STEPHEN
B. Dec. 24, 1927, Cleveland, OH
D. Nov. 30, 1991
Ohio State 6'2" 228 lbs.

1952	GB N	12	G
1953		12	G
1954		12	G
3 yrs.	36 games		

Bill Ryan
RYAN, WILLIAM
B. 1901
Deceased
Fordham 5'11" 190 lbs.

1924	ROC N	1	T
1924	CHIC N	1	T
1925	MIL N	1	T
2 yrs.	3 games		

Clarence Ryan
RYAN, CLARENCE D. (Cassie)
B. May 10, 1905, Mannington, WV
D. Jan. 6, 1981, West Virginia
West Virginia 5'6" 160 lbs.

| 1929 | BUF N | 9 | QB, HB, FB |

Dave Ryan
RYAN, DAVID
B. Feb. 4, 1923, Kaufman, TX
D. Dec. 5, 1988, Kaufman, TX
Hardin-Simmons 5'10" 190 lbs.

1945	DET N	10	HB
1946		11	HB
2 yrs.	21 games		

Ed Ryan
RYAN, EDWARD DENNIS
B. Dec. 29, 1925, Banff, Alb.
St. Mary's (California) 6'2" 200 lbs.

| 1948 | PIT N | 9 | E |

Frank Ryan
RYAN, FRANK BEALL
B. Jul. 12, 1936, Fort Worth, TX
Rice 6'3" 199 lbs.

1958	LA N	5	QB
1959		10	QB
1960		11	QB
1961		14	QB
1962	CLE N	11	QB
1963		13	QB
1964		14	QB
1965		12	QB
1966		14	QB
1967		13	QB
1968		7	QB

Frank Ryan continued

Year	Team	Games	Pos.
1969	WAS N	1	QB
1970		1	QB
13 yrs.	126 games		

Jim Ryan
RYAN, JAMES JOSEPH
B. May 18, 1957, Camden, NJ
William & Mary 6'1" 218 lbs.

1979	DEN N	16	LB
1980		16	LB
1981		16	LB
1982		9	LB
1983		15	LB
1984		16	LB
1985		16	LB
1986		16	LB
1987		14	LB
1988		16	LB
10 yrs.	150 games		

Joe Ryan
RYAN, JOSEPH
B. 1934
Villanova 6'2" 235 lbs.

| 1960 | NY A | | DE |

John Ryan
RYAN, JOHN J. (Sod)
B. 1906
Detroit 6'2" 205 lbs.

1929	CHIB N	5	T
1930	POR N	3	T
2 yrs.	8 games		

John Ryan
RYAN, JOHN RAYMOND (Rocky)
B. Jul. 5, 1932
Illinois 6'1" 202 lbs.

1956	PHI N	12	HB
1957		9	HB
1958		3	HB
1958	CHIB N	4	E
3 yrs.	28 games		

Kent Ryan
RYAN, ORSON KENT (Rip)
B. Feb. 3, 1915, Midvale, UT
Utah State 6'2" 193 lbs.

1938	DET N	7	HB, FB, QB
1939		6	HB, QB
1940		10	HB, FB
3 yrs.	23 games		

Pat Ryan
RYAN, PATRICK LEE
B. Sep. 16, 1955, Hutchinson, KS
Tennessee 6'3" 208 lbs.

1978	NYJ N	2	QB
1979		1	QB
1980		14	QB
1981		15	QB
1982		9	QB
1983		16	QB
1984		16	QB
1985		16	QB
1986		16	QB
1987		13	QB
1988		16	QB
1989		7	QB
1991	PHI N	4	QB
13 yrs.	145 games		

Tim Ryan
RYAN, TIMOTHY EDWARD
B. Sep. 8, 1967, Memphis, TN
Southern California 6'4" 268 lbs.

| 1990 | CHI N | 15 | DT |

Tim Ryan continued

Year	Team	Games	Pos.
1991		16	DE, DT
1992		16	DT
1993		11	DT
4 yrs.	58 games		

Tim Ryan
RYAN, TIMOTHY THOMAS
B. Sep. 2, 1968, Kansas City, MO
Notre Dame 6'2" 280 lbs.

1991	TB N	15	G
1992		16	G
1993		6	G
3 yrs.	37 games		

Larry Ryans
RYANS, LARRY BERNARD, JR.
B. Jul. 28, 1971, Greenwood, SC
Clemson 5'11" 182 lbs.

| 1996 | TB N | 3 | WR |

Tom Rychlec
RYCHLEC, THOMAS RICHARD
B. Sep. 11, 1934, Meriden, CT
American International 6'3" 220 lbs.

1958	DET N	12	E
1960	BUF A		OE
1961		14	OE
1962		6	OE
1963	DEN A	3	OE
5 yrs.	35 games		

Billy Ryckman
RYCKMAN, BILLY
B. Feb. 28, 1955, Lafayette, LA
Louisiana Tech 5'11" 172 lbs.

1977	ATL N	14	WR
1978		16	WR
1979		14	WR
3 yrs.	44 games		

Danny Ryczek
RYCZEK, DANIEL STANLEY
B. Aug. 24, 1949, Mentor, OH
Virginia 6'3" 248 lbs.

1973	WAS N	14	C
1974		14	C
1975		14	C
1976	TB N	14	C
1977		14	C
1978	LA N	16	C
1979		16	C
7 yrs.	102 games		

Paul Ryczek
RYCZEK, PAUL ANDREW
B. Jun. 25, 1952, Painesville, OH
Virginia 6'2" 231 lbs.

1974	ATL N	14	C
1975		14	C
1976		14	C
1977		14	C
1978		16	C
1979		16	C
1981	NO N	8	C
1987	PHI N	3	C
8 yrs.	99 games		

Ron Rydalch
RYDALCH, RONNIE JAMES (Dry Gulch)
B. Jan. 1, 1952, Tooele, UT
Utah 6'4" 259 lbs.

1975	CHI N	3	DT
1976		13	DT
1977		14	DT
1978		12	DT
1979		16	DT

Ron Rydalch continued

Year	Team	Games	Pos.
1980		16	DT
6 yrs.	74 games		

Nick Ryder
RYDER, NICHOLAS
B. Oct. 31, 1941, Nyack, NY
Miami (Florida) 6'0" 208 lbs.

1963	DET N	10	FB
1964		14	FB
2 yrs.	24 games		

Frank Rydzewski
RYDZEWSKI, FRANK XAVIER
B. Nov. 16, 1892, Chicago, IL
D. Oct., 1979, Chicago, IL
Notre Dame 6'1" 220 lbs.

1920	CLE A	3	C
1920	CHIT A	3	T
1920	HAM A	1	T
1921	CHIC A	8	T, C
1922	HAM A	8	C, T
1923		5	C, T
1923	CHIB N	1	C
1924	HAM A	4	C
1925		1	G
1925	MIL N	2	G, T
1926	HAM A	3	C, G
7 yrs.	39 games		

Julie Rykovich
RYKOVICH, JULIUS A.
B. Apr. 6, 1923, Gary, IN
D. Dec. 22, 1974, Merrillville, IN
Illinois/Notre Dame/Illinois 6'2" 204 lbs.

1947	BUF AA	13	HB
1948		6	HB
1948	CHI AA	6	HB
1949	CHIB N	11	HB
1950		12	HB
1951		12	HB
1952	WAS N	12	HB
1953		12	HB
7 yrs.	84 games		

Lou Rymkus
RYMKUS, LOUIS J.
B. Nov. 6, 1919, Royalton, IL
Notre Dame 6'4" 231 lbs.

1943	WAS N	10	T
1946	CLE AA	14	T
1947		13	T
1948		14	T
1949		12	T
1950	CLE N	12	T
1951		11	T
7 yrs.	86 games		

Mark Rypien
RYPIEN, MARK ROBERT
B. Oct. 2, 1962, Calgary, Alb.
Washington State 6'4" 234 lbs.

1988	WAS N	9	QB
1989		14	QB
1990		10	QB
1991		16	QB
1992		16	QB
1993		12	QB
1994	CLE N	7	QB
1995	STL N	11	QB
1996	PHI N	1	QB
9 yrs.	96 games		

Ted Rzempoluch
RZEMPOLUCH, TED C.
B. May 31, 1941, Jersey City, NJ
Virginia 6'1" 195 lbs.

| 1963 | WAS N | 6 | DB |

Year	Team	Games	Pos.

Kelly Saalfeld
SAALFELD, KELLY
B. Feb. 15, 1956, Columbus, NE
Nebraska 6'3" 246 lbs.

Year	Team		Games	Pos.
1980	NYG	N	7	C

Brad Saar
SAAR, BRAD
B. Feb. 24, 1963
Ball State 6'1" 220 lbs.

| 1987 | IND | N | 1 | LB |

Andy Sabados
SABADOS, ANDREW A.
B. Nov. 25, 1916, Aurora, IL
The Citadel 5'11" 209 lbs.

1939	CHIC	N	8	G
1940			10	G
2 yrs.	18 games			

Ron Sabal
SABAL, RONALD JOSEPH
B. Jul. 23, 1936
Purdue 6'2" 238 lbs.

1960	OAK	A		G
1961			14	OT
2 yrs.	14 games			

Lou Saban
SABAN, LOUIS H.
B. Oct. 13, 1921, Brookfield, IL
Indiana 6'0" 202 lbs.

1946	CLE	AA	14	FB
1947			14	FB
1948			14	C
1949			12	C
4 yrs.	54 games			

Joe Sabasteanski
SABASTEANSKI, JOSEPH E.
B. Feb. 24, 1921, Portland, ME
D. Jul., 1972
Fordham 6'0" 207 lbs.

1947	BOS	N	10	C, LB
1948			12	G, LB
1949	NYB	N	12	G, LB
3 yrs.	34 games			

Bill Sabatino
SABATINO, WILLIAM
B. Aug. 9, 1945, Alliance, OH
Colorado 6'3" 245 lbs.

1968	CLE	N	7	DT
1969	ATL	N	6	DT
2 yrs.	13 games			

Dwayne Sabb
SABB, DWAYNE IRVING
B. Oct. 9, 1969, Union City, NJ
New Hampshire 6'4" 248 lbs.

1992	NE	N	16	LB
1993			14	LB
1994			16	LB
1995			12	LB
1996			16	LB
5 yrs.	74 games			

Tino Sabucco
SABUCCO, TINO
B. Dec. 20, 1926
Wayne State/San Francisco 6'1" 206 lbs.

| 1949 | SF | AA | 10 | C |

Tony Sacca
SACCA, ANTHONY JOHN

Tony Sacca continued
B. Apr. 17, 1970, Delran, NJ
Penn State 6'5" 230 lbs.

| 1992 | PHX | N | 2 | QB |

Frank Sacco
SACCO, FRANK
B. Apr. 8, 1964
Fordham 6'4" 240 lbs.

| 1987 | NE | N | 2 | LB |

Lenny Sachs
SACHS, LEONARD DAVID
B. Aug. 7, 1897, Chicago, IL
D. Oct. 27, 1942, Chicago, IL
Loyola (Illinois)/DePaul 5'8" 177 lbs.

1920	CHIC	A	5	E
1921			8	E
1922	CHIC	N	7	E
1923	MIL	N	13	E
1924			2	E
1924	HAM	N	2	E
1925			4	E
1925	CHIC	N	2	E
1926	LOU	N	4	E
7 yrs.	47 games			

Frankie Sachse
SACHSE, FRANCIS MARION
B. Jul. 24, 1917, Brice, TX
D. Oct. 1, 1989, Dallas, TX
Texas 6'0" 197 lbs.

1943	BKN	N	5	HB
1944			6	HB
1945	BOS	N	8	HB
3 yrs.	19 games			

Jack Sachse
SACHSE, JACK CLARENCE
B. 1921
D. Jul., 1958
Southwestern (Texas)/Texas 6'0" 210 lbs.

| 1945 | BOS | N | 4 | C |

Jack Sack
SACKLOWSKI, JOHN
B. Feb. 2, 1902
D. Mar., 1980, Pittsburgh, PA
Pittsburgh 6'2" 190 lbs.

1923	COL	N	9	G
1926	CLE	N	5	G
1926	CAN	N	3	G
2 yrs.	17 games			

Norb Sacksteder
SACKSTEDER, NORBERT N.
B. Sep. 25, 1895
D. Jun., 1986, Florida
Dayton/Christian Brothers 5'9" 173 lbs.

1920	DAY	A	8	HB
1921	DET	A	6	HB
1922	CAN	N	11	HB, QB
1925			1	QB
4 yrs.	26 games			

Nick Sacrinty
SACRINTY, NICHOLAS WILLIAM
B. 1924
Wake Forest 5'11" 185 lbs.

| 1947 | CHIB | N | 10 | B |

Rod Saddler
SADDLER, RODERICK
B. Sep. 26, 1966, Atlanta, GA
Texas A&M 6'5" 276 lbs.

| 1987 | STL | N | 12 | DE |

Rod Saddler continued

1988	PHX	N	16	DE
1989			15	DE
1990			16	DE
1991			4	DE
1991	CIN	N	2	DE
5 yrs.	65 games			

Steve Sader
SADER, STEVE
B. 1921
none 5'11" 180 lbs.

| 1943 | P-P | N | 1 | B |

Troy Sadowski
SADOWSKI, ROBERT TROY
B. Dec. 8, 1965, Atlanta, GA
Georgia 6'5" 255 lbs.

1990	ATL	N	13	TE
1991	KC		14	TE
1992	NYJ	N	6	TE
1993			13	TE
1994	CIN	N	15	TE
1995			12	TE
1996			16	TE
7 yrs.	89 games			

Eddie Saenz
SAENZ, EDWIN M.
B. Sep. 21, 1923, Santa Barbara, CA
Loyola-Marymount/Southern California 5'11" 169 lbs.

1946	WAS	N	5	HB
1947			12	HB
1948			4	HB
1949			12	HB
1950			10	HB
1951			2	HB
6 yrs.	45 games			

Saint Saffold
SAFFOLD, SAINT SAMUEL
B. May 18, 1944, Leflore County, MS
San Jose State 6'4" 202 lbs.

| 1968 | CIN | A | 14 | SE |

Pio Sagapolutele
SAGAPOLUTELE, PIO ALIKA
B. Nov. 28, 1969, American Samoa
San Diego State 6'6" 297 lbs.

1991	CLE	N	15	DE, DT
1992			14	DE, DT
1993			8	DE
1994			12	DT
1995			15	DT
1996	NE	N	15	DT
6 yrs.	79 games			

Floyd Sagely
SAGLEY, FLOYD
B. Mar. 26, 1932, Van Buren, AR
Arkansas 6'1" 191 lbs.

1954	SF	N	12	OE, DB
1956			2	OE
1957	CHIC	N	10	DB
3 yrs.	24 games			

Ken Sager
SAGER, KEN
B. Oct. 15, 1963
Western Washington 6'4" 228 lbs.

| 1987 | SEA | N | 3 | TE |

Tony Sagnella
SAGNELLA, ANTHONY
B. Feb. 28, 1964

Tony Sagnella continued
Rutgers 6'5" 260 lbs.

| 1987 | WAS | N | 3 | DT |

Tom Saidock
SAIDOCK, THOMAS
B. Feb. 26, 1930, Detroit, MI
Michigan State 6'5" 261 lbs.

1957	PHI	N	11	T
1960	NY	A		DT
1961			14	DT
1962	BUF	A	2	DT
4 yrs.	27 games			

George Saimes
SAIMES, GEORGE T.
B. Sep. 1, 1941, Canton, OH
Michigan State 5'10" 188 lbs.

1963	BUF	A	14	DB
1964			14	DB
1965			14	DB
1966			14	DB
1967			14	DB
1968			13	DB
1969			8	S
1970	DEN	N	8	S
1971			13	S
1972			9	S
10 yrs.	121 games			

Pat Saindon
SAINDON, PATRICK ARTHUR
B. Mar. 3, 1961, Nice, France
Vanderbilt 6'3" 273 lbs.

1986	NO		8	G
1987	ATL		3	G
2 yrs.	11 games			

Bob St. Clair
ST. CLAIR, ROBERT BRUCE (Raw Meat)
B. Feb. 18, 1931, San Francisco, CA
San Francisco/Tulsa 6'9" 263 lbs.

1953	SF	N	10	T
1954			12	T
1955			12	T
1956			12	T
1957			5	T
1958			12	T
1959			12	T
1960			10	T
1961			12	OT
1962			8	OT
1963			14	OT
11 yrs.	119 games			

Mike St. Clair
ST. CLAIR, RICHARD MICHAEL
B. Sep. 2, 1953, Cleveland, OH
Grambling State 6'5" 248 lbs.

1976	CLE	N	14	DE
1977			11	DE
1978			16	DE, DT
1979			16	DE
1980	CIN	N	10	DE
1981			16	DE
1982			8	DE
7 yrs.	91 games			

Tom St. Germaine
ST. GERMAINE, THOMAS L.
B. 1885
Deceased
Carlisle/Howard 6'2" 250 lbs.

| 1922 | OOR | N | 5 | T, C, G |

Year	Team		Games	Pos.

Len St. Jean
ST. JEAN, LEONARD WAYNE
B. Oct. 27, 1941, Newberry, MI
Northern Michigan 6'1" 244 lbs.

Year	Team		Games	Pos.
1964	**BOS**	**A**	14	DE
1965			14	DE
1966			14	G
1967			14	G
1968			14	G
1969			14	G
1970	**BOS**	**N**	14	G
1971	**NE**	**N**	14	G
1972			14	G
1973			14	G
10 yrs.	140 games			

Herb St. John
ST. JOHN, HERBERT LEGRANDE
B. Jan. 17, 1926, Perry, FL
Georgia 5'10" 215 lbs.

Year	Team		Games	Pos.
1948	**BKN**	**AA**	10	G
1949	**CHI**	**AA**	11	G
2 yrs.	21 games			

Abdul Salaam
Born LAWRENCE FAULK
B. Feb. 12, 1953, New Brockton, AL
Kent State 6'2" 260 lbs.

Year	Team		Games	Pos.
1976	**NYJ**	**N**	14	DE, DT
1977			14	DT
1978			15	DT
1979			12	DT
1980			16	DT
1981			16	DT
1982			9	DT
1983			1	DT
8 yrs.	97 games			

Rashaan Salaam
SALAAM, RASHAAN
B. Oct. 8, 1974, San Diego, CA
Colorado 6'1" 226 lbs.

Year	Team		Games	Pos.
1995	**CHI**	**N**	16	RB
1996			12	RB
2 yrs.	28 games			

Andy Salata
SALATA, ANDREW J.
B. 1904
Deceased
Pittsburgh 5'10" 188 lbs.

Year	Team		Games	Pos.
1929	**ORA**	**N**	10	G
1930	**NEW**	**N**	10	G
2 yrs.	20 games			

Paul Salata
SALATA, PAUL THOMAS (Slats)
B. Oct. 17, 1926
Southern California 6'2" 191 lbs.

Year	Team		Games	Pos.
1949	**SF**	**AA**	12	E
1950	**SF**	**N**	4	E
1950	**BAL**	**N**	7	E
2 yrs.	23 games			

Jay Saldi
SALDI, JOHN JAY, IV
B. Oct. 8, 1954, White Plains, NY
South Carolina 6'3" 224 lbs.

Year	Team		Games	Pos.
1976	**DAL**	**N**	13	TE
1977			14	TE
1978			4	TE
1979			16	TE
1980			16	TE
1981			16	TE
1982			5	TE
1983	**CHI**	**N**	13	TE
1984			15	TE
9 yrs.	112 games			

Dan Saleaumua
SALEAUMUA, RAYMOND DANIEL
B. Nov. 11, 1964, San Diego, CA
Arizona State 6'0" 292 lbs.

Year	Team		Games	Pos.
1987	**DET**	**N**	9	NT
1988			16	NT
1989	**KC**	**N**	16	NT
1990			16	NT
1991			16	NT
1992			16	NT
1993			16	DT
1994			14	DT, DE
1995			16	DT
1996			15	DT
10 yrs.	150 games			

Eddie Salem
SALEM, EDWARD JOSEPH (Satchel)
B. 1928
Alabama 5'11" 193 lbs.

Year	Team		Games	Pos.
1951	**WAS**	**N**	12	QB

Harvey Salem
SALEM, HARVEY
B. Jan. 15, 1961, Berkeley, CA
California 6'6" 283 lbs.

Year	Team		Games	Pos.
1983	**HOU**	**N**	16	OT
1984			16	OT
1985			14	OT
1986			1	OT
1986	**DET**	**N**	13	OL
1987			11	OT, G
1988			16	G
1989			10	OT, G
1990			15	OT, G
1991	**DEN**	**N**	10	OT
1992	**GB**	**N**	4	G
10 yrs.	126 games			

Sam Salemi
SALEMI, SAMUEL (Smoke)
B. Jun. 4, 1903
D. Jul., 1969, Brooklyn, NY
Columbia/St. John's (New York)/Canisius 5'9" 180 lbs.

Year	Team		Games	Pos.
1928	**NYY**	**N**	5	HB

Sean Salisbury
SALISBURY, RICHARD SEAN
B. Mar. 9, 1963, Long Beach, CA
Southern California 6'5" 215 lbs.

Year	Team		Games	Pos.
1987	**IND**	**N**	2	QB
1992	**MIN**	**N**	10	QB
1993			11	QB
1994			1	QB
1996	**SD**	**N**	16	QB
5 yrs.	40 games			

Jerome Sally
SALLY, JEROME ELI
B. Feb. 24, 1959, Chicago, IL
Missouri 6'3" 270 lbs.

Year	Team		Games	Pos.
1982	**NYG**	**N**	4	NT
1983			16	NT
1984			16	NT
1985			16	NT
1986			16	NT
1987	**IND**	**N**	12	NT
1988	**KC**	**N**	3	NT
7 yrs.	83 games			

Brian Salonen
SALONEN, BRIAN SCOTT
B. Jul. 29, 1961, Glasgow, MT
Montana 6'3" 229 lbs.

Year	Team		Games	Pos.
1984	**DAL**	**N**	16	TE

Brian Salonen continued

Year	Team		Games	Pos.
1985			16	TE
2 yrs.	32 games			

Jim Salsbury
SALSBURY, JAMES WOODROW
B. Aug. 8, 1932, Los Angeles, CA
UCLA 6'1" 233 lbs.

Year	Team		Games	Pos.
1955	**DET**	**N**	12	G
1956			11	G
1957	**GB**	**N**	12	G
1958			12	G
4 yrs.	47 games			

Jack Salschneider
SALSCHNEIDER, JOHN
B. 1925
St. Thomas 5'10" 185 lbs.

Year	Team		Games	Pos.
1949	**NYG**	**N**	11	B

Bryant Salter
SALTER, BRYANT J.
B. Jan. 22, 1950, Pittsburgh, PA
Pittsburgh 6'4" 196 lbs.

Year	Team		Games	Pos.
1971	**SD**	**N**	14	CB
1972			14	S
1973			13	S
1974	**WAS**	**N**	3	S
1975			14	S
1976	**MIA**	**N**	12	S
1976	**BAL**	**N**	1	S
6 yrs.	71 games			

Chuck Sample
SAMPLE, CHARLES
B. Jan. 5, 1920, Green Bay, WI
Toledo 5'9" 205 lbs.

Year	Team		Games	Pos.
1942	**GB**	**N**	8	FB
1945			1	FB
2 yrs.	9 games			

Johnny Sample
SAMPLE, JOHN B., JR.
B. Jun. 15, 1937, Cape Charles, VA
Maryland-Eastern Shore 6'1" 203 lbs.

Year	Team		Games	Pos.
1958	**BAL**	**N**	12	DB
1959			12	DB
1960			11	DB
1961	**PIT**	**N**	14	DB
1962			6	DB
1963	**WAS**	**N**	2	DB
1964			14	DB
1965			13	DB
1966	**NY**	**A**	13	DB
1967			14	DB
1968			14	DB
11 yrs.	125 games			

Lawrence Sampleton
SAMPLETON, LAWRENCE
B. Sep. 25, 1959, Waelder, TX
Texas 6'5" 233 lbs.

Year	Team		Games	Pos.
1982	**PHI**	**N**	9	TE
1983			7	TE
1984			16	TE
1987	**MIA**	**N**	3	TE
4 yrs.	35 games			

Art Sampson
SAMPSON, ART
None 6'1" 206 lbs.

Year	Team		Games	Pos.
1921	**DAY**	**A**	7	G

Clint Sampson
SAMPSON, CLINTON BERNARD
B. Jan. 4, 1961, Los Angeles, CA

Clint Sampson continued
San Diego State 5'11" 183 lbs.

Year	Team		Games	Pos.
1983	**DEN**	**N**	16	WR
1984			12	WR
1985			16	WR
1986			15	WR
4 yrs.	59 games			

Eber Sampson
SAMPSON, EBER (Oats)
B. 1895
Deceased
None 6'0" 197 lbs.

Year	Team		Games	Pos.
1921	**MIN**	**A**	4	FB
1922	**MIN**	**N**	2	FB
1923			7	FB, HB
3 yrs.	13 games			

Greg Sampson
SAMPSON, RALPH GREGORY
B. Dec. 25, 1950, Bellingham, WA
Stanford 6'6" 266 lbs.

Year	Team		Games	Pos.
1972	**HOU**	**N**	14	DE, DT
1973			13	DT
1974			14	OT
1975			14	OT
1976			8	OT
1977			14	OT
1978			16	OT
7 yrs.	93 games			

Howard Sampson
SAMPSON, HOWARD EARL
B. Jul. 7, 1956, Baytown, TX
Arkansas 5'10" 185 lbs.

Year	Team		Games	Pos.
1978	**GB**	**N**	15	S
1979			16	S, CB
2 yrs.	31 games			

Ron Sams
SAMS, RONALD F., JR.
B. Apr. 12, 1961, Bridgeville, PA
Pittsburgh 6'3" 260 lbs.

Year	Team		Games	Pos.
1983	**GB**	**N**	5	G
1984	**MIN**	**N**	12	G
2 yrs.	17 games			

Michael Samson
SAMSON, MICHAEL
B. Feb. 17, 1973, Laurel, MS
Grambling State 6'3" 294 lbs.

Year	Team		Games	Pos.
1996	**PHI**	**N**	1	DT

Seneca Samson
SAMSON, SENECA GADSDEN
B. Nov. 10, 1899
D. Apr. 2, 1930, Wakefield, RI
Brown 5'8" 160 lbs.

Year	Team		Games	Pos.
1926	**PRO**	**N**	2	QB, HB

Don Samuel
SAMUEL, DONALD
B. Feb. 16, 1924
Oregon State 5'11" 190 lbs.

Year	Team		Games	Pos.
1949	**PIT**	**N**	5	HB
1950			1	HB
2 yrs.	6 games			

Chris Samuels
SAMUELS, CHRISTOPHER AUBURN
B. May 16, 1969, Montego Bay, Jamaica
Texas 5'10" 202 lbs.

Year	Team		Games	Pos.
1991	**SD**	**N**	3	RB

Year	Team	Games	Pos.

Terry Samuels
SAMUELS, TERRY
B. Sep. 27, 1970, Louisville, KY
Kentucky 6'2" 254 lbs.

Year	Team	Games	Pos.
1994	**ARI** N	16	TE
1995		4	TE
2 yrs.	20 games		

Tony Samuels
SAMUELS, ANDRE ANTONIO
B. Dec. 30, 1954, Tampa, FL
Florida A&M/Bethune-Cookman 6'4" 230 lbs.

Year	Team	Games	Pos.
1977	**KC** N	14	TE
1978		16	TE
1979		16	TE
1980		4	TE
1980	**TB** N	6	TE
4 yrs.	56 games		

Carl Samuelson
SAMUELSON, CARL CLINTON
B. Apr. 11, 1923, Grand Island, NE
Nebraska 6'4" 250 lbs.

Year	Team	Games	Pos.
1948	**PIT** N	11	T
1949		12	T
1950		8	T
1951		12	T
4 yrs.	43 games		

Bill Sanborn
SANBORN, WILLIAM
B. 1899
Deceased

Year	Team	Games	Pos.
1921	**TON** A	1	E

Johnny Sanchez
SANCHEZ, JOHN CLAUDE
B. Oct. 12, 1921, Los Angeles, CA
D. Sep. 11, 1992, Hayward, CA
San Francisco 6'3" 239 lbs.

Year	Team	Games	Pos.
1947	**CHI** AA	1	T
1947	**DET** N	3	T
1947	**WAS** N	4	T
1948		12	T
1949		2	T
1950	**NYG** N	12	T
4 yrs.	34 games		

Lupe Sanchez
SANCHEZ, LUPE
B. Oct. 28, 1961, Tulare, CA
UCLA 5'10" 192 lbs.

Year	Team	Games	Pos.
1986	**PIT** N	11	CB
1987		12	CB
1988		16	CB, S
3 yrs.	39 games		

Artie Sandberg
SANDBERG, ARTHUR W. (Swede, Carl)
B. Sep. 13, 1899, Minnesota
D. Jul., 1983, Elbow Lake, MN
None 192 lbs.

Year	Team	Games	Pos.
1926	**LA** N	6	HB, G
1929	**MIN** N	3	HB, QB
2 yrs.	9 games		

Sig Sandberg
SANDBERG, SIGURD E. (Sandy)
B. Jun. 14, 1910, Eddyville, IA
D. Apr. 10, 1989, St. Louis, MO
Iowa Wesleyan 6'2" 228 lbs.

Year	Team	Games	Pos.
1934	**C-S** N	3	T
1935	**PIT** N	10	T
1936		12	T, FB
1937		7	T

Sig Sandberg *continued*

Year	Team	Games	Pos.
1937	**BKN** N	3	T, G
4 yrs.	35 games		

Wayne Sandefur
SANDEFUR, RICHARD WAYNE
B. Aug. 1, 1912, Evansville, IN
Purdue 5'10" 195 lbs.

Year	Team	Games	Pos.
1936	**PIT** N	7	FB
1937		1	FB
2 yrs.	8 games		

Bill Sandeman
SANDEMAN, WILLIAM STEWART
B. Nov. 30, 1942, Providence, RI
Pacific 6'6" 254 lbs.

Year	Team	Games	Pos.
1966	**DAL** N	8	DT
1967	**NO** N	2	OT
1967	**ATL** N	13	OT
1968		4	OT
1969		13	OT
1970		6	OT
1971		14	OT
1972		14	OT
1973		12	OT
8 yrs.	86 games		

Mark Sander
SANDER, MARK LEONARD
B. Mar. 21, 1968, Louisville, KY
Louisville 6'2" 232 lbs.

Year	Team	Games	Pos.
1992	**MIA** N	12	LB

Barry Sanders
SANDERS, BARRY
B. Jul. 16, 1968, Wichita, KS
Oklahoma State 5'8" 203 lbs.

Year	Team	Games	Pos.
1989	**DET** N	15	RB
1990		16	RB
1991		15	RB
1992		16	RB
1993		11	RB
1994		16	RB
1995		16	RB
1996		16	RB
8 yrs.	121 games		

Bob Sanders
SANDERS, BOB
B. Jun. 9, 1943, Dallas, TX
North Texas State 6'3" 235 lbs.

Year	Team	Games	Pos.
1967	**ATL** N	9	LB

Charlie Sanders
SANDERS, CHARLES ALVIN
B. Aug. 25, 1946, Greensboro, NC
Minnesota 6'4" 227 lbs.

Year	Team	Games	Pos.
1968	**DET** N	14	TE
1969		14	TE
1970		14	TE
1971		13	TE
1972		9	TE
1973		14	TE
1974		14	TE
1975		13	TE
1976		13	TE
1977		10	TE
10 yrs.	128 games		

Chris Sanders
SANDERS, CHRIS
B. May 8, 1972, Denver, CO
Ohio State 6'0" 184 lbs.

Year	Team	Games	Pos.
1995	**HOU** N	16	WR
1996		16	WR
2 yrs.	32 games		

Chuck Sanders
SANDERS, CHARLES SAMUEL
B. Apr. 24, 1964, Pittsburgh, PA
Slippery Rock 6'1" 233 lbs.

Year	Team	Games	Pos.
1986	**PIT** N	14	RB
1987		5	RB
2 yrs.	19 games		

Clarence Sanders
SANDERS, CLARENCE
B. Dec. 28, 1952, Montgomery, AL
Cincinnati 6'4" 229 lbs.

Year	Team	Games	Pos.
1978	**KC** N	16	LB
1980		1	LB
2 yrs.	17 games		

Daryl Sanders
SANDERS, DARYL T.
B. Apr. 24, 1941, Canton, OH
Ohio State 6'5" 248 lbs.

Year	Team	Games	Pos.
1963	**DET** N	14	OT
1964		14	OT
1965		14	OT
1966		14	OT
4 yrs.	56 games		

Deion Sanders
SANDERS, DEION LUWYNN
(Neon, Prime Time)
B. Aug. 9, 1967, Fort Myers, FL
Florida State 6'0" 187 lbs.

Year	Team	Games	Pos.
1989	**ATL** N	15	CB
1990		16	CB
1991		15	CB
1992		13	CB
1993		11	CB
1994	**SF** N	14	CB
1995	**DAL** N	9	CB
1996		16	CB, WR
8 yrs.	109 games		

Eric Sanders
SANDERS, ERIC DOWNER
B. Oct. 22, 1958, Reno, NV
Nevada-Reno 6'7" 282 lbs.

Year	Team	Games	Pos.
1981	**ATL** N	16	OT
1982		9	OT
1983		16	OT
1984		10	OT
1985		16	OT
1986		8	OT
1986	**DET** N	3	OL
1987		12	OT, G
1988		16	OT, G
1989		16	OT, G
1990		16	OT, G
1991		14	OT, G
1992		6	OT
12 yrs.	158 games		

Frank Sanders
SANDERS, FRANK VONDEL
B. Feb. 17, 1973, Fort Lauderdale, FL
Auburn 6'1" 202 lbs.

Year	Team	Games	Pos.
1995	**ARI** N	16	WR
1996		16	WR
2 yrs.	32 games		

Gene Sanders
SANDERS, EUGENE
B. Nov. 10, 1956, New Orleans, LA
Texas A&M 6'3" 263 lbs.

Year	Team	Games	Pos.
1979	**TB** N	16	DT
1980		11	DE, DT
1981		16	G, OT
1982		4	OT
1983		12	OT
1984		16	OT

Gene Sanders *continued*

Year	Team	Games	Pos.
1985		2	OT
7 yrs.	77 games		

Glen Sanders
SANDERS, GLENELL
B. Nov. 4, 1966, New Orleans, LA
Louisiana Tech 6'0" 224 lbs.

Year	Team	Games	Pos.
1990	**CHI** N	2	LB
1991	**LARM** N	16	LB
1994	**DEN** N	1	LB
1995	**IND** N	9	LB
4 yrs.	28 games		

Jack Sanders
SANDERS, JOHN
B. Mar. 11, 1917, San Antonio, TX
D. Oct. 26, 1991
Southern Methodist 6'0" 219 lbs.

Year	Team	Games	Pos.
1940	**PIT** N	10	G, E, T
1941		10	G
1942		9	G
1945	**PHI** N	3	G
4 yrs.	32 games		

Joe Sanders
SANDERS, JOSEPH
B. May 26, 1901
D. Feb. 9, 1979, Greensboro, NC
Kentucky Wesleyan 5'10" 248 lbs.

Year	Team	Games	Pos.
1922	**EVA** N	2	G, E

John Sanders
SANDERS, JOHN MAURICE
B. Jan. 11, 1951, Chicago, IL
South Dakota 6'1" 177 lbs.

Year	Team	Games	Pos.
1974	**NE** N	14	S
1975		14	S
1976		2	S
1977	**PHI** N	14	S
1978		15	S
5 yrs.	59 games		

Ken Sanders
SANDERS, KENNETH ROY
B. Aug. 22, 1950, Valley Mills, TX
Howard Payne 6'5" 242 lbs.

Year	Team	Games	Pos.
1972	**DET** N	6	DE
1973		14	DE
1974		14	DE
1975		14	DE
1976		14	DE
1977		11	DE
1978		7	DE
1979		5	DE
1980	**MIN** N	6	DE
1981		9	DE
10 yrs.	100 games		

Lonnie Sanders
SANDERS, LONNIE, JR.
B. Nov. 6, 1941, Detroit, MI
Michigan State 6'3" 206 lbs.

Year	Team	Games	Pos.
1963	**WAS** N	14	DB
1964		14	DB
1965		7	DB
1966		9	DB
1967		13	DB
1968	**STL** N	13	DB
1969		1	CB
7 yrs.	71 games		

Paul Sanders
SANDERS, PAUL E.
B. Dec. 15, 1918, Otto, WY
Utah State 5'11" 192 lbs.

Year	Team	Games	Pos.
1944	**BOS** N	7	HB

Year	Team	Games	Pos.

Ricky Sanders
SANDERS, RICKY WAYNE
B. Sep. 30, 1960, Temple, TX
Southwest Texas State 5'11" 182 lbs.

Year	Team		Games	Pos.
1986	WAS	N	10	WR
1987			12	WR
1988			16	WR
1989			16	WR
1990			16	WR
1991			16	WR
1992			15	WR
1993			16	WR
1994	ATL	N	14	WR
1995			3	WR
10 yrs.	134 games			

Spec Sanders
SANDERS, ORBAN EUGENE
B. Jan. 26, 1920, Temple, OK
Georgia/North Carolina/Texas 5'11" 196 lbs.

Year	Team		Games	Pos.
1946	NY	AA	13	HB
1947			14	HB
1948			13	HB
1950	NYY	N	12	HB
4 yrs.	52 games			

Thomas Sanders
SANDERS, THOMAS
B. Jan. 4, 1962, Giddings, TX
Texas A&M 5'11" 203 lbs.

Year	Team		Games	Pos.
1985	CHI	N	15	RB
1986			12	RB
1987			12	RB
1988			16	RB
1989			16	RB
1990	PHI	N	10	RB
1991			5	RB
7 yrs.	90 games			

Reggie Sanderson
SANDERSON, REGINALD JOHN
B. Nov. 4, 1950, Galveston, TX
Stanford 5'10" 206 lbs.

Year	Team		Games	Pos.
1973	CHI	N	2	RB

Todd Sandham
SANDHAM, TODD
B. Dec. 3, 1963
Northeastern 6'3" 255 lbs.

Year	Team		Games	Pos.
1987	NE	N	2	G

Bill Sandifer
SANDIFER, WILLIAM PATRICK
B. Jan. 5, 1952, Quantico, VA
UCLA 6'6" 268 lbs.

Year	Team		Games	Pos.
1974	SF	N	5	DT
1975			13	DT
1976			13	DT
1977	SEA	N	1	DT
1978			15	DT
5 yrs.	47 games			

Dan Sandifer
SANDIFER, DANIEL PADGETT
B. Mar. 1, 1927, Shreveport, LA
D. Aug. 15, 1987, Shreveport, LA
Louisiana State 6'1" 190 lbs.

Year	Team		Games	Pos.
1948	WAS	N	12	HB, DB
1949			12	HB, DB
1950	SF	N	2	HB, DB
1950	DET	N	5	HB, DB
1950	PHI	N	5	HB, DB
1951			12	HB, DB
1952	GB	N	12	DB
1953			1	DB
1953	CHIC	N	4	DB
6 yrs.	65 games			

Curt Sandig
SANDIG, CURTIS WALTER
B. Jul. 12, 1918, Mart, TX
St. Mary's (Texas) 5'10" 173 lbs.

Year	Team		Games	Pos.
1942	PIT	N	11	HB
1946	BUF	AA	9	HB
2 yrs.	20 games			

Alex Sandusky
SANDUSKY, ALEXANDER VINCENT
B. Aug. 17, 1932, McKees Rocks, PA
Clarion State 6'1" 235 lbs.

Year	Team		Games	Pos.
1954	BAL	N	12	G
1955			12	G
1956			11	G
1957			12	G
1958			12	G
1959			12	G
1960			12	G
1961			14	G
1962			13	G
1963			14	G
1964			14	G
1965			14	G
1966		N	14	G
13 yrs.	166 games			

John Sandusky
SANDUSKY, JOHN T.
B. Dec. 28, 1925, Philadelphia, PA
Villanova 6'1" 251 lbs.

Year	Team		Games	Pos.
1950	CLE	N	12	T
1951			11	T
1952			11	T
1953			12	T
1954			12	T
1955			12	T
1956	GB	N	12	T
7 yrs.	82 games			

Mike Sandusky
SANDUSKY, MICHAEL
B. Mar. 14, 1935
Maryland 6'0" 231 lbs.

Year	Team		Games	Pos.
1957	PIT	N	12	G
1958			12	G
1959			11	G
1960			12	G
1961			12	G
1962			14	G
1963			13	G
1964			6	G
1965			12	G
9 yrs.	104 games			

Jim Sanford
SANFORD, JAMES L.
B. Dec. 25, 1898
D. Apr. 7, 1938
Lehigh 5'8" 195 lbs.

Year	Team		Games	Pos.
1924	DUL	N	1	T

Leo Sanford
SANFORD, OTTIS LEO
B. Oct. 4, 1929, Dallas, TX
Louisiana Tech 6'1" 224 lbs.

Year	Team		Games	Pos.
1951	CHIC	N	12	C, LB
1952			12	G, LB
1953			12	C, LB
1954			12	C, LB
1955			12	C, LB
1956			12	C, LB
1957			12	C, LB
1958	BAL	N	9	LB
8 yrs.	93 games			

Lucius Sanford
SANFORD, LUCIUS M., JR.
B. Feb. 14, 1956, Milledgeville, GA
Georgia Tech 6'2" 220 lbs.

Year	Team		Games	Pos.
1978	BUF	N	16	LB
1979			16	LB
1980			16	LB
1981			16	LB
1982			9	LB
1983			16	LB
1984			8	LB
1985			11	LB
1986			10	LB
1987	CLE	N	11	LB
10 yrs.	129 games			

Rick Sanford
SANFORD, RICHARD FRANCIS
B. Jan. 9, 1957, Rock Hill, SC
South Carolina 6'1" 192 lbs.

Year	Team		Games	Pos.
1979	NE	N	16	CB
1980			16	CB, S
1981			16	S
1982			9	CB, S
1983			16	S
1984			16	S
1985	SEA	N	5	S
7 yrs.	94 games			

Sandy Sanford
SANFORD, HAYWARD
B. Jun. 15, 1916, Plainview, AR
Alabama 6'1" 210 lbs.

Year	Team		Games	Pos.
1940	WAS	N	7	E

Stilwell Sanooke
SANOOKE, STILWELL
B. 1892
Deceased
Carlisle 5'8" 175 lbs.

Year	Team		Games	Pos.
1922	OOR	N	9	E

Ollie Sansen
SANSEN, OLIVER M.
B. Mar. 6, 1908, Alta, IA
D. Mar. 21, 1987, San Lorenzo, CA
Iowa 6'1" 193 lbs.

Year	Team		Games	Pos.
1932	BKN	N	10	FB, HB, QB
1933			10	HB, FB, E, QB
1934			11	HB, FB
1935			10	FB, HB, QB
4 yrs.	41 games			

Joe Santone
SANTONE, JOSEPH
B. Oct. 1, 1893, Italy
D. Oct., 1963
None 180 lbs.

Year	Team		Games	Pos.
1926	HAR	N	1	G

Frank Santora
SANTORA, FRANK
B. May 22, 1926, Garfield, NJ
None 5'10" 166 lbs.

Year	Team		Games	Pos.
1944	BOS	N	1	B

Dom Sanzotta
SANZOTTA, DOMINIC (Mickey)
B. Apr. 28, 1921, Geneva, OH
Case Western Reserve 5'9" 188 lbs.

Year	Team		Games	Pos.
1942	DET	N	10	FB, HB
1946			10	HB
2 yrs.	20 games			

Rick Sapienza
SAPIENZA, AMERICO

Rick Sapienza *continued*
B. Feb. 8, 1936
Villanova 5'11" 185 lbs.

Year	Team		Games	Pos.
1960	NY	A		DB

Jesse Sapolu
SAPOLU, JESSE
B. Mar. 10, 1961, Laie, Western Samoa
Hawaii 6'4" 264 lbs.

Year	Team		Games	Pos.
1983	SF	N	16	G
1984			1	G
1987			12	G, C
1988			16	G, C
1989			16	G, C
1990			16	C
1991			16	C
1992			16	C
1993			16	C
1994			14	G
1995			16	G, C
1996			16	C
12 yrs.	171 games			

Patrick Sapp
SAPP, PATRICK
B. May 11, 1973, Jacksonville, FL
Clemson 6'4" 258 lbs.

Year	Team		Games	Pos.
1996	SD	N	16	LB

Theron Sapp
SAPP, THERON COLEMAN
B. Jun. 15, 1935, Macon, GA
Georgia 6'1" 203 lbs.

Year	Team		Games	Pos.
1959	PHI	N	12	B
1960			5	B
1961			14	OB
1962			12	FB
1963			4	FB
1963	PIT	N	10	HB
1964			11	HB
1965			14	HB
7 yrs.	82 games			

Warren Sapp
SAPP, WARREN
B. Dec. 19, 1972, Plymouth, FL
Miami (Florida) 6'2" 281 lbs.

Year	Team		Games	Pos.
1995	TB	N	16	DT, DE
1996			15	DE
2 yrs.	31 games			

Al Sarafiny
SARAFINY, ALBERT JOSEPH
B. Sep. 2, 1906, Caspian, MI
D. Feb., 1981, Chicago, IL
St. Edward's 5'11" 235 lbs.

Year	Team		Games	Pos.
1933	GB	N	5	C

Tony Sarausky
SARAUSKY, ANTHONY OLGRID
B. Feb. 28, 1913, Cambridge, MA
D. Jun. 21, 1990, Littleton, WI
Fordham 5'11" 201 lbs.

Year	Team		Games	Pos.
1935	NYG	N	8	HB, QB, FB
1936			11	HB, QB
1937			4	B
1938	BKN	N	4	FB
4 yrs.	27 games			

Phil Sarboe
SARBOE, PHILIP J.
B. Aug. 22, 1912, Fairbanks, AK
D. Nov. 19, 1985, Spokane, WA
Washington State 5'10" 167 lbs.

Year	Team		Games	Pos.
1934	BOS	N	5	QB
1934	CHIC	N	12	QB
1935				QB

Year	Team		Games	Pos.

Phil Sarboe continued

1936			6	QB
1936	BKN	N	5	QB
3 yrs.	32 games			

Tony Sardisco
SARDISCO, ANTHONY GUY
B. Dec. 5, 1932, Shreveport, LA
Tulane 6'2" 226 lbs.

1956	WAS	N	7	G
1956	SF	N	2	G, LB
1960	BOS	A		LB
1961			13	G
1962			14	G
4 yrs.	36 games			

Broderick Sargent
SARGENT, BRODERICK LAWRENCE
B. Sep. 16, 1962, Waxahachie, TX
Baylor 5'10" 215 lbs.

1986	STL	N	16	RB
1987			15	FB
1989	DAL	N	14	RB
3 yrs.	45 games			

Kevin Sargent
SARGENT, KEVIN
B. Mar. 31, 1969, Bremerton, WA
Eastern Washington 6'6" 284 lbs.

1992	CIN	N	16	G, OT
1993			1	OT
1994			15	OT
1995			15	OT
4 yrs.	47 games			

Harvey Sark
SARK, HARVEY
B. Jan. 30, 1907
Phillips 210 lbs.

1931	NYG	N	3	G
1934	C-S	N	1	G
2 yrs.	4 games			

Charley Sarratt
SARRATT, CHARLES F.
B. Oct. 22, 1923, Oklahoma City, OK
Oklahoma 6'1" 185 lbs.

| 1948 | DET | N | 8 | QB |

Paul Sarringhaus
SARRINGHAUS, PAUL H.
B. Aug. 13, 1920, Hamilton, OH
Ohio State 6'0" 185 lbs.

| 1948 | DET | N | | HB |

Dan Sartin
SARTIN, DANIEL M.
B. Jun. 23, 1946, Gulfport, MS
Mississippi 6'1" 245 lbs.

| 1969 | SD | A | 13 | LB |

Martin Sartin
SARTIN, MARTIN
B. Mar. 9, 1963, Philadelphia, PA
Long Beach State 5'10" 202 lbs.

| 1987 | SD | N | 3 | RB |

Larry Sartori
SARTORI, LAWRENCE
B. Aug. 20, 1917, Sheppton, PA
D. Nov. 6, 1980, Paramus, NJ
Fordham 6'0" 208 lbs.

1942	DET	N	10	G
1945			1	G
2 yrs.	11 games			

Year	Team		Games	Pos.

Don Sasa
SASA, DON
B. Sep. 16, 1972, American Samoa
Washington State 6'3" 286 lbs.

1995	SD	N	5	DT
1996			4	DT
2 yrs.	9 games			

Doug Satcher
SATCHER, DOUGLAS
B. May 28, 1945, Sandersville, MS
Southern Mississippi 6'0" 221 lbs.

1966	BOS	A	14	LB
1967			14	LB
1968			14	LB
3 yrs.	42 games			

Ollie Satenstein
SATENSTEIN, BERNARD
B. 1906
New York University 6'0" 213 lbs.

1929	SI	N	4	G, E, T
1930			11	G
1931			11	G, T
1932			8	G, E
1933	NYG	N	9	G
5 yrs.	43 games			

Al Satterfield
SATTERFIELD, ALFRED NEAL
B. Nov. 28, 1921
D. Oct. 28, 1992, Greenville, TX
Vanderbilt 6'3" 225 lbs.

| 1947 | SF | AA | 12 | T |

Brian Satterfield
SATTERFIELD, BRIAN
B. Dec. 22, 1969, Blue Ridge, GA
North Alabama 6'0" 225 lbs.

| 1996 | GB | N | 1 | FB |

Howard Satterwhite
SATTERWHITE, HOWARD EUGENE
B. May 24, 1953, Monthalia, TX
Sam Houston State 5'11" 185 lbs.

1976	NYJ	N	12	WR
1977	BAL	N	1	WR
2 yrs.	13 games			

Craig Sauer
SAUER, CRAIG
B. Dec. 13, 1972, Sartell, MN
Minnesota 6'1" 226 lbs.

| 1996 | ATL | N | 16 | LB |

Eddie Sauer
SAUER, EDWARD A. (Tubby)
B. Nov. 27, 1898, Van Buren Township, OH
D. Feb., 1980, Dayton, OH
Miami (Ohio) 5'10" 246 lbs.

1920	DAY	A	8	T
1921			9	T
1921	CAN	A	1	G
1922	DAY	N	7	T
1922	AKR	N	2	T
1922	DAY	N	1	T
1923			8	T
1924			8	T
1925			8	T
1925	POT	N	1	T
1926	DAY	N	5	T
7 yrs.	58 games			

Year	Team		Games	Pos.

George Sauer
SAUER, GEORGE HENRY, SR.
B. Dec. 11, 1910, Stratton, NE
D. Feb. 5, 1994, Waco, TX
Nebraska 6'2" 208 lbs.

1935	GB	N	10	HB, FB
1936			10	HB
1937			2	HB
3 yrs.	22 games			

George Sauer
SAUER, GEORGE HENRY, JR.
B. Nov. 10, 1943, Sheboygan, WI
Texas 6'1" 199 lbs.

1965	NY	A	14	OE
1966			14	OE
1967			14	OE
1968			14	OE
1969			14	WR
1970	NYJ	N	14	WR
6 yrs.	84 games			

Todd Sauerbrun
SAUERBRUN, TODD
B. Jan. 20, 1971, Setauket, NY
West Virginia 5'10" 206 lbs.

1995	CHI	N	15	P
1996			16	P
2 yrs.	31 games			

Bill Saul
SAUL, WILLIAM NEAL
B. Nov. 19, 1940, Unionville, PA
Penn State 6'4" 225 lbs.

1962	BAL	N	14	LB
1963			14	LB
1964	PIT	N	13	LB
1966			14	LB
1967			14	LB
1968			3	LB
1969	NO	N	3	LB
7 yrs.	75 games			

Rich Saul
SAUL, RICHARD ROBERT
B. Feb. 5, 1948, Butler, PA
Michigan State 6'3" 241 lbs.

1970	LA	N	14	LB
1971			14	G
1972			14	C, G
1973			14	C, G
1974			14	C, G
1975			14	C, G
1976			14	C
1977			14	C
1978			16	C
1979			16	C
1980			16	C
1981			16	C
12 yrs.	176 games			

Ron Saul
SAUL, RONALD REED
B. Feb. 5, 1948, Butler, PA
Michigan State 6'2" 254 lbs.

1970	HOU	N	14	G
1971			3	G
1972			13	G
1973			3	G
1974			14	G
1975			14	G
1976	WAS	N	11	G
1977			14	G
1978			15	G
1979			15	G
1980			16	G
1981			10	G
12 yrs.	142 games			

Year	Team		Games	Pos.

Mac Sauls
SAULS, KIRBY M.
B. Aug. 15, 1945, Long Beach, CA
Southwest Texas State 6'0" 185 lbs.

1968	STL	N	6	DB
1969			4	S
2 yrs.	10 games			

Syl Saumer
SAUMER, SYLVESTER (Pete)
B. Apr. 30, 1912, St. Paul, MN
D. Jan., 1983, Reno, NV
St. Olaf 6'1" 195 lbs.

| 1934 | PIT | N | 3 | HB |
| 1934 | C-S | N | 3 | HB |

Cedric Saunders
SAUNDERS, CEDRIC
B. Sep. 30, 1972, Sarasota, FL
Ohio State 6'3" 240 lbs.

| 1995 | TB | N | 3 | TE |

Buck Saunders
SAUNDERS, WARD BISHOP
B. 1892
Deceased
California 6'1" 190 lbs.

| 1922 | TOL | N | 1 | HB |

John Saunders
SAUNDERS, JOHN
B. Apr. 29, 1950, Toledo, OH
Toledo 6'3" 198 lbs.

1972	BUF	N	2	S
1974	SF	N	4	CB, S
1975	DET	N	1	DB
1975	SF	N	3	CB, S
3 yrs.	10 games			

Russ Saunders
SAUNDERS, RUSSELL S.
B. 1906
D. Apr. 28, 1987, Burbank, CA
Southern California 5'9" 190 lbs.

| 1931 | GB | N | 9 | FB |

Sebastian Savage
SAVAGE, SEBASTIAN
B. Dec. 12, 1969, Carlisle, SC
North Carolina State 5'11" 196 lbs.

1994	WAS	N	1	DB
1995			2	CB, S
2 yrs.	3 games			

Tony Savage
SAVAGE, ANTHONY JOHN
B. Jul. 7, 1967, San Francisco, CA
Washington State 6'3" 300 lbs.

1990	SD	N	2	NT
1990			2	NT
1992	CIN	N	1	NT
2 yrs.	5 games			

Ollie Savatsky
SAVATSKY, OLIVER J.
B. May 13, 1912, Cleveland, OH
Miami (Ohio) 6'2" 215 lbs.

| 1937 | CLE | N | 1 | E |

George Savitsky
SAVITSKY, GEORGE M.
B. Jul. 30, 1924, New York, NY
Pennsylvania 6'2" 244 lbs.

1948	PHI	N	12	T
1949			12	T
2 yrs.	24 games			

Year	Team		Games	Pos.

Joe Savoldi
SAVOLDI, JOSEPH A. (Jumpin' Joe)
B. Mar. 5, 1908, Italy
D. Jan. 25, 1974, Cumberland Shores, KY
Notre Dame 5'11" 194 lbs.

Year	Team		Games	Pos.
1930	CHIB	N	3	FB

Buzz Sawyer
SAWYER, BUZZ
B. Nov. 18, 1962
Baylor 6'1" 201 lbs.

Year	Team		Games	Pos.
1987	DAL	N	3	P

Corey Sawyer
SAWYER, COREY
B. Oct. 4, 1971, Key West, FL
Florida State 5'11" 171 lbs.

Year	Team		Games	Pos.
1994	CIN	N	15	CB
1995			12	CB
1996			15	CB
3 yrs.	42 games			

Herm Sawyer
SAWYER, HERMAN W. (Speed)
B. Oct. 18, 1898
D. Sep., 1968, Bronx, NY
Syracuse 5'8" 170 lbs.

Year	Team		Games	Pos.
1922	ROC	N	3	QB, HB

John Sawyer
SAWYER, JOHN WESLEY
B. Jul. 26, 1953, Brookhaven, MS
Southern Mississippi 6'2" 230 lbs.

Year	Team		Games	Pos.
1975	HOU	N	8	TE
1976			14	TE
1977	SEA	N	14	TE
1978			11	TE
1980			16	TE
1981			16	TE
1982			7	TE
1983	WAS	N	7	TE
1983	DEN	N	7	TE
1984			10	TE
9 yrs.	110 games			

Jon Sawyer
SAWYER, JON
B. Apr. 6, 1965
Cincinnati 5'9" 175 lbs.

Year	Team		Games	Pos.
1987	NE	N	2	CB

Ken Sawyer
SAWYER, KENNETH L.
B. Jul. 22, 1952, Clearfield, PA
Syracuse 6'0" 192 lbs.

Year	Team		Games	Pos.
1974	CIN	N	12	DB

James Saxon
SAXON, JAMES ELIJAH
B. Mar. 23, 1966, Buford, SC
San Jose State 5'11" 215 lbs.

Year	Team		Games	Pos.
1988	KC	N	16	RB
1989			16	RB
1990			6	RB
1991			16	RB
1992	MIA	N	16	RB
1993			16	RB
1994			16	RB
1995	PHI	N	8	RB
8 yrs.	110 games			

Mike Saxon
SAXON, MIKE
B. Jul. 10, 1962, Arcadia, CA
San Diego State 6'3" 193 lbs.

Year	Team		Games	Pos.
1985	DAL	N	16	P

Mike Saxon *continued*

Year	Team		Games	Pos.
1986			16	P
1987			12	P
1988			16	P
1989			16	P
1990			16	P
1991			16	P
1992			16	P
1993	NE	N	16	P
1994	MIN	N	16	P
1995			16	P
11 yrs.	172 games			

Brian Saxton
SAXTON, PAUL BRIAN
B. Mar. 13, 1972, Whippany Park, NJ
Boston College 6'6" 256 lbs.

Year	Team		Games	Pos.
1996	NYG	N	16	TE

Jimmy Saxton
SAXTON, JAMES EVERETT, JR.
B. 1941
Texas 5'11" 173 lbs.

Year	Team		Games	Pos.
1962	DAL	A	13	HB

Gale Sayers
SAYERS, GALE EUGENE (The Kansas Comet)
B. May 30, 1943, Wichita, KS
Kansas 6'0" 199 lbs.

Year	Team		Games	Pos.
1965	CHI	N	14	HB
1966			14	HB
1967			13	RB
1968			9	RB
1969			14	RB
1970			2	RB
1971			2	RB
7 yrs.	68 games			

Ron Sayers
SAYERS, RONALD
B. Aug. 29, 1947, Wichita, KS
Nebraska-Omaha 6'1" 202 lbs.

Year	Team		Games	Pos.
1969	SD	A	7	RB

Sayforth
SAYFORTH
None

Year	Team		Games	Pos.
1926	PRO	N	1	HB

Ralph Sazio
SAZIO, RALPH JOSEPH
B. Jul. 22, 1922, Avellino, Italy
William & Mary 6'1" 220 lbs.

Year	Team		Games	Pos.
1948	BKN	AA	13	T

Ron Sbranti
SBRANTI, RON AL (Truck)
B. Oct. 24, 1944, Antioch, CA
Utah State 6'2" 230 lbs.

Year	Team		Games	Pos.
1966	DEN	A	14	LB

John Scafide
SCAFIDE, JOHN
B. Jun. 21, 1911
D. Oct., 1979, Bay St. Louis, MS
Tulane 6'0" 210 lbs.

Year	Team		Games	Pos.
1933	BOS	N	1	T

Charley Scales
SCALES, CHARLES
B. Jan. 11, 1938, Pittsburgh, PA
Indiana 5'11" 214 lbs.

Year	Team		Games	Pos.
1960	PIT	N	12	FB
1961			14	FB

Charley Scales *continued*

Year	Team		Games	Pos.
1962	CLE	N	14	FB
1963			14	HB
1964			14	HB
1965			14	FB
1966	ATL	N	5	RB
7 yrs.	87 games			

Dwight Scales
SCALES, DWIGHT
B. May 30, 1953, Little Rock, AR
Grambling State 6'2" 175 lbs.

Year	Team		Games	Pos.
1976	LA	N	14	WR
1977			12	WR
1978			13	WR
1979	NYG	N	15	WR
1981	SD	N	16	WR
1982			9	WR
1983			7	WR
1984	SEA	N	4	WR
8 yrs.	90 games			

Greg Scales
SCALES, GREG
B. May 9, 1966, Winston-Salem, NC
Wake Forest 6'4" 253 lbs.

Year	Team		Games	Pos.
1988	NO	N	12	TE
1989			14	TE
1990			16	TE
1991			2	TE
4 yrs.	44 games			

Hurles Scales
SCALES, HURLES
B. Dec. 1, 1950, Amarillo, TX
North Texas State 6'1" 200 lbs.

Year	Team		Games	Pos.
1974	CHI	N	2	DB
1974	STL	N	7	CB
1975	GB	N	8	DT
2 yrs.	17 games			

Ted Scalissi
SCALISSI, THEODORE GLENN
B. Oct. 26, 1921, Madison, WI
D. Jan. 6, 1987, Janesville, WI
Ripon 5'8" 173 lbs.

Year	Team		Games	Pos.
1947	CHI	AA	10	B

Johnny Scalzi
SCALZI, JOHN ANTHONY
B. Mar. 22, 1907, Stamford, CT
D. Sep. 27, 1962, Port Chester, NY
Georgetown (DC) 5'7" 168 lbs.

Year	Team		Games	Pos.
1931	BKN	N	6	FB, QB, HB

Jerry Scanlan
SCANLAN, JERRY
B. Jan. 4, 1957, Honolulu, HI
Hawaii 6'5" 270 lbs.

Year	Team		Games	Pos.
1980	WAS	N	3	OT
1981			3	OT
2 yrs.	6 games			

John Scanlon
SCANLON, JOHN
B. 1900, Illinois
Deceased
DePaul 185 lbs.

Year	Team		Games	Pos.
1921	CHIC	A	4	HB, G
1926	LOU	N	2	HB
2 yrs.	6 games			

Jack Scarbath
SCARBATH, JOHN C.
B. Aug. 12, 1930, Baltimore, MD
Maryland 6'2" 206 lbs.

Year	Team		Games	Pos.
1953	WAS	N	12	QB

Jack Scarbath *continued*

Year	Team		Games	Pos.
1954			10	QB
1956	PIT	N	12	QB
3 yrs.	34 games			

Sam Scarber
SCARBER, SAM W.
B. Jun. 24, 1949, St. Louis, MO
New Mexico 6'2" 232 lbs.

Year	Team		Games	Pos.
1975	SD	N	11	RB
1976			14	RB
2 yrs.	25 games			

John Scardina
SCARDINA, JOHN
B. Jul. 26, 1958, Milwaukee, WI
Lincoln (Missouri) 6'4" 265 lbs.

Year	Team		Games	Pos.
1987	MIN	N	3	OT

Carmen Scardine
SCARDINE, CARMEN
B. 1910
None

Year	Team		Games	Pos.
1932	CHIC	N	1	HB

Joe Scarpati
SCARPATI, JOSEPH H.
B. Mar. 5, 1943, Brooklyn, NY
North Carolina State 5'10" 185 lbs.

Year	Team		Games	Pos.
1964	PHI	N	12	DB
1965			14	DB
1966			14	DB
1967			14	DB
1968			14	DB
1969			14	S
1970	NO	N	14	S
7 yrs.	96 games			

Bill Scarpino
SCARPINO, WILLIAM
B. Apr. 23, 1898
D. Feb., 1983, South Des Moines, IA
Des Moines CC 5'11" 175 lbs.

Year	Team		Games	Pos.
1926	RI	A	2	E

Bob Scarpitto
SCARPITTO, ROBERT FRANK
B. Jan. 7, 1939, Rahway, NJ
Notre Dame 5'11" 194 lbs.

Year	Team		Games	Pos.
1961	SD	A	7	HB
1962	DEN	A	14	HB
1963			11	FL
1964			14	FL
1965			14	FL
1966			14	FL
1967			14	FL
1968	BOS	A	14	FL
8 yrs.	102 games			

Mike Scarry
SCARRY, MICHAEL J. (Mo)
B. Feb. 1, 1920, Duquesne, PA
Waynesburg 6'0" 214 lbs.

Year	Team		Games	Pos.
1944	CLE	N	10	C, G
1945			10	C
1946	CLE	AA	14	C
1947			11	C
4 yrs.	45 games			

Elmer Schaake
SCHAAKE, ELMER (Dutch)
B. 1911
Deceased
Kansas 5'11" 207 lbs.

Year	Team		Games	Pos.
1933	POR	N	0	FB, HB

Pete Schabarum
SCHABARUM, PETER FRANK
B. Jan. 9, 1929, Los Angeles, CA
California 5'11" 185 lbs.

Year	Team	Games	Pos.
1951	SF N	12	HB
1953		10	HB
1954		12	HB
3 yrs.	34 games		

Mike Schad
SCHAD, MICHAEL
B. Oct. 2, 1963, Trenton, Ont.
Queen's (Canada) 6'5" 290 lbs.

Year	Team	Games	Pos.
1987	LARM N	1	G
1988		6	G
1989	PHI N	16	G
1990		12	G
1992		14	G
1993		13	G
6 yrs.	62 games		

Don Schaefer
SCHAEFER, DONALD T.
B. Feb. 13, 1934, Pittsburgh, PA
Notre Dame 6'0" 210 lbs.

Year	Team	Games	Pos.
1956	PHI N	12	FB

Joe Schaffer
SCHAFFER, JOSEPH
B. 1938
Tennessee 6'0" 210 lbs.

Year	Team	Games	Pos.
1960	BUF A		LB

Pete Schaffnit
SCHAFFNIT, PETER
B. 1902
California 5'11" 180 lbs.

Year	Team	Games	Pos.
1926	LA N	9	HB, E, FB

Dick Schafrath
SCHAFRATH, RICHARD PHILLIP
B. Mar. 21, 1937, Canton, OH
Ohio State 6'3" 253 lbs.

Year	Team	Games	Pos.
1959	CLE N	12	DE, G
1960		12	OT
1961		13	OT
1962		14	OT
1963		14	OT
1964		14	OT
1965		14	OT
1966		13	OT
1967		14	OT
1968		14	OT
1969		14	OT
1970		14	OT
1971		14	OT
13 yrs.	176 games		

Duke Schamel
SCHAMEL, DUKE
B. Nov. 3, 1963
South Dakota 6'3" 235 lbs.

Year	Team	Games	Pos.
1987	MIA N	3	LB

Francis Schammel
SCHAMMEL, FRANCIS (Zud)
B. Aug. 26, 1910
D. Jan., 1973
Iowa 6'2" 235 lbs.

Year	Team	Games	Pos.
1937	GB N	8	G, E, T

Scott Schankweiler
SCHANKWEILER, SCOTT
B. Oct. 15, 1963, Sunbury, PA
Maryland 6'0" 225 lbs.

Year	Team	Games	Pos.
1987	BUF N	3	LB

Eddie Scharer
SCHARER, EDWARD
B. Jan. 6, 1902
D. May 5, 1989, Long Beach, CA
Detroit/Notre Dame 5'6" 165 lbs.

Year	Team	Games	Pos.
1926	DET N	12	QB, HB
1927	POT N	10	QB, HB
1928	DET N	8	HB, QB
3 yrs.	30 games		

Carl Schaukowitch
SCHAUKOWITCH, CARL
B. Feb. 14, 1951, Pittsburgh, PA
Penn State 6'2" 237 lbs.

Year	Team	Games	Pos.
1975	DEN N	11	G

Greg Schaum
SCHAUM, GREGORY JAMES
B. Jan. 1, 1954, Baltimore, MD
Michigan State 6'4" 246 lbs.

Year	Team	Games	Pos.
1976	DAL N	12	DT
1978	NE N	14	DE
2 yrs.	26 games		

Lee Scheib
SCHEIB, LEE RAYMOND (Skippy)
B. Jul. 28, 1903
D. Feb. 27, 1989, Saginaw, MI
West Virginia Wesleyan/Washington (MO) 6'2" 210 lbs.

Year	Team	Games	Pos.
1930	BKN N	6	C

Joe Schein
SCHEIN, JOSEPH
B. 1909, Brooklyn, NY
D. May 27, 1969, Providence, RI
Brown 5'10" 212 lbs.

Year	Team	Games	Pos.
1931	PRO N	11	T

Herb Schell
SCHELL, HERBERT PHILLIP
B. Jan. 5, 1902
D. Aug., 1985, Bexley, OH
Ohio State 175 lbs.

Year	Team	Games	Pos.
1924	COL N	5	HB, FB, QB

Ed Schenk
SCHENK, ED
B. Dec. 20, 1960
Baldwin-Wallace/Central Florida 6'4" 230 lbs.

Year	Team	Games	Pos.
1987	MIN N	3	TE

Nate Schenker
SCHENKER, NATHAN
B. 1918
Samford 6'2" 220 lbs.

Year	Team	Games	Pos.
1939	CLE N	3	T

Bernie Scherer
SCHERER, BERNARD JOSEPH
B. Jan. 28, 1913, Spencer, NE
Nebraska 6'1" 190 lbs.

Year	Team	Games	Pos.
1936	GB N	9	E
1937		9	E
1938		9	E
1939	PIT N	9	E
4 yrs.	36 games		

Abe Scheuer
SCHEUER, ABRAHAM (Babe)
B. 1912
New York University 6'3" 240 lbs.

Year	Team	Games	Pos.
1934	NYG N	1	T

Alex Schibanoff
SCHIBANOFF, ALEXANDER
B. Oct. 17, 1919, Freehold, NJ
Franklin & Marshall 6'1" 218 lbs.

Year	Team	Games	Pos.
1941	DET N	1	T
1942		6	T
2 yrs.	7 games		

Doyle Schick
SCHICK, DOYLE DEAN
B. Feb. 23, 1939, Lawrence, KS
Kansas 6'1" 210 lbs.

Year	Team	Games	Pos.
1961	WAS N	5	DB

Johnny Schiechl
SCHIECHL, JOHN GEORGE
B. Aug. 22, 1917, San Francisco, CA
D. Feb., 1964
Santa Clara 6'2" 244 lbs.

Year	Team	Games	Pos.
1941	PIT N	5	C
1942		1	C
1942	DET N	8	C
1945	CHIB N	9	C
1946		10	C
1947	SF AA	14	C
5 yrs.	47 games		

Ralph Schilling
SCHILLING, RALPH
B. Jul. 5, 1921, Morris, OK
Oklahoma City 6'3" 218 lbs.

Year	Team	Games	Pos.
1946	WAS N		E
1946	BUF AA	3	E
1 yr.	3 games		

Andy Schillinger
SCHILLINGER, ANDREW C.
B. Nov. 22, 1964, Lakewood, OH
Miami (Ohio) 5'11" 179 lbs.

Year	Team	Games	Pos.
1988	PHX N	3	WR

Steve Schimititisch
SCHIMITITISCH, STEPHEN G.
B. May 14, 1903, Vienna, Austria
D. Jun. 23, 1988, Wolfeboro, NH
Columbia 6'0" 195 lbs.

Year	Team	Games	Pos.
1926	NY A	9	C, G

Arthur Schimmel
SCHIMMEL, ARTHUR
None

Year	Team	Games	Pos.
1925	RI N	1	HB

Steve Schindler
SCHINDLER, STEVEN WAYNE
B. Jul. 24, 1954, Caldwell, NJ
Boston College 6'3" 256 lbs.

Year	Team	Games	Pos.
1977	DEN N	14	G
1978		14	G
2 yrs.	28 games		

Vic Schleich
SCHLEICH, VICTOR
B. 1921
Nebraska 6'3" 240 lbs.

Year	Team	Games	Pos.
1947	NY AA	11	T

Maury Schleicher
SCHLEICHER, MAURICE
B. Jul. 17, 1937, Allentown, PA
Penn State 6'3" 238 lbs.

Year	Team	Games	Pos.
1959	CHIC N	10	LB
1960	LA A		DE
1961	SD A	14	LB
1962		4	LB
4 yrs.	28 games		

Mark Schlereth
SCHLERETH, MARK
B. Jan. 25, 1966, Anchorage, AK
Idaho 6'3" 280 lbs.

Year	Team	Games	Pos.
1989	WAS N	6	C
1990		12	G
1991		16	G
1992		16	G
1993		9	G
1994		16	G
1995	DEN N	16	G
1996		14	G
8 yrs.	105 games		

Cory Schlesinger
SCHLESINGER, CORY
B. Jun. 23, 1972, Columbus, NE
Nebraska 6'0" 230 lbs.

Year	Team	Games	Pos.
1995	DET N	16	RB
1996		16	RB
2 yrs.	32 games		

Vin Schleusner
SCHLEUSNER, VINCENT L.
(Slice)
B. 1908
Iowa 6'3" 225 lbs.

Year	Team	Games	Pos.
1930	POR N	13	T
1931		11	T, G
2 yrs.	24 games		

Art Schlichter
SCHLICHTER, ARTHUR E.
B. Apr. 25, 1960, Washington Court House, OH
Ohio State 6'2" 210 lbs.

Year	Team	Games	Pos.
1982	BAL N	3	QB
1984	IND N	9	QB
1985		1	QB
3 yrs.	13 games		

Walt Schlinkman
SCHLINKMAN, WALTER GAYE
B. May 2, 1922, Channing, TX
D. Oct. 5, 1994, Weimar, TX
Texas Tech 5'8" 191 lbs.

Year	Team	Games	Pos.
1946	GB N	11	FB
1947		12	FB
1948		11	FB
1949		12	FB
4 yrs.	46 games		

Todd Schlopy
SCHLOPY, R. TODD
B. Jun. 17, 1962, Bradford, PA
Michigan 5'10" 168 lbs.

Year	Team	Games	Pos.
1987	BUF N	3	K

Herm Schmarr
SCHMARR, HERMAN
B. Oct. 1, 1915
D. Mar. 13, 1989, Bradenton, FL
Catholic 6'2" 210 lbs.

Year	Team	Games	Pos.
1943	BKN N	7	E, T

Art Schmaehl
SCHMAEHL, ARTHUR
B. Feb. 5, 1894
D. Dec., 1967, Chicago, IL
None 5'8" 170 lbs.

Year	Team	Games	Pos.
1921	GB A	6	FB, QB

Ray Schmautz
SCHMAUTZ, RAYMOND
B. 1943
San Diego State 6'1" 225 lbs.

Year	Team	Games	Pos.
1966	OAK A	10	LB

Year	Team		Games	Pos.

Jim Schmedding
SCHMEDDING, JAMES EDWARD
B. Feb. 10, 1946, San Diego, CA
Weber State 6'2" 250 lbs.

Year	Team		Games	Pos.
1968	SD	A	1	G
1969			14	G
1970	SD	N	9	G

3 yrs.   24 games

Bob Schmidt
SCHMIDT, ROBERT MALCOLM
B. Jul. 9, 1936, Rochester, MN
Minnesota 6'4" 248 lbs.

Year	Team		Games	Pos.
1959	NYG	N	12	T
1960			11	T
1961	HOU	A	12	C
1962			14	C
1963			14	C
1964	BOS	A	14	OT
1966	BUF	A	14	OT, C
1967			7	C

8 yrs.   98 games

George Schmidt
SCHMIDT, GEORGE
B. Oct. 28, 1927, Chicago, IL
Lewis 6'2" 230 lbs.

Year	Team		Games	Pos.
1953	CHIC	N	6	E

Henry Schmidt
SCHMIDT, HENRY
*Southern California/Trinity (Texas) 6'4'
245 lbs.*

Year	Team		Games	Pos.
1959	SF	N	12	DT
1960			12	DT
1961	SD	A	14	DT
1962			14	DE
1963			14	DT
1964			14	DT
1965	BUF	A	8	DT
1966	NY	A	11	DT

8 yrs.   99 games

Joe Schmidt
SCHMIDT, JOSEPH PAUL
B. Jan. 18, 1932, Pittsburgh, PA
Pittsburgh 6'1" 220 lbs.

Year	Team		Games	Pos.
1953	DET	N	11	LB
1954			12	LB
1955			12	LB
1956			12	LB
1957			12	LB
1958			12	LB
1959			12	LB
1960			10	LB
1961			14	LB
1962			14	LB
1963			10	LB
1964			9	LB
1965			14	LB

13 yrs.   154 games

John Schmidt
SCHMIDT, JOHN PETER
B. Apr. 3, 1917, Detroit, MI
Carnegie-Mellon 6'3" 210 lbs.

Year	Team		Games	Pos.
1940	PIT	N	1	G

Kermit Schmidt
SCHMIDT, KERMIT
B. 1909
California Poly (Pomona) 6'0" 200 lbs.

Year	Team		Games	Pos.
1933	CIN	N	5	E, FB

Roy Schmidt
SCHMIDT, ROY LEE
B. May 3, 1942, Colorado Springs, CO

Year	Team		Games	Pos.

Roy Schmidt continued
Long Beach State 6'3" 250 lbs.

Year	Team		Games	Pos.
1967	NO	N	10	G
1968			9	G
1969	ATL	N	9	G
1970	WAS	N	11	G
1971	MIN	N	4	G

5 yrs.   43 games

Terry Schmidt
SCHMIDT, TERRY RICHARD
B. May 28, 1952, Columbus, IN
Ball State 6'0" 177 lbs.

Year	Team		Games	Pos.
1974	NO	N	9	CB
1975			13	CB
1976	CHI	N	9	CB
1977			10	CB
1978			16	CB, S
1979			16	CB, S
1980			16	CB
1981			16	CB
1982			9	CB
1983			13	CB
1984			16	CB

11 yrs.   143 games

Joe Schmiesing
SCHMIESING, JOSEPH FRANK
B. Apr. 1, 1945, Melrose, MN
*Minnesota/New Mexico State 6'4" 253
lbs.*

Year	Team		Games	Pos.
1968	STL	N	14	DE, DT
1969			11	DE
1970			14	DT
1971			9	DE
1972	DET	N	5	DT
1973	BAL	N	14	DT
1974	NYJ	N	13	DE, DT

7 yrs.   80 games

Bob Schmit
SCHMIT, BOB
B. Jun. 28, 1950, Astoria, NY
Nebraska 6'1" 220 lbs.

Year	Team		Games	Pos.
1975	NYG	N	13	LB
1976			2	LB

2 yrs.   15 games

George Schmitt
SCHMITT, GEORGE PAUL
B. Mar. 6, 1961, Bryn Mawr, PA
Delaware 5'11" 193 lbs.

Year	Team		Games	Pos.
1983	STL	N	16	CB

John Schmitt
SCHMITT, JOHN CHARLES
B. Nov. 12, 1942, Brooklyn, NY
Hofstra 6'4" 253 lbs.

Year	Team		Games	Pos.
1964	NY	A	1	C
1965			2	C
1966			14	C
1967			14	C
1968			14	C
1969			14	C
1970	NYJ	N	14	C
1971			14	C
1972			14	C
1973			14	C
1974	GB	N	14	C

11 yrs.   129 games

Ted Schmitt
SCHMITT, THEODORE ALFRED
B. Oct. 2, 1916, Pittsburgh, PA
Pittsburgh 5'11" 216 lbs.

Year	Team		Games	Pos.
1938	PHI	N	10	G
1939			11	G

Year	Team		Games	Pos.

Ted Schmitt continued

Year	Team		Games	Pos.
1940			11	T, G

3 yrs.   32 games

Bob Schmitz
SCHMITZ, ROBERT
B. Sep. 10, 1938
Wisconsin/Montana State 6'1" 235 lbs.

Year	Team		Games	Pos.
1961	PIT	N	14	LB
1962			9	LB
1963			11	LB
1964			6	LB
1965			1	LB
1966			8	LB
1966	MIN	N	10	LB

6 yrs.   59 games

Steve Schnarr
SCHNARR, STEVE
B. Jul. 30, 1952, Philadelphia, PA
Otterbein 6'2" 216 lbs.

Year	Team		Games	Pos.
1975	BUF	N	12	RB

Don Schneider
SCHNEIDER, DONALD PAUL
B. Apr. 3, 1924, Crafton, PA
Pennsylvania 5'9" 170 lbs.

Year	Team		Games	Pos.
1948	BUF	AA	9	B

John Schneider
SCHNEIDER, JOHN J. (Pop)
B. Feb. 15, 1894
D. Jul., 1963
None 5'10" 180 lbs.

Year	Team		Games	Pos.
1920	COL	A	4	HB

Leroy Schneider
SCHNEIDER, LEROY
B. 1923
Tulane 5'11" 237 lbs.

Year	Team		Games	Pos.
1947	BKN	AA	1	T

Herm Schneidman
SCHNEIDMAN, HERMAN (Biff)
B. Nov. 22, 1913, Rock Island, IL
Iowa 5'11" 201 lbs.

Year	Team		Games	Pos.
1935	GB	N	11	QB, FB
1936			7	E, B
1937			11	QB, HB
1938			10	QB
1940	CHIC	N	6	B

5 yrs.   45 games

Bob Schnelker
**SCHNELKER, ROBERT
BERNARD**
B. Oct. 17, 1928, Galion, OH
Bowling Green 6'3" 214 lbs.

Year	Team		Games	Pos.
1953	PHI	N	8	E
1954	NYG	N	12	E
1955			12	E
1956			12	E
1957			12	E
1958			12	E
1959			11	E
1960			12	E
1961	PIT	N	14	OE

9 yrs.   105 games

Otto Schnellbacher
**SCHNELLBACHER, OTTO O.
(The Claw)**
B. Apr. 15, 1923, Sublette, KS
Kansas 6'2" 188 lbs.

Year	Team		Games	Pos.
1948	NY	AA	14	E
1949	B-NY	AA	12	E

Year	Team		Games	Pos.

Otto Schnellbacher continued

Year	Team		Games	Pos.
1950	NYG	N	12	HB
1951			12	HB

4 yrs.   50 games

John Schneller
SCHNELLER, JOHN B.
B. Nov. 1, 1911, Neenah, WI
D. Nov., 1978, Denver, CO
Wisconsin 6'2" 204 lbs.

Year	Team		Games	Pos.
1933	POR	N	9	E
1934	DET	N	13	E
1935			12	E, G
1936			12	E

4 yrs.   46 games

Mike Schnitker
SCHNITKER, JAMES MICHAEL
B. Dec. 30, 1946, Atchison County,
MO
Colorado 6'3" 243 lbs.

Year	Team		Games	Pos.
1969	DEN	A	7	G
1970	DEN	N	14	G
1971			13	G
1972			14	G
1973			14	G
1974			12	G

6 yrs.   74 games

Roy Schoemann
SCHOEMANN, LEROY
B. Aug. 30, 1914
D. May, 1972
Marquette 6'1" 192 lbs.

Year	Team		Games	Pos.
1938	GB	N	3	C

Tom Schoen
SCHOEN, TOM
B. Jan. 30, 1946, Cleveland, OH
Notre Dame 5'11" 185 lbs.

Year	Team		Games	Pos.
1970	CLE	N	4	S

Ray Schoenke
**SCHOENKE, RAYMOND
FREDERICK, JR.**
B. Sep. 10, 1941, Wahiawa, HI
Southern Methodist 6'3" 246 lbs.

Year	Team		Games	Pos.
1963	DAL	N	9	OT
1964			14	OT
1966	WAS	N	11	G
1967			14	G
1968			11	G
1969			13	G, OT
1970			14	G
1971			14	G
1972			14	G
1973			7	G
1974			14	G
1975			12	G

12 yrs.   145 games

Roy Scholl
SCHOLL, ROY F.
B. Sep. 15, 1904
D. Oct. 8, 1993, Topton, PA
Lehigh 5'8" 205 lbs.

Year	Team		Games	Pos.
1929	BOS	N	1	G

Bob Scholtz
SCHOLTZ, ROBERT JOSEPH
B. Dec. 25, 1937, Watertown, SD
Notre Dame 6'4" 250 lbs.

Year	Team		Games	Pos.
1960	DET	N	12	C
1961			14	C
1962			14	C
1963			9	C, OT
1964			11	C, OT

Bob Scholtz continued

Year	Team		Games	Pos.
1965	NYG	N	14	C
1966			7	C, OT

7 yrs. 81 games

Bruce Scholtz
SCHOLTZ, BRUCE DANIEL
B. Sep. 26, 1958, La Grange, TX
Texas 6'6" 241 lbs.

Year	Team		Games	Pos.
1982	SEA	N	9	LB
1983			16	LB
1984			16	LB
1985			16	LB
1986			16	LB
1987			8	LB
1988			15	LB
1989	NE	N	8	LB

8 yrs. 104 games

Turk Schonert
SCHONERT, TURK LEROY
B. Jan. 15, 1957, Torrance, CA
Stanford 6'1" 195 lbs.

Year	Team		Games	Pos.
1981	CIN	N	4	QB
1982			2	QB
1983			9	QB
1984			8	QB
1985			7	QB
1986	ATL	N	8	QB
1987	CIN	N	11	QB
1988			16	QB
1989			7	QB

9 yrs. 72 games

Ivan Schottel
SCHOTTEL, IVAN ESTIL
B. Oct. 11, 1921, Cosby, MO
Northwest Missouri State 6'2" 204 lbs.

Year	Team		Games	Pos.
1946	DET	N	10	DB
1948			6	E

2 yrs. 16 games

Marty Schottenheimer
SCHOTTENHEIMER, MARTIN EDWARD
B. Sep. 23, 1943, Canonsburg, PA
Pittsburgh 6'3" 225 lbs.

Year	Team		Games	Pos.
1965	BUF	A	14	LB
1966			14	LB
1967			14	LB
1968			14	LB
1969	BOS	A	11	LB
1970	BOS	N	12	LB

6 yrs. 79 games

Jim Schrader
SCHRADER, JAMES LEE
B. Jun. 27, 1932, Weston, WV
D. Jan. 16, 1972, Norristown, PA
Notre Dame 6'2" 244 lbs.

Year	Team		Games	Pos.
1954	WAS	N	10	C, T
1956			4	C
1957			12	C
1958			12	C
1959			12	C
1960			12	C
1961			14	C
1962	PHI	N	13	C, G
1963			13	C
1964			14	C

10 yrs. 116 games

Adam Schreiber
SCHREIBER, ADAM
B. Feb. 20, 1962, Galveston, TX
Texas 6'4" 281 lbs.

Year	Team		Games	Pos.
1984	SEA	N	6	G
1985	NO	N	1	G

Adam Schreiber continued

Year	Team		Games	Pos.
1986	PHI	N	9	G, C
1987			12	G, C
1988			6	G
1988	NYJ	N	7	G, C
1989			15	C, G
1990	MIN	N	16	C, G
1991			15	C, G
1992			16	C, G
1993			16	C, G
1994	NYG	N	16	C
1995			16	C
1996			15	C

13 yrs. 166 games

Larry Schreiber
SCHREIBER, LAWRENCE ANTHONY
B. Aug. 11, 1947, Covington, KY
Tennessee Tech 6'0" 206 lbs.

Year	Team		Games	Pos.
1971	SF	N	14	RB
1972			14	RB
1973			4	RB
1974			14	RB
1975			14	RB
1976	CHI	N	14	RB

6 yrs. 74 games

Bill Schroeder
SCHROEDER, WILLIAM H.
B. Apr. 11, 1924, Sheboygan, WI
Wisconsin 6'0" 190 lbs.

Year	Team		Games	Pos.
1946	CHI	AA	14	HB, DB
1947			12	HB, DB

2 yrs. 26 games

Gene Schroeder
SCHROEDER, EUGENE WILLARD
B. Mar. 3, 1929, Washington, DC
Virginia 6'3" 192 lbs.

Year	Team		Games	Pos.
1951	CHIB	N	12	E
1952			12	E
1954			3	E
1955			12	E
1956			11	E
1957			12	E

6 yrs. 62 games

Jay Schroeder
SCHROEDER, JAY BRIAN
B. Jun. 28, 1961, Milwaukee, WI
UCLA 6'4" 215 lbs.

Year	Team		Games	Pos.
1985	WAS	N	9	QB
1986			16	QB
1987			11	QB
1988	LARI	N	9	QB
1989			11	QB
1990			16	QB
1991			15	QB
1992			13	QB
1993	CIN	N	9	QB
1994	ARI	N	9	QB

10 yrs. 118 games

Bill Schroll
SCHROLL, WILLIAM CHARLES
B. Jan. 24, 1926, Alexandria, LA
Louisiana State 6'0" 214 lbs.

Year	Team		Games	Pos.
1949	BUF	AA	12	LB
1950	DET	N	12	FB, LB
1951	GB	N	12	LB

3 yrs. 36 games

Ken Schroy
SCHROY, KENNETH MICHAEL
B. Sep. 22, 1952, Valley Forge, PA
Maryland 6'2" 196 lbs.

Year	Team		Games	Pos.
1977	NYJ	N	14	S

Ken Schroy continued

Year	Team		Games	Pos.
1978			16	S, CB
1979			16	S
1980			14	S
1981			16	S
1982			9	S
1983			16	S
1984			12	S

8 yrs. 113 games

Jim Schuber
SCHUBER, JAMES B., JR.
B. Jun. 23, 1904
D. May, 1982, Naples, FL
Navy 5'8" 160 lbs.

Year	Team		Games	Pos.
1930	BKN	N	1	HB

Eric Schubert
SCHUBERT, ERIC JON
B. May 28, 1962, Abington, PA
Pittsburgh 5'8" 193 lbs.

Year	Team		Games	Pos.
1985	NYG	N	8	K
1986	STL	N	5	K
1987	NE	N	1	K

3 yrs. 14 games

Steve Schubert
SCHUBERT, STEVEN WILLIAM
B. Mar. 15, 1951, Brooklyn, NY
Massachusetts 5'10" 187 lbs.

Year	Team		Games	Pos.
1974	NE	N	10	WR
1975	CHI	N	12	WR
1976			14	WR
1977			13	WR
1978			13	WR
1979			14	WR

6 yrs. 76 games

Jake Schueble
SCHUEBLE, CHARLES JOHN
B. Sep. 28, 1917, Hondo, TX
Rice 6'0" 196 lbs.

Year	Team		Games	Pos.
1939	PHI	N	2	B

Karl Schuelke
SCHUELKE, KARL H., JR.
B. 1916
Wisconsin 5'10" 200 lbs.

Year	Team		Games	Pos.
1939	PIT	N	1	B

Charles Schuette
SCHUETTE, CHARLES W.
B. Apr. 4, 1922, Sheboygan, WI
Marquette 6'1" 206 lbs.

Year	Team		Games	Pos.
1948	BUF	AA	14	DB
1949			10	C, LB
1950	GB	N	12	LB
1951			12	C, LB

4 yrs. 48 games

Paul Schuette
SCHUETTE, PAUL A., JR.
B. Mar. 10, 1906, South Bend, IN
D. Oct. 20, 1960
Wisconsin 6'0" 220 lbs.

Year	Team		Games	Pos.
1928	NYG	N	4	G
1930	CHIB	N	11	G
1931			11	G
1932			1	G
1932	BOS	N	3	G

4 yrs. 30 games

Harry Schuh
SCHUH, HARRY FREDERICK
B. Sep. 25, 1942, Philadelphia, PA
Memphis State 6'2" 260 lbs.

Year	Team		Games	Pos.
1965	OAK	A	14	G

Harry Schuh continued

Year	Team		Games	Pos.
1966			14	G
1967			14	OT
1968			14	OT
1969			14	OT
1970	OAK	N	14	OT
1971	LA	N	14	OT
1972			14	OT
1973			14	OT
1974	GB	N	14	OT

10 yrs. 140 games

Jeff Schuh
SCHUH, JEFFREY JOHN
B. May 22, 1958, Crystal, MN
Minnesota 6'3" 230 lbs.

Year	Team		Games	Pos.
1981	CIN	N	16	LB
1982			9	LB
1983			16	LB
1984			16	LB
1985			16	LB
1986	GB	N	12	LB
1986	MIN	N	2	LB

6 yrs. 87 games

John Schuhmacher
SCHUHMACHER, JOHN
B. Sep. 23, 1955, Salem, OR
Southern California 6'3" 275 lbs.

Year	Team		Games	Pos.
1978	HOU	N	11	G
1981			16	G
1982			9	G
1983			1	OT
1984			16	G
1985			16	G

6 yrs. 69 games

Bill Schuler
SCHULER, WILLIAM MOUGHON
B. Oct. 18, 1922, Birmingham, AL
Yale 6'0" 215 lbs.

Year	Team		Games	Pos.
1947	NYG	N	11	T
1948			12	T

2 yrs. 23 games

Rick Schulte
SCHULTE, RICK
B. Jan. 24, 1963, Chicago, IL
Illinois 6'2" 265 lbs.

Year	Team		Games	Pos.
1987	BUF	N	3	G

Schultz
SCHULTZ
None 171 lbs.

Year	Team		Games	Pos.
1920	CHIC	A	1	FB

Bill Schultz
SCHULTZ, WILLIAM
B. May 1, 1967, Granada Hills, CA
Southern California 6'5" 303 lbs.

Year	Team		Games	Pos.
1990	IND	N	12	OT
1991			10	OT
1992			10	OT
1993			14	OT
1994	HOU	N	2	G
1995	DEN	N	2	OT

6 yrs. 50 games

Charley Schultz
SCHULTZ, CHARLES W.
B. Oct. 8, 1916, St. Paul, MN
Minnesota 6'3" 231 lbs.

Year	Team		Games	Pos.
1939	GB	N	8	T
1940			2	T
1941			11	T

3 yrs. 21 games

Year	Team	Games	Pos.

Chris Schultz
SCHULTZ, CHRIS
B. Feb. 18, 1960, Burlington, Ont.
Arizona 6'8" 280 lbs.

Year	Team		Games	Pos.
1983	**DAL**	N	5	OT
1985			16	OT
2 yrs.		21 games		

Elbie Schultz
SCHULTZ, EBERLE H.
B. Dec. 23, 1917, Eugene, OR
Oregon State 6'4" 252 lbs.

Year	Team		Games	Pos.
1940	PHI	N	11	G
1941	PIT	N	11	G, T
1942			11	T
1943	P-P	N	10	G, T
1944	C-P	N	10	G, T
1945	CLE	N	10	T
1946	LA	N	11	T
1947			12	T
8 yrs.		86 games		

John Schultz
SCHULTZ, JOHN A.
B. Jun. 10, 1953, Binghamton, MD
Maryland 5'10" 182 lbs.

Year	Team		Games	Pos.
1976	DEN	N	14	WR
1977			14	WR
1978			4	WR
3 yrs.		32 games		

Randy Schultz
SCHULTZ, RANDY
B. Nov. 17, 1943, Iowa Falls, IA
Deceased
Iowa State 5'11" 210 lbs.

Year	Team		Games	Pos.
1966	CLE	N	14	HB
1967	NO	N	8	RB
1968			9	RB
3 yrs.		31 games		

Pete Schultze
SCHULTZE, PETE
None 188 lbs.

Year	Team		Games	Pos.
1922	COL	N	1	FB

Jody Schulz
SCHULZ, JODY
B. Aug. 17, 1960, Easton, MD
East Carolina 6'3" 235 lbs.

Year	Team		Games	Pos.
1983	PHI	N	6	LB
1984			15	LB
1986			16	LB
1987			7	LB
4 yrs.		44 games		

Kurt Schulz
SCHULZ, KURT ERICH
B. Dec. 12, 1968, Wenatchee, WA
Eastern Washington 6'1" 206 lbs.

Year	Team		Games	Pos.
1992	BUF	N	8	S
1993			12	S
1994			16	S
1995			13	S
1996			15	S
5 yrs.		64 games		

Gregg Schumacher
SCHUMACHER, GREGG HAROLD
B. Jun. 30, 1942, Chicago, IL
Illinois 6'2" 240 lbs.

Year	Team		Games	Pos.
1967	LA	N	11	DE
1968			14	DE
2 yrs.		25 games		

Kurt Schumacher
SCHUMACHER, KURT
B. Dec. 26, 1952, Cleveland, OH
Ohio State 6'3" 252 lbs.

Year	Team		Games	Pos.
1975	NO	N	13	OT
1976			14	G
1977			14	G
1978	TB	N	4	G
4 yrs.		45 games		

Tex Schupbach
SCHUPBACH, ORRIN T., JR.
B. Mar. 9, 1917, El Paso, TX
West Texas State 6'5" 280 lbs.

Year	Team		Games	Pos.
1942	CLE	N	2	T
1943	BKN	N	2	T
2 yrs.		4 games		

Dick Schuster
SCHUSTER, RICHARD L.
B. Mar. 2, 1900
D. Feb. 8, 1980, Binghamton, NY
Penn State 6'1" 185 lbs.

Year	Team		Games	Pos.
1925	CAN	N	4	G

Scott Schutt
SCHUTT, SCOTT
B. Aug. 31, 1963
North Dakota State 6'4" 218 lbs.

Year	Team		Games	Pos.
1987	CIN	N	3	LB

Ray Schwab
SCHWAB, RAYMOND
B. Mar. 30, 1908, Missouri
D. May 3, 1988, Cheshire, CT
Oklahoma City 210 lbs.

Year	Team		Games	Pos.
1932	SI	N	1	E

Vic Schwall
SCHWALL, VICTOR HENRY
B. Jan. 21, 1925, Oak Park, IL
Northwestern 5'8" 188 lbs.

Year	Team		Games	Pos.
1947	CHIC	N	11	HB
1948			7	HB
1949			11	HB
1950			12	HB
4 yrs.		41 games		

Ade Schwammel
SCHWAMMEL, ADOLPHE JOHN (Tar)
B. Oct. 14, 1908, Los Angeles, CA
D. Nov. 18, 1979, Honolulu, HI
Oregon State 6'2" 225 lbs.

Year	Team		Games	Pos.
1934	GB	N	13	T
1935			10	T
1936			12	T
1943			3	T, G
1944			9	T
5 yrs.		47 games		

Jim Schwantz
SCHWANTZ, JAMES WILLIAM
B. Jan. 23, 1970, Arlington Heights, IL
Purdue 6'2" 231 lbs.

Year	Team		Games	Pos.
1992	CHI	N	1	LB
1994	DAL	N	7	LB
1995			16	LB
1996			16	LB
4 yrs.		40 games		

Bryan Schwartz
SCHWARTZ, BRYAN
B. Dec. 5, 1971, St. Lawrence, SD
Augustana (South Dakota) 6'4" 256 lbs.

Year	Team		Games	Pos.
1995	JAC	N	14	LB

Bryan Schwartz continued

Year	Team		Games	Pos.
1996			4	LB
2 yrs.		18 games		

Don Schwartz
SCHWARTZ, DONALD JEFFREY
B. Feb. 24, 1956, Billings, MT
Washington State 6'1" 191 lbs.

Year	Team		Games	Pos.
1978	NO	N	16	CB
1979			14	S
1980			16	S
1981	STL	N	5	S
4 yrs.		51 games		

Elmer Schwartz
SCHWARTZ, ELMER
B. 1907
Washington State 6'0" 212 lbs.

Year	Team		Games	Pos.
1931	POR	N	12	FB, HB
1932	CHIC	N	3	FB
1933	PIT	N	10	HB, FB
3 yrs.		25 games		

Perry Schwartz
SCHWARTZ, PERRY
B. Apr. 27, 1915, Chicago, IL
California 6'2" 199 lbs.

Year	Team		Games	Pos.
1938	BKN	N	10	E
1939			11	E
1940			11	E
1941			11	E
1942			11	E
1946	NY	AA	14	E
6 yrs.		68 games		

Ted Schwarzer
SCHWARZER, THEODORE
B. 1902
Centenary 5'11" 190 lbs.

Year	Team		Games	Pos.
1926	BUF	N	6	G, C

Brian Schweda
SCHWEDA, BRIAN CHRISTOPHER
B. Apr. 30, 1943, Kansas City, KS
Kansas 6'3" 240 lbs.

Year	Team		Games	Pos.
1966	CHI	N	14	DE
1967	NO	N	14	DE
1968			10	DE
3 yrs.		38 games		

John Schweder
SCHWEDER, JOHN A. (Bull)
B. Dec. 23, 1927, Bethlehem, PA
Pennsylvania 6'1" 224 lbs.

Year	Team		Games	Pos.
1950	BAL	N	11	G
1951	PIT	N	12	G
1952			12	G
1953			12	G
1954			12	G
1955			12	G
6 yrs.		71 games		

Ger Schwedes
SCHWEDES, GERHARD H.
B. 1939
Syracuse 6'1" 205 lbs.

Year	Team		Games	Pos.
1960	BOS	A		HB
1961			5	HB
2 yrs.		5 games		

Scott Schwedes
SCHWEDES, SCOTT ANDREW
B. Jun. 30, 1965, Syracuse, NY
Syracuse 6'0" 182 lbs.

Year	Team		Games	Pos.
1987	MIA	N	12	WR

Scott Schwedes continued

Year	Team		Games	Pos.
1988			16	WR
1989			9	WR
1990				WR
1990	SD	N	5	WR
1990	MIA	N		WR
4 yrs.		42 games		

Bob Schweickert
SCHWEICKERT, ROBERT LYNN
B. Sep. 17, 1942, Richmond, VA
Virginia Tech 6'1" 193 lbs.

Year	Team		Games	Pos.
1965	NY	A	3	HB
1967			3	FL
2 yrs.		6 games		

Dick Schweidler
SCHWEIDLER, RICHARD
B. Aug. 18, 1915
St. Louis 6'0" 182 lbs.

Year	Team		Games	Pos.
1938	CHIB	N		HB
1939			5	HB
1946			10	HB
3 yrs.		25 games		

Wilson Schwenk
SCHWENK, WILSON R. (Bud)
B. Aug. 26, 1919, St. Louis, MO
D. Oct. 1, 1980, St. Louis, MO
Illinois/Washington (Missouri) 6'2" 201 lbs.

Year	Team		Games	Pos.
1942	CHIC	N	10	QB
1946	CLE	AA	4	QB
1947	BAL	AA	14	QB
1948	NY	AA	8	QB
4 yrs.		36 games		

John Sciarra
SCIARRA, JOHN MICHAEL
B. Mar. 2, 1954, Los Angeles, CA
UCLA 5'11" 185 lbs.

Year	Team		Games	Pos.
1978	PHI	N	16	S
1979			16	S
1980			10	S
1981			8	S
1982			8	S
1983			10	S
6 yrs.		76 games		

Joe Scibelli
SCIBELLI, JOSEPH ALBERT
B. Apr. 19, 1939, Springfield, MA
Notre Dame 6'1" 256 lbs.

Year	Team		Games	Pos.
1961	LA	N	14	G
1962			14	G
1963			14	G
1964			14	G
1965			14	G
1966			14	G
1967			14	G
1968			14	G
1969			7	G
1970			14	G
1971			14	G
1972			13	G
1973			14	G
1974			14	G
1975			14	G
15 yrs.		202 games		

Willard Scissum
SCISSUM, WILLARD
B. Oct. 28, 1962, Huntsville, AL
Alabama 6'3" 275 lbs.

Year	Team		Games	Pos.
1987	WAS	N	3	G

Year	Team	Games	Pos.

Eric Scoggins
SCOGGINS, ERIC THOMAS
B. Jan. 23, 1959, Inglewood, CA
Southern California 6'2" 235 lbs.

Year	Team		Games	Pos.
1982	SF	N	3	LB

Ron Scoggins
SCOGGINS, RONALD ALONZO
B. Aug. 3, 1961
Nevada-Las Vegas 6'6" 305 lbs.

| 1987 | SEA | N | 3 | OT |

Nick Scollard
SCOLLARD, NICHOLAS M.
B. Apr. 3, 1920
D. Jan., 1985, Indianapolis, IN
St. Joseph's (Indiana) 6'4" 217 lbs.

1946	BOS	N	11	E
1947			12	E
1948			12	E
1949	NYB	N	12	E
4 yrs.	47 games			

Glenn Scolnik
SCOLNIK, GLENN
B. Jun. 16, 1951, Hammond, IN
Indiana 6'3" 190 lbs.

| 1973 | PIT | N | 2 | WR |

Bill Scott
SCOTT, WILLIAM JAMES
B. May 18, 1944, Laurel, MD
Idaho 6'0" 188 lbs.

| 1968 | CIN | A | 14 | DB |

Bo Scott
SCOTT, ROBERT M.
B. Mar. 30, 1943, Connellsville, PA
Ohio State 6'3" 213 lbs.

1969	CLE	N	13	RB
1970			13	RB
1971			14	RB
1972			12	RB
1973			7	RB
1974			14	RB
6 yrs.	73 games			

Bob Scott
SCOTT, ROBERT
B. Aug. 8, 1895
D. Aug., 1973, Phil Campbell, AL
None 195 lbs.

| 1926 | PRO | N | 6 | C, G, T |

Bobby Scott
SCOTT, ROBERT BENSON
B. Apr. 2, 1949, Chattanooga, TN
Tennessee 6'1" 198 lbs.

1973	NO	N	6	QB
1974			5	QB
1975			1	QB
1976			11	QB
1977			5	QB
1978			1	QB
1979			3	QB
1980			5	QB
1981			4	QB
1982			2	QB
10 yrs.	43 games			

Carlos Scott
SCOTT, CARLOS B.
B. Jul. 2, 1960, Hempstead, FL
Texas-El Paso 6'4" 285 lbs.

| 1983 | STL | N | 13 | C |
| 1984 | | | 16 | C |

Carlos Scott *continued*

| 1985 | | | 16 | C |
| 3 yrs. | 45 games | | | |

Chris Scott
SCOTT, CHRISTOPHER STERLING
B. Dec. 11, 1961, Berea, OH
Purdue 6'5" 245 lbs.

1984	IND	N	14	NT
1985			16	DE
1987			3	DE
3 yrs.	33 games			

Chuck Scott
SCOTT, CHARLES JOHN MILLER
B. May 24, 1963, Jacksonville, FL
Vanderbilt 6'2" 202 lbs.

1986	LARM	N	9	WR
1987	DAL	N	2	WR
2 yrs.	11 games			

Clarence Scott
SCOTT, CLARENCE
B. May 5, 1944, Norristown, PA
Morgan State 6'2" 204 lbs.

1969	BOS	A	14	S
1970	BOS	N	14	S
1971	NE	N	5	S
1972			10	S
4 yrs.	43 games			

Clarence Scott
SCOTT, CLARENCE B.
B. Apr. 9, 1949, Atlanta, GA
Kansas State 6'0" 182 lbs.

1971	CLE	N	13	DB
1972			14	CB
1973			14	CB
1974			14	CB
1975			14	CB
1976			14	CB
1977			13	CB
1978			16	CB
1979			16	CB
1980			16	S
1981			16	S
1982			9	S
1983			16	S
13 yrs.	185 games			

Clyde Scott
SCOTT, CLYDE L.
B. Aug. 29, 1924, Dixie, LA
Navy/Arkansas 6'0" 174 lbs.

1949	PHI	N	8	HB
1950			1	HB
1951			12	HB
1952			2	HB
1952	DET		5	HB
4 yrs.	28 games			

Darnay Scott
SCOTT, DARNAY
B. Jul. 7, 1972, St. Louis, MO
San Diego State 6'1" 185 lbs.

1994	CIN	N	16	WR
1995			16	WR
1996			16	WR
3 yrs.	48 games			

Dave Scott
SCOTT, DAVE
B. Dec. 26, 1953, Hackensack, NJ
Kansas 6'4" 270 lbs.

| 1976 | ATL | N | 13 | OT |

Dave Scott *continued*

1977			14	OT
1978			16	OT
1979			16	OT
1980			16	OT
1981			14	G
1982			9	G
7 yrs.	98 games			

Ed Scott
SCOTT, EDWARD
B. Feb. 15, 1961, New Orleans, LA
Grambling State 5'10" 182 lbs.

| 1987 | STL | N | 3 | S |

Freddie Scott
SCOTT, FREDDIE LEE, JR.
B. Aug. 26, 1974, Southfield, MS
Penn State 5'10" 189 lbs.

| 1996 | ATL | N | 10 | WR |

Freddie Scott
SCOTT, FREDDIE LEE, SR.
B. Aug. 5, 1952, Grady, AR
Amherst 6'2" 175 lbs.

1974	BAL	N	14	WR
1975			8	WR
1976			10	WR
1977			14	WR
1978	DET	N	16	WR
1979			16	WR
1980			16	WR
1981			16	WR
1982			9	WR
1983			15	WR
10 yrs.	132 games			

George Scott
SCOTT, GEORGE
B. Jul. 14, 1937
Miami (Ohio) 6'1" 180 lbs.

| 1959 | NYG | N | 7 | HB |

Herb Scott
SCOTT, HERBERT CARNELL, JR.
B. Jan. 18, 1953, Virginia Beach, VA
Virginia Union 6'2" 260 lbs.

1975	DAL	N	14	G
1976			14	G
1977			11	G
1978			16	G
1979			16	G
1980			16	G
1981			16	G
1982			6	G
1983			16	G
1984			15	G
10 yrs.	140 games			

Jack Scott
SCOTT, JOHN
B. Apr. 12, 1936, Ashland, KY
Ohio State 6'4" 260 lbs.

1960	BUF	A		DT
1961			7	DT
2 yrs.	7 games			

Jake Scott
SCOTT, JACOB E., III
B. Jul. 20, 1945, Greenwood, SC
Georgia 6'0" 188 lbs.

1970	MIA	N	14	S
1971			14	S
1972			14	S
1973			14	S
1974			14	S
1975			14	S

Jake Scott *continued*

1976	WAS	N	12	S
1977			14	S
1978			16	S
9 yrs.	126 games			

James Scott
SCOTT, JAMES
B. Mar. 28, 1952, Longview, TX
Henderson County JC 6'1" 190 lbs.

1976	CHI	N	11	WR
1977			14	WR
1978			15	WR
1979			10	WR
1980			15	WR
1982			5	WR
6 yrs.	70 games			

Joe Scott
SCOTT, JOSEPH
B. Mar. 17, 1926
San Francisco 6'1" 198 lbs.

1949	NYG	N	8	HB
1950			10	HB
1951			12	HB
1952			8	HB
1953			3	E
5 yrs.	41 games			

Johnny Scott
SCOTT, JOHN
B. 1895
Deceased
Lafayette 5'10" 176 lbs.

1920	BUF	A	2	HB
1921			7	QB, FB, HB
1922	BUF		1	HB
1923			2	HB
1926	PHI	A	9	QB
5 yrs.	21 games			

Kevin Scott
SCOTT, KEVIN BERNARD
B. Oct. 24, 1963, Fort Bragg, NC
Stanford 5'9" 179 lbs.

1988	SD	N	1	RB
1989	DAL	N	3	RB
2 yrs.	4 games			

Kevin Scott
SCOTT, KEVIN TOMMORSE
B. May 19, 1969, Phoenix, AZ
Stanford 5'9" 175 lbs.

1991	DET	N	16	CB
1992			16	CB
1993			12	CB
3 yrs.	44 games			

Lance Scott
SCOTT, LANCE
B. Feb. 15, 1972, Salt Lake City, UT
Utah 6'3" 285 lbs.

| 1995 | ARI | N | 1 | C |

Les Scott
SCOTT, LESTER
B. Dec. 20, 1898
Deceased
Hamline 5'10" 205 lbs.

1923	AKR	N	6	T, G, FB
1924	MIN	N	6	T, E
2 yrs.	12 games			

Lew Scott
SCOTT, LEWIS S.
B. Jun. 6, 1943, Bryn Mawr, PA

Year	Team	Games	Pos.

Lew Scott *continued*
Oregon State 5'10" 173 lbs.

1966	DEN	A	13	DB

Lindsay Scott
SCOTT, LINDSAY EUGENE
B. Dec. 6, 1960, Jesup, GA
Georgia 6'1" 194 lbs.

1982	NO	N	8	WR
1983			16	WR
1984			16	WR
1985			10	WR

4 yrs.   50 games

Malcolm Scott
SCOTT, MALCOLM M.
B. Jul. 10, 1961, New Orleans, LA
Louisiana State 6'5" 240 lbs.

1983	NYG	N	16	TE
1987	NO	N	3	TE

2 yrs.   19 games

Ned Scott
SCOTT, EDWARD
B. Mar. 13, 1901
D. Nov., 1987, Readlyn, IA
Monmouth 200 lbs.

1924	RI	N	9	T, G

Patrick Scott
SCOTT, PATRICK S.
B. Sep. 13, 1964, Shreveport, LA
Grambling State 5'10" 170 lbs.

1987	GB	N	8	WR
1988			16	WR

2 yrs.   24 games

Perry Scott
SCOTT, LEONARD PERRY, JR.
B. Aug. 17, 1917, East Orange, NJ
D. Apr. 4, 1988, Allentown, PA
Muhlenberg 6'2" 210 lbs.

1942	DET	N	7	E, T

Phil Scott
SCOTT, PHILIP
B. Apr. 11, 1906
D. Jan., 1975, Montclair Heights, NJ
None

1929	ORA	N	7	E

Prince Scott
SCOTT, PRINCE A.
B. Jun. 30, 1919, Grapevine, TX
Texas Tech 6'1" 190 lbs.

1946	MIA	AA	14	E

Ralph Scott
SCOTT, RALPH V.
B. Sep., 1897, Dewey Township, WI
D. Aug. 16, 1936, Hardin, MT
Wisconsin 6'2" 235 lbs.

1921	DEC	A	11	T
1922	CHIB	N	12	T
1923			12	T
1924			10	T, E
1925			11	G, T
1926	NY	A	8	T, G
1927	NYY	N	9	T, QB

7 yrs.   73 games

Randy Scott
SCOTT, RANDOLPH CHARLES
B. Jan. 31, 1959, Decatur, GA
Alabama 6'1" 225 lbs.

1981	GB	N	16	LB

Randy Scott *continued*

1982			9	LB
1983			6	LB
1984			16	LB
1985			16	LB
1986			15	LB
1987	MIN	N	2	LB

7 yrs.   80 games

Ronald Scott
SCOTT, RONALD
B. Mar. 3, 1963
Southern University 5'11" 200 lbs.

1987	MIA	N	3	RB

Sean Scott
SCOTT, SEAN
B. Apr. 10, 1966
Maryland 6'1" 226 lbs.

1988	DAL	N	5	LB

Stanley Scott
SCOTT, STANLEY
B. Jan. 30, 1964, Tampa, FL
Florida State 6'3" 255 lbs.

1987	MIA	N	3	DE

Todd Scott
SCOTT, TODD CARLTON
B. Jan. 23, 1968, Galveston, TX
Southwestern Louisiana 5'10" 190 lbs.

1991	MIN	N	16	CB
1992			16	CB
1993			13	S
1994			16	S
1995	NYJ	N	10	S
1995	TB	N	1	S
1996			2	S

6 yrs.   74 games

Tom Scott
SCOTT, TOM
B. Jun. 25, 1970, Burke County, NC
East Carolina 6'6" 330 lbs.

1993	CIN	N	13	OT

Tom Scott
SCOTT, THOMAS COSTER, JR.
B. Sep. 3, 1930, Baltimore, MD
Virginia 6'2" 219 lbs.

1953	PHI	N	12	E
1954			12	E
1955			12	E
1956			12	E
1957			12	E
1958			12	E
1959	NYG	N	11	LB
1960			12	LB
1961			13	LB
1962			14	LB
1963			14	LB
1964			14	LB

12 yrs.   150 games

Victor Scott
SCOTT, VICTOR RAMONE
B. Jun. 1, 1962, East St. Louis, IL
Colorado 6'0" 203 lbs.

1984	DAL	N	16	DB
1985			16	CB, S
1986			5	CB, S
1987			6	DB
1988			2	S

5 yrs.   45 games

Vince Scott
SCOTT, VINCENT JOSEPH
(Boomer)
B. Sep. 21, 1922, Le Roy, NY
D. Aug., 1979, Punta Gorda, FL
Notre Dame 5'8" 215 lbs.

1947	BUF	AA	14	G
1948			14	G

2 yrs.   28 games

Walter Scott
SCOTT, WALTER BERNARD
B. May 18, 1973, Augusta, GA
East Carolina 6'3" 285 lbs.

1996	NE	N	1	DE

Willie Scott
SCOTT, WILLIE LOUIS, JR.
B. Feb. 13, 1959, Newberry, SC
South Carolina 6'4" 245 lbs.

1981	KC	N	16	TE
1982			9	TE
1983			16	TE
1984			15	TE
1985			16	TE
1986	NE	N	14	TE
1987			9	TE
1988			3	TE

8 yrs.   98 games

Ben Scotti
SCOTTI, BENJAMIN JOSEPH
B. Jun. 9, 1937, Newark, NJ
Maryland 6'1" 185 lbs.

1959	WAS	N	11	DB
1960			11	DB
1961			14	DB
1962	PHI	N	14	DB
1963			9	DB
1964	SF	N	12	DB

6 yrs.   71 games

Colin Scotts
SCOTTS, COLIN ROBERT
B. Apr. 26, 1963, Sydney, Australia
Hawaii 6'5" 263 lbs.

1987	STL	N	7	DT

Bob Scrabis
SCRABIS, ROBERT
B. 1936
Penn State 6'3" 233 lbs.

1960	NY	A		QB
1961			11	QB
1962			6	QB

3 yrs.   17 games

Kirk Scrafford
SCRAFFORD, KIRK
B. Mar. 13, 1967, Billings, MT
Montana 6'6" 260 lbs.

1990	CIN	N	2	G, OT
1991			9	OT
1992			8	OT
1993	DEN	N	16	OT
1994			16	OT
1995	SF	N	5	OT, G
1996			6	OT

7 yrs.   72 games

Bucky Scribner
SCRIBNER, WILLIAM CHARLES
B. Jul. 11, 1960, Lawrence, KS
Kansas 6'0" 207 lbs.

1983	GB	N	16	P
1984			16	P
1987	MIN	N	4	P

Bucky Scribner *continued*

1988			16	P
1989			16	P

5 yrs.   68 games

Rob Scribner
SCRIBNER, ROBERT BRUCE
B. Apr. 9, 1951, Dallas, TX
UCLA 6'0" 200 lbs.

1973	LA	N	10	RB
1974			11	RB
1975			14	RB
1976			14	RB

4 yrs.   49 games

Tracy Scroggins
SCROGGINS, TRACY
B. Sep. 11, 1969, Checotah, OK
Tulsa 6'2" 255 lbs.

1992	DET	N	16	LB
1993			16	LB
1994			16	LB
1995			16	DE
1996			6	DE

5 yrs.   70 games

Ed Scruggs
SCRUGGS, EDWIN THEODORE
B. Apr. 18, 1923, Houston, TX
Rice 6'1" 195 lbs.

1947	BKN	AA	12	E
1948			14	E

2 yrs.   26 games

Ed Scrutchins
SCRUTCHINS, EDWARD
B. 1941
Toledo 6'3" 260 lbs.

1966	HOU	A	4	DE

Joe Scudero
SCUDERO, JOSEPH ANDREW
(Scooter)
B. Jul. 3, 1930, San Francisco, CA
San Francisco 5'10" 173 lbs.

1954	WAS	N	12	HB
1955			12	HB
1956			10	HB
1957			10	HB
1958			8	HB

5 yrs.   52 games

John Scully
SCULLY, JOHN
B. Aug. 2, 1958, Huntington, NY
Notre Dame 6'6" 262 lbs.

1981	ATL	N	16	C
1982			9	C
1983			16	C
1984			16	G
1985			8	G
1986			14	G
1987			12	G
1988			11	G
1990			10	G

9 yrs.   112 games

Mike Scully
SCULLY, MICHAEL JOHN
B. Nov. 1, 1965, Chicago, IL
Illinois 6'5" 280 lbs.

1988	WAS	N	1	C

Mike Scurlock
SCURLOCK, MICHAEL L.
B. Feb. 26, 1972, Casa Grande, AZ

Year	Team	Games	Pos.

Mike Scurlock continued

Arizona 5'10" 197 lbs.

Year	Team		Games	Pos.
1995	**STL**	**N**	14	CB
1996			16	CB
2 yrs.	30 games			

Stan Scuzerk

SCUZERK, STANLEY
B. Mar. 7, 1939, Cleveland, OH
Purdue 5'11" 229 lbs.

1963	**CLE**	**N**	9	LB
1964			14	LB
1965			11	LB
1966	**NYG**	**N**	11	LB
4 yrs.	45 games			

Todd Seabaugh

SEABAUGH, RAYMOND TODD
B. Mar. 16, 1961, Encino, CA
San Diego State 6'4" 220 lbs.

| 1984 | **PIT** | **N** | 16 | LB |

Charlie Seabright

SEABRIGHT, CHARLES EDWARD
(Lefty)
B. Feb. 13, 1918, McMechen, WV
D. Mar. 18, 1981, Bridgeport, OH
West Virginia 6'2" 204 lbs.

1941	**CLE**	**N**	7	QB
1946	**PIT**	**N**	10	QB
1947			12	QB
1948			12	QB
1949			12	QB
1950			10	QB
6 yrs.	63 games			

Malcolm Seabron

SEABRON, MALCOLM GREGORY
B. Dec. 29, 1972, San Francisco, CA
Fresno State 6'0" 194 lbs.

1994	**HOU**	**N**	13	WR
1995			15	WR
2 yrs.	28 games			

Tom Seabron

SEABRON, THOMAS HALL, JR.
B. May 24, 1957, Baltimore, MD
Michigan 6'3" 215 lbs.

1979	**SF**	**N**	16	LB
1980			6	LB
1980	**STL**	**N**	2	LB
2 yrs.	24 games			

Paul Seal

SEAL, PAUL NATHAN
B. Feb. 27, 1952, Detroit, MI
Michigan 6'4" 223 lbs.

1974	**NO**	**N**	14	TE
1975			14	TE
1976			14	TE
1977	**SF**	**N**	14	TE
1978			14	TE
1979			15	TE
6 yrs.	85 games			

Randy Sealby

SEALBY, RANDALL
B. May 16, 1960
Missouri 6'2" 230 lbs.

| 1987 | **NE** | **N** | 2 | LB |

Eugene Seale

SEALE, EUGENE
B. Jun. 3, 1964, Jasper, TX
Lamar 5'10" 247 lbs.

| 1987 | **HOU** | **N** | 9 | LB |

Eugene Seale continued

1988	16	LB
1989	15	LB
1990	15	LB
1991	15	LB
1992	9	LB
6 yrs.	79 games	

Sam Seale

SEALE, SAMUEL RICARDO
B. Oct. 6, 1962, Barbados
Western State (Colorado) 5'9" 182 lbs.

1984	**LARI**	**N**	12	WR, DB
1985			16	DB
1986			16	CB
1987			12	CB
1988	**SD**	**N**	14	CB
1989			13	CB
1990			16	CB
1991			16	CB
1992	**LARI**	**N**	5	CB
1993	**LARM**	**N**	1	CB
10 yrs.	121 games			

George Seals

SEALS, GEORGE EDWARD
B. Oct. 2, 1942, Higginsville, MO
Missouri 6'2" 259 lbs.

1964	**WAS**	**N**	12	DE
1965	**CHI**	**N**	14	DT, G
1966			14	DT, G
1967			14	G, OT
1968			14	OT
1969			14	G
1970			14	DT
1971			14	DT
1972	**KC**	**N**	11	DT
1973			13	DT
10 yrs.	134 games			

Leon Seals

SEALS, LEON
B. Jan. 30, 1964, New Orleans, LA
Jackson State 6'4" 266 lbs.

1987	**BUF**	**N**	13	DE
1988			16	DE
1989			16	DE
1990			16	DE
1991			16	DE
1992	**PHI**	**N**	5	DT
6 yrs.	82 games			

Ray Seals

SEALS, RAY
B. Jun. 17, 1965, Syracuse, NY
None 6'3" 273 lbs.

1989	**TB**	**N**	2	DE
1990			8	NT
1991			10	DE
1992			11	DE
1993			16	DE
1994	**PIT**	**N**	13	DE
1995			16	DE
7 yrs.	76 games			

Bill Searcey

SEARCEY, WILLIAM A.
B. Mar. 3, 1959, Savannah, GA
Alabama 6'1" 281 lbs.

| 1985 | **SD** | **N** | 1 | OT, G |

Leon Searcy

SEARCY, LEON
B. Dec. 21, 1969, Washington, DC
Miami (Florida) 6'3" 305 lbs.

1992	**PIT**	**N**	15	OT
1993			16	OT
1994			16	OT

Leon Searcy continued

1995			16	OT
1996	**JAC**	**N**	16	OT
5 yrs.	79 games			

Jimmy Sears

SEARS, JAMES HERBERT
B. Mar. 20, 1931, Los Angeles, CA
Southern California 5'11" 183 lbs.

1954	**CHIC**	**N**		HB
1957			12	HB
1958			12	HB
1960	**LA**	**A**		HB
1961	**DEN**	**A**	2	DB
5 yrs.	27 games			

Vic Sears

SEARS, VICTOR WILSON
B. Mar. 4, 1918, Ashwood, OR
Oregon State 6'3" 223 lbs.

1941	**PHI**	**N**	11	T
1942			11	T
1943	**P-P**	**N**	10	T
1945	**PHI**	**N**	10	T
1946			11	T
1947			7	T
1948			12	T
1949			11	T
1950			12	T
1951			12	T
1952			12	T
1953			12	T
12 yrs.	131 games			

George Seasholtz

SEASHOLTZ, GEORGE DONALD
(Dutch)
B. 1899
Deceased
Lafayette 5'8" 185 lbs.

1922	**MIL**	**N**	3	HB
1924	**KEN**	**N**	5	FB, HB, G
2 yrs.	8 games			

Junior Seau

SEAU, JUNIOR
B. Jan. 19, 1969, Samoa
Southern California 6'3" 250 lbs.

1990	**SD**	**N**	16	LB
1991			16	LB
1992			15	LB
1993			16	LB
1994			16	LB
1995			16	LB
1996			15	LB
7 yrs.	110 games			

Mark Seay

SEAY, MARK EDWARD
B. Apr. 11, 1967, Los Angeles, CA
Long Beach State 6'0" 175 lbs.

1993	**SD**	**N**	1	WR
1994			16	WR
1995			16	WR
1996	**PHI**	**N**	16	WR
4 yrs.	49 games			

Virgil Seay

SEAY, VIRGIL LEVAN
B. Jan. 1, 1958, Moultrie, GA
Troy State 6'5" 170 lbs.

1981	**WAS**	**N**	16	WR
1982			8	WR
1983			14	WR
1984			11	WR
1984	**ATL**	**N**	3	WR
4 yrs.	52 games			

Mike Sebastian

SEBASTIAN, MICHAEL J.
B. Jun. 7, 1910, Greensburg, PA
D. Jun. 28, 1989, Hemet, CA
Pittsburgh 5'11" 185 lbs.

1935	**PHI**	**N**	4	HB, FB
1935	**PIT**	**N**	2	HB
1937	**CLE**	**N**	1	HB
2 yrs.	7 games			

Nick Sebek

SEBEK, NICHOLAS
B. Oct. 11, 1927, Niagara Falls, NY
Indiana 6'1" 194 lbs.

| 1950 | **WAS** | **N** | 2 | QB |

Sam Sebo

SEBO, SAMUEL E.
B. 1906
D. Sep. 10, 1933
Syracuse 5'7" 165 lbs.

| 1930 | **NEW** | **N** | 2 | FB |

Herman Seborg

SEBORG, HERMAN (Porky)
B. 1907
Western Michigan 5'11" 195 lbs.

1930	**MIN**	**N**	6	QB, G
1930	**FRA**	**N**	1	HB
1930	**MIN**	**N**	1	QB
1930	**FRA**	**N**	2	HB
1930	**MIN**	**N**	1	HB
1930	**FRA**	**N**	1	HB
1930	**MIN**	**N**	1	G
1931	**FRA**	**N**	7	G
2 yrs.	20 games			

Walt Sechrist

SECHRIST, WALTER
B. Sep. 19, 1896, Indiana
D. Dec., 1977, Bradenton, FL
None 6'3" 258 lbs.

1920	**HAM**	**A**	1	G
1923	**HAM**	**N**	1	G
1924	**AKR**	**N**	1	G
1925	**FRA**	**N**	8	T, G
1925	**CLE**	**N**	3	T
1926	**HAM**	**N**	3	G
1926	**LOU**	**N**	1	G
1926	**HAM**	**N**	1	G
5 yrs.	19 games			

Joe Secord

SECORD, JOSEPH L.
B. Aug. 22, 1897, Green Bay, WI
D. Aug. 21, 1970, Green Bay, WI
None 190 lbs.

| 1922 | **GB** | **N** | 2 | C |

Scott Secules

SECULES, THOMAS WESCOTT
B. Nov. 8, 1964, Newport News, VA
Virginia 6'3" 219 lbs.

1989	**MIA**	**N**	15	QB
1990			16	QB
1991			14	QB
1993	**NE**	**N**	12	QB
4 yrs.	57 games			

Len Sedbrook

SEDBROOK, LEONARD (Twinkle)
B. Jan. 13, 1905
D. Apr., 1986, Oklahoma City, OK
Phillips 5'10" 174 lbs.

1928	**DET**	**N**	9	HB, QB
1929	**NYG**	**N**	15	HB, FB, QB
1930			15	HB, QB, FB

Year	Team	Games	Pos.

Len Sedbrook *continued*

Year	Team		Games	Pos.
1931			10	HB, QB, FB
4 yrs.	49 games			

Bob Sedlock
SEDLOCK, ROBERT
B. 1937
Georgia 6'4" 295 lbs.

Year	Team		Games	Pos.
1960	BUF	A		OT

Chris Sedoris
SEDORIS, CHRISTOPHER JUDE
B. Apr. 25, 1973, Louisville, KY
Purdue 6'3" 286 lbs.

Year	Team		Games	Pos.
1996	WAS	N	8	C

John Seedborg
SEEDBORG, JOHN
B. Jan. 23, 1943, Paso Robles, CA
Arizona State 6'0" 227 lbs.

Year	Team		Games	Pos.
1965	WAS	N	1	K

Frank Seeds
SEEDS, FRANK (Slippery)
B. Mar. 26, 1897
D. Oct., 1963, Pennsylvania
None 170 lbs.

Year	Team		Games	Pos.
1926	CAN	N	1	HB

George Seeman
SEEMAN, GEORGE MCHENRY
B. Apr. 3, 1916, Lincoln, NE
Nebraska 6'1" 195 lbs.

Year	Team		Games	Pos.
1940	GB	N	1	E

Maury Segal
SEGAL, MAURICE
B. 1902, England
Deceased
None

Year	Team		Games	Pos.
1925	CLE	N	5	E, HB, QB

Rocky Segretta
SEGRITO, ROCCO
B. 1897, Italy
Deceased
None

Year	Team		Games	Pos.
1926	HAR	N	1	E

Jason Sehorn
SEHORN, JASON
B. Apr. 15, 1971, Mount Shasta, CA
Southern California 6'2" 212 lbs.

Year	Team		Games	Pos.
1994	NYG	N	8	S
1995			14	CB, S
1996			16	CB
3 yrs.	38 games			

Dave Sehres
SEHRES, DAVID
B. 1900
Deceased
New York University 5'8" 160 lbs.

Year	Team		Games	Pos.
1926	BKN	A	4	HB, G

Ed Seibert
SEIBERT, EDWARD
B. Oct. 24, 1896
D. Jul., 1987, Indianapolis, IN
West Virginia 195 lbs.

Year	Team		Games	Pos.
1923	HAM	N	1	G

Ed Seibert
SEIBERT, EDWARD
B. Nov. 13, 1902
Otterbein 5'10" 190 lbs.

Year	Team		Games	Pos.
1927	DAY	N	3	T
1928			1	G
2 yrs.	4 games			

Champ Seibold
SEIBOLD, CHAMP C.
B. Dec. 5, 1912, Oshkosh, WI
D. Nov. 2, 1971, Oshkosh, WI
Ripon/Wisconsin/Wisconsin-Oshkosh 6'4" 238 lbs.

Year	Team		Games	Pos.
1934	GB	N	1	G
1935			7	T
1936			11	T
1937			10	T
1938			11	T
1940			10	T
1942	CHIC	N	11	T
7 yrs.	61 games			

Earl Seick
SEICK, FREDERICK EARL (Red)
B. Apr. 28, 1911, Lewiston, NY
D. Oct. 31, 1989
Manhattan 6'0" 195 lbs.

Year	Team		Games	Pos.
1942	NYG	N	8	G

Harry Seidelson
SEIDELSON, HARRY (Red)
B. Aug. 13, 1901
D. Jul., 1986, Pittsburgh, PA
Pittsburgh 6'1" 202 lbs.

Year	Team		Games	Pos.
1925	FRA	N	10	T, G
1926	AKR	N	7	G
2 yrs.	17 games			

Mike Seifert
SEIFERT, MICHAEL
B. Mar. 30, 1951, Kiel, WI
Wisconsin 6'3" 245 lbs.

Year	Team		Games	Pos.
1974	CLE	N	12	DE

Dexter Seigler
SEIGLER, DEXTER
B. Jan. 11, 1972, Avon Park, IL
Miami (Florida) 5'9" 178 lbs.

Year	Team		Games	Pos.
1996	SEA	N	12	CB

Paul Seiler
SEILER, PAUL HERMAN
B. Nov. 1, 1945, Algona, IA
Notre Dame 6'4" 258 lbs.

Year	Team		Games	Pos.
1967	NY	A	2	G, OT
1969			10	C, OT
1971	OAK	N	8	C, OT
1972			14	C, OT
1973			5	C, OT
5 yrs.	39 games			

Larry Seiple
SEIPLE, LARRY ROBERT
B. Feb. 14, 1945, Allentown, PA
Kentucky 6'0" 213 lbs.

Year	Team		Games	Pos.
1967	MIA	A	14	RB, P
1968			14	RB, P
1969			13	WR, P
1970	MIA	N	14	TE, P
1971			14	TE, P
1972			11	TE, P
1973			14	TE, P
1974			14	P, TE
1975			14	P, TE
1976			14	P, TE
1977			13	P, WR
11 yrs.	149 games			

Warren Seitz
SEITZ, WARREN TROY
B. Sep. 29, 1962, Kansas City, MO
Missouri 6'4" 223 lbs.

Year	Team		Games	Pos.
1986	PIT	N	16	WR
1987	NYG	N	2	WR
2 yrs.	18 games			

Gene Selawski
SELAWSKI, EUGENE FRANK
B. Nov. 28, 1935, Cleveland, OH
D. May 11, 1993, Duluth, GA
Purdue 6'4" 252 lbs.

Year	Team		Games	Pos.
1959	LA	N	12	T
1960	CLE	N	12	T
1961	SD	A	8	OT, G
3 yrs.	32 games			

Rob Selby
SELBY, ROBERT SETH
B. Oct. 11, 1967, Birmingham, AL
Auburn 6'3" 286 lbs.

Year	Team		Games	Pos.
1991	PHI	N	13	G, OT
1992			16	G, OT
1993			1	G
1994			2	OT, G
1995	ARI	N	7	OT, G
1996			13	G
6 yrs.	52 games			

Ron Selesky
SELESKY, RONALD
B. Sep. 4, 1965, New Brunswick, NJ
North Central 6'1" 266 lbs.

Year	Team		Games	Pos.
1987	MIN	N	2	G

Clarence Self
SELF, CLARENCE ELBERT
B. Oct. 10, 1925, Birmingham, AL
Wisconsin 5'8" 181 lbs.

Year	Team		Games	Pos.
1949	CHIC	N	12	HB
1950	DET	N	12	HB
1951			12	HB
1952	GB	N	12	HB
1954			12	HB
1955			2	HB
6 yrs.	62 games			

Andy Selfridge
SELFRIDGE, ANDREW PAUL
B. Jan. 12, 1949, Cleveland, OH
Virginia 6'4" 220 lbs.

Year	Team		Games	Pos.
1972	BUF	N	13	LB
1974	NYG	N	14	LB
1975			14	LB
1976	MIA	N	1	LB
1977	NYG	N	11	LB
5 yrs.	53 games			

Frank Seliger
SELIGER, FRANK H.
B. Aug. 31, 1891, Illinois
D. Aug., 1975, Hammond, IN
None 200 lbs.

Year	Team		Games	Pos.
1920	HAM	A	2	T
1921			1	G
2 yrs.	3 games			

Goldie Sellers
SELLERS, GOLDIE
B. Jan. 9, 1942, Winnsboro, LA
Grambling State 6'2" 198 lbs.

Year	Team		Games	Pos.
1966	DEN	A	14	DB
1967			13	DB
1968	KC	A	14	DB
1969			14	CB
4 yrs.	55 games			

Lance Sellers
SELLERS, LANCE KEVIN
B. Feb. 24, 1963, Seattle, WA
Boise State 6'1" 230 lbs.

Year	Team		Games	Pos.
1987	CIN	N	3	LB

Ron Sellers
SELLERS, RONALD
B. Feb. 5, 1947, Jacksonville, FL
Florida State 6'4" 196 lbs.

Year	Team		Games	Pos.
1969	BOS	A	12	WR
1970	BOS	N	13	WR
1971	NE	N	10	WR
1972	DAL	N	14	WR
1973	MIA	N	3	WR
5 yrs.	52 games			

Dewey Selmon
SELMON, DEWEY WILLIS
B. Nov. 19, 1953, Eufaula, OK
Oklahoma 6'1" 248 lbs.

Year	Team		Games	Pos.
1976	TB	N	12	DT
1977			14	DT
1978			16	LB
1979			15	LB
1980			15	LB
1982	SD		8	LB
6 yrs.	80 games			

Lee Roy Selmon
SELMON, LEE ROY
B. Oct. 20, 1954, Eufaula, OK
Oklahoma 6'3" 256 lbs.

Year	Team		Games	Pos.
1976	TB	N	8	DE
1977			14	DE
1978			14	DE
1979			16	DE
1980			16	DE
1981			14	DE
1982			9	DE
1983			14	DE
1984			16	DE
9 yrs.	121 games			

Harry Seltzer
SELTZER, HARRY
B. Mar. 26, 1919, Philadelphia, PA
D. Jul. 13, 1990
Morris Harvey 5'9" 195 lbs.

Year	Team		Games	Pos.
1942	DET	N	6	FB

Bernie Semes
SEMES, BERNARD
B. Jan. 29, 1919, Braddock, PA
Duquesne 5'7" 188 lbs.

Year	Team		Games	Pos.
1944	C, P	N	7	HB

Tony Semple
SEMPLE, ANTHONY LEE
B. Dec. 20, 1970, Springfield, IL
Memphis 6'4" 286 lbs.

Year	Team		Games	Pos.
1995	DET	N	16	G
1996			15	G
2 yrs.	31 games			

Robin Sendlein
SENDLEIN, ROBIN BRUNO
B. Dec. 1, 1958, Las Vegas, NV
Texas 6'3" 225 lbs.

Year	Team		Games	Pos.
1981	MIN	N	16	LB
1982			9	LB
1983			16	LB
1984			15	LB
1985	MIA	N	16	LB
5 yrs.	72 games			

Year	Team		Games	Pos.

Bill Senn
SENN, WILLIAM F.
B. Jul. 14, 1905
D. Sep. 5, 1973, Macomb, IL
Knox 6'0" 177 lbs.

Year	Team		Games	Pos.
1926	CHIB	N	15	HB, FB, QB
1927			13	HB, FB
1928			12	HB
1929			12	HB
1930			11	HB
1931			1	HB
1931	BKN	N	8	HB, QB
1934	C-S		3	HB
7 yrs.	75 games			

Frank Seno
SENO, FRANK
B. Feb. 15, 1921, Mendota, IL
D. Mar., 1974
George Washington 6'0" 191 lbs.

Year	Team		Games	Pos.
1943	WAS	N	10	HB
1944			10	HB
1945	CHIC	N	9	HB
1946			11	HB
1947	BOS	N	11	HB
1948			12	HB
1949	WAS	N	4	HB
7 yrs.	67 games			

Dean Sensenbaugher
SENSENBAUGHER, DEAN S.
B. Aug. 12, 1925, Midvale, OH
Ohio State/Army/Ohio State 5'9" 190 lbs.

Year	Team		Games	Pos.
1948	CLE	AA	11	B

Joe Senser
SENSER, JOSEPH SPENCE
B. Aug. 18, 1956, Philadelphia, PA
West Chester State 6'4" 240 lbs.

Year	Team		Games	Pos.
1980	MIN	N	16	TE
1981			16	TE
1982			9	TE
1984			8	TE
4 yrs.	49 games			

Mike Sensibaugh
SENSIBAUGH, JAMES MICHAEL
B. Jan. 3, 1949, Cincinnati, OH
Ohio State 5'11" 191 lbs.

Year	Team		Games	Pos.
1971	KC	N	7	S
1972			14	S
1973			14	S
1974			14	S
1975			14	S
1976	STL	N	14	S
1977			10	S
7 yrs.	87 games			

Rafael Septien
SEPTIEN, JOSE RAFAEL (MICHEL)
B. Dec. 12, 1953, Mexico City, Mexico
Southwestern Louisiana 5'10" 176 lbs.

Year	Team		Games	Pos.
1977	LA	N	14	K
1978	DAL	N	16	K
1979			16	K
1980			16	K
1981			16	K
1982			9	K
1983			16	K
1984			16	K
1985			16	K
1986			16	K
10 yrs.	151 games			

George Sergienko
SERGIENKO, GEORGE, JR.

George Sergienko continued
B. May 22, 1918, Chicopee, MA
D. Dec. 4, 1993, MA
American International 6'1" 248 lbs.

Year	Team		Games	Pos.
1943	BKN	N	10	T, G
1944			10	T
1945	BOS	N	10	T
1946	BKN	AA	7	T
4 yrs.	37 games			

Wash Serini
SERINI, WASHINGTON
B. Mar. 9, 1922, Tuckahoe, NY
D. Jun. 22, 1994
Kentucky 6'2" 236 lbs.

Year	Team		Games	Pos.
1948	CHIB	N	12	G
1949			12	G
1950			12	G
1951			12	G
1952	GB	N	11	G
5 yrs.	59 games			

Tom Sestak
SESTAK, THOMAS JOSEPH
B. Mar. 9, 1936, Gonzales, TX
McNeese State 6'5" 267 lbs.

Year	Team		Games	Pos.
1962	BUF	A	14	DT
1963			14	DT
1964			14	DT
1965			14	OT, DT
1966			14	DT
1967			14	DT
1968			12	DT
7 yrs.	96 games			

Joe Setcavage
SETCAVAGE, JOSEPH W.
B. Nov. 12, 1918
Duquesne 5'11" 190 lbs.

Year	Team		Games	Pos.
1943	BKN	N	10	QB

Joe Setron
SETRON, JOSEPH L.
B. Aug. 10, 1900, Buffalo, NY
D. Sep. 25, 1958, Cleveland, OH
West Virginia 5'9" 195 lbs.

Year	Team		Games	Pos.
1923	CLE	N	1	G

John Settle
SETTLE, JOHN R.
B. Jun. 2, 1965, Reidsville, NC
Appalachian State 5'9" 209 lbs.

Year	Team		Games	Pos.
1987	ATL	N	9	RB
1988			16	RB
1989			15	RB
1990			6	RB
4 yrs.	46 games			

Tony Settles
SETTLES, TONY
B. Aug. 29, 1964
Elon 6'3" 210 lbs.

Year	Team		Games	Pos.
1987	WAS	N	3	LB

Frank Seurer
SEURER, FRANK
B. Aug. 16, 1962, Huntington Beach, CA
Kansas 6'1" 195 lbs.

Year	Team		Games	Pos.
1986	KC	N	1	QB
1987			8	QB
2 yrs.	9 games			

Jeff Severson
SEVERSON, JEFFREY KENT
B. Sep. 16, 1949, Fargo, ND

Jeff Severson continued
Long Beach State 6'1" 183 lbs.

Year	Team		Games	Pos.
1972	WAS	N	12	S
1973	HOU	N	14	S
1974			14	S
1975	DEN	N	14	DB
1976	STL	N	14	S
1977			14	S
6 yrs.	82 games			

Jeff Sevy
SEVY, JEFFREY EVAN
B. Oct. 24, 1950, Palo Alto, CA
California 6'5" 259 lbs.

Year	Team		Games	Pos.
1975	CHI	N	14	OT
1976			14	OT
1977			12	OT, G
1978			14	OT
1979	SEA	N	4	OT
1980			15	OT
6 yrs.	73 games			

Harley Sewell
SEWELL, HARLEY EDWARD
B. Apr. 18, 1931, Arlington, TX
Texas 6'1" 230 lbs.

Year	Team		Games	Pos.
1953	DET	N	12	G
1954			12	G
1955			12	G
1956			12	G
1957			10	G
1958			12	G
1959			11	G
1960			12	G
1961			14	G
1962			13	G
1963	LA	N	2	G
11 yrs.	122 games			

Steve Sewell
SEWELL, STEVEN EDWARD
B. Apr. 2, 1963, San Francisco, CA
Oklahoma 6'3" 210 lbs.

Year	Team		Games	Pos.
1985	DEN	N	16	RB
1986			11	RB
1987			7	RB
1988			16	RB
1989			16	RB
1990			12	RB
1991			16	RB
7 yrs.	94 games			

Brent Sexton
SEXTON, RUSSELL BRENT
B. Jul. 23, 1953, Fayetteville, NC
Elon 6'1" 190 lbs.

Year	Team		Games	Pos.
1977	PIT	N	11	CB

Lin Sexton
SEXTON, LINWOOD B.
B. Apr. 26, 1926, Wichita, KS
Wichita State 6'0" 180 lbs.

Year	Team		Games	Pos.
1948	LA	AA	11	B

Frank Seyfrit
SEYFRIT, FRANK
B. Jul., 1893
Deceased
Notre Dame 5'10" 170 lbs.

Year	Team		Games	Pos.
1923	TOL	N	8	E
1924	HAM	N	5	E
2 yrs.	13 games			

Bob Seymour
SEYMOUR, ROBERT A.
B. Jun. 13, 1916, Wyandotte, OK
D. May, 1977, Golden, CO

Bob Seymour continued
Oklahoma 6'2" 205 lbs.

Year	Team		Games	Pos.
1940	WAS	N	9	FB
1941			10	HB
1942			10	FB
1943			10	FB
1944			10	FB
1945			10	FB
1946	LA	AA	13	HB
7 yrs.	72 games			

Jim Seymour
SEYMOUR, JAMES
B. Nov. 24, 1946, Detroit, MI
Notre Dame 6'4" 210 lbs.

Year	Team		Games	Pos.
1970	CHI	N	7	WR
1971			10	WR
1972			14	WR
3 yrs.	31 games			

Paul Seymour
SEYMOUR, PAUL CHRISTOPHER
B. Feb. 6, 1950, Detroit, MI
Michigan 6'5" 250 lbs.

Year	Team		Games	Pos.
1973	BUF	N	14	TE
1974			14	TE
1975			14	TE
1976			13	TE
1977			14	TE
5 yrs.	69 games			

Don Shackleford
SHACKLEFORD, DONALD
B. 1943
Pacific 6'4" 255 lbs.

Year	Team		Games	Pos.
1964	DEN	A	8	G

Sam Shade
SHADE, SAM
B. Jun. 14, 1973, Birmingham, AL
Alabama 6'1" 191 lbs.

Year	Team		Games	Pos.
1995	CIN	N	16	S
1996			12	S
2 yrs.	28 games			

Craig Shaffer
SHAFFER, CRAIG ALAN
B. Mar. 31, 1959, Terre Haute, IN
Indiana State 6'0" 230 lbs.

Year	Team		Games	Pos.
1982	STL	N	5	LB
1983			9	LB
1984			4	LB
3 yrs.	18 games			

George Shaffer
SHAFFER, GEORGE A.
B. 1910
Washington & Jefferson 6'0" 190 lbs.

Year	Team		Games	Pos.
1933	PIT	N	5	QB

Leland Shaffer
SHAFFER, LELAND K.
B. May 9, 1912, Minneola, KS
D. Jan. 24, 1993, Hillsboro Beach, FL
Kansas State 6'2" 203 lbs.

Year	Team		Games	Pos.
1935	NYG	N	12	HB, FB, QB
1936			10	FB
1937			10	FB
1938			11	FB
1939			9	FB, E
1940			11	HB, QB
1941			9	FB
1942			11	QB
1943			10	QB
1945			6	QB
10 yrs.	99 games			

Year	Team		Games	Pos.

Stanley Shakespeare
SHAKESPEARE, STANLEY
B. Feb. 5, 1963, Boynton Beach, FL
Miami (Florida) 5'11" 190 lbs.

| 1987 | TB | N | 1 | WR |

Henry Shank
SHANK, HENRY
B. May 29, 1896
D. Nov., 1977, Mount Erie, IL
None 5'9" 180 lbs.

| 1920 | DEC | A | 2 | HB |

Ron Shanklin
SHANKLIN, RONNIE EUGENE
B. Jan. 21, 1948, Hubbard, TX
North Texas State 6'1" 183 lbs.

1970	PIT	N	14	WR
1971			14	WR
1972			14	WR
1973			13	WR
1974			12	WR
1976	CHI	N	5	WR
6 yrs.	72 games			

Simon Shanks
SHANKS, SIMON
B. Oct. 16, 1971, Laurel, MS
Tennessee State 6'1" 215 lbs.

| 1995 | ARI | N | 15 | LB |

Shanley
SHANLEY
None 214 lbs.

| 1927 | DUL | N | 1 | T |

Jim Shanley
SHANLEY, JAMES
B. Jul. 27, 1936, Shelton, NE
Oregon 5'9" 174 lbs.

| 1958 | GB | N | 12 | HB |

Bobby Shann
SHANN, ROBERT ALLEN
B. Mar. 27, 1943, Andover, MA
Boston College 6'1" 189 lbs.

1965	PHI	N	4	DB
1967			6	DB
2 yrs.	10 games			

Carver Shannon
SHANNON, CARVER
B. 1938, Corinth, MS
Southern Illinois 6'1" 201 lbs.

1962	LA	N	12	DB
1963			14	DB
1964			12	DB
3 yrs.	38 games			

John Shannon
SHANNON, JOHN BYRON
B. Jan. 18, 1965, Lexington, KY
Kentucky 6'3" 269 lbs.

1988	CHI	N	13	DT
1989			12	DT
2 yrs.	25 games			

Randy Shannon
SHANNON, RANDY
B. Feb. 24, 1966, Miami, FL
Miami (Florida) 6'1" 221 lbs.

| 1989 | DAL | N | 16 | LB |

Jack Shapiro
SHAPIRO, JACK E. (Soapy)
B. Mar. 22, 1907, New York, NY
New York University 5'2" 126 lbs.

| 1929 | SI | N | 1 | QB |

Nate Share
SHARE, NATHAN
B. 1901
Deceased
Tufts 210 lbs.

1925	PRO	N	10	G
1926	BKN	A	2	T
2 yrs.	12 games			

Ed Sharkey
SHARKEY, EDWARD JOSEPH
B. Jul. 6, 1927, Brooklyn, NY
Duke/Nevada-Reno 6'3" 229 lbs.

1947	NY	AA	9	G
1948			10	G
1949	B-NY	AA	12	G
1950	NYY	N	12	G
1952	CLE	N	12	G
1953	BAL	N	12	G
1954	PHI	N	12	G, T
1955			7	G
1955	SF	N	5	G
1956			7	G
9 yrs.	98 games			

Ed Sharockman
SHAROCKMAN, EDWARD CHARLES
B. Nov. 4, 1939, St. Clair, PA
Pittsburgh 6'0" 200 lbs.

1962	MIN	N	14	DB
1963			14	DB
1964			14	DB
1965			14	DB
1966			11	DB
1967			14	DB
1968			14	DB
1969			11	CB
1970			14	CB
1971			14	CB
1972			7	CB
11 yrs.	141 games			

Dan Sharp
SHARP, DAN
B. Feb. 5, 1962, Dallas, TX
Texas Christian 6'2" 235 lbs.

| 1987 | ATL | N | 9 | TE |

Ev Sharp
SHARP, EVERETT
B. Jun. 25, 1919, Corinth, MS
California Poly (Pomona) 6'1" 223 lbs.

1944	WAS	N	6	T
1945			9	T
2 yrs.	15 games			

Rick Sharp
SHARP, RICH
B. Jun. 1, 1948, London, England
Washington 6'3" 264 lbs.

1970	PIT	N	14	DT, OT
1971			3	OT
1972	DEN	N	12	OT
3 yrs.	29 games			

Luis Sharpe
SHARPE, LUIS ERNESTO, JR.
B. Jun. 16, 1960, Havana, Cuba
UCLA 6'4" 275 lbs.

| 1982 | STL | N | 9 | OT |

Luis Sharpe continued
1983			16	OT
1984			16	OT
1985			16	OT
1986			16	OT
1987			12	OT
1988	PHX	N	16	OT
1989			14	OT
1990			16	OT
1991			16	OT
1992			15	OT
1993			16	OT
1994	ARI	N	11	OT
13 yrs.	189 games			

Shannon Sharpe
SHARPE, SHANNON
B. Jun. 26, 1968, Chicago, IL
Savannah State 6'2" 228 lbs.

1990	DEN	N	16	WR
1991			16	WR
1992			16	TE
1993			16	TE
1994			15	TE
1995			13	TE
1996			15	TE
7 yrs.	107 games			

Sterling Sharpe
SHARPE, STERLING
B. Apr. 6, 1965, Chicago, IL
South Carolina 5'11" 202 lbs.

1988	GB	N	16	WR
1989			16	WR
1990			16	WR
1991			16	WR
1992			16	WR
1993			16	WR
1994			16	WR
7 yrs.	112 games			

Tyrone Shavers
SHAVERS, TYRONE PERNELL
B. Jul. 14, 1967, Texarkana, TX
Lamar 6'3" 210 lbs.

| 1991 | CLE | N | 1 | WR |

Ben Shaw
SHAW, BENJAMIN
B. 1894, Ohio
Deceased
None

| 1923 | CAN | N | 1 | G |

Billy Shaw
SHAW, WILLIAM LEWIS
B. Dec. 15, 1938, Natchez, MS
Georgia Tech 6'3" 250 lbs.

1961	BUF	A	14	G
1962			14	G
1963			14	G
1964			14	G
1965			14	G
1966			14	G
1967			9	G
1968			13	G
1969			13	G
1979	DAL	N	16	C
1980			14	C
1981			3	C
12 yrs.	152 games			

Bob Shaw
SHAW, ROBERT
B. May 22, 1922, Richwood, OH
Ohio State 6'4" 226 lbs.

| 1945 | CLE | N | 5 | E |

Bob Shaw continued
1946	LA	N	10	E
1949			11	E
1950	CHIC	N	12	E
4 yrs.	38 games			

Bob Shaw
SHAW, ROBERT
B. Mar. 16, 1947, Wilson, NC
Winston-Salem State 6'0" 194 lbs.

| 1970 | NO | N | 4 | WR |

Charley Shaw
SHAW, CHARLES
B. 1927
Oklahoma State 6'2" 220 lbs.

| 1950 | SF | N | 6 | G |

Dennis Shaw
SHAW, DENNIS WENDELL
B. Mar. 3, 1947, Los Angeles, CA
Southern California/San Diego State 6'2" 213 lbs.

1970	BUF	N	14	QB
1971			14	QB
1972			14	QB
1973			4	QB
1974	STL	N	2	QB
1975			3	QB
6 yrs.	51 games			

Ed Shaw
SHAW, EDSON N.
B. Aug. 7, 1895
D. Oct., 1964, Omaha, NE
Nebraska 6'1" 203 lbs.

1920	RI	N	7	T
1922	CAN	N	11	FB, HB, T, G
1923	AKR	N	2	HB
3 yrs.	20 games			

Eric Shaw
SHAW, ERIC WENDELL
B. Sep. 17, 1971, Pensacola, FL
Florida State/Louisiana Tech 6'3" 248 lbs.

1992	CIN	N	11	LB
1993			14	LB
1994			3	LB
3 yrs.	28 games			

George Shaw
SHAW, GEORGE
B. Jul. 25, 1933, Portland, OR
Oregon 6'1" 183 lbs.

1955	BAL	N	12	QB
1956			5	QB
1957			7	QB
1958			12	QB
1959	NYG	N	5	QB
1960			9	QB
1961	MIN	N	8	QB
1962	DEN	A	13	QB
8 yrs.	71 games			

Glenn Shaw
SHAW, GLENN
B. Jul. 11, 1938, Paducah, KY
Kentucky 6'1" 210 lbs.

1960	CHI	N	12	HB
1962	LA	N	3	FB
1963	OAK	A	12	FB
1964			2	FB
4 yrs.	29 games			

Year	Team	Games	Pos.

Jesse Shaw
SHAW, JESSE
B. Jun. 11, 1907
D. Oct., 1965
Southern California 6'1" 198 lbs.

Year	Team		Games	Pos.
1931	CHIC	N	5	G

Nate Shaw
SHAW, NATHANIEL
B. May 20, 1945, San Diego, CA
Southern California 6'2" 205 lbs.

Year	Team		Games	Pos.
1969	LA	N	7	S
1970			8	S

2 yrs. 15 games

Pete Shaw
SHAW, KENNETH EDWARD
B. Aug. 25, 1954, Newark, NJ
Northwestern 5'10" 180 lbs.

Year	Team		Games	Pos.
1977	SD	N	14	S
1978			16	S
1979			16	S
1980			12	S
1981			16	S
1982	NYG	N	9	S
1983			15	S
1984			16	S

8 yrs. 114 games

Ricky Shaw
SHAW, RICKY ANDREW
B. Jul. 28, 1965, Westchester, NY
Oklahoma State 6'4" 240 lbs.

Year	Team		Games	Pos.
1988	NYG	N	14	LB
1989			7	LB
1989	PHI	N	8	LB
1990			8	LB

3 yrs. 37 games

Terrance Shaw
SHAW, TERRANCE
B. Nov. 11, 1973, Marshall, TX
Stephen F. Austin 5'11" 190 lbs.

Year	Team		Games	Pos.
1995	SD	N	16	CB
1996			16	CB

2 yrs. 32 games

Jerry Shay
SHAY, JEROME PAUL
B. Jul. 10, 1944, Gary, IN
Purdue 6'3" 244 lbs.

Year	Team		Games	Pos.
1966	MIN	N	14	DT
1967			1	DT
1968	ATL	N	14	DT
1969			14	DT
1970	NYG	N	14	DT
1971			6	DT

6 yrs. 63 games

Pat Shea
SHEA, PAT
B. Jun. 28, 1941, La Jolla, CA
Southern California 6'1" 241 lbs.

Year	Team		Games	Pos.
1962	SD	A	5	G
1963			14	G
1964			14	G
1965			8	G

4 yrs. 41 games

Al Sheard
SHEARD, ALFRED (Shag)
B. Nov. 17, 1898
D. Nov., 1980, Canton, NY
St. Lawrence 5'11" 177 lbs.

Year	Team		Games	Pos.
1923	ROC	N	4	QB
1924			7	QB, HB

Al Sheard continued

Year	Team	Games	Pos.
1925		7	HB

3 yrs. 18 games

Brad Shearer
SHEARER, STERLING BRADFORD
B. Aug. 10, 1955, Houston, TX
Texas 6'3" 249 lbs.

Year	Team		Games	Pos.
1978	CHI	N	15	DT
1980			13	DT
1981			6	DT

3 yrs. 34 games

Ron Shearer
SHEARER, RONALD
B. Sep. 12, 1905
Drake 6'0" 195 lbs.

Year	Team		Games	Pos.
1930	POR	N	1	T

Joe Shearin
SHEARIN, JOSEPH LESLIE
B. Apr. 16, 1960, Dallas, TX
Texas 6'4" 250 lbs.

Year	Team		Games	Pos.
1983	LARM	N	16	G
1984			15	G
1985	TB	N	10	G
1987	DAL	N	1	C

4 yrs. 42 games

Larry Shears
SHEARS, LARRY
B. Aug. 1, 1949, Mobile, AL
Lincoln (Missouri) 5'10" 185 lbs.

Year	Team		Games	Pos.
1971	ATL	N	9	CB, S
1972			1	CB

2 yrs. 10 games

Kenny Shedd
SHEDD, KENNY
B. Feb. 14, 1971, Davenport, IA
Northern Iowa 5'10" 170 lbs.

Year	Team		Games	Pos.
1996	OAK	N	16	WR

Ed Shedlosky
SHEDLOSKY, EDMOND
B. 1920
Tulsa/Fordham 6'0" 185 lbs.

Year	Team		Games	Pos.
1945	NYG	N	3	HB

Fred Sheehan
SHEEHAN, FREDERIC W.
B. Dec. 21, 1902, Abingdon, MA
D. Sep. 4, 1984, Dorchester, MA
Georgetown (DC) 6'2" 210 lbs.

Year	Team		Games	Pos.
1925	PRO	N	1	G

Jack Sheehy
SHEEHY, JOHN
B. Dec. 28, 1898
D. May, 1964
New York University 205 lbs.

Year	Team		Games	Pos.
1926	BKN	A	3	G, C

Paul Sheeks
SHEEKS, PAUL PRESTON
B. Oct. 18, 1889, Grand Rapids, ND
D. Sep. 17, 1968, Akron, OH
Dakota Wesleyan/South Dakota 5'8" 173 lbs.

Year	Team		Games	Pos.
1921	AKR	N	12	QB
1922	AKR	N	10	QB, E

2 yrs. 22 games

Chris Sheffield
SHEFFIELD, CHRISTOPHER JONATHAN
B. Jan. 9, 1963, Cairo, GA
Albany State 6'1" 185 lbs.

Year	Team		Games	Pos.
1986	PIT	N	10	CB
1987			5	CB
1987	DET	N	6	CB

2 yrs. 21 games

Ron Shegog
SHEGOG, RON
B. Mar. 2, 1964
Austin Peay 5'11" 190 lbs.

Year	Team		Games	Pos.
1987	NE		3	S

Vin Shekleton
SHEKLETON, VINCENT
B. 1896
Deceased
Colgate/Marquette 150 lbs.

Year	Team		Games	Pos.
1922	RAC	N	3	C

John Shelburne
SHELBURNE, JOHN A.
B. 1896
Deceased
Dartmouth 5'11" 200 lbs.

Year	Team		Games	Pos.
1922	HAM		8	FB

Willie Shelby
SHELBY, WILLIE E.
B. Jul. 24, 1953, Hattiesburg, MS
Alabama 5'11" 195 lbs.

Year	Team		Games	Pos.
1976	CIN	N	13	RB
1977			14	RB
1978	STL	N	3	RB

3 yrs. 30 games

Jim Sheldon
SHELDON, JAMES HURLON
B. Jan. 9, 1901, Oneonta, NY
D. Feb. 26, 1980, Round Hill, VA
Brown 5'11" 180 lbs.

Year	Team		Games	Pos.
1926	BKN	N	1	E

Art Shell
SHELL, ARTHUR
B. Nov. 26, 1946, Charleston, SC
Maryland-Eastern Shore 6'5" 267 lbs.

Year	Team		Games	Pos.
1968	OAK	A	14	OT
1969			14	OT
1970	OAK	N	14	OT
1971			14	OT
1972			14	OT
1973			14	OT
1974			14	OT
1975			14	OT
1976			14	OT
1977			16	OT
1978			16	OT
1979			11	OT
1980			16	OT
1981			16	OT
1982	LARI	N	8	OT

15 yrs. 207 games

Donnie Shell
SHELL, DONNIE
B. Aug. 26, 1952, Whitmire, SC
South Carolina State 5'11" 196 lbs.

Year	Team		Games	Pos.
1974	PIT	N	14	DB
1975			14	S
1976			14	S
1977			12	S
1978			16	S

Donnie Shell continued

Year	Team	Games	Pos.
1979		16	S
1980		16	S
1981		14	S
1982		9	S
1983		16	S
1984		16	S
1985		16	S
1986		15	S
1987		13	S

14 yrs. 201 games

Todd Shell
SHELL, TODD ANDREW
B. Jun. 24, 1962, Mesa, AZ
Brigham Young 6'4" 225 lbs.

Year	Team		Games	Pos.
1984	SF	N	16	LB
1985			15	LB
1986			1	LB
1987			6	LB

4 yrs. 38 games

Dexter Shelley
SHELLEY, DEXTER
B. Jun. 4, 1906
D. Dec., 1968, Austin, TX
Texas 5'11" 191 lbs.

Year	Team		Games	Pos.
1931	POR	N	2	HB
1931	PRO	N	8	HB, QB
1932	GB	N	2	FB, HB
1932	CHIC	N	2	HB

2 yrs. 14 games

Elbert Shelley
SHELLEY, ELBERT VERNELL
B. Dec. 24, 1964, Tyronza, AR
Arkansas State 5'11" 180 lbs.

Year	Team		Games	Pos.
1987	ATL	N	4	S
1988			12	S
1989			10	S
1990			12	S
1991			11	S
1992			13	CB
1993			16	CB
1994			16	CB
1995			13	CB
1996			12	CB

10 yrs. 119 games

Jonathan Shelley
SHELLEY, JONATHAN
B. Aug. 6, 1964, Vicksburg, MS
Mississippi 6'0" 176 lbs.

Year	Team		Games	Pos.
1987	SF	N	1	CB

Chris Shelling
SHELLING, CHRISTOPHER
B. Nov. 3, 1972, Columbus, GA
Auburn 5'10" 180 lbs.

Year	Team		Games	Pos.
1995	CIN	N	13	CB, S
1996			1	S

2 yrs. 14 games

Alec Shellogg
SHELLOGG, ALEXANDER FREDERICK
B. Feb. 17, 1914
D. Jul. 12, 1968
Notre Dame 6'0" 215 lbs.

Year	Team		Games	Pos.
1939	CHIB	N	1	T
1939	BKN	N	2	B, T

Anthony Shelton
SHELTON, ANTHONY LEVALA
B. Sep. 4, 1967, Fayetteville, TN
Tennessee State 6'1" 195 lbs.

Year	Team		Games	Pos.
1990	SD	N	14	CB

Year	Team		Games	Pos.

Anthony Shelton *continued*

Year	Team		Games	Pos.
1991			11	CB
2 yrs.	25 games			

Murray Shelton
SHELTON, MURRAY N.
B. Apr. 20, 1893, Dunkirk, NY
D. Aug., 1985, Columbia, MO
Cornell 6'1" 175 lbs.

Year	Team		Games	Pos.
1920	BUF	A	6	E

Richard Shelton
SHELTON, RICHARD EDDIE
B. Jan. 2, 1966, Marietta, GA
Liberty 5'10" 180 lbs.

Year	Team		Games	Pos.
1989	DEN	N	3	CB
1990	PIT	N	2	CB
1991			14	CB
1992			16	CB
1993			9	CB, S
5 yrs.	44 games			

Paul Shenefelt
SHENEFELT, PAUL JESSE
B. Mar. 4, 1911, Ames, IA
D. Oct. 30, 1988, Palm Beach Gardens, FL
Manchester 6'0" 195 lbs.

Year	Team		Games	Pos.
1934	CHIC	N	2	C

Charley Shepard
SHEPARD, CHARLES LAFAYETTE
B. Jul. 11, 1933, Dallas, TX
North Texas State 6'2" 215 lbs.

Year	Team		Games	Pos.
1956	PIT	N	12	FB

Derrick Shepard
SHEPARD, DERRICK LATHELL
B. Jan. 22, 1964, Odessa, TX
Oklahoma 5'10" 186 lbs.

Year	Team		Games	Pos.
1987	WAS		3	WR
1988			5	WR
1989	NO	N	4	WR
1989	DAL	N	11	WR
1990			8	WR
1991			6	WR
5 yrs.	37 games			

Bill Shepherd
SHEPHERD, WILLIAM L.
B. Dec. 4, 1911, Cherry Tree, PA
D. Mar. 8, 1967, Detroit, MI
Western Maryland 5'9" 199 lbs.

Year	Team		Games	Pos.
1935	BOS	N	7	QB, FB, HB
1935	DET	N	5	FB, HB
1936			12	FB
1937			11	QB, FB
1938			9	QB, HB
1939			11	FB
1940			3	FB
6 yrs.	58 games			

Johnny Shepherd
SHEPHERD, JOHNNY
B. Apr. 24, 1957, La Grange, NC
Livingston 5'10" 185 lbs.

Year	Team		Games	Pos.
1987	BUF	N	2	RB

Leslie Shepherd
SHEPHERD, LESLIE GLENARD
B. Nov. 3, 1969, Washington, DC
Temple 5'11" 189 lbs.

Year	Team		Games	Pos.
1994	WAS	N	3	WR
1995			14	WR
1996			12	WR
3 yrs.	29 games			

Ashley Sheppard
SHEPPARD, ASHLEY GUY
B. Jan. 21, 1969, Greenville, NC
Clemson 6'3" 243 lbs.

Year	Team		Games	Pos.
1993	MIN	N	10	LB
1994			7	LB
1995	JAC	N	2	LB
1995	MIN	N	1	LB
1995	STL	N	2	LB
3 yrs.	22 games			

Henry Sheppard
SHEPPARD, HENRY FOSSETT, JR.
B. Nov. 12, 1952, Cuero, TX
Southern Methodist 6'6" 255 lbs.

Year	Team		Games	Pos.
1976	CLE	N	14	OT, G
1977			13	OT, G
1978			14	G
1979			16	G
1980			16	OT
1981			9	G
6 yrs.	82 games			

Dave Sherer
SHERER, DAVID McDONALD, JR.
B. Feb. 14, 1937, Galion, OH
Southern Methodist 6'3" 218 lbs.

Year	Team		Games	Pos.
1959	BAL	N	12	E, P
1960	DAL	N	11	OE, P
2 yrs.	23 games			

Stan Sheriff
SHERIFF, STANLEY
B. 1931, San Francisco, CA
D. Jan. 16, 1993, Honolulu, HI
California Poly (San Luis Obispo) 6'1" 224 lbs.

Year	Team		Games	Pos.
1954	PIT	N	12	C
1956	SF	N	6	C, LB
1957			2	LB
1957	CLE	N	3	G
3 yrs.	23 games			

Jerry Sherk
SHERK, JERRY MARTIN
B. Jul. 7, 1948, Grants Pass, OR
Oklahoma State 6'4" 252 lbs.

Year	Team		Games	Pos.
1970	CLE	N	14	DT
1971			14	DT
1972			14	DT
1973			14	DT
1974			14	DT
1975			14	DT
1976			14	DT
1977			7	DT
1978			16	DT
1979			10	DT
1980			1	DT
1981			15	DT
12 yrs.	147 games			

Bob Sherlag
SHERLAG, ROBERT
B. Apr. 19, 1943, Chicago, IL
Memphis State 6'0" 197 lbs.

Year	Team		Games	Pos.
1966	ATL	N	9	FL

Allie Sherman
SHERMAN, ALEXANDER
B. Feb. 10, 1923, Brooklyn, NY
Brooklyn College 5'11" 170 lbs.

Year	Team		Games	Pos.
1943	P-P	N	9	QB
1944	PHI	N	10	QB
1945			10	QB
1946			11	QB
1947			11	QB
5 yrs.	51 games			

Bob Sherman
SHERMAN, ROBERT
B. Jul. 4, 1942
Iowa 6'2" 195 lbs.

Year	Team		Games	Pos.
1964	PIT	N	14	DB
1965			11	DB
2 yrs.	25 games			

Heath Sherman
SHERMAN, HEATH
B. Mar. 27, 1967, Wharton, TX
Texas A&I, Kingsville 6'0" 195 lbs.

Year	Team		Games	Pos.
1989	PHI	N	15	RB
1990			14	RB
1991			16	RB
1992			16	RB
1993			15	RB
5 yrs.	76 games			

Rod Sherman
SHERMAN, RODNEY JARVIS
B. Dec. 25, 1944, Pasadena, CA
Southern California 6'0" 190 lbs.

Year	Team		Games	Pos.
1967	OAK	A	13	WR
1968	CIN	A	13	FL
1969	OAK	A	14	WR
1970	OAK	N	14	WR
1971			11	WR
1972	DEN	N	14	WR
1973	LA	N	3	WR
7 yrs.	82 games			

Solly Sherman
SHERMAN, SAUL
B. Sep. 25, 1917, Chicago, IL
Chicago 6'1" 190 lbs.

Year	Team		Games	Pos.
1939	CHIB	N	7	QB
1940			7	QB
2 yrs.	14 games			

Tom Sherman
SHERMAN, TOM
B. Dec. 5, 1945, Bellevue, PA
Penn State 6'0" 190 lbs.

Year	Team		Games	Pos.
1968	BOS	A	14	QB, DB
1969			4	QB
1969	BUF	A	1	QB
2 yrs.	19 games			

Will Sherman
SHERMAN, WILLARD
B. Oct. 20, 1929, Weed, CA
St. Mary's (California) 6'2" 197 lbs.

Year	Team		Games	Pos.
1952	DAL	N	2	HB
1954	LA	N	12	HB
1955			12	HB
1956			12	HB
1957			10	HB
1958			11	HB
1959			10	HB
1960			10	HB
8 yrs.	79 games			

Mike Sherrard
SHERRARD, MICHAEL WATSON
B. Jun. 21, 1963, Oakland, CA
UCLA 6'2" 187 lbs.

Year	Team		Games	Pos.
1986	DAL	N	16	WR
1990	SF	N	7	WR
1991			16	WR
1992			16	WR
1993	NYG	N	6	WR
1994			16	WR
1995			13	WR
1996	DEN	N	15	WR
8 yrs.	105 games			

Bud Sherrod
SHERROD, HORACE M.
B. Dec. 2, 1927
D. Aug., 1980, Dallas, TX
Tennessee 6'0" 190 lbs.

Year	Team		Games	Pos.
1952	NYG	N	11	E

Gerry Sherry
SHERRY, GERRY
None

Year	Team		Games	Pos.
1926	LOU	N	1	FB

Tim Sherwin
SHERWIN, TIMOTHY THOMAS
B. May 4, 1958, Troy, NY
Boston College 6'6" 246 lbs.

Year	Team		Games	Pos.
1981	BAL	N	16	TE
1982			9	TE
1983			15	TE
1984	IND	N	16	TE
1985			9	TE
1986			7	TE
1987			8	TE
1988	NYG	N	3	TE
8 yrs.	83 games			

Rhoten Shetley
SHETLEY, RHOTEN NATHAN
B. Feb. 7, 1918, Newport, TN
D. Jan. 8, 1993, Greenville, SC
Furman 5'11" 208 lbs.

Year	Team		Games	Pos.
1940	BKN	N	11	QB
1941			11	QB
1942			3	QB
1946	BKN	AA	13	FB
4 yrs.	38 games			

James Shibest
SHIBEST, JAMES
B. Oct. 31, 1964
Arkansas 5'11" 187 lbs.

Year	Team		Games	Pos.
1987	ATL	N	1	WR

Joe Shield
SHIELD, JOSEPH MICHAEL
B. Jun. 26, 1962, Brattleboro, VT
Trinity (Connecticut) 6'1" 185 lbs.

Year	Team		Games	Pos.
1986	GB	N	3	QB

Billy Shields
SHIELDS, WILLIAM DEAN
B. Aug. 23, 1953, Vicksburg, MS
Georgia Tech 6'7" 266 lbs.

Year	Team		Games	Pos.
1975	SD	N	11	OT
1976			14	OT
1977			13	OT
1978			16	OT
1979			16	OT
1980			16	OT
1981			16	OT
1982			9	OT
1983			16	OT
1984	SF	N	11	OT
1985	NYJ	N	3	OT
1985	KC	N	2	OT
11 yrs.	143 games			

Burrell Shields
SHIELDS, BURRELL
B. Sep. 6, 1929, Cleveland, OH
John Carroll 6'2" 203 lbs.

Year	Team		Games	Pos.
1954	PIT	N	6	HB
1955	BAL	N	7	HB
2 yrs.	13 games			

Year	Team	Games	Pos.

Jon Shields
SHIELDS, JON
B. Apr. 30, 1964
Portland State 6'5" 293 lbs.

Year	Team		Games	Pos.
1987	DAL	N	1	OT, G

Lebron Shields
SHIELDS, LEBRON
B. Jul. 23, 1937, Walker County, GA
Tennessee 6'4" 243 lbs.

Year	Team		Games	Pos.
1960	BAL	N	12	T, G
1961	MIN	N	6	DE
2 yrs.		18 games		

Will Shields
SHIELDS, WILL HERTHIE
B. Sep. 15, 1971, Fort Riley, KS
Nebraska 6'2" 296 lbs.

Year	Team		Games	Pos.
1993	KC	N	16	G
1994			16	G
1995			16	G
1996			16	G
4 yrs.		64 games		

Dick Shiner
SHINER, RICHARD EARL, JR.
B. Jul. 18, 1942, Lebanon, PA
Maryland 6'0" 197 lbs.

Year	Team		Games	Pos.
1964	WAS	N	1	QB
1965			14	QB
1966			14	QB
1967	CLE	N	12	QB
1968	PIT	N	13	QB
1969			12	QB
1970	NYG	N	14	QB
1971	ATL	N	10	QB
1973			4	QB
1973	NE	N	4	QB
1974			14	QB
10 yrs.		112 games		

John Shinners
SHINNERS, JOHN JOSEPH
B. Mar. 1, 1947, Hartford, WI
Xavier (Ohio) 6'2" 255 lbs.

Year	Team		Games	Pos.
1969	NO	N	2	G
1970			9	G
1971			14	G
1972	BAL	N	8	G
1973	CIN	N	14	G
1974			13	G
1975			14	G
1976			13	G
1977				G
9 yrs.		87 games		

Don Shinnick
SHINNICK, DONALD DEE
B. May 15, 1935, Kansas City, MO
UCLA 6'0" 232 lbs.

Year	Team		Games	Pos.
1957	BAL	N	12	LB
1958			12	LB
1959			12	LB
1960			12	LB
1961			14	LB
1962			14	LB
1963			14	LB
1964			14	LB
1965			10	LB
1966			14	LB
1967			14	LB
1968			10	LB
1969			6	LB
13 yrs.		158 games		

Harry Shipkey
SHIPKEY, HARRY H.
B. Feb. 23, 1902

Harry Shipkey continued
D. Jul. 6, 1978, Palo Alto, CA
Stanford 6'2" 205 lbs.

Year	Team		Games	Pos.
1926	LA	A	14	T

Jerry Shipkey
SHIPKEY, GERALD WADE
B. Oct. 31, 1925, Fullerton, CA
Southern California/UCLA 6'1" 213 lbs.

Year	Team		Games	Pos.
1948	PIT	N	12	FB
1949			12	FB
1950			12	FB
1951			10	FB
1952			12	FB
1953	CHIB	N	8	FB
6 yrs.		66 games		

Billy Shipp
SHIPP, WILLIAM
B. Oct. 16, 1929, Mobile, AL
Alabama 6'5" 275 lbs.

Year	Team		Games	Pos.
1954	NYG	N	11	T

Jackie Shipp
SHIPP, JACKIE RENARDO
B. Mar. 19, 1962, Muskogee, OK
Oklahoma 6'2" 236 lbs.

Year	Team		Games	Pos.
1984	MIA	N	16	LB
1985			16	LB
1986			16	LB
1987			12	LB
1988			11	LB
1989	LARI	N	3	LB
6 yrs.		74 games		

Joe Shipp
SHIPP, JOSEPH DELANO
B. Jul. 25, 1955, Long Beach, CA
Southern California 6'4" 225 lbs.

Year	Team		Games	Pos.
1979	BUF	N	16	TE

Marshall Shires
SHIRES, ABRAHAM MARSHALL (Abe)
B. Feb. 12, 1917, Alderson, WV
D. Jul. 23, 1993, Sacramento, CA
Tennessee 6'2" 220 lbs.

Year	Team		Games	Pos.
1945	PHI	N	7	T

Fred Shirey
SHIREY, CHARLES FREDERICK
B. Jan. 12, 1916, Latrobe, PA
D. Nov. 1, 1961
Nebraska 6'2" 223 lbs.

Year	Team		Games	Pos.
1940	GB	N	3	T
1940	CLE	N	6	T
1941			3	T
2 yrs.		12 games		

Gary Shirk
SHIRK, GARY LEE
B. Feb. 23, 1950, Columbus, OH
Morehead State 6'1" 220 lbs.

Year	Team		Games	Pos.
1976	NYG	N	14	TE
1977			14	TE
1978			16	TE
1979			16	TE
1980			16	TE
1981			16	TE
1982			9	TE
7 yrs.		101 games		

John Shirk
SHIRK, JOHN
B. Jun. 24, 1917, Oklahoma City, OK
Oklahoma 6'4" 200 lbs.

Year	Team		Games	Pos.
1940	CHIC	N	11	E

George Shirkey
SHIRKEY, GEORGE
B. 1937
Stephen F. Austin 6'4" 252 lbs.

Year	Team		Games	Pos.
1960	HOU	A		DT
1961			7	DT
1962	OAK	A	14	DT
3 yrs.		21 games		

Marion Shirley
SHIRLEY, MARION V.
B. 1922
Oklahoma State/Oklahoma City 6'4" 260 lbs.

Year	Team		Games	Pos.
1948	NY	AA	13	T
1949	B-NY	AA	7	T
2 yrs.		20 games		

Clay Shiver
SHIVER, CLAY
B. Dec. 7, 1972, Tifton, GA
Florida State 6'2" 294 lbs.

Year	Team		Games	Pos.
1996	DAL	N	14	C

Rex Shiver
SHIVER, RAYMOND O.
B. Jan. 1, 1932, Miami, FL
Miami (Florida) 6'0" 190 lbs.

Year	Team		Games	Pos.
1956	LA	N	8	HB

Rick Shiver
SHIVER, RICK
None

Year	Team		Games	Pos.
1922	CHIC	N	1	FB

Sanders Shiver
SHIVER, SANDERS
B. Feb. 14, 1955, Gadsden, SC
Carson-Newman 6'2" 225 lbs.

Year	Team		Games	Pos.
1976	BAL	N	14	LB
1977			14	LB
1978			16	LB
1979			16	LB
1980			14	LB
1981			14	LB
1982			8	LB
1983			16	LB
1985	MIA	N	6	LB
9 yrs.		118 games		

Roy Shivers
SHIVERS, ROY L.
B. Jul. 5, 1942, Halley, AR
Utah State 6'0" 200 lbs.

Year	Team		Games	Pos.
1966	STL	N	13	HB
1967			9	RB
1968			14	RB
1969			12	RB
1970			12	RB
1971			11	RB
1972			2	RB
7 yrs.		73 games		

Boris Shlapak
SHLAPAK, BORIS W.
B. May 18, 1950, Chicago, IL
Michigan State 6'0" 165 lbs.

Year	Team		Games	Pos.
1972	BAL	N	8	K

Roger Shoals
SHOALS, ROGER RICHARD
B. Dec. 13, 1938, Baltimore, MD
Maryland 6'4" 256 lbs.

Year	Team		Games	Pos.
1963	CLE	N	2	OT
1964			14	OT
1965	DET	N	14	OT

Roger Shoals continued

Year	Team		Games	Pos.
1966			14	OT
1967			4	OT
1968			14	OT
1969			14	OT
1970			14	OT
1971	DEN	N	14	OT
9 yrs.		104 games		

Rod Shoate
SHOATE, RODERICK
B. Apr. 26, 1953, Spiro, OK
Oklahoma 6'1" 214 lbs.

Year	Team		Games	Pos.
1975	NE	N	4	LB
1977			14	LB
1978			16	LB
1979			14	LB
1980			16	LB
1981			16	LB
6 yrs.		80 games		

Arnie Shockley
JACKSON, PARNEL
B. Nov. 27, 1904
D. Aug., 1974, Melbourne, FL
Southwestern Oklahoma State 6'2" 220 lbs.

Year	Team		Games	Pos.
1929	BOS	N	5	T, G

Bill Shockley
SHOCKLEY, WILLIAM ALBERT, JR.
B. Mar. 13, 1937, West Chester, PA
West Chester State 6'0" 185 lbs.

Year	Team		Games	Pos.
1960	NY	A	14	HB, K
1961			6	HB, K
1961	BUF	A	2	HB
1962	NY	A	14	HB, K
1968	PIT	N	1	K
4 yrs.		37 games		

Hub Shoemake
SHOEMAKE, CHARLES HUBBARD
B. Sep. 29, 1899, Oskaloosa, IA
D. Mar. 10, 1984, Washington, DC
Lake Forest/Illinois/Bethany (West Virginia) 6'0" 186 lbs.

Year	Team		Games	Pos.
1920	DEC	A	3	G

Hal Shoener
SHOENER, HAROLD PHILLIP
B. Jan. 2, 1923, Reedsville, WV
D. Dec. 13, 1983, Oakland, CA
Iowa 6'3" 200 lbs.

Year	Team		Games	Pos.
1948	SF	AA	14	E
1949			12	E
1950	SF	N	12	E
3 yrs.		38 games		

Herb Shoener
SHOENER, HERBERT GEORGE
B. Jan. 2, 1923, Reedsville, WV
D. Dec. 24, 1985, Anaheim, CA
Lehigh/Iowa 6'3" 205 lbs.

Year	Team		Games	Pos.
1948	WAS	N	7	E
1949			11	E
2 yrs.		18 games		

Del Shofner
SHOFNER, DELBERT MARTIN
B. Dec. 11, 1934, Center, TX
Baylor 6'3" 188 lbs.

Year	Team		Games	Pos.
1957	LA	N	12	DB
1958			12	E
1959			12	E
1960			11	E

Year	Team	Games	Pos.

Del Shofner *continued*

Year	Team		Games	Pos.
1961	NYG	N	14	OE
1962			13	OE
1963			14	OE
1964			6	OE
1965			12	OE
1966			9	OE
1967			10	OE

11 yrs. 125 games

Jim Shofner
SHOFNER, JAMES
B. Dec. 18, 1935, Grapevine, TX
Texas Christian 6'2" 191 lbs.

1958	CLE	N	12	DB
1959			12	DB
1960			12	DB
1961			14	DB
1962			14	DB
1963				CB

6 yrs. 64 games

John Shonk
SHONK, JOHN J., III
B. Apr. 30, 1918, Charleston, WV
D. Apr. 26, 1984, Christiansburg, VA
West Virginia 6'1" 190 lbs.

1941	PHI	N	9	E

Chuck Shonta
SHONTA, CHARLES JOSEPH
B. Aug. 29, 1937, Detroit, MI
Eastern Michigan 6'0" 196 lbs.

1960	BOS	A	14	DB
1961			8	DB
1962			14	DB
1963			13	DB
1964			14	DB
1965			14	DB
1966			14	DB
1967			14	DB

8 yrs. 105 games

Al Shook
SHOOK, ALBERT
B. Jan. 15, 1898, Pierce City, MO
D. Apr. 14, 1984, Atchison, KS
None

1921	COL	A	2	G

Fred Shook
SHOOK, FREDERIC E.
B. Mar. 30, 1919, Fort Worth, TX
D. Apr. 16, 1992
Texas Christian 6'0" 218 lbs.

1941	CHIC	N	2	G, C

Laval Short
SHORT, LAVAL HOWARD, JR.
B. Sep. 29, 1958, Nashville, TN
Colorado 6'3" 250 lbs.

1980	DEN	N	15	DT
1981	TB	N	4	NT

2 yrs. 19 games

Jim Shorter
SHORTER, JAMES
B. Jun. 8, 1939, Montgomery, AL
Detroit 5'11" 184 lbs.

1962	CLE	N	9	DB
1963			11	CB
1964	WAS	N	14	DB
1965			13	DB
1966			13	DB
1967			13	DB
1969	PIT	N	14	CB

7 yrs. 87 games

George Shorthose
SHORTHOSE, GEORGE EDWARD
B. Dec. 22, 1961, Stanton, CA
Missouri 6'0" 196 lbs.

1985	KC	N	3	WR

Peter Shorts
SHORTS, PETER JOHN
B. Jul. 12, 1966, Clinton, WI
Illinois State 6'8" 278 lbs.

1989	NE	N	1	DE

Darin Shoulders
SHOULDERS, DARIN
B. May 23, 1968, Jackson, MS
Tulane 6'3" 288 lbs.

1991	IND	N	1	OT

Paul Shoults
SHOULTS, PAUL ARTHUR
B. Oct. 9, 1925, Washington Court House, OH
Miami (Ohio) 5'11" 178 lbs.

1949	NYB	N	12	B

Shriner
SHRINER
None

1921	CIN	A	1	E

Pete Shufelt
SHUFELT, PETER JULIAN
B. Oct. 28, 1969, Chicago, IL
Texas-El Paso 6'2" 241 lbs.

1994	NYG	N	4	LB

Clyde Shugart
SHUGART, CLYDE E.
B. Dec. 7, 1916, Elberon, IA
Iowa State 6'1" 221 lbs.

1939	WAS	N	11	G, T
1940			9	G
1941			9	G
1942			10	G
1943			10	T, G
1944			4	G

6 yrs. 53 games

Bret Shugarts
SHUGARTS, BRET
B. Feb. 17, 1960
Indiana (Pennsylvania) 6'2" 250 lbs.

1987	PIT	N	2	DE

Dave Shula
SHULA, DAVID DONALD
B. May 28, 1959, Lexington, KY
Dartmouth 5'11" 182 lbs.

1981	BAL	N	16	WR

Don Shula
SHULA, DONALD FRANCIS
B. Jan. 4, 1930, Painesville, OH
John Carroll 5'11" 190 lbs.

1951	CLE	N	12	HB
1952			5	HB
1953	BAL	N	12	HB
1954			12	HB
1955			9	HB
1956			12	HB
1957	WAS	N	11	HB

7 yrs. 73 games

Heath Shuler
SHULER, JOSEPH HEATH
B. Dec. 31, 1971, Bryson City, NC
Tennessee 6'2" 221 lbs.

1994	WAS	N	11	QB
1995			7	QB
1996			1	QB

3 yrs. 19 games

Mickey Shuler
SHULER, MICKEY CHARLES
B. Aug. 21, 1956, Harrisburg, PA
Penn State 6'3" 232 lbs.

1978	NYJ	N	16	TE
1979			16	TE
1980			16	TE
1981			6	TE
1982			9	TE
1983			16	TE
1984			16	TE
1985			16	TE
1986			16	TE
1987			11	TE
1988			15	TE
1989			7	TE
1990	PHI	N	16	TE
1991			4	TE

14 yrs. 180 games

Steve Shull
SHULL, STEVEN MARK
B. Mar. 27, 1958, Philadelphia, PA
William & Mary 6'1" 218 lbs.

1980	MIA	N	16	LB
1981			16	LB
1982			9	LB

3 yrs. 41 games

Johnny Shultz
SHULTZ, JOHN (Shebo)
B. Sep. 8, 1907
D. Jan., 1966
Temple 6'1" 189 lbs.

1930	FRA	N	5	HB, FB

Mike Shumann
SHUMANN, MICHAEL WILLIAM
B. Oct. 13, 1955, Louisville, KY
Florida State 6'0" 175 lbs.

1978	SF	N	6	WR
1979			16	WR
1980	TB	N	6	WR
1981	SF	N	13	WR
1982	STL	N	6	WR
1983			16	WR

6 yrs. 63 games

Mark Shumate
SHUMATE, MARK
B. Mar. 30, 1960, Poynette, WI
Wisconsin 6'5" 265 lbs.

1985	NYJ	N	4	DE
1985	GB	N	3	NT

Ron Shumon
SHUMON, RONALD
B. Dec. 11, 1955, Flint, MI
Wichita State 6'1" 230 lbs.

1978	CIN	N	13	LB

Mark Shupe
SHUPE, MARK
B. Apr. 25, 1962, Lafayette, IN
Arizona State 6'5" 285 lbs.

1987	BUF	N	2	C

Walt Shupp
SHUPP, WALTER
B. 1896
Deceased
Miami (Ohio) 6'0" 185 lbs.

1921	CIN	A	4	T, G

Marshall Shurnas
SHURNAS, MARSHALL
B. Apr. 1, 1922, St. Louis, MO
Missouri 6'1" 205 lbs.

1947	CLE	AA	11	E

Charlie Shurtcliffe
SHURTCLIFFE, CHARLES W. (Red)
B. Apr. 12, 1907
D. Sep., 1986, South Carolina
Marietta 160 lbs.

1929	BUF	N	3	HB

Bert Shurtleff
SHURTLEFF, BERTRAND LESLIE
B. Aug. 3, 1897, Adamsville, RI
D. Feb. 15, 1967, Anaheim, CA
Brown 5'11" 190 lbs.

1925	PRO	N	11	G
1929	BOS	N	4	C

2 yrs. 15 games

Hub Shurtz
SHURTZ, HUBERT
B. Jul. 1, 1923, Pinckneyville, IL
Louisiana State 6'3" 235 lbs.

1948	PIT	N	12	T

Don Shy
SHY, DONALD FREDERIC
B. Nov. 15, 1945, Cleveland, OH
San Diego State 6'1" 209 lbs.

1967	PIT	N	14	RB
1968			13	RB
1969	NO	N	14	RB
1971	CHI	N	11	RB
1972			13	RB
1973	STL	N	11	RB

6 yrs. 76 games

Les Shy
SHY, LES
B. Apr. 5, 1944, Cleveland, OH
Long Beach State 6'1" 202 lbs.

1966	DAL	N	11	HB
1967			13	RB
1968			14	RB
1969			14	RB
1970	NYG	N	13	RB

5 yrs. 65 games

Mike Siani
SIANI, MICHAEL JOSEPH
B. May 27, 1950, Staten Island, NY
Villanova 6'2" 196 lbs.

1972	OAK	N	14	WR
1973			14	WR
1974			5	WR
1975			14	WR
1976			14	WR
1977			12	WR
1978	BAL	N	7	WR
1979			9	WR
1980			10	WR

9 yrs. 99 games

Mike Siano
SIANO, MICHAEL

Year	Team		Games	Pos.

Mike Siano continued
B. Nov. 29, 1963, Philadelphia, PA
Syracuse 6'4" 220 lbs.

1987	PHI	N	3	WR

Tony Siano
SIANO, THOMAS ANTHONY
B. Jan. 10, 1907
D. Apr., 1986, Rochelle Park, NJ
Fordham 5'8" 172 lbs.

1932	BOS	N	9	C
1934	BKN	N	11	C
2 yrs.	20 games			

Jimmy Sidle
SIDLE, JAMES
B. Feb. 7, 1943
Auburn 6'2" 215 lbs.

1966	ATL	N	6	TE, RB

Alex Sidorik
SIDORIK, ALEXANDER THEODORE
B. Dec. 19, 1921, Hartford, CT
D. Apr., 1980, Amston, CT
Mississippi State 6'0" 248 lbs.

1947	BOS	N	12	T
1948	BAL	AA	9	T
1949			12	T
3 yrs.	33 games			

Wallie Sieb
SIEB, WALTER
B. May 6, 1899
D. Jan., 1974, Racine, WI
Ripon 5'10" 165 lbs.

1922	RAC	N	2	B

Johnny Siegal
SIEGAL, JOHN W.
B. May 15, 1918, Larksville, PA
Columbia 6'1" 203 lbs.

1939	CHIB	N	10	E
1940			8	E
1941			11	E
1942			11	E
1943			3	E
5 yrs.	43 games			

Herb Siegert
SIEGERT, HERBERT F.
B. Jan. 10, 1924, Pana, IL
Illinois 6'3" 216 lbs.

1949	WAS	N	12	G
1950			12	G
1951			12	G
3 yrs.	36 games			

Wayne Siegert
SIEGERT, WAYNE EWALD
B. Mar. 24, 1929, Pana, IL
Illinois 6'3" 225 lbs.

1951	NYY	N	3	T

Orville Siegfried
SIEGFRIED, ORVILLE
B. Feb. 19, 1903
D. May 28, 1965
Washington & Jefferson 5'10" 160 lbs.

1923	STL	N	7	HB, FB

Jules Siegle
SIEGLE, JULIUS J.
B. Feb. 16, 1923, East Chicago, IN
Northwestern 6'0" 210 lbs.

1948	NYG	N	3	FB

Larry Siemering
SIEMERING, LAWRENCE
B. 1914, San Francisco, CA
San Francisco 6'3" 206 lbs.

1935	BOS	N	11	C
1936			9	C
2 yrs.	20 games			

Clark Sieminski
SIEMINSKI, CLARK LEO
B. Jul. 3, 1940, Swoyersville, PA
Penn State 6'4" 262 lbs.

1963	SF	N	14	OT, DT
1964			14	OT
1965			14	DT
1966	ATL	N	14	DT
1967			14	DT
1968	DET	N	8	DT
6 yrs.	78 games			

Jeff Siemon
SIEMON, JEFFREY GLENN (The Minister of Defense)
B. Jun. 2, 1950, Rochester, MN
Stanford 6'2" 235 lbs.

1972	MIN	N	13	LB
1973			14	LB
1974			14	LB
1975			14	LB
1976			14	LB
1977			14	LB
1978			16	LB
1979			16	LB
1980			16	LB
1981			15	LB
1982			9	LB
11 yrs.	155 games			

Troy Sienkiewicz
SIENKIEWICZ, TROY ALLEN
B. May 27, 1972, Charleston, SC
New Mexico State 6'5" 310 lbs.

1996	SD	N	7	G

Steve Sieradzki
SIERADZKI, STEPHEN H.
B. Apr. 7, 1924
D. May, 1968
Michigan State 6'0" 194 lbs.

1948	NY	AA	2	B

Steve Sierocinski
SIEROCINSKI, STEPHEN PETER
B. 1922
None 6'3" 245 lbs.

1946	BOS	N	3	T

Herb Sies
SIES, DALE HERBERT
B. 1893
Deceased
Pittsburgh 6'1" 203 lbs.

1920	CLE	A	1	T
1921	DAY	A	9	G
1922	DAY	N	8	G
1923	RI	N	8	G, T, QB
1924	DAY	N	3	G
5 yrs.	29 games			

Eric Sievers
SIEVERS, ERIC SCOTT
B. Nov. 9, 1958, Urbana, IL
Maryland 6'4" 235 lbs.

1981	SD	N	16	TE
1982			9	TE
1983			16	TE
1984			14	TE

Eric Sievers continued

1985			16	TE
1986			9	TE
1987			12	TE
1988			5	TE
1988	LARM	N	1	TE
1989	NE	N	16	TE
1990			8	TE
10 yrs.	122 games			

Dom Sigillo
SIGILLO, DOMINIC
B. Mar. 7, 1913, Storrs, UT
Deceased
Xavier (Ohio) 6'0" 230 lbs.

1943	CHIB	N	6	T
1944			8	T, G
1945	DET	N	8	T
3 yrs.	22 games			

Ricky Siglar
SIGLAR, RICKY ALLAN
B. Jun. 14, 1966, Albuquerque, NM
San Jose State 6'7" 296 lbs.

1990	SF	N	16	OT
1993	KC	N	14	OT, G
1994			16	OT
1995			16	OT
1996			16	OT
5 yrs.	78 games			

Joe Signaigo
SIGNAIGO, JOSEPH SALVATORE
B. Feb. 9, 1923, Memphis, TN
Notre Dame 6'1" 220 lbs.

1948	NY	AA	14	G
1949	B-NY	AA	12	G
1950	NYY	N	12	G
3 yrs.	38 games			

Sig Sigurdson
SIGURDSON, SIGURD F.
B. Nov. 27, 1918, Seattle, WA
Pacific Lutheran 6'2" 206 lbs.

1947	BAL	AA	8	E

Vai Sikahema
SIKAHEMA, VAI
B. Aug. 29, 1962, Nukualofa, Tonga Islands
Brigham Young 5'9" 191 lbs.

1986	STL	N	16	RB
1987			15	HB
1988	PHX	N	12	RB
1989			16	RB
1990			16	RB
1991	GB	N	11	RB
1992	PHI	N	16	WR
1993			16	WR
8 yrs.	118 games			

Mike Sikich
SIKICH, MICHAEL P.
B. Mar. 13, 1949, Chicago, IL
Northwestern 6'2" 243 lbs.

1971	CLE	N	3	G

Rudy Sikich
SIKICH, RUDOLPH
B. 1921, Hibbing, MN
Minnesota 6'1" 220 lbs.

1945	CLE	N	6	T

Mike Sikora
SIKORA, MICHAEL W.
B. Nov. 29, 1926, Hammond, IN

Mike Sikora continued
Indiana/Oregon 6'2" 230 lbs.

1952	CHIC	N	9	G

Sam Silas
SILAS, SAMUEL LOUIS
B. Sep. 25, 1940, Homeland, FL
Southern Illinois 6'4" 251 lbs.

1963	STL	N	14	DT
1964			14	DT
1965			14	DT
1966			14	DT
1967			14	DT
1968	NYG	N	14	DT
1969	SF	N	4	DE
1970			12	DE, DT
8 yrs.	100 games			

Dan Sileo
SILEO, DANIEL WILLIAM
B. Jan. 3, 1964, Stamford, CT
Maryland/Cincinnati/Miami (Florida) 6'2" 282 lbs.

1987	TB	N	10	NT

Rich Siler
SILER, RICH
B. Nov. 1, 1963
Texas A&M 6'4" 240 lbs.

1987	MIA	N	1	TE

Joe Silipo
SILIPO, JOSEPH MARTIN
B. Dec. 31, 1957, Glen Cove, NY
Tulane 6'3" 295 lbs.

1987	BUF	N	1	C

Frank Sillin
Born FRANKLIN PAUL SILLEN
B. 1903
D. Dec. 30, 1932
Western Maryland 5'11" 179 lbs.

1921	DAY	A	1	HB
1927	DAY	N	7	HB
1928			4	HB, FB
1929			5	HB, FB
4 yrs.	17 games			

Milo Silvan
SILVAN, MILO
B. Oct. 2, 1973, Covington, LA
Tennessee 5'9" 176 lbs.

1996	TB	N	7	WR

Carl Silvestri
SILVESTRI, CARL
B. Mar. 27, 1943, Milwaukee, WI
Wisconsin 6'0" 195 lbs.

1965	STL	N	14	DB
1966	ATL	N	3	DB
2 yrs.	17 games			

Don Silvestri
SILVESTRI, DON
B. Dec. 25, 1968, Perkasie, PA
Pittsburgh 6'4" 205 lbs.

1995	NYJ	N	16	K
1996			12	K
2 yrs.	28 games			

Bill Simas
SIMAS, WILLIAM (Butch)
B. Aug. 31, 1908
D. May 24, 1989, Hermosa Beach, CA
St. Mary's (California) 6'0" 185 lbs.

1932	CHIC	N	7	B

Year	Team	Games	Pos.

Bill Simas continued

Year	Team	Games	Pos.
1933		3	B
2 yrs.	10 games		

Ken Simendinger
SIMENDINGER, KENNETH
B. 1899
D. May 26, 1972
Lehigh/Holy Cross 5'10" 175 lbs.

1926	HAR	N	2	HB

Don Simensen
SIMENSEN, DONALD ROY
B. Sep. 11, 1926, Minot, ND
D. Apr. 22, 1994, Fridley, MN
St. Thomas (Minnesota) 6'2" 220 lbs.

1951	LA	N	12	T
1952			12	T
2 yrs.	24 games			

John Simerson
SIMERSON, JOHN COOKE, JR.
B. Aug. 20, 1935, Honolulu, HI
D. Aug. 2, 1992
Purdue 6'3" 257 lbs.

1957	PHI	N	12	C
1958			4	C
1958	PIT	N	3	C, T
1960	HOU	A		C
1961	BOS	A	10	OT
4 yrs.	29 games			

Tracy Simien
SIMIEN, TRACY ANTHONY
B. May 21, 1967, Bay City, TX
Texas Christian 6'1" 248 lbs.

1991	KC	N	15	LB
1992			15	LB
1993			16	LB
1994			15	LB
1995			16	LB
1996			16	LB
6 yrs.	93 games			

Milt Simington
SIMINGTON, MILTON
B. Aug. 26, 1918, Wright City, OK
D. Jan. 18, 1943
Arkansas 6'2" 217 lbs.

1941	CLE	N	7	T, G
1942	PIT	N	11	G
2 yrs.	18 games			

Arnie Simkus
SIMKUS, ARNOLD
B. Mar. 25, 1943, Schlava, Germany
Michigan/Wayne State/New York University 6'4" 245 lbs.

1965	NY	A	1	DT
1967	MIN	N	11	DE
2 yrs.	12 games			

Mike Simmonds
SIMMONDS, MICHAEL TODD
B. Aug. 12, 1964, Belleville, IL
Indiana State 6'4" 285 lbs.

1989	TB	N	5	G

Bob Simmons
SIMMONS, ROBERT GATLING
B. Jul. 7, 1954, Temple, TX
Texas 6'4" 260 lbs.

1977	KC	N	14	OT
1978			16	OT
1979			16	G
1980			15	G

Bob Simmons continued

Year	Team	Games	Pos.
1981		4	G
1982		8	G
1983		15	G, OT
7 yrs.	88 games		

Cleo Simmons
SIMMONS, CLEO
B. Oct. 21, 1960, Mobile, AL
Jackson State 6'2" 225 lbs.

1983	DAL	N	11	TE

Clyde Simmons
SIMMONS, CLYDE
B. Aug. 4, 1964, Lanes, SC
Western Carolina 6'6" 275 lbs.

1986	PHI	N	16	DE
1987			12	DT, DE
1988			16	DE
1989			16	DE
1990			16	DE
1991			16	DE
1992			16	DE
1993			16	DE
1994	ARI	N	16	DE
1995			16	DE
1996	JAC	N	16	DE
11 yrs.	172 games			

Dave Simmons
SIMMONS, DAVID ALAN
B. Aug. 3, 1943, Elizabethtown, KY
Georgia Tech 6'4" 245 lbs.

1965	STL	N	14	LB
1966			6	LB
1967	NO	N	11	LB
1968	DAL	N	13	LB
4 yrs.	44 games			

Dave Simmons
SIMMONS, DAVID DEVONE
B. Jan. 19, 1957, Goldsboro, NC
North Carolina 6'4" 222 lbs.

1979	GB	N	16	LB
1980	DET	N	1	LB
1982	BAL	N	6	LB
1983	CHI	N	13	LB
4 yrs.	36 games			

Ed Simmons
SIMMONS, ED
B. Dec. 31, 1963, Seattle, WA
Eastern Washington 6'5" 292 lbs.

1987	WAS	N	5	OT
1988			16	OT
1989			16	OT
1990			13	OT
1991			6	OT
1992			16	OT
1993			13	OT
1994			16	OT
1995			16	OT
1996			11	OT
10 yrs.	128 games			

Floyd Simmons
SIMMONS, FLOYD WESTON
B. Feb. 19, 1925, Portland, OR
Notre Dame 6'1" 200 lbs.

1948	CHI	AA	11	B

Jack Simmons
SIMMONS, JOHN CHARLES
B. Oct. 8, 1925, Grosse Pointe, MI
D. Oct., 1978, Royal Oak, MI
Detroit 6'4" 236 lbs.

1948	BAL	AA	10	G

Jack Simmons continued

Year	Team	Games	Pos.
1949	DET	N	12	T
1950			12	C
1951	CHIC	N	12	C
1952			12	C
1953			12	C
1954			12	C
1955			12	C
1956			12	C
9 yrs.	106 games			

Jeff Simmons
SIMMONS, JEFFERY THOMAS
B. Jul. 6, 1960, Stockton, CA
Southern California 6'2" 197 lbs.

1983	LARM	N	3	WR

Jerry Simmons
SIMMONS, JERRY BERNARD
B. Nov. 14, 1942, Nichols, FL
Bethune-Cookman 6'1" 190 lbs.

1965	PIT	N	4	OE
1966			13	OE
1967	NO	N	2	SE
1967	ATL	N	12	OE
1968			14	OE
1969			2	WR
1969	CHI	N	8	WR
1971	DEN	N	14	WR
1972			9	WR
1973			9	WR
1974			14	WR
9 yrs.	101 games			

Jim Simmons
SIMMONS, JAMES A. (Jinks)
B. Apr. 17, 1902, Texas
D. Feb., 1984, Oklahoma
Southwestern Oklahoma State 6'0" 186 lbs.

1927	CLE	N	12	HB, FB, QB
1928	PRO	N	9	HB, FB
2 yrs.	21 games			

John Simmons
SIMMONS, JOHN CHRISTOPHER
B. Dec. 1, 1958, Little Rock, AR
Southern Methodist 5'11" 192 lbs.

1981	CIN	N	11	CB
1982			2	CB
1983			16	CB
1984			16	CB
1985			9	CB
1986			10	CB
1986	GB	N	6	CB
1987	IND	N	2	S
7 yrs.	72 games			

King Simmons
SIMMONS, KING DAVID
B. Feb. 12, 1963, Atlanta, GA
Texas Tech 6'2" 199 lbs.

1987	SD	N	3	S

Leon Simmons
SIMMONS, LEON
B. 1939
Grambling State 6'0" 225 lbs.

1963	DEN	A	2	LB

Marcello Simmons
SIMMONS, MARCELLO MUHAMMAD
B. Aug. 8, 1971, Tomball, TX
Southern Methodist 6'1" 180 lbs.

1993	CIN	N	16	CB

Michael Simmons
SIMMONS, MICHAEL G.
B. Nov. 14, 1965, Eupora, MS
Mississippi State 6'4" 269 lbs.

1989	NO	N	1	DE
1990			16	DE
2 yrs.	17 games			

Roy Simmons
SIMMONS, ROY FRANKLIN
B. Nov. 8, 1956, Savannah, GA
Georgia Tech 6'3" 264 lbs.

1979	NYG	N	16	G
1980			16	G
1981			16	G
1983	WAS	N	10	OT, G
4 yrs.	58 games			

Tony Simmons
SIMMONS, ANTHONY EARL
B. Dec. 18, 1962, Oakland, CA
Tennessee 6'4" 268 lbs.

1985	SD	N	13	DE
1987			3	DE
2 yrs.	16 games			

Stacey Simmons
SIMMONS, STACEY ANDREW
B. Aug. 5, 1968, Clearwater, FL
Florida 5'9" 183 lbs.

1990	IND	N	14	WR
1991	TB	N	14	WR
2 yrs.	28 games			

Victor Simmons
SIMMONS, VICTOR
B. May 9, 1964
Central State (Ohio) 6'2" 230 lbs.

1987	DAL	N	3	LB

Wayne Simmons
SIMMONS, WAYNE GENERAL
B. Dec. 15, 1969, Beaufort, SC
Clemson 6'3" 240 lbs.

1993	GB	N	14	LB
1994			12	LB
1995			16	LB
1996			16	LB
4 yrs.	58 games			

Bob Simms
SIMMS, ROBERT
B. Sep. 3, 1938
Rutgers 6'1" 223 lbs.

1960	NYG	N	9	DE
1961			14	DE
1962			3	LB
1962	PIT	N	5	LB
3 yrs.	31 games			

Phil Simms
SIMMS, PHILLIP
B. Nov. 3, 1956, Lebanon, KY
Morehead State 6'3" 215 lbs.

1979	NYG	N	12	QB
1980			13	QB
1981			10	QB
1983			2	QB
1984			16	QB
1985			16	QB
1986			16	QB
1987			9	QB
1988			15	QB
1989			15	QB
1990			14	QB
1991			6	QB
1992			4	QB

Year	Team	Games	Pos.

Phil Simms continued

Year	Team		Games	Pos.
1993			16	QB

14 yrs.   164 games

Bobby Simon
SIMON, BOBBY
B. Dec. 13, 1952, Mansfield, LA
Grambling State 6'3" 252 lbs.

1976	HOU	N	2	OT

Jim Simon
SIMON, JAMES E.
B. Mar. 22, 1940, Pittsburgh, PA
Miami (Florida) 6'5" 235 lbs.

1963	DET	N	13	DE, LB
1964			14	DE, LB
1965			14	G
1966	ATL	N	14	G, OT
1967			14	OT
1968			13	G

6 yrs.   82 games

Mike Simone
SIMONE, MICHAEL A.
B. May 20, 1950, Ravenna, OH
Stanford 6'0" 210 lbs.

1972	DEN	N	14	LB
1973			14	LB
1974			14	LB

3 yrs.   42 games

Len Simonetti
SIMONETTI, LEONARD
(Meatball)
B. Nov. 20, 1920, New Philadelphia, PA
D. Aug. 14, 1973, Denison, OH
Tennessee 5'11" 225 lbs.

1947	CLE	AA	14	T
1948			14	T

2 yrs.   28 games

Ed Simonini
SIMONINI, EDWARD
B. Feb. 2, 1954, Portsmouth, VA
Texas A&M 6'0" 211 lbs.

1976	BAL	N	14	LB
1977			14	LB
1978			16	LB
1979			13	LB
1980			16	LB
1981			1	LB
1982	NO	N	9	LB

7 yrs.   83 games

Jack Simons
SIMONS, JOHN
B. Dec. 26, 1899
D. Mar., 1972, Denison, IA
Hamline 5'11" 200 lbs.

1924	MIN	N	6	FB, E

Keith Simons
SIMONS, KEITH M.
B. Apr. 26, 1954, Belleville, MI
Minnesota 6'3" 254 lbs.

1976	KC	N	6	DT
1977			14	DT
1978	STL	N	13	DT
1979			16	DT

4 yrs.   49 games

Kevin Simons
SIMONS, KEVIN BRADLEY
B. Apr. 25, 1967, Miami, FL
Tennessee 6'3" 215 lbs.

1989	CLE	N	1	OT

Dave Simonson
SIMONSON, DAVID ARNOLD
B. May 2, 1952, Austin, MN
Minnesota 6'6" 248 lbs.

1974	BAL	N	13	OT
1975	NYG	N	2	OT
1976	HOU	N	2	OT
1976	SEA	N	5	OT
1977	DET	N	7	OT

4 yrs.   29 games

Ron Simpkins
SIMPKINS, RONALD BERNARD
B. Apr. 2, 1958, Detroit, MI
Michigan 6'1" 235 lbs.

1980	CIN	N	16	LB
1982			5	LB
1983			15	LB
1984			16	LB
1985			16	LB
1986			16	LB
1988	GB	N	7	LB

7 yrs.   91 games

Al Simpson
SIMPSON, ALLEN
B. Jul. 27, 1951, Port Arthur, TX
Colorado State 6'5" 255 lbs.

1975	NYG	N	13	OT
1976			10	OT

2 yrs.   23 games

Bill Simpson
SIMPSON, WILLIAM THOMAS
B. Dec. 5, 1951, Detroit, MI
Michigan State 6'1" 183 lbs.

1974	LA	N	14	S
1975			14	S
1976			14	S
1977			14	S
1978			16	S
1980	BUF	N	11	S
1981			16	S
1982			9	S

8 yrs.   108 games

Bob Simpson
SIMPSON, ROBERT
B. Mar. 29, 1954, Bloomington, IL
Colorado 6'5" 235 lbs.

1978	MIA	N	5	OT

Carl Simpson
SIMPSON, CARL WILHELM
B. Apr. 18, 1970, Baxley, GA
Florida State 6'2" 282 lbs.

1993	CHI	N	11	DT
1994			15	DT
1995			16	DT, DE
1996			16	DT

4 yrs.   58 games

Eber Simpson
SIMPSON, EBER EDWARD
B. Jul. 24, 1895, Oshkosh, WI
Wisconsin-Oshkosh/Wisconsin/Washington (Missouri) 155 lbs.

1923	STL	N	7	QB, HB

Howard Simpson
SIMPSON, HOWARD
B. 1943
Auburn 6'5" 230 lbs.

1964	MIN	N	3	DE

Jackie Simpson
SIMPSON, JACK M.
B. Aug. 20, 1937, Corinth, MS
Mississippi 6'1" 226 lbs.

1961	DEN	A	6	LB
1962	OAK	A	14	LB
1963			14	LB
1964			2	LB

4 yrs.   36 games

Jackie Simpson
SIMPSON, JACK MAYLEN
B. Apr. 2, 1934
D. Jun. 2, 1983, Pontiac, MI
Florida 5'10" 183 lbs.

1958	BAL	N	2	DB
1959			10	DB
1960			12	DB
1961	PIT	N	8	DB
1962			13	DB

5 yrs.   45 games

Jimmy Simpson
SIMPSON, JAMES FELIX
B. Oct. 6, 1897
D. Aug., 1979, Toledo, OH
Detroit 5'10" 160 lbs.

1922	TOL	N	3	HB, G, QB
1924	KEN	N	4	QB, HB

2 yrs.   7 games

Keith Simpson
SIMPSON, KEITH EDWARD
B. Mar. 9, 1956, Memphis, TN
Memphis State 6'1" 195 lbs.

1978	SEA	N	13	CB
1979			15	CB
1980			16	S
1981			12	S
1982			8	CB
1983			14	CB
1984			15	CB
1985			15	CB

8 yrs.   108 games

Mike Simpson
SIMPSON, MICHAEL HARRY
B. Mar. 13, 1947, Mena, AR
Houston 5'11" 172 lbs.

1970	SF	N	7	CB
1971			8	CB
1972			13	S, CB
1973			13	S

4 yrs.   41 games

Nate Simpson
SIMPSON, NATHANIEL JOSEPH
B. Nov. 30, 1954, Nashville, TN
Tennessee State 5'11" 189 lbs.

1977	GB	N	12	RB
1978			16	RB
1979			15	RB

3 yrs.   43 games

O.J. Simpson
SIMPSON, ORENTHAL JAMES
(The Juice)
B. Jul. 9, 1947, San Francisco, CA
Southern California 6'2" 211 lbs.

1969	BUF	A	13	RB
1970	BUF	N	8	RB
1971			14	RB
1972			14	RB
1973			14	RB
1974			14	RB
1975			14	RB
1976			14	RB

O.J. Simpson continued

1977			7	RB
1978	SF	N	10	RB
1979			13	RB

11 yrs.   135 games

Tim Simpson
SIMPSON, TIMOTHY JAMES
B. Mar. 5, 1969, Peoria, IL
Illinois 6'2" 296 lbs.

1994	PIT	N	3	G

Travis Simpson
SIMPSON, TRAVIS THERON
B. Nov. 19, 1963, Norman, OK
Oklahoma 6'3" 272 lbs.

1987	GB	N	3	C

Willie Simpson
SIMPSON, WILLIE
B. 1938
San Francisco State 6'0" 218 lbs.

1962	OAK	A	10	FB

Billy Sims
SIMS, BILLY RAY
B. Sep. 18, 1955, St. Louis, MO
Oklahoma 6'0" 212 lbs.

1980	DET	N	16	RB
1981			14	RB
1982			9	RB
1983			13	RB
1984			8	RB

5 yrs.   60 games

Darryl Sims
SIMS, DARRYL LEON
B. Jul. 23, 1961, Winston-Salem, NC
Wisconsin 6'3" 275 lbs.

1985	PIT	N	16	DE
1986			16	DE
1987	CLE	N	10	DE
1988			16	DE

4 yrs.   58 games

David Sims
SIMS, DAVID BERNARD
B. Oct. 26, 1955, Atlanta, GA
Georgia Tech 6'3" 216 lbs.

1977	SEA	N	14	RB
1978			12	RB
1979			3	FB

3 yrs.   29 games

George Sims
SIMS, GEORGE P. (Gabby)
B. Oct. 23, 1927, Afton, TX
Baylor 5'11" 170 lbs.

1949	LA	N	12	HB
1950			9	HB

2 yrs.   21 games

Jack Sims
SIMS, JACK
B. Apr. 21, 1962, San Mateo, CA
Hawaii 6'3" 260 lbs.

1987	SEA	N	3	G

Jimmy Sims
SIMS, JAMES
B. Dec. 18, 1950, Kountze, TX
Southern California 6'0" 195 lbs.

1976	TB	N	2	LB

Year	Team		Games	Pos.

Joe Sims
SIMS, JOE
B. Mar. 1, 1969, Sudbury, MA
Nebraska 6'3" 299 lbs.

Year	Team		Games	Pos.
1991	**ATL**	N	6	OT
1992	**GB**		15	OL
1993			13	OT, G
1994			15	OT
1995			4	OT
5 yrs.	53 games			

Keith Sims
SIMS, KEITH
B. Jun. 17, 1967, Baltimore, MD
Iowa State 6'2" 308 lbs.

Year	Team		Games	Pos.
1990	**MIA**	N	14	G
1991			12	G
1992			16	G
1993			16	G
1994			16	G
1995			16	G
1996			15	G
7 yrs.	105 games			

Ken Sims
SIMS, KEN
B. Nov. 9, 1963
Iowa 5'9" 177 lbs.

Year	Team		Games	Pos.
1987	**STL**	N	3	CB

Kenneth Sims
SIMS, KENNETH W.
B. Oct. 31, 1959, Kosse, TX
Texas 6'5" 272 lbs.

Year	Team		Games	Pos.
1983	**NE**	N	5	DE
1984			16	DE
1985			13	DE
1986			3	DE
1987			12	DE
1988			1	DE
1989			15	DE
7 yrs.	65 games			

Marvin Sims
SIMS, MARVIN
B. Jun. 18, 1957, Columbus, GA
Clemson 6'4" 236 lbs.

Year	Team		Games	Pos.
1980	**BAL**	N	16	FB
1981			16	FB
2 yrs.	32 games			

Mickey Sims
SIMS, ROBERT
B. Mar. 5, 1955, Union, SC
South Carolina State 6'5" 278 lbs.

Year	Team		Games	Pos.
1977	**CLE**	N	12	DT
1978			15	DT
1979			16	DT
3 yrs.	43 games			

Reggie Sims
SIMS, REGGIE
B. Jul. 30, 1962
Northern Illinois 6'4" 253 lbs.

Year	Team		Games	Pos.
1987	**CIN**	N	1	TE

Tom Sims
SIMS, THOMAS SIDNEY
B. Apr. 18, 1967, Detroit, MI
Western Michigan/Pittsburgh 6'2" 288 lbs.

Year	Team		Games	Pos.
1991	**KC**	N	14	NT
1992			12	NT
1993	**IND**	N	5	NT
1994			16	NT
4 yrs.	47 games			

Tommy Sims
SIMS, THOMAS EDWARD
B. Sep. 29, 1964, Americus, GA
Tennessee 6'0" 190 lbs.

Year	Team		Games	Pos.
1986	**IND**	N	1	CB, S

William Sims
SIMS, WILLIAM
B. Dec. 30, 1970, Frankfurt, Germany
Southwestern Louisiana 6'3" 265 lbs.

Year	Team		Games	Pos.
1994	**MIN**	N	8	LB

Michael Sinclair
SINCLAIR, MICHAEL GLENN
B. Jan. 31, 1968, Galveston, TX
Eastern New Mexico 6'4" 264 lbs.

Year	Team		Games	Pos.
1992	**SEA**	N	12	DE
1993			9	DE
1994			12	DE
1995			16	DE
1996			16	DE
5 yrs.	65 games			

Curt Singer
SINGER, CURT EDWARD
B. Nov. 4, 1961, Aliquippa, PA
Tennessee 6'5" 278 lbs.

Year	Team		Games	Pos.
1986	**SEA**	N	11	OT
1988	**DET**	N	3	OT
1989	**NYJ**	N	6	OT
1991	**SEA**	N	13	OT
4 yrs.	33 games			

Karl Singer
SINGER, KARL KENNETH
B. Oct. 12, 1943, Warren, OH
Purdue 6'3" 250 lbs.

Year	Team		Games	Pos.
1966	**BOS**	A	14	OT
1967			14	OT
1968			11	OT
3 yrs.	39 games			

Walt Singer
SINGER, WALTER
B. Dec. 6, 1912, Jersey City, NJ
D. Feb. 5, 1992
Syracuse 6'0" 198 lbs.

Year	Team		Games	Pos.
1935	**NYG**	N	10	E
1936			12	E
2 yrs.	22 games			

Bill Singletary
SINGLETARY, WILLIAM JAMES, JR. (Skip)
B. Mar. 18, 1951, Camden, NJ
Temple 6'2" 230 lbs.

Year	Team		Games	Pos.
1974	**NYG**	N	3	LB

Mike Singletary
SINGLETARY, MICHAEL (Samurai Mike)
B. Oct. 9, 1958, Houston, TX
Baylor 6'0" 230 lbs.

Year	Team		Games	Pos.
1981	**CHI**	N	16	LB
1982			9	LB
1983			16	LB
1984			16	LB
1985			16	LB
1986			14	LB
1987			12	LB
1988			16	LB
1989			16	LB
1990			16	LB
1991			16	LB
1992			16	LB
12 yrs.	179 games			

Reggie Singletary
SINGLETARY, REGGIE
B. Jan. 17, 1964, Whiteville, NC
North Carolina State 6'3" 279 lbs.

Year	Team		Games	Pos.
1986	**PHI**	N	16	DT
1987			12	G, OT
1988			16	G
1989			1	G, OT
1990			16	G, OT
5 yrs.	61 games			

Bill Singleton
SINGLETON, WILLIAM
B. Feb. 7, 1897
D. Oct., 1971, Illinois
Washington (Missouri) 5'9" 190 lbs.

Year	Team		Games	Pos.
1922	**HAM**	N	1	G

Chris Singleton
SINGLETON, CHRIS
B. Feb. 20, 1967, Parsippany, NJ
Arizona 6'2" 247 lbs.

Year	Team		Games	Pos.
1990	**NE**	N	13	LB
1991			12	LB
1992			8	LB
1993			8	LB
1993	**MIA**		9	LB
1994			11	LB
1995			16	LB
1996			14	LB
7 yrs.	91 games			

John Singleton
SINGLETON, JOHN EDWARD
B. Nov. 27, 1896, Gallipolis, OH
D. Oct. 23, 1937, Dayton, OH
None 5'11" 175 lbs.

Year	Team		Games	Pos.
1929	**DAY**	N	5	HB, QB

Nate Singleton
SINGLETON, NATE
B. Jul. 5, 1968, New Orleans, LA
Grambling State 5'11" 190 lbs.

Year	Team		Games	Pos.
1993	**SF**	N	16	WR
1994			16	WR
1995			6	WR
1996			2	WR
4 yrs.	40 games			

Ron Singleton
SINGLETON, RONALD LEE
B. Apr. 15, 1952, New Orleans, LA
Grambling State 6'7" 260 lbs.

Year	Team		Games	Pos.
1976	**SD**	N	13	OT
1977	**SF**	N	1	OT
1978			14	OT
1979			16	OT
1980			15	OT
5 yrs.	59 games			

Steve Sinko
SINKO, STEPHEN PATRICK
B. Sep. 15, 1910, Chisholm, MN
Duquesne 6'3" 232 lbs.

Year	Team		Games	Pos.
1934	**BOS**	N	10	T, G
1935			9	T
1936			11	T
3 yrs.	30 games			

Frank Sinkovitz
SINKOVITZ, FRANK BERNARD
B. May 20, 1923
D. Aug. 6, 1989, Baltimore, MD
Duke 6'1" 218 lbs.

Year	Team		Games	Pos.
1947	**PIT**		9	C
1948			9	C

Frank Sinkovitz continued

Year	Team		Games	Pos.
1949			12	C
1950			11	C
1951			12	C
1952			12	C
6 yrs.	65 games			

Frankie Sinkwich
SINKWICH, FRANCIS F.
B. Oct. 10, 1920, McKees Rocks, PA
D. Oct. 22, 1990, Athens, GA
Georgia 5'11" 190 lbs.

Year	Team		Games	Pos.
1943	**DET**	N	10	HB
1944			10	HB, QB
1946	**NY**	AA	4	HB
1947			3	B
1947	**BAL**	AA	8	B
4 yrs.	35 games			

Greg Sinnott
SINNOTT, EDWARD GREGORY
B. Aug. 29, 1964, Santa Cruz, CA
Utah State 6'7" 280 lbs.

Year	Team		Games	Pos.
1987	**LARM**	N	1	OT

John Sinnott
SINNOTT, JOHN DESMOND
B. Apr. 18, 1958, Wexford, Ireland
Brown 6'4" 275 lbs.

Year	Team		Games	Pos.
1982	**BAL**	N	9	OT

Brian Sipe
SIPE, BRIAN WINFIELD
B. Aug. 8, 1949, San Diego, CA
San Diego State 6'1" 193 lbs.

Year	Team		Games	Pos.
1974	**CLE**	N	10	QB
1975			7	QB
1976			14	QB
1977			9	QB
1978			16	QB
1979			16	QB
1980			16	QB
1981			16	QB
1982			6	QB
1983			16	QB
10 yrs.	126 games			

Tony Siragusa
SIRAGUSA, ANTHONY
B. May 14, 1967, Kenilworth, NJ
Pittsburgh 6'3" 301 lbs.

Year	Team		Games	Pos.
1990	**IND**	N	13	NT
1991			13	NT
1992			16	NT
1993			14	NT
1994			16	DT
1995			14	DT
1996			10	DT
7 yrs.	96 games			

George Sirochman
SIROCHMAN, GEORGE, JR.
B. Mar. 23, 1918, La Belle, PA
Duquesne 6'2" 215 lbs.

Year	Team		Games	Pos.
1942	**PIT**	N	2	G, C
1944	**DET**	N	8	G
2 yrs.	10 games			

Jerry Sisemore
SISEMORE, JERALD GRANT
B. Jul. 16, 1951, Olton, TX
Texas 6'4" 260 lbs.

Year	Team		Games	Pos.
1973	**PHI**	N	13	OT
1974			14	OT
1975			14	OT
1976			14	OT

Jerry Sisemore *continued*

Year	Team		Games	Pos.
1977			14	G
1978			16	G
1979			16	G, OT
1980			16	OT
1981			16	OT
1982			7	OT
1983			14	OT
1984			2	OT

12 yrs.   156 games

John Sisk

SISK, JOHN, JR.
B. Jul. 15, 1941, Milwaukee, WI
*Marquette/Miami (Florida) 6'3"
195 lbs.*

Year	Team		Games	Pos.
1964	CHI	N	3	HB, DB

Johnny Sisk

SISK, JOHN M., SR. (Big Train)
B. Dec. 11, 1906, New Haven, CT
D. May 27, 1986, Wauwatosa, WI
St. Viator/Marquette 6'2" 197 lbs.

Year	Team		Games	Pos.
1932	CHIB	N	11	HB
1933			13	HB, QB, FB
1934			8	HB
1935			12	HB, FB
1936			10	HB

5 yrs.   54 games

Brian Sisley

SISLEY, BRIAN
B. Jan. 18, 1964
South Dakota State 6'4" 235 lbs.

Year	Team		Games	Pos.
1987	NYG	N	3	DE

Scott Sisson

SISSON, SCOTT O'NEAL
B. Jul. 21, 1971, Marietta, GA
Georgia Tech 6'0" 197 lbs.

Year	Team		Games	Pos.
1993	NE	N	13	K
1996	MIN	N	16	K

2 yrs.   29 games

Manny Sistrunk

SISTRUNK, MANUEL
B. Jun. 16, 1947, Montgomery, AL
Arkansas-Pine Bluff 6'5" 269 lbs.

Year	Team		Games	Pos.
1970	WAS	N	10	DT
1971			14	DT
1972			12	DT
1973			12	DT
1974			1	DT
1975			13	DT
1976	PHI		14	DT
1977			14	DT
1978			16	DE
1979			16	DE

10 yrs.   122 games

Otis Sistrunk

SISTRUNK, OTIS (Mars)
B. Sep. 18, 1947, Columbus, GA
None 6'4" 265 lbs.

Year	Team		Games	Pos.
1972	OAK	N	14	DT
1973			14	DT
1974			14	DT
1975			14	DT
1976			14	DT
1977			12	DE
1978			16	DE

7 yrs.   98 games

Vince Sites

SITES, VINCENT J.
B. Jul. 9, 1912, Pittston, PA
D. Sep. 12, 1983, San Diego, CA

Vince Sites *continued*

Pittsburgh 6'2" 215 lbs.

Year	Team		Games	Pos.
1936	PIT	N	10	E
1937			7	E

2 yrs.   17 games

Emil Sitko

SITKO, EMIL MARTIN (Red)
B. Sep. 7, 1923, Fort Wayne, IN
D. Dec. 15, 1973, Fort Wayne, IN
Notre Dame 5'8" 183 lbs.

Year	Team		Games	Pos.
1950	SF	N	8	HB
1951	CHIC	N	11	B
1952			12	B

3 yrs.   31 games

Jim Sivell

SIVELL, RALPH JAMES (Happy)
B. Mar. 12, 1914, Chipley, GA
Auburn 5'9" 205 lbs.

Year	Team		Games	Pos.
1938	BKN	N	11	G
1939			9	G
1940			11	G
1941			11	G
1942			8	G
1944			1	G
1944	NYG	N	9	G
1945			9	G
1946	MIA	AA	10	G

8 yrs.   79 games

Mike Siwek

SIWEK, MIKE JOSEPH
B. Apr. 12, 1948, Mishawaka, IN
Western Michigan 6'3" 260 lbs.

Year	Team		Games	Pos.
1970	STL	N	2	DT

Jimmie Skaggs

SKAGGS, JIMMIE LEE
B. Jan. 3, 1940, Wetumka, OK
Washington 6'2" 246 lbs.

Year	Team		Games	Pos.
1963	PHI	N	3	DT
1964			14	G
1965			14	OT
1966			14	OT, G
1967			14	G
1969			7	G
1970			14	G
1971			10	G
1972			10	G

9 yrs.   100 games

Paul Skansi

SKANSI, PAUL ANTHONY
B. Jan. 11, 1961, Tacoma, WA
Washington 5'11" 186 lbs.

Year	Team		Games	Pos.
1983	PIT	N	15	WR
1984	SEA	N	7	WR
1985			12	WR
1986			16	WR
1987			12	WR
1988			16	WR
1989			16	WR
1990			16	WR
1991			5	WR

9 yrs.   115 games

Daryle Skaugstad

SKAUGSTAD, DARYLE
B. Apr. 8, 1957, Seattle, WA
California 6'5" 254 lbs.

Year	Team		Games	Pos.
1981	HOU	N	16	DT
1982			9	NT
1983	SF	N	3	NT
1983	GB	N	9	NT

3 yrs.   37 games

Gil Skeate

SKEATE, GILBERT
B. May 19, 1901
D. Jan., 1952
Gonzaga 5'10" 190 lbs.

Year	Team		Games	Pos.
1927	GB	N	2	FB

Doug Skene

SKENE, DOUG
B. Jun. 17, 1970, Fairview, TX
Michigan 6'6" 294 lbs.

Year	Team		Games	Pos.
1994	NE	N	6	G

Joe Skibinski

SKIBINSKI, JOSEPH J.
B. Oct. 23, 1928, Chicago, IL
Purdue 5'11" 236 lbs.

Year	Team		Games	Pos.
1952	CLE	N	12	G
1955	GB	N	12	G
1956			12	G

3 yrs.   36 games

John Skibinski

SKIBINSKI, JOHN JOSEPH
B. Apr. 27, 1955, Chicago, IL
Purdue 6'0" 222 lbs.

Year	Team		Games	Pos.
1978	CHI	N	16	RB
1979			1	RB
1980			16	RB
1981			11	RB

4 yrs.   44 games

Gerald Skinner

SKINNER, GERALD LYNN
B. Sep. 12, 1954, Malvern, AR
Arkansas 6'4" 260 lbs.

Year	Team		Games	Pos.
1978		N	15	OT

Lew Skinner

SKINNER, LEWIS B.
B. Nov., 1898
Deceased
None

Year	Team		Games	Pos.
1920	HAM	A	1	G, C
1922	EVA	N	1	FB, T

2 yrs.   2 games

Joe Skladany

SKLADANY, JOSEPH P. (Mugsy)
B. May, 1911, Larksville, PA
D. Aug. 9, 1972, Pittsburgh, PA
Pittsburgh 5'10" 210 lbs.

Year	Team		Games	Pos.
1934	PIT	N	12	E

Leo Skladany

SKLADANY, LEO B.
B. Aug. 9, 1927, Larksville, PA
Pittsburgh 6'1" 208 lbs.

Year	Team		Games	Pos.
1949	PHI	N	3	E
1950	NYG	N	4	E

2 yrs.   7 games

Tom Skladany

SKLADANY, THOMAS EDWARD
B. Jun. 29, 1955, Bethel Park, PA
Ohio State 5'11" 192 lbs.

Year	Team		Games	Pos.
1978	DET	N	16	P
1979			2	P
1980			16	P
1981			16	P
1982			7	P
1983	PHI	N	4	P

6 yrs.   61 games

John Sklopan

SKLOPAN, JOHN
B. 1941
Southern Mississippi 5'11" 190 lbs.

Year	Team		Games	Pos.
1963	DEN	A	3	DB

Stan Skoczen

SKOCZEN, STANLEY EDWARD
B. Oct. 12, 1920, Independence, OH
Case Western Reserve 5'11" 187 lbs.

Year	Team		Games	Pos.
1944	CLE	N		B

Bob Skoglund

SKOGLUND, ROBERT W.
B. Jul. 29, 1925, Chicago, IL
Notre Dame 6'1" 198 lbs.

Year	Team		Games	Pos.
1947	GB	N	9	E

Nick Skorich

SKORICH, NICHOLAS L.
B. Jun. 26, 1921, Bellaire, OH
Cincinnati 5'9" 197 lbs.

Year	Team		Games	Pos.
1946	PIT	N	8	G
1947			12	G
1948			12	G

3 yrs.   32 games

Bob Skoronski

SKORONSKI, ROBERT F.
B. Mar. 5, 1934, Ansonia, CT
Indiana 6'3" 249 lbs.

Year	Team		Games	Pos.
1956	GB	N	12	T
1959			12	T
1960			12	T
1961			13	OT
1962			13	OT
1963			14	OT
1964			14	C, OT
1965			14	OT, C
1966			14	OT
1967			14	OT
1968			14	OT

11 yrs.   146 games

Ed Skoronski

SKORONSKI, EDMUND J.
B. Oct. 15, 1911, Chicago, IL
Georgetown (DC)/Purdue 6'2" 213 lbs.

Year	Team		Games	Pos.
1935	PIT	N	3	C
1936			12	E
1937	BKN	N	5	G, T
1937	CLE	N	3	T, C

3 yrs.   23 games

John Skorupan

SKORUPAN, JOHN PAUL
B. May 17, 1951, Beaver, PA
Penn State 6'2" 222 lbs.

Year	Team		Games	Pos.
1973	BUF	N	14	LB
1974			6	LB
1975			14	LB
1976			14	LB
1977			2	LB
1978	NYG	N	16	LB
1979			14	LB
1980			12	LB

8 yrs.   92 games

Jim Skow

SKOW, JAMES JEFFREY
B. Jun. 29, 1963, Omaha, NE
Nebraska 6'3" 253 lbs.

Year	Team		Games	Pos.
1986	CIN	N	16	DE
1987			12	DE
1988			16	DE
1989			11	DE
1990	TB	N	12	DE

Jim Skow continued

Year	Team		Games	Pos.
1991	**SEA**	**N**	11	DE
1992	**SD**	**N**	1	DE
1992	**LARM**	**N**	4	DE

7 yrs. 83 games

Greg Skrepenak

SKREPENAK, GREGORY A.
B. Jan. 31, 1970, Wilkes-Barre, PA
Michigan 6'6" 315 lbs.

Year	Team		Games	Pos.
1992	**LARI**	**N**	10	OT
1994			12	OT, G
1995	**OAK**	**N**	14	OT
1996	**CAR**	**N**	16	G

4 yrs. 52 games

Dave Skudin

SKUDIN, DAVID
B. Jan. 22, 1905
D. Apr. 14, 1972, Freeport, NY
New York University 5'11" 195 lbs.

Year	Team		Games	Pos.
1929	**SI**	**N**	6	G, E

Lou Slaby

SLABY, LOUIS
B. Dec. 13, 1941, Salem, OR
Pittsburgh 6'2" 235 lbs.

Year	Team		Games	Pos.
1964	**NYG**	**N**	14	LB
1965			12	LB
1966	**DET**	**N**	13	LB

3 yrs. 39 games

Fritz Slackford

SLACKFORD, FREDERICK J.
B. Mar., 1894
Deceased
Notre Dame 6'0" 180 lbs.

Year	Team		Games	Pos.
1920	**DAY**	**A**	5	FB, HB, G
1921	**CAN**	**A**	10	HB, FB, E

2 yrs. 15 games

Chris Slade

SLADE, CHRISTOPHER CARROLL
B. Jan. 30, 1971, Newport News, VA
Virginia 6'4" 232 lbs.

Year	Team		Games	Pos.
1993	**NE**	**N**	16	LB
1994			16	LB
1995			16	LB
1996			16	LB

4 yrs. 64 games

George Slagle

SLAGLE, GEORGE
B. Aug. 9, 1898, South Dakota
D. Apr., 1983, Hollister, ID
None

Year	Team		Games	Pos.
1926	**LOU**	**N**	1	G

Duke Slater

SLATER, FREDERICK WAYMAN
B. Dec. 9, 1898, Normal, IL
D. Aug. 14, 1966, Chicago, IL
Iowa 6'1" 215 lbs.

Year	Team		Games	Pos.
1922	**RI**	**N**	7	T
1922	**MIL**	**N**	2	T
1923	**RI**	**N**	8	T
1924			8	T
1925			11	T
1926	**RI**	**A**	9	T
1926	**CHIC**	**N**	2	T
1927			11	T
1928			6	T
1929			13	T
1930			13	T
1931			9	T

10 yrs. 99 games

Howie Slater

SLATER, HOWARD WHITMAN (Dukes)
B. Mar. 9, 1903, Deer Park, WA
Washington State 5'10" 186 lbs.

Year	Team		Games	Pos.
1926	**MIL**	**N**	9	FB

Jackie Slater

SLATER, JACKIE RAY
B. May 27, 1954, Jackson, MS
Jackson State 6'4" 278 lbs.

Year	Team		Games	Pos.
1976	**LA**	**N**	14	G
1977			14	OT
1978			16	G
1979			16	G, OT
1980			15	OT
1981			11	OT
1982	**LARM**	**N**	9	OT
1983			16	OT
1984			7	OT
1985			16	OT
1986			16	OT
1987			12	OT
1988			16	OT
1989			16	OT
1990			15	OT
1991			13	OT
1992			16	OT
1993			8	OT
1994			12	OT
1995	**STL**	**N**	1	OT

20 yrs. 259 games

Mark Slater

SLATER, MARK WILLIAM
B. Feb. 1, 1955, Crosby, ND
Minnesota 6'2" 256 lbs.

Year	Team		Games	Pos.
1978	**SD**	**N**	9	C
1979	**PHI**	**N**	16	C
1980			16	C
1981			16	C
1982			9	C
1983			16	C

6 yrs. 82 games

Walt Slater

SLATER, WALTER
B. 1920
Tennessee 5'11" 187 lbs.

Year	Team		Games	Pos.
1947	**PIT**	**N**	11	HB

Mike Slaton

SLATON, MICHAEL LEE
B. Sep. 25, 1964, Sacramento, CA
South Dakota 6'2" 194 lbs.

Year	Team		Games	Pos.
1987	**MIN**	**N**	1	CB, S

Tony Slaton

SLATON, TONY TYRONE
B. Apr. 12, 1961, Merced, CA
Southern California 6'3" 265 lbs.

Year	Team		Games	Pos.
1985	**LARM**	**N**	13	C
1986			14	C
1987			11	C
1988			15	C, G
1989			15	G

5 yrs. 68 games

Chuck Slaughter

SLAUGHTER, CHUCK GARY
B. Nov. 21, 1958, Conway, SC
South Carolina 6'5" 260 lbs.

Year	Team		Games	Pos.
1982	**NO**	**N**	1	OT

Mickey Slaughter

SLAUGHTER, MILTON EUGENE
B. Aug. 22, 1941, Monroe, LA

Mickey Slaughter continued

Louisiana Tech 6'0" 190 lbs.

Year	Team		Games	Pos.
1963	**DEN**	**A**	13	QB
1964			14	QB
1965			10	QB
1966			3	QB

4 yrs. 40 games

Webster Slaughter

SLAUGHTER, WEBSTER M.
B. Oct. 19, 1964, Stockton, CA
San Diego State 6'0" 170 lbs.

Year	Team		Games	Pos.
1986	**CLE**	**N**	16	WR
1987			12	WR
1988			8	WR
1989			16	WR
1990			16	WR
1991			16	WR
1992	**HOU**	**N**	12	WR
1993			14	WR
1994			16	WR
1995	**KC**	**N**	16	WR
1996	**NYJ**	**N**	10	WR

11 yrs. 152 games

Leroy Sledge

SLEDGE, LEROY JAMES, JR.
B. Oct. 11, 1946, Richmond, VA
Bakersfield JC 6'2" 230 lbs.

Year	Team		Games	Pos.
1971	**HOU**	**N**	6	RB

Elmer Sleight

SLEIGHT, ELMER N. (Red)
B. Jul. 8, 1907
D. Aug., 1978, Naples, FL
Purdue 6'2" 226 lbs.

Year	Team		Games	Pos.
1930	**GB**	**N**	10	T, E
1931			13	T, E

2 yrs. 23 games

Richard Sligh

SLIGH, RICHARD ELLIS
B. Aug. 18, 1944, Newberry, SC
North Carolina Central 7'0" 300 lbs.

Year	Team		Games	Pos.
1967	**OAK**	**A**	8	DT

Steve Slivinski

SLIVINSKI, STEPHEN P.
B. Aug. 23, 1917, Cicero, IL
Washington 5'10" 214 lbs.

Year	Team		Games	Pos.
1939	**WAS**	**N**	11	G
1940			10	G
1941			11	G
1942			11	G
1943			9	G

5 yrs. 52 games

Bonnie Sloan

SLOAN, BONNIE RYAN
B. Jun. 1, 1948, Lebanon, TN
Austin Peay 6'5" 260 lbs.

Year	Team		Games	Pos.
1973	**STL**	**N**	4	DT

David Sloan

SLOAN, DAVID LYLE
B. Jun. 8, 1972, Fresno, CA
New Mexico 6'6" 254 lbs.

Year	Team		Games	Pos.
1995	**DET**	**N**	16	TE
1996			4	TE

2 yrs. 20 games

Dwight Sloan

SLOAN, DWIGHT (Paddlefoot)
B. 1915, Van Buren, AR
Arkansas 5'10" 180 lbs.

Year	Team		Games	Pos.
1938	**CHIC**	**N**	10	HB, QB

Dwight Sloan continued

Year	Team		Games	Pos.
1939	**DET**	**N**	10	QB
1940			11	FB, QB, HB

3 yrs. 31 games

Steve Sloan

SLOAN, STEPHEN CHARLES
B. Aug. 19, 1944, Austin, TN
Alabama 6'0" 185 lbs.

Year	Team		Games	Pos.
1966	**ATL**	**N**	3	QB
1967			5	QB

2 yrs. 8 games

Pete Slone

SLONE, PETER J.
B. Dec. 23, 1896, Pennsylvania
D. Aug., 1962
None 5'8" 180 lbs.

Year	Team		Games	Pos.
1921	**MUN**	**A**	1	E

Phil Slosburg

SLOSBURG, PHILIP J.
B. Oct. 30, 1926, Philadelphia, PA
Temple 5'10" 170 lbs.

Year	Team		Games	Pos.
1948	**BOS**	**N**	12	B
1949	**NYB**	**N**	3	B

2 yrs. 15 games

Elmer Slough

SLOUGH, ELMER (Ben)
B. Jul. 19, 1903
Oklahoma 5'8" 160 lbs.

Year	Team		Games	Pos.
1926	**BUF**	**N**	8	HB, FB

Greg Slough

SLOUGH, GREG C.
B. Feb. 26, 1948, Detroit, MI
Southern California 6'3" 230 lbs.

Year	Team		Games	Pos.
1971	**OAK**	**N**	13	LB
1972			9	LB

2 yrs. 22 games

Emil Slovacek

SLOVACEK, EMIL
B. Feb. 26, 1963
Stephen F. Austin 6'3" 300 lbs.

Year	Team		Games	Pos.
1987	**SD**	**N**	2	OT

Marty Slovak

SLOVAK, MARTIN (The Elliston Eel)
B. Dec. 25, 1916, Newport, MI
Deceased
Toledo 5'9" 179 lbs.

Year	Team		Games	Pos.
1939	**CLE**	**N**	9	HB
1940			9	HB, FB
1941			7	HB

3 yrs. 25 games

Scott Slutzker

SLUTZKER, SCOTT
B. Dec. 20, 1972, Hasbrouck Heights, NJ
Iowa 6'4" 250 lbs.

Year	Team		Games	Pos.
1996	**IND**	**N**	15	TE

Bill Slyker

SLYKER, WILLIAM V.
B. Feb. 14, 1899, Huron, OH
D. Sep. 1, 1949, Evansville, IN
Ohio State 6'1" 175 lbs.

Year	Team		Games	Pos.
1922	**EVA**	**N**	1	E

Year	Team	Games	Pos.

Stan Smagala
SMAGALA, STANLEY ADAM
B. Apr. 6, 1968, Chicago, IL
Notre Dame 5'10" 184 lbs.

Year	Team	Games	Pos.
1990	DAL	N	3	CB
1991		8	S

2 yrs. 11 games

Donovan Small
SMALL, DONOVAN O.
B. Jul. 10, 1964
Minnesota 5'11" 190 lbs.

| 1987 | HOU | N | 1 | S |

Eldridge Small
SMALL, ELDRIDGE
B. Aug. 2, 1949, Houston, TX
Texas A&I, Kingsville 6'1" 190 lbs.

1972	NYG	N	14	WR
1973		8	CB
1974		12	CB

3 yrs. 34 games

Fred Small
SMALL, JOHN FREDRICK
B. Jul. 15, 1963, Los Angeles, CA
Washington 5'11" 227 lbs.

| 1985 | PIT | N | 16 | LB |

George Small
SMALL, GEORGE MICHAEL
B. Nov. 18, 1956, Shreveport, LA
North Carolina A&T 6'2" 260 lbs.

| 1980 | NYG | N | 7 | G |

Gerald Small
SMALL, GERALD DAVID
B. Aug. 10, 1956, Washington, DC
San Jose State 5'11" 190 lbs.

1978	MIA	N	16	CB
1979		16	CB
1980		16	CB
1981		16	CB
1982		9	CB
1983		15	CB
1984	ATL	N	16	CB

7 yrs. 104 games

Jessie Small
SMALL, JESSIE
B. Nov. 30, 1966, Boston, GA
Eastern Kentucky 6'3" 239 lbs.

1989	PHI	N	16	LB
1990		15	LB
1991		16	LB
1992	PHX	N	6	LB

4 yrs. 53 games

John Small
SMALL, JOHN KENNETH
B. Nov. 20, 1946, Lumberton, NC
The Citadel 6'5" 260 lbs.

1970	ATL	N	10	LB
1971		14	LB, DT
1972		9	DT
1973	DET	N	1	DT
1974		13	LB

5 yrs. 47 games

Torrance Small
SMALL, TORRANCE RAMON
B. Sep. 6, 1970, Tampa, FL
Alcorn State 6'3" 201 lbs.

1992	NO	N	13	WR
1993		11	WR
1994		16	WR

Torrance Small continued

| 1995 | | 16 | WR |
| 1996 | | 16 | WR |

5 yrs. 72 games

Fred Smalls
SMALLS, FREDERICK
B. Jan. 7, 1963, Beaufort, SC
West Virginia 6'3" 225 lbs.

| 1987 | PHI | N | 3 | LB |

Metz Smeach
SMEACH, METZGER
B. Jun. 1, 1895
D. May, 1985, Garrettsville, OH
Georgetown (DC) 6'3" 195 lbs.

| 1921 | WAS | A | 4 | T |

Eric Smedley
SMEDLEY, ERIC
B. Jul. 23, 1973, Charleston, WV
Indiana 5'11" 199 lbs.

| 1996 | BUF | N | 6 | S |

Joel Smeenge
SMEENGE, JOEL ANDREW
B. Apr. 1, 1968, Holland, MI
Western Michigan 6'5" 253 lbs.

1990	NO	N	15	DE
1991		14	DE
1992		11	DE
1993		16	DE
1994		16	LB
1995	JAC	N	15	DE, LB
1996		10	DE

7 yrs. 97 games

Rudy Smeja
SMEJA, RUDOLPH M.
B. Dec. 1, 1920, Chicago, IL
D. Oct., 1982
Michigan 6'2" 195 lbs.

1944	CHIB	N	9	E
1945		8	E
1946	PHI	N	11	E

3 yrs. 28 games

Don Smerek
SMEREK, DONALD FREDERICK
B. Dec. 10, 1957, Waterford, MI
Nevada-Reno 6'7" 260 lbs.

1981	DAL	N	2	DE
1982		7	DT
1983		15	DT
1984		16	DT
1985		10	DT
1986		11	DT
1987		8	DT

7 yrs. 69 games

Fred Smerlas
SMERLAS, FREDERICK C.
B. Apr. 8, 1957, Waltham, MA
Boston College 6'3" 277 lbs.

1979	BUF	N	13	DT
1980		16	NT
1981		16	NT
1982		9	NT
1983		16	NT
1984		16	NT
1985		16	NT
1986		16	NT
1987		12	NT
1988		16	NT
1989		16	NT
1990	SF	N	16	NT
1991	NE	N	16	NT

Fred Smerlas continued

| 1992 | | 16 | NT |

14 yrs. 210 games

Dave Smigelsky
SMIGELSKY, DAVID WILLIAM
B. Jul. 3, 1959, Perth Amboy, NJ
Virginia Tech 5'11" 180 lbs.

| 1982 | ATL | N | 6 | P |

Bronko Smilanich
SMILANICH, BRONKO M.
B. 1916
Arizona 5'11" 180 lbs.

| 1939 | CLE | N | 2 | HB |

Tommie Smiley
SMILEY, TOMMIE B., JR.
B. Feb. 18, 1944, Port Arthur, TX
Arizona/Lamar 6'1" 235 lbs.

1968	CIN	A	8	FB
1969	DEN	A	14	RB
1970	HOU	N	7	RB

3 yrs. 29 games

Aaron Smith
SMITH, AARON CLAYTON
B. Aug. 10, 1962, Los Angeles, CA
Utah State 6'2" 223 lbs.

| 1984 | DEN | N | 10 | LB |

Al Smith
SMITH, AL FREDERICK
B. Nov. 26, 1964, Los Angeles, CA
California Poly (Pomona)/Utah State 6'1" 214 lbs.

1987	HOU	N	12	LB
1988		16	LB
1989		15	LB
1990		15	LB
1991		16	LB
1992		16	LB
1993		16	LB
1994		16	LB
1995		2	LB
1996		1	LB

10 yrs. 125 games

Allen Smith
SMITH, ALLEN
B. Oct. 7, 1942, Chattanooga, TN
Findlay 5'11" 195 lbs.

| 1966 | NY | A | 1 | HB |

Allen Smith
SMITH, ALLEN DUNCAN
B. Nov. 20, 1942, Fort Valley, GA
Fort Valley State 6'0" 200 lbs.

| 1966 | BUF | A | 14 | HB |
| 1967 | | 5 | RB |

2 yrs. 19 games

Allen Smith
SMITH, HOUSTON ALLEN
B. Mar. 29, 1922
D. Oct. 18, 1970, Hattiesburg, MS
Mississippi 6'2" 218 lbs.

| 1947 | CHIB | N | 12 | E |
| 1948 | | 10 | E |

2 yrs. 22 games

Anthony Smith
SMITH, ANTHONY WAYNE
B. Jun. 28, 1967, Elizabeth City, NC
Alabama/Arizona 6'3" 265 lbs.

| 1991 | LARI | N | 16 | DE |

Anthony Smith continued

1992		15	DE
1993		16	DE
1994		16	DE
1995	OAK	N	16	DE
1996		6	DE

6 yrs. 85 games

Artie Smith
SMITH, ARTHUR HENRY THOMPSON
B. Apr. 20, 1956, Honolulu, HI
Hawaii 6'1" 222 lbs.

| 1980 | DEN | N | 2 | LB |

Artie Smith
SMITH, ARTIE ENLOW
B. May 15, 1970, Stillwater, OK
Louisiana Tech 6'4" 303 lbs.

1993	SF	N	16	DE
1994		2	DE
1994	CIN	N	7	DT
1995		16	DE, DT
1996		16	DT

4 yrs. 57 games

Barry Smith
SMITH, BARRETT BENJAMIN
B. Jan. 15, 1951, West Palm Beach, FL
Florida State 6'1" 190 lbs.

1973	GB	N	14	WR
1974		14	WR
1975		14	WR
1976	TB	N	13	WR

4 yrs. 55 games

Barty Smith
SMITH, BARTON ELLIOTT
B. Mar. 23, 1952, Richmond, VA
Richmond 6'4" 240 lbs.

1974	GB	N	8	RB
1975		14	RB
1976		8	RB
1977		14	RB
1978		16	RB
1979		6	RB
1980		1	RB

7 yrs. 67 games

Ben Smith
SMITH, BEN H. (Big Ben)
B. Jun. 16, 1911, Haleyville, AL
Deceased
Alabama 6'3" 208 lbs.

1933	GB	N	9	E
1934	PIT	N	11	E
1935		10	E
1937	WAS	N	10	E

4 yrs. 40 games

Ben Smith
SMITH, BENJAMIN J.
B. May 14, 1967, Warner Robins, GA
Georgia 5'11" 184 lbs.

1990	PHI	N	16	S
1991		10	CB, S
1993		13	CB, S
1994	DEN	N	14	CB
1995	ARI	N	2	CB
1996		2	CB

6 yrs. 57 games

Bill Smith
SMITH, WILLIAM ARLEY
B. Jan. 3, 1912, Seattle, WA
D. Jun. 24, 1988, Desert Hot Springs, CA
Washington 6'1" 198 lbs.

| 1934 | CHIC | N | 11 | E, B |

Year	Team		Games	Pos.

Bill Smith continued

Year	Team		Games	Pos.
1935			12	E
1936			11	E
1937			9	E
1938			11	E
1939			11	E
6 yrs.	65 games			

Bill Smith
SMITH, WILLIAM GERALD
(Earthquake)
B. Oct. 23, 1926, Lexington, NC
North Carolina 6'2" 250 lbs.

1948	CHI	AA	2	T
1948	LA	AA	10	T
1 yr.	12 games			

Billy Ray Smith
SMITH, BILLY RAY, SR.
B. Jan. 27, 1935, Augusta, AR
Arkansas 6'4" 240 lbs.

1957	LA	N	12	DE
1958	PIT	N	12	DE
1959			6	DE
1960			12	DE
1961	BAL	N	14	DT
1962			13	DT
1964			13	DT
1965			14	DT
1966			14	DT
1967			14	DT
1968			14	DT
1969			14	DT
1970			14	DT
13 yrs.	166 games			

Billy Ray Smith
SMITH, BILLY RAY, JR.
B. Aug. 10, 1961, Fayetteville, AR
Arkansas 6'3" 235 lbs.

1983	SD	N	16	LB
1984			16	LB
1985			15	LB
1986			16	LB
1987			12	LB
1988			9	LB
1989			16	LB
1990			11	LB
1991			14	LB
1992			1	LB
10 yrs.	126 games			

Blaine Smith
SMITH, BLAINE
B. Dec. 22, 1959, Houston, TX
Southern Methodist 5'10" 190 lbs.

1987	KC	N	3	S

Bob Smith
SMITH, ROBERT
B. Feb. 23, 1933, Council Bluffs, IA
Nebraska 5'10" 195 lbs.

1955	CLE	N	12	HB
1956			2	HB
1956	PHI	N	4	HB
2 yrs.	18 games			

Bob Smith
SMITH, ROBERT
B. Dec. 28, 1945, Williamson, WV
Miami (Ohio) 6'0" 180 lbs.

1968	HOU	A	6	DB

Bob Smith
SMITH, ROBERT LEE
B. Feb. 28, 1929, Houston, TX
Texas A&M 6'0" 205 lbs.

1953	DET	N	3	FB

Bob Smith continued

1954			11	FB
2 yrs.	14 games			

Bobby Smith
SMITH, BOBBY
B. Jul. 5, 1938, Plain Dealing, LA
UCLA 6'0" 193 lbs.

1962	LA	N	14	DB
1963			14	DB
1964			14	DB
1965			7	DB
1965	DET	N	6	DB
1966			14	DB
5 yrs.	69 games			

Bobby Smith
SMITH, BOBBY
B. May 18, 1942, Corpus Christi, TX
North Texas State 6'0" 203 lbs.

1964	BUF	A	14	HB
1965			14	HB
1966	PIT	N	8	RB
3 yrs.	36 games			

Brad Smith
SMITH, BRAD
B. Sep. 5, 1969, Houston, TX
Texas Christian 6'2" 228 lbs.

1993	CIN	N	7	LB

Brady Smith
SMITH, BRADY MCKAY
B. Jun. 5, 1973, Royal Oak, MI
Colorado State 6'5" 260 lbs.

1996	NO	N	16	DE

Brian Smith
SMITH, BRIAN MARK
B. Apr. 23, 1966, Brooklyn, NY
Auburn 6'6" 242 lbs.

1989	LARM	N	3	LB
1990			16	LB, DT
2 yrs.	19 games			

Bruce Smith
SMITH, BRUCE BERNARD
B. Jun. 18, 1963, Norfolk, VA
Virginia Tech 6'4" 283 lbs.

1985	BUF	N	16	DE
1986			16	DE
1987			12	DE
1988			12	DE
1989			16	DE
1990			16	DE
1991			5	DE
1992			15	DE
1993			16	DE
1994			15	DE
1995			15	DE
1996			16	DE
12 yrs.	170 games			

Bruce Smith
SMITH, BRUCE P. (Boo)
B. Feb. 8, 1920, Faribault, MN
D. Aug. 28, 1967, Alexandria, MN
Minnesota 6'0" 197 lbs.

1945	GB	N	3	HB
1946			6	HB
1947			10	HB
1948			4	HB
1948	LA	N	8	HB
4 yrs.	31 games			

Bubba Smith
SMITH, CHARLES AARON
B. Feb. 28, 1945, Orange, TX
Michigan State 6'7" 280 lbs.

1967	BAL	N	13	DE, DT
1968			14	DE
1969			14	DE
1970			14	DE
1971			14	DE
1973	OAK	N	14	DE
1974			14	DE
1975	HOU	N	12	DE
1976			4	DE
9 yrs.	113 games			

Byron Smith
SMITH, BYRON KEITH
B. Dec. 21, 1962, Los Angeles, CA
California 6'5" 272 lbs.

1984	IND	N	3	DE
1985			16	DE
2 yrs.	19 games			

Carl Smith
SMITH, CARL E.
B. 1935
Tennessee 6'0" 200 lbs.

1960	BUF	A		FB

Cedric Smith
SMITH, CEDRIC C. (Pat)
B. Aug. 9, 1895
D. Nov., 1976, Delray Beach, FL
Michigan 6'0" 198 lbs.

1920	BUF	A	6	FB, HB
1921			11	FB
1923	BUF	N	1	FB
3 yrs.	18 games			

Cedric Smith
SMITH, CEDRIC DELON
B. May 27, 1968, Enterprise, AL
Florida 5'10" 223 lbs.

1990	MIN	N	15	RB
1991	NO	N	6	RB
1994	WAS	N	14	RB
1995			6	RB
1996	ARI	N	15	RB
5 yrs.	56 games			

Charley Smith
SMITH, CHARLES
B. 1933, Sweetwater, TX
Abilene Christian 6'2" 205 lbs.

1956	SF	N	12	E

Charlie Smith
SMITH, CHARLES
B. Jul. 26, 1950, Monroe, LA
Grambling State 6'1" 185 lbs.

1974	PHI	N	14	WR
1975			14	WR
1976			14	WR
1977			14	WR
1978			14	WR
1979			16	WR
1980			16	WR
1981			16	WR
8 yrs.	118 games			

Charlie Smith
SMITH, CHARLES HARLIN
B. Mar. 13, 1924, Aldrich, MO
Georgia 5'11" 170 lbs.

1947	CHIC	N	7	HB

Charlie Smith
SMITH, CHARLES HENRY
B. Jan. 18, 1946, Natchez, MS
Utah 6'1" 205 lbs.

1968	OAK	A	14	RB
1969			14	RB
1970	OAK	N	14	RB
1971			8	RB
1972			14	RB
1973			14	RB
1974			13	RB
1975	SD	N	4	RB
8 yrs.	95 games			

Chris Smith
SMITH, CHRIS MONTANE
B. Jun. 1, 1963, Cincinnati, OH
Notre Dame 6'1" 222 lbs.

1986	KC	N	1	RB
1987			3	RB
2 yrs.	4 games			

Chuck Smith
SMITH, CHARLES HENRY
B. Dec. 21, 1969, Athens, GA
Tennessee 6'2" 248 lbs.

1992	ATL	N	16	DE
1993			15	DE
1994			15	DE
1995			14	DE
1996			15	DE
5 yrs.	75 games			

Clyde Smith
SMITH, CLYDE W.
B. Jul. 17, 1904, Steelville, MO
D. Dec., 1982, Lawrenceville, IL
Missouri 5'10" 181 lbs.

1925	KC	N	1	G
1926			9	C
1927	CLE	N	12	C
1928	PRO	N	11	C
4 yrs.	33 games			

Dallis Smith
SMITH, DALLIS
B. Jul. 31, 1965
Valdosta State 5'11" 170 lbs.

1987	SEA	N	3	S

Dan Smith
SMITH, DANIEL
B. 1935
Northeastern Oklahoma 5'10" 180 lbs.

1961	DEN	A	4	DB

Darrin Smith
SMITH, DARRIN ANDREW
B. Apr. 15, 1970, Miami, FL
Miami (Florida) 6'1" 227 lbs.

1993	DAL	N	16	LB
1994			16	LB
1995			9	LB
1996			16	LB
4 yrs.	57 games			

Daryl Smith
SMITH, DARYL DIMITRI
B. May 8, 1963, Opelika, AL
North Alabama 5'9" 186 lbs.

1987	CIN	N	3	CB
1988			7	CB
1989	MIN	N	5	CB
3 yrs.	15 games			

Year	Team	Games	Pos.

Daryle Smith
SMITH, DARYLE RAY
B. Jan. 18, 1964, Knoxville, TN
Tennessee 6'5" 277 lbs.

Year	Team		Games	Pos.
1987	DAL	N	9	OT
1988			14	OT
1989	CLE	N	4	OT
1990	PHI	N	3	OT
1991			14	OT
1992			16	OT
6 yrs.	60 games			

Dave Smith
SMITH, DAVID
B. Mar. 23, 1937, Milwaukee, WI
Ripon 6'1" 209 lbs.

Year	Team		Games	Pos.
1960	HOU	A	14	FB
1961			14	FB
1962			14	FB
1963			14	FB
1964			9	FB
5 yrs.	65 games			

Dave Smith
SMITH, DAVID
B. Dec. 9, 1947, Salt Lake City, UT
Utah 6'0" 210 lbs.

Year	Team		Games	Pos.
1970	SD	N	7	RB

Dave Smith
SMITH, DAVID ALLAN
B. Dec. 12, 1964, Hammond, IN
Southern Illinois 6'7" 290 lbs.

Year	Team		Games	Pos.
1988	CIN	N	14	OT

Dave Smith
SMITH, DAVID LEWIS
B. May 18, 1947, New York, NY
Waynesburg/Indiana (Pennsylvania) 6'2" 205 lbs.

Year	Team		Games	Pos.
1970	PIT	N	14	WR
1971			14	WR
1972			6	WR
1972	HOU	N	2	WR
1973	KC	N	3	WR
4 yrs.	39 games			

Dennis Smith
SMITH, DENNIS
B. Feb. 3, 1959, Santa Monica, CA
Southern California 6'3" 200 lbs.

Year	Team		Games	Pos.
1981	DEN	N	16	S
1982			8	S
1983			14	S
1984			15	S
1985			13	S
1986			14	S
1987			6	S
1988			11	S
1989			14	S
1990			15	S
1991			16	S
1992			16	S
1993			14	S
1994			12	S
14 yrs.	184 games			

Dennis Smith
SMITH, DENNIS
B. Feb. 14, 1967, Hemet, CA
Utah 6'0" 230 lbs.

Year	Team		Games	Pos.
1990	PHX	N	4	RB

Detron Smith
SMITH, DETRON NEGIL
B. Feb. 25, 1974, Dallas, TX
Texas A&M 5'9" 231 lbs.

Year	Team		Games	Pos.
1996	DEN	N	13	RB

Dick Smith
SMITH, RICHARD HENRY
B. Jun. 18, 1944, Hamilton, OH
Northwestern 6'0" 205 lbs.

Year	Team		Games	Pos.
1967	WAS	N	10	DB
1968			10	DB, HB
2 yrs.	20 games			

Dick Smith
SMITH, RICHARD S.
B. Jan. 29, 1912
D. Apr. 5, 1980, New Canaan, CT
Ohio State 6'2" 225 lbs.

Year	Team		Games	Pos.
1933	CHIB	N	1	E

Don Smith
SMITH, DONALD (Dinny)
None

Year	Team		Games	Pos.
1930	NEW	N	3	G

Don Smith
SMITH, DONALD
B. 1943
Florida A&M 6'4" 240 lbs.

Year	Team		Games	Pos.
1967	DEN	A	2	G

Don Smith
SMITH, DONALD LOREN
B. May 9, 1957, Oakland, CA
Miami (Florida) 6'5" 260 lbs.

Year	Team		Games	Pos.
1979	ATL	N	16	DE
1980			16	DE
1981			16	NT
1982			9	NT
1983			14	NT
1984			16	DT
1985	BUF	N	16	NT
1986			5	NT
1987	NYJ	N	3	DE
9 yrs.	111 games			

Don Smith
SMITH, DONALD MICHAEL
B. Oct. 30, 1963, Hamilton, MS
Mississippi State 5'11" 195 lbs.

Year	Team		Games	Pos.
1988	TB	N	10	RB
1989			11	RB
1990	BUF	N	16	RB
3 yrs.	37 games			

Donald Smith
SMITH, DONALD RAY
B. Feb. 21, 1968, Danville, VA
Liberty 5'11" 189 lbs.

Year	Team		Games	Pos.
1991	DAL	N	3	CB, S

Donnell Smith
SMITH, DONNELL
B. May 25, 1949, Lakeland, FL
Southern University 6'4" 247 lbs.

Year	Team		Games	Pos.
1971	GB	N	5	DE
1973	NE	N	12	DE
1974			11	DE
3 yrs.	28 games			

Doug Smith
SMITH, CARL DOUGLAS
B. Nov. 25, 1956, Columbus, OH
Bowling Green 6'3" 259 lbs.

Year	Team		Games	Pos.
1978	LA	N	16	C
1979			4	C, G
1980			8	C, G
1981			16	C, G
1982	LARM	N	9	C, G
1983			14	C
1984			16	C
1985			13	C

Doug Smith continued

Year	Team	Games	Pos.
1986		16	C
1987		12	C
1988		16	C
1989		16	C
1990		16	C
1991		15	C
14 yrs.	187 games		

Doug Smith
SMITH, DOUGLAS
B. Feb. 4, 1963
Ohio State 6'0" 192 lbs.

Year	Team		Games	Pos.
1987	NYG	N	3	CB

Doug Smith
SMITH, DOUGLAS ARTHUR
B. Jun. 13, 1959, Mesic, NC
Auburn 6'4" 294 lbs.

Year	Team		Games	Pos.
1985	HOU	N	11	NT
1986			13	NT
1987			14	DT
1988			12	NT
1989			15	NT
1990			14	NT
1991			15	DT
1992			6	DT
8 yrs.	100 games			

Duke Smith
SMITH, DUKE
None 6'0" 195 lbs.

Year	Team		Games	Pos.
1922	GB	N	2	E

Ed Smith
SMITH, ED
B. Oct. 23, 1950, Nassau, Bahamas
Colorado College 6'5" 241 lbs.

Year	Team		Games	Pos.
1973	DEN	N	5	DE
1974			14	DE
2 yrs.	19 games			

Ed Smith
SMITH, EDWARD
B. Jun. 17, 1913, New York, NY
New York University 6'2" 207 lbs.

Year	Team		Games	Pos.
1936	BOS	N	8	FB
1937	GB	N	1	B
2 yrs.	9 games			

Ed Smith
SMITH, HENRY EDWARD, IV
B. May 18, 1957, Knoxville, TN
Vanderbilt 6'2" 217 lbs.

Year	Team		Games	Pos.
1980	BAL	N	16	LB
1981			16	LB
2 yrs.	32 games			

Ed Smith
SMITH, OSCAR EDWIN, JR.
B. Jul. 20, 1923, Fort Monroe, VA
Texas-El Paso 6'3" 185 lbs.

Year	Team		Games	Pos.
1948	GB	N	12	HB
1949	NYB	N	8	B
2 yrs.	20 games			

Elliot Smith
SMITH, ELLIOT
B. Aug. 14, 1967, Jackson, MS
Alcorn State 6'2" 192 lbs.

Year	Team		Games	Pos.
1989	SD	N	2	CB, S
1990	DEN	N	9	CB
2 yrs.	11 games			

Emmitt Smith
SMITH, EMMITT

Emmitt Smith continued
B. May 15, 1969, Pensacola, FL
Florida 5'9" 203 lbs.

Year	Team		Games	Pos.
1990	DAL	N	16	RB
1991			16	RB
1992			16	RB
1993			14	RB
1994			15	RB
1995			16	RB
1996			15	RB
7 yrs.	108 games			

Ernie Smith
SMITH, ERNEST
B. 1933
Compton JC 6'3" 190 lbs.

Year	Team		Games	Pos.
1955	SF	N	1	HB
1956			3	HB
2 yrs.	4 games			

Ernie Smith
SMITH, ERNEST FREDERICK
B. Nov. 26, 1909, Spearfish, SD
D. Apr. 25, 1985, Altadena, CA
Southern California 6'2" 224 lbs.

Year	Team		Games	Pos.
1935	GB	N	12	T
1936			12	T, G
1937			11	T
1939			6	T
4 yrs.	41 games			

Fernando Smith
SMITH, FERNANDO DEWITT
B. Aug. 2, 1971, Flint, MI
Jackson State 6'6" 270 lbs.

Year	Team		Games	Pos.
1994	MIN	N	7	DE
1995			12	DE
1996			16	DE
3 yrs.	35 games			

Fletcher Smith
SMITH, FLETCHER LEON
B. Oct. 10, 1943, Hearne, TX
Tennessee State 6'2" 182 lbs.

Year	Team		Games	Pos.
1966	KC	A	11	DB
1967			13	DB
1968	CIN	A	14	DB
1969			14	CB
1970	CIN	N	14	CB
1971			14	CB
6 yrs.	80 games			

Francis Smith
SMITH, FRANCIS
B. 1903
Holy Cross 5'8" 189 lbs.

Year	Team		Games	Pos.
1926	BOS	A	5	C, E

Frankie Smith
SMITH, FRANKIE
B. Oct. 8, 1968, Groesbeck, TX
Baylor 5'9" 186 lbs.

Year	Team		Games	Pos.
1993	MIA	N	5	CB
1994			13	CB, S
1995			11	CB
1996	SF	N	14	CB
4 yrs.	43 games			

Franky Smith
SMITH, FRANKY LEE
B. Jan. 16, 1956, Birmingham, AL
Alabama A&M 6'6" 279 lbs.

Year	Team		Games	Pos.
1980	KC	N	4	OT

Gary Smith
SMITH, GARY LOVELL

Year	Team		Games	Pos.

Gary Smith *continued*
B. Jan. 27, 1960, Bitburg AFB, Germany
Virginia Tech 6'2" 265 lbs.

1984	CIN	N	8	G

Gaylon Smith
SMITH, GAYLON
B. Jul. 15, 1916, Lonoke, AR
Southwestern (Memphis) 5'11" 202 lbs.

1940	CLE	N	11	QB, HB
1941			4	FB
1942			10	FB, HB
1946	CLE	AA	14	FB
4 yrs.		39 games		

Gene Smith
SMITH, HENRY EUGENE
B. Sep. 25, 1905, Montgomery, AL
D. Dec. 10, 1979, Atlanta, GA
Georgia 6'9" 190 lbs.

1930	FRA	N	1	G
1930	POR	N	4	C, G
1 yr.		5 games		

George Smith
SMITH, GEORGE
B. 1921
Villanova 6'1" 200 lbs.

1943	CHIC	N	3	B

George Smith
SMITH, GEORGE WILLIAM
B. Jun. 13, 1914, Los Angeles, CA
D. Mar. 5, 1986, Walnut Creek, CA
California 6'2" 220 lbs.

1937	WAS	N	7	C
1941			9	C
1942			3	C
1943			9	C
1944	BKN	N	10	C
1945	BOS	N	10	C
1947	SF	AA	10	C
7 yrs.		58 games		

Gordon Smith
SMITH, GORDON CHILTON
B. Apr. 9, 1939, Douglas, AZ
Arizona State/Missouri 6'2" 211 lbs.

1961	MIN	N	9	OE
1962			5	OE
1963			14	OE
1964			12	OE
1965			14	OE
5 yrs.		54 games		

Greg Smith
SMITH, GREGORY
B. Oct. 22, 1959, Chicago, IL
Kansas 6'3" 261 lbs.

1984	MIN	N	16	NT

Hal Smith
SMITH, HAL
B. 1936
UCLA 6'5" 250 lbs.

1960	BOS	A		DT
1960	DEN	A		DT
1961	OAK	A	8	DT
2 yrs.		8 games		

Hank Smith
SMITH, HENRY
B. Jul. 3, 1893
D. Feb., 1985, Buffalo, NY
None 6'1" 190 lbs.

1920	ROC	A	1	G

Hank Smith *continued*

1921			6	G, C
1922	ROC	N	5	T, C, HB
1923			2	C
1923	RI	N	3	G
1924	ROC	N	6	C
1925			5	C
6 yrs.		28 games		

Harry Smith
SMITH, HARRY E.
B. Aug. 26, 1918, Russellville, MO
Southern California 5'11" 215 lbs.

1940	DET	N	10	T, G

Herman Smith
SMITH, HERMAN
B. Jan. 25, 1971, Fort Lauderdale, FL
Portland State 6'5" 261 lbs.

1995	TB	N	3	DE
1996			5	DE
2 yrs.		8 games		

Holden Smith
SMITH, HOLDEN EUGENE
B. Nov. 5, 1958, San Jose, CA
California 6'1" 191 lbs.

1982	BAL	N	3	WR

Hugh Smith
SMITH, HUGH
B. 1938
Kansas 6'4" 215 lbs.

1962	WAS	N	2	OE

Irv Smith
SMITH, IRVIN MARTIN
B. Oct. 13, 1971, Trenton, NJ
Notre Dame 6'3" 246 lbs.

1993	NO	N	16	TE
1994			16	TE
1995			16	TE
1996			7	TE
4 yrs.		55 games		

Jack Smith
SMITH, JACK
B. Dec. 4, 1947, Ocilla, GA
Memphis State/Troy State 6'4" 204 lbs.

1971	PHI	N	5	DB

Jack Smith
SMITH, JOHN
B. Aug. 11, 1917, Los Angeles, CA
Stanford 6'1" 200 lbs.

1942	PHI	N	6	E, T
1943	WAS	N	5	E
2 yrs.		11 games		

Jackie Smith
SMITH, JACKIE LARUE
B. Feb. 23, 1940, Columbia, MS
Northwestern State (Louisiana) 6'4" 225 lbs.

1963	STL	N	14	HB
1964			14	OE, P
1965			14	OE, P
1966			14	TE, P
1967			14	TE
1968			14	TE
1969			14	TE
1970			14	TE
1971			9	TE
1972			14	TE
1973			14	TE
1974			14	TE
1975			9	TE

Jackie Smith *continued*

1976			12	TE
1977			14	TE
1978	DAL	N	12	TE
16 yrs.		210 games		

J.D. Smith
SMITH, J.D.
B. Jul. 19, 1932, Greenville, SC
North Carolina A&T 6'1" 205 lbs.

1956	CHIB		12	HB
1956	SF	N	5	HB
1957			12	HB
1958			12	FB
1959			12	HB
1960			12	HB
1961			14	HB
1962			14	HB
1963			14	HB
1964			2	FB
1965	DAL	N	14	FB
1966			14	FB
11 yrs.		137 games		

J.D. Smith
SMITH, JAMES (Jetstream)
B. 1938
Compton JC 6'0" 215 lbs.

1960	OAK	A	14	FB
1961	CHI	N	3	HB
2 yrs.		17 games		

J.D. Smith
SMITH, JESSE D.
B. May 27, 1936, Redland Springs, TX
Rice 6'5" 250 lbs.

1959	PHI	N	11	T
1960			12	T
1961			14	OT
1962			14	OT
1963			14	OT
1964	DET	N	7	OT
1966			14	OT
7 yrs.		86 games		

Jeff Smith
SMITH, JEFF
B. Nov. 12, 1943, Freeport, LA
Southern California 6'0" 237 lbs.

1966	NYG	N	14	LB

Jeff Smith
SMITH, JEFF
B. May 25, 1973, Decatur, TN
Tennessee 6'3" 334 lbs.

1996	KC	N	1	C

Jeff Smith
SMITH, JEFF K.
B. Mar. 22, 1962, Wichita, KS
Nebraska 5'9" 201 lbs.

1985	KC	N	13	RB
1986			15	RB
1987	TB	N	12	RB
1988			16	RB
4 yrs.		56 games		

Jeff Smith
SMITH, JEFFREY
B. May 4, 1962
Earlham 6'4" 248 lbs.

1987	CIN	N	3	DE

Jeff Smith
SMITH, JEFFREY
B. Dec. 28, 1962
Tennessee 6'3" 240 lbs.

1987	NYG	N	3	TE

Jerry Smith
SMITH, GERALD THOMAS
B. Jul. 19, 1944, Eugene, OR
Arizona State 6'2" 209 lbs.

1965	WAS	N	14	OE
1966			14	TE
1967			14	TE
1968			13	TE
1969			14	TE
1970			14	TE
1971			8	TE
1972			14	TE
1973			13	TE
1974			14	TE
1975			14	TE
1976			13	TE
1977			9	TE
13 yrs.		168 games		

Jerry Smith
SMITH, JEROME A.
B. Sep. 9, 1930, Dayton, OH
Wisconsin 6'1" 230 lbs.

1952	SF	N	12	G
1953			12	G
1956			2	G
1956	GB	N	3	G
3 yrs.		29 games		

Jim Smith
SMITH, JAMES
B. 1924
Colorado 6'4" 270 lbs.

1947	LA	AA	7	T

Jim Smith
SMITH, JAMES ARTHUR, JR.
B. Jul. 20, 1955, Harvey, IL
Michigan 6'2" 205 lbs.

1977	PIT	N	14	WR
1978			9	WR
1979			15	WR
1980			12	WR
1981			15	WR
1982			8	WR
1985	LARI		6	WR
7 yrs.		79 games		

Jim Smith
SMITH, JAMES MCCOY
B. Nov. 4, 1946, Yazoo, MS
Oregon 6'3" 195 lbs.

1968	WAS	N	14	DB

Jim Smith
SMITH, JAMES ROBERT (Masked Marvel)
B. Aug. 20, 1925, Ranger, TX
Iowa 6'1" 191 lbs.

1948	BUF	AA	3	B
1948	BKN	AA	10	B
1949	CHI	AA	3	B
1949	DET	N	12	HB
1950			12	HB
1951			12	HB
1952			12	HB
1953			12	HB
6 yrs.		76 games		

Jimmy Smith
SMITH, JAMES
B. Sep. 25, 1960, Kankakee, IL
Elon 6'0" 205 lbs.

1984	WAS	N	1	RB
1984	LARI	N	7	RB
1 yr.		8 games		

Year	Team	Games	Pos.

Jimmy Smith
SMITH, JAMES
B. 1961
Purdue 5'11" 190 lbs.

1987	MIN	N	1	RB

Jimmy Smith
SMITH, JAMES EARL
B. Jul. 12, 1945, Stockton, CA
Utah State 6'3" 190 lbs.

1969	DEN	A	2	S

Jimmy Smith
SMITH, JIMMY LEE, JR.
B. Feb. 9, 1969, Detroit, MI
Jackson State 6'1" 205 lbs.

1992	DAL	N	7	WR
1994	PHI	N	1	WR
1995	JAC	N	16	WR
1996			16	WR
4 yrs.	40 games			

Jim Ray Smith
SMITH, JAMES RAY, SR.
B. Feb. 27, 1932, West Columbia, TX
Baylor 6'3" 241 lbs.

1956	CLE	N	6	DE
1957			12	G
1958			12	G
1959			12	G
1960			12	G
1961			14	G
1962			13	G
1963	DAL	N	8	G
1964			4	G, OT
9 yrs.	93 games			

Joe Smith
SMITH, JOE H.
B. Jul. 23, 1922, Electra, TX
Deceased
Texas Tech 6'1" 183 lbs.

1948	BAL	AA	12	E

Joey Smith
SMITH, JOEY
B. May 30, 1969, Knoxville, TN
Louisville 5'10" 177 lbs.

1991	NYG	N	1	WR
1992			16	WR
2 yrs.	17 games			

John Smith
SMITH, JOHN HENRY
B. Jan. 27, 1956, Tuskegee, AL
Tennessee State 6'0" 175 lbs.

1979	CLE	N	6	WR

John Smith
SMITH, JOHN MICHAEL
B. Dec. 30, 1949, Leafield, England
Southampton (England) 6'0" 186 lbs.*

1974	NE	N	14	K
1975			14	K
1976			14	K
1977			14	K
1978			3	K
1979			16	K
1980			16	K
1981			16	K
1982			4	K
1983			5	K
10 yrs.	116 games			

Johnny Ray Smith
SMITH, JOHNNY RAY

Johnny Ray Smith cont.
B. Sep. 7, 1957, Crockett, TX
Lamar 5'9" 185 lbs.

1982	TB	N	9	S
1983			16	CB
1984	SD	N	1	CB
3 yrs.	26 games			

J.T. Smith
SMITH, JOHN THOMAS
B. Oct. 29, 1955, Leonard, TX
North Texas State 6'2" 185 lbs.

1978	WAS	N	6	WR
1978	KC	N	6	WR
1979			16	WR
1980			16	WR
1981			16	WR
1982			5	WR
1983			9	WR
1984			15	WR
1985	STL	N	14	WR
1986			16	WR
1987			15	WR
1988	PHX	N	16	WR
1989			9	WR
1990			13	WR
13 yrs.	172 games			

Ken Smith
SMITH, KEN JAMES
B. Oct. 16, 1960, Indianapolis, IN
Evansville/Miami (Ohio) 6'1" 285 lbs.

1987	CIN	N	3	G

Ken Smith
SMITH, KENNETH L.
B. Jul. 25, 1951, Houston, TX
New Mexico 6'4" 225 lbs.

1973	CLE	N	13	TE

Kendal Smith
SMITH, KENDAL CARSON
B. Nov. 23, 1965, San Mateo, CA
Utah State 5'9" 189 lbs.

1989	CIN	N	11	WR
1990			9	WR
2 yrs.	20 games			

Kevin Smith
SMITH, KEVIN ANTHONY
B. Apr. 2, 1967, Newport, RI
Rhode Island 5'11" 204 lbs.

1991	PIT	N	16	S

Kevin Smith
SMITH, KEVIN LINN
B. Jul. 25, 1969, Bakersfield, CA
UCLA 6'4" 255 lbs.

1992	LARI	N	1	TE
1993			10	TE
1994			3	TE
1996	GB	N	1	TE
4 yrs.	15 games			

Kevin Smith
SMITH, KEVIN REY
B. Apr. 7, 1970, Orange, TX
Texas A&M 5'11" 177 lbs.

1992	DAL	N	16	CB
1993			16	CB
1994			16	CB
1995			1	CB
1996			16	CB
5 yrs.	65 games			

Lamar Smith
SMITH, LAMAR
B. Nov. 29, 1970, Fort Wayne, IN
Houston 5'11" 230 lbs.

1994	SEA	N	2	RB
1995			13	RB
1996			16	RB
3 yrs.	31 games			

Lance Smith
SMITH, LANCE
B. Jan. 1, 1963, Kannapolis, NC
Louisiana State 6'2" 279 lbs.

1985	STL	N	14	G
1986			15	G
1987			15	OT
1988	PHX	N	16	G
1989			16	OT, G
1990			16	G
1991			16	G
1992			16	G
1993			16	G
1994	NYG	N	13	G
1995			13	G
1996			16	G
12 yrs.	182 games			

Larry Smith
SMITH, LARRY
B. Feb. 7, 1965
Kentucky 6'1" 200 lbs.

1987	HOU	N	3	LB

Larry Smith
SMITH, WILLIAM LAWRENCE
B. Sep. 2, 1947, Tampa, FL
Florida 6'3" 220 lbs.

1969	LA	N	14	RB
1970			11	RB
1971			14	RB
1972			12	RB
1973			14	RB
1974	WAS	N	6	RB
6 yrs.	71 games			

Laverne Smith
SMITH, LAVERNE
B. Sep. 12, 1954, Greenwood, MS
Kansas 5'10" 193 lbs.

1977	PIT	N	7	RB

Len Smith
SMITH, LEONARD M. (Fat)
B. Dec. 14, 1896
Deceased
Wisconsin 5'11" 195 lbs.

1923	RAC	N	2	T
1923	CHIC	N	1	G
1923	RAC	N	7	T
1924			10	T
2 yrs.	20 games			

Leonard Smith
SMITH, LEONARD PHILLIP
B. Sep. 2, 1960, New Orleans, LA
McNeese State 5'11" 200 lbs.

1983	STL	N	16	CB
1984			12	S
1985			16	S
1986			16	S
1987			15	S
1988	PHX	N	3	S
1988	BUF	N	13	S
1989			15	S
1990			16	S
1991			16	S
9 yrs.	138 games			

Lucious Smith
SMITH, LUCIOUS IRVIN
B. Jan. 17, 1957, Columbus, GA
San Diego State/Fullerton State 5'10" 190 lbs.

1980	LA	N	16	CB
1981			16	CB
1982	LARM	N	8	CB
1983	KC	N	16	CB
1984	BUF	N	4	CB
1984	SD	N	9	CB
1985			5	CB
6 yrs.	74 games			

Lyman Smith
SMITH, LYMAN SCOTT-WILLIAM
B. Sep. 24, 1956, Portland, OR
Duke 6'5" 250 lbs.

1978	MIN	N	11	DT

Marty Smith
SMITH, MARTY J.
B. Oct. 20, 1953, Pattison, MS
Louisville 6'3" 250 lbs.

1976	BUF	N	14	DT

Marv Smith
SMITH, MARVIN M.
B. Apr. 15, 1898
D. Apr. 24, 1986, Muncie, IN
Purdue 5'11" 185 lbs.

1921	CAN	A	1	HB

Matt Smith
SMITH, MATT
B. Sep. 1, 1965
West Virginia 6'2" 234 lbs.

1987	DEN	N	3	LB

Michael Smith
SMITH, MICHAEL CHARLES, JR.
B. Nov. 21, 1970, New Orleans, LA
Kansas State 5'8" 160 lbs.

1992	KC	N	2	WR

Mike Smith
SMITH, MICHAEL T.
B. Apr. 28, 1958, Bastrop, LA
Grambling State 5'10" 194 lbs.

1980	ATL	N	5	WR

Mike Smith
SMITH, MICHAEL WAYNE
B. Oct. 24, 1962, Houston, TX
Texas-El Paso 6'0" 171 lbs.

1985	MIA	N	7	CB, S
1986			14	CB
1987			8	CB
3 yrs.	29 games			

Milt Smith
SMITH, MILTON (Snuffy)
B. Dec. 22, 1918
D. Oct. 1, 1988, Landrum, SC
UCLA 6'3" 185 lbs.

1945	PHI	N	5	E

Monte Smith
SMITH, MONTE GENE
B. Apr. 24, 1967, Madison, WI
North Dakota 6'5" 270 lbs.

1989	DEN	N	14	G

Year	Team	Games	Pos.

Neil Smith
SMITH, NEIL
B. Apr. 10, 1966, New Orleans, LA
Nebraska 6'4" 271 lbs.

Year	Team		Games	Pos.
1988	KC	N	13	DE
1989			15	DE
1990			16	DE
1991			16	DE
1992			16	DE
1993			16	DE
1994			14	DE
1995			16	DE
1996			16	DE
9 yrs.	138 games			

Noland Smith
SMITH, NOLAND (Super Gnat)
B. Oct. 20, 1943, Jackson, MS
Tennessee State 5'6" 155 lbs.

Year	Team		Games	Pos.
1967	KC	A	14	FL
1968			12	FL
1969				FL
1969	SF	N	7	RB
3 yrs.	33 games			

Oke Smith
SMITH, OKLA E. (Oak)
B. Feb. 27, 1894
D. May 2, 1974, Long Beach, CA
Drake 6'2" 185 lbs.

Year	Team		Games	Pos.
1920	RI	A	7	E, FB
1921			6	E
2 yrs.	13 games			

Olin Smith
SMITH, OLIN BASHFORD
B. Mar. 25, 1900
Ohio Wesleyan 6'1" 230 lbs.

Year	Team		Games	Pos.
1924	CLE	N	8	T, G

Ollie Smith
SMITH, OLLIE P.
B. Mar. 8, 1949, Jackson, MS
Tennessee State 6'2" 198 lbs.

Year	Team		Games	Pos.
1973	BAL	N	7	WR
1974			1	WR
1976	GB	N	13	WR
1977			12	WR
4 yrs.	33 games			

Orland Smith
SMITH, ORLAND FRANCIS
B. Nov. 5, 1905, Gorham, NE
D. Aug., 1977, Esmond, RI
Brown 5'11" 203 lbs.

Year	Team		Games	Pos.
1927	PRO	N	13	T, G
1928			9	T, E
1929			9	T, G, E
3 yrs.	31 games			

Oscar Smith
SMITH, OSCAR E.
B. Apr. 5, 1963, Tampa, FL
Nicholls State 5'9" 203 lbs.

Year	Team		Games	Pos.
1986	DET	N	2	RB

Otis Smith
SMITH, OTIS
B. Oct. 22, 1965, New Orleans, LA
Missouri 5'11" 184 lbs.

Year	Team		Games	Pos.
1991	PHI	N	15	CB
1992			16	CB
1993			15	CB
1994			16	CB, S
1995	NYJ	N	11	CB
1996			11	CB
1996	NE	N	2	CB
6 yrs.	86 games			

Paul Smith
SMITH, PAUL EDWARD
B. Aug. 13, 1945, Ada, OK
New Mexico 6'3" 254 lbs.

Year	Team		Games	Pos.
1968	DEN	A	12	DE
1969			14	DE
1970	DEN	N	14	DT
1971			14	DT
1972			14	DT
1973			14	DT
1974			2	DT
1975			13	DT
1976			11	DT
1977			12	DT
1978			11	DT
1979	WAS	N	15	DE
1980			16	DE
13 yrs.	162 games			

Perry Smith
SMITH, EALTHON PERRY
B. Mar. 29, 1952, Spartanburg, SC
Mesa (Colorado)/Colorado State 6'1" 193 lbs.

Year	Team		Games	Pos.
1973	GB	N	8	CB
1974			12	CB
1975			14	CB
1976			13	CB
1977	STL	N	3	CB
1978			16	CB
1979			16	S
1980	DEN	N	14	CB
1981			12	CB
9 yrs.	108 games			

Phil Smith
SMITH, PHILLIP KEITH
B. Apr. 28, 1960, Los Angeles, CA
San Diego State 6'3" 188 lbs.

Year	Team		Games	Pos.
1983	BAL	N	1	WR
1984	IND	N	16	WR
1986	PHI	N	3	WR
3 yrs.	20 games			

Quintin Smith
SMITH, QUINTIN
B. Aug. 17, 1968, Houston, TX
Kansas 5'10" 172 lbs.

Year	Team		Games	Pos.
1990	CHI	N	4	WR

Ralph Smith
SMITH, RALPH ALLON
B. Dec. 1, 1939, Brookhaven, MS
Mississippi 6'2" 214 lbs.

Year	Team		Games	Pos.
1962	PHI	N	13	OE
1963			14	OE
1964			11	OE
1965	CLE	N	14	OE
1966			14	TE
1967			14	TE
1968			14	TE
1969	ATL	N	14	TE
8 yrs.	108 games			

Ray Smith
SMITH, RAYMOND
B. 1900
Lebanon Valley

Year	Team		Games	Pos.
1926	BKN	A	3	HB, QB

Ray Smith
SMITH, RAYMOND H.
B. 1908
Tulsa/Missouri 5'10" 195 lbs.

Year	Team		Games	Pos.
1930	PRO	N	9	C
1931			10	C
1933	PHI	N	7	C
3 yrs.	26 games			

Ray Gene Smith
SMITH, RAY GENE
B. Nov. 27, 1928, Anadarko, OK
Midwestern State 5'10" 187 lbs.

Year	Team		Games	Pos.
1954	CHIB	N	7	HB
1955			12	HB
1956			4	FB
1957			5	HB
4 yrs.	28 games			

Red Smith
SMITH, RICHARD PAUL
B. May 18, 1904, Brokaw, WI
D. Mar. 8, 1978, Toledo, OH
Lawrence/Notre Dame 5'10" 192 lbs.

Year	Team		Games	Pos.
1927	GB	N	5	G, E
1928	NYG	N	1	E
1928	NYY	N	10	HB, QB, E, FB
1929	GB	N	6	QB, G
1930	NEW	N	7	QB, HB
1931	NYG	N	9	QB, FB, HB, G
5 yrs.	38 games			

Reggie Smith
SMITH, REGGIE
B. Jul. 15, 1956, Kinston, NC
North Carolina Central 5'4" 168 lbs.

Year	Team		Games	Pos.
1980	ATL	N	8	WR
1981			15	WR
1987	NYJ	N	1	WR
3 yrs.	24 games			

Reggie Smith
SMITH, REGINALD LENARD
B. Aug. 29, 1961, Chicago, IL
Kansas 6'5" 295 lbs.

Year	Team		Games	Pos.
1987	TB	N	3	OT
1987	ATL	N	1	OT
1 yr.	4 games			

Ricky Smith
SMITH, RICKY
B. Jul. 20, 1960, Quincy, FL
Alabama State 6'0" 180 lbs.

Year	Team		Games	Pos.
1982	NE	N	9	CB
1983			16	CB, S
1984			1	CB, S
1984	WAS	N	11	CB
1987	DET	N	12	CB
4 yrs.	49 games			

Rico Smith
SMITH, RICO LOUIS
B. Jan. 14, 1969, Compton, CA
Colorado 6'0" 185 lbs.

Year	Team		Games	Pos.
1992	CLE	N	10	WR
1993			10	WR
1994			5	WR
1995			5	WR
4 yrs.	30 games			

Riley Smith
SMITH, RILEY H. (General)
B. Jul. 14, 1911, Carrollton, MS
Alabama 6'2" 200 lbs.

Year	Team		Games	Pos.
1936	BOS	N	12	QB, HB
1937	WAS	N	11	QB
1938			7	QB
3 yrs.	30 games			

Robert Smith
SMITH, ROBERT BENJAMIN
B. Dec. 3, 1962, Bogalusa, LA
Grambling State 6'7" 270 lbs.

Year	Team		Games	Pos.
1985	MIN	N	16	DE

Robert Smith
SMITH, ROBERT SCOTT
B. Mar. 4, 1972, Euclid, OH
Ohio State 6'0" 195 lbs.

Year	Team		Games	Pos.
1993	MIN	N	10	RB
1994			14	RB
1995			9	RB
1996			8	RB
4 yrs.	41 games			

Rod Smith
SMITH, ROD
B. May 15, 1970, Texarkana, AR
Missouri Southern 6'0" 183 lbs.

Year	Team		Games	Pos.
1995	DEN	N	16	WR
1996			10	WR
2 yrs.	26 games			

Rod Smith
SMITH, RODNEY MARC
B. Mar. 12, 1970, St. Paul, MN
Notre Dame 5'11" 187 lbs.

Year	Team		Games	Pos.
1992	NE	N	16	CB
1993			16	CB
1994			16	CB, S
1995	CAR	N	16	CB
1996			8	CB
5 yrs.	72 games			

Ron Smith
SMITH, RONALD
B. May 3, 1943, Chicago, IL
Wisconsin 6'1" 191 lbs.

Year	Team		Games	Pos.
1965	CHI	N	14	DB
1966	ATL	N	14	DB
1967			13	DB, FL
1968	LA	N	14	DB
1969			14	S
1970	CHI	N	14	S
1971			14	S
1972			14	CB
1973	SD	N	14	S
1974	OAK	N	14	DB
10 yrs.	139 games			

Ron Smith
SMITH, RONALD CHRISTOPHER
B. Jun. 27, 1942, Richmond, VA
Richmond 6'5" 220 lbs.

Year	Team		Games	Pos.
1965	LA	N	14	QB
1966	PIT	N	9	QB
2 yrs.	23 games			

Ronnie Smith
SMITH, RONNIE BERNARD
B. Nov. 20, 1956, Lakeland, FL
San Diego State 6'0" 185 lbs.

Year	Team		Games	Pos.
1978	LA	N	16	WR
1979			12	WR
1980	SD	N	15	WR
1981			9	WR
1981	PHI	N	3	WR
1982			9	WR
1983			2	WR
6 yrs.	66 games			

Royce Smith
SMITH, ROYCE LIONEL
B. Jun. 7, 1949, Savannah, GA
Georgia 6'3" 250 lbs.

Year	Team		Games	Pos.
1972	NO	N	10	G
1973			14	G
1974	ATL	N	14	G
1975			14	G
1976			10	G
5 yrs.	62 games			

Year	Team	Games	Pos.

Russ Smith
SMITH, EUGENE RUSSELL
B. Nov. 11, 1895
D. Jul. 7, 1958
Navy/Illinois 5'10" 220 lbs.

Year	Team		Games	Pos.
1921	DEC	A	11	G
1922	CHIB	N	10	G, C
1923	CAN	N	1	G
1923	MIL	N	4	G
1923	CHIC	N	1	T
1923	MIL	N	4	G
1924			1	G
1924	CLE		5	G, C
1925	DET		9	G
1925	CHIB	N	3	C
1926	HAM	N	3	G, T

6 yrs. 52 games

Russ Smith
SMITH, RUSSELL CONWAY
B. Aug. 4, 1944, Bronxville, NY
Miami (Florida) 6'1" 214 lbs.

Year	Team		Games	Pos.
1967	SD	A	12	RB
1968			14	RB
1969			14	RB
1970	SD	N	9	RB

4 yrs. 49 games

Sammie Smith
SMITH, SAMMIE LEE
B. May 16, 1967, Orlando, FL
Florida State 6'2" 226 lbs.

Year	Team		Games	Pos.
1989	MIA	N	13	RB
1990			16	RB
1991			12	RB
1992	DEN	N	3	RB

4 yrs. 44 games

Sean Smith
SMITH, SEAN LAMAR
B. Mar. 27, 1965, Bogalusa, LA
Grambling State 6'4" 280 lbs.

Year	Team		Games	Pos.
1987	CHI	N	10	DE
1988			9	DE
1989	DAL	N	2	DT
1989	TB	N	3	DE
1989	LARM	N	2	DT
1990	NE	N	15	DE
1991			2	DE

5 yrs. 43 games

Sherman Smith
SMITH, SHERMAN
B. Nov. 1, 1954, Youngstown, OH
Miami (Ohio) 6'4" 222 lbs.

Year	Team		Games	Pos.
1976	SEA	N	14	RB
1977			14	RB
1978			12	RB
1979			16	RB
1980			3	RB
1981			16	RB
1982			9	RB
1983	SD	N	13	RB

8 yrs. 95 games

Sid Smith
SMITH, SIDNEY E.
B. Jul. 6, 1948, Wichita, KS
Southern California 6'4" 260 lbs.

Year	Team		Games	Pos.
1970	KC	N	14	OT
1971			14	OT
1972			14	OT
1974	HOU	N	14	C, OT

4 yrs. 56 games

Steve Smith
SMITH, STEVEN ANTHONY
B. Aug. 30, 1964, Washington, DC

Steve Smith continued
Penn State 6'1" 232 lbs.

Year	Team		Games	Pos.
1987	LARI	N	7	RB
1988			16	RB
1989			16	RB
1990			16	RB
1991			16	RB
1992			16	RB
1993			16	RB
1994	SEA	N	16	RB
1995			10	RB

9 yrs. 129 games

Steve Smith
SMITH, STEPHEN CONANT
B. May 29, 1944, St. Louis, MO
Michigan 6'5" 246 lbs.

Year	Team		Games	Pos.
1966	PIT	N	3	TE
1966	SF	N	3	DE
1968	MIN	N	14	DE
1969			14	DE
1970			14	OT
1971	PHI	N	14	OT
1972			14	OT
1973			14	OT
1974			13	OT

8 yrs. 103 games

Stu Smith
SMITH, STUART M.
B. Feb. 3, 1915
D. Nov., 1969
Bucknell 6'0" 195 lbs.

Year	Team		Games	Pos.
1937	PIT	N	10	FB, HB, E
1938			11	FB, QB, HB

2 yrs. 21 games

Thomas Smith
SMITH, THOMAS LEE, JR.
B. Dec. 5, 1970, Gates, NC
North Carolina 5'11" 188 lbs.

Year	Team		Games	Pos.
1993	BUF	N	16	CB
1994			16	CB
1995			16	CB
1996			16	CB

4 yrs. 64 games

Tim Smith
SMITH, TIM
B. Mar. 20, 1957, Tucson, AZ
Nebraska 6'2" 280 lbs.

Year	Team		Games	Pos.
1980	HOU	N	16	WR
1981			4	WR
1982			9	WR
1983			16	WR
1984			16	WR
1985			16	WR
1986			13	WR

7 yrs. 90 games

Timmy Smith
SMITH, TIMMY
B. Jan. 21, 1964, Hobbs, NM
Texas Tech 5'11" 216 lbs.

Year	Team		Games	Pos.
1987	WAS	N	7	RB
1988			14	RB
1994	ATL	N	4	RB

3 yrs. 25 games

Tody Smith
SMITH, LAWRENCE EDWARD
B. Dec. 24, 1948, Orange, TX
Michigan State/Southern California 6'5" 248 lbs.

Year	Team		Games	Pos.
1971	DAL	N	7	DE
1972			10	DE
1973	HOU	N	14	DE
1974			14	DE

Tody Smith continued

Year	Team		Games	Pos.
1975			13	DE
1976			9	DE
1976	BUF	N	2	DE

6 yrs. 69 games

Tom Smith
SMITH, THOMAS ERIC
B. Oct. 4, 1949, Waterloo, IA
Iowa/Miami (Florida) 6'1" 216 lbs.

Year	Team		Games	Pos.
1973	MIA	N	2	RB

Tommie Smith
SMITH, TOMMIE
B. Jun. 5, 1944, Clarksville, TN
San Jose State 6'4" 190 lbs.

Year	Team		Games	Pos.
1969	CIN	A	2	WR

Tony Smith
SMITH, TONY
B. Jun. 29, 1970, Chicago, IL
Southern Mississippi 6'1" 214 lbs.

Year	Team		Games	Pos.
1992	ATL	N	14	RB
1993			15	RB

2 yrs. 29 games

Torin Smith
SMITH, TORIN
B. Sep. 30, 1961
Mesa JC 6'4" 230 lbs.

Year	Team		Games	Pos.
1987	NYG	N	1	DE

Truett Smith
SMITH, TRUETT HENRY
B. Mar. 27, 1924
Mississippi State/Wyoming 6'2" 208 lbs.

Year	Team		Games	Pos.
1950	PIT	N	9	QB
1951			11	QB

2 yrs. 20 games

Vernice Smith
SMITH, VERNICE CARLTON
B. Oct. 24, 1965, Orlando, FL
Florida A&M 6'2" 295 lbs.

Year	Team		Games	Pos.
1990	PHX	N	11	OT, G
1991			14	G, OT
1992			12	G
1993	CHI	N	6	G
1993	WAS	N	8	G
1994			4	G
1995			9	G, C

6 yrs. 64 games

Vitamin Smith
SMITH, VERDA T., JR. (Vitamin T)
B. Oct. 30, 1923, Sweetwater, TX
Abilene Christian 5'8" 179 lbs.

Year	Team		Games	Pos.
1949	LA	N	12	HB
1950			12	HB
1951			12	HB
1952			12	HB
1953			11	HB

5 yrs. 59 games

Vinson Smith
SMITH, VINSON ROBERT
B. Jul. 3, 1965, Statesville, NC
East Carolina 6'2" 228 lbs.

Year	Team		Games	Pos.
1988	ATL	N	3	LB
1990	DAL	N	16	LB
1991			13	LB
1992			16	LB
1993	CHI	N	16	LB
1994			12	LB
1995			16	LB
1996			15	LB

8 yrs. 107 games

Waddell Smith
SMITH, WADDELL
B. Aug. 24, 1955, New Orleans, LA
Kansas 6'2" 180 lbs.

Year	Team		Games	Pos.
1984	DAL	N	2	WR

Warren Smith
SMITH, WARREN
B. 1895, Minnesota
Deceased
Western Michigan 175 lbs.

Year	Team		Games	Pos.
1921	GB	A	2	G

Wayne Smith
SMITH, WAYNE LESTER
B. May 9, 1957, Chicago, IL
Wisconsin-La Crosse/Purdue 6'0" 170 lbs.

Year	Team		Games	Pos.
1980	DET	N	16	S
1981			16	S
1982			5	DB
1982	STL	N	1	CB
1983			16	CB
1984			16	CB
1985			16	CB
1986			16	CB
1987	MIN	N	6	CB

8 yrs. 108 games

Wes Smith
SMITH, WES
B. Jun. 24, 1963
East Texas State 6'1" 190 lbs.

Year	Team		Games	Pos.
1987	GB	N	1	WR

Wilfred Smith
SMITH, WILFRED (Big)
B. Apr. 7, 1899, Milroy, IN
D. Aug. 3, 1976, Chicago, IL
DePauw 6'4" 203 lbs.

Year	Team		Games	Pos.
1920	MUN	A	1	G
1921			2	T
1922	LOU	N	1	T
1923	CHIC	N	1	E
1923	HAM	N	5	G, E
1924	CHIC	N	6	T, E
1925			13	E, G, C

6 yrs. 29 games

Willie Smith
SMITH, WILLIE
B. 1938
Michigan 6'2" 255 lbs.

Year	Team		Games	Pos.
1960	DEN	A		OT
1961	OAK	A	14	G

2 yrs. 14 games

Willie Smith
SMITH, WILLIE
B. Aug. 6, 1964, Jacksonville, FL
Miami (Florida) 6'2" 235 lbs.

Year	Team		Games	Pos.
1987	MIA	N	3	TE

Willis Smith
SMITH, WILLIS M. (Wee Willie)
B. Jul. 2, 1910, Lexington, NE
Deceased
Idaho 5'6" 148 lbs.

Year	Team		Games	Pos.
1934	NYG	N	9	QB

Zeke Smith
SMITH, ZEKE
B. Jun. 3, 1936, Walker Springs, AL
Auburn 6'2" 233 lbs.

Year	Team		Games	Pos.
1960	BAL	N	12	E, LB
1961	NYG	N	12	G

2 yrs. 24 games

Year	Team	Games	Pos.

Bill Smithson
SMITHSON, WILLIAM B.
Syracuse

1921	SYR	A	3	E, C, G

Mark Smolinski
SMOLINSKI, MARK WAYNE
B. May 9, 1939, Alpena, MI
Wyoming 6'0" 218 lbs.

1961	BAL	N	14	FB
1962			14	FB
1963	NY	A	14	FB
1964			14	FB
1965			12	FB
1966			14	FB
1967			13	RB
1968			14	RB

8 yrs. 109 games

Raymond Smoot
SMOOT, RAYMOND EUGENE
B. Jul. 24, 1970, Leesville, LA
Louisiana State 6'4" 305 lbs.

1993	SD	N	2	G, OT

Howard Smothers
SMOTHERS, HOWARD
B. Nov. 16, 1973, Jacksonville, FL
Bethune-Cookman 6'3" 285 lbs.

1995	PHI	N	1	WR

Dave Smukler
SMUKLER, DAVID (Dynamite)
B. May 28, 1914, Gloversville, NY
D. Feb. 22, 1971, Los Angeles, CA
Temple 6'1" 226 lbs.

1936	PHI	N	10	FB, HB
1937			11	FB, HB
1938			11	FB
1939			4	FB
1944	BOS	N	2	FB

5 yrs. 38 games

Bill Smyth
SMYTH, WILLIAM KRANTZ
B. Apr. 8, 1922, Batavia, OH
D. Nov. 6, 1966
Cincinnati/Penn State/Cincinnati 6'3" 243 lbs.

1947	LA	N	12	T
1948			11	E
1949			12	E
1950			11	E

4 yrs. 46 games

Lou Smythe
SMYTHE, LOUIS LEHMAN (Hammer)
B. 1899
Deceased
Texas/Centre 6'1" 200 lbs.

1920	CAN	A	6	HB, FB
1921			6	HB, FB
1922	CAN	N	5	HB
1923			12	HB
1924	ROC	N	1	FB
1925			7	HB, FB
1925	FRA	N	3	HB
1926			4	HB
1926	HAR	N	5	FB
1926	PRO	N	3	HB

7 yrs. 52 games

Norm Snead
SNEAD, NORMAN BAILEY
B. Jul. 31, 1939, Halifax County, VA
Wake Forest 6'4" 215 lbs.

1961	WAS	N	14	QB

Norm Snead continued

1962			14	QB
1963			14	QB
1964	PHI	N	12	QB
1965			11	QB
1966			10	QB
1967			14	QB
1968			11	QB
1969			13	QB
1970			14	QB
1971	MIN	N	7	QB
1972	NYG	N	14	QB
1973			10	QB
1974			5	QB
1974	SF	N	3	QB
1975			9	QB
1976	NYG	N	3	QB

16 yrs. 178 games

Bob Sneddon
SNEDDON, ROBERT LEE
B. Jul. 9, 1921, Ogden, UT
Weber State/St. Mary's (California) 5'10" 180 lbs.

1944	WAS	N	9	B
1945	DET	N	1	HB
1946	LA	AA	11	HB

3 yrs. 21 games

Donald Snell
SNELL, DONALD WAYNE
B. Apr. 13, 1965
Virginia Tech 6'2" 177 lbs.

1987	SEA	N	1	WR

George Snell
SNELL, GEORGE A.
B. 1897
Deceased
Penn State 5'10" 185 lbs.

1926	BKN	N	11	FB, HB
1927	BUF	N	1	HB

2 yrs. 12 games

Matt Snell
SNELL, MATHEWS
B. Aug. 18, 1941, Garfield, GA
Ohio State 6'2" 220 lbs.

1964	NY	A	14	FB
1965			14	FB
1966			12	FB
1967			7	RB
1968			14	RB
1969			14	RB
1970	NYJ	N	3	RB
1971			5	RB
1972			4	RB

9 yrs. 87 games

Ray Snell
SNELL, RAY MICHAEL
B. Feb. 24, 1958, Baltimore, MD
Wisconsin 6'4" 260 lbs.

1980	TB	N	13	G, OT
1981			16	G
1982			7	G
1983			9	G, OT
1984	PIT	N	13	OT
1985			5	OT
1985	DET	N	2	G

6 yrs. 65 games

Ken Snelling
SNELLING, KENNETH E.
B. 1919
UCLA 6'2" 210 lbs.

1945	GB	N	2	FB

Jim Sniadecki
SNIADECKI, JAMES BERT
B. Mar. 23, 1947, South Bend, IN
Indiana 6'2" 224 lbs.

1969	SF	N	14	LB
1970			14	LB
1971			14	LB
1972			2	LB
1973			14	LB

5 yrs. 58 games

Malcolm Snider
SNIDER, MALCOLM PRATT
B. Apr. 5, 1947, Battle Creek, MI
Michigan State 6'5" 250 lbs.

1969	ATL	N	14	G, OT
1970			14	G
1971			13	OT
1972	GB	N	14	G
1973			14	G
1974			14	G

6 yrs. 83 games

Ron Snidow
SNIDOW, RONALD WAYNE
B. Dec. 30, 1941, Newport News, VA
Oregon 6'4" 249 lbs.

1963	WAS	N	13	DT
1964			14	DE
1965			14	DE, P
1966			14	DE
1967			14	DE
1968	CLE	N	13	DE
1969			14	DE
1970			14	DE
1971			13	DE
1972			3	DE

10 yrs. 126 games

Angelo Snipes
SNIPES, ANGELO BERNARD
B. Jan. 11, 1963, Atlanta, GA
West Georgia 6'0" 222 lbs.

1986	WAS	N	10	LB
1986	SD	N	6	LB
1987			2	LB
1987	KC	N	4	LB
1988			15	LB
1989			2	LB

4 yrs. 39 games

Lee Snoots
SNOOTS, JOHN LEE
B. Aug. 12, 1892
D. Nov., 1968, Columbus, OH
none 5'9" 185 lbs.

1920	COL	A	3	HB
1922	COL	N	7	HB, FB
1923			10	FB
1925			1	HB

4 yrs. 21 games

Matt Snorton
SNORTON, HICKMAN MATTHEW
B. Sep. 26, 1942, Crofton, KY
Michigan State 6'5" 250 lbs.

1964	DEN	A	5	OE

Jack Snow
SNOW, JACK THOMAS
B. Jan. 25, 1943, Rock Springs, WY
Notre Dame 6'2" 195 lbs.

1965	LA	N	14	OE
1966			14	OE
1967			14	OE
1968			14	OE
1969			14	WR

Jack Snow continued

1970			14	WR
1971			14	WR
1972			14	WR
1973			14	WR
1974			14	WR
1975			10	WR

11 yrs. 150 games

Percy Snow
SNOW, PERCY LEE
B. Nov. 5, 1967, Canton, OH
Michigan State 6'2" 248 lbs.

1990	KC	N	15	LB
1992			15	LB
1993	CHI	N	10	LB

3 yrs. 40 games

Cal Snowden
SNOWDEN, CALVIN REGINALD
B. Nov. 29, 1946, Washington, DC
Indiana 6'4" 247 lbs.

1969	STL	N	7	DE
1970			14	DE
1971	BUF	N	14	DE
1972	SD	N	8	DE
1973			4	DE

5 yrs. 47 games

Jim Snowden
SNOWDEN, JAMES JOHN
B. Jan. 12, 1942, Youngstown, OH
Notre Dame 6'3" 255 lbs.

1965	WAS	N	14	OT
1966			14	OT
1967			14	OT
1968			14	OT
1969			14	OT
1970			14	OT
1971			14	OT

7 yrs. 98 games

Al Snyder
SNYDER, ALBERT
B. 1942, Baltimore, MD
Holy Cross 6'0" 195 lbs.

1964	BOS	A	2	FL
1966	BAL	N	5	FL
1966	NYG	N	5	FL

2 yrs. 12 games

Bill Snyder
SNYDER, WILLIAM HOWARD (Bull)
B. Oct. 29, 1911, London, OH
D. Oct., 1973
Ohio University 6'2" 230 lbs.

1934	PIT	N	5	G, T
1935			7	G, T

2 yrs. 12 games

Bob Snyder
SNYDER, ROBERT A.
B. Feb. 6, 1913, Fremont, OH
D. Nov. 13, 1990
Ohio University 6'0" 200 lbs.

1937	CLE	N	10	HB
1938			10	HB
1939	CHIB	N	8	HB
1940			11	QB
1941			10	QB
1943			10	QB

6 yrs. 59 games

Gerry Snyder
SNYDER, GERALD T. (Snitz)
B. Aug. 6, 1905

777

Year	Team		Games	Pos.

Gerry Snyder *continued*
D. Jun., 1983, Brooklyn Heights, OH
Maryland 5'8" 190 lbs.

Year	Team		Games	Pos.
1929	NYG	N	13	HB, FB, QB
1930	SI	N	7	FB, QB, HB
2 yrs.	20 games			

Jim Snyder
SNYDER, J.E.
B. Jan., 1909
None 162 lbs.

| 1925 | MIL | N | 1 | HB |

Loren Snyder
SNYDER, LOREN
B. Nov. 28, 1963
Northern Colorado 6'4" 207 lbs.

| 1987 | DAL | N | 2 | QB |

Lum Snyder
SNYDER, KENNETH DAVID
B. Aug. 12, 1930, Cleveland, TN
D. Oct. 11, 1985
Georgia Tech 6'5" 228 lbs.

1952	PHI	N	11	T
1953			12	T
1954			12	T
1955			12	T
1958			12	T
5 yrs.	59 games			

Pat Snyder
SNYDER, PATRICK
B. Nov. 23, 1963
Purdue 6'1" 225 lbs.

| 1991 | IND | N | 1 | C |

Todd Snyder
SNYDER, JAMES TODD
B. Oct. 12, 1948, Athens, OH
Ohio University 6'2" 187 lbs.

1970	ATL	N	12	WR
1971			6	WR
1972			14	WR
3 yrs.	32 games			

Hank Soar
SOAR, ALBERT HENRY
B. Aug. 17, 1914, Alton, RI
Providence 6'2" 209 lbs.

1937	NYG	N	9	FB, QB, HB
1938			11	HB, FB
1939			11	HB
1940			10	HB
1941			11	B
1942			11	HB
1943			4	HB, FB
1944			3	FB, HB
1946			11	B
9 yrs.	81 games			

Phil Sobocinski
SOBOCINSKI, PHILIP
B. Jul. 2, 1945, Wauwatosa, WI
Wisconsin 6'3" 235 lbs.

| 1968 | ATL | N | 7 | C |

Joe Soboleski
SOBOLESKI, JOSEPH ROBERT
B. Aug. 22, 1926
Michigan 6'0" 213 lbs.

1949	CHI	AA	5	G
1949	WAS	N	7	G
1950	DET	N	12	G
1952	DAL	N	1	G
3 yrs.	25 games			

Bryan Sochia
SOCHIA, BRYAN
B. Jul. 21, 1961, Massena, NY
Northwestern Oklahoma State 6'3" 270 lbs.

1983	HOU	N	12	NT
1984			16	NT
1985			16	NT
1986	MIA	N	6	NT
1987			12	NT, DE
1988			16	NT
1989			16	NT
1990			5	NT
1991			3	NT
1991	DEN	N	10	DL
1992			16	NT, DE
10 yrs.	128 games			

John Sodaski
SODASKI, JOHN JOSEPH, JR.
B. Jan. 14, 1948, Phoenixville, PA
Villanova 6'1" 214 lbs.

1970	PIT	N	3	S
1972	PHI	N	4	LB
1973			14	LB
3 yrs.	21 games			

Alec Sofish
SOFISH, ALEXANDER
Grove City 6'2" 200 lbs.

| 1931 | PRO | N | 11 | G |

Ben Sohn
SOHN, BENJAMIN
B. Sep. 16, 1918, San Diego, CA
Southern California 6'2" 220 lbs.

| 1941 | NYG | N | 11 | G, T |

Benny Sohn
SOHN, BENJAMIN
B. Nov. 18, 1911
D. Nov., 1969
Washington 5'8" 170 lbs.

| 1934 | C-S | N | 2 | B |

Kurt Sohn
SOHN, KURT
B. Jun. 26, 1957, Ithaca, NY
North Carolina State/Fordham 5'11" 180 lbs.

1981	NYJ	N	16	WR
1982			9	WR
1984			5	WR
1985			15	WR
1986			15	WR
1987			12	WR
1988			15	WR
7 yrs.	87 games			

Bob Soleau
SOLEAU, ROBERT
B. Apr. 2, 1941
William & Mary 6'2" 235 lbs.

| 1964 | PIT | N | 14 | LB |

Ariel Solomon
SOLOMON, ARIEL MACE
B. Jul. 16, 1968, Brooklyn, NY
Colorado 6'5" 283 lbs.

1991	PIT	N	5	OT
1992			4	OT
1993			16	C, OT
1994			16	C
1995			4	C
1996	MIN	N	16	C
6 yrs.	61 games			

Freddie Solomon
SOLOMON, FREDDIE (Fabulous)
B. Jan. 11, 1953, Sumter, SC
Tampa 5'11" 184 lbs.

1975	MIA	N	14	RB, WR
1976			10	WR
1977			13	WR
1978	SF	N	16	WR
1979			15	WR
1980			16	WR
1981			15	WR
1982			9	WR
1983			13	WR
1984			14	WR
1985			16	WR
11 yrs.	151 games			

Freddie Solomon
SOLOMON, FREDDIE
B. Aug. 15, 1972, Gainesville, FL
South Carolina State 5'10" 180 lbs.

| 1996 | PHI | N | 12 | WR |

Jesse Solomon
SOLOMON, JESSE HOWARD
B. Nov. 4, 1963, Madison, FL
Florida State 6'0" 235 lbs.

1986	MIN	N	13	LB
1987			12	LB
1988			16	LB
1989			4	LB
1989	DAL	N	11	LB
1990			9	LB
1991	TB	N	13	LB
1992	ATL	N	16	LB
1993			16	LB
1994	MIA	N	6	LB
9 yrs.	116 games			

Roland Solomon
SOLOMON, ROLAND HOWARD
B. Feb. 6, 1956, Fort Worth, TX
Utah 6'0" 193 lbs.

1980	DAL	N	10	CB
1980	BUF	N	1	CB
1981	DEN	N	4	CB
2 yrs.	15 games			

Ron Solt
SOLT, RONALD MATTHEW
B. May 19, 1962, Bainbridge, MD
Maryland 6'3" 279 lbs.

1984	IND	N	16	G
1985			15	G
1986			16	G
1987			12	G
1988			1	G
1988	PHI	N	1	G
1989			15	G
1990			15	G
1991			15	G
1992	IND	N	6	G
9 yrs.	116 games			

Gordie Soltau
SOLTAU, GORDON LEROY
B. Jan. 25, 1925, Duluth, MN
Minnesota 6'2" 195 lbs.

1950	SF	N	12	OE, K
1951			12	OE, K
1952			11	OE, K
1953			12	OE, K
1954			10	OE, K
1955			12	OE, K
1956			12	OE, K
1957			12	OE, K
1958			12	OE, K
9 yrs.	105 games			

Bob Soltis
SOLTIS, ROBERT L.
B. 1936
Minnesota 6'2" 205 lbs.

1960	BOS	A		DB
1961			3	DB
2 yrs.	3 games			

George Somers
SOMERS, GEORGE A.
B. Oct. 5, 1915, Fountain Springs, PA
La Salle/Pennsylvania 6'2" 253 lbs.

1939	PHI	N	9	T
1940			10	T
1941	PIT	N	10	T
1942			11	T
4 yrs.	40 games			

Donnie Sommer
SOMMER, DONALD
B. Feb. 1, 1964, Corsicana, TX
Texas-El Paso 6'4" 290 lbs.

| 1987 | BUF | N | 3 | OT |

Mike Sommer
SOMMER, MICHAEL SANDOR
B. Oct. 9, 1934, Washington, DC
George Washington 5'11" 190 lbs.

1958	WAS	N	2	HB
1959			1	HB
1960	BAL	N	1	HB
1963	OAK	A	4	HB
4 yrs.	8 games			

Jack Sommers
SOMMERS, JOHN
B. 1919
UCLA 6'3" 232 lbs.

| 1947 | WAS | N | 8 | C |

Eddie Songin
SONGIN, EDWARD (Butch)
B. 1924, Walpole, MA
Boston College 6'2" 200 lbs.

1960	BOS	A	14	QB
1961			14	QB
1962	NY	A	7	QB
3 yrs.	35 games			

Treg Songy
SONGY, TREG
B. Jun. 15, 1962, New Orleans, LA
Tulane 6'2" 200 lbs.

| 1987 | NYJ | N | 2 | CB |

Gus Sonnenberg
SONNENBERG, GUSTAVE
(Dynamite, Iron Duke)
B. Mar. 6, 1898, Ewen, MI
D. Sep. 12, 1944, Great Lakes NTS, IL
Dartmouth/Detroit 5'6" 196 lbs.

1923	COL		10	T, HB
1923	BUF	N	1	T
1925	DET		12	T
1926			12	T, G
1927	PRO	N	14	T
1928			11	T, HB
1930			1	T
6 yrs.	61 games			

Ross Sorce
SORCE, ROSS P., JR.
B. 1920
Deceased
Georgetown (DC) 6'4" 255 lbs.

| 1945 | PIT | N | 1 | T |

Year	Team		Games	Pos.

Glen Sorenson
SORENSON, GLEN G.
B. Feb. 29, 1920, Salt Lake City, UT
D. Feb. 26, 1972, Salt Lake City, UT
Utah State 6'0" 217 lbs.

Year	Team		Games	Pos.
1943	**GB**	**N**	6	G
1944			10	G
1945			10	G
3 yrs.	26 games			

Jim Sorey
SOREY, JAMES
B. Sep. 5, 1936, Marianna, FL
Texas Southern 6'4" 278 lbs.

Year	Team		Games	Pos.
1960	**BUF**	**A**		DT
1961			14	DT
1962			14	DT
3 yrs.	28 games			

Revie Sorey
SOREY, REVIE CEE, JR.
B. Sep. 10, 1953, Brooklyn, NY
Illinois 6'2" 262 lbs.

Year	Team		Games	Pos.
1975	**CHI**	**N**	14	G
1976			5	G
1977			14	G
1978			16	G
1979			16	G
1980			16	G
1981			15	G
1983			3	G
8 yrs.	99 games			

Henry Sorrell
SORRELL, HENRY THOMAS
B. Jun. 10, 1943, Talladega, AL
Tennessee-Chattanooga 6'1" 215 lbs.

Year	Team		Games	Pos.
1967	**DEN**	**A**	10	LB

Bill Sortet
SORTET, WILBUR JOHN
B. Jun. 25, 1912, Vincennes, IN
West Virginia 6'1" 187 lbs.

Year	Team		Games	Pos.
1933	**PIT**	**N**	9	E
1934			12	E, B
1935			12	E
1936			12	E
1937			9	E
1938			8	E
1939			11	E
1940			11	E
8 yrs.	84 games			

Rick Sortun
SORTUN, HENRIK MARTIN
B. Sep. 26, 1942, Tacoma, WA
Washington 6'2" 234 lbs.

Year	Team		Games	Pos.
1964	**STL**	**N**	14	G
1965			13	G
1966			14	G
1967			13	G
1968			14	G
1969			14	G
6 yrs.	82 games			

Lou Sossamon
SOSSAMON, LOUIS CODY
B. Jun. 2, 1921, Gaffney, SC
South Carolina 6'1" 207 lbs.

Year	Team		Games	Pos.
1946	**NY**	**AA**	14	C
1947			14	C
1948			14	C
3 yrs.	42 games			

Frank Souchak
SOUCHAK, FRANK
B. 1915, Berwick, PA

Frank Souchak continued
Pittsburgh 6'0" 205 lbs.

Year	Team		Games	Pos.
1939	**PIT**	**N**	4	E

Cecil Souders
SOUDERS, CECIL B.
B. Jan. 3, 1921, Bucyrus, OH
Ohio State 6'1" 210 lbs.

Year	Team		Games	Pos.
1947	**DET**	**N**	11	E
1948			12	E
1949			12	T, E
3 yrs.	35 games			

Ronnie South
SOUTH, RONNIE LEE
B. May 8, 1945
Arkansas 6'1" 195 lbs.

Year	Team		Games	Pos.
1968	**NO**	**N**	4	QB, P

Tommy Southard
SOUTHARD, TOMMY
B. Jun. 29, 1955
Furman 6'0" 185 lbs.

Year	Team		Games	Pos.
1978	**STL**	**N**		WR

Robert Sowell
SOWELL, ROBERT DONNELL, JR.
B. Jun. 23, 1961, Columbus, OH
Howard 5'11" 175 lbs.

Year	Team		Games	Pos.
1983	**MIA**	**N**	16	DB
1984			16	CB, S
1985			10	CB
1987			3	CB
4 yrs.	45 games			

Rich Sowells
SOWELLS, RICHARD ALLEN
B. Oct. 27, 1948, Prairie View, TX
Alcorn State 6'0" 179 lbs.

Year	Team		Games	Pos.
1971	**NYJ**	**N**	8	DB
1972			11	CB
1973			12	CB
1974			14	CB
1975			14	CB
1976			10	CB
1977	**HOU**	**N**	10	DB
7 yrs.	79 games			

Vic Spadaccini
SPADACCINI, VICTOR M.
B. Mar. 2, 1916, Keewatin, MN
D. Apr., 1981, St. Paul, MN
Minnesota 6'0" 222 lbs.

Year	Team		Games	Pos.
1938	**CLE**	**N**	10	QB, HB
1939			11	QB
1940			9	QB
3 yrs.	30 games			

Joe Spagna
SPAGNA, JOSEPH (Butch)
B. May 15, 1897, New York, NY
D. Dec. 11, 1948, Philadelphia, PA
Brown/Lehigh 6'0" 215 lbs.

Year	Team		Games	Pos.
1920	**CLE**	**A**	3	T
1920	**BUF**	**A**	3	T
1921			4	T, G
1924	**FRA**	**N**	14	G
1925			7	G
1926	**PHI**	**A**	10	G
5 yrs.	41 games			

John Spagnola
SPAGNOLA, JOHN STEPHEN
B. Aug. 1, 1957, Bethlehem, PA
Yale 6'4" 241 lbs.

Year	Team		Games	Pos.
1979	**PHI**	**N**	16	TE

John Spagnola continued

Year	Team		Games	Pos.
1980			16	TE
1981			11	TE
1982			9	TE
1984			16	TE
1985			16	TE
1986			15	TE
1987			12	TE
1988	**SEA**	**N**	16	TE
1989	**GB**	**N**	6	TE
10 yrs.	133 games			

Dick Spain
SPAIN, RICHARD R.
B. May, 1893
D. Oct. 3, 1948
None 5'8" 180 lbs.

Year	Team		Games	Pos.
1921	**EVA**	**A**	1	C
1922	**EVA**	**A**	2	C
2 yrs.	3 games			

Gene Spangler
SPANGLER, EUGENE DOUGLAS
B. Dec. 17, 1922, Huntington, AR
Tulsa 5'10" 195 lbs.

Year	Team		Games	Pos.
1946	**DET**	**N**	6	HB

Gary Spani
SPANI, GARY L.
B. Jan. 9, 1956, Satanta, KS
Kansas State 6'2" 239 lbs.

Year	Team		Games	Pos.
1978	**KC**	**N**	14	LB
1979			16	LB
1980			16	LB
1981			16	LB
1982			8	LB
1983			10	LB
1984			14	LB
1985			14	LB
1986			16	LB
9 yrs.	124 games			

Frank Spaniel
SPANIEL, FRANCIS J.
B. May 21, 1928, Vandergrift, PA
D. Oct. 27, 1994, North Fort Myers, FL
Notre Dame 5'10" 185 lbs.

Year	Team		Games	Pos.
1950	**WAS**	**N**	6	HB
1950	**BAL**	**N**	6	HB
1 yr.	12 games			

Gary Spann
SPANN, GARY
B. Feb. 3, 1963
Texas Christian 6'1" 216 lbs.

Year	Team		Games	Pos.
1987	**KC**	**N**	2	LB

Dave Sparenberg
SPARENBERG, DAVID
B. May 28, 1959, Chatham, Ont.
Western Ontario 6'3" 257 lbs.

Year	Team		Games	Pos.
1987	**CLE**	**N**	1	G

Al Sparkman
SPARKMAN, ALAN TEMPLE
B. Feb. 17, 1926, Baltimore, MD
Texas A&M 6'6" 253 lbs.

Year	Team		Games	Pos.
1948	**LA**	**N**	12	T
1949			4	T
2 yrs.	16 games			

Dave Sparks
SPARKS, DAVID
B. 1928
D. Dec. 5, 1954, Arlington, VA

Dave Sparks continued
South Carolina 6'1" 229 lbs.

Year	Team		Games	Pos.
1951	**SF**	**N**	8	G
1954	**WAS**	**N**	10	T
2 yrs.	18 games			

Phillippi Sparks
SPARKS, PHILLIPPI DWAINE
B. Apr. 15, 1969, Phoenix, AZ
Arizona State 5'11" 186 lbs.

Year	Team		Games	Pos.
1992	**NYG**	**N**	16	CB
1993			5	CB
1994			11	CB
1995			16	CB
1996			14	CB
5 yrs.	62 games			

Al Sparlis
SPARLIS, ALBERT ALEXANDER
B. May 20, 1920, Los Angeles, CA
UCLA 5'11" 185 lbs.

Year	Team		Games	Pos.
1946	**GB**	**N**	3	G

Ed Sparr
SPARR, EDWIN A.
B. Jul. 29, 1898, Hazelhurst, WI
D. May 19, 1974, St. Clair Shores, MI
Carroll (Wisconsin) 5'11" 210 lbs.

Year	Team		Games	Pos.
1926	**RAC**	**N**	2	T, G

Jim Spavital
SPAVITAL, JAMES J.
B. Sep. 15, 1926, Oklahoma City, OK
D. Mar. 7, 1993, Stillwater, OK
Oklahoma State 6'1" 210 lbs.

Year	Team		Games	Pos.
1949	**LA**	**AA**	12	FB
1950	**BAL**	**N**	11	FB
2 yrs.	23 games			

Glen Spear
SPEAR, GLEN (Farmer)
B. Jan. 18, 1900
D. Dec., 1971, Sutton, NE
Drake 5'10" 185 lbs.

Year	Team		Games	Pos.
1926	**KC**	**N**	10	FB, HB, E

Ernest Spears
SPEARS, ERNEST
B. Nov. 6, 1967, Oceanside, CA
Southern California 5'11" 192 lbs.

Year	Team		Games	Pos.
1990	**NO**	**N**	16	S

Marcus Spears
SPEARS, MARCUS DEWAYNE
B. Sep. 28, 1971, Baton Rouge, LA
Northwestern Louisiana 6'4" 305 lbs.

Year	Team		Games	Pos.
1996	**CHI**	**N**	9	G

Ron Spears
SPEARS, RONALD DARNELL
B. Nov. 23, 1959, Los Angeles, CA
San Diego State 6'6" 255 lbs.

Year	Team		Games	Pos.
1982	**NE**	**N**	7	DE
1983			1	DE
1983	**GB**	**N**	13	DE
2 yrs.	21 games			

Emmett Specht
SPECHT, EMMETT
B. 1894
Deceased
None 5'9" 170 lbs.

Year	Team		Games	Pos.
1920	**HAM**	**A**		HB

779

Year	Team	Games	Pos.

Dutch Speck
SPECK, NORMAN H.
B. 1886, Canton, OH
D. Nov. 18, 1952, Canton, OH
none 5'10" 220 lbs.

Year	Team		Games	Pos.
1920	CAN	A	4	G, C
1921			7	G, C, T
1922	CAN	N	11	C, G
1923			6	C, G
1924	AKR	N	1	G
1925	CAN	N	5	G, C
1926			8	G, C

7 yrs. 42 games

Mac Speedie
SPEEDIE, MAC CURTIS
B. Jan. 12, 1920, Odell, IL
D. Mar. 12, 1993, Laguna Hills, CA
Utah 6'3" 203 lbs.

Year	Team		Games	Pos.
1946	CLE	AA	14	E
1947			14	E
1948			12	E
1949			12	E
1950	CLE	N	12	E
1951			10	E
1952			12	E

7 yrs. 86 games

Cliff Speegle
SPEEGLE, CLIFTON
B. 1918, Oklahoma City, OK
Oklahoma 6'1" 195 lbs.

Year	Team		Games	Pos.
1945	CHIC	N	8	C

Harry Speelman
SPEELMAN, HARRY E.
B. 1916
Deceased
Michigan State 5'11" 220 lbs.

Year	Team		Games	Pos.
1940	DET	N	4	G, T

Del Speer
SPEER, DEL
B. Feb. 1, 1970, Miami, FL
Florida 6'0" 196 lbs.

Year	Team		Games	Pos.
1993	CLE	N	16	CB, S
1994			8	S
1994	SEA	N	1	S

2 yrs. 25 games

Dick Speights
SPEIGHTS, RICHARD
B. Jun. 30, 1946
Wyoming 5'11" 175 lbs.

Year	Team		Games	Pos.
1968	SD	A	2	DB

Jeff Spek
SPEK, JEFF MARTIN
B. Oct. 1, 1960, Calgary, Alb.
Nevada-Las Vegas/San Diego State 6'3" 240 lbs.

Year	Team		Games	Pos.
1986	TB	N	2	TE

Frank Spellacy
SPELLACY, FRANK
B. 1901, New York State
Deceased
None

Year	Team		Games	Pos.
1922	BUF	N	1	E

Alonzo Spellman
SPELLMAN, ALONZO ROBERT
B. Sep. 27, 1971, Mount Holly, NJ
Ohio State 6'4" 280 lbs.

Year	Team		Games	Pos.
1992	CHI		15	DE
1993			16	DE

Alonzo Spellman continued

Year	Team	Games	Pos.
1994		16	DE
1995		16	DE
1996		16	DE

5 yrs. 79 games

Jack Spellman
SPELLMAN, JOHN FRANKLIN
B. Jun. 14, 1899, Middletown, CT
D. Aug. 1, 1966, Mangula, Zimbabwe
Brown 5'10" 201 lbs.

Year	Team		Games	Pos.
1925	PRO	N	9	T, FB, E
1926			12	HB, T, FB
1927			14	E, T, HB
1928			11	E, T
1929			12	E, T
1930			11	E
1931			11	E
1932	BOS	N	7	E, G, T

8 yrs. 87 games

Julian Spence
SPENCE, JULIAN
B. May 5, 1928, Austin, TX
D. Mar. 6, 1990, Clear Lake City, TX
Sam Houston State 5'11" 170 lbs.

Year	Team		Games	Pos.
1956	CHIC	N	8	HB
1957	SF	N	5	HB
1960	HOU	A	7	DB
1961			10	DB

4 yrs. 21 games

Darryl Spencer
SPENCER, DARRYL EUGENE
B. Mar. 21, 1970, Merritt Island, FL
Miami (Florida) 5'8" 172 lbs.

Year	Team		Games	Pos.
1994	ATL	N	8	WR
1995			5	WR

2 yrs. 13 games

Herbie Spencer
SPENCER, HERBERT SEABROOK
B. Sep. 23, 1959, Charleston, SC
Newberry 6'3" 230 lbs.

Year	Team		Games	Pos.
1987	ATL	N	3	LB

Jim Spencer
SPENCER, JAMES
B. Nov. 1, 1901
D. Feb., 1972, Cleveland, OH
Dayton 6'0" 205 lbs.

Year	Team		Games	Pos.
1928	DAY	N	6	G
1929			6	G

2 yrs. 12 games

Jimmy Spencer
SPENCER, JAMES ARTHUR, JR.
B. Mar. 29, 1969, Manning, SC
Florida 5'9" 180 lbs.

Year	Team		Games	Pos.
1992	NO	N	16	CB
1993			16	CB
1994			16	CB
1995			16	CB
1996	CIN	N	15	CB

5 yrs. 79 games

Joe Spencer
SPENCER, JOSEPH EMERSON
B. Aug. 15, 1923, Cleveland County, OK
Deceased
Oklahoma State 6'3" 239 lbs.

Year	Team		Games	Pos.
1948	BKN	AA	13	T
1949	CLE	AA	11	T
1950	GB	N	12	T
1951			12	T

4 yrs. 48 games

Maurice Spencer
SPENCER, THURMON MAURICE
B. Jun. 15, 1952, Winston-Salem, NC
North Carolina Central 6'0" 176 lbs.

Year	Team		Games	Pos.
1974	STL	N	7	CB
1974	NO	N	5	DB
1975			14	DB
1976			14	CB
1978			16	CB

4 yrs. 56 games

Ollie Spencer
SPENCER, OLIVER L.
B. Apr. 17, 1931, Ulysses, KS
D. Apr. 28, 1991, Ukiah, CA
Kansas 6'2" 245 lbs.

Year	Team		Games	Pos.
1953	DET	N	12	T
1956			12	T
1957	GB	N	12	T
1958			12	T
1959	DET	N	12	T
1960			12	T
1961				G
1963	OAK	A	14	G

8 yrs. 86 games

Tim Spencer
SPENCER, TIMOTHY
B. Dec. 10, 1960, Martins Ferry, OH
Ohio State 6'2" 224 lbs.

Year	Team		Games	Pos.
1985	SD	N	16	RB
1986			14	RB
1987			12	FB
1988			16	RB
1989			16	RB
1990			4	RB

6 yrs. 78 games

Todd Spencer
SPENCER, TODD LAMONT
B. Jul. 20, 1962, Portland, OR
Southern California 6'0" 210 lbs.

Year	Team		Games	Pos.
1984	PIT	N	7	RB
1985			16	RB
1987	SD	N	3	RB

3 yrs. 26 games

Willie Spencer
SPENCER, WILLIE THOMAS
B. Jan. 28, 1953, Massillon, OH
none 6'3" 235 lbs.

Year	Team		Games	Pos.
1976	MIN	N	3	RB
1977	NYG	N	13	RB
1978			15	RB

3 yrs. 31 games

George Speth
SPETH, GEORGE CARL
B. Jul. 25, 1918, Buffalo, NY
Murray State 6'2" 220 lbs.

Year	Team		Games	Pos.
1942	DET	N	11	T

Cotton Speyrer
SPEYRER, CHARLES WAYNE
B. Apr. 29, 1949, Port Arthur, TX
Texas 6'0" 175 lbs.

Year	Team		Games	Pos.
1972	BAL	N	5	WR
1973			14	WR
1974			14	WR
1975	MIA	N	4	WR

4 yrs. 37 games

Rob Spicer
SPICER, ROBIN E.
B. Jul. 20, 1951, Detroit, MI
Indiana 6'4" 227 lbs.

Year	Team		Games	Pos.
1973	NYJ	N	13	LB

Clarence Spiegel
SPIEGEL, CLARENCE ADOLPH (Rip)
B. Jul. 12, 1898
D. May 28, 1970, Evansville, IN
Campion 5'11" 190 lbs.

Year	Team		Games	Pos.
1921	EVA	A	5	T, G
1922	EVA	N	1	HB

2 yrs. 6 games

Chris Spielman
SPIELMAN, CHRIS
B. Oct. 11, 1965, Canton, OH
Ohio State 6'0" 247 lbs.

Year	Team		Games	Pos.
1988	DET	N	16	LB
1989			16	LB
1990			12	LB
1991			16	LB
1992			16	LB
1993			16	LB
1994			16	LB
1995			16	LB
1996	BUF	N	16	LB

9 yrs. 140 games

Bob Spiers
SPIERS, ROBERT H.
B. Jan. 4, 1895
D. Jul. 8, 1984, Naples, FL
Ohio State 5'11" 193 lbs.

Year	Team		Games	Pos.
1922	AKR	N	10	T
1925	CLE	N	3	T
1926	CLE	A	5	T, G

3 yrs. 18 games

Irving Spikes
SPIKES, IRVING
B. Dec. 21, 1970, Ocean Springs, MS
Northeast Louisiana 5'8" 215 lbs.

Year	Team		Games	Pos.
1994	MIA	N	12	RB
1995			9	RB
1996			15	RB

3 yrs. 36 games

Jack Spikes
SPIKES, JACK ERWIN
B. Feb. 5, 1938, Big Spring, TX
Texas Christian 6'2" 221 lbs.

Year	Team		Games	Pos.
1960	DAL	A	13	FB
1961			6	FB
1962			10	FB
1963	KC	A	14	FB
1964			7	FB
1965	HOU	A	14	FB
1966	BUF	A	14	RB
1967			7	RB

8 yrs. 85 games

John Spilis
SPILIS, JOHN
B. Oct. 14, 1947, Chicago, IL
Northern Illinois 6'3" 205 lbs.

Year	Team		Games	Pos.
1969	GB	N	12	WR
1970			14	WR
1971			14	WR

3 yrs. 40 games

Phil Spiller
SPILLER, PHILLIP A.
B. Apr. 2, 1945, Santa Monica, CA
Los Angeles State 6'0" 195 lbs.

Year	Team		Games	Pos.
1967	STL	N	14	DB
1968	ATL	N	7	DB
1968	CIN	A	4	DB

2 yrs. 25 games

Year	Team	Games	Pos.

Ray Spillers
SPILLERS, EUELL RAY (Brush)
B. Sep. 11, 1914
D. Jul., 1972, Fayetteville, AR
Arkansas 6'3" 218 lbs.

Year	Team		Games	Pos.
1937	PHI	N	10	T

Marc Spindler
SPINDLER, MARC RUDOLPH
B. Nov. 28, 1969, West Scranton, PA
Pittsburgh 6'5" 286 lbs.

Year	Team		Games	Pos.
1990	DET	N	3	NT
1991			16	DT, DE
1992			13	NT, DE
1993			16	DE
1994			9	NT
1995	NYJ	N	10	DT
1996			15	DT
7 yrs.	82 games			

Jack Spinks
SPINKS, JOHN
B. Aug. 15, 1930, Toomsuba, MS
D. Sep. 29, 1994, Jackson, MS
Alcorn State 6'0" 236 lbs.

Year	Team		Games	Pos.
1952	PIT	N	10	FB
1953	CHIC	N	3	B
1955	GB	N	6	G
1956			1	G
1956	NYG	N	3	G
1957			7	G
5 yrs.	30 games			

Art Spinney
SPINNEY, ARTHUR
B. Nov. 8, 1927, Saugus, MA
D. May 27, 1994
Boston College 6'0" 230 lbs.

Year	Team		Games	Pos.
1950	BAL	N	2	E
1953			12	E
1954			12	G
1955			12	G
1956			11	G
1957			11	G
1958			12	G
1959			12	G
1960			10	G
9 yrs.	94 games			

Johnny Spirida
SPIRIDA, JOHN MARTIN
B. Nov. 4, 1914
D. Apr., 1966
St. Anselm's 6'0" 195 lbs.

Year	Team		Games	Pos.
1939	WAS	N	9	E, QB

Bobby Spitulski
SPITULSKI, BOB
B. Sep. 10, 1969, Toledo, OH
Central Florida 6'3" 235 lbs.

Year	Team		Games	Pos.
1992	SEA	N	4	LB
1993			6	LB
1994			16	LB
3 yrs.	26 games			

Andy Spiva
SPIVA, HOWARD ANDREW
B. Feb. 6, 1955, Chattanooga, TN
D. Apr. 3, 1979, Atlanta, GA
Tennessee 6'2" 218 lbs.

Year	Team		Games	Pos.
1977	ATL	N	13	LB

Mike Spivey
SPIVEY, MICHAEL JAMES
B. Mar. 10, 1954, Houston, TX
Colorado 6'0" 196 lbs.

Year	Team		Games	Pos.
1977	CHI	N	14	CB

Mike Spivey continued

Year	Team		Games	Pos.
1978			16	CB
1979			16	CB
1980	OAK	N	9	S
1980	NO	N	2	CB
1981			12	CB
1982	ATL	N	8	CB
6 yrs.	77 games			

Sebron Spivey
SPIVEY, SEBRON
B. Aug. 2, 1964
Southern Illinois 5'11" 180 lbs.

Year	Team		Games	Pos.
1987	DAL	N	2	WR

Bob Sponaugle
SPONAUGLE, ROBERT R.
B. Jan. 31, 1928, Harrisburg, PA
D. Nov. 19, 1986, Hershey, PA
Pennsylvania 6'1" 203 lbs.

Year	Team		Games	Pos.
1949	NYB	N	2	E

Danny Spradlin
SPRADLIN, DANNY RAY
B. Mar. 3, 1959, Maryville, TN
Tennessee 6'1" 228 lbs.

Year	Team		Games	Pos.
1981	DAL	N	16	LB
1982			9	LB
1983	TB	N	16	LB
1984			15	LB
1985	STL	N	8	LB
5 yrs.	64 games			

Hal Springer
SPRINGER, HAROLD
B. May 10, 1922, Albuquerque, NM
D. May, 1981, Staten Island, NY
Central Oklahoma 6'4" 212 lbs.

Year	Team		Games	Pos.
1945	NYG	N	7	E

Kirk Springs
SPRINGS, KIRK EDWARD
B. Aug. 16, 1958, Cincinnati, OH
Miami (Ohio) 6'0" 196 lbs.

Year	Team		Games	Pos.
1981	NYJ	N	10	CB, S
1982			9	S, CB
1983			16	S, CB
1984			16	S, CB
1985			16	S
5 yrs.	67 games			

Ron Springs
SPRINGS, RONALD EDWARD
B. Nov. 4, 1956, Williamsburg, VA
Ohio State 6'2" 225 lbs.

Year	Team		Games	Pos.
1979	DAL	N	16	RB
1980			15	RB
1981			16	FB
1982			9	RB
1983			16	RB
1984			16	RB
1985	TB	N	12	RB
1986			12	RB
8 yrs.	112 games			

Bill Springsteen
SPRINGSTEEN, WILLIAM (Kid)
B. 1901
Deceased
Lehigh 6'0" 193 lbs.

Year	Team		Games	Pos.
1925	FRA	N	18	C
1926			17	E, C
1927	CHIC	N	11	C, E
1928			5	E
4 yrs.	51 games			

Ed Sprinkle
SPRINKLE, EDWARD A.
B. Sep. 3, 1923, Abilene, TX
Hardin-Simmons/Navy 6'1" 206 lbs.

Year	Team		Games	Pos.
1944	CHIB	N	9	G, T, C
1945			6	G
1946			11	E, FB, QB
1948			10	E
1949			12	E
1950			12	E
1951			12	E
1952			12	E
1953			12	E
1954			12	E
1955			12	E
11 yrs.	120 games			

Hugh Sprinkle
SPRINKLE, HUBERT O.
B. 1897
D. Dec. 11, 1961
Missouri/Carnegie-Mellon 6'2" 220 lbs.

Year	Team		Games	Pos.
1923	AKR	N	2	T, G
1924			5	T
1925	CLE	N	6	T
3 yrs.	13 games			

Dennis Sproul
SPROUL, DENNIS EUGENE
B. Jul. 17, 1956, Downey, CA
Arizona State 6'2" 210 lbs.

Year	Team		Games	Pos.
1978	GB		6	QB

Jim Spruill
SPRUILL, JAMES WINFRED
B. Feb. 26, 1923, Dublin, TX
Rice 6'3" 225 lbs.

Year	Team		Games	Pos.
1948	BAL	AA	14	T
1949			12	T
2 yrs.	26 games			

Steve Spurrier
SPURRIER, STEPHEN ORR, SR.
B. Apr. 20, 1945, Johnson City, TN
Florida 6'2" 202 lbs.

Year	Team		Games	Pos.
1967	SF	N	14	QB, P
1968			14	QB, P
1969			6	QB, P
1970			14	QB, P
1971			6	QB, P
1972			13	QB
1973			11	QB
1974			2	QB
1975			11	QB
1976	TB	N	14	QB
10 yrs.	105 games			

Jack Squirek
SQUIREK, JACK STEVE
B. Feb. 16, 1959, Cleveland, OH
Illinois 6'4" 230 lbs.

Year	Team		Games	Pos.
1982	LARI	N	9	LB
1983			16	LB
1984			12	LB
1985			16	LB
1986	MIA	N	2	LB
5 yrs.	55 games			

Seaman Squyres
SQUYRES, CHARLES SEAMAN (Cob)
B. Mar. 2, 1910
D. Nov., 1979, Houston, TX
Rice 6'3" 200 lbs.

Year	Team		Games	Pos.
1933	CIN	N	4	HB

Brian Stablein
STABLEIN, BRIAN
B. Apr. 14, 1970, Erie, PA
Ohio State 6'1" 185 lbs.

Year	Team		Games	Pos.
1994	IND	N	1	WR
1995			15	WR
1996			16	WR
3 yrs.	32 games			

Ken Stabler
STABLER, KEN MICHAEL (Snake)
B. Dec. 25, 1945, Foley, AL
Alabama 6'3" 210 lbs.

Year	Team		Games	Pos.
1970	OAK	N	3	QB
1971			14	QB
1972			14	QB
1973			14	QB
1974			14	QB
1975			12	QB
1976			13	QB
1977			14	QB
1978			16	QB
1979			16	QB
1980	HOU	N	16	QB
1981			13	QB
1982	NO	N	8	QB
1983			14	QB
1984			3	QB
15 yrs.	184 games			

Ed Stacco
STACCO, EDWARD ADAM
B. Apr. 16, 1925, Carbondale, PA
Colgate 6'2" 261 lbs.

Year	Team		Games	Pos.
1947	DET	N	10	T
1948	WAS	N	4	T
2 yrs.	14 games			

Ray Stachowicz
STACHOWICZ, RAYMOND M.
B. Mar. 6, 1959, Cleveland, OH
Michigan State 6'0" 185 lbs.

Year	Team		Games	Pos.
1981	GB	N	16	P
1982			9	P
1983	CHI	N	2	P
3 yrs.	27 games			

Rich Stachowski
STACHOWSKI, RICHARD C.
B. Mar. 19, 1961, Los Angeles, CA
California 6'4" 245 lbs.

Year	Team		Games	Pos.
1983	DEN	N	14	NT

Jack Stackpool
STACKPOOL, JOHN L.
B. Sep. 5, 1918, Chicago, IL
D. Aug. 20, 1976, Lincoln City, OR
Washington 6'1" 207 lbs.

Year	Team		Games	Pos.
1942	PHI	N	7	HB, FB

Billy Stacy
STACY, BILLY MCGOVERN
B. Jul. 30, 1936, Drew, MS
Mississippi State 6'1" 191 lbs.

Year	Team		Games	Pos.
1959	CHIC	N	12	DB
1960	STL	N	11	DB
1961			13	DB
1962			13	DB
1963			9	DB
5 yrs.	58 games			

Jim Stacy
STACY, JAMES WILLIAM (Red)
B. Mar. 4, 1912, Hollis, OK
Oklahoma 6'2" 210 lbs.

Year	Team		Games	Pos.
1935	DET	N	11	T, G
1936			10	T, G

Year	Team		Games	Pos.

Jim Stacy continued

Year	Team		Games	Pos.
1937			8	T, G
3 yrs.	29 games			

Siran Stacy
STACY, SIRAN
B. Aug. 6, 1968, Geneva, AL
Alabama 5'11" 203 lbs.

1992	PHI	N	16	RB

John Stadnik
STADNIK, JOHN STEVEN
B. Feb. 18, 1959, Chicago, IL
Western Illinois 6'4" 275 lbs.

1987	SD	N	3	OT

Spike Staff
STAFF, EDGAR JONATHAN
B. Mar. 13, 1892, Brockton, MA
D. Feb. 14, 1970, Providence, RI
Brown 6'0" 210 lbs.

1925	PRO	N	1	G

Dick Stafford
STAFFORD, RICHARD WADE
B. Aug. 21, 1940
Texas Tech 6'4" 253 lbs.

1962	PHI	N	7	OT, DT
1963			4	DE, DT
2 yrs.	11 games			

Harry Stafford
STAFFORD, ALBERT HARRISON
B. Jun. 18, 1912, Austin, TX
Texas 5'11" 205 lbs.

1934	NYG	N	6	HB

Jon Staggers
STAGGERS, JONATHAN L., JR.
B. Dec. 14, 1948, Richmond, VA
Missouri 5'10" 185 lbs.

1970	PIT	N	12	WR
1971			14	WR
1972	GB	N	14	WR
1973			14	WR
1974			14	WR
1975	DET	N	5	WR
6 yrs.	73 games			

Jeff Staggs
STAGGS, JEFFREY HUGH
B. May 14, 1944, Elgin, IL
San Diego State 6'2" 242 lbs.

1967	SD	A	14	LB
1968			12	LB
1969			13	LB
1970	SD	N	14	DE
1971			5	DE
1972	STL	N	8	LB
1973			13	LB
1974	SD	N	3	LB
8 yrs.	82 games			

Ed Stahl
STAHL, EDWARD H. (Jake)
B. 1893
Deceased
Pittsburgh 5'11" 185 lbs.

1920	CLE	A	3	G
1921	DAY	A	1	T
1921	CLE	A	1	G
2 yrs.	5 games			

Dick Stahlman
STAHLMAN, RICHARD F.

Dick Stahlman continued

B. Oct. 20, 1902
D. May 11, 1970, Chicago, IL
DePaul/Northwestern 6'2" 219 lbs.

1924	HAM	N	1	T
1924	KC	N	1	T
1924	KEN	N	4	G, T
1924	AKR	N	2	T
1925			8	T
1926	RI	A	9	T
1926	CHI	A	4	T, G
1927	NYG	N	10	E, T, G
1930			6	T, G
1931	GB	N	14	T, E
1932			13	T, G
1933	CHIB	N	8	T
8 yrs.	80 games			

Brenden Stai
STAI, BRENDEN
B. Mar. 30, 1972, Phoenix, AZ
Nebraska 6'4" 305 lbs.

1995	PIT	N	15	G
1996			9	G
2 yrs.	24 games			

Jerry Stalcup
STALCUP, JERRY NEWELL
B. Nov. 19, 1938, Rockford, IL
Wisconsin 6'0" 230 lbs.

1960	LA	N	12	G
1961	DEN	A	8	LB
1962			14	LB
3 yrs.	34 games			

Bill Staley
STALEY, WILLIAM P.
B. Sep. 9, 1946, Walnut Creek, CO
Utah State 6'3" 249 lbs.

1968	CIN	A	12	DT
1969			11	DT
1970	CHI	N	11	DT
1971			11	DT
1972			4	DT
5 yrs.	49 games			

Don Stallings
STALLINGS, ALVA DONALD
B. Nov. 18, 1938, Rocky Mount, NC
North Carolina 6'4" 250 lbs.

1960	WAS	N	9	T

Larry Stallings
STALLINGS, LARRY JOSEPH
B. Dec. 11, 1941, Evansville, IN
Georgia Tech 6'2" 230 lbs.

1963	STL	N	14	LB
1964			8	LB
1965			7	LB
1966			14	LB
1967			13	LB
1968			14	LB
1969			14	LB
1970			14	LB
1971			14	LB
1972			13	LB
1973			14	LB
1974			14	LB
1975			13	LB
1976			14	LB
14 yrs.	180 games			

Ramondo Stallings
STALLINGS, RAMONDO ANTONIO
B. Nov. 21, 1971, Winston-Salem, NC
San Diego State 6'7" 285 lbs.

1994	CIN	N	6	DE

Ramondo Stallings cont.

1995			13	DE, DT
1996			12	DE
3 yrs.	31 games			

Robert Stallings
STALLINGS, ROBERT RAY
B. Feb. 23, 1964, McComb, MS
Southern Mississippi 6'6" 250 lbs.

1986	STL	N	3	TE

Dave Stalls
STALLS, DAVID MILTON
B. Sep. 19, 1955, Madison, WI
Northern Colorado 6'4" 245 lbs.

1977	DAL	N	11	DT
1978			16	DT, DE
1979			16	DT, DE
1980	TB	N	15	DE
1981			16	DE
1982			9	DE
1983			6	DE
1983	LARI	N	6	NT
1985			4	DT
8 yrs.	99 games			

John Stallworth
STALLWORTH, JOHNNY LEE
B. Jul. 15, 1952, Tuscaloosa, AL
Alabama A&M 6'2" 190 lbs.

1974	PIT	N	13	WR
1975			11	WR
1976			8	WR
1977			14	WR
1978			16	WR
1979			16	WR
1980			3	WR
1981			16	WR
1982			9	WR
1983			4	WR
1984			16	WR
1985			16	WR
1986			11	WR
1987			12	WR
14 yrs.	165 games			

Ron Stallworth
STALLWORTH, RONALD TOBIAS
B. Feb. 25, 1966, Pensacola, FL
Auburn 6'5" 262 lbs.

1989	NYJ	N	16	DE
1990			16	DE
2 yrs.	32 games			

Tim Stallworth
STALLWORTH, TIM
B. Aug. 26, 1966, Pacoima, CA
Washington State 5'10" 185 lbs.

1990	DEN	N	1	WR

Sylvester Stamps
STAMPS, SYLVESTER
B. Feb. 24, 1961, Vicksburg, MS
Jackson State 5'7" 172 lbs.

1984	ATL	N	10	RB
1985			2	RB
1986			14	RB
1987			7	RB
1988			4	RB
1989	TB	N	10	RB
6 yrs.	47 games			

Frank Stams
STAMS, FRANK MICHAEL
B. Jul. 17, 1965, Akron, OH
Notre Dame 6'2" 240 lbs.

1989	LARM	N	16	LB

Frank Stams continued

1990			14	LB
1991			5	LB
1992	CLE	N	12	LB
1993			14	LB
1994			16	LB
1995	KC	N	1	LB
1995	CLE	N	4	LB
7 yrs.	82 games			

Harry Stanback
STANBACK, HARRY
B. Aug. 17, 1958, Rockingham, NC
North Carolina 6'5" 255 lbs.

1982	BAL	N	2	DE

Haskel Stanback
STANBACK, HASKEL LAVON
B. Mar. 19, 1952, Kannapolis, NC
Tennessee 6'0" 210 lbs.

1974	ATL	N	13	RB
1975			14	RB
1976			14	RB
1977			14	RB
1978			15	RB
1979			13	RB
6 yrs.	83 games			

Jeff Stanciel
STANCIEL, JEFFREY
B. May 4, 1947, Moorhead, MS
Mississippi Valley State 6'0" 192 lbs.

1969	ATL	N	2	RB

Norm Standlee
STANDLEE, NORMAN S.
B. Jul. 19, 1919, Downey, CA
D. Jan. 4, 1981, CA
Stanford 6'2" 238 lbs.

1941	CHIB	N	9	FB
1946	SF	AA	13	FB
1947			14	FB
1948			14	FB
1949			12	FB
1950	SF	N	11	FB
1951			11	FB
1952			1	FB
8 yrs.	85 games			

Dick Stanfel
STANFEL, RICHARD ANTHONY
B. Jul. 20, 1927, San Francisco, CA
San Francisco 6'3" 236 lbs.

1952	DET	N	12	G
1953			12	G
1954			6	G
1955			9	G
1956	WAS	N	11	G
1957			12	G
1958			11	G
7 yrs.	73 games			

Bill Stanfill
STANFILL, WILLIAM THOMAS
B. Jan. 13, 1947, Cairo, GA
Georgia 6'5" 251 lbs.

1969	MIA	A	13	DE
1970	MIA	N	14	DE
1971			14	DE
1972			14	DE
1973			14	DE
1974			14	DE
1975			13	DE
1976			14	DE
8 yrs.	110 games			

Year	Team	Games	Pos.

Scott Stankavage
STANKAVAGE, L. SCOTT
B. Jul. 5, 1962, Philadelphia, PA
North Carolina 6'1" 192 lbs.

Year	Team		Games	Pos.
1984	DEN	N	1	QB
1987	MIA	N	3	QB
2 yrs.	4 games			

Basil Stanley
STANLEY, B.L.
B. Feb. 8, 1896
D. Jul. 17, 1975, San Francisco, CA
Wabash/Notre Dame/Illinois/St. Mary's
5'9" 195 lbs.

Year	Team		Games	Pos.
1924	RI	N	1	G

Buster Stanley
STANLEY, WALTER
B. May 14, 1970, Youngstown, OH
Michigan 6'2" 283 lbs.

Year	Team		Games	Pos.
1994	NE	N	6	NT

C.B. Stanley
STANLEY, CLAIR B.
B. Jan. 25, 1919
D. Apr., 1977, Tulsa, OK
Tulsa 6'4" 225 lbs.

Year	Team		Games	Pos.
1946	BUF	AA	13	T

Israel Stanley
STANLEY, ISRAEL DAMON
B. Apr. 21, 1970, San Diego, CA
Arizona State 6'3" 260 lbs.

Year	Team		Games	Pos.
1995	NO	N	14	DE

Walter Stanley
STANLEY, WALTER
B. Nov. 5, 1962, Chicago, IL
Colorado/Mesa (Colorado) 5'9" 179 lbs.

Year	Team		Games	Pos.
1985	GB	N	14	WR
1986			16	WR
1987			12	WR
1988			7	WR
1989	DET	N	14	WR
1990	WAS	N	9	WR
1992	SD	N	1	WR
1992	NE	N	13	WR
7 yrs.	86 games			

Don Stansauk
STANSAUK, DONALD J.
B. Apr. 2, 1925, Los Angeles, CA
Denver 6'1" 255 lbs.

Year	Team		Games	Pos.
1950	GB	N	11	T

Bill Stanton
STANTON, WILLIAM MCK.
B. 1925, Rowland, NC
North Carolina State 6'2" 210 lbs.

Year	Team		Games	Pos.
1949	BUF	AA	10	E

Hank Stanton
STANTON, HENRY R.
B. Aug. 24, 1920
D. Apr. 11, 1975, Phoenix, AZ
Arizona 6'2" 200 lbs.

Year	Team		Games	Pos.
1946	NY	AA	6	E
1947			9	E
2 yrs.	15 games			

Jack Stanton
STANTON, JOHN
B. Jun. 6, 1938, Bridgeville, PA
North Carolina State 6'1" 180 lbs.

Year	Team		Games	Pos.
1961	PIT	N	2	HB

Ken Starch
STARCH, KENNETH
B. Mar. 5, 1954, La Crosse, WI
Wisconsin 5'11" 210 lbs.

Year	Team		Games	Pos.
1976	GB	N	6	RB

Tony Stargell
STARGELL, TONY
B. Aug. 7, 1966, La Grange, GA
Tennessee State 5'11" 190 lbs.

Year	Team		Games	Pos.
1990	NYJ	N	16	CB
1991			16	CB
1992	IND	N	13	DB
1993			16	CB
1994	TB	N	10	CB
1995			14	CB
1996	KC	N	8	CB
7 yrs.	93 games			

Chad Stark
STARK, CHAD WILLIAM
B. Apr. 4, 1964, Decorah, IA
North Dakota State 6'1" 220 lbs.

Year	Team		Games	Pos.
1987	SEA	N	2	RB

Howie Stark
STARK, HOWARD B.
B. Dec. 20, 1896
D. Mar., 1981, Wisconsin
Wisconsin 6'0" 210 lbs.

Year	Team		Games	Pos.
1923	RAC	N	3	T

Rohn Stark
STARK, ROHN TAYLOR
B. May 4, 1959, Minneapolis, MN
Florida State 6'3" 200 lbs.

Year	Team		Games	Pos.
1982	BAL	N	9	P
1983			16	P
1984	IND	N	16	P
1985			16	P
1986			16	P
1987			12	P
1988			16	P
1989			16	P
1990			16	P
1991			16	P
1992			16	P
1993			16	P
1994			16	P
1995	PIT	N	16	P
1996	CAR	N	16	P
15 yrs.	229 games			

George Starke
STARKE, GEORGE LAWRENCE
B. Jul. 18, 1948, New York, NY
Columbia 6'5" 255 lbs.

Year	Team		Games	Pos.
1973	WAS	N	14	OT
1974			14	OT
1975			14	OT
1976			14	OT
1977			14	OT
1978			9	OT
1979			16	OT
1980			13	OT
1981			14	OT
1982			9	OT
1983			16	OT
1984			9	OT
12 yrs.	156 games			

Marshall Starks
STARKS, MARSHALL L.
B. 1939
Illinois 6'0" 190 lbs.

Year	Team		Games	Pos.
1963	NY	A	14	DB
1964			4	DB
2 yrs.	18 games			

Timothy Starks
STARKS, TIMOTHY
B. Dec. 30, 1963, Mobile, AL
Kent State 5'9" 175 lbs.

Year	Team		Games	Pos.
1987	MIN	N	1	CB, S

John Starnes
STARNES, JOHN
B. Dec. 25, 1962
North Texas State 6'3" 185 lbs.

Year	Team		Games	Pos.
1987	ATL	N	1	P

Paul Staroba
STAROBA, PAUL LOUIS
B. Jan. 20, 1949, Flint, MI
Michigan 6'3" 204 lbs.

Year	Team		Games	Pos.
1972	CLE	N	8	WR
1973	GB	N	2	WR
2 yrs.	10 games			

Bart Starr
STARR, BRYAN BARTLETT
B. Jan. 9, 1934, Montgomery, AL
Alabama 6'1" 197 lbs.

Year	Team		Games	Pos.
1956	GB	N	9	QB
1957			12	QB
1958			12	QB
1959			12	QB
1960			12	QB
1961			14	QB
1962			14	QB
1963			13	QB
1964			14	QB
1965			14	QB
1966			14	QB
1967			14	QB
1968			13	QB
1969			12	QB
1970			12	QB
1971			5	QB
16 yrs.	198 games			

Ben Starrett
STARRETT, BENJAMIN L.
B. Nov. 19, 1918, San Francisco, CA
St. Mary's (California) 5'11" 213 lbs.

Year	Team		Games	Pos.
1941	PIT	N	4	B
1942	GB	N	5	QB
1943			6	B
1944			9	QB, FB
1945			8	QB
5 yrs.	32 games			

Stephen Starring
STARRING, STEPHEN DALE
B. Jul. 30, 1961, Baton Rouge, LA
McNeese State 5'10" 172 lbs.

Year	Team		Games	Pos.
1983	NE	N	15	WR
1984			16	WR
1985			16	WR
1986			14	WR
1987			11	WR
1988	TB	N	6	WR
1988	DET	N	6	WR
6 yrs.	84 games			

Leo Stasica
STASICA, LEO W.
B. Jun. 15, 1916, Rockford, IL
D. Sep., 1982, Denver, CO
Colorado 5'11" 185 lbs.

Year	Team		Games	Pos.
1941	BKN	N	6	B
1943	WAS	N	5	B
1944	BOS	N	7	B
3 yrs.	18 games			

Stan Stasica
STASICA, STANLEY J.
B. 1921
South Carolina/Illinois 5'10" 175 lbs.

Year	Team		Games	Pos.
1946	MIA	AA	1	HB

Randy Staten
STATEN, RANDOLPH WILBERT
B. Dec. 24, 1944, Charlotte, NC
Minnesota 6'1" 225 lbs.

Year	Team		Games	Pos.
1967	NYG	N	14	G

Robert Staten
STATEN, ROBERT
B. Nov. 23, 1969, Shibuta, MS
Jackson State 5'11" 240 lbs.

Year	Team		Games	Pos.
1996	TB	N	6	RB

Larry Station
STATION, LARRY WILSON, JR.
B. Dec. 5, 1963, Omaha, NE
Iowa 5'11" 227 lbs.

Year	Team		Games	Pos.
1986	PIT	N	6	LB

Jim Staton
STATON, JAMES
B. May 23, 1927, Ansonville, NC
D. Sep. 16, 1993, Greensboro, NC
Wake Forest 6'4" 246 lbs.

Year	Team		Games	Pos.
1951	WAS	N	8	T

Art Statuto
STATUTO, ARTHUR G.
B. Jul. 17, 1925, Saugus, MA
Notre Dame 6'2" 221 lbs.

Year	Team		Games	Pos.
1948	BUF	AA	14	C
1949			12	C
1950	LA	N	12	C
3 yrs.	38 games			

Roger Staubach
STAUBACH, ROGER THOMAS
B. Feb. 5, 1942, Cincinnati, OH
Navy 6'2" 198 lbs.

Year	Team		Games	Pos.
1969	DAL	N	6	QB
1970			8	QB
1971			13	QB
1972			4	QB
1973			14	QB
1974			14	QB
1975			14	QB
1976			14	QB
1977			14	QB
1978			15	QB
1979			16	QB
11 yrs.	132 games			

Scott Stauch
STAUCH, SCOTT
B. Jan. 3, 1959, Seattle, WA
UCLA 5'11" 204 lbs.

Year	Team		Games	Pos.
1981	NO	N	10	RB

Jason Staurovsky
STAUROVSKY, JASON CHARLES
B. Mar. 23, 1963, Tulsa, OK
Tulsa 5'9" 169 lbs.

Year	Team		Games	Pos.
1987	STL	N	2	K
1988	NE	N	8	K
1989			7	K
1990			16	K
1991			9	K
1992	NYJ	N	4	K
6 yrs.	46 games			

783

Year	Team		Games	Pos.

Ernie Stautner
STAUTNER, ERNEST ALFRED
B. Apr. 20, 1925, Kham, Germany
Boston College 6'1" 230 lbs.

Year	Team		Games	Pos.
1950	PIT	N	12	T
1951			12	T
1952			10	T
1953			8	T
1954			12	T
1955			12	T
1956			12	T
1958			12	T, E
1959			12	T
1960			12	E
1961			14	DT
1962			14	DE
1963			14	DE

13 yrs. 156 games

Odell Stautzenberger
STAUTZENBERGER, WELDON ODELL
B. 1925
Texas A&M 6'0" 218 lbs.

Year	Team		Games	Pos.
1949	BUF	AA	9	G

Joe Staysniak
STAYSNIAK, JOSEPH ANDREW
B. Dec. 8, 1966, Elyria, OH
Ohio State 6'5" 298 lbs.

Year	Team		Games	Pos.
1991	BUF	N	2	OT
1992	KC		6	G
1993	IND	N	14	OT
1994			16	G
1995			16	G
1996	ARI	N	9	OT, G

6 yrs. 63 games

John Steber
STEBER, JOHN WARREN, III
B. Sep. 12, 1923, Mobile, AL
D. Oct., 1975
Vanderbilt/Georgia Tech 6'0" 225 lbs.

Year	Team		Games	Pos.
1946	WAS	N	11	G
1947			12	G
1948			12	G
1949			9	G
1950			12	G

5 yrs. 56 games

Troy Stedman
STEDMAN, TROY M.
B. May 19, 1965, Cedar Falls, IA
Washburn 6'3" 243 lbs.

Year	Team		Games	Pos.
1988	KC	N	5	LB

Joel Steed
STEED, JOEL EDWARD
B. Feb. 17, 1969, Frankfurt, Germany
Colorado 6'2" 290 lbs.

Year	Team		Games	Pos.
1992	PIT	N	11	NT
1993			14	NT
1994			16	NT
1995			12	NT
1996			16	NT

5 yrs. 69 games

Chuck Steele
STEELE, CHUCK
B. Jun. 22, 1964, Los Angeles, CA
California 6'1" 255 lbs.

Year	Team		Games	Pos.
1987	DET	N	3	C

Cliff Steele
STEELE, CLIFFORD
B. 1898
Deceased

Cliff Steele continued
Syracuse/Fordham 5'8" 150 lbs.

Year	Team		Games	Pos.
1921	ROC	A	1	FB
1922	ROC	N	1	QB
1922	AKR	N	4	QB, FB

2 yrs. 6 games

Ernie Steele
STEELE, ERNEST
B. Nov. 2, 1917, Bothell, WA
Washington 6'0" 187 lbs.

Year	Team		Games	Pos.
1942	PHI	N	10	HB
1943	P-P	N	10	HB
1944	PHI	N	9	HB
1945			7	HB
1946			9	HB
1947			12	HB
1948			12	HB

7 yrs. 69 games

Red Steele
STEELE, PERCY D.
B. Aug. 9, 1897, McArthur, OH
D. Mar. 28, 1974, Ojai, CA
Miami (Ohio)/Harvard 6'0" 176 lbs.

Year	Team		Games	Pos.
1921	CAN	A	9	E

Robert Steele
STEELE, ROBERT HUGH
B. Aug. 2, 1956, Columbus, GA
North Alabama 6'4" 196 lbs.

Year	Team		Games	Pos.
1978	DAL	N	14	WR
1979	MIN	N	16	WR

2 yrs. 30 games

Anthony Steels
STEELS, WILLIAM ANTHONY
B. Jan. 8, 1959, Sacramento, CA
Nebraska 5'9" 200 lbs.

Year	Team		Games	Pos.
1985	SD	N	6	RB
1985	BUF	N	9	RB
1987	SD	N	2	RB

2 yrs. 17 games

Frank Steen
STEEN, FRANK
B. Apr. 1, 1914
D. Oct., 1984, Greenville, TX
Rice 6'1" 190 lbs.

Year	Team		Games	Pos.
1939	GB	N	3	E

Jim Steen
STEEN, JAMES
B. Mar. 28, 1913, Brooklyn, NY
D. Nov. 23, 1983, Detroit, MI
Syracuse 6'2" 205 lbs.

Year	Team		Games	Pos.
1935	DET	N	9	T
1936			11	T

2 yrs. 20 games

Dick Steere
STEERE, RICHARD EDWARD
B. Mar. 2, 1927, Chicago, IL
Drake 6'4" 240 lbs.

Year	Team		Games	Pos.
1951	PHI	N	5	T

Jim Steffen
STEFFEN, JAMES WILLIAM
B. May 1, 1936, Orange, CA
Occidental/UCLA 6'0" 196 lbs.

Year	Team		Games	Pos.
1959	DET	N	9	DB
1960			12	DB
1961	WAS	N	14	DB
1962			14	DB
1963			13	DB
1964			14	DB

Jim Steffen continued

Year	Team		Games	Pos.
1965			14	DB

7 yrs. 90 games

Milt Stegall
STEGALL, MILT
B. Jan. 25, 1970, Cincinnati, OH
Miami (Ohio) 6'0" 184 lbs.

Year	Team		Games	Pos.
1992	CIN	N	16	WR
1993			4	WR
1994			1	WR

3 yrs. 21 games

Larry Stegent
STEGENT, LARRY R.
B. Dec. 1, 1947, Houston, TX
Texas A&M 6'1" 200 lbs.

Year	Team		Games	Pos.
1971	STL		7	RB

Pete Steger
STEGER, PETER
B. Nov., 1896
Deceased
None

Year	Team		Games	Pos.
1921	CHIC	A	6	HB, FB

Ron Stehouwer
STEHOUWER, RONALD
B. Feb. 4, 1937
Colorado State 6'2" 232 lbs.

Year	Team		Games	Pos.
1960	PIT	N	12	G
1961			14	G
1962			14	G
1963			14	G
1964			14	G

5 yrs. 68 games

Bill Stein
STEIN, WILLIAM E. (Red)
B. May 28, 1899
D. Aug., 1983, Two Harbors, WI
Fordham 6'0" 190 lbs.

Year	Team		Games	Pos.
1923	DUL		6	G
1924			6	G, T
1925			3	C
1926			13	C, G
1927			1	C
1928	CHIC	N	2	C
1929			3	G, C

7 yrs. 34 games

Bob Stein
STEIN, ROBERT ALLEN
B. Jan. 22, 1948, Minneapolis, MN
Minnesota 6'2" 235 lbs.

Year	Team		Games	Pos.
1969	KC	A	14	LB
1970	KC	N	14	LB
1971			14	LB
1972			8	LB
1973	LA	N	13	LB
1974			14	LB
1975	SD	N	3	LB
1975	MIN	N	9	LB

7 yrs. 89 games

Herb Stein
STEIN, HERBERT ALFRED
B. Mar. 27, 1898, Warren, OH
D. Nov. 3, 1980, North Jackson, OH
Pittsburgh 6'1" 186 lbs.

Year	Team		Games	Pos.
1921	BUF	A	1	G
1922	TOL	N	9	G, T, C
1924	FRA	N	13	C, E
1925	POT	N	12	C
1926			10	C
1928			10	C, G, E

6 yrs. 55 games

Russ Stein
STEIN, RUSSELL FREDERICK
B. Apr. 21, 1896, Warren, OH
D. Jun. 1, 1970, Niles, OH
Washington & Jefferson 6'1" 210 lbs.

Year	Team		Games	Pos.
1922	TOL	N	6	T, G
1924	FRA	N	13	T, C
1925	POT	N	10	T
1926	CAN	N	8	E

4 yrs. 37 games

Sammy Stein
STEIN, SAMUEL
B. Apr. 1, 1905
D. Mar. 30, 1966, Las Vegas, NV
None 6'0" 195 lbs.

Year	Team		Games	Pos.
1926	NEW	A	2	E
1929	SI	N	9	E, HB
1930			12	E
1931	NYG	N	8	E, T
1932	BKN	N	1	E

5 yrs. 32 games

Larry Steinbach
STEINBACH, LAWRENCE J.
B. Dec. 23, 1900, New Rockford, ND
D. 1967, Carrington, ND
St. Thomas (Minnesota) 6'0" 220 lbs.

Year	Team		Games	Pos.
1930	CHIB	N	11	T
1931			4	T
1931	CHIC	N	2	T
1932			7	G, E
1933			1	T
1933	PHI	N	4	T

4 yrs. 29 games

Don Steinbrunner
STEINBRUNNER, DONALD THOMAS
B. Apr. 5, 1932, Bellingham, WA
D. Jul. 20, 1967, Kontum, Vietnam
Washington State 6'3" 220 lbs.

Year	Team		Games	Pos.
1953	CLE	N	8	T

Rebel Steiner
STEINER, ROY
B. Aug. 27, 1927, Ensley, AL
Alabama 6'0" 185 lbs.

Year	Team		Games	Pos.
1950	GB	N	12	DB
1951			12	DB

2 yrs. 24 games

Al Steinfeld
STEINFELD, ALAN A.
B. Oct. 28, 1958, Brooklyn, NY
C.W. Post 6'5" 256 lbs.

Year	Team		Games	Pos.
1982	KC	N	7	OT, C
1983	HOU	N	8	G
1983	NYG	N	5	C

2 yrs. 20 games

Fred Steinfort
STEINFORT, FREDERICK W.
B. Nov. 3, 1953, Wetter, Germany
Boston College 5'11" 180 lbs.

Year	Team		Games	Pos.
1976	OAK	N	7	K
1977	ATL	N	7	K
1978			6	K
1979	DEN	N	1	K
1980			16	K
1981			16	K
1983	NE	N	9	K
1986	BUF	N	2	K

8 yrs. 64 games

Gil Steinke
STEINKE, GILBERT ERWIN

Gil Steinke continued

B. May 3, 1919, Ganado, TX
D. May 10, 1995, Texas
Texas A&I, Kingsville 6'0" 175 lbs.

Year	Team		Games	Pos.
1945	PHI	N	7	HB
1946			10	HB
1947			6	HB
1948			2	HB
4 yrs.	25 games			

Bill Steinkemper

STEINKEMPER, WILLIAM JACOB
B. Dec. 27, 1913, Hanna, OK
D. 1972
Notre Dame 6'2" 220 lbs.

Year	Team		Games	Pos.
1943	CHIB	N	10	T

Dean Steinkuhler

STEINKUHLER, DEAN
B. Jan. 27, 1961, Burr, NE
Nebraska 6'3" 283 lbs.

Year	Team		Games	Pos.
1984	HOU	N	10	OT
1986			16	G
1987			11	OT, G
1988			16	OT, G
1989			16	OT
1990			15	OT
1991			16	OT
7 yrs.	100 games			

Ken Steinmetz

STEINMETZ, KENNETH C.
B. Aug. 7, 1924, Providence, RI
none 6'0" 188 lbs.

Year	Team		Games	Pos.
1944	BOS	N	6	FB, QB
1945			10	FB
2 yrs.	16 games			

Greg Stemrick

STEMRICK, GREGORY EARL, SR.
B. Oct. 25, 1951, Cincinnati, OH
Colorado State 5'11" 185 lbs.

Year	Team		Games	Pos.
1975	HOU	N	11	CB
1976			14	CB
1977			9	CB
1978			16	CB
1979			16	CB
1980			16	CB
1981			16	CB
1982			8	CB
1983	NO	N	11	CB
9 yrs.	117 games			

Jan Stenerud

STENERUD, JAN
B. Nov. 26, 1942, Fetsund, Norway
Montana State 6'2" 187 lbs.

Year	Team		Games	Pos.
1967	KC	A	14	K
1968			14	K
1969			14	K
1970	KC	N	14	K
1971			14	K
1972			14	K
1973			14	K
1974			14	K
1975			14	K
1976			14	K
1977			14	K
1978			16	K
1979			16	K
1980	GB	N	4	K
1981			16	K
1982			9	K
1983			16	K
1984	MIN	N	16	K
1985			16	K
19 yrs.	263 games			

Brian Stenger

STENGER, BRIAN F.
B. Jan. 16, 1947, Euclid, OH
Notre Dame 6'4" 226 lbs.

Year	Team		Games	Pos.
1969	PIT	N	14	LB
1970			7	LB
1971			14	LB
1972			14	LB
1973	NE	N	10	LB
5 yrs.	59 games			

Paul Stenn

STENKO, PAUL
B. Jul. 12, 1918, Berwick, PA
Villanova 6'2" 242 lbs.

Year	Team		Games	Pos.
1942	NYG	N	11	T
1946	WAS	N	8	T
1947	PIT	N	11	T
1948	CHIB	N	12	T
1949			11	T
1950			12	T
1951			12	T
7 yrs.	77 games			

Fred Stennett

STENNETT, FREDERICK F. (Stud)
B. Feb. 8, 1907
D. Aug. 23, 1989, Ventura, CA
St. Mary's (California) 6'0" 194 lbs.

Year	Team		Games	Pos.
1931	POR	N	9	HB, QB
1932	CHIC	N	1	HB
2 yrs.	10 games			

Mike Stensrud

STENSRUD, MICHAEL IVER
B. Feb. 19, 1956, Forest City, IA
Iowa State 6'5" 280 lbs.

Year	Team		Games	Pos.
1979	HOU	N	6	DE
1980			16	DE
1981			16	DE
1982			9	DE
1983			16	NT
1984			16	NT
1985			16	NT
1986	MIN	N	11	DT
1987	TB	N	12	NT
1988	KC	N	13	NT
1989	WAS	N	8	DT
11 yrs.	139 games			

Steve Stenstrom

STENSTROM, STEVE
B. Dec. 23, 1971, El Toro, CA
Stanford 6'2" 200 lbs.

Year	Team		Games	Pos.
1995	CHI	N	2	QB
1996			1	QB
2 yrs.	3 games			

Joe Stepanek

STEPANEK, JOSEPH P.
B. Nov. 6, 1963, Marshalltown, IA
Minnesota 6'5" 268 lbs.

Year	Team		Games	Pos.
1987	MIN	N	1	DT

Scott Stephen

STEPHEN, SCOTT
B. Jun. 18, 1964, Los Angeles, CA
Arizona State 6'2" 237 lbs.

Year	Team		Games	Pos.
1987	GB	N	8	LB
1988			8	LB
1989			16	LB
1990			16	LB
1991			16	LB
1992	LARM	N	16	LB
6 yrs.	80 games			

Bill Stephens

STEPHENS, WILLIAM ALEXANDER
B. Jul. 28, 1904, New York, NY
D. Jul. 25, 1993, Claremont, CA
Brown 5'8" 185 lbs.

Year	Team		Games	Pos.
1926	BKN	N	5	C

Bill Stephens

STEPHENS, WILLIAM SAMUEL
B. Jun. 16, 1903
D. Mar., 1980, Dilltown, PA
Bucknell 6'0" 185 lbs.

Year	Team		Games	Pos.
1926	BOS	A	5	T, G, C

Bruce Stephens

STEPHENS, BRUCE ANTHONY
B. Oct. 31, 1956, Columbus, GA
Columbia 5'9" 170 lbs.

Year	Team		Games	Pos.
1978	NYJ	N	6	WR, CB

Calvin Stephens

STEPHENS, CALVIN
B. Oct. 25, 1957, Kings Mountain, NC
South Carolina 6'2" 285 lbs.

Year	Team		Games	Pos.
1992	NE	N	14	G

Darnell Stephens

STEPHENS, DARNELL
B. Jan. 29, 1973, San Antonio, TX
Clemson 5'11" 253 lbs.

Year	Team		Games	Pos.
1995	TB	N	12	LB
1996			1	LB
2 yrs.	13 games			

Hal Stephens

STEPHENS, HAL FRANKLIN
B. Apr. 14, 1961, Whiteville, NC
East Carolina 6'4" 252 lbs.

Year	Team		Games	Pos.
1985	DET	N	1	NT
1985	KC	N	1	DE

Harold Stephens

STEPHENS, HAROLD
B. 1939
Hardin-Simmons 5'11" 175 lbs.

Year	Team		Games	Pos.
1962	NY	A	6	QB

Jamain Stephens

STEPHENS, JAMAIN
B. Jan. 9, 1974, Lumberton, NC
North Carolina A&T 6'5" 315 lbs.

Year	Team		Games	Pos.
1996	PIT	N	1	OT

John Stephens

STEPHENS, JOHN MILTON
B. Feb. 23, 1966, Shreveport, LA
Northwestern State (Louisiana) 6'1" 220 lbs.

Year	Team		Games	Pos.
1988	NE	N	16	RB
1989			14	RB
1990			16	RB
1991			14	RB
1992			16	RB
1993	GB	N	5	RB
1993	KC	N	7	RB
6 yrs.	88 games			

Johnny Stephens

STEPHENS, JOHN BAILEY
B. Jan. 15, 1915, Parkersburg, WV
Marshall 6'1" 190 lbs.

Year	Team		Games	Pos.
1938	CLE	N	11	E

Larry Stephens

STEPHENS, LAWRENCE CLIFTON
B. Sep. 24, 1938, Buda, TX
Texas 6'4" 245 lbs.

Year	Team		Games	Pos.
1960	CLE	N	12	DT
1961			14	DT
1962	LA	N	14	DE
1963	DAL	N	14	DE
1964			13	DE
1965			13	DE
1966			14	DE
1967			9	DE
8 yrs.	103 games			

Louis Stephens

STEPHENS, LOUIS EDWARD (Red)
B. May 10, 1930, Denver, CO
San Francisco 6'0" 230 lbs.

Year	Team		Games	Pos.
1955	WAS	N	11	G
1956			11	G
1957			12	G
1958			12	G
1959			12	G
1960			12	G
6 yrs.	70 games			

Mac Stephens

STEPHENS, MAC
B. Jan. 20, 1968, Akron, OH
Minnesota 6'3" 220 lbs.

Year	Team		Games	Pos.
1990	NYJ	N	2	LB
1991	MIN	N	3	LB
2 yrs.	5 games			

Ray Stephens

STEPHENS, LESLIE R.
B. Dec. 16, 1902
D. Feb., 1987, Queens, NY
Idaho 5'11" 190 lbs.

Year	Team		Games	Pos.
1926	LA	A	10	C
1927	NYY	N	10	C, G
2 yrs.	20 games			

Rich Stephens

STEPHENS, RICHARD SCOTT
B. Jan. 1, 1965, St. Louis, MO
Tulsa 6'7" 300 lbs.

Year	Team		Games	Pos.
1993	LARI	N	16	G
1995	OAK	N	13	OT, G
2 yrs.	29 games			

Rod Stephens

STEPHENS, RODREQUIS LA'VANT
B. Jun. 14, 1966, Atlanta, GA
Georgia Tech 6'1" 237 lbs.

Year	Team		Games	Pos.
1989	SEA	N	10	LB
1990			4	LB
1991			16	LB
1992			16	LB
1993			13	LB
1994			16	LB
1995	WAS	N	16	LB
1996			16	LB
8 yrs.	107 games			

Santo Stephens

STEPHENS, SANTO SEAN
B. Jun. 16, 1969, Washington, DC
Temple 6'4" 232 lbs.

Year	Team		Games	Pos.
1993	KC	N	16	LB
1994	CIN	N	14	LB
1995	JAC	N	13	LB
3 yrs.	43 games			

Year	Team	Games	Pos.

Steve Stephens
STEPHENS, STEVE B.
B. Mar. 4, 1957, Tampa, FL
Oklahoma State 6'3" 227 lbs.

Year	Team		Games	Pos.
1981	NYJ	N	16	TE

Tom Stephens
STEPHENS, THOMAS G.
B. 1935, Galveston, TX
Syracuse 6'1" 207 lbs.

Year	Team		Games	Pos.
1960	BOS	A		OE
1961			9	OE
1962			3	OE
1963			14	OE
1964			14	DB, OE
5 yrs.	40 games			

Dave Stephenson
STEPHENSON, JAMES DAVID
(Trapper)
B. Oct. 22, 1925, Clendenin, WV
D. Jul. 19, 1975, Charleston, WV
Tennessee/West Virginia 6'2" 232 lbs.

Year	Team		Games	Pos.
1950	LA	N	12	G
1951	GB	N	12	G
1952			11	G
1953			12	C
1954			12	C
1955			2	C
6 yrs.	61 games			

Dwight Stephenson
STEPHENSON, DWIGHT EUGENE
B. Nov. 20, 1957, Murfreesboro, NC
Alabama 6'2" 255 lbs.

Year	Team		Games	Pos.
1980	MIA	N	16	C
1981			16	C
1982			9	C
1983			16	C
1984			16	C
1985			16	C
1986			16	C
1987			9	C
8 yrs.	114 games			

Kay Stephenson
STEPHENSON, GEORGE KAY
B. Dec. 17, 1944, De Funiak Springs, FL
Florida 6'1" 208 lbs.

Year	Team		Games	Pos.
1967	SD	A	7	QB
1968	BUF	A	1	QB
2 yrs.	8 games			

Mark Stepnoski
STEPNOSKI, MARK MATTHEW
B. Jan. 20, 1967, Erie, PA
Pittsburgh 6'2" 269 lbs.

Year	Team		Games	Pos.
1989	DAL	N	16	G
1990			16	C, G
1991			16	C
1992			14	C
1993			13	C
1994			16	C
1995	HOU	N	16	C
1996			16	C
8 yrs.	123 games			

Mike Steponovich
STEPONOVICH, MICHAEL M.
B. Dec. 1, 1908
D. May 24, 1974, Inglewood, CA
St. Mary's (California) 5'9" 205 lbs.

Year	Team		Games	Pos.
1933	BOS	N	1	G

Tony Steponovich
STEPONOVICH, TONY ANDREW
B. 1907
Southern California 5'11" 185 lbs.

Year	Team		Games	Pos.
1930	MIN	N	7	E, G, C
1930	FRA	N	2	E
1930	MIN	N	1	E
1930	FRA	N	1	E
1930	MIN	N	1	E

Jack Steptoe
STEPTOE, JACK EUGENE
B. Jan. 21, 1956, Los Angeles, CA
Utah 6'1" 175 lbs.

Year	Team		Games	Pos.
1978	SF	N	6	WR

John Sterling
STERLING, JOHN
B. Sep. 15, 1964
Central Oklahoma 6'2" 203 lbs.

Year	Team		Games	Pos.
1987	GB	N	2	RB

Ed Sternaman
STERNAMAN, EDWARD CARL
(Dutch)
B. Feb. 9, 1895, Chicago, IL
D. Feb. 1, 1973, Chicago, IL
Illinois 5'8" 177 lbs.

Year	Team		Games	Pos.
1920	DEC	A	8	HB
1921			11	HB
1922	CHIB	N	11	HB, QB
1923			12	HB
1924			11	HB
1925			15	HB, FB, QB
1926			14	FB, QB, HB
1927			5	HB, FB
8 yrs.	87 games			

Joey Sternaman
STERNAMAN, JOSEPH THEODORE
B. Feb. 1, 1900, Springfield, IL
D. Mar. 10, 1988, Oak Park, IL
Illinois 5'6" 152 lbs.

Year	Team		Games	Pos.
1922	CHIB	N	12	QB
1923	DUL	N	7	QB, HB
1923	CHIB	N	4	QB
1924			11	QB
1925			15	QB
1926	CHI	A	14	QB
1927	CHIB	N	14	QB
1928			13	QB
1929			15	QB, HB
1930			9	QB
9 yrs.	114 games			

Gil Sterr
STERR, GIL (Pee Wee)
B. Jul. 30, 1900
D. Mar. 12, 1975
Carroll (Wisconsin) 5'6" 151 lbs.

Year	Team		Games	Pos.
1926	RAC	N	3	QB

Bill Stetz
STETZ, WILLIAM A.
B. Sep. 28, 1945, Milwaukee, WI
Boston College 6'3" 250 lbs.

Year	Team		Games	Pos.
1967	PHI	N	2	G

Bob Steuber
STEUBER, ROBERT J.
B. Oct. 25, 1921, Wenonah, NJ
Deceased
Missouri 6'2" 200 lbs.

Year	Team		Games	Pos.
1943	CHIB	N	1	B
1946	CLE	AA	6	HB
1947	LA	AA	3	B

Bob Steuber continued

Year	Team		Games	Pos.
1948	BUF	AA	9	B
4 yrs.	19 games			

Todd Steussie
STEUSSIE, TODD EDWARD
B. Dec. 1, 1970, Canoga Park, CA
California 6'6" 298 lbs.

Year	Team		Games	Pos.
1994	MIN		16	OT
1995			16	OT
1996			16	OT
3 yrs.	48 games			

Billy Stevens
STEVENS, WILLIAM
B. Aug. 27, 1945, Galveston, TX
Texas-El Paso 6'3" 195 lbs.

Year	Team		Games	Pos.
1968	GB	N	1	QB
1969			1	QB
2 yrs.	2 games			

Don Stevens
STEVENS, DONALD
B. May 25, 1928, Massillon, OH
D. Apr., 1976, Struthers, OH
Illinois 5'9" 176 lbs.

Year	Team		Games	Pos.
1952	PHI	N	11	HB
1954			4	HB
2 yrs.	15 games			

Howard Stevens
STEVENS, HOWARD MELVIN, JR. (Mighty Mite)
B. Feb. 9, 1950, Harrisonburg, VA
Randolph-Macon/Louisville 5'5" 167 lbs.

Year	Team		Games	Pos.
1973	NO	N	14	RB
1974			14	RB
1975	BAL	N	12	RB
1976			14	RB
1977			12	RB
5 yrs.	66 games			

Mark Stevens
STEVENS, MARK
B. Feb. 19, 1962, Passaic, NJ
Utah 6'1" 190 lbs.

Year	Team		Games	Pos.
1987	SF	N	2	QB

Matt Stevens
STEVENS, MATT
B. Jun. 15, 1973, Chapel Hill, NC
Appalachian State 6'0" 206 lbs.

Year	Team		Games	Pos.
1996	BUF	N	13	CB

Matt Stevens
STEVENS, MATTHEW ANTHONY
B. Jul. 30, 1964, Sulphur, LA
UCLA 6'0" 190 lbs.

Year	Team		Games	Pos.
1987	KC	N	3	QB

Pete Stevens
STEVENS, PETER P.
B. Jun. 18, 1909, Wilkes-Barre, PA
D. May 5, 1989, Melbourne, FL
Temple 6'0" 215 lbs.

Year	Team		Games	Pos.
1936	PHI	N	4	C

Richard Stevens
STEVENS, RICHARD GLENN
B. Feb. 23, 1949, Dublin, TX
Baylor 6'4" 241 lbs.

Year	Team		Games	Pos.
1970	PHI	N	14	OT
1971			14	OT
1972			7	OT

Richard Stevens continued

Year	Team		Games	Pos.
1973			11	OT
1974			14	OT
5 yrs.	60 games			

Art Stevenson
STEVENSON, ARTHUR
B. Dec. 27, 1897
D. Jun., 1986, New York State
Fordham 6'0" 190 lbs.

Year	Team		Games	Pos.
1926	NYG	N	2	C, T
1926	BKN	N	2	C
1928	NYY	N	1	C
2 yrs.	5 games			

Mark Stevenson
STEVENSON, MARK
B. Feb., 1893
Deceased
None 196 lbs.

Year	Team		Games	Pos.
1922	COL	N	8	G, C

Mark Stevenson
STEVENSON, MARK OLIVER
B. Feb. 24, 1958, Waukegan, IL
Missouri/Western Illinois 6'3" 285 lbs.

Year	Team		Games	Pos.
1985	DET	N	2	OT, G

Ralph Stevenson
STEVENSON, RALPH L.
B. Apr. 11, 1917
D. Jul. 7, 1987, Norman, OK
Oklahoma 5'10" 196 lbs.

Year	Team		Games	Pos.
1940	CLE	N	3	G

Norris Steverson
STEVERSON, NORRIS
B. Jul. 20, 1910
Arizona State 5'10" 185 lbs.

Year	Team		Games	Pos.
1934	C-S		5	QB, HB

Dean Steward
STEWARD, HAROLD DEAN
B. Jul. 12, 1923
D. Jul. 8, 1979, Budd Lake, NJ
Ursinus 6'0" 210 lbs.

Year	Team		Games	Pos.
1943	P-P	N	6	B, E
1994	MIA	N	16	S
2 yrs.	22 games			

Andrew Stewart
STEWART, ANDREW
B. Nov. 20, 1965, Jamaica
Cincinnati 6'5" 265 lbs.

Year	Team		Games	Pos.
1989	CLE	N	16	DE

Charlie Stewart
STEWART, CHARLES E.
B. Jul. 13, 1890
D. Jul., 1969, Batavia, NY
Colgate 5'9" 160 lbs.

Year	Team		Games	Pos.
1923	AKR	N	2	G

James Stewart
STEWART, JAMES
B. Dec. 8, 1971, Vero Beach, FL
Miami (Florida) 6'2" 245 lbs.

Year	Team		Games	Pos.
1995	MIN	N	4	RB

James Stewart
STEWART, JAMES OTTIS
B. Dec. 27, 1971, Morristown, TN
Tennessee 6'1" 221 lbs.

Year	Team		Games	Pos.
1995	JAC	N	14	RB

Year	Team		Games	Pos.

James Stewart continued

Year	Team		Games	Pos.
1996			13	RB
2 yrs.	27 games			

Jimmy Stewart
STEWART, JIMMY
B. Oct. 15, 1954, St. Louis, MO
Tulsa 5'11" 190 lbs.

1977	NO	N	9	S
1979	DET	N	5	S
2 yrs.	14 games			

Joe Stewart
STEWART, JOE L.
B. Nov. 18, 1955, Evanston, IL
Missouri 5'11" 180 lbs.

1978	OAK	N	16	WR
1979			3	WR
2 yrs.	19 games			

Kordell Stewart
STEWART, KORDELL (Slash)
B. Oct. 16, 1972, New Orleans, LA
Colorado 6'1" 212 lbs.

1995	PIT	N	10	QB, WR
1996			16	QB, WR
2 yrs.	26 games			

Mark Stewart
STEWART, MARK ANTHONY
B. Oct. 13, 1959, Palo Alto, CA
Washington 6'3" 232 lbs.

1984	MIN	N	4	LB

Michael Stewart
STEWART, MICHAEL
B. Jul. 12, 1965, Atascadero, CA
Fresno State 5'11" 195 lbs.

1987	LARM	N	12	S
1988			16	S
1989			16	S
1990			16	S
1991			11	S
1992			16	S
1993			16	S
1995	MIA	N	16	S
1996			9	S
9 yrs.	128 games			

Ralph Stewart
STEWART, RALPH E.
B. Dec. 10, 1925, St. Louis, MO
North Carolina/Missouri 6'0" 205 lbs.

1947	NY	AA	9	C
1948			1	C
1948	BAL	AA	14	C
2 yrs.	24 games			

Rayna Stewart
STEWART, RAYNA
B. Jun. 18, 1973, Oklahoma City, OK
Northern Arizona 5'10" 192 lbs.

1996	HOU	N	15	CB

Ryan Stewart
STEWART, RYAN
B. Sep. 30, 1973, Moncks Corner, SC
Georgia Tech 6'1" 207 lbs.

1996	DET	N	14	S

Steve Stewart
STEWART, STEVEN ANDREW
B. May 1, 1956, Minneapolis, MN
Minnesota 6'2" 219 lbs.

1978	ATL	N	12	LB

Steve Stewart continued

1979	GB	N	3	LB
2 yrs.	15 games			

Vaughn Stewart
STEWART, VAUGHN MORTON
B. Jan. 16, 1920, Anniston, AL
Alabama 6'1" 190 lbs.

1943	BKN	N	1	C
1943	CHIC	N	9	C
1944	BKN	N	9	C
2 yrs.	19 games			

Wayne Stewart
STEWART, WAYNE A.
B. Aug. 18, 1947, Cochrane, Ont.
California 6'7" 214 lbs.

1969	NY	A	14	TE
1970	NYJ	N	7	TE
1971			3	TE
1972			14	TE
1974	SD	N	14	TE
5 yrs.	52 games			

Walt Stickel
STICKEL, WALTER E.
B. Mar. 31, 1922, Philadelphia, PA
D. Dec. 6, 1987, Tequesta, FL
Tulsa/Pennsylvania 6'3" 247 lbs.

1946	CHIB	N	10	T
1947			12	T
1948			10	T
1949			12	T
1950	PHI	N	12	T
1951			11	T
6 yrs.	67 games			

Monty Stickles
STICKLES, MONTFORD ANTHONY
B. Aug. 16, 1938, Kingston, NY
Notre Dame 6'4" 232 lbs.

1960	SF	N	12	E
1961			14	OE
1962			14	OE
1963			12	OE
1964			14	OE
1965			14	TE
1966			14	TE
1967			8	TE
1968	NO	N	13	TE
9 yrs.	115 games			

Howard Stidham
STIDHAM, HOWARD
B. Dec. 17, 1954, Radcliffe, KY
Tennessee Tech 6'2" 214 lbs.

1977	SF	N	4	LB

Dave Stief
STIEF, DAVE
B. Jan. 29, 1956, Portland, OR
Portland State 6'3" 195 lbs.

1978	STL	N	15	WR
1979			16	WR
1980			16	WR
1981			12	WR
1982			9	S, CB
1983	WAS	N	3	WR
6 yrs.	71 games			

Jim Stienke
STIENKE, JAMES LEE
B. Nov. 7, 1950, Houston, TX
Southwest Texas State 5'11" 183 lbs.

1973	CLE	N	7	CB
1974	NYG	N	13	CB

Jim Stienke continued

1975			14	CB
1976			13	CB
1977			14	CB
1978	ATL	N	5	DB
6 yrs.	66 games			

Terry Stieve
STIEVE, TERRY ALLAN
B. Mar. 10, 1954, Baraboo, WI
Wisconsin 6'2" 251 lbs.

1976	NO	N	14	G
1977			14	G
1978	STL	N	16	G
1979			14	G
1981			16	G
1982			9	G
1983			16	G
1984			14	G
8 yrs.	113 games			

Jim Stifler
STIFLER, JAMES MADISON
B. Aug. 25, 1901, Swarthmore, PA
D. Jul. 17, 1954, Boston, MA
Brown 5'10" 175 lbs.

1926	PRO	N	7	E, HB
1927			2	E
2 yrs.	9 games			

Jim Stiger
STIGER, JAMES EDWARD
B. Jan. 7, 1941, Carthage, TX
D. Dec. 14, 1981, Lompoc, CA
Washington 5'11" 204 lbs.

1963	DAL	N	14	HB
1964			14	HB
1965			5	FB
1965	LA	N	11	FB
1966			14	FB
1967			5	RB
5 yrs.	63 games			

Art Still
STILL, ARTHUR BARRY
B. Dec. 5, 1955, Camden, NJ
Kentucky 6'7" 253 lbs.

1978	KC	N	16	DE
1979			16	DE
1980			16	DE
1981			11	DE
1982			9	DE
1983			15	DE
1984			16	DE
1985			9	DE
1986			16	DE
1987			12	DE
1988	BUF	N	15	DE
1989			16	DE
12 yrs.	167 games			

Bryan Still
STILL, BRYAN ANDREI
B. Jun. 3, 1974, Newport News, VA
Virginia Tech 5'11" 174 lbs.

1996	SD	N	16	WR

Jim Still
STILL, JAMES EDWARD, JR.
B. Mar. 5, 1924, Columbia, SC
Georgia Tech 6'3" 193 lbs.

1948	BUF	AA	12	B
1949			9	B
2 yrs.	21 games			

Ken Stills
STILLS, KENNETH LEE

Ken Stills continued
B. Sep. 6, 1963, Oceanside, CA
Wisconsin 5'10" 186 lbs.

1985	GB	N	8	CB, S
1986			16	CB, S
1987			11	DB
1988			14	CB, S
1989			16	CB, S
1990	MIN	N	12	S
6 yrs.	77 games			

Roger Stillwell
STILLWELL, ROGER HOWARD
B. Nov. 17, 1951, Santa Monica, CA
Stanford 6'5" 259 lbs.

1975	CHI	N	13	DT
1976			13	DT
1977			5	DE
3 yrs.	31 games			

Pete Stinchcomb
STINCHCOMB, GAYLORD R.
B. Jun. 24, 1895, Fostoria, OH
D. Aug. 24, 1973, Findlay, OH
Ohio State 5'8" 155 lbs.

1921	DEC	A	11	HB, QB
1922	CHIB	N	12	HB, FB
1923	COL	N	7	HB, QB
1923	CLE	N	1	HB
1926	LOU	N	3	HB, QB
4 yrs.	34 games			

Tom Stincic
STINCIC, THOMAS D.
B. Nov. 24, 1946, Cleveland, OH
Michigan 6'2" 229 lbs.

1969	DAL	N	14	LB
1970			14	LB
1971			7	LB
1972	NO	N	7	LB
4 yrs.	42 games			

Darryl Stingley
STINGLEY, DARRYL FLOYD
B. Sep. 18, 1951, Chicago, IL
Purdue 6'0" 194 lbs.

1973	NE	N	14	WR
1974			5	WR
1975			14	WR
1976			13	WR
1977			14	WR
5 yrs.	60 games			

Jim Stinnette
STINNETTE, JAMES EDWARD
B. Mar. 12, 1938, Corvallis, OR
Oregon State 6'1" 230 lbs.

1962	DEN	A	10	FB

Lemuel Stinson
STINSON, LEMUEL DALE
B. May 10, 1966, Houston, TX
Texas Tech 5'9" 159 lbs.

1988	CHI	N	15	CB, S
1989			12	CB, S
1990			10	CB, S
1991			16	CB
1992			16	CB
5 yrs.	69 games			

Carel Stith
STITH, CAREL LEWIS
B. May 24, 1945, Lincoln, NE
Nebraska 6'5" 257 lbs.

1967	HOU	A	14	DE
1968			3	DE

Year	Team	Games	Pos.

Carel Stith *continued*

Year	Team	Games	Pos.
1969		14	DT
3 yrs.	31 games		

Howie Stith
STITH, HOWARD
B. Jan., 1896
Deceased
None

1921	LOU	A	1	G

Bill Stits
STITS, WILLIAM DAVID
B. Jul. 26, 1931, Lomita, CA
UCLA 6'0" 194 lbs.

1954	DET	N	12	HB
1955			12	HB
1956			12	HB
1957	SF	N	12	HB
1958			12	HB
1959	WAS	N	5	HB
1959	NYG	N	5	HB
1960			12	HB
7 yrs.	82 games			

Bill Stobbs
STOBBS, WILLIAM THOMAS
B. May 28, 1896
D. Nov. 14, 1968, Norfolk, VA
Washington & Jefferson 5'7" 165 lbs.

1921	DET	A	7	QB

Herb Stock
STOCK, HERBERT
B. Sep. 3, 1899
Deceased
Kenyon 6'0" 182 lbs.

1924	COL	N	7	HB, FB, G

John Stock
STOCK, JOHN
B. 1934
Pittsburgh 6'2" 210 lbs.

1956	PIT	N	2	E

Mark Stock
STOCK, MARK ANTHONY
B. Apr. 27, 1966, Canton, OH
Virginia Military Institute 5'11" 177 lbs.

1989	PIT	N	8	WR
1993	WAS	N	3	WR
1996	IND	N	14	WR
3 yrs.	25 games			

Ralph Stockemer
STOCKEMER, RALPH
B. Dec. 20, 1962
Baylor 6'1" 212 lbs.

1987	KC	N	2	RB

Herschel Stockton
STOCKTON, HERSCHEL (Mule)
B. 1914
McMurry 6'1" 214 lbs.

1937	PHI	N	11	G
1938			11	G
2 yrs.	22 games			

Hust Stockton
STOCKTON, HOUSTON
B. 1902
D. 1967
Gonzaga 5'11" 193 lbs.

1925	FRA	N	14	FB, HB

Hust Stockton *continued*

Year	Team	Games	Pos.
1926			16	FB, HB
1928			13	FB, HB
1929	PRO	N	1	HB
1929	BOS	N	8	HB, FB
4 yrs.	52 games			

Eric Stocz
STOCZ, ERIC
B. May 25, 1974, Cortland, OH
Westminster 6'3" 278 lbs.

1996	DET	N	1	TE

Earl Stoecklein
STOECKLEIN, EARL
B. Oct. 1, 1896
D. Jan., 1975, Monroe, CT
None 6'2" 205 lbs.

1920	DAY	A	2	G

Terry Stoepel
STOEPEL, TERRY
B. Feb. 8, 1945, Cincinnati, OH
Tulsa 6'4" 235 lbs.

1967	CHI	N	6	TE
1970	HOU	N	14	TE
2 yrs.	20 games			

John Stofa
STOFA, JOHN CARL
B. Jun. 29, 1942, Johnstown, PA
Buffalo 6'3" 210 lbs.

1966	MIA	A	7	QB
1967			1	QB
1968	CIN	A	10	QB
1969	MIA	A	1	QB
1970	MIA	N	8	QB
5 yrs.	27 games			

Ken Stofer
STOFER, KENNETH LAMONT
B. Aug. 10, 1919, Lakewood, OH
Cornell 5'9" 188 lbs.

1946	BUF	AA	11	HB

Eddie Stofko
STOFKO, EDWARD
B. 1920
St. Francis (Pennsylvania) 6'1" 192 lbs.

1945	PIT	N	2	HB

Frank Stojack
STOJACK, FRANK NICHOLAS (Toughie)
B. Feb. 11, 1912, Wycliffe, B.C.
D. Aug. 30, 1987, Tacoma, WA
Washington State 5'10" 194 lbs.

1935	BKN	N	12	G
1936			11	G
2 yrs.	23 games			

Eric Stokes
STOKES, ERIC
B. Jan. 13, 1962
Northeastern 5'4" 255 lbs.

1987	NE	N	1	G

Fred Stokes
STOKES, LOUIS FRED
B. Mar. 14, 1964, Vidalia, GA
Georgia Southern 6'3" 268 lbs.

1987	LARM	N	8	DE
1988			5	DE
1989	WAS	N	16	DE

Fred Stokes *continued*

Year	Team	Games	Pos.
1990			16	DE
1991			16	DE
1992			16	DE
1993	LARM	N	15	DE
1994			16	DE
1995	STL	N	16	DE
1996	NO	N	9	DE
10 yrs.	133 games			

Jesse Stokes
STOKES, JESSE V. (J.V.)
B. Aug. 27, 1946, Kerrville, TX
Corpus Christi 6'0" 190 lbs.

1968	DEN	A	2	DB

J.J. Stokes
STOKES, JERAL JAMAL
B. Oct. 6, 1972, San Diego, CA
UCLA 6'4" 217 lbs.

1995	SF	N	12	WR
1996			6	WR
2 yrs.	18 games			

Lee Stokes
STOKES, LEE JAMES, JR. (Dixie)
B. Aug. 24, 1913, Shreveport, LA
D. Dec., 1967
Centenary 6'0" 205 lbs.

1937	DET	N	11	C
1938			10	C
1943	CHIC	N	8	C
3 yrs.	29 games			

Sims Stokes
STOKES, SIMS
B. Apr. 18, 1944, Mobile, AL
Kansas/Northern Arizona 6'1" 198 lbs.

1967	DAL	N	3	OE

Tim Stokes
STOKES, TIMOTHY PAUL
B. Mar. 16, 1950, Oakland, CA
Oregon 6'5" 252 lbs.

1974	LA	N	6	OT
1975	WAS	N	5	OT
1976			14	OT
1977			14	OT
1978	GB	N	16	OT
1979			16	OT
1980			15	OT
1981	NYG	N	3	OT
1981	GB	N	7	OT
1982			9	OT
9 yrs.	105 games			

Eric Stolberg
STOLBERG, ERIC C.
B. Dec. 13, 1947, Massillon, OH
Indiana 6'2" 180 lbs.

1971	NE	N	1	WR

Anton Stolfa
STOLFA, ANTON (Butch)
B. Sep. 6, 1917
D. Mar., 1976
Luther 6'0" 195 lbs.

1939	CHIB	N	1	QB

Tommy Stolhandske
STOLHANDSKE, CARL TOMMY
B. 1932, Baytown, TX
Texas 6'2" 210 lbs.

1955	SF	N	12	E

Bryan Stoltenberg
STOLTENBERG, BRYAN
B. Aug. 25, 1972, Kearney, NE
Colorado 6'1" 293 lbs.

1996	SD	N	9	C

Avatus Stone
STONE, AVATUS HARRY
B. Apr. 21, 1931, Washington, DC
Syracuse 6'1" 195 lbs.

1958	BAL	N	1	HB

Billy Stone
STONE, WILLIAM JOHN
B. Oct. 25, 1925, Peoria, IL
Bradley 6'0" 191 lbs.

1949	BAL	AA	12	B
1950	BAL	N	9	HB
1951	CHIB	N	12	HB
1952			10	HB
1953			12	HB
1954			12	HB
6 yrs.	67 games			

Donnie Stone
STONE, EDWARD DONALD
B. Jan. 5, 1937, Fayetteville, AR
Arkansas 6'2" 205 lbs.

1961	DEN	A	14	HB
1962			11	HB
1963			14	HB
1964			9	HB
1965	BUF	A	14	FB
1966	HOU	A	5	FB
6 yrs.	67 games			

Dwight Stone
STONE, DWIGHT
B. Jan. 28, 1964, Florala, AL
Middle Tennessee State 6'0" 188 lbs.

1987	PIT	N	14	RB
1988			16	RB
1989			16	RB
1990			16	WR, RB
1991			16	WR, RB
1992			15	RB, WR
1993			16	WR, RB
1994			16	WR, RB
1995	CAR	N	16	WR
1996			15	WR
10 yrs.	155 games			

Jack Stone
STONE, JACK
B. 1937
Oregon 6'2" 245 lbs.

1960	DAL	A		OT
1961	OAK	A	14	OT
1962			14	OT
3 yrs.	28 games			

Ken Stone
STONE, KENNETH BERNARD, JR.
B. Sep. 14, 1950, Cincinnati, OH
Vanderbilt 6'1" 180 lbs.

1973	BUF	N	6	DB
1973	WAS	N	4	DB
1974			14	S
1975			3	S
1976	TB	N	14	S
1977	STL	N	14	DB
1978			14	S
1979			16	S
1980			16	S
8 yrs.	101 games			

Year	Team		Games	Pos.

Ron Stone
STONE, RON
B. Jul. 20, 1971, West Roxbury, MA
Boston College 6'5" 309 lbs.

Year	Team		Games	Pos.
1994	DAL	N	15	G
1995			16	G, OT
1996	NYG	N	16	G
3 yrs.	47 games			

John Stonebreaker
STONEBREAKER, JOHN S.
B. Apr. 25, 1918, Frankfort, IN
Southern California 6'3" 200 lbs.

1942	GB	N	9	E

Mike Stonebreaker
STONEBREAKER, MICHAEL DAVID
B. Jan. 14, 1967, Baltimore, MD
Notre Dame 6'0" 226 lbs.

1991	CHI	N	16	LB
1994	NO	N	2	LB
2 yrs.	18 games			

Steve Stonebreaker
STONEBREAKER, STEVEN T.
B. Oct. 28, 1938, Moline, IL
D. Mar. 28, 1945, River Ridge, LA
Detroit 6'3" 223 lbs.

1962	MIN	N	14	OE
1963			14	LB
1964	BAL	N	14	LB
1965			14	LB
1966			4	LB
1967	NO	N	10	LB
1968			14	LB
7 yrs.	84 games			

Don Stonesifer
STONESIFER, DONALD HUMPHREY
B. Jan. 29, 1927, Chicago, IL
Northwestern 6'0" 200 lbs.

1951	CHIC	N	12	E
1952			12	E
1953			12	E
1954			12	E
1955			12	E
1956			12	E
6 yrs.	72 games			

Mike Stoops
STOOPS, MICHAEL
B. Dec. 13, 1961, Youngstown, OH
Iowa 6'1" 185 lbs.

1987	CHI	N	3	S

Jack Storer
STORER, JOHN W.
B. 1901
D. Jan. 15, 1927
Lehigh 5'10" 163 lbs.

1924	FRA	N	13	HB

Ed Storm
STORM, EDWARD
B. Oct. 2, 1907, Salinas, CA
D. 1980, Castroville, CA
Santa Clara 6'1" 195 lbs.

1934	PHI	N	11	FB, HB, QB
1935			11	HB, QB, FB
2 yrs.	22 games			

Greg Storr
STORR, GREG SCOTT
B. Oct. 16, 1960, Reading, PA

Greg Storr *continued*
Boston College 6'2" 225 lbs.

1987	MIA	N	3	LB

Bill Story
STORY, WILLIAM FRANK
B. Nov. 21, 1951, Memphis, TN
Southern Illinois 6'3" 245 lbs.

1975	KC	N	14	OT, G

Hal Stotsberry
STOTSBERRY, HAROLD
B. 1906
Xavier (Ohio) 6'1" 235 lbs.

1930	BKN	N	2	T

Rich Stotter
STOTTER, RICHARD LEE
B. Apr. 5, 1945, Cleveland, OH
Houston 6'0" 225 lbs.

1968	HOU	A	3	LB

Cliff Stoudt
STOUDT, CLIFFORD LEWIS
B. Mar. 27, 1955, Oberlin, OH
Youngstown State 6'4" 215 lbs.

1980	PIT	N	6	QB
1981			2	QB
1982			6	QB
1983			16	QB
1986	STL	N	5	QB
1987			12	QB
1988	PHX	N	16	QB
1989	MIA	N	16	QB
8 yrs.	79 games			

Kelly Stouffer
STOUFFER, KELLY WAYNE
B. Jul. 6, 1964, Scottsbluff, NE
Colorado State 6'3" 210 lbs.

1988	SEA	N	8	QB
1989			3	QB
1991			2	QB
1992			9	QB
4 yrs.	22 games			

Glen Stough
STOUGH, GLEN
B. 1921
Duke 6'5" 240 lbs.

1945	PIT	N	10	T

Pete Stout
STOUT, PETER
B. Jun. 1, 1923, Throckmorton, TX
North Texas/Texas Christian 6'0" 201 lbs.

1949	WAS	N	8	FB
1950			8	FB
2 yrs.	16 games			

Dick Stovall
STOVALL, RICHARD S.
B. Jun. 4, 1922, Albany, TX
Abilene Christian 6'0" 202 lbs.

1947	DET	N	11	C, LB
1948			10	G, LB
1949	WAS	N	10	G, LB
3 yrs.	31 games			

Jerry Stovall
STOVALL, JERRY LANE
B. Apr. 30, 1941, West Monroe, LA
Louisiana State 6'2" 201 lbs.

1963	STL	N	14	DB, HB, P

Jerry Stovall *continued*

Year	Team		Games	Pos.
1964			14	DB, P
1965			10	DB, P
1966			14	DB, P
1967			14	DB
1968			4	DB
1969			10	S
1970			11	S
1971			6	S
9 yrs.	97 games			

Jeff Stover
STOVER, JEFF OWEN
B. May 22, 1958, Corning, CA
Oregon 6'5" 275 lbs.

1982	SF	N	9	DT
1983			16	DE
1984			6	NT
1985			16	NT
1986			15	DE
1987			12	DE
1988			7	DE
7 yrs.	81 games			

Matt Stover
STOVER, JOHN MATTHEW
B. Jan. 27, 1968, Dallas, TX
Louisiana Tech 5'11" 178 lbs.

1991	CLE	N	16	K
1992			16	K
1993			16	K
1994			16	K
1995			16	K
1996	BAL	N	16	K
6 yrs.	96 games			

Stewart Stover
STOVER, STEWART (Smokey)
B. Aug. 24, 1938, McPherson, KS
Northeast Louisiana 6'0" 229 lbs.

1960	DAL	A	14	LB
1961			14	LB
1962			14	LB
1963	KC	A	14	LB
1964			14	LB
1965			14	LB
1966			14	LB
7 yrs.	98 games			

Otto Stowe
STOWE, OTTO
B. Feb. 25, 1949, Chicago, IL
Iowa State 6'2" 188 lbs.

1971	MIA	N	12	WR
1972			9	WR
1973	DAL	N	7	WR
1974	DEN	N	8	WR
4 yrs.	36 games			

Tyronne Stowe
STOWE, TYRONNE KEVIN
B. May 31, 1965, Passaic, NJ
Rutgers 6'1" 242 lbs.

1987	PIT	N	13	LB
1988			10	LB
1989			16	LB
1990			15	LB
1991	PHX	N	13	LB
1992			15	LB
1993			15	LB
1994	WAS	N	16	LB
1995	SEA	N	6	LB
9 yrs.	119 games			

Tommie Stowers
STOWERS, TOMMIE
B. Nov. 18, 1966, Kansas City, MO
Missouri 6'3" 240 lbs.

1992	NO	N	12	TE

Tommie Stowers *continued*

Year	Team		Games	Pos.
1993			4	TE
1994	KC	N	1	TE
3 yrs.	17 games			

Pete Stoyanovich
STOYANOVICH, PETE
B. Apr. 28, 1967, Dearborn, MI
Indiana 5'10" 180 lbs.

1989	MIA	N	16	K
1990			16	K
1991			14	K
1992			16	K
1993			16	K
1994			16	K
1995			16	K
1996	KC	N	16	K
8 yrs.	126 games			

Mike Strachan
STRACHAN, MICHAEL DAVID
B. May 24, 1953, Miami, FL
Iowa State 6'0" 199 lbs.

1975	NO	N	11	RB
1976			10	RB
1977			13	RB
1978			15	RB
1979			10	RB
1980			3	RB
6 yrs.	62 games			

Steve Strachan
STRACHAN, STEPHEN MICHAEL
B. Mar. 22, 1963, Everett, MA
Boston College 6'1" 221 lbs.

1985	LARI	N	4	RB
1986			16	RB
1987			11	RB
1988			16	RB
1989			16	RB
5 yrs.	63 games			

Charlie Strack
STRACK, CHARLES
B. 1902
Deceased
Colgate/Oklahoma State 6'0" 215 lbs.

1928	CHIC	N	3	G

Tim Stracka
STRACKA, TIMOTHY T.
B. Sep. 27, 1959, Madison, WI
Wisconsin 6'3" 225 lbs.

1983	CLE	N	13	TE
1984			6	TE
2 yrs.	19 games			

John Strada
STRADA, JOHN
B. Nov. 13, 1952, Kansas City, MO
William Jewell 6'3" 230 lbs.

1974	NYG	N	1	TE
1974	KC	N	11	TE
1 yr.	12 games			

Red Strader
STRADER, NORMAN PARKER
B. Dec. 21, 1904, Newton, NJ
D. May 26, 1956
St. Mary's (California) 5'9" 200 lbs.

1926	CHI	A	12	HB, FB
1927	CHIC	N	5	HB, FB
2 yrs.	17 games			

Year	Team	Games	Pos.

Troy Stradford
STRADFORD, TROY EDWIN
B. Sep. 11, 1964, Elizabeth, NJ
Boston College 5'9" 192 lbs.

Year	Team		Games	Pos.
1987	**MIA**	N	12	RB
1988			15	RB
1989			7	RB
1990			14	RB
1991	**KC**	N	10	RB
1992	**LARM**	N	2	RB
1992	**DET**	N	6	RB
6 yrs.	66 games			

Ray Straham
STRAHAM, RAYMOND
B. 1943
Texas Southern 6'6" 250 lbs.

Year	Team		Games	Pos.
1965	**HOU**	A	4	DE

Art Strahan
STRAHAN, ART
B. 1944
Texas Southern 6'5" 266 lbs.

Year	Team		Games	Pos.
1968	**ATL**	N	4	DT

Michael Strahan
STRAHAN, MICHAEL ANTHONY
B. Nov. 21, 1971, Houston, TX
Texas Southern 6'4" 275 lbs.

Year	Team		Games	Pos.
1993	**NYG**	N	9	DE
1994			15	DE
1995			15	DE
1996			16	DE
4 yrs.	55 games			

Clem Stralka
STRALKA, CLEMENT FRANK
B. May 19, 1914, Glen Lyon, PA
D. Jan. 10, 1994, Denver, CO
Georgetown (DC) 5'10" 215 lbs.

Year	Team		Games	Pos.
1938	**WAS**	N	9	G, T
1939			10	G
1940			10	G
1941			10	G
1942			11	G, T
1945			3	G
1946			11	HB
7 yrs.	64 games			

Mike Stramiello
STRAMIELLO, MICHAEL, JR.
B. 1907
Colgate 6'1" 198 lbs.

Year	Team		Games	Pos.
1930	**BKN**	N	12	E
1931			13	E, G
1932			2	E
1932	**SI**	N	5	E
1934	**BKN**	N	2	E
4 yrs.	34 games			

Eli Strand
STRAND, ELI S.
B. Feb. 11, 1943, Mount Vernon, NY
Iowa State 6'2" 250 lbs.

Year	Team		Games	Pos.
1966	**PIT**	N	8	G
1967	**NO**	N	14	G
2 yrs.	22 games			

Lief Strand
STRAND, LIEF R.
B. Jan. 6, 1899
D. Apr., 1968, Minneapolis, MN
Fordham/Minnesota 6'0" 210 lbs.

Year	Team		Games	Pos.
1924	**DUL**	N	6	C

Bob Stransky
STRANSKY, ROBERT
B. 1936
Colorado 6'1" 190 lbs.

Year	Team		Games	Pos.
1960	**DEN**	A		HB

Dutch Strasser
STRASSER, CLARENCE
B. Oct. 22, 1900
D. Mar., 1965
Findlay

Year	Team		Games	Pos.
1925	**CAN**	N	3	E

Mike Stratton
STRATTON, DAVID MICHAEL
B. Apr. 10, 1941, Vonore, TN
Tennessee 6'3" 236 lbs.

Year	Team		Games	Pos.
1962	**BUF**	A	12	LB
1963			14	LB
1964			14	LB
1965			14	LB
1966			14	LB
1967			14	LB
1968			14	LB
1969			14	LB
1970	**BUF**	N	9	LB
1971			13	LB
1972			10	LB
1973	**SD**	N	14	LB
12 yrs.	156 games			

Jimmy Strausbaugh
STRAUSBAUGH, JAMES EDWIN
B. Feb. 25, 1918, Chillicothe, OH
D. Nov. 25, 1991
Ohio State 5'9" 190 lbs.

Year	Team		Games	Pos.
1946	**CHIC**	N	11	HB

Dutch Strauss
STRAUSS, J. ARTHUR
B. Jan. 1, 1897
D. Aug. 10, 1969, Enid, OK
Phillips 5'10" 205 lbs.

Year	Team		Games	Pos.
1923	**TOL**	N	6	FB, HB
1924	**KC**	N	7	FB
2 yrs.	13 games			

Tom Strauthers
STRAUTHERS, THOMAS
B. Apr. 6, 1961, Wesson, MS
Jackson State 6'4" 262 lbs.

Year	Team		Games	Pos.
1983	**PHI**	N	4	DE
1984			16	DE
1985			16	DE
1986			11	DE
1988	**DET**	N	10	DE
1989	**MIN**	N	12	DE
1990			13	DE
1991			15	DE
8 yrs.	97 games			

Don Straw
STRAW, DONALD M.
B. Nov. 22, 1896
D. Jul. 31, 1961
Washington & Jefferson 5'11" 210 lbs.

Year	Team		Games	Pos.
1920	**DET**	A	1	G
1921			1	G
2 yrs.	2 games			

Les Strayhorn
STRAYHORN, LES
B. Sep. 1, 1951, Trenton, NC
East Carolina 5'10" 205 lbs.

Year	Team		Games	Pos.
1973	**DAL**	N	11	RB
1974			13	RB
2 yrs.	24 games			

Eric Streater
STREATER, ERIC
B. Mar. 21, 1964, Sylvia, NC
North Carolina 5'11" 165 lbs.

Year	Team		Games	Pos.
1987	**TB**	N	3	WR

George Streeter
STREETER, GEORGE LEON
B. Aug. 28, 1967, Chicago, IL
Notre Dame 6'2" 212 lbs.

Year	Team		Games	Pos.
1989	**CHI**	N	4	CB, S
1990	**IND**	N	4	DB
2 yrs.	8 games			

Rich Strenger
STRENGER, RICHARD GENE
B. Mar. 10, 1960, Port Washington, WI
Michigan 6'7" 280 lbs.

Year	Team		Games	Pos.
1983	**DET**	N	16	OT
1984			1	OT
1985			13	OT
1986			16	OT
1987			3	OT
5 yrs.	49 games			

Bill Stribling
STRIBLING, MAJURE B.
B. Nov. 5, 1927, Edinburg, MS
Mississippi 6'1" 206 lbs.

Year	Team		Games	Pos.
1951	**NYG**	N	6	E
1952			12	E
1953			12	E
1955	**PHI**	N	12	E
1956			2	E
1957			12	E
6 yrs.	56 games			

Tony Stricker
STRICKER, ANTHONY
B. 1941
Colorado 6'0" 185 lbs.

Year	Team		Games	Pos.
1963	**NY**	A	12	DB

Bill Strickland
STRICKLAND, WILLIAM
B. Sep. 14, 1898
D. Jan., 1976, Quincy, IL
Lombard 190 lbs.

Year	Team		Games	Pos.
1923	**MIL**	N	2	G

Bishop Strickland
STRICKLAND, BISHOP
B. 1929
South Carolina 5'10" 195 lbs.

Year	Team		Games	Pos.
1951	**SF**	N	9	FB

Dave Strickland
STRICKLAND, DAVID
B. 1932
Memphis State 6'0" 220 lbs.

Year	Team		Games	Pos.
1960	**DEN**	A		G

Fred Strickland
STRICKLAND, FREDRICK WILLIAM, JR.
B. Aug. 15, 1966, Ringwood, NJ
Purdue 6'2" 243 lbs.

Year	Team		Games	Pos.
1988	**LARM**	N	16	LB
1989			12	LB
1990			5	LB
1991			14	LB
1992			15	LB
1993	**MIN**	N	16	LB
1994	**GB**	N	16	LB
1995			14	LB
1996	**DAL**	N	16	LB
9 yrs.	124 games			

Larry Strickland
STRICKLAND, LAWRENCE
B. Sep. 3, 1931, Tyler, TX
D. Aug. 28, 1979, Tyler, TX
North Texas State 6'4" 248 lbs.

Year	Team		Games	Pos.
1954	**CHIB**	N	12	C
1955			12	C
1956			11	C
1957			11	C
1958			12	C
1959			3	C
6 yrs.	61 games			

Bill Striegel
STRIEGEL, WILLIAM J.
B. May 28, 1936
Pacific 6'2" 235 lbs.

Year	Team		Games	Pos.
1959	**PHI**	N	12	G
1960	**BOS**	A		OT
1960	**OAK**	A		OT
2 yrs.	12 games			

Art Stringer
STRINGER, ART
B. Jan. 30, 1954, Troy, AL
Ball State 6'1" 223 lbs.

Year	Team		Games	Pos.
1977	**HOU**	N	14	LB
1978			7	LB
1979			9	LB
1980			8	LB
1981			5	LB
5 yrs.	43 games			

Bob Stringer
STRINGER, ROBERT
B. Oct. 8, 1929, Shawnee, OK
Tulsa 6'1" 197 lbs.

Year	Team		Games	Pos.
1952	**PHI**	N	12	FB
1953			12	FB
2 yrs.	24 games			

Gene Stringer
STRINGER, EUGENE
B. May 29, 1903
D. Jun., 1985, Pueblo, CO
John Carroll 6'0" 200 lbs.

Year	Team		Games	Pos.
1925	**CLE**	N	10	HB, FB, T, QB, E

Korey Stringer
STRINGER, KOREY
B. May 8, 1974, Warren, OH
Ohio State 6'4" 332 lbs.

Year	Team		Games	Pos.
1995	**MIN**	N	16	OT
1996			16	OT
2 yrs.	32 games			

Scott Stringer
STRINGER, SCOTT
B. Aug. 5, 1951, Tracy, CA
California 5'11" 180 lbs.

Year	Team		Games	Pos.
1974	**STL**	N	5	CB

Hal Stringert
STRINGERT, HAROLD LLOYD
B. Jan. 5, 1952, Honolulu, HI
Willamette/Hawaii 5'11" 185 lbs.

Year	Team		Games	Pos.
1975	**SD**	N	6	CB
1976			11	CB
1977			14	CB
1978			13	CB
1979			15	CB
1980			10	CB
6 yrs.	69 games			

Joe Stringfellow
STRINGFELLOW, JOE ELBERT

Year	Team	Games	Pos.

Joe Stringfellow continued
B. Mar. 10, 1920, Meridian, MS
Southern Mississippi 6'0" 185 lbs.

Year	Team	Games	Pos.
1942	DET N	9	E, B

Don Strock
STROCK, DONALD JOSEPH
B. Nov. 27, 1950, Pottstown, PA
Virginia Tech 6'5" 220 lbs.

Year	Team	Games	Pos.
1974	MIA N	1	QB
1975		6	QB
1976		4	QB
1977		4	QB
1978		16	QB
1979		16	QB
1980		16	QB
1981		16	QB
1982		9	QB
1983		15	QB
1984		16	QB
1985		16	QB
1986		16	QB
1987		12	QB
1988	CLE N	4	QB
15 yrs.	167 games		

Woody Strode
STRODE, WOODROW WILSON
B. 1915, Los Angeles, CA
D. Dec. 31, 1994, Glendora, CA
UCLA 6'3" 205 lbs.

Year	Team	Games	Pos.
1946	LA N	10	E

Mike Strofolino
STROFOLINO, MICHAEL JAMES
B. Feb. 6, 1944, Brooklyn, NY
Villanova 6'2" 223 lbs.

Year	Team	Games	Pos.
1965	LA N	9	LB
1965	BAL N	12	LB
1966	STL N	8	LB
1967		1	LB
1968		14	LB
4 yrs.	44 games		

George Strohmeyer
STROHMEYER, GEORGE FERDINAND, II
B. Jan. 27, 1924, Kansas City, MO
D. Jan. 12, 1992
Texas A&M/Notre Dame 5'10" 205 lbs.

Year	Team	Games	Pos.
1948	BKN AA	14	C
1949	CHI AA	12	C
2 yrs.	26 games		

Frank Strom
STROM, FRANK E.
B. Aug. 29, 1916, Ballinger, TX
D. Jun. 8, 1992, Clinton, OK
Tulsa 6'2" 252 lbs.

Year	Team	Games	Pos.
1944	BKN N	8	T

Rick Strom
STROM, RICHARD JAMES
B. Mar. 11, 1965, Pittsburgh, PA
Georgia Tech 6'2" 210 lbs.

Year	Team	Games	Pos.
1989	PIT N	3	QB
1990		6	QB
1994	BUF N	1	QB
3 yrs.	10 games		

Mike Stromberg
STROMBERG, MICHAEL
B. May 25, 1945, Brooklyn, NY
Temple 6'2" 235 lbs.

Year	Team	Games	Pos.
1968	NY A	2	LB

Jim Strong
STRONG, JAMES HAROLD, JR.
B. Dec. 12, 1946, San Antonio, TX
Houston 6'1" 204 lbs.

Year	Team	Games	Pos.
1970	SF N	3	RB
1971	NO N	14	RB
1972		14	RB
3 yrs.	31 games		

Ken Strong
STRONG, ELMER KENNETH, JR.
B. Aug. 6, 1906, West Haven, CT
D. Oct. 5, 1979, New York, NY
New York University 6'0" 206 lbs.

Year	Team	Games	Pos.
1929	SI N	10	FB, HB
1930		12	HB, FB, QB
1931		11	HB, FB, QB
1932		10	HB
1933	NYG N	14	HB
1934		13	HB, QB
1935		11	HB, QB, FB
1939		9	HB
1944		10	HB, FB, QB
1945		9	HB
1946		11	HB, FB
1947		10	FB
12 yrs.	130 games		

Mack Strong
STRONG, MACK
B. Sep. 11, 1971, Fort Benning, GA
Georgia 6'0" 211 lbs.

Year	Team	Games	Pos.
1994	SEA N	8	RB
1995		16	RB
1996		14	RB
3 yrs.	38 games		

Ray Strong
STRONG, RAYMOND
B. May 7, 1956, Berkeley, CA
Nevada-Las Vegas 5'9" 184 lbs.

Year	Team	Games	Pos.
1978	ATL N	14	RB
1979		6	RB
1980		16	RB
1981		16	RB
1982		9	RB
5 yrs.	61 games		

William Strong
STRONG, WILLIAM
B. Nov. 3, 1971, Chester, SC
North Carolina State 5'10" 191 lbs.

Year	Team	Games	Pos.
1995	NO N	1	CB
1996		10	CB
2 yrs.	11 games		

Breck Stroschein
STROSCHEIN, BRECK
B. 1930
Deceased
UCLA 6'1" 205 lbs.

Year	Team	Games	Pos.
1951	NYY N	11	E

Aubrey Strosnider
STROSNIDER, AUBREY
B. May 9, 1904
Dayton 6'1" 205 lbs.

Year	Team	Games	Pos.
1928	DAY N	1	T

Vince Stroth
STROTH, VINCE M.
B. Nov. 25, 1960, San Jose, CA
Brigham Young 6'3" 259 lbs.

Year	Team	Games	Pos.
1985	SF N	1	OT
1987	HOU N	9	G
1988		6	OT
3 yrs.	16 games		

Deon Strother
STROTHER, DEON
B. Apr. 12, 1972, Saginaw, MI
Southern California 5'11" 213 lbs.

Year	Team	Games	Pos.
1994	DEN N	2	RB

Jack Stroud
STROUD, JOHN
B. Jan. 29, 1928, Fresno, CA
D. Jun. 1, 1994, Flemington, NJ
Tennessee 6'1" 235 lbs.

Year	Team	Games	Pos.
1953	NYG N	12	G
1954		6	G
1955		12	G
1956		11	G
1957		11	G
1958		7	E
1959		12	G
1960		12	G
1961		12	G
1962		14	G
1963		14	OT
1964		9	OT
12 yrs.	132 games		

Morris Stroud
STROUD, MORRIS, JR. (Rocket)
B. May 17, 1946, Miami, FL
Clark 6'9" 250 lbs.

Year	Team	Games	Pos.
1970	KC N	14	TE
1971		14	TE
1972		14	TE
1973		14	TE
1974		14	TE
5 yrs.	70 games		

Art Strozier
STROZIER, ARTHUR
B. May 23, 1946, Kansas City, KS
Kansas State 6'2" 220 lbs.

Year	Team	Games	Pos.
1970	SD N	14	TE
1971		6	TE
2 yrs.	20 games		

Wilbur Strozier
STROZIER, WILBUR LAMAR
B. Nov. 12, 1964, La Grange, TX
Georgia 6'4" 255 lbs.

Year	Team	Games	Pos.
1987	SEA N	12	TE
1988	SD N	6	TE
2 yrs.	18 games		

George Strugar
STRUGAR, GEORGE RALPH
B. Apr. 2, 1934, Cle Elum, WA
Washington 6'5" 259 lbs.

Year	Team	Games	Pos.
1957	LA N	9	T
1958		12	T
1959		11	T
1960		11	T
1961		14	DT
1962	PIT N	1	DT
1962	NY A	12	DT
1963		8	DT
7 yrs.	78 games		

Art Strutt
STRUTT, ARTHUR E.
B. Dec. 4, 1912, Mingo Junction, OH
Duquesne 6'0" 202 lbs.

Year	Team	Games	Pos.
1935	PIT N	9	HB, FB
1936		10	HB
2 yrs.	19 games		

Dan Stryzinski
STRYZINSKI, DANIEL THOMAS
B. May 15, 1965, Indianapolis, IN

Dan Stryzinski continued
Indiana 6'1" 193 lbs.

Year	Team	Games	Pos.
1990	PIT N	16	P
1991		16	P
1992	TB N	16	P
1993		16	P
1994		16	P
1995	ATL N	16	P
1996		16	P
7 yrs.	112 games		

Justin Strzelczyk
STRZELCZYK, JUSTIN CONRAD
B. Aug. 18, 1968, Seneca, NY
Maine 6'5" 298 lbs.

Year	Team	Games	Pos.
1990	PIT N	16	OT
1991		16	OT
1992		16	OT
1993		16	OT
1994		15	G, OT
1995		16	G, OT
1996		16	G
7 yrs.	111 games		

Johnny Strzykalski
STRZYKALSKI, JOHN (Strike)
B. Dec. 14, 1922
Marquette 5'9" 190 lbs.

Year	Team	Games	Pos.
1946	SF AA	13	HB
1947		14	B
1948		14	B
1949		7	B
1950	SF N	12	HB
1951		11	HB
1952		10	HB
7 yrs.	81 games		

Jim Stuart
STUART, JAMES
B. Jul. 2, 1919, Hermiston, OR
D. Dec., 1985, Stanfield, OR
Oregon 6'0" 212 lbs.

Year	Team	Games	Pos.
1941	WAS N	6	G, T

Roy Stuart
STUART, ROY J.
B. Jul. 25, 1920, Shawnee, OK
Tulsa 5'8" 188 lbs.

Year	Team	Games	Pos.
1942	CLE N	9	G
1943	DET N	6	G
1946	BUF AA	9	G
3 yrs.	24 games		

Dana Stubblefield
STUBBLEFIELD, DANA WILLIAM
B. Nov. 14, 1970, Cleves, OH
Kansas 6'2" 302 lbs.

Year	Team	Games	Pos.
1993	SF N	16	DE
1994		14	DT
1995		16	DT
1996		15	DT
4 yrs.	61 games		

Danny Stubbs
STUBBS, DANIEL, II
B. Jan. 3, 1965, Long Branch, NJ
Miami (Florida) 6'4" 260 lbs.

Year	Team	Games	Pos.
1988	SF N	16	DE
1989		16	DE
1990	DAL N	16	DE
1991		9	DE
1991	CIN N	7	DE
1992		16	DE
1993		16	DE
1994	PHI N	16	DE
1996	MIA N	16	DE
8 yrs.	128 games		

Year	Team	Games	Pos.

Henry Stuckey
STUCKEY, HENRY
B. Aug. 24, 1950, Oakland, CA
Missouri 6'1" 180 lbs.

Year	Team		Games	Pos.
1973	MIA	N	6	DB
1974			14	CB
1975	NYG	N	4	CB
1976			3	CB
4 yrs.	27 games			

Jim Stuckey
STUCKEY, JAMES
B. Jun. 21, 1958, Cayce, SC
Clemson 6'4" 251 lbs.

Year	Team		Games	Pos.
1980	SF	N	16	DT
1981			15	DE
1982			9	DE
1983			16	DE
1984			16	DE
1985			15	DE
1986			1	DE
1986	NYJ	N	5	DE
7 yrs.	93 games			

Mark Studaway
STUDAWAY, MARK WAYNE
B. Sep. 20, 1960, Memphis, TN
Tennessee 6'3" 260 lbs.

Year	Team		Games	Pos.
1984	HOU	N	6	DE
1985	TB	N	6	DE
1987	ATL	N	2	DE
3 yrs.	14 games			

Dave Studdard
STUDDARD, DAVID DERALD
B. Nov. 22, 1955, San Antonio, TX
Texas 6'4" 260 lbs.

Year	Team		Games	Pos.
1979	DEN	N	16	OT
1980			16	OT
1981			16	OT
1982			9	OT
1983			16	OT
1984			16	OT
1985			16	OT
1986			15	OT
1987			14	OT
1988			11	OT
10 yrs.	145 games			

Les Studdard
STUDDARD, LESLIE ELVIN
B. Dec. 14, 1958, El Paso, TX
Texas 6'4" 260 lbs.

Year	Team		Games	Pos.
1982	KC	N	9	C
1983	HOU	N	6	C
2 yrs.	15 games			

Vern Studdard
STUDDARD, VERNON AARON, JR.
B. Apr. 30, 1948, Columbia, MS
Mississippi 5'11" 175 lbs.

Year	Team		Games	Pos.
1971	NYJ	N	7	WR

Darren Studstill
STUDSTILL, DARREN HENRY
B. Aug. 9, 1970, Palm Beach Gardens, FL
West Virginia 6'1" 186 lbs.

Year	Team		Games	Pos.
1994	DAL	N	1	S
1995	JAC	N	8	S
1996			7	S
3 yrs.	16 games			

Pat Studstill
STUDSTILL, PATRICK LEWIS
B. Jun. 4, 1938, Shreveport, LA

Pat Studstill continued
Houston 6'1" 176 lbs.

Year	Team		Games	Pos.
1961	DET	N	14	FL
1962			14	FL
1964			14	FL
1965			14	FL, P
1966			14	FL, P
1967			7	FL, P
1968	LA	N	14	FL, P
1969			14	WR, P
1970			14	WR, P
1971			14	WR, P
1972	NE	N	14	P, WR
11 yrs.	147 games			

Scott Studwell
STUDWELL, JOHN SCOTT
B. Aug. 27, 1954, Evansville, IN
Illinois 6'2" 228 lbs.

Year	Team		Games	Pos.
1977	MIN	N	14	LB
1978			13	LB
1979			14	LB
1980			16	LB
1981			16	LB
1982			8	LB
1983			16	LB
1984			16	LB
1985			14	LB
1986			15	LB
1987			12	LB
1988			16	LB
1989			16	LB
1990			16	LB
14 yrs.	202 games			

Mel Stuessy
STUESSY, MELVIN
B. Aug. 8, 1901
D. Oct., 1980, Bull Valley, IL
St. Edward's 5'9" 180 lbs.

Year	Team		Games	Pos.
1926	CHIC	N	1	G

Harry Stuhldreher
STUHLDREHER, HARRY AUGUSTUS
B. Oct. 14, 1901, Massillon, OH
D. Jan. 26, 1965, Pittsburgh, PA
Notre Dame 5'7" 165 lbs.

Year	Team		Games	Pos.
1926	BKN	A	4	QB
1926	BKN	N	1	HB
1 yr.	5 games			

Charlie Stukes
STUKES, CHARLES
B. Sep. 13, 1943, Chesapeake, VA
Maryland-Eastern Shore 6'3" 212 lbs.

Year	Team		Games	Pos.
1967	BAL	N	14	DB
1968			14	DB
1969			14	CB
1970			11	CB
1971			14	CB
1972			12	CB
1973	LA	N	14	CB
1974			14	CB
8 yrs.	107 games			

Cecil Sturgeon
STURGEON, CECIL
B. Jun. 27, 1919, Carnduff, Sask.
D. Feb., 1972
North Dakota State 6'2" 254 lbs.

Year	Team		Games	Pos.
1941	PHI	N	9	T, E

Lyle Sturgeon
STURGEON, LYLE
B. Jan. 18, 1914, Saskatchewan
Deceased

Lyle Sturgeon continued
North Dakota State 6'3" 250 lbs.

Year	Team		Games	Pos.
1937	GB	N	7	T

Oscar Sturgis
STURGIS, OSCAR
B. Jan. 12, 1971, Hamlet, NC
North Carolina 6'5" 280 lbs.

Year	Team		Games	Pos.
1995	DAL	N	1	DE

Jerry Sturm
STURM, JERRY GORDON
B. Dec. 31, 1936, English, IN
Illinois 6'3" 257 lbs.

Year	Team		Games	Pos.
1961	DEN	A	14	OT
1962			14	OT
1963			14	C
1964			14	C
1965			14	G
1966			14	G
1967	NO	N	7	OT
1968			14	OT
1969			14	OT
1970			10	C
1971	HOU	N	12	C
1972	PHI	N	1	C
12 yrs.	142 games			

Fred Sturt
STURT, FREDERICK NEIL
B. Jan. 6, 1951, Toledo, OH
Bowling Green 6'4" 255 lbs.

Year	Team		Games	Pos.
1974	WAS	N	7	G, OT
1976	NE	N	14	G
1977			14	G
1978			1	G
1978	NO	N	12	G
1979			16	G
1980			15	G
1981			16	G
7 yrs.	95 games			

Dick Sturtridge
STURTRIDGE, RICHARD N.
B. Mar. 8, 1904
D. Dec. 4, 1978, Los Angeles, CA
DePauw 5'8" 171 lbs.

Year	Team		Games	Pos.
1928	CHIB	N	10	HB
1929			2	HB
2 yrs.	12 games			

Joe Stydahar
STYDAHAR, JOSEPH LEE (Jumbo Joe)
B. Mar. 16, 1912, Kaylor, PA
D. Mar. 23, 1977, Beckley, WV
Pittsburgh/West Virginia 6'4" 233 lbs.

Year	Team		Games	Pos.
1936	CHIB	N	12	T
1937			10	T
1938			11	T
1939			11	T
1940			10	T
1941			7	T
1942			9	T
1945			3	T
1946			11	T, E
9 yrs.	84 games			

Lorenzo Styles
STYLES, LORENZO
B. Jan. 31, 1974, Columbus, OH
Ohio State 6'1" 244 lbs.

Year	Team		Games	Pos.
1995	ATL	N	12	LB
1996			16	LB
2 yrs.	28 games			

Andy Stynchula
STYNCHULA, ANDREW RALPH
B. Jan. 7, 1939, Latrobe, PA
Deceased
Penn State 6'3" 252 lbs.

Year	Team		Games	Pos.
1960	WAS	N	12	E
1961			14	DE
1962			13	DE
1963			14	DE
1964	NYG	N	14	DT, DE
1965			11	DE
1966	BAL	N	8	DE
1967			13	DT, DE
1968	DAL	N	5	DE
9 yrs.	104 games			

Nick Subis
SUBIS, NICHOLAS ALEXANDER
B. Dec. 24, 1967, Inglewood, CA
San Diego State 6'4" 278 lbs.

Year	Team		Games	Pos.
1991	DEN	N	16	OT, G

Larry Suchy
SUCHY, LAWRENCE
B. Jul. 12, 1946
Mississippi College 5'11" 180 lbs.

Year	Team		Games	Pos.
1968	ATL	N	1	DB

Paul Suchy
SUCHY, PAUL
B. Mar. 28, 1904
D. Nov., 1986, Inverness, IL
None 188 lbs.

Year	Team		Games	Pos.
1925	CLE	N	2	E

Bob Suci
SUCI, ROBERT L.
B. 1940
Michigan State 5'10" 182 lbs.

Year	Team		Games	Pos.
1962	HOU	A	6	DB
1963	BOS	A	14	DB
2 yrs.	20 games			

Steve Sucic
SUCIC, STEPHEN
B. Apr. 21, 1921, Chicago, IL
Illinois 6'0" 207 lbs.

Year	Team		Games	Pos.
1946	LA	N	4	FB
1947	BOS	N	3	FB
1947	DET	N	5	HB
1948			3	FB
3 yrs.	15 games			

Ray Suess
SUESS, RAYMOND
B. Aug. 8, 1903
D. Aug., 1970, Santa Ana, CA
None 204 lbs.

Year	Team		Games	Pos.
1926	DUL	N	6	T, E, G
1927			9	G, T
2 yrs.	15 games			

Bob Suffridge
SUFFRIDGE, ROBERT LEE
B. Apr. 1, 1919, Knoxville TN
D. Mar. 3, 1974, Knoxville, TN
Tennessee 6'0" 205 lbs.

Year	Team		Games	Pos.
1941	PHI	N	10	G
1945			10	G
2 yrs.	20 games			

Leo Sugar
SUGAR, LEO TATEUSZ
B. Apr. 6, 1929, Flint, MI
Purdue 6'1" 214 lbs.

Year	Team		Games	Pos.
1954	CHIC	N	12	E
1955			12	E

Year	Team		Games	Pos.

Leo Sugar continued

Year	Team		Games	Pos.
1956			12	E
1957			12	E
1958			12	E
1959			12	E
1960	STL	N	12	E
1961	PHI	N	14	DE
1962	DET	N	6	DE

9 yrs.   104 games

Shafer Suggs

SUGGS, SHAFER
B. Apr. 28, 1953, Elkhart, IN
Ball State 6'1" 200 lbs.

1976	NYJ	N	11	S, CB
1977			9	CB, S
1978			16	S
1979			16	S
1980			4	S

5 yrs.   56 games

Walter Suggs

SUGGS, WILLIAM WALTER, JR.
B. May 15, 1939, Hattiesburg, MS
Mississippi State 6'5" 257 lbs.

1962	HOU	A	14	OT
1963			14	OT
1964			14	OT
1965			14	OT
1966			14	OT
1967			14	OT
1968			14	OT
1969			14	OT
1970	HOU	N	14	OT
1971			11	OT

10 yrs.   137 games

Matt Suhey

SUHEY, MATTHEW JEROME
B. Jul. 7, 1958, Bellefonte, PA
Penn State 5'11" 215 lbs.

1980	CHI	N	16	RB
1981			15	RB
1982			9	RB
1983			16	RB
1984			16	RB
1985			16	RB
1986			16	RB
1987			12	FB
1988			16	RB
1989			16	RB

10 yrs.   148 games

Steve Suhey

SUHEY, STEVEN JOSEPH
B. Jan. 8, 1922
D. Jan. 8, 1977, State College, PA
Penn State 5'11" 215 lbs.

| 1948 | PIT | N | 12 | G |
| 1949 | | | 12 | G |

2 yrs.   24 games

Joe Sulatis

SULATIS, JOSEPH
B. Jun. 20, 1921, Hoboken, NJ
D. Feb. 8, 1980, Point Pleasant, NJ
none 6'2" 212 lbs.

1943	NYG	N	7	B, E
1944			6	HB
1945			8	HB
1946	BOS	N	3	FB
1947	NYG	N	11	E
1948			12	E
1949			12	B
1950			12	G
1951			12	G
1952			12	G
1953			12	E

11 yrs.   107 games

George Sulima

SULIMA, GEORGE
B. Feb. 27, 1928
D. Oct. 31, 1987, Burlington, VT
Boston University 6'2" 200 lbs.

1952	PIT	N	12	E
1953			10	E
1954			12	E

3 yrs.   34 games

John Sullins

SULLINS, JOHN ROBERTSON
B. Sep. 7, 1969, Oxford, MS
Alabama 6'1" 225 lbs.

| 1992 | DEN | N | 6 | LB |

Bob Sullivan

SULLIVAN, ROBERT
B. 1925
Iowa 5'9" 191 lbs.

| 1947 | PIT | N | 3 | HB |
| 1948 | BKN | AA | 2 | HB |

2 yrs.   5 games

Bob Sullivan

SULLIVAN, ROBERT JOSEPH
B. Aug. 15, 1923
D. Jun. 19, 1981, Boston, MA
Holy Cross 5'10" 190 lbs.

| 1948 | SF | AA | 13 | B |

Carl Sullivan

SULLIVAN, CARL JEFFREY
B. Apr. 30, 1962, San Jose, CA
San Jose State 6'4" 248 lbs.

| 1987 | GB | N | 3 | DE |

Chris Sullivan

SULLIVAN, CHRISTOPHER PATRICK
B. Mar. 14, 1973, North Attleboro, MA
Boston College 6'4" 279 lbs.

| 1996 | NE | N | 16 | DE |

Dan Sullivan

SULLIVAN, DANIEL JOSEPH
B. Sep. 1, 1939, Dorchester, MA
Boston College 6'3" 250 lbs.

1962	BAL	N	14	OT
1963			7	OT
1964			14	OT, G
1965			14	OT, G
1966			13	G
1967			14	G
1968			14	G
1969			10	G
1970			14	G
1971			12	G
1972			14	G

11 yrs.   140 games

Dave Sullivan

SULLIVAN, DAVE
B. Jan. 13, 1949, Steelton, PA
Virginia 5'11" 185 lbs.

| 1973 | CLE | N | 1 | WR |
| 1974 | | | 6 | WR |

2 yrs.   7 games

Frank Sullivan

SULLIVAN, FRANK JOSEPH
B. Aug. 6, 1912, Nashville, TN
D. Jun., 1956
Loyola (Louisiana) 6'3" 206 lbs.

| 1935 | CHIB | N | 10 | C |
| 1936 | | | 3 | C |

Dave Sullivan continued

1937			8	C
1938			10	C, G
1939			10	C, G
1940	PIT	N	9	C

6 yrs.   50 games

George Sullivan

SULLIVAN, GEORGE ALBERT
B. 1926
Notre Dame 6'2" 205 lbs.

| 1948 | BOS | | 1 | E |

George Sullivan

SULLIVAN, GEORGE H.
B. Mar. 15, 1897
D. Jul. 5, 1989, Woodbury, NJ
Pennsylvania 5'9" 170 lbs.

1924	FRA	N	6	HB, QB
1925			15	HB, FB, E
1926	PHI	A	7	HB, E

3 yrs.   28 games

Gerry Sullivan

SULLIVAN, GERALD B.
B. Jan. 15, 1952, Oak Park, IL
Illinois 6'4" 250 lbs.

1974	CLE	N	13	OT
1975			14	OT
1976			14	OT
1977			13	C, OT
1978			16	C, OT
1979			16	C, OT
1980			16	C, OT
1981			16	C, OT

8 yrs.   118 games

Hew Sullivan

SULLIVAN, HAROLD C. (Red)
B. Mar. 2, 1898
D. Oct., 1975, Minneapolis, MN
None 185 lbs.

| 1926 | DUL | N | 1 | G |

Jack Sullivan

SULLIVAN, JOHN (Torchy)
None 170 lbs.

| 1921 | BUF | A | 2 | E |

Jack Sullivan

SULLIVAN, JOHN HENRY
B. Nov. 12, 1891, Holyoke, MA
Deceased
North Carolina State 170 lbs.

| 1921 | WAS | A | 2 | FB, HB |

Jim Sullivan

SULLIVAN, JAMES EDMUND
B. Aug. 29, 1944, Detroit, MI
Lincoln (Missouri) 6'4" 240 lbs.

| 1970 | ATL | N | 7 | DL |

John Sullivan

SULLIVAN, JOHN LLOYD
B. Oct. 15, 1961, Hartford, CA
California 6'1" 196 lbs.

1986	GB	N	6	DB
1986	SD	N	9	DB
1987	SF	N	1	S

2 yrs.   16 games

John Sullivan

SULLIVAN, JOHN PATRICK
B. Oct. 1, 1956, Massapequa Park, NY
Illinois 6'1" 223 lbs.

| 1979 | NYJ | N | 12 | LB |

John Sullivan continued

| 1980 | | | 16 | LB |

2 yrs.   28 games

Kent Sullivan

SULLIVAN, KENT ALLEN
B. May 15, 1964, Plymouth, IN
California Lutheran 5'10" 197 lbs.

1991	HOU	N	1	P
1992	KC	N	1	P
1993	HOU	N	1	P
1993	SD	N	2	P

3 yrs.   5 games

Mike Sullivan

SULLIVAN, MIKE
B. Dec. 22, 1967, Chicago, IL
Miami (Florida) 6'3" 290 lbs.

1992	TB	N	9	G
1993			11	G
1994			15	G
1995			12	G, C

4 yrs.   47 games

Pat Sullivan

SULLIVAN, PATRICK
B. Jan. 18, 1950, Birmingham, AL
Auburn 6'0" 200 lbs.

1972	ATL	N	14	QB
1973			4	QB
1974			6	QB
1975			6	QB

4 yrs.   30 games

Steve Sullivan

SULLIVAN, STEPHEN (Paddy)
B. Jul. 1, 1897
D. Aug., 1969, Concord, CA
Montana 5'11" 180 lbs.

1922	MIL	N	2	QB, HB
1922	EVA	N	1	QB
1922	HAM	N	2	QB, HB
1923			3	HB
1924			1	E

3 yrs.   9 games

Tom Sullivan

SULLIVAN, THOMAS ASHLEY
B. Mar. 5, 1950, Jacksonville, FL
Miami (Florida) 6'0" 190 lbs.

1972	PHI	N	12	RB
1973			13	RB
1974			14	RB
1975			14	RB
1976			13	RB
1977			14	RB
1978	CLE	N		RB

7 yrs.   80 games

Sully

SULLY
None

| 1925 | PRO | N | 1 | FB |

Ivory Sully

SULLY, IVORY ULYSSES
B. Jun. 20, 1957, Salisbury, MD
Delaware 6'0" 200 lbs.

1979	LA	N	8	S, CB
1980			16	S, CB
1981			16	S
1982	LARM	N	9	S
1983			16	S
1984			16	S
1985	TB	N	16	S
1986			16	S
1987	DET	N	11	S

9 yrs.   124 games

Dave Suminski
SUMINSKI, DAVID
B. Aug. 18, 1931, Ashland, WI
Wisconsin 5'11" 230 lbs.

Year	Team	Games	Pos.
1953	WAS N	2	G
1953	CHIC N	6	G
1 yr.	8 games		

Tony Sumler
SUMLER, TONY
B. Apr. 10, 1956, Detroit, MI
Wichita State 5'10" 185 lbs.

Year	Team	Games	Pos.
1978	DET N	1	DB

Pat Summerall
SUMMERALL, GEORGE ALLEN
B. May 10, 1930, Lake City, FL
Arkansas 6'4" 228 lbs.

Year	Team	Games	Pos.
1952	DET N	2	E
1953	CHIC N	12	E, K
1954		12	E, K
1955		11	E, K
1956		12	E, K
1957		12	E, K
1958	NYG N	10	E, K
1959		12	E, K
1960		12	E, K
1961		14	OE, K
10 yrs.	109 games		

Carl Summerell
SUMMERELL, CARL
B. Dec. 6, 1951, Virginia Beach, VA
East Carolina 6'4" 208 lbs.

Year	Team	Games	Pos.
1974	NYG N	7	QB
1975		3	QB
2 yrs.	10 games		

Bob Summerhays
SUMMERHAYS, ROBERT W.
B. Mar. 19, 1927, Salt Lake City, UT
Utah 6'1" 210 lbs.

Year	Team	Games	Pos.
1949	GB N	12	FB
1950		11	FB
1951		12	FB
3 yrs.	35 games		

Don Summers
SUMMERS, DONALD O.
B. Feb. 22, 1961, Grants Pass, OR
Oregon Tech/Boise State 6'4" 230 lbs.

Year	Team	Games	Pos.
1984	DEN N	16	TE
1985		2	TE
1987	GB N	3	TE
3 yrs.	21 games		

Freddie Summers
SUMMERS, FREDERICK S.
B. Feb. 16, 1947, Columbia, SC
Wake Forest 6'1" 180 lbs.

Year	Team	Games	Pos.
1969	CLE N	9	CB, S
1970		12	CB
1971		1	S
3 yrs.	22 games		

Jim Summers
SUMMERS, JAMES, III
B. Dec. 23, 1945, Orangeburg, SC
Michigan State 5'10" 175 lbs.

Year	Team	Games	Pos.
1967	DEN A	11	DB

Wilbur Summers
SUMMERS, WILBUR
B. Aug. 6, 1954, Irvington, NJ
Louisville 6'4" 220 lbs.

Year	Team	Games	Pos.
1977	DET N	13	P

Charlie Sumner
SUMNER, CHARLES EDWARD
B. Oct. 19, 1930, Radford, VA
William & Mary 6'1" 194 lbs.

Year	Team	Games	Pos.
1955	CHIB N	10	DB
1958		12	DB
1959		12	DB
1960	CHI N	12	DB
1961	MIN N	13	DB
1962		14	DB
6 yrs.	73 games		

Walt Sumner
SUMNER, WALTER HERMAN
B. Feb. 2, 1947, Ocilla, GA
Florida State 6'1" 188 lbs.

Year	Team	Games	Pos.
1969	CLE N	14	S, CB
1970		12	S, CB
1971		14	CB
1972		13	S
1973		13	S
1974		10	DB
6 yrs.	76 games		

Tony Sumpter
SUMPTER, ANTHONY B.
B. Sep. 13, 1923, Fletcher, OK
Cameron 6'1" 215 lbs.

Year	Team	Games	Pos.
1946	CHI AA	12	G
1947		1	G
2 yrs.	13 games		

Milt Sunde
SUNDE, MILTON JOHN
B. Feb. 1, 1942, Minneapolis, MN
Minnesota 6'2" 245 lbs.

Year	Team	Games	Pos.
1964	MIN N	14	G
1965		14	G
1966		14	G, C
1967		10	G
1968		14	G
1969		14	G
1970		14	G
1971		14	G
1972		14	G
1973		14	G
1974		11	G
11 yrs.	147 games		

Sundquist
SUNDQUIST
None

Year	Team	Games	Pos.
1925	DUL N	1	T

Ian Sunter
SUNTER, IAN
B. Dec. 21, 1952, Dundee, Scotland
None 6'1" 215 lbs.

Year	Team	Games	Pos.
1976	DET N	3	K
1980	CIN N	10	K
2 yrs.	13 games		

Steve Superick
SUPERICK, STEVE
B. Aug. 9, 1963
West Virginia 5'11" 204 lbs.

Year	Team	Games	Pos.
1987	HOU N	2	P

Len Supulski
SUPULSKI, LEONARD
B. Dec. 15, 1920, Kingston, PA
D. 1944
Dickinson 6'0" 175 lbs.

Year	Team	Games	Pos.
1942	PHI N	9	E

Zeke Surabian
SURABIAN, ZAREH F.
B. Jan. 19, 1904
D. Jan. 5, 1984, Watertown, MA
Williams 5'10" 195 lbs.

Year	Team	Games	Pos.
1926	BOS A	4	T

Nick Susoeff
SUSOEFF, NICHOLAS
B. Apr. 15, 1921, Umapine, OR
D. Jan. 31, 1967, Palo Alto, CA
Washington State 6'1" 211 lbs.

Year	Team	Games	Pos.
1946	SF AA	6	E
1947		14	E
1948		13	E
1949		11	E
4 yrs.	44 games		

Ed Susteric
SUSTERIC, EDWARD
B. Jan. 7, 1922, Cleveland, OH
Findlay 6'0" 205 lbs.

Year	Team	Games	Pos.
1949	CLE AA	11	B

George Sutch
SUTCH, GEORGE RUSSELL, JR.
B. Aug. 28, 1921, Jeffersonville, PA
Rochester/Temple 6'1" 205 lbs.

Year	Team	Games	Pos.
1946	CHIC N	3	B

Don Sutherin
SUTHERIN, DONALD P.
B. Feb. 29, 1936, Empire, OH
Ohio State 5'10" 193 lbs.

Year	Team	Games	Pos.
1959	NYG N	2	HB
1959	PIT N	6	HB
1960		4	HB
2 yrs.	12 games		

Doug Sutherland
SUTHERLAND, DOUGLAS A.
B. Apr. 1, 1948, Superior, WI
Wisconsin-Superior 6'3" 250 lbs.

Year	Team	Games	Pos.
1970	NO N	10	G
1971	MIN N	11	G
1972		14	DE, DT
1973		9	DT
1974		14	DT
1975		14	DT
1976		14	DT
1977		14	DT
1978		16	DT
1979		16	DT
1980		16	DT
1981	SEA N	16	DT
12 yrs.	164 games		

John Sutro
SUTRO, JOHN ROBERT
B. May 8, 1940
San Jose State 6'4" 245 lbs.

Year	Team	Games	Pos.
1962	SF N	5	OT

Eddie Sutter
SUTTER, EDWARD LEE
B. Oct. 3, 1969, Peoria, IL
Northwestern 6'3" 240 lbs.

Year	Team	Games	Pos.
1993	CLE N	15	LB
1994		16	LB
1995		16	LB
1996	BAL N	16	LB
4 yrs.	63 games		

Archie Sutton
SUTTON, ARCHIE MICHAEL
B. Nov. 2, 1942, New Orleans, LA

Archie Sutton *continued*
Illinois 6'4" 263 lbs.

Year	Team	Games	Pos.
1965	MIN N	14	OT
1966		3	OT
1967		2	OT
3 yrs.	19 games		

Ed Sutton
SUTTON, EDWARD C.
B. Mar. 16, 1935, Sylva, NC
North Carolina 6'1" 205 lbs.

Year	Team	Games	Pos.
1957	WAS N	12	HB
1958		10	HB
1959		11	HB
1960	NYG N	12	HB
4 yrs.	45 games		

Eric Sutton
SUTTON, ERIC
B. Oct. 24, 1972, Torrance, CA
San Diego State 5'10" 169 lbs.

Year	Team	Games	Pos.
1996	WAS N	4	CB

Frank Sutton
SUTTON, FRANK
B. Mar. 29, 1964
Jackson State 6'3" 280 lbs.

Year	Team	Games	Pos.
1987	NYG N	2	OT

Joe Sutton
SUTTON, JOSEPH
B. Apr. 26, 1924, Philadelphia, PA
Temple 5'11" 180 lbs.

Year	Team	Games	Pos.
1949	BUF AA	9	HB
1950	PHI N	9	HB
1951		11	HB
3 yrs.	29 games		

Jon Sutton
SUTTON, JONATHAN E.
B. Jan. 1, 1957, New Orleans, LA
New Mexico 6'1" 195 lbs.

Year	Team	Games	Pos.
1987	NO N	2	CB, S

Mickey Sutton
SUTTON, MICKEY
B. Jul. 17, 1943
Auburn 6'0" 190 lbs.

Year	Team	Games	Pos.
1966	HOU A	5	DB

Mickey Sutton
SUTTON, WILLIAM
B. Aug. 28, 1960, Greenville, MS
Montana 5'8" 167 lbs.

Year	Team	Games	Pos.
1986	LARM N	16	CB
1987		12	CB
1988		15	CB
1989	GB N	4	CB
1989	BUF N	12	CB
1990	LARM N	7	CB, S
5 yrs.	66 games		

Mitch Sutton
SUTTON, MITCHELL
B. May 10, 1951, Stone Mountain, GA
Kansas 6'4" 260 lbs.

Year	Team	Games	Pos.
1974	PHI N	14	DT
1975		4	DT
2 yrs.	18 games		

Reggie Sutton
SUTTON, REGGIE
B. Feb. 16, 1965, Miami, FL
Miami (Florida) 5'10" 180 lbs.

Year	Team	Games	Pos.
1987	NO N	11	CB

Year	Team		Games	Pos.

Reggie Sutton *continued*

Year	Team		Games	Pos.
1988			15	CB
2 yrs.	26 games			

Ricky Sutton
SUTTON, FREDERICK DEWAYNE
B. Apr. 27, 1971, Atlanta, GA
Auburn 6'2" 281 lbs.

1993	PIT	N	7	DE, DT

Harland Svare
SVARE, HARLAND JAMES
B. Nov. 15, 1930, Clarksville, MN
Washington State 6'0" 214 lbs.

1953	LA	N	10	G
1954			10	G
1955	NYG	N	12	G
1956			11	E
1957			12	E
1958			10	E
1959			12	LB
1960			12	LB
8 yrs.	89 games			

Earl Svendsen
SVENDSEN, EARL G. (Bud)
B. Feb. 7, 1915, Minneapolis, MN
D. Aug. 6, 1996, Edina, MN
Minnesota 6'1" 190 lbs.

1937	GB	N	8	C
1939			10	C
1940	BKN	N	11	C
1941			11	C
1942			4	C
1943			10	C
6 yrs.	54 games			

George Svendsen
SVENDSEN, GEORGE P., JR.
B. Mar. 22, 1913, Minneapolis, MN
Oregon/Minnesota 6'4" 230 lbs.

1935	GB	N	9	C
1936			11	C
1937			11	C
1940			10	C
1941			10	C
5 yrs.	51 games			

Paul Sverchek
SVERCHEK, PAUL
B. May 9, 1961, San Luis Obispo, CA
California Poly (San Luis Obispo) 6'3" 252 lbs.

1984	MIN	N	3	NT

Bob Svihus
SVIHUS, ROBERT C.
B. Jun. 21, 1943, Los Angeles, CA
Southern California 6'4" 245 lbs.

1965	OAK	A	14	OT
1966			14	OT
1967			14	OT
1968			14	OT
1969			13	OT
1970	OAK	A	13	OT
1971	NYJ	N	14	OT
1972			14	OT
1973			12	OT
9 yrs.	122 games			

Bill Svoboda
SVOBODA, WILLIAM R.
B. Jul. 12, 1928, Wichita Falls, TX
D. Jun. 20, 1980, Houma, LA
Tulane 6'0" 210 lbs.

1950	CHIC	N	11	LB

Bill Svoboda *continued*

Year	Team		Games	Pos.
1951			12	FB, LB
1952			10	LB
1953			12	LB
1954	NYG	N	11	LB
1955			12	LB
1956			11	LB
1957			11	LB
1958			10	LB
9 yrs.	100 games			

Alton Swain
SWAIN, ALTON (Judge)
B. Oct. 2, 1899
D. Mar., 1976, Arlington, TX
Trinity (Texas) 6'1" 190 lbs.

1926	BUF	N	3	E

Bill Swain
SWAIN, WILLIAM STEVEN
B. Feb. 22, 1941, Dickinson, ND
Oregon 6'2" 229 lbs.

1963	LA	N	14	LB
1964	MIN	N	14	LB
1965	NYG	N	14	LB
1967			14	LB
1968	DET	N	13	LB
1969			14	LB
6 yrs.	83 games			

John Swain
SWAIN, JOHN WESLEY
B. Sep. 4, 1959, Miami, FL
Miami (Florida) 6'1" 194 lbs.

1981	MIN	N	12	CB
1982			9	CB
1983			14	CB
1984			15	CB
1985	MIA	N	6	CB
1985	PIT	N	9	CB
1986			11	CB
1987	MIA	N	1	CB
7 yrs.	77 games			

Russ Swan
SWAN, RUSSELL S.
B. Mar. 30, 1963
Virginia 6'4" 225 lbs.

1987	DAL	N	5	LB

Karl Swanke
SWANKE, KARL VANCE
B. Dec. 29, 1957, Elmhurst, IL
Boston College 6'6" 260 lbs.

1980	GB	N	16	OT, C
1981			4	OT, C
1982			8	OT, C
1983			16	OT, C
1984			15	OT, C
1985			15	OT
1986			10	OT, C
7 yrs.	84 games			

Charles Swann
SWANN, CHARLES
B. Oct. 29, 1970, Memphis, TN
Indiana State 6'1" 188 lbs.

1994	DEN	N	14	CB

Eric Swann
SWANN, ERIC JERROD
B. Aug. 16, 1970, Pinehurst, NC
Wake Technical CC 6'4" 310 lbs.*

1991	PHX	N	12	DE
1992			16	DE, DT
1993			9	DE, DT
1994	ARI	N	16	DT

Eric Swann *continued*

Year	Team		Games	Pos.
1995			13	DT
1996			16	DT
6 yrs.	82 games			

Lynn Swann
SWANN, LYNN CURTIS
B. Mar. 7, 1962, Alcoa, TN
Southern California 6'0" 180 lbs.

1974	PIT	N	12	WR
1975			14	WR
1976			12	WR
1977			14	WR
1978			16	WR
1979			13	WR
1980			13	WR
1981			13	WR
1982			9	WR
9 yrs.	116 games			

Eric Swanson
SWANSON, ERIC CHARLES
B. Aug. 25, 1963, San Bernardino, CA
Tennessee 5'11" 186 lbs.

1986	STL	N	9	WR

Evar Swanson
SWANSON, ERNEST EVAR
B. Oct. 15, 1902, De Kalb, IL
D. Jul. 17, 1973, Galesburg, IL
Lombard 5'9" 168 lbs.

1924	MIL	N	9	E
1925	RI	N	2	E
1925	CHIC	N	1	E
1926			3	HB, E
1927			7	E
4 yrs.	22 games			

Shane Swanson
SWANSON, SHANE
B. Oct. 4, 1962, Tracy, CA
Nebraska 5'9" 200 lbs.

1987	DEN	N	3	WR

Terry Swanson
SWANSON, TERRY G.
B. Jan. 8, 1944, Cambridge, MA
Massachusetts 6'0" 210 lbs.

1967	BOS	A	14	P
1968			10	P
1969	CIN	A	2	P
3 yrs.	26 games			

George Swarn
SWARN, GEORGE
B. Feb. 15, 1964, Cincinnati, OH
Miami (Ohio) 5'10" 205 lbs.

1987	CLE	N	1	RB

Gregg Swartwoudt
SWARTWOUDT, GREGG H.
B. 1964
North Dakota 6'3" 275 lbs.

1987	NYG	N	1	OT

Dick Swatland
SWATLAND, RICHARD THOMAS
B. Oct. 8, 1945, Stamford, CT
Notre Dame 6'3" 245 lbs.

1968	HOU	A	4	G

Harry Swayne
SWAYNE, HARRY
B. Feb. 2, 1965, Philadelphia, PA
Rutgers 6'5" 268 lbs.

1987	TB	N	8	DE

Harry Swayne *continued*

Year	Team		Games	Pos.
1988			10	DE
1989			16	OT
1990			10	OT
1991	SD	N	12	OT
1992			16	OT
1993			11	OT
1994			16	OT
1995			16	OT
1996			16	OT
10 yrs.	131 games			

Calvin Sweeney
SWEENEY, CALVIN EUGENE
B. Jan. 12, 1955, Riverside, CA
California-Riverside/Southern California 6'2" 188 lbs.

1980	PIT	N	14	WR
1981			14	WR
1982			7	WR
1983			16	WR
1984			9	WR
1985			16	WR
1986			16	WR
1987			9	WR
8 yrs.	101 games			

Jake Sweeney
SWEENEY, JAKE
B. May 25, 1922, Cincinnati, OH
Cincinnati 6'3" 240 lbs.

1944	CHIB	N	7	T

Jim Sweeney
SWEENEY, JAMES JOSEPH
B. Aug. 8, 1962, Pittsburgh, PA
Pittsburgh 6'4" 277 lbs.

1984	NYJ	N	10	G, C
1985			16	G, C
1986			16	G, OT, C
1987			12	OT
1988			16	OT, G
1989			16	C, OT, G
1990			16	C
1991			16	C, G
1992			16	C, G
1993			16	C, G
1994			16	C
1995	SEA	N	16	C
1996	PIT	N	16	C
13 yrs.	198 games			

Kevin Sweeney
SWEENEY, KEVIN JOSEPH
B. Nov. 16, 1963, Bozeman, MT
Fresno State 6'0" 191 lbs.

1987	DAL	N	3	QB
1988			3	QB
2 yrs.	6 games			

Neal Sweeney
SWEENEY, NEAL
B. Jun. 13, 1945, Van Nuys, CA
Tulsa 6'2" 170 lbs.

1967	DEN	A	10	OE

Steve Sweeney
SWEENEY, STEVEN
B. Sep. 6, 1950, Bozeman, MT
California 6'3" 205 lbs.

1973	OAK	A	14	TE

Walt Sweeney
SWEENEY, WALTER FRANCIS
B. Apr. 18, 1941, Cohasset, MA
Syracuse 6'3" 256 lbs.

1963	SD	A	14	G

Year	Team		Games	Pos.

Walt Sweeney *continued*

Year	Team		Games	Pos.
1964			14	G
1965			14	G
1966			14	G
1967			14	G
1968			14	G
1969			14	G
1970	SD	N	14	G
1971			14	G
1972			14	G
1973			14	G
1974	WAS	N	14	G
1975			14	G

13 yrs.   182 games

Fred Sweet
SWEET, FREDERICK
B. Aug. 17, 1901, Philadelphia, PA
D. Oct. 31, 1976
Brown 5'10" 165 lbs.

Year	Team		Games	Pos.
1925	PRO	N	8	HB, FB, E
1926			8	HB, FB, QB

2 yrs.   16 games

Joe Sweet
SWEET, JOSEPH LAMAR
B. Jul. 5, 1948, Lakeland, FL
Tennessee State 6'2" 196 lbs.

Year	Team		Games	Pos.
1972	LA	N	11	WR
1973			8	WR
1974	NE	N	4	WR
1975	SD	N	11	WR

4 yrs.   34 games

Tony Sweet
SWEET, TONY
B. Dec. 13, 1963
Montclair State 6'4" 240 lbs.

Year	Team		Games	Pos.
1987	NYJ	N	3	TE

Karl Sweetan
SWEETAN, KARL ROBERT
B. Oct. 2, 1942, Dallas, TX
Texas A&M/Wake Forest/Navarro JC 6'1" 203 lbs.

Year	Team		Games	Pos.
1966	DET	N	10	QB
1967			10	QB
1968	NO	N	5	QB
1969	LA	N	5	QB
1970			6	QB

5 yrs.   36 games

Fred Sweetland
SWEETLAND, FREDERICK G.
(Buck)
B. Nov., 1893, Everett, MA
Deceased
Washington & Lee/Fordham 5'10" 175 lbs.

Year	Team		Games	Pos.
1920	AKR	A	2	HB
1921	NY	A	1	FB

2 yrs.   3 games

Bob Sweiger
SWEIGER, ROBERT M.
B. Jun. 20, 1919
D. Nov., 1975
Minnesota 6'0" 209 lbs.

Year	Team		Games	Pos.
1946	NY	AA	13	HB, LB
1947			14	HB, LB
1948			14	HB, LB
1949	CHI	AA	12	HB, LB

4 yrs.   53 games

Bob Swenson
SWENSON, ROBERT CHARLES
B. Jul. 1, 1953, Stockton, CA

Bob Swenson *continued*
California 6'3" 222 lbs.

Year	Team		Games	Pos.
1975	DEN	N	14	LB
1976			14	LB
1977			14	LB
1978			16	LB
1979			16	LB
1981			16	LB
1982			4	LB
1983			2	LB

8 yrs.   96 games

Merwin Swenson
SWENSON, MERWIN WILLIAM
(Swede)
B. May 12, 1898
Deceased
Chicago/Dartmouth 6'1" 196 lbs.

Year	Team		Games	Pos.
1926	CHI	A	7	G

Bill Swiacki
SWIACKI, WILLIAM ADAM
B. Oct. 2, 1922, Southbridge, MA
D. Jul. 7, 1976, Sturbridge, MA
Columbia 6'2" 196 lbs.

Year	Team		Games	Pos.
1948	NYG	N	12	E
1949			12	E
1950			12	E
1951	DET	N	12	E
1952			11	E

5 yrs.   59 games

Phil Swiadon
SWIADON, PHILIP EDWARD
B. Dec. 5, 1914
New York University 6'0" 220 lbs.

Year	Team		Games	Pos.
1943	BKN	N	3	T, G

Larry Swider
SWIDER, LAWRENCE
B. Feb. 1, 1955, Limestone, ME
Pittsburgh 6'2" 195 lbs.

Year	Team		Games	Pos.
1979	DET	N	14	P
1980	STL	N	16	P
1981	TB	N	13	P
1982			9	P

4 yrs.   52 games

Doug Swift
SWIFT, DOUGLAS A.
B. Oct. 24, 1948, Syracuse, NY
Amherst 6'3" 228 lbs.

Year	Team		Games	Pos.
1970	MIA	N	14	LB
1971			14	LB
1972			14	LB
1973			14	LB
1974			8	LB
1975			14	LB

6 yrs.   78 games

Dennis Swilley
SWILLEY, DENNIS NEAL
B. Jun. 28, 1955, Bossier City, LA
Texas A&M 6'3" 260 lbs.

Year	Team		Games	Pos.
1977	MIN	N	14	G
1978			14	G
1979			16	G
1980			16	G
1981			16	G
1982			9	C
1983			16	C
1985			16	C
1986			16	C
1987			6	C

10 yrs.   139 games

Pat Swilling
SWILLING, PAT
B. Oct. 25, 1964, Toccoa, GA
Georgia Tech 6'3" 242 lbs.

Year	Team		Games	Pos.
1986	NO	N	16	LB
1987			12	LB
1988			15	LB
1989			16	LB
1990			16	LB
1991			16	LB
1992			16	LB
1993	DET	N	14	LB
1994			16	LB
1995	OAK	N	16	DE
1996			16	DE

11 yrs.   169 games

Wayne Swinford
SWINFORD, LENIS WAYNE
B. May 3, 1943, Anniston, AL
Georgia 6'0" 194 lbs.

Year	Team		Games	Pos.
1965	SF	N	14	DB
1966			7	FL
1967			5	FL

3 yrs.   26 games

Jim Swink
SWINK, JAMES
B. 1936
Texas Christian 6'1" 195 lbs.

Year	Team		Games	Pos.
1960	DAL	A		HB

Clovis Swinney
SWINNEY, CLOVIS
B. Aug. 17, 1945, Mexico, MO
Arkansas/Arkansas State 6'3" 240 lbs.

Year	Team		Games	Pos.
1970	NO	N	14	DE
1971	NYJ	N	4	DE
1971	HOU	N	4	DT

2 yrs.   22 games

Bob Swisher
SWISHER, ROBERT E.
B. Jul. 14, 1914, Victoria, IL
D. Sep., 1979, Memphis, TN
Northwestern 5'11" 163 lbs.

Year	Team		Games	Pos.
1938	CHIB	N	6	HB, FB
1939			10	HB
1940			9	HB
1941			11	HB
1945			3	HB

5 yrs.   39 games

Mike Swistowicz
SWISTOWICZ, MICHAEL PAUL
B. Apr. 22, 1927, Chicago, IL
Notre Dame 5'10" 185 lbs.

Year	Team		Games	Pos.
1950	NYY	N	1	B
1950	CHIC	N	9	HB, FB

Marvin Switzer
SWITZER, MARVIN DUANE
B. Oct. 28, 1954, Bogue, KS
Kansas State 6'1" 192 lbs.

Year	Team		Games	Pos.
1978	BUF	N	10	S

Veryl Switzer
SWITZER, VERYL A.
B. Aug. 6, 1932, Nicodemus, KS
Kansas State 5'11" 190 lbs.

Year	Team		Games	Pos.
1954	GB	N	12	HB
1955			12	HB

2 yrs.   24 games

Craig Swoope
SWOOPE, CRAIG AVERY

Craig Swoope *continued*
B. Feb. 3, 1964, Fort Pierce, FL
Illinois 6'1" 200 lbs.

Year	Team		Games	Pos.
1986	TB	N	15	CB, S
1987			1	S
1987	IND	N	3	DB
1988			11	CB, S

3 yrs.   30 games

Patrick Swoopes
SWOOPES, PATRICK ROAMAN
B. Mar. 4, 1964, Florence, AL
Mississippi State 6'4" 280 lbs.

Year	Team		Games	Pos.
1987	NO	N	9	NT
1989			15	NT
1991	KC	N	4	DE
1991	MIA	N	3	DE

3 yrs.   31 games

Jeff Sydner
SYDNER, JEFF
B. Nov. 11, 1969, Columbus, OH
Hawaii 5'6" 170 lbs.

Year	Team		Games	Pos.
1992	PHI	N	15	WR
1993			4	WR
1994			16	WR
1995	NYJ	N	6	WR

4 yrs.   41 games

Harry Sydney
SYDNEY, HARRY FLANROY, III
B. Jun. 26, 1959, Petersburg, VA
Kansas 6'0" 217 lbs.

Year	Team		Games	Pos.
1987	SF	N	14	RB
1988			16	RB
1989			7	RB
1990			16	RB
1991			16	RB
1992	GB	N	16	RB

6 yrs.   85 games

Willie Sydnor
SYDNOR, GEORGE ROSS
B. Mar. 21, 1959, Bryn Mawr, PA
Northwestern/Villanova/Syracuse 5'11" 170 lbs.

Year	Team		Games	Pos.
1982	PIT	N	7	WR

Al Sykes
SYKES, ALFRED
B. Dec. 20, 1947, Tallahassee, FL
Florida A&M 6'3" 160 lbs.

Year	Team		Games	Pos.
1971	NE	N	4	WR

Bob Sykes
SYKES, ROBERT
B. Mar. 15, 1927, Oakland, CA
San Jose State 6'1" 218 lbs.

Year	Team		Games	Pos.
1952	WAS	N	3	FB

Gene Sykes
SYKES, EUGENE CHARLES
B. Sep. 26, 1941, New Orleans, LA
Louisiana State 6'1" 196 lbs.

Year	Team		Games	Pos.
1963	BUF	A	9	DB
1964			10	DB
1965			4	DB
1967	DEN	A	4	DB

4 yrs.   27 games

John Sykes
SYKES, JOHN
B. Mar. 13, 1950, Baltimore, MD
Morgan State 5'11" 195 lbs.

Year	Team		Games	Pos.
1972	SD	N	2	WR

Johnny Sylvester
SYLVESTER, JOHN J.
B. Jan. 14, 1923, Norristown, PA
Temple 6'0" 183 lbs.

Year	Team		Games	Pos.
1947	NY	AA	7	B
1948	BAL	AA	12	B
2 yrs.	19 games			

Steve Sylvester
SYLVESTER, STEVEN PHILLIP
B. Mar. 4, 1953, Cincinnati, OH
Notre Dame 6'4" 261 lbs.

Year	Team		Games	Pos.
1975	OAK	N	11	G
1976			14	C, G
1977			14	C
1978			16	C
1979			16	C, G
1980			7	G, C, OT
1981			15	C, G
1982	LARI	N	5	C, G
1983			9	C, G
9 yrs.	107 games			

John Symank
SYMANK, JOHN RICHARD
B. Aug. 31, 1935, La Grange, TX
Florida 5'11" 180 lbs.

Year	Team		Games	Pos.
1957	GB	N	12	DB
1958			12	DB
1959			12	DB
1960			12	DB
1961			14	DB
1962			14	DB
1963	STL	N	13	DB
7 yrs.	89 games			

Stan Sytsma
SYTSMA, STANLEY ALLEN
B. May 3, 1956, Glendale, AZ
Minnesota 6'2" 200 lbs.

Year	Team		Games	Pos.
1980	ATL	N	2	LB

Len Szafaryn
SZAFARYN, LEONARD ADOLPH
B. Jan. 19, 1928, Ambridge, PA
D. Sep. 22, 1990, Baden, PA
North Carolina 6'2" 226 lbs.

Year	Team		Games	Pos.
1949	WAS	N	12	T
1950	GB	N	12	G
1953			7	G
1954			12	T
1955			12	T
1956			12	G
1957	PHI	N	1	T
1958			7	T
8 yrs.	75 games			

Paul Szakash
SZAKASH, PAUL MICHAEL
(Socko)
B. May 5, 1914, Chicago, IL
D. Oct. 24, 1984, Missoula, MT
Montana 6'0" 213 lbs.

Year	Team		Games	Pos.
1938	DET	N	7	FB
1939			11	QB, FB, HB
1941			7	E
1942			10	E, QB
4 yrs.	35 games			

Rich Szaro
SZARO, RICHARD JULIAN
B. Mar. 7, 1948, Rzeszow, Poland
Harvard 5'11" 204 lbs.

Year	Team		Games	Pos.
1975	NO	N	11	K
1976			14	K
1977			14	K
1978			4	K

Rich Szaro continued

Year	Team		Games	Pos.
1979	NYJ	N	1	K
5 yrs.	44 games			

Joe Szczecko
SZCZECKO, JOSEPH
B. Aug. 25, 1942, Lahr, Germany
Northwestern 6'0" 245 lbs.

Year	Team		Games	Pos.
1966	ATL	N	12	DT
1967			13	DT
1968			10	DT
1968	NYG	N	10	DT
1969			14	DT
4 yrs.	59 games			

Walt Szot
SZOT, WALTER STANLEY
B. Mar. 30, 1920, Clifton, NJ
D. Nov. 3, 1981, Passaic, NJ
Bucknell 6'1" 222 lbs.

Year	Team		Games	Pos.
1946	CHIC	N	9	T
1947			12	T
1948			12	T
1949	PIT	N	12	T
1950			11	T
5 yrs.	56 games			

Dave Szott
SZOTT, DAVID ANDREW
B. Dec. 12, 1967, Passaic, NJ
Penn State 6'4" 285 lbs.

Year	Team		Games	Pos.
1990	KC	N	16	G
1991			1	G
1992			16	G
1993			14	G
1994			16	G, OT
1995			16	G
1996			16	G
7 yrs.	95 games			

Dave Szymakowski
SZYMAKOWSKI, DAVID
B. Mar. 15, 1946, Bethlehem, PA
West Texas State 6'2" 198 lbs.

Year	Team		Games	Pos.
1968	NO	N	3	FL

Dick Szymanski
SZYMANSKI, RICHARD FRANK
B. Oct. 7, 1932, Toledo, OH
Notre Dame 6'3" 233 lbs.

Year	Team		Games	Pos.
1955	BAL	N	12	C
1957			5	C
1958			8	C
1959			12	LB, C
1960			12	LB
1961			14	C
1962			14	C
1963			14	C
1964			14	C
1965			10	C
1966			14	C
1967			14	C
1968			14	C
13 yrs.	157 games			

Frank Szymanski
SZYMANSKI, FRANCIS STANISLAUS
B. Jul. 6, 1923, Detroit, MI
D. Apr. 26, 1987
Notre Dame 6'0" 220 lbs.

Year	Team		Games	Pos.
1945	DET	N	4	C
1946			11	C
1947			12	C
1948	PHI	N	9	C
1949	CHIB	N	11	C
5 yrs.	47 games			

Jim Szymanski
SZYMANSKI, JIM
B. Sep. 7, 1967, Sterling Heights, MI
Michigan State 6'5" 268 lbs.

Year	Team		Games	Pos.
1990	DEN	N	6	DE
1991			1	DE
2 yrs.	7 games			

Paul Tabor
TABOR, PAUL CARROL
B. Nov. 30, 1956, Little Rock, AR
Oklahoma 6'4" 241 lbs.

Year	Team		Games	Pos.
1980	CHI	N	16	C, G

Phil Tabor
TABOR, PHILIP
B. Nov. 30, 1956, Houston, TX
Oklahoma 6'4" 255 lbs.

Year	Team		Games	Pos.
1979	NYG	N	15	DE
1980			16	DT
1981			16	DT
1982			9	DE
4 yrs.	56 games			

Doyle Tackett
TACKETT, DOYLE LEE
B. Aug. 22, 1925
Louisiana State 6'0" 205 lbs.

Year	Team		Games	Pos.
1946	BKN	AA	14	HB, DB
1947			10	HB, DB
1948			1	HB, DB
3 yrs.	25 games			

Charles Tackwell
TACKWELL, CHARLES O.
(Cookie)
B. Mar. 27, 1906
D. Aug., 1984, Columbia City, IN
Kansas State 6'2" 215 lbs.

Year	Team		Games	Pos.
1930	FRA	N	15	E, T
1930	MIN	N	1	E
1931	FRA	N	7	T
1931	CHIB	N	5	T, E
1932			10	E
1933			3	E
1933	CIN	N	5	E
1934	C-S	N	8	E
5 yrs.	54 games			

Joe Taffoni
TAFFONI, JOSEPH
B. Mar. 27, 1945, Brownsville, PA
*West Virginia/Tennessee-Martin 6'3"
251 lbs.*

Year	Team		Games	Pos.
1967	CLE	N	14	G
1968			13	G
1969			14	OT
1970			14	OT
1972	NYG	N	14	OT
1973			9	OT
6 yrs.	78 games			

Jerry Tagge
TAGGE, JERRY LEE
B. Apr. 12, 1950, Omaha, NE
Nebraska 6'2" 218 lbs.

Year	Team		Games	Pos.
1972	GB	N	4	QB
1973			7	QB
1974			6	QB
3 yrs.	17 games			

John Tagliaferri
TAGLIAFERRI, JOHN
B. Apr. 13, 1964
Cornell 5'11" 195 lbs.

Year	Team		Games	Pos.
1987	MIA	N	3	RB

Joe Taibi
TAIBI, JOE
B. Feb. 22, 1963
Idaho 6'5" 265 lbs.

Year	Team		Games	Pos.
1987	NYG	N	3	DE

Art Tait
TAIT, ARTHUR WILLIAM
B. 1929
Mississippi State 5'11" 205 lbs.

Year	Team		Games	Pos.
1951	NYY	N	12	E
1952	DAL	N	8	E
2 yrs.	20 games			

Bob Talamini
TALAMINI, ROBERT GUY
B. Jan. 8, 1939, Louisville, KY
Kentucky 6'1" 249 lbs.

Year	Team		Games	Pos.
1960	HOU	A	10	G
1961			14	G
1962			14	G
1963			14	G
1964			14	G
1965			14	G
1966			14	G
1967			14	G
1968	NY	A	14	G
9 yrs.	122 games			

Diron Talbert
TALBERT, DIRON VESTER
B. Jul. 1, 1944, Pascagoula, MS
Texas 6'5" 252 lbs.

Year	Team		Games	Pos.
1967	LA	N	2	DT
1968			14	DT
1969			14	DT
1970			14	DT
1971	WAS	N	14	DT
1972			14	DT
1973			14	DT
1974			14	DT
1975			14	DT
1976			14	DT
1977			14	DT
1978			12	DT
1979			14	DT
1980			16	DT
14 yrs.	186 games			

Don Talbert
TALBERT, DONALD LARRY
B. Mar. 1, 1939, Louisville, MS
Texas 6'5" 248 lbs.

Year	Team		Games	Pos.
1962	DAL	N	14	LB
1965			14	OT
1966	ATL	N	12	OT
1967			12	OT
1968			14	OT
1969	NO	N	14	OT
1970			14	OT
1971	DAL	N	9	OT
8 yrs.	103 games			

John Talbot
TALBOT, JOHN ORECHIA
B. Apr. 27, 1900, South Weymouth, MA
D. Dec. 5, 1981, Keene, NH
Brown 6'2" 182 lbs.

Year	Team		Games	Pos.
1926	PRO	N	2	E

Jim Talbott
TALBOTT, JAMES S.
B. Jul. 26, 1893
D. Nov., 1972, Hollywood, FL
North Dakota

Year	Team		Games	Pos.
1920	HAM	A	1	HB

Year	Team	Games	Pos.

Don Talcott
TALCOTT, DON
B. May 21, 1921, Grass Valley, CA
Nevada-Reno 6'2" 235 lbs.

Year	Team	Games	Pos.
1947	PHI	N	8	T

George Taliaferro
TALIAFERRO, GEORGE
B. Jan. 8, 1927, Halls, TN
Indiana 5'11" 196 lbs.

Year	Team		Games	Pos.
1949	LA	AA	11	B
1950	NYY	N	12	B
1951			12	B
1952	DAL	N	12	HB
1953	BAL	N	11	HB
1954			10	HB
1955	PHI	N	3	HB

7 yrs.   71 games

Mike Taliaferro
TALIAFERRO, MYRON EUGENE
B. Jul. 26, 1941, Houston, TX
Illinois 6'2" 206 lbs.

Year	Team		Games	Pos.
1964	NY	A	14	QB
1965			14	QB
1966			14	QB
1967			3	QB
1968	BOS	A	7	QB
1969			14	QB
1970	BOS	N	11	QB
1972	BUF	N	5	QB

8 yrs.   82 games

Dave Tallant
TALLANT, DAVID
B. Aug., 1896, Pennsylvania
Deceased
Muskingum/Grove City 6'1" 205 lbs.

Year	Team		Games	Pos.
1921	HAM	A	5	T
1922	HAM	N	3	T
1923			6	T
1924			1	T
1925			3	T

5 yrs.   18 games

Ben Talley
TALLEY, BENJAMIN JERMAINE
B. Jul. 14, 1972, Griffin, GA
Tennessee 6'3" 248 lbs.

Year	Team		Games	Pos.
1995	NYG	N	4	LB

Darryl Talley
TALLEY, DARRYL VICTOR
B. Jul. 10, 1960, Cleveland, OH
West Virginia 6'4" 231 lbs.

Year	Team		Games	Pos.
1983	BUF	N	16	LB
1984			16	LB
1985			16	LB
1986			16	LB
1987			12	LB
1988			16	LB
1989			16	LB
1990			16	LB
1991			16	LB
1992			16	LB
1993			16	LB
1994			16	LB
1995	ATL	N	16	LB
1996	MIN	N	12	LB

14 yrs.   216 games

John Talley
TALLEY, JOHN THOMAS
B. Dec. 19, 1964, Cleveland, OH
West Virginia 6'5" 245 lbs.

Year	Team		Games	Pos.
1990	CLE	N	14	TE
1991			3	TE

2 yrs.   17 games

Stan Talley
TALLEY, ROBERT STANLEY
B. Sep. 5, 1958, Dallas, TX
Texas Christian 6'5" 220 lbs.

Year	Team		Games	Pos.
1987	LARI	N	12	P

Charlie Tallman
TALLMAN, CHARLES W.
B. Jan. 9, 1896, New York State
D. Apr., 1970, Franklin, NJ
None

Year	Team		Games	Pos.
1921	TON	A	1	T

Ken Talton
TALTON, KENNETH B.
B. Jun. 25, 1957, Mansfield, OH
Cornell 6'0" 205 lbs.

Year	Team		Games	Pos.
1980	KC	N	2	RB

Ben Tamburello
TAMBURELLO, BEN ALLEN, JR.
B. Sep. 9, 1964, Birmingham, AL
Auburn 6'3" 278 lbs.

Year	Team		Games	Pos.
1987	PHI	N	2	C, G
1988			16	G, C
1989			16	G, C
1990			16	G, C

4 yrs.   50 games

Sam Tamburo
TAMBURO, SAMUEL J.
B. Jul. 1, 1926, New Kensington, PA
Penn State 6'2" 200 lbs.

Year	Team		Games	Pos.
1949	NYB	N	12	E

Ralph Tamm
TAMM, RALPH EARL
B. Mar. 11, 1966, Philadelphia, PA
West Chester 6'4" 280 lbs.

Year	Team		Games	Pos.
1990	CLE	N	16	G, C
1991			1	G, C
1991	WAS	N	2	G
1991	CIN	N	1	G
1992	SF	N	14	C, G
1993			16	G, C
1994			1	G
1995	DEN	N	13	G, C
1996			10	C

7 yrs.   74 games

George Tandy
TANDY, GEORGE WASHINGTON (Yank)
B. Nov. 27, 1893, Jacksonville, IL
D. May, 1969, Springfield, IL
North Carolina 6'1" 210 lbs.

Year	Team		Games	Pos.
1921	CLE	A	5	C

James Tanguay
TANGUAY, JAMES
B. 1910
New York University 6'0" 190 lbs.

Year	Team		Games	Pos.
1933	PIT	N	3	HB

Steve Tannen
TANNEN, STEVE
B. Jul. 23, 1948, Miami, FL
Florida 6'1" 194 lbs.

Year	Team		Games	Pos.
1970	NYJ	N	14	DB
1971			11	CB
1972			13	CB, S
1973			9	CB
1974			14	S, CB

5 yrs.   61 games

Bob Tanner
TANNER, ROBERT E.
B. Sep. 27, 1907, Fairmont, MN
D. Nov. 17, 1994
Minnesota 6'0" 190 lbs.

Year	Team		Games	Pos.
1930	FRA	N	11	E, T

Hamp Tanner
TANNER, HAMPTON
B. 1930
Georgia 6'2" 280 lbs.

Year	Team		Games	Pos.
1951	SF	N	12	T
1952	DAL	N	11	T

2 yrs.   23 games

John Tanner
TANNER, JOHN PORTER (Hump)
B. Aug. 5, 1900
D. Nov., 1976, Detroit, MI
Centre 5'5" 165 lbs.

Year	Team		Games	Pos.
1922	TOL	N	2	HB
1923	CLE	N	6	QB, HB
1924			2	HB, FB

3 yrs.   10 games

John Tanner
TANNER, JOHN VANCE
B. Mar. 8, 1945, Orlando, FL
Tennessee Tech 6'4" 231 lbs.

Year	Team		Games	Pos.
1971	SD	N	14	LB
1973	NE	N	14	LB
1974			14	LB

3 yrs.   42 games

Maa Tanuvasa
TANUVASA, MAA JUNIOR
B. Nov. 6, 1970, American Samoa
Hawaii 6'2" 277 lbs.

Year	Team		Games	Pos.
1995	DEN	N	1	DT
1996			16	DT

2 yrs.   17 games

George Tarasovic
TARASOVIC, GEORGE
B. May 6, 1930, Granville, NY
Louisiana State 6'4" 245 lbs.

Year	Team		Games	Pos.
1952	PIT	N	12	E
1953			12	E
1956			12	C, LB, E
1957			12	E
1958			12	E
1959			12	E
1960			12	E
1961			12	DE
1962			14	LB
1963			8	LB
1964	PHI	N	11	DE
1965			14	DE
1966	DEN	A	6	DE

13 yrs.   149 games

Bruce Tarbox
TARBOX, BRUCE B.
B. May 10, 1939
Syracuse 6'2" 230 lbs.

Year	Team		Games	Pos.
1961	LA	N	14	G

Richard Tardits
TARDITS, RICHARD
B. Jul. 30, 1965, Biarritz, France
Georgia 6'2" 228 lbs.

Year	Team		Games	Pos.
1990	NE	N	2	LB
1991			16	LB
1992			9	LB

3 yrs.   27 games

Fran Tarkenton
TARKENTON, FRANCIS ASBURY (The Scrambler)
B. Feb. 3, 1940, Richmond, VA
Georgia 6'1" 190 lbs.

Year	Team		Games	Pos.
1961	MIN	N	14	QB
1962			14	QB
1963			14	QB
1964			14	QB
1965			14	QB
1966			14	QB
1967	NYG	N	14	QB
1968			14	QB
1969			14	QB
1970			14	QB
1971			13	QB
1972	MIN	N	14	QB
1973			14	QB
1974			13	QB
1975			14	QB
1976			13	QB
1977			9	QB
1978			16	QB

18 yrs.   246 games

Jerry Tarr
TARR, GERALD
B. 1940, Bakersfield, CA
Oregon 6'0" 190 lbs.

Year	Team		Games	Pos.
1962	DEN	A	14	OE

Jim Tarr
TARR, JAMES L.
B. 1907
Missouri 6'2" 190 lbs.

Year	Team		Games	Pos.
1931	CLE	N	1	E

Bob Tarrant
TARRANT, ROBERT
B. Apr. 4, 1914
D. Dec. 16, 1991, Danbury, CT
Pittsburg State 6'0" 180 lbs.

Year	Team		Games	Pos.
1936	NYG	N	1	E

Jim Tarrant
TARRANT, JAMES ROBERT, JR.
B. Feb. 18, 1921, Birmingham, AL
Samford/Tennessee 5'9" 160 lbs.

Year	Team		Games	Pos.
1946	MIA	AA	4	QB

John Tarver
TARVER, JOHN ANDREW
B. Jan. 1, 1949, Bakersfield, CA
Colorado 6'3" 224 lbs.

Year	Team		Games	Pos.
1972	NE	N	8	RB
1973			12	RB
1974			14	RB
1975	PHI	N	8	RB

4 yrs.   42 games

Carl Taseff
TASEFF, CARL
B. Sep. 28, 1928, Cleveland, OH
John Carroll 5'11" 182 lbs.

Year	Team		Games	Pos.
1951	CLE	N	9	HB
1953	BAL	N	9	HB
1954			12	HB
1955			10	HB
1956			12	HB
1957			4	HB
1958			12	HB
1959			12	HB
1960			12	HB
1961				DB
1961	PHI	N		DB
1962	BUF	A	11	DB

11 yrs.   103 games

Year	Team		Games	Pos.

Steve Tasker
TASKER, STEVE
B. Apr. 10, 1962, Leoti, KS
Northwestern 5'9" 185 lbs.

Year	Team		Games	Pos.
1985	HOU	N	7	RB
1986			2	WR
1986	BUF	N	7	WR
1987			12	WR
1988			14	WR
1989			16	WR
1990			16	WR
1991			16	WR
1992			15	WR
1993			15	WR
1994			14	WR
1995			13	WR
1996			8	WR
12 yrs.	155 games			

Damon Tassos
TASSOS, DAMON G. (Greek)
B. Dec. 5, 1923, San Antonio, TX
Texas A&M 6'1" 224 lbs.

Year	Team		Games	Pos.
1945	DET	N	9	G
1946			11	G
1947	GB	N	3	G
1948			11	G
1949			12	G
5 yrs.	46 games			

Bob Tatarek
TATAREK, ROBERT FRANCIS
B. Jul. 3, 1946, Greensburg, PA
Miami (Florida) 6'4" 260 lbs.

Year	Team		Games	Pos.
1968	BUF	A	14	DT
1969			14	DT
1970	BUF	N	4	DT
1971			14	DT
1972			1	DT
1972	DET	N	2	DT
5 yrs.	49 games			

David Tate
TATE, DAVID
B. Nov. 22, 1964, Denver, CO
Colorado 6'0" 177 lbs.

Year	Team		Games	Pos.
1988	CHI	N	16	CB, S
1989			14	CB, S
1990			16	S
1991			16	S
1992			16	S
1993	NYG	N	14	S
1994	IND	N	16	S, CB
1995			16	S
1996			10	S
9 yrs.	134 games			

Frank Tate
TATE, FRANKLIN
B. Nov. 14, 1952, Gastonia, NC
North Carolina Central 6'3" 225 lbs.

Year	Team		Games	Pos.
1975	SD	N	4	LB

John Tate
TATE, JOHN
B. May 1, 1953, Mobile, AL
Jackson State 6'2" 230 lbs.

Year	Team		Games	Pos.
1976	NYG	N	2	LB

Lars Tate
TATE, LARS JAMEL
B. Feb. 2, 1966, Indianapolis, IN
Georgia 6'2" 215 lbs.

Year	Team		Games	Pos.
1988	TB	N	15	RB
1989			15	RB
1990	CHI	N	2	RB
3 yrs.	32 games			

Rodney Tate
TATE, RODNEY DANE
B. Feb. 14, 1959, Okmulgee, OK
Texas 5'11" 190 lbs.

Year	Team		Games	Pos.
1982	CIN	N	9	RB
1983			12	RB
1984	ATL	N	7	RB
3 yrs.	28 games			

Willy Tate
TATE, WILLY
B. Sep. 7, 1972, Fontana, CA
Oregon 6'3" 243 lbs.

Year	Team		Games	Pos.
1996	TB	N	13	TE

Pete Tatman
TATMAN, PETE
B. Apr. 27, 1945, North Platte, NE
Nebraska 6'1" 220 lbs.

Year	Team		Games	Pos.
1967	MIN	N	5	RB

Jack Tatum
TATUM, JOHN DAVID (The Assassin)
B. Nov. 18, 1948, Cherryville, NC
Ohio State 5'10" 203 lbs.

Year	Team		Games	Pos.
1971	OAK	N	14	DB
1972			14	S
1973			13	S
1974			10	DB
1975			13	S
1976			14	S
1977			11	S
1978			15	S
1979			16	S
1980	HOU	N	16	S
10 yrs.	136 games			

Jess Tatum
TATUM, JESS
B. Oct. 8, 1914
D. Feb. 4, 1992
North Carolina State 6'1" 215 lbs.

Year	Team		Games	Pos.
1938	PIT	N	5	E

Mosi Tatupu
TATUPU, MOSIULA F.
B. Apr. 26, 1955, Pago Pago, American Samoa
Southern California 6'0" 227 lbs.

Year	Team		Games	Pos.
1978	NE	N	16	RB
1979			16	RB
1980			16	RB
1981			16	RB
1982			9	RB
1983			16	RB
1984			16	RB
1985			16	RB
1986			16	RB
1987			12	RB
1988			16	RB
1989			14	RB
1990			15	RB
1991	LARM	N	5	RB
14 yrs.	199 games			

Biff Taugher
TAUGHER, CLAUDE
B. Mar., 1895
Deceased
Carroll (Wisconsin)/Marquette 5'10" 180 lbs.

Year	Team		Games	Pos.
1922	GB	N	2	FB

Terry Tausch
TAUSCH, TERRY WAYNE
B. Feb. 5, 1959, New Braunfels, TX

Terry Tausch continued
Texas 6'5" 275 lbs.

Year	Team		Games	Pos.
1982	MIN	N	2	OT
1983			10	OT
1984			16	OT
1985			16	OT
1986			16	OT
1987			5	OT
1988			16	G
1989	SF	N	9	G
8 yrs.	90 games			

Junior Tautalatasi
TAUTALATASI, TAIVALE, JR.
B. Mar. 24, 1962, Oakland, CA
Washington State 5'10" 207 lbs.

Year	Team		Games	Pos.
1986	PHI	N	16	RB
1987			12	RB
1988			10	RB
1989	DAL	N	13	RB
4 yrs.	51 games			

John Tautolo
TAUTOLO, JOHN WILLIAM
B. May 29, 1959, Long Beach, CA
UCLA 6'3" 260 lbs.

Year	Team		Games	Pos.
1982	NYG	N	1	G
1983			6	G
1987	LARI	N	3	G
3 yrs.	10 games			

Terry Tautolo
TAUTOLO, TERRY L.
B. Aug. 30, 1954, Corona, CA
UCLA 6'2" 235 lbs.

Year	Team		Games	Pos.
1976	PHI	N	13	LB
1977			14	LB
1978			16	LB
1979			16	LB
1980	SF	N	14	LB
1981			5	LB
1981	DET	N	11	LB
1982			2	LB
1983	MIA	N	9	LB
1984	DET	N	4	LB
9 yrs.	104 games			

John Tavener
TAVENER, JOHN H.
B. Jan. 10, 1921
D. Sep. 19, 1993
Indiana 6'0" 225 lbs.

Year	Team		Games	Pos.
1946	MIA	AA	3	C

Aaron Taylor
TAYLOR, AARON MATTHEW
B. Nov. 14, 1972, San Francisco, CA
Notre Dame 6'4" 305 lbs.

Year	Team		Games	Pos.
1995	GB	N	16	G
1996			16	G
2 yrs.	32 games			

Alphonso Taylor
TAYLOR, ALPHONSO
B. Sep. 7, 1969, Trenton, NJ
Temple 6'6" 350 lbs.

Year	Team		Games	Pos.
1993	DEN	N	3	DT

Altie Taylor
TAYLOR, ALTIE
B. Sep. 29, 1947, Pittsburg, CA
Utah State 5'10" 199 lbs.

Year	Team		Games	Pos.
1969	DET	N	10	RB
1970			14	RB
1971			14	RB
1972			13	RB
1973			13	RB

Altie Taylor continued

Year	Team		Games	Pos.
1974			13	RB
1975			14	RB
1976	HOU	N	11	RB
8 yrs.	102 games			

Billy Taylor
TAYLOR, WILLIAM TURNER
B. Jul. 6, 1956, San Antonio, TX
Texas Tech 6'0" 215 lbs.

Year	Team		Games	Pos.
1978	NYG	N	13	RB
1979			16	RB
1980			12	RB
1981			5	RB
1981	NYJ	N	3	RB
1982	LARI	N	1	RB
5 yrs.	50 games			

Bob Taylor
TAYLOR, ROBERT
B. Feb. 5, 1940, Columbia, SC
Maryland-Eastern Shore 6'3" 238 lbs.

Year	Team		Games	Pos.
1963	NYG	N	14	DE
1964			14	DE, DT
2 yrs.	28 games			

Bobby Taylor
TAYLOR, ROBERT
B. Dec. 28, 1973, Houston, TX
Notre Dame 6'3" 208 lbs.

Year	Team		Games	Pos.
1995	PHI	N	16	CB
1996			16	CB
2 yrs.	32 games			

Brian Taylor
TAYLOR, BRIAN TEON
B. Oct. 1, 1967, New Orleans, LA
Oregon State 5'10" 185 lbs.

Year	Team		Games	Pos.
1989	CHI	N	5	RB
1991	BUF	N	3	CB
2 yrs.	8 games			

Bruce Taylor
TAYLOR, BRUCE LAWRENCE
B. May 28, 1948, Perth Amboy, NJ
Boston University 6'0" 184 lbs.

Year	Team		Games	Pos.
1970	SF	N	14	S
1971			14	CB
1972			14	CB
1973			14	CB
1974			14	CB
1975			12	CB
1976			13	CB
1977			14	CB
8 yrs.	109 games			

Charley Taylor
TAYLOR, CHARLES ROBERT
B. Sep. 28, 1941, Grand Prairie, TX
Arizona State 6'3" 210 lbs.

Year	Team		Games	Pos.
1964	WAS	N	14	HB
1965			13	HB
1966			14	HB
1967			12	OE
1968			14	OE
1969			14	WR
1970			10	WR
1971			5	WR
1972			14	WR
1973			14	WR
1974			14	WR
1975			14	WR
1977			12	WR
13 yrs.	164 games			

Charlie Taylor
TAYLOR, CHARLES A.

Year	Team	Games	Pos.

Charlie Taylor *continued*
B. Jan. 12, 1920, Tupelo, AR
D. Jan., 1977, Santa Fe, NM
Ouachita Baptist 5'10" 210 lbs.

| 1944 | BKN | N | 9 | QB, G |

Chuck Taylor
TAYLOR, CHARLES ALBERT
B. Jan. 24, 1920, Portland, OR
D. May 6, 1994, Stanford, CA
Stanford 5'11" 205 lbs.

| 1946 | MIA | AA | 14 | G |

Cliff Taylor
TAYLOR, CLIFTON
B. May 10, 1952, Memphis, TN
Memphis State 6'0" 198 lbs.

1974	CHI	N	14	RB
1976	GB	N	7	RB
2 yrs.	21 games

Corky Taylor
TAYLOR, CECIL R.
B. 1934
Kansas State 5'10" 189 lbs.

1955	LA	N	10	HB
1957			2	HB
2 yrs.	12 games

Craig Taylor
TAYLOR, CRAIG
B. Jan. 3, 1966, Elizabeth, NJ
West Virginia 5'11" 224 lbs.

1989	CIN	N	12	RB
1990			12	RB
1991			12	RB
3 yrs.	36 games

David Taylor
TAYLOR, DAVID MERRITT
B. Oct. 17, 1949, Statesville, NC
Catawba 6'4" 260 lbs.

1973	BAL	N	13	OT
1974			14	OT
1975			14	OT
1976			14	OT
1977			14	OT
1979			3	OT
6 yrs.	72 games

Ed Taylor
TAYLOR, EVERETT EARL
B. May 13, 1953, Memphis, TN
Memphis State 6'0" 174 lbs.

1975	NYJ	N	14	CB
1976			11	S, CB
1977			14	CB, S
1978			16	CB
1979			4	CB
1979	MIA	N	5	CB
1980			16	CB
1981			6	CB
7 yrs.	86 games

Erk Taylor
TAYLOR, ERQUIET (Babe)
B. 1908
D. Nov. 2, 1959
Auburn 6'2" 210 lbs.

| 1931 | SI | N | 7 | G, T |

Gene Taylor
TAYLOR, EUGENE
B. Nov. 12, 1962, Oakland, CA
Fresno State 6'2" 189 lbs.

| 1987 | TB | N | 8 | WR |

Gene Taylor *continued*

1988			4	WR
1991	NE	N	1	WR
3 yrs.	13 games

Greg Taylor
TAYLOR, GREGORY O.
B. Oct. 23, 1958, Richmond, VA
Virginia 5'8" 175 lbs.

| 1982 | NE | N | 1 | RB |

Hosea Taylor
TAYLOR, HOSEA, JR.
B. Dec. 3, 1958, Jefferson, TX
Houston 6'5" 260 lbs.

1981	BAL	N	16	DE
1983			4	DE
2 yrs.	20 games

Hugh Taylor
TAYLOR, HUGH WILSON (Bones)
B. Jul. 6, 1923, Wynne, AR
D. Oct. 31, 1992, Wynne, AR
Tulane/Oklahoma City 6'4" 194 lbs.

1947	WAS	N	10	E
1948			12	E
1949			12	E
1950			12	E
1951			12	E
1952			12	E
1953			12	E
1954			12	E
8 yrs.	94 games

James Taylor
TAYLOR, JAMES MICHAEL (J.T.)
B. Aug. 12, 1956, Peoria, IL
Missouri 6'4" 265 lbs.

1978	NO	N	16	OT
1979			16	OT
1980			13	OT
1981			12	OT
4 yrs.	57 games

Jay Taylor
TAYLOR, EMANUEL JAY
B. Nov. 8, 1967, San Diego, CA
San Jose State 5'9" 170 lbs.

1989	PHX	N	16	CB
1990			16	CB
1991			16	CB
1993	KC	N	15	CB
1994			16	CB, S
5 yrs.	79 games

Jesse Taylor
TAYLOR, JESSE
B. May 26, 1948, Latrobe, PA
Cincinnati 6'0" 200 lbs.

| 1972 | SD | N | 14 | RB |

Jim Taylor
TAYLOR, JIM GLEN
B. Jun. 27, 1934, Rowden, TX
Baylor 6'2" 232 lbs.

1956	PIT	N	12	C
1957	CHIC	N	5	C, LB
1958			12	C, LB
3 yrs.	29 games

Jim Taylor
TAYLOR, JAMES CHARLES
B. Sep. 20, 1935, Baton Rouge, LA
Louisiana State 6'0" 214 lbs.

| 1958 | GB | N | 12 | FB |
| 1959 | | | 12 | FB |

Jim Taylor *continued*

1960			12	FB
1961			14	FB
1962			14	FB
1963			14	FB
1964			13	FB
1965			13	FB
1966			14	FB
1967	NO	N	14	RB
10 yrs.	132 games

Jim Bob Taylor
TAYLOR, JIM BOB
B. Sep. 9, 1959, San Antonio, TX
Southern Methodist/Georgia Tech 6'2" 197 lbs.

| 1983 | BAL | N | 8 | QB |

Joe Taylor
TAYLOR, JOSEPH
B. Dec. 27, 1940, Miami, FL
North Carolina A&T 6'2" 189 lbs.

1967	CHI	N	14	DB
1968			14	DB
1969			14	CB, S
1970			1	CB
1971			13	CB
1972			14	CB
1973			14	CB
1974			14	CB
8 yrs.	98 games

John Taylor
TAYLOR, JOHN GREGORY
B. Mar. 31, 1962, Pennsauken, NJ
Delaware State 6'1" 185 lbs.

1987	SF	N	12	WR
1988			12	WR
1989			15	WR
1990			14	WR
1991			14	WR
1992			9	WR
1993			16	WR
1994			15	WR
1995			12	WR
9 yrs.	121 games

Johnny Taylor
TAYLOR, JOHNNY HERBERT
B. Jun. 21, 1961, Seattle, WA
Hawaii 6'4" 235 lbs.

1984	ATL	N	2	LB
1985			15	LB
1986			5	LB
1986	MIA	N	1	LB
1987	SD	N	7	LB
4 yrs.	30 games

Keith Taylor
TAYLOR, KEITH GERARD
B. Dec. 21, 1964, Pennsauken, NJ
Illinois 5'11" 193 lbs.

1988	IND	N	3	DB
1989			16	CB, S
1990			16	CB, S
1991			16	CB, S
1992	NO	N	16	S
1993			16	S
1994	WAS	N	1	S
1995			16	S
1996			3	S
9 yrs.	103 games

Kenny Taylor
TAYLOR, KENNETH DANIEL
B. Sep. 2, 1963, San Jose, CA
Oregon State 6'1" 196 lbs.

| 1985 | CHI | N | 16 | CB |

Kenny Taylor *continued*

| 1986 | SD | N | 14 | CB |
| 2 yrs. | 30 games |

Kitrick Taylor
TAYLOR, KITRICK LAVELL
B. Jul. 22, 1964, Los Angeles, CA
Washington State 5'10" 194 lbs.

1988	KC	N	16	WR
1989	NE	N	4	WR
1990	SD	N	3	WR
1991			12	WR
1992	GB	N	10	WR
1993	DEN	N	2	WR
6 yrs.	47 games

Lawrence Taylor
TAYLOR, LAWRENCE (L.T.)
B. Feb. 4, 1959, Williamsburg, VA
North Carolina 6'3" 241 lbs.

1981	NYG	N	16	LB
1982			9	LB
1983			16	LB
1984			16	LB
1985			16	LB
1986			16	LB
1987			12	LB
1988			12	LB
1989			16	LB
1990			16	LB
1991			14	LB
1992			9	LB
1993			16	LB
13 yrs.	184 games

Lenny Taylor
TAYLOR, LENNY MOORE
B. Feb. 15, 1961, Miami, FL
Tennessee 6'0" 183 lbs.

1984	GB	N	2	WR
1987	ATL	N	3	WR
2 yrs.	5 games

Lionel Taylor
TAYLOR, LIONEL THOMAS
B. Aug. 15, 1936, Kansas City, MO
New Mexico Highlands 6'2" 215 lbs.

1959	CHIB	N	8	E
1960	DEN	A	12	OE
1961			14	OE
1962			14	OE
1963			14	OE
1964			14	OE
1965			14	OE
1966			14	OE
1967	HOU	A	8	OE
1968			9	OE
10 yrs.	121 games

Malcolm Taylor
TAYLOR, MALCOLM
B. Jun. 20, 1960, Crystal Springs, MS
Tennessee State 6'6" 278 lbs.

1982	HOU	N	9	DE
1983			16	DE
1986			3	DE
1987	LARI	N	12	DT
1988			15	DT
1989	ATL	N	13	DE
6 yrs.	68 games

Mike Taylor
TAYLOR, MICHAEL
B. Sep. 21, 1949, Detroit, MI
Michigan 6'1" 230 lbs.

1972	NYJ	N	14	LB
1973			8	LB
2 yrs.	22 games

Year	Team	Games	Pos.

Mike Taylor
TAYLOR, MICHAEL RAY
B. May 5, 1945, San Francisco, CA
Southern California 6'4" 247 lbs.

Year	Team		Games	Pos.
1968	PIT	N	14	OT
1969			9	OT
1969	NO	N	1	OT
1970	WAS	N	11	OT
1971	WAS	N	6	OT
1973	STL	N	6	OT
5 yrs.	47 games			

Otis Taylor
TAYLOR, OTIS, JR.
B. Aug. 11, 1942, Houston, TX
Prairie View A&M 6'2" 215 lbs.

Year	Team		Games	Pos.
1965	KC	A	14	OE
1966			14	OE
1967			14	FL
1968			11	FL
1969			11	WR
1970	KC	N	13	WR
1971			14	WR
1972			14	WR
1973			14	WR
1974			10	WR
1975			1	WR
11 yrs.	130 games			

Rob Taylor
TAYLOR, ROBERT WAYNE
B. Nov. 14, 1960, St. Charles, IL
Northwestern 6'6" 293 lbs.

Year	Team		Games	Pos.
1986	TB	N	16	OT
1987			5	OT
1988			16	OT
1989			16	OT
1990			16	OT
1991			16	OT
1992			9	OT
1993			16	OT
8 yrs.	110 games			

Roger Taylor
TAYLOR, ROGER WAYNE
B. Jan. 5, 1958, Shawnee, OK
Oklahoma State 6'6" 271 lbs.

Year	Team		Games	Pos.
1981	KC	N	13	WR

Rosey Taylor
TAYLOR, ROOSEVELT
B. Jul. 4, 1937, New Orleans, LA
Grambling State 5'11" 186 lbs.

Year	Team		Games	Pos.
1961	CHI	N	14	DB
1962			14	DB
1963			14	DB
1964			14	DB
1965			14	DB
1966			14	DB
1967			14	DB
1968			14	DB
1969			6	S
1969	SF	N	8	S
1970			14	S
1971			12	S
1972	WAS	N	14	DB
12 yrs.	166 games			

Sammy Taylor
TAYLOR, SAMUEL
B. Apr. 23, 1940, Houston, TX
Grambling State 6'0" 190 lbs.

Year	Team		Games	Pos.
1965	SD	A	12	OE

Steve Taylor
TAYLOR, STEVEN
B. Dec. 27, 1953, Fort Worth, TX
Kansas 6'3" 204 lbs.

Year	Team		Games	Pos.
1976	KC	N	14	CB

Tarzan Taylor
TAYLOR, JOHN L.
B. Jan. 10, 1895, Superior, WI
D. May 1, 1971, Green Bay, WI
Ohio State 5'11" 173 lbs.

Year	Team		Games	Pos.
1921	DEC	A	11	G
1922	CAN	A	11	G
1926	BKN	A	4	G
1926	BKN	N	2	G
3 yrs.	28 games			

Terry Taylor
TAYLOR, TERRY
B. Jul. 18, 1961, Warren, OH
Southern Illinois 5'10" 188 lbs.

Year	Team		Games	Pos.
1984	SEA	N	16	CB
1985			16	CB
1986			16	CB
1987			12	CB
1988			14	CB
1989	DET	N	15	CB
1990			2	CB
1991			13	CB
1992	CLE	N	16	CB
1993			10	CB
1994	SEA	N	5	CB
1995	ATL	N	16	CB
12 yrs.	151 games			

Tom Taylor
TAYLOR, THOMAS
B. Sep. 14, 1962, Acton, CA
Georgia Tech 6'3" 265 lbs.

Year	Team		Games	Pos.
1987	LARM	N	3	LB

Troy Taylor
TAYLOR, TROY SCOTT
B. Apr. 5, 1968, Downey, CA
California 6'4" 200 lbs.

Year	Team		Games	Pos.
1990	NYJ	N	4	QB
1991			5	QB
2 yrs.	9 games			

Willie Taylor
TAYLOR, WILLIE T.
B. Dec. 9, 1955, Montclair, NJ
Pittsburgh 6'1" 179 lbs.

Year	Team		Games	Pos.
1978	GB	N	1	WR

Jimmy Tays
TAYS, JAMES ELMER
B. Mar. 10, 1899, Michigan
D. Jun., 1986, Champaign, IL
Penn State/Chicago 5'8" 174 lbs.

Year	Team		Games	Pos.
1925	CHIC	N	9	HB, F, QB
1926	CHI	A	1	HB
1927	DAY	N	7	QB, HB
1930	NEW	N	1	HB
1930	SI	N	4	FB, HB, QB
4 yrs.	22 games			

Guy Teafatiller
TEAFATILLER, GUY
B. May 10, 1964, Downey, CA
Illinois 6'2" 260 lbs.

Year	Team		Games	Pos.
1987	CHI	N	3	DT

George Teague
TEAGUE, GEORGE THEO
B. Feb. 18, 1971, Lansing, MI
Alabama 6'1" 187 lbs.

Year	Team		Games	Pos.
1993	GB	N	16	CB, S
1994			16	S
1995			15	S
1996	DAL	N	16	S
4 yrs.	63 games			

Matthew Teague
TEAGUE, MATTHEW NATHANIEL
B. Oct. 22, 1958, Cincinnati, OH
Prairie View A&M 6'5" 240 lbs.

Year	Team		Games	Pos.
1981	ATL	N	11	DE

Pat Teague
TEAGUE, PAT
B. Oct. 22, 1963
North Carolina State 6'1" 250 lbs.

Year	Team		Games	Pos.
1987	TB	N	1	LB

Jimmy Teal
TEAL, JAMES FRANKLIN
B. May 14, 1950, Baltimore, MD
Purdue 6'3" 225 lbs.

Year	Team		Games	Pos.
1973	DET	N	14	LB

Jimmy Teal
TEAL, JIMMY DEWAYNE
B. Aug. 18, 1962, Lufkin, TX
Texas A&M 5'10" 170 lbs.

Year	Team		Games	Pos.
1985	BUF	N	3	WR
1986			5	WR
1987	SEA	N	4	WR
1988			2	WR
4 yrs.	14 games			

Willie Teal
TEAL, WILLIE, JR.
B. Dec. 20, 1957, Texarkana, TX
Louisiana State 5'10" 195 lbs.

Year	Team		Games	Pos.
1980	MIN	N	1	CB
1981			16	CB
1982			9	CB
1983			16	CB
1984			11	CB
1985			16	CB
1986			11	CB
1987	LARI	N	1	CB
8 yrs.	81 games			

Larry Tearry
TEARRY, LARRY WAYNE
B. Apr. 24, 1956, Erwin, NC
Wake Forest 6'3" 260 lbs.

Year	Team		Games	Pos.
1978	DET	N	14	C
1979			11	C
2 yrs.	25 games			

Gus Tebell
TEBELL, GUSTAVE KENNETH
B. Sep. 6, 1897, St. Charles, IL
D. May 28, 1969
Wisconsin 5'10" 170 lbs.

Year	Team		Games	Pos.
1923	COL	N	10	E
1924			2	FB, E
2 yrs.	12 games			

John Teerlinck
TEERLINCK, JOHN L.
B. Apr. 9, 1951, Rochester, NY
Western Illinois 6'5" 248 lbs.

Year	Team		Games	Pos.
1974	SD	N	14	DT
1975			6	DT
2 yrs.	20 games			

Al Teeter
TEETER, ALLEN M.
B. 1908
Minnesota 6'1" 202 lbs.

Year	Team		Games	Pos.
1932	SI	N	4	E

Mike Teeter
TEETER, MICHAEL LEE
B. Oct. 4, 1967, Grand Haven, MI
Michigan 6'2" 269 lbs.

Year	Team		Games	Pos.
1991	MIN	N	1	DT
1993	HOU	N	14	DT
1994			14	DE, DT
3 yrs.	29 games			

Len Teeuws
TEEUWS, LEONARD
B. Apr. 19, 1927, Oak Park, IL
Tulane 6'4" 242 lbs.

Year	Team		Games	Pos.
1952	LA	N	12	T
1953			12	T
1954	CHIC	N	12	T
1955			12	T
1956			12	T
1957			12	T
6 yrs.	72 games			

Lance Teichelman
TEICHELMAN, LANCE THEODORE
B. Oct. 21, 1970, San Antonio, TX
Texas A&M 6'4" 274 lbs.

Year	Team		Games	Pos.
1994	IND	N	1	DT

Mike Teifke
TEIFKE, MIKE
B. Dec. 29, 1963
Akron 6'4" 255 lbs.

Year	Team		Games	Pos.
1987	CLE	N	3	C

John Teltschik
TELTSCHIK, JOHN ROBERT
B. Mar. 8, 1964, Floresville, TX
Texas 6'2" 212 lbs.

Year	Team		Games	Pos.
1986	PHI	N	16	P
1987			12	P
1988			16	P
1989			10	P
4 yrs.	54 games			

Jim Temp
TEMP, JAMES ARTHUR
B. Oct. 10, 1933, La Crosse, WI
Wisconsin 6'4" 245 lbs.

Year	Team		Games	Pos.
1957	GB	N	12	E
1958			12	E
1959			12	E
1960			7	E
4 yrs.	43 games			

Mark Temple
TEMPLE, MARK
B. 1912
Oregon 5'10" 175 lbs.

Year	Team		Games	Pos.
1936	BKN	N	7	B
1936	BOS	N	2	B
1 yr.	9 games			

Garth Ten Napel
TEN NAPEL, GARTH
B. Mar. 27, 1954, Los Angeles, CA
Texas A&M 6'1" 213 lbs.

Year	Team		Games	Pos.
1976	DET	N	14	LB
1977			14	LB
1978	ATL	N	1	LB
3 yrs.	29 games			

Derek Tennell
TENNELL, DEREK WAYNE
B. Feb. 12, 1964, Los Angeles, CA
UCLA 6'5" 245 lbs.

Year	Team		Games	Pos.
1987	CLE	N	11	TE

Year	Team		Games	Pos.

Derek Tennell *continued*

Year	Team		Games	Pos.
1988			16	TE
1989			14	TE
1991	DET	N	15	TE
1992	MIN	N	3	TE
1993			16	TE
6 yrs.	75 games			

Bob Tenner
TENNER, ROBERT JOHNSON
B. Jun. 1, 1913, Minneapolis, MN
D. Nov. 17, 1984, Minneapolis, MN
Minnesota 6'0" 212 lbs.

1935	GB	N	11	E

Steve Tensi
TENSI, STEPHEN MICHAEL
B. Dec. 8, 1942, Cincinnati, OH
Florida State 6'5" 213 lbs.

1965	SD	A	1	QB
1966			14	QB
1967	DEN	A	14	QB
1968			7	QB
1969			13	QB
1970	DEN		7	QB
6 yrs.	56 games			

Lou Tepe
TEPE, LOUIS
B. Jun. 18, 1930
Duke 6'2" 208 lbs.

1953	PIT	N	10	C
1954			12	C
1955			12	C
3 yrs.	34 games			

Tony Teresa
TERESA, ANTHONY
B. Dec. 8, 1933, Pittsburg, CA
D. Oct. 16, 1984, Salinas, CA
San Jose State 5'9" 188 lbs.

1960	OAK	A	14	HB

Joe Tereshinski
TERESHINSKI, JOSEPH PETER, SR.
B. Dec. 7, 1923, Glen Lyon, PA
Georgia 6'2" 215 lbs.

1947	WAS	N	11	E
1948			11	E
1949			9	E
1950			12	E
1951			12	E
1952			12	E
1953			12	E
1954			7	E
8 yrs.	86 games			

George Terlep
TERLEP, GEORGE RUDOLPH (Duke)
B. Apr. 12, 1923, Elkhart, IN
Notre Dame 5'10" 180 lbs.

1946	BUF	AA	12	QB
1947			11	QB
1948			3	QB
1948	CLE	AA	9	QB
3 yrs.	35 games			

Marv Terrell
TERRELL, MARVIN, JR. (Bo)
B. 1938
Mississippi 6'1" 236 lbs.

1960	DAL	A		G
1961			3	G
1962			12	G

Marv Terrell *continued*

Year	Team		Games	Pos.
1963	KC	A	14	G
4 yrs.	29 games			

Pat Terrell
TERRELL, PATRICK CHRISTOPHER
B. Mar. 18, 1968, Memphis, TN
Notre Dame 6'0" 195 lbs.

1990	LARM	N	15	S
1991			16	S
1992			15	S
1993			13	S
1994	NYJ	N	16	S
1995	CAR	N	16	S
1996			16	S
7 yrs.	107 games			

Ray Terrell
TERRELL, RAYMOND WILLARD
B. Jun. 29, 1919, Water Valley, MS
Mississippi 6'0" 185 lbs.

1946	CLE	AA	9	HB
1947	BAL	AA	10	HB
1947	CLE	AA	3	HB
2 yrs.	22 games			

Doug Terry
TERRY, DOUGLAS MAURICE
B. Feb. 10, 1968, Dumas, AR
Kansas 5'11" 192 lbs.

1992	KC		16	CB, S
1993			15	S
1994			10	S
1995			16	S
4 yrs.	57 games			

Joe Terry
TERRY, JOE
B. May 7, 1965
Hayward State 6'2" 222 lbs.

1987	SEA	N	2	LB

Nat Terry
TERRY, NAT
B. Jul. 20, 1956, Tampa, FL
Florida State 5'11" 165 lbs.

1978	PIT	N	6	CB
1978	DET	N	4	CB
1 yr.	10 games			

Ryan Terry
TERRY, RYAN
B. Sep. 20, 1971, Fort Bragg, NC
Iowa 5'11" 203 lbs.

1995	ARI	N	15	RB
1996			5	RB
2 yrs.	20 games			

Rudy Tersch
TERSCH, RUDY
B. 1896
Deceased
None 192 lbs.

1921	MIN	A	2	G
1922	MIN	N	4	T, E
1923			8	T
3 yrs.	14 games			

Ray Tesser
TESSER, RAYMOND
B. 1910
Carnegie-Mellon 6'2" 204 lbs.

1933	PIT	N	11	E
1934			12	E
2 yrs.	23 games			

Vinny Testaverde
TESTAVERDE, VINCENT FRANK
B. Nov. 13, 1963, Brooklyn, NY
Miami (Florida) 6'5" 217 lbs.

1987	TB	N	6	QB
1988			15	QB
1989			14	QB
1990			15	QB
1991			13	QB
1992			14	QB
1993	CLE	N	10	QB
1994			14	QB
1995			13	QB
1996	BAL	N	16	QB
10 yrs.	130 games			

Don Testerman
TESTERMAN, DONALD RAY
B. Nov. 7, 1952, Danville, VA
Virginia Tech/Lenoir-Rhyne/Clemson 6'2" 231 lbs.

1976	SEA	N	14	RB
1977			14	RB
1978			16	RB
1980	MIA	N	5	RB
4 yrs.	49 games			

Deral Teteak
TETEAK, DERAL
B. Dec. 11, 1929, Oconto, WI
Wisconsin 5'10" 210 lbs.

1952	GB	N	12	G
1953			7	G
1954			6	G
1955			12	G
1956			12	G
5 yrs.	49 games			

Lee Tevis
TEVIS, LEE KESSLER
B. Sep. 29, 1921
George Washington/Miami (Ohio) 5'11" 190 lbs.

1947	BKN	AA	8	B
1948			14	B
2 yrs.	22 games			

Lowell Tew
TEW, LOWELL WILLIAM (Dusty)
B. Jan. 2, 1927, Waynesboro, MS
D. Mar., 1981
Alabama 5'11" 195 lbs.

1948	NY	AA	14	B
1949	B-NY	AA	1	B
2 yrs.	15 games			

Al Thacker
THACKER, ALVIN MONROE
B. Mar. 1, 1919, Kayford, WV
Morris Harvey 5'10" 200 lbs.

1942	PHI	N	1	G

Tom Tharp
THARP, THOMAS (Corky)
B. 1932
Alabama 5'10" 180 lbs.

1960	NY	A		DB

Larry Tharpe
THARPE, LARRY
B. Nov. 19, 1970, Macon, GA
Tennessee State 6'4" 299 lbs.

1992	DET	N	11	OT
1993			5	OT
1995	ARI	N	11	OT
3 yrs.	27 games			

Richard Tharpe
THARPE, RICHARD
B. Oct. 31, 1960, Central Islip, NY
Louisville 6'3" 255 lbs.

1987	BUF	N	3	DE

Galand Thaxton
THAXTON, GALAND W.
B. Oct. 23, 1964, Mildinhall, England
Wyoming 6'1" 242 lbs.

1989	ATL	N	16	LB
1991	SD	N	14	LB
2 yrs.	30 games			

James Thaxton
THAXTON, JAMES IVORY
B. Jan. 11, 1949, Brownsville, TN
Tennessee State 6'2" 241 lbs.

1973	SD	N	10	TE
1974	CLE	N	12	TE
1976	NO	N	11	TE
1977			14	TE
1978	STL	N	5	TE
5 yrs.	52 games			

Harry Thayer
THAYER, HARRY J. (Hobo)
B. 1907
Tennessee 6'1" 215 lbs.

1933	POR	N	9	T, G

Tom Thayer
THAYER, THOMAS ALLEN
B. Aug. 16, 1961, Joliet, IL
Notre Dame 6'4" 271 lbs.

1985	CHI	N	16	G, C
1986			16	G, C
1987			11	G
1988			16	G
1989			16	G
1990			16	G
1991			16	G
1992			16	G
1993	MIA	N	3	C, G
9 yrs.	126 games			

Joe Theismann
THEISMANN, JOSEPH ROBERT
B. Sep. 9, 1949, New Brunswick, NJ
Notre Dame 6'0" 195 lbs.

1974	WAS	N	9	QB
1975			14	QB
1976			14	QB
1977			14	QB
1978			16	QB
1979			16	QB
1980			16	QB
1981			16	QB
1982			9	QB
1983			16	QB
1984			16	QB
1985			11	QB
12 yrs.	167 games			

Harry Theofiledes
THEOFILEDES, ARIS HARRY
B. Apr. 19, 1944, Homestead, PA
Waynesburg 5'10" 180 lbs.

1968	WAS	N	5	QB

Jim Thibaut
THIBAUT, JAMES P.
B. 1919
Tulane 5'11" 205 lbs.

1946	BUF	AA	3	FB

Year	Team	Games	Pos.

Jim Thibert
THIBERT, JAMES GERALD
B. Jun. 14, 1940, Toledo, OH
Toledo 6'3" 230 lbs.

Year	Team	Games	Pos.
1965	**DEN**	A	13	LB

Carl Thiele
THIELE, CARL L. (Dutch)
B. Nov. 19, 1892, Dayton, OH
D. Jul., 1986
Denison 6'1" 195 lbs.

Year	Team	Games	Pos.
1920	**DAY**	A	8	E
1921		7	E
1922	**DAY**	N	7	E
1923		8	E
4 yrs.	30 games		

R.C. Thielemann
THIELEMANN, RAY CHARLES
B. Aug. 12, 1955, Houston, TX
Arkansas 6'4" 260 lbs.

Year	Team	Games	Pos.
1977	**ATL**	N	14	G, C
1978		16	G
1979		11	G
1980		16	G
1981		16	G
1982		9	G
1983		14	G
1984		16	G
1985	**WAS**	N	3	G
1986		14	G
1987		12	G
1988		14	G
12 yrs.	155 games		

John Thierry
THIERRY, JOHN FITZGERALD
B. Sep. 4, 1971, Opelousas, LA
Alcorn State 6'4" 250 lbs.

Year	Team	Games	Pos.
1994	**CHI**	N	16	DE
1995		16	DE
1996		16	DE
3 yrs.	48 games		

Yancey Thigpen
THIGPEN, YANCEY DIRK
B. Aug. 15, 1969, Tarboro, NC
Winston-Salem State 6'1" 208 lbs.

Year	Team	Games	Pos.
1991	**SD**	N	4	WR
1992	**PIT**	N	12	WR
1993		12	WR
1994		15	WR
1995		16	WR
1996		6	WR
6 yrs.	65 games		

Aaron Thomas
THOMAS, AARON N.
B. Nov. 7, 1937, Dierks, AR
Oregon State 6'3" 209 lbs.

Year	Team	Games	Pos.
1961	**SF**	N	14	OE
1962		2	OE
1962	**NYG**	N	12	OE
1963		14	OE
1964		14	OE, FL
1965		13	OE, FL
1966		14	TE
1967		14	TE
1968		12	TE
1969		9	WR
1970		14	WR
10 yrs.	132 games		

Al Thomas
THOMAS, AL
None

Year	Team	Games	Pos.
1926	**HAR**	N	5	HB, QB

Andre Thomas
THOMAS, ANDRE
B. Nov. 26, 1960, Tupelo, MS
Mississippi 6'0" 205 lbs.

Year	Team	Games	Pos.
1987	**MIN**	N	1	RB

Ben Thomas
THOMAS, BENJAMIN, JR.
B. Jul. 2, 1961, Ashburn, GA
Auburn 6'4" 276 lbs.

Year	Team	Games	Pos.
1985	**NE**	N	15	DE
1986		4	DE
1986	**GB**	N	9	DE, NT
1988	**PIT**	N	8	DE
1989	**ATL**	N	16	DE
1991	**LARM**	N	2	DE
5 yrs.	54 games		

Bill Thomas
THOMAS, WILLIAM G. (Whitey)
B. Aug. 17, 1895
D. Aug., 1978, Lavallette, NJ
Penn State 5'10" 170 lbs.

Year	Team	Games	Pos.
1924	**FRA**	N	14	E
1926	**PHI**	A	10	E
2 yrs.	24 games		

Bill Thomas
THOMAS, WILLIAM JEFFREY
B. Aug. 7, 1949, Ossining, NY
Boston College 6'2" 225 lbs.

Year	Team	Games	Pos.
1972	**DAL**	N	7	RB
1973	**HOU**	N	6	RB
1974	**KC**	N	14	RB
3 yrs.	27 games		

Blair Thomas
THOMAS, BLAIR
B. Oct. 7, 1967, Philadelphia, PA
Penn State 5'10" 195 lbs.

Year	Team	Games	Pos.
1990	**NYJ**	N	15	RB
1991		16	RB
1992		9	RB
1993		11	RB
1994	**NE**	N	4	RB
1994	**DAL**	N	2	RB
1995	**CAR**	N	7	RB
6 yrs.	64 games		

Bob Thomas
THOMAS, BOB
B. Aug. 23, 1948, Pittsburgh, PA
Arizona State 5'10" 201 lbs.

Year	Team	Games	Pos.
1971	**LA**	N	6	RB
1972		14	RB
1973	**SD**	N	14	RB
1974		14	RB
4 yrs.	48 games		

Bob Thomas
THOMAS, ROBERT RANDALL
B. Aug. 7, 1952, Rochester, NY
Notre Dame 5'10" 175 lbs.

Year	Team	Games	Pos.
1975	**CHI**	N	14	K
1976		14	K
1977		14	K
1978		16	K
1979		16	K
1980		16	K
1981		2	K
1982	**DET**	N	2	K
1982	**CHI**	N	2	K
1983		16	K
1984		16	K
1985	**SD**	N	15	K
1986	**NYG**	N	1	K
12 yrs.	144 games		

Broderick Thomas
THOMAS, BRODERICK
B. Feb. 20, 1967, Houston, TX
Nebraska 6'4" 248 lbs.

Year	Team	Games	Pos.
1989	**TB**	N	16	LB
1990		16	LB
1991		16	LB
1992		16	LB
1993		16	LB
1994	**DET**	N	16	LB
1995	**MIN**	N	16	LB
1996	**DAL**	N	16	LB
8 yrs.	128 games		

Cal Thomas
THOMAS, CALVIN
B. Jul. 1, 1915
D. Apr. 14, 1982, Harper Woods, MI
Tulsa 6'2" 210 lbs.

Year	Team	Games	Pos.
1939	**DET**	N	5	T, E
1940		7	T, B
2 yrs.	12 games		

Calvin Thomas
THOMAS, CALVIN LEWIS
B. Jan. 7, 1960, St. Louis, MO
Illinois 5'11" 245 lbs.

Year	Team	Games	Pos.
1982	**CHI**	N	6	RB
1983		13	RB
1984		16	RB
1985		13	RB
1986		16	RB
1987		12	FB
1988		1	RB
1988	**DEN**	N	2	RB
7 yrs.	79 games		

Carl Thomas
THOMAS, CARL H. (Whitey)
B. Mar. 2, 1897, Philadelphia, PA
D. Oct. 30, 1961
Pennsylvania 5'10" 195 lbs.

Year	Team	Games	Pos.
1921	**ROC**	A	6	T, G, C
1922	**BUF**	N	10	T, HB
1923		9	T, FB, G
3 yrs.	25 games		

Carlton Thomas
THOMAS, CARLTON FITZGERALD
B. Nov. 25, 1963, Portsmouth, VA
Elizabeth City State 6'0" 190 lbs.

Year	Team	Games	Pos.
1987	**KC**	N	4	CB

Charlie Thomas
THOMAS, CHARLES
B. Nov. 27, 1948, Houston, TX
Tennessee State 5'9" 180 lbs.

Year	Team	Games	Pos.
1975	**NO**	N	4	RB
1975	**KC**	N	7	RB

Chris Thomas
THOMAS, CHRIS ERIC
B. Jul. 16, 1971, Ventura, CA
Cal Poly (San Luis Obispo) 6'1" 180 lbs.

Year	Team	Games	Pos.
1995	**SF**	N	14	WR

Chuck Thomas
THOMAS, CHARLES
B. Feb. 24, 1960, Houston, TX
Oklahoma 6'3" 277 lbs.

Year	Team	Games	Pos.
1985	**ATL**	N	4	C, G
1987	**SF**	N	7	C, G
1988		16	C
1989		16	C
1990		16	C
1991		12	C

Chuck Thomas *continued*

Year	Team	Games	Pos.
1992		2	C
7 yrs.	73 games		

Clendon Thomas
THOMAS, BOBBY CLENDON
B. Dec. 28, 1935, Oklahoma City, OK
Oklahoma 6'2" 196 lbs.

Year	Team	Games	Pos.
1958	**LA**	N	6	DB
1959		10	DB
1960		12	HB, DB
1961		13	DB
1962	**PIT**	N	14	DB
1963		13	DB
1964		14	DB
1965		14	OE, DB
1966		14	DB
1967		13	DB
1968		14	DB
11 yrs.	137 games		

Curtland Thomas
THOMAS, CURTLAND PARRISH
B. Feb. 19, 1962, St. Louis, MO
Missouri 6'0" 183 lbs.

Year	Team	Games	Pos.
1987	**NO**	N	2	WR

Damon Thomas
THOMAS, DAMON ANDREW
B. Dec. 15, 1970, Clovis, CA
Wayne State (Nebraska) 6'2" 215 lbs.

Year	Team	Games	Pos.
1994	**BUF**	N	3	WR
1995		14	WR
2 yrs.	17 games		

Dave Thomas
THOMAS, DAVE
B. Aug. 25, 1968, Miami, FL
Tennessee 6'2" 208 lbs.

Year	Team	Games	Pos.
1993	**DAL**	N	12	CB
1994		16	CB
1995	**JAC**	N	15	CB
1996		9	CB
4 yrs.	52 games		

Dee Thomas
THOMAS, DERWARD HEITH
B. Nov. 7, 1967, Morgan City, LA
Nicholls State 5'10" 176 lbs.

Year	Team	Games	Pos.
1990	**HOU**	N	6	CB, S

Derrick Thomas
THOMAS, DERRICK LEROY
B. Mar. 8, 1965, Paducah, KY
Arkansas 6'0" 232 lbs.

Year	Team	Games	Pos.
1987	**TB**	N	1	RB

Derrick Thomas
THOMAS, DERRICK VINCENT
B. Jan. 1, 1967, Miami, FL
Alabama 6'3" 237 lbs.

Year	Team	Games	Pos.
1989	**KC**	N	16	LB
1990		15	LB
1991		16	LB
1992		16	LB
1993		16	LB
1994		16	LB
1995		15	LB
1996		16	LB
8 yrs.	126 games		

Donnie Thomas
THOMAS, DONALD M.
B. Mar. 12, 1953, Michigan City, IN
Indiana 6'2" 245 lbs.

Year	Team	Games	Pos.
1976	**NE**	N	3	LB

Year	Team	Games	Pos.

Doug Thomas
THOMAS, DOUGLAS SANDY
B. Sep. 18, 1969, Rockingham, NC
Clemson 5'10" 178 lbs.

Year	Team		Games	Pos.
1991	SEA	N	11	WR
1992			12	WR
1993			16	WR
3 yrs.	39 games			

Duane Thomas
THOMAS, DUANE
B. Jun. 21, 1947, Dallas, TX
West Texas State 6'1" 215 lbs.

Year	Team		Games	Pos.
1970	DAL	N	14	RB
1971			11	RB
1973	WAS	N	13	RB
1974			1	RB
4 yrs.	39 games			

Earl Thomas
THOMAS, EARL LEWIS
B. Oct. 4, 1948, Greenville, TX
Houston 6'3" 219 lbs.

Year	Team		Games	Pos.
1971	CHI	N	11	TE
1972			14	TE
1973			14	TE
1974	STL	N	14	WR
1975			11	WR
1976	HOU	N	7	WR
6 yrs.	71 games			

Earlie Thomas
THOMAS, EARLIE
B. Dec. 11, 1945, Denton, TX
Colorado State 6'1" 190 lbs.

Year	Team		Games	Pos.
1970	NYJ	N	14	DB
1971			13	CB
1972			14	CB
1973			12	CB
1974			8	CB
1975	DEN	N	10	CB
6 yrs.	71 games			

Ed Thomas
THOMAS, EDWARD LEE
B. May 4, 1966, New Orleans, LA
Houston 6'3" 240 lbs.

Year	Team		Games	Pos.
1990	TB	N	7	TE
1991			6	TE
2 yrs.	13 games			

Emmitt Thomas
THOMAS, EMMITT EARL
B. Jun. 3, 1943, Angleton, TX
Bishop 6'2" 192 lbs.

Year	Team		Games	Pos.
1966	KC	A	14	DB
1967			11	DB
1968			14	DB
1969			14	CB
1970	KC	N	14	CB
1971			14	CB
1972			14	CB
1973			14	CB
1974			14	CB
1975			14	CB
1976			14	CB
1977			14	CB
1978			16	CB
13 yrs.	181 games			

Enid Thomas
THOMAS, ENID
B. 1901
Deceased
Slippery Rock/Pennsylvania 5'8" 170 lbs.

Year	Team		Games	Pos.
1926	HAR	N	2	HB

Eric Thomas
THOMAS, ERIC JASON
B. Sep. 11, 1964, Tucson, AZ
Tulane 5'11" 181 lbs.

Year	Team		Games	Pos.
1987	CIN	N	12	CB
1988			16	CB
1989			16	CB
1990			4	CB
1991			16	CB
1992			16	CB
1993	NYJ	N	11	CB
1994			2	CB
1995	DEN	N	14	CB
9 yrs.	107 games			

Fred Thomas
THOMAS, FRED
B. Sep. 11, 1973, Grand Rapids, MI
Miss. Valley State/Mississippi/Tenn.-
Martin 5'9" 172 lbs.*

Year	Team		Games	Pos.
1996	SEA	N	15	CB

Garth Thomas
THOMAS, GARTH
B. Nov. 26, 1963, Bellevue, WA
Washington 6'3" 260 lbs.

Year	Team		Games	Pos.
1987	SEA	N	1	G

Gene Thomas
THOMAS, EUGENE WARREN
B. Sep. 1, 1942, Barberton, OH
Florida A&M 6'1" 210 lbs.

Year	Team		Games	Pos.
1966	KC	A	14	HB
1967			14	RB
1968	BOS	A		RB
1968	OAK	A		RB
3 yrs.	28 games			

George Thomas
THOMAS, GEORGE CARROLL
B. Mar. 4, 1928, Fairland, OK
D. May 23, 1989, Scottsdale, AZ
Oklahoma 6'1" 183 lbs.

Year	Team		Games	Pos.
1950	WAS	N	12	HB
1951			12	HB
1952	NYG	N	7	HB
3 yrs.	31 games			

George Thomas
THOMAS, GEORGE RAY, JR.
B. Jul. 11, 1964, Riverside, CA
Nevada-Las Vegas 5'9" 169 lbs.

Year	Team		Games	Pos.
1989	ATL	N	16	WR
1990			13	WR
1991			12	WR
1992			5	WR
1992	TB	N	5	WR
4 yrs.	51 games			

Henry Thomas
THOMAS, HENRY
B. Feb. 12, 1964
Southwest Texas State 6'2" 275 lbs.

Year	Team		Games	Pos.
1987	NO	N	3	G

Henry Thomas
THOMAS, HENRY LEE, JR.
B. Jan. 12, 1965, Houston, TX
Louisiana State 6'2" 273 lbs.

Year	Team		Games	Pos.
1987	MIN	N	12	NT
1988			15	NT
1989			14	NT
1990			16	DT
1991			16	NT
1992			16	DT
1993			13	DT
1994			16	DT

Henry Thomas *continued*

Year	Team		Games	Pos.
1995	DET	N	16	DE, DT
1996			15	DT
10 yrs.	149 games			

Hollis Thomas
THOMAS, HOLLIS
B. Jan. 10, 1974, St. Louis, MO
Northern Illinois 6'0" 306 lbs.

Year	Team		Games	Pos.
1996	PHI	N	16	DT

Ike Thomas
THOMAS, ISAAC
B. Nov. 4, 1947, Newton, LA
Bishop 6'2" 194 lbs.

Year	Team		Games	Pos.
1971	DAL	N	7	CB
1972	GB	N	12	CB
1973			13	CB
1975	BUF	N	5	DB
4 yrs.	37 games			

Jesse Thomas
THOMAS, JESSE L.
B. May 23, 1928, Guthrie, OK
Michigan State 5'10" 180 lbs.

Year	Team		Games	Pos.
1955	BAL	N	12	DB
1956			11	DB
1957			10	DB
1960	LA	A		DB
4 yrs.	33 games			

Jewerl Thomas
THOMAS, JEWERL, JR.
B. Sep. 10, 1957, Hanford, CA
UCLA/San Jose State 5'10" 229 lbs.

Year	Team		Games	Pos.
1980	LA	N	16	RB
1981			15	RB
1982	LARM	N	8	FB
1983	KC	N	10	RB
1984	SD	N	7	RB
5 yrs.	56 games			

Jim Thomas
THOMAS, JAMES
B. 1917
Oklahoma 5'11" 200 lbs.

Year	Team		Games	Pos.
1939	CHIC	N	5	G

Jimmy Thomas
THOMAS, JIMMY
B. Aug. 17, 1947, Greenville, TX
Texas-Arlington 6'1" 215 lbs.

Year	Team		Games	Pos.
1969	SF	N	14	RB
1970			14	RB
1971			10	WR, RB
1972			14	WR
1973			11	RB
5 yrs.	63 games			

Joe Thomas
THOMAS, JOSEPH EARL
B. Mar. 25, 1963, Lafayette, LA
Mississippi Valley State 5'11" 175 lbs.

Year	Team		Games	Pos.
1987	NO	N	1	WR

John Thomas
THOMAS, JOHN H., JR.
B. Mar. 6, 1964
Toledo 6'4" 280 lbs.

Year	Team		Games	Pos.
1987	NYJ	N	3	OT

John Thomas
THOMAS, JOHN LOUIS
B. Jan. 25, 1935, Tyler, TX
Pacific 6'4" 246 lbs.

Year	Team		Games	Pos.
1958	SF	N	12	T

John Thomas *continued*

Year	Team		Games	Pos.
1959			12	T
1960			9	T
1961			14	OT
1962			14	OT, LB
1963			14	LB
1964			14	G
1965			14	G
1966			14	G
1967			5	G
10 yrs.	122 games			

Johnny Thomas
THOMAS, JOHNNY, JR.
B. Aug. 3, 1964, Houston, TX
Baylor 5'9" 188 lbs.

Year	Team		Games	Pos.
1988	WAS	N	4	CB
1989	SD	N	13	CB
1990	WAS	N	4	CB
1992			16	CB
1993			16	CB
1994			16	CB
1995	CLE	N	16	CB
1996	PHI	N	8	CB
8 yrs.	93 games			

J.T. Thomas
THOMAS, JAMES, JR.
B. Apr. 22, 1951, Macon, GA
Florida State 6'2" 196 lbs.

Year	Team		Games	Pos.
1973	PIT	N	14	DB
1974			14	CB, S
1975			14	CB
1976			14	CB
1977			14	CB
1979			14	CB
1980			16	CB
1981			16	S, CB
1982	DEN	N	9	S
9 yrs.	125 games			

J.T. Thomas
THOMAS, JOHNNY LE'MON
B. Dec. 15, 1971, San Bernardino, CA
Arizona State 5'10" 173 lbs.

Year	Team		Games	Pos.
1995	STL	N	15	WR
1996			16	WR
2 yrs.	31 games			

Kelly Thomas
THOMAS, KELLY SCOTT
B. Sep. 9, 1960, Lynwood, CA
Southern California 6'6" 270 lbs.

Year	Team		Games	Pos.
1983	TB	N	14	OT
1984			10	OT
1987	LARM	N	3	OT
3 yrs.	27 games			

Ken Thomas
THOMAS, KENNETH RAY
B. Dec. 21, 1959, Hanford, CA
San Jose State 5'9" 211 lbs.

Year	Team		Games	Pos.
1983	KC	N	14	RB

Kevin Thomas
THOMAS, KEVIN ALAN
B. Jul. 27, 1964, Tucson, AZ
Arizona State 6'2" 265 lbs.

Year	Team		Games	Pos.
1988	TB	N	10	C

Lamar Thomas
THOMAS, LAMAR NATHANIEL
B. Feb. 12, 1970, Ocala, FL
Miami (Florida) 6'1" 170 lbs.

Year	Team		Games	Pos.
1993	TB	N	14	WR
1994			10	WR
1995			11	WR

Year	Team	Games	Pos.

Lamar Thomas continued

Year	Team	Games	Pos.
1996	MIA	N	9	WR

4 yrs. 44 games

Lavale Thomas
THOMAS, LAVALE ALVIN
B. Dec. 12, 1963, Los Angeles, CA
Fresno State 6'0" 205 lbs.

| 1988 | GB | N | 1 | RB |

Lee Thomas
THOMAS, LEE EDWARD
B. Mar. 12, 1946, Karnack, TX
Jackson State 6'5" 246 lbs.

1971	SD	N	9	DE
1972			14	DE
1973	CIN	N	9	DE

3 yrs. 32 games

Louis Thomas
THOMAS, LOUIS T. (Speedy)
B. Apr. 13, 1947, Houston, TX
Utah 6'1" 174 lbs.

1969	CIN	A	14	WR
1970	CIN	N	14	WR
1971			12	WR
1972			11	WR
1973	NO	N	6	WR
1974			1	WR

6 yrs. 58 games

Lynn Thomas
THOMAS, LYNN
B. Jul. 9, 1959, Pascagoula, MS
Pittsburgh 5'11" 181 lbs.

| 1981 | SF | N | 15 | CB |
| 1982 | | | 9 | CB |

2 yrs. 24 games

Mark Thomas
THOMAS, MARK ANDREW
B. May 6, 1969, Lilburn, GA
North Carolina State 6'5" 273 lbs.

1993	SF	N	11	DE
1994			8	DE
1995	CAR	N	10	DE
1996			12	DE

4 yrs. 41 games

Markus Thomas
THOMAS, MARKUS
B. Jul. 12, 1970
Eastern Kentucky 5'10" 192 lbs.

| 1994 | PHI | N | 1 | RB |

Mike Thomas
THOMAS, MALCOLM
B. Jul. 17, 1953, Greenville, TX
Oklahoma/Nevada-Las Vegas 5'11" 190 lbs.

1975	WAS	N	14	RB
1976			13	RB
1977			13	RB
1978			13	RB
1979	SD	N	14	RB
1980			10	RB

6 yrs. 77 games

Norris Thomas
THOMAS, NORRIS LEE
B. May 3, 1954, Inverness, MS
Southern California 5'11" 178 lbs.

1977	MIA	N	14	CB
1978			16	CB
1979			16	CB
1980	TB	N	16	CB

Norris Thomas continued

1981			16	CB
1982			9	CB
1983			10	CB
1984			15	CB

8 yrs. 112 games

Orlanda Thomas
THOMAS, ORLANDA
B. Oct. 21, 1972, Crowley, LA
Southwestern Louisiana 6'1" 209 lbs.

| 1995 | MIN | N | 16 | S |
| 1996 | | | 16 | S |

2 yrs. 32 games

Pat Thomas
THOMAS, PATRICK SHANE
B. Sep. 1, 1954, Plano, TX
Texas A&M 5'9" 181 lbs.

1976	LA	N	14	CB
1977			14	CB
1978			16	CB
1979			8	CB
1980			14	CB
1981			12	CB
1982	LARM	N	9	CB

7 yrs. 87 games

Ralph Thomas
THOMAS, RALPH WARNER
B. Dec. 6, 1927, Kenosha, WI
San Francisco 5'11" 190 lbs.

1952	CHIC	N	8	E
1955	WAS	N	12	E
1956			12	E

3 yrs. 32 games

Rex Thomas
THOMAS, REX
B. 1903
Tulsa/St. John's (New York) 5'9" 174 lbs.

1926	BKN	N	10	HB
1927	CLE	N	13	HB
1928	DET	N	10	HB, FB
1930	BKN	N	6	HB, QB
1931			7	HB, QB

5 yrs. 46 games

Ricky Thomas
THOMAS, RICKY
B. Mar. 29, 1965
Alabama 6'0" 185 lbs.

| 1987 | SEA | N | 1 | S |

Robb Thomas
THOMAS, ROBB DOUGLAS
B. Mar. 29, 1966, Portland, OR
Oregon State 5'11" 174 lbs.

1989	KC	N	8	WR
1990			16	WR
1991			15	WR
1992	SEA	N	15	WR
1993			16	WR
1994			16	WR
1995			15	WR
1996	TB	N	12	WR

8 yrs. 113 games

Rodell Thomas
THOMAS, RODELL
B. Aug. 2, 1958, Quincy, FL
Alabama State 6'1" 227 lbs.

1981	MIA	N	3	LB
1981	SEA	N	11	LB
1982			8	LB
1983	MIA	N	16	LB

Rodell Thomas continued

| 1984 | | | 14 | LB |

4 yrs. 52 games

Rodney Thomas
THOMAS, RODNEY LAMAR
B. Dec. 21, 1965, Los Angeles, CA
Brigham Young 5'10" 190 lbs.

1988	MIA	N	12	CB
1989			16	CB
1990			15	CB
1991	LARM	N	3	CB

4 yrs. 46 games

Rodney Thomas
THOMAS, RODNEY DEJUANE
B. Mar. 30, 1973, Groveton, TX
Texas A&M 5'10" 213 lbs.

| 1995 | HOU | N | 16 | RB |
| 1996 | | | 16 | RB |

2 yrs. 32 games

Russ Thomas
THOMAS, JOHN RUSSEL
B. Jul. 24, 1924, Griffithsville, WV
D. Mar. 19, 1991, Detroit, MI
Ohio State 6'3" 237 lbs.

1946	DET	N	11	T
1947			12	T
1948			12	T
1949			9	T

4 yrs. 44 games

Sean Thomas
THOMAS, SEAN
B. Apr. 12, 1962, Sacramento, CA
Texas Christian 5'11" 190 lbs.

| 1985 | CIN | N | 5 | CB, S |
| 1985 | ATL | N | 6 | DB |

Skip Thomas
THOMAS, ALONZO (Doctor Death)
B. Feb. 7, 1950, Higginsville, MO
Southern California 6'1" 205 lbs.

1972	OAK	N	14	DB
1973			14	CB, S
1974			14	DB
1975			14	DB
1976			14	CB
1977			12	CB

6 yrs. 82 games

Spencer Thomas
THOMAS, SPENCER
B. Mar. 9, 1951, Kansas City, KS
Washburn 6'2" 185 lbs.

| 1975 | WAS | N | 14 | S |
| 1976 | BAL | N | 2 | CB |

2 yrs. 16 games

Stan Thomas
THOMAS, STAN
B. Oct. 28, 1968, El Centro, CA
Texas 6'5" 296 lbs.

1991	CHI	N	15	OT
1992			11	OT
1993	HOU	N	14	OT
1994			15	OT

4 yrs. 55 games

Thurman Thomas
THOMAS, THURMAN
B. May 16, 1966, Houston, TX
Oklahoma State 5'10" 198 lbs.

| 1988 | BUF | N | 15 | RB |

Thurman Thomas continued

1989			16	RB
1990			16	RB
1991			15	RB
1992			16	RB
1993			16	RB
1994			15	RB
1995			14	RB
1996			15	RB

9 yrs. 138 games

Todd Thomas
THOMAS, TODD R.
B. Dec. 2, 1959, Mankato, MN
North Dakota 6'5" 262 lbs.

| 1981 | KC | N | 15 | OT, C |

Vern Thomas
THOMAS, VERNON P.
B. Feb. 2, 1898
D. Apr., 1973, Richland, NY
None 155 lbs.

| 1920 | ROC | A | 1 | E |

William Thomas
THOMAS, WILLIAM HARRISON, JR.
B. Aug. 13, 1968, Amarillo, TX
Texas A&M 6'2" 218 lbs.

1991	PHI	N	16	LB
1992			16	LB
1993			16	LB
1994			16	LB
1995			16	LB
1996			16	LB

6 yrs. 96 games

Zach Thomas
THOMAS, ZACH
B. Sep. 1, 1973, Lubbock, TX
Texas Tech 5'11" 231 lbs.

| 1996 | MIA | N | 16 | LB |

Zack Thomas
THOMAS, ZACHARY DWAYNE
B. Sep. 8, 1960, Cocoa, FL
South Carolina State 6'0" 182 lbs.

1983	DEN	N	16	WR
1984			12	WR
1984	TB	N	2	WR

2 yrs. 30 games

Rick Thomaselli
THOMASELLI, RICH
B. Feb. 26, 1957, Follansbee, WV
West Virginia Wesleyan 6'1" 185 lbs.

| 1981 | HOU | N | 12 | RB |
| 1982 | | | 9 | RB |

2 yrs. 21 games

Bobby Thomason
THOMASON, ROBERT LEE
B. Mar. 26, 1928, Palos, AL
Virginia Military Institute 6'1" 196 lbs.

1949	LA	N	6	QB
1951	GB	N	11	QB
1952	PHI	N	12	QB
1953			12	QB
1954			10	QB
1955			10	QB
1956			12	QB
1957			12	QB

8 yrs. 85 games

Jeff Thomason
THOMASON, JEFFREY DAVID

Year	Team		Games	Pos.

Jeff Thomason continued

B. Dec. 30, 1969, San Diego, CA
Oregon 6'4" 233 lbs.

Year	Team		Games	Pos.
1992	CIN	N	4	TE
1993			3	TE
1995	GB	N	16	TE
1996			16	TE
4 yrs.	39 games			

Jim Thomason
THOMASON, JAMES N.
B. Oct. 4, 1919
D. Jun. 2, 1989, Lyons, TX
Texas A&M 6'0" 200 lbs.

| 1945 | DET | N | 5 | HB |

John Thomason
THOMASON, JOHN GRIFFIN (Stumpy)
B. Feb. 24, 1906, Atlanta, GA
D. Apr. 20, 1989, Thomasville, NC
Georgia Tech 5'7" 189 lbs.

Year	Team		Games	Pos.
1930	BKN	N	6	HB, QB
1931			13	HB, QB
1932			7	HB
1933			9	HB, FB
1934			8	FB, HB
1935			1	QB
1935	PHI	N	7	QB, HB
1936			12	HB, FB
7 yrs.	63 games			

Leon Thomasson
THOMASSON, LEON
B. Jun. 20, 1963
Texas Southern 5'11" 190 lbs.

| 1987 | ATL | N | 3 | CB |

Chris Thome
THOME, CHRISTOPHER JOHN
B. Jan. 15, 1969, St. Cloud, MN
Minnesota 6'4" 280 lbs.

Year	Team		Games	Pos.
1991	CLE	N	7	C
1992			3	C
2 yrs.	10 games			

Alvie Thompson
THOMPSON, ALVIS
B. Jan. 22, 1901
Lombard/Nebraska 6'2" 210 lbs.

Year	Team		Games	Pos.
1925	KC	N	8	T
1926			2	T, G
2 yrs.	10 games			

Anthony Thompson
THOMPSON, ANTHONY
B. Jun. 19, 1967, Stantonsburg, NC
East Carolina 6'1" 227 lbs.

| 1990 | DEN | N | 10 | LB |

Anthony Thompson
THOMPSON, ANTHONY
B. Apr. 8, 1967, Terre Haute, IN
Indiana 5'11" 207 lbs.

Year	Team		Games	Pos.
1990	PHX	N	13	RB
1991			16	RB
1992			1	RB
1992	LARM	N	7	LB
3 yrs.	37 games			

Arland Thompson
THOMPSON, ARLAND LEE
B. Sep. 19, 1957, Lockney, TX
Baylor 6'3" 265 lbs.

| 1980 | DEN | N | 2 | G |
| 1981 | GB | N | 10 | G |

Arland Thompson continued

Year	Team		Games	Pos.
1982	BAL	N	3	G
1987	KC	N	3	G
4 yrs.	18 games			

Aundra Thompson
THOMPSON, AUNDRA (Boomer)
B. Jan. 2, 1953, Dallas, TX
East Texas State 6'1" 186 lbs.

Year	Team		Games	Pos.
1977	GB	N	14	WR
1978			15	WR
1979			15	WR
1980			15	WR
1981			3	WR
1981	SD	N	1	WR
1981	NO	N	10	WR
1982			9	WR
6 yrs.	83 games			

Bennie Thompson
THOMPSON, BENNIE
B. Feb. 10, 1963, New Orleans, LA
Grambling State 6'0" 200 lbs.

Year	Team		Games	Pos.
1989	NO	N	2	S
1990			16	S
1991			16	S
1992	KC	N	16	S
1993			16	S
1994	CLE	N	16	S
1995			13	S
1996	BAL	N	16	S
8 yrs.	111 games			

Bill Thompson
THOMPSON, WILLIAM
B. 1907
None 182 lbs.

| 1925 | MIL | N | 1 | C |

Billy Thompson
THOMPSON, WILLIAM ALLEN
B. Oct. 10, 1946, Greenville, SC
Maryland-Eastern Shore 6'1" 200 lbs.

Year	Team		Games	Pos.
1969	DEN	A	14	CB
1970	DEN	N	9	CB
1971			14	CB
1972			14	CB
1973			14	CB
1974			14	S
1975			14	S
1976			14	S
1977			14	S
1978			16	S
1979			16	S
1980			16	S
1981			16	S
13 yrs.	185 games			

Bobby Thompson
THOMPSON, BOBBY
B. Jan. 16, 1947, Raleigh, NC
Oklahoma 5'11" 195 lbs.

Year	Team		Games	Pos.
1975	DET	N	14	RB
1976			14	RB
2 yrs.	28 games			

Bobby Lee Thompson
THOMPSON, ROBERT LEE
B. Mar. 30, 1939, Minden, LA
Arizona 5'10" 179 lbs.

Year	Team		Games	Pos.
1964	DET	N	14	HB, DB
1965			11	DB
1966			14	DB
1967			12	DB
1968			14	DB
1969	NO	N	7	S
6 yrs.	72 games			

Broderick Thompson
THOMPSON, BRODERICK
B. Aug. 14, 1960, Birmingham, AL
Kansas 6'5" 291 lbs.

Year	Team		Games	Pos.
1985	DAL	N	11	G
1987	SD	N	8	G
1988			16	G, OT
1989			16	G, OT
1990			16	G, OT
1991			16	G, OT
1992			12	G, OT
1993	PHI	N	10	OT, G
1994			14	OT
1995	DEN	N	16	OT
1996			16	OT
11 yrs.	151 games			

Bryant Thompson
THOMPSON, GEORGE BRYANT (Tiny)
B. 1899
Deceased
Syracuse 5'10" 233 lbs.

Year	Team		Games	Pos.
1921	SYR	A	1	G
1922	ROC	N	5	G
2 yrs.	6 games			

Craig Thompson
THOMPSON, CRAIG ANTONIO
B. Jan. 13, 1969, Hartsville, SC
North Carolina A&T 6'2" 244 lbs.

Year	Team		Games	Pos.
1992	CIN	N	16	TE
1993			13	TE
2 yrs.	29 games			

Darrell Thompson
THOMPSON, DARRELL ALEXANDER
B. Nov. 23, 1967, Rochester, MN
Minnesota 6'0" 215 lbs.

Year	Team		Games	Pos.
1990	GB	N	16	RB
1991			13	RB
1992			7	RB
1993			16	RB
1994			8	RB
5 yrs.	60 games			

Dave Thompson
THOMPSON, DAVID (Chubby)
B. Nov. 17, 1897
Deceased
Denison 5'10" 215 lbs.

| 1921 | CIN | A | 1 | HB |

Dave Thompson
THOMPSON, DAVID WAYNE
B. Feb. 1, 1949, Langdale, AL
Clemson 6'4" 271 lbs.

Year	Team		Games	Pos.
1971	DET	N	14	G, C
1972			7	C
1973			14	C
1974	NO	N	14	C
1975			7	OT
5 yrs.	56 games			

Del Thompson
THOMPSON, DELBERT RAY
B. Feb. 21, 1958, Kermit, TX
Texas/Texas-El Paso 6'0" 203 lbs.

| 1982 | KC | N | 6 | RB |

Don Thompson
THOMPSON, DONALD
B. Oct. 7, 1939
Richmond 6'4" 230 lbs.

| 1962 | BAL | N | 10 | DE |
| 1963 | | | 14 | DE |

Don Thompson continued

Year	Team		Games	Pos.
1964	PHI	N	3	DE
3 yrs.	27 games			

Don Thompson
THOMPSON, ROBERT DONALD
B. Dec. 29, 1903
D. Aug., 1973, Los Angeles, CA
Redlands 6'2" 205 lbs.

| 1926 | LA | N | 10 | G |

Donnell Thompson
THOMPSON, LAWRENCE DONNELL
B. Oct. 27, 1958, Lumberton, NC
North Carolina 6'4" 270 lbs.

Year	Team		Games	Pos.
1981	BAL	N	13	DE
1982			9	DE
1983			14	DE
1984	IND	N	10	DE
1985			14	DE
1986			16	DE
1987			12	DE
1988			16	DE
1989			16	DE
1990			12	DE
1991			14	DE
11 yrs.	146 games			

Emmuel Thompson
THOMPSON, EMMUEL LEE
B. Nov. 15, 1959, Houston, TX
Texas A&I, Kingsville 5'10" 180 lbs.

| 1987 | HOU | N | 3 | CB |

Ernie Thompson
THOMPSON, ERNIE
B. Oct. 25, 1969, Terre Haute, IN
Indiana 5'11" 230 lbs.

Year	Team		Games	Pos.
1991	LARM	N	3	RB
1993	KC	N	16	RB
2 yrs.	19 games			

Gary Thompson
THOMPSON, GARY
B. Feb. 23, 1959, Castro Valley, CA
San Jose State 6'0" 180 lbs.

Year	Team		Games	Pos.
1983	BUF	N	16	CB
1984			8	CB
1987	WAS	N	1	CB
3 yrs.	25 games			

George Thompson
THOMPSON, GEORGE D.
B. Aug. 31, 1899
D. Aug., 1965
Iowa 6'1" 210 lbs.

Year	Team		Games	Pos.
1923	RI	N	7	G
1924			9	G, T
1925			11	G, HB
3 yrs.	27 games			

Hal Thompson
THOMPSON, HAROLD C. (Buck)
B. Oct. 18, 1922, Manasquan, NJ
Delaware 6'1" 205 lbs.

Year	Team		Games	Pos.
1947	BKN	AA	12	E
1948			9	E
2 yrs.	21 games			

Harry Thompson
THOMPSON, HAROLD JULIUS
B. Jan. 8, 1926, Memphis, TN
UCLA 6'2" 225 lbs.

| 1950 | LA | N | 12 | G |
| 1951 | | | 12 | G |

Year	Team	Games	Pos.

Harry Thompson *continued*

Year	Team		Games	Pos.
1952			12	G
1953			8	G
1954			12	G
1955	CHIC	N	11	G
6 yrs.	67 games			

Jack Thompson
THOMPSON, JACK
B. May 19, 1956, Tutuwila, American Samoa
Washington State 6'3" 217 lbs.

Year	Team		Games	Pos.
1979	CIN	N	9	QB
1980			14	QB
1981			8	QB
1982			1	QB
1983	TB	N	14	QB
1984			5	QB
6 yrs.	51 games			

James Thompson
THOMPSON, JAMES, III
B. Jan. 9, 1953, Memphis, TN
Memphis State 6'0" 178 lbs.

1978	NYG	N	13	WR

Jesse Thompson
THOMPSON, JESSE, III
B. Mar. 12, 1956, Merced, CA
California 6'1" 185 lbs.

1978	DET	N	11	WR
1980			11	WR
2 yrs.	22 games			

Jim Thompson
THOMPSON, JAMES L.
B. Dec. 4, 1940, Peoria, IL
Southern Illinois 6'3" 255 lbs.

1965	DEN	A	4	DT

John Thompson
THOMPSON, JOHN WASHINGTON, JR.
B. Jan. 18, 1957, Jackson, MS
Weber State/Utah State 6'3" 228 lbs.

1979	GB	N	16	TE
1980			7	TE
1981			2	TE
1982			9	TE
4 yrs.	34 games			

Johnny Thompson
THOMPSON, JOHN H.
B. 1906
Lafayette 5'10" 215 lbs.

1929	FRA	N	2	G

Kenny Thompson
THOMPSON, KENNETH WAYNE
B. Dec. 6, 1958, Snyder, TX
Utah State 6'1" 178 lbs.

1982	STL	N	1	WR
1983			5	WR
2 yrs.	6 games			

Leonard Thompson
THOMPSON, LEONARD I.
B. Jul. 28, 1952, Oklahoma City, OK
Oklahoma State 5'11" 190 lbs.

1975	DET	N	14	RB
1976			14	RB
1977			14	WR, RB
1978			16	WR
1979			15	WR
1980			16	WR
1981			16	WR

Leonard Thompson *cont.*

Year	Team	Games	Pos.
1982		9	WR
1983		13	WR
1984		16	WR
1985		16	WR
1986		16	WR
12 yrs.	175 games		

Leroy Thompson
THOMPSON, ULYS LEROY
B. Feb. 3, 1968, Knoxville, TN
Penn State 5'10" 215 lbs.

Year	Team		Games	Pos.
1991	PIT	N	13	RB
1992			15	RB
1993			15	RB
1994	NE	N	16	RB
1995	KC	N	16	RB
1996	TB	N	5	RB
6 yrs.	80 games			

Marty Thompson
THOMPSON, GLENN MARTIN
B. Dec. 9, 1969, Whittier, LA
Fresno State 6'3" 243 lbs.

1993	DET	N	6	TE

Mike Thompson
THOMPSON, MIKE
B. Dec. 22, 1972, Portage, WI
Wisconsin 6'3" 276 lbs.

1995	JAC	N	1	DT

Norm Thompson
THOMPSON, NORMAN JACK
B. Mar. 5, 1945, San Francisco, CA
Utah 6'1" 179 lbs.

Year	Team		Games	Pos.
1971	STL	N	14	CB
1972			12	CB
1973			11	CB
1974			12	CB, S
1975			14	CB
1976			13	CB
1977	BAL	N	14	CB
1978			13	CB
8 yrs.	103 games			

Reyna Thompson
THOMPSON, REYNA ONALD
B. Aug. 28, 1963, Dallas, TX
Baylor 6'0" 194 lbs.

Year	Team		Games	Pos.
1986	MIA	N	16	S
1987			9	CB
1988			16	CB
1989	NYG	N	16	CB
1990			16	CB
1991			12	CB
1992			16	CB, S
1993	NE	N	15	CB
8 yrs.	116 games			

Ricky Thompson
THOMPSON, RICKY D.
B. May 15, 1954, El Paso, TX
Baylor 6'0" 176 lbs.

Year	Team		Games	Pos.
1976	BAL	N	9	WR
1977			5	WR
1978	WAS	N	16	WR
1979			15	WR
1980			16	WR
1981			16	WR
1982	STL	N	3	WR
7 yrs.	80 games			

Robert Thompson
THOMPSON, ROBERT C.
B. Feb. 4, 1960, Chicago, IL
Michigan 6'3" 225 lbs.

1983	TB	N	10	LB

Robert Thompson *continued*

Year	Team	Games	Pos.
1984		9	LB
2 yrs.	19 games		

Robert Thompson
THOMPSON, ROBERT L.
B. Sep. 9, 1962, Hollywood, FL
Youngstown State 5'9" 168 lbs.

1987	DEN	N	2	WR

Rocky Thompson
SYMONDS-THOMPSON, RALPH GARY
B. Nov. 8, 1947, Paget, Bermuda
West Texas State 5'11" 200 lbs.

Year	Team		Games	Pos.
1971	NYG	N	14	RB
1972			14	RB
1973			1	RB
3 yrs.	29 games			

Russ Thompson
THOMPSON, RUSSELL J.
B. May 10, 1912, Whitney, NE
Chadron State/Nebraska 6'5" 249 lbs.

Year	Team		Games	Pos.
1936	CHIB	N	9	T
1937			11	T
1938			10	T
1939			11	T
1940	PHI	N	11	T
5 yrs.	52 games			

Steve Thompson
THOMPSON, STEVE
B. Feb. 12, 1945, Seattle, WA
Washington 6'5" 244 lbs.

Year	Team		Games	Pos.
1968	NY	A	4	DE, DT
1969			14	DE
1970	NYJ	N	12	DT
1972			5	DT
1973			8	DT
5 yrs.	43 games			

Steve Thompson
THOMPSON, STEVEN K.
B. Jun. 24, 1965
Minnesota 6'2" 275 lbs.

1987	WAS	N	1	DT

Ted Thompson
THOMPSON, TED CLARENCE
B. Jan. 17, 1953, Atlanta, GA
Southern Methodist 6'1" 219 lbs.

Year	Team		Games	Pos.
1975	HOU	N	14	DE
1976			14	LB
1977			14	LB
1978			16	LB
1979			16	LB
1980			15	LB
1981			16	LB
1982			9	LB
1983			16	LB
1984			16	LB
10 yrs.	146 games			

Tom Thompson
THOMPSON, THOMAS
B. Sep. 22, 1951, Oxford, MS
Southern Illinois 6'1" 205 lbs.

1974	SD	N	12	RB

Tommy Thompson
THOMPSON, THOMAS WRIGHT
B. Jan. 6, 1927, Jersey City, NJ
D. Oct. 1, 1990, Baltimore, MD
William & Mary 6'1" 221 lbs.

1949	CLE	AA	8	C

Tommy Thompson *continued*

Year	Team		Games	Pos.
1950	CLE	N	12	C
1951			12	C
1952			12	C
1953			9	C
5 yrs.	53 games			

Tommy Thompson
THOMPSON, TOMMY
B. Apr. 27, 1972, Ventura, CA
Oregon 5'9" 192 lbs.

1995	SF	N	16	P
1996			16	P
2 yrs.	32 games			

Tommy Thompson
THOMPSON, TOMMYE PRYOR
B. Aug. 15, 1916, Hutchinson, KS
D. Apr. 21, 1989, Calico Rock, AR
Tulsa 6'1" 192 lbs.

Year	Team		Games	Pos.
1940	PIT	N	11	QB
1941	PHI	N	11	QB
1942			11	QB
1945			8	QB
1946			10	QB
1947			12	QB
1948			12	QB
1949			12	QB
1950			12	QB
9 yrs.	99 games			

Tuffy Thompson
THOMPSON, CLARENCE L.
B. Jun. 29, 1914
D. Nov., 1986, Burnsville, MN
Minnesota 5'11" 172 lbs.

Year	Team		Games	Pos.
1937	PIT	N	7	HB, E
1938			9	HB
1939	GB	N	1	HB
3 yrs.	17 games			

Vince Thompson
THOMPSON, VINCENT
B. Feb. 21, 1957, Trenton, NJ
Villanova 6'0" 230 lbs.

1981	DET	N	13	RB
1983			10	RB
2 yrs.	23 games			

Warren Thompson
THOMPSON, WARREN
B. Apr. 13, 1964
Oklahoma State 6'3" 241 lbs.

1987	NYG	N	3	LB

Weegie Thompson
THOMPSON, WILLIS HOPE
B. Mar. 12, 1961, Pensacola, FL
Florida State 6'6" 212 lbs.

Year	Team		Games	Pos.
1984	PIT	N	16	WR
1985			16	WR
1986			16	WR
1987			12	WR
1988			16	WR
1989			16	WR
6 yrs.	92 games			

Woody Thompson
THOMPSON, ALEXANDER WOODROW
B. Aug. 20, 1952, Erie, PA
Miami (Florida) 6'1" 228 lbs.

1975	ATL	N	14	RB
1976			7	RB
1977			14	RB
3 yrs.	35 games			

Year	Team		Games	Pos.

Art Thoms
THOMS, ARTHUR WILLIAM, JR.
B. Oct. 20, 1946, Teaneck, NJ
Syracuse 6'5" 251 lbs.

Year	Team		Games	Pos.
1969	OAK	A	12	DT
1970	OAK	N	6	DT
1971			14	DT
1972			14	DT
1973			14	DT
1974			14	DT
1975			13	DT
1977	PHI	N	14	DE, NT
8 yrs.	101 games			

Fred Thomsen
THOMSEN, FREDERICK C.
B. 1897, Minden, AR
Deceased
Nebraska 5'11" 170 lbs.

Year	Team		Games	Pos.
1924	RI	N	9	E

Bob Thornbladh
THORNBLADH, BOB
B. Sep. 19, 1952, Cleveland, OH
Michigan 6'1" 220 lbs.

Year	Team		Games	Pos.
1974	KC	N	14	RB

Al Thornburg
THORNBURG, ALVIN
B. 1901
D. Apr. 20, 1949
Iowa State 5'10" 170 lbs.

Year	Team		Games	Pos.
1926	CLE	A	3	C

Claude Thornhill
THORNHILL, CLAUDE EARL
(Tiny)
B. Apr. 14, 1893, Richmond, VA
D. Jun. 28, 1956, Berkeley, CA
Pittsburgh 5'11" 185 lbs.

Year	Team		Games	Pos.
1920	CLE	A	7	T, G
1920	BUF	A	2	T
1 yr.	9 games			

Bill Thornton
THORNTON, WILLIAM ALBERT
B. Sep. 20, 1939, Toledo, OH
Nebraska 6'1" 214 lbs.

Year	Team		Games	Pos.
1963	STL	N	14	FB
1964			13	FB
1965			14	FB
1967			5	RB
4 yrs.	46 games			

Bruce Thornton
THORNTON, BRUCE EDWARD
B. Feb. 14, 1958, Detroit, MI
Illinois 6'5" 265 lbs.

Year	Team		Games	Pos.
1979	DAL	N	16	DT
1980			13	DT
1981			12	DE, DT
1982	STL	N	6	DT
4 yrs.	47 games			

Bubba Thornton
THORNTON, CHARLES GARLAND
B. Mar. 9, 1947, Fort Worth, TX
Texas Christian 6'0" 175 lbs.

Year	Team		Games	Pos.
1969	BUF	A	14	WR

Dick Thornton
THORNTON, HARRY RICHARD
B. Feb. 4, 1908, Chicago, IL
D. Nov. 15, 1973
Missouri-Rolla 5'8" 165 lbs.

Year	Team		Games	Pos.
1933	PHI	N	4	QB

George Thornton
THORNTON, GEORGE RENARDO
B. Apr. 27, 1968, Montgomery, AL
Alabama 6'3" 300 lbs.

Year	Team		Games	Pos.
1991	SD	N	16	DT
1992			16	DT
1993	NYG	N	5	DE
3 yrs.	37 games			

Jack Thornton
THORNTON, LAWRENCE JACKSON
B. 1945
Auburn 6'1" 230 lbs.

Year	Team		Games	Pos.
1966	MIA	A	6	LB

James Thornton
THORNTON, JAMES MICHAEL
(Robocop)
B. Feb. 8, 1965, Santa Rosa, CA
Fullerton State 6'2" 242 lbs.

Year	Team		Games	Pos.
1988	CHI	N	16	TE
1989			16	TE
1990			16	TE
1991			16	TE
1993	NYJ	N	13	TE
1994			16	TE
1995	HOU	N	4	TE
7 yrs.	97 games			

John Thornton
THORNTON, JOHN EARVIN
B. Jun. 28, 1969, Flint, MI
Cincinnati 6'3" 303 lbs.

Year	Team		Games	Pos.
1991	CLE	N	5	DE, DT

Reggie Thornton
THORNTON, REGINALD ORLANDO
B. Sep. 26, 1967, Detroit, MI
Bowling Green 5'10" 170 lbs.

Year	Team		Games	Pos.
1991	IND	N	5	WR
1993	CIN	N	1	WR
2 yrs.	6 games			

Rupe Thornton
THORNTON, RUPERT V.
B. 1919
Santa Clara 5'10" 205 lbs.

Year	Team		Games	Pos.
1946	SF	AA	11	G
1947			14	T
2 yrs.	25 games			

Sidney Thornton
THORNTON, SIDNEY
B. Sep. 2, 1954, New Orleans, LA
Northwestern State (Louisiana) 5'11" 230 lbs.

Year	Team		Games	Pos.
1977	PIT	N	13	RB
1978			16	RB
1979			13	RB
1980			12	RB
1981			16	RB
1982			4	RB
6 yrs.	74 games			

Don Thorp
THORP, DONALD KEVIN
B. Jul. 10, 1962, Chicago, IL
Illinois 6'4" 248 lbs.

Year	Team		Games	Pos.
1984	NO	N	5	NT
1987	IND	N	6	DL
1988			1	NT
1988	KC	N	3	DE, NT
3 yrs.	15 games			

Jack Thorpe
THORPE, JACK (Deadeye)
B. 1899
Deceased
None 6'0" 210 lbs.

Year	Team		Games	Pos.
1922	OOR	N	1	FB
1923			7	G, HB, C, T
2 yrs.	8 games			

Jim Thorpe
THORPE, JAMES FRANCIS
(Bright Path)
B. May 28, 1887, Prague, OK
D. Mar. 28, 1953, Long Beach, CA
Carlisle 6'1" 201 lbs.

Year	Team		Games	Pos.
1920	CAN	A	6	HB, FB
1921	CLE	A	5	HB
1922	OOR	N	4	HB
1923			9	HB
1924	RI	N	9	HB
1925	NYG	N	3	HB
1925	RI	N	2	HB
1926	CAN	N	9	HB, E, FB
1928	CHIC	N	1	E
8 yrs.	48 games			

Wilfred Thorpe
THORPE, WILFRED
Arkansas 6'3" 205 lbs.

Year	Team		Games	Pos.
1941	CLE	N	5	G, E, T
1942			11	G
2 yrs.	16 games			

Bruce Threadgill
THREADGILL, BRUCE CRAIG
B. May 7, 1956, Nocona, TX
Mississippi State 6'0" 190 lbs.

Year	Team		Games	Pos.
1978	SF	N	14	S

Cliff Thrift
THRIFT, CLIFFORD RAY
B. May 3, 1956, Dallas, TX
East Central Oklahoma 6'2" 235 lbs.

Year	Team		Games	Pos.
1979	SD	N	16	LB
1980			15	LB
1981			7	LB
1982			9	LB
1983			6	LB
1984			16	LB
1985	CHI	N	16	LB
1986	LARM	N	12	LB
8 yrs.	97 games			

Jim Thrower
THROWER, JAMES FREDERICK
B. Nov. 6, 1947, Camden, AR
East Texas State 6'2" 194 lbs.

Year	Team		Games	Pos.
1970	PHI	N	5	DB
1971			14	CB
1972			5	CB
1973	DET	N	10	CB
1974			12	CB
5 yrs.	46 games			

Willie Thrower
THROWER, WILLIE L.
B. Mar. 22, 1930, New Kensington, PA
Michigan State 5'11" 182 lbs.

Year	Team		Games	Pos.
1953	CHIB	N	1	QB

Baptiste Thunder
THUNDER, BAPTISTE
None 5'10" 215 lbs.

Year	Team		Games	Pos.
1922	OOR	N	1	T

Bob Thurbon
THURBON, ROBERT W.
B. Feb. 22, 1918, Erie, PA
Pittsburgh 5'10" 176 lbs.

Year	Team		Games	Pos.
1943	P-P	N	10	QB
1944	C-P	N	10	HB
1946	BUF	AA	2	HB
3 yrs.	22 games			

Brian Thure
THURE, BRIAN
B. Sep. 3, 1973, Downey, CA
California 6'5" 300 lbs.

Year	Team		Games	Pos.
1995	WAS	N	4	OT

Steve Thurlow
THURLOW, STEPHEN CHARLES
B. Apr. 25, 1942, Long Beach, CA
Stanford 6'3" 217 lbs.

Year	Team		Games	Pos.
1964	NYG	N	11	HB
1965			14	HB
1966			1	HB
1966	WAS	N	13	RB
1967			6	RB
1968			6	RB
5 yrs.	51 games			

Dennis Thurman
THURMAN, DENNIS LEE
B. Apr. 13, 1956, Los Angeles, CA
Southern California 5'11" 178 lbs.

Year	Team		Games	Pos.
1978	DAL	N	16	CB
1979			16	CB
1980			16	CB
1981			16	S
1982			9	CB
1983			16	CB
1984			16	CB
1985			16	CB
1986	STL	N	16	S
9 yrs.	137 games			

John Thurman
THURMAN, JOHN C. (Hackle)
B. Feb. 9, 1900
D. Mar., 1976, Pasadena, CA
Pennsylvania 6'1" 225 lbs.

Year	Team		Games	Pos.
1926	LA	N	10	T

Junior Thurman
THURMAN, ULYSSES
B. Sep. 8, 1964
Southern California 6'0" 180 lbs.

Year	Team		Games	Pos.
1987	NO	N	3	CB, S

Fuzzy Thurston
THURSTON, FRED CHARLES
B. Dec. 29, 1933, Altoona, WI
Valparaiso 6'1" 247 lbs.

Year	Team		Games	Pos.
1958	BAL	N	4	G
1959	GB	N	12	G
1960			12	G
1961			14	G
1962			14	G
1963			14	G
1964			11	G
1965			14	G
1966			12	G
1967			9	G
10 yrs.	116 games			

John Tice
TICE, JOHN
B. Jun. 22, 1960, Bay Shore, NY
Maryland 6'5" 246 lbs.

Year	Team		Games	Pos.
1983	NO	N	16	TE
1984			10	TE

Year	Team		Games	Pos.

John Tice continued

Year	Team		Games	Pos.
1985			16	TE
1986			16	TE
1987			12	TE
1988			15	TE
1989			15	TE
1990			16	TE
1991			15	TE
1992			3	TE
10 yrs.	134 games			

Mike Tice
TICE, MICHAEL PETER
B. Feb. 2, 1959, Bay Shore, NY
Maryland 6'7" 246 lbs.

1981	SEA	N	16	TE
1982			9	TE
1983			15	TE
1984			16	TE
1985			9	TE
1986			16	TE
1987			12	TE
1988			16	TE
1989	WAS	N	16	TE
1990	SEA	N	5	TE
1991			16	TE
1992	MIN	N	12	TE
1993			16	TE
1995			2	TE
14 yrs.	176 games			

Glenn Tidd
TIDD, GLENN
B. Apr. 23, 1894
D. Oct., 1978, Dayton, OH
none 5'11" 202 lbs.

1921	DAY	A	4	G, C, T
1922	DAY	N	4	C, HB
1923			5	G, C, T
1924			8	C, G
4 yrs.	21 games			

Sam Tidmore
TIDMORE, SAMUEL E.
B. Oct. 28, 1938, Decatur, IL
Ohio State 6'1" 223 lbs.

1962	CLE	N	13	LB
1963			5	LB
2 yrs.	18 games			

Billy Tidwell
TIDWELL, BILLY R.
B. Aug. 3, 1930, Hearne, TX
D. Dec. 19, 1990, Trinity, TX
Texas A&M 5'9" 178 lbs.

1954	SF	N	10	HB

Travis Tidwell
TIDWELL, TRAVIS VAUGHN
B. Feb. 5, 1925, Florence, AL
Auburn 5'10" 185 lbs.

1950	NYG	N	8	QB
1951			6	QB
2 yrs.	14 games			

Festus Tierney
TIERNEY, FESTUS P.
B. Jul. 1, 1899
D. Aug., 1973, Minneapolis, MN
Minnesota 6'1" 198 lbs.

1922	HAM	N	6	G, T
1923	MIN	N	8	G
1924			6	G
1925	MIL	N	3	G, T
4 yrs.	23 games			

Leo Tierney
TIERNEY, CLARENCE LEO, III
B. Jan. 28, 1954, San Antonio, TX
Georgia Tech 6'3" 248 lbs.

1978	CLE	N	2	C
1978	NYG	N	5	C
1 yr.	7 games			

Van Tiffin
TIFFIN, VAN
B. Sep. 6, 1965, Red Bay, AL
Alabama 5'9" 155 lbs.

1987	TB	N	3	K
1987	MIA	N	1	K
1 yr.	4 games			

Mark Tigges
TIGGES, MARK
B. Feb. 5, 1964
Western Illinois 6'3" 290 lbs.

1987	CIN	N	3	OT

Calvin Tiggle
TIGGLE, CALVIN BERNARD
B. Nov. 10, 1968, Fort Washington, MD
Georgia Tech 6'1" 235 lbs.

1991	TB	N	16	LB
1992			8	LB
2 yrs.	24 games			

Mike Tilleman
TILLEMAN, MICHAEL JOHN
B. Mar. 30, 1944, Chinook, MT
Montana 6'5" 275 lbs.

1966	MIN	N	12	DT
1967	NO	N	14	DT
1968			14	DT
1969			14	DT
1970			14	DT
1971	HOU	N	14	DT
1972			14	DT
1973	ATL	N	13	DT
1974			12	DT
1975			14	DT
1976			14	DT
11 yrs.	149 games			

Jim Tiller
TILLER, JAMES T.
B. 1939
Purdue 5'9" 165 lbs.

1962	NY	A	11	HB

Morgan Tiller
TILLER, MORGAN JOHN
B. Oct. 13, 1919, Trinidad, CO
D. Dec., 1983, Vienna, VA
Denver 6'1" 195 lbs.

1941	PIT	N	1	E
1944	BOS	N	4	E
1945	PIT	N	10	E
3 yrs.	15 games			

Emmett Tilley
TILLEY, EMMETT
B. Feb. 13, 1961, Durham, NC
Duke 5'11" 240 lbs.

1983	MIA	N	6	LB

Pat Tilley
TILLEY, PATRICK LEE
B. Feb. 15, 1953, Shreveport, LA
Louisiana Tech 5'10" 176 lbs.

1976	STL	N	13	WR
1977			14	WR

Pat Tilley continued

Year	Team		Games	Pos.
1978			16	WR
1979			16	WR
1980			14	WR
1981			16	WR
1982			9	WR
1983			16	WR
1984			16	WR
1985			16	WR
1986			1	WR
11 yrs.	147 games			

Ed Tillison
TILLISON, ED
B. Feb. 12, 1969, Pearl River, LA
Northwest Missouri State 6'0" 225 lbs.

1992	DET	N	6	RB

Alonzo Tillman
TILLMAN, ALONZO M. (Pete)
B. May 9, 1923, Mangum, OK
Oklahoma 6'0" 210 lbs.

1949	BAL	AA	11	C

Andre Tillman
TILLMAN, ANDRE
B. Nov. 1, 1952, Dallas, TX
Texas Tech 6'5" 230 lbs.

1975	MIA	N	14	TE
1976			14	TE
1977			14	TE
1978			16	TE
4 yrs.	58 games			

Cedric Tillman
TILLMAN, CEDRIC CORNEL
B. Jul. 22, 1970, Natchez, MS
Alcorn State 6'2" 204 lbs.

1992	DEN	N	9	WR
1993			14	WR
1994			16	WR
1995	JAC	N	13	WR
4 yrs.	52 games			

Faddie Tillman
TILLMAN, FADDIE CHARLES
B. Oct. 2, 1948, Dallas, TX
Boise State 6'5" 230 lbs.

1972	NO	N	1	DT

Lawyer Tillman
TILLMAN, LAWYER JAMES, JR.
B. May 20, 1966, Mobile, AL
Auburn 6'5" 230 lbs.

1989	CLE	N	14	WR
1992			11	WR
1993			7	WR
1995	CAR	N	5	TE
4 yrs.	37 games			

Lewis Tillman
TILLMAN, LEWIS
B. Apr. 16, 1966, Oklahoma City, OK
Jackson State 6'0" 195 lbs.

1989	NYG	N	16	RB
1990			16	RB
1991			16	RB
1992			16	RB
1993			16	RB
1994	CHI	N	16	RB
1995			13	RB
7 yrs.	109 games			

Rusty Tillman
TILLMAN, RUSSELL ARTHUR
B. Feb. 27, 1946, Beloit, WI

Rusty Tillman continued
Arizona/Northern Arizona 6'2" 230 lbs.

Year	Team		Games	Pos.
1970	WAS	N	14	LB
1971			9	LB
1972			14	LB
1973			14	LB
1974			14	LB
1975			14	LB
1976			14	LB
1977			14	LB
8 yrs.	107 games			

Spencer Tillman
TILLMAN, SPENCER ALLEN
B. Apr. 21, 1964, Tulsa, OK
Oklahoma 5'11" 206 lbs.

1987	HOU	N	5	RB
1988			16	RB
1989	SF	N	15	RB
1990			16	RB
1991			16	RB
1992	HOU	N	16	RB
1993			15	RB
1994			16	RB
8 yrs.	115 games			

Tony Tillmon
TILLMON, TONY V.
B. Sep. 12, 1963
Texas 5'10" 170 lbs.

1987	LARI	N	3	CB

Ron Tilton
TILTON, RONALD JOHN
B. Aug. 9, 1963, Homestead, FL
Florida/Tulane 6'4" 250 lbs.

1986	WAS	N	7	G

Bob Timberlake
TIMBERLAKE, ROBERT
B. Oct. 18, 1943, Middletown, OH
Michigan 6'4" 220 lbs.

1965	NYG	N	13	QB, K

George Timberlake
TIMBERLAKE, GEORGE R.
B. Nov. 3, 1932, Long Beach, CA
Southern California 6'1" 220 lbs.

1955	GB	N	6	G

Ken Times
TIMES, KEN
B. Jan. 26, 1957, Deerfield Beach, FL
Southern University 6'2" 246 lbs.

1980	SF	N	3	DT
1981	STL	N	2	DT
2 yrs.	5 games			

Kirk Timmer
TIMMER, KIRK
B. Dec. 18, 1963, Butte, MT
Michigan State 6'3" 242 lbs.

1987	DAL	N	1	LB

Adam Timmerman
TIMMERMAN, ADAM LARRY
B. Aug. 14, 1971, Cherokee, IA
South Dakota State 6'4" 289 lbs.

1995	GB	N	13	G
1996			16	G
2 yrs.	29 games			

Charlie Timmons
TIMMONS, CHARLES TRUMAN
B. Feb. 8, 1917, Piedmont, SC

Year	Team	Games	Pos.

Charlie Timmons *continued*
Clemson/Georgia 5'10" 210 lbs.

Year	Team	Games	Pos.
1946	BKN	AA	13	FB

Michael Timpson
TIMPSON, MICHAEL DWAIN
B. Jun. 6, 1967, Baxley, GA
Penn State 5'10" 175 lbs.

Year	Team	Games	Pos.
1989	NE	N	2	WR
1990			5	WR
1991			16	WR
1992			16	WR
1993			16	WR
1994			15	WR
1995	CHI	N	16	WR
1996			15	WR
8 yrs.	101 games		

Tim Tindale
TINDALE, TIM
B. Apr. 15, 1971, London, Ont.
Western Ontario 5'10" 220 lbs.

Year	Team	Games	Pos.
1995	BUF	N	16	RB
1996			14	RB
2 yrs.	30 games		

Mick Tingelhoff
TINGELHOFF, HENRY MICHAEL
B. May 22, 1940, Lexington, NE
Nebraska 6'1" 237 lbs.

Year	Team	Games	Pos.
1962	MIN	N	14	LB
1963			14	C
1964			14	C
1965			14	C
1966			14	C
1967			14	C
1968			14	C
1969			14	C
1970			14	C
1971			14	C
1972			14	C
1973			14	C
1974			14	C
1975			14	C
1976			14	C
1977			14	C
1978			16	C
17 yrs.	240 games		

Gerald Tinker
TINKER, GERALD ALEXANDER
B. Jan. 19, 1951, Miami, FL
Memphis State/Kent State 5'9" 173 lbs.

Year	Team	Games	Pos.
1974	ATL	N	13	WR
1975			8	WR
1975	GB	N	6	WR
2 yrs.	27 games		

Bob Tinsley
TINSLEY, ROBERT PORTER, JR.
(Buddy)
B. Aug. 16, 1924, Damon, TX
Baylor 6'4" 245 lbs.

Year	Team	Games	Pos.
1949	LA	AA	10	T

Gaynell Tinsley
TINSLEY, GAYNELL C. (Gus)
B. Feb. 1, 1915, Ruple, LA
Louisiana State 6'1" 198 lbs.

Year	Team	Games	Pos.
1937	CHIC	N	11	E
1938			11	E
1940			7	E
3 yrs.	29 games		

Jess Tinsley
TINSLEY, JESS D.
B. Aug. 4, 1906

Jess Tinsley *continued*
D. Apr., 1977, Blevins, AR
Louisiana State 6'0" 201 lbs.

Year	Team	Games	Pos.
1929	CHIC	N	12	T, E
1930			9	T
1931			6	T
1932			10	T
1933			11	T, E
5 yrs.	48 games		

Keith Tinsley
TINSLEY, KEITH
B. Mar. 31, 1965
Pittsburgh 5'9" 184 lbs.

Year	Team	Games	Pos.
1987	CLE	N	3	WR

Pete Tinsley
TINSLEY, ELIJAH POPE, JR.
B. Mar. 16, 1913, Sumter, SC
Georgia 5'8" 205 lbs.

Year	Team	Games	Pos.
1938	GB	N	8	G, B
1939			8	G
1940			7	G
1941			9	G, T
1942			9	G
1943			10	G
1944			10	G
1945			10	G
8 yrs.	71 games		

Scott Tinsley
TINSLEY, SCOTT
B. Nov. 14, 1959, Oklahoma City, OK
Southern California 6'2" 195 lbs.

Year	Team	Games	Pos.
1987	PHI	N	3	QB

Sid Tinsley
TINSLEY, SIDNEY W.
B. Aug. 16, 1924
Clemson 5'9" 168 lbs.

Year	Team	Games	Pos.
1945	PIT	N	9	HB

Andre Tippett
TIPPETT, ANDRE BERNARD
B. Dec. 27, 1959, Birmingham, AL
Iowa 6'3" 240 lbs.

Year	Team	Games	Pos.
1982	NE	N	9	LB
1983			15	LB
1984			16	LB
1985			16	LB
1986			11	LB
1987			13	LB
1988			12	LB
1990			13	LB
1991			16	LB
1992			14	LB
1993			16	LB
11 yrs.	151 games		

Kenny Tippins
TIPPINS, KEN
B. Jul. 22, 1966, Adel, GA
Middle Tennessee State 6'1" 229 lbs.

Year	Team	Games	Pos.
1989	DAL	N	6	LB
1990	ATL	N	16	LB
1991			16	LB
1992			16	LB
1993			14	LB
1994			16	LB
1995			16	LB
7 yrs.	100 games		

Dave Tipton
TIPTON, DAVID JOSEPH
B. Dec. 10, 1953, Superior, WI
Western Illinois 6'1" 253 lbs.

Year	Team	Games	Pos.
1975	NE	N	4	DT

Dave Tipton *continued*

Year	Team	Games	Pos.
1976			8	DT
2 yrs.	12 games		

Dave Tipton
TIPTON, DAVID LANCE
B. Apr. 23, 1949, Hollister, CA
Stanford 6'6" 242 lbs.

Year	Team	Games	Pos.
1971	NYG	N	5	DT
1972			14	DE
1973			6	DE
1974	SD	N	11	DE
1975			14	DE
1976	SEA	N	12	DE
6 yrs.	62 games		

Howie Tipton
TIPTON, HOWARD DURWARD
B. Apr. 19, 1911, Los Angeles, CA
D. Mar., 1966
Southern California 5'11" 186 lbs.

Year	Team	Games	Pos.
1933	CHIC	N	10	HB, G
1934			10	G, E
1935			8	G
1936			12	G, E
1937			11	QB
5 yrs.	51 games		

Rico Tipton
TIPTON, RICO
B. Jul. 31, 1961, Pittsburg, CA
Washington State 6'2" 240 lbs.

Year	Team	Games	Pos.
1987	SEA	N	3	LB

Bob Titchenal
TITCHENAL, ROBERT A.
B. Oct. 17, 1917, Ventura, CA
San Jose State 6'2" 194 lbs.

Year	Team	Games	Pos.
1940	WAS	N	10	C
1941			10	C
1942			10	C, E
1946	SF	AA	14	E
1947	LA	AA	14	E, C
5 yrs.	58 games		

Glen Titensor
TITENSOR, GLEN WESTON
B. Feb. 21, 1958, Bellflower, CA
UCLA/Brigham Young 6'4" 270 lbs.

Year	Team	Games	Pos.
1981	DAL	N	16	OT
1982			4	G
1983			15	C, G
1984			15	C
1985			16	G
1986			16	G
1988			10	G
7 yrs.	92 games		

Herb Titmas
TITMAS, HERBERT J.
B. 1907
Deceased
Syracuse 5'8" 165 lbs.

Year	Team	Games	Pos.
1931	PRO	N	10	QB, HB

Y.A. Tittle
TITTLE, YELBERTON
ABRAHAM (Ya-Ya, The Bald Eagle)
B. Oct. 24, 1926, Marshall, TX
Louisiana State 6'0" 182 lbs.

Year	Team	Games	Pos.
1948	BAL	AA	14	QB
1949			11	QB
1950	BAL	N	12	QB
1951	SF	N	12	QB
1952			12	QB
1953			10	QB
1954			12	QB

Y.A. Tittle *continued*

Year	Team	Games	Pos.
1955			12	QB
1956			10	QB
1957			12	QB
1958			11	QB
1959			10	QB
1960			9	QB
1961	NYG	N	13	QB
1962			14	QB
1963			13	QB
1964			14	QB
17 yrs.	201 games		

George Titus
TITUS, GEORGE T.
B. Jan. 7, 1922, Brooklyn, NY
Holy Cross 5'10" 185 lbs.

Year	Team	Games	Pos.
1946	PIT	N	11	C

Si Titus
TITUS, SILAS J.
B. Sep. 23, 1918, Brooklyn, NY
Deceased
Holy Cross 6'0" 195 lbs.

Year	Team	Games	Pos.
1940	BKN	N	4	C
1941			7	G, C
1942			9	G, C
1945	PIT	N	9	C
4 yrs.	29 games		

Casey Tiumalu
TIUMALU, CASEY
B. Jun. 19, 1961
Brigham Young 5'8" 206 lbs.

Year	Team	Games	Pos.
1987	LARM	N	3	RB

Robbie Tobeck
TOBECK, ROBBIE
B. Mar. 6, 1970, Tarpon Springs, FL
Washington State 6'4" 275 lbs.

Year	Team	Games	Pos.
1994	ATL	N	6	C
1995			16	G, C
1996			16	C
3 yrs.	38 games		

Dave Tobey
TOBEY, DAVID MORGAN
B. Mar. 17, 1943, Portland, OR
Oregon 6'3" 230 lbs.

Year	Team	Games	Pos.
1966	MIN	N	14	LB
1967			2	LB
1968	DEN	A	7	LB
3 yrs.	23 games		

Bill Tobin
TOBIN, WILLIAM
B. 1941
Missouri 5'11" 210 lbs.

Year	Team	Games	Pos.
1963	HOU	A	10	HB

Elgie Tobin
TOBIN, ELGIN W. (Yegg)
B. May, 1885
Deceased
Penn State 5'9" 160 lbs.

Year	Team	Games	Pos.
1920	AKR	A	1	QB
1921			8	QB
2 yrs.	9 games		

George Tobin
TOBIN, GEORGE EDWARD
B. 1921
Notre Dame 5'10" 205 lbs.

Year	Team	Games	Pos.
1947	NYG	N	11	G

Year	Team	Games	Pos.

Jimmy Tobin
TOBIN, JIMMY (Doc)
B. 1899
Deceased
None

1925	DUL	N	1	E

Leo Tobin
TOBIN, LEAMAN
B. Mar., 1890
Deceased
Grove City 5'9" 220 lbs.

1921	AKR	A	8	G

Steve Tobin
TOBIN, STEVE A.
B. Mar. 29, 1957, Breckenridge, MN
Minnesota 6'4" 258 lbs.

1980	NYG	N	4	C

Nelson Toburen
TOBUREN, NELSON
B. Nov. 24, 1938, Boulder, CO
Wichita State 6'3" 235 lbs.

1961	GB	N	14	LB
1962			10	LB
2 yrs.	24 games

Dick Todd
TODD, RICHARD S.
B. Oct. 2, 1914, Thrall, TX
Texas A&M 5'11" 172 lbs.

1939	WAS	N	10	HB
1940			10	HB
1941			7	FB
1942			10	FB
1945			6	HB
1946			9	HB
1947			11	HB
1948			12	HB
8 yrs.	75 games

Jim Todd
TODD, JAMES
B. Mar. 2, 1943, Wabash, IN
Ball State 5'11" 195 lbs.

1966	DET	N	10	RB

Larry Todd
TODD, LARRY
B. Oct. 7, 1942, Memphis, TN
Arizona State 6'1" 185 lbs.

1965	OAK	A	14	RB
1966			14	OE
1967			5	RB
1968			3	RB
1969			11	RB
1970	OAK	N	10	RB
6 yrs.	57 games

Richard Todd
TODD, RICHARD
B. Nov. 19, 1953, Birmingham, AL
Alabama 6'2" 210 lbs.

1976	NYJ	N	13	QB
1977			12	QB
1978			5	QB
1979			15	QB
1980			16	QB
1981			16	QB
1982			9	QB
1983			16	QB
1984	NO	N	15	QB
1985			2	QB
10 yrs.	119 games

Jeff Toews
TOEWS, JEFFREY MARK
B. Nov. 4, 1957, San Jose, CA
Washington 6'3" 255 lbs.

1979	MIA	N	11	OT
1980			7	G
1981			9	G
1982			9	G
1983			8	G
1984			16	G
1985			11	G, C
7 yrs.	71 games

Loren Toews
TOEWS, LOREN JAMES
B. Nov. 3, 1951, Dinuba, CA
California 6'3" 220 lbs.

1973	PIT	N	14	LB
1974			14	LB
1975			14	LB
1976			14	LB
1977			14	LB
1978			11	LB
1979			11	LB
1980			16	LB
1981			16	LB
1982			9	LB
1983			16	LB
11 yrs.	149 games

Joe Tofflemire
TOFFLEMIRE, JOSEPH SALVATORE
B. Jul. 7, 1965, Los Angeles, CA
Arizona 6'2" 274 lbs.

1990	SEA	N	16	C
1992			16	C
1994			1	C
3 yrs.	33 games

Joe Tofil
TOFIL, JOSEPH J.
B. Mar. 15, 1918, Campbell, OH
D. May, 1973
Indiana 6'1" 205 lbs.

1942	BKN	N	11	E, B

Brendan Toibin
TOIBIN, BRENDAN
B. Feb. 2, 1964, Columbia, SC
Richmond 6'0" 205 lbs.

1987	WAS	N	1	K

Charley Tolar
TOLAR, CHARLES (Tuna)
B. Sep. 5, 1937
Northwestern State (Louisiana) 5'7" 199 lbs.

1960	HOU	A	14	FB
1961			14	FB
1962			14	FB
1963			14	FB
1964			14	FB
1965			11	FB
1966			14	FB
7 yrs.	95 games

Jim Tolbert
TOLBERT, LOVE JAMES
B. Mar. 12, 1944, Fairfield, AL
Lincoln (Missouri) 6'3" 207 lbs.

1966	SD	A	1	DB
1967			14	DB
1968			12	DB
1969			4	CB
1970	SD	N	14	CB
1971			12	S
1972	HOU	N	4	CB

Jim Tolbert continued

1973	STL	N	13	S
1974			12	S, CB
1975			14	CB, S
1976	SD	N	4	CB
11 yrs.	104 games

Tony Tolbert
TOLBERT, TONY LEWIS
B. Dec. 29, 1967, Tuskegee, AL
Texas-El Paso 6'6" 261 lbs.

1989	DAL	N	16	DE
1990			16	DE
1991			16	DE
1992			16	DE
1993			16	DE
1994			16	DE
1995			16	DE
1996			16	DE
8 yrs.	128 games

Ken Toler
TOLER, KENNETH PACK
B. Apr. 9, 1959, Greenville, MS
Mississippi 6'2" 195 lbs.

1981	NE	N	16	WR
1982			9	WR
2 yrs.	25 games

Alvin Toles
TOLES, ALVIN
B. Mar. 23, 1963, Barnesville, GA
Tennessee 6'1" 227 lbs.

1985	NO	N	16	LB
1986			16	LB
1987			12	LB
1988			11	LB
4 yrs.	55 games

Stuart Tolle
TOLLE, STUART
B. Feb. 7, 1962, Columbus, OH
Bowling Green 6'3" 245 lbs.

1987	DET	N	1	NT

Charlie Tollefson
TOLLEFSON, CHARLES W.
B. Feb. 28, 1917, Elk Point, SD
D. Aug. 20, 1989, Green Bay, WI
Iowa 6'0" 215 lbs.

1944	GB	N	6	G
1945			9	G
1946			2	G
3 yrs.	17 games

Tommy Tolleson
TOLLESON, THOMAS
B. Jan. 30, 1943, Birmingham, AL
Alabama 6'0" 185 lbs.

1966	ATL	N	8	FL

Ed Tolley
TOLLEY, EDGAR A.
B. 1902, Ohio
Deceased
None 175 lbs.

1929	DAY	N	1	G

Billy Joe Tolliver
TOLLIVER, BILLY JOE
B. Feb. 7, 1966, Dallas, TX
Texas Tech 6'1" 218 lbs.

1989	SD	N	5	QB
1990			15	QB
1991	ATL	N	7	QB
1992			9	QB

Billy Joe Tolliver continued

1993			7	QB
1994	HOU	N	11	QB
6 yrs.	54 games

Mel Tom
TOM, MELVIN M.
B. Aug. 4, 1941, Honolulu, HI
Hawaii/San Jose State 6'4" 247 lbs.

1967	PHI	N	14	DE
1968			14	DE
1969			14	DE
1970			14	DE
1971			14	DE
1972			14	DE
1973			4	DE
1973	CHI	N	5	DE
1974			14	DE
1975			6	DE
9 yrs.	113 games

Army Tomaini
TOMAINI, AMADEO FREDERICK
B. Feb. 5, 1918, Long Branch, NJ
Catawba 6'0" 235 lbs.

1945	NYG	N	8	T

Johnny Tomaini
TOMAINI, JOHN
B. Jul. 19, 1902, Long Branch, NJ
D. Jul., 1985, Spring Lake, NJ
Georgetown (DC) 6'0" 195 lbs.

1929	ORA	N	11	E
1930	NEW	N	11	E, T
1930	BKN	N	2	E
1931			8	E, QB
3 yrs.	32 games

Lou Tomasetti
TOMASETTI, LOUIS VINCENT (Babe)
B. Jan. 8, 1916, Old Forge, PA
Bucknell 6'0" 198 lbs.

1939	PIT	N	11	HB
1940			10	HB
1941	DET	N	4	HB
1941	PHI	N	6	HB
1942			10	FB
1946	BUF	AA	14	HB
1947			13	HB
1948			14	HB
1949			12	HB
8 yrs.	94 games

Andy Tomasic
TOMASIC, ANDREW JOHN
B. Dec. 10, 1919, Hokendauqua, PA
Temple 6'0" 175 lbs.

1942	PIT	N	11	HB
1946			4	HB
2 yrs.	15 games

Pat Tomberlin
TOMBERLIN, HOWARD PATRICK
B. Jan. 29, 1966, Jacksonville, FL
Florida State 6'2" 312 lbs.

1990	IND	N	16	OT
1993	TB	N	2	G, OT
2 yrs.	18 games

Mike Tomczak
TOMCZAK, MICHAEL
B. Oct. 23, 1962, Calumet City, IL
Ohio State 6'1" 196 lbs.

1985	CHI	N	6	QB
1986			13	QB

Mike Tomczak *continued*

Year	Team		Games	Pos.
1987			12	QB
1988			14	QB
1989			16	QB
1990			16	QB
1991	GB	N	12	QB
1992	CLE	N	12	QB
1993	PIT	N	7	QB
1994			6	QB
1995			7	QB
1996			16	QB
12 yrs.	137 games			

Tommy Tomlin
TOMLIN, JOHN THOMAS
(Dowie)
B. Sep., 1893, Virginia
D. May 11, 1953, Woodstock, NY
Syracuse 5'10" 196 lbs.

Year	Team		Games	Pos.
1920	AKR	A	9	G
1921			6	G
1921	HAM	A	2	G
1922	MIL	N	5	G
1925	NYG	N	9	G, T
1926			4	G
5 yrs.	34 games			

Dick Tomlinson
TOMLINSON, RICHARD
B. Aug. 5, 1928
Kansas 6'1" 205 lbs.

Year	Team		Games	Pos.
1950	PIT	N	11	G
1951			12	G
2 yrs.	23 games			

Clarence Tommerson
TOMMERSON, CLARENCE L.
B. Apr. 8, 1915, La Crosse, WI
Wisconsin 6'2" 196 lbs.

Year	Team		Games	Pos.
1938	PIT	N	3	HB, FB
1939			1	B
2 yrs.	4 games			

Bob Toneff
TONEFF, ROBERT
B. Jun. 23, 1930, Detroit, MI
Notre Dame 6'2" 260 lbs.

Year	Team		Games	Pos.
1952	SF	N	12	T
1954			10	T
1955			11	T
1956			12	G, T
1957			12	T
1958			12	E
1959	WAS	N	12	T
1960			12	T
1961			14	DT
1962			14	DT
1963			14	DT
1964			14	DT
12 yrs.	149 games			

Mario Tonelli
TONELLI, MARIO GEORGE
(Motts)
B. Mar. 28, 1917, Lemont, IL
Notre Dame 5'11" 200 lbs.

Year	Team		Games	Pos.
1940	CHIC	N	9	FB

Tony Tonelli
TONELLI, AMERIGO
B. Sep. 1, 1917
D. Jan. 30, 1987, Newport Beach, CA
Southern California 6'0" 210 lbs.

Year	Team		Games	Pos.
1939	DET	N	9	C, G

Ed Toner
TONER, EDWARD W.

Ed Toner *continued*

B. Sep. 11, 1944, Reading, MA
Massachusetts 6'3" 250 lbs.

Year	Team		Games	Pos.
1967	BOS	A	14	DT
1968			5	DT, LB
1969			9	DT
3 yrs.	28 games			

Ed Toner
TONER, EDWARD WILLIAM
B. Mar. 22, 1968, Lynn, MA
Boston College 6'0" 240 lbs.

Year	Team		Games	Pos.
1992	IND	N	8	RB
1993			16	RB
1994			9	RB
3 yrs.	33 games			

Tom Toner
TONER, THOMAS EDWARD
B. Jan. 25, 1950, Woburn, MA
Idaho State 6'3" 233 lbs.

Year	Team		Games	Pos.
1973	GB	N	14	LB
1975			14	LB
1976			11	LB
1977			14	LB
4 yrs.	53 games			

Anthony Toney
TONEY, ANTHONY
B. Sep. 23, 1962, Salinas, CA
Texas A&M 6'0" 227 lbs.

Year	Team		Games	Pos.
1986	PHI	N	12	RB
1987			11	FB
1988			15	RB
1989			14	RB
1990			15	RB
5 yrs.	67 games			

Marco Tongue
TONGUE, MARCO CHARLES
B. Apr. 6, 1960, Annapolis, MD
Bowie State 5'9" 174 lbs.

Year	Team		Games	Pos.
1983	BAL	N	7	CB

Reggie Tongue
TONGUE, REGINALD CLINTON
B. Apr. 11, 1973, Baltimore, MD
Oregon State 6'0" 201 lbs.

Year	Team		Games	Pos.
1996	KC	N	16	CB

Clayton Tonnemaker
TONNEMAKER, FRANK CLAYTON
B. Jun. 8, 1928, Ogilvie, MN
Deceased
Minnesota 6'2" 237 lbs.

Year	Team		Games	Pos.
1950	GB	N	12	C
1953			12	C
1954			12	C
3 yrs.	36 games			

Charley Toogood
TOOGOOD, CHARLES WAYNE
B. Jul. 16, 1927
Nebraska 6'0" 232 lbs.

Year	Team		Games	Pos.
1951	LA		8	T
1952			10	T
1953			12	T
1954			12	T
1955			12	T
1956			7	T
1957	CHIC	N	6	G, T
7 yrs.	67 games			

Pat Toomay
TOOMAY, PATRICK JAY

Pat Toomay *continued*

B. May 17, 1945, Pomona, CA
Vanderbilt 6'4" 245 lbs.

Year	Team		Games	Pos.
1970	DAL	N	14	DE
1971			14	DE
1972			14	DE
1973			14	DE
1974			14	DE
1975	BUF	N	14	DE
1976	TB	N	14	DE
1977	OAK	N	14	DE
1978			16	DE
1979			14	DE
10 yrs.	142 games			

Amani Toomer
TOOMER, AMANI
B. Sep. 8, 1974, Berkeley, CA
Michigan 6'3" 202 lbs.

Year	Team		Games	Pos.
1996	NYG	N	7	WR

Al Toon
TOON, AL LEE, JR.
B. Apr. 30, 1963, Newport News, VA
Wisconsin 6'4" 205 lbs.

Year	Team		Games	Pos.
1985	NYJ	N	15	WR
1986			16	WR
1987			12	WR
1988			15	WR
1989			11	WR
1990			14	WR
1991			15	WR
1992			9	WR
8 yrs.	107 games			

Chief Toorock
TOOROCK, CHIEF
B. 1902
Deceased
New York University 5'9" 180 lbs.

Year	Team		Games	Pos.
1926	BKN	N	1	HB

Jeff Tootle
TOOTLE, JEFF
None

Year	Team		Games	Pos.
1987	NYG	N	3	LB

Ted Topor
TOPOR, TED R.
B. May 1, 1930, East Chicago, IN
Michigan 6'1" 210 lbs.

Year	Team		Games	Pos.
1955	DET	N	6	LB

Bob Topp
TOPP, EUGENE ROBERT
B. Apr. 22, 1932, Kalamazoo, MI
Michigan 6'2" 190 lbs.

Year	Team		Games	Pos.
1954	NYG	N	6	E

Stacey Toran
TORAN, STACEY J.
B. Nov. 10, 1961, Indianapolis, IN
D. 1989
Notre Dame 6'2" 200 lbs.

Year	Team		Games	Pos.
1984	LARI	N	16	S
1985			16	S
1986			16	S
1987			12	S
1988			12	S
5 yrs.	72 games			

LaVerne Torczon
TORCZON, LAVERNE
B. Jan. 1, 1936, Columbus, NE
Nebraska 6'2" 243 lbs.

Year	Team		Games	Pos.
1960	BUF	A	14	DE

LaVerne Torczon *continued*

Year	Team		Games	Pos.
1961			14	DE
1962			4	DE
1962	NY	A	10	DE
1963			14	DE
1964			14	DE
1965			14	DE
1966	MIA	A	14	DE
7 yrs.	98 games			

LaVern Torgeson
TORGESON, LAVERN EARL
B. Feb. 28, 1929, Lacrosse, WA
Washington State 6'0" 215 lbs.

Year	Team		Games	Pos.
1951	DET	N	12	C
1952			12	C
1953			11	C
1954			12	C, LB
1955	WAS	N	11	C
1956			12	C
1957			12	C
7 yrs.	82 games			

Eric Torkelson
TORKELSON, ERIC GROVE
B. Mar. 3, 1952, Burnt Hills, NY
Connecticut 6'2" 196 lbs.

Year	Team		Games	Pos.
1974	GB	N	14	RB
1975			14	RB
1976			14	RB
1977			14	RB
1978			14	RB
1979			14	RB
1981			8	RB
7 yrs.	92 games			

Jack Torrence
TORRENCE, JACK (Baby Jack)
B. Jun. 20, 1913
D. Nov. 10, 1969
Louisiana State 6'3" 285 lbs.

Year	Team		Games	Pos.
1939	CHIB	N	8	T, G
1940			7	T, G
2 yrs.	15 games			

Gino Torretta
TORRETTA, GINO LOUIS
B. Aug. 10, 1970, Pinole Valley, CA
Miami (Florida) 6'2" 215 lbs.

Year	Team		Games	Pos.
1993	MIN	N	1	QB
1996	SEA	N	2	QB
2 yrs.	3 games			

Bob Torrey
TORREY, ROBERT
B. Jan. 30, 1957, Ceres, NY
Penn State 6'4" 231 lbs.

Year	Team		Games	Pos.
1979	NYG	N	6	RB
1979	MIA	N	7	FB
1980	PHI	N	1	FB
2 yrs.	14 games			

Fran Toscani
TOSCANI, FRANCIS (Bud)
B. Apr. 19, 1909
D. Jun., 1966
St. Mary's (California) 5'10" 168 lbs.

Year	Team		Games	Pos.
1932	BKN	N	3	HB
1932	CHIC	N	3	HB
1 yr.	6 games			

Flavio Tosi
TOSI, FLAVIO JOSEPH
B. Apr. 30, 1912, Beverly, MA
Boston College 6'1" 191 lbs.

Year	Team		Games	Pos.
1934	BOS	N	9	E
1935			11	E

Year	Team	Games	Pos.

Flavio Tosi continued

Year	Team		Games	Pos.
1936			7	E
3 yrs.	27 games			

Johnny Tosi
TOSI, JOHN
B. 1915
Niagara 5'10" 225 lbs.

Year	Team		Games	Pos.
1939	PIT	N	3	C, G
1939	BKN	N	1	G
1944	PHI	N	1	T
2 yrs.	5 games			

Tom Toth
TOTH, THOMAS JEFFREY
B. May 23, 1962, Chicago, IL
Western Michigan 6'5" 279 lbs.

Year	Team		Games	Pos.
1986	MIA	N	13	OT
1987			12	OT
1988			9	G
1989			16	G
1990	SD	N	1	G
5 yrs.	51 games			

Zollie Toth
TOTH, ZOLLIE ANTHONY
(Tugboat)
B. Jan. 26, 1924, Pocahontas, VA
Louisiana State 6'2" 218 lbs.

Year	Team		Games	Pos.
1950	NYY	N	11	B
1951			10	B
1952	DAL	N	12	FB
1954	BAL	N	12	FB
4 yrs.	45 games			

Willie Totten
TOTTEN, WILLIE
B. Jul. 4, 1962, Leflore, MS
Mississippi Valley State 6'2" 195 lbs.

Year	Team		Games	Pos.
1987	BUF	N	2	QB

Darrell Toussaint
TOUSSAINT, DARRELL
B. Oct. 3, 1958, Chicago, IL
Northwestern State (Louisiana) 6'0" 175 lbs.

Year	Team		Games	Pos.
1987	NO	N	2	CB, S

Steve Tovar
TOVAR, STEVEN ERIC
B. Apr. 25, 1970, Elyria, OH
Ohio State 6'3" 244 lbs.

Year	Team		Games	Pos.
1993	CIN	N	16	LB
1994			16	LB
1995			14	LB
1996			13	LB
4 yrs.	59 games			

Steve Towle
TOWLE, STEPHEN RICHARDS
B. Oct. 23, 1953, Kansas City, KS
Kansas 6'2" 233 lbs.

Year	Team		Games	Pos.
1975	MIA	N	14	LB
1976			14	LB
1977			1	LB
1978			13	LB
1979			16	LB
1980			9	LB
6 yrs.	67 games			

Dan Towler
TOWLER, DANIEL LEE (Deacon Dan)
B. Mar. 6, 1928, Donora, PA
Washington & Jefferson 6'2" 225 lbs.

Year	Team		Games	Pos.
1950	LA	N	12	FB

Dan Towler continued

Year	Team		Games	Pos.
1951			12	FB
1952			12	FB
1953			12	FB
1954			12	FB
1955			7	FB
6 yrs.	67 games			

Willie Townes
TOWNES, WILLIE CARROLL
B. Jul. 21, 1943, Hattiesburg, MS
Tulsa 6'5" 263 lbs.

Year	Team		Games	Pos.
1966	DAL	N	13	DT
1967			14	DE, DT
1968			5	DE
1970	NO	N	6	DT
4 yrs.	38 games			

Bobby Towns
TOWNS, ROBERT
B. Mar. 17, 1938, Elberton, GA
Georgia 6'1" 180 lbs.

Year	Team		Games	Pos.
1960	STL	N	4	HB
1961	BOS	A	2	DB
2 yrs.	6 games			

Morris Towns
TOWNS, MORRIS
B. Jan. 10, 1954, St. Louis, MO
Missouri 6'4" 270 lbs.

Year	Team		Games	Pos.
1977	HOU	N	1	OT
1978			16	OT
1979			16	OT
1980			16	OT
1981			16	OT, G
1982			9	OT, G
1983			14	OT
1984	WAS	N	4	OT
8 yrs.	92 games			

JoJo Townsell
TOWNSELL, JOSEPH RAY
B. Nov. 4, 1960, Reno, NV
UCLA 5'9" 180 lbs.

Year	Team		Games	Pos.
1985	NYJ	N	16	WR
1986			14	WR
1987			12	WR
1988			16	WR
1989			16	WR
1990			9	WR
6 yrs.	83 games			

Andre Townsend
TOWNSEND, ANDRE
B. Oct. 8, 1962, Chicago, IL
Mississippi 6'3" 265 lbs.

Year	Team		Games	Pos.
1984	DEN	N	16	NT
1985			16	DE, NT
1986			16	DE, NT
1987			12	DE, NT
1988			16	DE, NT
1989			13	DE, NT
1990			15	DE, NT
7 yrs.	104 games			

Brian Townsend
TOWNSEND, BRIAN LEWIS
B. Nov. 7, 1968, Cincinnati, OH
Cincinnati 6'3" 242 lbs.

Year	Team		Games	Pos.
1992	CIN	N	3	RB

Curtis Townsend
TOWNSEND, CURTIS
B. Jan. 20, 1955, Montgomery, AL
Arkansas 6'1" 229 lbs.

Year	Team		Games	Pos.
1978	STL	N	9	LB

Greg Townsend
TOWNSEND, GREG
B. Nov. 3, 1961, Los Angeles, CA
Texas Christian 6'3" 262 lbs.

Year	Team		Games	Pos.
1983	LARI	N	16	DE
1984			16	DE
1985			16	DE
1986			15	DE
1987			13	DE
1988			16	DE
1989			16	LB, DE
1990			16	DE
1991			16	DE
1992			14	DE
1993			16	DE
1994	PHI	N	16	DE
12 yrs.	186 games			

Otto Townsend
TOWNSEND, OTTO
None 190 lbs.

Year	Team		Games	Pos.
1922	MIN	N	2	T, G

John Tracey
TRACEY, JOHN JOSEPH
B. Jun. 27, 1933, Philadelphia, PA
D. Sep. 18, 1978, Medford Lakes, NJ
Texas A&M 6'3" 225 lbs.

Year	Team		Games	Pos.
1959	CHIC	N	8	OE
1960	STL	N	12	LB
1961	PHI	N	9	OE
1962	BUF	A	12	LB, OE
1963			14	LB
1964			14	LB
1965			14	LB
1966			14	LB
1967			13	LB
9 yrs.	110 games			

Tom Tracy
TRACY, JOHN THOMAS (The Bomb)
B. Sep. 7, 1934, Birmingham, AL
Tennessee 5'9" 205 lbs.

Year	Team		Games	Pos.
1956	DET	N	4	FB
1957			9	FB
1958	PIT	N	12	HB
1959			12	HB
1960			12	FB, HB
1961			14	HB
1962			4	HB
1963			6	HB
1963	WAS	N	8	HB
1964			14	HB
9 yrs.	95 games			

George Trafton
TRAFTON, GEORGE (Beast)
B. Dec. 6, 1896, Chicago, IL
D. Sep. 5, 1971, Los Angeles, CA
Notre Dame 6'1" 231 lbs.

Year	Team		Games	Pos.
1920	DEC	A	8	C
1921			10	C
1923	CHIB	N	13	C
1924			11	C
1925			15	C
1926			15	C
1927			14	C
1928			9	C
1929			11	C
1930			14	C, G
1931			11	C
1932			10	C
12 yrs.	141 games			

John Trahan
TRAHAN, JOHN
B. Apr. 19, 1961, Grand Forks, ND
Southern Colorado 5'9" 160 lbs.

Year	Team		Games	Pos.
1987	KC	N	3	WR

Mike Trainor
TRAINOR, MICHAEL J.
B. Dec. 18, 1899, New York State
D. Apr., 1980, Lake Success, NY
Canisius 5'9" 165 lbs.

Year	Team		Games	Pos.
1923	BUF	N	12	HB, QB
1924			11	HB
2 yrs.	23 games			

Allen Trammell
TRAMMELL, ALLEN
B. Jul. 19, 1942
Florida 6'0" 190 lbs.

Year	Team		Games	Pos.
1966	HOU	A	3	DB

Steve Trapilo
TRAPILO, STEPHEN PAUL
B. Sep. 20, 1964, Boston, MA
Boston College 6'5" 290 lbs.

Year	Team		Games	Pos.
1987	NO	N	11	G
1988			9	G
1989			16	G
1990			16	G
1992			5	G
5 yrs.	57 games			

James Trapp
TRAPP, JAMES HAROLD
B. Dec. 28, 1969, Greenville, SC
Clemson 6'0" 180 lbs.

Year	Team		Games	Pos.
1993	LARI	N	14	CB
1994			16	CB
1995	OAK	N	14	CB
1996			12	CB
4 yrs.	56 games			

Richard Trapp
TRAPP, RICHARD
B. Sep. 21, 1946, Lynwood, CA
Florida 6'1" 174 lbs.

Year	Team		Games	Pos.
1968	BUF	A	14	OE
1969	SD	A	8	WR
2 yrs.	22 games			

Orville Trask
TRASK, ORVILLE
B. 1935
Rice 6'4" 250 lbs.

Year	Team		Games	Pos.
1960	HOU	A		DT
1961			14	DT
1962	OAK	A	7	DT
3 yrs.	21 games			

Herb Travenio
TRAVENIO, HERBERT
B. 1931
none 6'0" 218 lbs.

Year	Team		Games	Pos.
1964	SD	A	3	K
1965			14	K
2 yrs.	17 games			

Ed Travis
TRAVIS, J. EDWARD (Brick)
B. Jul. 17, 1897
D. Sep. 18, 1982, St. Louis, MO
Tarkio/Missouri 6'1" 205 lbs.

Year	Team		Games	Pos.
1921	RI	A	4	T
1923	STL	N	7	T
2 yrs.	11 games			

Leslie Travis
TRAVIS, LESLIE M.
Syracuse

Year	Team		Games	Pos.
1921	SYR	A	2	E

Year	Team	Games	Pos.

John Travis
TRAVIS, JOHN
B. Aug. 23, 1943, San Jose, CA
San Jose State 6'1" 216 lbs.

1966	SD	A	6	K

Mack Travis
TRAVIS, MACK
B. Jul. 3, 1970, Las Vegas, NV
California 6'1" 280 lbs.

1993	DET	N	4	NT

Keith Traylor
TRAYLOR, BYRON KEITH
B. Sep. 3, 1969, Malvern, AR
Oklahoma/Central Oklahoma 6'2" 260 lbs.

1991	DEN	N	16	LB
1992			16	LB
1993	GB	N	5	LB
1995	KC	N	16	DT
1996			15	DT
5 yrs.	68 games			

Jerry Traynham
TRAYNHAM, JERRY FRANCIS
B. Jan. 23, 1939
Southern California 5'10" 190 lbs.

1961	DEN	A	2	HB

Wade Traynham
TRAYNHAM, WADE LANIER
B. Feb. 3, 1942, Hampton, VA
Frederick 6'2" 218 lbs.

1966	ATL	N	2	K
1967			14	K
2 yrs.	16 games			

Mark Traynowicz
TRAYNOWICZ, MARK JOSEPH
B. Nov. 20, 1962, Omaha, NE
Nebraska 6'5" 277 lbs.

1985	BUF	N	14	OT, G
1986			16	G
1987			11	G
1988			4	G
1988	PHX	N	5	G
1989			2	OT
5 yrs.	52 games			

Barney Traynor
TRAYNOR, BERNARD P.
B. Nov. 24, 1896
D. Aug. 26, 1980
Colgate 6'1" 190 lbs.

1925	MIL	N	5	C

John Treadway
TREADWAY, JOHN CHARLES
B. Aug. 21, 1920, Berings, TX
Hardin-Simmons 6'5" 258 lbs.

1948	NYG	N	12	T
1949	DET	N	7	T
2 yrs.	19 games			

David Treadwell
TREADWELL, DAVID MARK
B. Feb. 27, 1965, Columbia, SC
Clemson 6'1" 175 lbs.

1989	DEN	N	16	K
1990			16	K
1991			16	K
1992			16	K
1993	NYG	N	16	K
1994			13	K
6 yrs.	93 games			

Herb Treat
TREAT, C. HERBERT
B. Dec. 16, 1900, Cambridge, MA
Deceased
Boston College/Princeton 6'0" 190 lbs.

1926	BOS	A	5	T

Ivan Trebotich
TREBOTICH, IVAN PETER (Buzz)
B. Dec. 30, 1920, Oakland, CA
D. Aug. 4, 1992, Napa, CA
St. Mary's (California) 5'10" 208 lbs.

1944	DET	N	6	DB
1945			9	LB
1947	BAL	AA	2	LB
3 yrs.	17 games			

Brian Treggs
TREGGS, BRIAN
B. Jun. 11, 1970, Los Angeles, CA
California 5'9" 161 lbs.

1992	SEA	N	2	WR

Greg Tremble
TREMBLE, GREGORY DESHAWN
B. Apr. 16, 1972, Warner Robins, GA
Georgia 5'11" 188 lbs.

1995	DAL	N	7	S
1995	PHI	N	4	S
1 yr.	11 games			

Jack Triggs
TRIGGS, JOHN
B. Jan. 11, 1903
Providence 6'0" 200 lbs.

1926	PRO	N	2	FB

Frank Trigillo
TRIGILLO, FRANK J.
B. 1919
Alfred/Vermont 5'11" 200 lbs.

1946	LA	AA	1	FB
1946	MIA	AA	7	FB
1 yr.	8 games			

Steve Trimble
TRIMBLE, STEVEN GARFIELD
B. May 11, 1958, Cumberland, MD
Maryland 5'10" 181 lbs.

1981	DEN	N	3	CB, S
1982			6	CB
1983			5	S
1987	CHI	N	3	S, CB
4 yrs.	17 games			

Wayne Trimble
TRIMBLE, WAYNE ALLEN
B. Dec. 10, 1944, Cullman, AL
Alabama 6'3" 203 lbs.

1967	SF	N	1	DB

Bill Triplett
TRIPLETT, WILLIAM CLARENCE
B. May 4, 1940, Shaw, MS
Miami (Ohio) 6'2" 212 lbs.

1962	STL	N	13	HB, FB
1963			13	HB
1965			14	HB
1966			8	HB
1967	NYG	N	11	RB
1968	DET	N	12	RB
1969			14	RB
1970			14	RB
1971			14	RB

Bill Triplett continued

1972			14	RB
10 yrs.	127 games			

Mel Triplett
TRIPLETT, MELVIN
B. Dec. 24, 1931, Indianola, MS
Toledo 6'1" 215 lbs.

1955	NYG	N	12	FB
1956			12	FB
1957			10	FB
1958			12	FB
1959			11	FB
1960			12	FB
1961	MIN	N	14	FB
1962			14	FB
8 yrs.	97 games			

Wally Triplett
TRIPLETT, WALLACE, III
B. Apr. 18, 1926, La Mott, PA
Penn State 5'10" 175 lbs.

1949	DET	N	11	HB
1950			7	HB
1952	CHIC	N	2	HB
1953			4	HB
4 yrs.	24 games			

Paul Tripoli
TRIPOLI, PAUL RANDALL
B. Dec. 14, 1961, Utica, NY
Alabama 6'0" 197 lbs.

1987	TB	N	13	S

Charley Trippi
TRIPPI, CHARLES LOUIS
B. Dec. 14, 1922, Pittston, PA
Georgia 6'0" 186 lbs.

1947	CHIC	N	11	HB
1948			12	HB
1949			12	HB
1950			12	HB
1951			12	HB
1952			12	HB
1953			12	HB
1954			12	HB
1955			5	HB
9 yrs.	100 games			

John Tripson
TRIPSON, JOHN ROBERT
B. Sep. 17, 1919, Madero, TX
Mississippi State 6'3" 210 lbs.

1941	DET	N	11	T

Frank Tripucka
TRIPUCKA, FRANCIS JOSEPH
B. Dec. 8, 1927, Bloomfield, NJ
Notre Dame 6'2" 192 lbs.

1949	DET	N	6	QB
1950	CHIC	N	11	QB
1951			3	QB
1952			2	QB
1952	DAL	N	6	QB
1960	DEN	A	14	QB
1961			14	QB
1962			14	QB
1963			2	QB
8 yrs.	72 games			

Rick Trocano
TROCANO, RICK CHARLES
B. Apr. 4, 1959, Cleveland, OH
Pittsburgh 6'0" 188 lbs.

1981	CLE	N	6	QB
1982			2	QB
2 yrs.	8 games			

Bob Trocolor
TROCOLOR, ROBERT G.
B. Mar. 31, 1919, Oak Hill, TX
D. Jul. 27, 1984, Franklin Lakes, NJ
Alabama/Long Island 6'2" 207 lbs.

1942	NYG	N	7	B
1943			5	B
1944	BKN	N	2	B
3 yrs.	14 games			

Gene Trosch
TROSCH, EUGENE L.
B. Jun. 7, 1945, Steubenville, OH
Miami (Florida) 6'7" 277 lbs.

1967	KC	A	14	DE
1969			13	DE
2 yrs.	27 games			

Milt Trost
TROST, MILTON FRANK (Bud)
B. Mar. 4, 1913, Detroit, MI
D. Apr. 2, 1986, Zephyrsville, FL
Marquette 6'1" 206 lbs.

1935	CHIB	N	4	T
1936			10	T
1937			10	T, G
1938			10	T
1939			9	T
1940	PHI	N	7	T
6 yrs.	50 games			

Bill Troup
TROUP, PAUL WILLIAM, III
B. Apr. 2, 1952, Pittsburgh, PA
Virginia/South Carolina 6'5" 218 lbs.

1974	BAL	N	1	QB
1976			14	QB
1977			14	QB
1978			12	QB
1980	GB	N	2	QB
5 yrs.	43 games			

David Trout
TROUT, DAVID MARSHALL
B. Nov. 12, 1957, Mount Pleasant, PA
Pittsburgh 5'6" 165 lbs.

1981	PIT	N	16	K
1987			3	K
2 yrs.	19 games			

Ray Trowbridge
TROWBRIDGE, RAYMOND
B. Nov. 25, 1895
D. Nov., 1966, Venice, CA
Boston College/Purdue 170 lbs.

1920	CLE	A	2	E
1921	NY	A	2	E
2 yrs.	4 games			

Billy Truax
TRUAX, WILLIAM FREDERICK
B. Jul. 15, 1943, Gulfport, MS
Louisiana State 6'5" 238 lbs.

1964	LA	N	10	OE
1965			14	OE
1966			14	TE
1967			14	TE
1968			14	TE
1969			14	TE
1970			14	TE
1971	DAL	N	12	TE
1972			6	TE
1973			2	TE
10 yrs.	114 games			

Dalton Truax
TRUAX, DALTON

Year	Team		Games	Pos.

Dalton Truax continued

B. Jan. 17, 1935, New Orleans, LA
Tulane 6'2" 235 lbs.

Year	Team		Games	Pos.
1960	OAK	A		OT

Ken Truckenmiller

TRUCKENMILLER, KENNETH
B. Oct. 14, 1903
D. Apr. 29, 1973
Cornell (Iowa) 6'1" 190 lbs.

Year	Team		Games	Pos.
1926	RI	A	3	G

Jack Trudeau

TRUDEAU, JACK FRANCIS
B. Sep. 9, 1962, Forest Lake, MN
Illinois 6'3" 213 lbs.

Year	Team		Games	Pos.
1986	IND	N	12	QB
1987			10	QB
1988			2	QB
1989			13	QB
1990			6	QB
1991			2	QB
1992			11	QB
1993			5	QB
1994	NYJ	N	5	QB
1995	CAR	N	1	QB

10 yrs. 67 games

Hal Truesdell

TRUESDELL, HAROLD
B. 1907
D. 1932
Hamline 6'0" 200 lbs.

Year	Team		Games	Pos.
1930	MIN	N	1	T

Dave Truitt

TRUITT, DAVID
B. Feb. 18, 1964
North Carolina 6'4" 232 lbs.

Year	Team		Games	Pos.
1987	WAS	N	1	TE

Greg Truitt

TRUITT, GREG
B. Dec. 8, 1965, Sarasota, FL
Penn State 6'0" 235 lbs.

Year	Team		Games	Pos.
1994	CIN	N	16	C
1995			16	C
1996			16	C

3 yrs. 48 games

Olanda Truitt

TRUITT, OLANDA
B. Jan. 4, 1971, Birmingham, AL
Pittsburgh/Mississippi State 6'0" 186 lbs.

Year	Team		Games	Pos.
1993	MIN	N	8	WR
1994	WAS	N	9	WR
1995			5	WR
1996	OAK	N	10	WR

4 yrs. 32 games

Don Trull

TRULL, DONALD DEAN
B. Oct. 20, 1941, Oklahoma City, OK
Baylor 6'1" 189 lbs.

Year	Team		Games	Pos.
1964	HOU	A	14	QB
1965			14	QB
1966			14	QB
1967			3	QB
1967	BOS	A	10	QB
1968	HOU	A	11	QB
1969			14	QB

6 yrs. 80 games

Bob Trumpy

TRUMPY, ROBERT T., JR. (Trump)
B. Mar. 6, 1945, Springfield, IL

Bob Trumpy continued

Illinois/Utah 6'6" 226 lbs.

Year	Team		Games	Pos.
1968	CIN	A	14	SE
1969			14	WR, TE
1970	CIN	N	11	TE
1971			14	TE
1972			12	TE
1973			14	TE
1974			13	TE
1975			11	TE
1976			13	TE
1977			14	TE

10 yrs. 130 games

Eric Truvillion

TRUVILLION, ERIC
B. Jun. 18, 1959, New York, NY
Florida A&M 6'4" 205 lbs.

Year	Team		Games	Pos.
1987	DET	N	3	WR

Eddie Tryon

TRYON, JOSEPH EDWARD
B. Jul. 25, 1900, Medford, MA
D. May 1, 1982, St. Petersburg, FL
Colgate 5'8" 180 lbs.

Year	Team		Games	Pos.
1926	NY	A	12	HB, FB
1927	NYY	A	14	HB, FB, QB

2 yrs. 26 games

Chalmers Tschappatt

TSCHAPPATT, JOHN CHALMERS
B. Jun., 1896
Deceased
West Virginia Wesleyan 5'11" 180 lbs.

Year	Team		Games	Pos.
1921	DAY	A	2	T

John Tsoutsouvas

TSOUTSOUVAS, JOHN SAMUEL
B. Oct. 8, 1917, Madera, CA
Oregon State 6'0" 205 lbs.

Year	Team		Games	Pos.
1940	DET	N	3	C, G

Lou Tsoutsouvas

TSOUTSOUVAS, LOUIS SAMUEL
B. Jul. 4, 1915, Fresno, CA
Stanford 5'11" 210 lbs.

Year	Team		Games	Pos.
1938	PIT	N	4	C

Esera Tuaolo

TUAOLO, ESERA TAVAI
B. Jul. 11, 1968, Honolulu, HI
Oregon State 6'2" 284 lbs.

Year	Team		Games	Pos.
1991	GB	N	16	NT
1992			4	NT
1992	MIN	N	5	DT
1993			11	DT
1994			16	NT
1995			16	NT
1996			14	DT

6 yrs. 82 games

Natu Tuatagaloa

TUATAGALOA, GERARDUS MAURITIUS NATUITASINA
B. May 25, 1966, San Francisco, CA
California 6'4" 274 lbs.

Year	Team		Games	Pos.
1989	CIN	N	14	NT
1990			16	DE
1991			16	DE
1992	SEA	N	14	DE
1993			16	DE
1995	HOU	N	2	DE

6 yrs. 78 games

Jerry Tubbs

TUBBS, GERALD
B. Jan. 23, 1935, Throckmorton, TX
Oklahoma 6'2" 221 lbs.

Year	Team		Games	Pos.
1957	CHIC	N	11	C
1958			7	LB
1958	SF	N	4	LB
1959			12	LB
1960	DAL	N	12	LB
1961			14	LB
1962			13	LB
1963			14	LB
1964			13	LB
1965			14	LB
1966			4	LB

10 yrs. 118 games

Winfred Tubbs

TUBBS, WINFRED O'NEAL
B. Sep. 24, 1970, Hollywood, FL
Texas 6'4" 250 lbs.

Year	Team		Games	Pos.
1994	NO	N	13	LB
1995			7	LB
1996			16	LB

3 yrs. 36 games

Bill Tucker

TUCKER, BILL
B. Sep. 14, 1943, Union, SC
Tennessee State 6'2" 221 lbs.

Year	Team		Games	Pos.
1967	SF	N	14	RB
1968			14	RB
1969			13	RB, TE
1970			14	RB
1971	CHI	N	14	RB

5 yrs. 69 games

Bob Tucker

TUCKER, ROBERT LOUIS, SR.
B. Jun. 8, 1945, Hazleton, PA
Bloomsburg State 6'3" 230 lbs.

Year	Team		Games	Pos.
1970	NYG	N	14	TE
1971			12	TE
1972			14	TE
1973			14	TE
1974			13	TE
1975			13	TE
1976			14	TE
1977			5	TE
1977	MIN	N	8	TE
1978			16	TE
1979			16	TE
1980			16	TE

11 yrs. 155 games

Erroll Tucker

TUCKER, ERROLL R.
B. Jul. 6, 1964, Pittsburgh, PA
Utah 5'8" 170 lbs.

Year	Team		Games	Pos.
1988	BUF	N	9	CB, S
1989			4	CB, S
1989	NE	N	5	CB

2 yrs. 18 games

Gary Tucker

TUCKER, GARY
B. Feb. 19, 1945, Shelbyville, TN
Tennessee-Chattanooga 5'11" 195 lbs.

Year	Team		Games	Pos.
1968	MIA	A	14	RB

Mark Tucker

TUCKER, MARK
B. Apr. 29, 1968, Spokane, WA
Southern California 6'3" 290 lbs.

Year	Team		Games	Pos.
1994	ARI	N	16	G

Travis Tucker

TUCKER, TRAVIS TYRONE
B. Sep. 19, 1963, Brooklyn, NY
Southern Connecticut State 6'3" 240 lbs.

Year	Team		Games	Pos.
1985	CLE	N	16	TE
1986			16	TE
1987			4	TE

3 yrs. 36 games

Wendell Tucker

TUCKER, WENDELL EDWARD
B. Sep. 4, 1943, Philadelphia, PA
South Carolina State 5'10" 185 lbs.

Year	Team		Games	Pos.
1967	LA	N	7	OE
1968			10	OE
1969			14	WR
1970			12	WR

4 yrs. 43 games

Phil Tuckett

TUCKETT, PHILIP
B. Apr. 27, 1946, Eugene, OR
Weber State 6'0" 180 lbs.

Year	Team		Games	Pos.
1968	SD	A	1	OE

Dick Tuckey

TUCKEY, RICHARD
B. Sep. 29, 1914
D. Dec., 1974, Naugatuck, CT
Manhattan 6'2" 205 lbs.

Year	Team		Games	Pos.
1938	WAS	N	3	FB
1938	CLE	N	4	HB

1 yr. 7 games

Anthony Tuggle

TUGGLE, ANTHONY IVAN
B. Sep. 13, 1963, Baker, LA
Southern University/Nicholls State 6'1" 211 lbs.

Year	Team		Games	Pos.
1985	PIT	N	2	DB
1987			2	CB

2 yrs. 4 games

Jessie Tuggle

TUGGLE, JESSIE LLOYD
B. Feb. 14, 1965, Spalding County, GA
Valdosta State 5'11" 226 lbs.

Year	Team		Games	Pos.
1987	ATL	N	12	LB
1988			16	LB
1989			16	LB
1990			16	LB
1991			16	LB
1992			15	LB
1993			16	LB
1994			16	LB
1995			16	LB
1996			16	LB

10 yrs. 155 games

John Tuggle

TUGGLE, JOHN
B. Jan. 31, 1961, Honolulu, HI
California 6'1" 210 lbs.

Year	Team		Games	Pos.
1983	NYG	N	16	RB

Manu Tuiasosopo

TUIASOSOPO, MANU'ULA ASOVALU
B. Aug. 30, 1957, Los Angeles, CA
UCLA 6'3" 260 lbs.

Year	Team		Games	Pos.
1979	SEA	N	16	DT
1980			16	DT
1981			16	DT

Year	Team	Games	Pos.

Manu Tuiasosopo *continued*

Year	Team		Games	Pos.
1982			9	DT
1983			16	NT
1984	**SF**	N	16	NT
1985			15	NT
1986			15	NT

8 yrs.   119 games

Navy Tuiasosopo
TUIASOSOPO, NAVY ASOAOGA
B. May 24, 1965, American Samoa
Utah State 6'2" 285 lbs.

1987	**LARM**	N	3	RB

Mark Tuinei
TUINEI, MARK PULEMAU
B. Mar. 31, 1960, Nanakuli, HI
UCLA/Hawaii 6'5" 291 lbs.

1983	**DAL**	N	10	DT
1984			16	DT
1985			16	C
1986			16	C
1987			8	C
1988			5	C
1989			16	C
1990			13	OT
1991			12	OT
1992			15	OT
1993			15	OT
1994			15	OT
1995			16	OT
1996			15	OT

14 yrs.   189 games

Tom Tuinei
TUINEI, TUMUA
B. Feb. 21, 1958, Oceanside, CA
Hawaii 6'4" 250 lbs.

1980	**DET**	N	12	DT

Peter Tuipulotu
TUIPULOTU, PETER
B. Feb. 20, 1969, Nukualofa, Tonga
Islands
Brigham Young 5'11" 210 lbs.

1992	**SD**	N	6	RB

Walter Tullis
TULLIS, WALTER
B. Apr. 12, 1953, Americus, GA
Delaware State 6'0" 170 lbs.

1978	**GB**	N	16	WR
1979			16	WR

2 yrs.   32 games

Willie Tullis
TULLIS, WILLIE
B. Apr. 5, 1958, Newville, AL
Southern Mississippi/Troy State 6'0" 190 lbs.

1981	**HOU**	N	16	CB
1982			9	CB, S
1983			16	CB
1984			16	CB
1985	**NO**	N	14	CB
1986			7	CB
1987	**IND**	N	12	CB
1988			16	CB

8 yrs.   106 games

Darrell Tully
TULLY, DARRELL DEAN
B. Dec. 14, 1917, Henryetta, OK
East Texas State 6'1" 200 lbs.

1939	**DET**	N	9	QB, HB

George Tully
TULLY, GEORGE C.
B. Mar. 12, 1904
D. May 1, 1980, Worcester, MA
Dartmouth 5'10" 180 lbs.

1926	**PHI**	A	10	E
1927	**FRA**	N	1	E

2 yrs.   11 games

Tom Tumulty
TUMULTY, THOMAS PATRICK
B. Feb. 11, 1973, Penn Hills, PA
Pittsburgh 6'2" 242 lbs.

1996	**CIN**	N	16	LB

Emlen Tunnell
TUNNELL, EMLEN LEWIS (The Gremlin)
B. Mar. 29, 1925, Bryn Mawr, PA
D. Jul. 22, 1975, Pleasantville, NY
Toledo/Iowa 6'1" 193 lbs.

1948	**NYG**	N	8	HB, DB
1949			12	HB, DB
1950			12	DB
1951			12	DB
1952			12	DB
1953			12	DB
1954			12	DB
1955			12	DB
1956			12	DB
1957			12	DB
1958			12	DB
1959	**GB**	N	12	DB
1960			12	DB
1961			13	DB

14 yrs.   165 games

Tom Tupa
TUPA, THOMAS JOSEPH
B. Feb. 6, 1966, Cleveland, OH
Ohio State 6'4" 220 lbs.

1988	**PHX**	N	2	QB, P
1989			13	QB, P
1990			15	QB, P
1991			11	QB, P
1992	**IND**	N	3	QB, P
1994	**CLE**	N	16	P
1995			16	P
1996	**NE**	N	16	P

8 yrs.   92 games

Jeff Tupper
TUPPER, JEFF
B. Dec. 26, 1962, Joplin, MO
Oklahoma 6'5" 269 lbs.

1986	**PHI**	N	3	DE
1987	**DEN**	N	4	NT

2 yrs.   7 games

Frank Turbert
TURBERT, FRANCIS
B. Sep. 7, 1918
D. Aug., 1987, Hollywood, FL
Duke/Morris Harvey 5'11" 200 lbs.

1944	**BOS**	N	5	HB

Dan Turk
TURK, DANIEL ANTHONY
B. Jun. 25, 1962, Milwaukee, WI
Drake/Wisconsin 6'4" 286 lbs.

1985	**PIT**	N	1	C
1986			16	C
1987	**TB**	N	13	C
1988			12	C
1989	**LARI**	N	16	C
1990			16	C
1991			16	C
1992			16	C

Dan Turk *continued*

1993			16	C
1994			16	C
1995	**OAK**	N	16	C
1996			16	C

12 yrs.   170 games

Godwin Turk
TURK, GODWIN LEE
B. Oct. 15, 1950, Houston, TX
California/Southern University 6'3" 230 lbs.

1975	**NYJ**	N	14	LB
1976	**DEN**	N	13	LB
1977			13	LB
1978			16	LB

4 yrs.   56 games

Matt Turk
TURK, MATT
B. Jun. 16, 1968, Greenfield, WI
Wisconsin-Whitewater 6'5" 230 lbs.

1995	**WAS**	N	16	P
1996			16	P

2 yrs.   32 games

Doug Turley
TURLEY, DOUGLAS P.
B. Nov. 25, 1918, Nanticoke, PA
D. Nov. 1, 1992, Wilmington, DE
Scranton 6'2" 215 lbs.

1944	**WAS**	N	7	E
1945			10	E
1946			10	E
1947			12	E
1948			12	E

5 yrs.   51 games

John Turley
TURLEY, JOHN
B. Nov. 20, 1912, Delaware, OH
D. Jul., 1977, Dayton, OH
Ohio Wesleyan 5'10" 183 lbs.

1935	**PIT**	N	10	QB
1936			4	QB

2 yrs.   14 games

Guy Turnbow
TURNBOW, GUY
B. Mar. 28, 1908
D. Oct., 1975, Oxford, MS
Mississippi 6'2" 217 lbs.

1933	**PHI**	N	9	T, E
1934			2	T

2 yrs.   11 games

Jesse Turnbow
TURNBOW, JESSE
B. Oct. 8, 1956, Cincinnati, OH
Tennessee 6'7" 272 lbs.

1978	**CLE**	N	16	DT

Renaldo Turnbull
TURNBULL, RENALDO ANTONIO
B. Jan. 5, 1966, St. Thomas, Virgin Islands
West Virginia 6'4" 252 lbs.

1990	**NO**	N	16	DE
1991			16	DE
1992			14	DE
1993			15	DE
1994			16	DE
1995			15	DE
1996			12	DE

7 yrs.   104 games

Bake Turner
TURNER, BAKE
B. Jul. 22, 1940, Apine, TX
Texas Tech 6'0" 180 lbs.

1962	**BAL**	N	14	HB
1963	**NY**	A	14	OE
1964			14	OE
1965			13	OE
1966			14	OE
1967			8	OE
1968			13	OE
1969			14	WR
1970	**BOS**	N	14	WR

9 yrs.   118 games

Bill Turner
TURNER, WILLIAM
B. Mar. 5, 1960
Boston College 6'4" 245 lbs.

1987	**NE**	N	2	DE
1990	**MIA**	N	14	DE
1991			13	DE
1992			16	DE

4 yrs.   45 games

Buff Turner
TURNER, MILTON
B. Jan., 1891, Maryland
Deceased
None 188 lbs.

1921	**WAS**	A	3	T

Bulldog Turner
TURNER, CLYDE D.
B. Mar. 10, 1919, Sweetwater, TX
Hardin-Simmons 6'1" 237 lbs.

1940	**CHIB**	N	11	C
1941			11	C
1942			11	C
1943			10	C
1944			10	C
1945			2	C
1946			11	C
1947			12	C
1948			12	C
1949			12	C
1950			12	C
1951			12	C
1952			12	T

13 yrs.   138 games

Calvin Turner
TURNER, CALVIN EUGENE
B. Apr. 10, 1960, Fairmont, WV
West Virginia 6'4" 270 lbs.

1987	**TB**	N	3	LB

Cecil Turner
TURNER, CECIL ANGELO
B. Apr. 2, 1944, Washington, DC
California Poly (San Luis Obispo) 5'10" 172 lbs.

1968	**CHI**	N	14	WR
1969			9	WR
1970			14	WR
1971			14	WR
1972			14	WR
1973			11	WR

6 yrs.   76 games

Clem Turner
TURNER, CLEMENT
B. May 28, 1945, Cincinnati, OH
Cincinnati 6'1" 238 lbs.

1969	**CIN**	A	14	RB
1970	**DEN**	N	11	RB
1971			14	RB
1972			12	RB

4 yrs.   51 games

Year	Team	Games	Pos.

Daryl Turner
TURNER, DARYL
B. Dec. 15, 1961, Wadley, GA
Michigan State 6'3" 196 lbs.

Year	Team		Games	Pos.
1984	SEA	N	16	WR
1985			16	WR
1986			15	WR
1987			12	WR
4 yrs.		59 games		

Deacon Turner
TURNER, DAVID
B. Jan. 2, 1955, Jackson, MS
San Diego State 5'11" 211 lbs.

Year	Team		Games	Pos.
1978	CIN	N	16	RB
1979			16	RB
1980			12	RB
3 yrs.		44 games		

Dwain Turner
TURNER, DWAIN FITZGERALD
B. Oct. 7, 1964, Houston, TX
Rice 6'0" 290 lbs.

Year	Team		Games	Pos.
1987	HOU	N	1	NT

Eric Turner
TURNER, ERIC RAY
B. Sep. 20, 1968, Ventura, CA
UCLA 6'1" 207 lbs.

Year	Team		Games	Pos.
1991	CLE	N	8	S
1992			15	S
1993			16	S
1994			16	S
1995			8	S
1996	BAL	N	14	S
6 yrs.		77 games		

Floyd Turner
TURNER, FLOYD
B. May 29, 1966, Shreveport, LA
Northwestern State (Louisiana) 5'11" 188 lbs.

Year	Team		Games	Pos.
1989	NO	N	13	WR
1990			16	WR
1991			16	WR
1992			2	WR
1993			10	WR
1994	IND	N	16	WR
1995			14	WR
1996	BAL	N	11	WR
8 yrs.		98 games		

Hal Turner
TURNER, HAROLD
B. 1930
Tennessee State 6'2" 235 lbs.

Year	Team		Games	Pos.
1954	DET	N	3	E

Herschel Turner
TURNER, HERSCHEL
B. Jun. 17, 1942, Houston, KY
Kentucky 6'3" 230 lbs.

Year	Team		Games	Pos.
1964	STL	N	14	G
1965			13	G, OT
2 yrs.		27 games		

Jay Turner
TURNER, JAY LEWIS
B. Jul. 11, 1914, Springfield, MO
D. Nov., 1960
George Washington 5'10" 202 lbs.

Year	Team		Games	Pos.
1938	WAS	N	8	QB, HB
1939			8	HB
2 yrs.		16 games		

Jim Turner
TURNER, JAMES BAYARD
B. Mar. 28, 1941, Martinez, CA
Utah State 6'2" 206 lbs.

Year	Team		Games	Pos.
1964	NY	A	14	K
1965			14	K, QB
1966			14	K, QB
1967			14	K
1968			14	K, QB
1969			14	K, QB
1970	NYJ	N	14	K, QB
1971	DEN	N	14	K
1972			14	K
1973			14	K
1974			14	K
1975			14	K
1976			14	K
1977			14	K
1978			16	K
1979			16	K
16 yrs.		228 games		

Jim Turner
TURNER, JAMES (Buddy)
B. Apr. 18, 1899
D. Jun., 1971, Chicago, IL
Northwestern 5'8" 165 lbs.

Year	Team		Games	Pos.
1923	MIL	N	3	HB

Jim Turner
TURNER, JAMES K.
B. Jan. 14, 1912
Oklahoma State 6'2" 210 lbs.

Year	Team		Games	Pos.
1937	CLE	N	7	C

Jimmie Turner
TURNER, JIMMIE
B. Feb. 16, 1962, Vienna, GA
Presbytarian 6'2" 215 lbs.

Year	Team		Games	Pos.
1984	DAL	N	5	LB

Jimmy Turner
TURNER, JIMMY LEE
B. Jun. 15, 1959, Sherman, TX
UCLA 6'0" 187 lbs.

Year	Team		Games	Pos.
1983	CIN	N	16	CB
1984			16	CB
1985			16	CB
1986			8	CB
1986	ATL	N	6	CB
1987			2	CB
5 yrs.		64 games		

John Turner
TURNER, JOHN (Tiny)
B. 1895
Deceased
Ohio State 6'0" 190 lbs.

Year	Team		Games	Pos.
1920	DAY	A	7	G, C
1921	ROC	A	1	T
2 yrs.		8 games		

John Turner
TURNER, JOHN, JR.
B. Feb. 22, 1956, Miami, FL
Miami (Florida) 6'0" 199 lbs.

Year	Team		Games	Pos.
1978	MIN	N	14	CB
1979			16	CB
1980			16	CB
1981			13	CB
1982			9	CB
1983			16	CB
1984	SD	N	15	DB
1985	MIN	N	15	CB
1987			2	CB, S
9 yrs.		116 games		

J.T. Turner
TURNER, JAMES DENIS
B. Apr. 17, 1953, Moultrie, GA
Duke 6'3" 251 lbs.

Year	Team		Games	Pos.
1977	NYG	N	13	DT
1978			16	G
1979			16	G
1980			16	G
1981			16	G
1982			9	G
1983			16	G
1984	WAS	N	1	G, OT
8 yrs.		103 games		

Keena Turner
TURNER, KEENA
B. Oct. 22, 1958, Chicago, IL
Purdue 6'2" 211 lbs.

Year	Team		Games	Pos.
1980	SF		16	LB
1981			16	LB
1982			9	LB
1983			15	LB
1984			16	LB
1985			15	LB
1986			16	LB
1987			10	LB
1988			11	LB
1989			13	LB
1990			16	LB
11 yrs.		153 games		

Kevin Turner
TURNER, KEVIN RAY
B. Feb. 5, 1958, Fremont, CA
Pacific 6'2" 225 lbs.

Year	Team		Games	Pos.
1980	NYG	N	3	LB
1981	WAS	N	4	LB
1981	SEA	N	8	LB
1982	CLE	N	8	LB
3 yrs.		23 games		

Kevin Turner
TURNER, PAUL KEVIN
B. Jun. 12, 1969, Prattville, AL
Alabama 6'0" 224 lbs.

Year	Team		Games	Pos.
1992	NE	N	16	RB
1993			16	RB
1994			16	RB
1995	PHI	N	2	RB
1996			16	FB
5 yrs.		66 games		

Marcus Turner
TURNER, MARCUS JARED
B. Jan. 13, 1966, Harbor City, CA
UCLA 6'0" 190 lbs.

Year	Team		Games	Pos.
1989	PHX	N	14	DB
1990			16	CB, S
1991			3	CB, S
1992	NYJ	N	16	CB, S
1993			16	CB, S
1994			16	CB
1995			6	CB
7 yrs.		87 games		

Maurice Turner
TURNER, MAURICE ANTOINE
B. Sep. 10, 1960, Salt Lake City, UT
Utah State 5'11" 200 lbs.

Year	Team		Games	Pos.
1984	MIN	N	13	RB
1985			10	RB
1987	NYJ	N	2	RB
3 yrs.		25 games		

Mike Turner
TURNER, JERRY MICHAEL
B. Sep. 10, 1960, Oceanside, CA
Louisiana State 6'3" 255 lbs.

Year	Team		Games	Pos.
1987	MIN	N	2	CB, S

Nate Turner
TURNER, NATE
B. May 28, 1969, Chicago, IL
Nebraska 6'1" 255 lbs.

Year	Team		Games	Pos.
1993	BUF	N	13	RB
1994			13	RB
1995	CAR	N	2	RB
3 yrs.		28 games		

Odessa Turner
TURNER, ODESSA
B. Oct. 12, 1964, Monroe, LA
Northwestern State (Louisiana) 6'3" 205 lbs.

Year	Team		Games	Pos.
1987	NYG	N	7	WR
1988			4	WR
1989			13	WR
1990			4	WR
1991			16	WR
1992	SF	N	16	WR
1993			7	WR
7 yrs.		67 games		

Rich Turner
TURNER, RICHARD JUNIOR
B. Feb. 14, 1959, Hugo, OK
Oklahoma 6'2" 260 lbs.

Year	Team		Games	Pos.
1981	GB	N	16	NT
1982			9	NT
1983			6	NT
3 yrs.		31 games		

Ricky Turner
TURNER, RICKY
B. May 14, 1962, Harbor City, CA
Washington State 6'0" 190 lbs.

Year	Team		Games	Pos.
1988	IND	N	4	QB

Robert Turner
TURNER, ROBERT D.
B. Mar. 6, 1954, Wynnewood, OK
Oklahoma State 5'11" 200 lbs.

Year	Team		Games	Pos.
1978	HOU	N	4	RB

Rocky Turner
TURNER, HARLEY
B. Aug. 6, 1950, Augusta, GA
Tennessee-Chattanooga 6'0" 195 lbs.

Year	Team		Games	Pos.
1972	NYJ	N	8	WR
1973			13	WR
2 yrs.		21 games		

Sam Turner
TURNER, SAMUEL (Bumps)
B. Apr. 16, 1902, Richardson, TX
D. Aug., 1976, Windsor, VA
None 170 lbs.

Year	Team		Games	Pos.
1921	WAS	A	2	G

Scott Turner
TURNER, SCOTT
B. Feb. 26, 1972, Richardson, TX
Illinois 5'9" 178 lbs.

Year	Team		Games	Pos.
1995	WAS	N	16	CB
1996			16	CB
2 yrs.		32 games		

T.J. Turner
TURNER, THOMAS JAMES
B. May 16, 1963, Lufkin, TX
Houston 6'4" 276 lbs.

Year	Team		Games	Pos.
1986	MIA	N	16	NT
1987			12	DE
1988			16	DE
1989			14	DE
4 yrs.		58 games		

Vernon Turner
TURNER, VERNON MAURICE
B. Jna. 6, 1967, Brooklyn, NY
Carson-Newman 5'8" 185 lbs.

Year	Team		Games	Pos.
1990	BUF	N	1	WR
1991	LARM	N	15	WR
1992			12	WR
1993	DET	N	7	WR
1993	TB	N	1	WR
1994			13	RB
1995	DET	N	6	RB
6 yrs.	55 games			

Vince Turner
TURNER, VINCENT
B. 1943
Missouri 5'11" 190 lbs.

Year	Team		Games	Pos.
1964	NY	A	6	DB

Wylie Turner
TURNER, WYLIE
B. Apr. 19, 1957, Dallas, TX
Angelo State 5'10" 182 lbs.

Year	Team		Games	Pos.
1979	GB	N	12	DB
1980			16	CB, S
1985			3	RB
3 yrs.	31 games			

Tom Turnure
TURNURE, THOMAS WILLIAM
B. Jul. 9, 1957, Seattle, WA
Washington 6'4" 253 lbs.

Year	Team		Games	Pos.
1980	DET	N	3	C
1981			16	C
1982			9	C
1983			16	C
1985			6	G, C
1986			13	G, C
6 yrs.	63 games			

Miles Turpin
TURPIN, MILES JOHN
B. May 15, 1964, Minneapolis, MN
California 6'4" 232 lbs.

Year	Team		Games	Pos.
1986	GB	N	1	LB
1987	TB	N	3	LB
2 yrs.	4 games			

Willie Turral
TURRAL, WILLIE
B. Feb. 1, 1964, Tallahassee, FL
New Mexico 5'10" 190 lbs.

Year	Team		Games	Pos.
1987	PHI	N	1	RB

Silvio Tursi
TURSI, SILVIO V.
B. Jan. 4, 1901
Muhlenberg 5'7" 165 lbs.

Year	Team		Games	Pos.
1926	NEW		3	E

Melvin Tuten
TUTEN, MELVIN EUGENE
B. Nov. 11, 1971, Washington, DC
Syracuse 6'6" 305 lbs.

Year	Team		Games	Pos.
1995	CIN	N	16	OT
1996			16	OT
2 yrs.	32 games			

Rick Tuten
TUTEN, RICHARD LAMAR
B. Jan. 5, 1965, Perry, FL
Miami (Florida)/Florida State 6'2" 220 lbs.

Year	Team		Games	Pos.
1989	PHI	N	2	P
1990	BUF	N	14	P
1991	SEA	N	10	P

Rick Tuten continued

Year	Team		Games	Pos.
1992			16	P
1993			16	P
1994			16	P
1995			16	P
1996			16	P
8 yrs.	106 games			

Tom Tutson
TUTSON, THOMAS
B. May 20, 1958, Jacksonville, FL
South Carolina State 6'1" 180 lbs.

Year	Team		Games	Pos.
1983	ATL	N	10	CB

George Tuttle
TUTTLE, GEORGE K.
B. Jan. 14, 1905, Minneapolis, MN
D. Oct., 1986, Minneapolis, MN
Minnesota 5'11" 180 lbs.

Year	Team		Games	Pos.
1927	GB	N	1	E

Orville Tuttle
TUTTLE, JAMES ORVILLE
B. Sep. 18, 1912, Licking, MO
Phillips/Oklahoma State 5'9" 210 lbs.

Year	Team		Games	Pos.
1937	NYG	N	11	G
1938			11	G
1939			11	G
1940			11	G
1941			11	G
1946			5	G
6 yrs.	60 games			

Perry Tuttle
TUTTLE, PERRY WARREN
B. Aug. 2, 1959, Lexington, NC
Clemson 6'0" 178 lbs.

Year	Team		Games	Pos.
1982	BUF	N	7	WR
1983			9	WR
1984	TB	N	3	WR
1984	ATL	N	5	WR
3 yrs.	24 games			

Frank Twedell
TWEDELL, FRANCIS
B. May 29, 1917
D. May, 1969
Minnesota 5'11" 220 lbs.

Year	Team		Games	Pos.
1939	GB	N	3	G, B

Rodney Tweet
TWEET, RODNEY
B. Feb. 20, 1964
South Dakota 6'1" 195 lbs.

Year	Team		Games	Pos.
1987	CIN	N	2	WR

Howard Twilley
TWILLEY, HOWARD JAMES, JR.
B. Dec. 25, 1943, Houston, TX
Tulsa 5'10" 183 lbs.

Year	Team		Games	Pos.
1966	MIA	A	6	SE
1967			14	OE
1968			14	OE
1969			4	WR
1970	MIA	N	14	WR
1971			14	WR
1972			13	WR
1973			6	WR
1974			13	WR
1975			14	WR
1976			8	WR
11 yrs.	120 games			

Darren Twombly
TWOMBLY, DARREN

Darren Twombly continued
B. May 14, 1965
Boston College 6'4" 270 lbs.

Year	Team		Games	Pos.
1987	NE	N	1	C

Andre Tyler
TYLER, ANDRE MIGUEL
B. Jul. 17, 1959, Tucson, AZ
Stanford 6'0" 180 lbs.

Year	Team		Games	Pos.
1983	TB	N	14	WR

Maurice Tyler
TYLER, MAURICE MICHAEL
B. Jul. 19, 1950, Baltimore, MD
Morgan State 6'0" 189 lbs.

Year	Team		Games	Pos.
1972	BUF	N	14	S
1973	DEN	N	14	DB
1974			14	S
1975	SD	N	13	S
1976	DET	N	9	S
1977	NYJ	N	14	CB
1978	NYG	N	8	S
7 yrs.	86 games			

Pete Tyler
TYLER, PETER
B. 1914
Hardin-Simmons 5'11" 190 lbs.

Year	Team		Games	Pos.
1937	CHIC	N	6	HB, QB
1938			9	QB, HB
2 yrs.	15 games			

Rob Tyler
TYLER, ROBERT
B. Oct. 12, 1965, Savannah, GA
South Carolina State 6'5" 257 lbs.

Year	Team		Games	Pos.
1989	SEA	N	9	TE

Toussaint Tyler
TYLER, TOUSSAINT L'OVERTURE
B. Mar. 19, 1959, Los Angeles, CA
Washington 6'2" 220 lbs.

Year	Team		Games	Pos.
1981	NO	N	15	RB
1982			2	RB
2 yrs.	17 games			

Wendell Tyler
TYLER, WENDELL AVERY
B. May 20, 1955, Shreveport, LA
UCLA 5'10" 205 lbs.

Year	Team		Games	Pos.
1977	LA	N	14	RB
1978			2	RB
1979			16	RB
1980			4	RB
1981			15	RB
1982	LARM	N	9	RB
1983	SF	N	14	RB
1984			16	RB
1985			13	RB
1986			5	RB
10 yrs.	108 games			

Rich Tylski
TYLSKI, RICHARD LEE
B. Feb. 27, 1971, San Diego, CA
Utah State 6'5" 309 lbs.

Year	Team		Games	Pos.
1996	JAC	N	16	G

Scott Tyner
TYNER, SCOTT
B. Apr. 11, 1972, Houston, TX
Oklahoma State 6'1" 189 lbs.

Year	Team		Games	Pos.
1994	ATL	N	6	P, K

Layne Tynes
TYNES, DAVID LAYNE (Buddy, Cowboy)
B. Feb. 26, 1902
D. Nov. 28, 1984, Anchorage, AK
Texas 6'0" 185 lbs.

Year	Team		Games	Pos.
1924	COL	N	6	FB, HB
1925			8	HB, FB
2 yrs.	14 games			

Jim Tyree
TYREE, JAMES E.
B. 1922
Oklahoma 6'3" 204 lbs.

Year	Team		Games	Pos.
1948	BOS	N	12	E

Jim Tyrer
TYRER, JAMES EFFLO
B. Feb. 25, 1939, Newark, OH
Ohio State 6'6" 283 lbs.

Year	Team		Games	Pos.
1961	DAL	A	14	OT
1962			14	OT
1963	KC	A	14	OT
1964			14	OT
1965			14	OT
1966			14	OT
1967			14	OT
1968			14	OT
1969			14	OT
1970	KC	N	14	OT
1971			14	OT
1972			14	OT
1973			12	OT
1974	WAS	N	14	OT
14 yrs.	194 games			

Joe Tyrrell
TYRRELL, JOSEPH P.
B. Apr. 6, 1929, Philadelphia, PA
D. Jun. 10, 1994, Philadelphia, PA
Temple 5'11" 216 lbs.

Year	Team		Games	Pos.
1952	PHI	N	2	G

Tim Tyrrell
TYRRELL, TIMOTHY G.
B. Feb. 19, 1961, Chicago, IL
Northern Illinois 6'1" 204 lbs.

Year	Team		Games	Pos.
1984	ATL	N	11	RB
1985			16	RB
1986			3	RB
1986	LARM	N	6	RB
1987			11	RB
1988			12	RB
1989	PIT	N	7	RB
6 yrs.	66 games			

Dick Tyson
TYSON, RICHARD HAL
B. Jan. 5, 1943, Kansas City, MO
Tulsa 6'2" 245 lbs.

Year	Team		Games	Pos.
1966	OAK	A	3	G
1967	DEN	A	7	G
2 yrs.	10 games			

Mitch Ucovich
UCOVICH, MITCHELL A.
B. Jan. 27, 1915, San Jose, CA
D. Dec. 1, 1989, San Jose, CA
San Jose State 5'11" 208 lbs.

Year	Team		Games	Pos.
1944	WAS	N	9	G, T
1945	CHIC	N	1	T
2 yrs.	10 games			

Keith Uecker
UECKER, RICHARD KEITH
B. Jun. 29, 1960, Hollywood, FL
Auburn 6'5" 260 lbs.

Year	Team		Games	Pos.
1982	DEN	N	5	G

Year	Team		Games	Pos.

Keith Uecker *continued*

Year	Team		Games	Pos.
1983			16	OT
1984	**GB**	N	6	OL
1985			8	G, OT
1987			8	OL
1988			16	G, OT
1990			13	G, OT
1991			14	OT

8 yrs.   86 games

Rocky Ugoccioni
UGOCCIONI, ENRICO
B. Apr. 19, 1918, New London, CT
Murray State 6'0" 195 lbs.

| 1944 | **BKN** | N | 10 | E |

Jeff Uhlenhake
UHLENHAKE, JEFFREY ALAN
B. Jan. 28, 1966, Indianapolis, IN
Ohio State 6'3" 282 lbs.

1989	**MIA**	N	16	C
1990			16	C
1991			13	C
1992			13	C
1993			5	C
1994	**NO**	N	16	C
1995			14	C
1996	**WAS**	N	12	C

8 yrs.   105 games

Steve Uhrinyak
UHRINYAK, STEVEN J.
B. 1915
Franklin & Marshall 6'2" 218 lbs.

| 1939 | **WAS** | N | 1 | G |

Eddie Ulinski
ULINSKI, EDWARD FRANKLIN
B. Dec. 7, 1919, Pittsburgh, PA
Marshall 5'11" 203 lbs.

1946	**CLE**	AA	14	G
1947			14	G
1948			14	G
1949			12	G

4 yrs.   54 games

Harry Ulinski
ULINSKI, HARRY JOHN
B. Apr. 4, 1925, Pittsburgh, PA
Kentucky 6'4" 229 lbs.

1950	**WAS**	N	12	C
1951			12	C
1953			12	C
1954			12	C
1955			12	C
1956			12	C

6 yrs.   72 games

Jiggs Ullery
ULLERY, WILLIAM W.
B. 1897
D. Dec. 20, 1989, Harrisburg, PA
Penn State 6'0" 200 lbs.

| 1922 | **DAY** | N | 7 | HB, FB |

Mike Ulmer
ULMER, MICHAEL WALTER
B. Dec. 28, 1954, York, NE
Doane 6'0" 190 lbs.

| 1980 | **CHI** | N | 3 | S |
| 1987 | **PHI** | N | 1 | CB, S |

2 yrs.   4 games

Chuck Ulrich
ULRICH, CHARLES, JR.
B. Dec. 14, 1929, Chicago, IL

Chuck Ulrich *continued*
Illinois 6'4" 243 lbs.

1954	**CHIC**	N	11	T
1955			12	T
1956			5	T
1957			11	T
1958			12	T

5 yrs.   51 games

Hub Ulrich
ULRICH, HUBERT J., JR.
B. Dec. 12, 1920
D. Mar., 1974
Kansas 6'0" 205 lbs.

| 1946 | **MIA** | AA | 14 | E |

Mike Ulufale
ULUFALE, MIKE
B. Feb. 1, 1972, Honolulu, HI
Brigham Young 6'4" 282 lbs.

| 1996 | **DAL** | N | 3 | DT |

Frank Umont
UMONT, FRANK WILLIAM
B. Nov. 17, 1917, Staten Island, NY
D. Jan. 20, 1991, Fort Lauderdale, FL
None 5'11" 218 lbs.

1943	**NYG**	N	1	T
1944			6	G, FB
1945			8	G

3 yrs.   15 games

Rich Umphrey
UMPHREY, RICHARD VERN, III
B. Dec. 13, 1958, Garden Grove, CA
Utah/Colorado 6'3" 260 lbs.

1982	**NYG**	N	9	C
1983			10	C
1984			15	C
1985	**SD**	N	11	C, G

4 yrs.   45 games

Forest Underwood
UNDERWOOD, FOREST
B. Dec. 8, 1913, West Union, WV
D. Oct. 26, 1967, Grantsville, WV
Davis & Elkins 6'1" 190 lbs.

| 1937 | **CLE** | N | 3 | T, G |

Jack Underwood
UNDERWOOD, JOHN
B. Aug., 1897
D. Duluth., MN
None 6'0" 200 lbs.

1924	**DUL**	N	6	E
1925			2	E
1926			12	E
1927	**POT**	N	1	E
1927	**BUF**	N	3	E
1929	**CHIC**	N	10	G, C

5 yrs.   34 games

John Underwood
UNDERWOOD, JOHN A., JR. (Big Heavy)
B. 1899
D. 1932
Rice 6'7" 265 lbs.

| 1923 | **MIL** | N | 13 | G |

Olen Underwood
UNDERWOOD, OLEN ULESUS
B. May 25, 1942, Holly Grove, TX
Texas 6'1" 224 lbs.

| 1965 | **NYG** | N | 10 | LB |
| 1966 | **HOU** | A | 11 | LB |

Olen Underwood *continued*

1967			14	LB
1968			14	LB
1969			14	LB
1970	**HOU**	N	12	LB
1971	**DEN**	N	14	LB

7 yrs.   89 games

Joe Ungerer
UNGERER, JOSEPH
B. Dec. 10, 1916, Bethlehem, PA
D. Jul. 15, 1990, Absecon, NJ
Fordham 6'0" 243 lbs.

| 1944 | **WAS** | N | 6 | T |
| 1945 | | | 10 | T |

2 yrs.   16 games

Johnny Unitas
UNITAS, JOHN CONSTANTINE
B. May 7, 1933, Pittsburgh, PA
Louisville 6'1" 194 lbs.

1956	**BAL**	N	12	QB
1957			12	QB
1958			10	QB
1959			12	QB
1960			12	QB
1961			14	QB
1962			14	QB
1963			14	QB
1964			14	QB
1965			11	QB
1966			14	QB
1967			14	QB
1968			5	QB
1969			13	QB
1970			14	QB
1971			13	QB
1972			8	QB
1973	**SD**	N	5	QB

18 yrs.   211 games

Pong Unitas
UNITAS, MATTHEW
B. Sep. 13, 1895
D. Oct., 1972, Baltimore, MD
None 180 lbs.

| 1921 | **WAS** | A | 3 | G |

Terry Unrein
UNREIN, TERRANCE LYNN
B. Oct. 24, 1962, Brighton, CO
Colorado State 6'5" 283 lbs.

| 1986 | **SD** | N | 12 | DE |
| 1987 | | | 9 | NT |

2 yrs.   21 games

Morris Unutoa
UNUTOA, MORRIS
B. Mar. 10, 1971, Torrance, CA
Brigham Young 6'1" 284 lbs.

| 1996 | **PHI** | N | 16 | C |

Eric Unverzagt
UNVERZAGT, ERIC
B. Dec. 18, 1972, Central Islip, NY
Wisconsin 6'1" 236 lbs.

| 1996 | **SEA** | N | 7 | LB |

Rick Upchurch
UPCHURCH, RICHARD
B. May 20, 1952, Toledo, OH
Minnesota 5'10" 173 lbs.

1975	**DEN**	N	14	WR
1976			13	WR
1977			14	WR
1978			12	WR
1979			16	WR

Rick Upchurch *continued*

1980			16	WR
1981			13	WR
1982			9	WR
1983			12	WR

9 yrs.   119 games

Tuufuli Uperesa
UPERESA, TUUFULI
B. Jan. 20, 1948, American Samoa
Montana 6'3" 255 lbs.

| 1971 | **PHI** | N | 2 | OT |

Gene Upshaw
UPSHAW, EUGENE
B. Aug. 15, 1945, Robstown, TX
Texas A&I, Kingsville 6'5" 255 lbs.

1967	**OAK**	A	14	G, OT
1968			14	G, OT
1969			14	G
1970	**OAK**	N	14	G
1971			14	G
1972			14	G
1973			14	G
1974			14	G
1975			14	G
1976			14	G
1977			14	G
1978			16	G
1979			16	G
1980			16	G
1981			15	G

15 yrs.   217 games

Marv Upshaw
UPSHAW, MARVIN ALLEN
B. Nov. 22, 1946, Robstown, TX
Trinity (Texas) 6'3" 253 lbs.

1968	**CLE**	N	14	DE
1969			14	DE, DT
1970	**KC**	N	6	DT
1971			14	DT
1972			14	DT
1973			14	DE
1974			14	DE
1975			14	DT
1976	**STL**	N	4	DT

9 yrs.   98 games

Regan Upshaw
UPSHAW, REGAN
B. Aug. 12, 1975, Detroit, MI
California 6'4" 260 lbs.

| 1996 | **TB** | N | 16 | DE |

Andy Uram
URAM, ANDREW
B. Mar. 21, 1915, Minneapolis, MN
D. Dec. 8, 1984, Green Bay, WI
Minnesota 5'10" 188 lbs.

1938	**GB**	N	11	HB
1939			9	HB
1940			10	HB
1941			11	HB
1942			10	HB
1943			7	HB

6 yrs.   58 games

Alex Urban
URBAN, ALEXANDER W. (Jeep)
B. Jul. 16, 1917, Bessemer, PA
South Carolina 6'3" 207 lbs.

1941	**GB**	N	6	E
1944			4	E, B
1945			1	E

3 yrs.   11 games

Year Team	Games	Pos.

Frank Urban
URBAN, FRANK
B. 1900
Deceased
MIT 6'0" 190 lbs.

Year	Team		Games	Pos.
1926	RI	A	2	E

Gasper Urban
URBAN, GASPER GEORGE
B. Mar. 18, 1923, Lynn, MA
Notre Dame 6'1" 215 lbs.

Year	Team		Games	Pos.
1948	CHI	AA	14	G

Luke Urban
URBAN, LOUIS JOHN
B. Mar. 22, 1898, Fall River, MA
D. Dec. 7, 1980, Somerset, MA
Boston College 5'8" 165 lbs.

Year	Team		Games	Pos.
1921	BUF	A	12	E
1922	BUF	N	9	E
1923			11	E
3 yrs.	32 games			

Jim Urbanek
URBANEK, JAMES E.
B. Apr. 18, 1945, Oxford, MS
Mississippi 6'4" 270 lbs.

Year	Team		Games	Pos.
1968	MIA	A	8	DE

Scott Urch
URCH, SCOTT E.
B. Jul. 2, 1965
Virginia 6'2" 270 lbs.

Year	Team		Games	Pos.
1987	NYG	N	3	G

Emil Uremovich
UREMOVICH, EMIL P.
B. Sep. 26, 1916, Gary, IN
D. Apr. 22, 1994
Indiana 6'2" 233 lbs.

Year	Team		Games	Pos.
1941	DET	N	10	T
1942			11	T
1945			8	T
1946			11	T
1948	CHI	AA	8	T
5 yrs.	48 games			

Herm Urenda
URENDA, HERMAN
B. 1940
Pacific 5'11" 170 lbs.

Year	Team		Games	Pos.
1963	OAK	A	2	DB, OE

Claude Urevig
UREVIG, CLAUDE
None

Year	Team		Games	Pos.
1934	PHI	N	1	T

Rube Ursella
URSELLA, REUBEN
B. Jan. 11, 1890
D. Feb., 1980, Minneapolis, MN
None 5'9" 172 lbs.

Year	Team		Games	Pos.
1920	RI	A	4	QB
1921	MIN	A	4	QB
1924	RI		7	HB, QB
1925			10	HB, QB, FB, E
1926	AKR	N	7	HB, QB
1926	HAM	N	1	HB
1929	MIN	N	7	QB, HB
6 yrs.	40 games			

Darryl Usher
USHER, DARRYL
B. Jan. 3, 1965, Los Angeles, CA

Darryl Usher continued
Illinois 5'8" 170 lbs.

Year	Team		Games	Pos.
1989	SD	N	6	WR
1989	PHX	N	7	WR

Eddie Usher
USHER, EDWARD T.
B. Jun. 19, 1898
D. Apr., 1973, Bradenton, FL
Michigan 5'11" 192 lbs.

Year	Team		Games	Pos.
1921	BUF	A	1	E
1922	RI	N	5	HB
1922	GB	N	5	HB
1924			1	HB
1924	KC	N	6	HB, FB, QB
3 yrs.	18 games			

Lou Usher
USHER, LOUIS C.
B. 1898
Deceased
Syracuse 6'2" 240 lbs.

Year	Team		Games	Pos.
1920	ROC	A	1	T
1921			1	G
1921	DEC	A	3	G, T
1923	HAM		3	T
1923	CHIB	N	8	T, G
1924	HAM	N	1	T
1924	KEN	N	5	T, C
1924	MIL	N	5	G
1926	HAM	N	4	T
5 yrs.	31 games			

Mike Utley
UTLEY, MICHAEL GERALD
B. Dec. 20, 1965, Seattle, WA
Washington State 6'6" 288 lbs.

Year	Team		Games	Pos.
1989	DET	N	5	G, OT
1990			16	G, OT
1991			9	G
3 yrs.	30 games			

Ben Utt
UTT, BENJAMIN MICHAEL
B. Jun. 13, 1959, Richmond, CA
Georgia Tech 6'5" 271 lbs.

Year	Team		Games	Pos.
1982	BAL	N	9	G
1983			16	G
1984	IND	N	16	G
1985			16	G
1986			9	G
1987			12	G
1988			16	G
1989			16	G
8 yrs.	110 games			

Iheanyi Uwaezuoke
UWAEZUOKE, IHEANYI
B. Jul. 24, 1973, Lagos, Nigeria
California 6'2" 195 lbs.

Year	Team		Games	Pos.
1996	SF	N	14	WR

Walt Uzdavinis
UZDAVINIS, WALTER A.
B. Jun. 19, 1912, Middleboro, MA
Fordham 6'2" 210 lbs.

Year	Team		Games	Pos.
1937	CLE	N	7	E

Sam Vacanti
VACANTI, SAMUEL F.
B. Mar. 20, 1922, Omaha, NE
D. Dec. 17, 1981, Omaha, NE
Iowa/Purdue/Nebraska 5'11" 203 lbs.

Year	Team		Games	Pos.
1947	CHI	AA	13	B
1948			9	B
1948	BAL	AA	5	B
1949			12	B
3 yrs.	39 games			

Ted Vactor
VACTOR, THEODORE FRANCIS
B. May 27, 1944, Washington, PA
Nebraska 6'0" 185 lbs.

Year	Team		Games	Pos.
1969	WAS	N	14	CB
1970			14	CB
1971			14	CB
1972			14	CB
1973			9	CB
1975	CHI	N	4	CB
6 yrs.	69 games			

Pete Vainowski
VAINOWSKI, PETER
B. Sep. 7, 1902
D. Jul., 1957, Illinois
None 200 lbs.

Year	Team		Games	Pos.
1926	LOU	N	1	G

Dom Vairo
VAIRO, DOMINIC MARTIN
B. Nov. 2, 1913, Calumet, MI
Notre Dame 6'2" 203 lbs.

Year	Team		Games	Pos.
1935	GB	N	1	E

Vern Valdez
VALDEZ, VERNON
B. 1936
California-San Diego 5'11" 190 lbs.

Year	Team		Games	Pos.
1960	LA	N	9	DB
1961	BUF	A	13	DB
1962	OAK	A	10	DB
3 yrs.	32 games			

Ira Valentine
VALENTINE, IRA LYNN
B. Jun. 4, 1963, Marshall, TX
Texas A&M 6'0" 212 lbs.

Year	Team		Games	Pos.
1987	HOU	N	7	RB

Zack Valentine
VALENTINE, ZACHARY BERNARD
B. May 29, 1957, Edenton, NC
East Carolina 6'2" 222 lbs.

Year	Team		Games	Pos.
1979	PIT	N	16	LB
1980			16	LB
1981			16	LB
1982	PHI	N	8	LB
4 yrs.	56 games			

Joe Valerio
VALERIO, JOSEPH WILLIAM
B. Feb. 11, 1969, Swarthmore, PA
Pennsylvania 6'5" 293 lbs.

Year	Team		Games	Pos.
1992	KC	N	16	OT
1993			13	OT, C
1994			16	OT, C
1995			16	OT, C
1996	STL	N	1	OL
5 yrs.	62 games			

Emilio Vallez
VALLEZ, EMILIO
B. Apr. 30, 1946, Belen, NM
New Mexico 6'2" 210 lbs.

Year	Team		Games	Pos.
1968	CHI	N	6	LB, TE
1969			2	TE
2 yrs.	8 games			

Norm Van Brocklin
VAN BROCKLIN, NORMAN (The Dutchman)
B. Mar. 15, 1926, Eagle Butte, SD
D. May 2, 1983, Social Circle, GA
Oregon 6'1" 199 lbs.

Year	Team		Games	Pos.
1949	LA	N	8	QB, P

Norm Van Brocklin cont.

Year	Team		Games	Pos.
1950			12	QB, P
1951			12	QB, P
1952			12	QB, P
1953			12	QB, P
1954			12	QB, P
1955			12	QB, P
1956			12	QB, P
1957			12	QB, P
1958	PHI	N	12	QB, P
1959			12	QB, P
1960			12	QB, P
12 yrs.	140 games			

Ebert Van Buren
VAN BUREN, EBERT HARRY
B. Dec. 6, 1924, Tela, Honduras
Louisiana State 6'2" 210 lbs.

Year	Team		Games	Pos.
1951	PHI	N	12	FB
1952			12	HB
1953			12	FB
3 yrs.	36 games			

Steve Van Buren
VAN BUREN, STEPHEN W.
B. Dec. 20, 1920, Tela, Honduras
Louisiana State 6'0" 203 lbs.

Year	Team		Games	Pos.
1944	PHI	N	9	HB
1945			10	HB
1946			9	HB
1947			12	HB
1948			11	HB
1949			12	HB
1950			10	HB
1951			10	HB
8 yrs.	83 games			

Joe Vance
VANCE, JOSEPH ALBERT (Sandy)
B. Sep. 16, 1905, Devine, TX
D. Jul. 4, 1978, Devine, TX
Southwest Texas State/Texas 6'1" 180 lbs.

Year	Team		Games	Pos.
1931	BKN	N	11	HB, QB, FB

Matt Vanderbeek
VANDERBEEK, MATTHEW JAMES
B. Aug. 16, 1967, Saugatuck, MI
Michigan State 6'3" 254 lbs.

Year	Team		Games	Pos.
1990	IND	N	16	DE
1991			5	LB
1992			15	LB
1993	DAL	N	16	LB
1994			12	LB
1995	WAS	N	16	LB
1996			1	LB
7 yrs.	81 games			

Skip Vanderbundt
VANDERBUNDT, WILLIAM GERARD
B. Dec. 4, 1946, Martinez, CA
Oregon State 6'3" 227 lbs.

Year	Team		Games	Pos.
1969	SF	N	14	LB
1970			12	LB
1971			14	LB
1972			14	LB
1973			9	LB
1974			14	LB
1975			14	LB
1976			14	LB
1977			14	LB
1978	NO	N	15	LB
10 yrs.	134 games			

Ron Vander Kelen
VANDER KELEN, RONALD

Year	Team		Games	Pos.

Ron Vander Kelen continued

B. Nov. 6, 1939, Green Bay, WI
Wisconsin 6'1" 186 lbs.

Year	Team		Games	Pos.
1963	MIN	N	6	QB
1964			5	QB
1965			4	QB
1966			3	QB
1967			11	QB
5 yrs.	29 games			

George Vander Loo

VANDER LOO, V.B. (Viv)
B. 1898
Deceased
Iowa State 5'10" 191 lbs.

1921	RI	A	4	FB

Mark Vander Poel

VANDER POEL, JOHN MARK
B. Mar. 5, 1968, Upland, CA
Colorado 6'7" 303 lbs.

1991	IND	N	10	OT
1992			13	OT
2 yrs.	23 games			

Phil Vandersea

VANDERSEA, PHILLIP JOHN
B. Feb. 25, 1943, Whitinsville, MA
Massachusetts 6'3" 228 lbs.

1966	GB	N	14	LB
1967	NO	N	8	LB
1968	GB	N	10	TE, LB
1969			14	TE, LB
4 yrs.	46 games			

Al Vandeweghe

VANDEWEGHE, ALFRED B.
B. 1921, Teaneck, NJ
William & Mary 5'11" 200 lbs.

1946	BUF	AA	5	E

Randy Van Divier

VAN DIVIER, RANDY LEE
B. Jun. 5, 1958, Anaheim, CA
Washington 6'5" 275 lbs.

1981	BAL	N	16	OT
1982	LARI	N	1	G
2 yrs.	17 games			

Bob Van Doren

VAN DOREN, ROBERT
B. 1929, Baltimore, MD
Southern California 6'3" 215 lbs.

1953	SF	N	10	E

Bob Van Duyne

VAN DUYNE, ROBERT SCOTT
B. May 15, 1952, San Bernardino, CA
Idaho 6'5" 243 lbs.

1974	BAL	N	14	G
1975			14	G
1976			14	G
1977			9	G, OT
1978			14	G, OT
1979			16	G, OT
1980			7	G
7 yrs.	88 games			

Alex Van Dyke

VAN DYKE, FRANK ALEXANDER
B. Jul. 24, 1974, Sacramento, CA
Nevada 6'0" 200 lbs.

1996	NYJ	N	15	WR

Bruce Van Dyke

VAN DYKE, BRUCE ROBERT
B. Aug. 6, 1944, Lancaster, CA
Missouri 6'2" 248 lbs.

1966	PHI	N	4	G
1967	PIT	N	14	G
1968			14	G
1969			14	G
1970			14	G
1971			12	G
1972			13	G
1973			14	G
1975	GB	N	14	G
1976			14	G
10 yrs.	127 games			

Jimmy Van Dyke

VAN DYKE, JAMES (Slim Jimmy)
B. Dec. 2, 1898
D. Aug., 1980, Louisville, KY
None 5'7" 140 lbs.

1921	LOU	A	1	QB
1922	LOU	N	2	HB
1923			1	QB
3 yrs.	4 games			

Ralph Van Dyke

VAN DYKE, RALPH W., III
B. Jan. 19, 1964, Chicago Heights, IL
Southern Illinois 6'6" 273 lbs.

1987	CLE	N	2	OT

Chase Van Dyne

VAN DYNE, CHARLES M.
B. Feb. 12, 1901
D. Sep., 1962
Missouri 6'1" 194 lbs.

1925	BUF	N	8	T, G

Mark van Eeghen

VAN EEGHEN, MARK
B. Apr. 19, 1952, Cambridge, MA
Colgate 6'2" 224 lbs.

1974	OAK	N	14	RB
1975			14	RB
1976			14	RB
1977			14	RB
1978			16	RB
1979			16	RB
1980			16	RB
1981			8	RB
1982	NE	N	9	RB
1983			15	RB
10 yrs.	136 games			

Hal Van Every

VAN EVERY, HAROLD
B. Feb. 10, 1918, Minnetonka Beach, MN
Minnesota 6'0" 195 lbs.

1940	GB	N	9	HB
1941			11	HB
2 yrs.	20 games			

Tim Van Galder

VAN GALDER, TIMOTHY SCOTT
B. May 26, 1944, Racine, WI
Iowa State 6'1" 190 lbs.

1972	STL	N	5	QB

Billy Van Heusen

VAN HEUSEN, WILLIAM P.
B. Aug. 27, 1946, New Rochelle, NY
Maryland 6'1" 200 lbs.

1968	DEN	A	13	OE, P
1969			5	WR, P

Billy Van Heusen continued

1970	DEN	N	14	WR, K
1971			14	WR, K
1972			14	WR, K
1973			14	WR, P
1974			14	P, WR
1975			14	WR, P
1976			7	WR, P
9 yrs.	109 games			

Charlie Van Horn

VAN HORN, CHARLES E.
B. 1902
Washington & Lee 6'2" 185 lbs.

1927	BUF	N	2	FB
1929	ORA	N	3	HB
2 yrs.	5 games			

Doug Van Horn

VAN HORN, DOUGLAS CLAYDON
B. Jun. 24, 1944, Sedalia, MO
Ohio State 6'2" 245 lbs.

1966	DET	N	14	G
1968	NYG	N	3	G
1969			14	G
1970			14	G
1971			12	G
1972			14	G
1973			14	G
1974			14	G
1975			14	OT
1976			14	OT
1977			14	OT
1978			16	OT
1979			15	OT
13 yrs.	172 games			

Keith Van Horne

VAN HORNE, KEITH
B. Nov. 6, 1957, Mount Lebanon, PA
Southern California 6'6" 280 lbs.

1981	CHI	N	14	OT
1982			9	OT
1983			14	OT
1984			14	OT
1985			16	OT
1986			16	OT
1987			12	OT
1988			15	OT
1989			15	OT
1990			16	OT
1991			16	OT
1992			16	OT
1993			13	OT
13 yrs.	186 games			

Sean Vanhorse

VANHORSE, SEAN JOSEPH
B. Jul. 22, 1968, Baltimore, MD
Howard 5'10" 180 lbs.

1992	SD	N	16	CB
1993			15	CB
1994			16	CB
1995	DET	N	14	CB
1996	MIN	N	9	CB
5 yrs.	70 games			

Ed Van Meter

VAN METER, ED
B. 1901
Deceased
None 6'1" 212 lbs.

1921	WAS	A	2	G

Norwood Vann

VANN, NORWOOD JACOB, JR.
B. Feb. 18, 1962, Philadelphia, PA

Norwood Vann continued

East Carolina 6'1" 225 lbs.

1984	LARM	N	16	LB
1985			8	LB
1986			16	LB
1987			11	LB
1988	LARI	N	1	LB
5 yrs.	52 games			

Jeff Van Note

VAN NOTE, JEFFREY ALOYSIUS
B. Feb. 7, 1946, South Orange, NJ
Kentucky 6'2" 260 lbs.

1969	ATL	N	1	C
1970			14	C
1971			14	C
1972			14	C
1973			14	C
1974			14	C
1975			14	C
1976			10	C
1977			14	C
1978			16	C
1979			16	C
1980			16	C
1981			16	C
1982			9	C
1983			16	C
1984			16	C
1985			16	C
1986			15	C
18 yrs.	245 games			

Tamarick Vanover

VANOVER, TAMARICK
B. Feb. 25, 1974, Tallahassee, FL
Florida State 5'11" 213 lbs.

1995	KC	N	15	WR
1996			13	WR
2 yrs.	28 games			

Vernon Vanoy

VANOY, VERNON
B. Dec. 31, 1948, Kansas City, MO
Kansas 6'3" 270 lbs.

1971	NYG	N	6	DT
1972	GB	N	13	DT
1973	HOU	N	1	DT
3 yrs.	20 games			

Alex Van Pelt

VAN PELT, GREGORY ALEXANDER
B. May 1, 1970, Grafton, WV
Pittsburgh 6'1" 219 lbs.

1995	BUF	N	1	QB
1996			1	QB
2 yrs.	2 games			

Brad Van Pelt

VAN PELT, BRAD ALAN
B. Apr. 5, 1951, Owosso, MI
Michigan State 6'5" 235 lbs.

1973	NYG	N	5	LB
1974			12	LB
1975			14	LB
1976			14	LB
1977			14	LB
1978			14	LB
1979			16	LB
1980			15	LB
1981			14	LB
1982			9	LB
1983			16	LB
1984	LARI	N	9	LB
1985			16	LB
1986	CLE	N	16	LB
14 yrs.	184 games			

Year	Team		Games	Pos.

Dick Van Raaphorst
VAN RAAPHORST, RICHARD WILLIAM
B. Dec. 10, 1942, Port Huron, MI
Ohio State 5'11" 215 lbs.

Year	Team		Games	Pos.
1964	DAL	N	14	K
1966	SD	A	14	K
1967			14	K
3 yrs.	42 games			

Jeff Van Raaphorst
VAN RAAPHORST, JEFFREY RICHARD
B. Dec. 7, 1963
Arizona State 6'1" 210 lbs.

Year	Team		Games	Pos.
1987	ATL	N	2	QB

Clyde Van Sickle
VAN SICKLE, CLYDE
B. 1905
Arkansas 6'1" 220 lbs.

Year	Team		Games	Pos.
1930	FRA	N	11	G
1932	GB	N	1	G
1933			6	G
3 yrs.	18 games			

Fred Vant Hull
VANT HULL, FREDERICK N.
B. Aug. 21, 1920, Winnipeg, Man.
D. Apr. 10, 1975, Minneapolis, MN
Minnesota 6'0" 214 lbs.

Year	Team		Games	Pos.
1942	GB	N	10	T, G

Art Van Tone
VAN TONE, ARTHUR
B. Sep. 30, 1918, Ottawa, OH
D. Aug. 9, 1990, Conyers, GA
Southern Mississippi 5'10" 185 lbs.

Year	Team		Games	Pos.
1943	DET	N	10	HB
1944			10	HB
1945			2	HB
1946	BKN	AA	9	HB
4 yrs.	31 games			

Pete Van Valkenberg
VAN VALKENBERG, PETE
B. May 19, 1950, Sandy, UT
Brigham Young 6'2" 194 lbs.

Year	Team		Games	Pos.
1973	BUF	N	13	RB
1974	GB	N	6	RB
1974	CHI	N	6	RB
2 yrs.	25 games			

Jim Van Wagner
VAN WAGNER, JAMES PARKER
B. May 3, 1955, Ann Arbor, MI
Michigan Tech 6'0" 202 lbs.

Year	Team		Games	Pos.
1978	NO	N	5	RB

Fred Vanzo
VANZO, FREDERICK G.
(Chopper)
B. Jan. 8, 1916, Universal, IN
D. Feb. 7, 1976, Minneapolis, MN
Northwestern 6'2" 230 lbs.

Year	Team		Games	Pos.
1938	DET	N	10	HB
1939			10	HB
1940			10	HB
1941			6	QB, HB
1941	CHIC	N	3	QB
4 yrs.	39 games			

Mike Varajon
VARAJON, MICHAEL JOSEPH
B. Jul. 12, 1964, Detroit, MI
Toledo 6'1" 232 lbs.

Year	Team		Games	Pos.
1987	SF	N	3	RB

Tommy Vardell
VARDELL, THOMAS ARTHUR
B. Feb. 20, 1969, El Cajon, CA
Stanford 6'2" 238 lbs.

Year	Team		Games	Pos.
1992	CLE	N	14	RB
1993			16	RB
1994			5	RB
1995			5	RB
1996	SF	N	11	RB
5 yrs.	51 games			

Johnny Vardian
VARDIAN, JOHN J.
B. Sep. 25, 1921, Johnstown, PA
D. Aug. 8, 1989, Tampa, FL
none 5'8" 167 lbs.

Year	Team		Games	Pos.
1946	MIA	AA	6	HB
1947	BAL	AA	14	HB
1948			12	HB
3 yrs.	32 games			

Larry Vargo
VARGO, LAWRENCE F.
B. Apr. 5, 1939, Iron Mountain, MI
Detroit 6'3" 212 lbs.

Year	Team		Games	Pos.
1962	DET	N	9	OE
1963			14	OE
1964	MIN	N	14	DB
1965			13	DB
1966	NYG	N	7	DB
5 yrs.	57 games			

Frank Varrichione
VARRICHIONE, FRANK
B. Jan. 14, 1932, Natick, MA
Notre Dame 6'1" 234 lbs.

Year	Team		Games	Pos.
1955	PIT	N	12	T
1956			12	T
1957			12	T
1958			12	T
1959			12	T
1960			12	T
1961	LA	N	14	OT
1962			12	OT
1963			14	OT
1964			10	OT
1965			11	OT
11 yrs.	133 games			

Mike Varty
VARTY, MICHAEL S.
B. Feb. 10, 1952, Detroit, MI
Northwestern 6'1" 223 lbs.

Year	Team		Games	Pos.
1974	WAS	N	1	LB
1975	BAL	N	6	LB
2 yrs.	7 games			

Vic Vasicek
VASICEK, VICTOR F.
B. May 5, 1926, Austin, TX
Southern California/Texas 5'11" 223 lbs.

Year	Team		Games	Pos.
1949	BUF	AA	12	G
1950	LA	N	12	G
2 yrs.	24 games			

Roy Vassau
VASSAU, ROY E. (Tiny)
B. Dec., 1893
Deceased
St. Thomas (Minnesota) 6'0" 220 lbs.

Year	Team		Games	Pos.
1923	MIL	N	1	T

Arunas Vasys
VASYS, ARUNAS BRUNO
B. Aug. 18, 1943, Lithuania
Notre Dame 6'2" 232 lbs.

Year	Team		Games	Pos.
1966	PHI	N	10	LB

Arunas Vasys continued

Year	Team		Games	Pos.
1967			9	LB
1968			3	LB
3 yrs.	22 games			

Randy Vataha
VATAHA, RANDEL EDWARD
B. Dec. 4, 1948, Santa Monica, CA
Stanford 5'10" 173 lbs.

Year	Team		Games	Pos.
1971	NE	N	14	WR
1972			14	WR
1973			14	WR
1974			14	WR
1975			14	WR
1976			12	WR
1977	GB	N	6	WR
7 yrs.	88 games			

Harp Vaughan
VAUGHAN, JOHN J.
B. Nov. 19, 1904
D. Dec. 27, 1978, Jacksonville, FL
Indiana (Pennsylvania) 5'7" 150 lbs.

Year	Team		Games	Pos.
1933	PIT	N	8	HB, QB, FB
1934			11	QB, HB, FB
2 yrs.	19 games			

Pug Vaughan
VAUGHAN, CHARLES WESLEY
B. Mar. 18, 1911, Knoxville, TN
D. Mar., 1968, Detroit, MI
Tennessee 5'11" 181 lbs.

Year	Team		Games	Pos.
1935	DET	N	6	QB, HB
1936	CHIC	N	12	HB, QB
2 yrs.	18 games			

Ruben Vaughan
VAUGHAN, RUBEN CHARLES, JR.
B. Aug. 6, 1956, Los Angeles, CA
Colorado 6'2" 255 lbs.

Year	Team		Games	Pos.
1979	SF	N	13	DT
1982	LARI	N	9	NT
1984	MIN	N	5	NT
3 yrs.	27 games			

Bill Vaughn
VAUGHN, WILLIAM
B. Jan. 10, 1902
D. Apr., 1971, Mesquite, TX
Southern Methodist 5'10" 192 lbs.

Year	Team		Games	Pos.
1926	BUF	N	9	FB, HB

Bob Vaughn
VAUGHN, ROBERT CURTIS
B. Jun. 8, 1945, Memphis, TN
Mississippi 6'4" 240 lbs.

Year	Team		Games	Pos.
1968	DEN	A	1	G

Clarence Vaughn
VAUGHN, CLARENCE
B. Jul. 17, 1964, Chicago, IL
Northern Illinois 6'0" 202 lbs.

Year	Team		Games	Pos.
1987	WAS	N	5	S
1988			14	S
1989			16	S
1990			1	S
1991			12	S
5 yrs.	48 games			

Jon Vaughn
VAUGHN, JONATHAN STEWART
B. Mar. 12, 1970, Florissant, MO
Michigan 5'9" 203 lbs.

Year	Team		Games	Pos.
1991	NE	N	16	RB
1992			16	RB

Jon Vaughn continued

Year	Team		Games	Pos.
1993	SEA	N	16	RB
1994			10	RB
1994	KC	N	3	RB
4 yrs.	61 games			

Tommy Vaughn
VAUGHN, THOMAS ROBERT
B. Feb. 28, 1943, Troy, OH
Iowa State 5'11" 192 lbs.

Year	Team		Games	Pos.
1965	DET	N	14	DB
1966			13	DB
1967			14	DB
1968			13	DB
1969			14	S
1970			11	S
1971			9	S
7 yrs.	88 games			

Teddy Vaught
VAUGHT, THOMAS
B. Jul. 19, 1932, Littlefield, TX
Texas Christian 6'0" 208 lbs.

Year	Team		Games	Pos.
1955	SF	N	1	E

Elton Veals
VEALS, ELTON ALVIN
B. Mar. 26, 1961, Baton Rouge, LA
Tulane 5'11" 223 lbs.

Year	Team		Games	Pos.
1984	PIT	N	15	RB

Craig Veasey
VEASEY, ANTHONY CRAIG
B. Dec. 25, 1965, Clear Lake City, TX
Houston 6'2" 283 lbs.

Year	Team		Games	Pos.
1990	PIT	N	10	NT
1991			13	DT, DE
1992	HOU	N	4	DT
1993			1	DE, DT
1993	MIA	N	14	NT
1994			12	NT
1995	HOU	N	15	DT, DE
6 yrs.	69 games			

Norton Vedder
VEDDER, NORTON (Orrin)
B. Jul. 7, 1899
D. Oct., 1986
None 5'7" 165 lbs.

Year	Team		Games	Pos.
1927	BUF	N	2	FB

Alan Veingrad
VEINGRAD, ALAN STUART
B. Jul. 24, 1963, Brooklyn, NY
East Texas State 6'5" 277 lbs.

Year	Team		Games	Pos.
1986	GB	N	16	OT, G
1987			11	G, OT
1989			16	OT
1990			16	OT
1991	DAL	N	16	OT
1992			11	G, OT
6 yrs.	86 games			

John Vella
VELLA, JOHN
B. Apr. 21, 1950, Cleveland, OH
Southern California 6'4" 258 lbs.

Year	Team		Games	Pos.
1972	OAK	N	14	OT
1973			14	OT
1974			13	OT
1975			13	OT
1976			14	OT
1977			5	OT
1979			11	OT
1980	MIN	N	8	OT
8 yrs.	92 games			

Year	Team		Games	Pos.

Jim Vellone
VELLONE, JAMES CARL
B. Aug. 2, 1944, Camp Lejeune, NC
Southern California 6'2" 255 lbs.

Year	Team		Games	Pos.
1966	MIN	N	14	G, OT
1967			14	G
1968			14	G, OT
1969			13	G
1970			11	G
5 yrs.	66 games			

Fred Venturelli
VENTURELLI, FRED
B. Aug. 22, 1917
D. Jan. 20, 1990, Racine, WI
None 5'11" 235 lbs.

Year	Team		Games	Pos.
1948	CHIB	N		K

Sam Venuto
VENUTO, SAMUEL
B. Nov. 2, 1927, Havertown, PA
Guilford 6'1" 195 lbs.

Year	Team		Games	Pos.
1952	WAS	N	3	HB

Clarence Verdin
VERDIN, CLARENCE
B. Jun. 14, 1953, New Orleans, LA
Southwestern Louisiana 5'8" 160 lbs.

Year	Team		Games	Pos.
1986	WAS	N	8	WR
1987			3	WR
1988	IND	N	16	WR
1989			16	WR
1990			15	WR
1991			16	WR
1992			16	WR
1993			16	WR
1994	ATL	N	12	WR
9 yrs.	118 games			

Ed Vereb
VEREB, ED
B. 1933
Maryland 6'0" 190 lbs.

Year	Team		Games	Pos.
1960	WAS	N	9	HB

Carl Vereen
VEREEN, CARL H.
B. Jan. 27, 1936, Miami, FL
Georgia Tech 6'2" 247 lbs.

Year	Team		Games	Pos.
1957	GB	N	12	T

George Vergara
VERGARA, GEORGE W. (Zip)
B. Mar. 18, 1901
D. Aug. 13, 1982, Montrose, NY
Fordham/Notre Dame 6'1" 190 lbs.

Year	Team		Games	Pos.
1925	GB	N	12	E

Chris Verhulst
VERHULST, CHRISTOPHER SEAN
B. May 19, 1966, Sacramento, CA
Chico State 6'2" 249 lbs.

Year	Team		Games	Pos.
1988	HOU	N	1	TE
1989			16	TE
1990	DEN	N	11	TE
3 yrs.	28 games			

Garin Veris
VERIS, GARIN LEE
B. Feb. 27, 1963, Chillicothe, OH
Stanford 6'4" 255 lbs.

Year	Team		Games	Pos.
1985	NE	N	16	DE
1986			16	DE
1987			12	DE
1988			11	DE

Garin Veris continued

Year	Team		Games	Pos.
1990			7	DE
1991			16	DE
1992	SF	N	10	DE
7 yrs.	88 games			

Norm Verry
VERRY, DAVID NORMAN
B. Sep. 18, 1922, Hanford, CA
Southern California 6'1" 240 lbs.

Year	Team		Games	Pos.
1946	CHI	AA	10	T
1947			1	T
2 yrs.	11 games			

David Verser
VERSER, DAVID
B. Mar. 1, 1958, Kansas City, KS
Kansas 6'1" 200 lbs.

Year	Team		Games	Pos.
1981	CIN	N	16	WR
1982			9	WR
1983			13	WR
1984			11	WR
1985	TB	N	1	WR
1987	CLE	N	2	WR
6 yrs.	52 games			

Mike Verstegen
VERSTEGEN, MIKE
B. Oct. 24, 1971, Appleton, WI
Wisconsin 6'6" 311 lbs.

Year	Team		Games	Pos.
1996	NO	N	9	OT

Brian Vertefeuille
VERTEFEUILLE, BRIAN LEONEL
B. Apr. 4, 1951, Willimantic, CT
Idaho State 6'3" 252 lbs.

Year	Team		Games	Pos.
1974	SD	N	14	OT

Billy Vessels
VESSELS, BILLY DALE
B. Mar. 22, 1931, Cleveland, OK
Oklahoma 6'0" 190 lbs.

Year	Team		Games	Pos.
1956	BAL	N	12	HB

John Vesser
VESSER, JOHN MARTIN
B. Oct. 1, 1900, Coeur d'Alene, ID
Idaho 6'0" 186 lbs.

Year	Team		Games	Pos.
1926	LA	A	7	E
1927	CHIC	N	10	E
1930			8	E
1931			1	E
4 yrs.	26 games			

Joe Vetrano
VETRANO, JOSEPH GEORGE
B. Oct. 15, 1918, Neptune, NJ
D. May 9, 1995, San Francisco, CA
Southern Mississippi 5'9" 170 lbs.

Year	Team		Games	Pos.
1946	SF	AA	13	HB
1947			14	B
1948			14	B
1949			12	B
4 yrs.	53 games			

Jack Vetter
VETTER, JACK ROBBINS
B. Oct. 30, 1920, Kansas City, MO
McPherson 6'2" 198 lbs.

Year	Team		Games	Pos.
1942	BKN	N	5	B

Roy Vexall
VEXALL, ROY
B. Jun. 6, 1902
D. May, 1982, Blaine, MN

Roy Vexall continued
None 190 lbs.

Year	Team		Games	Pos.
1924	DUL	N	2	FB, QB
1925			1	FB
2 yrs.	3 games			

Walt Vezmar
VEZMAR, WALTER
B. Jan. 1, 1925, Detroit, MI
D. May, 1981, Pollock, LA
Michigan State 5'11" 235 lbs.

Year	Team		Games	Pos.
1946	DET	N	11	G
1947			2	G
2 yrs.	13 games			

David Viaene
VIAENE, DAVID RONALD
B. Jul. 14, 1965, Appleton, WI
Minnesota-Duluth 6'5" 300 lbs.

Year	Team		Games	Pos.
1989	NE	N	16	OT
1990			4	OT
1992	GB	N	1	OT
3 yrs.	21 games			

Dick Vick
VICK, RICHARD D. (Dutch)
B. Apr. 16, 1892
D. Sep., 1980, Bozeman, MT
Washington & Jefferson 5'9" 167 lbs.

Year	Team		Games	Pos.
1924	KEN	N	4	HB, FB, QB
1925	DET	N	11	QB, HB, FB
1926			6	QB, HB
1926	CAN	N	7	QB, HB
3 yrs.	28 games			

Ernie Vick
VICK, HENRY ARTHUR
B. Jul. 2, 1900, Toledo, OH
D. Jul. 16, 1980, Ann Arbor, MI
Michigan 5'10" 190 lbs.

Year	Team		Games	Pos.
1925	DET	N	9	C
1927	CHIB	N	10	C
1928			1	C
1928	DET	N	6	G, T
3 yrs.	26 games			

Roger Vick
VICK, ROGER
B. Aug. 11, 1964, Conroe, TX
Texas A&M 6'3" 232 lbs.

Year	Team		Games	Pos.
1987	NYJ	N	12	RB
1988			16	RB
1989			16	RB
1990	PHI	N	14	RB
4 yrs.	58 games			

Kipp Vickers
VICKERS, KIPP
B. Aug. 27, 1969, Holiday, FL
Miami (Florida) 6'2" 288 lbs.

Year	Team		Games	Pos.
1995	IND	N	9	OT
1996			10	OT
2 yrs.	19 games			

Gene Vidal
VIDAL, EUGENE L.
B. Apr. 13, 1895, Madison, SD
D. Mar. 20, 1969
Nebraska/South Dakota/Army 5'10" 180 lbs.

Year	Team		Games	Pos.
1921	WAS	A	2	FB

Vic Vidoni
VIDONI, VICTOR JOSEPH (Putt)
B. Dec. 9, 1912, Fostoria, OH
Duquesne 6'1" 210 lbs.

Year	Team		Games	Pos.
1935	PIT	N	12	E, G

Vic Vidoni continued

Year	Team		Games	Pos.
1936			2	E
2 yrs.	14 games			

Tommy Vigorito
VIGORITO, THOMAS J.
B. Oct. 23, 1959, Passaic, NJ
Virginia 5'10" 195 lbs.

Year	Team		Games	Pos.
1981	MIA	N	16	RB
1982			9	RB
1983			1	RB
1985			9	RB
4 yrs.	35 games			

Danny Villa
VILLA, DANIEL
B. Sep. 21, 1964, Nogales, AZ
Arizona State 6'5" 305 lbs.

Year	Team		Games	Pos.
1987	NE	N	11	OT
1988			16	OT
1989			15	OT
1990			16	OT
1991			10	G
1992	PHX	N	16	G, OT
1993	KC	N	13	G
1994			14	G
1995			16	G
1996			16	G
10 yrs.	143 games			

Vince Villanucci
VILLANUCCI, VINCE
B. May 30, 1964, Lorain, OH
Bowling Green 6'2" 265 lbs.

Year	Team		Games	Pos.
1987	GB	N	2	NT

Danny Villanueva
VILLANUEVA, DANIEL DARIO
B. Nov. 5, 1937, Tucumcari, NM
New Mexico State 5'11" 202 lbs.

Year	Team		Games	Pos.
1960	LA	N	12	K
1961			14	K, P
1962			14	P, K
1963			14	K, P
1964			14	P, K
1965	DAL	N	14	K, P
1966			14	K, P
1967			14	P, K
8 yrs.	110 games			

Phil Villapiano
VILLAPIANO, PHILIP JAMES
B. Feb. 26, 1949, Long Branch, NJ
Bowling Green 6'1" 222 lbs.

Year	Team		Games	Pos.
1971	OAK	N	14	LB
1972			14	LB
1973			14	LB
1974			14	LB
1975			14	LB
1976			14	LB
1977			2	LB
1978			16	LB
1979			16	LB
1980	BUF	N	16	LB
1981			16	LB
1982			9	LB
1983			4	LB
13 yrs.	163 games			

Chris Villarrial
VILLARRIAL, CHRIS
B. Jun. 9, 1973, Hummelstown, PA
Indiana (Pennsylvania) 6'4" 300 lbs.

Year	Team		Games	Pos.
1996	CHI	N	14	C

Theo Viltz
VILTZ, THEOPHILE A.

Year	Team	Games	Pos.

Theo Viltz *continued*
B. Apr. 20, 1943
Southern California 6'2" 190 lbs.

1966	HOU	A	14	DB

Adam Vinatieri
VINATIERI, ADAM
B. Dec. 28, 1972, Yankton, SD
South Dakota State 6'0" 200 lbs.

1996	NE	N	16	K

Ralph Vince
VINCE, RALPH D.
B. Mar. 18, 1900, Vinci, Italy
Washington & Jefferson 5'8" 175 lbs.

1923	CLE	N	7	G
1925			8	G, E
1926	CLE	A	1	G

3 yrs. 16 games

Shawn Vincent
VINCENT, SHAWN DAVID
B. Jun. 2, 1968, Bellaire, OH
Akron 5'10" 180 lbs.

1991	PIT	N	10	CB

Ted Vincent
VINCENT, TED
B. Aug. 10, 1956, O'Fallon, MO
Wichita State 6'4" 264 lbs.

1978	CIN	N	16	DT
1979	SF	N	16	DT
1980			12	DT

3 yrs. 44 games

Troy Vincent
VINCENT, TROY
B. Jun. 8, 1970, Trenton, NJ
Wisconsin 6'0" 191 lbs.

1992	MIA	N	15	CB
1993			13	CB
1994			13	CB
1995			16	CB
1996	PHI	N	16	CB

5 yrs. 73 games

Paul Vinnola
VINNOLA, PAUL PETER
B. Aug. 24, 1922, Denver, CO
Santa Clara 5'10" 180 lbs.

1946	LA	AA	13	HB

Fernandus Vinson
VINSON, FERNANDUS LAMAR
B. Nov. 3, 1968, Montgomery, AL
North Carolina State 5'10" 197 lbs.

1991	CIN	N	13	S
1992			13	S
1993			16	S
1994			16	S

4 yrs. 58 games

Kenny Vinyard
VINYARD, KENNY
B. Jun. 18, 1947, Amarillo, TX
Texas Tech 5'10" 190 lbs.

1970	ATL	N	14	K

Scott Virkus
VIRKUS, SCOTT
B. Sep. 7, 1959, Palo Alto, CA
Purdue 6'5" 270 lbs.

1983	BUF	N	15	DE
1984			2	DE
1984	NE	N	5	DE

Scott Virkus *continued*

1984	IND	N	1	DE
1985			15	DE

3 yrs. 38 games

George Visger
VISGER, GEORGE ANTHONY
B. Sep. 26, 1958, Stockton, CA
Colorado 6'4" 250 lbs.

1980	SF	N	3	DT

Larry Visnic
VISNIC, LAWRENCE
B. Apr. 7, 1919, Jacobsburg, OH
St. Benedict's (Kansas) 5'11" 190 lbs.

1943	NYG	N	8	G
1944			5	G
1945			8	G

3 yrs. 21 games

Lionel Vital
VITAL, LIONEL
B. Jul. 15, 1963, Loreauville, LA
Nicholls State 5'9" 195 lbs.

1987	WAS	N	3	RB

Sandro Vitiello
VITIELLO, SANDRO
B. Feb. 21, 1958, Broccastella, Italy
Massachusetts 6'2" 197 lbs.

1980	CIN	N	2	K

Mark Vlasic
VLASIC, MARK RICHARD
B. Oct. 25, 1963, Rochester, PA
Iowa 6'3" 206 lbs.

1987	SD	N	1	QB
1988			2	QB
1990			6	QB
1991	KC	N	6	QB

4 yrs. 15 games

Joe Vodicka
VODICKA, JOSEPH J.
B. Mar. 4, 1921, Chicago, IL
D. Feb., 1985, Chicago, IL
Illinois Tech 5'10" 189 lbs.

1943	CHIB	N	3	HB
1945			4	HB
1945	CHIC	N	4	HB

2 yrs. 11 games

Evan Vogds
VOGDS, EVAN EDWARD (Red)
B. Feb. 10, 1923, Johnsburg, WI
Wisconsin 5'10" 210 lbs.

1946	CHI	AA	14	G
1947			13	G
1948	GB	N	12	G
1949			12	G

4 yrs. 51 games

Bob Vogel
VOGEL, ROBERT LOUIS
B. Sep. 23, 1941, Columbus, OH
Ohio State 6'5" 248 lbs.

1963	BAL	N	14	OT
1964			14	OT
1965			13	OT
1966			14	OT
1967			14	OT
1968			14	OT
1969			14	OT
1970			14	OT
1971			14	OT
1972			14	OT

10 yrs. 139 games

Paul Vogel
VOGEL, PAUL
B. Feb. 22, 1961, New York, NY
South Carolina 6'1" 220 lbs.

1987	HOU	N	1	LB

Carroll Vogelear
VOGELEAR, CARROLL ROBERT
B. Apr. 8, 1920, Idyllwild, CA
D. Dec. 7, 1967, Palm Springs, CA
Loyola (California)/San Francisco 6'3" 253 lbs.

1947	BOS	N	12	T
1948			12	T
1949	NYB	N	12	T
1950	NYY	N	10	T

4 yrs. 46 games

Tim Vogler
VOGLER, TIMOTHY GENE
B. Oct. 2, 1956, Troy, OH
Ohio State 6'3" 265 lbs.

1979	BUF	N	10	C
1980			10	C
1981			14	C
1982			6	C
1983			16	C
1984			14	C, G
1985			14	C
1986			9	G
1987			12	OL
1988			10	G

10 yrs. 117 games

Bob Voight
VOIGHT, BOB
B. 1937
Los Angeles State 6'5" 265 lbs.

1961	OAK	A	14	DT

Mike Voight
VOIGHT, MIKE
B. Feb. 28, 1954, Norfolk, VA
North Carolina 6'0" 214 lbs.

1977	HOU	N	14	RB

Walter Voight
VOIGHT, WALTER
B. Apr. 15, 1895
D. May, 1972
None 5'8" 200 lbs.

1920	CHIT	A	6	G, C
1921	HAM	A	3	C, HB, G
1921	CHIC	A	1	G

2 yrs. 10 games

Stu Voigt
VOIGT, STUART ALAN (Chainsaw)
B. Aug. 12, 1948, Madison, WI
Wisconsin 6'1" 223 lbs.

1970	MIN	N	3	TE
1971			12	TE
1972			14	TE
1973			13	TE
1974			14	TE
1975			13	TE
1976			14	TE
1977			14	TE
1978			15	TE
1979			16	TE
1980			3	TE

11 yrs. 131 games

Otto Vokaty
VOKATY, OTTO (Lefty)
B. 1909
Heidelberg 6'1" 191 lbs.

1931	CLE	N	8	FB, HB

Otto Vokaty *continued*

1932	NYG	N	5	FB, HB
1933	CHIC	N	1	FB, HB
1934	C-S	N	3	FB, HB

4 yrs. 17 games

Elmer Volgenau
VOLGENAU, ELMER P.
B. Aug. 2, 1900
D. Dec. 6, 1955, Clarence Compact, NY
Colgate 6'2" 190 lbs.

1924	ROC	N	1	G, T

Rick Volk
VOLK, RICHARD ROBERT
B. Mar. 15, 1945, Toledo, OH
Michigan 6'3" 195 lbs.

1967	BAL	N	14	DB
1968			14	DB
1969			14	S
1970			12	S
1971			14	S
1972			14	S
1973			14	S
1974			13	S
1975			13	S
1976	NYG	N	8	S
1977	MIA	N	3	S
1978			16	S

12 yrs. 150 games

Jim Vollenweider
VOLLENWEIDER, JAMES STEPHEN
B. Sep. 2, 1939
Miami (Florida) 6'1" 210 lbs.

1962	SF	N	14	HB
1963			13	FB

2 yrs. 27 games

Bill Volok
VOLOK, WILLIAM JAMES
B. Mar. 23, 1910, Lucas, KS
D. Aug. 6, 1991, Drumright, OK
Tulsa 6'2" 215 lbs.

1934	CHIC	N	10	G
1935			12	G, T
1936			12	G
1937			11	G
1938			11	G

5 yrs. 56 games

Pete Volz
VOLZ, PETE (The Caveman)
B. Jan. 13, 1897
D. Nov., 1957
Northwestern 190 lbs.

1920	CHIT	A	1	E
1921	CIN	A	4	E

2 yrs. 5 games

Wilbur Volz
VOLZ, WILBUR
B. Jan. 1, 1924, Edwardsville IL
Missouri 6'0" 192 lbs.

1949	BUF	AA	8	B

Kimo Von Oelhoffen
VON OELHOFFEN, KIMO
B. Jan. 30, 1971, Kaunakakai, HI
Hawaii/Boise State 6'4" 300 lbs.

1994	CIN	N	7	DT
1995			16	DT
1996			10	DT

3 yrs. 33 games

Year	Team	Games	Pos.

Uwe von Schamann
VON SCHAMANN, UWE DETLEF WALTER
B. Apr. 23, 1956, Berlin, Germany
Oklahoma 6'0" 192 lbs.

Year	Team		Games	Pos.
1979	MIA	N	16	K, P
1980			16	K
1981			16	K
1982			9	K
1983			16	K
1984			16	K

6 yrs.   89 games

Andy Von Sonn
VON SONN, ANDREW
B. Nov. 5, 1940, Los Angeles, CA
UCLA 6'2" 223 lbs.

1964	LA	N	14	LB

Don Vosberg
VOSBERG, DONALD THEODORE
B. Oct. 3, 1919, Dubuque, IA
Marquette 6'2" 188 lbs.

1941	NYG	N	7	E

Lloyd Voss
VOSS, LLOYD JOHN
B. Feb. 13, 1942, Adrian, MN
Nebraska 6'4" 256 lbs.

1964	GB	N	14	DE
1965			14	DE
1966	PIT	N	14	DT
1967			13	DT
1968			14	DE
1969			14	DE
1970			14	DE
1971			13	DE
1972	DEN	N	13	DE

9 yrs.   123 games

Tillie Voss
VOSS, WALTER C.
B. Mar. 28, 1897
D. Dec. 14, 1975, Florida
Detroit 6'3" 207 lbs.

1921	DET	A	7	E, T
1921	BUF	A	4	T
1922	RI	N	7	E
1922	AKR	N	2	E, T
1923	TOL	N	8	T, E
1924	GB	N	11	E
1925	DET	N	10	E
1926	NYG	N	12	E
1927	CHIB	N	11	E
1928			13	E
1929	DAY	N	1	T
1929	BUF	N	8	E

9 yrs.   94 games

Ed Voytek
VOYTEK, EDWARD LOUIS
B. Apr. 4, 1935, Cleveland, OH
Purdue 6'2" 235 lbs.

1957	WAS	N	12	G
1958			12	G

2 yrs.   24 games

Milt Vucinich
VUCINICH, MILTON CHRISTERFER
B. Nov. 1, 1920, San Francisco, CA
Stanford 6'0" 215 lbs.

1945	CHIB	N	3	C

Tom Waddle
WADDLE, GREGORY THOMAS

Tom Waddle *continued*
B. Feb. 20, 1967, Cincinnati, OH
Boston College 6'0" 181 lbs.

1989	CHI	N	3	WR
1990			5	WR
1991			16	WR
1992			12	WR
1993			15	WR
1994			9	WR

6 yrs.   60 games

Billy Waddy
WADDY, BILLY DEAN
B. Feb. 19, 1954, Wharton, TX
Colorado 5'11" 185 lbs.

1977	LA	N	14	WR
1978			11	WR
1979			13	WR
1980			15	WR
1981			15	WR
1982	LARM	N	3	WR
1984	MIN	N	4	WR

7 yrs.   75 games

Ray Waddy
WADDY, RAYMOND
B. Aug. 21, 1956, Freeport, TX
Texas A&I, Kingsville 5'11" 175 lbs.

1979	WAS	N	16	CB
1980			7	CB

2 yrs.   23 games

Billy Wade
WADE, WILLIAM JAMES, JR.
B. Oct. 4, 1930, Nashville, TN
Vanderbilt 6'2" 204 lbs.

1954	LA	N	10	QB
1955			7	QB
1956			12	QB
1957			5	QB
1958			12	QB
1959			12	QB
1960			11	QB
1961	CHI	N	13	QB
1962			14	QB
1963			14	QB
1964			11	QB
1965			5	QB
1966			2	QB

13 yrs.   128 games

Bob Wade
WADE, ROBERT PERNELL
B. Dec. 9, 1944, Baltimore, MD
Morgan State 6'2" 200 lbs.

1968	PIT	N	14	DB
1969	WAS	N	13	S
1970	DEN	N	3	CB

3 yrs.   30 games

Charlie Wade
WADE, CHARLES GARNELL
B. Feb. 23, 1950, Nashville, TN
Tennessee State 5'10" 163 lbs.

1974	CHI	N	14	WR
1975	GB	N	2	WR
1977	KC	N	5	WR

3 yrs.   21 games

Jim Wade
WADE, JAMES
B. Feb. 14, 1926, Talihina, OK
Oklahoma City 5'11" 175 lbs.

1949	NYB	N	10	B

Tommy Wade
WADE, THOMAS VIRGIL

Tommy Wade *continued*
B. Mar. 23, 1942, Henderson, TX
Texas 6'2" 195 lbs.

1964	PIT	N	1	QB
1965			4	QB

2 yrs.   5 games

Henry Waechter
WAECHTER, HENRY CARL
B. Feb. 13, 1959, Epworth, IA
Nebraska 6'5" 275 lbs.

1982	CHI	N	9	DE
1983	BAL	N	11	DE
1984	IND	N	1	DE
1984	CHI	N	2	DT
1985			13	DT
1986			16	DT
1987	WAS	N	1	DT

6 yrs.   53 games

Carl Wafer
WAFER, CARL
B. Jan. 17, 1951, Magnolia AR
Tennessee State 6'3" 250 lbs.

1974	GB	N	1	C

Clint Wager
WAGER, CLINTON B.
B. Jan. 20, 1922, Winona, MN
St. Mary's (Minnesota) 6'6" 218 lbs.

1942	CHIB	N	7	E
1943	CHIC	N	5	E
1944	C-P	N	8	E
1945	CHIC	N	3	E

4 yrs.   23 games

John Wager
WAGER, JOHN (Popeye, Red)
B. 1904, Mount Carmel, IL
D. 1982
Carthage 5'11" 203 lbs.

1931	POR	N	9	C, G
1932			10	G, C
1933			10	C, G

3 yrs.   29 games

Harmon Wages
WAGES, HARMON LEON
B. May 18, 1946, Jacksonville, FL
Florida 6'1" 214 lbs.

1968	ATL	N	13	RB
1969			14	RB
1970			13	RB
1971			14	RB
1973			6	RB

5 yrs.   60 games

Barry Wagner
WAGNER, BARRY
B. 1968
Alabama A&M 6'3" 213 lbs.

1992	CHI	N	1	WR

Bryan Wagner
WAGNER, BRYAN J.
B. Mar. 28, 1962, Escondido, CA
California Lutheran/Cal. State–Northridge 6'2" 198 lbs.

1987	CHI	N	10	P
1988			16	P
1989	CLE	N	16	P
1990			16	P
1991	NE	N	3	P
1992	GB	N	7	P
1993			16	P
1994	SD	N	14	P

Bryan Wagner *continued*

1995	NE	N	8	P

9 yrs.   106 games

Buff Wagner
WAGNER, ALMORE C.
B. Feb. 21, 1897, Marinette, WI
D. Feb., 1962
Carroll (Wisconsin) 5'9" 165 lbs.

1921	GB	A	4	HB, QB

Lowell Wagner
WAGNER, LOWELL R.
B. 1924
Southern California 6'0" 194 lbs.

1946	NY	AA	13	HB
1947			7	B
1948			14	B
1949	SF	AA	10	B
1950	SF	N	12	HB
1951			12	HB
1952			12	HB
1953			10	HB
1955			1	HB

9 yrs.   91 games

Mike Wagner
WAGNER, MICHAEL ROBERT
B. Jun. 22, 1949, Waukegan, IL
Western Illinois 6'1" 200 lbs.

1971	PIT	N	12	DB
1972			14	S
1973			14	S
1974			13	S
1975			12	S
1976			14	S
1977			3	S
1978			14	S
1979			8	S
1980			15	S

10 yrs.   119 games

Ray Wagner
WAGNER, RAYMOND JOHN
B. Feb. 25, 1902
Columbia 5'10" 172 lbs.

1929	ORA	N	1	E
1930	NEW	N	4	E, HB
1931	BKN	N	6	E, T

3 yrs.   11 games

Ray Wagner
WAGNER, RAYMOND L.
B. Nov. 15, 1957, Altoona, PA
Kent State 6'3" 290 lbs.

1982	CIN	N	4	OT

Sid Wagner
WAGNER, SIDNEY P.
B. Oct. 29, 1912, Lansing, MI
D. Nov., 1972, Alpena, MI
Michigan State 5'11" 192 lbs.

1936	DET	N	6	G
1937			11	G, T
1938			11	G

3 yrs.   28 games

Steve Wagner
WAGNER, STEVEN JOHN
B. Apr. 18, 1954, Milwaukee, WI
Wisconsin 6'2" 206 lbs.

1976	GB	N	11	S
1977			14	S
1978			16	S
1979			16	CB
1980	PHI	N	4	S

5 yrs.   61 games

Year	Team		Games	Pos.

Danny Wagoner
WAGONER, DANIEL WRIGHT
B. Dec. 12, 1959, High Point, NC
Kansas 5'10" 180 lbs.

Year	Team		Games	Pos.
1982	DET	N	1	CB, S
1983			14	CB, S
1984			1	CB, S
1984	MIN	N	4	S
1985	ATL	N	14	DB
4 yrs.	34 games			

Jim Wagstaff
WAGSTAFF, JAMES
B. Jun. 12, 1936, American Falls, ID
Idaho State 6'2" 192 lbs.

Year	Team		Games	Pos.
1959	CHIC	N	3	DB
1960	BUF	A		DB
1961			14	DB
3 yrs.	17 games			

Jim Wahler
WAHLER, JAMES JOSEPH
B. Jul. 29, 1966, San Jose, CA
UCLA 6'4" 272 lbs.

Year	Team		Games	Pos.
1989	PHX	N	13	DT
1990			16	DT
1991			15	NT
1992			5	NT
1992	WAS	N	5	DT
1993			8	DT
5 yrs.	62 games			

Loyd Wainscott
WAINSCOTT, LOYD DALE
B. Oct. 26, 1946, Texas City, TX
Texas 6'1" 235 lbs.

Year	Team		Games	Pos.
1969	HOU	A	14	LB
1970	HOU	N	11	LB
2 yrs.	25 games			

Frank Wainright
WAINRIGHT, FRANK WESLEY
B. Oct. 10, 1967, Peoria, IL
Northern Colorado 6'3" 236 lbs.

Year	Team		Games	Pos.
1991	NO	N	14	TE
1992			13	TE
1993			16	TE
1995	PHI	N	7	TE
1995	MIA	N	6	TE
1996			16	TE
5 yrs.	72 games			

Carl Waite
WAITE, CARL (Rusty)
B. Feb. 27, 1902
D. Oct., 1961
Rutgers/Georgetown (DC) 5'9" 205 lbs.

Year	Team		Games	Pos.
1928	FRA	N	7	E, HB
1929	ORA	N	11	HB, FB, T
1930	NEW	N	5	HB, QB, E
3 yrs.	23 games			

Will Waite
WAITE, WILLARD
B. Jan. 4, 1893
D. Jan., 1964, Cleveland, OH
None 6'2" 200 lbs.

Year	Team		Games	Pos.
1920	COL	A	5	C
1921			7	G, HB, T
2 yrs.	12 games			

Van Waiters
WAITERS, VAN ALLEN
B. Feb. 27, 1965, Coral Gables, FL
Indiana 6'4" 243 lbs.

Year	Team		Games	Pos.
1988	CLE	N	16	LB
1989			16	LB

Van Waiters continued

Year	Team		Games	Pos.
1990			16	LB
1991			16	LB
1992	MIN	N	16	LB
5 yrs.	80 games			

Alex Waits
WAITS, ALEX
B. Jun. 21, 1968, Glasgow, Scotland
Texas 6'2" 208 lbs.

Year	Team		Games	Pos.
1991	SEA	N	3	P

Larry Walbridge
WALBRIDGE, LYMAN
B. Sep. 11, 1897
D. Jan. 11, 1982, Pelham Manor, NY
Lafayette/Fordham 5'11" 200 lbs.

Year	Team		Games	Pos.
1925	NYG	N	2	C

Mark Walczak
WALCZAK, MARK CHARLES
B. Apr. 26, 1962, Rochester, NY
Arizona 6'6" 246 lbs.

Year	Team		Games	Pos.
1987	BUF	N	2	TE
1987	IND	N	8	TE
1988	PHX	N	16	TE
1989	SD	N	6	TE
1991			1	TE
4 yrs.	33 games			

Stan Waldemore
WALDEMORE, STANLEY
B. Feb. 20, 1955, Newark, NJ
Nebraska 6'4" 258 lbs.

Year	Team		Games	Pos.
1978	NYJ	N	4	G, OT
1979			16	G, OT
1980			16	G, OT, C
1981			16	C, OT, G
1982			9	G, C, OT
1983			4	G, C, OT
1984			14	G, OT
7 yrs.	79 games			

Bobby Walden
WALDEN, ROBERT EARL, SR.
B. Mar. 9, 1938, Boston, GA
Georgia 6'0" 192 lbs.

Year	Team		Games	Pos.
1964	MIN	N	14	P
1965			14	P
1966			14	P
1967			14	P
1968	PIT	N	14	P
1969			14	P
1970			13	P
1971			14	P
1972			14	P
1973			14	P
1974			14	P
1975			14	P
1976			14	P
1977			13	P
14 yrs.	194 games			

Tim Waldron
WALDRON, AUSTIN (Pinky)
B. 1903
Deceased
Gonzaga 195 lbs.

Year	Team		Games	Pos.
1927	CHIC	N	5	G, T, C

Rob Waldrop
WALDROP, ROBERT F.
B. Dec. 1, 1971, Atlanta, GA
Arizona 6'1" 276 lbs.

Year	Team		Games	Pos.
1994	KC	N	3	DT

Kerwin Waldroup
WALDROUP, KERWIN
B. Aug. 1, 1974, Chicago, IL
Michigan/Central State (Ohio) 6'3" 260 lbs.

Year	Team		Games	Pos.
1996	DET	N	16	DT

Ralph Waldsmith
WALDSMITH, RALPH GEORGE (Fat)
B. Aug. 7, 1892, Akron, OH
D. Jul. 7, 1925, Wilkes-Barre, PA
Akron 225 lbs.

Year	Team		Games	Pos.
1921	CLE	A	3	C
1922	CAN	N	5	G, C
2 yrs.	8 games			

Mark Walen
WALEN, MARK HARTLEY
B. Mar. 10, 1963, San Francisco, CA
UCLA 6'5" 262 lbs.

Year	Team		Games	Pos.
1987	DAL	N	9	DT
1988			15	DT
2 yrs.	24 games			

Billy Walik
WALIK, WILLIAM S.
B. Nov. 8, 1947, New Haven, CT
Villanova 5'11" 180 lbs.

Year	Team		Games	Pos.
1970	PHI	N	14	WR
1971			8	WR
1972			10	WR
3 yrs.	32 games			

Adam Walker
WALKER, ADAM
B. Apr. 9, 1963, New York, NY
Carthage 5'11" 220 lbs.

Year	Team		Games	Pos.
1987	MIN	N	2	RB

Adam Walker
WALKER, ADAM
B. Jun. 7, 1968, Pittsburgh, PA
Pittsburgh 6'1" 210 lbs.

Year	Team		Games	Pos.
1992	SF	N	1	RB
1993			10	RB
1994			8	RB
1995			13	RB
1996	PHI	N	13	RB
5 yrs.	45 games			

Billy Walker
WALKER, WILLIAM B.
B. Sep. 16, 1920, Richmond, VA
Virginia Military Institute 6'0" 220 lbs.

Year	Team		Games	Pos.
1944	BOS	N	10	G
1945			5	G
2 yrs.	15 games			

Bracey Walker
WALKER, BRACEY WORDELL
B. Oct. 28, 1970, Spring Lake, NC
North Carolina 5'10" 200 lbs.

Year	Team		Games	Pos.
1994	KC	N	2	S
1994	CIN	N	8	S
1995			14	S
1996			16	S
3 yrs.	40 games			

Bruce Walker
WALKER, BRUCE
B. Jul. 18, 1972, Compton, CA
UCLA 6'4" 310 lbs.

Year	Team		Games	Pos.
1995	NE	N	11	NT

Brian Walker
WALKER, BRIAN
B. May 31, 1972, Colorado Springs, CO
Washington State 6'2" 186 lbs.

Year	Team		Games	Pos.
1996	WAS	N	16	S

Byron Walker
WALKER, BYRON BURNEIL
B. Jul. 28, 1960, Scott AFB, IL
The Citadel 6'4" 190 lbs.

Year	Team		Games	Pos.
1982	SEA	N	9	WR
1983			16	WR
1984			16	WR
1985			16	WR
1986			1	WR
5 yrs.	58 games			

Chuck Walker
WALKER, CHARLES DAVID
B. Aug. 10, 1941, Uniontown, PA
Duke 6'2" 249 lbs.

Year	Team		Games	Pos.
1964	STL	N	3	DE
1965			14	DE
1966			14	DT
1967			13	DT
1968			14	DT
1969			14	DE
1970			11	DE
1971			11	DE
1972			2	DT
1972	ATL	N	11	DT
1973			14	DT
1974			14	DT
1975			10	DT
12 yrs.	145 games			

Clarence Walker
WALKER, CLARENCE
B. 1939, De Quincy, LA
Southern Illinois 6'1" 205 lbs.

Year	Team		Games	Pos.
1963	DEN	A	1	HB

Cleo Walker
WALKER, CLEO FRANKLIN
B. Feb. 7, 1948, Columbus, GA
Louisville 6'3" 220 lbs.

Year	Team		Games	Pos.
1970	GB	N	14	C, LB
1971	ATL	N	10	LB
2 yrs.	24 games			

Darnell Walker
WALKER, DARNELL ROBERT
B. Jan. 17, 1970, St. Louis, MO
Oklahoma 5'8" 164 lbs.

Year	Team		Games	Pos.
1993	ATL	N	15	CB
1994			16	CB
1995			16	CB
1996			15	CB
4 yrs.	62 games			

Derrick Walker
WALKER, DERRICK NORVAL
B. Jun. 23, 1967, Glenwood, IL
Michigan 6'1" 244 lbs.

Year	Team		Games	Pos.
1990	SD	N	16	TE
1991			16	TE
1992			16	TE
1993			12	TE
1994	KC	N	15	TE
1995			16	TE
1996			11	TE
7 yrs.	102 games			

Doak Walker
WALKER, EWELL DOAK, JR.
B. Jan. 1, 1927, Dallas, TX

Year	Team	Games	Pos.

Doak Walker *continued*
Southern Methodist 5'11" 173 lbs.

Year	Team		Games	Pos.
1950	**DET**	N	12	HB
1951			12	HB
1952			7	HB
1953			12	HB
1954			12	HB
1955			12	HB
6 yrs.	67 games			

Donnie Walker
WALKER, DONNIE MACK
B. Dec. 26, 1950, Bronx, NY
Central State (Ohio) 6'1" 182 lbs.

1973	**BUF**	N	11	CB
1974			14	S
1975	**NYJ**	N	2	CB
3 yrs.	27 games			

Dwight Walker
WALKER, DWIGHT GERARD
B. Jan. 10, 1959, Metairie, LA
Nicholls State 5'10" 185 lbs.

1982	**CLE**	N	9	RB
1983			16	RB, WR
1984			11	RB
1987	**NO**	N	2	WR
4 yrs.	38 games			

Elliott Walker
WALKER, ELLIOTT
B. Sep. 10, 1956, Indianola, MS
Pittsburgh 5'11" 193 lbs.

| 1978 | **SF** | N | 9 | RB |

Fulton Walker
WALKER, FULTON LUTHER, JR.
B. Apr. 30, 1958, Martinsburg, WV
West Virginia 5'11" 193 lbs.

1981	**MIA**	N	16	CB
1982			9	CB
1983			15	CB
1984			12	CB
1985			2	CB
1985	**LARI**	N	13	S
1986			14	S
6 yrs.	81 games			

Gary Walker
WALKER, GARY
B. Feb. 28, 1973, Lavonia, GA
Auburn 6'2" 285 lbs.

1995	**HOU**	N	15	DT
1996			16	DT
2 yrs.	31 games			

Gary Walker
WALKER, GARY WAYNE
B. Dec. 15, 1963
Boston University 6'3" 283 lbs.

| 1987 | **DAL** | N | 1 | OT, G |

Glen Walker
WALKER, GLEN JOE
B. Jan. 16, 1952, Torrance, CA
Southern California 6'1" 210 lbs.

1977	**LA**	N	14	P, K
1978			16	P, K
2 yrs.	30 games			

Herschel Walker
WALKER, HERSCHEL
B. Mar. 3, 1962, Wrightsville, GA
Georgia 6'1" 225 lbs.

| 1986 | **DAL** | N | 16 | RB |
| 1987 | | | 12 | RB |

Herschel Walker *continued*

1988			16	RB
1989			5	RB
1989	**MIN**	N	11	RB
1990			16	RB
1991			15	RB
1992	**PHI**	N	16	RB
1993			16	RB
1994			16	RB
1995	**NYG**	N	16	RB
1996	**DAL**	N	16	RB
11 yrs.	171 games			

Homer Walker
WALKER, HOMER D. (Bear)
B. Jan. 17, 1903
D. Sep., 1986, Austin, TX
Baylor 5'10" 195 lbs.

| 1926 | **RI** | A | 7 | E |

Jackie Walker
WALKER, JACKIE A.
B. Nov. 3, 1962, Monroe, LA
Jackson State 6'5" 250 lbs.

1986	**TB**	N	15	LB
1987			12	LB
1988			16	LB
1989			14	TE
4 yrs.	57 games			

James Walker
WALKER, JAMES CHARLES
B. Dec. 9, 1958, Muskogee, OK
Kansas State 6'1" 250 lbs.

| 1983 | **KC** | N | 4 | LB |

Jay Walker
WALKER, JEWELL JAY
B. Jan. 24, 1972, Los Angeles, CA
Howard 6'3" 230 lbs.

| 1996 | **MIN** | N | 2 | QB |

Jeff Walker
WALKER, JEFFREY LYNN
B. Jan. 22, 1963, Jonesboro, AR
Memphis State 6'4" 295 lbs.

1986	**SD**	N	16	G
1988	**NO**	N	1	OT
1989			13	G
3 yrs.	30 games			

Jimmy Walker
WALKER, JAMES
B. Dec. 30, 1956, Camden, AR
Arkansas 6'2" 265 lbs.

| 1987 | **MIN** | N | 2 | DT |

John Walker
WALKER, JOHN WAYNE
B. Sep. 12, 1961, Omaha, NE
Nebraska-Omaha 6'6" 270 lbs.

| 1987 | **KC** | N | 3 | DL |

Kenny Walker
WALKER, KENNY WAYNE
B. Apr. 6, 1967, Crane, TX
Nebraska 6'3" 260 lbs.

1991	**DEN**	N	16	DE, NT
1992			15	DE, DT
2 yrs.	31 games			

Kevin Walker
WALKER, KEVIN CORNELIUS
B. Oct. 20, 1963, Greensboro, NC
East Carolina 5'11" 180 lbs.

| 1986 | **TB** | N | 4 | CB, S |

Kevin Walker *continued*

| 1987 | | | 3 | CB |
| 2 yrs. | 7 games | | | |

Kevin Walker
WALKER, KEVIN P.
B. Dec. 24, 1965, Denville, NJ
Maryland 6'2" 238 lbs.

1988	**CIN**	N	3	LB
1989			16	LB
1990			16	LB
1991			5	LB
1992			4	LB
5 yrs.	44 games			

Louie Walker
WALKER, LOUIE
B. Jul. 23, 1952, Los Angeles, CA
Colorado State 6'1" 216 lbs.

| 1974 | **DAL** | N | 8 | LB |

Malcolm Walker
WALKER, MALCOLM E.
B. May 24, 1943, Dallas, TX
Rice 6'4" 249 lbs.

1966	**DAL**	N	5	C, LB
1967			14	C, OT
1968			14	C, OT
1969			14	C, OT
1970	**GB**	N	14	LB
5 yrs.	61 games			

Marquis Walker
WALKER, MARQUIS ROSHE
B. Jul. 6, 1972, St. Louis, MO
Southeast Missouri State 5'10" 173 lbs.

1996	**WAS**	N	1	CB
1996	**STL**	N	8	CB
1 yr.	9 games			

Mickey Walker
WALKER, GEORGE MICKEY
B. Oct. 14, 1939, Petoskey, MI
Michigan State 6'0" 232 lbs.

1961	**NYG**	N	14	LB
1962			14	G
1963			13	LB
1964			7	G
1965			4	G
5 yrs.	52 games			

Mike Walker
WALKER, JOSEPH MICHAEL
B. Nov. 7, 1949, Texarkana, AR
Tulane 6'4" 235 lbs.

| 1971 | **NO** | N | 5 | DE |

Mike Walker
WALKER, MICHAEL
B. Oct. 18, 1949, Lancaster, England
none 6'0" 190 lbs.

| 1972 | **NE** | N | 8 | K |

Paul Walker
WALKER, PAUL FREDERICK
B. Jul. 29, 1925, Springfield MO
D. Oct. 20, 1972, West Hartford, CT
Yale 6'3" 210 lbs.

| 1948 | **NYG** | N | 12 | E |

Quentin Walker
WALKER, LAQUENTIN
ANTONIO
B. Aug. 27, 1961, Teaneck, NJ
Virginia 6'1" 205 lbs.

| 1984 | **STL** | N | 3 | RB |

Randy Walker
WALKER, RANDALL PAUL
B. Aug. 29, 1951, Shreveport, LA
Northwestern State (Louisiana) 5'10" 177 lbs.

| 1974 | **GB** | N | 14 | P |

Rick Walker
WALKER, RICHARD
B. May 28, 1955, Santa Ana, CA
UCLA 6'3" 236 lbs.

1977	**CIN**	N	6	TE
1978			15	TE
1979			10	TE
1980	**WAS**	N	15	TE
1981			16	TE
1982			9	TE
1983			16	TE
1984			16	TE
1985			16	TE
9 yrs.	119 games			

Robert Walker
WALKER, ROBERT
B. Jun. 26, 1972, Huntington, WV
West Virginia 5'11" 180 lbs.

| 1996 | **NYG** | N | 1 | RB |

Sammy Walker
WALKER, SAMMY WILLIAM
B. Jan. 20, 1969, McKinney, TX
Texas Tech 5'11" 197 lbs.

1991	**PIT**	N	2	TE
1992			16	CB
1993	**GB**	N	8	CB
3 yrs.	26 games			

Tim Walker
WALKER, TIMOTHY ALAN
B. May 12, 1958, Hartford, CT
Savannah State 6'1" 230 lbs.

| 1980 | **SEA** | N | 16 | LB |

Tony Walker
WALKER, TONY MAURICE
B. Apr. 2, 1968, Birmingham, AL
Southeast Missouri State 6'3" 235 lbs.

1990	**IND**	N	14	LB
1991			16	LB
1992			13	LB
3 yrs.	43 games			

Val Joe Walker
WALKER, VAL JOE
B. Jan. 7, 1930, Tahoka, TX
Southern Methodist 6'1" 179 lbs.

1953	**GB**	N	12	HB
1954			10	HB
1955			12	HB
1956			12	HB
1957	**SF**	N	12	HB
5 yrs.	58 games			

Wayne Walker
WALER, RONALD WAYNE
B. Dec. 27, 1966, Waco, TX
Texas Tech 5'8" 162 lbs.

| 1989 | **SD** | N | 13 | WR |

Wayne Walker
WALKER, WAYNE
B. Oct. 14, 1944, Shreveport, LA
Northwestern Louisiana State 6'2" 215 lbs.

1967	**KC**	A	4	P
1968	**HOU**	A	8	K, P
2 yrs.	12 games			

Year	Team	Games	Pos.

Wayne Walker
WALKER, WAYNE HARRISON
B. Sep. 30, 1936, Boise, ID
Idaho 6'2" 225 lbs.

Year	Team	Games	Pos.
1958	**DET** N	12	LB
1959		9	LB, K
1960		12	LB
1961		14	LB, K
1962		14	LB, K
1963		14	LB, K
1964		14	LB, K
1965		14	LB, K
1966		13	LB, K
1967		14	LB, K
1968		14	LB, K
1969		14	LB
1970		14	LB
1971		14	LB, K
1972		14	LB
15 yrs.	200 games		

Wesley Walker
WALKER, WESLEY DARCEL
B. May 26, 1955, San Bernardino, CA
California 6'0" 178 lbs.

Year	Team	Games	Pos.
1977	**NYJ** N	14	WR
1978		16	WR
1979		9	WR
1980		10	WR
1981		13	WR
1982		9	WR
1983		16	WR
1984		12	WR
1985		12	WR
1986		16	WR
1987		5	WR
1988		16	WR
1989		6	WR
13 yrs.	154 games		

Willie Walker
WALKER, WILLIE
B. Sep. 15, 1942, Anguilla, MS
Tennessee State 6'3" 200 lbs.

Year	Team	Games	Pos.
1966	**DET** N	9	FL

Eddie Wall
WALESKI, EDWARD
B. Feb. 1, 1906
D. Jan., 1978, Delray Beach, FL
Allegheny/Grove City 5'9" 170 lbs.

Year	Team	Games	Pos.
1930	**FRA** N	6	T

Aaron Wallace
WALLACE, AARON
B. Apr. 17, 1967, Paris, TX
Texas A&M 6'3" 236 lbs.

Year	Team	Games	Pos.
1990	**LARI** N	16	LB
1991		16	LB
1992		16	LB
1993		16	LB
1994		16	LB
1995	**OAK** N	13	DE
6 yrs.	93 games		

Beverly Wallace
WALLACE, BEVERLY WILLIAM
B. Mar. 7, 1923
Compton JC 6'2" 180 lbs.

Year	Team	Games	Pos.
1947	**SF** AA	4	B
1948		10	B
1949		9	B
3 yrs.	23 games		

Bob Wallace
WALLACE, ROBERT
B. Oct. 7, 1945, Phoenix, AZ
Texas-El Paso 6'3" 213 lbs.

Year	Team	Games	Pos.
1968	**CHI** N	12	FL, TE

Bob Wallace *continued*

Year	Team	Games	Pos.
1969		14	WR
1970		5	WR
1971		14	WR
1972		14	TE
5 yrs.	59 games		

Calvin Wallace
WALLACE, CALVIN
B. Apr. 17, 1965
West Virginia Tech 6'3" 230 lbs.

Year	Team	Games	Pos.
1987	**GB** N	1	DE

Dutch Wallace
WALLACE, CLARENCE
B. Apr. 18, 1900, Akron, OH
D. Feb., 1977, Akron, OH
None 6'0" 208 lbs.

Year	Team	Games	Pos.
1923	**AKR** N	5	G, T
1924		7	G, C, E
1925	**CLE** N	11	G, T
1926	**CAN** N	7	G
1926	**AKR** N	1	G
4 yrs.	31 games		

Gordon Wallace
WALLACE, GORDON LEWIS
B. Aug. 6, 1899
Deceased
Rochester 5'10" 170 lbs.

Year	Team	Games	Pos.
1923	**ROC** N	2	HB
1924		1	C
2 yrs.	3 games		

Henry Wallace
WALLACE, HENRY
B. 1938
Pacific 6'0" 195 lbs.

Year	Team	Games	Pos.
1960	**LA** A		DB

Jackie Wallace
WALLACE, JACKIE
B. Mar. 13, 1951, New Orleans, LA
Arizona 6'3" 197 lbs.

Year	Team	Games	Pos.
1974	**MIN** N	14	DB
1975	**BAL** N	14	S
1976		14	S
1977	**LA**	10	DB
1978		14	S, CB
1979		4	S
6 yrs.	70 games		

John Wallace
WALLACE, JOHN J.
B. Sep. 5, 1904
D. Aug., 1981, Niagara Falls, NY
Notre Dame 6'0" 180 lbs.

Year	Team	Games	Pos.
1928	**CHIB** N	12	E
1929	**DAY** N	4	E
2 yrs.	16 games		

Ray Wallace
WALLACE, RAYMOND DURYEA
B. Dec. 3, 1963, Indianapolis, IN
Purdue 6'0" 224 lbs.

Year	Team	Games	Pos.
1986	**HOU** N	8	FB
1987		12	FB
1989	**PIT** N	9	RB
3 yrs.	29 games		

Rod Wallace
WALLACE, RODNEY ALLAN
B. Feb. 10, 1949, Pueblo, CO
New Mexico 6'5" 255 lbs.

Year	Team	Games	Pos.
1971	**DAL** N	11	G
1972		14	G
1973		12	G
3 yrs.	37 games		

Roger Wallace
WALLACE, ROGER LEE
B. Jul. 22, 1952, Urbana, OH
Bowling Green 5'11" 180 lbs.

Year	Team	Games	Pos.
1976	**NYG** N	3	WR

Stan Wallace
WALLACE, STANLEY HOWARD
B. Nov. 15, 1931, Hillsboro, IL
Illinois 6'3" 208 lbs.

Year	Team	Games	Pos.
1954	**CHIB** N	7	HB
1956		6	HB
1957		12	HB
1958		12	HB
4 yrs.	37 games		

Steve Wallace
WALLACE, BARRON STEVEN
B. Dec. 27, 1964, Atlanta, GA
Auburn 6'5" 276 lbs.

Year	Team	Games	Pos.
1986	**SF** N	16	OT
1987		11	OT
1988		16	OT
1989		16	OT
1990		16	OT
1991		16	OT
1992		16	OT
1993		15	OT
1994		15	OT
1995		13	OT
1996		16	OT
11 yrs.	166 games		

Bill Waller
WALLER, WILLIAM H. (Blondy)
B. Dec. 2, 1914
D. Nov., 1979
Illinois 6'1" 190 lbs.

Year	Team	Games	Pos.
1938	**BKN** N	10	E

Ron Waller
WALLER, RONALD
B. Feb. 14, 1933, Hastings, FL
Maryland 5'11" 180 lbs.

Year	Team	Games	Pos.
1955	**LA** N	12	HB
1956		9	HB
1957		11	HB
1958		10	HB
1960	**LA** A		HB
5 yrs.	42 games		

Brett Wallerstedt
WALLERSTEDT, BRETT ROBERT
B. Nov. 24, 1970, Tacoma, WA
Arizona State 6'1" 240 lbs.

Year	Team	Games	Pos.
1993	**PHX** N	7	LB
1994	**CIN** N	10	LB
1995		11	LB
3 yrs.	28 games		

James Wallis
WALLIS, JAMES J.
B. Oct. 19, 1902
D. Jun., 1977, Lynn, MA
Holy Cross 5'10" 180 lbs.

Year	Team	Games	Pos.
1926	**BOS** A	6	QB, HB, FB

Fred Wallner
WALLNER, FREDERICK WILLIAM
B. Apr. 12, 1928, Greenfield, MA
Notre Dame 6'2" 231 lbs.

Year	Team	Games	Pos.
1951	**CHIC** N	12	G
1952		7	G
1954		12	G
1955		12	G
1960	**HOU** A		G
5 yrs.	43 games		

Craig Walls
WALLS, CRAIG STEVENS, SR.
B. Dec. 24, 1958, Pittsburgh, PA
Indiana 6'1" 215 lbs.

Year	Team	Games	Pos.
1987	**BUF** N	3	LB

Everson Walls
WALLS, EVERSON COLLINS
B. Dec. 28, 1959, Dallas, TX
Grambling State 6'1" 194 lbs.

Year	Team	Games	Pos.
1981	**DAL** N	16	CB
1982		9	CB
1983		16	CB
1984		16	CB
1985		16	CB
1986		16	CB
1987		12	CB
1988		16	CB
1989		16	CB
1990	**NYG** N	16	CB
1991		14	CB
1992		6	CB, S
1992	**CLE** N	10	CB, S
1993		7	CB
13 yrs.	186 games		

Henry Walls
WALLS, HENRY
B. Feb. 13, 1964, Lexington, NC
Clemson 6'2" 220 lbs.

Year	Team	Games	Pos.
1987	**NYJ** N	3	LB

Herkie Walls
WALLS, MCCUREY HERCULES
B. Jul. 18, 1961, Garland, TX
Texas 5'8" 160 lbs.

Year	Team	Games	Pos.
1983	**HOU** N	16	WR
1984		14	WR
1985		6	WR
1987	**TB** N	2	WR
4 yrs.	38 games		

Wesley Walls
WALLS, CHARLES WESLEY
B. Feb. 26, 1966, Batesville, MS
Mississippi 6'5" 246 lbs.

Year	Team	Games	Pos.
1989	**SF** N	16	TE
1990		16	TE
1991		15	TE
1993		6	TE
1994	**NO** N	15	TE
1995		16	TE
1996	**CAR** N	16	TE
7 yrs.	100 games		

Will Walls
WALLS, WILLIAM
B. Dec. 8, 1914, Lonoke, AR
D. Jan. 2, 1993, Dallas, TX
Texas Christian 6'4" 214 lbs.

Year	Team	Games	Pos.
1937	**NYG** N	11	E
1938		4	E
1939		10	E
1941		11	E
1942		11	E
1943		8	E
6 yrs.	55 games		

Laurie Walquist
WALQUIST, LAWRENCE W.
B. Mar. 9, 1898
D. Sep. 28, 1985, Deerfield Lake, IL
Illinois 5'8" 167 lbs.

Year	Team	Games	Pos.
1922	**CHIB** N	11	HB, FB
1924		9	HB
1925		15	HB, FB
1926		15	HB, FB
1927		14	HB
1928		12	HB

Year	Team		Games	Pos.

Laurie Walquist continued

Year	Team		Games	Pos.
1929			13	HB, QB
1930			10	HB, QB
1931			10	QB
9 yrs.	109 games			

Bill Walsh
WALSH, WILLIAM HENRY
B. Sep. 8, 1927, Phillipsburg, NJ
Notre Dame 6'2" 230 lbs.

1949	PIT	N	12	C
1950			12	C
1951			12	C
1952			12	C
1954			12	C
5 yrs.	60 games			

Chris Walsh
WALSH, CHRISTOPHER LEE
B. Dec. 12, 1968, Cleveland, OH
Stanford 6'1" 185 lbs.

1992	BUF	N	2	WR
1993			3	WR
1994	MIN	N	10	WR
1995			16	WR
1996			15	WR
5 yrs.	46 games			

Ed Walsh
WALSH, EDWARD
B. 1936
Widener 6'4" 243 lbs.

1961	NY	A	6	OT

Jimmy Walsh
WALSH, JIM
B. Dec. 17, 1956, Burlingame, CA
San Jose State 5'11" 220 lbs.

1980	SEA	N	4	FB

Steve Walsh
WALSH, STEPHEN JOHN
B. Dec. 1, 1966, St. Paul, MN
Miami (Florida) 6'2" 200 lbs.

1989	DAL	N	8	QB
1990			1	QB
1990	NO	N	12	QB
1991			8	QB
1993			2	QB
1994	CHI	N	12	QB
1995			1	QB
1996	STL	N	3	QB
7 yrs.	47 games			

Ward Walsh
WALSH, WARD
B. Nov. 21, 1949, Paradise, CA
Colorado 6'0" 213 lbs.

1971	HOU	N	12	RB
1972			6	RB
1972	GB	N	2	RB
2 yrs.	20 games			

Bullets Walson
WALSON, CHARLES
B. Jan. 6, 1893
D. Dec., 1963
None 174 lbs.

1921	WAS	A	3	QB

Bobby Walston
WALSTON, ROBERT HAROLD
B. Oct. 17, 1928, Columbus, OH
D. Oct. 7, 1987, Roselle, IL
Georgia 6'0" 190 lbs.

1951	PHI	N	12	E, K
1952			12	E, K

Bobby Walston continued

Year	Team		Games	Pos.
1953			12	E, K
1954			12	E, K
1955			12	E, K
1956			12	E, K
1957			12	E, K
1958			12	E, K
1959			12	E, K
1960			12	E, K
1961			14	OE, K
1962			14	OE, K
12 yrs.	148 games			

Dave Walter
WALTER, DAVID
B. Dec. 9, 1964, West Branch, MI
Michigan Tech 6'3" 230 lbs.

1987	CIN	N	3	QB

Joe Walter
WALTER, JOSEPH FOLLMANN, JR.
B. Jun. 18, 1963, Dallas, TX
Texas Tech 6'6" 290 lbs.

1985	CIN	N	14	OT
1986			15	OT
1987			12	OT
1988			16	OT
1989			10	OT
1990			16	OT
1991			15	OT
1992			16	OT
1993			16	OT
1995			16	OT
1996			16	OT
11 yrs.	162 games			

Mike Walter
WALTER, MICHAEL DAVID
B. Nov. 30, 1960, Salem, OR
Oregon 6'3" 240 lbs.

1983	DAL	N	15	LB
1984	SF	N	16	LB
1985			14	LB
1986			16	LB
1987			12	LB
1988			16	LB
1989			16	LB
1990			3	LB
1991			11	LB
1992			15	LB
1993			15	LB
11 yrs.	149 games			

Walters
WALTERS
None

1924	KEN	N	3	HB

Chal Walters
WALTERS, CHALMERS
B. Mar. 19, 1900
D. Aug. 28, 1992
Washington 5'9" 190 lbs.

1926	LA	A	11	C

Dale Walters
WALTERS, DALE JAMES
B. Jun. 21, 1961, Dighton, KS
Rice 6'0" 200 lbs.

1987	CLE	N	2	P

Danny Walters
WALTERS, DANNY EUGENE
B. Nov. 4, 1960, Prescott, AR
Arkansas 6'1" 186 lbs.

1983	SD	N	16	CB
1984			8	CB

Danny Walters continued

Year	Team		Games	Pos.
1985			16	CB
1986			2	CB
1987			12	CB
5 yrs.	54 games			

Joey Walters
WALTERS, JOEY LAVERNE
B. Oct. 29, 1958, Florence, SC
Clemson 5'11" 175 lbs.

1987	HOU	N	5	WR

Les Walters
WALTERS, LESTER K.
B. Feb. 13, 1937, Palmyra, PA
Penn State 6'0" 185 lbs.

1958	WAS	N	8	HB

Pete Walters
WALTERS, PETER
B. Mar. 17, 1959, Shepherdsville, KY
Western Kentucky 6'2" 265 lbs.

1987	PHI	N	3	G

Rod Walters
WALTERS, WAYNE RODERICK, II
B. Feb. 27, 1954, Lansing, MI
Iowa 6'3" 258 lbs.

1976	KC	N	14	G
1978			16	G, OT
1979			16	G, OT
1980			6	G
1980	MIA	N	1	G
1980	DET	N	2	G
4 yrs.	55 games			

Stan Walters
WALTERS, STANLEY PETER
B. May 27, 1948, Rutherford, NJ
Syracuse 6'6" 270 lbs.

1972	CIN	N	8	OT
1973			4	OT
1974			14	OT
1975	PHI	N	14	OT
1976			14	OT
1977			14	OT
1978			16	OT
1979			16	OT
1980			16	OT
1981			16	OT
1982			9	OT
1983			12	OT
12 yrs.	153 games			

Tommy Walters
WALTERS, THOMAS H.
B. Jun. 11, 1942, Petal, MS
Southern Mississippi 6'2" 195 lbs.

1964	WAS	N	13	DB
1965			14	DB
1966			12	DB
1967			10	DB
4 yrs.	49 games			

Len Walterscheid
WALTERSCHEID, LEONARD RAYMOND
B. Sep. 13, 1954, Gainesville, TX
Southern Utah State 5'11" 189 lbs.

1977	CHI	N	14	DB
1978			14	S
1979			16	S
1980			15	S
1981			6	S
1982			9	S
1983	BUF	N	3	S
7 yrs.	77 games			

Alvin Walton
WALTON, ALVIN EARL
B. Mar. 14, 1964, Riverside, CA
Kansas 6'0" 180 lbs.

1986	WAS	N	16	S
1987			12	S
1988			16	S
1989			13	S
1990			16	S
1991			4	S
6 yrs.	77 games			

Bruce Walton
WALTON, BRUCE
B. Jun. 14, 1951, San Diego, CA
UCLA 6'6" 250 lbs.

1973	DAL	N	7	G, OT
1974			13	G
1975			13	OT
3 yrs.	33 games			

Chuck Walton
WALTON, CHARLES RICHARD
B. Jul. 7, 1941, Canon City, CO
Iowa State 6'3" 253 lbs.

1967	DET	N	14	G
1968			14	G
1969			14	G
1970			14	G
1971			14	G
1972			10	G
1973			4	G
1974			14	G
8 yrs.	98 games			

Frank Walton
WALTON, FRANK JOSEPH (Tiger)
B. Dec. 25, 1911, Beaver Falls, PA
D. Sep., 1953, Beaver Falls, PA
Pittsburgh 5'11" 230 lbs.

1934	BOS	N	12	G
1944	WAS	N	10	G, B
1945			3	G
3 yrs.	25 games			

Joe Walton
WALTON, JOSEPH FRANK
B. Dec. 15, 1935, Beaver Falls, PA
Pittsburgh 5'11" 202 lbs.

1957	WAS	N	12	E
1958			12	E
1959			9	E
1960			12	E
1961	NYG	N	12	OE
1962			14	OE
1963			12	OE
7 yrs.	83 games			

Johnnie Walton
WALTON, JOHNNIE B.
B. Oct. 4, 1947, Elizabeth City, NC
Elizabeth City State 6'2" 210 lbs.

1976	PHI	N	3	QB
1978			4	QB
1979			8	QB
3 yrs.	15 games			

Larry Walton
WALTON, LARRY JAMES
B. Feb. 8, 1947, Johnstown, PA
Arizona State 6'0" 181 lbs.

1969	DET	N	14	WR
1970			13	WR
1971			14	WR
1972			14	WR
1973			13	WR
1974			13	WR
1976			14	WR
1978	BUF	N	12	WR
8 yrs.	107 games			

Year	Team	Games	Pos.

Riley Walton
WALTON, RILEY
B. Aug. 6, 1962, Nashville, TN
Tennessee State 6'4" 245 lbs.

Year	Team		Games	Pos.
1987	KC	N	2	TE

Sam Walton
WALTON, SAM T., JR.
B. Jan. 3, 1943, Memphis, TN
East Texas State 6'5" 270 lbs.

Year	Team		Games	Pos.
1968	NY	A	14	OT
1969			6	OT
1971	HOU	N	14	OT

3 yrs. 34 games

Wayne Walton
WALTON, GERALD WAYNE
B. Oct. 15, 1948, Waco, TX
Abilene Christian 6'5" 252 lbs.

Year	Team		Games	Pos.
1971	NYG	N	14	OT, C
1973	KC	N	14	OL
1974			9	G, OT

3 yrs. 37 games

Whip Walton
WALTON, WHIP
B. Jul. 16, 1955, Corona, CA
San Diego State 6'2" 225 lbs.

Year	Team		Games	Pos.
1980	NYG	N	3	LB

George Wanless
WANLESS, GEORGE
B. Jul., 1898
Deceased
None 5'8" 160 lbs.

Year	Team		Games	Pos.
1922	LOU	N	1	G
1923			2	HB, E

2 yrs. 3 games

Hal Wantland
WANTLAND, HOWELL SMITH
B. 1945
Tennessee 6'0" 195 lbs.

Year	Team		Games	Pos.
1966	MIA	A	2	DB

Ward
WARD
None

Year	Team		Games	Pos.
1920	HAM	A	2	QB, HB

Ward
WARD
None

Year	Team		Games	Pos.
1921	SYR	A	1	FB

Bill Ward
WARD, WILLIAM C.
B. Feb. 19, 1921, Sequim, WA
D. Dec. 3, 1992, Bellingham, WA
Washington State/Washington 6'0" 230 lbs.

Year	Team		Games	Pos.
1946	WAS	N	9	QB
1947	DET	N	4	G
1948			12	G
1949			12	G

4 yrs. 37 games

Bill Ward
WARD, WILLIAM H.
B. 1898
Pennsylvania 6'0" 212 lbs.

Year	Team		Games	Pos.
1921	BUF	A	9	T, G

Carl Ward
WARD, CARL DAVIS
B. Jul. 26, 1944, Hartselle, AL
Michigan 5'9" 180 lbs.

Year	Team		Games	Pos.
1967	CLE	N	14	DB
1968			14	DB
1969	NO	N	2	S

3 yrs. 30 games

Chris Ward
WARD, CHRISTOPHER LAMAR
B. Dec. 16, 1955, Cleveland, OH
Ohio State 6'3" 280 lbs.

Year	Team		Games	Pos.
1978	NYJ	N	16	OT, G
1979			16	OT
1980			14	OT
1981			16	OT
1982			9	OT
1983			16	OT
1984	NO	N	13	OT

7 yrs. 100 games

Dave Ward
WARD, DAVID
B. Mar. 10, 1964, Helena, AR
Southern Arkansas 6'2" 231 lbs.

Year	Team		Games	Pos.
1987	CIN	N	3	LB
1989	NE	N	16	LB

2 yrs. 19 games

David Ward
WARD, DAVID (Nubbin)
B. Oct. 13, 1906
D. Jun., 1975, Toppenish, WA
Haskell/New Mexico 5'10" 195 lbs.

Year	Team		Games	Pos.
1933	BOS	N	1	E

Elmer Ward
WARD, ELMER HENRY (Bear)
B. Oct. 13, 1912, Willard, UT
Deceased
Utah State 6'2" 215 lbs.

Year	Team		Games	Pos.
1935	DET	N	11	C, G

Jim Ward
WARD, JAMES EDGAR HAROLD
B. Jul. 16, 1944, Gaithersburg, MD
Gettysburg 6'2" 197 lbs.

Year	Team		Games	Pos.
1967	BAL	N	6	QB
1968			5	QB
1971	PHI	N	2	QB

3 yrs. 13 games

John Ward
WARD, JOHN HENRY
B. May 27, 1948, Enid, OK
Oklahoma State 6'4" 258 lbs.

Year	Team		Games	Pos.
1970	MIN	N	14	DT
1971			14	DE
1972			14	DE
1973			8	G
1975			14	C, G
1976	TB	N	4	G, C
1976	CHI		10	OL

6 yrs. 78 games

Johnny Ward
WARD, JOHN
B. 1907
Southern California 6'1" 215 lbs.

Year	Team		Games	Pos.
1930	MIN	N	9	T
1930	FRA	N	5	T

1 yr. 14 games

Paul Ward
WARD, PAUL

Paul Ward *continued*
B. Jan. 20, 1937, Santa Fe, NM
Whitworth 6'3" 247 lbs.

Year	Team		Games	Pos.
1961	DET	N	8	DT
1962			6	DT

2 yrs. 14 games

Duane Wardlow
WARDLOW, DUANE
B. 1932
Washington 6'4" 215 lbs.

Year	Team		Games	Pos.
1954	LA	N	12	E
1956			9	E

2 yrs. 21 games

Andre Ware
WARE, ANDRE
B. Jul. 31, 1968, Galveston, TX
Houston 6'2" 205 lbs.

Year	Team		Games	Pos.
1990	DET	N	4	QB
1991			1	QB
1992			4	QB
1993			5	QB

4 yrs. 14 games

Charlie Ware
WARE, CHARLES
B. Mar. 2, 1918, Atlanta, GA
Birmingham-Southern 6'3" 245 lbs.

Year	Team		Games	Pos.
1944	BKN	N	6	T

Derek Ware
WARE, DEREK GENE
B. Sep. 17, 1967, Sacramento, CA
Texas A&M/Central Oklahoma 6'2" 255 lbs.

Year	Team		Games	Pos.
1992	PHX	N	15	TE
1993			16	TE
1994	ARI	N	15	TE
1995	CIN	N	7	TE
1996	DAL	N	4	TE

5 yrs. 57 games

Timmie Ware
WARE, TIMMIE EUGENE
B. Apr. 2, 1963, Los Angeles, CA
Southern California 5'10" 171 lbs.

Year	Team		Games	Pos.
1986	SD	N	9	WR
1987			12	WR
1989	LARI	N	13	WR

3 yrs. 34 games

War Eagle
WAR EAGLE
None 195 lbs.

Year	Team		Games	Pos.
1922	OOR	N	5	T, G

Paul Warfield
WARFIELD, PAUL D.
B. Nov. 28, 1942, Warren, OH
Ohio State 6'0" 188 lbs.

Year	Team		Games	Pos.
1964	CLE	N	14	FL
1965			1	OE
1966			14	OE
1967			14	OE
1968			14	OE
1969			14	WR
1970	MIA	N	11	WR
1971			14	WR
1972			12	WR
1973			14	WR
1974			9	WR
1976	CLE	N	14	WR
1977			12	WR

13 yrs. 157 games

Ernie Warlick
WARLICK, ERNEST
B. Jan. 31, 1932, Washington, DC
North Carolina Central 6'4" 234 lbs.

Year	Team		Games	Pos.
1962	BUF	A	14	OE
1963			14	OE
1964			14	OE
1965			14	OE

4 yrs. 56 games

Jim Warne
WARNE, JAMES
B. Nov. 27, 1964, Phoenix, AZ
Arizona State 6'7" 315 lbs.

Year	Team		Games	Pos.
1987	DET	N	3	OT

Charley Warner
WARNER, CHARLES
B. Apr. 14, 1940, Granger, TX
Prairie View A&M 5'11" 178 lbs.

Year	Team		Games	Pos.
1963	KC	A	14	DB
1964			5	DB
1964	BUF	A	4	DB
1965			14	DB
1966			14	DB

4 yrs. 51 games

Curt Warner
WARNER, CURT
B. Mar. 18, 1961, Wyoming, WV
Penn State 5'11" 205 lbs.

Year	Team		Games	Pos.
1983	SEA	N	16	RB
1984			1	RB
1985			16	RB
1986			16	RB
1987			12	RB
1988			16	RB
1989			16	RB
1990	LARM	N	7	RB

8 yrs. 100 games

Dave Warnke
WARNKE, DAVID
B. 1960
Augsburg 5'11" 185 lbs.

Year	Team		Games	Pos.
1983	TB	N	1	K

Buist Warren
WARREN, BUIST
B. 1917
Tennessee 5'11" 175 lbs.

Year	Team		Games	Pos.
1945	PHI	N	1	HB
1945	PIT	N	8	HB

1 yr. 9 games

Chris Warren
WARREN, CHRISTOPHER COLLINS, JR.
B. Jan. 24, 1967, Silver Spring, MD
Ferrum 6'2" 225 lbs.

Year	Team		Games	Pos.
1990	SEA	N	16	RB
1991			16	RB
1992			16	RB
1993			14	RB
1994			16	RB
1995			16	RB
1996			14	RB

7 yrs. 108 games

Dewey Warren
WARREN, MADISON DEWEY
B. May 7, 1945, Savannah, GA
Tennessee 6'0" 205 lbs.

Year	Team		Games	Pos.
1968	CIN	A	7	QB

Year	Team		Games	Pos.

Don Warren
WARREN, DON
B. May 5, 1956, Bellingham, WA
San Diego State 6'4" 240 lbs.

Year	Team		Games	Pos.
1979	WAS	N	16	TE
1980			13	TE
1981			16	TE
1982			9	TE
1983			13	TE
1984			16	TE
1985			16	TE
1986			16	TE
1987			12	TE
1988			14	TE
1989			15	TE
1990			16	TE
1991			10	TE
1992			11	TE
14 yrs.		193 games		

Frank Warren
WARREN, FRANK WILLIAM, III
B. Sep. 14, 1959, Birmingham, AL
Auburn 6'4" 285 lbs.

Year	Team		Games	Pos.
1981	NO	N	16	DE
1982			9	DE
1983			16	DE
1984			16	DE
1985			16	DE
1986			16	DE
1987			12	DE
1988			16	DE
1989			16	DE
1991			16	DE
1992			16	DE
1993			8	DE
1994			16	NT, DE
13 yrs.		189 games		

Jimmy Warren
WARREN, JAMES DAVID
B. Jul. 20, 1939, Ferriday, LA
Illinois 5'11" 178 lbs.

Year	Team		Games	Pos.
1964	SD	A	14	DB
1965			14	DB
1966	MIA	A	14	DB
1967			14	DB
1968			14	DB
1969			13	CB
1970	OAK	N	10	DB
1972			7	DB
1973			10	CB, S
1974			14	DB
1977			2	CB
11 yrs.		126 games		

John Warren
WARREN, JOHN SHEPPARD
B. Nov. 8, 1960, Jesup, GA
Tennessee 6'0" 207 lbs.

Year	Team		Games	Pos.
1983	DAL	N	9	P
1984			3	P
2 yrs.		12 games		

Lamont Warren
WARREN, LAMONT
B. Jan. 14, 1973, Indianapolis, IN
Colorado 5'11" 194 lbs.

Year	Team		Games	Pos.
1994	IND	N	11	RB
1995			12	RB
1996			13	RB
3 yrs.		36 games		

Morrie Warren
WARREN, MORRISON FULBRIGHT (Dit)
B. Dec. 6, 1923, Marlin, TX
Arizona State 5'11" 208 lbs.

Year	Team		Games	Pos.
1948	BKN	AA	2	B

Terrence Warren
WARREN, TERRENCE LEE
B. Aug. 2, 1969, Suffolk, VA
Hampton Institute 6'1" 200 lbs.

Year	Team		Games	Pos.
1993	SEA	N	2	WR
1994			14	WR
1995	SF	N	1	WR
3 yrs.		17 games		

Vince Warren
WARREN, VINCENT LEO
B. Feb. 18, 1963, Little Rock, AR
San Diego State 6'0" 180 lbs.

Year	Team		Games	Pos.
1986	NYG	N	4	WR

Xavier Warren
WARREN, XAVIER
B. Aug. 12, 1964
Tulsa 6'1" 250 lbs.

Year	Team		Games	Pos.
1987	PIT	N	2	DE

Caleb Warrington
WARRINGTON, CALEB VAN (Tex)
B. Mar. 21, 1921, Dover, DE
D. Sep. 21, 1993
William & Mary/Auburn 6'2" 210 lbs.

Year	Team		Games	Pos.
1946	BKN	AA	12	C
1947			13	C, G
1948			14	C, G
3 yrs.		39 games		

Earl Warweg
WARWEG, EARL O.
B. Jan. 11, 1892
D. Dec. 7, 1979, Newburg, IL

Year	Team		Games	Pos.
1921	EVA	A	1	HB

Lonnie Warwick
WARWICK, LONNIE PRESTON
B. Feb. 26, 1942, Mount Hope, WV
Tennessee/Tennessee Tech 6'3" 235 lbs.

Year	Team		Games	Pos.
1965	MIN	N	14	LB
1966			12	LB
1967			14	LB
1968			14	LB
1969			14	LB
1970			14	LB
1971			4	LB
1972			6	LB
1973	ATL	N	14	LB
1974			14	LB
10 yrs.		120 games		

Ron Warzeka
WARZEKA, RONALD
B. 1931
Montana State 6'4" 250 lbs.

Year	Team		Games	Pos.
1960	OAK	A		DT

Alvin Washington
WASHINGTON, ALVIN KENT
B. Sep. 25, 1958, Erie, PA
Ohio State 6'3" 255 lbs.

Year	Team		Games	Pos.
1981	NYJ	N	16	LB

Anthony Washington
WASHINGTON, ANTHONY WAYNE
B. Feb. 4, 1958, San Francisco, CA
California/Fresno State 6'2" 204 lbs.

Year	Team		Games	Pos.
1981	PIT	N	16	CB
1982			9	CB
1983	WAS	N	16	CB
1984			16	CB
4 yrs.		57 games		

Brian Washington
WASHINGTON, BRIAN WAYNE
B. Sep. 10, 1965, Richmond, VA
Nebraska 6'0" 210 lbs.

Year	Team		Games	Pos.
1988	CLE	N	4	S
1990	NYJ	N	14	S
1991			16	S
1992			16	S
1993			16	S
1994			15	S
1995	KC	N	16	S
1996			16	S
8 yrs.		125 games		

Charles Washington
WASHINGTON, CHARLES EDWIN
B. Oct. 8, 1966, Shreveport, LA
Texas/Cameron 6'1" 208 lbs.

Year	Team		Games	Pos.
1989	IND	N	16	CB, S
1990	KC	N	16	CB, S
1991			16	CB
1992	ATL	N	14	DB
1993			6	S
1994			16	S
6 yrs.		74 games		

Chris Washington
WASHINGTON, CHRIS
B. Mar. 6, 1962, Jackson, MS
Iowa State 6'4" 231 lbs.

Year	Team		Games	Pos.
1984	TB	N	16	LB
1985			16	LB
1986			16	LB
1987			12	LB
1988			16	LB
1990	PHX	N	8	LB
6 yrs.		84 games		

Chuck Washington
WASHINGTON, CHARLES
B. Jan. 9, 1964
Arkansas 5'11" 186 lbs.

Year	Team		Games	Pos.
1987	GB	N	3	CB, S

Clarence Washington
WASHINGTON, CLARENCE CORNELIUS, JR.
B. Dec. 23, 1946, Little Rock, AR
Arkansas-Pine Bluff 6'3" 265 lbs.

Year	Team		Games	Pos.
1969	PIT	N	13	DT
1970			14	DT
2 yrs.		27 games		

Clyde Washington
WASHINGTON, CLYDE
B. Mar. 21, 1938
Purdue 6'0" 202 lbs.

Year	Team		Games	Pos.
1960	BOS	A		DB
1961			14	DB
1963	NY	A	14	DB
1964			8	DB
1965			14	DB
5 yrs.		50 games		

Dave Washington
WASHINGTON, DAVID EUGENE
B. Dec. 28, 1940, Los Angeles, CA
Southern California 6'4" 228 lbs.

Year	Team		Games	Pos.
1968	DEN	A	2	TE

Dave Washington
WASHINGTON, DAVID V.
B. Sep. 12, 1948, Tuscaloosa, AL
Alcorn State 6'5" 224 lbs.

Year	Team		Games	Pos.
1970	DEN	N	13	LB
1971			14	LB

Dave Washington *continued*

Year	Team		Games	Pos.
1972	BUF	N	14	LB, TE
1973			7	TE
1974			14	LB, TE
1975	SF	N	14	LB
1976			14	LB
1977			9	LB
1978	DET	N	16	LB
1979			7	LB
1980	NO	N	16	LB
11 yrs.		138 games		

Dewayne Washington
WASHINGTON, DEWAYNE NERON
B. Dec. 27, 1972, Durham, NC
North Carolina State 5'11" 192 lbs.

Year	Team		Games	Pos.
1994	MIN	N	16	CB
1995			15	CB
1996			16	CB
3 yrs.		47 games		

Dick Washington
WASHINGTON, RICHARD
B. Feb. 15, 1945, Savannah, GA
Bethune-Cookman 6'1" 205 lbs.

Year	Team		Games	Pos.
1968	MIA	A	4	RB

Eric Washington
WASHINGTON, ERIC CHRISTOPHER
B. Apr. 22, 1950, Washington, DC
Texas-El Paso 6'2" 190 lbs.

Year	Team		Games	Pos.
1972	STL	N	6	DB
1973			9	CB
2 yrs.		15 games		

Fred Washington
WASHINGTON, FREDERICK
B. Jun. 14, 1944, Marlin, TX
North Texas State 6'5" 268 lbs.

Year	Team		Games	Pos.
1968	WAS	N	1	OT

Gene Washington
WASHINGTON, EUGENE
B. Jan. 25, 1944, La Porte, TX
Michigan State 6'3" 212 lbs.

Year	Team		Games	Pos.
1967	MIN	N	14	OE
1968			14	OE
1969			14	WR
1970			14	WR
1971			13	WR
1972			12	WR
1973	DEN	N	14	WR
7 yrs.		95 games		

Gene Washington
WASHINGTON, EUGENE HENRY
B. Jun. 6, 1953, Gadsden, SC
Georgia 5'9" 170 lbs.

Year	Team		Games	Pos.
1979	NYG	N	2	WR

Gene Washington
WASHINGTON, GENE ALDEN
B. Jan. 14, 1947, Tuscaloosa, AL
Stanford 6'1" 185 lbs.

Year	Team		Games	Pos.
1969	SF	N	14	WR
1970			13	WR
1971			14	WR
1972			14	WR
1973			13	WR
1974			14	WR
1975			14	WR
1976			14	WR
1977			14	WR
1979	DET	N	16	WR
10 yrs.		140 games		

Year Team	Games	Pos.
Year Team	Games	Pos.
Year Team	Games	Pos.
Year Team	Games	Pos.

Harry Washington
WASHINGTON, HARRY
B. Jul. 30, 1956, Tacoma, WA
Colorado State 6'0" 180 lbs.

Year	Team		Games	Pos.
1978	MIN	N	10	WR
1979	CHI	N	5	WR

2 yrs.   15 games

James Washington
WASHINGTON, JAMES MCARTHUR
B. Jan. 10, 1965, Los Angeles, CA
UCLA 6'1" 196 lbs.

Year	Team		Games	Pos.
1988	LARM	N	16	S
1989			8	S
1990	DAL	N	15	S
1991			16	S
1992			16	S
1993			14	S
1994			16	S
1995	WAS	N	12	S

8 yrs.   113 games

Joe Washington
WASHINGTON, JOE DAN (Little Joe)
B. Sep. 24, 1953, Crockett, TX
Oklahoma 5'10" 181 lbs.

Year	Team		Games	Pos.
1977	SD	N	13	RB
1978	BAL	N	16	RB
1979			15	RB
1980			16	RB
1981	WAS	N	14	RB
1982			7	RB
1983			15	RB
1984			7	RB
1985	ATL	N	16	RB

9 yrs.   119 games

Joe Washington
WASHINGTON, JOSEPH
B. Nov. 23, 1950, Baton Rouge, LA
Illinois State 5'9" 180 lbs.

Year	Team		Games	Pos.
1973	ATL	N	9	RB

John Washington
WASHINGTON, JOHN
B. Feb. 20, 1963, Houston, TX
Oklahoma State 6'4" 280 lbs.

Year	Team		Games	Pos.
1986	NYG	N	16	DE
1987			12	DE
1988			16	DE
1989			16	DE
1990			16	DE
1991			12	DE
1992	ATL	N	3	DE
1993	NE	N	16	DE

8 yrs.   119 games

Keith Washington
WASHINGTON, KEITH
B. Dec. 18, 1973, Dallas, TX
Nevada-Las Vegas 6'4" 270 lbs.

Year	Team		Games	Pos.
1996	DET	N	12	DE

Kenny Washington
WASHINGTON, KENNETH STANLEY (Dusky Meteor)
B. Aug. 31, 1918, Los Angeles, CA
D. Jun. 24, 1971, Los Angeles, CA
UCLA 6'1" 212 lbs.

Year	Team		Games	Pos.
1946	LA	N	6	HB
1947			11	HB
1948			10	HB

3 yrs.   27 games

Lionel Washington
WASHINGTON, LIONEL
B. Oct. 21, 1960, New Orleans, LA
Tulane 6'0" 186 lbs.

Year	Team		Games	Pos.
1983	STL	N	16	CB
1984			15	CB
1985			5	CB
1986			16	CB
1987	LARI	N	11	CB
1988			12	CB
1989			16	CB
1990			15	CB
1991			16	CB
1992			16	CB
1993			16	CB
1994			12	CB
1995	DEN	N	16	CB
1996			14	CB

14 yrs.   196 games

Mark Washington
WASHINGTON, MARK HENRY
B. Dec. 28, 1947, Chicago, IL
Morgan State 5'10" 187 lbs.

Year	Team		Games	Pos.
1970	DAL	N	14	CB
1971			2	CB
1972			10	CB
1973			14	CB
1974			13	CB
1975			14	CB
1976			13	CB
1977			14	CB
1978			13	CB
1979	NE	N	12	CB

10 yrs.   119 games

Marvin Washington
WASHINGTON, MARVIN ANDREW
B. Oct. 22, 1965, Denver, CO
Texas-El Paso/Idaho 6'6" 270 lbs.

Year	Team		Games	Pos.
1989	NYJ	N	16	DE
1990			16	DT, DE
1991			15	DE, DT
1992			16	DE
1993			16	DE
1994			15	DE
1995			16	DE, DT
1996			14	DE

8 yrs.   124 games

Mickey Washington
WASHINGTON, MICKEY LYNN
B. Jul. 8, 1968, Galveston, TX
Texas A&M 5'9" 187 lbs.

Year	Team		Games	Pos.
1990	NE	N	9	CB
1991			16	CB
1992	WAS	N	3	CB
1993	BUF	N	16	CB
1994			16	CB
1995	JAC	N	16	CB
1996			16	CB

7 yrs.   92 games

Mike Washington
WASHINGTON, MICHAEL LEE
B. Jul. 1, 1953, Montgomery, AL
Alabama 6'3" 196 lbs.

Year	Team		Games	Pos.
1976	TB	N	5	DB
1977			14	CB
1978			16	CB
1979			15	CB
1980			16	CB
1981			14	CB
1982			8	CB
1983			14	CB
1984			1	CB

9 yrs.   103 games

Robert Washington
WASHINGTON, ROBERT
B. Apr. 2, 1963
Alcorn State 6'4" 251 lbs.

Year	Team		Games	Pos.
1987	PIT	N	3	OT

Ronnie Washington
WASHINGTON, RONNIE CARROLL
B. Jul. 29, 1963, Monroe, LA
Northeast Louisiana 6'1" 244 lbs.

Year	Team		Games	Pos.
1985	ATL	N	16	LB
1987	LARI	N	2	LB
1989	IND	N	2	LB

3 yrs.   20 games

Russ Washington
WASHINGTON, RUSSELL EUGENE
B. Dec. 17, 1946, Kansas City, MO
Missouri 6'7" 290 lbs.

Year	Team		Games	Pos.
1968	SD	A	14	DT
1969			14	DT
1970	SD	N	14	OT
1971			14	OT
1972			14	OT
1973			14	OT
1974			14	OT
1975			14	OT
1976			14	OT
1977			14	OT
1978			14	OT
1979			16	OT
1980			6	OT
1981			13	OT
1982			9	OT

15 yrs.   200 games

Sam Washington
WASHINGTON, SAMUEL LEE, JR.
B. Mar. 7, 1960, Tampa, FL
Mississippi Valley State 5'9" 180 lbs.

Year	Team		Games	Pos.
1982	PIT	N	4	CB
1983			16	S
1984			14	CB
1985			7	CB
1985	CIN	N	8	CB

4 yrs.   49 games

Ted Washington
WASHINGTON, TED, JR.
B. Apr. 13, 1968, Tampa, FL
Louisville 6'4" 299 lbs.

Year	Team		Games	Pos.
1991	SF	N	16	DL
1992			16	NT, DE
1993			12	NT
1994	DEN	N	16	NT
1995	BUF	N	16	NT
1996			16	DT

6 yrs.   92 games

Ted Washington
WASHINGTON, THEODORE BERNARD
B. Feb. 16, 1948, Tampa, FL
Mississippi Valley State 6'1" 243 lbs.

Year	Team		Games	Pos.
1973	NYJ	N	1	LB
1974	HOU	N	14	LB
1975			14	LB
1976			13	LB
1977			14	LB
1978			15	LB
1979			15	LB
1980			16	LB
1981			16	LB
1982			9	LB

10 yrs.   128 games

Teddy Washington
WASHINGTON, HAROLD
B. 1945
San Diego State 5'11" 210 lbs.

Year	Team		Games	Pos.
1968	CIN	A	1	RB

Tim Washington
WASHINGTON, TIMOTHY BERNARD
B. Nov. 7, 1959, Fresno, CA
D. Jan. 7, 1992, Fremont, CA
Fresno State 5'9" 184 lbs.

Year	Team		Games	Pos.
1982	SF	N	1	DB
1982	KC	N	1	DB

1 yr.   2 games

Vic Washington
WASHINGTON, VICTOR ARNOLD
B. Mar. 23, 1946, Plainfield, NJ
Wyoming 5'10" 196 lbs.

Year	Team		Games	Pos.
1971	SF	N	14	RB
1972			13	RB
1973			13	RB
1974	HOU	N	11	RB
1975	BUF	N	13	RB
1976			2	RB

6 yrs.   66 games

Jim Waskiewicz
WASKIEWICZ, JAMES A.
B. Feb. 10, 1944, Milwaukee, WI
Wichita State 6'4" 237 lbs.

Year	Team		Games	Pos.
1966	NY	A	14	C, LB
1967			13	OT, LB
1969	ATL	N	12	C

3 yrs.   39 games

Lloyd Wasserbach
WASSERBACH, LLOYD G.
B. 1921, Wisconsin
Wisconsin 5'11" 205 lbs.

Year	Team		Games	Pos.
1946	CHI	AA	12	T
1947			5	T

2 yrs.   17 games

Bob Waterfield
WATERFIELD, ROBERT STANTON (Rifle)
B. Jul. 26, 1920, Elmira, NY
D. Mar. 25, 1983, Burbank, CA
UCLA 6'1" 196 lbs.

Year	Team		Games	Pos.
1945	CLE	N	10	QB, P
1946	LA	N	11	QB, P
1947			12	QB, P
1948			11	QB, P
1949			12	QB, P
1950			12	QB, P
1951			11	QB, P
1952			12	QB, P

8 yrs.   91 games

Andre Waters
WATERS, ANDRE
B. Mar. 10, 1962, Belle Glade, FL
Cheyney State 5'11" 189 lbs.

Year	Team		Games	Pos.
1984	PHI	N	16	CB
1985			16	CB
1986			12	S
1987			12	S
1988			16	S
1989			16	S
1990			14	S
1991			16	S
1992			6	S
1993			9	S
1994	ARI	N	12	S
1995			8	S

12 yrs.   157 games

Year	Team		Games	Pos.

Bobby Waters
WATERS, ROBERT LEE
B. Jun. 22, 1938, Millen, GA
Presbyterian 6'2" 184 lbs.

1960	**SF**	**N**	8	QB
1961			8	QB
1962			7	QB
1963			7	QB
4 yrs.	30 games			

Charlie Waters
WATERS, CHARLES TUTAN
B. Sep. 10, 1948, Miami, FL
Clemson 6'1" 195 lbs.

1970	**DAL**	**N**	14	CB
1971			14	S
1972			14	S
1973			14	CB
1974			14	CB
1975			14	S
1976			14	S
1977			14	S
1978			16	S
1980			16	S
1981			16	S
11 yrs.	160 games			

Dale Waters
WATERS, DALE BERNARD
B. May 27, 1909, Henry County, IN
Florida 6'2" 212 lbs.

1931	**POR**	**N**	2	C
1931	**CLE**	**N**	7	E, T, HB
1932	**BOS**	**N**	9	T
1933			10	G, E
3 yrs.	28 games			

Mike Waters
WATERS, ROBERT MICHAEL
B. Mar. 15, 1962, San Diego, CA
San Diego State 6'2" 225 lbs.

1986	**PHI**	**N**	5	FB
1987	**NO**	**N**	5	FB
2 yrs.	10 games			

Jerry Watford
WATFORD, GERALD RAY
B. Dec. 19, 1930, Gadsden, AL
D. Mar., 1993
Alabama 6'3" 205 lbs.

1953	**CHIC**	**N**	12	G
1954			12	G
2 yrs.	24 games			

Pete Wathen
WATHEN, CHAPEZE
B. 1903
Kentucky 175 lbs.

| 1922 | **EVA** | **N** | 2 | E, HB |

Bobby Watkins
WATKINS, BOBBY LAWRENCE
B. May 31, 1960, Cottonwood, ID
Southwest Texas State 5'10" 184 lbs.

1982	**DET**	**N**	9	CB, S
1983			16	CB, S
1984			16	CB
1985			16	S, CB
1986			5	CB
1987			5	CB
1988			16	CB, S
7 yrs.	83 games			

Bobby Watkins
WATKINS, ROBERT ARCHIBALD
B. Mar. 30, 1932, New Bedford, MA
Ohio State 5'10" 196 lbs.

| 1955 | **CHIB** | **N** | 12 | HB |

Bobby Watkins continued

1956			9	HB
1957			12	HB
1958	**CHIC**	**N**	5	HB
4 yrs.	38 games			

Foster Watkins
WATKINS, FOSTER FORREST
(Flippin')
B. Nov. 17, 1917, Memphis, TN
West Texas State 5'9" 163 lbs.

1940	**PHI**	**N**	9	QB
1941			11	QB
2 yrs.	20 games			

Gordon Watkins
WATKINS, GORDON C. (Coot)
B. Aug. 31, 1907
D. Aug., 1944
Georgia Tech 6'1" 220 lbs.

1930	**FRA**	**N**	3	E
1930	**MIN**	**N**	1	T
1930	**FRA**	**N**	2	E, T
1930	**MIN**	**N**	1	T
1931	**BKN**	**N**	7	T, G
2 yrs.	14 games			

Kendell Watkins
WATKINS, KENDELL MAIRO
B. Mar. 8, 1973, Jackson, MS
Mississippi State 6'1" 305 lbs.

| 1995 | **DAL** | **N** | 15 | TE |

Larry Watkins
WATKINS, LAWRENCE
B. Oct. 5, 1946, Bessemer, AL
Alcorn State 6'2" 226 lbs.

1969	**DET**	**N**	14	RB
1970	**PHI**	**N**	11	RB
1971			12	RB
1972			14	RB
1973	**BUF**	**N**	14	RB
1974			10	RB
1975	**NYG**	**N**	14	RB
1976			13	RB
1977			9	RB
9 yrs.	111 games			

Tommy Watkins
WATKINS, THOMAS
B. Oct. 23, 1937, West Memphis, AR
Iowa State 6'1" 195 lbs.

1961	**CLE**	**N**	10	HB
1962	**DET**	**N**	13	HB
1963			13	HB
1964			14	HB
1965			11	HB
1967			13	RB
1968	**PIT**	**N**	1	RB
7 yrs.	75 games			

Allen Watson
WATSON, ALLEN
B. Nov. 4, 1944, Blackwood, Wales
Newport (Wales) 5'10" 165 lbs.*

| 1970 | **PIT** | **N** | 4 | K |

Dave Watson
WATSON, CARL DAVID
B. 1941
Georgia Tech 6'1" 225 lbs.

1963	**BOS**	**A**	14	G
1964			14	G
2 yrs.	28 games			

Ed Watson
WATSON, EDWARD
B. May 8, 1945, Coushatta, LA
Grambling State 6'2" 222 lbs.

| 1969 | **HOU** | **A** | 3 | LB |

Jim Watson
WATSON, JIM
B. Mar. 26, 1961, Stockton, CA
Pacific 6'0" 205 lbs.

| 1945 | **WAS** | **N** | 4 | C |

Joe Watson
WATSON, JOSEPH LAVERNE
B. Aug. 19, 1925, Sherman, TX
Rice 6'3" 235 lbs.

| 1950 | **DET** | **N** | 8 | C |

John Watson
WATSON, JOHNNY A.
B. Jan. 11, 1949, Palo Alto, CA
Oklahoma 6'4" 246 lbs.

1971	**SF**	**N**	14	OT
1972			14	OT
1973			14	OT
1974			13	G, OT
1975			14	G
1976			11	G, OT
1977	**NO**	**N**	5	OT
1978			5	OT
1979			5	OT
9 yrs.	95 games			

Louis Watson
WATSON, LOUIS
B. Jan. 11, 1963, Mobile, AL
Mississippi Valley State 5'11" 175 lbs.

| 1987 | **CLE** | **N** | | WR |

Mike Watson
WATSON, MICHAEL EUGENE
B. Oct. 27, 1955, Clarksburg, WV
Miami (Ohio) 6'6" 272 lbs.

| 1977 | **NO** | **N** | 1 | OT |

Pete Watson
WATSON, PETER
B. Sep. 19, 1950, New York, NY
Tufts 6'1" 210 lbs.

| 1972 | **CIN** | **N** | 1 | TE |

Rat Watson
WATSON, GRADY
B. May 12, 1899
D. Apr., 1985, Edmond, OK
Southwestern (Texas)/Texas 5'9" 181 lbs.

1922	**TOL**	**N**	7	QB, HB
1923			5	QB, HB, FB
1924	**KC**	**N**	1	HB
1924	**HAM**	**N**	3	QB
1925			2	FB, HB
1927	**BUF**	**N**	3	HB, E, FB
5 yrs.	21 games			

Remi Watson
WATSON, REMI
B. Aug. 11, 1964
Bethune-Cookman 6'0" 174 lbs.

| 1987 | **CLE** | **N** | | WR |

Sid Watson
WATSON, SIDNEY JOHN
B. May 4, 1932, Andover, MA
Northeastern 5'11" 187 lbs.

| 1955 | **PIT** | **N** | 12 | HB |

Sid Watson continued

1956			12	HB
1957			11	HB
1958	**WAS**	**N**	10	HB
4 yrs.	45 games			

Steve Watson
WATSON, STEPHEN ROSS
B. May 28, 1957, Baltimore, MD
Temple 6'4" 195 lbs.

1979	**DEN**	**N**	16	WR
1980			16	WR
1981			16	WR
1982			9	WR
1983			16	WR
1984			16	WR
1985			16	WR
1986			16	WR
1987			5	WR
9 yrs.	126 games			

Tim Watson
WATSON, JAMES TIMOTHY
B. Aug. 13, 1970, Fort Valley, GA
Howard 6'1" 213 lbs.

1993	**KC**	**N**	4	S
1994			1	S
1995			4	S
1995	**NYG**	**N**	1	S
3 yrs.	10 games			

Joe Watt
WATT, JOSEPH CHESSAR
B. Jun. 18, 1919, Montreal, Que.
D. Apr., 1984, Monroe, NY
Syracuse 5'11" 184 lbs.

1947	**BOS**	**N**	1	HB
1947	**DET**	**N**	8	HB
1948			12	HB
1949	**NYB**	**N**	5	HB
3 yrs.	26 games			

Walt Watt
WATT, WALTER
B. 1922
Miami (Florida) 6'0" 187 lbs.

| 1945 | **CHIC** | **N** | 4 | HB |

Frank Wattelet
WATTELET, FRANK
B. Oct. 25, 1958, Paola, KS
Kansas 6'0" 185 lbs.

1981	**NO**	**N**	16	S
1982			9	S
1983			16	S
1984			16	S
1985			16	S
1986			16	S
1987			2	S
1987	**LARM**	**N**	5	S
1988			2	S
8 yrs.	98 games			

Bob Watters
WATTERS, ROBERT LEE (Beck)
B. 1936
Lincoln (Missouri) 6'4" 247 lbs.

1962	**NY**	**A**	12	DE
1963			12	DE
1964			5	DE
3 yrs.	29 games			

Len Watters
WATTERS, LEONARD A. (Cupid)
B. May 4, 1898, Dubuque, IA
D. Dec. 10, 1986, Florida
Springfield 5'10" 185 lbs.

| 1924 | **BUF** | **N** | 8 | E |

Year	Team	Games	Pos.

Orlando Watters
WATTERS, ORLANDO
B. Oct. 26, 1971, Anniston, AL
Arkansas 5'11" 177 lbs.

Year	Team	Games	Pos.
1994	**SEA** N	16	CB

Ricky Watters
WATTERS, RICHARD JAMES
B. Apr. 7, 1969, Harrisburg, PA
Notre Dame 6'1" 212 lbs.

Year	Team	Games	Pos.
1992	**SF** N	14	RB
1993		13	RB
1994		16	RB
1995	**PHI** N	16	RB
1996		16	RB
5 yrs.	75 games		

Scott Watters
WATTERS, SCOTT
B. Jan. 1, 1965, Columbus, OH
Wittenberg 6'2" 230 lbs.

Year	Team	Games	Pos.
1987	**BUF** N	3	LB

Bob Watts
WATTS, ROBERT
B. Jun. 16, 1954, New York, NY
Boston College 6'3" 218 lbs.

Year	Team	Games	Pos.
1978	**OAK** N	2	LB

Damon Watts
WATTS, DAMON
B. Apr. 8, 1972, Indianapolis, IN
Indiana 5'10" 173 lbs.

Year	Team	Games	Pos.
1994	**IND** N	16	CB
1995		13	CB
1996		10	CB
3 yrs.	39 games		

Elbert Watts
WATTS, ELBERT
B. Mar. 20, 1963, Carson, CA
Oklahoma/Southern California 6'1" 205 lbs.

Year	Team	Games	Pos.
1986	**GB** N	9	CB

George Watts
WATTS, GEORGE
B. Jul. 12, 1918, McAdenville, NC
D. 1991
Appalachian State 6'1" 225 lbs.

Year	Team	Games	Pos.
1942	**WAS** N	6	T

Randy Watts
WATTS, RANDY
B. Jun. 22, 1963, Sandersville, GA
East Carolina/Catawba 6'6" 275 lbs.

Year	Team	Games	Pos.
1987	**DAL** N	5	DE, DT

Rickey Watts
WATTS, RICKEY RICARDO
B. May 16, 1957, Longview, TX
Tulsa 6'1" 203 lbs.

Year	Team	Games	Pos.
1979	**CHI** N	16	WR
1980		15	WR
1981		12	WR
1982		9	WR
1983		4	WR
5 yrs.	56 games		

Ted Watts
WATTS, TED
B. May 29, 1958, Tarpon Springs, FL
Texas Tech 6'0" 190 lbs.

Year	Team	Games	Pos.
1981	**OAK** N	16	CB
1982	**LARI**	9	CB

Year	Team	Games	Pos.

Ted Watts continued

Year	Team	Games	Pos.
1983		16	CB
1984		16	CB
1985	**NYG** N	16	CB
1987	**SD** N	1	S
6 yrs.	74 games		

Charles Way
WAY, CHARLES CHRISTOPHER
B. Dec. 27, 1972, Philadelphia, PA
Virginia 6'0" 236 lbs.

Year	Team	Games	Pos.
1995	**NYG** N	16	RB
1996		16	RB
2 yrs.	32 games		

Charlie Way
WAY, CHARLES A. (Pie)
B. Dec. 29, 1897, Embreeville, PA
D. Jan. 31, 1988, Honeybrook, PA
Penn State 5'8" 144 lbs.

Year	Team	Games	Pos.
1921	**CAN** A	6	HB
1924	**FRA** A	13	HB
1926	**PHI** A	7	HB, QB
3 yrs.	26 games		

Dave Waymer
WAYMER, DAVID BENJAMIN, JR.
B. Jul. 1, 1958, Brooklyn, NY
D. May 30, 1993, Mooresville, NC
Notre Dame 6'1" 195 lbs.

Year	Team	Games	Pos.
1980	**NO** N	16	CB
1981		16	CB
1982		9	CB
1983		16	CB
1984		16	CB
1985		16	CB
1986		16	CB
1987		12	CB
1988		16	CB
1989		16	S
1990	**SF** N	16	S
1991		16	S
1992	**LARI**	16	S
13 yrs.	197 games		

Russ Wayt
WAYT, RUSSELL
B. Oct. 6, 1942, Oklahoma City, OK
Rice 6'4" 235 lbs.

Year	Team	Games	Pos.
1965	**DAL** N	9	LB

Bob Wear
WEAR, ROBERT F.
B. Jan. 5, 1919, Yeagerstown, PA
D. Apr. 22, 1992, Martinsburg, PA
Penn State 5'11" 205 lbs.

Year	Team	Games	Pos.
1942	**PHI** N	3	C, G

Jim Weatherall
WEATHERALL, JAMES PRESTON
B. Oct. 26, 1929, Graham, TX
D. Aug. 2, 1992, Oklahoma City, OK
Oklahoma 6'4" 245 lbs.

Year	Team	Games	Pos.
1955	**PHI** N	12	T
1956		12	T
1957		12	T
1958	**WAS** N	9	T
1959	**DET** N	8	T
1960		12	T
6 yrs.	65 games		

Jim Weatherford
WEATHERFORD, JAMES
B. Aug. 16, 1946, Athens, TN
Tennessee 5'10" 180 lbs.

Year	Team	Games	Pos.
1969	**ATL** N	14	CB, S

Year	Team	Games	Pos.

Gerry Weatherly
WEATHERLY, GERALD CRAFT (Bones)
B. Dec. 26, 1928, Houston, TX
Rice 6'5" 218 lbs.

Year	Team	Games	Pos.
1950	**CHIB** N	6	C
1952		5	C
1953		12	C
1954		12	C
4 yrs.	35 games		

Jim Weatherly
WEATHERLY, JAMES
B. Apr. 13, 1952, Hazen, AR
Mount San Antonio JC 6'3" 245 lbs.

Year	Team	Games	Pos.
1976	**ATL** N	3	C

Carl Weathers
WEATHERS, CARL
B. Jan. 14, 1948, New Orleans, LA
San Diego State 6'2" 220 lbs.

Year	Team	Games	Pos.
1970	**OAK** N	7	LB
1971		1	LB
2 yrs.	8 games		

Clarence Weathers
WEATHERS, CLARENCE
B. Jan. 10, 1962, Green Pond, SC
Delaware State 5'9" 170 lbs.

Year	Team	Games	Pos.
1983	**NE** N	16	WR
1984		9	WR
1985	**CLE** N	13	WR
1986		16	WR
1987		12	WR
1988		16	WR
1989	**IND** N	4	WR
1989	**KC** N	11	WR
1990	**GB** N	14	WR
1991		14	WR
9 yrs.	125 games		

Curtis Weathers
WEATHERS, CURTIS L.
B. Sep. 16, 1956, Memphis, TN
Mississippi 6'5" 230 lbs.

Year	Team	Games	Pos.
1979	**CLE** N	16	TE
1980		10	TE
1981		13	LB
1982		7	LB
1983		16	LB
1984		16	LB
1985		16	LB
7 yrs.	94 games		

Guy Weathers
WEATHERS, GUY B. (Cop)
B. Jun. 9, 1898
D. Sep. 27, 1964
Baylor 5'9" 230 lbs.

Year	Team	Games	Pos.
1926	**BUF** N	5	G

Robert Weathers
WEATHERS, ROBERT JAMES
B. Sep. 13, 1960, Westfield, NY
Arizona State 6'2" 220 lbs.

Year	Team	Games	Pos.
1982	**NE** N	6	RB
1983		15	RB
1984		2	RB
1985		16	RB
1986		5	RB
5 yrs.	44 games		

Cephus Weatherspoon
WEATHERSPOON, CEPHUS, JR.
B. Jun. 14, 1948, Meridian, MS
Fort Lewis 6'1" 182 lbs.

Year	Team	Games	Pos.
1972	**NO** N	1	WR

Year	Team	Games	Pos.

Chuck Weatherspoon
WEATHERSPOON, JOHNNY, JR.
B. Jul. 31, 1968, Hinesville, GA
Houston 5'7" 230 lbs.

Year	Team	Games	Pos.
1991	**TB** N	4	RB

Jim Weatherwax
WEATHERWAX, JAMES MICHAEL
B. Jan. 9, 1943, Porterville, CA
Los Angeles State 6'7" 265 lbs.

Year	Team	Games	Pos.
1966	**GB** N	14	DT
1967		14	DT
1969		6	DT
3 yrs.	34 games		

Charles Weaver
WEAVER, CHARLES A. (Buck)
B. Mar. 4, 1907
D. May, 1972
Chicago 6'4" 235 lbs.

Year	Team	Games	Pos.
1930	**CHIC** N	6	G, E, T
1930	**POR** N	4	G
1 yr.	10 games		

Charlie Weaver
WEAVER, CHARLES EARL
B. Jul. 12, 1949, Greenwood, MS
Southern California 6'2" 223 lbs.

Year	Team	Games	Pos.
1971	**DET** N	14	LB
1972		14	LB
1973		13	LB
1974		14	LB
1975		12	LB
1976		14	LB
1977		14	LB
1978		16	LB
1979		8	LB
1980		16	LB
1981		7	LB
1981	**WAS** N	5	LB
11 yrs.	147 games		

Emanuel Weaver
WEAVER, EMANUEL, III
B. Jun. 28, 1960, New Orleans, LA
South Carolina State 6'4" 260 lbs.

Year	Team	Games	Pos.
1982	**CIN** N	5	NT
1987	**ATL** N	2	NT
2 yrs.	7 games		

Gary Weaver
WEAVER, GARY LYNN
B. Mar. 13, 1949, Florence, AL
Fresno State 6'1" 225 lbs.

Year	Team	Games	Pos.
1973	**OAK** N	10	LB
1974		14	LB
1975	**GB** N	14	LB
1976		14	LB
1977		5	LB
1978		16	LB
1979		14	LB
7 yrs.	87 games		

Herman Weaver
WEAVER, WILLIAM HERMAN (Thunder Foot)
B. Nov. 17, 1948, Villa Rica, GA
Tennessee 6'4" 210 lbs.

Year	Team	Games	Pos.
1970	**DET** N	14	P
1971		13	P
1972		14	P
1973		14	P
1974		14	P
1975		14	P
1976		14	P

Year	Team	Games	Pos.

Herman Weaver continued

Year	Team	Games	Pos.
1977	SEA N	13	P
1978		16	P
1979		16	P
1980		16	P
11 yrs.	158 games		

Jim Weaver

WEAVER, JAMES REDWICK (Red)
B. Jul. 19, 1897
D. Nov. 23, 1968, Mayfield, KY
Centre 5'10" 165 lbs.

Year	Team	Games	Pos.
1923	COL N	9	C
1926	CLE A	5	C
2 yrs.	14 games		

John Weaver

WEAVER, JOHN DEAN
B. Mar. 31, 1926, Dayton, OH
Miami (Ohio) 6'2" 215 lbs.

Year	Team	Games	Pos.
1949	NYB N	12	G

Larrye Weaver

WEAVER, LARRYE
B. Nov. 17, 1931, Monte Vista, CO
Antelope JC/Fullerton JC 5'11" 190 lbs.

Year	Team	Games	Pos.
1955	NYG N	6	HB

Webb

WEBB
None

Year	Team	Games	Pos.
1921	TON A	1	FB

Allan Webb

WEBB, ALLAN
B. Jan. 22, 1935, Washington, DC
Arnold 5'11" 180 lbs.

Year	Team	Games	Pos.
1961	NYG N	10	HB, DB
1962		14	DB
1963		7	DB
1964		14	DB
1965		3	DB
5 yrs.	48 games		

Art Webb

WEBB, ARTHUR
B. Feb. 17, 1893
D. Apr., 1973, Cleveland, OH
None 5'10" 210 lbs.

Year	Team	Games	Pos.
1920	ROC A	1	G
1922	MIL N	7	T
2 yrs.	8 games		

Chuck Webb

WEBB, CHARLES EUGENE
B. Nov. 17, 1969, Toledo, OH
Tennessee 5'9" 201 lbs.

Year	Team	Games	Pos.
1991	GB N	2	RB

Don Webb

WEBB, DONALD WAYNE
B. May 22, 1939, Jefferson City, MO
Iowa State 5'10" 196 lbs.

Year	Team	Games	Pos.
1961	BOS A	14	DB
1962		14	DB
1964		14	DB
1965		14	DB
1966		14	DB
1967		14	DB
1968		10	DB
1969		14	S
1970	BOS N	14	S
1971	NE N	12	S
10 yrs.	134 games		

George Webb

WEBB, GEORGE L.
B. Jun. 2, 1916
Texas Tech 6'1" 180 lbs.

Year	Team	Games	Pos.
1943	BKN N	8	E

Jimmy Webb

WEBB, JAMES ROGERS
B. Apr. 13, 1952, Jackson, MS
Mississippi State 6'5" 246 lbs.

Year	Team	Games	Pos.
1975	SF N	14	DT
1976		14	DT
1977		14	DT
1978		16	DT
1979		16	DT
1980		16	DT
1981	SD N	16	DT
7 yrs.	106 games		

Ken Webb

WEBB, KENNETH
B. Aug. 15, 1935, Decatur, GA
Presbyterian 5'11" 207 lbs.

Year	Team	Games	Pos.
1958	DET N	12	HB
1959		12	HB
1960		12	HB
1961		11	HB
1962		14	FB
1963	CLE N	12	FB
6 yrs.	73 games		

Richmond Webb

WEBB, RICHMOND JEWEL
B. Jan. 11, 1967, Dallas, TX
Texas A&M 6'6" 298 lbs.

Year	Team	Games	Pos.
1990	MIA N	16	OT
1991		14	OT
1992		16	OT
1993		16	OT
1994		16	OT
1995		16	OT
1996		16	OT
7 yrs.	110 games		

Dutch Webber

WEBBER, HOWARD (Cowboy)
B. Dec. 15, 1901
D. Jun., 1985, Ulysses, KS
Kansas State 6'2" 190 lbs.

Year	Team	Games	Pos.
1924	KC N	9	E
1925		8	E
1925	CLE N	4	E
1926	HAR N	8	E
1926	NYG N	2	E
1926	KC N	1	E
1927	CLE N	3	E, HB
1928	GB N	4	E, FB
1930	PRO N	1	E
1930	NEW N	3	E
6 yrs.	43 games		

Harry Webber

WEBBER, HARRY (Obe)
B. Oct. 18, 1892, South Dakota
D. Oct., 1970, Salinas, CA
Morningside 173 lbs.

Year	Team	Games	Pos.
1920	RI A	2	E
1923	RI N	2	G, E
2 yrs.	4 games		

Charlie Weber

WEBER, CHARLES
B. Jan. 5, 1891
D. Feb., 1974, Queens, NY
Colgate 6'1" 203 lbs.

Year	Team	Games	Pos.
1926	BKN N	7	G

Chuck Weber

WEBER, CHARLES
B. Mar. 26, 1930, Philadelphia, PA
West Chester State 6'1" 229 lbs.

Year	Team	Games	Pos.
1955	CLE N	12	G
1956		4	E
1956	CHIC N	5	E
1957		12	E
1958		10	MG
1959	PHI N	12	LB
1960		12	LB
1961			LB
7 yrs.	67 games		

Dick Weber

WEBER, RICHARD
B. 1919
St. Louis 5'11" 195 lbs.

Year	Team	Games	Pos.
1945	DET N	3	HB

Alex Webster

WEBSTER, ALEXANDER (Big Red)
B. Apr. 19, 1931, Kearny, NJ
North Carolina State 6'3" 218 lbs.

Year	Team	Games	Pos.
1955	NYG N	12	HB
1956		12	HB
1957		11	HB
1958		9	HB
1959		10	HB
1960		8	HB
1961		14	HB
1962		14	FB
1963		7	FB
1964		12	RB
10 yrs.	109 games		

Cornell Webster

WEBSTER, CORNELL PRESTON
B. Nov. 2, 1954, Greeneville, TN
California/Tulsa 6'0" 180 lbs.

Year	Team	Games	Pos.
1977	SEA N	14	S
1978		15	S
1979		15	CB
1980		8	CB
4 yrs.	52 games		

Dave Webster

WEBSTER, DAVID
B. 1938
Prairie View A&M 6'4" 218 lbs.

Year	Team	Games	Pos.
1960	DAL A		DB
1961		14	DB
2 yrs.	14 games		

Elnardo Webster

WEBSTER, ELNARDO JULIAN
B. Dec. 23, 1969, Gorizia, Italy
Rutgers 6'2" 243 lbs.

Year	Team	Games	Pos.
1992	PIT N	3	LB

George Webster

WEBSTER, GEORGE D.
B. Nov. 25, 1945, Anderson, SC
Michigan State 6'4" 225 lbs.

Year	Team	Games	Pos.
1967	HOU A	14	LB
1968		14	LB
1969		14	LB
1970	HOU N	7	LB
1971		10	LB
1972		5	LB
1972	PIT N	6	LB
1973		12	LB
1974	NE N	14	LB
1975		10	LB
1976		13	LB
10 yrs.	119 games		

John Webster

THOMAS, JOHN WEBSTER
B. Dec. 13, 1900
D. Aug., 1977, Woodstock, IL
Jamestown/Chicago 6'1" 188 lbs.

Year	Team	Games	Pos.
1924	RAC N	2	FB

Kevin Webster

WEBSTER, KEVIN
B. Mar. 6, 1962, Berwyn, IL
Northern Iowa 6'2" 260 lbs.

Year	Team	Games	Pos.
1987	MIN N	3	C

Larry Webster

WEBSTER, LARRY MELVIN, JR.
B. Jan. 18, 1969, Elkton, MD
Maryland 6'5" 289 lbs.

Year	Team	Games	Pos.
1992	MIA N	16	DE
1993		13	DT
1994		15	DE, DT
1995	CLE N	10	DT
4 yrs.	54 games		

Mike Webster

WEBSTER, MICHAEL LEWIS
B. Mar. 18, 1952, Tomahawk, WI
Wisconsin 6'1" 252 lbs.

Year	Team	Games	Pos.
1974	PIT N	14	C, G
1975		14	C, G
1976		14	C, G
1977		14	C, G
1978		16	C
1979		16	C
1980		16	C
1981		16	C
1982		9	C
1983		16	C
1984		16	C
1985		16	C
1986		12	C
1987		15	C
1988		16	C
1989	KC N	16	C
1990		9	C
17 yrs.	245 games		

Tim Webster

WEBSTER, TIM
B. Sep. 11, 1949, Grove, OK
Arkansas 6'0" 195 lbs.

Year	Team	Games	Pos.
1971	GB N	4	K

Mike Weddington

WEDDINGTON, MICHAEL WAYNE
B. Oct. 9, 1960, Belton, TX
Oklahoma 6'4" 245 lbs.

Year	Team	Games	Pos.
1986	GB N	3	LB
1987		12	LB
1988		16	LB
1989		15	LB
1990		6	LB
5 yrs.	52 games		

Dick Wedel

WEDEL, RICHARD WESLEY (Bud)
B. May 29, 1923, Toledo, OH
Wake Forest 5'11" 205 lbs.

Year	Team	Games	Pos.
1948	CHIC N	1	G

Herman Wedemeyer

WEDEMEYER, HERMAN JOHN (Squirmin' Herman)
B. May 20, 1924, Hilo, HI
St. Mary's (California) 5'10" 178 lbs.

Year	Team	Games	Pos.
1948	LA AA	14	B

Year	Team	Games	Pos.

Herman Wedemeyer *cont.*

Year	Team		Games	Pos.
1949	BAL	AA	11	B
2 yrs.	25 games			

Tad Weed

WEED, THURLOW
B. 1933, Columbus, OH
Ohio State 5'5" 140 lbs.

1955	PIT	N	6	K

Don Weedon

WEEDON, JOHN DONALD
B. Jan. 13, 1919
D. Nov. 19, 1981
Texas 5'11" 220 lbs.

1947	PHI	N	12	G

George Weeks

WEEKS, GEORGE E.
B. Dec. 16, 1918
D. Mar., 1960, Florence, AL
Alabama 6'2" 200 lbs.

1944	BKN	N	4	E, B

Norris Weese

WEESE, NORRIS LEE
B. Aug. 12, 1951, Baton Rouge, LA
D. Jan. 20, 1995, Denver, CO
Mississippi 6'1" 195 lbs.

1976	DEN	N	14	QB
1977			14	QB
1978			13	QB
1979			16	QB
4 yrs.	57 games			

Bill Wegener

WEGENER, WILLIAM (Bucky)
B. 1941
Missouri 5'10" 245 lbs.

1962	HOU	A	4	G
1963			14	G
2 yrs.	18 games			

Mike Weger

WEGER, MICHAEL ROY
B. Oct. 2, 1945, Dallas, TX
Bowling Green 6'2" 197 lbs.

1967	DET	N	14	DB
1968			14	DB
1969			13	S
1970			14	S
1971			14	S
1972			14	S
1973			12	S
1975			13	S
1976	HOU	N	4	S
1977			11	S
10 yrs.	123 games			

Ted Wegert

WEGERT, THEODORE ADDISON
B. Apr. 17, 1932
D. Feb., 1986, West Palm Beach, FL
none 5'11" 202 lbs.

1955	PHI	N	7	HB
1956			7	HB
1960	BUF	A		HB
3 yrs.	14 games			

Ray Wehba

WEHBA, RAYMOND
B. Aug. 16, 1916, Sherman, TX
Southern California 6'0" 215 lbs.

1943	BKN	N	10	E
1944	GB	N	10	E
2 yrs.	20 games			

Roger Wehrli

WEHRLI, ROGER RUSSEL
B. Nov. 26, 1947, St. Louis, MO
Missouri 6'1" 192 lbs.

1969	STL	N	13	S
1970			14	CB
1971			13	CB
1972			14	CB, S
1973			11	CB, S
1974			14	CB
1975			14	CB
1976			14	CB
1977			14	CB
1978			16	CB
1979			16	CB
1980			16	CB
1981			16	CB
1982			8	CB
14 yrs.	193 games			

Bert Weidner

WEIDNER, BERT
B. Jan. 20, 1966, Eden, NY
Kent State 6'3" 284 lbs.

1990	MIA	N	8	NT
1991			15	C
1992			16	C, G
1993			16	G, C
1994			15	G
1995			12	G, C
6 yrs.	82 games			

Lee Weigel

WEIGEL, LEE
B. Nov. 15, 1963
Wisconsin-Eau Claire 5'11" 220 lbs.

1987	GB	N	2	RB

Jack Weil

WEIL, JACK LEE
B. Mar. 16, 1962, Denver, CO
Wyoming 5'11" 175 lbs.

1986	DEN	N	6	P
1987	WAS	N	3	P
2 yrs.	9 games			

Chuck Weimer

WEIMER, CHARLES (Dutch)
B. 1906
Wilmington 5'9" 178 lbs.

1929	BUF	N	9	HB, QB
1930	BKN	N	11	HB, FB, QB
1931	CLE	N	6	HB, QB
3 yrs.	26 games			

Henry Weinberg

WEINBERG, HENRY
B. 1911
Duquesne 5'7" 190 lbs.

1934	PIT	N	8	G

Saul Weinberg

WEINBERG, SAUL
B. 1895
Deceased
Case Western Reserve 5'9" 165 lbs.

1923	CLE	N	2	HB, T

Al Weiner

WEINER, ALBERT
B. Nov. 13, 1910
D. Feb., 1980, Philadelphia, PA
Muhlenberg 5'9" 180 lbs.

1934	PHI	N	6	FB

Art Weiner

WEINER, ART EDWARD
B. Apr. 16, 1924, Newark, NJ
North Carolina 6'3" 212 lbs.

1950	NYY	N	12	E

Bernie Weiner

WEINER, BERNARD
B. Jan. 24, 1918, Newark, NJ
D. Apr., 1990, Passaic, NJ
Kansas State 5'11" 222 lbs.

1942	BKN	N	10	G, T

Arnie Weinmeister

WEINMEISTER, ARNOLD G.
B. Mar. 23, 1923, Rhine, Sask.
Washington 6'4" 235 lbs.

1948	NY	AA	14	T
1949	B-NY	AA	11	T
1950	NYG	N	10	T
1951			12	T
1952			12	T
1953			12	T
6 yrs.	71 games			

Izzy Weinstock

WEINSTOCK, ISADORE
B. Jun. 27, 1913, Wilkes-Barre, PA
Pittsburgh 6'0" 211 lbs.

1935	PHI	N	11	QB, FB
1937	PIT	N	11	FB, QB
1938			2	QB
3 yrs.	24 games			

Ed Weir

WEIR, EDWARD S.
B. Mar. 14, 1903, Superior, WI
D. May 15, 1991, Lincoln, NE
Nebraska 5'10" 192 lbs.

1926	FRA	N	4	T
1927			18	T, E
1928			14	T, E, G
3 yrs.	36 games			

Joe Weir

WEIR, JOSEPH
B. Aug. 26, 1905, Superior, WI
D. Feb., 1986, Sioux City, IA
Nebraska 5'11" 185 lbs.

1927	FRA	N	12	E

Sammy Weir

WEIR, SAMMY
B. Mar. 18, 1941, Walnut Ridge, AR
Arkansas State 5'9" 170 lbs.

1965	HOU	A	9	FL
1966	NY	A	11	OE
2 yrs.	20 games			

Ed Weisacosky

WEISACOSKY, EDWARD L.
B. May 4, 1944, Pottsville, PA
Miami (Florida) 6'0" 228 lbs.

1967	NYG	A	14	LB
1968	MIA	A	8	LB
1969			14	LB
1970	MIA	N	3	LB
1971	NE	N	14	LB
1972			14	LB
6 yrs.	67 games			

Heinie Weisenbaugh

WEISENBAUGH, HENRY A.
B. Mar. 12, 1914, Tarentum, PA
Pittsburgh 5'11" 190 lbs.

1935	PIT	N	5	HB

Heinie Weisenbaugh *cont.*

1935	BOS	N	4	FB, QB
1936			8	HB
2 yrs.	17 games			

Dick Weisgerber

WEISGERBER, RICHARD
B. Feb. 19, 1915, Kearny, NJ
D. Jun. 1, 1984, Sturgeon Bay, WI
Willamette 5'10" 200 lbs.

1938	GB	N	4	QB, FB
1939			3	QB
1940			10	QB
1942			9	QB
4 yrs.	26 games			

Clayton Weishuhn

WEISHUHN, CLAYTON CHARLES
B. Oct. 7, 1959, San Angelo, TX
Angelo State 6'2" 220 lbs.

1982	NE	N	9	LB
1983			16	LB
1984			1	LB
1986			4	LB
1987	GB	N	9	LB
5 yrs.	39 games			

Howie Weiss

WEISS, HOWARD WILLIAM (Howitzer)
B. Oct. 12, 1917, Fort Atkinson, WI
Wisconsin 6'0" 210 lbs.

1939	DET	N	9	FB
1940			11	FB
2 yrs.	20 games			

Johnny Weiss

WEISS, JOHN
B. Feb. 17, 1922, Jersey City, NJ
D. Aug., 1976
None 6'3" 198 lbs.

1944	NYG	N	10	E
1945			10	E
1946			7	E
3 yrs.	27 games			

Ron Weissenhofer

WEISSENHOFER, RON
B. Feb. 3, 1964
Notre Dame 6'3" 235 lbs.

1987	NO	N	1	LB

Tripp Welborne

WELBORNE, SULLIVAN ANTHONY
B. Nov. 20, 1968, Reidsville, NC
Michigan 6'0" 205 lbs.

1992	MIN	N	2	WR

Claxton Welch

WELCH, CLAXTON NATHANIEL
B. Jul. 3, 1947, Portland, OR
Oregon 5'11" 202 lbs.

1969	DAL	N	6	RB
1970	NO	N	1	RB
1970	DAL	N	9	RB
1971			14	RB
1973	NE	N	2	RB
4 yrs.	32 games			

Gibby Welch

WELCH, GILBERT L.
B. Dec. 24, 1904, Parkersburg, WV
D. Feb. 10, 1984, Pittsburgh, PA
Pittsburgh 5'11" 178 lbs.

1928	NYY	N	13	QB, HB

Year	Team	Games	Pos.

Gibby Welch continued

Year	Team	Games	Pos.
1929	**PRO**	N	12	QB, HB, FB
2 yrs.	25 games		

Herb Welch
WELCH, HERB DOYAN
B. Jan. 12, 1961, Los Angeles, CA
UCLA 5'11" 180 lbs.

1985	**NYG**	N	16	CB, S
1986		16	CB, S
1987		12	S
1989	**WAS**	N	9	S
1990	**DET**	N	16	S
1991		10	S
6 yrs.	79 games		

Jim Welch
WELCH, JAMES EVAN
B. Mar. 17, 1938, Anson, TX
Southern Methodist 6'0" 191 lbs.

1960	**BAL**	N	11	DB
1961		14	DB
1962		13	DB
1963		14	DB
1964		13	DB
1965		14	DB
1966		11	DB
1967		10	DB
1968	**DET**	N	14	DB
9 yrs.	114 games		

Hal Weldin
WELDIN, HAROLD G.
B. May 25, 1908
D. Dec. 15, 1988, Hilton Head, SC
Northwestern 6'0" 198 lbs.

| 1934 | **C-S** | N | 1 | C |

Casey Weldon
WELDON, WILLIAM CASEY
B. Feb. 3, 1968, Americus, GA
Florida State 6'1" 200 lbs.

1993	**TB**	N	3	QB
1994		3	QB
1995		16	QB
1996		3	QB
4 yrs.	25 games		

John Weldon
WELDON, JOHN (Bodie)
B. 1895
Deceased
Lafayette 5'7" 165 lbs.

| 1920 | **BUF** | A | 5 | HB |

Larry Weldon
WELDON, LAWRENCE
B. Jun. 15, 1917, Sumter, SC
D. Aug. 17, 1990, Virginia Beach, VA
Presbyterian 6'0" 198 lbs.

1944	**WAS**	N	7	QB
1945		4	QB
2 yrs.	11 games		

Joe Wellborn
WELLBORN, JOSEPH HOLLER
B. Jun. 3, 1944
Texas A&M 6'2" 215 lbs.

| 1966 | **NYG** | N | 7 | C |

Bub Weller
WELLER, RAYMOND F.
B. 1902
Nebraska 6'4" 224 lbs.

| 1923 | **STL** | N | 7 | T |
| 1924 | **MIL** | N | 13 | T |

Bub Weller continued

Year	Team	Games	Pos.
1925	**CHIC**	N	3	T
1926		12	T, E, G
1927		11	T, E
1928	**FRA**	N	15	T, G
6 yrs.	61 games		

Louis Weller
WELLER, LOUIS (Rabbit)
B. Mar. 2, 1904
D. Apr. 17, 1979, Albuquerque, NM
Haskell 5'6" 150 lbs.

| 1933 | **BOS** | N | 7 | HB, QB |

Gary Wellman
WELLMAN, GARY JAMES
B. Aug. 9, 1967, Syracuse, NY
Southern California 5'9" 168 lbs.

1992	**HOU**	N	9	WR
1993		11	WR
1994		8	WR
3 yrs.	28 games		

Mike Wellman
WELLMAN, MICHAEL JAY
B. Jul. 15, 1956, Newton, KS
Kansas 6'3" 253 lbs.

1979	**GB**	N	16	C
1980		4	C
2 yrs.	20 games		

Arthur Wells
WELLS, ARTHUR LEE
B. Feb. 1, 1963, Shreveport, LA
Grambling State 6'4" 235 lbs.

| 1987 | **TB** | N | 2 | TE |

Billy Wells
WELLS, WILLIAM PRESCOTT
B. Dec. 7, 1931, Menominee, WI
Michigan State 5'9" 176 lbs.

1954	**WAS**	N	12	HB
1956		7	HB
1957		1	HB
1957	**PIT**	N	10	HB
1958	**PHI**	N	12	HB
1960	**BOS**	A		HB
5 yrs.	42 games		

Bob Wells
WELLS, ROBERT
B. Aug. 4, 1945, New York, NY
D. Aug. 7, 1994
Johnson C. Smith 6'4" 273 lbs.

1968	**SD**	A	2	OT
1969		14	OT
1970	**SD**	N	4	OT
3 yrs.	20 games		

Dana Wells
WELLS, DANA C., JR.
B. Aug. 5, 1966, Phoenix, AZ
Arizona 6'0" 270 lbs.

| 1989 | **CIN** | N | 1 | NT |

Dean Wells
WELLS, DONALD DEAN
B. Jul. 20, 1970, Louisville, KY
Kentucky 6'3" 238 lbs.

1993	**SEA**	N	14	LB
1994		15	LB
1995		14	LB
1996		16	LB
4 yrs.	59 games		

Don Wells
WELLS, DONALD RAY
B. Jul. 12, 1922, Waycross, GA
D. Feb. 14, 1989, Stuart, FL
Georgia 6'2" 200 lbs.

1946	**GB**	N	11	E
1947		12	E
1948		12	E
3 yrs.	35 games		

Harold Wells
WELLS, HAROLD
B. Nov. 26, 1938, St. Louis, MO
Purdue 6'2" 221 lbs.

1965	**PHI**	N	14	LB
1966		14	LB
1967		14	LB
1968		14	LB
4 yrs.	56 games		

Joel Wells
WELLS, JOEL WHITLOCK
B. Nov. 26, 1935
Clemson 6'1" 198 lbs.

| 1961 | **NYG** | N | 14 | HB |

Kent Wells
WELLS, KENT E.
B. Jul. 25, 1967, Lincoln, NE
Nebraska 6'4" 295 lbs.

| 1990 | **NYG** | N | 6 | DT |

Mike Wells
WELLS, MICHAEL EUGENE
B. Jun. 18, 1951, Normal, IL
Illinois 6'5" 225 lbs.

| 1977 | **CIN** | N | 7 | QB |

Mike Wells
WELLS, MIKE
B. Jan. 22, 1962
San Diego State 6'3" 233 lbs.

| 1987 | **SF** | N | 1 | TE |

Mike Wells
WELLS, MIKE ALLAN
B. Jan. 6, 1971, Arnold, MO
Iowa 6'3" 287 lbs.

1994	**DET**	N	3	DE
1995		15	DE, DT
1996		16	DT
3 yrs.	34 games		

Norm Wells
WELLS, NORMAN EDWARD
B. Nov. 8, 1957, Detroit, MI
Northwestern 6'5" 261 lbs.

| 1980 | **DAL** | N | 3 | DT |

Terence Wells
WELLS, TERENCE
B. Apr. 20, 1951, Wade, MS
Southern Mississippi 5'11" 195 lbs.

1974	**HOU**	N	6	RB
1975	**GB**	N	14	RB
2 yrs.	20 games		

Warren Wells
WELLS, WARREN
B. Nov. 14, 1942, Franklin, LA
Texas Southern 6'1" 191 lbs.

1964	**DET**	N	9	OE
1967	**OAK**	A	13	OE
1968		14	OE
1969		14	WR

Warren Wells continued

Year	Team	Games	Pos.
1970	**OAK**	N	14	WR
5 yrs.	64 games		

Doug Wellsandt
WELLSANDT, DOUGLAS D.
B. Feb. 9, 1967, Moses Lake, WA
Washington State 6'3" 248 lbs.

| 1990 | **NYJ** | N | 16 | TE |

Woodchuck Welmas
WELMAS, WOODCHUCK
B. 1893
Deceased
Carlisle 5'7" 180 lbs.

| 1923 | **OOR** | N | 2 | E |

Jim Welsh
WELSH, JAMES
B. Sep. 17, 1902
D. Feb. 12, 1958
Colgate 5'11" 250 lbs.

1923	**ROC**	N	2	G
1924	**FRA**	N	10	G, C
1925		8	G, T
1926	**POT**	N	13	G, T
4 yrs.	33 games		

Tom Welter
WELTER, TOM
B. Feb. 24, 1964
Nebraska 6'5" 280 lbs.

| 1987 | **STL** | N | 3 | OT |

Larry Weltman
WELTMAN, LAWRENCE
B. Jun., 1898, Pittsfield, MA
Deceased
Syracuse 5'10" 150 lbs.

| 1922 | **ROC** | N | 4 | QB, HB, T |

Don Wemple
WEMPLE, DONALD L.
B. Oct. 14, 1917, Gloversville, NY
D. Jun. 23, 1943, India
Colgate 6'2" 195 lbs.

| 1941 | **BKN** | N | 11 | E |

Marty Wendell
WENDELL, MARTIN P.
B. 1927, Chicago, IL
Notre Dame 5'10" 215 lbs.

| 1949 | **CHI** | AA | 10 | G |

Jack Wender
WENDER, JACK
B. May 31, 1954, San Francisco, CA
Fresno State 6'0" 210 lbs.

| 1977 | **TB** | N | 2 | RB |

Hal Wendler
WENDLER, HAROLD W. (Windy)
B. Jan. 20, 1902
D. Aug. 25, 1984, Baton Rouge, LA
Ohio State 5'10" 175 lbs.

| 1926 | **AKR** | N | 8 | HB, QB |
| 1926 | **HAM** | N | 1 | QB |

Joe Wendlick
WENDLICK, JOSEPH P.
B. Dec. 14, 1915, Portland, OR
Oregon State 6'0" 207 lbs.

1940	**PHI**	N	9	E
1941	**PIT**	N	11	E
2 yrs.	20 games		

Joe Wendryhoski
WENDRYHOSKI, JOSEPH STANLEY
B. Mar. 1, 1939, West Frankfort, IL
Illinois 6'2" 245 lbs.

Year	Team	Games	Pos.
1964	**LA** N	13	C
1965		4	C
1966		14	C
1967	**NO** N	14	C
1968		14	C

5 yrs. 59 games

Ken Wendt
WENDT, KENNETH
B. Jun. 24, 1908
Marquette 6'0" 195 lbs.

Year	Team	Games	Pos.
1932	**CHIC** N	1	G

Al Wenglikowski
WENGLIKOWSKI, ALAN LEE
B. Aug. 3, 1960, Franklin, OH
Pittsburgh 6'1" 220 lbs.

Year	Team	Games	Pos.
1984	**BUF** N	5	LB
1987		1	LB

2 yrs. 6 games

Obe Wenig
WENIG, OBE
B. 1896
Deceased
Morningside 5'10" 190 lbs.

Year	Team	Games	Pos.
1921	**RI** A	7	E
1922	**RI** N	5	E

2 yrs. 12 games

Ad Wenke
WENKE, ADOLPH E.
B. Jan. 22, 1898
D. Mar. 3, 1961
Nebraska 6'4" 195 lbs.

Year	Team	Games	Pos.
1923	**MIL** N	12	T

Cy Wentworth
WENTWORTH, SHIRLEY P.
B. Jan. 2, 1904, Salem, MA
D. Jan. 19, 1986, Salem, MA
New Hampshire 5'10" 165 lbs.

Year	Team	Games	Pos.
1925	**PRO** N	12	HB
1926		8	HB, FB
1929	**BOS** N	6	QB, HB

3 yrs. 26 games

Barney Wentz
WENTZ, BYRON W.
B. Apr. 21, 1901, Shenandoah, PA
D. 1963
Penn State 5'11" 204 lbs.

Year	Team	Games	Pos.
1925	**POT** N	12	FB
1926		14	FB, HB
1927		12	FB, HB
1928		2	FB, HB

4 yrs. 40 games

Jeff Wenzel
WENZEL, JEFF
B. Oct. 21, 1963, New Orleans, LA
Tulane 6'7" 270 lbs.

Year	Team	Games	Pos.
1987	**PHI** N	3	OT

Ralph Wenzel
WENZEL, RALPH
B. Jul. 22, 1918, Perla, AR
Tulane 6'0" 205 lbs.

Year	Team	Games	Pos.
1942	**PIT** N	4	E

Ralph Wenzel
WENZEL, RALPH RICHARD
B. Mar. 13, 1943, San Mateo, CA
San Diego State 6'3" 244 lbs.

Year	Team	Games	Pos.
1966	**PIT** N	6	G
1967		13	G
1968		14	G
1969		8	G
1970		14	G
1972	**SD** N	14	G
1973		14	G

7 yrs. 83 games

Dick Werder
WERDER, RICHARD IRVING
B. Jul. 31, 1922, Buffalo, NY
Georgetown 5'9" 210 lbs.

Year	Team	Games	Pos.
1948	**NY** AA	3	G

Gerry Werder
WERDER, GERALD (Red)
B. Oct., 1894
Deceased
Dayton 185 lbs.

Year	Team	Games	Pos.
1921	**TON** A	1	C

Bob Werl
WERL, ROBERT
B. Jan. 7, 1943
Miami (Florida) 6'3" 240 lbs.

Year	Team	Games	Pos.
1966	**NY** A	8	G, DE

Clyde Werner
WERNER, CLYDE LEROY
B. Dec. 10, 1947, Munising, MI
Washington 6'4" 227 lbs.

Year	Team	Games	Pos.
1970	**KC** N	14	LB
1972		14	LB
1973		14	LB
1974		14	LB
1976		14	LB

5 yrs. 70 games

Greg Werner
WERNER, GREGORY ALAN
B. Oct. 21, 1966, Batesville, IN
DePauw 6'4" 236 lbs.

Year	Team	Games	Pos.
1989	**NYJ** N	10	TE

Matt Werner
WERNER, MATT
B. Jun. 14, 1971, Westwood, NJ
UCLA 6'3" 265 lbs.

Year	Team	Games	Pos.
1994	**SEA** N	1	DE

Ray Wersching
WERSCHING, RAIMUND
B. Aug. 21, 1950, Mondsee, Austria
California 5'11" 215 lbs.

Year	Team	Games	Pos.
1973	**SD** N	14	K
1974		14	K
1975		14	K
1976		9	K
1977	**SF** N	10	K
1978		16	K
1979		16	K
1980		16	K
1981		16	K
1982		9	K
1983		16	K
1984		16	K
1985		16	K
1986		16	K
1987		12	K

15 yrs. 210 games

Mule Werwaiss
WERWAISS, ELBERT
B. 1904, Connecticut
Deceased
None 235 lbs.

Year	Team	Games	Pos.
1926	**HAR** N	8	T, G

Al Wesbecher
WESBECHER, ALOYSIUS A.
B. Nov. 3, 1892
D. Mar. 27, 1966, Greensburg, PA
Washington & Jefferson 5'10" 190 lbs.

Year	Team	Games	Pos.
1920	**CLE** A	4	C

Bull Wesley
WESLEY, CECIL OLEN (Rat)
B. 1902
D. Tuscaloosa., AL
Alabama 6'1" 190 lbs.

Year	Team	Games	Pos.
1926	**PRO** N	7	G, FB
1927		10	C, G
1928	**NYG** N	5	C
1930	**POR** N	13	C, G, T

4 yrs. 35 games

Ricky Wesson
WESSON, RICKY CHARLES
B. Jun. 29, 1955, Dallas, TX
Southern Methodist 5'9" 163 lbs.

Year	Team	Games	Pos.
1977	**KC** N	14	WR

Belf West
WEST, DAVID BELFORD (Hi)
B. May 7, 1896, Hamilton, NY
D. Sep. 11, 1973, Hamilton, NY
Colgate 6'2" 200 lbs.

Year	Team	Games	Pos.
1921	**CAN** A	9	T

Bill West
WEST, WILLIAM
B. Mar. 3, 1947, Steubenville, OH
Tennessee State 5'10" 185 lbs.

Year	Team	Games	Pos.
1972	**DEN** N	8	CB

Charlie West
WEST, CHARLES
B. Aug. 31, 1946, Big Spring, TX
San Angelo/Texas-El Paso 6'1" 194 lbs.

Year	Team	Games	Pos.
1968	**MIN** N	14	DB
1969		14	CB
1970		14	S
1971		14	CB
1972		14	DB
1973		5	S, CB
1974	**DET** N	13	S, CB
1975		14	S, CB
1976		14	S
1977		13	S
1978	**DEN** N	16	S
1979		16	S

12 yrs. 161 games

David West
WEST, DAVID
B. 1938
Central State (Ohio) 6'3" 190 lbs.

Year	Team	Games	Pos.
1963	**NY** A	2	DB

Derek West
WEST, DEREK
B. Mar. 28, 1972, Denver, CO
Colorado 6'8" 303 lbs.

Year	Team	Games	Pos.
1995	**IND** N	3	OT
1996		1	OT

2 yrs. 4 games

Ed West
WEST, EDWARD LEE, III
B. Aug. 2, 1961, Colbert County, AL
Auburn 6'1" 243 lbs.

Year	Team	Games	Pos.
1984	**GB** N	16	TE
1985		16	TE
1986		16	TE
1987		12	TE
1988		16	TE
1989		13	TE
1990		16	TE
1991		16	TE
1992		16	TE
1993		16	TE
1994		16	TE
1995	**PHI** N	16	TE
1996		16	TE

13 yrs. 199 games

Hodges West
WEST, HODGES (Burr)
B. Sep. 30, 1918, Knoxville, TN
Tennessee 6'1" 220 lbs.

Year	Team	Games	Pos.
1941	**PHI** N	10	T

Jeff West
WEST, JEFFREY HAROLD
B. Apr. 6, 1953, Wheeling, VA
Cincinnati 6'3" 214 lbs.

Year	Team	Games	Pos.
1975	**STL** N	14	TE, P
1976	**SD** N	6	P, TE
1977		14	P, TE
1978		16	P, TE
1979		16	P, TE
1981	**SEA** N	15	P
1982		9	P
1983		16	P
1984		16	P
1985		2	P

10 yrs. 124 games

Mel West
WEST, MELVIN G.
B. 1939
Missouri 5'9" 190 lbs.

Year	Team	Games	Pos.
1961	**BOS** A	4	HB
1961	**NY** A	9	HB
1962		3	HB

2 yrs. 16 games

Pat West
WEST, PATRICK MICHAEL
B. Feb. 21, 1923, Florence, PA
Pittsburgh/Southern California 6'0" 201 lbs.

Year	Team	Games	Pos.
1945	**CLE** N	10	FB
1946	**LA** N	10	FB
1947		12	FB
1948		4	FB
1948	**GB** N	3	FB

4 yrs. 39 games

Robert West
WEST, ROBERT
B. Oct. 3, 1950, San Diego, CA
San Diego State 6'4" 218 lbs.

Year	Team	Games	Pos.
1972	**KC** N	11	WR
1973		8	WR
1974	**SF** N	10	WR

3 yrs. 29 games

Ronnie West
WEST, RONNIE LEE
B. Jun. 23, 1968, Pineview, GA
Valdosta State/Pittsburg State 6'1" 215 lbs.*

Year	Team	Games	Pos.
1992	**MIN** N	13	WR

Year	Team		Games	Pos.

Stan West
WEST, STANLEY B.
B. Sep. 22, 1926, Weatherford, OK
Oklahoma 6'2" 239 lbs.

Year	Team		Games	Pos.
1950	LA	N	12	G
1951			12	G
1952			12	G
1953			12	G
1954			9	G
1955	NYG	N	11	G
1956	CHIC	N	11	C
1957			5	C
8 yrs.	84 games			

Troy West
WEST, TROY H.
B. Aug. 26, 1961, Los Angeles, CA
Southern California 6'1" 205 lbs.

Year	Team		Games	Pos.
1987	PHI	N	3	S

Walt West
WEST, WALTER J.
B. Oct. 26, 1918, Burgettstown, PA
D. Sep. 13, 1984, Carlsbad, CA
Pittsburgh 6'0" 197 lbs.

Year	Team		Games	Pos.
1944	CLE	N	8	FB

Willie West
WEST, WILLIE T.
B. May 1, 1938, Lexington, MS
Oregon 5'10" 188 lbs.

Year	Team		Games	Pos.
1960	STL	N	7	HB
1961			14	DB
1962	BUF	A	12	DB
1963			14	DB
1964	DEN	A	7	DB
1964	NY	A	3	DB
1965			14	DB
1966	MIA	A	14	DB
1967			7	DB
1968			13	DB
9 yrs.	105 games			

Don Westbrook
WESTBROOK, DONALD JOSEPH, JR.
B. Nov. 1, 1952, Cheyenne, WY
Nebraska 5'10" 185 lbs.

Year	Team		Games	Pos.
1977	NE	N	13	WR
1978			16	WR
1979			16	WR
1980			14	WR
1981			12	WR
5 yrs.	71 games			

Michael Westbrook
WESTBROOK, MICHAEL
B. Jul. 7, 1972, Detroit, MI
Colorado 6'3" 215 lbs.

Year	Team		Games	Pos.
1995	WAS	N	11	WR
1996			11	WR
2 yrs.	22 games			

Greg Westbrooks
WESTBROOKS, GREGORY MELVIN
B. Feb. 24, 1953, Chicago, IL
Mesa (Colorado)/Colorado 6'2" 217 lbs.

Year	Team		Games	Pos.
1975	NO	N	14	LB
1976			14	LB
1977			7	LB
1978	STL	N	10	LB
1978	OAK	N	1	LB
1979			4	LB
1979	LA	N	5	LB
1980	OAK	N	1	LB
1980	LA	N	6	LB
6 yrs.	62 games			

Cleve Wester
WESTER, CLEVE
B. Jun. 14, 1964
Concordia (Nebraska) 5'8" 188 lbs.

Year	Team		Games	Pos.
1987	DET	N	3	RB

Westey
WESTEY
None

Year	Team		Games	Pos.
1925	MIL	N	1	G

Bob Westfall
WESTFALL, ROBERT BARTON
B. May 5, 1919, Ann Arbor, MI
D. Oct. 23, 1980, Adrian, MI
Michigan 5'8" 190 lbs.

Year	Team		Games	Pos.
1944	DET	N	10	FB, HB
1945			9	FB
1946			10	FB
1947			12	FB
4 yrs.	41 games			

Ed Westfall
WESTFALL, EDGAR
B. Nov. 8, 1909
D. Oct., 1963
Ohio Wesleyan 5'9" 170 lbs.

Year	Team		Games	Pos.
1932	BOS	N	2	HB
1933			3	HB
1933	PIT	N	6	HB
2 yrs.	11 games			

Dick Westmoreland
WESTMORELAND, RICHARD CARL
B. Feb. 17, 1941, Charlotte, NC
North Carolina A&T 6'1" 191 lbs.

Year	Team		Games	Pos.
1963	SD	A	14	DB
1964			14	DB
1965			4	DB
1966	MIA	A	14	DB
1967			14	DB
1968			11	DB
1969			10	CB
7 yrs.	81 games			

Jeff Weston
WESTON, JEFFREY GRAHAM
B. Apr. 10, 1956, Jersey City, NJ
Notre Dame 6'5" 265 lbs.

Year	Team		Games	Pos.
1979	NYG	N	16	G
1980			6	G
1981			14	G
1982			1	OT
4 yrs.	37 games			

Rhondy Weston
WESTON, RHONDY
B. Jun. 7, 1966, Belle Glade, FL
Florida 6'5" 275 lbs.

Year	Team		Games	Pos.
1989	TB	N	13	DE

Joe Westoupal
WESTOUPAL, JOSEPH
B. 1903, West Point, NE
Nebraska 6'3" 203 lbs.

Year	Team		Games	Pos.
1926	KC	N	4	C
1928	DET	N	8	C
1929	NYG	N	15	C
1930			16	C
4 yrs.	43 games			

Ryan Wetnight
WETNIGHT, RYAN SCOTT
B. Nov. 5, 1970, Fresno, CA
Stanford 6'2" 228 lbs.

Year	Team		Games	Pos.
1993	CHI	N	10	TE

Ryan Wetnight continued

Year	Team		Games	Pos.
1994			11	TE
1995			12	TE
1996			11	TE
4 yrs.	44 games			

Bob Wetoska
WETOSKA, ROBERT STEPHEN
B. Aug. 22, 1937, Minneapolis, MN
Notre Dame 6'3" 241 lbs.

Year	Team		Games	Pos.
1960	CHI	N	12	T
1961			14	G
1962			14	G
1963			14	OT
1964			14	OT
1965			14	OT
1966			14	OT
1967			12	OT
1968			14	OT
1969			6	OT
10 yrs.	128 games			

Chet Wetterlund
WETTERLUND, CHESTER
B. Mar. 19, 1918, Chicago, IL
D. Sep. 5, 1944
Illinois Wesleyan 6'2" 185 lbs.

Year	Team		Games	Pos.
1942	DET	N	6	HB

Max Wettstein
WETTSTEIN, MAX
B. Jul. 3, 1944, Leesburg, FL
Florida State 6'3" 217 lbs.

Year	Team		Games	Pos.
1966	DEN	A	2	TE

Harlan Wetz
WETZ, HARLAN HENRY
B. Sep. 15, 1925
D. Nov. 14, 1983
Texas 6'5" 265 lbs.

Year	Team		Games	Pos.
1947	BKN	AA	11	T

Damon Wetzel
WETZEL, DAMON HENRY (Buzz)
B. Nov. 7, 1910, Roseville, OH
D. Oct., 1985
Ohio State 5'10" 190 lbs.

Year	Team		Games	Pos.
1935	CHIB	N	1	FB
1935	PIT	N	9	FB
1 yr.	10 games			

Marty Wetzel
WETZEL, MARTIN
B. Jan. 29, 1958, New Orleans, LA
Tulane 6'3" 235 lbs.

Year	Team		Games	Pos.
1981	NYJ	N	5	LB

Ron Wetzel
WETZEL, RON JOSEPH
B. Nov. 10, 1960, Pittsburgh, PA
Arizona State 6'5" 242 lbs.

Year	Team		Games	Pos.
1983	KC	N	16	TE

Bill Whalen
WHALEN, WILLIAM
B. Sep. 11, 1900
D. Jan., 1975, Chicago, IL
None 5'7" 165 lbs.

Year	Team		Games	Pos.
1920	CHIC	A	4	C
1922	CHIC	N	3	C, T
1923			1	C
1924			1	C
4 yrs.	9 games			

Jerry Whalen
WHALEN, GERALD CORNELIUS
B. Apr. 23, 1928, Buffalo, NY
D. Nov., 1973, Buffalo, NY
Canisius 6'1" 235 lbs.

Year	Team		Games	Pos.
1948	BUF	AA	7	C

Jim Whalen
WHALEN, JAMES FRANCIS, JR.
B. May 20, 1943, Cambridge, MA
Boston College 6'2" 210 lbs.

Year	Team		Games	Pos.
1965	BOS	A	14	OE
1966			14	OE
1967			14	TE
1968			14	TE
1969			14	TE
1970	DEN	N	14	TE
1971			3	TE
1971	PHI	N	2	TE
7 yrs.	89 games			

Ben Whaley
WHALEY, BENJAMIN F.
B. Oct. 14, 1926, Richmond, VA
Virginia State 5'11" 210 lbs.

Year	Team		Games	Pos.
1949	LA	AA	3	G

Tom Wham
WHAM, THOMAS ARTHUR
B. Nov. 22, 1923, Greenville, SC
Furman 6'2" 217 lbs.

Year	Team		Games	Pos.
1949	CHIC	N	12	E
1950			11	E
1951			12	E
3 yrs.	35 games			

Hogan Wharton
WHARTON, HOGAN
B. 1936
Houston 6'2" 248 lbs.

Year	Team		Games	Pos.
1960	HOU	A		G
1961			14	G
1962			4	G
1963			14	G
4 yrs.	32 games			

Jim Whatley
WHATLEY, JAMES W.
B. Mar. 11, 1913, Tuscaloosa, AL
Alabama 6'5" 223 lbs.

Year	Team		Games	Pos.
1936	BKN	N	11	T, E
1937			11	T, G
1938			10	T
3 yrs.	32 games			

Warren Wheat
WHEAT, WARREN
B. May 13, 1967, Phoenix, AZ
Brigham Young 6'6" 274 lbs.

Year	Team		Games	Pos.
1989	SEA	N	2	G
1991			14	G
2 yrs.	16 games			

Tyrone Wheatley
WHEATLEY, TYRONE
B. Jan. 19, 1972, Inkster, MI
Michigan 6'0" 227 lbs.

Year	Team		Games	Pos.
1995	NYG	N	13	RB
1996			14	RB
2 yrs.	27 games			

Dwight Wheeler
WHEELER, DWIGHT
B. Jan. 13, 1955, Memphis, TN
Tennessee State 6'3" 270 lbs.

Year	Team		Games	Pos.
1978	NE	N	2	OT

Year	Team		Games	Pos.

Dwight Wheeler continued

Year	Team		Games	Pos.
1979			13	OT
1980			16	OT
1981			16	OT
1982			9	OT
1983			16	C
1984	LARI	N	4	OL
1987			4	C, G
1987	SD	N	3	G, OT
1988	LARI	N	8	C, OT

9 yrs.   91 games

Ernie Wheeler

WHEELER, ERNEST
B. Jan. 28, 1915, Fargo, ND
D. Jun., 1982, Detroit Lakes, MN
North Dakota State 6'1" 190 lbs.

Year	Team		Games	Pos.
1939	PIT	N	5	HB
1939	CHIC	N	2	HB
1942			3	HB

2 yrs.   10 games

Kyle Wheeler

WHEELER, KYLE (Cowboy)
B. Apr., 1898, Stiles Township, WI
Deceased
Ripon 5'9" 180 lbs.

Year	Team		Games	Pos.
1921	GB	A	3	E
1922	GB	N	9	E
1923			10	E

3 yrs.   22 games

Leonard Wheeler

WHEELER, LEONARD TYRONE
B. Jan. 15, 1969, Toccoa, GA
Mississippi/Troy State 5'11" 189 lbs.*

Year	Team		Games	Pos.
1992	CIN	N	16	CB
1993			16	CB
1995			16	CB, S
1996			13	CB

4 yrs.   61 games

Manch Wheeler

WHEELER, MANCH
B. 1939
Maine 6'0" 190 lbs.

Year	Team		Games	Pos.
1962	BUF	A	4	QB

Mark Wheeler

WHEELER, MARK
B. Jun. 15, 1964
Kentucky 6'2" 232 lbs.

Year	Team		Games	Pos.
1987	DET	N	3	TE

Mark Wheeler

WHEELER, MARK
B. Apr. 1, 1970, San Marcos, TX
Texas A&M 6'2" 280 lbs.

Year	Team		Games	Pos.
1992	TB	N	16	NT
1993			10	NT
1994			15	NT
1995			14	DT
1996	NE	N	16	DT

5 yrs.   71 games

Ron Wheeler

WHEELER, RONALD WAYNE
B. Sep. 5, 1958, Oakland, CA
Washington 6'5" 235 lbs.

Year	Team		Games	Pos.
1987	LARI	N	3	TE

Ted Wheeler

WHEELER, TED
B. Sep. 16, 1945, Detroit, MI
West Texas State 6'3" 240 lbs.

Year	Team		Games	Pos.
1967	STL	N	3	TE

Ted Wheeler continued

Year	Team		Games	Pos.
1968			5	G
1970	CHI	N	6	G

3 yrs.   14 games

Wayne Wheeler

WHEELER, WAYNE B., JR.
B. Mar. 28, 1950, Orlando, FL
Alabama 6'2" 180 lbs.

Year	Team		Games	Pos.
1974	CHI	N	13	WR

Ernie Wheelwright

WHEELWRIGHT, ERNEST
B. Nov. 28, 1939, Columbus, OH
Southern Illinois 6'3" 235 lbs.

Year	Team		Games	Pos.
1964	NYG	N	11	FB
1965			13	FB
1966	ATL		14	RB
1967			3	RB
1967	NO	N	12	RB
1968			12	RB
1969			13	RB
1970			4	RB

7 yrs.   82 games

Tom Whelan

WHELAN, THOMAS JOSEPH
B. Jan. 3, 1894, Lynn, MA
D. Jun. 26, 1957, Boston, MA
Dartmouth/Georgetown (DC) 5'10" 180 lbs.

Year	Team		Games	Pos.
1920	CAN	A	7	E
1921	CLE	A	2	C

2 yrs.   9 games

Tommy Whelan

WHELAN, THOMAS (Moose)
B. Oct. 20, 1909
D. Jan., 1976, Pittsburgh, PA
Catholic 5'8" 165 lbs.

Year	Team		Games	Pos.
1933	PIT	N	1	HB

Larry Whigham

WHIGHAM, LARRY JEROME
B. Jun. 23, 1972, Hattiesburg, MS
Northeast Louisiana 6'2" 199 lbs.

Year	Team		Games	Pos.
1994	NE	N	12	S
1995			16	S
1996			16	S

3 yrs.   44 games

Ray Whipple

WHIPPLE, RAYMOND
B. Nov. 14, 1893
D. Dec., 1973, Crest Hill, IL
Notre Dame 5'9" 170 lbs.

Year	Team		Games	Pos.
1920	DET	A	3	E

John Whire

WHIRE, J.J. (Jodie)
B. Jun. 11, 1910
D. Feb., 1983, Albany, GA
Georgia 6'1" 185 lbs.

Year	Team		Games	Pos.
1933	PHI	N	2	FB

Ken Whisenhunt

WHISENHUNT, KENNETH MOORE
B. Feb. 28, 1962, Atlanta, GA
Georgia Tech 6'3" 237 lbs.

Year	Team		Games	Pos.
1985	ATL	N	16	TE
1986			16	TE
1987			7	TE
1988			16	TE
1990	WAS	N	2	TE
1991	NYJ	N	7	TE

Ken Whisenhunt continued

Year	Team		Games	Pos.
1992			10	TE

7 yrs.   74 games

Bill Whitaker

WHITAKER, WILLIAM ANDREW
B. Jan. 18, 1959, Kansas City, MO
Missouri 6'0" 182 lbs.

Year	Team		Games	Pos.
1981	GB	N	16	CB, S
1982			9	S
1983	STL	N	7	LB
1984			7	LB

4 yrs.   39 games

Creston Whitaker

WHITAKER, CRESTON
B. Aug. 12, 1947, Quincy, IL
North Texas State 6'2" 187 lbs.

Year	Team		Games	Pos.
1972	NO	N		WR

Danta Whitaker

WHITAKER, DANTA ANTONIO
B. Mar. 14, 1964, Atlanta, GA
Mississippi Valley State 6'4" 248 lbs.

Year	Team		Games	Pos.
1990	KC	N	16	TE
1992	MIN	N	12	TE
1993	CHI	N	5	TE

3 yrs.   33 games

Frank Whitcomb

WHITCOMB, FRANK E.
B. Dec. 7, 1896
D. Aug. 23, 1977, Fulton, NY
Syracuse 6'3" 217 lbs.

Year	Team		Games	Pos.
1921	ROC	A	2	G, T

Adrian White

WHITE, ADRIAN DARNELL
B. Apr. 6, 1964, Orange Park, FL
Southern Illinois/Florida 6'0" 200 lbs.

Year	Team		Games	Pos.
1987	NYG	N	6	S
1988			16	S
1989			15	S
1991			14	CB, S
1992	GB	N	15	S
1993	NE	N	5	CB, S

6 yrs.   71 games

Alberto White

WHITE, ALBERTO
B. Apr. 8, 1971, Miami, FL
Texas Southern 6'3" 245 lbs.

Year	Team		Games	Pos.
1994	LARI	N	8	DE
1995	STL	N	2	DE
1996			3	DE

3 yrs.   13 games

Allie White

WHITE, THOMAS ALLISON
B. Mar. 23, 1915, Crosby, TX
Texas Christian 5'11" 212 lbs.

Year	Team		Games	Pos.
1939	PHI	N		G, T

Andre White

WHITE, ANDRE MOSES
B. Oct. 7, 1944, Winter Park, FL
Florida A&M 6'5" 225 lbs.

Year	Team		Games	Pos.
1967	DEN	A	14	TE
1968	CIN	A	3	TE
1968	SD	A	8	TE

2 yrs.   25 games

Art White

WHITE, ARTHUR P. (Tarzan)
B. Dec. 6, 1915, Lockhart, AL

Art White continued

Deceased
Alabama 5'9" 217 lbs.

Year	Team		Games	Pos.
1937	NYG	N	11	G
1938			10	G
1939			5	G
1940	CHIC	N	10	G, E
1941			9	G
1945	NYG	N	5	G

6 yrs.   50 games

Bob White

WHITE, LOREN ROBERT
B. 1938
Ohio State 6'2" 220 lbs.

Year	Team		Games	Pos.
1960	HOU	A		FB

Bob White

WHITE, ROBERT
B. Sep. 28, 1903
D. Jul., 1982, Louisville, KY
None 150 lbs.

Year	Team		Games	Pos.
1923	LOU	N	2	E

Bob White

WHITE, ROBERT A.
B. Apr. 9, 1963, Fitchburg, MA
Rhode Island 6'5" 272 lbs.

Year	Team		Games	Pos.
1987	DAL	N	5	G
1988			12	G
1989			8	C

3 yrs.   25 games

Bob White

WHITE, ROBERT W.
B. 1929
Stanford 5'11" 176 lbs.

Year	Team		Games	Pos.
1951	SF	N	12	HB
1952			12	HB
1955	CLE	N	8	HB
1955	BAL	N	3	HB

3 yrs.   35 games

Brad White

WHITE, BRADLEY DEE
B. Aug. 18, 1958, Rexburg, ID
Tennessee 6'2" 250 lbs.

Year	Team		Games	Pos.
1981	TB	N	16	DT, DE
1982			9	NT
1983			16	NT
1984	IND		15	NT
1985			16	NT
1987	MIN	N	1	DT

6 yrs.   73 games

Charles White

WHITE, CHARLES RAYMOND
B. Jan. 22, 1958, Los Angeles, CA
Southern California 5'10" 190 lbs.

Year	Team		Games	Pos.
1980	CLE	N	14	RB
1981			16	RB
1982			9	RB
1984			10	RB
1985	LARM	N	16	RB
1986			16	RB
1987			15	RB
1988			12	RB

8 yrs.   108 games

Charlie White

WHITE, CHARLES F.
B. Aug. 31, 1953, Suffern, NY
Bethune-Cookman 6'0" 222 lbs.

Year	Team		Games	Pos.
1977	NYJ	N	13	RB
1978	TB	N	7	RB

2 yrs.   20 games

Year	Team		Games	Pos.

Chris White
WHITE, CHRIS
B. Mar. 1, 1962
Tennessee 6'3" 200 lbs.

Year	Team		Games	Pos.
1987	SEA	N	1	S

Craig White
WHITE, CRAIG C.
B. Oct. 8, 1961, St. Joseph, MO
Missouri 6'1" 194 lbs.

Year	Team		Games	Pos.
1984	BUF	N	14	WR

Danny White
WHITE, WILFORD DANIEL
B. Feb. 9, 1952, Mesa, AZ
Arizona State 6'3" 195 lbs.

Year	Team		Games	Pos.
1976	DAL	N	14	QB, P
1977			14	QB, P
1978			16	QB, P
1979			16	QB, P
1980			16	QB, P
1981			16	QB, P
1982			9	QB, P
1983			16	QB, P
1984			14	QB, P
1985			14	QB, P
1986			7	QB
1987			11	QB
1988			3	QB

13 yrs. 166 games

Daryl White
WHITE, ROBERT DARYL
B. Oct. 12, 1951, Newark, NJ
Nebraska 6'3" 250 lbs.

Year	Team		Games	Pos.
1974	DET	N	10	G

David White
WHITE, DAVID
B. Feb. 27, 1970, New Orleans, LA
Nebraska 6'2" 235 lbs.

Year	Team		Games	Pos.
1993	NE	N	6	LB
1995	BUF	N	15	LB
1996			16	LB

3 yrs. 37 games

Dwayne White
WHITE, DWAYNE ALLEN
B. Feb. 10, 1967, Philadelphia, PA
Alcorn State 6'2" 311 lbs.

Year	Team		Games	Pos.
1990	NYJ	N	11	G
1991			16	G
1992			16	G
1993			15	G
1994			16	G
1995	STL	N	15	G
1996			16	G

7 yrs. 105 games

Dwight White
WHITE, DWIGHT LYNN (Mad Dog)
B. Jul. 30, 1949, Hampton, VA
East Texas State 6'4" 253 lbs.

Year	Team		Games	Pos.
1971	PIT	N	14	DE
1972			14	DE
1973			14	DE
1974			14	DE
1975			14	DE
1976			9	DE
1977			14	DE
1978			15	DE
1979			11	DE
1980			7	DE

10 yrs. 126 games

Year	Team		Games	Pos.

Ed White
WHITE, EDWARD ALVIN
B. Apr. 4, 1947, La Mesa, CA
California 6'2" 275 lbs.

Year	Team		Games	Pos.
1969	MIN	N	14	G, DT
1970			14	G
1971			14	G
1972			14	G
1973			14	G
1974			13	G
1975			13	G
1976			13	G
1977			13	G
1978	SD	N	15	G
1979			16	G
1980			16	G
1981			16	G
1982			9	G
1983			16	G
1984			15	G
1985			16	G

17 yrs. 241 games

Ellery White
WHITE, ELLERY
None 175 lbs.

Year	Team		Games	Pos.
1926	LA	N	8	HB, FB

Freeman White
WHITE, FREEMAN, II
B. Dec. 17, 1943, Montgomery, AL
Nebraska 6'5" 225 lbs.

Year	Team		Games	Pos.
1966	NYG	N	14	TE
1967			14	OE, LB
1968			14	DB, LB
1969			13	TE, S

4 yrs. 55 games

Gene White
WHITE, EUGENE
B. Jun. 21, 1932, Greensboro, NC
Georgia 6'2" 205 lbs.

Year	Team		Games	Pos.
1954	GB	N	8	E

Gene White
WHITE, EUGENE
B. 1940
Florida A&M 6'1" 197 lbs.

Year	Team		Games	Pos.
1962	OAK	A	7	HB

Gene White
WHITE, EUGENE G.
B. 1919
D. Apr. 24, 1989
Indiana 6'0" 205 lbs.

Year	Team		Games	Pos.
1946	BUF	AA	1	G

Gerald White
WHITE, GERALD E.
B. Dec. 9, 1964
Michigan 5'11" 223 lbs.

Year	Team		Games	Pos.
1987	DAL	N	3	RB

Harvey White
WHITE, HARVEY
B. 1938
Clemson 6'1" 190 lbs.

Year	Team		Games	Pos.
1960	BOS	A		QB

James White
WHITE, JAMES C. (Duck)
B. Oct. 26, 1953, Hot Springs, AR
Oklahoma State 6'3" 265 lbs.

Year	Team		Games	Pos.
1976	MIN	N	14	DT
1977			14	DT

Year	Team		Games	Pos.

James White *continued*

Year	Team		Games	Pos.
1978			16	DT
1979			16	DT
1980			16	DT
1981			16	DT
1982			9	DT
1983			16	NT

8 yrs. 117 games

Jan White
WHITE, JAN
B. Oct. 6, 1948, Harrisburg, PA
Ohio State 6'2" 216 lbs.

Year	Team		Games	Pos.
1971	BUF	N	13	TE
1972			14	TE

2 yrs. 27 games

Jeff White
WHITE, JEFFREY CHARLES
B. Jun. 10, 1948, Bronxville, NY
Texas-El Paso 5'11" 170 lbs.

Year	Team		Games	Pos.
1973	NE	N	11	K

Jeris White
WHITE, JERIS JEROME
B. Sep. 3, 1952, Fort Worth, TX
Hawaii 5'11" 183 lbs.

Year	Team		Games	Pos.
1974	MIA	N	14	DB
1975			14	DB
1976			14	CB
1977	TB	N	14	CB
1978			16	CB
1979			16	CB
1980	WAS	N	16	CB
1981			16	CB
1982			9	CB

9 yrs. 129 games

Jim White
WHITE, JAMES
B. Sep. 5, 1948, Chicago, IL
Colorado State 6'3" 257 lbs.

Year	Team		Games	Pos.
1972	NE	N	13	DE
1974	HOU	N	14	DE
1975			14	DE
1976			1	DE
1976	SEA	N	2	DE
1976	DEN	N	7	DE

4 yrs. 51 games

Jim White
WHITE, JAMES JOSEPH
B. Feb. 28, 1920
D. Apr., 1987, Dumont, NJ
Notre Dame 6'2" 227 lbs.

Year	Team		Games	Pos.
1946	NYG	N	11	T
1947			11	T
1948			11	T
1949			11	T
1950			11	T

5 yrs. 55 games

John White
WHITE, JOHN
B. 1939
Texas Southern 6'4" 230 lbs.

Year	Team		Games	Pos.
1960	HOU	A	4	OE
1961			14	OE

2 yrs. 18 games

Lawrence White
WHITE, LAWRENCE
B. Jun. 3, 1963
Dana 6'2" 187 lbs.

Year	Team		Games	Pos.
1987	CHI	N	2	WR

Year	Team		Games	Pos.

Lee White
WHITE, LEE ANDREW
B. May 9, 1946, Las Vegas, NV
Weber State 6'4" 238 lbs.

Year	Team		Games	Pos.
1968	NY	A	1	RB
1969			14	RB
1970	NYJ	N	14	RB
1971	LA	N	7	RB
1972	SD	N	8	RB

5 yrs. 44 games

Leon White
WHITE, THOMAS LEON
B. Oct. 4, 1963, San Diego, CA
Brigham Young 6'3" 240 lbs.

Year	Team		Games	Pos.
1986	CIN	N	16	LB
1987			12	LB
1988			16	LB
1989			16	LB
1990			16	LB
1991			16	LB
1992	LARM	N	1	LB
1993			14	LB

8 yrs. 107 games

Lorenzo White
WHITE, LORENZO MAURICE
B. Apr. 12, 1966, Hollywood, FL
Michigan State 5'11" 209 lbs.

Year	Team		Games	Pos.
1988	HOU	N	11	RB
1989			16	RB
1990			16	RB
1991			13	RB
1992			16	RB
1993			8	RB
1994			16	RB
1995	CLE	N	13	RB

8 yrs. 109 games

Lyman White
WHITE, LYMAN D., JR.
B. Jan. 3, 1959, Lafayette, LA
Louisiana State 6'0" 217 lbs.

Year	Team		Games	Pos.
1981	ATL	N	16	LB
1982			2	LB

2 yrs. 18 games

Marsh White
WHITE, MARSH R.
B. Apr. 1, 1953, Bonham, TX
Arkansas 6'2" 220 lbs.

Year	Team		Games	Pos.
1975	NYG	N	14	RB
1976			14	RB

2 yrs. 28 games

Mike White
WHITE, JAMES MICHAEL
B. Aug. 11, 1957, Augusta, GA
Albany State 6'5" 266 lbs.

Year	Team		Games	Pos.
1979	CIN	N	16	DT
1980			15	DT
1981	SEA	N	15	DT
1982			5	DT

4 yrs. 51 games

Paul White
WHITE, PAUL
B. Sep. 17, 1948, San Antonio, TX
Texas-El Paso 6'0" 200 lbs.

Year	Team		Games	Pos.
1970	STL	N	5	RB
1971			6	RB

2 yrs. 11 games

Paul White
WHITE, PAUL C.
B. Nov. 13, 1921
D. Jun. 3, 1947, Atlanta, GA

Year	Team	Games	Pos.

Paul White continued
Michigan 6'1" 183 lbs.

Year	Team		Games	Pos.
1947	PIT	N	11	HB

Phil White
WHITE, PHILLIP E. (Doc)
B. May 17, 1900
D. May, 1982, Oklahoma City, OK
Oklahoma 6'2" 210 lbs.

1925	KC	N	8	GB, QB, FB
1925	NYG	N	3	FB
1927			12	HB, FB

2 yrs. 23 games

Ralph White
WHITE, RALPH
B. Nov. 18, 1902
D. Mar., 1982, Riverhead, NY
New York University 175 lbs.

1927	BUF	N	2	E

Randy White
WHITE, RANDY LEE (Manster)
B. Jan. 15, 1953, Wilmington, DE
Maryland 6'4" 260 lbs.

1975	DAL	N	14	DE, DT, LB
1976			14	LB
1977			14	DT
1978			16	DT
1979			15	DT
1980			16	DT
1981			16	DT
1982			9	DT
1983			16	DT
1984			16	DT
1985			16	DT
1986			16	DT
1987			15	DT
1988			16	DT

14 yrs. 209 games

Ray White
WHITE, RAYMOND C.
B. May 5, 1949, Weymouth, MA
Syracuse 6'1" 227 lbs.

1971	SD	N	14	LB
1972			4	LB
1975	STL	N	14	LB
1976			6	LB

4 yrs. 38 games

Reggie White
WHITE, REGINALD EUGENE
B. Mar. 22, 1970, Baltimore, MD
North Carolina A&T 6'4" 296 lbs.

1992	SD	N	3	DT
1993			8	DT
1994			11	DT, DE
1995	NE	N	16	NT

4 yrs. 38 games

Reggie White
WHITE, REGINALD HOWARD
(The Minister of Defense)
B. Dec. 19, 1961, Chattanooga, TN
Tennessee 6'5" 285 lbs.

1985	PHI	N	13	DT
1986			16	DT
1987			12	DE, DT
1988			16	DE
1989			16	DE
1990			16	DE
1991			16	DE
1992			16	DE
1993	GB	N	16	DE
1994			16	DE, DT
1995			15	DE, DT
1996			16	DE

12 yrs. 184 games

Robb White
WHITE, ROBB
B. May 26, 1965, Aberdeen, SD
South Dakota 6'4" 270 lbs.

1988	NYG	N	1	DE
1989			1	DE
1990	TB	N	7	DE

3 yrs. 9 games

Robert White
WHITE, ROBERT
B. Nov. 24, 1962
Lamar 6'2" 180 lbs.

1987	HOU	N	3	CB

Roy White
WHITE, ROY E. (Buck)
B. Feb. 18, 1901, Brownwood, TX
D. May 15, 1993, San Antonio, TX
Howard Payne/Valparaiso 6'0" 195 lbs.

1925	CHIB	N	9	FB, HB
1926	CHI	A	14	FB, HB
1927	CHIB	N	13	FB, HB
1928			13	FB
1929			10	FB, T

5 yrs. 59 games

Russell White
WHITE, RUSSELL LAMAR
B. Dec. 15, 1970, Pacoima, CA
California 5'11" 216 lbs.

1993	LARM	N	5	RB

Sammy White
WHITE, SAMMY
B. Mar. 16, 1954, Winnsboro, LA
Grambling State 5'11" 195 lbs.

1976	MIN	N	14	WR
1977			14	WR
1978			16	WR
1979			15	WR
1980			16	WR
1981			16	WR
1982			7	WR
1983			11	WR
1984			13	WR
1985			6	WR

10 yrs. 128 games

Sheldon White
WHITE, SHELDON DARNELL
B. Mar. 1, 1965, Dayton, OH
Miami (Ohio) 5'11" 188 lbs.

1988	NYG	N	16	CB, S
1989			16	CB, S
1990	DET	N	3	CB
1991			16	CB
1992			13	CB
1993	CIN	N	8	CB

6 yrs. 72 games

Sherman White
WHITE, SHERMAN EUGENE
B. Oct. 6, 1948, Manchester, NH
California 6'5" 251 lbs.

1972	CIN	N	13	DE
1973			13	DE
1974			14	DE
1975			14	DE
1976	BUF	N	13	DE
1977			14	DE
1978			16	DE
1979			15	DE
1980			15	DE
1981			16	DE
1982			9	DE
1983			8	DE

12 yrs. 158 games

Stan White
WHITE, STANLEY CLEVE
B. Aug. 14, 1971, Birmingham, AL
Auburn 6'2" 218 lbs.

1996	NYG	N	1	QB

Stan White
WHITE, STANLEY RAY
B. Oct. 24, 1949, Dover, OH
Ohio State 6'1" 224 lbs.

1972	BAL	N	14	LB
1973			14	LB
1974			14	LB
1975			14	LB
1976			14	LB
1977			14	LB
1978			12	LB
1979			16	LB
1980	DET	N	16	LB
1981			16	LB
1982			9	LB

11 yrs. 153 games

Steve White
WHITE, STEVE
B. Oct. 25, 1973, Memphis, TN
Tennessee 6'2" 246 lbs.

1996	TB	N	4	DE, LB

Walter White
WHITE, WALTER LEE
B. Jul. 19, 1951, Charlottesville, VA
Maryland 6'3" 216 lbs.

1975	KC	N	14	TE
1976			14	TE
1977			13	TE
1978			16	TE
1979			6	TE

5 yrs. 63 games

Whizzer White
WHITE, BYRON RAYMOND
B. Jun. 8, 1917, Fort Collins, CO
Colorado 6'1" 187 lbs.

1938	PIT	N	11	HB, QB
1940	DET	N	11	HB, QB
1941			11	HB, QB

3 yrs. 33 games

Wilbur White
WHITE, WILBUR MCKEE (Mac)
B. Feb. 22, 1890, Hillsboro, OH
D. Feb., 1974, Hillsboro, OH
Marietta 6'0" 178 lbs.

1922	TOL	N	7	E, FB
1923			8	E, T, G, HB

2 yrs. 15 games

Wilbur White
WHITE, WILBUR WALTER (Red)
B. Apr. 30, 1912, Seibert, CO
D. Apr., 1968
Colorado State 6'0" 187 lbs.

1935	BKN	N	8	HB
1936	DET	N	3	HB

2 yrs. 11 games

Wilford White
WHITE, WILFORD PARLEY
(Whizzer)
B. Sep. 26, 1928, Mesa, AZ
Arizona State 5'9" 172 lbs.

1951	CHIB	N	11	HB
1952			6	HB

2 yrs. 17 games

William White
WHITE, WILLIAM EUGENE
B. Feb. 19, 1966, Lima, OH
Ohio State 5'10" 191 lbs.

1988	DET	N	16	CB
1989			15	CB
1990			16	CB, S
1991			16	CB
1992			16	CB, S
1993			16	S
1994	KC	N	15	S
1995			16	S
1996			11	S

9 yrs. 137 games

White Cloud
JONES, HORATIO
B. Oct. 23, 1888, Cattaraugus
Reservation, NY
D. Sep. 8, 1985, Lewiston, NY
Haskell

1922	OOR	N	2	E

Marv Whited
WHITED, MARVIN
B. Jul. 26, 1918, Crowell, TX
Deceased
Oklahoma 5'10" 208 lbs.

1942	WAS	N	5	B
1945			10	G

2 yrs. 15 games

Mike Whited
WHITED, MICHAEL DOUGLAS
B. Mar. 30, 1958, Chico, CA
Pacific 6'4" 250 lbs.

1980	DET	N	16	OT

Bud Whitehead
WHITEHEAD, RUBEN ANGUS
B. Jan. 1, 1939, Marianna, FL
Florida State 6'0" 184 lbs.

1961	SD	A	9	DB
1962			14	DB
1963			14	DB
1964			12	DB
1965			14	DB
1966			14	DB
1967			14	DB
1968			1	DB

8 yrs. 92 games

David Whitehurst
WHITEHURST, CHARLES DAVID
B. Apr. 27, 1955, Baumhaulder,
Germany
Furman 6'2" 204 lbs.

1977	GB	N	7	QB
1978			16	QB
1979			13	QB
1980			2	QB
1981			8	QB
1982			3	QB
1983			4	QB

7 yrs. 53 games

Sam Whiteman
WHITEMAN, SAM W.
B. Sep. 29, 1901
Deceased
Missouri 5'9" 195 lbs.

1926	CHI	A	10	HB, FB

Vic Whitemarsh
WHITEMARSH, VICTOR L.
B. Mar., 1896, Detroit, MI

Year	Team		Games	Pos.

Vic Whitemarsh *continued*
Deceased
Syracuse 190 lbs.

| 1921 | DET | A | 2 | E |

A.D. Whitfield
WHITFIELD, A.D.
B. Sep. 2, 1943, Rosebud, TX
North Texas State 5'10" 200 lbs.

1965	DAL	N	2	FB
1966	WAS	N	14	RB
1967			13	RB
1968			10	RB
4 yrs.	39 games			

Bob Whitfield
WHITFIELD, BOB
B. Oct. 18, 1971, Carson, CA
Stanford 6'5" 298 lbs.

1992	ATL	N	11	OT
1993			16	OT
1994			16	OT
1995			16	OT
1996			16	OT
5 yrs.	75 games			

Blake Whitlach
WHITLACH, BLAKE
B. Oct. 13, 1955, Baton Rouge, LA
Louisiana State 6'1" 233 lbs.

| 1978 | NYJ | N | 4 | LB |

Curtis Whitley
WHITLEY, CURTIS WAYNE
B. May 10, 1969, Lowgrounds, NC
Clemson 6'1" 288 lbs.

1992	SD	N	3	C
1993			15	C
1994			12	C, G
1995	CAR	N	16	C
1996			11	C
5 yrs.	57 games			

Hall Whitley
WHITLEY, HALL
B. 1936
Texas A&I, Kingsville 6'2" 225 lbs.

| 1960 | NY | A | | LB |

Wilson Whitley
WHITLEY, WILSON
B. Apr. 28, 1955, Brenham, TX
D. Oct. 25, 1992, Marietta, GA
Houston 6'3" 265 lbs.

1977	CIN	N	13	DT
1978			16	DT
1979			14	DT
1980			16	DT
1981			14	NT
1982			9	NT
6 yrs.	82 games			

Bob Whitlow
WHITLOW, ROBERT E.
B. Feb. 15, 1936, Shelbyville, IN
Arizona 6'1" 236 lbs.

1960	WAS	N	12	G
1961	DET	N	6	C, G
1962			14	C, G
1963			14	C
1964			12	C
1965			9	C
1966	ATL	N	11	C
1968	CLE	N	14	C
8 yrs.	92 games			

Ken Whitlow
WHITLOW, KENNETH M.
B. Nov. 30, 1917
D. Nov., 1969
Rice 6'1" 190 lbs.

| 1946 | MIA | AA | 13 | C |

S.J. Whitman
WHITMAN, S.J. LAVERNE
B. Aug. 17, 1926, Hollis, OK
Tulsa 5'11" 185 lbs.

1951	CHIC	N	12	B
1952			10	B
1953			3	B
1953	CHIB	N	10	HB
1954			8	HB
4 yrs.	43 games			

David Whitmore
WHITMORE, DAVID
B. Jul. 6, 1967, Daingerfield, TX
Stephen F. Austin 6'0" 235 lbs.

1990	NYG	N	16	S
1991	SF	N	11	S
1992			16	S
1993	KC	N	6	S
1994			12	S
1995	PHI	N	3	S
6 yrs.	64 games			

Nat Whitmyer
WHITMYER, NATHANIEL
B. Aug. 31, 1940, Washington, DC
Washington 6'0" 182 lbs.

1963	LA	N	7	DB
1966	SD	A	14	DB
2 yrs.	21 games			

Dave Whitsell
WHITSELL, DAVID A.
B. Jul. 14, 1938, Shelby, MI
Indiana 6'0" 189 lbs.

1958	DET	N	12	DB
1959			12	DB
1960			11	DB
1961	CHI	N	14	DB
1962			14	DB
1963			14	DB
1964			14	DB
1965			14	DB
1966			14	DB
1967	NO	N	14	DB
1968			14	DB
1969			14	S
12 yrs.	161 games			

Bobby Whitten
WHITTEN, BOBBY
B. May 7, 1959, Junction City, KS
Kansas 6'3" 265 lbs.

| 1981 | CIN | N | 1 | OT |

Todd Whitten
WHITTEN, TODD
B. Feb. 16, 1965
Stephen F. Austin 6'0" 185 lbs.

| 1987 | NE | N | 1 | QB |

Jesse Whittenton
WHITTENTON, URSHELL
B. May 9, 1934, Big Springs, TX
Texas-El Paso 6'0" 193 lbs.

1956	LA	N	12	DB
1957			12	DB
1958	GB	N	8	DB
1959			12	DB

Jesse Whittenton *continued*

1960			12	DB
1961			14	DB
1962			14	DB
1963			14	DB
1964			14	DB
9 yrs.	112 games			

Cary Whittingham
WHITTINGHAM, CARY
B. May 30, 1963, San Luis Obispo, CA
Brigham Young 6'2" 230 lbs.

| 1987 | LARM | N | 3 | LB |

Fred Whittingham
WHITTINGHAM, FRED
B. Feb. 4, 1939, Boston, MA
Brigham Young/California Poly (SLO) 6'1" 240 lbs.

1964	LA	N	5	G
1966	PHI	N	14	LB
1967	NO	N	7	LB
1968			13	LB
1969	DAL	N	7	LB
1970	BOS	N	13	LB
1971	PHI	N	4	LB
7 yrs.	63 games			

Kyle Whittingham
WHITTINGHAM, KYLE DAVID
B. Nov. 21, 1959, San Luis Obispo, CA
Brigham Young 6'0" 232 lbs.

| 1987 | LARM | N | 3 | LB |

Arthur Whittington
WHITTINGTON, ARTHUR LEE
B. Sep. 4, 1955, Cuero, TX
Southern Methodist 5'11" 181 lbs.

1978	OAK	N	16	RB
1979			9	RB
1980			15	RB
1981			16	RB
1982	BUF	N	2	RB
5 yrs.	58 games			

Bernard Whittington
WHITTINGTON, BERNARD
B. Jul. 20, 1971, St. Louis, MO
Indiana 6'6" 257 lbs.

1994	IND	N	13	DE
1995			16	DE
1996			16	DE
3 yrs.	45 games			

C.L. Whittington
WHITTINGTON, COLUMBUS LORENZO
B. Aug. 1, 1952, Beaumont, TX
Prairie View A&M 6'1" 200 lbs.

1974	HOU	N	14	DB
1975			14	S
1976			14	S
1978			12	DB
4 yrs.	54 games			

Mike Whittington
WHITTINGTON, MICHAEL SCOTT
B. Aug. 9, 1958, Miami, FL
Notre Dame 6'2" 220 lbs.

1980	NYG	N	16	LB
1981			6	LB
1982			9	LB
1983			8	LB
4 yrs.	39 games			

Ricky Whittle
WHITTLE, RICKY JEROME
B. Dec. 21, 1971, Fresno, CA
Oregon 5'9" 200 lbs.

| 1996 | NO | N | 10 | RB |

Mike Whitwell
WHITWELL, MICHAEL CARROLL
B. Nov. 14, 1958, Kenedy, TX
Texas A&M 6'0" 175 lbs.

1982	CLE	N	9	WR
1983			16	S
2 yrs.	25 games			

Johnny Wiatrak
WIATRAK, JOHN P.
B. 1913
Washington 6'0" 220 lbs.

| 1939 | DET | N | 1 | C |

Ossie Wiberg
WIBERG, OSCAR M. (Swede)
B. Oct. 11, 1904
D. Aug. 14, 1989, Gering, NE
Nebraska Wesleyan 5'11" 207 lbs.

1927	CLE	N	10	HB, FB, G
1928	DET	N	10	HB
1930	NYG	N	17	HB, FB
1932	BKN	N	6	HB, QB
1933	CIN	N	1	B
5 yrs.	44 games			

Murray Wichard
WICHARD, MURRAY
B. Nov. 16, 1963
Frostburg State 6'2" 260 lbs.

| 1987 | NE | N | 3 | DE |

Tom Wickert
WICKERT, THOMAS KIRK
B. Apr. 5, 1952, Astoria, OK
Washington State 6'4" 248 lbs.

1974	MIA	N	13	G
1975	NO	N	1	OT
1976			7	OT
1977	DET	N	1	OT
1977	KC	N	5	OT, G
4 yrs.	27 games			

Lloyd Wickett
WICKETT, LLOYD MELDRUM
B. Apr. 3, 1920, Ontario
Oregon State 6'1" 208 lbs.

1943	DET	N	4	T
1946			10	T
2 yrs.	14 games			

Bob Wicks
WICKS, ROBERT BLAINE
B. Jul. 24, 1950, Pasadena, CA
Utah State 6'3" 200 lbs.

1972	STL	N	9	WR
1974	GB	N	1	WR
1974	NO	N	5	WR
2 yrs.	15 games			

Ron Widby
WIDBY, GEORGE RONALD
B. Mar. 9, 1945, Knoxville, TN
Tennessee 6'4" 212 lbs.

1968	DAL	N	13	P
1969			14	P
1970			14	P
1971			14	P
1972	GB	N	14	P

Year	Team	Games	Pos.

Ron Widby *continued*

Year	Team		Games	Pos.
1973			12	P
6 yrs.	81 games			

Dave Widell
WIDELL, DAVID HAROLD
B. May 14, 1965, Hartford, CT
Boston College 6'6" 296 lbs.

Year	Team		Games	Pos.
1988	DAL	N	14	OT
1989			15	OT
1990	DEN		16	OT
1991			16	OT
1992			16	OT
1993			15	C, OT
1994			16	C
1995	JAC	N	16	C
1996			15	C
9 yrs.	139 games			

Doug Widell
WIDELL, DOUGLAS JOSEPH
B. Sep. 23, 1966, Hartford, CT
Boston College 6'4" 287 lbs.

Year	Team		Games	Pos.
1989	DEN	N	16	G
1990			16	G
1991			16	G
1992			16	G
1993	GB	N	16	G
1994	DET	N	16	G
1995			12	G
1996	IND	N	16	G
8 yrs.	124 games			

Chet Widerquist
WIDERQUIST, CHESTER C.
B. Sep. 23, 1895, Illinois
D. Jul., 1976, Rock Island, IL
Northwestern/Washington & Jefferson 6'1" 219 lbs.

Year	Team		Games	Pos.
1923	MIL	N	2	T
1924			13	T
1925	RI	N	11	T, G
1926	RI	A	8	G
1926	CHIC	N	1	G
1928			3	T
1928	DET	N	3	G, T
1928	CHIC	N	3	T
1928	DET	N	1	G
1929	MIN	N	9	T
6 yrs.	54 games			

Corey Widmer
WIDMER, COREY EDWARD
B. Dec. 25, 1968, Alexandria, VA
Montana State 6'3" 276 lbs.

Year	Team		Games	Pos.
1992	NYG	N	8	NT
1993			11	DE
1994			16	LB
1995			16	LB
1996			16	LB
5 yrs.	67 games			

Ed Widseth
WIDSETH, EDWIN C.
B. Jan. 5, 1912, Gonvick, MN
Minnesota 6'1" 223 lbs.

Year	Team		Games	Pos.
1937	NYG	N	11	T
1938			11	T
1939			11	T
1940			11	T
4 yrs.	44 games			

Ralph Wiedich
WIEDICH, RALPH H.
B. 1902
Emporia State 6'1" 205 lbs.

Year	Team		Games	Pos.
1924	KC	N	2	T
1926	RI	A	3	C
2 yrs.	5 games			

Eric Wiegand
WIEGAND, ERIC
B. Mar. 13, 1964
Missouri-Rolla 6'2" 260 lbs.

Year	Team		Games	Pos.
1987	ATL	N	2	C

Zach Wiegert
WIEGERT, ZACH
B. Aug. 16, 1972, Fremont, NE
Nebraska 6'4" 311 lbs.

Year	Team		Games	Pos.
1995	STL	N	5	OT, G
1996			16	OT
2 yrs.	21 games			

Casey Wiegmann
WIEGMANN, CASEY
B. Jul. 20, 1973, Parkersburg, IA
Iowa 6'3" 290 lbs.

Year	Team		Games	Pos.
1996	IND	N	1	C

Joe Wiehl
WIEHL, JOSEPH JOHN (Tiny)
B. Jan. 30, 1910, Coal Center, PA
Washington & Jefferson/Duquesne 5'11" 254 lbs.

Year	Team		Games	Pos.
1935	PIT	N	3	T

Bob Wiese
WIESE, ROBERT LEE
B. Jan. 25, 1923, Jamestown, ND
D. Nov., 1971
Michigan 6'3" 198 lbs.

Year	Team		Games	Pos.
1947	DET	N	12	FB
1948			4	FB
2 yrs.	16 games			

Ray Wietecha
WIETECHA, RAYMOND W.
B. Nov. 4, 1928, East Chicago, IN
Michigan State/Northwestern 6'1" 225 lbs.

Year	Team		Games	Pos.
1953	NYG	N	12	C
1954			12	C
1955			12	C
1956			12	C
1957			12	C
1958			12	C
1959			12	C
1960			12	C
1961			14	C
1962			14	C
10 yrs.	124 games			

John Wiethe
WIETHE, JOHN ALBERT (Socko)
B. Oct. 17, 1912, Cincinnati, OH
D. May 3, 1989, Cincinnati, OH
Xavier (Ohio) 6'0" 198 lbs.

Year	Team		Games	Pos.
1939	DET	N	11	G
1940			11	G
1941			7	G
1942			7	G
4 yrs.	36 games			

Paul Wiggin
WIGGIN, PAUL DAVID
B. Nov. 18, 1934, Modesto, CA
Stanford 6'3" 245 lbs.

Year	Team		Games	Pos.
1957	CLE	N	12	E
1958			12	E
1959			12	E
1960			12	E
1961			14	DE
1962			14	DE
1963			14	DE
1964			14	DE
1965			14	DE

Paul Wiggin *continued*

Year	Team		Games	Pos.
1966			14	DE
1967			14	DE
11 yrs.	146 games			

Gene Wiggs
WIGGS, EUGENE O.
B. 1900, Tennessee
Deceased

Year	Team		Games	Pos.
1921	LOU	A	2	G

Hubert Wiggs
WIGGS, HUBERT
B. 1896
Deceased
Vanderbilt 5'8" 183 lbs.

Year	Team		Games	Pos.
1921	LOU	A	1	T
1922	LOU	A	3	FB, T
1923			3	FB
3 yrs.	7 games			

Bill Wightkin
WIGHTKIN, WILLIAM JOHN
B. Jul. 28, 1927, Detroit, MI
Notre Dame 6'3" 235 lbs.

Year	Team		Games	Pos.
1950	CHIB	N	12	E
1951			10	E
1952			11	E
1953			12	E
1954			12	T
1955			12	T
1956			12	T
1957			11	T
8 yrs.	92 games			

John Wilbur
WILBUR, JOHN LEONARD
B. May 21, 1943, San Diego, CA
Stanford 6'3" 245 lbs.

Year	Team		Games	Pos.
1966	DAL	N	8	G, OT
1967			14	G
1968			14	G
1969			14	G
1970	LA	N	8	G
1971	WAS	N	14	G
1972			14	G
1973			14	G
8 yrs.	100 games			

Barry Wilburn
WILBURN, BARRY TODD
B. Dec. 9, 1963, Memphis, TN
Mississippi 6'3" 186 lbs.

Year	Team		Games	Pos.
1985	WAS	N	16	S
1986			16	CB
1987			12	CB
1988			10	CB
1989			8	CB
1992	CLE	N	6	CB
1995	PHI	N	16	S
1996			7	CB
8 yrs.	91 games			

J.R. Wilburn
WILBURN, JOHNNIE RICHARD
B. Apr. 27, 1943, San Diego, CA
South Carolina 6'2" 190 lbs.

Year	Team		Games	Pos.
1966	PIT	N	14	OE
1967			14	OE
1968			2	OE
1969			10	WR
1970			6	WR, TE
5 yrs.	46 games			

Steve Wilburn
WILBURN, STEPHEN T.
B. Feb. 25, 1961, Chicago, IL

Steve Wilburn *continued*
Illinois State 6'4" 266 lbs.

Year	Team		Games	Pos.
1987	NE	N	3	DE

Mike Wilcher
WILCHER, MIKE
B. Mar. 20, 1960, Washington, DC
North Carolina 6'3" 238 lbs.

Year	Team		Games	Pos.
1983	LARM	N	15	LB
1984			15	LB
1985			16	LB
1986			16	LB
1987			12	LB
1988			16	LB
1989			16	LB
1990			16	LB
1991	SD	N	2	LB
9 yrs.	124 games			

Solomon Wilcots
WILCOTS, SOLOMON
B. Oct. 9, 1964, Los Angeles, CA
Colorado 5'11" 189 lbs.

Year	Team		Games	Pos.
1987	CIN	N	12	CB
1988			16	CB
1989			16	CB
1990			16	S
1991	MIN	N	16	S
1992	PIT	N	16	S
6 yrs.	92 games			

Dave Wilcox
WILCOX, DAVID
B. Sep. 29, 1942, Ontario, OR
Oregon 6'3" 235 lbs.

Year	Team		Games	Pos.
1964	SF	N	14	LB
1965			14	LB
1966			14	LB
1967			14	LB
1968			14	LB
1969			14	LB
1970			13	LB
1971			14	LB
1972			14	LB
1973			14	LB
1974			14	LB
11 yrs.	153 games			

John Wilcox
WILCOX, JOHN (Firpo)
B. Apr. 23, 1903
Oklahoma 6'0" 220 lbs.

Year	Team		Games	Pos.
1926	BUF	N	10	T
1930	SI	N	3	T
2 yrs.	13 games			

John Wilcox
WILCOX, JOHN DALE
B. Mar. 15, 1938
Oregon 6'5" 230 lbs.

Year	Team		Games	Pos.
1960	PHI	N	12	E, T

Ned Wilcox
WILCOX, EDMUND QUINCY
B. Feb. 7, 1904
D. Sep., 1968
Swarthmore 5'11" 185 lbs.

Year	Team		Games	Pos.
1926	FRA	N	12	HB, QB
1927			14	FB, HB
2 yrs.	26 games			

George Wilde
WILDE, GEORGE HALL
B. Mar. 16, 1923, Olney, TX
D. May, 1975
Texas A&M 6'1" 193 lbs.

Year	Team		Games	Pos.
1947	WAS	N	9	HB

Year	Team		Games	Pos.

Bert Wilder
WILDER, ALBERT GREEN
B. Apr. 14, 1939, Greensboro, NC
North Carolina State 6'3" 245 lbs.

Year	Team		Games	Pos.
1964	NY	A	14	DE
1965			14	DE
1966			14	DE
1967			13	DE, DT
4 yrs.	55 games			

Hal Wilder
WILDER, HAROLD (Bo)
B. Feb. 8, 1893
D. Feb. 5, 1989, Lincoln, NE
Nebraska 5'10" 175 lbs.

Year	Team		Games	Pos.
1923	STL	N	2	G, E

James Wilder
WILDER, JAMES CURTIS
B. May 12, 1958, Sikeston, MO
Missouri 6'3" 224 lbs.

Year	Team		Games	Pos.
1981	TB	N	16	RB
1982			9	RB
1983			10	RB
1984			16	RB
1985			16	RB
1986			12	RB
1987			12	RB
1988			7	RB
1989			15	RB
1990	WAS	N	1	RB
1990	DET	N	15	RB
10 yrs.	129 games			

Dick Wildung
WILDUNG, RICHARD K.
B. Aug. 16, 1921, Scotland, SD
Minnesota 6'0" 221 lbs.

Year	Team		Games	Pos.
1946	GB	N	11	G
1947			3	G
1948			12	T
1949			12	T
1950			12	T
1951			12	T
1953			12	T
7 yrs.	74 games			

Charles Wiley
WILEY, CHARLES KENNEDY
B. Dec. 9, 1964
Nevada-Las Vegas 6'2" 268 lbs.

Year	Team		Games	Pos.
1987	SEA	N	1	NT

Jack Wiley
WILEY, JOHN
B. 1921
Waynesburg 5'11" 208 lbs.

Year	Team		Games	Pos.
1946	PIT	N	11	T
1947			11	T
1948			12	T
1949			12	T
1950			11	T
5 yrs.	57 games			

Cole Wilging
WILGING, COLEMAN
B. 1912
D. Mar. 10, 1973, Cincinnati, OH
Xavier (Ohio) 6'3" 205 lbs.

Year	Team		Games	Pos.
1934	C-S	N	4	E

Erik Wilhelm
WILHELM, ERIK BRADLEY
B. Nov. 16, 1965, Dayton, OH
Oregon State 6'3" 213 lbs.

Year	Team		Games	Pos.
1989	CIN	N	6	QB
1990			7	QB

Erik Wilhelm *continued*

Year	Team		Games	Pos.
1991			4	QB
1993			1	QB
1994			2	QB
1995			1	QB
1996			3	QB
7 yrs.	24 games			

Elmer Wilkens
WILKENS, ELMER S. (Swede)
B. Jan. 25, 1901
D. Mar., 1967, Fort Wayne, IN
Indiana 5'9" 170 lbs.

Year	Team		Games	Pos.
1925	GB	N	7	E

Basil Wilkerson
WILKERSON, BASIL
B. Jan. 22, 1907, Alex, OK
D. Sep., 1967
Oklahoma City 215 lbs.

Year	Team		Games	Pos.
1932	BOS	N	5	E, T, G
1932	SI	N	1	E
1934	C-S	N	1	E
2 yrs.	7 games			

Bruce Wilkerson
WILKERSON, BRUCE ALAN
B. Jul. 28, 1964, Loudon, TN
Tennessee 6'5" 289 lbs.

Year	Team		Games	Pos.
1987	LARI	N	11	G
1988			16	G
1989			16	G, OT
1990			8	OT
1991			16	OT
1992			15	OT
1993			14	OT
1994			11	OT
1995	JAC	N	10	OT
1996	GB	N	14	OT
10 yrs.	131 games			

Daryl Wilkerson
WILKERSON, DARYL WAYNE
B. Sep. 25, 1958, Houston, TX
Houston 6'4" 255 lbs.

Year	Team		Games	Pos.
1981	BAL	N	5	DT

Doug Wilkerson
WILKERSON, DOUGLAS
B. Mar. 27, 1947, Fayetteville, NC
North Carolina Central 6'3" 256 lbs.

Year	Team		Games	Pos.
1970	HOU	N	9	G
1971	SD	N	14	G
1972			14	G
1973			14	G
1974			14	G
1975			14	G
1976			14	G
1977			14	G
1978			16	G
1979			12	G
1980			16	G
1981			16	G
1982			9	G
1983			12	G
1984			16	G
15 yrs.	204 games			

Eric Wilkerson
WILKERSON, ERIC LASHAWN
B. Dec. 19, 1966, Cleveland, OH
Kent State 5'9" 185 lbs.

Year	Team		Games	Pos.
1989	PIT	N	1	WR

Reggie Wilkes
WILKES, REGINALD WAYMAN
B. May 27, 1956, Pine Bluff, AR

Reggie Wilkes *continued*
Georgia Tech 6'4" 240 lbs.

Year	Team		Games	Pos.
1978	PHI	N	16	LB
1979			16	LB
1980			16	LB
1981			14	LB
1982			9	LB
1983			14	LB
1984			14	LB
1985			16	LB
1986	ATL	N	16	LB
1987			6	LB
10 yrs.	137 games			

Willie Wilkin
WILKIN, WILBUR B. (Wee Willie)
B. Apr. 21, 1916, Bingham, UT
D. May 16, 1973, Palo Alto, CA
St. Mary's (California) 6'4" 261 lbs.

Year	Team		Games	Pos.
1938	WAS	N	11	T
1939			11	T
1940			11	T
1941			11	T
1942			11	T
1943			9	T
1946	CHI	AA	10	T
7 yrs.	74 games			

David Wilkins
WILKINS, DAVID
B. Feb. 24, 1969, Cincinnati, OH
Eastern Kentucky 6'4" 240 lbs.

Year	Team		Games	Pos.
1992	SF	N	13	DE, LB

Dick Wilkins
WILKINS, RICHARD M.
B. Sep. 28, 1925, Portland, OR
Oregon 6'2" 194 lbs.

Year	Team		Games	Pos.
1949	LA	AA	11	E
1952	DAL	N	12	E
1954	NYG	N	6	E
3 yrs.	29 games			

Gabe Wilkins
WILKINS, GABRIEL NICHOLAS
B. Sep. 1, 1971, Cowpens, SC
Gardner-Webb 6'4" 292 lbs.

Year	Team		Games	Pos.
1994	GB	N	15	DE
1995			13	DT, DE
1996			16	DT
3 yrs.	44 games			

Gary Wilkins
WILKINS, GARY CLIFTON
B. Nov. 23, 1963, West Palm Beach, FL
Georgia Tech 6'1" 235 lbs.

Year	Team		Games	Pos.
1986	BUF	N	16	FB
1987			1	RB
1988	ATL	N	14	TE
1989			13	TE
1990			13	TE
1991			6	TE
6 yrs.	63 games			

Jeff Wilkins
WILKINS, JEFF
B. Apr. 19, 1972, Youngstown, OH
Youngstown State 6'1" 180 lbs.

Year	Team		Games	Pos.
1994	PHI	N	6	K
1995	SF	N	7	K
1996			16	K
3 yrs.	29 games			

Roy Wilkins
WILKINS, ROY LEE
B. Dec. 26, 1933, Murray County, GA

Roy Wilkins *continued*
Georgia 6'3" 224 lbs.

Year	Team		Games	Pos.
1958	LA	N	12	E, LB
1959			12	LB
1961	WAS	N	14	LB
3 yrs.	38 games			

Bob Wilkinson
WILKINSON, ROBERT R.
B. Oct. 8, 1926
UCLA 6'3" 215 lbs.

Year	Team		Games	Pos.
1951	NYG	N	12	E
1952			7	E
2 yrs.	19 games			

Dan Wilkinson
WILKINSON, DAN
B. Mar. 13, 1973, Dayton, OH
Ohio State 6'5" 300 lbs.

Year	Team		Games	Pos.
1994	CIN	N	16	DT
1995			14	DT, DE
1996			16	DT
3 yrs.	46 games			

Jerry Wilkinson
WILKINSON, GERALD EDWARD
B. Feb. 27, 1956, San Francisco, CA
Oregon State 6'9" 248 lbs.

Year	Team		Games	Pos.
1979	LA	N	16	DE
1980	CLE	N	7	DE
1980	SF	N	6	DE
2 yrs.	29 games			

Jim Wilks
WILKS, JIMMY RAY
B. Mar. 12, 1958, Los Angeles, CA
California/San Diego State 6'5" 269 lbs.

Year	Team		Games	Pos.
1981	NO	N	16	DT
1982			8	NT
1983			16	DE
1984			16	DE
1985			16	DE
1986			16	DE
1987			12	DE
1988			16	DE
1989			16	DE
1990			15	NT
1991			16	NT
1992			12	NT
1993			8	NT
13 yrs.	183 games			

Erwin Will
WILL, ERWIN A., JR.
B. Jan. 14, 1943
Dayton 6'5" 270 lbs.

Year	Team		Games	Pos.
1965	PHI	N	4	OT

Ken Willard
WILLARD, KENNETH HENDERSON
B. Jul. 14, 1943, Richmond, VA
North Carolina 6'2" 225 lbs.

Year	Team		Games	Pos.
1965	SF	N	14	FB
1966			14	FB
1967			13	RB
1968			14	RB
1969			14	RB
1970			14	RB
1971			14	RB
1972			14	RB
1973			14	RB
1974	STL	N	14	RB
10 yrs.	139 games			

Henry Willegalle
WILLEGALLE, HENRY MINARD

845

Year	Team	Games	Pos.

Henry Willegalle *continued*
B. Jun. 9, 1901
D. Jun., 1964, Minneapolis, MN
Carleton 5'11" 190 lbs.

Year	Team	Games	Pos.
1929	MIN N	8	HB, QB, FB, E

Willert
WILLERT
None

1922	HAM N	1	C

Norm Willey
WILLEY, NORMAN EARLE
(Wildman)
B. Aug. 22, 1927, Hastings, WV
Marshall 6'2" 224 lbs.

1950	PHI N	12	E
1951		11	E
1952		12	G, E
1953		12	E
1954		12	E
1955		12	E
1956		9	E
1957		12	E
8 yrs.	92 games		

Gerald Willhite
WILLHITE, GERALD WILLIAM
B. May 30, 1959, Sacramento, CA
San Jose State 5'10" 200 lbs.

1982	DEN N	9	RB
1983		8	RB
1984		16	RB
1985		15	RB
1986		16	RB
1987		3	RB
1988		11	RB
7 yrs.	78 games		

Kevin Willhite
WILLHITE, ALFRED KEVIN
B. May 11, 1963, Sacramento, CA
Oregon 5'11" 208 lbs.

1987	GB N	3	RB

A.D. Williams
WILLIAMS, A.D.
B. 1933
Pacific 6'2" 210 lbs.

1959	GB N	12	E
1960	CLE N	12	E
1961	MIN N	13	OE
3 yrs.	37 games		

Aeneas Williams
WILLIAMS, AENEAS
DEMETRIUS
B. Jan. 29, 1968, New Orleans, LA
Southern University 5'10" 187 lbs.

1991	PHX N	16	CB
1992		16	CB
1993		16	CB
1994	ARI N	16	CB
1995		16	CB
1996		16	CB
6 yrs.	96 games		

Al Williams
WILLIAMS, ALPHONSO
B. Feb. 4, 1962, Vidalia, GA
Nevada-Reno 5'10" 180 lbs.

1987	SD N	3	WR

Albert Williams
WILLIAMS, ALBERT
B. Sep. 7, 1964, San Antonio, TX

Albert Williams *continued*
Texas-El Paso 6'3" 229 lbs.

1987	PIT N	3	LB

Alfred Williams
WILLIAMS, ALFRED HAMILTON
B. Nov. 6, 1968, Houston, TX
Colorado 6'6" 240 lbs.

1991	CIN N	16	LB
1992		15	LB
1993		16	LB
1994		16	DE
1995	SF N	16	DE
1996	DEN N	16	DE
6 yrs.	95 games		

Allen Williams
WILLIAMS, ALLEN
B. Sep. 17, 1972, Thomasville, GA
Georgia 5'10" 205 lbs.

1995	DET N	5	RB

Alonzo Williams
WILLIAMS, ALONZO
B. Aug. 9, 1963
Mesa (Colorado) 5'10" 192 lbs.

1987	LARM N	3	RB

Art Williams
WILLIAMS, ARTHUR V. (Pop)
B. Sep. 26, 1905
D. Feb., 1979, Dexter, ME
Connecticut 6'0" 207 lbs.

1928	PRO N	7	FB, HB
1929		11	HB, FB, QB, E
1930		11	HB, QB
1931		7	HB
4 yrs.	36 games		

Ben Williams
WILLIAMS, ROBERT JERRY
B. Sep. 1, 1954, Yazoo City, MS
Mississippi 6'3" 260 lbs.

1976	BUF N	13	DT
1977		14	DT
1978		16	DE
1979		16	DE
1980		16	DE
1981		16	DE
1982		9	DE
1983		16	DE
1984		15	DE
1985		16	DE
10 yrs.	147 games		

Bernard Williams
WILLIAMS, BENNIE BERNARD
B. Jul. 18, 1972, Memphis, TN
Georgia 6'8" 317 lbs.

1994	PHI N	16	OT

Billy Williams
WILLIAMS, BILLY LOUIS
B. Jun. 7, 1971, Alcoa, TN
Tennessee 5'11" 175 lbs.

1996	STL N	1	WR

Bobby Williams
WILLIAMS, ROBERT
B. Jan. 2, 1930, Cumberland, MD
Notre Dame 6'1" 197 lbs.

1951	CHIB N	8	QB
1952		11	QB
1955		10	QB
3 yrs.	29 games		

Bobby Ray Williams
WILLIAMS, BOBBY RAY
B. Feb. 28, 1942, Geiger, AL
Central Oklahoma 6'1" 195 lbs.

1966	STL N	14	DB
1967		14	DB
1969	DET N	13	CB
1970		14	CB
1971		14	CB
5 yrs.	69 games		

Boyd Williams
WILLIAMS, BOYD
B. 1922
Syracuse 6'3" 218 lbs.

1947	PHI N	6	C

Brent Williams
WILLIAMS, BRENT DIONE
B. Oct. 23, 1964, Flint, MI
Toledo 6'3" 278 lbs.

1986	NE N	16	DE
1987		12	DE
1988		16	DE
1989		16	DE
1990		16	DE
1991		16	DE
1992		16	DE
1993		13	DE
1994	SEA N	10	DE
1995		11	DE
1996	NYJ N	5	DE
11 yrs.	147 games		

Brian Williams
WILLIAMS, BRIAN KEITH
B. Oct. 14, 1957, New Orleans, LA
Southern 6'5" 240 lbs.

1982	NE N	1	TE

Brian Williams
WILLIAMS, BRIAN MARCEE
B. Dec. 17, 1972, Dallas, TX
Southern California 6'1" 238 lbs.

1995	GB N	13	LB
1996		16	LB
2 yrs.	29 games		

Brian Williams
WILLIAMS, BRIAN SCOTT
B. Jun. 8, 1966, Mount Lebanon, PA
Minnesota 6'5" 300 lbs.

1989	NYG N	14	G
1990		14	C, G
1991		14	C, G
1992		13	C, G
1993		16	C, G
1994		14	C
1995		16	C
1996		14	C
8 yrs.	117 games		

Brooks Williams
WILLIAMS, KIM BROOKS
B. Dec. 7, 1954, Baltimore, MD
North Carolina 6'4" 226 lbs.

1978	NO N	16	TE
1979		16	TE
1980		12	TE
1981		7	TE
1981	CHI N	5	TE
1982		9	TE
1983	NE N	13	TE
6 yrs.	78 games		

Byron Williams
WILLIAMS, BYRON K.

Byron Williams *continued*
B. Oct. 31, 1960, Texarkana, TX
Texas-Arlington 6'2" 180 lbs.

1983	PHI N	2	WR
1983	NYG N	5	WR
1984		16	WR
1985		16	WR
3 yrs.	139 games		

Calvin Williams
WILLIAMS, CALVIN JOHN, JR.
B. Mar. 3, 1967, Baltimore, MD
Purdue 5'11" 181 lbs.

1990	PHI N	16	WR
1991		12	WR
1992		16	WR
1993		16	WR
1994		16	WR
1995		16	WR
1996		1	WR
1996	BAL N	7	WR
7 yrs.	100 games		

Charlie Williams
WILLIAMS, CHARLES
B. Sep. 14, 1953, Magee, MS
Jackson State 6'1" 180 lbs.

1978	PHI N	7	CB

Charlie Williams
WILLIAMS, CHARLIE
B. Feb. 2, 1972, Detroit, MI
Bowling Green 6'0" 190 lbs.

1995	DAL N	16	S
1996		7	S
2 yrs.	23 games		

Chris Williams
WILLIAMS, CHRIS
B. Nov. 23, 1968, Chelsea, MA
American International 6'3" 304 lbs.

1991	PHX N	15	NT

Chris Williams
WILLIAMS, CHRIS ALBANY
B. Jan. 2, 1959, Alexander, LA
Louisiana State 6'0" 197 lbs.

1982	BUF N	5	CB
1983		16	CB
2 yrs.	21 games		

Clancy Williams
WILLIAMS, CLARENCE
B. Sep. 24, 1942, Beaumont, TX
Washington State 6'2" 197 lbs.

1965	LA N	12	DB
1966		14	DB
1967		14	DB
1968		14	DB
1969		14	CB
1970		5	CB
1971		6	CB
1972		9	CB
8 yrs.	88 games		

Clarence Williams
WILLIAMS, CLARENCE (Big Cat)
B. Sep. 3, 1946, Brazoria, TX
Prairie View A&M 6'5" 255 lbs.

1970	GB N	14	DE
1971		14	DE
1972		14	DE
1973		14	DE
1974		14	DE
1975		14	DE
1976		14	DE
1977		14	DE
8 yrs.	112 games		

Clarence Williams
WILLIAMS, CLARENCE
B. Jan. 25, 1955, Oakley, SC
D. Sep. 17, 1994, Columbia, SC
South Carolina 5'9" 196 lbs.

Year	Team		Games	Pos.
1977	SD	N	14	RB
1978			10	RB
1979			16	RB
1980			13	RB
1981			14	RB
5 yrs.	67 games			

Clarence Williams
WILLIAMS, CLARENCE (Butch)
B. Aug. 7, 1969, Los Angeles, CA
Washington State 6'2" 240 lbs.

Year	Team		Games	Pos.
1993	CLE	N	7	TE

Clyde Williams
WILLIAMS, CLYDE A.
B. Jul. 27, 1940, Shreveport, LA
Southern University 6'2" 252 lbs.

Year	Team		Games	Pos.
1967	STL	N	9	OT
1968			10	OT
1969			13	OT, G
1970			14	OT
1971			14	G
5 yrs.	60 games			

Clyde Williams
WILLIAMS, CLYDE W.
B. Apr. 2, 1910
D. Aug., 1961
Georgia Tech 6'2" 210 lbs.

Year	Team		Games	Pos.
1935	PHI	N	3	T, G

Cy Williams
WILLIAMS, BURTON C.
B. Apr. 12, 1902, Florida
D. Dec. 13, 1975, Richmond, CA
Florida 6'0" 200 lbs.

Year	Team		Games	Pos.
1926	NEW	A	4	T
1929	SI		9	T
1930			12	T
1932	BKN	N	1	T
4 yrs.	26 games			

Dan Williams
WILLIAMS, DAN
B. Dec. 15, 1969, Ypsilanti, MI
Tennessee State/Toledo 6'4" 290 lbs.

Year	Team		Games	Pos.
1993	DEN	N	13	DE
1994			13	DT, DE
1995			6	DE
1996			15	DT
4 yrs.	47 games			

Darryl Williams
WILLIAMS, DARRYL EDWIN
B. Jan. 1, 1970, Miami, FL
Miami (Florida) 6'0" 191 lbs.

Year	Team		Games	Pos.
1992	CIN	N	16	S
1993			16	S
1994			16	S
1995			16	S
1996	SEA	N	16	S
5 yrs.	80 games			

Dave Williams
WILLIAMS, DAVID
B. Mar. 10, 1954, Minden, LA
Colorado 6'2" 210 lbs.

Year	Team		Games	Pos.
1977	SF	N	12	RB
1978			16	RB
1979	CHI	N	14	RB
1980			16	RB
1981			8	RB
5 yrs.	66 games			

Dave Williams
WILLIAMS, DAVID LAVERNE
B. Aug. 10, 1945, Cedar Rapids, IA
Washington 6'2" 205 lbs.

Year	Team		Games	Pos.
1967	STL	N	14	FL
1968			12	FL
1969			14	WR
1970			14	WR
1971			13	WR
1972	SD	N	12	WR
1973			6	WR
1973	PIT	N	1	WR
7 yrs.	86 games			

David Williams
WILLIAMS, DAVID LAMAR
B. Jun. 10, 1963, Los Angeles, CA
Illinois 6'3" 190 lbs.

Year	Team		Games	Pos.
1986	TB	N	15	WR
1987	LARI	N	3	WR
2 yrs.	18 games			

David Williams
WILLIAMS, DAVID WAYNE
B. Jun. 21, 1966, Mulberry, FL
Florida 6'5" 292 lbs.

Year	Team		Games	Pos.
1989	HOU	N	14	OT
1990			15	OT
1991			16	OT
1992			16	OT
1993			15	OT
1994			16	OT
1995			10	OT
1996	NYJ	N	14	OT
8 yrs.	116 games			

Del Williams
WILLIAMS, DELANO R.
B. Nov. 9, 1945, Live Oak, FL
Florida State 6'2" 250 lbs.

Year	Team		Games	Pos.
1967	NO	N	14	G
1968			14	G
1969			14	G
1970			14	C
1971			14	C
1972			8	G
1973			14	G
7 yrs.	92 games			

Delvin Williams
WILLIAMS, DELVIN, JR.
B. Apr. 17, 1951, Houston, TX
Kansas 6'0" 197 lbs.

Year	Team		Games	Pos.
1974	SF	N	13	RB
1975			14	RB
1976			13	RB
1977			14	RB
1978	MIA	N	16	RB
1979			14	RB
1980			15	RB
7 yrs.	99 games			

DeMise Williams
WILLIAMS, DEMISE
B. Jul. 9, 1964
Oklahoma State 6'1" 225 lbs.

Year	Team		Games	Pos.
1987	LARI	N	1	S

Derwin Williams
WILLIAMS, DERRICK DAWAYNE
B. May 6, 1961, Brownwood, TX
New Mexico 6'1" 185 lbs.

Year	Team		Games	Pos.
1985	NE	N	16	WR
1986			16	WR
1987			10	WR
3 yrs.	42 games			

Doc Williams
WILLIAMS, DANIEL A.
B. 1898
D. Apr. 14, 1991, St. Paul, MN
None 210 lbs.

Year	Team		Games	Pos.
1923	DUL	N	6	G
1924			6	G
1925			3	G
1926			12	G
4 yrs.	27 games			

Dokie Williams
WILLIAMS, DARRYL EUGENE
B. Aug. 25, 1960, Oceanside, CA
UCLA 5'11" 180 lbs.

Year	Team		Games	Pos.
1983	LARI	N	16	WR
1984			16	WR
1985			16	WR
1986			15	WR
1987			11	WR
5 yrs.	74 games			

Don Williams
WILLIAMS, DONALD
B. May 23, 1919, Claude, TX
Texas 5'8" 210 lbs.

Year	Team		Games	Pos.
1941	PIT	N	6	G

Donnie Williams
WILLIAMS, CHARLES DONELL
B. Mar. 12, 1948, Dallas, TX
Prairie View A&M 6'3" 210 lbs.

Year	Team		Games	Pos.
1970	LA	N	13	CB

Doug Williams
WILLIAMS, DOUG
B. Oct. 1, 1962, Cincinnati, OH
Texas A&M 6'5" 286 lbs.

Year	Team		Games	Pos.
1986	HOU	N	15	OT, G
1987			7	OT, G
2 yrs.	22 games			

Doug Williams
WILLIAMS, DOUGLAS LEE
B. Aug. 9, 1955, Zachary, LA
Grambling State 6'4" 220 lbs.

Year	Team		Games	Pos.
1978	TB	N	10	QB
1979			16	QB
1980			16	QB
1981			16	QB
1982			9	QB
1986	WAS	N	1	QB
1987			5	QB
1988			11	QB
1989			4	QB
9 yrs.	88 games			

Ed Williams
WILLIAMS, EDWARD
B. Jun. 19, 1950, Oklahoma City, OK
Langston 6'2" 245 lbs.

Year	Team		Games	Pos.
1974	CIN	N	14	RB
1975			14	RB
1976	TB	N	12	RB
1977			14	RB
4 yrs.	54 games			

Ed Williams
WILLIAMS, EDWARD EUGENE
B. Sep. 8, 1961, Odessa, TX
Texas 6'4" 244 lbs.

Year	Team		Games	Pos.
1984	NE	N	14	LB
1985			13	LB
1986			8	LB
1987			12	LB
1990			15	LB
5 yrs.	62 games			

Ellery Williams
WILLIAMS, ELLERY
B. 1926
Santa Clara 6'0" 185 lbs.

Year	Team		Games	Pos.
1950	NYG	N	12	E

Eric Williams
WILLIAMS, ERIC D.
B. Jun. 17, 1955, Los Angeles, CA
Southern California 6'2" 222 lbs.

Year	Team		Games	Pos.
1977	STL	N	14	LB
1978			13	LB
1979			16	LB
1980			12	LB
1981			15	LB
1982	LARM	N	3	LB
1983			11	LB
1984	SD	N	13	LB
8 yrs.	97 games			

Eric Williams
WILLIAMS, ERIC MICHAEL
B. Feb. 24, 1962, Stockton, CA
Washington State 6'4" 282 lbs.

Year	Team		Games	Pos.
1984	DET	N	12	DT
1985			12	DT
1986			16	NT
1987			11	NT
1988			16	NT
1989			16	DE
1990	WAS	N	13	DT
1991			15	DT
1992			6	DE
1993			4	DT
10 yrs.	121 games			

Eric Williams
WILLIAMS, ERIC THOMAS
B. Mar. 21, 1960, Raleigh, NC
North Carolina State 6'1" 188 lbs.

Year	Team		Games	Pos.
1983	PIT	N	3	S
1984			16	S
1985			14	S
1986			16	S
1987	DET	N	1	CB
5 yrs.	50 games			

Erik Williams
WILLIAMS, ERIK GEORGE
B. Sep. 7, 1968, Philadelphia, PA
Central State (Ohio) 6'6" 231 lbs.

Year	Team		Games	Pos.
1991	DAL	N	11	OT
1992			16	OT
1993			16	OT
1994			7	OT
1995			15	OT
1996			16	OT
6 yrs.	81 games			

Erwin Williams
WILLIAMS, ERWIN
B. Jun. 21, 1947, Portsmouth, VA
Maryland-Eastern Shore 6'5" 215 lbs.

Year	Team		Games	Pos.
1969	PIT	N	9	LB

Eugene Williams
WILLIAMS, EUGENE
B. Jun. 15, 1960, Longview, TX
Tulsa 6'1" 220 lbs.

Year	Team		Games	Pos.
1982	SEA	N	9	LB
1983			4	LB
2 yrs.	13 games			

Frank Williams
WILLIAMS, FRANK
B. 1932
Pepperdine 6'2" 215 lbs.

Year	Team		Games	Pos.
1961	LA	N	2	FB

Year	Team	Games	Pos.

Frank Williams
WILLIAMS, FRANK P.
B. Feb. 27, 1922, Bountiful, UT
Utah State 6'0" 212 lbs.

Year	Team		Games	Pos.
1948	NYG	N	9	FB

Fred Williams
WILLIAMS, FRED
B. Feb. 8, 1929, Little Rock, AR
Arkansas 6'4" 249 lbs.

Year	Team		Games	Pos.
1952	CHIB	N	12	T
1953			12	T
1954			12	T
1955			12	T
1956			12	T
1957			12	T
1958			12	T
1959			11	T
1960	CHI	N	12	T
1961			14	DT
1962			14	DT
1963			5	DT
1964	WAS		14	DT
1965			14	DT

14 yrs. 168 games

Gardner Williams
WILLIAMS, GARDNER
B. Dec. 11, 1961, Washington, DC
St. Mary's (California) 6'2" 199 lbs.

Year	Team		Games	Pos.
1984	DET	N	3	CB, S

Garland Williams
WILLIAMS, GARLAND H. (Bulldog)
B. Aug. 21, 1921
Deceased
Georgia 6'3" 220 lbs.

Year	Team		Games	Pos.
1947	BKN	AA	14	T
1948			12	T

2 yrs. 26 games

Gary Williams
WILLIAMS, GARY LEON
B. Sep. 4, 1959, Wilmington, OH
Ohio State 6'2" 215 lbs.

Year	Team		Games	Pos.
1984	CIN	N	8	WR

Gene Williams
WILLIAMS, GENE
B. Oct. 14, 1968, Blair, NE
Iowa State 6'2" 308 lbs.

Year	Team		Games	Pos.
1991	MIA	N	10	G
1992			5	G
1993	CLE	N	16	OT, G
1994			16	OT, G
1995	ATL		12	G
1996			10	G

6 yrs. 69 games

Gerald Williams
WILLIAMS, GERALD
B. Sep. 3, 1962, Waycross, GA
Auburn 6'3" 281 lbs.

Year	Team		Games	Pos.
1986	PIT	N	16	DT, NT
1987			9	NT
1988			16	DE, NT
1989			16	NT
1990			16	NT
1991			16	NT
1992			10	NT
1993			10	NT
1994			11	DE
1995	CAR	N	16	DE
1996			16	DE

11 yrs. 152 games

Gerard Williams
WILLIAMS, GERARD ANTHONY
B. May 25, 1952, Oklahoma City, OK
Langston 6'1" 184 lbs.

Year	Team		Games	Pos.
1976	WAS	N	14	CB
1977			14	CB
1978			16	CB
1979	SF		15	CB
1980			4	CB
1980	STL	N	4	CB

5 yrs. 67 games

Grant Williams
WILLIAMS, GRANT
B. May 10, 1974, Hattiesburg, MS
Louisiana Tech 6'7" 323 lbs.

Year	Team		Games	Pos.
1996	SEA	N	8	OT

Greg Williams
WILLIAMS, GREG
B. Aug. 1, 1959, Greenville, MS
Mississippi State 5'11" 185 lbs.

Year	Team		Games	Pos.
1982	WAS	N	9	S
1983			16	CB, S
1984			16	S
1985			16	S

4 yrs. 57 games

Harvey Williams
WILLIAMS, HARVEY LAVANCE
B. Apr. 22, 1967, Hempstead, TX
Louisiana State 6'2" 226 lbs.

Year	Team		Games	Pos.
1991	KC	N	14	RB
1992			14	RB
1993			7	RB
1994	LARI		16	RB
1995	OAK		16	RB
1996			13	RB

6 yrs. 80 games

Henry Williams
WILLIAMS, HENRY JAMES
B. Dec. 2, 1956, Greensboro, AL
San Diego State 5'10" 180 lbs.

Year	Team		Games	Pos.
1979	OAK	N	16	CB
1983	LARM	N	6	CB
1983	SD	N	1	CB

2 yrs. 23 games

Henry Williams
WILLIAMS, HENRY L. (Gizmo)
B. May 31, 1962, Memphis, TN
East Carolina 5'6" 185 lbs.

Year	Team		Games	Pos.
1989	PHI	N	13	WR

Herb Williams
WILLIAMS, HERBERT EARL
B. Aug. 3, 1958, Lafayette, LA
Southern University 6'0" 198 lbs.

Year	Team		Games	Pos.
1980	SF	N	9	CB
1981	STL	N	3	CB
1982			7	CB, S

3 yrs. 19 games

Howie Williams
WILLIAMS, HOWARD LEE
B. Dec. 4, 1936, Spartanburg, SC
Howard 6'2" 188 lbs.

Year	Team		Games	Pos.
1962	GB	N	3	DB
1963			7	DB
1963	SF		14	DB
1964	OAK	A	12	DB
1965			14	DB
1966			14	DB
1967			13	DB
1968			13	DB

Howie Williams continued
Howie Williams continued

Year	Team		Games	Pos.
1969			14	S

8 yrs. 104 games

Ike Williams
WILLIAMS, IVAN A.
B. Jan. 3, 1903
D. May, 1977, Flint, TX
Georgia Tech 5'10" 180 lbs.

Year	Team		Games	Pos.
1926	NEW	A	4	FB, QB
1929	SI	N	6	HB, QB

2 yrs. 10 games

Inky Williams
WILLIAMS, JAY MAYO
B. 1897
D. Jan. 2, 1980, Chicago, IL
Brown 5'11" 165 lbs.

Year	Team		Games	Pos.
1921	HAM	A	5	E
1921	CAN	A	1	E
1922	HAM		6	E
1923			6	E
1924			3	E
1924	DAY	N	1	E
1925	HAM		4	E
1925	CLE	N	9	E
1926	HAM		3	E

6 yrs. 38 games

Jack Williams
WILLIAMS, JACK G. (Tex)
B. Aug. 21, 1919, Lancaster, PA
Auburn 5'11" 193 lbs.

Year	Team		Games	Pos.
1942	PHI	N	3	T, C-B
1946	MIA	AA	6	C

2 yrs. 9 games

Jake Williams
WILLIAMS, JACOB CRAWFORD
B. 1904
Texas Christian 6'0" 205 lbs.

Year	Team		Games	Pos.
1929	CHIC	N	6	T, G
1930			8	T
1931			8	T
1932			8	T
1933			11	T

5 yrs. 41 games

James Williams
WILLIAMS, JAMES (J.D.)
B. Nov. 22, 1963
Fresno State 5'10" 174 lbs.

Year	Team		Games	Pos.
1987	SEA	N	1	RB

James Williams
WILLIAMS, JAMES EARL
B. Mar. 30, 1967, Osceola, AR
Fresno State 5'10" 185 lbs.

Year	Team		Games	Pos.
1990	BUF	N	16	CB
1991			8	CB
1992			15	CB
1993			15	CB, S
1994	ARI	N	15	CB
1996	SF	N	1	CB

6 yrs. 70 games

James Williams
WILLIAMS, JAMES EDWARD
B. Oct. 10, 1968, Natchez, MS
Mississippi State 6'0" 230 lbs.

Year	Team		Games	Pos.
1990	NO	N	14	LB
1991			16	LB
1992			16	LB
1993			16	LB
1994			16	LB
1995	JAC	N	12	LB

6 yrs. 90 games

James Williams
WILLIAMS, JAMES OTIS (Big Cat)
B. Mar. 29, 1968, Pittsburgh, PA
Cheyney State 6'7" 315 lbs.

Year	Team		Games	Pos.
1991	CHI	N	14	DE
1992			5	DT
1993			3	OT
1994			16	OT
1995			16	OT
1996			16	OT

6 yrs. 70 games

Jamie Williams
WILLIAMS, JAMIE
B. Feb. 25, 1960, Vero Beach, FL
Nebraska 6'4" 241 lbs.

Year	Team		Games	Pos.
1983	STL	N	1	TE
1984	HOU	N	16	TE
1985			16	TE
1986			16	TE
1987			12	TE
1988			16	TE
1989	SF		3	TE
1990			16	TE
1991			16	TE
1992			16	TE
1993			16	TE
1994	LARI	N	16	TE

12 yrs. 160 games

Jarvis Williams
WILLIAMS, JARVIS ERIC
B. May 16, 1964, Palatka, FL
Florida 5'11" 196 lbs.

Year	Team		Games	Pos.
1988	MIA	N	16	S
1989			16	S
1990			16	S
1991			11	S
1992			16	S
1993			16	S
1994	NYG	N	13	S

7 yrs. 104 games

Jay Williams
WILLIAMS, JAY
B. Oct. 13, 1971, Washington, DC
Wake Forest 6'3" 266 lbs.

Year	Team		Games	Pos.
1995	STL	N	6	DE, DT
1996			2	DT, DE

2 yrs. 8 games

Jeff Williams
WILLIAMS, JEFFREY
B. May 7, 1943, High Springs, FL
Oklahoma State 6'1" 210 lbs.

Year	Team		Games	Pos.
1966	MIN	N	3	RB

Jeff Williams
WILLIAMS, JEFFREY SCOTT
B. Apr. 15, 1955, Gloucester, MA
Rhode Island 6'4" 258 lbs.

Year	Team		Games	Pos.
1977	LA	N	1	G
1978	WAS	N	7	OT
1979			16	OT
1980			15	G
1981	SD	N	12	OT
1982	CHI	N	5	G

6 yrs. 56 games

Jerrol Williams
WILLIAMS, JERROL LYNN
B. Jul. 5, 1967, Las Vegas, NV
Purdue 6'5" 240 lbs.

Year	Team		Games	Pos.
1989	PIT	N	16	LB
1990			16	LB
1991			16	LB
1992			16	LB
1993	SD	N	6	LB

Year	Team	Games	Pos.

Column 1

Jerrol Williams continued

Year	Team	Games	Pos.
1994	KC	N	6	LB
1996	BAL	N	9	LB
7 yrs.	85 games		

Jerry Williams
WILLIAMS, JEROME RALPH
B. Nov. 1, 1923, Spokane, WA
Washington State 5'10" 175 lbs.

1949	LA	N	12	HB
1950			12	HB
1951			10	HB
1952			12	HB
1953	PHI	N	12	HB
1954			11	HB
6 yrs.	69 games		

Jim Williams
WILLIAMS, JAMES
B. Jan. 6, 1945
Alcorn State 6'1" 190 lbs.

| 1969 | CIN | A | 3 | WR, CB |

Jimmy Williams
WILLIAMS, JAMES HENRY
B. Nov. 15, 1960, Washington, DC
Nebraska 6'3" 228 lbs.

1982	DET	N	6	LB
1983			16	LB
1984			16	LB
1985			16	LB
1986			10	LB
1987			12	LB
1988			5	LB
1989			16	LB
1990			10	LB
1990	MIN	N	4	LB
1991			12	LB
1992	TB	N	16	LB
1993			11	LB
12 yrs.	150 games		

Joe Williams
WILLIAMS, JOE
B. Mar. 30, 1947, Center, TX
Wyoming 6'0" 194 lbs.

1971	DAL	N	12	RB
1972	NO	N	14	RB
2 yrs.	26 games		

Joe Williams
WILLIAMS, JOE
B. Mar. 5, 1965
Grambling State 6'4" 237 lbs.

| 1987 | PIT | N | 3 | LB |

Joe Williams
WILLIAMS, JOSEPH A.
B. 1898
Deceased
Lafayette 6'0" 238 lbs.

1923	CAN	N	8	G, E
1925	NYG	N	9	G
1926			11	G, T
3 yrs.	28 games		

Joe Williams
WILLIAMS, JOSEPH JOHN
(Jumpin' Joe)
B. 1914
Ohio State 5'9" 178 lbs.

1937	CLE	N	1	FB
1939	PIT	N	1	B
2 yrs.	2 games		

Column 2

Joel Williams
WILLIAMS, JOEL
B. Dec. 13, 1956, Miami, FL
Wisconsin-La Crosse 6'1" 222 lbs.

1979	ATL	N	16	LB
1980			16	LB
1981			10	LB
1982			9	LB
1983	PHI	N	16	LB
1984			16	LB
1985			7	LB
1986	ATL	N	15	LB
1987			8	LB
1988			14	LB
1989			10	LB
11 yrs.	137 games		

Joel Williams
WILLIAMS, JOEL DAVID
B. Mar. 16, 1965, Pittsburgh, PA
Notre Dame 6'3" 242 lbs.

| 1987 | MIA | N | 3 | TE |

Joel Williams
WILLIAMS, JOEL HERSCHEL
B. Mar. 18, 1962, San Angelo, TX
Texas 6'1" 220 lbs.

1948	SF	AA	14	C
1950	BAL		12	C
2 yrs.	26 games		

John Williams
WILLIAMS, JOHN ALAN
B. Oct. 26, 1960, Muskegon, MI
Wisconsin 5'11" 213 lbs.

1985	DAL	N	8	RB
1985	SEA	N	2	RB
1986	NO	N	7	FB
1987	IND	N	2	RB
3 yrs.	19 games		

John Williams
WILLIAMS, JOHN MCKAY
B. Oct. 27, 1947, Jackson, MS
Minnesota 6'3" 257 lbs.

1968	BAL	N	14	DE
1969			13	G
1970			14	G
1971			14	G
1972	LA	N	14	OT, G
1973			14	OT, G
1974			14	OT
1975			14	OT
1976			14	OT
1977			14	OT
1978			16	OT
1979			11	OT
12 yrs.	166 games		

John L. Williams
WILLIAMS, JOHN L.
B. Nov. 23, 1964, Palatka, FL
Florida 5'11" 228 lbs.

1986	SEA	N	16	RB
1987			12	FB
1988			16	RB
1989			15	RB
1990			16	RB
1991			16	RB
1992			16	RB
1993			16	RB
1994	PIT	N	15	RB
1995			12	RB
10 yrs.	150 games		

Johnny Williams
WILLIAMS, JOHN ELLIOTT
B. Jun. 30, 1927, Los Angeles, CA

Column 3

Johnny Williams continued
Southern California 5'11" 177 lbs.

1952	WAS	N	12	HB
1953			12	HB
1954	SF	N	10	HB
3 yrs.	34 games		

Jon Williams
WILLIAMS, JONATHAN
B. Jun. 1, 1961, Somerville, NJ
Penn State 5'9" 200 lbs.

| 1984 | NE | N | 9 | RB |

Karl Williams
WILLIAMS, KARL
B. Apr. 10, 1971, Rowlett, TX
Texas A&M-Kingsville 5'10" 163 lbs.

| 1996 | TB | N | 16 | WR |

Keith Williams
WILLIAMS, KEITH
B. Sep. 30, 1964, St. Louis, MO
Southeast Missouri State 5'10" 173 lbs.

| 1986 | ATL | N | 12 | RB |

Kendall Williams
WILLIAMS, KENDALL EDWIN
B. Feb. 7, 1959, Long Beach, CA
Arizona State 5'9" 189 lbs.

| 1983 | BAL | N | 16 | CB |

Kevin Williams
WILLIAMS, KEVIN DELEON
B. Feb. 17, 1970, Marshall, TX
UCLA 6'1" 215 lbs.

| 1993 | GB | N | 3 | RB |

Kevin Williams
WILLIAMS, KEVIN J.
B. Nov. 28, 1961, San Diego, CA
Iowa State 5'9" 170 lbs.

1985	WAS	N	12	CB
1986	BUF	N	1	CB
1988	WAS	N	5	CB
3 yrs.	18 games		

Kevin Williams
WILLIAMS, KEVIN LEWIS
B. Jan. 7, 1958, Los Angeles, CA
D. Feb. 1, 1996, Cajon Junction, CA
Southern California 5'8" 164 lbs.

| 1981 | BAL | N | 11 | RB |

Kevin Williams
WILLIAMS, KEVIN RAY
B. Jan. 25, 1971, Dallas, TX
Miami (Florida) 5'9" 192 lbs.

1993	DAL	N	16	WR
1994			15	WR
1995			16	WR
1996			11	WR
4 yrs.	58 games		

Larry Williams
WILLIAMS, LAWRENCE RICHARD, II
B. Jul. 3, 1963, Orange, CA
Notre Dame 6'5" 290 lbs.

1986	CLE	N	16	G
1987			12	G
1988			14	G
1991	NO	N	6	G
1992	NE	N	13	G
5 yrs.	61 games		

Column 4

Lawrence Williams
WILLIAMS, LAWRENCE DOUGLAS
B. Sep. 3, 1953, Wichita Falls, TX
Texas Tech 5'10" 174 lbs.

1976	KC	N	13	WR
1977			6	WR
1977	CLE	N	3	WR
2 yrs.	22 games		

Lee Williams
WILLIAMS, LEE ERIC
B. Oct. 15, 1962, Fort Lauderdale, FL
Bethune-Cookman 6'6" 269 lbs.

1984	SD	N	8	DE
1985			16	DE
1986			16	DE
1987			12	DE
1988			16	DE
1989			16	DE
1990			16	DE
1991	HOU	N	16	DE, DT
1992			16	DE, DT
1993			14	DE, DT
10 yrs.	140 games		

Leonard Williams
WILLIAMS, LEONARD, JR.
B. Jun. 27, 1960, Greensboro, NC
Western Carolina 6'0" 205 lbs.

| 1987 | BUF | N | 2 | RB |

Lester Williams
WILLIAMS, LESTER
B. Jan. 19, 1959, Miami, FL
Miami (Florida) 6'3" 272 lbs.

1982	NE	N	9	NT
1983			15	NT
1984			7	NT
1985			9	NT
1986	SD	N	4	DE
1987	SEA	N	2	NT
6 yrs.	46 games		

Mark Williams
WILLIAMS, MARK ANTHONY
B. May 17, 1971, Camp Springs, MD
Ohio State 6'3" 229 lbs.

1994	GB	N	16	LB
1995	JAC	N	11	LB
1996	STL	N	2	LB
1996	TB	N	1	LB
3 yrs.	30 games		

Marvin Williams
WILLIAMS, MARVIN
B. Oct. 11, 1963
Fullerton State 6'3" 235 lbs.

| 1987 | WAS | N | 2 | TE |

Maxie Williams
WILLIAMS, MAXIE FOY
B. Jun. 28, 1940, Granite Falls, NC
Southeastern Louisiana 6'4" 247 lbs.

1965	HOU	A	14	OT
1966	MIA	A	14	OT
1967			14	OT
1968			14	OT, G
1969			14	G
1970	MIA	N	13	G
6 yrs.	83 games		

Michael Williams
WILLIAMS, MICHAEL DEAN
B. May 28, 1970, Los Angeles, CA
UCLA 5'10" 185 lbs.

| 1995 | SF | N | 3 | CB |

Year	Team		Games	Pos.

Mike Williams
WILLIAMS, MICHAEL
B. Aug. 27, 1959, Lafayette, AL
Alabama A&M 6'4" 245 lbs.

Year	Team		Games	Pos.
1982	WAS	N	6	TE
1983			7	TE
1984			1	TE
3 yrs.	14 games			

Mike Williams
WILLIAMS, MICHAEL
B. Jul. 16, 1961, Atmore, AL
Mississippi College 6'2" 217 lbs.

Year	Team		Games	Pos.
1983	PHI	N	15	RB
1984			16	RB
1987	ATL	N	3	RB
3 yrs.	34 games			

Mike Williams
WILLIAMS, MICHAEL ANTHONY
B. Oct. 14, 1957, New Kingston, PA
New Mexico 6'3" 222 lbs.

Year	Team		Games	Pos.
1979	KC	N	14	FB
1980			16	RB
1981			3	RB
3 yrs.	33 games			

Mike Williams
WILLIAMS, MIKE
B. Oct. 9, 1966, Mount Kisco, NY
Northeastern 5'10" 177 lbs.

Year	Team		Games	Pos.
1989	DET	N	1	WR
1991	MIA	N	3	WR
1992			15	WR
1993			13	WR
1994			15	WR
1995			12	WR
6 yrs.	59 games			

Mike Williams
WILLIAMS, MIKELL HERMAN
B. Nov. 22, 1953, New Orleans, LA
Louisiana State 5'10" 186 lbs.

Year	Team		Games	Pos.
1975	SD	N	14	DB
1976			14	CB
1977			10	CB
1978			16	CB
1979			16	CB
1980			14	CB
1981			14	CB
1982			9	CB
1983	LARM	N	2	CB
9 yrs.	109 games			

Moe Williams
WILLIAMS, MOE
B. Jul. 26, 1974, Columbus, GA
Kentucky 6'1" 203 lbs.

Year	Team		Games	Pos.
1996	MIN	N	9	RB

Monk Williams
WILLIAMS, CHARLES LEE
B. Feb. 15, 1945, Shreveport, LA
Arkansas-Pine Bluff 5'7" 155 lbs.

Year	Team		Games	Pos.
1968	CIN	A		WR

Newton Williams
WILLIAMS, NEWTON DENNIS
B. May 10, 1959, Charlotte, NC
Arizona State 5'10" 204 lbs.

Year	Team		Games	Pos.
1982	SF	N	6	RB
1983	BAL	N	16	RB
2 yrs.	22 games			

Oliver Williams
WILLIAMS, OLIVER LAVELL, JR.
B. Oct. 17, 1960, Chicago, IL
Illinois 6'3" 191 lbs.

Year	Team		Games	Pos.
1985	IND	N	8	WR
1986			3	WR
1987	HOU	N	3	WR
3 yrs.	14 games			

Perry Williams
WILLIAMS, PERRY
B. Apr. 2, 1964, Cartersville, GA
Clemson 6'1" 200 lbs.

Year	Team		Games	Pos.
1987	NE	N	3	CB

Perry Williams
WILLIAMS, PERRY ANDREWS
B. Dec. 11, 1946, Cincinnati, OH
Purdue 6'2" 220 lbs.

Year	Team		Games	Pos.
1969	GB	N	14	RB
1970			14	RB
1971			14	RB
1972			14	RB
1973			14	RB
1974	CHI	N	14	RB
6 yrs.	84 games			

Perry Williams
WILLIAMS, PERRY LAMAR
B. May 12, 1961, Hamlet, NC
North Carolina State 6'2" 203 lbs.

Year	Team		Games	Pos.
1984	NYG	N	16	CB
1985			16	CB
1986			16	CB
1987			10	CB
1988			16	CB
1989			16	CB
1990			16	CB
1991			16	CB
1992			16	CB
1993			8	CB
10 yrs.	146 games			

Pryor Williams
WILLIAMS, PRYOR (Pig Iron)
B. Dec. 26, 1893
Deceased
Vanderbilt 6'1" 226 lbs.

Year	Team		Games	Pos.
1921	DET	A	3	G, C

Ralph Williams
WILLIAMS, RALPH
B. Mar. 27, 1958, Monroe, LA
Southern University 6'3" 276 lbs.

Year	Team		Games	Pos.
1982	HOU	N	7	OT
1983			1	G
1985	NO	N	16	OT
1986			6	OT
4 yrs.	30 games			

Ray Williams
WILLIAMS, RAYMOND
B. Nov. 9, 1965
Rhode Island 5'11" 180 lbs.

Year	Team		Games	Pos.
1987	PIT	N	1	CB, S

Ray Williams
WILLIAMS, RAYMOND DARRELL
B. Sep. 22, 1958, Welch, WV
Washington State 5'9" 170 lbs.

Year	Team		Games	Pos.
1980	DET	N	6	RB

Reggie Williams
WILLIAMS, REGINALD
B. Sep. 19, 1954, Flint, MI
Dartmouth 6'0" 228 lbs.

Year	Team		Games	Pos.
1976	CIN	N	14	LB

Reggie Williams *continued*

Year	Team		Games	Pos.
1977			14	LB
1978			16	LB
1979			12	LB
1980			14	LB
1981			16	LB
1982			9	LB
1983			16	LB
1984			16	LB
1985			16	LB
1986			16	LB
1987			15	LB
1988			16	LB
1989			16	LB
14 yrs.	206 games			

Rex Williams
WILLIAMS, REX B. (Pinky)
B. Jul. 16, 1916
D. Nov., 1980, Rogers, AR
Texas Tech 6'2" 203 lbs.

Year	Team		Games	Pos.
1945	DET	N	1	C

Richard Williams
WILLIAMS, RICHARD, JR.
B. Jan. 30, 1952, Campville, FL
Abilene Christian 5'11" 170 lbs.

Year	Team		Games	Pos.
1974	NO	N	2	WR

Richard Williams
WILLIAMS, RICHARD
B. Aug. 13, 1960, Eustis, FL
Memphis State 6'0" 205 lbs.

Year	Team		Games	Pos.
1983	ATL	N	14	RB
1984			1	RB
2 yrs.	15 games			

Ricky Williams
WILLIAMS, RICKY C.
B. Apr. 27, 1960, Santa Monica, CA
Langston 6'1" 195 lbs.

Year	Team		Games	Pos.
1985	LARI	N	2	CB
1987			1	CB
2 yrs.	3 games			

Robert Williams
WILLIAMS, ROBERT ANTHONY
B. Sep. 26, 1962, Chicago, IL
Eastern Illinois 5'11" 202 lbs.

Year	Team		Games	Pos.
1984	PIT	N	2	S

Robert Williams
WILLIAMS, ROBERT COLE
B. Oct. 2, 1962, Galveston, TX
Baylor 5'10" 188 lbs.

Year	Team		Games	Pos.
1987	DAL	N	11	DB
1988			16	CB, S
1989			13	CB
1990			16	CB
1991			16	CB
1992			9	CB
1993			4	S
7 yrs.	85 games			

Roger Williams
WILLIAMS, ROGER
B. Jul. 1, 1946, Jeanerette, LA
Grambling State 5'10" 180 lbs.

Year	Team		Games	Pos.
1971	LA	N	4	WR
1972			14	S
2 yrs.	18 games			

Rollie Williams
WILLIAMS, ROLLAND F.
B. Oct. 11, 1897
D. Apr., 1968, North Liberty, IA

Rollie Williams *continued*
Wisconsin 5'8" 170 lbs.

Year	Team		Games	Pos.
1923	RAC	N	2	HB

Ronnie Williams
WILLIAMS, RONNIE
B. Jan. 19, 1966, Wichita Falls, TX
Oklahoma State 6'3" 259 lbs.

Year	Team		Games	Pos.
1993	MIA	N	11	TE
1994			14	TE
1995			16	TE
1996	SEA	N	14	TE
4 yrs.	55 games			

Roy Williams
WILLIAMS, ROY
B. Apr. 30, 1937, Moorhead, MN
Pacific 6'7" 265 lbs.

Year	Team		Games	Pos.
1963	SF	N	7	DT

Sam Williams
WILLIAMS, SAMUEL F.
B. Mar. 9, 1931, Dansville, MI
Michigan State 6'5" 235 lbs.

Year	Team		Games	Pos.
1959	LA	N	12	E
1960	DET	N	12	E
1961			12	DE
1962			13	DE
1963			14	DE
1964			14	DE
1965			14	DE
1966	ATL	N	14	DE
1967			14	DE
9 yrs.	119 games			

Scott Williams
WILLIAMS, EDMUND SCOTT
B. Jul. 21, 1962, Charlotte, NC
Georgia 6'2" 234 lbs.

Year	Team		Games	Pos.
1986	DET	N	16	RB
1987			5	FB
1988			11	RB
3 yrs.	32 games			

Sherman Williams
WILLIAMS, SHERMAN
B. Aug. 13, 1973, Mobile, AL
Alabama 5'8" 190 lbs.

Year	Team		Games	Pos.
1995	DAL	N	12	RB
1996			15	RB
2 yrs.	27 games			

Sid Williams
WILLIAMS, SIDNEY
B. Mar. 3, 1942, Shreveport, LA
Southern University 6'2" 235 lbs.

Year	Team		Games	Pos.
1964	CLE	N	14	DE
1965			14	DE
1966			13	LB
1967	WAS	N	10	LB
1968	BAL	N	12	LB
1969	PIT	N	13	LB
6 yrs.	76 games			

Stan Williams
WILLIAMS, STANLEY N.
B. 1929
Baylor 6'2" 195 lbs.

Year	Team		Games	Pos.
1952	DAL	N	12	E, HB

Stepfret Williams
WILLIAMS, STEPFRET
B. Jun. 14, 1973, Minden, LA
Northeast Louisiana 6'0" 170 lbs.

Year	Team		Games	Pos.
1996	DAL	N	6	WR

Year	Team		Games	Pos.

Steve Williams
WILLIAMS, STEVEN
B. Jan. 12, 1951, Columbia, SC
Western Carolina 6'6" 260 lbs.

1974	BAL	N	12	DE

Ted Williams
WILLIAMS, THEODORE PATRICK
B. Jun. 3, 1917, Bay Bulls, Nfld.
D. Oct. 30, 1993, Gloucester, MA
Boston College 5'11" 183 lbs.

1942	PHI	N	10	FB
1944	BOS	N	9	HB, G
2 yrs.	19 games			

Terry Williams
WILLIAMS, TERRANCE
B. Oct. 14, 1965, Homestead, FL
Bethune-Cookman 5'11" 197 lbs.

1988	NYJ	N	8	CB
1989			3	CB
2 yrs.	11 games			

Toby Williams
WILLIAMS, TOBIAS
B. Nov. 19, 1959, Washington, DC
Nebraska 6'4" 270 lbs.

1983	NE	N	16	DE
1984			16	DE
1985			5	DE
1986			16	DE
1987			12	NT
1988			15	NT
6 yrs.	80 games			

Tom Williams
WILLIAMS, WILLIAM THOMAS
B. Jul. 21, 1948, Hempstead, NY
California-Davis 6'4" 250 lbs.

1970	SD	N	14	TE

Travis Williams
WILLIAMS, TRAVIS
B. Jan. 14, 1946, El Dorado, AR
Arizona State 6'1" 210 lbs.

1967	GB	N	14	RB
1968			14	RB
1969			13	RB
1970			7	RB
1971	LA	N	14	RB
5 yrs.	62 games			

Travis Williams
WILLIAMS, TRAVIS B.
B. Jan. 5, 1892, Boonville, IN
D. Nov., 1986, Evansville, IN
Indiana 6'0" 200 lbs.

1921	EVA	A	3	HB

Tyrone Williams
WILLIAMS, TYRONE
B. Mar. 26, 1970, Halifax, N.S.
Western Ontario 6'5" 220 lbs.

1993	DAL	N	5	WR

Tyrone Williams
WILLIAMS, TYRONE
B. May 31, 1973, Bradenton, FL
Nebraska 5'11" 190 lbs.

1996	GB	N	16	CB

Van Williams
WILLIAMS, GEORGE VAN
B. Mar. 15, 1959, Johnson City, TN

Van Williams continued
East Tennessee State/Carson-Newman 6'0" 210 lbs.

1983	BUF	N	16	RB
1984			16	RB
1985			2	RB
1987	NYG	N	3	RB
4 yrs.	37 games			

Vaughn Williams
WILLIAMS, VAUGHN AARON
B. Dec. 14, 1961, Denver, CO
Stanford 6'2" 193 lbs.

1984	IND	N	10	DB

Vince Williams
WILLIAMS, VINCE BERNARD
B. Oct. 24, 1959, Tacoma, WA
Oregon 6'0" 231 lbs.

1982	SF	N	2	FB
1983			1	RB
2 yrs.	3 games			

Wally Williams
WILLIAMS, WALLY JAMES, JR.
B. Feb. 19, 1971, Tallahassee, FL
Florida A&M 6'2" 300 lbs.

1993	CLE	N	2	C
1994			12	G, C
1995			16	G, C
1996	BAL	N	15	C
4 yrs.	45 games			

Walt Williams
WILLIAMS, WALT
B. Jul. 10, 1954, Bedford Hills, NY
Ashland/New Mexico State 6'0" 185 lbs.

1977	DET	N	14	DB
1978			15	S
1979			12	CB
1980			16	CB
1981	MIN	N	16	CB
1982			1	CB
1982	CHI	N	4	CB
1983			15	CB
7 yrs.	93 games			

Walt Williams
WILLIAMS, WALTER L.
B. 1919
D. Aug. 8, 1990
Boston University 6'1" 194 lbs.

1946	CHI	AA	14	HB
1947	BOS	N	10	HB
2 yrs.	24 games			

Wandy Williams
WILLIAMS, WANQUALIN
B. Jan. 3, 1946, Brooklyn, NY
Kansas/Hofstra 6'0" 192 lbs.

1969	DEN	A	11	RB
1970	DEN	N	1	RB
2 yrs.	12 games			

Warren Williams
WILLIAMS, WARREN, JR.
B. Jul. 29, 1965, Fort Myers, FL
Miami (Florida) 6'0" 209 lbs.

1988	PIT	N	15	RB
1989			5	RB
1990			14	RB
1991			16	RB
1992			16	RB
1993	IND	N	5	RB
6 yrs.	71 games			

Willie Williams
WILLIAMS, WILLIE
B. Aug. 6, 1967, Houston, TX
Louisiana State 6'6" 300 lbs.

1991	PHX	N	16	OT
1994	NO	N	16	OT
2 yrs.	32 games			

Willie Williams
WILLIAMS, WILLIE ALBERT
B. Dec. 29, 1942, Atlanta, GA
Grambling State 6'0" 190 lbs.

1965	NYG	N	14	DB
1966	OAK	A	7	DB
1967	NYG	N	6	DB
1968			14	DB
1969			14	CB
1970			14	CB
1971			10	CB
1972			14	CB
1973			14	CB
9 yrs.	107 games			

Willie Williams
WILLIAMS, WILLIE JAMES, JR.
B. Dec. 26, 1970, Columbia, SC
Western Carolina 5'9" 188 lbs.

1993	PIT	N	16	CB
1994			16	CB
1995			16	CB
1996			15	CB
4 yrs.	63 games			

Win Williams
WILLIAMS, D. WINDELL
B. Mar. 10, 1923, Fort Towson, OK
D. May 13, 1992, Houston, TX
Rice/Southwestern Louisiana/Rice 6'2" 185 lbs.

1948	BAL	AA	14	E
1949			12	E
2 yrs.	26 games			

Carlton Williamson
WILLIAMSON, CARLTON
B. Jun. 12, 1958, Atlanta, GA
Pittsburgh 6'0" 204 lbs.

1981	SF	N	16	CB
1982			8	S
1983			9	S
1984			15	S
1985			16	S
1986			16	S
1987			8	S
7 yrs.	88 games			

Ernie Williamson
WILLIAMSON, ERNEST WARRINER
B. Sep. 9, 1922, Crewe, VA
Newport News Apprentice/North Carolina 6'4" lbs.

1947	WAS	N	9	T
1949	LA	AA	12	T
2 yrs.	21 games			

Fred Williamson
WILLIAMSON, FREDERICK (The Hammer)
B. Mar. 5, 1938, Gary, IN
Northwestern/California 6'2" 210 lbs.

1960	PIT	N	11	HB
1961	OAK	A	14	DB
1962			14	DB
1963			14	DB
1965	KC	A	14	DB
1966			12	DB
1967			11	DB
7 yrs.	90 games			

Greg Williamson
WILLIAMSON, GREG
B. May 11, 1964, Long Beach, CA
Fresno State 5'11" 190 lbs.

1987	LARM	N	3	CB

John Williamson
WILLIAMSON, JOHN ROBERT "J.R."
B. Oct. 9, 1942, El Dorado, AR
Louisiana Tech 6'2" 220 lbs.

1964	OAK	A	14	LB
1965			14	LB
1966			13	LB
1968	BOS	A	14	LB
1969			14	LB, C
1970	BOS	N	11	LB, C
6 yrs.	80 games			

Matt Willig
WILLIG, MATT
B. Jan. 21, 1969, Whittier, CA
Southern California 6'8" 305 lbs.

1993	NYJ	N	3	OT
1994			16	OT, G
1995	NYJ	N	15	OT
1996	ATL	N	13	OT
4 yrs.	47 games			

Larry Willingham
WILLINGHAM, LARRY LEVI
B. Dec. 22, 1948, Cullman, AL
Auburn 6'1" 190 lbs.

1971	STL	N	9	CB, S
1972			11	S
2 yrs.	20 games			

Bill Willis
WILLIS, WILLIAM K.
B. Oct. 5, 1921, Columbus, OH
Ohio State 6'2" 213 lbs.

1946	CLE	AA	13	G
1947			13	G
1948			14	G
1949			12	G
1950	CLE	N	12	G
1951			12	G
1952			12	G
1953			11	G
8 yrs.	99 games			

Chester Willis
WILLIS, CHESTER
B. May 2, 1958, Elberton, GA
Auburn 5'11" 195 lbs.

1981	OAK	N	15	RB
1982	LARI	N	8	RB
1983			13	RB
1984			16	RB
4 yrs.	52 games			

Donald Willis
WILLIS, DONALD KIRK
B. Jul. 15, 1973, Goleta, CA
North Carolina A&T 6'3" 330 lbs.

1996	NO	N	4	G

Fred Willis
WILLIS, FREDERICK FRANCIS, III
B. Dec. 9, 1947, Natick, MA
Boston College 6'0" 209 lbs.

1971	CIN	N	14	RB
1972			5	RB
1972	HOU	N	8	RB
1973			14	RB
1974			10	RB

Year	Team	Games	Pos.

Fred Willis *continued*

Year	Team	Games	Pos.
1975		13	RB
1976		13	RB
6 yrs.	77 games		

Jamal Willis
WILLIS, JAMAL
B. Dec. 12, 1972, Lawton, OK
Brigham Young 6'2" 218 lbs.

1995	SF	N	12	RB

James Willis
WILLIS, JAMES EDWARD, III
B. Sep. 2, 1972, Huntsville, AL
Auburn 6'2" 235 lbs.

1993	GB	N	13	LB
1994			12	LB
1995	PHI	N	5	LB
1996			16	LB
4 yrs.	46 games			

Keith Willis
WILLIS, KEITH
B. Jul. 29, 1959, Newark, NJ
Northwestern 6'1" 260 lbs.

1982	PIT	N	9	DE
1983			14	DE
1984			12	DE
1985			16	DE
1986			16	DE
1987			11	DE
1989			16	DE
1990			16	DE
1991			16	DE
1992	BUF	N	12	DE
1993	WAS	N	1	DE
11 yrs.	139 games			

Ken Willis
WILLIS, ROBERT KENNETH
B. Oct. 6, 1966, Owensboro, KY
Kentucky 5'11" 189 lbs.

1990	DAL	N	16	K
1991			16	K
1992	TB	N	9	K
1992	NYG	N	6	K
3 yrs.	47 games			

Larry Willis
WILLIS, LARRY LEE
B. Jul. 18, 1948, Phoenix, AZ
Texas-El Paso 5'11" 170 lbs.

1973	WAS	N	1	S

Len Willis
WILLIS, LEONARD LEROY
B. Mar. 4, 1953, Washington, DC
Ohio State 5'11" 183 lbs.

1976	MIN	N	14	WR
1977	NO	N	7	WR
1977	BUF	N	4	WR
1978			4	WR
1979			7	WR
4 yrs.	36 games			

Mitch Willis
WILLIS, OTIS MITCHELL
B. Mar. 16, 1962, Dallas, TX
Southern Methodist 6'8" 278 lbs.

1985	LARI	N	11	NT
1986			16	DT
1987			10	DT
1988			2	DT
1988	ATL	N	9	NT
4 yrs.	48 games			

Peter Tom Willis
WILLIS, PETER TOM
B. Jan. 4, 1967, Morris, AL
Florida State 6'2" 188 lbs.

1990	CHI	N	3	QB
1991			4	QB
1992			9	QB
1993			5	QB
4 yrs.	21 games			

Ladell Wills
WILLS, LADELL
B. May 30, 1962, Flint, MI
Jackson State 6'3" 240 lbs.

1987	NYJ	N	3	LB

Joe Willson
WILLSON, JOSEPH P.
B. 1902
Deceased
Pennsylvania 5'11" 185 lbs.

1926	BUF	N	6	G

Osborn Willson
WILLSON, OSBORN PUTNAM
(Diddie)
B. Jan. 17, 1911, Crosby, PA
D. Jan., 1961
Pennsylvania 5'10" 196 lbs.

1933	PHI	N	5	G, E
1934			11	G
1935			10	G
3 yrs.	26 games			

Ray Wilmer
WILMER, BONNIE RAY
B. Jun. 27, 1962, Pineville, LA
Louisiana Tech 6'2" 190 lbs.

1984	SEA	N	3	S

Trevor Wilmot
WILMOT, TREVOR
B. Oct. 30, 1972, Evanston, IL
Indiana 6'2" 220 lbs.

1995	IND	N	7	LB

Klaus Wilmsmeyer
WILMSMEYER, KLAUS
B. Dec. 4, 1967, Mississauga, Ont.
Louisville 6'1" 210 lbs.

1992	SF	N	15	P
1993			15	P
1994			16	P
1995	NO	N	16	P
1996			16	P
5 yrs.	78 games			

Jeff Wilner
WILNER, JEFFREY SCOTT
B. Dec. 31, 1971, East Meadow, NY
Wesleyan (Connecticut) 6'4" 253 lbs.

1994	GB	N	11	TE
1995			2	TE
2 yrs.	13 games			

Frank Wilsbach
WILSBACH, FRANK W.
B. 1904
D. Dec. 16, 1959
Bucknell 6'2" 215 lbs.

1925	FRA	N	4	G, FB

Wilson
WILSON
None

1926	HAR	N	1	HB

Abe Wilson
WILSON, ABE
B. Oct. 6, 1899
D. May, 1981, Everett, MA
Washington 5'10" 192 lbs.

1926	LA	A	12	G
1928	PRO	N	9	G
1929			10	G, C, T
3 yrs.	31 games			

Ben Wilson
WILSON, BENJAMIN IVERY
B. Mar. 9, 1939, Houston, TX
Southern California 6'0" 225 lbs.

1963	LA	N	13	FB
1964			14	HB
1965			14	HB
1967	GB	N	14	RB
4 yrs.	55 games			

Bernard Wilson
WILSON, BERNARD
B. Aug. 15, 1955, Daytona Beach, FL
Vanderbilt 6'0" 180 lbs.

1979	PHI	N	14	S
1980			16	S
1981			15	S
1982			8	S
1983			16	S
1984			16	S
1985			16	S, CB
1986			16	S, CB
1987			1	CB
1987	ATL	N	8	S
9 yrs.	126 games			

Bernard Wilson
WILSON, BERNARD
B. Aug. 17, 1970, Nashville, TN
Tennessee State 6'2" 295 lbs.

1993	TB	N	13	NT
1994			1	DT
1994	ARI	N	13	DT
1995			16	DT
1996			16	DT
4 yrs.	59 games			

Billy Wilson
WILSON, WILLIAM GENE
B. Feb. 3, 1927, Sayre, OK
San Jose State 6'3" 191 lbs.

1951	SF	N	9	E
1952			9	E
1953			12	E
1954			12	E
1955			12	E
1956			12	E
1957			11	E
1958			9	E
1959			10	E
1960			4	E
10 yrs.	100 games			

Billy Wilson
WILSON, WILLIAM STANTON
B. May 8, 1912, Union, OR
D. Dec., 1972, Renton, WA
Gonzaga 5'10" 184 lbs.

1935	CHIC	N	11	E
1936			12	E
1937			11	E, B
1938	PIT	N	3	E
4 yrs.	37 games			

Bobby Wilson
WILSON, BOBBY
B. Mar. 4, 1968, Chicago, IL
Michigan State 6'2" 289 lbs.

1991	WAS	N	16	DT

Bobby Wilson *continued*

Year	Team	Games	Pos.
1992			5	DT
1993			12	DT
1994			9	DT
4 yrs.	42 games			

Bobby Wilson
WILSON, ROBERT EDWARD, JR.
B. Aug. 16, 1913, Corsicana, TX
Southern Methodist 5'9" 147 lbs.

1936	BKN	N	12	HB

Brett Wilson
WILSON, BRETT
B. Dec. 29, 1960, La Grange, IL
Illinois 6'0" 220 lbs.

1987	MIN	N	3	RB

Butch Wilson
WILSON, GEORGE MARVIN
B. Sep. 18, 1941, Birmingham, AL
Alabama 6'2" 223 lbs.

1963	BAL	N	2	OE
1964			11	OE
1965			14	OE
1966			14	TE
1967			13	TE
1968	NYG	N	14	TE
1969			14	TE
7 yrs.	82 games			

Camp Wilson
WILSON, WARREN CAMP
B. Mar. 29, 1922, Pecos, TX
Hardin-Simmons/Tulsa 6'2" 201 lbs.

1946	DET	N	10	FB
1947			12	FB
1948			11	FB
1949			12	FB
4 yrs.	45 games			

Charles Wilson
WILSON, CHARLES JOSEPH
B. Jul. 1, 1968, Tallahassee, FL
Memphis State 5'9" 174 lbs.

1990	GB	N	15	WR
1991			15	WR
1992	TB	N	2	WR
1993			15	WR
1994			14	WR
1995	NYJ	N	15	WR
6 yrs.	76 games			

Darrell Wilson
WILSON, DARRELL
B. Jul. 28, 1958, Camden, NJ
Connecticut 5'11" 180 lbs.

1981	NE	N	1	CB

Darryal Wilson
WILSON, DARRYAL E.
B. Sep. 19, 1960, Florence, AL
Tennessee 6'0" 182 lbs.

1983	NE	N	9	WR

Dave Wilson
WILSON, DAVID CARLTON
B. Apr. 27, 1959, Anaheim, CA
Illinois 6'3" 206 lbs.

1981	NO	N	11	QB
1983			8	QB
1984			5	QB
1985			10	QB
1986			14	QB
1987			4	QB
1988			1	QB
7 yrs.	53 games			

Year	Team		Games	Pos.

David Wilson
WILSON, DAVID ALAN
B. Jun. 10, 1970, Los Angeles, CA
California 5'10" 192 lbs.

Year	Team		Games	Pos.
1992	**NE**	**N**	1	S
1992	**MIN**	**N**	3	S
1 yr.	4 games			

Don Wilson
WILSON, DONALD ALLEN
B. Jul. 21, 1961, Washington, DC
North Carolina State 6'2" 190 lbs.

Year	Team		Games	Pos.
1984	**BUF**	**N**	16	S
1985			16	S
2 yrs.	32 games			

Drip Wilson
WILSON, DRIP
B. 1903
Deceased
None

Year	Team		Games	Pos.
1931	**CLE**	**N**	1	C

Earl Wilson
WILSON, EARL
B. Sep. 13, 1958, Long Branch, NJ
Kentucky 6'4" 280 lbs.

Year	Team		Games	Pos.
1985	**SD**	**N**	16	DE
1986			16	DE
1987			1	DE
3 yrs.	33 games			

Eddie Wilson
WILSON, EDWARD A.
B. Aug. 14, 1940, Redding, CA
Arizona 6'0" 190 lbs.

Year	Team		Games	Pos.
1962	**DAL**	**A**	14	QB
1963	**KC**	**A**	14	QB
1965	**BOS**	**A**	14	QB
3 yrs.	42 games			

Eric Wilson
WILSON, ERIC
B. Oct. 17, 1963, Charlottesville, VA
Maryland 6'1" 247 lbs.

Year	Team		Games	Pos.
1985	**BUF**	**N**	14	LB
1987	**WAS**	**N**	3	LB
2 yrs.	17 games			

Frank Wilson
WILSON, FRANK H.
B. Oct. 11, 1958, Austin, TX
Rice 6'2" 233 lbs.

Year	Team		Games	Pos.
1982	**PIT**	**N**	1	TE, RB

Gene Wilson
WILSON, OLLIE EUGENE
B. Jun. 24, 1926, Arp, TX
Southern Methodist 5'10" 178 lbs.

Year	Team		Games	Pos.
1947	**GB**	**N**	9	E
1948			12	E
2 yrs.	21 games			

George Wilson
WILSON, GEORGE, JR.
B. 1945
Xavier (Ohio) 6'1" 190 lbs.

Year	Team		Games	Pos.
1966	**MIA**	**A**	14	QB

George Wilson
WILSON, GEORGE SCHLY
(Wildcat)
B. 1901, Everett, MA
D. Dec. 27, 1963, San Francisco, CA
Washington 5'11" 200 lbs.

Year	Team		Games	Pos.
1926	**LA**	**A**	14	HB

George Wilson continued

Year	Team		Games	Pos.
1927	**PRO**	**N**	14	HB, FB
1928			11	HB
1929			11	HB, FB
4 yrs.	50 games			

George Wilson
WILSON, GEORGE WILLIAM
B. Feb. 3, 1914, Chicago, IL
D. Nov. 23, 1978, Detroit, MI
Northwestern 6'1" 199 lbs.

Year	Team		Games	Pos.
1937	**CHIB**	**N**	11	E
1938			10	E
1939			10	E
1940			11	E
1941			10	E
1942			11	E
1943			10	E
1944			10	E
1945			9	E
1946			9	E
10 yrs.	101 games			

Gordon Wilson
WILSON, GORDON
B. Nov. 23, 1915, Fort Towson, OK
Texas Western 6'0" 228 lbs.

Year	Team		Games	Pos.
1941	**CLE**	**N**	1	G
1942	**CHIC**	**N**	10	G
1943			10	G
1944	**BKN**	**N**	7	G, C
1945	**CHIC**	**N**	9	G
5 yrs.	37 games			

Harry Wilson
WILSON, HARRY EDWARD
B. Sep. 28, 1944, Steubenville OH
Nebraska 5'11" 204 lbs.

Year	Team		Games	Pos.
1967	**PHI**	**N**	3	RB
1969			2	RB
1970			1	RB
3 yrs.	6 games			

Jack Wilson
WILSON, JACK WILLIAM
B. 1918
Baylor 6'0" 200 lbs.

Year	Team		Games	Pos.
1946	**LA**	**N**	9	HB
1947			1	HB
2 yrs.	10 games			

J.C. Wilson
WILSON, JAMES C.
B. Mar. 11, 1956, Cleveland, OH
Tampa/Pittsburgh 6'0" 177 lbs.

Year	Team		Games	Pos.
1978	**HOU**	**N**	16	CB, S
1979			16	CB, S
1980			16	CB
1981			16	CB
1982			7	CB
1983			13	CB
6 yrs.	84 games			

Jerrel Wilson
WILSON, JERREL DOUGLAS
B. Oct. 4, 1941, New Orleans, LA
Southern Mississippi 6'4" 222 lbs.

Year	Team		Games	Pos.
1963	**KC**	**A**	14	FB, P
1964			14	HB, P
1965			14	HB, P
1966			14	HB, P
1967			10	RB, P
1968			14	P, RB
1969			14	P
1970	**KC**	**N**	14	P
1971			14	P
1972			14	P
1973			14	P

Jerrel Wilson continued

Year	Team		Games	Pos.
1974			14	P
1975			11	P
1976			14	P
1977			14	P
1978	**NE**	**N**	14	P
16 yrs.	217 games			

Jerry Wilson
WILSON, JERRY
B. Jul. 17, 1973, Lake Charles, LA
Southern University 5'10" 184 lbs.

Year	Team		Games	Pos.
1996	**MIA**	**N**	2	CB

Jerry Wilson
WILSON, JERRY ROSCOE
B. Dec. 9, 1936
Auburn 6'3" 238 lbs.

Year	Team		Games	Pos.
1959	**PHI**	**N**	12	E
1960			4	E
1960	**SF**	**N**	6	LB
2 yrs.	22 games			

Jim Wilson
WILSON, JAMES MILLIGAN
B. Aug. 14, 1941, Pittsburgh, PA
Georgia 6'3" 257 lbs.

Year	Team		Games	Pos.
1965	**SF**	**N**	11	G, OT
1966			14	G
1967	**ATL**	**N**	7	G
1968	**LA**	**N**	14	G
4 yrs.	46 games			

Joe Wilson
WILSON, JOSEPH
B. Aug. 11, 1950, Raeford, NC
Holy Cross 5'10" 210 lbs.

Year	Team		Games	Pos.
1973	**CIN**	**N**	13	RB
1974	**NE**	**N**	14	RB
2 yrs.	27 games			

Johnny Wilson
WILSON, JOHN S.
B. Nov. 2, 1915, Dover, OH
Case Western Reserve 6'3" 203 lbs.

Year	Team		Games	Pos.
1939	**CLE**	**N**	11	E
1940			10	E
1941			11	E
1942			4	E
4 yrs.	36 games			

Karl Wilson
WILSON, KARL WENDELL
B. Sep. 10, 1964, Amite, LA
Louisiana State 6'4" 273 lbs.

Year	Team		Games	Pos.
1987	**SD**	**N**	7	DE
1988			13	DE
1989	**PHX**	**N**	16	DE
1990	**MIA**	**N**	16	DE
1991	**LARM**	**N**	13	DE
1992	**NYJ**	**N**	2	DL
1993			5	DT, DE
1993	**MIA**	**N**	2	DT
1993	**SF**	**N**	5	DE
1994	**TB**	**N**	14	DE
1995	**BUF**	**N**	9	DE
9 yrs.	102 games			

Larry Wilson
WILSON, LAWRENCE FRANK
B. Mar. 24, 1938, Rigby, ID
Utah 6'0" 190 lbs.

Year	Team		Games	Pos.
1960	**STL**	**N**	11	DB
1961			11	DB
1962			14	DB
1963			14	DB
1964			14	DB

Larry Wilson continued

Year	Team		Games	Pos.
1965			10	DB
1966			14	DB
1967			14	DB
1968			14	DB
1969			14	S
1970			13	S
1971			14	S
1972			12	S
13 yrs.	169 games			

Lee Wilson
WILSON, LELAND
B. Jul. 24, 1905
D. Oct., 1970, Clarion, IA
Cornell (Iowa) 5'11" 184 lbs.

Year	Team		Games	Pos.
1929	**MIN**	**N**	9	E, HB
1930			8	E
1931	**FRA**	**N**	5	E
3 yrs.	22 games			

Marc Wilson
WILSON, MARC DOUGLAS
B. Feb. 15, 1957, Bremerton, WA
Brigham Young 6'6" 207 lbs.

Year	Team		Games	Pos.
1980	**OAK**	**N**	2	QB
1981			13	QB
1982	**LARI**	**N**	8	QB
1983			10	QB
1984			16	QB
1985			16	QB
1986			16	QB
1987			15	QB
1989	**NE**	**N**	14	QB
1990			16	QB
10 yrs.	126 games			

Marcus Wilson
WILSON, EDMOND MARCUS
B. Apr. 16, 1968, Rochester, NY
Virginia 6'1" 200 lbs.

Year	Team		Games	Pos.
1991	**LARI**	**N**	1	RB
1992	**GB**	**N**	6	RB
1993			16	RB
1994			12	RB
1995			14	RB
5 yrs.	49 games			

Mike Wilson
WILSON, GEORGE BOWNAN, JR.
B. Jul. 18, 1905, Glenside, PA
D. May 3, 1990, Bryn Mawr, PA
Lafayette 5'10" 175 lbs.

Year	Team		Games	Pos.
1929	**FRA**	**N**	19	HB, FB, QB, T

Mike Wilson
WILSON, MICHAEL DEFOREST
B. Oct. 20, 1947, Wilmington, OH
Dayton 6'1" 243 lbs.

Year	Team		Games	Pos.
1969	**CIN**	**A**	3	G
1970	**CIN**	**N**	14	G
1971	**BUF**	**N**	5	G
1975	**KC**	**N**	4	G
4 yrs.	26 games			

Mike Wilson
WILSON, MICHAEL RUBEN
B. Dec. 19, 1958, Los Angeles, CA
Washington State 6'3" 213 lbs.

Year	Team		Games	Pos.
1981	**SF**	**N**	16	WR
1982			6	WR
1983			15	WR
1984			13	WR
1985			16	WR
1986			11	WR
1987			11	WR
1988			16	WR
1989			16	WR

Year	Team		Games	Pos.

Mike Wilson *continued*

Year	Team		Games	Pos.
1990			16	WR

10 yrs.   136 games

Mike Wilson
WILSON, MICHAEL S.
B. Nov. 19, 1946, Washington, DC
Western Illinois 5'11" 185 lbs.

1969	STL	N	3	CB

Mike Wilson
WILSON, SAMUEL MARSHALL
B. Dec. 2, 1896, Edge Hill, PA
D. May 16, 1978, Boynton Beach, FL
Lehigh 5'10" 166 lbs.

1922	BUF	N	4	E
1922	ROC	N	1	E
1923	RI		6	E
1924			8	E
1926	RI	A	8	E, C

4 yrs.   27 games

Mike Wilson
WILSON, WILLIAM MIKE
B. May 28, 1955, Norfolk, VA
Georgia 6'5" 275 lbs.

1978	CIN	N	9	OT
1979			16	OT
1980			16	OT
1981			16	OT
1982			9	OT
1983			16	OT
1984			16	OT
1985			16	OT
1986	SEA	N	16	OT
1987			12	OT
1988			16	OT
1989			16	OT

12 yrs.   174 games

Milt Wilson
WILSON, MILT
None 215 lbs.

1923	AKR	N	5	T, G
1924			1	G

2 yrs.   6 games

Milt Wilson
WILSON, MILTON R.
Wisconsin-Oshkosh 5'10" 200 lbs.

1921	GB	A	6	G

Mule Wilson
WILSON, FAYE
B. 1902
Deceased
Texas A&M 5'11" 192 lbs.

1926	BUF	N	9	HB, QB
1927	NYG	N	13	HB, FB, QB
1928			13	HB
1929			7	HB
1930			10	HB
1930	SI	N	2	HB
1931	GB	N	12	HB
1932	POR	N	10	HB, FB
1933			5	HB, FB

8 yrs.   81 games

Nemiah Wilson
WILSON, NEMIAH
B. Apr. 6, 1943, Baton Rouge, LA
Grambling State 6'0" 186 lbs.

1965	DEN	A	9	DB
1966			14	DB
1967			14	DB
1968	OAK	A	1	DB
1969			14	CB

Nemiah Wilson *continued*

1970	OAK	N	14	CB
1971			13	DB
1972			14	CB
1973			13	DB
1974			12	DB
1975	CHI	N	7	CB

11 yrs.   125 games

Otis Wilson
WILSON, OTIS RAY
B. Sep. 15, 1957, New York, NY
Syracuse/Louisville 6'2" 227 lbs.

1980	CHI	N	16	LB
1981			15	LB
1982			9	LB
1983			16	LB
1984			15	LB
1985			16	LB
1986			15	LB
1987			7	LB
1989	LARI	N	1	LB

9 yrs.   110 games

Percy Wilson
WILSON, PERCY
B. 1890
D. Sep. 20, 1936
None 150 lbs.

1920	DET	A	4	QB

Ray Wilson
WILSON, RAY
B. Aug. 26, 1971, Panama City, FL
New Mexico 6'2" 202 lbs.

1994	NO	N	3	S
1994	GB	N	3	S

1 yr.   6 games

Robert Wilson
WILSON, ROBERT EUGENE
B. Jan. 13, 1969, Houston, TX
Texas A&M 6'0" 240 lbs.

1991	TB	N	16	RB
1994	DAL	N	2	RB
1994	MIA	N	2	RB
1995			16	RB
1996			15	RB

4 yrs.   51 games

Sheddrick Wilson
WILSON, SHEDDRICK
B. Nov. 23, 1973, Thomasville, GA
Louisiana State 6'2" 210 lbs.

1996	HOU	N	11	WR

Stanley Wilson
WILSON, STANLEY T.
B. Aug. 23, 1961, Los Angeles, CA
Oklahoma 5'10" 210 lbs.

1983	CIN	N	10	RB
1984			1	RB
1986			10	RB
1988			15	RB

4 yrs.   36 games

Steve Wilson
WILSON, STEVE ALAN
B. May 19, 1954, Fort Sill, OK
Georgia 6'4" 266 lbs.

1976	TB	N	12	OT
1977			14	OT
1978			16	G
1979			16	C
1980			15	C
1981			15	C
1982			8	C

Steve Wilson *continued*

1983			10	C
1984			16	C
1985			5	C

10 yrs.   127 games

Steve Wilson
WILSON, STEVEN ANTHONY
B. Aug. 24, 1957, Los Angeles, CA
Howard 5'10" 195 lbs.

1979	DAL	N	16	WR
1980			16	CB
1981			16	CB
1982	DEN	N	8	CB
1983			16	CB
1984			15	CB
1985			14	CB
1986			16	CB
1987			11	CB
1988			12	CB

10 yrs.   140 games

Stu Wilson
WILSON, STUART
B. Mar. 31, 1905
D. Dec., 1963, Pennsylvania
Washington & Jefferson 6'2" 209 lbs.

1932	SI	N	10	HB, E, FB

Ted Wilson
WILSON, TED
B. Jul. 14, 1964, Zephyr Hills, FL
Central Florida 5'9" 170 lbs.

1987	WAS	N	3	WR

Tim Wilson
WILSON, TIM
B. Jan. 14, 1954, New Castle, DE
Deceased
Maryland 6'3" 220 lbs.

1977	HOU	N	10	RB
1978			16	RB
1979			16	RB
1980			16	RB
1981			16	RB
1982			9	RB
1983	NO	N	6	RB
1984			12	FB

8 yrs.   101 games

Tommy Wilson
WILSON, THOMAS LEE
(Touchdown Tommy)
B. Sep. 1, 1932, Stamford, CT
none 6'0" 203 lbs.

1956	LA	N	12	HB
1957			11	HB
1958			12	HB
1959			12	HB
1960			11	HB
1961			11	HB, FB
1962	CLE	N	14	HB
1963	MIN	N	8	HB

8 yrs.   91 games

Troy Wilson
WILSON, TROY
B. Sep. 19, 1965, Lubbock, TX
Notre Dame 5'10" 170 lbs.

1987	CLE	N	3	CB

Troy Wilson
WILSON, TROY
B. Nov. 22, 1970, Topeka, KS
Pittsburg State 6'4" 235 lbs.

1993	SF	N	10	DE
1994			11	DE

Troy Wilson *continued*

1995	DEN	N	3	DE

3 yrs.   24 games

Wade Wilson
WILSON, CHARLES WADE
B. Feb. 1, 1959, Greenville, TX
East Texas State 6'3" 211 lbs.

1981	MIN	N	3	QB
1983			1	QB
1984			8	QB
1985			4	QB
1986			9	QB
1987			12	QB
1988			14	QB
1989			14	QB
1990			6	QB
1991			5	QB
1992	ATL	N	9	QB
1993	NO	N	14	QB
1994			4	QB
1995	DAL	N	7	QB
1996			3	QB

15 yrs.   113 games

Walter Wilson
WILSON, WALTER JAMES
B. Oct. 6, 1966, Baltimore, MD
East Carolina 5'10" 185 lbs.

1990	SD	N	14	WR

Wayne Wilson
WILSON, WAYNE MACARTHUR
B. Sep. 4, 1957, Montgomery County, MD
Shepherd 6'3" 218 lbs.

1979	NO	N	14	FB
1980			15	FB
1981			16	FB
1982			8	RB
1983			14	RB
1984			14	RB
1985			16	FB
1986	MIN	N	7	FB
1986	NO	N	5	FB
1987	WAS	N	2	RB

9 yrs.   111 games

Ab Wimberly
WIMBERLY, ABNER PERRY
B. May 4, 1926, Oak Ridge, LA
D. Sep. 19, 1976, Oak Ridge, LA
Louisiana State 6'1" 213 lbs.

1949	LA	AA	12	E
1950	GB	N	11	E
1951			12	E
1952			12	E

4 yrs.   47 games

By Wimberly
WIMBERLY, BYRON A.
B. Sep. 3, 1892
D. May 11, 1956
Washington & Jefferson 6'2" 200 lbs.

1925	DET	N	11	T, G

Derek Wimberly
WIMBERLY, DEREK NATHANIEL
B. Jan. 4, 1964, Miami, FL
Purdue 6'4" 270 lbs.

1987	MIA	N	3	DE

Gary Wimmer
WIMMER, GARY E.
B. Mar. 9, 1961, Pocatello, ID
Stanford 6'2" 225 lbs.

1983	SEA	N	3	LB

Year	Team		Games	Pos.

Jeff Winans
WINANS, JEFF DOW
B. Oct. 12, 1951, Turlock, CA
Southern California 6'5" 263 lbs.

Year	Team		Games	Pos.
1973	BUF	N	9	DT
1975			11	DE
1976	NO	N	3	DT
1977	TB	N	11	G
1978			1	OT, G
5 yrs.	35 games			

Tydus Winans
WINANS, TYDUS ORAN
B. Jul. 26, 1972, Los Angeles, CA
Fresno State 5'11" 180 lbs.

Year	Team		Games	Pos.
1994	WAS	N	15	WR
1995			8	WR
1996	CIN	N	2	WR
3 yrs.	25 games			

Ernie Winburn
WINBURN, ERNEST
B. Apr., 1897, Missouri
Deceased
Central Missouri State 5'11" 175 lbs.

Year	Team		Games	Pos.
1923	STL	N	1	E

Bill Windauer
WINDAUER, WILLIAM JOSEPH
B. Nov. 22, 1949, Chicago, IL
Iowa 6'3" 248 lbs.

Year	Team		Games	Pos.
1973	BAL	N	2	DT
1974			9	DT
1975	MIA	N	1	DT
1975	NYG	N	4	DT
1976	ATL	N	3	DT
4 yrs.	19 games			

Joe Windbiel
WINDBIEL, JOSEPH C.
B. Mar. 6, 1897
D. Jun. 25, 1971, Fort Lauderdale, FL
Dayton 6'1" 220 lbs.

Year	Team		Games	Pos.
1921	EVA	A	5	C
1922	EVA	N	1	HB
2 yrs.	6 games			

Sammy Winder
WINDER, SAMMY
B. Jul. 15, 1959, Madison, MS
Southern Mississippi 5'11" 203 lbs.

Year	Team		Games	Pos.
1982	DEN	N	8	RB
1983			14	RB
1984			16	RB
1985			14	RB
1986			16	RB
1987			12	RB
1988			16	RB
1989			16	RB
1990			15	RB
9 yrs.	127 games			

David Windham
WINDHAM, DAVID ROGERS
B. Mar. 14, 1961, Mobile, AL
Jackson State 6'2" 240 lbs.

Year	Team		Games	Pos.
1987	WAS	N	3	LB

Bob Windsor
WINDSOR, ROBERT EDWARD
B. Dec. 19, 1942, Washington, DC
Kentucky 6'4" 227 lbs.

Year	Team		Games	Pos.
1967	SF	N	14	TE
1968			14	TE
1969			14	TE
1970			14	TE

Bob Windsor continued

Year	Team		Games	Pos.
1971			13	TE
1972	NE	N	14	TE
1973			13	TE
1974			7	TE
1975			14	TE
9 yrs.	117 games			

Vern Winfield
WINFIELD, VERNON HALL
B. Aug. 27, 1949, Norfolk, VA
Minnesota 6'2" 248 lbs.

Year	Team		Games	Pos.
1972	PHI	N	9	G
1973			5	G
2 yrs.	14 games			

Carl Winfrey
WINFREY, CARL
B. Mar. 27, 1949, Chicago, IL
Wisconsin 6'0" 230 lbs.

Year	Team		Games	Pos.
1971	MIN	N	14	LB
1972	PIT	N	1	LB
2 yrs.	15 games			

Stan Winfrey
WINFREY, STANLEY (Mule)
B. Feb. 20, 1953, Forrest City, AR
Arkansas State 5'11" 223 lbs.

Year	Team		Games	Pos.
1975	MIA	N	11	RB
1976			14	RB
1977			3	RB
1977	TB	N	2	RB
3 yrs.	30 games			

Elmer Wingate
WINGATE, ELMER
B. 1929
Maryland 6'3" 230 lbs.

Year	Team		Games	Pos.
1953	BAL	N	12	E

Heath Wingate
WINGATE, HEATH
B. Dec. 5, 1944, Toledo, OH
Bowling Green 6'2" 240 lbs.

Year	Team		Games	Pos.
1967	WAS	N	8	C

Leonard Wingate
WINGATE, LEONARD
B. Nov. 3, 1961, Charleston, SC
South Carolina State 6'3" 265 lbs.

Year	Team		Games	Pos.
1987	ATL	N	1	DE

Blake Wingle
WINGLE, BLAKE LEO
B. Apr. 17, 1960, Pottsville, CA
California Poly (San Luis Obispo) 6'2" 267 lbs.

Year	Team		Games	Pos.
1983	PIT	N	16	G
1984			15	G
1985			3	G
1985	GB	N	2	G
1987	CLE	N	3	G
4 yrs.	39 games			

Rich Wingo
WINGO, RICHARD ALLEN
B. Jul. 16, 1956, Elkhart, IN
Alabama 6'1" 230 lbs.

Year	Team		Games	Pos.
1979	GB	N	16	LB
1981			16	LB
1982			5	LB
1983			16	LB
1984			16	LB
5 yrs.	69 games			

Dean Wink
WINK, DEAN ALBERT
B. Sep. 25, 1944, Moville, IA
Yankton 6'4" 246 lbs.

Year	Team		Games	Pos.
1967	PHI	N	5	DE
1968			7	DE
2 yrs.	12 games			

Bob Winkel
WINKEL, ROBERT A.
B. Oct. 23, 1955, Paducah, KY
Kentucky 6'4" 251 lbs.

Year	Team		Games	Pos.
1979	NYJ		15	DL
1980			16	DT, DE
2 yrs.	31 games			

Ben Winkleman
WINKLEMAN, BENJAMIN
B. Feb. 28, 1899
Deceased
Arkansas 180 lbs.

Year	Team		Games	Pos.
1922	MIL	N	1	E
1923			13	E, HB, FB
1924			13	HB, FB, E
3 yrs.	27 games			

Bernie Winkler
WINKLER, BERNARD A.
B. Dec. 5, 1925, The Grove, TX
Texas Tech/Millsaps/Texas Tech 6'1" 232 lbs.

Year	Team		Games	Pos.
1948	LA	AA	4	T

Francis Winkler
WINKLER, FRANCIS
B. Oct. 20, 1946, Memphis, TN
Memphis State 6'3" 230 lbs.

Year	Team		Games	Pos.
1968	GB	N	7	DE
1969			14	DE
2 yrs.	21 games			

Jim Winkler
WINKLER, JAMES C.
B. 1929
Deceased
Texas A&M 6'2" 250 lbs.

Year	Team		Games	Pos.
1952	LA	N	12	T
1953	BAL	N	9	G
2 yrs.	21 games			

Joe Winkler
WINKLER, J.C.
B. 1922
Purdue 6'1" 200 lbs.

Year	Team		Games	Pos.
1945	CLE	N	8	C

Randy Winkler
WINKLER, RANDOLPH STANLEY
B. Jul. 18, 1943, Temple, TX
Tarleton State 6'5" 258 lbs.

Year	Team		Games	Pos.
1967	DET	N	8	OT
1968	ATL	N	12	OT, G
1971	GB	N	5	G
3 yrs.	25 games			

Bryant Winn
WINN, BRYANT
B. Nov. 7, 1961, Memphis, TN
Houston 6'4" 231 lbs.

Year	Team		Games	Pos.
1987	DEN	N	3	LB

Bill Winneshick
WINNESHICK, WILLIAM
B. 1894

Bill Winneshick continued
Deceased
Carlisle 5'8" 180 lbs.

Year	Team		Games	Pos.
1922	OOR	N	4	C

Jason Winrow
WINROW, JASON
B. Jan. 16, 1971, Bridgeton, NJ
Ohio State 6'4" 321 lbs.

Year	Team		Games	Pos.
1994	NYG	N	1	G

Bob Winslow
WINSLOW, ROBERT E.
B. 1916
Southern California 6'1" 205 lbs.

Year	Team		Games	Pos.
1940	DET	N	8	E
1940	BKN	N	2	E
1 yr.	10 games			

Doug Winslow
WINSLOW, CHARLES DOUGLAS
B. Jul. 19, 1951, Runnells, IA
Drake 5'11" 181 lbs.

Year	Team		Games	Pos.
1973	NO	N	12	WR
1976	WAS	N	5	WR
2 yrs.	17 games			

George Winslow
WINSLOW, GEORGE ARTHUR
B. Jul. 28, 1963, Philadelphia, PA
Wisconsin/Villanova 6'4" 203 lbs.

Year	Team		Games	Pos.
1987	CLE	N	5	P
1989	NO	N	5	P
2 yrs.	10 games			

Kellen Winslow
WINSLOW, KELLEN BOSWELL
B. Nov. 5, 1957, St. Louis, MO
Missouri 6'5" 250 lbs.

Year	Team		Games	Pos.
1979	SD	N	7	TE
1980			16	TE
1981			16	TE
1982			9	TE
1983			16	TE
1984			7	TE
1985			10	TE
1986			16	TE
1987			12	TE
9 yrs.	109 games			

Paul Winslow
WINSLOW, PAUL
B. Feb. 28, 1938, Elizabeth City, NC
North Carolina Central 5'11" 200 lbs.

Year	Team		Games	Pos.
1960	GB	N	12	HB

Charlie Winston
WINSTON, CHARLES S.
B. Jun., 1890
Deceased
Purdue 6'1" 185 lbs.

Year	Team		Games	Pos.
1920	DAY	A	5	G

De Mond Winston
WINSTON, EDWARD DEMOND
B. Sep. 14, 1968, Birmingham, AL
Vanderbilt 6'2" 239 lbs.

Year	Team		Games	Pos.
1990	NO	N	16	LB
1992			15	LB
1993			16	LB
1994			3	LB
4 yrs.	50 games			

Dennis Winston
WINSTON, DENNIS EDWARD

Year	Team		Games	Pos.

Dennis Winston *continued*
(Dirt)
B. Oct. 25, 1955, Forrest City, AR
Arkansas 6'0" 228 lbs.

Year	Team		Games	Pos.
1977	PIT	N	13	LB
1978			16	LB
1979			16	LB
1980			14	LB
1981			14	LB
1982	NO	N	9	LB
1983			16	LB
1984			16	LB
1985			4	LB
1985	PIT	N	10	LB
1986			16	LB

10 yrs.   144 games

Kelton Winston
WINSTON, KELTON EARL
B. Oct. 22, 1940, San Diego, CA
Wiley 6'0" 195 lbs.

Year	Team		Games	Pos.
1967	LA	N	9	DB
1968			11	DB

2 yrs.   20 games

Lloyd Winston
WINSTON, LLOYD LEONARD
B. Sep. 22, 1939
Southern California 6'2" 215 lbs.

Year	Team		Games	Pos.
1962	SF	N	2	FB
1963			4	FB

2 yrs.   6 games

Roy Winston
WINSTON, ROY CHARLES
(Moonie)
B. Sep. 15, 1940, Baton Rouge, LA
Louisiana State 6'1" 228 lbs.

Year	Team		Games	Pos.
1962	MIN	N	13	LB
1963			14	LB
1964			14	LB
1965			14	LB
1966			12	LB
1967			14	LB
1968			14	LB
1969			14	LB
1970			14	LB
1971			14	LB
1972			13	LB
1973			13	LB
1974			11	LB
1975			9	LB
1976			7	LB

15 yrs.   190 games

Bill Winter
WINTER, WILLIAM
B. Jan. 28, 1940, Milbank, SD
St. Olaf 6'4" 220 lbs.

Year	Team		Games	Pos.
1962	NYG	N	11	LB
1963			10	LB
1964			12	LB

3 yrs.   33 games

Blaise Winter
WINTER, BLAISE
B. Jan. 31, 1962, Blauvelt, NY
Syracuse 6'3" 279 lbs.

Year	Team		Games	Pos.
1984	IND	N	16	NT
1986	SD	N	4	DE
1987			3	NT
1988	GB	N	16	DE
1989			16	DE, NT
1990			13	DE, NT
1992	SD	N	16	DT
1993			16	DT
1994			2	DE, DT

9 yrs.   102 games

Year	Team		Games	Pos.

Leon Winterheimer
WINTERHEIMER, LEON
None 6'1" 240 lbs.

Year	Team		Games	Pos.
1921	EVA	A	1	T
1922	EVA	N	2	G

2 yrs.   3 games

Chet Winters
WINTERS, CHESTER
B. Oct. 22, 1960, Chicago, IL
Oklahoma 5'11" 204 lbs.

Year	Team		Games	Pos.
1983	GB	N	4	RB

Frank Winters
WINTERS, FRANK MITCHELL
B. Jan. 23, 1964, Hoboken, NJ
Eastern Utah/Western Illinois 6'3" 290 lbs.

Year	Team		Games	Pos.
1987	CLE	N	12	C
1988			16	C
1989	NYG	N	15	C
1990	KC	N	16	C, G
1991			16	C
1992	GB	N	16	C, G
1993			16	C, G
1994			16	C, G
1995			16	C
1996			16	C

10 yrs.   155 games

Jay Winters
WINTERS, JULIAN JOHN
B. Sep. 10, 1903
D. Apr., 1985, Bucyrus, OH
Ohio Wesleyan 5'7" 145 lbs.

Year	Team		Games	Pos.
1926	CLE	A	3	QB

Sonny Winters
WINTERS, LINDELL
B. 1900
Deceased
Ohio Wesleyan 5'9" 155 lbs.

Year	Team		Games	Pos.
1923	COL	N	10	QB, HB
1924			8	QB

2 yrs.   18 games

Wimpy Winther
WINTHER, RICHARD LEW
B. Oct. 22, 1947, Charles City, IA
Mississippi 6'3" 260 lbs.

Year	Team		Games	Pos.
1971	GB	N	11	C
1972	NO	N	5	C

2 yrs.   16 games

Don Wiper
WIPER, DONALD WILLIAM
B. Jul. 8, 1900, Columbus, OH
D. Nov., 1961
Ohio State 5'10" 150 lbs.

Year	Team		Games	Pos.
1922	COL	N	2	QB

Denny Wirgowski
WIRGOWSKI, DENNIS
B. Sep. 20, 1947, Bay City, MI
Purdue 6'5" 253 lbs.

Year	Team		Games	Pos.
1970	BOS	N	14	DE
1971	NE	N	9	DE
1972			14	DE
1973	PHI	N	13	DE

4 yrs.   50 games

Terrence Wisdom
WISDOM, TERRENCE
B. Dec. 4, 1971, Brooklyn, NY
Syracuse 6'4" 300 lbs.

Year	Team		Games	Pos.
1995	NYJ	N	5	G

Year	Team		Games	Pos.

Wise
WISE
None

Year	Team		Games	Pos.
1921	TON	A	1	QB

Mike Wise
WISE, MIKE
B. Jun. 5, 1964, Greenbrae, CA
D. Aug., 1992, CA
California-Davis 6'7" 271 lbs.

Year	Team		Games	Pos.
1986	LARI	N	6	DE
1988			16	DE
1989			16	DE
1990			13	DE
1991	CLE	N	3	DE

5 yrs.   54 games

Phil Wise
WISE, PHILLIP VAUGHN
B. Apr. 25, 1949, Omaha, NE
Nebraska-Omaha 6'0" 192 lbs.

Year	Team		Games	Pos.
1971	NYJ	N	14	DB
1972			9	S
1973			8	S
1974			14	S
1975			5	S
1976			12	S
1977	MIN	N	13	S
1978			16	S
1979			1	S

9 yrs.   92 games

Gary Wisener
WISENER, GARY
B. 1938, Fort Smith, AR
Baylor 6'1" 206 lbs.

Year	Team		Games	Pos.
1960	DAL	N	10	OE, DB
1961	HOU	A	5	DB

2 yrs.   15 games

Jeff Wiska
WISKA, JEFFREY ROLLAND
B. Oct. 17, 1959, Detroit, MI
Michigan State 6'3" 260 lbs.

Year	Team		Games	Pos.
1986	CLE	N	1	G
1987	MIA	N	3	G

2 yrs.   4 games

Pete Wismann
WISMANN, PETER
B. Oct. 9, 1923
Miami (Ohio)/Washington (Missouri)/St. Louis 6'0" 218 lbs.

Year	Team		Games	Pos.
1949	SF	AA	12	C
1950	SF	N	12	C
1951			9	C
1952			12	C

4 yrs.   45 games

Leo Wisniewski
WISNIEWSKI, LEO JOSEPH
B. Nov. 6, 1959, Hancock, MI
Penn State 6'2" 263 lbs.

Year	Team		Games	Pos.
1982	BAL	N	7	DT
1983			15	NT
1984	IND	N	14	NT

3 yrs.   36 games

Steve Wisniewski
WISNIEWSKI, STEPHEN ADAM
B. Apr. 7, 1967, Rutland, VT
Penn State 6'4" 285 lbs.

Year	Team		Games	Pos.
1989	LARI	N	15	G
1990			15	G
1991			15	G
1992			16	G
1993			16	G

Year	Team		Games	Pos.

Steve Wisniewski *continued*

Year	Team		Games	Pos.
1994			16	G
1995	OAK	N	16	G
1996			16	G

8 yrs.   126 games

Zeke Wissinger
WISSINGER, ZONAR A. (Doc)
B. Oct. 30, 1903
D. Nov., 1963, Pennsylvania
Pittsburgh 6'0" 195 lbs.

Year	Team		Games	Pos.
1926	POT	N	5	T, G

Al Wistert
WISTERT, ALBERT ALEXANDER
B. Dec. 28, 1920, Chicago, IL
Michigan 6'1" 214 lbs.

Year	Team		Games	Pos.
1943	P-P	N	10	T
1944	PHI	N	8	T
1945			10	T
1946			9	T
1947			12	T
1948			12	T
1949			12	T
1950			11	T
1951			12	T

9 yrs.   96 games

Al Witcher
WITCHER, ALBERT T.
B. 1937
Baylor 6'1" 200 lbs.

Year	Team		Games	Pos.
1960	HOU	A		OE

Dick Witcher
WITCHER, DICK VERNON
B. Oct. 10, 1944, Salinas, CA
UCLA 6'3" 205 lbs.

Year	Team		Games	Pos.
1966	SF	N	14	FL
1967			14	FL
1968			14	FL, TE
1969			14	WR
1970			11	WR
1971			14	WR
1972			14	WR
1973			14	TE

8 yrs.   109 games

Derrick Witherspoon
WITHERSPOON, DERRICK
B. Feb. 14, 1971, Sumter, SC
Clemson 5'10" 197 lbs.

Year	Team		Games	Pos.
1995	PHI	N	15	RB
1996			16	RB

2 yrs.   31 games

Cal Withrow
WITHROW, JAMES CALVIN
B. Jul. 4, 1945, Portsmouth, OH
Kentucky 6'0" 240 lbs.

Year	Team		Games	Pos.
1970	SD	N	4	C
1971	GB	N	14	C
1972			14	C
1973			14	C
1974	STL	N	12	C

5 yrs.   58 games

Mike Withycombe
WITHYCOMBE, MIKE
B. Nov. 18, 1964, Meridian, MS
Fresno State 6'5" 295 lbs.

Year	Team		Games	Pos.
1988	NYJ	N	6	OT
1989			5	G, OT
1991	PIT	N	2	C, G
1991	CIN	N	3	OT
1992			14	OT

4 yrs.   30 games

Year	Team		Games	Pos.

John Witkowski
WITKOWSKI, JOHN JOSEPH
B. Jun. 18, 1962, Flushing, NY
Columbia 6'1" 205 lbs.

Year	Team		Games	Pos.
1984	**DET**	**N**	3	QB
1988			2	QB
2 yrs.	5 games			

Jon Witman
WITMAN, JON DOYLE
B. Jun. 1, 1972, Wrightsville, PA
Penn State 6'1" 242 lbs.

Year	Team		Games	Pos.
1996	**PIT**	**N**	16	RB

Billy Witt
WITT, BILLY
B. Apr. 15, 1964
North Alabama 6'5" 265 lbs.

Year	Team		Games	Pos.
1987	**BUF**	**N**	2	DE

Mel Witt
WITT, MELVIN
B. Nov. 23, 1945, Fort Worth, TX
Texas-Arlington 6'3" 261 lbs.

Year	Team		Games	Pos.
1967	**BOS**	**A**	1	DT
1968			14	DT
1969			6	DE
1970	**BOS**	**N**	14	DE
4 yrs.	35 games			

Earl Witte
WITTE, EARL
B. 1908
Gustavus Adolphus 6'0" 188 lbs.

Year	Team		Games	Pos.
1934	**GB**	**N**	4	QB

Mark Witte
WITTE, MARK STEVEN
B. Dec. 3, 1959, Corpus Christi, TX
North Texas State 6'3" 240 lbs.

Year	Team		Games	Pos.
1983	**TB**	**N**	16	TE
1984			16	TE
1985			16	TE
1987	**DET**	**N**	3	TE
4 yrs.	51 games			

Mike Witteck
WITTECK, MIKE
B. 1964
Northwestern 6'2" 225 lbs.

Year	Team		Games	Pos.
1987	**NYJ**	**N**	3	LB

John Wittenborn
WITTENBORN, JOHN OTIS
B. Mar. 1, 1936, Sparta, IL
Southeast Missouri State 6'2" 238 lbs.

Year	Team		Games	Pos.
1958	**SF**	**N**	12	G
1959			12	G
1960			4	G
1960	**PHI**	**N**	8	G
1961			14	G
1962			14	G
1964	**HOU**	**A**	5	DE
1965			14	G
1966			14	G
1967			14	K
1968			6	K
10 yrs.	117 games			

Ray Witter
WITTER, RAYMOND C.
B. Nov. 23, 1896
D. Feb., 1975, Canandaigua, NY
Syracuse/Alfred 5'10" 183 lbs.

Year	Team		Games	Pos.
1921	**ROC**	**A**	5	E
1922	**ROC**		1	FB

Ray Witter continued

Year	Team		Games	Pos.
1923			3	G, C, FB
3 yrs.	9 games			

Tom Wittum
WITTUM, THOMAS HOWARD
B. Jan. 11, 1950, Berwyn, IL
Northern Illinois 6'1" 191 lbs.

Year	Team		Games	Pos.
1973	**SF**	**N**	14	P
1974			14	P
1975			14	P
1976			14	P
1977			14	P, K
5 yrs.	70 games			

Cas Witucki
WITUCKI, CASMIR LEO (Slug)
B. May 26, 1928, South Bend, IN
Indiana 5'11" 245 lbs.

Year	Team		Games	Pos.
1950	**WAS**	**N**	12	G
1951			12	G
1953			11	G
1954			12	G
1955			2	G
1956			5	G
6 yrs.	54 games			

Alex Wizbicki
WIZBICKI, ALEX JOHN
B. Oct. 6, 1921, Brooklyn, NY
Dartmouth/Holy Cross 5'11" 188 lbs.

Year	Team		Games	Pos.
1947	**BUF**	**AA**	13	B
1948			9	B
1949			12	B
1950	**GB**	**N**	11	HB
4 yrs.	45 games			

Ernie Woerner
WOERNER, ERWIN
B. May 26, 1906
D. Dec. 26, 1972, Atlantic Highlands, NJ
Bucknell 5'8" 200 lbs.

Year	Team		Games	Pos.
1930	**NEW**	**N**	7	T

Scott Woerner
WOERNER, SCOTT ALLISON
B. Dec. 18, 1958, Baytown, TX
Georgia 6'0" 195 lbs.

Year	Team		Games	Pos.
1981	**ATL**	**N**	16	CB, S
1987	**NO**	**N**	1	S
2 yrs.	17 games			

Dave Wohlabaugh
WOHLABAUGH, DAVID VINCENT
B. Apr. 13, 1972, Lackawanna, NY
Syracuse 6'3" 304 lbs.

Year	Team		Games	Pos.
1995	**NE**	**N**	11	C
1996			16	C
2 yrs.	27 games			

Richie Woit
WOIT, RICHARD
B. 1931
Arkansas State 5'8" 175 lbs.

Year	Team		Games	Pos.
1955	**DET**	**N**	1	HB

Johnny Woitt
WOITT, JOHN
B. Jun. 29, 1946, Yakima, WA
Mississippi State 5'11" 172 lbs.

Year	Team		Games	Pos.
1968	**SF**	**N**	14	DB
1969			14	CB
2 yrs.	28 games			

Alex Wojciechowicz
WOJCIECHOWICZ, ALEXANDER FRANCIS (Wojo)
B. Aug. 12, 1915, South River, NJ
D. Jul. 13, 1992, Forked River, NJ
Fordham 5'11" 217 lbs.

Year	Team		Games	Pos.
1938	**DET**	**N**	11	C
1939			11	C
1940			11	C
1941			9	C
1942			11	C
1943			9	C
1944			10	C
1945			10	C
1946			3	C
1946	**PHI**	**N**	7	C
1947			12	C
1948			10	C
1949			12	C
1950			7	C
13 yrs.	133 games			

John Wojciechowski
WOJCIECHOWSKI, JOHN STANLEY
B. Jul. 30, 1963, Detroit, MI
Michigan State 6'4" 271 lbs.

Year	Team		Games	Pos.
1987	**CHI**	**N**	4	G
1988			16	G
1989			13	G
1990			13	G, OT
1991			16	G
1992			16	G
1993			14	G
7 yrs.	92 games			

Greg Wojcik
WOJCIK, GREGORY STEVEN
B. Jan. 27, 1946, Jamestown, ND
Southern California 6'6" 268 lbs.

Year	Team		Games	Pos.
1971	**LA**	**N**	10	DT
1972	**SD**		7	DT
1973			10	DT
1975			6	DT
4 yrs.	33 games			

Al Wolden
WOLDEN, ALLEN
B. Apr. 11, 1965
Bemidji State 6'3" 232 lbs.

Year	Team		Games	Pos.
1987	**CHI**	**N**	3	RB

Dick Wolf
WOLF, RICHARD
B. Aug., 1900
D. Jun. 28, 1967
Miami (Ohio) 5'8" 160 lbs.

Year	Team		Games	Pos.
1923	**CLE**	**N**	5	FB, HB
1924			6	HB, QB, E
1925			14	QB, HB
1926	**CLE**	**A**	5	QB
1927	**CLE**	**N**	1	HB
5 yrs.	31 games			

James Wolf
WOLF, JAMES
B. Apr. 4, 1952, Warren, TX
Prairie View A&M 6'3" 240 lbs.

Year	Team		Games	Pos.
1974	**PIT**	**N**	11	DE
1976	**KC**	**N**	14	DE
2 yrs.	25 games			

Joe Wolf
WOLF, JOSEPH FRANCIS
B. Dec. 28, 1966, Allentown, PA
Boston College 6'5" 288 lbs.

Year	Team		Games	Pos.
1989	**PHX**	**N**	16	G
1990			15	OT, G

Joe Wolf continued

Year	Team		Games	Pos.
1991			8	OT
1992			3	G
1993			8	G
1994	**ARI**	**N**	8	OT, G
1995			7	OT, G
1996			16	G
8 yrs.	81 games			

Hugh Wolfe
WOLFE, HUGH OTHELLO (Red)
B. 1913
Texas 6'0" 205 lbs.

Year	Team		Games	Pos.
1938	**NYG**	**N**	8	FB

Wayne Wolff
WOLFF, WAYNE
B. Jan. 28, 1938, Greensburg, PA
Wake Forest 6'2" 243 lbs.

Year	Team		Games	Pos.
1961	**BUF**	**A**	2	G

Craig Wolfley
WOLFLEY, CRAIG ALAN
B. May 19, 1958, Buffalo, NY
Syracuse 6'1" 269 lbs.

Year	Team		Games	Pos.
1980	**PIT**	**N**	16	G
1981			16	G
1982			9	G
1983			14	G
1984			9	G
1985			13	G
1986			9	G
1987			12	G
1988			16	G
1989			15	G, OT
1990	**MIN**	**N**	8	G, OT
1991			16	G
12 yrs.	153 games			

Ron Wolfley
WOLFLEY, RONALD PAUL
B. Oct. 14, 1962, Blasdell, NY
West Virginia 6'0" 224 lbs.

Year	Team		Games	Pos.
1985	**STL**	**N**	16	RB
1986			16	RB
1987			12	FB
1988	**PHX**	**N**	16	RB
1989			16	RB
1990			13	RB
1991			16	RB
1992	**CLE**	**N**	15	RB
1993			16	RB
1995	**STL**	**N**	9	RB
10 yrs.	145 games			

Oscar Wolford
WOLFORD, OSCAR
B. Mar. 14, 1897, West Virginia
D. Feb., 1977, Sugar Creek, WV
None 6'0" 188 lbs.

Year	Team		Games	Pos.
1920	**COL**	**A**	4	C
1921			8	C
1922	**COL**		8	C, G, E
1924			4	G, FB, E, T
4 yrs.	24 games			

Will Wolford
WOLFORD, WILLIAM CHARLES
B. May 18, 1964, Louisville, KY
Vanderbilt 6'5" 289 lbs.

Year	Team		Games	Pos.
1986	**BUF**	**N**	16	OT
1987			12	OT
1988			16	OT
1989			16	OT
1990			14	OT
1991			15	OT
1992			16	OT
1993	**IND**	**N**	12	OT

Year	Team	Games	Pos.

Will Wolford *continued*

1994			16	OT
1995			16	OT
1996	PIT	N	16	OT

11 yrs. 165 games

Bill Wolski
WOLSKI, WILLIAM
B. May 23, 1944, Muskegon, MI
Notre Dame 5'11" 203 lbs.

1966	ATL	N	2	RB

Clem Woltman
WOLTMAN, CLEMENT J.
B. 1916
D. Jan. 16, 1988
Purdue 6'1" 214 lbs.

1938	PHI	N	10	T
1939			11	T
1940			10	T, G

3 yrs. 31 games

Bruce Womack
WOMACK, BRUCE LARIMORE
B. May 12, 1929, Floydada, TX
West Texas State 6'3" 210 lbs.

1951	DET	N	3	G

Jeff Womack
WOMACK, JEFFREY
B. Jun. 26, 1963, McMinnville, TN
Memphis State 5'9" 188 lbs.

1987	MIN	N	2	RB

Joe Womack
WOMACK, JOSEPH
B. Dec. 10, 1936
Los Angeles State 5'9" 210 lbs.

1962	PIT	N	11	HB

Royce Womble
WOMBLE, ROYCE CULLEN
B. Aug. 12, 1931, Webb, TX
North Texas State 6'0" 185 lbs.

1954	BAL	N	12	HB
1955			3	HB
1956			12	HB
1957			10	HB
1960	LA	A		HB

5 yrs. 37 games

Bill Wondolowski
WONDOLOWSKI, WILLIAM
B. Nov. 29, 1946, Jersey City, NJ
Eastern Montana 5'10" 168 lbs.

1969	SF	N	1	WR

George Wonsley
WONSLEY, GEORGE IVORY
B. Nov. 23, 1960, Moss Point, MS
Mississippi State 6'2" 218 lbs.

1984	IND	N	14	RB
1985			16	RB
1986			16	RB
1987			11	RB
1988			16	RB
1989	NE	N	5	RB

6 yrs. 78 games

Nathan Wonsley
WONSLEY, NATHAN, JR.
B. Dec. 7, 1963, Moss Point, MS
Mississippi 5'10" 190 lbs.

1986	TB	N	10	RB

Otis Wonsley
WONSLEY, OTIS
B. Aug. 13, 1957, Pascagoula, MS
Alcorn State 5'10" 205 lbs.

1981	WAS	N	15	RB
1982			9	RB
1983			16	RB
1984			16	RB
1985			16	RB

5 yrs. 72 games

Wood
WOOD
None

1920	DET	A	1	FB

Bill Wood
WOOD, WILLIAM
B. 1939
West Virginia Wesleyan 5'11" 190 lbs.

1963	NY	A	1	DB

Bo Wood
WOOD, CHARLES HENRY
B. Jan. 24, 1945, Camden, NJ
North Carolina 6'3" 225 lbs.

1967	ATL	N	14	DE

Bobby Wood
WOOD, ROBERT H.
B. 1916
Deceased
Alabama 6'2" 230 lbs.

1940	CHIC	N	1	T
1940	GB	N	1	T

1 yr. 2 games

Duane Wood
WOOD, DUANE
B. Sep. 20, 1937
Oklahoma State 6'1" 196 lbs.

1960	DAL	A		DB
1961			14	DB
1962			14	DB
1963	KC		14	DB
1964			14	DB

5 yrs. 56 games

Dick Wood
WOOD, RICHARD M.
B. Feb. 2, 1936, Lanett, AL
Auburn 6'5" 202 lbs.

1962	SD	A	6	QB
1962	DEN		1	QB
1963	NY		12	QB
1965	OAK	A	14	QB
1966	MIA	A	14	QB

4 yrs. 47 games

Gary Wood
WOOD, GARY F.
B. Feb. 5, 1942, Taylor, NY
D. Mar. 2, 1994, Long Island, NY
Cornell 5'11" 188 lbs.

1964	NYG	N	12	QB
1965			9	QB
1966			14	QB
1967	NO	N	3	QB
1968	NYG	N		QB
1969		N		QB

6 yrs. 38 games

Marv Wood
WOOD, MARVIN (Sam, Hard)
B. Nov. 28, 1900
D. Dec., 1973, Bloomington, IN

California 6'0" 190 lbs.

1924	KEN	N	4	FB, E, G, HB

Mike Wood
WOOD, MICHAEL STEPHEN
B. Sep. 3, 1954, Kirkwood, MO
Southeast Missouri State 5'11" 199 lbs.

1978	MIN	N	7	P
1978	STL	N	8	P
1979			3	K
1979	SD	N	9	K
1980			1	K
1981	BAL	N	16	K
1982			6	K

5 yrs. 50 games

Richard Wood
WOOD, RICHARD MARLON
(Batman)
B. May 31, 1953, Elizabeth, NJ
Southern California 6'2" 221 lbs.

1975	NYJ	N	14	LB
1976	TB	N	14	LB
1977			14	LB
1978			16	LB
1979			16	LB
1980			16	LB
1981			16	LB
1982			9	LB
1983			16	LB
1984			16	LB

10 yrs. 147 games

Willie Wood
WOOD, WILLIAM VERNELL
B. Dec. 23, 1936, Washington, DC
Southern California 5'10" 189 lbs.

1960	GB	N	12	DB
1961			14	DB
1962			14	DB
1963			14	DB
1964			14	DB
1965			14	DB
1966			14	DB
1967			14	DB
1968			14	DB
1969			14	S
1970			14	S
1971			14	S

12 yrs. 166 games

Al Woodall
WOODALL, AL
B. Dec. 7, 1945, Erwin, NC
Duke 6'5" 202 lbs.

1969	NY	A	4	QB
1970	NYJ	N	10	QB
1971			5	QB
1973			9	QB
1974			3	QB

5 yrs. 31 games

Lee Woodall
WOODALL, LEE
B. Oct. 31, 1969, Carlisle, PA
West Chester 6'0" 220 lbs.

1994	SF	N	15	LB
1995			16	LB
1996			16	LB

3 yrs. 47 games

Ken Woodard
WOODARD, KENNETH EMIL
B. Jan. 22, 1960, Detroit, MI
Tuskegee Institute 6'1" 218 lbs.

1982	DEN	N	9	LB
1983			16	LB

Ken Woodard *continued*

1984			16	LB
1985			16	LB
1986			16	LB
1987	PIT	N	7	LB
1988	SD	N	8	LB
1989			1	LB

8 yrs. 104 games

Marc Woodard
WOODARD, MARC
B. Feb. 21, 1970, Kosciusko, MS
Mississippi State 6'0" 234 lbs.

1994	PHI	N	15	LB
1995			16	LB
1996			16	LB

3 yrs. 47 games

Ray Woodard
WOODARD, RAYMOND LEE
B. Aug. 20, 1961, Corrigan, TX
Texas 6'6" 290 lbs.

1987	DEN	N	3	DE
1987	KC	N	5	DE

1 yr. 8 games

Dennis Woodberry
WOODBERRY, DENNIS EARL
B. Apr. 22, 1961, Texarkana, AR
Southern Arkansas 5'10" 183 lbs.

1986	ATL	N	7	CB
1987	WAS	N	12	CB
1988			12	CB, S

3 yrs. 31 games

John Woodcock
WOODCOCK, JOHN MAURER
B. Mar. 19, 1954, Eureka, CA
New Mexico/Hawaii 6'3" 252 lbs.

1976	DET	N	14	DT
1977			14	DT
1978			16	DT
1980			8	DT
1981	SD	N	12	DE
1982			6	DE

6 yrs. 70 games

Shawn Wooden
WOODEN, SHAWN
B. Oct. 23, 1973, Willow Grove, PA
Notre Dame 5'11" 186 lbs.

1996	MIA	N	16	CB

Terry Wooden
WOODEN, TERRENCE TYLON
B. Jan. 14, 1967, Hartford, CT
Syracuse 6'3" 236 lbs.

1990	SEA	N	8	LB
1991			16	LB
1992			8	LB
1993			16	LB
1994			16	LB
1995			16	LB
1996			9	LB

7 yrs. 89 games

Tom Woodeshick
WOODESHICK, THOMAS
(Woody)
B. Dec. 3, 1941, Wilkes-Barre, PA
West Virginia 6'0" 219 lbs.

1963	PHI	N	14	HB
1964			13	HB
1965			12	FB
1966			14	FB
1967			14	RB
1968			14	RB

Year	Team	Games	Pos.

Tom Woodeshick *continued*

1969		12	RB
1970		6	RB
1971		11	RB
1972	STL N	4	RB

10 yrs. 114 games

Howie Woodin
WOODIN, HOWARD LEE
(Whitey)
B. Nov. 29, 1894, Fort Atkinson, WI
D. Feb. 9, 1974, Green Bay, WI
Marquette 5'10" 208 lbs.

1922	RAC N	4	T, G
1922	GB N	6	G
1923		10	G
1924		11	G
1925		10	G, C
1926		12	G
1927		7	G
1928		10	G, T
1929		4	G
1930		8	G
1931		2	G

10 yrs. 84 games

David Woodley
WOODLEY, DAVID EUGENE
B. Oct. 25, 1958, Shreveport, LA
Louisiana State 6'2" 210 lbs.

1980	MIA N	13	QB
1981		15	QB
1982		9	QB
1983		5	QB
1984	PIT N	7	QB
1985		9	QB

6 yrs. 58 games

Richard Woodley
WOODLEY, RICHARD
B. Jan. 13, 1972, La Marque, TX
Texas Christian 5'9" 180 lbs.

| 1996 | DET N | 11 | CB |

Doug Woodlief
WOODLIEF, DOUGLAS EUGENE
B. Sep. 4, 1943, Marianna, FL
Memphis State 6'3" 231 lbs.

1965	LA N	14	LB
1966		14	LB
1967		13	LB
1968		14	LB
1969		14	LB

5 yrs. 69 games

John Woodring
WOODRING, JOHN
B. Apr. 4, 1959, Philadelphia, PA
Brown 6'2" 230 lbs.

1981	NYJ N	12	LB
1982		9	LB
1983		14	LB
1984		15	LB
1985		2	LB

5 yrs. 52 games

Dwayne Woodruff
WOODRUFF, DWAYNE DONZELL
B. Feb. 18, 1957, Bowling Green, KY
Louisville 5'11" 195 lbs.

1979	PIT N	16	CB
1980		16	CB
1981		16	CB, S
1982		9	CB, S
1983		15	CB
1984		16	CB
1985		12	CB

Dwayne Woodruff *continued*

1987		12	CB
1988		14	CB
1989		16	CB
1990		15	CB

11 yrs. 157 games

Jim Woodruff
WOODRUFF, JAMES L.
B. Aug. 3, 1903
D. Dec., 1971, Atlanta, GA
None 6'3" 210 lbs.

| 1926 | CHIC N | 1 | E |
| 1929 | BUF N | 6 | E, C, T |

2 yrs. 7 games

Lee Woodruff
WOODRUFF, LEE T. (Cowboy)
B. 1907
Mississippi 6'0" 202 lbs.

1931	PRO N	10	FB, HB
1932	BOS N	7	HB, QB
1933	PHI N	9	HB, FB

3 yrs. 26 games

Tony Woodruff
WOODRUFF, TONY DEWAYNE
B. Nov. 12, 1958, Hazen, AR
Fresno State 6'0" 175 lbs.

1982	PHI N	2	WR
1983		6	WR
1984		16	WR

3 yrs. 24 games

Carl Woods
WOODS, CARL FRANK
B. Oct. 22, 1964
Vanderbilt 5'11" 200 lbs.

| 1987 | NE N | 2 | RB |

Chris Woods
WOODS, CHRISTOPHER WYATT
B. Jul. 19, 1962, Birmingham, AL
Auburn 5'11" 190 lbs.

1987	LARI N	9	WR
1988		2	WR
1989	DEN N	1	WR

3 yrs. 12 games

Don Woods
WOODS, DONALD RAY
B. Feb. 17, 1951, Denton, TX
New Mexico Highlands/New Mexico 6'1" 209 lbs.

1974	SD N	12	RB
1975		5	RB
1976		11	RB
1977		14	RB
1978		16	RB
1979		15	RB
1980		2	RB
1980	SF N	10	RB

7 yrs. 85 games

Gerry Woods
WOODS, GERALD (Flash)
B. Apr. 16, 1902
Butler 6'0" 180 lbs.

| 1926 | COL N | 2 | HB |

Glenn Woods
WOODS, GLENN
B. Jan. 7, 1945, Kilgore, TX
Prairie View A&M 6'4" 250 lbs.

| 1969 | HOU A | 7 | DE |

Ickey Woods
WOODS, ELBERT
B. Feb. 28, 1966, Fresno, CA
Nevada-Las Vegas 6'2" 232 lbs.

1988	CIN N	16	RB
1989		2	RB
1990		10	RB
1991		9	RB

4 yrs. 37 games

Jerome Woods
WOODS, JEROME
B. Mar. 17, 1973, Memphis, TN
Memphis 6'2" 198 lbs.

| 1996 | KC N | 16 | S |

Jerry Woods
WOODS, JERRY LEE
B. Feb. 13, 1966, Dyersburg, TN
Northern Michigan 5'10" 187 lbs.

| 1989 | DET N | 2 | CB |
| 1990 | GB N | 16 | S |

2 yrs. 18 games

Jimmy Woods
WOODS, JAMES
B. May 5, 1894
D. Dec., 1966, Salamanca, NY
None 5'9" 196 lbs.

1920	ROC A	1	G
1921		3	G, T
1922	ROC N	1	T
1923		4	C, G, T
1924		5	T, C, G

5 yrs. 14 games

Larry Woods
WOODS, LAWRENCE DOBIE
B. May 11, 1948, Rogersville, AL
Tennessee State 6'6" 265 lbs.

1971	DET N	1	DT
1972		12	DT
1973	MIA N	3	DT
1974	NYJ N	14	DT
1975		12	DT
1976	SEA N	6	DT

6 yrs. 48 games

Mike Woods
WOODS, MICHAEL
B. Nov. 1, 1954, Cleveland, OH
Tampa/Cincinnati 6'2" 233 lbs.

1979	BAL N	16	LB
1980		13	LB
1981		7	LB

3 yrs. 36 games

Rick Woods
WOODS, RICK L.
B. Nov. 16, 1959, Boise, ID
Boise State 6'0" 196 lbs.

1982	PIT N	5	S
1983		15	S
1984		15	S
1985		16	S
1986		15	S, CB
1987	TB N	5	S

6 yrs. 71 games

Rob Woods
WOODS, ALEX ROBERT
B. Oct. 3, 1965, Fayetteville, NC
Eastern Wash./Cal-Santa Barbara/Arizona 6'5" 295 lbs.

| 1991 | CLE N | 2 | OT |

Robert Woods
WOODS, ROBERT CHRISTOPHER
B. Jul. 3, 1955, New Orleans, LA
Grambling State 5'7" 170 lbs.

| 1978 | HOU N | 3 | WR |

Robert Woods
WOODS, ROBERT EARL
B. Jul. 26, 1950, Florence, AL
Tennessee State 6'4" 259 lbs.

1973	NYJ N	14	OT
1974		14	OT
1975		14	OT
1976		10	OT
1977		2	OT
1977	NO N	4	OL
1978		16	G
1979		15	G
1980		10	G

8 yrs. 99 games

Tony Woods
WOODS, CLINTON ANTHONY
B. Mar. 14, 1966, Fort Lee, VA
Oklahoma 6'4" 274 lbs.

| 1989 | CHI N | 15 | DE |

Tony Woods
WOODS, STANLEY ANTHONY
B. Sep. 11, 1965, Newark NJ
Pittsburgh 6'4" 259 lbs.

1987	SEA N	12	LB
1988		16	LB
1989		16	LB
1990		16	LB
1991		14	DE
1992		15	DE
1993	LARM N	13	DE
1994	WAS N	15	DE
1995		16	DE
1996		13	DE

10 yrs. 146 games

Keith Woodside
WOODSIDE, KEITH A.
B. Jul. 29, 1964, Natchez, MS
Texas A&M 5'11" 203 lbs.

1988	GB N	16	RB
1989		16	RB
1990		16	RB
1991		16	RB

4 yrs. 64 games

Abe Woodson
WOODSON, ABRAHAM BENJAMIN
B. Feb. 15, 1934, Jackson, MS
Illinois 5'11" 188 lbs.

1958	SF N	9	DB
1959		12	DB
1960		12	DB
1961		14	DB
1962		14	DB
1963		14	DB
1964		14	DB
1965	STL N	13	DB
1966		14	DB

9 yrs. 116 games

Darren Woodson
WOODSON, DARREN RAY
B. Apr. 25, 1969, Phoenix, AZ
Arizona State 6'1" 215 lbs.

1992	DAL N	16	S
1993		16	S
1994		16	S
1995		16	S

Year	Team	Games	Pos.

Darren Woodson *continued*

Year	Team		Games	Pos.
1996			16	S
5 yrs.	80 games			

Freddie Woodson
WOODSON, FREDDIE
Florida A&M 6'2" 250 lbs.

Year	Team		Games	Pos.
1967	MIA	A	12	G
1968			14	G, DE
1969			1	G, DT
3 yrs.	27 games			

Marv Woodson
WOODSON, MARVIN LEWIS
B. Sep. 19, 1941, Hattiesburg, MS
Indiana 6'0" 195 lbs.

Year	Team		Games	Pos.
1964	PIT	N	4	DB
1965			13	DB
1966			14	DB
1967			14	DB
1968			14	DB
1969			8	S
1969	NO	N	5	S
6 yrs.	72 games			

Rod Woodson
WOODSON, RODERICK KEVIN
B. Mar. 10, 1965, Fort Wayne, IN
Purdue 6'0" 198 lbs.

Year	Team		Games	Pos.
1987	PIT	N	8	S, CB
1988			16	CB, S
1989			15	CB
1990			16	CB
1991			15	CB
1992			16	CB
1993			16	CB
1994			15	CB
1995			1	CB
1996			16	CB
10 yrs.	134 games			

Dick Woodward
WOODWARD, RICHARD E.
B. Jul. 26, 1926, Britt, IA
Iowa 6'2" 224 lbs.

Year	Team		Games	Pos.
1949	LA	AA	12	C
1950	NYG	N	12	C
1951			11	C
1952	WAS	N	9	C
1953	NYG	N	12	C
5 yrs.	56 games			

Scott Woolf
WOOLF, SCOTT
B. Dec. 26, 1961
Mount Union 6'1" 190 lbs.

Year	Team		Games	Pos.
1987	LARI	N	1	QB

Butch Woolfolk
WOOLFOLK, HAROLD
B. Mar. 1, 1960, Milwaukee, WI
Michigan 6'1" 215 lbs.

Year	Team		Games	Pos.
1982	NYG	N	9	RB
1983			16	RB
1984			15	RB
1985	HOU	N	16	RB
1986			10	RB
1987	DET	N	12	RB
6 yrs.	78 games			

Donnell Woolford
WOOLFORD, DONNELL
B. Jan. 6, 1966, Baltimore, MD
Clemson 5'9" 187 lbs.

Year	Team		Games	Pos.
1989	CHI	N	13	CB, S
1990			13	CB
1991			15	CB

Donnell Woolford *continued*

Year	Team		Games	Pos.
1992			16	CB
1993			16	CB
1994			16	CB
1995			9	CB
1996			15	CB
8 yrs.	113 games			

Gary Woolford
WOOLFORD, GARY S.
B. May 4, 1954, Cairo, IL
Western Illinois/Florida State 6'0" 182 lbs.

Year	Team		Games	Pos.
1980	NYG	N	12	S

Rolly Woolsey
WOOLSEY, ROLAND BERT
B. Aug. 11, 1953, Provo, UT
Boise State 6'1" 182 lbs.

Year	Team		Games	Pos.
1975	DAL	N	14	CB
1976	SEA	N	14	CB
1977	CLE	N	14	S
1978	STL	N	2	S
4 yrs.	44 games			

John Wooten
WOOTEN, JOHN
B. Dec. 5, 1936, Clarksville, TX
Colorado 6'3" 250 lbs.

Year	Team		Games	Pos.
1959	CLE	N	12	G
1960			12	G
1962			14	G
1963			14	G
1964			14	G
1965			14	G
1966			14	G
1968	WAS	N	14	G
8 yrs.	108 games			

Mike Wooten
WOOTEN, MICHAEL
B. Oct. 23, 1962, Roanoke, VA
Virginia Military Institute 6'3" 260 lbs.

Year	Team		Games	Pos.
1987	WAS	N	3	C

Ron Wooten
WOOTEN, RONALD J.
B. Jun. 28, 1959, Bourne, MS
North Carolina 6'4" 275 lbs.

Year	Team		Games	Pos.
1982	NE	N	9	G
1983			16	G
1984			16	G
1985			14	G
1986			16	G
1987			13	G
1988			14	G
7 yrs.	98 games			

Tito Wooten
WOOTEN, TITO
B. Dec. 12, 1971, Goldsboro, NC
North Carolina/Northeast Louisiana 6'0" 181 lbs.

Year	Team		Games	Pos.
1994	NYG	N	16	S
1995			16	S, CB
1996			13	S
3 yrs.	45 games			

Barry Word
WORD, BARRY QUENTIN
B. Jul. 17, 1964, Long Island, VA
Virginia 6'2" 240 lbs.

Year	Team		Games	Pos.
1987	NO	N	12	RB
1988			2	RB
1990	KC	N	16	RB
1991			16	RB
1992			12	RB

Barry Word *continued*

Year	Team		Games	Pos.
1993	MIN	N	13	RB
1994	ARI	N	1	RB
7 yrs.	72 games			

Roscoe Word
WORD, ROSCOE
B. Jul. 24, 1952, Pine Bluff, AR
Jackson State 5'11" 170 lbs.

Year	Team		Games	Pos.
1974	NYJ	N	14	DB
1975			14	CB
1976			2	CB
1976	BUF	N	1	DB
1976	NYG	N	4	DB
1976	TB	N	2	CB
3 yrs.	37 games			

Jim Worden
WORDEN, JAMES
B. 1916
Waynesburg 5'10" 180 lbs.

Year	Team		Games	Pos.
1945	CLE	N	5	HB

Neil Worden
WORDEN, NEIL JAMES
B. Jul. 1, 1931, Milwaukee, WI
Notre Dame 5'10" 198 lbs.

Year	Team		Games	Pos.
1954	PHI	N	12	FB
1957			12	FB
2 yrs.	24 games			

Stu Worden
WORDEN, STUART
B. May 6, 1907
D. Mar., 1978, Mineral, VA
Hampden-Sydney 6'0" 210 lbs.

Year	Team		Games	Pos.
1930	BKN	N	11	T, G
1932			11	G
1933			10	G
1934			11	G, C
4 yrs.	43 games			

Joe Work
WORK, JOSEPH
B. Jan. 25, 1900
D. Oct., 1979, Adena, OH
Miami (Ohio) 5'10" 177 lbs.

Year	Team		Games	Pos.
1923	CLE	N	7	E
1925			4	E
2 yrs.	11 games			

Blake Workman
WORKMAN, BLAKE (Sheriff)
B. Aug. 12, 1908
D. Jun., 1983, Opelousas, LA
Tulsa 5'11" 185 lbs.

Year	Team		Games	Pos.
1934	C, S	N	3	QB

Harry Workman
WORKMAN, HARRY HALL (Hoge)
B. Sep. 25, 1899, Huntington, WV
D. May 20, 1972, Fort Myers, FL
Ohio State 5'11" 173 lbs.

Year	Team		Games	Pos.
1924	CLE	N	9	HB, FB
1931			9	QB, HB
1932	NYG	N	1	B
3 yrs.	19 games			

Vince Workman
WORKMAN, VINCE
B. May 9, 1968, Buffalo, NY
Ohio State 5'10" 193 lbs.

Year	Team		Games	Pos.
1989	GB	N	15	RB
1990			15	RB
1991			16	RB
1992			10	RB

Vince Workman *continued*

Year	Team		Games	Pos.
1993	TB	N	16	RB
1994			15	RB
1995	CAR	N	9	RB
1995	IND	N	1	RB
1996			9	RB
8 yrs.	106 games			

Tim Worley
WORLEY, TIMOTHY ASHLEY
B. Sep. 24, 1966, Lumberton, NC
Georgia 6'2" 228 lbs.

Year	Team		Games	Pos.
1989	PIT	N	15	RB
1990			11	RB
1991			2	RB
1993			5	RB
1993	CHI	N	10	RB
1994			5	RB
5 yrs.	48 games			

Barron Wortham
WORTHAM, BARRON WINFRED
B. Nov. 1, 1969, Everman, TX
Texas-El Paso 5'11" 244 lbs.

Year	Team		Games	Pos.
1994	HOU	N	16	LB
1995			16	LB
1996			15	LB
3 yrs.	47 games			

Naz Worthen
WORTHEN, NASRALLAH ONEA
B. Mar. 27, 1966, Jacksonville, FL
North Carolina State 5'8" 177 lbs.

Year	Team		Games	Pos.
1989	KC	N	10	WR
1990			9	WR
2 yrs.	19 games			

Keith Wortman
WORTMAN, KEITH DELANE
B. Jul. 20, 1950, Billings, MT
Nebraska 6'2" 259 lbs.

Year	Team		Games	Pos.
1972	GB	N	13	G
1973			8	G
1974			12	G
1975			14	G
1976	STL	N	3	G
1977			14	G
1978			14	G
1979			13	G
1980			2	OT
1981			4	OT
10 yrs.	97 games			

John Woudenberg
WOUDENBERG, JOHN WILLIAM
B. May 25, 1918, Denver, CO
Denver/St. Mary's 6'3" 226 lbs.

Year	Team		Games	Pos.
1940	PIT	N	7	T, E
1941			11	T
1942			11	T
1946	SF	AA	14	T
1947			14	T
1948			14	T
1949			12	T
7 yrs.	83 games			

Mike Woulfe
WOULFE, MIKE JEROME
B. Aug. 14, 1939
Colorado 6'2" 225 lbs.

Year	Team		Games	Pos.
1962	PHI	N	13	LB

John Wozniak
WOZNIAK, JOHN EDWARD
B. Aug. 2, 1921, Arnold City, PA
D. Aug., 1982, Tuscaloosa, AL
Alabama 6'0" 218 lbs.

Year	Team		Games	Pos.
1948	BKN	AA	14	G

Year	Team	Games	Pos.

John Wozniak continued

Year	Team		Games	Pos.
1949	B-NY	AA	12	G
1950	NYY	N	12	G
1951			12	G
1952	DAL	N	12	G

5 yrs.   62 games

Lud Wray
WRAY, JAMES R. LUDLOW
B. Feb. 7, 1894, Philadelphia, PA
D. Jul. 24, 1967, Philadelphia, PA
Pennsylvania 6'0" 180 lbs.

Year	Team		Games	Pos.
1920	BUF	A	6	C
1921			7	C

2 yrs.   13 games

Darryl Wren
WREN, DARRYL
B. Jan. 25, 1957, Tulsa, OK
Pittsburg State 6'0" 188 lbs.

Year	Team		Games	Pos.
1993	NE	N	12	CB
1994			8	CB

2 yrs.   20 games

Junior Wren
WREN, LOWE, JR.
B. Dec. 10, 1930, Kansas City, MO
Missouri 6'0" 192 lbs.

Year	Team		Games	Pos.
1956	CLE	N	12	DB
1957			12	DB
1958			12	DB
1959			12	DB
1960	PIT	N	12	DB
1961	NY	A	2	DB

6 yrs.   62 games

Ab Wright
WRIGHT, ALBERT OWEN
B. Nov. 16, 1905, Terlton, OK
Oklahoma State 6'1" 190 lbs.

Year	Team		Games	Pos.
1930	FRA	N	3	HB

Adrian Wright
WRIGHT, ADRIAN
B. Oct. 13, 1961, Charleston, WV
Virginia Union 6'1" 230 lbs.

Year	Team		Games	Pos.
1987	TB	N		FB

Alexander Wright
WRIGHT, ALEXANDER
B. Jul. 19, 1967, Albany, GA
Auburn 6'0" 189 lbs.

Year	Team		Games	Pos.
1990	DAL	N	15	WR
1991			16	WR
1992			3	WR
1992	LARI	N	10	WR
1993			15	WR
1994			16	WR
1995	STL	N	8	WR
1996			3	WR

7 yrs.   86 games

Alvin Wright
WRIGHT, ALVIN
B. Feb. 5, 1961, Wedowee, AL
Jacksonville State 6'2" 270 lbs.

Year	Team		Games	Pos.
1986	LARM	N	4	NT
1987			15	NT
1988			16	NT
1989			16	NT
1990			16	NT
1991			13	DT
1992	CLE	N	3	DT

7 yrs.   83 games

Charles Wright
WRIGHT, CHARLES JAMES
B. Apr. 3, 1964, Carthage, MO
Tulsa 5'9" 178 lbs.

Year	Team		Games	Pos.
1987	STL	N	3	CB
1988	DAL	N	3	CB, S

2 yrs.   6 games

Dana Wright
WRIGHT, DANA
B. Jun. 2, 1963, Ravenna, OH
Findlay 6'1" 219 lbs.

Year	Team		Games	Pos.
1987	CIN	N	5	RB

Elmo Wright
WRIGHT, ELMO
B. Jul. 3, 1949, Brazoria, TX
Houston 6'0" 190 lbs.

Year	Team		Games	Pos.
1971	KC	N	14	WR
1972			7	WR
1973			11	WR
1974			13	WR
1975	HOU	N	2	WR
1975	NE	N	4	WR

5 yrs.   51 games

Eric Wright
WRIGHT, ERIC C.
B. Apr. 18, 1959, St. Louis, MO
Missouri 6'1" 183 lbs.

Year	Team		Games	Pos.
1981	SF	N	16	CB
1982			7	CB
1983			16	CB
1984			16	CB
1985			16	CB
1986			2	CB
1987			2	CB
1988			15	CB
1989			11	CB
1990			9	CB

10 yrs.   110 games

Eric Wright
WRIGHT, ERIC LAMON
B. Aug. 4, 1969, Pittsburg, TX
Stephen F. Austin 6'0" 196 lbs.

Year	Team		Games	Pos.
1992	CHI	N	13	WR

Ernie Wright
WRIGHT, ERNEST HENRY
B. Nov. 6, 1939, Toledo, OH
Ohio State 6'4" 268 lbs.

Year	Team		Games	Pos.
1960	LA	A	14	OT
1961	SD	A	14	OT
1962			14	OT
1963			14	OT
1964			14	OT
1965			14	OT
1966			13	OT
1967			14	OT
1968	CIN	A	14	OT
1969			14	OT
1970	CIN	N	14	OT
1971			7	OT
1972	SD	N	14	OT

13 yrs.   174 games

Felix Wright
WRIGHT, FELIX CARL
B. Jun. 22, 1959, Carthage, MO
Drake 6'2" 190 lbs.

Year	Team		Games	Pos.
1985	CLE	N	16	S
1986			16	CB, S
1987			12	CB, S
1988			16	S
1989			16	S
1990			16	S
1991	MIN	N	16	S

Felix Wright continued

Year	Team		Games	Pos.
1992			13	S

8 yrs.   121 games

George Wright
WRIGHT, GEORGE WAYNE
B. Mar. 3, 1947, Houston, TX
Sam Houston State 6'3" 262 lbs.

Year	Team		Games	Pos.
1970	BAL	N	1	DT
1971			10	DT
1972	CLE	N	4	DT

3 yrs.   15 games

Gordon Wright
WRIGHT, GORDON
B. Dec. 5, 1943, Freeport, NY
Delaware State 6'3" 245 lbs.

Year	Team		Games	Pos.
1967	PHI	N	3	G
1969	NY	A	2	G

2 yrs.   5 games

James Wright
WRIGHT, JAMES EARL
B. 1939
Memphis State 5'11" 190 lbs.

Year	Team		Games	Pos.
1964	DEN	A	10	DB

James Wright
WRIGHT, JAMES WILLIE
B. Sep. 1, 1956, Fort Hood, TX
Texas Christian 6'3" 240 lbs.

Year	Team		Games	Pos.
1978	ATL	N	15	TE
1980	DEN	N	1	TE
1981			16	TE
1982			9	TE
1983			6	TE
1984			16	TE
1985			16	TE

7 yrs.   79 games

Jeff Wright
WRIGHT, JEFF DEE
B. Jun. 13, 1963, San Bernardino, CA
Tulsa/Central Missouri State 6'2" 270 lbs.

Year	Team		Games	Pos.
1988	BUF	N	15	NT
1989			15	NT
1990			16	NT
1991			9	NT
1992			16	NT
1993			15	NT
1994			12	NT

7 yrs.   98 games

Jeff Wright
WRIGHT, JEFFREY RALPH
B. Jun. 13, 1949, Edna, MN
Minnesota 5'11" 190 lbs.

Year	Team		Games	Pos.
1971	MIN	N	14	DB
1972			13	S
1973			14	S
1974			11	S
1975			3	S
1976			14	S
1977			14	S

7 yrs.   83 games

Jim Wright
WRIGHT, JIM SID
B. 1921
North Texas/Southern Methodist 6'1" 222 lbs.

Year	Team		Games	Pos.
1947	BOS	N	12	G

John Wright
WRIGHT, JOHN OLIVER (Red)

John Wright continued

B. Jul. 13, 1921, Baltimore, MD
Maryland 5'11" 225 lbs.

Year	Team		Games	Pos.
1947	BAL	AA	13	B

John Wright
WRIGHT, JOHN WILLIAM, SR.
B. Jan. 11, 1946, Oak Park, IL
Illinois 6'0" 196 lbs.

Year	Team		Games	Pos.
1968	ATL	N	5	FL
1969	DET	N	14	WR

2 yrs.   19 games

Johnnie Wright
WRIGHT, JOHNNIE LEE
B. Sep. 13, 1958, Fort Myers, FL
South Carolina 6'2" 210 lbs.

Year	Team		Games	Pos.
1982	BAL	N	7	RB

Keith Wright
WRIGHT, WILLIAM KEITH
B. Jan. 30, 1956, Mercedes, TX
Memphis State 5'10" 174 lbs.

Year	Team		Games	Pos.
1978	CLE	N	16	WR
1979			5	WR
1980			12	WR

3 yrs.   33 games

Lonnie Wright
WRIGHT, LONNIE
B. Jan. 23, 1945, Newark NJ
Colorado State* 6'2" 205 lbs.

Year	Team		Games	Pos.
1966	DEN	A	14	DB
1967			12	DB

2 yrs.   26 games

Louis Wright
WRIGHT, LOUIS DONNEL
B. Jan. 31, 1953, Gilmer, TX
Arizona State/San Jose State 6'3" 200 lbs.

Year	Team		Games	Pos.
1975	DEN	N	11	CB
1976			14	CB
1977			14	CB
1978			16	CB
1979			16	CB
1980			15	CB
1981			8	CB
1982			9	CB
1983			16	CB
1984			16	CB
1985			15	CB
1986			16	CB

12 yrs.   166 games

Nate Wright
WRIGHT, NATHANIEL
B. Dec. 21, 1947, Madison, FL
San Diego State 5'11" 180 lbs.

Year	Team		Games	Pos.
1969	ATL	N	3	CB
1969	STL	N	10	CB
1970			14	CB
1971	MIN	N	4	CB
1972			14	CB
1973			14	CB
1974			14	CB
1975			14	CB
1976			14	CB
1977			14	CB
1978			16	CB
1979			10	CB
1980			16	CB

12 yrs.   157 games

Ralph Wright
WRIGHT, RALPH
B. Jan. 16, 1908

Year	Team	Games	Pos.

Ralph Wright continued
Kentucky 6'0" 230 lbs.

Year	Team	Games	Pos.
1933	BKN	N	4	T

Randy Wright
WRIGHT, RANDALL STEVEN
B. Jan. 12, 1961, St. Charles, IL
Wisconsin 6'2" 200 lbs.

Year	Team		Games	Pos.
1984	GB	N	8	QB
1985			7	QB
1986			16	QB
1987			9	QB
1988			8	QB

5 yrs. 48 games

Rayfield Wright
WRIGHT, LARRY RAYFIELD (The Big Cat)
B. Aug. 23, 1945, Griffin, GA
Fort Valley State 6'7" 254 lbs.

Year	Team		Games	Pos.
1967	DAL	N	10	TE
1968			14	TE, OT
1969			14	OT
1970			14	OT
1971			14	OT
1972			14	OT
1973			12	OT
1974			14	OT
1975			13	OT
1976			14	OT
1977			2	OT
1978			15	OT
1979			16	OT

13 yrs. 166 games

Steve Wright
WRIGHT, STEPHEN HOUGH
B. Apr. 8, 1959, St. Louis, MO
Northern Iowa 6'6" 269 lbs.

Year	Team		Games	Pos.
1981	DAL	N	16	OT
1982			9	OT
1983	BAL	N	13	G
1984	IND	N	16	OT
1987	LARI	N	9	OT
1988			15	OT
1989			16	OT
1990			16	OT
1991			16	OT
1992			7	OT

10 yrs. 133 games

Steve Wright
WRIGHT, STEPHEN THOMAS
B. Jul. 17, 1942, Birmingham, AL
Alabama 6'6" 250 lbs.

Year	Team		Games	Pos.
1964	GB	N	14	DE
1965			14	DE
1966			14	OT
1967			14	OT
1968	NYG	N	10	OT
1969			2	OT
1970	WAS	N	14	OT
1971	CHI	N	14	OT
1972	STL	N	5	OT

9 yrs. 101 games

Sylvester Wright
WRIGHT, SYLVESTER
B. Dec. 30, 1971, Detroit, MI
Kansas 6'2" 244 lbs.

Year	Team		Games	Pos.
1995	PHI	N	6	LB
1996			16	LB

2 yrs. 22 games

Ted Wright
WRIGHT, WELDON G.
B. Nov. 15, 1913, Savoy, TX
North Texas State 6'0" 185 lbs.

Year	Team		Games	Pos.
1934	BOS	N	8	HB

Ted Wright continued

Year	Team		Games	Pos.
1935			6	QB, HB
1935	BKN	N	2	HB, QB

2 yrs. 16 games

Terry Wright
WRIGHT, TERRY
B. Jul. 17, 1965, Phoenix, AZ
Temple 6'0" 195 lbs.

Year	Team		Games	Pos.
1987	IND	N	13	DB
1988			8	CB, S

2 yrs. 21 games

Toby Wright
WRIGHT, TOBY LIN
B. Nov. 19, 1970, Phoenix, AZ
Nebraska 5'11" 203 lbs.

Year	Team		Games	Pos.
1994	LARM	N	16	S
1995	STL	N	16	S
1996			12	S

3 yrs. 44 games

Willie Wright
WRIGHT, WILLIE DON
B. Mar. 9, 1968, Riverton, WY
Wyoming 6'4" 240 lbs.

Year	Team		Games	Pos.
1992	PHX	N	9	LB

Tim Wrightman
WRIGHTMAN, TIMOTHY JON
B. Mar. 27, 1960, Harbor City, CA
UCLA 6'3" 237 lbs.

Year	Team		Games	Pos.
1985	CHI	N	16	TE
1986			16	TE

2 yrs. 32 games

Al Wukits
WUKITS, ALBERT R.
B. Dec. 16, 1918, Millville, PA
D. Nov., 1971
Duquesne 6'3" 213 lbs.

Year	Team		Games	Pos.
1943	P-P	N	9	C
1944	C-P	N	10	C, G
1945	PIT		3	C
1946	BUF	AA	8	C
1946	MIA	AA	7	C

4 yrs. 37 games

Jim Wulff
WULFF, JAMES F.
B. Mar. 22, 1936, Chicago, IL
Michigan State 6'1" 185 lbs.

Year	Team		Games	Pos.
1960	WAS	N	9	DB
1961			8	DB

2 yrs. 17 games

Harry Wunsch
WUNSCH, HARRY F.
B. Nov. 20, 1910
D. Apr., 1954
Notre Dame 5'11" 212 lbs.

Year	Team		Games	Pos.
1934	GB	N	2	G

Freddy Wyant
WYANT, FREDERICK
B. Apr. 26, 1934, Weston, WV
West Virginia 6'0" 200 lbs.

Year	Team		Games	Pos.
1956	WAS	N	10	QB

Alvin Wyatt
WYATT, ALVIN
B. Dec. 13, 1947, Jacksonville, FL
Bethune-Cookman 5'10" 183 lbs.

Year	Team		Games	Pos.
1970	OAK	N	11	S
1971	BUF	N	14	CB
1972			14	CB

Alvin Wyatt continued

Year	Team		Games	Pos.
1973	HOU	N	4	S

4 yrs. 43 games

Doug Wyatt
WYATT, JOHN DOUGLAS
B. Oct. 18, 1946, Tyler, TX
Tulsa 6'1" 195 lbs.

Year	Team		Games	Pos.
1970	NO	N	14	S
1971			12	S
1972			14	S
1973	DET	N	6	S
1974			12	S

5 yrs. 58 games

Kervin Wyatt
WYATT, KERVIN D.
B. Oct. 17, 1957, Washington, DC
Maryland 6'2" 235 lbs.

Year	Team		Games	Pos.
1980	NYG	N	4	LB

Kevin Wyatt
WYATT, KEVIN MICHAEL
B. Mar. 14, 1964, Norfolk, VA
Arkansas 5'10" 190 lbs.

Year	Team		Games	Pos.
1986	SD	N	16	CB
1987	KC	N	2	CB

2 yrs. 18 games

Willie Wyatt
WYATT, WILLIE PORTER
B. Sep. 27, 1967, Birmingham, AL
Alabama 6'0" 275 lbs.

Year	Team		Games	Pos.
1990	TB	N	7	DE

Sam Wyche
WYCHE, SAMUEL DAVID
B. Jan. 5, 1945, Atlanta, GA
Furman 6'4" 214 lbs.

Year	Team		Games	Pos.
1968	CIN	A	3	QB
1969			7	QB
1970	CIN	N	13	QB
1971	WAS	N	1	QB
1972			7	QB
1974	DET	N	14	QB
1976	STL	N	1	QB

7 yrs. 46 games

Frank Wycheck
WYCHECK, FRANK
B. Oct. 14, 1971, Philadelphia, PA
Maryland 6'3" 235 lbs.

Year	Team		Games	Pos.
1993	WAS	N	9	TE
1994			9	TE
1995	HOU	N	16	TE
1996			16	TE

4 yrs. 50 games

Craig Wycinski
WYCINSKY, CRAIG P.
B. Jan. 4, 1948, Detroit, MI
Michigan State 6'3" 243 lbs.

Year	Team		Games	Pos.
1972	CLE	N	6	G

Doug Wycoff
WYCOFF, STEPHEN DOUGLAS
B. Sep. 6, 1903, St. Louis, MO
D. Oct., 1981, Atlanta, GA
Georgia Tech 6'0" 206 lbs.

Year	Team		Games	Pos.
1926	NEW	A	5	HB, FB
1927	NYG	N	11	HB, FB
1929	SI		9	HB, QB, FB
1930			12	FB, HB, QB
1931	NYG	N	12	FB, HB
1932	SI	N	12	FB, HB
1934	BOS	N	12	FB, QB, HB

7 yrs. 73 games

Frank Wydo
WYDO, FRANK
B. Jun. 15, 1924, Footedale, PA
D. Feb. 17, 1979, Uniontown, PA
Duquesne/Cornell 6'4" 225 lbs.

Year	Team		Games	Pos.
1947	PIT	N	12	T
1948			12	T
1949			12	T
1950			12	T
1951			12	T
1952	PHI	N	12	T
1953			12	T
1954			12	T
1955			12	T
1956			12	T
1957			12	T

11 yrs. 132 games

John Wyhonic
WYHONIC, JOHN
B. Dec. 22, 1920, Tiltonville, OH
D. Jul. 17, 1989, Arcadia, FL
Alabama 6'0" 213 lbs.

Year	Team		Games	Pos.
1946	PHI	N	11	G
1947			12	G
1948	BUF	AA	12	G
1949			3	G

4 yrs. 38 games

Lee Wykoff
WYKOFF, LEE
B. Mar. 10, 1898
D. Apr. 30, 1974, Kansas City, KS
Washburn 6'1" 195 lbs.

Year	Team		Games	Pos.
1923	STL	N	3	HB, FB

Pudge Wyland
WYLAND, GUIDO B.
B. Jun., 1891
D. Dec. 8, 1974, Moline, IL
Iowa 5'10" 180 lbs.

Year	Team		Games	Pos.
1920	RI	A	7	G

Arnie Wyman
WYMAN, ARNOLD D.
B. Aug., 1895
Deceased
Minnesota 5'11" 172 lbs.

Year	Team		Games	Pos.
1920	RI	A	6	FB, HB

Dave Wyman
WYMAN, DAVID MATTHEW
B. Mar. 31, 1964, San Diego, CA
Stanford 6'2" 245 lbs.

Year	Team		Games	Pos.
1987	SEA	N	4	LB
1988			16	LB
1989			16	LB
1990			8	LB
1991			6	LB
1992			11	LB
1993	DEN	N	16	LB
1994			4	LB
1995			11	LB

9 yrs. 92 games

Devin Wyman
WYMAN, DEVIN
B. Aug. 29, 1973, East Palo Alto, CA
Kentucky State 6'7" 307 lbs.

Year	Team		Games	Pos.
1996	NE	N	9	DT

Will Wynn
WYNN, WILLIAM
B. Jan. 15, 1949, Apex, NC
Tennessee State 6'4" 244 lbs.

Year	Team		Games	Pos.
1973	PHI	N	12	DE
1974			14	DE
1975			14	DE

Year	Team	Games	Pos.

Will Wynn *continued*

Year	Team		Games	Pos.
1976			14	DE
1977	WAS	N	1	DE
5 yrs.	55 games			

Chet Wynne
WYNNE, CHESTER ALLEN
B. Nov. 23, 1898
D. Jul. 17, 1967, Chicago, IL
Notre Dame 6'0" 180 lbs.

1922	ROC	N	2	FB, HB

Elmer Wynne
WYNNE, ELMER BURTON
B. Jan. 20, 1901, Long Island, KS
D. Nov. 10, 1989, Denver, CO
Nebraska/Notre Dame 6'1" 193 lbs.

1928	CHIB	N	10	FB
1929	DAY	N	5	FB
2 yrs.	15 games			

Harry Wynne
WYNNE, HARRY CLAYTON
B. Jul. 10, 1920, Senatobia, MS
Arkansas 6'4" 203 lbs.

1944	BOS	N	10	E
1945	NYG	N	5	E
2 yrs.	15 games			

Pete Wysocki
WYSOCKI, PETER JOSEPH
B. Oct. 3, 1948, Detroit, MI
Western Michigan 6'2" 225 lbs.

1975	WAS	N	13	LB
1976			14	LB
1977			13	LB
1978			16	LB
1979			16	LB
1980			16	LB
6 yrs.	88 games			

Izzy Yablok
YABLOK, JULES (Indian)
B. Jul. 28, 1907
D. Aug. 15, 1983, Encino, CA
Colgate 5'10" 172 lbs.

1930	BKN	N	7	QB, HB
1931			6	QB, FB
1931	SI	N	7	QB, HB
2 yrs.	20 games			

Vinnie Yablonski
YABLONSKI, VENTAN CONSTANTINE
B. Mar. 4, 1923, Worcester, MA
Fordham/Columbia 5'8" 195 lbs.

1948	CHIC	N	12	FB
1949			12	FB
1950			11	FB
1951			4	B
4 yrs.	39 games			

John Yaccino
YACCINO, JOHN
B. 1938
Pittsburgh 6'0" 190 lbs.

1962	BUF	A	3	DB

Joe Yackanich
YACKANICH, JOSEPH
B. Mar. 31, 1922
D. Aug., 1969
Fordham 5'10" 205 lbs.

1946	NY	AA	11	G
1947			14	G
1948			1	G
3 yrs.	26 games			

Ray Yagiello
YAGIELLO, RAYMOND W.
B. Sep. 21, 1923, Orange, NJ
Franklin & Marshall/Catawba 6'0" 220 lbs.

1948	LA	N	12	G
1949			12	G
2 yrs.	24 games			

Ray Yakavonis
YAKAVONIS, RAY
B. Jan. 20, 1957, Wilkes-Barre, PA
East Stroudsburg State 6'4" 248 lbs.

1981	MIN	N	15	DE
1982			2	DE
1983			2	NT
1983	KC	N	2	NT
3 yrs.	21 games			

Bill Yanchar
YANCHAR, BILL
B. Mar. 25, 1948, Euclid, OH
Purdue 6'3" 250 lbs.

1970	CLE	N	5	DT

Carlos Yancy
YANCY, CARLOS DELANIO
B. Jun. 24, 1970, Sarasota, FL
Georgia 6'1" 185 lbs.

1995	NE	N	4	CB

Ron Yankowski
YANKOWSKI, RONALD WILLIAM
B. Oct. 22, 1946, Arlington, MA
Kansas State 6'5" 244 lbs.

1971	STL	N	12	DE
1972			10	DE
1973			14	DE
1974			14	DE
1975			13	DE
1976			5	DE
1977			14	DE
1978			16	DE
1979			16	DE
1980			14	DE
10 yrs.	128 games			

Eric Yarber
YARBER, ERIC LAMONE
B. Sep. 22, 1963, Chicago, IL
Idaho 5'8" 156 lbs.

1986	WAS	N	2	WR
1987			12	WR
2 yrs.	14 games			

Ryan Yarborough
YARBOROUGH, RYAN
B. Apr. 26, 1971, Baltimore, MD
Wyoming 6'2" 190 lbs.

1994	NYJ	N	13	WR
1995			16	WR
2 yrs.	29 games			

Jim Yarbrough
YARBROUGH, JAMES
B. Nov. 20, 1963
Murray State 6'0" 195 lbs.

1987	NYG	N	3	S

Jim Yarbrough
YARBROUGH, JAMES KELLEY (Punjab)
B. Oct. 28, 1946, Charlotte, NC
Florida 6'6" 261 lbs.

1969	DET	N	13	OT
1970			12	OT
1971			14	OT

Jim Yarbrough *continued*

1972			13	OT
1973			10	OT
1974			12	OT
1975			13	OT
1976			11	OT
1977			13	OT
9 yrs.	111 games			

George Yarno
YARNO, GEORGE ANTHONY
B. Aug. 12, 1957, Spokane, WA
Washington State 6'2" 260 lbs.

1979	TB	N	15	G
1980			16	G
1981			16	G, C
1982			9	G
1983			14	G, OT
1985			12	OL
1986			16	G, OT
1987			11	G, OT
1988	ATL	N	16	C
1989	HOU	N	11	C
10 yrs.	136 games			

John Yarno
YARNO, JOHN
B. Dec. 17, 1954, Spokane, WA
Idaho 6'5" 251 lbs.

1977	SEA	N	10	C
1978			13	C
1979			16	C
1980			15	C
1981			11	C
1982			9	C
6 yrs.	74 games			

Tommy Yarr
YARR, THOMAS CORNELIUS
B. 1908, Dabob, WA
D. Dec. 24, 1941, Chicago, IL
Notre Dame 5'10" 205 lbs.

1933	CHIC	N	8	C, T, G

Ron Yary
YARY, ANTHONY RONALD
B. Aug. 16, 1946, Chicago, IL
Southern California 6'6" 256 lbs.

1968	MIN	N	14	OT
1969			11	OT
1970			14	OT
1971			14	OT
1972			14	OT
1973			14	OT
1974			14	OT
1975			14	OT
1976			14	OT
1977			14	OT
1978			16	OT
1979			16	OT
1980			14	OT
1981			16	OT
1982	LARM	N	8	OT
15 yrs.	207 games			

Bob Yates
YATES, ROBERT E.
B. 1939
Syracuse 6'3" 233 lbs.

1960	BOS	A		DT
1961			14	C
1962			14	C
1963			14	C
1964			12	OT
1965			14	OT
6 yrs.	68 games			

Howie Yeager
YEAGER, HOWARD LEON

Howie Yeager *continued*
B. Feb. 19, 1915, Orosi, CA
California-Santa Barbara 5'11" 173 lbs.

1941	NYG	N	10	HB

Jim Yeager
YEAGER, JAMES R. (Dutch)
B. Mar. 17, 1903
D. Dec., 1966, Cliffside Park, NJ
Lehigh 6'1" 230 lbs.

1926	BKN	N	10	T, G

Bill Yearby
YEARBY, WILLIAM M.
B. Jul. 24, 1944, Birmingham, AL
Michigan 6'3" 235 lbs.

1966	NY	A	9	TE

Jeff Yeates
YEATES, JEFFREY LEE
B. Aug. 3, 1951, Buffalo, NY
Boston College 6'3" 246 lbs.

1974	BUF	N	10	DT
1975			13	DT
1976			3	DT
1976	ATL	N	2	DT
1977			13	DT
1978			16	DT
1979			16	DT
1980			16	DE
1981			16	DE
1982			9	DE
1983			16	DE
1984			8	DE
11 yrs.	138 games			

Phil Yeboah-Kodie
YEBOAH-KODIE, PHIL ANTHONY
B. Jan. 22, 1971, Montreal, Que., Canada
Penn State 6'2" 225 lbs.

1996	IND	N	2	LB

Don Yeisley
YEISLEY, DONALD
B. Jan. 21, 1904
D. Oct., 1971, Victor, IA
Chicago 6'1" 185 lbs.

1928	CHIC	N	3	E

Billy Yelverton
YELVERTON, BILLY G.
B. 1934
Mississippi 6'4" 220 lbs.

1960	DEN	A		DE

Dick Yelvington
YELVINGTON, RICHARD, JR.
B. Jul. 27, 1928
Georgia 6'2" 232 lbs.

1952	NYG	N	7	T
1953			12	T
1954			12	T
1955			11	T
1956			12	T
1957			8	T
6 yrs.	62 games			

Garo Yepremian
YEPREMIAN, GARABED SARKIS
B. Jun. 2, 1944, Larnaca, Cyprus
none 5'8" 172 lbs.

1966	DET	N	9	K
1967			8	K
1970	MIA	N	13	K
1971			14	K

Garo Yepremian *continued*

Year	Team		Games	Pos.
1972			14	K
1973			14	K
1974			14	K
1975			14	K
1976			14	K
1977			14	K
1978			16	K
1979	NO	N	14	K
1980	TB	N	16	K
1981			3	K
14 yrs.	177 games			

Howard Yerges
YERGES, HOWARD E.
Also played as **LITTLEBOY**
B. 1896
Deceased
Ohio State 5'9" 155 lbs.

Year	Team		Games	Pos.
1920	COL	A	1	HB

Tom Yewcic
YEWCIC, THOMAS J.
B. May 9, 1932, Conemaugh, PA
Michigan State 5'11" 185 lbs.

Year	Team		Games	Pos.
1961	BOS	A	14	QB
1962			14	QB
1963			14	QB
1964			14	QB
1965			14	QB
1966			7	QB
6 yrs.	77 games			

John Yezerski
YEZERSKI, JOHN G.
B. Sep. 22, 1914
D. Jan., 1979, Boring, OR
St. Mary's (California) 6'4" 240 lbs.

Year	Team		Games	Pos.
1936	BKN	N	9	T

Dave Yohn
YOHN, DAVID
B. Oct. 10, 1937
Gettysburg 6'0" 223 lbs.

Year	Team		Games	Pos.
1962	BAL	N	4	LB
1963	NY	A	14	LB
2 yrs.	18 games			

Mack Yoho
YOHO, MACK
B. Jun. 14, 1936, Reader, WV
Miami (Ohio) 6'2" 239 lbs.

Year	Team		Games	Pos.
1960	BUF	A	14	DE
1961			14	DE
1962			14	DE
1963			14	DE
4 yrs.	42 games			

Frank Yokas
YOKAS, FRANK P.
B. Feb. 27, 1924, Rock Island, IL
None 5'11" 210 lbs.

Year	Team		Games	Pos.
1946	LA	AA	12	G
1947	BAL	AA	13	G
2 yrs.	25 games			

John Yonakor
YONAKOR, JOHN JOSEPH
B. Aug. 4, 1921, Boston, MA
Notre Dame 6'5" 222 lbs.

Year	Team		Games	Pos.
1946	CLE	AA	14	E
1947			14	E
1948			14	E
1949			12	E
1950	NYY	N	8	E
1952	WAS	N	12	E
6 yrs.	74 games			

Wally Yonamine
YONAMINE, WALLACE
B. 1924, Maui, HI
None 5'9" 180 lbs.

Year	Team		Games	Pos.
1947	SF	AA	12	B

Jim Youel
YOUEL, JAMES S.
B. Feb. 13, 1922, Vinton, IA
Iowa 6'0" 175 lbs.

Year	Team		Games	Pos.
1946	WAS	N	8	QB
1947			6	QB
1948	BOS	N	6	QB
1948	WAS	N	2	QB
3 yrs.	22 games			

Maury Youmans
YOUMANS, MAURICE E.
B. Oct. 18, 1936, Eagle Bay, NY
Syracuse 6'6" 253 lbs.

Year	Team		Games	Pos.
1960	CHI	N	8	T
1961			14	DT, DE
1962			6	DE
1964	DAL	N	14	DE
1965			14	DE
5 yrs.	56 games			

Len Younce
YOUNCE, LEONARD A.
B. Jan. 8, 1917, Dayton, OR
Oregon State 6'1" 208 lbs.

Year	Team		Games	Pos.
1941	NYG	N	11	G
1943			10	G
1944			10	G
1946			11	G
1947			12	G
1948			11	G
6 yrs.	65 games			

Adrian Young
YOUNG, MATTHEW ADRIAN
B. Jan. 31, 1946, Dublin, Ireland
Southern California 6'1" 230 lbs.

Year	Team		Games	Pos.
1968	PHI	N	10	LB
1969			13	LB
1970			14	LB
1971			2	LB
1972			1	LB
1972	DET	N	10	LB
1973	CHI	N	2	LB
6 yrs.	52 games			

Al Young
YOUNG, ALFRED
B. Aug. 24, 1949, Norway, SC
South Carolina State 6'1" 195 lbs.

Year	Team		Games	Pos.
1971	PIT	N	1	WR
1972			14	WR
2 yrs.	15 games			

Al Young
YOUNG, JOHN A.
B. Apr. 28, 1902
D. Mar. 14, 1980, Corning, CA
California 5'10" 180 lbs.

Year	Team		Games	Pos.
1926	LA	N	7	HB, FB, E

Almon Young
YOUNG, ALMON
B. Jul. 3, 1962, Eustis, FL
Bethune-Cookman 6'3" 290 lbs.

Year	Team		Games	Pos.
1987	HOU	N	3	G

Andre Young
YOUNG, ANDRE BENOISE
B. Nov. 22, 1960, West Monroe, LA

Andre Young *continued*

Louisiana Tech 6'0" 203 lbs.

Year	Team		Games	Pos.
1982	SD	N	8	S
1983			15	S
1984			13	S
3 yrs.	36 games			

Anthony Young
YOUNG, ANTHONY RICARDO
B. Oct. 8, 1963, Columbia, SC
Temple 5'11" 187 lbs.

Year	Team		Games	Pos.
1985	IND	N	13	S

Ben Young
YOUNG, BENJAMIN
B. Jan. 13, 1960, Toledo, OH
Texas-Arlington 6'4" 225 lbs.

Year	Team		Games	Pos.
1983	ATL	N	11	TE

Bill Young
YOUNG, WILLIAM A., JR.
(Bubbles)
B. May 20, 1914, North Little Rock, AR
D. Jan. 21, 1994
Alabama 6'1" 247 lbs.

Year	Team		Games	Pos.
1937	WAS	N	5	T
1938			11	G, T
1939			8	G
1940			9	G, T
1941			8	T
1942			9	T
6 yrs.	50 games			

Billy Young
YOUNG, WILLIAM G.
B. Dec. 17, 1901
D. Jul. 29, 1971, Kenton, OH
Ohio State 5'10" 210 lbs.

Year	Team		Games	Pos.
1929	GB	N	2	T

Bob Young
YOUNG, ROBERT ALLEN
B. Sep. 3, 1942, Marshall, TX
Texas/Southwest Texas State/Howard Payne 6'2" 269 lbs.

Year	Team		Games	Pos.
1966	DEN	A	11	DT
1967			5	G
1968			14	G
1969			14	G
1970	DEN	N	14	G
1971	HOU	N	14	G
1972	STL	N	14	G
1973			13	G
1974			9	G
1975			12	G
1976			14	G
1977			14	G
1978			16	G
1979			13	G
1980	HOU	N	15	G
1981	NO	N	2	G
16 yrs.	194 games			

Bryant Young
YOUNG, BRYANT COLBY
B. Jan. 27, 1972, Chicago Heights, IL
Notre Dame 6'2" 276 lbs.

Year	Team		Games	Pos.
1994	SF	N	16	DT
1995			12	DT
1996			16	DT
3 yrs.	44 games			

Buddy Young
YOUNG, CLAUDE HENRY K.
B. Jan. 5, 1926, Chicago, IL
D. Sep. 4, 1983, Dallas, TX

Buddy Young *continued*

Illinois 5'5" 173 lbs.

Year	Team		Games	Pos.
1947	NY	AA	14	HB, DB
1948			12	HB, DB
1949	B, NY	AA	12	HB
1950	NYY	N	12	HB
1951			12	HB
1952	DAL	N	12	HB
1953	BAL	N	10	HB
1954			10	HB
1955			11	HB
9 yrs.	105 games			

Charle Young
YOUNG, CHARLE EDWARD
B. Feb. 5, 1951, Fresno, CA
Southern California 6'4" 235 lbs.

Year	Team		Games	Pos.
1973	PHI	N	14	TE
1974			14	TE
1975			14	TE
1976			14	TE
1977	LA	N	14	TE
1978			16	TE
1979			15	TE
1980	SF	N	16	TE
1981			16	TE
1982			9	TE
1983	SEA	N	16	TE
1984			15	TE
1985			14	TE
13 yrs.	187 games			

Charley Young
YOUNG, CHARLES LEE
B. Oct. 13, 1952, Raleigh, NC
North Carolina State 6'1" 213 lbs.

Year	Team		Games	Pos.
1974	DAL	N	14	RB
1975			12	RB
1976			11	RB
3 yrs.	37 games			

Dave Young
YOUNG, DAVID J.
B. Feb. 9, 1959, Akron, OH
Purdue 6'5" 240 lbs.

Year	Team		Games	Pos.
1981	NYG	N	11	TE
1983	BAL	N	1	TE
1984	IND	N	13	TE
3 yrs.	25 games			

Dick Young
YOUNG, RICHARD
B. Aug. 25, 1930, Trumbull, CT
Tennessee-Chattanooga 5'11" 210 lbs.

Year	Team		Games	Pos.
1955	BAL	N	10	FB
1956			12	FB
1957	PIT	N	11	FB
3 yrs.	33 games			

Duane Young
YOUNG, CURTIS DUANE
B. May 29, 1968, Kalamazoo, MI
Michigan State 6'1" 266 lbs.

Year	Team		Games	Pos.
1991	SD	N	7	TE
1992			16	TE
1993			16	TE
1994			14	TE
1995			16	TE
5 yrs.	69 games			

Fredd Young
YOUNG, FREDD
B. Nov. 14, 1961, Dallas, TX
New Mexico State 6'1" 233 lbs.

Year	Team		Games	Pos.
1984	SEA	N	16	LB
1985			16	LB
1986			15	LB
1987			13	LB

Year	Team	Games	Pos.

Fredd Young continued

Year	Team	Games	Pos.
1988	IND N	15	LB
1989		15	LB
1990		11	LB
7 yrs.	101 games		

George Young
YOUNG, GEORGE D. (Pordy)
B. May 10, 1924, Wilkes-Barre, PA
D. Sep. 21, 1969, Chicago, IL
Baldwin-Wallace/Georgia 6'3" 214 lbs.

Year	Team	Games	Pos.
1946	CLE AA	13	E
1947		13	E
1948		14	E
1949		9	E
1950	CLE N	12	E
1951		12	E
1952		12	E
1953		12	E
8 yrs.	97 games		

Glen Young
YOUNG, GLEN
B. Oct. 11, 1960, Greenwood, MS
Mississippi State 6'2" 205 lbs.

Year	Team	Games	Pos.
1983	PHI N	16	WR
1984	CLE N	2	WR
1985		15	WR
1987		10	WR
1988		15	WR
5 yrs.	58 games		

Glen Young
YOUNG, GLEN
B. May 2, 1969, Scarborough, Ont.
Syracuse 6'3" 235 lbs.

Year	Team	Games	Pos.
1995	SD N	16	LB
1996		6	LB
2 yrs.	22 games		

Glenn Young
YOUNG, GLENN C.
B. Dec. 22, 1930, Woodstock, IL
Purdue 6'2" 205 lbs.

Year	Team	Games	Pos.
1956	GB N	4	HB

Herm Young
YOUNG, HERMAN D.
B. Mar. 21, 1906
D. Jun., 1985, Bradenton, FL
Detroit 5'11" 178 lbs.

Year	Team	Games	Pos.
1930	PRO N	3	E

James Young
YOUNG, JAMES
B. Jul. 8, 1950, Houston, TX
Texas Southern 6'2" 260 lbs.

Year	Team	Games	Pos.
1977	HOU N	13	DE
1978		16	DE
1979		11	DE
3 yrs.	40 games		

Jim Young
YOUNG, JAMES NORMAN
B. Jun. 6, 1943, Hamilton, Ont.
Queen's (Canada) 6'0" 205 lbs.

Year	Team	Games	Pos.
1965	MIN N	2	HB
1966		4	HB
2 yrs.	6 games		

Joe Young
YOUNG, JOSEPH A.
B. 1935
Arizona 6'3" 245 lbs.

Year	Team	Games	Pos.
1960	DEN A		DE
1961		6	DE
2 yrs.	6 games		

Kevin Young
YOUNG, KEVIN
B. Nov. 8, 1964
Utah State 6'5" 265 lbs.

Year	Team	Games	Pos.
1987	NO N	1	DE

Les Young
YOUNG, LESLIE
B. 1905, Austin, MN
Macalester/North Dakota 6'1" 190 lbs.

Year	Team	Games	Pos.
1927	PRO N	2	FB

Lonnie Young
YOUNG, LONNIE
B. Jul. 18, 1963, Flint, MI
Michigan State 6'1" 182 lbs.

Year	Team	Games	Pos.
1985	STL N	16	CB, S
1986		13	CB, S
1987		12	S
1988	PHX N	12	S
1989		10	S
1990		16	CB, S
1991	NYJ N	12	CB, S
1992		13	CB, S
1993		9	S, CB
1994	SD N	12	CB, S
1995	NYJ N	7	S
1996		15	S
12 yrs.	147 games		

Mike Young
YOUNG, MICHAEL DAVID
B. Feb. 21, 1962, Hanford, CA
UCLA 6'1" 185 lbs.

Year	Team	Games	Pos.
1985	LARM N	15	WR
1986		16	WR
1987		12	WR
1988		7	WR
1989	DEN N	16	WR
1990		16	WR
1991		16	WR
1992		3	WR
1993	PHI N	10	WR
1994	KC N	2	WR
10 yrs.	113 games		

Mitch Young
YOUNG, MITCHELL
B. Jul. 18, 1962, Coldwater, MS
Arkansas State 6'4" 260 lbs.

Year	Team	Games	Pos.
1987	ATL N	1	DT

Paul Young
YOUNG, PAUL
B. Dec. 28, 1908
D. Oct., 1978, Cambridge, NE
Oklahoma 6'4" 195 lbs.

Year	Team	Games	Pos.
1933	GB N	2	C

Randy Young
YOUNG, RANDALL
B. Jul. 4, 1954, Montgomery, AL
Iowa State 6'5" 250 lbs.

Year	Team	Games	Pos.
1976	TB N	8	DT

Renard Young
YOUNG, RENARD F.
B. Jul. 31, 1961, Los Angeles, CA
Nevada-Las Vegas/San Diego State 5'10" 184 lbs.

Year	Team	Games	Pos.
1987	SEA N	3	CB

Rickey Young
YOUNG, RICKEY DARNELL
B. Dec. 7, 1953, Mobile, Al
Jackson State 6'2" 195 lbs.

Year	Team	Games	Pos.
1975	SD N	14	RB

Rickey Young continued

Year	Team	Games	Pos.
1976		14	RB
1977		14	RB
1978	MIN N	16	RB
1979		16	RB
1980		16	RB
1981		16	RB
1982		9	RB
1983		16	RB
9 yrs.	131 games		

Robert Young
YOUNG, ROBERT
B. Jan. 29, 1969, Jackson, MS
Mississippi State 6'6" 275 lbs.

Year	Team	Games	Pos.
1991	LARM N	16	DT
1992		11	DT
1993		6	DE
1994		16	DE
1995	STL N	14	DE
1996	HOU N	15	DE
6 yrs.	78 games		

Rodney Young
YOUNG, RODNEY MENARD
B. Jan. 25, 1973, Grambling, LA
Louisiana State 6'1" 206 lbs.

Year	Team	Games	Pos.
1995	NYG N	10	S
1996		12	S
2 yrs.	22 games		

Roynell Young
YOUNG, ROYNELL
B. Dec. 1, 1957, New Orleans, LA
Alcorn State 6'1" 184 lbs.

Year	Team	Games	Pos.
1980	PHI N	16	CB
1981		13	CB
1982		9	CB
1983		16	CB
1984		7	CB
1985		14	CB
1986		16	CB
1987		11	CB
1988		15	CB
9 yrs.	117 games		

Russ Young
YOUNG, RUSSELL CHARLES
B. Sep. 15, 1902, Bryan, OH
D. May 13, 1984, Roseville, CA
Dayton 6'0" 190 lbs.

Year	Team	Games	Pos.
1925	DAY N	4	FB, G

Sam Young
YOUNG, LLOYD
B. May 27, 1903, Austin, MN
D. Jul., 1978, Austin, MN
Macalester/North Dakota 5'8" 192 lbs.

Year	Team	Games	Pos.
1925	PRO N	11	G, T
1926		13	G, E, T
1927		1	G
1929	MIN N	8	C, G, T
1930		2	G
5 yrs.	35 games		

Steve Young
YOUNG, STEVE
B. Oct. 11, 1961, Salt Lake City, UT
Brigham Young 6'2" 200 lbs.

Year	Team	Games	Pos.
1985	TB N	5	QB
1986		14	QB
1987	SF N	8	QB
1988		11	QB
1989		10	QB
1990		6	QB
1991		11	QB
1992		16	QB
1993		16	QB

Steve Young continued

Year	Team	Games	Pos.
1994		16	QB
1995		11	QB
1996		12	QB
12 yrs.	136 games		

Steve Young
YOUNG, STEVE
B. Jul. 18, 1953, Spokane, WA
Colorado 6'8" 271 lbs.

Year	Team	Games	Pos.
1976	TB N	13	OT
1977	MIA N	14	OT
2 yrs.	27 games		

Theo Young
YOUNG, THEO THOMAS
B. Apr. 25, 1965, Newport, AR
Arkansas 6'2" 237 lbs.

Year	Team	Games	Pos.
1987	PIT N	12	TE

Tyrone Young
YOUNG, TYRONE DONNIVE
B. Apr. 29, 1960, Ocala, FL
Florida 6'6" 190 lbs.

Year	Team	Games	Pos.
1983	NO N	16	WR
1984		16	WR
2 yrs.	32 games		

Waddy Young
YOUNG, WALTER ROLAND
B. Sep. 4, 1916, Ponca City, OK
D. Jan. 9, 1945, Tokyo, Japan
Oklahoma 6'3" 205 lbs.

Year	Team	Games	Pos.
1939	BKN N	11	E
1940		11	E
2 yrs.	22 games		

Wilbur Young
YOUNG, WILBUR EUGENE, JR.
B. Apr. 20, 1949, New York, NY
William Penn 6'6" 289 lbs.

Year	Team	Games	Pos.
1971	KC N	14	DT
1972		14	DT, DE
1973		13	DT
1974		14	DE
1975		13	DE
1976		14	DE
1977		13	DE
1978	SD N	10	DE
1979		16	DE
1980		14	DE
1981	WAS N	7	DT
1981	SD N	5	DT
1982		9	DT
12 yrs.	156 games		

Willie Young
YOUNG, WILLIAM JOSEPH
(Sugar Bear)
B. Jun. 27, 1943, Ruston, LA
Grambling State 6'0" 259 lbs.

Year	Team	Games	Pos.
1966	NYG N	14	OT
1967		14	OT
1968		14	OT
1969		14	OT
1970		13	OT
1971		14	OT
1972		14	OT
1973		14	OT
1974		12	OT
1975		12	OT
10 yrs.	135 games		

Willie Young
YOUNG, WILLIE
B. Nov. 12, 1947, Jefferson, MS
Alcorn State 6'4" 270 lbs.

Year	Team	Games	Pos.
1971	BUF N	14	OT

Year	Team	Games	Pos.

Willie Young continued

Year	Team		Games	Pos.
1972			1	OT
1973	MIA	N	1	OT
3 yrs.	16 games			

George Youngblood
YOUNG, GEORGE ALTON
B. Jan. 4, 1945, Los Angeles, CA
Los Angeles State 6'3" 204 lbs.

Year	Team		Games	Pos.
1966	LA	N	14	DB
1967	CLE	N	11	DB
1967	NO		12	DB
1968			4	DB
1969	CHI	N	14	S
4 yrs.	55 games			

Jack Youngblood
YOUNGBLOOD, HERBERT JACKSON, III
B. Jan. 26, 1950, Monticello, FL
Florida 6'4" 248 lbs.

Year	Team		Games	Pos.
1971	LA	N	14	DE
1972			14	DE
1973			14	DE
1974			14	DE
1975			14	DE
1976			14	DE
1977			14	DE
1978			16	DE
1979			16	DE
1980			16	DE
1981			16	DE
1982	LARM	N	9	DE
1983			16	DE
1984			15	DE
14 yrs.	202 games			

Jim Youngblood
YOUNGBLOOD, JIMMY LEE
B. Feb. 23, 1950, Union, SC
Tennessee Tech 6'3" 237 lbs.

Year	Team		Games	Pos.
1973	LA	N	14	LB
1974			14	LB
1975			14	LB
1976			14	LB
1977			14	LB
1978			16	LB
1979			16	LB
1980			15	LB
1981			16	LB
1982	LARM	N	7	LB
1983			7	LB
1984			5	LB
1984	WAS	N	4	LB
12 yrs.	156 games			

Sid Youngelman
YOUNGELMAN, SIDNEY
B. Dec. 1, 1931, Newark, NJ
D. Jan. 12, 1991, Lake Hiawatha, NJ
Alabama 6'3" 257 lbs.

Year	Team		Games	Pos.
1955	SF	N	8	T
1956	PHI	N	12	T
1957			12	T
1958			5	T
1959	CLE	N	12	T
1960	NY	A		DT
1961			14	DT
1962	BUF	A	14	DT
1963			14	DT
9 yrs.	91 games			

Tank Younger
YOUNGER, PAUL
B. Jun. 25, 1928, Grambling, LA
Grambling State 6'3" 225 lbs.

Year	Team		Games	Pos.
1949	LA	N	11	HB
1950			12	HB
1951			12	FB

Year	Team	Games	Pos.

Tank Younger continued

Year	Team		Games	Pos.
1952			12	HB, FB
1953			12	FB
1954			8	FB
1955			8	FB
1956			12	FB
1957			12	FB
1958	PIT	N	12	FB
10 yrs.	112 games			

Frank Youngfleish
YOUNGFLEISH, FRANK (Yank)
B. May 7, 1896, Pottsville, PA
Deceased
Villanova 5'9" 190 lbs.

Year	Team		Games	Pos.
1926	POT	N	9	C, G
1927			6	C, G
2 yrs.	15 games			

Swede Youngstrom
YOUNGSTROM, ADOLPH F.
B. May 24, 1897, Waltham, MA
D. Aug. 5, 1968, Lexington, MA
Dartmouth 6'1" 187 lbs.

Year	Team		Games	Pos.
1920	BUF	A	6	G
1921			12	G
1921	CAN	A	1	G
1922	BUF	N	10	G, E
1923			12	G
1924			11	G, T, C
1925			9	G
1925	CLE	N	1	G
1926	FRA	N	14	T, G
1927			14	T, G
8 yrs.	90 games			

Mike Yount
YOUNT, MYRON EDWARD
B. Apr. 18, 1894, Indiana
D. Jan., 1964
Franklin (Indiana) 6'1" 205 lbs.

Year	Team		Games	Pos.
1921	MUN	A	2	T

Frank Youso
YOUSO, FRANK MICHAEL
B. Jul. 5, 1936, International Falls, MN
Minnesota 6'4" 257 lbs.

Year	Team		Games	Pos.
1958	NYG	N	12	T
1959			12	T
1960			12	T
1961	MIN	N	14	OT
1962			13	OT
1963	OAK	A	4	OT
1964			14	OT
1965			11	OT
8 yrs.	92 games			

John Yovicsin
YOVICSIN, JOHN M.
B. Oct. 17, 1918
D. Sep. 13, 1989, Hyannis, MA
Gettysburg 6'3" 195 lbs.

Year	Team		Games	Pos.
1944	PHI	N	1	E

Walt Yowarsky
YOWARSKY, WALTER
B. May 10, 1928, Cleveland, OH
Kentucky 6'2" 234 lbs.

Year	Team		Games	Pos.
1951	WAS	N	11	E
1954			11	E
1955	NYG	N	10	E
1955	DET	N	2	E
1956	NYG	N	11	E
1957			11	E
1958	SF	N	8	E
6 yrs.	64 games			

Year	Team	Games	Pos.

John Yurchey
YURCHEY, JOHN HENRY
B. Nov. 12, 1917, Bridgeville, PA
Duquesne 5'11" 188 lbs.

Year	Team		Games	Pos.
1940	PIT	N	1	B

Steve Zabel
ZABEL, STEVEN GREGORY
B. Mar. 20, 1948, Minneapolis, MN
Oklahoma 6'4" 233 lbs.

Year	Team		Games	Pos.
1970	PHI	N	14	TE
1971			14	LB, TE
1972			7	LB
1973			11	LB
1974			14	LB
1975	NE	N	13	LB
1976			14	LB
1977			11	LB
1978			11	LB
1979	BAL	N	15	LB
10 yrs.	124 games			

Kenny Zachary
ZACHARY, KENNY R.
B. Nov. 19, 1963, Sapulpa, OK
Oklahoma State 6'0" 222 lbs.

Year	Team		Games	Pos.
1987	SD	N	3	RB

Tony Zackery
ZACKERY, ANTHONY EUGENE
B. Nov. 20, 1966, Seattle, WA
Washington 6'2" 195 lbs.

Year	Team		Games	Pos.
1989	ATL	N	1	S
1990	NE	N	2	S
1991			16	S
3 yrs.	19 games			

Frank Zadworney
ZADWORNEY, FRANK S.
B. 1917
Ohio State 6'2" 202 lbs.

Year	Team		Games	Pos.
1940	BKN	N	3	B

Paul Zaeske
ZAESKE, PAUL A.
B. Dec. 4, 1945, Sioux City, IA
North Park 6'2" 200 lbs.

Year	Team		Games	Pos.
1969	HOU	A	6	WR
1970	HOU	N	5	WR
2 yrs.	11 games			

Bert Zagers
ZAGERS, ALBERT ALDON
B. Jan. 30, 1933, Fremont, MI
D. Sep. 2, 1992, Traverse City, MI
Michigan State 5'10" 185 lbs.

Year	Team		Games	Pos.
1955	WAS	N	11	HB
1957			11	HB
1958			10	HB
3 yrs.	32 games			

Ernie Zalejski
ZALEJSKI, ERNEST R.
B. Nov. 23, 1925, South Bend, IN
Notre Dame 6'0" 185 lbs.

Year	Team		Games	Pos.
1950	BAL	N	12	HB

John Zamberlin
ZAMBERLIN, JOHN
B. Feb. 13, 1956, Tacoma, WA
Pacific Lutheran 6'2" 231 lbs.

Year	Team		Games	Pos.
1979	NE	N	16	LB
1980			16	LB
1981			16	LB
1982			8	LB
1983	KC	N	14	LB

Year	Team	Games	Pos.

John Zamberlin continued

Year	Team		Games	Pos.
1984			8	LB
6 yrs.	78 games			

Carl Zander
ZANDER, CARL AUGUST, JR.
B. Mar. 23, 1963, Mendham, NJ
Tennessee 6'2" 235 lbs.

Year	Team		Games	Pos.
1985	CIN	N	16	LB
1986			16	LB
1987			12	LB
1988			16	LB
1989			16	LB
1990			16	LB
1991			14	LB
7 yrs.	106 games			

Emanuel Zanders
ZANDERS, EMANUEL
B. Jul. 31, 1951, Demopolis, AL
Jackson State 6'1" 251 lbs.

Year	Team		Games	Pos.
1974	NO	N	10	G
1975			14	G
1976			14	G
1977			14	G
1978			3	G
1979			16	G
1980			16	G
1981	CHI	N	12	G
8 yrs.	99 games			

Mike Zandofsky
ZANDOFSKY, MICHAEL LESLIE
B. Nov. 30, 1965, Corvallis, OR
Washington 6'2" 298 lbs.

Year	Team		Games	Pos.
1989	PHX	N	15	G, OT
1990	SD	N	13	G
1991			10	G
1992			15	C, G
1993			16	G
1994	ATL	N	16	G
1995			12	G
1996			14	G
8 yrs.	111 games			

Silvio Zaninelli
ZANINELLI, SILVIO DAVID
B. Dec. 9, 1913, Reading, PA
D. Jan., 1979, Weirton, WV
Duquesne 5'10" 207 lbs.

Year	Team		Games	Pos.
1934	PIT	N	11	QB, FB, HB
1935			11	FB
1936			12	QB, FB
1937			10	QB
4 yrs.	44 games			

Bill Zapalac
ZAPALAC, WILLIAM FRANK, JR.
B. Sep. 1, 1948, Bellville, TX
Texas 6'4" 225 lbs.

Year	Team		Games	Pos.
1971	NYJ	N	14	LB, DE
1972			6	LB, DE
1973			13	DE, LB
3 yrs.	33 games			

Joe Zapustas
ZAPUSTAS, JOSEPH JOHN
B. Jul. 25, 1907, Boston, MA
Fordham 6'0" 198 lbs.

Year	Team		Games	Pos.
1933	NYG	N	2	E

Gust Zarnas
ZARNAS, GUSTAVE C.
B. 1915
Ohio State 5'10" 220 lbs.

Year	Team		Games	Pos.
1938	CHIB	N	10	G
1939	BKN	N	4	G

Year	Team	Games	Pos.

Gust Zarnas *continued*

Year	Team		Games	Pos.
1939	**GB**	N	4	G
1940			9	G

3 yrs. 27 games

Carroll Zaruba
ZARUBA, CARROLL
B. 1934
Nebraska 5'9" 210 lbs.

Year	Team		Games	Pos.
1960	**DAL**	A		DB

Rob Zatechka
ZATECHKA, ROBERT
B. Dec. 1, 1971, Lansing, MI
Nebraska 6'4" 307 lbs.

Year	Team		Games	Pos.
1995	**NYG**	N	16	G
1996			15	G

2 yrs. 31 games

Roger Zatkoff
ZATKOFF, ROGER
B. Mar. 25, 1931, Hamtramck, MI
Michigan 6'2" 216 lbs.

Year	Team		Games	Pos.
1953	**GB**	N	12	T
1954			12	T
1955			12	T
1956			12	T
1957	**DET**	N	12	LB
1958			12	LB

6 yrs. 72 games

Godfrey Zaunbrechner
ZAUNBRECHNER, GODFREY WINSTON
B. Dec. 17, 1946, Crowley, LA
Louisiana State 6'4" 238 lbs.

Year	Team		Games	Pos.
1971	**MIN**	N	5	C
1972			7	C
1973			6	C

3 yrs. 18 games

Jerry Zawadzkas
ZAWADZKAS, GERALD
B. Jan. 3, 1946, Torrington, CT
Columbia 6'4" 220 lbs.

Year	Team		Games	Pos.
1967	**DET**	N	2	TE

Dave Zawatson
ZAWATSON, DAVID F.
B. Apr. 13, 1966, Cleveland, OH
California 6'4" 275 lbs.

Year	Team		Games	Pos.
1989	**CHI**	N	4	OT
1990	**NYJ**	N	16	G, OT
1991	**MIA**	N	2	OT

3 yrs. 22 games

Rich Zecher
ZECHER, RICHARD FREDERICK
B. Oct. 14, 1943, Alameda, CA
Utah State 6'2" 240 lbs.

Year	Team		Games	Pos.
1965	**OAK**	A	14	OT
1966	**MIA**	A	14	DT
1967			7	DT
1967	**BUF**	A	5	DT

3 yrs. 40 games

Henry Zehrer
ZEHRER, HENRY CHRISTIAN
B. Dec. 20, 1905, New Britain, CT
D. Mar. 16, 1955, Putnam, CT
None 175 lbs.

Year	Team		Games	Pos.
1926	**HAR**	N	6	FB, HB

Eric Zeier
ZEIER, ERIC ROYCE

Eric Zeier *continued*
B. Sep. 6, 1972, Marietta, GA
Georgia 6'0" 205 lbs.

Year	Team		Games	Pos.
1995	**CLE**	N	7	QB
1996	**BAL**	N	1	QB

2 yrs. 8 games

Dusty Zeigler
ZEIGLER, CURTIS DUSTIN
B. Sep. 27, 1973, Rincon, GA
Notre Dame 6'5" 298 lbs.

Year	Team		Games	Pos.
1996	**BUF**	N	2	G

Mike Zele
ZELE, MICHAEL ROBERT
B. Jul. 3, 1956, Cleveland, OH
Kent State 6'3" 236 lbs.

Year	Team		Games	Pos.
1979	**ATL**	N	13	DT
1980			11	DT
1981			14	DT
1982			9	NT
1983			4	NT

5 yrs. 51 games

Connie Zelencik
ZELENCIK, CONRAD JAMES
B. Apr. 3, 1955, Calumet City, IL
Purdue 6'4" 245 lbs.

Year	Team		Games	Pos.
1977	**BUF**	N	14	C

Frank Zelencik
ZELENCIK, FRANK
B. Jan. 17, 1915
D. Mar., 1976, Newark, AR
Oglethorpe 6'1" 220 lbs.

Year	Team		Games	Pos.
1939	**CHIC**	N	9	T

Ray Zellars
ZELLARS, RAYMOND MARK
B. Mar. 25, 1973, Pittsburgh, PA
Notre Dame 5'11" 221 lbs.

Year	Team		Games	Pos.
1995	**NO**	N	12	RB
1996			9	FB

2 yrs. 21 games

Jerry Zeller
ZELLER, GERALD T.
B. Jun. 3, 1898, Ohio
D. Nov., 1968, Columbus, OH
Purdue/Illinois 5'11" 170 lbs.

Year	Team		Games	Pos.
1921	**EVA**	A	4	HB, QB

Joe Zeller
ZELLER, JOSEPH THOMAS
B. May 2, 1908, East Chicago, IN
D. Sep., 1983, Chicago, IL
Indiana 6'1" 203 lbs.

Year	Team		Games	Pos.
1932	**GB**	N	14	G, T
1933	**CHIB**	N	11	G, E
1934			11	G
1935			11	G
1936			11	G
1937			11	G, T
1938			10	G, E

7 yrs. 79 games

Bob Zeman
ZEMAN, EDWARD ROBERT
B. Feb. 22, 1937, Wheaton, IL
Wisconsin 6'1" 202 lbs.

Year	Team		Games	Pos.
1960	**LA**	A	12	DB
1961	**SD**	A	14	DB
1962	**DEN**	A	14	DB
1963			14	DB
1965	**SD**	A	14	DB
1966			14	DB

6 yrs. 82 games

Ed Zeman
ZEMAN, ED
B. Sep. 25, 1963
Fort Lewis (Colorado) 6'1" 195 lbs.

Year	Team		Games	Pos.
1987	**LARM**	N	3	CB, S

Joaquin Zendejas
ZENDEJAS, JOAQUIN (CAMPOS)
B. Jan. 14, 1960, Curimeo Michoacan, Mexico
La Verne 5'11" 176 lbs.

Year	Team		Games	Pos.
1983	**NE**	N	2	K

Luis Zendejas
ZENDEJAS, LUIS FERNANDO
B. Oct. 22, 1961, Mexico City, Mexico
Arizona State 5'9" 190 lbs.

Year	Team		Games	Pos.
1987	**DAL**	N	2	K
1988			2	K
1988	**PHI**	N	12	K
1989			8	K
1989	**DAL**	N	7	K

3 yrs. 31 games

Max Zendejas
ZENDEJAS, MAXIMILIAN JAVIER
B. Sep. 2, 1963, Curimeo Michoacan, Mexico
Arizona 5'11" 184 lbs.

Year	Team		Games	Pos.
1986	**WAS**	N	9	K
1987	**GB**	N	10	K
1988			8	K

3 yrs. 27 games

Tony Zendejas
ZENDEJAS, TONY
B. May 15, 1960, Curimeo Michoacan, Mexico
Nevada-Reno 5'8" 165 lbs.

Year	Team		Games	Pos.
1985	**HOU**	N	14	K
1986			15	K
1987			13	K
1988			16	K
1989			16	K
1990			7	K
1991	**LARM**	N	16	K
1992			16	K
1993			16	K
1994			16	K
1995	**ATL**	N	1	K
1995	**SF**	N	3	K

11 yrs. 149 games

Coleman Zeno
ZENO, COLEMAN
B. Nov. 18, 1946, New Orleans, LA
Grambling State 6'4" 210 lbs.

Year	Team		Games	Pos.
1971	**NYG**	N	2	WR

Joe Zeno
ZENO, JOSEPH
B. Jun. 14, 1919, Brooklyn, NY
D. Jan. 8, 1992, Sacramento, CA
Holy Cross 5'10" 234 lbs.

Year	Team		Games	Pos.
1942	**WAS**	N	7	G
1943			8	T, G
1944			10	T
1947	**BOS**	N	2	G

4 yrs. 27 games

Lance Zeno
ZENO, LANCE MICHAEL
B. Apr. 15, 1967, Hollywood, CA
UCLA 6'4" 279 lbs.

Year	Team		Games	Pos.
1992	**CLE**	N	3	C
1993			2	C
1993	**GB**	N	5	C

2 yrs. 10 games

Mike Zentic
ZENTIC, MIKE
B. Nov. 22, 1963
Oklahoma State 6'3" 255 lbs.

Year	Team		Games	Pos.
1987	**DAL**	N	3	C

Harold Zerbe
ZERBE, HAROLD
B. 1901
Deceased
None 165 lbs.

Year	Team		Games	Pos.
1926	**CAN**	N	1	E

Jeff Zgonina
ZGONINA, JEFFREY MARC
B. May 24, 1970, Lake Grove, IL
Purdue 6'1" 284 lbs.

Year	Team		Games	Pos.
1993	**PIT**	N	5	DE, DT
1994			16	DT
1995	**CAR**	N	2	DT
1996	**ATL**	N	8	DT

4 yrs. 31 games

Frank Ziegler
ZIEGLER, FRANK R.
B. Oct. 1, 1923, College Park, GA
Georgia Tech 5'11" 175 lbs.

Year	Team		Games	Pos.
1949	**PHI**	N	10	HB
1950			12	HB
1951			12	HB
1952			11	HB
1953			12	HB

5 yrs. 57 games

Paul Ziegler
ZIEGLER, PAUL K.
B. Sep., 1898, Pleasant Township, OH
None 5'10" 185 lbs.

Year	Team		Games	Pos.
1922	**COL**	N	5	HB, G

Dave Ziff
ZIFF, DAVID
B. Jan. 18, 1902, Massachusetts
D. Oct. 17, 1977, New York, NY
Syracuse/Carson-Newman 6'0" 195 lbs.

Year	Team		Games	Pos.
1925	**ROC**	N	4	E
1926	**BKN**	N	7	E

2 yrs. 11 games

Jack Zilly
ZILLY, JOHN JYNUS
B. Nov. 11, 1921, Southington, CT
Notre Dame 6'2" 212 lbs.

Year	Team		Games	Pos.
1947	**LA**	N	12	E
1948			12	E
1949			12	E
1950			12	E
1951			4	E
1952	**PHI**	N	12	E

6 yrs. 64 games

Geno Zimmerlink
ZIMMERLINK, GENO
B. Mar. 23, 1963
Virginia 6'3" 222 lbs.

Year	Team		Games	Pos.
1987	**ATL**	N	3	TE

Corl Zimmerman
ZIMMERMAN, CORL
B. Feb. 22, 1899
Mount Union 6'0" 185 lbs.

Year	Team		Games	Pos.
1927	**DAY**	N	4	G, T
1928			4	G
1929			4	G

3 yrs. 12 games

Year	Team	Games	Pos.

Don Zimmerman
ZIMMERMAN, DONALD (Float)
B. Nov. 22, 1949, Monroe, LA
Arkansas-Pine Bluff/Northeastern La.
6'3" 195 lbs.

Year	Team		Games	Pos.
1973	PHI	N	14	WR
1974			14	WR
1975			10	WR
1976			14	WR
1976	GB	N	2	WR
4 yrs.	54 games			

Gary Zimmerman
ZIMMERMAN, GARY WAYNE
B. Dec. 13, 1961, Fullerton, CA
Oregon 6'6" 284 lbs.

Year	Team		Games	Pos.
1986	MIN	N	16	OT
1987			12	OT
1988			16	OT
1989			16	OT
1990			16	OT
1991			16	OT
1992			16	OT
1993	DEN	N	16	OT
1994			16	OT
1995			16	OT
1996			14	OT
11 yrs.	170 games			

Giff Zimmerman
ZIMMERMAN, GIFFORD GUY
B. Aug. 25, 1900, Akron, OH
D. Nov. 27, 1968, Akron, OH
Syracuse 5'10" 180 lbs.

Year	Team		Games	Pos.
1924	AKR	N	2	HB
1925	CAN	N	6	HB
2 yrs.	8 games			

Jeff Zimmerman
ZIMMERMAN, JEFFREY ALAN
B. Jan. 10, 1965, Enid, OK
Florida 6'3" 316 lbs.

Year	Team		Games	Pos.
1987	DAL	N	11	OT
1988			1	OT
1989			16	G
1990			6	G
4 yrs.	34 games			

Roy Zimmerman
ZIMMERMAN, HENRY LEROY, JR.
B. Feb. 20, 1918, Tonganoxie, KS
D. Mar. 27, 1992, Oxford, IA
San Jose State 6'2" 201 lbs.

Year	Team		Games	Pos.
1940	WAS	N	6	HB
1941			9	HB, FB
1942			7	HB
1943	P, P		10	QB
1944	PHI	N	10	QB
1945			10	QB
1946			11	QB
1947	DET	N	12	QB
1948	BOS	N	9	QB
9 yrs.	84 games			

Bob Zimny
ZIMNY, ROBERT JOHN
B. Oct. 11, 1921, Chicago, IL
Indiana 6'1" 233 lbs.

Year	Team		Games	Pos.
1945	CHIC	N	10	T
1946			11	T
1947			7	T
1948			12	T
1949			12	T
5 yrs.	52 games			

Walt Zirinsky
ZIRINSKY, WALTER J.
B. 1921
Lafayette 5'11" 187 lbs.

Year	Team		Games	Pos.
1945	CLE	N	5	HB

Vince Zizak
ZIZAK, VINCENT AUGUSTINE
B. Aug. 8, 1908, Camden, NJ
D. Aug., 1973, Upper Darby, PA
Villanova 5'8" 208 lbs.

Year	Team		Games	Pos.
1934	PHI	N	7	T, G
1935			4	G, T
1936			10	G
1937			2	G
4 yrs.	23 games			

Mickey Zofko
ZOFKO, MICKEY JOSEPH
B. Jun. 8, 1949, Melbourne, FL
Auburn 6'3" 195 lbs.

Year	Team		Games	Pos.
1971	DET	N	11	RB
1972			14	RB
1973			8	RB
1974			4	RB
1974	NYG	N	7	RB
4 yrs.	44 games			

Jon Zogg
ZOGG, JON F.
B. Nov. 19, 1960, San Jose, CA
San Jose State 6'4" 290 lbs.

Year	Team		Games	Pos.
1987	LARI	N	1	G

Clyde Zoia
ZOIA, CLYDE
B. May, 1896, Illinois
Notre Dame 5'7" 175 lbs.

Year	Team		Games	Pos.
1920	CHIC	A	6	G
1921			8	G
1922	CHIC	N	8	G
1923			11	G
4 yrs.	33 games			

Scott Zolak
ZOLAK, SCOTT DAVID
B. Dec. 13, 1967, Pittsburgh, PA
Maryland 6'5" 222 lbs.

Year	Team		Games	Pos.
1992	NE	N	6	QB
1993			3	QB
1994			16	QB
1995			16	QB
1996			3	QB
5 yrs.	44 games			

Dick Zoll
ZOLL, RICHARD M.
B. Dec. 10, 1913, Green Bay, WI
Indiana 5'11" 218 lbs.

Year	Team		Games	Pos.
1937	CLE	N	11	G, T
1938			10	T
2 yrs.	21 games			

Marty Zoll
ZOLL, MARTIN A.
B. Nov. 12, 1900, Howard, WI
D. Oct., 1967, Green Bay, WI
None 5'9" 185 lbs.

Year	Team		Games	Pos.
1921	GB	A	1	G
1922	GB	N	1	G
2 yrs.	2 games			

Eric Zomalt
ZOMALT, ERIC LEE
B. Aug. 9, 1972, Los Angeles, CA
California 5'11" 197 lbs.

Year	Team		Games	Pos.
1994	PHI	N	12	S
1995			15	S
1996			3	S
1996	NYJ	N	10	S
3 yrs.	40 games			

Joe Zombek
ZOMBEK, JOSEPH
B. Dec. 24, 1932
Pittsburgh 6'1" 195 lbs.

Year	Team		Games	Pos.
1954	PIT	N	8	E

Lou Zontini
ZONTINI, LOUIS ROGERS
B. Aug. 30, 1917, Alliance, OH
D. Aug. 6, 1986, Cleveland, OH
Notre Dame 5'9" 189 lbs.

Year	Team		Games	Pos.
1940	CHIC	N	8	B, T
1941			7	B
1944	CLE	N	9	B
1946	BUF	AA	14	FB
4 yrs.	38 games			

John Zook
ZOOK, JOHN
B. Sep. 24, 1947, Garden City, KS
Kansas 6'5" 248 lbs.

Year	Team		Games	Pos.
1969	ATL	N	14	DE
1970			14	DE
1971			14	DE
1972			14	DE
1973			14	DE
1974			14	DE
1975			14	DE
1976	STL	N	13	DE
1977			12	DE
1978			16	DE
1979			5	DE
11 yrs.	144 games			

Frank Zoppetti
ZOPPETTI, FRANK
B. Nov. 16, 1916
D. Aug., 1985, Burgettstown, PA
Duquesne 5'11" 185 lbs.

Year	Team		Games	Pos.
1941	PIT	N	4	B

Mike Zordich
ZORDICH, MICHAEL EDWARD
B. Oct. 12, 1963, Youngstown, OH
Penn State 5'11" 207 lbs.

Year	Team		Games	Pos.
1987	NYJ	N	10	S
1988			16	S
1989	PHX	N	16	S
1990			16	CB, S
1991			16	S
1992			16	S
1993			16	S
1994	PHI	N	16	S
1995			15	S
1996			16	S
10 yrs.	153 games			

Chris Zorich
ZORICH, CHRISTOPHER ROBERT
B. Mar. 13, 1969, Chicago, IL
Notre Dame 6'1" 273 lbs.

Year	Team		Games	Pos.
1991	CHI	N	12	DT

Chris Zorich continued

Year	Team		Games	Pos.
1992			16	DT
1993			16	DT
1994			16	DT
1995			16	DT
5 yrs.	76 games			

George Zorich
ZORICH, GEORGE
B. Nov. 24, 1915, Wakefield, MI
D. Oct. 14, 1967, Rensselaer, IN
Northwestern 6'2" 213 lbs.

Year	Team		Games	Pos.
1944	CHIB	N	10	G
1945			8	G
1946			1	G
1946	MIA	AA	6	G
1947	BAL	AA	11	G
4 yrs.	36 games			

Jim Zorn
ZORN, JAMES ARTHUR (Zig Zag)
B. May 10, 1953, Whittier, CA
California Poly (Pomona) 6'2" 200 lbs.

Year	Team		Games	Pos.
1976	SEA	N	14	QB
1977			10	QB
1978			16	QB
1979			16	QB
1980			16	QB
1981			13	QB
1982			9	QB
1983			16	QB
1984			16	QB
1985	GB	N	13	QB
1987	TB	N	1	QB
11 yrs.	140 games			

Vic Zucco
ZUCCO, VICTOR A.
B. Sep. 4, 1935, Renton, PA
Wayne State (Michigan)/Michigan State 6'0" 187 lbs.

Year	Team		Games	Pos.
1957	CHIB	N	12	HB
1958			12	HB
1959			2	HB
1960	CHI	N	12	HB
4 yrs.	38 games			

Dave Zuidmulder
ZUIDMULDER, DAVID
B. Feb. 4, 1906, New Franken, WI
D. Jun. 8, 1978, Green Bay, WI
St. Ambrose/Georgetown (DC) 5'9" 175 lbs.

Year	Team		Games	Pos.
1930	GB	N	4	HB
1931			1	HB
2 yrs.	5 games			

Charlie Zunker
ZUNKER, CHARLES
B. Aug. 23, 1908
D. Jun., 1963
Southwest Texas State 6'4" 227 lbs.

Year	Team		Games	Pos.
1934	C-S	N	3	T

Al Zupek
ZUPEK, ALBERT E.
B. Jan. 12, 1922, Racine, WI
D. Jun. 16, 1980, Burlington, IA
Lawrence 6'1" 205 lbs.

Year	Team		Games	Pos.
1946	GB	N	3	QB

Merle Zuver
ZUVER, MERLE
B. 1906
Nebraska 6'1" 198 lbs.

Year	Team		Games	Pos.
1930	GB	N	10	G, C

Year Team	Games Pos.	Year Team	Games Pos.	Year Team	Games Pos.	Year Team	Games Pos.

Tony Zuzzio
ZUZZIO, ANTHONY JOSEPH
B. Aug. 5, 1916, Irvington, NJ
Muhlenberg 5'11" 210 lbs.

Year	Team		Games	Pos.
1942	DET	N	2	G

Jim Zyntell
ZYNTELL, IGNATIUS JAMES
B. Apr. 27, 1910, Boston, MA
D. Nov. 13, 1992, Brighton, MA
Holy Cross 6'1" 200 lbs.

Year	Team		Games	Pos.
1933	NYG	N	1	G
1933	PHI	N	8	G
1934			7	G
1935			7	G
3 yrs.	23 games			

PART EIGHT

Scoring Register
Rushing Register
Passing Register
Receiving Register
Interceptions Register
Punting Register

Introduction To Statistical Registers

The NFL first compiled statistics in 1932 for rushing, passing, receiving, and punting. Through 1934 we have only a few leaders, plus more complete figures for the New York Giants and the Chicago Bears for 1933 and '34, culled from newspapers and programs. The accuracy of these stats is sometimes questionable, too.

For example, take the rushing leader of 1932. Press releases at the end of the season listed Dutch Clark of Portsmouth as the leader, with 581 yards, followed by Cliff Battles of Boston, with 576. A few years later, though, when the league started including lists of annual leaders in its guides, Bob Campiglio of Staten Island turned up as the 1932 leader, with 504 yards. Decades passed before Battles was returned to the top spot. And what about Clark? Today the generally accepted total for him is 461 yards; but it's certainly not a sure thing.

What we've tried to do with this book is to bring together all the final statistics that are available. Most of these are the official statistics of each league. In several cases there are unofficial statistics reconstructed and compiled especially for this book.

A Brief History of Professional Football Statistics

By the time the National Football League was formed in 1920, the average game summary that appeared in newspapers across the country had evolved into a more or less standard form that owed much to baseball box scores. The game starters and substitutions were listed, followed by the scoring-by-quarters totals for the teams. Below that came the number of touchdowns scored by each player (in whatever order the writer desired that day, and not showing how it was scored—rushing, passing, etc.), number of extra points made (very rarely how many attempts), number of field goals made (again, rarely how many attempts), and how many safeties (usually who was tackled for the safety but not who made the tackle). Last came a list of the officiating crew!

Some papers, usually in the NFL's smaller cities (such as Canton, Rock Island, Pottsville, and Green Bay) occasionally printed some team totals like first downs, penalty yards, and pass completions—or play-by-play accounts of varying completeness.

Then came Ned Irish. Irish, who's more famous for his involvement with basketball's New York Knicks (which earned him a spot in the Basketball Hall of Fame), was hired by the NFL to head the league's Press Bureau. One of the first tasks he set out was for the league to start compiling statistics, something no organization had ever attempted in football. (The NCAA didn't start compiling stats until 1936.)

We really don't know how successful Irish's first efforts were. The NFL didn't publish a record manual until 1935, and few newspapers printed the league's press releases containing the stats; what they did print was usually just the top five or ten in selected categories. For instance, until research for this book began, we thought only scoring, rushing, passing, and receiving statistics were kept for individual players in 1932. That was

before we discovered a couple of year-end reports listing Dick Nesbitt of the Bears as the leading punter, with a 42.4-yard average.

Even in 1935, when Spalding published the NFL's first record manual and rule book, only rudimentary team statistics and top tens in scoring, rushing, passing, and receiving were printed. It wasn't until the 1937 manual that complete lists were published for these four categories. Field goal attempts made their appearance for the 1938 season, punting reappeared with numbers for the 1939 season, punt returns and interceptions debuted in 1941, kickoff returns in 1942, fumbles in 1945, and sacks in 1982.

Interceptions were actually compiled for the first time in 1940, but for some reason they weren't included in the year-end stats or the following year's Spalding Guide. As a result, all we have for that season are the three league leaders, the Giants' team leaders, and complete figures for the Redskins and the Bears. Likewise, kickoff returns were compiled in 1941, but only the top five returners were released at the end of the season.

The records of the NFL were still somewhat erratic until 1961, when the league (at the insistence of newly appointed commissioner Pete Rozelle) hired the Elias Sports Bureau to take over the task of compiling the official statistics for the league.

The statistics for the American Football League were the charge of the league's publicity director. This changed after the announcement of the league's merger with the NFL, and Elias took over the AFL's statistics for the league's three final seasons, 1967 to '69.

As for team statistics, many stats have come and gone—and sometimes come back—over the years. Also, the statistics have changed and expanded with additional categories.

The following is a listing of which individual statistics were officially recorded by the league.

Scoring

	NFL	AAFC	AFL
Touchdowns (Total)	*1936–1996	1946–1949	1960–1969
Touchdowns Rushing	∞1967–1996	1946–1949	1960–1969
Touchdowns Pass Receiving	1941–1996	1946–1949	1960–1969
Touchdowns Other	∞1967–1996	∞	1964–1969
Field Goals Made	†1935–1996	1946–1949	1960–1969
Field Goals Attempted	†1939–1996	1946–1949	1960–1969
Extra Points Made	*1936–1996	1946–1949	1960–1969
Extra Points Attempted	††1938–1996	1946–1949	–1969
Two–Point Extra Points Made	1994–1996	n/a	1960–1969
Safeties	1946–1996		–1969
Points Scored	*1936–1996	1946–1949	1960–1969

Rushing

	NFL	AAFC	AFL
Attempts	*1936–1996	1946–1949	1960–1969
Net Yards Rushing	*1936–1996	1946–1949	1960–1969
Long Gain	1941–1996	§§	1961–1969
Touchdowns	∞1944–1996	1946–1949	1960–1969

Passing

Attempts	*1936–1996	1946–1949	1960–1969
Compeletions	*1936–1996	1946–1949	1960–1969
Gross Yards Passing	*1936–1996	1946–1949	1960–1969
Touchdowns	1939/1941–1996	1946–1949	1960–1969
Interceptions	*1936–1996	1946–1949	1960–1969
Long Gain	1941–1996	§§	1965–1969
Times Sacked	1969–1996	##	1969
Yards Lost	1969–1996	##	1969
Rating Points	1973–1996		

Receiving

Receptions	*1936–1996	1946–1949	1960–1969
Yards	*1936–1996	1946–1949	1960–1969
Long Gain	1941–1996	§§	1961–1969
Touchdowns	1937–1996	1946–1949	1960–1969

Interceptions

Interceptions	#1941–1996	1946–1949	1960–1969
Yards	#1941–1996	1946–1949	1960–1969
Long Gain	1941–1996	§§	1961–1969
Touchdowns	1941–1996	1946–1949	1960–1969

Punting §

Net Punts	1939–1996	1946–1949	1960–1969
Gross Yards	1967–1996	1947–1949	1960–1969
Long Punt	1939–1996	§§	1961–1969
Total Punts	1939–1996	1946–1949	1967–1969
Punts Blocked	1941–1996	1946–1949	1967–1969
Touchbacks	1976–1996		
Inside 20	1976–1996		

*	League leaders available for 1932–1935.
†	League leaders available for 1932–1934.
§	League leader (average only) available for 1932; gross average available 1939–1966; rounded off to whole yard 1939–1940.
∞	Touchdowns rushing and by other means (returns and recoveries) were combined as touchdown running through 1943. The AAFC also recorded touchdowns in this manner.
#	League leaders available for 1940.
**	League leaders available for 1941.
††	Individuals who didn't score but attempted an extra point not listed until 1969.
§§	League printed list of longest plays with a minimum yardage required to be included in each listing.
##	League recorded sacks as rushing plays.
n/a	not applicable

SCORING REGISTER

Year	Team		TD	1XP	2XP	FG	FGA	SAF	Pts

George Blanda

Year	Team		TD	1XP	2XP	FG	FGA	SAF	Pts
1949	**CHIB**	**N**	1	0		7	15	0	27
1950			0	0		6	15	0	18
1951			0	26		6	17	0	44
1952			1	30		6	25	0	54
1953			0	27		7	20	0	48
1954			0	23		8	16	0	47
1955			2	37		11	16	0	82
1956			0	**45**		12	**28**	0	81
1957			1	23		14	**26**	0	71
1958			0	36		11	23	0	69
1960	**HOU**	**A**	4	46	0	15	**34**	0	115
1961			0	**64**	0	16	26	0	112
1962			0	**48**	0	11	26	0	81
1963			0	39	0	9	22	0	66
1964			0	37	0	13	29	0	76
1965			0	28	0	11	21	0	61
1966			0	39	0	16	30	0	87
1967	**OAK**	**A**	0	**56**	0	20	30	0	**116**
1968			0	**54**	0	21	34	0	117
1969			0	**45**	0	20	37	0	105
1970	**OAK**	**N**	0	36		16	29	0	84
1971			0	41		15	22	0	86
1972			0	**44**		17	26	0	95
1973			0	31		23	33	0	100
1974			0	**44**		11	17	0	77
1975			0	44		13	21	0	83
Career			9	**943**	0	335	**638**	0	**2002**
Playoffs			0	**49**	0	**22**	**39**	0	115

Key

Team — The team (and league) the player played for.
TD — Touchdowns
1XP — Points after touchdown
2XP — 2 point conversions
FG — Field goals
FGA — Field goals attempted
SAF — Safeties
PTS — Total number of points scored

In addition, boldface numbers indicate that the player led the league in that category that season. For example, Blanda's 116 points scored in 1967 are boldfaced, meaning that he led the league in scoring that year. Also, boldfaced career and playoff stats indicate all-time highs. Blanda's 2002 points scored indicate that he is the all-time career leader in this category.

Fay Abbott

Year	Team		TD	1XP	2XP	FG	FGA	SAF	Pts
1921	DAY	A	1	0		0		0	6
1925	DAY	N	0	0		1		0	3
1928			0	0		1		0	3
Career			1	0		2		0	12

Vince Abbott

Year	Team		TD	1XP	2XP	FG	FGA	SAF	Pts
1987	SD	N	0	22		13	22	0	61
1988			0	15		8	12	0	39
Career			0	37		21	34	0	100

Karim Abdul-Jabbar

Year	Team		TD	1XP	2XP	FG	FGA	SAF	Pts
1996	MIA	N	11	0	0	0	0	0	66

Walter Abercrombie

Year	Team		TD	1XP	2XP	FG	FGA	SAF	Pts
1982	PIT	N	2	0		0	0	0	12
1983			7	0		0	0	0	42
1984			1	0		0	0	0	6
1985			9	0		0	0	0	54
1986			8	0		0	0	0	48
1987			2	0		0	0	0	12
Career			29	0		0	0	0	174

Danny Abramowicz

Year	Team		TD	1XP	2XP	FG	FGA	SAF	Pts
1967	NO	N	6	0		0	0	0	36
1968			7	0		0	0	0	42
1969			7	0		0	0	0	42
1970			5	0		0	0	0	30
1971			5	0		0	0	0	30
1972			7	0		0	0	0	42
1973	SF	N	1	0		0	0	0	6
1974			1	0		0	0	0	6
Career			39	0		0	0	0	234

Nate Abrams

Year	Team		TD	1XP	2XP	FG	FGA	SAF	Pts
1921	GB	A	1	0		0		0	6

George Abramson

Year	Team		TD	1XP	2XP	FG	FGA	SAF	Pts
1925	GB	N	0	2		2		0	8

Dick Abrell

Year	Team		TD	1XP	2XP	FG	FGA	SAF	Pts
1920	DAY	A	1	2		0		0	8

Dick Absher

Year	Team		TD	1XP	2XP	FG	FGA	SAF	Pts
1967	WAS	N	0	4		0	1	0	4

Ron Acks

Year	Team		TD	1XP	2XP	FG	FGA	SAF	Pts
1969	ATL	N	1	0		0	0	0	6

Mike Adamle

Year	Team		TD	1XP	2XP	FG	FGA	SAF	Pts
1971	KC	N	1	0		0	0	0	6
1972			1	0		0	0	0	6
1974	NYJ	N	2	0		0	0	0	12
1975	CHI	N	1	0		0	0	0	6
1976			1	0		0	0	1	8
Career			6	0		0	0	1	38

Tony Adamle

Year	Team		TD	1XP	2XP	FG	FGA	SAF	Pts
1947	CLE	AA	1	0		0	0	0	6
1948			1	0		0	0	0	6
Career			2	0		0	0	0	12

Chet Adams

Year	Team		TD	1XP	2XP	FG	FGA	SAF	Pts
1939	CLE	N	0	5		0	0	0	5
1940			0	7		1	5	0	10
1941			0	13		1	2	0	16
1942			0	14		3	6	0	23
1943	GB	N	0	0		1	6	0	3
1946	CLE	AA	2	5		0	0	0	17
1947			0	1		1	1	0	4
1949	BUF	AA	0	32		4	11	0	44
1950	NYY	N	0	45		2	9	0	51
Career			2	122		13	40	0	173
Playoffs			0	3		0	1	0	3

Curtis Adams

Year	Team		TD	1XP	2XP	FG	FGA	SAF	Pts
1985	SD	N	1	0		0	0	0	6
1986			4	0		0	0	0	24
1987			1	0		0	0	0	6
1988			1	0		0	0	0	6
Career			7	0		0	0	0	42

David Adams

Year	Team		TD	1XP	2XP	FG	FGA	SAF	Pts
1987	DAL	N	1	0		0	0	0	6

George Adams

Year	Team		TD	1XP	2XP	FG	FGA	SAF	Pts
1985	NYG	N	4	0		0	0	0	24
1987			2	0		0	0	0	12
1990	NE	N	1	0		0	0	0	6
Career			7	0		0	0	0	42

John Adams

Year	Team		TD	1XP	2XP	FG	FGA	SAF	Pts
1961	CHI	N	1	0		0	0	0	6
1962			3	0		0	0	0	18
Career			4	0		0	0	0	24

O'Neal Adams

Year	Team		TD	1XP	2XP	FG	FGA	SAF	Pts
1942	NYG	N	4	0		0	0	0	24
1943			2	0		0	0	0	12
1944			1	0		0	0	0	6
1946	BKN	AA	2	0		0	0	0	12
Career			9	0		0	0	0	54

Sam Adams

Year	Team		TD	1XP	2XP	FG	FGA	SAF	Pts
1995	SEA	N	0	0	0	0	0	1	2

Stefon Adams

Year	Team		TD	1XP	2XP	FG	FGA	SAF	Pts
1989	LARI	N	0	0		0	0	1	2

Willis Adams

Year	Team		TD	1XP	2XP	FG	FGA	SAF	Pts
1983	CLE	N	2	0		0	0	0	12

Herb Adderley

Year	Team		TD	1XP	2XP	FG	FGA	SAF	Pts
1962	GB	N	2	0		0	0	0	12
1963			1	0		0	0	0	6
1965			3	0		0	0	0	18
1966			1	0		0	0	0	6
1967			1	0		0	0	0	6
1969			1	0		0	0	0	6
Career			9	0		0	0	0	54
Playoffs			1	0		0	0	0	6

Tom Addison

Year	Team		TD	1XP	2XP	FG	FGA	SAF	Pts
1962	BOS	A	1	0	0	0	0	0	6

Mark Adickes

Year	Team		TD	1XP	2XP	FG	FGA	SAF	Pts
1987	KC	N	1	0		0	0	0	6

Bob Adkins

Year	Team		TD	1XP	2XP	FG	FGA	SAF	Pts
1940	GB	N	2	1		0	1	0	13
1941			0	3		0	0	0	3
Career			2	4		0	1	0	16

Ben Agajanian

Year	Team		TD	1XP	2XP	FG	FGA	SAF	Pts
1945	PIT	N	0	1		4	4	0	13
1947	LA	AA	0	39		**15**	**24**	0	84
1948			0	31		5	15	0	46
1949	NYG	N	0	35		8	13	0	59
1953	LA	N	0	36		10	24	0	66
1954	NYG	N	0	35		13	**25**	0	74
1955			0	32		10	15	0	62
1956			0	23		5	13	0	38
1957			0	32		10	18	0	62
1960	LA	A	0	46	0	13	24	0	85
1961	DAL-GB	N	0	15		4	11	0	27
1962	OAK	A	0	10	0	5	14	0	25
1964	SD	A	0	8	0	2	4	0	14
Career			0	343	0	104	204	0	655
Playoffs			0	6	0	5	6	0	21

Sam Agee

Year	Team		TD	1XP	2XP	FG	FGA	SAF	Pts
1938	CHIC	N	1	0		0		0	6
1939			1	0		0	0	0	6
Career			2	0		0	0	0	12

Tommie Agee

Year	Team		TD	1XP	2XP	FG	FGA	SAF	Pts
1990	DAL	N	1	0		0	0	0	6
1991			1	0		0	0	0	6
Career			2	0		0	0	0	12

Ray Agnew

Year	Team		TD	1XP	2XP	FG	FGA	SAF	Pts
1996	NYG	N	1	0	0	0	0	0	6

Louie Aguiar

Year	Team		TD	1XP	2XP	FG	FGA	SAF	Pts
1991	NYJ	N	0	0		1	2	0	3

Joe Aguirre

Year	Team		TD	1XP	2XP	FG	FGA	SAF	Pts
1941	WAS	N	2	8		2	5	0	26
1943			7	6		0	2	0	48

Joe Aguirre *continued*

Year	Team		TD	1XP	2XP	FG	FGA	SAF	Pts
1944			4	15		4	6	0	51
1945			0	23		**7**	**13**	0	44
1946	LA	AA	2	31		4	11	0	55
1947			4	0		0	0	0	24
1948			9	2		0	0	0	56
1949			1	0		0	0	0	6
Career			29	85		17	37	0	310
Playoffs			1	3		0	2	0	9

Dave Ahrens

Year	Team		TD	1XP	2XP	FG	FGA	SAF	Pts
1981	STL	N	1	0		0	0	0	6

Carl Aikens

Year	Team		TD	1XP	2XP	FG	FGA	SAF	Pts
1987	LARI	N	3	0		0	0	0	18

Troy Aikman

Year	Team		TD	1XP	2XP	FG	FGA	SAF	Pts
1990	DAL	N	1	0		0	0	0	6
1991			1	0		0	0	0	6
1992			1	0		0	0	0	6
1994			1	0	0	0	0	0	6
1995			1	0	0	0	0	0	6
1996			1	0	0	0	0	0	6
Career			6	0	0	0	0	0	36
Playoffs			1	0	0	0	0	0	6

Al Akins

Year	Team		TD	1XP	2XP	FG	FGA	SAF	Pts
1946	CLE	AA	1	0		0	0	0	6
1947	BKN	AA	2	0		0	0	0	12
Career			3	0		0	0	0	18

Frank Akins

Year	Team		TD	1XP	2XP	FG	FGA	SAF	Pts
1944	WAS	N	1	0		0	0	0	6
1945			6	0		0	0	0	36
Career			7	0		0	0	0	42

Mike Akiu

Year	Team		TD	1XP	2XP	FG	FGA	SAF	Pts
1985	HOU	N	1	0		0	0	0	6

Frankie Albert

Year	Team		TD	1XP	2XP	FG	FGA	SAF	Pts
1946	SF	AA	4	0		0	0	0	24
1947			5	0		0	0	0	30
1948			8	1		0	0	0	49
1949			3	0		0	0	0	18
1950	SF	N	3	0		0	0	0	18
1951			3	0		0	0	0	18
1952			1	0		0	0	0	6
Career			27	1		0	0	0	163

Bill Albright

Year	Team		TD	1XP	2XP	FG	FGA	SAF	Pts
1953	NYG	N	1	0		0	0	0	6

Ki Aldrich

Year	Team		TD	1XP	2XP	FG	FGA	SAF	Pts
1941	WAS	N	0	4		1	3	0	7
1942			1	0		0	0	0	6
1946			1	0		0	0	0	6
Career			2	4		1	3	0	19

Bennie Aldridge

Year	Team		TD	1XP	2XP	FG	FGA	SAF	Pts
1952	SF	N	1	0		0	0	0	6

Lionel Aldridge

Year	Team		TD	1XP	2XP	FG	FGA	SAF	Pts
1964	GB	N	1	0		0	0	0	6

Charles Alexander

Year	Team		TD	1XP	2XP	FG	FGA	SAF	Pts
1979	CIN	N	1	0		0	0	0	6
1980			2	0		0	0	0	12
1981			3	0		0	0	0	18
1982			2	0		0	0	0	12
1983			3	0		0	0	0	18
1984			2	0		0	0	0	12
1985			2	0		0	0	0	12
Career			15	0		0	0	0	90
Playoffs			2	0		0	0	0	12

Derrick Alexander

Year	Team		TD	1XP	2XP	FG	FGA	SAF	Pts
1994	CLE	N	2	0	1	0	0	0	14
1995			1	0	0	0	0	0	6
1996	BAL	N	9	0	1	0	0	0	56
Career			12	0	2	0	0	0	76

Jeff Alexander

Year	Team		TD	1XP	2XP	FG	FGA	SAF	Pts
1989	DEN	N	2	0		0	0	0	12

Joe Alexander

Year	Team	Lg	TD	1XP	2XP	FG	FGA	SAF	Pts
1925	NYG	N	1	0		0		0	6
1926			2	0		0		0	12
1927			1	0		0		0	6
Career			4	0		0		0	24

John Alexander

Year	Team	Lg	TD	1XP	2XP	FG	FGA	SAF	Pts
1926	NYG	N	1	0		0		0	6

Kermit Alexander

Year	Team	Lg	TD	1XP	2XP	FG	FGA	SAF	Pts
1964	SF	N	1	0		0	0	0	6
1966			2	0		0	0	0	12
1968			1	0		0	0	0	6
1970	LA	N	1	0		0	0	0	6
1971			1	0		0	0	0	6
Career			6	0		0	0	0	36

Mike Alexander

Year	Team	Lg	TD	1XP	2XP	FG	FGA	SAF	Pts
1989	LARI	N	1	0		0	0	0	6

Ray Alexander

Year	Team	Lg	TD	1XP	2XP	FG	FGA	SAF	Pts
1984	DEN	N	1	0		0	0	0	6
1988	DAL	N	6	0		0	0	0	36
Career			7	0		0	0	0	42

Vincent Alexander

Year	Team	Lg	TD	1XP	2XP	FG	FGA	SAF	Pts
1987	NO	N	1	0		0	0	0	6

Willie Alexander

Year	Team	Lg	TD	1XP	2XP	FG	FGA	SAF	Pts
1977	HOU	N	1	0		0	0	0	6

Julie Alfonse

Year	Team	Lg	TD	1XP	2XP	FG	FGA	SAF	Pts
1938	CLE	N	2	0		0	0	0	12

Bruce Alford

Year	Team	Lg	TD	1XP	2XP	FG	FGA	SAF	Pts
1947	NY	AA	7	0		0	0	0	42
1948			3	0		0	0	0	18
1949	B-NY	AA	1	0		0	0	0	6
1950	NYY	N	1	0		0	0	0	6
Career			12	0		0	0	0	72

Bruce Alford

Year	Team	Lg	TD	1XP	2XP	FG	FGA	SAF	Pts
1967	WAS	N	0	3		0	2	0	3
1968	BUF	A	0	15	0	14	24	0	57
1969			0	23	0	17	26	0	74
Career			0	41	0	31	52	0	134

Gene Alford

Year	Team	Lg	TD	1XP	2XP	FG	FGA	SAF	Pts
1931	POR	N	2	0		0		0	12
1933			1	0		0		0	6
1934	C-S	N	0	3		1		0	6
Career			3	3		1		0	24

Raul Allegre

Year	Team	Lg	TD	1XP	2XP	FG	FGA	SAF	Pts
1983	BAL	N	0	22		30	35	0	112
1984	IND	N	0	14		11	18	0	47
1985			0	36		16	26	0	84
1986	NYG	N	0	33		24	32	0	105
1987			0	25		17	27	0	76
1988			0	14		10	11	0	44
1989			0	23		20	26	0	83
1990			0	9		4	5	0	21
1991	NYG-NYJ	N	0	7		5	6	0	22
Career			0	183		137	186	0	594
Playoffs			0	15		5	5	0	30

Anthony Allen

Year	Team	Lg	TD	1XP	2XP	FG	FGA	SAF	Pts
1985	ATL	N	2	0		0	0	0	12
1986			2	0		0	0	0	12
1987	WAS	N	3	0		0	0	0	18
1988			1	0		0	0	0	6
Career			8	0		0	0	0	48

Carl Allen

Year	Team	Lg	TD	1XP	2XP	FG	FGA	SAF	Pts
1948	BKN	AA	1	0		0	0	0	6

Carl Allen

Year	Team	Lg	TD	1XP	2XP	FG	FGA	SAF	Pts
1980	STL	N	1	0		0	0	0	6

Chuck Allen

Year	Team	Lg	TD	1XP	2XP	FG	FGA	SAF	Pts
1961	SD	A	1	0	0	0	0	0	6
1963			1	0	0	0	0	0	6
Career			2	0	0	0	0	0	12

Don Allen

Year	Team	Lg	TD	1XP	2XP	FG	FGA	SAF	Pts
1960	DEN	A	1	0	0	0	0	0	6

Duane Allen

Year	Team	Lg	TD	1XP	2XP	FG	FGA	SAF	Pts
1961	LA	N	2	0		0	0	0	12
1962			2	0		0	0	0	12
1964			1	0		0	0	0	6
Career			5	0		0	0	0	30

Eric Allen

Year	Team	Lg	TD	1XP	2XP	FG	FGA	SAF	Pts
1990	PHI	N	1	0		0	0	0	6
1993			4	0		0	0	0	24
Career			5	0		0	0	0	30
Playoffs			1	0		0	0	0	6

Gary Allen

Year	Team	Lg	TD	1XP	2XP	FG	FGA	SAF	Pts
1982	HOU	N	1	0		0	0	0	6
1983	DAL	N	1	0		0	0	0	6
Career			2	0		0	0	0	12

Jerry Allen

Year	Team	Lg	TD	1XP	2XP	FG	FGA	SAF	Pts
1967	WAS	N	4	0		0	0	0	24
1968			5	0		0	0	0	30
Career			9	0		0	0	0	54

Jimmy Allen

Year	Team	Lg	TD	1XP	2XP	FG	FGA	SAF	Pts
1978	DET	N	1	0		0	0	0	6

Marcus Allen

Year	Team	Lg	TD	1XP	2XP	FG	FGA	SAF	Pts
1982	LARI	N	**14**	0		0	0	0	**84**
1983			12	0		0	0	0	72
1984			**18**	0		0	0	0	108
1985			14	0		0	0	0	84
1986			7	0		0	0	0	42
1987			5	0		0	0	0	30
1988			8	0		0	0	0	48
1989			2	0		0	0	0	12
1990			13	0		0	0	0	78
1991			2	0		0	0	0	12
1992			3	0		0	0	0	18
1993	KC	N	15	0		0	0	0	90
1994			7	0	1	0	0	0	44
1995			5	0	0	0	0	0	30
1996			9	0	0	0	0	0	54
Career			134	0	1	0	0	0	806
Playoffs			13	0	0	0	0	0	78

Marvin Allen

Year	Team	Lg	TD	1XP	2XP	FG	FGA	SAF	Pts
1989	NE	N	1	0		0	0	0	6
1990			1	0		0	0	0	6
Career			2	0		0	0	0	12

Nate Allen

Year	Team	Lg	TD	1XP	2XP	FG	FGA	SAF	Pts
1975	SF	N	1	0		0	0	0	6
1976	MIN	N	1	0		0	0	0	6
Career			2	0		0	0	0	12

Terry Allen

Year	Team	Lg	TD	1XP	2XP	FG	FGA	SAF	Pts
1991	MIN	N	3	0		0	0	0	18
1992			15	0		0	0	0	90
1994			8	0	1	0	0	0	50
1995	WAS	N	11	0	0	0	0	0	66
1996			**21**	0	0	0	0	0	126
Career			58	0	1	0	0	0	350
Playoffs			1	0	0	0	0	0	6

Jim Allison

Year	Team	Lg	TD	1XP	2XP	FG	FGA	SAF	Pts
1966	SD	A	2	0	0	0	0	0	12

Neely Allison

Year	Team	Lg	TD	1XP	2XP	FG	FGA	SAF	Pts
1926	BUF	N	1	0		0		0	6

Lyneal Alston

Year	Team	Lg	TD	1XP	2XP	FG	FGA	SAF	Pts
1987	PIT	N	2	0		0	0	0	12

Mack Alston

Year	Team	Lg	TD	1XP	2XP	FG	FGA	SAF	Pts
1973	HOU	N	4	0		0	0	0	24
1974			3	0		0	0	0	18
1975			4	0		0	0	0	24
1976			1	0		0	0	0	6
1978	BAL	N	2	0		0	0	0	12
1979			1	0		0	0	0	6
Career			15	0		0	0	0	90

Mike Alstott

Year	Team	Lg	TD	1XP	2XP	FG	FGA	SAF	Pts
1996	TB	N	6	0	0	0	0	0	36

Wilson Alvarez

Year	Team	Lg	TD	1XP	2XP	FG	FGA	SAF	Pts
1981	SEA	N	0	14		3	7	0	23

Lance Alworth

Year	Team	Lg	TD	1XP	2XP	FG	FGA	SAF	Pts
1962	SD	A	3	0	0	0	0	0	18
1963			11	0	0	0	0	0	66
1964			**15**	0	0	0	0	0	90
1965			**14**	0	0	0	0	0	84
1966			**13**	0	0	0	0	0	78
1967			9	0	0	0	0	0	54
1968			10	0	1	0	0	0	62
1969			4	0	0	0	0	0	24
1970	SD	N	4	0		0	0	0	24
1971	DAL	N	2	0		0	0	0	12
1972			2	0		0	0	0	12
Career			87	0	1	0	0	0	524
Playoffs			2	0	0	0	0	0	12

Lyle Alzado

Year	Team	Lg	TD	1XP	2XP	FG	FGA	SAF	Pts
1978	DEN	N	0	0		0	0	1	2
1983	LARI	N	0	0		0	0	1	2
1985			1	0		0	0	1	8
Career			1	0		0	0	3	12

Ashley Ambrose

Year	Team	Lg	TD	1XP	2XP	FG	FGA	SAF	Pts
1996	CIN	N	1	0	0	0	0	0	6

Alan Ameche

Year	Team	Lg	TD	1XP	2XP	FG	FGA	SAF	Pts
1955	BAL	N	**9**	0		0	0	0	54
1956			8	0		0	0	0	48
1957			7	0		0	0	0	42
1958			9	0		0	0	0	54
1959			8	0		0	0	0	48
1960			3	0		0	0	0	18
Career			44	0		0	0	0	264
Playoffs			2	0		0	0	0	12

George Amundson

Year	Team	Lg	TD	1XP	2XP	FG	FGA	SAF	Pts
1974	HOU	N	5	0		0	0	0	30

Kimble Anders

Year	Team	Lg	TD	1XP	2XP	FG	FGA	SAF	Pts
1993	KC	N	1	0		0	0	0	6
1994			3	0	0	0	0	0	18
1995			3	0	0	0	0	0	18
1996			4	0	0	0	0	0	24
Career			11	0	0	0	0	0	66
Playoffs			1	0	0	0	0	0	6

Morten Andersen

Year	Team	Lg	TD	1XP	2XP	FG	FGA	SAF	Pts
1982	NO	N	0	6		2	5	0	12
1983			0	37		18	24	0	91
1984			0	34		20	27	0	94
1985			0	27		31	35	0	120
1986			0	30		26	30	0	108
1987			0	37		**28**	**36**	0	121
1988			0	32		26	36	0	110
1989			0	44		20	29	0	104
1990			0	29		21	27	0	92
1991			0	38		25	32	0	113
1992			0	33		29	34	0	120
1993			0	33		28	35	0	117
1994			0	32	0	28	**39**	0	116
1995	ATL	N	0	29	0	31	37	0	122
1996			0	31	0	22	29	0	97
Career			0	472	0	355	455	0	1537
Playoffs			0	7	0	9	11	0	34

Alfred Anderson

Year	Team	Lg	TD	1XP	2XP	FG	FGA	SAF	Pts
1979	PIT	N	1	0		0	0	0	6
1984	MIN	N	3	0		0	0	0	18
1985			5	0		0	0	0	30
1986			4	0		0	0	0	24
1987			2	0		0	0	0	12
1988			8	0		0	0	0	48
1989			2	0		0	0	0	12
1990			2	0		0	0	0	12
1991			1	0		0	0	0	6
Career			28	0		0	0	0	168
Playoffs			2	0		0	0	0	12

Bill Anderson

Year	Team	Lg	TD	1XP	2XP	FG	FGA	SAF	Pts
1958	**WAS**	**N**	2	0		0	0	0	12
1959			6	0		0	0	0	36
1960			3	0		0	0	0	18
1962			2	0		0	0	0	12
1963			1	0		0	0	0	6
1965	**GB**	**N**	1	0		0	0	0	6
Career			15	0		0	0	0	90

Bobby Anderson

Year	Team	Lg	TD	1XP	2XP	FG	FGA	SAF	Pts
1970	**DEN**	**N**	4	0		0	0	0	24
1971			4	0		0	0	0	24
1972			2	0		0	0	0	12
1973			1	0		0	0	0	6
Career			11	0		0	0	0	66

Brad Anderson

Year	Team	Lg	TD	1XP	2XP	FG	FGA	SAF	Pts
1984	**CHI**	**N**	1	0		0	0	0	6

Chet Anderson

Year	Team	Lg	TD	1XP	2XP	FG	FGA	SAF	Pts
1967	**PIT**	**N**	2	0		0	0	0	12

Cliff Anderson

Year	Team	Lg	TD	1XP	2XP	FG	FGA	SAF	Pts
1952	**CHIC**	**N**	2	0		0	0	0	12

Dick Anderson

Year	Team	Lg	TD	1XP	2XP	FG	FGA	SAF	Pts
1967	**NO**	**N**	0	0		0	0	1	2

Dick Anderson

Year	Team	Lg	TD	1XP	2XP	FG	FGA	SAF	Pts
1968	**MIA**	**A**	1	0	0	0	0	0	6
1972	**MIA**	**N**	1	0		0	0	0	6
1973			2	0		0	0	0	12
Career			4	0	0	0	0	0	24
Playoffs			1	0	0	0	0	0	6

Donny Anderson

Year	Team	Lg	TD	1XP	2XP	FG	FGA	SAF	Pts
1966	**GB**	**N**	3	0		0	0	0	18
1967			9	0		0	0	0	54
1968			6	0		0	0	0	36
1969			2	0		0	0	0	12
1970			5	0		0	0	0	30
1971			6	0		0	0	0	36
1972	**STL**	**N**	6	0		0	0	0	36
1973			13	0		0	0	0	78
1974			6	0		0	0	0	36
Career			56	0		0	0	0	336
Playoffs			2	0		0	0	0	12

Eddie Anderson

Year	Team	Lg	TD	1XP	2XP	FG	FGA	SAF	Pts
1923	**CHIC**	**N**	1	0		0		0	6
1925			1	0		0		0	6
Career			2	0		0			12

Eddie Anderson

Year	Team	Lg	TD	1XP	2XP	FG	FGA	SAF	Pts
1989	**LARI**	**N**	2	0		0	0	0	12
1992			1	0		0	0	0	6
Career			3	0		0	0	0	18

Ezz Anderson

Year	Team	Lg	TD	1XP	2XP	FG	FGA	SAF	Pts
1947	**LA**	**AA**	1	0		0	0	0	6

Flipper Anderson

Year	Team	Lg	TD	1XP	2XP	FG	FGA	SAF	Pts
1989	**LARM**	**N**	5	0		0	0	0	30
1990			4	0		0	0	0	24
1991			1	0		0	0	0	6
1992			7	0		0	0	0	42
1993			4	0		0	0	0	24
1994			5	0	0	0	0	0	30
1995	**IND**	**N**	2	0	0	0	0	0	12
Career			28	0	0	0	0	0	168
Playoffs			2	0	0	0	0	0	12

Gary Anderson

Year	Team	Lg	TD	1XP	2XP	FG	FGA	SAF	Pts
1985	**SD**	**N**	7	0		0	0	0	42
1986			9	0		0	0	0	54
1987			5	0		0	0	0	30
1988			3	0		0	0	0	18
1990	**TB**	**N**	5	0		0	0	0	30
1991			1	0		0	0	0	6
1992			1	0		0	0	0	6
1993			1	0		0	0	0	6
Career			32	0		0	0	0	192

Gary Anderson

Year	Team	Lg	TD	1XP	2XP	FG	FGA	SAF	Pts
1982	**PIT**	**N**	0	22		10	12	0	52
1983			0	38		27	31	0	119
1984			0	45		24	32	0	117
1985			0	40		**33**	**42**	0	139
1986			0	32		21	32	0	95
1987			0	21		22	27	0	87
1988			0	34		28	36	0	118
1989			0	28		21	30	0	91
1990			0	32		20	25	0	92
1991			0	31		23	33	0	100
1992			0	29		28	36	0	113
1993			0	32		28	30	0	116
1994			0	32	0	24	29	0	104
1995	**PHI**	**N**	0	32	0	22	30	0	98
1996			0	40	0	25	29	0	115
Career			0	488	0	356	454	0	1556
Playoffs			0	30	0	19	25	0	87

Jamal Anderson

Year	Team	Lg	TD	1XP	2XP	FG	FGA	SAF	Pts
1995	**ATL**	**N**	1	0	0	0	0	0	6
1996			6	0	0	0	0	0	36
Career			7	0	0	0	0	0	42

Jesse Anderson

Year	Team	Lg	TD	1XP	2XP	FG	FGA	SAF	Pts
1991	**TB**	**N**	2	0		0	0	0	12

John Anderson

Year	Team	Lg	TD	1XP	2XP	FG	FGA	SAF	Pts
1979	**GB**	**N**	0	1		1	1	0	4
1983			1	0		0	0	0	6
Career			1	1		1	1	0	10

Ken Anderson

Year	Team	Lg	TD	1XP	2XP	FG	FGA	SAF	Pts
1971	**CIN**	**N**	1	0		0	0	0	6
1972			3	0		0	0	0	18
1974			2	0		0	0	0	12
1975			2	0		0	0	0	12
1976			1	0		0	0	0	6
1977			2	0		0	0	0	12
1978			1	0		0	0	0	6
1979			2	0		0	0	0	12
1981			1	0		0	0	0	6
1982			4	0		0	0	0	24
1983			1	0		0	0	0	6
Career			20	0		0	0	0	120
Playoffs			1	0		0	0	0	6

Kim Anderson

Year	Team	Lg	TD	1XP	2XP	FG	FGA	SAF	Pts
1983	**BAL**	**N**	1	0		0	0	0	6

Larry Anderson

Year	Team	Lg	TD	1XP	2XP	FG	FGA	SAF	Pts
1978	**PIT**	**N**	1	0		0	0	0	6
1983	**BAL**	**N**	1	0		0	0	0	6
Career			2	0		0	0	0	12

Marcus Anderson

Year	Team	Lg	TD	1XP	2XP	FG	FGA	SAF	Pts
1981	**CHI**	**N**	2	0		0	0	0	12

Max Anderson

Year	Team	Lg	TD	1XP	2XP	FG	FGA	SAF	Pts
1968	**BUF**	**A**	3	0	0	0	0	0	18
1969			1	0	0	0	0	0	6
Career			4	0	0	0	0	0	24

Neal Anderson

Year	Team	Lg	TD	1XP	2XP	FG	FGA	SAF	Pts
1986	**CHI**	**N**	1	0		0	0	0	6
1987			6	0		0	0	0	36
1988			12	0		0	0	0	72
1989			15	0		0	0	0	90
1990			13	0		0	0	0	78
1991			9	0		0	0	0	54
1992			11	0		0	0	0	66
1993			4	0		0	0	0	24
Career			71	0		0	0	0	426
Playoffs			1	0		0	0	0	6

Ockie Anderson

Year	Team	Lg	TD	1XP	2XP	FG	FGA	SAF	Pts
1920	**BUF**	**A**	2	1		0		0	13
1921			**7**	0		0		0	42
1922	**BUF**	**N**	1	0		0		0	6
Career			10	1		0		0	61

O.J. Anderson

Year	Team	Lg	TD	1XP	2XP	FG	FGA	SAF	Pts
1979	**STL**	**N**	10	0		0	0	0	60
1980			9	0		0	0	0	54

O.J. Anderson *continued*

Year	Team	Lg	TD	1XP	2XP	FG	FGA	SAF	Pts
1981			9	0		0	0	0	54
1982			3	0		0	0	0	18
1983			6	0		0	0	0	36
1984			8	0		0	0	0	48
1985			4	0		0	0	0	24
1986	**STL-NYG**	**N**	3	0		0	0	0	18
1988	**NYG**	**N**	8	0		0	0	0	48
1989			14	0		0	0	0	84
1990			11	0		0	0	0	66
1991			1	0		0	0	0	6
Career			86	0		0	0	0	516
Playoffs			3	0		0	0	0	18

Ralph Anderson

Year	Team	Lg	TD	1XP	2XP	FG	FGA	SAF	Pts
1958	**CHIB**	**N**	1	0		0	0	0	6
1960	**LA**	**A**	5	0	0	0	0	0	30
Career			6	0	0	0	0	0	36

Ralph Anderson

Year	Team	Lg	TD	1XP	2XP	FG	FGA	SAF	Pts
1972	**PIT**	**N**	0	0		0	0	1	2

Richie Anderson

Year	Team	Lg	TD	1XP	2XP	FG	FGA	SAF	Pts
1994	**NYJ**	**N**	2	0	0	0	0	0	12
1996			1	0	0	0	0	0	6
Career			3	0	0	0	0	0	18

Stevie Anderson

Year	Team	Lg	TD	1XP	2XP	FG	FGA	SAF	Pts
1995	**ARI**	**N**	1	0	2	0	0	0	10

Taz Anderson

Year	Team	Lg	TD	1XP	2XP	FG	FGA	SAF	Pts
1961	**STL**	**N**	3	0		0	0	0	18
1962			3	0		0	0	0	18
1966	**ATL**	**N**	3	0		0	0	0	18
1967			1	0		0	0	0	6
Career			10	0		0	0	0	60

Billy Andrews

Year	Team	Lg	TD	1XP	2XP	FG	FGA	SAF	Pts
1970	**CLE**	**N**	1	0		0	0	0	6

John Andrews

Year	Team	Lg	TD	1XP	2XP	FG	FGA	SAF	Pts
1973	**BAL**	**N**	1	0		0	0	0	6

Roy Andrews

Year	Team	Lg	TD	1XP	2XP	FG	FGA	SAF	Pts
1924	**KC**	**N**	0	1		1		0	4
1925			0	1		1		0	4
1926			0	1		0		0	1
Career			0	3		2		0	9

William Andrews

Year	Team	Lg	TD	1XP	2XP	FG	FGA	SAF	Pts
1979	**ATL**	**N**	5	0		0	0	0	30
1980			5	0		0	0	0	30
1981			12	0		0	0	0	72
1982			7	0		0	0	0	42
1983			11	0		0	0	0	66
1986			1	0		0	0	0	6
Career			41	0		0	0	0	246
Playoffs			1	0		0	0	0	6

George Andrie

Year	Team	Lg	TD	1XP	2XP	FG	FGA	SAF	Pts
1965	**DAL**	**N**	1	0		0	0	0	6
1966			1	0		0	0	0	6
1969			0	0		0	0	1	2
Career			2	0		0	0	1	14
Playoffs			1	0		0	0	0	6

Teddy Andrulewicz

Year	Team	Lg	TD	1XP	2XP	FG	FGA	SAF	Pts
1930	**NEW**	**N**	1	0		0		0	6

Elmer Angsman

Year	Team	Lg	TD	1XP	2XP	FG	FGA	SAF	Pts
1946	**CHIC**	**N**	2	0		0	0	0	12
1947			8	0		0	0	0	48
1948			9	0		0	0	0	54
1949			6	0		0	0	0	36
1950			2	0		0	0	0	12
1951			4	0		0	0	0	24
1952			1	0		0	0	0	6
Career			32	0		0	0	0	192
Playoffs			2	0		0	0	0	12

Dunc Annan

Year	Team	Lg	TD	1XP	2XP	FG	FGA	SAF	Pts
1920	**CHIT**	**A**	1	0		0		0	6
1922	**TOL**	**N**	5	1		0		0	31

Dunc Annan *continued*

Year	Team		TD	1XP	2XP	FG	FGA	SAF	Pts
1925	AKR	N	1	0		0		0	6
Career			7	1		0		0	43

Tyrone Anthony

Year	Team		TD	1XP	2XP	FG	FGA	SAF	Pts
1984	NO	N	1	0		0	0	0	6

Scott Appleton

Year	Team		TD	1XP	2XP	FG	FGA	SAF	Pts
1967	SD	A	1	0	0	0	0	0	6

Fred Arbanas

Year	Team		TD	1XP	2XP	FG	FGA	SAF	Pts
1962	DAL	A	6	0	0	0	0	0	36
1963	KC	A	6	0	0	0	0	0	36
1964			8	0	0	0	0	0	48
1965			4	0	0	0	0	0	24
1966			4	0	1	0	0	0	26
1967			5	0	0	0	0	0	30
1970	KC	N	1	0		0	0	0	6
Career			34	0	1	0	0	0	206
Playoffs			1	0	0	0	0	0	6

Charles Arbuckle

Year	Team		TD	1XP	2XP	FG	FGA	SAF	Pts
1992	IND	N	1	0		0	0	0	6

David Archer

Year	Team		TD	1XP	2XP	FG	FGA	SAF	Pts
1985	ATL	N	2	0		0	0	0	12

Troy Archer

Year	Team		TD	1XP	2XP	FG	FGA	SAF	Pts
1978	NYG	N	1	0		0	0	0	6

Joe Arenas

Year	Team		TD	1XP	2XP	FG	FGA	SAF	Pts
1951	SF	N	4	0		0	0	0	24
1952			1	0		0	0	0	6
1953			7	0		0	0	0	42
1955			2	0		0	0	0	12
1956			3	0		0	0	0	18
1957			1	0		0	0	0	6
Career			18	0		0	0	0	108

Bob Argus

Year	Team		TD	1XP	2XP	FG	FGA	SAF	Pts
1922	ROC	N	1	0		0		0	6

Obed Ariri

Year	Team		TD	1XP	2XP	FG	FGA	SAF	Pts
1984	TB	N	0	38		19	26	0	95
1987	WAS	N	0	6		3	5	0	15
Career			0	44		22	31	0	110

Justin Armour

Year	Team		TD	1XP	2XP	FG	FGA	SAF	Pts
1995	BUF	N	3	0	0	0	0	0	18

Jessie Armstead

Year	Team		TD	1XP	2XP	FG	FGA	SAF	Pts
1995	NYG	N	1	0	0	0	0	0	6

Adger Armstrong

Year	Team		TD	1XP	2XP	FG	FGA	SAF	Pts
1981	HOU	N	1	0		0	0	0	6
1983	TB	N	2	0		0	0	0	12
1984			5	0		0	0	0	30
1985			1	0		0	0	0	6
Career			9	0		0	0	0	54

Graham Armstrong

Year	Team		TD	1XP	2XP	FG	FGA	SAF	Pts
1947	BUF	AA	0	8		0	1	0	8
1948			0	15		0	1	0	15
Career			0	23		0	2	0	23
Playoffs			0	5		0	0	0	5

Johnny Armstrong

Year	Team		TD	1XP	2XP	FG	FGA	SAF	Pts
1923	RI	N	2	0		0		0	12
1924			1	1		0		0	7
1925			4	1		0		0	25
1926	RI	A	1	0		0		0	6
Career			8	2		0		0	50

Neill Armstrong

Year	Team		TD	1XP	2XP	FG	FGA	SAF	Pts
1947	PHI	N	2	0		0	0	0	12
1948			3	0		0	0	0	18
1949			5	0		0	0	0	30
1950			1	0		0	0	0	6
Career			11	0		0	0	0	66

Otis Armstrong

Year	Team		TD	1XP	2XP	FG	FGA	SAF	Pts
1973	DEN	N	1	0		0	0	0	6
1974			12	0		0	0	0	72
1976			6	0		0	0	0	36

Otis Armstrong *continued*

Year	Team		TD	1XP	2XP	FG	FGA	SAF	Pts
1977			4	0		0	0	0	24
1978			2	0		0	0	0	12
1979			3	0		0	0	0	18
1980			4	0		0	0	0	24
Career			32	0		0	0	0	192
Playoffs			1	0		0	0	0	6

Tyji Armstrong

Year	Team		TD	1XP	2XP	FG	FGA	SAF	Pts
1992	TB	N	1	0		0	0	0	6
1993			1	0		0	0	0	6
1994			1	0	0	0	0	0	6
Career			3	0	0	0	0	0	18

Mark Arneson

Year	Team		TD	1XP	2XP	FG	FGA	SAF	Pts
1979	STL	N	1	0		0	0	0	6

Jon Arnett

Year	Team		TD	1XP	2XP	FG	FGA	SAF	Pts
1957	LA	N	6	0		0	0	0	36
1958			7	0		0	0	0	42
1959			4	0		0	0	0	24
1960			4	0		0	0	0	24
1961			5	0		0	0	0	30
1962			2	0		0	0	0	12
1963			2	0		0	0	0	12
1964	CHI	N	3	0		0	0	0	18
1965			5	0		0	0	0	30
1966			1	0		0	0	0	6
Career			39	0		0	0	0	234

Jay Arnold

Year	Team		TD	1XP	2XP	FG	FGA	SAF	Pts
1938	PHI	N	4	3		0		0	27
1939			1	0		0	0	0	6
Career			5	3		0	0	0	33

Walt Arnold

Year	Team		TD	1XP	2XP	FG	FGA	SAF	Pts
1980	LA	N	1	0		0	0	0	6
1981			2	0		0	0	0	12
1983	HOU	N	1	0		0	0	0	6
1984	KC	N	1	0		0	0	0	6
1985			1	0		0	0	0	6
1986			2	0		0	0	0	12
Career			8	0		0	0	0	48

Rick Arrington

Year	Team		TD	1XP	2XP	FG	FGA	SAF	Pts
1970	PHI	N	1	0		0	0	0	6

Arrowhead

Year	Team		TD	1XP	2XP	FG	FGA	SAF	Pts
1923	OOR	N	2	0		0		0	12

Lee Artoe

Year	Team		TD	1XP	2XP	FG	FGA	SAF	Pts
1940	CHIB	N	0	1		1	1	0	4
1941			0	3		1	7	0	6
1942			1	20		0	1	0	26
1945			0	0		0	1	0	0
1946	LA	AA	0	1		0	0	0	1
Career			1	25		2	10	0	37
Playoffs			1	1		0	2	0	7

Herman Arvie

Year	Team		TD	1XP	2XP	FG	FGA	SAF	Pts
1996	BAL	N	1	0	0	0	0	0	6

Doug Asad

Year	Team		TD	1XP	2XP	FG	FGA	SAF	Pts
1960	OAK	A	1	0	0	0	0	0	6
1961			2	0	0	0	0	0	12
Career			3	0	0	0	0	0	18

Willie Asbury

Year	Team		TD	1XP	2XP	FG	FGA	SAF	Pts
1966	PIT	N	9	0		0	0	0	54
1967			4	0		0	0	0	24
Career			13	0		0	0	0	78

Jamie Asher

Year	Team		TD	1XP	2XP	FG	FGA	SAF	Pts
1996	WAS	N	4	0	0	0	0	0	24

Walker Lee Ashley

Year	Team		TD	1XP	2XP	FG	FGA	SAF	Pts
1988	MIN	N	1	0		0	0	0	6

Marion Ashmore

Year	Team		TD	1XP	2XP	FG	FGA	SAF	Pts
1926	MIL	N	0	2		0		0	2

Josh Ashton

Year	Team		TD	1XP	2XP	FG	FGA	SAF	Pts
1972	NE	N	4	0		0	0	0	24

Joe Aska

Year	Team		TD	1XP	2XP	FG	FGA	SAF	Pts
1996	OAK	N	1	0	0	0	0	0	6

Bert Askson

Year	Team		TD	1XP	2XP	FG	FGA	SAF	Pts
1976	GB	N	1	0		0	0	0	6

Jack Atchason

Year	Team		TD	1XP	2XP	FG	FGA	SAF	Pts
1960	HOU	A	1	0	0	0	0	0	6

Pete Athas

Year	Team		TD	1XP	2XP	FG	FGA	SAF	Pts
1971	NYG	N	1	0		0	0	0	6

Dale Atkeson

Year	Team		TD	1XP	2XP	FG	FGA	SAF	Pts
1954	WAS	N	3	0		0	0	0	18
1955			2	0		0	0	0	12
1956			1	0		0	0	0	6
Career			6	0		0	0	0	36

Billy Atkins

Year	Team		TD	1XP	2XP	FG	FGA	SAF	Pts
1960	BUF	A	0	27	0	6	13	0	45
1961			1	29	0	2	6	0	41
Career			1	56	0	8	19	0	86

Bob Atkins

Year	Team		TD	1XP	2XP	FG	FGA	SAF	Pts
1971	HOU	N	1	0		0	0	0	6

Dave Atkins

Year	Team		TD	1XP	2XP	FG	FGA	SAF	Pts
1973	SF	N	1	0		0	0	0	6

Doug Atkins

Year	Team		TD	1XP	2XP	FG	FGA	SAF	Pts
1963	CHI	N	0	0		0	0	1	2

Pervis Atkins

Year	Team		TD	1XP	2XP	FG	FGA	SAF	Pts
1962	LA	N	1	0		0	0	0	6
1963			1	0		0	0	0	6
1964	WAS	N	1	0		0	0	0	6
Career			3	0		0	0	0	18

Steve Atkins

Year	Team		TD	1XP	2XP	FG	FGA	SAF	Pts
1979	GB	N	1	0		0	0	0	6
1980			2	0		0	0	0	12
Career			3	0		0	0	0	18

George Atkinson

Year	Team		TD	1XP	2XP	FG	FGA	SAF	Pts
1968	OAK	A	3	0	0	0	0	0	18
1969			1	0	0	0	0	0	6
1971	OAK	N	1	0		0	0	0	6
1973			2	0		0	0	0	12
Career			7	0	0	0	0	0	42
Playoffs			1	0	0	0	0	0	6

Jess Atkinson

Year	Team		TD	1XP	2XP	FG	FGA	SAF	Pts
1985	NYG-STL	N	1	17		10	18	0	53
1986	WAS	N	0	3		0	0	0	3
1987			0	1		1	1	0	4
Career			1	21		11	19	0	60
Playoffs			0	4		6	6	0	22

Reggie Attache

Year	Team		TD	1XP	2XP	FG	FGA	SAF	Pts
1922	OOR	N	0	0		0		0	0

John Atwood

Year	Team		TD	1XP	2XP	FG	FGA	SAF	Pts
1948	NYG	N	1	0		0	0	0	6

Joe Auer

Year	Team		TD	1XP	2XP	FG	FGA	SAF	Pts
1964	BUF	A	3	0	0	0	0	0	18
1966	MIA	A	9	0	0	0	0	0	54
1967			3	0	0	0	0	0	18
Career			15	0	0	0	0	0	90

Mike Augustyniak

Year	Team		TD	1XP	2XP	FG	FGA	SAF	Pts
1981	NYJ	N	1	0		0	0	0	6
1982			4	0		0	0	0	24
1983			3	0		0	0	0	18
Career			8	0		0	0	0	48

Cliff Austin

Year	Team		TD	1XP	2XP	FG	FGA	SAF	Pts
1985	ATL	N	1	0		0	0	0	6
1986			1	0		0	0	0	6
1987	TB	N	1	0		0	0	0	6
Career			3	0		0	0	0	18

Jim Austin

Year	Team		TD	1XP	2XP	FG	FGA	SAF	Pts
1938	BKN	N	1	0		0	0	0	6

Chuck Avedisian

Year	Team		TD	1XP	2XP	FG	FGA	SAF	Pts
1943	**NYG**	**N**	1	0		0	0	0	6
1944			1	0		0	0	0	6
Career			2	0		0	0	0	12

Bob Avellini

Year	Team		TD	1XP	2XP	FG	FGA	SAF	Pts
1975	**CHI**	**N**	1	0		0	0	0	6
1976			1	0		0	0	0	6
1977			1	0		0	0	0	6
1978			2	0		0	0	0	12
Career			5	0		0	0	0	30

John Aveni

Year	Team		TD	1XP	2XP	FG	FGA	SAF	Pts
1959	**CHIB**	**N**	0	28		10	19	0	58
1960	**CHI**	**N**	0	23		7	16	0	44
1961	**WAS**	**N**	1	21		5	28	0	42
Career			1	72		22	63	0	144

Steve Avery

Year	Team		TD	1XP	2XP	FG	FGA	SAF	Pts
1995	**PIT**	**N**	1	0	0	0	0	0	6

Rob Awalt

Year	Team		TD	1XP	2XP	FG	FGA	SAF	Pts
1987	**STL**	**N**	6	0		0	0	0	36
1988	**PHX**	**N**	4	0		0	0	0	24
Career			10	0		0	0	0	60

Al Babartsky

Year	Team		TD	1XP	2XP	FG	FGA	SAF	Pts
1939	**CHIC**	**N**	1	0		0	0	0	6

Charlie Babb

Year	Team		TD	1XP	2XP	FG	FGA	SAF	Pts
Playoffs			1	0	0	0	0	0	6

Gene Babb

Year	Team		TD	1XP	2XP	FG	FGA	SAF	Pts
1957	**SF**	**N**	3	0		0	0	0	18
1960	**DAL**	**N**	1	0		0	0	0	6
1962	**HOU**	**A**	1	0	0	0	0	0	6
Career			5	0	0	0	0	0	30

Bob Babich

Year	Team		TD	1XP	2XP	FG	FGA	SAF	Pts
1971	**SD**	**N**	1	0		0	0	0	6

Carl Bacchus

Year	Team		TD	1XP	2XP	FG	FGA	SAF	Pts
1927	**CLE**	**N**	3	0		0		0	18
1928	**DET**	**N**	4	0		0		0	24
Career			7	0		0		0	42

Coy Bacon

Year	Team		TD	1XP	2XP	FG	FGA	SAF	Pts
1970	**LA**	**N**	1	0		0	0	0	6
1973	**SD**	**N**	1	0		0	0	0	6
1976	**CIN**	**N**	0	0		0	0	1	2
Career			2	0		0	0	1	14

Frank Bacon

Year	Team		TD	1XP	2XP	FG	FGA	SAF	Pts
1920	**DAY**	**A**	**5**	2		0		0	**32**
1921			6	0		0		0	36
1922	**DAY**	**N**	1	0		0		0	6
1923			1	0		0		0	6
1924			1	0		0		0	6
Career			14	2		0		0	86

Rick Badanjek

Year	Team		TD	1XP	2XP	FG	FGA	SAF	Pts
1987	**ATL**	**N**	1	0		0	0	0	6

Red Badgro

Year	Team		TD	1XP	2XP	FG	FGA	SAF	Pts
1927	**NYY**	**N**	1	0		0		0	6
1930	**NYG**	**N**	3	0		0		0	18
1933			3	0		0		0	18
1934			1	0		0		0	6
Career			8	0		0		0	48
Playoffs			1	0		0	0	0	6

Steve Bagarus

Year	Team		TD	1XP	2XP	FG	FGA	SAF	Pts
1945	**WAS**	**N**	6	0		0	0	0	36
1946			3	0		0	0	0	18
1948			1	0		0	0	0	6
Career			10	0		0	0	0	60
Playoffs			1	0		0	0	0	6

Herm Bagby

Year	Team		TD	1XP	2XP	FG	FGA	SAF	Pts
1926	**BKN**	**N**	3	0		0		0	18

Eddie Bagdon

Year	Team		TD	1XP	2XP	FG	FGA	SAF	Pts
1952	**WAS**	**N**	0	4		1	3	0	7

Billy Baggett

Year	Team		TD	1XP	2XP	FG	FGA	SAF	Pts
1952	**DAL**	**N**	1	0		0	0	0	6

Pete Bahan

Year	Team		TD	1XP	2XP	FG	FGA	SAF	Pts
1923	**CLE**	**N**	0	0		0		0	0

Chris Bahr

Year	Team		TD	1XP	2XP	FG	FGA	SAF	Pts
1976	**CIN**	**N**	0	39		14	27	0	81
1977			0	25		19	27	0	82
1978			0	26		16	30	0	74
1979			0	40		13	23	0	79
1980	**OAK**	**N**	0	41		19	37	0	98
1981			0	27		14	24	0	69
1982	**LARI**	**N**	0	**32**		10	16	0	62
1983			0	51		21	27	0	114
1984			0	40		20	27	0	100
1985			0	40		20	32	0	100
1986			0	36		21	28	0	99
1987			0	27		19	29	0	84
1988			0	37		18	29	0	91
1989	**SD**	**N**	0	29		17	25	0	80
Career			0	490		241	381	0	1213
Playoffs			0	33		14	18	0	75

Matt Bahr

Year	Team		TD	1XP	2XP	FG	FGA	SAF	Pts
1979	**PIT**	**N**	0	**50**		18	30	0	104
1980			0	39		19	28	0	96
1981	**SF-CLE**	**N**	0	34		15	26	0	79
1982	**CLE**	**N**	0	17		7	15	0	38
1983			0	38		21	24	0	101
1984			0	25		24	32	0	97
1985			0	35		14	18	0	77
1986			0	30		20	26	0	90
1987			0	9		4	5	0	21
1988			0	32		24	29	0	104
1989			0	40		16	24	0	88
1990	**NYG**	**N**	0	29		17	23	0	80
1991			0	24		22	29	0	90
1992			0	29		16	21	0	77
1993	**PHI-NE**	**N**	0	28		13	18	0	67
1994	**NE**	**N**	0	36	0	27	34	0	117
1995			0	27	0	23	33	0	96
Career			0	522	0	300	415	0	1422
Playoffs			0	40	0	21	25	0	103

Aaron Bailey

Year	Team		TD	1XP	2XP	FG	FGA	SAF	Pts
1995	**IND**	**N**	4	0	0	0	0	0	24
1996			1	0	0	0	0	0	6
Career			5	0	0	0	0	0	30
Playoffs			1	0	0	0	0	0	6

By Bailey

Year	Team		TD	1XP	2XP	FG	FGA	SAF	Pts
1952	**DET**	**N**	2	0		0	0	0	12

Carlton Bailey

Year	Team		TD	1XP	2XP	FG	FGA	SAF	Pts
Playoffs			1	0	0	0	0	0	6

Johnny Bailey

Year	Team		TD	1XP	2XP	FG	FGA	SAF	Pts
1990	**CHI**	**N**	1	0		0	0	0	6
1991			1	0		0	0	0	6
1992	**PHX**	**N**	2	0		0	0	0	12
1993			2	0		0	0	0	12
1994	**LARM**	**N**	1	0	0	0	0	0	6
1995	**STL**	**N**	2	0	1	0	0	0	14
Career			9	0	1	0	0	0	56

Mark Bailey

Year	Team		TD	1XP	2XP	FG	FGA	SAF	Pts
1977	**KC**	**N**	3	0		0	0	0	18

Robert Bailey

Year	Team		TD	1XP	2XP	FG	FGA	SAF	Pts
1992	**LARM**	**N**	1	0		0	0	0	6
1994			1	0	0	0	0	0	6
Career			2	0	0	0	0	0	12

Stacey Bailey

Year	Team		TD	1XP	2XP	FG	FGA	SAF	Pts
1982	**ATL**	**N**	1	0		0	0	0	6
1983			6	0		0	0	0	36
1984			6	0		0	0	0	36
1987			3	0		0	0	0	18
1988			2	0		0	0	0	12
Career			18	0		0	0	0	108

Tom Bailey

Year	Team		TD	1XP	2XP	FG	FGA	SAF	Pts
1971	**PHI**	**N**	1	0		0	0	0	6

Tom Bailey *continued*

Year	Team		TD	1XP	2XP	FG	FGA	SAF	Pts
1973			1	0		0	0	0	6
Career			2	0		0	0	0	12

Victor Bailey

Year	Team		TD	1XP	2XP	FG	FGA	SAF	Pts
1993	**PHI**	**N**	1	0		0	0	0	6
1994			1	0	0	0	0	0	6
Career			2	0	0	0	0	0	12

Bill Baird

Year	Team		TD	1XP	2XP	FG	FGA	SAF	Pts
1963	**NY**	**A**	1	0	0	0	0	0	6
1964			1	0	0	0	0	0	6
1966			1	0	0	0	0	0	6
Career			3	0	0	0	0	0	18

Art Baker

Year	Team		TD	1XP	2XP	FG	FGA	SAF	Pts
1961	**BUF**	**A**	3	0	0	0	0	0	18
1962			1	0	0	0	0	0	6
Career			4	0	0	0	0	0	24

Bullet Baker

Year	Team		TD	1XP	2XP	FG	FGA	SAF	Pts
1926	**NY**	**A**	1	0		0		0	6
1927	**NYY**	**N**	1	0		0		0	6
1931	**SI**	**N**	0	0		0		0	0
Career			2	0		0		0	12

Conway Baker

Year	Team		TD	1XP	2XP	FG	FGA	SAF	Pts
1937	**CHIC**	**N**	0	6		0		0	6
1943			1	5		1	2	0	14
1944	**C-P**	**N**	0	11		0	0	0	11
1945	**CHIC**	**N**	0	0		0	1	0	0
Career			1	22		1	3	0	31

Frank Baker

Year	Team		TD	1XP	2XP	FG	FGA	SAF	Pts
1931	**GB**	**N**	1	0		0		0	6

Jesse Baker

Year	Team		TD	1XP	2XP	FG	FGA	SAF	Pts
1979	**HOU**	**N**	1	0		0	0	0	6
1987			0	0		0	0	1	2
Career			1	0		0	0	1	8

Johnny Baker

Year	Team		TD	1XP	2XP	FG	FGA	SAF	Pts
1964	**HOU**	**A**	1	0	0	0	0	0	6

Melvin Baker

Year	Team		TD	1XP	2XP	FG	FGA	SAF	Pts
1974	**MIA**	**N**	2	0		0	0	0	12

Myron Baker

Year	Team		TD	1XP	2XP	FG	FGA	SAF	Pts
1993	**CHI**	**N**	2	0		0	0	0	12

Ralph Baker

Year	Team		TD	1XP	2XP	FG	FGA	SAF	Pts
1971	**NYJ**	**N**	0	1		0	0	0	1
1973			1	0		0	0	0	6
1974			1	0		0	0	0	6
Career			2	1		0	0	0	13

Sam Baker

Year	Team		TD	1XP	2XP	FG	FGA	SAF	Pts
1953	**WAS**	**N**	1	0		0	0	0	6
1956			0	16		**17**	25	0	67
1957			1	29		14	23	0	**77**
1958			0	25		13	26	0	64
1959			0	21		10	22	0	51
1960	**CLE**	**N**	0	**44**		12	20	0	80
1962	**DAL**	**N**	0	**50**		14	27	0	92
1963			0	38		9	20	0	65
1964	**PHI**	**N**	0	36		16	26	0	84
1965			0	38		9	23	0	65
1966			0	38		18	25	0	92
1967			0	45		12	19	0	81
1968			0	17		19	30	0	74
1969			0	31		16	30	0	79
Career			2	428		179	316	0	977

Stephen Baker

Year	Team		TD	1XP	2XP	FG	FGA	SAF	Pts
1987	**NYG**	**N**	2	0		0	0	0	12
1988			7	0		0	0	0	42
1989			2	0		0	0	0	12
1990			4	0		0	0	0	24
1991			4	0		0	0	0	24
1992			2	0		0	0	0	12
Career			21	0		0	0	0	126
Playoffs			2	0		0	0	0	12

Terry Baker

Year	Team		TD	1XP	2XP	FG	FGA	SAF	Pts
1965	LA	N	3	0		0	0	0	18

Tony Baker

Year	Team		TD	1XP	2XP	FG	FGA	SAF	Pts
1969	NO	N	2	0		0	0	0	12
1970			1	0		0	0	0	6
1971			1	0		0	0	0	6
1973	LA	N	7	0		0	0	0	42
1974			5	0		0	0	0	30
1975	SD	N	1	0		0	0	0	6
Career			17	0		0	0	0	102
Playoffs			1	0		0	0	0	6

Jim Bakken

Year	Team		TD	1XP	2XP	FG	FGA	SAF	Pts
1962	STL	N	0	0		0	1	0	0
1963			0	44		11	21	0	77
1964			0	40		**25**	**38**	0	115
1965			0	33		21	31	0	96
1966			0	27		23	40	0	96
1967			0	36		**27**	39	0	**117**
1968			0	40		15	24	0	85
1969			0	38		12	24	0	74
1970			0	37		20	32	0	97
1971			0	24		21	32	0	87
1972			0	19		14	22	0	61
1973			0	31		23	32	0	100
1974			0	30		13	22	0	69
1975			0	40		19	24	0	97
1976			0	33		20	27	0	93
1977			0	35		7	16	0	56
1978			0	27		11	22	0	60
Career			0	534		282	447	0	1380
Playoffs			0	4		1	2	0	7

Ed Balatti

Year	Team		TD	1XP	2XP	FG	FGA	SAF	Pts
1946	SF	AA	1	2		0	0	0	8
1947			2	1		0	0	0	13
Career			3	3		0	0	0	21

Frank Balazs

Year	Team		TD	1XP	2XP	FG	FGA	SAF	Pts
1940	GB	N	1	0		0	0	0	6
1941	GB-CHIC	N	0	1		0	0	0	1
Career			1	1		0	0	0	7

Mike Baldassin

Year	Team		TD	1XP	2XP	FG	FGA	SAF	Pts
1977	SF	N	1	0		0	0	0	6

Al Baldwin

Year	Team		TD	1XP	2XP	FG	FGA	SAF	Pts
1947	BUF	AA	7	0		0	0	0	42
1948			8	0		0	0	0	48
1949			7	0		0	0	0	42
1950	GB	N	3	0		0	0	0	18
Career			25	0		0	0	0	150
Playoffs			2	0		0	0	0	12

Burr Baldwin

Year	Team		TD	1XP	2XP	FG	FGA	SAF	Pts
1947	LA	AA	1	0		0	0	0	6

Randy Baldwin

Year	Team		TD	1XP	2XP	FG	FGA	SAF	Pts
1993	CLE	N	1	0		0	0	0	6
1994			1	0	0	0	0	0	6
Career			2	0	0	0	0	0	12

Tom Baldwin

Year	Team		TD	1XP	2XP	FG	FGA	SAF	Pts
1985	NYJ	N	1	0		0	0	0	6

Eric Ball

Year	Team		TD	1XP	2XP	FG	FGA	SAF	Pts
1989	CIN	N	3	0		0	0	0	18
1990			2	0		0	0	0	12
1991			1	0		0	0	0	6
1992			4	0		0	0	0	24
1993			1	0		0	0	0	6
Career			11	0		0	0	0	66
Playoffs			1	0		0	0	0	6

Jerry Ball

Year	Team		TD	1XP	2XP	FG	FGA	SAF	Pts
1991	DET	N	0	0		0	0	1	2
1992			1	0		0	0	0	6
1996	OAK	N	1	0	0	0	0	0	6
Career			2	0	0	0	0	1	14

Larry Ball

Year	Team		TD	1XP	2XP	FG	FGA	SAF	Pts
1975	DET	N	1	0		0	0	0	6

Gary Ballman

Year	Team		TD	1XP	2XP	FG	FGA	SAF	Pts
1963	PIT	N	6	0		0	0	0	36
1964			7	0		0	0	0	42
1965			8	0		0	0	0	48
1966			5	0		0	0	0	30
1967	PHI	N	7	0		0	0	0	42
1968			4	0		0	0	0	24
1969			2	0		0	0	0	12
1970			3	0		0	0	0	18
Career			42	0		0	0	0	252

Pete Banaszak

Year	Team		TD	1XP	2XP	FG	FGA	SAF	Pts
1967	OAK	A	2	0	0	0	0	0	12
1968			5	0	0	0	0	0	30
1969			3	0	0	0	0	0	18
1970	OAK	N	2	0		0	0	0	12
1971			8	0		0	0	0	48
1972			1	0		0	0	0	6
1974			5	0		0	0	0	30
1975			16	0		0	0	0	96
1976			5	0		0	0	0	30
1977			5	0		0	0	0	30
Career			52	0	0	0	0	0	312
Playoffs			6	0	0	0	0	0	36

Bruno Banducci

Year	Team		TD	1XP	2XP	FG	FGA	SAF	Pts
1950	SF	N	1	0		0	0	0	6

Tony Banfield

Year	Team		TD	1XP	2XP	FG	FGA	SAF	Pts
1962	HOU	A	1	0	0	0	0	0	6

Emil Banjavic

Year	Team		TD	1XP	2XP	FG	FGA	SAF	Pts
1942	DET	N	1	0		0	0	0	6

Carl Banks

Year	Team		TD	1XP	2XP	FG	FGA	SAF	Pts
1988	NYG	N	1	0		0	0	0	6
1989			1	0		0	0	0	6
Career			2	0		0	0	0	12

Chip Banks

Year	Team		TD	1XP	2XP	FG	FGA	SAF	Pts
1983	CLE	N	1	0		0	0	0	6

Estes Banks

Year	Team		TD	1XP	2XP	FG	FGA	SAF	Pts
1968	CIN	A	1	0	0	0	0	0	6

Fred Banks

Year	Team		TD	1XP	2XP	FG	FGA	SAF	Pts
1985	CLE	N	2	0		0	0	0	12
1987	MIA	N	1	0		0	0	0	6
1988			2	0		0	0	0	12
1989			1	0		0	0	0	6
1991			1	0		0	0	0	6
1992			3	0		0	0	0	18
Career			10	0		0	0	0	60

Gordon Banks

Year	Team		TD	1XP	2XP	FG	FGA	SAF	Pts
1987	DAL	N	1	0		0	0	0	6

Tony Banks

Year	Team		TD	1XP	2XP	FG	FGA	SAF	Pts
1996	STL	N	0	0	1	0	0	0	2

Warren Bankston

Year	Team		TD	1XP	2XP	FG	FGA	SAF	Pts
1969	PIT	N	1	0		0	0	0	6
1970			2	0		0	0	0	12
1975	OAK	N	1	0		0	0	0	6
1976			1	0		0	0	0	6
Career			5	0		0	0	0	30
Playoffs			1	0		0	0	0	6

Vincent Banonis

Year	Team		TD	1XP	2XP	FG	FGA	SAF	Pts
1947	CHIC	N	1	0		0	0	0	6
1949			1	0		0	0	0	6
Career			2	0		0	0	0	12

Jack Banta

Year	Team		TD	1XP	2XP	FG	FGA	SAF	Pts
1941	PHI	N	1	0		0	0	0	6
1944			3	0		0	0	0	18
1945			1	0		0	0	0	6
1946	LA	N	1	0		0	0	0	6
1947			1	0		0	0	0	6
Career			7	0		0	0	0	42

Gary Barbaro

Year	Team		TD	1XP	2XP	FG	FGA	SAF	Pts
1977	KC	N	1	0		0	0	0	6
1979			1	0		0	0	0	6

Gary Barbaro *continued*

Year	Team		TD	1XP	2XP	FG	FGA	SAF	Pts
1982			1	0		0	0	0	6
Career			3	0		0	0	0	18

Marion Barber

Year	Team		TD	1XP	2XP	FG	FGA	SAF	Pts
1983	NYJ	N	2	0		0	0	0	12
1984			2	0		0	0	0	12
Career			4	0		0	0	0	24

Mike Barber

Year	Team		TD	1XP	2XP	FG	FGA	SAF	Pts
1977	HOU	N	1	0		0	0	0	6
1978			3	0		0	0	0	18
1979			3	0		0	0	0	18
1980			5	0		0	0	0	30
1981			1	0		0	0	0	6
1982	LARM	N	1	0		0	0	0	6
1983			3	0		0	0	0	18
Career			17	0		0	0	0	102
Playoffs			2	0		0	0	0	12

Mike Barber

Year	Team		TD	1XP	2XP	FG	FGA	SAF	Pts
1990	CIN	N	1	0		0	0	0	6
1991			1	0		0	0	0	6
Career			2	0		0	0	0	12

Stew Barber

Year	Team		TD	1XP	2XP	FG	FGA	SAF	Pts
1961	BUF	A	1	0	0	0	0	0	6

Ken Barefoot

Year	Team		TD	1XP	2XP	FG	FGA	SAF	Pts
1968	WAS	N	1	0		0	0	0	6

Ed Barker

Year	Team		TD	1XP	2XP	FG	FGA	SAF	Pts
1953	PIT	N	1	0		0	0	0	6
1954	WAS	N	3	0		0	0	0	18
Career			4	0		0	0	0	24

Leo Barker

Year	Team		TD	1XP	2XP	FG	FGA	SAF	Pts
1988	CIN	N	1	0		0	0	0	6

Ralph Barkman

Year	Team		TD	1XP	2XP	FG	FGA	SAF	Pts
1929	ORA	N	0	1		0		0	1

Rod Barksdale

Year	Team		TD	1XP	2XP	FG	FGA	SAF	Pts
1986	LARI	N	2	0		0	0	0	12
1987	DAL	N	1	0		0	0	0	6
Career			3	0		0	0	0	18

Jerome Barkum

Year	Team		TD	1XP	2XP	FG	FGA	SAF	Pts
1972	NYJ	N	2	0		0	0	0	12
1973			6	0		0	0	0	36
1974			3	0		0	0	0	18
1975			5	0		0	0	0	30
1976			1	0		0	0	0	6
1977			6	0		0	0	0	36
1978			3	0		0	0	0	18
1979			4	0		0	0	0	24
1980			1	0		0	0	0	6
1981			7	0		0	0	0	42
1982			1	0		0	0	0	6
1983			1	0		0	0	0	6
Career			40	0		0	0	0	240

George Barna

Year	Team		TD	1XP	2XP	FG	FGA	SAF	Pts
1929	FRA	N	1	0		0		0	6

Hap Barnard

Year	Team		TD	1XP	2XP	FG	FGA	SAF	Pts
Playoffs			1	0	0	0	0	0	6

Al Barnes

Year	Team		TD	1XP	2XP	FG	FGA	SAF	Pts
1972	DET	N	1	0		0	0	0	6
1973			1	0		0	0	0	6
Career			2	0		0	0	0	12

Benny Barnes

Year	Team		TD	1XP	2XP	FG	FGA	SAF	Pts
1973	DAL	N	0	0		0	0	2	4
1979			1	0		0	0	0	6
1981			1	0		0	0	0	6
Career			2	0		0	0	2	16

Billy Ray Barnes

Year	Team		TD	1XP	2XP	FG	FGA	SAF	Pts
1957	PHI	N	2	0		0	0	0	12
1958			7	0		0	0	0	42
1959			9	0		0	0	0	54
1960			6	0		0	0	0	36

Billy Ray Barnes *continued*

Year	Team		TD	1XP	2XP	FG	FGA	SAF	Pts
1961			4	0		0	0	0	24
1962	WAS	N	3	0		0	0	0	18
1963			6	0		0	0	0	36
1966	MIN	N	1	0		0	0	0	6
Career			38	0		0	0	0	228
Playoffs			1	0		0	0	0	6

Erich Barnes

Year	Team		TD	1XP	2XP	FG	FGA	SAF	Pts
1958	CHIB	N	2	0		0	0	0	12
1961	NYG	N	3	0		0	0	0	18
1964			2	0		0	0	0	12
1968	CLE	N	1	0		0	0	0	6
1969			1	0		0	0	0	6
1970			1	0		0	0	0	6
Career			10	0		0	0	0	60

Gary Barnes

Year	Team		TD	1XP	2XP	FG	FGA	SAF	Pts
1966	ATL	N	1	0		0	0	0	6
1967			1	0		0	0	0	6
Career			2	0		0	0	0	12

Larry Barnes

Year	Team		TD	1XP	2XP	FG	FGA	SAF	Pts
1960	OAK	A	0	37	0	6	25	0	55

Larry Barnes

Year	Team		TD	1XP	2XP	FG	FGA	SAF	Pts
1978	PHI	N	1	0		0	0	0	6
1979			1	0		0	0	0	6
Career			2	0		0	0	0	12

Lew Barnes

Year	Team		TD	1XP	2XP	FG	FGA	SAF	Pts
1986	CHI	N	1	0		0	0	0	6

Pete Barnes

Year	Team		TD	1XP	2XP	FG	FGA	SAF	Pts
1971	SD	N	1	0		0	0	0	6

Walt Barnes

Year	Team		TD	1XP	2XP	FG	FGA	SAF	Pts
1948	PHI	N	0	0		0	0	1	2

Buster Barnett

Year	Team		TD	1XP	2XP	FG	FGA	SAF	Pts
1981	BUF	N	1	0		0	0	0	6

Fred Barnett

Year	Team		TD	1XP	2XP	FG	FGA	SAF	Pts
1990	PHI	N	8	0		0	0	0	48
1991			4	0		0	0	0	24
1992			6	0		0	0	0	36
1994			5	0	0	0	0	0	30
1995			5	0	1	0	0	0	32
1996	MIA	N	3	0	0	0	0	0	18
Career			31	0	1	0	0	0	188
Playoffs			3	0	0	0	0	0	18

Oliver Barnett

Year	Team		TD	1XP	2XP	FG	FGA	SAF	Pts
1991	ATL	N	1	0		0	0	0	6

Tim Barnett

Year	Team		TD	1XP	2XP	FG	FGA	SAF	Pts
1991	KC	N	5	0		0	0	0	30
1992			4	0		0	0	0	24
1993			1	0		0	0	0	6
Career			10	0		0	0	0	60
Playoffs			1	0		0	0	0	6

Tom Barnett

Year	Team		TD	1XP	2XP	FG	FGA	SAF	Pts
1959	PIT	N	2	0		0	0	0	12

Eppie Barney

Year	Team		TD	1XP	2XP	FG	FGA	SAF	Pts
1968	CLE	N	2	0		0	0	0	12

Lem Barney

Year	Team		TD	1XP	2XP	FG	FGA	SAF	Pts
1967	DET	N	3	0		0	0	0	18
1968			2	0		0	0	0	12
1969			1	0		0	0	0	6
1970			3	0		0	0	0	18
1971			1	0		0	0	0	6
1976			1	0		0	0	0	6
Career			11	0		0	0	0	66

Milton Barney

Year	Team		TD	1XP	2XP	FG	FGA	SAF	Pts
1987	ATL	N	2	0		0	0	0	12

Dan Barnhart

Year	Team		TD	1XP	2XP	FG	FGA	SAF	Pts
1934	PHI	N	0	0		0		0	0

Roy Barni

Year	Team		TD	1XP	2XP	FG	FGA	SAF	Pts
1955	WAS	N	1	0		0	0	0	6

Len Barnum

Year	Team		TD	1XP	2XP	FG	FGA	SAF	Pts
1938	NYG	N	1	0		0		0	6
1939			2	3		3	7	0	24
1940			0	6		1	4	0	9
1941	PHI	N	0	2		2	6	0	8
1942			0	7		3	7	0	16
Career			3	18		9	24	0	63

Pete Barnum

Year	Team		TD	1XP	2XP	FG	FGA	SAF	Pts
1926	COL	N	1	0		0		0	6

Malcolm Barnwell

Year	Team		TD	1XP	2XP	FG	FGA	SAF	Pts
1981	OAK	N	1	0		0	0	0	6
1983	LARI	N	1	0		0	0	0	6
1984			2	0		0	0	0	12
Career			4	0		0	0	0	24
Playoffs			1	0		0	0	0	6

Shorty Barr

Year	Team		TD	1XP	2XP	FG	FGA	SAF	Pts
1923	RAC	N	1	0		0		0	6
1924			0	0		1		0	3
1926			0	0		0		0	0
Career			1	0		1		0	9

Terry Barr

Year	Team		TD	1XP	2XP	FG	FGA	SAF	Pts
1958	DET	N	1	0		0	0	0	6
1959			1	0		0	0	0	6
1960			2	0		0	0	0	12
1961			6	0		0	0	0	36
1962			3	0		0	0	0	18
1963			13	0		0	0	0	78
1964			9	0		0	0	0	54
1965			3	0		0	0	0	18
Career			38	0		0	0	0	228
Playoffs			1	0		0	0	0	6

Jan Barrett

Year	Team		TD	1XP	2XP	FG	FGA	SAF	Pts
1964	OAK	A	2	0	0	0	0	0	12

Jeff Barrett

Year	Team		TD	1XP	2XP	FG	FGA	SAF	Pts
1936	BKN	N	1	0		0		0	6
1937			3	0		0		0	18
1938			2	0		0	0	0	12
Career			6	0		0	0	0	36

John Barrett

Year	Team		TD	1XP	2XP	FG	FGA	SAF	Pts
1924	AKR	N	1	0		0		0	6
1926	DET	N	1	0		0		0	6
Career			2	0		0		0	12

Johnny Barrett

Year	Team		TD	1XP	2XP	FG	FGA	SAF	Pts
1920	CHIT	A	0	0		1		0	3

Reggie Barrett

Year	Team		TD	1XP	2XP	FG	FGA	SAF	Pts
1992	DET	N	1	0		0	0	0	6

Tom Barrington

Year	Team		TD	1XP	2XP	FG	FGA	SAF	Pts
1968	NO	N	1	0		0	0	0	6
1969			1	0		0	0	0	6
1970			2	0		0	0	0	12
Career			4	0		0	0	0	24

Jim Barron

Year	Team		TD	1XP	2XP	FG	FGA	SAF	Pts
1921	ROC	A	1	0		0		0	6

Norm Barry

Year	Team		TD	1XP	2XP	FG	FGA	SAF	Pts
1921	GB	A	1	0		0		0	6

Odell Barry

Year	Team		TD	1XP	2XP	FG	FGA	SAF	Pts
1964	DEN	A	1	0	0	0	0	0	6

Paul Barry

Year	Team		TD	1XP	2XP	FG	FGA	SAF	Pts
1950	LA	N	2	0		0	0	0	12
1952			1	0		0	1	0	6
Career			3	0		0	1	0	18

Steve Bartalo

Year	Team		TD	1XP	2XP	FG	FGA	SAF	Pts
1987	TB	N	1	0		0	0	0	6

Steve Bartkowski

Year	Team		TD	1XP	2XP	FG	FGA	SAF	Pts
1975	ATL	N	2	0		0	0	0	12

Steve Bartkowski *continued*

Year	Team		TD	1XP	2XP	FG	FGA	SAF	Pts
1976			1	0		0	0	0	6
1978			2	0		0	0	0	12
1979			2	0		0	0	0	12
1980			2	0		0	0	0	12
1982			1	0		0	0	0	6
1983			1	0		0	0	0	6
Career			11	0		0	0	0	66

Don Barton

Year	Team		TD	1XP	2XP	FG	FGA	SAF	Pts
1953	GB	N	1	0		0	0	0	6

Mike Bartrum

Year	Team		TD	1XP	2XP	FG	FGA	SAF	Pts
1996	NE	N	1	0	0	0	0	0	6

Mike Basca

Year	Team		TD	1XP	2XP	FG	FGA	SAF	Pts
1941	PHI	N	1	9		1	2	0	18

Brian Baschnagel

Year	Team		TD	1XP	2XP	FG	FGA	SAF	Pts
1977	CHI	N	1	0		0	0	0	6
1979			2	0		0	0	0	12
1980			2	0		0	0	0	12
1981			3	0		0	0	0	18
1982			2	0		0	0	0	12
Career			10	0		0	0	0	60

Myrt Basing

Year	Team		TD	1XP	2XP	FG	FGA	SAF	Pts
1923	GB	N	2	0		0		0	12
1925			6	0		0		0	36
1926			1	0		0		0	6
Career			9	0		0		0	54

Billy Bass

Year	Team		TD	1XP	2XP	FG	FGA	SAF	Pts
1947	CHI	AA	2	0		0	0	0	12

Dick Bass

Year	Team		TD	1XP	2XP	FG	FGA	SAF	Pts
1961	LA	N	5	0		0	0	0	30
1962			8	0		0	0	0	48
1963			5	0		0	0	0	30
1964			2	0		0	0	0	12
1965			4	0		0	0	0	24
1966			8	0		0	0	0	48
1967			7	0		0	0	0	42
1968			3	0		0	0	0	18
Career			42	0		0	0	0	252

Don Bass

Year	Team		TD	1XP	2XP	FG	FGA	SAF	Pts
1978	CIN	N	5	0		0	0	0	30
1979			3	0		0	0	0	18
1980			6	0		0	0	0	36
Career			14	0		0	0	0	84
Playoffs			1	0		0	0	0	6

Glenn Bass

Year	Team		TD	1XP	2XP	FG	FGA	SAF	Pts
1961	BUF	A	3	0	0	0	0	0	18
1962			4	0	0	0	0	0	24
1963			1	0	0	0	0	0	6
1964			7	0	0	0	0	0	42
1965			1	0	0	0	0	0	6
1967	HOU	A	1	0	0	0	0	0	6
Career			17	0	0	0	0	0	102

Mike Bass

Year	Team		TD	1XP	2XP	FG	FGA	SAF	Pts
1971	WAS	N	1	0		0	0	0	6
1972			1	0		0	0	0	6
1973			1	0		0	0	0	6
1974			1	0		0	0	0	6
Career			4	0		0	0	0	24
Playoffs			1	0		0	0	0	6

Mo Bassett

Year	Team		TD	1XP	2XP	FG	FGA	SAF	Pts
1954	CLE	N	6	0		0	0	0	36
1955			3	0		0	0	0	18
1956			2	0		0	0	0	12
Career			11	0		0	0	0	66

Dick Bassi

Year	Team		TD	1XP	2XP	FG	FGA	SAF	Pts
1938	CHIB	N	1	0		0	0	0	6

Marv Bateman

Year	Team		TD	1XP	2XP	FG	FGA	SAF	Pts
1973	DAL	N	0	1		0	0	0	1

Mario Bates

Year	Team		TD	1XP	2XP	FG	FGA	SAF	Pts
1994	NO	N	6	0	0	0	0	0	36

Mario Bates *continued*

Year	Team		TD	1XP	2XP	FG	FGA	SAF	Pts
1995			7	0	0	0	0	0	42
1996			4	0	0	0	0	0	24
Career			17	0	0	0	0	0	102

Michael Bates

Year	Team		TD	1XP	2XP	FG	FGA	SAF	Pts
1994	**SEA**	**N**	1	0	0	0	0	0	6
1996	**CAR**	**N**	1	0	0	0	0	0	6
Career			2	0	0	0	0	0	12

Ron Battle

Year	Team		TD	1XP	2XP	FG	FGA	SAF	Pts
1982	**LARM**	**N**	1	0		0	0	0	6

Cliff Battles

Year	Team		TD	1XP	2XP	FG	FGA	SAF	Pts
1932	**BOS**	**N**	4	0		0		0	24
1933			4	0		1		0	27
1934			7	1		0		0	43
1935			2	0		0		0	12
1936			7	0		0		0	42
1937	**WAS**	**N**	**7**	0		0		0	42
Career			31	1		1		0	190
Playoffs			1	0		0	0	0	6

Greg Baty

Year	Team		TD	1XP	2XP	FG	FGA	SAF	Pts
1986	**NE**	**N**	2	0		0	0	0	12
1987			2	0		0	0	0	12
1991	**MIA**	**N**	1	0		0	0	0	6
1992			1	0		0	0	0	6
1993			1	0		0	0	0	6
1994			1	0	0	0	0	0	6
Career			8	0	0	0	0	0	48

Hank Bauer

Year	Team		TD	1XP	2XP	FG	FGA	SAF	Pts
1977	**SD**	**N**	1	0		0	0	0	6
1978			9	0		0	0	0	54
1979			8	0		0	0	0	48
1980			1	0		0	0	0	6
1981			1	0		0	0	0	6
Career			20	0		0	0	0	120

Sammy Baugh

Year	Team		TD	1XP	2XP	FG	FGA	SAF	Pts
1937	**WAS**	**N**	1	0		0		0	6
1942			1	0		0	0	0	6
1945			0	1		0	0	0	1
1946			1	0		0	0	0	6
1947			2	0		0	0	0	12
1948			1	0		0	0	0	6
1949			2	0		0	0	0	12
1950			1	0		0	0	0	6
Career			9	1		0	0	0	55

Maxie Baughan

Year	Team		TD	1XP	2XP	FG	FGA	SAF	Pts
1965	**PHI**	**N**	1	0		0	0	0	6

Charlie Baumann

Year	Team		TD	1XP	2XP	FG	FGA	SAF	Pts
1991	**MIA-NE**	**N**	0	15		9	12	0	42
1992	**NE**	**N**	0	22		11	17	0	55
Career			0	37		20	29	0	97

Bob Baumhower

Year	Team		TD	1XP	2XP	FG	FGA	SAF	Pts
1978	**MIA**	**N**	1	0		0	0	0	6
1984			1	0		0	0	0	6
Career			2	0		0	0	0	12

Mark Bavaro

Year	Team		TD	1XP	2XP	FG	FGA	SAF	Pts
1985	**NYG**	**N**	4	0		0	0	0	24
1986			4	0		0	0	0	24
1987			8	0		0	0	0	48
1988			4	0		0	0	0	24
1989			3	0		0	0	0	18
1990			5	0		0	0	0	30
1992	**CLE**	**N**	2	0		0	0	0	12
1993	**PHI**	**N**	6	0		0	0	0	36
1994			3	0	0	0	0	0	18
Career			39	0	0	0	0	0	234
Playoffs			3	0	0	0	0	0	18

Bibbles Bawel

Year	Team		TD	1XP	2XP	FG	FGA	SAF	Pts
1952	**PHI**	**N**	1	0		0	0	0	6
1955			2	0		0	0	0	12
Career			3	0		0	0	0	18

Brad Baxter

Year	Team		TD	1XP	2XP	FG	FGA	SAF	Pts
1990	**NYJ**	**N**	6	0		0	0	0	36

Brad Baxter *continued*

Year	Team		TD	1XP	2XP	FG	FGA	SAF	Pts
1991			11	0		0	0	0	66
1992			6	0		0	0	0	36
1993			7	0		0	0	0	42
1994			4	0	0	0	0	0	24
1995			1	0	0	0	0	0	6
Career			35	0	0	0	0	0	210

Fred Baxter

Year	Team		TD	1XP	2XP	FG	FGA	SAF	Pts
1993	**NYJ**	**N**	1	0		0	0	0	6
1994			1	0	0	0	0	0	6
1995			1	0	0	0	0	0	6
Career			3	0	0	0	0	0	18

Martin Bayless

Year	Team		TD	1XP	2XP	FG	FGA	SAF	Pts
1994	**WAS**	**N**	1	0	0	0	0	0	6

Craig Baynham

Year	Team		TD	1XP	2XP	FG	FGA	SAF	Pts
1967	**DAL**	**N**	1	0		0	0	0	6
1968			8	0		0	0	0	48
Career			9	0		0	0	0	54
Playoffs			3	0		0	0	0	18

Pat Beach

Year	Team		TD	1XP	2XP	FG	FGA	SAF	Pts
1982	**BAL**	**N**	1	0		0	0	0	6
1983			1	0		0	0	0	6
1985	**IND**	**N**	6	0		0	0	0	36
1986			1	0		0	0	0	6
1989			2	0		0	0	0	12
1990			1	0		0	0	0	6
1992	**PHI**	**N**	2	0		0	0	0	12
Career			14	0		0	0	0	84
Playoffs			1	0		0	0	0	6

Sanjay Beach

Year	Team		TD	1XP	2XP	FG	FGA	SAF	Pts
1992	**GB**	**N**	1	0		0	0	0	6
1993	**SF**	**N**	1	0		0	0	0	6
Career			2	0		0	0	0	12

Walter Beach

Year	Team		TD	1XP	2XP	FG	FGA	SAF	Pts
1960	**BOS**	**A**	1	0	0	0	0	0	6
1964	**CLE**	**N**	1	0		0	0	0	6
Career			2	0	0	0	0	0	12

Alyn Beals

Year	Team		TD	1XP	2XP	FG	FGA	SAF	Pts
1946	**SF**	**AA**	10	1		0	0	0	61
1947			10	0		0	0	0	60
1948			14	0		0	0	0	84
1949			**12**	1		0	0	0	**73**
1950	**SF**	**N**	3	0		0	0	0	18
Career			49	2		0	0	0	296

Autry Beamon

Year	Team		TD	1XP	2XP	FG	FGA	SAF	Pts
1975	**MIN**	**N**	0	0		0	0	1	2
1977	**SEA**	**N**	1	0		0	0	0	6
Career			1	0		0	0	1	8

Bubba Bean

Year	Team		TD	1XP	2XP	FG	FGA	SAF	Pts
1976	**ATL**	**N**	3	0		0	0	0	18
1978			4	0		0	0	0	24
1979			1	0		0	0	0	6
Career			8	0		0	0	0	48
Playoffs			1	0		0	0	0	6

John Beasley

Year	Team		TD	1XP	2XP	FG	FGA	SAF	Pts
1967	**MIN**	**N**	4	0		0	0	0	24
1969			5	0		0	0	0	30
1970			2	0		0	0	0	12
1972			1	0		0	0	0	6
1973	**MIN-NO**	**N**	2	0		0	0	0	12
Career			14	0		0	0	0	84

Terry Beasley

Year	Team		TD	1XP	2XP	FG	FGA	SAF	Pts
1974	**SF**	**N**	3	0		0	0	0	18

Pete Beathard

Year	Team		TD	1XP	2XP	FG	FGA	SAF	Pts
1965	**KC**	**A**	4	0	1	0	0	0	26
1966			1	0	0	0	0	0	6
1967	**HOU**	**A**	1	0	0	0	0	0	6
1968			2	0	0	0	0	0	12
1969			2	0	0	0	0	0	12
1973	**KC**	**N**	1	0		0	0	0	6
Career			11	0	1	0	0	0	68

Chuck Beatty

Year	Team		TD	1XP	2XP	FG	FGA	SAF	Pts
1970	**PIT**	**N**	1	0		0	0	0	6

Al Beauchamp

Year	Team		TD	1XP	2XP	FG	FGA	SAF	Pts
1968	**CIN**	**A**	1	0	0	0	0	0	6
1970	**CIN**	**N**	1	0		0	0	0	6
1971			1	0		0	0	0	6
Career			3	0	0	0	0	0	18

Joe Beauchamp

Year	Team		TD	1XP	2XP	FG	FGA	SAF	Pts
1968	**SD**	**A**	2	0	0	0	0	0	12
1972	**SD**	**N**	1	0		0	0	0	6
Career			3	0	0	0	0	0	18

Hub Bechtol

Year	Team		TD	1XP	2XP	FG	FGA	SAF	Pts
1947	**BAL**	**AA**	1	0		0	0	0	6

Braden Beck

Year	Team		TD	1XP	2XP	FG	FGA	SAF	Pts
1971	**HOU**	**N**	0	1		1	2	0	4

Wayland Becker

Year	Team		TD	1XP	2XP	FG	FGA	SAF	Pts
1935	**BKN**	**N**	1	0		0		0	6
1936	**GB**	**N**	1	0		0		0	6
Career			2	0		0		0	12

Art Beckley

Year	Team		TD	1XP	2XP	FG	FGA	SAF	Pts
1926	**DAY**	**N**	0	0		1		0	3

Brad Beckman

Year	Team		TD	1XP	2XP	FG	FGA	SAF	Pts
1989	**ATL**	**N**	1	0		0	0	0	6

Ed Beckman

Year	Team		TD	1XP	2XP	FG	FGA	SAF	Pts
1978	**KC**	**N**	0	0		0	0	1	2
1984			1	0		0	0	0	6
Career			1	0		0	0	1	8

Chuck Bednarik

Year	Team		TD	1XP	2XP	FG	FGA	SAF	Pts
1953	**PHI**	**N**	1	0		0	0	0	6

Hal Bedsole

Year	Team		TD	1XP	2XP	FG	FGA	SAF	Pts
1964	**MIN**	**N**	5	0		0	0	0	30
1965			3	0		0	0	0	18
Career			8	0		0	0	0	48

Don Beebe

Year	Team		TD	1XP	2XP	FG	FGA	SAF	Pts
1989	**BUF**	**N**	2	0		0	0	0	12
1990			1	0		0	0	0	6
1991			6	0		0	0	0	36
1992			2	0		0	0	0	12
1993			3	0		0	0	0	18
1994			4	0	0	0	0	0	24
1995	**CAR**	**N**	1	0	0	0	0	0	6
1996	**GB**	**N**	6	0	0	0	0	0	36
Career			25	0	0	0	0	0	150
Playoffs			3	0	0	0	0	0	18

Willie Beecher

Year	Team		TD	1XP	2XP	FG	FGA	SAF	Pts
1987	**MIA**	**N**	0	12		3	4	0	21

Tom Beer

Year	Team		TD	1XP	2XP	FG	FGA	SAF	Pts
1968	**DEN**	**A**	1	0	0	0	0	0	6
1971	**NE**	**N**	3	0		0	0	0	18
Career			4	0	0	0	0	0	24

Bull Behman

Year	Team		TD	1XP	2XP	FG	FGA	SAF	Pts
1925	**FRA**	**N**	2	12		5		0	39
1929			0	0		0		0	0
Career			2	12		5		0	39

Jim Beirne

Year	Team		TD	1XP	2XP	FG	FGA	SAF	Pts
1968	**HOU**	**A**	4	0	0	0	0	0	24
1969			4	0	1	0	0	0	26
1970	**HOU**	**N**	1	0		0	0	0	6
1971			1	0		0	0	0	6
1972			1	0		0	0	0	6
Career			11	0	1	0	0	0	68

Bill Belanich

Year	Team		TD	1XP	2XP	FG	FGA	SAF	Pts
1927	**DAY**	**N**	1	0		0		0	6

Bunny Belden

Year	Team		TD	1XP	2XP	FG	FGA	SAF	Pts
1930	**CHIC**	**N**	3	0		0		0	18
1931			3	0		0		0	18
Career			6	0		0		0	36

Steve Belichick

Year	Team		TD	1XP	2XP	FG	FGA	SAF	Pts
1941	DET	N	3	0		0	0	0	18

Bill Belk

Year	Team		TD	1XP	2XP	FG	FGA	SAF	Pts
1968	SF	N	1	0		0	0	0	6
1974			1	0		0	0	0	6
Career			2	0		0	0	0	12

Rocky Belk

Year	Team		TD	1XP	2XP	FG	FGA	SAF	Pts
1983	CLE	N	2	0		0	0	0	12

Bill Bell

Year	Team		TD	1XP	2XP	FG	FGA	SAF	Pts
1971	ATL	N	0	29		13	21	0	68
1972			0	31		16	30	0	79
1973	NE	N	0	4		1	4	0	7
Career			0	64		30	55	0	154

Bob Bell

Year	Team		TD	1XP	2XP	FG	FGA	SAF	Pts
1971	DET	N	1	0		0	0	0	6

Bobby Bell

Year	Team		TD	1XP	2XP	FG	FGA	SAF	Pts
1964	KC	A	1	0	0	0	0	0	6
1965			1	0	0	0	0	0	6
1966			1	0	0	0	0	0	6
1967			1	0	0	0	0	0	6
1969			1	0	0	0	0	0	6
1970	KC	N	1	0		0	0	0	6
1971			1	0		0	0	0	6
1972			1	0		0	0	0	6
1974			1	0		0	0	0	6
Career			9	0	0	0	0	0	54

Coleman Bell

Year	Team		TD	1XP	2XP	FG	FGA	SAF	Pts
1995	WAS	N	1	0	0	0	0	0	6

Eddie Bell

Year	Team		TD	1XP	2XP	FG	FGA	SAF	Pts
1956	PHI	N	1	0		0	0	0	6

Eddie Bell

Year	Team		TD	1XP	2XP	FG	FGA	SAF	Pts
1970	NYJ	N	2	0		0	0	0	12
1971			1	0		0	0	0	6
1972			2	0		0	0	0	12
1973			2	0		0	0	0	12
1974			1	0		0	0	0	6
1975			4	0		0	0	0	24
Career			12	0		0	0	0	72

Gordon Bell

Year	Team		TD	1XP	2XP	FG	FGA	SAF	Pts
1976	NYG	N	2	0		0	0	0	12

Greg Bell

Year	Team		TD	1XP	2XP	FG	FGA	SAF	Pts
1984	BUF	N	8	0		0	0	0	48
1985			9	0		0	0	0	54
1986			6	0		0	0	0	36
1987	LARM	N	1	0		0	0	0	6
1988			**18**	0		0	0	0	108
1989			15	0		0	0	0	90
1990	LARI	N	1	0		0	0	0	6
Career			58	0		0	0	0	348
Playoffs			1	0		0	0	0	6

Jerry Bell

Year	Team		TD	1XP	2XP	FG	FGA	SAF	Pts
1983	TB	N	1	0		0	0	0	6
1984			4	0		0	0	0	24
1985			2	0		0	0	0	12
Career			7	0		0	0	0	42

Nick Bell

Year	Team		TD	1XP	2XP	FG	FGA	SAF	Pts
1991	LARI	N	3	0		0	0	0	18
1992			3	0		0	0	0	18
1993			1	0		0	0	0	6
Career			7	0		0	0	0	42

Richard Bell

Year	Team		TD	1XP	2XP	FG	FGA	SAF	Pts
1990	PIT	N	1	0		0	0	0	6

Ricky Bell

Year	Team		TD	1XP	2XP	FG	FGA	SAF	Pts
1977	TB	N	1	0		0	0	0	6
1978			6	0		0	0	0	36
1979			9	0		0	0	0	54
1980			3	0		0	0	0	18
Career			19	0		0	0	0	114
Playoffs			2	0		0	0	0	12

Theo Bell

Year	Team		TD	1XP	2XP	FG	FGA	SAF	Pts
1976	PIT	N	1	0		0	0	0	6
1978			1	0		0	0	0	6
1980			2	0		0	0	0	12
1981	TB	N	2	0		0	0	0	12
1983			2	0		0	0	0	12
Career			8	0		0	0	0	48

Todd Bell

Year	Team		TD	1XP	2XP	FG	FGA	SAF	Pts
1981	CHI	N	1	0		0	0	0	6
1984			1	0		0	0	0	6
Career			2	0		0	0	0	12

Rodney Bellinger

Year	Team		TD	1XP	2XP	FG	FGA	SAF	Pts
1986	BUF	N	1	0		0	0	0	6

Joe Bellino

Year	Team		TD	1XP	2XP	FG	FGA	SAF	Pts
1966	BOS	A	1	0	0	0	0	0	6

Jason Belser

Year	Team		TD	1XP	2XP	FG	FGA	SAF	Pts
1996	IND	N	2	0	0	0	0	0	12

Horace Belton

Year	Team		TD	1XP	2XP	FG	FGA	SAF	Pts
1979	KC	N	1	0		0	0	0	6
1980			2	0		0	0	0	12
Career			3	0		0	0	0	18

Willie Belton

Year	Team		TD	1XP	2XP	FG	FGA	SAF	Pts
1971	ATL	N	1	0		0	0	0	6

Jesse Bendross

Year	Team		TD	1XP	2XP	FG	FGA	SAF	Pts
1985	SD	N	2	0		0	0	0	12

Rolf Benirschke

Year	Team		TD	1XP	2XP	FG	FGA	SAF	Pts
1977	SD	N	0	21		17	23	0	72
1978			0	37		18	22	0	91
1979			0	12		4	4	0	24
1980			0	46		24	36	0	118
1981			0	**55**		19	26	0	112
1982			0	**32**		16	22	0	80
1983			0	43		15	24	0	88
1984			0	41		17	26	0	92
1985			0	2		0	0	0	2
1986			0	39		16	25	0	87
Career			0	328		146	208	0	766
Playoffs			0	16		7	12	0	37

Chuck Bennett

Year	Team		TD	1XP	2XP	FG	FGA	SAF	Pts
1930	POR	N	6	0		0		0	36

Cornelius Bennett

Year	Team		TD	1XP	2XP	FG	FGA	SAF	Pts
1990	BUF	N	1	0		0	0	0	6
1991			1	0		0	0	0	6
1995			1	0	0	0	0	0	6
Career			3	0	0	0	0	0	18

Donnell Bennett

Year	Team		TD	1XP	2XP	FG	FGA	SAF	Pts
1994	KC	N	2	0	0	0	0	0	12

Edgar Bennett

Year	Team		TD	1XP	2XP	FG	FGA	SAF	Pts
1993	GB	N	10	0		0	0	0	60
1994			9	0	0	0	0	0	54
1995			7	0	0	0	0	0	42
1996			3	0	2	0	0	0	22
Career			29	0	2	0	0	0	178
Playoffs			5	0	0	0	0	0	30

Lewis Bennett

Year	Team		TD	1XP	2XP	FG	FGA	SAF	Pts
1987	NYG	N	1	0		0	0	0	6

Roy Bennett

Year	Team		TD	1XP	2XP	FG	FGA	SAF	Pts
1988	SD	N	1	0		0	0	0	6

Tony Bennett

Year	Team		TD	1XP	2XP	FG	FGA	SAF	Pts
1992	GB	N	1	0		0	0	0	6
1994	IND	N	1	0	0	0	0	0	6
1995			1	0	0	0	0	1	8
Career			3	0	0	0	0	1	20

Woody Bennett

Year	Team		TD	1XP	2XP	FG	FGA	SAF	Pts
1979	NYJ	N	1	0		0	0	0	6
1980	MIA	N	1	0		0	0	0	6
1983			2	0		0	0	0	12
1984			8	0		0	0	0	48

Woody Bennett *continued*

Year	Team		TD	1XP	2XP	FG	FGA	SAF	Pts
1985			1	0		0	0	0	6
Career			13	0		0	0	0	78
Playoffs			4	0		0	0	0	24

Albert Bentley

Year	Team		TD	1XP	2XP	FG	FGA	SAF	Pts
1985	IND	N	2	0		0	0	0	12
1986			3	0		0	0	0	18
1987			9	0		0	0	0	54
1988			3	0		0	0	0	18
1989			5	0		0	0	0	30
1990			6	0		0	0	0	36
Career			28	0		0	0	0	168
Playoffs			1	0		0	0	0	6

Ray Bentley

Year	Team		TD	1XP	2XP	FG	FGA	SAF	Pts
1992	CIN	N	1	0		0	0	0	6

Jim Benton

Year	Team		TD	1XP	2XP	FG	FGA	SAF	Pts
1938	CLE	N	6	0		0	0	0	36
1939			8	0		0	0	0	48
1940			3	0		0	0	0	18
1942			1	0		0	0	0	6
1943	CHIB	N	3	0		0	0	0	18
1944	CLE	N	7	0		0	0	0	42
1945			8	0		0	0	0	48
1946	LA	N	6	0		0	0	0	36
1947			6	0		0	0	0	36
Career			48	0		0	0	0	288
Playoffs			2	0		0	0	0	12

George Benyola

Year	Team		TD	1XP	2XP	FG	FGA	SAF	Pts
1987	NYG	N	0	3		3	5	0	12

Karl Bernard

Year	Team		TD	1XP	2XP	FG	FGA	SAF	Pts
1987	DET	N	2	0		0	0	0	12

Frank Bernardi

Year	Team		TD	1XP	2XP	FG	FGA	SAF	Pts
1955	CHIC	N	1	0		0	0	0	6
1956			1	0		0	0	0	6
Career			2	0		0	0	0	12

Ed Bernet

Year	Team		TD	1XP	2XP	FG	FGA	SAF	Pts
1955	PIT	N	1	0		0	0	0	6

Rod Bernstine

Year	Team		TD	1XP	2XP	FG	FGA	SAF	Pts
1987	SD	N	1	0		0	0	0	6
1989			2	0		0	0	0	12
1990			4	0		0	0	0	24
1991			8	0		0	0	0	48
1992			4	0		0	0	0	24
1993	DEN	N	4	0		0	0	0	24
1995			1	0	0	0	0	0	6
Career			24	0	0	0	0	0	144

Bob Berry

Year	Team		TD	1XP	2XP	FG	FGA	SAF	Pts
1968	ATL	N	2	0		0	0	0	12
1972			2	0		0	0	0	12
Career			4	0		0	0	0	24

Charlie Berry

Year	Team		TD	1XP	2XP	FG	FGA	SAF	Pts
1925	POT	N	6	**29**		3		0	**74**
1926			3	0		0		0	18
Career			9	29		3		0	92

Connie Mack Berry

Year	Team		TD	1XP	2XP	FG	FGA	SAF	Pts
1942	CHIB	N	2	0		0	0	0	12
1943			2	0		0	0	0	12
1944			6	0		0	0	0	36
Career			10	0		0	0	0	60

George Berry

Year	Team		TD	1XP	2XP	FG	FGA	SAF	Pts
1925	AKR	N	1	0		0		0	6

Howard Berry

Year	Team		TD	1XP	2XP	FG	FGA	SAF	Pts
1921	ROC	A	2	1		2		0	19

Ray Berry

Year	Team		TD	1XP	2XP	FG	FGA	SAF	Pts
1989	MIN	N	0	0		0	0	1	2

Raymond Berry

Year	Team		TD	1XP	2XP	FG	FGA	SAF	Pts
1956	BAL	N	2	0		0	0	0	12
1957			6	0		0	0	0	36
1958			9	0		0	0	0	54

Raymond Berry *continued*

Year	Team		TD	1XP	2XP	FG	FGA	SAF	Pts
1959			**14**	0		0	0	0	84
1960			10	0		0	0	0	60
1962			3	0		0	0	0	18
1963			3	0		0	0	0	18
1964			6	0		0	0	0	36
1965			7	0		0	0	0	42
1966			7	0		0	0	0	42
1967			1	0		0	0	0	6
Career			68	0		0	0	0	408
Playoffs			1	0		0	0	0	6

Rex Berry

Year	Team		TD	1XP	2XP	FG	FGA	SAF	Pts
1953	**SF**	**N**	1	0		0	0	0	6
1954			1	0		0	0	0	6
1955			1	0		0	0	0	6
Career			3	0		0	0	0	18

Royce Berry

Year	Team		TD	1XP	2XP	FG	FGA	SAF	Pts
1970	**CIN**	**N**	2	0		0	0	0	12

Angelo Bertelli

Year	Team		TD	1XP	2XP	FG	FGA	SAF	Pts
1946	**LA**	**AA**	1	0		0	0	0	6
1947	**CHI**	**AA**	0	0		0	1	0	0
Career			1	0		0	1	0	6

Jim Bertelsen

Year	Team		TD	1XP	2XP	FG	FGA	SAF	Pts
1972	**LA**	**N**	6	0		0	0	0	36
1973			5	0		0	0	0	30
1974			2	0		0	0	0	12
1975			3	0		0	0	0	18
1976			2	0		0	0	0	12
Career			18	0		0	0	0	108

Jim Bertoglio

Year	Team		TD	1XP	2XP	FG	FGA	SAF	Pts
1926	**COL**	**N**	1	0		0		0	6

Don Bessillieu

Year	Team		TD	1XP	2XP	FG	FGA	SAF	Pts
1980	**MIA**	**N**	1	0		0	0	0	6

Greg Best

Year	Team		TD	1XP	2XP	FG	FGA	SAF	Pts
1983	**PIT**	**N**	1	0		0	0	0	6

Elvin Bethea

Year	Team		TD	1XP	2XP	FG	FGA	SAF	Pts
1969	**HOU**	**A**	0	0	0	0	0	1	2
1974	**HOU**	**N**	1	0		0	0	0	6
1975			0	0		0	0	1	2
Career			1	0	0	0	0	2	10

James Betterson

Year	Team		TD	1XP	2XP	FG	FGA	SAF	Pts
1977	**PHI**	**N**	1	0		0	0	0	6

Jerome Bettis

Year	Team		TD	1XP	2XP	FG	FGA	SAF	Pts
1993	**LARM**	**N**	7	0		0	0	0	42
1994			4	0	2	0	0	0	28
1995	**STL**	**N**	3	0	0	0	0	0	18
1996	**PIT**	**N**	11	0	0	0	0	0	66
Career			25	0	2	0	0	0	154
Playoffs			2	0	0	0	0	0	12

Steve Beuerlein

Year	Team		TD	1XP	2XP	FG	FGA	SAF	Pts
1994	**ARI**	**N**	1	0	0	0	0	0	6

Dwight Beverly

Year	Team		TD	1XP	2XP	FG	FGA	SAF	Pts
1987	**NO**	**N**	2	0		0	0	0	12

Randy Beverly

Year	Team		TD	1XP	2XP	FG	FGA	SAF	Pts
1968	**NY**	**A**	1	0	0	0	0	0	6

Dean Biasucci

Year	Team		TD	1XP	2XP	FG	FGA	SAF	Pts
1984	**IND**	**N**	0	13		3	5	0	22
1986			0	26		13	25	0	65
1987			0	24		24	27	0	96
1988			0	39		25	32	0	114
1989			0	31		21	27	0	94
1990			0	32		17	24	0	83
1991			0	14		15	26	0	59
1992			0	24		16	29	0	72
1993			0	15		26	31	0	93
1994			0	37	0	16	24	0	85
1995	**STL**	**N**	0	13	0	9	12	0	40
Career			0	268	0	185	262	0	823
Playoffs			0	3	0	0	0	0	3

Dick Bielski

Year	Team		TD	1XP	2XP	FG	FGA	SAF	Pts
1955	**PHI**	**N**	1	23		9	23	0	56
1956			1	0		0	1	0	6
1957			2	0		0	2	0	12
1958			1	0		0	0	0	6
1959			1	0		0	5	0	6
1960	**DAL**	**N**	1	0		0	0	0	6
1961			3	10		6	9	0	46
1962	**BAL**	**N**	2	25		11	25	0	70
Career			12	58		26	65	0	208

Eric Bieniemy

Year	Team		TD	1XP	2XP	FG	FGA	SAF	Pts
1992	**SD**	**N**	3	0		0	0	0	18
1993			1	0		0	0	0	6
1995	**CIN**	**N**	3	0	0	0	0	0	18
1996			2	0	0	0	0	0	12
Career			9	0	0	0	0	0	54

Scotty Bierce

Year	Team		TD	1XP	2XP	FG	FGA	SAF	Pts
1920	**AKR**	**A**	0	0		0		1	2
1921			2	0		0		0	12
1922	**AKR**	**N**	2	0		0		0	12
1923	**CLE-BUF**	**N**	3	0		0		0	18
Career			7	0		0		1	44

Verlon Biggs

Year	Team		TD	1XP	2XP	FG	FGA	SAF	Pts
1972	**WAS**	**N**	1	0		0	0	0	6
1973			1	0		0	0	0	6
Career			2	0		0	0	0	12

Fred Biletnikoff

Year	Team		TD	1XP	2XP	FG	FGA	SAF	Pts
1966	**OAK**	**A**	3	0	0	0	0	0	18
1967			5	0	0	0	0	0	30
1968			7	0	0	0	0	0	42
1969			12	0	0	0	0	0	72
1970	**OAK**	**N**	7	0		0	0	0	42
1971			9	0		0	0	0	54
1972			7	0		0	0	0	42
1973			4	0		0	0	0	24
1974			7	0		0	0	0	42
1975			2	0		0	0	0	12
1976			7	0		0	0	0	42
1977			5	0		0	0	0	30
1978			2	0		0	0	0	12
Career			77	0	0	0	0	0	462
Playoffs			10	0	0	0	0	0	60

Lewis Billups

Year	Team		TD	1XP	2XP	FG	FGA	SAF	Pts
1988	**CIN**	**N**	1	0		0	0	0	6

Don Bingham

Year	Team		TD	1XP	2XP	FG	FGA	SAF	Pts
1956	**CHIB**	**N**	1	0		0	0	0	6

Gregg Bingham

Year	Team		TD	1XP	2XP	FG	FGA	SAF	Pts
1977	**HOU**	**N**	1	0		0	0	0	6

John Binotto

Year	Team		TD	1XP	2XP	FG	FGA	SAF	Pts
1942	**PIT**	**N**	0	1		0	0	0	1

Rodger Bird

Year	Team		TD	1XP	2XP	FG	FGA	SAF	Pts
1968	**OAK**	**A**	1	0	0	0	0	0	6

J.J. Birden

Year	Team		TD	1XP	2XP	FG	FGA	SAF	Pts
1990	**KC**	**N**	3	0		0	0	0	18
1991			2	0		0	0	0	12
1992			3	0		0	0	0	18
1993			2	0		0	0	0	12
1994			4	0	1	0	0	0	26
1995	**ATL**	**N**	1	0	0	0	0	0	6
1996			2	0	0	0	0	0	12
Career			17	0	1	0	0	0	104
Playoffs			3	0	0	0	0	0	18

Danny Birdwell

Year	Team		TD	1XP	2XP	FG	FGA	SAF	Pts
1962	**OAK**	**A**	0	0	0	0	1	0	0
1967			0	0	0	0	0	1	2
Career			0	0	0	0	1	1	2

Tom Birney

Year	Team		TD	1XP	2XP	FG	FGA	SAF	Pts
1979	**GB**	**N**	0	7		7	9	0	28
1980			0	14		6	12	0	32
Career			0	21		13	21	0	60

Bill Bishop

Year	Team		TD	1XP	2XP	FG	FGA	SAF	Pts
1958	**CHIB**	**N**	1	0		0	0	0	6

Blaine Bishop

Year	Team		TD	1XP	2XP	FG	FGA	SAF	Pts
1995	**HOU**	**N**	1	0	0	0	0	0	6

Don Bishop

Year	Team		TD	1XP	2XP	FG	FGA	SAF	Pts
1962	**DAL**	**N**	1	0		0	0	0	6

Richard Bishop

Year	Team		TD	1XP	2XP	FG	FGA	SAF	Pts
1978	**NE**	**N**	0	0		0	0	1	2

Don Bitterlich

Year	Team		TD	1XP	2XP	FG	FGA	SAF	Pts
1976	**SEA**	**N**	0	7		1	4	0	10

Charlie Bivins

Year	Team		TD	1XP	2XP	FG	FGA	SAF	Pts
1961	**CHI**	**N**	1	0		0	0	0	6
1962			1	0		0	0	0	6
1964			1	0		0	0	0	6
1965			2	0		0	0	0	12
1967	**PIT**	**N**	1	0		0	0	0	6
Career			6	0		0	0	0	36

Eric Bjornson

Year	Team		TD	1XP	2XP	FG	FGA	SAF	Pts
1996	**DAL**	**N**	3	0	1	0	0	0	20

Bill Blackburn

Year	Team		TD	1XP	2XP	FG	FGA	SAF	Pts
1946	**CHIC**	**N**	1	0		0	0	1	8
1948			2	0		0	0	0	12
1949			1	0		0	0	0	6
Career			4	0		0	0	1	26

Todd Blackledge

Year	Team		TD	1XP	2XP	FG	FGA	SAF	Pts
1984	**KC**	**N**	1	0		0	0	0	6
1988	**PIT**	**N**	1	0		0	0	0	6
Career			2	0		0	0	0	12

Hugh Blacklock

Year	Team		TD	1XP	2XP	FG	FGA	SAF	Pts
1920	**DEC**	**A**	0	6		0		0	6
1921			0	2		0		0	2
Career			0	8		0		0	8

Don Blackmon

Year	Team		TD	1XP	2XP	FG	FGA	SAF	Pts
1985	**NE**	**N**	0	0		0	0	2	4

Robert Blackmon

Year	Team		TD	1XP	2XP	FG	FGA	SAF	Pts
1993	**SEA**	**N**	1	0		0	0	0	6
1996			1	0	0	0	0	0	6
Career			2	0	0	0	0	0	12

Richard Blackmore

Year	Team		TD	1XP	2XP	FG	FGA	SAF	Pts
1982	**PHI**	**N**	1	0		0	0	0	6

Glenn Blackwood

Year	Team		TD	1XP	2XP	FG	FGA	SAF	Pts
1982	**MIA**	**N**	1	0		0	0	0	6

Lyle Blackwood

Year	Team		TD	1XP	2XP	FG	FGA	SAF	Pts
1978	**BAL**	**N**	2	0		0	0	0	12

Bennie Blades

Year	Team		TD	1XP	2XP	FG	FGA	SAF	Pts
1992	**DET**	**N**	1	0		0	0	0	6
1995			0	0	0	0	0	1	2
1996			1	0	0	0	0	0	6
Career			2	0	0	0	0	1	14

Brian Blades

Year	Team		TD	1XP	2XP	FG	FGA	SAF	Pts
1988	**SEA**	**N**	8	0		0	0	0	48
1989			5	0		0	0	0	30
1990			3	0		0	0	0	18
1991			2	0		0	0	0	12
1992			1	0		0	0	0	6
1993			3	0		0	0	0	18
1994			4	0	1	0	0	0	26
1995			4	0	0	0	0	0	24
1996			2	0	0	0	0	0	12
Career			32	0	1	0	0	0	194

Joe Blahak

Year	Team		TD	1XP	2XP	FG	FGA	SAF	Pts
1975	**MIN**	**N**	0	0		0	0	1	2

Russ Blailock

Year	Team		TD	1XP	2XP	FG	FGA	SAF	Pts
1923	**MIL**	**N**	1	0		0		0	6
1925	**AKR**	**N**	0	2		1		0	5
Career			1	2		1		0	11

George Blair

Year	Team	Lg	TD	1XP	2XP	FG	FGA	SAF	Pts
1961	SD	A	0	42	0	13	27	0	81
1962			0	31	0	17	20	0	82
1963			0	44	0	17	27	0	95
1964			0	5	0	3	5	0	14
Career			0	122	0	50	79	0	272
Playoffs			0	6	0	2	4	0	12

Matt Blair

Year	Team	Lg	TD	1XP	2XP	FG	FGA	SAF	Pts
1977	MIN	N	1	0		0	0	0	6
1978			1	0		0	0	0	6
Career			2	0		0	0	0	12

Jeff Blake

Year	Team	Lg	TD	1XP	2XP	FG	FGA	SAF	Pts
1994	CIN	N	1	0	1	0	0	0	8
1995			2	0	1	0	0	0	14
1996			2	0	0	0	0	0	12
Career			5	0	2	0	0	0	34

Ricky Blake

Year	Team	Lg	TD	1XP	2XP	FG	FGA	SAF	Pts
1991	DAL	N	1	0		0	0	0	6

Cary Blanchard

Year	Team	Lg	TD	1XP	2XP	FG	FGA	SAF	Pts
1992	NYJ	N	0	17		16	22	0	65
1993			0	31		17	26	0	82
1995	IND	N	0	25	0	19	24	0	82
1996			0	27	0	36	40	0	135
Career			0	100	0	88	112	0	364
Playoffs			0	9	0	4	7	0	21

Carl Bland

Year	Team	Lg	TD	1XP	2XP	FG	FGA	SAF	Pts
1986	DET	N	2	0		0	0	0	12
1987			1	0		0	0	0	6
1988			2	0		0	0	0	12
1989	GB	N	2	0		0	0	0	12
Career			7	0		0	0	0	42

George Blanda

Year	Team	Lg	TD	1XP	2XP	FG	FGA	SAF	Pts
1949	CHIB	N	1	0		7	15	0	27
1950			0	0		6	15	0	18
1951			0	26		6	17	0	44
1952			1	30		6	25	0	54
1953			0	27		7	20	0	48
1954			0	23		8	16	0	47
1955			2	37		11	16	0	82
1956			0	**45**		12	**28**	0	81
1957			1	23		14	**26**	0	71
1958			0	36		11	23	0	69
1960	HOU	A	4	46	0	15	**34**	0	115
1961			0	**64**	0	16	26	0	112
1962			0	**48**	0	11	26	0	81
1963			0	39	0	9	22	0	66
1964			0	37	0	13	29	0	76
1965			0	28	0	11	21	0	61
1966			0	39	0	16	30	0	87
1967	OAK	A	0	**56**	0	20	30	0	**116**
1968			0	**54**	0	21	34	0	117
1969			0	**45**	0	20	37	0	105
1970	OAK	N	0	36		16	29	0	84
1971			0	41		15	22	0	86
1972			0	**44**		17	26	0	95
1973			0	31		23	33	0	100
1974			0	**44**		11	17	0	77
1975			0	44		13	21	0	83
Career			9	**943**	0	335	**638**	0	**2002**
Playoffs			0	**49**	0	**22**	**39**	0	115

Sid Blanks

Year	Team	Lg	TD	1XP	2XP	FG	FGA	SAF	Pts
1964	HOU	A	7	0	0	0	0	0	42
1966			2	0	0	0	0	0	12
1967			2	0	0	0	0	0	12
Career			11	0	0	0	0	0	66

Scott Blanton

Year	Team	Lg	TD	1XP	2XP	FG	FGA	SAF	Pts
1996	WAS	N	0	40	0	26	32	0	118

Anthony Blaylock

Year	Team	Lg	TD	1XP	2XP	FG	FGA	SAF	Pts
1990	CLE	N	1	0		0	0	0	6

Tony Blazine

Year	Team	Lg	TD	1XP	2XP	FG	FGA	SAF	Pts
1938	CHIC	N	1	0		0		0	6

Mel Bleeker

Year	Team	Lg	TD	1XP	2XP	FG	FGA	SAF	Pts
1944	PHI	N	8	0		0	0	0	48

Mel Bleeker *continued*

Year	Team	Lg	TD	1XP	2XP	FG	FGA	SAF	Pts
1945			2	0		0	0	0	12
1947	LA	N	1	0		0	0	0	6
Career			11	0		0	0	0	66

Bob Bleier

Year	Team	Lg	TD	1XP	2XP	FG	FGA	SAF	Pts
1987	NE	N	1	0		0	0	0	6

Rocky Bleier

Year	Team	Lg	TD	1XP	2XP	FG	FGA	SAF	Pts
1974	PIT	N	2	0		0	0	0	12
1975			2	0		0	0	0	12
1976			5	0		0	0	0	30
1977			4	0		0	0	0	24
1978			6	0		0	0	0	36
1979			4	0		0	0	0	24
1980			2	0		0	0	0	12
Career			25	0		0	0	0	150
Playoffs			6	0		0	0	0	36

Dennis Bligen

Year	Team	Lg	TD	1XP	2XP	FG	FGA	SAF	Pts
1985	NYJ	N	1	0		0	0	0	6
1986			1	0		0	0	0	6
1987			1	0		0	0	0	6
Career			3	0		0	0	0	18

Harry Bliss

Year	Team	Lg	TD	1XP	2XP	FG	FGA	SAF	Pts
1921	COL	A	0	1		0		0	1

Johnny Blood

Year	Team	Lg	TD	1XP	2XP	FG	FGA	SAF	Pts
1926	DUL	N	2	0		0		0	12
1927			1	0		0		0	6
1928	POT	N	3	1		0		0	19
1929	GB	N	5	0		1		0	33
1930			5	0		0		0	30
1931			**13**	0		0		0	**78**
1932			4	0		0		0	24
1933			3	1		0		0	19
1935			4	0		0		0	24
1936			3	1		0		0	19
1937	PIT	N	5	0		0		0	30
1938			0	0		0		0	0
Career			48	3		1		0	294

Al Bloodgood

Year	Team	Lg	TD	1XP	2XP	FG	FGA	SAF	Pts
1925	KC	N	0	2		2		0	8
1926			3	5		8		0	47
1927	CLE	N	**6**	6		1		0	45
1928	NYG	N	1	0		0		0	6
Career			10	13		11		0	106

Alvin Blount

Year	Team	Lg	TD	1XP	2XP	FG	FGA	SAF	Pts
1987	DAL	N	3	0		0	0	0	18

Eric Blount

Year	Team	Lg	TD	1XP	2XP	FG	FGA	SAF	Pts
1993	PHX	N	1	0		0	0	0	6

Lamar Blount

Year	Team	Lg	TD	1XP	2XP	FG	FGA	SAF	Pts
1946	MIA	AA	1	0		0	0	0	6

Mel Blount

Year	Team	Lg	TD	1XP	2XP	FG	FGA	SAF	Pts
1972	PIT	N	1	0		0	0	0	6
1974			1	0		0	0	0	6
1981			1	0		0	0	0	6
1983			1	0		0	0	0	6
Career			4	0		0	0	0	24

Al Blozis

Year	Team	Lg	TD	1XP	2XP	FG	FGA	SAF	Pts
1943	NYG	N	1	0		0	0	0	6

Forrest Blue

Year	Team	Lg	TD	1XP	2XP	FG	FGA	SAF	Pts
1971	SF	N	1	0		0	0	0	6

Luther Blue

Year	Team	Lg	TD	1XP	2XP	FG	FGA	SAF	Pts
1977	DET	N	1	0		0	0	0	6
1978			2	0		0	0	0	12
1979			1	0		0	0	0	6
Career			4	0		0	0	0	24

Jimmy Blumenstock

Year	Team	Lg	TD	1XP	2XP	FG	FGA	SAF	Pts
1947	NYG	N	2	0		0	0	0	12

Herb Blumer

Year	Team	Lg	TD	1XP	2XP	FG	FGA	SAF	Pts
1925	CHIC	N	2	0		0		0	12

Ronnie Blye

Year	Team	Lg	TD	1XP	2XP	FG	FGA	SAF	Pts
1968	NYG	N	1	0		0	0	0	6

Dwaine Board

Year	Team	Lg	TD	1XP	2XP	FG	FGA	SAF	Pts
1983	SF	N	1	0		0	0	0	6

Tony Boddie

Year	Team	Lg	TD	1XP	2XP	FG	FGA	SAF	Pts
1987	DEN	N	1	0		0	0	0	6

Billy Boedecker

Year	Team	Lg	TD	1XP	2XP	FG	FGA	SAF	Pts
1946	CHI	AA	1	0		0	0	0	6
1947	CLE	AA	5	0		0	0	0	30
1948			5	0		0	0	0	30
1949			3	0		0	0	0	18
Career			14	0		0	0	0	84

George Bogue

Year	Team	Lg	TD	1XP	2XP	FG	FGA	SAF	Pts
1930	CHIC	N	0	1		0		0	1

Dewey Bohling

Year	Team	Lg	TD	1XP	2XP	FG	FGA	SAF	Pts
1960	NY	A	6	0	0	0	0	0	36
1961	BUF	A	3	0	0	0	0	0	18
Career			9	0	0	0	0	0	54

Novo Bojovic

Year	Team	Lg	TD	1XP	2XP	FG	FGA	SAF	Pts
1985	STL	N	0	11		3	7	0	20

Kim Bokamper

Year	Team	Lg	TD	1XP	2XP	FG	FGA	SAF	Pts
1978	MIA	N	0	0		0	0	1	2
1983			1	0		0	0	0	6
Career			1	0		0	0	1	8

George Bolan

Year	Team	Lg	TD	1XP	2XP	FG	FGA	SAF	Pts
1922	CHIB	N	2	0		0		0	12

Leroy Bolden

Year	Team	Lg	TD	1XP	2XP	FG	FGA	SAF	Pts
1958	CLE	N	1	0		0	0	0	6

Rickey Bolden

Year	Team	Lg	TD	1XP	2XP	FG	FGA	SAF	Pts
1988	CLE	N	1	0		0	0	0	6

Chase Boldt

Year	Team	Lg	TD	1XP	2XP	FG	FGA	SAF	Pts
1922	LOU	N	1	0		0		0	6

Jim Bolger

Year	Team	Lg	TD	1XP	2XP	FG	FGA	SAF	Pts
1926	BKN	A	1	0		0		0	6

Nick Bolkovac

Year	Team	Lg	TD	1XP	2XP	FG	FGA	SAF	Pts
1953	PIT	N	1	27		4	12	0	45
1954			0	3		3	4	0	12
Career			1	30		7	16	0	57

Ron Bolton

Year	Team	Lg	TD	1XP	2XP	FG	FGA	SAF	Pts
1976	CLE	N	1	0		0	0	0	6
Playoffs			1	0	0	0	0	0	6

Lynn Bomar

Year	Team	Lg	TD	1XP	2XP	FG	FGA	SAF	Pts
1925	NY	N	3	0		0		0	18
1926			2	0		0		0	12
Career			5	0		0		0	30

Bourbon Bondurant

Year	Team	Lg	TD	1XP	2XP	FG	FGA	SAF	Pts
1921	EVA	A	0	6		0		0	6

Chris Boniol

Year	Team	Lg	TD	1XP	2XP	FG	FGA	SAF	Pts
1994	DAL	N	0	48	0	22	29	0	114
1995			0	46	0	27	28	0	127
1996			0	24	0	32	36	0	120
Career			0	118	0	81	93	0	361
Playoffs			0	24	0	13	14	0	63

Glen Bonner

Year	Team	Lg	TD	1XP	2XP	FG	FGA	SAF	Pts
1974	SD	N	4	0		0	0	0	24

Steve Bono

Year	Team	Lg	TD	1XP	2XP	FG	FGA	SAF	Pts
1987	PIT	N	1	0		0	0	0	6
1993	SF	N	1	0		0	0	0	6
1995	KC	N	5	0	0	0	0	0	30
Career			7	0	0	0	0	0	42

Vaughn Booker

Year	Team	Lg	TD	1XP	2XP	FG	FGA	SAF	Pts
1995	KC	N	1	0	0	0	0	0	6

Johnny Bookman

Year	Team	Lg	TD	1XP	2XP	FG	FGA	SAF	Pts
1957	NYG	N	1	0		0	0	0	6

Jack Boone

Year	Team	Lg	TD	1XP	2XP	FG	FGA	SAF	Pts
1942	CLE	N	1	0		0	0	0	6

J.R. Boone

Year	Team	Lg	TD	1XP	2XP	FG	FGA	SAF	Pts
1948	CHIB	N	7	0		0	0	0	42
1949			3	0		0	0	0	18
1952	SF	N	1	0		0	0	0	6
1953	GB	N	1	0		0	0	0	6
Career			12	0		0	0	0	72

Dick Booth

Year	Team	Lg	TD	1XP	2XP	FG	FGA	SAF	Pts
1941	DET	N	1	0		0	0	0	6
1945			1	0		0	0	0	6
Career			2	0		0	0	0	12

Emerson Boozer

Year	Team	Lg	TD	1XP	2XP	FG	FGA	SAF	Pts
1966	NY	A	6	0	0	0	0	0	36
1967			**13**	0	0	0	0	0	78
1968			5	0	0	0	0	0	30
1969			4	0	0	0	0	0	24
1970	NYJ	N	5	0		0	0	0	30
1971			6	0		0	0	0	36
1972			**14**	0		0	0	0	84
1973			6	0		0	0	0	36
1974			5	0		0	0	0	30
1975			1	0		0	0	0	6
Career			65	0	0	0	0	0	390
Playoffs			1	0	0	0	0	0	6

Kenny Bordelon

Year	Team	Lg	TD	1XP	2XP	FG	FGA	SAF	Pts
1979	NO	N	1	0		0	0	0	6

Mike Boryla

Year	Team	Lg	TD	1XP	2XP	FG	FGA	SAF	Pts
1976	PHI	N	2	0		0	0	0	12

Cap Boso

Year	Team	Lg	TD	1XP	2XP	FG	FGA	SAF	Pts
1987	CHI	N	2	0		0	0	0	12
1989			1	0		0	0	0	6
1990			1	0		0	0	0	6
Career			4	0		0	0	0	24

Don Bosseler

Year	Team	Lg	TD	1XP	2XP	FG	FGA	SAF	Pts
1957	WAS	N	7	0		0	0	0	42
1958			4	0		0	0	0	24
1959			3	0		0	0	0	18
1960			2	0		0	0	0	12
1961			3	0		0	0	0	18
1962			2	0		0	0	0	12
1963			2	0		0	0	0	12
Career			23	0		0	0	0	138

Keith Bostic

Year	Team	Lg	TD	1XP	2XP	FG	FGA	SAF	Pts
1984	HOU	N	1	0		0	0	0	6

Lew Bostick

Year	Team	Lg	TD	1XP	2XP	FG	FGA	SAF	Pts
1939	CLE	N	0	2		0	0	0	2

Lee Bouggess

Year	Team	Lg	TD	1XP	2XP	FG	FGA	SAF	Pts
1970	PHI	N	4	0		0	0	0	24
1971			3	0		0	0	0	18
1973			1	0		0	0	0	6
Career			8	0		0	0	0	48

Gil Bouley

Year	Team	Lg	TD	1XP	2XP	FG	FGA	SAF	Pts
1947	LA	N	1	0		0	0	0	6

Matt Bouza

Year	Team	Lg	TD	1XP	2XP	FG	FGA	SAF	Pts
1982	BAL	N	2	0		0	0	0	12
1985	IND	N	2	0		0	0	0	12
1986			5	0		0	0	0	30
1987			4	0		0	0	0	24
1988			4	0		0	0	0	24
Career			17	0		0	0	0	102

Tony Bova

Year	Team	Lg	TD	1XP	2XP	FG	FGA	SAF	Pts
1943	P-P	N	5	0		0	0	0	30
1944	C-P	N	2	0		0	0	0	12
1947	PIT	N	0	0		0	0	1	2
Career			7	0		0	0	1	44

Bill Bowman

Year	Team	Lg	TD	1XP	2XP	FG	FGA	SAF	Pts
1954	DET	N	5	0		0	0	0	30
1956			2	0		0	0	0	12
Career			7	0		0	0	0	42
Playoffs			1	0		0	0	0	6

Jim Bowman

Year	Team	Lg	TD	1XP	2XP	FG	FGA	SAF	Pts
Playoffs			1	0	0	0	0	0	6

Kevin Bowman

Year	Team	Lg	TD	1XP	2XP	FG	FGA	SAF	Pts
1987	PHI	N	1	0		0	0	0	6

Arda Bowser

Year	Team	Lg	TD	1XP	2XP	FG	FGA	SAF	Pts
1922	CAN	N	2	2		0		0	14

Cloyce Box

Year	Team	Lg	TD	1XP	2XP	FG	FGA	SAF	Pts
1949	DET	N	4	0		0	0	0	24
1950			11	0		0	0	0	66
1952			**15**	0		0	0	0	90
1953			2	0		0	0	0	12
Career			32	0		0	0	0	192

Bill Boyd

Year	Team	Lg	TD	1XP	2XP	FG	FGA	SAF	Pts
1930	CHIC	N	2	0		0		0	12

Bob Boyd

Year	Team	Lg	TD	1XP	2XP	FG	FGA	SAF	Pts
1950	LA	N	4	0		0	0	0	24
1951			1	0		0	0	0	6
1953			4	0		0	0	0	24
1954			6	0		0	0	0	36
1955			3	0		0	0	0	18
1956			7	0		0	0	0	42
1957			3	0		0	0	0	18
Career			28	0		0	0	0	168

Bobby Boyd

Year	Team	Lg	TD	1XP	2XP	FG	FGA	SAF	Pts
1963	BAL	N	1	0		0	0	0	6
1965			1	0		0	0	0	6
1966			1	0		0	0	0	6
1967			1	0		0	0	0	6
1968			1	0		0	0	0	6
Career			5	0		0	0	0	30

Dennis Boyd

Year	Team	Lg	TD	1XP	2XP	FG	FGA	SAF	Pts
1981	SEA	N	1	0		0	0	0	6

Elmo Boyd

Year	Team	Lg	TD	1XP	2XP	FG	FGA	SAF	Pts
1978	SF	N	1	0		0	0	0	6

Greg Boyd

Year	Team	Lg	TD	1XP	2XP	FG	FGA	SAF	Pts
1982	DEN	N	0	0		0	0	1	2
1983	GB	N	0	0		0	0	1	2
Career			0	0		0	0	2	4

Sam Boyd

Year	Team	Lg	TD	1XP	2XP	FG	FGA	SAF	Pts
1939	PIT	N	2	0		0	0	0	12

Max Boydston

Year	Team	Lg	TD	1XP	2XP	FG	FGA	SAF	Pts
1955	CHIC	N	1	0		0	0	0	6
1956			2	0		0	0	0	12
1958			1	0		0	0	0	6
1960	DAL	A	3	0	0	0	0	0	18
1961			1	0	0	0	0	0	6
Career			8	0	0	0	0	0	48

Mark Boyer

Year	Team	Lg	TD	1XP	2XP	FG	FGA	SAF	Pts
1986	IND	N	1	0		0	0	0	6
1988			2	0		0	0	0	12
1989			2	0		0	0	0	12
1990	NYJ	N	1	0		0	0	0	6
Career			6	0		0	0	0	36

Garland Boyette

Year	Team	Lg	TD	1XP	2XP	FG	FGA	SAF	Pts
1971	HOU	N	1	0		0	0	0	6

Deral Boykin

Year	Team	Lg	TD	1XP	2XP	FG	FGA	SAF	Pts
1993	LARM	N	1	0		0	0	0	6

Greg Boykin

Year	Team	Lg	TD	1XP	2XP	FG	FGA	SAF	Pts
1978	SF	N	2	0		0	0	0	12

Jim Boylan

Year	Team	Lg	TD	1XP	2XP	FG	FGA	SAF	Pts
1963	MIN	N	1	0		0	0	0	6

Benny Boynton

Year	Team	Lg	TD	1XP	2XP	FG	FGA	SAF	Pts
1921	ROC-WAS	A	4	12		1		0	39
1924	BUF	N	6	11		4		0	59
Career			10	23		5		0	98

Ordell Braase

Year	Team	Lg	TD	1XP	2XP	FG	FGA	SAF	Pts
1962	BAL	N	1	0		0	0	0	6
1967			1	0		0	0	0	6
Career			2	0		0	0	0	12

Bill Brace

Year	Team	Lg	TD	1XP	2XP	FG	FGA	SAF	Pts
1920	BUF	A	1	0		0		0	6

Bill Bradley

Year	Team	Lg	TD	1XP	2XP	FG	FGA	SAF	Pts
1969	PHI	N	1	0		0	0	0	6

Danny Bradley

Year	Team	Lg	TD	1XP	2XP	FG	FGA	SAF	Pts
1987	DET	N	2	0		0	0	0	12

Luther Bradley

Year	Team	Lg	TD	1XP	2XP	FG	FGA	SAF	Pts
1978	DET	N	1	0		0	0	0	6

Jim Bradshaw

Year	Team	Lg	TD	1XP	2XP	FG	FGA	SAF	Pts
1926	LA	A	1	0		0		0	6

Jim Bradshaw

Year	Team	Lg	TD	1XP	2XP	FG	FGA	SAF	Pts
1964	PIT	N	2	0		0	0	0	12
1965			1	0		0	0	0	6
1966			1	0		0	0	0	6
Career			4	0		0	0	0	24

Morris Bradshaw

Year	Team	Lg	TD	1XP	2XP	FG	FGA	SAF	Pts
1975	OAK	N	4	0		0	0	0	24
1976			1	0		0	0	0	6
1978			2	0		0	0	0	12
1980			1	0		0	0	0	6
1981			3	0		0	0	0	18
1982	NE	N	1	0		0	0	0	6
Career			12	0		0	0	0	72

Terry Bradshaw

Year	Team	Lg	TD	1XP	2XP	FG	FGA	SAF	Pts
1970	PIT	N	1	0		0	0	0	6
1971			5	0		0	0	0	30
1972			7	0		0	0	0	42
1973			3	0		0	0	0	18
1974			2	0		0	0	0	12
1975			3	0		0	0	0	18
1976			3	0		0	0	0	18
1977			3	0		0	0	0	18
1978			1	0		0	0	0	6
1980			2	0		0	0	0	12
1981			2	0		0	0	0	12
Career			32	0		0	0	0	192
Playoffs			3	0		0	0	0	18

Wes Bradshaw

Year	Team	Lg	TD	1XP	2XP	FG	FGA	SAF	Pts
1926	RI	A	1	1		0		0	7

Kerry Brady

Year	Team	Lg	TD	1XP	2XP	FG	FGA	SAF	Pts
1987	DAL	N	0	1		0	0	0	1

Kyle Brady

Year	Team	Lg	TD	1XP	2XP	FG	FGA	SAF	Pts
1995	NYJ	N	2	0	0	0	0	0	12
1996			1	0	1	0	0	0	8
Career			3	0	1	0	0	0	20

Mike Bragg

Year	Team	Lg	TD	1XP	2XP	FG	FGA	SAF	Pts
1974	WAS	N	0	7		1	1	0	10
Playoffs			0	1	0	1	1	0	4

John Bramlett

Year	Team	Lg	TD	1XP	2XP	FG	FGA	SAF	Pts
1965	DEN	A	2	0	0	0	0	0	12
1966			1	0	0	0	0	0	6
Career			3	0	0	0	0	0	18

Mark Brammer

Year	Team	Lg	TD	1XP	2XP	FG	FGA	SAF	Pts
1980	BUF	N	4	0		0	0	0	24
1981			2	0		0	0	0	12
1982			2	0		0	0	0	12
1983			2	0		0	0	0	12
Career			10	0		0	0	0	60

Cliff Branch

Year	Team	Lg	TD	1XP	2XP	FG	FGA	SAF	Pts
1973	OAK	N	3	0		0	0	0	18

Cliff Branch *continued*

Year	Team		TD	1XP	2XP	FG	FGA	SAF	Pts
1974			13	0		0	0	0	78
1975			9	0		0	0	0	54
1976			12	0		0	0	0	72
1977			6	0		0	0	0	36
1978			1	0		0	0	0	6
1979			6	0		0	0	0	36
1980			7	0		0	0	0	42
1981			1	0		0	0	0	6
1982	LARI	N	4	0		0	0	0	24
1983			5	0		0	0	0	30
Career			67	0		0	0	0	402
Playoffs			5	0		0	0	0	30

Reggie Branch

Year	Team		TD	1XP	2XP	FG	FGA	SAF	Pts
1987	WAS	N	1	0		0	0	0	6

David Brandon

Year	Team		TD	1XP	2XP	FG	FGA	SAF	Pts
1987	SD	N	1	0		0	0	0	6
1991	CLE	N	1	0		0	0	0	6
1992			2	0		0	0	0	12
Career			4	0		0	0	0	24

Jim Brandt

Year	Team		TD	1XP	2XP	FG	FGA	SAF	Pts
1953	PIT	N	3	0		0	0	0	18
1954			1	0		0	0	0	6
Career			4	0		0	0	0	24

Chris Brantley

Year	Team		TD	1XP	2XP	FG	FGA	SAF	Pts
1996	BUF	N	1	0	0	0	0	0	6

Zeke Bratkowski

Year	Team		TD	1XP	2XP	FG	FGA	SAF	Pts
1954	CHIB	N	1	0		0	0	0	6
1961	LA	N	3	0		0	0	0	18
1971	GB	N	1	0		0	0	0	6
Career			5	0		0	0	0	30

Melvin Bratton

Year	Team		TD	1XP	2XP	FG	FGA	SAF	Pts
1989	DEN	N	4	0		0	0	0	24
1990			4	0		0	0	0	24
Career			8	0		0	0	0	48
Playoffs			2	0		0	0	0	12

Hez Braxton

Year	Team		TD	1XP	2XP	FG	FGA	SAF	Pts
1962	SD	A	1	0	1	0	0	0	8

Jim Braxton

Year	Team		TD	1XP	2XP	FG	FGA	SAF	Pts
1972	BUF	N	6	0		0	0	0	36
1973			4	0		0	0	0	24
1974			4	0		0	0	0	24
1975			13	0		0	0	0	78
1977			2	0		0	0	0	12
1978	MIA	N	2	0		0	0	0	12
Career			31	0		0	0	0	186

Tyrone Braxton

Year	Team		TD	1XP	2XP	FG	FGA	SAF	Pts
1989	DEN	N	1	0		0	0	0	6
1991			1	0		0	0	0	6
1996			1	0	0	0	0	0	6
Career			3	0	0	0	0	0	18

Larry Braziel

Year	Team		TD	1XP	2XP	FG	FGA	SAF	Pts
1979	BAL	N	2	0		0	0	0	12

Bill Bredde

Year	Team		TD	1XP	2XP	FG	FGA	SAF	Pts
1954	CHIC	N	1	0		0	0	0	6

John Bredice

Year	Team		TD	1XP	2XP	FG	FGA	SAF	Pts
1956	PHI	N	1	0		0	0	0	6

Ed Breding

Year	Team		TD	1XP	2XP	FG	FGA	SAF	Pts
1967	WAS	N	0	0		0	0	1	2

Jim Breech

Year	Team		TD	1XP	2XP	FG	FGA	SAF	Pts
1979	OAK	N	0	41		18	27	0	95
1980	CIN	N	0	11		4	7	0	23
1981			0	49		22	32	0	115
1982			0	25		14	18	0	67
1983			0	39		16	23	0	87
1984			0	37		22	31	0	103
1985			0	48		24	33	0	120
1986			0	50		17	32	0	101
1987			0	25		24	30	0	97
1988			0	**56**		11	16	0	89

Jim Breech *continued*

Year	Team		TD	1XP	2XP	FG	FGA	SAF	Pts
1989			0	37		12	14	0	73
1990			0	41		17	21	0	92
1991			0	27		23	29	0	96
1992			0	31		19	27	0	88
Career			0	517		243	340	0	1246
Playoffs			0	24		9	11	0	51

Louis Breeden

Year	Team		TD	1XP	2XP	FG	FGA	SAF	Pts
1981	CIN	N	1	0		0	0	0	6
1986			1	0		0	0	0	6
Career			2	0		0	0	0	12

Wayne Brenkert

Year	Team		TD	1XP	2XP	FG	FGA	SAF	Pts
1923	AKR	N	2	0		0		0	12
1924			3	0		0		0	18
Career			5	0		0		0	30

Brian Brennan

Year	Team		TD	1XP	2XP	FG	FGA	SAF	Pts
1984	CLE	N	3	0		0	0	0	18
1985			1	0		0	0	0	6
1986			7	0		0	0	0	42
1987			6	0		0	0	0	36
1988			1	0		0	0	0	6
1990			2	0		0	0	0	12
1991			1	0		0	0	0	6
1992	CIN	N	1	0		0	0	0	6
Career			22	0		0	0	0	132
Playoffs			4	0		0	0	0	24

Matt Brennan

Year	Team		TD	1XP	2XP	FG	FGA	SAF	Pts
1925	NYG	N	0	0		1		0	3
1926	BKN	N	1	2		1		0	11
Career			1	2		2		0	14

Willie Brennan

Year	Team		TD	1XP	2XP	FG	FGA	SAF	Pts
1924	CHIC	N	1	0		0		0	6

Hoby Brenner

Year	Team		TD	1XP	2XP	FG	FGA	SAF	Pts
1983	NO	N	3	0		0	0	0	18
1984			6	0		0	0	0	36
1985			3	0		0	0	0	18
1987			2	0		0	0	0	12
1989			4	0		0	0	0	24
1990			2	0		0	0	0	12
1993			1	0		0	0	0	6
Career			21	0		0	0	0	126

Jeep Brett

Year	Team		TD	1XP	2XP	FG	FGA	SAF	Pts
1937	PIT	N	1	0		0		0	6

Brooke Brewer

Year	Team		TD	1XP	2XP	FG	FGA	SAF	Pts
1922	AKR	N	1	0		0		0	6

Chris Brewer

Year	Team		TD	1XP	2XP	FG	FGA	SAF	Pts
1987	CHI	N	3	0		0	0	0	18

Dewell Brewer

Year	Team		TD	1XP	2XP	FG	FGA	SAF	Pts
1994	IND	N	1	0	0	0	0	0	6

John Brewer

Year	Team		TD	1XP	2XP	FG	FGA	SAF	Pts
1952	PHI	N	2	0		0	0	0	12
1953			1	0		0	0	0	6
Career			3	0		0	0	0	18

Johnny Brewer

Year	Team		TD	1XP	2XP	FG	FGA	SAF	Pts
1962	CLE	N	2	0		0	0	0	12
1964			3	0		0	0	0	18
1965			1	0		0	0	0	6
1967			1	0		0	0	0	6
Career			7	0		0	0	0	42

Darrel Brewster

Year	Team		TD	1XP	2XP	FG	FGA	SAF	Pts
1952	CLE	N	1	0		0	0	0	6
1953			4	0		0	0	0	24
1954			4	0		0	0	0	24
1955			6	0		0	0	0	36
1956			1	0		0	0	0	6
1957			2	0		0	0	0	12
1958			1	0		0	0	0	6
1959	PIT	N	2	0		0	0	0	12
Career			21	0		0	0	0	126
Playoffs			1	0		0	0	0	6

Harry Brian

Year	Team		TD	1XP	2XP	FG	FGA	SAF	Pts
1926	HAR	N	1	0		0		0	6

Frank Briante

Year	Team		TD	1XP	2XP	FG	FGA	SAF	Pts
1929	SI	N	1	0		0		0	6
1930	NEW	N	1	0		0		0	6
Career			2	0		0		0	12

George Brickley

Year	Team		TD	1XP	2XP	FG	FGA	SAF	Pts
1920	CLE	A	1	0		0		0	6

Doug Brien

Year	Team		TD	1XP	2XP	FG	FGA	SAF	Pts
1994	SF	N	0	**60**	0	15	20	0	105
1995	SF-NO	N	0	35	0	19	29	0	92
1996	NO	N	0	18	0	21	25	0	81
Career			0	113	0	55	74	0	278
Playoffs			0	17	0	2	3	0	23

Bob Briggs

Year	Team		TD	1XP	2XP	FG	FGA	SAF	Pts
1969	SD	A	1	0	0	0	0	0	6
1972	CLE	N	1	0		0	0	0	6
Career			2	0	0	0	0	0	12

Leon Bright

Year	Team		TD	1XP	2XP	FG	FGA	SAF	Pts
1981	NYG	N	2	0		0	0	0	12

James Brim

Year	Team		TD	1XP	2XP	FG	FGA	SAF	Pts
1987	MIN	N	3	0		0	0	0	18

Mike Brim

Year	Team		TD	1XP	2XP	FG	FGA	SAF	Pts
1992	NYJ	N	1	0		0	0	0	6
1993	CIN	N	1	0		0	0	0	6
Career			2	0		0	0	0	12

Walt Brindley

Year	Team		TD	1XP	2XP	FG	FGA	SAF	Pts
1922	RI	N	0	0		0		0	0

Larry Brink

Year	Team		TD	1XP	2XP	FG	FGA	SAF	Pts
1950	LA	N	0	0		0	0	1	2
1954	CHIB	N	1	0		0	0	0	6
Career			1	0		0	0	1	8
Playoffs			1	0		0	0	0	6

Larry Brinson

Year	Team		TD	1XP	2XP	FG	FGA	SAF	Pts
1977	DAL	N	1	0		0	0	0	6
1978			2	0		0	0	0	12
1980	SEA	N	1	0		0	0	0	6
Career			4	0		0	0	0	24

Vincent Brisby

Year	Team		TD	1XP	2XP	FG	FGA	SAF	Pts
1993	NE	N	2	0		0	0	0	12
1994			5	0	0	0	0	0	30
1995			3	0	0	0	0	0	18
Career			10	0	0	0	0	0	60

Marlin Briscoe

Year	Team		TD	1XP	2XP	FG	FGA	SAF	Pts
1968	DEN	A	3	0	0	0	0	0	18
1969	BUF	A	5	0	0	0	0	0	30
1970	BUF	N	8	0		0	0	0	48
1971			5	0		0	0	0	30
1972	MIA	N	4	0		0	0	0	24
1973			2	0		0	0	0	12
1974			1	0		0	0	0	6
1975	DET	N	4	0		0	0	0	24
1976	NE	N	1	0		0	0	0	6
Career			33	0	0	0	0	0	198

Bubby Brister

Year	Team		TD	1XP	2XP	FG	FGA	SAF	Pts
1986	PIT	N	1	0		0	0	0	6
1988			6	0		0	0	0	36
Career			7	0		0	0	0	42

Willie Brister

Year	Team		TD	1XP	2XP	FG	FGA	SAF	Pts
1975	NYJ	N	1	0		0	0	0	6

Obie Bristow

Year	Team		TD	1XP	2XP	FG	FGA	SAF	Pts
1925	KC	N	0	0		0		0	0

Gene Brito

Year	Team		TD	1XP	2XP	FG	FGA	SAF	Pts
1952	WAS	N	2	0		0	0	0	12

Charley Britt

Year	Team		TD	1XP	2XP	FG	FGA	SAF	Pts
1960	LA	N	1	0		0	0	0	6

James Britt

Year	Team		TD	1XP	2XP	FG	FGA	SAF	Pts
1986	ATL	N	1	0		0	0	0	6

Maury Britt

Year	Team		TD	1XP	2XP	FG	FGA	SAF	Pts
1941	DET	N	1	0		0	0	0	6

Earl Britton

Year	Team		TD	1XP	2XP	FG	FGA	SAF	Pts
1926	BKN	A	1	0		0		0	6
1927	DAY	N	0	0		1		0	3
1928			0	0		0		0	0
Career			1	0		1		0	9

Charley Brock

Year	Team		TD	1XP	2XP	FG	FGA	SAF	Pts
1939	GB	N	1	0		0	0	0	6
1942			1	0		0	0	0	6
1945			2	0		0	0	0	12
Career			4	0		0	0	0	24

Lou Brock

Year	Team		TD	1XP	2XP	FG	FGA	SAF	Pts
1941	GB	N	2	0		0	0	0	12
1942			3	2		0	1	0	20
1943			3	0		0	0	0	18
1944			5	0		0	0	0	30
1945			3	0		0	0	0	18
Career			16	2		0	1	0	98

Matt Brock

Year	Team		TD	1XP	2XP	FG	FGA	SAF	Pts
1995	NYJ	N	1	0	0	0	0	0	6

Pete Brock

Year	Team		TD	1XP	2XP	FG	FGA	SAF	Pts
1976	NE	N	1	0		0	0	0	6

Jeff Brockhaus

Year	Team		TD	1XP	2XP	FG	FGA	SAF	Pts
1987	SF	N	0	11		3	6	0	20

John Brockington

Year	Team		TD	1XP	2XP	FG	FGA	SAF	Pts
1971	GB	N	5	0		0	0	0	30
1972			9	0		0	0	0	54
1973			3	0		0	0	0	18
1974			5	0		0	0	0	30
1975			8	0		0	0	0	48
1976			2	0		0	0	0	12
1977	KC	N	2	0		0	0	0	12
Career			34	0		0	0	0	204

Bob Brodhead

Year	Team		TD	1XP	2XP	FG	FGA	SAF	Pts
1960	BUF	A	0	0	1	0	0	0	2

John Brodie

Year	Team		TD	1XP	2XP	FG	FGA	SAF	Pts
1958	SF	N	1	0		0	0	0	6
1960			1	0		0	0	0	6
1961			2	0		0	0	0	12
1962			4	0		0	0	0	24
1964			2	0		0	0	0	12
1965			1	0		0	0	0	6
1966			3	0		0	0	0	18
1967			1	0		0	0	0	6
1970			2	0		0	0	0	12
1971			3	0		0	0	0	18
1972			1	0		0	0	0	6
1973			1	0		0	0	0	6
Career			22	0		0	0	0	132
Playoffs			1	0		0	0	0	6

J.W. Brodnax

Year	Team		TD	1XP	2XP	FG	FGA	SAF	Pts
1960	DEN	A	1	0	0	0	0	0	6

Tommy Brooker

Year	Team		TD	1XP	2XP	FG	FGA	SAF	Pts
1962	DAL	A	3	33	0	12	22	0	87
1963	KC	A	0	20	0	6	15	0	38
1964			0	**46**	0	8	17	0	70
1965			0	37	0	13	30	0	76
1966			0	13	0	2	2	0	19
Career			3	149	0	41	86	0	290
Playoffs			0	2	0	2	3	0	8

Mitchell Brookins

Year	Team		TD	1XP	2XP	FG	FGA	SAF	Pts
1984	BUF	N	1	0		0	0	0	6

Bill Brooks

Year	Team		TD	1XP	2XP	FG	FGA	SAF	Pts
1986	IND	N	8	0		0	0	0	48
1987			3	0		0	0	0	18
1988			3	0		0	0	0	18
1989			4	0		0	0	0	24

Bill Brooks *continued*

Year	Team		TD	1XP	2XP	FG	FGA	SAF	Pts
1990			5	0		0	0	0	30
1991			4	0		0	0	0	24
1992			1	0		0	0	0	6
1993	BUF	N	5	0		0	0	0	30
1994			2	0	0	0	0	0	12
1995			11	0	0	0	0	0	66
Career			46	0	0	0	0	0	276
Playoffs			2	0	0	0	0	0	12

Billy Brooks

Year	Team		TD	1XP	2XP	FG	FGA	SAF	Pts
1977	CIN	N	4	0		0	0	0	24
1978			2	0		0	0	0	12
1979			1	0		0	0	0	6
Career			7	0		0	0	0	42

James Brooks

Year	Team		TD	1XP	2XP	FG	FGA	SAF	Pts
1981	SD	N	6	0		0	0	0	36
1982			6	0		0	0	0	36
1983			3	0		0	0	0	18
1984	CIN	N	4	0		0	0	0	24
1985			12	0		0	0	0	72
1986			9	0		0	0	0	54
1987			3	0		0	0	0	18
1988			14	0		0	0	0	84
1989			9	0		0	0	0	54
1990			9	0		0	0	0	54
1991			4	0		0	0	0	24
Career			79	0		0	0	0	474
Playoffs			4	0		0	0	0	24

Michael Brooks

Year	Team		TD	1XP	2XP	FG	FGA	SAF	Pts
1989	DEN	N	0	0		0	0	1	2
1992			1	0		0	0	0	6
Career			1	0		0	0	1	8

Reggie Brooks

Year	Team		TD	1XP	2XP	FG	FGA	SAF	Pts
1993	WAS	N	3	0		0	0	0	18
1994			2	0	0	0	0	0	12
1996	TB	N	2	0	0	0	0	0	12
Career			7	0	0	0	0	0	42

Robert Brooks

Year	Team		TD	1XP	2XP	FG	FGA	SAF	Pts
1992	GB	N	1	0		0	0	0	6
1993			1	0		0	0	0	6
1994			6	0	0	0	0	0	36
1995			13	0	0	0	0	0	78
1996			4	0	0	0	0	0	24
Career			25	0	0	0	0	0	150
Playoffs			4	0	0	0	0	0	24

Mal Bross

Year	Team		TD	1XP	2XP	FG	FGA	SAF	Pts
1926	LA	A	3	2		0		0	20

Walter Broughton

Year	Team		TD	1XP	2XP	FG	FGA	SAF	Pts
1987	BUF	N	1	0		0	0	0	6

Steve Broussard

Year	Team		TD	1XP	2XP	FG	FGA	SAF	Pts
1990	ATL	N	4	0		0	0	0	24
1991			5	0		0	0	0	30
1992			2	0		0	0	0	12
1993			1	0		0	0	0	6
1994	CIN	N	2	0	1	0	0	0	14
1995	SEA	N	1	0	0	0	0	0	6
1996			1	0	0	0	0	0	6
Career			16	0	1	0	0	0	98

Angie Brovelli

Year	Team		TD	1XP	2XP	FG	FGA	SAF	Pts
1933	PIT	N	2	2		0		0	14
1934			1	0		0		0	6
Career			3	2		0		0	20

Aaron Brown

Year	Team		TD	1XP	2XP	FG	FGA	SAF	Pts
1971	KC	N	1	0		0	0	0	6

A.B. Brown

Year	Team		TD	1XP	2XP	FG	FGA	SAF	Pts
1991	NYJ	N	1	0		0	0	0	6

Andre Brown

Year	Team		TD	1XP	2XP	FG	FGA	SAF	Pts
1989	MIA	N	5	0		0	0	0	30

Bill Brown

Year	Team		TD	1XP	2XP	FG	FGA	SAF	Pts
1962	MIN	N	1	0		0	0	0	6
1963			8	0		0	0	0	48

Bill Brown *continued*

Year	Team		TD	1XP	2XP	FG	FGA	SAF	Pts
1964			16	0		0	0	0	96
1965			7	0		0	0	0	42
1966			6	0		0	0	0	36
1967			5	0		0	0	0	30
1968			14	0		0	0	0	84
1969			3	0		0	0	0	18
1970			2	0		0	0	0	12
1971			2	0		0	0	0	12
1972			8	0		0	0	0	48
1973			4	0		0	0	0	24
Career			76	0		0	0	0	456
Playoffs			3	0		0	0	0	18

Bob Brown

Year	Team		TD	1XP	2XP	FG	FGA	SAF	Pts
1972	NO	N	1	0		0	0	0	6

Bob Brown

Year	Team		TD	1XP	2XP	FG	FGA	SAF	Pts
1972	GB	N	0	0		0	0	1	2

Cedric Brown

Year	Team		TD	1XP	2XP	FG	FGA	SAF	Pts
1980	TB	N	1	0		0	0	0	6
1981			2	0		0	0	0	12
Career			3	0		0	0	0	18

Charlie Brown

Year	Team		TD	1XP	2XP	FG	FGA	SAF	Pts
1967	NO	N	2	0		0	0	0	12
1968			1	0		0	0	0	6
Career			3	0		0	0	0	18

Charlie Brown

Year	Team		TD	1XP	2XP	FG	FGA	SAF	Pts
1982	WAS	N	8	0		0	0	0	48
1983			8	0		0	0	0	48
1984			3	0		0	0	0	18
1985	ATL	N	2	0		0	0	0	12
1986			4	0		0	0	0	24
Career			25	0		0	0	0	150
Playoffs			3	0		0	0	0	18

Corwin Brown

Year	Team		TD	1XP	2XP	FG	FGA	SAF	Pts
1996	NE	N	1	0	0	0	0	0	6

Curtis Brown

Year	Team		TD	1XP	2XP	FG	FGA	SAF	Pts
1977	BUF	N	1	0		0	0	0	6
1978			5	0		0	0	0	30
1979			4	0		0	0	0	24
1980			3	0		0	0	0	18
1981			1	0		0	0	0	6
1983	HOU	N	1	0		0	0	0	6
Career			15	0		0	0	0	90

Dave Brown

Year	Team		TD	1XP	2XP	FG	FGA	SAF	Pts
1976	SEA	N	0	0		0	0	1	2
1977			1	0		0	0	0	6
1984			2	0		0	0	0	12
1985			1	0		0	0	0	6
1986			1	0		0	0	0	6
Career			5	0		0	0	1	32

Dave Brown

Year	Team		TD	1XP	2XP	FG	FGA	SAF	Pts
1994	NYG	N	2	0	0	0	0	0	12
1995			4	0	0	0	0	0	24
Career			6	0	0	0	0	0	36

Derek Brown

Year	Team		TD	1XP	2XP	FG	FGA	SAF	Pts
1993	NO	N	3	0		0	0	0	18
1994			4	0	0	0	0	0	24
1995			2	0	0	0	0	0	12
Career			9	0	0	0	0	0	54

Ed Brown

Year	Team		TD	1XP	2XP	FG	FGA	SAF	Pts
1955	CHIB	N	2	0		0	0	0	12
1956			2	0		0	0	0	12
1957			1	0		0	0	0	6
1958			3	0		0	0	0	18
1959			1	0		0	0	0	6
1960	CHI	N	2	0		0	0	0	12
1961			0	1		1	2	0	4
1963	PIT	N	2	0		0	0	0	12
1964			2	0		0	0	0	12
Career			15	1		1	2	0	94

Eddie Brown

Year	Team		TD	1XP	2XP	FG	FGA	SAF	Pts
1976	WAS	N	1	0		0	0	0	6

Eddie Brown

Year	Team	TD	1XP	2XP	FG	FGA	SAF	Pts
1985	CIN N	8	0		0	0	0	48
1986		4	0		0	0	0	24
1987		3	0		0	0	0	18
1988		9	0		0	0	0	54
1989		6	0		0	0	0	36
1990		9	0		0	0	0	54
1991		2	0		0	0	0	12
Career		41	0		0	0	0	246

Fred Brown

Year	Team	TD	1XP	2XP	FG	FGA	SAF	Pts
1961	BUF A	2	0	0	0	0	0	12
1963		1	0		0	0	0	6
Career		3	0		0	0	0	18

Gary Brown

Year	Team	TD	1XP	2XP	FG	FGA	SAF	Pts
1991	HOU N	1	0		0	0	0	6
1992		1	0		0	0	0	6
1993		8	0		0	0	0	48
1994		5	0		0	0	0	30
Career		15	0		0	0	0	90
Playoffs		1	0		0	0	0	6

George Brown

Year	Team	TD	1XP	2XP	FG	FGA	SAF	Pts
1923	AKR N	0	0		0		1	2

Gordon Brown

Year	Team	TD	1XP	2XP	FG	FGA	SAF	Pts
1987	IND N	1	0		0	0	0	6

Greg Brown

Year	Team	TD	1XP	2XP	FG	FGA	SAF	Pts
1981	PHI N	1	0		0	0	0	6
1982		1	0		0	0	0	6
1986		0	0		0	0	1	2
Career		2	0		0	0	1	14

Hardy Brown

Year	Team	TD	1XP	2XP	FG	FGA	SAF	Pts
1948	BKN AA	2	25		0	1	0	37
1950	BAL N	0	0		0	0	0	0
1954	SF N	1	0		0	0	0	6
Career		3	25		0	1	0	43

Ivory Lee Brown

Year	Team	TD	1XP	2XP	FG	FGA	SAF	Pts
1992	PHX N	2	0		0	0	0	12

J.B. Brown

Year	Team	TD	1XP	2XP	FG	FGA	SAF	Pts
1992	MIA N	1	0		0	0	0	6

Jesse Brown

Year	Team	TD	1XP	2XP	FG	FGA	SAF	Pts
1926	POT N	1	0		0		0	6

Jim Brown

Year	Team	TD	1XP	2XP	FG	FGA	SAF	Pts
1957	CLE N	10	0		0	0	0	60
1958		18	0		0	0	0	108
1959		14	0		0	0	0	84
1960		11	0		0	0	0	66
1961		10	0		0	0	0	60
1962		18	0		0	0	0	108
1963		15	0		0	0	0	90
1964		9	0		0	0	0	54
1965		21	0		0	0	0	126
Career		126	0		0	0	0	756
Playoffs		1	0		0	0	0	6

John Brown

Year	Team	TD	1XP	2XP	FG	FGA	SAF	Pts
1949	LA AA	2	0		0	0	0	12

Ken Brown

Year	Team	TD	1XP	2XP	FG	FGA	SAF	Pts
1972	CLE N	2	0		0	0	0	12
1974		6	0		0	0	0	36
1975		1	0		0	0	0	6
Career		9	0		0	0	0	54

Larry Brown

Year	Team	TD	1XP	2XP	FG	FGA	SAF	Pts
1969	WAS N	4	0		0	0	0	24
1970		7	0		0	0	0	42
1971		6	0		0	0	0	36
1972		12	0		0	0	0	72
1973		14	0		0	0	0	84
1974		7	0		0	0	0	42
1975		5	0		0	0	0	30
Career		55	0		0	0	0	330
Playoffs		2	0		0	0	0	12

Larry Brown

Year	Team	TD	1XP	2XP	FG	FGA	SAF	Pts
1971	PIT N	1	0		0	0	0	6
1972		1	0		0	0	0	6
1974		1	0		0	0	0	6
1975		1	0		0	0	0	6
1979		1	0		0	0	0	6
Career		5	0		0	0	0	30
Playoffs		2	0		0	0	0	12

Larry Brown

Year	Team	TD	1XP	2XP	FG	FGA	SAF	Pts
1995	DAL N	2	0	0	0	0	0	12

Marc Brown

Year	Team	TD	1XP	2XP	FG	FGA	SAF	Pts
1987	BUF N	1	0		0	0	0	6

Otto Brown

Year	Team	TD	1XP	2XP	FG	FGA	SAF	Pts
1971	NYG N	1	0		0	0	0	6

Preston Brown

Year	Team	TD	1XP	2XP	FG	FGA	SAF	Pts
1982	NE N	1	0		0	0	0	6

Ray Brown

Year	Team	TD	1XP	2XP	FG	FGA	SAF	Pts
1974	ATL N	1	0		0	0	0	6
1975		1	0		0	0	0	6
Career		2	0		0	0	0	12

Reggie Brown

Year	Team	TD	1XP	2XP	FG	FGA	SAF	Pts
1994	HOU N	0	0	1	0	0	0	2

Robert Brown

Year	Team	TD	1XP	2XP	FG	FGA	SAF	Pts
1984	GB N	1	0		0	0	0	6
1985		0	0		0	0	1	2
Career		1	0		0	0	1	8

Roger Brown

Year	Team	TD	1XP	2XP	FG	FGA	SAF	Pts
1962	DET N	0	0		0	0	2	4
1965		0	0		0	0	1	2
Career		0	0		0	0	3	6

Ron Brown

Year	Team	TD	1XP	2XP	FG	FGA	SAF	Pts
1984	LARM N	4	0		0	0	0	24
1985		6	0		0	0	0	36
1986		3	0		0	0	0	18
1987		3	0		0	0	0	18
1989		1	0		0	0	0	6
Career		17	0		0	0	0	102

Steve Brown

Year	Team	TD	1XP	2XP	FG	FGA	SAF	Pts
1983	HOU N	1	0		0	0	0	6
1988		1	0		0	0	0	6
Career		2	0		0	0	0	12

Ted Brown

Year	Team	TD	1XP	2XP	FG	FGA	SAF	Pts
1979	MIN N	1	0		0	0	0	6
1980		10	0		0	0	0	60
1981		8	0		0	0	0	48
1982		3	0		0	0	0	18
1983		11	0		0	0	0	66
1984		6	0		0	0	0	36
1985		10	0		0	0	0	60
1986		4	0		0	0	0	24
Career		53	0		0	0	0	318
Playoffs		3	0		0	0	0	18

Terry Brown

Year	Team	TD	1XP	2XP	FG	FGA	SAF	Pts
1973	MIN N	1	0		0	0	0	6
1975		1	0		0	0	0	6
Career		2	0		0	0	0	12
Playoffs		1	0		0	0	0	6

Theotis Brown

Year	Team	TD	1XP	2XP	FG	FGA	SAF	Pts
1979	STL N	7	0		0	0	0	42
1980		2	0		0	0	0	12
1981	STL-SEA N	8	0		0	0	0	48
1982	SEA N	2	0		0	0	0	12
1983	KC N	10	0		0	0	0	60
1984		4	0		0	0	0	24
Career		33	0		0	0	0	198

Tim Brown

Year	Team	TD	1XP	2XP	FG	FGA	SAF	Pts
1988	LARI N	7	0		0	0	0	42
1990		3	0		0	0	0	18
1991		6	0		0	0	0	36
1992		7	0		0	0	0	42

Tim Brown continued

Year	Team	TD	1XP	2XP	FG	FGA	SAF	Pts
1993		8	0		0	0	0	48
1994		9	0	0	0	0	0	54
1995	OAK N	10	0	0	0	0	0	60
1996		9	0	0	0	0	0	54
Career		59	0		0	0	0	354
Playoffs		2	0		0	0	0	12

Timmy Brown

Year	Team	TD	1XP	2XP	FG	FGA	SAF	Pts
1960	PHI N	4	0		0	0	0	24
1961		5	0		0	0	0	30
1962		13	0		0	0	0	78
1963		11	0		0	0	0	66
1964		10	0		0	0	0	60
1965		9	0		0	0	0	54
1966		8	0		0	0	0	48
1967		2	0		0	0	0	12
1968	BAL N	2	0		0	0	0	12
Career		64	0		0	0	0	384
Playoffs		1	0		0	0	0	6

Tom Brown

Year	Team	TD	1XP	2XP	FG	FGA	SAF	Pts
1942	PIT N	1	0		0	0	0	6

Tom Brown

Year	Team	TD	1XP	2XP	FG	FGA	SAF	Pts
1968	GB N	2	0		0	0	0	12

Troy Brown

Year	Team	TD	1XP	2XP	FG	FGA	SAF	Pts
1995	NE N	1	0		0	0	0	6

Tyrone Brown

Year	Team	TD	1XP	2XP	FG	FGA	SAF	Pts
1996	ATL N	1	0		0	0	0	6

Vincent Brown

Year	Team	TD	1XP	2XP	FG	FGA	SAF	Pts
1992	NE N	2	0		0	0	0	12

Willie Brown

Year	Team	TD	1XP	2XP	FG	FGA	SAF	Pts
1965	LA N	1	0		0	0	0	6

Willie Brown

Year	Team	TD	1XP	2XP	FG	FGA	SAF	Pts
1967	OAK A	1	0		0	0	0	6
1968		1	0		0	0	0	6
Career		2	0		0	0	0	12
Playoffs		3	0		0	0	0	18

Joey Browner

Year	Team	TD	1XP	2XP	FG	FGA	SAF	Pts
1984	MIN N	1	0		0	0	0	6
1985		1	0		0	0	0	6
1986		1	0		0	0	0	6
1990		1	0		0	0	0	6
Career		4	0		0	0	0	24

Keith Browner

Year	Team	TD	1XP	2XP	FG	FGA	SAF	Pts
1988	SD N	1	0		0	0	0	6

Ross Browner

Year	Team	TD	1XP	2XP	FG	FGA	SAF	Pts
1983	CIN N	0	1		0	0	0	1
1985		0	0		0	0	1	2
Career		0	1		0	0	1	3

Darrick Brownlow

Year	Team	TD	1XP	2XP	FG	FGA	SAF	Pts
1995	WAS N	0	0	0	0	0	1	2

Dick Brubaker

Year	Team	TD	1XP	2XP	FG	FGA	SAF	Pts
1960	BUF A	1	0		0	0	0	6

Aundray Bruce

Year	Team	TD	1XP	2XP	FG	FGA	SAF	Pts
1995	OAK N	1	0		0	0	0	6

Gail Bruce

Year	Team	TD	1XP	2XP	FG	FGA	SAF	Pts
1951	SF N	0	1		0	0	0	1

Isaac Bruce

Year	Team	TD	1XP	2XP	FG	FGA	SAF	Pts
1994	LARM N	3	0		0	0	0	18
1995	STL N	13	0	1	0	0	0	80
1996		7	0		0	0	0	42
Career		23	0	1	0	0	0	140

Hank Bruder

Year	Team	TD	1XP	2XP	FG	FGA	SAF	Pts
1931	GB N	3	0		0		0	18
1932		4	0		0		0	24
1933		3	0		0		0	18
1934		3	4		0		0	22
1935		1	0		0		0	6

Hank Bruder *continued*

Year	Team	Lg	TD	1XP	2XP	FG	FGA	SAF	Pts
1937			1	0		0		0	6
1939			1	0		0	0	0	6
Career			16	4		0	0	0	100

Woody Bruder

Year	Team	Lg	TD	1XP	2XP	FG	FGA	SAF	Pts
1925	**BUF-FRA**	**N**	1	2		0		0	8
1926	**FRA**	**N**	3	1		0		0	19
Career			4	3		0		0	27

Bob Brudzinski

Year	Team	Lg	TD	1XP	2XP	FG	FGA	SAF	Pts
1978	**LA**	**N**	1	0		0	0	0	6
1985	**MIA**	**N**	1	0		0	0	0	6
Career			2	0		0	0	0	12

Mark Bruener

Year	Team	Lg	TD	1XP	2XP	FG	FGA	SAF	Pts
1995	**PIT**	**N**	3	0	0	0	0	0	18
1996			0	0	1	0	0	0	2
Career			3	0	1	0	0	0	20

Bob Bruer

Year	Team	Lg	TD	1XP	2XP	FG	FGA	SAF	Pts
1979	**SF**	**N**	1	0		0	0	0	6
1981	**MIN**	**N**	3	0		0	0	0	18
1982			2	0		0	0	0	12
1983			2	0		0	0	0	12
Career			8	0		0	0	0	48

Boyd Brumbaugh

Year	Team	Lg	TD	1XP	2XP	FG	FGA	SAF	Pts
1938	**BKN**	**N**	1	0		0	0	0	6
1939	**PIT**	**N**	3	0		0	0	0	18
1941			2	0		0	0	0	12
Career			6	0		0	0	0	36

Carl Brumbaugh

Year	Team	Lg	TD	1XP	2XP	FG	FGA	SAF	Pts
1930	**CHIB**	**N**	2	1		0		0	13
1931			1	0		0		0	6
1933			0	0		0		0	0
1934			2	3		0		0	15
1936			2	0		0		0	12
Career			7	4		0		0	46

Don Brumm

Year	Team	Lg	TD	1XP	2XP	FG	FGA	SAF	Pts
1965	**STL**	**N**	1	0		0	0	0	6
1968			1	0		0	0	0	6
Career			2	0		0	0	0	12

Mark Brunell

Year	Team	Lg	TD	1XP	2XP	FG	FGA	SAF	Pts
1994	**GB**	**N**	1	0	0	0	0	0	6
1995	**JAC**	**N**	4	0	0	0	0	0	24
1996			3	0	2	0	0	0	22
Career			8	0	2	0	0	0	52

Bob Brunet

Year	Team	Lg	TD	1XP	2XP	FG	FGA	SAF	Pts
1968	**WAS**	**N**	1	0		0	0	0	6
1972			2	0		0	0	0	12
1975			1	0		0	0	0	6
Career			4	0		0	0	0	24

Fred Bruney

Year	Team	Lg	TD	1XP	2XP	FG	FGA	SAF	Pts
1962	**BOS**	**A**	1	0	0	0	0	0	6

Scott Brunner

Year	Team	Lg	TD	1XP	2XP	FG	FGA	SAF	Pts
1982	**NYG**	**N**	1	0		0	0	0	6

Larry Brunson

Year	Team	Lg	TD	1XP	2XP	FG	FGA	SAF	Pts
1974	**KC**	**N**	2	0		0	0	0	12
1975			2	0		0	0	0	12
1976			1	0		0	0	0	6
1979	**OAK**	**N**	1	0		0	0	0	6
Career			6	0		0	0	0	36

Ross Brupbacher

Year	Team	Lg	TD	1XP	2XP	FG	FGA	SAF	Pts
1971	**CHI**	**N**	1	0		0	0	0	6
1972			1	0		0	0	0	6
Career			2	0		0	0	0	12

Tedy Bruschi

Year	Team	Lg	TD	1XP	2XP	FG	FGA	SAF	Pts
1996	**NE**	**N**	1	0	0	0	0	0	6

Johnny Bryan

Year	Team	Lg	TD	1XP	2XP	FG	FGA	SAF	Pts
1923	**CHIB**	**N**	4	0		0		0	24
1924			3	0		0		0	18
1925			1	0		0		0	6

Johnny Bryan *continued*

Year	Team	Lg	TD	1XP	2XP	FG	FGA	SAF	Pts
1926	**MIL**	**N**	1	0		0		0	6
Career			9	0		0		0	54

Rick Bryan

Year	Team	Lg	TD	1XP	2XP	FG	FGA	SAF	Pts
1984	**ATL**	**N**	0	0		0	0	1	2
1985			0	1		0	0	0	1
Career			0	1		0	0	1	3

Bill Bryant

Year	Team	Lg	TD	1XP	2XP	FG	FGA	SAF	Pts
1977	**NYG**	**N**	1	0		0	0	0	6

Bobby Bryant

Year	Team	Lg	TD	1XP	2XP	FG	FGA	SAF	Pts
1968	**MIN**	**N**	1	0		0	0	0	6
1970			1	0		0	0	0	6
1972			1	0		0	0	0	6
1973			1	0		0	0	0	6
Career			4	0		0	0	0	24
Playoffs			2	0		0	0	0	12

Cullen Bryant

Year	Team	Lg	TD	1XP	2XP	FG	FGA	SAF	Pts
1973	**LA**	**N**	1	0		0	0	0	6
1974			1	0		0	0	0	6
1975			2	0		0	0	0	12
1976			3	0		0	0	0	18
1978			7	0		0	0	0	42
1979			5	0		0	0	0	30
1980			6	0		0	0	0	36
1981			1	0		0	0	0	6
Career			26	0		0	0	0	156
Playoffs			3	0		0	0	0	18

Domingo Bryant

Year	Team	Lg	TD	1XP	2XP	FG	FGA	SAF	Pts
1988	**HOU**	**N**	1	0		0	0	0	6

Hubie Bryant

Year	Team	Lg	TD	1XP	2XP	FG	FGA	SAF	Pts
1971	**NE**	**N**	1	0		0	0	0	6

Jeff Bryant

Year	Team	Lg	TD	1XP	2XP	FG	FGA	SAF	Pts
1984	**SEA**	**N**	0	0		0	0	1	2

Kelvin Bryant

Year	Team	Lg	TD	1XP	2XP	FG	FGA	SAF	Pts
1986	**WAS**	**N**	7	0		0	0	0	42
1987			6	0		0	0	0	36
1988			6	0		0	0	0	36
1990			1	0		0	0	0	6
Career			20	0		0	0	0	120
Playoffs			2	0		0	0	0	12

Buck Buchanan

Year	Team	Lg	TD	1XP	2XP	FG	FGA	SAF	Pts
1968	**KC**	**A**	0	0	0	0	0	1	2

Charles Buchanan

Year	Team	Lg	TD	1XP	2XP	FG	FGA	SAF	Pts
1988	**CLE**	**N**	0	0		0	0	1	2

Ray Buchanan

Year	Team	Lg	TD	1XP	2XP	FG	FGA	SAF	Pts
1994	**IND**	**N**	3	0	0	0	0	0	18

Willie Buchanon

Year	Team	Lg	TD	1XP	2XP	FG	FGA	SAF	Pts
1972	**GB**	**N**	1	0		0	0	0	6
1977			1	0		0	0	0	6
1978			1	0		0	0	0	6
Career			3	0		0	0	0	18

Frank Bucher

Year	Team	Lg	TD	1XP	2XP	FG	FGA	SAF	Pts
1925	**POT**	**N**	2	0		0		0	12

Howard Buck

Year	Team	Lg	TD	1XP	2XP	FG	FGA	SAF	Pts
1922	**GB**	**N**	0	3		1		0	6
1923			0	5		6		0	23
1924			0	8		3		0	17
1925			0	8		0		0	8
Career			0	24		10		0	54

Vince Buck

Year	Team	Lg	TD	1XP	2XP	FG	FGA	SAF	Pts
1992	**NO**	**N**	1	0		0	0	0	6

Bill Buckler

Year	Team	Lg	TD	1XP	2XP	FG	FGA	SAF	Pts
1926	**CHIB**	**N**	0	1		0		0	1
1932			0	1		0		0	1
Career			0	2		0		0	2

Ralph Buckley

Year	Team	Lg	TD	1XP	2XP	FG	FGA	SAF	Pts
1930	**SI**	**N**	1	0		0		0	6

Terrell Buckley

Year	Team	Lg	TD	1XP	2XP	FG	FGA	SAF	Pts
1992	**GB**	**N**	2	0	0	0	0	0	12
1996	**MIA**	**N**	1	0	0	0	0	0	6
Career			3	0	0	0	0	0	18

Ted Bucklin

Year	Team	Lg	TD	1XP	2XP	FG	FGA	SAF	Pts
1927	**CHIC**	**N**	1	0		0		0	6

Tom Buckman

Year	Team	Lg	TD	1XP	2XP	FG	FGA	SAF	Pts
1969	**DEN**	**A**	1	0	0	0	0	0	6

Brentson Buckner

Year	Team	Lg	TD	1XP	2XP	FG	FGA	SAF	Pts
1995	**PIT**	**N**	1	0	0	0	0	0	6

Frank Budd

Year	Team	Lg	TD	1XP	2XP	FG	FGA	SAF	Pts
1962	**PHI**	**N**	1	0		0	0	0	6

Johnny Budd

Year	Team	Lg	TD	1XP	2XP	FG	FGA	SAF	Pts
1926	**FRA**	**N**	0	12		6		0	30
1928	**POT**	**N**	0	3		0		0	3
Career			0	15		6		0	33

Ted Buffalo

Year	Team	Lg	TD	1XP	2XP	FG	FGA	SAF	Pts
1923	**OOR**	**N**	1	0		0		0	6

Doug Buffone

Year	Team	Lg	TD	1XP	2XP	FG	FGA	SAF	Pts
1967	**CHI**	**N**	1	0		0	0	0	6

Danny Buggs

Year	Team	Lg	TD	1XP	2XP	FG	FGA	SAF	Pts
1977	**WAS**	**N**	1	0		0	0	0	6
1978			2	0		0	0	0	12
1979			1	0		0	0	0	6
Career			4	0		0	0	0	24

Drew Buie

Year	Team	Lg	TD	1XP	2XP	FG	FGA	SAF	Pts
1971	**OAK**	**N**	2	0		0	0	0	12

Ray Buivid

Year	Team	Lg	TD	1XP	2XP	FG	FGA	SAF	Pts
1937	**CHIB**	**N**	1	0		0		0	6

Glenn Bujnoch

Year	Team	Lg	TD	1XP	2XP	FG	FGA	SAF	Pts
1977	**CIN**	**N**	1	0		0	0	0	6

Joe Bukant

Year	Team	Lg	TD	1XP	2XP	FG	FGA	SAF	Pts
1939	**PHI**	**N**	3	0		0	0	0	18
1940			1	0		0	0	0	6
Career			4	0		0	0	0	24

Fred Bukaty

Year	Team	Lg	TD	1XP	2XP	FG	FGA	SAF	Pts
1961	**DEN**	**A**	5	0	1	0	0	0	32

Rudy Bukich

Year	Team	Lg	TD	1XP	2XP	FG	FGA	SAF	Pts
1953	**LA**	**N**	1	0		0	0	0	6
1961	**PIT**	**N**	2	0		0	0	0	12
1963	**CHI**	**N**	1	0		0	0	0	6
1965			3	0		0	0	0	18
1966			2	0		0	0	0	12
Career			9	0		0	0	0	54

George Buksar

Year	Team	Lg	TD	1XP	2XP	FG	FGA	SAF	Pts
1949	**CHI**	**AA**	1	0		0	0	0	6
1952	**WAS**	**N**	0	15		3	7	0	24
Career			1	15		3	7	0	30

Norm Bulaich

Year	Team	Lg	TD	1XP	2XP	FG	FGA	SAF	Pts
1970	**BAL**	**N**	3	0		0	0	0	18
1971			10	0		0	0	0	60
1972			1	0		0	0	0	6
1973	**PHI**	**N**	4	0		0	0	0	24
1975	**MIA**	**N**	10	0		0	0	0	60
1976			4	0		0	0	0	24
1977			4	0		0	0	0	24
1978			2	0		0	0	0	12
1979			3	0		0	0	0	18
Career			41	0		0	0	0	246
Playoffs			2	0		0	0	0	12

Chet Bulger

Year	Team	Lg	TD	1XP	2XP	FG	FGA	SAF	Pts
1943	**CHIC**	**N**	0	1		0	0	0	1
1945			1	0		0	0	0	6
Career			1	1		0	0	0	7

Ronnie Bull

Year	Team	Lg	TD	1XP	2XP	FG	FGA	SAF	Pts
1962	**CHI**	**N**	1	0		0	0	0	6

Year	Team		TD	1XP	2XP	FG	FGA	SAF	Pts

Ronnie Bull *continued*
1963			3	0		0	0	0	18
1964			1	0		0	0	0	6
1965			4	0		0	0	0	24
1967			1	0		0	0	0	6
1968			3	0		0	0	0	18
1971	PHI	N	1	0		0	0	0	6
Career			14	0		0	0	0	84

Scott Bull
1976	SF	N	2	0		0	0	0	12
1978			1	0		0	0	0	6
Career			3	0		0	0	0	18

Amos Bullocks
1962	DAL	N	3	0		0	0	0	18
1963			2	0		0	0	0	12
1966	PIT	N	2	0		0	0	0	12
Career			7	0		0	0	0	42

Rex Bumgardner
1948	BUF	AA	2	0		0	0	0	12
1949			5	0		0	0	0	30
1950	CLE	N	3	0		0	0	0	18
1951			2	0		0	0	0	12
Career			12	0		0	0	0	72
Playoffs			2	0		0	0	0	12

Jarrod Bunch
1992	NYG	N	4	0		0	0	0	24
1993			3	0		0	0	0	18
Career			7	0		0	0	0	42

Nick Buoniconti
1963	BOS	A	1	0	0	0	0	0	6
1967			0	0	0	0	0	1	2
1973	MIA	N	1	0	0	0	0	0	6
Career			2	0	0	0	0	1	14

Cornell Burbage
| 1987 | DAL | N | 2 | 0 | | 0 | 0 | 0 | 12 |

Jerry Burch
| 1961 | OAK | A | 1 | 0 | 0 | 0 | 0 | 0 | 6 |

Chris Burford
1960	DAL	A	5	0	0	0	0	0	30
1961			5	0	0	0	0	0	30
1962			12	0	0	0	0	0	72
1963	KC	A	9	0	1	0	0	0	56
1964			7	0	0	0	0	0	42
1965			6	0	0	0	0	0	36
1966			8	0	0	0	0	0	48
1967			3	0	0	0	0	0	18
Career			55	0	1	0	0	0	332

Adrian Burk
1950	BAL	N	1	0		0	0	0	6
1951	PHI	N	1	0		0	0	0	6
1953			3	0		0	0	0	18
1955			2	0		0	0	0	12
Career			7	0		0	0	0	42

Don Burke
| 1952 | SF | N | 1 | 0 | | 0 | 0 | 0 | 6 |

Mike Burke
| 1974 | LA | N | 0 | 1 | | 0 | 0 | 0 | 1 |

Randy Burke
1978	BAL	N	0	0		0	0	1	2
1980			3	0		0	0	0	18
Career			3	0		0	0	1	20

Vern Burke
1965	SF	N	1	0		0	0	0	6
1966	ATL	N	1	0		0	0	0	6
Career			2	0		0	0	0	12

Chris Burkett
1986	BUF	N	4	0		0	0	0	24
1987			4	0		0	0	0	24
1988			1	0		0	0	0	6
1989	NYJ	N	1	0		0	0	0	6

Chris Burkett *continued*
1991			5	0		0	0	0	30
1992			1	0		0	0	0	6
1993			4	0		0	0	0	24
Career			20	0		0	0	0	120
Playoffs			1	0		0	0	0	6

Jeff Burkett
| 1947 | CHIC | N | 1 | 0 | | 0 | 0 | 0 | 6 |

Randy Burks
| 1976 | CHI | N | 1 | 0 | | 0 | 0 | 0 | 6 |

Alex Burl
| 1956 | CHIC | N | 1 | 0 | | 0 | 0 | 0 | 6 |

Gary Burley
| 1978 | CIN | N | 0 | 0 | | 0 | 0 | 1 | 2 |

Bobby Burnett
| 1966 | BUF | A | 8 | 0 | 0 | 0 | 0 | 0 | 48 |

Dale Burnett
1930	NYG	N	6	4		0	0	0	40
1931			3	0		0	0	0	18
1932			1	0		0	0	0	6
1933			4	0		0	0	0	24
1934			2	0		0	0	0	12
1935			6	0		0	0	0	36
1936			3	0		0	0	0	18
1937			1	0		0	0	0	6
1938			1	0		0	0	0	6
Career			27	4		0	0	0	166

Hank Burnine
| 1956 | PHI | N | 2 | 0 | | 0 | 0 | 0 | 12 |

Bob Burns
| 1974 | NYJ | N | 1 | 0 | | 0 | 0 | 0 | 6 |

Leon Burns
1971	SD	N	1	0		0	0	0	6
1972	STL	N	2	0		0	0	0	12
Career			3	0		0	0	0	18

Clinton Burrell
| 1982 | CLE | N | 1 | 0 | | 0 | 0 | 0 | 6 |

George Burrell
| 1969 | DEN | A | 1 | 0 | 0 | 0 | 0 | 0 | 6 |

Ode Burrell
1964	HOU	A	1	0	0	0	0	0	6
1965			7	0	2	0	0	0	46
1966			5	0	0	0	0	0	30
Career			13	0	2	0	0	0	82

Bo Burris
| 1968 | NO | N | 1 | 0 | | 0 | 0 | 0 | 6 |

Jeff Burris
| Playoffs | | | 1 | 0 | 0 | 0 | 0 | 0 | 6 |

Ken Burrough
1970	NO	N	2	0		0	0	0	12
1971	HOU	N	1	0		0	0	0	6
1972			4	0		0	0	0	24
1973			3	0		0	0	0	18
1974			2	0		0	0	0	12
1975			8	0		0	0	0	48
1976			7	0		0	0	0	42
1977			8	0		0	0	0	48
1978			2	0		0	0	0	12
1979			6	0		0	0	0	36
1981			7	0		0	0	0	42
Career			50	0		0	0	0	300
Playoffs			1	0		0	0	0	6

Jim Burroughs
| 1982 | BAL | N | 1 | 0 | | 0 | 0 | 0 | 6 |

Curtis Burrow
| 1988 | GB | N | 0 | 2 | | 0 | 1 | 0 | 2 |

Ken Burrow
1971	ATL	N	6	0		0	0	0	36
1972			5	0		0	0	0	30
1973			7	0		0	0	0	42
1974			1	0		0	0	0	6
1975			2	0		0	0	0	12
Career			21	0		0	0	0	126

Harry Burrus
1946	NY	AA	1	0		0	0	0	6
1947			2	0		0	0	0	12
1948	BKN	AA	1	2		0	0	0	8
Career			4	2		0	0	0	26

Lloyd Burruss
1981	KC	N	1	0		0	0	0	6
1986			4	0		0	0	0	24
Career			5	0		0	0	0	30

Jimmy Burson
1964	STL	N	1	0		0	0	0	6
1968	ATL	N	1	0		0	0	0	6
Career			2	0		0	0	0	12

Jim Burt
| 1988 | NYG | N | 1 | 0 | | 0 | 0 | 0 | 6 |

Russ Burt
| 1924 | BUF | N | 1 | 0 | | 0 | | 0 | 6 |

Larry Burton
1975	NO	N	2	0		0	0	0	12
1976			2	0		0	0	0	12
1978	SD	N	3	0		0	0	0	18
Career			7	0		0	0	0	42

Leon Burton
| 1960 | NY | A | 3 | 0 | | 0 | 0 | 0 | 18 |

Ron Burton
1960	BOS	A	1	0		0	0	0	6
1961			3	0		0	0	0	18
1962			7	0		0	0	0	42
1964			5	0		0	0	0	30
1965			3	0		0	0	0	18
Career			19	0		0	0	0	114

Sam Busich
1936	BOS	N	1	1		1	0	0	10
1943	DET	N	0	1		0	0	0	1
Career			1	2		1	0	0	11

Dexter Bussey
1975	DET	N	4	0		0	0	0	24
1976			3	0		0	0	0	18
1977			5	0		0	0	0	30
1978			6	0		0	0	0	36
1979			1	0		0	0	0	6
1980			3	0		0	0	0	18
1983			1	0		0	0	0	6
1989	CIN	N	1	0		0	0	0	6
1990			1	0		0	0	0	6
Career			25	0		0	0	0	150

Wendell Butcher
| 1938 | BKN | N | 1 | 0 | | 0 | | 0 | 6 |

Dick Butkus
1969	CHI	N	0	0		0	0	1	2
1971			0	1		0	0	0	1
1972			0	1		0	0	0	1
1973			1	0		0	0	0	6
Career			1	2		0	0	1	10

Bill Butler
1959	GB	N	1	0		0	0	0	6
1961	PIT	N	1	0		0	0	0	6
1962	MIN	N	1	0		0	0	0	6
1963			1	0		0	0	0	6
Career			4	0		0	0	0	24

Bill Butler
| 1972 | NO | N | 2 | 0 | | 0 | 0 | 0 | 12 |

Bill Butler *continued*

Year	Team		TD	1XP	2XP	FG	FGA	SAF	Pts
1973			3	0		0	0	0	18
Career			5	0		0	0	0	30

Bobby Butler

Year	Team		TD	1XP	2XP	FG	FGA	SAF	Pts
1986	**ATL**	**N**	1	0		0	0	0	6
1989			1	0		0	0	0	6
1990			2	0		0	0	0	12
Career			4	0		0	0	0	24

Gary Butler

Year	Team		TD	1XP	2XP	FG	FGA	SAF	Pts
1973	**KC**	**N**	2	0		0	0	0	12

Jack Butler

Year	Team		TD	1XP	2XP	FG	FGA	SAF	Pts
1951	**PIT**	**N**	1	0		0	0	0	6
1952			2	0		0	0	0	12
1953			2	0		0	0	0	12
1954			2	0		0	0	0	12
1956			2	0		0	0	0	12
Career			9	0		0	0	0	54

Jerry Butler

Year	Team		TD	1XP	2XP	FG	FGA	SAF	Pts
1979	**BUF**	**N**	4	0		0	0	0	24
1980			6	0		0	0	0	36
1981			8	0		0	0	0	48
1982			4	0		0	0	0	24
1983			3	0		0	0	0	18
1985			2	0		0	0	0	12
1986			2	0		0	0	0	12
Career			29	0		0	0	0	174
Playoffs			1	0		0	0	0	6

Jim Butler

Year	Team		TD	1XP	2XP	FG	FGA	SAF	Pts
1965	**PIT**	**N**	1	0		0	0	0	6
1966			4	0		0	0	0	24
1968	**ATL**	**N**	2	0		0	0	0	12
1969			5	0		0	0	0	30
1970			1	0		0	0	0	6
1971			4	0		0	0	0	24
Career			17	0		0	0	0	102

Johnny Butler

Year	Team		TD	1XP	2XP	FG	FGA	SAF	Pts
1943	**P-P**	**N**	3	0		0	0	0	18
1944	**C-P**	**N**	2	0		0	0	0	12
1945	**PHI**	**N**	1	0		0	0	0	6
Career			6	0		0	0	0	36

Kevin Butler

Year	Team		TD	1XP	2XP	FG	FGA	SAF	Pts
1985	**CHI**	**N**	0	51		31	37	0	**144**
1986			0	36		28	**41**	0	120
1987			0	28		19	28	0	85
1988			0	37		15	19	0	82
1989			0	43		15	19	0	88
1990			0	36		26	37	0	114
1991			0	32		19	29	0	89
1992			0	34		19	26	0	91
1993			0	21		27	36	0	102
1994			0	24	0	21	29	0	87
1995			0	45	0	23	31	0	114
1996	**ARI**	**N**	0	17	0	14	17	0	59
Career			0	404	0	257	349	0	1175
Playoffs			0	23	0	17	25	0	74

LeRoy Butler

Year	Team		TD	1XP	2XP	FG	FGA	SAF	Pts
1993	**GB**	**N**	1	0		0	0	0	6
1996			1	0	0	0	0	0	6
Career			2	0	0	0	0	0	12

Mike Butler

Year	Team		TD	1XP	2XP	FG	FGA	SAF	Pts
1979	**GB**	**N**	1	0		0	0	0	6

Ray Butler

Year	Team		TD	1XP	2XP	FG	FGA	SAF	Pts
1980	**BAL**	**N**	2	0		0	0	0	12
1981			9	0		0	0	0	54
1982			2	0		0	0	0	12
1983			3	0		0	0	0	18
1984	**IND**	**N**	6	0		0	0	0	36
1985			2	0		0	0	0	12
1986	**SEA**	**N**	4	0		0	0	0	24
1987			5	0		0	0	0	30
1988			4	0		0	0	0	24
Career			37	0		0	0	0	222

Skip Butler

Year	Team		TD	1XP	2XP	FG	FGA	SAF	Pts
1971	**NO**	**N**	0	5		1	5	0	8
1972	**HOU**	**N**	0	15		12	19	0	51
1973			0	21		15	24	0	66
1974			0	29		9	19	0	56
1975			0	31		18	30	0	85
1976			0	24		16	27	0	72
1977			0	2		0	3	0	2
Career			0	127		71	127	0	340

Sol Butler

Year	Team		TD	1XP	2XP	FG	FGA	SAF	Pts
1924	**HAM-AKR**	**N**	2	0		0		0	12

Greg Buttle

Year	Team		TD	1XP	2XP	FG	FGA	SAF	Pts
1976	**NYJ**	**N**	1	0		0	0	0	6
1977			1	0		0	0	0	6
1981			0	0		0	0	1	2
1984			1	0		0	0	0	6
Career			3	0		0	0	1	20

Marion Butts

Year	Team		TD	1XP	2XP	FG	FGA	SAF	Pts
1989	**SD**	**N**	9	0		0	0	0	54
1990			8	0		0	0	0	48
1991			7	0		0	0	0	42
1992			4	0		0	0	0	24
1993			4	0		0	0	0	24
1994	**NE**	**N**	8	0	0	0	0	0	48
1995	**HOU**	**N**	4	0	0	0	0	0	24
Career			44	0	0	0	0	0	264
Playoffs			1	0	0	0	0	0	6

Keith Byars

Year	Team		TD	1XP	2XP	FG	FGA	SAF	Pts
1986	**PHI**	**N**	1	0		0	0	0	6
1987			4	0		0	0	0	24
1988			10	0		0	0	0	60
1989			5	0		0	0	0	30
1990			3	0		0	0	0	18
1991			4	0		0	0	0	24
1992			3	0		0	0	0	18
1993	**MIA**	**N**	6	0		0	0	0	36
1994			7	0	0	0	0	0	42
1995			3	0	0	0	0	0	18
1996	**NE**	**N**	2	0	1	0	0	0	14
Career			48	0	1	0	0	0	290
Playoffs			2	0	0	0	0	0	12

Rick Byas

Year	Team		TD	1XP	2XP	FG	FGA	SAF	Pts
1977	**ATL**	**N**	1	0		0	0	0	6
1978			1	0		0	0	0	6
1979			1	0		0	0	0	6
Career			3	0		0	0	0	18

Earnest Byner

Year	Team		TD	1XP	2XP	FG	FGA	SAF	Pts
1984	**CLE**	**N**	3	0		0	0	0	18
1985			10	0		0	0	0	60
1986			4	0		0	0	0	24
1987			10	0		0	0	0	60
1988			5	0		0	0	0	30
1989	**WAS**	**N**	9	0		0	0	0	54
1990			7	0		0	0	0	42
1991			5	0		0	0	0	30
1992			7	0		0	0	0	42
1993			1	0		0	0	0	6
1994	**CLE**	**N**	2	0	0	0	0	0	12
1995			4	0	0	0	0	0	24
1996	**BAL**	**N**	5	0	0	0	0	0	30
Career			72	0	0	0	0	0	432
Playoffs			8	0	0	0	0	0	48

Butch Byrd

Year	Team		TD	1XP	2XP	FG	FGA	SAF	Pts
1964	**BUF**	**A**	1	0	0	0	0	0	6
1966			2	0	0	0	0	0	12
1968			1	0	0	0	0	0	6
1969			1	0	0	0	0	0	6
1970	**BUF**	**N**	1	0		0	0	0	6
Career			6	0	0	0	0	0	36
Playoffs			1	0	0	0	0	0	6

Dennis Byrd

Year	Team		TD	1XP	2XP	FG	FGA	SAF	Pts
1990	**NYJ**	**N**	0	0		0	0	1	2

Gill Byrd

Year	Team		TD	1XP	2XP	FG	FGA	SAF	Pts
1984	**SD**	**N**	2	0		0	0	0	12

Carl Byrum

Year	Team		TD	1XP	2XP	FG	FGA	SAF	Pts
1986	**BUF**	**N**	1	0		0	0	0	6

Larry Cabrelli

Year	Team		TD	1XP	2XP	FG	FGA	SAF	Pts
1941	**PHI**	**N**	1	0		0	0	0	6
1942			1	0		0	0	0	6
1943	**P-P**	**N**	2	0		0	0	0	12
1944	**PHI**	**N**	1	0		0	0	0	6
1946			1	0		0	0	0	6
Career			6	0		0	0	0	36

Ernie Caddel

Year	Team		TD	1XP	2XP	FG	FGA	SAF	Pts
1933	**POR**	**N**	5	0		0		0	30
1934	**DET**	**N**	6	0		0		0	36
1935			6	0		0		0	36
1936			5	0		0		0	30
1937			3	0		0		0	18
1938			1	0		0	0	0	6
Career			26	0		0	0	0	156
Playoffs			1	0		0	0	0	6

George Cafego

Year	Team		TD	1XP	2XP	FG	FGA	SAF	Pts
1944	**BOS**	**N**	1	0		0	0	0	6

Lee Roy Caffey

Year	Team		TD	1XP	2XP	FG	FGA	SAF	Pts
1963	**PHI**	**N**	1	0		0	0	0	6
1965	**GB**	**N**	1	0		0	0	0	6
1966			1	0		0	0	0	6
Career			3	0		0	0	0	18

Chris Cagle

Year	Team		TD	1XP	2XP	FG	FGA	SAF	Pts
1931	**NYG**	**N**	1	0		0		0	6
1932			4	0		0		0	24
1933	**BKN**	**N**	0	0		0		0	0
1934			0	0		0		0	0
Career			5	0		0		0	30

Bill Cahill

Year	Team		TD	1XP	2XP	FG	FGA	SAF	Pts
1973	**BUF**	**N**	1	0		0	0	0	6

Tiny Cahoon

Year	Team		TD	1XP	2XP	FG	FGA	SAF	Pts
1927	**GB**	**N**	1	0		0		0	6

Jim Cain

Year	Team		TD	1XP	2XP	FG	FGA	SAF	Pts
1950	**DET**	**N**	1	0		0	0	0	6

J.V. Cain

Year	Team		TD	1XP	2XP	FG	FGA	SAF	Pts
1974	**STL**	**N**	1	0		0	0	0	6
1975			1	0		0	0	0	6
1976			5	0		0	0	0	30
1977			2	0		0	0	0	12
Career			9	0		0	0	0	54

Lynn Cain

Year	Team		TD	1XP	2XP	FG	FGA	SAF	Pts
1979	**ATL**	**N**	4	0		0	0	0	24
1980			9	0		0	0	0	54
1981			6	0		0	0	0	36
1982			2	0		0	0	0	12
1983			1	0		0	0	0	6
1984			3	0		0	0	0	18
Career			25	0		0	0	0	150
Playoffs			1	0		0	0	0	6

Pete Calac

Year	Team		TD	1XP	2XP	FG	FGA	SAF	Pts
1920	**CAN**	**A**	2	0		0		0	12
1921	**CLE**	**A**	3	0		0		0	18
1922	**OOR**	**N**	2	0		0		0	12
1924	**BUF**	**N**	2	0		0		0	12
Career			9	0		0		0	54

Ralph Calacagni

Year	Team		TD	1XP	2XP	FG	FGA	SAF	Pts
1947	**PIT**	**N**	0	0		0	0	1	2

Bruce Caldwell

Year	Team		TD	1XP	2XP	FG	FGA	SAF	Pts
1928	**NYG**	**N**	1	0		1		0	9

Mike Caldwell

Year	Team		TD	1XP	2XP	FG	FGA	SAF	Pts
1995	**CLE**	**N**	1	0	0	0	0	0	6
1996	**BAL**	**N**	1	0	0	0	0	0	6
Career			2	0	0	0	0	0	12

Ravin Caldwell

Year	Team		TD	1XP	2XP	FG	FGA	SAF	Pts
1988	**WAS**	**N**	0	0		0	0	1	2

Jamie Caleb

Year	Team		TD	1XP	2XP	FG	FGA	SAF	Pts
1960	CLE	N	1	0		0	0	0	6

Don Calhoun

Year	Team		TD	1XP	2XP	FG	FGA	SAF	Pts
1975	NE	N	2	0		0	0	0	12
1976			1	0		0	0	0	6
1977			4	0		0	0	0	24
1978			1	0		0	0	0	6
1979			6	0		0	0	0	36
1980			9	0		0	0	0	54
1981			2	0		0	0	0	12
Career			25	0		0	0	0	150

Rick Calhoun

Year	Team		TD	1XP	2XP	FG	FGA	SAF	Pts
1987	LARI	N	1	0		0	0	0	6

Jim Callahan

Year	Team		TD	1XP	2XP	FG	FGA	SAF	Pts
1946	DET	N	2	0		0	0	0	12

Lee Calland

Year	Team		TD	1XP	2XP	FG	FGA	SAF	Pts
1967	ATL	N	1	0		0	0	0	6

Len Calligaro

Year	Team		TD	1XP	2XP	FG	FGA	SAF	Pts
1944	NYG	N	1	0		0	0	0	6

Bill Callihan

Year	Team		TD	1XP	2XP	FG	FGA	SAF	Pts
1943	DET	N	4	0		0	0	0	24
1945			1	25		0	0	0	31
Career			5	25		0	0	0	55

Chris Calloway

Year	Team		TD	1XP	2XP	FG	FGA	SAF	Pts
1990	PIT	N	1	0		0	0	0	6
1991			1	0		0	0	0	6
1992	NYG	N	1	0		0	0	0	6
1993			3	0		0	0	0	18
1994			2	0	0	0	0	0	12
1995			3	0	0	0	0	0	18
1996			4	0	0	0	0	0	24
Career			15	0	0	0	0	0	90

Tony Calvelli

Year	Team		TD	1XP	2XP	FG	FGA	SAF	Pts
1940	DET	N	1	0		0	0	0	6

Rich Camarillo

Year	Team		TD	1XP	2XP	FG	FGA	SAF	Pts
1992	PHX	N	0	0		0	0	0	0

Al Campana

Year	Team		TD	1XP	2XP	FG	FGA	SAF	Pts
1950	CHIB	N	1	0		0	0	0	6
1952			1	0		0	0	0	6
Career			2	0		0	0	0	12
Playoffs			1	0		0	0	0	6

Earl Campbell

Year	Team		TD	1XP	2XP	FG	FGA	SAF	Pts
1978	HOU	N	13	0		0	0	0	78
1979			**19**	0		0	0	0	114
1980			13	0		0	0	0	78
1981			10	0		0	0	0	60
1982			2	0		0	0	0	12
1983			12	0		0	0	0	72
1984			4	0		0	0	0	24
1985	NO	N	1	0		0	0	0	6
Career			74	0		0	0	0	444
Playoffs			4	0		0	0	0	24

Glenn Campbell

Year	Team		TD	1XP	2XP	FG	FGA	SAF	Pts
1929	NYG	N	1	0		0		0	6
1930			4	0		0		0	24
1931			2	0		0		0	12
1933			1	0		0		0	6
Career			8	0		0		0	48

Jeff Campbell

Year	Team		TD	1XP	2XP	FG	FGA	SAF	Pts
1990	DET	N	2	0		0	0	0	12
1992			1	0		0	0	0	6
1994	DEN	N	1	0	0	0	0	0	6
Career			4	0	0	0	0	0	24

John Campbell

Year	Team		TD	1XP	2XP	FG	FGA	SAF	Pts
1965	PIT	N	1	0		0	0	0	6

Milt Campbell

Year	Team		TD	1XP	2XP	FG	FGA	SAF	Pts
1957	CLE	N	1	0		0	0	0	6

Scott Campbell

Year	Team		TD	1XP	2XP	FG	FGA	SAF	Pts
1987	ATL	N	2	0		0	0	0	12

Sonny Campbell

Year	Team		TD	1XP	2XP	FG	FGA	SAF	Pts
1970	ATL	N	2	0		0	0	0	12

Woody Campbell

Year	Team		TD	1XP	2XP	FG	FGA	SAF	Pts
1967	HOU	A	6	0	0	0	0	0	36
1968			6	0	0	0	0	0	36
1969			1	0	0	0	0	0	6
1970	HOU	N	1	0		0	0	0	6
1971			1	0		0	0	0	6
Career			15	0	0	0	0	0	90

Billy Campfield

Year	Team		TD	1XP	2XP	FG	FGA	SAF	Pts
1979	PHI	N	4	0		0	0	0	24
1980			3	0		0	0	0	18
1981			4	0		0	0	0	24
1982			1	0		0	0	0	6
Career			12	0		0	0	0	72
Playoffs			1	0		0	0	0	6

Bob Campiglio

Year	Team		TD	1XP	2XP	FG	FGA	SAF	Pts
1932	SI	N	3	0		0		0	18

Larry Canada

Year	Team		TD	1XP	2XP	FG	FGA	SAF	Pts
1978	DEN	N	3	0		0	0	0	18
1981			4	0		0	0	0	24
Career			7	0		0	0	0	42

Tony Canadeo

Year	Team		TD	1XP	2XP	FG	FGA	SAF	Pts
1941	GB	N	3	0		0	0	0	18
1942			3	0		0	0	0	18
1943			5	0		0	0	0	30
1947			2	0		0	0	0	12
1948			4	0		0	0	0	24
1949			4	0		0	0	0	24
1950			4	0		0	0	0	24
1951			3	0		0	0	0	18
1952			3	0		0	0	0	18
Career			31	0		0	0	0	186

Justin Canale

Year	Team		TD	1XP	2XP	FG	FGA	SAF	Pts
1967	BOS	A	0	1	0	0	0	0	1

Pat Cannamela

Year	Team		TD	1XP	2XP	FG	FGA	SAF	Pts
1952	DAL	N	0	8		0	1	0	8

Billy Cannon

Year	Team		TD	1XP	2XP	FG	FGA	SAF	Pts
1960	HOU	A	7	0	0	0	0	0	42
1961			15	0	0	0	0	0	90
1962			13	0	1	0	0	0	80
1964	OAK	A	8	0	0	0	0	0	48
1966			2	0	0	0	0	0	12
1967			10	0	0	0	0	0	60
1968			6	0	0	0	0	0	36
1969			2	0	0	0	0	0	12
1970	KC	N	2	0		0	0	0	12
Career			65	0	1	0	0	0	392
Playoffs			4	0	0	0	0	0	24

Leo Cantor

Year	Team		TD	1XP	2XP	FG	FGA	SAF	Pts
1942	NYG	N	2	0		0	0	0	12
1945	CHIC	N	5	0		0	0	0	30
Career			7	0		0	0	0	42

Bill Capece

Year	Team		TD	1XP	2XP	FG	FGA	SAF	Pts
1981	TB	N	0	30		15	24	0	75
1982			0	14		18	23	0	68
1983			0	23		10	23	0	53
Career			0	67		43	70	0	196
Playoffs			0	2		1	1	0	5

Wayne Capers

Year	Team		TD	1XP	2XP	FG	FGA	SAF	Pts
1983	PIT	N	1	0		0	0	0	6
1985	IND	N	5	0		0	0	0	30
Career			6	0		0	0	0	36
Playoffs			1	0		0	0	0	6

Warren Capone

Year	Team		TD	1XP	2XP	FG	FGA	SAF	Pts
1976	NO	N	1	0		0	0	0	6

Bob Cappadona

Year	Team		TD	1XP	2XP	FG	FGA	SAF	Pts
1966	BOS	A	1	0	1	0	0	0	8

Bob Cappadona *continued*

Year	Team		TD	1XP	2XP	FG	FGA	SAF	Pts
1967			1	0	0	0	0	0	6
1968	BUF	A	3	0	1	0	0	0	20
Career			5	0	2	0	0	0	34

Gino Cappelletti

Year	Team		TD	1XP	2XP	FG	FGA	SAF	Pts
1960	BOS	A	0	30	3	8	21	0	60
1961			8	48	0	**17**	**32**	0	**147**
1962			5	38	0	20	37	0	128
1963			2	35	0	**22**	**38**	0	**113**
1964			7	36	1	**25**	**39**	0	**155**
1965			9	27	0	17	27	0	**132**
1966			6	35	0	16	32	0	**119**
1967			3	29	0	16	31	0	95
1968			2	26	0	15	27	0	83
1969			0	26	0	14	34	0	68
1970	BOS	N	0	12		6	15	0	30
Career			42	342	4	176	333	0	1130
Playoffs			0	3	0	5	6	0	18

John Cappelletti

Year	Team		TD	1XP	2XP	FG	FGA	SAF	Pts
1975	LA	N	6	0		0	0	0	36
1976			2	0		0	0	0	12
1977			6	0		0	0	0	36
1978			4	0		0	0	0	24
1980	SD	N	5	0		0	0	0	30
1981			5	0		0	0	0	30
Career			28	0		0	0	0	168
Playoffs			1	0		0	0	0	6

Joe Caravello

Year	Team		TD	1XP	2XP	FG	FGA	SAF	Pts
1990	SD	N	1	0		0	0	0	6

Lloyd Cardwell

Year	Team		TD	1XP	2XP	FG	FGA	SAF	Pts
1937	DET	N	1	0		0		0	6
1938			5	0		0		0	30
1939			3	0		0	0	0	18
1940			3	0		0	0	0	18
1942			1	0		0	0	0	6
Career			13	0		0	0	0	78

Bob Carey

Year	Team		TD	1XP	2XP	FG	FGA	SAF	Pts
1952	LA	N	2	0		0	0	0	12
1954			0	2		1	1	0	5
1956			1	0		0	0	0	6
Career			3	2		1	1	0	23

Harland Carl

Year	Team		TD	1XP	2XP	FG	FGA	SAF	Pts
1956	CHIB	N	1	0		0	0	0	6

Cody Carlson

Year	Team		TD	1XP	2XP	FG	FGA	SAF	Pts
1988	HOU	N	1	0		0	0	0	6
1992			1	0		0	0	0	6
1993			2	0		0	0	0	12
Career			4	0		0	0	0	24

Roy Carlson

Year	Team		TD	1XP	2XP	FG	FGA	SAF	Pts
1928	CHIB	N	1	0		0		0	6

Wray Carlton

Year	Team		TD	1XP	2XP	FG	FGA	SAF	Pts
1960	BUF	A	11	0	0	0	0	0	66
1961			4	0	0	0	0	0	24
1962			2	0	0	0	0	0	12
1964			1	0	0	0	0	0	6
1965			7	0	0	0	0	0	42
1966			6	0	0	0	0	0	36
1967			3	0	0	0	0	0	18
Career			34	0	0	0	0	0	204
Playoffs			1	0	0	0	0	0	6

Al Carmichael

Year	Team		TD	1XP	2XP	FG	FGA	SAF	Pts
1953	GB	N	1	0		0	0	0	6
1955			2	0		0	0	0	12
1956			2	0		0	0	0	12
1957			1	0		0	0	0	6
1958			1	0		0	0	0	6
1960	DEN	A	7	0	0	0	0	0	42
Career			14	0	0	0	0	0	84

Harold Carmichael

Year	Team		TD	1XP	2XP	FG	FGA	SAF	Pts
1972	PHI	N	2	0		0	0	0	12
1973			9	0		0	0	0	54
1974			8	0		0	0	0	48
1975			7	0		0	0	0	42

Harold Carmichael *continued*

Year	Team		TD	1XP	2XP	FG	FGA	SAF	Pts
1976			5	0		0	0	0	30
1977			7	0		0	0	0	42
1978			8	0		0	0	0	48
1979			11	0		0	0	0	66
1980			9	0		0	0	0	54
1981			6	0		0	0	0	36
1982			4	0		0	0	0	24
1983			3	0		0	0	0	18
Career			79	0		0	0	0	474
Playoffs			6	0		0	0	0	36

Ray Carnelly

Year	Team		TD	1XP	2XP	FG	FGA	SAF	Pts
1939	**BKN**	**N**	0	0		0	1	0	0

John Carney

Year	Team		TD	1XP	2XP	FG	FGA	SAF	Pts
1988	**TB**	**N**	0	6		2	5	0	12
1990	**SD**	**N**	0	27		19	21	0	84
1991			0	31		19	29	0	88
1992			0	35		26	32	0	113
1993			0	31		31	40	0	124
1994			0	33	0	**34**	38	0	**135**
1995			0	32	0	21	26	0	95
1996			0	31	0	29	36	0	118
Career			0	226	0	181	227	0	769
Playoffs			0	9	0	7	8	0	30

Brett Carolan

Year	Team		TD	1XP	2XP	FG	FGA	SAF	Pts
1996	**MIA**	**N**	1	0	0	0	0	0	6

Reg Carolan

Year	Team		TD	1XP	2XP	FG	FGA	SAF	Pts
1962	**SD**	**A**	1	0	0	0	0	0	6
1964	**KC**	**A**	1	0	0	0	0	0	6
1965			0	0	1	0	0	0	2
1966			3	0	0	0	0	0	18
1967			0	0	1	0	0	0	2
Career			5	0	2	0	0	0	34

J.C. Caroline

Year	Team		TD	1XP	2XP	FG	FGA	SAF	Pts
1956	**CHIB**	**N**	4	0		0	0	0	24
1958			1	0		0	0	0	6
1960	**CHI**	**N**	1	0		0	0	0	6
Career			6	0		0	0	0	36

Ken Carpenter

Year	Team		TD	1XP	2XP	FG	FGA	SAF	Pts
1950	**CLE**	**N**	1	0		0	0	0	6
1951			6	0		0	0	0	36
1952			5	0		0	0	0	30
1953			5	0		0	0	0	30
1960	**DEN**	**A**	1	0	0	0	0	0	6
Career			18	0	0	0	0	0	108
Playoffs			1	0	0	0	0	0	6

Lew Carpenter

Year	Team		TD	1XP	2XP	FG	FGA	SAF	Pts
1953	**DET**	**N**	1	0		0	0	0	6
1954			5	0		0	0	0	30
1955			8	0		0	0	0	48
1957	**CLE**	**N**	4	0		0	0	0	24
1958			2	0		0	0	0	12
1959	**GB**	**N**	1	0		0	0	0	6
Career			21	0		0	0	0	126
Playoffs			1	0		0	0	0	6

Preston Carpenter

Year	Team		TD	1XP	2XP	FG	FGA	SAF	Pts
1957	**CLE**	**N**	3	0		0	0	0	18
1958			1	0		0	0	0	6
1959			2	0		0	0	0	12
1960	**PIT**	**N**	2	0		0	0	0	12
1961			4	0		0	0	0	24
1962			4	0		0	0	0	24
1963			1	0		0	0	0	6
1964	**WAS**	**N**	3	0		0	0	0	18
1966	**MIN**	**N**	4	0		0	0	0	24
Career			24	0		0	0	0	144

Rob Carpenter

Year	Team		TD	1XP	2XP	FG	FGA	SAF	Pts
1977	**HOU**	**N**	1	0		0	0	0	6
1978			5	0		0	0	0	30
1979			4	0		0	0	0	24
1980			3	0		0	0	0	18
1981	**HOU-NYG**	**N**	6	0		0	0	0	36
1982	**NYG**	**N**	1	0		0	0	0	6
1983			6	0		0	0	0	36

Rob Carpenter *continued*

Year	Team		TD	1XP	2XP	FG	FGA	SAF	Pts
1984			8	0		0	0	0	48
Career			34	0		0	0	0	204
Playoffs			1	0		0	0	0	6

Rob Carpenter

Year	Team		TD	1XP	2XP	FG	FGA	SAF	Pts
1992	**NYJ**	**N**	1	0		0	0	0	6
Playoffs			1	0	0	0	0	0	6

Ron Carpenter

Year	Team		TD	1XP	2XP	FG	FGA	SAF	Pts
1974	**CIN**	**N**	0	0		0	0	1	2

Ed Carr

Year	Team		TD	1XP	2XP	FG	FGA	SAF	Pts
1948	**SF**	**AA**	2	0		0	0	0	12
1949			7	0		0	0	0	42
Career			9	0		0	0	0	54

Freddie Carr

Year	Team		TD	1XP	2XP	FG	FGA	SAF	Pts
1976	**GB**	**N**	1	0		0	0	0	6

Gregg Carr

Year	Team		TD	1XP	2XP	FG	FGA	SAF	Pts
1987	**PIT**	**N**	0	0		0	0	1	2

Harlan Carr

Year	Team		TD	1XP	2XP	FG	FGA	SAF	Pts
1927	**BUF-POT**	**N**	3	0		0		0	18

Henry Carr

Year	Team		TD	1XP	2XP	FG	FGA	SAF	Pts
1966	**NYG**	**N**	1	0		0	0	0	6

Jimmy Carr

Year	Team		TD	1XP	2XP	FG	FGA	SAF	Pts
1960	**PHI**	**N**	1	0		0	0	0	6

Roger Carr

Year	Team		TD	1XP	2XP	FG	FGA	SAF	Pts
1975	**BAL**	**N**	2	0		0	0	0	12
1976			11	0		0	0	0	66
1977			1	0		0	0	0	6
1978			6	0		0	0	0	36
1979			1	0		0	0	0	6
1980			5	0		0	0	0	30
1981			3	0		0	0	0	18
1982	**SEA**	**N**	2	0		0	0	0	12
Career			31	0		0	0	0	186
Playoffs			1	0		0	0	0	6

Mark Carrier

Year	Team		TD	1XP	2XP	FG	FGA	SAF	Pts
1987	**TB**	**N**	3	0		0	0	0	18
1988			5	0		0	0	0	30
1989			9	0		0	0	0	54
1990			4	0		0	0	0	24
1991			2	0		0	0	0	12
1992			4	0		0	0	0	24
1993	**CLE**	**N**	5	0		0	0	0	30
1994			6	0	0	0	0	0	36
1995	**CAR**	**N**	3	0	0	0	0	0	18
1996			6	0	0	0	0	0	36
Career			47	0	0	0	0	0	282
Playoffs			1	0	0	0	0	0	6

Mark Carrier

Year	Team		TD	1XP	2XP	FG	FGA	SAF	Pts
1993	**CHI**	**N**	1	0		0	0	0	6

Darren Carrington

Year	Team		TD	1XP	2XP	FG	FGA	SAF	Pts
1992	**SD**	**N**	1	0		0	0	0	6

Bird Carroll

Year	Team		TD	1XP	2XP	FG	FGA	SAF	Pts
1921	**CAN**	**A**	1	0		0		0	6
1922	**CAN**	**N**	1	1		0		0	7
1923			1	1		0		0	7
Career			3	2		0		0	20

Jay Carroll

Year	Team		TD	1XP	2XP	FG	FGA	SAF	Pts
1984	**TB**	**N**	1	0		0	0	0	6

Vic Carroll

Year	Team		TD	1XP	2XP	FG	FGA	SAF	Pts
1936	**BOS**	**N**	1	0		0		0	6
1941	**WAS**	**N**	1	0		0	0	0	6
1944	**NYG**	**N**	1	0		0	0	0	6
1947			2	0		0	0	0	12
Career			5	0		0	0	0	30

Wesley Carroll

Year	Team		TD	1XP	2XP	FG	FGA	SAF	Pts
1991	**NO**	**N**	1	0		0	0	0	6
1992			2	0		0	0	0	12
Career			3	0		0	0	0	18

Paul Ott Carruth

Year	Team		TD	1XP	2XP	FG	FGA	SAF	Pts
1986	**GB**	**N**	4	0		0	0	0	24
1987			4	0		0	0	0	24
Career			8	0		0	0	0	48

Carlos Carson

Year	Team		TD	1XP	2XP	FG	FGA	SAF	Pts
1981	**KC**	**N**	1	0		0	0	0	6
1982			2	0		0	0	0	12
1983			7	0		0	0	0	42
1984			4	0		0	0	0	24
1985			4	0		0	0	0	24
1986			4	0		0	0	0	24
1987			7	0		0	0	0	42
1988			3	0		0	0	0	18
1989			1	0		0	0	0	6
Career			33	0		0	0	0	198

Harry Carson

Year	Team		TD	1XP	2XP	FG	FGA	SAF	Pts
1979	**NYG**	**N**	1	0		0	0	0	6
1986			1	0		0	0	0	6
Career			2	0		0	0	0	12
Playoffs			1	0		0	0	0	6

Johnny Carson

Year	Team		TD	1XP	2XP	FG	FGA	SAF	Pts
1955	**WAS**	**N**	3	0		0	0	0	18
1956			3	0		0	0	0	18
1957			3	0		0	0	0	18
1958			2	0		0	0	0	12
1960	**HOU**	**A**	4	0	0	0	0	0	24
Career			15	0	0	0	0	0	90

Kern Carson

Year	Team		TD	1XP	2XP	FG	FGA	SAF	Pts
1965	**NY**	**A**	2	0	0	0	0	0	12

Allen Carter

Year	Team		TD	1XP	2XP	FG	FGA	SAF	Pts
1975	**NE**	**N**	1	0		0	0	0	6

Anthony Carter

Year	Team		TD	1XP	2XP	FG	FGA	SAF	Pts
1985	**MIN**	**N**	8	0		0	0	0	48
1986			7	0		0	0	0	42
1987			7	0		0	0	0	42
1988			6	0		0	0	0	36
1989			4	0		0	0	0	24
1990			8	0		0	0	0	48
1991			6	0		0	0	0	36
1992			3	0		0	0	0	18
1993			5	0		0	0	0	30
1994	**DET**	**N**	3	0	0	0	0	0	18
Career			57	0	0	0	0	0	342
Playoffs			2	0	0	0	0	0	12

Cris Carter

Year	Team		TD	1XP	2XP	FG	FGA	SAF	Pts
1987	**PHI**	**N**	2	0		0	0	0	12
1988			7	0		0	0	0	42
1989			11	0		0	0	0	66
1990	**MIN**	**N**	3	0		0	0	0	18
1991			5	0		0	0	0	30
1992			6	0		0	0	0	36
1993			9	0		0	0	0	54
1994			7	0	2	0	0	0	46
1995			17	0	0	0	0	0	102
1996			10	0	0	0	0	0	60
Career			77	0	2	0	0	0	466
Playoffs			3	0	1	0	0	0	20

Dale Carter

Year	Team		TD	1XP	2XP	FG	FGA	SAF	Pts
1992	**KC**	**N**	3	0		0	0	0	18
1996			1	0	0	0	0	0	6
Career			4	0	0	0	0	0	24

Dexter Carter

Year	Team		TD	1XP	2XP	FG	FGA	SAF	Pts
1990	**SF**	**N**	1	0		0	0	0	6
1991			4	0		0	0	0	24
1992			1	0		0	0	0	6
1993			2	0		0	0	0	12
1994			1	0	0	0	0	0	6
1995			1	0	0	0	0	0	6
1996			1	0	0	0	0	0	6
Career			11	0	0	0	0	0	66

Gerald Carter

Year	Team		TD	1XP	2XP	FG	FGA	SAF	Pts
1983	**TB**	**N**	2	0		0	0	0	12
1984			5	0		0	0	0	30
1985			3	0		0	0	0	18

Year	Team		TD	1XP	2XP	FG	FGA	SAF	Pts

Gerald Carter continued
1986			2	0		0	0	0	12
1987			5	0		0	0	0	30
Career			17	0		0	0	0	102

Jim Carter
| 1973 | GB | N | 1 | 0 | | 0 | 0 | 0 | 6 |

Joe Carter
1933	PHI	N	2	1		0		0	13
1934			4	0		0		0	24
1935			2	0		0		0	12
1936			1	0		0		0	6
1937			3	0		0		0	18
1938			8	0		0		0	48
1939			2	0		0	0	0	12
1942	GB	N	1	0		0	0	0	6
Career			23	1		0	0	0	139

Joe Carter
| 1984 | MIA | N | 1 | 0 | | 0 | 0 | 0 | 6 |

Kevin Carter
| 1995 | STL | N | 0 | 0 | 0 | 0 | 0 | 1 | 2 |

Ki-Jana Carter
| 1996 | CIN | N | 9 | 0 | 0 | 0 | 0 | 0 | 54 |

Louis Carter
1976	TB	N	1	0		0	0	0	6
1977			2	0		0	0	0	12
1978			1	0		0	0	0	6
Career			4	0		0	0	0	24

Michael Carter
| Playoffs | | | 1 | 0 | 0 | 0 | 0 | 0 | 6 |

Pat Carter
1991	LARM	N	2	0		0	0	0	12
1992			3	0		0	0	0	18
1993			1	0		0	0	0	6
1994	HOU	N	1	0	0	0	0	0	6
1996	ARI	N	1	0	0	0	0	0	6
Career			8	0	0	0	0	0	48

Rodney Carter
1987	PIT	N	3	0		0	0	0	18
1988			5	0		0	0	0	30
1989			4	0		0	0	0	24
Career			12	0		0	0	0	72

Rubin Carter
| 1979 | DEN | N | 1 | 0 | | 0 | 0 | 0 | 6 |

Tom Carter
| 1995 | WAS | N | 1 | 0 | 0 | 0 | 0 | 0 | 6 |

Tony Carter
| 1995 | CHI | N | 1 | 0 | 0 | 0 | 0 | 0 | 6 |

Virgil Carter
1968	CHI	N	4	0		0	0	0	24
1970	CIN	N	2	0		0	0	0	12
1971			0	1		0	0	0	1
1972			2	0		0	0	0	12
Career			8	1		0	0	0	49

Maurice Carthon
| 1988 | NYG | N | 3 | 0 | | 0 | 0 | 0 | 18 |
| Playoffs | | | 1 | 0 | 0 | 0 | 0 | 0 | 6 |

Charlie Cartin
| 1925 | FRA | N | 1 | 0 | | 0 | 0 | | 6 |

Mel Carver
1982	TB	N	2	0		0	0	0	12
1983			1	0		0	0	0	6
Career			3	0		0	0	0	18

Larry Carwell
1968	HOU	A	1	0	0	0	0	0	6
1971	NE	N	1	0	0	0	0	0	6
1972			1	0		0	0	0	6
Career			3	0	0	0	0	0	18

Ken Casanega
| 1946 | SF | AA | 2 | 0 | | 0 | 0 | 0 | 12 |

Tommy Casanova
1972	CIN	N	1	0		0	0	0	6
1976			3	0		0	0	0	18
Career			4	0		0	0	0	24

Rick Casares
1955	CHIB	N	5	0		0	0	0	30
1956			14	0		0	0	0	84
1957			6	0		0	0	0	36
1958			3	0		0	0	0	18
1959			12	0		0	0	0	72
1960	CHI	N	5	0		0	0	0	30
1961			8	0		0	0	0	48
1962			3	0		0	0	0	18
1963			1	0		0	0	0	6
1964			2	0		0	0	0	12
1966	MIA	A	1	0	0	0	0	0	6
Career			60	0	0	0	0	0	360
Playoffs			1	0	0	0	0	0	6

Ernie Case
| 1947 | BAL | AA | 0 | 1 | 1 | 1 | 0 | | 4 |

Scott Case
1984	ATL	N	0	0		0	0	1	2
1990			1	0		0	0	0	6
Career			1	0		0	0	1	8

Al Casey
| 1923 | STL | N | 2 | 0 | | 0 | | 0 | 12 |

Bernie Casey
1961	SF	N	1	0		0	0	0	6
1962			6	0		0	0	0	36
1963			7	0		0	0	0	42
1964			4	0		0	0	0	24
1965			8	0		0	0	0	48
1966			1	0		0	0	0	6
1967	LA	N	8	0		0	0	0	48
1968			5	0		0	0	0	30
Career			40	0		0	0	0	240
Playoffs			1	0		0	0	0	6

Tom Casey
| 1948 | NY | AA | 1 | 0 | | 0 | 0 | 0 | 6 |

Keith Cash
1991	PIT	N	1	0		0	0	0	6
1992	KC	N	2	0		0	0	0	12
1993			4	0		0	0	0	24
1994			2	0	0	0	0	0	12
1995			1	0	0	0	0	0	6
Career			10	0	0	0	0	0	60
Playoffs			1	0	0	0	0	0	6

Kerry Cash
1992	IND	N	3	0		0	0	0	18
1993			3	0		0	0	0	18
1994			1	0	0	0	0	0	6
1995	OAK	N	2	0	0	0	0	0	12
Career			9	0	0	0	0	0	54

Ken Casner
| 1952 | LA | N | 1 | 0 | | 0 | 0 | 0 | 6 |

Jim Cason
1948	SF	AA	3	0		0	0	0	18
1949			1	0		0	0	0	6
1950	SF	N	4	0		0	0	0	24
1951			1	0		0	0	0	6
1955	LA	N	1	0		0	0	0	6
Career			10	0		0	0	0	60

Cy Casper
| 1935 | PIT | N | 3 | 0 | | 0 | | 0 | 18 |

Dave Casper
1974	OAK	N	3	0		0	0	0	18
1975			1	0		0	0	0	6
1976			10	0		0	0	0	60
1977			6	0		0	0	0	36

Dave Casper continued
1978			10	0		0	0	0	60
1979			3	0		0	0	0	18
1980	OAK-HOU	N	4	0		0	0	0	24
1981	HOU	N	8	0		0	0	0	48
1982			6	0		0	0	0	36
1984	LARI	N	2	0		0	0	0	12
Career			53	0		0	0	0	318
Playoffs			7	0		0	0	0	42

Howard Cassady
1957	DET	N	6	0		0	0	0	36
1958			7	0		0	0	0	42
1959			5	0		0	0	0	30
1960			2	0		0	0	0	12
1961			2	0		0	0	0	12
1962	PHI	N	2	0		0	0	0	12
Career			24	0		0	0	0	144
Playoffs			1	0		0	0	0	6

Dick Cassiano
| 1940 | BKN | N | 2 | 0 | | 0 | 0 | 1 | 14 |

Mike Casteel
| 1922 | RI | N | 1 | 0 | | 0 | | 0 | 6 |

Rich Caster
1970	NYJ	N	3	0		0	0	0	18
1971			6	0		0	0	0	36
1972			10	0		0	0	0	60
1973			4	0		0	0	0	24
1974			7	0		0	0	0	42
1975			4	0		0	0	0	24
1976			1	0		0	0	0	6
1977			1	0		0	0	0	6
1978	HOU	N	5	0		0	0	0	30
1979			1	0		0	0	0	6
1980			3	0		0	0	0	18
Career			45	0		0	0	0	270

Jim Castiglia
1941	PHI	N	4	0		0	0	0	24
1946			1	0		0	0	0	6
1947	BAL-WAS	AA-N	6	0		0	0	0	36
1948	WAS	N	2	0		0	0	0	12
Career			13	0		0	0	0	78

Jeremiah Castille
| 1983 | TB | N | 1 | 0 | | 0 | 0 | 0 | 6 |

Sam Cathcart
| 1949 | SF | AA | 1 | 0 | | 0 | 0 | 0 | 6 |

Knute Cauldwell
| 1925 | AKR | N | 0 | 4 | | 0 | | 0 | 4 |

Matt Cavanaugh
| 1981 | NE | N | 3 | 0 | | 0 | 0 | 0 | 18 |

John Cavosie
1932	POR	N	3	0		0		0	18
1933			1	1		1		0	10
Career			4	1		1		0	28

Les Caywood
| 1930 | NYG | N | 1 | 0 | | 0 | | 0 | 6 |

Chuck Cecil
| 1995 | HOU | N | 1 | 0 | 0 | 0 | 0 | 0 | 6 |

Jimmy Cefalo
1978	MIA	N	3	0		0	0	0	18
1979			3	0		0	0	0	18
1980			1	0		0	0	0	6
1981			3	0		0	0	0	18
1982			1	0		0	0	0	6
1984			2	0		0	0	0	12
Career			13	0		0	0	0	78
Playoffs			2	0		0	0	0	12

Bob Celeri
1951	NYY	N	1	0		0	0	0	6
1952	DAL	N	1	0		0	0	0	6
Career			2	0		0	0	0	12

Larry Centers

Year	Team		TD	1XP	2XP	FG	FGA	SAF	Pts
1992	PHX	N	2	0		0	0	0	12
1993			3	0		0	0	0	18
1994	ARI	N	7	0	0	0	0	0	42
1995			4	0	0	0	0	0	24
1996			9	0	0	0	0	0	54
Career			25	0	0	0	0	0	150

Jeff Chadwick

Year	Team		TD	1XP	2XP	FG	FGA	SAF	Pts
1983	DET	N	4	0		0	0	0	24
1984			3	0		0	0	0	18
1985			3	0		0	0	0	18
1986			5	0		0	0	0	30
1988			3	0		0	0	0	18
1990	SEA	N	4	0		0	0	0	24
1991			3	0		0	0	0	18
1992	LARM	N	3	0		0	0	0	18
Career			28	0		0	0	0	168

Pat Chaffey

Year	Team		TD	1XP	2XP	FG	FGA	SAF	Pts
1991	ATL	N	1	0		0	0	0	6
1992	NYJ	N	1	0		0	0	0	6
1993			1	0		0	0	0	6
Career			3	0		0	0	0	18

Dan Chamberlain

Year	Team		TD	1XP	2XP	FG	FGA	SAF	Pts
1960	BUF	A	4	0	0	0	0	0	24

Guy Chamberlin

Year	Team		TD	1XP	2XP	FG	FGA	SAF	Pts
1921	DEC	A	3	0		0		0	18
1922	CAN	N	**7**	0		0		0	42
1923			2	0		0		0	12
1924	CLE	N	2	0		0		0	12
1925	FRA	N	2	0		0		1	14
1926			1	0		0		0	6
Career			17	0		0		1	104

Rusty Chambers

Year	Team		TD	1XP	2XP	FG	FGA	SAF	Pts
1975	NO	N	1	0		0	0	0	6

Ed Champagne

Year	Team		TD	1XP	2XP	FG	FGA	SAF	Pts
1950	LA	N	1	0		0	0	0	6

Jim Champion

Year	Team		TD	1XP	2XP	FG	FGA	SAF	Pts
1950	NYY	N	0	0		0	0	1	2

Al Chandler

Year	Team		TD	1XP	2XP	FG	FGA	SAF	Pts
1976	NE	N	3	0		0	0	0	18
1978	STL	N	4	0		0	0	0	24
1979			2	0		0	0	0	12
Career			9	0		0	0	0	54

Bob Chandler

Year	Team		TD	1XP	2XP	FG	FGA	SAF	Pts
1972	BUF	N	5	0		0	0	0	30
1973			3	1		0	0	0	19
1974			1	0		0	0	0	6
1975			6	0		0	0	0	36
1976			10	0		0	0	0	60
1977			4	0		0	0	0	24
1978			5	0		0	0	0	30
1980	OAK	N	10	0		0	0	0	60
1981			4	0		0	0	0	24
Career			48	1		0	0	0	289

Chris Chandler

Year	Team		TD	1XP	2XP	FG	FGA	SAF	Pts
1988	IND	N	3	0		0	0	0	18
1989			1	0		0	0	0	6
1990	TB	N	1	0		0	0	0	6
1992	PHX	N	1	0		0	0	0	6
1994	LARM	N	1	0	0	0	0	0	6
1995	HOU	N	2	0	1	0	0	0	14
Career			9	0	1	0	0	0	56

Don Chandler

Year	Team		TD	1XP	2XP	FG	FGA	SAF	Pts
1956	NYG	N	0	3		0	0	0	3
1959			0	2		0	1	0	2
1962			0	47		19	28	0	104
1963			0	**52**		18	29	0	**106**
1964			0	27		9	20	0	54
1965	GB	N	0	37		17	26	0	88
1966			0	41		12	28	0	77
1967			0	39		19	29	0	96
Career			0	248		94	161	0	530
Playoffs			0	24		10	15	0	54

Edgar Chandler

Year	Team		TD	1XP	2XP	FG	FGA	SAF	Pts
1970	BUF	N	1	0		0	0	0	6
1971			0	0		0	0	1	2
Career			1	0		0	0	1	8

Thornton Chandler

Year	Team		TD	1XP	2XP	FG	FGA	SAF	Pts
1986	DAL	N	2	0		0	0	0	12
1987			1	0		0	0	0	6
1988			1	0		0	0	0	6
Career			4	0		0	0	0	24

Wes Chandler

Year	Team		TD	1XP	2XP	FG	FGA	SAF	Pts
1978	NO	N	2	0		0	0	0	12
1979			6	0		0	0	0	36
1980			6	0		0	0	0	36
1981	NO-SD	N	6	0		0	0	0	36
1982	SD	N	9	0		0	0	0	54
1983			5	0		0	0	0	30
1984			6	0		0	0	0	36
1985			10	0		0	0	0	60
1986			4	0		0	0	0	24
1987			2	0		0	0	0	12
Career			56	0		0	0	0	336
Playoffs			1	0		0	0	0	6

Lynn Chandnois

Year	Team		TD	1XP	2XP	FG	FGA	SAF	Pts
1951	PIT	N	7	0		0	0	0	42
1952			5	0		0	0	0	30
1953			4	0		0	0	0	24
1954			1	0		0	0	0	6
1955			5	0		0	0	0	30
1956			5	0		0	0	0	30
Career			27	0		0	0	0	162

Clarence Chapman

Year	Team		TD	1XP	2XP	FG	FGA	SAF	Pts
1977	NO	N	1	0		0	0	0	6

Chappelle

Year	Team		TD	1XP	2XP	FG	FGA	SAF	Pts
1920	CHIC	A	1	0		0		0	6

Jack Chapple

Year	Team		TD	1XP	2XP	FG	FGA	SAF	Pts
1965	SF	N	1	0		0	0	0	6

Bob Chappuis

Year	Team		TD	1XP	2XP	FG	FGA	SAF	Pts
1948	BKN	AA	1	0		0	0	0	6

John Charles

Year	Team		TD	1XP	2XP	FG	FGA	SAF	Pts
1967	BOS	A	1	0	0	0	0	0	6
1969			1	0	0	0	0	0	6
Career			2	0	0	0	0	0	12

Mike Charles

Year	Team		TD	1XP	2XP	FG	FGA	SAF	Pts
1983	MIA	N	0	0		0	0	1	2

Carl Charon

Year	Team		TD	1XP	2XP	FG	FGA	SAF	Pts
1962	BUF	A	2	0	0	0	0	0	12
1963			1	0	0	0	0	0	6
Career			3	0	0	0	0	0	18

Cliff Chatman

Year	Team		TD	1XP	2XP	FG	FGA	SAF	Pts
1982	NYG	N	2	0		0	0	0	12

Barney Chavous

Year	Team		TD	1XP	2XP	FG	FGA	SAF	Pts
1982	DEN	N	0	0		0	0	1	2
1983			1	0		0	0	0	6
Career			1	0		0	0	1	8

Lloyd Cheatham

Year	Team		TD	1XP	2XP	FG	FGA	SAF	Pts
1942	CHIC	N	1	0		0	0	0	6
1946	NY	AA	1	0		0	0	0	6
1947			2	0		0	0	0	12
Career			4	0		0	0	0	24

Deron Cherry

Year	Team		TD	1XP	2XP	FG	FGA	SAF	Pts
1985	KC	N	1	0		0	0	0	6
1986			2	0		0	0	0	12
Career			3	0		0	0	0	18

Tony Cherry

Year	Team		TD	1XP	2XP	FG	FGA	SAF	Pts
1987	SF	N	1	0		0	0	0	6

Wes Chesson

Year	Team		TD	1XP	2XP	FG	FGA	SAF	Pts
1972	ATL	N	1	0		0	0	0	6

Wes Chesson *continued*

Year	Team		TD	1XP	2XP	FG	FGA	SAF	Pts
1973			1	0		0	0	0	6
Career			2	0		0	0	0	12

Raymond Chester

Year	Team		TD	1XP	2XP	FG	FGA	SAF	Pts
1970	OAK	N	7	0		0	0	0	42
1971			7	0		0	0	0	42
1972			8	0		0	0	0	48
1973	BAL	N	1	0		0	0	0	6
1974			1	0		0	0	0	6
1975			3	0		0	0	0	18
1976			3	0		0	0	0	18
1977			3	0		0	0	0	18
1978	OAK	N	2	0		0	0	0	12
1979			8	0		0	0	0	48
1980			4	0		0	0	0	24
1981			1	0		0	0	0	6
Career			48	0		0	0	0	288
Playoffs			1	0		0	0	0	6

George Cheverko

Year	Team		TD	1XP	2XP	FG	FGA	SAF	Pts
1947	NYG	N	3	0		0	0	0	18

Fred Chicken

Year	Team		TD	1XP	2XP	FG	FGA	SAF	Pts
1920	RI	A	3	0		0		0	18

Freddie Childress

Year	Team		TD	1XP	2XP	FG	FGA	SAF	Pts
1991	NE	N	1	0		0	0	0	6

Joe Childress

Year	Team		TD	1XP	2XP	FG	FGA	SAF	Pts
1956	CHIC	N	1	0		0	0	0	6
1957			1	0		0	0	0	6
1958			4	0		0	0	0	24
1959			1	0		0	0	0	6
1960	STL	N	2	0		0	0	0	12
1962			1	0		0	0	0	6
1963			4	0		0	0	0	24
1964			2	0		0	0	0	12
Career			16	0		0	0	0	96

Ray Childress

Year	Team		TD	1XP	2XP	FG	FGA	SAF	Pts
1990	HOU	N	0	0		0	0	1	2
1992			1	0		0	0	0	6
1993			1	0		0	0	0	6
Career			2	0		0	0	1	14

Clarence Childs

Year	Team		TD	1XP	2XP	FG	FGA	SAF	Pts
1964	NYG	N	1	0		0	0	0	6
1966			1	0		0	0	0	6
Career			2	0		0	0	0	12

Henry Childs

Year	Team		TD	1XP	2XP	FG	FGA	SAF	Pts
1976	NO	N	4	0		0	0	0	24
1977			9	0		0	0	0	54
1978			4	0		0	0	0	24
1979			5	0		0	0	0	30
1980			6	0		0	0	0	36
1981	LA	N	1	0		0	0	0	6
Career			29	0		0	0	0	174

Jimmy Childs

Year	Team		TD	1XP	2XP	FG	FGA	SAF	Pts
1978	STL	N	1	0		0	0	0	6

Bill Chipley

Year	Team		TD	1XP	2XP	FG	FGA	SAF	Pts
1947	BOS	N	1	0		0	0	0	6
1948			2	0		0	0	0	12
1949	NYB	N	2	0		0	0	0	12
Career			5	0		0	0	0	30

John Chirico

Year	Team		TD	1XP	2XP	FG	FGA	SAF	Pts
1987	NYJ	N	1	0		0	0	0	6

Mark Chmura

Year	Team		TD	1XP	2XP	FG	FGA	SAF	Pts
1995	GB	N	7	0	1	0	0	0	44
Playoffs			2	0	1	0	0	0	14

Max Choboian

Year	Team		TD	1XP	2XP	FG	FGA	SAF	Pts
1966	DEN	A	2	0	0	0	0	0	12

Wayne Chrebet

Year	Team		TD	1XP	2XP	FG	FGA	SAF	Pts
1995	NYJ	N	4	0	0	0	0	0	24
1996			3	0	0	0	0	0	18
Career			7	0	0	0	0	0	42

Frank Christensen

Year	Team		TD	1XP	2XP	FG	FGA	SAF	Pts
1934	**DET**	**N**	2	0		0		0	12
1935			1	2		0		0	8
1936			1	0		0		0	6
Career			4	2		0		0	26

George Christensen

Year	Team		TD	1XP	2XP	FG	FGA	SAF	Pts
1931	**POR**	**N**	0	0		0		1	2

Todd Christensen

Year	Team		TD	1XP	2XP	FG	FGA	SAF	Pts
1980	**OAK**	**N**	1	0		0	0	0	6
1981			2	0		0	0	1	14
1982	**LARI**	**N**	4	0		0	0	0	24
1983			12	0		0	0	0	72
1984			7	0		0	0	0	42
1985			6	0		0	0	0	36
1986			8	0		0	0	0	48
1987			2	0		0	0	0	12
Career			42	0		0	0	1	254
Playoffs			1	0		0	0	0	6

Bob Christian

Year	Team		TD	1XP	2XP	FG	FGA	SAF	Pts
1995	**CAR**	**N**	1	0	1	0	0	0	8

Jack Christiansen

Year	Team		TD	1XP	2XP	FG	FGA	SAF	Pts
1951	**DET**	**N**	4	0		0	0	0	24
1952			4	0		0	0	0	24
1953			1	0		0	0	0	6
1954			2	0		0	0	0	12
1956			1	0		0	0	0	6
1957			1	0		0	0	0	6
Career			13	0		0	0	0	78

Marty Christiansen

Year	Team		TD	1XP	2XP	FG	FGA	SAF	Pts
1940	**CHIC**	**N**	1	0		0	0	0	6

Oscar Christianson

Year	Team		TD	1XP	2XP	FG	FGA	SAF	Pts
1921	**MIN**	**A**	1	0		0		0	6

Steve Christie

Year	Team		TD	1XP	2XP	FG	FGA	SAF	Pts
1990	**TB**	**N**	0	27		23	27	0	96
1991			0	22		15	20	0	67
1992	**BUF**	**N**	0	43		24	30	0	115
1993			0	36		23	32	0	105
1994			0	38	0	24	28	0	110
1995			0	33	0	31	40	0	126
1996			0	33	0	24	29	0	105
Career			0	232	0	164	206	0	724
Playoffs			0	28	0	20	23	0	88

Floyd Christman

Year	Team		TD	1XP	2XP	FG	FGA	SAF	Pts
1925	**BUF**	**N**	1	0		0		0	6

Paul Christman

Year	Team		TD	1XP	2XP	FG	FGA	SAF	Pts
1945	**CHIC**	**N**	1	0		0	0	0	6
1946			3	0		0	0	0	18
1947			2	0		0	0	0	12
1948			1	0		0	0	0	6
1950	**GB**	**N**	1	0		0	0	0	6
Career			8	0		0	0	0	48

Jim Christopherson

Year	Team		TD	1XP	2XP	FG	FGA	SAF	Pts
1962	**MIN**	**N**	0	28		11	20	0	61

Ryan Christopherson

Year	Team		TD	1XP	2XP	FG	FGA	SAF	Pts
1995	**JAC**	**N**	1	0	0	0	0	0	6

Dick Christy

Year	Team		TD	1XP	2XP	FG	FGA	SAF	Pts
1960	**BOS**	**A**	6	0	0	0	0	0	36
1961	**NY**	**A**	5	0	0	0	0	0	30
1962			8	0	0	0	0	0	48
1963			1	0	0	0	0	0	6
Career			20	0	0	0	0	0	120

Bob Cifers

Year	Team		TD	1XP	2XP	FG	FGA	SAF	Pts
1946	**DET**	**N**	4	0		0	0	0	24
1948	**PIT**	**N**	1	0		0	0	0	6
Career			5	0		0	0	0	30

Ed Cifers

Year	Team		TD	1XP	2XP	FG	FGA	SAF	Pts
1941	**WAS**	**N**	1	0		0	0	0	6
1942			3	0		0	0	0	18
1947	**CHIB**	**N**	2	0		0	0	0	12
Career			6	0		0	0	0	36

Larry Cipa

Year	Team		TD	1XP	2XP	FG	FGA	SAF	Pts
1974	**NO**	**N**	1	0		0	0	0	6

Darryl Clack

Year	Team		TD	1XP	2XP	FG	FGA	SAF	Pts
1988	**DAL**	**N**	1	0		0	0	0	6
1989			2	0		0	0	0	12
Career			3	0		0	0	0	18

Rickey Claitt

Year	Team		TD	1XP	2XP	FG	FGA	SAF	Pts
1980	**WAS**	**N**	2	0		0	0	0	12

Jack Clancy

Year	Team		TD	1XP	2XP	FG	FGA	SAF	Pts
1967	**MIA**	**A**	2	0	0	0	0	0	12
1969			1	0	0	0	0	0	6
1970	**GB**	**N**	2	0		0	0	0	12
Career			5	0	0	0	0	0	30

Stu Clancy

Year	Team		TD	1XP	2XP	FG	FGA	SAF	Pts
1931	**SI**	**N**	1	0		0		0	6
1932	**NYG**	**N**	1	0		0		0	6
1933			3	0		0		0	18
1935			1	0		0		0	6
Career			6	0		0		0	36

Algy Clark

Year	Team		TD	1XP	2XP	FG	FGA	SAF	Pts
1931	**CLE**	**N**	2	0		0		0	12
1932	**BOS**	**N**	1	0		0		0	6
1933	**CIN**	**N**	0	3		4		0	15
1934	**C-S**	**N**	0	0		1		0	3
Career			3	3		5		0	36

Allan Clark

Year	Team		TD	1XP	2XP	FG	FGA	SAF	Pts
1979	**NE**	**N**	2	0		0	0	0	12
1980			2	0		0	0	0	12
Career			4	0		0	0	0	24

Beryl Clark

Year	Team		TD	1XP	2XP	FG	FGA	SAF	Pts
1940	**CHIC**	**N**	0	3		0	0	0	3

Boobie Clark

Year	Team		TD	1XP	2XP	FG	FGA	SAF	Pts
1973	**CIN**	**N**	8	0		0	0	0	48
1974			6	0		0	0	0	36
1975			4	0		0	0	0	24
1976			8	0		0	0	0	48
1977			1	0		0	0	0	6
1987	**NO**	**N**	0	0		0	0	1	2
Career			27	0		0	0	1	164
Playoffs			1	0		0	0	0	6

Derrick Clark

Year	Team		TD	1XP	2XP	FG	FGA	SAF	Pts
1994	**DEN**	**N**	3	0	0	0	0	0	18

Dutch Clark

Year	Team		TD	1XP	2XP	FG	FGA	SAF	Pts
1931	**POR**	**N**	9	6		0		0	60
1932			6	**10**		**3**		0	**55**
1934	**DET**	**N**	8	13		4		0	73
1935			6	**16**		1		0	**55**
1936			7	**19**		4		0	**73**
1937			6	6		1		0	45
1938			0	2		2	2	0	8
Career			42	72		15	2	0	369
Playoffs			1	1		0	0	0	7

Dwight Clark

Year	Team		TD	1XP	2XP	FG	FGA	SAF	Pts
1980	**SF**	**N**	8	0		0	0	0	48
1981			4	0		0	0	0	24
1982			5	0		0	0	0	30
1983			8	0		0	0	0	48
1984			6	0		0	0	0	36
1985			10	0		0	0	0	60
1986			2	0		0	0	0	12
1987			5	0		0	0	0	30
Career			48	0		0	0	0	288
Playoffs			3	0		0	0	0	18

Gary Clark

Year	Team		TD	1XP	2XP	FG	FGA	SAF	Pts
1985	**WAS**	**N**	5	0		0	0	0	30
1986			7	0		0	0	0	42
1987			7	0		0	0	0	42
1988			7	0		0	0	0	42
1989			9	0		0	0	0	54
1990			8	0		0	0	0	48
1991			10	0		0	0	0	60
1992			5	0		0	0	0	30

Gary Clark *continued*

Year	Team		TD	1XP	2XP	FG	FGA	SAF	Pts
1993	**PHX**	**N**	4	0		0	0	0	24
1994	**ARI**	**N**	1	0	0	0	0	0	6
1995	**MIA**	**N**	2	0	0	0	0	0	12
Career			65	0	0	0	0	0	390
Playoffs			6	0	0	0	0	0	36

Hal Clark

Year	Team		TD	1XP	2XP	FG	FGA	SAF	Pts
1923	**ROC**	**N**	1	0		0		0	6

Harry Clark

Year	Team		TD	1XP	2XP	FG	FGA	SAF	Pts
1940	**CHIB**	**N**	3	0		0	0	0	18
1941			0	1		0	0	0	1
1942			6	0		0	0	0	36
1943			10	0		0	0	0	60
1946	**LA**	**AA**	2	0		0	0	0	12
1947			2	0		0	0	0	12
Career			23	1		0	0	0	139
Playoffs			4	0		0	0	0	24

Jessie Clark

Year	Team		TD	1XP	2XP	FG	FGA	SAF	Pts
1983	**GB**	**N**	1	0		0	0	0	6
1984			6	0		0	0	0	36
1985			7	0		0	0	0	42
1987			1	0		0	0	0	6
Career			15	0		0	0	0	90

Jimmy Clark

Year	Team		TD	1XP	2XP	FG	FGA	SAF	Pts
1934	**PIT**	**N**	1	0		0		0	6

Kelvin Clark

Year	Team		TD	1XP	2XP	FG	FGA	SAF	Pts
1983	**NO**	**N**	1	0		0	0	0	6

Kevin Clark

Year	Team		TD	1XP	2XP	FG	FGA	SAF	Pts
1987	**DEN**	**N**	1	0		0	0	0	6

Louis Clark

Year	Team		TD	1XP	2XP	FG	FGA	SAF	Pts
1988	**SEA**	**N**	1	0		0	0	0	6
1989			1	0		0	0	0	6
1991			2	0		0	0	0	12
1992			1	0		0	0	0	6
Career			5	0		0	0	0	30

Mike Clark

Year	Team		TD	1XP	2XP	FG	FGA	SAF	Pts
1963	**PHI**	**N**	0	29		7	15	0	50
1964	**PIT**	**N**	0	28		13	25	0	67
1965			0	19		11	19	0	52
1966			0	34		21	32	0	97
1967			0	35		12	22	0	71
1968	**DAL**	**N**	0	**54**		17	29	0	105
1969			0	43		20	36	0	103
1970			0	35		18	27	0	89
1971			0	**47**		13	25	0	86
1973			0	1		1	2	0	4
Career			0	325		133	232	0	724
Playoffs			0	14		9	14	0	41

Robert Clark

Year	Team		TD	1XP	2XP	FG	FGA	SAF	Pts
1988	**NO**	**N**	2	0		0	0	0	12
1989	**DET**	**N**	2	0		0	0	0	12
1990			8	0		0	0	0	48
1991			6	0		0	0	0	36
Career			18	0		0	0	0	108

Vinnie Clark

Year	Team		TD	1XP	2XP	FG	FGA	SAF	Pts
1993	**ATL**	**N**	1	0		0	0	0	6

Wayne Clark

Year	Team		TD	1XP	2XP	FG	FGA	SAF	Pts
1974	**CIN**	**N**	1	0		0	0	0	6

Willie Clark

Year	Team		TD	1XP	2XP	FG	FGA	SAF	Pts
1996	**SD**	**N**	1	0	0	0	0	0	6

Frank Clarke

Year	Team		TD	1XP	2XP	FG	FGA	SAF	Pts
1960	**DAL**	**N**	3	0		0	0	0	18
1961			9	0		0	0	0	54
1962			14	0		0	0	0	84
1963			10	0		0	0	0	60
1964			5	0		0	0	0	30
1965			4	0		0	0	0	24
1966			4	0		0	0	0	24
1967			2	0		0	0	0	12
Career			51	0		0	0	0	306
Playoffs			1	0		0	0	0	6

Hagood Clarke

Year	Team		TD	1XP	2XP	FG	FGA	SAF	Pts
1964	**BUF**	**A**	1	0	0	0	0	0	6
1966			1	0	0	0	0	0	6
1968			1	0	0	0	0	0	6
Career			3	0	0	0	0	0	18

Ken Clarke

Year	Team		TD	1XP	2XP	FG	FGA	SAF	Pts
1981	**PHI**	**N**	0	0		0	0	1	2

Leon Clarke

Year	Team		TD	1XP	2XP	FG	FGA	SAF	Pts
1956	**LA**	**N**	4	0		0	0	0	24
1957			4	0		0	0	0	24
1958			5	0		0	0	0	30
1960	**CLE**	**N**	4	0		0	0	0	24
1961			2	0		0	0	0	12
Career			19	0		0	0	0	114

Stu Clarkson

Year	Team		TD	1XP	2XP	FG	FGA	SAF	Pts
1946	**CHIB**	**N**	1	0		0	0	0	6

Bobby Clatterbuck

Year	Team		TD	1XP	2XP	FG	FGA	SAF	Pts
1954	**NYG**	**N**	1	0		0	0	0	6

Boyd Clay

Year	Team		TD	1XP	2XP	FG	FGA	SAF	Pts
1940	**CLE**	**N**	0	0		0	1	0	0
1941			0	1		1	2	0	4
1942			0	4		0	0	0	4
Career			0	5		1	3	0	8

Randy Clay

Year	Team		TD	1XP	2XP	FG	FGA	SAF	Pts
1950	**NYG**	**N**	2	0		1	1	0	15
1953			1	20		2	7	0	32
Career			3	20		3	8	0	47
Playoffs			0	0		1	1	0	3

Walt Clay

Year	Team		TD	1XP	2XP	FG	FGA	SAF	Pts
1946	**CHI**	**AA**	1	0		0	0	0	6
1948	**LA**	**AA**	4	0		0	0	0	24
Career			5	0		0	0	0	30

Willie Clay

Year	Team		TD	1XP	2XP	FG	FGA	SAF	Pts
1993	**DET**	**N**	2	0		0	0	0	12
1994			1	0	0	0	0	0	6
Career			3	0	0	0	0	0	18

Raymond Clayborn

Year	Team		TD	1XP	2XP	FG	FGA	SAF	Pts
1977	**NE**	**N**	3	0		0	0	1	20
1985			1	0		0	0	0	6
1987			1	0		0	0	0	6
Career			5	0		0	0	1	32

Harvey Clayton

Year	Team		TD	1XP	2XP	FG	FGA	SAF	Pts
1983	**PIT**	**N**	1	0		0	0	0	6

Mark Clayton

Year	Team		TD	1XP	2XP	FG	FGA	SAF	Pts
1983	**MIA**	**N**	2	0		0	0	0	12
1984			**18**	0		0	0	0	108
1985			4	0		0	0	0	24
1986			10	0		0	0	0	60
1987			7	0		0	0	0	42
1988			14	0		0	0	0	84
1989			9	0		0	0	0	54
1990			3	0		0	0	0	18
1991			12	0		0	0	0	72
1992			3	0		0	0	0	18
1993	**GB**	**N**	3	0		0	0	0	18
Career			85	0		0	0	0	510
Playoffs			3	0		0	0	0	18

Cal Clemens

Year	Team		TD	1XP	2XP	FG	FGA	SAF	Pts
1936	**GB**	**N**	0	1		0		0	1

Johnny Clement

Year	Team		TD	1XP	2XP	FG	FGA	SAF	Pts
1941	**CHIC**	**N**	1	0		0	0	0	6
1946	**PIT**	**N**	1	0		0	0	0	6
1947			4	0		0	0	0	24
1948			2	0		0	0	0	12
1949	**CHI**	**AA**	5	0		0	0	0	30
Career			13	0		0	0	0	78

Vin Clements

Year	Team		TD	1XP	2XP	FG	FGA	SAF	Pts
1973	**NYG**	**N**	2	0		0	0	0	12

Craig Clemons

Year	Team		TD	1XP	2XP	FG	FGA	SAF	Pts
1975	**CHI**	**N**	1	0		0	0	0	6

Topper Clemons

Year	Team		TD	1XP	2XP	FG	FGA	SAF	Pts
1987	**PHI**	**N**	1	0		0	0	0	6

Mike Clendenen

Year	Team		TD	1XP	2XP	FG	FGA	SAF	Pts
1987	**DEN**	**N**	0	7		3	4	0	16

Einar Cleve

Year	Team		TD	1XP	2XP	FG	FGA	SAF	Pts
1922	**MIN**	**N**	1	0		0		0	6
1923			1	0		0		0	6
Career			2	0		0		0	12

Doug Cline

Year	Team		TD	1XP	2XP	FG	FGA	SAF	Pts
1960	**HOU**	**A**	2	0	0	0	0	0	12
1961			2	0	0	0	0	0	12
1966			1	0	0	0	0	0	6
Career			5	0	0	0	0	0	30

Ollie Cline

Year	Team		TD	1XP	2XP	FG	FGA	SAF	Pts
1949	**BUF**	**AA**	3	0		0	0	0	18
1950	**DET**	**N**	2	0		0	0	0	12
1952			1	0		0	0	0	6
1953			1	0		0	0	0	6
Career			7	0		0	0	0	42

Tony Cline

Year	Team		TD	1XP	2XP	FG	FGA	SAF	Pts
1996	**BUF**	**N**	1	0	0	0	0	0	6
Playoffs			1	0	0	0	0	0	6

Dextor Clinkscale

Year	Team		TD	1XP	2XP	FG	FGA	SAF	Pts
1983	**DAL**	**N**	1	0		0	0	0	6

Joey Clinkscales

Year	Team		TD	1XP	2XP	FG	FGA	SAF	Pts
1987	**PIT**	**N**	1	0		0	0	0	6

Jack Cloud

Year	Team		TD	1XP	2XP	FG	FGA	SAF	Pts
1950	**GB**	**N**	3	0		0	0	0	18
1951			2	0		0	0	0	12
1953	**WAS**	**N**	1	0		0	0	0	6
Career			6	0		0	0	0	36

Rich Coady

Year	Team		TD	1XP	2XP	FG	FGA	SAF	Pts
1970	**CHI**	**N**	1	0		0	0	0	6

Bert Coan

Year	Team		TD	1XP	2XP	FG	FGA	SAF	Pts
1964	**KC**	**A**	2	0	0	0	0	0	12
1965			3	0	0	0	0	0	18
1966			9	0	0	0	0	0	54
1967			4	0	0	0	0	0	24
1968			1	0	0	0	0	0	6
Career			19	0	0	0	0	0	114

Ben Coates

Year	Team		TD	1XP	2XP	FG	FGA	SAF	Pts
1991	**NE**	**N**	1	0		0	0	0	6
1992			3	0		0	0	0	18
1993			8	0		0	0	0	48
1994			7	0	0	0	0	0	42
1995			6	0	0	0	0	0	36
1996			9	0	1	0	0	0	56
Career			34	0	1	0	0	0	206
Playoffs			1	0	0	0	0	0	6

Ray Coates

Year	Team		TD	1XP	2XP	FG	FGA	SAF	Pts
1948	**NYG**	**N**	3	0		0	0	0	18
1949			1	0		0	0	0	6
Career			4	0		0	0	0	24

Marvin Cobb

Year	Team		TD	1XP	2XP	FG	FGA	SAF	Pts
1975	**CIN**	**N**	1	0		0	0	0	6

Reggie Cobb

Year	Team		TD	1XP	2XP	FG	FGA	SAF	Pts
1990	**TB**	**N**	2	0		0	0	0	12
1991			7	0		0	0	0	42
1992			9	0		0	0	0	54
1993			4	0		0	0	0	24
1994	**GB**	**N**	4	0	0	0	0	0	24
1996	**NYJ**	**N**	1	0	0	0	0	0	6
Career			27	0	0	0	0	0	162

Red Cochran

Year	Team		TD	1XP	2XP	FG	FGA	SAF	Pts
1947	**CHIC**	**N**	2	0		0	0	0	12
1949			4	0		0	0	0	24
Career			6	0		0	0	0	36

Tom Cochran

Year	Team		TD	1XP	2XP	FG	FGA	SAF	Pts
1949	**WAS**	**N**	1	0		0	0	0	6

Don Cockroft

Year	Team		TD	1XP	2XP	FG	FGA	SAF	Pts
1968	**CLE**	**N**	0	46		18	24	0	100
1969			0	**45**		12	23	0	81
1970			0	34		12	22	0	70
1971			0	34		15	28	0	79
1972			0	28		22	27	0	94
1973			0	24		22	31	0	90
1974			0	29		14	16	0	71
1975			0	21		17	23	0	72
1976			0	27		15	28	0	72
1977			0	30		17	23	0	81
1978			0	37		19	28	0	94
1979			0	38		17	29	0	89
1980			0	39		16	26	0	87
Career			0	432		216	328	0	1080
Playoffs			0	12		5	11	0	27

Sherman Cocroft

Year	Team		TD	1XP	2XP	FG	FGA	SAF	Pts
1989	**TB**	**N**	0	0		0	0	1	2

Ed Cody

Year	Team		TD	1XP	2XP	FG	FGA	SAF	Pts
1947	**GB**	**N**	2	0		0	0	0	12
1948			0	11		0	0	0	11
1949	**CHIB**	**N**	1	0		0	0	0	6
Career			3	11		0	0	0	29

Mike Cofer

Year	Team		TD	1XP	2XP	FG	FGA	SAF	Pts
1987	**NO**	**N**	0	5		1	1	0	8
1988	**SF**	**N**	0	40		27	**38**	0	121
1989			0	49		29	36	0	**136**
1990			0	39		24	36	0	111
1991			0	49		14	28	0	91
1992			0	**53**		18	27	0	107
1993			0	**59**		16	26	0	107
1995	**IND**	**N**	0	9	0	4	9	0	21
Career			0	303	0	133	201	0	702
Playoffs			0	42	0	12	19	0	78

Pat Coffee

Year	Team		TD	1XP	2XP	FG	FGA	SAF	Pts
1937	**CHIC**	**N**	1	0		0		0	6
1938			2	0		0		0	12
Career			3	0		0		0	18

Junior Coffey

Year	Team		TD	1XP	2XP	FG	FGA	SAF	Pts
1966	**ATL**	**N**	5	0		0	0	0	30
1967			5	0		0	0	0	30
1969	**ATL-NY**	**N**	5	0		0	0	0	30
Career			15	0		0	0	0	90

Paul Coffman

Year	Team		TD	1XP	2XP	FG	FGA	SAF	Pts
1979	**GB**	**N**	4	0		0	0	0	24
1980			3	0		0	0	0	18
1981			4	0		0	0	0	24
1982			2	0		0	0	0	12
1983			11	0		0	0	0	66
1984			9	0		0	0	0	54
1985			6	0		0	0	0	36
1986	**KC**	**N**	2	0		0	0	0	12
1987			1	0		0	0	0	6
Career			42	0		0	0	0	252

Gail Cogdill

Year	Team		TD	1XP	2XP	FG	FGA	SAF	Pts
1960	**DET**	**N**	1	0		0	0	0	6
1961			6	0		0	0	0	36
1962			8	0		0	0	0	48
1963			10	0		0	0	0	60
1964			3	0		0	0	0	18
1966			1	0		0	0	0	6
1967			1	0		0	0	0	6
1969	**ATL**	**N**	5	0		0	0	0	30
1970			1	0		0	0	0	6
Career			36	0		0	0	0	216

Art Coglizer

Year	Team		TD	1XP	2XP	FG	FGA	SAF	Pts
1926	**NY**	**A**	0	9		1		0	12

Angelo Coia

Year	Team		TD	1XP	2XP	FG	FGA	SAF	Pts
1960	**CHI**	**N**	4	0		0	0	0	24
1961			3	0		0	0	0	18
1962			4	0		0	0	0	24
1963			1	0		0	0	0	6
1964	**WAS**	**N**	5	0		0	0	0	30
1965			3	0		0	0	0	18
Career			20	0		0	0	0	120

Rondy Colbert

Year	Team		TD	1XP	2XP	FG	FGA	SAF	Pts
1975	NYG	N	1	0		0	0	0	6

Jim Colclough

Year	Team		TD	1XP	2XP	FG	FGA	SAF	Pts
1960	BOS	A	9	0	0	0	0	0	54
1961			9	0	0	0	0	0	54
1962			10	0	0	0	0	0	60
1963			3	0	0	0	0	0	18
1964			5	0	2	0	0	0	34
1965			3	0	0	0	0	0	18
Career			39	0	2	0	0	0	238

Eddie Cole

Year	Team		TD	1XP	2XP	FG	FGA	SAF	Pts
1980	DET	N	0	0		0	0	1	2

Emerson Cole

Year	Team		TD	1XP	2XP	FG	FGA	SAF	Pts
1951	CLE	N	1	0		0	0	0	6

John Cole

Year	Team		TD	1XP	2XP	FG	FGA	SAF	Pts
1940	PHI	N	0	3		1	1	0	6

Larry Cole

Year	Team		TD	1XP	2XP	FG	FGA	SAF	Pts
1968	DAL	N	2	0		0	0	0	12
1969			1	0		0	0	0	6
1980			1	0		0	0	0	6
Career			4	0		0	0	0	24

Terry Cole

Year	Team		TD	1XP	2XP	FG	FGA	SAF	Pts
1968	BAL	N	3	0		0	0	0	18
1969			3	0		0	0	0	18
Career			6	0		0	0	0	36

Tom Colella

Year	Team		TD	1XP	2XP	FG	FGA	SAF	Pts
1944	CLE	N	3	0		1	1	0	21
1945			4	0		0	0	0	24
1946	CLE	AA	3	0		0	0	0	18
1947			4	0		0	0	0	24
1948			1	0		0	0	0	6
Career			15	0		1	1	0	93

Al Coleman

Year	Team		TD	1XP	2XP	FG	FGA	SAF	Pts
1972	PHI	N	0	0		0	0	1	2

Andre Coleman

Year	Team		TD	1XP	2XP	FG	FGA	SAF	Pts
1994	SD	N	2	0	0	0	0	0	12
1995			3	0	0	0	0	0	18
1996			2	0	0	0	0	0	12
Career			7	0	0	0	0	0	42
Playoffs			1	0	0	0	0	0	6

Lincoln Coleman

Year	Team		TD	1XP	2XP	FG	FGA	SAF	Pts
1993	DAL	N	2	0		0	0	0	12
1994			1	0	0	0	0	0	6
Career			3	0	0	0	0	0	18

Monte Coleman

Year	Team		TD	1XP	2XP	FG	FGA	SAF	Pts
1981	WAS	N	1	0		0	0	0	6
1984			1	0		0	0	0	6
1989			1	0		0	0	0	6
1993			1	0		0	0	0	6
Career			4	0		0	0	0	24

Pat Coleman

Year	Team		TD	1XP	2XP	FG	FGA	SAF	Pts
1991	HOU	N	1	0		0	0	0	6
1994			1	0	0	0	0	0	6
Career			2	0	0	0	0	0	12

Ronnie Coleman

Year	Team		TD	1XP	2XP	FG	FGA	SAF	Pts
1974	HOU	N	1	0		0	0	0	6
1975			5	0		0	0	0	30
1976			6	0		0	0	0	36
1977			6	0		0	0	0	36
1978			2	0		0	0	0	12
1979			1	0		0	0	0	6
1980			1	0		0	0	0	6
1981			1	0		0	0	0	6
Career			23	0		0	0	0	138

Jimmy Collier

Year	Team		TD	1XP	2XP	FG	FGA	SAF	Pts
Playoffs			1	0	0	0	0	0	6

Mike Collier

Year	Team		TD	1XP	2XP	FG	FGA	SAF	Pts
1975	PIT	N	4	0		0	0	0	24
1979	BUF	N	2	0		0	0	0	12
Career			6	0		0	0	0	36

Tim Collier

Year	Team		TD	1XP	2XP	FG	FGA	SAF	Pts
1977	KC	N	1	0		0	0	0	6
1983	SF	N	1	0		0	0	0	6
Career			2	0		0	0	0	12

Andre Collins

Year	Team		TD	1XP	2XP	FG	FGA	SAF	Pts
1991	WAS	N	1	0		0	0	0	6
1994			2	0	0	0	0	0	12
Career			3	0	0	0	0	0	18

Dwight Collins

Year	Team		TD	1XP	2XP	FG	FGA	SAF	Pts
1984	MIN	N	1	0		0	0	0	6

Gary Collins

Year	Team		TD	1XP	2XP	FG	FGA	SAF	Pts
1962	CLE	N	2	0		0	0	0	12
1963			13	0		0	0	0	78
1964			8	0		0	0	0	48
1965			10	0		0	0	0	60
1966			12	0		0	0	0	72
1967			7	0		0	0	0	42
1969			11	0		0	0	0	66
1970			4	0		0	0	0	24
1971			3	0		0	0	0	18
Career			70	0		0	0	0	420
Playoffs			5	0		0	0	0	30

Kerry Collins

Year	Team		TD	1XP	2XP	FG	FGA	SAF	Pts
1995	CAR	N	3	0	0	0	0	0	18
1996			0	0	1	0	0	0	2
Career			3	0	1	0	0	0	20

Larry Collins

Year	Team		TD	1XP	2XP	FG	FGA	SAF	Pts
1978	CLE	N	1	0		0	0	0	6

Mark Collins

Year	Team		TD	1XP	2XP	FG	FGA	SAF	Pts
1988	NYG	N	0	0		0	0	1	2
1993			1	0		0	0	0	6
1994	KC	N	1	0	0	0	0	0	6
1995			1	0	0	0	0	0	6
Career			3	0	0	0	0	1	20

Shawn Collins

Year	Team		TD	1XP	2XP	FG	FGA	SAF	Pts
1989	ATL	N	3	0		0	0	0	18
1990			2	0		0	0	0	12
Career			5	0		0	0	0	30

Tony Collins

Year	Team		TD	1XP	2XP	FG	FGA	SAF	Pts
1981	NE	N	7	0		0	0	0	42
1982			3	0		0	0	0	18
1983			10	0		0	0	0	60
1984			5	0		0	0	0	30
1985			5	0		0	0	0	30
1986			8	0		0	0	0	48
1987			6	0		0	0	0	36
Career			44	0		0	0	0	264
Playoffs			1	0		0	0	0	6

Cris Collinsworth

Year	Team		TD	1XP	2XP	FG	FGA	SAF	Pts
1981	CIN	N	8	0		0	0	0	48
1982			1	0		0	0	0	6
1983			5	0		0	0	0	30
1984			6	0		0	0	0	36
1985			5	0		0	0	0	30
1986			10	0		0	0	0	60
1988			1	0		0	0	0	6
Career			36	0		0	0	0	216
Playoffs			1	0		0	0	0	6

Mickey Colmer

Year	Team		TD	1XP	2XP	FG	FGA	SAF	Pts
1946	BKN	AA	1	0		0	0	0	6
1947			10	0		0	0	0	60
1948			10	0		0	0	0	60
Career			21	0		0	0	0	126

Lloyd Colteryahn

Year	Team		TD	1XP	2XP	FG	FGA	SAF	Pts
1955	BAL	N	3	0		0	0	0	18

Jim Colvin

Year	Team		TD	1XP	2XP	FG	FGA	SAF	Pts
1963	BAL	N	0	0		0	0	1	2

Neal Colzie

Year	Team		TD	1XP	2XP	FG	FGA	SAF	Pts
1978	OAK	N	1	0		0	0	0	6
1981	TB	N	1	0		0	0	0	6
Career			2	0		0	0	0	12

Bill Combs

Year	Team		TD	1XP	2XP	FG	FGA	SAF	Pts
1942	PHI	N	1	0		0	0	0	6

Chris Combs

Year	Team		TD	1XP	2XP	FG	FGA	SAF	Pts
1980	STL	N	1	0		0	0	0	6

Marty Comer

Year	Team		TD	1XP	2XP	FG	FGA	SAF	Pts
1946	BUF	AA	1	0		0	0	0	6
1947			1	0		0	0	0	6
1948			1	0		0	0	0	6
Career			3	0		0	0	0	18

Irv Comp

Year	Team		TD	1XP	2XP	FG	FGA	SAF	Pts
1943	GB	N	4	0		0	0	0	24
1944			3	0		0	0	0	18
1945			2	0		0	0	0	12
1946			1	0		0	0	0	6
Career			10	0		0	0	0	60

Tony Compagno

Year	Team		TD	1XP	2XP	FG	FGA	SAF	Pts
1946	PIT	N	1	0		0	0	0	6
1947			5	0		0	0	0	30
1948			1	0		0	0	0	6
Career			7	0		0	0	0	42

Dick Compton

Year	Team		TD	1XP	2XP	FG	FGA	SAF	Pts
1965	HOU	A	2	0	0	0	0	0	12
1967	PIT	N	1	0		0	0	0	6
1968			1	0		0	0	0	6
Career			4	0	0	0	0	0	24

Jack Concannon

Year	Team		TD	1XP	2XP	FG	FGA	SAF	Pts
1964	PHI	N	1	0		0	0	0	6
1966			2	0		0	0	0	12
1967	CHI	N	3	0		0	0	0	18
1968			2	0		0	0	0	12
1969			1	0		0	0	0	6
1970			2	0		0	0	0	12
1974	GB	N	1	0		0	0	0	6
Career			12	0		0	0	0	72

Merl Condit

Year	Team		TD	1XP	2XP	FG	FGA	SAF	Pts
1940	PIT	N	1	0		0	0	0	6
1941	BKN	N	4	11		2	11	0	41
1942			3	10		3	6	0	37
1943			2	0		0	3	0	12
1945	WAS	N	3	1		0	0	0	19
1946	PIT	N	1	4		0	2	0	10
Career			14	26		5	22	0	125

Fred Cone

Year	Team		TD	1XP	2XP	FG	FGA	SAF	Pts
1951	GB	N	1	29		5	7	0	44
1952			3	32		1	1	0	53
1953			6	23		5	16	0	74
1954			0	27		9	16	0	54
1955			0	30		**16**	**24**	0	78
1956			4	33		5	8	0	72
1957			2	26		12	17	0	74
1960	DAL	N	0	21		6	13	0	39
Career			16	221		59	102	0	488

Charlie Conerly

Year	Team		TD	1XP	2XP	FG	FGA	SAF	Pts
1948	NYG	N	5	0		0	0	0	30
1950			1	0		0	0	0	6
1951			1	0		0	0	0	6
1952			0	2		0	0	0	2
1954			1	1		0	0	0	7
1955			0	1		0	0	0	1
1957			1	0		0	0	0	6
1959			1	0		0	0	0	6
Career			10	4		0	0	0	64
Playoffs			1	0		0	0	0	6

Larry Conjar

Year	Team		TD	1XP	2XP	FG	FGA	SAF	Pts
1968	PHI	N	0	0		0	0	1	2

Bill Conkright

Year	Team		TD	1XP	2XP	FG	FGA	SAF	Pts
1938	CHIB	N	1	0		0	0	0	6

George Conn

Year	Team		TD	1XP	2XP	FG	FGA	SAF	Pts
1920	CLE	A	1	0		0		0	6

Clyde Conner

Year	Team		TD	1XP	2XP	FG	FGA	SAF	Pts
1956	SF	N	1	0		0	0	0	6
1957			4	0		0	0	0	24

Clyde Conner *continued*

Year	Team		TD	1XP	2XP	FG	FGA	SAF	Pts
1958			5	0		0	0	0	30
1959			1	0		0	0	0	6
1960			2	0		0	0	0	12
1961			1	0		0	0	0	6
1962			4	0		0	0	0	24
Career			18	0		0	0	0	108

Dan Conners

Year	Team		TD	1XP	2XP	FG	FGA	SAF	Pts
1966	OAK	A	1	0	0	0	0	0	6
1967			2	0	0	0	0	0	12
1969			2	0	0	0	0	0	12
Career			5	0	0	0	0	0	30

Dutch Connor

Year	Team		TD	1XP	2XP	FG	FGA	SAF	Pts
1925	PRO	N	0	2		0		0	2

George Connor

Year	Team		TD	1XP	2XP	FG	FGA	SAF	Pts
1955	CHIB	N	1	0		0	0	0	6

Larry Conover

Year	Team		TD	1XP	2XP	FG	FGA	SAF	Pts
1923	CAN	N	0	1		0		0	1

Scott Conover

Year	Team		TD	1XP	2XP	FG	FGA	SAF	Pts
1994	DET	N	1	0	0	0	0	0	6

Bobby Joe Conrad

Year	Team		TD	1XP	2XP	FG	FGA	SAF	Pts
1958	CHIC	N	0	33		6	17	0	51
1959			6	30		6	9	0	84
1960	STL	N	0	28		2	5	0	34
1961			3	4		0	1	0	22
1962			4	0		0	1	0	24
1963			10	0		0	0	0	60
1964			6	0		0	0	0	36
1965			5	0		0	0	0	30
1966			2	0		0	0	0	12
1967			2	0		0	0	0	12
1968			4	0		0	0	0	24
Career			42	95		14	33	0	389

Curtis Conway

Year	Team		TD	1XP	2XP	FG	FGA	SAF	Pts
1993	CHI	N	2	0		0	0	0	12
1994			2	0	1	0	0	0	14
1995			12	0	0	0	0	0	72
1996			7	0	0	0	0	0	42
Career			23	0	1	0	0	0	140

Dave Conway

Year	Team		TD	1XP	2XP	FG	FGA	SAF	Pts
1971	GB	N	0	5		0	1	0	5

Jimmy Conzelman

Year	Team		TD	1XP	2XP	FG	FGA	SAF	Pts
1920	DEC	A	1	0		1		0	9
1921	RI	A	2	0		1		0	15
1922	RI-MIL	N	8	0		2		0	54
1923	MIL	N	3	2		0		0	20
1924			1	0		0		0	6
1925	DET	N	3	0		0		0	18
1926			2	1		0		0	13
1927	PRO	N	4	0		0		0	24
1928			2	1		0		0	13
1929			1	0		0		0	6
Career			27	4		4		0	178

Anthony Cook

Year	Team		TD	1XP	2XP	FG	FGA	SAF	Pts
1995	HOU	N	0	0	0	0	0	1	2

Dave Cook

Year	Team		TD	1XP	2XP	FG	FGA	SAF	Pts
1934	CHIC	N	0	1		1		0	4
1935			1	0		0		0	6
Career			1	1		1		0	10

Fred Cook

Year	Team		TD	1XP	2XP	FG	FGA	SAF	Pts
1975	BAL	N	1	0		0	0	0	6

Greg Cook

Year	Team		TD	1XP	2XP	FG	FGA	SAF	Pts
1969	CIN	A	1	0	0	0	0	0	6

Marv Cook

Year	Team		TD	1XP	2XP	FG	FGA	SAF	Pts
1990	NE	N	5	0		0	0	0	30
1991			3	0		0	0	0	18
1992			2	0		0	0	0	12
1993			1	0		0	0	0	6
1994	CHI	N	1	0	0	0	0	0	6
1995	STL	N	1	0	0	0	0	0	6
Career			13	0	0	0	0	0	78

Ted Cook

Year	Team		TD	1XP	2XP	FG	FGA	SAF	Pts
1947	DET	N	1	0		0	0	0	6
1949	GB	N	1	0		0	0	0	6
1950			3	0		0	0	0	18
Career			5	0		0	0	0	30

Toi Cook

Year	Team		TD	1XP	2XP	FG	FGA	SAF	Pts
1989	NO	N	1	0		0	0	0	6
1992			1	0		0	0	0	6
Career			2	0		0	0	0	12

Ed Cooke

Year	Team		TD	1XP	2XP	FG	FGA	SAF	Pts
1962	NY	A	1	0	0	0	0	0	6
1964	DEN	A	1	0	0	0	0	0	6
Career			2	0	0	0	0	0	12

Johnie Cooks

Year	Team		TD	1XP	2XP	FG	FGA	SAF	Pts
1983	BAL	N	1	0		0	0	0	6

Bob Coolbaugh

Year	Team		TD	1XP	2XP	FG	FGA	SAF	Pts
1961	OAK	A	4	0	1	0	0	0	26

Adrian Cooper

Year	Team		TD	1XP	2XP	FG	FGA	SAF	Pts
1991	PIT	N	2	0		0	0	0	12
1992			3	0		0	0	0	18
Career			5	0		0	0	0	30
Playoffs			1	0		0	0	0	6

Bill Cooper

Year	Team		TD	1XP	2XP	FG	FGA	SAF	Pts
1961	SF	N	1	0		0	0	0	6

Earl Cooper

Year	Team		TD	1XP	2XP	FG	FGA	SAF	Pts
1980	SF	N	9	0		0	0	0	54
1981			1	0		0	0	0	6
1982			1	0		0	0	0	6
1983			3	0		0	0	0	18
1984			4	0		0	0	0	24
Career			18	0		0	0	0	108
Playoffs			1	0		0	0	0	6

Joe Cooper

Year	Team		TD	1XP	2XP	FG	FGA	SAF	Pts
1984	HOU	N	0	13		11	13	0	46
1986	NYG	N	0	4		2	4	0	10
Career			0	17		13	17	0	56

Thurlow Cooper

Year	Team		TD	1XP	2XP	FG	FGA	SAF	Pts
1960	NY	A	3	0	1	0	0	0	20
1961			4	0	0	0	1	0	24
1962			1	0	1	0	0	0	8
Career			8	0	2	0	1	0	52

Frank Cope

Year	Team		TD	1XP	2XP	FG	FGA	SAF	Pts
1941	NYG	N	1	0		0	0	0	6

Danny Copeland

Year	Team		TD	1XP	2XP	FG	FGA	SAF	Pts
1992	WAS	N	1	0		0	0	0	6

Horace Copeland

Year	Team		TD	1XP	2XP	FG	FGA	SAF	Pts
1993	TB	N	4	0		0	0	0	24
1994			0	0	1	0	0	0	2
1995			2	0	0	0	0	0	12
Career			6	0	1	0	0	0	38

Russell Copeland

Year	Team		TD	1XP	2XP	FG	FGA	SAF	Pts
1993	BUF	N	1	0		0	0	0	6
1994			1	0	0	0	0	0	6
1995			1	0	0	0	0	0	6
Career			3	0	0	0	0	0	18

Charlie Copley

Year	Team		TD	1XP	2XP	FG	FGA	SAF	Pts
1920	AKR	A	0	**12**		1		0	15
1921			0	10		0		0	10
1922	AKR-MIL	N	0	1		0		0	1
Career			0	23		1		0	26

Al Coppage

Year	Team		TD	1XP	2XP	FG	FGA	SAF	Pts
1940	CHIC	N	1	0		0	0	0	6
1947	BUF	AA	2	0		0	0	0	12
Career			3	0		0	0	0	18

George Corbett

Year	Team		TD	1XP	2XP	FG	FGA	SAF	Pts
1932	CHIB	N	1	1		0		0	7
1935			0	0		1		0	3
1936			1	0		0		0	6

George Corbett *continued*

Year	Team		TD	1XP	2XP	FG	FGA	SAF	Pts
1938			1	0		0	0	0	6
Career			3	1		1	0	0	22

Jim Corbett

Year	Team		TD	1XP	2XP	FG	FGA	SAF	Pts
1977	CIN	N	1	0		0	0	0	6

Art Corcoran

Year	Team		TD	1XP	2XP	FG	FGA	SAF	Pts
1921	CLE	A	1	0		0		0	6
1922	AKR	N	0	0		0		0	0
Career			1	0		0		0	6

Ollie Cordill

Year	Team		TD	1XP	2XP	FG	FGA	SAF	Pts
1940	CLE	N	2	0		0	0	0	12

Chuck Corgan

Year	Team		TD	1XP	2XP	FG	FGA	SAF	Pts
1924	KC	N	4	2		0		0	26
1925			1	0		0		0	6
Career			5	2		0		0	32

John Corker

Year	Team		TD	1XP	2XP	FG	FGA	SAF	Pts
1980	HOU	N	1	0		0	0	0	6

Bo Cornell

Year	Team		TD	1XP	2XP	FG	FGA	SAF	Pts
1977	BUF	N	1	0		0	0	0	6

Fred Cornwell

Year	Team		TD	1XP	2XP	FG	FGA	SAF	Pts
1984	DAL	N	1	0		0	0	0	6
1985			1	0		0	0	0	6
Career			2	0		0	0	0	12

Frank Corral

Year	Team		TD	1XP	2XP	FG	FGA	SAF	Pts
1978	LA	N	0	31		**29**	**43**	0	**118**
1979			0	36		13	25	0	75
1980			0	51		16	30	0	99
1981			0	36		17	26	0	87
Career			0	154		75	124	0	379
Playoffs			0	9		7	11	0	30

Quentin Coryatt

Year	Team		TD	1XP	2XP	FG	FGA	SAF	Pts
1994	IND	N	1	0	0	0	0	0	6

Red Corzine

Year	Team		TD	1XP	2XP	FG	FGA	SAF	Pts
1933	CIN	N	1	0		0		0	6
1934	C-S	N	1	0		0		0	6
1935	NYG	N	1	0		0		0	6
1936			1	0		0		0	6
1937			1	0		0		0	6
Career			5	0		0		0	30

Doug Cosbie

Year	Team		TD	1XP	2XP	FG	FGA	SAF	Pts
1980	DAL	N	1	0		0	0	0	6
1981			5	0		0	0	0	30
1982			4	0		0	0	0	24
1983			6	0		0	0	0	36
1984			4	0		0	0	0	24
1985			6	0		0	0	0	36
1986			1	0		0	0	0	6
1987			3	0		0	0	0	18
Career			30	0		0	0	0	180
Playoffs			3	0		0	0	0	18

Bruce Coslet

Year	Team		TD	1XP	2XP	FG	FGA	SAF	Pts
1969	CIN	A	1	0	0	0	0	0	6
1970	CIN	N	1	0		0	0	0	6
1971			4	0		0	0	0	24
1972			1	0		0	0	0	6
1976			2	0		0	0	0	12
Career			9	0	0	0	0	0	54

Dave Costa

Year	Team		TD	1XP	2XP	FG	FGA	SAF	Pts
1972	SD	N	0	0		0	0	1	2

Paul Costa

Year	Team		TD	1XP	2XP	FG	FGA	SAF	Pts
1966	BUF	A	3	0	0	0	0	0	18
1967			2	0	0	0	0	0	12
1968			2	0	0	0	0	0	12
Career			7	0	0	0	0	0	42

Vince Costello

Year	Team		TD	1XP	2XP	FG	FGA	SAF	Pts
1961	CLE	N	1	0		0	0	0	6
1962			1	0		0	0	0	6
Career			2	0		0	0	0	12

Jeff Cothran

Year	Team	Lg	TD	1XP	2XP	FG	FGA	SAF	Pts
1994	CIN	N	1	0	0	0	0	0	6
1996			1	0	0	0	0	0	6
Career			2	0	0	0	0	0	12

Paige Cothren

Year	Team	Lg	TD	1XP	2XP	FG	FGA	SAF	Pts
1957	LA	N	0	**38**		11	19	0	71
1958			0	42		**14**	25	0	84
1959	PHI	N	0	1		8	18	0	25
Career			0	81		33	62	0	180

Craig Cotton

Year	Team	Lg	TD	1XP	2XP	FG	FGA	SAF	Pts
1972	DET	N	1	0		0	0	0	6

Tex Coulter

Year	Team	Lg	TD	1XP	2XP	FG	FGA	SAF	Pts
1947	NYG	N	1	0		0	0	0	6

Johnny Counts

Year	Team	Lg	TD	1XP	2XP	FG	FGA	SAF	Pts
1962	NYG	N	1	0		0	0	0	6

Gerry Courtney

Year	Team	Lg	TD	1XP	2XP	FG	FGA	SAF	Pts
1942	BKN	N	1	0		0	0	0	6

Larry Coutre

Year	Team	Lg	TD	1XP	2XP	FG	FGA	SAF	Pts
1950	GB	N	3	0		0	0	0	18

Bob Cowan

Year	Team	Lg	TD	1XP	2XP	FG	FGA	SAF	Pts
1947	CLE	AA	3	0		0	0	0	18
1948			5	0		0	0	0	30
Career			8	0		0	0	0	48

Gerry Cowhig

Year	Team	Lg	TD	1XP	2XP	FG	FGA	SAF	Pts
1948	LA	N	2	0		0	0	0	12
1949			2	0		0	0	0	12
1951	PHI	N	1	0		0	0	0	6
Career			5	0		0	0	0	30

Aaron Cox

Year	Team	Lg	TD	1XP	2XP	FG	FGA	SAF	Pts
1988	LARM	N	5	0		0	0	0	30
1989			3	0		0	0	0	18
Career			8	0		0	0	0	48

Arthur Cox

Year	Team	Lg	TD	1XP	2XP	FG	FGA	SAF	Pts
1983	ATL	N	1	0		0	0	0	6
1984			3	0		0	0	0	18
1985			2	0		0	0	0	12
1986			1	0		0	0	0	6
1989	SD	N	2	0		0	0	0	12
1990			1	0		0	0	0	6
Career			10	0		0	0	0	60

Bryan Cox

Year	Team	Lg	TD	1XP	2XP	FG	FGA	SAF	Pts
1996	CHI	N	1	0	0	0	0	0	6

Fred Cox

Year	Team	Lg	TD	1XP	2XP	FG	FGA	SAF	Pts
1963	MIN	N	0	39		12	24	0	75
1964			0	40		21	33	0	103
1965			0	44		**23**	**35**	0	113
1966			0	34		18	33	0	88
1967			0	26		17	33	0	77
1968			0	31		19	29	0	88
1969			0	43		**26**	37	0	**121**
1970			0	35		**30**	**46**	0	**125**
1971			0	25		22	32	0	91
1972			0	34		21	33	0	97
1973			0	33		21	35	0	96
1974			0	32		12	20	0	68
1975			0	46		13	17	0	85
1976			0	32		19	31	0	89
1977			0	25		8	17	0	49
Career			0	519		282	455	0	1365
Playoffs			0	37		11	18	0	70

Steve Cox

Year	Team	Lg	TD	1XP	2XP	FG	FGA	SAF	Pts
1981	CLE	N	0	0		0	1	0	0
1982			0	0		0	1	0	0
1983			0	0		1	1	0	3
1984			0	0		1	3	0	3
1985	WAS	N	0	0		0	1	0	0
1986			0	0		3	6	0	9
1987			0	3		1	2	0	6
Career			0	3		6	15	0	21
Playoffs			0	0		0	1	0	0

Claude Crabb

Year	Team	Lg	TD	1XP	2XP	FG	FGA	SAF	Pts
1963	WAS	N	1	0		0	0	0	6

Clyde Crabtree

Year	Team	Lg	TD	1XP	2XP	FG	FGA	SAF	Pts
1930	FRA	N	2	1		0		0	13

Eric Crabtree

Year	Team	Lg	TD	1XP	2XP	FG	FGA	SAF	Pts
1967	DEN	A	5	0	0	0	0	0	30
1968			5	0	0	0	0	0	30
1969	CIN	A	7	0	0	0	0	0	42
1970	CIN	N	2	0		0	0	0	12
1971	CIN-NE	N	3	0		0	0	0	18
Career			22	0	0	0	0	0	132

Donnie Craft

Year	Team	Lg	TD	1XP	2XP	FG	FGA	SAF	Pts
1982	HOU	N	4	0		0	0	0	24

Russ Craft

Year	Team	Lg	TD	1XP	2XP	FG	FGA	SAF	Pts
1947	PHI	N	1	0		0	0	0	6
1948			2	0		0	0	0	12
1949			1	0		0	0	0	6
1950			1	0		0	0	0	6
1952			1	0		0	0	0	6
1954	PIT	N	1	0		0	0	0	6
Career			7	0		0	0	0	42
Playoffs			1	0		0	0	0	6

Dobie Craig

Year	Team	Lg	TD	1XP	2XP	FG	FGA	SAF	Pts
1962	OAK	A	4	0	0	0	0	0	24
1963			2	0	0	0	0	0	12
1964	HOU	A	1	0	0	0	0	0	6
Career			7	0	0	0	0	0	42

Larry Craig

Year	Team	Lg	TD	1XP	2XP	FG	FGA	SAF	Pts
1945	GB	N	1	0		0	0	0	6

Neal Craig

Year	Team	Lg	TD	1XP	2XP	FG	FGA	SAF	Pts
1972	CIN	N	1	0		0	0	0	6
1974	BUF	N	1	0		0	0	0	6
Career			2	0		0	0	0	12
Playoffs			1	0		0	0	0	6

Roger Craig

Year	Team	Lg	TD	1XP	2XP	FG	FGA	SAF	Pts
1983	SF	N	12	0		0	0	0	72
1984			10	0		0	0	0	60
1985			15	0		0	0	0	90
1986			7	0		0	0	0	42
1987			4	0		0	0	0	24
1988			10	0		0	0	0	60
1989			7	0		0	0	0	42
1990			1	0		0	0	0	6
1991	LARI	N	1	0		0	0	0	6
1992	MIN	N	4	0		0	0	0	24
1993			2	0		0	0	0	12
Career			73	0		0	0	0	438
Playoffs			9	0		0	0	0	54

Steve Craig

Year	Team	Lg	TD	1XP	2XP	FG	FGA	SAF	Pts
1974	MIN	N	1	0		0	0	0	6

Carl Cramer

Year	Team	Lg	TD	1XP	2XP	FG	FGA	SAF	Pts
1921	AKR	A	6	1		0		0	37
1922	AKR	N	6	0		0		0	36
1924			1	0		1		0	9
Career			13	1		1		0	82

Paul Crane

Year	Team	Lg	TD	1XP	2XP	FG	FGA	SAF	Pts
1968	NY	A	0	0	0	0	0	1	2
1969			2	0	0	0	0	0	12
Career			2	0	0	0	0	1	14

Jack Crangle

Year	Team	Lg	TD	1XP	2XP	FG	FGA	SAF	Pts
1923	CHIC	N	3	0		0		0	18

Aaron Craver

Year	Team	Lg	TD	1XP	2XP	FG	FGA	SAF	Pts
1991	MIA	N	1	0		0	0	0	6
1994			0	0	1	0	0	0	2
1995	DEN	N	6	0	0	0	0	0	36
1996			3	0	0	0	0	0	18
Career			10	0	1	0	0	0	62
Playoffs			1	0	0	0	0	0	6

Charles Crawford

Year	Team	Lg	TD	1XP	2XP	FG	FGA	SAF	Pts
1986	PHI	N	1	0		0	0	0	6

Jim Crawford

Year	Team	Lg	TD	1XP	2XP	FG	FGA	SAF	Pts
1960	BOS	A	2	0	1	0	1	0	14
1962			4	0	1	0	0	0	26
1963			1	0	0	0	0	0	6
Career			7	0	2	0	1	0	46

Dick Crayne

Year	Team	Lg	TD	1XP	2XP	FG	FGA	SAF	Pts
1936	BKN	N	1	1		0		0	7
1937			0	0		1		0	3
Career			1	1		1		0	10

Milan Creighton

Year	Team	Lg	TD	1XP	2XP	FG	FGA	SAF	Pts
1931	CHIC	N	1	0		0		0	6

Ted Cremer

Year	Team	Lg	TD	1XP	2XP	FG	FGA	SAF	Pts
1947	DET	N	1	0		0	0	0	6

Willis Crenshaw

Year	Team	Lg	TD	1XP	2XP	FG	FGA	SAF	Pts
1964	STL	N	1	0		0	0	0	6
1965			1	0		0	0	0	6
1968			7	0		0	0	0	42
1969			3	0		0	0	0	18
1970	DEN	N	6	0		0	0	0	36
Career			18	0		0	0	0	108

Bobby Crespino

Year	Team	Lg	TD	1XP	2XP	FG	FGA	SAF	Pts
1961	CLE	N	1	0		0	0	0	6
1963			1	0		0	0	0	6
1965	NYG	N	4	0		0	0	0	24
1966			2	0		0	0	0	12
1967			1	0		0	0	0	6
Career			9	0		0	0	0	54

Joe Cribbs

Year	Team	Lg	TD	1XP	2XP	FG	FGA	SAF	Pts
1980	BUF	N	12	0		0	0	0	72
1981			10	0		0	0	0	60
1982			3	0		0	0	0	18
1983			10	0		0	0	0	60
1985			1	0		0	0	0	6
1986	SF	N	5	0		0	0	0	30
1987			2	0		0	0	0	12
Career			43	0		0	0	0	258
Playoffs			3	0		0	0	0	18

Bernie Crimmins

Year	Team	Lg	TD	1XP	2XP	FG	FGA	SAF	Pts
1945	GB	N	1	0		0	0	0	6

Hal Crisler

Year	Team	Lg	TD	1XP	2XP	FG	FGA	SAF	Pts
1946	BOS	N	5	0		0	0	0	30
1947			2	0		0	0	0	12
1948	WAS	N	6	0		0	0	0	36
1949			4	0		0	0	0	24
1950	BAL	N	5	0		0	0	0	30
Career			22	0		0	0	0	132

Ray Criswell

Year	Team	Lg	TD	1XP	2XP	FG	FGA	SAF	Pts
1988	TB	N	0	1		0	0	0	1

Ken Criter

Year	Team	Lg	TD	1XP	2XP	FG	FGA	SAF	Pts
1973	DEN	N	0	0		0	0	1	2

Ray Crittenden

Year	Team	Lg	TD	1XP	2XP	FG	FGA	SAF	Pts
1993	NE	N	1	0		0	0	0	6
1994			3	0	0	0	0	0	18
Career			4	0	0	0	0	0	24

Jack Crittendon

Year	Team	Lg	TD	1XP	2XP	FG	FGA	SAF	Pts
1954	CHIC	N	0	0		0	1	0	0

Bobby Crockett

Year	Team	Lg	TD	1XP	2XP	FG	FGA	SAF	Pts
1966	BUF	A	3	0	0	0	0	0	18

Monte Crockett

Year	Team	Lg	TD	1XP	2XP	FG	FGA	SAF	Pts
1960	BUF	A	1	0	0	0	0	0	6

Ray Crockett

Year	Team	Lg	TD	1XP	2XP	FG	FGA	SAF	Pts
1990	DET	N	1	0		0	0	0	6
1991			1	0		0	0	0	6
1995	DEN	N	1	0	0	0	0	0	6
Career			3	0	0	0	0	0	18

Zack Crockett

Year	Team	Lg	TD	1XP	2XP	FG	FGA	SAF	Pts
1996	IND	N	1	0	0	0	0	0	6
Playoffs			2	0	0	0	0	0	12

Mike Croel

Year	Team		TD	1XP	2XP	FG	FGA	SAF	Pts
1993	**DEN**	**N**	1	0		0	0	0	6

Abe Croft

Year	Team		TD	1XP	2XP	FG	FGA	SAF	Pts
1944	**CHIB**	**N**	2	0		0	0	0	12

Nolan Cromwell

Year	Team		TD	1XP	2XP	FG	FGA	SAF	Pts
1978	**LA**	**N**	2	0		0	0	0	12
1979			1	0		0	0	0	6
1980			1	1		0	0	0	7
1982	**LARM**	**N**	1	0		0	0	0	6
1983			1	0		0	0	0	6
1984			1	0		0	0	0	6
1986			1	0		0	0	0	6
Career			8	1		0	0	0	49

Bill Cronin

Year	Team		TD	1XP	2XP	FG	FGA	SAF	Pts
1926	**BOS**	**A**	1	0		0		0	6
1927	**PRO**	**N**	2	0		0		0	12
Career			3	0		0		0	18

Bill Cronin

Year	Team		TD	1XP	2XP	FG	FGA	SAF	Pts
1966	**MIA**	**A**	1	0	0	0	0	0	6

Jack Cronin

Year	Team		TD	1XP	2XP	FG	FGA	SAF	Pts
1928	**PRO**	**N**	3	0		0		0	18
1929			1	0		0		0	6
Career			4	0		0		0	24

Tommy Cronin

Year	Team		TD	1XP	2XP	FG	FGA	SAF	Pts
1922	**GB**	**N**	1	0		0		0	6

Corey Croom

Year	Team		TD	1XP	2XP	FG	FGA	SAF	Pts
1993	**NE**	**N**	1	0		0	0	0	6

Billy Cross

Year	Team		TD	1XP	2XP	FG	FGA	SAF	Pts
1951	**CHIC**	**N**	6	0		0	0	0	36
1952			4	0		0	0	0	24
1953			2	0		0	0	0	12
Career			12	0		0	0	0	72

Howard Cross

Year	Team		TD	1XP	2XP	FG	FGA	SAF	Pts
1989	**NYG**	**N**	1	0		0	0	0	6
1991			2	0		0	0	0	12
1992			2	0		0	0	0	12
1993			5	0		0	0	0	30
1994			4	0	0	0	0	0	24
1996			1	0	0	0	0	0	6
Career			15	0	0	0	0	0	90
Playoffs			1	0	0	0	0	0	6

Irv Cross

Year	Team		TD	1XP	2XP	FG	FGA	SAF	Pts
1964	**PHI**	**N**	1	0		0	0	0	6
1966	**LA**	**N**	1	0		0	0	0	6
Career			2	0		0	0	0	12

Leon Crosswhite

Year	Team		TD	1XP	2XP	FG	FGA	SAF	Pts
1973	**DET**	**N**	1	0		0	0	0	6
1974			1	0		0	0	0	6
Career			2	0		0	0	0	12

Ray Crouse

Year	Team		TD	1XP	2XP	FG	FGA	SAF	Pts
1984	**GB**	**N**	1	0		0	0	0	6

John David Crow

Year	Team		TD	1XP	2XP	FG	FGA	SAF	Pts
1958	**CHIC**	**N**	6	0		0	0	0	36
1959			7	0		0	0	0	42
1960	**STL**	**N**	9	0		0	0	0	54
1961			4	0		0	0	0	24
1962			17	0		0	0	0	102
1964			8	0		0	0	0	48
1965	**SF**	**N**	9	0		0	0	0	54
1966			4	0		0	0	0	24
1967			5	0		0	0	0	30
1968			5	0		0	0	0	30
Career			74	0		0	0	0	444

Lindon Crow

Year	Team		TD	1XP	2XP	FG	FGA	SAF	Pts
1959	**NYG**	**N**	1	0		0	0	0	6
1960			1	0		0	0	0	6
1962	**LA**	**N**	1	0		0	0	0	6
1963			0	0		0	0	1	2
Career			3	0		0	0	1	20

Wayne Crow

Year	Team		TD	1XP	2XP	FG	FGA	SAF	Pts
1961	**OAK**	**A**	2	0	1	0	0	0	14
1962	**BUF**	**A**	2	0	0	0	0	0	12
Career			4	0	1	0	0	0	26

Paul Crowe

Year	Team		TD	1XP	2XP	FG	FGA	SAF	Pts
1948	**SF**	**AA**	2	0		0	0	0	12
1949	**LA**	**AA**	1	0		0	0	0	6
Career			3	0		0	0	0	18

Jim Crowley

Year	Team		TD	1XP	2XP	FG	FGA	SAF	Pts
1925	**GB**	**N**	1	0		0		0	6

Joe Crowley

Year	Team		TD	1XP	2XP	FG	FGA	SAF	Pts
1944	**BOS**	**N**	3	0		0	0	0	18

Rae Crowther

Year	Team		TD	1XP	2XP	FG	FGA	SAF	Pts
1925	**FRA**	**N**	3	0		0		0	18

Dwayne Crump

Year	Team		TD	1XP	2XP	FG	FGA	SAF	Pts
1975	**STL**	**N**	1	0		0	0	0	6

George Crump

Year	Team		TD	1XP	2XP	FG	FGA	SAF	Pts
1982	**NE**	**N**	0	0		0	0	1	2

Harry Crump

Year	Team		TD	1XP	2XP	FG	FGA	SAF	Pts
1963	**BOS**	**A**	5	0	0	0	0	0	30

Carlester Crumpler

Year	Team		TD	1XP	2XP	FG	FGA	SAF	Pts
1995	**SEA**	**N**	1	0	0	0	0	0	6

Dwayne Crutchfield

Year	Team		TD	1XP	2XP	FG	FGA	SAF	Pts
1982	**NYJ**	**N**	1	0		0	0	0	6
1983			3	0		0	0	0	18
1984	**LARM**	**N**	2	0		0	0	0	12
Career			6	0		0	0	0	36
Playoffs			1	0		0	0	0	6

Larry Csonka

Year	Team		TD	1XP	2XP	FG	FGA	SAF	Pts
1968	**MIA**	**A**	7	0	0	0	0	0	42
1969			3	0	0	0	0	0	18
1970	**MIA**	**N**	6	0		0	0	0	36
1971			8	0		0	0	0	48
1972			6	0		0	0	0	36
1973			5	0		0	0	0	30
1974			9	0		0	0	0	54
1976	**NYG**	**N**	4	0		0	0	0	24
1977			1	0		0	0	0	6
1978			6	0		0	0	0	36
1979	**MIA**	**N**	13	0		0	0	0	78
Career			68	0	0	0	0	0	408
Playoffs			10	0	0	0	0	0	60

Walt Cudzik

Year	Team		TD	1XP	2XP	FG	FGA	SAF	Pts
1960	**BOS**	**A**	0	0	0	0	1	0	0

Ward Cuff

Year	Team		TD	1XP	2XP	FG	FGA	SAF	Pts
1937	**NYG**	**N**	4	0		2		0	30
1938			2	**18**		**5**	9	0	45
1939			2	6		**7**	**16**	0	39
1940			2	9		5	8	0	36
1941			2	19		5	13	0	46
1942			2	18		3	11	0	39
1943			3	26		**3**	9	0	53
1944			2	2		1	4	0	17
1946	**CHIC**	**N**	2	28		5	12	0	55
1947	**GB**	**N**	0	30		**7**	**16**	0	51
Career			21	156		43	98	0	411
Playoffs			1	2		2	5	0	14

Curley Culp

Year	Team		TD	1XP	2XP	FG	FGA	SAF	Pts
1975	**HOU**	**N**	1	0		0	0	0	6

Rodney Culver

Year	Team		TD	1XP	2XP	FG	FGA	SAF	Pts
1992	**IND**	**N**	9	0		0	0	0	54
1993			5	0		0	0	0	30
1995	**SD**	**N**	3	0	0	0	0	0	18
Career			17	0	0	0	0	0	102

Bennie Cunningham

Year	Team		TD	1XP	2XP	FG	FGA	SAF	Pts
1976	**PIT**	**N**	1	0		0	0	0	6
1977			2	0		0	0	0	12
1978			2	0		0	0	0	12
1979			4	0		0	0	0	24

Bennie Cunningham *continued*

Year	Team		TD	1XP	2XP	FG	FGA	SAF	Pts
1980			2	0		0	0	0	12
1981			3	0		0	0	0	18
1982			2	0		0	0	0	12
1983			3	0		0	0	0	18
1984			1	0		0	0	0	6
Career			20	0		0	0	0	120
Playoffs			2	0		0	0	0	12

Cookie Cunningham

Year	Team		TD	1XP	2XP	FG	FGA	SAF	Pts
1926	**CLE**	**A**	2	0		0		0	12

Doug Cunningham

Year	Team		TD	1XP	2XP	FG	FGA	SAF	Pts
1967	**SF**	**N**	2	0		0	0	0	12
1969			3	0		0	0	0	18
1970			3	0		0	0	0	18
1971			1	0		0	0	0	6
1973			1	0		0	0	0	6
Career			10	0		0	0	0	60

Jay Cunningham

Year	Team		TD	1XP	2XP	FG	FGA	SAF	Pts
1967	**BOS**	**A**	1	0	0	0	0	0	6

Jim Cunningham

Year	Team		TD	1XP	2XP	FG	FGA	SAF	Pts
1961	**WAS**	**N**	2	0		0	0	0	12
1962			2	0		0	0	0	12
1963			1	0		0	0	0	6
Career			5	0		0	0	0	30

Randall Cunningham

Year	Team		TD	1XP	2XP	FG	FGA	SAF	Pts
1986	**PHI**	**N**	5	0		0	0	0	30
1987			3	0		0	0	0	18
1988			6	0		0	0	0	36
1989			4	0		0	0	0	24
1990			5	0		0	0	0	30
1992			5	0		0	0	0	30
1993			1	0		0	0	0	6
1994			3	0	0	0	0	0	18
Career			32	0	0	0	0	0	192
Playoffs			1	0	0	0	0	0	6

Rick Cunningham

Year	Team		TD	1XP	2XP	FG	FGA	SAF	Pts
1996	**OAK**	**N**	1	0	0	0	0	0	6

Sam Cunningham

Year	Team		TD	1XP	2XP	FG	FGA	SAF	Pts
1973	**NE**	**N**	5	0		0	0	0	30
1974			11	0		0	0	0	66
1975			8	0		0	0	0	48
1976			3	0		0	0	0	18
1977			5	0		0	0	0	30
1978			8	0		0	0	0	48
1979			5	0		0	0	0	30
1981			4	0		0	0	0	24
Career			49	0		0	0	0	294

Gary Cuozzo

Year	Team		TD	1XP	2XP	FG	FGA	SAF	Pts
1967	**NO**	**N**	1	0		0	0	0	6

Pat Curran

Year	Team		TD	1XP	2XP	FG	FGA	SAF	Pts
1970	**LA**	**N**	1	0		0	0	0	6
1971			1	0		0	0	0	6
1973			1	0		0	0	0	6
1975	**SD**	**N**	0	1		0	0	0	1
1976			1	0		0	0	0	6
1978			2	0		0	0	0	12
Career			6	1		0	0	0	37

Dan Currie

Year	Team		TD	1XP	2XP	FG	FGA	SAF	Pts
1961	**GB**	**N**	1	0		0	0	0	6

Bill Currier

Year	Team		TD	1XP	2XP	FG	FGA	SAF	Pts
1983	**NYG**	**N**	1	0		0	0	0	6

Don Currivan

Year	Team		TD	1XP	2XP	FG	FGA	SAF	Pts
1943	**CHIC**	**N**	2	0		0	0	0	12
1944	**C-P**	**N**	2	0		0	0	0	12
1945	**BOS**	**N**	4	0		0	0	0	24
1946			4	0		0	0	0	24
1947			10	0		0	0	0	60
1948	**LA**	**N**	4	0		0	0	0	24
1949			1	0		0	0	0	6
Career			27	0		0	0	0	162

Buddy Curry

Year	Team		TD	1XP	2XP	FG	FGA	SAF	Pts
1980	ATL	N	1	0		0	0	0	6
1981			1	0		0	0	0	6
Career			2	0		0	0	0	12

Roy Curry

Year	Team		TD	1XP	2XP	FG	FGA	SAF	Pts
1963	PIT	N	1	0		0	0	0	6

Don Curtin

Year	Team		TD	1XP	2XP	FG	FGA	SAF	Pts
1926	MIL	N	0	1		2		0	7

Isaac Curtis

Year	Team		TD	1XP	2XP	FG	FGA	SAF	Pts
1973	CIN	N	9	0		0	0	0	54
1974			10	0		0	0	0	60
1975			7	0		0	0	0	42
1976			6	0		0	0	0	36
1977			2	0		0	0	0	12
1978			3	0		0	0	0	18
1979			8	0		0	0	0	48
1980			3	0		0	0	0	18
1981			2	0		0	0	0	12
1982			1	0		0	0	0	6
1983			2	0		0	0	0	12
Career			53	0		0	0	0	318
Playoffs			2	0		0	0	0	12

Mike Curtis

Year	Team		TD	1XP	2XP	FG	FGA	SAF	Pts
1966	BAL	N	1	0		0	0	0	6
1968			1	0		0	0	0	6
1972			1	0		0	0	0	6
Career			3	0		0	0	0	18
Playoffs			1	0		0	0	0	6

Harry Curzon

Year	Team		TD	1XP	2XP	FG	FGA	SAF	Pts
1925	HAM-BUF	N	1	0		0		0	6

Bill Daddio

Year	Team		TD	1XP	2XP	FG	FGA	SAF	Pts
1941	CHIC	N	0	8		4	8	0	20
1942			1	8		**5**	10	0	29
1946	BUF	AA	0	3		0	0	0	3
Career			1	19		9	18	0	52

Carroll Dale

Year	Team		TD	1XP	2XP	FG	FGA	SAF	Pts
1960	LA	N	3	0		0	0	0	18
1961			2	0		0	0	0	12
1962			3	0		0	0	0	18
1963			7	0		0	0	0	42
1964			2	0		0	0	0	12
1965	GB	N	2	0		0	0	0	12
1966			7	0		0	0	0	42
1967			5	0		0	0	0	30
1968			8	0		0	0	0	48
1969			6	0		0	0	0	36
1970			2	0		0	0	0	12
1971			4	0		0	0	0	24
1972			1	0		0	0	0	6
Career			52	0		0	0	0	312
Playoffs			3	0		0	0	0	18

Jeff Dale

Year	Team		TD	1XP	2XP	FG	FGA	SAF	Pts
1985	SD	N	1	0		0	0	0	6

Bill Daley

Year	Team		TD	1XP	2XP	FG	FGA	SAF	Pts
1947	CHI	AA	4	0		0	0	0	24
1948	NY	AA	1	0		0	0	0	6
Career			5	0		0	0	0	30

Brad Daluiso

Year	Team		TD	1XP	2XP	FG	FGA	SAF	Pts
1991	ATL	N	0	2		2	3	0	8
1992	DEN	N	0	0		0	1	0	0
1993	NYG	N	0	0		1	3	0	3
1994			0	5	0	11	11	0	38
1995			0	28	0	20	28	0	88
1996			0	22	0	24	27	0	94
Career			0	57	0	58	73	0	231

Boley Dancewicz

Year	Team		TD	1XP	2XP	FG	FGA	SAF	Pts
1947	BOS	N	1	0		0	0	0	6
1948			1	0		0	0	0	6
Career			2	0		0	0	0	12

Joe Danelo

Year	Team		TD	1XP	2XP	FG	FGA	SAF	Pts
1975	GB	N	0	20		11	16	0	53
1976	NYG	N	0	20		8	21	0	44

Joe Danelo *continued*

Year	Team		TD	1XP	2XP	FG	FGA	SAF	Pts
1977			0	19		14	23	0	61
1978			0	27		21	29	0	90
1979			0	28		9	20	0	55
1980			0	27		16	24	0	75
1981			0	31		24	**38**	0	103
1982			0	18		12	21	0	54
1983	BUF	N	0	33		10	20	0	63
1984			0	17		8	16	0	41
Career			0	240		133	228	0	639
Playoffs			0	6		1	3	0	9

George Daney

Year	Team		TD	1XP	2XP	FG	FGA	SAF	Pts
1969	KC	A	1	0	0	0	0	0	6

Eugene Daniel

Year	Team		TD	1XP	2XP	FG	FGA	SAF	Pts
1986	IND	N	1	0		0	0	0	6
1988			1	0		0	0	0	6
1995			1	0	0	0	0	0	6
1996			1	0	0	0	0	0	6
Career			4	0	0	0	0	0	24
Playoffs			1	0	0	0	0	0	6

Willie Daniel

Year	Team		TD	1XP	2XP	FG	FGA	SAF	Pts
1962	PIT	N	1	0		0	0	0	6
1965			1	0		0	0	0	6
Career			2	0		0	0	0	12

Clem Daniels

Year	Team		TD	1XP	2XP	FG	FGA	SAF	Pts
1961	OAK	A	2	0	0	0	0	0	12
1962			8	0	0	0	0	0	48
1963			8	0	0	0	0	0	48
1964			8	0	0	0	0	0	48
1965			12	0	0	0	0	0	72
1966			10	0	0	0	0	0	60
1967			6	0	0	0	0	0	36
Career			54	0	0	0	0	0	324

Gary Danielson

Year	Team		TD	1XP	2XP	FG	FGA	SAF	Pts
1980	DET	N	2	0		0	0	0	12
1981			2	0		0	0	0	12
1984			4	0		0	0	0	24
Career			8	0		0	0	0	48

Rick Danmeier

Year	Team		TD	1XP	2XP	FG	FGA	SAF	Pts
1978	MIN	N	0	36		12	19	0	72
1979			0	28		13	22	0	67
1980			0	33		16	26	0	81
1981			0	34		21	25	0	97
1982			0	23		8	14	0	47
Career			0	154		70	106	0	364
Playoffs			0	7		4	5	0	19

Ed Danowski

Year	Team		TD	1XP	2XP	FG	FGA	SAF	Pts
1935	NYG	N	2	0		0		0	12
1937			1	0		0		0	6
1938			1	0		0		0	6
Career			4	0		0		0	24
Playoffs			1	0		0	0	0	6

Paul Darby

Year	Team		TD	1XP	2XP	FG	FGA	SAF	Pts
1980	NYJ	N	1	0		0	0	0	6

Thom Darden

Year	Team		TD	1XP	2XP	FG	FGA	SAF	Pts
1974	CLE	N	1	0		0	0	0	6
1977			1	0		0	0	0	6
1979			1	0		0	0	0	6
Career			3	0		0	0	0	18

Bernie Darling

Year	Team		TD	1XP	2XP	FG	FGA	SAF	Pts
1929	GB	N	0	0		0		1	2

Dick Daugherty

Year	Team		TD	1XP	2XP	FG	FGA	SAF	Pts
1957	LA	N	1	0		0	0	1	8
1958			1	0		0	0	0	6
Career			2	0		0	0	1	14

Red Daum

Year	Team		TD	1XP	2XP	FG	FGA	SAF	Pts
1922	AKR	N	2	0		0		0	12
1925			1	0		0		0	6
Career			3	0		0		0	18

Charles Davenport

Year	Team		TD	1XP	2XP	FG	FGA	SAF	Pts
1992	PIT	N	1	0		0	0	0	6

Ron Davenport

Year	Team		TD	1XP	2XP	FG	FGA	SAF	Pts
1985	MIA	N	13	0		0	0	0	78
1986			1	0		0	0	0	6
1987			2	0		0	0	0	12
1989			1	0		0	0	0	6
Career			17	0		0	0	0	102
Playoffs			2	0		0	0	0	12

Stan David

Year	Team		TD	1XP	2XP	FG	FGA	SAF	Pts
1984	BUF	N	1	0		0	0	0	6

Bill Davidson

Year	Team		TD	1XP	2XP	FG	FGA	SAF	Pts
1937	PIT	N	4	0		0		0	24

Cotton Davidson

Year	Team		TD	1XP	2XP	FG	FGA	SAF	Pts
1960	DAL	A	1	8	0	1	1	0	17
1961			1	20	0	0	2	0	26
1962	OAK	A	3	4	0	1	2	0	25
1963			4	0	0	0	0	0	24
1964			2	0	0	0	0	0	12
Career			11	32	0	2	5	0	104

Kenny Davidson

Year	Team		TD	1XP	2XP	FG	FGA	SAF	Pts
1993	PIT	N	1	0		0	0	0	6

Al Davis

Year	Team		TD	1XP	2XP	FG	FGA	SAF	Pts
1971	PHI	N	1	0		0	0	0	6

Anthony Davis

Year	Team		TD	1XP	2XP	FG	FGA	SAF	Pts
1977	TB	N	1	0		0	0	0	6

Ben Davis

Year	Team		TD	1XP	2XP	FG	FGA	SAF	Pts
1967	CLE	N	1	0		0	0	0	6
1975	DET	N	1	0		0	0	0	6
Career			2	0		0	0	0	12

Bill Davis

Year	Team		TD	1XP	2XP	FG	FGA	SAF	Pts
1941	CHIC	N	1	0		0	0	0	6

Bob Davis

Year	Team		TD	1XP	2XP	FG	FGA	SAF	Pts
1938	CLE	N	0	0		0	0	0	0
1942	PHI	N	3	0		0	0	0	18
1944	BOS	N	1	0		0	0	0	6
1946			1	0		0	0	0	6
Career			5	0		0	0	0	30

Bob Davis

Year	Team		TD	1XP	2XP	FG	FGA	SAF	Pts
1946	PIT	N	1	0		0	0	0	6

Bob Davis

Year	Team		TD	1XP	2XP	FG	FGA	SAF	Pts
1968	HOU	A	1	0	0	0	0	0	6
1971	NYJ	N	1	0		0	0	0	6
Career			2	0	0	0	0	0	12

Brian Davis

Year	Team		TD	1XP	2XP	FG	FGA	SAF	Pts
1991	SEA	N	1	0		0	0	0	6

Bruce Davis

Year	Team		TD	1XP	2XP	FG	FGA	SAF	Pts
1984	CLE	N	2	0		0	0	0	12

Charlie Davis

Year	Team		TD	1XP	2XP	FG	FGA	SAF	Pts
1976	TB	N	1	0		0	0	0	6

Charlie Davis

Year	Team		TD	1XP	2XP	FG	FGA	SAF	Pts
1977	STL	N	1	0		0	0	0	6

Clarence Davis

Year	Team		TD	1XP	2XP	FG	FGA	SAF	Pts
1971	OAK	N	2	0		0	0	0	12
1972			6	0		0	0	0	36
1973			4	0		0	0	0	24
1974			3	0		0	0	0	18
1975			5	0		0	0	0	30
1976			3	0		0	0	0	18
1977			5	0		0	0	0	30
Career			28	0		0	0	0	168
Playoffs			3	0		0	0	0	18

Corby Davis

Year	Team		TD	1XP	2XP	FG	FGA	SAF	Pts
1938	CLE	N	3	1		0	0	0	19
1939			1	4		1	2	0	13
Career			4	5		1	2	0	32

Darrell Davis

Year	Team		TD	1XP	2XP	FG	FGA	SAF	Pts
1990	NYJ	N	1	0		0	0	0	6

Dave Davis

Year	Team		TD	1XP	2XP	FG	FGA	SAF	Pts
1972	**GB**	**N**	1	0		0	0	0	6

Eric Davis

Year	Team		TD	1XP	2XP	FG	FGA	SAF	Pts
1993	**SF**	**N**	2	0		0	0	0	12
1995			1	0	0	0	0	0	6
Career			3	0	0	0	0	0	18
Playoffs			1	0	0	0	0	0	6

Gary Davis

Year	Team		TD	1XP	2XP	FG	FGA	SAF	Pts
1976	**MIA**	**N**	1	0		0	0	0	6
1977			3	0		0	0	0	18
1978			3	0		0	0	0	18
1979			1	0		0	0	0	6
Career			8	0		0	0	0	48

Glenn Davis

Year	Team		TD	1XP	2XP	FG	FGA	SAF	Pts
1950	**LA**	**N**	7	0		0	0	0	42
1951			2	0		0	0	0	12
Career			9	0		0	0	0	54
Playoffs			1	0		0	0	0	6

Greg Davis

Year	Team		TD	1XP	2XP	FG	FGA	SAF	Pts
1987	**ATL**	**N**	0	6		3	4	0	15
1988			0	25		19	30	0	82
1989	**NE-ATL**	**N**	0	25		23	34	0	94
1990	**ATL**	**N**	0	40		22	33	0	108
1991	**PHX**	**N**	0	19		21	30	0	82
1992			0	28		13	26	0	67
1993			0	37		21	28	0	100
1994	**ARI**	**N**	0	17	0	20	26	0	77
1995			0	19	0	30	39	0	109
1996			0	12	0	9	14	0	39
Career			0	228	0	181	264	0	773

Harper Davis

Year	Team		TD	1XP	2XP	FG	FGA	SAF	Pts
1949	**LA**	**AA**	1	0		0	0	0	6
1950	**CHIB**	**N**	1	0		0	0	0	6
Career			2	0		0	0	0	12

Harrison Davis

Year	Team		TD	1XP	2XP	FG	FGA	SAF	Pts
1974	**SD**	**N**	2	0		0	0	0	12

Henry Davis

Year	Team		TD	1XP	2XP	FG	FGA	SAF	Pts
1972	**PIT**	**N**	1	0		0	0	0	6

James Davis

Year	Team		TD	1XP	2XP	FG	FGA	SAF	Pts
1982	**LARI**	**N**	1	0		0	0	0	6

Jerry Davis

Year	Team		TD	1XP	2XP	FG	FGA	SAF	Pts
1948	**CHIC**	**N**	2	0		0	0	0	12
1949			1	0		0	0	0	6
1952	**DAL**	**N**	1	0		0	0	0	6
Career			4	0		0	0	0	24

Joe Davis

Year	Team		TD	1XP	2XP	FG	FGA	SAF	Pts
1946	**BKN**	**AA**	1	1		0	0	0	7

Johnny Davis

Year	Team		TD	1XP	2XP	FG	FGA	SAF	Pts
1978	**TB**	**N**	3	0		0	0	0	18
1979			2	0		0	0	0	12
1980			1	0		0	0	0	6
1981	**SF**	**N**	7	0		0	0	0	42
1982	**CLE**	**N**	1	0		0	0	0	6
1984			1	0		0	0	0	6
Career			15	0		0	0	0	90
Playoffs			1	0		0	0	0	6

Kenneth Davis

Year	Team		TD	1XP	2XP	FG	FGA	SAF	Pts
1986	**GB**	**N**	1	0		0	0	0	6
1987			3	0		0	0	0	18
1988			1	0		0	0	0	6
1989	**BUF**	**N**	3	0		0	0	0	18
1990			5	0		0	0	0	30
1991			5	0		0	0	0	30
1992			6	0		0	0	0	36
1993			6	0		0	0	0	36
1994			2	0	0	0	0	0	12
Career			32	0	0	0	0	0	192
Playoffs			7	0	0	0	0	0	42

Lamar Davis

Year	Team		TD	1XP	2XP	FG	FGA	SAF	Pts
1946	**MIA**	**AA**	2	0		0	0	0	12
1947	**BAL**	**AA**	2	0		0	0	0	12

Lamar Davis *continued*

Year	Team		TD	1XP	2XP	FG	FGA	SAF	Pts
1948			7	0		0	0	0	42
1949			1	0		0	0	0	6
Career			12	0		0	0	0	72

Mike Davis

Year	Team		TD	1XP	2XP	FG	FGA	SAF	Pts
1982	**LARI**	**N**	1	0		0	0	0	6

Milt Davis

Year	Team		TD	1XP	2XP	FG	FGA	SAF	Pts
1957	**BAL**	**N**	2	0		0	0	0	12
1959			1	0		0	0	0	6
Career			3	0		0	0	0	18

Oliver Davis

Year	Team		TD	1XP	2XP	FG	FGA	SAF	Pts
1978	**CLE**	**N**	1	0		0	0	0	6

Red Davis

Year	Team		TD	1XP	2XP	FG	FGA	SAF	Pts
1933	**PHI**	**N**	1	3		0		0	9

Reuben Davis

Year	Team		TD	1XP	2XP	FG	FGA	SAF	Pts
1989	**TB**	**N**	1	0		0	0	0	6
1995	**SD**	**N**	0	0	0	0	0	1	2
Career			1	0	0	0	0	1	8
Playoffs			0	0	0	0	0	1	2

Russell Davis

Year	Team		TD	1XP	2XP	FG	FGA	SAF	Pts
1980	**PIT**	**N**	1	0		0	0	0	6
1981			1	0		0	0	0	6
Career			2	0		0	0	0	12

Stephen Davis

Year	Team		TD	1XP	2XP	FG	FGA	SAF	Pts
1996	**WAS**	**N**	2	0	0	0	0	0	12

Steve Davis

Year	Team		TD	1XP	2XP	FG	FGA	SAF	Pts
1972	**PIT**	**N**	1	0		0	0	0	6
1973			3	0		0	0	0	18
1974			3	0		0	0	0	18
1975	**NYJ**	**N**	1	0		0	0	0	6
1976			3	0		0	0	0	18
Career			11	0		0	0	0	66

Terrell Davis

Year	Team		TD	1XP	2XP	FG	FGA	SAF	Pts
1995	**DEN**	**N**	8	0	0	0	0	0	48
1996			15	0	0	0	0	0	90
Career			23	0	0	0	0	0	138
Playoffs			1	0	1	0	0	0	8

Tommy Davis

Year	Team		TD	1XP	2XP	FG	FGA	SAF	Pts
1959	**SF**	**N**	0	31		12	26	0	67
1960			0	21		**19**	**32**	0	78
1961			0	44		12	22	0	80
1962			0	36		10	23	0	66
1963			0	24		10	31	0	54
1964			0	30		8	25	0	54
1965			0	**52**		17	27	0	103
1966			0	38		16	31	0	86
1967			0	33		14	33	0	75
1968			0	26		9	16	0	53
1969			0	13		3	10	0	22
Career			0	348		130	276	0	738

Tony Davis

Year	Team		TD	1XP	2XP	FG	FGA	SAF	Pts
1976	**CIN**	**N**	1	0		0	0	0	6
1977			2	0		0	0	0	12
1978			2	0		0	0	0	12
1980	**TB**	**N**	1	0		0	0	0	6
Career			6	0		0	0	0	36

Van Davis

Year	Team		TD	1XP	2XP	FG	FGA	SAF	Pts
1948	**NY**	**AA**	1	0		0	0	0	6

Wendell Davis

Year	Team		TD	1XP	2XP	FG	FGA	SAF	Pts
1989	**CHI**	**N**	3	0		0	0	0	18
1990			3	0		0	0	0	18
1991			6	0		0	0	0	36
1992			2	0		0	0	0	12
Career			14	0		0	0	0	84

Willie Davis

Year	Team		TD	1XP	2XP	FG	FGA	SAF	Pts
1960	**GB**	**N**	1	0		0	0	0	6
1962			1	0		0	0	0	6
1963			0	0		0	0	1	2
1967			0	0		0	0	1	2
Career			2	0		0	0	2	16

Willie Davis

Year	Team		TD	1XP	2XP	FG	FGA	SAF	Pts
1992	**KC**	**N**	3	0		0	0	0	18
1993			7	0		0	0	0	42
1994			5	0	1	0	0	0	32
1995			5	0	0	0	0	0	30
1996	**HOU**	**N**	6	0	0	0	0	0	36
Career			26	0	1	0	0	0	158
Playoffs			1	0	0	0	0	0	6

Joe Dawkins

Year	Team		TD	1XP	2XP	FG	FGA	SAF	Pts
1970	**HOU**	**N**	2	0		0	0	0	12
1971			2	0		0	0	0	12
1972	**DEN**	**N**	2	0		0	0	0	12
1973			2	0		0	0	0	12
1974	**NYG**	**N**	5	0		0	0	0	30
1975			2	0		0	0	0	12
1976	**HOU**	**N**	1	0		0	0	0	6
Career			16	0		0	0	0	96

Julius Dawkins

Year	Team		TD	1XP	2XP	FG	FGA	SAF	Pts
1983	**BUF**	**N**	1	0		0	0	0	6
1984			2	0		0	0	0	12
Career			3	0		0	0	0	18

Sean Dawkins

Year	Team		TD	1XP	2XP	FG	FGA	SAF	Pts
1993	**IND**	**N**	1	0		0	0	0	6
1994			5	0	0	0	0	0	30
1995			3	0	0	0	0	0	18
1996			1	0	0	0	0	0	6
Career			10	0	0	0	0	0	60
Playoffs			1	0	0	0	0	0	6

Lawrence Dawsey

Year	Team		TD	1XP	2XP	FG	FGA	SAF	Pts
1991	**TB**	**N**	4	0		0	0	0	24
1992			1	0		0	0	0	6
1994			1	0	0	0	0	0	6
Career			6	0	0	0	0	0	36

Dale Dawson

Year	Team		TD	1XP	2XP	FG	FGA	SAF	Pts
1987	**MIN**	**N**	0	4		1	5	0	7
1988	**PHI-GB**	**N**	0	4		3	6	0	13
Career			0	8		4	11	0	20

Gib Dawson

Year	Team		TD	1XP	2XP	FG	FGA	SAF	Pts
1953	**GB**	**N**	1	0		0	0	0	6

Lake Dawson

Year	Team		TD	1XP	2XP	FG	FGA	SAF	Pts
1994	**KC**	**N**	2	0	0	0	0	0	12
1995			5	0	0	0	0	0	30
1996			1	0	0	0	0	0	6
Career			8	0	0	0	0	0	48
Playoffs			1	0	0	0	0	0	6

Len Dawson

Year	Team		TD	1XP	2XP	FG	FGA	SAF	Pts
1957	**PIT**	**N**	0	0		0	1	0	0
1962	**DAL**	**A**	3	0	0	0	0	0	18
1963	**KC**	**A**	2	0	0	0	0	0	12
1964			2	0	0	0	0	0	12
1965			2	0	0	0	0	0	12
Career			9	0	0	0	1	0	54
Playoffs			1	0	0	0	0	0	6

Lin Dawson

Year	Team		TD	1XP	2XP	FG	FGA	SAF	Pts
1982	**NE**	**N**	1	0		0	0	0	6
1983			1	0		0	0	0	6
1984			4	0		0	0	0	24
1988			2	0		0	0	0	12
Career			8	0		0	0	0	48
Playoffs			1	0		0	0	0	6

Rhett Dawson

Year	Team		TD	1XP	2XP	FG	FGA	SAF	Pts
1972	**HOU**	**N**	1	0		0	0	0	6

Harry Dayhoff

Year	Team		TD	1XP	2XP	FG	FGA	SAF	Pts
1924	**FRA**	**N**	2	0		0		0	12

Fred Dean

Year	Team		TD	1XP	2XP	FG	FGA	SAF	Pts
1977	**SD**	**N**	2	0		0	0	0	12

Randy Dean

Year	Team		TD	1XP	2XP	FG	FGA	SAF	Pts
1979	**NYG**	**N**	1	0		0	0	0	6

Ted Dean

Year	Team		TD	1XP	2XP	FG	FGA	SAF	Pts
1960	**PHI**	**N**	3	0		0	0	0	18

Ted Dean *continued*

Year	Team		TD	1XP	2XP	FG	FGA	SAF	Pts
1961			3	0		0	0	0	18
Career			6	0		0	0	0	36
Playoffs			1	0		0	0	0	6

Vernon Dean

Year	Team		TD	1XP	2XP	FG	FGA	SAF	Pts
1983	WAS	N	1	0		0	0	0	6
1984			2	0		0	0	0	12
1988	SEA	N	1	0		0	0	0	6
Career			4	0		0	0	0	24

Steve DeBerg

Year	Team		TD	1XP	2XP	FG	FGA	SAF	Pts
1978	SF	N	1	0		0	0	0	6
1982	DEN	N	1	0		0	0	0	6
1983			1	0		0	0	0	6
1984	TB	N	2	0		0	0	0	12
1986			1	0		0	0	0	6
1988	KC	N	1	0		0	0	0	6
Career			7	0		0	0	0	42

Bill deCorrevont

Year	Team		TD	1XP	2XP	FG	FGA	SAF	Pts
1946	DET	N	2	0		0	0	0	12
1947	CHIC	N	1	0		0	0	0	6
Career			3	0		0	0	0	18

Walt DeGree

Year	Team		TD	1XP	2XP	FG	FGA	SAF	Pts
1921	DET	A	0	0		1		0	3

Paul Dekker

Year	Team		TD	1XP	2XP	FG	FGA	SAF	Pts
1953	WAS	N	1	0		0	0	0	6

Joe Delaney

Year	Team		TD	1XP	2XP	FG	FGA	SAF	Pts
1981	KC	N	3	0		0	0	0	18

Bob DeLauer

Year	Team		TD	1XP	2XP	FG	FGA	SAF	Pts
1946	LA	N	0	0		0	2	0	0

Al Del Greco

Year	Team		TD	1XP	2XP	FG	FGA	SAF	Pts
1984	GB	N	0	34		9	12	0	61
1985			0	38		19	26	0	95
1986			0	29		17	27	0	80
1987	GB-STL	N	0	19		9	15	0	46
1988	PHX	N	0	42		12	21	0	78
1989			0	28		18	26	0	82
1990			0	31		17	27	0	82
1991	HOU	N	0	16		10	13	0	46
1992			0	41		21	27	0	104
1993			0	39		29	34	0	126
1994			0	18	0	16	20	0	66
1995			0	33	0	27	31	0	114
1996			0	35	0	32	38	0	131
Career			0	403	0	236	317	0	1111
Playoffs			0	12	0	5	7	0	27

Steve DeLine

Year	Team		TD	1XP	2XP	FG	FGA	SAF	Pts
1988	SD	N	0	12		6	8	0	30
1989	PHI	N	0	3		3	7	0	12
Career			0	15		9	15	0	42

Spiro Dellerba

Year	Team		TD	1XP	2XP	FG	FGA	SAF	Pts
1947	CLE	AA	1	0		0	0	0	6

Johnny Dell Isola

Year	Team		TD	1XP	2XP	FG	FGA	SAF	Pts
1938	NYG	N	0	0		0		1	2

Jack Deloplaine

Year	Team		TD	1XP	2XP	FG	FGA	SAF	Pts
1976	PIT	N	2	0		0	0	0	12

Robert Delpino

Year	Team		TD	1XP	2XP	FG	FGA	SAF	Pts
1988	LARM	N	2	0		0	0	0	12
1989			2	0		0	0	0	12
1990			4	0		0	0	0	24
1991			10	0		0	0	0	60
1992			1	0		0	0	0	6
1993	DEN	N	8	0		0	0	0	48
Career			27	0		0	0	0	162

Jack Del Rio

Year	Team		TD	1XP	2XP	FG	FGA	SAF	Pts
1985	NO	N	1	0		0	0	0	6
1989	DAL	N	1	0		0	0	0	6
1992	MIN	N	1	0		0	0	0	6
Career			3	0		0	0	0	18

Tom Dempsey

Year	Team		TD	1XP	2XP	FG	FGA	SAF	Pts
1969	NO	N	0	33		22	**41**	0	99
1970			0	16		18	34	0	70
1971	PHI	N	0	13		12	17	0	49
1972			0	11		20	35	0	71
1973			0	34		24	40	0	106
1974			0	26		10	16	0	56
1975	LA	N	0	31		21	26	0	94
1976			0	36		17	26	0	87
1977	HOU	N	0	8		4	6	0	20
1978	BUF	N	0	36		10	13	0	66
1979			0	8		1	4	0	11
Career			0	252		159	258	0	729
Playoffs			0	9		0	4	0	9

Vern Den Herder

Year	Team		TD	1XP	2XP	FG	FGA	SAF	Pts
1978	MIA	N	1	0		0	0	0	6

Preston Dennard

Year	Team		TD	1XP	2XP	FG	FGA	SAF	Pts
1979	LA	N	4	0		0	0	0	24
1980			6	0		0	0	0	36
1981			4	0		0	0	0	24
1982	LARM	N	2	0		0	0	0	12
1983			5	0		0	0	0	30
1984	BUF	N	7	0		0	0	0	42
1985	GB	N	2	0		0	0	0	12
Career			30	0		0	0	0	180
Playoffs			3	0		0	0	0	18

Mike Dennery

Year	Team		TD	1XP	2XP	FG	FGA	SAF	Pts
1975	OAK	N	0	0		0	0	1	2

Vince Dennery

Year	Team		TD	1XP	2XP	FG	FGA	SAF	Pts
1941	NYG	N	1	0		0	0	0	6

Austin Denney

Year	Team		TD	1XP	2XP	FG	FGA	SAF	Pts
1968	CHI	N	2	0		0	0	0	12
1969			1	0		0	0	0	6
Career			3	0		0	0	0	18

Mike Dennis

Year	Team		TD	1XP	2XP	FG	FGA	SAF	Pts
1981	NYG	N	1	0		0	0	0	6

Doug Dennison

Year	Team		TD	1XP	2XP	FG	FGA	SAF	Pts
1974	DAL	N	4	0		0	0	0	24
1975			7	0		0	0	0	42
1976			6	0		0	0	0	36
1977			1	0		0	0	0	6
1978			1	0		0	0	0	6
Career			19	0		0	0	0	114
Playoffs			2	0		0	0	0	12

Glenn Dennison

Year	Team		TD	1XP	2XP	FG	FGA	SAF	Pts
1984	NYJ	N	1	0		0	0	0	6

Al Denson

Year	Team		TD	1XP	2XP	FG	FGA	SAF	Pts
1964	DEN	A	1	0	1	0	0	0	8
1966			3	0	0	0	0	0	18
1967			11	0	0	0	0	0	66
1968			5	0	0	0	0	0	30
1969			10	0	0	0	0	0	60
1970	DEN	N	2	0		0	0	0	12
Career			32	0	1	0	0	0	194

Moses Denson

Year	Team		TD	1XP	2XP	FG	FGA	SAF	Pts
1974	WAS	N	2	0		0	0	0	12
Playoffs			1	0	0	0	0	0	6

Richard Dent

Year	Team		TD	1XP	2XP	FG	FGA	SAF	Pts
1985	CHI	N	1	0		0	0	0	6
1990			1	0		0	0	0	6
1996	IND	N	0	0	0	0	0	1	2
Career			2	0	0	0	0	1	14

Jerry DePoyster

Year	Team		TD	1XP	2XP	FG	FGA	SAF	Pts
1968	DET	N	0	18		3	15	0	27

Lee DeRamus

Year	Team		TD	1XP	2XP	FG	FGA	SAF	Pts
1996	NO	N	1	0	0	0	0	0	6

Dean Derby

Year	Team		TD	1XP	2XP	FG	FGA	SAF	Pts
1957	PIT	N	2	3		2	4	0	21

Al DeRogatis

Year	Team		TD	1XP	2XP	FG	FGA	SAF	Pts
1949	NYG	N	1	0		0	0	0	6
1950			1	0		0	0	0	6
Career			2	0		0	0	0	12

Brian DeRoo

Year	Team		TD	1XP	2XP	FG	FGA	SAF	Pts
1979	BAL	N	1	0		0	0	0	6

Dan DeSantis

Year	Team		TD	1XP	2XP	FG	FGA	SAF	Pts
1941	PHI	N	0	1		0	0	0	1

Chuck DeShane

Year	Team		TD	1XP	2XP	FG	FGA	SAF	Pts
1945	DET	N	2	0		0	0	0	12
1946			0	10		0	1	0	10
Career			2	10		0	1	0	22

Versil Deskin

Year	Team		TD	1XP	2XP	FG	FGA	SAF	Pts
1936	CHIC	N	1	0		0		0	6
1937			1	0		0		0	6
Career			2	0		0		0	12

Darrell Dess

Year	Team		TD	1XP	2XP	FG	FGA	SAF	Pts
1967	NYG	N	1	0		0	0	0	6

Fred DeStefano

Year	Team		TD	1XP	2XP	FG	FGA	SAF	Pts
1924	CHIC	N	1	0		0		0	6

Harold Deters

Year	Team		TD	1XP	2XP	FG	FGA	SAF	Pts
1967	DAL	N	0	9		1	4	0	12

Ty Detmer

Year	Team		TD	1XP	2XP	FG	FGA	SAF	Pts
1996	PHI	N	1	0	0	0	0	0	6

Chuck Detwiler

Year	Team		TD	1XP	2XP	FG	FGA	SAF	Pts
1970	SD	N	1	0		0	0	0	6

Mark Devlin

Year	Team		TD	1XP	2XP	FG	FGA	SAF	Pts
1920	CLE	A	0	0		0		0	0

Jim Dewar

Year	Team		TD	1XP	2XP	FG	FGA	SAF	Pts
1947	CLE	AA	1	0		0	0	0	6

Billy Dewell

Year	Team		TD	1XP	2XP	FG	FGA	SAF	Pts
1941	CHIC	N	1	0		0	0	0	6
1945			1	0		0	0	0	6
1946			7	0		0	0	0	42
1947			4	0		0	0	0	24
1948			2	0		0	0	0	12
1949			2	0		0	0	0	12
Career			17	0		0	0	0	102

Herb DeWitz

Year	Team		TD	1XP	2XP	FG	FGA	SAF	Pts
1927	CLE	N	2	0		0		0	12

Rufe DeWitz

Year	Team		TD	1XP	2XP	FG	FGA	SAF	Pts
1924	KC	N	0	1		1		0	4
1926			1	0		0		0	6
Career			1	1		1		0	10

Willard Dewveall

Year	Team		TD	1XP	2XP	FG	FGA	SAF	Pts
1959	CHIB	N	3	0		0	0	0	18
1960	CHI	N	5	0		0	0	0	30
1961	HOU	A	3	0	0	0	0	0	18
1962			5	0	0	0	0	0	30
1963			7	0	0	0	0	0	42
1964			4	0	0	0	0	0	24
Career			27	0	0	0	0	0	162
Playoffs			1	0	0	0	0	0	6

Buddy Dial

Year	Team		TD	1XP	2XP	FG	FGA	SAF	Pts
1959	PIT	N	6	0		0	0	0	36
1960			9	0		0	0	0	54
1961			12	0		0	0	0	72
1962			6	0		0	0	0	36
1963			9	0		0	0	0	54
1965	DAL	N	1	0		0	0	0	6
1966			1	0		0	0	0	6
Career			44	0		0	0	0	264

Dorne Dibble

Year	Team		TD	1XP	2XP	FG	FGA	SAF	Pts
1951	DET	N	6	0		0	0	0	36
1953			3	0		0	0	0	18
1954			6	0		0	0	0	36
1955			2	0		0	0	0	12

Dorne Dibble *continued*

Year	Team		TD	1XP	2XP	FG	FGA	SAF	Pts
1956			2	0		0	0	0	12
Career			19	0		0	0	0	114

Anthony Dickerson

Year	Team		TD	1XP	2XP	FG	FGA	SAF	Pts
1983	DAL	N	0	0		0	0	1	2

Eric Dickerson

Year	Team		TD	1XP	2XP	FG	FGA	SAF	Pts
1983	LARM	N	20	0		0	0	0	120
1984			14	0		0	0	0	84
1985			12	0		0	0	0	72
1986			11	0		0	0	0	66
1987	LARI-IND	N	6	0		0	0	0	36
1988	IND	N	15	0		0	0	0	90
1989			8	0		0	0	0	48
1990			4	0		0	0	0	24
1991			3	0		0	0	0	18
1992	LARI	N	3	0		0	0	0	18
Career			96	0		0	0	0	576
Playoffs			4	0		0	0	0	24

Curtis Dickey

Year	Team		TD	1XP	2XP	FG	FGA	SAF	Pts
1980	BAL	N	13	0		0	0	0	78
1981			10	0		0	0	0	60
1982			1	0		0	0	0	6
1983			7	0		0	0	0	42
1984	IND	N	3	0		0	0	0	18
1986	CLE	N	6	0		0	0	0	36
Career			40	0		0	0	0	240

Eldridge Dickey

Year	Team		TD	1XP	2XP	FG	FGA	SAF	Pts
1971	OAK	N	1	0		0	0	0	6

Lynn Dickey

Year	Team		TD	1XP	2XP	FG	FGA	SAF	Pts
1973	HOU	N	0	1		0	0	0	1
1976	GB	N	1	0		0	0	0	6
1980			1	0		0	0	0	6
1983			3	0		0	0	0	18
1984			3	0		0	0	0	18
1985			1	0		0	0	0	6
Career			9	1		0	0	0	55

Bo Dickinson

Year	Team		TD	1XP	2XP	FG	FGA	SAF	Pts
1960	DAL	A	1	0	0	0	0	0	6
1961			5	0	2	0	0	0	34
1962	DEN	A	4	0	0	0	0	0	24
1963	HOU	A	1	0	0	0	0	0	6
Career			11	0	2	0	0	0	70

Chuck Dicus

Year	Team		TD	1XP	2XP	FG	FGA	SAF	Pts
1971	SD	N	1	0		0	0	0	6
1972			2	0		0	0	0	12
Career			3	0		0	0	0	18

Clint Didier

Year	Team		TD	1XP	2XP	FG	FGA	SAF	Pts
1982	WAS	N	1	0		0	0	0	6
1983			5	0		0	0	0	30
1984			5	0		0	0	0	30
1985			4	0		0	0	0	24
1986			4	0		0	0	0	24
1987			1	0		0	0	0	6
1988	GB	N	1	0		0	0	0	6
1989			1	0		0	0	0	6
Career			22	0		0	0	0	132
Playoffs			2	0		0	0	0	12

Dave Diehl

Year	Team		TD	1XP	2XP	FG	FGA	SAF	Pts
1940	DET	N	1	0		0	0	0	6
1944			4	0		0	0	0	24
Career			5	0		0	0	0	30

Wally Diehl

Year	Team		TD	1XP	2XP	FG	FGA	SAF	Pts
1928	FRA	N	5	0		0		0	30
1929			6	0		0		0	36
1930			0	0		0		0	0
Career			11	0		0		0	66

Doug Dieken

Year	Team		TD	1XP	2XP	FG	FGA	SAF	Pts
1971	CLE	N	0	0		0	0	1	2
1983			1	0		0	0	0	6
Career			1	0		0	0	1	8

Scott Dierking

Year	Team		TD	1XP	2XP	FG	FGA	SAF	Pts
1977	NYJ	N	1	0		0	0	0	6
1978			4	0		0	0	0	24

Scott Dierking *continued*

Year	Team		TD	1XP	2XP	FG	FGA	SAF	Pts
1979			3	0		0	0	0	18
1980			7	0		0	0	0	42
1981			2	0		0	0	0	12
1982			2	0		0	0	0	12
1983			3	0		0	0	0	18
1984	TB	N	1	0		0	0	0	6
Career			23	0		0	0	0	138
Playoffs			1	0		0	0	0	6

John Diettrich

Year	Team		TD	1XP	2XP	FG	FGA	SAF	Pts
1987	HOU	N	0	5		6	6	0	23

Trent Dilfer

Year	Team		TD	1XP	2XP	FG	FGA	SAF	Pts
1995	TB	N	2	0	0	0	0	0	12

Ken Dilger

Year	Team		TD	1XP	2XP	FG	FGA	SAF	Pts
1995	IND	N	4	0	0	0	0	0	24
1996			4	0	0	0	0	0	24
Career			8	0	0	0	0	0	48
Playoffs			1	0	0	0	0	0	6

Bobby Dillon

Year	Team		TD	1XP	2XP	FG	FGA	SAF	Pts
1953	GB	N	1	0		0	0	0	6
1954			1	0		0	0	0	6
1956			1	0		0	0	0	6
1957			1	0		0	0	0	6
1958			1	0		0	0	0	6
Career			5	0		0	0	0	30

Steve Dils

Year	Team		TD	1XP	2XP	FG	FGA	SAF	Pts
1988	ATL	N	1	0		0	0	0	6

Lavern Dilweg

Year	Team		TD	1XP	2XP	FG	FGA	SAF	Pts
1927	GB	N	2	0		0		0	12
1929			3	0		0		0	18
1930			3	0		0		0	18
1931			4	1		0		0	25
1932			0	1		0		0	1
1934			2	0		0		0	12
Career			14	2		0		0	86

Babe Dimancheff

Year	Team		TD	1XP	2XP	FG	FGA	SAF	Pts
1946	BOS	N	1	0		0	0	0	6
1947	CHIC	N	4	0		0	0	0	24
1948			4	0		0	0	0	24
1949			4	0		0	0	0	24
1952	CHIB	N	2	0		0	0	0	12
Career			15	0		0	0	0	90

Charles Dimry

Year	Team		TD	1XP	2XP	FG	FGA	SAF	Pts
1991	DEN	N	1	0		0	0	0	6

Mike Dingle

Year	Team		TD	1XP	2XP	FG	FGA	SAF	Pts
1991	CIN	N	1	0		0	0	0	6

Bob Dinsmore

Year	Team		TD	1XP	2XP	FG	FGA	SAF	Pts
1926	PHI	A	1	2		3		0	17

Mike Dirks

Year	Team		TD	1XP	2XP	FG	FGA	SAF	Pts
1970	PHI	N	1	0		0	0	0	6

Cris Dishman

Year	Team		TD	1XP	2XP	FG	FGA	SAF	Pts
1988	HOU	N	1	0		0	0	0	6
1989			1	0		0	0	0	6
1991			1	0		0	0	0	6
1993			1	0		0	0	0	6
1994			1	0	0	0	0	0	6
Career			5	0	0	0	0	0	30

Mike Ditka

Year	Team		TD	1XP	2XP	FG	FGA	SAF	Pts
1961	CHI	N	12	0		0	0	0	72
1962			6	0		0	0	0	36
1963			8	0		0	0	0	48
1964			6	0		0	0	0	36
1965			2	0		0	0	0	12
1966			2	0		0	0	0	12
1967	PHI	N	2	0		0	0	0	12
1968			2	0		0	0	0	12
1969	DAL	N	3	0		0	0	0	18
1971			1	0		0	0	0	6
1972			1	0		0	0	0	6
Career			45	0		0	0	0	270
Playoffs			1	0		0	0	0	6

Al Dixon

Year	Team		TD	1XP	2XP	FG	FGA	SAF	Pts
1978	NYG	N	3	0		0	0	0	18
1980	KC	N	1	0		0	0	0	6
1981			2	0		0	0	0	12
1982			2	0		0	0	0	12
Career			8	0		0	0	0	48

Floyd Dixon

Year	Team		TD	1XP	2XP	FG	FGA	SAF	Pts
1986	ATL	N	2	0		0	0	0	12
1987			5	0		0	0	0	30
1988			2	0		0	0	0	12
1989			2	0		0	0	0	12
1990			4	0		0	0	0	24
1991			1	0		0	0	0	6
Career			16	0		0	0	0	96

Gerald Dixon

Year	Team		TD	1XP	2XP	FG	FGA	SAF	Pts
1995	CLE	N	1	0	0	0	0	0	6

Hewritt Dixon

Year	Team		TD	1XP	2XP	FG	FGA	SAF	Pts
1963	DEN	A	2	0	0	0	0	0	12
1964			1	0	0	0	0	0	6
1965			2	0	0	0	0	0	12
1966	OAK	A	9	0	0	0	0	0	54
1967			7	0	0	0	0	0	42
1968			4	0	1	0	0	0	26
1969			1	0	0	0	0	0	6
1970	OAK	N	2	0		0	0	0	12
Career			28	0	1	0	0	0	170
Playoffs			1	0	0	0	0	0	6

James Dixon

Year	Team		TD	1XP	2XP	FG	FGA	SAF	Pts
1989	DAL	N	3	0		0	0	0	18

Randy Dixon

Year	Team		TD	1XP	2XP	FG	FGA	SAF	Pts
1989	IND	N	1	0		0	0	0	6

Zack Dixon

Year	Team		TD	1XP	2XP	FG	FGA	SAF	Pts
1981	BAL	N	1	0		0	0	0	6
1982			1	0		0	0	0	6
1983	SEA	N	1	0		0	0	0	6
1984			2	0		0	0	0	12
Career			5	0		0	0	0	30

Dinger Doane

Year	Team		TD	1XP	2XP	FG	FGA	SAF	Pts
1922	MIL	N	1	0		0		0	6
1923			2	0		0		0	12
1924			4	0		0		0	24
1925	DET	N	5	0		0		0	30
1926			3	0		0		0	18
Career			15	0		0		0	90

Glenn Dobbs

Year	Team		TD	1XP	2XP	FG	FGA	SAF	Pts
1946	BKN	AA	6	0		0	0	0	36
1947	BKN-LA	AA	2	0		0	0	0	12
1948	LA	AA	4	0		0	0	0	24
1949			3	0		0	0	0	18
Career			15	0		0	0	0	90

Bob Dobelstein

Year	Team		TD	1XP	2XP	FG	FGA	SAF	Pts
1947	NYG	N	1	0		0	0	0	6
1948			1	0		0	0	0	6
Career			2	0		0	0	0	12

Conrad Dobler

Year	Team		TD	1XP	2XP	FG	FGA	SAF	Pts
1977	STL	N	1	0		0	0	0	6

Al Dodd

Year	Team		TD	1XP	2XP	FG	FGA	SAF	Pts
1969	NO	N	1	0		0	0	0	6
1970			2	0		0	0	0	12
1974	ATL	N	1	0		0	0	0	6
Career			4	0		0	0	0	24

Dale Dodrill

Year	Team		TD	1XP	2XP	FG	FGA	SAF	Pts
1952	PIT	N	1	0		0	0	0	6
1953			1	0		0	0	0	6
Career			2	0		0	0	0	12

John Doehring

Year	Team		TD	1XP	2XP	FG	FGA	SAF	Pts
1932	CHIB	N	1	0		0		0	6
1933			0	0		0		0	0
Career			1	0		0			6

Jack Dolbin

Year	Team		TD	1XP	2XP	FG	FGA	SAF	Pts
1975	DEN	N	4	0		0	0	0	24

Jack Dolbin *continued*

Year	Team		TD	1XP	2XP	FG	FGA	SAF	Pts
1976			1	0		0	0	0	6
1977			3	0		0	0	0	18
Career			8	0		0	0	0	48
Playoffs			1	0		0	0	0	6

Chris Doleman

Year	Team		TD	1XP	2XP	FG	FGA	SAF	Pts
1986	MIN	N	1	0		0	0	0	6
1990			0	0		0	0	1	2
1992			1	0		0	0	1	8
1996	SF	N	1	0	0	0	0	0	6
Career			3	0	0	0	0	2	22

Don Doll

Year	Team		TD	1XP	2XP	FG	FGA	SAF	Pts
1949	DET	N	2	0		0	0	0	12
1950			1	0		0	0	0	6
Career			3	0		0	0	0	18

Marty Domres

Year	Team		TD	1XP	2XP	FG	FGA	SAF	Pts
1969	SD	A	4	0	0	0	0	0	24
1972	BAL	N	1	0		0	0	0	6
1973			2	0		0	0	0	12
1974			2	0		0	0	0	12
1975			1	0		0	0	0	6
Career			10	0	0	0	0	0	60

Tom Domres

Year	Team		TD	1XP	2XP	FG	FGA	SAF	Pts
1969	HOU	A	1	0	0	0	0	0	6

Oscar Donahue

Year	Team		TD	1XP	2XP	FG	FGA	SAF	Pts
1962	MIN	N	1	0		0	0	0	6

Jeff Donaldson

Year	Team		TD	1XP	2XP	FG	FGA	SAF	Pts
1986	HOU	N	1	0		0	0	0	6

Doug Donley

Year	Team		TD	1XP	2XP	FG	FGA	SAF	Pts
1983	DAL	N	2	0		0	0	0	12
1984			2	0		0	0	0	12
Career			4	0		0	0	0	24

Roger Donnahoo

Year	Team		TD	1XP	2XP	FG	FGA	SAF	Pts
1960	NY	A	2	0	0	0	0	0	12

Rick Donnelly

Year	Team		TD	1XP	2XP	FG	FGA	SAF	Pts
1986	ATL	N	0	1		0	0	0	1

Mike Donohoe

Year	Team		TD	1XP	2XP	FG	FGA	SAF	Pts
1968	ATL	N	1	0		0	0	0	6
1970			1	0		0	0	0	6
Career			2	0		0	0	0	12

Bill Donohue

Year	Team		TD	1XP	2XP	FG	FGA	SAF	Pts
1927	FRA	N	2	0		0		0	12

Art Donovan

Year	Team		TD	1XP	2XP	FG	FGA	SAF	Pts
1953	BAL	N	0	0		0	0	1	2

Jim Dooley

Year	Team		TD	1XP	2XP	FG	FGA	SAF	Pts
1953	CHIB	N	4	0		0	0	0	24
1954			7	0		0	0	0	42
1957			1	0		0	0	0	6
1959			3	0		0	0	0	18
1960	CHI	N	1	0		0	0	0	6
Career			16	0		0	0	0	96

Dan Doornink

Year	Team		TD	1XP	2XP	FG	FGA	SAF	Pts
1978	NYG	N	1	0		0	0	0	6
1979	SEA	N	9	0		0	0	0	54
1980			5	0		0	0	0	30
1981			5	0		0	0	0	30
1983			4	0		0	0	0	24
1984			2	0		0	0	0	12
Career			26	0		0	0	0	156
Playoffs			1	0		0	0	0	6

Jim Doran

Year	Team		TD	1XP	2XP	FG	FGA	SAF	Pts
1951	DET	N	2	0		0	0	0	12
1952			1	0		0	0	0	6
1954			4	0		0	0	0	24
1955			2	0		0	0	0	12
1957			5	0		0	0	0	30
1958			4	0		0	0	0	24
1959			2	0		0	0	0	12
1960	DAL	N	3	0		0	0	0	18

Jim Doran *continued*

Year	Team		TD	1XP	2XP	FG	FGA	SAF	Pts
1961			2	0		0	0	0	12
Career			25	0		0	0	0	150
Playoffs			2	0		0	0	0	12

Torin Dorn

Year	Team		TD	1XP	2XP	FG	FGA	SAF	Pts
1991	LARI	N	0	0		0	0	1	2
1995	STL	N	2	0	0	0	0	0	12
Career			2	0	0	0	0	1	14

Al Dorow

Year	Team		TD	1XP	2XP	FG	FGA	SAF	Pts
1954	WAS	N	3	0		0	0	0	18
1957	PHI	N	2	0		0	0	0	12
1960	NY	A	7	0	0	0	0	0	42
1961			4	0	0	0	0	0	24
Career			16	0	0	0	0	0	96

Tony Dorsett

Year	Team		TD	1XP	2XP	FG	FGA	SAF	Pts
1977	DAL	N	13	0		0	0	0	78
1978			10	0		0	0	0	60
1979			7	0		0	0	0	42
1980			11	0		0	0	0	66
1981			6	0		0	0	0	36
1982			5	0		0	0	0	30
1983			9	0		0	0	0	54
1984			7	0		0	0	0	42
1985			10	0		0	0	0	60
1986			6	0		0	0	0	36
1987			2	0		0	0	0	12
1988	DEN	N	5	0		0	0	0	30
Career			91	0		0	0	0	546
Playoffs			10	0		0	0	0	60

Dean Dorsey

Year	Team		TD	1XP	2XP	FG	FGA	SAF	Pts
1988	PHI-GB	N	0	12		5	10	0	27

Dick Dorsey

Year	Team		TD	1XP	2XP	FG	FGA	SAF	Pts
1962	OAK	A	2	0	0	0	0	0	12

Larry Dorsey

Year	Team		TD	1XP	2XP	FG	FGA	SAF	Pts
1977	SD	N	2	0		0	0	0	12
1978	KC	N	2	0		0	0	0	12
Career			4	0		0	0	0	24

Reggie Doss

Year	Team		TD	1XP	2XP	FG	FGA	SAF	Pts
1985	LARM	N	0	0		0	0	1	2

Al Dotson

Year	Team		TD	1XP	2XP	FG	FGA	SAF	Pts
1969	OAK	A	0	0	0	0	0	1	2

Santana Dotson

Year	Team		TD	1XP	2XP	FG	FGA	SAF	Pts
1992	TB	N	1	0		0	0	0	6

Kayo Dottley

Year	Team		TD	1XP	2XP	FG	FGA	SAF	Pts
1951	CHIB	N	4	0		0	0	0	24
1952			4	0		0	0	0	24
1953			1	0		0	0	0	6
Career			9	0		0	0	0	54

Phil Dougherty

Year	Team		TD	1XP	2XP	FG	FGA	SAF	Pts
1938	CHIC	N	1	0		0		0	6

Glenn Doughty

Year	Team		TD	1XP	2XP	FG	FGA	SAF	Pts
1973	BAL	N	4	0		0	0	0	24
1974			2	0		0	0	0	12
1975			4	0		0	0	0	24
1976			5	0		0	0	0	30
1977			4	0		0	0	0	24
1978			3	0		0	0	0	18
1979			2	0		0	0	0	12
Career			24	0		0	0	0	144
Playoffs			1	0		0	0	0	6

Ben Douglas

Year	Team		TD	1XP	2XP	FG	FGA	SAF	Pts
1933	BKN	N	1	0		0		0	6

Hugh Douglas

Year	Team		TD	1XP	2XP	FG	FGA	SAF	Pts
1996	NYJ	N	1	0	0	0	0	0	6

Leland Douglas

Year	Team		TD	1XP	2XP	FG	FGA	SAF	Pts
1987	MIA	N	1	0		0	0	0	6

Merrill Douglas

Year	Team		TD	1XP	2XP	FG	FGA	SAF	Pts
1959	CHIB	N	2	0		0	0	0	12

Omar Douglas

Year	Team		TD	1XP	2XP	FG	FGA	SAF	Pts
1995	NYG	N	1	0	0	0	0	0	6

Bobby Douglass

Year	Team		TD	1XP	2XP	FG	FGA	SAF	Pts
1969	CHI	N	2	0		0	0	0	12
1971			3	1		0	0	0	19
1972			8	0		0	0	0	48
1973			5	0		0	0	0	30
1974			1	0		0	0	0	6
1975			1	0		0	0	0	6
1976	NO	N	2	0		0	0	0	12
Career			22	1		0	0	0	133

Maurice Douglass

Year	Team		TD	1XP	2XP	FG	FGA	SAF	Pts
1996	NYG	N	1	0	0	0	0	0	6

Mike Douglass

Year	Team		TD	1XP	2XP	FG	FGA	SAF	Pts
1983	GB	N	2	0		0	0	0	12
1985			1	0		0	0	0	6
Career			3	0		0	0	0	18

Bob Dove

Year	Team		TD	1XP	2XP	FG	FGA	SAF	Pts
1946	CHI	AA	1	0		0	0	0	6
1947			1	0		0	0	0	6
Career			2	0		0	0	0	12

Woody Dow

Year	Team		TD	1XP	2XP	FG	FGA	SAF	Pts
1938	PHI	N	1	0		0		0	6

Jerry Dowd

Year	Team		TD	1XP	2XP	FG	FGA	SAF	Pts
1939	CLE	N	1	0		0	0	0	6

Harry Dowda

Year	Team		TD	1XP	2XP	FG	FGA	SAF	Pts
1949	WAS	N	3	0		0	0	0	18
1950			1	0		0	0	0	6
1952			1	0		0	0	0	6
1953			1	0		0	0	0	6
Career			6	0		0	0	0	36

Marcus Dowdell

Year	Team		TD	1XP	2XP	FG	FGA	SAF	Pts
1993	NO	N	1	0		0	0	0	6
1996	ARI	N	2	0	0	0	0	0	12
Career			3	0	0	0	0	0	18

Mike Dowdle

Year	Team		TD	1XP	2XP	FG	FGA	SAF	Pts
1966	SF	N	1	0		0	0	0	6

Boyd Dowler

Year	Team		TD	1XP	2XP	FG	FGA	SAF	Pts
1959	GB	N	4	0		0	0	0	24
1960			2	0		0	0	0	12
1961			3	0		0	0	0	18
1962			2	0		0	0	0	12
1963			6	0		0	0	0	36
1964			5	0		0	0	0	30
1965			4	0		0	0	0	24
1967			4	0		0	0	0	24
1968			6	0		0	0	0	36
1969			4	0		0	0	0	24
Career			40	0		0	0	0	240
Playoffs			5	0		0	0	0	30

Brian Dowling

Year	Team		TD	1XP	2XP	FG	FGA	SAF	Pts
1972	NE	N	3	0		0	0	0	18

Michael Downs

Year	Team		TD	1XP	2XP	FG	FGA	SAF	Pts
1982	DAL	N	1	0		0	0	0	6
1983			1	0		0	0	0	6
1984			1	0		0	0	0	6
Career			3	0		0	0	0	18

Eddie Doyle

Year	Team		TD	1XP	2XP	FG	FGA	SAF	Pts
1924	FRA	N	2	0		0		0	12
1925	POT	N	1	0		0		0	6
Career			3	0		0		0	18

Ted Doyle

Year	Team		TD	1XP	2XP	FG	FGA	SAF	Pts
1945	PIT	N	1	0		0	0	0	6

D.J. Dozier

Year	Team		TD	1XP	2XP	FG	FGA	SAF	Pts
1987	MIN	N	7	0		0	0	0	42
1988			2	0		0	0	0	12
Career			9	0		0	0	0	54
Playoffs			1	0		0	0	0	6

Johnny Drake

Year	Team		TD	1XP	2XP	FG	FGA	SAF	Pts
1937	**CLE**	**N**	5	0		0		0	30
1938			1	0		0	0	0	6
1939			9	0		0	0	0	54
1940			**9**	2		0	1	0	56
1941			3	0		0	0	0	18
Career			27	2		0	1	0	164

Troy Drayton

Year	Team		TD	1XP	2XP	FG	FGA	SAF	Pts
1993	**LARM**	**N**	4	0		0	0	0	24
1994			6	0	0	0	0	0	36
1995	**STL**	**N**	4	0	0	0	0	0	24
1996	**MIA**	**N**	0	0	1	0	0	0	2
Career			14	0	1	0	0	0	86

Chuck Drazenovich

Year	Team		TD	1XP	2XP	FG	FGA	SAF	Pts
1950	**WAS**	**N**	1	0		0	0	0	6
1951			3	0		0	0	0	18
1952			3	0		0	0	0	18
1953			1	0		0	0	0	6
Career			8	0		0	0	0	48

Fred Dreher

Year	Team		TD	1XP	2XP	FG	FGA	SAF	Pts
1938	**CHIB**	**N**	1	0		0	0	0	6

Chris Dressel

Year	Team		TD	1XP	2XP	FG	FGA	SAF	Pts
1983	**HOU**	**N**	4	0		0	0	0	24
1984			2	0		0	0	0	12
1985			1	0		0	0	0	6
1989	**KC**	**N**	1	0		0	0	0	6
Career			8	0		0	0	0	48

Chuck Dressen

Year	Team		TD	1XP	2XP	FG	FGA	SAF	Pts
1922	**RAC**	**N**	2	0		0		0	12

Doug Dressler

Year	Team		TD	1XP	2XP	FG	FGA	SAF	Pts
1971	**CIN**	**N**	1	0		0	0	0	6
1972			7	0		0	0	0	42
1974			2	0		0	0	0	12
1975	**KC**	**N**	1	0		0	0	0	6
Career			11	0		0	0	0	66

Willie Drewrey

Year	Team		TD	1XP	2XP	FG	FGA	SAF	Pts
1988	**HOU**	**N**	1	0		0	0	0	6
1989	**TB**	**N**	1	0		0	0	0	6
1990			1	0		0	0	0	6
1991			2	0		0	0	0	12
1992			2	0		0	0	0	12
Career			7	0		0	0	0	42
Playoffs			1	0		0	0	0	6

Ted Drews

Year	Team		TD	1XP	2XP	FG	FGA	SAF	Pts
1926	**BKN**	**A**	0	0		0		0	0
1928	**CHIB**	**N**	0	1		0		0	1
Career			0	1		0		0	1

Wally Dreyer

Year	Team		TD	1XP	2XP	FG	FGA	SAF	Pts
1950	**GB**	**N**	1	0		0	0	0	6

Paddy Driscoll

Year	Team		TD	1XP	2XP	FG	FGA	SAF	Pts
1920	**CHIC**	**A**	2	4		0		0	16
1921			3	4		1		0	25
1922	**CHIC**	**N**	2	5		**8**		0	41
1923			7	6		10		0	78
1924			2	7		7		0	40
1925			4	10		**11**		0	67
1926	**CHIB**	**N**	6	14		**12**		0	**86**
1927			5	7		2		0	43
1928			2	9		0		0	21
1929			1	3		0		0	9
Career			34	69		51		0	426

Robert Drummond

Year	Team		TD	1XP	2XP	FG	FGA	SAF	Pts
1989	**PHI**	**N**	1	0		0	0	0	6
1990			1	0		0	0	0	6
1991			2	0		0	0	0	12
Career			4	0		0	0	0	24

Hoot Drury

Year	Team		TD	1XP	2XP	FG	FGA	SAF	Pts
1931	**CHIB**	**N**	1	0		0		0	6

Fred Dryer

Year	Team		TD	1XP	2XP	FG	FGA	SAF	Pts
1973	**LA**	**N**	0	0		0	0	2	4
1975			1	0		0	0	0	6
Career			1	0		0	0	2	10

Ron Drzewiecki

Year	Team		TD	1XP	2XP	FG	FGA	SAF	Pts
1955	**CHIB**	**N**	1	0		0	0	0	6

Elbert Dubenion

Year	Team		TD	1XP	2XP	FG	FGA	SAF	Pts
1960	**BUF**	**A**	8	0	0	0	0	0	48
1961			8	0	0	0	0	0	48
1962			6	0	0	0	0	0	36
1963			4	0	0	0	0	0	24
1964			10	0	0	0	0	0	60
1965			1	0	0	0	0	0	6
1966			2	0	0	0	0	0	12
Career			39	0	0	0	0	0	234
Playoffs			2	0	0	0	0	0	12

Tom Dublinski

Year	Team		TD	1XP	2XP	FG	FGA	SAF	Pts
1954	**DET**	**N**	1	0		0	0	0	6

Doug DuBose

Year	Team		TD	1XP	2XP	FG	FGA	SAF	Pts
1988	**SF**	**N**	2	0		0	0	0	12

Jimmy DuBose

Year	Team		TD	1XP	2XP	FG	FGA	SAF	Pts
1978	**TB**	**N**	4	0		0	0	0	24

Kenny Duckett

Year	Team		TD	1XP	2XP	FG	FGA	SAF	Pts
1982	**NO**	**N**	2	0		0	0	0	12
1983			2	0		0	0	0	12
Career			4	0		0	0	0	24

Bobby Duckworth

Year	Team		TD	1XP	2XP	FG	FGA	SAF	Pts
1983	**SD**	**N**	5	0		0	0	0	30
1984			4	0		0	0	0	24
1985	**LARM**	**N**	3	0		0	0	0	18
1986			1	0		0	0	0	6
Career			13	0		0	0	0	78

Joe Duckworth

Year	Team		TD	1XP	2XP	FG	FGA	SAF	Pts
1947	**WAS**	**N**	3	0		0	0	0	18

Joe Dudek

Year	Team		TD	1XP	2XP	FG	FGA	SAF	Pts
1987	**DEN**	**N**	2	0		0	0	0	12

Andy Dudish

Year	Team		TD	1XP	2XP	FG	FGA	SAF	Pts
1947	**BAL**	**AA**	2	0		0	0	0	12

Bill Dudley

Year	Team		TD	1XP	2XP	FG	FGA	SAF	Pts
1942	**PIT**	**N**	6	0		0	0	0	36
1945			3	2		0	0	0	20
1946			5	12		2	7	0	48
1947	**DET**	**N**	11	0		0	0	0	66
1948			7	0		0	0	0	42
1949			6	30		5	14	0	81
1950	**WAS**	**N**	3	31		5	10	0	64
1951			3	21		10	13	0	69
1953			0	25		11	22	0	58
Career			44	121		33	66	0	484

Paul Dudley

Year	Team		TD	1XP	2XP	FG	FGA	SAF	Pts
1962	**NYG**	**N**	1	0		0	0	0	6

Rickey Dudley

Year	Team		TD	1XP	2XP	FG	FGA	SAF	Pts
1996	**OAK**	**N**	4	0	0	0	0	0	24

Dave Duerson

Year	Team		TD	1XP	2XP	FG	FGA	SAF	Pts
1990	**NYG**	**N**	1	0		0	0	0	6

Joe Dufek

Year	Team		TD	1XP	2XP	FG	FGA	SAF	Pts
1984	**BUF**	**N**	1	0		0	0	0	6

Pat Duffy

Year	Team		TD	1XP	2XP	FG	FGA	SAF	Pts
1929	**DAY**	**N**	0	1		0		0	1

Fred Dugan

Year	Team		TD	1XP	2XP	FG	FGA	SAF	Pts
1960	**DAL**	**N**	1	0		0	0	0	6
1961	**WAS**	**N**	4	0		0	0	0	24
1962			5	0		0	0	0	30
1963			3	0		0	0	0	18
Career			13	0		0	0	0	78

Jack Dugger

Year	Team		TD	1XP	2XP	FG	FGA	SAF	Pts
1946	**BUF**	**AA**	1	0		0	0	0	6

Paul Duhart

Year	Team		TD	1XP	2XP	FG	FGA	SAF	Pts
1944	**GB**	**N**	4	0		0	0	0	24
1945	**PIT**	**N**	1	0		0	0	0	6
Career			5	0		0	0	0	30

A.J. Duhe

Year	Team		TD	1XP	2XP	FG	FGA	SAF	Pts
1978	**MIA**	**N**	0	0		0	0	1	2
Playoffs			1	0	0	0	0	0	6

Bobby Duhon

Year	Team		TD	1XP	2XP	FG	FGA	SAF	Pts
1968	**NYG**	**N**	4	0		0	0	0	24
1970			1	0		0	0	0	6
1971			1	0		0	0	0	6
Career			6	0		0	0	0	36

Mike Dumas

Year	Team		TD	1XP	2XP	FG	FGA	SAF	Pts
1991	**HOU**	**N**	1	0		0	0	0	6

Billy DuMoe

Year	Team		TD	1XP	2XP	FG	FGA	SAF	Pts
1921	**GB**	**A**	2	0		0		0	12

Jim Dunaway

Year	Team		TD	1XP	2XP	FG	FGA	SAF	Pts
1966	**BUF**	**A**	1	0	0	0	0	0	6

Jubilee Dunbar

Year	Team		TD	1XP	2XP	FG	FGA	SAF	Pts
1973	**NO**	**N**	4	0		0	0	0	24

Vaughn Dunbar

Year	Team		TD	1XP	2XP	FG	FGA	SAF	Pts
1992	**NO**	**N**	3	0		0	0	0	18
1995	**JAC**	**N**	2	0	0	0	0	0	12
Career			5	0	0	0	0	0	30

Brian Duncan

Year	Team		TD	1XP	2XP	FG	FGA	SAF	Pts
1976	**CLE**	**N**	1	0		0	0	0	6
1977			1	0		0	0	0	6
Career			2	0		0	0	0	12

Clyde Duncan

Year	Team		TD	1XP	2XP	FG	FGA	SAF	Pts
1985	**STL**	**N**	1	0		0	0	0	6

Curtis Duncan

Year	Team		TD	1XP	2XP	FG	FGA	SAF	Pts
1987	**HOU**	**N**	5	0		0	0	0	30
1988			1	0		0	0	0	6
1989			5	0		0	0	0	30
1990			1	0		0	0	0	6
1991			4	0		0	0	0	24
1992			1	0		0	0	0	6
1993			3	0		0	0	0	18
Career			20	0		0	0	0	120
Playoffs			2	0		0	0	0	12

Jim Duncan

Year	Team		TD	1XP	2XP	FG	FGA	SAF	Pts
1969	**BAL**	**N**	1	0		0	0	0	6
1970			1	0		0	0	0	6
Career			2	0		0	0	0	12

Rick Duncan

Year	Team		TD	1XP	2XP	FG	FGA	SAF	Pts
1967	**DEN**	**A**	0	3	0	2	5	0	9

Speedy Duncan

Year	Team		TD	1XP	2XP	FG	FGA	SAF	Pts
1965	**SD**	**A**	2	0	0	0	0	0	12
1966			1	0	0	0	0	0	6
1967			3	0	0	0	0	0	18
1968			1	0	0	0	0	0	6
1969			1	0	0	0	0	0	6
1971	**WAS**	**N**	1	0		0	0	0	6
Career			9	0	0	0	0	0	54

David Dunn

Year	Team		TD	1XP	2XP	FG	FGA	SAF	Pts
1995	**CIN**	**N**	1	0	0	0	0	0	6
1996			2	0	0	0	0	0	12
Career			3	0	0	0	0	0	18

Jason Dunn

Year	Team		TD	1XP	2XP	FG	FGA	SAF	Pts
1996	**PHI**	**N**	2	0	0	0	0	0	12

Perry Lee Dunn

Year	Team		TD	1XP	2XP	FG	FGA	SAF	Pts
1964	**DAL**	**N**	1	0		0	0	0	6
1965			3	0		0	0	0	18
1968	**ATL**	**N**	3	0		0	0	0	18
Career			7	0		0	0	0	42

Red Dunn

Year	Team		TD	1XP	2XP	FG	FGA	SAF	Pts
1924	**MIL**	**N**	2	14		7		0	47
1925	**CHIC**	**N**	3	8		0		0	26
1926			0	3		4		0	15
1927	**GB**	**N**	1	7		0		0	13
1928			0	1		0		0	1
1929			0	11		1		0	14
1930			0	**14**		0		0	14

Year	Team		TD	1XP	2XP	FG	FGA	SAF	Pts

Red Dunn *continued*

Year	Team		TD	1XP	2XP	FG	FGA	SAF	Pts
1931			0	**15**	0		0	0	15
Career			6	73	12		0		145

Pat Dunsmore

| 1984 | CHI | N | 1 | 0 | | 0 | 0 | 0 | 6 |
| Playoffs | | | 1 | 0 | 0 | 0 | 0 | 0 | 6 |

Bill Dunstan

| 1974 | PHI | N | 1 | 0 | | 0 | 0 | 0 | 6 |

Elwyn Dunstan

| 1941 | CLE | N | 1 | 0 | | 0 | 0 | 0 | 6 |

Reggie Dupard

1987	NE	N	3	0		0	0	0	18
1988			2	0		0	0	0	12
1989			1	0		0	0	0	6
Career			6	0		0	0	0	36

Mark Duper

1983	MIA	N	10	0		0	0	0	60
1984			8	0		0	0	0	48
1985			3	0		0	0	0	18
1986			11	0		0	0	0	66
1987			8	0		0	0	0	48
1988			1	0		0	0	0	6
1989			1	0		0	0	0	6
1990			5	0		0	0	0	30
1991			5	0		0	0	0	30
1992			7	0		0	0	0	42
Career			59	0		0	0	0	354
Playoffs			5	0		0	0	0	30

L.G. Dupre

1955	BAL	N	1	0		0	0	0	6
1956			4	0		0	0	0	24
1957			4	0		0	0	0	24
1958			3	0		0	0	0	18
1959			1	0		0	0	0	6
1960	DAL	N	5	0		0	0	0	30
Career			18	0		0	0	0	108

Billy Joe Dupree

1973	DAL	N	5	0		0	0	0	30
1974			4	0		0	0	0	24
1975			1	0		0	0	0	6
1976			2	0		0	0	0	12
1977			3	0		0	0	0	18
1978			9	0		0	0	0	54
1979			5	0		0	0	0	30
1980			7	0		0	0	0	42
1981			2	0		0	0	0	12
1982			3	0		0	0	0	18
1983			1	0		0	0	0	6
Career			42	0		0	0	0	252
Playoffs			4	0		0	0	0	24

Marcus Dupree

| 1991 | LARM | N | 1 | 0 | | 0 | 0 | 0 | 6 |

Don Durdan

| 1946 | SF | AA | 1 | 0 | | 0 | 0 | 0 | 6 |

Charlie Durkee

1967	NO	N	0	27		14	32	0	69
1968			0	27		19	**37**	0	84
1971			0	24		16	23	0	72
1972			0	9		3	9	0	18
Career			0	87		52	101	0	243

John Durko

| 1944 | PHI | N | 1 | 0 | | 0 | 0 | | 6 |

Mark Dusbabek

| 1990 | MIN | N | 0 | 0 | | 0 | 0 | 1 | 2 |

Brad Dusek

1975	WAS	N	1	0		0	0	0	6
1976			1	0		0	0	0	6
1978			1	0		0	0	0	6
Career			3	0		0	0	0	18

Bill Dutton

| 1946 | PIT | N | 2 | 0 | | 0 | 0 | 0 | 12 |

John Dutton

1980	DAL	N	1	0		0	0	0	6
1981			0	0		0	0	1	2
1984			0	0		0	0	1	2
Career			1	0		0	0	2	10

Ben Dvorak

| 1921 | MIN | A | 2 | 0 | | 0 | | 0 | 12 |

Jack Dwyer

1952	LA	N	2	0		0	0	0	12
1953			1	0		0	0	0	6
1954			1	0		0	0	0	6
Career			4	0		0	0	0	24

Mike Dyal

| 1989 | LARI | N | 2 | 0 | | 0 | 0 | 0 | 12 |

Les Dye

1944	WAS	N	2	0		0	0	0	12
1945			2	0		0	0	0	12
Career			4	0		0	0	0	24

Henry Dyer

1968	LA	N	1	0		0	0	0	6
1969	WAS	N	1	0		0	0	0	6
Career			2	0		0	0	0	12

Ken Dyer

| 1968 | SD | A | 1 | 0 | | 0 | 0 | 0 | 6 |

Hart Lee Dykes

1989	NE	N	5	0		0	0	0	30
1990			2	0		0	0	0	12
Career			7	0		0	0	0	42

Eagle Feather

| 1922 | OOR | N | 1 | 0 | | 0 | | 0 | 6 |

Larry Eaglin

| 1973 | HOU | N | 1 | 0 | | 0 | 0 | 0 | 6 |

Kay Eakin

| 1941 | NYG | N | 1 | 0 | | 0 | 1 | 0 | 6 |

Ralph Earhart

1948	GB	N	3	0		0	0	0	18
1949			1	0		0	0	0	6
Career			4	0		0	0	0	24

Robin Earl

1977	CHI	N	1	0		0	0	0	6
1980			3	0		0	0	0	18
1981			1	0		0	0	0	6
Career			5	0		0	0	0	30

Quinn Early

1988	SD	N	4	0		0	0	0	24
1990			1	0		0	0	0	6
1991	NO	N	2	0		0	0	0	12
1992			5	0		0	0	0	30
1993			6	0		0	0	0	36
1994			4	0	0	0	0	0	24
1995			8	0	0	0	0	0	48
1996	BUF	N	4	0	1	0	0	0	26
Career			34	0	1	0	0	0	206
Playoffs			1	0	0	0	0	0	6

Jug Earps

| 1923 | GB | N | 0 | 0 | | 0 | 0 | | 0 |

Kenny Easley

1981	SEA	N	1	0		0	0	0	6
1984			2	0		0	0	0	12
Career			3	0		0	0	0	18

Walt Easley

| 1981 | SF | N | 1 | 0 | | 0 | 0 | 0 | 6 |

Tony Eason

| 1984 | NE | N | 5 | 0 | | 0 | 0 | 0 | 30 |

Tony Eason *continued*

| 1985 | | | 1 | 0 | | 0 | 0 | 0 | 6 |
| Career | | | 6 | 0 | | 0 | 0 | 0 | 36 |

Ron East

| 1975 | CLE | N | 0 | 0 | | 0 | 0 | 1 | 2 |

Scott Eaton

| 1969 | NYG | N | 1 | 0 | | 0 | 0 | 0 | 6 |

Harry Ebding

1932	POR	N	1	0		0	0	0	6
1934	DET	N	2	0		0	0	0	12
1935			1	0		0	0	0	6
1936			4	0		0	0	0	24
1937			3	0		0	0	0	18
Career			11	0		0	0	0	66

Rick Eber

| 1969 | SD | A | 1 | 0 | | 0 | 0 | 0 | 6 |

Ray Ebli

1946	BUF	AA	1	0		0	0	0	6
1947	CHI	AA	1	0		0	0	0	6
Career			2	0		0	0	0	12

Byron Eby

| 1930 | POR | N | 1 | 0 | | 0 | | 0 | 6 |

Ox Eckhardt

| 1928 | NYG | N | 3 | 1 | | 0 | | 0 | 19 |

Jerry Eckwood

1979	TB	N	2	0		0	0	0	12
1980			3	0		0	0	0	18
1981			2	0		0	0	0	12
Career			7	0		0	0	0	42

Nick Eddy

1969	DET	N	3	0		0	0	0	18
1970			1	0		0	0	0	6
1972			1	0		0	0	0	6
Career			5	0		0	0	0	30

Booker Edgerson

1968	BUF	A	2	0		0	0	0	12
1969			1	0		0	0	0	6
Career			3	0	0	0	0	0	18

Bob Edler

| 1923 | CLE | N | 1 | 0 | | 0 | | 0 | 6 |

Bobby Joe Edmonds

| 1986 | SEA | N | 1 | 0 | | 0 | 0 | 0 | 6 |

Ferrell Edmunds

1988	MIA	N	3	0		0	0	0	18
1989			3	0		0	0	0	18
1990			1	0		0	0	0	6
1991			2	0		0	0	0	12
1992			1	0		0	0	0	6
1993	SEA	N	2	0		0	0	0	12
Career			12	0		0	0	0	72

Al Edwards

| 1991 | BUF | N | 2 | 0 | | 0 | 0 | 0 | 12 |

Anthony Edwards

1992	PHX	N	1	0		0	0	0	6
1993			1	0		0	0	0	6
1995	ARI	N	2	0	0	0	0	0	12
1996			1	0		0	0	0	6
Career			5	0	0	0	0	0	30

Antonio Edwards

1993	SEA	N	0	0		0	0	1	2
1995			1	0		0	0	0	6
Career			1	0	0	0	0	1	8

Brad Edwards

1988	MIN	N	1	0		0	0	0	6
1992	WAS	N	1	0		0	0	0	6
Career			2	0		0	0	0	12

Bud Edwards

Year	Team		TD	1XP	2XP	FG	FGA	SAF	Pts
1930	**PRO**	**N**	1	0		0		0	6

Cid Edwards

Year	Team		TD	1XP	2XP	FG	FGA	SAF	Pts
1968	**STL**	**N**	1	0		0	0	0	6
1969			3	0		0	0	0	18
1970			2	0		0	0	0	12
1971			4	0		0	0	0	24
1972	**SD**	**N**	7	0		0	0	0	42
1973			1	0		0	0	0	6
1975	**CHI**	**N**	1	0		0	0	0	6
Career			19	0		0	0	0	114

Danny Edwards

Year	Team		TD	1XP	2XP	FG	FGA	SAF	Pts
1949	**CHI**	**AA**	4	0		0	0	0	24
1950	**NYY**	**N**	6	0		0	0	0	36
1951			3	0		0	0	0	18
1953	**BAL**	**N**	3	0		0	0	0	18
1954			1	0		0	0	0	6
Career			17	0		0	0	0	102

Dave Edwards

Year	Team		TD	1XP	2XP	FG	FGA	SAF	Pts
1967	**DAL**	**N**	1	0		0	0	0	6

Dave Edwards

Year	Team		TD	1XP	2XP	FG	FGA	SAF	Pts
1986	**PIT**	**N**	0	0		0	0	1	2

Dixon Edwards

Year	Team		TD	1XP	2XP	FG	FGA	SAF	Pts
1991	**DAL**	**N**	1	0		0	0	0	6

Eddie Edwards

Year	Team		TD	1XP	2XP	FG	FGA	SAF	Pts
1986	**CIN**	**N**	1	0		0	0	0	6

Glen Edwards

Year	Team		TD	1XP	2XP	FG	FGA	SAF	Pts
1973	**PIT**	**N**	1	0		0	0	0	6
1974			1	0		0	0	0	6
1980	**SD**	**N**	1	0		0	0	0	6
Career			3	0		0	0	0	18

Herman Edwards

Year	Team		TD	1XP	2XP	FG	FGA	SAF	Pts
1978	**PHI**	**N**	1	0		0	0	0	6
1985			1	0		0	0	0	6
Career			2	0		0	0	0	12

Kelvin Edwards

Year	Team		TD	1XP	2XP	FG	FGA	SAF	Pts
1987	**DAL**	**N**	4	0		0	0	0	24

Stan Edwards

Year	Team		TD	1XP	2XP	FG	FGA	SAF	Pts
1983	**HOU**	**N**	1	0		0	0	0	6
1984			1	0		0	0	0	6
1985			1	0		0	0	0	6
Career			3	0		0	0	0	18

Turk Edwards

Year	Team		TD	1XP	2XP	FG	FGA	SAF	Pts
1932	**BOS**	**N**	1	0		0		0	6
1937	**WAS**	**N**	0	0		0		1	2
1938			1	0		0	0	0	6
1939			0	0		0	0	0	0
Career			2	0		0	0	1	14

Ron Egloff

Year	Team		TD	1XP	2XP	FG	FGA	SAF	Pts
1978	**DEN**	**N**	1	0		0	0	0	6
1981			1	0		0	0	0	6
1983			2	0		0	0	0	12
Career			4	0		0	0	0	24

Patrick Egu

Year	Team		TD	1XP	2XP	FG	FGA	SAF	Pts
1989	**NE**	**N**	1	0		0	0	0	6

Mike Eischeid

Year	Team		TD	1XP	2XP	FG	FGA	SAF	Pts
1966	**OAK**	**A**	0	37	0	11	26	0	70

Alfred Eissler

Year	Team		TD	1XP	2XP	FG	FGA	SAF	Pts
1920	**CHIT**	**A**	1	0		0		0	6

Carl Ekern

Year	Team		TD	1XP	2XP	FG	FGA	SAF	Pts
1985	**LARM**	**N**	1	0		0	0	0	6

Cleveland Elam

Year	Team		TD	1XP	2XP	FG	FGA	SAF	Pts
1976	**SF**	**N**	1	0		0	0	0	6

Jason Elam

Year	Team		TD	1XP	2XP	FG	FGA	SAF	Pts
1993	**DEN**	**N**	0	41		26	35	0	119
1994			0	29	0	30	37	0	119
1995			0	39	0	31	38	0	132

Jason Elam *continued*

Year	Team		TD	1XP	2XP	FG	FGA	SAF	Pts
1996			0	46	0	21	28	0	109
Career			0	155	0	108	138	0	479
Playoffs			0	4	0	1	1	0	7

Monroe Eley

Year	Team		TD	1XP	2XP	FG	FGA	SAF	Pts
1977	**ATL**	**N**	1	0		0	0	0	6

Don Eliason

Year	Team		TD	1XP	2XP	FG	FGA	SAF	Pts
1946	**BOS**	**N**	0	0		0	0	0	0

Chief Elkins

Year	Team		TD	1XP	2XP	FG	FGA	SAF	Pts
1928	**FRA**	**N**	2	1		0		0	13
1929	**CHIC**	**N**	0	0		1		0	3
Career			2	1		1		0	16

Larry Elkins

Year	Team		TD	1XP	2XP	FG	FGA	SAF	Pts
1966	**HOU**	**A**	3	0	0	0	0	0	18

Henry Ellard

Year	Team		TD	1XP	2XP	FG	FGA	SAF	Pts
1983	**LARM**	**N**	1	0		0	0	0	6
1984			8	0		0	0	0	48
1985			6	0		0	0	0	36
1986			4	0		0	0	0	24
1987			3	0		0	0	0	18
1988			10	0		0	0	0	60
1989			8	0		0	0	0	48
1990			4	0		0	0	0	24
1991			3	0		0	0	0	18
1992			3	0		0	0	0	18
1993			2	0		0	0	0	12
1994	**WAS**	**N**	6	0	0	0	0	0	36
1995			5	0	0	0	0	0	30
1996			2	0	0	0	0	0	12
Career			65	0	0	0	0	0	390
Playoffs			1	0	0	0	0	0	6

Carl Eller

Year	Team		TD	1XP	2XP	FG	FGA	SAF	Pts
1964	**MIN**	**N**	1	0		0	0	0	6
1965			0	0		0	0	1	2
1977			0	0		0	0	1	2
Career			1	0		0	0	2	10
Playoffs			0	0		0	0	1	2

Gary Ellerson

Year	Team		TD	1XP	2XP	FG	FGA	SAF	Pts
1985	**GB**	**N**	2	0		0	0	0	12
1986			3	0		0	0	0	18
1987	**DET**	**N**	4	0		0	0	0	24
Career			9	0		0	0	0	54

Al Elliott

Year	Team		TD	1XP	2XP	FG	FGA	SAF	Pts
1922	**RAC**	**N**	2	0		0		0	12
1923			2	0		0		0	12
1924			1	0		0		0	6
Career			5	0		0		0	30

Carl Elliott

Year	Team		TD	1XP	2XP	FG	FGA	SAF	Pts
1951	**GB**	**N**	5	0		0	0	0	36
1952			1	0		0	0	0	6
1953			1	0		0	0	0	6
Career			7	0		0	0	0	48

Doc Elliott

Year	Team		TD	1XP	2XP	FG	FGA	SAF	Pts
1922	**CAN**	**N**	2	0		0		0	12
1923			6	0		0		0	36
1924	**CLE**	**N**	6	1		1		0	40
1925			2	5		3		0	26
1926	**CLE**	**A**	0	4		2		0	10
1931	**CLE**	**N**	1	0		0		0	6
Career			17	10		6		0	130

John Elliott

Year	Team		TD	1XP	2XP	FG	FGA	SAF	Pts
1970	**NYJ**	**N**	0	0		0	0	1	2

Lenvil Elliott

Year	Team		TD	1XP	2XP	FG	FGA	SAF	Pts
1973	**CIN**	**N**	2	0		0	0	0	12
1974			2	0		0	0	0	12
1975			4	0		0	0	0	24
1976			3	0		0	0	0	18
1977			1	0		0	0	0	6
1979	**SF**	**N**	3	0		0	0	0	18
1980			3	0		0	0	0	18
Career			18	0		0	0	0	108
Playoffs			1	0		0	0	0	6

Lin Elliott

Year	Team		TD	1XP	2XP	FG	FGA	SAF	Pts
1992	**DAL**	**N**	0	47		24	35	0	119
1993			0	2		2	4	0	8
1994	**KC**	**N**	0	30	0	25	30	0	105
1995			0	34	0	24	30	0	106
Career			0	113	0	75	99	0	338
Playoffs			0	17	0	5	9	0	32

Allan Ellis

Year	Team		TD	1XP	2XP	FG	FGA	SAF	Pts
1976	**CHI**	**N**	1	0		0	0	0	6

Craig Ellis

Year	Team		TD	1XP	2XP	FG	FGA	SAF	Pts
1987	**LARI**	**N**	2	0		0	0	0	12

Gerry Ellis

Year	Team		TD	1XP	2XP	FG	FGA	SAF	Pts
1980	**GB**	**N**	8	0		0	0	0	48
1981			7	0		0	0	0	42
1982			1	0		0	0	0	6
1983			6	0		0	0	0	36
1984			6	0		0	0	0	36
1985			5	0		0	0	0	30
1986			2	0		0	0	0	12
Career			35	0		0	0	0	210
Playoffs			1	0		0	0	0	6

Ken Ellis

Year	Team		TD	1XP	2XP	FG	FGA	SAF	Pts
1971	**GB**	**N**	1	0		0	0	0	6
1972			2	0		0	0	0	12
1973			1	0		0	0	0	6
1974			1	0		0	0	0	6
Career			5	0		0	0	0	30

Ray Ellis

Year	Team		TD	1XP	2XP	FG	FGA	SAF	Pts
1987	**CLE**	**N**	1	0		0	0	0	6

Jerry Ellison

Year	Team		TD	1XP	2XP	FG	FGA	SAF	Pts
1995	**TB**	**N**	5	0	0	0	0	0	30

Willie Ellison

Year	Team		TD	1XP	2XP	FG	FGA	SAF	Pts
1968	**LA**	**N**	7	0		0	0	0	42
1969			2	0		0	0	0	12
1970			7	0		0	0	0	42
1971			4	0		0	0	0	24
1972			6	0		0	0	0	36
1973	**KC**	**N**	2	0		0	0	0	12
1974			2	0		0	0	0	12
Career			30	0		0	0	0	180

Bud Ellor

Year	Team		TD	1XP	2XP	FG	FGA	SAF	Pts
1930	**NEW**	**N**	1	0		0		0	6

Swede Ellstrom

Year	Team		TD	1XP	2XP	FG	FGA	SAF	Pts
1934	**PHI**	**N**	1	0		0		0	6

Dave Elmendorf

Year	Team		TD	1XP	2XP	FG	FGA	SAF	Pts
1974	**LA**	**N**	2	0		0	0	0	12

Neil Elshire

Year	Team		TD	1XP	2XP	FG	FGA	SAF	Pts
1985	**MIN**	**N**	0	0		0	0	1	2

Leo Elter

Year	Team		TD	1XP	2XP	FG	FGA	SAF	Pts
1955	**WAS**	**N**	4	0		0	0	0	24
1956			2	0		0	0	0	12
1957			3	0		0	0	0	18
1958	**PIT**	**N**	2	0		0	0	0	12
Career			11	0		0	0	0	66

John Elway

Year	Team		TD	1XP	2XP	FG	FGA	SAF	Pts
1983	**DEN**	**N**	1	0		0	0	0	6
1984			1	0		0	0	0	6
1986			2	0		0	0	0	12
1987			4	0		0	0	0	24
1988			1	0		0	0	0	6
1989			3	0		0	0	0	18
1990			3	0		0	0	0	18
1991			6	0		0	0	0	36
1992			2	0		0	0	0	12
1994			4	0	0	0	0	0	24
1995			1	0	1	0	0	0	8
1996			4	0	0	0	0	0	24
Career			32	0	1	0	0	0	194
Playoffs			4	0	0	0	0	0	24

Bert Emanuel

Year	Team		TD	1XP	2XP	FG	FGA	SAF	Pts
1994	**ATL**	**N**	4	0	0	0	0	0	24

Bert Emanuel *continued*

Year	Team		TD	1XP	2XP	FG	FGA	SAF	Pts
1995			5	0	0	0	0	0	30
1996			6	0	0	0	0	0	36
Career			15	0	0	0	0	0	90

Frank Emanuel

Year	Team		TD	1XP	2XP	FG	FGA	SAF	Pts
1968	**MIA**	**A**	1	0	0	0	0	0	6

John Embree

Year	Team		TD	1XP	2XP	FG	FGA	SAF	Pts
1969	**DEN**	**A**	5	0	0	0	0	0	30

Mel Embree

Year	Team		TD	1XP	2XP	FG	FGA	SAF	Pts
1953	**BAL**	**N**	1	0		0	0	0	6

Frank Emmons

Year	Team		TD	1XP	2XP	FG	FGA	SAF	Pts
1940	**PHI**	**N**	2	0		0	0	0	12

Steve Emtman

Year	Team		TD	1XP	2XP	FG	FGA	SAF	Pts
1992	**IND**	**N**	1	0		0	0	0	6

Tiny Engebretsen

Year	Team		TD	1XP	2XP	FG	FGA	SAF	Pts
1932	**CHIB**	**N**	0	**10**		1		0	13
1933	**PIT**	**N**	0	0		1		0	3
1935	**GB**	**N**	0	1		0		0	1
1936			0	2		5		0	17
1937			0	5		1		0	8
1938			0	9		2	2	0	15
1939			0	**18**		4	8	0	30
1940			0	8		1	5	0	11
1941			0	0		1	3	0	3
Career			0	53		16	18	0	101
Playoffs			0	5		2	2	0	11

Wuert Engelmann

Year	Team		TD	1XP	2XP	FG	FGA	SAF	Pts
1930	**GB**	**N**	3	0		0		0	18
1931			4	0		0		0	24
1932			1	0		0		0	6
1933			2	0		0		0	12
Career			10	0		0		0	60

Doug English

Year	Team		TD	1XP	2XP	FG	FGA	SAF	Pts
1977	**DET**	**N**	0	0		0	0	1	2
1979			0	0		0	0	1	2
1983			0	0		0	0	2	4
Career			0	0		0	0	**4**	8

Bobby Engram

Year	Team		TD	1XP	2XP	FG	FGA	SAF	Pts
1996	**CHI**	**N**	6	0	0	0	0	0	36

Hunter Enis

Year	Team		TD	1XP	2XP	FG	FGA	SAF	Pts
1960	**DAL**	**A**	3	0	0	0	0	0	18
1961	**SD**	**A**	2	0	0	0	0	0	12
Career			5	0	0	0	0	0	30

Fred Enke

Year	Team		TD	1XP	2XP	FG	FGA	SAF	Pts
1949	**DET**	**N**	1	0		0	0	0	6

Rex Enright

Year	Team		TD	1XP	2XP	FG	FGA	SAF	Pts
1926	**GB**	**N**	1	0		0		0	6
1927			4	0		0		0	24
Career			5	0		0		0	30

Bill Enyart

Year	Team		TD	1XP	2XP	FG	FGA	SAF	Pts
1969	**BUF**	**A**	3	0	0	0	0	0	18
1970	**BUF**	**N**	1	0		0	0	0	6
Career			4	0	0	0	0	0	24

Bobby Epps

Year	Team		TD	1XP	2XP	FG	FGA	SAF	Pts
1955	**NYG**	**N**	2	0		0	0	0	12

Phillip Epps

Year	Team		TD	1XP	2XP	FG	FGA	SAF	Pts
1982	**GB**	**N**	2	0		0	0	0	12
1983			1	0		0	0	0	6
1984			3	0		0	0	0	18
1985			4	0		0	0	0	24
1986			4	0		0	0	0	24
1987			2	0		0	0	0	12
Career			16	0		0	0	0	96

Dick Erdlitz

Year	Team		TD	1XP	2XP	FG	FGA	SAF	Pts
1942	**PHI**	**N**	1	8		0	0	0	14
1946	**MIA**	**AA**	1	22		2	7	0	34
Career			2	30		2	7	0	48

Rich Erenberg

Year	Team		TD	1XP	2XP	FG	FGA	SAF	Pts
1984	**PIT**	**N**	3	0		0	0	0	18
1985			3	0		0	0	0	18
1986			4	0		0	0	0	24
Career			10	0		0	0	0	60
Playoffs			1	0		0	0	0	6

Craig Erickson

Year	Team		TD	1XP	2XP	FG	FGA	SAF	Pts
1994	**TB**	**N**	1	0	0	0	0	0	6

Hal Erickson

Year	Team		TD	1XP	2XP	FG	FGA	SAF	Pts
1923	**MIL**	**N**	1	0		0		0	6
1924			3	0		0		0	18
1925	**CHIC**	**N**	6	0		0		0	36
1926			1	0		0		0	6
1928			1	0		0		0	6
1929	**MIN**	**N**	0	1		1		0	4
Career			12	1		1		0	76

Tom Erlandson

Year	Team		TD	1XP	2XP	FG	FGA	SAF	Pts
1966	**MIA**	**A**	1	0	0	0	0	0	6

Jack Ernst

Year	Team		TD	1XP	2XP	FG	FGA	SAF	Pts
1925	**POT**	**N**	3	0		0		0	18
1926			1	0		0		0	6
1927			0	0		0		0	0
1928			2	0		0		0	12
1929	**BOS**	**N**	0	1		0		0	1
1930	**FRA**	**N**	1	0		0		0	6
Career			7	1		0		0	43

Ricky Ervins

Year	Team		TD	1XP	2XP	FG	FGA	SAF	Pts
1991	**WAS**	**N**	4	0		0	0	0	24
1992			2	0		0	0	0	12
1994			4	0	0	0	0	0	24
Career			10	0	0	0	0	0	60
Playoffs			1	0	0	0	0	0	6

Russell Erxleben

Year	Team		TD	1XP	2XP	FG	FGA	SAF	Pts
1979	**NO**	**N**	0	4		2	2	0	10
1980			0	2		2	5	0	8
1982			0	1		0	1	0	1
Career			0	7		4	8	0	19

Len Eshmont

Year	Team		TD	1XP	2XP	FG	FGA	SAF	Pts
1946	**SF**	**AA**	9	0		0	0	0	54
1947			2	0		0	0	0	12
1948			2	0		0	0	0	12
1949			2	0		0	0	0	12
Career			15	0		0	0	0	90

Boomer Esiason

Year	Team		TD	1XP	2XP	FG	FGA	SAF	Pts
1984	**CIN**	**N**	2	0		0	0	0	12
1985			1	0		0	0	0	6
1986			1	0		0	0	0	6
1988			1	0		0	0	0	6
1993	**NYJ**	**N**	1	0		0	0	0	6
1996	**ARI**	**N**	1	0	1	0	0	0	8
Career			7	0	1	0	0	0	44
Playoffs			1	0	0	0	0	0	6

Mike Esposito

Year	Team		TD	1XP	2XP	FG	FGA	SAF	Pts
1976	**ATL**	**N**	2	0		0	0	0	12

Ron Essink

Year	Team		TD	1XP	2XP	FG	FGA	SAF	Pts
1980	**SEA**	**N**	1	0		0	0	0	6

Carl Etelman

Year	Team		TD	1XP	2XP	FG	FGA	SAF	Pts
1926	**BOS**	**A**	0	0		1		0	3

Joe Ethridge

Year	Team		TD	1XP	2XP	FG	FGA	SAF	Pts
1949	**GB**	**N**	0	1		1	2	0	4

Bob Etter

Year	Team		TD	1XP	2XP	FG	FGA	SAF	Pts
1968	**ATL**	**N**	0	17		11	21	0	50
1969			0	33		15	30	0	78
Career			0	50		26	51	0	128

Bobby Evans

Year	Team		TD	1XP	2XP	FG	FGA	SAF	Pts
1965	**HOU**	**A**	1	0	0	0	0	0	6

Byron Evans

Year	Team		TD	1XP	2XP	FG	FGA	SAF	Pts
1990	**PHI**	**N**	1	0		0	0	0	6
1993			1	0		0	0	0	6
Career			2	0		0	0	0	12

Charlie Evans

Year	Team		TD	1XP	2XP	FG	FGA	SAF	Pts
1971	**NYG**	**N**	5	0		0	0	0	30
1972			5	0		0	0	0	30
1973			1	0		0	0	0	6
1974	**WAS**	**N**	2	0		0	0	0	12
Career			13	0		0	0	0	78

Chuck Evans

Year	Team		TD	1XP	2XP	FG	FGA	SAF	Pts
1995	**MIN**	**N**	2	0	0	0	0	0	12

Doug Evans

Year	Team		TD	1XP	2XP	FG	FGA	SAF	Pts
1996	**GB**	**N**	1	0	0	0	0	0	6

Earl Evans

Year	Team		TD	1XP	2XP	FG	FGA	SAF	Pts
1925	**CHIC**	**N**	1	0		0		0	6

Fred Evans

Year	Team		TD	1XP	2XP	FG	FGA	SAF	Pts
1947	**BUF-CHI**	**AA**	2	0		0	0	0	12
1948	**CHIB**	**N**	2	0		0	0	0	12
Career			4	0		0	0	0	24

Jerry Evans

Year	Team		TD	1XP	2XP	FG	FGA	SAF	Pts
1994	**DEN**	**N**	2	0	0	0	0	0	12
1995			1	0	0	0	0	0	6
Career			3	0	0	0	0	0	18

Ray Evans

Year	Team		TD	1XP	2XP	FG	FGA	SAF	Pts
1948	**PIT**	**N**	2	0		0	0	0	12

Reggie Evans

Year	Team		TD	1XP	2XP	FG	FGA	SAF	Pts
1983	**WAS**	**N**	4	0		0	0	0	24

Vince Evans

Year	Team		TD	1XP	2XP	FG	FGA	SAF	Pts
1979	**CHI**	**N**	1	0		0	0	0	6
1980			8	0		0	0	0	48
1981			3	0		0	0	0	18
1983			1	0		0	0	0	6
1987	**LARI**	**N**	1	0		0	0	0	6
Career			14	0		0	0	0	84

Eric Everett

Year	Team		TD	1XP	2XP	FG	FGA	SAF	Pts
1989	**PHI**	**N**	1	0		0	0	0	6

Jim Everett

Year	Team		TD	1XP	2XP	FG	FGA	SAF	Pts
1986	**LARM**	**N**	1	0		0	0	0	6
1987			1	0		0	0	0	6
1989			1	0		0	0	0	6
1990			1	0		0	0	0	6
Career			4	0		0	0	0	24

Nuu Faaola

Year	Team		TD	1XP	2XP	FG	FGA	SAF	Pts
1987	**NYJ**	**N**	2	0		0	0	0	12

Eric Fairs

Year	Team		TD	1XP	2XP	FG	FGA	SAF	Pts
1988	**HOU**	**N**	0	0		0	0	1	2

Derrick Faison

Year	Team		TD	1XP	2XP	FG	FGA	SAF	Pts
1990	**LARM**	**N**	1	0		0	0	0	6

Earl Faison

Year	Team		TD	1XP	2XP	FG	FGA	SAF	Pts
1963	**SD**	**A**	0	0	1	0	0	0	2
1964			1	0	0	0	0	0	6
1965			1	0	0	0	0	0	6
Career			2	0	1	0	0	0	14

Guil Falcon

Year	Team		TD	1XP	2XP	FG	FGA	SAF	Pts
1921	**CAN**	**A**	3	0		0		0	18
1922	**TOL**	**N**	1	0		0		0	6
1924	**HAM**	**N**	2	0		0		0	12
Career			6	0		0		0	36

Tony Falkenstein

Year	Team		TD	1XP	2XP	FG	FGA	SAF	Pts
1943	**GB**	**N**	1	0		0	0	0	6

Gary Famiglietti

Year	Team		TD	1XP	2XP	FG	FGA	SAF	Pts
1939	**CHIB**	**N**	0	1		0	0	0	1
1940			4	0		0	0	0	24
1941			1	0		0	0	0	6
1942			7	0		0	0	0	42
1943			2	0		0	0	0	12
1944			3	0		0	0	0	18
1945			3	0		0	0	0	18
1946	**BOS**	**N**	4	0		0	1	0	24
Career			24	1		0	1	0	145
Playoffs			1	0		0	0	0	6

Mike Fanning

Year	Team		TD	1XP	2XP	FG	FGA	SAF	Pts
1983	DET	N	0	0		0	0	1	2

Chris Farasopoulas

Year	Team		TD	1XP	2XP	FG	FGA	SAF	Pts
1972	NYJ	N	1	0		0	0	0	6

Andy Farkas

Year	Team		TD	1XP	2XP	FG	FGA	SAF	Pts
1938	WAS	N	6	1		0	0	0	37
1939			**11**	2		0	1	0	**68**
1941			3	0		0	0	0	18
1942			6	3		0	0	0	39
1943			9	0		0	0	0	54
1945	DET	N	2	0		0	0	0	12
Career			37	6		0	1	0	228
Playoffs			6	0		0	0	0	36

George Farmer

Year	Team		TD	1XP	2XP	FG	FGA	SAF	Pts
1970	CHI	N	2	0		0	0	0	12
1971			5	0		0	0	0	30
1972			2	0		0	0	0	12
1973			1	0		0	0	0	6
Career			10	0		0	0	0	60

George Farmer

Year	Team		TD	1XP	2XP	FG	FGA	SAF	Pts
1982	LARM	N	2	0		0	0	0	12
1983			5	0		0	0	0	30
Career			7	0		0	0	0	42
Playoffs			1	0		0	0	0	6

Tom Farmer

Year	Team		TD	1XP	2XP	FG	FGA	SAF	Pts
1946	LA	N	1	0		0	0	0	6
1947	WAS	N	1	0		0	0	0	6
1948			3	0		0	0	0	18
Career			5	0		0	0	0	30

John Farquhar

Year	Team		TD	1XP	2XP	FG	FGA	SAF	Pts
Playoffs			0	0	1	0	0	0	2

Mel Farr

Year	Team		TD	1XP	2XP	FG	FGA	SAF	Pts
1967	DET	N	6	0		0	0	0	36
1968			7	0		0	0	0	42
1969			4	0		0	0	0	24
1970			11	0		0	0	0	66
1971			1	0		0	0	0	6
1972			3	0		0	0	0	18
1973			4	0		0	0	0	24
Career			36	0		0	0	0	216

Mike Farr

Year	Team		TD	1XP	2XP	FG	FGA	SAF	Pts
1991	DET	N	1	0		0	0	0	6

Miller Farr

Year	Team		TD	1XP	2XP	FG	FGA	SAF	Pts
1967	HOU	A	3	0	0	0	0	0	18
1968			2	0	0	0	0	0	12
1970	STL	N	1	0		0	0	0	6
Career			6	0	0	0	0	0	36

Scrapper Farrell

Year	Team		TD	1XP	2XP	FG	FGA	SAF	Pts
1938	BKN	N	3	0		0		0	18

Bo Farrington

Year	Team		TD	1XP	2XP	FG	FGA	SAF	Pts
1961	CHI	N	4	0		0	0	0	24
1962			1	0		0	0	0	6
1963			2	0		0	0	0	12
Career			7	0		0	0	0	42

Marshall Faulk

Year	Team		TD	1XP	2XP	FG	FGA	SAF	Pts
1994	IND	N	12	0	0	0	0	0	72
1995			14	0	0	0	0	0	84
1996			7	0	0	0	0	0	42
Career			33	0	0	0	0	0	198

Mike Faulkerson

Year	Team		TD	1XP	2XP	FG	FGA	SAF	Pts
1996	CHI	N	1	0	0	0	0	0	6

Christian Fauria

Year	Team		TD	1XP	2XP	FG	FGA	SAF	Pts
1995	SEA	N	1	0	0	0	0	0	6
1996			1	0	0	0	0	0	6
Career			2	0	0	0	0	0	12

Frank Fausch

Year	Team		TD	1XP	2XP	FG	FGA	SAF	Pts
1921	EVA	A	3	0		0		0	18
1922	EVA	N	0	0		0		0	0
Career			3	0		0		0	18

George Faust

Year	Team		TD	1XP	2XP	FG	FGA	SAF	Pts
1939	CHIC	N	0	1		0	1	0	1

Brett Favre

Year	Team		TD	1XP	2XP	FG	FGA	SAF	Pts
1992	GB	N	1	0		0	0	0	6
1993			1	0		0	0	0	6
1994			2	0	0	0	0	0	12
1995			3	0	0	0	0	0	18
1996			2	0	0	0	0	0	12
Career			9	0	0	0	0	0	54
Playoffs			1	0	0	0	0	0	6

Ricky Feacher

Year	Team		TD	1XP	2XP	FG	FGA	SAF	Pts
1979	CLE	N	1	0		0	0	0	6
1980			4	0		0	0	0	24
1981			3	0		0	0	0	18
1982			3	0		0	0	0	18
1983			3	0		0	0	0	18
1984			1	0		0	0	0	6
Career			15	0		0	0	0	90
Playoffs			1	0		0	0	0	6

Tom Feamster

Year	Team		TD	1XP	2XP	FG	FGA	SAF	Pts
1956	BAL	N	0	24		0	3	0	24

Tom Fears

Year	Team		TD	1XP	2XP	FG	FGA	SAF	Pts
1948	LA	N	5	0		0	0	0	30
1949			9	0		0	0	0	54
1950			7	0		0	0	0	42
1951			3	6		0	0	0	24
1952			6	0		0	0	0	36
1953			4	5		1	1	0	32
1954			3	1		0	0	0	19
1955			2	0		0	3	0	12
Career			39	12		1	4	0	249
Playoffs			5	0		0	0	0	30

Tiny Feather

Year	Team		TD	1XP	2XP	FG	FGA	SAF	Pts
1928	DET	N	7	0		0		0	42
1929	NYG	N	3	0		0		0	18
1930			1	0		0		0	6
1931			0	0		0		0	0
Career			11	0		0		0	66

Beattie Feathers

Year	Team		TD	1XP	2XP	FG	FGA	SAF	Pts
1934	CHIB	N	**9**	0		0		0	54
1935			3	0		0		0	18
1936			2	0		0		0	12
1937			1	0		0		0	6
1938	BKN	N	2	0		0	0	0	12
Career			17	0		0	0	0	102

Al Feeney

Year	Team		TD	1XP	2XP	FG	FGA	SAF	Pts
1920	CAN	A	0	8		1		0	11
1921			0	7		0		0	7
Career			0	15		1		0	18

Gene Fekete

Year	Team		TD	1XP	2XP	FG	FGA	SAF	Pts
1946	CLE	AA	1	0		0	0	0	6

Gene Felker

Year	Team		TD	1XP	2XP	FG	FGA	SAF	Pts
1952	DAL	N	1	0		0	0	0	6

Happy Feller

Year	Team		TD	1XP	2XP	FG	FGA	SAF	Pts
1971	PHI	N	0	10		6	20	0	28
1972	NO	N	0	10		6	11	0	28
1973			0	7		4	12	0	19
Career			0	27		16	43	0	75

Ron Fellows

Year	Team		TD	1XP	2XP	FG	FGA	SAF	Pts
1983	DAL	N	2	0		0	0	0	12
1986			1	0		0	0	0	6
Career			3	0		0	0	0	18

Dick Felt

Year	Team		TD	1XP	2XP	FG	FGA	SAF	Pts
1961	NY	A	1	0	0	0	0	0	6

Ralph Felton

Year	Team		TD	1XP	2XP	FG	FGA	SAF	Pts
1954	WAS	N	0	16		1	2	0	19

Bobby Felts

Year	Team		TD	1XP	2XP	FG	FGA	SAF	Pts
1966	DET	N	2	0		0	0	0	12

Gary Fencik

Year	Team		TD	1XP	2XP	FG	FGA	SAF	Pts
1981	CHI	N	1	0		0	0	0	6

Chuck Fenenbock

Year	Team		TD	1XP	2XP	FG	FGA	SAF	Pts
1943	DET	N	1	0		0	0	0	6
1945			2	0		0	0	0	12
1946	LA	AA	4	0		0	0	0	24
1947			6	0		0	0	0	36
1948	CHI	AA	1	0		0	0	0	6
Career			14	0		0	0	0	84

Gill Fenerty

Year	Team		TD	1XP	2XP	FG	FGA	SAF	Pts
1990	NO	N	2	0		0	0	0	12
1991			5	0		0	0	0	30
Career			7	0		0	0	0	42

Bob Fenimore

Year	Team		TD	1XP	2XP	FG	FGA	SAF	Pts
1947	CHIB	N	3	0		0	0	0	18

Carl Fennema

Year	Team		TD	1XP	2XP	FG	FGA	SAF	Pts
1948	NYG	N	1	0		0	0	0	6

Derrick Fenner

Year	Team		TD	1XP	2XP	FG	FGA	SAF	Pts
1989	SEA	N	1	0		0	0	0	6
1990			15	0		0	0	0	90
1991			4	0		0	0	0	24
1992	CIN	N	8	0		0	0	0	48
1993			1	0		0	0	0	6
1994			2	0	0	0	0	0	12
1995	OAK	N	3	0	0	0	0	0	18
1996			8	0	0	0	0	0	48
Career			42	0	0	0	0	0	252

Lee Fenner

Year	Team		TD	1XP	2XP	FG	FGA	SAF	Pts
1922	DAY	N	0	0		1		0	3
1924			1	0		0		0	6
Career			1	0		1		0	9

Rick Fenney

Year	Team		TD	1XP	2XP	FG	FGA	SAF	Pts
1987	MIN	N	2	0		0	0	0	12
1988			3	0		0	0	0	18
1989			6	0		0	0	0	36
1990			2	0		0	0	0	12
Career			13	0		0	0	0	78
Playoffs			1	0		0	0	0	6

Duke Fergersen

Year	Team		TD	1XP	2XP	FG	FGA	SAF	Pts
1977	SEA	N	2	0		0	0	0	12

Bob Ferguson

Year	Team		TD	1XP	2XP	FG	FGA	SAF	Pts
1963	PIT	N	1	0		0	0	0	6

Charley Ferguson

Year	Team		TD	1XP	2XP	FG	FGA	SAF	Pts
1961	CLE	N	1	0		0	0	0	6
1962	MIN	N	6	0		0	0	0	36
1963	BUF	A	3	0	0	0	0	0	18
1965			2	0	0	0	0	0	12
1966			1	0	0	0	0	0	6
Career			13	0	0	0	0	0	78

Howie Ferguson

Year	Team		TD	1XP	2XP	FG	FGA	SAF	Pts
1955	GB	N	4	0		0	0	0	24
1957			2	0		0	0	0	12
1958			1	0		0	0	0	6
1960	LA	A	6	0	0	0	0	0	36
Career			13	0	0	0	0	0	78

Joe Ferguson

Year	Team		TD	1XP	2XP	FG	FGA	SAF	Pts
1973	BUF	N	2	0		0	0	0	12
1974			2	0		0	0	0	12
1975			1	0		0	0	0	6
1977			2	0		0	0	0	12
1979			1	0		0	0	0	6
1981			1	0		0	0	0	6
1982			2	0		0	0	0	12
1985	DET	N	1	0		0	0	0	6
Career			12	0		0	0	0	72

Vagas Ferguson

Year	Team		TD	1XP	2XP	FG	FGA	SAF	Pts
1980	NE	N	2	0		0	0	0	12
1981			3	0		0	0	0	18
Career			5	0		0	0	0	30

Ron Fernandes

Year	Team		TD	1XP	2XP	FG	FGA	SAF	Pts
1976	BAL	N	0	0		0	0	1	2

Mervyn Fernandez

Year	Team		TD	1XP	2XP	FG	FGA	SAF	Pts
1988	LARI	N	4	0		0	0	0	24
1989			9	0		0	0	0	54
1990			5	0		0	0	0	30
1991			1	0		0	0	0	6
Career			19	0		0	0	0	114
Playoffs			1	0		0	0	0	6

Vince Ferragamo

Year	Team		TD	1XP	2XP	FG	FGA	SAF	Pts
1980	LA	N	1	0		0	0	0	6
1982	LARM	N	1	0		0	0	0	6
1985	BUF	N	1	0		0	0	0	6
Career			3	0		0	0	0	18

Jack Ferrante

Year	Team		TD	1XP	2XP	FG	FGA	SAF	Pts
1944	PHI	N	1	0		0	0	0	6
1945			7	0		0	0	0	42
1946			4	0		0	0	0	24
1947			4	0		0	0	0	24
1948			7	0		0	0	0	42
1949			5	0		0	0	0	30
1950			3	0		0	0	0	18
Career			31	0		0	0	0	186
Playoffs			1	0		0	0	0	6

Bobby Ferrell

Year	Team		TD	1XP	2XP	FG	FGA	SAF	Pts
1976	SF	N	1	0		0	0	0	6
1977			1	0		0	0	0	6
1978			1	0		0	0	0	6
Career			3	0		0	0	0	18

Earl Ferrell

Year	Team		TD	1XP	2XP	FG	FGA	SAF	Pts
1983	STL	N	1	0		0	0	0	6
1984			2	0		0	0	0	12
1985			4	0		0	0	0	24
1986			3	0		0	0	0	18
1987			7	0		0	0	0	42
1988	PHX	N	9	0		0	0	0	54
1989			6	0		0	0	0	36
Career			32	0		0	0	0	192

Neil Ferris

Year	Team		TD	1XP	2XP	FG	FGA	SAF	Pts
1952	WAS	N	1	0		0	0	0	6

Lou Ferry

Year	Team		TD	1XP	2XP	FG	FGA	SAF	Pts
1952	PIT	N	1	0		0	0	0	6
1953			0	0		0	0	1	2
Career			1	0		0	0	1	8

Gus Fetz

Year	Team		TD	1XP	2XP	FG	FGA	SAF	Pts
1923	CHIB	N	1	0		0		0	6

Ross Fichtner

Year	Team		TD	1XP	2XP	FG	FGA	SAF	Pts
1963	CLE	N	1	0		0	0	0	6
1965			1	0		0	0	0	6
1966			1	0		0	0	0	6
Career			3	0		0	0	0	18

Jitter Fields

Year	Team		TD	1XP	2XP	FG	FGA	SAF	Pts
1987	KC	N	1	0		0	0	0	6

Frank Filchock

Year	Team		TD	1XP	2XP	FG	FGA	SAF	Pts
1938	WAS	N	1	0		0	0	0	6
1939			1	0		0	0	0	6
1940			2	0		0	0	0	12
1941			2	0		0	0	0	12
1946	NYG	N	2	0		0	0	0	12
Career			8	0		0	0	0	48

Jim Files

Year	Team		TD	1XP	2XP	FG	FGA	SAF	Pts
1970	NYG	N	0	0		0	0	1	2
1972			1	0		0	0	0	6
Career			1	0		0	0	1	8

Steve Filipowicz

Year	Team		TD	1XP	2XP	FG	FGA	SAF	Pts
1945	NYG	N	2	0		0	0	0	12
1946			3	0		0	0	0	18
Career			5	0		0	0	0	30
Playoffs			1	0		0	0	0	6

Gene Filipski

Year	Team		TD	1XP	2XP	FG	FGA	SAF	Pts
1956	NYG	N	1	0		0	0	0	6

John Fina

Year	Team		TD	1XP	2XP	FG	FGA	SAF	Pts
1992	BUF	N	1	0		0	0	0	6

Jim Finks

Year	Team		TD	1XP	2XP	FG	FGA	SAF	Pts
1949	PIT	N	2	0		0	0	0	12
1951			1	0		0	0	0	6
1952			5	0		0	0	0	30
1953			2	0		0	0	0	12
1955			4	0		0	0	0	24
Career			14	0		0	0	0	84

Jack Finn

Year	Team		TD	1XP	2XP	FG	FGA	SAF	Pts
1924	FRA	N	2	2		2		0	20

Tom Finnin

Year	Team		TD	1XP	2XP	FG	FGA	SAF	Pts
1954	BAL	N	0	0		0	0	1	2

Clete Fischer

Year	Team		TD	1XP	2XP	FG	FGA	SAF	Pts
1949	NYG	N	1	0		0	0	0	6

Pat Fischer

Year	Team		TD	1XP	2XP	FG	FGA	SAF	Pts
1964	STL	N	3	0		0	0	0	18
1967			1	0		0	0	0	6
1971	WAS	N	1	0		0	0	0	6
Career			5	0		0	0	0	30

Joe Fishback

Year	Team		TD	1XP	2XP	FG	FGA	SAF	Pts
1991	ATL	N	1	0		0	0	0	6

Dick Fishel

Year	Team		TD	1XP	2XP	FG	FGA	SAF	Pts
1933	BKN	N	1	0		0		0	6

Bob Fisher

Year	Team		TD	1XP	2XP	FG	FGA	SAF	Pts
1980	CHI	N	2	0		0	0	0	12

Jeff Fisher

Year	Team		TD	1XP	2XP	FG	FGA	SAF	Pts
1981	CHI	N	1	0		0	0	0	6

Alex Fishman

Year	Team		TD	1XP	2XP	FG	FGA	SAF	Pts
1921	EVA	A	1	0		0		0	6

Bill Fisk

Year	Team		TD	1XP	2XP	FG	FGA	SAF	Pts
1941	DET	N	2	0		0	0	0	12
1946	SF	AA	1	0		0	0	0	6
Career			3	0		0	0	0	18

Fitzgerald

Year	Team		TD	1XP	2XP	FG	FGA	SAF	Pts
1920	DET	A	1	0		0		0	6

Paul Fitzgibbons

Year	Team		TD	1XP	2XP	FG	FGA	SAF	Pts
1926	DUL	N	1	0		0		0	6
1930	GB	N	3	0		0		0	18
1931			0	1		0		0	1
Career			4	1		0		0	25

Bob Fitzke

Year	Team		TD	1XP	2XP	FG	FGA	SAF	Pts
1925	FRA	N	1	0		0		0	6

Scott Fitzkee

Year	Team		TD	1XP	2XP	FG	FGA	SAF	Pts
1979	PHI	N	1	0		0	0	0	6
1980			2	0		0	0	0	12
1982	SD	N	1	0		0	0	0	6
Career			4	0		0	0	0	24

Terrence Flagler

Year	Team		TD	1XP	2XP	FG	FGA	SAF	Pts
1989	SF	N	1	0		0	0	0	6
1990	PHX	N	2	0		0	0	0	12
Career			3	0		0	0	0	18

Dick Flaherty

Year	Team		TD	1XP	2XP	FG	FGA	SAF	Pts
1926	GB	N	2	0		0		0	12

Pat Flaherty

Year	Team		TD	1XP	2XP	FG	FGA	SAF	Pts
1926	BKN	A	1	0		0		0	6

Ray Flaherty

Year	Team		TD	1XP	2XP	FG	FGA	SAF	Pts
1927	NYY	N	4	0		0		0	24
1928			1	0		0		0	6
1929	NYG	N	8	1		0		0	49
1931			2	0		0		0	12
1932			5	0		0		0	30

Ray Flaherty *continued*

Year	Team		TD	1XP	2XP	FG	FGA	SAF	Pts
1934			1	0		0		0	6
Career			21	1		0		0	127

Hoot Flanagan

Year	Team		TD	1XP	2XP	FG	FGA	SAF	Pts
1925	POT	N	7	0		0		0	42

Jim Flanigan

Year	Team		TD	1XP	2XP	FG	FGA	SAF	Pts
1995	CHI	N	2	0	0	0	0	0	12
1996			1	0	0	0	0	0	6
Career			3	0	0	0	0	0	18
Playoffs			1	0	0	0	0	0	6

Paul Flatley

Year	Team		TD	1XP	2XP	FG	FGA	SAF	Pts
1963	MIN	N	4	0		0	0	0	24
1964			3	0		0	0	0	18
1965			7	0		0	0	0	42
1966			3	0		0	0	0	18
1969	ATL	N	6	0		0	0	0	36
1970			1	0		0	0	0	6
Career			24	0		0	0	0	144

Jack Flavin

Year	Team		TD	1XP	2XP	FG	FGA	SAF	Pts
1923	BUF	N	2	0		0		0	12

Bill Fleckenstein

Year	Team		TD	1XP	2XP	FG	FGA	SAF	Pts
1928	CHIB	N	1	0		0		0	6

George Fleming

Year	Team		TD	1XP	2XP	FG	FGA	SAF	Pts
1961	OAK	A	1	24	0	11	26	0	63

Marv Fleming

Year	Team		TD	1XP	2XP	FG	FGA	SAF	Pts
1963	GB	N	2	0		0	0	0	12
1965			2	0		0	0	0	12
1966			2	0		0	0	0	12
1967			1	0		0	0	0	6
1968			3	0		0	0	0	18
1969			2	0		0	0	0	12
1971	MIA	N	2	0		0	0	0	12
1972			1	0		0	0	0	6
1974			1	0		0	0	0	6
Career			16	0		0	0	0	96
Playoffs			1	0		0	0	0	6

Mack Flenniken

Year	Team		TD	1XP	2XP	FG	FGA	SAF	Pts
1930	CHIC	N	3	0		0		0	18
1931	NYG	N	1	0		0		0	6
Career			4	0		0		0	24

Chris Fletcher

Year	Team		TD	1XP	2XP	FG	FGA	SAF	Pts
1971	SD	N	1	0		0	0	0	6

Simon Fletcher

Year	Team		TD	1XP	2XP	FG	FGA	SAF	Pts
1990	DEN	N	0	0		0	0	1	2

Terrell Fletcher

Year	Team		TD	1XP	2XP	FG	FGA	SAF	Pts
1995	SD	N	1	0	0	0	0	0	6
1996			2	0	0	0	0	0	12
Career			3	0	0	0	0	0	18

Tom Flick

Year	Team		TD	1XP	2XP	FG	FGA	SAF	Pts
1986	SD	N	1	0		0	0	0	6

Mike Flores

Year	Team		TD	1XP	2XP	FG	FGA	SAF	Pts
1993	PHI	N	0	0		0	0	1	2

Tom Flores

Year	Team		TD	1XP	2XP	FG	FGA	SAF	Pts
1960	OAK	A	3	0	0	0	0	0	18
1961			1	0	0	0	0	0	6
1966			1	0	0	0	0	0	6
Career			5	0	0	0	0	0	30

Charlie Flowers

Year	Team		TD	1XP	2XP	FG	FGA	SAF	Pts
1960	LA	A	2	0	0	0	0	0	12
1961	SD	A	3	0	0	0	0	0	18
Career			5	0	0	0	0	0	30

Keith Flowers

Year	Team		TD	1XP	2XP	FG	FGA	SAF	Pts
1952	DAL	N	0	3		0	0	0	3

Kenny Flowers

Year	Team		TD	1XP	2XP	FG	FGA	SAF	Pts
1989	ATL	N	1	0		0	0	0	6

Bobby Jack Floyd

Year	Team		TD	1XP	2XP	FG	FGA	SAF	Pts
1952	GB	N	1	0		0	0	0	6

Don Floyd

Year	Team		TD	1XP	2XP	FG	FGA	SAF	Pts
1962	HOU	A	1	0	0	0	0	0	6
1964			1	0	0	0	0	0	6
Career			2	0	0	0	0	0	12

John Floyd

Year	Team		TD	1XP	2XP	FG	FGA	SAF	Pts
1979	SD	N	1	0		0	0	0	6
1980			1	0		0	0	0	6
Career			2	0		0	0	0	12

Malcolm Floyd

Year	Team		TD	1XP	2XP	FG	FGA	SAF	Pts
1996	HOU	N	1	0	0	0	0	0	6

William Floyd

Year	Team		TD	1XP	2XP	FG	FGA	SAF	Pts
1994	SF	N	6	0	0	0	0	0	36
1995			3	0	0	0	0	0	18
1996			3	0	0	0	0	0	18
Career			12	0	0	0	0	0	72
Playoffs			5	0	0	0	0	0	30

Darren Flutie

Year	Team		TD	1XP	2XP	FG	FGA	SAF	Pts
1988	SD	N	2	0		0	0	0	12

Doug Flutie

Year	Team		TD	1XP	2XP	FG	FGA	SAF	Pts
1986	CHI	N	1	0		0	0	0	6
1988	NE	N	1	0		0	0	0	6
Career			2	0		0	0	0	12

Don Flynn

Year	Team		TD	1XP	2XP	FG	FGA	SAF	Pts
1960	DAL	A	1	0	0	0	1	0	6

Tom Flynn

Year	Team		TD	1XP	2XP	FG	FGA	SAF	Pts
1986	NYG	N	1	0		0	0	0	6
1987			1	0		0	0	0	6
1988			1	0		0	0	0	6
Career			3	0		0	0	0	18

Hank Foldberg

Year	Team		TD	1XP	2XP	FG	FGA	SAF	Pts
1948	BKN	AA	1	0		0	0	0	6

Steve Foley

Year	Team		TD	1XP	2XP	FG	FGA	SAF	Pts
1984	DEN	N	2	0		0	0	0	12

Tim Foley

Year	Team		TD	1XP	2XP	FG	FGA	SAF	Pts
1973	MIA	N	2	0		0	0	0	12
1974			0	0		0	0	1	2
Career			2	0		0	0	1	14

Lee Folkins

Year	Team		TD	1XP	2XP	FG	FGA	SAF	Pts
1962	DAL	N	6	0		0	0	0	36
1963			4	0		0	0	0	24
1965	PIT	N	1	0		0	0	0	6
Career			11	0		0	0	0	66

Steve Folsom

Year	Team		TD	1XP	2XP	FG	FGA	SAF	Pts
1988	DAL	N	2	0		0	0	0	12
1989			2	0		0	0	0	12
Career			4	0		0	0	0	24

Art Folz

Year	Team		TD	1XP	2XP	FG	FGA	SAF	Pts
1923	CHIC	N	1	1		0		0	7
1925			4	0		0		0	24
Career			5	1		0		0	31

Al Fontenot

Year	Team		TD	1XP	2XP	FG	FGA	SAF	Pts
1995	CHI	N	0	0	0	0	0	1	2

Herman Fontenot

Year	Team		TD	1XP	2XP	FG	FGA	SAF	Pts
1986	CLE	N	2	0		0	0	0	12
1988			2	0		0	0	0	12
1989	GB	N	4	0		0	0	0	24
1990			1	0		0	0	0	6
Career			9	0		0	0	0	54
Playoffs			2	0		0	0	0	12

Wayne Fontes

Year	Team		TD	1XP	2XP	FG	FGA	SAF	Pts
1962	NY	A	1	0	0	0	0	0	6

Adrian Ford

Year	Team		TD	1XP	2XP	FG	FGA	SAF	Pts
1926	PHI	A	3	0		0		0	18

Adrian Ford *continued*

Year	Team		TD	1XP	2XP	FG	FGA	SAF	Pts
1927	FRA	N	2	0		0		0	12
Career			5	0		0		0	30

Bernard Ford

Year	Team		TD	1XP	2XP	FG	FGA	SAF	Pts
1989	DAL	N	1	0		0	0	0	6
1990	HOU	N	1	0		0	0	0	6
Career			2	0		0	0	0	12

Cole Ford

Year	Team		TD	1XP	2XP	FG	FGA	SAF	Pts
1995	OAK	N	0	17	0	8	9	0	41
1996			0	36	0	24	31	0	108
Career			0	53	0	32	40	0	149

Fred Ford

Year	Team		TD	1XP	2XP	FG	FGA	SAF	Pts
1960	LA	A	2	0	0	0	0	0	12

Garrett Ford

Year	Team		TD	1XP	2XP	FG	FGA	SAF	Pts
1968	DEN	A	1	0	0	0	0	0	6

Henry Ford

Year	Team		TD	1XP	2XP	FG	FGA	SAF	Pts
1956	PIT	N	2	0		0	0	0	12

Jim Ford

Year	Team		TD	1XP	2XP	FG	FGA	SAF	Pts
1971	NO	N	2	0		0	0	0	12

Len Ford

Year	Team		TD	1XP	2XP	FG	FGA	SAF	Pts
1948	LA	AA	7	0		0	0	0	42
1949			1	0		0	0	0	6
1952	CLE	N	1	0		0	0	0	6
1954			0	0		0	0	1	2
Career			9	0		0	0	1	56

Brian Forde

Year	Team		TD	1XP	2XP	FG	FGA	SAF	Pts
1989	NO	N	0	0		0	0	1	2

Jim Fordham

Year	Team		TD	1XP	2XP	FG	FGA	SAF	Pts
1944	CHIB	N	4	0		0	0	0	24
1945			1	0		0	0	0	6
Career			5	0		0	0	0	30

Chuck Foreman

Year	Team		TD	1XP	2XP	FG	FGA	SAF	Pts
1973	MIN	N	6	0		0	0	0	36
1974			**15**	0		0	0	0	90
1975			22	0		0	0	0	132
1976			**14**	0		0	0	0	84
1977			9	0		0	0	0	54
1978			7	0		0	0	0	42
1979			2	0		0	0	0	12
1980	NE	N	1	0		0	0	0	6
Career			76	0		0	0	0	456
Playoffs			7	0		0	0	0	42

Bill Forester

Year	Team		TD	1XP	2XP	FG	FGA	SAF	Pts
1959	GB	N	0	0		0	0	1	2

Fred Forsberg

Year	Team		TD	1XP	2XP	FG	FGA	SAF	Pts
1971	DEN	N	1	0		0	0	0	6

Bob Forte

Year	Team		TD	1XP	2XP	FG	FGA	SAF	Pts
1947	GB	N	3	0		0	0	0	18
1948			1	0		0	0	0	6
Career			4	0		0	0	0	24

Ike Forte

Year	Team		TD	1XP	2XP	FG	FGA	SAF	Pts
1976	NE	N	2	0		0	0	0	12
1977			2	0		0	0	0	12
1979	WAS	N	1	0		0	0	0	6
1980			2	0		0	0	0	12
Career			7	0		0	0	0	42

Danny Fortmann

Year	Team		TD	1XP	2XP	FG	FGA	SAF	Pts
1942	CHIB	N	1	0		0	0	0	6

Joe Fortunato

Year	Team		TD	1XP	2XP	FG	FGA	SAF	Pts
1956	CHIB	N	1	0		0	0	0	6
1957			1	0		0	0	0	6
1966	CHI	N	1	0		0	0	0	6
Career			3	0		0	0	0	18

Bill Fortune

Year	Team		TD	1XP	2XP	FG	FGA	SAF	Pts
1924	HAM	N	0	0		0		0	0

Barry Foster

Year	Team		TD	1XP	2XP	FG	FGA	SAF	Pts
1990	PIT	N	1	0		0	0	0	6
1991			2	0		0	0	0	12
1992			11	0		0	0	0	66
1993			9	0		0	0	0	54
1994			5	0	0	0	0	0	30
Career			28	0	0	0	0	0	168

Bob Foster

Year	Team		TD	1XP	2XP	FG	FGA	SAF	Pts
1922	RAC	N	3	0		0		0	18

Geno Foster

Year	Team		TD	1XP	2XP	FG	FGA	SAF	Pts
1965	SD	A	2	0	0	0	0	0	12
1966			3	0	0	0	0	0	18
1968			1	0	0	0	0	0	6
1969			1	0	0	0	0	0	6
Career			7	0	0	0	0	0	42

Roy Foster

Year	Team		TD	1XP	2XP	FG	FGA	SAF	Pts
Playoffs			1	0	0	0	0	0	6

Wally Foster

Year	Team		TD	1XP	2XP	FG	FGA	SAF	Pts
1925	BUF	N	0	1		0		0	1

Will Foster

Year	Team		TD	1XP	2XP	FG	FGA	SAF	Pts
1973	NE	N	1	0		0	0	0	6

John Fourcade

Year	Team		TD	1XP	2XP	FG	FGA	SAF	Pts
1989	NO	N	1	0		0	0	0	6
1990			1	0		0	0	0	6
Career			2	0		0	0	0	12

Dan Fouts

Year	Team		TD	1XP	2XP	FG	FGA	SAF	Pts
1974	SD	N	1	0		0	0	0	6
1975			2	0		0	0	0	12
1978			2	0		0	0	0	12
1979			2	0		0	0	0	12
1980			2	0		0	0	0	12
1982			1	0		0	0	0	6
1983			1	0		0	0	0	6
1987			2	0		0	0	0	12
Career			13	0		0	0	0	78

Willmer Fowler

Year	Team		TD	1XP	2XP	FG	FGA	SAF	Pts
1960	BUF	A	1	0	0	0	0	0	6

Chas Fox

Year	Team		TD	1XP	2XP	FG	FGA	SAF	Pts
1986	STL	N	1	0		0	0	0	6

Sam Fox

Year	Team		TD	1XP	2XP	FG	FGA	SAF	Pts
1945	NYG	N	2	0		0	0	0	12

Tim Fox

Year	Team		TD	1XP	2XP	FG	FGA	SAF	Pts
1978	NE	N	0	0		0	0	1	2

Dick Frahm

Year	Team		TD	1XP	2XP	FG	FGA	SAF	Pts
1932	SI	N	0	2		0		0	2

Pete Franceschi

Year	Team		TD	1XP	2XP	FG	FGA	SAF	Pts
1946	SF	AA	2	0		0	0	0	12

Gene Francis

Year	Team		TD	1XP	2XP	FG	FGA	SAF	Pts
1926	CHIC	N	1	0		0		0	6

James Francis

Year	Team		TD	1XP	2XP	FG	FGA	SAF	Pts
1990	CIN	N	1	0		0	0	1	8
1992			1	0		0	0	0	6
1996			1	0	0	0	0	0	6
Career			3	0	0	0	0	1	20

Joe Francis

Year	Team		TD	1XP	2XP	FG	FGA	SAF	Pts
1958	GB	N	1	0		0	0	0	6

Jon Francis

Year	Team		TD	1XP	2XP	FG	FGA	SAF	Pts
1987	LARM	N	2	0		0	0	0	12

Phil Francis

Year	Team		TD	1XP	2XP	FG	FGA	SAF	Pts
1979	SF	N	1	0		0	0	0	6

Ron Francis

Year	Team		TD	1XP	2XP	FG	FGA	SAF	Pts
1987	DAL	N	1	0		0	0	0	6

Russ Francis

Year	Team		TD	1XP	2XP	FG	FGA	SAF	Pts
1975	NE	N	4	0		0	0	0	24

Russ Francis *continued*

Year	Team	Lg	TD	1XP	2XP	FG	FGA	SAF	Pts
1976			3	0		0	0	0	18
1977			4	0		0	0	0	24
1978			4	0		0	0	0	24
1979			5	0		0	0	0	30
1980			8	0		0	0	0	48
1982	SF	N	2	0		0	0	0	12
1983			4	0		0	0	0	24
1984			2	0		0	0	0	12
1985			3	0		0	0	0	18
1986			1	0		0	0	0	6
Career			40	0		0	0	0	240
Playoffs			3	0		0	0	0	18

Sam Francis

Year	Team	Lg	TD	1XP	2XP	FG	FGA	SAF	Pts
1937	CHIB	N	1	1		0		0	7
1938			3	0		0	0	0	18
1939	PIT	N	1	0		0	0	0	6
1940	BKN	N	1	0		0	1	0	6
Career			6	1		0	1	0	37

Wallace Francis

Year	Team	Lg	TD	1XP	2XP	FG	FGA	SAF	Pts
1973	BUF	N	2	0		0	0	0	12
1975	ATL	N	4	0		0	0	0	24
1977			1	0		0	0	0	6
1978			3	0		0	0	0	18
1979			8	0		0	0	0	48
1980			7	0		0	0	0	42
1981			5	0		0	0	0	30
Career			30	0		0	0	0	180
Playoffs			2	0		0	0	0	12

George Franck

Year	Team	Lg	TD	1XP	2XP	FG	FGA	SAF	Pts
1941	NYG	N	4	0		0	0	0	24
1946			1	0		0	0	0	6
1947			3	0		0	0	0	18
Career			8	0		0	0	0	48
Playoffs			1	0		0	0	0	6

Brian Franco

Year	Team	Lg	TD	1XP	2XP	FG	FGA	SAF	Pts
1987	CLE	N	0	2		3	4	0	11

Donald Frank

Year	Team	Lg	TD	1XP	2XP	FG	FGA	SAF	Pts
1991	SD	N	1	0		0	0	0	6
1993			1	0		0	0	0	6
Career			2	0		0	0	0	12

John Frank

Year	Team	Lg	TD	1XP	2XP	FG	FGA	SAF	Pts
1984	SF	N	1	0		0	0	0	6
1985			1	0		0	0	0	6
1986			2	0		0	0	0	12
1987			3	0		0	0	0	18
1988			3	0		0	0	0	18
Career			10	0		0	0	0	60
Playoffs			2	0		0	0	0	12

Ike Frankian

Year	Team	Lg	TD	1XP	2XP	FG	FGA	SAF	Pts
1933	BOS	N	1	0		0		0	6
1935	NYG	N	1	0		0		0	6
Career			2	0		0		0	12
Playoffs			1	0		0		0	6

Andra Franklin

Year	Team	Lg	TD	1XP	2XP	FG	FGA	SAF	Pts
1981	MIA	N	8	0		0	0	0	48
1982			7	0		0	0	0	42
1983			8	0		0	0	0	48
Career			23	0		0	0	0	138
Playoffs			2	0		0	0	0	12

Bobby Franklin

Year	Team	Lg	TD	1XP	2XP	FG	FGA	SAF	Pts
1960	CLE	N	2	0		0	0	0	12
1961			1	0		0	0	0	6
Career			3	0		0	0	0	18

Byron Franklin

Year	Team	Lg	TD	1XP	2XP	FG	FGA	SAF	Pts
1983	BUF	N	4	0		0	0	0	24
1984			4	0		0	0	0	24
1986	SEA	N	2	0		0	0	0	12
Career			10	0		0	0	0	60

Cleveland Franklin

Year	Team	Lg	TD	1XP	2XP	FG	FGA	SAF	Pts
1980	BAL	N	2	0		0	0	0	12
1981			1	0		0	0	0	6
Career			3	0		0	0	0	18

Pat Franklin

Year	Team	Lg	TD	1XP	2XP	FG	FGA	SAF	Pts
1986	TB	N	2	0		0	0	0	12

Paul Franklin

Year	Team	Lg	TD	1XP	2XP	FG	FGA	SAF	Pts
1931	CHIB	N	1	0		0		0	6

Red Franklin

Year	Team	Lg	TD	1XP	2XP	FG	FGA	SAF	Pts
1935	BKN	N	3	0		0		0	18
1936			1	0		0		0	6
Career			4	0		0		0	24

Tony Franklin

Year	Team	Lg	TD	1XP	2XP	FG	FGA	SAF	Pts
1979	PHI	N	0	36		23	31	0	105
1980			0	48		16	31	0	96
1981			0	41		20	31	0	101
1982			0	23		6	9	0	41
1983			0	24		15	26	0	69
1984	NE	N	0	42		22	28	0	108
1985			0	40		24	30	0	112
1986			0	44		**32**	**41**	0	**140**
1987			0	37		15	26	0	82
1988	MIA	N	0	6		4	11	0	18
Career			0	341		177	264	0	872
Playoffs			0	27		16	22	0	75

Ray Frankowski

Year	Team	Lg	TD	1XP	2XP	FG	FGA	SAF	Pts
1946	LA	AA	1	0		0	0	0	6

Jim Fraser

Year	Team	Lg	TD	1XP	2XP	FG	FGA	SAF	Pts
1962	DEN	A	0	2	0	0	0	0	2

Al Frazier

Year	Team	Lg	TD	1XP	2XP	FG	FGA	SAF	Pts
1961	DEN	A	8	0	1	0	0	0	50
1962			3	0	0	0	0	0	18
Career			11	0	1	0	0	0	68

Charlie Frazier

Year	Team	Lg	TD	1XP	2XP	FG	FGA	SAF	Pts
1962	HOU	A	1	0	0	0	0	0	6
1963			1	0	0	0	0	0	6
1964			2	0	0	0	0	0	12
1965			6	0	0	0	0	0	36
1966			12	0	0	0	0	0	72
1967			1	0	0	0	0	0	6
1969	BOS	A	7	0	0	0	0	0	42
Career			30	0	0	0	0	0	180
Playoffs			1	0	0	0	0	0	6

Leslie Frazier

Year	Team	Lg	TD	1XP	2XP	FG	FGA	SAF	Pts
1983	CHI	N	1	0		0	0	0	6
1985			1	0		0	0	0	6
Career			2	0		0	0	0	12

Paul Frazier

Year	Team	Lg	TD	1XP	2XP	FG	FGA	SAF	Pts
1989	NO	N	1	0		0	0	0	6

Willie Frazier

Year	Team	Lg	TD	1XP	2XP	FG	FGA	SAF	Pts
1964	HOU	A	1	0	0	0	0	0	6
1965			8	0	0	0	0	0	48
1966	SD	A	2	0	0	0	0	0	12
1967			10	0	0	0	0	0	60
1968			3	0	0	0	0	0	18
1970	SD	N	8	0		0	0	0	48
1972	KC	N	5	0		0	0	0	30
Career			37	0	0	0	0	0	222

Rob Frederickson

Year	Team	Lg	TD	1XP	2XP	FG	FGA	SAF	Pts
1995	OAK	N	1	0	0	0	0	0	6

Tucker Frederickson

Year	Team	Lg	TD	1XP	2XP	FG	FGA	SAF	Pts
1965	NYG	N	6	0		0	0	0	36
1967			2	0		0	0	0	12
1968			3	0		0	0	0	18
1969			1	0		0	0	0	6
1970			4	0		0	0	0	24
1971			1	0		0	0	0	6
Career			17	0		0	0	0	102

Antonio Freeman

Year	Team	Lg	TD	1XP	2XP	FG	FGA	SAF	Pts
1995	GB	N	1	0	0	0	0	0	6
1996			9	0	0	0	0	0	54
Career			10	0	0	0	0	0	60
Playoffs			4	0	0	0	0	0	24

Phil Freeman

Year	Team	Lg	TD	1XP	2XP	FG	FGA	SAF	Pts
1986	TB	N	2	0		0	0	0	12
1987			2	0		0	0	0	12
Career			4	0		0	0	0	24

Steve Freeman

Year	Team	Lg	TD	1XP	2XP	FG	FGA	SAF	Pts
1975	BUF	N	1	0		0	0	0	6
1979			1	0		0	0	0	6
1980			1	0		0	0	0	6
Career			3	0		0	0	0	18

Walt French

Year	Team	Lg	TD	1XP	2XP	FG	FGA	SAF	Pts
1925	POT	N	5	0		0		0	30

Gus Frerotte

Year	Team	Lg	TD	1XP	2XP	FG	FGA	SAF	Pts
1995	WAS	N	1	0	0	0	0	0	6

Mitch Frerotte

Year	Team	Lg	TD	1XP	2XP	FG	FGA	SAF	Pts
1992	BUF	N	2	0		0	0	0	12
Playoffs			1	0	0	0	0	0	6

Mike Friede

Year	Team	Lg	TD	1XP	2XP	FG	FGA	SAF	Pts
1981	NYG	N	1	0		0	0	0	6

Andy Friedman

Year	Team	Lg	TD	1XP	2XP	FG	FGA	SAF	Pts
1921	SYR	A	1	0		0		0	6

Benny Friedman

Year	Team	Lg	TD	1XP	2XP	FG	FGA	SAF	Pts
1927	CLE	N	2	11		0		0	23
1928	DET	N	4	**19**		0		0	43
1929	NYG	N	2	**20**		0		0	32
1930			6	10		1		0	49
1931			2	0		0		0	12
1932	BKN	N	0	4		1		0	7
1933			0	6		0		0	6
Career			16	70		2		0	172

David Frisch

Year	Team	Lg	TD	1XP	2XP	FG	FGA	SAF	Pts
1996	MIN	N	1	0	0	0	0	0	6

Ted Fritsch

Year	Team	Lg	TD	1XP	2XP	FG	FGA	SAF	Pts
1942	GB	N	0	1		4	5	0	13
1943			4	0		0	2	0	24
1944			5	0		0	0	0	30
1945			8	0		3	8	0	57
1946			**10**	13		**9**	**17**	0	**100**
1947			6	2		6	13	0	56
1948			1	5		6	16	0	29
1949			1	11		5	**20**	0	32
1950			0	30		3	17	0	39
Career			35	62		36	98	0	380
Playoffs			2	0		0	0	0	12

Toni Fritsch

Year	Team	Lg	TD	1XP	2XP	FG	FGA	SAF	Pts
1971	DAL	N	0	2		5	8	0	17
1972			0	36		21	36	0	99
1973			0	**43**		18	28	0	97
1975			0	38		**22**	**35**	0	104
1976	SD	N	0	11		6	12	0	29
1977	HOU	N	0	19		12	16	0	55
1978			0	31		14	18	0	73
1979			0	41		21	25	0	104
1980			0	26		19	24	0	83
1981			0	32		15	22	0	77
1982	NO	N	0	8		4	7	0	20
Career			0	287		157	231	0	758
Playoffs			0	26		20	25	0	86

Stan Fritts

Year	Team	Lg	TD	1XP	2XP	FG	FGA	SAF	Pts
1975	CIN	N	10	0		0	0	0	60
1976			3	0		0	0	0	18
Career			13	0		0	0	0	78
Playoffs			1	0		0	0	0	6

William Frizzell

Year	Team	Lg	TD	1XP	2XP	FG	FGA	SAF	Pts
1990	PHI	N	1	0		0	0	0	6

Ed Frutig

Year	Team	Lg	TD	1XP	2XP	FG	FGA	SAF	Pts
1945	DET	N	1	0		0	0	0	6
1946			2	0		0	0	0	12
Career			3	0		0	0	0	18

Wes Fry

Year	Team	Lg	TD	1XP	2XP	FG	FGA	SAF	Pts
1926	NY	A	2	0		0		0	12

Wes Fry *continued*

Year	Team		TD	1XP	2XP	FG	FGA	SAF	Pts
1927	**NYY**	**N**	4	1		0		0	25
Career			6	1		0		0	37

Irving Fryar

Year	Team		TD	1XP	2XP	FG	FGA	SAF	Pts
1984	**NE**	**N**	1	0		0	0	0	6
1985			10	0		0	0	0	60
1986			7	0		0	0	0	42
1987			5	0		0	0	0	30
1988			5	0		0	0	0	30
1989			3	0		0	0	0	18
1990			4	0		0	0	0	24
1991			3	0		0	0	0	18
1992			4	0		0	0	0	24
1993	**MIA**	**N**	5	0		0	0	0	30
1994			7	0	2	0	0	0	46
1995			8	0	0	0	0	0	48
1996	**PHI**	**N**	11	0	0	0	0	0	66
Career			73	0	2	0	0	0	442
Playoffs			2	0	0	0	0	0	12

Jean Fugett

Year	Team		TD	1XP	2XP	FG	FGA	SAF	Pts
1973	**DAL**	**N**	3	0		0	0	0	18
1974			1	0		0	0	0	6
1975			3	0		0	0	0	18
1976	**WAS**	**N**	6	0		0	0	0	36
1977			5	0		0	0	0	30
1978			7	0		0	0	0	42
1979			3	0		0	0	0	18
Career			28	0		0	0	0	168

David Fulcher

Year	Team		TD	1XP	2XP	FG	FGA	SAF	Pts
1988	**CIN**	**N**	1	0		0	0	0	6
1990			0	0		0	0	1	2
1991			1	0		0	0	0	6
Career			2	0		0	0	1	14

Charley Fuller

Year	Team		TD	1XP	2XP	FG	FGA	SAF	Pts
1961	**OAK**	**A**	2	0	0	0	0	0	12

Corey Fuller

Year	Team		TD	1XP	2XP	FG	FGA	SAF	Pts
1995	**MIN**	**N**	1	0	0	0	0	0	6

Frank Fuller

Year	Team		TD	1XP	2XP	FG	FGA	SAF	Pts
1960	**STL**	**N**	0	0		0	0	1	2

Jeff Fuller

Year	Team		TD	1XP	2XP	FG	FGA	SAF	Pts
1987	**SF**	**N**	0	0		0	0	1	2
Playoffs			1	0	0	0	0	0	6

Larry Fuller

Year	Team		TD	1XP	2XP	FG	FGA	SAF	Pts
1944	**WAS**	**N**	1	0		0	0	0	6

Mike Fuller

Year	Team		TD	1XP	2XP	FG	FGA	SAF	Pts
1975	**SD**	**N**	1	0		0	0	0	6
1976			0	1		0	0	0	1
1977			2	0		0	0	0	12
1978			1	0		0	0	0	6
Career			4	1		0	0	0	25

Steve Fuller

Year	Team		TD	1XP	2XP	FG	FGA	SAF	Pts
1979	**KC**	**N**	1	0		0	0	0	6
1980			4	0		0	0	0	24
1984	**CHI**	**N**	1	0		0	0	0	6
1985			5	0		0	0	0	30
Career			11	0		0	0	0	66

William Fuller

Year	Team		TD	1XP	2XP	FG	FGA	SAF	Pts
1992	**HOU**	**N**	1	0		0	0	0	6
1994	**PHI**	**N**	0	0	0	0	0	1	2
Career			1	0	0	0	0	1	8

Brent Fullwood

Year	Team		TD	1XP	2XP	FG	FGA	SAF	Pts
1987	**GB**	**N**	5	0		0	0	0	30
1988			8	0		0	0	0	48
1989			5	0		0	0	0	30
1990			1	0		0	0	0	6
Career			19	0		0	0	0	114

John Fuqua

Year	Team		TD	1XP	2XP	FG	FGA	SAF	Pts
1970	**PIT**	**N**	9	0		0	0	0	54
1971			5	0		0	0	0	30
1972			4	0		0	0	0	24
1973			2	0		0	0	0	12

John Fuqua *continued*

Year	Team		TD	1XP	2XP	FG	FGA	SAF	Pts
1974			2	0		0	0	0	12
1975			1	0		0	0	0	6
1976			1	0		0	0	0	6
Career			24	0		0	0	0	144

Ray Fuqua

Year	Team		TD	1XP	2XP	FG	FGA	SAF	Pts
1935	**BKN**	**N**	1	0		0		0	6
1936			0	0		0		0	0
Career			1	0		0		0	6

Roman Gabriel

Year	Team		TD	1XP	2XP	FG	FGA	SAF	Pts
1963	**LA**	**N**	3	0		0	0	0	18
1964			1	0		0	0	0	6
1965			2	0		0	0	0	12
1966			3	0		0	0	0	18
1967			6	0		0	0	0	36
1968			4	0		0	0	0	24
1969			5	0		0	0	0	30
1970			1	0		0	0	0	6
1971			2	0		0	0	0	12
1972			1	0		0	0	0	6
1973	**PHI**	**N**	1	0		0	0	0	6
1975			1	0		0	0	0	6
Career			30	0		0	0	0	180

Mike Gaechter

Year	Team		TD	1XP	2XP	FG	FGA	SAF	Pts
1962	**DAL**	**N**	1	0		0	0	0	6
1965			1	0		0	0	0	6
Career			2	0		0	0	0	12

Derrick Gaffney

Year	Team		TD	1XP	2XP	FG	FGA	SAF	Pts
1978	**NYJ**	**N**	3	0		0	0	0	18
1979			1	0		0	0	0	6
1980			2	0		0	0	0	12
1982			1	0		0	0	0	6
Career			7	0		0	0	0	42
Playoffs			1	0		0	0	0	6

Jim Gaffney

Year	Team		TD	1XP	2XP	FG	FGA	SAF	Pts
1946	**WAS**	**N**	1	0		0	0	0	6

Jeff Gaffney

Year	Team		TD	1XP	2XP	FG	FGA	SAF	Pts
1987	**SD**	**N**	0	4		3	6	0	13

Monk Gafford

Year	Team		TD	1XP	2XP	FG	FGA	SAF	Pts
1946	**MIA**	**AA**	5	0		0	0	0	30
1947	**BKN**	**AA**	1	0		0	0	0	6
1948			5	0		0	0	0	30
Career			11	0		0	0	0	66

Bobby Gage

Year	Team		TD	1XP	2XP	FG	FGA	SAF	Pts
1949	**PIT**	**N**	3	0		0	0	0	18
1950			5	0		0	0	0	30
Career			8	0		0	0	0	48

Bob Gagliano

Year	Team		TD	1XP	2XP	FG	FGA	SAF	Pts
1989	**DET**	**N**	4	0		0	0	0	24

Bob Gain

Year	Team		TD	1XP	2XP	FG	FGA	SAF	Pts
1952	**CLE**	**N**	0	3		0	0	0	3
1960			1	0		0	0	0	6
Career			1	3		0	0	0	9

Derrick Gainer

Year	Team		TD	1XP	2XP	FG	FGA	SAF	Pts
1990	**CLE**	**N**	1	0		0	0	0	6
Playoffs			1	0	0	0	0	0	6

Clark Gaines

Year	Team		TD	1XP	2XP	FG	FGA	SAF	Pts
1976	**NYJ**	**N**	5	0		0	0	0	30
1977			4	0		0	0	0	24
1978			2	0		0	0	0	12
1980			3	0		0	0	0	18
Career			14	0		0	0	0	84

Lawrence Gaines

Year	Team		TD	1XP	2XP	FG	FGA	SAF	Pts
1976	**DET**	**N**	5	0		0	0	0	30
1978			1	0		0	0	0	6
Career			6	0		0	0	0	36

Wendall Gaines

Year	Team		TD	1XP	2XP	FG	FGA	SAF	Pts
1995	**ARI**	**N**	2	0	0	0	0	0	12

Blane Gaison

Year	Team		TD	1XP	2XP	FG	FGA	SAF	Pts
1983	**ATL**	**N**	1	0		0	0	0	6

Bob Gaiters

Year	Team		TD	1XP	2XP	FG	FGA	SAF	Pts
1961	**NYG**	**N**	7	0		0	0	0	42
1963	**DEN**	**A**	1	0	0	0	0	0	6
Career			8	0	0	0	0	0	48

Bill Gaiver

Year	Team		TD	1XP	2XP	FG	FGA	SAF	Pts
1923	**RI**	**N**	4	0		0		0	24

Hokie Gajan

Year	Team		TD	1XP	2XP	FG	FGA	SAF	Pts
1983	**NO**	**N**	4	0		0	0	0	24
1984			7	0		0	0	0	42
1985			2	0		0	0	0	12
Career			13	0		0	0	0	78

Scott Galbraith

Year	Team		TD	1XP	2XP	FG	FGA	SAF	Pts
1992	**CLE**	**N**	1	0		0	0	0	6
1993	**DAL**	**N**	1	0		0	0	0	6
1995	**WAS**	**N**	2	0	0	0	0	0	12
1996			2	0	0	0	0	0	12
Career			6	0	0	0	0	0	36
Playoffs			1	0	0	0	0	0	6

Tony Galbreath

Year	Team		TD	1XP	2XP	FG	FGA	SAF	Pts
1976	**NO**	**N**	8	0		0	0	0	48
1977			3	0		0	0	0	18
1978			7	0		0	0	0	42
1979			10	1		2	3	0	67
1980			5	0		0	0	0	30
1981	**MIN**	**N**	2	0		0	0	0	12
1982			1	0		0	0	0	6
1983			6	0		0	0	0	36
1985	**NYG**	**N**	1	0		0	0	0	6
Career			43	1		2	3	0	265

Willie Galimore

Year	Team		TD	1XP	2XP	FG	FGA	SAF	Pts
1957	**CHIB**	**N**	7	0		0	0	0	42
1958			12	0		0	0	0	72
1959			3	0		0	0	0	18
1960	**CHI**	**N**	1	0		0	0	0	6
1961			7	0		0	0	0	42
1962			2	0		0	0	0	12
1963			5	0		0	0	0	30
Career			37	0		0	0	0	222
Playoffs			1	0		0	0	0	6

Hugh Gallarneau

Year	Team		TD	1XP	2XP	FG	FGA	SAF	Pts
1941	**CHIB**	**N**	11	0		0	0	0	66
1942			7	0		0	0	0	42
1945			3	0		0	0	0	18
1946			8	0		0	0	0	48
1947			6	0		0	0	0	36
Career			35	0		0	0	0	210
Playoffs			1	0		0	0	0	6

Chan Gallegos

Year	Team		TD	1XP	2XP	FG	FGA	SAF	Pts
1962	**OAK**	**A**	0	0	0	0	0	0	0

Jim Gallery

Year	Team		TD	1XP	2XP	FG	FGA	SAF	Pts
1987	**STL**	**N**	0	30		9	19	0	57
1989	**CIN**	**N**	0	13		2	6	0	19
Career			0	43		11	25	0	76

David Galloway

Year	Team		TD	1XP	2XP	FG	FGA	SAF	Pts
1983	**STL**	**N**	0	0		0	0	1	2

Joey Galloway

Year	Team		TD	1XP	2XP	FG	FGA	SAF	Pts
1995	**SEA**	**N**	9	0	0	0	0	0	54
1996			8	0	0	0	0	0	48
Career			17	0	0	0	0	0	102

Lu Gambino

Year	Team		TD	1XP	2XP	FG	FGA	SAF	Pts
1948	**BAL**	**AA**	1	0		0	0	0	6
1949			1	0		0	0	0	6
Career			2	0		0	0	0	12

Kenny Gamble

Year	Team		TD	1XP	2XP	FG	FGA	SAF	Pts
1989	**KC**	**N**	1	0		0	0	0	6

R.C. Gamble

Year	Team		TD	1XP	2XP	FG	FGA	SAF	Pts
1968	**BOS**	**A**	2	0	0	0	0	0	12

Billy Gambrell

Year	Team	Lg	TD	1XP	2XP	FG	FGA	SAF	Pts
1964	STL	N	2	0		0	0	0	12
1965			2	0		0	0	0	12
1966			5	0		0	0	0	30
1967			2	0		0	0	0	12
1968	DET	N	7	0		0	0	0	42
Career			18	0		0	0	0	108

Sonny Gandee

Year	Team	Lg	TD	1XP	2XP	FG	FGA	SAF	Pts
1952	DET	N	0	0		0	0	1	2
1955			1	0		0	0	0	6
Career			1	0		0	0	1	8

Mike Gann

Year	Team	Lg	TD	1XP	2XP	FG	FGA	SAF	Pts
1985	ATL	N	1	0		0	0	0	6
1986			0	0		0	0	1	2
1988			1	0		0	0	0	6
Career			2	0		0	0	1	14

Rich Gannon

Year	Team	Lg	TD	1XP	2XP	FG	FGA	SAF	Pts
1990	MIN	N	1	0		0	0	0	6
1991			2	0		0	0	0	12
1993	WAS	N	1	0		0	0	0	6
1995	KC	N	1	0	0	0	0	0	6
Career			5	0	0	0	0	0	30

Earl Gant

Year	Team	Lg	TD	1XP	2XP	FG	FGA	SAF	Pts
1979	KC	N	1	0		0	0	0	6

Reuben Gant

Year	Team	Lg	TD	1XP	2XP	FG	FGA	SAF	Pts
1975	BUF	N	2	0		0	0	0	12
1976			3	0		0	0	0	18
1977			2	0		0	0	0	12
1978			5	0		0	0	0	30
1979			2	0		0	0	0	12
1980			1	0		0	0	0	6
Career			15	0		0	0	0	90

Milt Gantenbein

Year	Team	Lg	TD	1XP	2XP	FG	FGA	SAF	Pts
1931	GB	N	1	0		0		0	6
1933			1	0		0		0	6
1935			1	0		0		0	6
1936			1	0		0		0	6
1937			2	0		0		0	12
1938			1	0		0		0	6
1939			1	0		0	0	0	6
Career			8	0		0	0	0	48
Playoffs			2	0		0	0	0	12

Greg Gantt

Year	Team	Lg	TD	1XP	2XP	FG	FGA	SAF	Pts
1974	NYJ	N	0	1		0	0	0	1

Bubba Garcia

Year	Team	Lg	TD	1XP	2XP	FG	FGA	SAF	Pts
1980	KC	N	1	0		0	0	0	6

Eddie Garcia

Year	Team	Lg	TD	1XP	2XP	FG	FGA	SAF	Pts
1984	GB	N	0	14		3	9	0	23

Teddy Garcia

Year	Team	Lg	TD	1XP	2XP	FG	FGA	SAF	Pts
1988	NE	N	0	11		6	13	0	29
1989	MIN	N	0	8		1	5	0	11
1990	HOU	N	0	26		14	20	0	68
Career			0	45		21	38	0	108
Playoffs			0	2		0	0	0	2

Ron Gardin

Year	Team	Lg	TD	1XP	2XP	FG	FGA	SAF	Pts
1970	BAL	N	1	0		0	0	0	6

Carwell Gardner

Year	Team	Lg	TD	1XP	2XP	FG	FGA	SAF	Pts
1991	BUF	N	4	0		0	0	0	24
1992			2	0		0	0	0	12
1993			1	0		0	0	0	6
1994			4	0	0	0	0	0	24
1995			1	0	1	0	0	0	8
1996	BAL	N	0	0	1	0	0	0	2
Career			12	0	2	0	0	0	76
Playoffs			1	0	0	0	0	0	6

Milt Gardner

Year	Team	Lg	TD	1XP	2XP	FG	FGA	SAF	Pts
1925	GB	N	1	0		0		0	6

Don Garlin

Year	Team	Lg	TD	1XP	2XP	FG	FGA	SAF	Pts
1949	SF	AA	1	0		0	0	0	6
Playoffs			1	0	0	0	0	0	6

Bill Garnaas

Year	Team	Lg	TD	1XP	2XP	FG	FGA	SAF	Pts
1946	PIT	N	1	0		0	0	0	6
1947			2	0		0	0	0	12
Career			3	0		0	0	0	18

Charlie Garner

Year	Team	Lg	TD	1XP	2XP	FG	FGA	SAF	Pts
1994	PHI	N	3	0	0	0	0	0	18
1995			6	0	0	0	0	0	36
1996			1	0	0	0	0	0	6
Career			10	0	0	0	0	0	60
Playoffs			1	0	0	0	0	0	6

Alvin Garrett

Year	Team	Lg	TD	1XP	2XP	FG	FGA	SAF	Pts
1980	NYG	N	1	0		0	0	0	6
1983	WAS	N	1	0		0	0	0	6
Career			2	0		0	0	0	12
Playoffs			5	0		0	0	0	30

Bill Garrett

Year	Team	Lg	TD	1XP	2XP	FG	FGA	SAF	Pts
1950	CHIB	N	1	0		0	0	0	6

Carl Garrett

Year	Team	Lg	TD	1XP	2XP	FG	FGA	SAF	Pts
1969	BOS	A	7	0	0	0	0	0	42
1970	BOS	N	4	0		0	0	0	24
1971	NE	N	2	0		0	0	0	12
1972			5	0		0	0	0	30
1973	CHI	N	5	0		0	0	0	30
1974			2	0		0	0	0	12
1975	NYJ	N	6	0		0	0	0	36
1976	OAK	N	1	0		0	0	0	6
1977			3	0		0	0	0	18
Career			35	0	0	0	0	0	210

J.D. Garrett

Year	Team	Lg	TD	1XP	2XP	FG	FGA	SAF	Pts
1964	BOS	A	2	0	0	0	0	0	12
1965			3	0	0	0	0	0	18
1967			1	0	0	0	0	0	6
Career			6	0	0	0	0	0	36

Mike Garrett

Year	Team	Lg	TD	1XP	2XP	FG	FGA	SAF	Pts
1966	KC	A	8	0	0	0	0	0	48
1967			10	0	0	0	0	0	60
1968			6	0	0	0	0	0	36
1969			8	0	0	0	0	0	48
1970	SD	N	2	0		0	0	0	12
1971			7	0		0	0	0	42
1972			7	0		0	0	0	42
1973			1	0		0	0	0	6
Career			49	0	0	0	0	0	294
Playoffs			3	0	0	0	0	0	18

Reggie Garrett

Year	Team	Lg	TD	1XP	2XP	FG	FGA	SAF	Pts
1975	PIT	N	1	0		0	0	0	6

Thurman Garrett

Year	Team	Lg	TD	1XP	2XP	FG	FGA	SAF	Pts
1947	CHIB	N	0	0		0	1	0	0

Gary Garrison

Year	Team	Lg	TD	1XP	2XP	FG	FGA	SAF	Pts
1966	SD	A	4	0	0	0	0	0	24
1967			2	0	0	0	0	0	12
1968			10	0	0	0	0	0	60
1969			7	0	0	0	0	0	42
1970	SD	N	12	0		0	0	0	72
1971			6	0		0	0	0	36
1972			7	0		0	0	0	42
1973			2	0		0	0	0	12
1974			5	0		0	0	0	30
1975			2	0		0	0	0	12
1976			1	0		0	0	0	6
Career			58	0	0	0	0	0	348

Walt Garrison

Year	Team	Lg	TD	1XP	2XP	FG	FGA	SAF	Pts
1966	DAL	N	1	0		0	0	0	6
1968			5	0		0	0	0	30
1969			2	0		0	0	0	12
1970			5	0		0	0	0	30
1971			2	0		0	0	0	12
1972			10	0		0	0	0	60
1973			8	0		0	0	0	48
1974			6	0		0	0	0	36
Career			39	0		0	0	0	234
Playoffs			3	0		0	0	0	18

Gregg Garrity

Year	Team	Lg	TD	1XP	2XP	FG	FGA	SAF	Pts
1983	PIT	N	1	0		0	0	0	6
1986	PHI	N	1	0		0	0	0	6
1987			2	0		0	0	0	12
1988			1	0		0	0	0	6
1989			2	0		0	0	0	12
Career			7	0		0	0	0	42

Larry Garron

Year	Team	Lg	TD	1XP	2XP	FG	FGA	SAF	Pts
1961	BOS	A	6	0	0	0	0	0	36
1962			6	0	0	0	0	0	36
1963			4	0	0	0	0	0	24
1964			9	0	0	0	0	0	54
1965			2	0	0	0	0	0	12
1966			9	0	0	0	0	0	54
1967			5	0	0	0	0	0	30
1968			1	0	0	0	0	0	6
Career			42	0	0	0	0	0	252
Playoffs			3	0	0	0	0	0	18

Frank Garvey

Year	Team	Lg	TD	1XP	2XP	FG	FGA	SAF	Pts
1925	PRO	N	2	0		0		0	12
1926			0	1		0		0	1
Career			2	1		0		0	13

Cleveland Gary

Year	Team	Lg	TD	1XP	2XP	FG	FGA	SAF	Pts
1989	LARM	N	1	0		0	0	0	6
1990			15	0		0	0	0	90
1991			1	0		0	0	0	6
1992			10	0		0	0	0	60
1993			2	0		0	0	0	12
Career			29	0		0	0	0	174

Sammy Garza

Year	Team	Lg	TD	1XP	2XP	FG	FGA	SAF	Pts
1987	STL	N	1	0		0	0	0	6

Sam Gash

Year	Team	Lg	TD	1XP	2XP	FG	FGA	SAF	Pts
1992	NE	N	1	0		0	0	0	6
1993			1	0		0	0	0	6
1995			1	0	0	0	0	0	6
1996			2	0	1	0	0	0	14
Career			5	0	1	0	0	0	32

Thane Gash

Year	Team	Lg	TD	1XP	2XP	FG	FGA	SAF	Pts
1989	CLE	N	2	0		0	0	0	12

Mark Gastineau

Year	Team	Lg	TD	1XP	2XP	FG	FGA	SAF	Pts
1983	NYJ	N	1	0		0	0	0	6
1984			1	0		0	0	0	6
Career			2	0		0	0	0	12

Frank Gatski

Year	Team	Lg	TD	1XP	2XP	FG	FGA	SAF	Pts
1946	CLE	AA	1	0		0	0	0	6

Dennis Gaubatz

Year	Team	Lg	TD	1XP	2XP	FG	FGA	SAF	Pts
1964	DET	N	0	0		0	0	1	2

Willie Gault

Year	Team	Lg	TD	1XP	2XP	FG	FGA	SAF	Pts
1983	CHI	N	8	0		0	0	0	48
1984			6	0		0	0	0	36
1985			2	0		0	0	0	12
1986			5	0		0	0	0	30
1987			7	0		0	0	0	42
1988	LARI	N	2	0		0	0	0	12
1989			4	0		0	0	0	24
1990			3	0		0	0	0	18
1991			4	0		0	0	0	24
1992			4	0		0	0	0	24
Career			45	0		0	0	0	270
Playoffs			3	0		0	0	0	18

Steve Gaunty

Year	Team	Lg	TD	1XP	2XP	FG	FGA	SAF	Pts
1979	KC	N	1	0		0	0	0	6

Prentice Gautt

Year	Team	Lg	TD	1XP	2XP	FG	FGA	SAF	Pts
1960	CLE	N	1	0		0	0	0	6
1961	STL	N	6	0		0	0	0	36
1962			2	0		0	0	0	12
1964			2	0		0	0	0	12
1965			2	0		0	0	0	12
1966			2	0		0	0	0	12
1967			2	0		0	0	0	12
Career			17	0		0	0	0	102

Chuck Gavin

Year	Team	Lg	TD	1XP	2XP	FG	FGA	SAF	Pts
1961	DEN	A	1	0	0	0	0	0	6

Pat Gavin

Year	Team	Lg	TD	1XP	2XP	FG	FGA	SAF	Pts
1922	RI-BUF	N	6	0		0		0	36
1924	RI	N	7	0		0		0	42
Career			13	0		0		0	78

Momcilo Gavric

Year	Team	Lg	TD	1XP	2XP	FG	FGA	SAF	Pts
1969	SF	N	0	22		3	11	0	31

Blenda Gay

Year	Team	Lg	TD	1XP	2XP	FG	FGA	SAF	Pts
1974	SD	N	1	0		0	0	0	6

Everett Gay

Year	Team	Lg	TD	1XP	2XP	FG	FGA	SAF	Pts
1988	DAL	N	1	0		0	0	0	6

William Gay

Year	Team	Lg	TD	1XP	2XP	FG	FGA	SAF	Pts
1979	DET	N	1	0		0	0	0	6

Shaun Gayle

Year	Team	Lg	TD	1XP	2XP	FG	FGA	SAF	Pts
1987	CHI	N	1	0		0	0	0	6
1995	SD	N	2	0	0	0	0	0	12
Career			3	0	0	0	0	0	18
Playoffs			1	0	0	0	0	0	6

Bob Geddes

Year	Team	Lg	TD	1XP	2XP	FG	FGA	SAF	Pts
1974	NE	N	1	0		0	0	0	6

Gene Gedman

Year	Team	Lg	TD	1XP	2XP	FG	FGA	SAF	Pts
1953	DET	N	3	0		0	0	0	18
1956			8	0		0	0	0	48
1957			3	0		0	0	0	18
1958			7	0		0	0	0	42
Career			21	0		0	0	0	126
Playoffs			2	0		0	0	0	12

Chris Gedney

Year	Team	Lg	TD	1XP	2XP	FG	FGA	SAF	Pts
1994	CHI	N	3	0	0	0	0	0	18

Mark Gehring

Year	Team	Lg	TD	1XP	2XP	FG	FGA	SAF	Pts
1987	HOU	N	1	0		0	0	0	6

Bruce Gehrke

Year	Team	Lg	TD	1XP	2XP	FG	FGA	SAF	Pts
1948	NYG	N	1	0		0	0	0	6

Erwin Gehrke

Year	Team	Lg	TD	1XP	2XP	FG	FGA	SAF	Pts
1926	BOS	A	0	1		1		0	4

Fred Gehrke

Year	Team	Lg	TD	1XP	2XP	FG	FGA	SAF	Pts
1945	CLE	N	8	0		0	0	0	48
1946	LA	N	5	0		0	0	0	30
1947			1	4		1	1	0	13
1948			3	1		0	0	0	19
1949			5	2		0	1	0	32
1950	SF	N	2	0		0	0	0	12
Career			24	7		1	2	0	154

Chuck Gelatka

Year	Team	Lg	TD	1XP	2XP	FG	FGA	SAF	Pts
1938	NYG	N	2	0		0		0	12

Pete Gent

Year	Team	Lg	TD	1XP	2XP	FG	FGA	SAF	Pts
1965	DAL	N	2	0		0	0	0	12
1966			1	0		0	0	0	6
1967			1	0		0	0	0	6
Career			4	0		0	0	0	24

Dale Gentry

Year	Team	Lg	TD	1XP	2XP	FG	FGA	SAF	Pts
1946	LA	AA	5	0		0	0	0	30
1947			2	0		0	0	0	12
Career			7	0		0	0	0	42

Dennis Gentry

Year	Team	Lg	TD	1XP	2XP	FG	FGA	SAF	Pts
1984	CHI	N	1	0		0	0	0	6
1985			3	0		0	0	0	18
1986			3	0		0	0	0	18
1987			2	0		0	0	0	12
1988			4	0		0	0	0	24
1989			1	0		0	0	0	6
1990			2	0		0	0	0	12
Career			16	0		0	0	0	96

Bill George

Year	Team	Lg	TD	1XP	2XP	FG	FGA	SAF	Pts
1953	CHIB	N	0	0		0	1	0	0

Bill George *continued*

Year	Team	Lg	TD	1XP	2XP	FG	FGA	SAF	Pts
1954			0	13		4	6	0	25
1958			0	1		0	0	0	1
1961	CHI	N	0	0		0	1	0	0
Career			0	14		4	8	0	26

Eddie George

Year	Team	Lg	TD	1XP	2XP	FG	FGA	SAF	Pts
1996	HOU	N	8	0	0	0	0	0	48

Jeff George

Year	Team	Lg	TD	1XP	2XP	FG	FGA	SAF	Pts
1990	IND	N	1	0		0	0	0	6
1992			1	0		0	0	0	6
Career			2	0		0	0	0	12

Ray George

Year	Team	Lg	TD	1XP	2XP	FG	FGA	SAF	Pts
1939	DET	N	0	0		0		1	2

Tom Geredine

Year	Team	Lg	TD	1XP	2XP	FG	FGA	SAF	Pts
1973	ATL	N	1	0		0	0	0	6
1976	LA	N	1	0		0	0	0	6
Career			2	0		0	0	0	12

Roy Gerela

Year	Team	Lg	TD	1XP	2XP	FG	FGA	SAF	Pts
1969	HOU	A	0	29	0	19	40	0	86
1970	HOU	N	0	23		18	32	0	77
1971	PIT	N	0	27		17	27	0	78
1972			0	35		28	41	0	119
1973			0	36		29	43	0	123
1974			0	33		20	29	0	93
1975			0	44		17	21	0	95
1976			0	40		14	26	0	82
1977			0	34		9	14	0	61
1978			0	44		12	26	0	80
1979	SD	N	0	6		1	7	0	9
Career			0	351	0	184	306	0	903
Playoffs			0	37	0	15	26	0	82

Joe Geri

Year	Team	Lg	TD	1XP	2XP	FG	FGA	SAF	Pts
1949	PIT	N	5	12		1	1	0	45
1950			3	22		8	14	0	64
1951			4	22		7	14	0	67
1952	CHIC	N	0	22		2	18	0	28
Career			12	78		18	47	0	204

Jimmy German

Year	Team	Lg	TD	1XP	2XP	FG	FGA	SAF	Pts
1939	WAS	N	2	0		0	0	0	12

Willie Germany

Year	Team	Lg	TD	1XP	2XP	FG	FGA	SAF	Pts
1975	HOU	N	1	0		0	0	0	6

Bill Geyer

Year	Team	Lg	TD	1XP	2XP	FG	FGA	SAF	Pts
1943	CHIB	N	4	0		0	0	0	24

Milt Ghee

Year	Team	Lg	TD	1XP	2XP	FG	FGA	SAF	Pts
1920	CHIT	A	0	0		0		0	0
1921	CLE	A	2	0		0		0	12
Career			2	0		0		0	12

Louie Giammona

Year	Team	Lg	TD	1XP	2XP	FG	FGA	SAF	Pts
1976	NYJ	N	1	0		0	0	0	6
1980	PHI	N	5	0		0	0	0	30
1981			2	0		0	0	0	12
1982			1	0		0	0	0	6
Career			9	0		0	0	0	54

Hal Giancanelli

Year	Team	Lg	TD	1XP	2XP	FG	FGA	SAF	Pts
1953	PHI	N	6	0		0	0	0	36
1954			4	0		0	0	0	24
1955			3	0		0	0	0	18
1956			1	0		0	0	0	6
Career			14	0		0	0	0	84

Mario Giannelli

Year	Team	Lg	TD	1XP	2XP	FG	FGA	SAF	Pts
1949	PHI	N	0	0		0	0	1	2

Nick Giaquinto

Year	Team	Lg	TD	1XP	2XP	FG	FGA	SAF	Pts
1980	MIA	N	2	0		0	0	0	12
1981	MIA-WAS	N	2	0		0	0	0	12
1983	WAS	N	1	0		0	0	0	6
Career			5	0		0	0	0	30

Jim Gibbons

Year	Team	Lg	TD	1XP	2XP	FG	FGA	SAF	Pts
1958	DET	N	2	0		0	0	0	12
1959			1	0		0	0	0	6

Jim Gibbons *continued*

Year	Team	Lg	TD	1XP	2XP	FG	FGA	SAF	Pts
1960			2	0		0	0	0	12
1961			1	0		0	0	0	6
1962			2	0		0	0	0	12
1963			1	0		0	0	0	6
1964			8	0		0	0	0	48
1965			2	0		0	0	0	12
1966			1	0		0	0	0	6
Career			20	0		0	0	0	120

Claude Gibson

Year	Team	Lg	TD	1XP	2XP	FG	FGA	SAF	Pts
1961	SD	A	0	0	1	0	0	0	2
1962			1	0	0	0	0	0	6
1963	OAK	A	2	0	0	0	0	0	12
1965			1	0	0	0	0	0	6
Career			4	0	1	0	0	0	26

Frank Gifford

Year	Team	Lg	TD	1XP	2XP	FG	FGA	SAF	Pts
1953	NYG	N	7	2		1	5	0	47
1954			3	0		0	0	0	18
1955			7	0		0	0	0	42
1956			9	8		1	2	0	65
1957			9	0		0	0	0	54
1958			10	0		0	0	0	60
1959			7	0		0	0	0	42
1960			7	0		0	0	0	42
1962			8	0		0	0	0	48
1963			7	0		0	0	0	42
1964			4	0		0	0	0	24
Career			78	10		2	7	0	484
Playoffs			4	0		0	0	0	24

Sean Gilbert

Year	Team	Lg	TD	1XP	2XP	FG	FGA	SAF	Pts
1994	LARM	N	0	0	0	0	0	1	2

Wally Gilbert

Year	Team	Lg	TD	1XP	2XP	FG	FGA	SAF	Pts
1923	DUL	N	1	0		0		0	6
1924			1	1		3		0	16
1925			0	0		0		0	0
Career			2	1		3		0	22

Cookie Gilchrist

Year	Team	Lg	TD	1XP	2XP	FG	FGA	SAF	Pts
1962	BUF	A	15	14	0	8	20	0	128
1963			14	0	0	0	0	0	84
1964			6	0	0	0	0	0	36
1965	DEN	A	7	0	0	0	0	0	42
1966	MIA	A	1	0	0	0	0	0	6
Career			43	14	0	8	20	0	296
Playoffs			1	0	0	0	0	0	6

Johnny Gildea

Year	Team	Lg	TD	1XP	2XP	FG	FGA	SAF	Pts
1937	PIT	N	1	0		0		0	6
1938	NYG	N	0	0		0		0	0
Career			1	0		0		0	6
Playoffs			0	0		0		0	0

Jimmie Giles

Year	Team	Lg	TD	1XP	2XP	FG	FGA	SAF	Pts
1978	TB	N	2	0		0	0	0	12
1979			7	0		0	0	0	42
1980			4	0		0	0	0	24
1981			6	0		0	0	0	36
1982			3	0		0	0	0	18
1983			1	0		0	0	0	6
1984			2	0		0	0	0	12
1985			8	0		0	0	0	48
1986	TB-DET	N	4	0		0	0	0	24
1987	PHI	N	1	0		0	0	0	6
1988			1	0		0	0	0	6
1989			2	0		0	0	0	12
Career			41	0		0	0	0	246
Playoffs			1	0		0	0	0	6

Owen Gill

Year	Team	Lg	TD	1XP	2XP	FG	FGA	SAF	Pts
1985	IND	N	2	0		0	0	0	12
1986			1	0		0	0	0	6
Career			3	0		0	0	0	18

Jim Gillette

Year	Team	Lg	TD	1XP	2XP	FG	FGA	SAF	Pts
1944	CLE	N	2	0		0	0	0	12
1945			1	0		0	0	0	6
1946	BOS	N	2	0		0	0	0	12
1947	GB	N	1	0		0	0	0	6
Career			6	0		0	0	0	36
Playoffs			1	0		0	0	0	6

Walker Gillette

Year	Team		TD	1XP	2XP	FG	FGA	SAF	Pts
1971	SD	N	2	0		0	0	0	12
1972	STL	N	2	0		0	0	0	12
1973			1	0		0	0	0	6
1974	NYG	N	3	0		0	0	0	18
1975			2	0		0	0	0	12
1976			2	0		0	0	0	12
Career			12	0		0	0	0	72

Joe Gilliam

Year	Team		TD	1XP	2XP	FG	FGA	SAF	Pts
1974	PIT	N	1	0		0	0	0	6

John Gilliam

Year	Team		TD	1XP	2XP	FG	FGA	SAF	Pts
1967	NO	N	2	0		0	0	0	12
1969	STL	N	10	0		0	0	0	60
1970			6	0		0	0	0	36
1971			3	0		0	0	0	18
1972	MIN	N	7	0		0	0	0	42
1973			9	0		0	0	0	54
1974			5	0		0	0	0	30
1975			7	0		0	0	0	42
1976	ATL	N	2	0		0	0	0	12
1977	NO	N	1	0		0	0	0	6
Career			52	0		0	0	0	312
Playoffs			5	0		0	0	0	30

Hank Gillo

Year	Team		TD	1XP	2XP	FG	FGA	SAF	Pts
1922	RAC	N	5	4		6		0	**52**
1923			2	8		8		0	44
1924			3	6		8		0	48
1926			0	0		0		0	0
Career			10	18		22		0	144

Horace Gillom

Year	Team		TD	1XP	2XP	FG	FGA	SAF	Pts
1948	CLE	AA	1	0		0	0	0	6
1950	CLE	N	1	0		0	0	0	6
1951			1	0		0	0	0	6
1952			1	0		0	0	0	6
Career			4	0		0	0	0	24

Harry Gilmer

Year	Team		TD	1XP	2XP	FG	FGA	SAF	Pts
1950	WAS	N	1	0		0	0	0	6
1952			1	0		0	0	0	6
Career			2	0		0	0	0	12

Hubie Ginn

Year	Team		TD	1XP	2XP	FG	FGA	SAF	Pts
1972	MIA	N	1	0		0	0	0	6
1974			2	0		0	0	0	12
Career			3	0		0	0	0	18

Paul Gipson

Year	Team		TD	1XP	2XP	FG	FGA	SAF	Pts
1969	ATL	N	1	0		0	0	0	6
1970			3	0		0	0	0	18
Career			4	0		0	0	0	24

Earl Girard

Year	Team		TD	1XP	2XP	FG	FGA	SAF	Pts
1949	GB	N	1	0		0	0	0	6
1951			2	0		0	0	0	12
1952	DET	N	4	0		0	0	0	24
1954			7	0		0	0	0	42
1957	PIT	N	4	2		1	3	0	29
Career			18	2		1	3	0	113

Ernest Givins

Year	Team		TD	1XP	2XP	FG	FGA	SAF	Pts
1986	HOU	N	4	0		0	0	0	24
1987			6	0		0	0	0	36
1988			5	0		0	0	0	30
1989			3	0		0	0	0	18
1990			9	0		0	0	0	54
1991			5	0		0	0	0	30
1992			10	0		0	0	0	60
1993			4	0		0	0	0	24
1994			2	0	0	0	0	0	12
1995	JAC	N	3	0	0	0	0	0	18
Career			51	0	0	0	0	0	306
Playoffs			8	0	0	0	0	0	48

Joe Glamp

Year	Team		TD	1XP	2XP	FG	FGA	SAF	Pts
1947	PIT	N	0	30		6	14	0	48
1948			3	26		4	10	0	56
1949			0	18		1	6	0	21
Career			3	74		11	30	0	125

Nesby Glasgow

Year	Team		TD	1XP	2XP	FG	FGA	SAF	Pts
1979	BAL	N	1	0		0	0	0	6
1989	SEA	N	1	0		0	0	0	6
Career			2	0		0	0	0	12

Bill Glass

Year	Team		TD	1XP	2XP	FG	FGA	SAF	Pts
1966	CLE	N	1	0		0	0	0	6
1968			1	0		0	0	0	6
Career			2	0		0	0	0	12

Chip Glass

Year	Team		TD	1XP	2XP	FG	FGA	SAF	Pts
1969	CLE	N	2	0		0	0	0	12
1970			2	0		0	0	0	12
1971			1	0		0	0	0	6
Career			5	0		0	0	0	30

Leland Glass

Year	Team		TD	1XP	2XP	FG	FGA	SAF	Pts
1972	GB	N	1	0		0	0	0	6

Bill Glassgow

Year	Team		TD	1XP	2XP	FG	FGA	SAF	Pts
1930	POR	N	5	4		0		0	34
1931	CHIC	N	1	0		0		0	6
Career			6	4		0		0	40

Bob Glazebrook

Year	Team		TD	1XP	2XP	FG	FGA	SAF	Pts
1982	ATL	N	1	0		0	0	0	6
Playoffs			1	0	0	0	0	0	6

Aaron Glenn

Year	Team		TD	1XP	2XP	FG	FGA	SAF	Pts
1996	NYJ	N	2	0	0	0	0	0	12

Kerry Glenn

Year	Team		TD	1XP	2XP	FG	FGA	SAF	Pts
1985	NYJ	N	1	0		0	0	0	6
1990	MIA	N	1	0		0	0	0	6
Career			2	0		0	0	0	12

Terry Glenn

Year	Team		TD	1XP	2XP	FG	FGA	SAF	Pts
1996	NE	N	6	0	0	0	0	0	36

Vencie Glenn

Year	Team		TD	1XP	2XP	FG	FGA	SAF	Pts
1987	SD	N	1	0		0	0	0	6
1989			1	0		0	0	0	6
1995	NYG	N	1	0	0	0	0	0	6
Career			3	0	0	0	0	0	18

Fred Glick

Year	Team		TD	1XP	2XP	FG	FGA	SAF	Pts
1963	HOU	A	1	0	0	0	0	0	6

Gary Glick

Year	Team		TD	1XP	2XP	FG	FGA	SAF	Pts
1956	PIT	N	0	16		4	7	0	28
1957			0	10		5	18	0	25
1958			1	0		0	0	0	6
1960	WAS	N	1	0		0	0	0	6
Career			2	26		9	25	0	65

Fred Gloden

Year	Team		TD	1XP	2XP	FG	FGA	SAF	Pts
1946	MIA	AA	1	0		0	0	0	6

Andrew Glover

Year	Team		TD	1XP	2XP	FG	FGA	SAF	Pts
1991	LARI	N	3	0		0	0	0	18
1992			1	0		0	0	0	6
1993			1	0		0	0	0	6
1994			2	0	0	0	0	0	12
1995	OAK	N	3	0	0	0	0	0	18
1996			1	0	0	0	0	0	6
Career			11	0	0	0	0	0	66

Tim Goad

Year	Team		TD	1XP	2XP	FG	FGA	SAF	Pts
1992	NE	N	1	0		0	0	0	6

Art Gob

Year	Team		TD	1XP	2XP	FG	FGA	SAF	Pts
1959	WAS	N	0	0		0	0	1	2

Les Goble

Year	Team		TD	1XP	2XP	FG	FGA	SAF	Pts
1954	CHIC	N	3	0		0	0	0	18

Ed Goddard

Year	Team		TD	1XP	2XP	FG	FGA	SAF	Pts
1937	BKN-CLE	N	2	1		0		0	13
1938	CLE	N	1	1		0	0	0	7
Career			3	2		0	0	0	20

Paul Goebel

Year	Team		TD	1XP	2XP	FG	FGA	SAF	Pts
1923	COL	N	1	2		0		0	8
1924			3	0		0		0	18

Paul Goebel *continued*

Year	Team		TD	1XP	2XP	FG	FGA	SAF	Pts
1926	NY	A	1	0		0		0	6
Career			5	2		0		0	32

Robert Goff

Year	Team		TD	1XP	2XP	FG	FGA	SAF	Pts
1992	NO	N	2	0		0	0	0	12

Charley Gogolak

Year	Team		TD	1XP	2XP	FG	FGA	SAF	Pts
1966	WAS	N	0	39		22	34	0	105
1967			0	3		1	4	0	6
1968			0	30		9	19	0	57
1970	BOS	N	0	5		2	7	0	11
1971	NE	N	0	28		12	21	0	64
1972			0	9		6	8	0	27
Career			0	114		52	93	0	270

Pete Gogolak

Year	Team		TD	1XP	2XP	FG	FGA	SAF	Pts
1964	BUF	A	0	45	0	19	29	0	102
1965			0	31	0	**28**	**46**	0	115
1966	NYG	N	0	29		16	28	0	77
1967			0	28		6	10	0	46
1968			0	36		14	24	0	78
1969			0	33		11	21	0	66
1970			0	32		25	41	0	107
1971			0	30		6	17	0	48
1972			0	34		21	31	0	97
1973			0	25		17	28	0	76
1974			0	21		10	19	0	51
Career			0	344	0	173	294	0	863
Playoffs			0	4	0	5	7	0	19

Marshall Goldberg

Year	Team		TD	1XP	2XP	FG	FGA	SAF	Pts
1939	CHIC	N	3	0		0	0	0	18
1940			3	0		0	0	0	18
1941			4	0		0	0	0	24
1942			2	0		0	0	0	12
1943			1	0		0	0	0	6
1946			4	0		0	0	0	24
Career			17	0		0	0	0	102

Buckets Goldenberg

Year	Team		TD	1XP	2XP	FG	FGA	SAF	Pts
1933	GB	N	**7**	0		0		0	42
1934			2	0		0		0	12
1937			1	0		0		0	6
Career			10	0		0		0	60

Joe Golding

Year	Team		TD	1XP	2XP	FG	FGA	SAF	Pts
1947	BOS	N	3	0		0	0	0	18
1948			6	0		0	0	0	36
1949	NYB	N	3	0		0	0	0	18
1950	NYY	N	2	0		0	0	0	12
Career			14	0		0	0	0	84

Earl Goldsmith

Year	Team		TD	1XP	2XP	FG	FGA	SAF	Pts
1921	EVA	A	1	0		0		0	6

Al Goldstein

Year	Team		TD	1XP	2XP	FG	FGA	SAF	Pts
1960	OAK	A	2	0	0	0	0	0	12

Ralph Goldston

Year	Team		TD	1XP	2XP	FG	FGA	SAF	Pts
1952	PHI	N	3	0		0	0	0	18

Archie Golembeski

Year	Team		TD	1XP	2XP	FG	FGA	SAF	Pts
1925	PRO	N	2	0		0		0	12
1926			1	0		0		0	6
Career			3	0		0		0	18

Bob Golic

Year	Team		TD	1XP	2XP	FG	FGA	SAF	Pts
1983	CLE	N	1	0		0	0	0	6

Bill Gompers

Year	Team		TD	1XP	2XP	FG	FGA	SAF	Pts
1948	BUF	AA	1	0		0	0	0	6
Playoffs			1	0	0	0	0	0	6

George Gonda

Year	Team		TD	1XP	2XP	FG	FGA	SAF	Pts
1942	PIT	N	2	0		0	0	0	12

Goose Gonsoulin

Year	Team		TD	1XP	2XP	FG	FGA	SAF	Pts
1962	DEN	A	1	0	0	0	0	0	6
1963			1	0	0	0	0	0	6
1965			0	0	1	0	0	0	2
Career			2	0	1	0	0	0	14

Bob Gonya
Year	Team		TD	1XP	2XP	FG	FGA	SAF	Pts
1934	PHI	N	1	0		0		0	6

Royce Goodbread
Year	Team		TD	1XP	2XP	FG	FGA	SAF	Pts
1930	FRA	N	1	0		0		0	6

Chris Goode
Year	Team		TD	1XP	2XP	FG	FGA	SAF	Pts
1990	IND	N	1	0		0	0	0	6

Kerry Goode
Year	Team		TD	1XP	2XP	FG	FGA	SAF	Pts
1988	TB	N	0	0		0	0	1	2

Rob Goode
Year	Team		TD	1XP	2XP	FG	FGA	SAF	Pts
1949	WAS	N	2	0		0	0	0	12
1950			6	0		0	0	0	36
1951			9	0		0	0	0	54
1954			1	0		0	0	0	6
Career			18	0		0	0	0	108

Eugene Goodlow
Year	Team		TD	1XP	2XP	FG	FGA	SAF	Pts
1983	NO	N	2	0		0	0	0	12
1984			3	0		0	0	0	18
1985			3	0		0	0	0	18
1986			2	0		0	0	0	12
Career			10	0		0	0	0	60

Les Goodman
Year	Team		TD	1XP	2XP	FG	FGA	SAF	Pts
1973	GB	N	1	0		0	0	0	6

Clyde Goodnight
Year	Team		TD	1XP	2XP	FG	FGA	SAF	Pts
1945	GB	N	4	0		0	0	0	24
1946			1	0		0	0	0	6
1947			6	0		0	0	0	36
1948			3	0		0	0	0	18
1950	WAS	N	2	0		0	0	0	12
Career			16	0		0	0	0	96

Ronnie Goodwin
Year	Team		TD	1XP	2XP	FG	FGA	SAF	Pts
1963	PHI	N	4	0		0	0	0	24
1964			3	0		0	0	0	18
1965			1	0		0	0	0	6
1966			1	0		0	0	0	6
Career			9	0		0	0	0	54

Tod Goodwin
Year	Team		TD	1XP	2XP	FG	FGA	SAF	Pts
1935	NYG	N	4	0		0		0	24
1936			2	0		0		0	12
Career			6	0		0		0	36

Alex Gordon
Year	Team		TD	1XP	2XP	FG	FGA	SAF	Pts
1991	CIN	N	0	0		0	0	1	2

Darrien Gordon
Year	Team		TD	1XP	2XP	FG	FGA	SAF	Pts
1994	SD	N	2	0	0	0	0	0	12
1996			1	0	0	0	0	0	6
Career			3	0	0	0	0	0	18

Dick Gordon
Year	Team		TD	1XP	2XP	FG	FGA	SAF	Pts
1965	CHI	N	3	0		0	0	0	18
1966			1	0		0	0	0	6
1967			5	0		0	0	0	30
1968			4	0		0	0	0	24
1969			4	0		0	0	0	24
1970			**13**	0		0	0	0	78
1971			5	0		0	0	0	30
1972	LA	N	1	0		0	0	0	6
Career			36	0		0	0	0	216

Larry Gordon
Year	Team		TD	1XP	2XP	FG	FGA	SAF	Pts
1981	MIA	N	0	0		0	0	1	2

Ken Gorgal
Year	Team		TD	1XP	2XP	FG	FGA	SAF	Pts
1954	CLE	N	1	0		0	0	0	6

Paul Gorrill
Year	Team		TD	1XP	2XP	FG	FGA	SAF	Pts
1926	COL	N	1	0		0		0	6

Bruce Gossett
Year	Team		TD	1XP	2XP	FG	FGA	SAF	Pts
1964	LA	N	0	31		18	24	0	85
1965			0	30		15	26	0	75
1966			0	29		**28**	**49**	0	**113**
1967			0	**48**		20	**43**	0	108
1968			0	37		17	31	0	88
1969			0	36		22	34	0	102

Bruce Gossett *continued*
Year	Team		TD	1XP	2XP	FG	FGA	SAF	Pts
1970	SF	N	0	39		21	31	0	102
1971			0	32		23	36	0	101
1972			0	41		18	29	0	95
1973			0	26		26	33	0	104
1974			0	25		11	24	0	58
Career			0	374		219	360	0	1031
Playoffs			0	13		6	13	0	31

Preston Gothard
Year	Team		TD	1XP	2XP	FG	FGA	SAF	Pts
1986	PIT	N	1	0		0	0	0	6
1987			1	0		0	0	0	6
1988			1	0		0	0	0	6
Career			3	0		0	0	0	18

Kurt Gouveia
Year	Team		TD	1XP	2XP	FG	FGA	SAF	Pts
1990	WAS	N	1	0		0	0	0	6
1993			1	0		0	0	0	6
Career			2	0		0	0	0	12

Paul Governali
Year	Team		TD	1XP	2XP	FG	FGA	SAF	Pts
1946	BOS	N	2	0		0	0	0	12
1947	NYG	N	2	0		0	0	0	12
Career			4	0		0	0	0	24

Cornell Gowdy
Year	Team		TD	1XP	2XP	FG	FGA	SAF	Pts
1987	PIT	N	1	0		0	0	0	6

Casimir Gozdowski
Year	Team		TD	1XP	2XP	FG	FGA	SAF	Pts
1922	TOL	N	2	0		0		0	12

Jim Grabowski
Year	Team		TD	1XP	2XP	FG	FGA	SAF	Pts
1966	GB	N	1	0		0	0	0	6
1967			3	0		0	0	0	18
1968			4	0		0	0	0	24
1969			2	0		0	0	0	12
1970			1	0		0	0	0	6
Career			11	0		0	0	0	66
Playoffs			1	0		0	0	0	6

Sam Graddy
Year	Team		TD	1XP	2XP	FG	FGA	SAF	Pts
1990	LARI	N	1	0		0	0	0	6
1991			1	0		0	0	0	6
1992			1	0		0	0	0	6
Career			3	0		0	0	0	18

Randy Gradishar
Year	Team		TD	1XP	2XP	FG	FGA	SAF	Pts
1975	DEN	N	1	0		0	0	0	6
1976			1	0		0	0	0	6
1978			1	0		0	0	0	6
1980			1	0		0	0	0	6
Career			4	0		0	0	0	24

Al Graham
Year	Team		TD	1XP	2XP	FG	FGA	SAF	Pts
1927	DAY	N	1	0		0		0	6
1929			1	0		0		0	6
Career			2	0		0		0	12

Art Graham
Year	Team		TD	1XP	2XP	FG	FGA	SAF	Pts
1963	BOS	A	5	0	0	0	0	0	30
1964			6	0	0	0	0	0	36
1966			4	0	0	0	0	0	24
1967			4	0	0	0	0	0	24
1968			1	0	0	0	0	0	6
Career			20	0	0	0	0	0	120

Hason Graham
Year	Team		TD	1XP	2XP	FG	FGA	SAF	Pts
1995	NE	N	2	0	0	0	0	0	12

Jeff Graham
Year	Team		TD	1XP	2XP	FG	FGA	SAF	Pts
1992	PIT	N	1	0		0	0	0	6
1994	CHI	N	5	0	1	0	0	0	32
1995			4	0	0	0	0	0	24
1996	NYJ	N	6	0	0	0	0	0	36
Career			16	0	1	0	0	0	98
Playoffs			1	0	0	0	0	0	6

Kenny Graham
Year	Team		TD	1XP	2XP	FG	FGA	SAF	Pts
1965	SD	A	1	0	0	0	0	0	6
1966			1	0	0	0	0	0	6
1967			1	0	0	0	0	0	6
1969			2	0	0	0	0	0	12
Career			5	0	0	0	0	0	30

Mike Graham
Year	Team		TD	1XP	2XP	FG	FGA	SAF	Pts
1948	LA	AA	1	0		0	0	0	6

Otto Graham
Year	Team		TD	1XP	2XP	FG	FGA	SAF	Pts
1946	CLE	AA	2	0		0	0	0	12
1947			1	0		0	0	0	6
1948			6	0		0	0	0	36
1949			3	0		0	0	0	18
1950	CLE	N	6	0		0	0	0	36
1951			4	0		0	0	0	24
1952			4	0		0	0	0	24
1953			6	0		0	0	0	36
1954			8	0		0	0	0	48
1955			6	0		0	0	0	36
Career			46	0		0	0	0	276
Playoffs			6	0		0	0	0	36

Scottie Graham
Year	Team		TD	1XP	2XP	FG	FGA	SAF	Pts
1993	MIN	N	3	0		0	0	0	18
1994			2	0	0	0	0	0	12
1995			2	0	0	0	0	0	12
Career			7	0	0	0	0	0	42

Ken Grandberry
Year	Team		TD	1XP	2XP	FG	FGA	SAF	Pts
1974	CHI	N	2	0		0	0	0	12

Sonny Grandelius
Year	Team		TD	1XP	2XP	FG	FGA	SAF	Pts
1953	NYG	N	1	0		0	0	0	6

Garland Grange
Year	Team		TD	1XP	2XP	FG	FGA	SAF	Pts
1929	CHIB	N	2	0		0		0	12
1930			0	1		0		0	1
1931			1	1		0		0	7
Career			3	2		0		0	20

Red Grange
Year	Team		TD	1XP	2XP	FG	FGA	SAF	Pts
1925	CHIB	N	3	0		0		0	18
1926	NY	A	8	2		0		0	50
1927	NYY	N	1	0		0		0	6
1929	CHIB	N	2	1		0		0	13
1930			8	1		0		0	49
1931			7	0		0		0	42
1932			**7**	0		0		0	42
1933			1	0		0		0	6
1934			3	0		0		0	18
Career			40	4		0		0	244

Hoyle Granger
Year	Team		TD	1XP	2XP	FG	FGA	SAF	Pts
1966	HOU	A	2	0	0	0	0	0	12
1967			9	0	0	0	0	0	54
1968			7	0	0	0	0	0	42
1969			4	0	0	0	0	0	24
1970	HOU	N	1	0		0	0	0	6
1971	NO	N	1	0		0	0	0	6
Career			24	0	0	0	0	0	144

Alan Grant
Year	Team		TD	1XP	2XP	FG	FGA	SAF	Pts
1990	IND	N	1	0		0	0	0	6

Bob Grant
Year	Team		TD	1XP	2XP	FG	FGA	SAF	Pts
1970	BAL	N	1	0		0	0	0	6

Bud Grant
Year	Team		TD	1XP	2XP	FG	FGA	SAF	Pts
1952	PHI	N	7	0		0	0	0	42

Darryl Grant
Year	Team		TD	1XP	2XP	FG	FGA	SAF	Pts
1984	WAS	N	1	0		0	0	0	6
Playoffs			1	0	0	0	0	0	6

Frank Grant
Year	Team		TD	1XP	2XP	FG	FGA	SAF	Pts
1973	WAS	N	1	0		0	0	0	6
1974			1	0		0	0	0	6
1975			8	0		0	0	0	48
1976			5	0		0	0	0	30
1977			3	0		0	0	0	18
Career			18	0		0	0	0	108
Playoffs			1	0		0	0	0	6

Hugh Grant
Year	Team		TD	1XP	2XP	FG	FGA	SAF	Pts
1928	CHIC	N	0	1		0		0	1

Otis Grant
Year	Team		TD	1XP	2XP	FG	FGA	SAF	Pts
1983	LARM	N	1	0		0	0	0	6

Larry Grantham

Year	Team		TD	1XP	2XP	FG	FGA	SAF	Pts
1962	NY	A	1	0	0	0	0	0	6
1963			1	0	0	0	0	0	6
1970	NYJ	N	1	0		0	0	0	6
Career			3	0	0	0	0	0	18

Willie Grate

Year	Team		TD	1XP	2XP	FG	FGA	SAF	Pts
1969	BUF	A	1	0	0	0	0	0	6
1970	BUF	N	2	0		0	0	0	12
Career			3	0	0	0	0	0	18

Ray Graves

Year	Team		TD	1XP	2XP	FG	FGA	SAF	Pts
1942	PHI	N	0	1		0	0	0	1

Earnest Gray

Year	Team		TD	1XP	2XP	FG	FGA	SAF	Pts
1979	NYG	N	4	0		0	0	0	24
1980			10	0		0	0	0	60
1981			2	0		0	0	0	12
1982			4	0		0	0	0	24
1983			5	0		0	0	0	30
1984			2	0		0	0	0	12
Career			27	0		0	0	0	162
Playoffs			1	0		0	0	0	6

Jerry Gray

Year	Team		TD	1XP	2XP	FG	FGA	SAF	Pts
1987	LARM	N	1	0		0	0	0	6
1988			1	0		0	0	0	6
1989			1	0		0	0	0	6
1991			1	0		0	0	0	6
Career			4	0		0	0	0	24

Johnnie Gray

Year	Team		TD	1XP	2XP	FG	FGA	SAF	Pts
1976	GB	N	1	0		0	0	0	6

Mel Gray

Year	Team		TD	1XP	2XP	FG	FGA	SAF	Pts
1971	STL	N	4	0		0	0	0	24
1973			7	0		0	0	0	42
1974			6	0		0	0	0	36
1975			11	0		0	0	0	66
1976			5	0		0	0	0	30
1977			5	0		0	0	0	30
1978			2	0		0	0	0	12
1979			1	0		0	0	0	6
1980			3	0		0	0	0	18
1981			2	0		0	0	0	12
Career			46	0		0	0	0	276
Playoffs			1	0		0	0	0	6

Mel Gray

Year	Team		TD	1XP	2XP	FG	FGA	SAF	Pts
1986	NO	N	1	0		0	0	0	6
1987			1	0		0	0	0	6
1988			1	0		0	0	0	6
1991	DET	N	1	0		0	0	0	6
1992			2	0		0	0	0	12
1993			1	0		0	0	0	6
1994			3	0	0	0	0	0	18
Career			10	0	0	0	0	0	60

Tim Gray

Year	Team		TD	1XP	2XP	FG	FGA	SAF	Pts
1977	KC	N	2	0		0	0	0	12

Dave Grayson

Year	Team		TD	1XP	2XP	FG	FGA	SAF	Pts
1961	DAL	A	1	0	0	0	0	0	6
1963	KC	A	1	0	0	0	0	0	6
1965	OAK	A	2	0	0	0	0	0	12
1968			1	0	0	0	0	0	6
1969			1	0	0	0	0	0	6
Career			6	0	0	0	0	0	36

David Grayson

Year	Team		TD	1XP	2XP	FG	FGA	SAF	Pts
1987	CLE	N	1	0		0	0	0	6
1989			2	0		0	0	0	12
Career			3	0		0	0	0	18

Elvis Grbac

Year	Team		TD	1XP	2XP	FG	FGA	SAF	Pts
1995	SF	N	2	0	0	0	0	0	12
1996			2	0	0	0	0	0	12
Career			4	0	0	0	0	0	24
Playoffs			1	0	0	0	0	0	6

Bobby Joe Green

Year	Team		TD	1XP	2XP	FG	FGA	SAF	Pts
1961	PIT	N	0	0		0	1	0	0

Boyce Green

Year	Team		TD	1XP	2XP	FG	FGA	SAF	Pts
1983	CLE	N	4	0		0	0	0	24
1984			1	0		0	0	0	6
1986	KC	N	4	0		0	0	0	24
Career			9	0		0	0	0	54

Cornell Green

Year	Team		TD	1XP	2XP	FG	FGA	SAF	Pts
1961	DAL	N	0	19		5	15	0	34
1963			1	0		0	0	0	6
1965			1	0		0	0	0	6
1966			1	0		0	0	0	6
1968			1	0		0	0	0	6
Career			4	19		5	15	0	58
Playoffs			1	0		0	0	0	6

Darrell Green

Year	Team		TD	1XP	2XP	FG	FGA	SAF	Pts
1984	WAS	N	1	0		0	0	0	6
1987			1	0		0	0	0	6
1990			1	0		0	0	0	6
1993			1	0		0	0	0	6
1994			1	0	0	0	0	0	6
1995			1	0	0	0	0	0	6
1996			1	0	0	0	0	0	6
Career			7	0	0	0	0	0	42
Playoffs			3	0	0	0	0	0	18

Dave Green

Year	Team		TD	1XP	2XP	FG	FGA	SAF	Pts
1975	CIN	N	0	40		10	21	0	70
1976	TB	N	0	11		8	14	0	35
1977			0	5		4	7	0	17
1978			0	0		1	1	0	3
Career			0	56		23	43	0	125
Playoffs			0	4		0	0	0	4

Eric Green

Year	Team		TD	1XP	2XP	FG	FGA	SAF	Pts
1990	PIT	N	7	0		0	0	0	42
1991			6	0		0	0	0	36
1992			2	0		0	0	0	12
1993			5	0		0	0	0	30
1994			4	0	0	0	0	0	24
1995	MIA	N	3	0	1	0	0	0	20
1996	BAL	N	1	0	0	0	0	0	6
Career			28	0	1	0	0	0	170
Playoffs			2	0	0	0	0	0	12

Ernie Green

Year	Team		TD	1XP	2XP	FG	FGA	SAF	Pts
1962	CLE	N	1	0		0	0	0	6
1963			3	0		0	0	0	18
1964			10	0		0	0	0	60
1965			4	0		0	0	0	24
1966			9	0		0	0	0	54
1967			6	0		0	0	0	36
1968			2	0		0	0	0	12
Career			35	0		0	0	0	210
Playoffs			1	0		0	0	0	6

Gary Green

Year	Team		TD	1XP	2XP	FG	FGA	SAF	Pts
1982	KC	N	1	0		0	0	0	6
1985	LARM	N	1	0		0	0	0	6
Career			2	0		0	0	0	12

Gaston Green

Year	Team		TD	1XP	2XP	FG	FGA	SAF	Pts
1990	LARM	N	2	0		0	0	0	12
1991	DEN	N	4	0		0	0	0	24
1992			2	0		0	0	0	12
Career			8	0		0	0	0	48

Harold Green

Year	Team		TD	1XP	2XP	FG	FGA	SAF	Pts
1990	CIN	N	2	0		0	0	0	12
1991			2	0		0	0	0	12
1992			2	0		0	0	0	12
1994			2	0	0	0	0	0	12
1995			3	0	0	0	0	0	18
1996	STL	N	5	0	1	0	0	0	32
Career			16	0	1	0	0	0	98
Playoffs			1	0	0	0	0	0	6

Hugh Green

Year	Team		TD	1XP	2XP	FG	FGA	SAF	Pts
1983	TB	N	2	0		0	0	0	12
Playoffs			1	0	0	0	0	0	6

Jacob Green

Year	Team		TD	1XP	2XP	FG	FGA	SAF	Pts
1983	SEA	N	1	0		0	0	0	6
1985			2	0		0	0	0	12

Jacob Green *continued*

Year	Team		TD	1XP	2XP	FG	FGA	SAF	Pts
1988			1	0		0	0	0	6
Career			4	0		0	0	0	24

Jessie Green

Year	Team		TD	1XP	2XP	FG	FGA	SAF	Pts
1980	SEA	N	1	0		0	0	0	6

Joe Green

Year	Team		TD	1XP	2XP	FG	FGA	SAF	Pts
1971	NYG	N	1	0		0	0	0	6

Johnny Green

Year	Team		TD	1XP	2XP	FG	FGA	SAF	Pts
1960	BUF	A	2	0	0	0	0	0	12
1961			1	0	0	0	0	0	6
1962	NY	A	3	0	0	0	0	0	18
Career			6	0	0	0	0	0	36

Johnny Green

Year	Team		TD	1XP	2XP	FG	FGA	SAF	Pts
1950	PHI	N	1	0		0	0	0	6

Mark Green

Year	Team		TD	1XP	2XP	FG	FGA	SAF	Pts
1989	CHI	N	1	0		0	0	0	6
1990			1	0		0	0	0	6
1991			3	0		0	0	0	18
1992			2	0		0	0	0	12
Career			7	0		0	0	0	42

Paul Green

Year	Team		TD	1XP	2XP	FG	FGA	SAF	Pts
1992	SEA	N	1	0		0	0	0	6
1993			1	0		0	0	0	6
1994			1	0	0	0	0	0	6
Career			3	0	0	0	0	0	18

Robert Green

Year	Team		TD	1XP	2XP	FG	FGA	SAF	Pts
1994	CHI	N	2	0	0	0	0	0	12
1995			3	0	0	0	0	0	18
Career			5	0	0	0	0	0	30

Roy Green

Year	Team		TD	1XP	2XP	FG	FGA	SAF	Pts
1979	STL	N	1	0		0	0	0	6
1980			1	0		0	0	0	6
1981			5	0		0	0	0	30
1982			3	0		0	0	0	18
1983			14	0		0	0	0	84
1984			12	0		0	0	0	72
1985			5	0		0	0	0	30
1986			6	0		0	0	0	36
1987			4	0		0	0	0	24
1988	PHX	N	7	0		0	0	0	42
1989			7	0		0	0	0	42
1990			4	0		0	0	0	24
Career			69	0		0	0	0	414

Sammy Green

Year	Team		TD	1XP	2XP	FG	FGA	SAF	Pts
1979	SEA	N	1	0		0	0	0	6

Tim Green

Year	Team		TD	1XP	2XP	FG	FGA	SAF	Pts
1990	ATL	N	0	0		0	0	1	2

Tony Green

Year	Team		TD	1XP	2XP	FG	FGA	SAF	Pts
1978	WAS	N	3	0		0	0	0	18

Van Green

Year	Team		TD	1XP	2XP	FG	FGA	SAF	Pts
1973	CLE	N	1	0		0	0	0	6
1974			1	0		0	0	0	6
Career			2	0		0	0	0	12

Willie Green

Year	Team		TD	1XP	2XP	FG	FGA	SAF	Pts
1991	DET	N	7	0		0	0	0	42
1992			5	0		0	0	0	30
1993			2	0		0	0	0	12
1995	CAR	N	6	0	0	0	0	0	36
1996			3	0	0	0	0	0	18
Career			23	0	0	0	0	0	138
Playoffs			4	0	0	0	0	0	24

Woody Green

Year	Team		TD	1XP	2XP	FG	FGA	SAF	Pts
1974	KC	N	4	0		0	0	0	24
1975			6	0		0	0	0	36
1976			1	0		0	0	0	6
Career			11	0		0	0	0	66

Danny Greene

Year	Team		TD	1XP	2XP	FG	FGA	SAF	Pts
1985	SEA	N	1	0		0	0	0	6

John Greene

Year	Team		TD	1XP	2XP	FG	FGA	SAF	Pts
1945	**DET**	**N**	5	0		0	0	0	30
1946			2	0		0	0	1	14
1947			5	0		0	0	0	30
1948			5	0		0	0	0	30
1949			7	0		0	0	0	42
1950			3	0		0	0	0	18
Career			27	0		0	0	1	164

Kevin Greene

Year	Team		TD	1XP	2XP	FG	FGA	SAF	Pts
1987	**LARM**	**N**	1	0		0	0	0	6
1988			0	0		0	0	1	2
1991			0	0		0	0	1	2
1992			0	0		0	0	1	2
1996	**CAR**	**N**	1	0	0	0	0	0	6
Career			2	0	0	0	0	3	18

Scott Greene

Year	Team		TD	1XP	2XP	FG	FGA	SAF	Pts
1996	**CAR**	**N**	1	0	0	0	0	0	6

Tiger Greene

Year	Team		TD	1XP	2XP	FG	FGA	SAF	Pts
1990	**GB**	**N**	1	0		0	0	0	6

Tony Greene

Year	Team		TD	1XP	2XP	FG	FGA	SAF	Pts
1972	**BUF**	**N**	1	0		0	0	0	6
1976			1	0		0	0	0	6
1977			0	0		0	0	1	2
Career			2	0		0	0	1	14

Tracy Greene

Year	Team		TD	1XP	2XP	FG	FGA	SAF	Pts
1994	**KC**	**N**	1	0	0	0	0	0	6

Tom Greenfield

Year	Team		TD	1XP	2XP	FG	FGA	SAF	Pts
1939	**GB**	**N**	1	0		0	0	0	6

Don Greenwood

Year	Team		TD	1XP	2XP	FG	FGA	SAF	Pts
1945	**CLE**	**N**	4	0		0	0	0	24
1946	**CLE**	**AA**	6	0		0	0	0	36
Career			10	0		0	0	0	60

L.C. Greenwood

Year	Team		TD	1XP	2XP	FG	FGA	SAF	Pts
1974	**PIT**	**N**	0	0		0	0	1	2

Charles Greer

Year	Team		TD	1XP	2XP	FG	FGA	SAF	Pts
1972	**DEN**	**N**	1	0		0	0	0	6

Jim Greer

Year	Team		TD	1XP	2XP	FG	FGA	SAF	Pts
1960	**DEN**	**A**	1	0	0	0	0	0	6

Terry Greer

Year	Team		TD	1XP	2XP	FG	FGA	SAF	Pts
1987	**SF**	**N**	1	0		0	0	0	6
1990	**DET**	**N**	3	0		0	0	0	18
Career			4	0		0	0	0	24

Ben Gregory

Year	Team		TD	1XP	2XP	FG	FGA	SAF	Pts
1968	**BUF**	**A**	1	0	0	0	0	0	6

Bruce Gregory

Year	Team		TD	1XP	2XP	FG	FGA	SAF	Pts
1926	**DET**	**N**	2	0		0		0	12

Hank Gremminger

Year	Team		TD	1XP	2XP	FG	FGA	SAF	Pts
1963	**GB**	**N**	1	0		0	0	0	6

Bob Gresham

Year	Team		TD	1XP	2XP	FG	FGA	SAF	Pts
1971	**NO**	**N**	6	0		0	0	0	36
1972			3	0		0	0	0	18
1973	**HOU**	**N**	4	0		0	0	0	24
1975	**NYJ**	**N**	1	0		0	0	0	6
Career			14	0		0	0	0	84

Marrio Grier

Year	Team		TD	1XP	2XP	FG	FGA	SAF	Pts
1996	**NE**	**N**	1	0	0	0	0	0	6

Roosevelt Grier

Year	Team		TD	1XP	2XP	FG	FGA	SAF	Pts
1960	**NYG**	**N**	0	0		0	0	1	2
1966	**LA**	**N**	0	0		0	0	1	2
Career			0	0		0	0	2	4

Bob Griese

Year	Team		TD	1XP	2XP	FG	FGA	SAF	Pts
1967	**MIA**	**A**	1	0	0	0	0	0	6
1968			1	0	0	0	0	0	6
1970	**MIA**	**N**	2	0		0	0	0	12
1972			1	0		0	0	0	6
1974			1	0		0	0	0	6

Bob Griese *continued*

Year	Team		TD	1XP	2XP	FG	FGA	SAF	Pts
1975			1	0		0	0	0	6
Career			7	0	0	0	0	0	42

Archie Griffin

Year	Team		TD	1XP	2XP	FG	FGA	SAF	Pts
1976	**CIN**	**N**	3	0		0	0	0	18
1978			3	0		0	0	0	18
1979			2	0		0	0	0	12
1981			4	0		0	0	0	24
1982			1	0		0	0	0	6
Career			13	0		0	0	0	78
Playoffs			1	0		0	0	0	6

Bob Griffin

Year	Team		TD	1XP	2XP	FG	FGA	SAF	Pts
1955	**LA**	**N**	0	0		0	0	1	2

Don Griffin

Year	Team		TD	1XP	2XP	FG	FGA	SAF	Pts
1986	**SF**	**N**	1	0		0	0	0	6
1991			1	0		0	0	0	6
Career			2	0		0	0	0	12

James Griffin

Year	Team		TD	1XP	2XP	FG	FGA	SAF	Pts
1983	**CIN**	**N**	1	0		0	0	0	6
1984			1	0		0	0	0	6
1985			1	0		0	0	0	6
Career			3	0		0	0	0	18

Jim Griffin

Year	Team		TD	1XP	2XP	FG	FGA	SAF	Pts
1968	**CIN**	**A**	1	0	0	0	0	0	6

John Griffin

Year	Team		TD	1XP	2XP	FG	FGA	SAF	Pts
1965	**DEN**	**A**	2	0	0	0	0	0	12

Keith Griffin

Year	Team		TD	1XP	2XP	FG	FGA	SAF	Pts
1985	**WAS**	**N**	3	0		0	0	0	18
1987			1	0		0	0	0	6
1988			1	0		0	0	0	6
Career			5	0		0	0	0	30

Larry Griffin

Year	Team		TD	1XP	2XP	FG	FGA	SAF	Pts
1992	**PIT**	**N**	1	0		0	0	0	6

Ray Griffin

Year	Team		TD	1XP	2XP	FG	FGA	SAF	Pts
1979	**CIN**	**N**	1	0		0	0	0	6
1980			2	0		0	0	0	12
Career			3	0		0	0	0	18

Forrest Griffith

Year	Team		TD	1XP	2XP	FG	FGA	SAF	Pts
1950	**NYG**	**N**	2	0		0	0	0	12

Homer Griffith

Year	Team		TD	1XP	2XP	FG	FGA	SAF	Pts
1934	**CHIC**	**N**	2	0		0		0	12

Howard Griffith

Year	Team		TD	1XP	2XP	FG	FGA	SAF	Pts
1994	**LARM**	**N**	1	0	0	0	0	0	6
1995	**CAR**	**N**	2	0	0	0	0	0	12
1996			2	0	0	0	0	0	12
Career			5	0	0	0	0	0	30
Playoffs			1	0	0	0	0	0	6

Johnny Grigas

Year	Team		TD	1XP	2XP	FG	FGA	SAF	Pts
1943	**CHIC**	**N**	3	0		0	0	0	18
1944	**C-P**	**N**	3	0		0	0	0	18
1945	**BOS**	**N**	2	0		0	0	0	12
1946			3	0		0	0	0	18
Career			11	0		0	0	0	66

Forrest Grigg

Year	Team		TD	1XP	2XP	FG	FGA	SAF	Pts
1950	**CLE**	**N**	0	9		1	2	0	12
1952	**DAL**	**N**	0	9		0	3	0	9
Career			0	18		1	5	0	21

Tex Grigg

Year	Team		TD	1XP	2XP	FG	FGA	SAF	Pts
1920	**CAN**	**A**	1	0		0		0	6
1921			1	0		0		0	6
1923	**CAN**	**N**	4	0		0		0	24
1925	**ROC**	**N**	0	2		0		0	2
Career			6	2		0		0	38

Billy Griggs

Year	Team		TD	1XP	2XP	FG	FGA	SAF	Pts
1987	**NYJ**	**N**	1	0		0	0	0	6
Playoffs			1	0	0	0	0	0	6

Hal Griggs

Year	Team		TD	1XP	2XP	FG	FGA	SAF	Pts
1926	**AKR**	**N**	3	0		0		0	18

Frank Grigonis

Year	Team		TD	1XP	2XP	FG	FGA	SAF	Pts
1942	**DET**	**N**	1	0		0	0	0	6

Bob Grim

Year	Team		TD	1XP	2XP	FG	FGA	SAF	Pts
1967	**MIN**	**N**	1	0		0	0	0	6
1969			1	0		0	0	0	6
1971			7	0		0	0	0	42
1972	**NYG**	**N**	1	0		0	0	0	6
1973			2	0		0	0	0	12
1974			2	0		0	0	0	12
1975	**CHI**	**N**	2	0		0	0	0	12
Career			16	0		0	0	0	96

Billy Joe Grimes

Year	Team		TD	1XP	2XP	FG	FGA	SAF	Pts
1949	**LA**	**AA**	6	0		0	0	0	36
1950	**GB**	**N**	8	0		0	0	0	48
1951			2	0		0	0	0	12
Career			16	0		0	0	0	96

George Grimes

Year	Team		TD	1XP	2XP	FG	FGA	SAF	Pts
1948	**DET**	**N**	1	0		0	0	0	6

Steve Grogan

Year	Team		TD	1XP	2XP	FG	FGA	SAF	Pts
1975	**NE**	**N**	3	0		0	0	0	18
1976			13	0		0	0	0	78
1977			1	0		0	0	0	6
1978			5	0		0	0	0	30
1979			2	0		0	0	0	12
1980			1	0		0	0	0	6
1981			2	0		0	0	0	12
1982			1	0		0	0	0	6
1983			2	0		0	0	0	12
1985			2	0		0	0	0	12
1986			1	0		0	0	0	6
1987			2	0		0	0	0	12
1988			1	0		0	0	0	6
Career			36	0		0	0	0	216

Bill Groman

Year	Team		TD	1XP	2XP	FG	FGA	SAF	Pts
1960	**HOU**	**A**	12	0	0	0	0	0	72
1961			**18**	0	0	0	0	0	108
1962			3	0	0	0	0	0	18
1963	**DEN**	**A**	3	0	0	0	0	0	18
1964	**BUF**	**A**	1	0	0	0	0	0	6
Career			37	0	0	0	0	0	222
Playoffs			1	0	0	0	0	0	6

Mel Groomes

Year	Team		TD	1XP	2XP	FG	FGA	SAF	Pts
1949	**DET**	**N**	1	0		0	0	0	6

Elois Grooms

Year	Team		TD	1XP	2XP	FG	FGA	SAF	Pts
1977	**NO**	**N**	1	0		0	0	0	6
1979			0	0		0	0	1	2
1983	**STL**	**N**	1	0		0	0	0	6
Career			2	0		0	0	1	14

Earl Gros

Year	Team		TD	1XP	2XP	FG	FGA	SAF	Pts
1962	**GB**	**N**	2	0		0	0	0	12
1963			2	0		0	0	0	12
1964	**PHI**	**N**	2	0		0	0	0	12
1965			9	0		0	0	0	54
1966			9	0		0	0	0	54
1967	**PIT**	**N**	1	0		0	0	0	6
1968			6	0		0	0	0	36
1969			7	0		0	0	0	42
Career			38	0		0	0	0	228

Al Gross

Year	Team		TD	1XP	2XP	FG	FGA	SAF	Pts
1985	**CLE**	**N**	1	0		0	0	0	6
1986			1	0		0	0	0	6
Career			2	0		0	0	0	12

Burt Grossman

Year	Team		TD	1XP	2XP	FG	FGA	SAF	Pts
1990	**SD**	**N**	0	0		0	0	1	2
1992			0	0		0	0	2	4
Career			0	0		0	0	3	6

Jack Grossman

Year	Team		TD	1XP	2XP	FG	FGA	SAF	Pts
1932	**BKN**	**N**	5	0		0		0	30
1934			2	0		0		0	12

Jack Grossman *continued*

Year	Team		TD	1XP	2XP	FG	FGA	SAF	Pts
1935			2	1		0		0	13
Career			9	1		0		0	55

Randy Grossman

Year	Team		TD	1XP	2XP	FG	FGA	SAF	Pts
1975	**PIT**	**N**	1	0		0	0	0	6
1976			1	0		0	0	0	6
1978			1	0		0	0	0	6
1979			1	0		0	0	0	6
1981			1	0		0	0	0	6
Career			5	0		0	0	0	30
Playoffs			1	0		0	0	0	6

Rex Grossman

Year	Team		TD	1XP	2XP	FG	FGA	SAF	Pts
1948	**BAL**	**AA**	0	43		**10**	18	0	73
1949			0	19		6	11	0	37
1950	**BAL**	**N**	0	16		0	3	0	16
Career			0	78		16	32	0	126
Playoffs			0	2		1	2	0	5

George Grosvenor

Year	Team		TD	1XP	2XP	FG	FGA	SAF	Pts
1936	**CHIC**	**N**	5	0		0		0	30
1937			2	0		0		0	12
Career			7	0		0		0	42

Jeff Groth

Year	Team		TD	1XP	2XP	FG	FGA	SAF	Pts
1981	**NO**	**N**	1	0		0	0	0	6
1982			1	0		0	0	0	6
1983			1	0		0	0	0	6
1985			2	0		0	0	0	12
Career			5	0		0	0	0	30

Roger Grove

Year	Team		TD	1XP	2XP	FG	FGA	SAF	Pts
1931	**GB**	**N**	1	2		0		0	8
1932			3	5		0		0	23
1933			0	8		0		0	8
1934			4	1		0		0	25
Career			8	16		0		0	64

Lou Groza

Year	Team		TD	1XP	2XP	FG	FGA	SAF	Pts
1946	**CLE**	**AA**	0	**45**		**13**	**29**	0	**84**
1947			0	39		7	19	0	60
1948			0	51		8	**19**	0	75
1949			0	34		2	9	0	40
1950	**CLE**	**N**	1	29		**13**	**19**	0	74
1951			0	**43**		10	**23**	0	73
1952			0	32		**19**	**33**	0	89
1953			0	39		**23**	**26**	0	108
1954			0	37		**16**	24	0	85
1955			0	**44**		11	22	0	77
1956			0	18		11	20	0	51
1957			0	32		**15**	22	0	77
1958			0	36		8	19	0	60
1959			0	33		5	16	0	48
1961			0	37		16	23	0	85
1962			0	33		14	31	0	75
1963			0	40		15	23	0	85
1964			0	49		22	33	0	115
1965			0	45		16	25	0	93
1966			0	51		9	23	0	78
1967			0	43		11	23	0	76
Career			1	810		264	481	0	1608
Playoffs			0	44		13	28	0	83

Frank Grube

Year	Team		TD	1XP	2XP	FG	FGA	SAF	Pts
1928	**NYY**	**N**	0	1		0		0	1

Al Grygo

Year	Team		TD	1XP	2XP	FG	FGA	SAF	Pts
1944	**CHIB**	**N**	2	0		0	0	0	12
1945			1	0		0	0	0	6
Career			3	0		0	0	0	18

Darrell Grymes

Year	Team		TD	1XP	2XP	FG	FGA	SAF	Pts
1987	**DET**	**N**	2	0		0	0	0	12

Albert Guarnieri

Year	Team		TD	1XP	2XP	FG	FGA	SAF	Pts
1924	**BUF**	**N**	2	1		0		0	13

Pete Gudauskas

Year	Team		TD	1XP	2XP	FG	FGA	SAF	Pts
1940	**CLE**	**N**	0	1		0	0	0	1
1944	**CHIB**	**N**	0	**36**		0	0	0	36
1945			0	27		1	2	0	30
Career			0	64		1	2	0	67

Dick Guesman

Year	Team		TD	1XP	2XP	FG	FGA	SAF	Pts
1961	**NY**	**A**	0	24	0	5	15	0	39
1962			0	2	0	0	1	0	2
1963			0	30	0	9	24	0	57
1964	**DEN**	**A**	0	13	0	6	22	0	31
Career			0	69	0	20	62	0	129

Terry Guess

Year	Team		TD	1XP	2XP	FG	FGA	SAF	Pts
1996	**NO**	**N**	1	0	0	0	0	0	6

Roy Guffey

Year	Team		TD	1XP	2XP	FG	FGA	SAF	Pts
1926	**BUF**	**N**	1	0		0		0	6

Ralph Guglielmi

Year	Team		TD	1XP	2XP	FG	FGA	SAF	Pts
1955	**WAS**	**N**	1	0		0	0	0	6
1961	**STL**	**N**	1	0		0	0	0	6
Career			2	0		0	0	0	12

Eric Guliford

Year	Team		TD	1XP	2XP	FG	FGA	SAF	Pts
1995	**CAR**	**N**	2	0	0	0	0	0	12

George Gulyanics

Year	Team		TD	1XP	2XP	FG	FGA	SAF	Pts
1947	**CHIB**	**N**	4	0		0	0	0	24
1948			5	0		0	0	0	30
1949			6	0		0	0	0	36
1950			2	0		0	0	0	12
1951			4	0		0	0	0	24
Career			21	0		0	0	0	126
Playoffs			1	0		0	0	0	6

Mike Guman

Year	Team		TD	1XP	2XP	FG	FGA	SAF	Pts
1980	**LA**	**N**	4	0		0	0	0	24
1981			4	0		0	0	0	24
1982	**LARM**	**N**	2	0		0	0	0	12
1983			4	0		0	0	0	24
1984			1	0		0	0	0	6
1987			1	0		0	0	0	6
Career			16	0		0	0	0	96

Harry Gunner

Year	Team		TD	1XP	2XP	FG	FGA	SAF	Pts
1968	**CIN**	**A**	0	0	0	0	0	1	2
1969			1	0	0	0	0	0	6
Career			1	0	0	0	0	1	8

Mike Gussie

Year	Team		TD	1XP	2XP	FG	FGA	SAF	Pts
1940	**BKN**	**N**	1	0		0	0	0	6

Jim Gustafson

Year	Team		TD	1XP	2XP	FG	FGA	SAF	Pts
1986	**MIN**	**N**	2	0		0	0	0	12
1988			1	0		0	0	0	6
1989			2	0		0	0	0	12
Career			5	0		0	0	0	30

Grant Guthrie

Year	Team		TD	1XP	2XP	FG	FGA	SAF	Pts
1970	**BUF**	**N**	0	24		10	19	0	54
1971			0	8		3	10	0	17
Career			0	32		13	29	0	71

Ace Gutowsky

Year	Team		TD	1XP	2XP	FG	FGA	SAF	Pts
1932	**POR**	**N**	3	0		0		0	18
1933			1	1		0		0	7
1934	**DET**	**N**	5	0		0		0	30
1935			2	0		0		0	12
1936			6	0		0		0	36
1937			1	0		0		0	6
1938			2	0		0		0	12
Career			20	1		0		0	121
Playoffs			1	0		0	0	0	6

Ray Guy

Year	Team		TD	1XP	2XP	FG	FGA	SAF	Pts
1976	**OAK**	**N**	0	0		0	0	0	0

Joe Guyon

Year	Team		TD	1XP	2XP	FG	FGA	SAF	Pts
1920	**CAN**	**A**	1	0		0		0	6
1921	**CLE**	**A**	3	10		0		0	28
1922	**OOR**	**N**	5	3		0		0	33
1923			2	0		0		0	12
Career			11	13		0		0	79

Bruno Haas

Year	Team		TD	1XP	2XP	FG	FGA	SAF	Pts
1921	**CLE**	**A**	1	0		0		0	6

Dale Hackbart

Year	Team		TD	1XP	2XP	FG	FGA	SAF	Pts
1961	**WAS**	**N**	2	0		0	0	0	12

Dale Hackbart *continued*

Year	Team		TD	1XP	2XP	FG	FGA	SAF	Pts
1966	**MIN**	**N**	1	0		0	0	0	6
1967			1	0		0	0	0	6
Career			4	0		0	0	0	24

Dino Hackett

Year	Team		TD	1XP	2XP	FG	FGA	SAF	Pts
1988	**KC**	**N**	0	0		0	0	1	2

Joey Hackett

Year	Team		TD	1XP	2XP	FG	FGA	SAF	Pts
1988	**GB**	**N**	1	0		0	0	0	6

Elmer Hackney

Year	Team		TD	1XP	2XP	FG	FGA	SAF	Pts
1940	**PHI**	**N**	1	0		0	0	0	6
1941	**PIT**	**N**	1	0		0	0	0	6
1942	**DET**	**N**	2	0		0	0	0	12
1943			3	0		0	0	0	18
1944			5	0		0	0	0	30
Career			12	0		0	0	0	72

Michael Haddix

Year	Team		TD	1XP	2XP	FG	FGA	SAF	Pts
1983	**PHI**	**N**	2	0		0	0	0	12
1984			1	0		0	0	0	6
1989	**GB**	**N**	1	0		0	0	0	6
1990			2	0		0	0	0	12
Career			6	0		0	0	0	36

Wayne Haddix

Year	Team		TD	1XP	2XP	FG	FGA	SAF	Pts
1990	**TB**	**N**	3	0		0	0	0	18

Al Haddon

Year	Team		TD	1XP	2XP	FG	FGA	SAF	Pts
1925	**DET**	**N**	4	0		0		0	24
1926			1	0		0		0	6
Career			5	0		0		0	30

Pat Haden

Year	Team		TD	1XP	2XP	FG	FGA	SAF	Pts
1976	**LA**	**N**	4	0		0	0	0	24
1977			2	0		0	0	0	12
Career			6	0		0	0	0	36
Playoffs			1	0		0	0	0	6

John Hadl

Year	Team		TD	1XP	2XP	FG	FGA	SAF	Pts
1962	**SD**	**A**	1	0	0	0	0	0	6
1964			1	0	0	0	0	0	6
1965			1	0	0	0	0	0	6
1966			2	0	0	0	0	0	12
1967			3	0	0	0	0	0	18
1968			2	0	0	0	0	0	12
1969			2	0	0	0	0	0	12
1970	**SD**	**N**	1	0		0	0	0	6
1971			1	0		0	0	0	6
1972			1	0		0	0	0	6
1977	**HOU**	**N**	1	0		0	0	0	6
Career			16	0	0	0	0	0	96
Playoffs			1	0	0	0	0	0	6

James Hadnot

Year	Team		TD	1XP	2XP	FG	FGA	SAF	Pts
1980	**KC**	**N**	2	0		0	0	0	12
1981			3	0		0	0	0	18
Career			5	0		0	0	0	30

Mike Haffner

Year	Team		TD	1XP	2XP	FG	FGA	SAF	Pts
1968	**DEN**	**A**	1	0	0	0	0	0	6
1969			5	0	0	0	0	0	30
1970	**DEN**	**N**	1	0		0	0	0	6
Career			7	0	0	0	0	0	42

Roger Hagberg

Year	Team		TD	1XP	2XP	FG	FGA	SAF	Pts
1965	**OAK**	**A**	1	0	0	0	0	0	6
1966			1	0	0	0	0	0	6
1967			3	0	0	0	0	0	18
1968			2	0	0	0	0	0	12
1969			1	0	0	0	0	0	6
Career			8	0	0	0	0	0	48

Rudy Hagberg

Year	Team		TD	1XP	2XP	FG	FGA	SAF	Pts
1929	**BUF**	**N**	3	0		0		0	18
1930	**BKN**	**N**	1	0		0		0	6
Career			4	0		0		0	24

Jack Hagerty

Year	Team		TD	1XP	2XP	FG	FGA	SAF	Pts
1926	**NYG**	**N**	2	0		0		0	12
1927			3	0		0		0	18
1929			3	0		0		0	18
1930			5	0		0		0	30

Jack Hagerty *continued*

Year	Team		TD	1XP	2XP	FG	FGA	SAF	Pts
1932			0	2		0		0	2
Career			13	2		0		0	80

Isaac Hagins

Year	Team		TD	1XP	2XP	FG	FGA	SAF	Pts
1979	**TB**	**N**	3	0		0	0	0	18
1980			2	0		0	0	0	12
Career			5	0		0	0	0	30

Scott Hagler

Year	Team		TD	1XP	2XP	FG	FGA	SAF	Pts
1987	**SEA**	**N**	0	4		2	2	0	10

Mac Haik

Year	Team		TD	1XP	2XP	FG	FGA	SAF	Pts
1968	**HOU**	**A**	8	0	0	0	0	0	48
1969			1	0	0	0	0	0	6
Career			9	0	0	0	0	0	54

Hinkey Haines

Year	Team		TD	1XP	2XP	FG	FGA	SAF	Pts
1925	**NYG**	**N**	3	0		0		0	18
1926			6	0		0		0	36
1927			**6**	0		0		0	36
1928			6	0		0		0	30
1929	**SI**	**N**	2	0		0		0	12
Career			23	0		0		0	132

Russell Hairston

Year	Team		TD	1XP	2XP	FG	FGA	SAF	Pts
1987	**PIT**	**N**	1	0		0	0	0	6

Chuck Hajek

Year	Team		TD	1XP	2XP	FG	FGA	SAF	Pts
1934	**PHI**	**N**	0	1		0		0	1

Ali Haji-Sheikh

Year	Team		TD	1XP	2XP	FG	FGA	SAF	Pts
1983	**NYG**	**N**	0	22		**35**	42	0	127
1984			0	32		17	33	0	83
1985			0	5		2	5	0	11
1986	**ATL**	**N**	0	7		9	12	0	34
1987	**WAS**	**N**	0	29		13	19	0	68
Career			0	95		76	111	0	323
Playoffs			0	13		5	9	0	28

George Halas

Year	Team		TD	1XP	2XP	FG	FGA	SAF	Pts
1920	**DEC**	**A**	2	0		0		0	12
1921			3	0		0		0	18
1922	**CHIB**	**N**	2	2		0		0	14
1923			1	0		0		0	6
1927			3	0		0		0	18
1928			1	0		0		0	6
Career			12	2		0		0	74

Chris Hale

Year	Team		TD	1XP	2XP	FG	FGA	SAF	Pts
1992	**BUF**	**N**	0	0		0	0	1	2

Charles Haley

Year	Team		TD	1XP	2XP	FG	FGA	SAF	Pts
1988	**SF**	**N**	0	0		0	0	1	2
1989			1	0		0	0	0	6
Career			1	0		0	0	1	8

Dick Haley

Year	Team		TD	1XP	2XP	FG	FGA	SAF	Pts
1959	**WAS**	**N**	1	0		0	0	0	6
1963	**PIT**	**N**	1	0		0	0	0	6
Career			2	0		0	0	0	12

Eddie Halicki

Year	Team		TD	1XP	2XP	FG	FGA	SAF	Pts
1929	**FRA**	**N**	6	6		1		0	45
1930			4	5		0		0	29
Career			10	11		1		0	74

Alvin Hall

Year	Team		TD	1XP	2XP	FG	FGA	SAF	Pts
1981	**DET**	**N**	1	0		0	0	0	6
1982			1	0		0	0	0	6
Career			2	0		0	0	0	12

Charlie Hall

Year	Team		TD	1XP	2XP	FG	FGA	SAF	Pts
1974	**CLE**	**N**	1	0		0	0	0	6
1975			1	0		0	0	0	6
Career			2	0		0	0	0	12

Delton Hall

Year	Team		TD	1XP	2XP	FG	FGA	SAF	Pts
1987	**PIT**	**N**	2	0		0	0	0	12

Dino Hall

Year	Team		TD	1XP	2XP	FG	FGA	SAF	Pts
1979	**CLE**	**N**	1	0		0	0	0	6
1982			1	0		0	0	0	6
Career			2	0		0	0	0	12

Forrest Hall

Year	Team		TD	1XP	2XP	FG	FGA	SAF	Pts
1948	**SF**	**AA**	2	0		0	0	0	12

Galen Hall

Year	Team		TD	1XP	2XP	FG	FGA	SAF	Pts
1962	**WAS**	**N**	1	0		0	0	0	6
1963	**NY**	**A**	1	0	0	0	0	0	6
Career			2	0	0	0	0	0	12

Johnny Hall

Year	Team		TD	1XP	2XP	FG	FGA	SAF	Pts
1940	**CHIC**	**N**	5	0		0	0	0	30
1941			4	0		0	0	0	24
1943			1	0		0	0	0	6
Career			10	0		0	0	0	60

Ken Hall

Year	Team		TD	1XP	2XP	FG	FGA	SAF	Pts
1959	**CHIC**	**N**	2	0		0	0	0	12
1960	**HOU**	**A**	1	0	0	0	0	0	6
1961			1	0	0	0	0	0	6
Career			4	0	0	0	0	0	24

Parker Hall

Year	Team		TD	1XP	2XP	FG	FGA	SAF	Pts
1939	**CLE**	**N**	2	0		0	0	0	12
1940			1	0		0	0	0	6
1941			2	0		0	0	0	12
1942			1	0		0	0	0	6
Career			6	0		0	0	0	36

Rhett Hall

Year	Team		TD	1XP	2XP	FG	FGA	SAF	Pts
1996	**PHI**	**N**	1	0	0	0	0	0	6

Ron Hall

Year	Team		TD	1XP	2XP	FG	FGA	SAF	Pts
1987	**TB**	**N**	1	0		0	0	0	6
1989			2	0		0	0	0	12
1990			2	0		0	0	0	12
1992			4	0		0	0	0	24
1993			1	0		0	0	0	6
Career			10	0		0	0	0	60

Ronnie Hall

Year	Team		TD	1XP	2XP	FG	FGA	SAF	Pts
1962	**BOS**	**A**	1	0	0	0	0	0	6

Tom Hall

Year	Team		TD	1XP	2XP	FG	FGA	SAF	Pts
1963	**DET**	**N**	1	0		0	0	0	6
1964	**MIN**	**N**	2	0		0	0	0	12
1965			2	0		0	0	0	12
1966			2	0		0	0	0	12
1968			1	0		0	0	0	6
Career			8	0		0	0	0	48

Willie Hall

Year	Team		TD	1XP	2XP	FG	FGA	SAF	Pts
1977	**OAK**	**N**	1	0		0	0	0	6

Windlan Hall

Year	Team		TD	1XP	2XP	FG	FGA	SAF	Pts
1973	**SF**	**N**	2	0		0	0	0	12

Death Halladay

Year	Team		TD	1XP	2XP	FG	FGA	SAF	Pts
1923	**RAC**	**N**	1	0		0		0	6
1924			1	0		0		0	6
Career			2	0		0		0	12

Ty Hallock

Year	Team		TD	1XP	2XP	FG	FGA	SAF	Pts
1993	**DET**	**N**	2	0		0	0	0	12

Jack Ham

Year	Team		TD	1XP	2XP	FG	FGA	SAF	Pts
1972	**PIT**	**N**	1	0		0	0	0	6
1973			1	0		0	0	0	6
Career			2	0		0	0	0	12

Johnny Haman

Year	Team		TD	1XP	2XP	FG	FGA	SAF	Pts
1940	**CLE**	**N**	1	0		0	0	0	6

Tex Hamer

Year	Team		TD	1XP	2XP	FG	FGA	SAF	Pts
1924	**FRA**	**N**	**12**	0		0		0	72
1925			7	3		0		0	45
1926			2	3		0		0	15
Career			21	6		0		0	132

Keith Hamilton

Year	Team		TD	1XP	2XP	FG	FGA	SAF	Pts
1993	**NYG**	**N**	0	0		0	0	1	2

Ray Hamilton

Year	Team		TD	1XP	2XP	FG	FGA	SAF	Pts
1944	**CLE**	**N**	1	0		0	0	0	6
1947	**LA**	**N**	1	0		0	0	0	6
Career			2	0		0	0	0	12

Ray Hamilton

Year	Team		TD	1XP	2XP	FG	FGA	SAF	Pts
1975	**NE**	**N**	1	0		0	0	0	6

Mal Hammack

Year	Team		TD	1XP	2XP	FG	FGA	SAF	Pts
1955	**CHIC**	**N**	2	0		0	0	0	12
1958			1	0		0	0	0	6
1959			1	0		0	0	0	6
1960	**STL**	**N**	2	0		0	0	0	12
1961			1	0		0	0	0	6
1962			1	0		0	0	0	6
Career			8	0		0	0	0	48

Bobby Hammond

Year	Team		TD	1XP	2XP	FG	FGA	SAF	Pts
1977	**NYG**	**N**	4	0		0	0	0	24
1978			3	0		0	0	0	18
1980	**WAS**	**N**	1	0		0	0	0	6
Career			8	0		0	0	0	48

Kim Hammond

Year	Team		TD	1XP	2XP	FG	FGA	SAF	Pts
1969	**BOS**	**A**	0	0	1	0	0	0	2

Dan Hampton

Year	Team		TD	1XP	2XP	FG	FGA	SAF	Pts
1986	**CHI**	**N**	0	0		0	0	1	2

Dave Hampton

Year	Team		TD	1XP	2XP	FG	FGA	SAF	Pts
1969	**GB**	**N**	7	0		0	0	0	42
1970			1	0		0	0	0	6
1971			5	0		0	0	0	30
1972	**ATL**	**N**	7	0		0	0	0	42
1973			5	0		0	0	0	30
1974			2	0		0	0	0	12
1975			6	0		0	0	0	36
1976	**PHI**	**N**	1	0		0	0	0	6
Career			34	0		0	0	0	204

Lorenzo Hampton

Year	Team		TD	1XP	2XP	FG	FGA	SAF	Pts
1985	**MIA**	**N**	3	0		0	0	0	18
1986			12	0		0	0	0	72
1987			1	0		0	0	0	6
1988			12	0		0	0	0	72
Career			28	0		0	0	0	168

Rodney Hampton

Year	Team		TD	1XP	2XP	FG	FGA	SAF	Pts
1990	**NYG**	**N**	4	0		0	0	0	24
1991			10	0		0	0	0	60
1992			14	0		0	0	0	84
1993			5	0		0	0	0	30
1994			6	0	1	0	0	0	38
1995			10	0	1	0	0	0	62
1996			1	0	0	0	0	0	6
Career			50	0	2	0	0	0	304
Playoffs			2	0	0	0	0	0	12

James Hamrick

Year	Team		TD	1XP	2XP	FG	FGA	SAF	Pts
1987	**KC**	**N**	0	4		2	2	0	10

Chris Hanburger

Year	Team		TD	1XP	2XP	FG	FGA	SAF	Pts
1968	**WAS**	**N**	1	0		0	0	0	6
1969			1	0		0	0	0	6
1971			1	0		0	0	0	6
1972			1	0		0	0	0	6
1974			1	0		0	0	0	6
Career			5	0		0	0	0	30

Anthony Hancock

Year	Team		TD	1XP	2XP	FG	FGA	SAF	Pts
1982	**KC**	**N**	1	0		0	0	0	6
1983			1	0		0	0	0	6
1984			1	0		0	0	0	6
1985			2	0		0	0	0	12
Career			5	0		0	0	0	30

Mike Hancock

Year	Team		TD	1XP	2XP	FG	FGA	SAF	Pts
1973	**WAS**	**N**	2	0		0	0	0	12

Larry Hand

Year	Team		TD	1XP	2XP	FG	FGA	SAF	Pts
1967	**DET**	**N**	2	0		0	0	0	12
1970			1	0		0	0	0	6
Career			3	0		0	0	0	18

Carl Hanke

Year	Team		TD	1XP	2XP	FG	FGA	SAF	Pts
1921	**HAM**	**A**	1	0		0		0	6
1924	**CHIC**	**N**	2	0		0		0	12
Career			3	0		0		0	18

Ray Hanken

Year	Team		TD	1XP	2XP	FG	FGA	SAF	Pts
1938	NYG	N	2	0		0		0	12

Merton Hanks

Year	Team		TD	1XP	2XP	FG	FGA	SAF	Pts
1992	SF	N	1	0		0	0	0	6
1993			1	0		0	0	0	6
1995			1	0	0	0	0	0	6
Career			3	0	0	0	0	0	18

John Hannah

Year	Team		TD	1XP	2XP	FG	FGA	SAF	Pts
1974	NE	N	1	0		0	0	0	6

Chuck Hanneman

Year	Team		TD	1XP	2XP	FG	FGA	SAF	Pts
1937	DET	N	1	0		0		0	6
1938			1	0		0		0	6
1939			2	5		4	5	0	29
1940			0	10		2	4	0	16
1941			1	4		1	4	0	13
Career			5	19		7	13	0	70

Dave Hanner

Year	Team		TD	1XP	2XP	FG	FGA	SAF	Pts
1959	GB	N	0	0		0	0	1	2

Tom Hannon

Year	Team		TD	1XP	2XP	FG	FGA	SAF	Pts
1980	MIN	N	1	0		0	0	0	6
1981			0	0		0	0	2	4
Career			1	0		0	0	2	10

Frank Hanny

Year	Team		TD	1XP	2XP	FG	FGA	SAF	Pts
1923	CHIB	N	1	0		0		0	6
1924			1	0		0		0	6
1925			1	0		0		0	6
1926			4	0		0		0	24
1928	PRO	N	1	0		0		0	6
1929			0	1		0		0	1
Career			8	1		0		0	49

Terry Hanratty

Year	Team		TD	1XP	2XP	FG	FGA	SAF	Pts
1971	PIT	N	1	0		0	0	0	6

Don Hansen

Year	Team		TD	1XP	2XP	FG	FGA	SAF	Pts
1971	ATL	N	1	0		0	0	0	6

Wayne Hansen

Year	Team		TD	1XP	2XP	FG	FGA	SAF	Pts
1954	CHIB	N	1	0		0	0	0	6

Jason Hanson

Year	Team		TD	1XP	2XP	FG	FGA	SAF	Pts
1992	DET	N	0	30		21	26	0	93
1993			0	28		34	43	0	130
1994			0	39	0	18	27	0	93
1995			0	**48**	0	28	34	0	132
1996			0	36	0	12	17	0	72
Career			0	181	0	113	147	0	520
Playoffs			0	7	0	2	3	0	13

Tom Hanson

Year	Team		TD	1XP	2XP	FG	FGA	SAF	Pts
1932	SI	N	1	0		0		0	6
1933	PHI	N	4	0		0		0	24
1934			8	0		0		0	48
1936			1	0		0		0	6
1937			1	0		0		0	6
Career			15	0		0		0	90

Chet Hanulak

Year	Team		TD	1XP	2XP	FG	FGA	SAF	Pts
1954	CLE	N	4	0		0	0	0	24
1957			3	0		0	0	0	18
Career			7	0		0	0	0	42
Playoffs			1	0		0	0	0	6

Merle Hapes

Year	Team		TD	1XP	2XP	FG	FGA	SAF	Pts
1942	NYG	N	5	0		0	0	0	30
1946			5	0		0	0	0	30
Career			10	0		0	0	0	60

Jim Harbaugh

Year	Team		TD	1XP	2XP	FG	FGA	SAF	Pts
1988	CHI	N	1	0		0	0	0	6
1989			3	0		0	0	0	18
1990			4	0		0	0	0	24
1991			2	0		0	0	0	12
1992			1	0		0	0	0	6
1993			4	0		0	0	0	24
1995	IND	N	2	0	0	0	0	0	12

Jim Harbaugh *continued*

Year	Team		TD	1XP	2XP	FG	FGA	SAF	Pts
1996			1	0	0	0	0	0	6
Career			18	0	0	0	0	0	108
Playoffs			1	0	0	0	0	0	6

Buddy Hardeman

Year	Team		TD	1XP	2XP	FG	FGA	SAF	Pts
1979	WAS	N	1	0		0	0	0	6

Don Hardeman

Year	Team		TD	1XP	2XP	FG	FGA	SAF	Pts
1975	HOU	N	5	0		0	0	0	30
1976			1	0		0	0	0	6
1977			3	0		0	0	0	18
1979	BAL	N	4	0		0	0	0	24
Career			13	0		0	0	0	78

Mike Harden

Year	Team		TD	1XP	2XP	FG	FGA	SAF	Pts
1984	DEN	N	1	0		0	0	0	6
1985			1	0		0	0	0	6
1986			3	0		0	0	0	18
Career			5	0		0	0	0	30

Pat Harder

Year	Team		TD	1XP	2XP	FG	FGA	SAF	Pts
1946	CHIC	N	5	5		0	0	0	35
1947			7	39		**7**	10	0	**102**
1948			6	**53**		7	**17**	0	**110**
1949			8	**45**		3	5	0	**102**
1950			1	22		4	9	0	40
1951	DET	N	8	0		3	5	0	57
1952			3	34		11	23	0	85
Career			38	198		35	69	0	531
Playoffs			2	10		2	4	0	28

Cedrick Hardman

Year	Team		TD	1XP	2XP	FG	FGA	SAF	Pts
1973	SF	N	0	0		0	0	1	2
1981	OAK	N	1	0		0	0	0	6
Career			1	0		0	0	1	8

Bruce Hardy

Year	Team		TD	1XP	2XP	FG	FGA	SAF	Pts
1978	MIA	N	2	0		0	0	0	12
1979			3	0		0	0	0	18
1980			2	0		0	0	0	12
1982			2	0		0	0	0	12
1984			5	0		0	0	0	30
1985			4	0		0	0	0	24
1986			5	0		0	0	0	30
1987			2	0		0	0	0	12
Career			25	0		0	0	0	150
Playoffs			4	0		0	0	0	24

Carroll Hardy

Year	Team		TD	1XP	2XP	FG	FGA	SAF	Pts
1955	SF	N	4	0		0	0	0	24

Charley Hardy

Year	Team		TD	1XP	2XP	FG	FGA	SAF	Pts
1960	OAK	A	3	0	0	0	0	0	18
1961			4	0	0	0	0	0	24
Career			7	0	0	0	0	0	42

David Hardy

Year	Team		TD	1XP	2XP	FG	FGA	SAF	Pts
1987	LARI	N	0	7		0	1	0	7

Jim Hardy

Year	Team		TD	1XP	2XP	FG	FGA	SAF	Pts
1949	CHIC	N	1	0		0	0	0	6
1950			1	0		0	0	0	6
1952	DET	N	0	1		0	0	0	1
Career			2	1		0	0	0	13

Larry Hardy

Year	Team		TD	1XP	2XP	FG	FGA	SAF	Pts
1978	NO	N	1	0		0	0	0	6
1979			1	0		0	0	0	6
1981			1	0		0	0	0	6
1982			1	0		0	0	0	6
1984			1	0		0	0	0	6
1985			2	0		0	0	0	12
Career			7	0		0	0	0	42

Cecil Hare

Year	Team		TD	1XP	2XP	FG	FGA	SAF	Pts
1942	WAS	N	2	0		0	0	0	12

Ray Hare

Year	Team		TD	1XP	2XP	FG	FGA	SAF	Pts
1941	WAS	N	1	0		0	0	0	6
1942			2	0		0	0	0	12
1944	BKN	N	1	0		0	0	0	6
Career			4	0		0	0	0	24

Edd Hargett

Year	Team		TD	1XP	2XP	FG	FGA	SAF	Pts
1971	NO	N	1	0		0	0	0	6

Jimmy Hargrove

Year	Team		TD	1XP	2XP	FG	FGA	SAF	Pts
1981	CIN	N	1	0		0	0	0	6
1987	GB	N	1	0		0	0	0	6
Career			2	0		0	0	0	12

Jimmy Hargrove

Year	Team		TD	1XP	2XP	FG	FGA	SAF	Pts
1967	MIN	N	1	0		0	0	0	6

Marvin Hargrove

Year	Team		TD	1XP	2XP	FG	FGA	SAF	Pts
1990	PHI	N	1	0		0	0	0	6

Chic Harley

Year	Team		TD	1XP	2XP	FG	FGA	SAF	Pts
1921	DEC	A	0	0		0		0	0

Clarence Harmon

Year	Team		TD	1XP	2XP	FG	FGA	SAF	Pts
1977	WAS	N	1	0		0	0	0	6
1978			1	0		0	0	0	6
1979			5	0		0	0	0	30
1980			8	0		0	0	0	48
1982			1	0		0	0	0	6
Career			16	0		0	0	0	96

Derrick Harmon

Year	Team		TD	1XP	2XP	FG	FGA	SAF	Pts
1984	SF	N	1	0		0	0	0	6
1986			1	0		0	0	0	6
Career			2	0		0	0	0	12

Ronnie Harmon

Year	Team		TD	1XP	2XP	FG	FGA	SAF	Pts
1986	BUF	N	1	0		0	0	0	6
1987			4	0		0	0	0	24
1988			4	0		0	0	0	24
1989			4	0		0	0	0	24
1990	SD	N	2	0		0	0	0	12
1991			2	0		0	0	0	12
1992			4	0		0	0	0	24
1993			2	0		0	0	0	12
1994			2	0	3	0	0	0	18
1995			6	0	0	0	0	0	36
1996	HOU	N	3	0	0	0	0	0	18
Career			34	0	3	0	0	0	210

Tommy Harmon

Year	Team		TD	1XP	2XP	FG	FGA	SAF	Pts
1946	LA	N	5	0		0	0	0	30
1947			4	0		0	0	0	24
Career			9	0		0	0	0	54

Alvin Harper

Year	Team		TD	1XP	2XP	FG	FGA	SAF	Pts
1991	DAL	N	1	0		0	0	0	6
1992			4	0		0	0	0	24
1993			5	0		0	0	0	30
1994			8	0	0	0	0	0	48
1995	TB	N	2	0	0	0	0	0	12
1996			1	0	0	0	0	0	6
Career			21	0	0	0	0	0	126
Playoffs			4	0	0	0	0	0	24

Bruce Harper

Year	Team		TD	1XP	2XP	FG	FGA	SAF	Pts
1977	NYJ	N	1	0		0	0	0	6
1978			5	0		0	0	0	30
1979			2	0		0	0	0	12
1980			3	0		0	0	0	18
1981			5	0		0	0	0	30
1982			1	0		0	0	0	6
1983			3	0		0	0	0	18
1984			1	0		0	0	0	6
Career			21	0		0	0	0	126

Darrell Harper

Year	Team		TD	1XP	2XP	FG	FGA	SAF	Pts
1960	BUF	A	0	1	0	2	3	0	7

Dwayne Harper

Year	Team		TD	1XP	2XP	FG	FGA	SAF	Pts
1992	SEA	N	1	0		0	0	0	6

Jack Harper

Year	Team		TD	1XP	2XP	FG	FGA	SAF	Pts
1967	MIA	A	4	0	0	0	0	0	24

Maurice Harper

Year	Team		TD	1XP	2XP	FG	FGA	SAF	Pts
1937	PHI	N	1	0		0		0	6

Michael Harper

Year	Team		TD	1XP	2XP	FG	FGA	SAF	Pts
1987	NYJ	N	2	0		0	0	0	12

Roland Harper

Year	Team		TD	1XP	2XP	FG	FGA	SAF	Pts
1975	CHI	N	1	0		0	0	0	6
1976			3	0		0	0	0	18
1978			8	0		0	0	0	48
1980			5	0		0	0	0	30
1981			1	0		0	0	0	6
Career			18	0		0	0	0	108

Charley Harraway

Year	Team		TD	1XP	2XP	FG	FGA	SAF	Pts
1968	CLE	N	1	0		0	0	0	6
1969	WAS	N	9	0		0	0	0	54
1970			5	0		0	0	0	30
1971			2	0		0	0	0	12
1972			6	0		0	0	0	36
1973			4	0		0	0	0	24
Career			27	0		0	0	0	162
Playoffs			1	0		0	0	0	6

Willard Harrell

Year	Team		TD	1XP	2XP	FG	FGA	SAF	Pts
1975	GB	N	3	0		0	0	0	18
1976			4	0		0	0	0	24
1977			2	0		0	0	0	12
1978	STL	N	1	0		0	0	0	6
1980			3	0		0	0	0	18
1981			2	0		0	0	0	12
1984			1	0		0	0	0	6
Career			16	0		0	0	0	96

John Harrington

Year	Team		TD	1XP	2XP	FG	FGA	SAF	Pts
1947	CHI	AA	3	0		0	0	0	18

Perry Harrington

Year	Team		TD	1XP	2XP	FG	FGA	SAF	Pts
1980	PHI	N	1	0		0	0	0	6
1981			2	0		0	0	0	12
1982			1	0		0	0	0	6
1983			1	0		0	0	0	6
1985	STL	N	1	0		0	0	0	6
Career			6	0		0	0	0	36
Playoffs			1	0		0	0	0	6

Al Harris

Year	Team		TD	1XP	2XP	FG	FGA	SAF	Pts
1981	CHI	N	1	0		0	0	0	6
1989	PHI	N	0	0		0	0	1	2
Career			1	0		0	0	1	8

Bill Harris

Year	Team		TD	1XP	2XP	FG	FGA	SAF	Pts
1968	ATL	N	1	0		0	0	0	6

Bo Harris

Year	Team		TD	1XP	2XP	FG	FGA	SAF	Pts
1982	CIN	N	1	0		0	0	0	6

Bob Harris

Year	Team		TD	1XP	2XP	FG	FGA	SAF	Pts
1987	KC	N	1	0		0	0	0	6

Cliff Harris

Year	Team		TD	1XP	2XP	FG	FGA	SAF	Pts
1975	DAL	N	1	0		0	0	0	6

Corey Harris

Year	Team		TD	1XP	2XP	FG	FGA	SAF	Pts
1995	SEA	N	1	0	0	0	0	0	6

Darryl Harris

Year	Team		TD	1XP	2XP	FG	FGA	SAF	Pts
1988	MIN	N	1	0		0	0	0	6

Dick Harris

Year	Team		TD	1XP	2XP	FG	FGA	SAF	Pts
1960	LA	A	1	0	0	0	0	0	6
1961	SD	A	3	0	0	0	0	0	18
1963			1	0	0	0	0	0	6
Career			5	0	0	0	0	0	30

Duriel Harris

Year	Team		TD	1XP	2XP	FG	FGA	SAF	Pts
1976	MIA	N	1	0		0	0	0	6
1977			5	0		0	0	0	30
1978			3	0		0	0	0	18
1979			3	0		0	0	0	18
1980			2	0		0	0	0	12
1981			2	0		0	0	0	12
1982			1	0		0	0	0	6
1983			1	0		0	0	0	6
1984	CLE	N	2	0		0	0	0	12
Career			20	0		0	0	0	120

Eric Harris

Year	Team		TD	1XP	2XP	FG	FGA	SAF	Pts
1982	KC	N	1	0		0	0	0	6

Franco Harris

Year	Team		TD	1XP	2XP	FG	FGA	SAF	Pts
1972	PIT	N	11	0		0	0	0	66
1973			3	0		0	0	0	18
1974			6	0		0	0	0	36
1975			11	0		0	0	0	66
1976			14	0		0	0	0	84
1977			11	0		0	0	0	66
1978			8	0		0	0	0	48
1979			12	0		0	0	0	72
1980			6	0		0	0	0	36
1981			9	0		0	0	0	54
1982			2	0		0	0	0	12
1983			7	0		0	0	0	42
Career			100	0		0	0	0	600
Playoffs			18	0		0	0	0	108

Harry Harris

Year	Team		TD	1XP	2XP	FG	FGA	SAF	Pts
1920	AKR	A	1	0		0		0	6

Ike Harris

Year	Team		TD	1XP	2XP	FG	FGA	SAF	Pts
1976	STL	N	1	0		0	0	0	6
1977			3	0		0	0	0	18
1978	NO	N	4	0		0	0	0	24
1979			2	0		0	0	0	12
1980			6	0		0	0	0	36
Career			16	0		0	0	0	96

Jack Harris

Year	Team		TD	1XP	2XP	FG	FGA	SAF	Pts
1925	GB	N	1	0		0		0	6
1926			2	0		0		0	12
Career			3	0		0		0	18

Jackie Harris

Year	Team		TD	1XP	2XP	FG	FGA	SAF	Pts
1991	GB	N	3	0		0	0	0	18
1992			2	0		0	0	0	12
1993			4	0		0	0	0	24
1994	TB	N	3	0	1	0	0	0	20
1995			1	0	0	0	0	0	6
1996			1	0	1	0	0	0	8
Career			14	0	2	0	0	0	88

James Harris

Year	Team		TD	1XP	2XP	FG	FGA	SAF	Pts
1974	LA	N	5	0		0	0	0	30
1975			1	0		0	0	0	6
1976			2	0		0	0	0	12
1977	SD	N	2	0		0	0	0	12
Career			10	0		0	0	0	60

James Harris

Year	Team		TD	1XP	2XP	FG	FGA	SAF	Pts
1994	MIN	N	1	0	0	0	0	0	6

Jimmy Harris

Year	Team		TD	1XP	2XP	FG	FGA	SAF	Pts
1957	PHI	N	1	0		0	0	0	6

Joe Harris

Year	Team		TD	1XP	2XP	FG	FGA	SAF	Pts
1979	LA	N	1	0		0	0	0	6
1981			1	0		0	0	0	6
Career			2	0		0	0	0	12

John Harris

Year	Team		TD	1XP	2XP	FG	FGA	SAF	Pts
1981	SEA	N	2	0		0	0	0	12

Ken Harris

Year	Team		TD	1XP	2XP	FG	FGA	SAF	Pts
1923	DUL	N	0	0		0		0	0

Leonard Harris

Year	Team		TD	1XP	2XP	FG	FGA	SAF	Pts
1989	HOU	N	2	0		0	0	0	12
1990			3	0		0	0	0	18
1992			2	0		0	0	0	12
1993			1	0		0	0	0	6
Career			8	0		0	0	0	48

Leroy Harris

Year	Team		TD	1XP	2XP	FG	FGA	SAF	Pts
1977	MIA	N	4	0		0	0	0	24
1978			2	0		0	0	0	12
1979	PHI	N	2	0		0	0	0	12
1980			4	0		0	0	0	24
1982			2	0		0	0	0	12
Career			14	0		0	0	0	84
Playoffs			1	0		0	0	0	6

M.L. Harris

Year	Team		TD	1XP	2XP	FG	FGA	SAF	Pts
1981	CIN	N	2	0		0	0	0	12
1982			3	0		0	0	0	18

M.L. Harris continued

Year	Team		TD	1XP	2XP	FG	FGA	SAF	Pts
1983			2	0		0	0	0	12
1984			2	0		0	0	0	12
1985			1	0		0	0	0	6
Career			10	0		0	0	0	60
Playoffs			1	0		0	0	0	6

Raymont Harris

Year	Team		TD	1XP	2XP	FG	FGA	SAF	Pts
1994	CHI	N	1	0	0	0	0	0	6
1996			5	0	0	0	0	0	30
Career			6	0	0	0	0	0	36
Playoffs			1	0	0	0	0	0	6

Rickie Harris

Year	Team		TD	1XP	2XP	FG	FGA	SAF	Pts
1965	WAS	N	2	0		0	0	0	12
1966			1	0		0	0	0	6
1969			1	0		0	0	0	6
Career			4	0		0	0	0	24

Tim Harris

Year	Team		TD	1XP	2XP	FG	FGA	SAF	Pts
1988	GB	N	1	0		0	0	2	10

Wendell Harris

Year	Team		TD	1XP	2XP	FG	FGA	SAF	Pts
1962	BAL	N	0	6		1	3	0	9
1966	NYG	N	1	0		0	0	0	6
1967			0	2		0	1	0	2
Career			1	8		1	4	0	17

William Harris

Year	Team		TD	1XP	2XP	FG	FGA	SAF	Pts
1989	TB	N	1	0		0	0	0	6

Dwight Harrison

Year	Team		TD	1XP	2XP	FG	FGA	SAF	Pts
1971	DEN	N	2	0		0	0	0	12
1973	BUF	N	1	0		0	0	0	6
Career			3	0		0	0	0	18

Ed Harrison

Year	Team		TD	1XP	2XP	FG	FGA	SAF	Pts
1926	BKN	A	1	0		0		0	6

James Harrison

Year	Team		TD	1XP	2XP	FG	FGA	SAF	Pts
1972	CHI	N	3	0		0	0	0	18
1973			3	0		0	0	0	18
1974			1	0		0	0	0	6
Career			7	0		0	0	0	42

Kenny Harrison

Year	Team		TD	1XP	2XP	FG	FGA	SAF	Pts
1977	SF	N	1	0		0	0	0	6

Marvin Harrison

Year	Team		TD	1XP	2XP	FG	FGA	SAF	Pts
1996	IND	N	8	0	0	0	0	0	48

Nolan Harrison

Year	Team		TD	1XP	2XP	FG	FGA	SAF	Pts
1992	LARI	N	0	0		0	0	1	2

Reggie Harrison

Year	Team		TD	1XP	2XP	FG	FGA	SAF	Pts
1974	PIT	N	1	0		0	0	0	6
1975			3	0		0	0	0	18
1976			4	0		0	0	0	24
Career			8	0		0	0	0	48
Playoffs			3	0		0	0	1	20

Emile Harry

Year	Team		TD	1XP	2XP	FG	FGA	SAF	Pts
1986	KC	N	1	0		0	0	0	6
1988			1	0		0	0	0	6
1989			2	0		0	0	0	12
1990			2	0		0	0	0	12
1991			3	0		0	0	0	18
Career			9	0		0	0	0	54

Douglas Hart

Year	Team		TD	1XP	2XP	FG	FGA	SAF	Pts
1965	GB	N	1	0		0	0	0	6
1966			1	0		0	0	0	6
1969			1	0		0	0	0	6
1970			1	0		0	0	0	6
1971			1	0		0	0	1	8
Career			5	0		0	0	1	32

Harold Hart

Year	Team		TD	1XP	2XP	FG	FGA	SAF	Pts
1974	OAK	N	3	0		0	0	0	18
1975			4	0		0	0	0	24
Career			7	0		0	0	0	42

Jim Hart

Year	Team		TD	1XP	2XP	FG	FGA	SAF	Pts
1967	STL	N	3	0		0	0	0	18

Jim Hart *continued*

Year	Team	TD	1XP	2XP	FG	FGA	SAF	Pts
1968		6	0		0	0	0	36
1969		2	0		0	0	0	12
1974		2	0		0	0	0	12
1975		1	0		0	0	0	6
1978		2	0		0	0	0	12
Career		16	0		0	0	0	96

Leon Hart

Year	Team	TD	1XP	2XP	FG	FGA	SAF	Pts
1950	DET N	1	0		0	0	0	6
1951		12	0		0	0	0	72
1952		4	0		0	0	0	24
1953		7	0		0	0	0	42
1954		1	0		0	0	0	6
1955		1	0		0	0	0	6
1956		6	0		0	0	0	36
Career		32	0		0	0	0	192
Playoffs		1	0		0	0	0	6

Tommy Hart

Year	Team	TD	1XP	2XP	FG	FGA	SAF	Pts
1971	SF N	1	0		0	0	0	6
1975		1	0		0	0	0	6
1976		0	0		0	0	1	2
1978	CHI N	0	0		0	0	1	2
Career		2	0		0	0	2	16

Mike Hartenstine

Year	Team	TD	1XP	2XP	FG	FGA	SAF	Pts
1975	CHI N	0	0		0	0	1	2
1976		1	0		0	0	0	6
1983		1	0		0	0	0	6
Career		2	0		0	0	1	14

Frank Hartley

Year	Team	TD	1XP	2XP	FG	FGA	SAF	Pts
1994	CLE N	1	0	0	0	0	0	6
1995		1	0	0	0	0	0	6
Career		2	0	0	0	0	0	12

Howard Hartley

Year	Team	TD	1XP	2XP	FG	FGA	SAF	Pts
1948	WAS N	1	0		0	0	0	6

Fred Hartman

Year	Team	TD	1XP	2XP	FG	FGA	SAF	Pts
1947	CHIB N	1	0		0	0	0	6

John Harty

Year	Team	TD	1XP	2XP	FG	FGA	SAF	Pts
1985	SF N	0	0		0	0	1	2

John Harvey

Year	Team	TD	1XP	2XP	FG	FGA	SAF	Pts
1990	TB N	1	0		0	0	0	6

Ken Harvey

Year	Team	TD	1XP	2XP	FG	FGA	SAF	Pts
1988	PHX N	0	0		0	0	1	2

Maurice Harvey

Year	Team	TD	1XP	2XP	FG	FGA	SAF	Pts
1982	GB N	1	0		0	0	0	6

Don Hasselbeck

Year	Team	TD	1XP	2XP	FG	FGA	SAF	Pts
1977	NE N	4	0		0	0	0	24
1980		4	0		0	0	0	24
1981		6	0		0	0	0	36
1982		1	0		0	0	0	6
1983	LARI N	2	0		0	0	0	12
1985	NYG N	1	0		0	0	0	6
Career		18	0		0	0	0	108
Playoffs		2	0		0	0	0	12

Andre Hastings

Year	Team	TD	1XP	2XP	FG	FGA	SAF	Pts
1994	PIT N	2	0	0	0	0	0	12
1995		2	0	0	0	0	0	12
1996		6	0	0	0	0	0	36
Career		10	0	0	0	0	0	60

James Hasty

Year	Team	TD	1XP	2XP	FG	FGA	SAF	Pts
1989	NYJ N	1	0		0	0	0	6
1995	KC N	1	0	0	0	0	0	6
1996		1	0	0	0	0	0	6
Career		3	0	0	0	0	0	18

Russ Hathaway

Year	Team	TD	1XP	2XP	FG	FGA	SAF	Pts
1921	DAY A	0	12		4		0	24
1922	DAY N	0	9		2		0	15
1923		0	1		3		0	10
1924		0	3		1		0	6
1926	POT N	0	3		0		0	3

Russ Hathaway *continued*

Year	Team	TD	1XP	2XP	FG	FGA	SAF	Pts
1927	BUF N	0	0		0		0	0
Career		0	28		10		0	58

Art Hauser

Year	Team	TD	1XP	2XP	FG	FGA	SAF	Pts
1957	LA N	1	0		0	0	0	6

Earl Hauser

Year	Team	TD	1XP	2XP	FG	FGA	SAF	Pts
1921	CIN A	1	0		0		0	6

Sam Havrilak

Year	Team	TD	1XP	2XP	FG	FGA	SAF	Pts
1969	BAL N	1	0		0	0	0	6
1972		6	0		0	0	0	36
Career		7	0		0	0	0	42

Alex Hawkins

Year	Team	TD	1XP	2XP	FG	FGA	SAF	Pts
1960	BAL N	5	0		0	0	0	30
1961		5	0		0	0	0	30
1962		4	0		0	0	0	24
1964		1	0		0	0	0	6
1965		1	0		0	0	0	6
1966	ATL N	2	0		0	0	0	12
1967	BAL N	4	0		0	0	0	24
Career		22	0		0	0	0	132

Ben Hawkins

Year	Team	TD	1XP	2XP	FG	FGA	SAF	Pts
1967	PHI N	10	0		0	0	0	60
1968		5	0		0	0	0	30
1969		8	0		0	0	0	48
1970		4	0		0	0	0	24
1971		5	0		0	0	0	30
1972		1	0		0	0	0	6
Career		33	0		0	0	0	198

Clarence Hawkins

Year	Team	TD	1XP	2XP	FG	FGA	SAF	Pts
1979	OAK N	1	0		0	0	0	6

Courtney Hawkins

Year	Team	TD	1XP	2XP	FG	FGA	SAF	Pts
1992	TB N	2	0		0	0	0	12
1993		5	0		0	0	0	30
1994		5	0	0	0	0	0	30
1996		1	0	0	0	0	0	6
Career		13	0	0	0	0	0	78

Frank Hawkins

Year	Team	TD	1XP	2XP	FG	FGA	SAF	Pts
1982	LARI N	3	0		0	0	0	18
1983		8	0		0	0	0	48
1984		3	0		0	0	0	18
1985		4	0		0	0	0	24
Career		18	0		0	0	0	108
Playoffs		4	0		0	0	0	24

Mike Hawkins

Year	Team	TD	1XP	2XP	FG	FGA	SAF	Pts
1979	NE N	1	0		0	0	0	6

Rip Hawkins

Year	Team	TD	1XP	2XP	FG	FGA	SAF	Pts
1962	MIN N	0	0		0	0	1	2
1964		2	0		0	0	0	12
1965		1	0		0	0	0	6
Career		3	0		0	0	1	20

Les Haws

Year	Team	TD	1XP	2XP	FG	FGA	SAF	Pts
1924	FRA N	4	0		0		0	24
1925		1	0		0		0	6
Career		5	0		0		0	30

Greg Hawthorne

Year	Team	TD	1XP	2XP	FG	FGA	SAF	Pts
1979	PIT N	1	0		0	0	0	6
1980		4	0		0	0	0	24
1981		2	0		0	0	0	12
1982		3	0		0	0	0	18
1985	NE N	1	0		0	0	0	6
Career		11	0		0	0	0	66

Ken Haycraft

Year	Team	TD	1XP	2XP	FG	FGA	SAF	Pts
1929	MIN N	2	0		0		0	12

Aaron Hayden

Year	Team	TD	1XP	2XP	FG	FGA	SAF	Pts
1995	SD N	3	0	0	0	0	0	18

Leo Hayden

Year	Team	TD	1XP	2XP	FG	FGA	SAF	Pts
1972	STL N	1	0		0	0	0	6

Bob Hayes

Year	Team	TD	1XP	2XP	FG	FGA	SAF	Pts
1965	DAL N	13	0		0	0	0	78
1966		13	0		0	0	0	78
1967		11	0		0	0	0	66
1968		12	0		0	0	0	72
1969		4	0		0	0	0	24
1970		11	0		0	0	0	66
1971		8	0		0	0	0	48
1973		3	0		0	0	0	18
1974		1	0		0	0	0	6
Career		76	0		0	0	0	456
Playoffs		2	0		0	0	0	12

Dave Hayes

Year	Team	TD	1XP	2XP	FG	FGA	SAF	Pts
1921	RI A	1	0		0		0	6

Jeff Hayes

Year	Team	TD	1XP	2XP	FG	FGA	SAF	Pts
1986	CIN N	1	0		0	0	0	6

Jonathan Hayes

Year	Team	TD	1XP	2XP	FG	FGA	SAF	Pts
1985	KC N	1	0		0	0	0	6
1987		2	0		0	0	0	12
1988		1	0		0	0	0	6
1989		2	0		0	0	0	12
1990		1	0		0	0	0	6
1991		2	0		0	0	0	12
1992		2	0		0	0	0	12
1993		1	0		0	0	0	6
1994	PIT N	1	0	0	0	0	0	6
Career		13	0	0	0	0	0	78

Larry Hayes

Year	Team	TD	1XP	2XP	FG	FGA	SAF	Pts
1961	NYG N	1	0		0	0	0	6

Lester Hayes

Year	Team	TD	1XP	2XP	FG	FGA	SAF	Pts
1979	OAK N	2	0		0	0	0	12
1980		1	0		0	0	0	6
1985	LARI N	1	0		0	0	0	6
1986		1	0		0	0	0	6
Career		5	0		0	0	0	30
Playoffs		2	0		0	0	0	12

Luther Hayes

Year	Team	TD	1XP	2XP	FG	FGA	SAF	Pts
1961	SD A	3	0	0	0	0	0	18

Ray Hayes

Year	Team	TD	1XP	2XP	FG	FGA	SAF	Pts
1961	MIN N	2	0		0	0	0	12

Tom Hayes

Year	Team	TD	1XP	2XP	FG	FGA	SAF	Pts
1971	ATL N	3	0		0	0	0	18
1973		2	0		0	0	0	12
1976	SD N	1	0		0	0	0	6
Career		6	0		0	0	0	36

Wendell Hayes

Year	Team	TD	1XP	2XP	FG	FGA	SAF	Pts
1965	DEN A	7	0	1	0	0	0	44
1966		1	0	0	0	0	0	6
1967		4	0	1	0	0	0	26
1968	KC A	5	0	0	0	0	0	30
1969		4	0	0	0	0	0	24
1970	KC N	5	0	0	0	0	0	30
1971		2	0	0	0	0	0	12
1972		3	0	0	0	0	0	18
1973		2	0	0	0	0	0	12
1974		2	0	0	0	0	0	12
Career		35	0	2	0	0	0	214
Playoffs		1	0	0	0	0	0	6

Alvin Haymond

Year	Team	TD	1XP	2XP	FG	FGA	SAF	Pts
1965	BAL N	1	0		0	0	0	6
1966		1	0		0	0	0	6
1968	PHI N	2	0		0	0	0	12
1970	LA N	1	0		0	0	0	6
Career		5	0		0	0	0	30

Abner Haynes

Year	Team	TD	1XP	2XP	FG	FGA	SAF	Pts
1960	DAL A	12	0		0	0	0	72
1961		13	0		0	0	0	78
1962		19	0		0	0	0	114
1963	KC A	6	0		0	0	0	36
1964		8	0		0	0	0	48
1965	DEN A	6	0		0	0	0	36
1966		3	0		0	0	0	18

Abner Haynes *continued*

Year	Team	Lg	TD	1XP	2XP	FG	FGA	SAF	Pts
1967	MIA	A	2	0	0	0	0	0	12
Career			69	0	0	0	0	0	414
Playoffs			2	0	0	0	0	0	12

Hall Haynes

Year	Team	Lg	TD	1XP	2XP	FG	FGA	SAF	Pts
1950	WAS	N	1	0		0	0	0	6

James Haynes

Year	Team	Lg	TD	1XP	2XP	FG	FGA	SAF	Pts
1986	NO	N	1	0		0	0	0	6

Mark Haynes

Year	Team	Lg	TD	1XP	2XP	FG	FGA	SAF	Pts
1987	DEN	N	1	0		0	0	0	6
Playoffs			1	0	0	0	0	0	6

Michael Haynes

Year	Team	Lg	TD	1XP	2XP	FG	FGA	SAF	Pts
1988	ATL	N	4	0		0	0	0	24
1989			4	0		0	0	0	24
1991			11	0		0	0	0	66
1992			10	0		0	0	0	60
1993			4	0		0	0	0	24
1994	NO	N	5	0	0	0	0	0	30
1995			4	0	0	0	0	0	24
1996			4	0	1	0	0	0	26
Career			46	0	1	0	0	0	278
Playoffs			2	0	0	0	0	0	12

Mike Haynes

Year	Team	Lg	TD	1XP	2XP	FG	FGA	SAF	Pts
1976	NE	N	2	0		0	0	0	12
1978			1	0		0	0	0	6
1980			1	0		0	0	0	6
1984	LARI	N	1	0		0	0	0	6
Career			5	0		0	0	0	30

George Hays

Year	Team	Lg	TD	1XP	2XP	FG	FGA	SAF	Pts
1952	PIT	N	2	0		0	0	0	12

Tracy Hayworth

Year	Team	Lg	TD	1XP	2XP	FG	FGA	SAF	Pts
1991	DET	N	1	0		0	0	0	6

Matt Hazeltine

Year	Team	Lg	TD	1XP	2XP	FG	FGA	SAF	Pts
1958	SF	N	1	0		0	0	0	6
1959			1	0		0	0	0	6
1966			1	0		0	0	0	6
Career			3	0		0	0	0	18

Andy Headen

Year	Team	Lg	TD	1XP	2XP	FG	FGA	SAF	Pts
1984	NYG	N	1	0		0	0	0	6

Sherrill Headrick

Year	Team	Lg	TD	1XP	2XP	FG	FGA	SAF	Pts
1961	DAL	A	2	0	0	0	0	0	12
1963	KC	A	1	0	0	0	0	0	6
Career			3	0	0	0	0	0	18

Ed Healey

Year	Team	Lg	TD	1XP	2XP	FG	FGA	SAF	Pts
1921	RI	A	1	0		0		0	6

Walt Heap

Year	Team	Lg	TD	1XP	2XP	FG	FGA	SAF	Pts
1947	LA	AA	2	0		0	0	0	12
1948			1	0		0	0	0	6
Career			3	0		0	0	0	18

Herman Heard

Year	Team	Lg	TD	1XP	2XP	FG	FGA	SAF	Pts
1984	KC	N	4	0		0	0	0	24
1985			6	0		0	0	0	36
1986			2	0		0	0	0	12
1987			3	0		0	0	0	18
1989			1	0		0	0	0	6
Career			16	0		0	0	0	96

Les Hearden

Year	Team	Lg	TD	1XP	2XP	FG	FGA	SAF	Pts
1924	GB	N	1	0		0		0	6

Garrison Hearst

Year	Team	Lg	TD	1XP	2XP	FG	FGA	SAF	Pts
1993	PHX	N	1	0		0	0	0	6
1994	ARI	N	1	0	0	0	0	0	6
1995			2	0	0	0	0	0	12
1996	CIN	N	1	0	1	0	0	0	8
Career			5	0	1	0	0	0	32

Larry Heater

Year	Team	Lg	TD	1XP	2XP	FG	FGA	SAF	Pts
1980	NYG	N	3	0		0	0	0	18

Leon Heath

Year	Team	Lg	TD	1XP	2XP	FG	FGA	SAF	Pts
1952	WAS	N	3	0		0	0	0	18
1953			4	0		0	0	0	24
Career			7	0		0	0	0	42

Stan Heath

Year	Team	Lg	TD	1XP	2XP	FG	FGA	SAF	Pts
1949	GB	N	1	0		0	0	0	6

Bobby Hebert

Year	Team	Lg	TD	1XP	2XP	FG	FGA	SAF	Pts
1985	NO	N	1	0		0	0	0	6
1996	ATL	N	1	0	0	0	0	0	6
Career			2	0	0	0	0	0	12

Vaughn Hebron

Year	Team	Lg	TD	1XP	2XP	FG	FGA	SAF	Pts
1993	PHI	N	3	0		0	0	0	18
1994			2	0	0	0	0	0	12
Career			5	0	0	0	0	0	30
Playoffs			1	0	0	0	0	0	6

Ralph Heck

Year	Team	Lg	TD	1XP	2XP	FG	FGA	SAF	Pts
1971	NYG	N	1	0		0	0	0	6

Norb Hecker

Year	Team	Lg	TD	1XP	2XP	FG	FGA	SAF	Pts
1951	LA	N	1	0		0	1	0	6
1955	WAS	N	1	2		0	1	0	8
1956			1	0		0	0	0	6
Career			3	2		0	2	0	20

Johnny Hector

Year	Team	Lg	TD	1XP	2XP	FG	FGA	SAF	Pts
1983	NYJ	N	1	0		0	0	0	6
1984			1	0		0	0	0	6
1985			6	0		0	0	0	36
1986			8	0		0	0	0	48
1987			11	0		0	0	0	66
1988			10	0		0	0	0	60
1989			5	0		0	0	0	30
1990			2	0		0	0	0	12
Career			44	0		0	0	0	264
Playoffs			1	0		0	0	0	6

Gene Heeter

Year	Team	Lg	TD	1XP	2XP	FG	FGA	SAF	Pts
1963	NY	A	1	0	0	0	0	0	6
1964			1	0	0	0	0	0	6
Career			2	0	0	0	0	0	12

Victor Heflin

Year	Team	Lg	TD	1XP	2XP	FG	FGA	SAF	Pts
1985	MIA	N	1	0		0	0	0	6
1986	TB	N	1	0		0	0	0	6
Career			2	0		0	0	0	12

Mike Hegman

Year	Team	Lg	TD	1XP	2XP	FG	FGA	SAF	Pts
1980	DAL	N	1	0		0	0	0	6
1983			1	0		0	0	0	6
Career			2	0		0	0	0	12
Playoffs			1	0		0	0	0	6

Johnny Heimsch

Year	Team	Lg	TD	1XP	2XP	FG	FGA	SAF	Pts
1926	MIL	N	3	0		0		0	18

Lakei Heimuli

Year	Team	Lg	TD	1XP	2XP	FG	FGA	SAF	Pts
1987	CHI	N	1	0		0	0	0	6

Mel Hein

Year	Team	Lg	TD	1XP	2XP	FG	FGA	SAF	Pts
1938	NYG	N	1	0		0		0	6

Ken Heineman

Year	Team	Lg	TD	1XP	2XP	FG	FGA	SAF	Pts
1940	CLE	N	0	1		0	0	0	1

Don Heinrich

Year	Team	Lg	TD	1XP	2XP	FG	FGA	SAF	Pts
1955	NYG	N	2	0		0	0	0	12
1957			2	0		0	0	0	12
1958			1	0		0	0	0	6
Career			5	0		0	0	0	30

Paul Held

Year	Team	Lg	TD	1XP	2XP	FG	FGA	SAF	Pts
1954	PIT	N	0	14		3	5	0	23

Ron Heller

Year	Team	Lg	TD	1XP	2XP	FG	FGA	SAF	Pts
1986	TB	N	1	0		0	0	0	6

Ron Heller

Year	Team	Lg	TD	1XP	2XP	FG	FGA	SAF	Pts
1987	SF	N	3	0		0	0	0	18
1989	ATL	N	1	0		0	0	0	6

Ron Heller *continued*

Year	Team	Lg	TD	1XP	2XP	FG	FGA	SAF	Pts
1990	SEA	N	1	0		0	0	0	6
Career			5	0		0	0	0	30

Warren Heller

Year	Team	Lg	TD	1XP	2XP	FG	FGA	SAF	Pts
1934	PIT	N	1	0		0		0	6
1936			3	0		0		0	18
Career			4	0		0		0	24

Jerry Helluin

Year	Team	Lg	TD	1XP	2XP	FG	FGA	SAF	Pts
1953	CLE	N	1	0		0	0	0	6

Jack Helms

Year	Team	Lg	TD	1XP	2XP	FG	FGA	SAF	Pts
1946	DET	N	0	4		3	4	0	13

Herb Henderson

Year	Team	Lg	TD	1XP	2XP	FG	FGA	SAF	Pts
1921	EVA	A	4	5		0		0	29

Jerome Henderson

Year	Team	Lg	TD	1XP	2XP	FG	FGA	SAF	Pts
1995	PHI	N	1	0	0	0	0	0	6

John Henderson

Year	Team	Lg	TD	1XP	2XP	FG	FGA	SAF	Pts
1965	DET	N	1	0		0	0	0	6
1969	MIN	N	5	0		0	0	0	30
1970			2	0		0	0	0	12
1972			2	0		0	0	0	12
Career			10	0		0	0	0	60

Jon Henderson

Year	Team	Lg	TD	1XP	2XP	FG	FGA	SAF	Pts
1969	PIT	N	3	0		0	0	0	18
1970	WAS	N	3	0		0	0	0	18
Career			6	0		0	0	0	36

Keith Henderson

Year	Team	Lg	TD	1XP	2XP	FG	FGA	SAF	Pts
1989	SF	N	1	0		0	0	0	6
1991			2	0		0	0	0	12
1992	MIN	N	1	0		0	0	0	6
Career			4	0		0	0	0	24

Thomas Henderson

Year	Team	Lg	TD	1XP	2XP	FG	FGA	SAF	Pts
1975	DAL	N	1	0		0	0	0	6
1976			0	0		0	0	1	2
1977			1	0		0	0	0	6
Career			2	0		0	0	1	14
Playoffs			1	0		0	0	0	6

William Henderson

Year	Team	Lg	TD	1XP	2XP	FG	FGA	SAF	Pts
1996	GB	N	1	0	0	0	0	0	6

Wymon Henderson

Year	Team	Lg	TD	1XP	2XP	FG	FGA	SAF	Pts
1990	DEN	N	1	0		0	0	0	6
1992			1	0		0	0	0	6
Career			2	0		0	0	0	12

John Hendren

Year	Team	Lg	TD	1XP	2XP	FG	FGA	SAF	Pts
1920	CAN	A	1	0		0		0	6
1921	CLE	A	1	0		0		0	6
Career			2	0		0			12

Dutch Hendrian

Year	Team	Lg	TD	1XP	2XP	FG	FGA	SAF	Pts
1923	AKR-CAN	N	1	1		0		0	7
1924	GB	N	3	0		1		0	21
1925	NYG	N	2	1		3		0	22
Career			6	2		4		0	50

Ted Hendricks

Year	Team	Lg	TD	1XP	2XP	FG	FGA	SAF	Pts
1970	BAL	N	1	0		0	0	0	6
1971			1	0		0	0	0	6
1973			1	0		0	0	0	6
1974	GB	N	0	0		0	0	1	2
1975	OAK	N	0	0		0	0	1	2
1976			0	0		0	0	1	2
1979			1	0		0	0	0	6
1980			0	0		0	0	1	2
Career			4	0		0	0	**4**	32

Steve Hendrickson

Year	Team	Lg	TD	1XP	2XP	FG	FGA	SAF	Pts
1991	SD	N	2	0		0	0	0	12
Playoffs			1	0	0	0	0	0	6

Manny Hendrix

Year	Team	Lg	TD	1XP	2XP	FG	FGA	SAF	Pts
1991	DAL	N	0	0		0	0	1	2

John Hendy

Year	Team	Lg	TD	1XP	2XP	FG	FGA	SAF	Pts
1985	SD	N	1	0		0	0	0	6

Jerry Hennessy

Year	Team	Lg	TD	1XP	2XP	FG	FGA	SAF	Pts
1952	WAS	N	0	0		0	0	1	2

Charley Hennigan

Year	Team	Lg	TD	1XP	2XP	FG	FGA	SAF	Pts
1960	HOU	A	6	0	0	0	0	0	36
1961			12	0	0	0	0	0	72
1962			8	0	0	0	0	0	48
1963			10	0	0	0	0	0	60
1964			8	0	0	0	0	0	48
1965			4	0	0	0	0	0	24
1966			3	0	0	0	0	0	18
Career			51	0	0	0	0	0	306

Bernard Henry

Year	Team	Lg	TD	1XP	2XP	FG	FGA	SAF	Pts
1983	BAL	N	4	0		0	0	0	24
1984	IND	N	2	0		0	0	0	12
Career			6	0		0	0	0	36

Pete Henry

Year	Team	Lg	TD	1XP	2XP	FG	FGA	SAF	Pts
1920	CAN	A	1	0		0		0	6
1922	CAN	N	0	4		2		0	10
1923			1	**25**		9		0	**58**
1925			0	5		1		0	8
1926			0	3		0		0	3
1927	POT	N	0	1		2		0	7
1928			0	2		0		0	2
Career			2	40		14		0	94

Wally Henry

Year	Team	Lg	TD	1XP	2XP	FG	FGA	SAF	Pts
1978	PHI	N	1	0		0	0	0	6
1981			2	0		0	0	0	12
Career			3	0		0	0	0	18

Dick Hensley

Year	Team	Lg	TD	1XP	2XP	FG	FGA	SAF	Pts
1952	PIT	N	2	0		0	0	0	12
1953	CHIB	N	0	0		0	0	1	2
Career			2	0		0	0	1	14

Craig Hentrich

Year	Team	Lg	TD	1XP	2XP	FG	FGA	SAF	Pts
1995	GB	N	0	5	0	3	5	0	14

Arnie Herber

Year	Team	Lg	TD	1XP	2XP	FG	FGA	SAF	Pts
1930	GB	N	1	0		0		0	6
1931			1	0		0		0	6
1932			2	0		0		0	12
1933			0	1		0		0	1
1935			0	1		0		0	1
1938			2	0		0		0	12
1939			1	0		0	0	0	6
Career			7	2		0	0	0	44

Bill Herchman

Year	Team	Lg	TD	1XP	2XP	FG	FGA	SAF	Pts
1957	SF	N	1	0		0	0	0	6

Joe Hergert

Year	Team	Lg	TD	1XP	2XP	FG	FGA	SAF	Pts
1960	BUF	A	1	0	0	2	4	0	12
1961			0	0	0	6	14	0	18
Career			1	0	0	8	18	0	30

Don Herndon

Year	Team	Lg	TD	1XP	2XP	FG	FGA	SAF	Pts
1960	NY	A	1	0	0	0	0	0	6

Ken Herock

Year	Team	Lg	TD	1XP	2XP	FG	FGA	SAF	Pts
1963	OAK	A	3	0	0	0	0	0	18
1964			2	0	0	0	0	0	12
Career			5	0	0	0	0	0	30

Efren Herrera

Year	Team	Lg	TD	1XP	2XP	FG	FGA	SAF	Pts
1974	DAL	N	0	33		8	13	0	57
1976			0	34		18	23	0	88
1977			0	**39**		18	29	0	93
1978	SEA	N	0	40		13	21	0	79
1979			0	43		19	23	0	100
1980			0	33		20	31	0	93
1981			0	23		12	17	0	59
1982	BUF	N	0	11		8	14	0	35
Career			0	256		116	171	0	604
Playoffs			0	10		7	10	0	31

George Herring

Year	Team	Lg	TD	1XP	2XP	FG	FGA	SAF	Pts
1961	DEN	A	2	0	0	0	0	0	12

Mark Herrmann

Year	Team	Lg	TD	1XP	2XP	FG	FGA	SAF	Pts
1982	DEN	N	1	0		0	0	0	6

Don Herrmann

Year	Team	Lg	TD	1XP	2XP	FG	FGA	SAF	Pts
1969	NYG	N	5	0		0	0	0	30
1970			2	0		0	0	0	12
1971			1	0		0	0	0	6
1972			5	0		0	0	0	30
1973			2	0		0	0	0	12
1975	NO	N	1	0		0	0	0	6
Career			16	0		0	0	0	96

Jeff Herrod

Year	Team	Lg	TD	1XP	2XP	FG	FGA	SAF	Pts
1993	IND	N	1	0		0	0	0	6
1996			1	0	0	0	0	0	6
Career			2	0	0	0	0	0	12

Mack Herron

Year	Team	Lg	TD	1XP	2XP	FG	FGA	SAF	Pts
1973	NE	N	4	0		0	0	0	24
1974			12	0		0	0	0	72
Career			16	0		0	0	0	96

Wally Hess

Year	Team	Lg	TD	1XP	2XP	FG	FGA	SAF	Pts
1920	HAM	A	1	0		0		0	6
1924	HAM	N	0	0		0		0	0
1925			1	0		0		0	6
Career			2	0		0		0	12

Jessie Hester

Year	Team	Lg	TD	1XP	2XP	FG	FGA	SAF	Pts
1985	LARI	N	5	0		0	0	0	30
1986			6	0		0	0	0	36
1990	IND	N	6	0		0	0	0	36
1991			5	0		0	0	0	30
1992			1	0		0	0	0	6
1993			1	0		0	0	0	6
1994	LARM	N	3	0	0	0	0	0	18
1995	STL	N	3	0	0	0	0	0	18
Career			30	0	0	0	0	0	180
Playoffs			1	0	0	0	0	0	6

Jim Hester

Year	Team	Lg	TD	1XP	2XP	FG	FGA	SAF	Pts
1968	NO	N	2	0		0	0	0	12
1969			1	0		0	0	0	6
Career			3	0		0	0	0	18

Bill Hewitt

Year	Team	Lg	TD	1XP	2XP	FG	FGA	SAF	Pts
1932	CHIB	N	1	0		0		0	6
1933			3	0		0		0	18
1934			5	0		0		0	30
1936			7	0		0		0	42
1937	PHI	N	5	0		0		0	30
1938			4	0		0		0	24
1939			1	0		0	0	0	6
Career			26	0		0	0	0	156

Craig Heyward

Year	Team	Lg	TD	1XP	2XP	FG	FGA	SAF	Pts
1988	NO	N	1	0		0	0	0	6
1989			1	0		0	0	0	6
1990			4	0		0	0	0	24
1991			5	0		0	0	0	30
1992			3	0		0	0	0	18
1994	ATL	N	8	0	0	0	0	0	48
1995			8	0	0	0	0	0	48
1996			3	0	0	0	0	0	18
Career			33	0	0	0	0	0	198
Playoffs			1	0	0	0	0	0	6

Ralph Heywood

Year	Team	Lg	TD	1XP	2XP	FG	FGA	SAF	Pts
1946	CHI	AA	4	0		0	0	0	24
1947	DET	N	2	0		0	0	0	12
1948	BOS	N	3	0		0	0	0	18
1949	NYB	N	4	0		0	0	0	24
Career			13	0		0	0	0	78

Bo Hickey

Year	Team	Lg	TD	1XP	2XP	FG	FGA	SAF	Pts
1967	DEN	A	5	0	0	0	0	0	30

Red Hickey

Year	Team	Lg	TD	1XP	2XP	FG	FGA	SAF	Pts
1941	CLE	N	4	0		0	0	0	24
1946	LA	N	3	0		0	0	0	18
1947			2	0		0	0	0	12
1948			7	0		0	0	0	42
Career			16	0		0	0	0	96

Herman Hickman

Year	Team	Lg	TD	1XP	2XP	FG	FGA	SAF	Pts
1933	BKN	N	0	2		2		0	8

Dwight Hicks

Year	Team	Lg	TD	1XP	2XP	FG	FGA	SAF	Pts
1981	SF	N	2	0		0	0	0	12
1983			2	0		0	0	0	12
Career			4	0		0	0	0	24

Tom Hicks

Year	Team	Lg	TD	1XP	2XP	FG	FGA	SAF	Pts
1979	CHI	N	1	0		0	0	0	6

Victor Hicks

Year	Team	Lg	TD	1XP	2XP	FG	FGA	SAF	Pts
1980	LA	N	3	0		0	0	0	18

Alex Higdon

Year	Team	Lg	TD	1XP	2XP	FG	FGA	SAF	Pts
1988	ATL	N	2	0		0	0	0	12

Bob Higgins

Year	Team	Lg	TD	1XP	2XP	FG	FGA	SAF	Pts
1920	CAN	A	1	0		0		0	6
1921			2	2		0		0	14
Career			3	2		0		0	20

Mark Higgs

Year	Team	Lg	TD	1XP	2XP	FG	FGA	SAF	Pts
1990	MIA	N	1	0		0	0	0	6
1991			4	0		0	0	0	24
1992			7	0		0	0	0	42
1993			3	0		0	0	0	18
Career			15	0		0	0	0	90

Alonzo Highsmith

Year	Team	Lg	TD	1XP	2XP	FG	FGA	SAF	Pts
1987	HOU	N	2	0		0	0	0	12
1988			2	0		0	0	0	12
1989			6	0		0	0	0	36
Career			10	0		0	0	0	60

Don Highsmith

Year	Team	Lg	TD	1XP	2XP	FG	FGA	SAF	Pts
1971	OAK	N	1	0		0	0	0	6
1972			1	0		0	0	0	6
Career			2	0		0	0	0	12

Ben Hightower

Year	Team	Lg	TD	1XP	2XP	FG	FGA	SAF	Pts
1942	CLE	N	3	0		0	0	0	18
1943	DET	N	1	0		0	0	0	6
Career			4	0		0	0	0	24

Wally Hilgenberg

Year	Team	Lg	TD	1XP	2XP	FG	FGA	SAF	Pts
1972	MIN	N	1	0		0	0	0	6
1973			1	0		0	0	0	6
1974			0	0		0	0	1	2
Career			2	0		0	0	1	14

Bruce Hill

Year	Team	Lg	TD	1XP	2XP	FG	FGA	SAF	Pts
1987	TB	N	2	0		0	0	0	12
1988			9	0		0	0	0	54
1989			5	0		0	0	0	30
1990			5	0		0	0	0	30
1991			2	0		0	0	0	12
Career			23	0		0	0	0	138

Calvin Hill

Year	Team	Lg	TD	1XP	2XP	FG	FGA	SAF	Pts
1969	DAL	N	8	0		0	0	0	48
1970			4	0		0	0	0	24
1971			11	0		0	0	0	66
1972			9	0		0	0	0	54
1973			6	0		0	0	0	36
1974			7	0		0	0	0	42
1976	WAS	N	1	0		0	0	0	6
1977			1	0		0	0	0	6
1978	CLE	N	7	0		0	0	0	42
1979			3	0		0	0	0	18
1980			6	0		0	0	0	36
1981			2	0		0	0	0	12
Career			65	0		0	0	0	390
Playoffs			3	0		0	0	0	18

Charlie Hill

Year	Team	Lg	TD	1XP	2XP	FG	FGA	SAF	Pts
1925	KC	N	4	0		0		0	24
1926			1	0		0		0	6
Career			5	0		0		0	30

David Hill

Year	Team	Lg	TD	1XP	2XP	FG	FGA	SAF	Pts
1976	DET	N	5	0		0	0	0	30
1977			2	0		0	0	0	12

David Hill *continued*

Year	Team		TD	1XP	2XP	FG	FGA	SAF	Pts
1978			4	0		0	0	0	24
1979			3	0		0	0	0	18
1980			1	0		0	0	0	6
1981			4	0		0	0	0	24
1982			4	0		0	0	0	24
1983	LARM	N	2	0		0	0	0	12
1984			1	0		0	0	0	6
1985			1	0		0	0	0	6
1986			1	0		0	0	0	6
Career			28	0		0	0	0	168
Playoffs			2	0		0	0	0	12

Derek Hill

Year	Team		TD	1XP	2XP	FG	FGA	SAF	Pts
1989	PIT	N	1	0		0	0	0	6

Don Hill

Year	Team		TD	1XP	2XP	FG	FGA	SAF	Pts
1929	CHIC	N	1	0		0		0	6

Drew Hill

Year	Team		TD	1XP	2XP	FG	FGA	SAF	Pts
1979	LA	N	1	0		0	0	0	6
1980			3	0		0	0	0	18
1981			3	0		0	0	0	18
1984	LARM	N	4	0		0	0	0	24
1985	HOU	N	9	0		0	0	0	54
1986			5	0		0	0	0	30
1987			6	0		0	0	0	36
1988			10	0		0	0	0	60
1989			8	0		0	0	0	48
1990			5	0		0	0	0	30
1991			4	0		0	0	0	24
1992	ATL	N	3	0		0	0	0	18
Career			61	0		0	0	0	366
Playoffs			1	0		0	0	0	6

Eddie Hill

Year	Team		TD	1XP	2XP	FG	FGA	SAF	Pts
1979	LA	N	2	0		0	0	0	12
1981	MIA	N	2	0		0	0	0	12
Career			4	0		0	0	0	24

Eric Hill

Year	Team		TD	1XP	2XP	FG	FGA	SAF	Pts
1991	PHX	N	1	0		0	0	0	6

Fred Hill

Year	Team		TD	1XP	2XP	FG	FGA	SAF	Pts
1968	PHI	N	3	0		0	0	0	18
1969			1	0		0	0	0	6
1970			1	0		0	0	0	6
Career			5	0		0	0	0	30

Greg Hill

Year	Team		TD	1XP	2XP	FG	FGA	SAF	Pts
1986	KC	N	1	0		0	0	0	6

Greg Hill

Year	Team		TD	1XP	2XP	FG	FGA	SAF	Pts
1994	KC	N	1	0	0	0	0	0	6
1995			1	0	0	0	0	0	6
1996			5	0	0	0	0	0	30
Career			7	0	0	0	0	0	42

Harlon Hill

Year	Team		TD	1XP	2XP	FG	FGA	SAF	Pts
1954	CHIB	N	**12**	0		0	0	0	72
1955			**9**	0		0	0	0	54
1956			11	0		0	0	0	66
1957			2	0		0	0	0	12
1958			3	0		0	0	0	18
1959			3	0		0	0	0	18
Career			40	0		0	0	0	240

Harold Hill

Year	Team		TD	1XP	2XP	FG	FGA	SAF	Pts
1939	BKN	N	0	0		0		1	2

Harry Hill

Year	Team		TD	1XP	2XP	FG	FGA	SAF	Pts
1923	TOL	N	3	0		0		0	18
1924	KC	N	1	0		0		0	6
1925			1	0		0		0	6
1926	NYG	N	2	0		0		0	12
Career			7	0		0		0	42

Ike Hill

Year	Team		TD	1XP	2XP	FG	FGA	SAF	Pts
1971	BUF	N	2	0		0	0	0	12
1973	CHI	N	2	0		0	0	0	12
1974			1	0		0	0	0	6
Career			5	0		0	0	0	30

Irv Hill

Year	Team		TD	1XP	2XP	FG	FGA	SAF	Pts
1932	CHIC	N	3	4		0		0	22

Jack Hill

Year	Team		TD	1XP	2XP	FG	FGA	SAF	Pts
1961	DEN	A	0	16	0	5	15	0	31

J.D. Hill

Year	Team		TD	1XP	2XP	FG	FGA	SAF	Pts
1971	BUF	N	2	0		0	0	0	12
1972			5	0		0	0	0	30
1974			6	0		0	0	0	36
1975			7	0		0	0	0	42
1977	DET	N	1	0		0	0	0	6
Career			21	0		0	0	0	126

Jerry Hill

Year	Team		TD	1XP	2XP	FG	FGA	SAF	Pts
1963	BAL	N	6	0		0	0	0	36
1964			6	0		0	0	0	36
1965			5	0		0	0	0	30
1967			2	0		0	0	0	12
1968			2	0		0	0	0	12
1969			2	0		0	0	0	12
1970			2	0		0	0	0	12
Career			25	0		0	0	0	150
Playoffs			1	0		0	0	0	6

Jim Hill

Year	Team		TD	1XP	2XP	FG	FGA	SAF	Pts
1975	CLE	N	1	0		0	0	0	6

Jimmy Hill

Year	Team		TD	1XP	2XP	FG	FGA	SAF	Pts
1959	CHIC	N	1	0		0	0	0	6
1960	STL	N	1	0		0	0	0	6
1961			1	0		0	0	0	6
1963			1	0		0	0	0	6
Career			4	0		0	0	0	24

King Hill

Year	Team		TD	1XP	2XP	FG	FGA	SAF	Pts
1959	CHIC	N	5	0		0	0	0	30
1962	PHI	N	1	0		0	0	0	6
1965			2	0		0	0	0	12
Career			8	0		0	0	0	48

Lonzell Hill

Year	Team		TD	1XP	2XP	FG	FGA	SAF	Pts
1987	NO	N	2	0		0	0	0	12
1988			7	0		0	0	0	42
1989			4	0		0	0	0	24
Career			13	0		0	0	0	78

Mack Lee Hill

Year	Team		TD	1XP	2XP	FG	FGA	SAF	Pts
1964	KC	A	6	0	0	0	0	0	36
1965			3	0	0	0	0	0	18
Career			9	0	0	0	0	0	54

Randal Hill

Year	Team		TD	1XP	2XP	FG	FGA	SAF	Pts
1991	PHX	N	1	0		0	0	0	6
1992			3	0		0	0	0	18
1993			4	0		0	0	0	24
1996	MIA	N	4	0	0	0	0	0	24
Career			12	0	0	0	0	0	72
Playoffs			1	0	0	0	0	0	6

Sean Hill

Year	Team		TD	1XP	2XP	FG	FGA	SAF	Pts
1996	MIA	N	1	0	0	0	0	0	6

Tony Hill

Year	Team		TD	1XP	2XP	FG	FGA	SAF	Pts
1978	DAL	N	6	0		0	0	0	36
1979			10	0		0	0	0	60
1980			8	0		0	0	0	48
1981			4	0		0	0	0	24
1982			1	0		0	0	0	6
1983			7	0		0	0	0	42
1984			5	0		0	0	0	30
1985			7	0		0	0	0	42
1986			3	0		0	0	0	18
Career			51	0		0	0	0	306
Playoffs			4	0		0	0	0	24

Travis Hill

Year	Team		TD	1XP	2XP	FG	FGA	SAF	Pts
1994	CLE	N	1	0	0	0	0	0	6

Ira Hillary

Year	Team		TD	1XP	2XP	FG	FGA	SAF	Pts
1988	CIN	N	1	0		0	0	0	6
1989			1	0		0	0	0	6
Career			2	0		0	0	0	12

Jerry Hillebrand

Year	Team		TD	1XP	2XP	FG	FGA	SAF	Pts
1963	NYG	N	1	0		0	0	0	6
1965			1	0		0	1	0	6
1966			1	0		0	0	0	6
Career			3	0		0	1	0	18

Billy Hillenbrand

Year	Team		TD	1XP	2XP	FG	FGA	SAF	Pts
1946	CHI	AA	8	0		0	0	0	48
1947	BAL	AA	10	0		0	0	0	60
1948			13	0		0	0	0	78
Career			31	0		0	0	0	186

Dalton Hilliard

Year	Team		TD	1XP	2XP	FG	FGA	SAF	Pts
1986	NO	N	5	0		0	0	0	30
1987			8	0		0	0	0	48
1988			6	0		0	0	0	36
1989			**18**	0		0	0	0	108
1990			1	0		0	0	0	6
1991			5	0		0	0	0	30
1992			7	0		0	0	0	42
1993			3	0		0	0	0	18
Career			53	0		0	0	0	318
Playoffs			1	0		0	0	0	6

Carl Hilton

Year	Team		TD	1XP	2XP	FG	FGA	SAF	Pts
1987	MIN	N	2	0		0	0	0	12
1988			1	0		0	0	0	6
Career			3	0		0	0	0	18
Playoffs			2	0		0	0	0	12

John Hilton

Year	Team		TD	1XP	2XP	FG	FGA	SAF	Pts
1966	PIT	N	4	0		0	0	0	24
1967			5	0		0	0	0	30
1968			1	0		0	0	0	6
1970	GB	N	4	0		0	0	0	24
1972	DET	N	1	0		0	0	0	6
1973			1	0		0	0	0	6
Career			16	0		0	0	0	96

Roy Hilton

Year	Team		TD	1XP	2XP	FG	FGA	SAF	Pts
1968	BAL	N	1	0		0	0	0	6
1974	NYG	N	1	0		0	0	0	6
Career			2	0		0	0	0	12

Stan Hindman

Year	Team		TD	1XP	2XP	FG	FGA	SAF	Pts
1968	SF	N	1	0		0	0	0	6

Bryan Hinkle

Year	Team		TD	1XP	2XP	FG	FGA	SAF	Pts
1983	PIT	N	1	0		0	0	0	6
1984			1	0		0	0	0	6
1991			1	0		0	0	0	6
Career			3	0		0	0	0	18

Clarke Hinkle

Year	Team		TD	1XP	2XP	FG	FGA	SAF	Pts
1932	GB	N	3	1		0		0	19
1933			2	0		2		0	18
1934			2	5		3		0	26
1935			2	0		2		0	18
1936			5	1		0		0	31
1937			**7**	9		2		0	57
1938			7	7		3	9	0	**58**
1939			5	2		1	10	0	35
1940			3	3		**9**	**14**	0	48
1941			6	2		**6**	**14**	0	56
Career			42	30		28	47	0	366
Playoffs			2	0		0	1	0	12

Jack Hinkle

Year	Team		TD	1XP	2XP	FG	FGA	SAF	Pts
1943	P-P	N	4	0		0	0	0	24
1944	PHI	N	3	0		0	0	0	18
Career			7	0		0	0	0	42

Chuck Hinton

Year	Team		TD	1XP	2XP	FG	FGA	SAF	Pts
1964	PIT	N	1	0		0	0	0	6
1967			1	0		0	0	0	6
Career			2	0		0	0	0	12

Eddie Hinton

Year	Team		TD	1XP	2XP	FG	FGA	SAF	Pts
1969	BAL	N	1	0		0	0	0	6
1970			7	0		0	0	0	42
1971			2	0		0	0	0	12
1972			1	0		0	0	0	6

Eddie Hinton *continued*

Year	Team	Lg	TD	1XP	2XP	FG	FGA	SAF	Pts
1973	**HOU**	**N**	1	0		0	0	0	6
Career			12	0		0	0	0	72
Playoffs			1	0		0	0	0	6

J.W. Hinton

Year	Team	Lg	TD	1XP	2XP	FG	FGA	SAF	Pts
1932	**SI**	**N**	1	0		0		0	6

Eric Hipple

Year	Team	Lg	TD	1XP	2XP	FG	FGA	SAF	Pts
1981	**DET**	**N**	7	0		0	0	0	42
1983			3	0		0	0	0	18
1985			2	0		0	0	0	12
1989			1	0		0	0	0	6
Career			13	0		0	0	0	78

Ed Hirsch

Year	Team	Lg	TD	1XP	2XP	FG	FGA	SAF	Pts
1947	**BUF**	**AA**	1	0		0	0	0	6
Playoffs			1	0		0	0	0	6

Elroy Hirsch

Year	Team	Lg	TD	1XP	2XP	FG	FGA	SAF	Pts
1946	**CHI**	**AA**	6	0		0	0	0	36
1947			4	0		0	0	0	24
1948			1	0		0	0	0	6
1949	**LA**	**N**	6	0		0	0	0	36
1950			7	5		0	0	0	47
1951			**17**	0		0	0	0	**102**
1952			4	0		0	0	0	24
1953			4	4		0	0	0	28
1954			3	0		0	0	0	18
1955			2	0		0	0	0	12
1956			6	0		0	0	0	36
1957			6	0		0	0	0	36
Career			66	9		0	0	0	405

Terry Hoage

Year	Team	Lg	TD	1XP	2XP	FG	FGA	SAF	Pts
1985	**NO**	**N**	1	0		0	0	0	6
1988	**PHI**	**N**	1	0		0	0	0	6
Career			2	0		0	0	0	12

Joe Hoague

Year	Team	Lg	TD	1XP	2XP	FG	FGA	SAF	Pts
1941	**PIT**	**N**	2	0		0	0	0	12
1942			1	0		0	0	0	6
Career			3	0		0	0	0	18

Dick Hoak

Year	Team	Lg	TD	1XP	2XP	FG	FGA	SAF	Pts
1962	**PIT**	**N**	4	0		0	0	0	24
1963			7	0		0	0	0	42
1964			5	0		0	0	0	30
1965			6	0		0	0	0	36
1966			1	0		0	0	0	6
1967			2	0		0	0	0	12
1968			4	0		0	0	0	24
1969			3	0		0	0	0	18
1970			1	0		0	0	0	6
Career			33	0		0	0	0	198

Leroy Hoard

Year	Team	Lg	TD	1XP	2XP	FG	FGA	SAF	Pts
1990	**CLE**	**N**	3	0		0	0	0	18
1991			11	0		0	0	0	66
1992			1	0		0	0	0	6
1994			9	0	0	0	0	0	54
1996	**MIN**	**N**	3	0	0	0	0	0	18
Career			27	0	0	0	0	0	162
Playoffs			1	0	0	0	0	0	6

Billy Hobbs

Year	Team	Lg	TD	1XP	2XP	FG	FGA	SAF	Pts
1971	**PHI**	**N**	1	0		0	0	0	6

Daryl Hobbs

Year	Team	Lg	TD	1XP	2XP	FG	FGA	SAF	Pts
1995	**OAK**	**N**	3	0	0	0	0	0	18
1996			3	0	0	0	0	0	18
Career			6	0	0	0	0	0	36

Stephen Hobbs

Year	Team	Lg	TD	1XP	2XP	FG	FGA	SAF	Pts
1990	**WAS**	**N**	1	0		0	0	0	6

Liffort Hobley

Year	Team	Lg	TD	1XP	2XP	FG	FGA	SAF	Pts
1987	**MIA**	**N**	1	0		0	0	0	6
1988			1	0		0	0	0	6
Career			2	0		0	0	0	12

Ben Hobson

Year	Team	Lg	TD	1XP	2XP	FG	FGA	SAF	Pts
1926	**BUF**	**N**	1	0		0		0	6

Floyd Hodge

Year	Team	Lg	TD	1XP	2XP	FG	FGA	SAF	Pts
1983	**ATL**	**N**	4	0		0	0	0	24

Herman Hodges

Year	Team	Lg	TD	1XP	2XP	FG	FGA	SAF	Pts
1939	**BKN**	**N**	1	0		0	0	0	6

Dick Hoerner

Year	Team	Lg	TD	1XP	2XP	FG	FGA	SAF	Pts
1947	**LA**	**N**	2	0		0	0	0	12
1948			6	0		0	0	0	36
1949			6	0		0	0	0	36
1950			11	0		0	0	0	66
1951			7	0		0	0	0	42
1952	**DAL**	**N**	2	0		0	0	0	12
Career			34	0		0	0	0	204
Playoffs			3	0		0	0	0	18

Bob Hoernschemeyer

Year	Team	Lg	TD	1XP	2XP	FG	FGA	SAF	Pts
1947	**CHI-BKN**	**AA**	6	0		0	0	0	36
1948	**BKN**	**AA**	7	0		0	0	0	42
1949	**CHI**	**AA**	2	0		0	0	0	12
1950	**DET**	**N**	2	0		0	0	0	12
1951			5	0		0	0	0	30
1952			4	0		0	0	0	24
1953			9	0		0	0	0	54
1954			3	0		0	0	0	18
1955			1	0		0	0	0	6
Career			39	0		0	0	0	234
Playoffs			1	0		0	0	0	6

George Hoey

Year	Team	Lg	TD	1XP	2XP	FG	FGA	SAF	Pts
1971	**STL**	**N**	1	0		0	0	0	6

Paul Hofer

Year	Team	Lg	TD	1XP	2XP	FG	FGA	SAF	Pts
1976	**SF**	**N**	1	0		0	0	0	6
1978			7	0		0	0	0	42
1979			9	0		0	0	0	54
1980			3	0		0	0	0	18
1981			1	0		0	0	0	6
Career			21	0		0	0	0	126

Bob Hoffman

Year	Team	Lg	TD	1XP	2XP	FG	FGA	SAF	Pts
1946	**LA**	**N**	3	0		0	0	0	18
1947			3	0		0	0	0	18
1948			5	0		0	0	0	30
Career			11	0		0	0	0	66

Dalton Hoffman

Year	Team	Lg	TD	1XP	2XP	FG	FGA	SAF	Pts
1964	**HOU**	**A**	1	0	0	0	0	0	6

John Hoffman

Year	Team	Lg	TD	1XP	2XP	FG	FGA	SAF	Pts
1949	**CHIB**	**N**	3	0		0	0	0	18
1950			3	0		0	0	0	18
1951			2	0		0	0	0	12
1953			4	0		0	0	0	24
1954			2	0		0	0	0	12
1955			1	0		0	0	1	8
1956			2	0		0	0	0	12
Career			17	0		0	0	1	104

John Hoffman

Year	Team	Lg	TD	1XP	2XP	FG	FGA	SAF	Pts
1969	**WAS**	**N**	1	0		0	0	0	6

Darrell Hogan

Year	Team	Lg	TD	1XP	2XP	FG	FGA	SAF	Pts
1952	**PIT**	**N**	1	0		0	0	0	6

Mike Hogan

Year	Team	Lg	TD	1XP	2XP	FG	FGA	SAF	Pts
1977	**PHI**	**N**	1	0		0	0	0	6
1978			5	0		0	0	0	30
1980	**NYG-PHI**	**N**	2	0		0	0	0	12
Career			8	0		0	0	0	48

Paul Hogan

Year	Team	Lg	TD	1XP	2XP	FG	FGA	SAF	Pts
1924	**AKR**	**N**	0	2		1		0	5
1925	**CAN**	**N**	0	0		0		0	0
1926	**NY-FRA**	**N**	0	5		0		0	5
1927	**CHIC**	**N**	1	0		0		0	6
Career			1	7		1		0	16

Merril Hoge

Year	Team	Lg	TD	1XP	2XP	FG	FGA	SAF	Pts
1987	**PIT**	**N**	1	0		0	0	0	6
1988			6	0		0	0	0	36
1989			8	0		0	0	0	48
1990			10	0		0	0	0	60

Merril Hoge *continued*

Year	Team	Lg	TD	1XP	2XP	FG	FGA	SAF	Pts
1991			3	0		0	0	0	18
1992			1	0		0	0	0	6
1993			5	0		0	0	0	30
Career			34	0		0	0	0	204
Playoffs			2	0		0	0	0	12

Gary Hogeboom

Year	Team	Lg	TD	1XP	2XP	FG	FGA	SAF	Pts
1985	**DAL**	**N**	1	0		0	0	0	6
1986	**IND**	**N**	1	0		0	0	0	6
1988			1	0		0	0	0	6
1989	**PHX**	**N**	1	0		0	0	0	6
Career			4	0		0	0	0	24

Al Hoisington

Year	Team	Lg	TD	1XP	2XP	FG	FGA	SAF	Pts
1960	**OAK**	**A**	2	0	0	0	0	0	12

Steve Hokuf

Year	Team	Lg	TD	1XP	2XP	FG	FGA	SAF	Pts
1934	**BOS**	**N**	0	1		1		0	4

Steve Holden

Year	Team	Lg	TD	1XP	2XP	FG	FGA	SAF	Pts
1974	**CLE**	**N**	3	0		0	0	0	18
1976			1	0		0	0	0	6
Career			4	0		0	0	0	24

Jamie Holland

Year	Team	Lg	TD	1XP	2XP	FG	FGA	SAF	Pts
1988	**SD**	**N**	2	0		0	0	0	12

John Holland

Year	Team	Lg	TD	1XP	2XP	FG	FGA	SAF	Pts
1975	**BUF**	**N**	1	0		0	0	0	6
1976			3	0		0	0	0	18
Career			4	0		0	0	0	24

John Hollar

Year	Team	Lg	TD	1XP	2XP	FG	FGA	SAF	Pts
1949	**WAS**	**N**	2	0		0	0	0	12

Tommy Holleran

Year	Team	Lg	TD	1XP	2XP	FG	FGA	SAF	Pts
1922	**TOL**	**N**	0	0		0		0	0
1923	**BUF**	**N**	2	0		0		0	12
Career			2	0		0		0	12

Ron Holliday

Year	Team	Lg	TD	1XP	2XP	FG	FGA	SAF	Pts
1973	**SD**	**N**	0	1		0	0	0	1

Mike Hollis

Year	Team	Lg	TD	1XP	2XP	FG	FGA	SAF	Pts
1995	**JAC**	**N**	0	27	0	20	27	0	87
1996			0	27	0	30	36	0	117
Career			0	54	0	50	63	0	204
Playoffs			0	6	0	8	9	0	30

Randy Holloway

Year	Team	Lg	TD	1XP	2XP	FG	FGA	SAF	Pts
1980	**MIN**	**N**	0	0		0	0	1	2
1981			1	0		0	0	0	6
Career			1	0		0	0	1	8

Bob Holly

Year	Team	Lg	TD	1XP	2XP	FG	FGA	SAF	Pts
1985	**ATL**	**N**	1	0		0	0	0	6

Bernie Holm

Year	Team	Lg	TD	1XP	2XP	FG	FGA	SAF	Pts
1931	**POR**	**N**	2	0		0		0	12

Rodney Holman

Year	Team	Lg	TD	1XP	2XP	FG	FGA	SAF	Pts
1982	**CIN**	**N**	1	0		0	0	0	6
1984			1	0		0	0	0	6
1985			7	0		0	0	0	42
1986			2	0		0	0	0	12
1987			2	0		0	0	0	12
1988			3	0		0	0	0	18
1989			9	0		0	0	0	54
1990			5	0		0	0	0	30
1991			2	0		0	0	0	12
1992			2	0		0	0	0	12
1993	**DET**	**N**	2	0		0	0	0	12
Career			36	0		0	0	0	216

Walt Holmer

Year	Team	Lg	TD	1XP	2XP	FG	FGA	SAF	Pts
1929	**CHIB**	**N**	0	0		1		0	3
1930			3	0		0		0	18
1931	**CHIC**	**N**	0	0		0		0	0
1932			1	2		0		0	8
1933	**BOS**	**N**	1	0		0		0	6
Career			5	2		1		0	35

Darick Holmes

Year	Team		TD	1XP	2XP	FG	FGA	SAF	Pts
1995	**BUF**	**N**	4	0	0	0	0	0	24
1996			5	0	1	0	0	0	32
Career			9	0	1	0	0	0	56
Playoffs			1	0	0	0	0	0	6

Don Holmes

Year	Team		TD	1XP	2XP	FG	FGA	SAF	Pts
1989	**PHX**	**N**	1	0		0	0	0	6

Jack Holmes

Year	Team		TD	1XP	2XP	FG	FGA	SAF	Pts
1980	**NO**	**N**	3	0		0	0	0	18
1981			2	0		0	0	0	12
Career			5	0		0	0	0	30

Jerry Holmes

Year	Team		TD	1XP	2XP	FG	FGA	SAF	Pts
1983	**NYJ**	**N**	2	0		0	0	0	12
1989	**DET**	**N**	1	0		0	0	0	6
Career			3	0		0	0	0	18

Mike Holmes

Year	Team		TD	1XP	2XP	FG	FGA	SAF	Pts
1975	**SF**	**N**	1	0		0	0	0	6

Robert Holmes

Year	Team		TD	1XP	2XP	FG	FGA	SAF	Pts
1968	**KC**	**A**	7	0	0	0	0	0	42
1969			5	0	0	0	0	0	30
1970	**KC**	**N**	4	0		0	0	0	24
1971	**HOU**	**N**	4	0		0	0	0	24
1973	**SD**	**N**	7	0		0	0	0	42
Career			27	0	0	0	0	0	162
Playoffs			1	0	0	0	0	0	6

Tom Holmoe

Year	Team		TD	1XP	2XP	FG	FGA	SAF	Pts
1986	**SF**	**N**	2	0		0	0	0	12

Pete Holohan

Year	Team		TD	1XP	2XP	FG	FGA	SAF	Pts
1983	**SD**	**N**	2	0		0	0	0	12
1984			1	0		0	0	0	6
1985			3	0		0	0	0	18
1986			1	0		0	0	0	6
1988	**LARM**	**N**	3	0		0	0	0	18
1989			2	0		0	0	0	12
1990			2	0		0	0	0	12
1991	**KC**	**N**	2	0		0	0	0	12
Career			16	0		0	0	0	96
Playoffs			1	0		0	0	0	6

Mike Holovak

Year	Team		TD	1XP	2XP	FG	FGA	SAF	Pts
1946	**LA**	**N**	3	0		0	0	0	18
1947	**CHIB**	**N**	1	0		0	0	0	6
1948			2	0		0	0	0	12
Career			6	0		0	0	0	36

Mike Holston

Year	Team		TD	1XP	2XP	FG	FGA	SAF	Pts
1981	**HOU**	**N**	2	0		0	0	0	12
1982			1	0		0	0	0	6
1984			1	0		0	0	0	6
Career			4	0		0	0	0	24

Harry Holt

Year	Team		TD	1XP	2XP	FG	FGA	SAF	Pts
1983	**CLE**	**N**	3	0		0	0	0	18
1985			1	0		0	0	0	6
1986			2	0		0	0	0	12
Career			6	0		0	0	0	36

Issiac Holt

Year	Team		TD	1XP	2XP	FG	FGA	SAF	Pts
1986	**MIN**	**N**	1	0		0	0	0	6
1988			0	0		0	0	1	2
1989			1	0		0	0	0	6
1990	**DAL**	**N**	1	0		0	0	0	6
1992			0	0		0	0	1	2
Career			3	0		0	0	2	22

Glenn Holtzman

Year	Team		TD	1XP	2XP	FG	FGA	SAF	Pts
1958	**LA**	**N**	0	0		0	0	1	2

Dennis Homan

Year	Team		TD	1XP	2XP	FG	FGA	SAF	Pts
1968	**DAL**	**N**	1	0		0	0	0	6
1972	**KC**	**N**	1	0		0	0	0	6
Career			2	0		0	0	0	12

Henry Homan

Year	Team		TD	1XP	2XP	FG	FGA	SAF	Pts
1925	**FRA**	**N**	2	0		0		0	12
1926			3	0		0		0	18
1927			2	0		0		0	12

Henry Homan *continued*

Year	Team		TD	1XP	2XP	FG	FGA	SAF	Pts
1928			1	0		0		0	6
1929			2	0		0		0	12
Career			10	0		0		0	60

Estus Hood

Year	Team		TD	1XP	2XP	FG	FGA	SAF	Pts
1981	**GB**	**N**	1	0		0	0	0	6

Fair Hooker

Year	Team		TD	1XP	2XP	FG	FGA	SAF	Pts
1970	**CLE**	**N**	2	0		0	0	0	12
1971			1	0		0	0	0	6
1972			2	0		0	0	0	12
1973			2	0		0	0	0	12
1974			1	0		0	0	0	6
Career			8	0		0	0	0	48
Playoffs			1	0		0	0	0	6

Roland Hooks

Year	Team		TD	1XP	2XP	FG	FGA	SAF	Pts
1978	**BUF**	**N**	3	0		0	0	0	18
1979			6	0		0	0	0	36
1980			1	0		0	0	0	6
1981			5	0		0	0	0	30
Career			15	0		0	0	0	90

Trell Hooper

Year	Team		TD	1XP	2XP	FG	FGA	SAF	Pts
1987	**MIA**	**N**	1	0		0	0	0	6

Mel Hoover

Year	Team		TD	1XP	2XP	FG	FGA	SAF	Pts
1984	**PHI**	**N**	2	0		0	0	0	12

Roy Hopkins

Year	Team		TD	1XP	2XP	FG	FGA	SAF	Pts
1969	**HOU**	**A**	5	0	0	0	0	0	30
1970	**HOU**	**N**	3	0		0	0	0	18
Career			8	0	0	0	0	0	48

Wes Hopkins

Year	Team		TD	1XP	2XP	FG	FGA	SAF	Pts
1985	**PHI**	**N**	1	0		0	0	0	6

Harry Hopp

Year	Team		TD	1XP	2XP	FG	FGA	SAF	Pts
1941	**DET**	**N**	1	0		0	0	0	6
1943			9	0		0	0	0	54
1946	**BUF-MIA**	**AA**	3	0		0	0	0	18
Career			13	0		0	0	0	78

Don Horn

Year	Team		TD	1XP	2XP	FG	FGA	SAF	Pts
1969	**GB**	**N**	1	0		0	0	0	6

Sam Horner

Year	Team		TD	1XP	2XP	FG	FGA	SAF	Pts
1961	**WAS**	**N**	1	0		0	0	0	6

Clarence Horning

Year	Team		TD	1XP	2XP	FG	FGA	SAF	Pts
1920	**DET**	**A**	0	0		0		0	0
1921	**BUF**	**A**	1	0		0		0	6
1922	**TOL**	**N**	1	0		0		0	6
Career			2	0		0		0	12

Paul Hornung

Year	Team		TD	1XP	2XP	FG	FGA	SAF	Pts
1957	**GB**	**N**	3	0		0	4	0	18
1958			2	22		11	21	0	67
1959			7	31		7	17	0	**94**
1960			**15**	41		15	28	0	**176**
1961			10	41		15	22	0	**146**
1962			7	14		6	10	0	74
1964			5	41		12	**38**	0	107
1965			8	0		0	0	0	48
1966			5	0		0	0	0	30
Career			62	190		66	140	0	760
Playoffs			3	5		5	6	0	38

Ethan Horton

Year	Team		TD	1XP	2XP	FG	FGA	SAF	Pts
1985	**KC**	**N**	4	0		0	0	0	24
1987	**LARI**	**N**	1	0		0	0	0	6
1989			1	0		0	0	0	6
1990			3	0		0	0	0	18
1991			5	0		0	0	0	30
1992			2	0		0	0	0	12
1993			1	0		0	0	0	6
1994	**WAS**	**N**	3	0	0	0	0	0	18
Career			20	0	0	0	0	0	120
Playoffs			2	0	0	0	0	0	12

Ray Horton

Year	Team		TD	1XP	2XP	FG	FGA	SAF	Pts
1983	**CIN**	**N**	1	0		0	0	0	6
1984			1	0		0	0	0	6

Ray Horton *continued*

Year	Team		TD	1XP	2XP	FG	FGA	SAF	Pts
1991	**DAL**	**N**	2	0		0	0	0	12
1992			1	0		0	0	0	6
Career			5	0		0	0	0	30

Les Horvath

Year	Team		TD	1XP	2XP	FG	FGA	SAF	Pts
1948	**LA**	**N**	1	0		0	0	0	6
1949	**CLE**	**AA**	3	0		0	0	0	18
Career			4	0		0	0	0	24

Arnie Horween

Year	Team		TD	1XP	2XP	FG	FGA	SAF	Pts
1922	**CHIC**	**N**	4	0		1		0	27
1923			0	3		2		0	9
Career			4	3		3		0	36

Ralph Horween

Year	Team		TD	1XP	2XP	FG	FGA	SAF	Pts
1921	**CHIC**	**A**	0	0		1		0	3
1922	**CHIC**	**N**	0	1		3		0	10
1923			2	0		0		0	12
Career			2	1		4		0	25

Bob Hoskins

Year	Team		TD	1XP	2XP	FG	FGA	SAF	Pts
Playoffs			1	0	0	0	0	0	6

Jeff Hostetler

Year	Team		TD	1XP	2XP	FG	FGA	SAF	Pts
1989	**NYG**	**N**	2	0		0	0	0	12
1990			2	0		0	0	0	12
1991			2	0		0	0	0	12
1992			3	0		0	0	0	18
1993	**LARI**	**N**	5	0		0	0	0	30
1994			2	0	0	0	0	0	12
1996	**OAK**	**N**	1	0	0	0	0	0	6
Career			17	0	0	0	0	0	102
Playoffs			1	0	0	0	0	0	6

Bill Houle

Year	Team		TD	1XP	2XP	FG	FGA	SAF	Pts
1924	**MIN**	**N**	0	1		0		0	1

Kevin House

Year	Team		TD	1XP	2XP	FG	FGA	SAF	Pts
1980	**TB**	**N**	5	0		0	0	0	30
1981			9	0		0	0	0	54
1982			2	0		0	0	0	12
1983			5	0		0	0	0	30
1984			5	0		0	0	0	30
1985			5	0		0	0	0	30
1986	**LARM**	**N**	2	0		0	0	0	12
1987			1	0		0	0	0	6
Career			34	0		0	0	0	204
Playoffs			1	0		0	0	0	6

Bobby Houston

Year	Team		TD	1XP	2XP	FG	FGA	SAF	Pts
1992	**NYJ**	**N**	1	0		0	0	0	6

Jim Houston

Year	Team		TD	1XP	2XP	FG	FGA	SAF	Pts
1964	**CLE**	**N**	1	0		0	0	0	6
1966			1	1		0	0	0	7
1967			2	0		0	0	0	12
Career			4	1		0	0	0	25

Ken Houston

Year	Team		TD	1XP	2XP	FG	FGA	SAF	Pts
1967	**HOU**	**A**	3	0	0	0	0	0	18
1968			2	0	0	0	0	0	12
1969			1	0	0	0	0	0	6
1971	**HOU**	**N**	5	0		0	0	0	30
1974	**WAS**	**N**	1	0		0	0	0	6
Career			12	0	0	0	0	0	72

Rich Houston

Year	Team		TD	1XP	2XP	FG	FGA	SAF	Pts
1971	**NYG**	**N**	4	0		0	0	0	24
1972			3	0		0	0	0	18
Career			7	0		0	0	0	42

Don Hover

Year	Team		TD	1XP	2XP	FG	FGA	SAF	Pts
1979	**WAS**	**N**	1	0		0	0	0	6

Bob Howard

Year	Team		TD	1XP	2XP	FG	FGA	SAF	Pts
1930	**NYG**	**N**	1	0		0		0	6

Bobby Howard

Year	Team		TD	1XP	2XP	FG	FGA	SAF	Pts
1986	**TB**	**N**	1	0		0	0	0	6
1987			1	0		0	0	0	6
Career			2	0		0	0	0	12

Bobby Howard

Year	Team		TD	1XP	2XP	FG	FGA	SAF	Pts
1975	NE	N	1	0		0	0	0	6

Desmond Howard

Year	Team		TD	1XP	2XP	FG	FGA	SAF	Pts
1992	WAS	N	1	0		0	0	0	6
1994			5	0	1	0	0	0	32
1995	JAC	N	1	0	0	0	0	0	6
1996	GB	N	3	0	0	0	0	0	18
Career			10	0	1	0	0	0	62
Playoffs			2	0	0	0	0	0	12

Erik Howard

Year	Team		TD	1XP	2XP	FG	FGA	SAF	Pts
1995	NYJ	N	0	0	0	0	0	1	2

Gene Howard

Year	Team		TD	1XP	FG	FGA	SAF	Pts
1971	LA	N	1	0	0	0	0	6
1972			1	0	0	0	0	6
Career			2	0	0	0	0	12

Lynn Howard

Year	Team		TD	1XP	FG	SAF	Pts
1921	GB	A	1	0	0	0	6

Percy Howard

Year	Team		TD	1XP	2XP	FG	FGA	SAF	Pts
Playoffs			1	0	0	0	0	0	6

Ron Howard

Year	Team		TD	1XP	FG	FGA	SAF	Pts
1977	SEA	N	1	0	0	0	0	6
1978			1	0	0	0	0	6
Career			2	0	0	0	0	12

Thomas Howard

Year	Team		TD	1XP	FG	FGA	SAF	Pts
1980	KC	N	1	0	0	0	0	6
1981			1	0	0	0	0	6
1984	STL	N	1	0	0	0	0	6
Career			3	0	0	0	0	18

Sherman Howard

Year	Team		TD	1XP	FG	FGA	SAF	Pts
1949	B-NY	AA	3	0	0	0	0	18
1950	NYY	N	9	0	0	0	0	54
1951			7	0	0	0	0	42
1952	CLE	N	3	0	0	0	0	18
Career			22	0	0	0	0	132
Playoffs			1	0	0	0	0	6

William Howard

Year	Team		TD	1XP	FG	FGA	SAF	Pts
1988	TB	N	1	0	0	0	0	6
1989			2	0	0	0	0	12
Career			3	0	0	0	0	18

Earl Howell

Year	Team		TD	1XP	FG	FGA	SAF	Pts
1949	LA	AA	2	0	0	0	0	12

Jim Lee Howell

Year	Team		TD	1XP	FG	FGA	SAF	Pts
1938	NYG	N	2	0	0		0	12
1939			2	0	0	0	0	12
1940			2	0	0	0	0	12
1941			1	0	0	0	0	6
Career			7	0	0	0	0	42

Steve Howell

Year	Team		TD	1XP	FG	SAF	Pts
1980	MIA	N	1	0	0	0	6

Bobby Howfield

Year	Team		TD	1XP	2XP	FG	FGA	SAF	Pts
1968	DEN	A	0	30	0	9	18	0	57
1969			0	36	0	13	29	0	75
1970	DEN	N	0	27		18	32	0	81
1971	NYJ	N	0	25		8	19	0	49
1972			0	40		27	37	0	121
1973			0	27		17	24	0	78
1974			0	8		6	7	0	26
Career			0	193	0	98	166	0	487

Ian Howfield

Year	Team		TD	1XP	FG	FGA	SAF	Pts
1991	HOU	N	0	25	13	18	0	64

Chuck Howley

Year	Team		TD	1XP	FG	FGA	SAF	Pts
1966	DAL	N	1	0	0	0	0	6
1967			1	0	0	0	0	6
1968			1	0	0	0	0	6
Career			3	0	0	0	0	18
Playoffs			1	0	0	0	0	6

Billy Howton

Year	Team		TD	1XP	FG	FGA	SAF	Pts
1952	GB	N	13	0	0	0	0	78

Billy Howton *continued*

Year	Team		TD	1XP	FG	FGA	SAF	Pts
1953			4	0	0	0	0	24
1954			2	0	0	0	0	12
1955			5	0	0	0	0	30
1956			12	0	0	0	0	72
1957			5	0	0	0	0	30
1958			2	0	0	0	0	12
1959	CLE	N	1	0	0	0	0	6
1960	DAL	N	4	0	0	0	0	24
1961			4	0	0	0	0	24
1962			6	0	0	0	0	36
1963			3	0	0	0	0	18
Career			61	0	0	0	0	366

Cal Hubbard

Year	Team		TD	1XP	FG	SAF	Pts
1930	GB	N	1	0	0	0	6
1935			1	0	0	0	6
Career			2	0	0	0	12

Marv Hubbard

Year	Team		TD	1XP	FG	FGA	SAF	Pts
1970	OAK	N	1	0	0	0	0	6
1971			6	0	0	0	0	36
1972			4	0	0	0	0	24
1973			6	0	0	0	0	36
1974			4	0	0	0	0	24
1975			2	0	0	0	0	12
1977	DET	N	1	0	0	0	0	6
Career			24	0	0	0	0	144
Playoffs			3	0	0	0	0	18

Wes Hubbard

Year	Team		TD	1XP	FG	SAF	Pts
1935	BKN	N	1	0	0	0	6

Frank Hubbell

Year	Team		TD	1XP	FG	FGA	SAF	Pts
1947	LA	N	2	0	0	0	0	12
1948			1	0	0	0	0	6
1949			1	0	0	0	0	6
Career			4	0	0	0	0	24

Brad Hubbert

Year	Team		TD	1XP	2XP	FG	FGA	SAF	Pts
1967	SD	A	4	0	0	0	0	0	24
1968			2	0	0	0	0	0	12
1969			4	0	0	0	0	0	24
1970	SD	N	1	0		0	0	0	6
Career			11	0	0	0	0	0	66

Pooley Hubert

Year	Team		TD	1XP	FG	SAF	Pts
1926	NY	A	2	0	0	0	12

Harlan Huckleby

Year	Team		TD	1XP	FG	FGA	SAF	Pts
1980	GB	N	1	0	0	0	0	6
1981			8	0	0	0	0	48
1983			4	0	0	0	0	24
Career			13	0	0	0	0	78

Billy Hudson

Year	Team		TD	1XP	2XP	FG	FGA	SAF	Pts
1961	SD	A	1	0	0	0	0	0	6

Gordon Hudson

Year	Team		TD	1XP	FG	FGA	SAF	Pts
1986	SEA	N	1	0	0	0	0	6

Johnnie Hudson

Year	Team		TD	1XP	FG	SAF	Pts
1921	WAS	A	1	0	0	0	6

Carlos Huerta

Year	Team		TD	1XP	2XP	FG	FGA	SAF	Pts
1996	CHI-STL	N	0	5	0	4	7	0	17

Gary Huff

Year	Team		TD	1XP	FG	FGA	SAF	Pts
1974	CHI	N	2	0	0	0	0	12

Sam Huff

Year	Team		TD	1XP	FG	FGA	SAF	Pts
1957	NYG	N	1	0	0	0	0	6
1959			1	0	0	0	0	6
1961			1	0	0	0	0	6
1963			1	0	0	0	0	6
1969	WAS	N	1	0	0	0	0	6
Career			5	0	0	0	0	30

Ken Huffine

Year	Team		TD	1XP	FG	SAF	Pts
1921	DEC	A	2	0	0	0	12
1922	DAY	N	3	0	0	0	18
Career			5	0	0	0	30

Dave Huffman

Year	Team		TD	1XP	FG	FGA	SAF	Pts
1983	MIN	N	1	0	0	0	0	6

Dick Huffman

Year	Team		TD	1XP	FG	FGA	SAF	Pts
1947	LA	N	1	0	0	0	0	6

Frank Huffman

Year	Team		TD	1XP	FG	FGA	SAF	Pts
1940	CHIC	N	0	0	0	1	0	2

Vern Huffman

Year	Team		TD	1XP	FG	SAF	Pts
1937	DET	N	1	0	0	0	6
1938			1	0	0	0	6
Career			2	0	0	0	12

Bernie Hughes

Year	Team		TD	1XP	FG	SAF	Pts
1932	BOS	N	0	5	0	0	5

Danan Hughes

Year	Team		TD	1XP	2XP	FG	FGA	SAF	Pts
1995	KC	N	1	0	0	0	0	0	6
1996			1	0	0	0	0	0	6
Career			2	0	0	0	0	0	12

David Hughes

Year	Team		TD	1XP	FG	FGA	SAF	Pts
1981	SEA	N	2	0	0	0	0	12
1982			1	0	0	0	0	6
1983			2	0	0	0	0	12
1984			2	0	0	0	0	12
Career			7	0	0	0	0	42
Playoffs			1	0	0	0	0	6

Dennis Hughes

Year	Team		TD	1XP	FG	FGA	SAF	Pts
1970	PIT	N	3	0	0	0	0	18

Denny Hughes

Year	Team		TD	1XP	FG	SAF	Pts
1925	POT	N	0	2	0	0	2

Randy Hughes

Year	Team		TD	1XP	FG	FGA	SAF	Pts
1975	DAL	N	1	0	0	0	0	6

Tyrone Hughes

Year	Team		TD	1XP	2XP	FG	FGA	SAF	Pts
1993	NO	N	3	0		0	0	0	18
1994			4	0	0	0	0	0	24
Career			7	0	0	0	0	0	42

Tommy Hughitt

Year	Team		TD	1XP	FG	SAF	Pts
1920	BUF	A	1	3	0	0	9
1921			3	2	0	0	20
1922	BUF	N	2	0	0	0	12
1923			1	0	1	0	9
Career			7	5	1	0	50

George Hughley

Year	Team		TD	1XP	FG	FGA	SAF	Pts
1965	WAS	N	1	0	0	0	0	6

Mike Hull

Year	Team		TD	1XP	FG	FGA	SAF	Pts
1969	CHI	N	1	0	0	0	0	6

Vivian Hultman

Year	Team		TD	1XP	FG	SAF	Pts
1925	DET	N	1	0	0	0	6
1926			1	0	0	0	6
1927	POT	N	1	0	0	0	6
Career			3	0	0	0	18

Don Hultz

Year	Team		TD	1XP	FG	FGA	SAF	Pts
1963	MIN	N	1	0	0	0	0	6
1967	PHI		1	0	0	0	0	6
Career			2	0	0	0	0	12

Dick Humbert

Year	Team		TD	1XP	FG	FGA	SAF	Pts
1941	PHI	N	3	0	0	0	0	18
1946			3	0	0	0	0	18
Career			6	0	0	0	0	36

Mike Humiston

Year	Team		TD	1XP	FG	FGA	SAF	Pts
1984	IND	N	0	0	0	0	1	2

Bobby Humphery

Year	Team		TD	1XP	FG	FGA	SAF	Pts
1984	NYJ	N	2	0	0	0	0	12
1986			1	0	0	0	1	8
1987			1	0	0	0	0	6
1990	LARM	N	1	0	0	0	0	6
Career			5	0	0	0	1	32

Bobby Humphrey

Year	Team		TD	1XP	2XP	FG	FGA	SAF	Pts
1989	DEN	N	8	0		0	0	0	48
1990			7	0		0	0	0	42
1992	MIA	N	2	0		0	0	0	12
Career			17	0		0	0	0	102

Claude Humphrey

Year	Team		TD	1XP	2XP	FG	FGA	SAF	Pts
1969	ATL	N	1	0		0	0	0	6
1972			0	0		0	0	1	2
1976			0	0		0	0	1	2
Career			1	0		0	0	2	10

Ronald Humphrey

Year	Team		TD	1XP	2XP	FG	FGA	SAF	Pts
1994	IND	N	1	0	0	0	0	0	6

Bob Humphreys

Year	Team		TD	1XP	2XP	FG	FGA	SAF	Pts
1967	DEN	A	0	18	0	7	15	0	39
1968			0	1	0	1	5	0	4
Career			0	19	0	8	20	0	43

Stan Humphries

Year	Team		TD	1XP	2XP	FG	FGA	SAF	Pts
1990	WAS	N	2	0		0	0	0	12
1992	SD	N	4	0		0	0	0	24
1995			1	0	0	0	0	0	6
Career			7	0	0	0	0	0	42

James Hundon

Year	Team		TD	1XP	2XP	FG	FGA	SAF	Pts
1996	CIN	N	1	0	0	0	0	0	6

Ricky Hunley

Year	Team		TD	1XP	2XP	FG	FGA	SAF	Pts
1987	DEN	N	1	0		0	0	0	6

Chuck Hunsinger

Year	Team		TD	1XP	2XP	FG	FGA	SAF	Pts
1950	CHIB	N	2	0		0	0	0	12
1951			4	0		0	0	0	24
1952			2	0		0	0	0	12
Career			8	0		0	0	0	48

Bobby Hunt

Year	Team		TD	1XP	2XP	FG	FGA	SAF	Pts
1964	KC	A	1	0	0	0	0	0	6
1968	CIN	A	1	0	0	0	0	0	6
Career			2	0	0	0	0	0	12

George Hunt

Year	Team		TD	1XP	2XP	FG	FGA	SAF	Pts
1973	BAL	N	0	22		16	28	0	70
1975	NYG	N	0	24		6	11	0	42
Career			0	46		22	39	0	112

Jim Hunt

Year	Team		TD	1XP	2XP	FG	FGA	SAF	Pts
1963	BOS	A	1	0	0	0	0	0	6
1966			1	0	0	0	0	0	6
1967			0	0	0	0	0	1	2
Career			2	0	0	0	0	1	14

Sam Hunt

Year	Team		TD	1XP	2XP	FG	FGA	SAF	Pts
1976	NE	N	1	0		0	0	0	6

Al Hunter

Year	Team		TD	1XP	2XP	FG	FGA	SAF	Pts
1977	SEA	N	1	0		0	0	0	6
1978			2	0		0	0	0	12
1979			1	0		0	0	0	6
Career			4	0		0	0	0	24

Eddie Hunter

Year	Team		TD	1XP	2XP	FG	FGA	SAF	Pts
1987	NYJ	N	2	0		0	0	0	12

George Hunter

Year	Team		TD	1XP	2XP	FG	FGA	SAF	Pts
1965	WAS	N	1	0		0	0	0	6

Herman Hunter

Year	Team		TD	1XP	2XP	FG	FGA	SAF	Pts
1985	PHI	N	2	0		0	0	0	12
1986	DET	N	1	0		0	0	0	6
Career			3	0		0	0	0	18

James Hunter

Year	Team		TD	1XP	2XP	FG	FGA	SAF	Pts
1976	DET	N	1	0		0	0	0	6

Monty Hunter

Year	Team		TD	1XP	2XP	FG	FGA	SAF	Pts
Playoffs			1	0	0	0	0	0	6

Patrick Hunter

Year	Team		TD	1XP	2XP	FG	FGA	SAF	Pts
1991	SEA	N	1	0		0	0	0	6

Scott Hunter

Year	Team		TD	1XP	2XP	FG	FGA	SAF	Pts
1971	GB	N	4	0		0	0	0	24
1972			5	0		0	0	0	30
1973			1	0		0	0	0	6
1976	ATL	N	1	0		0	0	0	6
1977			1	0		0	0	0	6
1979	DET	N	1	0		0	0	0	6
Career			13	0		0	0	0	78

Stan Hunter

Year	Team		TD	1XP	2XP	FG	FGA	SAF	Pts
1987	NYJ	N	1	0		0	0	0	6

Tony Hunter

Year	Team		TD	1XP	2XP	FG	FGA	SAF	Pts
1983	BUF	N	3	0		0	0	0	18
1984			2	0		0	0	0	12
1985	LARM	N	4	0		0	0	0	24
Career			9	0		0	0	0	54

Tom Hupke

Year	Team		TD	1XP	2XP	FG	FGA	SAF	Pts
1937	DET	N	1	0		0		0	6

John Hurlburt

Year	Team		TD	1XP	2XP	FG	FGA	SAF	Pts
1924	CHIC	N	3	0		0		0	18

Bill Hurley

Year	Team		TD	1XP	2XP	FG	FGA	SAF	Pts
1982	NO	N	1	0		0	0	0	6

Maurice Hurst

Year	Team		TD	1XP	2XP	FG	FGA	SAF	Pts
1989	NE	N	1	0		0	0	0	6

Michael Husted

Year	Team		TD	1XP	2XP	FG	FGA	SAF	Pts
1993	TB	N	0	27		16	22	0	75
1994			0	20	0	23	35	0	89
1995			0	25	0	19	26	0	82
1996			0	18	0	25	32	0	93
Career			0	90	0	83	115	0	339

Tom Hutchinson

Year	Team		TD	1XP	2XP	FG	FGA	SAF	Pts
1965	CLE	N	2	0		0	0	0	12

Anthony Hutchison

Year	Team		TD	1XP	2XP	FG	FGA	SAF	Pts
1983	CHI	N	1	0		0	0	0	6
1984			1	0		0	0	0	6
Career			2	0		0	0	0	12

Gerry Huth

Year	Team		TD	1XP	2XP	FG	FGA	SAF	Pts
1959	PHI	N	1	0		0	0	0	6

Don Hutson

Year	Team		TD	1XP	2XP	FG	FGA	SAF	Pts
1935	GB	N	**7**	1		0		0	43
1936			**9**	0		0		0	54
1937			**7**	0		0		1	44
1938			**9**	3		0		0	57
1939			6	2		0	0	1	40
1940			7	15		0	0	0	**57**
1941			**12**	**20**		1	1	0	**95**
1942			**17**	**33**		1	4	0	**138**
1943			**12**	36		**3**	5	0	**117**
1944			**9**	**31**		0	3	0	**85**
1945			10	31		2	4	0	97
Career			105	172		7	17	2	827
Playoffs			1	4		0	0	0	10

John Huzvar

Year	Team		TD	1XP	2XP	FG	FGA	SAF	Pts
1952	PHI	N	2	0		0	0	0	12
1953	BAL	N	5	0		0	0	0	30
Career			7	0		0	0	0	42

Donald Igwebuike

Year	Team		TD	1XP	2XP	FG	FGA	SAF	Pts
1985	TB	N	0	30		22	32	0	96
1986			0	26		17	24	0	77
1987			0	24		14	18	0	66
1988			0	21		19	25	0	78
1989			0	33		22	28	0	99
1990	MIN	N	0	19		14	16	0	61
Career			0	153		108	143	0	477

Ted Illman

Year	Team		TD	1XP	2XP	FG	FGA	SAF	Pts
1926	LA	A	1	1		0		0	7

Tut Imlay

Year	Team		TD	1XP	2XP	FG	FGA	SAF	Pts
1926	LA	N	4	0		0		0	24

Bob Ingalls

Year	Team		TD	1XP	2XP	FG	FGA	SAF	Pts
1942	GB	N	1	0		0	0	0	6

Darryl Ingram

Year	Team		TD	1XP	2XP	FG	FGA	SAF	Pts
1989	MIN	N	1	0		0	0	0	6

Mark Ingram

Year	Team		TD	1XP	2XP	FG	FGA	SAF	Pts
1988	NYG	N	1	0		0	0	0	6
1989			1	0		0	0	0	6
1990			5	0		0	0	0	30
1991			3	0		0	0	0	18
1992			1	0		0	0	0	6
1993	MIA	N	6	0		0	0	0	36
1994			6	0	0	0	0	0	36
1995	GB	N	3	0	0	0	0	0	18
Career			26	0	0	0	0	0	156

Einar Irgens

Year	Team		TD	1XP	2XP	FG	FGA	SAF	Pts
1922	MIN	N	0	1		0		0	1
1923			0	0		0		0	0
Career			0	1		0		0	1

Gerald Irons

Year	Team		TD	1XP	2XP	FG	FGA	SAF	Pts
1977	CLE	N	1	0		0	0	0	6

Le Roy Irvin

Year	Team		TD	1XP	2XP	FG	FGA	SAF	Pts
1981	LA	N	3	0		0	0	0	18
1982	LARM	N	1	0		0	0	0	6
1984			2	0		0	0	0	12
1985			1	0		0	0	0	6
1986			3	0		0	0	0	18
1987			1	0		0	0	0	6
Career			11	0		0	0	0	66

Michael Irvin

Year	Team		TD	1XP	2XP	FG	FGA	SAF	Pts
1988	DAL	N	5	0		0	0	0	30
1989			2	0		0	0	0	12
1990			5	0		0	0	0	30
1991			8	0		0	0	0	48
1992			7	0		0	0	0	42
1993			7	0		0	0	0	42
1994			6	0	0	0	0	0	36
1995			10	0	0	0	0	0	60
1996			2	0	1	0	0	0	14
Career			52	0	1	0	0	0	314
Playoffs			8	0	0	0	0	0	48

Tex Irvin

Year	Team		TD	1XP	2XP	FG	FGA	SAF	Pts
1933	NYG	N	1	0		0		0	6

Don Irwin

Year	Team		TD	1XP	2XP	FG	FGA	SAF	Pts
1936	BOS	N	2	0		0		0	12
1937	WAS	N	2	0		0		0	12
1938			1	0		0	0	0	6
1939			1	0		0	0	0	6
Career			6	0		0	0	0	36

Wilmer Isabel

Year	Team		TD	1XP	2XP	FG	FGA	SAF	Pts
1923	COL	N	2	0		0		0	12

Cecil Isbell

Year	Team		TD	1XP	2XP	FG	FGA	SAF	Pts
1938	GB	N	2	0		0		0	12
1939			2	3		0	0	0	15
1940			4	0		0	0	0	24
1941			1	0		0	0	0	6
1942			1	0		0	0	0	6
Career			10	3		0	0	0	63

John Isenbarger

Year	Team		TD	1XP	2XP	FG	FGA	SAF	Pts
1970	SF	N	1	0		0	0	0	6
1972			1	0		0	0	0	6
Career			2	0		0	0	0	12

Qadry Ismail

Year	Team		TD	1XP	2XP	FG	FGA	SAF	Pts
1993	MIN	N	1	0		0	0	0	6
1994			5	0	0	0	0	0	30
1995			3	0	0	0	0	0	18
1996			3	0	0	0	0	0	18
Career			12	0	0	0	0	0	72

Raghib Ismail

Year	Team		TD	1XP	2XP	FG	FGA	SAF	Pts
1993	LARI	N	1	0		0	0	0	6
1994			5	0	0	0	0	0	30

Raghib Ismail *continued*

Year	Team		TD	1XP	2XP	FG	FGA	SAF	Pts
1995	OAK	N	3	0	0	0	0	0	18
1996	CAR	N	1	0	0	0	0	0	6
Career			10	0	0	0	0	0	60

Rickey Isom

Year	Team		TD	1XP	2XP	FG	FGA	SAF	Pts
1987	MIA	N	1	0		0	0	0	6

Duke Iverson

Year	Team		TD	1XP	2XP	FG	FGA	SAF	Pts
1950	NYY	N	1	0		0	0	1	8

Eddie Lee Ivery

Year	Team		TD	1XP	2XP	FG	FGA	SAF	Pts
1980	GB	N	4	0		0	0	0	24
1981			1	0		0	0	0	6
1982			10	0		0	0	0	60
1983			3	0		0	0	0	18
1984			7	0		0	0	0	42
1985			4	0		0	0	0	24
1986			1	0		0	0	0	6
Career			30	0		0	0	0	180
Playoffs			2	0		0	0	0	12

Horace Ivory

Year	Team		TD	1XP	2XP	FG	FGA	SAF	Pts
1978	NE	N	11	0		0	0	0	66
1979			3	0		0	0	0	18
1980			3	0		0	0	0	18
1982	SEA	N	1	0		0	0	0	6
Career			18	0		0	0	0	108

Pop Ivy

Year	Team		TD	1XP	2XP	FG	FGA	SAF	Pts
1941	CHIC	N	2	0		0	0	0	12
1942			0	2		0	0	0	2
1946			1	0		0	0	0	6
1947			0	0		0	1	0	0
Career			3	2		0	1	0	20

Eric Jack

Year	Team		TD	1XP	2XP	FG	FGA	SAF	Pts
1994	ATL	N	1	0	0	0	0	0	6

Chris Jacke

Year	Team		TD	1XP	2XP	FG	FGA	SAF	Pts
1989	GB	N	0	42		22	28	0	108
1990			0	28		23	30	0	97
1991			0	31		18	24	0	85
1992			0	30		22	29	0	96
1993			0	35		31	37	0	128
1994			0	41	0	19	26	0	98
1995			0	43	0	17	23	0	94
1996			0	**51**	0	21	27	0	114
Career			0	301	0	173	224	0	820
Playoffs			0	28	0	15	22	0	73

Alfred Jackson

Year	Team		TD	1XP	2XP	FG	FGA	SAF	Pts
1978	ATL	N	2	0		0	0	0	12
1980			7	0		0	0	0	42
1981			7	0		0	0	0	42
1982			1	0		0	0	0	6
1983			3	0		0	0	0	18
1984			2	0		0	0	0	12
Career			22	0		0	0	0	132

Alfred Jackson

Year	Team		TD	1XP	2XP	FG	FGA	SAF	Pts
1995	MIN	N	1	0	0	0	0	0	6

Andrew Jackson

Year	Team		TD	1XP	2XP	FG	FGA	SAF	Pts
1987	HOU	N	1	0		0	0	0	6

Billy Jackson

Year	Team		TD	1XP	2XP	FG	FGA	SAF	Pts
1981	KC	N	11	0		0	0	0	66
1982			3	0		0	0	0	18
1983			2	0		0	0	0	12
1984			2	0		0	0	0	12
Career			18	0		0	0	0	108

Bo Jackson

Year	Team		TD	1XP	2XP	FG	FGA	SAF	Pts
1987	LARI	N	6	0		0	0	0	36
1988			3	0		0	0	0	18
1989			4	0		0	0	0	24
1990			5	0		0	0	0	30
Career			18	0		0	0	0	108

Bob Jackson

Year	Team		TD	1XP	2XP	FG	FGA	SAF	Pts
1950	NYG	N	2	0		0	0	0	12

Bob Jackson

Year	Team		TD	1XP	2XP	FG	FGA	SAF	Pts
1962	SD	A	7	0	0	0	0	0	42
1963			4	0	0	0	0	0	24
1964	HOU	A	3	0	0	0	0	0	18
1965			2	0	0	0	0	0	12
Career			16	0	0	0	0	0	96

Bobby Jackson

Year	Team		TD	1XP	2XP	FG	FGA	SAF	Pts
1979	NYJ	N	1	0		0	0	0	6
1982			2	0		0	0	0	12
Career			3	0		0	0	0	18

Calvin Jackson

Year	Team		TD	1XP	2XP	FG	FGA	SAF	Pts
1996	MIA	N	1	0	0	0	0	0	6

Charles Jackson

Year	Team		TD	1XP	2XP	FG	FGA	SAF	Pts
1983	KC	N	1	0		0	0	0	6

Earnest Jackson

Year	Team		TD	1XP	2XP	FG	FGA	SAF	Pts
1984	SD	N	9	0		0	0	0	54
1985	PHI	N	6	0		0	0	0	36
1986	PIT	N	5	0		0	0	0	30
1987			1	0		0	0	0	6
1988			3	0		0	0	0	18
Career			24	0		0	0	0	144

Ernie Jackson

Year	Team		TD	1XP	2XP	FG	FGA	SAF	Pts
1972	NO	N	1	0		0	0	0	6

Frank Jackson

Year	Team		TD	1XP	2XP	FG	FGA	SAF	Pts
1961	DAL	A	5	0	0	0	0	0	30
1962			4	0	0	0	0	0	24
1963	KC	A	9	0	0	0	0	0	54
1964			9	0	0	0	0	0	54
1965			1	0	0	0	0	0	6
1966	MIA	A	2	0	0	0	0	0	12
1967			1	0	0	0	0	0	6
Career			31	0	0	0	0	0	186

Greg Jackson

Year	Team		TD	1XP	2XP	FG	FGA	SAF	Pts
1994	PHI	N	1	0	0	0	0	0	6
1995			1	0	0	0	0	0	6
Career			2	0	0	0	0	0	12

Harold Jackson

Year	Team		TD	1XP	2XP	FG	FGA	SAF	Pts
1969	PHI	N	9	0		0	0	0	54
1970			5	0		0	0	0	30
1971			3	0		0	0	0	18
1972			4	0		0	0	0	24
1973	LA	N	13	0		0	0	0	78
1974			5	0		0	0	0	30
1975			7	0		0	0	0	42
1976			5	0		0	0	0	30
1977			6	0		0	0	0	36
1978	NE	N	6	0		0	0	0	36
1979			7	0		0	0	0	42
1980			5	0		0	0	0	30
1983	SEA	N	1	0		0	0	0	6
Career			76	0		0	0	0	456
Playoffs			5	0		0	0	0	30

Jazz Jackson

Year	Team		TD	1XP	2XP	FG	FGA	SAF	Pts
1974	NYJ	N	2	0		0	0	0	12

Jeff Jackson

Year	Team		TD	1XP	2XP	FG	FGA	SAF	Pts
1984	ATL	N	1	0		0	0	0	6

Jim Jackson

Year	Team		TD	1XP	2XP	FG	FGA	SAF	Pts
1966	SF	N	1	0		0	0	0	6

John Jackson

Year	Team		TD	1XP	2XP	FG	FGA	SAF	Pts
1992	PHX	N	1	0		0	0	0	6

Johnnie Jackson

Year	Team		TD	1XP	2XP	FG	FGA	SAF	Pts
1989	SF	N	1	0		0	0	0	6

Keith Jackson

Year	Team		TD	1XP	2XP	FG	FGA	SAF	Pts
1988	PHI	N	6	0		0	0	0	36
1989			3	0		0	0	0	18
1990			6	0		0	0	0	36
1991			5	0		0	0	0	30
1992	MIA	N	5	0		0	0	0	30
1993			6	0		0	0	0	36

Keith Jackson *continued*

Year	Team		TD	1XP	2XP	FG	FGA	SAF	Pts
1994			7	0	1	0	0	0	44
1995	GB	N	1	0	0	0	0	0	6
1996			10	0	0	0	0	0	60
Career			49	0	1	0	0	0	296
Playoffs			6	0	0	0	0	0	36

Kenny Jackson

Year	Team		TD	1XP	2XP	FG	FGA	SAF	Pts
1984	PHI	N	1	0		0	0	0	6
1985			1	0		0	0	0	6
1986			6	0		0	0	0	36
1987			3	0		0	0	0	18
Career			11	0		0	0	0	66

Kirby Jackson

Year	Team		TD	1XP	2XP	FG	FGA	SAF	Pts
1987	LARM	N	1	0		0	0	0	6
1989	BUF	N	1	0		0	0	0	6
Career			2	0		0	0	0	12

Leroy Jackson

Year	Team		TD	1XP	2XP	FG	FGA	SAF	Pts
1962	WAS	N	1	0		0	0	0	6

Louis Jackson

Year	Team		TD	1XP	2XP	FG	FGA	SAF	Pts
1981	NYG	N	1	0		0	0	0	6

Mark Jackson

Year	Team		TD	1XP	2XP	FG	FGA	SAF	Pts
1986	DEN	N	1	0		0	0	0	6
1987			2	0		0	0	0	12
1988			6	0		0	0	0	36
1989			2	0		0	0	0	12
1990			5	0		0	0	0	30
1991			1	0		0	0	0	6
1992			8	0		0	0	0	48
1993	NYG	N	4	0		0	0	0	24
1994	IND	N	1	0	0	0	0	0	6
Career			30	0	0	0	0	0	180
Playoffs			2	0	0	0	0	0	12

Mark Jackson

Year	Team		TD	1XP	2XP	FG	FGA	SAF	Pts
1987	STL	N	1	0		0	0	0	6

Michael Jackson

Year	Team		TD	1XP	2XP	FG	FGA	SAF	Pts
1991	CLE	N	2	0		0	0	0	12
1992			7	0		0	0	0	42
1993			8	0		0	0	0	48
1994			2	0	0	0	0	0	12
1995			9	0	0	0	0	0	54
1996	BAL	N	14	0	2	0	0	0	88
Career			42	0	2	0	0	0	256

Monte Jackson

Year	Team		TD	1XP	2XP	FG	FGA	SAF	Pts
1975	LA	N	1	0		0	0	0	6
1976			3	0		0	0	0	18
Career			4	0		0	0	0	24

Pete Jackson

Year	Team		TD	1XP	2XP	FG	FGA	SAF	Pts
1928	DET	N	2	0		0		0	12

Randy Jackson

Year	Team		TD	1XP	2XP	FG	FGA	SAF	Pts
1972	BUF	N	1	0		0	0	0	6

Richard Jackson

Year	Team		TD	1XP	2XP	FG	FGA	SAF	Pts
1967	DEN	A	0	0	0	0	0	1	2

Rickey Jackson

Year	Team		TD	1XP	2XP	FG	FGA	SAF	Pts
1988	NO	N	0	0		0	0	1	2

Robert Jackson

Year	Team		TD	1XP	2XP	FG	FGA	SAF	Pts
1984	CIN	N	1	0		0	0	0	6
1985			1	0		0	0	0	6
Career			2	0		0	0	0	12

Steve Jackson

Year	Team		TD	1XP	2XP	FG	FGA	SAF	Pts
1993	HOU	N	1	0		0	0	0	6
1996			0	0	0	0	0	1	2
Career			1	0	0	0	0	1	8

Terry Jackson

Year	Team		TD	1XP	2XP	FG	FGA	SAF	Pts
1978	NYG	N	1	0		0	0	0	6
1979			1	0		0	0	0	6
1981			1	0		0	0	0	6
1983			1	0		0	0	0	6

Terry Jackson *continued*

Year	Team	Lg	TD	1XP	2XP	FG	FGA	SAF	Pts
1984	SEA	N	1	0		0	0	0	6
Career			5	0		0	0	0	30

Tom Jackson

Year	Team	Lg	TD	1XP	2XP	FG	FGA	SAF	Pts
1976	DEN	N	1	0		0	0	0	6
1977			1	0		0	0	0	6
1978			1	0		0	0	0	6
Career			3	0		0	0	0	18

Vestee Jackson

Year	Team	Lg	TD	1XP	2XP	FG	FGA	SAF	Pts
1990	CHI	N	1	0		0	0	0	6
1992	MIA	N	1	0		0	0	0	6
Career			2	0		0	0	0	12

Wilbur Jackson

Year	Team	Lg	TD	1XP	2XP	FG	FGA	SAF	Pts
1974	SF	N	2	0		0	0	0	12
1976			2	0		0	0	0	12
1977			7	0		0	0	0	42
1979			2	0		0	0	0	12
1980	WAS	N	4	0		0	0	0	24
Career			17	0		0	0	0	102

Willie Jackson

Year	Team	Lg	TD	1XP	2XP	FG	FGA	SAF	Pts
1995	JAC	N	5	0	1	0	0	0	32
1996			3	0	1	0	0	0	20
Career			8	0	2	0	0	0	52

Allen Jacobs

Year	Team	Lg	TD	1XP	2XP	FG	FGA	SAF	Pts
1966	NYG	N	1	0		0	0	0	6

Dave Jacobs

Year	Team	Lg	TD	1XP	2XP	FG	FGA	SAF	Pts
1979	NYJ	N	0	10		5	9	0	25
1981	CLE	N	0	9		4	12	0	21
1987	PHI	N	0	2		3	5	0	11
Career			0	21		12	26	0	57

Jack Jacobs

Year	Team	Lg	TD	1XP	2XP	FG	FGA	SAF	Pts
1947	GB	N	1	0		0	0	0	6
1948			1	0		0	0	0	6
Career			2	0		0	0	0	12

Joe Jacoby

Year	Team	Lg	TD	1XP	2XP	FG	FGA	SAF	Pts
1984	WAS	N	1	0		0	0	0	6

Harry Jacunski

Year	Team	Lg	TD	1XP	2XP	FG	FGA	SAF	Pts
1939	GB	N	2	0		0	0	0	12
1942			1	0		0	0	0	6
1943			3	0		0	0	0	18
Career			6	0		0	0	0	36

Jeff Jaeger

Year	Team	Lg	TD	1XP	2XP	FG	FGA	SAF	Pts
1987	CLE	N	0	33		14	22	0	75
1989	LARI	N	0	34		23	34	0	103
1990			0	40		15	20	0	85
1991			0	29		29	34	0	116
1992			0	28		15	26	0	73
1993			0	27		**35**	**44**	0	**132**
1994			0	31	0	22	28	0	97
1995	OAK	N	0	22	0	13	18	0	61
1996	CHI	N	0	23	0	19	23	0	80
Career			0	267	0	185	249	0	822
Playoffs			0	10	0	6	7	0	28

Harry Jagade

Year	Team	Lg	TD	1XP	2XP	FG	FGA	SAF	Pts
1949	BAL	AA	2	0		0	0	0	12
1952	CLE	N	3	0		0	0	0	18
1953			4	0		0	0	0	24
1954	CHIB	N	3	0		0	0	0	18
1955			2	0		0	0	0	12
Career			14	0		0	0	0	84
Playoffs			2	0		0	0	0	12

George Jakowenko

Year	Team	Lg	TD	1XP	2XP	FG	FGA	SAF	Pts
1976	BUF	N	0	21		12	17	0	57

Claudis James

Year	Team	Lg	TD	1XP	2XP	FG	FGA	SAF	Pts
1968	GB	N	2	0		0	0	0	12

Craig James

Year	Team	Lg	TD	1XP	2XP	FG	FGA	SAF	Pts
1984	NE	N	1	0		0	0	0	6
1985			7	0		0	0	0	42
1986			4	0		0	0	0	24

Craig James *continued*

Year	Team	Lg	TD	1XP	2XP	FG	FGA	SAF	Pts
1988			1	0		0	0	0	6
Career			13	0		0	0	0	78
Playoffs			1	0		0	0	0	6

Dick James

Year	Team	Lg	TD	1XP	2XP	FG	FGA	SAF	Pts
1956	WAS	N	3	0		0	0	0	18
1958			1	0		0	0	0	6
1959			4	0		0	0	0	24
1960			6	0		0	0	0	36
1961			5	0		0	0	0	30
1962			5	0		0	0	0	30
1963			6	0		0	0	0	36
1964	NYG	N	4	0		0	0	0	24
Career			34	0		0	0	0	204

Garry James

Year	Team	Lg	TD	1XP	2XP	FG	FGA	SAF	Pts
1986	DET	N	3	0		0	0	0	18
1987			4	0		0	0	0	24
1988			7	0		0	0	0	42
Career			14	0		0	0	0	84

Lionel James

Year	Team	Lg	TD	1XP	2XP	FG	FGA	SAF	Pts
1984	SD	N	1	0		0	0	0	6
1985			8	0		0	0	0	48
1987			6	0		0	0	0	36
1988			1	0		0	0	0	6
Career			16	0		0	0	0	96

Lynn James

Year	Team	Lg	TD	1XP	2XP	FG	FGA	SAF	Pts
1991	CIN	N	1	0		0	0	0	6

Robert James

Year	Team	Lg	TD	1XP	2XP	FG	FGA	SAF	Pts
1971	BUF	N	1	0		0	0	0	6

Roland James

Year	Team	Lg	TD	1XP	2XP	FG	FGA	SAF	Pts
1980	NE	N	1	0		0	0	0	6
1984			0	0		0	0	1	2
Career			1	0		0	0	1	8

Ron James

Year	Team	Lg	TD	1XP	2XP	FG	FGA	SAF	Pts
1972	PHI	N	1	0		0	0	0	6
1973			1	0		0	0	0	6
1974			2	0		0	0	0	12
1975			2	0		0	0	0	12
Career			6	0		0	0	0	36

Tommy James

Year	Team	Lg	TD	1XP	2XP	FG	FGA	SAF	Pts
1949	CLE	AA	1	0		0	0	0	6
1953	CLE	N	1	0		0	0	0	6
Career			2	0		0	0	0	12
Playoffs			0	0		0	0	0	0

George Jamison

Year	Team	Lg	TD	1XP	2XP	FG	FGA	SAF	Pts
1987	DET	N	0	0		0	0	1	2
1988			2	0		0	0	0	12
1993			1	0		0	0	0	6
Career			3	0		0	0	1	20

Bobby Jancik

Year	Team	Lg	TD	1XP	2XP	FG	FGA	SAF	Pts
1964	HOU	A	1	0	0	0	0	0	6

Len Janiak

Year	Team	Lg	TD	1XP	2XP	FG	FGA	SAF	Pts
1940	CLE	N	0	0		0	0	0	0
1942			1	0		0	0	0	6
Career			1	0		0	0	0	6

Tommy Janik

Year	Team	Lg	TD	1XP	2XP	FG	FGA	SAF	Pts
1964	DEN	A	1	0	0	0	0	0	6
1966	BUF	A	2	0	0	0	0	0	12
1967			2	0	0	0	0	0	12
1968			1	0	0	0	0	0	6
Career			6	0	0	0	0	0	36

Ed Jankowski

Year	Team	Lg	TD	1XP	2XP	FG	FGA	SAF	Pts
1937	GB	N	4	1		0		0	25
1938			2	2		0		0	14
1939			2	0		0	0	0	12
1940			2	0		0	0	0	12
1941			0	1		1	1	0	4
Career			10	4		1	1	0	67
Playoffs			1	0		0	0	0	6

Vic Janowicz

Year	Team	Lg	TD	1XP	2XP	FG	FGA	SAF	Pts
1954	WAS	N	0	9		4	8	0	21
1955			7	28		6	20	0	88
Career			7	37		10	28	0	109

Val Jansante

Year	Team	Lg	TD	1XP	2XP	FG	FGA	SAF	Pts
1946	PIT	N	1	0		0	0	0	6
1947			5	0		0	0	1	32
1948			3	0		0	0	0	18
1949			4	0		0	0	0	24
Career			13	0		0	0	1	80

Pete Jaquess

Year	Team	Lg	TD	1XP	2XP	FG	FGA	SAF	Pts
1964	HOU	A	1	0	0	0	0	0	6
1966	MIA	A	1	0	0	0	0	0	6
Career			2	0	0	0	0	0	12

Mike Jarmoluk

Year	Team	Lg	TD	1XP	2XP	FG	FGA	SAF	Pts
1947	CHIB	N	1	0		0	0	0	6
1952	PHI	N	2	0		0	0	0	12
Career			3	0		0	0	0	18

Ray Jarvis

Year	Team	Lg	TD	1XP	2XP	FG	FGA	SAF	Pts
1975	DET	N	4	0		0	0	0	24
1976			5	0		0	0	0	30
1977			1	0		0	0	0	6
1979	NE	N	1	0		0	0	0	6
Career			11	0		0	0	0	66

Dick Jauron

Year	Team	Lg	TD	1XP	2XP	FG	FGA	SAF	Pts
1973	DET	N	1	0		0	0	0	6
1978	CIN	N	1	0		0	0	0	6
Career			2	0		0	0	0	12

Ron Jaworski

Year	Team	Lg	TD	1XP	2XP	FG	FGA	SAF	Pts
1974	LA	N	1	0		0	0	0	6
1975			2	0		0	0	0	12
1976			1	0		0	0	0	6
1977	PHI	N	5	0		0	0	0	30
1979			2	0		0	0	0	12
1980			1	0		0	0	0	6
1983			1	0		0	0	0	6
1984			1	0		0	0	0	6
1985			2	0		0	0	0	12
Career			16	0		0	0	0	96
Playoffs			1	0		0	0	0	6

Jim Jeffcoat

Year	Team	Lg	TD	1XP	2XP	FG	FGA	SAF	Pts
1984	DAL	N	1	0		0	0	0	6
1985			1	0		0	0	0	6
1987			1	0		0	0	0	6
1989			1	0		0	0	0	6
Career			4	0		0	0	0	24

Billy Jefferson

Year	Team	Lg	TD	1XP	2XP	FG	FGA	SAF	Pts
1941	DET	N	2	0		0	0	0	12

James Jefferson

Year	Team	Lg	TD	1XP	2XP	FG	FGA	SAF	Pts
1989	SEA	N	1	0		0	0	0	6

John Jefferson

Year	Team	Lg	TD	1XP	2XP	FG	FGA	SAF	Pts
1978	SD	N	13	0		0	0	0	78
1979			10	0		0	0	0	60
1980			13	0		0	0	0	78
1981	GB	N	4	0		0	0	0	24
1983			7	0		0	0	0	42
Career			47	0		0	0	0	282
Playoffs			2	0		0	0	0	12

Roy Jefferson

Year	Team	Lg	TD	1XP	2XP	FG	FGA	SAF	Pts
1965	PIT	N	1	0		0	0	0	6
1966			4	0		0	0	0	24
1967			4	0		0	0	0	24
1968			12	0		0	0	0	72
1969			9	0		0	0	0	54
1970	BAL	N	7	0		0	0	0	42
1971	WAS	N	4	0		0	0	0	24
1972			3	0		0	0	0	18
1973			1	0		0	0	0	6
1974			4	0		0	0	0	24
1975			2	0		0	0	0	12
1976			2	0		0	0	0	12
Career			53	0		0	0	0	318
Playoffs			4	0		0	0	0	24

Shawn Jefferson

Year	Team		TD	1XP	2XP	FG	FGA	SAF	Pts
1991	SD	N	1	0		0	0	0	6
1992			2	0		0	0	0	12
1993			2	0		0	0	0	12
1994			3	0	0	0	0	0	18
1995			2	0	0	0	0	0	12
1996	NE	N	4	0	0	0	0	0	24
Career			14	0	0	0	0	0	84
Playoffs			1	0	0	0	0	0	6

Haywood Jeffires

Year	Team		TD	1XP	2XP	FG	FGA	SAF	Pts
1988	HOU	N	1	0		0	0	0	6
1989			2	0		0	0	0	12
1990			8	0		0	0	0	48
1991			7	0		0	0	0	42
1992			9	0		0	0	0	54
1993			6	0		0	0	0	36
1994			6	0	3	0	0	0	42
1995			8	0	0	0	0	0	48
1996	NO	N	3	0	0	0	0	0	18
Career			50	0	3	0	0	0	306
Playoffs			3	0	0	0	0	0	18

Jon Jelacic

Year	Team		TD	1XP	2XP	FG	FGA	SAF	Pts
1963	OAK	A	2	0	0	0	0	0	12

Bob Jencks

Year	Team		TD	1XP	2XP	FG	FGA	SAF	Pts
1963	CHI	N	0	35		1	10	0	38
1964			0	29		3	7	0	38
1965	WAS	N	0	29		10	22	0	59
Career			0	93		14	39	0	135
Playoffs			0	2		0	0	0	2

Alfred Jenkins

Year	Team		TD	1XP	2XP	FG	FGA	SAF	Pts
1975	ATL	N	6	0		0	0	0	36
1976			6	0		0	0	0	36
1977			4	0		0	0	0	24
1979			3	0		0	0	0	18
1980			6	0		0	0	0	36
1981			13	0		0	0	0	78
1982			1	0		0	0	0	6
1983			1	0		0	0	0	6
Career			40	0		0	0	0	240
Playoffs			1	0		0	0	0	6

Carlos Jenkins

Year	Team		TD	1XP	2XP	FG	FGA	SAF	Pts
1992	MIN	N	2	0		0	0	0	12

Izel Jenkins

Year	Team		TD	1XP	2XP	FG	FGA	SAF	Pts
1988	PHI	N	0	0		0	0	1	2

Jack Jenkins

Year	Team		TD	1XP	2XP	FG	FGA	SAF	Pts
1943	WAS	N	0	1		0	0	0	1
1946			1	0		0	0	0	6
Career			1	1		0	0	0	7

James Jenkins

Year	Team		TD	1XP	2XP	FG	FGA	SAF	Pts
1994	WAS	N	4	0	0	0	0	0	24

Ken Jenkins

Year	Team		TD	1XP	2XP	FG	FGA	SAF	Pts
1984	DET	N	1	0		0	0	0	6

Melvin Jenkins

Year	Team		TD	1XP	2XP	FG	FGA	SAF	Pts
1992	DET	N	1	0		0	0	0	6
Playoffs			2	0	0	0	0	0	12

Keith Jennings

Year	Team		TD	1XP	2XP	FG	FGA	SAF	Pts
1992	CHI	N	1	0		0	0	0	6
1994			3	0	0	0	0	0	18
1995			6	0	0	0	0	0	36
Career			10	0	0	0	0	0	60
Playoffs			1	0	0	0	0	0	6

Lou Jennings

Year	Team		TD	1XP	2XP	FG	FGA	SAF	Pts
1929	PRO	N	0	3		0		0	3
1930	POR	N	0	0		0		0	0
Career			0	3		0		0	3

Stanford Jennings

Year	Team		TD	1XP	2XP	FG	FGA	SAF	Pts
1984	CIN	N	5	0		0	0	0	30
1985			4	0		0	0	0	24
1986			1	0		0	0	0	6
1987			3	0		0	0	0	18
1988			2	0		0	0	0	12

Stanford Jennings *continued*

Year	Team		TD	1XP	2XP	FG	FGA	SAF	Pts
1989			3	0		0	0	0	18
1990			1	0		0	0	0	6
1992	TB	N	1	0		0	0	0	6
Career			20	0		0	0	0	120
Playoffs			2	0		0	0	0	12

Bob Jensen

Year	Team		TD	1XP	2XP	FG	FGA	SAF	Pts
1948	CHI	AA	1	0		0	0	0	6

Derrick Jensen

Year	Team		TD	1XP	2XP	FG	FGA	SAF	Pts
1979	OAK	N	1	0		0	0	0	6
1980			1	0		0	0	0	6
1981			4	0		0	0	0	24
1983	LARI	N	1	0		0	0	0	6
1984			2	0		0	0	0	12
Career			9	0		0	0	0	54
Playoffs			1	0		0	0	0	6

Jim Jensen

Year	Team		TD	1XP	2XP	FG	FGA	SAF	Pts
1977	DEN	N	1	0		0	0	0	6
1979			2	0		0	0	0	12
1980			3	0		0	0	0	18
1982	GB	N	1	0		0	0	0	6
Career			7	0		0	0	0	42
Playoffs			1	0		0	0	1	8

Jim Jensen

Year	Team		TD	1XP	2XP	FG	FGA	SAF	Pts
1984	MIA	N	2	0		0	0	0	12
1985			1	0		0	0	0	6
1986			1	0		0	0	0	6
1987			1	0		0	0	0	6
1988			5	0		0	0	0	30
1989			6	0		0	0	0	36
1990			1	0		0	0	0	6
1991			2	0		0	0	0	12
Career			19	0		0	0	0	114

Mark Jerue

Year	Team		TD	1XP	2XP	FG	FGA	SAF	Pts
1986	LARM	N	1	0		0	0	0	6

Ron Jessie

Year	Team		TD	1XP	2XP	FG	FGA	SAF	Pts
1971	DET	N	2	0		0	0	1	14
1972			4	0		0	0	0	24
1973			4	0		0	0	0	24
1974			4	0		0	0	0	24
1975	LA	N	3	0		0	0	0	18
1976			6	0		0	0	0	36
1978			4	0		0	0	0	24
1979			2	0		0	0	0	12
1980	BUF	N	1	0		0	0	0	6
Career			30	0		0	0	1	182
Playoffs			1	0		0	0	0	6

Tim Jessie

Year	Team		TD	1XP	2XP	FG	FGA	SAF	Pts
1987	WAS	N	1	0		0	0	0	6

Billy Jessup

Year	Team		TD	1XP	2XP	FG	FGA	SAF	Pts
1951	SF	N	1	0		0	0	0	6
1952			1	0		0	0	0	6
1954			3	0		0	0	0	18
1958			1	0		0	0	0	6
1960	DEN	A	1	0	0	0	0	0	6
Career			7	0	0	0	0	0	42

Bob Jeter

Year	Team		TD	1XP	2XP	FG	FGA	SAF	Pts
1966	GB	N	2	0		0	0	0	12

Gary Jeter

Year	Team		TD	1XP	2XP	FG	FGA	SAF	Pts
1986	LARM	N	0	0		0	0	1	2

Perry Jeter

Year	Team		TD	1XP	2XP	FG	FGA	SAF	Pts
1956	CHIB	N	3	0		0	0	0	18

James Jett

Year	Team		TD	1XP	2XP	FG	FGA	SAF	Pts
1993	LARI	N	3	0		0	0	0	18
1995	OAK	N	1	0	0	0	0	0	6
1996			4	0	0	0	0	0	24
Career			8	0	0	0	0	0	48
Playoffs			1	0	0	0	0	0	6

Bob Jewett

Year	Team		TD	1XP	2XP	FG	FGA	SAF	Pts
1958	CHIB	N	1	0		0	0	0	6

Art Jocher

Year	Team		TD	1XP	2XP	FG	FGA	SAF	Pts
1940	BKN	N	1	0		0	0	0	6

Jim Jodat

Year	Team		TD	1XP	2XP	FG	FGA	SAF	Pts
1977	LA	N	2	0		0	0	0	12
1979			1	0		0	0	0	6
1980	SEA	N	6	0		0	0	0	36
1981			1	0		0	0	0	6
Career			10	0		0	0	0	60
Playoffs			1	0		0	0	0	6

Billy Joe

Year	Team		TD	1XP	2XP	FG	FGA	SAF	Pts
1963	DEN	A	5	0	0	0	0	0	30
1964			2	0	1	0	0	0	14
1965	BUF	A	6	0	0	0	0	0	36
1966	MIA	A	1	0	1	0	0	0	8
1967	NY	A	2	0	0	0	0	0	12
1968			3	0	0	0	0	0	18
Career			19	0	2	0	0	0	118

Herb Joesting

Year	Team		TD	1XP	2XP	FG	FGA	SAF	Pts
1929	MIN	N	2	0		0		0	12
1930	MIN-FRA	N	4	0		0		0	24
1931	FRA-CHIB	N	2	0		0		0	12
Career			8	0		0		0	48

Ove Johansson

Year	Team		TD	1XP	2XP	FG	FGA	SAF	Pts
1977	PHI	N	0	1		1	4	0	4

Paul Johns

Year	Team		TD	1XP	2XP	FG	FGA	SAF	Pts
1981	SEA	N	1	0		0	0	0	6
1982			1	0		0	0	0	6
1983			5	0		0	0	0	30
1984			2	0		0	0	0	12
Career			9	0		0	0	0	54
Playoffs			1	0		0	0	0	6

A.J. Johnson

Year	Team		TD	1XP	2XP	FG	FGA	SAF	Pts
1989	WAS	N	1	0		0	0	0	6
1993			1	0		0	0	0	6
Career			2	0		0	0	0	12

Andy Johnson

Year	Team		TD	1XP	2XP	FG	FGA	SAF	Pts
1975	NE	N	4	0		0	0	0	24
1976			10	0		0	0	0	60
1978			3	0		0	0	0	18
1979			1	0		0	0	0	6
1980			3	0		0	0	0	18
1981			1	0		0	0	0	6
Career			22	0		0	0	0	132
Playoffs			1	0		0	0	0	6

Anthony Johnson

Year	Team		TD	1XP	2XP	FG	FGA	SAF	Pts
1990	IND	N	2	0		0	0	0	12
1992			3	0		0	0	0	18
1993			1	0		0	0	0	6
1995	CAR	N	1	0	0	0	0	0	6
1996			6	0	0	0	0	0	36
Career			13	0	0	0	0	0	78

Bert Johnson

Year	Team		TD	1XP	2XP	FG	FGA	SAF	Pts
1938	CHIB	N	2	0		0	0	0	12
1941	CHIC	N	1	0		0	0	0	6
1942	PHI	N	2	0		0	0	0	12
Career			5	0		0	0	0	30

Bill Johnson

Year	Team		TD	1XP	2XP	FG	FGA	SAF	Pts
1949	SF	AA	1	0		0	0	0	6

Bill Johnson

Year	Team		TD	1XP	2XP	FG	FGA	SAF	Pts
1987	CIN	N	1	0		0	0	0	6

Billy Johnson

Year	Team		TD	1XP	2XP	FG	FGA	SAF	Pts
1974	HOU	N	3	0		0	0	0	18
1975			5	0		0	0	0	30
1976			4	0		0	0	0	24
1977			7	0		0	0	0	42
1979			1	0		0	0	0	6
1980			2	0		0	0	0	12
1983	ATL	N	5	0		0	0	0	30
1984			3	0		0	0	0	18
1985			5	0		0	0	0	30
Career			35	0		0	0	0	210

Bobby Johnson

Year	Team		TD	1XP	2XP	FG	FGA	SAF	Pts
1983	**NO**	**N**	1	0		0	0	0	6

Bobby Lee Johnson

Year	Team		TD	1XP	2XP	FG	FGA	SAF	Pts
1984	**NYG**	**N**	7	0		0	0	0	42
1985			8	0		0	0	0	48
1986			5	0		0	0	0	30
Career			20	0		0	0	0	120
Playoffs			1	0		0	0	0	6

Brad Johnson

Year	Team		TD	1XP	2XP	FG	FGA	SAF	Pts
1996	**MIN**	**N**	1	0	0	0	0	0	6
Playoffs			1	0	0	0	0	0	6

Butch Johnson

Year	Team		TD	1XP	2XP	FG	FGA	SAF	Pts
1976	**DAL**	**N**	2	0		0	0	0	12
1977			1	0		0	0	0	6
1979			1	0		0	0	0	6
1980			4	0		0	0	0	24
1981			5	0		0	0	0	30
1982			3	0		0	0	0	18
1983			3	0		0	0	0	18
1984	**DEN**	**N**	6	0		0	0	0	36
1985			3	0		0	0	0	18
Career			28	0		0	0	0	168
Playoffs			4	0		0	0	0	24

Cecil Johnson

Year	Team		TD	1XP	2XP	FG	FGA	SAF	Pts
1943	**BKN**	**N**	2	0		0	0	0	12

Charles Johnson

Year	Team		TD	1XP	2XP	FG	FGA	SAF	Pts
1994	**PIT**	**N**	3	0	0	0	0	0	18
1996			3	0	1	0	0	0	20
Career			6	0	1	0	0	0	38

Charley Johnson

Year	Team		TD	1XP	2XP	FG	FGA	SAF	Pts
1962	**STL**	**N**	3	0		0	0	0	18
1963			1	0		0	0	0	6
1964			2	0		0	0	0	12
1965			1	0		0	0	0	6
1966			2	0		0	0	0	12
1969			1	0		0	0	0	6
Career			10	0		0	0	0	60

Charlie Johnson

Year	Team		TD	1XP	2XP	FG	FGA	SAF	Pts
1982	**MIN**	**N**	1	0		0	0	0	6
1983			1	0		0	0	0	6
Career			2	0		0	0	0	12

Curley Johnson

Year	Team		TD	1XP	2XP	FG	FGA	SAF	Pts
1960	**DAL**	**A**	2	0	1	0	1	0	14
1965	**NY**	**A**	1	0	0	0	0	0	6
1966			1	0	0	0	0	0	6
Career			4	0	1	0	1	0	26

Curtis Johnson

Year	Team		TD	1XP	2XP	FG	FGA	SAF	Pts
1971	**MIA**	**N**	1	0		0	0	0	6
1973			0	0		0	0	1	2
Career			1	0		0	0	1	8

Damone Johnson

Year	Team		TD	1XP	2XP	FG	FGA	SAF	Pts
1987	**LARM**	**N**	2	0		0	0	0	12
1988			6	0		0	0	0	36
1989			5	0		0	0	0	30
1990			3	0		0	0	0	18
1991			2	0		0	0	0	12
Career			18	0		0	0	0	108
Playoffs			2	0		0	0	0	12

Dan Johnson

Year	Team		TD	1XP	2XP	FG	FGA	SAF	Pts
1983	**MIA**	**N**	4	0		0	0	0	24
1984			3	0		0	0	0	18
1985			3	0		0	0	0	18
1986			4	0		0	0	0	24
1987			2	0		0	0	0	12
Career			16	0		0	0	0	96
Playoffs			3	0		0	0	0	18

Daryl Johnson

Year	Team		TD	1XP	2XP	FG	FGA	SAF	Pts
1969	**BOS**	**A**	1	0	0	0	0	1	8

Dennis Johnson

Year	Team		TD	1XP	2XP	FG	FGA	SAF	Pts
1978	**BUF**	**N**	2	0		0	0	0	12

Dick Johnson

Year	Team		TD	1XP	2XP	FG	FGA	SAF	Pts
1963	**KC**	**A**	1	0	0	0	0	0	6

D.J. Johnson

Year	Team		TD	1XP	2XP	FG	FGA	SAF	Pts
1990	**PIT**	**N**	1	0		0	0	0	6

Don Johnson

Year	Team		TD	1XP	2XP	FG	FGA	SAF	Pts
1953	**PHI**	**N**	7	0		0	0	0	42

Essex Johnson

Year	Team		TD	1XP	2XP	FG	FGA	SAF	Pts
1968	**CIN**	**A**	3	0	0	0	0	0	18
1970	**CIN**	**N**	4	0		0	0	0	24
1971			6	0		0	0	0	36
1972			6	0		0	0	0	36
1973			7	0		0	0	0	42
1974			1	0		0	0	0	6
1975			2	0		0	0	0	12
1976	**TB**	**N**	2	0		0	0	0	12
Career			31	0	0	0	0	0	186

Farnham Johnson

Year	Team		TD	1XP	2XP	FG	FGA	SAF	Pts
1948	**CHI**	**AA**	0	2		0	0	0	2

Flip Johnson

Year	Team		TD	1XP	2XP	FG	FGA	SAF	Pts
1988	**BUF**	**N**	1	0		0	0	0	6
1989			1	0		0	0	0	6
Career			2	0		0	0	0	12

Frank Johnson

Year	Team		TD	1XP	2XP	FG	FGA	SAF	Pts
1920	**AKR**	**A**	1	0		0		0	6

Gary Johnson

Year	Team		TD	1XP	2XP	FG	FGA	SAF	Pts
1978	**SD**	**N**	1	0		0	0	0	6
1981			1	0		0	0	0	6
1982			0	0		0	0	1	2
1984	**SF**	**N**	1	0		0	0	1	8
Career			3	0		0	0	2	22

Glenn Johnson

Year	Team		TD	1XP	2XP	FG	FGA	SAF	Pts
1949	**GB**	**N**	1	0		0	0	0	6

Greg Johnson

Year	Team		TD	1XP	2XP	FG	FGA	SAF	Pts
1977	**TB**	**N**	1	0		0	0	0	6

Greggory Johnson

Year	Team		TD	1XP	2XP	FG	FGA	SAF	Pts
1981	**SEA**	**N**	1	0		0	0	0	6

Harvey Johnson

Year	Team		TD	1XP	2XP	FG	FGA	SAF	Pts
1946	**NY**	**AA**	0	36		6	8	0	54
1947			0	**49**		7	8	0	70
1948			0	37		2	7	0	43
1949	**B-NY**	**AA**	0	25		**7**	**15**	0	46
1951	**NYY**	**N**	0	31		6	14	0	49
Career			0	178		28	52	0	262
Playoffs			0	1		2	2	0	7

Herb Johnson

Year	Team		TD	1XP	2XP	FG	FGA	SAF	Pts
1954	**NYG**	**N**	2	0		0	0	0	12

Jack Johnson

Year	Team		TD	1XP	2XP	FG	FGA	SAF	Pts
1937	**DET**	**N**	1	0		0		0	6
1940			1	0		0	0	0	6
Career			2	0		0	0	0	12

Jerry Johnson

Year	Team		TD	1XP	2XP	FG	FGA	SAF	Pts
1922	**RI**	**N**	1	6		1		0	15

Jimmie Johnson

Year	Team		TD	1XP	2XP	FG	FGA	SAF	Pts
1990	**WAS**	**N**	2	0		0	0	0	12
1991			2	0		0	0	0	12
Career			4	0		0	0	0	24

Jimmy Johnson

Year	Team		TD	1XP	2XP	FG	FGA	SAF	Pts
1962	**SF**	**N**	4	0		0	0	0	24
1966			1	0		0	0	0	6
1970			1	0		0	0	1	8
Career			6	0		0	0	1	38

Joe Johnson

Year	Team		TD	1XP	2XP	FG	FGA	SAF	Pts
1948	**NYG**	**N**	2	0		0	0	0	12

Joe Johnson

Year	Team		TD	1XP	2XP	FG	FGA	SAF	Pts
1954	**GB**	**N**	1	0		0	0	0	6

Joe Johnson *continued*

Year	Team		TD	1XP	2XP	FG	FGA	SAF	Pts
1955			1	0		0	0	0	6
1957			1	0		0	0	0	6
1958			1	0		0	0	0	6
1960	**BOS**	**A**	3	0	0	0	0	0	18
1961			1	0	0	0	0	0	6
Career			8	0	0	0	0	0	48

Joe Johnson

Year	Team		TD	1XP	2XP	FG	FGA	SAF	Pts
1989	**WAS**	**N**	1	0		0	0	0	6
1992	**MIN**	**N**	1	0		0	0	0	6
Career			2	0		0	0	0	12

John Johnson

Year	Team		TD	1XP	2XP	FG	FGA	SAF	Pts
1992	**SF**	**N**	1	0		0	0	0	6

John Henry Johnson

Year	Team		TD	1XP	2XP	FG	FGA	SAF	Pts
1954	**SF**	**N**	9	0		0	0	0	54
1955			1	0		0	0	0	6
1956			2	0		0	0	0	12
1957	**DET**	**N**	5	0		0	0	0	30
1959			3	0		0	0	0	18
1960	**PIT**	**N**	3	0		0	0	0	18
1961			7	0		0	0	0	42
1962			9	0		0	0	0	54
1963			5	0		0	0	0	30
1964			8	0		0	0	0	48
1966	**HOU**	**A**	3	0	0	0	0	0	18
Career			55	0	0	0	0	0	330

Johnnie Johnson

Year	Team		TD	1XP	2XP	FG	FGA	SAF	Pts
1980	**LA**	**N**	1	0		0	0	0	6
1983	**LARM**	**N**	2	0		0	0	0	12
1985			1	0		0	0	0	6
1987			1	0		0	0	0	6
Career			5	0		0	0	0	30

Johnny Johnson

Year	Team		TD	1XP	2XP	FG	FGA	SAF	Pts
1990	**PHX**	**N**	5	0		0	0	0	30
1991			6	0		0	0	0	36
1992			6	0		0	0	0	36
1993	**NYJ**	**N**	4	0		0	0	0	24
1994			5	0	0	0	0	0	30
Career			26	0	0	0	0	0	156

Ken Johnson

Year	Team		TD	1XP	2XP	FG	FGA	SAF	Pts
1980	**BUF**	**N**	0	0		0	0	1	2

Kenny Johnson

Year	Team		TD	1XP	2XP	FG	FGA	SAF	Pts
1979	**NYG**	**N**	1	0		0	0	0	6

Kenny Johnson

Year	Team		TD	1XP	2XP	FG	FGA	SAF	Pts
1981	**ATL**	**N**	2	0		0	0	0	12
1983			2	0		0	0	0	12
Career			4	0		0	0	0	24

Kermit Johnson

Year	Team		TD	1XP	2XP	FG	FGA	SAF	Pts
1976	**SF**	**N**	1	0		0	0	0	6

Kevin Johnson

Year	Team		TD	1XP	2XP	FG	FGA	SAF	Pts
1995	**PHI**	**N**	1	0	0	0	0	0	6

Keyshawn Johnson

Year	Team		TD	1XP	2XP	FG	FGA	SAF	Pts
1996	**NYJ**	**N**	8	0	1	0	0	0	50

Lee Johnson

Year	Team		TD	1XP	2XP	FG	FGA	SAF	Pts
1988	**CIN**	**N**	0	0		1	2	0	3
1989			0	0		0	0	0	0
1991			0	0		1	3	0	3
1992			0	0		0	1	0	0
Career			0	0		2	6	0	6

LeShon Johnson

Year	Team		TD	1XP	2XP	FG	FGA	SAF	Pts
1996	**ARI**	**N**	4	0	0	0	0	0	24

Levi Johnson

Year	Team		TD	1XP	2XP	FG	FGA	SAF	Pts
1974	**DET**	**N**	3	0		0	0	0	18
1975			1	0		0	0	0	6
1976			1	0		0	0	0	6
Career			5	0		0	0	0	30

Lonnie Johnson

Year	Team		TD	1XP	2XP	FG	FGA	SAF	Pts
1995	**BUF**	**N**	1	0	0	0	0	0	6

Marshall Johnson

Year	Team		TD	1XP	2XP	FG	FGA	SAF	Pts
1975	BAL	N	2	0		0	0	0	12
Playoffs			1	0	0	0	0	0	6

Maurice Johnson

Year	Team		TD	1XP	2XP	FG	FGA	SAF	Pts
1991	PHI	N	2	0		0	0	0	12
1994			2	0	0	0	0	0	12
Career			4	0	0	0	0	0	24

Mike Johnson

Year	Team		TD	1XP	2XP	FG	FGA	SAF	Pts
1990	CLE	N	1	0		0	0	0	6
1992			1	0		0	0	0	6
1994	DET	N	1	0		0	0	0	6
Career			3	0	0	0	0	0	18

Monte Johnson

Year	Team		TD	1XP	2XP	FG	FGA	SAF	Pts
1979	OAK	N	1	0		0	0	0	6

Norm Johnson

Year	Team		TD	1XP	2XP	FG	FGA	SAF	Pts
1982	SEA	N	0	13		10	14	0	43
1983			0	49		18	25	0	103
1984			0	50		20	24	0	110
1985			0	40		14	25	0	82
1986			0	42		22	35	0	108
1987			0	40		15	20	0	85
1988			0	39		22	28	0	105
1989			0	27		15	25	0	72
1990			0	33		23	32	0	102
1991	ATL	N	0	38		19	23	0	95
1992			0	39		18	22	0	93
1993			0	34		26	27	0	112
1994			0	32	0	21	25	0	95
1995	PIT	N	0	39	0	34	41	0	141
1996			0	37	0	23	30	0	106
Career			0	552	0	300	396	0	1452
Playoffs			0	28	0	22	26	0	94

Pat Johnson

Year	Team		TD	1XP	2XP	FG	FGA	SAF	Pts
1995	MIA	N	1	0	0	0	0	0	6

Pepper Johnson

Year	Team		TD	1XP	2XP	FG	FGA	SAF	Pts
1988	NYG	N	1	0		0	0	0	6
1989			1	0		0	0	0	6
Career			2	0		0	0	0	12

Pete Johnson

Year	Team		TD	1XP	2XP	FG	FGA	SAF	Pts
1977	CIN	N	4	0		0	0	0	24
1978			7	0		0	0	0	42
1979			15	0		0	0	0	90
1980			7	0		0	0	0	42
1981			16	0		0	0	0	96
1982			7	0		0	0	0	42
1983			14	0		0	0	0	84
1984	SD-MIA	N	12	0		0	0	0	72
Career			82	0		0	0	0	492
Playoffs			2	0		0	0	0	12

Randy Johnson

Year	Team		TD	1XP	2XP	FG	FGA	SAF	Pts
1966	ATL	N	4	0		0	0	0	24
1967			1	0		0	0	0	6
1968			1	0		0	0	0	6
1969			1	0		0	0	0	6
1972	NYG	N	1	0		0	0	0	6
1973			1	0		0	0	0	6
1976	GB	N	1	0		0	0	0	6
Career			10	0		0	0	0	60

Reggie Johnson

Year	Team		TD	1XP	2XP	FG	FGA	SAF	Pts
1991	DEN	N	1	0		0	0	0	6
1992			1	0		0	0	0	6
1993			1	0		0	0	0	6
1995	PHI	N	2	0	0	0	0	0	12
1996	KC	N	1	0		0	0	0	6
Career			6	0	0	0	0	0	36
Playoffs			1	0	1	0	0	0	8

Richard Johnson

Year	Team		TD	1XP	2XP	FG	FGA	SAF	Pts
1969	HOU	A	1	0	0	0	0	0	6

Richard Johnson

Year	Team		TD	1XP	2XP	FG	FGA	SAF	Pts
1990	HOU	N	1	0		0	0		6

Richard Johnson

Year	Team		TD	1XP	2XP	FG	FGA	SAF	Pts
1989	DET	N	8	0		0	0	0	48
1990			6	0		0	0	0	36
Career			14	0		0	0	0	84

Ron Johnson

Year	Team		TD	1XP	2XP	FG	FGA	SAF	Pts
1986	PHI	N	1	0		0	0	0	6
1988			2	0		0	0	0	12
1989			1	0		0	0	0	6
Career			4	0		0	0	0	24

Ron Johnson

Year	Team		TD	1XP	2XP	FG	FGA	SAF	Pts
1969	CLE	N	7	0		0	0	0	42
1970	NYG	N	12	0		0	0	0	72
1971			1	0		0	0	0	6
1972			14	0		0	0	0	84
1973			9	0		0	0	0	54
1974			6	0		0	0	0	36
1975			6	0		0	0	0	36
Career			55	0		0	0	0	330

Ron Johnson

Year	Team		TD	1XP	2XP	FG	FGA	SAF	Pts
1983	PIT	N	1	0		0	0	0	6

Rudy Johnson

Year	Team		TD	1XP	2XP	FG	FGA	SAF	Pts
1964	SF	N	1	0		0	0	0	6

Sammy Johnson

Year	Team		TD	1XP	2XP	FG	FGA	SAF	Pts
1974	SF	N	2	0		0	0	0	12
1975			3	0		0	0	0	18
1976			2	0		0	0	0	12
1977	MIN	N	2	0		0	0	0	12
Career			9	0		0	0	0	54
Playoffs			2	0		0	0	0	12

Tony Johnson

Year	Team		TD	1XP	2XP	FG	FGA	SAF	Pts
1996	NO	N	1	0	0	0	0	0	6

Tracy Johnson

Year	Team		TD	1XP	2XP	FG	FGA	SAF	Pts
1990	ATL	N	4	0		0	0	0	24
1993	SEA	N	1	0		0	0	0	6
1994			2	0	0	0	0	0	12
1995			1	0	0	0	0	0	6
Career			8	0	0	0	0	0	48
Playoffs			1	0	0	0	0	0	6

Troy Johnson

Year	Team		TD	1XP	2XP	FG	FGA	SAF	Pts
1987	STL	N	2	0		0	0	0	12

Trumaine Johnson

Year	Team		TD	1XP	2XP	FG	FGA	SAF	Pts
1985	SD	N	1	0		0	0	0	6
1986			1	0		0	0	0	6
1987	BUF	N	2	0		0	0	0	12
Career			4	0		0	0	0	24

Vance Johnson

Year	Team		TD	1XP	2XP	FG	FGA	SAF	Pts
1985	DEN	N	3	0		0	0	0	18
1986			2	0		0	0	0	12
1987			7	0		0	0	0	42
1988			5	0		0	0	0	30
1989			7	0		0	0	0	42
1990			3	0		0	0	0	18
1991			3	0		0	0	0	18
1992			2	0		0	0	0	12
1993			5	0		0	0	0	30
Career			37	0		0	0	0	222
Playoffs			4	0		0	0	0	24

Walter Johnson

Year	Team		TD	1XP	2XP	FG	FGA	SAF	Pts
1969	CLE	N	1	0		0	0	0	6
1970			0	0		0	0	1	2
1971			1	0		0	0	0	6
Career			2	0		0	0	1	14

Luke Johnsos

Year	Team		TD	1XP	2XP	FG	FGA	SAF	Pts
1929	CHIB	N	3	0		0		0	18
1930			4	4		0		0	28
1931			1	4		1		0	13
1932			4	2		0		0	26
1933			3	0		0		0	18
1934			1	0		0		0	6
1935			4	0			0		24

Luke Johnsos *continued*

Year	Team		TD	1XP	2XP	FG	FGA	SAF	Pts
1936			2	0		0		0	12
Career			22	10		1		0	145

Chet Johnston

Year	Team		TD	1XP	2XP	FG	FGA	SAF	Pts
1934	C-S	N	1	0		0		0	6
1935	GB	N	1	0		0		0	6
1936			1	0		0		0	6
1939	PIT	N	2	0		0	0	0	12
Career			5	0		0	0	0	30

Daryl Johnston

Year	Team		TD	1XP	2XP	FG	FGA	SAF	Pts
1989	DAL	N	3	0		0	0	0	18
1990			2	0		0	0	0	12
1991			1	0		0	0	0	6
1992			2	0		0	0	0	12
1993			4	0		0	0	0	24
1994			4	0	0	0	0	0	24
1995			3	0	0	0	0	0	18
1996			1	0	0	0	0	0	6
Career			20	0	0	0	0	0	120
Playoffs			3	0	0	0	0	0	18

Jimmy Johnston

Year	Team		TD	1XP	2XP	FG	FGA	SAF	Pts
1939	WAS	N	1	1		0	0	0	7
1940			7	0		0	0	0	42
Career			8	1		0	0	0	49

Mark Johnston

Year	Team		TD	1XP	2XP	FG	FGA	SAF	Pts
1961	HOU	A	1	0	0	0	0	0	6
1963			1	0	0	0	0	0	6
Career			2	0	0	0	0	0	12

Preston Johnston

Year	Team		TD	1XP	2XP	FG	FGA	SAF	Pts
1946	MIA-BUF	AA	3	1		0	0	0	19

Lance Johnstone

Year	Team		TD	1XP	2XP	FG	FGA	SAF	Pts
1996	OAK	N	1	0	0	0	0	0	6

Charlie Joiner

Year	Team		TD	1XP	2XP	FG	FGA	SAF	Pts
1970	HOU	N	3	0		0	0	0	18
1971			7	0		0	0	0	42
1972			2	0		0	0	0	12
1974	CIN	N	1	0		0	0	0	6
1975			5	0		0	0	0	30
1976	SD	N	7	0		0	0	0	42
1977			6	0		0	0	0	36
1978			1	0		0	0	0	6
1979			4	0		0	0	0	24
1980			4	0		0	0	0	24
1981			7	0		0	0	0	42
1983			3	0		0	0	0	18
1984			6	0		0	0	0	36
1985			7	0		0	0	0	42
1986			2	0		0	0	0	12
Career			65	0		0	0	0	390
Playoffs			5	0		0	0	0	30

Art Jones

Year	Team		TD	1XP	2XP	FG	FGA	SAF	Pts
1941	PIT	N	5	0		0	0	0	30

Ben Jones

Year	Team		TD	1XP	2XP	FG	FGA	SAF	Pts
1923	CAN	N	6	0		0		0	36
1924	CLE	N	5	1		0		0	31
1925	CAN-FRA	N	4	0		0		0	24
1926	FRA	N	8	0		0		0	48
1927	CHIC	N	2	0		0		0	12
Career			25	1		0		0	151

Bert Jones

Year	Team		TD	1XP	2XP	FG	FGA	SAF	Pts
1974	BAL	N	4	0		0	0	0	24
1975			3	0		0	0	0	18
1976			2	0		0	0	0	12
1977			2	0		0	0	0	12
1979			1	0		0	0	0	6
1980			2	0		0	0	0	12
Career			14	0		0	0	0	84

Bill Jones

Year	Team		TD	1XP	2XP	FG	FGA	SAF	Pts
1990	KC	N	5	0		0	0	0	30
1991			1	0		0	0	0	6
Career			6	0		0	0	0	36

SCORING

Bob Jones

Year	Team		TD	1XP	2XP	FG	FGA	SAF	Pts
1967	CHI	N	1	0		0	0	0	6

Bobby Jones

Year	Team		TD	1XP	2XP	FG	FGA	SAF	Pts
1979	NYJ	N	1	0		0	0	0	6
1981			2	0		0	0	0	12
1983	CLE	N	4	0		0	0	0	24
Career			7	0		0	0	0	42
Playoffs			1	0		0	0	0	6

Brent Jones

Year	Team		TD	1XP	2XP	FG	FGA	SAF	Pts
1988	SF	N	2	0		0	0	0	12
1989			4	0		0	0	0	24
1990			5	0		0	0	0	30
1992			4	0		0	0	0	24
1993			3	0		0	0	0	18
1994			9	0	1	0	0	0	56
1995			3	0	0	0	0	0	18
1996			1	0	0	0	0	0	6
Career			31	0	1	0	0	0	188
Playoffs			5	0	0	0	0	0	30

Brian Jones

Year	Team		TD	1XP	2XP	FG	FGA	SAF	Pts
1996	NO	N	1	0	0	0	0	0	6

Bruce Jones

Year	Team		TD	1XP	2XP	FG	FGA	SAF	Pts
1928	GB	N	1	0		0		0	6

Calvin Jones

Year	Team		TD	1XP	2XP	FG	FGA	SAF	Pts
1976	DEN	N	1	0		0	0	0	6

Cedric Jones

Year	Team		TD	1XP	2XP	FG	FGA	SAF	Pts
1983	NE	N	1	0		0	0	0	6
1984			3	0		0	0	0	18
1985			3	0		0	0	0	18
1986			1	0		0	0	0	6
1987			3	0		0	0	0	18
1988			1	0		0	0	0	6
1989			6	0		0	0	0	36
Career			18	0		0	0	0	108

Charlie Jones

Year	Team		TD	1XP	2XP	FG	FGA	SAF	Pts
1996	SD	N	4	0	0	0	0	0	24

Chris T. Jones

Year	Team		TD	1XP	2XP	FG	FGA	SAF	Pts
1996	PHI	N	5	0	0	0	0	0	30

Clint Jones

Year	Team		TD	1XP	2XP	FG	FGA	SAF	Pts
1967	MIN	N	1	0		0	0	0	6
1968			1	0		0	0	0	6
1969			3	0		0	0	0	18
1970			9	0		0	0	0	54
1971			4	0		0	0	0	24
1972			2	0		0	0	0	12
1973	SD	N	1	0		0	0	0	6
Career			21	0		0	0	0	126
Playoffs			1	0		0	0	0	6

Dante Jones

Year	Team		TD	1XP	2XP	FG	FGA	SAF	Pts
1993	CHI	N	1	0		0	0	0	6

Deacon Jones

Year	Team		TD	1XP	2XP	FG	FGA	SAF	Pts
1965	LA	N	0	0		0	0	1	2
1967			0	0		0	0	1	2
1974	WAS	N	0	1		0	0	0	1
Career			0	1		0	0	2	5

Doug Jones

Year	Team		TD	1XP	2XP	FG	FGA	SAF	Pts
1977	BUF	N	1	0		0	0	0	6

Drew Jones

Year	Team		TD	1XP	2XP	FG	FGA	SAF	Pts
1975	NO	N	1	0		0	0	0	6

Dub Jones

Year	Team		TD	1XP	2XP	FG	FGA	SAF	Pts
1947	BKN	AA	1	0		0	0	0	6
1948	CLE	AA	3	0		0	0	0	18
1949			5	0		0	0	0	30
1950	CLE	N	11	0		0	0	0	66
1951			12	0		0	0	0	72
1952			6	0		0	0	0	36
1954			2	0		0	0	0	12
1955			1	0		0	0	0	6
Career			41	0		0	0	0	246
Playoffs			4	0		0	0	0	24

Edgar Jones

Year	Team		TD	1XP	2XP	FG	FGA	SAF	Pts
1946	CLE	AA	6	0		0	0	0	36
1947			6	0		0	0	0	36
1948			10	0		0	0	0	60
1949			7	0		0	0	0	42
Career			29	0		0	0	0	174
Playoffs			5	0		0	0	0	30

Ernie Jones

Year	Team		TD	1XP	2XP	FG	FGA	SAF	Pts
1979	NYG	N	1	0		0	0	0	6

Ernie Jones

Year	Team		TD	1XP	2XP	FG	FGA	SAF	Pts
1988	PHX	N	3	0		0	0	0	18
1989			3	0		0	0	0	18
1990			4	0		0	0	0	24
1991			4	0		0	0	0	24
1992			4	0		0	0	0	24
1993	LARM	N	2	0		0	0	0	12
Career			20	0		0	0	0	120

Ezell Jones

Year	Team		TD	1XP	2XP	FG	FGA	SAF	Pts
1969	BOS	A	0	0	0	0	0	1	2

Fred Jones

Year	Team		TD	1XP	2XP	FG	FGA	SAF	Pts
Playoffs			2	0	0	0	0	0	12

Gary Jones

Year	Team		TD	1XP	2XP	FG	FGA	SAF	Pts
1995	NYJ	N	1	0	0	0	0	0	6

Gordon Jones

Year	Team		TD	1XP	2XP	FG	FGA	SAF	Pts
1979	TB	N	1	0		0	0	0	6
1980			5	0		0	0	0	30
1981			1	0		0	0	0	6
1982			1	0		0	0	0	6
Career			8	0		0	0	0	48
Playoffs			1	0		0	0	0	6

Greg Jones

Year	Team		TD	1XP	2XP	FG	FGA	SAF	Pts
1970	BUF	N	2	0		0	0	0	12
1971			1	0		0	0	0	6
Career			3	0		0	0	0	18

Hassan Jones

Year	Team		TD	1XP	2XP	FG	FGA	SAF	Pts
1986	MIN	N	4	0		0	0	0	24
1987			2	0		0	0	0	12
1988			5	0		0	0	0	30
1989			1	0		0	0	0	6
1990			7	0		0	0	0	42
1991			1	0		0	0	0	6
1992			4	0		0	0	0	24
Career			24	0		0	0	0	144
Playoffs			3	0		0	0	0	18

Harvey Jones

Year	Team		TD	1XP	2XP	FG	FGA	SAF	Pts
1944	CLE	N	1	0		0	0	0	6
1945			1	0		0	0	0	6
Career			2	0		0	0	0	12

Henry Jones

Year	Team		TD	1XP	2XP	FG	FGA	SAF	Pts
1992	BUF	N	2	0		0	0	0	12
1993			1	0		0	0	1	8
Career			3	0		0	0	1	20

Homer Jones

Year	Team		TD	1XP	2XP	FG	FGA	SAF	Pts
1965	NYG	N	6	0		0	0	0	36
1966			8	0		0	0	0	48
1967			**14**	0		0	0	0	84
1968			7	0		0	0	0	42
1969			1	0		0	0	0	6
1970	CLE	N	2	0		0	0	0	12
Career			38	0		0	0	0	228

James Jones

Year	Team		TD	1XP	2XP	FG	FGA	SAF	Pts
1981	DAL	N	1	0		0	0	0	6
1984			1	0		0	0	0	6
Career			2	0		0	0	0	12
Playoffs			1	0		0	0	0	6

James Jones

Year	Team		TD	1XP	2XP	FG	FGA	SAF	Pts
1983	DET	N	7	0		0	0	0	42
1984			8	0		0	0	0	48
1985			9	0		0	0	0	54
1986			9	0		0	0	0	54

James Jones *continued*

Year	Team		TD	1XP	2XP	FG	FGA	SAF	Pts
1991	SEA	N	3	0		0	0	0	18
Career			36	0		0	0	0	216

James Jones

Year	Team		TD	1XP	2XP	FG	FGA	SAF	Pts
1991	CLE	N	1	0		0	0	1	8
1992			1	0		0	0	0	6
1993			1	0		0	0	0	6
1996	BAL	N	1	0	0	0	0	0	6
Career			4	0	0	0	0	1	26

Jimmie Jones

Year	Team		TD	1XP	2XP	FG	FGA	SAF	Pts
Playoffs			1	0	0	0	0	0	6

Jimmie Lee Jones

Year	Team		TD	1XP	2XP	FG	FGA	SAF	Pts
1974	DET	N	1	0		0	0	0	6

Jimmy Jones

Year	Team		TD	1XP	2XP	FG	FGA	SAF	Pts
1965	CHI	N	4	0		0	0	0	24
1966			5	0		0	0	0	30
1968	DEN	A	2	0	0	0	0	0	12
Career			11	0	0	0	0	0	66

Joe Jones

Year	Team		TD	1XP	2XP	FG	FGA	SAF	Pts
1976	CLE	N	1	0		0	0	0	6

Joe Jones

Year	Team		TD	1XP	2XP	FG	FGA	SAF	Pts
1987	IND	N	1	0		0	0	0	6

Johnny Jones

Year	Team		TD	1XP	2XP	FG	FGA	SAF	Pts
1980	NYJ	N	3	0		0	0	0	18
1981			3	0		0	0	0	18
1982			2	0		0	0	0	12
1983			4	0		0	0	0	24
1984			1	0		0	0	0	6
Career			13	0		0	0	0	78

Keith Jones

Year	Team		TD	1XP	2XP	FG	FGA	SAF	Pts
1989	CLE	N	1	0		0	0	0	6

Keith Jones

Year	Team		TD	1XP	2XP	FG	FGA	SAF	Pts
1989	ATL	N	6	0		0	0	0	36
1990			1	0		0	0	0	6
Career			7	0		0	0	0	42

Larry Jones

Year	Team		TD	1XP	2XP	FG	FGA	SAF	Pts
1974	WAS	N	1	0		0	0	0	6
1975			1	0		0	0	0	6
Career			2	0		0	0	0	12

Leroy Jones

Year	Team		TD	1XP	2XP	FG	FGA	SAF	Pts
1977	SD	N	1	0		0	0	0	6

Mike Jones

Year	Team		TD	1XP	2XP	FG	FGA	SAF	Pts
1984	MIN	N	1	0		0	0	0	6
1985			4	0		0	0	0	24
1986	NO	N	3	0		0	0	0	18
1987			3	0		0	0	0	18
Career			11	0		0	0	0	66

Mike Jones

Year	Team		TD	1XP	2XP	FG	FGA	SAF	Pts
1991	MIN	N	2	0		0	0	0	12

Mike Jones

Year	Team		TD	1XP	2XP	FG	FGA	SAF	Pts
1995	OAK	N	1	0	0	0	0	0	6

Reggie Jones

Year	Team		TD	1XP	2XP	FG	FGA	SAF	Pts
1992	NO	N	1	0		0	0	0	6

Rod Jones

Year	Team		TD	1XP	2XP	FG	FGA	SAF	Pts
1987	KC	N	1	0		0	0	0	6

Roger Jones

Year	Team		TD	1XP	2XP	FG	FGA	SAF	Pts
1992	TB	N	1	0		0	0	0	6
1995	CIN	N	1	0	0	0	0	0	6
Career			2	0	0	0	0	0	12

Rulon Jones

Year	Team		TD	1XP	2XP	FG	FGA	SAF	Pts
1980	DEN	N	0	0		0	0	1	2
1983			0	0		0	0	1	2
1984			1	0		0	0	0	6
1986			0	0		0	0	1	2
Career			1	0		0	0	3	12
Playoffs			0	0		0	0	1	2

Sean Jones

Year	Team	Lg	TD	1XP	2XP	FG	FGA	SAF	Pts
1995	GB	N	1	0	0	0	0	0	6

Steve Jones

Year	Team	Lg	TD	1XP	2XP	FG	FGA	SAF	Pts
1975	STL	N	3	0		0	0	0	18
1976			9	0		0	0	0	54
1977			3	0		0	0	0	18
1978			2	0		0	0	0	12
Career			17	0		0	0	0	102
Playoffs			1	0		0	0	0	6

Thurman Jones

Year	Team	Lg	TD	1XP	2XP	FG	FGA	SAF	Pts
1942	BKN	N	0	1		0	0	0	1

Tom Jones

Year	Team	Lg	TD	1XP	2XP	FG	FGA	SAF	Pts
1932	NYG	N	1	0		0		0	6

Tony Jones

Year	Team	Lg	TD	1XP	2XP	FG	FGA	SAF	Pts
1990	HOU	N	6	0		0	0	0	36
1991			2	0		0	0	0	12
1992	ATL	N	1	0		0	0	0	6
Career			9	0		0	0	0	54

Willie Jones

Year	Team	Lg	TD	1XP	2XP	FG	FGA	SAF	Pts
1980	OAK	N	1	0		0	0	0	6
1981			1	0		0	0	0	6
Career			2	0		0	0	0	12

Andrew Jordan

Year	Team	Lg	TD	1XP	2XP	FG	FGA	SAF	Pts
1994	MIN	N	0	0	1	0	0	0	2
1995			2	0	0	0	0	0	12
1996			0	0	1	0	0	0	2
Career			2	0	2	0	0	0	16

Brian Jordan

Year	Team	Lg	TD	1XP	2XP	FG	FGA	SAF	Pts
1991	ATL	N	0	0		0	0	2	4

Buford Jordan

Year	Team	Lg	TD	1XP	2XP	FG	FGA	SAF	Pts
1986	NO	N	1	0		0	0	0	6
1987			2	0		0	0	0	12
1988			1	0		0	0	0	6
1989			3	0		0	0	0	18
1991			3	0		0	0	0	18
Career			10	0		0	0	0	60

Charles Jordan

Year	Team	Lg	TD	1XP	2XP	FG	FGA	SAF	Pts
1995	GB	N	2	0	0	0	0	0	12

Curtis Jordan

Year	Team	Lg	TD	1XP	2XP	FG	FGA	SAF	Pts
1982	WAS	N	1	0		0	0	0	6
1984			1	0		0	0	0	6
Career			2	0		0	0	0	12

Darin Jordan

Year	Team	Lg	TD	1XP	2XP	FG	FGA	SAF	Pts
1988	PIT	N	1	0		0	0	0	6
1991	SF	N	0	0		0	0	1	2
Career			1	0		0	0	1	8

Henry Jordan

Year	Team	Lg	TD	1XP	2XP	FG	FGA	SAF	Pts
1964	GB	N	1	0		0	0	0	6

Lee Roy Jordan

Year	Team	Lg	TD	1XP	2XP	FG	FGA	SAF	Pts
1966	DAL	N	1	0		0	0	0	6
1967			1	0		0	0	1	8
1973			1	0		0	0	0	6
Career			3	0		0	0	1	20

Randy Jordan

Year	Team	Lg	TD	1XP	2XP	FG	FGA	SAF	Pts
1995	JAC	N	1	0	0	0	0	0	6

Steve Jordan

Year	Team	Lg	TD	1XP	2XP	FG	FGA	SAF	Pts
1983	MIN	N	2	0		0	0	0	12
1984			3	0		0	0	0	18
1986			6	0		0	0	0	36
1987			2	0		0	0	0	12
1988			5	0		0	0	0	30
1989			3	0		0	0	0	18
1990			3	0		0	0	0	18
1991			2	0		0	0	0	12
1992			2	0		0	0	0	12
1993			1	0		0	0	0	6
Career			29	0		0	0	0	174
Playoffs			1	0		0	0	0	6

Steve Jordan

Year	Team	Lg	TD	1XP	2XP	FG	FGA	SAF	Pts
1987	IND	N	0	7		3	5	0	16

Tony Jordan

Year	Team	Lg	TD	1XP	2XP	FG	FGA	SAF	Pts
1988	PHX	N	3	0		0	0	0	18
1989			2	0		0	0	0	12
Career			5	0		0	0	0	30

Tim Jorden

Year	Team	Lg	TD	1XP	2XP	FG	FGA	SAF	Pts
1992	PIT	N	2	0		0	0	0	12

Carl Jorgensen

Year	Team	Lg	TD	1XP	2XP	FG	FGA	SAF	Pts
1935	PHI	N	0	1		1		0	4

James Joseph

Year	Team	Lg	TD	1XP	2XP	FG	FGA	SAF	Pts
1991	PHI	N	3	0		0	0	0	18
1993			1	0		0	0	0	6
1994			3	0	0	0	0	0	18
Career			7	0	0	0	0	0	42

Red Joseph

Year	Team	Lg	TD	1XP	2XP	FG	FGA	SAF	Pts
1930	POR	N	1	0		0		0	6

Les Josephson

Year	Team	Lg	TD	1XP	2XP	FG	FGA	SAF	Pts
1964	LA	N	4	0		0	0	0	24
1966			1	0		0	0	0	6
1967			8	0		0	0	0	48
1969			2	0		0	0	0	12
1970			5	0		0	0	0	30
1971			5	0		0	0	0	30
1972			1	0		0	0	0	6
1973			2	0		0	0	0	12
Career			28	0		0	0	0	168

Seth Joyner

Year	Team	Lg	TD	1XP	2XP	FG	FGA	SAF	Pts
1987	PHI	N	1	0		0	0	0	6
1991			2	0		0	0	0	12
1992			2	0		0	0	0	12
Career			5	0		0	0	0	30

Saxon Judd

Year	Team	Lg	TD	1XP	2XP	FG	FGA	SAF	Pts
1946	BKN	AA	5	0		0	0	0	30
1947			1	0		0	0	0	6
1948			2	0		0	0	0	12
Career			8	0		0	0	0	48

William Judson

Year	Team	Lg	TD	1XP	2XP	FG	FGA	SAF	Pts
1984	MIA	N	1	0		0	0	0	6
1985			1	0		0	0	0	6
Career			2	0		0	0	0	12

E.J. Junior

Year	Team	Lg	TD	1XP	2XP	FG	FGA	SAF	Pts
1988	PHX	N	1	0		0	0	0	6

Steve Junker

Year	Team	Lg	TD	1XP	2XP	FG	FGA	SAF	Pts
1957	DET	N	4	0		0	0	0	24
1962	WAS	N	2	0		0	0	0	12
Career			6	0		0	0	0	36
Playoffs			3	0		0	0	0	18

Trey Junkin

Year	Team	Lg	TD	1XP	2XP	FG	FGA	SAF	Pts
1985	LARI	N	1	0		0	0	0	6
1988			2	0		0	0	0	12
1989			2	0		0	0	0	12
1992	SEA	N	1	0		0	0	0	6
1994			1	0	0	0	0	0	6
Career			7	0	0	0	0	0	42

Sonny Jurgensen

Year	Team	Lg	TD	1XP	2XP	FG	FGA	SAF	Pts
1957	PHI	N	2	0		0	0	0	12
1962			2	0		0	0	0	12
1963			1	0		0	0	0	6
1964	WAS	N	3	0		0	0	0	18
1965			2	0		0	0	0	12
1967			2	0		0	0	0	12
1968			1	0		0	0	0	6
1969			1	0		0	0	0	6
1970			1	0		0	0	0	6
Career			15	0		0	0	0	90

Tom Jurich

Year	Team	Lg	TD	1XP	2XP	FG	FGA	SAF	Pts
1978	NO	N	0	2		0	3	0	2

Charlie Justice

Year	Team	Lg	TD	1XP	2XP	FG	FGA	SAF	Pts
1950	WAS	N	2	0		0	0	0	18
1952			1	0		0	0	0	6
1953			4	0		0	0	0	24
1954			3	0		0	0	0	18
Career			10	0		0	0	0	66

Ed Justice

Year	Team	Lg	TD	1XP	2XP	FG	FGA	SAF	Pts
1937	WAS	N	3	0		0		0	18
1938			1	0		0	0	0	6
1939			3	0		0	0	0	18
1940			2	0		0	0	0	12
1941			1	0		0	0	0	6
1942			1	0		0	0	0	6
Career			11	0		0	0	0	66
Playoffs			1	0		0	0	0	6

Sid Justin

Year	Team	Lg	TD	1XP	2XP	FG	FGA	SAF	Pts
1979	LA	N	1	0		0	0	0	6

Steve Juzwik

Year	Team	Lg	TD	1XP	2XP	FG	FGA	SAF	Pts
1942	WAS	N	2	3		0	0	0	15
1946	BUF	AA	7	0		0	0	0	42
1947			1	28		2	3	0	40
1948	CHI	AA	0	5		0	0	0	5
Career			10	36		2	3	0	102

Vyto Kab

Year	Team	Lg	TD	1XP	2XP	FG	FGA	SAF	Pts
1982	PHI	N	1	0		0	0	0	6
1983			1	0		0	0	0	6
1984			3	0		0	0	0	18
Career			5	0		0	0	0	30

Mike Kabealo

Year	Team	Lg	TD	1XP	2XP	FG	FGA	SAF	Pts
1944	CLE	N	1	0		0	0	0	6

Mike Kadish

Year	Team	Lg	TD	1XP	2XP	FG	FGA	SAF	Pts
1974	BUF	N	0	0		0	0	1	2
1975			1	0		0	0	0	6
Career			1	0		0	0	1	8

Mort Kaer

Year	Team	Lg	TD	1XP	2XP	FG	FGA	SAF	Pts
1931	FRA	N	1	0		0		0	6

Mark Kafentzis

Year	Team	Lg	TD	1XP	2XP	FG	FGA	SAF	Pts
1984	IND	N	1	0		0	0	0	6

Eddie Kahn

Year	Team	Lg	TD	1XP	2XP	FG	FGA	SAF	Pts
1937	WAS	N	1	0		0		0	6

George Kakasic

Year	Team	Lg	TD	1XP	2XP	FG	FGA	SAF	Pts
1936	PIT	N	1	1		2		0	13
1937			0	3		0		0	3
Career			1	4		2		0	16

Tommy Kalmanir

Year	Team	Lg	TD	1XP	2XP	FG	FGA	SAF	Pts
1949	LA	N	2	0		0	0	0	12
1950			1	0		0	0	0	6
1951			2	0		0	0	0	12
1953	BAL	N	1	0		0	0	0	6
Career			6	0		0	0	0	36

John Kamana

Year	Team	Lg	TD	1XP	2XP	FG	FGA	SAF	Pts
1987	ATL	N	1	0		0	0	0	6

Rick Kane

Year	Team	Lg	TD	1XP	2XP	FG	FGA	SAF	Pts
1977	DET	N	4	0		0	0	0	24
1978			2	0		0	0	0	12
1979			5	0		0	0	0	30
1981			3	0		0	0	0	18
Career			14	0		0	0	0	84

Tommy Kane

Year	Team	Lg	TD	1XP	2XP	FG	FGA	SAF	Pts
1990	SEA	N	4	0		0	0	0	24
1991			2	0		0	0	0	12
1992			3	0		0	0	0	18
Career			9	0		0	0	0	54

Al Kanya

Year	Team	Lg	TD	1XP	2XP	FG	FGA	SAF	Pts
1931	SI	N	1	0		0		0	6

Ave Kaplan

Year	Team	Lg	TD	1XP	2XP	FG	FGA	SAF	Pts
1923	MIN	N	1	3		3		0	18

Ave Kaplan *continued*

Year	Team		TD	1XP	2XP	FG	FGA	SAF	Pts
1926	RI	A	0	2		0		0	2
Career			1	5		3		0	20

Sam Kaplan

Year	Team		TD	1XP	2XP	FG	FGA	SAF	Pts
1921	WAS	A	1	1		0		0	7

Joe Kapp

Year	Team		TD	1XP	2XP	FG	FGA	SAF	Pts
1967	MIN	N	2	0		0	0	0	12
1968			3	0		0	0	0	18
Career			5	0		0	0	0	30
Playoffs			2	0		0	0	0	12

George Karamatic

Year	Team		TD	1XP	2XP	FG	FGA	SAF	Pts
1938	WAS	N	1	2		1	2	0	11

John Karcis

Year	Team		TD	1XP	2XP	FG	FGA	SAF	Pts
1932	BKN	N	1	0		0		0	6
1935			1	0		0		0	6
1936	PIT	N	2	1		0		0	13
1937			3	0		0		0	18
1938	NYG	N	5	0		0		0	30
Career			12	1		0		0	73

Carl Karilivacz

Year	Team		TD	1XP	2XP	FG	FGA	SAF	Pts
1954	DET	N	1	0		0	0	0	6
1958	NYG	N	1	0		0	0	0	6
Career			2	0		0	0	0	12

Rich Karlis

Year	Team		TD	1XP	2XP	FG	FGA	SAF	Pts
1982	DEN	N	0	15		11	13	0	48
1983			0	33		21	25	0	96
1984			0	38		21	28	0	101
1985			0	41		23	38	0	110
1986			0	44		20	28	0	104
1987			0	37		18	25	0	91
1988			0	36		23	36	0	105
1989	MIN	N	0	27		**31**	39	0	120
1990	DET	N	0	12		4	7	0	24
Career			0	283		172	239	0	799
Playoffs			0	20		14	20	0	62

Abe Karnofsky

Year	Team		TD	1XP	2XP	FG	FGA	SAF	Pts
1945	PHI	N	2	0		0	0	0	12
1946	BOS	N	3	0		0	0	0	18
Career			5	0		0	0	0	30

Bill Karr

Year	Team		TD	1XP	2XP	FG	FGA	SAF	Pts
1933	CHIB	N	4	0		0		0	24
1934			1	0		0		0	6
1935			6	0		0		0	36
1936			3	0		0		0	18
1937			2	0		0		0	12
1938			4	0		0	0	0	24
Career			20	0		0	0	0	120
Playoffs			2	0		0	0	0	12

Alex Karras

Year	Team		TD	1XP	2XP	FG	FGA	SAF	Pts
1962	DET	N	0	0		0	0	1	2

Johnny Karras

Year	Team		TD	1XP	2XP	FG	FGA	SAF	Pts
1952	CHIC	N	1	0		0	0	0	6

John Kasay

Year	Team		TD	1XP	2XP	FG	FGA	SAF	Pts
1991	SEA	N	0	27		25	31	0	102
1992			0	14		14	22	0	56
1993			0	29		23	28	0	98
1994			0	25	0	20	24	0	85
1995	CAR	N	0	27	0	26	33	0	105
1996			0	34	0	**37**	**45**	0	**145**
Career			0	156	0	145	183	0	591
Playoffs			0	3	0	6	6	0	21

Tony Kaska

Year	Team		TD	1XP	2XP	FG	FGA	SAF	Pts
1936	BKN	N	1	0		0		0	6

Ed Kasky

Year	Team		TD	1XP	2XP	FG	FGA	SAF	Pts
1942	PHI	N	0	0		0	1	0	0

Chuck Kassel

Year	Team		TD	1XP	2XP	FG	FGA	SAF	Pts
1927	FRA	N	2	0		0		0	12
1928			1	0		0		0	6
1929	CHIC	N	2	0		0		0	12
1931			1	0		0		0	6

Chuck Kassel *continued*

Year	Team		TD	1XP	2XP	FG	FGA	SAF	Pts
1932			1	0		0		0	6
Career			7	0		0		0	42

Jim Katcavage

Year	Team		TD	1XP	2XP	FG	FGA	SAF	Pts
1958	NYG	N	0	0		0	0	1	2
1961			0	0		0	0	1	2
1963			1	0		0	0	0	6
1965			0	0		0	0	1	2
Career			1	0		0	0	3	12

Eric Kattus

Year	Team		TD	1XP	2XP	FG	FGA	SAF	Pts
1986	CIN	N	1	0		0	0	0	6
1987			2	0		0	0	0	12
1990			2	0		0	0	0	12
Career			5	0		0	0	0	30
Playoffs			1	0		0	0	0	6

Mel Kaufman

Year	Team		TD	1XP	2XP	FG	FGA	SAF	Pts
1983	WAS	N	2	0		0	0	0	12

Napoleon Kaufman

Year	Team		TD	1XP	2XP	FG	FGA	SAF	Pts
1995	OAK	N	2	0	0	0	0	0	12
1996			2	0	0	0	0	0	12
Career			4	0	0	0	0	0	24

Jerry Kauric

Year	Team		TD	1XP	2XP	FG	FGA	SAF	Pts
1990	CLE	N	0	24		14	20	0	66

Ken Kavanaugh

Year	Team		TD	1XP	2XP	FG	FGA	SAF	Pts
1940	CHIB	N	3	0		0	0	0	18
1941			6	1		0	0	0	37
1945			6	0		0	0	0	36
1946			5	0		0	0	0	30
1947			13	0		0	0	0	78
1948			7	0		0	0	0	42
1949			9	0		0	0	0	54
1950			3	0		0	0	0	18
Career			52	1		0	0	0	313
Playoffs			3	0		0	0	0	18

Eddie Kaw

Year	Team		TD	1XP	2XP	FG	FGA	SAF	Pts
1924	BUF	N	2	0		0		0	12

Eddie Kawal

Year	Team		TD	1XP	2XP	FG	FGA	SAF	Pts
1935	CHIB	N	1	0		0		0	6

Clarence Kay

Year	Team		TD	1XP	2XP	FG	FGA	SAF	Pts
1984	DEN	N	3	0		0	0	0	18
1985			3	0		0	0	0	18
1986			1	0		0	0	0	6
1988			4	0		0	0	0	24
1989			2	0		0	0	0	12
Career			13	0		0	0	0	78
Playoffs			2	0		0	0	0	12

Jim Keane

Year	Team		TD	1XP	2XP	FG	FGA	SAF	Pts
1946	CHIB	N	3	0		0	0	0	18
1947			10	0		0	0	0	60
1948			3	0		0	0	0	18
1949			6	0		0	0	0	36
1951			1	0		0	0	0	6
1952	GB	N	1	0		0	0	0	6
Career			24	0		0	0	0	144

Tom Keane

Year	Team		TD	1XP	2XP	FG	FGA	SAF	Pts
1948	LA	N	2	0		0	0	0	12
1950			1	0		0	0	0	6
1955	CHIC	N	0	0		0	1	0	0
Career			3	0		0	1	0	18

Jim Kearney

Year	Team		TD	1XP	2XP	FG	FGA	SAF	Pts
1969	KC	A	1	0	0	0	0	0	6
1972	KC	N	4	0		0	0	0	24
Career			5	0	0	0	0	0	30

Chris Keating

Year	Team		TD	1XP	2XP	FG	FGA	SAF	Pts
1984	BUF	N	1	0		0	0	0	6

Stan Keck

Year	Team		TD	1XP	2XP	FG	FGA	SAF	Pts
1923	CLE	N	0	1		2		0	7

Joe Keeble

Year	Team		TD	1XP	2XP	FG	FGA	SAF	Pts
1937	CLE	N	1	0		0		0	6

Jack Keefer

Year	Team		TD	1XP	2XP	FG	FGA	SAF	Pts
1926	PRO	N	3	2		0		0	20

Mark Keel

Year	Team		TD	1XP	2XP	FG	FGA	SAF	Pts
1987	SEA	N	1	0		0	0	0	6

Bob Keene

Year	Team		TD	1XP	2XP	FG	FGA	SAF	Pts
1944	DET	N	2	0		0	0	0	12

Jim Kekeris

Year	Team		TD	1XP	2XP	FG	FGA	SAF	Pts
1947	PHI	N	0	2		0	1	0	2

Bill Kellagher

Year	Team		TD	1XP	2XP	FG	FGA	SAF	Pts
1946	CHI	AA	3	0		0	0	0	18
1948			1	0		0	0	0	6
Career			4	0		0	0	0	24

Kenny Keller

Year	Team		TD	1XP	2XP	FG	FGA	SAF	Pts
1956	PHI	N	4	0		0	0	0	24

Ernie Kellerman

Year	Team		TD	1XP	2XP	FG	FGA	SAF	Pts
1969	CLE	N	1	0		0	0	0	6

Billy Kelley

Year	Team		TD	1XP	2XP	FG	FGA	SAF	Pts
1949	GB	N	1	0		0	0	0	6

Chris Kelley

Year	Team		TD	1XP	2XP	FG	FGA	SAF	Pts
1987	CLE	N	0	1		0	0	0	1

Frank Kelley

Year	Team		TD	1XP	2XP	FG	FGA	SAF	Pts
1927	CLE	N	3	0		0		0	18

Bill Kellogg

Year	Team		TD	1XP	2XP	FG	FGA	SAF	Pts
1924	FRA	N	3	0		0		0	18
1925	ROC	N	2	0		0		0	12
Career			5	0		0		0	30

Clarence Kellogg

Year	Team		TD	1XP	2XP	FG	FGA	SAF	Pts
1936	CHIC	N	0	6		1		0	9

Bill Kelly

Year	Team		TD	1XP	2XP	FG	FGA	SAF	Pts
1927	NYY	N	3	0		0		0	18
1928			2	0		0		0	12
1929	FRA	N	1	0		0		0	6
1930	BKN	N	1	0		0		0	6
Career			7	0		0		0	42

Bob Kelly

Year	Team		TD	1XP	2XP	FG	FGA	SAF	Pts
1947	LA	AA	3	0		0	0	0	18

Jim Kelly

Year	Team		TD	1XP	2XP	FG	FGA	SAF	Pts
1964	PIT	N	1	0		0	0	0	6
1967	PHI	N	4	0		0	0	0	24
Career			5	0		0	0	0	30

Jim Kelly

Year	Team		TD	1XP	2XP	FG	FGA	SAF	Pts
1989	BUF	N	2	0		0	0	0	12
1991			1	0		0	0	0	6
1992			1	0		0	0	0	6
1994			1	0	0	0	0	0	6
1996			2	0	0	0	0	0	12
Career			7	0	0	0	0	0	42

John Kelly

Year	Team		TD	1XP	2XP	FG	FGA	SAF	Pts
1933	BKN	N	**7**	1		0		0	43
1934			1	0		0		0	6
Career			8	1		0		0	49

Leroy Kelly

Year	Team		TD	1XP	2XP	FG	FGA	SAF	Pts
1964	CLE	N	1	0		0	0	0	6
1965			2	0		0	0	0	12
1966			**16**	0		0	0	0	96
1967			13	0		0	0	0	78
1968			**20**	0		0	0	0	**120**
1969			10	0		0	0	0	60
1970			8	0		0	0	0	48
1971			12	0		0	0	0	72
1972			5	0		0	0	0	30
1973			3	0		0	0	0	18
Career			90	0		0	0	0	540
Playoffs			3	0		0	0	0	18

Mose Kelsch

Year	Team		TD	1XP	2XP	FG	FGA	SAF	Pts
1933	PIT	N	0	2		3		0	11

Mose Kelsch *continued*

Year	Team		TD	1XP	2XP	FG	FGA	SAF	Pts
1934			0	2		1		0	5
Career			0	4		4		0	16

Mark Kelso

Year	Team		TD	1XP	2XP	FG	FGA	SAF	Pts
1987	BUF	N	1	0		0	0	0	6
1988			1	0		0	0	0	6
1989			1	0		0	0	0	6
Career			3	0		0	0	0	18

Jack Kemp

Year	Team		TD	1XP	2XP	FG	FGA	SAF	Pts
1960	LA	A	8	0	0	0	0	0	48
1961	SD	A	6	0	0	0	0	0	36
1962	SD-BUF	A	2	0	0	0	0	0	12
1963	BUF	A	8	0	0	0	0	0	48
1964			5	0	0	0	0	0	30
1965			4	0	0	0	0	0	24
1966			5	0	0	0	0	0	30
1967			2	0	1	0	0	0	14
Career			40	0	1	0	0	0	242
Playoffs			1	0	0	0	0	0	6

Jeff Kemp

Year	Team		TD	1XP	2XP	FG	FGA	SAF	Pts
1984	LARM	N	1	0		0	0	0	6

Perry Kemp

Year	Team		TD	1XP	2XP	FG	FGA	SAF	Pts
1987	CLE	N	2	0		0	0	0	12
1989	GB	N	2	0		0	0	0	12
1990			2	0		0	0	0	12
1991			2	0		0	0	0	12
Career			8	0		0	0	0	48

Florian Kempf

Year	Team		TD	1XP	2XP	FG	FGA	SAF	Pts
1982	HOU	N	0	16		4	6	0	28
1983			0	33		17	21	0	84
1984			0	14		4	6	0	26
1987	NO	N	0	1		4	5	0	13
Career			0	64		29	38	0	151

Herb Kempton

Year	Team		TD	1XP	2XP	FG	FGA	SAF	Pts
1921	CAN	A	1	0		0		0	6

Jim Kendrick

Year	Team		TD	1XP	2XP	FG	FGA	SAF	Pts
1925	HAM-BUF	N	1	3		3		0	18
1926	BUF	N	2	4		0		0	16
Career			3	7		3		0	34

Vince Kendrick

Year	Team		TD	1XP	2XP	FG	FGA	SAF	Pts
1974	ATL	N	1	0		0	0	0	6

Ken Kennard

Year	Team		TD	1XP	2XP	FG	FGA	SAF	Pts
1977	HOU	N	0	0		0	0	1	2

George Kenneally

Year	Team		TD	1XP	2XP	FG	FGA	SAF	Pts
1927	POT	N	1	0		0		0	6
1928			1	0		0		0	6
1929	BOS	N	0	1		0		0	1
Career			2	1		0		0	13

Bob Kennedy

Year	Team		TD	1XP	2XP	FG	FGA	SAF	Pts
1946	NY	AA	2	0		0	0	0	12
1947			1	0		0	0	0	6
1948			1	0		0	0	0	6
1949	B-NY	AA	6	0		0	0	0	36
Career			10	0		0	0	0	60

Jimmie Kennedy

Year	Team		TD	1XP	2XP	FG	FGA	SAF	Pts
1975	BAL	N	1	0		0	0	0	6

Mike Kennedy

Year	Team		TD	1XP	2XP	FG	FGA	SAF	Pts
1983	BUF	N	1	0		0	0	0	6

Bill Kenney

Year	Team		TD	1XP	2XP	FG	FGA	SAF	Pts
1981	KC	N	1	0		0	0	0	6
1983			3	0		0	0	0	18
1985			1	0		0	0	0	6
Career			5	0		0	0	0	30

Eddie Kennison

Year	Team		TD	1XP	2XP	FG	FGA	SAF	Pts
1996	STL	N	11	0	0	0	0	0	66

Ralph Kercheval

Year	Team		TD	1XP	2XP	FG	FGA	SAF	Pts
1934	BKN	N	3	6		4		0	36
1935			2	8		5		0	35
1936			3	4		5		0	37
1937			1	1		2		0	13
1938			1	7		**5**	**13**	0	28
1939			0	3		6	13	0	21
1940			0	3		4	11	0	15
Career			10	32		31	37	0	185

Gary Kerkorian

Year	Team		TD	1XP	2XP	FG	FGA	SAF	Pts
1952	PIT	N	0	35		4	9	0	47
1954	BAL	N	1	11		5	10	0	32
1955			1	0		1	2	0	9
1956			0	1		0	0	0	1
Career			2	47		10	21	0	89

Bill Kern

Year	Team		TD	1XP	2XP	FG	FGA	SAF	Pts
1929	GB	N	0	0		0		1	2

Jimmy Keyes

Year	Team		TD	1XP	2XP	FG	FGA	SAF	Pts
1968	MIA	A	0	30	0	7	16	0	51

Leroy Keyes

Year	Team		TD	1XP	2XP	FG	FGA	SAF	Pts
1969	PHI	N	3	0		0	0	0	18

Jon Keyworth

Year	Team		TD	1XP	2XP	FG	FGA	SAF	Pts
1974	DEN	N	10	0		0	0	0	60
1975			4	0		0	0	0	24
1976			4	0		0	0	0	24
1977			1	0		0	0	0	6
1978			4	0		0	0	0	24
1979			1	0		0	0	0	6
1980			1	0		0	0	0	6
Career			25	0		0	0	0	150
Playoffs			1	0		0	0	0	6

Bob Khayat

Year	Team		TD	1XP	2XP	FG	FGA	SAF	Pts
1960	WAS	N	0	19		15	23	0	64
1962			0	38		11	25	0	71
1963			0	33		12	26	0	69
Career			0	90		38	74	0	204

Walt Kichefski

Year	Team		TD	1XP	2XP	FG	FGA	SAF	Pts
1941	PIT	N	1	0		0	0	0	6

John Kidd

Year	Team		TD	1XP	2XP	FG	FGA	SAF	Pts
1993	SD	N	1	0		0	0	0	6

Blair Kiel

Year	Team		TD	1XP	2XP	FG	FGA	SAF	Pts
1990	GB	N	1	0		0	0	0	6

Walt Kiesling

Year	Team		TD	1XP	2XP	FG	FGA	SAF	Pts
1928	POT	N	0	0		0		1	2

George Kiick

Year	Team		TD	1XP	2XP	FG	FGA	SAF	Pts
1945	PIT	N	1	0		0	0	0	6

Jim Kiick

Year	Team		TD	1XP	2XP	FG	FGA	SAF	Pts
1968	MIA	A	4	0	0	0	0	0	24
1969			10	0	0	0	0	0	60
1970	MIA	N	6	0		0	0	0	36
1971			3	0		0	0	0	18
1972			6	0		0	0	0	36
1974			2	0		0	0	0	12
1976	DEN	N	2	0		0	0	0	12
Career			33	0	0	0	0	0	198
Playoffs			6	0	0	0	0	0	36

Rodger Kiley

Year	Team		TD	1XP	2XP	FG	FGA	SAF	Pts
1923	CHIC	N	1	0		0		0	6

Glenn Killinger

Year	Team		TD	1XP	2XP	FG	FGA	SAF	Pts
1926	PHI	A	1	0		0		0	6

Billy Kilmer

Year	Team		TD	1XP	2XP	FG	FGA	SAF	Pts
1961	SF	N	10	0		0	0	0	60
1962			6	0		0	0	0	36
1967	NO	N	1	0		0	0	0	6
1968			2	0		0	0	0	12
1971	WAS	N	2	0		0	0	0	12
1975			1	0		0	0	0	6
Career			22	0		0	0	0	132

David Kilson

Year	Team		TD	1XP	2XP	FG	FGA	SAF	Pts
1983	BUF	N	1	0		0	0	0	6

John Kimbrough

Year	Team		TD	1XP	2XP	FG	FGA	SAF	Pts
1946	LA	AA	7	0		0	0	0	42
1947			11	0		0	0	0	66
1948			5	0		0	0	0	30
Career			23	0		0	0	0	138

John Kimbrough

Year	Team		TD	1XP	2XP	FG	FGA	SAF	Pts
1977	BUF	N	3	0		0	0	0	18

Billy Kinard

Year	Team		TD	1XP	2XP	FG	FGA	SAF	Pts
1956	CLE	N	1	0		0	0	0	6

Frank Kinard

Year	Team		TD	1XP	2XP	FG	FGA	SAF	Pts
1938	BKN	N	0	0		0		1	2
1939			0	7		0	0	0	7
1941			1	3		0	0	0	9
1943			1	8		1	1	0	17
1944			0	9		0	0	0	9
Career			2	27		1	1	1	44

Terry Kinard

Year	Team		TD	1XP	2XP	FG	FGA	SAF	Pts
1987	NYG	N	1	0		0	0	0	6
1989			1	0		0	0	0	6
1990	HOU	N	1	0		0	0	0	6
Career			3	0		0	0	0	18

Jim Kincaid

Year	Team		TD	1XP	2XP	FG	FGA	SAF	Pts
1954	WAS	N	0	1		0	0	0	1

Brian Kinchen

Year	Team		TD	1XP	2XP	FG	FGA	SAF	Pts
1993	CLE	N	2	0		0	0	0	12
1994			1	0	0	0	0	0	6
1996	BAL	N	1	0	0	0	0	0	6
Career			4	0	0	0	0	0	24

Todd Kinchen

Year	Team		TD	1XP	2XP	FG	FGA	SAF	Pts
1992	LARM	N	2	0		0	0	0	12
1993			1	0		0	0	0	6
1994			4	0	0	0	0	0	24
1995	STL	N	4	0	0	0	0	0	24
Career			11	0	0	0	0	0	66

George Kinderdine

Year	Team		TD	1XP	2XP	FG	FGA	SAF	Pts
1920	DAY	A	0	**12**		0		0	12

Don Kindt

Year	Team		TD	1XP	2XP	FG	FGA	SAF	Pts
1947	CHIB	N	2	0		0	0	0	12
1948			2	0		0	0	0	12
1950			1	0		0	0	0	6
1951			1	0		0	0	0	6
1952			0	0		0	0	1	2
1953			1	0		0	0	0	6
Career			7	0		0	0	1	44

Don Kindt

Year	Team		TD	1XP	2XP	FG	FGA	SAF	Pts
1987	CHI	N	1	0		0	0	0	6

Steve Kiner

Year	Team		TD	1XP	2XP	FG	FGA	SAF	Pts
1973	NE	N	0	0		0	0	1	2

Andy King

Year	Team		TD	1XP	2XP	FG	FGA	SAF	Pts
1920	AKR	A	0	0		0		0	0
1921			1	3		0		0	9
1922	AKR	N	3	3		0		0	21
1923	CHIC	N	1	1		0		0	7
1925	HAM	N	0	1		0		0	1
Career			5	8		0		0	38

Angelo King

Year	Team		TD	1XP	2XP	FG	FGA	SAF	Pts
1987	DET	N	1	0		0	0	0	6

Charley King

Year	Team		TD	1XP	2XP	FG	FGA	SAF	Pts
1968	CIN	A	1	0	0	0	0	0	6

Claude King

Year	Team		TD	1XP	2XP	FG	FGA	SAF	Pts
1961	HOU	A	3	0	0	0	0	0	18
1962	BOS	A	1	0	0	0	0	0	6
Career			4	0	0	0	0	0	24

Dick King

Year	Team		TD	1XP	2XP	FG	FGA	SAF	Pts
1923	STL	N	0	2		0		0	2

Emmett King

Year	Team		TD	1XP	2XP	FG	FGA	SAF	Pts
1954	CHIC	N	1	0		0	0	0	6

Fay King

Year	Team	Lg	TD	1XP	2XP	FG	FGA	SAF	Pts
1946	**BUF**	**AA**	6	0		0	0	0	36
1947			6	0		0	0	0	36
1948	**CHI**	**AA**	7	0		0	0	0	42
1949			1	0		0	0	0	6
Career			20	0		0	0	0	120

Horace King

Year	Team	Lg	TD	1XP	2XP	FG	FGA	SAF	Pts
1975	**DET**	**N**	2	0		0	0	0	12
1977			1	0		0	0	0	6
1978			6	0		0	0	0	36
1979			1	0		0	0	0	6
1980			2	0		0	0	0	12
1981			1	0		0	0	0	6
1982			1	0		0	0	0	6
Career			14	0		0	0	0	84

Kenny King

Year	Team	Lg	TD	1XP	2XP	FG	FGA	SAF	Pts
1980	**OAK**	**N**	4	0		0	0	0	24
1982	**LARI**	**N**	2	0		0	0	0	12
1983			2	0		0	0	0	12
Career			8	0		0	0	0	48
Playoffs			3	0		0	0	0	18

Linden King

Year	Team	Lg	TD	1XP	2XP	FG	FGA	SAF	Pts
1989	**LARI**	**N**	1	0		0	0	0	6

Phil King

Year	Team	Lg	TD	1XP	2XP	FG	FGA	SAF	Pts
1958	**NYG**	**N**	1	0		0	0	0	6
1959			1	0		0	0	0	6
1962			2	0		0	0	0	12
1963			8	0		0	0	0	48
1964	**PIT**	**N**	2	0		0	0	0	12
1965	**MIN**	**N**	1	0		0	0	0	6
1966			1	0		0	0	0	6
Career			16	0		0	0	0	96

Shawn King

Year	Team	Lg	TD	1XP	2XP	FG	FGA	SAF	Pts
1996	**CAR**	**N**	1	0	0	0	0	0	6

Larry Kinnebrew

Year	Team	Lg	TD	1XP	2XP	FG	FGA	SAF	Pts
1983	**CIN**	**N**	3	0		0	0	0	18
1984			10	0		0	0	0	60
1985			10	0		0	0	0	60
1986			9	0		0	0	0	54
1987			8	0		0	0	0	48
1989	**BUF**	**N**	6	0		0	0	0	36
1990			1	0		0	0	0	6
Career			47	0		0	0	0	282

Jeff Kinney

Year	Team	Lg	TD	1XP	2XP	FG	FGA	SAF	Pts
1972	**KC**	**N**	1	0		0	0	0	6
1973			1	0		0	0	0	6
1974			1	0		0	0	0	6
1975			2	0		0	0	0	12
1976	**BUF**	**N**	1	0		0	0	0	6
Career			6	0		0	0	0	36

Carl Kinscherf

Year	Team	Lg	TD	1XP	2XP	FG	FGA	SAF	Pts
1943	**NYG**	**N**	1	0		0	0	0	6

Terry Kirby

Year	Team	Lg	TD	1XP	2XP	FG	FGA	SAF	Pts
1993	**MIA**	**N**	6	0		0	0	0	36
1994			2	0	1	0	0	0	14
1995			7	0	0	0	0	0	42
1996	**SF**	**N**	4	0	0	0	0	0	24
Career			19	0	1	0	0	0	116
Playoffs			2	0	0	0	0	0	12

Levon Kirkland

Year	Team	Lg	TD	1XP	2XP	FG	FGA	SAF	Pts
1993	**PIT**	**N**	1	0		0	0	0	6

Frank Kirkleski

Year	Team	Lg	TD	1XP	2XP	FG	FGA	SAF	Pts
1927	**POT**	**N**	1	0		0		0	6
1929	**ORA**	**N**	2	0		0		0	12
1930	**NEW**	**N**	1	0		0		0	6
Career			4	0		0		0	24

Roger Kirkman

Year	Team	Lg	TD	1XP	2XP	FG	FGA	SAF	Pts
1933	**PHI**	**N**	1	2		0		0	8
1934			1	5		0		0	11
Career			2	7		0		0	19

Lou Kirouac

Year	Team	Lg	TD	1XP	2XP	FG	FGA	SAF	Pts
1966	**ATL**	**N**	0	19		9	18	0	46

Ben Kish

Year	Team	Lg	TD	1XP	2XP	FG	FGA	SAF	Pts
1943	**P-P**	**N**	2	0		0	0	0	12
1944	**PHI**	**N**	1	1		0	0	0	7
1948			1	0		0	0	0	6
Career			4	1		0	0	0	25

Ed Kissell

Year	Team	Lg	TD	1XP	2XP	FG	FGA	SAF	Pts
1952	**PIT**	**N**	0	0		0	2	0	0
1954			0	8		2	4	0	14
Career			0	8		2	6	0	14

John Kissell

Year	Team	Lg	TD	1XP	2XP	FG	FGA	SAF	Pts
1950	**CLE**	**N**	0	0		0	0	1	2

Vito Kissell

Year	Team	Lg	TD	1XP	2XP	FG	FGA	SAF	Pts
1950	**BAL**	**N**	0	11		0	1	0	11

Paul Kittredge

Year	Team	Lg	TD	1XP	2XP	FG	FGA	SAF	Pts
1929	**BOS**	**N**	2	0		0		0	12

John Kitzmiller

Year	Team	Lg	TD	1XP	2XP	FG	FGA	SAF	Pts
1931	**NYG**	**N**	4	3		0		0	27

Bob Klein

Year	Team	Lg	TD	1XP	2XP	FG	FGA	SAF	Pts
1969	**LA**	**N**	1	0		0	0	0	6
1971			4	0		0	0	0	24
1972			1	0		0	0	0	6
1973			2	0		0	0	0	12
1974			4	0		0	0	0	24
1975			2	0		0	0	0	12
1976			1	0		0	0	0	6
1977	**SD**	**N**	1	0		0	0	0	6
1978			2	0		0	0	0	12
1979			5	0		0	0	0	30
Career			23	0		0	0	0	138
Playoffs			2	0		0	0	0	12

Rocky Klever

Year	Team	Lg	TD	1XP	2XP	FG	FGA	SAF	Pts
1984	**NYJ**	**N**	1	0		0	0	0	6
1985			2	0		0	0	0	12
Career			3	0		0	0	0	18

Ed Klewicki

Year	Team	Lg	TD	1XP	2XP	FG	FGA	SAF	Pts
1935	**DET**	**N**	2	0		0		0	12
1937			1	0		0		0	6
Career			3	0		0		0	18

Harry Kline

Year	Team	Lg	TD	1XP	2XP	FG	FGA	SAF	Pts
1939	**NYG**	**N**	1	0		0	0	0	6

Chuck Klingbeil

Year	Team	Lg	TD	1XP	2XP	FG	FGA	SAF	Pts
1991	**MIA**	**N**	1	0		0	0	0	6

Dave Klug

Year	Team	Lg	TD	1XP	2XP	FG	FGA	SAF	Pts
1982	**KC**	**N**	1	0		0	0	0	6

Pete Kmetovic

Year	Team	Lg	TD	1XP	2XP	FG	FGA	SAF	Pts
1947	**DET**	**N**	2	0		0	0	0	12

Gary Knafelc

Year	Team	Lg	TD	1XP	2XP	FG	FGA	SAF	Pts
1955	**GB**	**N**	8	0		0	0	0	48
1956			6	0		0	0	0	36
1957			2	0		0	0	0	12
1958			1	0		0	0	0	6
1959			4	0		0	0	0	24
1963	**SF**	**N**	2	0		0	0	0	12
Career			23	0		0	0	0	138

Gayle Knief

Year	Team	Lg	TD	1XP	2XP	FG	FGA	SAF	Pts
1970	**BOS**	**N**	1	0		0	0	0	6

Curt Knight

Year	Team	Lg	TD	1XP	2XP	FG	FGA	SAF	Pts
1969	**WAS**	**N**	0	35		16	27	0	83
1970			0	33		20	27	0	93
1971			0	27		**29**	**49**	0	114
1972			0	40		14	30	0	82
1973			0	37		22	42	0	103
Career			0	172		101	175	0	475
Playoffs			0	8		11	14	0	41

David Knight

Year	Team	Lg	TD	1XP	2XP	FG	FGA	SAF	Pts
1973	**NYJ**	**N**	1	0		0	0	0	6
1974			4	0		0	0	0	24
1976			2	0		0	0	0	12
Career			7	0		0	0	0	42

Kurt Knoff

Year	Team	Lg	TD	1XP	2XP	FG	FGA	SAF	Pts
1980	**MIN**	**N**	1	0		0	0	0	6

Oscar Knop

Year	Team	Lg	TD	1XP	2XP	FG	FGA	SAF	Pts
1920	**CHIT**	**A**	1	0		0		0	6
1923	**CHIB**	**N**	2	0		0		0	12
1924			1	0		0		0	6
1925			2	0		0		0	12
1926			1	0		0		0	6
1927			1	0		0		0	6
Career			8	0		0		0	48

George Koch

Year	Team	Lg	TD	1XP	2XP	FG	FGA	SAF	Pts
1947	**BUF**	**AA**	1	0		0	0	0	6

Roger Kochman

Year	Team	Lg	TD	1XP	2XP	FG	FGA	SAF	Pts
1963	**BUF**	**A**	1	0	0	0	0	0	6

Dave Kocourek

Year	Team	Lg	TD	1XP	2XP	FG	FGA	SAF	Pts
1960	**LA**	**A**	1	0	0	0	0	0	6
1961	**SD**	**A**	4	0	0	0	0	0	24
1962			4	0	1	0	0	0	26
1963			5	0	1	0	0	0	32
1964			5	0	0	0	0	0	30
1965			2	0	0	0	0	0	12
1966	**MIA**	**A**	2	0	0	0	0	0	12
1967	**OAK**	**A**	0	0	1	0	0	0	2
1968			1	0	0	0	0	0	6
Career			24	0	3	0	0	0	150
Playoffs			2	0	0	0	0	0	12

Bob Koehler

Year	Team	Lg	TD	1XP	2XP	FG	FGA	SAF	Pts
1920	**DEC**	**A**	2	0		0		0	12
1921	**CHIC**	**A**	1	2		0		0	8
1922	**CHIC**	**N**	2	0		0		0	12
1923			1	0		0		0	6
1924			1	0		0		0	6
1925			4	0		0		0	24
Career			11	2		0		0	68

Matt Kofler

Year	Team	Lg	TD	1XP	2XP	FG	FGA	SAF	Pts
1985	**IND**	**N**	1	0		0	0	0	6

Bob Kohrs

Year	Team	Lg	TD	1XP	2XP	FG	FGA	SAF	Pts
1983	**PIT**	**N**	0	0		0	0	1	2

Mike Koken

Year	Team	Lg	TD	1XP	2XP	FG	FGA	SAF	Pts
1933	**CHIC**	**N**	0	1		0		0	1

Louie Kolls

Year	Team	Lg	TD	1XP	2XP	FG	FGA	SAF	Pts
1920	**HAM**	**A**	0	1		0		0	1
1924	**RI**	**N**	0	0		0		0	0
Career			0	1		0		0	1

Jeff Komlo

Year	Team	Lg	TD	1XP	2XP	FG	FGA	SAF	Pts
1979	**DET**	**N**	2	0		0	0	0	12

John Koniszewski

Year	Team	Lg	TD	1XP	2XP	FG	FGA	SAF	Pts
1948	**WAS**	**N**	0	0		0	0	1	2

Kenny Konz

Year	Team	Lg	TD	1XP	2XP	FG	FGA	SAF	Pts
1954	**CLE**	**N**	2	3		0	0	0	15
1955			1	0		0	0	0	6
1956			1	0		0	0	0	6
1958			1	0		0	0	0	6
Career			5	3		0	0	0	33

George Koonce

Year	Team	Lg	TD	1XP	2XP	FG	FGA	SAF	Pts
1996	**GB**	**N**	1	0	0	0	0	0	6

Dave Kopay

Year	Team	Lg	TD	1XP	2XP	FG	FGA	SAF	Pts
1964	**SF**	**N**	2	0		0	0	0	12
1965			4	0		0	0	0	24
1966			2	0		0	0	0	12
Career			8	0		0	0	0	48

Joe Kopcha

Year	Team	Lg	TD	1XP	2XP	FG	FGA	SAF	Pts
1935	**CHIB**	**N**	0	0		1		0	3

Walt Koppisch
Year	Team	Lg	TD	1XP	2XP	FG	FGA	SAF	Pts
1926	NYG	N	0	0		0		0	0

Ken Kortas
Year	Team	Lg	TD	1XP	2XP	FG	FGA	SAF	Pts
1967	PIT	N	1	0		0	0	0	6

Steve Korte
Year	Team	Lg	TD	1XP	2XP	FG	FGA	SAF	Pts
1983	NO	N	1	0		0	0	0	6

Bernie Kosar
Year	Team	Lg	TD	1XP	2XP	FG	FGA	SAF	Pts
1985	CLE	N	1	0		0	0	0	6
1987			1	0		0	0	0	6
1988			1	0		0	0	0	6
1989			1	0		0	0	0	6
1995	MIA	N	1	0	0	0	0	0	6
Career			5	0	0	0	0	0	30

Stan Kosel
Year	Team	Lg	TD	1XP	2XP	FG	FGA	SAF	Pts
1939	BKN	N	1	0		0	0	0	6

Gary Kosins
Year	Team	Lg	TD	1XP	2XP	FG	FGA	SAF	Pts
1972	CHI	N	1	0		0	0	0	6
1974			1	0		0	0	0	6
Career			2	0		0	0	0	12

Tony Kostos
Year	Team	Lg	TD	1XP	2XP	FG	FGA	SAF	Pts
1928	FRA	N	0	2		0		0	2
1929			1	0		0		0	6
1930			1	0		0		0	6
Career			2	2		0		0	14

Eddie Kotal
Year	Team	Lg	TD	1XP	2XP	FG	FGA	SAF	Pts
1925	GB	N	1	0		0		0	6
1926			2	0		0		0	12
1927			1	0		0		0	6
1928			3	0		0		0	18
1929			3	0		0		0	18
Career			10	0		0		0	60

Doug Kotar
Year	Team	Lg	TD	1XP	2XP	FG	FGA	SAF	Pts
1974	NYG	N	4	0		0	0	0	24
1975			6	0		0	0	0	36
1976			3	0		0	0	0	18
1977			2	0		0	0	0	12
1978			2	0		0	0	0	12
1979			3	0		0	0	0	18
1981			1	0		0	0	0	6
Career			21	0		0	0	0	126

Rich Kotite
Year	Team	Lg	TD	1XP	2XP	FG	FGA	SAF	Pts
1968	PIT	N	2	0		0	0	0	12
1969	NYG	N	1	0		0	0	0	6
1971			2	0		0	0	0	12
Career			5	0		0	0	0	30

Marty Kottler
Year	Team	Lg	TD	1XP	2XP	FG	FGA	SAF	Pts
1933	PIT	N	1	0		0		0	6

Johnny Kovatch
Year	Team	Lg	TD	1XP	2XP	FG	FGA	SAF	Pts
1938	CLE	N	1	0		0	0	0	6

Johnny Kovatch
Year	Team	Lg	TD	1XP	2XP	FG	FGA	SAF	Pts
1942	WAS	N	1	0		0	0	0	6

Walt Kowalczyk
Year	Team	Lg	TD	1XP	2XP	FG	FGA	SAF	Pts
1958	PHI	N	1	0		0	0	0	6
1960	DAL	N	2	0		0	0	0	12
Career			3	0		0	0	0	18

Andy Kowalski
Year	Team	Lg	TD	1XP	2XP	FG	FGA	SAF	Pts
1944	BKN	N	1	0		0	0	0	6

Ernie Koy
Year	Team	Lg	TD	1XP	2XP	FG	FGA	SAF	Pts
1967	NYG	N	5	0		0	0	0	30
1968			4	0		0	0	0	24
1969			6	0		0	0	0	36
Career			15	0		0	0	0	90

Ted Koy
Year	Team	Lg	TD	1XP	2XP	FG	FGA	SAF	Pts
1971	BUF	N	1	0		0	0	0	6

Brian Kozlowski
Year	Team	Lg	TD	1XP	2XP	FG	FGA	SAF	Pts
1996	NYG	N	1	0	0	0	0	0	6

Glen Kozlowski
Year	Team	Lg	TD	1XP	2XP	FG	FGA	SAF	Pts
1987	CHI	N	3	0		0	0	0	18

Mike Kozlowski
Year	Team	Lg	TD	1XP	2XP	FG	FGA	SAF	Pts
1981	MIA	N	1	0		0	0	0	6
1983			2	0		0	0	0	12
Career			3	0		0	0	0	18

George Kracum
Year	Team	Lg	TD	1XP	2XP	FG	FGA	SAF	Pts
1941	BKN	N	3	0		0	0	0	18

Greg Kragen
Year	Team	Lg	TD	1XP	2XP	FG	FGA	SAF	Pts
1989	DEN	N	1	0		0	0	0	6
1995	CAR	N	1	0	0	0	0	0	6
Career			2	0	0	0	0	0	12

Erik Kramer
Year	Team	Lg	TD	1XP	2XP	FG	FGA	SAF	Pts
1991	DET	N	1	0		0	0	0	6
1995	CHI	N	1	0	0	0	0	0	6
Career			2	0	0	0	0	0	12

Jerry Kramer
Year	Team	Lg	TD	1XP	2XP	FG	FGA	SAF	Pts
1962	GB	N	0	38		9	11	0	65
1963			0	43		16	34	0	91
1968			0	9		4	9	0	21
Career			0	90		29	54	0	177
Playoffs			0	1		3	3	0	10

Kent Kramer
Year	Team	Lg	TD	1XP	2XP	FG	FGA	SAF	Pts
1966	SF	N	3	0		0	0	0	18
1967	NO	N	2	0		0	0	0	12
1969	MIN	N	1	0		0	0	0	6
1971	PHI	N	1	0		0	0	0	6
1972			1	0		0	0	0	6
Career			8	0		0	0	0	48

Ron Kramer
Year	Team	Lg	TD	1XP	2XP	FG	FGA	SAF	Pts
1961	GB	N	4	0		0	0	0	24
1962			7	0		0	0	0	42
1963			4	0		0	0	0	24
1965	DET	N	1	0		0	0	0	6
Career			16	0		0	0	0	96
Playoffs			2	0		0	0	0	12

Tommy Kramer
Year	Team	Lg	TD	1XP	2XP	FG	FGA	SAF	Pts
1979	MIN	N	1	0		0	0	0	6
1980			1	0		0	0	0	6
1982			3	0		0	0	0	18
1984			1	0		0	0	0	6
1986			1	0		0	0	0	6
1987			2	0		0	0	0	12
Career			9	0		0	0	0	54

Larry Krause
Year	Team	Lg	TD	1XP	2XP	FG	FGA	SAF	Pts
1970	GB	N	1	0		0	0	0	6

Max Krause
Year	Team	Lg	TD	1XP	2XP	FG	FGA	SAF	Pts
1933	NYG	N	1	1		0		0	7
1936			1	0		0		0	6
1937	WAS	N	1	0		0		0	6
1938			3	0		0	0	0	18
Career			6	1		0	0	0	37
Playoffs			1	0		0	0	0	6

Paul Krause
Year	Team	Lg	TD	1XP	2XP	FG	FGA	SAF	Pts
1964	WAS	N	1	0		0	0	0	6
1965			1	0		0	0	0	6
1969	MIN	N	1	0		0	0	0	6
1972			2	0		0	0	0	12
1975			1	0		0	0	0	6
Career			6	0		0	0	0	36
Playoffs			1	0		0	0	0	6

Barry Krauss
Year	Team	Lg	TD	1XP	2XP	FG	FGA	SAF	Pts
1982	BAL	N	1	0		0	0	0	6

Rich Kraynak
Year	Team	Lg	TD	1XP	2XP	FG	FGA	SAF	Pts
1984	PHI	N	1	0		0	0	0	6

Steve Kreider
Year	Team	Lg	TD	1XP	2XP	FG	FGA	SAF	Pts
1981	CIN	N	5	0		0	0	0	30
1982			1	1		0	0	0	7
1983			1	0		0	0	0	6
1984			1	0		0	0	0	6

Steve Kreider *continued*
Year	Team	Lg	TD	1XP	2XP	FG	FGA	SAF	Pts
1985			1	1		0	0	0	7
Career			9	2		0	0	0	56

Walt Kreinheder
Year	Team	Lg	TD	1XP	2XP	FG	FGA	SAF	Pts
1922	AKR	N	0	1		0		0	1

Rich Kreitling
Year	Team	Lg	TD	1XP	2XP	FG	FGA	SAF	Pts
1960	CLE	N	3	0		0	0	0	18
1961			3	0		0	0	0	18
1962			3	0		0	0	0	18
1963			6	0		0	0	0	36
1964	CHI	N	2	0		0	0	0	12
Career			17	0		0	0	0	102

Karl Kremser
Year	Team	Lg	TD	1XP	2XP	FG	FGA	SAF	Pts
1969	MIA	A	0	26	0	13	22	0	65
1970	MIA	N	0	2		0	1	0	2
Career			0	28	0	13	23	0	67

Keith Krepfle
Year	Team	Lg	TD	1XP	2XP	FG	FGA	SAF	Pts
1976	PHI	N	1	0		0	0	0	6
1977			3	0		0	0	0	18
1978			3	0		0	0	0	18
1979			3	0		0	0	0	18
1980			4	0		0	0	0	24
1981			5	0		0	0	0	30
Career			19	0		0	0	0	114
Playoffs			1	0		0	0	0	6

Joe Kresky
Year	Team	Lg	TD	1XP	2XP	FG	FGA	SAF	Pts
1932	BOS	N	0	0		0		1	2

Al Kreuz
Year	Team	Lg	TD	1XP	2XP	FG	FGA	SAF	Pts
1926	PHI	A	1	4		8		0	34

Dave Krieg
Year	Team	Lg	TD	1XP	2XP	FG	FGA	SAF	Pts
1981	SEA	N	1	0		0	0	0	6
1983			2	0		0	0	0	12
1984			3	0		0	0	0	18
1985			1	0		0	0	0	6
1986			1	0		0	0	0	6
1987			2	0		0	0	0	12
1992	KC	N	2	0		0	0	0	12
1996	CHI	N	1	0	0	0	0	0	6
Career			13	0	0	0	0	0	78
Playoffs			1	0	0	0	0	0	6

Bob Krieger
Year	Team	Lg	TD	1XP	2XP	FG	FGA	SAF	Pts
1941	PHI	N	2	0		0	0	0	12

Gary Kroner
Year	Team	Lg	TD	1XP	2XP	FG	FGA	SAF	Pts
1965	DEN	A	0	32	0	13	29	0	71
1966			0	20	0	14	25	0	62
1967			0	5	0	2	2	0	11
Career			0	57	0	29	56	0	144

Mike Kruczek
Year	Team	Lg	TD	1XP	2XP	FG	FGA	SAF	Pts
1976	PIT	N	2	0		0	0	0	12

Al Krueger
Year	Team	Lg	TD	1XP	2XP	FG	FGA	SAF	Pts
1941	WAS	N	1	0		0	0	0	6
1946	LA	AA	1	0		0	0	0	6
Career			2	0		0	0	0	12

Charlie Krueger
Year	Team	Lg	TD	1XP	2XP	FG	FGA	SAF	Pts
1959	SF	N	0	0		0	0	1	2
1960			0	0		0	0	1	2
1961			0	0		0	0	1	2
1965			1	0		0	0	0	6
Career			1	0		0	0	3	12

Larry Krutko
Year	Team	Lg	TD	1XP	2XP	FG	FGA	SAF	Pts
1959	PIT	N	4	0		0	0	0	24

Gary Kubiak
Year	Team	Lg	TD	1XP	2XP	FG	FGA	SAF	Pts
1983	DEN	N	1	0		0	0	0	6
1984			1	0		0	0	0	6
Career			2	0		0	0	0	12
Playoffs			1	0		0	0	0	6

Bert Kuczynski
Year	Team	Lg	TD	1XP	2XP	FG	FGA	SAF	Pts
1946	PHI	N	1	0		0	0	0	6

Waddy Kuehl

Year	Team		TD	1XP	2XP	FG	FGA	SAF	Pts
1920	RI	A	3	0		0		0	18
1921	DET-BUF	A	2	0		0		0	12
1922	BUF	N	3	1		0		0	19
1923	RI	N	4	0		0		0	24
Career			12	1		0		0	73

Oscar Kuehner

Year	Team		TD	1XP	2XP	FG	FGA	SAF	Pts
1920	COL	A	0	1		0		0	1

Ray Kuffel

Year	Team		TD	1XP	2XP	FG	FGA	SAF	Pts
1948	CHI	AA	3	0		0	0	0	18

Joe Kuharich

Year	Team		TD	1XP	2XP	FG	FGA	SAF	Pts
1940	CHIC	N	0	0		0	1	0	0
1945			0	12		0	3	0	12
Career			0	12		0	4	0	12

Joe Kulbacki

Year	Team		TD	1XP	2XP	FG	FGA	SAF	Pts
1960	BUF	A	1	0	0	0	0	0	6

Vic Kulbitski

Year	Team		TD	1XP	2XP	FG	FGA	SAF	Pts
1946	BUF	AA	2	0		0	0	0	12
1947			5	1		0	0	0	31
1948			1	8		0	0	0	14
Career			8	9		0	0	0	57

Ralph Kurek

Year	Team		TD	1XP	2XP	FG	FGA	SAF	Pts
1966	CHI	N	1	0		0	0	0	6
1968			1	0		0	0	0	6
Career			2	0		0	0	0	12

Jamie Kurisko

Year	Team		TD	1XP	2XP	FG	FGA	SAF	Pts
1987	NYJ	N	1	0		0	0	0	6

Howie Kurnick

Year	Team		TD	1XP	2XP	FG	FGA	SAF	Pts
1979	CIN	N	1	0		0	0	0	6

Johnny Kusko

Year	Team		TD	1XP	2XP	FG	FGA	SAF	Pts
1936	PHI	N	1	0		0		0	6

Mal Kutner

Year	Team		TD	1XP	2XP	FG	FGA	SAF	Pts
1946	CHIC	N	5	0		0	0	0	30
1947			8	0		0	0	0	48
1948			**15**	0		0	0	0	90
1949			5	0		0	0	0	30
Career			33	0		0	0	0	198

Fulton Kuykendall

Year	Team		TD	1XP	2XP	FG	FGA	SAF	Pts
1981	ATL	N	1	0		0	0	0	6

John Kuzman

Year	Team		TD	1XP	2XP	FG	FGA	SAF	Pts
1946	SF	AA	1	0		0	0	0	6

Ted Kwalick

Year	Team		TD	1XP	2XP	FG	FGA	SAF	Pts
1969	SF	N	1	0		0	0	0	6
1970			1	0		0	0	0	6
1971			5	0		0	0	0	30
1972			9	0		0	0	0	54
1973			5	0		0	0	0	30
1974			2	0		0	0	0	12
Career			23	0		0	0	0	138

Aaron Kyle

Year	Team		TD	1XP	2XP	FG	FGA	SAF	Pts
1976	DAL	N	0	0		0	0	1	2

John Kyle

Year	Team		TD	1XP	2XP	FG	FGA	SAF	Pts
1923	CLE	N	1	0		0		0	6

Steve Lach

Year	Team		TD	1XP	2XP	FG	FGA	SAF	Pts
1942	CHIC	N	4	1		0	0	0	25
1946	PIT	N	5	0		0	0	0	30
1947			9	0		0	0	0	54
Career			18	1		0	0	0	109

Sean LaChapelle

Year	Team		TD	1XP	2XP	FG	FGA	SAF	Pts
1996	KC	N	2	0	0	0	0	0	12

Rick Lackman

Year	Team		TD	1XP	2XP	FG	FGA	SAF	Pts
1935	PHI	N	0	1		0		0	1

Ken Lacy

Year	Team		TD	1XP	2XP	FG	FGA	SAF	Pts
1984	KC	N	4	0		0	0	0	24

Greg LaFleur

Year	Team		TD	1XP	2XP	FG	FGA	SAF	Pts
1981	STL	N	2	0		0	0	0	12
1982			1	0		0	0	0	6
Career			3	0		0	0	0	18

Morris LaGrand

Year	Team		TD	1XP	2XP	FG	FGA	SAF	Pts
1975	KC	N	1	0		0	0	0	6

Hal Lahar

Year	Team		TD	1XP	2XP	FG	FGA	SAF	Pts
1941	CHIB	N	0	1		1	1	0	4

Warren Lahr

Year	Team		TD	1XP	2XP	FG	FGA	SAF	Pts
1949	CLE	AA	1	0		0	0	0	6
1950	CLE	N	2	0		0	0	0	12
1951			2	0		0	0	0	12
1954			1	0		0	0	0	6
Career			6	0		0	0	0	36
Playoffs			1	0		0	0	0	6

Scott Laidlaw

Year	Team		TD	1XP	2XP	FG	FGA	SAF	Pts
1976	DAL	N	4	0		0	0	0	24
1977			1	0		0	0	0	6
1978			4	0		0	0	0	24
1979			3	0		0	0	0	18
Career			12	0		0	0	0	72
Playoffs			4	0		0	0	0	24

Bruce Laird

Year	Team		TD	1XP	2XP	FG	FGA	SAF	Pts
1975	BAL	N	0	0		0	0	1	2
Playoffs			1	0	0	0	0	0	6

Jim Laird

Year	Team		TD	1XP	2XP	FG	FGA	SAF	Pts
1920	ROC	A	0	0		2		0	6
1921	ROC-CAN	A	6	0		0		0	36
1922	BUF	N	4	0		0		0	24
1925	PRO	N	3	2		3		0	29
Career			13	2		5		0	95

Carnell Lake

Year	Team		TD	1XP	2XP	FG	FGA	SAF	Pts
1995	PIT	N	1	0	0	0	0	0	6
1996			2	0	0	0	0	0	12
Career			3	0	0	0	0	0	18
Playoffs			0	0	0	0	0	1	2

Roland Lakes

Year	Team		TD	1XP	2XP	FG	FGA	SAF	Pts
1969	SF	N	1	0		0	0	0	6

Peter Lamana

Year	Team		TD	1XP	2XP	FG	FGA	SAF	Pts
1946	CHI	AA	1	0		0	0	0	6

Joe Lamas

Year	Team		TD	1XP	2XP	FG	FGA	SAF	Pts
1942	PIT	N	1	0		0	0	0	6

Roddy Lamb

Year	Team		TD	1XP	2XP	FG	FGA	SAF	Pts
1925	RI	N	5	3		0		0	33
1926	CHIC	N	1	1		0		0	7
1927			1	0		0		0	6
Career			7	4		0		0	46

Curly Lambeau

Year	Team		TD	1XP	2XP	FG	FGA	SAF	Pts
1921	GB	A	2	7		3		0	28
1922	GB	N	4	3		1		0	30
1923			3	0		0		0	18
1924			1	1		1		0	10
1925			0	5		1		0	8
1926			0	4		0		0	4
1927			2	0		0		0	12
1928			0	0		0		0	0
Career			12	20		6		0	110

Pete Lammons

Year	Team		TD	1XP	2XP	FG	FGA	SAF	Pts
1966	NY	A	4	0	0	0	0	0	24
1967			2	0	0	0	0	0	12
1968			3	0	0	0	0	0	18
1969			2	0	0	0	0	0	12
1970	NYJ	N	2	0		0	0	0	12
1971			1	0		0	0	0	6
Career			14	0	0	0	0	0	84
Playoffs			1	0	0	0	0	0	6

Daryle Lamonica

Year	Team		TD	1XP	2XP	FG	FGA	SAF	Pts
1963	BUF	A	0	0	1	0	0	0	2
1964			6	0	2	0	0	0	40
1965			1	0	0	0	0	0	6

Daryle Lamonica *continued*

Year	Team		TD	1XP	2XP	FG	FGA	SAF	Pts
1966			1	0	0	0	0	0	6
1967	OAK	A	4	0	0	0	0	0	24
1968			1	0	0	0	0	0	6
1969			1	0	0	0	0	0	6
Career			14	0	3	0	0	0	90
Playoffs			1	0	0	0	0	0	6

Chuck Lamson

Year	Team		TD	1XP	2XP	FG	FGA	SAF	Pts
1966	LA	N	1	0		0	0	0	6

Mel Land

Year	Team		TD	1XP	2XP	FG	FGA	SAF	Pts
1965	PHI	N	1	0		0	0	0	6

Walt Landers

Year	Team		TD	1XP	2XP	FG	FGA	SAF	Pts
1978	GB	N	1	0		0	0	0	6
1979			1	0		0	0	0	6
Career			2	0		0	0	0	12

Greg Landry

Year	Team		TD	1XP	2XP	FG	FGA	SAF	Pts
1968	DET	N	1	0		0	0	0	6
1969			1	0		0	0	0	6
1970			1	0		0	0	0	6
1971			3	0		0	0	0	18
1972			9	0		0	0	0	54
1973			2	0		0	0	0	12
1974			1	0		0	0	0	6
1976			1	0		0	0	0	6
1980	BAL	N	1	0		0	0	0	6
1981			1	0		0	0	0	6
1984	CHI	N	1	0		0	0	0	6
Career			22	0		0	0	0	132

Tom Landry

Year	Team		TD	1XP	2XP	FG	FGA	SAF	Pts
1950	NYG	N	1	0		0	0	0	6
1951			3	0		0	0	0	18
1952			2	0		0	0	0	12
Career			6	0		0	0	0	36

Night Train Lane

Year	Team		TD	1XP	2XP	FG	FGA	SAF	Pts
1952	LA	N	2	0		0	0	1	14
1953			2	0		0	0	0	12
1955	CHIC	N	1	0		0	0	0	6
1956			1	0		0	0	0	6
1959			1	0		0	0	0	6
1960	DET	N	1	0		0	0	0	6
Career			8	0		0	0	1	50

Eric Lane

Year	Team		TD	1XP	2XP	FG	FGA	SAF	Pts
1984	SEA	N	5	0		0	0	0	30
1986			2	0		0	0	0	12
Career			7	0		0	0	0	42

MacArthur Lane

Year	Team		TD	1XP	2XP	FG	FGA	SAF	Pts
1969	STL	N	1	0		0	0	0	6
1970			**13**	0		0	0	0	78
1971			3	0		0	0	0	18
1972	GB	N	3	0		0	0	0	18
1973			2	0		0	0	0	12
1974			6	0		0	0	0	36
1975	KC	N	2	0		0	0	0	12
1976			6	0		0	0	0	36
1977			1	0		0	0	0	6
Career			37	0		0	0	0	222

David Lang

Year	Team		TD	1XP	2XP	FG	FGA	SAF	Pts
1992	LARM	N	6	0		0	0	0	36

Gene Lang

Year	Team		TD	1XP	2XP	FG	FGA	SAF	Pts
1984	DEN	N	3	0		0	0	0	18
1985			7	0		0	0	0	42
1986			3	0		0	0	0	18
1987			4	0		0	0	0	24
1988	ATL	N	1	0		0	0	0	6
1989			2	0		0	0	0	12
Career			20	0		0	0	0	120
Playoffs			2	0		0	0	0	12

Izzy Lang

Year	Team		TD	1XP	2XP	FG	FGA	SAF	Pts
1966	PHI	N	1	0		0	0	0	6
1967			5	0		0	0	0	30
1968			1	0		0	0	0	6
Career			7	0		0	0	0	42

Irv Langhoff

Year	Team		TD	1XP	2XP	FG	FGA	SAF	Pts
1922	RAC	N	1	2		0		0	8

Reggie Langhorne

Year	Team		TD	1XP	2XP	FG	FGA	SAF	Pts
1986	CLE	N	1	0		0	0	0	6
1987			1	0		0	0	0	6
1988			8	0		0	0	0	48
1989			2	0		0	0	0	12
1990			2	0		0	0	0	12
1991			2	0		0	0	0	12
1992	IND	N	1	0		0	0	0	6
1993			3	0		0	0	0	18
Career			20	0		0	0	0	120
Playoffs			2	0		0	0	0	12

Willie Lanier

Year	Team		TD	1XP	2XP	FG	FGA	SAF	Pts
1968	KC	A	1	0	0	0	0	0	6
1973	KC	N	1	0		0	0	0	6
1974			0	0		0	0	1	2
Career			2	0	0	0	0	1	14

Mike Lansford

Year	Team		TD	1XP	2XP	FG	FGA	SAF	Pts
1982	LARM	N	0	23		9	15	0	50
1983			0	9		6	9	0	27
1984			0	37		25	33	0	112
1985			0	38		22	29	0	104
1986			0	34		17	24	0	85
1987			0	36		17	21	0	87
1988			0	45		24	32	0	117
1989			0	**51**		23	30	0	120
1990			0	42		15	24	0	87
Career			0	315		158	217	0	789
Playoffs			0	14		9	12	0	41

Ralph Lanum

Year	Team		TD	1XP	2XP	FG	FGA	SAF	Pts
1920	DEC	A	1	0		0		0	6
1923	CHIB	N	1	0		0		0	6
Career			2	0		0		0	12

Ted Lapka

Year	Team		TD	1XP	2XP	FG	FGA	SAF	Pts
1944	WAS	N	1	0		0	0	0	6
1946			1	0		0	0	0	6
Career			2	0		0	0	0	12
Playoffs			1	0		0	0	0	6

Benny LaPresta

Year	Team		TD	1XP	2XP	FG	FGA	SAF	Pts
1933	BOS	N	0	1		0		0	1

Bob Laraba

Year	Team		TD	1XP	2XP	FG	FGA	SAF	Pts
1961	SD	A	3	1	0	0	0	0	19

Steve Largent

Year	Team		TD	1XP	2XP	FG	FGA	SAF	Pts
1976	SEA	N	4	0		0	0	0	24
1977			10	0		0	0	0	60
1978			8	0		0	0	0	48
1979			9	0		0	0	0	54
1980			6	0		0	0	0	36
1981			10	0		0	0	0	60
1982			3	0		0	0	0	18
1983			11	0		0	0	0	66
1984			12	0		0	0	0	72
1985			6	1		0	0	0	37
1986			9	0		0	0	0	54
1987			8	0		0	0	0	48
1988			2	0		0	0	0	12
1989			3	1		0	0	0	19
Career			101	2		0	0	0	608
Playoffs			4	0		0	0	0	24

Jack Larscheid

Year	Team		TD	1XP	2XP	FG	FGA	SAF	Pts
1960	OAK	A	2	0	0	0	0	0	12

Bill Larson

Year	Team		TD	1XP	2XP	FG	FGA	SAF	Pts
1980	GB	N	1	0		0	0	0	6

Pete Larson

Year	Team		TD	1XP	2XP	FG	FGA	SAF	Pts
1967	WAS	N	1	0		0	0	0	6
1968			2	0		0	0	0	12
Career			3	0		0	0	0	18

Yale Lary

Year	Team		TD	1XP	2XP	FG	FGA	SAF	Pts
1952	DET	N	1	0		0	0	0	6
1953			1	0		0	0	0	6
1956			1	0		0	0	0	6

Yale Lary *continued*

Year	Team		TD	1XP	2XP	FG	FGA	SAF	Pts
1958			1	0		0	0	0	6
1959			1	0		0	0	0	6
1963			1	0		0	0	0	6
Career			6	0		0	0	0	36

Johnny Lascari

Year	Team		TD	1XP	2XP	FG	FGA	SAF	Pts
1942	NYG	N	1	0		0	1	0	6

Jim Lash

Year	Team		TD	1XP	2XP	FG	FGA	SAF	Pts
1975	MIN	N	4	0		0	0	0	24
Playoffs			1	0	0	0	0	0	6

Tim Lashar

Year	Team		TD	1XP	2XP	FG	FGA	SAF	Pts
1987	CHI	N	0	10		3	4	0	19

Derrick Lassic

Year	Team		TD	1XP	2XP	FG	FGA	SAF	Pts
1993	DAL	N	3	0		0	0	0	18

Lamar Lathon

Year	Team		TD	1XP	2XP	FG	FGA	SAF	Pts
1991	HOU	N	1	0		0	0	0	6
1994			0	0	0	0	0	1	2
Career			1	0	0	0	0	1	8

Don Latimer

Year	Team		TD	1XP	2XP	FG	FGA	SAF	Pts
1980	DEN	N	1	0		0	0	0	6

Jerry Latin

Year	Team		TD	1XP	2XP	FG	FGA	SAF	Pts
1975	STL	N	1	0		0	0	0	6
1976			1	0		0	0	0	6
1977			2	0		0	0	0	12
Career			4	0		0	0	0	24

Tony Latone

Year	Team		TD	1XP	2XP	FG	FGA	SAF	Pts
1925	POT	N	**8**	0		0		0	48
1926			4	0		0		0	24
1928			3	0		0		0	18
1929	BOS	N	9	0		0		0	54
1930	PRO	N	3	0		0		0	18
Career			27	0		0		0	162

Chuck Latourette

Year	Team		TD	1XP	2XP	FG	FGA	SAF	Pts
1968	STL	N	1	0		0	0	0	6
1970			1	0		0	0	0	6
Career			2	0		0	0	0	12

Greg Latta

Year	Team		TD	1XP	2XP	FG	FGA	SAF	Pts
1975	CHI	N	3	0		0	0	0	18
1977			4	0		0	0	0	24
Career			7	0		0	0	0	42

Johnny Lattner

Year	Team		TD	1XP	2XP	FG	FGA	SAF	Pts
1954	PIT	N	7	0		0	0	0	42

Hal Lauer

Year	Team		TD	1XP	2XP	FG	FGA	SAF	Pts
1922	RI	N	5	1		0		0	31
1926	DET	N	1	0		0		0	6
Career			6	1		0		0	37

Ted Laux

Year	Team		TD	1XP	2XP	FG	FGA	SAF	Pts
1943	P-P	N	0	2		0	0	0	2

Dante Lavelli

Year	Team		TD	1XP	2XP	FG	FGA	SAF	Pts
1946	CLE	AA	8	0		0	0	0	48
1947			9	0		0	0	0	54
1948			5	0		0	0	0	30
1949			7	0		0	0	0	42
1950	CLE	N	5	0		0	0	0	30
1951			6	0		0	0	0	36
1952			4	0		0	0	0	24
1953			6	0		0	0	0	36
1954			7	0		0	0	0	42
1955			4	0		0	0	0	24
1956			1	0		0	0	0	6
Career			62	0		0	0	0	372
Playoffs			5	0		0	0	0	30

Joe Lavender

Year	Team		TD	1XP	2XP	FG	FGA	SAF	Pts
1974	PHI	N	2	0		0	0	0	12
1975			1	0		0	0	0	6
1980	WAS	N	1	0		0	0	0	6
Career			4	0		0	0	0	24

Robert Lavette

Year	Team		TD	1XP	2XP	FG	FGA	SAF	Pts
1986	DAL	N	1	0		0	0	0	6

Ty Law

Year	Team		TD	1XP	2XP	FG	FGA	SAF	Pts
1996	NE	N	1	0	0	0	0	0	6

Al Lawler

Year	Team		TD	1XP	2XP	FG	FGA	SAF	Pts
1948	CHIB	N	0	3		1	1	0	6

Amos Lawrence

Year	Team		TD	1XP	2XP	FG	FGA	SAF	Pts
1981	SF	N	2	0		0	0	0	12

Jimmy Lawrence

Year	Team		TD	1XP	2XP	FG	FGA	SAF	Pts
1937	CHIC	N	1	0		0		0	6
1938			3	0		0		0	18
Career			4	0		0		0	24

Rolland Lawrence

Year	Team		TD	1XP	2XP	FG	FGA	SAF	Pts
1975	ATL	N	1	0		0	0	0	6
1979			1	0		0	0	0	6
Career			2	0		0	0	0	12

Joe Laws

Year	Team		TD	1XP	2XP	FG	FGA	SAF	Pts
1934	GB	N	2	0		0		0	12
1935			1	0		0		0	6
1936			3	0		0		0	18
1937			2	0		0		0	12
1938			2	0		0		0	12
1939			4	0		0	0	0	24
1940			1	0		0	0	0	6
1941			1	0		0	0	0	6
1942			1	0		0	0	0	6
1944			4	0		0	0	0	24
Career			21	0		0	0	0	126
Playoffs			1	0		0	0	0	6

Jim Lawson

Year	Team		TD	1XP	2XP	FG	FGA	SAF	Pts
1926	LA	A	0	4		2		0	10

Roger Lawson

Year	Team		TD	1XP	2XP	FG	FGA	SAF	Pts
1972	CHI	N	1	0		0	0	0	6

Pete Layden

Year	Team		TD	1XP	2XP	FG	FGA	SAF	Pts
1948	NY	AA	3	0		0	0	0	18
1949	B-NY	AA	1	0		0	0	0	6
1950	NYY	N	0	3		0	0	0	3
Career			4	3		0	0	0	27

Bobby Layne

Year	Team		TD	1XP	2XP	FG	FGA	SAF	Pts
1948	CHIB	N	1	0		0	1	0	6
1949	NYB	N	3	0		0	0	0	18
1950	DET	N	4	1		0	0	0	25
1951			1	0		0	0	0	6
1952			1	2		0	0	0	8
1954			2	0		0	0	0	12
1956			5	33		12	15	0	**99**
1957			0	25		6	11	0	43
1958	DET-PIT	N	3	1		0	0	0	19
1959	PIT	N	2	32		11	17	0	77
1960			2	21		5	6	0	48
1961			0	5		0	0	0	5
1962			1	0		0	0	0	6
Career			25	120		34	50	0	372
Playoffs			1	0		0	0	0	6

Bill Lazetich

Year	Team		TD	1XP	2XP	FG	FGA	SAF	Pts
1939	CLE	N	1	0		0	0	0	6
1942			2	0		0	0	0	12
Career			3	0		0	0	0	18

Pat Leahy

Year	Team		TD	1XP	2XP	FG	FGA	SAF	Pts
1974	NYJ	N	0	18		6	11	0	36
1975			0	27		13	21	0	66
1976			0	16		11	16	0	49
1977			0	18		15	25	0	63
1978			0	41		22	30	0	107
1979			0	12		8	13	0	36
1980			0	36		14	22	0	78
1981			0	38		25	36	0	113
1982			0	26		11	17	0	59
1983			0	36		16	24	0	84
1984			0	38		17	24	0	89
1985			0	43		26	34	0	121
1986			0	44		16	19	0	92

Pat Leahy *continued*

Year	Team		TD	1XP	2XP	FG	FGA	SAF	Pts
1987			0	31		18	22	0	85
1988			0	43		23	28	0	112
1989			0	29		14	21	0	71
1990			0	32		23	26	0	101
1991			0	30		26	37	0	108
Career			0	558		304	426	0	1470
Playoffs			0	19		8	10	0	43

Roosevelt Leaks

Year	Team		TD	1XP	2XP	FG	FGA	SAF	Pts
1975	**BAL**	**N**	1	0		0	0	0	6
1976			7	0		0	0	0	42
1977			4	0		0	0	0	24
1978			4	0		0	0	0	24
1979			1	0		0	0	0	6
1980	**BUF**	**N**	3	0		0	0	0	18
1981			6	0		0	0	0	36
1982			5	0		0	0	0	30
1983			1	0		0	0	0	6
Career			32	0		0	0	0	192
Playoffs			2	0		0	0	0	12

Tom Leary

Year	Team		TD	1XP	2XP	FG	FGA	SAF	Pts
1929	**SI**	**N**	2	0		0		1	14
1930	**NEW**	**N**	2	0		0		0	12
Career			4	0		0		1	26

Allan Leavitt

Year	Team		TD	1XP	2XP	FG	FGA	SAF	Pts
1977	**TB**	**N**	0	5		5	10	0	20

Eddie LeBaron

Year	Team		TD	1XP	2XP	FG	FGA	SAF	Pts
1952	**WAS**	**N**	2	6		0	0	0	18
1953			2	0		0	0	0	12
1955			4	0		0	0	0	24
1960	**DAL**	**N**	1	0		0	0	0	6
Career			9	6		0	0	0	60

Dick LeBeau

Year	Team		TD	1XP	2XP	FG	FGA	SAF	Pts
1962	**DET**	**N**	2	0		0	0	0	12
1963			1	0		0	0	0	6
1965			1	0		0	0	0	6
Career			4	0		0	0	0	24

Mike LeBlanc

Year	Team		TD	1XP	2XP	FG	FGA	SAF	Pts
1987	**NE**	**N**	1	0		0	0	0	6

Bill Leckonby

Year	Team		TD	1XP	2XP	FG	FGA	SAF	Pts
1940	**BKN**	**N**	2	0		0	0	0	12
1941			1	0		0	0	0	6
Career			3	0		0	0	0	18

Jim LeClair

Year	Team		TD	1XP	2XP	FG	FGA	SAF	Pts
1967	**DEN**	**A**	1	0	0	0	0	0	6

Jim LeClair

Year	Team		TD	1XP	2XP	FG	FGA	SAF	Pts
1979	**CIN**	**N**	1	0		0	0	0	6

Roger LeClerc

Year	Team		TD	1XP	2XP	FG	FGA	SAF	Pts
1961	**CHI**	**N**	0	40		10	24	0	70
1962			0	36		13	27	0	75
1963			0	0		13	23	0	39
1964			0	0		10	16	0	30
1965			0	**52**		11	26	0	85
1966			0	24		18	30	0	78
1967	**DEN**	**A**	0	2	0	1	6	0	5
Career			0	154	0	76	152	0	382
Playoffs			0	0	0	0	2	0	0

Terry LeCount

Year	Team		TD	1XP	2XP	FG	FGA	SAF	Pts
1979	**MIN**	**N**	2	0		0	0	0	12
1981			2	0		0	0	0	12
1982			1	0		0	0	0	6
1983			2	0		0	0	0	12
Career			7	0		0	0	0	42

Homer Ledbetter

Year	Team		TD	1XP	2XP	FG	FGA	SAF	Pts
1932	**SI**	**N**	2	0		0		0	12

Monte Ledbetter

Year	Team		TD	1XP	2XP	FG	FGA	SAF	Pts
1967	**HOU-BUF**	**A**	2	0	0	0	0	0	12
1968	**BUF**	**A**	1	0	0	0	0	0	6
Career			3	0	0	0	0	0	18

Toy Ledbetter

Year	Team		TD	1XP	2XP	FG	FGA	SAF	Pts
1950	**PHI**	**N**	3	0		0	0	0	18
1953			3	0		0	0	0	18
1954			4	0		0	0	0	24
1955			1	0		0	0	0	6
Career			11	0		0	0	0	66

Amp Lee

Year	Team		TD	1XP	2XP	FG	FGA	SAF	Pts
1992	**SF**	**N**	4	0		0	0	0	24
1993			3	0		0	0	0	18
1994	**MIN**	**N**	2	0	0	0	0	0	12
1995			3	0	0	0	0	0	18
1996			2	0	0	0	0	0	12
Career			14	0	0	0	0	0	84
Playoffs			1	0	0	0	0	0	6

Bob Lee

Year	Team		TD	1XP	2XP	FG	FGA	SAF	Pts
1970	**MIN**	**N**	1	0		0	0	0	6
1971			1	0		0	0	0	6
1974	**ATL**	**N**	1	0		0	0	0	6
Career			3	0		0	0	0	18

Carl Lee

Year	Team		TD	1XP	2XP	FG	FGA	SAF	Pts
1988	**MIN**	**N**	2	0		0	0	0	12

Gary Lee

Year	Team		TD	1XP	2XP	FG	FGA	SAF	Pts
1988	**DET**	**N**	1	0		0	0	0	6

Hilary Lee

Year	Team		TD	1XP	2XP	FG	FGA	SAF	Pts
1933	**CIN**	**N**	0	0		1		0	3
1934	**C-S**	**N**	0	1		0		0	1
Career			0	1		1		0	4

Jacky Lee

Year	Team		TD	1XP	2XP	FG	FGA	SAF	Pts
1964	**DEN**	**A**	3	0	0	0	0	0	18

John Lee

Year	Team		TD	1XP	2XP	FG	FGA	SAF	Pts
1986	**STL**	**N**	0	14		8	13	0	38

Ken Lee

Year	Team		TD	1XP	2XP	FG	FGA	SAF	Pts
1972	**BUF**	**N**	1	0		0	0	0	6

Mark Lee

Year	Team		TD	1XP	2XP	FG	FGA	SAF	Pts
1981	**GB**	**N**	1	0		0	0	0	6
Playoffs			1	0	0	0	0	0	6

Ron Lee

Year	Team		TD	1XP	2XP	FG	FGA	SAF	Pts
1976	**BAL**	**N**	1	0		0	0	0	6
1977			3	0		0	0	0	18
1978			2	0		0	0	0	12
Career			6	0		0	0	0	36
Playoffs			2	0		0	0	0	12

Ronnie Lee

Year	Team		TD	1XP	2XP	FG	FGA	SAF	Pts
1980	**MIA**	**N**	2	0		0	0	0	12
1981			1	0		0	0	0	6
Career			3	0		0	0	0	18
Playoffs			1	0		0	0	0	6

Willie Lee

Year	Team		TD	1XP	2XP	FG	FGA	SAF	Pts
1977	**KC**	**N**	1	0		0	0	0	6

Tuffy Leemans

Year	Team		TD	1XP	2XP	FG	FGA	SAF	Pts
1936	**NYG**	**N**	2	0		0		0	12
1937			1	0		0		0	6
1938			4	0		0		0	24
1939			5	0		0	0	0	30
1940			1	0		0	0	0	6
1941			4	0		0	0	0	24
1942			3	0		0	0	0	18
Career			20	0		0	0	0	120
Playoffs			1	0		0	0	0	6

Gil LeFebvre

Year	Team		TD	1XP	2XP	FG	FGA	SAF	Pts
1933	**CIN**	**N**	1	0		0		0	6

Clyde LeForce

Year	Team		TD	1XP	2XP	FG	FGA	SAF	Pts
1948	**DET**	**N**	5	0		0	0	0	30
1949			1	0		0	0	0	6
Career			6	0		0	0	0	36

Dick Leftridge

Year	Team		TD	1XP	2XP	FG	FGA	SAF	Pts
1966	**PIT**	**N**	2	0		0	0	0	12

Earl Leggett

Year	Team		TD	1XP	2XP	FG	FGA	SAF	Pts
1959	**CHIB**	**N**	0	0		0	0	1	2

Chris Lehrer

Year	Team		TD	1XP	2XP	FG	FGA	SAF	Pts
1921	**SYR**	**A**	0	1		0		0	1

Jake Leicht

Year	Team		TD	1XP	2XP	FG	FGA	SAF	Pts
1948	**BAL**	**AA**	2	0		0	0	0	12

Jeff Leiding

Year	Team		TD	1XP	2XP	FG	FGA	SAF	Pts
1986	**IND**	**N**	0	0		0	0	1	2
1987			0	0		0	0	1	2
Career			0	0		0	0	2	4

Charlie Leigh

Year	Team		TD	1XP	2XP	FG	FGA	SAF	Pts
1968	**CLE**	**N**	1	0		0	0	0	6
1973	**MIA**	**N**	1	0		0	0	0	6
Career			2	0		0	0	0	12

Walt LeJeune

Year	Team		TD	1XP	2XP	FG	FGA	SAF	Pts
1922	**AKR**	**N**	4	0		0		0	24

Frank LeMaster

Year	Team		TD	1XP	2XP	FG	FGA	SAF	Pts
1975	**PHI**	**N**	1	0		0	0	0	6
1978			1	0		0	0	0	6
1981			1	0		0	0	0	6
Career			3	0		0	0	0	18

Bruce Lemmerman

Year	Team		TD	1XP	2XP	FG	FGA	SAF	Pts
1969	**ATL**	**N**	1	0		0	0	0	6

Lawren Lentz

Year	Team		TD	1XP	2XP	FG	FGA	SAF	Pts
1920	**DAY**	**A**	1	0		0		0	6

Bobby Leo

Year	Team		TD	1XP	2XP	FG	FGA	SAF	Pts
1967	**BOS**	**A**	1	0	0	0	0	0	6

Jim Leo

Year	Team		TD	1XP	2XP	FG	FGA	SAF	Pts
1962	**MIN**	**N**	0	0		0	0	1	2

Jim Leonard

Year	Team		TD	1XP	2XP	FG	FGA	SAF	Pts
1934	**PHI**	**N**	1	0		0		0	6
1935			1	0		0		0	6
1936			1	0		0		0	6
Career			3	0		0		0	18

Tony Leonard

Year	Team		TD	1XP	2XP	FG	FGA	SAF	Pts
1976	**SF**	**N**	1	0		0	0	0	6
1978			1	0		0	0	0	6
Career			2	0		0	0	0	12

Darrell Lester

Year	Team		TD	1XP	2XP	FG	FGA	SAF	Pts
1966	**DEN**	**A**	1	0	0	0	0	0	6

Tim Lester

Year	Team		TD	1XP	2XP	FG	FGA	SAF	Pts
1995	**PIT**	**N**	1	0	0	0	0	0	6
1996			1	0	0	0	0	0	6
Career			2	0	0	0	0	0	12

Dorsey Levens

Year	Team		TD	1XP	2XP	FG	FGA	SAF	Pts
1995	**GB**	**N**	7	0	0	0	0	0	42
1996			10	0	0	0	0	0	60
Career			17	0	0	0	0	0	102
Playoffs			3	0	0	0	0	0	18

Jim Levey

Year	Team		TD	1XP	2XP	FG	FGA	SAF	Pts
1935	**PIT**	**N**	4	0		0		0	24

Jerry LeVias

Year	Team		TD	1XP	2XP	FG	FGA	SAF	Pts
1969	**HOU**	**A**	5	0	0	0	0	0	30
1970	**HOU**	**N**	5	0		0	0	0	30
1971	**SD**	**N**	1	0		0	0	0	6
1973			3	0		0	0	0	18
Career			14	0	0	0	0	0	84

Len Levy

Year	Team		TD	1XP	2XP	FG	FGA	SAF	Pts
1946	**LA**	**N**	1	0		0	0	0	6

Verne Lewellen

Year	Team		TD	1XP	2XP	FG	FGA	SAF	Pts
1924	**GB**	**N**	2	0		0		0	12
1925			4	1		0		0	25
1926			7	0		0		0	42
1927			5	0		0		0	30

Verne Lewellen *continued*

Year	Team	TD	1XP	2XP	FG	FGA	SAF	Pts
1928		9	0		0		0	54
1929		8	1		0		0	49
1930		9	0		0		0	54
1931		6	0		0		0	36
1932		1	0		0		0	6
Career		51	2		0		0	308

Albert Lewis

Year	Team	TD	1XP	2XP	FG	FGA	SAF	Pts
1985	KC N	1	0	0	0	0	0	6
1988		0	0	0	0	0	1	2
1993		1	0	0	0	0	0	6
Career		2	0	0	0	0	1	14
Playoffs		1	0	0	0	0		6

Art Lewis

Year	Team	TD	1XP	2XP	FG	FGA	SAF	Pts
1921	CIN A	0	1		0		0	1

Art Lewis

Year	Team	TD	1XP	2XP	FG	FGA	SAF	Pts
1936	NYG N	1	0		0		0	6

Cliff Lewis

Year	Team	TD	1XP	2XP	FG	FGA	SAF	Pts
1949	CLE AA	1	0		0		0	6

Danny Lewis

Year	Team	TD	1XP	2XP	FG	FGA	SAF	Pts
1959	DET N	2	0	0	0	0	0	12
1960		2	0	0	0	0	0	12
1961		4	0	0	0	0	0	24
1962		7	0	0	0	0	0	42
1963		2	0	0	0	0	0	12
1964		2	0	0	0	0	0	12
1965	WAS N	4	0	0	0	0	0	24
1966	NYG N	1	0	0	0	0	0	6
Career		24	0	0	0	0	0	144

Darren Lewis

Year	Team	TD	1XP	2XP	FG	FGA	SAF	Pts
1992	CHI N	5	0	0	0	0	0	30

Darryll Lewis

Year	Team	TD	1XP	2XP	FG	FGA	SAF	Pts
1991	HOU N	1	0	0	0	0	0	6
1993		1	0	0	0	0	0	6
1995		1	0	0	0	0	0	6
1996		1	0	0	0	0	0	6
Career		4	0	0	0	0	0	24

Dave Lewis

Year	Team	TD	1XP	2XP	FG	FGA	SAF	Pts
1979	TB N	1	0	0	0	0	0	6

David Lewis

Year	Team	TD	1XP	2XP	FG	FGA	SAF	Pts
1984	DET N	3	0	0	0	0	0	18
1985		3	0	0	0	0	0	18
1986		1	0	0	0	0	0	6
1987	MIA N	1	0	0	0	0	0	6
Career		8	0	0	0	0	0	48

D.D. Lewis

Year	Team	TD	1XP	2XP	FG	FGA	SAF	Pts
1973	DAL N	1	0	0	0	0	0	6

Ernie Lewis

Year	Team	TD	1XP	2XP	FG	FGA	SAF	Pts
1946	CHI AA	1	0	0	0	0	0	6
1949		1	0	0	0	0	0	6
Career		2	0	0	0	0	0	12

Frank Lewis

Year	Team	TD	1XP	2XP	FG	FGA	SAF	Pts
1972	PIT N	5	0	0	0	0	0	30
1973		3	0	0	0	0	0	18
1974		4	0	0	0	0	0	24
1975		2	0	0	0	0	0	12
1976		2	0	0	0	0	0	12
1977		1	0	0	0	0	0	6
1978	BUF N	7	0	0	0	0	0	42
1979		2	0	0	0	0	0	12
1980		6	0	0	0	0	0	36
1981		4	0	0	0	0	0	24
1982		2	0	0	0	0	0	12
1983		3	0	0	0	0	0	18
Career		41	0	0	0	0	0	246
Playoffs		5	0		0	0		30

Gary Lewis

Year	Team	TD	1XP	2XP	FG	FGA	SAF	Pts
1964	SF N	1	0	0	0	0	0	6
1965		3	0	0	0	0	0	18
1966		3	0	0	0	0	0	18
1967		7	0	0	0	0	0	42
1968		4	0	0	0	0	0	24
Career		18	0	0	0	0	0	108

Gary Lewis

Year	Team	TD	1XP	2XP	FG	FGA	SAF	Pts
1983	GB N	2	0	0	0	0	0	12

Greg Lewis

Year	Team	TD	1XP	2XP	FG	FGA	SAF	Pts
1991	DEN N	4	0	0	0	0	0	24
1992		4	0	0	0	0	0	24
Career		8	0	0	0	0	0	48
Playoffs		2	0	0	0	0	0	12

Jermaine Lewis

Year	Team	TD	1XP	2XP	FG	FGA	SAF	Pts
1996	BAL N	1	0	0	0	0	0	6

Joe Lewis

Year	Team	TD	1XP	2XP	FG	FGA	SAF	Pts
1960	PIT N	1	0	0	0	0	0	6

Leo Lewis

Year	Team	TD	1XP	2XP	FG	FGA	SAF	Pts
1982	MIN N	3	0	0	0	0	0	18
1984		4	0	0	0	0	0	24
1985		3	0	0	0	0	0	18
1986		2	0	0	0	0	0	12
1987		3	0	0	0	0	0	18
1988		1	0	0	0	0	0	6
1989		1	0	0	0	0	0	6
Career		17	0	0	0	0	0	102
Playoffs		1	0	0	0	0	0	6

Mark Lewis

Year	Team	TD	1XP	2XP	FG	FGA	SAF	Pts
1986	GB N	2	0	0	0	0	0	12
1988	DET N	1	0	0	0	0	0	6
Career		3	0	0	0	0	0	18

Mike Lewis

Year	Team	TD	1XP	2XP	FG	FGA	SAF	Pts
1972	ATL N	0	0	0	0	0	1	2
1979		0	0	0	0	0	1	2
Career		0	0	0	0	0	2	4

Mo Lewis

Year	Team	TD	1XP	2XP	FG	FGA	SAF	Pts
1994	NYJ N	2	0	0	0	0	0	12
1995		1	0	0	0	0	0	6
Career		3	0	0	0	0	0	18

Nate Lewis

Year	Team	TD	1XP	2XP	FG	FGA	SAF	Pts
1990	SD N	3	0	0	0	0	0	18
1991		4	0	0	0	0	0	24
1992		4	0	0	0	0	0	24
1993		4	0	0	0	0	0	24
1994	CHI N	1	0	0	0	0	0	6
Career		16	0	0	0	0	0	96

Reggie Lewis

Year	Team	TD	1XP	2XP	FG	FGA	SAF	Pts
1983	NO N	1	0	0	0	0	0	6

Thomas Lewis

Year	Team	TD	1XP	2XP	FG	FGA	SAF	Pts
1995	NYG N	2	0	0	0	0	0	12
1996		4	0	0	0	0	0	24
Career		6	0	0	0	0	0	36

Tim Lewis

Year	Team	TD	1XP	2XP	FG	FGA	SAF	Pts
1984	GB N	1	0	0	0	0	0	6
1985		1	0	0	0	0	0	6
Career		2	0	0	0	0	0	12

Tiny Lewis

Year	Team	TD	1XP	2XP	FG	FGA	SAF	Pts
1930	POR N	2	10		0		0	22

Will Lewis

Year	Team	TD	1XP	2XP	FG	FGA	SAF	Pts
1980	SEA N	1	0	0	0	0		6

Woodley Lewis

Year	Team	TD	1XP	2XP	FG	FGA	SAF	Pts
1950	LA N	1	0	0	0	0		6
1952		2	0	0	0	0		12
1953		2	0	0	0	0		12
1954		1	0	0	0	0		6
1957	CHIC N	5	0	0	0	0		30
1958		4	0	0	0	0		24
1959		3	0	0	0	0		18
Career		18	0	0	0	0		108

John Leypoldt

Year	Team	TD	1XP	2XP	FG	FGA	SAF	Pts
1971	BUF N	0	12		9	15	0	39
1972		0	29		16	24	0	77
1973		0	27		21	30	0	90
1974		0	25		19	33	0	82
1975		0	51		9	16	0	78
1976	BUF-SEA N	0	22		8	15	0	46
1977	SEA N	0	33		9	18	0	60
1978	NO N	0	4		2	3	0	10
Career		0	203		93	154	0	482
Playoffs		0	2		0	0	0	2

Carl Lidberg

Year	Team	TD	1XP	2XP	FG	FGA	SAF	Pts
1926	GB N	4	0		0		0	24
1929		2	0		0		0	12
1930		1	0		0		0	6
Career		7	0		0		0	42

Frank Liebel

Year	Team	TD	1XP	2XP	FG	FGA	SAF	Pts
1943	NYG N	3	0	0	0	0	0	18
1944		6	0	0	0	0	0	36
1945		10	0	0	0	0	0	60
1946		4	0	0	0	0	0	24
1947		1	0	0	0	0	0	6
Career		24	0	0	0	0	0	144
Playoffs		1	0	0	0	0	0	6

Joe Lillard

Year	Team	TD	1XP	2XP	FG	FGA	SAF	Pts
1932	CHIC N	0	2		0	0		2
1933		2	1		2	0		19
Career		2	3		2	0		21

Bob Lilly

Year	Team	TD	1XP	2XP	FG	FGA	SAF	Pts
1963	DAL N	1	0	0	0	0	0	6
1965		1	0	0	0	0	0	6
1969		1	0	0	0	0	0	6
1971		1	0	0	0	0	0	6
Career		4	0	0	0	0	0	24

Verl Lillywhite

Year	Team	TD	1XP	2XP	FG	FGA	SAF	Pts
1948	SF AA	3	0	0	0	0	0	18
1949		4	0	0	0	0	0	24
1951	SF N	2	0	0	0	0	0	12
Career		9	0	0	0	0	0	54
Playoffs		1	0	0	0	0	0	6

Jeremy Lincoln

Year	Team	TD	1XP	2XP	FG	FGA	SAF	Pts
1993	CHI N	1	0		0	0	0	6

Keith Lincoln

Year	Team	TD	1XP	2XP	FG	FGA	SAF	Pts
1961	SD A	3	0	0	0	0	0	18
1962		4	0	0	0	0	0	24
1963		8	0	0	0	0	0	48
1964		6	16	0	5	12	0	67
1965		7	0	0	0	0	0	42
1966		3	0	0	0	0	0	18
1967	BUF A	9	0	0	0	0	0	54
Career		40	16	0	5	12	0	271
Playoffs		2	1		0	0	0	13

Mike Lind

Year	Team	TD	1XP	2XP	FG	FGA	SAF	Pts
1964	SF N	7	0		0	0	0	42
1965	PIT N	2	0		0	0	0	12
Career		9	0		0	0	0	54

Dale Lindsey

Year	Team	TD	1XP	2XP	FG	FGA	SAF	Pts
1970	CLE N	1	0	0	0	0	0	6
Playoffs		1	0	0	0	0	0	6

Jim Lindsey

Year	Team	TD	1XP	2XP	FG	FGA	SAF	Pts
1966	MIN N	3	0		0	0	0	18
1968		4	0		0	0	0	24
1969		2	0		0	0	0	12
1970		1	0		0	0	0	6
1971		1	0		0	0	0	6
Career		11	0		0	0	0	66

Menz Lindsey

Year	Team	TD	1XP	2XP	FG	FGA	SAF	Pts
1921	EVA A	2	0		0		0	12

Vic Lindskog

Year	Team	TD	1XP	2XP	FG	FGA	SAF	Pts
1944	PHI N	1	0		0	0	0	6

Toni Linhart

Year	Team		TD	1XP	2XP	FG	FGA	SAF	Pts
1972	NO	N	0	5		2	5	0	11
1974	BAL	N	0	22		12	20	0	58
1975			0	**51**		10	18	0	81
1976			0	**49**		20	27	0	109
1977			0	32		17	26	0	83
1978			0	27		8	17	0	51
1979	BAL-NYJ	N	0	14		6	14	0	32
Career			0	200		75	127	0	425
Playoffs			0	7		2	2	0	13

Larry Linne

Year	Team		TD	1XP	2XP	FG	FGA	SAF	Pts
1987	NE	N	2	0		0	0	0	12

Joe Lintzenich

Year	Team		TD	1XP	2XP	FG	FGA	SAF	Pts
1931	CHIB	N	2	0		0		0	12

Augie Lio

Year	Team		TD	1XP	2XP	FG	FGA	SAF	Pts
1941	DET	N	1	12		0	5	0	18
1942			0	5		0	4	0	5
1943			0	21		2	**11**	0	27
1944	BOS	N	0	10		2	8	0	16
1945			0	15		4	5	0	27
1946	PHI	N	1	27		6	11	0	51
1947	BAL	AA	0	19		3	8	0	28
Career			2	109		17	52	0	172

Ronnie Lippett

Year	Team		TD	1XP	2XP	FG	FGA	SAF	Pts
1987	NE	N	2	0		0	0	0	12

Louis Lipps

Year	Team		TD	1XP	2XP	FG	FGA	SAF	Pts
1984	PIT	N	11	0		0	0	0	66
1985			15	0		0	0	0	90
1986			3	0		0	0	0	18
1988			6	0		0	0	0	36
1989			6	0		0	0	0	36
1990			3	0		0	0	0	18
1991			2	0		0	0	0	12
Career			46	0		0	0	0	276
Playoffs			2	0		0	0	0	12

Gene Lipscomb

Year	Team		TD	1XP	2XP	FG	FGA	SAF	Pts
1960	BAL	N	0	0		0	0	1	2

Don Lisbon

Year	Team		TD	1XP	2XP	FG	FGA	SAF	Pts
1963	SF	N	2	0		0	0	0	12
1964			1	0		0	0	0	6
Career			3	0		0	0	0	18

Pete Liske

Year	Team		TD	1XP	2XP	FG	FGA	SAF	Pts
1970	DEN	N	1	0		0	0	0	6
1971	PHI	N	1	0		0	0	0	6
Career			2	0		0	0	0	12

David Little

Year	Team		TD	1XP	2XP	FG	FGA	SAF	Pts
1985	PHI	N	1	0		0	0	0	6

Floyd Little

Year	Team		TD	1XP	2XP	FG	FGA	SAF	Pts
1967	DEN	A	2	0	0	0	0	0	12
1968			5	0	0	0	0	0	30
1969			7	0	0	0	0	0	42
1970	DEN	N	3	0		0	0	0	18
1971			6	0		0	0	0	36
1972			13	0		0	0	0	78
1973			13	0		0	0	0	78
1974			1	0		0	0	0	6
1975			4	0		0	0	0	24
1989	PHI	N	1	0		0	0	0	6
Career			55	0	0	0	0	0	330

Steve Little

Year	Team		TD	1XP	2XP	FG	FGA	SAF	Pts
1979	STL	N	0	24		10	19	0	54
1980			0	17		3	8	0	26
Career			0	41		13	27	0	80

Carl Littlefield

Year	Team		TD	1XP	2XP	FG	FGA	SAF	Pts
1938	CLE	N	1	0		0	0	0	6

Joe Little Twig

Year	Team		TD	1XP	2XP	FG	FGA	SAF	Pts
1923	OOR	N	0	1		0		0	1
1924	RI	N	1	0		0		0	6
1925			1	0		0		0	6
Career			2	1		0		0	13

Virgil Livers

Year	Team		TD	1XP	2XP	FG	FGA	SAF	Pts
1975	CHI	N	1	0		0	0	0	6
1978			1	0		0	0	0	6
Career			2	0		0	0	0	12

Andy Livingston

Year	Team		TD	1XP	2XP	FG	FGA	SAF	Pts
1964	CHI	N	1	0		0	0	0	6
1965			2	0		0	0	0	12
1969	NO	N	8	0		0	0	0	48
Career			11	0		0	0	0	66

Cliff Livingston

Year	Team		TD	1XP	2XP	FG	FGA	SAF	Pts
1955	NYG	N	1	0		0	0	0	6

Dale Livingston

Year	Team		TD	1XP	2XP	FG	FGA	SAF	Pts
1968	CIN	A	0	20	0	13	26	0	59
1970	GB	N	0	19		15	28	0	64
Career			0	39	0	28	54	0	123

Howie Livingston

Year	Team		TD	1XP	2XP	FG	FGA	SAF	Pts
1944	NYG	N	3	0		0	0	0	18
1945			5	0		0	0	0	30
1946			3	0		0	0	0	18
1947			3	0		0	0	0	18
1949	WAS	N	1	0		0	0	0	6
1950	WAS-SF	N	5	0		0	0	0	30
Career			20	0		0	0	0	120

Mike Livingston

Year	Team		TD	1XP	2XP	FG	FGA	SAF	Pts
1973	KC	N	2	0		0	0	0	12
1975			2	0		0	0	0	12
1976			2	0		0	0	0	12
1977			1	0		0	0	0	6
1978			1	0		0	0	0	6
Career			8	0		0	0	0	48

Walt Livingston

Year	Team		TD	1XP	2XP	FG	FGA	SAF	Pts
1960	BOS	A	1	0	0	0	0	0	6

Warren Livingston

Year	Team		TD	1XP	2XP	FG	FGA	SAF	Pts
1964	DAL	N	1	0		0	0	0	6

Bob Livingstone

Year	Team		TD	1XP	2XP	FG	FGA	SAF	Pts
1948	CHI	AA	2	0		0	0	0	12
1949	BUF	AA	1	0		0	0	0	6
Career			3	0		0	0	0	18

Dave Lloyd

Year	Team		TD	1XP	2XP	FG	FGA	SAF	Pts
1965	PHI	N	0	7		1	2	0	10

Charles Lockett

Year	Team		TD	1XP	2XP	FG	FGA	SAF	Pts
1987	PIT	N	1	0		0	0	0	6
1988			1	0		0	0	0	6
Career			2	0		0	0	0	12

J.W. Lockett

Year	Team		TD	1XP	2XP	FG	FGA	SAF	Pts
1961	SF-DAL	N	3	0		0	0	0	18
1962	DAL	N	3	0		0	0	0	18
1963	BAL	N	1	0		0	0	0	6
1964	WAS	N	3	0		0	0	0	18
Career			10	0		0	0	0	60

Eugene Lockhart

Year	Team		TD	1XP	2XP	FG	FGA	SAF	Pts
1985	DAL	N	1	0		0	0	0	6
1989			1	0		0	0	0	6
Career			2	0		0	0	0	12

Spider Lockhart

Year	Team		TD	1XP	2XP	FG	FGA	SAF	Pts
1968	NYG	N	2	0		0	0	0	12
1972			1	0		0	0	0	6
Career			3	0		0	0	0	18

Mike Lodish

Year	Team		TD	1XP	2XP	FG	FGA	SAF	Pts
1992	BUF	N	1	0		0	0	0	6
1994			1	0	0	0	0	0	6
Career			2	0	0	0	0	0	12

James Lofton

Year	Team		TD	1XP	2XP	FG	FGA	SAF	Pts
1978	GB	N	6	0		0	0	0	36
1979			4	0		0	0	0	24
1980			4	0		0	0	0	24
1981			8	0		0	0	0	48
1982			5	0		0	0	0	30
1983			8	0		0	0	0	48

James Lofton *continued*

Year	Team		TD	1XP	2XP	FG	FGA	SAF	Pts
1984			7	0		0	0	0	42
1985			4	0		0	0	0	24
1986			4	0		0	0	0	24
1987	LARI	N	5	0		0	0	0	30
1989	BUF	N	3	0		0	0	0	18
1990			4	0		0	0	0	24
1991			8	0		0	0	0	48
1992			6	0		0	0	0	36
Career			76	0		0	0	0	456
Playoffs			9	0		0	0	0	54

Oscar Lofton

Year	Team		TD	1XP	2XP	FG	FGA	SAF	Pts
1960	BOS	A	4	0	0	0	0	0	24

Dave Logan

Year	Team		TD	1XP	2XP	FG	FGA	SAF	Pts
1977	CLE	N	1	0		0	0	0	6
1978			4	0		0	0	0	24
1979			7	0		0	0	0	42
1980			4	0		0	0	0	24
1981			4	0		0	0	0	24
1982			2	0		0	0	0	12
1983			2	0		0	0	0	12
Career			24	0		0	0	0	144

Dave Logan

Year	Team		TD	1XP	2XP	FG	FGA	SAF	Pts
1980	TB	N	1	0		0	0	0	6
1981			1	0		0	0	0	6
1983			1	0		0	0	0	6
1984			1	0		0	0	0	6
Career			4	0		0	0	0	24

Jerry Logan

Year	Team		TD	1XP	2XP	FG	FGA	SAF	Pts
1964	BAL	N	1	0		0	0	0	6
1965			2	0		0	0	0	12
1967			1	0		0	0	0	6
1970			2	0		0	0	0	12
Career			6	0		0	0	0	36

Marc Logan

Year	Team		TD	1XP	2XP	FG	FGA	SAF	Pts
1987	CIN	N	1	0		0	0	0	6
1989	MIA	N	2	0		0	0	0	12
1990			2	0		0	0	0	12
1992	SF	N	1	0		0	0	0	6
1993			7	0		0	0	0	42
1994			2	0	0	0	0	0	12
1995	WAS	N	3	0	0	0	0	0	18
1996			2	0	0	0	0	0	12
Career			20	0	0	0	0	0	120
Playoffs			1	0	0	0	0	0	6

Obert Logan

Year	Team		TD	1XP	2XP	FG	FGA	SAF	Pts
1965	DAL	N	1	0		0	0	0	6

John Lohmeyer

Year	Team		TD	1XP	2XP	FG	FGA	SAF	Pts
1973	KC	N	1	0		0	0	0	6
1976			0	0		0	0	1	2
Career			1	0		0	0	1	8

Chip Lohmiller

Year	Team		TD	1XP	2XP	FG	FGA	SAF	Pts
1988	WAS	N	0	40		19	26	0	97
1989			0	41		29	**40**	0	128
1990			0	41		30	**40**	0	131
1991			0	**56**		**31**	**43**	0	**149**
1992			0	30		**30**	**40**	0	120
1993			0	24		16	28	0	72
1994			0	30	0	20	28	0	90
1995	NO	N	0	11	0	8	14	0	35
1996	STL	N	0	28	0	21	25	0	91
Career			0	301	0	204	284	0	913
Playoffs			0	19	0	12	18	0	55

Neil Lomax

Year	Team		TD	1XP	2XP	FG	FGA	SAF	Pts
1981	STL	N	2	0		0	0	0	12
1982			1	0		0	0	0	6
1983			2	0		0	0	0	12
1984			3	0		0	0	0	18
1986			1	0		0	0	0	6
1988	PHX	N	1	0		0	0	0	6
Career			10	0		0	0	0	60

Bob Long

Year	Team		TD	1XP	2XP	FG	FGA	SAF	Pts
1965	GB	N	4	0		0	0	0	24
1968	ATL	N	4	0		0	0	0	24

Bob Long continued

Year	Team	TD	1XP	2XP	FG	FGA	SAF	Pts
1969	WAS N	1	0		0	0	0	6
1970	LA N	1	0		0	0	0	6
Career		10	0		0	0	0	60

Bob Long

Year	Team	TD	1XP	2XP	FG	FGA	SAF	Pts
1955	DET N	0	0		0	0	1	2

Carson Long

Year	Team	TD	1XP	2XP	FG	FGA	SAF	Pts
1977	BUF N	0	13		7	11	0	34

Cutter Long

Year	Team	TD	1XP	2XP	FG	FGA	SAF	Pts
1953	NYG N	2	0		0	0	1	14
1954		2	0		0	0	0	12
1955		1	0		0	0	0	6
Career		5	0		0	0	1	32

Kevin Long

Year	Team	TD	1XP	2XP	FG	FGA	SAF	Pts
1978	NYJ N	10	0		0	0	0	60
1979		7	0		0	0	0	42
1980		6	0		0	0	0	36
1981		5	0		0	0	0	30
Career		28	0		0	0	0	168
Playoffs		1	0		0	0	0	6

Louie Long

Year	Team	TD	1XP	2XP	FG	FGA	SAF	Pts
1931	POR N	1	0			0	0	6

Paul Longua

Year	Team	TD	1XP	2XP	FG	FGA	SAF	Pts
1929	ORA N	1	0			0	0	6

Jack Lookabaugh

Year	Team	TD	1XP	2XP	FG	FGA	SAF	Pts
1947	WAS N	1	0		0	0	0	6

Ace Loomis

Year	Team	TD	1XP	2XP	FG	FGA	SAF	Pts
1952	GB N	1	0		0	0	0	6

Don Looney

Year	Team	TD	1XP	2XP	FG	FGA	SAF	Pts
1940	PHI N	5	0		0	0	0	30
1941	PIT N	1	0		0	0	0	6
1942		1	0		0	0	0	6
Career		7	0		0	0	0	42

Joe Don Looney

Year	Team	TD	1XP	2XP	FG	FGA	SAF	Pts
1964	BAL N	2	0		0	0	0	12
1965	DET N	6	0		0	0	0	36
1966	DET-WAS N	4	0		0	0	0	24
1967	WAS N	1	0		0	0	0	6
Career		13	0		0	0	0	78

Karl Lorch

Year	Team	TD	1XP	2XP	FG	FGA	SAF	Pts
1979	WAS N	1	0		0	0	0	6

Tony Lorick

Year	Team	TD	1XP	2XP	FG	FGA	SAF	Pts
1964	BAL N	4	0		0	0	0	24
1965		3	0		0	0	0	18
1966		3	0		0	0	0	18
1967		6	0		0	0	0	36
1968	NO N	3	0		0	0	0	18
Career		19	0		0	0	0	114

Billy Lothridge

Year	Team	TD	1XP	2XP	FG	FGA	SAF	Pts
1964	DAL N	1	0		0	0	0	6

Billy Lott

Year	Team	TD	1XP	2XP	FG	FGA	SAF	Pts
1960	OAK A	6	0	1	0	0	0	38
1961	BOS A	11	0	0	0	0	0	66
1963		4	0	0	0	0	0	24
Career		21	0	1	0	0	0	128

Ronnie Lott

Year	Team	TD	1XP	2XP	FG	FGA	SAF	Pts
1981	SF N	3	0		0	0	0	18
1982		1	0		0	0	0	6
1986		1	0		0	0	0	6
Career		5	0		0	0	0	30
Playoffs		2	0		0	0	0	12

Tom Louderback

Year	Team	TD	1XP	2XP	FG	FGA	SAF	Pts
1961	OAK A	1	0	0	0	0	0	6

John Love

Year	Team	TD	1XP	2XP	FG	FGA	SAF	Pts
1967	WAS N	3	10		2	7	0	34
1972	LA N	1	0		0	0	0	6
Career		4	10		2	7	0	40

Randy Love

Year	Team	TD	1XP	2XP	FG	FGA	SAF	Pts
1983	STL N	3	0		0	0	0	18
1984		2	0		0	0	0	12
Career		5	0		0	0	0	30

Edwin Lovelady

Year	Team	TD	1XP	2XP	FG	FGA	SAF	Pts
1987	NYG N	2	0		0	0	0	12

John LoVetere

Year	Team	TD	1XP	2XP	FG	FGA	SAF	Pts
1960	LA N	1	0		0	0	0	6

Derek Loville

Year	Team	TD	1XP	2XP	FG	FGA	SAF	Pts
1995	SF N	13	0	1	0	0	0	80
1996		4	0	0	0	0	0	24
Career		17	0	1	0	0	0	104
Playoffs		1	0	0	0	0	0	6

Fritz Lovin

Year	Team	TD	1XP	2XP	FG	FGA	SAF	Pts
1929	MIN N	1	0			0	0	6

Frank LoVuolo

Year	Team	TD	1XP	2XP	FG	FGA	SAF	Pts
1949	NYG N	1	0			0	0	6

Gary Lowe

Year	Team	TD	1XP	2XP	FG	FGA	SAF	Pts
1961	DET N	0	0		0	0	1	2

Paul Lowe

Year	Team	TD	1XP	2XP	FG	FGA	SAF	Pts
1960	LA A	11	0	0	0	0	0	60
1961	SD A	9	0	0	0	0	0	54
1963		10	0	0	0	0	0	60
1964		5	0	0	0	0	0	30
1965		8	0	0	0	0	0	48
1966		3	0	0	0	0	0	18
1967		1	0	0	0	0	0	6
Career		47	0	0	0	0	0	276
Playoffs		2	0	0	0	0	0	12

Woodrow Lowe

Year	Team	TD	1XP	2XP	FG	FGA	SAF	Pts
1979	SD N	2	0		0	0	0	12
1980		1	0		0	0	0	6
1984		1	0		0	0	0	6
Career		4	0		0	0	0	24

Michael Lowery

Year	Team	TD	1XP	2XP	FG	FGA	SAF	Pts
1996	CHI N	1	0	0	0	0	0	6

Nick Lowery

Year	Team	TD	1XP	2XP	FG	FGA	SAF	Pts
1978	NE N	0	7		0	1	0	7
1980	KC N	0	37		20	26	0	97
1981		0	37		26	36	0	115
1982		0	17		19	24	0	74
1983		0	44		24	30	0	116
1984		0	35		23	33	0	104
1985		0	35		24	27	0	107
1986		0	43		19	26	0	100
1987		0	26		19	23	0	83
1988		0	23		27	32	0	104
1989		0	34		24	33	0	106
1990		0	37		34	37	0	139
1991		0	35		25	30	0	110
1992		0	39		22	24	0	105
1993		0	37		23	29	0	106
1994	NYJ N	0	26	0	20	23	0	86
1995		0	24	0	17	21	0	75
1996		0	26	0	17	24	0	77
Career		0	562	0	383	479	0	1711
Playoffs		0	13	0	8	12	0	37

Russ Lowther

Year	Team	TD	1XP	2XP	FG	FGA	SAF	Pts
1945	PIT N	0	0		0	0	0	0

Dick Lucas

Year	Team	TD	1XP	2XP	FG	FGA	SAF	Pts
1961	PHI N	5	0		0	0	0	30
1962		1	0		0	0	0	6
Career		6	0		0	0	0	36

Richie Lucas

Year	Team	TD	1XP	2XP	FG	FGA	SAF	Pts
1960	BUF A	3	0	0	0	0	0	18
1961		1	0	3	0	0	0	12
Career		4	0	3	0	0	0	30

Mike Lucci

Year	Team	TD	1XP	2XP	FG	FGA	SAF	Pts
1966	DET N	1	0		0	0	0	6
1967		1	0		0	0	0	6

Mike Lucci continued

Year	Team	TD	1XP	2XP	FG	FGA	SAF	Pts
1971		2	0		0	0	0	12
Career		4	0		0	0	0	24

Derrel Luce

Year	Team	TD	1XP	2XP	FG	FGA	SAF	Pts
1976	BAL N	1	0		0	0	0	6
1978		1	0		0	0	0	6
Career		2	0		0	0	0	12

Johnny Lucente

Year	Team	TD	1XP	2XP	FG	FGA	SAF	Pts
1945	PIT N	2	0		0	0	0	12

Oliver Luck

Year	Team	TD	1XP	2XP	FG	FGA	SAF	Pts
1984	HOU N	1	0		0	0	0	6

Terry Luck

Year	Team	TD	1XP	2XP	FG	FGA	SAF	Pts
1977	CLE N	1	0		0	0	0	6

Mick Luckhurst

Year	Team	TD	1XP	2XP	FG	FGA	SAF	Pts
1981	ATL N	0	51		21	33	0	114
1982		0	21		10	14	0	51
1983		0	43		17	22	0	94
1984		0	31		20	27	0	91
1985		0	29		24	31	0	101
1986		0	21		14	24	0	63
1987		0	17		9	13	0	44
Career		0	213		115	164	0	558
Playoffs		1	3		1	1	0	12

Sid Luckman

Year	Team	TD	1XP	2XP	FG	FGA	SAF	Pts
1939	CHIB N	1	0		0	0	0	6
1941		1	0		0	0	0	6
1942		1	0		0	0	0	6
1943		1	0		0	0	0	6
1944		1	0		0	0	0	6
1947		1	1		0	0	0	7
Career		6	1		0	0	0	37
Playoffs		2	0		0	0	0	12

Nolan Luhn

Year	Team	TD	1XP	2XP	FG	FGA	SAF	Pts
1945	GB N	1	0		0	0	0	6
1946		2	0		0	0	1	14
1947		7	0		0	0	0	42
1948		2	0		0	0	0	12
1949		1	0		0	0	0	6
Career		13	0		0	0	1	80

Johnny Lujack

Year	Team	TD	1XP	2XP	FG	FGA	SAF	Pts
1948	CHIB N	1	44		0	3	0	50
1949		2	42		1	1	0	57
1950		11	34		3	5	0	109
1951		7	10		0	0	0	52
Career		21	130		4	9	0	268
Playoffs		0	2		0	0	0	2

Steve Luke

Year	Team	TD	1XP	2XP	FG	FGA	SAF	Pts
1978	GB N	1	0		0	0	0	6

Jim Lukens

Year	Team	TD	1XP	2XP	FG	FGA	SAF	Pts
1949	BUF AA	2	0		0	0	0	12

Roy Lumpkin

Year	Team	TD	1XP	2XP	FG	FGA	SAF	Pts
1930	POR N	3	0		0		0	18
1931		1	0		0		0	6
1932		1	0		0		0	6
1933		1	0		0		0	6
1934	DET N	2	0		0		0	12
Career		8	0		0		0	48

Sean Lumpkin

Year	Team	TD	1XP	2XP	FG	FGA	SAF	Pts
1995	NO N	1	0	0	0	0	0	6

Bill Lund

Year	Team	TD	1XP	2XP	FG	FGA	SAF	Pts
1946	CLE AA	3	0		0	0	0	18
1947		3	0		0	0	0	18
Career		6	0		0	0	0	36

Bob Lundell

Year	Team	TD	1XP	2XP	FG	FGA	SAF	Pts
1930	SI N	1	0		0		0	6

Lamar Lundy

Year	Team	TD	1XP	2XP	FG	FGA	SAF	Pts
1957	LA N	3	0		0	0	0	18
1958		3	0		0	0	0	18
1960		1	0		0	0	0	6

Lamar Lundy *continued*

Year	Team		TD	1XP	2XP	FG	FGA	SAF	Pts
1964			1	0		0	0	0	6
1966			1	0		0	0	0	6
Career			9	0		0	0	0	54

Jerry Lunz

Year	Team		TD	1XP	2XP	FG	FGA	SAF	Pts
1926	CHIC	N	1	0		0		0	6

Herb Lusk

Year	Team		TD	1XP	2XP	FG	FGA	SAF	Pts
1977	PHI	N	3	0		0	0	0	18

Booth Lusteg

Year	Team		TD	1XP	2XP	FG	FGA	SAF	Pts
1966	BUF	A	0	**41**	0	19	**38**	0	98
1967	MIA	A	0	18	0	7	12	0	39
1968	PIT	N	0	26		8	20	0	50
1969	GB	N	0	12		1	5	0	15
Career			0	97	0	35	75	0	202
Playoffs			0	1	0	0	0	0	1

Todd Lyght

Year	Team		TD	1XP	2XP	FG	FGA	SAF	Pts
1994	LARM	N	1	0	0	0	0	0	6
1995	STL	N	1	0	0	0	0	0	6
1996			1	0	0	0	0	0	6
Career			3	0	0	0	0	0	18

Lenny Lyles

Year	Team		TD	1XP	2XP	FG	FGA	SAF	Pts
1958	BAL	N	4	0		0	0	0	24
1959	SF	N	1	0		0	0	0	6
1960			1	0		0	0	0	6
1963	BAL	N	1	0		0	0	0	6
1967			1	0		0	0	0	6
Career			8	0		0	0	0	48

Robert Lyles

Year	Team		TD	1XP	2XP	FG	FGA	SAF	Pts
1986	HOU	N	1	0		0	0	0	6
1987			1	0		0	0	0	6
Career			2	0		0	0	0	12

Link Lyman

Year	Team		TD	1XP	2XP	FG	FGA	SAF	Pts
1923	CAN	N	1	0		0		0	6
1924	CLE	N	4	1		0		0	25
1931	CHIB	N	1	0		0		0	6
Career			6	1		0		0	37

Dick Lynch

Year	Team		TD	1XP	2XP	FG	FGA	SAF	Pts
1960	NYG	N	1	0		0	0	0	6
1962			2	0		0	0	0	12
1963			3	0		0	0	0	18
1965			1	0		0	0	0	6
Career			7	0		0	0	0	42

Eddie Lynch

Year	Team		TD	1XP	2XP	FG	FGA	SAF	Pts
1927	PRO	N	1	0		0		0	6

Eric Lynch

Year	Team		TD	1XP	2XP	FG	FGA	SAF	Pts
1993	DET	N	2	0		0	0	0	12

Fran Lynch

Year	Team		TD	1XP	2XP	FG	FGA	SAF	Pts
1968	DEN	A	4	0	0	0	0	0	24
1969			2	0	0	0	0	0	12
1970	DEN	N	1	0		0	0	0	6
1971			1	0		0	0	1	8
1972			2	0		0	0	0	12
1975			4	0		0	0	0	24
Career			14	0	0	0	0	1	86

Jim Lynch

Year	Team		TD	1XP	2XP	FG	FGA	SAF	Pts
1968	KC	A	1	0	0	0	0	0	6

Lorenzo Lynch

Year	Team		TD	1XP	2XP	FG	FGA	SAF	Pts
1991	PHX	N	1	0		0	0	0	6
1993			1	0		0	0	0	6
1995	ARI	N	1	0	0	0	0	0	6
Career			3	0	0	0	0	0	18

Johnny Lynn

Year	Team		TD	1XP	2XP	FG	FGA	SAF	Pts
1979	NYJ	N	1	0		0	0	0	6
1983			1	0		0	0	0	6
Career			2	0		0	0	0	12

Marty Lyons

Year	Team		TD	1XP	2XP	FG	FGA	SAF	Pts
1987	NYJ	N	0	0		0	0	1	2
1988			0	0		0	0	1	2
Career			0	0		0	0	2	4

Mitch Lyons

Year	Team		TD	1XP	2XP	FG	FGA	SAF	Pts
1996	ATL	N	1	0	0	0	0	0	6

Rob Lytle

Year	Team		TD	1XP	2XP	FG	FGA	SAF	Pts
1977	DEN	N	2	0		0	0	0	12
1978			2	0		0	0	0	12
1979			4	0		0	0	0	24
1980			1	0		0	0	0	6
1981			5	0		0	0	0	30
Career			14	0		0	0	0	84
Playoffs			2	0		0	0	0	12

Bill Maas

Year	Team		TD	1XP	2XP	FG	FGA	SAF	Pts
1987	KC	N	1	0		0	0	0	6
1988			0	0		0	0	1	2
1989			1	0		0	0	0	6
1990			0	0		0	0	1	2
Career			2	0		0	0	2	16

Ken MacAfee

Year	Team		TD	1XP	2XP	FG	FGA	SAF	Pts
1954	NYG	N	8	0		0	0	0	48
1955			1	0		0	0	0	6
1956			4	0		0	0	0	24
1957			2	0		0	0	0	12
1958			2	0		0	0	0	12
1959	WAS	N	1	0		0	0	0	6
Career			18	0		0	0	0	108

Ken MacAfee

Year	Team		TD	1XP	2XP	FG	FGA	SAF	Pts
1978	SF	N	1	0		0	0	0	6
1979			4	0		0	0	0	24
Career			5	0		0	0	0	30

Jay MacDowell

Year	Team		TD	1XP	2XP	FG	FGA	SAF	Pts
1946	PHI	N	0	0		0	0	1	2

Bill Mack

Year	Team		TD	1XP	2XP	FG	FGA	SAF	Pts
1961	PIT	N	2	0		0	0	0	12
1962			2	0		0	0	0	12
1963			3	0		0	0	0	18
1964	PHI	N	1	0		0	0	0	6
Career			8	0		0	0	0	48

Cedric Mack

Year	Team		TD	1XP	2XP	FG	FGA	SAF	Pts
1988	PHX	N	1	0		0	0	0	6

Kevin Mack

Year	Team		TD	1XP	2XP	FG	FGA	SAF	Pts
1985	CLE	N	10	0		0	0	0	60
1986			10	0		0	0	0	60
1987			6	0		0	0	0	36
1988			3	0		0	0	0	18
1989			1	0		0	0	0	6
1990			7	0		0	0	0	42
1991			10	0		0	0	0	60
1992			6	0		0	0	0	36
1993			1	0		0	0	0	6
Career			54	0		0	0	0	324
Playoffs			2	0		0	0	0	12

Milton Mack

Year	Team		TD	1XP	2XP	FG	FGA	SAF	Pts
1993	TB	N	1	0		0	0	0	6

Earsell Mackbee

Year	Team		TD	1XP	2XP	FG	FGA	SAF	Pts
1967	MIN	N	2	0		0	0	0	12

Dee Mackey

Year	Team		TD	1XP	2XP	FG	FGA	SAF	Pts
1962	BAL	N	4	0		0	0	0	24
1963	NY	A	3	0	0	0	0	0	18
1965			1	0	1	0	0	0	8
Career			8	0	1	0	0	0	50

John Mackey

Year	Team		TD	1XP	2XP	FG	FGA	SAF	Pts
1963	BAL	N	7	0		0	0	0	42
1964			2	0		0	0	0	12
1965			7	0		0	0	0	42
1966			9	0		0	0	0	54
1967			3	0		0	0	0	18
1968			5	0		0	0	0	30
1969			2	0		0	0	0	12
1970			3	0		0	0	0	18
Career			38	0		0	0	0	228
Playoffs			2	0		0	0	0	12

Kyle Mackey

Year	Team		TD	1XP	2XP	FG	FGA	SAF	Pts
1987	MIA	N	2	0		0	0	0	12

Jacque MacKinnon

Year	Team		TD	1XP	2XP	FG	FGA	SAF	Pts
1962	SD	A	2	0	0	0	0	0	12
1963			4	0	0	0	0	0	24
1964			2	0	0	0	0	0	12
1966			6	0	0	0	0	0	36
1967			2	0	0	0	0	0	12
1968			6	0	1	0	0	0	38
Career			22	0	1	0	0	0	134

Bill Mackrides

Year	Team		TD	1XP	2XP	FG	FGA	SAF	Pts
1947	PHI	N	1	0		0	0	0	6
1949			1	0		0	0	0	6
1953	PIT	N	1	0		0	0	0	6
Career			3	0		0	0	0	18

Bob MacLeod

Year	Team		TD	1XP	2XP	FG	FGA	SAF	Pts
1939	CHIB	N	5	0		0	0	0	30

Jim MacMurdo

Year	Team		TD	1XP	2XP	FG	FGA	SAF	Pts
1936	PHI	N	1	0		0		0	6

Eddie Macon

Year	Team		TD	1XP	2XP	FG	FGA	SAF	Pts
1952	CHIB	N	2	0		0	0	0	12
1953			3	0		0	0	0	18
1960	OAK	A	1	0	0	0	0	0	6
Career			6	0	0	0	0	0	36

Elmer Madarik

Year	Team		TD	1XP	2XP	FG	FGA	SAF	Pts
1947	DET	N	1	0		0	0	0	6

Lloyd Madden

Year	Team		TD	1XP	2XP	FG	FGA	SAF	Pts
1940	CHIC	N	3	0		0	0	0	18

Bob Maddox

Year	Team		TD	1XP	2XP	FG	FGA	SAF	Pts
1974	CIN	N	1	0		0	0	0	6

Calvin Magee

Year	Team		TD	1XP	2XP	FG	FGA	SAF	Pts
1985	TB	N	3	0		0	0	0	18
1986			5	0		0	0	0	30
1987			3	0		0	0	0	18
Career			11	0		0	0	0	66

Archie Maggiolo

Year	Team		TD	1XP	2XP	FG	FGA	SAF	Pts
1949	DET	N	1	0		0	0	0	6

Dante Magnani

Year	Team		TD	1XP	2XP	FG	FGA	SAF	Pts
1940	CLE	N	1	0		0	0	0	6
1941			2	0		0	0	0	12
1942			5	0		0	0	0	30
1943	CHIB	N	4	0		0	0	0	24
1946			1	0		0	0	0	6
1947	LA	N	1	0		0	0	0	6
1948			1	0		0	0	0	6
Career			15	0		0	0	0	90
Playoffs			3	0		0	0	0	18

Paul Maguire

Year	Team		TD	1XP	2XP	FG	FGA	SAF	Pts
1960	LA	A	1	0	0	0	0	0	6

Bruce Maher

Year	Team		TD	1XP	2XP	FG	FGA	SAF	Pts
1960	DET	N	0	0		0	0	1	2
1963			0	0		0	0	1	2
1967			0	0		0	0	1	2
Career			0	0		0	0	3	6

Frank Mahoney

Year	Team		TD	1XP	2XP	FG	FGA	SAF	Pts
1925	CHIC	N	1	1		0		0	7
1926			2	0		0		0	12
Career			3	1		0			19

Al Mahrt

Year	Team		TD	1XP	2XP	FG	FGA	SAF	Pts
1920	DAY	A	1	0		0		0	6
1921			1	0		0		0	6
1922	DAY	N	1	0		0		0	6
Career			3	0		0		0	18

Armin Mahrt

Year	Team		TD	1XP	2XP	FG	FGA	SAF	Pts
1924	DAY	N	1	0		0		0	6
1925	POT	N	1	0		0		0	6
Career			2	0		0		0	12

Lou Mahrt

Year	Team	Lg	TD	1XP	2XP	FG	FGA	SAF	Pts
1926	DAY	N	0	0		0		0	0

Gil Mains

Year	Team	Lg	TD	1XP	2XP	FG	FGA	SAF	Pts
1955	DET	N	1	0		0	0	0	6

Jack Maitland

Year	Team	Lg	TD	1XP	2XP	FG	FGA	SAF	Pts
1970	BAL	N	2	0		0	0	0	12
1971	NE	N	1	0		0	0	0	6
Career			3	0		0	0	0	18

Don Majkowski

Year	Team	Lg	TD	1XP	2XP	FG	FGA	SAF	Pts
1988	GB	N	1	0		0	0	0	6
1989			5	0		0	0	0	36
1990			1	0		0	0	0	6
1991			2	0		0	0	0	12
1994	IND	N	3	0	0	0	0	0	18
Career			12	0	0	0	0	0	78

Bill Malinchak

Year	Team	Lg	TD	1XP	2XP	FG	FGA	SAF	Pts
1967	DET	N	4	0		0	0	0	24
1972	WAS	N	1	0		0	0	1	8
Career			5	0		0	0	1	32

John Mallory

Year	Team	Lg	TD	1XP	2XP	FG	FGA	SAF	Pts
1968	PHI	N	1	0		0	0	0	6
1970	ATL	N	2	0		0	0	0	12
1971			1	0		0	0	0	6
Career			4	0		0	0	0	24

Ray Mallouf

Year	Team	Lg	TD	1XP	2XP	FG	FGA	SAF	Pts
1948	CHIC	N	1	0		0	0	0	6

Les Malloy

Year	Team	Lg	TD	1XP	2XP	FG	FGA	SAF	Pts
1931	CHIC	N	2	0		0		0	12

Art Malone

Year	Team	Lg	TD	1XP	2XP	FG	FGA	SAF	Pts
1970	ATL	N	1	0		0	0	0	6
1971			8	0		0	0	0	48
1972			10	0		0	0	0	60
1973			3	0		0	0	0	18
1974			2	0		0	0	0	12
1976	PHI	N	1	0		0	0	0	6
Career			25	0		0	0	0	150

Benny Malone

Year	Team	Lg	TD	1XP	2XP	FG	FGA	SAF	Pts
1974	MIA	N	3	0		0	0	0	18
1975			3	0		0	0	0	18
1976			4	0		0	0	0	24
1977			5	0		0	0	0	30
1978			1	0		0	0	0	6
1979	WAS	N	4	0		0	0	0	24
Career			20	0		0	0	0	120
Playoffs			1	0		0	0	0	6

Charley Malone

Year	Team	Lg	TD	1XP	2XP	FG	FGA	SAF	Pts
1934	BOS	N	2	0		0		0	12
1935			2	0		0		0	12
1936			1	0		0		0	6
1937	WAS	N	4	0		0		0	24
1938			1	0		0	0	0	6
1939			3	0		0	0	0	18
Career			13	0		0	0	0	78

Mark Malone

Year	Team	Lg	TD	1XP	2XP	FG	FGA	SAF	Pts
1981	PIT	N	3	0		0	0	0	18
1984			3	0		0	0	0	18
1985			1	0		0	0	0	6
1986			5	0		0	0	0	30
1987			3	0		0	0	0	18
1988	SD	N	4	0		0	0	0	24
Career			19	0		0	0	0	114

Norm Maloney

Year	Team	Lg	TD	1XP	2XP	FG	FGA	SAF	Pts
1948	SF	AA	1	1		0	0	0	7

Red Maloney

Year	Team	Lg	TD	1XP	2XP	FG	FGA	SAF	Pts
1925	PRO	N	1	4		3		0	19
1926	NY	A	2	0		0		0	12
1927	NYY	N	1	0		0		0	6
Career			4	4		3		0	37

Mike Mamula

Year	Team	Lg	TD	1XP	2XP	FG	FGA	SAF	Pts
1996	PHI	N	1	0	0	0	0	0	6

Massimo Manca

Year	Team	Lg	TD	1XP	2XP	FG	FGA	SAF	Pts
1987	CIN	N	0	3		1	2	0	6

Jack Manders

Year	Team	Lg	TD	1XP	2XP	FG	FGA	SAF	Pts
1933	CHIB	N	0	**14**		**6**		0	32
1934			3	**29**		**10**		0	**77**
1935			0	**16**		1		0	19
1936			4	17		**7**		0	62
1937			5	15		**8**		0	**69**
1938			3	10		3	9	0	37
1939			4	17		3	7	0	50
1940			0	17		2	3	0	23
Career			19	135		40	19	0	369
Playoffs			2	7		5	10	0	34

Pug Manders

Year	Team	Lg	TD	1XP	2XP	FG	FGA	SAF	Pts
1939	BKN	N	2	0		0	0	0	12
1940			6	0		0	0	0	36
1941			7	0		0	0	0	42
1942			6	0		0	0	0	36
1943			4	0		0	0	0	24
1944			5	0		0	1	0	30
1945	BOS	N	6	0		0	0	0	36
1946	NY	AA	3	0		0	0	0	18
Career			39	0		0	1	0	234

Jim Mandich

Year	Team	Lg	TD	1XP	2XP	FG	FGA	SAF	Pts
1970	MIA	N	1	0		0	0	0	6
1971			1	0		0	0	0	6
1972			3	0		0	0	0	18
1973			4	0		0	0	0	24
1974			6	0		0	0	0	36
1975			4	0		0	0	0	24
1976			4	0		0	0	0	24
Career			23	0		0	0	0	138
Playoffs			1	0		0	0	0	6

Pete Mandley

Year	Team	Lg	TD	1XP	2XP	FG	FGA	SAF	Pts
1985	DET	N	1	0		0	0	0	6
1986			1	0		0	0	0	6
1987			7	0		0	0	0	42
1988			5	0		0	0	0	30
1989	KC	N	1	0		0	0	0	6
Career			15	0		0	0	0	90

Joe Maniaci

Year	Team	Lg	TD	1XP	2XP	FG	FGA	SAF	Pts
1937	BKN	N	2	5		2		0	23
1938	CHIB	N	3	11		1	3	0	32
1939			5	4		1	2	0	37
1940			3	1		0	0	0	19
1941			3	8		1	1	0	29
Career			16	29		5	6	0	140
Playoffs			1	2		0	0	0	8

Dexter Manley

Year	Team	Lg	TD	1XP	2XP	FG	FGA	SAF	Pts
1986	WAS	N	1	0		0	0	0	6
1989			0	0		0	0	1	2
Career			1	0		0	0	1	8

Bob Mann

Year	Team	Lg	TD	1XP	2XP	FG	FGA	SAF	Pts
1948	DET	N	3	0		0	0	0	18
1949			4	0		0	0	0	24
1950	GB	N	1	0		0	0	0	6
1951			8	0		0	0	0	48
1952			6	0		0	0	0	36
1953			2	0		0	0	0	12
Career			24	0		0	0	0	144

Charles Mann

Year	Team	Lg	TD	1XP	2XP	FG	FGA	SAF	Pts
1983	WAS	N	0	0		0	0	1	2

Dave Mann

Year	Team	Lg	TD	1XP	2XP	FG	FGA	SAF	Pts
1955	CHIC	N	5	0		1	1	0	33
1956			1	0		0	0	0	6
Career			6	0		1	1	0	39

Errol Mann

Year	Team	Lg	TD	1XP	2XP	FG	FGA	SAF	Pts
1968	GB	N	0	4		0	3	0	4
1969	DET	N	0	26		25	37	0	101
1970			0	**41**		20	29	0	101
1971			0	37		22	37	0	103
1972			0	38		20	29	0	98
1973			0	14		13	19	0	53
1974			0	23		23	32	0	92

Errol Mann *continued*

Year	Team	Lg	TD	1XP	2XP	FG	FGA	SAF	Pts
1975			0	25		14	21	0	67
1976	DET-OAK	N	0	35		8	21	0	59
1977	OAK	N	0	**39**		20	28	0	**99**
1978			0	33		12	20	0	69
Career			0	315		177	276	0	846
Playoffs			0	14		6	9	0	32

Archie Manning

Year	Team	Lg	TD	1XP	2XP	FG	FGA	SAF	Pts
1971	NO	N	4	0		0	0	0	24
1972			2	0		0	0	0	12
1973			2	0		0	0	0	12
1974			1	0		0	0	0	6
1975			1	0		0	0	0	6
1977			5	0		0	0	0	30
1978			1	0		0	0	0	6
1979			2	0		0	0	0	12
Career			18	0		0	0	0	108

Joe Manning

Year	Team	Lg	TD	1XP	2XP	FG	FGA	SAF	Pts
1926	HAR	N	3	0		0		0	18

Tim Manoa

Year	Team	Lg	TD	1XP	2XP	FG	FGA	SAF	Pts
1988	CLE	N	2	0		0	0	0	12
1989			5	0		0	0	0	30
1991	IND	N	1	0		0	0	0	6
Career			8	0		0	0	0	48
Playoffs			1	0		0	0	0	6

Jerry Mansfield

Year	Team	Lg	TD	1XP	2XP	FG	FGA	SAF	Pts
1920	RI	A	1	0		0		0	6

Ray Mansfield

Year	Team	Lg	TD	1XP	2XP	FG	FGA	SAF	Pts
Playoffs			0	2	0	0	0	0	2

Ed Manske

Year	Team	Lg	TD	1XP	2XP	FG	FGA	SAF	Pts
1935	PHI	N	4	0		0		0	24
1937	CHIB	N	4	0		0		0	24
1938	PIT-CHIB	N	3	0		0		0	18
1939	CHIB	N	2	0		0	0	0	12
Career			13	0		0	0	0	78
Playoffs			1	0		0	0	0	6

Tillie Manton

Year	Team	Lg	TD	1XP	2XP	FG	FGA	SAF	Pts
1936	NYG	N	1	15		0		0	21
1937			0	12		5		0	27
1938	WAS	N	0	2		1	4	0	5
1943	BKN	N	0	0		0	1	0	0
Career			1	29		6	5	0	53

Lionel Manuel

Year	Team	Lg	TD	1XP	2XP	FG	FGA	SAF	Pts
1984	NYG	N	4	0		0	0	0	24
1985			5	0		0	0	0	30
1986			3	0		0	0	0	18
1987			6	0		0	0	0	36
1988			4	0		0	0	0	24
1989			1	0		0	0	0	6
Career			23	0		0	0	0	138
Playoffs			1	0		0	0	0	6

Frank Manumaleuga

Year	Team	Lg	TD	1XP	2XP	FG	FGA	SAF	Pts
1980	KC	N	1	0		0	0	0	6

Gary Marangi

Year	Team	Lg	TD	1XP	2XP	FG	FGA	SAF	Pts
1976	BUF	N	2	0		0	0	0	12

Gino Marchetti

Year	Team	Lg	TD	1XP	2XP	FG	FGA	SAF	Pts
1952	DAL	N	1	0		0	0	0	6
1957	BAL	N	1	0		0	0	0	6
1961			0	0		0	0	1	2
1963			1	0		0	0	0	6
Career			3	0		0	0	1	20

Ted Marchibroda

Year	Team	Lg	TD	1XP	2XP	FG	FGA	SAF	Pts
1955	PIT	N	1	0		0	0	0	6
1956			2	0		0	0	0	12
Career			3	0		0	0	0	18

Chester Marcol

Year	Team	Lg	TD	1XP	2XP	FG	FGA	SAF	Pts
1972	GB	N	0	29		**33**	**48**	0	**128**
1973			0	19		21	35	0	82
1974			0	19		**25**	**39**	0	**94**
1975			0	0		1	1	0	3
1976			0	24		10	19	0	54

Chester Marcol *continued*

Year	Team	TD	1XP	2XP	FG	FGA	SAF	Pts
1977		0	11		13	21	0	50
1978		0	30		11	19	0	63
1979		0	16		4	10	0	28
1980	GB-HOU N	1	8		3	4	0	23
Career		1	156		121	196	0	525
Playoffs		0	0		1	1	0	3

Joe Marconi

Year	Team	TD	1XP	2XP	FG	FGA	SAF	Pts
1956	LA N	7	0		0	0	0	42
1957		4	0		0	0	0	24
1958		1	0		0	0	0	6
1959		5	0		0	0	0	30
1960		3	0		0	0	0	18
1961		4	0		0	0	0	24
1962	CHI N	6	0		0	0	0	36
1963		4	0		0	0	0	24
1964		5	0		0	0	0	30
Career		39	0		0	0	0	234

Andrew Marefos

Year	Team	TD	1XP	2XP	FG	FGA	SAF	Pts
1941	NYG N	2	6		4	5	0	30
1942		1	0		0	2	0	6
1946	LA AA	4	2		0	0	0	26
Career		7	8		4	7	0	62

Jodie Marek

Year	Team	TD	1XP	2XP	FG	FGA	SAF	Pts
1943	BKN N	0	0		0	1	0	0

Bob Margarita

Year	Team	TD	1XP	2XP	FG	FGA	SAF	Pts
1944	CHIB N	4	0		0	0	0	24
1945		5	0		0	0	0	30
Career		9	0		0	0	0	54

Ken Margerum

Year	Team	TD	1XP	2XP	FG	FGA	SAF	Pts
1981	CHI N	1	0		0	0	0	6
1982		3	0		0	0	0	18
1983		2	0		0	0	0	12
1985		2	0		0	0	0	12
Career		8	0		0	0	0	48

Joe Margucci

Year	Team	TD	1XP	2XP	FG	FGA	SAF	Pts
1947	DET N	2	0		0	0	0	12
1948		5	0		0	0	0	30
Career		7	0		0	0	0	42

Ed Marinaro

Year	Team	TD	1XP	2XP	FG	FGA	SAF	Pts
1972	MIN N	1	0		0	0	0	6
1973		4	0		0	0	0	24
1974		2	0		0	0	0	12
1975		4	0		0	0	0	24
1976	NYJ N	2	0		0	0	0	12
Career		13	0		0	0	0	78

Dan Marino

Year	Team	TD	1XP	2XP	FG	FGA	SAF	Pts
1983	MIA N	2	0		0	0	0	12
1987		1	0		0	0	0	6
1989		2	0		0	0	0	12
1991		1	0		0	0	0	6
1993		1	0		0	0	0	6
1994		1	0	0	0	0	0	6
Career		8	0	0	0	0	0	48
Playoffs		1	0	0	0	0	0	6

Brock Marion

Year	Team	TD	1XP	2XP	FG	FGA	SAF	Pts
1995	DAL N	1	0	0	0	0	0	6

Fred Marion

Year	Team	TD	1XP	2XP	FG	FGA	SAF	Pts
1986	NE N	1	0		0	0		6

Phil Marion

Year	Team	TD	1XP	2XP	FG	FGA	SAF	Pts
1925	DET N	4	0		0	0		24

Cliff Marker

Year	Team	TD	1XP	2XP	FG	FGA	SAF	Pts
1926	CAN N	1	0		0	0		6

Larry Marks

Year	Team	TD	1XP	2XP	FG	FGA	SAF	Pts
1926	NY A	2	0		0	0		12
1927	NYY N	0	0		0	0		0
1928	GB N	2	0		0	0		12
Career		4	0		0	0		24

Steve Maronic

Year	Team	TD	1XP	2XP	FG	FGA	SAF	Pts
1940	DET N	0	0		0	1	0	0

John Marquart

Year	Team	TD	1XP	2XP	FG	FGA	SAF	Pts
1921	CHIC A	1	0		0	0		6

Aaron Marsh

Year	Team	TD	1XP	2XP	FG	FGA	SAF	Pts
1968	BOS A	4	0	0	0	0	0	24

Amos Marsh

Year	Team	TD	1XP	2XP	FG	FGA	SAF	Pts
1961	DAL N	3	0		0	0	0	18
1962		9	0		0	0	0	54
1963		5	0		0	0	0	30
1964		2	0		0	0	0	12
1965	DET N	8	0		0	0	0	48
1966		3	0		0	0	0	18
1967		3	0		0	0	0	18
Career		33	0		0	0	0	198

Doug Marsh

Year	Team	TD	1XP	2XP	FG	FGA	SAF	Pts
1980	STL N	4	0		0	0		24
1981		1	0		0	0		6
1983		8	0		0	0		48
1984		5	0		0	0		30
1985		1	0		0	0		6
Career		19	0		0	0		114

Al Marshall

Year	Team	TD	1XP	2XP	FG	FGA	SAF	Pts
1974	NE N	1	0		0	0		6

Anthony Marshall

Year	Team	TD	1XP	2XP	FG	FGA	SAF	Pts
1995	CHI N	1	0	0	0	0		6

Arthur Marshall

Year	Team	TD	1XP	2XP	FG	FGA	SAF	Pts
1992	DEN N	1	0		0	0		6
1993		2	0		0	0		12
1995	NYG N	1	0	0	0	0		6
Career		4	0	0	0	0		24

Bobby Marshall

Year	Team	TD	1XP	2XP	FG	FGA	SAF	Pts
1920	RI A	0	3		0	0		3

Ed Marshall

Year	Team	TD	1XP	2XP	FG	FGA	SAF	Pts
1976	NYG N	3	0		0	0		18

Henry Marshall

Year	Team	TD	1XP	2XP	FG	FGA	SAF	Pts
1976	KC N	3	0		0	0		18
1977		4	0		0	0		24
1978		2	0		0	0		12
1979		2	0		0	0		12
1980		6	0		0	0		36
1981		4	0		0	0		24
1982		3	0		0	0		18
1983		6	0		0	0		36
1984		4	0		0	0		24
1986		1	0		0	0		6
Career		35	0		0	0		210

Jim Marshall

Year	Team	TD	1XP	2XP	FG	FGA	SAF	Pts
1963	MIN N	1	0		0	0	0	6
1968		0	0		0	0	1	2
Career		1	0		0	0	1	8

Leonard Marshall

Year	Team	TD	1XP	2XP	FG	FGA	SAF	Pts
1983	NYG N	0	0		0	0	1	2
1989		0	0		0	0	1	2
Career		0	0		0	0	2	4

Randy Marshall

Year	Team	TD	1XP	2XP	FG	FGA	SAF	Pts
1970	ATL N	1	0		0	0		6

Wilber Marshall

Year	Team	TD	1XP	2XP	FG	FGA	SAF	Pts
1986	CHI N	2	0		0	0		12
1991	WAS N	1	0	0	0	0		6
1992		1	0		0	0		6
Career		4	0		0	0		24
Playoffs		1	0		0	0		6

Paul Martha

Year	Team	TD	1XP	2XP	FG	FGA	SAF	Pts
1968	PIT N	1	0		0	0		6

Aaron Martin

Year	Team	TD	1XP	2XP	FG	FGA	SAF	Pts
1964	LA N	1	0		0	0		6
1965		1	0		0	0		6
1966	PHI N	1	0		0	0		6
Career		3	0		0	0		18

Abe Martin

Year	Team	TD	1XP	2XP	FG	FGA	SAF	Pts
1932	CHIC N	2	0		0	0		12

Amos Martin

Year	Team	TD	1XP	2XP	FG	FGA	SAF	Pts
1974	MIN N	1	0		0	0	0	6

Billy Martin

Year	Team	TD	1XP	2XP	FG	FGA	SAF	Pts
1962	CHI N	1	0		0	0	0	6

Billy Martin

Year	Team	TD	1XP	2XP	FG	FGA	SAF	Pts
1967	ATL N	3	0		0	0	0	18
1968	MIN N	1	0		0	0	0	6
Career		4	0		0	0	0	24
Playoffs		1	0		0	0	0	6

Blanche Martin

Year	Team	TD	1XP	2XP	FG	FGA	SAF	Pts
1960	LA A	1	0		0	0	0	6

Chris Martin

Year	Team	TD	1XP	2XP	FG	FGA	SAF	Pts
1984	MIN N	1	0		0	0	0	6
1988		1	0		0	0	0	6
1990	KC N	1	0		0	0	0	6
1991		1	0		0	0	0	6
Career		4	0		0	0	0	24

Curtis Martin

Year	Team	TD	1XP	2XP	FG	FGA	SAF	Pts
1995	NE N	15	0	1	0	0	0	92
1996		17	0	1	0	0	0	104
Career		32	0	2	0	0	0	196
Playoffs		5	0	0	0	0	0	30

Eric Martin

Year	Team	TD	1XP	2XP	FG	FGA	SAF	Pts
1985	NO N	4	0		0	0	0	24
1986		5	0		0	0	0	30
1987		7	0		0	0	0	42
1988		7	0		0	0	0	42
1989		8	0		0	0	0	48
1990		5	0		0	0	0	30
1991		4	0		0	0	0	24
1992		5	0		0	0	0	30
1993		3	0		0	0	0	18
1994	KC N	1	0		0	0	0	6
Career		49	0		0	0	0	294
Playoffs		1	0		0	0	0	6

Frank Martin

Year	Team	TD	1XP	2XP	FG	FGA	SAF	Pts
1945	BOS N	1	0		0	0		6

George Martin

Year	Team	TD	1XP	2XP	FG	FGA	SAF	Pts
1977	NYG N	1	0		0	0		6
1978		1	0		0	0		6
1980		1	0		0	0		6
1981		2	0		0	0		12
1985		1	0		0	0		6
1986		1	0		0	0		6
Career		7	0		0	0		42
Playoffs		0	0		0	0	1	2

Harvey Martin

Year	Team	TD	1XP	2XP	FG	FGA	SAF	Pts
1979	DAL N	0	0		0	0	1	2
1981		0	0		0	0	1	2
Career		0	0		0	0	2	4

Ike Martin

Year	Team	TD	1XP	2XP	FG	FGA	SAF	Pts
1920	CAN A	1	0		0	0		6

Jim Martin

Year	Team	TD	1XP	2XP	FG	FGA	SAF	Pts
1953	DET N	0	4		2	4	0	10
1954		0	0		1	6	0	3
1955		0	0		1	0	0	0
1956		0	3		4	10	0	15
1957		0	5		7	14	0	26
1958		0	28		7	19	0	49
1959		0	0		7	16	0	21
1960		0	26		13	24	0	65
1961		0	25		15	30	0	70
1963	BAL N	0	32		24	39	0	104
1964	WAS N	0	35		12	28	0	71
Career		0	158		92	191	0	434
Playoffs		0	12		2	3	0	18

John Martin

Year	Team	TD	1XP	2XP	FG	FGA	SAF	Pts
1941	CHIC N	2	0		0	0	0	12

John Martin *continued*

Year	Team		TD	1XP	2XP	FG	FGA	SAF	Pts
1945	**BOS**	**N**	2	0		0	0	0	12
Career			4	0		0	0	0	24

Kelvin Martin

Year	Team		TD	1XP	2XP	FG	FGA	SAF	Pts
1988	**DAL**	**N**	3	0		0	0	0	18
1989			2	0		0	0	0	12
1991			1	0		0	0	0	6
1992			5	0		0	0	0	30
1993	**SEA**	**N**	5	0		0	0	0	30
1994			1	0	0	0	0	0	6
1996	**DAL**	**N**	1	0	0	0	0	0	6
Career			18	0	0	0	0	0	108
Playoffs			1	0	0	0	0	0	6

Mike Martin

Year	Team		TD	1XP	2XP	FG	FGA	SAF	Pts
1987	**CIN**	**N**	3	0		0	0	0	18
1988			1	0		0	0	0	6
1989			2	0		0	0	0	12
Career			6	0		0	0	0	36

Robbie Martin

Year	Team		TD	1XP	2XP	FG	FGA	SAF	Pts
1981	**DET**	**N**	1	0		0	0	0	6
1983			1	0		0	0	0	6
1985	**IND**	**N**	1	0		0	0	0	6
Career			3	0		0	0	0	18

Rod Martin

Year	Team		TD	1XP	2XP	FG	FGA	SAF	Pts
1980	**OAK**	**N**	1	0		0	0	0	6
1982	**LARI**	**N**	1	0		0	0	0	6
1983			2	0		0	0	0	12
1984			2	0		0	0	1	14
Career			6	0		0	0	1	38

Sammy Martin

Year	Team		TD	1XP	2XP	FG	FGA	SAF	Pts
1988	**NE**	**N**	1	0		0	0	0	6
1990			1	0		0	0	0	6
Career			2	0		0	0	0	12

Tony Martin

Year	Team		TD	1XP	2XP	FG	FGA	SAF	Pts
1990	**MIA**	**N**	2	0		0	0	0	12
1991			2	0		0	0	0	12
1992			2	0		0	0	0	12
1993			3	0		0	0	0	18
1994	**SD**	**N**	7	0	0	0	0	0	42
1995			6	0	0	0	0	0	36
1996			14	0	0	0	0	0	84
Career			36	0	0	0	0	0	216
Playoffs			3	0	0	0	0	0	18

Vern Martin

Year	Team		TD	1XP	2XP	FG	FGA	SAF	Pts
1942	**PIT**	**N**	2	0		0	0	0	12

Roy Martineau

Year	Team		TD	1XP	2XP	FG	FGA	SAF	Pts
1923	**BUF**	**N**	1	0		0		0	6

Rich Martini

Year	Team		TD	1XP	2XP	FG	FGA	SAF	Pts
1979	**OAK**	**N**	2	0		0	0	0	12

John Martinkovic

Year	Team		TD	1XP	2XP	FG	FGA	SAF	Pts
1952	**GB**	**N**	2	0		0	0	0	12

Phil Martinovich

Year	Team		TD	1XP	2XP	FG	FGA	SAF	Pts
1939	**DET**	**N**	0	0		3	6	0	9
1940	**CHIB**	**N**	0	0		2	2	0	6
1946	**BKN**	**AA**	0	21		5	10	0	36
1947			0	22		3	20	0	31
Career			0	43		13	38	0	82
Playoffs			0	1		0	1	0	1

Lonnie Marts

Year	Team		TD	1XP	2XP	FG	FGA	SAF	Pts
1992	**KC**	**N**	1	0		0	0	0	6

Russell Maryland

Year	Team		TD	1XP	2XP	FG	FGA	SAF	Pts
1992	**DAL**	**N**	1	0		0	0	0	6

Len Masini

Year	Team		TD	1XP	2XP	FG	FGA	SAF	Pts
1947	**SF**	**AA**	2	0		0	0	0	12

Matt Maslowski

Year	Team		TD	1XP	2XP	FG	FGA	SAF	Pts
1971	**LA**	**N**	1	0		0	0	0	6

Joel Mason

Year	Team		TD	1XP	2XP	FG	FGA	SAF	Pts
1943	**GB**	**N**	2	0		0	0	0	12

Larry Mason

Year	Team		TD	1XP	2XP	FG	FGA	SAF	Pts
1987	**CLE**	**N**	3	0		0	0	0	18
1988	**GB**	**N**	1	0		0	0	0	6
Career			4	0		0	0	0	24

Sam Mason

Year	Team		TD	1XP	2XP	FG	FGA	SAF	Pts
1925	**MIL**	**N**	0	1		0		0	1

Tommy Mason

Year	Team		TD	1XP	2XP	FG	FGA	SAF	Pts
1961	**MIN**	**N**	3	0		0	0	0	18
1962			8	0		0	0	0	48
1963			9	0		0	0	0	54
1964			5	0		0	0	0	30
1965			11	0		0	0	0	66
1966			3	0		0	0	0	18
1968	**LA**	**N**	3	0		0	0	0	18
1969			2	0		0	0	0	12
1970			1	0		0	0	0	6
Career			45	0		0	0	0	270

Robert Massey

Year	Team		TD	1XP	2XP	FG	FGA	SAF	Pts
1992	**PHX**	**N**	3	0		0	0	0	18

Rick Massie

Year	Team		TD	1XP	2XP	FG	FGA	SAF	Pts
1987	**DEN**	**N**	4	0		0	0	0	24

Billy Masters

Year	Team		TD	1XP	2XP	FG	FGA	SAF	Pts
1967	**BUF**	**A**	2	0	0	0	0	0	12
1969			1	0	0	0	0	0	6
1970	**DEN**	**N**	2	0		0	0	0	12
1971			1	0		0	0	0	6
1972			3	0		0	0	0	18
1975	**KC**	**N**	3	0		0	0	0	18
1976			3	0		0	0	0	18
Career			15	0	0	0	0	0	90

Bernie Masterson

Year	Team		TD	1XP	2XP	FG	FGA	SAF	Pts
1934	**CHIB**	**N**	1	1		0		0	7
1935			1	0		0		0	6
1936			2	0		0		0	12
1937			1	0		0		0	6
1939			2	0		0	0	0	12
1940			1	1		0	0	0	7
Career			8	2		0	0	0	50

Bob Masterson

Year	Team		TD	1XP	2XP	FG	FGA	SAF	Pts
1938	**WAS**	**N**	1	5		1	1	0	14
1939			1	6		1	6	0	15
1940			4	15		1	2	0	42
1941			1	8		3	6	0	23
1942			2	17		1	5	0	32
1943			3	20		1	5	0	41
1944	**BKN**	**N**	1	0		0	5	0	6
1945	**BOS**	**N**	0	0		0	1	0	0
1946	**NY**	**AA**	0	0		0	1	0	0
Career			13	71		8	32	0	173
Playoffs			0	8		0	1	0	8

John Mastrangelo

Year	Team		TD	1XP	2XP	FG	FGA	SAF	Pts
1947	**PIT**	**N**	1	0		0	0	0	6

Ed Matesic

Year	Team		TD	1XP	2XP	FG	FGA	SAF	Pts
1934	**PHI**	**N**	1	1		0		0	7
1935			1	0		0		0	6
Career			2	1		0		0	13

Jack Matheson

Year	Team		TD	1XP	2XP	FG	FGA	SAF	Pts
1943	**DET**	**N**	1	0		0	0	0	6
1944			3	0		0	0	0	18
1945			2	0		0	0	1	14
Career			6	0		0	0	1	38

Ned Mathews

Year	Team		TD	1XP	2XP	FG	FGA	SAF	Pts
1941	**DET**	**N**	1	0		0	0	0	6
1943			3	0		0	0	0	18
1945	**BOS**	**N**	1	0		0	0	0	6
1946	**CHI**	**AA**	3	0		0	0	0	18
1947	**SF**	**AA**	5	0		0	0	0	30
Career			13	0		0	0	0	78

Neil Mathews

Year	Team		TD	1XP	2XP	FG	FGA	SAF	Pts
1920	**CHIT**	**A**	0	1		0		0	1

Ray Mathews

Year	Team		TD	1XP	2XP	FG	FGA	SAF	Pts
1951	**PIT**	**N**	1	0		0	0	0	6
1952			7	1		0	0	0	43
1953			7	0		0	0	1	44
1954			8	0		0	0	0	48
1955			7	0		0	0	0	42
1956			5	0		0	0	0	30
1957			4	0		0	0	0	24
1958			4	0		0	0	0	24
Career			43	1		0	0	1	261

Bill Mathis

Year	Team		TD	1XP	2XP	FG	FGA	SAF	Pts
1960	**NY**	**A**	2	0	0	0	0	0	12
1961			8	0	0	0	0	0	48
1962			3	0	0	0	0	0	18
1963			2	0	0	0	0	0	12
1964			4	0	0	0	0	0	24
1965			6	0	0	0	0	0	36
1966			3	0	0	0	0	0	18
1967			7	0	2	0	0	0	46
1968			6	0	1	0	0	0	38
1969			5	0	0	0	0	0	30
Career			46	0	3	0	0	0	282

Terance Mathis

Year	Team		TD	1XP	2XP	FG	FGA	SAF	Pts
1990	**NYJ**	**N**	1	0		0	0	0	6
1991			1	0		0	0	0	6
1992			4	0		0	0	0	24
1993			1	0		0	0	0	6
1994	**ATL**	**N**	11	0	2	0	0	0	70
1995			9	0	3	0	0	0	60
1996			7	0	1	0	0	0	44
Career			34	0	**6**	0	0	0	216

Bruce Mathison

Year	Team		TD	1XP	2XP	FG	FGA	SAF	Pts
1985	**BUF**	**N**	1	0		0	0	0	6

Charlie Mathys

Year	Team		TD	1XP	2XP	FG	FGA	SAF	Pts
1921	**HAM**	**A**	0	0		1		0	3
1922	**GB**	**N**	2	0		1		0	15
1923			1	0		0		0	6
1924			2	0		0		0	12
1925			0	0		0		0	0
1926			0	0		0		0	0
Career			5	0		2		0	36

Trevor Matich

Year	Team		TD	1XP	2XP	FG	FGA	SAF	Pts
1991	**NYJ**	**N**	1	0		0	0	0	6

Ollie Matson

Year	Team		TD	1XP	2XP	FG	FGA	SAF	Pts
1952	**CHIC**	**N**	9	0		0	0	0	54
1954			9	0		0	0	0	54
1955			5	0		0	0	0	30
1956			8	0		0	0	0	48
1957			9	0		0	0	0	54
1958			10	0		0	0	0	60
1959	**LA**	**N**	6	0		0	0	0	36
1960			1	0		0	0	0	6
1961			5	0		0	0	0	30
1962			1	0		0	0	0	6
1964	**PHI**	**N**	5	0		0	0	0	30
1965			3	0		0	0	0	18
1966			2	0		0	0	0	12
Career			73	0		0	0	0	438

Archie Matsos

Year	Team		TD	1XP	2XP	FG	FGA	SAF	Pts
1960	**BUF**	**A**	1	0	0	0	0	0	6

Tom Matte

Year	Team		TD	1XP	2XP	FG	FGA	SAF	Pts
1962	**BAL**	**N**	3	0		0	0	0	18
1963			5	0		0	0	0	30
1964			1	0		0	0	0	6
1965			1	0		0	0	0	6
1966			3	0		0	0	0	18
1967			12	0		0	0	0	72
1968			10	0		0	0	0	60
1969			**13**	0		0	0	0	78
1971			8	0		0	0	0	48
1972			1	0		0	0	0	6
Career			57	0		0	0	0	342
Playoffs			3	0		0	0	0	18

Al Matthews

Year	Team		TD	1XP	2XP	FG	FGA	SAF	Pts
1973	**GB**	**N**	1	0		0	0	0	6

Al Matthews *continued*

Year	Team	Lg	TD	1XP	2XP	FG	FGA	SAF	Pts
1976	SEA	N	1	0		0	0	0	6
Career			2	0		0	0	0	12

Allama Matthews

Year	Team	Lg	TD	1XP	2XP	FG	FGA	SAF	Pts
1985	ATL	N	1	0		0	0	0	6

Aubrey Matthews

Year	Team	Lg	TD	1XP	2XP	FG	FGA	SAF	Pts
1987	ATL	N	3	0		0	0	0	18
1988	GB	N	2	0		0	0	0	12
1990	DET	N	1	0		0	0	0	6
1994			3	0	0	0	0	0	18
Career			9	0	0	0	0	0	54

Bo Matthews

Year	Team	Lg	TD	1XP	2XP	FG	FGA	SAF	Pts
1974	SD	N	4	0		0	0	0	24
1975			3	0		0	0	0	18
1976			4	0		0	0	0	24
1979			1	0		0	0	0	6
Career			12	0		0	0	0	72

Clay Matthews

Year	Team	Lg	TD	1XP	2XP	FG	FGA	SAF	Pts
1987	CLE	N	1	0		0	0	0	6
1989			1	0		0	0	0	6
Career			2	0		0	0	0	12

Ira Matthews

Year	Team	Lg	TD	1XP	2XP	FG	FGA	SAF	Pts
1979	OAK	N	1	0		0	0	0	6

Shane Matthews

Year	Team	Lg	TD	1XP	2XP	FG	FGA	SAF	Pts
1996	CHI	N	1	0	0	0	0	0	6

Harry Mattos

Year	Team	Lg	TD	1XP	2XP	FG	FGA	SAF	Pts
1937	CLE	N	1	2		0		0	8

John Matuszak

Year	Team	Lg	TD	1XP	2XP	FG	FGA	SAF	Pts
1975	KC	N	1	0		0	0	0	6

Carl Mauck

Year	Team	Lg	TD	1XP	2XP	FG	FGA	SAF	Pts
1972	SD	N	1	0		0	0	0	6

Tuffy Maul

Year	Team	Lg	TD	1XP	2XP	FG	FGA	SAF	Pts
1926	LA	N	2	3		2		0	21

Rich Mauti

Year	Team	Lg	TD	1XP	2XP	FG	FGA	SAF	Pts
1978	NO	N	2	0		0	0	0	12

Brett Maxie

Year	Team	Lg	TD	1XP	2XP	FG	FGA	SAF	Pts
1987	NO	N	0	0		0	0	1	2
1989			1	0		0	0	0	6
1990			1	0		0	0	0	6
1991			1	0		0	0	0	6
Career			3	0		0	0	1	20

Alvin Maxson

Year	Team	Lg	TD	1XP	2XP	FG	FGA	SAF	Pts
1974	NO	N	3	0		0	0	0	18
1975			3	0		0	0	0	18
1976			1	0		0	0	0	6
Career			7	0		0	0	0	42

Bill May

Year	Team	Lg	TD	1XP	2XP	FG	FGA	SAF	Pts
1937	CHIC	N	0	4		2		0	10
1938			0	0		0		0	0
Career			0	4		2		0	10

Ray May

Year	Team	Lg	TD	1XP	2XP	FG	FGA	SAF	Pts
1968	PIT	N	1	0		0	0	0	6

Doug Mayberry

Year	Team	Lg	TD	1XP	2XP	FG	FGA	SAF	Pts
1962	MIN	N	2	0		0	0	0	12

James Mayberry

Year	Team	Lg	TD	1XP	2XP	FG	FGA	SAF	Pts
1979	ATL	N	2	0		0	0	0	12

Derrick Mayes

Year	Team	Lg	TD	1XP	2XP	FG	FGA	SAF	Pts
1996	GB	N	2	0	0	0	0	0	12

Rueben Mayes

Year	Team	Lg	TD	1XP	2XP	FG	FGA	SAF	Pts
1986	NO	N	8	0		0	0	0	48
1987			5	0		0	0	0	30
1988			3	0		0	0	0	18
1990			7	0		0	0	0	42
Career			23	0		0	0	0	138

Lindy Mayhew

Year	Team	Lg	TD	1XP	2XP	FG	FGA	SAF	Pts
1937	PIT	N	0	0		0		1	2

Martin Mayhew

Year	Team	Lg	TD	1XP	2XP	FG	FGA	SAF	Pts
1991	WAS	N	1	0		0	0	0	6
1995	TB	N	1	0	0	0	0	0	6
Career			2	0	0	0	0	0	12

Gene Mayl

Year	Team	Lg	TD	1XP	2XP	FG	FGA	SAF	Pts
1926	DAY	N	2	0		0		0	12

Don Maynard

Year	Team	Lg	TD	1XP	2XP	FG	FGA	SAF	Pts
1960	NY	A	6	0	0	0	0	0	36
1961			8	0	0	0	0	0	48
1962			8	0	0	0	0	0	48
1963			9	0	0	0	0	0	54
1964			8	0	0	0	0	0	48
1965			**14**	0	0	0	0	0	84
1966			5	0	0	0	0	0	30
1967			10	0	1	0	0	0	62
1968			10	0	0	0	0	0	60
1969			6	0	1	0	0	0	38
1971	NYJ	N	2	0	0	0	0	0	12
1972			2	0	0	0	0	0	12
Career			88	0	2	0	0	0	532
Playoffs			2	0	0	0	0	0	12

Lew Mayne

Year	Team	Lg	TD	1XP	2XP	FG	FGA	SAF	Pts
1946	BKN	AA	2	0		0	0	0	12
1947	CLE	AA	3	0		0	0	0	18
Career			5	0		0	0	0	30

Alvoid Mays

Year	Team	Lg	TD	1XP	2XP	FG	FGA	SAF	Pts
1995	PIT	N	1	0	0	0	0	0	6

Jerry Mays

Year	Team	Lg	TD	1XP	2XP	FG	FGA	SAF	Pts
1963	KC	A	1	0	0	0	0	0	6

Frank Maznicki

Year	Team	Lg	TD	1XP	2XP	FG	FGA	SAF	Pts
1942	CHIB	N	2	21		4	5	0	45
1946			0	25		4	9	0	37
1947	BOS	N	2	19		2	2	0	37
Career			4	65		10	16	0	119
Playoffs			0	3		1	2	0	6

Vince Mazza

Year	Team	Lg	TD	1XP	2XP	FG	FGA	SAF	Pts
1948	BUF	AA	1	0		0	0	0	6

Gino Mazzanti

Year	Team	Lg	TD	1XP	2XP	FG	FGA	SAF	Pts
1950	BAL	N	1	0		0	0	0	6

Tim Mazzetti

Year	Team	Lg	TD	1XP	2XP	FG	FGA	SAF	Pts
1978	ATL	N	0	18		13	16	0	57
1979			0	31		13	25	0	70
1980			0	46		19	27	0	103
Career			0	95		45	68	0	230
Playoffs			0	7		4	5	0	19

Dean McAdams

Year	Team	Lg	TD	1XP	2XP	FG	FGA	SAF	Pts
1941	BKN	N	0	3		2	3	0	9
1942			0	2		0	0	0	2
Career			0	5		2	3	0	11

Derrick McAdoo

Year	Team	Lg	TD	1XP	2XP	FG	FGA	SAF	Pts
1987	STL	N	4	0		0	0	0	24

Fred McAfee

Year	Team	Lg	TD	1XP	2XP	FG	FGA	SAF	Pts
1991	NO	N	2	0		0	0	0	12
1992			1	0		0	0	0	6
1993			1	0		0	0	0	6
1994	ARI-PIT	N	2	0	0	0	0	0	12
1995	PIT	N	1	0	0	0	0	0	6
Career			7	0	0	0	0	0	42

George McAfee

Year	Team	Lg	TD	1XP	2XP	FG	FGA	SAF	Pts
1940	CHIB	N	3	0		0	0	0	18
1941			**12**	0		0	0	0	72
1945			4	0		0	0	0	24
1946			3	0		0	0	0	18
1947			4	0		0	0	0	24
1948			8	0		0	0	0	48
1949			5	0		0	0	0	30
Career			39	0		0	0	0	234
Playoffs			2	0		0	0	0	12

Wes McAfee

Year	Team	Lg	TD	1XP	2XP	FG	FGA	SAF	Pts
1941	PHI	N	1	2		0	0	0	8

James McAlister

Year	Team	Lg	TD	1XP	2XP	FG	FGA	SAF	Pts
1975	PHI	N	3	0		0	0	0	18
1978	NE	N	2	0		0	0	0	12
Career			5	0		0	0	0	30

Kevin McArthur

Year	Team	Lg	TD	1XP	2XP	FG	FGA	SAF	Pts
Playoffs			1	0	0	0	0	0	6

Jack McAuliffe

Year	Team	Lg	TD	1XP	2XP	FG	FGA	SAF	Pts
1926	GB	N	0	0		0		0	0

Charlie McBride

Year	Team	Lg	TD	1XP	2XP	FG	FGA	SAF	Pts
1936	CHIC	N	1	0		0		0	6

Jack McBride

Year	Team	Lg	TD	1XP	2XP	FG	FGA	SAF	Pts
1925	NY	N	2	7		2		0	25
1926	NYG	N	5	**15**		1		0	48
1927			**6**	**15**		2		0	**57**
1928			0	2		0		0	2
1929	PRO	N	0	6		0		0	6
1930	BKN	N	8	8		0		0	**56**
1931			3	1		0		0	19
1932	NYG	N	1	0		0		0	6
1933			0	6		0		0	6
1934			0	1		0		0	1
Career			25	61		5		0	226

Oscar McBride

Year	Team	Lg	TD	1XP	2XP	FG	FGA	SAF	Pts
1995	ARI	N	2	0	0	0	0	0	12

Richie McCabe

Year	Team	Lg	TD	1XP	2XP	FG	FGA	SAF	Pts
1955	PIT	N	1	0		0	0	0	6

Don McCafferty

Year	Team	Lg	TD	1XP	2XP	FG	FGA	SAF	Pts
1946	NYG	N	1	0		0	0	0	6

Ed McCaffrey

Year	Team	Lg	TD	1XP	2XP	FG	FGA	SAF	Pts
1992	NYG	N	5	0		0	0	0	30
1993			2	0		0	0	0	12
1994	SF	N	2	0	0	0	0	0	12
1995	DEN	N	2	0	1	0	0	0	14
1996			7	0	0	0	0	0	42
Career			18	0	1	0	0	0	110
Playoffs			1	0	0	0	0	0	6

Don McCall

Year	Team	Lg	TD	1XP	2XP	FG	FGA	SAF	Pts
1967	NO	N	2	0		0	0	0	12
1968			6	0		0	0	0	36
1969	PIT	N	1	0		0	0	0	6
1970	NO	N	1	0		0	0	0	6
Career			10	0		0	0	0	60

Reese McCall

Year	Team	Lg	TD	1XP	2XP	FG	FGA	SAF	Pts
1978	BAL	N	2	0		0	0	0	12
1979			4	0		0	0	0	24
1980			5	0		0	0	0	30
1981			2	0		0	0	0	12
Career			13	0		0	0	0	78

Napoleon McCallum

Year	Team	Lg	TD	1XP	2XP	FG	FGA	SAF	Pts
1986	LARI	N	1	0		0	0	0	6
1991			1	0		0	0	0	6
1993			3	0		0	0	0	18
1994			1	0	0	0	0	0	6
Career			6	0	0	0	0	0	36
Playoffs			5	0	0	0	0	0	30

Keith McCants

Year	Team	Lg	TD	1XP	2XP	FG	FGA	SAF	Pts
1994	ARI	N	1	0	0	0	0	0	6
1995			1	0	0	0	0	0	6
Career			2	0	0	0	0	0	12

Keenan McCardell

Year	Team	Lg	TD	1XP	2XP	FG	FGA	SAF	Pts
1993	CLE	N	4	0		0	0	0	24
1995			4	0		0	0	0	24
1996	JAC	N	3	0	2	0	0	0	22
Career			11	0	2	0	0	0	70
Playoffs			2	0	0	0	0	0	12

Brendan McCarthy

Year	Team	Lg	TD	1XP	2XP	FG	FGA	SAF	Pts
1968	ATL-DEN	N-A	3	0	0	0	0	0	18

Jim McCarthy

Year	Team	Lg	TD	1XP	2XP	FG	FGA	SAF	Pts
1946	BKN	AA	3	5		0	1	0	23
1948	CHI	AA	0	21		2	3	0	27
1949			0	21		6	13	0	39
Career			3	47		8	17	0	89

Vince McCarthy

Year	Team	Lg	TD	1XP	2XP	FG	FGA	SAF	Pts
1924	RI	N	1	1		0		0	7
1925			2	0		0		0	12
Career			3	1		0		0	19

Don McCauley

Year	Team	Lg	TD	1XP	2XP	FG	FGA	SAF	Pts
1971	BAL	N	2	0		0	0	0	12
1972			5	0		0	0	0	30
1973			2	0		0	0	0	12
1974			1	0		0	0	0	6
1975			11	0		0	0	0	66
1976			11	0		0	0	0	66
1977			8	0		0	0	0	48
1978			5	0		0	0	0	30
1979			6	0		0	0	0	36
1980			5	0		0	0	0	30
1981			2	0		0	0	0	12
Career			58	0		0	0	0	348

Thomas McCauley

Year	Team	Lg	TD	1XP	2XP	FG	FGA	SAF	Pts
1970	ATL	N	1	0		0	0	0	6

Bob McChesney

Year	Team	Lg	TD	1XP	2XP	FG	FGA	SAF	Pts
1938	WAS	N	1	0		0	0	0	6
1939			1	0		0	0	0	6
1940			1	0		0	0	0	6
1941			2	0		0	0	0	12
1942			1	0		0	0	0	6
Career			6	0		0	0	0	36

Bob McChesney

Year	Team	Lg	TD	1XP	2XP	FG	FGA	SAF	Pts
1950	NYG	N	6	0		0	0	0	36
1951			2	0		0	0	0	12
1952			6	0		0	0	0	36
Career			14	0		0	0	0	84

Cliff McClain

Year	Team	Lg	TD	1XP	2XP	FG	FGA	SAF	Pts
1971	NYJ	N	2	0		0	0	0	12

Clint McClain

Year	Team	Lg	TD	1XP	2XP	FG	FGA	SAF	Pts
1941	NYG	N	2	0		0	0	0	12

Dewey McClain

Year	Team	Lg	TD	1XP	2XP	FG	FGA	SAF	Pts
1978	ATL	N	0	0		0	0	1	2

Jack McClairen

Year	Team	Lg	TD	1XP	2XP	FG	FGA	SAF	Pts
1957	PIT	N	2	0		0	0	0	12
1958			1	0		0	0	0	6
Career			3	0		0	0	0	18

Brent McClanahan

Year	Team	Lg	TD	1XP	2XP	FG	FGA	SAF	Pts
1974	MIN	N	1	0		0	0	0	6
1975			1	0		0	0	0	6
1976			5	0		0	0	0	30
1977			3	0		0	0	0	18
Career			10	0		0	0	0	60
Playoffs			1	0		0	0	0	6

Billy McClard

Year	Team	Lg	TD	1XP	2XP	FG	FGA	SAF	Pts
1972	SD	N	0	2		3	6	0	11
1973	NO	N	0	9		13	24	0	48
1974			0	19		9	16	0	46
1975			0	1		1	5	0	4
Career			0	31		26	51	0	109

Willie McClendon

Year	Team	Lg	TD	1XP	2XP	FG	FGA	SAF	Pts
1979	CHI	N	1	0		0	0	0	6
1980			1	0		0	0	0	6
Career			2	0		0	0	0	12

Curtis McClinton

Year	Team	Lg	TD	1XP	2XP	FG	FGA	SAF	Pts
1962	DAL	A	2	0	0	0	0	0	12
1963	KC	A	6	0	0	0	0	0	36
1964			3	0	1	0	0	0	20
1965			9	0	0	0	0	0	54
1966			9	0	0	0	0	0	54

Curtis McClinton *continued*

Year	Team	Lg	TD	1XP	2XP	FG	FGA	SAF	Pts
1967			3	0	1	0	0	0	20
Career			32	0	2	0	0	0	196
Playoffs			1	0	0	0	0	0	6

Mike McCloskey

Year	Team	Lg	TD	1XP	2XP	FG	FGA	SAF	Pts
1983	HOU	N	1	0		0	0	0	6
1984			1	0		0	0	0	6
1985			1	0		0	0	0	6
Career			3	0		0	0	0	18

David McCluskey

Year	Team	Lg	TD	1XP	2XP	FG	FGA	SAF	Pts
1987	CIN	N	1	0		0	0	0	6

Bill McColl

Year	Team	Lg	TD	1XP	2XP	FG	FGA	SAF	Pts
1952	CHIB	N	2	0		0	0	0	12
1953			5	0		0	0	0	30
1954			2	0		0	0	0	12
1955			4	0		0	0	0	24
1956			4	0		0	0	0	24
1957			1	0		0	0	0	6
1958			8	0		0	0	0	48
Career			26	0		0	0	0	156

Milt McColl

Year	Team	Lg	TD	1XP	2XP	FG	FGA	SAF	Pts
1985	SF	N	1	0		0	0	0	6

Phil McConkey

Year	Team	Lg	TD	1XP	2XP	FG	FGA	SAF	Pts
1984	NYG	N	1	0		0	0	0	6
1985			1	0		0	0	0	6
1986			1	0		0	0	0	6
Career			3	0		0	0	0	18
Playoffs			2	0		0	0	0	12

Darris McCord

Year	Team	Lg	TD	1XP	2XP	FG	FGA	SAF	Pts
1962	DET	N	0	0		0	0	1	2
1963			1	0		0	0	0	6
Career			1	0		0	0	1	8

Felix McCormick

Year	Team	Lg	TD	1XP	2XP	FG	FGA	SAF	Pts
1929	ORA	N	0	0		1		0	3

Frank McCormick

Year	Team	Lg	TD	1XP	2XP	FG	FGA	SAF	Pts
1920	AKR	A	3	0		0		0	18
1921			3	0		0		0	18
Career			6	0		0		0	36

Tom McCormick

Year	Team	Lg	TD	1XP	2XP	FG	FGA	SAF	Pts
1955	LA	N	1	0		0	0	0	6

Mike McCoy

Year	Team	Lg	TD	1XP	2XP	FG	FGA	SAF	Pts
1975	GB	N	1	0		0	0	0	6

Fred McCrary

Year	Team	Lg	TD	1XP	2XP	FG	FGA	SAF	Pts
1995	PHI	N	1	0	0	0	0	0	6

Greg McCrary

Year	Team	Lg	TD	1XP	2XP	FG	FGA	SAF	Pts
1977	ATL	N	1	0		0	0	0	6
1978	SD	N	1	0		0	0	0	6
1979			0	0		0	0	1	2
1980			2	0		0	0	0	12
Career			4	0		0	0	1	26

Hurdis McCrary

Year	Team	Lg	TD	1XP	2XP	FG	FGA	SAF	Pts
1929	GB	N	4	0		0		0	24
1930			6	0		0		0	36
1931			1	0		0		0	6
1932			1	0		0		0	6
Career			12	0		0		0	72

Bruce McCray

Year	Team	Lg	TD	1XP	2XP	FG	FGA	SAF	Pts
1987	CHI	N	1	0		0	0	0	6

Prentice McCray

Year	Team	Lg	TD	1XP	2XP	FG	FGA	SAF	Pts
1976	NE	N	2	0		0	0	0	12

Loaird McCreary

Year	Team	Lg	TD	1XP	2XP	FG	FGA	SAF	Pts
1977	MIA	N	1	0		0	0	0	6
1978			2	0		0	0	0	12
Career			3	0		0	0	0	18

Earl McCullouch

Year	Team	Lg	TD	1XP	2XP	FG	FGA	SAF	Pts
1968	DET	N	5	0		0	0	0	30
1969			5	0		0	0	0	30

Earl McCullouch *continued*

Year	Team	Lg	TD	1XP	2XP	FG	FGA	SAF	Pts
1970			4	0		0	0	0	24
1971			3	0		0	0	0	18
1972			1	0		0	0	0	6
1973			1	0		0	0	0	6
Career			19	0		0	0	0	114

Hugh McCullough

Year	Team	Lg	TD	1XP	2XP	FG	FGA	SAF	Pts
1939	PIT	N	1	0		0	0	0	6
1940	CHIC	N	3	1		0	1	0	19
Career			4	1		0	1	0	25

Sam McCullum

Year	Team	Lg	TD	1XP	2XP	FG	FGA	SAF	Pts
1974	MIN	N	3	0		0	0	0	18
1976	SEA	N	4	0		0	0	0	24
1977			1	0		0	0	0	6
1978			3	0		0	0	0	18
1979			4	0		0	0	0	24
1980			6	0		0	0	0	36
1981			3	0		0	0	0	18
1983	MIN	N	2	0		0	0	0	12
Career			26	0		0	0	0	156
Playoffs			1	0		0	0	0	6

Lawrence McCutcheon

Year	Team	Lg	TD	1XP	2XP	FG	FGA	SAF	Pts
1973	LA	N	5	0		0	0	0	30
1974			5	0		0	0	0	30
1975			3	0		0	0	0	18
1976			11	0		0	0	0	66
1977			9	0		0	0	0	54
1978			2	0		0	0	0	12
1980	SEA	N	4	0		0	0	0	24
Career			39	0		0	0	0	234
Playoffs			2	0		0	0	0	12

Ed McDaniel

Year	Team	Lg	TD	1XP	2XP	FG	FGA	SAF	Pts
1964	NY	A	1	0	0	0	0	0	6

Johnny McDaniel

Year	Team	Lg	TD	1XP	2XP	FG	FGA	SAF	Pts
1976	CIN	N	1	0		0	0	0	6
1978	WAS	N	4	0		0	0	0	24
1979			2	0		0	0	0	12
Career			7	0		0	0	0	42

Terry McDaniel

Year	Team	Lg	TD	1XP	2XP	FG	FGA	SAF	Pts
1990	LARI	N	1	0		0	0	0	6
1993			1	0		0	0	0	6
1994			3	0	0	0	0	0	18
1995	OAK	N	1	0	0	0	0	0	6
1996			1	0	0	0	0	0	6
Career			7	0	0	0	0	0	42

Gary McDermott

Year	Team	Lg	TD	1XP	2XP	FG	FGA	SAF	Pts
1968	BUF	A	4	0	1	0	0	0	26

Ron McDole

Year	Team	Lg	TD	1XP	2XP	FG	FGA	SAF	Pts
1971	WAS	N	1	0		0	0	0	6
1975			1	0		0	0	0	6
1976			0	0		0	0	1	2
Career			2	0		0	0	1	14

Don McDonald

Year	Team	Lg	TD	1XP	2XP	FG	FGA	SAF	Pts
1944	PHI	N	1	0		0	0	0	6
1945			1	0		0	0	0	6
Career			2	0		0	0	0	12

Don McDonald

Year	Team	Lg	TD	1XP	2XP	FG	FGA	SAF	Pts
1961	BUF	A	1	0	0	0	0	0	6

Dwight McDonald

Year	Team	Lg	TD	1XP	2XP	FG	FGA	SAF	Pts
1975	SD	N	3	0		0	0	0	18
1976			4	0		0	0	0	24
1978			1	0		0	0	0	6
Career			8	0		0	0	0	48

James McDonald

Year	Team	Lg	TD	1XP	2XP	FG	FGA	SAF	Pts
1983	LARM	N	1	0		0	0	0	6
1987			2	0		0	0	0	12
Career			3	0		0	0	0	18

Keith McDonald

Year	Team	Lg	TD	1XP	2XP	FG	FGA	SAF	Pts
1987	HOU	N	1	0		0	0	0	6

Les McDonald

Year	Team	Lg	TD	1XP	2XP	FG	FGA	SAF	Pts
1937	**CHIB**	**N**	4	0		0		0	24
1938			1	1		0	0	0	7
1939			3	0		0	0	0	18
Career			8	1		0	0	0	49

Paul McDonald

Year	Team	Lg	TD	1XP	2XP	FG	FGA	SAF	Pts
1984	**CLE**	**N**	1	0		0	0	0	6

Ray McDonald

Year	Team	Lg	TD	1XP	2XP	FG	FGA	SAF	Pts
1967	**WAS**	**N**	4	0		0	0	0	24

Tim McDonald

Year	Team	Lg	TD	1XP	2XP	FG	FGA	SAF	Pts
1989	**PHX**	**N**	1	0		0	0	0	6
1994	**SF**	**N**	2	0	0	0	0	0	12
1995			2	0	0	0	0	0	12
Career			5	0	0	0	0	0	30

Tommy McDonald

Year	Team	Lg	TD	1XP	2XP	FG	FGA	SAF	Pts
1957	**PHI**	**N**	3	0		0	0	0	18
1958			9	0		0	0	0	54
1959			11	0		0	0	0	66
1960			13	0		0	0	0	78
1961			13	0		0	0	0	78
1962			10	0		0	0	0	60
1963			8	0		0	0	0	48
1964	**DAL**	**N**	2	0		0	0	0	12
1965	**LA**	**N**	9	0		0	0	0	54
1966			2	0		0	0	0	12
1967	**ATL**	**N**	4	0		0	0	0	24
1968	**CLE**	**N**	1	0		0	0	0	6
Career			85	0		0	0	0	510
Playoffs			1	0		0	0	0	6

Walt McDonald

Year	Team	Lg	TD	1XP	2XP	FG	FGA	SAF	Pts
1948	**BKN**	**AA**	1	0		0	0	0	6

Mickey McDonnell

Year	Team	Lg	TD	1XP	2XP	FG	FGA	SAF	Pts
1925	**DUL**	**N**	1	0		0		0	6
1926	**CHIC**	**N**	2	0		0		0	12
1929			2	0		0		0	12
Career			5	0		0		0	30

Coley McDonough

Year	Team	Lg	TD	1XP	2XP	FG	FGA	SAF	Pts
1939	**PIT**	**N**	1	0		0	0	0	6
1940			1	0		0	0	0	6
Career			2	0		0	0	0	12

Paul McDonough

Year	Team	Lg	TD	1XP	2XP	FG	FGA	SAF	Pts
1939	**CLE**	**N**	1	0		0	0	0	6
1940			1	0		0	0	0	6
1941			2	0		0	0	0	12
Career			4	0		0	0	0	24

Gerry McDougall

Year	Team	Lg	TD	1XP	2XP	FG	FGA	SAF	Pts
1962	**SD**	**A**	3	0	0	0	0	0	18
1963			1	0	0	0	0	0	6
1964			2	0	1	0	0	0	14
Career			6	0	1	0	0	0	38

Anthony McDowell

Year	Team	Lg	TD	1XP	2XP	FG	FGA	SAF	Pts
1992	**TB**	**N**	2	0		0	0	0	12
1993			1	0		0	0	0	6
1994			1	0	0	0	0	0	6
Career			4	0	0	0	0	0	24

Bubba McDowell

Year	Team	Lg	TD	1XP	2XP	FG	FGA	SAF	Pts
1989	**HOU**	**N**	0	0		0	0	1	2
1991			1	0		0	0	0	6
1992			1	0		0	0	0	6
Career			2	0		0	0	1	14
Playoffs			1	0		0	0	0	6

O.J. McDuffie

Year	Team	Lg	TD	1XP	2XP	FG	FGA	SAF	Pts
1993	**MIA**	**N**	2	0		0	0	0	12
1994			3	0	0	0	0	0	18
1995			8	0	1	0	0	0	50
1996			8	0	0	0	0	0	48
Career			21	0	1	0	0	0	128
Playoffs			1	0	1	0	0	0	8

Hugh McElhenny

Year	Team	Lg	TD	1XP	2XP	FG	FGA	SAF	Pts
1952	**SF**	**N**	10	0		0	0	0	60
1953			5	0		0	0	0	30

Hugh McElhenny *continued*

Year	Team	Lg	TD	1XP	2XP	FG	FGA	SAF	Pts
1954			6	0		0	0	0	36
1955			6	0		0	0	0	36
1956			8	0		0	0	0	48
1957			3	0		0	0	0	18
1958			8	0		0	0	0	48
1959			4	0		0	0	0	24
1960			1	0		0	0	0	6
1961	**MIN**	**N**	7	0		0	0	0	42
1963	**NYG**	**N**	2	0		0	0	0	12
Career			60	0		0	0	0	360
Playoffs			1	0		0	0	0	6

Leeland McElroy

Year	Team	Lg	TD	1XP	2XP	FG	FGA	SAF	Pts
1996	**ARI**	**N**	2	0	0	0	0	0	12

Vann McElroy

Year	Team	Lg	TD	1XP	2XP	FG	FGA	SAF	Pts
1987	**LARI**	**N**	1	0		0	0	0	6

Bill McElwain

Year	Team	Lg	TD	1XP	2XP	FG	FGA	SAF	Pts
1926	**CHIC**	**N**	1	0		0		0	6

Doug McEnulty

Year	Team	Lg	TD	1XP	2XP	FG	FGA	SAF	Pts
1943	**CHIB**	**N**	1	0		0	0	0	6
1944			1	0		0	0	0	6
Career			2	0		0	0	0	12

Craig McEwen

Year	Team	Lg	TD	1XP	2XP	FG	FGA	SAF	Pts
1990	**SD**	**N**	3	0		0	0	0	18
1991			3	0		0	0	0	18
Career			6	0		0	0	0	36

Banks McFadden

Year	Team	Lg	TD	1XP	2XP	FG	FGA	SAF	Pts
1940	**BKN**	**N**	3	0		0	0	0	18

Paul McFadden

Year	Team	Lg	TD	1XP	2XP	FG	FGA	SAF	Pts
1984	**PHI**	**N**	0	26		**30**	**37**	0	116
1985			0	29		25	30	0	104
1986			0	26		20	31	0	86
1987			0	36		16	26	0	84
1988	**NYG**	**N**	0	25		14	19	0	67
1989	**ATL**	**N**	0	18		15	20	0	63
Career			0	160		120	163	0	520

Thad McFadden

Year	Team	Lg	TD	1XP	2XP	FG	FGA	SAF	Pts
1987	**BUF**	**N**	1	0		0	0	0	6

Bud McFadin

Year	Team	Lg	TD	1XP	2XP	FG	FGA	SAF	Pts
1955	**LA**	**N**	0	0		1	5	0	3
1956			1	0		1	4	0	9
1962	**DEN**	**A**	1	0	0	0	0	0	6
1963			1	0	0	0	0	0	6
Career			3	0	0	2	9	0	24

Jim McFarland

Year	Team	Lg	TD	1XP	2XP	FG	FGA	SAF	Pts
1971	**STL**	**N**	2	0		0	0	0	12
1973			1	0		0	0	0	6
Career			3	0		0	0	0	18

Kay McFarland

Year	Team	Lg	TD	1XP	2XP	FG	FGA	SAF	Pts
1963	**SF**	**N**	1	0		0	0	0	6
1965			1	0		0	0	0	6
1966			1	0		0	0	0	6
1968			1	0		0	0	0	6
Career			4	0		0	0	0	24

Nyle McFarlane

Year	Team	Lg	TD	1XP	2XP	FG	FGA	SAF	Pts
1960	**OAK**	**A**	2	0	0	0	0	0	12

Ben McGee

Year	Team	Lg	TD	1XP	2XP	FG	FGA	SAF	Pts
1967	**PIT**	**N**	1	0		0	0	0	6

Buford McGee

Year	Team	Lg	TD	1XP	2XP	FG	FGA	SAF	Pts
1984	**SD**	**N**	6	0		0	0	0	36
1985			3	0		0	0	0	18
1986			7	0		0	0	0	42
1987	**LARM**	**N**	1	0		0	0	0	6
1988			3	0		0	0	0	18
1989			5	0		0	0	0	30
1990			5	0		0	0	0	30
Career			30	0		0	0	0	180

Max McGee

Year	Team	Lg	TD	1XP	2XP	FG	FGA	SAF	Pts
1954	**GB**	**N**	9	0		0	0	0	54

Max McGee *continued*

Year	Team	Lg	TD	1XP	2XP	FG	FGA	SAF	Pts
1957			1	0		0	0	0	6
1958			7	0		0	0	0	42
1959			5	0		0	0	0	30
1960			4	0		0	0	0	24
1961			7	0		0	0	0	42
1962			3	0		0	0	0	18
1963			6	0		0	0	0	36
1964			7	0		0	0	0	42
1965			1	0		0	0	0	6
1966			1	0		0	0	0	6
Career			51	0		0	0	0	306
Playoffs			4	0		0	0	0	24

Tim McGee

Year	Team	Lg	TD	1XP	2XP	FG	FGA	SAF	Pts
1986	**CIN**	**N**	1	0		0	0	0	6
1987			1	0		0	0	0	6
1988			6	0		0	0	0	36
1989			8	0		0	0	0	48
1990			1	0		0	0	0	6
1991			4	0		0	0	0	24
1992			3	0		0	0	0	18
1993	**WAS**	**N**	3	0		0	0	0	18
1994	**CIN**	**N**	1	0	0	0	0	0	6
Career			28	0	0	0	0	0	168

Tony McGee

Year	Team	Lg	TD	1XP	2XP	FG	FGA	SAF	Pts
1994	**CIN**	**N**	1	0	0	0	0	0	6
1995			4	0	0	0	0	0	24
1996			4	0	0	0	0	0	24
Career			9	0	0	0	0	0	54

Willie McGee

Year	Team	Lg	TD	1XP	2XP	FG	FGA	SAF	Pts
1976	**SF**	**N**	4	0		0	0	0	24

John McGeever

Year	Team	Lg	TD	1XP	2XP	FG	FGA	SAF	Pts
1962	**DEN**	**A**	1	0	0	0	0	0	6

Rich McGeorge

Year	Team	Lg	TD	1XP	2XP	FG	FGA	SAF	Pts
1970	**GB**	**N**	2	0		0	0	0	12
1971			4	0		0	0	0	24
1972			2	0		0	0	0	12
1973			1	0		0	0	0	6
1975			1	0		0	0	0	6
1976			1	0		0	0	0	6
1977			1	0		0	0	0	6
1978			1	0		0	0	0	6
Career			13	0		0	0	0	78

Mike McGill

Year	Team	Lg	TD	1XP	2XP	FG	FGA	SAF	Pts
1970	**MIN**	**N**	1	0		0	0	0	6

Ralph McGill

Year	Team	Lg	TD	1XP	2XP	FG	FGA	SAF	Pts
1975	**SF**	**N**	1	0		0	0	0	6
1976			1	0		0	0	0	6
Career			2	0		0	0	0	12

Willie McGinest

Year	Team	Lg	TD	1XP	2XP	FG	FGA	SAF	Pts
1996	**NE**	**N**	2	0	0	0	0	0	12

Joe McGlone

Year	Team	Lg	TD	1XP	2XP	FG	FGA	SAF	Pts
1926	**BOS**	**A**	0	1		0		0	1

Rob McGovern

Year	Team	Lg	TD	1XP	2XP	FG	FGA	SAF	Pts
1989	**KC**	**N**	0	0		0	0	1	2

Reggie McGowan

Year	Team	Lg	TD	1XP	2XP	FG	FGA	SAF	Pts
1987	**NYG**	**N**	1	0		0	0	0	6

Mark McGrath

Year	Team	Lg	TD	1XP	2XP	FG	FGA	SAF	Pts
1984	**WAS**	**N**	1	0		0	0	0	6

Lamar McGriggs

Year	Team	Lg	TD	1XP	2XP	FG	FGA	SAF	Pts
1993	**MIN**	**N**	1	0		0	0	0	6

Mike McGruder

Year	Team	Lg	TD	1XP	2XP	FG	FGA	SAF	Pts
1993	**SF**	**N**	1	0		0	0	0	6

Lamar McHan

Year	Team	Lg	TD	1XP	2XP	FG	FGA	SAF	Pts
1954	**CHIC**	**N**	1	0		0	0	0	6
1955			2	0		0	0	0	12
1956			5	0		0	0	0	30
1957			2	0		0	0	0	12
1958			1	0		0	0	0	6

Lamar McHan *continued*

Year	Team		TD	1XP	2XP	FG	FGA	SAF	Pts
1960	GB	N	1	0		0	0	0	6
Career			12	0		0	0	0	72

Pat McHugh

Year	Team		TD	1XP	2XP	FG	FGA	SAF	Pts
1947	PHI	N	2	0		0	0	0	12
1949			1	0		0	0	0	6
Career			3	0		0	0	0	18
Playoffs			1	0		0	0	0	6

Don McIlhenny

Year	Team		TD	1XP	2XP	FG	FGA	SAF	Pts
1956	DET	N	5	0		0	0	0	30
1957	GB	N	3	0		0	0	0	18
1958			2	0		0	0	0	12
1959			2	0		0	0	0	12
1960	DAL	N	2	0		0	0	0	12
Career			14	0		0	0	0	84

Pat McInally

Year	Team		TD	1XP	2XP	FG	FGA	SAF	Pts
1977	CIN	N	3	0		0	0	0	18
1980			2	0		0	0	0	12
Career			5	0		0	0	0	30

Nick McInerney

Year	Team		TD	1XP	2XP	FG	FGA	SAF	Pts
1925	CHIC	N	1	0		0		0	6

Joe McIntosh

Year	Team		TD	1XP	2XP	FG	FGA	SAF	Pts
1987	ATL	N	1	0		0	0	0	6

Guy McIntyre

Year	Team		TD	1XP	2XP	FG	FGA	SAF	Pts
1985	SF	N	1	0		0	0	0	6
1988			1	0		0	0	0	6
Career			2	0		0	0	0	12

Secedrik McIntyre

Year	Team		TD	1XP	2XP	FG	FGA	SAF	Pts
1977	ATL	N	1	0		0	0	0	6

Bill McKalip

Year	Team		TD	1XP	2XP	FG	FGA	SAF	Pts
1931	POR	N	4	0		0		0	24

John McKay

Year	Team		TD	1XP	2XP	FG	FGA	SAF	Pts
1976	TB	N	1	0		0	0	0	6
1978			1	0		0	0	0	6
Career			2	0		0	0	0	12

Roy McKay

Year	Team		TD	1XP	2XP	FG	FGA	SAF	Pts
1945	GB	N	2	0		0	0	0	12
1946			1	2		0	0	0	8
1947			0	1		0	0	0	1
Career			3	3		0	0	0	21

Paul McKee

Year	Team		TD	1XP	2XP	FG	FGA	SAF	Pts
1947	WAS	N	2	0		0	0	0	12

Marlin McKeever

Year	Team		TD	1XP	2XP	FG	FGA	SAF	Pts
1964	LA	N	1	0		0	0	0	6
1965			4	0		0	0	0	24
1966			1	0		0	0	0	6
Career			6	0		0	0	0	36

Keith McKeller

Year	Team		TD	1XP	2XP	FG	FGA	SAF	Pts
1989	BUF	N	2	0		0	0	0	12
1990			5	0		0	0	0	30
1991			3	0		0	0	0	18
1993			1	0		0	0	0	6
Career			11	0		0	0	0	66

Hugh McKinnis

Year	Team		TD	1XP	2XP	FG	FGA	SAF	Pts
1974	CLE	N	2	0		0	0	0	12
1975			4	0		0	0	0	24
1976	SEA	N	4	0		0	0	0	24
Career			10	0		0	0	0	60

Dennis McKinnon

Year	Team		TD	1XP	2XP	FG	FGA	SAF	Pts
1983	CHI	N	5	0		0	0	0	30
1984			3	0		0	0	0	18
1985			7	0		0	0	0	42
1987			3	0		0	0	0	18
1988			4	0		0	0	0	24
1989			3	0		0	0	0	18
1990	DAL	N	1	0		0	0	0	6
Career			26	0		0	0	0	156
Playoffs			4	0		0	0	0	24

James McKnight

Year	Team		TD	1XP	2XP	FG	FGA	SAF	Pts
1994	SEA	N	1	0	0	0	0	0	6

Ted McKnight

Year	Team		TD	1XP	2XP	FG	FGA	SAF	Pts
1978	KC	N	7	0		0	0	0	42
1979			8	0		0	0	0	48
1980			3	0		0	0	0	18
1981			5	0		0	0	0	30
Career			23	0		0	0	0	138

Tim McKyer

Year	Team		TD	1XP	2XP	FG	FGA	SAF	Pts
1986	SF	N	1	0		0	0	0	6
1995	CAR	N	1	0	0	0	0	0	6
Career			2	0	0	0	0	0	12

Mayes McLain

Year	Team		TD	1XP	2XP	FG	FGA	SAF	Pts
1930	POR	N	7	0		0		0	42
1931	SI	N	2	0		0		0	12
Career			9	0		0		0	54

Steve McLaughlin

Year	Team		TD	1XP	2XP	FG	FGA	SAF	Pts
1995	STL	N	0	17	0	8	16	0	41

Ray McLean

Year	Team		TD	1XP	2XP	FG	FGA	SAF	Pts
1940	CHIB	N	4	1		0	0	0	25
1941			3	0		0	0	0	18
1942			9	0		0	0	0	54
1943			3	0		0	0	0	18
1944			7	0		0	0	0	42
1946			3	0		0	0	0	18
1947			1	**44**		0	1	0	50
Career			30	45		0	1	0	225
Playoffs			0	1		0	0	0	1

Dana McLemore

Year	Team		TD	1XP	2XP	FG	FGA	SAF	Pts
1982	SF	N	1	0		0	0	0	6
1983			1	0		0	0	0	6
1984			2	0		0	0	0	12
1987			1	0		0	0	0	6
Career			5	0		0	0	0	30

Emmett McLemore

Year	Team		TD	1XP	2XP	FG	FGA	SAF	Pts
1923	OOR	N	1	1		0		0	7

Bob McLeod

Year	Team		TD	1XP	2XP	FG	FGA	SAF	Pts
1961	HOU	A	2	0	0	0	0	0	12
1962			6	0	0	0	0	0	36
1963			5	0	0	0	0	0	30
1964			2	0	0	0	0	0	12
1965			1	0	0	0	0	0	6
1966			3	0	0	0	0	0	18
Career			19	0	0	0	0	0	114

Harold McLinton

Year	Team		TD	1XP	2XP	FG	FGA	SAF	Pts
1974	WAS	N	1	0		0	0	0	6

Jim McMahon

Year	Team		TD	1XP	2XP	FG	FGA	SAF	Pts
1982	CHI	N	1	0		0	0	0	6
1983			3	0		0	0	0	18
1984			2	0		0	0	0	12
1985			4	0		0	0	0	24
1986			1	0		0	0	0	6
1987			2	0		0	0	0	12
1988			4	0		0	0	0	24
1991	PHI	N	1	0		0	0	0	6
Career			18	0		0	0	0	108
Playoffs			3	0		0	0	0	18

John McMakin

Year	Team		TD	1XP	2XP	FG	FGA	SAF	Pts
1972	PIT	N	1	0		0	0	0	6
1973			1	0		0	0	0	6
1976	SEA	N	2	0		0	0	0	12
Career			4	0		0	0	0	24

Steve McMichael

Year	Team		TD	1XP	2XP	FG	FGA	SAF	Pts
1985	CHI	N	0	0		0	0	1	2
1986			0	0		0	0	1	2
1988			0	0		0	0	1	2
Career			0	0		0	0	3	6

Erik McMillan

Year	Team		TD	1XP	2XP	FG	FGA	SAF	Pts
1988	NYJ	N	2	0		0	0	0	12
1989			3	0		0	0	0	18

Erik McMillan *continued*

Year	Team		TD	1XP	2XP	FG	FGA	SAF	Pts
1991			2	0		0	0	0	12
Career			7	0		0	0	0	42

Randy McMillan

Year	Team		TD	1XP	2XP	FG	FGA	SAF	Pts
1981	BAL	N	4	0		0	0	0	24
1982			1	0		0	0	0	6
1983			6	0		0	0	0	36
1984	IND	N	5	0		0	0	0	30
1985			7	0		0	0	0	42
1986			3	0		0	0	0	18
Career			26	0		0	0	0	156

Audrey McMillian

Year	Team		TD	1XP	2XP	FG	FGA	SAF	Pts
1992	MIN	N	2	0		0	0	0	12
1993			1	0		0	0	0	6
Career			3	0		0	0	0	18

Bo McMillin

Year	Team		TD	1XP	2XP	FG	FGA	SAF	Pts
1922	MIL	N	1	0		0		0	6
1923			0	0		0		0	0
Career			1	0		0		0	6

Jim McMillin

Year	Team		TD	1XP	2XP	FG	FGA	SAF	Pts
1962	DEN	A	2	0	0	0	0	0	12
1963	OAK	A	1	0	0	0	0	0	6
1964	DEN	A	1	0	0	0	0	0	6
Career			4	0	0	0	0	0	24

Greg McMurtry

Year	Team		TD	1XP	2XP	FG	FGA	SAF	Pts
1991	NE	N	2	0		0	0	0	12
1992			1	0		0	0	0	6
1993			1	0		0	0	0	6
1994	CHI	N	1	0	0	0	0	0	6
Career			5	0	0	0	0	0	30

Steve McNair

Year	Team		TD	1XP	2XP	FG	FGA	SAF	Pts
1996	HOU	N	2	0	0	0	0	0	12

Todd McNair

Year	Team		TD	1XP	2XP	FG	FGA	SAF	Pts
1989	KC	N	1	0		0	0	0	6
1990			2	0		0	0	0	12
1991			1	0		0	0	0	6
1992			2	0		0	0	0	12
1993			2	0		0	0	0	12
1995	HOU	N	1	0	0	0	0	0	6
1996	KC	N	1	0	0	0	0	0	6
Career			10	0	0	0	0	0	60

Frank McNally

Year	Team		TD	1XP	2XP	FG	FGA	SAF	Pts
1933	CHIC	N	1	0		0		1	8

Bob McNamara

Year	Team		TD	1XP	2XP	FG	FGA	SAF	Pts
1960	DEN	A	2	0	0	0	0	0	12

Tom McNamara

Year	Team		TD	1XP	2XP	FG	FGA	SAF	Pts
1923	TOL	N	0	0		1		0	3

Sean McNanie

Year	Team		TD	1XP	2XP	FG	FGA	SAF	Pts
1987	BUF	N	1	0		0	0	0	6

Don McNeal

Year	Team		TD	1XP	2XP	FG	FGA	SAF	Pts
1982	MIA	N	1	0		0	0	0	6
1984			1	0		0	0	0	6
Career			2	0		0	0	0	12

Travis McNeal

Year	Team		TD	1XP	2XP	FG	FGA	SAF	Pts
1991	SEA	N	1	0		0	0	0	6
1993	LARM	N	1	0		0	0	0	6
Career			2	0		0	0	0	12

Charlie McNeil

Year	Team		TD	1XP	2XP	FG	FGA	SAF	Pts
1961	SD	A	2	0	0	0	0	0	12

Clifton McNeil

Year	Team		TD	1XP	2XP	FG	FGA	SAF	Pts
1964	CLE	N	1	0		0	0	0	6
1966			2	0		0	0	0	12
1967			2	0		0	0	0	12
1968	SF	N	7	0		0	0	0	42
1969			3	0		0	0	0	18
1970	NYG	N	5	0		0	0	0	30
1971	NYG-WAS	N	3	0		0	0	0	18
Career			23	0		0	0	0	138

Fred McNeil

Year	Team	TD	1XP	2XP	FG	FGA	SAF	Pts
1978	MIN N	1	0		0	0	0	6

Freeman McNeil

Year	Team	TD	1XP	2XP	FG	FGA	SAF	Pts
1981	NYJ N	3	0		0	0	0	18
1982		7	0		0	0	0	42
1983		4	0		0	0	0	24
1984		6	0		0	0	0	36
1985		5	0		0	0	0	30
1986		6	0		0	0	0	36
1987		1	0		0	0	0	6
1988		7	0		0	0	0	42
1989		3	0		0	0	0	18
1990		6	0		0	0	0	36
1991		2	0		0	0	0	12
Career		50	0		0	0	0	300
Playoffs		4	0		0	0	0	24

Gerald McNeil

Year	Team	TD	1XP	2XP	FG	FGA	SAF	Pts
1986	CLE N	2	0		0	0	0	12
1987		2	0		0	0	0	12
Career		4	0		0	0	0	24

Rod McNeill

Year	Team	TD	1XP	2XP	FG	FGA	SAF	Pts
1974	NO N	1	0		0	0	0	6
1975		4	0		0	0	0	24
Career		5	0		0	0	0	30

Paul McNulty

Year	Team	TD	1XP	2XP	FG	FGA	SAF	Pts
1925	CHIC N	1	0		0		0	6

Bill McPeak

Year	Team	TD	1XP	2XP	FG	FGA	SAF	Pts
1954	PIT N	0	0		0	0	1	2
1956		0	0		0	0	1	2
1957		0	0		0	0	1	2
Career		0	0		0	0	3	6

Buck McPhail

Year	Team	TD	1XP	2XP	FG	FGA	SAF	Pts
1953	BAL N	0	21	2	5	0		27

Hal McPhail

Year	Team	TD	1XP	2XP	FG	FGA	SAF	Pts
1934	BOS N	3	4		0		0	22

Leon McQuay

Year	Team	TD	1XP	2XP	FG	FGA	SAF	Pts
1974	NYG N	1	0		0	0	0	6

Bennie McRae

Year	Team	TD	1XP	2XP	FG	FGA	SAF	Pts
1963	CHI N	1	0		0	0	0	6
1965		1	0		0	0	0	6
1967		2	0		0	0	0	12
Career		4	0		0	0	0	24

Rod McSwain

Year	Team	TD	1XP	2XP	FG	FGA	SAF	Pts
1986	NE N	1	0		0	0	0	6

Warren McVea

Year	Team	TD	1XP	2XP	FG	FGA	SAF	Pts
1968	CIN A	3	0		0	0	0	18
1969	KC A	7	0		0	0	0	42
1971	KC N	3	0		0	0	0	18
Career		13	0		0	0	0	78

Bill McWatters

Year	Team	TD	1XP	2XP	FG	FGA	SAF	Pts
1964	MIN N	1	0		0	0	0	6

Johnny McWilliams

Year	Team	TD	1XP	2XP	FG	FGA	SAF	Pts
1996	ARI N	1	0	0	0	0	0	6

Mike Meade

Year	Team	TD	1XP	2XP	FG	FGA	SAF	Pts
1983	GB N	3	0		0	0	0	18

Eddie Meador

Year	Team	TD	1XP	2XP	FG	FGA	SAF	Pts
1960	LA N	1	0		0	0	0	6
1965		1	0		0	0	0	6
1967		2	0		0	0	0	12
1969		2	0		0	0	0	12
Career		6	0		0	0	0	36

Johnny Meads

Year	Team	TD	1XP	2XP	FG	FGA	SAF	Pts
1992	HOU N	1	0		0	0	0	6

Natrone Means

Year	Team	TD	1XP	2XP	FG	FGA	SAF	Pts
1993	SD N	8	0		0	0	0	48
1994		12	0		0	0	0	72
1995		5	0		0	0	0	30

Natrone Means *continued*

Year	Team	TD	1XP	2XP	FG	FGA	SAF	Pts
1996	JAC N	3	0	0	0	0	0	18
Career		28	0	0	0	0	0	168
Playoffs		4	0	0	0	0	0	24

Karl Mecklenburg

Year	Team	TD	1XP	2XP	FG	FGA	SAF	Pts
1989	DEN N	1	0		0	0	0	6
1990		1	0		0	0	1	8
Career		2	0		0	0	1	14

Herb Meeker

Year	Team	TD	1XP	2XP	FG	FGA	SAF	Pts
1930	PRO N	2	1		1		0	16
1931		0	1		0		0	1
Career		2	2		1		0	17

Dave Meggett

Year	Team	TD	1XP	2XP	FG	FGA	SAF	Pts
1989	NYG N	5	0		0	0	0	30
1990		2	0		0	0	0	12
1991		5	0		0	0	0	30
1992		3	0		0	0	0	18
1993		1	0		0	0	0	6
1994		6	0	0	0	0	0	36
1995	NE N	2	0	2	0	0	0	16
1996		1	0	0	0	0	0	6
Career		25	0	2	0	0	0	154

Charlie Mehelich

Year	Team	TD	1XP	2XP	FG	FGA	SAF	Pts
1951	PIT N	0	0		0	0	1	2

Lance Mehl

Year	Team	TD	1XP	2XP	FG	FGA	SAF	Pts
1983	NYJ N	1	0		0	0	0	6

Steve Meilinger

Year	Team	TD	1XP	2XP	FG	FGA	SAF	Pts
1956	WAS N	5	0		0	0	0	30
1957		2	0		0	0	0	12
1958	GB N	1	0		0	0	0	6
Career		8	0		0	0	0	48

Dale Meinert

Year	Team	TD	1XP	2XP	FG	FGA	SAF	Pts
1964	STL N	1	0		0	0	0	6

Jim Mello

Year	Team	TD	1XP	2XP	FG	FGA	SAF	Pts
1948	CHI AA	1	0		0	0	0	6

John Mellus

Year	Team	TD	1XP	2XP	FG	FGA	SAF	Pts
1940	NYG N	1	0		0	0	0	6
1946	SF AA	0	1		0	1	0	1
Career		1	1		0	1	0	7

Melvin

Year	Team	TD	1XP	2XP	FG	FGA	SAF	Pts
1921	CIN A	1	0		0		0	6

Chuck Mercein

Year	Team	TD	1XP	2XP	FG	FGA	SAF	Pts
1965	NYG N	2	0		0	2	0	12
1967	NY-GB N	1	2		0	1	0	8
1968	GB N	1	7		2	5	0	19
1970	NYJ N	1	0		0	0	0	6
Career		5	9		2	8	0	45
Playoffs		1	0		0	0	0	6

Ken Mercer

Year	Team	TD	1XP	2XP	FG	FGA	SAF	Pts
1927	FRA N	2	8		5		1	37
1928		6	2		0		0	38
1929		1	6		2		0	18
Career		9	16		7		1	93

Mike Mercer

Year	Team	TD	1XP	2XP	FG	FGA	SAF	Pts
1961	MIN N	0	36		9	21	0	63
1962		0	3		0	5	0	3
1963	OAK A	0	47	0	8	21	0	71
1964		0	34	0	15	24	0	79
1965		0	35	0	9	15	0	62
1966	OAK-KC A	0	35	0	21	30	0	98
1967	BUF A	0	25	0	16	27	0	73
1968	BUF-GB A-N	0	16	0	7	16	0	37
1969	GB N	0	23		5	17	0	38
1970	SD N	0	34		12	19	0	70
Career		0	288	0	102	195	0	594
Playoffs		0	5	0	2	4	0	11

Don Meredith

Year	Team	TD	1XP	2XP	FG	FGA	SAF	Pts
1961	DAL N	1	0		0	0	0	6
1963		3	0		0	0	0	18
1964		4	0		0	0	0	24

Don Meredith *continued*

Year	Team	TD	1XP	2XP	FG	FGA	SAF	Pts
1965		1	0		0	0	0	6
1966		5	0		0	0	0	30
1968		1	0		0	0	0	6
Career		15	0		0	0	0	90

Guido Merkens

Year	Team	TD	1XP	2XP	FG	FGA	SAF	Pts
1979	HOU N	1	0		0	0	0	6
1981	NO N	1	0		0	0	0	6
1985		1	0		0	0	0	6
Career		3	0		0	0	0	18

Jim Merlo

Year	Team	TD	1XP	2XP	FG	FGA	SAF	Pts
1976	NO N	2	0		0	0	0	12
1977		1	0		0	0	0	6
Career		3	0		0	0	0	18

Sam Merriman

Year	Team	TD	1XP	2XP	FG	FGA	SAF	Pts
1985	SEA N	1	0		0	0	0	6

Mike Merriweather

Year	Team	TD	1XP	2XP	FG	FGA	SAF	Pts
1983	PIT N	1	0		0	0	0	6
1985		1	0		0	0	0	6
1989	MIN N	1	0		0	0	1	8
1990		1	0		0	0	0	6
1991		1	0		0	0	0	6
Career		5	0		0	0	1	32

Jerry Mertens

Year	Team	TD	1XP	2XP	FG	FGA	SAF	Pts
1959	SF N	1	0		0	0	0	6

Bus Mertes

Year	Team	TD	1XP	2XP	FG	FGA	SAF	Pts
1946	LA AA	1	0		0	0	0	6
1947	BAL AA	2	0		0	0	0	12
1948		4	0		0	0	0	24
1949		1	0		0	0	0	6
Career		8	0		0	0	0	48
Playoffs		2	0		0	0	0	12

Frank Mestnik

Year	Team	TD	1XP	2XP	FG	FGA	SAF	Pts
1960	STL N	3	0		0	0	0	18
1961		2	0		0	0	0	12
Career		5	0		0	0	0	30

Eric Metcalf

Year	Team	TD	1XP	2XP	FG	FGA	SAF	Pts
1989	CLE N	10	0		0	0	0	60
1990		4	0		0	0	0	24
1992		7	0		0	0	0	42
1993		5	0		0	0	0	30
1994		7	0	0	0	0	0	42
1995	ATL N	10	0	0	0	0	0	60
1996		6	0	0	0	0	0	36
Career		49	0	0	0	0	0	294
Playoffs		2	0	0	0	0	0	12

Terry Metcalf

Year	Team	TD	1XP	2XP	FG	FGA	SAF	Pts
1973	STL N	2	0		0	0	0	12
1974		8	0		0	0	0	48
1975		13	0		0	0	0	78
1976		7	0		0	0	0	42
1977		6	0		0	0	0	36
Career		36	0		0	0	0	216
Playoffs		1	0		0	0	0	6

Russ Method

Year	Team	TD	1XP	2XP	FG	FGA	SAF	Pts
1924	DUL N	1	0		0		0	6
1926		1	0		0		0	6
1927		1	0		0		0	6
Career		3	0		0		0	18

Pete Metzelaars

Year	Team	TD	1XP	2XP	FG	FGA	SAF	Pts
1983	SEA N	1	0		0	0	0	6
1985	BUF N	1	0		0	0	0	6
1986		4	0		0	0	0	24
1988		1	0		0	0	0	6
1989		2	0		0	0	0	12
1990		1	0		0	0	0	6
1991		2	0		0	0	0	12
1992		6	0		0	0	0	36
1993		4	0		0	0	0	24
1994		5	0		0	0	0	30
1995	CAR N	3	0		0	0	0	18
Career		30	0		0	0	0	180
Playoffs		2	0		0	0	0	12

Fred Meyer

Year	Team		TD	1XP	2XP	FG	FGA	SAF	Pts
1942	**PHI**	**N**	1	0		0	0	0	6
1945			1	0		0	0	0	6
Career			2	0		0	0	0	12

Paul Meyers

Year	Team		TD	1XP	2XP	FG	FGA	SAF	Pts
1923	**RAC**	**N**	1	0		0		0	6

Rich Miano

Year	Team		TD	1XP	2XP	FG	FGA	SAF	Pts
1987	**NYJ**	**N**	1	0		0	0	0	6

Al Michaels

Year	Team		TD	1XP	2XP	FG	FGA	SAF	Pts
1923	**AKR**	**N**	0	0		1		0	3
1924			1	0		0		0	6
1925	**CLE**	**N**	0	0		0		0	0
1926	**CLE**	**A**	0	0		0		0	0
Career			1	0		1		0	9

Lou Michaels

Year	Team		TD	1XP	2XP	FG	FGA	SAF	Pts
1958	**LA**	**N**	1	0		0	0	0	6
1959			0	12		8	17	0	36
1960			0	1		2	3	0	7
1961	**PIT**	**N**	0	27		15	26	0	72
1962			0	32		**26**	**42**	0	110
1963			0	32		21	**41**	0	95
1964	**BAL**	**N**	0	**53**		17	35	0	104
1965			0	48		17	28	1	101
1966			0	35		21	39	0	98
1967			0	46		20	37	0	106
1968			0	48		18	28	0	102
1969			0	33		14	31	0	75
1971	**GB**	**N**	0	19		8	14	0	43
Career			1	386		187	341	1	955
Playoffs			0	9		4	8	0	21

Walt Michaels

Year	Team		TD	1XP	2XP	FG	FGA	SAF	Pts
1951	**GB**	**N**	0	0		0	1	0	0
1953	**CLE**	**N**	1	0		0	0	0	6
1955			1	0		0	0	0	6
Career			2	0		0	1	0	12

Art Michalik

Year	Team		TD	1XP	2XP	FG	FGA	SAF	Pts
1955	**PIT**	**N**	0	9		1	12	0	12
1956			0	0		0	1	0	0
Career			0	9		1	13	0	12

Mike Michalske

Year	Team		TD	1XP	2XP	FG	FGA	SAF	Pts
1931	**GB**	**N**	1	0		0		0	6
1932			1	0		0		0	6
Career			2	0		0		0	12

Mike Michel

Year	Team		TD	1XP	2XP	FG	FGA	SAF	Pts
1977	**MIA**	**N**	0	0		0	0	0	0
1978	**PHI**	**N**	0	9		0	0	0	9
Career			0	9		0	0	0	9
Playoffs			0	1		0	2	0	1

Bobby Micho

Year	Team		TD	1XP	2XP	FG	FGA	SAF	Pts
1987	**DEN**	**N**	2	0		0	0	0	12

Mike Micka

Year	Team		TD	1XP	2XP	FG	FGA	SAF	Pts
1946	**BOS**	**N**	1	0		0	0	0	6

Terry Mickens

Year	Team		TD	1XP	2XP	FG	FGA	SAF	Pts
1996	**GB**	**N**	2	0	0	0	0	0	12

Dave Middleton

Year	Team		TD	1XP	2XP	FG	FGA	SAF	Pts
1955	**DET**	**N**	5	0		0	0	0	30
1956			5	0		0	0	0	30
1957			2	0		0	0	0	12
1958			3	0		0	0	0	18
1959			2	0		0	0	0	12
1961	**MIN**	**N**	2	0		0	0	0	12
Career			19	0		0	0	0	114
Playoffs			1	0		0	0	0	6

Frank Middleton

Year	Team		TD	1XP	2XP	FG	FGA	SAF	Pts
1984	**IND**	**N**	2	0		0	0	0	12
1985			1	0		0	0	0	6
1987	**SD**	**N**	1	0		0	0	0	6
Career			4	0		0	0	0	24

Ron Middleton

Year	Team		TD	1XP	2XP	FG	FGA	SAF	Pts
1989	**CLE**	**N**	1	0		0	0	0	6

Ron Middleton *continued*

Year	Team		TD	1XP	2XP	FG	FGA	SAF	Pts
1993	**WAS**	**N**	2	0		0	0	0	12
Career			3	0		0	0	0	18
Playoffs			1	0		0	0	0	6

Terdell Middleton

Year	Team		TD	1XP	2XP	FG	FGA	SAF	Pts
1977	**GB**	**N**	1	0		0	0	0	6
1978			12	0		0	0	0	72
1979			3	0		0	0	0	18
1980			2	0		0	0	0	12
1981			1	0		0	0	0	6
Career			19	0		0	0	0	114

Saul Mielziner

Year	Team		TD	1XP	2XP	FG	FGA	SAF	Pts
1933	**BKN**	**N**	0	0		0		0	0

Nick Mike-Mayer

Year	Team		TD	1XP	2XP	FG	FGA	SAF	Pts
1973	**ATL**	**N**	0	34		26	38	0	112
1974			0	12		9	16	0	39
1975			0	30		4	10	0	42
1976			0	20		10	21	0	50
1977	**ATL-PHI**	**N**	0	14		10	22	0	44
1978	**PHI**	**N**	0	21		8	17	0	45
1979	**BUF**	**N**	0	17		20	29	0	99
1980			0	37		13	23	0	76
1981			0	37		14	24	0	79
1982			0	4		1	4	0	7
Career			0	226		115	204	0	593
Playoffs			0	9		1	4	0	12

Steve Mike-Mayer

Year	Team		TD	1XP	2XP	FG	FGA	SAF	Pts
1975	**SF**	**N**	0	27		14	28	0	69
1976			0	26		16	28	0	74
1977	**DET**	**N**	0	19		8	19	0	43
1978	**NO**	**N**	0	18		6	13	0	36
1979	**BAL**	**N**	0	28		11	20	0	61
1980			0	43		12	23	0	79
Career			0	161		67	131	0	362

Mike Mikulak

Year	Team		TD	1XP	2XP	FG	FGA	SAF	Pts
1934	**CHIC**	**N**	4	0		0		0	24
1935			1	0		0		0	6
Career			5	0		0		0	30

Glyn Milburn

Year	Team		TD	1XP	2XP	FG	FGA	SAF	Pts
1993	**DEN**	**N**	3	0		0	0	0	18
1994			4	0	0	0	0	0	24
Career			7	0	0	0	0	0	42

Ostell Miles

Year	Team		TD	1XP	2XP	FG	FGA	SAF	Pts
1993	**CIN**	**N**	1	0		0	0	0	6

Keith Millard

Year	Team		TD	1XP	2XP	FG	FGA	SAF	Pts
1989	**MIN**	**N**	1	0		0	0	0	6

Hugh Millen

Year	Team		TD	1XP	2XP	FG	FGA	SAF	Pts
1991	**NE**	**N**	1	0		0	0	0	6

Alan Miller

Year	Team		TD	1XP	2XP	FG	FGA	SAF	Pts
1960	**BOS**	**A**	3	0	0	0	0	0	18
1961	**OAK**	**A**	7	0	0	0	0	0	42
1962			1	0	0	0	0	0	6
1963			5	0	0	0	0	0	30
1965			4	0	0	0	0	0	24
Career			20	0	0	0	0	0	120

Anthony Miller

Year	Team		TD	1XP	2XP	FG	FGA	SAF	Pts
1988	**SD**	**N**	4	0		0	0	0	24
1989			11	0		0	0	0	66
1990			7	0		0	0	0	42
1991			3	0		0	0	0	18
1992			8	0		0	0	0	48
1993			7	0		0	0	0	42
1994	**DEN**	**N**	5	0	1	0	0	0	32
1995			14	0	0	0	0	0	84
1996			4	0	0	0	0	0	24
Career			63	0	1	0	0	0	380

Bill Miller

Year	Team		TD	1XP	2XP	FG	FGA	SAF	Pts
1963	**BUF**	**A**	3	0	0	0	0	0	18
1967	**OAK**	**A**	6	0	0	0	0	0	36
1968			1	0	0	0	0	0	6
Career			10	0	0	0	0	0	60
Playoffs			3	0	0	0	0	0	18

Candy Miller

Year	Team		TD	1XP	2XP	FG	FGA	SAF	Pts
1922	**CAN**	**N**	1	0		0		0	6

Chris Miller

Year	Team		TD	1XP	2XP	FG	FGA	SAF	Pts
1988	**ATL**	**N**	1	0		0	0	0	6
1989			0	0		1	1	0	3
1990			1	0		0	0	0	6
Career			2	0		1	1	0	15

Clark Miller

Year	Team		TD	1XP	2XP	FG	FGA	SAF	Pts
1965	**SF**	**N**	1	0		0	0	0	6

Cleo Miller

Year	Team		TD	1XP	2XP	FG	FGA	SAF	Pts
1975	**CLE**	**N**	1	0		0	0	0	6
1976			4	0		0	0	0	24
1977			5	0		0	0	0	30
1978			1	0		0	0	0	6
1979			1	0		0	0	0	6
1980			3	0		0	0	0	18
1981			2	0		0	0	0	12
Career			17	0		0	0	0	102

Dan Miller

Year	Team		TD	1XP	2XP	FG	FGA	SAF	Pts
1982	**NE-BAL**	**N**	0	9		6	11	0	27

Eddie Miller

Year	Team		TD	1XP	2XP	FG	FGA	SAF	Pts
1939	**NYG**	**N**	1	0		0	0	0	6
1940			1	0		0	0	0	6
Career			2	0		0	0	0	12

Heinie Miller

Year	Team		TD	1XP	2XP	FG	FGA	SAF	Pts
1920	**BUF**	**A**	0	0		0		0	0
1921			3	0		0		0	18
Career			3	0		0		0	18

Jamir Miller

Year	Team		TD	1XP	2XP	FG	FGA	SAF	Pts
1996	**ARI**	**N**	1	0	0	0	0	0	6

Jim Miller

Year	Team		TD	1XP	2XP	FG	FGA	SAF	Pts
1930	**BKN**	**N**	1	0		0		0	6

Johnny Miller

Year	Team		TD	1XP	2XP	FG	FGA	SAF	Pts
1956	**WAS**	**N**	0	0		0	0	1	2

Junior Miller

Year	Team		TD	1XP	2XP	FG	FGA	SAF	Pts
1980	**ATL**	**N**	9	0		0	0	0	54
1981			3	0		0	0	0	18
1982			1	0		0	0	0	6
1984	**NO**	**N**	1	0		0	0	0	6
Career			14	0		0	0	0	84

Kevin Miller

Year	Team		TD	1XP	2XP	FG	FGA	SAF	Pts
1978	**MIN**	**N**	1	0		0	0	0	6

Les Miller

Year	Team		TD	1XP	2XP	FG	FGA	SAF	Pts
1987	**SD**	**N**	1	0		0	0	0	6
1990			2	0		0	0	0	12
Career			3	0		0	0	0	18

Mark Miller

Year	Team		TD	1XP	2XP	FG	FGA	SAF	Pts
1978	**CLE**	**N**	1	0		0	0	0	6

Ookie Miller

Year	Team		TD	1XP	2XP	FG	FGA	SAF	Pts
1936	**CHIB**	**N**	1	0		0		0	6

Paul Miller

Year	Team		TD	1XP	2XP	FG	FGA	SAF	Pts
1936	**GB**	**N**	3	0		0		0	18
1937			1	0		0		0	6
Career			4	0		0		0	24

Primo Miller

Year	Team		TD	1XP	2XP	FG	FGA	SAF	Pts
1937	**CLE**	**N**	1	0		0		0	6

Robert Miller

Year	Team		TD	1XP	2XP	FG	FGA	SAF	Pts
1975	**MIN**	**N**	1	0		0	0	0	6
1976			1	0		0	0	0	6
1978			3	0		0	0	0	18
1979			2	0		0	0	0	12
1980			1	0		0	0	0	6
Career			8	0		0	0	0	48

Scott Miller

Year	Team		TD	1XP	2XP	FG	FGA	SAF	Pts
1994	**MIA**	**N**	1	0	0	0	0	0	6

Scott Miller *continued*

Year	Team		TD	1XP	2XP	FG	FGA	SAF	Pts
1996			1	0	0	0	0	0	6
Career			2	0	0	0	0	0	12

Solomon Miller

Year	Team		TD	1XP	2XP	FG	FGA	SAF	Pts
1986	**NYG**	**N**	2	0		0	0	0	12

Terry Miller

Year	Team		TD	1XP	2XP	FG	FGA	SAF	Pts
1978	**BUF**	**N**	7	0		0	0	0	42
1979			1	0		0	0	0	6
Career			8	0		0	0	0	48

Tom Miller

Year	Team		TD	1XP	2XP	FG	FGA	SAF	Pts
1943	**P-P**	**N**	1	0		0	0	0	6
1944	**PHI**	**N**	1	0		0	0	0	6
Career			2	0		0	0	0	12

Willie Miller

Year	Team		TD	1XP	2XP	FG	FGA	SAF	Pts
1975	**CLE**	**N**	1	0		0	0	0	6
1978	**LA**	**N**	5	0		0	0	0	30
1979			1	0		0	0	0	6
1980			8	0		0	0	0	48
1982	**LARM**	**N**	1	0		0	0	0	6
Career			16	0		0	0	0	96
Playoffs			1	0		0	0	0	6

James Milling

Year	Team		TD	1XP	2XP	FG	FGA	SAF	Pts
1990	**ATL**	**N**	1	0		0	0	0	6

Bob Millman

Year	Team		TD	1XP	2XP	FG	FGA	SAF	Pts
1926	**POT**	**N**	1	0		0		0	6

Wayne Millner

Year	Team		TD	1XP	2XP	FG	FGA	SAF	Pts
1937	**WAS**	**N**	3	0		0		0	18
1938			1	0		0	0	0	6
1939			4	0		0	0	0	24
1940			3	0		0	0	0	18
1945			2	0		0	0	0	12
Career			13	0		0	0	0	78
Playoffs			2	0		0	0	0	12

Ernie Mills

Year	Team		TD	1XP	2XP	FG	FGA	SAF	Pts
1991	**PIT**	**N**	2	0		0	0	0	12
1992			3	0		0	0	0	18
1993			1	0		0	0	0	6
1994			1	0	0	0	0	0	6
1995			8	0	0	0	0	0	48
1996			1	0	0	0	0	0	6
Career			16	0	0	0	0	0	96
Playoffs			2	0	0	0	0	0	12

Joe Mills

Year	Team		TD	1XP	2XP	FG	FGA	SAF	Pts
1922	**AKR**	**N**	1	1		0		0	7

Sam Mills

Year	Team		TD	1XP	2XP	FG	FGA	SAF	Pts
1992	**NO**	**N**	1	0		0	0	0	6
1993			1	0		0	0	0	6
1995	**CAR**	**N**	1	0	0	0	0	0	6
1996			1	0	0	0	0	0	6
Career			4	0	0	0	0	0	24

Stan Mills

Year	Team		TD	1XP	2XP	FG	FGA	SAF	Pts
1923	**GB**	**N**	3	0		0		0	18
1924	**AKR**	**N**	1	0		0		0	6
Career			4	0		0		0	24

Brian Milne

Year	Team		TD	1XP	2XP	FG	FGA	SAF	Pts
1996	**CIN**	**N**	1	0	0	0	0	0	6

Charley Milstead

Year	Team		TD	1XP	2XP	FG	FGA	SAF	Pts
1961	**HOU**	**A**	0	1	0	0	0	0	1

Eugene Milton

Year	Team		TD	1XP	2XP	FG	FGA	SAF	Pts
1968	**MIA**	**A**	1	0	0	0	0	0	6
1969			1	0	0	0	0	0	6
Career			2	0	0	0	0	0	12

Chris Mims

Year	Team		TD	1XP	2XP	FG	FGA	SAF	Pts
1992	**SD**	**N**	0	0		0	0	1	2

David Mims

Year	Team		TD	1XP	2XP	FG	FGA	SAF	Pts
1993	**ATL**	**N**	1	0		0	0	0	6

Hank Minarik

Year	Team		TD	1XP	2XP	FG	FGA	SAF	Pts
1951	**PIT**	**N**	1	0		0	0	0	6

Charles Mincy

Year	Team		TD	1XP	2XP	FG	FGA	SAF	Pts
1992	**KC**	**N**	3	0		0	0	0	18

Tom Miner

Year	Team		TD	1XP	2XP	FG	FGA	SAF	Pts
1958	**PIT**	**N**	0	31		**14**	**28**	0	73

Gene Mingo

Year	Team		TD	1XP	2XP	FG	FGA	SAF	Pts
1960	**DEN**	**A**	6	33	0	**18**	28	0	**123**
1961			2	11	0	3	10	0	32
1962			4	32	0	**27**	**39**	0	**137**
1963			0	35	0	16	30	0	83
1964	**DEN-OAK**	**A**	1	9	0	8	12	0	39
1965	**OAK**	**A**	0	0	0	8	19	0	24
1966	**MIA**	**A**	0	23	0	10	22	0	53
1967	**MIA-WAS**	**A-N**	0	29		5	16	0	44
1969	**PIT**	**N**	0	26		12	26	0	62
1970			0	17		5	18	0	32
Career			13	215	0	112	220	0	629

Kevin Miniefield

Year	Team		TD	1XP	2XP	FG	FGA	SAF	Pts
Playoffs			1	0	0	0	0	0	6

Frank Minini

Year	Team		TD	1XP	2XP	FG	FGA	SAF	Pts
1947	**CHIB**	**N**	2	0		0	0	0	12
1948			5	0		0	0	0	30
Career			7	0		0	0	0	42

Tony Minisi

Year	Team		TD	1XP	2XP	FG	FGA	SAF	Pts
1948	**NYG**	**N**	2	0		0	0	0	12

Randy Minniear

Year	Team		TD	1XP	2XP	FG	FGA	SAF	Pts
1967	**NYG**	**N**	2	0		0	0	0	12
1968			2	0		0	0	0	12
1969			1	0		0	0	0	6
1970	**CLE**	**N**	1	0		0	0	0	6
Career			6	0		0	0	0	36

Frank Minnifield

Year	Team		TD	1XP	2XP	FG	FGA	SAF	Pts
1986	**CLE**	**N**	1	0		0	0	0	6
1988			1	0		0	0	0	6
Career			2	0		0	0	0	12
Playoffs			1	0		0	0	0	6

Barry Minter

Year	Team		TD	1XP	2XP	FG	FGA	SAF	Pts
1995	**CHI**	**N**	1	0	0	0	0	0	6

Cedric Minter

Year	Team		TD	1XP	2XP	FG	FGA	SAF	Pts
1984	**NYJ**	**N**	2	0		0	0	0	12

Rick Mirer

Year	Team		TD	1XP	2XP	FG	FGA	SAF	Pts
1993	**SEA**	**N**	3	0		0	0	0	18
1995			1	0	0	0	0	0	6
1996			2	0	0	0	0	0	12
Career			6	0	0	0	0	0	36

Dave Mishel

Year	Team		TD	1XP	2XP	FG	FGA	SAF	Pts
1931	**CLE**	**N**	0	1		0		0	1

John Mistler

Year	Team		TD	1XP	2XP	FG	FGA	SAF	Pts
1981	**NYG**	**N**	1	0		0	0	0	6
1982			2	0		0	0	0	12
Career			3	0		0	0	0	18
Playoffs			1	0		0	0	0	6

Gene Mitcham

Year	Team		TD	1XP	2XP	FG	FGA	SAF	Pts
1958	**PHI**	**N**	1	0		0	0	0	6

Bobby Mitchell

Year	Team		TD	1XP	2XP	FG	FGA	SAF	Pts
1958	**CLE**	**N**	6	0		0	0	0	36
1959			10	0		0	0	0	60
1960			12	0		0	0	0	72
1961			10	0		0	0	0	60
1962	**WAS**	**N**	12	0		0	0	0	72
1963			8	0		0	0	0	48
1964			10	0		0	0	0	60
1965			6	0		0	0	0	36
1966			10	0		0	0	0	60
1967			7	0		0	0	0	42
Career			91	0		0	0	0	546

Brian Mitchell

Year	Team		TD	1XP	2XP	FG	FGA	SAF	Pts
1990	**WAS**	**N**	1	0		0	0	0	6
1991			2	0		0	0	0	12
1992			1	0		0	0	0	6
1993			3	0		0	0	0	18
1994			3	0	1	0	0	0	20
1995			3	0	0	0	0	0	18
Career			13	0	1	0	0	0	80
Playoffs			1	0	0	0	0	0	6

Charlie Mitchell

Year	Team		TD	1XP	2XP	FG	FGA	SAF	Pts
1963	**DEN**	**A**	1	0	0	0	0	0	6
1964			6	0	0	0	0	0	36
1966			2	0	0	0	0	0	12
Career			9	0	0	0	0	0	54

Devon Mitchell

Year	Team		TD	1XP	2XP	FG	FGA	SAF	Pts
1988	**DET**	**N**	1	0		0	0	0	6

Gran Mitchell

Year	Team		TD	1XP	2XP	FG	FGA	SAF	Pts
1937	**BKN**	**N**	1	0		0		0	6

Jim Mitchell

Year	Team		TD	1XP	2XP	FG	FGA	SAF	Pts
1969	**ATL**	**N**	4	0		0	0	0	24
1970			7	0		0	0	0	42
1971			6	0		0	0	0	36
1972			4	0		0	0	0	24
1974			1	0		0	0	0	6
1975			5	0		0	0	0	30
1978			2	0		0	0	0	12
1979			2	0		0	0	0	12
Career			31	0		0	0	0	186
Playoffs			1	0		0	0	0	6

Jim Mitchell

Year	Team		TD	1XP	2XP	FG	FGA	SAF	Pts
1974	**DET**	**N**	0	0		0	0	1	2

Johnny Mitchell

Year	Team		TD	1XP	2XP	FG	FGA	SAF	Pts
1992	**NYJ**	**N**	1	0		0	0	0	6
1993			6	0		0	0	0	36
1994			4	0	0	0	0	0	24
1995			5	0	0	0	0	0	30
Career			16	0	0	0	0	0	96

Leroy Mitchell

Year	Team		TD	1XP	2XP	FG	FGA	SAF	Pts
1973	**DEN**	**N**	1	0		0	0	0	6

Lydell Mitchell

Year	Team		TD	1XP	2XP	FG	FGA	SAF	Pts
1972	**BAL**	**N**	2	0		0	0	0	12
1973			2	0		0	0	0	12
1974			7	0		0	0	0	42
1975			15	0		0	0	0	90
1976			8	0		0	0	0	48
1977			7	0		0	0	0	42
1978	**SD**	**N**	5	0		0	0	0	30
1979			1	0		0	0	0	6
Career			47	0		0	0	0	282
Playoffs			1	0		0	0	0	6

Mack Mitchell

Year	Team		TD	1XP	2XP	FG	FGA	SAF	Pts
1976	**CLE**	**N**	0	0		0	0	1	2

Paul Mitchell

Year	Team		TD	1XP	2XP	FG	FGA	SAF	Pts
1947	**LA**	**AA**	1	0		0	0	0	6

Pete Mitchell

Year	Team		TD	1XP	2XP	FG	FGA	SAF	Pts
1995	**JAC**	**N**	2	0	0	0	0	0	12
1996			1	0	0	0	0	0	6
Career			3	0	0	0	0	0	18

Scott Mitchell

Year	Team		TD	1XP	2XP	FG	FGA	SAF	Pts
1994	**DET**	**N**	1	0	0	0	0	0	6
1995			4	0	0	0	0	0	24
1996			4	0	0	0	0	0	24
Career			9	0	0	0	0	0	54

Shannon Mitchell

Year	Team		TD	1XP	2XP	FG	FGA	SAF	Pts
1995	**SD**	**N**	1	0	0	0	0	0	6

Stan Mitchell

Year	Team		TD	1XP	2XP	FG	FGA	SAF	Pts
1967	**MIA**	**A**	4	0	0	0	0	0	24
1968			4	0	0	0	0	0	24
1970	**MIA**	**N**	1	0		0	0	0	6
Career			9	0	0	0	0	0	54

Stump Mitchell

Year	Team		TD	1XP	2XP	FG	FGA	SAF	Pts
1981	STL	N	2	0		0	0	0	12
1982			1	0		0	0	0	6
1983			3	0		0	0	0	18
1984			11	0		0	0	0	66
1985			10	0		0	0	0	60
1986			5	0		0	0	0	30
1987			5	0		0	0	0	30
1988	PHX	N	5	0		0	0	0	30
Career			42	0		0	0	0	252

Tom Mitchell

Year	Team		TD	1XP	2XP	FG	FGA	SAF	Pts
1966	OAK	A	1	0	0	0	0	0	6
1968	BAL	N	4	0		0	0	0	24
1969			3	0		0	0	0	18
1970			4	0		0	0	0	24
1972			4	0		0	0	0	24
1973			4	0		0	0	0	24
1975	SF	N	3	0		0	0	0	18
1976			1	0		0	0	0	6
Career			24	0	0	0	0	0	144
Playoffs			1	0	0	0	0	0	6

Willie Mitchell

Year	Team		TD	1XP	2XP	FG	FGA	SAF	Pts
1965	KC	A	2	0	0	0	0	0	12
1966			1	0	0	0	0	0	6
1967			1	0	0	0	0	0	6
Career			4	0	0	0	0	0	24

Billy Mixon

Year	Team		TD	1XP	2XP	FG	FGA	SAF	Pts
1953	SF	N	1	0		0	0	0	6

Kelly Moan

Year	Team		TD	1XP	2XP	FG	FGA	SAF	Pts
1939	CLE	N	0	1		0	0	0	1

Orson Mobley

Year	Team		TD	1XP	2XP	FG	FGA	SAF	Pts
1986	DEN	N	1	0		0	0	0	6
1987			1	0		0	0	0	6
1988			2	0		0	0	0	12
Career			4	0		0	0	0	24
Playoffs			1	0		0	0	0	6

Rudy Mobley

Year	Team		TD	1XP	2XP	FG	FGA	SAF	Pts
1947	BAL	AA	2	0		0	0	0	12

Stacey Mobley

Year	Team		TD	1XP	2XP	FG	FGA	SAF	Pts
1987	LARM	N	1	0		0	0	0	6

Dick Modzelewski

Year	Team		TD	1XP	2XP	FG	FGA	SAF	Pts
1954	WAS	N	0	0		0	0	1	2
1961	NYG	N	0	0		0	0	1	2
Career			0	0		0	0	2	4

Ed Modzelewski

Year	Team		TD	1XP	2XP	FG	FGA	SAF	Pts
1952	PIT	N	3	0		0	0	0	18
1955	CLE	N	8	0		0	0	0	48
1956			2	0		0	0	0	12
1959			1	0		0	0	0	6
Career			14	0		0	0	0	84

Hal Moe

Year	Team		TD	1XP	2XP	FG	FGA	SAF	Pts
1933	CHIC	N	2	0		0		0	12

Dicky Moegle

Year	Team		TD	1XP	2XP	FG	FGA	SAF	Pts
1955	SF	N	5	0		0	0	0	30
1956			1	0		0	0	0	6
1957			1	0		0	0	0	6
Career			7	0		0	0	0	42

Tim Moffett

Year	Team		TD	1XP	2XP	FG	FGA	SAF	Pts
1987	SD	N	1	0		0	0	0	6

Johnny Mohardt

Year	Team		TD	1XP	2XP	FG	FGA	SAF	Pts
1922	CHIC	N	1	0		0		0	6
1923			1	0		0		0	6
1924	RAC	N	0	0		0		0	0
1925	CHIB	N	1	0		0		0	6
1926	CHI	A	4	0		0		0	24
Career			7	0		0		0	42

Chris Mohr

Year	Team		TD	1XP	2XP	FG	FGA	SAF	Pts
1989	TB	N	0	1		0	0	0	1

Louie Mohs

Year	Team		TD	1XP	2XP	FG	FGA	SAF	Pts
1923	MIN	N	1	0		0		0	6

Frank Molden

Year	Team		TD	1XP	2XP	FG	FGA	SAF	Pts
1965	LA	N	1	0		0	0	0	6

Bo Molenda

Year	Team		TD	1XP	2XP	FG	FGA	SAF	Pts
1927	NYY	N	1	1		0		0	7
1928	NYY-GB	N	1	3		0		0	9
1929	GB	N	3	2		0		0	20
1930			3	4		0		0	22
1931			3	3		0		0	21
1932	NYG	N	0	4		0		0	4
1933			3	0		0		0	18
1934			0	2		0		0	2
1935			1	5		0		0	11
Career			15	24		0		0	114
Playoffs			0	1		0	0	0	1

Keith Molesworth

Year	Team		TD	1XP	2XP	FG	FGA	SAF	Pts
1931	CHIB	N	1	0		0		0	6
1932			3	0		0		0	18
1933			1	0		0		0	6
1934			1	0		0		0	6
1935			4	0		0		0	24
1937			0	1		0		0	1
Career			10	1		0		0	61

Lou Molinet

Year	Team		TD	1XP	2XP	FG	FGA	SAF	Pts
1927	FRA	N	1	1		0		0	7

Bob Momsen

Year	Team		TD	1XP	2XP	FG	FGA	SAF	Pts
1952	SF	N	0	0		0	0	1	2

Jim Monachino

Year	Team		TD	1XP	2XP	FG	FGA	SAF	Pts
1951	SF	N	2	0		0	0	0	12
1955	WAS	N	2	0		0	0	0	12
Career			4	0		0	0	0	24

Regis Monahan

Year	Team		TD	1XP	2XP	FG	FGA	SAF	Pts
1936	DET	N	1	0		0		0	6
1937			0	5		5		0	20
1938			0	2		4	5	0	14
1939	CHIC	N	0	1		1	1	0	4
Career			1	8		10	6	0	44

Art Monk

Year	Team		TD	1XP	2XP	FG	FGA	SAF	Pts
1980	WAS	N	3	0		0	0	0	18
1981			6	0		0	0	0	36
1982			1	0		0	0	0	6
1983			5	0		0	0	0	30
1984			7	0		0	0	0	42
1985			2	0		0	0	0	12
1986			4	0		0	0	0	24
1987			6	0		0	0	0	36
1988			5	0		0	0	0	30
1989			8	0		0	0	0	48
1990			5	0		0	0	0	30
1991			8	0		0	0	0	48
1992			3	0		0	0	0	18
1993			2	0		0	0	0	12
1994	NYJ	N	3	0	0	0	0	0	18
Career			68	0	0	0	0	0	408
Playoffs			7	0	0	0	0	0	42

Bob Monnett

Year	Team		TD	1XP	2XP	FG	FGA	SAF	Pts
1933	GB	N	5	10		0		0	40
1934			2	6		4		0	30
1935			1	2		1		0	11
1936			0	3		0		0	3
1937			1	0		0		0	6
1938			0	7		0		0	7
Career			9	28		5		0	97
Playoffs			1	0		0	0	0	6

Carl Monroe

Year	Team		TD	1XP	2XP	FG	FGA	SAF	Pts
1984	SF	N	1	0		0	0	0	6
1985			1	0		0	0	0	6
1987			1	0		0	0	0	6
Career			3	0		0	0	0	18
Playoffs			1	0		0	0	0	6

Tommy Mont

Year	Team		TD	1XP	2XP	FG	FGA	SAF	Pts
1948	WAS	N	1	0		0	0	0	6

Tommy Mont *continued*

Year	Team		TD	1XP	2XP	FG	FGA	SAF	Pts
1949			2	0		0	0	0	12
Career			3	0		0	0	0	18

Joe Montana

Year	Team		TD	1XP	2XP	FG	FGA	SAF	Pts
1980	SF	N	2	0		0	0	0	12
1981			2	0		0	0	0	12
1982			1	0		0	0	0	6
1983			2	0		0	0	0	12
1984			2	0		0	0	0	12
1985			3	0		0	0	0	18
1987			1	0		0	0	0	6
1988			3	0		0	0	0	18
1989			3	0		0	0	0	18
1990			1	0		0	0	0	6
Career			20	0		0	0	0	120
Playoffs			2	0		0	0	0	12

Alton Montgomery

Year	Team		TD	1XP	2XP	FG	FGA	SAF	Pts
1995	ATL	N	1	0	0	0	0	0	6

Cleo Montgomery

Year	Team		TD	1XP	2XP	FG	FGA	SAF	Pts
1984	LARI	N	1	0		0	0	0	6

Cliff Montgomery

Year	Team		TD	1XP	2XP	FG	FGA	SAF	Pts
1934	BKN	N	0	0		0		0	0

Mike Montgomery

Year	Team		TD	1XP	2XP	FG	FGA	SAF	Pts
1971	SD	N	3	0		0	0	0	18
1972	DAL	N	3	0		0	0	0	18
1973			3	0		0	0	0	18
1974	HOU	N	1	0		0	0	0	6
Career			10	0		0	0	0	60

Randy Montgomery

Year	Team		TD	1XP	2XP	FG	FGA	SAF	Pts
1972	DEN	N	1	0		0	0	0	6

Tyrone Montgomery

Year	Team		TD	1XP	2XP	FG	FGA	SAF	Pts
1994	LARI	N	1	0	0	0	0	0	6

Wilbert Montgomery

Year	Team		TD	1XP	2XP	FG	FGA	SAF	Pts
1977	PHI	N	3	0		0	0	0	18
1978			10	0		0	0	0	60
1979			14	0		0	0	0	84
1980			10	0		0	0	0	60
1981			10	0		0	0	0	60
1982			9	0		0	0	0	54
1984			2	0		0	0	0	12
Career			58	0		0	0	0	348
Playoffs			6	0		0	0	0	36

Keith Moody

Year	Team		TD	1XP	2XP	FG	FGA	SAF	Pts
1976	BUF	N	1	0		0	0	0	6
1977			1	0		0	0	0	6
1978			1	0		0	0	0	6
Career			3	0		0	0	0	18

Warren Moon

Year	Team		TD	1XP	2XP	FG	FGA	SAF	Pts
1984	HOU	N	1	0		0	0	0	6
1986			2	0		0	0	0	12
1987			3	0		0	0	0	18
1988			5	0		0	0	0	30
1989			4	0		0	0	0	24
1990			2	0		0	0	0	12
1991			2	0		0	0	0	12
1992			1	0		0	0	0	6
1993			1	0		0	0	0	6
Career			21	0		0	0	0	126

Jim Mooney

Year	Team		TD	1XP	2XP	FG	FGA	SAF	Pts
1930	NEW	N	0	2		0		0	2
1931	BKN	N	0	1		0		0	1
Career			0	3		0		0	3

Tipp Mooney

Year	Team		TD	1XP	2XP	FG	FGA	SAF	Pts
1944	CHIB	N	1	0		0	0	0	6

Alvin Moore

Year	Team		TD	1XP	2XP	FG	FGA	SAF	Pts
1983	BAL	N	1	0		0	0	0	6
1984	IND	N	2	0		0	0	0	12
1985	DET	N	5	0		0	0	0	30
Career			8	0		0	0	0	48

Bill Moore

Year	Team	TD	1XP	2XP	FG	FGA	SAF	Pts
1932	CHIC N	1	0		0		0	6

Bill Moore

Year	Team	TD	1XP	2XP	FG	FGA	SAF	Pts
1939	DET N	1	0		0		0	6

Blake Moore

Year	Team	TD	1XP	2XP	FG	FGA	SAF	Pts
1984	GB N	1	0		0	0	0	6
1985		1	0		0	0	0	6
Career		2	0		0	0	0	12

Bob Moore

Year	Team	TD	1XP	2XP	FG	FGA	SAF	Pts
1972	OAK N	1	0		0	0	0	6
1973		4	0		0	0	0	24
1974		2	0		0	0	0	12
Career		7	0		0	0	0	42
Playoffs		1	0		0	0	0	6

Booker Moore

Year	Team	TD	1XP	2XP	FG	FGA	SAF	Pts
1983	BUF N	1	0		0	0	0	6
1985		1	0		0	0	0	6
Career		2	0		0	0	0	12

Dave Moore

Year	Team	TD	1XP	2XP	FG	FGA	SAF	Pts
1993	TB N	1	0		0	0	0	6
1996		3	0		0	0	0	18
Career		4	0		0	0	0	24

Derrick Moore

Year	Team	TD	1XP	2XP	FG	FGA	SAF	Pts
1993	DET N	4	0		0	0	0	24
1994		4	0		0	0	0	24
1995	CAR N	4	0		0	0	0	24
Career		12	0		0	0	0	72
Playoffs		1	0		0	0	0	6

Dinty Moore

Year	Team	TD	1XP	2XP	FG	FGA	SAF	Pts
1927	POT N	2	0		0		0	12

Henry Moore

Year	Team	TD	1XP	2XP	FG	FGA	SAF	Pts
Playoffs		1	0		0		0	6

Herman Moore

Year	Team	TD	1XP	2XP	FG	FGA	SAF	Pts
1992	DET N	4	0		0	0	0	24
1993		6	0		0	0	0	36
1994		11	0		0	0	0	66
1995		14	0		0	0	0	84
1996		9	0	1	0	0	0	56
Career		44	0	1	0	0	0	266
Playoffs		2	0	1	0	0	0	14

Jeff Moore

Year	Team	TD	1XP	2XP	FG	FGA	SAF	Pts
1979	SEA N	2	0		0	0	0	12
1982	SF N	8	0		0	0	0	48
1983		1	0		0	0	0	6
1984	WAS N	2	0		0	0	0	12
Career		13	0		0	0	0	78

Jeff Moore

Year	Team	TD	1XP	2XP	FG	FGA	SAF	Pts
1980	LA N	1	0		0	0	0	6

Lenny Moore

Year	Team	TD	1XP	2XP	FG	FGA	SAF	Pts
1956	BAL N	9	0		0	0	0	54
1957		11	0		0	0	0	66
1958		14	0		0	0	0	84
1959		8	0		0	0	0	48
1960		13	0		0	0	0	78
1961		15	0		0	0	0	90
1962		4	0		0	0	0	24
1963		4	0		0	0	0	24
1964		20	0		0	0	0	120
1965		8	0		0	0	0	48
1966		3	0		0	0	0	18
1967		4	0		0	0	0	24
Career		113	0		0	0	0	678
Playoffs		1	0		0	0	0	6

Leroy Moore

Year	Team	TD	1XP	2XP	FG	FGA	SAF	Pts
1961	BOS A	1	0	0	0	0	0	6
1962	BUF A	1	0	0	0	0	0	6
Career		2	0	0	0	0	0	12

Malcolm Moore

Year	Team	TD	1XP	2XP	FG	FGA	SAF	Pts
1987	LARM N	1	0		0	0	0	6

Manfred Moore

Year	Team	TD	1XP	2XP	FG	FGA	SAF	Pts
1974	SF N	2	0		0	0	0	12

Nat Moore

Year	Team	TD	1XP	2XP	FG	FGA	SAF	Pts
1974	MIA N	2	0		0	0	0	12
1975		4	0		0	0	0	24
1976		4	0		0	0	0	24
1977		13	0		0	0	0	78
1978		10	0		0	0	0	60
1979		6	0		0	0	0	36
1980		7	0		0	0	0	42
1981		2	0		0	0	0	12
1982		1	0		0	0	0	6
1983		6	0		0	0	0	36
1984		6	0		0	0	0	36
1985		7	0		0	0	0	42
1986		7	0		0	0	0	42
Career		75	0		0	0	0	450
Playoffs		4	0		0	0	0	24

Paul Moore

Year	Team	TD	1XP	2XP	FG	FGA	SAF	Pts
1940	DET N	1	0		0	0	0	6

Ricky Moore

Year	Team	TD	1XP	2XP	FG	FGA	SAF	Pts
1986	BUF N	1	0		0	0	0	6

Rob Moore

Year	Team	TD	1XP	2XP	FG	FGA	SAF	Pts
1990	NYJ N	6	0		0	0	0	36
1991		5	0		0	0	0	30
1992		4	0		0	0	0	24
1993		1	0		0	0	0	6
1994		6	0	2	0	0	0	40
1995	ARI N	5	0	1	0	0	0	32
1996		4	0	1	0	0	0	26
Career		31	0	4	0	0	0	194

Robert Moore

Year	Team	TD	1XP	2XP	FG	FGA	SAF	Pts
1987	ATL N	1	0		0	0	0	6
1988		1	0		0	0	0	6
Career		2	0		0	0	0	12

Ron Moore

Year	Team	TD	1XP	2XP	FG	FGA	SAF	Pts
1993	PHX N	9	0		0	0	0	54
1994	ARI N	5	0	1	0	0	0	32
Career		14	0	1	0	0	0	86

Stevon Moore

Year	Team	TD	1XP	2XP	FG	FGA	SAF	Pts
1992	CLE N	1	0		0	0	0	6
1993		1	0		0	0	0	6
Career		2	0		0	0	0	12

Tom Moore

Year	Team	TD	1XP	2XP	FG	FGA	SAF	Pts
1960	GB N	5	0		0	0	0	30
1961		2	0		0	0	0	12
1962		7	0		0	0	0	42
1963		8	0		0	0	0	48
1964		4	0		0	0	0	24
1965		1	0		0	0	0	6
1966	LA N	4	0		0	0	0	24
Career		31	0		0	0	0	186

Wilbur Moore

Year	Team	TD	1XP	2XP	FG	FGA	SAF	Pts
1940	WAS N	3	0		0	0	0	18
1941		1	0		0	0	0	6
1942		2	0		0	0	0	12
1943		9	0		0	0	0	54
1944		7	0		0	0	0	42
1945		2	0		0	0	0	12
Career		24	0		0	0	0	144
Playoffs		1	0		0	0	0	6

Will Moore

Year	Team	TD	1XP	2XP	FG	FGA	SAF	Pts
1995	NE N	1	0	0	0	0	0	6

Zeke Moore

Year	Team	TD	1XP	2XP	FG	FGA	SAF	Pts
1967	HOU A	1	0	0	0	0	0	6
1969		1	0	0	0	0	0	6
1974	HOU N	1	0	0	0	0	0	6
1977		1	0	0	0	0	0	6
Career		4	0	0	0	0	0	24

Emery Moorehead

Year	Team	TD	1XP	2XP	FG	FGA	SAF	Pts
1977	NYG N	1	0		0	0	0	6

Emery Moorehead continued

Year	Team	TD	1XP	2XP	FG	FGA	SAF	Pts
1982	CHI N	5	0		0	0	0	30
1983		3	0		0	0	0	18
1984		1	0		0	0	0	6
1985		1	0		0	0	0	6
1986		1	0		0	0	0	6
1987		1	0		0	0	0	6
1988		2	0		0	0	0	12
Career		15	0		0	0	0	90

Gonzalo Morales

Year	Team	TD	1XP	2XP	FG	FGA	SAF	Pts
1948	PIT N	1	0		0	0	0	6

Fran Moran

Year	Team	TD	1XP	2XP	FG	FGA	SAF	Pts
1926	FRA N	5	3		0		0	33
1927	FRA-CHIC N	2	4	3			0	25
1929	NYG N	5	0		0		0	30
1930		4	3		0		0	27
1931		4	8	1			0	35
1932		1	1		0		0	7
1933		1	1		0		0	7
Career		22	20	4			0	164

Doug Moreau

Year	Team	TD	1XP	2XP	FG	FGA	SAF	Pts
1967	MIA A	3	0	0	0	0	0	18
1968		3	6	1	3	0		27
Career		6	6	1	3	0		45

John Morelli

Year	Team	TD	1XP	2XP	FG	FGA	SAF	Pts
1944	BOS N	2	0		0	0	0	12

Tim Moresco

Year	Team	TD	1XP	2XP	FG	FGA	SAF	Pts
1979	NYJ N	0	0		0	0	1	2

Arnold Morgado

Year	Team	TD	1XP	2XP	FG	FGA	SAF	Pts
1978	KC N	7	0		0	0	0	42
1979		4	0		0	0	0	24
1980		5	0		0	0	0	30
Career		16	0		0	0	0	96

Anthony Morgan

Year	Team	TD	1XP	2XP	FG	FGA	SAF	Pts
1991	CHI N	2	0		0	0	0	12
1992		2	0		0	0	0	12
1994	GB N	4	0	0	0	0	0	24
1995		4	0	0	0	0	0	24
Career		12	0	0	0	0	0	72

Dennis Morgan

Year	Team	TD	1XP	2XP	FG	FGA	SAF	Pts
1974	DAL N	1	0		0	0	0	6

Melvin Morgan

Year	Team	TD	1XP	2XP	FG	FGA	SAF	Pts
1976	CIN N	1	0		0	0	0	6

Mike Morgan

Year	Team	TD	1XP	2XP	FG	FGA	SAF	Pts
1964	PHI N	1	0		0	0	0	6
1970	NO N	1	0		0	0	0	6
Career		2	0		0	0	0	12

Stanley Morgan

Year	Team	TD	1XP	2XP	FG	FGA	SAF	Pts
1977	NE N	3	0		0	0	0	18
1978		5	0		0	0	0	30
1979		13	0		0	0	0	78
1980		6	0		0	0	0	36
1981		6	0		0	0	0	36
1982		3	0		0	0	0	18
1983		2	0		0	0	0	12
1984		5	0		0	0	0	30
1985		5	0		0	0	0	30
1986		10	0		0	0	0	60
1987		3	0		0	0	0	18
1988		4	0		0	0	0	24
1989		3	0		0	0	0	18
1990	IND N	5	0		0	0	0	30
Career		73	0		0	0	0	438
Playoffs		3	0		0	0	0	18

Larry Moriarty

Year	Team	TD	1XP	2XP	FG	FGA	SAF	Pts
1983	HOU N	3	0		0	0	0	18
1984		7	0		0	0	0	42
1985		3	0		0	0	0	18
1986		1	0		0	0	0	6
1987	KC N	1	0		0	0	0	6
Career		15	0		0	0	0	90

Pat Moriarty

Year	Team		TD	1XP	2XP	FG	FGA	SAF	Pts
1979	CLE	N	2	0		0	0	0	12

Tom Moriarty

Year	Team		TD	1XP	2XP	FG	FGA	SAF	Pts
1978	ATL	N	1	0		0	0	0	6

Milt Morin

Year	Team		TD	1XP	2XP	FG	FGA	SAF	Pts
1966	CLE	N	3	0		0	0	0	18
1968			5	0		0	0	0	30
1970			1	0		0	0	0	6
1971			2	0		0	0	0	12
1972			1	0		0	0	0	6
1973			1	0		0	0	0	6
1974			3	0		0	0	0	18
Career			16	0		0	0	0	96
Playoffs			2	0		0	0	0	12

Mike Moroski

Year	Team		TD	1XP	2XP	FG	FGA	SAF	Pts
1979	ATL	N	1	0		0	0	0	6
1986	SF	N	1	0		0	0	0	6
Career			2	0		0	0	0	12

Earl Morrall

Year	Team		TD	1XP	2XP	FG	FGA	SAF	Pts
1957	PIT	N	2	0		0	0	0	12
1960	DET	N	1	0		0	0	0	6
1962			1	0		0	0	0	6
1963			1	0		0	0	0	6
1967	NYG	N	1	0		0	0	0	6
1968	BAL	N	1	0		0	0	0	6
1972	MIA	N	1	0		0	0	0	6
Career			8	0		0	0	0	48

Bam Morris

Year	Team		TD	1XP	2XP	FG	FGA	SAF	Pts
1994	PIT	N	7	0	0	0	0	0	42
1995			9	0	0	0	0	0	54
1996	BAL	N	5	0	0	0	0	0	30
Career			21	0	0	0	0	0	126
Playoffs			4	0	0	0	0	0	24

Glenn Morris

Year	Team		TD	1XP	2XP	FG	FGA	SAF	Pts
1940	DET	N	0	0		0		1	2

Jack Morris

Year	Team		TD	1XP	2XP	FG	FGA	SAF	Pts
1958	LA	N	1	0		0	0	0	6
1959			0	15		3	8	0	24
Career			1	15		3	8	0	30

Jamie Morris

Year	Team		TD	1XP	2XP	FG	FGA	SAF	Pts
1988	WAS	N	2	0		0	0	0	12
1989			2	0		0	0	0	12
Career			4	0		0	0	0	24

Joe Morris

Year	Team		TD	1XP	2XP	FG	FGA	SAF	Pts
1982	NYG	N	1	0		0	0	0	6
1983			1	0		0	0	0	6
1984			4	0		0	0	0	24
1985			21	0		0	0	0	126
1986			15	0		0	0	0	90
1987			3	0		0	0	0	18
1988			5	0		0	0	0	30
1991	CLE	N	2	0		0	0	0	12
Career			52	0		0	0	0	312
Playoffs			4	0		0	0	0	24

Johnny Morris

Year	Team		TD	1XP	2XP	FG	FGA	SAF	Pts
1958	CHIB	N	2	0		0	0	0	12
1959			3	0		0	0	0	18
1960	CHI	N	6	0		0	0	0	36
1961			4	0		0	0	0	24
1962			5	0		0	0	0	30
1963			2	0		0	0	0	12
1964			10	0		0	0	0	60
1965			4	0		0	0	0	24
1967			1	0		0	0	0	6
Career			37	0		0	0	0	222

Larry Morris

Year	Team		TD	1XP	2XP	FG	FGA	SAF	Pts
1955	LA	N	1	0		0	0	0	6
1959	CHIB	N	1	0		0	0	0	6
Career			2	0		0	0	0	12

Lee Morris

Year	Team		TD	1XP	2XP	FG	FGA	SAF	Pts
1987	GB	N	1	0		0	0	0	6

Max Morris

Year	Team		TD	1XP	2XP	FG	FGA	SAF	Pts
1947	CHI	AA	2	0		0	0	0	12
1948	BKN	AA	1	0		0	0	0	6
Career			3	0		0	0	0	18

Mercury Morris

Year	Team		TD	1XP	2XP	FG	FGA	SAF	Pts
1969	MIA	A	2	0		0	0	0	12
1970	MIA	N	1	0		0	0	0	6
1971			2	0		0	0	0	12
1972			12	0		0	0	0	72
1973			10	0		0	0	0	60
1974			2	0		0	0	0	12
1975			4	0		0	0	0	24
1976	SD	N	2	0		0	0	0	12
Career			35	0		0	0	0	210
Playoffs			1	0		0	0	0	6

Randall Morris

Year	Team		TD	1XP	2XP	FG	FGA	SAF	Pts
1986	SEA	N	1	0		0	0	0	6

Reilly Morris

Year	Team		TD	1XP	2XP	FG	FGA	SAF	Pts
1961	OAK	A	1	0		0	0	0	6

Ron Morris

Year	Team		TD	1XP	2XP	FG	FGA	SAF	Pts
1987	CHI	N	1	0		0	0	0	6
1988			4	0		0	0	0	24
1989			1	0		0	0	0	6
1990			3	0		0	0	0	18
Career			9	0		0	0	0	54
Playoffs			1	0		0	0	0	6

Wayne Morris

Year	Team		TD	1XP	2XP	FG	FGA	SAF	Pts
1976	STL	N	4	0		0	0	0	24
1977			9	0		0	0	0	54
1978			2	0		0	0	0	12
1979			9	0		0	0	0	54
1980			7	0		0	0	0	42
1981			5	0		0	0	0	30
1982			4	0		0	0	0	24
1983			2	0		0	0	0	12
1984	SD	N	1	0		0	0	0	6
Career			43	0		0	0	0	258

Charlie Morrison

Year	Team		TD	1XP	2XP	FG	FGA	SAF	Pts
1926	BOS	A	1	0		0		0	6

Darryl Morrison

Year	Team		TD	1XP	2XP	FG	FGA	SAF	Pts
1994	WAS	N	1	0	0	0	0	0	6

Duke Morrison

Year	Team		TD	1XP	2XP	FG	FGA	SAF	Pts
1926	LA	A	2	0		0		0	12

Fred Morrison

Year	Team		TD	1XP	2XP	FG	FGA	SAF	Pts
1950	CHIB	N	1	0		0	0	0	6
1952			4	0		0	0	0	24
1953			2	0		0	0	0	12
1954	CLE	N	2	0		0	0	0	12
1955			3	0		0	0	0	18
1956			2	0		0	0	0	12
Career			14	0		0	0	0	84
Playoffs			2	0		0	0	0	12

Joe Morrison

Year	Team		TD	1XP	2XP	FG	FGA	SAF	Pts
1959	NYG	N	2	0		0	0	0	12
1960			5	0		0	0	0	30
1961			2	0		0	0	0	12
1962			3	0		0	0	0	18
1963			10	0		0	0	0	60
1964			3	0		0	0	0	18
1965			5	0		0	0	0	30
1966			8	0		0	0	0	48
1967			9	0		0	0	0	54
1968			6	0		0	0	0	36
1969			1	0		0	0	0	66
1971			1	0		0	0	0	6
Career			55	0		0	0	0	390

Ram Morrison

Year	Team		TD	1XP	2XP	FG	FGA	SAF	Pts
1926	LA	A	1	0		0		0	6

Reece Morrison

Year	Team		TD	1XP	2XP	FG	FGA	SAF	Pts
1968	CLE	N	2	0		0	0	0	12
1969			1	0		0	0	0	6

Reece Morrison continued

Year	Team		TD	1XP	2XP	FG	FGA	SAF	Pts
1970			1	0		0	0	0	6
Career			4	0		0	0	0	24

Frank Morrissey

Year	Team		TD	1XP	2XP	FG	FGA	SAF	Pts
1922	BUF	N	0	8		2		0	14
1923			0	7		8		0	31
1924			0	0		2		0	6
Career			0	15		12		0	51

Bob Morrow

Year	Team		TD	1XP	2XP	FG	FGA	SAF	Pts
1941	CHIC	N	1	0		0	0	0	6
1942			1	0		0	0	0	6
1943			2	0		0	0	0	12
Career			4	0		0	0	0	24

Jim Morrow

Year	Team		TD	1XP	2XP	FG	FGA	SAF	Pts
1921	CAN	A	1	0		0		0	6

Russ Morrow

Year	Team		TD	1XP	2XP	FG	FGA	SAF	Pts
1946	BKN	AA	2	0		0	0	0	12

Bobby Morse

Year	Team		TD	1XP	2XP	FG	FGA	SAF	Pts
1989	NO	N	1	0		0	0	0	6

Ray Morse

Year	Team		TD	1XP	2XP	FG	FGA	SAF	Pts
1937	DET	N	1	0				0	6

Craig Morton

Year	Team		TD	1XP	2XP	FG	FGA	SAF	Pts
1968	DAL	N	2	0		0	0	0	12
1969			1	0		0	0	0	6
1971			1	0		0	0	0	6
1972			2	0		0	0	0	12
1977	DEN	N	4	0		0	0	0	24
1979			1	0		0	0	0	6
1980			1	0		0	0	0	6
Career			12	0		0	0	0	72
Playoffs			1	0		0	0	0	6

Jack Morton

Year	Team		TD	1XP	2XP	FG	FGA	SAF	Pts
1946	LA	AA	1	0		0	0	0	6

Johnnie Morton

Year	Team		TD	1XP	2XP	FG	FGA	SAF	Pts
1994	DET	N	2	0	0	0	0	0	12
1995			8	0	0	0	0	0	48
1996			6	0	0	0	0	0	36
Career			16	0	0	0	0	0	96
Playoffs			1	0	0	0	0	0	6

Michael Morton

Year	Team		TD	1XP	2XP	FG	FGA	SAF	Pts
1987	SEA	N	1	0		0	0	0	6

Jim Moscrip

Year	Team		TD	1XP	2XP	FG	FGA	SAF	Pts
1938	DET	N	1	6		0		0	12
1939			1	9		0	1	0	15
Career			2	15		0	1	0	27

Mark Moseley

Year	Team		TD	1XP	2XP	FG	FGA	SAF	Pts
1970	PHI	N	0	25		14	25	0	67
1971	HOU	N	0	25		16	26	0	73
1972			0	2		1	2	0	5
1974	WAS	N	0	27		18	30	0	81
1975			0	37		16	25	0	85
1976			0	31		22	34	0	97
1977			0	19		21	37	0	82
1978			0	30		19	30	0	87
1979			0	39		25	33	0	114
1980			0	27		18	33	0	81
1981			0	38		19	30	0	95
1982			0	16		20	21	0	76
1983			0	62		33	47	0	161
1984			0	48		24	31	0	120
1985			0	31		22	34	0	97
1986	WAS-CLE	N	0	25		12	19	0	61
Career			0	482		300	457	0	1382
Playoffs			0	31		17	31	0	82

Dom Moselle

Year	Team		TD	1XP	2XP	FG	FGA	SAF	Pts
1951	GB	N	3	0		0	0	0	18
1954	PHI	N	3	0		0	0	0	18
Career			6	0		0	0	0	36

Rick Moser

Year	Team		TD	1XP	2XP	FG	FGA	SAF	Pts
1979	PIT	N	1	0		0	0	0	6
1981			1	0		0	0	0	6
Career			2	0		0	0	0	12

Haven Moses

Year	Team		TD	1XP	2XP	FG	FGA	SAF	Pts
1968	BUF	A	2	0	0	0	0	0	12
1969			5	0	0	0	0	0	30
1970	BUF	N	2	0		0	0	0	12
1971			2	0		0	0	0	12
1972	DEN	N	5	0		0	0	0	30
1972	BUF-DEN	N	6	0		0	0	0	36
1973	DEN	N	9	0		0	0	0	54
1974			2	0		0	0	0	12
1975			2	0		0	0	0	12
1976			7	0		0	0	0	42
1977			4	0		0	0	0	24
1978			5	0		0	0	0	30
1979			6	0		0	0	0	36
1980			4	0		0	0	0	24
1981			1	0		0	0	0	6
Career			62	0	0	0	0	0	372
Playoffs			2	0	0	0	0	0	12

Anthony Mosley

Year	Team		TD	1XP	2XP	FG	FGA	SAF	Pts
1987	CHI	N	1	0		0	0	0	6

Mike Mosley

Year	Team		TD	1XP	2XP	FG	FGA	SAF	Pts
1983	BUF	N	3	0		0	0	0	18

Norm Mosley

Year	Team		TD	1XP	2XP	FG	FGA	SAF	Pts
1948	PIT	N	1	0		0	0	0	6

Eddie Moss

Year	Team		TD	1XP	2XP	FG	FGA	SAF	Pts
1975	STL	N	1	0		0	0	0	6

Paul Moss

Year	Team		TD	1XP	2XP	FG	FGA	SAF	Pts
1933	PIT	N	2	0		0		0	12
1934	C-S	N	1	0		0		0	6
Career			3	0		0		0	18

Roland Moss

Year	Team		TD	1XP	2XP	FG	FGA	SAF	Pts
1971	NE	N	2	0		0	0	0	12

Winston Moss

Year	Team		TD	1XP	2XP	FG	FGA	SAF	Pts
1987	TB	N	1	0		0	0	0	6

Kelley Mote

Year	Team		TD	1XP	2XP	FG	FGA	SAF	Pts
1947	DET	N	1	0		0	0	0	6
1950	NYG	N	1	0		0	0	0	6
1951			4	0		0	0	0	24
Career			6	0		0	0	0	36

Bob Motl

Year	Team		TD	1XP	2XP	FG	FGA	SAF	Pts
1946	CHI	AA	1	0		0	0	0	6

Marion Motley

Year	Team		TD	1XP	2XP	FG	FGA	SAF	Pts
1946	CLE	AA	6	0		0	0	0	36
1947			10	0		0	0	0	60
1948			7	0		0	0	0	42
1949			8	0		0	0	0	48
1950	CLE	N	4	0		0	0	0	24
1951			1	0		0	0	0	6
1952			3	0		0	0	0	18
Career			39	0		0	0	0	234
Playoffs			5	0		0	0	0	30

Eric Moulds

Year	Team		TD	1XP	2XP	FG	FGA	SAF	Pts
1996	BUF	N	3	0	0	0	0	0	18

Zeke Mowatt

Year	Team		TD	1XP	2XP	FG	FGA	SAF	Pts
1983	NYG	N	1	0		0	0	0	6
1984			6	0		0	0	0	36
1986			2	0		0	0	0	12
1987			1	0		0	0	0	6
1988			1	0		0	0	0	6
1991			1	0		0	0	0	6
Career			12	0		0	0	0	72
Playoffs			2	0		0	0	0	12

Paul Moyer

Year	Team		TD	1XP	2XP	FG	FGA	SAF	Pts
1983	SEA	N	1	0		0	0	0	6
1986			1	0		0	0	0	6
Career			2	0		0	0	0	12

Dick Moynihan

Year	Team		TD	1XP	2XP	FG	FGA	SAF	Pts
1927	FRA	N	0	0		1		0	3

Tim Moynihan

Year	Team		TD	1XP	2XP	FG	FGA	SAF	Pts
1932	CHIC	N	2	0		0		0	12

Bob Mrosko

Year	Team		TD	1XP	2XP	FG	FGA	SAF	Pts
1990	NYG	N	1	0		0	0	0	6

Larry Mucker

Year	Team		TD	1XP	2XP	FG	FGA	SAF	Pts
1979	TB	N	5	0		0	0	0	30

Frank Muehlheuser

Year	Team		TD	1XP	2XP	FG	FGA	SAF	Pts
1948	BOS	N	1	0		0	0	0	6
1949	NYB	N	1	0		0	0	0	6
Career			2	0		0	0	0	12

Ed Muelhaupt

Year	Team		TD	1XP	2XP	FG	FGA	SAF	Pts
1961	BUF	A	1	0	0	0	0	0	6

Jamie Mueller

Year	Team		TD	1XP	2XP	FG	FGA	SAF	Pts
1987	BUF	N	2	0		0	0	0	12
1990			3	0		0	0	0	18
Career			5	0		0	0	0	30

Vance Mueller

Year	Team		TD	1XP	2XP	FG	FGA	SAF	Pts
1987	LARI	N	1	0		0	0	0	6
1989			4	0		0	0	0	24
Career			5	0		0	0	0	30

Joe Muha

Year	Team		TD	1XP	2XP	FG	FGA	SAF	Pts
1947	PHI	N	2	0		1	5	0	15
1948			1	0		0	5	0	6
1949			1	5		0	1	0	11
1950			1	0		0	5	0	6
Career			5	5		1	16	0	38

Calvin Muhammad

Year	Team		TD	1XP	2XP	FG	FGA	SAF	Pts
1982	LARI	N	1	0		0	0	0	6
1983			2	0		0	0	0	12
1984	WAS	N	4	0		0	0	0	24
1985			1	0		0	0	0	6
Career			8	0		0	0	0	48

Mushin Muhammad

Year	Team		TD	1XP	2XP	FG	FGA	SAF	Pts
1996	CAR	N	1	0	0	0	0	0	6

Horst Muhlmann

Year	Team		TD	1XP	2XP	FG	FGA	SAF	Pts
1969	CIN	A	0	32	0	16	24	0	80
1970	CIN	N	0	33		25	37	0	108
1971			0	31		20	36	0	91
1972			0	30		27	40	0	111
1973			0	31		21	31	0	94
1974			0	32		11	18	0	65
1975	PHI	N	0	21		20	29	0	81
1976			0	18		11	16	0	51
1977			0	17		3	8	0	26
Career			0	245	0	154	239	0	707
Playoffs			0	1	0	3	4	0	10

Mike Mularkey

Year	Team		TD	1XP	2XP	FG	FGA	SAF	Pts
1984	MIN	N	2	0		0	0	0	12
1985			1	0		0	0	0	6
1986			2	0		0	0	0	12
1989	PIT	N	1	0		0	0	0	6
1990			3	0		0	0	0	18
Career			9	0		0	0	0	54

Joe Mulbarger

Year	Team		TD	1XP	2XP	FG	FGA	SAF	Pts
1921	COL	A	1	0		0		0	6

Herb Mul-Key

Year	Team		TD	1XP	2XP	FG	FGA	SAF	Pts
1972	WAS	N	1	0		0	0	0	6
1973			1	0		0	0	0	6
Career			2	0		0	0	0	12

Tom Mullady

Year	Team		TD	1XP	2XP	FG	FGA	SAF	Pts
1980	NYG	N	2	0		0	0	0	12
1981			1	0		0	0	0	6
1983			1	0		0	0	0	6
Career			4	0		0	0	0	24
Playoffs			1	0		0	0	0	6

Verne Mullen

Year	Team		TD	1XP	2XP	FG	FGA	SAF	Pts
1926	CHIB	N	1	0		0		0	6

Carl Mulleneaux

Year	Team		TD	1XP	2XP	FG	FGA	SAF	Pts
1938	GB	N	2	0		0		0	12
1939			1	0		0	0	1	8
1940			7	0		0	0	0	42
1941			2	0		0	0	0	12
Career			12	0		0	0	1	74
Playoffs			1	0		0	0	0	6

Brick Muller

Year	Team		TD	1XP	2XP	FG	FGA	SAF	Pts
1926	LA	N	1	0		0		0	6

Eric Mullins

Year	Team		TD	1XP	2XP	FG	FGA	SAF	Pts
1984	HOU	N	1	0		0	0	0	6

Gerry Mullins

Year	Team		TD	1XP	2XP	FG	FGA	SAF	Pts
1972	PIT	N	1	0		0	0	0	6
1974			1	0		0	0	0	6
1975			1	0		0	0	0	6
Career			3	0		0	0	0	18
Playoffs			1	0		0	0	0	6

Noah Mullins

Year	Team		TD	1XP	2XP	FG	FGA	SAF	Pts
1948	CHIB	N	6	0		0	0	0	36
1949	NYG	N	1	0		0	0	0	6
Career			7	0		0	0	0	42

Nick Mumley

Year	Team		TD	1XP	2XP	FG	FGA	SAF	Pts
1960	NY	A	1	0	0	0	0	0	6

Lloyd Mumphord

Year	Team		TD	1XP	2XP	FG	FGA	SAF	Pts
1970	MIA	N	2	0		0	0	0	12
1972			1	0		0	0	0	6
Career			3	0		0	0	0	18

Mike Munchak

Year	Team		TD	1XP	2XP	FG	FGA	SAF	Pts
1986	HOU	N	1	0		0	0	0	6

Chuck Muncie

Year	Team		TD	1XP	2XP	FG	FGA	SAF	Pts
1976	NO	N	2	0		0	0	0	12
1977			7	0		0	0	0	42
1978			7	0		0	0	0	42
1979			11	0		0	0	0	66
1980	NO-SD	N	6	0		0	0	0	36
1981	SD	N	**19**	0		0	0	0	114
1982			9	0		0	0	0	54
1983			13	0		0	0	0	78
Career			74	0		0	0	0	444
Playoffs			3	0		0	0	0	18

Lyle Munn

Year	Team		TD	1XP	2XP	FG	FGA	SAF	Pts
1926	KC	N	1	0		0		0	6
1929	NYG	N	0	1		0		0	1
Career			1	1		0		0	7

George Munns

Year	Team		TD	1XP	2XP	FG	FGA	SAF	Pts
1921	CIN	A	0	1		0		0	1

Anthony Munoz

Year	Team		TD	1XP	2XP	FG	FGA	SAF	Pts
1984	CIN	N	1	0		0	0	0	6
1986			2	0		0	0	0	12
1987			1	0		0	0	0	6
Career			4	0		0	0	0	24

Nelson Munsey

Year	Team		TD	1XP	2XP	FG	FGA	SAF	Pts
1972	BAL	N	1	0		0	0	0	6
1975			1	0		0	0	0	6
Career			2	0		0	0	0	12

Bill Munson

Year	Team		TD	1XP	2XP	FG	FGA	SAF	Pts
1965	LA	N	1	0		0	0	0	6
1968	DET	N	1	0		0	0	0	6
1974			1	0		0	0	0	6
Career			3	0		0	0	0	18

Les Murdock

Year	Team		TD	1XP	2XP	FG	FGA	SAF	Pts
1967	NYG	N	0	13		4	9	0	25

Kevin Murphy

Year	Team		TD	1XP	2XP	FG	FGA	SAF	Pts
1988	TB	N	1	0		0	0	0	6

Mark Murphy

Year	Team		TD	1XP	2XP	FG	FGA	SAF	Pts
1985	GB	N	1	0		0	0	0	6

Eddie Murray

Year	Team		TD	1XP	2XP	FG	FGA	SAF	Pts
1980	DET	N	0	35		27	42	0	116
1981			0	46		25	35	0	121
1982			0	16		11	12	0	49
1983			0	38		25	32	0	113
1984			0	31		20	27	0	91
1985			0	31		26	31	0	109
1986			0	31		18	25	0	85
1987			0	21		20	32	0	81
1988			0	22		20	21	0	82
1989			0	36		20	21	0	96
1990			0	34		13	19	0	73
1991			0	40		19	28	0	97
1992	KC-TB	N	0	13		5	9	0	28
1993	DAL	N	0	38		28	33	0	122
1994	PHI	N	0	33	0	21	25	0	96
1995	WAS	N	0	33		27	36	0	114
Career			0	498	0	325	428	0	1473
Playoffs			0	20	0	11	14	0	53

Franny Murray

Year	Team		TD	1XP	2XP	FG	FGA	SAF	Pts
1939	PHI	N	3	8		2	4	0	32
1940			0	6		0	10	0	6
Career			3	14		2	5	0	38

Jab Murray

Year	Team		TD	1XP	2XP	FG	FGA	SAF	Pts
1922	RAC	N	0	1		0		0	1

Walter Murray

Year	Team		TD	1XP	2XP	FG	FGA	SAF	Pts
1987	IND	N	3	0		0	0	0	18

Adrian Murrell

Year	Team		TD	1XP	2XP	FG	FGA	SAF	Pts
1993	NYJ	N	1	0		0	0	0	6
1995			3	0		0	0	0	18
1996			7	0		0	0	0	42
Career			11	0		0	0	0	66

Don Murry

Year	Team		TD	1XP	2XP	FG	FGA	SAF	Pts
1925	CHIB	N	1	0		0		0	6
1929			0	0		0		1	2
Career			1	0		0		1	8

George Murtagh

Year	Team		TD	1XP	2XP	FG	FGA	SAF	Pts
1929	NYG	N	1	0		0		0	6

Jim Musick

Year	Team		TD	1XP	2XP	FG	FGA	SAF	Pts
1932	BOS	N	1	0		0		0	6
1933			5	11		1		0	44
1935			2	2		0		0	14
Career			8	13		1		0	64

Johnny Musso

Year	Team		TD	1XP	2XP	FG	FGA	SAF	Pts
1976	CHI	N	4	0		0	0	1	26
1977			2	0		0	0	0	12
Career			6	0		0	0	1	38

Brad Muster

Year	Team		TD	1XP	2XP	FG	FGA	SAF	Pts
1988	CHI	N	1	0		0	0	0	6
1989			8	0		0	0	0	48
1990			6	0		0	0	0	36
1991			7	0		0	0	0	42
1992			5	0		0	0	0	30
1993	NO	N	3	0		0	0	0	18
1994			1	0		0	0	0	6
Career			31	0		0	0	0	186

Najee Mustafaa

Year	Team		TD	1XP	2XP	FG	FGA	SAF	Pts
1989	MIN	N	1	0		0	0	0	6
1991			1	0		0	0	0	6
1993	CLE	N	1	0		0	0	0	6
Career			3	0		0	0	0	18
Playoffs			1	0		0	0	0	6

Chet Mutryn

Year	Team		TD	1XP	2XP	FG	FGA	SAF	Pts
1946	BUF	AA	5	0		0	0	0	30
1947			12	1		0	0	0	73
1948			16	0		0	0	0	96
1949			5	0		0	0	0	30
1950	BAL	N	4	0		0	0	0	24
Career			42	1		0	0	0	253
Playoffs			2	0		0	0	0	12

Jim Mutscheller

Year	Team		TD	1XP	2XP	FG	FGA	SAF	Pts
1955	BAL	N	7	0		0	0	0	42
1956			6	0		0	0	0	36
1957			8	0		0	0	0	48
1958			7	0		0	0	0	42
1959			8	0		0	0	0	48
1960			2	0		0	0	0	12
1961			2	0		0	0	0	12
Career			40	0		0	0	0	240

Brad Myers

Year	Team		TD	1XP	2XP	FG	FGA	SAF	Pts
1953	LA	N	3	0		0	0	0	18

Chip Myers

Year	Team		TD	1XP	2XP	FG	FGA	SAF	Pts
1969	CIN	A	2	0	0	0	0	0	12
1970	CIN	N	1	0		0	0	0	6
1971			1	0		0	0	0	6
1972			3	0		0	0	0	18
1974			1	0		0	0	0	6
1975			3	0		0	0	0	18
1976			1	0		0	0	0	6
Career			12	0		0	0	0	72

Cy Myers

Year	Team		TD	1XP	2XP	FG	FGA	SAF	Pts
1922	TOL	N	0	1		0		0	1

Jack Myers

Year	Team		TD	1XP	2XP	FG	FGA	SAF	Pts
1948	PHI	N	1	0		0	0	0	6
1949			1	0		0	0	0	6
1952	LA	N	1	0		0	0	0	6
Career			3	0		0	0	0	18

Tommy Myers

Year	Team		TD	1XP	2XP	FG	FGA	SAF	Pts
1975	NO	N	1	0		0	0	0	6
1976			1	0		0	0	0	6
1977			1	0		0	0	0	6
1978			1	0		0	0	0	6
1979			1	0		0	0	0	6
Career			5	0		0	0	0	30

Steve Myhra

Year	Team		TD	1XP	2XP	FG	FGA	SAF	Pts
1957	BAL	N	0	14		4	6	0	26
1958			0	48		4	10	0	60
1959			0	50		6	17	0	68
1960			0	35		9	19	0	62
1961			0	33		21	39	0	96
Career			0	180		44	91	0	312
Playoffs			0	6		2	4	0	12

Jesse Myles

Year	Team		TD	1XP	2XP	FG	FGA	SAF	Pts
1983	DEN	N	1	0		0	0	0	6
Playoffs			1	0	0	0	0	0	6

Chip Myrtle

Year	Team		TD	1XP	2XP	FG	FGA	SAF	Pts
1968	DEN	A	0	0	0	0	0	1	2

Gern Nagler

Year	Team		TD	1XP	2XP	FG	FGA	SAF	Pts
1953	CHIC	N	6	0		0	0	0	36
1955			3	0		0	0	0	18
1956			4	0		0	0	0	24
1957			4	0		0	0	0	24
1958			5	0		0	0	0	30
1959	PIT	N	2	0		0	0	0	12
1960	CLE	N	3	0		0	0	0	18
1961			1	0		0	0	0	6
Career			28	0		0	0	0	168

Bronko Nagurski

Year	Team		TD	1XP	2XP	FG	FGA	SAF	Pts
1930	CHIB	N	5	0		0		0	30
1931			2	0		0		0	12
1932			4	0		0		0	24
1933			1	1		0		0	7
1934			7	1		0		0	43
1935			1	0		0		0	6
1936			3	1		0		0	19
1937			1	0		0		0	6
1943			1	0		0		0	6
Career			25	3		0	0	0	153
Playoffs			2	0		0	0	0	12

John Naioti

Year	Team		TD	1XP	2XP	FG	FGA	SAF	Pts
1945	PIT	N	0	4		0	0	0	4

Rob Nairne

Year	Team		TD	1XP	2XP	FG	FGA	SAF	Pts
1979	DEN	N	1	0		0	0	0	6

Joe Namath

Year	Team		TD	1XP	2XP	FG	FGA	SAF	Pts
1966	NY	A	2	0	0	0	0	0	12
1967			1	0	0	0	0	0	6
1968			2	0	0	0	0	0	12
1969			2	0	0	0	0	0	12
1974	NYJ	N	1	0		0	0	0	6
Career			8	0	0	0	0	0	48

Jim Nance

Year	Team		TD	1XP	2XP	FG	FGA	SAF	Pts
1965	BOS	A	5	0		0	0	0	30
1966			11	0		0	0	0	66
1967			8	0		0	0	0	48
1968			4	0		0	0	0	24
1969			6	0		0	0	0	36
1970	BOS	N	7	0		0	0	0	42
1971	NE	N	5	0		0	0	0	30
Career			46	0		0	0	0	276

Bob Nash

Year	Team		TD	1XP	2XP	FG	FGA	SAF	Pts
1920	AKR	A	3	0		0		0	18
1921	BUF	A	1	0		0		0	6
Career			4	0		0		0	24

Joe Nash

Year	Team		TD	1XP	2XP	FG	FGA	SAF	Pts
1984	SEA	N	1	0		0	0	0	6
1993			1	0		0	0	0	6
Career			2	0		0	0	0	12

Tom Nash

Year	Team		TD	1XP	2XP	FG	FGA	SAF	Pts
1929	GB	N	1	0		0		0	6
1930			1	0		0		0	6
1931			1	0		0		0	6
1932			0	0		0		2	4
1933	BKN	N	2	0		0		0	12
Career			5	0		0		2	34

Tony Nathan

Year	Team		TD	1XP	2XP	FG	FGA	SAF	Pts
1979	MIA	N	3	0		0	0	0	18
1980			6	0		0	0	0	36
1981			8	0		0	0	0	48
1982			1	0		0	0	0	6
1983			4	0		0	0	0	24
1984			3	0		0	0	0	18
1985			6	0		0	0	0	36
1986			2	0		0	0	0	12
Career			33	0		0	0	0	198
Playoffs			5	0		0	0	0	30

Ricky Nattiel

Year	Team		TD	1XP	2XP	FG	FGA	SAF	Pts
1987	DEN	N	2	0		0	0	0	12
1988			1	0		0	0	0	6
1989			1	0		0	0	0	6
1990			2	0		0	0	0	12
1991			2	0		0	0	0	12
Career			8	0		0	0	0	48
Playoffs			2	0		0	0	0	12

Clem Neacy

Year	Team		TD	1XP	2XP	FG	FGA	SAF	Pts
1924	MIL	N	2	0		0		0	12
1925			1	0		0		0	6
Career			3	0		0		0	18

Ed Neal

Year	Team		TD	1XP	2XP	FG	FGA	SAF	Pts
1947	GB	N	1	0		0	0	0	6

Frankie Neal

Year	Team		TD	1XP	2XP	FG	FGA	SAF	Pts
1987	GB	N	3	0		0	0	0	18

Lorenzo Neal

Year	Team		TD	1XP	2XP	FG	FGA	SAF	Pts
1993	NO	N	1	0		0	0	0	6
1994			1	0	0	0	0	0	6
1995			1	0	0	0	0	0	6
1996			2	0	0	0	0	0	12
Career			5	0	0	0	0	0	30

Louis Neal

Year	Team		TD	1XP	2XP	FG	FGA	SAF	Pts
1973	ATL	N	1	0		0	0	0	6

Ray Neal

Year	Team		TD	1XP	2XP	FG	FGA	SAF	Pts
1925	HAM	N	1	0		0		0	6

Richard Neal

Year	Team		TD	1XP	2XP	FG	FGA	SAF	Pts
1972	**NO**	**N**	1	0		0	0	0	6

Speedy Neal

Year	Team		TD	1XP	2XP	FG	FGA	SAF	Pts
1984	**BUF**	**N**	1	0		0	0	0	6

Derrick Ned

Year	Team		TD	1XP	2XP	FG	FGA	SAF	Pts
1993	**NO**	**N**	1	0		0	0	0	6

Joe Nedney

Year	Team		TD	1XP	2XP	FG	FGA	SAF	Pts
1996	**MIA**	**N**	0	35	0	18	29	0	89

Fred Negus

Year	Team		TD	1XP	2XP	FG	FGA	SAF	Pts
1948	**CHI**	**AA**	1	0		0	0	0	6
1949			1	0		0	0	0	6
Career			2	0		0	0	0	12

Renaldo Nehemiah

Year	Team		TD	1XP	2XP	FG	FGA	SAF	Pts
1982	**SF**	**N**	1	0		0	0	0	6
1983			1	0		0	0	0	6
1984			2	0		0	0	0	12
Career			4	0		0	0	0	24

Steve Neils

Year	Team		TD	1XP	2XP	FG	FGA	SAF	Pts
1979	**STL**	**N**	1	0		0	0	0	6

Mike Nelms

Year	Team		TD	1XP	2XP	FG	FGA	SAF	Pts
1981	**WAS**	**N**	2	0		0	0	0	12

Bill Nelsen

Year	Team		TD	1XP	2XP	FG	FGA	SAF	Pts
1965	**PIT**	**N**	1	0		0	0	0	6
1968	**CLE**	**N**	1	0		0	0	0	6
Career			2	0		0	0	0	12

Al Nelson

Year	Team		TD	1XP	2XP	FG	FGA	SAF	Pts
1966	**PHI**	**N**	1	0		0	0	0	6
1971			2	0		0	0	0	12
Career			3	0		0	0	0	18

Andy Nelson

Year	Team		TD	1XP	2XP	FG	FGA	SAF	Pts
1958	**BAL**	**N**	1	0		0	0	0	6
1959			1	0		0	0	0	6
1963			1	0		0	0	0	6
Career			3	0		0	0	0	18

Benny Nelson

Year	Team		TD	1XP	2XP	FG	FGA	SAF	Pts
1964	**HOU**	**A**	1	0	0	0	0	0	6

Bob Nelson

Year	Team		TD	1XP	2XP	FG	FGA	SAF	Pts
1945	**DET**	**N**	0	0		1	4	0	3
1946	**LA**	**AA**	0	3		2	6	0	9
1947			2	0		0	0	0	12
1949			0	34		3	6	0	43
Career			2	37		6	16	0	67

Chuck Nelson

Year	Team		TD	1XP	2XP	FG	FGA	SAF	Pts
1983	**LARM**	**N**	0	33		5	11	0	48
1984	**BUF**	**N**	0	14		3	5	0	23
1986	**MIN**	**N**	0	44		22	28	0	110
1987			0	36		13	24	0	75
1988			0	48		20	25	0	108
Career			0	175		63	93	0	364
Playoffs			0	13		10	11	0	43

Darrin Nelson

Year	Team		TD	1XP	2XP	FG	FGA	SAF	Pts
1983	**MIN**	**N**	1	0		0	0	0	6
1984			4	0		0	0	0	24
1985			6	0		0	0	0	36
1986			7	0		0	0	0	42
1987			2	0		0	0	0	12
1988			1	0		0	0	0	6
1991			2	0		0	0	0	12
Career			23	0		0	0	0	138

Derrie Nelson

Year	Team		TD	1XP	2XP	FG	FGA	SAF	Pts
1983	**SD**	**N**	1	0		0	0	0	6

Jimmy Nelson

Year	Team		TD	1XP	2XP	FG	FGA	SAF	Pts
1946	**MIA**	**AA**	2	0		0	0	0	12

Lee Nelson

Year	Team		TD	1XP	2XP	FG	FGA	SAF	Pts
1983	**STL**	**N**	1	0		0	0	0	6

Ralph Nelson

Year	Team		TD	1XP	2XP	FG	FGA	SAF	Pts
1975	**WAS**	**N**	1	0		0	0	0	6
1976	**SEA**	**N**	1	0		0	0	0	6
Career			2	0		0	0	0	12

Terry Nelson

Year	Team		TD	1XP	2XP	FG	FGA	SAF	Pts
1977	**LA**	**N**	3	0		0	0	0	18
1978			1	0		0	0	0	6
1979			3	0		0	0	0	18
Career			7	0		0	0	0	42

Jerry Nemecek

Year	Team		TD	1XP	2XP	FG	FGA	SAF	Pts
1931	**BKN**	**N**	1	0		0		0	6

Steve Nemeth

Year	Team		TD	1XP	2XP	FG	FGA	SAF	Pts
1946	**CHI**	**AA**	0	32		9	12	0	59
1947	**BAL**	**AA**	0	1		0	1	0	1
Career			0	33		9	13	0	60

Dick Nesbitt

Year	Team		TD	1XP	2XP	FG	FGA	SAF	Pts
1930	**CHIB**	**N**	1	0		0		0	6
1931			2	0		0		0	12
1932			2	0		0		0	12
1933	**CHIC**	**N**	1	0		0		0	6
Career			6	0		0		0	36

Al Nesser

Year	Team		TD	1XP	2XP	FG	FGA	SAF	Pts
1921	**AKR**	**A**	1	0		0		0	6
1922	**AKR**	**N**	1	0		0		0	6
1923			1	0		0		0	6
1925	**CLE**	**N**	1	0		0		0	6
Career			4	0		0		0	24

Frank Nesser

Year	Team		TD	1XP	2XP	FG	FGA	SAF	Pts
1920	**COL**	**A**	0	0		0		0	0
1921			0	1		0		0	1
1922	**COL**	**N**	1	0		0		0	6
Career			1	1		0		0	7

Fred Nesser

Year	Team		TD	1XP	2XP	FG	FGA	SAF	Pts
1921	**COL**	**A**	1	0		0		0	6

Doug Nettles

Year	Team		TD	1XP	2XP	FG	FGA	SAF	Pts
1977	**BAL**	**N**	0	0		0	0	1	2

Jim Nettles

Year	Team		TD	1XP	2XP	FG	FGA	SAF	Pts
1965	**PHI**	**N**	1	0		0	0	0	6
1966			1	0		0	0	0	6
1967			1	0		0	0	0	6
1971	**LA**	**N**	1	0		0	0	0	6
Career			4	0		0	0	0	24

Keith Neubert

Year	Team		TD	1XP	2XP	FG	FGA	SAF	Pts
1989	**NYJ**	**N**	1	0		0	0	0	6

Rick Neuheisel

Year	Team		TD	1XP	2XP	FG	FGA	SAF	Pts
1987	**SD**	**N**	1	1		0	0	0	7

Bob Neuman

Year	Team		TD	1XP	2XP	FG	FGA	SAF	Pts
1935	**CHIC**	**N**	1	0		0		0	6

Tom Neumann

Year	Team		TD	1XP	2XP	FG	FGA	SAF	Pts
1963	**BOS**	**A**	1	0	0	0	0	0	6

Ernie Nevers

Year	Team		TD	1XP	2XP	FG	FGA	SAF	Pts
1926	**DUL**	**N**	8	11		4		0	71
1927			4	7		0		0	31
1929	**CHIC**	**N**	**12**	10		1		0	**85**
1930			6	9		1		0	48
1931			8	**15**		1		0	66
Career			38	52		7		0	301

Tom Newberry

Year	Team		TD	1XP	2XP	FG	FGA	SAF	Pts
1986	**LARM**	**N**	1	0		0	0	0	6

Robert Newhouse

Year	Team		TD	1XP	2XP	FG	FGA	SAF	Pts
1972	**DAL**	**N**	1	0		0	0	0	6
1973			2	0		0	0	0	12
1974			3	0		0	0	0	18
1975			2	0		0	0	0	12
1976			3	0		0	0	0	18
1977			4	0		0	0	0	24
1978			10	0		0	0	0	60

Robert Newhouse *continued*

Year	Team		TD	1XP	2XP	FG	FGA	SAF	Pts
1979			4	0		0	0	0	24
1980			6	0		0	0	0	36
1982			1	0		0	0	0	6
Career			36	0		0	0	0	216
Playoffs			3	0		0	0	0	18

Bob Newland

Year	Team		TD	1XP	2XP	FG	FGA	SAF	Pts
1972	**NO**	**N**	2	0		0	0	0	12
1973			4	0		0	0	0	24
1974			2	0		0	0	0	12
Career			8	0		0	0	0	48

Anthony Newman

Year	Team		TD	1XP	2XP	FG	FGA	SAF	Pts
1991	**LARM**	**N**	1	0		0	0	0	6
1994			1	0	0	0	0	0	6
Career			2	0	0	0	0	0	12

Harry Newman

Year	Team		TD	1XP	2XP	FG	FGA	SAF	Pts
1933	**NYG**	**N**	4	5		1		0	32
1934			4	5		3		0	38
1935			0	3		2		0	9
Career			8	13		6		0	79

Olin Newman

Year	Team		TD	1XP	2XP	FG	FGA	SAF	Pts
1925	**AKR**	**N**	1	1		0		0	7

Pat Newman

Year	Team		TD	1XP	2XP	FG	FGA	SAF	Pts
1993	**NO**	**N**	1	0		0	0	0	6

Don Newmeyer

Year	Team		TD	1XP	2XP	FG	FGA	SAF	Pts
1926	**LA**	**N**	0	2		0		0	2

Billy Newsome

Year	Team		TD	1XP	2XP	FG	FGA	SAF	Pts
1971	**BAL**	**N**	1	0		0	0	0	6

Craig Newsome

Year	Team		TD	1XP	2XP	FG	FGA	SAF	Pts
Playoffs			1	0	0	0	0	0	6

Ozzie Newsome

Year	Team		TD	1XP	2XP	FG	FGA	SAF	Pts
1978	**CLE**	**N**	4	0		0	0	0	24
1979			9	0		0	0	0	54
1980			3	0		0	0	0	18
1981			6	0		0	0	0	36
1982			3	0		0	0	0	18
1983			6	0		0	0	0	36
1984			5	0		0	0	0	30
1985			5	0		0	0	0	30
1986			3	0		0	0	0	18
1988			2	0		0	0	0	12
1989			1	0		0	0	0	6
1990			2	0		0	0	0	12
Career			49	0		0	0	0	294
Playoffs			1	0		0	0	0	6

Timmy Newsome

Year	Team		TD	1XP	2XP	FG	FGA	SAF	Pts
1980	**DAL**	**N**	2	0		0	0	0	12
1982			2	0		0	0	0	12
1983			6	0		0	0	0	36
1984			5	0		0	0	0	30
1985			3	0		0	0	0	18
1986			5	0		0	0	0	30
1987			4	0		0	0	0	24
1988			3	0		0	0	0	18
Career			30	0		0	0	0	180
Playoffs			3	0		0	0	0	18

Vince Newsome

Year	Team		TD	1XP	2XP	FG	FGA	SAF	Pts
1989	**LARM**	**N**	1	0		0	0	0	6
1991	**CLE**	**N**	1	0		0	0	0	6
Career			2	0		0	0	0	12

Chuck Newton

Year	Team		TD	1XP	2XP	FG	FGA	SAF	Pts
1939	**PHI**	**N**	1	0		0	0	0	6

Tim Newton

Year	Team		TD	1XP	2XP	FG	FGA	SAF	Pts
1989	**MIN**	**N**	1	0		0	0	0	6

Tom Newton

Year	Team		TD	1XP	2XP	FG	FGA	SAF	Pts
1978	**NYJ**	**N**	2	0		0	0	0	12
1979			6	0		0	0	0	36
1981			1	0		0	0	0	6
Career			9	0		0	0	0	54

Armand Niccolai

Year	Team		TD	1XP	2XP	FG	FGA	SAF	Pts
1934	PIT	N	0	1		3		0	10
1935			0	10		**6**		0	28
1936			0	7		**7**		0	28
1937			0	5		4		0	17
1938			0	10		1	5	0	13
1939			0	15		3	8	0	24
1940			0	6		6	**14**	0	24
1941			0	8		2	4	0	14
1942			0	9		2	**14**	0	15
Career			0	71		34	45	0	173

Al Nichelini

Year	Team		TD	1XP	2XP	FG	FGA	SAF	Pts
1935	CHIC	N	4	0		0		0	24
1936			1	0		0		0	6
Career			5	0		0		0	30

Mark Nichols

Year	Team		TD	1XP	2XP	FG	FGA	SAF	Pts
1981	DET	N	1	0		0	0	0	6
1982			2	0		0	0	0	12
1983			1	0		0	0	0	6
1984			1	0		0	0	0	6
1985			4	0		0	0	0	24
Career			9	0		0	0	0	54

Sid Nichols

Year	Team		TD	1XP	2XP	FG	FGA	SAF	Pts
1920	RI	A	1	3		0		0	9
1921			1	0		0		0	6
Career			2	3		0		0	15

Elbie Nickel

Year	Team		TD	1XP	2XP	FG	FGA	SAF	Pts
1948	PIT	N	1	0		0	0	0	6
1949			3	0		0	0	0	18
1950			4	0		0	0	0	24
1951			3	0		0	0	0	18
1952			9	0		0	0	0	54
1953			4	0		0	0	0	24
1954			5	0		0	0	0	30
1955			2	0		0	0	0	12
1956			5	0		0	0	0	30
1957			1	0		0	0	0	6
Career			37	0		0	0	0	222

Frank Niehaus

Year	Team		TD	1XP	2XP	FG	FGA	SAF	Pts
1925	AKR	N	1	0		0		0	6

Hans Nielson

Year	Team		TD	1XP	2XP	FG	FGA	SAF	Pts
1981	CHI	N	0	8		0	2	0	8

Walt Nielson

Year	Team		TD	1XP	2XP	FG	FGA	SAF	Pts
1940	NYG	N	1	0		0	0	0	6

Laurie Niemi

Year	Team		TD	1XP	2XP	FG	FGA	SAF	Pts
1953	WAS	N	1	0		0	0	0	6

John Niland

Year	Team		TD	1XP	2XP	FG	FGA	SAF	Pts
1972	DAL	N	1	0		0	0	0	6

Jim Ninowski

Year	Team		TD	1XP	2XP	FG	FGA	SAF	Pts
1960	DET	N	5	0		0	0	0	30
1961			5	0		0	0	0	30
Career			10	0		0	0	0	60

Ray Nitschke

Year	Team		TD	1XP	2XP	FG	FGA	SAF	Pts
1960	GB	N	1	0		0	0	0	6
1967			1	0		0	0	0	6
Career			2	0		0	0	0	12

Bjorn Nittmo

Year	Team		TD	1XP	2XP	FG	FGA	SAF	Pts
1989	NYG	N	0	12		9	12	0	39

Doyle Nix

Year	Team		TD	1XP	2XP	FG	FGA	SAF	Pts
1960	LA	A	1	0	0	0	0	0	6

Jack Nix

Year	Team		TD	1XP	2XP	FG	FGA	SAF	Pts
1950	SF	N	0	1		0	0	0	1

Kent Nix

Year	Team		TD	1XP	2XP	FG	FGA	SAF	Pts
1967	PIT	N	2	0		0	0	0	12

Jeff Nixon

Year	Team		TD	1XP	2XP	FG	FGA	SAF	Pts
1980	BUF	N	1	0		0	0	0	6

Tory Nixon

Year	Team		TD	1XP	2XP	FG	FGA	SAF	Pts
1986	SF	N	1	0		0	0	0	6

Tommy Nobis

Year	Team		TD	1XP	2XP	FG	FGA	SAF	Pts
1967	ATL	N	1	0		0	0	0	6
1972			1	0		0	0	0	6
Career			2	0		0	0	0	12

Brian Noble

Year	Team		TD	1XP	2XP	FG	FGA	SAF	Pts
1991	GB	N	1	0		0	0	0	6

Dave Noble

Year	Team		TD	1XP	2XP	FG	FGA	SAF	Pts
1924	CLE	N	6	0		0		0	36
1925			6	0		0		0	36
1926	CLE	A	5	0		0		0	30
Career			17	0		0		0	102

James Noble

Year	Team		TD	1XP	2XP	FG	FGA	SAF	Pts
1987	IND	N	2	0		0	0	0	12

George Nock

Year	Team		TD	1XP	2XP	FG	FGA	SAF	Pts
1970	NYJ	N	6	0		0	0	0	36
1971			5	0		0	0	0	30
Career			11	0		0	0	0	66

Terry Nofsinger

Year	Team		TD	1XP	2XP	FG	FGA	SAF	Pts
1965	STL	N	1	0		0	0	0	6
1966			2	0		0	0	0	12
Career			3	0		0	0	0	18

Al Noga

Year	Team		TD	1XP	2XP	FG	FGA	SAF	Pts
1990	MIN	N	2	0		0	0	0	12

Niko Noga

Year	Team		TD	1XP	2XP	FG	FGA	SAF	Pts
1987	STL	N	1	0		0	0	0	6

Pete Noga

Year	Team		TD	1XP	2XP	FG	FGA	SAF	Pts
1987	STL	N	1	0		0	0	0	6

Dick Nolan

Year	Team		TD	1XP	2XP	FG	FGA	SAF	Pts
1954	NYG	N	0	0		0	0	1	2

Earl Nolan

Year	Team		TD	1XP	2XP	FG	FGA	SAF	Pts
1937	CHIC	N	0	0		0		0	0

Chuck Noll

Year	Team		TD	1XP	2XP	FG	FGA	SAF	Pts
1955	CLE	N	1	0		0	0	1	8
1956			1	0		0	0	0	6
Career			2	0		0	0	1	14

Ray Nolting

Year	Team		TD	1XP	2XP	FG	FGA	SAF	Pts
1936	CHIB	N	1	0		0		0	6
1937			2	0		0		0	12
1938			2	0		0	0	0	12
1939			4	0		0	0	0	24
1940			2	0		0	0	0	12
1941			1	0		0	0	0	6
1942			3	0		0	0	0	18
1943			1	0		0	0	0	6
Career			16	0		0	0	0	96
Playoffs			1	0		0	0	0	6

Leo Nomellini

Year	Team		TD	1XP	2XP	FG	FGA	SAF	Pts
1951	SF	N	1	0		0	0	0	6
1957			0	0		0	0	1	2
1960			0	0		0	0	1	2
Career			1	0		0	0	2	10

Danny Noonan

Year	Team		TD	1XP	2XP	FG	FGA	SAF	Pts
1988	DAL	N	1	0		0	0	1	8

Jerry Noonan

Year	Team		TD	1XP	2XP	FG	FGA	SAF	Pts
1921	ROC	A	3	0		0		0	18
1924	ROC	N	1	0		0		0	6
Career			4	0		0		0	24

Karl Noonan

Year	Team		TD	1XP	2XP	FG	FGA	SAF	Pts
1966	MIA	A	1	0	0	0	0	0	6
1967			1	0	0	0	0	0	6
1968			11	0	0	0	0	0	66
1969			3	0	0	0	0	0	18
1970	MIA	N	1	0		0	0	0	6
Career			17	0	0	0	0	0	102

Keith Nord

Year	Team		TD	1XP	2XP	FG	FGA	SAF	Pts
1980	MIN	N	1	0		0	0	0	6

Erik Norgard

Year	Team		TD	1XP	2XP	FG	FGA	SAF	Pts
1996	HOU	N	1	0	0	0	0	0	6

Pettis Norman

Year	Team		TD	1XP	2XP	FG	FGA	SAF	Pts
1963	DAL	N	3	0		0	0	0	18
1964			2	0		0	0	0	12
1965			3	0		0	0	0	18
1967			2	0		0	0	0	12
1968			1	0		0	0	0	6
1969			3	0		0	0	0	18
1971	SD	N	1	0		0	0	0	6
Career			15	0		0	0	0	90

Will Norman

Year	Team		TD	1XP	2XP	FG	FGA	SAF	Pts
1928	POT	N	1	0		0		0	6

Ulysses Norris

Year	Team		TD	1XP	2XP	FG	FGA	SAF	Pts
1979	DET	N	1	0		0	0	0	6
1983			7	0		0	0	0	42
Career			8	0		0	0	0	48

John North

Year	Team		TD	1XP	2XP	FG	FGA	SAF	Pts
1948	BAL	AA	2	0		0	0	0	12
1949			4	0		0	0	0	24
Career			6	0		0	0	0	36

Gabe Northern

Year	Team		TD	1XP	2XP	FG	FGA	SAF	Pts
1996	BUF	N	1	0	0	0	0	0	6

Don Norton

Year	Team		TD	1XP	2XP	FG	FGA	SAF	Pts
1960	LA	A	5	0	0	0	0	0	30
1961	SD	A	6	0	0	0	0	0	36
1962			7	0	0	0	0	0	42
1963			1	0	0	0	0	0	6
1964			6	0	0	0	0	0	36
1965			2	0	0	0	0	0	12
Career			27	0	0	0	0	0	162
Playoffs			1	0	0	0	0	0	6

Jerry Norton

Year	Team		TD	1XP	2XP	FG	FGA	SAF	Pts
1954	PHI	N	1	0		0	0	0	6
1955			3	0		0	0	0	18
1957			1	0		0	0	0	6
1961	STL	N	2	0		0	0	0	12
1962	DAL	N	1	0		0	0	0	6
Career			8	0		0	0	0	48

Jim Norton

Year	Team		TD	1XP	2XP	FG	FGA	SAF	Pts
1967	HOU	A	1	0	0	0	0	0	6

Ken Norton

Year	Team		TD	1XP	2XP	FG	FGA	SAF	Pts
1995	SF	N	2	0	0	0	0	0	12
Playoffs			1	0	0	0	0	0	6

Marty Norton

Year	Team		TD	1XP	2XP	FG	FGA	SAF	Pts
1922	MIN	N	2	0		0		0	12
1924			2	0		0		0	12
1925	GB	N	6	0		0		0	36
1926	RI	A	1	0		0		0	6
Career			11	0		0		0	66

Scott Norwood

Year	Team		TD	1XP	2XP	FG	FGA	SAF	Pts
1985	BUF	N	0	23		13	17	0	62
1986			0	32		17	27	0	83
1987			0	31		10	15	0	61
1988			0	33		**32**	37	0	**129**
1989			0	46		23	30	0	115
1990			0	**50**		20	29	0	110
1991			0	**56**		18	29	0	110
Career			0	271		133	184	0	670
Playoffs			0	27		13	18	0	66

Don Nottingham

Year	Team		TD	1XP	2XP	FG	FGA	SAF	Pts
1971	BAL	N	6	0		0	0	0	36
1972			3	0		0	0	0	18
1973			1	0		0	0	0	6
1974	MIA	N	8	0		0	0	0	48
1975			12	0		0	0	0	72
1976			3	0		0	0	0	18

Don Nottingham *continued*

Year	Team		TD	1XP	2XP	FG	FGA	SAF	Pts
1977			2	0		0	0	0	12
Career			35	0		0	0	0	210
Playoffs			2	0		0	0	0	12

Jay Novacek

Year	Team		TD	1XP	2XP	FG	FGA	SAF	Pts
1987	**STL**	**N**	3	0		0	0	0	18
1988	**PHX**	**N**	4	0		0	0	0	24
1989			1	0		0	0	0	6
1990	**DAL**	**N**	4	0		0	0	0	24
1991			4	0		0	0	0	24
1992			6	0		0	0	0	36
1993			2	0		0	0	0	12
1994			2	0	0	0	0	0	12
1995			5	0	1	0	0	0	32
Career			31	0	1	0	0	0	188
Playoffs			6	0	0	0	0	0	36

Eddie Novak

Year	Team		TD	1XP	2XP	FG	FGA	SAF	Pts
1921	**RI**	**A**	1	0		0		0	6
1924	**MIN**	**N**	0	1		0		0	1
1925	**RI**	**N**	1	0		0		0	6
Career			2	1		0		0	13

Jack Novak

Year	Team		TD	1XP	2XP	FG	FGA	SAF	Pts
1976	**TB**	**N**	1	0		0	0	0	6

Brent Novoselsky

Year	Team		TD	1XP	2XP	FG	FGA	SAF	Pts
1989	**MIN**	**N**	2	0		0	0	0	12

Ray Novotny

Year	Team		TD	1XP	2XP	FG	FGA	SAF	Pts
1930	**POR**	**N**	1	0		0		0	6

Bob Nowaskey

Year	Team		TD	1XP	2XP	FG	FGA	SAF	Pts
1940	**CHIB**	**N**	2	0		0	0	0	12
1941			2	1		0	0	0	13
1946	**LA**	**AA**	4	0		0	0	0	24
Career			8	1		0	0	0	49

Tom Nowatzke

Year	Team		TD	1XP	2XP	FG	FGA	SAF	Pts
1965	**DET**	**N**	2	0		0	0	0	12
1966			7	0		0	0	0	42
1967			6	0		0	0	0	36
1968			1	0		0	0	0	6
1970	**BAL**	**N**	1	0		0	0	0	6
Career			17	0		0	0	0	102
Playoffs			1	0		0	0	0	6

Bob Nussbaumer

Year	Team		TD	1XP	2XP	FG	FGA	SAF	Pts
1947	**WAS**	**N**	4	0		0	0	0	24
1948			1	0		0	0	0	6
Career			5	0		0	0	0	30

Jerry Nuzum

Year	Team		TD	1XP	2XP	FG	FGA	SAF	Pts
1949	**PIT**	**N**	7	0		0	0	0	42
1950			2	0		0	0	0	12
1951			1	0		0	0	0	6
Career			10	0		0	0	0	60

Mally Nydahl

Year	Team		TD	1XP	2XP	FG	FGA	SAF	Pts
1929	**MIN**	**N**	2	2		0		0	14
1930	**MIN-FRA**	**N**	2	1		0		0	13
Career			4	3		0		0	27

Bernie Nygren

Year	Team		TD	1XP	2XP	FG	FGA	SAF	Pts
1946	**LA**	**AA**	1	0		0	0	0	6

Carleton Oats

Year	Team		TD	1XP	2XP	FG	FGA	SAF	Pts
1967	**OAK**	**A**	1	0	0	0	0	0	6

Terry Obee

Year	Team		TD	1XP	2XP	FG	FGA	SAF	Pts
1993	**CHI**	**N**	3	0		0	0	0	18

Harry O'Boyle

Year	Team		TD	1XP	2XP	FG	FGA	SAF	Pts
1928	**GB**	**N**	1	8		**3**		0	23
1932			0	7		0		0	7
Career			1	15		3		0	30

Ed O'Bradovich

Year	Team		TD	1XP	2XP	FG	FGA	SAF	Pts
1966	**CHI**	**N**	1	0		0	0	0	6
1969			0	0		0	0	1	2
Career			1	0		0	0	1	8

Jim Obradovich

Year	Team		TD	1XP	2XP	FG	FGA	SAF	Pts
1975	**NYG**	**N**	1	0		0	0	0	6
1978	**TB**	**N**	3	0		0	0	0	18
1979			1	0		0	0	0	6
1981			1	0		0	0	0	6
1983			1	0		0	0	0	6
Career			7	0		0	0	0	42

Davey O'Brien

Year	Team		TD	1XP	2XP	FG	FGA	SAF	Pts
1939	**PHI**	**N**	1	0		0	0	0	6
1940			1	0		0	0	0	6
Career			2	0		0	0	0	12

Jack O'Brien

Year	Team		TD	1XP	2XP	FG	FGA	SAF	Pts
1955	**PIT**	**N**	2	0		0	0	0	12

Jim O'Brien

Year	Team		TD	1XP	2XP	FG	FGA	SAF	Pts
1970	**BAL**	**N**	0	36		19	34	0	93
1971			0	35		20	29	0	95
1972			2	24		13	31	0	75
1973	**DET**	**N**	0	14		8	14	0	38
Career			2	109		60	108	0	301
Playoffs			0	8		6	14	0	26

Grattan O'Connell

Year	Team		TD	1XP	2XP	FG	FGA	SAF	Pts
1926	**HAR**	**N**	1	0		0		0	6

Milt O'Connell

Year	Team		TD	1XP	2XP	FG	FGA	SAF	Pts
1924	**FRA**	**N**	1	0		0		0	6

Tommy O'Connell

Year	Team		TD	1XP	2XP	FG	FGA	SAF	Pts
1956	**CLE**	**N**	2	0		0	0	0	12
1957			1	0		0	0	0	6
1960	**BUF**	**A**	1	0	1	0	1	0	8
Career			4	0	1	0	1	0	26

Bill O'Connor

Year	Team		TD	1XP	2XP	FG	FGA	SAF	Pts
1948	**BUF**	**AA**	2	0		0	0	0	12
Playoffs			1	0	0	0	0	0	6

Curly Oden

Year	Team		TD	1XP	2XP	FG	FGA	SAF	Pts
1926	**PRO**	**N**	**9**	1		0		0	55
1927			2	0		0		0	12
1928			4	3		0		0	27
1930			0	1		0		0	1
1931			1	0		0		0	6
Career			16	5		0		0	101

Cliff Odom

Year	Team		TD	1XP	2XP	FG	FGA	SAF	Pts
1990	**MIA**	**N**	1	0		0	0	0	6

Steve Odom

Year	Team		TD	1XP	2XP	FG	FGA	SAF	Pts
1974	**GB**	**N**	3	0		0	0	0	18
1975			5	0		0	0	0	30
1976			2	0		0	0	0	12
1977			3	0		0	0	0	18
1978			2	0		0	0	0	12
Career			15	0		0	0	0	90

Nate Odomes

Year	Team		TD	1XP	2XP	FG	FGA	SAF	Pts
1990	**BUF**	**N**	1	0		0	0	0	6
1991			1	0		0	0	0	6
1993			1	0		0	0	0	6
Career			3	0		0	0	0	18

Riley Odoms

Year	Team		TD	1XP	2XP	FG	FGA	SAF	Pts
1972	**DEN**	**N**	1	0		0	0	0	6
1973			7	0		0	0	0	42
1974			6	0		0	0	0	36
1975			4	0		0	0	0	24
1976			5	0		0	0	0	30
1977			3	0		0	0	0	18
1978			6	0		0	0	0	36
1979			1	0		0	0	0	6
1980			6	0		0	0	0	36
1981			5	0		0	0	0	30
Career			44	0		0	0	0	264
Playoffs			1	0		0	0	0	6

Pat O'Donahue

Year	Team		TD	1XP	2XP	FG	FGA	SAF	Pts
1952	**SF**	**N**	1	1		0	0	0	7

Dicky O'Donnell

Year	Team		TD	1XP	2XP	FG	FGA	SAF	Pts
1923	**DUL**	**N**	1	0		0		0	6

Dicky O'Donnell *continued*

Year	Team		TD	1XP	2XP	FG	FGA	SAF	Pts
1925	**GB**	**N**	1	0		0		0	6
1926			2	0		0		0	12
1928			1	0		0		0	6
1931	**BKN**	**N**	1	0		0		0	6
Career			6	0		0		0	36

Neil O'Donnell

Year	Team		TD	1XP	2XP	FG	FGA	SAF	Pts
1991	**PIT**	**N**	1	0		0	0	0	6
1992			1	0		0	0	0	6
1994			1	0	0	0	0	0	6
Career			3	0	0	0	0	0	18

Neil O'Donoghue

Year	Team		TD	1XP	2XP	FG	FGA	SAF	Pts
1977	**BUF**	**N**	0	4		2	6	0	10
1978	**TB**	**N**	0	25		13	23	0	64
1979			0	30		11	19	0	63
1980	**STL**	**N**	0	18		11	15	0	51
1981			0	36		19	32	0	93
1982			0	15		8	13	0	39
1983			0	45		15	28	0	90
1984			0	48		23	35	0	117
1985			0	19		10	18	0	49
Career			0	240		112	189	0	576
Playoffs			0	4		2	5	0	10

Urban Odson

Year	Team		TD	1XP	2XP	FG	FGA	SAF	Pts
1946	**GB**	**N**	0	0		0	0	1	2

Johnny Oehler

Year	Team		TD	1XP	2XP	FG	FGA	SAF	Pts
1933	**PIT**	**N**	0	0		0		1	2

Arnie Oehlrich

Year	Team		TD	1XP	2XP	FG	FGA	SAF	Pts
1928	**FRA**	**N**	2	0		0		0	12
1929			1	0		0		0	6
Career			3	0		0		0	18

Jonathan Ogden

Year	Team		TD	1XP	2XP	FG	FGA	SAF	Pts
1996	**BAL**	**N**	1	0	0	0	0	0	6

Ray Ogden

Year	Team		TD	1XP	2XP	FG	FGA	SAF	Pts
1967	**ATL**	**N**	1	0		0	0	0	6
1968			2	0		0	0	0	12
1970	**CHI**	**N**	1	0		0	0	0	6
Career			4	0		0	0	0	24

Ross O'Hanley

Year	Team		TD	1XP	2XP	FG	FGA	SAF	Pts
1964	**BOS**	**A**	1	0	0	0	0	0	6

Christian Okoye

Year	Team		TD	1XP	2XP	FG	FGA	SAF	Pts
1987	**KC**	**N**	3	0		0	0	0	18
1988			3	0		0	0	0	18
1989			12	0		0	0	0	72
1990			7	0		0	0	0	42
1991			9	0		0	0	0	54
1992			6	0		0	0	0	36
Career			40	0		0	0	0	240

Cliff Olander

Year	Team		TD	1XP	2XP	FG	FGA	SAF	Pts
1979	**SD**	**N**	0	1		0	1	0	1

Doug Oldershaw

Year	Team		TD	1XP	2XP	FG	FGA	SAF	Pts
1941	**NYG**	**N**	1	0		0	0	0	6

Chris Oldham

Year	Team		TD	1XP	2XP	FG	FGA	SAF	Pts
1995	**PIT**	**N**	1	0	0	0	0	0	6

Jim Oldham

Year	Team		TD	1XP	2XP	FG	FGA	SAF	Pts
1926	**RAC**	**N**	1	0		0		0	6

Ray Oldham

Year	Team		TD	1XP	2XP	FG	FGA	SAF	Pts
1980	**DET**	**N**	1	0		0	0	0	6
1982			1	0		0	0	0	6
Career			2	0		0	0	0	12

Bill Olds

Year	Team		TD	1XP	2XP	FG	FGA	SAF	Pts
1973	**BAL**	**N**	2	0		0	0	0	12
1974			3	0		0	0	0	18
1975			4	0		0	0	0	24
1976	**PHI**	**N**	1	0		0	0	0	6
Career			10	0		0	0	0	60

Stan Oleniczak

Year	Team		TD	1XP	2XP	FG	FGA	SAF	Pts
1935	**PIT**	**N**	1	0		0		0	6

Elmer Oliphant

Year	Team		TD	1XP	2XP	FG	FGA	SAF	Pts
1921	BUF	A	1	**26**		**5**		0	**47**

Mike Oliphant

Year	Team		TD	1XP	2XP	FG	FGA	SAF	Pts
1989	CLE	N	1	0		0	0	0	6

Chip Oliver

Year	Team		TD	1XP	2XP	FG	FGA	SAF	Pts
1969	OAK	A	1	0	0	0	0	0	6

Hubie Oliver

Year	Team		TD	1XP	2XP	FG	FGA	SAF	Pts
1981	PHI	N	1	0		0	0	0	6
1983			3	0		0	0	0	18
Career			4	0		0	0	0	24

Louis Oliver

Year	Team		TD	1XP	2XP	FG	FGA	SAF	Pts
1992	MIA	N	1	0		0	0	0	6
1993			1	0		0	0	0	6
Career			2	0		0	0	0	12

Winslow Oliver

Year	Team		TD	1XP	2XP	FG	FGA	SAF	Pts
1996	CAR	N	1	0	0	0	0	0	6

Neal Olkewicz

Year	Team		TD	1XP	2XP	FG	FGA	SAF	Pts
1981	WAS	N	1	0		0	0	0	6

Merlin Olsen

Year	Team		TD	1XP	2XP	FG	FGA	SAF	Pts
1962	LA	N	1	0		0	0	0	6

Johnny Olszewski

Year	Team		TD	1XP	2XP	FG	FGA	SAF	Pts
1953	CHIC	N	5	0		0	0	0	30
1954			2	0		0	0	0	12
1955			1	0		0	0	0	6
1956			2	0		0	0	0	12
1957			2	0		0	0	0	12
1958	WAS	N	2	0		0	0	0	12
1959			1	0		0	0	0	6
1960			3	0		0	0	0	18
1962	DEN	A	1	0	0	0	0	0	6
Career			19	0	0	0	0	0	114

Russ Oltz

Year	Team		TD	1XP	2XP	FG	FGA	SAF	Pts
1921	HAM	A	1	0		0		0	6

Joe O'Malley

Year	Team		TD	1XP	2XP	FG	FGA	SAF	Pts
1955	PIT	N	1	0		0	0	0	6

Ken O'Neal

Year	Team		TD	1XP	2XP	FG	FGA	SAF	Pts
1987	NO	N	1	0		0	0	0	6

Leslie O'Neal

Year	Team		TD	1XP	2XP	FG	FGA	SAF	Pts
1986	SD	N	1	0		0	0	0	6

Chuck O'Neil

Year	Team		TD	1XP	2XP	FG	FGA	SAF	Pts
1921	EVA	A	0	0		0		0	0

Ed O'Neil

Year	Team		TD	1XP	2XP	FG	FGA	SAF	Pts
1975	DET	N	1	0		0	0	0	6
1976			1	0		0	0	0	6
1977			1	0		0	0	0	6
Career			3	0		0	0	0	18

Pat O'Neill

Year	Team		TD	1XP	2XP	FG	FGA	SAF	Pts
1994	NE	N	0	0	0	0	1	0	0

Red O'Neill

Year	Team		TD	1XP	2XP	FG	FGA	SAF	Pts
1926	HAR	N	1	0		0		0	6

Tip O'Neill

Year	Team		TD	1XP	2XP	FG	FGA	SAF	Pts
1922	DAY	N	1	0		0		0	6

Larry Onesti

Year	Team		TD	1XP	2XP	FG	FGA	SAF	Pts
1965	HOU	A	1	0	0	0	0	0	6

Johnny O'Quinn

Year	Team		TD	1XP	2XP	FG	FGA	SAF	Pts
1950	CHIB	N	1	0		0	0	0	6

Joe Orduna

Year	Team		TD	1XP	2XP	FG	FGA	SAF	Pts
1972	NYG	N	2	0		0	0	0	12
1973			1	0		0	0	0	6
1974	BAL	N	1	0		0	0	0	6
Career			4	0		0	0	0	24

Bob Oristaglio

Year	Team		TD	1XP	2XP	FG	FGA	SAF	Pts
1951	CLE	N	1	0		0	0	0	6

Bo Orlando

Year	Team		TD	1XP	2XP	FG	FGA	SAF	Pts
1993	HOU	N	1	0		0	0	0	6

Dan Orlich

Year	Team		TD	1XP	2XP	FG	FGA	SAF	Pts
1950	GB	N	1	0		0	0	0	6

Charlie O'Rourke

Year	Team		TD	1XP	2XP	FG	FGA	SAF	Pts
1942	CHIB	N	1	0		0	0	0	6
1946	LA	AA	1	0		0	0	0	6
1947			1	0		0	0	0	6
1948	BAL	AA	1	0		0	0	0	6
Career			4	0		0	0	0	24

Jimmy Orr

Year	Team		TD	1XP	2XP	FG	FGA	SAF	Pts
1958	PIT	N	7	0		0	0	0	42
1959			5	0		0	0	0	30
1960			4	0		0	0	0	24
1961	BAL	N	4	0		0	0	0	24
1962			11	0		0	0	0	66
1963			5	0		0	0	0	30
1964			6	0		0	0	0	36
1965			10	0		0	0	0	60
1966			3	0		0	0	0	18
1967			1	0		0	0	0	6
1968			6	0		0	0	0	36
1969			2	0		0	0	0	12
1970			2	0		0	0	0	12
Career			66	0		0	0	0	396

Terry Orr

Year	Team		TD	1XP	2XP	FG	FGA	SAF	Pts
1986	WAS	N	1	0		0	0	0	6
1988			2	0		0	0	0	12
1991			4	0		0	0	0	24
1992			3	0		0	0	0	18
Career			10	0		0	0	0	60

Ralph Ortega

Year	Team		TD	1XP	2XP	FG	FGA	SAF	Pts
1977	ATL	N	1	0		0	0	0	6

Keith Ortego

Year	Team		TD	1XP	2XP	FG	FGA	SAF	Pts
1986	CHI	N	2	0		0	0	0	12

Dave Osborn

Year	Team		TD	1XP	2XP	FG	FGA	SAF	Pts
1965	MIN	N	2	0		0	0	0	12
1966			3	0		0	0	0	18
1967			3	0		0	0	0	18
1969			8	0		0	0	0	48
1970			6	0		0	0	0	36
1971			6	0		0	0	0	36
1972			3	0		0	0	0	18
1974			4	0		0	0	0	24
1975			1	0		0	0	0	6
Career			36	0		0	0	0	216
Playoffs			5	0		0	0	0	30

Jim Osborne

Year	Team		TD	1XP	2XP	FG	FGA	SAF	Pts
1982	CHI	N	0	0		0	0	1	2

Richard Osborne

Year	Team		TD	1XP	2XP	FG	FGA	SAF	Pts
1976	NYJ	N	1	0		0	0	0	6

Tom Osborne

Year	Team		TD	1XP	2XP	FG	FGA	SAF	Pts
1961	WAS	N	2	0		0	0	0	12

Bill Osmanski

Year	Team		TD	1XP	2XP	FG	FGA	SAF	Pts
1939	CHIB	N	8	0		0	0	0	48
1940			3	0		0	0	0	18
1941			4	0		0	0	0	24
1943			1	0		0	0	0	6
1946			5	0		0	0	0	30
Career			21	0		0	0	0	126
Playoffs			1	0		0	0	0	6

Joe Osmanski

Year	Team		TD	1XP	2XP	FG	FGA	SAF	Pts
1946	CHIB	N	2	0		0	0	0	12
1947			1	0		0	0	0	6
1948			1	0		0	0	0	6
1949	NYB	N	2	0		0	0	0	12
Career			6	0		0	0	0	36

Jimmy Ostendarp

Year	Team		TD	1XP	2XP	FG	FGA	SAF	Pts
1950	NYG	N	2	0		0	0	0	12

Jim Otis

Year	Team		TD	1XP	2XP	FG	FGA	SAF	Pts
1971	KC	N	2	0		0	0	0	12
1973	STL	N	1	0		0	0	0	6
1974			1	0		0	0	0	6
1975			6	0		0	0	0	36
1976			2	0		0	0	0	12
1977			2	0		0	0	0	12
1978			8	0		0	0	0	48
Career			22	0		0	0	0	132
Playoffs			2	0		0	0	0	12

Lowell Otte

Year	Team		TD	1XP	2XP	FG	FGA	SAF	Pts
1926	NY	A	1	0		0		0	6
1927	BUF	N	0	0		0		1	2
Career			1	0		0		1	8

Gus Otto

Year	Team		TD	1XP	2XP	FG	FGA	SAF	Pts
1965	OAK	A	2	0	0	0	0	0	12

John Outlaw

Year	Team		TD	1XP	2XP	FG	FGA	SAF	Pts
1971	NE	N	1	0		0	0	0	6
1973	PHI	N	1	0		0	0	0	6
Career			2	0		0	0	0	12

David Overstreet

Year	Team		TD	1XP	2XP	FG	FGA	SAF	Pts
1983	MIA	N	3	0		0	0	0	18

Al Owen

Year	Team		TD	1XP	2XP	FG	FGA	SAF	Pts
1939	NYG	N	1	0		0	0	0	6

Tom Owen

Year	Team		TD	1XP	2XP	FG	FGA	SAF	Pts
1974	SF	N	1	0		0	0	0	6

Artie Owens

Year	Team		TD	1XP	2XP	FG	FGA	SAF	Pts
1976	SD	N	1	0		0	0	0	6
1979			2	0		0	0	0	12
Career			3	0		0	0	0	18

Brig Owens

Year	Team		TD	1XP	2XP	FG	FGA	SAF	Pts
1966	WAS	N	2	0		0	0	0	12
1967			1	2		0	2	0	8
1973			2	0		0	0	0	12
Career			5	2		0	2	0	32

Burgess Owens

Year	Team		TD	1XP	2XP	FG	FGA	SAF	Pts
1973	NYJ	N	1	0		0	0	0	6
1974			2	0		0	0	0	12
1978			1	0		0	0	0	6
1980	OAK	N	1	0		0	0	0	6
1981			1	0		0	0	0	6
Career			6	0		0	0	0	36

Don Owens

Year	Team		TD	1XP	2XP	FG	FGA	SAF	Pts
1959	PHI	N	1	0		0	0	0	6

James Owens

Year	Team		TD	1XP	2XP	FG	FGA	SAF	Pts
1979	SF	N	1	0		0	0	0	6
1980			1	0		0	0	0	6
1981	TB	N	3	0		0	0	0	18
1982			1	0		0	0	0	6
1983			6	0		0	0	0	36
1984			1	0		0	0	0	6
Career			13	0		0	0	0	78

Jim Owens

Year	Team		TD	1XP	2XP	FG	FGA	SAF	Pts
1950	BAL	N	1	0		0	0	0	6

Joe Owens

Year	Team		TD	1XP	2XP	FG	FGA	SAF	Pts
1970	SD	N	0	0		0	0	1	2
1972	NO	N	0	0		0	0	1	2
Career			0	0		0	0	2	4

Luke Owens

Year	Team		TD	1XP	2XP	FG	FGA	SAF	Pts
1960	STL	N	0	0		0	0	1	2

Morris Owens

Year	Team		TD	1XP	2XP	FG	FGA	SAF	Pts
1976	TB	N	6	0		0	0	0	36
1977			3	0		0	0	0	18
1978			5	0		0	0	0	30
Career			14	0		0	0	0	84

R.C. Owens

Year	Team		TD	1XP	2XP	FG	FGA	SAF	Pts
1957	SF	N	5	0		0	0	0	30
1958			1	0		0	0	0	6

R.C. Owens *continued*

Year	Team	TD	1XP	2XP	FG	FGA	SAF	Pts
1959		3	0		0	0	0	18
1960		6	0		0	0	0	36
1961		6	0		0	0	0	36
1962	BAL N	2	0		0	0	0	12
Career		23	0		0	0	0	138
Playoffs		1	0		0	0	0	6

Steve Owens

Year	Team	TD	1XP	2XP	FG	FGA	SAF	Pts
1970	DET N	2	0		0	0	0	12
1971		10	0		0	0	0	60
1972		4	0		0	0	0	24
1973		3	0		0	0	0	18
1974		3	0		0	0	0	18
Career		22	0		0	0	0	132

Terrell Owens

Year	Team	TD	1XP	2XP	FG	FGA	SAF	Pts
1996	SF N	4	0	0	0	0	0	24

Tinker Owens

Year	Team	TD	1XP	2XP	FG	FGA	SAF	Pts
1976	NO N	1	0		0	0	0	6
1978		2	0		0	0	0	12
1979		1	0		0	0	0	6
Career		4	0		0	0	0	24

Jim Pace

Year	Team	TD	1XP	2XP	FG	FGA	SAF	Pts
1958	SF N	2	0		0	0	0	12

Bob Paffrath

Year	Team	TD	1XP	2XP	FG	FGA	SAF	Pts
1946	BKN-MIA AA	2	0		0	0	0	12

Alan Page

Year	Team	TD	1XP	2XP	FG	FGA	SAF	Pts
1969	MIN N	1	0	0	0	0	0	6
1970		1	0	0	0	0	0	6
1971		0	0	0	0	0	2	4
1980	CHI N	1	0	0	0	0	1	8
Career		3	0	0	0	0	3	24
Playoffs		0	0	0	0	0	1	2

Mike Pagel

Year	Team	TD	1XP	2XP	FG	FGA	SAF	Pts
1982	BAL N	1	0		0	0	0	6
1984	IND N	1	0		0	0	0	6
1985		2	0		0	0	0	12
Career		4	0		0	0	0	24

Joe Pagliei

Year	Team	TD	1XP	2XP	FG	FGA	SAF	Pts
1960	NY A	1	0	0	0	0	0	6

Louie Pahl

Year	Team	TD	1XP	2XP	FG	FGA	SAF	Pts
1923	MIN N	1	0		0		0	6

Stephone Paige

Year	Team	TD	1XP	2XP	FG	FGA	SAF	Pts
1983	KC N	6	0		0	0	0	36
1984		4	0		0	0	0	24
1985		10	0		0	0	0	60
1986		11	0		0	0	0	66
1987		4	0		0	0	0	24
1988		7	0		0	0	0	42
1989		2	0		0	0	0	12
1990		5	0		0	0	0	30
Career		49	0		0	0	0	294
Playoffs		1	0		0	0	0	6

Tony Paige

Year	Team	TD	1XP	2XP	FG	FGA	SAF	Pts
1984	NYJ N	8	0		0	0	0	48
1985		10	0		0	0	0	60
1986		2	0		0	0	0	12
1990	MIA N	6	0		0	0	0	36
1991		1	0		0	0	0	6
1992		2	0		0	0	0	12
Career		29	0		0	0	0	174
Playoffs		2	0		0	0	0	12

Mike Palm

Year	Team	TD	1XP	2XP	FG	FGA	SAF	Pts
1926	NYG N	1	0		0		0	6

David Palmer

Year	Team	TD	1XP	2XP	FG	FGA	SAF	Pts
1995	MIN N	1	0	0	0	0	0	6
1996		1	0	0	0	0	0	6
Career		2	0	0	0	0	0	12

Paul Palmer

Year	Team	TD	1XP	2XP	FG	FGA	SAF	Pts
1987	KC N	2	0		0	0	0	12
1988		6	0		0	0	0	36

Paul Palmer *continued*

Year	Team	TD	1XP	2XP	FG	FGA	SAF	Pts
1989	DAL N	2	0		0	0	0	12
Career		10	0		0	0	0	60

John Paluck

Year	Team	TD	1XP	2XP	FG	FGA	SAF	Pts
1956	WAS N	1	0		0	0	0	6
1964		0	0		0	0	1	2
Career		1	0		0	0	1	8

Hal Pangle

Year	Team	TD	1XP	2XP	FG	FGA	SAF	Pts
1936	CHIC N	1	0		0		0	6
1937		2	0		0		0	12
Career		3	0		0		0	18

Ernie Pannell

Year	Team	TD	1XP	2XP	FG	FGA	SAF	Pts
1941	GB N	1	0		0	0	0	6

Nick Papac

Year	Team	TD	1XP	2XP	FG	FGA	SAF	Pts
1961	OAK A	1	0	0	0	0	0	6

George Papach

Year	Team	TD	1XP	2XP	FG	FGA	SAF	Pts
1948	PIT N	3	0		0	0	0	18

Oran Pape

Year	Team	TD	1XP	2XP	FG	FGA	SAF	Pts
1930	MIN N	2	0		0		0	12
1931	PRO	3	0		0		0	18
1932	BOS-SI N	1	0		0		0	6
Career		6	0		0		0	36

Johnny Papit

Year	Team	TD	1XP	2XP	FG	FGA	SAF	Pts
1952	WAS N	1	0		0	0	0	6
1953	GB N	1	0		0	0	0	6
Career		2	0		0	0	0	12

Jack Pardee

Year	Team	TD	1XP	2XP	FG	FGA	SAF	Pts
1962	LA N	1	0		0	0	1	8
1967		2	0		0	0	0	12
1968		2	0		0	0	0	12
1971	WAS N	1	0		0	0	0	6
Career		6	0		0	0	1	38

Paul Pardonner

Year	Team	TD	1XP	2XP	FG	FGA	SAF	Pts
1934	CHIC N	0	0		1	0		3
1935		0	1		1	0		4
Career		0	1		2	0		7

Curt Pardridge

Year	Team	TD	1XP	2XP	FG	FGA	SAF	Pts
1987	SEA N	1	0		0	0	0	6

Bob Paremore

Year	Team	TD	1XP	2XP	FG	FGA	SAF	Pts
1963	STL N	2	0		0	0	0	12

Babe Parilli

Year	Team	TD	1XP	2XP	FG	FGA	SAF	Pts
1952	GB N	1	0		0	0	0	6
1953		4	0		0	0	0	24
1957		2	0		0	0	0	12
1960	OAK A	1	0	0	0	0	0	6
1961	BOS A	5	0	1	0	0	0	32
1962		2	0	0	0	0	0	12
1963		5	0	0	0	0	0	30
1964		2	0	0	0	0	0	12
1966		1	0	0	0	0	0	6
1968	NY A	1	0	0	0	0	0	6
Career		24	0	1	0	0	0	146

Don Parish

Year	Team	TD	1XP	2XP	FG	FGA	SAF	Pts
1970	STL N	1	0		0	0	0	6

Ace Parker

Year	Team	TD	1XP	2XP	FG	FGA	SAF	Pts
1937	BKN N	2	1		0		0	13
1938		4	5		0		0	29
1939		5	0		1	5	0	33
1940		5	**19**		0		0	49
1946	NY AA	4	0		0		0	24
Career		20	25		1	5	0	148

Andy Parker

Year	Team	TD	1XP	2XP	FG	FGA	SAF	Pts
1986	LARI N	1	0		0	0	0	6
1989	SD N	1	0		0	0	0	6
Career		2	0		0	0	0	12

Anthony Parker

Year	Team	TD	1XP	2XP	FG	FGA	SAF	Pts
1992	MIN N	1	0		0	0	0	6
1994		3	0		0	0	0	18

Anthony Parker *continued*

Year	Team	TD	1XP	2XP	FG	FGA	SAF	Pts
1995	STL N	1	0		0	0	0	6
1996		2	0		0	0	0	12
Career		7	0		0	0	0	42

Buddy Parker

Year	Team	TD	1XP	2XP	FG	FGA	SAF	Pts
1937	CHIC N	1	1		0		0	7
1938		2	0		0		0	12
1940		1	3		0	1	0	9
1941		0	0		0	0	0	0
Career		4	4		0	1	0	28
Playoffs		1	0		0	0		6

Joel Parker

Year	Team	TD	1XP	2XP	FG	FGA	SAF	Pts
1974	NO N	4	0		0	0	0	24
1975		2	0		0	0	0	12
Career		6	0		0	0	0	36

Robert Parker

Year	Team	TD	1XP	2XP	FG	FGA	SAF	Pts
1987	KC N	1	0		0	0	0	6

Rodney Parker

Year	Team	TD	1XP	2XP	FG	FGA	SAF	Pts
1980	PHI N	1	0		0	0	0	6
1981		2	0		0	0	0	12
Career		3	0		0	0	0	18

Billy Parks

Year	Team	TD	1XP	2XP	FG	FGA	SAF	Pts
1971	SD N	4	0		0	0	0	24
1972	DAL N	1	0		0	0	0	6
1973	HOU N	1	0		0	0	0	6
1974		1	0		0	0	0	6
Career		7	0		0	0	0	42
Playoffs		1	0		0	0	0	6

Dave Parks

Year	Team	TD	1XP	2XP	FG	FGA	SAF	Pts
1964	SF N	8	0		0	0	0	48
1965		12	0		0	0	0	72
1966		5	0		0	0	0	30
1967		2	0		0	0	0	12
1969	NO N	3	0		0	0	0	18
1970		2	0		0	0	0	12
1971		5	0		0	0	0	30
1972		6	0		0	0	0	36
1973	HOU N	1	0		0	0	0	6
Career		44	0		0	0	0	264

Ed Parks

Year	Team	TD	1XP	2XP	FG	FGA	SAF	Pts
1939	WAS N	0	0		0	0	1	0

Bernie Parmalee

Year	Team	TD	1XP	2XP	FG	FGA	SAF	Pts
1994	MIA N	7	0	1	0	0	0	44
1995		10	0	0	0	0	0	60
Career		17	0	1	0	0	0	104
Playoffs		1	0	0	0	0	0	6

Jim Parmer

Year	Team	TD	1XP	2XP	FG	FGA	SAF	Pts
1948	PHI N	3	0		0	0	0	18
1949		5	0		0	0	0	30
1950		8	0		0	0	0	48
1951		2	0		0	0	0	12
1953		2	0		0	0	0	12
1955		1	0		0	0	0	6
Career		21	0		0	0	0	126

Gary Parris

Year	Team	TD	1XP	2XP	FG	FGA	SAF	Pts
1977	CLE N	5	0		0	0	0	30
1979	STL N	0	1		0	0	0	1
Career		5	1		0	0	0	31

Bernie Parrish

Year	Team	TD	1XP	2XP	FG	FGA	SAF	Pts
1959	CLE N	1	0		0	0	0	6
1960		1	0		0	0	0	6
1961		1	0		0	0	0	6
1964		1	0		0	0	0	6
Career		4	0		0	0	0	24

Lemar Parrish

Year	Team	TD	1XP	2XP	FG	FGA	SAF	Pts
1970	CIN N	3	0		0	0	0	18
1971		2	0		0	0	0	12
1972		3	0		0	0	0	18
1973		1	0		0	0	0	6
1974		3	0		0	0	0	18
1977		1	0		0	0	0	6
Career		13	0		0	0	0	78

Rick Parros

Year	Team		TD	1XP	2XP	FG	FGA	SAF	Pts
1981	**DEN**	**N**	3	0		0	0	0	18
1982			3	0		0	0	0	18
1983			3	0		0	0	0	18
1984			2	0		0	0	0	12
1987	**SEA**	**N**	1	0		0	0	0	6
Career			12	0		0	0	0	72

Ara Parseghian

Year	Team		TD	1XP	2XP	FG	FGA	SAF	Pts
1948	**CLE**	**AA**	2	0		0	0	0	12

Bob Parsons

Year	Team		TD	1XP	2XP	FG	FGA	SAF	Pts
1972	**CHI**	**N**	1	0		0	0	0	6
1973			1	0		0	0	0	6
1974			1	0		0	0	0	6
1975			1	0		0	0	0	6
Career			4	0		0	0	0	24

Earle Parsons

Year	Team		TD	1XP	2XP	FG	FGA	SAF	Pts
1946	**SF**	**AA**	2	0		0	0	0	12
1947			2	0		0	0	0	12
Career			4	0		0	0	0	24

Dennis Partee

Year	Team		TD	1XP	2XP	FG	FGA	SAF	Pts
1968	**SD**	**A**	0	40	0	22	32	0	106
1969			0	33	0	15	28	0	78
1971	**SD**	**N**	0	36		17	29	0	87
1972			0	26		15	25	0	71
1973			0	4		1	2	0	7
1974			0	26		1	5	0	29
Career			0	165	0	71	121	0	378

Lou Partlow

Year	Team		TD	1XP	2XP	FG	FGA	SAF	Pts
1920	**DAY**	**A**	3	0		0		0	18
1921			1	0		0		0	6
1922	**DAY**	**N**	1	0		0		0	6
1924			2	0		0		0	12
Career			7	0		0		0	42

Bill Paschal

Year	Team		TD	1XP	2XP	FG	FGA	SAF	Pts
1943	**NYG**	**N**	**12**	0		0	0	0	72
1944			**9**	0		0	0	0	54
1945			2	0		0	0	0	12
1946			6	0		0	0	0	36
1947	**BOS**	**N**	1	0		0	0	0	6
1948			5	0		0	0	0	30
Career			35	0		0	0	0	210

Doug Paschal

Year	Team		TD	1XP	2XP	FG	FGA	SAF	Pts
1980	**MIN**	**N**	1	0		0	0	0	6

Gordon Paschka

Year	Team		TD	1XP	2XP	FG	FGA	SAF	Pts
1943	**P-P**	**N**	0	2		0	0	0	2
1947	**NYG**	**N**	2	0		0	0	0	12
Career			2	2		0	0	0	14

Keith Paskett

Year	Team		TD	1XP	2XP	FG	FGA	SAF	Pts
1987	**GB**	**N**	1	0		0	0	0	6

Joe Pasqua

Year	Team		TD	1XP	2XP	FG	FGA	SAF	Pts
1942	**CLE**	**N**	0	1		0	0	0	1
1943	**WAS**	**N**	0	1		0	0	0	1
Career			0	2		0	0	0	2

Ralph Pasquariello

Year	Team		TD	1XP	2XP	FG	FGA	SAF	Pts
1950	**LA**	**N**	1	0		0	0	0	6
1951	**CHIC**	**N**	1	0		0	0	0	6
Career			2	0		0	0	0	12

Dan Pastorini

Year	Team		TD	1XP	2XP	FG	FGA	SAF	Pts
1971	**HOU**	**N**	3	0		0	0	0	18
1972			2	0		0	0	0	12
1975			1	0		0	0	0	6
1977			2	0		0	0	0	12
Career			8	0		0	0	0	48

Alan Pastrana

Year	Team		TD	1XP	2XP	FG	FGA	SAF	Pts
1970	**DEN**	**N**	1	0		0	0	0	6

Loyd Pate

Year	Team		TD	1XP	2XP	FG	FGA	SAF	Pts
1970	**BUF**	**N**	1	0		0	0	0	6

Rupert Pate

Year	Team		TD	1XP	2XP	FG	FGA	SAF	Pts
1942	**PHI**	**N**	1	0		0	0	0	6

Dennis Patera

Year	Team		TD	1XP	2XP	FG	FGA	SAF	Pts
1968	**SF**	**N**	0	10		2	8	0	16

Frank Patrick

Year	Team		TD	1XP	2XP	FG	FGA	SAF	Pts
1938	**CHIC**	**N**	1	8		1	4	0	17
1939			1	1		0	0	0	7
Career			2	9		1	4	0	24

Wayne Patrick

Year	Team		TD	1XP	2XP	FG	FGA	SAF	Pts
1969	**BUF**	**A**	3	0	0	0	0	0	18
1970	**BUF**	**N**	1	0		0	0	0	6
1971			1	0		0	0	0	6
1972			1	0		0	0	0	6
Career			6	0	0	0	0	0	36

Maury Patt

Year	Team		TD	1XP	2XP	FG	FGA	SAF	Pts
1940	**CLE**	**N**	1	0		0	0	0	6
1941			1	0		0	0	0	6
Career			2	0		0	0	0	12

Billy Patterson

Year	Team		TD	1XP	2XP	FG	FGA	SAF	Pts
1939	**CHIB**	**N**	0	1		0	0	0	1

Elvis Patterson

Year	Team		TD	1XP	2XP	FG	FGA	SAF	Pts
1985	**NYG**	**N**	1	0		0	0	0	6
1987	**SD**	**N**	1	0		0	0	0	6
1991	**LARI**	**N**	1	0		0	0	0	6
1992			1	0		0	0	0	6
Career			4	0		0	0	0	24

Paul Patterson

Year	Team		TD	1XP	2XP	FG	FGA	SAF	Pts
1949	**CHI**	**AA**	4	0		0	0	0	24

Shawn Patterson

Year	Team		TD	1XP	2XP	FG	FGA	SAF	Pts
1990	**GB**	**N**	1	0		0	0	0	6

Cliff Patton

Year	Team		TD	1XP	2XP	FG	FGA	SAF	Pts
1947	**PHI**	**N**	0	36		3	14	0	45
1948			0	50		**8**	12	0	74
1949			0	42		**9**	18	0	69
1950			0	32		8	17	0	56
1951	**CHIC**	**N**	0	19		5	8	0	34
Career			0	179		33	69	0	278
Playoffs			0	9		0	3	0	9

Jimmy Patton

Year	Team		TD	1XP	2XP	FG	FGA	SAF	Pts
1955	**NYG**	**N**	2	0		0	0	0	12
1957			1	0		0	0	0	6
1961			1	0		0	0	0	6
Career			4	0		0	0	0	24

Ricky Patton

Year	Team		TD	1XP	2XP	FG	FGA	SAF	Pts
1978	**ATL**	**N**	2	0		0	0	0	12
1981	**SF**	**N**	5	0		0	0	0	30
Career			7	0		0	0	0	42
Playoffs			1	0		0	0	0	6

Don Paul

Year	Team		TD	1XP	2XP	FG	FGA	SAF	Pts
1950	**CHIC**	**N**	2	0		0	0	0	12
1951			6	0		0	0	0	36
1952			1	0		0	0	0	6
1953			2	0		0	0	0	12
1955	**CLE**	**N**	1	0		0	0	0	6
1956			1	0		0	0	0	6
1957			1	0		0	0	0	6
Career			14	0		0	0	0	84
Playoffs			1	0		0	0	0	6

Whitney Paul

Year	Team		TD	1XP	2XP	FG	FGA	SAF	Pts
1980	**KC**	**N**	1	0		0	0	0	6
1981			1	0		0	0	0	6
Career			2	0		0	0	0	12

Dainard Paulson

Year	Team		TD	1XP	2XP	FG	FGA	SAF	Pts
1964	**NY**	**A**	1	0	0	0	0	0	6

Bryce Paup

Year	Team		TD	1XP	2XP	FG	FGA	SAF	Pts
1991	**GB**	**N**	0	0		0	0	1	2
1994			1	0	0	0	0	0	6
Career			1	0	0	0	0	1	8

Ted Pavelec

Year	Team		TD	1XP	2XP	FG	FGA	SAF	Pts
1942	**DET**	**N**	0	0		1	2	0	3

Ken Payne

Year	Team		TD	1XP	2XP	FG	FGA	SAF	Pts
1976	**GB**	**N**	4	0		0	0	0	24
1977			1	0		0	0	0	6
1978	**PHI**	**N**	1	0		0	0	0	6
Career			6	0		0	0	0	36

Eddie Payton

Year	Team		TD	1XP	2XP	FG	FGA	SAF	Pts
1977	**DET**	**N**	2	0		0	0	0	12
1981	**MIN**	**N**	1	0		0	0	0	6
Career			3	0		0	0	0	18

Walter Payton

Year	Team		TD	1XP	2XP	FG	FGA	SAF	Pts
1975	**CHI**	**N**	7	0		0	0	0	42
1976			13	0		0	0	0	78
1977			**16**	0		0	0	0	96
1978			11	0		0	0	0	66
1979			16	0		0	0	0	96
1980			7	0		0	0	0	42
1981			8	0		0	0	0	48
1982			1	0		0	0	0	6
1983			8	0		0	0	0	48
1984			11	0		0	0	0	66
1985			11	0		0	0	0	66
1986			11	0		0	0	0	66
1987			5	0		0	0	0	30
Career			125	0		0	0	0	750
Playoffs			2	0		0	0	0	12

Larry Peace

Year	Team		TD	1XP	2XP	FG	FGA	SAF	Pts
1941	**BKN**	**N**	0	1		0	0	0	1

Elvis Peacock

Year	Team		TD	1XP	2XP	FG	FGA	SAF	Pts
1980	**LA**	**N**	9	0		0	0	0	54

Johnny Peacock

Year	Team		TD	1XP	2XP	FG	FGA	SAF	Pts
1969	**HOU**	**A**	1	0	0	0	0	0	6
1970	**HOU**	**N**	1	0		0	0	0	6
Career			2	0	0	0	0	0	12

Clarence Peaks

Year	Team		TD	1XP	2XP	FG	FGA	SAF	Pts
1957	**PHI**	**N**	1	0		0	0	0	6
1958			5	0		0	0	0	30
1959			3	0		0	0	0	18
1960			3	0		0	0	0	18
1961			5	0		0	0	0	30
1962			3	0		0	0	0	18
1963			2	0		0	0	0	12
1964	**PIT**	**N**	2	0		0	0	0	12
Career			24	0		0	0	0	144

Harley Pearce

Year	Team		TD	1XP	2XP	FG	FGA	SAF	Pts
1926	**COL**	**N**	1	0		0		0	6

Walt Pearce

Year	Team		TD	1XP	2XP	FG	FGA	SAF	Pts
1920	**DEC**	**A**	1	0		0		0	6
1921			2	0		0		0	12
1922	**CHIB**	**N**	1	0		0		0	6
Career			4	0		0		0	24

Barry Pearson

Year	Team		TD	1XP	2XP	FG	FGA	SAF	Pts
1973	**PIT**	**N**	3	0		0	0	0	18
1974	**KC**	**N**	1	0		0	0	0	6
1975			3	0		0	0	0	18
Career			7	0		0	0	0	42
Playoffs			1	0		0	0	0	6

Dennis Pearson

Year	Team		TD	1XP	2XP	FG	FGA	SAF	Pts
1978	**ATL**	**N**	1	0		0	0	0	6

Drew Pearson

Year	Team		TD	1XP	2XP	FG	FGA	SAF	Pts
1973	**DAL**	**N**	2	0		0	0	0	12
1974			3	0		0	0	0	18
1975			8	0		0	0	0	48
1976			7	0		0	0	0	42
1977			2	0		0	0	0	12
1978			3	0		0	0	0	18
1979			8	0		0	0	0	48
1980			6	0		0	0	0	36
1981			3	0		0	0	0	18
1982			3	0		0	0	0	18
1983			5	0		0	0	0	30
Career			50	0		0	0	0	300
Playoffs			8	0		0	0	0	48

Year	Team		TD	1XP	2XP	FG	FGA	SAF	Pts

J.C. Pearson
Year	Team		TD	1XP	2XP	FG	FGA	SAF	Pts
1989	KC	N	1	0	0	0	0		6

Lindy Pearson
| 1950 | DET | N | 2 | 0 | 0 | 0 | 0 | | 12 |

Preston Pearson
1968	BAL	N	4	0	0	0	0		24
1970	PIT	N	2	0	0	0	0		12
1971			3	0	0	0	0		18
1973			4	0	0	0	0		24
1974			4	0	0	0	0		24
1975	DAL	N	4	0	0	0	0		24
1976			3	0	0	0	0		18
1977			5	0	0	0	0		30
1979			2	0	0	0	0		12
1980			2	0	0	0	0		12
Career			33	0	0	0	0		198
Playoffs			3	0	0	0	0		18

Brent Pease
1987	HOU	N	1	0	0	0	0		6
1988			1	0	0	0	0		6
Career			2	0	0	0	0		12

George Pease
1926	NY	A	2	0		0	0		12
1929	ORA	N	1	0		0	0		6
Career			3	0		0	0		18

Win Pedersen
| 1941 | NYG | N | 0 | 0 | | 1 | 1 | 0 | 3 |

Danny Peebles
| 1990 | TB | N | 1 | 0 | | 0 | 0 | 0 | 6 |

Jim Peebles
1946	WAS	N	1	0		0	2	0	6
1947			0	0		0	1	0	0
1948			0	1		0	0	0	1
Career			1	1		0	3	0	7

Rodney Peete
1989	DET	N	4	0	0	0	0		24
1990			6	0	0	0	0		36
1991			2	0	0	0	0		12
1993			1	0	0	0	0		6
1995	PHI	N	1	0	0	0	0		6
1996			1	0	0	0	0		6
Career			15	0	0	0	0		90

Brian Peets
| 1979 | SEA | N | 1 | 0 | | 0 | 0 | 0 | 6 |

Erric Pegram
1991	ATL	N	1	0		0	0	0	6
1993			3	0		0	0	0	18
1994			1	0	0	0	0	0	6
1995	PIT	N	6	0	1	0	0	0	38
1996			2	0	0	0	0	0	12
Career			13	0	1	0	0	0	80

Doug Pelfrey
1993	CIN	N	0	13		24	31	0	85
1994			0	24	0	28	33	0	108
1995			0	34	0	29	36	0	121
1996			0	41	0	23	28	0	110
Career			0	112	0	104	128	0	424

Ray Pelfrey
1951	GB	N	5	0		0	0	0	30
1952	DAL	N	2	0		0	0	0	12
1953	NYG	N	3	0		0	0	0	18
Career			10	0		0	0	0	60

Bob Pellegrini
| 1965 | WAS | N | 1 | 0 | | 0 | 0 | 0 | 6 |

Bill Pellington
| 1959 | BAL | N | 1 | 0 | | 0 | 0 | 0 | 6 |

Steve Pelluer
| 1986 | DAL | N | 1 | 0 | 0 | 0 | 0 | | 6 |
| 1987 | | | 1 | 0 | 0 | 0 | 0 | | 6 |

Steve Pelluer *continued*
Year	Team		TD	1XP	2XP	FG	FGA	SAF	Pts
1988			2	0	0	0	0		12
1989	KC	N	2	0	0	0	0		12
Career			6	0	0	0	0		36

Chris Penn
| 1996 | KC | N | 5 | 0 | 0 | 0 | 0 | 0 | 30 |

Jesse Penn
| 1985 | DAL | N | 1 | 0 | | 0 | 0 | 0 | 6 |

Tom Pennington
| 1962 | DAL | A | 0 | 13 | 0 | 2 | 5 | 0 | 19 |

Carlos Pennywell
1979	NE	N	1	0		0	0	0	6
1980			1	0		0	0	0	6
1981			1	0		0	0	0	6
Career			3	0		0	0	0	18

Robert Pennywell
1977	ATL	N	1	0		0	0	0	6
1979			1	0		0	0	0	6
Career			2	0		0	0	0	12

Mac Percival
1967	CHI	N	0	26		13	26	0	65
1968			0	25		25	36	0	100
1969			0	26		8	21	0	50
1970			0	28		20	34	0	88
1971			0	18		15	33	0	63
1972			0	26		12	24	0	62
1973			0	10		6	8	0	28
1974	DAL	N	0	4		2	8	0	10
Career			0	163		101	190	0	466

John Pergine
| 1975 | WAS | N | 1 | 0 | | 0 | 0 | 0 | 6 |

Bob Perina
1946	NY	AA	1	0		0	0	0	6
1947	BKN	AA	4	0		0	0	0	24
Career			5	0		0	0	0	30

Pete Perini
| 1954 | CHIB | N | 0 | 1 | | 0 | 0 | 0 | 1 |

Art Perkins
1962	LA	N	2	0		0	0	0	12
1963			4	0		0	0	0	24
Career			6	0		0	0	0	36

Bruce Perkins
| 1990 | TB | N | 2 | 0 | | 0 | 0 | 0 | 12 |

Don Perkins
1961	DAL	N	5	0		0	0	0	30
1962			7	0		0	0	0	42
1963			7	0		0	0	0	42
1964			6	0		0	0	0	36
1966			8	0		0	0	0	48
1967			6	0		0	0	0	36
1968			6	0		0	0	0	36
Career			45	0		0	0	0	270
Playoffs			3	0		0	0	0	18

Don Perkins
1944	GB	N	2	0		0	0	0	12
1945	GB-CHIB	N	2	0		0	0	0	12
Career			4	0		0	0	0	24

Johnny Perkins
1978	NYG	N	3	0		0	0	0	18
1979			4	0		0	0	0	24
1980			3	0		0	0	0	18
1981			6	0		0	0	0	36
1982			2	0		0	0	0	12
Career			18	0		0	0	0	108
Playoffs			2	0		0	0	0	12

Ray Perkins
1967	BAL	N	2	0		0	0	0	12
1968			1	0		0	0	0	6
1969			3	0		0	0	0	18

Ray Perkins *continued*
Year	Team		TD	1XP	2XP	FG	FGA	SAF	Pts
1970			1	0		0	0	0	6
1971			4	0		0	0	0	24
Career			11	0		0	0	0	66
Playoffs			1	0		0	0	0	6

Brett Perriman
1988	NO	N	2	0		0	0	0	12
1990			2	0		0	0	0	12
1991	DET	N	1	0		0	0	0	6
1992			4	0		0	0	0	24
1993			2	0		0	0	0	12
1994			4	0	2	0	0	0	28
1995			9	0	1	0	0	0	56
1996			5	0	0	0	0	0	30
Career			29	0	3	0	0	0	180
Playoffs			2	0	0	0	0		12

Benny Perrin
| 1983 | STL | N | 1 | 0 | | 0 | 0 | 0 | 6 |

Jack Perrin
| 1926 | HAR | N | 0 | 3 | | 1 | | 0 | 6 |

Lonnie Perrin
1976	DEN	N	2	0		0	0	0	12
1977			4	0		0	0	0	24
1978			5	0		0	0	0	30
Career			11	0		0	0	0	66

Darren Perry
| 1996 | PIT | N | 1 | 0 | 0 | 0 | 0 | 0 | 6 |

Jerry Perry
1957	DET	N	0	0		0	1	0	2
1958			0	1		4	4	0	13
1959			0	18		3	7	0	27
1960	STL	N	0	5		13	20	0	44
1961			0	30		7	16	0	51
1962			0	38		5	12	0	53
Career			0	92		32	59	1	190

Joe Perry
1948	SF	AA	12	0		0	0	0	72
1949			11	0		0	0	0	66
1950	SF	N	6	0		0	0	0	36
1951			4	0		0	0	0	24
1952			8	0		0	0	0	48
1953			13	0		0	3	0	78
1954			8	6		1	3	0	57
1955			3	0		0	0	0	18
1956			3	0		0	0	0	18
1957			3	0		0	0	0	18
1958			5	0		0	0	0	30
1959			3	0		0	0	0	18
1960			1	0		0	0	0	6
1961	BAL	N	4	0		0	0	0	24
Career			84	6		1	6	0	513

Leon Perry
1980	NYG	N	2	0		0	0	0	12
1981			1	0		0	0	0	6
Career			3	0		0	0	0	18

Lowell Perry
| 1956 | PIT | N | 2 | 0 | | 0 | 0 | 0 | 12 |

Mario Perry
| 1987 | LARI | N | 1 | 0 | | 0 | 0 | 0 | 6 |

Michael Dean Perry
| 1988 | CLE | N | 1 | 0 | | 0 | 0 | 0 | 6 |

Rod Perry
1978	LA	N	3	0		0	0	0	18
1980			1	0		0	0	0	6
Career			4	0		0	0	0	24

Scott Perry
| 1978 | CIN | N | 3 | 0 | | 0 | 0 | 0 | 18 |

Vernon Perry
| Playoffs | | | 1 | 0 | 0 | 0 | 0 | 0 | 6 |

William Perry

Year	Team		TD	1XP	2XP	FG	FGA	SAF	Pts
1985	CHI	N	3	0		0	0	0	18
Playoffs			1	0	0	0	0	0	6

Bob Perryman

Year	Team		TD	1XP	2XP	FG	FGA	SAF	Pts
1988	NE	N	6	0		0	0	0	36
1989			2	0		0	0	0	12
1990			1	0		0	0	0	6
Career			9	0		0	0	0	54

John Petchel

Year	Team		TD	1XP	2XP	FG	FGA	SAF	Pts
1944	CLE	N	1	0		0	0	0	6

Boni Petcoff

Year	Team		TD	1XP	2XP	FG	FGA	SAF	Pts
1924	COL	N	0	0		0		1	2

Forest Peters

Year	Team		TD	1XP	2XP	FG	FGA	SAF	Pts
1930	PRO	N	2	7		**2**		0	25
1931	BKN	N	0	2		0		0	2
Career			2	9		2		0	27

Volney Peters

Year	Team		TD	1XP	2XP	FG	FGA	SAF	Pts
1952	CHIC	N	1	0		0	0	0	6

Jim Peterson

Year	Team		TD	1XP	2XP	FG	FGA	SAF	Pts
1975	LA	N	1	0		0	0	0	6

Ken Peterson

Year	Team		TD	1XP	2XP	FG	FGA	SAF	Pts
1936	DET	N	3	0		0		0	18

Nelson Peterson

Year	Team		TD	1XP	2XP	FG	FGA	SAF	Pts
1938	CLE	N	2	2		2	2	0	20

Todd Peterson

Year	Team		TD	1XP	2XP	FG	FGA	SAF	Pts
1994	ARI	N	0	4	0	2	4	0	10
1995	SEA	N	0	40	0	23	28	0	109
1996			0	27	0	28	34	0	111
Career			0	71	0	53	66	0	230

Richie Petitbon

Year	Team		TD	1XP	2XP	FG	FGA	SAF	Pts
1959	CHIB	N	1	0		0	0	0	6
1962	CHI	N	1	0		0	0	0	6
1963			1	0		0	0	0	6
Career			3	0		0	0	0	18

Elmer Petrie

Year	Team		TD	1XP	2XP	FG	FGA	SAF	Pts
1922	TOL	N	2	0		0		0	12

Bill Petrilas

Year	Team		TD	1XP	2XP	FG	FGA	SAF	Pts
1944	NYG	N	2	0		0	0	0	12

Stan Petry

Year	Team		TD	1XP	2XP	FG	FGA	SAF	Pts
1990	KC	N	1	0		0	0	0	6

Neal Petties

Year	Team		TD	1XP	2XP	FG	FGA	SAF	Pts
1964	BAL	N	1	0		0	0	0	6

John Petty

Year	Team		TD	1XP	2XP	FG	FGA	SAF	Pts
1942	CHIB	N	2	0		0	0	0	12

Bob Pfohl

Year	Team		TD	1XP	2XP	FG	FGA	SAF	Pts
1948	BAL	AA	6	0		0	0	0	36
1949			2	0		0	0	0	12
Career			8	0		0	0	0	48

Art Pharmer

Year	Team		TD	1XP	2XP	FG	FGA	SAF	Pts
1930	MIN-FRA	N	1	6		0		0	12

Bob Phelan

Year	Team		TD	1XP	2XP	FG	FGA	SAF	Pts
1922	TOL	N	2	0		0		0	12

Don Phelps

Year	Team		TD	1XP	2XP	FG	FGA	SAF	Pts
1950	CLE	N	3	0		0	0	0	18
1951			1	0		0	0	0	6
Career			4	0		0	0	0	24

Todd Philcox

Year	Team		TD	1XP	2XP	FG	FGA	SAF	Pts
1993	CLE	N	1	0		0	0	0	6

Charles Phillips

Year	Team		TD	1XP	2XP	FG	FGA	SAF	Pts
1978	OAK	N	3	0		0	0	0	18

Jason Phillips

Year	Team		TD	1XP	2XP	FG	FGA	SAF	Pts
1989	DET	N	1	0		0	0	0	6

Jason Phillips *continued*

Year	Team		TD	1XP	2XP	FG	FGA	SAF	Pts
1992	ATL	N	1	0		0	0	0	6
Career			2	0		0	0	0	12

Jess Phillips

Year	Team		TD	1XP	2XP	FG	FGA	SAF	Pts
1969	CIN	A	3	0	0	0	0	0	18
1970	CIN	N	5	0		0	0	0	30
1971			1	0		0	0	0	6
1972			1	0		0	0	0	6
1974	NO	N	2	0		0	0	0	12
1975	OAK	N	1	0		0	0	0	6
1976	NE	N	1	0		0	0	0	6
1977			1	0		0	0	0	6
Career			15	0	0	0	0	0	90
Playoffs			1	0	0	0	0	0	6

Jim Phillips

Year	Team		TD	1XP	2XP	FG	FGA	SAF	Pts
1958	LA	N	2	0		0	0	0	12
1959			4	0		0	0	0	24
1960			8	0		0	0	0	48
1961			5	0		0	0	0	30
1962			5	0		0	0	0	30
1963			1	0		0	0	0	6
1964			2	0		0	0	0	12
1965	MIN	N	1	0		0	0	0	6
1966			3	0		0	0	0	18
1967			3	0		0	0	0	18
Career			34	0		0	0	0	204

Lawrence Phillips

Year	Team		TD	1XP	2XP	FG	FGA	SAF	Pts
1996	STL	N	5	0	0	0	0	0	30

Mel Phillips

Year	Team		TD	1XP	2XP	FG	FGA	SAF	Pts
1970	SF	N	1	0		0	0	0	6

Reggie Phillips

Year	Team		TD	1XP	2XP	FG	FGA	SAF	Pts
Playoffs			1	0	0	0	0	0	6

Rod Phillips

Year	Team		TD	1XP	2XP	FG	FGA	SAF	Pts
1976	LA	N	1	0		0	0	0	6
1977			1	0		0	0	0	6
1979	STL	N	1	0		0	0	0	6
Career			3	0		0	0	0	18

Ed Philpott

Year	Team		TD	1XP	2XP	FG	FGA	SAF	Pts
1968	BOS	A	1	0	0	0	0	0	6

Dino Philyaw

Year	Team		TD	1XP	2XP	FG	FGA	SAF	Pts
1996	CAR	N	1	0	0	0	0	0	6

Mike Phipps

Year	Team		TD	1XP	2XP	FG	FGA	SAF	Pts
1972	CLE	N	5	0		0	0	0	30
1973			5	0		0	0	0	30
1974			1	0		0	0	0	6
1980	CHI	N	2	0		0	0	0	12
Career			13	0		0	0	0	78
Playoffs			1	0		0	0	0	6

Alex Piasecky

Year	Team		TD	1XP	2XP	FG	FGA	SAF	Pts
1943	WAS	N	1	0		0	0	0	6

Bill Piccolo

Year	Team		TD	1XP	2XP	FG	FGA	SAF	Pts
1945	NYG	N	1	0		0	0	0	6

Brian Piccolo

Year	Team		TD	1XP	2XP	FG	FGA	SAF	Pts
1968	CHI	N	2	0		0	0	0	12
1969			3	0		0	0	0	18
Career			5	0		0	0	0	30

Lou Piccone

Year	Team		TD	1XP	2XP	FG	FGA	SAF	Pts
1976	NYJ	N	1	0		0	0	0	6
1977	BUF	N	2	0		0	0	0	12
1978			2	0		0	0	1	14
1979			2	0		0	0	0	12
Career			7	0		0	0	1	44

Bob Pickard

Year	Team		TD	1XP	2XP	FG	FGA	SAF	Pts
1974	DET	N	1	0		0	0	0	6

Carl Pickens

Year	Team		TD	1XP	2XP	FG	FGA	SAF	Pts
1992	CIN	N	2	0		0	0	0	12
1993			6	0		0	0	0	36
1994			11	0	0	0	0	0	66
1995			17	0	0	0	0	0	102

Carl Pickens *continued*

Year	Team		TD	1XP	2XP	FG	FGA	SAF	Pts
1996			12	0	1	0	0	0	74
Career			48	0	1	0	0	0	290

Aaron Pierce

Year	Team		TD	1XP	2XP	FG	FGA	SAF	Pts
1994	NYG	N	4	0	0	0	0	0	24
1996			2	0	0	0	0	0	12
Career			6	0	0	0	0	0	36

Al Pierotti

Year	Team		TD	1XP	2XP	FG	FGA	SAF	Pts
1920	CLE	A	0	2		0		0	2

Nick Pietrosante

Year	Team		TD	1XP	2XP	FG	FGA	SAF	Pts
1959	DET	N	3	0		0	0	0	18
1960			8	0		0	0	0	48
1961			5	0		0	0	0	30
1962			4	0		0	0	0	24
1963			5	0		0	0	0	30
1964			4	0		0	0	0	24
1965			1	0		0	0	0	6
Career			30	0		0	0	0	180

Bert Piggott

Year	Team		TD	1XP	2XP	FG	FGA	SAF	Pts
1947	LA	AA	1	0		0	0	0	6

Pete Pihos

Year	Team		TD	1XP	2XP	FG	FGA	SAF	Pts
1947	PHI	N	8	0		0	0	0	48
1948			11	0		0	0	0	66
1949			4	0		0	0	0	24
1950			6	0		0	0	0	36
1951			5	0		0	0	0	30
1952			2	0		0	0	0	12
1953			10	0		0	0	0	60
1954			10	0		0	0	0	60
1955			7	0		0	0	0	42
Career			63	0		0	0	0	378
Playoffs			1	0		0	0	0	6

Joe Pilconis

Year	Team		TD	1XP	2XP	FG	FGA	SAF	Pts
1936	PHI	N	1	0		0		0	6
1937			1	0		0		0	6
Career			2	0		0		0	12

Frank Pillow

Year	Team		TD	1XP	2XP	FG	FGA	SAF	Pts
1988	TB	N	1	0		0	0	0	6

Erny Pinckert

Year	Team		TD	1XP	2XP	FG	FGA	SAF	Pts
1933	BOS	N	1	0		0		0	6
1934			1	0		0		0	6
1937	WAS	N	1	0		0		0	6
Career			3	0		0		0	18

Stan Pincura

Year	Team		TD	1XP	2XP	FG	FGA	SAF	Pts
1938	CLE	N	1	0		0	0	0	6

Cyril Pinder

Year	Team		TD	1XP	2XP	FG	FGA	SAF	Pts
1969	PHI	N	1	0		0	0	0	6
1970			2	0		0	0	0	12
1971	CHI	N	1	0		0	0	0	6
1972			3	0		0	0	0	18
Career			7	0		0	0	0	42

Johnny Pingel

Year	Team		TD	1XP	2XP	FG	FGA	SAF	Pts
1939	DET	N	1	0		0	0	0	6

Allen Pinkett

Year	Team		TD	1XP	2XP	FG	FGA	SAF	Pts
1986	HOU	N	3	0		0	0	0	18
1987			2	0		0	0	0	12
1988			9	0		0	0	0	54
1989			2	0		0	0	0	12
1991			10	0		0	0	0	60
Career			26	0		0	0	0	156
Playoffs			2	0		0	0	0	12

Reggie Pinkney

Year	Team		TD	1XP	2XP	FG	FGA	SAF	Pts
1977	DET	N	1	0		0	0	0	6

Ray Pinney

Year	Team		TD	1XP	2XP	FG	FGA	SAF	Pts
1981	PIT	N	1	0		0	0	0	6
1982			1	0		0	0	0	6
Career			2	0		0	0	0	12

Hank Piro

Year	Team		TD	1XP	2XP	FG	FGA	SAF	Pts
1941	PHI	N	1	0		0	0	0	6

Joe Pisarcik

Year	Team		TD	1XP	2XP	FG	FGA	SAF	Pts
1977	NYG	N	2	0	0	0	0	0	12
1978			1	0	0	0	0	0	6
1984	PHI	N	2	0	0	0	0	0	12
Career			5	0	0	0	0	0	30

Danny Pittman

Year	Team		TD	1XP	2XP	FG	FGA	SAF	Pts
1983	NYG	N	1	0	0	0	0	0	6

Elijah Pitts

Year	Team		TD	1XP	2XP	FG	FGA	SAF	Pts
1961	GB	N	1	0	0	0	0	0	6
1962			2	0	0	0	0	0	12
1963			6	0	0	0	0	0	36
1964			2	0	0	0	0	0	12
1965			5	0	0	0	0	0	30
1966			10	0	0	0	0	0	60
1967			6	0	0	0	0	0	36
1968			2	0	0	0	0	0	12
1969			1	0	0	0	0	0	6
Career			35	0	0	0	0	0	210
Playoffs			3	0	0	0	0	0	18

Frank Pitts

Year	Team		TD	1XP	2XP	FG	FGA	SAF	Pts
1966	KC	A	1	0	0	0	0	0	6
1967			2	0	0	0	0	0	12
1968			6	0	0	0	0	0	36
1969			2	0	0	0	0	0	12
1970	KC	N	2	0	0	0	0	0	12
1971	CLE	N	4	0	0	0	0	0	24
1972			8	0	0	0	0	0	48
1973			4	0	0	0	0	0	24
Career			29	0	0	0	0	0	174

Mike Pitts

Year	Team		TD	1XP	2XP	FG	FGA	SAF	Pts
1986	ATL	N	1	0	0	0	0	0	6

Ron Pitts

Year	Team		TD	1XP	2XP	FG	FGA	SAF	Pts
1986	BUF	N	1	0	0	0	0	0	6
1988	GB	N	1	0	0	0	0	0	6
Career			2	0	0	0	0	0	12

Dave Pivec

Year	Team		TD	1XP	2XP	FG	FGA	SAF	Pts
1967	LA	N	1	0	0	0	0	0	6
1968			0	0	0	0	0	1	2
Career			1	0	0	0	0	1	8

Doug Plank

Year	Team		TD	1XP	2XP	FG	FGA	SAF	Pts
1981	CHI	N	0	0	0	0	0	1	2

Tony Plansky

Year	Team		TD	1XP	2XP	FG	FGA	SAF	Pts
1928	NYG	N	1	0	0	0	0	0	6
1929			9	2	2	0	0	0	62
Career			10	2	2	0	0	0	68

Dick Plasman

Year	Team		TD	1XP	2XP	FG	FGA	SAF	Pts
1937	CHIB	N	1	2	0	0	0	0	8
1938			1	0	0	0	0	0	6
1939			3	3	0	1	0	0	21
1940			2	3	0	0	0	0	15
1941			0	6	0	0	0	0	6
Career			7	14	0	1	0	0	56
Playoffs			0	1	0	0	0	0	1

George Platukas

Year	Team		TD	1XP	2XP	FG	FGA	SAF	Pts
1939	PIT	N	3	0	0	0	0	0	18
1940			2	0	0	0	0	0	12
1942	CLE	N	2	0	0	0	0	0	12
Career			7	0	0	0	0	0	42

Anthony Pleasant

Year	Team		TD	1XP	2XP	FG	FGA	SAF	Pts
1993	CLE	N	0	0	0	0	0	1	2

Milt Plum

Year	Team		TD	1XP	2XP	FG	FGA	SAF	Pts
1958	CLE	N	4	2	0	0	0	0	26
1959			1	0	0	0	0	0	6
1960			2	0	0	0	0	0	12
1961			1	0	0	0	0	0	6
1962	DET	N	1	0	0	5	12	0	21
1963			0	13	1	4	0	0	16
1964			1	0	0	0	0	0	6
1965			3	0	0	0	0	0	18
1966			0	1	0	0	0	0	1
Career			13	16	6	16	0	0	112

Gary Plummer

Year	Team		TD	1XP	2XP	FG	FGA	SAF	Pts
1990	SD	N	2	0	0	0	0	0	12

Tony Plummer

Year	Team		TD	1XP	2XP	FG	FGA	SAF	Pts
1973	ATL	N	0	0	0	0	0	1	2

Jim Plunkett

Year	Team		TD	1XP	2XP	FG	FGA	SAF	Pts
1972	NE	N	1	0	0	0	0	0	6
1973			5	0	0	0	0	0	30
1974			2	0	0	0	0	0	12
1975			1	0	0	0	0	0	6
1977	SF	N	1	0	0	0	0	0	6
1980	OAK	N	2	0	0	0	0	0	12
1981			1	0	0	0	0	0	6
1984	LARI	N	1	0	0	0	0	0	6
Career			14	0	0	0	0	0	84
Playoffs			1	0	0	0	0	0	6

Ray Poage

Year	Team		TD	1XP	2XP	FG	FGA	SAF	Pts
1963	MIN	N	2	0	0	0	0	0	12
1964	PHI	N	1	0	0	0	0	0	6
1965			5	0	0	0	0	0	30
1969	NO	N	4	0	0	0	0	0	24
1970			1	0	0	0	0	0	6
Career			13	0	0	0	0	0	78

Ed Podolak

Year	Team		TD	1XP	2XP	FG	FGA	SAF	Pts
1970	KC	N	4	0	0	0	0	0	24
1971			9	0	0	0	0	0	54
1972			6	0	0	0	0	0	36
1973			3	0	0	0	0	0	18
1974			3	0	0	0	0	0	18
1975			5	0	0	0	0	0	30
1976			5	0	0	0	0	0	30
1977			5	0	0	0	0	0	30
Career			40	0	0	0	0	0	240
Playoffs			2	0	0	0	0	0	12

Jim Podoley

Year	Team		TD	1XP	2XP	FG	FGA	SAF	Pts
1957	WAS	N	6	0	0	0	0	0	36
1958			4	0	0	0	0	0	24
1959			2	0	0	0	0	0	12
1960			1	0	0	0	0	0	6
Career			13	0	0	0	0	0	78

Johnnie Poe

Year	Team		TD	1XP	2XP	FG	FGA	SAF	Pts
1983	NO	N	1	0	0	0	0	0	6
1985			1	0	0	0	0	0	6
1987			1	0	0	0	0	0	6
Career			3	0	0	0	0	0	18

Dick Poillon

Year	Team		TD	1XP	2XP	FG	FGA	SAF	Pts
1942	WAS	N	0	2	1	2	0		5
1946			1	21	6	16	0		45
1947			6	37	4	6	0		85
1948			3	33	5	7	0		66
1949			0	34	4	7	0		46
Career			10	127	20	38	0		247

John Polanski

Year	Team		TD	1XP	2XP	FG	FGA	SAF	Pts
1946	LA	AA	2	0	0	0	0	0	12

Al Pollard

Year	Team		TD	1XP	2XP	FG	FGA	SAF	Pts
1952	PHI	N	1	0	0	0	0	0	6
1953			0	1	0	2	0		1
Career			1	1	0	2	0		7

Bob Pollard

Year	Team		TD	1XP	2XP	FG	FGA	SAF	Pts
1977	NO	N	1	0	0	0	0	0	6

Frank Pollard

Year	Team		TD	1XP	2XP	FG	FGA	SAF	Pts
1981	PIT	N	2	0	0	0	0	0	12
1982			2	0	0	0	0	0	12
1983			4	0	0	0	0	0	24
1984			6	0	0	0	0	0	36
1985			3	0	0	0	0	0	18
1987			3	0	0	0	0	0	18
Career			20	0	0	0	0	0	120
Playoffs			2	0	0	0	0	0	12

Fritz Pollard

Year	Team		TD	1XP	2XP	FG	FGA	SAF	Pts
1920	AKR	A	4	0	0	0		0	24
1921			7	0	0	0		0	42
1922	MIL	N	3	2	0	0		0	20

Fritz Pollard *continued*

Year	Team		TD	1XP	2XP	FG	FGA	SAF	Pts
1923	HAM	N	0	1	0	0		1	1
1925	AKR	N	2	0	0	0		0	12
1926			0	0	0	0		0	0
Career			16	3	0	0			99

Marcus Pollard

Year	Team		TD	1XP	2XP	FG	FGA	SAF	Pts
1996	IND	N	1	0	0	0	0	0	6

Red Pollock

Year	Team		TD	1XP	2XP	FG	FGA	SAF	Pts
1935	CHIB	N	4	0	0	0		0	24

Fran Polsfoot

Year	Team		TD	1XP	2XP	FG	FGA	SAF	Pts
1950	CHIC	N	6	0	0	0	0	0	36
1951			4	0	0	0	0	0	24
Career			10	0	0	0	0	0	60

Randy Poltl

Year	Team		TD	1XP	2XP	FG	FGA	SAF	Pts
1976	DEN	N	1	0	0	0	0	0	6

David Pool

Year	Team		TD	1XP	2XP	FG	FGA	SAF	Pts
1992	NE	N	1	0	0	0	0	0	6

Hamp Pool

Year	Team		TD	1XP	2XP	FG	FGA	SAF	Pts
1941	CHIB	N	1	0	0	0	0	0	6
1942			5	0	0	0	0	0	30
1943			6	0	0	0	0	0	36
Career			12	0	0	0	0	0	72
Playoffs			1	0	0	0	0	0	6

Barney Poole

Year	Team		TD	1XP	2XP	FG	FGA	SAF	Pts
1950	NYY	N	1	0	0	0	0	0	6

Jim Poole

Year	Team		TD	1XP	2XP	FG	FGA	SAF	Pts
1937	NYG	N	2	0	0	0		0	12
1938			1	0	0	0		0	6
1940			3	0	0	0		0	18
1941			3	0	0	0		0	18
1945	CHIC	N	2	0	0	0		0	12
1946	NYG	N	3	0	0	0		0	18
Career			14	0	0	0		0	84

Larry Poole

Year	Team		TD	1XP	2XP	FG	FGA	SAF	Pts
1976	CLE	N	1	0	0	0	0	0	6
1977			4	0	0	0	0	0	24
Career			5	0	0	0	0	0	30

Nathan Poole

Year	Team		TD	1XP	2XP	FG	FGA	SAF	Pts
1983	DEN	N	4	0	0	0	0	0	24
1987			1	0	0	0	0	0	6
Career			5	0	0	0	0	0	30

Ray Poole

Year	Team		TD	1XP	2XP	FG	FGA	SAF	Pts
1947	NYG	N	4	0	0	0	0	0	24
1948			4	0	0	0	0	1	26
1949			1	0	0	0	0	0	6
1950			0	30	5	11	0		45
1951			0	30	12	16	0		66
1952			0	26	10	17	0		56
Career			9	86	27	44	1		223

Steve Poole

Year	Team		TD	1XP	2XP	FG	FGA	SAF	Pts
1976	NYJ	N	1	0	0	0	0	0	6

Bucky Pope

Year	Team		TD	1XP	2XP	FG	FGA	SAF	Pts
1964	LA	N	10	0	0	0	0	0	60
1966			1	0	0	0	0	0	6
1967			2	0	0	0	0	0	12
Career			13	0	0	0	0	0	78

Lew Pope

Year	Team		TD	1XP	2XP	FG	FGA	SAF	Pts
1933	CIN	N	1	0	0	0		0	6

Marquez Pope

Year	Team		TD	1XP	2XP	FG	FGA	SAF	Pts
1996	SF	N	1	0	0	0	0	0	6

Milt Popovich

Year	Team		TD	1XP	2XP	FG	FGA	SAF	Pts
1939	CHIC	N	1	0	0	0	0	0	6

Ted Popson

Year	Team		TD	1XP	2XP	FG	FGA	SAF	Pts
1996	SF	N	6	0	0	0	0	0	36

Tracy Porter

Year	Team		TD	1XP	2XP	FG	FGA	SAF	Pts
1981	DET	N	1	0	0	0	0	0	6

Tracy Porter *continued*

Year	Team	Lg	TD	1XP	2XP	FG	FGA	SAF	Pts
1984	**IND**	**N**	2	0		0	0	0	12
Career			3	0		0	0	0	18

David Posey

Year	Team	Lg	TD	1XP	2XP	FG	FGA	SAF	Pts
1978	**NE**	**N**	0	29		11	22	0	62
Playoffs			0	2	0	0	1	0	2

Dickie Post

Year	Team	Lg	TD	1XP	2XP	FG	FGA	SAF	Pts
1967	**SD**	**A**	8	0	0	0	0	0	48
1968			3	0	0	0	0	0	18
1969			6	0	0	0	0	0	36
1970	**SD**	**N**	1	0		0	0	0	6
1971	**DEN**	**N**	1	0		0	0	0	6
Career			19	0	0	0	0	0	114

Johnny Poto

Year	Team	Lg	TD	1XP	2XP	FG	FGA	SAF	Pts
1947	**BOS**	**N**	1	0		0	0	0	6

Earl Potteiger

Year	Team	Lg	TD	1XP	2XP	FG	FGA	SAF	Pts
1994	**IND**	**N**	2	0	0	0	0	0	12

Bob Potts

Year	Team	Lg	TD	1XP	2XP	FG	FGA	SAF	Pts
1926	**FRA**	**N**	1	0		0		0	6

Roosevelt Potts

Year	Team	Lg	TD	1XP	2XP	FG	FGA	SAF	Pts
1995	**IND**	**N**	1	0	0	0	0	0	6

Ernie Pough

Year	Team	Lg	TD	1XP	2XP	FG	FGA	SAF	Pts
1976	**PIT**	**N**	1	0		0	0	0	6

Art Powell

Year	Team	Lg	TD	1XP	2XP	FG	FGA	SAF	Pts
1959	**PHI**	**N**	1	0		0	0	0	6
1960	**NY**	**A**	**14**	0	0	0	0	0	84
1961			5	0	0	0	0	0	30
1962			8	0	0	0	0	0	48
1963	**OAK**	**A**	**16**	0	0	0	0	0	96
1964			11	0	0	0	0	0	66
1965			12	0	0	0	0	0	72
1966			11	0	0	0	0	0	66
1967	**BUF**	**A**	4	0	0	0	0	0	24
Career			82	0	0	0	0	0	492

Charley Powell

Year	Team	Lg	TD	1XP	2XP	FG	FGA	SAF	Pts
1952	**SF**	**N**	0	0		0	0	1	2

Darnell Powell

Year	Team	Lg	TD	1XP	2XP	FG	FGA	SAF	Pts
1978	**NYJ**	**N**	1	0		0	0	0	6

Warren Powers

Year	Team	Lg	TD	1XP	2XP	FG	FGA	SAF	Pts
1967	**OAK**	**A**	2	0	0	0	0	0	12

Warren Powers

Year	Team	Lg	TD	1XP	2XP	FG	FGA	SAF	Pts
1991	**DEN**	**N**	1	0		0	0	0	6

Bob Pratt

Year	Team	Lg	TD	1XP	2XP	FG	FGA	SAF	Pts
1977	**BAL**	**N**	1	0		0	0	0	6

John Prchlik

Year	Team	Lg	TD	1XP	2XP	FG	FGA	SAF	Pts
1951	**DET**	**N**	0	0		0	0	1	2

Gene Prebola

Year	Team	Lg	TD	1XP	2XP	FG	FGA	SAF	Pts
1960	**OAK**	**A**	2	0	0	0	0	0	12
1961	**DEN**	**A**	1	0	1	0	0	0	8
1962			1	0	1	0	0	0	8
1963			2	0	1	0	0	0	14
Career			6	0	3	0	0	0	42

Steve Preece

Year	Team	Lg	TD	1XP	2XP	FG	FGA	SAF	Pts
1969	**NO**	**N**	1	0		0	0	0	6
1970	**PHI**	**N**	1	0		0	0	0	6
1973	**LA**	**N**	1	0		0	0	0	6
Career			3	0		0	0	0	18

Merv Pregulman

Year	Team	Lg	TD	1XP	2XP	FG	FGA	SAF	Pts
1948	**DET**	**N**	0	26		2	6	0	32

Hal Prescott

Year	Team	Lg	TD	1XP	2XP	FG	FGA	SAF	Pts
1949	**NYB**	**N**	1	0		0	0	0	6

Glenn Presnell

Year	Team	Lg	TD	1XP	2XP	FG	FGA	SAF	Pts
1931	**POR**	**N**	4	8		1		0	35
1932			2	1		0		0	13
1933			6	12		5		0	**63**

Glenn Presnell *continued*

Year	Team	Lg	TD	1XP	2XP	FG	FGA	SAF	Pts
1934	**DET**	**N**	7	9		4		0	63
1935			2	4		4		0	28
1936			1	6		1		0	15
Career			22	40		15		0	217
Playoffs			0	1		0	0	0	1

Jim Prestel

Year	Team	Lg	TD	1XP	2XP	FG	FGA	SAF	Pts
1964	**MIN**	**N**	1	0		0	0	0	6
1965			0	0		0	0	1	2
Career			1	0		0	0	1	8

Dave Preston

Year	Team	Lg	TD	1XP	2XP	FG	FGA	SAF	Pts
1978	**DEN**	**N**	2	0		0	0	0	12
1979			2	0		0	0	0	12
1980			4	0		0	0	0	24
1981			3	0		0	0	0	18
1983			2	0		0	0	0	12
Career			13	0		0	0	0	78
Playoffs			2	0		0	0	0	12

Roell Preston

Year	Team	Lg	TD	1XP	2XP	FG	FGA	SAF	Pts
1995	**ATL**	**N**	1	0	0	0	0	0	6
1996			1	0	0	0	0	0	6
Career			2	0	0	0	0	0	12

Charley Price

Year	Team	Lg	TD	1XP	2XP	FG	FGA	SAF	Pts
1940	**DET**	**N**	2	4		0	0	0	16

Eddie Price

Year	Team	Lg	TD	1XP	2XP	FG	FGA	SAF	Pts
1950	**NYG**	**N**	4	0		0	0	0	24
1951			7	0		0	0	0	42
1952			5	0		0	0	0	30
1953			3	0		0	0	0	18
1954			5	0		0	0	0	30
Career			24	0		0	0	0	144

Elex Price

Year	Team	Lg	TD	1XP	2XP	FG	FGA	SAF	Pts
1976	**NO**	**N**	1	0		0	0	0	6
1980			1	0		0	0	0	6
Career			2	0		0	0	0	12

Ernie Price

Year	Team	Lg	TD	1XP	2XP	FG	FGA	SAF	Pts
1975	**DET**	**N**	0	0		0	0	1	2

Jim Price

Year	Team	Lg	TD	1XP	2XP	FG	FGA	SAF	Pts
1991	**LARM**	**N**	2	0		0	0	0	12
1992			2	0		0	0	0	12
Career			4	0		0	0	0	24

Mitchell Price

Year	Team	Lg	TD	1XP	2XP	FG	FGA	SAF	Pts
1990	**CIN**	**N**	1	0		0	0	0	6
1991			1	0		0	0	0	6
Career			2	0		0	0	0	12

Sam Price

Year	Team	Lg	TD	1XP	2XP	FG	FGA	SAF	Pts
1967	**MIA**	**A**	2	0	0	0	0	0	12

Billy Pricer

Year	Team	Lg	TD	1XP	2XP	FG	FGA	SAF	Pts
1958	**BAL**	**N**	1	0		0	0	0	6
1960			2	0		0	0	0	12
Career			3	0		0	0	0	18

Tom Pridemore

Year	Team	Lg	TD	1XP	2XP	FG	FGA	SAF	Pts
1981	**ATL**	**N**	1	0		0	0	0	6

James Primus

Year	Team	Lg	TD	1XP	2XP	FG	FGA	SAF	Pts
1988	**ATL**	**N**	1	0		0	0	0	6

Dom Principe

Year	Team	Lg	TD	1XP	2XP	FG	FGA	SAF	Pts
1946	**BKN**	**AA**	2	0		0	0	0	12

Mike Prindle

Year	Team	Lg	TD	1XP	2XP	FG	FGA	SAF	Pts
1987	**DET**	**N**	0	6		6	7	0	24

Mike Prior

Year	Team	Lg	TD	1XP	2XP	FG	FGA	SAF	Pts
1989	**IND**	**N**	1	0		0	0	0	6

Bill Pritchard

Year	Team	Lg	TD	1XP	2XP	FG	FGA	SAF	Pts
1927	**PRO**	**N**	1	3		0		0	9
1928	**NYY**	**N**	1	1		0		0	7
Career			2	4		0		0	16

Bosh Pritchard

Year	Team	Lg	TD	1XP	2XP	FG	FGA	SAF	Pts
1942	**PHI**	**N**	1	0		0	0	0	6
1946			6	0		0	0	0	36
1947			4	0		0	0	0	24
1948			8	0		0	0	0	48
1949			5	0		0	0	0	30
1951	**NYG**	**N**	1	0		0	0	0	6
Career			25	0		0	0	0	150
Playoffs			1	0		0	0	0	6

Mike Pritchard

Year	Team	Lg	TD	1XP	2XP	FG	FGA	SAF	Pts
1991	**ATL**	**N**	2	0		0	0	0	12
1992			5	0		0	0	0	30
1993			7	0		0	0	0	42
1994	**DEN**	**N**	1	0	0	0	0	0	6
1995			3	0	0	0	0	0	18
1996	**SEA**	**N**	1	0	0	0	0	0	6
Career			19	0	0	0	0	0	114

Ron Pritchard

Year	Team	Lg	TD	1XP	2XP	FG	FGA	SAF	Pts
1970	**HOU**	**N**	0	0		0	0	1	2

Billy Pritchett

Year	Team	Lg	TD	1XP	2XP	FG	FGA	SAF	Pts
1976	**ATL**	**N**	1	0		0	0	0	6

Stanley Pritchett

Year	Team	Lg	TD	1XP	2XP	FG	FGA	SAF	Pts
1996	**MIA**	**N**	2	0	0	0	0	0	12

Steve Pritko

Year	Team	Lg	TD	1XP	2XP	FG	FGA	SAF	Pts
1943	**NYG**	**N**	1	0		0	0	0	6
1944	**CLE**	**N**	3	0		0	0	0	18
1945			4	0		0	0	0	24
1946	**LA**	**N**	2	0		0	0	0	12
1948	**BOS**	**N**	1	0		0	0	0	6
1949	**GB**	**N**	2	0		0	0	0	12
1950			2	0		0	0	0	12
Career			15	0		0	0	0	90

Dewey Proctor

Year	Team	Lg	TD	1XP	2XP	FG	FGA	SAF	Pts
1946	**NY**	**AA**	2	0		0	0	0	12
1947			1	0		0	0	0	6
1948	**CHI**	**AA**	1	0		0	0	0	6
Career			4	0		0	0	0	24

Ricky Proehl

Year	Team	Lg	TD	1XP	2XP	FG	FGA	SAF	Pts
1990	**PHX**	**N**	4	0		0	0	0	24
1991			2	0		0	0	0	12
1992			3	0		0	0	0	18
1993			7	0		0	0	0	42
1994	**ARI**	**N**	5	0	0	0	0	0	30
1996	**SEA**	**N**	2	0	0	0	0	0	12
Career			23	0	0	0	0	0	138

Joe Profit

Year	Team	Lg	TD	1XP	2XP	FG	FGA	SAF	Pts
1971	**ATL**	**N**	1	0		0	0	0	6
1973			2	0		0	0	0	12
Career			3	0		0	0	0	18

Eddie Prokop

Year	Team	Lg	TD	1XP	2XP	FG	FGA	SAF	Pts
1946	**NY**	**AA**	3	0		0	0	0	18
1947			5	0		0	0	0	30
1948	**CHI**	**AA**	4	0		0	0	0	24
1949	**B-NY**	**AA**	2	0		0	0	0	12
Career			14	0		0	0	0	84

Joe Prokop

Year	Team	Lg	TD	1XP	2XP	FG	FGA	SAF	Pts
1989	**NYJ**	**N**	1	0		0	0	0	6

Greg Pruitt

Year	Team	Lg	TD	1XP	2XP	FG	FGA	SAF	Pts
1973	**CLE**	**N**	5	0		0	0	0	30
1974			5	0		0	0	0	30
1975			9	0		0	0	0	54
1976			5	0		0	0	0	30
1977			4	0		0	0	0	24
1978			5	0		0	0	0	30
1979			1	0		0	0	0	6
1980			5	0		0	0	0	30
1981			4	0		0	0	0	24
1982	**LARI**	**N**	1	0		0	0	0	6
1983			3	0		0	0	0	18
Career			47	0		0	0	0	282

James Pruitt

Year	Team	Lg	TD	1XP	2XP	FG	FGA	SAF	Pts
1986	**MIA**	**N**	3	0		0	0	0	18

James Pruitt *continued*

Year	Team		TD	1XP	2XP	FG	FGA	SAF	Pts
1987			3	0		0	0	0	18
1989	IND	N	1	0		0	0	0	6
1990	MIA	N	3	0		0	0	0	18
Career			10	0		0	0	0	60

Mike Pruitt

Year	Team		TD	1XP	2XP	FG	FGA	SAF	Pts
1977	CLE	N	1	0		0	0	0	6
1978			5	0		0	0	0	30
1979			11	0		0	0	0	66
1980			6	0		0	0	0	36
1981			8	0		0	0	0	48
1982			3	0		0	0	0	18
1983			12	0		0	0	0	72
1984			6	0		0	0	0	36
1985	KC	N	2	0		0	0	0	12
1986			2	0		0	0	0	12
Career			56	0		0	0	0	336

Jim Psaltis

Year	Team		TD	1XP	2XP	FG	FGA	SAF	Pts
1955	CHIC	N	1	0		0	0	0	6

Jethro Pugh

Year	Team		TD	1XP	2XP	FG	FGA	SAF	Pts
1967	DAL	N	0	0		0	0	1	2
1968			0	0		0	0	1	2
Career			0	0		0	0	2	4

Marion Pugh

Year	Team		TD	1XP	2XP	FG	FGA	SAF	Pts
1941	NYG	N	0	0		0	0	0	0
1946	MIA	AA	2	0		0	0	0	12
Career			2	0		0	0	0	12

Alfred Pupunu

Year	Team		TD	1XP	2XP	FG	FGA	SAF	Pts
1994	SD	N	2	0	0	0	0	0	12
1996			1	0	0	0	0	0	6
Career			3	0	0	0	0	0	18
Playoffs			2	0	1	0	0	0	14

Mike Purdy

Year	Team		TD	1XP	2XP	FG	FGA	SAF	Pts
1922	MIL	N	1	0		0		0	6

Pid Purdy

Year	Team		TD	1XP	2XP	FG	FGA	SAF	Pts
1926	GB	N	0	14		2		0	20
1927			1	1		1		0	10
Career			1	15		3		0	30

Dave Pureifory

Year	Team		TD	1XP	2XP	FG	FGA	SAF	Pts
1975	GB	N	0	2		0	0	1	4

Johnny Pyeatt

Year	Team		TD	1XP	2XP	FG	FGA	SAF	Pts
1960	DEN	A	1	0	0	0	0	0	6

Bob Pylman

Year	Team		TD	1XP	2XP	FG	FGA	SAF	Pts
1938	PHI	N	1	0		0		0	6

Jeff Queen

Year	Team		TD	1XP	2XP	FG	FGA	SAF	Pts
1970	SD	N	2	0		0	0	0	12
1971			7	0		0	0	0	42
1974	HOU	N	1	0		0	0	0	6
Career			10	0		0	0	0	60

Jeff Query

Year	Team		TD	1XP	2XP	FG	FGA	SAF	Pts
1989	GB	N	2	0		0	0	0	12
1990			3	0		0	0	0	18
1992	CIN	N	3	0		0	0	0	18
1993			4	0		0	0	0	24
Career			12	0		0	0	0	72

Mike Quick

Year	Team		TD	1XP	2XP	FG	FGA	SAF	Pts
1982	PHI	N	1	0		0	0	0	6
1983			13	0		0	0	0	78
1984			9	0		0	0	0	54
1985			11	0		0	0	0	66
1986			9	0		0	0	0	54
1987			11	0		0	0	0	66
1988			4	0		0	0	0	24
1989			2	0		0	0	0	12
1990			1	0		0	0	0	6
Career			61	0		0	0	0	366

Frank Quillen

Year	Team		TD	1XP	2XP	FG	FGA	SAF	Pts
1946	CHI	AA	2	0		0	0	0	12
1947			1	0		0	0	0	6
Career			3	0		0	0	0	18

Skeets Quinlan

Year	Team		TD	1XP	2XP	FG	FGA	SAF	Pts
1952	LA	N	3	0		0	0	0	18
1953			6	0		0	0	0	36
1954			6	0		0	0	0	36
1955			1	0		0	0	0	6
Career			16	0		0	0	0	96
Playoffs			1	0		0	0	0	6

Ed Quirk

Year	Team		TD	1XP	2XP	FG	FGA	SAF	Pts
1948	WAS	N	4	0		0	0	0	24
1949			1	0		0	0	0	6
Career			5	0		0	0	0	30

Warren Rabb

Year	Team		TD	1XP	2XP	FG	FGA	SAF	Pts
1961	BUF	A	0	0	1	0	0	0	2
1962			3	0	1	0	0	0	20
Career			3	0	2	0	0	0	22

Frank Racis

Year	Team		TD	1XP	2XP	FG	FGA	SAF	Pts
1926	POT	N	1	0		0		0	6
1927			1	0		0		0	6
1930	PRO	N	1	0		0		0	6
Career			3	0		0		0	18

George Radachowsky

Year	Team		TD	1XP	2XP	FG	FGA	SAF	Pts
1989	NYJ	N	1	0		0	0	0	6

John Rade

Year	Team		TD	1XP	2XP	FG	FGA	SAF	Pts
1983	ATL	N	1	0		0	0	0	6
1985			1	0		0	0	0	6
Career			2	0		0	0	0	12

Scott Radecic

Year	Team		TD	1XP	2XP	FG	FGA	SAF	Pts
1984	KC	N	1	0		0	0	0	6

Bill Rademacher

Year	Team		TD	1XP	2XP	FG	FGA	SAF	Pts
1969	BOS	A	3	0	0	0	0	0	18

Vic Radzevich

Year	Team		TD	1XP	2XP	FG	FGA	SAF	Pts
1926	HAR	N	0	2		1		0	5

Mike Rae

Year	Team		TD	1XP	2XP	FG	FGA	SAF	Pts
1976	OAK	N	1	0		0	0	0	6
1977			1	0		0	0	0	6
Career			2	0		0	0	0	12

George Ragsdale

Year	Team		TD	1XP	2XP	FG	FGA	SAF	Pts
1978	TB	N	2	0		0	0	0	12

Pat Ragusa

Year	Team		TD	1XP	2XP	FG	FGA	SAF	Pts
1987	NYJ	N	0	7		2	4	0	13

Steve Raible

Year	Team		TD	1XP	2XP	FG	FGA	SAF	Pts
1976	SEA	N	2	0		0	0	0	12
1978			1	0		0	0	1	8
1979			1	0		0	0	0	6
Career			4	0		0	0	1	26

Larry Rakestraw

Year	Team		TD	1XP	2XP	FG	FGA	SAF	Pts
1967	CHI	N	2	0		0	0	0	12

Derrick Ramsey

Year	Team		TD	1XP	2XP	FG	FGA	SAF	Pts
1979	OAK	N	3	0		0	0	0	18
1981			4	0		0	0	0	24
1983	NE	N	6	0		0	0	0	36
1984			7	0		0	0	0	42
1985			1	0		0	0	0	6
Career			21	0		0	0	0	126
Playoffs			1	0		0	0	0	6

Garrard Ramsey

Year	Team		TD	1XP	2XP	FG	FGA	SAF	Pts
1949	CHIC	N	0	0		0	0	1	2

Herschel Ramsey

Year	Team		TD	1XP	2XP	FG	FGA	SAF	Pts
1938	PHI	N	1	0		0	0	0	6
1939			1	0		0	0	0	6
Career			2	0		0	0	0	12

Nate Ramsey

Year	Team		TD	1XP	2XP	FG	FGA	SAF	Pts
1969	PHI	N	1	0		0	0	0	6

Ray Ramsey

Year	Team		TD	1XP	2XP	FG	FGA	SAF	Pts
1947	CHI	AA	10	0		0	0	0	60
1948	BKN	AA	3	0		0	0	0	18

Ray Ramsey *continued*

Year	Team		TD	1XP	2XP	FG	FGA	SAF	Pts
1949	CHI	AA	4	0		0	0	0	24
1953	CHIC	N	1	0		0	0	0	6
Career			18	0		0	0	0	108

Steve Ramsey

Year	Team		TD	1XP	2XP	FG	FGA	SAF	Pts
1972	DEN	N	2	0		0	0	0	12

Tom Ramsey

Year	Team		TD	1XP	2XP	FG	FGA	SAF	Pts
1987	NE	N	1	0		0	0	0	6

Eason Ramson

Year	Team		TD	1XP	2XP	FG	FGA	SAF	Pts
1978	STL	N	1	0		0	0	0	6
1980	SF	N	2	0		0	0	0	12
1983			1	0		0	0	0	6
1985	BUF	N	1	0		0	0	0	6
Career			5	0		0	0	0	30

Proc Randels

Year	Team		TD	1XP	2XP	FG	FGA	SAF	Pts
1927	CLE	N	2	0		0		0	12
1928	DET	N	1	0		0		0	6
Career			3	0		0		0	18

Sonny Randle

Year	Team		TD	1XP	2XP	FG	FGA	SAF	Pts
1959	CHIC	N	1	0		0	0	0	6
1960	STL	N	**15**	0		0	0	0	90
1961			9	0		0	0	0	54
1962			7	0		0	0	0	42
1963			12	0		0	0	0	72
1964			5	0		0	0	0	30
1965			9	0		0	0	0	54
1966			2	0		0	0	0	12
1967	SF	N	4	0		0	0	0	24
1968			1	0		0	0	0	6
Career			65	0		0	0	0	390

Tate Randle

Year	Team		TD	1XP	2XP	FG	FGA	SAF	Pts
1985	IND	N	0	0		0	0	1	2

Al Randolph

Year	Team		TD	1XP	2XP	FG	FGA	SAF	Pts
1966	SF	N	1	0		0	0	0	6
1970			0	0		0	0	1	2
Career			1	0		0	0	1	8

Keith Ranspot

Year	Team		TD	1XP	2XP	FG	FGA	SAF	Pts
1942	GB	N	1	0		0	0	0	6
1944	BOS	N	3	0		0	1	0	18
Career			4	0		0	1	0	24

Bob Rapp

Year	Team		TD	1XP	2XP	FG	FGA	SAF	Pts
1922	COL	N	1	0		0		0	6
1923			5	0		0		0	30
1924			5	0		0		0	30
1925			2	0		0		0	12
1926			0	0		0		0	0
Career			13	0		0		0	78

Herb Rapp

Year	Team		TD	1XP	2XP	FG	FGA	SAF	Pts
1931	SI	N	0	0		0		1	2

Walter Rasby

Year	Team		TD	1XP	2XP	FG	FGA	SAF	Pts
1995	CAR	N	0	0	1	0	0	0	2

Ahmad Rashad

Year	Team		TD	1XP	2XP	FG	FGA	SAF	Pts
1972	STL	N	3	0		0	0	0	18
1973			3	0		0	0	0	18
1974	BUF	N	6	0		0	0	0	36
1976	MIN	N	3	0		0	0	0	18
1977			2	0		0	0	0	12
1978			8	0		0	0	0	48
1979			9	0		0	0	0	54
1980			5	0		0	0	0	30
1981			7	0		0	0	0	42
Career			46	0		0	0	0	276
Playoffs			1	0		0	0	0	6

Kenyon Rasheed

Year	Team		TD	1XP	2XP	FG	FGA	SAF	Pts
1993	NYG	N	1	0		0	0	0	6

Randy Rasmussen

Year	Team		TD	1XP	2XP	FG	FGA	SAF	Pts
1972	NYJ	N	1	0		0	0	0	6

Wayne Rasmussen

Year	Team		TD	1XP	2XP	FG	FGA	SAF	Pts
1965	DET	N	2	0		0	0	0	12

Bo Rather

Year	Team		TD	1XP	2XP	FG	FGA	SAF	Pts
1974	CHI	N	3	0		0	0	0	18
1975			2	0		0	0	0	12
1977			2	0		0	0	0	12
Career			7	0		0	0	0	42

Tom Rathman

Year	Team		TD	1XP	2XP	FG	FGA	SAF	Pts
1986	SF	N	1	0		0	0	0	6
1987			4	0		0	0	0	24
1988			2	0		0	0	0	12
1989			2	0		0	0	0	12
1990			7	0		0	0	0	42
1991			6	0		0	0	0	36
1992			9	0		0	0	0	54
1993			3	0		0	0	0	18
Career			34	0		0	0	0	204
Playoffs			5	0		0	0	0	30

George Ratterman

Year	Team		TD	1XP	2XP	FG	FGA	SAF	Pts
1947	BUF	AA	1	0		0	0	0	6
1948			3	0		0	0	0	18
1949			4	0		0	0	0	24
1950	NYY	N	3	0		0	0	0	18
1954	CLE	N	1	0		0	0	0	6
1955			1	0		0	0	0	6
1956			1	0		0	0	0	6
Career			14	0		0	0	0	84

John Rauch

Year	Team		TD	1XP	2XP	FG	FGA	SAF	Pts
1949	NYB	N	1	0		0	0	0	6

Bob Ravensburg

Year	Team		TD	1XP	2XP	FG	FGA	SAF	Pts
1949	CHIC	N	3	0		0	0	0	18

Darrol Ray

Year	Team		TD	1XP	2XP	FG	FGA	SAF	Pts
1980	NYJ	N	2	0		0	0	0	12
1981			2	0		0	0	0	12
Career			4	0		0	0	0	24
Playoffs			1	0		0	0	0	6

David Ray

Year	Team		TD	1XP	2XP	FG	FGA	SAF	Pts
1970	LA	N	0	34		29	45	0	121
1971			0	37		18	29	0	91
1972			0	31		24	41	0	103
1973			0	40		**30**	**47**	0	**130**
1974			0	25		9	16	0	52
Career			0	167		110	178	0	497
Playoffs			0	3		6	11	0	21

Eddie Ray

Year	Team		TD	1XP	2XP	FG	FGA	SAF	Pts
1973	ATL	N	11	0		0	0	0	66

Corey Raymond

Year	Team		TD	1XP	2XP	FG	FGA	SAF	Pts
1996	DET	N	1	0	0	0	0	0	6

Frank Reagan

Year	Team		TD	1XP	2XP	FG	FGA	SAF	Pts
1941	NYG	N	4	0		0	0	0	24
1946			2	0		0	0	0	12
1949	PHI	N	1	0		0	0	0	6
1950			1	0		0	0	0	6
Career			8	0		0	0	0	48

Tommy Reamon

Year	Team		TD	1XP	2XP	FG	FGA	SAF	Pts
1976	KC	N	5	0		0	0	0	30

Gary Reasons

Year	Team		TD	1XP	2XP	FG	FGA	SAF	Pts
1989	NYG	N	0	0		0	0	1	2

John Reaves

Year	Team		TD	1XP	2XP	FG	FGA	SAF	Pts
1972	PHI	N	1	0		0	0	0	6
1975	CIN	N	2	0		0	0	0	12
Career			3	0		0	0	0	18

Ken Reaves

Year	Team		TD	1XP	2XP	FG	FGA	SAF	Pts
1968	ATL	N	1	0		0	0	0	6

Paul Rebseaman

Year	Team		TD	1XP	2XP	FG	FGA	SAF	Pts
1927	POT	N	1	0		0		0	6

Bert Rechichar

Year	Team		TD	1XP	2XP	FG	FGA	SAF	Pts
1953	BAL	N	3	0		5	13	0	33
1954			0	1		6	13	0	19
1955			0	25		10	**24**	0	55
1956			0	8		3	13	0	17

Bert Rechichar *continued*

Year	Team		TD	1XP	2XP	FG	FGA	SAF	Pts
1957			0	22		3	13	0	31
1958			1	0		1	4	0	9
1959			0	0		0	1	0	0
1960	PIT	N	0	6		3	7	0	15
Career			4	62		31	88	0	179
Playoffs			0	0		0	1	0	0

Barry Redden

Year	Team		TD	1XP	2XP	FG	FGA	SAF	Pts
1983	LARM	N	2	0		0	0	0	12
1986			5	0		0	0	0	30
1988	SD	N	3	0		0	0	0	18
1989	CLE	N	1	0		0	0	0	6
Career			11	0		0	0	0	66

Gus Redman

Year	Team		TD	1XP	2XP	FG	FGA	SAF	Pts
1922	DAY	N	1	0		0		0	6
1924			0	0		0		0	0
Career			1	0		0		0	6

Rick Redman

Year	Team		TD	1XP	2XP	FG	FGA	SAF	Pts
1966	SD	A	1	0	0	0	0	0	6

Rudy Redmond

Year	Team		TD	1XP	2XP	FG	FGA	SAF	Pts
1972	DET	N	1	0		0	0	0	6

Beasley Reece

Year	Team		TD	1XP	2XP	FG	FGA	SAF	Pts
1981	NYG	N	1	0		0	0	0	6

Danny Reece

Year	Team		TD	1XP	2XP	FG	FGA	SAF	Pts
1976	TB	N	1	0		0	0	0	6

Don Reece

Year	Team		TD	1XP	2XP	FG	FGA	SAF	Pts
1946	MIA	AA	2	0		0	0	0	12

Alvin Reed

Year	Team		TD	1XP	2XP	FG	FGA	SAF	Pts
1967	HOU	A	1	0	0	0	0	0	6
1968			5	0	0	0	0	0	30
1969			2	0	0	0	0	0	12
1970	HOU	N	2	0		0	0	0	12
1971			1	0		0	0	0	6
1974	WAS	N	1	0		0	0	0	6
1975			2	0		0	0	0	12
Career			14	0	0	0	0	0	84
Playoffs			1	0	0	0	0	0	6

Andre Reed

Year	Team		TD	1XP	2XP	FG	FGA	SAF	Pts
1985	BUF	N	5	0		0	0	0	30
1986			7	0		0	0	0	42
1987			5	0		0	0	0	30
1988			6	0		0	0	0	36
1989			9	0		0	0	0	54
1990			8	0		0	0	0	48
1991			10	0		0	0	0	60
1992			3	0		0	0	0	18
1993			6	0		0	0	0	36
1994			8	0	0	0	0	0	48
1995			3	0	0	0	0	0	18
1996			6	0	0	0	0	0	36
Career			76	0	0	0	0	0	456
Playoffs			9	0	0	0	0	0	54

Bob Reed

Year	Team		TD	1XP	2XP	FG	FGA	SAF	Pts
1962	MIN	N	1	0		0	0	0	6

Dick Reed

Year	Team		TD	1XP	2XP	FG	FGA	SAF	Pts
1926	LA	A	0	4		2		0	10

Frank Reed

Year	Team		TD	1XP	2XP	FG	FGA	SAF	Pts
1978	ATL	N	0	0		0	0	1	2
1980			1	0		0	0	0	6
Career			1	0		0	0	1	8

Jake Reed

Year	Team		TD	1XP	2XP	FG	FGA	SAF	Pts
1994	MIN	N	4	0	0	0	0	0	24
1995			9	0	0	0	0	0	54
1996			7	0	0	0	0	0	42
Career			20	0	0	0	0	0	120

Joe Reed

Year	Team		TD	1XP	2XP	FG	FGA	SAF	Pts
1975	DET	N	1	0		0	0	0	6
1976			1	0		0	0	0	6
Career			2	0		0	0	0	12

J.T. Reed

Year	Team		TD	1XP	2XP	FG	FGA	SAF	Pts
1937	CHIC	N	1	0		0		0	6

Max Reed

Year	Team		TD	1XP	2XP	FG	FGA	SAF	Pts
1926	FRA	N	1	0		0		0	6

Oscar Reed

Year	Team		TD	1XP	2XP	FG	FGA	SAF	Pts
1969	MIN	N	3	0		0	0	0	18
1970			1	0		0	0	0	6
1971			1	0		0	0	0	6
1972			2	0		0	0	0	12
1973			3	0		0	0	0	18
1974			1	0		0	0	0	6
Career			11	0		0	0	0	66

Tony Reed

Year	Team		TD	1XP	2XP	FG	FGA	SAF	Pts
1977	KC	N	2	0		0	0	0	12
1978			6	0		0	0	0	36
1979			1	0		0	0	0	6
1980			1	0		0	0	0	6
Career			10	0		0	0	0	60

Archie Reese

Year	Team		TD	1XP	2XP	FG	FGA	SAF	Pts
1982	LARI	N	1	0		0	0	0	6

Dave Reese

Year	Team		TD	1XP	2XP	FG	FGA	SAF	Pts
1920	DAY	A	3	0		0		0	18
1921			1	0		0		0	6
Career			4	0		0		0	24

Don Reese

Year	Team		TD	1XP	2XP	FG	FGA	SAF	Pts
1975	MIA	N	0	0		0	0	1	2
1980	NO	N	1	0		0	0	0	6
Career			1	0		0	0	1	8

Hank Reese

Year	Team		TD	1XP	2XP	FG	FGA	SAF	Pts
1935	PHI	N	0	4		1		0	7
1936			0	3		2		0	9
1937			0	3		0		0	3
1938			0	10		1	6	0	13
1939			0	1		2	4	0	7
Career			0	21		6	10	0	39

Lloyd Reese

Year	Team		TD	1XP	2XP	FG	FGA	SAF	Pts
1946	CHIB	N	2	0		0	0	0	12

Bryan Reeves

Year	Team		TD	1XP	2XP	FG	FGA	SAF	Pts
1994	ARI	N	1	0	0	0	0	0	6

Dan Reeves

Year	Team		TD	1XP	2XP	FG	FGA	SAF	Pts
1965	DAL	N	3	0		0	0	0	18
1966			**16**	0		0	0	0	96
1967			11	0		0	0	0	66
1968			5	0		0	0	0	30
1969			5	0		0	0	0	30
1970			2	0		0	0	0	12
1971			0	1		0	0	0	1
Career			42	1		0	0	0	253
Playoffs			1	0		0	0	0	6

Walter Reeves

Year	Team		TD	1XP	2XP	FG	FGA	SAF	Pts
1993	PHX	N	1	0		0	0	0	6
1994	CLE	N	1	0	0	0	0	0	6
1995			1	0	0	0	0	0	6
Career			3	0	0	0	0	0	18

John Reger

Year	Team		TD	1XP	2XP	FG	FGA	SAF	Pts
1957	PIT	N	1	0		0	0	0	6
1964	WAS	N	1	0		0	0	0	6
1966			1	0		0	0	0	6
Career			3	0		0	0	0	18

Bill Reichardt

Year	Team		TD	1XP	2XP	FG	FGA	SAF	Pts
1952	GB	N	1	5		5	20	0	26

Lou Reichel

Year	Team		TD	1XP	2XP	FG	FGA	SAF	Pts
1926	COL	N	0	2		0		0	2

Jerry Reichow

Year	Team		TD	1XP	2XP	FG	FGA	SAF	Pts
1956	DET	N	1	0		0	0	0	6
1957			3	0		0	0	0	18
1959			1	0		0	0	0	6
1961	MIN	N	11	0		0	0	0	66
1962			3	0		0	0	0	18

Jerry Reichow *continued*

Year	Team		TD	1XP	2XP	FG	FGA	SAF	Pts
1963			3	0		0	0	0	18
1964			2	0		0	0	0	12
Career			24	0		0	0	0	144

Floyd Reid

Year	Team		TD	1XP	2XP	FG	FGA	SAF	Pts
1950	GB	N	3	0		0	0	0	18
1952			4	0		0	0	0	24
1953			3	0		0	0	0	18
1954			5	0		0	0	0	30
1955			3	0		0	0	0	18
Career			18	0		0	0	0	108

Mike Reilly

Year	Team		TD	1XP	2XP	FG	FGA	SAF	Pts
1969	MIN	N	1	0		0	0	0	6

Mike Reinfeldt

Year	Team		TD	1XP	2XP	FG	FGA	SAF	Pts
1982	HOU	N	1	0		0	0	0	6

Billy Reinhard

Year	Team		TD	1XP	2XP	FG	FGA	SAF	Pts
1947	LA	AA	1	0		0	0	0	6
1948			2	0		0	0	0	12
Career			3	0		0	0	0	18

Bob Reinhard

Year	Team		TD	1XP	2XP	FG	FGA	SAF	Pts
1946	LA	AA	1	0		0	0	0	6
1947			1	0		0	0	0	6
1950	LA	N	1	0		0	0	0	6
Career			3	0		0	0	0	18

Bill Reissig

Year	Team		TD	1XP	2XP	FG	FGA	SAF	Pts
1938	BKN	N	0	0		2	2	0	6
1939			0	0		1	1	0	3
Career			0	0		3	3	0	9

Albie Reisz

Year	Team		TD	1XP	2XP	FG	FGA	SAF	Pts
1944	CLE	N	2	0		0	0	0	12

Johnny Rembert

Year	Team		TD	1XP	2XP	FG	FGA	SAF	Pts
1985	NE	N	1	0		0	0	0	6
1986			1	0		0	0	0	6
Career			2	0		0	0	0	12
Playoffs			1	0		0	0	0	6

Reggie Rembert

Year	Team		TD	1XP	2XP	FG	FGA	SAF	Pts
1991	CIN	N	1	0		0	0	0	6

Dick Renfro

Year	Team		TD	1XP	2XP	FG	FGA	SAF	Pts
1946	SF	AA	3	0		0	0	0	18

Mel Renfro

Year	Team		TD	1XP	2XP	FG	FGA	SAF	Pts
1964	DAL	N	2	0		0	0	0	12
1965			2	0		0	0	0	12
1966			1	0		0	0	0	6
1973			1	0		0	0	0	6
Career			6	0		0	0	0	36

Mike Renfro

Year	Team		TD	1XP	2XP	FG	FGA	SAF	Pts
1978	HOU	N	2	0		0	0	0	12
1979			2	0		0	0	0	12
1980			1	0		0	0	0	6
1981			1	0		0	0	0	6
1982			3	0		0	0	0	18
1983			2	0		0	0	0	12
1984	DAL	N	2	0		0	0	0	12
1985			8	0		0	0	0	48
1986			3	0		0	0	0	18
1987			4	0		0	0	0	24
Career			28	0		0	0	0	168
Playoffs			1	0		0	0	0	6

Ray Renfro

Year	Team		TD	1XP	2XP	FG	FGA	SAF	Pts
1953	CLE	N	9	0		0	0	0	54
1954			1	0		0	0	0	6
1955			8	0		0	0	0	48
1956			4	0		0	0	0	24
1957			6	0		0	0	0	36
1958			6	0		0	0	0	36
1959			6	0		0	0	0	36
1960			4	0		0	0	0	24
1961			6	0		0	0	0	36
1962			4	0		0	0	0	24
1963			1	0		0	0	0	6
Career			55	0		0	0	0	330
Playoffs			3	0		0	0	0	18

Neil Rengel

Year	Team		TD	1XP	2XP	FG	FGA	SAF	Pts
1930	FRA	N	0	0		0		0	0

Bobby Renn

Year	Team		TD	1XP	2XP	FG	FGA	SAF	Pts
1961	NY	A	1	0	0	0	0	0	6

Pug Rentner

Year	Team		TD	1XP	2XP	FG	FGA	SAF	Pts
1934	BOS	N	1	0		0		0	6
1935			2	1		0		0	13
1936			3	0		0		0	18
1937	CHIB	N	1	0		0		0	6
Career			7	1		0		0	43
Playoffs			1	0		0	0	0	6

Lance Rentzel

Year	Team		TD	1XP	2XP	FG	FGA	SAF	Pts
1965	MIN	N	1	0		0	0	0	6
1967	DAL	N	8	0		0	0	0	48
1968			6	0		0	0	0	36
1969			**13**	0		0	0	0	78
1970			5	0		0	0	0	30
1971	LA	N	6	0		0	0	0	36
1972			2	0		0	0	0	12
1974			1	0		0	0	0	6
Career			42	0		0	0	0	252
Playoffs			2	0		0	0	0	12

Joe Repko

Year	Team		TD	1XP	2XP	FG	FGA	SAF	Pts
1947	PIT	N	1	0		0	0	0	6

Pete Retzlaff

Year	Team		TD	1XP	2XP	FG	FGA	SAF	Pts
1958	PHI	N	2	0		0	0	0	12
1959			1	0		0	0	0	6
1960			5	0		0	0	0	30
1961			8	0		0	0	0	48
1962			3	0		0	0	0	18
1963			4	0		0	0	0	24
1964			8	0		0	0	0	48
1965			10	0		0	0	0	60
1966			6	0		0	0	0	36
Career			47	0		0	0	0	282

Fuad Reveiz

Year	Team		TD	1XP	2XP	FG	FGA	SAF	Pts
1985	MIA	N	0	50		22	27	0	116
1986			0	**52**		14	22	0	94
1987			0	28		9	11	0	55
1988			0	31		8	12	0	55
1990	SD-MIN	N	0	26		13	19	0	65
1991	MIN	N	0	34		17	24	0	85
1992			0	45		19	25	0	102
1993			0	27		26	35	0	105
1994			0	30	0	**34**	**39**	0	132
1995			0	44	0	26	36	0	122
Career			0	367	0	188	250	0	931
Playoffs			0	7	0	4	6	0	19

Bill Reynolds

Year	Team		TD	1XP	2XP	FG	FGA	SAF	Pts
1944	BKN	N	1	0		0	0	0	6

Billy Reynolds

Year	Team		TD	1XP	2XP	FG	FGA	SAF	Pts
1953	CLE	N	3	0		0	0	0	18
1954			2	0		0	0	0	12
1957			1	0		0	0	0	6
1958	PIT	N	1	0		0	0	0	6
1960	OAK	A	0	0	0	0	0	0	0
Career			7	0	0	0	0	0	42

Chuck Reynolds

Year	Team		TD	1XP	2XP	FG	FGA	SAF	Pts
1970	CLE	N	0	0		0	0	1	2

Jack Reynolds

Year	Team		TD	1XP	2XP	FG	FGA	SAF	Pts
1979	LA	N	1	0		0	0	0	6

M.C. Reynolds

Year	Team		TD	1XP	2XP	FG	FGA	SAF	Pts
1961	BUF	A	4	0	0	0	0	0	24

Ricky Reynolds

Year	Team		TD	1XP	2XP	FG	FGA	SAF	Pts
1989	TB	N	2	0		0	0	0	12
1992			1	0		0	0	0	6
1994	NE	N	2	0	0	0	0	0	12
Career			5	0	0	0	0	0	30

Tom Reynolds

Year	Team		TD	1XP	2XP	FG	FGA	SAF	Pts
1972	NE	N	2	0		0	0	0	12

Errict Rhett

Year	Team		TD	1XP	2XP	FG	FGA	SAF	Pts
1994	TB	N	7	0	1	0	0	0	44
1995			11	0	0	0	0	0	66
1996			4	0	0	0	0	0	24
Career			22	0	1	0	0	0	134

Ray Rhodes

Year	Team		TD	1XP	2XP	FG	FGA	SAF	Pts
1975	NYG	N	6	0		0	0	0	36
1976			1	0		0	0	0	6
Career			7	0		0	0	0	42

Jerry Rhome

Year	Team		TD	1XP	2XP	FG	FGA	SAF	Pts
1970	HOU	N	1	0		0	0	0	6

Paul Riblett

Year	Team		TD	1XP	2XP	FG	FGA	SAF	Pts
1932	BKN	N	1	0		0		0	6
1933			1	0		0		0	6
1934			1	0		0		0	6
Career			3	0		0		0	18

Benny Ricardo

Year	Team		TD	1XP	2XP	FG	FGA	SAF	Pts
1976	BUF-DET	N	0	21		11	18	0	54
1978	DET	N	0	32		20	28	0	92
1979			0	25		10	18	0	55
1980	NO	N	0	31		10	17	0	61
1981			0	24		13	25	0	63
1983	MIN	N	0	33		25	33	0	108
1984	SD	N	0	5		3	3	0	14
Career			0	171		92	142	0	447

Jim Ricca

Year	Team		TD	1XP	2XP	FG	FGA	SAF	Pts
1954	WAS	N	1	0		0	0	1	8

Allen Rice

Year	Team		TD	1XP	2XP	FG	FGA	SAF	Pts
1984	MIN	N	2	0		0	0	0	12
1985			4	0		0	0	0	24
1986			5	0		0	0	0	30
1987			2	0		0	0	0	12
1988			6	0		0	0	0	36
Career			19	0		0	0	0	114
Playoffs			1	0		0	0	0	6

Floyd Rice

Year	Team		TD	1XP	2XP	FG	FGA	SAF	Pts
1973	SD	N	1	0		0	0	0	6

Jerry Rice

Year	Team		TD	1XP	2XP	FG	FGA	SAF	Pts
1985	SF	N	4	0		0	0	0	24
1986			16	0		0	0	0	96
1987			**23**	0		0	0	0	**138**
1988			10	0		0	0	0	60
1989			17	0		0	0	0	102
1990			13	0		0	0	0	78
1991			14	0		0	0	0	84
1992			11	0		0	0	0	66
1993			**16**	0		0	0	0	96
1994			15	0	1	0	0	0	92
1995			17	0	1	0	0	0	104
1996			9	0	0	0	0	0	54
Career			**165**	0	2	0	0	0	994
Playoffs			18	0	0	0	0	0	108

Herb Rich

Year	Team		TD	1XP	2XP	FG	FGA	SAF	Pts
1950	BAL	N	2	0		0	0	0	12
1952	LA	N	1	0		0	0	0	6
1953			1	0		0	0	0	6
Career			4	0		0	0	0	24

Stanley Richard

Year	Team		TD	1XP	2XP	FG	FGA	SAF	Pts
1994	SD	N	2	0	0	0	0	0	12

Curvin Richards

Year	Team		TD	1XP	2XP	FG	FGA	SAF	Pts
1992	DAL	N	1	0		0	0	0	6

Golden Richards

Year	Team		TD	1XP	2XP	FG	FGA	SAF	Pts
1973	DAL	N	1	0		0	0	0	6
1974			5	0		0	0	0	30
1975			5	0		0	0	0	30
1976			3	0		0	0	0	18
1977			3	0		0	0	0	18
1979	CHI	N	1	0		0	0	0	6
Career			18	0		0	0	0	108
Playoffs			4	0		0	0	0	24

Kink Richards

Year	Team		TD	1XP	2XP	FG	FGA	SAF	Pts
1933	NYG	N	**7**	1		0		0	43

Kink Richards *continued*

Year	Team	Lg	TD	1XP	2XP	FG	FGA	SAF	Pts
1934			2	1		0		0	13
1935			4	1		1		0	28
1936			2	0		0		0	12
1937			3	0		0		0	18
1938			0	2		0		0	2
1939			1	0		0	0	0	6
Career			19	5		1	0	0	122

Perry Richards

Year	Team	Lg	TD	1XP	2XP	FG	FGA	SAF	Pts
1959	**CHIC**	**N**	1	0		0	0	0	6
1961	**BUF**	**A**	3	0	0	0	0	0	18
Career			4	0	0	0	0	0	24

Al Richardson

Year	Team	Lg	TD	1XP	2XP	FG	FGA	SAF	Pts
1980	**ATL**	**N**	1	0		0	0	0	6

Bucky Richardson

Year	Team	Lg	TD	1XP	2XP	FG	FGA	SAF	Pts
1994	**HOU**	**N**	1	0	0	0	0	0	6

Gloster Richardson

Year	Team	Lg	TD	1XP	2XP	FG	FGA	SAF	Pts
1967	**KC**	**A**	2	0	0	0	0	0	12
1968			6	0	0	0	0	0	36
1969			2	0	0	0	0	0	12
1970	**KC**	**N**	2	0		0	0	0	12
1971	**DAL**	**N**	3	0		0	0	0	18
1973	**CLE**	**N**	1	0		0	0	0	6
1974			2	0		0	0	0	12
Career			18	0	0	0	0	0	108
Playoffs			1	0	0	0	0	0	6

Jerry Richardson

Year	Team	Lg	TD	1XP	2XP	FG	FGA	SAF	Pts
1959	**BAL**	**N**	3	0		0	0	0	18
1960			1	0		0	0	0	6
Career			4	0		0	0	0	24
Playoffs			1	0		0	0	0	6

Mike Richardson

Year	Team	Lg	TD	1XP	2XP	FG	FGA	SAF	Pts
1969	**HOU**	**A**	0	0	1	0	0	0	2
1970	**HOU**	**N**	3	0		0	0	0	18
Career			3	0	1	0	0	0	20

Mike Richardson

Year	Team	Lg	TD	1XP	2XP	FG	FGA	SAF	Pts
1985	**CHI**	**N**	1	0		0	0	0	6

Tony Richardson

Year	Team	Lg	TD	1XP	2XP	FG	FGA	SAF	Pts
1996	**KC**	**N**	1	0	0	0	0	0	6

Willie Richardson

Year	Team	Lg	TD	1XP	2XP	FG	FGA	SAF	Pts
1965	**BAL**	**N**	1	0		0	0	0	6
1966			2	0		0	0	0	12
1967			8	0		0	0	0	48
1968			8	0		0	0	0	48
1969			3	0		0	0	0	18
1970	**MIA**	**N**	1	0		0	0	0	6
1971	**BAL**	**N**	2	0		0	0	0	12
Career			25	0		0	0	0	150
Playoffs			1	0		0	0	0	6

Les Richter

Year	Team	Lg	TD	1XP	2XP	FG	FGA	SAF	Pts
1954	**LA**	**N**	0	38		8	15	0	62
1955			0	30		13	**24**	0	69
1956			0	36		8	15	0	60
1959			0	0		0	1	0	0
1960			0	2		0	0	0	2
Career			0	106		29	55	0	193
Playoffs			0	2		0	0	0	2

Pat Richter

Year	Team	Lg	TD	1XP	2XP	FG	FGA	SAF	Pts
1963	**WAS**	**N**	3	0		0	0	0	18
1965			2	0		0	0	0	12
1968			9	0		0	0	0	54
Career			14	0		0	0	0	84

Harold Ricks

Year	Team	Lg	TD	1XP	2XP	FG	FGA	SAF	Pts
1987	**TB**	**N**	1	0		0	0	0	6

Louis Riddick

Year	Team	Lg	TD	1XP	2XP	FG	FGA	SAF	Pts
1993	**CLE**	**N**	0	0		0	0	1	2

Ray Riddick

Year	Team	Lg	TD	1XP	2XP	FG	FGA	SAF	Pts
1942	**GB**	**N**	1	0		0	0	0	6

Robb Riddick

Year	Team	Lg	TD	1XP	2XP	FG	FGA	SAF	Pts
1986	**BUF**	**N**	5	0		0	0	0	30

Robb Riddick *continued*

Year	Team	Lg	TD	1XP	2XP	FG	FGA	SAF	Pts
1987			8	0		0	0	1	50
1988			14	0		0	0	0	84
Career			27	0		0	0	1	164
Playoffs			1	0		0	0	0	6

Preston Ridlehuber

Year	Team	Lg	TD	1XP	2XP	FG	FGA	SAF	Pts
1966	**ATL**	**N**	2	0		0	0	0	12
1968	**OAK**	**A**	1	0	0	0	0	0	6
Career			3	0	0	0	0	0	18

Jimmy Ridlon

Year	Team	Lg	TD	1XP	2XP	FG	FGA	SAF	Pts
1964	**DAL**	**N**	2	0		0	0	0	12

Dick Rifenburg

Year	Team	Lg	TD	1XP	2XP	FG	FGA	SAF	Pts
1950	**DET**	**N**	1	0		0	0	0	6

Dick Riffle

Year	Team	Lg	TD	1XP	2XP	FG	FGA	SAF	Pts
1938	**PHI**	**N**	1	0		0		0	6
1940			5	0		0	0	0	30
1941	**PIT**	**N**	2	0		0	0	0	12
1942			4	1		0	0	0	25
Career			12	1		0	0	0	73

John Riggins

Year	Team	Lg	TD	1XP	2XP	FG	FGA	SAF	Pts
1971	**NYJ**	**N**	3	0		0	0	0	18
1972			8	0		0	0	0	48
1973			4	0		0	0	0	24
1974			7	0		0	0	0	42
1975			9	0		0	0	0	54
1976	**WAS**	**N**	4	0		0	0	0	24
1977			2	0		0	0	0	12
1978			5	0		0	0	0	30
1979			12	0		0	0	0	72
1981			13	0		0	0	0	78
1982			3	0		0	0	0	18
1983			**24**	0		0	0	0	144
1984			14	0		0	0	0	84
1985			8	0		0	0	0	48
Career			116	0		0	0	0	696
Playoffs			12	0		0	0	0	72

Bob Riggle

Year	Team	Lg	TD	1XP	2XP	FG	FGA	SAF	Pts
1966	**ATL**	**N**	1	0		0	0	0	6

Gerald Riggs

Year	Team	Lg	TD	1XP	2XP	FG	FGA	SAF	Pts
1982	**ATL**	**N**	5	0		0	0	0	30
1983			8	0		0	0	0	48
1984			13	0		0	0	0	78
1985			10	0		0	0	0	60
1986			9	0		0	0	0	54
1987			2	0		0	0	0	12
1988			1	0		0	0	0	6
1989	**WAS**	**N**	4	0		0	0	0	24
1990			6	0		0	0	0	36
1991			11	0		0	0	0	66
Career			69	0		0	0	0	414
Playoffs			6	0		0	0	0	36

Ken Riley

Year	Team	Lg	TD	1XP	2XP	FG	FGA	SAF	Pts
1975	**CIN**	**N**	1	0		0	0	0	6
1976			1	0		0	0	0	6
1982			1	0		0	0	0	6
1983			2	0		0	0	0	12
Career			5	0		0	0	0	30

Preston Riley

Year	Team	Lg	TD	1XP	2XP	FG	FGA	SAF	Pts
1972	**SF**	**N**	1	0		0	0	0	6

Bill Ring

Year	Team	Lg	TD	1XP	2XP	FG	FGA	SAF	Pts
1981	**SF**	**N**	1	0		0	0	0	6
1982			1	0		0	0	0	6
1983			2	0		0	0	0	12
1984			3	0		0	0	0	18
1985			1	0		0	0	0	6
Career			8	0		0	0	0	48
Playoffs			1	0		0	0	0	6

Alan Risher

Year	Team	Lg	TD	1XP	2XP	FG	FGA	SAF	Pts
1987	**GB**	**N**	1	0		0	0	0	6

Elliot Risley

Year	Team	Lg	TD	1XP	2XP	FG	FGA	SAF	Pts
1921	**HAM**	**A**	0	2		0		0	2

Andre Rison

Year	Team	Lg	TD	1XP	2XP	FG	FGA	SAF	Pts
1989	**IND**	**N**	4	0		0	0	0	24
1990	**ATL**	**N**	10	0		0	0	0	60
1991			12	0		0	0	0	72
1992			11	0		0	0	0	66
1993			15	0		0	0	0	90
1994			8	0	1	0	0	0	50
1995	**CLE**	**N**	3	0	0	0	0	0	18
1996	**JAC-GB**	**N**	3	0	0	0	0	0	18
Career			66	0	1	0	0	0	398
Playoffs			3	0	0	0	0	0	18

Del Ritchhart

Year	Team	Lg	TD	1XP	2XP	FG	FGA	SAF	Pts
1936	**DET**	**N**	1	0		0		0	6

Ron Rivera

Year	Team	Lg	TD	1XP	2XP	FG	FGA	SAF	Pts
1985	**CHI**	**N**	1	0		0	0	0	6

Reggie Rivers

Year	Team	Lg	TD	1XP	2XP	FG	FGA	SAF	Pts
1992	**DEN**	**N**	4	0		0	0	0	24
1993			2	0		0	0	1	14
1994			2	0	0	0	0	0	12
Career			8	0	0	0	0	1	50

Ron Rivers

Year	Team	Lg	TD	1XP	2XP	FG	FGA	SAF	Pts
1995	**DET**	**N**	1	0	0	0	0	0	6
Playoffs			1	0	1	0	0	0	8

John Roach

Year	Team	Lg	TD	1XP	2XP	FG	FGA	SAF	Pts
1960	**STL**	**N**	1	0		0	0	0	6
1961	**GB**	**N**	1	0		0	0	0	6
Career			2	0		0	0	0	12

Rollin Roach

Year	Team	Lg	TD	1XP	2XP	FG	FGA	SAF	Pts
1927	**CHIC**	**N**	1	0		0		0	6

Carl Roaches

Year	Team	Lg	TD	1XP	2XP	FG	FGA	SAF	Pts
1981	**HOU**	**N**	1	0		0	0	0	6
1983			1	0		0	0	0	6
Career			2	0		0	0	0	12

Oscar Roan

Year	Team	Lg	TD	1XP	2XP	FG	FGA	SAF	Pts
1975	**CLE**	**N**	3	0		0	0	0	18
1976			4	0		0	0	0	24
1977			2	0		0	0	0	12
Career			9	0		0	0	0	54

Harry Robb

Year	Team	Lg	TD	1XP	2XP	FG	FGA	SAF	Pts
1921	**CAN**	**A**	1	0		0		0	6
1922	**CAN**	**N**	3	0		0		0	18
1923			1	0		0		0	6
1925			3	0		0		0	18
1926			2	1		0		0	13
Career			10	1		0		0	61

Stan Robb

Year	Team	Lg	TD	1XP	2XP	FG	FGA	SAF	Pts
1926	**CAN**	**N**	1	0		0		0	6

Austin Robbins

Year	Team	Lg	TD	1XP	2XP	FG	FGA	SAF	Pts
1995	**OAK**	**N**	1	0	0	0	0	0	6

Randy Robbins

Year	Team	Lg	TD	1XP	2XP	FG	FGA	SAF	Pts
1984	**DEN**	**N**	1	0		0	0	0	6
1989			1	0		0	0	0	6
Career			2	0		0	0	0	12

Bo Roberson

Year	Team	Lg	TD	1XP	2XP	FG	FGA	SAF	Pts
1961	**SD**	**A**	3	0	0	0	0	0	18
1962	**OAK**	**A**	7	0	1	0	0	0	44
1963			3	0	0	0	0	0	18
1964			1	0	0	0	0	0	6
1965	**BUF**	**A**	3	0	0	0	0	0	18
1966	**MIA**	**A**	2	0	0	0	0	0	12
Career			19	0	1	0	0	0	116

Alfredo Roberts

Year	Team	Lg	TD	1XP	2XP	FG	FGA	SAF	Pts
1989	**KC**	**N**	1	0		0	0	0	6
1991	**DAL**	**N**	1	0		0	0	0	6
Career			2	0		0	0	0	12

C.R. Roberts

Year	Team	Lg	TD	1XP	2XP	FG	FGA	SAF	Pts
1959	**SF**	**N**	1	0		0	0	0	6
1960			2	0		0	0	0	12
1961			1	0		0	0	0	6
Career			4	0		0	0	0	24

Gene Roberts

Year	Team	Lg	TD	1XP	2XP	FG	FGA	SAF	Pts
1947	**NYG**	**N**	1	0		0	0	0	6
1948			3	0		0	0	0	18
1949			**17**	0		0	0	0	**102**
1950			5	0		0	0	1	32
Career			26	0		0	0	1	158

Guy Roberts

Year	Team	Lg	TD	1XP	2XP	FG	FGA	SAF	Pts
1926	**CLE**	**A**	0	0		1		0	3

Jack Roberts

Year	Team	Lg	TD	1XP	2XP	FG	FGA	SAF	Pts
1933	**PHI**	**N**	1	0		0		0	6

Walt Roberts

Year	Team	Lg	TD	1XP	2XP	FG	FGA	SAF	Pts
1964	**CLE**	**N**	1	0		0	0	0	6
1965			4	0		0	0	0	24
1967	**NO**	**N**	5	0		0	0	0	30
1970	**WAS**	**N**	1	0		0	0	0	6
Career			11	0		0	0	0	66

Wooky Roberts

Year	Team	Lg	TD	1XP	2XP	FG	FGA	SAF	Pts
1922	**CAN**	**N**	1	0		0		0	6
1923			2	0		0		0	12
1924	**CLE**	**N**	3	1		0		0	19
1926	**FRA**	**N**	1	0		0		0	6
Career			7	1		0		0	43

Isiah Robertson

Year	Team	Lg	TD	1XP	2XP	FG	FGA	SAF	Pts
1973	**LA**	**N**	1	0		0	0	0	6
1975			1	0		0	0	0	6
1978			1	0		0	0	0	6
1979	**BUF**	**N**	1	0		0	0	0	6
Career			4	0		0	0	0	24
Playoffs			1	0		0	0	0	6

Jimmy Robertson

Year	Team	Lg	TD	1XP	2XP	FG	FGA	SAF	Pts
1925	**AKR**	**N**	2	1		0		0	13

Marcus Robertson

Year	Team	Lg	TD	1XP	2XP	FG	FGA	SAF	Pts
1993	**HOU**	**N**	1	0		0	0	0	6

Paul Robeson

Year	Team	Lg	TD	1XP	2XP	FG	FGA	SAF	Pts
1922	**MIL**	**N**	2	0		0		0	12

Bo Robinson

Year	Team	Lg	TD	1XP	2XP	FG	FGA	SAF	Pts
1979	**DET**	**N**	2	0		0	0	0	12
1982	**ATL**	**N**	2	0		0	0	0	12
1984	**NE**	**N**	1	0		0	0	0	6
Career			5	0		0	0	0	30

Charley Robinson

Year	Team	Lg	TD	1XP	2XP	FG	FGA	SAF	Pts
1954	**BAL**	**N**	1	0		0	0	0	6

Dave Robinson

Year	Team	Lg	TD	1XP	2XP	FG	FGA	SAF	Pts
1973	**WAS**	**N**	1	0		0	0	0	6

Eddie Robinson

Year	Team	Lg	TD	1XP	2XP	FG	FGA	SAF	Pts
1923	**HAM**	**N**	1	1		0		0	7
1925			1	0		0		0	6
Career			2	1		0		0	13

Eddie Robinson

Year	Team	Lg	TD	1XP	2XP	FG	FGA	SAF	Pts
1995	**HOU**	**N**	1	0	0	0	0	0	6

Eugene Robinson

Year	Team	Lg	TD	1XP	2XP	FG	FGA	SAF	Pts
1987	**SEA**	**N**	1	0		0	0	0	6
1990			1	0		0	0	0	6
Career			2	0		0	0	0	12

Greg Robinson

Year	Team	Lg	TD	1XP	2XP	FG	FGA	SAF	Pts
1993	**LARI**	**N**	1	0		0	0	0	6
1996	**STL**	**N**	1	0	0	0	0	0	6
Career			2	0	0	0	0	0	12

Jerry Robinson

Year	Team	Lg	TD	1XP	2XP	FG	FGA	SAF	Pts
1962	**SD**	**A**	3	0	0	0	0	0	18
1963			2	0	0	0	0	0	12
Career			5	0	0	0	0	0	30

Jerry Robinson

Year	Team	Lg	TD	1XP	2XP	FG	FGA	SAF	Pts
1980	**PHI**	**N**	1	0		0	0	0	6
1986	**LARI**	**N**	2	0		0	0	0	12
1990			1	0		0	0	0	6
Career			4	0		0	0	0	24

Jimmy Robinson

Year	Team	Lg	TD	1XP	2XP	FG	FGA	SAF	Pts
1976	**NYG**	**N**	1	0		0	0	0	6
1977			3	0		0	0	0	18
1978			2	0		0	0	0	12
Career			6	0		0	0	0	36

Johnnie Robinson

Year	Team	Lg	TD	1XP	2XP	FG	FGA	SAF	Pts
1966	**DET**	**N**	1	0		0	0	0	6

Johnny Robinson

Year	Team	Lg	TD	1XP	2XP	FG	FGA	SAF	Pts
1960	**DAL**	**A**	9	0	0	0	0	0	54
1961			7	0	0	0	0	0	42
1966	**KC**	**A**	1	0	0	0	0	0	6
1970	**KC**	**N**	1	0		0	0	0	6
Career			18	0	0	0	0	0	108

Johnny Robinson

Year	Team	Lg	TD	1XP	2XP	FG	FGA	SAF	Pts
1981	**OAK**	**N**	0	0		0	0	1	2

Matt Robinson

Year	Team	Lg	TD	1XP	2XP	FG	FGA	SAF	Pts
1979	**NYJ**	**N**	1	0		0	0	0	6
1980	**DEN**	**N**	3	0		0	0	0	18
Career			4	0		0	0	0	24

Paul Robinson

Year	Team	Lg	TD	1XP	2XP	FG	FGA	SAF	Pts
1968	**CIN**	**A**	9	0	0	0	0	0	54
1969			4	0	0	0	0	0	24
1970	**CIN**	**N**	7	0		0	0	0	42
1971			1	0		0	0	0	6
1972	**HOU**	**N**	3	0		0	0	0	18
1973			2	0		0	0	0	12
Career			26	0	0	0	0	0	156

Rex Robinson

Year	Team	Lg	TD	1XP	2XP	FG	FGA	SAF	Pts
1982	**NE**	**N**	0	5		1	2	0	8

Shelton Robinson

Year	Team	Lg	TD	1XP	2XP	FG	FGA	SAF	Pts
1983	**SEA**	**N**	2	0		0	0	0	12

Stacy Robinson

Year	Team	Lg	TD	1XP	2XP	FG	FGA	SAF	Pts
1986	**NYG**	**N**	2	0		0	0	0	12
1987			2	0		0	0	0	12
1988			3	0		0	0	0	18
Career			7	0		0	0	0	42

Virgil Robinson

Year	Team	Lg	TD	1XP	2XP	FG	FGA	SAF	Pts
1971	**NO**	**N**	2	0		0	0	0	12

Terry Robiskie

Year	Team	Lg	TD	1XP	2XP	FG	FGA	SAF	Pts
1977	**OAK**	**N**	1	0		0	0	0	6
1978			2	0		0	0	0	12
1980	**MIA**	**N**	2	0		0	0	0	12
Career			5	0		0	0	0	30

Marshall Robnett

Year	Team	Lg	TD	1XP	2XP	FG	FGA	SAF	Pts
1944	**C-P**	**N**	0	1		0	2	0	1

Andy Robustelli

Year	Team	Lg	TD	1XP	2XP	FG	FGA	SAF	Pts
1952	**LA**	**N**	2	0		0	0	0	12
1954			1	0		0	0	0	6
1955			2	0		0	0	0	12
1956	**NYG**	**N**	0	0		0	0	1	2
Career			5	0		0	0	1	32

Doug Roby

Year	Team	Lg	TD	1XP	2XP	FG	FGA	SAF	Pts
1923	**CLE**	**N**	1	1		0		0	7

Hank Rockwell

Year	Team	Lg	TD	1XP	2XP	FG	FGA	SAF	Pts
1940	**CLE**	**N**	1	0		0	0	0	6

Mirro Roder

Year	Team	Lg	TD	1XP	2XP	FG	FGA	SAF	Pts
1973	**CHI**	**N**	0	11		8	16	0	35
1974			0	17		9	13	0	44
1976	**TB**	**N**	0	0		0	3	0	0
Career			0	28		17	32	0	79

John Roderick

Year	Team	Lg	TD	1XP	2XP	FG	FGA	SAF	Pts
1966	**MIA**	**A**	1	0	0	0	0	0	6

Del Rodgers

Year	Team	Lg	TD	1XP	2XP	FG	FGA	SAF	Pts
1982	**GB**	**N**	3	0		0	0	0	18
1984			1	0		0	0	0	6
1987	**SF**	**N**	1	0		0	0	0	6
Career			5	0		0	0	0	30

Hosea Rodgers

Year	Team	Lg	TD	1XP	2XP	FG	FGA	SAF	Pts
1949	**LA**	**AA**	5	0		0	0	0	30

John Rodgers

Year	Team	Lg	TD	1XP	2XP	FG	FGA	SAF	Pts
1982	**PIT**	**N**	1	0		0	0	0	6

Willie Rodgers

Year	Team	Lg	TD	1XP	2XP	FG	FGA	SAF	Pts
1972	**HOU**	**N**	2	0		0	0	0	12
1974			5	0		0	0	0	30
1975			1	0		0	0	1	8
Career			8	0		0	0	1	50

Kelly Rodriguez

Year	Team	Lg	TD	1XP	2XP	FG	FGA	SAF	Pts
1930	**FRA**	**N**	0	0		0		0	0

Johnny Roepke

Year	Team	Lg	TD	1XP	2XP	FG	FGA	SAF	Pts
1928	**FRA**	**N**	1	1		1		0	10

Fritz Roessler

Year	Team	Lg	TD	1XP	2XP	FG	FGA	SAF	Pts
1922	**RAC**	**N**	1	0		0		0	6

John Rogalla

Year	Team	Lg	TD	1XP	2XP	FG	FGA	SAF	Pts
1945	**PHI**	**N**	0	1		0	0	0	1

Fran Rogel

Year	Team	Lg	TD	1XP	2XP	FG	FGA	SAF	Pts
1950	**PIT**	**N**	4	0		0	0	0	24
1951			3	0		0	0	0	18
1952			3	0		0	0	0	18
1953			2	0		0	0	0	12
1954			2	0		0	0	0	12
1955			2	0		0	0	0	12
1956			2	0		0	0	0	12
1957			1	0		0	0	0	6
Career			19	0		0	0	0	114

Charley Rogers

Year	Team	Lg	TD	1XP	2XP	FG	FGA	SAF	Pts
1927	**FRA**	**N**	4	0		0		0	24
1928			3	0		0		0	18
Career			7	0		0		0	42

Doug Rogers

Year	Team	Lg	TD	1XP	2XP	FG	FGA	SAF	Pts
Playoffs			1	0	0	0	0	0	6

George Rogers

Year	Team	Lg	TD	1XP	2XP	FG	FGA	SAF	Pts
1981	**NO**	**N**	13	0		0	0	0	78
1982			3	0		0	0	0	18
1983			5	0		0	0	0	30
1984			2	0		0	0	0	12
1985	**WAS**	**N**	7	0		0	0	0	42
1986			**18**	0		0	0	0	108
1987			6	0		0	0	0	36
Career			54	0		0	0	0	324
Playoffs			2	0		0	0	0	12

Jimmy Rogers

Year	Team	Lg	TD	1XP	2XP	FG	FGA	SAF	Pts
1980	**NO**	**N**	3	0		0	0	0	18
1982			2	0		0	0	0	12
Career			5	0		0	0	0	30

Tracy Rogers

Year	Team	Lg	TD	1XP	2XP	FG	FGA	SAF	Pts
1992	**KC**	**N**	1	0		0	0	0	6

George Rogge

Year	Team	Lg	TD	1XP	2XP	FG	FGA	SAF	Pts
1931	**CHIC**	**N**	1	0		0		0	6

George Rohleder

Year	Team	Lg	TD	1XP	2XP	FG	FGA	SAF	Pts
1925	**COL**	**N**	0	1		3		0	10
1926	**AKR**	**N**	0	2		1		0	5
Career			0	3		4		0	15

Herm Rohrig

Year	Team	Lg	TD	1XP	2XP	FG	FGA	SAF	Pts
1941	**GB**	**N**	0	1		1	1	0	4

John Rokisky

Year	Team	Lg	TD	1XP	2XP	FG	FGA	SAF	Pts
1946	**CLE**	**AA**	0	1		0	0	0	1
1947	**CHI**	**AA**	0	33		4	8	0	45
Career			0	34		4	8	0	46

Johnny Roland

Year	Team	Lg	TD	1XP	2XP	FG	FGA	SAF	Pts
1966	**STL**	**N**	6	0		0	0	0	36
1967			11	0		0	0	0	66
1968			2	0		0	0	0	12
1969			6	0		0	0	0	36
1970			5	0		0	0	0	30

Johnny Roland *continued*

Year	Team		TD	1XP	2XP	FG	FGA	SAF	Pts
1972			4	0		0	0	0	24
1973	NYG	N	2	0		0	0	0	12
Career			36	0		0	0	0	216

Butch Rolle

Year	Team		TD	1XP	2XP	FG	FGA	SAF	Pts
1987	BUF	N	2	0		0	0	0	12
1988			2	0		0	0	0	12
1989			1	0		0	0	0	6
1990			3	0		0	0	0	18
1991			2	0		0	0	0	12
1993	PHX	N	1	0		0	0	0	6
Career			11	0		0	0	0	66

Dave Rolle

Year	Team		TD	1XP	2XP	FG	FGA	SAF	Pts
1960	DEN	A	3	0	0	0	0	0	18

Nick Roman

Year	Team		TD	1XP	2XP	FG	FGA	SAF	Pts
1972	CLE	N	1	0		0	0	0	6

Steve Romanik

Year	Team		TD	1XP	2XP	FG	FGA	SAF	Pts
1951	CHIB	N	1	0		0	0	0	6
1953	CHIC	N	1	0		0	0	0	6
1954			1	0		0	0	0	6
Career			3	0		0	0	0	18

Rudy Romboli

Year	Team		TD	1XP	2XP	FG	FGA	SAF	Pts
1948	BOS	N	1	0		0	0	0	6

Stan Rome

Year	Team		TD	1XP	2XP	FG	FGA	SAF	Pts
1981	KC	N	1	0		0	0	0	6

Tony Romeo

Year	Team		TD	1XP	2XP	FG	FGA	SAF	Pts
1962	BOS	A	1	0	0	0	0	0	6
1963			2	0	0	0	0	0	12
1964			4	0	0	0	0	0	24
1965			2	0	0	0	0	0	12
1966			0	0	1	0	0	0	2
Career			9	0	1	0	0	0	56

Charles Romes

Year	Team		TD	1XP	2XP	FG	FGA	SAF	Pts
1978	BUF	N	1	0		0	0	0	6
1979			1	0		0	0	0	6
Career			2	0		0	0	0	12
Playoffs			1	0		0	0	0	6

Dick Romey

Year	Team		TD	1XP	2XP	FG	FGA	SAF	Pts
1926	CHI	A	1	0		0		0	6

Milt Romney

Year	Team		TD	1XP	2XP	FG	FGA	SAF	Pts
1923	RAC	N	1	0		0		0	6
1924			1	0		0		0	6
1926	CHIB	N	4	1		0		0	25
1927			1	0		0		0	6
1928			2	1		0		0	13
Career			9	2		0		0	56

Gene Ronzani

Year	Team		TD	1XP	2XP	FG	FGA	SAF	Pts
1933	CHIB	N	1	0		0		0	6
1934			3	0		0		0	18
1935			2	3		0		0	15
1936			2	0		0		0	12
1937			1	0		0		0	6
Career			9	3		0		0	57

Bill Rooney

Year	Team		TD	1XP	2XP	FG	FGA	SAF	Pts
1924	DUL	N	2	0		0		0	12
1925	NYG	N	1	0		0		0	6
Career			3	0		0		0	18

Cobb Rooney

Year	Team		TD	1XP	2XP	FG	FGA	SAF	Pts
1924	DUL	N	0	0		0		0	0
1926			1	0		0		0	6
1927			1	0		0		0	6
1929	CHIC	N	3	0		0		0	18
1930			1	0		0		0	6
Career			6	0		0		0	36

Joe Rooney

Year	Team		TD	1XP	2XP	FG	FGA	SAF	Pts
1923	DUL	N	1	0		0		0	6
1924			1	0		0		0	6
1925	RI	N	1	0		0		0	6
1926	DUL	N	1	0		0		0	6
1927			3	0		0		0	18

Joe Rooney *continued*

Year	Team		TD	1XP	2XP	FG	FGA	SAF	Pts
1928	POT	N	1	0		0		0	6
Career			8	0		0		0	48

Jim Root

Year	Team		TD	1XP	2XP	FG	FGA	SAF	Pts
1953	CHIC	N	1	0		0	0	0	6
1956			2	0		0	0	0	12
Career			3	0		0	0	0	18

Durwood Roquemore

Year	Team		TD	1XP	2XP	FG	FGA	SAF	Pts
1983	KC	N	1	0		0	0	0	6

Sal Rosato

Year	Team		TD	1XP	2XP	FG	FGA	SAF	Pts
1945	WAS	N	2	0		0	0	0	12
1946			2	0		0	0	0	12
1947			1	0		0	0	0	6
Career			5	0		0	0	0	30

Al Rose

Year	Team		TD	1XP	2XP	FG	FGA	SAF	Pts
1931	PRO	N	3	0		0		0	18
1932	GB	N	2	0		0		0	12
1933			1	0		0		0	6
1934			2	0		0		0	12
Career			8	0		0		0	48

Gene Rose

Year	Team		TD	1XP	2XP	FG	FGA	SAF	Pts
1929	CHIC	N	1	0		0		0	6
1930			4	1		0		0	25
Career			5	1		0		0	31

George Rose

Year	Team		TD	1XP	2XP	FG	FGA	SAF	Pts
1964	MIN	N	1	0		0	0	0	6

Joe Rose

Year	Team		TD	1XP	2XP	FG	FGA	SAF	Pts
1981	MIA	N	2	0		0	0	0	12
1982			2	0		0	0	0	12
1983			3	0		0	0	0	18
1984			2	0		0	0	0	12
1985			4	0		0	0	0	24
Career			13	0		0	0	0	78
Playoffs			2	0		0	0	0	12

Ken Rose

Year	Team		TD	1XP	2XP	FG	FGA	SAF	Pts
1992	PHI	N	1	0		0	0	0	6

Timm Rosenbach

Year	Team		TD	1XP	2XP	FG	FGA	SAF	Pts
1990	PHX	N	3	0		0	0	0	18

Ken Roskie

Year	Team		TD	1XP	2XP	FG	FGA	SAF	Pts
1948	GB	N	1	0		0	0	0	6

Alvin Ross

Year	Team		TD	1XP	2XP	FG	FGA	SAF	Pts
1987	PHI	N	1	0		0	0	0	6

Dan Ross

Year	Team		TD	1XP	2XP	FG	FGA	SAF	Pts
1979	CIN	N	1	0		0	0	0	6
1980			4	0		0	0	0	24
1981			5	0		0	0	0	30
1982			3	0		0	0	0	18
1983			3	0		0	0	0	18
1985	SEA	N	2	0		0	0	0	12
1986	GB	N	1	0		0	0	0	6
Career			19	0		0	0	0	114
Playoffs			3	0		0	0	0	18

Dave Ross

Year	Team		TD	1XP	2XP	FG	FGA	SAF	Pts
1960	NY	A	1	0	0	0	0	0	6

Jermaine Ross

Year	Team		TD	1XP	2XP	FG	FGA	SAF	Pts
1994	LARM	N	1	0	0	0	0	0	6
1996	STL	N	1	0	0	0	0	0	6
Career			2	0	0	0	0	0	12

Kevin Ross

Year	Team		TD	1XP	2XP	FG	FGA	SAF	Pts
1984	KC	N	1	0		0	0	0	6
1986			1	0		0	0	0	6
1987			1	0		0	0	0	6
1990			1	0		0	0	0	6
1992			1	0		0	0	0	6
1995	ATL	N	1	0	0	0	0	0	6
Career			6	0	0	0	0	0	36

Willie Ross

Year	Team		TD	1XP	2XP	FG	FGA	SAF	Pts
1964	BUF	A	1	0	0	0	0	0	6

Kyle Rote

Year	Team		TD	1XP	2XP	FG	FGA	SAF	Pts
1951	NYG	N	1	0		0	0	0	6
1952			4	0		0	0	0	24
1953			6	0		0	0	0	36
1954			2	0		0	0	0	12
1955			8	0		0	0	0	48
1956			4	0		0	0	0	24
1957			3	0		0	0	0	18
1958			3	0		0	0	0	18
1959			4	0		0	0	0	24
1960			10	0		0	0	0	60
1961			7	0		0	0	0	42
Career			52	0		0	0	0	312
Playoffs			1	0		0	0	0	6

Tobin Rote

Year	Team		TD	1XP	2XP	FG	FGA	SAF	Pts
1951	GB	N	3	0		0	0	0	18
1952			3	0		0	0	0	18
1954			8	0		0	0	0	48
1955			5	0		0	0	0	30
1956			11	0		0	0	0	66
1957	DET	N	1	0		0	0	0	6
1958			3	0		0	0	0	18
1959			2	0		0	0	0	12
1963	SD	A	2	0	0	0	0	0	12
Career			38	0	0	0	0	0	228
Playoffs			2	0	0	0	0	0	12

George Roudebush

Year	Team		TD	1XP	2XP	FG	FGA	SAF	Pts
1920	DAY	A	1	0		1		0	9
1921			1	0		0		0	6
Career			2	0		1		0	15

Tubby Rousch

Year	Team		TD	1XP	2XP	FG	FGA	SAF	Pts
1922	TOL	N	1	0		0		0	6

Lee Rouson

Year	Team		TD	1XP	2XP	FG	FGA	SAF	Pts
1986	NYG	N	3	0		0	0	0	18
1987			1	0		0	0	0	6
Career			4	0		0	0	0	24

John Roveto

Year	Team		TD	1XP	2XP	FG	FGA	SAF	Pts
1981	CHI	N	0	19		10	18	0	49
1982			0	10		4	13	0	22
Career			0	29		14	31	0	71

Bob Rowe

Year	Team		TD	1XP	2XP	FG	FGA	SAF	Pts
1969	STL	N	1	0		0	0	0	6

Harmon Rowe

Year	Team		TD	1XP	2XP	FG	FGA	SAF	Pts
1951	NYG	N	0	0		0	0	1	2

John Rowser

Year	Team		TD	1XP	2XP	FG	FGA	SAF	Pts
1971	PIT	N	1	0		0	0	0	6
1973			1	0		0	0	0	6
1976	DEN	N	2	0		0	0	0	12
Career			4	0		0	0	0	24

Mazio Royster

Year	Team		TD	1XP	2XP	FG	FGA	SAF	Pts
1993	TB	N	1	0		0	0	0	6

Mike Rozier

Year	Team		TD	1XP	2XP	FG	FGA	SAF	Pts
1985	HOU	N	8	0		0	0	0	48
1986			4	0		0	0	0	24
1987			3	0		0	0	0	18
1988			11	0		0	0	0	66
1989			2	0		0	0	0	12
1990	ATL	N	3	0		0	0	0	18
Career			31	0		0	0	0	186
Playoffs			2	0		0	0	0	12

Rob Rubick

Year	Team		TD	1XP	2XP	FG	FGA	SAF	Pts
1982	DET	N	1	0		0	0	0	6
1983			1	0		0	0	0	6
1984			1	0		0	0	0	6
1987			1	0		0	0	0	6
Career			4	0		0	0	0	24

Martin Ruby

Year	Team		TD	1XP	2XP	FG	FGA	SAF	Pts
1949	B-NY	AA	1	0		0	0	0	6
1950	NYY	N	0	0		0	0	1	2
Career			1	0		0	0	1	8

Eddie Rucinski

Year	Team		TD	1XP	2XP	FG	FGA	SAF	Pts
1941	BKN	N	1	0		0	0	0	6
1942			1	0		0	0	0	6
1943	CHIC	N	3	0		0	0	0	18
1944	C-P	N	1	0		0	0	0	6
1945	CHIC	N	2	0		0	0	0	12
Career			8	0		0	0	0	48

Reggie Rucker

Year	Team		TD	1XP	2XP	FG	FGA	SAF	Pts
1970	DAL	N	1	0		0	0	0	6
1971			1	0		0	0	0	6
1972	NE	N	3	0		0	0	0	18
1973			3	0		0	0	0	18
1974			4	0		0	0	0	24
1975	CLE	N	3	0		0	0	0	18
1976			8	0		0	0	0	48
1977			2	0		0	0	0	12
1978			8	0		0	0	0	48
1979			6	0		0	0	0	36
1980			4	0		0	0	0	24
1981			1	0		0	0	0	6
Career			44	0		0	0	0	264

Guy Ruff

Year	Team		TD	1XP	2XP	FG	FGA	SAF	Pts
Playoffs			1	0	0	0	0	0	6

Emmett Ruh

Year	Team		TD	1XP	2XP	FG	FGA	SAF	Pts
1921	COL	A	1	1		2		0	13
1922	COL	N	1	0		0		0	6
Career			2	1		2		0	19

Homer Ruh

Year	Team		TD	1XP	2XP	FG	FGA	SAF	Pts
1920	COL	A	1	0		0		0	6
1921			1	0		0		0	6
Career			2	0		0		0	12

Tommy Runnels

Year	Team		TD	1XP	2XP	FG	FGA	SAF	Pts
1956	WAS	N	1	0		0	0	0	6

Marion Rushing

Year	Team		TD	1XP	2XP	FG	FGA	SAF	Pts
1964	STL	N	0	0		0	0	1	2

Andy Russell

Year	Team		TD	1XP	2XP	FG	FGA	SAF	Pts
1966	PIT	N	1	1		0	0	0	7
1973			1	0		0	0	0	6
Career			2	1		0	0	0	13
Playoffs			1	0		0	0	0	6

Bo Russell

Year	Team		TD	1XP	2XP	FG	FGA	SAF	Pts
1939	WAS	N	1	15		1	6	0	24
1940			0	11		1	1	0	14
Career			1	26		2	7	0	38

Booker Russell

Year	Team		TD	1XP	2XP	FG	FGA	SAF	Pts
1979	OAK	N	4	0		0	0	0	24
1981	PHI	N	4	0		0	0	0	24
Career			8	0		0	0	0	48

Derek Russell

Year	Team		TD	1XP	2XP	FG	FGA	SAF	Pts
1991	DEN	N	1	0		0	0	0	6
1993			4	0		0	0	0	24
1994			1	0	0	0	0	0	6
1996	HOU	N	2	0	0	0	0	0	12
Career			8	0	0	0	0	0	48
Playoffs			1	0	0	0	0	0	6

Doug Russell

Year	Team		TD	1XP	2XP	FG	FGA	SAF	Pts
1934	CHIC	N	2	0		0		0	12
1937			2	0		0		0	12
1938			1	0		0		0	6
1939	CLE	N	1	0		0	0	0	6
Career			6	0		0	0	0	36

Jack Russell

Year	Team		TD	1XP	2XP	FG	FGA	SAF	Pts
1946	NY	AA	4	0		0	0	0	24
1947			3	0		0	0	0	18
1948			6	0		0	0	0	36
1949	B-NY	AA	2	0		0	0	0	12
1950	NYY	N	3	0		0	0	0	18
Career			18	0		0	0	0	108

Leonard Russell

Year	Team		TD	1XP	2XP	FG	FGA	SAF	Pts
1991	NE	N	4	0		0	0	0	24
1992			2	0		0	0	0	12

Leonard Russell *continued*

Year	Team		TD	1XP	2XP	FG	FGA	SAF	Pts
1993			7	0		0	0	0	42
1994	DEN	N	9	0	0	0	0	0	54
1996	SD	N	7	0	0	0	0	0	42
Career			29	0	0	0	0	0	174

Wade Russell

Year	Team		TD	1XP	2XP	FG	FGA	SAF	Pts
1987	CIN	N	1	0		0	0	0	6

Ed Rutkowski

Year	Team		TD	1XP	2XP	FG	FGA	SAF	Pts
1963	BUF	A	1	0	0	0	0	0	6
1964			1	0	0	0	0	0	6
1965			1	0	0	0	0	0	6
1966			2	0	0	0	0	0	12
1968			1	0	0	0	0	0	6
Career			6	0	0	0	0	0	36

Jeff Rutledge

Year	Team		TD	1XP	2XP	FG	FGA	SAF	Pts
1990	WAS	N	1	0		0	0	0	6

Roger Ruzek

Year	Team		TD	1XP	2XP	FG	FGA	SAF	Pts
1987	DAL	N	0	26		22	25	0	92
1988			0	27		12	22	0	63
1989	DAL-PHI	N	0	28		13	22	0	67
1990	PHI	N	0	45		21	29	0	108
1991			0	27		28	33	0	111
1992			0	40		16	25	0	88
1993			0	13		8	10	0	37
Career			0	206		120	166	0	566
Playoffs			0	6		5	6	0	21

Clarence Ryan

Year	Team		TD	1XP	2XP	FG	FGA	SAF	Pts
1929	BUF	N	2	0		0		0	12

Dave Ryan

Year	Team		TD	1XP	2XP	FG	FGA	SAF	Pts
1945	DET	N	2	0		1	3	0	15
1946			2	0		0	0	0	12
Career			4	0		1	3	0	27

Frank Ryan

Year	Team		TD	1XP	2XP	FG	FGA	SAF	Pts
1959	LA	N	1	0		0	0	0	6
1960			2	0		0	0	0	12
1962	CLE	N	1	0		0	0	0	6
1963			2	0		0	0	0	12
1964			1	0		0	0	0	6
Career			7	0		0	0	0	42

Jim Ryan

Year	Team		TD	1XP	2XP	FG	FGA	SAF	Pts
1987	DEN	N	0	0		0	0	1	2

John Ryan

Year	Team		TD	1XP	2XP	FG	FGA	SAF	Pts
1957	PHI	N	2	0		0	0	0	12

Kent Ryan

Year	Team		TD	1XP	2XP	FG	FGA	SAF	Pts
1939	DET	N	2	0		0	0	0	12

Pat Ryan

Year	Team		TD	1XP	2XP	FG	FGA	SAF	Pts
1983	NYJ	N	0	1		0	0	0	1
1984			0	1		0	0	0	1
1987			1	0		0	0	0	6
Career			1	2		0	0	0	8

Tom Rychlec

Year	Team		TD	1XP	2XP	FG	FGA	SAF	Pts
1961	BUF	A	2	0	0	0	0	0	12
1962			1	0	0	0	0	0	6
Career			3	0	0	0	0	0	18

Billy Ryckman

Year	Team		TD	1XP	2XP	FG	FGA	SAF	Pts
1977	ATL	N	1	0		0	0	0	6
1978			2	0		0	0	0	12
1979			2	0		0	0	0	12
Career			5	0		0	0	0	30

Nick Ryder

Year	Team		TD	1XP	2XP	FG	FGA	SAF	Pts
1963	DET	N	1	0		0	0	0	6
1964			1	0		0	0	0	6
Career			2	0		0	0	0	12

Julie Rykovich

Year	Team		TD	1XP	2XP	FG	FGA	SAF	Pts
1947	BUF	AA	4	0		0	0	0	24
1948	BUF-CHI	AA	6	0		0	1	0	36
1949	CHIB	N	8	0		0	0	0	48
1950			7	0		0	0	0	42
1951			4	0		0	0	0	24

Julie Rykovich *continued*

Year	Team		TD	1XP	2XP	FG	FGA	SAF	Pts
1952	WAS	N	2	1		0	0	0	13
1953			1	0		0	0	0	6
Career			32	1		0	1	0	193

Lou Rymkus

Year	Team		TD	1XP	2XP	FG	FGA	SAF	Pts
1943	WAS	N	2	0		0	0	0	12

Mark Rypien

Year	Team		TD	1XP	2XP	FG	FGA	SAF	Pts
1988	WAS	N	1	0		0	0	0	6
1989			1	0		0	0	0	6
1991			1	0		0	0	0	6
1992			2	0		0	0	0	12
1993			3	0		0	0	0	18
Career			8	0		0	0	0	48
Playoffs			1	0		0	0	0	6

Lou Saban

Year	Team		TD	1XP	2XP	FG	FGA	SAF	Pts
1947	CLE	AA	0	10		0	0	0	10
1949			1	11		0	2	0	17
Career			1	21		0	2	0	27
Playoffs			1	1		0	0	0	7

Lenny Sachs

Year	Team		TD	1XP	2XP	FG	FGA	SAF	Pts
1920	CHIC	A	2	0		0		0	12
1921			1	0		0		0	6
1923	MIL	N	2	0		0		0	12
Career			5	0		0		0	30

Norb Sacksteder

Year	Team		TD	1XP	2XP	FG	FGA	SAF	Pts
1920	DAY	A	3	0		0		0	18
1922	CAN	N	4	0		0		0	24
Career			7	0		0		0	42

Rod Saddler

Year	Team		TD	1XP	2XP	FG	FGA	SAF	Pts
1988	PHX	N	1	0		0	0	0	6
1991			1	0		0	0	0	6
Career			2	0		0	0	0	12

Eddie Saenz

Year	Team		TD	1XP	2XP	FG	FGA	SAF	Pts
1946	WAS	N	4	0		0	0	0	24
1947			6	0		0	0	0	36
1950			2	0		0	0	0	12
Career			12	0		0	0	0	72

George Saimes

Year	Team		TD	1XP	2XP	FG	FGA	SAF	Pts
1965	BUF	A	1	0	0	0	0	0	6

Mike St. Clair

Year	Team		TD	1XP	2XP	FG	FGA	SAF	Pts
1981	CIN	N	1	0		0	0	0	6

Rashaan Salaam

Year	Team		TD	1XP	2XP	FG	FGA	SAF	Pts
1995	CHI	N	10	0	0	0	0	0	60
1996			4	0	0	0	0	0	24
Career			14	0	0	0	0	0	84

Paul Salata

Year	Team		TD	1XP	2XP	FG	FGA	SAF	Pts
1949	SF	AA	4	0		0	0	0	24
1950	BAL	N	2	0		0	0	0	12
Career			6	0		0	0	0	36
Playoffs			1	0		0	0	0	6

Jay Saldi

Year	Team		TD	1XP	2XP	FG	FGA	SAF	Pts
1977	DAL	N	3	0		0	0	0	18
1978			2	0		0	0	0	12
1979			1	0		0	0	0	6
1980			1	0		0	0	0	6
1981			1	0		0	0	0	6
Career			8	0		0	0	0	48
Playoffs			1	0		0	0	0	6

Dan Saleaumua

Year	Team		TD	1XP	2XP	FG	FGA	SAF	Pts
1990	KC	N	1	0		0	0	0	6
1991			0	0		0	0	1	2
1993			1	0		0	0	0	6
1996			0	0	0	0	0	1	2
Career			2	0	0	0	0	2	16

Sam Salemi

Year	Team		TD	1XP	2XP	FG	FGA	SAF	Pts
1928	NYY	N	1	0		0		0	6

Jack Salschneider

Year	Team		TD	1XP	2XP	FG	FGA	SAF	Pts
1949	NYG	N	1	0		0	0	0	6

Chuck Sample

Year	Team		TD	1XP	2XP	FG	FGA	SAF	Pts
1942	GB	N	5	0		0	0	0	30

Johnny Sample

Year	Team		TD	1XP	2XP	FG	FGA	SAF	Pts
1960	BAL	N	1	0		0	0	0	6
1961	PIT	N	2	0		0	0	0	12
1964	WAS	N	1	0		0	0	0	6
1967	NY	A	1	0	0	0	0	0	6
1968			1	0	0	0	0	0	6
Career			6	0	0	0	0	0	36
Playoffs			1	0	0	0	0	0	6

Clint Sampson

Year	Team		TD	1XP	2XP	FG	FGA	SAF	Pts
1983	DEN	N	3	0		0	0	0	18
1984			1	0		0	0	0	6
1985			4	0		0	0	0	24
Career			8	0		0	0	0	48

Eber Sampson

Year	Team		TD	1XP	2XP	FG	FGA	SAF	Pts
1921	MIN	A	2	0		0		0	12
1923	MIN	N	1	0		0		0	6
Career			3	0		0		0	18

Don Samuel

Year	Team		TD	1XP	2XP	FG	FGA	SAF	Pts
1949	PIT	N	1	0		0	0	0	6

Tony Samuels

Year	Team		TD	1XP	2XP	FG	FGA	SAF	Pts
1979	KC	N	1	0		0	0	0	6
1980			2	0		0	0	0	12
Career			3	0		0	0	0	18

Carl Samuelson

Year	Team		TD	1XP	2XP	FG	FGA	SAF	Pts
1949	PIT	N	1	0		0	0	1	8

Lupe Sanchez

Year	Team		TD	1XP	2XP	FG	FGA	SAF	Pts
1986	PIT	N	1	0		0	0	0	6

Barry Sanders

Year	Team		TD	1XP	2XP	FG	FGA	SAF	Pts
1989	DET	N	14	0		0	0	0	84
1990			**16**	0		0	0	0	96
1991			**17**	0		0	0	0	102
1992			10	0		0	0	0	60
1993			3	0		0	0	0	18
1994			8	0	0	0	0	0	48
1995			12	0	0	0	0	0	72
1996			11	0	0	0	0	0	66
Career			91	0	0	0	0	0	546
Playoffs			1	0	0	0	0	0	6

Charlie Sanders

Year	Team		TD	1XP	2XP	FG	FGA	SAF	Pts
1968	DET	N	1	0		0	0	0	6
1969			3	0		0	0	0	18
1970			6	0		0	0	0	36
1971			5	0		0	0	0	30
1972			2	0		0	0	0	12
1973			2	0		0	0	0	12
1974			3	0		0	0	0	18
1975			3	0		0	0	0	18
1976			5	0		0	0	0	30
1977			1	0		0	0	0	6
Career			31	0		0	0	0	186

Chris Sanders

Year	Team		TD	1XP	2XP	FG	FGA	SAF	Pts
1995	HOU	N	9	0	0	0	0	0	54
1996			4	0	0	0	0	0	24
Career			13	0	0	0	0	0	78

Chuck Sanders

Year	Team		TD	1XP	2XP	FG	FGA	SAF	Pts
1987	PIT	N	1	0		0	0	0	6

Deion Sanders

Year	Team		TD	1XP	2XP	FG	FGA	SAF	Pts
1989	ATL	N	1	0		0	0	0	6
1990			3	0		0	0	0	18
1991			2	0		0	0	0	12
1992			3	0		0	0	0	18
1993			1	0		0	0	0	6
1994	SF	N	3	0	0	0	0	0	18
1996	DAL	N	2	0	0	0	0	0	12
Career			15	0	0	0	0	0	90
Playoffs			1	0	0	0	0	0	6

Frank Sanders

Year	Team		TD	1XP	2XP	FG	FGA	SAF	Pts
1995	ARI	N	2	0	2	0	0	0	16

Frank Sanders *continued*

Year	Team		TD	1XP	2XP	FG	FGA	SAF	Pts
1996			4	0	0	0	0	0	24
Career			6	0	2	0	0	0	40

Jack Sanders

Year	Team		TD	1XP	2XP	FG	FGA	SAF	Pts
1941	PIT	N	0	5		0	0	0	5
1942			0	7		0	0	0	7
Career			0	12		0	0	0	12

John Sanders

Year	Team		TD	1XP	2XP	FG	FGA	SAF	Pts
1974	NE	N	1	0		0	0	0	6
1978	PHI	N	1	0		0	0	0	6
Career			2	0		0	0	0	12

Ricky Sanders

Year	Team		TD	1XP	2XP	FG	FGA	SAF	Pts
1986	WAS	N	2	0		0	0	0	12
1987			3	0		0	0	0	18
1988			12	0		0	0	0	72
1989			4	0		0	0	0	24
1990			3	0		0	0	0	18
1991			6	0		0	0	0	36
1992			3	0		0	0	0	18
1993			4	0		0	0	0	24
1994	ATL	N	1	0	0	0	0	0	6
Career			38	0	0	0	0	0	228
Playoffs			2	0	0	0	0	0	12

Spec Sanders

Year	Team		TD	1XP	2XP	FG	FGA	SAF	Pts
1946	NY	AA	**12**	0		0	0	0	72
1947			**19**	0		0	0	0	**114**
1948			9	0		0	0	0	54
Career			40	0		0	0	0	240
Playoffs			1	0		0	0	0	6

Thomas Sanders

Year	Team		TD	1XP	2XP	FG	FGA	SAF	Pts
1985	CHI	N	1	0		0	0	0	6
1986			5	0		0	0	0	30
1987			1	0		0	0	0	6
1988			3	0		0	0	0	18
1989			2	0		0	0	0	12
1990	PHI	N	1	0		0	0	0	6
1991			1	0		0	0	0	6
Career			14	0		0	0	0	84

Dan Sandifer

Year	Team		TD	1XP	2XP	FG	FGA	SAF	Pts
1948	WAS	N	4	0		0	0	0	24
1949			3	0		0	0	0	18
1951	PHI	N	2	0		0	0	0	12
Career			9	0		0	0	0	54

Curt Sandig

Year	Team		TD	1XP	2XP	FG	FGA	SAF	Pts
1942	PIT	N	4	0		0	0	0	24
1946	BUF	AA	1	0		0	0	0	6
Career			5	0		0	0	0	30

Leo Sanford

Year	Team		TD	1XP	2XP	FG	FGA	SAF	Pts
1953	CHIC	N	1	0		0	0	0	6
1955			1	0		0	0	0	6
Career			2	0		0	0	0	12

Lucius Sanford

Year	Team		TD	1XP	2XP	FG	FGA	SAF	Pts
1979	BUF	N	1	0		0	0	0	6
1980			1	0		0	0	0	6
1984			1	0		0	0	0	6
Career			3	0		0	0	0	18

Rick Sanford

Year	Team		TD	1XP	2XP	FG	FGA	SAF	Pts
1979	NE	N	1	0		0	0	0	6
1980			1	0		0	0	0	6
1982			1	0		0	0	0	6
Career			3	0		0	0	0	18

Sandy Sanford

Year	Team		TD	1XP	2XP	FG	FGA	SAF	Pts
1940	WAS	N	0	3		0	2	0	3

Ollie Sansen

Year	Team		TD	1XP	2XP	FG	FGA	SAF	Pts
1932	BKN	N	1	0		0		0	6
1933			1	0		0		0	6
Career			2	0		0		0	12

Theron Sapp

Year	Team		TD	1XP	2XP	FG	FGA	SAF	Pts
1959	PHI	N	1	0		0	0	0	6
1961			1	0		0	0	0	6
1962			2	0		0	0	0	12

Theron Sapp *continued*

Year	Team		TD	1XP	2XP	FG	FGA	SAF	Pts
1963	PIT	N	1	0		0	0	0	6
Career			5	0		0	0	0	30

Warren Sapp

Year	Team		TD	1XP	2XP	FG	FGA	SAF	Pts
1995	TB	N	1	0	0	0	0	0	6

Tony Sarausky

Year	Team		TD	1XP	2XP	FG	FGA	SAF	Pts
1935	NYG	N	1	1		0		0	7
1936			1	1		1		0	10
Career			2	2		1		0	17

Phil Sarboe

Year	Team		TD	1XP	2XP	FG	FGA	SAF	Pts
1934	CHIC	N	0	0		0		0	0
1935			2	0		0		0	12
Career			2	0		0		0	12

Broderick Sargent

Year	Team		TD	1XP	2XP	FG	FGA	SAF	Pts
1989	DAL	N	1	0		0	0	0	6

Martin Sartin

Year	Team		TD	1XP	2XP	FG	FGA	SAF	Pts
1987	SD	N	1	0		0	0	0	6

Doug Satcher

Year	Team		TD	1XP	2XP	FG	FGA	SAF	Pts
1968	BOS	A	0	0	0	0	0	1	2

George Sauer

Year	Team		TD	1XP	2XP	FG	FGA	SAF	Pts
1935	GB	N	4	0		0		0	24
1936			3	0		0		0	18
Career			7	0		0		0	42

George Sauer

Year	Team		TD	1XP	2XP	FG	FGA	SAF	Pts
1965	NY	A	2	0	0	0	0	0	12
1966			5	0	1	0	0	0	32
1967			6	0	1	0	0	0	38
1968			3	0	0	0	0	0	18
1969			8	0	0	0	0	0	48
1970	NYJ	N	4	0		0	0	0	24
Career			28	0	2	0	0	0	172

Bill Saul

Year	Team		TD	1XP	2XP	FG	FGA	SAF	Pts
1962	BAL	N	0	0		0	0	1	2

Syl Saumer

Year	Team		TD	1XP	2XP	FG	FGA	SAF	Pts
1934	C-S	N	1	0		0		0	6

Russ Saunders

Year	Team		TD	1XP	2XP	FG	FGA	SAF	Pts
1931	GB	N	1	0		0		0	6

Joe Savoldi

Year	Team		TD	1XP	2XP	FG	FGA	SAF	Pts
1930	CHIB	N	1	0		0		0	6

Corey Sawyer

Year	Team		TD	1XP	2XP	FG	FGA	SAF	Pts
1994	CIN	N	1	0	0	0	0	0	6

John Sawyer

Year	Team		TD	1XP	2XP	FG	FGA	SAF	Pts
1975	HOU	N	1	0		0	0	0	6
1976			1	0		0	0	0	6
Career			2	0		0	0	0	12

James Saxon

Year	Team		TD	1XP	2XP	FG	FGA	SAF	Pts
1988	KC	N	2	0		0	0	0	12
1989			3	0		0	0	0	18
Career			5	0		0	0	0	30

Gale Sayers

Year	Team		TD	1XP	2XP	FG	FGA	SAF	Pts
1965	CHI	N	**22**	0		0	0	0	**132**
1966			12	0		0	0	0	72
1967			12	0		0	0	0	72
1968			2	0		0	0	0	12
1969			8	0		0	0	0	48
Career			56	0		0	0	0	336

Charley Scales

Year	Team		TD	1XP	2XP	FG	FGA	SAF	Pts
1962	CLE	N	3	0		0	0	0	18
1963			1	0		0	0	0	6
1964			1	0		0	0	0	6
Career			5	0		0	0	0	30

Dwight Scales

Year	Team		TD	1XP	2XP	FG	FGA	SAF	Pts
1976	LA	N	1	0		0	0	0	6
1977			1	0		0	0	0	6
1978			1	0		0	0	0	6
1981	SD	N	1	0		0	0	0	6

Dwight Scales *continued*

Year	Team		TD	1XP	2XP	FG	FGA	SAF	Pts
1982			1	0		0	0	0	6
Career			5	0		0	0	0	30

Greg Scales

Year	Team		TD	1XP	2XP	FG	FGA	SAF	Pts
1988	**NO**	**N**	1	0		0	0	0	6
1990			1	0		0	0	0	6
Career			2	0		0	0	0	12

Ted Scalissi

Year	Team		TD	1XP	2XP	FG	FGA	SAF	Pts
1947	**CHI**	**AA**	2	0		0	0	0	12

John Scanlon

Year	Team		TD	1XP	2XP	FG	FGA	SAF	Pts
1921	**CHIC**	**A**	1	0		0		0	6

Sam Scarber

Year	Team		TD	1XP	2XP	FG	FGA	SAF	Pts
1975	**SD**	**N**	2	0		0	0	0	12
1976			2	0		0	0	0	12
Career			4	0		0	0	0	24

Joe Scarpati

Year	Team		TD	1XP	2XP	FG	FGA	SAF	Pts
1964	**PHI**	**N**	1	0		0	0	0	6
1967			1	0		0	0	0	6
1969			1	0		0	0	0	6
Career			3	0		0	0	0	18

Bob Scarpitto

Year	Team		TD	1XP	2XP	FG	FGA	SAF	Pts
1961	**SD**	**A**	2	0	0	0	0	0	12
1962	**DEN**	**A**	6	0	0	0	0	0	36
1963			5	0	0	0	0	0	30
1964			4	0	0	0	0	0	24
1965			5	0	0	0	0	0	30
1966			5	0	1	0	0	0	32
1968	**BOS**	**A**	1	0	0	0	0	0	6
Career			28	0	1	0	0	0	170

Elmer Schaake

Year	Team		TD	1XP	2XP	FG	FGA	SAF	Pts
1933	**POR**	**N**	1	0		0		0	6

Pete Schabarum

Year	Team		TD	1XP	2XP	FG	FGA	SAF	Pts
1951	**SF**	**N**	2	0		0	0	0	12
1954			1	0		0	0	0	6
Career			3	0		0	0	0	18

Don Schaefer

Year	Team		TD	1XP	2XP	FG	FGA	SAF	Pts
1956	**PHI**	**N**	2	0		0	0	0	12

Francis Schammel

Year	Team		TD	1XP	2XP	FG	FGA	SAF	Pts
1937	**GB**	**N**	1	0		0		0	6

Eddie Scharer

Year	Team		TD	1XP	2XP	FG	FGA	SAF	Pts
1926	**DET**	**N**	1	0		0		0	6
1928			0	1		0		0	1
Career			1	1		0		0	7

Herb Schell

Year	Team		TD	1XP	2XP	FG	FGA	SAF	Pts
1924	**COL**	**N**	1	0		1		0	9

Bernie Scherer

Year	Team		TD	1XP	2XP	FG	FGA	SAF	Pts
1936	**GB**	**N**	1	0		0		0	6
1937			1	0		0		0	6
1938			1	0		0		0	6
Career			3	0		0		0	18

Vin Schleusner

Year	Team		TD	1XP	2XP	FG	FGA	SAF	Pts
1930	**POR**	**N**	1	0		0		0	6

Art Schlichter

Year	Team		TD	1XP	2XP	FG	FGA	SAF	Pts
1984	**IND**	**N**	1	0		0	0	0	6

Walt Schlinkman

Year	Team		TD	1XP	2XP	FG	FGA	SAF	Pts
1946	**GB**	**N**	1	0		0	0	0	6
1947			2	0		0	0	0	12
1948			4	0		0	0	0	24
Career			7	0		0	0	0	42

Todd Schlopy

Year	Team		TD	1XP	2XP	FG	FGA	SAF	Pts
1987	**BUF**	**N**	0	1		2	5	0	7

Art Schmaehl

Year	Team		TD	1XP	2XP	FG	FGA	SAF	Pts
1921	**GB**	**A**	2	0		0		0	12

George Schmidt

Year	Team		TD	1XP	2XP	FG	FGA	SAF	Pts
1953	**CHIC**	**N**	0	0		0	0	1	2

Hank Schmidt

Year	Team		TD	1XP	2XP	FG	FGA	SAF	Pts
1964	**SD**	**A**	1	0	0	0	0	0	6

Joe Schmidt

Year	Team		TD	1XP	2XP	FG	FGA	SAF	Pts
1960	**DET**	**N**	2	0		0	0	0	12
1961			1	0		0	0	0	6
Career			3	0		0	0	0	18

Terry Schmidt

Year	Team		TD	1XP	2XP	FG	FGA	SAF	Pts
1974	**NO**	**N**	1	0		0	0	0	6
1979	**CHI**	**N**	1	0		0	0	0	6
1983			1	0		0	0	0	6
Career			3	0		0	0	0	18

Bob Schmitz

Year	Team		TD	1XP	2XP	FG	FGA	SAF	Pts
1939	**PHI**	**N**	1	0		0	0	0	6
1962	**PIT**	**N**	1	0		0	0	0	6
1963			0	0		0	0	1	2
Career			2	0		0	0	1	14

Herm Schneidman

Year	Team		TD	1XP	2XP	FG	FGA	SAF	Pts
1936	**GB**	**N**	1	0		0		0	6
1937			1	0		0		0	6
Career			2	0		0		0	12

Bob Schnelker

Year	Team		TD	1XP	2XP	FG	FGA	SAF	Pts
1954	**NYG**	**N**	8	0		0	0	0	48
1955			3	0		0	0	0	18
1956			1	0		0	0	0	6
1957			5	0		0	0	0	30
1958			5	0		0	0	0	30
1959			6	0		0	0	0	36
1960			2	0		0	0	0	12
1961	**MIN-PIT**	**N**	4	0		0	0	0	24
Career			34	0		0	0	0	204
Playoffs			1	0		0	0	0	6

Otto Schnellbacher

Year	Team		TD	1XP	2XP	FG	FGA	SAF	Pts
1948	**NY**	**AA**	1	0		0	0	0	6
1951	**NYG**	**N**	2	0		0	0	0	12
Career			3	0		0	0	0	18

John Schneller

Year	Team		TD	1XP	2XP	FG	FGA	SAF	Pts
1935	**DET**	**N**	2	0		0		0	12
1936			1	0		0		0	6
Career			3	0		0		0	18

Tom Schoen

Year	Team		TD	1XP	2XP	FG	FGA	SAF	Pts
1962	**NY**	**A**	0	29	0	13	26	0	68

Bruce Scholtz

Year	Team		TD	1XP	2XP	FG	FGA	SAF	Pts
1982	**SEA**	**N**	1	0		0	0	0	6

Turk Schonert

Year	Team		TD	1XP	2XP	FG	FGA	SAF	Pts
1983	**CIN**	**N**	2	0		0	0	0	12
1984			1	0		0	0	0	6
1986	**ATL**	**N**	1	0		0	0	0	6
Career			4	0		0	0	0	24

Ivan Schottel

Year	Team		TD	1XP	2XP	FG	FGA	SAF	Pts
1946	**DET**	**N**	1	0		0	0	0	6

Marty Schottenheimer

Year	Team		TD	1XP	2XP	FG	FGA	SAF	Pts
1967	**BUF**	**A**	1	0	0	0	0	0	6

Larry Schreiber

Year	Team		TD	1XP	2XP	FG	FGA	SAF	Pts
1971	**SF**	**N**	1	1		0	0	0	7
1972			3	0		0	0	0	18
1974			4	0		0	0	0	24
1975			6	0		0	0	0	36
Career			14	1		0	0	0	85
Playoffs			3	0		0	0	0	18

Bill Schroeder

Year	Team		TD	1XP	2XP	FG	FGA	SAF	Pts
1947	**CHI**	**AA**	3	0		0	0	0	18

Gene Schroeder

Year	Team		TD	1XP	2XP	FG	FGA	SAF	Pts
1951	**CHIB**	**N**	3	0		0	0	0	18
1952			6	0		0	0	0	36
1954			1	0		0	0	0	6
1955			2	0		0	0	0	12
1956			1	0		0	0	0	6
Career			13	0		0	0	0	78

Jay Schroeder

Year	Team		TD	1XP	2XP	FG	FGA	SAF	Pts
1986	**WAS**	**N**	1	0		0	0	0	6
1987			3	0		0	0	0	18
1988	**LARI**	**N**	1	0		0	0	0	6
Career			5	0		0	0	0	30

Ken Schroy

Year	Team		TD	1XP	2XP	FG	FGA	SAF	Pts
1980	**NYJ**	**N**	1	0		0	0	0	6

Eric Schubert

Year	Team		TD	1XP	2XP	FG	FGA	SAF	Pts
1985	**NYG**	**N**	0	26		10	13	0	56
1986	**STL**	**N**	0	9		3	11	0	18
1987	**NE**	**N**	0	1		1	2	0	4
Career			0	36		14	26	0	78
Playoffs			0	2		1	5	0	5

Steve Schubert

Year	Team		TD	1XP	2XP	FG	FGA	SAF	Pts
1974	**NE**	**N**	1	0		0	0	0	6
1977	**CHI**	**N**	1	0		0	0	0	6
1978			1	0		0	0	0	6
1979			1	0		0	0	0	6
Career			4	0		0	0	0	24
Playoffs			1	0		0	0	0	6

Charles Schuette

Year	Team		TD	1XP	2XP	FG	FGA	SAF	Pts
1948	**BUF**	**AA**	1	0		0	0	0	6

Bill Schultz

Year	Team		TD	1XP	2XP	FG	FGA	SAF	Pts
1992	**IND**	**N**	1	0		0	0	0	6

Elbie Schultz

Year	Team		TD	1XP	2XP	FG	FGA	SAF	Pts
1944	**C-P**	**N**	1	0		0	0	0	6

Randy Schultz

Year	Team		TD	1XP	2XP	FG	FGA	SAF	Pts
1967	**NO**	**N**	2	0		0	0	0	12

Kurt Schulz

Year	Team		TD	1XP	2XP	FG	FGA	SAF	Pts
1995	**BUF**	**N**	1	0	0	0	0	0	6

Scott Schutt

Year	Team		TD	1XP	2XP	FG	FGA	SAF	Pts
1987	**CIN**	**N**	0	0		0	0	1	2

Vic Schwall

Year	Team		TD	1XP	2XP	FG	FGA	SAF	Pts
1948	**CHIC**	**N**	1	0		0	0	0	6
1949			2	0		0	0	0	12
Career			3	0		0	0	0	18

Ade Schwammel

Year	Team		TD	1XP	2XP	FG	FGA	SAF	Pts
1934	**GB**	**N**	0	0		1		0	3
1935			0	3		4		0	15
1936			0	5		1		0	8
Career			0	8		6		0	26

Elmer Schwartz

Year	Team		TD	1XP	2XP	FG	FGA	SAF	Pts
1931	**POR**	**N**	3	0		0		0	18

Perry Schwartz

Year	Team		TD	1XP	2XP	FG	FGA	SAF	Pts
1938	**BKN**	**N**	1	0		0	0	0	6
1939			3	0		0	0	0	18
1940			3	0		0	0	0	18
1941			2	0		0	0	0	12
1942			1	0		0	0	0	6
Career			10	0		0	0	0	60

Scott Schwedes

Year	Team		TD	1XP	2XP	FG	FGA	SAF	Pts
1989	**MIA**	**N**	2	0		0	0	0	12
1990			1	0		0	0	0	6
Career			3	0		0	0	0	18

Dick Schweidler

Year	Team		TD	1XP	2XP	FG	FGA	SAF	Pts
1946	**CHIB**	**N**	3	0		0	0	0	18

Wilson Schwenk

Year	Team		TD	1XP	2XP	FG	FGA	SAF	Pts
1942	**CHIC**	**N**	2	0		0	0	0	12
1946	**CLE**	**AA**	1	0		0	0	0	6
1947	**BAL**	**AA**	1	0		0	0	0	6
Career			4	0		0	0	0	24

John Sciarra

Year	Team		TD	1XP	2XP	FG	FGA	SAF	Pts
1978	**PHI**	**N**	2	0		0	0	0	12

Nick Scollard

Year	Team		TD	1XP	2XP	FG	FGA	SAF	Pts
1946	**BOS**	**N**	2	21		0	1	0	33
1947			0	2		1	4	0	5

Nick Scollard *continued*

Year	Team	Lg	TD	1XP	2XP	FG	FGA	SAF	Pts
1948			0	8		2	3	0	14
1949	NYB	N	2	18		3	10	0	39
Career			4	49		6	18	0	91

Bo Scott

Year	Team	Lg	TD	1XP	2XP	FG	FGA	SAF	Pts
1970	CLE	N	11	0		0	0	0	66
1971			10	0		0	0	0	60
1972			2	0		0	0	0	12
1973			1	0		0	0	0	6
Career			24	0		0	0	0	144
Playoffs			2	0		0	0	0	12

Bobby Scott

Year	Team	Lg	TD	1XP	2XP	FG	FGA	SAF	Pts
1976	NO	N	1	0		0	0	0	6

Clarence Scott

Year	Team	Lg	TD	1XP	2XP	FG	FGA	SAF	Pts
1972	CLE	N	1	0		0	0	0	6
1973			1	0		0	0	0	6
1977			1	0		0	0	0	6
Career			3	0		0	0	0	18

Clyde Scott

Year	Team	Lg	TD	1XP	2XP	FG	FGA	SAF	Pts
1949	PHI	N	3	0		0	0	0	18
1951			4	0		0	0	0	24
Career			7	0		0	0	0	42

Darnay Scott

Year	Team	Lg	TD	1XP	2XP	FG	FGA	SAF	Pts
1994	CIN	N	5	0	0	0	0	0	30
1995			5	0	0	0	0	0	30
1996			5	0	0	0	0	0	30
Career			15	0	0	0	0	0	90

Freddie Scott

Year	Team	Lg	TD	1XP	2XP	FG	FGA	SAF	Pts
1977	BAL	N	2	0		0	0	0	12
1978	DET	N	2	0		0	0	0	12
1979			5	0		0	0	0	30
1980			5	0		0	0	0	30
1981			5	0		0	0	0	30
1982			1	0		0	0	0	6
1983			1	0		0	0	0	6
Career			21	0		0	0	0	126

Jake Scott

Year	Team	Lg	TD	1XP	2XP	FG	FGA	SAF	Pts
1970	MIA	N	1	0		0	0	0	6

James Scott

Year	Team	Lg	TD	1XP	2XP	FG	FGA	SAF	Pts
1976	CHI	N	6	0		0	0	0	36
1977			3	0		0	0	0	18
1978			5	0		0	0	0	30
1979			3	0		0	0	0	18
1980			3	0		0	0	0	18
Career			20	0		0	0	0	120

Joe Scott

Year	Team	Lg	TD	1XP	2XP	FG	FGA	SAF	Pts
1948	NYG	N	5	0		0	0	0	30
1949			7	0		0	0	0	42
1950			3	0		0	0	0	18
1951			3	0		0	0	0	18
1952			4	0		0	0	0	24
Career			22	0		0	0	0	132

Johnny Scott

Year	Team	Lg	TD	1XP	2XP	FG	FGA	SAF	Pts
1921	BUF	A	5	0		0		0	30
1926	PHI	A	0	0		0		0	0
Career			5	0		0		0	30

Lindsay Scott

Year	Team	Lg	TD	1XP	2XP	FG	FGA	SAF	Pts
1984	NO	N	1	0		0	0	0	6

Patrick Scott

Year	Team	Lg	TD	1XP	2XP	FG	FGA	SAF	Pts
1988	GB	N	1	0		0	0	0	6

Prince Scott

Year	Team	Lg	TD	1XP	2XP	FG	FGA	SAF	Pts
1946	MIA	AA	2	0		0	0	0	12

Ralph Scott

Year	Team	Lg	TD	1XP	2XP	FG	FGA	SAF	Pts
1921	DEC	A	1	0		0		0	6
1923	CHIB	N	0	1		0		0	1
Career			1	1		0		0	7

Ronald Scott

Year	Team	Lg	TD	1XP	2XP	FG	FGA	SAF	Pts
1987	MIA	N	3	0		0	0	0	18

Todd Scott

Year	Team	Lg	TD	1XP	2XP	FG	FGA	SAF	Pts
1992	MIN	N	1	0		0	0	0	6

Tom Scott

Year	Team	Lg	TD	1XP	2XP	FG	FGA	SAF	Pts
1953	PHI	N	1	0		0	0	0	6
1960	NYG	N	1	0		0	0	0	6
1961			1	0		0	0	0	6
Career			3	0		0	0	0	18

Victor Scott

Year	Team	Lg	TD	1XP	2XP	FG	FGA	SAF	Pts
1985	DAL	N	1	0		0	0	0	6

Willie Scott

Year	Team	Lg	TD	1XP	2XP	FG	FGA	SAF	Pts
1981	KC	N	1	0		0	0	0	6
1982			1	0		0	0	0	6
1983			6	0		0	0	0	36
1984			3	0		0	0	0	18
1986	NE	N	3	0		0	0	0	18
1987			2	0		0	0	0	12
Career			16	0		0	0	0	96

Bob Scrabis

Year	Team	Lg	TD	1XP	2XP	FG	FGA	SAF	Pts
1961	NY	A	1	0	0	0	0	0	6

Rob Scribner

Year	Team	Lg	TD	1XP	2XP	FG	FGA	SAF	Pts
1974	LA	N	1	0		0	0	0	6
1975			2	0		0	0	0	12
1976			1	0		0	0	0	6
Career			4	0		0	0	0	24

Tracy Scroggins

Year	Team	Lg	TD	1XP	2XP	FG	FGA	SAF	Pts
1995	DET	N	1	0	0	0	0	0	6

Joe Scudero

Year	Team	Lg	TD	1XP	2XP	FG	FGA	SAF	Pts
1954	WAS	N	1	0		0	0	0	6
1955			2	0		0	0	0	12
Career			3	0		0	0	0	18

Charlie Seabright

Year	Team	Lg	TD	1XP	2XP	FG	FGA	SAF	Pts
1946	PIT	N	1	0		0	0	0	6
1947			1	0		0	0	0	6
1948			1	0		0	0	0	6
1950			1	0		0	0	0	6
Career			4	0		0	0	0	24

Malcolm Seabron

Year	Team	Lg	TD	1XP	2XP	FG	FGA	SAF	Pts
1995	HOU	N	1	0	0	0	0	0	6

Paul Seal

Year	Team	Lg	TD	1XP	2XP	FG	FGA	SAF	Pts
1974	NO	N	4	0		0	0	0	24
1975			1	0		0	0	0	6
1977	SF	N	1	0		0	0	0	6
1978			2	0		0	0	0	12
Career			8	0		0	0	0	48

Eugene Seale

Year	Team	Lg	TD	1XP	2XP	FG	FGA	SAF	Pts
1987	HOU	N	1	0		0	0	0	6
1988			0	0		0	0	1	2
1989			1	0		0	0	0	6
Career			2	0		0	0	1	14

Sam Seale

Year	Team	Lg	TD	1XP	2XP	FG	FGA	SAF	Pts
1985	LARI	N	1	0		0	0	0	6
1988	SD	N	1	0		0	0	0	6
Career			2	0		0	0	0	12

George Seals

Year	Team	Lg	TD	1XP	2XP	FG	FGA	SAF	Pts
1971	CHI	N	1	0		0	0	0	6

Leon Seals

Year	Team	Lg	TD	1XP	2XP	FG	FGA	SAF	Pts
1988	BUF	N	1	0		0	0	0	6

Ray Seals

Year	Team	Lg	TD	1XP	2XP	FG	FGA	SAF	Pts
1993	TB	N	1	0		0	0	0	6

Jimmy Sears

Year	Team	Lg	TD	1XP	2XP	FG	FGA	SAF	Pts
1957	CHIC	N	1	0		0	0	0	6
1958			2	0		0	0	0	12
Career			3	0		0	0	0	18

Vic Sears

Year	Team	Lg	TD	1XP	2XP	FG	FGA	SAF	Pts
1942	PHI	N	1	0		0	0	0	6
1952			1	0		0	0	0	6
Career			2	0		0	0	0	12

George Seasholtz

Year	Team	Lg	TD	1XP	2XP	FG	FGA	SAF	Pts
1924	KEN	N	2	0		0		0	12

Junior Seau

Year	Team	Lg	TD	1XP	2XP	FG	FGA	SAF	Pts
1995	SD	N	1	0	0	0	0	0	6

Mark Seay

Year	Team	Lg	TD	1XP	2XP	FG	FGA	SAF	Pts
1994	SD	N	6	0	0	0	0	0	36
1995			3	0	1	0	0	0	20
Career			9	0	1	0	0	0	56
Playoffs			1	0	1	0	0	0	8

Virgil Seay

Year	Team	Lg	TD	1XP	2XP	FG	FGA	SAF	Pts
1981	WAS	N	3	0		0	0	0	18
1983			1	0		0	0	0	6
1984			1	0		0	0	0	6
Career			5	0		0	0	0	30

Walt Sechrist

Year	Team	Lg	TD	1XP	2XP	FG	FGA	SAF	Pts
1924	AKR	N	0	1		0		0	1
1926	HAM	N	0	0		1		0	3
Career			0	1		1		0	4

Scott Secules

Year	Team	Lg	TD	1XP	2XP	FG	FGA	SAF	Pts
1991	MIA	N	1	0		0	0	0	6

Len Sedbrook

Year	Team	Lg	TD	1XP	2XP	FG	FGA	SAF	Pts
1928	DET	N	4	0		0		0	24
1929	NYG	N	11	0		0		0	66
1930			8	0		0		0	48
1931			2	0		0		0	12
Career			25	0		0		0	150

Jason Sehorn

Year	Team	Lg	TD	1XP	2XP	FG	FGA	SAF	Pts
1996	NYG	N	1	0	0	0	0	0	6

Champ Seibold

Year	Team	Lg	TD	1XP	2XP	FG	FGA	SAF	Pts
1942	CHIC	N	1	0		0	0	0	6

Larry Seiple

Year	Team	Lg	TD	1XP	2XP	FG	FGA	SAF	Pts
1968	MIA	A	1	0	0	0	0	0	6
1969			5	0	0	0	0	0	30
1976	MIA	N	1	0		0	0	0	6
Career			7	0	0	0	0	0	42

Clarence Self

Year	Team	Lg	TD	1XP	2XP	FG	FGA	SAF	Pts
1950	DET	N	1	0		0	0	0	6

Goldie Sellers

Year	Team	Lg	TD	1XP	2XP	FG	FGA	SAF	Pts
1966	DEN	A	2	0	0	0	0	0	12
1967			1	0	0	0	0	0	6
1968	KC	A	1	0	0	0	0	0	6
1969			1	0	0	0	0	0	6
Career			5	0	0	0	0	0	30

Ron Sellers

Year	Team	Lg	TD	1XP	2XP	FG	FGA	SAF	Pts
1969	BOS	A	6	0	0	0	0	0	36
1970	BOS	N	4	0		0	0	0	24
1971	NE	N	3	0		0	0	0	18
1972	DAL	N	5	0		0	0	0	30
Career			18	0	0	0	0	0	108
Playoffs			1	0	0	0	0	0	6

Lee Roy Selmon

Year	Team	Lg	TD	1XP	2XP	FG	FGA	SAF	Pts
1979	TB	N	1	0		0	0	0	6

Bill Senn

Year	Team	Lg	TD	1XP	2XP	FG	FGA	SAF	Pts
1926	CHIB	N	7	2		0		0	44
1927			6	0		0		0	36
1928			5	1		0		0	31
1929			4	0		0		0	24
1930			1	0		0		0	6
1931			1	1		0		0	7
1934	C-S	N	0	0		1		0	3
Career			24	4		1		0	151

Frank Seno

Year	Team	Lg	TD	1XP	2XP	FG	FGA	SAF	Pts
1945	CHIC	N	2	0		0	0	0	12
1946			2	0		0	0	0	12
1947	BOS	N	2	0		0	0	0	12
1948			3	0		0	0	0	18
Career			9	0		0	0	0	54

Dean Sensenbaugher

Year	Team	Lg	TD	1XP	2XP	FG	FGA	SAF	Pts
1948	CLE	AA	1	0		0	0	0	6
1949	NYB	N	1	0		0	0	0	6
Career			2	0		0	0	0	12

Joe Senser

Year	Team	Lg	TD	1XP	2XP	FG	FGA	SAF	Pts
1980	MIN	N	7	0		0	0	0	42
1981			8	0		0	0	0	48
1982			1	0		0	0	0	6
Career			16	0		0	0	0	96

Mike Sensibaugh

Year	Team	Lg	TD	1XP	2XP	FG	FGA	SAF	Pts
1976	STL	N	1	0		0	0	0	6
1977			1	0		0	0	0	6
Career			2	0		0	0	0	12

Rafael Septien

Year	Team	Lg	TD	1XP	2XP	FG	FGA	SAF	Pts
1977	LA	N	0	32		18	30	0	86
1978	DAL	N	0	**46**		16	26	0	94
1979			0	40		19	29	0	97
1980			0	**59**		11	17	0	92
1981			0	40		**27**	35	0	**121**
1982			0	28		10	14	0	58
1983			0	57		22	27	0	123
1984			0	33		23	29	0	102
1985			0	42		19	28	0	99
1986			0	43		15	21	0	88
Career			0	420		180	256	0	960
Playoffs			0	41		18	20	0	95

Wash Serini

Year	Team	Lg	TD	1XP	2XP	FG	FGA	SAF	Pts
1950	CHIB	N	0	0		0	0	1	2

Tom Sestak

Year	Team	Lg	TD	1XP	2XP	FG	FGA	SAF	Pts
1962	BUF	A	1	0	0	0	0	0	6
1964			1	0	0	0	0	0	6
1967			1	0	0	0	0	0	6
Career			3	0	0	0	0	0	18

John Settle

Year	Team	Lg	TD	1XP	2XP	FG	FGA	SAF	Pts
1988	ATL	N	8	0		0	0	0	48
1989			5	0		0	0	0	30
Career			13	0		0	0	0	78

Harley Sewell

Year	Team	Lg	TD	1XP	2XP	FG	FGA	SAF	Pts
1954	DET	N	1	0		0	0	0	6

Steve Sewell

Year	Team	Lg	TD	1XP	2XP	FG	FGA	SAF	Pts
1985	DEN	N	5	0		0	0	0	30
1986			2	0		0	0	0	12
1987			3	0		0	0	0	18
1988			6	0		0	0	0	36
1989			3	0		0	0	0	18
1990			3	0		0	0	0	18
1991			4	0		0	0	0	24
Career			26	0		0	0	0	156
Playoffs			1	0		0	0	0	6

Frank Seyfrit

Year	Team	Lg	TD	1XP	2XP	FG	FGA	SAF	Pts
1923	TOL	N	1	0		0		0	6

Bob Seymour

Year	Team	Lg	TD	1XP	2XP	FG	FGA	SAF	Pts
1940	WAS	N	4	0		0	0	0	24
1941			4	0		0	0	0	24
1942			1	0		0	0	0	6
1943			2	0		0	0	0	12
1944			6	0		0	0	0	36
1945			3	0		0	0	0	18
1946	LA	AA	3	0		0	0	0	18
Career			23	0		0	0	0	138
Playoffs			1	0		0	0	0	6

Jim Seymour

Year	Team	Lg	TD	1XP	2XP	FG	FGA	SAF	Pts
1970	CHI	N	4	0		0	0	0	24
1972			1	0		0	0	0	6
Career			5	0		0	0	0	30

Paul Seymour

Year	Team	Lg	TD	1XP	2XP	FG	FGA	SAF	Pts
1974	BUF	N	2	0		0	0	0	12
1975			1	0		0	0	0	6
Career			3	0		0	0	0	18
Playoffs			1	0		0	0	0	6

Leland Shaffer

Year	Team	Lg	TD	1XP	2XP	FG	FGA	SAF	Pts
1936	NYG	N	1	0		0		0	6
1938			2	0		0		0	12
1940			3	0		0	0	0	18
Career			6	0		0	0	0	36

Ron Shanklin

Year	Team	Lg	TD	1XP	2XP	FG	FGA	SAF	Pts
1970	PIT	N	4	0		0	0	0	24
1971			6	0		0	0	0	36
1972			3	0		0	0	0	18
1973			10	0		0	0	0	60
1974			1	0		0	0	0	6
Career			24	0		0	0	0	144

Bobby Shann

Year	Team	Lg	TD	1XP	2XP	FG	FGA	SAF	Pts
1965	PHI	N	1	0		0	0	0	6

Carver Shannon

Year	Team	Lg	TD	1XP	2XP	FG	FGA	SAF	Pts
1963	LA	N	1	0		0	0	0	6

Ed Sharockman

Year	Team	Lg	TD	1XP	2XP	FG	FGA	SAF	Pts
1962	MIN	N	1	0		0	0	0	6
1963			1	0		0	0	0	6
1965			1	0		0	0	0	6
1970			3	0		0	0	0	18
Career			6	0		0	0	0	36

Luis Sharpe

Year	Team	Lg	TD	1XP	2XP	FG	FGA	SAF	Pts
1990	PHX	N	1	0		0	0	0	6

Shannon Sharpe

Year	Team	Lg	TD	1XP	2XP	FG	FGA	SAF	Pts
1990	DEN	N	1	0		0	0	0	6
1991			1	0		0	0	0	6
1992			2	0		0	0	0	12
1993			9	0		0	0	0	54
1994			4	0	2	0	0	0	28
1995			4	0	0	0	0	0	24
1996			10	0	0	0	0	0	60
Career			31	0	2	0	0	0	190
Playoffs			2	0	0	0	0	0	12

Sterling Sharpe

Year	Team	Lg	TD	1XP	2XP	FG	FGA	SAF	Pts
1988	GB	N	1	0		0	0	0	6
1989			13	0		0	0	0	78
1990			6	0		0	0	0	36
1991			4	0		0	0	0	24
1992			13	0		0	0	0	78
1993			11	0		0	0	0	66
1994			18	0	0	0	0	0	108
Career			66	0	0	0	0	0	396
Playoffs			4	0	0	0	0	0	24

Bob Shaw

Year	Team	Lg	TD	1XP	2XP	FG	FGA	SAF	Pts
1946	LA	N	3	0		0	0	0	18
1949			6	0		0	0	0	36
1950	CHIC	N	**12**	0		0	0	0	72
Career			21	0		0	0	0	126

Ed Shaw

Year	Team	Lg	TD	1XP	2XP	FG	FGA	SAF	Pts
1922	CAN	N	5	8		2		0	44

George Shaw

Year	Team	Lg	TD	1XP	2XP	FG	FGA	SAF	Pts
1955	BAL	N	3	0		0	0	0	18
1957			1	0		0	0	0	6
1958			1	0		0	0	0	6
1962	DEN	A	1	0	0	0	0	0	6
Career			6	0	0	0	0	0	36

Glenn Shaw

Year	Team	Lg	TD	1XP	2XP	FG	FGA	SAF	Pts
1963	OAK	A	2	0	0	0	0	0	12
1964			2	0	0	0	0	0	12
Career			4	0	0	0	0	0	24

Al Sheard

Year	Team	Lg	TD	1XP	2XP	FG	FGA	SAF	Pts
1923	ROC	N	0	0		0		0	0
1924			0	1		0		0	1
1925			2	0		0		0	12
Career			2	1		0		0	13

Kenny Shedd

Year	Team	Lg	TD	1XP	2XP	FG	FGA	SAF	Pts
1996	OAK	N	1	0	0	0	0	1	8

Paul Sheeks

Year	Team	Lg	TD	1XP	2XP	FG	FGA	SAF	Pts
1921	AKR	A	1	1		2		0	13

Paul Sheeks *continued*

Year	Team	Lg	TD	1XP	2XP	FG	FGA	SAF	Pts
1922	AKR	N	0	8		4		0	20
Career			1	9		6		0	33

Willie Shelby

Year	Team	Lg	TD	1XP	2XP	FG	FGA	SAF	Pts
1976	CIN	N	1	0		0	0	0	6
1977			1	0		0	0	0	6
Career			2	0		0	0	0	12

Donnie Shell

Year	Team	Lg	TD	1XP	2XP	FG	FGA	SAF	Pts
1978	PIT	N	1	0		0	0	0	6
1984			1	0		0	0	0	6
1987			2	0		0	0	0	12
Career			4	0		0	0	0	24

Todd Shell

Year	Team	Lg	TD	1XP	2XP	FG	FGA	SAF	Pts
1984	SF	N	1	0		0	0	0	6

Dexter Shelley

Year	Team	Lg	TD	1XP	2XP	FG	FGA	SAF	Pts
1931	PRO	N	0	4		0		0	4

Richard Shelton

Year	Team	Lg	TD	1XP	2XP	FG	FGA	SAF	Pts
1991	PIT	N	1	0		0	0	0	6

Derrick Shepard

Year	Team	Lg	TD	1XP	2XP	FG	FGA	SAF	Pts
1989	NO-DAL	N	2	0		0	0	0	12

Bill Shepherd

Year	Team	Lg	TD	1XP	2XP	FG	FGA	SAF	Pts
1935	BOS-DET	N	4	1		0		0	25
1936	DET	N	2	1		0		0	13
1937			3	7		2		0	31
1938			3	2		1	2	0	23
1939			3	0		0	0	0	18
Career			15	11		3	2	0	110

Leslie Shepherd

Year	Team	Lg	TD	1XP	2XP	FG	FGA	SAF	Pts
1995	WAS	N	3	0	0	0	0	0	18
1996			5	0	0	0	0	0	30
Career			8	0	0	0	0	0	48

Jerry Sherk

Year	Team	Lg	TD	1XP	2XP	FG	FGA	SAF	Pts
1977	CLE	N	0	0		0	0	1	2

Bob Sherlag

Year	Team	Lg	TD	1XP	2XP	FG	FGA	SAF	Pts
1966	ATL	N	1	0		0	0	0	6

Allie Sherman

Year	Team	Lg	TD	1XP	2XP	FG	FGA	SAF	Pts
1944	PHI	N	1	0		0	0	0	6
1945			1	0		0	0	0	6
1947			1	0		0	0	0	6
Career			3	0		0	0	0	18

Heath Sherman

Year	Team	Lg	TD	1XP	2XP	FG	FGA	SAF	Pts
1989	PHI	N	2	0		0	0	0	12
1990			4	0		0	0	0	24
1992			6	0		0	0	0	36
1993			2	0		0	0	0	12
Career			14	0		0	0	0	84
Playoffs			1	0		0	0	0	6

Rod Sherman

Year	Team	Lg	TD	1XP	2XP	FG	FGA	SAF	Pts
1967	OAK	A	1	0	0	0	0	0	6
1968	CIN	A	1	4	0	0	1	0	10
1971	OAK	N	1	0		0	0	0	6
1972	DEN	N	3	0		0	0	0	18
Career			6	4	0	0	1	0	40
Playoffs			3	0	0	0	0	0	18

Solly Sherman

Year	Team	Lg	TD	1XP	2XP	FG	FGA	SAF	Pts
1939	CHIB	N	1	0		0	0	0	6

Will Sherman

Year	Team	Lg	TD	1XP	2XP	FG	FGA	SAF	Pts
1956	LA	N	2	0		0	0	0	12
1958			2	0		0	0	0	12
Career			4	0		0	0	0	24

Mike Sherrard

Year	Team	Lg	TD	1XP	2XP	FG	FGA	SAF	Pts
1986	DAL	N	5	0		0	0	0	30
1990	SF	N	2	0		0	0	0	12
1991			2	0		0	0	0	12
1992			1	0		0	0	0	6
1993	NYG	N	2	0		0	0	0	12
1994			6	0	0	0	0	0	36
1995			4	0	0	0	0	0	24

Mike Sherrard *continued*

Year	Team		TD	1XP	2XP	FG	FGA	SAF	Pts
1996	DEN	N	1	0	0	0	0	0	6
Career			23	0	0	0	0	0	138
Playoffs			1	0	0	0	0	0	6

Bud Sherrod

Year	Team		TD	1XP	2XP	FG	FGA	SAF	Pts
1952	NYG	N	1	0		0	0	0	6

Tim Sherwin

Year	Team		TD	1XP	2XP	FG	FGA	SAF	Pts
1982	BAL	N	1	0		0	0	0	6
1986	IND	N	1	0		0	0	0	6
1987			1	0		0	0	0	6
Career			3	0		0	0	0	18

Rhoten Shetley

Year	Team		TD	1XP	2XP	FG	FGA	SAF	Pts
1940	BKN	N	1	0		0	0	0	6
1941			1	0		0	0	0	6
1942			1	0		0	0	0	6
Career			3	0		0	0	0	18

Lebron Shields

Year	Team		TD	1XP	2XP	FG	FGA	SAF	Pts
1960	BAL	N	0	0		0	0	1	2

Dick Shiner

Year	Team		TD	1XP	2XP	FG	FGA	SAF	Pts
1969	PIT	N	1	0		0	0	0	6
1971	ATL	N	1	0		0	0	0	6
Career			2	0		0	0	0	12

Don Shinnick

Year	Team		TD	1XP	2XP	FG	FGA	SAF	Pts
Playoffs			1	0	0	0	0	0	6

Jerry Shipkey

Year	Team		TD	1XP	2XP	FG	FGA	SAF	Pts
1948	PIT	N	8	0		0	0	0	48
1949			5	0		0	0	0	30
1950			3	0		0	0	0	18
1951			1	0		0	0	0	6
Career			17	0		0	0	0	102

Joe Shipp

Year	Team		TD	1XP	2XP	FG	FGA	SAF	Pts
1979	BUF	N	1	0		0	0	0	6

Gary Shirk

Year	Team		TD	1XP	2XP	FG	FGA	SAF	Pts
1976	NYG	N	1	0		0	0	0	6
1977			2	0		0	0	0	12
1978			2	0		0	0	0	12
1979			2	0		0	0	0	12
1980			1	0		0	0	0	6
1981			3	0		0	0	0	18
Career			11	0		0	0	0	66

Sanders Shiver

Year	Team		TD	1XP	2XP	FG	FGA	SAF	Pts
1980	BAL	N	1	0		0	0	0	6

Roy Shivers

Year	Team		TD	1XP	2XP	FG	FGA	SAF	Pts
1966	STL	N	1	0		0	0	0	6
1967			1	0		0	0	0	6
1968			7	0		0	0	0	42
1969			3	0		0	0	0	18
1970			2	0		0	0	0	12
1971			1	0		0	0	0	6
Career			15	0		0	0	0	90

Boris Shlapak

Year	Team		TD	1XP	2XP	FG	FGA	SAF	Pts
1972	BAL	N	0	4		0	8	0	4

Roger Shoals

Year	Team		TD	1XP	2XP	FG	FGA	SAF	Pts
1964	CLE	N	1	0		0	0	0	6

Rod Shoate

Year	Team		TD	1XP	2XP	FG	FGA	SAF	Pts
1980	NE	N	1	0		0	0	0	6

Bill Shockley

Year	Team		TD	1XP	2XP	FG	FGA	SAF	Pts
1960	NY	A	2	**47**	0	9	21	0	86
1961	NY-BUF	A	0	13	0	4	9	0	25
1968	PIT	N	0	2		0	1	0	2
Career			2	62	0	13	31	0	113

Hal Shoener

Year	Team		TD	1XP	2XP	FG	FGA	SAF	Pts
1948	SF	AA	3	0		0	0	0	18

Herb Shoener

Year	Team		TD	1XP	2XP	FG	FGA	SAF	Pts
1949	WAS	N	1	0		0	0	0	6

Del Shofner

Year	Team		TD	1XP	2XP	FG	FGA	SAF	Pts
1958	LA	N	8	0		0	0	0	48
1959			7	0		0	0	0	42
1960			1	0		0	0	0	6
1961	NYG	N	11	0		0	0	0	66
1962			12	0		0	0	0	72
1963			9	0		0	0	0	54
1965			2	0		0	0	0	12
1967			1	0		0	0	0	6
Career			51	0		0	0	0	306

Chuck Shonta

Year	Team		TD	1XP	2XP	FG	FGA	SAF	Pts
1960	BOS	A	1	0	0	0	0	0	6

Jim Shorter

Year	Team		TD	1XP	2XP	FG	FGA	SAF	Pts
1965	WAS	N	1	0		0	0	0	6

Mickey Shuler

Year	Team		TD	1XP	2XP	FG	FGA	SAF	Pts
1978	NYJ	N	3	0		0	0	0	18
1979			3	0		0	0	0	18
1980			2	0		0	0	0	12
1982			3	0		0	0	0	18
1983			1	0		0	0	0	6
1984			6	0		0	0	0	36
1985			7	0		0	0	0	42
1986			4	0		0	0	0	24
1987			3	0		0	0	0	18
1988			5	0		0	0	0	30
Career			37	0		0	0	0	222
Playoffs			2	0		0	0	0	12

Johnny Shultz

Year	Team		TD	1XP	2XP	FG	FGA	SAF	Pts
1930	FRA	N	0	0		0		0	0

Mike Shumann

Year	Team		TD	1XP	2XP	FG	FGA	SAF	Pts
1979	SF	N	4	0		0	0	0	24
1980	TB	N	1	0		0	0	0	6
Career			5	0		0	0	0	30
Playoffs			1	0		0	0	0	6

Don Shy

Year	Team		TD	1XP	2XP	FG	FGA	SAF	Pts
1967	PIT	N	5	0		0	0	0	30
1968			1	0		0	0	0	6
1969	NO	N	2	0		0	0	0	12
1970	CHI	N	1	0		0	0	0	6
1971			2	0		0	0	0	12
1972			1	0		0	0	0	6
1973	STL	N	2	0		0	0	0	12
Career			14	0		0	0	0	84

Les Shy

Year	Team		TD	1XP	2XP	FG	FGA	SAF	Pts
1966	DAL	N	1	0		0	0	0	6
1968			1	0		0	0	0	6
1969			2	0		0	0	0	12
Career			4	0		0	0	0	24

Mike Siani

Year	Team		TD	1XP	2XP	FG	FGA	SAF	Pts
1972	OAK	N	5	0		0	0	0	30
1973			3	0		0	0	0	18
1974			1	0		0	0	0	6
1976			2	0		0	0	0	12
1977			2	0		0	0	0	12
1978	BAL	N	1	0		0	0	0	6
1979			2	0		0	0	0	12
1980			1	0		0	0	0	6
Career			17	0		0	0	0	102
Playoffs			3	0		0	0	0	18

Mike Siano

Year	Team		TD	1XP	2XP	FG	FGA	SAF	Pts
1987	PHI	N	1	0		0	0	0	6

Wallie Sieb

Year	Team		TD	1XP	2XP	FG	FGA	SAF	Pts
1922	RAC	N	2	1		0		0	13

Johnny Siegal

Year	Team		TD	1XP	2XP	FG	FGA	SAF	Pts
1939	CHIB	N	1	0		0	0	0	6
1940			1	0		0	0	0	6
1941			3	0		0	0	0	18
1942			2	0		0	0	0	12
Career			7	0		0	0	0	42

Larry Siemering

Year	Team		TD	1XP	2XP	FG	FGA	SAF	Pts
1936	BOS	N	1	0		0		0	6

Herb Sies

Year	Team		TD	1XP	2XP	FG	FGA	SAF	Pts
1923	RI	N	0	8		3		0	17
1924	DAY	N	0	0		1		0	3
Career			0	8		4		0	20

Eric Sievers

Year	Team		TD	1XP	2XP	FG	FGA	SAF	Pts
1981	SD	N	3	0		0	0	0	18
1982			1	0		0	0	0	6
1983			3	0		0	0	0	18
1984			3	0		0	0	0	18
1985			6	0		0	0	0	36
Career			16	0		0	0	0	96
Playoffs			1	0		0	0	0	6

Vai Sikahema

Year	Team		TD	1XP	2XP	FG	FGA	SAF	Pts
1986	STL	N	3	0		0	0	0	18
1987			1	0		0	0	0	6
1992	PHI	N	1	0		0	0	0	6
Career			5	0		0	0	0	30

Frank Sillin

Year	Team		TD	1XP	2XP	FG	FGA	SAF	Pts
1928	DAY	N	1	0		0		0	6

Milt Simington

Year	Team		TD	1XP	2XP	FG	FGA	SAF	Pts
1942	PIT	N	0	1		1	1	0	4

Clyde Simmons

Year	Team		TD	1XP	2XP	FG	FGA	SAF	Pts
1988	PHI	N	1	0		0	0	1	8
1989			1	0		0	0	0	6
1990			1	0		0	0	0	6
1991			1	0		0	0	0	6
1995	ARI	N	1	0	0	0	0	0	6
Career			5	0	0	0	0	1	32
Playoffs			1	0	0	0	0	0	6

Floyd Simmons

Year	Team		TD	1XP	2XP	FG	FGA	SAF	Pts
1948	CHI	AA	2	0		0	0	0	12

Jerry Simmons

Year	Team		TD	1XP	2XP	FG	FGA	SAF	Pts
1966	PIT	N	1	0		0	0	0	6
1967	ATL	N	2	0		0	0	0	12
1971	DEN	N	1	0		0	0	0	6
1972			2	0		0	0	0	12
1973			1	0		0	0	0	6
1974			2	0		0	0	0	12
Career			9	0		0	0	0	54

Jim Simmons

Year	Team		TD	1XP	2XP	FG	FGA	SAF	Pts
1927	CLE	N	5	0		0		0	30

John Simmons

Year	Team		TD	1XP	2XP	FG	FGA	SAF	Pts
1984	CIN	N	1	0		0	0	0	6
1986	GB	N	1	0		0	0	0	6
Career			2	0		0	0	0	12

Phil Simms

Year	Team		TD	1XP	2XP	FG	FGA	SAF	Pts
1979	NYG	N	1	0		0	0	0	6
1980			1	0		0	0	0	6
1986			1	0		0	0	0	6
1989			1	0		0	0	0	6
1990			1	0		0	0	0	6
1991			1	0		0	0	0	6
Career			6	0		0	0	0	36

Bill Simpson

Year	Team		TD	1XP	2XP	FG	FGA	SAF	Pts
1980	BUF	N	0	0		0	0	1	2
Playoffs			1	0	0	0	0	0	6

Eber Simpson

Year	Team		TD	1XP	2XP	FG	FGA	SAF	Pts
1923	STL	N	0	0		0		0	0

Jackie Simpson

Year	Team		TD	1XP	2XP	FG	FGA	SAF	Pts
1962	OAK	A	0	6	0	3	10	0	15

Jimmy Simpson

Year	Team		TD	1XP	2XP	FG	FGA	SAF	Pts
1924	KEN	N	0	0		0		0	0

Keith Simpson

Year	Team		TD	1XP	2XP	FG	FGA	SAF	Pts
1978	SEA	N	1	0		0	0	0	6
1984			2	0		0	0	0	12
Career			3	0		0	0	0	18

Mike Simpson

Year	Team		TD	1XP	2XP	FG	FGA	SAF	Pts
1972	SF	N	1	0		0	0	0	6

Nate Simpson

Year	Team		TD	1XP	2XP	FG	FGA	SAF	Pts
1979	GB	N	1	0		0	0	0	6

O.J. Simpson

Year	Team		TD	1XP	2XP	FG	FGA	SAF	Pts
1969	BUF	A	5	0	0	0	0	0	30
1970	BUF	N	6	0		0	0	0	36
1971			5	0		0	0	0	30
1972			6	0		0	0	0	36
1973			12	0		0	0	0	72
1974			4	0		0	0	0	24
1975			**23**	0		0	0	0	**138**
1976			9	0		0	0	0	54
1978	SF	N	3	0		0	0	0	18
1979			3	0		0	0	0	18
Career			76	0	0	0	0	0	456
Playoffs			1	0	0	0	0	0	6

Billy Sims

Year	Team		TD	1XP	2XP	FG	FGA	SAF	Pts
1980	DET	N	**16**	0		0	0	0	96
1981			15	0		0	0	0	90
1982			4	0		0	0	0	24
1983			7	0		0	0	0	42
1984			5	0		0	0	0	30
Career			47	0		0	0	0	282
Playoffs			2	0		0	0	0	12

David Sims

Year	Team		TD	1XP	2XP	FG	FGA	SAF	Pts
1977	SEA	N	8	0		0	0	0	48
1978			**15**	0		0	0	0	90
Career			23	0		0	0	0	138

George Sims

Year	Team		TD	1XP	2XP	FG	FGA	SAF	Pts
1949	LA	N	1	0		0	0	0	6

Marvin Sims

Year	Team		TD	1XP	2XP	FG	FGA	SAF	Pts
1980	BAL	N	2	0		0	0	0	12

Walt Singer

Year	Team		TD	1XP	2XP	FG	FGA	SAF	Pts
1935	NYG	N	1	0		0		0	6
1936			1	0		0		0	6
Career			2	0		0		0	12

Chris Singleton

Year	Team		TD	1XP	2XP	FG	FGA	SAF	Pts
1992	NE	N	1	0		0	0	0	6

Nate Singleton

Year	Team		TD	1XP	2XP	FG	FGA	SAF	Pts
1993	SF	N	1	0		0	0	0	6
1994			2	0	0	0	0	0	12
1995			1	0	0	0	0	0	6
Career			4	0	0	0	0	0	24

Frank Sinkovitz

Year	Team		TD	1XP	2XP	FG	FGA	SAF	Pts
1947	PIT	N	1	0		0	0	0	6

Frankie Sinkwich

Year	Team		TD	1XP	2XP	FG	FGA	SAF	Pts
1943	DET	N	2	0		0	1	0	12
1944			6	24		2	8	0	66
Career			8	24		2	9	0	78

Brian Sipe

Year	Team		TD	1XP	2XP	FG	FGA	SAF	Pts
1974	CLE	N	4	0		0	0	0	24
1976			0	1		0	0	0	1
1978			3	0		0	0	0	18
1979			2	0		0	0	0	12
1980			1	0		0	0	0	6
1981			1	0		0	0	0	6
Career			11	1		0	0	0	67

Johnny Sisk

Year	Team		TD	1XP	2XP	FG	FGA	SAF	Pts
1933	CHIB	N	1	0		0		0	6
1934			1	0		0		0	6
1935			1	0		0		0	6
Career			3	0		0		0	18

Scott Sisson

Year	Team		TD	1XP	2XP	FG	FGA	SAF	Pts
1993	NE	N	0	15		14	26	0	57
1996	MIN	N	0	30	0	22	29	0	96
Career			0	45	0	36	55	0	153
Playoffs			0	1	0	0	0	0	1

Otis Sistrunk

Year	Team		TD	1XP	2XP	FG	FGA	SAF	Pts
1974	OAK	N	0	0		0	0	1	2

Emil Sitko

Year	Team		TD	1XP	2XP	FG	FGA	SAF	Pts
1950	SF	N	2	0		0	0	0	12
1952	CHIC	N	1	0		0	0	0	6
Career			3	0		0	0	0	18

Paul Skansi

Year	Team		TD	1XP	2XP	FG	FGA	SAF	Pts
1985	SEA	N	1	0		0	0	0	6
1987			1	0		0	0	0	6
1988			1	0		0	0	0	6
1989			5	0		0	0	0	30
1990			2	0		0	0	0	12
Career			10	0		0	0	0	60

Joe Skladany

Year	Team		TD	1XP	2XP	FG	FGA	SAF	Pts
1934	PIT	N	2	0		0		0	12

Leo Skladany

Year	Team		TD	1XP	2XP	FG	FGA	SAF	Pts
Playoffs			1	0	0	0	0	0	6

Ed Skoronski

Year	Team		TD	1XP	2XP	FG	FGA	SAF	Pts
1936	PIT	N	1	0		0		0	6

John Skorupan

Year	Team		TD	1XP	2XP	FG	FGA	SAF	Pts
1979	NYG	N	0	0		0	0	1	2

Fritz Slackford

Year	Team		TD	1XP	2XP	FG	FGA	SAF	Pts
1921	CAN	A	1	0		0		0	6

Chris Slade

Year	Team		TD	1XP	2XP	FG	FGA	SAF	Pts
1995	NE	N	1	0	0	0	0	0	6

Duke Slater

Year	Team		TD	1XP	2XP	FG	FGA	SAF	Pts
1929	CHIC	N	1	0		0		0	6

Howie Slater

Year	Team		TD	1XP	2XP	FG	FGA	SAF	Pts
1926	MIL	N	1	0		0		0	6

Mickey Slaughter

Year	Team		TD	1XP	2XP	FG	FGA	SAF	Pts
1963	DEN	A	1	0	0	0	0	0	6
1964			0	0	1	0	0	0	2
Career			1	0	1	0	0	0	8

Webster Slaughter

Year	Team		TD	1XP	2XP	FG	FGA	SAF	Pts
1986	CLE	N	5	0		0	0	0	30
1987			7	0		0	0	0	42
1988			3	0		0	0	0	18
1989			6	0		0	0	0	36
1990			4	0		0	0	0	24
1991			3	0		0	0	0	18
1992	HOU	N	4	0		0	0	0	24
1993			5	0		0	0	0	30
1994			2	0	0	0	0	0	12
1995	KC	N	4	0	0	0	0	0	24
1996	NYJ	N	2	0	0	0	0	0	12
Career			45	0	0	0	0	0	270
Playoffs			6	0	0	0	0	0	36

Leroy Sledge

Year	Team		TD	1XP	2XP	FG	FGA	SAF	Pts
1971	HOU	N	1	0		0	0	0	6

David Sloan

Year	Team		TD	1XP	2XP	FG	FGA	SAF	Pts
1995	DET	N	1	0	0	0	0	0	6
Playoffs			2	0	0	0	0	0	12

Dwight Sloan

Year	Team		TD	1XP	2XP	FG	FGA	SAF	Pts
1939	DET	N	4	0		0		0	24

Phil Slosburg

Year	Team		TD	1XP	2XP	FG	FGA	SAF	Pts
1949	NYB	N	1	0		0	0	0	6

Elmer Slough

Year	Team		TD	1XP	2XP	FG	FGA	SAF	Pts
1926	BUF	N	2	0		0		0	12

Marty Slovak

Year	Team		TD	1XP	2XP	FG	FGA	SAF	Pts
1940	CLE	N	1	0		0	0	0	6

Bill Slyker

Year	Team		TD	1XP	2XP	FG	FGA	SAF	Pts
1922	EVA	N	1	0		0		0	6

Gerald Small

Year	Team		TD	1XP	2XP	FG	FGA	SAF	Pts
1978	MIA	N	1	0		0	0	0	6

Torrance Small

Year	Team		TD	1XP	2XP	FG	FGA	SAF	Pts
1992	NO	N	3	0		0	0	0	18

Torrance Small *continued*

Year	Team		TD	1XP	2XP	FG	FGA	SAF	Pts
1993			1	0		0	0	0	6
1994			5	0	1	0	0	0	32
1995			6	0	0	0	0	0	36
1996			3	0	0	0	0	0	18
Career			18	0	1	0	0	0	110

Metz Smeach

Year	Team		TD	1XP	2XP	FG	FGA	SAF	Pts
1921	WAS	A	1	0		0		0	6

Rudy Smeja

Year	Team		TD	1XP	2XP	FG	FGA	SAF	Pts
1944	CHIB	N	1	0		0	0	0	6

Fred Smerlas

Year	Team		TD	1XP	2XP	FG	FGA	SAF	Pts
1979	BUF	N	1	0		0	0	0	6

Tommie Smiley

Year	Team		TD	1XP	2XP	FG	FGA	SAF	Pts
1968	CIN	A	1	0	0	0	0	0	6
1969	DEN	A	4	0	0	0	0	0	24
Career			5	0	0	0	0	0	30

Al Smith

Year	Team		TD	1XP	2XP	FG	FGA	SAF	Pts
1991	HOU	N	1	0		0	0	0	6

Anthony Smith

Year	Team		TD	1XP	2XP	FG	FGA	SAF	Pts
1994	LARI	N	1	0	0	0	0	0	6

Barry Smith

Year	Team		TD	1XP	2XP	FG	FGA	SAF	Pts
1973	GB	N	2	0		0	0	0	12
1974			1	0		0	0	0	6
1975			1	0		0	0	0	6
Career			4	0		0	0	0	24

Barty Smith

Year	Team		TD	1XP	2XP	FG	FGA	SAF	Pts
1975	GB	N	5	0		0	0	0	30
1976			5	0		0	0	0	30
1977			3	0		0	0	0	18
1978			4	0		0	0	0	24
1979			4	0		0	0	0	24
Career			21	0		0	0	0	126

Bill Smith

Year	Team		TD	1XP	2XP	FG	FGA	SAF	Pts
1934	CHIC	N	3	4		1		0	25
1935			2	5		**6**		0	35
1936			1	2		1		0	11
1937			1	3		0		0	9
1938			1	4		2	2	0	16
1939			4	6		2	8	0	36
Career			12	24		12	10	0	132

Billy Ray Smith

Year	Team		TD	1XP	2XP	FG	FGA	SAF	Pts
1989	SD	N	1	0		0	0	0	6

Bob Smith

Year	Team		TD	1XP	2XP	FG	FGA	SAF	Pts
1955	CLE	N	1	0		0	0	0	6

Bobby Smith

Year	Team		TD	1XP	2XP	FG	FGA	SAF	Pts
1964	LA	N	2	0		0	0	0	12

Bobby Smith

Year	Team		TD	1XP	2XP	FG	FGA	SAF	Pts
1964	BUF	A	4	0	0	0	0	0	24
1965			1	0	0	0	0	0	6
Career			5	0	0	0	0	0	30

Bruce Smith

Year	Team		TD	1XP	2XP	FG	FGA	SAF	Pts
1947	GB	N	2	0		0	0	1	14

Bruce Smith

Year	Team		TD	1XP	2XP	FG	FGA	SAF	Pts
1987	BUF	N	1	0		0	0	0	6
1988			0	0		0	0	1	2
Career			1	0		0	0	1	8
Playoffs			0	0		0	0	1	2

Carl Smith

Year	Team		TD	1XP	2XP	FG	FGA	SAF	Pts
1960	BUF	A	1	0	0	0	0	0	6

Cedric Smith

Year	Team		TD	1XP	2XP	FG	FGA	SAF	Pts
1920	BUF	A	4	0		0		0	24
1921			3	0		0		0	18
Career			7	0		0		0	42

Cedric Smith

Year	Team		TD	1XP	2XP	FG	FGA	SAF	Pts
1994	WAS	N	1	0	0	0	0	0	6

Cedric Smith *continued*

Year	Team		TD	1XP	2XP	FG	FGA	SAF	Pts
1996	ARI	N	2	0	0	0	0	0	12
Career			3	0	0	0	0	0	18

Charlie Smith

Year	Team		TD	1XP	2XP	FG	FGA	SAF	Pts
1968	OAK	A	7	0	0	0	0	0	42
1969			4	0	0	0	0	0	24
1970	OAK	N	5	0		0	0	0	30
1971			1	0		0	0	0	6
1972			10	0		0	0	0	60
1973			5	0		0	0	0	30
1974			2	0		0	0	0	12
Career			34	0	0	0	0	0	204
Playoffs			3	0	0	0	0	0	18

Charlie Smith

Year	Team		TD	1XP	2XP	FG	FGA	SAF	Pts
1975	PHI	N	6	0		0	0	0	36
1976			5	0		0	0	0	30
1977			4	0		0	0	0	24
1978			2	0		0	0	0	12
1979			1	0		0	0	0	6
1980			3	0		0	0	0	18
1981			4	0		0	0	0	24
Career			25	0		0	0	0	150
Playoffs			1	0		0	0	0	6

Chuck Smith

Year	Team		TD	1XP	2XP	FG	FGA	SAF	Pts
1994	ATL	N	1	0	0	0	0	0	6

Darrin Smith

Year	Team		TD	1XP	2XP	FG	FGA	SAF	Pts
1994	DAL	N	1	0	0	0	0	0	6

Dave Smith

Year	Team		TD	1XP	2XP	FG	FGA	SAF	Pts
1960	HOU	A	7	0	0	0	0	0	42
1961			3	0	0	0	0	0	18
1962			3	0	0	0	0	0	18
1963			5	0	0	0	0	0	30
Career			18	0	0	0	0	0	108
Playoffs			1	0	0	0	0	0	6

Dave Smith

Year	Team		TD	1XP	2XP	FG	FGA	SAF	Pts
1970	PIT	N	2	0		0	0	0	12
1971			5	0		0	0	0	30
Career			7	0		0	0	0	42

Dennis Smith

Year	Team		TD	1XP	2XP	FG	FGA	SAF	Pts
1984	DEN	N	1	0		0	0	0	6

Don Smith

Year	Team		TD	1XP	2XP	FG	FGA	SAF	Pts
1988	TB	N	1	0		0	0	0	6
1990	BUF	N	2	0		0	0	0	12
Career			3	0		0	0	0	18
Playoffs			1	0		0	0	0	6

Ed Smith

Year	Team		TD	1XP	2XP	FG	FGA	SAF	Pts
1936	BOS	N	0	0		1		0	3

Emmitt Smith

Year	Team		TD	1XP	2XP	FG	FGA	SAF	Pts
1990	DAL	N	11	0		0	0	0	66
1991			13	0		0	0	0	78
1992			**19**	0		0	0	0	114
1993			10	0		0	0	0	60
1994			**22**	0	0	0	0	0	132
1995			**25**	0	0	0	0	0	**150**
1996			15	0	0	0	0	0	90
Career			115	0	0	0	0	0	690
Playoffs			**20**	0	0	0	0	0	**120**

Ernie Smith

Year	Team		TD	1XP	2XP	FG	FGA	SAF	Pts
1935	GB	N	0	11		1		0	14
1936			0	17		4		1	31
1937			0	11		1		0	14
1939			0	3		0	0	0	3
Career			0	42		6	0	1	62
Playoffs			0	3		1	1	0	6

Fletcher Smith

Year	Team		TD	1XP	2XP	FG	FGA	SAF	Pts
1966	KC	A	0	2	0	0	0	0	2

Gaylon Smith

Year	Team		TD	1XP	2XP	FG	FGA	SAF	Pts
1939	CLE	N	2	0		0	0	0	12
1942			2	0		0	0	0	12
1946	CLE	AA	5	0		0	0	0	30
Career			9	0		0	0	0	54

George Smith

Year	Team		TD	1XP	2XP	FG	FGA	SAF	Pts
1942	WAS	N	0	0		0	1	0	0

Gordon Smith

Year	Team		TD	1XP	2XP	FG	FGA	SAF	Pts
1961	MIN	N	4	0		0	0	0	24
1962			1	0		0	0	0	6
1963			2	0		0	0	0	12
1964			1	0		0	0	0	6
1965			5	0		0	0	0	30
Career			13	0		0	0	0	78

Hank Smith

Year	Team		TD	1XP	2XP	FG	FGA	SAF	Pts
1922	ROC	N	1	0		0		0	6

Irv Smith

Year	Team		TD	1XP	2XP	FG	FGA	SAF	Pts
1993	NO	N	2	0		0	0	0	12
1994			3	0	0	0	0	0	18
1995			3	0	1	0	0	0	20
Career			8	0	1	0	0	0	50

Jackie Smith

Year	Team		TD	1XP	2XP	FG	FGA	SAF	Pts
1963	STL	N	2	0		0	0	0	12
1964			4	0		0	0	0	24
1965			2	0		0	0	0	12
1966			3	0		0	0	0	18
1967			9	0		0	0	0	54
1968			5	0		0	0	0	30
1969			1	0		0	0	0	6
1970			4	0		0	0	0	24
1971			4	0		0	0	0	24
1972			2	0		0	0	0	12
1973			1	0		0	0	0	6
1974			3	0		0	0	0	18
1975			2	0		0	0	0	12
1977			1	0		0	0	0	6
Career			43	0		0	0	0	258
Playoffs			1	0		0	0	0	6

J.D. Smith

Year	Team		TD	1XP	2XP	FG	FGA	SAF	Pts
1958	SF	N	3	0		0	0	0	18
1959			11	0		0	0	0	66
1960			6	0		0	0	0	36
1961			9	0		0	0	0	54
1962			7	0		0	0	0	42
1963			6	0		0	0	0	36
1965	DAL	N	3	0		0	0	0	18
1966			1	0		0	0	0	6
Career			46	0		0	0	0	276

J.D. Smith

Year	Team		TD	1XP	2XP	FG	FGA	SAF	Pts
1960	PHI	N	1	0		0	0	0	6

J.D. Smith

Year	Team		TD	1XP	2XP	FG	FGA	SAF	Pts
1960	OAK	A	8	0	1	0	0	0	50

Jeff Smith

Year	Team		TD	1XP	2XP	FG	FGA	SAF	Pts
1985	KC	N	2	0		0	0	0	12
1986			6	0		0	0	0	36
1987	TB	N	4	0		0	0	0	24
Career			12	0		0	0	0	72
Playoffs			1	0		0	0	0	6

Jerry Smith

Year	Team		TD	1XP	2XP	FG	FGA	SAF	Pts
1965	WAS	N	2	0		0	0	0	12
1966			6	0		0	0	0	36
1967			12	0		0	0	0	72
1968			6	0		0	0	0	36
1969			9	0		0	0	0	54
1970			9	0		0	0	0	54
1971			1	0		0	0	0	6
1972			7	0		0	0	0	42
1974			3	0		0	0	0	18
1975			3	0		0	0	0	18
1976			2	0		0	0	0	12
Career			60	0		0	0	0	360
Playoffs			1	0		0	0	0	6

Jim Smith

Year	Team		TD	1XP	2XP	FG	FGA	SAF	Pts
1949	DET	N	1	0		0	0	0	6
1950			1	0		0	0	0	6
1952			1	0		0	0	0	6
Career			3	0		0	0	0	18

Jim Smith

Year	Team		TD	1XP	2XP	FG	FGA	SAF	Pts
1968	WAS	N	1	0		0	0	0	6

Jim Smith

Year	Team		TD	1XP	2XP	FG	FGA	SAF	Pts
1978	PIT	N	2	0		0	0	0	12
1979			2	0		0	0	0	12
1980			9	0		0	0	0	54
1981			7	0		0	0	0	42
1982			4	0		0	0	0	24
1985	LARI	N	1	0		0	0	0	6
Career			25	0		0	0	0	150

Jimmy Smith

Year	Team		TD	1XP	2XP	FG	FGA	SAF	Pts
1995	JAC	N	5	0	0	0	0	0	30
1996			7	0	0	0	0	0	42
Career			12	0	0	0	0	0	72
Playoffs			2	0	0	0	0	0	12

Joe Smith

Year	Team		TD	1XP	2XP	FG	FGA	SAF	Pts
1948	BAL	AA	1	0		0	0	0	6

John Smith

Year	Team		TD	1XP	2XP	FG	FGA	SAF	Pts
1974	NE	N	0	42		16	22	0	90
1975			0	33		9	17	0	60
1976			0	42		15	25	0	87
1977			0	33		15	21	0	78
1978			0	6		1	1	0	9
1979			0	46		23	**33**	0	**115**
1980			0	51		26	34	0	**129**
1981			0	37		15	24	0	82
1982			0	6		5	8	0	21
1983			0	12		3	6	0	21
Career			0	308		128	191	0	692
Playoffs			0	4		2	3	0	10

J.T. Smith

Year	Team		TD	1XP	2XP	FG	FGA	SAF	Pts
1979	KC	N	5	0		0	0	0	30
1980			4	0		0	0	0	24
1981			2	0		0	0	0	12
1982			1	0		0	0	0	6
1985	STL	N	1	0		0	0	0	6
1986			6	0		0	0	0	36
1987			8	0		0	0	0	48
1988	PHX	N	5	0		0	0	0	30
1989			5	0		0	0	0	30
1990			2	0		0	0	0	12
Career			39	0		0	0	0	234

Kendal Smith

Year	Team		TD	1XP	2XP	FG	FGA	SAF	Pts
1989	CIN	N	1	0		0	0	0	6

Kevin Smith

Year	Team		TD	1XP	2XP	FG	FGA	SAF	Pts
1993	DAL	N	1	0		0	0	0	6

Lamar Smith

Year	Team		TD	1XP	2XP	FG	FGA	SAF	Pts
1996	SEA	N	8	0	3	0	0	0	54

Larry Smith

Year	Team		TD	1XP	2XP	FG	FGA	SAF	Pts
1969	LA	N	3	0		0	0	0	18
1970			2	0		0	0	0	12
1971			5	0		0	0	0	30
1972			3	0		0	0	0	18
1973			2	0		0	0	0	12
1974	WAS	N	1	0		0	0	0	6
Career			16	0		0	0	0	96

Leonard Smith

Year	Team		TD	1XP	2XP	FG	FGA	SAF	Pts
1984	STL	N	1	0		0	0	0	6
1987			1	0		0	0	0	6
1990	BUF	N	1	0		0	0	0	6
Career			3	0		0	0	0	18

Lucious Smith

Year	Team		TD	1XP	2XP	FG	FGA	SAF	Pts
1983	KC	N	1	0		0	0	0	6

Neil Smith

Year	Team		TD	1XP	2XP	FG	FGA	SAF	Pts
1989	KC	N	1	0		0	0	0	6
1992			1	0		0	0	0	6
Career			2	0		0	0	0	12

Noland Smith

Year	Team		TD	1XP	2XP	FG	FGA	SAF	Pts
1967	KC	A	1	0	0	0	0	0	6
1968			1	0	0	0	0	0	6
Career			2	0	0	0	0	0	12

Olin Smith

Year	Team	Lg	TD	1XP	2XP	FG	FGA	SAF	Pts
1924	CLE	N	1	2		0		0	8

Ollie Smith

Year	Team	Lg	TD	1XP	2XP	FG	FGA	SAF	Pts
1976	GB	N	1	0		0	0	0	6

Otis Smith

Year	Team	Lg	TD	1XP	2XP	FG	FGA	SAF	Pts
1991	PHI	N	1	0		0	0	0	6
1995	NYJ	N	1	0	0	0	0	0	6
Career			2	0	0	0	0	0	12
Playoffs			1	0	0	0	0	0	6

Paul Smith

Year	Team	Lg	TD	1XP	2XP	FG	FGA	SAF	Pts
1975	DEN	N	1	0		0	0	0	6

Phil Smith

Year	Team	Lg	TD	1XP	2XP	FG	FGA	SAF	Pts
1984	IND	N	1	0		0	0	0	6

Ralph Smith

Year	Team	Lg	TD	1XP	2XP	FG	FGA	SAF	Pts
1963	PHI	N	1	0		0	0	0	6
1966	CLE	N	3	0		0	0	0	18
1967			2	0		0	0	0	12
Career			6	0		0	0	0	36

Red Smith

Year	Team	Lg	TD	1XP	2XP	FG	FGA	SAF	Pts
1928	NYY	N	3	2		0		0	20
1930	NEW	N	0	1		0		0	1
1931	NYG	N	0	2		0		0	2
Career			3	5		0		0	23

Ricky Smith

Year	Team	Lg	TD	1XP	2XP	FG	FGA	SAF	Pts
1982	NE	N	1	0		0	0	0	6
1987	DET	N	1	0		0	0	0	6
Career			2	0		0	0	0	12

Rico Smith

Year	Team	Lg	TD	1XP	2XP	FG	FGA	SAF	Pts
1995	CLE	N	1	0	0	0	0	0	6

Riley Smith

Year	Team	Lg	TD	1XP	2XP	FG	FGA	SAF	Pts
1936	BOS	N	2	14		4		0	38
1937	WAS	N	3	**22**		5		0	55
1938			1	3		2	5	0	15
Career			6	39		11	5	0	108
Playoffs			0	4		0	1	0	4

Robert Smith

Year	Team	Lg	TD	1XP	2XP	FG	FGA	SAF	Pts
1993	MIN	N	2	0		0	0	0	12
1994			1	0	0	0	0	0	6
1995			5	0	1	0	0	0	32
1996			3	0	0	0	0	0	18
Career			11	0	1	0	0	0	68

Rod Smith

Year	Team	Lg	TD	1XP	2XP	FG	FGA	SAF	Pts
1995	DEN	N	1	0	0	0	0	0	6
1996			2	0	0	0	0	0	12
Career			3	0	0	0	0	0	18

Ron Smith

Year	Team	Lg	TD	1XP	2XP	FG	FGA	SAF	Pts
1967	ATL	N	1	0		0	0	0	6
1968	LA	N	1	0		0	0	0	6
1969			1	0		0	0	0	6
1972	CHI	N	1	0		0	0	0	6
1973	SD	N	2	0		0	0	0	12
Career			6	0		0	0	0	36

Ronnie Smith

Year	Team	Lg	TD	1XP	2XP	FG	FGA	SAF	Pts
1979	LA	N	1	0		0	0	0	6
1981	SD	N	2	0		0	0	0	12
1982	PHI	N	1	0		0	0	0	6
Career			4	0		0	0	0	24
Playoffs			3	0		0	0	0	18

Russ Smith

Year	Team	Lg	TD	1XP	2XP	FG	FGA	SAF	Pts
1967	SD	A	1	0	0	0	0	0	6
1968			4	0	0	0	0	0	24
1969			2	0	0	0	0	0	12
1970	SD	N	3	0		0	0	0	18
Career			10	0	0	0	0	0	60

Sammie Smith

Year	Team	Lg	TD	1XP	2XP	FG	FGA	SAF	Pts
1989	MIA	N	6	0		0	0	0	36
1990			9	0		0	0	0	54
1991			1	0		0	0	0	6
Career			16	0		0	0	0	96

Sean Smith

Year	Team	Lg	TD	1XP	2XP	FG	FGA	SAF	Pts
1989	TB	N	0	0		0	0	1	2

Sherman Smith

Year	Team	Lg	TD	1XP	2XP	FG	FGA	SAF	Pts
1976	SEA	N	5	0		0	0	0	30
1977			6	0		0	0	0	36
1978			7	0		0	0	0	42
1979			15	0		0	0	0	90
1980			1	0		0	0	0	6
1981			4	0		0	0	0	24
Career			38	0		0	0	0	228

Steve Smith

Year	Team	Lg	TD	1XP	2XP	FG	FGA	SAF	Pts
1971	PHI	N	1	0		0	0	0	6

Steve Smith

Year	Team	Lg	TD	1XP	2XP	FG	FGA	SAF	Pts
1988	LARI	N	9	0		0	0	0	54
1989			1	0		0	0	0	6
1990			5	0		0	0	0	30
1991			2	0		0	0	0	12
1992			1	0		0	0	0	6
1994	SEA	N	3	0	0	0	0	0	18
1995			1	0	0	0	0	0	6
Career			22	0	0	0	0	0	132

Tim Smith

Year	Team	Lg	TD	1XP	2XP	FG	FGA	SAF	Pts
1983	HOU	N	6	0		0	0	0	36
1984			4	0		0	0	0	24
1985			2	0		0	0	0	12
Career			12	0		0	0	0	72

Timmy Smith

Year	Team	Lg	TD	1XP	2XP	FG	FGA	SAF	Pts
1988	WAS	N	3	0		0	0	0	18
Playoffs			2	0		0	0	0	12

Tony Smith

Year	Team	Lg	TD	1XP	2XP	FG	FGA	SAF	Pts
1992	ATL	N	2	0		0	0	0	12
1993			1	0		0	0	0	6
Career			3	0		0	0	0	18

Vitamin Smith

Year	Team	Lg	TD	1XP	2XP	FG	FGA	SAF	Pts
1949	LA	N	4	0		0	0	0	24
1950			8	0		0	0	0	48
1951			2	0		0	0	0	12
1952			6	0		0	0	0	36
1953			3	0		0	0	0	18
Career			23	0		0	0	0	138
Playoffs			1	0		0	0	0	6

Willie Smith

Year	Team	Lg	TD	1XP	2XP	FG	FGA	SAF	Pts
1987	MIA	N	1	0		0	0	0	6

Willis Smith

Year	Team	Lg	TD	1XP	2XP	FG	FGA	SAF	Pts
1934	NYG	N	2	0		0		0	12

Mark Smolinski

Year	Team	Lg	TD	1XP	2XP	FG	FGA	SAF	Pts
1961	BAL	N	1	0		0	0	0	6
1962			2	0		0	0	0	12
1963	NY	A	5	0	0	0	0	0	30
1964			1	0	0	0	0	0	6
1966			3	0	0	0	0	0	18
1967			4	0	0	0	0	0	24
1968			1	0	0	0	0	0	6
Career			17	0	0	0	0	0	102

Dave Smukler

Year	Team	Lg	TD	1XP	2XP	FG	FGA	SAF	Pts
1936	PHI	N	0	2		1		0	5
1937			1	8		1		0	17
1938			2	6		0		0	18
Career			3	16		2		0	40

Bill Smyth

Year	Team	Lg	TD	1XP	2XP	FG	FGA	SAF	Pts
1948	LA	N	1	0		0	0	0	6

Lou Smythe

Year	Team	Lg	TD	1XP	2XP	FG	FGA	SAF	Pts
1921	CAN	A	1	0		0		0	6
1922	CAN	N	0	0		0		0	0
1923			**7**	0		0		0	42
1925	ROC-FRA	N	2	0		0		0	12
1926	HAR	N	1	0		0		0	6
Career			11	0		0		0	66

Norm Snead

Year	Team	Lg	TD	1XP	2XP	FG	FGA	SAF	Pts
1961	WAS	N	3	0		0	0	0	18

Norm Snead *continued*

Year	Team	Lg	TD	1XP	2XP	FG	FGA	SAF	Pts
1962			3	0		0	0	0	18
1963			2	0		0	0	0	12
1964	PHI	N	2	0		0	0	0	12
1965			3	0		0	0	0	18
1966			1	0		0	0	0	6
1967			2	0		0	0	0	12
1969			2	0		0	0	0	12
1970			3	0		0	0	0	18
1971	MIN	N	1	0		0	0	0	6
1975	SF	N	1	0		0	0	0	6
Career			23	0		0	0	0	138

George Snell

Year	Team	Lg	TD	1XP	2XP	FG	FGA	SAF	Pts
1926	BKN	N	1	0		0		0	6

Matt Snell

Year	Team	Lg	TD	1XP	2XP	FG	FGA	SAF	Pts
1964	NY	A	6	0	0	0	0	0	36
1965			4	0	0	0	0	0	24
1966			8	0	0	0	0	0	48
1968			7	0	0	0	0	0	42
1969			5	0	0	0	0	0	30
1970	NYJ	N	1	0		0	0	0	6
Career			31	0	0	0	0	0	186
Playoffs			1	0	0	0	0	0	6

Malcolm Snider

Year	Team	Lg	TD	1XP	2XP	FG	FGA	SAF	Pts
1969	ATL	N	1	0		0	0	0	6

Ron Snidow

Year	Team	Lg	TD	1XP	2XP	FG	FGA	SAF	Pts
1970	CLE	N	0	0		0	0	1	2

Lee Snoots

Year	Team	Lg	TD	1XP	2XP	FG	FGA	SAF	Pts
1922	COL	N	1	0		0		0	6
1923			1	0		0		0	6
Career			2	0		0		0	12

Jack Snow

Year	Team	Lg	TD	1XP	2XP	FG	FGA	SAF	Pts
1965	LA	N	3	0		0	0	0	18
1966			3	0		0	0	0	18
1967			8	0		0	0	0	48
1968			3	0		0	0	0	18
1969			6	0		0	0	0	36
1970			7	0		0	0	0	42
1971			5	0		0	0	0	30
1972			4	0		0	0	0	24
1973			2	0		0	0	0	12
1974			3	0		0	0	0	18
1975			1	0		0	0	0	6
Career			45	0		0	0	0	270

Bob Snyder

Year	Team	Lg	TD	1XP	2XP	FG	FGA	SAF	Pts
1937	CLE	N	1	7		1		1	18
1938			0	7		1	2	0	10
1939	CHIB	N	0	1		1	1	0	4
1940			0	4		1	4	0	7
1941			0	**20**		2	2	0	26
1943			0	**39**		2	7	0	45
Career			1	78		8	16	1	110
Playoffs			0	8		5	5	0	23

Gerry Snyder

Year	Team	Lg	TD	1XP	2XP	FG	FGA	SAF	Pts
1929	NYG	N	3	0		0		0	18

Todd Snyder

Year	Team	Lg	TD	1XP	2XP	FG	FGA	SAF	Pts
1970	ATL	N	2	0		0	0	0	12

Hank Soar

Year	Team	Lg	TD	1XP	2XP	FG	FGA	SAF	Pts
1937	NYG	N	2	2		1		0	17
1938			2	1		0		0	13
1939			3	2		0	1	0	20
1940			2	0		0	1	0	12
1941			0	3		0	0	0	3
1942			1	2		0	2	0	8
Career			10	10		1	4	0	73
Playoffs			1	0		0	0	0	6

Bryan Sochia

Year	Team	Lg	TD	1XP	2XP	FG	FGA	SAF	Pts
1990	MIA	N	1	0		0	0	0	6

Kurt Sohn

Year	Team	Lg	TD	1XP	2XP	FG	FGA	SAF	Pts
1985	NYJ	N	4	0		0	0	0	24
1986			2	0		0	0	0	12
1987			2	0		0	0	0	12

Kurt Sohn continued

Year	Team	TD	1XP	2XP	FG	FGA	SAF	Pts
1988		2	0		0	0	0	12
Career		10	0		0	0	0	60

Freddie Solomon

Year	Team	TD	1XP	2XP	FG	FGA	SAF	Pts
1975	MIA N	3	0		0	0	0	18
1976		4	0		0	0	0	24
1977		2	0		0	0	0	12
1978	SF N	3	0		0	0	0	18
1979		8	0		0	0	0	48
1980		10	0		0	0	0	60
1981		8	0		0	0	0	48
1982		3	0		0	0	0	18
1983		4	0		0	0	0	24
1984		11	0		0	0	0	66
1985		1	0		0	0	0	6
Career		57	0		0	0	0	342
Playoffs		6	0		0	0	0	36

Jesse Solomon

Year	Team	TD	1XP	2XP	FG	FGA	SAF	Pts
1988	MIN N	1	0		0	0	0	6

Gordie Soltau

Year	Team	TD	1XP	2XP	FG	FGA	SAF	Pts
1950	SF N	1	26		4	7	0	44
1951		7	30		6	18	0	90
1952		7	34		6	12	0	**94**
1953		6	**48**		10	15	0	**114**
1954		2	31		11	18	0	76
1955		1	27		3	12	0	42
1956		1	26		13	20	0	71
1957		0	33		9	15	0	60
1958		0	29		8	21	0	53
Career		25	284		70	138	0	644
Playoffs		0	3		2	2	0	9

George Somers

Year	Team	TD	1XP	2XP	FG	FGA	SAF	Pts
1940	PHI N	0	1		2	9	0	7
1941	PIT N	0	0		0	2	0	0
1942		0	1		0	1	0	1
Career		0	2		2	12	0	8

Mike Sommer

Year	Team	TD	1XP	2XP	FG	FGA	SAF	Pts
1959	BAL N	2	0		0	0	0	12

Jack Sommers

Year	Team	TD	1XP	2XP	FG	FGA	SAF	Pts
1947	WAS N	0	0		0	1	0	0

Eddie Songin

Year	Team	TD	1XP	2XP	FG	FGA	SAF	Pts
1960	BOS A	2	0		0	0	0	12

Gus Sonnenberg

Year	Team	TD	1XP	2XP	FG	FGA	SAF	Pts
1923	COL N	1	0		0	0	0	6
1925	DET	0	12		5	0	0	27
1926		0	7		9	0	0	34
1927	PRO N	0	7		3	0	0	16
1928		0	7		1	0	0	10
Career		1	33		18	0	0	93

Glen Sorenson

Year	Team	TD	1XP	2XP	FG	FGA	SAF	Pts
1943	GB N	0	0		0	2	0	0
1944		0	1		0	2	0	1
1945		0	0		0	1	0	0
Career		0	1		0	5	0	1

Bill Sortet

Year	Team	TD	1XP	2XP	FG	FGA	SAF	Pts
1934	PIT N	1	0		0	0	0	6
1936		1	0		0	0	0	6
1937		1	0		0	0	0	6
1938		4	0		0	0	0	24
1939		1	0		0	0	0	6
Career		8	0		0	0	0	48

Lou Sossamon

Year	Team	TD	1XP	2XP	FG	FGA	SAF	Pts
1947	NY AA	1	0		0	0	0	6

Cecil Souders

Year	Team	TD	1XP	2XP	FG	FGA	SAF	Pts
1947	DET N	1	0		0	0	0	6

Rich Sowells

Year	Team	TD	1XP	2XP	FG	FGA	SAF	Pts
1973	NYJ N	1	0		0	0	0	6

Vic Spadaccini

Year	Team	TD	1XP	2XP	FG	FGA	SAF	Pts
1939	CLE N	1	12		0	0	0	18

Vic Spadaccini continued

Year	Team	TD	1XP	2XP	FG	FGA	SAF	Pts
1940		3	5		0	0	0	23
Career		4	17		0	0	0	41

Joe Spagna

Year	Team	TD	1XP	2XP	FG	FGA	SAF	Pts
1924	FRA N	1	0		0		0	6

John Spagnola

Year	Team	TD	1XP	2XP	FG	FGA	SAF	Pts
1980	PHI N	3	0		0	0	0	18
1982		2	0		0	0	0	12
1984		1	0		0	0	0	6
1985		5	0		0	0	0	30
1986		1	0		0	0	0	6
1987		2	0		0	0	0	12
1988	SEA N	1	0		0	0	0	6
Career		15	0		0	0	0	90

Gary Spani

Year	Team	TD	1XP	2XP	FG	FGA	SAF	Pts
1980	KC N	2	0		0	0	0	12
1981		1	0		0	0	0	6
Career		3	0		0	0	0	18

Frank Spaniel

Year	Team	TD	1XP	2XP	FG	FGA	SAF	Pts
1950	BAL N	2	0		0	0	0	12

Jim Spavital

Year	Team	TD	1XP	2XP	FG	FGA	SAF	Pts
1950	BAL N	3	0		0	0	0	18

Glen Spear

Year	Team	TD	1XP	2XP	FG	FGA	SAF	Pts
1926	KC N	1	0		0		0	6

Marcus Spears

Year	Team	TD	1XP	2XP	FG	FGA	SAF	Pts
1996	CHI N	1	0		0	0	0	6

Emmett Specht

Year	Team	TD	1XP	2XP	FG	FGA	SAF	Pts
1920	HAM A	0	0		0	0	0	0

Mac Speedie

Year	Team	TD	1XP	2XP	FG	FGA	SAF	Pts
1946	CLE AA	7	1		0	0	0	43
1947		7	0		0	0	0	42
1948		4	0		0	0	0	24
1949		7	0		0	0	0	42
1950	CLE N	1	0		0	0	0	6
1951		3	0		0	0	0	18
1952		5	0		0	0	0	30
Career		34	1		0	0	0	205

Jack Spellman

Year	Team	TD	1XP	2XP	FG	FGA	SAF	Pts
1925	PRO N	1	0		0		0	6

Jimmy Spencer

Year	Team	TD	1XP	2XP	FG	FGA	SAF	Pts
1996	CIN N	1	0	0	0	0	0	6

Tim Spencer

Year	Team	TD	1XP	2XP	FG	FGA	SAF	Pts
1985	SD N	10	0		0	0	0	60
1986		6	0		0	0	0	36
1989		3	0		0	0	0	18
Career		19	0		0	0	0	114

Willie Spencer

Year	Team	TD	1XP	2XP	FG	FGA	SAF	Pts
1977	NYG N	3	0		0	0	0	18
1978		2	0		0	0	0	12
Career		5	0		0	0	0	30

Cotton Speyrer

Year	Team	TD	1XP	2XP	FG	FGA	SAF	Pts
1973	BAL N	5	0		0	0	0	30
1974		1	0		0	0	0	6
Career		6	0		0	0	0	36

Chris Spielman

Year	Team	TD	1XP	2XP	FG	FGA	SAF	Pts
1994	DET N	1	0	0	0	0	0	6

Irving Spikes

Year	Team	TD	1XP	2XP	FG	FGA	SAF	Pts
1994	MIA N	2	0	0	0	0	0	12
1995		2	0	0	0	0	0	12
1996		4	0	0	0	0	0	24
Career		8	0	0	0	0	0	48

Jack Spikes

Year	Team	TD	1XP	2XP	FG	FGA	SAF	Pts
1960	DAL A	5	34	0	13	31	0	103
1961		5	10	1	4	13	0	54
1962		1	1	0	0	0	0	7
1963	KC A	3	23	0	2	13	0	47
1965	HOU A	3	6	0	1	2	0	27

Jack Spikes continued

Year	Team	TD	1XP	2XP	FG	FGA	SAF	Pts
1966	BUF A	4	0	0	0	0	0	24
Career		21	74	1	20	59	0	262

John Spilis

Year	Team	TD	1XP	2XP	FG	FGA	SAF	Pts
1971	GB N	1	0		0	0	0	6

Mike Spivey

Year	Team	TD	1XP	2XP	FG	FGA	SAF	Pts
1978	CHI N	1	0		0	0	0	6

Kirk Springs

Year	Team	TD	1XP	2XP	FG	FGA	SAF	Pts
1983	NYJ N	1	0		0	0	0	6

Ron Springs

Year	Team	TD	1XP	2XP	FG	FGA	SAF	Pts
1979	DAL N	3	0		0	0	0	18
1980		7	0		0	0	0	42
1981		12	0		0	0	0	72
1982		4	0		0	0	0	24
1983		8	0		0	0	0	48
1984		4	0		0	0	0	24
Career		38	0		0	0	0	228
Playoffs		3	0		0	0	0	18

Ed Sprinkle

Year	Team	TD	1XP	2XP	FG	FGA	SAF	Pts
1946	CHIB N	3	0		0	0	0	18
1948		3	0		0	0	0	18
1949		0	0		0	0	1	2
1951		2	0		0	0	0	12
1952		1	0		0	0	0	6
1953		1	0		0	0	0	6
Career		10	0		0	0	1	62

Steve Spurrier

Year	Team	TD	1XP	2XP	FG	FGA	SAF	Pts
1973	SF N	2	0		0	0	0	12

Jack Squirek

Year	Team	TD	1XP	2XP	FG	FGA	SAF	Pts
Playoffs		1	0		0	0	0	6

Brian Stablein

Year	Team	TD	1XP	2XP	FG	FGA	SAF	Pts
1996	IND N	1	0	0	0	0	0	6

Ken Stabler

Year	Team	TD	1XP	2XP	FG	FGA	SAF	Pts
1971	OAK N	2	0		0	0	0	12
1974		1	0		0	0	0	6
1976		1	0		0	0	0	6
Career		4	0		0	0	0	24
Playoffs		2	0		0	0	0	12

Billy Stacy

Year	Team	TD	1XP	2XP	FG	FGA	SAF	Pts
1959	CHIC N	2	0		0	0	0	12
1960	STL N	1	0		0	0	0	6
1961		4	0		0	0	0	24
Career		7	0		0	0	0	42

Jon Staggers

Year	Team	TD	1XP	2XP	FG	FGA	SAF	Pts
1970	PIT N	1	0		0	0	0	6
1971		1	0		0	0	0	6
1972	GB N	2	0		0	0	0	12
1973		4	0		0	0	0	24
1974		1	0		0	0	0	6
1975	DET N	2	0		0	0	0	12
Career		11	0		0	0	0	66

Larry Stallings

Year	Team	TD	1XP	2XP	FG	FGA	SAF	Pts
1965	STL N	1	0		0	0	0	6
1969		1	0		0	0	0	6
1971		1	0		0	0	0	6
Career		3	0		0	0	0	18

John Stallworth

Year	Team	TD	1XP	2XP	FG	FGA	SAF	Pts
1974	PIT N	1	0		0	0	0	6
1975		4	0		0	0	0	24
1976		3	0		0	0	0	18
1977		7	0		0	0	0	42
1978		9	0		0	0	0	54
1979		8	0		0	0	0	48
1980		1	0		0	0	0	6
1981		5	0		0	0	0	30
1982		7	0		0	0	0	42
1984		11	0		0	0	0	66
1985		5	0		0	0	0	30
1986		1	0		0	0	0	6

John Stallworth *continued*

Year	Team		TD	1XP	2XP	FG	FGA	SAF	Pts
1987			2	0		0	0	0	12
Career			64	0		0	0	0	384
Playoffs			12	0		0	0	0	72

Sylvester Stamps

Year	Team		TD	1XP	2XP	FG	FGA	SAF	Pts
1986	ATL	N	1	0		0	0	0	6
1987			1	0		0	0	0	6
1989	TB	N	1	0		0	0	0	6
Career			3	0		0	0	0	18

Haskel Stanback

Year	Team		TD	1XP	2XP	FG	FGA	SAF	Pts
1974	ATL	N	1	0		0	0	0	6
1975			5	0		0	0	0	30
1976			4	0		0	0	0	24
1977			6	0		0	0	0	36
1978			5	0		0	0	0	30
1979			5	0		0	0	0	30
Career			26	0		0	0	0	156

Norm Standlee

Year	Team		TD	1XP	2XP	FG	FGA	SAF	Pts
1941	CHIB	N	5	0		0	0	0	30
1946	SF	AA	2	0		0	0	0	12
1947			8	0		0	0	0	48
1948			3	0		0	0	0	18
1949			4	0		0	0	0	24
1950	SF	N	1	0		0	0	0	6
Career			23	0		0	0	0	138
Playoffs			4	0		0	0	0	24

Bill Stanfill

Year	Team		TD	1XP	2XP	FG	FGA	SAF	Pts
1969	MIA	A	2	0	0	0	0	0	12

Walter Stanley

Year	Team		TD	1XP	2XP	FG	FGA	SAF	Pts
1986	GB	N	3	0		0	0	0	18
1987			3	0		0	0	0	18
Career			6	0		0	0	0	36

Marshall Starks

Year	Team		TD	1XP	2XP	FG	FGA	SAF	Pts
1963	NY	A	1	0	0	0	0	0	6

Paul Staroba

Year	Team		TD	1XP	2XP	FG	FGA	SAF	Pts
1972	CLE	N	1	0		0	0	0	6

Bart Starr

Year	Team		TD	1XP	2XP	FG	FGA	SAF	Pts
1957	GB	N	3	0		0	0	0	18
1958			1	0		0	0	0	6
1961			1	0		0	0	0	6
1962			1	0		0	0	0	6
1964			3	0		0	0	0	18
1965			1	0		0	0	0	6
1966			2	0		0	0	0	12
1968			1	0		0	0	0	6
1970			1	0		0	0	0	6
1971			1	0		0	0	0	6
Career			15	0		0	0	0	90
Playoffs			1	0		0	0	0	6

Ben Starrett

Year	Team		TD	1XP	2XP	FG	FGA	SAF	Pts
1944	GB	N	2	0		0	0	0	12

Stephen Starring

Year	Team		TD	1XP	2XP	FG	FGA	SAF	Pts
1983	NE	N	2	0		0	0	0	12
1984			4	0		0	0	0	24
1986			2	0		0	0	0	12
1987			3	0		0	0	0	18
Career			11	0		0	0	0	66

Roger Staubach

Year	Team		TD	1XP	2XP	FG	FGA	SAF	Pts
1969	DAL	N	1	0		0	0	0	6
1971			2	0		0	0	0	12
1973			3	0		0	0	0	18
1974			3	0		0	0	0	18
1975			4	0		0	0	0	24
1976			3	0		0	0	0	18
1977			3	0		0	0	0	18
1978			1	0		0	0	0	6
Career			20	0		0	0	0	120

Jason Staurovsky

Year	Team		TD	1XP	2XP	FG	FGA	SAF	Pts
1987	STL	N	0	6		1	3	0	9
1988	NE	N	0	14		7	11	0	35
1989			0	14		14	17	0	56
1990			0	19		16	22	0	67

Jason Staurovsky *continued*

Year	Team		TD	1XP	2XP	FG	FGA	SAF	Pts
1991			0	10		13	19	0	49
1992	NYJ	N	0	6		3	8	0	15
Career			0	69		54	80	0	231

Ernie Stautner

Year	Team		TD	1XP	2XP	FG	FGA	SAF	Pts
1950	PIT	N	0	0		0	0	1	2
1958			0	0		0	0	1	2
1962			0	0		0	0	1	2
Career			0	0		0	0	3	6

Cliff Steele

Year	Team		TD	1XP	2XP	FG	FGA	SAF	Pts
1922	ROC	N	0	1		0		0	1

Ernie Steele

Year	Team		TD	1XP	2XP	FG	FGA	SAF	Pts
1942	PHI	N	2	1		0	0	0	13
1943	P-P	N	7	0		0	0	0	42
1944	PHI	N	5	0		0	0	0	30
1945			2	0		0	0	0	12
1946			1	0		0	0	0	6
1947			1	0		0	0	0	6
1948			2	0		0	0	0	12
Career			20	1		0	0	0	121

Jim Steffen

Year	Team		TD	1XP	2XP	FG	FGA	SAF	Pts
1962	WAS	N	1	0		0	0	0	6
1963			1	0		0	0	0	6
Career			2	0		0	0	0	12

Bob Stefik

Year	Team		TD	1XP	2XP	FG	FGA	SAF	Pts
1948	BUF	AA	0	0		0	0	0	0

Milt Stegall

Year	Team		TD	1XP	2XP	FG	FGA	SAF	Pts
1992	CIN	N	1	0		0	0	0	6

Bob Stein

Year	Team		TD	1XP	2XP	FG	FGA	SAF	Pts
1971	KC	N	0	0		0	1	0	0

Herb Stein

Year	Team		TD	1XP	2XP	FG	FGA	SAF	Pts
1924	FRA	N	0	1		0		0	1

Russ Stein

Year	Team		TD	1XP	2XP	FG	FGA	SAF	Pts
1922	TOL	N	0	2		1		0	5
1924	FRA	N	0	12		1		0	15
Career			0	14		2		0	20

Sammy Stein

Year	Team		TD	1XP	2XP	FG	FGA	SAF	Pts
1929	SI	N	1	0		0		0	6
1930			1	0		0		0	6
Career			2	0		0		0	12

Rebel Steiner

Year	Team		TD	1XP	2XP	FG	FGA	SAF	Pts
1950	GB	N	1	0		0	0	0	6

Fred Steinfort

Year	Team		TD	1XP	2XP	FG	FGA	SAF	Pts
1976	OAK	N	0	16		4	8	0	28
1977	ATL	N	0	13		6	11	0	31
1978			0	8		3	10	0	17
1980	DEN	N	0	32		26	34	0	110
1981			0	36		17	30	0	87
1983	BUF-NE	N	0	17		7	21	0	38
Career			0	122		63	114	0	311
Playoffs			0	0		0	1	0	0

Gil Steinke

Year	Team		TD	1XP	2XP	FG	FGA	SAF	Pts
1945	PHI	N	1	0		0	0	0	6
1946			4	0		0	0	0	24
1947			1	0		0	0	0	6
Career			6	0		0	0	0	36

Greg Stemrick

Year	Team		TD	1XP	2XP	FG	FGA	SAF	Pts
1977	HOU	N	1	0		0	0	0	6

Jan Stenerud

Year	Team		TD	1XP	2XP	FG	FGA	SAF	Pts
1967	KC	A	0	45	0	**21**	**36**	0	108
1968			0	39	0	30	40	0	129
1969			0	38	0	27	35	0	119
1970	KC	N	0	26		**30**	42	0	116
1971			0	32		26	44	0	110
1972			0	32		21	36	0	95
1973			0	21		24	38	0	93
1974			0	24		17	24	0	75
1975			0	30		**22**	32	0	96
1976			0	27		21	**38**	0	90

Jan Stenerud *continued*

Year	Team		TD	1XP	2XP	FG	FGA	SAF	Pts
1977			0	27		8	18	0	51
1978			0	25		20	30	0	85
1979			0	28		12	23	0	64
1980	GB	N	0	3		3	5	0	12
1981			0	35		22	24	0	101
1982			0	25		13	18	0	64
1983			0	52		21	26	0	115
1984	MIN	N	0	30		20	23	0	90
1985			0	41		15	26	0	86
Career			0	580	0	373	558	0	1699
Playoffs			0	15	0	13	21	0	54

Joe Stepanek

Year	Team		TD	1XP	2XP	FG	FGA	SAF	Pts
1987	MIN	N	0	0		0	0	1	2

John Stephens

Year	Team		TD	1XP	2XP	FG	FGA	SAF	Pts
1988	NE	N	5	0		0	0	0	30
1989			7	0		0	0	0	42
1990			3	0		0	0	0	18
1991			2	0		0	0	0	12
1992			2	0		0	0	0	12
1993	GB	N	1	0		0	0	0	6
Career			20	0		0	0	0	120

Larry Stephens

Year	Team		TD	1XP	2XP	FG	FGA	SAF	Pts
1960	CLE	N	1	0		0	0	0	6

Rod Stephens

Year	Team		TD	1XP	2XP	FG	FGA	SAF	Pts
1993	SEA	N	1	0		0	0	2	10

Tom Stephens

Year	Team		TD	1XP	2XP	FG	FGA	SAF	Pts
1960	BOS	A	3	0	0	0	0	0	18
1961			3	0	0	0	0	0	18
Career			6	0	0	0	0	0	36

Jack Steptoe

Year	Team		TD	1XP	2XP	FG	FGA	SAF	Pts
1978	SF	N	1	0		0	0	0	6

Ed Sternaman

Year	Team		TD	1XP	2XP	FG	FGA	SAF	Pts
1920	DEC	A	1	1		**3**		0	16
1921			2	9		**5**		0	36
1922	CHIB	N	2	5		6		0	35
1923			5	7		5		0	52
1924			3	2		1		0	23
1925			1	0		0		0	6
1926			1	3		1		0	12
Career			15	27		21		0	180

Joey Sternaman

Year	Team		TD	1XP	2XP	FG	FGA	SAF	Pts
1922	CHIB	N	6	2		0		0	38
1923	DUL-CHIB	N	2	4		6		0	34
1924	CHIB	N	6	12		**9**		0	**75**
1925			6	17		3		0	62
1926	CHI	A	3	7		**9**		0	52
1927	CHIB	N	2	4		0		0	16
1928			5	5		0		0	35
1929			0	8		0		0	8
1930			1	5		0		0	11
Career			31	64		27		0	331

Bob Steuber

Year	Team		TD	1XP	2XP	FG	FGA	SAF	Pts
1948	BUF	AA	3	20		1	2	0	41

Don Stevens

Year	Team		TD	1XP	2XP	FG	FGA	SAF	Pts
1952	PHI	N	1	0		0	0	0	6

Howard Stevens

Year	Team		TD	1XP	2XP	FG	FGA	SAF	Pts
1973	NO	N	2	0		0	0	0	12
1974			1	0		0	0	0	6
1976	BAL	N	1	0		0	0	0	6
Career			4	0		0	0	0	24

Mark Stevens

Year	Team		TD	1XP	2XP	FG	FGA	SAF	Pts
1987	SF	N	1	0		0	0	0	6

James Stewart

Year	Team		TD	1XP	2XP	FG	FGA	SAF	Pts
1995	JAC	N	3	0	0	0	0	0	18
1996			10	0	0	0	0	0	60
Career			13	0	0	0	0	0	78

Kordell Stewart

Year	Team		TD	1XP	2XP	FG	FGA	SAF	Pts
1995	PIT	N	2	0	0	0	0	0	12

Kordell Stewart *continued*

Year	Team	Lg	TD	1XP	2XP	FG	FGA	SAF	Pts
1996			8	0	0	0	0	0	48
Career			10	0	0	0	0	0	60
Playoffs			3	0	0	0	0	0	18

Michael Stewart

Year	Team	Lg	TD	1XP	2XP	FG	FGA	SAF	Pts
1987	LARM	N	0	0		0	0	1	2
1989			1	0		0	0	0	6
Career			1	0		0	0	1	8

Wayne Stewart

Year	Team	Lg	TD	1XP	2XP	FG	FGA	SAF	Pts
1972	NYJ	N	1	0		0	0	0	6
1974	SD	N	1	0		0	0	0	6
Career			2	0		0	0	0	12

Walt Stickel

Year	Team	Lg	TD	1XP	2XP	FG	FGA	SAF	Pts
1951	PHI	N	0	0		0	0	1	2

Monty Stickles

Year	Team	Lg	TD	1XP	2XP	FG	FGA	SAF	Pts
1961	SF	N	5	0		0	0	0	30
1962			3	0		0	0	0	18
1964			3	0		0	0	0	18
1965			1	0		0	0	0	6
1966			2	0		0	0	0	12
1968	NO	N	2	0		0	0	0	12
Career			16	0		0	0	0	96

Dave Stief

Year	Team	Lg	TD	1XP	2XP	FG	FGA	SAF	Pts
1978	STL	N	4	0		0	0	0	24
1981			1	0		0	0	0	6
Career			5	0		0	0	0	30

Jim Stienke

Year	Team	Lg	TD	1XP	2XP	FG	FGA	SAF	Pts
1976	NYG	N	1	0		0	0	0	6

Jim Stiger

Year	Team	Lg	TD	1XP	2XP	FG	FGA	SAF	Pts
1963	DAL	N	1	0		0	0	0	6
1964			2	0		0	0	0	12
1966	LA	N	1	0		0	0	0	6
Career			4	0		0	0	0	24

Ken Stills

Year	Team	Lg	TD	1XP	2XP	FG	FGA	SAF	Pts
1986	GB	N	1	0		0	0	0	6

Pete Stinchcomb

Year	Team	Lg	TD	1XP	2XP	FG	FGA	SAF	Pts
1921	DEC	A	4	0		0		0	24
1922	CHIB	N	3	0		0		0	18
Career			7	0		0		0	42

Darryl Stingley

Year	Team	Lg	TD	1XP	2XP	FG	FGA	SAF	Pts
1973	NE	N	2	0		0	0	0	12
1974			2	0		0	0	0	12
1975			2	0		0	0	0	12
1976			4	0		0	0	0	24
1977			6	0		0	0	0	36
Career			16	0		0	0	0	96

Jim Stinnette

Year	Team	Lg	TD	1XP	2XP	FG	FGA	SAF	Pts
1961	DEN	A	1	0	0	0	0	0	6
1962			1	0	0	0	0	0	6
Career			2	0	0	0	0	0	12

Lemuel Stinson

Year	Team	Lg	TD	1XP	2XP	FG	FGA	SAF	Pts
1989	CHI	N	1	0		0	0	0	6
1991			1	0		0	0	0	6
Career			2	0		0	0	0	12

Bill Stits

Year	Team	Lg	TD	1XP	2XP	FG	FGA	SAF	Pts
1955	DET	N	1	0		0	0	0	6

Hust Stockton

Year	Team	Lg	TD	1XP	2XP	FG	FGA	SAF	Pts
1925	FRA	N	0	0		0		0	0
1926			2	0		0		0	12
1928			4	0		0		0	24
1929	PRO-BOS	N	1	0		0		0	6
Career			7	0		0		0	42

John Stofa

Year	Team	Lg	TD	1XP	2XP	FG	FGA	SAF	Pts
1967	MIA	A	1	0	0	0	0	0	6

Fred Stokes

Year	Team	Lg	TD	1XP	2XP	FG	FGA	SAF	Pts
1989	WAS	N	0	0		0	0	1	2

J.J. Stokes

Year	Team	Lg	TD	1XP	2XP	FG	FGA	SAF	Pts
1995	SF	N	4	0	0	0	0	0	24

Lee Stokes

Year	Team	Lg	TD	1XP	2XP	FG	FGA	SAF	Pts
1943	CHIC	N	0	5		1	3	0	8

Billy Stone

Year	Team	Lg	TD	1XP	2XP	FG	FGA	SAF	Pts
1949	BAL	AA	8	0		0	0	0	48
1950	BAL	N	5	0		0	0	0	30
1951	CHIB	N	2	0		0	0	0	12
1952			4	0		0	0	0	24
1953			6	0		0	0	0	36
1954			6	0		0	0	0	36
Career			31	0		0	0	0	186

Donnie Stone

Year	Team	Lg	TD	1XP	2XP	FG	FGA	SAF	Pts
1961	DEN	A	8	0	0	0	0	0	48
1962			5	0	0	0	0	0	30
1963			4	0	0	0	0	0	24
Career			17	0	0	0	0	0	102

Dwight Stone

Year	Team	Lg	TD	1XP	2XP	FG	FGA	SAF	Pts
1988	PIT	N	2	0		0	0	0	12
1990			1	0		0	0	0	6
1991			5	0		0	0	0	30
1992			3	0		0	0	0	18
1993			3	0		0	0	0	18
1994			0	0	1	0	0	0	2
Career			14	0	1	0	0	0	86

Ken Stone

Year	Team	Lg	TD	1XP	2XP	FG	FGA	SAF	Pts
1973	WAS	N	1	0		0	0	0	6

Steve Stonebreaker

Year	Team	Lg	TD	1XP	2XP	FG	FGA	SAF	Pts
1962	MIN	N	1	0		0	0	0	6
1964	BAL	N	1	0		0	0	0	6
Career			2	0		0	0	0	12

Don Stonesifer

Year	Team	Lg	TD	1XP	2XP	FG	FGA	SAF	Pts
1951	CHIC	N	2	0		0	0	0	12
1953			2	0		0	0	0	12
1954			3	0		0	0	0	18
1955			5	0		0	0	0	30
1956			2	0		0	0	0	12
Career			14	0		0	0	0	84

Jack Storer

Year	Team	Lg	TD	1XP	2XP	FG	FGA	SAF	Pts
1924	FRA	N	8	0		0		0	48

Ed Storm

Year	Team	Lg	TD	1XP	2XP	FG	FGA	SAF	Pts
1934	PHI	N	2	0		0		0	12

Cliff Stoudt

Year	Team	Lg	TD	1XP	2XP	FG	FGA	SAF	Pts
1983	PIT	N	4	0		0	0	0	24

Pete Stout

Year	Team	Lg	TD	1XP	2XP	FG	FGA	SAF	Pts
1949	WAS	N	6	0		0	0	0	36

Jerry Stovall

Year	Team	Lg	TD	1XP	2XP	FG	FGA	SAF	Pts
1964	STL	N	1	0		0	0	0	6
1966			1	0		0	0	0	6
Career			2	0		0	0	0	12

Matt Stover

Year	Team	Lg	TD	1XP	2XP	FG	FGA	SAF	Pts
1991	CLE	N	0	33		16	22	0	81
1992			0	29		21	29	0	92
1993			0	36		16	22	0	84
1994			0	32	0	26	28	0	110
1995			0	26	0	29	33	0	113
1996	BAL	N	0	34	0	19	25	0	91
Career			0	190	0	127	159	0	571
Playoffs			0	2	0	3	5	0	11

Otto Stowe

Year	Team	Lg	TD	1XP	2XP	FG	FGA	SAF	Pts
1971	MIA	N	1	0		0	0	0	6
1972			2	0		0	0	0	12
1973	DAL	N	6	0		0	0	0	36
1974	DEN	N	1	0		0	0	0	6
Career			10	0		0	0	0	60

Tyronne Stowe

Year	Team	Lg	TD	1XP	2XP	FG	FGA	SAF	Pts
1990	PIT	N	0	0		0	0	1	2

Tommie Stowers

Year	Team	Lg	TD	1XP	2XP	FG	FGA	SAF	Pts
1993	NO	N	0	0		0	0	1	2

Pete Stoyanovich

Year	Team	Lg	TD	1XP	2XP	FG	FGA	SAF	Pts
1989	MIA	N	0	38		19	26	0	95
1990			0	37		21	25	0	100
1991			0	28		**31**	37	0	121
1992			0	34		**30**	37	0	**124**
1993			0	37		24	32	0	109
1994			0	35	0	24	31	0	107
1995			0	37	0	27	34	0	118
1996	KC	N	0	34	0	17	24	0	85
Career			0	280	0	193	246	0	859
Playoffs			0	19	0	7	10	0	40

Mike Strachan

Year	Team	Lg	TD	1XP	2XP	FG	FGA	SAF	Pts
1975	NO	N	2	0		0	0	0	12
1976			2	0		0	0	0	12
1978			4	0		0	0	0	24
1979			6	0		0	0	0	36
Career			14	0		0	0	0	84

Steve Strachan

Year	Team	Lg	TD	1XP	2XP	FG	FGA	SAF	Pts
1988	LARI	N	1	0		0	0	0	6

Red Strader

Year	Team	Lg	TD	1XP	2XP	FG	FGA	SAF	Pts
1927	CHIC	N	1	0		0		0	6

Troy Stradford

Year	Team	Lg	TD	1XP	2XP	FG	FGA	SAF	Pts
1987	MIA	N	7	0		0	0	0	42
1988			3	0		0	0	0	18
1989			1	0		0	0	0	6
1990			1	0		0	0	0	6
Career			12	0		0	0	0	72

Michael Strahan

Year	Team	Lg	TD	1XP	2XP	FG	FGA	SAF	Pts
1995	NYG	N	0	0	0	0	0	1	2

Mike Stramiello

Year	Team	Lg	TD	1XP	2XP	FG	FGA	SAF	Pts
1930	BKN	N	1	6		0		0	12
1931			1	0		0		0	6
Career			2	6		0		0	18

Lief Strand

Year	Team	Lg	TD	1XP	2XP	FG	FGA	SAF	Pts
1924	DUL	N	0	0		0		1	2

Mike Stratton

Year	Team	Lg	TD	1XP	2XP	FG	FGA	SAF	Pts
1963	BUF	A	1	0	0	0	0	0	6
1966			1	0	0	0	0	0	6
Career			2	0	0	0	0	0	12

Jimmy Strausbaugh

Year	Team	Lg	TD	1XP	2XP	FG	FGA	SAF	Pts
1946	CHIC	N	3	0		0	0	0	18

Dutch Strauss

Year	Team	Lg	TD	1XP	2XP	FG	FGA	SAF	Pts
1924	KC	N	1	0		0		0	6

Les Strayhorn

Year	Team	Lg	TD	1XP	2XP	FG	FGA	SAF	Pts
1973	DAL	N	1	0		0	0	0	6

Eric Streater

Year	Team	Lg	TD	1XP	2XP	FG	FGA	SAF	Pts
1987	TB	N	2	0		0	0	0	12

Bill Stribling

Year	Team	Lg	TD	1XP	2XP	FG	FGA	SAF	Pts
1951	NYG	N	2	0		0	0	0	12
1952			5	0		0	0	0	30
1955	PHI	N	6	0		0	0	0	36
1957			1	0		0	0	0	6
Career			14	0		0	0	0	84

Don Strock

Year	Team	Lg	TD	1XP	2XP	FG	FGA	SAF	Pts
1975	MIA	N	1	0		0	0	0	6
1976			1	0		0	0	0	6
Career			2	0		0	0	0	12

Jim Strong

Year	Team	Lg	TD	1XP	2XP	FG	FGA	SAF	Pts
1971	NO	N	3	0		0	0	0	18

Ken Strong

Year	Team	Lg	TD	1XP	2XP	FG	FGA	SAF	Pts
1929	SI	N	5	9		0		0	39
1930			7	8		1		0	53
1931			7	5		**2**		0	53
1932			2	3		0		0	15
1933	NYG	N	5	**14**		5		0	59

Ken Strong *continued*

Year	Team		TD	1XP	2XP	FG	FGA	SAF	Pts
1934			6	7		4		0	55
1935			1	11		4		0	29
1939			0	7		4	8	0	19
1944			0	23		**6**	**12**	0	41
1945			0	23		6	**13**	0	41
1946			0	32		4	9	0	44
1947			0	24		2	5	0	30
Career			33	166		38	47	0	478
Playoffs			4	9		1	2	0	36

Mack Strong

Year	Team		TD	1XP	2XP	FG	FGA	SAF	Pts
1994	**SEA**	**N**	2	0	0	0	0	0	12
1995			4	0	0	0	0	0	24
Career			6	0	0	0	0	0	36

Ray Strong

Year	Team		TD	1XP	2XP	FG	FGA	SAF	Pts
1978	**ATL**	**N**	2	0		0	0	0	12
1980			1	0		0	0	0	6
Career			3	0		0	0	0	18

Morris Stroud

Year	Team		TD	1XP	2XP	FG	FGA	SAF	Pts
1970	**KC**	**N**	1	0		0	0	0	6
1971			1	0		0	0	0	6
1972			1	0		0	0	0	6
1973			2	0		0	0	0	12
1974			2	0		0	0	0	12
Career			7	0		0	0	0	42

Art Strutt

Year	Team		TD	1XP	2XP	FG	FGA	SAF	Pts
1935	**PIT**	**N**	1	0		0		0	6
1936			1	0		0		0	6
Career			2	0		0		0	12

Johnny Strzykalski

Year	Team		TD	1XP	2XP	FG	FGA	SAF	Pts
1946	**SF**	**AA**	2	0		0	0	0	12
1947			8	0		0	0	0	48
1948			11	0		0	0	0	66
1949			4	0		0	0	0	24
1950	**SF**	**N**	3	0		0	0	0	18
1951			3	0		0	0	0	18
Career			31	0		0	0	0	186

Jim Stuckey

Year	Team		TD	1XP	2XP	FG	FGA	SAF	Pts
1980	**SF**	**N**	0	0		0	0	1	2

Dave Studdard

Year	Team		TD	1XP	2XP	FG	FGA	SAF	Pts
1979	**DEN**	**N**	1	0		0	0	0	6
1986			1	0		0	0	0	6
Career			2	0		0	0	0	12

Pat Studstill

Year	Team		TD	1XP	2XP	FG	FGA	SAF	Pts
1961	**DET**	**N**	1	0		0	0	0	6
1962			4	0		0	0	0	24
1964			1	0		0	0	0	6
1965			3	0		0	0	0	18
1966			5	0		0	0	0	30
1967			2	0		0	0	0	12
1968	**LA**	**N**	1	0		0	0	0	6
1970			2	0		0	0	0	12
Career			19	0		0	0	0	114

Harry Stuhldreher

Year	Team		TD	1XP	2XP	FG	FGA	SAF	Pts
1926	**BKN**	**A**	0	1		0		0	1

Charlie Stukes

Year	Team		TD	1XP	2XP	FG	FGA	SAF	Pts
1968	**BAL**	**N**	1	0		0	0	0	6

Dick Sturtridge

Year	Team		TD	1XP	2XP	FG	FGA	SAF	Pts
1928	**CHIB**	**N**	3	1		0		0	19

Joe Stydahar

Year	Team		TD	1XP	2XP	FG	FGA	SAF	Pts
1936	**CHIB**	**N**	0	3		0		0	3
1939			0	4		0	0	0	4
1941			0	4		0	0	0	4
1942			0	5		0	0	0	5
1946			0	12		0	2	0	12
Career			0	28		0	2	0	28
Playoffs			0	4		0	0	0	4

Andy Stynchula

Year	Team		TD	1XP	2XP	FG	FGA	SAF	Pts
1964	**NYG**	**N**	0	1		0	0	0	1
1965			0	12		3	7	0	21
Career			0	13		3	7	0	22

Bob Suci

Year	Team		TD	1XP	2XP	FG	FGA	SAF	Pts
1963	**BOS**	**A**	2	0	0	0	0	0	12

Leo Sugar

Year	Team		TD	1XP	2XP	FG	FGA	SAF	Pts
1954	**CHIC**	**N**	1	0		0	0	0	6
1957			2	0		0	0	0	12
Career			3	0		0	0	0	18

Shafer Suggs

Year	Team		TD	1XP	2XP	FG	FGA	SAF	Pts
1979	**NYJ**	**N**	1	0		0	0	0	6

Matt Suhey

Year	Team		TD	1XP	2XP	FG	FGA	SAF	Pts
1981	**CHI**	**N**	3	0		0	0	0	18
1982			3	0		0	0	0	18
1983			5	0		0	0	0	30
1984			6	0		0	0	0	36
1985			2	0		0	0	0	12
1986			2	0		0	0	0	12
1988			2	0		0	0	0	12
1989			2	0		0	0	0	12
Career			25	0		0	0	0	150
Playoffs			1	0		0	0	0	6

Joe Sulatis

Year	Team		TD	1XP	2XP	FG	FGA	SAF	Pts
1948	**NYG**	**N**	2	0		0	0	0	12

George Sulima

Year	Team		TD	1XP	2XP	FG	FGA	SAF	Pts
1952	**PIT**	**N**	1	0		0	0	0	6
1954			1	0		0	0	0	6
Career			2	0		0	0	0	12

Bob Sullivan

Year	Team		TD	1XP	2XP	FG	FGA	SAF	Pts
1947	**PIT**	**N**	2	0		0	0	0	12

Bob Sullivan

Year	Team		TD	1XP	2XP	FG	FGA	SAF	Pts
1948	**SF**	**AA**	1	0		0	0	0	6

George Sullivan

Year	Team		TD	1XP	2XP	FG	FGA	SAF	Pts
1924	**FRA**	**N**	5	0		0		0	30
1925			3	0		0		0	18
Career			8	0		0		0	48

Jack Sullivan

Year	Team		TD	1XP	2XP	FG	FGA	SAF	Pts
1921	**WAS**	**A**	0	0		0		0	0

Tom Sullivan

Year	Team		TD	1XP	2XP	FG	FGA	SAF	Pts
1973	**PHI**	**N**	5	0		0	0	0	30
1974			12	0		0	0	0	72
1976			3	0		0	0	0	18
1977			2	0		0	0	0	12
Career			22	0		0	0	0	132

Ivory Sully

Year	Team		TD	1XP	2XP	FG	FGA	SAF	Pts
1984	**LARM**	**N**	0	0		0	0	1	2

Pat Summerall

Year	Team		TD	1XP	2XP	FG	FGA	SAF	Pts
1953	**CHIC**	**N**	0	23		9	24	0	50
1954			0	21		8	18	0	45
1955			1	23		8	19	0	53
1956			0	30		10	22	0	60
1957			0	24		6	17	0	42
1958	**NYG**	**N**	0	28		12	23	0	64
1959			0	30		**20**	**29**	0	90
1960			0	32		13	26	0	71
1961			0	**46**		14	34	0	88
Career			1	257		100	212	0	563
Playoffs			0	4		5	5	0	19

Bob Summerhays

Year	Team		TD	1XP	2XP	FG	FGA	SAF	Pts
1951	**GB**	**N**	1	0		0	0	0	6

Don Summers

Year	Team		TD	1XP	2XP	FG	FGA	SAF	Pts
1987	**GB**	**N**	1	0		0	0	0	6

Charlie Sumner

Year	Team		TD	1XP	2XP	FG	FGA	SAF	Pts
1958	**CHIB**	**N**	1	0		0	0	0	6

Walt Sumner

Year	Team		TD	1XP	2XP	FG	FGA	SAF	Pts
1969	**CLE**	**N**	1	0		0	0	0	6
Playoffs			1	0	0	0	0	0	6

Ian Sunter

Year	Team		TD	1XP	2XP	FG	FGA	SAF	Pts
1980	**CIN**	**N**	0	15		11	20	0	48

Len Supulski

Year	Team		TD	1XP	2XP	FG	FGA	SAF	Pts
1942	**PHI**	**N**	1	0		0	0	0	6

Nick Susoeff

Year	Team		TD	1XP	2XP	FG	FGA	SAF	Pts
1947	**SF**	**AA**	2	0		0	0	0	12
1948			1	0		0	0	0	6
1949			1	0		0	0	0	6
Career			4	0		0	0	0	24

Ed Susteric

Year	Team		TD	1XP	2XP	FG	FGA	SAF	Pts
1949	**CLE**	**AA**	1	0		0	0	0	6

Don Sutherin

Year	Team		TD	1XP	2XP	FG	FGA	SAF	Pts
1959	**PIT**	**N**	0	0		0	1	0	0

Ed Sutton

Year	Team		TD	1XP	2XP	FG	FGA	SAF	Pts
1957	**WAS**	**N**	6	0		0	0	0	36
1958			3	0		0	0	0	18
1959			1	0		0	0	0	6
Career			10	0		0	0	0	60

Joe Sutton

Year	Team		TD	1XP	2XP	FG	FGA	SAF	Pts
1949	**BUF**	**AA**	1	0		0	0	0	6

Reggie Sutton

Year	Team		TD	1XP	2XP	FG	FGA	SAF	Pts
1987	**NO**	**N**	1	0		0	0	0	6

Harland Svare

Year	Team		TD	1XP	2XP	FG	FGA	SAF	Pts
1959	**NYG**	**N**	1	0		0	0	0	6

Earl Svendsen

Year	Team		TD	1XP	2XP	FG	FGA	SAF	Pts
1939	**GB**	**N**	1	0		0	0	0	6

Alton Swain

Year	Team		TD	1XP	2XP	FG	FGA	SAF	Pts
1926	**BUF**	**N**	1	0		0		0	6

Bill Swain

Year	Team		TD	1XP	2XP	FG	FGA	SAF	Pts
1968	**DET**	**N**	1	0		0	0	0	6

Karl Swanke

Year	Team		TD	1XP	2XP	FG	FGA	SAF	Pts
1981	**GB**	**N**	1	0		0	0	0	6

Eric Swann

Year	Team		TD	1XP	2XP	FG	FGA	SAF	Pts
1992	**PHX**	**N**	0	0		0	0	1	2
1993			0	0		0	0	1	2
1994	**ARI**	**N**	0	0	0	0	0	1	2
Career			0	0	0	0	0	3	6

Lynn Swann

Year	Team		TD	1XP	2XP	FG	FGA	SAF	Pts
1974	**PIT**	**N**	3	0		0	0	0	18
1975			11	0		0	0	0	66
1976			3	0		0	0	0	18
1977			7	0		0	0	0	42
1978			11	0		0	0	0	66
1979			6	0		0	0	0	36
1980			7	0		0	0	0	42
1981			5	0		0	0	0	30
Career			53	0		0	0	0	318
Playoffs			9	0		0	0	0	54

Evar Swanson

Year	Team		TD	1XP	2XP	FG	FGA	SAF	Pts
1924	**MIL**	**N**	3	0		0		0	18
1926	**CHIC**	**N**	0	1		0		0	1
1927			0	2		1		0	5
Career			3	3		1			24

Shane Swanson

Year	Team		TD	1XP	2XP	FG	FGA	SAF	Pts
1987	**DEN**	**N**	1	0		0	0	0	6

Calvin Sweeney

Year	Team		TD	1XP	2XP	FG	FGA	SAF	Pts
1980	**PIT**	**N**	1	0		0	0	0	6
1983			5	0		0	0	0	30
1986			1	0		0	0	0	6
Career			7	0		0	0	0	42

Steve Sweeney

Year	Team		TD	1XP	2XP	FG	FGA	SAF	Pts
1973	**OAK**	**N**	1	0		0	0	0	6

Fred Sweet

Year	Team		TD	1XP	2XP	FG	FGA	SAF	Pts
1925	**PRO**	**N**	0	1		2		0	7
1926			0	1		0		0	1
Career			0	2		2		0	8

Year	Team		TD	1XP	2XP	FG	FGA	SAF	Pts
Joe Sweet									
1972	LA	N	1	0		0	0	1	8
Karl Sweetan									
1966	DET	N	1	0		0	0	0	6
1967			1	0		0	0	0	6
Career			2	0		0	0	0	12
Fred Sweetland									
1920	AKR	A	1	0		0		0	6
Bob Sweiger									
1946	NY	AA	1	0		0	0	0	6
1947			2	0		0	0	0	12
Career			3	0		0	0	0	18
Bob Swenson									
1979	DEN	N	1	0		0	0	0	6
Bill Swiacki									
1948	NYG	N	10	0		0	0	0	60
1949			4	0		0	0	0	24
1950			3	0		0	0	0	18
1952	DET	N	1	0		0	0	0	6
Career			18	0		0	0	0	108
Pat Swilling									
1991	NO	N	1	0		0	0	0	6
Bob Swisher									
1939	CHIB	N	3	0		0	0	0	18
1941			3	0		0	0	0	18
Career			6	0		0	0	0	36
Playoffs			1	0		0	0	0	6
Veryl Switzer									
1954	GB	N	4	0		0	0	0	24
1955			1	0		0	0	0	6
Career			5	0		0	0	0	30
Harry Sydney									
1990	SF	N	3	0		0	0	0	18
1991			7	0		0	0	0	42
1992	GB	N	3	0		0	0	0	18
Career			13	0		0	0	0	78
John Symank									
1963	STL	N	1	0		0	0	0	6
Len Szafaryn									
1955	GB	N	1	0		0	0	0	6
Paul Szakash									
1939	DET	N	0	0		0	0	0	0
Rich Szaro									
1975	NO	N	0	17		10	16	0	47
1976			0	25		18	23	0	79
1977			0	29		5	12	0	44
1978			0	9		4	6	0	21
1979	NYJ	N	0	2		0	2	0	2
Career			0	82		37	59	0	193
Dick Szymanski									
1959	BAL	N	1	0		0	0	0	6
Doyle Tackett									
1946	BKN	AA	2	0		0	0	0	12
Charles Tackwell									
1930	FRA	N	1	1		0		0	7
1931	FRA-CHIB	N	0	3		0		0	3
1932	CHIB	N	0	3		0		0	3
Career			1	7		0		0	13
Jerry Tagge									
1972	GB	N	1	0		0	0	0	6
1973			2	0		0	0	0	12
Career			3	0		0	0	0	18
John Tagliaferri									
1987	MIA	N	1	0		0	0	0	6

Year	Team		TD	1XP	2XP	FG	FGA	SAF	Pts
Art Tait									
1951	NYY	N	2	0		0	0	0	12
George Taliaferro									
1949	LA	AA	7	0		0	0	0	42
1950	NYY	N	9	0		0	0	0	54
1951			5	0		0	0	0	30
1952	DAL	N	2	0		0	0	0	12
1953	BAL	N	4	0		0	0	0	24
1954			1	0		0	0	0	6
Career			28	0		0	0	0	168
Mike Taliaferro									
1966	NY	A	0	0	1	0	0	0	2
Darryl Talley									
1990	BUF	N	1	0		0	0	0	6
1993			1	0		0	0	0	6
Career			2	0		0	0	0	12
Playoffs			1	0		0	0	0	6
Ralph Tamm									
1993	SF	N	1	0		0	0	0	6
James Tanguay									
1933	PIT	N	0	0		0		0	0
Steve Tannen									
1970	NYJ	N	1	0		0	0	0	6
Bob Tanner									
1930	FRA	N	2	0		0		0	12
Hamp Tanner									
1951	SF	N	0	0		0	0	1	2
John Tanner									
1923	CLE	N	1	2		0		0	8
1924			2	0		0		0	12
Career			3	2		0		0	20
John Tanner									
1974	NE	N	1	0		0	0	0	6
George Tarasovic									
1959	PIT	N	1	0		0	0	0	6
1965	PHI	N	2	0		0	0	0	12
Career			3	0		0	0	0	18
Fran Tarkenton									
1961	MIN	N	5	0		0	0	0	30
1962			2	0		0	0	0	12
1963			1	0		0	0	0	6
1964			2	0		0	0	0	12
1965			1	0		0	0	0	6
1966			4	0		0	0	0	24
1967	NYG	N	2	0		0	0	0	12
1968			3	0		0	0	0	18
1970			2	0		0	0	0	12
1971			3	0		0	0	0	18
1973	MIN	N	1	0		0	0	0	6
1974			2	0		0	0	0	12
1975			2	0		0	0	0	12
1976			1	0		0	0	0	6
1978			1	0		0	0	0	6
Career			32	0		0	0	0	192
Playoffs			1	0		0	0	0	6
Jerry Tarr									
1962	DEN	A	2	0	0	0	0	0	12
John Tarver									
1972	NE	N	2	0		0	0	0	12
1973			4	0		0	0	0	24
1974			2	0		0	0	0	12
Career			8	0		0	0	0	48
Carl Taseff									
1951	CLE	N	2	0		0	0	0	12
1953	BAL	N	2	0		0	0	0	12
1954			1	0		0	0	0	6
1956			2	0		0	0	0	12
1959			1	0		0	0	0	6
Career			8	0		0	0	0	48

Year	Team		TD	1XP	2XP	FG	FGA	SAF	Pts
Steve Tasker									
1987	BUF	N	0	0		0	0	1	2
1990			2	0		0	0	0	12
1991			1	0		0	0	0	6
1995			3	0	0	0	0	0	18
1996			3	0	0	0	0	0	18
Career			9	0	0	0	0	1	56
Playoffs			1	0	0	0	0	0	6
Damon Tassos									
1946	DET	N	0	3		0	1	0	3
Lars Tate									
1988	TB	N	8	0		0	0	0	48
1989			9	0		0	0	0	54
Career			17	0		0	0	0	102
Jack Tatum									
1972	OAK	N	1	0		0	0	0	6
Mosi Tatupu									
1980	NE	N	3	0		0	0	0	18
1981			3	0		0	0	0	18
1983			5	0		0	0	0	30
1984			4	0		0	0	0	24
1985			2	0		0	0	0	12
1986			2	0		0	0	0	12
1988			2	0		0	0	0	12
Career			21	0		0	0	0	126
Playoffs			1	0		0	0	0	6
Biff Taugher									
1922	GB	N	1	0		0		0	6
Junior Tautalatasi									
1986	PHI	N	2	0		0	0	0	12
Altie Taylor									
1970	DET	N	4	0		0	0	0	24
1971			5	0		0	0	0	30
1972			6	0		0	0	0	36
1973			5	0		0	0	0	30
1974			6	0		0	0	0	36
1975			4	0		0	0	0	24
Career			30	0		0	0	0	180
Billy Taylor									
1979	NYG	N	11	0		0	0	0	66
1980			4	0		0	0	0	24
1981			2	0		0	0	0	12
Career			17	0		0	0	0	102
Bruce Taylor									
1970	SF	N	1	0		0	0	0	6
1971			1	0		0	0	0	6
Career			2	0		0	0	0	12
Charley Taylor									
1964	WAS	N	10	0		0	0	0	60
1965			6	0		0	0	0	36
1966			15	0		0	0	0	90
1967			9	0		0	0	0	54
1968			5	0		0	0	0	30
1969			8	0		0	0	0	48
1970			8	0		0	0	0	48
1971			4	0		0	0	0	24
1972			7	0		0	0	0	42
1973			7	0		0	0	0	42
1974			5	0		0	0	0	30
1975			6	0		0	0	0	36
Career			90	0		0	0	0	540
Playoffs			2	0		0	0	0	12
Cliff Taylor									
1974	CHI	N	1	0		0	0	0	6
1976	GB	N	1	0		0	0	0	6
Career			2	0		0	0	0	12
Corky Taylor									
1955	LA	N	2	0		0	0	0	12
Craig Taylor									
1989	CIN	N	5	0		0	0	0	30
1990			3	0		0	0	0	18

Craig Taylor *continued*

Year	Team		TD	1XP	2XP	FG	FGA	SAF	Pts
1991			2	0		0	0	0	12
Career			10	0		0	0	0	60

Hosea Taylor

Year	Team		TD	1XP	2XP	FG	FGA	SAF	Pts
1981	**BAL**	**N**	0	0		0	0	1	2

Hugh Taylor

Year	Team		TD	1XP	2XP	FG	FGA	SAF	Pts
1947	**WAS**	**N**	6	0		0	0	0	36
1948			3	0		0	0	0	18
1949			9	0		0	0	0	54
1950			9	0		0	0	0	54
1951			3	0		0	0	0	18
1952			12	0		0	0	0	72
1953			8	0		0	0	0	48
1954			8	0		0	0	0	48
Career			58	0		0	0	0	348

Jesse Taylor

Year	Team		TD	1XP	2XP	FG	FGA	SAF	Pts
1972	**SD**	**N**	1	0		0	0	0	6

Jim Taylor

Year	Team		TD	1XP	2XP	FG	FGA	SAF	Pts
1958	**GB**	**N**	2	0		0	0	0	12
1959			8	0		0	0	0	48
1960			11	0		0	0	0	66
1961			**16**	0		0	0	0	96
1962			**19**	0		0	0	0	**114**
1963			10	0		0	0	0	60
1964			15	0		0	0	0	90
1965			4	0		0	0	0	24
1966			6	0		0	0	0	36
1967	**NO**	**N**	2	0		0	0	0	12
Career			93	0		0	0	0	558
Playoffs			2	0		0	0	0	12

John Taylor

Year	Team		TD	1XP	2XP	FG	FGA	SAF	Pts
1987	**SF**	**N**	1	0		0	0	0	6
1988			4	0		0	0	0	24
1989			10	0		0	0	0	60
1990			7	0		0	0	0	42
1991			9	0		0	0	0	54
1992			3	0		0	0	0	18
1993			5	0		0	0	0	30
1994			5	0	0	0	0	0	30
1995			2	0	0	0	0	0	12
Career			46	0	0	0	0	0	276
Playoffs			6	0	0	0	0	0	36

Keith Taylor

Year	Team		TD	1XP	2XP	FG	FGA	SAF	Pts
1989	**IND**	**N**	1	0		0	0	0	6

Kitrick Taylor

Year	Team		TD	1XP	2XP	FG	FGA	SAF	Pts
1990	**SD**	**N**	1	0		0	0	0	6
1992	**GB**	**N**	1	0		0	0	0	6
Career			2	0		0	0	0	12

Lawrence Taylor

Year	Team		TD	1XP	2XP	FG	FGA	SAF	Pts
1982	**NYG**	**N**	1	0		0	0	0	6
1990			1	0		0	0	0	6
Career			2	0		0	0	0	12
Playoffs			1	0		0	0	0	6

Lenny Taylor

Year	Team		TD	1XP	2XP	FG	FGA	SAF	Pts
1987	**ATL**	**N**	1	0		0	0	0	6

Lionel Taylor

Year	Team		TD	1XP	2XP	FG	FGA	SAF	Pts
1960	**DEN**	**A**	12	0	0	0	0	0	72
1961			4	0	0	0	0	0	24
1962			4	0	0	0	0	0	24
1963			10	0	0	0	0	0	60
1964			7	0	0	0	0	0	42
1965			6	0	0	0	0	0	36
1966			1	0	0	0	0	0	6
1967	**HOU**	**A**	1	0	0	0	0	0	6
Career			45	0	0	0	0	0	270

Otis Taylor

Year	Team		TD	1XP	2XP	FG	FGA	SAF	Pts
1965	**KC**	**A**	5	0	0	0	0	0	30
1966			8	0	0	0	0	0	48
1967			12	0	0	0	0	0	72
1968			5	0	0	0	0	0	30
1969			7	0	0	0	0	0	42
1970	**KC**	**N**	3	0		0	0	0	18
1971			8	0		0	0	0	48

Otis Taylor *continued*

Year	Team		TD	1XP	2XP	FG	FGA	SAF	Pts
1972			6	0		0	0	0	36
1973			4	0		0	0	0	24
1974			2	0		0	0	0	12
Career			60	0	0	0	0	0	360
Playoffs			2	0	0	0	0	0	12

Rosey Taylor

Year	Team		TD	1XP	2XP	FG	FGA	SAF	Pts
1962	**CHI**	**N**	2	0		0	0	0	12
1963			1	0		0	0	0	6
1965			1	0		0	0	0	6
1967			1	0		0	0	0	6
1968			1	0		0	0	0	6
Career			6	0		0	0	0	36

Terry Taylor

Year	Team		TD	1XP	2XP	FG	FGA	SAF	Pts
1985	**SEA**	**N**	2	0		0	0	0	12
1988			1	0		0	0	0	6
Career			3	0		0	0	0	18

Troy Taylor

Year	Team		TD	1XP	2XP	FG	FGA	SAF	Pts
1990	**NYJ**	**N**	1	0		0	0	0	6

Jimmy Tays

Year	Team		TD	1XP	2XP	FG	FGA	SAF	Pts
1925	**CHIC**	**N**	1	0		0		0	6

George Teague

Year	Team		TD	1XP	2XP	FG	FGA	SAF	Pts
Playoffs			2	0	0	0	0	0	12

Jimmy Teal

Year	Team		TD	1XP	2XP	FG	FGA	SAF	Pts
1986	**BUF**	**N**	1	0		0	0	0	6
1987	**SEA**	**N**	2	0		0	0	0	12
Career			3	0		0	0	0	18

Willie Teal

Year	Team		TD	1XP	2XP	FG	FGA	SAF	Pts
1984	**MIN**	**N**	1	0		0	0	0	6
1985			1	0		0	0	0	6
Career			2	0		0	0	0	12

Gus Tebell

Year	Team		TD	1XP	2XP	FG	FGA	SAF	Pts
1923	**COL**	**N**	3	6		4		0	36
1924			0	3		1		0	6
Career			3	9		5		0	42

Mark Temple

Year	Team		TD	1XP	2XP	FG	FGA	SAF	Pts
1936	**BKN**	**N**	1	0		0		0	6

Derek Tennell

Year	Team		TD	1XP	2XP	FG	FGA	SAF	Pts
1987	**CLE**	**N**	3	0		0	0	0	18
1988			1	0		0	0	0	6
1989			1	0		0	0	0	6
Career			5	0		0	0	0	30
Playoffs			1	0		0	0	0	6

Tony Teresa

Year	Team		TD	1XP	2XP	FG	FGA	SAF	Pts
1960	**OAK**	**A**	10	0	0	0	0	0	60

Joe Tereshinski

Year	Team		TD	1XP	2XP	FG	FGA	SAF	Pts
1947	**WAS**	**N**	1	0		0	0	0	6
1948			1	0		0	0	0	6
1951			2	0		0	0	0	12
Career			4	0		0	0	0	24

George Terlep

Year	Team		TD	1XP	2XP	FG	FGA	SAF	Pts
1946	**BUF**	**AA**	1	0		0	0	0	6

Ray Terrell

Year	Team		TD	1XP	2XP	FG	FGA	SAF	Pts
1946	**CLE**	**AA**	1	0		0	0	0	6

Rudy Tersch

Year	Team		TD	1XP	2XP	FG	FGA	SAF	Pts
1923	**MIN**	**N**	1	0		0		0	6

Vinny Testaverde

Year	Team		TD	1XP	2XP	FG	FGA	SAF	Pts
1987	**TB**	**N**	1	0		0	0	0	6
1988			1	0		0	0	0	6
1990			1	0		0	0	0	6
1992			2	0		0	0	0	12
1994	**CLE**	**N**	2	0	0	0	0	0	12
1995			2	0	0	0	0	0	12
1996	**BAL**	**N**	2	0	1	0	0	0	14
Career			11	0	1	0	0	0	68

Don Testerman

Year	Team		TD	1XP	2XP	FG	FGA	SAF	Pts
1976	**SEA**	**N**	2	0		0	0	0	12

Don Testerman *continued*

Year	Team		TD	1XP	2XP	FG	FGA	SAF	Pts
1977			5	0		0	0	0	30
Career			7	0		0	0	0	42

Lee Tevis

Year	Team		TD	1XP	2XP	FG	FGA	SAF	Pts
1948	**BKN**	**AA**	0	4		2	7	0	10

Lowell Tew

Year	Team		TD	1XP	2XP	FG	FGA	SAF	Pts
1948	**NY**	**AA**	5	0		0	0	0	30
1949	**B-NY**	**AA**	1	0		0	0	0	6
Career			6	0		0	0	0	36

James Thaxton

Year	Team		TD	1XP	2XP	FG	FGA	SAF	Pts
1973	**SD**	**N**	2	0		0	0	0	12
1976	**NO**	**N**	1	0		0	0	0	6
1977			1	0		0	0	0	6
1978	**STL**	**N**	1	0		0	0	1	8
Career			5	0		0	0	1	32

Joe Theismann

Year	Team		TD	1XP	2XP	FG	FGA	SAF	Pts
1974	**WAS**	**N**	1	0		0	0	0	6
1976			1	0		0	0	0	6
1977			1	0		0	0	0	6
1978			1	0		0	0	0	6
1979			4	0		0	0	0	24
1980			3	0		0	0	0	18
1981			2	0		0	0	0	12
1983			1	0		0	0	0	6
1984			1	0		0	0	0	6
1985			2	0		0	0	0	12
Career			17	0		0	0	0	102

Jim Thibaut

Year	Team		TD	1XP	2XP	FG	FGA	SAF	Pts
1946	**BUF**	**AA**	1	0		0	0	0	6

Carl Thiele

Year	Team		TD	1XP	2XP	FG	FGA	SAF	Pts
1921	**DAY**	**A**	1	0		0		0	6
1922	**DAY**	**N**	1	0		0		0	6
Career			2	0		0		0	12

Yancey Thigpen

Year	Team		TD	1XP	2XP	FG	FGA	SAF	Pts
1993	**PIT**	**N**	3	0		0	0	0	18
1994			4	0	0	0	0	0	24
1995			5	0	0	0	0	0	30
1996			2	0	0	0	0	0	12
Career			14	0	0	0	0	0	84
Playoffs			2	0	0	0	0	0	12

Aaron Thomas

Year	Team		TD	1XP	2XP	FG	FGA	SAF	Pts
1961	**SF**	**N**	2	0		0	0	0	12
1963	**NYG**	**N**	3	0		0	0	0	18
1964			6	0		0	0	0	36
1965			5	0		0	0	0	30
1966			4	0		0	0	0	24
1967			9	0		0	0	0	54
1968			4	0		0	0	0	24
1969			3	0		0	0	0	18
1970			1	0		0	0	0	6
Career			37	0		0	0	0	222

Bill Thomas

Year	Team		TD	1XP	2XP	FG	FGA	SAF	Pts
1924	**FRA**	**N**	0	0		0		0	0

Blair Thomas

Year	Team		TD	1XP	2XP	FG	FGA	SAF	Pts
1990	**NYJ**	**N**	2	0		0	0	0	12
1991			4	0		0	0	0	24
1993			1	0		0	0	0	6
1994	**NE-DAL**	**N**	2	0	0	0	0	0	12
Career			9	0	0	0	0	0	54
Playoffs			2	0	0	0	0	0	12

Bob Thomas

Year	Team		TD	1XP	2XP	FG	FGA	SAF	Pts
1975	**CHI**	**N**	0	18		13	23	0	57
1976			0	27		12	25	0	63
1977			0	27		14	27	0	69
1978			0	26		17	22	0	77
1979			0	34		16	27	0	82
1980			0	35		13	18	0	74
1981			0	2		2	3	0	8
1982	**DET-CHI**	**N**	0	9		10	12	0	39
1983	**CHI**	**N**	0	35		14	25	0	77
1984			0	35		22	28	0	101
1985	**SD**	**N**	0	51		18	28	0	105

Bob Thomas *continued*

Year	Team		TD	1XP	2XP	FG	FGA	SAF	Pts
1986	NYG	N	0	4	0	1	0		4
Career			0	303	151	239	0		756
Playoffs			0	5	2	4	0		11

Bob Thomas

Year	Team		TD	1XP	2XP	FG	FGA	SAF	Pts
1972	LA	N	3	0	0	0	0		18
1973	SD	N	1	0	0	0	0		6
Career			4	0	0	0	0		24

Broderick Thomas

1992	TB	N	1	0		0	0	0	6

Calvin Thomas

Year	Team		TD	1XP	2XP	FG	FGA	SAF	Pts
1984	CHI	N	1	0		0	0	0	6
1985			4	0		0	0	0	24
Career			5	0		0	0	0	30
Playoffs			1	0		0	0	0	6

Carl Thomas

1922	BUF	N	1	0		0		0	6

Clendon Thomas

Year	Team		TD	1XP	2XP	FG	FGA	SAF	Pts
1960	LA	N	2	0		0	0	0	12
1964	PIT	N	1	0		0	0	0	6
1965			1	0		0	0	0	6
1966			1	0		0	0	0	6
Career			5	0		0	0	0	30

Derrick Thomas

Year	Team		TD	1XP	2XP	FG	FGA	SAF	Pts
1991	KC	N	1	0		0	0	0	6
1992			1	0		0	0	0	6
1993			1	0		0	0	0	6
1994			0	0	0	0	0	1	2
Career			3	0	0	0	0	1	20

Duane Thomas

Year	Team		TD	1XP	2XP	FG	FGA	SAF	Pts
1970	DAL	N	5	0		0	0	0	30
1971			13	0		0	0	0	78
1974	WAS	N	6	0		0	0	0	36
Career			24	0		0	0	0	144
Playoffs			5	0		0	0	0	30

Earl Thomas

Year	Team		TD	1XP	2XP	FG	FGA	SAF	Pts
1972	CHI	N	4	0		0	0	0	24
1973			4	0		0	0	0	24
1974	STL	N	5	0		0	0	0	30
1975			2	0		0	0	0	12
Career			15	0		0	0	0	90
Playoffs			1	0		0	0	0	6

Earlie Thomas

1970	NYJ	N	1	0		0	0	0	6

Emmitt Thomas

Year	Team		TD	1XP	2XP	FG	FGA	SAF	Pts
1967	KC	A	1	0	0	0	0	0	6
1969			1	0	0	0	0	0	6
1971	KC	N	1	0	0	0	0	0	6
1974			2	0		0	0	0	12
Career			5	0	0	0	0	0	30

Eric Thomas

1989	CIN	N	1	0		0	0	0	6

Gene Thomas

Year	Team		TD	1XP	2XP	FG	FGA	SAF	Pts
1966	KC	A	1	0	0	0	0	0	6
1967			3	0	0	0	0	0	18
1968	BOS	A	2	0	0	0	0	0	12
Career			6	0	0	0	0	0	36

George Thomas

1951	WAS	N	2	0		0	0	0	12

George Thomas

Year	Team		TD	1XP	2XP	FG	FGA	SAF	Pts
1990	ATL	N	1	0		0	0	0	6
1991			2	0		0	0	0	12
Career			3	0		0	0	0	18

Henry Thomas

Year	Team		TD	1XP	2XP	FG	FGA	SAF	Pts
1988	MIN	N	1	0		0	0	0	6
1989			1	0		0	0	0	6
1993			0	0		0	0	1	2
Career			2	0		0	0	1	14

Ike Thomas

1971	DAL	N	2	0		0	0	0	12

Jesse Thomas

1956	BAL	N	1	0		0	0	0	6

Jewerl Thomas

Year	Team		TD	1XP	2XP	FG	FGA	SAF	Pts
1980	LA	N	3	0		0	0	0	18
1984	SD	N	2	0		0	0	0	12
Career			5	0		0	0	0	30
Playoffs			1	0		0	0	0	6

Jimmy Thomas

Year	Team		TD	1XP	2XP	FG	FGA	SAF	Pts
1969	SF	N	6	0		0	0	0	36
1970			3	0		0	0	0	18
1971			1	0		0	0	0	6
1972			1	0		0	0	0	6
1973			1	0		0	0	0	6
Career			12	0		0	0	0	72

J.T. Thomas

Year	Team		TD	1XP	2XP	FG	FGA	SAF	Pts
1974	PIT	N	1	0		0	0	0	6
1975			1	0		0	0	0	6
Career			2	0		0	0	0	12

Ken Thomas

1983	KC	N	1	0		0	0	0	6

Lamar Thomas

Year	Team		TD	1XP	2XP	FG	FGA	SAF	Pts
1993	TB	N	2	0		0	0	0	12
1996	MIA	N	1	0	0	0	0	0	6
Career			3	0	0	0	0	0	18

Lavale Thomas

1987	GB	N	1	0		0	0	0	6

Louis Thomas

Year	Team		TD	1XP	2XP	FG	FGA	SAF	Pts
1969	CIN	A	4	0	0	0	0	0	24
1970	CIN	N	2	0	0	0	0	0	12
1971			2	0		0	0	0	12
1972			1	0		0	0	0	6
Career			9	0	0	0	0	0	54

Mike Thomas

Year	Team		TD	1XP	2XP	FG	FGA	SAF	Pts
1975	WAS	N	7	0		0	0	0	42
1976			9	0		0	0	0	54
1977			5	0		0	0	0	30
1978			5	0		0	0	0	30
1979	SD	N	1	0		0	0	0	6
1980			3	0		0	0	0	18
Career			30	0		0	0	0	180

Norris Thomas

1978	MIA	N	1	0		0	0	0	6

Orlanda Thomas

1995	MIN	N	2	0		0	0	0	12

Pat Thomas

1978	LA	N	1	0		0	0	0	6

Ralph Thomas

1955	WAS	N	3	0		0	0	0	18

Rex Thomas

Year	Team		TD	1XP	2XP	FG	FGA	SAF	Pts
1926	BKN	N	4	1		0	0	0	25
1927	CLE	N	3	0		0	0	0	18
1928	DET	N	3	0		0	0	0	18
1930	BKN	N	5	1		0	0	0	31
1931			1	0		0		0	6
Career			16	2		0		0	98

Robb Thomas

Year	Team		TD	1XP	2XP	FG	FGA	SAF	Pts
1989	KC	N	2	0		0	0	0	12
1990			4	0		0	0	0	24
1991			1	0		0	0	0	6
1995	SEA	N	1	0	0	0	0	0	6
1996	TB	N	2	0	0	0	0	0	12
Career			10	0	0	0	0	0	60

Rodell Thomas

1981	SEA	N	1	0		0	0	0	6

Rodney Thomas

Year	Team		TD	1XP	2XP	FG	FGA	SAF	Pts
1995	HOU	N	7	0	1	0	0	0	44
1996			1	0	0	0	0	0	6
Career			8	0	1	0	0	0	50

Skip Thomas

1974	OAK	N	1	0		0	0	0	6

Thurman Thomas

Year	Team		TD	1XP	2XP	FG	FGA	SAF	Pts
1988	BUF	N	2	0		0	0	0	12
1989			12	0		0	0	0	72
1990			13	0		0	0	0	78
1991			12	0		0	0	0	72
1992			12	0		0	0	0	72
1993			6	0		0	0	0	36
1994			9	0		0	0	0	54
1995			8	0		0	0	0	48
1996			8	0		0	0	0	48
Career			82	0		0	0	0	492
Playoffs			20	0		0	0	0	120

William Thomas

Year	Team		TD	1XP	2XP	FG	FGA	SAF	Pts
1995	PHI	N	1	0	0	0	0	0	6
1996			1	0	0	0	0	0	6
Career			2	0	0	0	0	0	12
Playoffs			1	0	0	0	0	0	6

Zach Thomas

1996	MIA	N	1	0	0	0	0	0	6

Zack Thomas

1983	DEN	N	1	0		0	0	0	6

Bobby Thomason

Year	Team		TD	1XP	2XP	FG	FGA	SAF	Pts
1953	PHI	N	1	0		0	0	0	6
1956			2	0		0	0	0	12
1957			3	0		0	0	0	18
Career			6	0		0	0	0	36

John Thomason

Year	Team		TD	1XP	2XP	FG	FGA	SAF	Pts
1930	BKN	N	4	0		0		0	24
1931			1	0		0		0	6
1932			1	0		0		0	6
1936	PHI	N	0	1		0		0	1
Career			6	1		0		0	37

Anthony Thompson

Year	Team		TD	1XP	2XP	FG	FGA	SAF	Pts
1990	PHX	N	4	0		0	0	0	24
1991			1	0		0	0	0	6
1992			1	0		0	0	0	6
Career			6	0		0	0	0	36

Aundra Thompson

Year	Team		TD	1XP	2XP	FG	FGA	SAF	Pts
1978	GB	N	2	0		0	0	0	12
1979			4	0		0	0	0	24
1980			2	0		0	0	0	12
1982	NO	N	1	0		0	0	0	6
Career			9	0		0	0	0	54

Billy Thompson

Year	Team		TD	1XP	2XP	FG	FGA	SAF	Pts
1969	DEN	A	1	0	0	0	0	0	6
1973	DEN	N	2	0		0	0	0	12
1974			1	0		0	0	0	6
1978			1	0		0	0	0	6
1979			1	0		0	0	0	6
1980			1	0		0	0	0	6
Career			7	0	0	0	0	0	42

Bobby Thompson

1975	DET	N	1	0		0	0	0	6

Craig Thompson

Year	Team		TD	1XP	2XP	FG	FGA	SAF	Pts
1992	CIN	N	2	0		0	0	0	12
1993			1	0		0	0	0	6
Career			3	0		0	0	0	18

Darrell Thompson

Year	Team		TD	1XP	2XP	FG	FGA	SAF	Pts
1990	GB	N	2	0		0	0	0	12
1991			1	0		0	0	0	6
1992			3	0		0	0	0	18
1993			3	0		0	0	0	18
Career			9	0		0	0	0	54

Don Thompson

Year	Team		TD	1XP	2XP	FG	FGA	SAF	Pts
1926	**LA**	**N**	2	0		0		0	12

Donnell Thompson

Year	Team		TD	1XP	2XP	FG	FGA	SAF	Pts
1983	**BAL**	**N**	0	0		0	0	1	2
1987	**IND**	**N**	1	0		0	0	0	6
Career			1	0		0	0	1	8

Ernie Thompson

Year	Team		TD	1XP	2XP	FG	FGA	SAF	Pts
1991	**LARM**	**N**	1	0		0	0	0	6

Hal Thompson

Year	Team		TD	1XP	2XP	FG	FGA	SAF	Pts
1948	**BKN**	**AA**	1	0		0	0	0	6

Jack Thompson

Year	Team		TD	1XP	2XP	FG	FGA	SAF	Pts
1979	**CIN**	**N**	5	0		0	0	0	30
1980			1	0		0	0	0	6
Career			6	0		0	0	0	36

Jesse Thompson

Year	Team		TD	1XP	2XP	FG	FGA	SAF	Pts
1978	**DET**	**N**	4	0		0	0	0	24

John Thompson

Year	Team		TD	1XP	2XP	FG	FGA	SAF	Pts
1982	**GB**	**N**	2	0		0	0	0	12

Leonard Thompson

Year	Team		TD	1XP	2XP	FG	FGA	SAF	Pts
1977	**DET**	**N**	2	0		0	0	0	12
1978			4	0		0	0	0	24
1979			2	0		0	0	0	12
1980			3	0		0	0	0	18
1981			4	0		0	0	0	24
1982			4	0		0	0	0	24
1983			4	0		0	0	0	24
1984			6	0		0	0	0	36
1985			5	0		0	0	0	30
1986			5	0		0	0	0	30
Career			39	0		0	0	0	234

Leroy Thompson

Year	Team		TD	1XP	2XP	FG	FGA	SAF	Pts
1992	**PIT**	**N**	1	0		0	0	0	6
1993			3	0		0	0	0	18
1994	**NE**	**N**	7	0	0	0	0	0	42
Career			11	0	0	0	0	0	66
Playoffs			1	0	0	0	0	0	6

Norm Thompson

Year	Team		TD	1XP	2XP	FG	FGA	SAF	Pts
1972	**STL**	**N**	2	0		0	0	0	12
1974			1	0		0	0	0	6
1975			1	0		0	0	0	6
Career			4	0		0	0	0	24

Reyna Thompson

Year	Team		TD	1XP	2XP	FG	FGA	SAF	Pts
1992	**NYG**	**N**	1	0		0	0	0	6

Ricky Thompson

Year	Team		TD	1XP	2XP	FG	FGA	SAF	Pts
1978	**WAS**	**N**	1	0		0	0	0	6
1979			4	0		0	0	0	24
1980			5	0		0	0	0	30
1981			4	0		0	0	0	24
Career			14	0		0	0	0	84

Rocky Thompson

Year	Team		TD	1XP	2XP	FG	FGA	SAF	Pts
1971	**NYG**	**N**	2	0		0	0	0	12
1972			1	0		0	0	0	6
Career			3	0		0	0	0	18

Ted Thompson

Year	Team		TD	1XP	2XP	FG	FGA	SAF	Pts
1980	**HOU**	**N**	0	4		0	0	0	4

Tommy Thompson

Year	Team		TD	1XP	2XP	FG	FGA	SAF	Pts
1941	**PHI**	**N**	1	0		0	0	0	6
1942			1	0		0	0	0	6
1947			2	0		0	0	0	12
1948			1	0		0	0	0	6
1949			2	0		0	0	0	12
Career			7	0		0	0	0	42

Tuffy Thompson

Year	Team		TD	1XP	2XP	FG	FGA	SAF	Pts
1937	**PIT**	**N**	1	0		0		0	6
1938			1	0		0		0	6
Career			2	0		0		0	12

Vince Thompson

Year	Team		TD	1XP	2XP	FG	FGA	SAF	Pts
1981	**DET**	**N**	1	0		0	0	0	6

Vince Thompson *continued*

Year	Team		TD	1XP	2XP	FG	FGA	SAF	Pts
1983			1	0		0	0	0	6
Career			2	0		0	0	0	12

Weegie Thompson

Year	Team		TD	1XP	2XP	FG	FGA	SAF	Pts
1984	**PIT**	**N**	3	0		0	0	0	18
1985			1	0		0	0	0	6
1986			5	0		0	0	0	30
1987			1	0		0	0	0	6
1988			1	0		0	0	0	6
Career			11	0		0	0	0	66

Woody Thompson

Year	Team		TD	1XP	2XP	FG	FGA	SAF	Pts
1977	**ATL**	**N**	1	0		0	0	0	6

Art Thoms

Year	Team		TD	1XP	2XP	FG	FGA	SAF	Pts
1974	**OAK**	**N**	1	0		0	0	0	6

Bill Thornton

Year	Team		TD	1XP	2XP	FG	FGA	SAF	Pts
1963	**STL**	**N**	1	0		0	0	0	6
1964			1	0		0	0	0	6
Career			2	0		0	0	0	12

James Thornton

Year	Team		TD	1XP	2XP	FG	FGA	SAF	Pts
1989	**CHI**	**N**	3	0		0	0	0	18
1990			1	0		0	0	0	6
1991			1	0		0	0	0	6
1993	**NYJ**	**N**	2	0		0	0	0	12
Career			7	0		0	0	0	42
Playoffs			1	0		0	0	0	6

Sidney Thornton

Year	Team		TD	1XP	2XP	FG	FGA	SAF	Pts
1977	**PIT**	**N**	2	0		0	0	0	12
1978			3	0		0	0	0	18
1979			10	0		0	0	0	60
1980			4	0		0	0	0	24
1981			4	0		0	0	0	24
1982			1	0		0	0	0	6
Career			24	0		0	0	0	144
Playoffs			1	0		0	0	0	6

Jim Thorpe

Year	Team		TD	1XP	2XP	FG	FGA	SAF	Pts
1920	**CAN**	**A**	0	0		**3**		0	9
1921	**CLE**	**A**	1	2		1		0	11
1922	**OOR**	**N**	3	0		0		0	18
1923			0	0		1		0	3
1924	**RI**	**N**	0	1		2		0	7
1926	**CAN**	**N**	2	0		0		0	12
Career			6	3		7		0	60

Bob Thurbon

Year	Team		TD	1XP	2XP	FG	FGA	SAF	Pts
1943	**P-P**	**N**	6	0		0	0	0	36
1944	**C-P**	**N**	5	0		0	0	0	30
Career			11	0		0	0	0	66

Steve Thurlow

Year	Team		TD	1XP	2XP	FG	FGA	SAF	Pts
1964	**NYG**	**N**	1	0		0	0	0	6
1965			5	0		0	0	0	30
Career			6	0		0	0	0	36

Dennis Thurman

Year	Team		TD	1XP	2XP	FG	FGA	SAF	Pts
1980	**DAL**	**N**	1	0		0	0	0	6
1982			1	0		0	0	0	6
1983			1	0		0	0	0	6
1984			1	0		0	0	0	6
1985			1	0		0	0	0	6
Career			5	0		0	0	0	30
Playoffs			1	0		0	0	0	6

John Tice

Year	Team		TD	1XP	2XP	FG	FGA	SAF	Pts
1983	**NO**	**N**	1	0		0	0	0	6
1984			1	0		0	0	0	6
1985			2	0		0	0	0	12
1986			3	0		0	0	0	18
1987			6	0		0	0	0	36
1988			1	0		0	0	0	6
1989			1	0		0	0	0	6
Career			15	0		0	0	0	90

Mike Tice

Year	Team		TD	1XP	2XP	FG	FGA	SAF	Pts
1984	**SEA**	**N**	3	0		0	0	0	18
1987			2	0		0	0	0	12
1991			4	0		0	0	0	24
1992	**MIN**	**N**	1	0		0	0	0	6

Mike Tice *continued*

Year	Team		TD	1XP	2XP	FG	FGA	SAF	Pts
1993			1	0		0	0	0	6
Career			11	0		0	0	0	66

Glenn Tidd

Year	Team		TD	1XP	2XP	FG	FGA	SAF	Pts
1922	**DAY**	**N**	1	0		0		0	6
1924			1	0		0		0	6
Career			2	0		0		0	12

Travis Tidwell

Year	Team		TD	1XP	2XP	FG	FGA	SAF	Pts
1950	**NYG**	**N**	2	0		0	0	0	12

Van Tiffin

Year	Team		TD	1XP	2XP	FG	FGA	SAF	Pts
1987	**TB-MIA**	**N**	0	11		5	7	0	26

Pat Tilley

Year	Team		TD	1XP	2XP	FG	FGA	SAF	Pts
1976	**STL**	**N**	1	0		0	0	0	6
1978			3	0		0	0	0	18
1979			6	0		0	0	0	36
1980			6	0		0	0	0	36
1981			3	0		0	0	0	18
1982			2	0		0	0	0	12
1983			5	0		0	0	0	30
1984			5	0		0	0	0	30
1985			6	0		0	0	0	36
Career			37	0		0	0	0	222
Playoffs			1	0		0	0	0	6

Andre Tillman

Year	Team		TD	1XP	2XP	FG	FGA	SAF	Pts
1976	**MIA**	**N**	1	0		0	0	0	6
1977			2	0		0	0	0	12
1978			3	0		0	0	0	18
Career			6	0		0	0	0	36

Cedric Tillman

Year	Team		TD	1XP	2XP	FG	FGA	SAF	Pts
1992	**DEN**	**N**	1	0		0	0	0	6
1993			2	0		0	0	0	12
1994			1	0	0	0	0	0	6
1995	**JAC**	**N**	3	0	0	0	0	0	18
Career			7	0	0	0	0	0	42

Lawyer Tillman

Year	Team		TD	1XP	2XP	FG	FGA	SAF	Pts
1989	**CLE**	**N**	3	0		0	0	0	18
1993			1	0		0	0	0	6
Career			4	0		0	0	0	24

Lewis Tillman

Year	Team		TD	1XP	2XP	FG	FGA	SAF	Pts
1990	**NYG**	**N**	1	0		0	0	0	6
1991			1	0		0	0	0	6
1993			3	0		0	0	0	18
1994	**CHI**	**N**	7	0	0	0	0	0	42
Career			12	0	0	0	0	0	72
Playoffs			2	0	0	0	0	0	12

Spencer Tillman

Year	Team		TD	1XP	2XP	FG	FGA	SAF	Pts
1987	**HOU**	**N**	1	0		0	0	0	6
1993			1	0		0	0	0	6
Career			2	0		0	0	0	12

Bob Timberlake

Year	Team		TD	1XP	2XP	FG	FGA	SAF	Pts
1965	**NYG**	**N**	0	21		1	15	0	24

Michael Timpson

Year	Team		TD	1XP	2XP	FG	FGA	SAF	Pts
1991	**NE**	**N**	2	0		0	0	0	12
1992			1	0		0	0	0	6
1993			2	0		0	0	0	12
1994			3	0	0	0	0	0	18
1995	**CHI**	**N**	3	0	0	0	0	0	18
Career			11	0	0	0	0	0	66

Tim Tindale

Year	Team		TD	1XP	2XP	FG	FGA	SAF	Pts
Playoffs			1	0	0	0	0	0	6

Gerald Tinker

Year	Team		TD	1XP	2XP	FG	FGA	SAF	Pts
1974	**ATL**	**N**	1	0		0	0	0	6
1975	**ATL-GB**	**N**	2	0		0	0	0	12
Career			3	0		0	0	0	18

Gaynell Tinsley

Year	Team		TD	1XP	2XP	FG	FGA	SAF	Pts
1937	**CHIC**	**N**	6	0		0		0	36
1938			1	0		0		0	6
1940			1	0		0	0	0	6
Career			8	0		0	0	0	48

Andre Tippett

Year	Team	Lg	TD	1XP	2XP	FG	FGA	SAF	Pts
1985	NE	N	1	0		0	0	0	6
1987			1	0		0	0	0	6
Career			2	0		0	0	0	12

Kenny Tippins

Year	Team	Lg	TD	1XP	2XP	FG	FGA	SAF	Pts
1991	ATL	N	1	0		0	0	0	6

Howie Tipton

Year	Team	Lg	TD	1XP	2XP	FG	FGA	SAF	Pts
1933	CHIC	N	1	0		0		0	6

Bob Titchenal

Year	Team	Lg	TD	1XP	2XP	FG	FGA	SAF	Pts
1946	SF	AA	2	0		0	0	0	12

Herb Titmas

Year	Team	Lg	TD	1XP	2XP	FG	FGA	SAF	Pts
1931	PRO	N	1	0		0		0	6

Y.A. Tittle

Year	Team	Lg	TD	1XP	2XP	FG	FGA	SAF	Pts
1948	BAL	AA	4	0		0	0	0	24
1949			2	0		0	0	0	12
1950	BAL	N	2	0		0	0	0	12
1951	SF	N	1	0		0	0	0	6
1953			6	0		0	0	0	36
1954			4	0		0	0	0	24
1956			4	0		0	0	0	24
1957			6	0		0	0	0	36
1958			2	0		0	0	0	12
1961	NYG	N	3	0		0	0	0	18
1962			2	0		0	0	0	12
1963			2	0		0	0	0	12
1964			1	0		0	0	0	6
Career			39	0		0	0	0	234

Robbie Tobeck

Year	Team	Lg	TD	1XP	2XP	FG	FGA	SAF	Pts
1996	ATL	N	1	0	0	0	0	0	6

Bill Tobin

Year	Team	Lg	TD	1XP	2XP	FG	FGA	SAF	Pts
1963	HOU	A	5	0	0	0	0	0	30

Elgie Tobin

Year	Team	Lg	TD	1XP	2XP	FG	FGA	SAF	Pts
1921	AKR	A	0	1		0		0	1

Dick Todd

Year	Team	Lg	TD	1XP	2XP	FG	FGA	SAF	Pts
1939	WAS	N	6	2		0	0	0	38
1940			**9**	0		0	0	0	54
1941			3	0		0	0	0	18
1942			5	2		0	0	0	32
1946			5	0		0	0	0	30
1948			7	0		0	0	0	42
Career			35	4		0	0	0	214

Larry Todd

Year	Team	Lg	TD	1XP	2XP	FG	FGA	SAF	Pts
1966	OAK	A	1	0	0	0	0	0	6
1967			2	0	0	0	0	0	12
1968			2	0	0	0	0	0	12
1969			2	0	0	0	0	0	12
Career			7	0	0	0	0	0	42

Richard Todd

Year	Team	Lg	TD	1XP	2XP	FG	FGA	SAF	Pts
1976	NYJ	N	1	0		0	0	0	6
1977			2	0		0	0	0	12
1979			5	0		0	0	0	30
1980			5	0		0	0	0	30
1982			1	0		0	0	0	6
Career			14	0		0	0	0	84

Loren Toews

Year	Team	Lg	TD	1XP	2XP	FG	FGA	SAF	Pts
1976	PIT	N	0	0		0	0	1	2
1980			0	0		0	0	1	2
Career			0	0		0	0	2	4

Brendan Toibin

Year	Team	Lg	TD	1XP	2XP	FG	FGA	SAF	Pts
1987	WAS	N	0	4		0	2	0	4

Charley Tolar

Year	Team	Lg	TD	1XP	2XP	FG	FGA	SAF	Pts
1960	HOU	A	3	0	0	0	0	0	18
1961			5	0	0	0	0	0	30
1962			8	0	0	0	0	0	48
1963			3	0	0	0	0	0	18
1964			4	0	0	0	0	0	24
Career			23	0	0	0	0	0	138
Playoffs			1	0	0	0	0	0	6

Tony Tolbert

Year	Team	Lg	TD	1XP	2XP	FG	FGA	SAF	Pts
1994	DAL	N	1	0	0	0	0	0	6

Ken Toler

Year	Team	Lg	TD	1XP	2XP	FG	FGA	SAF	Pts
1982	NE	N	2	0		0	0	0	12

Alvin Toles

Year	Team	Lg	TD	1XP	2XP	FG	FGA	SAF	Pts
1987	NO	N	1	0		0	0	0	6

Billy Joe Tolliver

Year	Team	Lg	TD	1XP	2XP	FG	FGA	SAF	Pts
1994	HOU	N	2	0	0	0	0	0	12

Johnny Tomaini

Year	Team	Lg	TD	1XP	2XP	FG	FGA	SAF	Pts
1929	ORA	N	0	1		0		0	1
1930	NEW	N	1	0		0		0	6
Career			1	1		0		0	7

Lou Tomasetti

Year	Team	Lg	TD	1XP	2XP	FG	FGA	SAF	Pts
1939	PIT	N	1	0		0	0	0	6
1940			2	0		0	0	0	12
1941	PHI	N	1	0		0	0	0	6
1946	BUF	AA	2	0		0	0	0	12
1947			3	0		0	0	0	18
1948			8	0		0	0	0	48
1949			3	0		0	0	0	18
Career			20	0		0	0	0	120
Playoffs			1	0		0	0	0	6

Andy Tomasic

Year	Team	Lg	TD	1XP	2XP	FG	FGA	SAF	Pts
1942	PIT	N	1	0		0	0	0	6

Mike Tomczak

Year	Team	Lg	TD	1XP	2XP	FG	FGA	SAF	Pts
1986	CHI	N	3	0		0	0	0	18
1987			1	0		0	0	0	6
1988			1	0		0	0	0	6
1989			1	0		0	0	0	6
1990			2	0		0	0	0	12
1991	GB	N	1	0		0	0	0	6
Career			9	0		0	0	0	54

Mario Tonelli

Year	Team	Lg	TD	1XP	2XP	FG	FGA	SAF	Pts
1940	CHIC	N	1	0		0	0	0	6

Tom Toner

Year	Team	Lg	TD	1XP	2XP	FG	FGA	SAF	Pts
1975	GB	N	0	0		0	0	1	2

Anthony Toney

Year	Team	Lg	TD	1XP	2XP	FG	FGA	SAF	Pts
1986	PHI	N	1	0		0	0	0	6
1987			6	0		0	0	0	36
1988			5	0		0	0	0	30
1989			3	0		0	0	0	18
1990			4	0		0	0	0	24
Career			19	0		0	0	0	114
Playoffs			1	0		0	0	0	6

Clayton Tonnemaker

Year	Team	Lg	TD	1XP	2XP	FG	FGA	SAF	Pts
1950	GB	N	0	1		0	0	0	1

Pat Toomay

Year	Team	Lg	TD	1XP	2XP	FG	FGA	SAF	Pts
1975	BUF	N	1	0		0	0	0	6

Amani Toomer

Year	Team	Lg	TD	1XP	2XP	FG	FGA	SAF	Pts
1996	NYG	N	2	0	0	0	0	0	12

Al Toon

Year	Team	Lg	TD	1XP	2XP	FG	FGA	SAF	Pts
1985	NYJ	N	3	0		0	0	0	18
1986			8	0		0	0	0	48
1987			5	0		0	0	0	30
1988			5	0		0	0	0	30
1989			2	0		0	0	0	12
1990			6	0		0	0	0	36
1992			2	0		0	0	0	12
Career			31	0		0	0	0	186
Playoffs			2	0		0	0	0	12

Bob Topp

Year	Team	Lg	TD	1XP	2XP	FG	FGA	SAF	Pts
1954	NYG	N	3	0		0	0	0	18

Stacey Toran

Year	Team	Lg	TD	1XP	2XP	FG	FGA	SAF	Pts
1985	LARI	N	1	0		0	0	0	6
1987			1	0		0	0	0	6
Career			2	0		0	0	0	12

La Verne Torczon

Year	Team	Lg	TD	1XP	2XP	FG	FGA	SAF	Pts
1964	NY	A	1	0	0	0	0	0	6

La Vern Torgeson

Year	Team	Lg	TD	1XP	2XP	FG	FGA	SAF	Pts
1952	DET	N	1	0		0	0	0	6

Eric Torkelson

Year	Team	Lg	TD	1XP	2XP	FG	FGA	SAF	Pts
1974	GB	N	1	0		0	0	0	6
1975			2	0		0	0	0	12
1976			2	0		0	0	0	12
1977			1	0		0	0	0	6
1979			3	0		0	0	0	18
Career			9	0		0	0	0	54

Bob Torrey

Year	Team	Lg	TD	1XP	2XP	FG	FGA	SAF	Pts
1979	MIA	N	1	0		0	0	0	6

Flavio Tosi

Year	Team	Lg	TD	1XP	2XP	FG	FGA	SAF	Pts
1935	BOS	N	1	0		0		0	6
1936			1	0		0		0	6
Career			2	0		0		0	12

Zollie Toth

Year	Team	Lg	TD	1XP	2XP	FG	FGA	SAF	Pts
1950	NYY	N	8	0		0	0	0	48
1951			4	0		0	0	0	24
1952	DAL	N	4	0		0	0	0	24
1954	BAL	N	1	0		0	0	0	6
Career			17	0		0	0	0	102

Dan Towler

Year	Team	Lg	TD	1XP	2XP	FG	FGA	SAF	Pts
1950	LA	N	6	0		0	0	0	36
1951			6	0		0	0	0	36
1952			10	0		0	0	0	60
1953			8	0		0	0	0	48
1954			11	0		0	0	0	66
1955			3	0		0	0	0	18
Career			44	0		0	0	0	264
Playoffs			2	0		0	0	0	12

Willie Townes

Year	Team	Lg	TD	1XP	2XP	FG	FGA	SAF	Pts
1966	DAL	N	0	0		0	0	1	2
1968			1	0		0	0	0	6
Career			1	0		0	0	1	8

JoJo Townsell

Year	Team	Lg	TD	1XP	2XP	FG	FGA	SAF	Pts
1986	NYJ	N	1	0		0	0	0	6
1987			1	0		0	0	0	6
1988			1	0		0	0	0	6
1989			5	0		0	0	0	30
Career			8	0		0	0	0	48

Andre Townsend

Year	Team	Lg	TD	1XP	2XP	FG	FGA	SAF	Pts
1986	DEN	N	1	0		0	0	0	6

Greg Townsend

Year	Team	Lg	TD	1XP	2XP	FG	FGA	SAF	Pts
1983	LARI	N	1	0		0	0	1	8
1986			0	0		0	0	1	2
1988			2	0		0	0	0	12
1990			1	0		0	0	0	6
Career			4	0		0	0	2	28

John Tracey

Year	Team	Lg	TD	1XP	2XP	FG	FGA	SAF	Pts
1960	STL	N	0	0		0	0	1	2
1963	BUF	A	0	0	1	0	0	0	2
Career			0	0	1	0	0	1	4
Playoffs			0	0	1	0	0	0	2

Tom Tracy

Year	Team	Lg	TD	1XP	2XP	FG	FGA	SAF	Pts
1958	PIT	N	9	0		0	0	0	54
1959			8	0		0	0	0	48
1960			9	0		3	6	0	63
1961			3	2		0	1	0	20
1963	PIT-WAS	N	1	2		0	0	0	8
1964	WAS	N	1	0		0	0	0	6
Career			31	4		3	7	0	199
Playoffs			2	0		0	0	0	12

Mike Trainor

Year	Team	Lg	TD	1XP	2XP	FG	FGA	SAF	Pts
1923	BUF	N	2	0		0		0	12
1924			1	0		0		0	6
Career			3	0		0		0	18

Herb Travenio

Year	Team	Lg	TD	1XP	2XP	FG	FGA	SAF	Pts
1964	SD	A	0	10	0	2	5	0	16

Herb Travenio *continued*

Year	Team	TD	1XP	2XP	FG	FGA	SAF	Pts
1965		0	40	0	18	30	0	94
Career		0	50	0	20	35	0	110
Playoffs		0	0	0	0	2	0	0

Wade Traynham

Year	Team	TD	1XP	2XP	FG	FGA	SAF	Pts
1966	ATL N	0	2		0	1	0	2
1967		0	22		7	18	0	43
Career		0	24		7	19	0	45

David Treadwell

Year	Team	TD	1XP	2XP	FG	FGA	SAF	Pts
1989	DEN N	0	39		27	33	0	120
1990		0	34		25	34	0	109
1991		0	31		27	36	0	112
1992		0	28		20	24	0	88
1993	NYG N	0	28		25	31	0	103
1994		0	22	0	11	17	0	55
Career		0	182	0	135	175	0	587
Playoffs		0	13	0	9	14	0	40

Frank Trigillo

Year	Team	TD	1XP	2XP	FG	FGA	SAF	Pts
1946	MIA AA	1	0		0	0	0	6

Bill Triplett

Year	Team	TD	1XP	2XP	FG	FGA	SAF	Pts
1963	STL N	8	0		0	0	0	48
1965		7	0		0	0	0	42
1967	NYG N	2	0		0	0	0	12
1969	DET N	4	0		0	0	0	24
1970		1	0		0	0	0	6
Career		22	0		0	0	0	132

Mel Triplett

Year	Team	TD	1XP	2XP	FG	FGA	SAF	Pts
1956	NYG N	6	0		0	0	0	36
1958		1	0		0	0	0	6
1959		1	0		0	0	0	6
1960		6	0		0	0	0	36
1961	MIN N	1	0		0	0	0	6
1962		3	0		0	0	0	18
Career		18	0		0	0	0	108
Playoffs		2	0		0	0	0	12

Wally Triplett

Year	Team	TD	1XP	2XP	FG	FGA	SAF	Pts
1949	DET N	2	0		0	0	0	12
1950		2	0		0	0	0	12
Career		4	0		0	0	0	24

Paul Tripoli

Year	Team	TD	1XP	2XP	FG	FGA	SAF	Pts
1987	TB N	1	0		0	0	0	6

Charley Trippi

Year	Team	TD	1XP	2XP	FG	FGA	SAF	Pts
1947	CHIC N	3	0		0	0	0	18
1948		10	0		0	0	0	60
1949		9	0		0	0	0	54
1950		4	0		0	0	0	24
1951		4	0		0	0	0	24
1952		4	0		0	0	0	24
1953		2	0		0	0	0	12
1954		1	0		0	0	0	6
Career		37	0		0	0	0	222
Playoffs		2	0		0	0	0	12

Frank Tripucka

Year	Team	TD	1XP	2XP	FG	FGA	SAF	Pts
1949	DET N	1	0		0	0	0	6
1950	CHIC N	1	0		0	0	0	6
1952	DAL N	3	0		0	0	0	18
1962	DEN A	1	0	0	0	0	0	6
Career		6	0	0	0	0	0	36

Bill Troup

Year	Team	TD	1XP	2XP	FG	FGA	SAF	Pts
1976	BAL N	1	0		0	0	0	6
1978		1	0		0	0	0	6
Career		2	0		0	0	0	12

David Trout

Year	Team	TD	1XP	2XP	FG	FGA	SAF	Pts
1981	PIT N	0	38		12	17	0	74
1987		0	10		0	2	0	10
Career		0	48		12	19	0	84

Billy Truax

Year	Team	TD	1XP	2XP	FG	FGA	SAF	Pts
1965	LA N	1	0		0	0	0	6
1966		1	0		0	0	0	6
1967		4	0		0	0	0	24
Career		6	0		0	0	0	36
Playoffs		1	0		0	0	0	6

Dalton Truax

Year	Team	TD	1XP	2XP	FG	FGA	SAF	Pts
1968	LA N	3	0		0	0	0	18
1969		5	0		0	0	0	30
1970		3	0		0	0	0	18
1971	DAL N	1	0		0	0	0	6
Career		12	0		0	0	0	72

Jack Trudeau

Year	Team	TD	1XP	2XP	FG	FGA	SAF	Pts
1986	IND N	1	0		0	0	0	6
1989		2	0		0	0	0	12
Career		3	0		0	0	0	18

Olanda Truitt

Year	Team	TD	1XP	2XP	FG	FGA	SAF	Pts
1994	WAS N	1	0	0	0	0	0	6
1995		1	0	0	0	0	0	6
Career		2	0	0	0	0	0	12

Don Trull

Year	Team	TD	1XP	2XP	FG	FGA	SAF	Pts
1965	HOU A	2	0	0	0	0	0	12
1966		7	0	0	0	0	0	42
1967	BOS A	3	0	0	0	0	0	18
1969	HOU A	2	0	0	0	0	0	12
Career		14	0	0	0	0	0	84

Bob Trumpy

Year	Team	TD	1XP	2XP	FG	FGA	SAF	Pts
1968	CIN A	3	0	0	0	0	0	18
1969		9	0	0	0	0	0	54
1970	CIN N	2	0	0	0	0	0	12
1971		3	0	0	0	0	0	18
1972		2	0	0	0	0	0	12
1973		5	0	0	0	0	0	30
1974		2	0	0	0	0	0	12
1975		1	0	0	0	0	0	6
1976		7	0	0	0	0	0	42
1977		1	0	0	0	0	0	6
Career		35	0	0	0	0	0	210

Eric Truvillion

Year	Team	TD	1XP	2XP	FG	FGA	SAF	Pts
1987	DET N	1	0		0	0	0	6

Eddie Tryon

Year	Team	TD	1XP	2XP	FG	FGA	SAF	Pts
1926	NY A	9	12		2		0	72
1927	NYY N	6	8		0		0	44
Career		15	20		2		0	116

Bill Tucker

Year	Team	TD	1XP	2XP	FG	FGA	SAF	Pts
1968	SF N	7	0		0	0	0	42
1969		4	0		0	0	0	24
1970		2	0		0	0	0	12
Career		13	0		0	0	0	78

Bob Tucker

Year	Team	TD	1XP	2XP	FG	FGA	SAF	Pts
1970	NYG N	5	0		0	0	0	30
1971		4	0		0	0	0	24
1972		5	0		0	0	0	30
1973		5	0		0	0	0	30
1974		2	0		0	0	0	12
1975		1	0		0	0	0	6
1976		1	0		0	0	0	6
1977	MIN N	2	0		0	0	0	12
1979		2	0		0	0	0	12
1980		1	0		0	0	0	6
Career		28	0		0	0	0	168

Wendell Tucker

Year	Team	TD	1XP	2XP	FG	FGA	SAF	Pts
1968	LA N	4	0		0	0	0	24
1969		7	0		0	0	0	42
Career		11	0		0	0	0	66

Dick Tuckey

Year	Team	TD	1XP	2XP	FG	FGA	SAF	Pts
1938	CLE N	0	2		0	0	0	2

Jessie Tuggle

Year	Team	TD	1XP	2XP	FG	FGA	SAF	Pts
1988	ATL N	1	0		0	0	0	6
1990		1	0		0	0	0	6
1991		1	0		0	0	0	6
1992		1	0		0	0	0	6
1995		1	0	0	0	0	0	6
Career		5	0	0	0	0	0	30

John Tuggle

Year	Team	TD	1XP	2XP	FG	FGA	SAF	Pts
1983	NYG N	1	0		0	0	0	6

Walter Tullis

Year	Team	TD	1XP	2XP	FG	FGA	SAF	Pts
1979	GB N	1	0		0	0	0	6

Willie Tullis

Year	Team	TD	1XP	2XP	FG	FGA	SAF	Pts
1981	HOU N	1	0		0	0	0	6

Darrell Tully

Year	Team	TD	1XP	2XP	FG	FGA	SAF	Pts
1939	DET N	1	0		0	0	0	6

George Tully

Year	Team	TD	1XP	2XP	FG	FGA	SAF	Pts
1926	PHI A	1	0		0	0	0	6

Emlen Tunnell

Year	Team	TD	1XP	2XP	FG	FGA	SAF	Pts
1948	NYG N	1	0		0	0	0	6
1949		3	0		0	0	0	18
1951		4	0		0	0	0	24
1955		1	0		0	0	0	6
1957		1	0		0	0	0	6
Career		10	0		0	0	0	60

Tom Tupa

Year	Team	TD	1XP	2XP	FG	FGA	SAF	Pts
1991	PHX N	1	0		0	0	0	6
1994	CLE N	0	0	3	0	0	0	6
Career		1	0	3	0	0	0	12

Doug Turley

Year	Team	TD	1XP	2XP	FG	FGA	SAF	Pts
1944	WAS N	1	0		0	0	0	6
1945		1	0		0	0	0	6
1947		1	0		0	0	0	6
1948		1	0		0	0	0	6
Career		4	0		0	0	0	24

Guy Turnbow

Year	Team	TD	1XP	2XP	FG	FGA	SAF	Pts
1933	PHI N	0	0		1		0	3

Bake Turner

Year	Team	TD	1XP	2XP	FG	FGA	SAF	Pts
1962	BAL N	1	0		0	0	0	6
1963	NY A	6	0		0	0	0	36
1964		9	0		0	0	0	54
1965		2	0		0	0	0	12
1968		2	0		0	0	0	12
1969		3	0		0	0	0	18
1970	BOS N	2	0		0	0	0	12
Career		25	0		0	0	0	150

Bulldog Turner

Year	Team	TD	1XP	2XP	FG	FGA	SAF	Pts
1942	CHIB N	2	0		0	0	0	12
1944		1	0		0	0	0	6
1947		1	0		0	0	0	6
Career		4	0		0	0	0	24
Playoffs		1	0		0	0	0	6

Cecil Turner

Year	Team	TD	1XP	2XP	FG	FGA	SAF	Pts
1968	CHI N	2	0		0	0	0	12
1970		4	0		0	0	0	24
Career		6	0		0	0	0	36

Clem Turner

Year	Team	TD	1XP	2XP	FG	FGA	SAF	Pts
1970	DEN N	2	0		0	0	0	12
1971		1	0		0	0	0	6
Career		3	0		0	0	0	18

Daryl Turner

Year	Team	TD	1XP	2XP	FG	FGA	SAF	Pts
1984	SEA N	10	0		0	0	0	60
1985		13	0		0	0	0	78
1986		7	0		0	0	0	42
1987		6	0		0	0	0	36
Career		36	0		0	0	0	216
Playoffs		1	0		0	0	0	6

Deacon Turner

Year	Team	TD	1XP	2XP	FG	FGA	SAF	Pts
1979	CIN N	1	0		0	0	0	6
1980		1	0		0	0	0	6
Career		2	0		0	0	0	12

Eric Turner

Year	Team	TD	1XP	2XP	FG	FGA	SAF	Pts
1991	CLE N	1	0		0	0	0	6
1994		1	0	0	0	0	0	6
Career		2	0	0	0	0	0	12

Floyd Turner

Year	Team	TD	1XP	2XP	FG	FGA	SAF	Pts
1989	NO N	1	0		0	0	0	6
1990		4	0		0	0	0	24
1991		8	0		0	0	0	48

Floyd Turner *continued*

Year	Team	Lg	TD	1XP	2XP	FG	FGA	SAF	Pts
1993			1	0		0	0	0	6
1994	**IND**	**N**	6	0	0	0	0	0	36
1995			4	0	2	0	0	0	28
1996	**BAL**	**N**	2	0	0	0	0	0	12
Career			26	0	2	0	0	0	160
Playoffs			3	0	0	0	0	0	18

Jim Turner

Year	Team	Lg	TD	1XP	2XP	FG	FGA	SAF	Pts
1964	**NY**	**A**	0	33	0	13	27	0	72
1965			0	31	0	20	34	0	91
1966			0	34	0	18	35	0	88
1967			0	36	0	17	32	0	87
1968			0	43	0	**34**	**46**	0	**145**
1969			0	33	0	**32**	**47**	0	**129**
1970	**NYJ**	**N**	0	28		19	35	0	85
1971	**DEN**	**N**	0	18		25	38	0	93
1972			0	37		20	29	0	97
1973			0	40		22	33	0	106
1974			0	35		11	21	0	68
1975			0	23		21	28	0	86
1976			0	36		15	21	0	81
1977			1	31		13	19	0	76
1978			0	31		11	22	0	64
1979			0	32		13	21	0	71
Career			1	521	0	304	488	0	1439
Playoffs			0	13	0	11	18	0	43

Jim Turner

Year	Team	Lg	TD	1XP	2XP	FG	FGA	SAF	Pts
1923	**MIL**	**N**	1	0		0		0	6

John Turner

Year	Team	Lg	TD	1XP	2XP	FG	FGA	SAF	Pts
1982	**MIN**	**N**	1	0		0	0	0	6

Keena Turner

Year	Team	Lg	TD	1XP	2XP	FG	FGA	SAF	Pts
1985	**SF**	**N**	1	0		0	0	0	6
1990			0	0		0	0	1	2
Career			1	0		0	0	1	8

Kevin Turner

Year	Team	Lg	TD	1XP	2XP	FG	FGA	SAF	Pts
1992	**NE**	**N**	2	0		0	0	0	12
1993			2	0		0	0	0	12
1994			3	0	0	0	0	0	18
1996	**PHI**	**N**	1	0	0	0	0	0	6
Career			8	0	0	0	0	0	48

Marcus Turner

Year	Team	Lg	TD	1XP	2XP	FG	FGA	SAF	Pts
1990	**PHX**	**N**	2	0		0	0	0	12
1994	**NYJ**	**N**	1	0	0	0	0	0	6
Career			3	0	0	0	0	0	18

Nate Turner

Year	Team	Lg	TD	1XP	2XP	FG	FGA	SAF	Pts
1994	**BUF**	**N**	1	0	0	0	0	0	6

Odessa Turner

Year	Team	Lg	TD	1XP	2XP	FG	FGA	SAF	Pts
1987	**NYG**	**N**	1	0		0	0	0	6
1988			1	0		0	0	0	6
1989			4	0		0	0	0	24
1992	**SF**	**N**	2	0		0	0	0	12
Career			8	0		0	0	0	48

Ricky Turner

Year	Team	Lg	TD	1XP	2XP	FG	FGA	SAF	Pts
1988	**IND**	**N**	2	0		0	0	0	12

Scott Turner

Year	Team	Lg	TD	1XP	2XP	FG	FGA	SAF	Pts
1996	**WAS**	**N**	1	0	0	0	0	0	6

Vernon Turner

Year	Team	Lg	TD	1XP	2XP	FG	FGA	SAF	Pts
1991	**LARM**	**N**	1	0		0	0	0	6
1994	**TB**	**N**	1	0	0	0	0	0	6
Career			2	0	0	0	0	0	12

Melvin Tuten

Year	Team	Lg	TD	1XP	2XP	FG	FGA	SAF	Pts
1995	**CIN**	**N**	1	0	0	0	0	0	6

Rick Tuten

Year	Team	Lg	TD	1XP	2XP	FG	FGA	SAF	Pts
1994	**SEA**	**N**	0	0	1	0	0	0	2

Perry Tuttle

Year	Team	Lg	TD	1XP	2XP	FG	FGA	SAF	Pts
1983	**BUF**	**N**	3	0		0	0	0	18

Howard Twilley

Year	Team	Lg	TD	1XP	2XP	FG	FGA	SAF	Pts
1967	**MIA**	**A**	2	0	0	0	0	0	12
1968			1	0	0	0	0	0	6

Howard Twilley *continued*

Year	Team	Lg	TD	1XP	2XP	FG	FGA	SAF	Pts
1969			1	0	0	0	0	0	6
1970	**MIA**	**N**	5	0		0	0	0	30
1971			4	0		0	0	0	24
1972			3	0		0	0	0	18
1974			2	0		0	0	0	12
1975			4	0		0	0	0	24
1976			1	0		0	0	0	6
Career			23	0	0	0	0	0	138
Playoffs			1	0	0	0	0	0	6

Maurice Tyler

Year	Team	Lg	TD	1XP	2XP	FG	FGA	SAF	Pts
1978	**NYG**	**N**	1	0		0	0	0	6

Pete Tyler

Year	Team	Lg	TD	1XP	2XP	FG	FGA	SAF	Pts
1937	**CHIC**	**N**	1	0		0		0	6
1938			1	0		0		0	6
Career			2	0		0		0	12

Wendell Tyler

Year	Team	Lg	TD	1XP	2XP	FG	FGA	SAF	Pts
1977	**LA**	**N**	3	0		0	0	0	18
1979			10	0		0	0	0	60
1981			17	0		0	0	0	102
1982	**LARM**	**N**	13	0		0	0	0	78
1983	**SF**	**N**	6	0		0	0	0	36
1984			9	0		0	0	0	54
1985			8	0		0	0	0	48
Career			66	0		0	0	0	396
Playoffs			3	0		0	0	0	18

Layne Tynes

Year	Team	Lg	TD	1XP	2XP	FG	FGA	SAF	Pts
1924	**COL**	**N**	2	0		0		0	12
1925			1	0		0		0	6
Career			3	0		0		0	18

Jim Tyree

Year	Team	Lg	TD	1XP	2XP	FG	FGA	SAF	Pts
1948	**BOS**	**N**	1	0		0	0	0	6

Rocky Ugoccioni

Year	Team	Lg	TD	1XP	2XP	FG	FGA	SAF	Pts
1944	**BKN**	**N**	1	0		0	0	0	6

Hub Ulrich

Year	Team	Lg	TD	1XP	2XP	FG	FGA	SAF	Pts
1946	**MIA**	**AA**	1	0		0	0	0	6

Jack Underwood

Year	Team	Lg	TD	1XP	2XP	FG	FGA	SAF	Pts
1924	**DUL**	**N**	2	0		0		0	12
1926			1	0		0		0	6
Career			3	0		0		0	18

Olen Underwood

Year	Team	Lg	TD	1XP	2XP	FG	FGA	SAF	Pts
1968	**HOU**	**A**	0	0	0	0	0	1	2

Johnny Unitas

Year	Team	Lg	TD	1XP	2XP	FG	FGA	SAF	Pts
1956	**BAL**	**N**	1	0		0	0	0	6
1957			1	0		0	0	0	6
1958			3	0		0	0	0	18
1959			2	0		0	0	0	12
1961			2	0		0	0	0	12
1964			2	0		0	0	0	12
1965			1	0		0	0	0	6
1966			1	0		0	0	0	6
Career			13	0		0	0	0	78
Playoffs			1	0		0	0	0	6

Rick Upchurch

Year	Team	Lg	TD	1XP	2XP	FG	FGA	SAF	Pts
1975	**DEN**	**N**	3	0		0	0	0	18
1976			6	0		0	0	0	36
1977			4	0		0	0	0	24
1978			2	0		0	0	0	12
1979			7	0		0	0	0	42
1980			3	0		0	0	0	18
1981			3	0		0	0	0	18
1982			5	0		0	0	0	30
1983			2	0		0	0	0	12
Career			35	0		0	0	0	210

Marv Upshaw

Year	Team	Lg	TD	1XP	2XP	FG	FGA	SAF	Pts
1974	**KC**	**N**	1	0		0	0	0	6

Andy Uram

Year	Team	Lg	TD	1XP	2XP	FG	FGA	SAF	Pts
1938	**GB**	**N**	2	0		0		0	12
1939			3	0		0	0	0	18
1940			3	1		0	0	0	19
1941			1	0		0	0	0	6

Andy Uram *continued*

Year	Team	Lg	TD	1XP	2XP	FG	FGA	SAF	Pts
1942			5	1		0	0	0	31
1943			2	0		0	0	0	12
Career			16	2		0	0	0	98

Alex Urban

Year	Team	Lg	TD	1XP	2XP	FG	FGA	SAF	Pts
1941	**GB**	**N**	1	0		0	0	0	6

Luke Urban

Year	Team	Lg	TD	1XP	2XP	FG	FGA	SAF	Pts
1921	**BUF**	**A**	1	0		0		0	6
1923	**BUF**	**N**	1	0		0		0	6
Career			2	0		0		0	12

Rube Ursella

Year	Team	Lg	TD	1XP	2XP	FG	FGA	SAF	Pts
1920	**RI**	**A**	1	5		1		0	14
1921	**MIN**	**A**	0	4		1		0	7
1924	**RI**	**N**	1	4		1		0	13
1925			0	2		3		0	11
1929	**MIN**	**N**	0	0		0		0	0
Career			2	15		6		0	45

Eddie Usher

Year	Team	Lg	TD	1XP	2XP	FG	FGA	SAF	Pts
1922	**RI-GB**	**N**	2	0		0		0	12

Iheanyi Uwaezuoke

Year	Team	Lg	TD	1XP	2XP	FG	FGA	SAF	Pts
1996	**SF**	**N**	1	0	0	0	0	0	6

Sam Vacanti

Year	Team	Lg	TD	1XP	2XP	FG	FGA	SAF	Pts
1947	**CHI**	**AA**	1	0		0	0	0	6
1948			2	0		0	0	0	12
1949	**BAL**	**AA**	0	3		0	2	0	3
Career			3	3		0	2	0	21

Ted Vactor

Year	Team	Lg	TD	1XP	2XP	FG	FGA	SAF	Pts
1973	**WAS**	**N**	1	0		0	0	0	6

Joe Valerio

Year	Team	Lg	TD	1XP	2XP	FG	FGA	SAF	Pts
1993	**KC**	**N**	1	0		0	0	0	6
1994			2	0	0	0	0	0	12
1995			1	0	0	0	0	0	6
Career			4	0	0	0	0	0	24

Norm Van Brocklin

Year	Team	Lg	TD	1XP	2XP	FG	FGA	SAF	Pts
1950	**LA**	**N**	1	0		0	0	0	6
1951			2	0		0	0	0	12
1956			1	0		0	0	0	6
1957			4	0		0	0	0	24
1958	**PHI**	**N**	1	0		0	0	0	6
1959			2	0		0	0	0	12
Career			11	0		0	0	0	66

Ebert Van Buren

Year	Team	Lg	TD	1XP	2XP	FG	FGA	SAF	Pts
1952	**PHI**	**N**	1	0		0	0	1	8

Steve Van Buren

Year	Team	Lg	TD	1XP	2XP	FG	FGA	SAF	Pts
1944	**PHI**	**N**	7	0		0	0	0	42
1945			**18**	2		0	0	0	**110**
1946			6	0		0	0	0	36
1947			**14**	0		0	0	0	84
1948			10	0		0	0	0	60
1949			12	0		0	0	0	72
1950			4	0		0	0	0	24
1951			6	0		0	0	0	36
Career			77	2		0	0	0	464
Playoffs			3	0		0	0	0	18

Joe Vance

Year	Team	Lg	TD	1XP	2XP	FG	FGA	SAF	Pts
1931	**BKN**	**N**	2	0		0		0	12

Skip Vanderbundt

Year	Team	Lg	TD	1XP	2XP	FG	FGA	SAF	Pts
1972	**SF**	**N**	3	0		0	0	0	18

Ron Vander Kelen

Year	Team	Lg	TD	1XP	2XP	FG	FGA	SAF	Pts
1967	**MIN**	**N**	1	0		0	0	0	6

Al Vandeweghe

Year	Team	Lg	TD	1XP	2XP	FG	FGA	SAF	Pts
1946	**BUF**	**AA**	2	0		0	0	0	12

Alex Van Dyke

Year	Team	Lg	TD	1XP	2XP	FG	FGA	SAF	Pts
1996	**NYJ**	**N**	1	0	0	0	0	0	6

Jimmy Van Dyke

Year	Team	Lg	TD	1XP	2XP	FG	FGA	SAF	Pts
1922	**LOU**	**N**	1	1		0		0	7

Mark van Eghen

Year	Team	Lg	TD	1XP	2XP	FG	FGA	SAF	Pts
1975	OAK	N	3	0		0	0	0	18
1976			3	0		0	0	0	18
1977			7	0		0	0	0	42
1978			10	0		0	0	0	60
1979			9	0		0	0	0	54
1980			5	0		0	0	0	30
1981			2	0		0	0	0	12
1982	NE	N	1	0		0	0	0	6
1983			2	0		0	0	0	12
Career			42	0		0	0	0	252
Playoffs			4	0		0	0	0	24

Hal Van Every

Year	Team	Lg	TD	1XP	2XP	FG	FGA	SAF	Pts
1941	GB	N	3	0		0	0	0	18
Playoffs			1	0	0	0	0	0	6

Billy Van Heusen

Year	Team	Lg	TD	1XP	2XP	FG	FGA	SAF	Pts
1968	DEN	A	3	0	0	0	0	0	18
1970	DEN	N	2	0		0	0	0	12
1972			1	0		0	0	0	6
1973			1	0		0	0	0	6
1974			4	0		0	0	0	24
1975			1	0		0	0	0	6
Career			12	0	0	0	0	0	72

Sean Vanhorse

Year	Team	Lg	TD	1XP	2XP	FG	FGA	SAF	Pts
1994	SD	N	1	0	0	0	0	0	6

Norwood Vann

Year	Team	Lg	TD	1XP	2XP	FG	FGA	SAF	Pts
1984	LARM	N	0	0		0	0	1	2

Tamarick Vanover

Year	Team	Lg	TD	1XP	2XP	FG	FGA	SAF	Pts
1995	KC	N	5	0	0	0	0	0	30
1996			2	0	0	0	0	0	12
Career			7	0	0	0	0	0	42

Dick Van Raaphorst

Year	Team	Lg	TD	1XP	2XP	FG	FGA	SAF	Pts
1964	DAL	N	0	28		14	29	0	70
1966	SD	A	0	39	0	16	31	0	87
1967			0	45	0	15	30	0	90
Career			0	112	0	45	90	0	247

Art Van Tone

Year	Team	Lg	TD	1XP	2XP	FG	FGA	SAF	Pts
1943	DET	N	1	0		0	0	0	6
1944			6	0		0	0	0	36
1946	BKN	AA	3	0		0	0	0	18
Career			10	0		0	0	0	60

Tommy Vardell

Year	Team	Lg	TD	1XP	2XP	FG	FGA	SAF	Pts
1993	CLE	N	4	0		0	0	0	24
1994			1	0	0	0	0	0	6
1996	SF	N	2	0	0	0	0	0	12
Career			7	0	0	0	0	0	42

Johnny Vardian

Year	Team	Lg	TD	1XP	2XP	FG	FGA	SAF	Pts
1947	BAL	AA	1	0		0	0	0	6

Larry Vargo

Year	Team	Lg	TD	1XP	2XP	FG	FGA	SAF	Pts
1963	DET	N	1	0		0	0	0	6

Randy Vataha

Year	Team	Lg	TD	1XP	2XP	FG	FGA	SAF	Pts
1971	NE	N	9	0		0	0	0	54
1972			2	0		0	0	0	12
1973			3	0		0	0	0	18
1974			3	0		0	0	0	18
1975			6	0		0	0	0	36
1976			1	0		0	0	0	6
Career			24	0		0	0	0	144

Harp Vaughan

Year	Team	Lg	TD	1XP	2XP	FG	FGA	SAF	Pts
1933	PIT	N	1	0		0		0	6

Jon Vaughn

Year	Team	Lg	TD	1XP	2XP	FG	FGA	SAF	Pts
1991	NE	N	3	0		0	0	0	18
1992			2	0		0	0	0	12
1994	SEA-KC	N	4	0	1	0	0	0	26
Career			9	0	1	0	0	0	56

Fred Venturelli

Year	Team	Lg	TD	1XP	2XP	FG	FGA	SAF	Pts
1948	CHIB	N	0	4		1	2	0	7

Sam Venuto

Year	Team	Lg	TD	1XP	2XP	FG	FGA	SAF	Pts
1952	WAS	N	1	0		0	0	0	6

Clarence Verdin

Year	Team	Lg	TD	1XP	2XP	FG	FGA	SAF	Pts
1988	IND	N	5	0		0	0	0	30
1989			2	0		0	0	0	12
1990			1	0		0	0	0	6
1991			1	0		0	0	0	6
1992			2	0		0	0	0	12
1993			1	0		0	0	0	6
Career			12	0		0	0	0	72

David Verser

Year	Team	Lg	TD	1XP	2XP	FG	FGA	SAF	Pts
1981	CIN	N	2	0		0	0	0	12
1982			1	0		0	0	0	6
Career			3	0		0	0	0	18

Billy Vessels

Year	Team	Lg	TD	1XP	2XP	FG	FGA	SAF	Pts
1956	BAL	N	3	0		0	0	0	18

John Vesser

Year	Team	Lg	TD	1XP	2XP	FG	FGA	SAF	Pts
1926	LA	A	1	0		0		0	6
1927	CHIC	N	1	0		0		0	6
Career			2	0		0		0	12

Joe Vetrano

Year	Team	Lg	TD	1XP	2XP	FG	FGA	SAF	Pts
1946	SF	AA	1	31		4	7	0	49
1947			0	38		4	12	0	50
1948			1	**62**		5	8	0	83
1949			0	**56**		3	7	0	65
Career			2	187		16	34	0	247
Playoffs			0	3		1	2	0	6

Dick Vick

Year	Team	Lg	TD	1XP	2XP	FG	FGA	SAF	Pts
1924	KEN	N	0	0		0		0	0
1925	DET	N	0	0		0		0	0
Career			0	0		0		0	0

Roger Vick

Year	Team	Lg	TD	1XP	2XP	FG	FGA	SAF	Pts
1987	NYJ	N	1	0		0	0	0	6
1988			3	0		0	0	0	18
1989			7	0		0	0	0	42
1990	PHI	N	1	0		0	0	0	6
Career			12	0		0	0	0	72

Tommy Vigorito

Year	Team	Lg	TD	1XP	2XP	FG	FGA	SAF	Pts
1981	MIA	N	4	0		0	0	0	24
1982			2	0		0	0	0	12
Career			6	0		0	0	0	36

Danny Villanueva

Year	Team	Lg	TD	1XP	2XP	FG	FGA	SAF	Pts
1960	LA	N	0	28		12	19	0	64
1961			0	32		13	27	0	71
1962			0	26		10	20	0	56
1963			0	25		9	17	0	52
1965	DAL	N	0	37		16	27	0	85
1966			0	**56**		17	31	0	107
1967			0	32		8	19	0	56
Career			0	236		85	160	0	491
Playoffs			0	12		4	5	0	24

Phil Villapiano

Year	Team	Lg	TD	1XP	2XP	FG	FGA	SAF	Pts
1972	OAK	N	1	0		0	0	0	6
1978			0	0		0	0	1	2
Career			1	0		0	0	1	8

Adam Vinatieri

Year	Team	Lg	TD	1XP	2XP	FG	FGA	SAF	Pts
1996	NE	N	0	39	0	27	35	0	120
Playoffs			0	9	0	2	3	0	15

Troy Vincent

Year	Team	Lg	TD	1XP	2XP	FG	FGA	SAF	Pts
1994	MIA	N	1	0	0	0	0	0	6
1995			1	0	0	0	0	0	6
1996	PHI	N	1	0	0	0	0	0	6
Career			3	0	0	0	0	0	18

Fernandus Vinson

Year	Team	Lg	TD	1XP	2XP	FG	FGA	SAF	Pts
1992	CIN	N	1	0		0	0	0	6

Kenny Vinyard

Year	Team	Lg	TD	1XP	2XP	FG	FGA	SAF	Pts
1970	ATL	N	0	23		9	25	0	50

Lionel Vital

Year	Team	Lg	TD	1XP	2XP	FG	FGA	SAF	Pts
1987	WAS	N	2	0		0	0	0	12

Sandro Vitiello

Year	Team	Lg	TD	1XP	2XP	FG	FGA	SAF	Pts
1980	CIN	N	0	1		0	2	0	1

Stu Voigt

Year	Team	Lg	TD	1XP	2XP	FG	FGA	SAF	Pts
1971	MIN	N	1	0		0	0	0	6
1972			2	0		0	0	0	12
1973			2	0		0	0	0	12
1974			5	0		0	0	0	30
1975			4	0		0	0	0	24
1976			1	0		0	0	0	6
1977			1	0		0	0	0	6
1979			2	0		0	0	0	12
Career			18	0		0	0	0	108
Playoffs			3	0		0	0	0	18

Otto Vokaty

Year	Team	Lg	TD	1XP	2XP	FG	FGA	SAF	Pts
1931	CLE	N	4	0		0		0	24

Rick Volk

Year	Team	Lg	TD	1XP	2XP	FG	FGA	SAF	Pts
1967	BAL	N	1	0		0	0	0	6

Jim Vollenweider

Year	Team	Lg	TD	1XP	2XP	FG	FGA	SAF	Pts
1963	SF	N	2	0		0	0	0	12

Bill Volok

Year	Team	Lg	TD	1XP	2XP	FG	FGA	SAF	Pts
1935	CHIC	N	1	0		0		0	6

Wilbur Volz

Year	Team	Lg	TD	1XP	2XP	FG	FGA	SAF	Pts
1949	BUF	AA	1	0		0	0	0	6

Uwe von Schamann

Year	Team	Lg	TD	1XP	2XP	FG	FGA	SAF	Pts
1979	MIA	N	0	36		21	29	0	99
1980			0	32		14	23	0	74
1981			0	37		24	31	0	109
1982			0	21		15	20	0	66
1983			0	45		18	27	0	99
1984			0	**66**		9	19	0	93
Career			0	237		101	149	0	540
Playoffs			0	32		9	15	0	59

Tillie Voss

Year	Team	Lg	TD	1XP	2XP	FG	FGA	SAF	Pts
1921	DET	A	1	2		0		0	8
1922	RI	N	2	6		0		0	18
1923	TOL	N	1	1		0		0	7
1924	GB	N	5	0		0		0	30
1928	CHIB	N	1	0		0		0	6
Career			10	9		0		0	69

Tom Waddle

Year	Team	Lg	TD	1XP	2XP	FG	FGA	SAF	Pts
1991	CHI	N	3	0		0	0	0	18
1992			4	0		0	0	0	24
1993			1	0		0	0	0	6
1994			1	0	0	0	0	0	6
Career			9	0	0	0	0	0	54
Playoffs			1	0	0	0	0	0	6

Billy Waddy

Year	Team	Lg	TD	1XP	2XP	FG	FGA	SAF	Pts
1977	LA	N	1	0		0	0	0	6
1978			1	0		0	0	0	6
1979			3	0		0	0	0	18
1980			5	0		0	0	0	30
Career			10	0		0	0	0	60
Playoffs			1	0		0	0	0	6

Billy Wade

Year	Team	Lg	TD	1XP	2XP	FG	FGA	SAF	Pts
1954	LA	N	1	0		0	0	0	6
1956			3	0		0	0	0	18
1958			2	0		0	0	0	12
1959			2	0		0	0	0	12
1960			2	0		0	0	0	12
1961	CHI	N	2	0		0	0	0	12
1962			5	0		0	0	0	30
1963			6	0		0	0	0	36
1964			1	0		0	0	0	6
Career			24	0		0	0	0	144
Playoffs			3	0		0	0	0	18

Charlie Wade

Year	Team	Lg	TD	1XP	2XP	FG	FGA	SAF	Pts
1974	CHI	N	1	0		0	0	0	6

Henry Waechter

Year	Team	Lg	TD	1XP	2XP	FG	FGA	SAF	Pts
1985	CHI	N	0	0		0	0	1	2
Playoffs			0	0	0	0	0	1	2

Harmon Wages

Year	Team	Lg	TD	1XP	2XP	FG	FGA	SAF	Pts
1968	ATL	N	1	0		0	0	0	6
1969			3	0		0	0	0	18

Year	Team		TD	1XP	2XP	FG	FGA	SAF	Pts

Harmon Wages *continued*
1970			3	0		0	0	0	18
1971			2	0		0	0	0	12
1973			1	0		0	0	0	6
Career			10	0		0	0	0	60

Lowell Wagner
1946	NY	AA	2	0		0	0	0	12
1947			1	0		0	0	0	6
1948			1	0		0	0	0	6
1949	SF	AA	1	0		0	0	0	6
Career			5	0		0	0	0	30

Mike Wagner
| 1973 | PIT | N | 1 | 0 | | 0 | 0 | 0 | 6 |

Jim Wagstaff
| 1960 | BUF | A | 1 | 0 | 0 | 0 | 0 | 0 | 6 |

Frank Wainright
| 1996 | MIA | N | 1 | 0 | 0 | 0 | 0 | 0 | 6 |

Carl Waite
1928	FRA	N	1	0		0		0	6
1929	ORA	N	1	0		0		0	6
1930	NEW	N	1	0		0		0	6
Career			3	0		0		0	18

Van Waiters
| 1989 | CLE | N | 1 | 0 | | 0 | 0 | 0 | 6 |

Billy Walik
| 1972 | PHI | N | 1 | 0 | | 0 | 0 | 0 | 6 |

Adam Walker
1994	SF	N	1	0	0	0	0	0	6
1995			1	0	0	0	0	0	6
Career			2	0	0	0	0	0	12
Playoffs			1	0	0	0	0	0	6

Byron Walker
1982	SEA	N	2	0		0	0	0	12
1983			2	0		0	0	0	12
1984			1	0		0	0	0	6
1985			3	0		0	0	0	18
Career			8	0		0	0	0	48

Darnell Walker
| 1994 | ATL | N | 1 | 0 | 0 | 0 | 0 | 0 | 6 |

Derrick Walker
1990	SD	N	1	0		0	0	0	6
1992			2	0		0	0	0	12
1993			1	0		0	0	0	6
1994	KC	N	2	0		0	0	0	12
1995			1	0		0	0	0	6
1996			1	0		0	0	0	6
Career			8	0		0	0	0	48
Playoffs			1	0		0	0	0	6

Doak Walker
1950	DET	N	11	38		8	18	0	128
1951			6	43		6	12	0	97
1952			0	5		3	5	0	14
1953			5	27		12	19	0	93
1954			5	43		11	17	0	106
1955			7	27		9	16	0	96
Career			34	183		49	87	0	534
Playoffs			2	3		2	4	0	21

Dwight Walker
| 1983 | CLE | N | 1 | 0 | | 0 | 0 | 0 | 6 |

Fulton Walker
1981	MIA	N	1	0		0	0	0	6
1986	LARI	N	1	0		0	0	0	6
Career			2	0		0	0	0	12
Playoffs			1	0		0	0	0	6

Herschel Walker
1986	DAL	N	14	0		0	0	0	84
1987			8	0		0	0	0	48
1988			7	0		0	0	0	42
1989	DAL-MIN	N	10	0		0	0	0	60

Herschel Walker *continued*
1990	MIN	N	9	0		0	0	0	54
1991			10	0		0	0	0	60
1992	PHI	N	10	0		0	0	0	60
1993			4	0		0	0	0	24
1994			8	0	0	0	0	0	48
1995	NYG	N	1	0	0	0	0	0	6
1996	DAL	N	1	0	0	0	0	0	6
Career			82	0	0	0	0	0	492

Kevin Walker
| 1987 | TB | N | 1 | 0 | | 0 | 0 | 0 | 6 |

Mike Walker
| 1972 | NE | N | 0 | 15 | | 2 | 8 | 0 | 21 |

Rick Walker
1978	CIN	N	2	0		0	0	0	12
1979			1	0		0	0	0	6
1980	WAS	N	1	0		0	0	0	6
1981			1	0		0	0	0	6
1982			1	0		0	0	0	6
1983			2	0		0	0	0	12
1984			1	0		0	0	0	6
Career			9	0		0	0	0	54

Val Joe Walker
| 1953 | GB | N | 1 | 0 | | 0 | 0 | 0 | 6 |

Wayne Walker
1958	DET	N	2	0		0	0	0	12
1959			0	5		0	0	0	5
1960			0	0		0	0	1	2
1961			0	6		0	3	0	6
1962			0	37		9	22	0	64
1963			0	29		9	22	0	56
1964			0	32		14	25	0	74
1965			0	33		8	22	0	57
1966			0	11		2	8	0	17
1967			0	11		5	15	0	26
1968			0	6		6	14	0	24
1971			0	2		0	0	0	2
Career			2	172		53	131	1	345

Wayne Walker
| 1968 | HOU | A | 0 | 26 | 0 | 8 | 16 | 0 | 50 |

Wayne Walker
| 1989 | SD | N | 1 | 0 | | 0 | 0 | 0 | 6 |

Wesley Walker
1977	NYJ	N	3	0		0	0	0	18
1978			8	0		0	0	0	48
1979			5	0		0	0	0	30
1980			1	0		0	0	0	6
1981			9	0		0	0	0	54
1982			6	0		0	0	0	36
1983			7	0		0	0	0	42
1984			7	0		0	0	0	42
1985			5	0		0	0	1	32
1986			12	0		0	0	0	72
1987			1	0		0	0	0	6
1988			7	0		0	0	0	42
Career			71	0		0	0	1	428
Playoffs			3	0		0	0	0	18

Beverly Wallace
| 1949 | SF | AA | 1 | 0 | | 0 | 0 | 0 | 6 |

Bob Wallace
1968	CHI	N	2	0		0	0	0	12
1969			5	0		0	0	0	30
1971			2	0		0	0	0	12
Career			9	0		0	0	0	54

Dutch Wallace
| 1924 | AKR | N | 0 | 2 | | 0 | | 0 | 2 |

Jackie Wallace
| 1975 | BAL | N | 2 | 0 | | 0 | 0 | 0 | 12 |

John Wallace
| 1928 | CHIB | N | 1 | 0 | | 0 | | 0 | 6 |

Ray Wallace
1986	HOU	N	5	0		0	0	0	30
1989	PIT	N	1	0		0	0	0	6
Career			6	0		0	0	0	36

Ron Waller
1955	LA	N	8	0		0	0	0	48
1956			1	0		0	0	0	6
Career			9	0		0	0	0	54
Playoffs			1	0		0	0	0	6

Everson Walls
| 1990 | NYG | N | 1 | 0 | | 0 | 0 | 0 | 6 |

Herkie Walls
1983	HOU	N	1	0		0	0	0	6
1984			1	0		0	0	0	6
Career			2	0		0	0	0	12

Wesley Walls
1989	SF	N	1	0		0	0	0	6
1994	NO	N	4	0	1	0	0	0	26
1995			4	0	1	0	0	0	26
1996	CAR	N	10	0	0	0	0	0	60
Career			19	0	2	0	0	0	118
Playoffs			1	0	0	0	0	0	6

Will Walls
1942	NYG	N	2	0		0	0	0	12
1943			2	0		0	0	0	12
Career			4	0		0	0	0	24

Laurie Walquist
1922	CHIB	N	0	0		0		0	0
1924			1	0		0		0	6
1925			3	0		0		0	18
1926			2	0		0		0	12
1927			1	0		0		0	6
1928			2	0		0		0	12
1929			3	0		0		0	18
1930			0	1		0		0	1
Career			12	1		0		0	73

Chris Walsh
| 1996 | MIN | N | 1 | 0 | 1 | 0 | 0 | 0 | 8 |

Steve Walsh
| 1994 | CHI | N | 1 | 0 | 0 | 0 | 0 | 0 | 6 |

Ward Walsh
1971	HOU	N	1	0		0	0	0	6
1972			1	0		0	0	0	6
Career			2	0		0	0	0	12

Bullets Walson
| 1921 | WAS | A | 2 | 1 | | 0 | | 0 | 13 |

Bobby Walston
1951	PHI	N	8	28		6	11	0	94
1952			3	31		11	20	0	82
1953			5	45		4	13	0	87
1954			11	36		4	10	0	114
1955			3	6		2	3	0	30
1956			3	17		6	13	0	53
1957			1	20		9	12	0	53
1958			3	31		6	14	0	67
1959			3	33		0	1	0	51
1960			4	39		14	20	0	105
1961			2	43		14	25	0	97
1962			0	36		4	15	0	48
Career			46	365		80	157	0	881
Playoffs			0	2		1	1	0	5

Tommy Walters
| 1965 | WAS | N | 1 | 0 | | 0 | 0 | 0 | 6 |

Len Walterscheid
| 1980 | CHI | N | 1 | 0 | | 0 | 0 | 0 | 6 |

Alvin Walton
1989	WAS	N	1	0		0	0	0	6
1990			1	0		0	0	0	6
Career			2	0		0	0	0	12

Joe Walton

Year	Team		TD	1XP	2XP	FG	FGA	SAF	Pts
1958	**WAS**	**N**	5	0		0	0	0	30
1959			3	0		0	0	0	18
1960			3	0		0	0	0	18
1961	**NYG**	**N**	2	0		0	0	0	12
1962			9	0		0	0	0	54
1963			6	0		0	0	0	36
Career			28	0		0	0	0	168

Larry Walton

Year	Team		TD	1XP	2XP	FG	FGA	SAF	Pts
1970	**DET**	**N**	5	0		0	0	0	30
1971			5	0		0	0	0	30
1972			6	0		0	0	0	36
1973			5	0		0	0	0	30
1974			3	0		0	0	0	18
1976			3	0		0	0	0	18
1978	**BUF**	**N**	1	0		0	0	0	6
Career			28	0		0	0	0	168

Bill Ward

Year	Team		TD	1XP	2XP	FG	FGA	SAF	Pts
1921	**BUF**	**A**	1	0		0		0	6

Carl Ward

Year	Team		TD	1XP	2XP	FG	FGA	SAF	Pts
1967	**CLE**	**N**	1	0		0	0	0	6

Derek Ware

Year	Team		TD	1XP	2XP	FG	FGA	SAF	Pts
1994	**ARI**	**N**	1	0	0	0	0	0	6

Paul Warfield

Year	Team		TD	1XP	2XP	FG	FGA	SAF	Pts
1964	**CLE**	**N**	9	0		0	0	0	54
1966			6	0		0	0	0	36
1967			8	0		0	0	0	48
1968			12	0		0	0	0	72
1969			10	0		0	0	0	60
1970	**MIA**	**N**	6	0		0	0	0	36
1971			11	0		0	0	0	66
1972			3	0		0	0	0	18
1973			11	0		0	0	0	66
1974			2	0		0	0	0	12
1976	**CLE**	**N**	6	0		0	0	0	36
1977			2	0		0	0	0	12
Career			86	0		0	0	0	516
Playoffs			5	0		0	0	0	30

Ernie Warlick

Year	Team		TD	1XP	2XP	FG	FGA	SAF	Pts
1962	**BUF**	**A**	2	0	0	0	0	0	12
1963			1	0	0	0	0	0	6
1965			1	0	0	0	0	0	6
Career			4	0	0	0	0	0	24
Playoffs			1	0	0	0	0	0	6

Charley Warner

Year	Team		TD	1XP	2XP	FG	FGA	SAF	Pts
1965	**BUF**	**A**	4	0	0	0	0	0	24
1966			1	0	0	0	0	0	6
Career			5	0	0	0	0	0	30

Curt Warner

Year	Team		TD	1XP	2XP	FG	FGA	SAF	Pts
1983	**SEA**	**N**	14	0		0	0	0	84
1985			9	0		0	0	0	54
1986			13	0		0	0	0	78
1987			10	0		0	0	0	60
1988			12	0		0	0	0	72
1989			4	0		0	0	0	24
1990	**LARM**	**N**	1	0		0	0	0	6
Career			63	0		0	0	0	378
Playoffs			2	0		0	0	0	12

Dave Warnke

Year	Team		TD	1XP	2XP	FG	FGA	SAF	Pts
1983	**TB**	**N**	0	1		0	1	0	1

Buist Warren

Year	Team		TD	1XP	2XP	FG	FGA	SAF	Pts
1945	**PIT**	**N**	2	0		0	0	0	12

Chris Warren

Year	Team		TD	1XP	2XP	FG	FGA	SAF	Pts
1990	**SEA**	**N**	1	0		0	0	0	6
1991			1	0		0	0	0	6
1992			3	0		0	0	0	18
1993			7	0		0	0	0	42
1994			11	0	1	0	0	0	68
1995			16	0	0	0	0	0	96
1996			5	0	1	0	0	0	32
Career			44	0	2	0	0	0	268

Don Warren

Year	Team		TD	1XP	2XP	FG	FGA	SAF	Pts
1981	**WAS**	**N**	1	0		0	0	0	6
1983			2	0		0	0	0	12
1985			1	0		0	0	0	6
1986			1	0		0	0	0	6
1989			1	0		0	0	0	6
1990			1	0		0	0	0	6
Career			7	0		0	0	0	42
Playoffs			1	0		0	0	0	6

Frank Warren

Year	Team		TD	1XP	2XP	FG	FGA	SAF	Pts
1985	**NO**	**N**	2	0		0	0	0	12
1989			0	0		0	0	1	2
1991			1	0		0	0	0	6
1993			1	0		0	0	0	6
Career			4	0		0	0	1	26

Jimmy Warren

Year	Team		TD	1XP	2XP	FG	FGA	SAF	Pts
1966	**MIA**	**A**	1	0	0	0	0	0	6
1967			1	0	0	0	0	0	6
1971	**OAK**	**N**	2	0		0	0	0	12
Career			4	0	0	0	0	0	24

Lamont Warren

Year	Team		TD	1XP	2XP	FG	FGA	SAF	Pts
1995	**IND**	**N**	1	0	0	0	0	0	6
1996			1	0	0	0	0	0	6
Career			2	0	0	0	0	0	12

Lonnie Warwick

Year	Team		TD	1XP	2XP	FG	FGA	SAF	Pts
1965	**MIN**	**N**	1	0		0	0	0	6

Brian Washington

Year	Team		TD	1XP	2XP	FG	FGA	SAF	Pts
1988	**CLE**	**N**	1	0		0	0	0	6
1992	**NYJ**	**N**	1	0		0	0	0	6
1993			1	0		0	0	0	6
1995	**KC**	**N**	1	0	0	0	0	0	6
Career			4	0	0	0	0	0	24

Dave Washington

Year	Team		TD	1XP	2XP	FG	FGA	SAF	Pts
1970	**DEN**	**N**	0	0		0	0	1	2
1974	**BUF**	**N**	2	0		0	0	0	12
1975	**SF**	**N**	1	0		0	0	0	6
Career			3	0		0	0	1	20

Dewayne Washington

Year	Team		TD	1XP	2XP	FG	FGA	SAF	Pts
1994	**MIN**	**N**	3	0	0	0	0	0	18
1996			1	0	0	0	0	0	6
Career			4	0	0	0	0	0	24

Gene Washington

Year	Team		TD	1XP	2XP	FG	FGA	SAF	Pts
1967	**MIN**	**N**	2	0		0	0	0	12
1968			6	0		0	0	0	36
1969			9	0		0	0	0	54
1970			4	0		0	0	0	24
1972			2	0		0	0	0	12
1973	**DEN**	**N**	3	0		0	0	0	18
Career			26	0		0	0	0	156
Playoffs			2	0		0	0	0	12

Gene Washington

Year	Team		TD	1XP	2XP	FG	FGA	SAF	Pts
1969	**SF**	**N**	3	0		0	0	0	18
1970			12	0		0	0	0	72
1971			4	0		0	0	0	24
1972			12	0		0	0	0	72
1973			2	0		0	0	0	12
1974			6	0		0	0	0	36
1975			9	0		0	0	0	54
1976			6	0		0	0	0	36
1977			5	0		0	0	0	30
1979	**DET**	**N**	1	0		0	0	0	6
Career			60	0		0	0	0	360
Playoffs			1	0		0	0	0	6

James Washington

Year	Team		TD	1XP	2XP	FG	FGA	SAF	Pts
Playoffs			1	0	0	0	0	0	6

Joe Washington

Year	Team		TD	1XP	2XP	FG	FGA	SAF	Pts
1978	**BAL**	**N**	2	0		0	0	0	12
1979			7	0		0	0	0	42
1980			4	0		0	0	0	24
1981	**WAS**	**N**	7	0		0	0	0	42
1982			2	0		0	0	0	12
1983			6	0		0	0	0	36
1984			1	0		0	0	0	6

Joe Washington *continued*

Year	Team		TD	1XP	2XP	FG	FGA	SAF	Pts
1985	**ATL**	**N**	2	0		0	0	0	12
Career			31	0		0	0	0	186

Kenny Washington

Year	Team		TD	1XP	2XP	FG	FGA	SAF	Pts
1946	**LA**	**N**	1	0		0	0	0	6
1947			5	0		0	0	0	30
1948			3	0		0	0	0	18
Career			9	0		0	0	0	54

Lionel Washington

Year	Team		TD	1XP	2XP	FG	FGA	SAF	Pts
1985	**STL**	**N**	1	0		0	0	0	6
1989	**LARI**	**N**	2	0		0	0	0	12
1994			1	0	0	0	0	0	6
Career			4	0	0	0	0	0	24

Mark Washington

Year	Team		TD	1XP	2XP	FG	FGA	SAF	Pts
1970	**DAL**	**N**	1	0		0	0	0	6
1972			0	0		0	0	1	2
Career			1	0		0	0	1	8

Marvin Washington

Year	Team		TD	1XP	2XP	FG	FGA	SAF	Pts
1992	**NYJ**	**N**	0	0		0	0	1	2

Mickey Washington

Year	Team		TD	1XP	2XP	FG	FGA	SAF	Pts
1993	**BUF**	**N**	1	0		0	0	0	6
1995	**JAC**	**N**	1	0	0	0	0	0	6
1996			1	0	0	0	0	0	6
Career			3	0	0	0	0	0	18

Mike Washington

Year	Team		TD	1XP	2XP	FG	FGA	SAF	Pts
1977	**TB**	**N**	1	0		0	0	0	6
1978			1	0		0	0	0	6
1979			1	0		0	0	0	6
1981			1	0		0	0	0	6
Career			4	0		0	0	0	24

Sam Washington

Year	Team		TD	1XP	2XP	FG	FGA	SAF	Pts
1984	**PIT**	**N**	2	0		0	0	0	12

Ted Washington

Year	Team		TD	1XP	2XP	FG	FGA	SAF	Pts
Playoffs			0	0	0	0	0	1	2

Vic Washington

Year	Team		TD	1XP	2XP	FG	FGA	SAF	Pts
1971	**SF**	**N**	7	0		0	0	0	42
1972			5	0		0	0	0	30
1973			8	0		0	0	0	48
1974	**HOU**	**N**	2	0		0	0	0	12
Career			22	0		0	0	0	132
Playoffs			1	0		0	0	0	6

Bob Waterfield

Year	Team		TD	1XP	2XP	FG	FGA	SAF	Pts
1945	**CLE**	**N**	5	**31**		1	3	0	64
1946	**LA**	**N**	1	**37**		6	9	0	61
1947			1	27		**7**	**16**	0	54
1948			0	38		6	11	0	56
1949			1	43		**9**	16	0	76
1950			1	**54**		7	14	0	81
1951			3	41		**13**	**23**	0	98
1952			1	**44**		11	18	0	83
Career			13	315		60	110	0	573
Playoffs			0	14		2	6	0	20

Andre Waters

Year	Team		TD	1XP	2XP	FG	FGA	SAF	Pts
1984	**PHI**	**N**	1	0		0	0	0	6
1989			1	0		0	0	0	6
Career			2	0		0	0	0	12

Bobby Waters

Year	Team		TD	1XP	2XP	FG	FGA	SAF	Pts
1961	**SF**	**N**	3	0		0	0	0	18

Charlie Waters

Year	Team		TD	1XP	2XP	FG	FGA	SAF	Pts
1972	**DAL**	**N**	1	0		0	0	0	6
1975			1	0		0	0	0	6
1977			1	0		0	0	0	6
1978			0	0		0	0	1	2
Career			3	0		0	0	1	20

Mike Waters

Year	Team		TD	1XP	2XP	FG	FGA	SAF	Pts
1987	**NO**	**N**	1	0		0	0	0	6

Bobby Watkins

Year	Team		TD	1XP	2XP	FG	FGA	SAF	Pts
1955	**CHIB**	**N**	8	0		0	0	0	48
1956			3	0		0	0	0	18

Bobby Watkins *continued*

Year	Team	TD	1XP	2XP	FG	FGA	SAF	Pts
1957		2	0		0	0	0	12
1958	CHIC N	1	0		0	0	0	6
Career		14	0		0	0	0	84

Foster Watkins

Year	Team	TD	1XP	2XP	FG	FGA	SAF	Pts
1940	PHI N	0	2		0	0	0	2

Larry Watkins

Year	Team	TD	1XP	2XP	FG	FGA	SAF	Pts
1969	DET N	1	0		0	0	0	6
1970	PHI N	1	0		0	0	0	6
1971		1	0		0	0	0	6
1972		1	0		0	0	0	6
1973	BUF N	3	0		0	0	0	18
1974		2	0		0	0	0	12
1975	NYG N	3	0		0	0	0	18
1976		1	0		0	0	0	6
Career		13	0		0	0	0	78

Tommy Watkins

Year	Team	TD	1XP	2XP	FG	FGA	SAF	Pts
1961	CLE N	1	0		0	0	0	6
1962	DET N	3	0		0	0	0	18
1963		4	0		0	0	0	24
1964		4	0		0	0	0	24
1967		5	0		0	0	0	30
Career		17	0		0	0	0	102

Allen Watson

Year	Team	TD	1XP	2XP	FG	FGA	SAF	Pts
1970	PIT N	0	7		5	10	0	22

Rat Watson

Year	Team	TD	1XP	2XP	FG	FGA	SAF	Pts
1922	TOL N	0	3		0		0	3
1923		0	1		0		0	1
Career		0	4		0		0	4

Sid Watson

Year	Team	TD	1XP	2XP	FG	FGA	SAF	Pts
1955	PIT N	1	0		0	0	0	6
1956		4	10	1	1	0		37
1958	WAS N	1	0		0	0	0	6
Career		6	10	1	1	0		49

Steve Watson

Year	Team	TD	1XP	2XP	FG	FGA	SAF	Pts
1981	DEN N	13	0		0	0	0	78
1982		2	0		0	0	0	12
1983		5	0		0	0	0	30
1984		7	0		0	0	0	42
1985		5	0		0	0	0	30
1986		3	0		0	0	0	18
1987		1	0		0	0	0	6
Career		36	0		0	0	0	216
Playoffs		1	0		0	0	0	6

Joe Watt

Year	Team	TD	1XP	2XP	FG	FGA	SAF	Pts
1947	DET N	2	0		0	0	0	12

Frank Wattelet

Year	Team	TD	1XP	2XP	FG	FGA	SAF	Pts
1984	NO N	2	0		0	0	0	12

Len Watters

Year	Team	TD	1XP	2XP	FG	FGA	SAF	Pts
1924	BUF N	1	0		0		0	6

Orlando Watters

Year	Team	TD	1XP	2XP	FG	FGA	SAF	Pts
1994	SEA N	1	0	0	0	0	0	6

Ricky Watters

Year	Team	TD	1XP	2XP	FG	FGA	SAF	Pts
1992	SF N	11	0		0	0	0	66
1993		11	0		0	0	0	66
1994		11	0		0	0	0	66
1995	PHI N	12	0		0	0	0	72
1996		13	0		0	0	0	78
Career		58	0		0	0	0	348
Playoffs		12	0		0	0	0	72

Rickey Watts

Year	Team	TD	1XP	2XP	FG	FGA	SAF	Pts
1979	CHI N	4	0		0	0	0	24
1980		2	0		0	0	0	12
1981		3	0		0	0	0	18
Career		9	0		0	0	0	54

Ted Watts

Year	Team	TD	1XP	2XP	FG	FGA	SAF	Pts
1981	OAK N	1	0		0	0	0	6

Charles Way

Year	Team	TD	1XP	2XP	FG	FGA	SAF	Pts
1995	NYG N	1	0	0	0	0	0	6

Charles Way *continued*

Year	Team	TD	1XP	2XP	FG	FGA	SAF	Pts
1996		2	0	0	0	0	0	12
Career		3	0	0	0	0	0	18

Charlie Way

Year	Team	TD	1XP	2XP	FG	FGA	SAF	Pts
1921	CAN A	1	0		0		0	6
1924	FRA N	4	0		0		0	24
1926	PHI A	2	0		0		0	12
Career		7	0		0		0	42

Dave Waymer

Year	Team	TD	1XP	2XP	FG	FGA	SAF	Pts
1988	NO N	1	0		0	0	0	6

Jim Weatherford

Year	Team	TD	1XP	2XP	FG	FGA	SAF	Pts
1969	ATL N	1	0		0	0	0	6

Gerry Weatherly

Year	Team	TD	1XP	2XP	FG	FGA	SAF	Pts
1950	CHIB N	2	0		0	0	0	12
1954		1	0		0	0	0	6
Career		3	0		0	0	0	18

Clarence Weathers

Year	Team	TD	1XP	2XP	FG	FGA	SAF	Pts
1983	NE N	3	0		0	0	0	18
1984		2	0		0	0	0	12
1985	CLE N	3	0		0	0	0	18
1987		2	0		0	0	0	12
1988		1	0		0	0	0	6
1990	GB N	1	0		0	0	0	6
Career		12	0		0	0	0	72

Robert Weathers

Year	Team	TD	1XP	2XP	FG	FGA	SAF	Pts
1982	NE N	1	0		0	0	0	6
1983		1	0		0	0	0	6
1985		1	0		0	0	0	6
1986		1	0		0	0	0	6
Career		4	0		0	0	0	24
Playoffs		1	0		0	0	0	6

Jim Weaver

Year	Team	TD	1XP	2XP	FG	FGA	SAF	Pts
1923	COL N	0	2		0		0	2

Don Webb

Year	Team	TD	1XP	2XP	FG	FGA	SAF	Pts
1961	BOS A	4	0	0	0	0	0	24

Ken Webb

Year	Team	TD	1XP	2XP	FG	FGA	SAF	Pts
1958	DET N	3	0		0	0	0	18
1959		2	0		0	0	0	12
1960		2	0		0	0	0	12
1961		1	0		0	0	0	6
1962		1	0		0	0	0	6
Career		9	0		0	0	0	54

Chuck Weber

Year	Team	TD	1XP	2XP	FG	FGA	SAF	Pts
1959	PHI N	1	0		0	0	0	6

Alex Webster

Year	Team	TD	1XP	2XP	FG	FGA	SAF	Pts
1955	NYG N	6	0		0	0	0	36
1956		10	0		0	0	0	60
1957		6	0		0	0	0	36
1958		6	0		0	0	0	36
1959		7	0		0	0	0	42
1961		5	0		0	0	0	30
1962		9	0		0	0	0	54
1963		4	0		0	0	0	24
1964		3	0		0	0	0	18
Career		56	0		0	0	0	336
Playoffs		2	0		0	0	0	12

Cornell Webster

Year	Team	TD	1XP	2XP	FG	FGA	SAF	Pts
1979	SEA N	1	0		0	0	0	6

Dave Webster

Year	Team	TD	1XP	2XP	FG	FGA	SAF	Pts
1960	DAL A	3	0	0	0	0	0	18

Tim Webster

Year	Team	TD	1XP	2XP	FG	FGA	SAF	Pts
1971	GB N	0	8		6	11	0	26

Herman Wedemeyer

Year	Team	TD	1XP	2XP	FG	FGA	SAF	Pts
1948	LA AA	2	0		0	0	0	12

Tad Weed

Year	Team	TD	1XP	2XP	FG	FGA	SAF	Pts
1955	PIT N	0	12		3	6	0	21

Norris Weese

Year	Team	TD	1XP	2XP	FG	FGA	SAF	Pts
1977	DEN N	1	0		0	0	0	6
1978		1	0		0	0	0	6
1979		3	0		0	0	0	18
Career		5	0		0	0	0	30

Mike Weger

Year	Team	TD	1XP	2XP	FG	FGA	SAF	Pts
1970	DET N	1	0		0	0	0	6
1971		1	0		0	0	0	6
Career		2	0		0	0	0	12

Ted Wegert

Year	Team	TD	1XP	2XP	FG	FGA	SAF	Pts
1955	PHI N	2	0		0	0	0	12
1956		1	0		0	0	0	6
1960	NY A	2	0	0	0	0	0	12
Career		5	0	0	0	0	0	30

Roger Wehrli

Year	Team	TD	1XP	2XP	FG	FGA	SAF	Pts
1974	STL N	1	0		0	0	0	6
1975		0	1		0	0	0	1
1979		1	0		0	0	0	6
1982		1	0		0	0	0	6
Career		3	1		0	0	0	19

Chuck Weimer

Year	Team	TD	1XP	2XP	FG	FGA	SAF	Pts
1929	BUF N	1	3		3		0	18
1930	BKN N	2	1		0		0	13
Career		3	4		3		0	31

Al Weiner

Year	Team	TD	1XP	2XP	FG	FGA	SAF	Pts
1934	PHI N	0	3		1		0	6

Art Weiner

Year	Team	TD	1XP	2XP	FG	FGA	SAF	Pts
1950	NYY N	6	0		0	0	0	36

Arnie Weinmeister

Year	Team	TD	1XP	2XP	FG	FGA	SAF	Pts
1952	NYG N	0	0		0	0	1	2

Izzy Weinstock

Year	Team	TD	1XP	2XP	FG	FGA	SAF	Pts
1937	PIT N	0	4		0		0	4

Ed Weir

Year	Team	TD	1XP	2XP	FG	FGA	SAF	Pts
1926	FRA N	0	2		1		0	5
1928		1	1		0		0	7
Career		1	3		1		0	12

Heinie Weisenbaugh

Year	Team	TD	1XP	2XP	FG	FGA	SAF	Pts
1935	PIT N	2	0		0		0	12

Dick Weisgerber

Year	Team	TD	1XP	2XP	FG	FGA	SAF	Pts
1942	GB N	0	2		0	0	0	2

Clayton Weishuhn

Year	Team	TD	1XP	2XP	FG	FGA	SAF	Pts
1983	NE N	1	0		0	0	0	6

Howie Weiss

Year	Team	TD	1XP	2XP	FG	FGA	SAF	Pts
1940	DET N	4	0		0	0	0	24

Johnny Weiss

Year	Team	TD	1XP	2XP	FG	FGA	SAF	Pts
1945	NYG N	1	0		0	0	0	6
1946		1	0		0	0	0	6
Career		2	0		0	0	0	12

Claxton Welch

Year	Team	TD	1XP	2XP	FG	FGA	SAF	Pts
1970	DAL N	1	0		0	0	0	6
1971		1	0		0	0	1	8
Career		2	0		0	0	1	14

Gibby Welch

Year	Team	TD	1XP	2XP	FG	FGA	SAF	Pts
1928	NYY N	7	0		0		0	42
1929	PRO N	6	0		0		0	36
Career		13	0		0		0	78

Jim Welch

Year	Team	TD	1XP	2XP	FG	FGA	SAF	Pts
1961	BAL N	1	0		0	0	0	6

Casey Weldon

Year	Team	TD	1XP	2XP	FG	FGA	SAF	Pts
1995	TB N	1	0	0	0	0	0	6

John Weldon

Year	Team	TD	1XP	2XP	FG	FGA	SAF	Pts
1920	BUF A	1	5		1		0	14

Larry Weldon

Year	Team	TD	1XP	2XP	FG	FGA	SAF	Pts
1944	WAS N	0	4		0	0	0	4

Year	Team		TD	1XP	2XP	FG	FGA	SAF	Pts

Bub Weller
| 1927 | CHIC | N | 1 | 2 | | 0 | | 0 | 8 |

Louis Weller
| 1933 | BOS | N | 2 | 1 | | 0 | | 0 | 13 |

Gary Wellman
| 1993 | HOU | N | 1 | 0 | | 0 | 0 | 0 | 6 |

Arthur Wells
| 1987 | TB | N | 1 | 0 | | 0 | 0 | 0 | 6 |

Billy Wells
1954	WAS	N	4	0		0	0	0	24
1956			2	0		0	0	0	12
1957	PIT	N	1	0		0	0	0	6
1958	PHI	N	1	0		0	0	0	6
1960	BOS	A	1	0		0	0	0	6
Career			9	0		0	0	0	54

Harold Wells
| 1966 | PHI | N | 1 | 0 | | 0 | 0 | | 6 |

Joel Wells
| 1961 | NYG | N | 2 | 0 | | 0 | 0 | | 12 |

Mike Wells
| 1987 | SF | N | 1 | 0 | | 0 | 0 | 0 | 6 |

Mike Wells
| 1996 | DET | N | 1 | 0 | | 0 | 0 | 0 | 6 |

Warren Wells
1967	OAK	A	6	0	0	0	0	0	36
1968			12	0	0	0	0	0	72
1969			14	0	0	0	0	0	84
1970	OAK		11	0		0	0	0	66
Career			43	0	0	0	0	0	258
Playoffs			3	0	0	0	0	0	18

Jim Welsh
1923	ROC	N	0	0		0		0	0
1924	FRA	N	0	17		7		0	38
1926	POT	N	0	15		5		0	30
Career			0	32		12		0	68

Larry Weltman
| 1922 | ROC | N | 0 | 0 | | 0 | | 0 | 0 |

Don Wemple
| 1941 | BKN | N | 1 | 0 | | 0 | 0 | 0 | 6 |

Obe Wenig
| 1921 | RI | A | 3 | 8 | | 0 | 0 | 0 | 26 |

Cy Wentworth
1925	PRO	N	3	0		0		0	18
1926			0	3		1		0	6
1929	BOS	N	3	6		0		0	24
Career			6	9		1		0	48

Barney Wentz
1925	POT	N	5	2		0		0	32
1926			9	0		0		0	54
1927			2	2		1		0	17
Career			16	4		1		0	103

Ray Wersching
1973	SD	N	0	15		11	25	0	48
1974			0	0		5	11	0	15
1975			0	20		12	24	0	56
1976			0	14		4	8	0	26
1977	SF	N	0	23		10	17	0	53
1978			0	24		15	23	0	69
1979			0	32		20	24	0	92
1980			0	33		15	19	0	78
1981			0	30		17	23	0	81
1982			0	23		12	17	0	59
1983			0	51		25	30	0	126
1984			0	56		25	35	0	**131**
1985			0	**52**		13	21	0	91
1986			0	41		25	35	0	116

Ray Wersching *continued*
1987			0	**44**		13	17	0	83
Career			0	458		222	329	0	1124
Playoffs			0	30		13	22	0	69

Belf West
| 1921 | CAN | A | 0 | 4 | | 1 | | 0 | 7 |

Charlie West
| 1968 | MIN | N | 1 | 0 | | 0 | 0 | 0 | 6 |

Ed West
1984	GB	N	5	0		0	0	0	30
1985			1	0		0	0	0	6
1986			1	0		0	0	0	6
1987			1	0		0	0	0	6
1988			3	0		0	0	0	18
1989			5	0		0	0	0	30
1990			5	0		0	0	0	30
1991			3	0		0	0	0	18
1994			2	0	1	0	0	0	14
1995	PHI	N	1	0	0	0	0	0	6
Career			27	0	1	0	0	0	164

Mel West
| 1961 | NY | A | 3 | 0 | 0 | 0 | 0 | 0 | 18 |

Pat West
1946	LA	N	1	0		0	0		6
1947			2	0		0	0		12
Career			3	0		0	0		18

Robert West
| 1972 | KC | N | 3 | 0 | | 0 | 0 | | 18 |

Walt West
| 1944 | CLE | N | 1 | 6 | | 0 | 0 | | 12 |

Willie West
1961	STL	N	1	0		0	0		6
1968	MIA	A	1	0		0	0		6
Career			2	0		0	0		12

Don Westbrook
1979	NE	N	1	0		0	0		6
1981			2	0		0	0		12
Career			3	0		0	0		18

Michael Westbrook
1995	WAS	N	2	0	0	0	0	0	12
1996			1	0	0	0	0	0	6
Career			3	0	0	0	0	0	18

Bob Westfall
1944	DET	N	5	0		0	0	0	30
1945			9	0		0	0	0	54
1946			1	0		0	0	0	6
1947			1	0		0	0	0	6
Career			16	0		0	0	0	96

Ed Westfall
| 1933 | BOS-PIT | N | 2 | 1 | | 0 | | 0 | 13 |

Dick Westmoreland
1966	MIA	A	1	0	0	0	0	0	6
1967			1	0	0	0	0	0	6
Career			2	0	0	0	0	0	12

Ryan Wetnight
1993	CHI	N	1	0		0	0	0	6
1994			1	0		0	0	0	6
1995			2	0		0	0	0	12
1996			1	0		0	0	0	6
Career			5	0		0	0	0	30

Damon Wetzel
| 1935 | PIT | N | 1 | 0 | | 0 | | 0 | 6 |

Jim Whalen
1966	BOS	A	4	0	0	0	0	0	24
1967			5	0	0	0	0	0	30
1968			7	0	0	0	0	0	42
1969			1	0	0	0	0	0	6

Jim Whalen *continued*
| 1970 | DEN | N | 3 | 0 | 0 | 0 | 0 | 0 | 18 |
| Career | | | 20 | 0 | 0 | 0 | 0 | 0 | 120 |

Tom Wham
1949	CHIC	N	1	0		0	0	0	6
1950			1	0		0	0	0	6
Career			2	0		0	0	0	12

Tyrone Wheatley
1995	NYG	N	3	0	0	0	0	0	18
1996			3	0	0	0	0	0	18
Career			6	0	0	0	0	0	36

Kyle Wheeler
| 1923 | GB | N | 1 | 0 | | 0 | | 0 | 6 |

Wayne Wheeler
| 1974 | CHI | N | 1 | 0 | | 0 | 0 | 0 | 6 |

Ernie Wheelwright
1964	NYG	N	3	0		0	0	0	18
1966	ATL	N	6	0		0	0	0	36
1967			1	0		0	0	0	6
1968	NO	N	1	0		0	0	0	6
1969			5	0		0	0	0	30
Career			16	0		0	0	0	96

Tom Whelan
| 1921 | CLE | A | 1 | 0 | | 0 | | 0 | 6 |

Ken Whisenhunt
1986	ATL	N	3	0		0	0	0	18
1987			1	0		0	0	0	6
1988			1	0		0	0	0	6
Career			5	0		0	0	0	30

Danta Whitaker
| 1990 | KC | N | 1 | 0 | | 0 | 0 | 0 | 6 |

Andre White
| 1967 | DEN | A | 0 | 0 | 0 | 0 | 0 | 1 | 2 |

Bob White
| 1952 | SF | N | 3 | 0 | | 0 | 0 | | 18 |

Charles White
1980	CLE	N	6	0		0	0	0	36
1981			1	0		0	0	0	6
1982			3	0		0	0	0	18
1985	LARM	N	3	0		0	0	0	18
1987			11	0		0	0	0	66
Career			24	0		0	0	0	144

Charlie White
| 1977 | NYJ | N | 2 | 0 | | 0 | 0 | 0 | 12 |

Danny White
1980	DAL	N	1	0		0	0	0	6
1983			5	0		0	0	0	30
1985			2	0		0	0	0	12
1986			1	0		0	0	0	6
1987			1	0		0	0	0	6
Career			10	0		0	0	0	60

David White
| 1996 | BUF | N | 1 | 0 | | 0 | 0 | 0 | 6 |

Dwight White
1973	PIT	N	0	0		0	0	1	2
1975			0	0		0	0	1	2
Career			0	0		0	0	2	4
Playoffs			0	0		0	0	1	2

Freeman White
| 1969 | NYG | N | 1 | 0 | | 0 | 0 | 0 | 6 |

Gene White
| 1962 | OAK | A | 1 | 0 | 1 | 0 | 0 | 0 | 8 |

Jan White
| 1972 | BUF | N | 2 | 0 | | 0 | 0 | 0 | 12 |

Jeff White

Year	Team	Lg	TD	1XP	2XP	FG	FGA	SAF	Pts
1973	NE	N	0	21		14	25	0	63

Jeris White

Year	Team	Lg	TD	1XP	2XP	FG	FGA	SAF	Pts
Playoffs			1	0	0	0	0	0	6

Jim White

Year	Team	Lg	TD	1XP	2XP	FG	FGA	SAF	Pts
1946	NYG	N	1	0		0	0	0	6
1947			1	0		0	0	0	6
1948			1	0		0	0	0	6
Career			3	0		0	0	0	18

John White

Year	Team	Lg	TD	1XP	2XP	FG	FGA	SAF	Pts
1961	HOU	A	1	0	0	0	0	0	6

Lee White

Year	Team	Lg	TD	1XP	2XP	FG	FGA	SAF	Pts
1970	NYJ	N	1	0		0	0	0	6

Leon White

Year	Team	Lg	TD	1XP	2XP	FG	FGA	SAF	Pts
1986	CIN	N	0	0		0	0	1	2
1989			1	0		0	0	0	6
Career			1	0		0	0	1	8

Lorenzo White

Year	Team	Lg	TD	1XP	2XP	FG	FGA	SAF	Pts
1988	HOU	N	1	0		0	0	0	6
1989			5	0		0	0	0	30
1990			12	0		0	0	0	72
1991			4	0		0	0	0	24
1992			8	0		0	0	0	48
1993			2	0		0	0	0	12
1994			4	0	0	0	0	0	24
1995	CLE	N	1	0	0	0	0	0	6
Career			37	0	0	0	0	0	222
Playoffs			1	0	0	0	0	0	6

Marsh White

Year	Team	Lg	TD	1XP	2XP	FG	FGA	SAF	Pts
1975	NYG	N	1	0		0	0	0	6
1976			1	0		0	0	0	6
Career			2	0		0	0	0	12

Phil White

Year	Team	Lg	TD	1XP	2XP	FG	FGA	SAF	Pts
1925	KC-NY	N	5	1		1		0	34
1927	NYG	N	3	1		0		0	19
Career			8	2		1		0	53

Randy White

Year	Team	Lg	TD	1XP	2XP	FG	FGA	SAF	Pts
Playoffs			0	0	0	0	0	1	2

Ray White

Year	Team	Lg	TD	1XP	2XP	FG	FGA	SAF	Pts
1971	SD	N	0	0		0	0	1	2
1972	CIN	N	0	0		0	0	1	2
Career			0	0		0	0	2	4

Reggie White

Year	Team	Lg	TD	1XP	2XP	FG	FGA	SAF	Pts
1987	PHI	N	1	0		0	0	0	6
1992			1	0		0	0	0	6
Career			2	0		0	0	0	12
Playoffs			0	0		0	0	1	2

Roy White

Year	Team	Lg	TD	1XP	2XP	FG	FGA	SAF	Pts
1925	CHIB	N	3	0		0		0	18
1926	CHI	A	1	0		0		0	6
1927	CHIB	N	2	0		0		0	12
1928			3	0		0		0	18
1929			2	0		0		0	12
Career			11	0		0		0	66

Sammy White

Year	Team	Lg	TD	1XP	2XP	FG	FGA	SAF	Pts
1976	MIN	N	10	0		0	0	0	60
1977			9	0		0	0	0	54
1978			9	0		0	0	0	54
1979			4	0		0	0	0	24
1980			5	0		0	0	0	30
1981			3	0		0	0	0	18
1982			5	0		0	0	0	30
1983			4	0		0	0	0	24
1984			1	0		0	0	0	6
Career			50	0		0	0	0	300
Playoffs			5	0		0	0	0	30

Sheldon White

Year	Team	Lg	TD	1XP	2XP	FG	FGA	SAF	Pts
1991	DET	N	1	0		0	0	0	6

Stan White

Year	Team	Lg	TD	1XP	2XP	FG	FGA	SAF	Pts
1973	BAL	N	1	0		0	0	0	6
1975			1	0		0	0	0	6
Career			2	0		0	0	0	12

Walter White

Year	Team	Lg	TD	1XP	2XP	FG	FGA	SAF	Pts
1975	KC	N	3	0		0	0	0	18
1976			7	0		0	0	0	42
1977			5	0		0	0	0	30
1978			1	0		0	0	0	6
Career			16	0		0	0	0	96

Whizzer White

Year	Team	Lg	TD	1XP	2XP	FG	FGA	SAF	Pts
1938	PIT	N	4	0		0		0	24
1940	DET	N	5	2		0	1	0	32
1941			4	0		0	0	0	24
Career			13	2		0	1	0	80

Wilford White

Year	Team	Lg	TD	1XP	2XP	FG	FGA	SAF	Pts
1951	CHIB	N	2	1		1	2	0	16
1952			0	1		2	3	0	7
Career			2	2		3	5	0	23

William White

Year	Team	Lg	TD	1XP	2XP	FG	FGA	SAF	Pts
1989	DET	N	1	0		0	0	0	6
1990			1	0		0	0	0	6
1991			1	0		0	0	0	6
Career			3	0		0	0	0	18

Bud Whitehead

Year	Team	Lg	TD	1XP	2XP	FG	FGA	SAF	Pts
1965	SD	A	1	0	0	0	0	0	6

David Whitehurst

Year	Team	Lg	TD	1XP	2XP	FG	FGA	SAF	Pts
1977	GB	N	1	0		0	0	0	6
1978			1	0		0	0	0	6
1979			4	0		0	0	0	24
1981			1	0		0	0	0	6
Career			7	0		0	0	0	42

A.D. Whitfield

Year	Team	Lg	TD	1XP	2XP	FG	FGA	SAF	Pts
1966	WAS	N	3	0		0	0	0	18
1967			3	0		0	0	0	18
Career			6	0		0	0	0	36

S.J. Whitman

Year	Team	Lg	TD	1XP	2XP	FG	FGA	SAF	Pts
1954	CHIB	N	1	0		0	0	0	6

Dave Whitsell

Year	Team	Lg	TD	1XP	2XP	FG	FGA	SAF	Pts
1963	CHI	N	1	0		0	0	0	6
1965			1	0		0	0	0	6
1967	NO	N	2	0		0	0	0	12
1968			1	0		0	0	0	6
Career			5	0		0	0	0	30

Jesse Whittenton

Year	Team	Lg	TD	1XP	2XP	FG	FGA	SAF	Pts
1956	LA	N	1	0		0	0	0	6
1961	GB	N	1	0		0	0	0	6
Career			2	0		0	0	0	12

Arthur Whittington

Year	Team	Lg	TD	1XP	2XP	FG	FGA	SAF	Pts
1978	OAK	N	7	0		0	0	0	42
1979			2	0		0	0	0	12
1980			4	0		0	0	0	24
1981			3	0		0	0	0	18
Career			16	0		0	0	0	96
Playoffs			1	0		0	0	0	6

C.L. Whittington

Year	Team	Lg	TD	1XP	2XP	FG	FGA	SAF	Pts
1976	HOU	N	1	0		0	0	0	6

Ossie Wiberg

Year	Team	Lg	TD	1XP	2XP	FG	FGA	SAF	Pts
1927	CLE	N	4	1		0		1	27
1928	DET	N	3	1		0		0	19
1930	NYG	N	4	6		0		0	30
1932	BKN	N	0	2		0		0	2
Career			11	10		0		1	78

Paul Wiggin

Year	Team	Lg	TD	1XP	2XP	FG	FGA	SAF	Pts
1960	CLE	N	1	0		0	0	0	6
1964			1	0		0	0	0	6
Career			2	0		0	0	0	12

Bill Wightkin

Year	Team	Lg	TD	1XP	2XP	FG	FGA	SAF	Pts
1951	CHIB	N	1	0		0	0	0	6

Bill Wightkin *continued*

Year	Team	Lg	TD	1XP	2XP	FG	FGA	SAF	Pts
1952			2	0		0	0	0	12
1953			1	0		0	0	0	6
Career			4	0		0	0	0	24

Barry Wilburn

Year	Team	Lg	TD	1XP	2XP	FG	FGA	SAF	Pts
1987	WAS	N	1	0		0	0	0	6
Playoffs			1	0	0	0	0	0	6

J.R. Wilburn

Year	Team	Lg	TD	1XP	2XP	FG	FGA	SAF	Pts
1967	PIT	N	5	0		0	0	0	30
1968			3	0		0	0	0	18
Career			8	0		0	0	0	48

Mike Wilcher

Year	Team	Lg	TD	1XP	2XP	FG	FGA	SAF	Pts
1987	LARM	N	1	0		0	0	0	6

Dave Wilcox

Year	Team	Lg	TD	1XP	2XP	FG	FGA	SAF	Pts
1965	SF	N	1	0		0	0	0	6
1974			1	0		0	0	0	6
Career			2	0		0	0	0	12

Ned Wilcox

Year	Team	Lg	TD	1XP	2XP	FG	FGA	SAF	Pts
1926	FRA	N	3	0		0		0	18
1927			2	0		0		0	12
Career			5	0		0		0	30

George Wilde

Year	Team	Lg	TD	1XP	2XP	FG	FGA	SAF	Pts
1947	WAS	N	1	0		0	0	0	6

James Wilder

Year	Team	Lg	TD	1XP	2XP	FG	FGA	SAF	Pts
1981	TB	N	5	0		0	0	0	30
1982			4	0		0	0	0	24
1983			6	0		0	0	0	36
1984			13	0		0	0	0	78
1985			10	0		0	0	0	60
1986			3	0		0	0	0	18
1987			1	0		0	0	0	6
1988			1	0		0	0	0	6
1989			3	0		0	0	0	18
1990	DET	N	1	0		0	0	0	6
Career			47	0		0	0	0	282

Dick Wildung

Year	Team	Lg	TD	1XP	2XP	FG	FGA	SAF	Pts
1947	GB	N	0	0		0	0	1	2

Reggie Wilkes

Year	Team	Lg	TD	1XP	2XP	FG	FGA	SAF	Pts
1981	PHI	N	0	1		0	0	0	1

Willie Wilkin

Year	Team	Lg	TD	1XP	2XP	FG	FGA	SAF	Pts
1939	WAS	N	0	0		0	0	0	0
1942			1	0		0	0	1	8
Career			1	0		0	0	1	8

Dick Wilkins

Year	Team	Lg	TD	1XP	2XP	FG	FGA	SAF	Pts
1949	LA	AA	3	0		0	0	0	18
1952	DAL	N	3	0		0	0	0	18
1954	NYG	N	1	0		0	0	0	6
Career			7	0		0	0	0	42

Gary Wilkins

Year	Team	Lg	TD	1XP	2XP	FG	FGA	SAF	Pts
1989	ATL	N	3	0		0	0	0	18
1990			2	0		0	0	0	12
1991			1	0		0	0	0	6
Career			6	0		0	0	0	36

Jeff Wilkins

Year	Team	Lg	TD	1XP	2XP	FG	FGA	SAF	Pts
1995	SF	N	0	27	0	12	13	0	63
1996			0	40	0	30	34	0	130
Career			0	67	0	42	47	0	193
Playoffs			0	6	0	1	1	0	9

Bob Wilkinson

Year	Team	Lg	TD	1XP	2XP	FG	FGA	SAF	Pts
1951	NYG	N	1	0		0	0	0	6
1952			2	0		0	0	0	12
Career			3	0		0	0	0	18

Ken Willard

Year	Team	Lg	TD	1XP	2XP	FG	FGA	SAF	Pts
1965	SF	N	9	0		0	0	0	54
1966			7	0		0	0	0	42
1967			6	0		0	0	0	36
1968			7	0		0	0	0	42
1969			10	0		0	0	0	60
1970			10	0		0	0	0	60

Ken Willard *continued*

Year	Team		TD	1XP	2XP	FG	FGA	SAF	Pts
1971			5	0		0	0	0	30
1972			5	0		0	0	0	30
1973			2	0		0	0	0	12
1974	STL	N	1	0		0	0	0	6
Career			62	0		0	0	0	372

Norm Willey

Year	Team		TD	1XP	2XP	FG	FGA	SAF	Pts
1950	PHI	N	1	0		0	0	0	6
1954			1	0		0	0	0	6
Career			2	0		0	0	0	12

Gerald Willhite

Year	Team		TD	1XP	2XP	FG	FGA	SAF	Pts
1982	DEN	N	2	0		0	0	0	12
1983			4	0		0	0	0	24
1984			2	0		0	0	0	12
1985			4	0		0	0	0	24
1986			9	0		0	0	0	54
1988			2	0		0	0	0	12
Career			23	0		0	0	0	138
Playoffs			1	0		0	0	0	6

A.D. Williams

Year	Team		TD	1XP	2XP	FG	FGA	SAF	Pts
1961	MIN	N	1	0		0	0	0	6

Aeneas Williams

Year	Team		TD	1XP	2XP	FG	FGA	SAF	Pts
1993	PHX	N	2	0		0	0	0	12
1995	ARI	N	3	0	0	0	0	0	18
1996			1	0	0	0	0	0	6
Career			6	0	0	0	0	0	36

Al Williams

Year	Team		TD	1XP	2XP	FG	FGA	SAF	Pts
1987	SD	N	1	0		0	0	0	6

Alfred Williams

Year	Team		TD	1XP	2XP	FG	FGA	SAF	Pts
1993	CIN	N	0	0		0	0	1	2
1994			0	0	0	0	0	1	2
Career			0	0	0	0	0	2	4

Art Williams

Year	Team		TD	1XP	2XP	FG	FGA	SAF	Pts
1928	PRO	N	4	0		0		0	24
1929			7	0		0		0	42
1930			2	0		0		0	12
Career			13	0		0		0	78

Ben Williams

Year	Team		TD	1XP	2XP	FG	FGA	SAF	Pts
1981	BUF	N	0	0		0	0	1	2

Bobby Ray Williams

Year	Team		TD	1XP	2XP	FG	FGA	SAF	Pts
1969	DET	N	1	0		0	0	0	6
1970			1	0		0	0	0	6
Career			2	0		0	0	0	12

Brent Williams

Year	Team		TD	1XP	2XP	FG	FGA	SAF	Pts
1986	NE	N	1	0		0	0	0	6
1990			1	0		0	0	0	6
Career			2	0		0	0	0	12

Brooks Williams

Year	Team		TD	1XP	2XP	FG	FGA	SAF	Pts
1980	NO	N	2	0		0	0	0	12

Byron Williams

Year	Team		TD	1XP	2XP	FG	FGA	SAF	Pts
1983	NYG	N	1	0		0	0	0	6
1984			2	0		0	0	0	12
Career			3	0		0	0	0	18

Calvin Williams

Year	Team		TD	1XP	2XP	FG	FGA	SAF	Pts
1990	PHI	N	9	0		0	0	0	54
1991			3	0		0	0	0	18
1992			7	0		0	0	0	42
1993			10	0		0	0	0	60
1994			3	0	0	0	0	0	18
1995			2	0	1	0	0	0	14
1996	BAL	N	1	0	0	0	0	0	6
Career			35	0	1	0	0	0	212
Playoffs			1	0	0	0	0	0	6

Clancy Williams

Year	Team		TD	1XP	2XP	FG	FGA	SAF	Pts
1966	LA	N	1	0		0	0	0	6
1970			1	0		0	0	0	6
Career			2	0		0	0	0	12

Clarence Williams

Year	Team		TD	1XP	2XP	FG	FGA	SAF	Pts
1972	GB	N	1	0		0	0	0	6

Clarence Williams

Year	Team		TD	1XP	2XP	FG	FGA	SAF	Pts
1977	SD	N	2	0		0	0	0	12
1979			12	0		0	0	0	72
1980			4	0		0	0	0	24
1981			1	0		0	0	0	6
Career			19	0		0	0	0	114
Playoffs			1	0		0	0	0	6

Darryl Williams

Year	Team		TD	1XP	2XP	FG	FGA	SAF	Pts
1993	CIN	N	1	0		0	0	0	6
1995			0	0	0	0	0	1	2
1996	SEA	N	1	0	0	0	0	0	6
Career			2	0	0	0	0	1	14

Dave Williams

Year	Team		TD	1XP	2XP	FG	FGA	SAF	Pts
1967	STL	N	5	0		0	0	0	30
1968			6	0		0	0	0	36
1969			7	0		0	0	0	42
1970			3	0		0	0	0	18
1971			1	0		0	0	0	6
1972	SD	N	3	0		0	0	0	18
Career			25	0		0	0	0	150

Dave Williams

Year	Team		TD	1XP	2XP	FG	FGA	SAF	Pts
1977	SF	N	1	0		0	0	0	6
1978			1	0		0	0	0	6
1979	CHI	N	6	0		0	0	0	36
1980			1	0		0	0	0	6
1981			2	0		0	0	0	12
Career			11	0		0	0	0	66

Delvin Williams

Year	Team		TD	1XP	2XP	FG	FGA	SAF	Pts
1974	SF	N	3	0		0	0	0	18
1975			4	0		0	0	0	24
1976			9	0		0	0	0	54
1977			9	0		0	0	0	54
1978	MIA	N	8	0		0	0	0	48
1979			4	0		0	0	0	24
1980			2	0		0	0	0	12
Career			39	0		0	0	0	234

Dokie Williams

Year	Team		TD	1XP	2XP	FG	FGA	SAF	Pts
1983	LARI	N	3	0		0	0	0	18
1984			4	0		0	0	0	24
1985			5	0		0	0	0	30
1986			8	0		0	0	0	48
1987			5	0		0	0	0	30
Career			25	0		0	0	0	150

Doug Williams

Year	Team		TD	1XP	2XP	FG	FGA	SAF	Pts
1978	TB	N	1	0		0	0	0	6
1979			2	0		0	0	0	12
1980			4	0		0	0	0	24
1981			4	0		0	0	0	24
1982			2	0		0	0	0	12
1987	WAS	N	1	0		0	0	0	6
1988			1	0		0	0	0	6
Career			15	0		0	0	0	90

Ed Williams

Year	Team		TD	1XP	2XP	FG	FGA	SAF	Pts
1974	CIN	N	4	0		0	0	0	24
1975			3	0		0	0	0	18
1976	TB	N	2	0		0	0	0	12
Career			9	0		0	0	0	54

Erwin Williams

Year	Team		TD	1XP	2XP	FG	FGA	SAF	Pts
1969	PIT	N	1	0		0	0	0	6

Frank Williams

Year	Team		TD	1XP	2XP	FG	FGA	SAF	Pts
1948	NYG	N	0	4		0	1	0	4

Gerald Williams

Year	Team		TD	1XP	2XP	FG	FGA	SAF	Pts
1994	PIT	N	1	0	0	0	0	0	6

Gerard Williams

Year	Team		TD	1XP	2XP	FG	FGA	SAF	Pts
1978	WAS	N	1	0		0	0	0	6

Harvey Williams

Year	Team		TD	1XP	2XP	FG	FGA	SAF	Pts
1991	KC	N	3	0		0	0	0	18
1992			1	0		0	0	0	6
1994	LARI	N	7	0	1	0	0	0	44
1995	OAK	N	9	0	0	0	0	0	54
Career			20	0	1	0	0	0	122

Inky Williams

Year	Team		TD	1XP	2XP	FG	FGA	SAF	Pts
1923	HAM	N	1	0		0		0	6

James Williams

Year	Team		TD	1XP	2XP	FG	FGA	SAF	Pts
1990	BUF	N	1	0		0	0	0	6

James Williams

Year	Team		TD	1XP	2XP	FG	FGA	SAF	Pts
1994	NO	N	1	0	0	0	0	0	6

Jamie Williams

Year	Team		TD	1XP	2XP	FG	FGA	SAF	Pts
1984	HOU	N	3	0		0	0	0	18
1985			1	0		0	0	0	6
1986			1	0		0	0	0	6
1987			3	0		0	0	0	18
1991	SF	N	1	0		0	0	0	6
1992			1	0		0	0	0	6
1993			1	0		0	0	0	6
Career			11	0		0	0	0	66

Jarvis Williams

Year	Team		TD	1XP	2XP	FG	FGA	SAF	Pts
1990	MIA	N	1	0		0	0	0	6

Jerrol Williams

Year	Team		TD	1XP	2XP	FG	FGA	SAF	Pts
1991	PIT	N	1	0		0	0	0	6

Jerry Williams

Year	Team		TD	1XP	2XP	FG	FGA	SAF	Pts
1949	LA	N	4	0		0	0	0	24
1950			2	0		0	0	0	12
1951			4	0		0	0	0	24
1953	PHI	N	4	0		0	0	0	24
1954			4	0		0	0	0	24
Career			18	0		0	0	0	108

Jimmy Williams

Year	Team		TD	1XP	2XP	FG	FGA	SAF	Pts
1990	DET	N	1	0		0	0	0	6

Joe Williams

Year	Team		TD	1XP	2XP	FG	FGA	SAF	Pts
1925	NY	N	1	0		0		0	6

Joe Williams

Year	Team		TD	1XP	2XP	FG	FGA	SAF	Pts
1971	DAL	N	1	0		0	0	0	6

Joel Williams

Year	Team		TD	1XP	2XP	FG	FGA	SAF	Pts
1950	BAL	N	1	0		0	0	0	6

Joel Williams

Year	Team		TD	1XP	2XP	FG	FGA	SAF	Pts
1980	ATL	N	1	0		0	0	1	8
1981			1	0		0	0	0	6
1986			1	0		0	0	0	6
Career			3	0		0	0	1	20

John L. Williams

Year	Team		TD	1XP	2XP	FG	FGA	SAF	Pts
1987	SEA	N	4	0		0	0	0	24
1988			7	0		0	0	0	42
1989			7	0		0	0	0	42
1990			3	0		0	0	0	18
1991			5	0		0	0	0	30
1992			3	0		0	0	0	18
1993			4	0		0	0	0	24
1994	PIT	N	3	0	0	0	0	0	18
1995			1	0	0	0	0	0	6
Career			37	0	0	0	0	0	222
Playoffs			4	0	0	0	0	0	24

Johnny Williams

Year	Team		TD	1XP	2XP	FG	FGA	SAF	Pts
1952	WAS	N	3	0		0	0	0	18

Karl Williams

Year	Team		TD	1XP	2XP	FG	FGA	SAF	Pts
1996	TB	N	1	0	0	0	0	0	6

Keith Williams

Year	Team		TD	1XP	2XP	FG	FGA	SAF	Pts
1986	ATL	N	1	0		0	0	0	6

Kevin Williams

Year	Team		TD	1XP	2XP	FG	FGA	SAF	Pts
1993	DAL	N	6	0		0	0	0	36
1994			2	0	0	0	0	0	12
1995			2	0	0	0	0	0	12
1996			1	0	0	0	0	0	6
Career			11	0	0	0	0	0	66

Lawrence Williams

Year	Team		TD	1XP	2XP	FG	FGA	SAF	Pts
1977	KC	N	1	0		0	0	0	6

Lee Williams

Year	Team		TD	1XP	2XP	FG	FGA	SAF	Pts
1984	SD	N	1	0		0	0	0	6
1987			0	0		0	0	1	2
Career			1	0		0	0	1	8

Mike Williams

Year	Team		TD	1XP	2XP	FG	FGA	SAF	Pts
1979	KC	N	3	0		0	0	0	18
1980			1	0		0	0	0	6
Career			4	0		0	0	0	24

Mike Williams

Year	Team		TD	1XP	2XP	FG	FGA	SAF	Pts
Playoffs			1	0	0	0	0	0	6

Oliver Williams

Year	Team		TD	1XP	2XP	FG	FGA	SAF	Pts
1985	IND	N	1	0		0	0	0	6
1987	HOU	N	1	0		0	0	0	6
Career			2	0		0	0	0	12

Perry Williams

Year	Team		TD	1XP	2XP	FG	FGA	SAF	Pts
1973	GB	N	1	0		0	0	0	6
1974	CHI	N	1	0		0	0	0	6
Career			2	0		0	0	0	12

Ray Williams

Year	Team		TD	1XP	2XP	FG	FGA	SAF	Pts
1980	DET	N	3	0		0	0	0	18

Reggie Williams

Year	Team		TD	1XP	2XP	FG	FGA	SAF	Pts
1977	CIN	N	2	0		0	0	0	12
1980			0	0		0	0	1	2
1982			0	0		0	0	1	2
1983			1	0		0	0	0	6
Career			3	0		0	0	2	22

Robert Williams

Year	Team		TD	1XP	2XP	FG	FGA	SAF	Pts
1991	DAL	N	1	0		0	0	0	6
1992			1	0		0	0	0	6
Career			2	0		0	0	0	12

Rollie Williams

Year	Team		TD	1XP	2XP	FG	FGA	SAF	Pts
1923	RAC	N	1	0		0		0	6

Ronnie Williams

Year	Team		TD	1XP	2XP	FG	FGA	SAF	Pts
1996	SEA	N	1	0	0	0	0	0	6
Playoffs			1	0	0	0	0	0	6

Sam Williams

Year	Team		TD	1XP	2XP	FG	FGA	SAF	Pts
1959	LA	N	0	0		0	0	1	2
1962	DET	N	2	0		0	0	0	12
1964			1	0		0	0	0	6
Career			3	0		0	0	1	20

Scott Williams

Year	Team		TD	1XP	2XP	FG	FGA	SAF	Pts
1986	DET	N	2	0		0	0	0	12
1987			1	0		0	0	0	6
1988			1	0		0	0	0	6
Career			4	0		0	0	0	24

Sherman Williams

Year	Team		TD	1XP	2XP	FG	FGA	SAF	Pts
1995	DAL	N	1	0	0	0	0	0	6

Sid Williams

Year	Team		TD	1XP	2XP	FG	FGA	SAF	Pts
1964	CLE	N	1	0		0	0	0	6

Stan Williams

Year	Team		TD	1XP	2XP	FG	FGA	SAF	Pts
1952	DAL	N	1	0		0	0	0	6

Ted Williams

Year	Team		TD	1XP	2XP	FG	FGA	SAF	Pts
1942	PHI	N	2	0		0	0	0	12
1944	BOS	N	1	0		0	0	0	6
Career			3	0		0	0	0	18

Travis Williams

Year	Team		TD	1XP	2XP	FG	FGA	SAF	Pts
1921	EVA	A	1	0		0		0	6

Travis Williams

Year	Team		TD	1XP	2XP	FG	FGA	SAF	Pts
1967	GB	N	6	0		0	0	0	36
1969			9	0		0	0	0	54
1970			2	0		0	0	0	12
1971	LA	N	1	0		0	0	0	6
Career			18	0		0	0	0	108
Playoffs			2	0		0	0	0	12

Van Williams

Year	Team		TD	1XP	2XP	FG	FGA	SAF	Pts
1984	BUF	N	1	0		0	0	0	6

Walt Williams

Year	Team		TD	1XP	2XP	FG	FGA	SAF	Pts
1946	CHI	AA	2	0		0	0	0	12

Walt Williams

Year	Team		TD	1XP	2XP	FG	FGA	SAF	Pts
1979	DET	N	1	0		0	0	0	6
1981	MIN	N	0	0		0	0	1	2
Career			1	0		0	0	1	8

Wandy Williams

Year	Team		TD	1XP	2XP	FG	FGA	SAF	Pts
1969	DEN	A	1	0	0	0	0	0	6

Warren Williams

Year	Team		TD	1XP	2XP	FG	FGA	SAF	Pts
1988	PIT	N	1	0		0	0	0	6
1989			1	0		0	0	0	6
1990			4	0		0	0	0	24
1991			4	0		0	0	0	24
Career			10	0		0	0	0	60

Willie Williams

Year	Team		TD	1XP	2XP	FG	FGA	SAF	Pts
1991	PHX	N	1	0		0	0	0	6

Willie Williams

Year	Team		TD	1XP	2XP	FG	FGA	SAF	Pts
1995	PIT	N	1	0	0	0	0	0	6

Win Williams

Year	Team		TD	1XP	2XP	FG	FGA	SAF	Pts
1948	BAL	AA	2	0		0	0	0	12
1949			1	0		0	0	0	6
Career			3	0		0	0	0	18

Carlton Williamson

Year	Team		TD	1XP	2XP	FG	FGA	SAF	Pts
1985	SF	N	1	0		0	0	0	6

Fred Williamson

Year	Team		TD	1XP	2XP	FG	FGA	SAF	Pts
1962	OAK	A	1	0	0	0	0	0	6
1967	KC	A	1	0	0	0	0	0	6
Career			2	0	0	0	0	0	12

Bill Willis

Year	Team		TD	1XP	2XP	FG	FGA	SAF	Pts
Playoffs			0	0	0	0	0	1	2

Chester Willis

Year	Team		TD	1XP	2XP	FG	FGA	SAF	Pts
1981	OAK	N	1	0		0	0	0	6

Fred Willis

Year	Team		TD	1XP	2XP	FG	FGA	SAF	Pts
1971	CIN	N	7	0		0	0	0	42
1972	HOU	N	2	0		0	0	0	12
1973			5	0		0	0	0	30
1974			4	0		0	0	0	24
1975			2	0		0	0	0	12
1976			3	0		0	0	0	18
Career			23	0		0	0	0	138

Ken Willis

Year	Team		TD	1XP	2XP	FG	FGA	SAF	Pts
1990	DAL	N	0	26		18	25	0	80
1991			0	37		27	39	0	118
1992	TB-NYG	N	0	27		10	16	0	57
Career			0	90		55	80	0	255
Playoffs			0	2		3	5	0	11

Klaus Wilmsmeyer

Year	Team		TD	1XP	2XP	FG	FGA	SAF	Pts
1996	NO	N	0	0	1	0	0	0	2

Ben Wilson

Year	Team		TD	1XP	2XP	FG	FGA	SAF	Pts
1963	LA	N	2	0		0	0	0	12
1964			6	0		0	0	0	36
1965			1	0		0	0	0	6
1967	GB	N	2	0		0	0	0	12
Career			11	0		0	0	0	66

Billy Wilson

Year	Team		TD	1XP	2XP	FG	FGA	SAF	Pts
1951	SF	N	3	0		0	0	0	18
1952			3	0		0	0	0	18
1953			10	0		0	0	0	60
1954			5	0		0	0	0	30
1955			7	0		0	0	0	42
1956			5	0		0	0	0	30
1957			6	0		0	0	0	36
1958			5	0		0	0	0	30
1959			4	0		0	0	0	24
1960			1	0		0	0	0	6
Career			49	0		0	0	0	294
Playoffs			1	0		0	0	0	6

Bobby Wilson

Year	Team		TD	1XP	2XP	FG	FGA	SAF	Pts
1936	BKN	N	4	0		0		0	24

Butch Wilson

Year	Team		TD	1XP	2XP	FG	FGA	SAF	Pts
1964	BAL	N	1	0		0	0	0	6
1966			2	0		0	0	0	12
Career			3	0		0	0	0	18

Camp Wilson

Year	Team		TD	1XP	2XP	FG	FGA	SAF	Pts
1946	DET	N	3	0		0	0	0	18
1948			2	0		0	0	0	12
1949			1	0		0	0	0	6
Career			6	0		0	0	0	36

Charles Wilson

Year	Team		TD	1XP	2XP	FG	FGA	SAF	Pts
1991	GB	N	2	0		0	0	0	12
1994	TB	N	6	0	0	0	0	0	36
1995	NYJ	N	4	0	0	0	0	0	24
Career			12	0	0	0	0	0	72

Dave Wilson

Year	Team		TD	1XP	2XP	FG	FGA	SAF	Pts
1983	NO	N	1	0		0	0	0	6
1986			1	0		0	0	0	6
Career			2	0		0	0	0	12

Don Wilson

Year	Team		TD	1XP	2XP	FG	FGA	SAF	Pts
1984	BUF	N	1	0		0	0	0	6
1985			1	0		0	0	0	6
Career			2	0		0	0	0	12

Eddie Wilson

Year	Team		TD	1XP	2XP	FG	FGA	SAF	Pts
1964	KC	A	1	0	0	0	0	0	6

George Wilson

Year	Team		TD	1XP	2XP	FG	FGA	SAF	Pts
1926	LA	A	4	0		0		0	24
1927	PRO	N	4	0		0		0	24
1928			5	0		0		0	30
1929			1	0		0		0	6
Career			14	0		0		0	84

George Wilson

Year	Team		TD	1XP	2XP	FG	FGA	SAF	Pts
1937	CHIB	N	1	0		0		0	6
1938			1	0		0	0	0	6
1940			1	0		0	0	0	6
1942			2	0		0	0	0	12
1943			5	0		0	0	0	30
1944			4	0		0	0	0	24
1945			3	0		0	0	0	18
1946			1	0		0	0	0	6
Career			18	0		0	0	0	108

George Wilson

Year	Team		TD	1XP	2XP	FG	FGA	SAF	Pts
1966	MIA	A	0	0	1	0	0	0	2

Jack Wilson

Year	Team		TD	1XP	2XP	FG	FGA	SAF	Pts
1946	LA	N	1	0		0	0	0	6

J.C. Wilson

Year	Team		TD	1XP	2XP	FG	FGA	SAF	Pts
1979	HOU	N	1	0		0	0	0	6

Jerrel Wilson

Year	Team		TD	1XP	2XP	FG	FGA	SAF	Pts
1965	KC	A	0	0	1	0	0	0	2
1966			0	0	1	0	0	0	2
1978	NE	N	0	0		0	0	0	0
Career			0	0	2	0	0	0	4

Johnny Wilson

Year	Team		TD	1XP	2XP	FG	FGA	SAF	Pts
1939	CLE	N	1	0		0	0	0	6
1940			1	0		0	0	0	6
1941			1	0		0	0	0	6
1942			2	0		0	0	0	12
Career			5	0		0	0	0	30

Karl Wilson

Year	Team		TD	1XP	2XP	FG	FGA	SAF	Pts
1989	PHX	N	0	0		0	0	1	2

Larry Wilson

Year	Team		TD	1XP	2XP	FG	FGA	SAF	Pts
1961	STL	N	0	0		0	0	1	2
1962			1	0		0	0	0	6
1963			2	0		0	0	0	12
1964			1	0		0	0	0	6
1965			1	0		0	0	0	6
1966			2	0		0	0	0	12

Larry Wilson *continued*

Year	Team		TD	1XP	2XP	FG	FGA	SAF	Pts
1969			1	0		0	0	0	6
Career			8	0		0	0	1	50

Marc Wilson

Year	Team		TD	1XP	2XP	FG	FGA	SAF	Pts
1981	OAK	N	2	0		0	0	0	12
1984	LARI	N	1	0		0	0	0	6
1985			2	0		0	0	0	12
Career			5	0		0	0	0	30

Mike Wilson

Year	Team		TD	1XP	2XP	FG	FGA	SAF	Pts
1923	RI	N	1	0		0		0	6
1924			1	0		0		0	6
Career			2	0		0		0	12

Mike Wilson

Year	Team		TD	1XP	2XP	FG	FGA	SAF	Pts
1929	FRA	N	0	0		0		0	0

Mike Wilson

Year	Team		TD	1XP	2XP	FG	FGA	SAF	Pts
1981	SF	N	1	0		0	0	0	6
1982			1	0		0	0	0	6
1984			1	0		0	0	0	6
1985			2	0		0	0	0	12
1986			1	0		0	0	0	6
1987			5	0		0	0	0	30
1988			3	0		0	0	0	18
1989			1	0		0	0	0	6
Career			15	0		0	0	0	90
Playoffs			2	0		0	0	0	12

Mule Wilson

Year	Team		TD	1XP	2XP	FG	FGA	SAF	Pts
1927	NYG	N	**6**	0		0		0	36
1928			1	1		0		0	7
1929			1	0		0		0	6
1930			4	0		0		0	24
1931	GB	N	2	0		0		0	12
Career			14	1		0		0	85

Nemiah Wilson

Year	Team		TD	1XP	2XP	FG	FGA	SAF	Pts
1965	DEN	A	1	0	0	0	0	0	6
1966			1	0	0	0	0	0	6
1967			2	0	0	0	0	0	12
Career			4	0	0	0	0	0	24

Otis Wilson

Year	Team		TD	1XP	2XP	FG	FGA	SAF	Pts
1982	CHI	N	1	0		0	0	0	6
1985			1	0		0	0	1	8
Career			2	0		0	0	1	14

Robert Wilson

Year	Team		TD	1XP	2XP	FG	FGA	SAF	Pts
1991	TB	N	2	0		0	0	0	12
1996	MIA	N	1	0	0	0	0	0	6
Career			3	0	0	0	0	0	18

Stanley Wilson

Year	Team		TD	1XP	2XP	FG	FGA	SAF	Pts
1983	CIN	N	2	0		0	0	0	12
1986			8	0		0	0	0	48
1988			3	0		0	0	0	18
Career			13	0		0	0	0	78
Playoffs			2	0		0	0	0	12

Steve Wilson

Year	Team		TD	1XP	2XP	FG	FGA	SAF	Pts
1986	DEN	N	1	0		0	0	0	6

Stu Wilson

Year	Team		TD	1XP	2XP	FG	FGA	SAF	Pts
1932	SI	N	1	3		1		0	12

Ted Wilson

Year	Team		TD	1XP	2XP	FG	FGA	SAF	Pts
1987	WAS	N	2	0		0	0	0	12

Tim Wilson

Year	Team		TD	1XP	2XP	FG	FGA	SAF	Pts
1977	HOU	N	3	0		0	0	0	18
1978			1	0		0	0	0	6
1979			3	0		0	0	0	18
1980			2	0		0	0	0	12
Career			9	0		0	0	0	54
Playoffs			1	0		0	0	0	6

Tommy Wilson

Year	Team		TD	1XP	2XP	FG	FGA	SAF	Pts
1956	LA	N	1	0		0	0	0	6
1957			4	0		0	0	0	24
1958			10	0		0	0	0	60
1959			1	0		0	0	0	6
1960			2	0		0	0	0	12

Tommy Wilson *continued*

Year	Team		TD	1XP	2XP	FG	FGA	SAF	Pts
1961			1	0		0	0	0	6
1962	CLE	N	1	0		0	0	0	6
1963	MIN	N	4	0		0	0	0	24
Career			24	0		0	0	0	144

Wade Wilson

Year	Team		TD	1XP	2XP	FG	FGA	SAF	Pts
1986	MIN	N	1	0		0	0	0	6
1987			5	0		0	0	0	30
1988			2	0		0	0	0	12
1989			1	0		0	0	0	6
Career			9	0		0	0	0	54

Wayne Wilson

Year	Team		TD	1XP	2XP	FG	FGA	SAF	Pts
1980	NO	N	2	0		0	0	0	12
1981			5	0		0	0	0	30
1982			5	0		0	0	0	30
1983			11	0		0	0	0	66
1984			4	0		0	0	0	24
1985			3	0		0	0	0	18
1987	WAS	N	2	0		0	0	0	12
Career			32	0		0	0	0	192

Ab Wimberly

Year	Team		TD	1XP	2XP	FG	FGA	SAF	Pts
1949	LA	AA	2	0		0	0	0	12

Tydus Winans

Year	Team		TD	1XP	2XP	FG	FGA	SAF	Pts
1994	WAS	N	2	0	1	0	0	0	14

Sammy Winder

Year	Team		TD	1XP	2XP	FG	FGA	SAF	Pts
1982	DEN	N	1	0		0	0	0	6
1983			3	0		0	0	0	18
1984			6	0		0	0	0	36
1985			8	0		0	0	0	48
1986			14	0		0	0	0	84
1987			7	0		0	0	0	42
1988			5	0		0	0	0	30
1989			2	0		0	0	0	12
1990			2	0		0	0	0	12
Career			48	0		0	0	0	288
Playoffs			3	0		0	0	0	18

Bob Windsor

Year	Team		TD	1XP	2XP	FG	FGA	SAF	Pts
1967	SF	N	3	0		0	0	0	18
1968			2	0		0	0	0	12
1969			2	0		0	0	0	12
1970			2	0		0	0	0	12
1972	NE	N	1	0		0	0	0	6
1973			4	0		0	0	0	24
1974			1	0		0	0	0	6
Career			15	0		0	0	0	90
Playoffs			1	0		0	0	0	6

Stan Winfrey

Year	Team		TD	1XP	2XP	FG	FGA	SAF	Pts
1976	MIA	N	2	0		0	0	0	12

Rich Wingo

Year	Team		TD	1XP	2XP	FG	FGA	SAF	Pts
1981	GB	N	0	1		0	0	0	1

Ben Winkleman

Year	Team		TD	1XP	2XP	FG	FGA	SAF	Pts
1923	MIL	N	3	9		6		0	45
1924			2	0		1		0	15
Career			5	9		7		0	60

Kellen Winslow

Year	Team		TD	1XP	2XP	FG	FGA	SAF	Pts
1979	SD	N	2	0		0	0	0	12
1980			9	0		0	0	0	54
1981			10	0		0	0	0	60
1982			6	0		0	0	0	36
1983			8	0		0	0	0	48
1984			2	0		0	0	0	12
1986			5	0		0	0	0	30
1987			3	0		0	0	0	18
Career			45	0		0	0	0	270
Playoffs			4	0		0	0	0	24

Paul Winslow

Year	Team		TD	1XP	2XP	FG	FGA	SAF	Pts
1960	GB	N	1	0		0	0	0	6

Dennis Winston

Year	Team		TD	1XP	2XP	FG	FGA	SAF	Pts
1979	PIT	N	1	0		0	0	0	6
1980			1	0		0	0	0	6
1984	NO	N	2	0		0	0	0	12
Career			4	0		0	0	0	24

Lloyd Winston

Year	Team		TD	1XP	2XP	FG	FGA	SAF	Pts
1963	SF	N	1	0		0	0	0	6

Roy Winston

Year	Team		TD	1XP	2XP	FG	FGA	SAF	Pts
1963	MIN	N	1	0		0	0	0	6
1970			1	0		0	0	0	6
1971			1	0		0	0	0	6
1973			0	0		0	0	1	2
Career			3	0		0	0	1	20

Sonny Winters

Year	Team		TD	1XP	2XP	FG	FGA	SAF	Pts
1923	COL	N	3	1		0		0	19
1924			1	5		1		0	14
Career			4	6		1		0	33

Phil Wise

Year	Team		TD	1XP	2XP	FG	FGA	SAF	Pts
1973	NYJ	N	1	0		0	0	0	6

Al Witcher

Year	Team		TD	1XP	2XP	FG	FGA	SAF	Pts
1960	HOU	A	1	0	0	0	0	0	6

Dick Witcher

Year	Team		TD	1XP	2XP	FG	FGA	SAF	Pts
1966	SF	N	1	0		0	0	0	6
1967			3	0		0	0	0	18
1968			2	0		0	0	0	12
1969			3	0		0	0	0	18
1970			2	0		0	0	0	12
1971			3	0		0	0	0	18
1972			1	0		0	0	0	6
Career			15	0		0	0	0	90
Playoffs			2	0		0	0	0	12

Derrick Witherspoon

Year	Team		TD	1XP	2XP	FG	FGA	SAF	Pts
1995	PHI	N	1	0	0	0	0	0	6
1996			2	0	0	0	0	0	12
Career			3	0	0	0	0	0	18

Jon Witman

Year	Team		TD	1XP	2XP	FG	FGA	SAF	Pts
Playoffs			1	0	0	0	0	0	6

Mel Witt

Year	Team		TD	1XP	2XP	FG	FGA	SAF	Pts
1968	BOS	A	1	0	0	0	0	0	6

John Wittenborn

Year	Team		TD	1XP	2XP	FG	FGA	SAF	Pts
1960	SF	N	0	0		0	3	0	0
1962	PHI	N	0	0		2	4	0	6
1967	HOU	A	0	30	0	14	28	0	72
1968			0	11	0	4	13	0	23
Career			0	41	0	20	48	0	101
Playoffs			0	1	0	0	0	0	1

Tom Wittum

Year	Team		TD	1XP	2XP	FG	FGA	SAF	Pts
1977	SF	N	0	2		1	2	0	5

Alex Wizbicki

Year	Team		TD	1XP	2XP	FG	FGA	SAF	Pts
1947	BUF	AA	1	0		0	0	0	6

Johnny Woitt

Year	Team		TD	1XP	2XP	FG	FGA	SAF	Pts
1969	SF	N	1	0		0	0	0	6

Alex Wojciechowicz

Year	Team		TD	1XP	2XP	FG	FGA	SAF	Pts
1940	DET	N	1	0		0	0	0	6

Dick Wolf

Year	Team		TD	1XP	2XP	FG	FGA	SAF	Pts
1923	CLE	N	1	0		0		0	6
1924			2	0		0		0	12
1925			1	0		0		0	6
1926	CLE	A	1	1		0		0	7
Career			5	1		0		0	31

Hugh Wolfe

Year	Team		TD	1XP	2XP	FG	FGA	SAF	Pts
1938	NYG	N	0	0		0		0	0

Ron Wolfley

Year	Team		TD	1XP	2XP	FG	FGA	SAF	Pts
1987	STL	N	1	0		0	0	0	6
1989	PHX	N	1	0		0	0	0	6
1992	CLE	N	1	0		0	0	0	6
1993			1	0		0	0	0	6
Career			4	0		0	0	0	24

Oscar Wolford

Year	Team		TD	1XP	2XP	FG	FGA	SAF	Pts
1921	COL	A	2	0		0		0	12

Jeff Womack

Year	Team		TD	1XP	2XP	FG	FGA	SAF	Pts
1987	MIN	N	1	0		0	0	0	6

Joe Womack

Year	Team		TD	1XP	2XP	FG	FGA	SAF	Pts
1962	PIT	N	5	0		0	0	0	30

Royce Womble

Year	Team		TD	1XP	2XP	FG	FGA	SAF	Pts
1954	BAL	N	3	0		0	0	0	18
1956			2	0		0	0	0	12
1960	LA	A	4	0	0	0	0	0	24
Career			9	0	0	0	0	0	54

George Wonsley

Year	Team		TD	1XP	2XP	FG	FGA	SAF	Pts
1985	IND	N	6	0		0	0	0	36
1986			1	0		0	0	0	6
1987			1	0		0	0	0	6
1988			1	0		0	0	0	6
Career			9	0		0	0	0	54

Nathan Wonsley

Year	Team		TD	1XP	2XP	FG	FGA	SAF	Pts
1986	TB	N	3	0		0	0	0	18

Otis Wonsley

Year	Team		TD	1XP	2XP	FG	FGA	SAF	Pts
1982	WAS	N	1	0		0	0	0	6
1984			4	0		0	0	0	24
Career			5	0		0	0	0	30

Duane Wood

Year	Team		TD	1XP	2XP	FG	FGA	SAF	Pts
1960	DAL	A	1	0	0	0	0	0	6
1963	KC	A	1	0	0	0	0	0	6
Career			2	0	0	0	0	0	12

Dick Wood

Year	Team		TD	1XP	2XP	FG	FGA	SAF	Pts
1963	NY	A	1	0	0	0	0	0	6
1964			1	0	0	0	0	0	6
1965	OAK	A	1	0	0	0	0	0	6
1966	MIA	A	1	0	0	0	0	0	6
Career			4	0	0	0	0	0	24

Gary Wood

Year	Team		TD	1XP	2XP	FG	FGA	SAF	Pts
1964	NYG	N	3	0		0	0	0	18
1965			0	1		0	0	0	1
1966			3	0		0	0	0	18
Career			6	1		0	0	0	37

Mike Wood

Year	Team		TD	1XP	2XP	FG	FGA	SAF	Pts
1979	STL-SD	N	0	34		13	21	0	73
1981	BAL	N	0	29		10	18	0	59
1982			0	6		6	10	0	24
Career			0	69		29	49	0	156
Playoffs			0	2		0	1	0	2

Richard Wood

Year	Team		TD	1XP	2XP	FG	FGA	SAF	Pts
1977	TB	N	2	0		0	0	0	12
1980			1	0		0	0	0	6
Career			3	0		0	0	0	18

Willie Wood

Year	Team		TD	1XP	2XP	FG	FGA	SAF	Pts
1961	GB	N	2	0		0	0	0	12
1964			1	1		0	1	0	7
1966			1	0		0	0	0	6
Career			4	1		0	1	0	25

Lee Woodall

Year	Team		TD	1XP	2XP	FG	FGA	SAF	Pts
1995	SF	N	1	0	0	0	0	0	6

Ken Woodard

Year	Team		TD	1XP	2XP	FG	FGA	SAF	Pts
1984	DEN	N	1	0		0	0	0	6
1986			1	0		0	0	0	6
Career			2	0		0	0	0	12

Terry Wooden

Year	Team		TD	1XP	2XP	FG	FGA	SAF	Pts
1994	SEA	N	1	0	0	0	0	0	6

Tom Woodeshick

Year	Team		TD	1XP	2XP	FG	FGA	SAF	Pts
1964	PHI	N	2	0		0	0	0	12
1966			5	0		0	0	0	30
1967			10	0		0	0	0	60
1968			3	0		0	0	0	18
1969			4	0		0	0	0	24
1970			2	0		0	0	0	12
1971			1	0		0	0	0	6
Career			27	0		0	0	0	162

Howie Woodin

Year	Team		TD	1XP	2XP	FG	FGA	SAF	Pts
1926	GB	N	0	1		0		0	1
1931			1	3		0		0	9
Career			1	4		0		0	10

David Woodley

Year	Team		TD	1XP	2XP	FG	FGA	SAF	Pts
1980	MIA	N	3	0		0	0	0	18
1981			4	0		0	0	0	24
1982			3	0		0	0	0	18
1985	PIT	N	2	0		0	0	0	12
Career			12	0		0	0	0	72
Playoffs			1	0		0	0	0	6

Dwayne Woodruff

Year	Team		TD	1XP	2XP	FG	FGA	SAF	Pts
1984	PIT	N	2	0		0	0	0	12
1987			1	0		0	0	0	6
1988			1	0		0	0	0	6
1989			1	0		0	0	0	6
Career			5	0		0	0	0	30

Jim Woodruff

Year	Team		TD	1XP	2XP	FG	FGA	SAF	Pts
1929	BUF	N	0	0		0		0	0

Lee Woodruff

Year	Team		TD	1XP	2XP	FG	FGA	SAF	Pts
1931	PRO	N	4	1		0		0	25
1933	PHI	N	2	0		0		0	12
Career			6	1		0		0	37

Tony Woodruff

Year	Team		TD	1XP	2XP	FG	FGA	SAF	Pts
1983	PHI	N	2	0		0	0	0	12
1984			3	0		0	0	0	18
Career			5	0		0	0	0	30

Carl Woods

Year	Team		TD	1XP	2XP	FG	FGA	SAF	Pts
1987	NE	N	1	0		0	0	0	6

Don Woods

Year	Team		TD	1XP	2XP	FG	FGA	SAF	Pts
1974	SD	N	10	0		0	0	0	60
1975			2	0		0	0	0	12
1976			4	0		0	0	0	24
1977			2	0		0	0	0	12
1978			3	0		0	0	0	18
Career			21	0		0	0	0	126

Ickey Woods

Year	Team		TD	1XP	2XP	FG	FGA	SAF	Pts
1988	CIN	N	15	0		0	0	0	90
1989			2	0		0	0	0	12
1990			6	0		0	0	0	36
1991			4	0		0	0	0	24
Career			27	0		0	0	0	162
Playoffs			4	0		0	0	0	24

Rick Woods

Year	Team		TD	1XP	2XP	FG	FGA	SAF	Pts
1983	PIT	N	1	0		0	0	0	6

Robert Woods

Year	Team		TD	1XP	2XP	FG	FGA	SAF	Pts
1978	HOU	N	2	0		0	0	0	12

Tony Woods

Year	Team		TD	1XP	2XP	FG	FGA	SAF	Pts
1995	WAS	N	1	0	0	0	0	0	6

Keith Woodside

Year	Team		TD	1XP	2XP	FG	FGA	SAF	Pts
1988	GB	N	5	0		0	0	0	30
1989			1	0		0	0	0	6
1990			1	0		0	0	0	6
1991			1	0		0	0	0	6
Career			8	0		0	0	0	48

Abe Woodson

Year	Team		TD	1XP	2XP	FG	FGA	SAF	Pts
1959	SF	N	1	0		0	0	0	6
1961			2	0		0	0	0	12
1962			2	0		0	0	0	12
1963			3	0		0	0	0	18
Career			8	0		0	0	0	48

Darren Woodson

Year	Team		TD	1XP	2XP	FG	FGA	SAF	Pts
1994	DAL	N	1	0	0	0	0	0	6
1995			1	0	0	0	0	0	6
Career			2	0	0	0	0	0	12

Marv Woodson

Year	Team		TD	1XP	2XP	FG	FGA	SAF	Pts
1965	PIT	N	1	0		0	0	0	6
1966			1	0		0	0	0	6
Career			2	0		0	0	0	12

Rod Woodson

Year	Team		TD	1XP	2XP	FG	FGA	SAF	Pts
1987	PIT	N	1	0		0	0	0	6
1988			1	0		0	0	0	6
1989			1	0		0	0	0	6
1990			1	0		0	0	0	6
1992			1	0		0	0	0	6
1993			1	0		0	0	0	6
1994			2	0	0	0	0	0	12
1996			2	0	0	0	0	0	12
Career			10	0	0	0	0	0	60

Dick Woodward

Year	Team		TD	1XP	2XP	FG	FGA	SAF	Pts
1949	LA	AA	1	0		0	0	0	6
1950	NYG	N	1	0		0	0	0	6
Career			2	0		0	0	0	12

Butch Woolfolk

Year	Team		TD	1XP	2XP	FG	FGA	SAF	Pts
1982	NYG	N	4	0		0	0	0	24
1983			4	0		0	0	0	24
1984			1	0		0	0	0	6
1985	HOU	N	5	0		0	0	0	30
1986			2	0		0	0	0	12
Career			16	0		0	0	0	96

Donnell Woolford

Year	Team		TD	1XP	2XP	FG	FGA	SAF	Pts
1996	CHI	N	1	0	0	0	0	0	6

Tito Wooten

Year	Team		TD	1XP	2XP	FG	FGA	SAF	Pts
1995	NYG	N	1	0	0	0	0	0	6
1996			1	0	0	0	0	1	8
Career			2	0	0	0	0	1	14

Barry Word

Year	Team		TD	1XP	2XP	FG	FGA	SAF	Pts
1987	NO	N	2	0		0	0	0	12
1990	KC	N	4	0		0	0	0	24
1991			4	0		0	0	0	24
1992			4	0		0	0	0	24
1993	MIN	N	2	0		0	0	0	12
Career			16	0		0	0	0	96
Playoffs			1	0		0	0	0	6

Neil Worden

Year	Team		TD	1XP	2XP	FG	FGA	SAF	Pts
1954	PHI	N	1	0		0	0	0	6

Joe Work

Year	Team		TD	1XP	2XP	FG	FGA	SAF	Pts
1924	CLE	N	1	0		0		0	6

Harry Workman

Year	Team		TD	1XP	2XP	FG	FGA	SAF	Pts
1924	CLE	N	0	16		3		0	25
1931			0	2		0		0	2
Career			0	18		3		0	27

Vince Workman

Year	Team		TD	1XP	2XP	FG	FGA	SAF	Pts
1989	GB	N	1	0		0	0	0	6
1990			1	0		0	0	0	6
1991			11	0		0	0	0	66
1992			2	0		0	0	0	12
1993	TB	N	4	0		0	0	0	24
1995	CAR	N	1	0	0	0	0	0	6
Career			20	0	0	0	0	0	120

Tim Worley

Year	Team		TD	1XP	2XP	FG	FGA	SAF	Pts
1989	PIT	N	5	0		0	0	0	30
1993	CHI	N	2	0		0	0	0	12
1994			1	0	0	0	0	0	6
Career			8	0	0	0	0	0	48
Playoffs			1	0	0	0	0	0	6

Junior Wren

Year	Team		TD	1XP	2XP	FG	FGA	SAF	Pts
1956	CLE	N	0	0		0	0	1	2
1959			1	0		0	0	0	6
Career			1	0		0	0	1	8

Adrian Wright

Year	Team		TD	1XP	2XP	FG	FGA	SAF	Pts
1987	TB	N	1	0		0	0	0	6

Alexander Wright

Year	Team		TD	1XP	2XP	FG	FGA	SAF	Pts
1990	DAL	N	1	0		0	0	0	6
1991			1	0		0	0	0	6
1992	LARI	N	2	0		0	0	0	12
1993			4	0		0	0	0	24
1994			2	0	0	0	0	0	12
1995	STL	N	2	0	0	0	0	0	12
Career			12	0	0	0	0	0	72

Elmo Wright

Year	Team	Lg	TD	1XP	2XP	FG	FGA	SAF	Pts
1971	KC	N	3	0		0	0	0	18
1973			2	0		0	0	0	12
1974			2	0		0	0	0	12
Career			7	0		0	0	0	42

Eric Wright

Year	Team	Lg	TD	1XP	2XP	FG	FGA	SAF	Pts
1983	SF	N	2	0		0	0	0	12

Felix Wright

Year	Team	Lg	TD	1XP	2XP	FG	FGA	SAF	Pts
1986	CLE	N	1	0		0	0	0	6
1987			1	0		0	0	0	6
1989			1	0		0	0	0	6
Career			3	0		0	0	0	18

James Wright

Year	Team	Lg	TD	1XP	2XP	FG	FGA	SAF	Pts
1981	DEN	N	1	0		0	0	0	6
1982			1	0		0	0	0	6
1984			1	0		0	0	0	6
1985			1	0		0	0	0	6
Career			4	0		0	0	0	24
Playoffs			1	0		0	0	0	6

John Wright

Year	Team	Lg	TD	1XP	2XP	FG	FGA	SAF	Pts
1969	DET	N	3	0		0	0	0	18

Keith Wright

Year	Team	Lg	TD	1XP	2XP	FG	FGA	SAF	Pts
1980	CLE	N	3	0		0	0	0	18

Louis Wright

Year	Team	Lg	TD	1XP	2XP	FG	FGA	SAF	Pts
1977	DEN	N	1	0		0	0	0	6
1979			1	0		0	0	0	6
1984			1	0		0	0	0	6
1985			1	0		0	0	0	6
Career			4	0		0	0	0	24

Nate Wright

Year	Team	Lg	TD	1XP	2XP	FG	FGA	SAF	Pts
1977	MIN	N	1	0		0	0	0	6
Playoffs			1	0	0	0	0	0	6

Randy Wright

Year	Team	Lg	TD	1XP	2XP	FG	FGA	SAF	Pts
1986	GB	N	1	0		0	0	0	6
1988			2	0		0	0	0	12
Career			3	0		0	0	0	18

Rayfield Wright

Year	Team	Lg	TD	1XP	2XP	FG	FGA	SAF	Pts
1968	DAL	N	1	0		0	0	0	6

Ted Wright

Year	Team	Lg	TD	1XP	2XP	FG	FGA	SAF	Pts
1934	BOS	N	1	2		0		0	8
1935			0	1		0		0	1
Career			1	3		0		0	9

Toby Wright

Year	Team	Lg	TD	1XP	2XP	FG	FGA	SAF	Pts
1994	LARM	N	1	0	0	0	0	0	6
1995	STL	N	1	0	0	0	0	0	6
1996			1	0	0	0	0	0	6
Career			3	0	0	0	0	0	18

Tim Wrightman

Year	Team	Lg	TD	1XP	2XP	FG	FGA	SAF	Pts
1985	CHI	N	1	0		0	0	0	6

Al Wukits

Year	Team	Lg	TD	1XP	2XP	FG	FGA	SAF	Pts
1943	P-P	N	1	0		0	0	0	6

Alvin Wyatt

Year	Team	Lg	TD	1XP	2XP	FG	FGA	SAF	Pts
1970	OAK	N	1	0		0	0	0	6
1971	BUF	N	1	0		0	0	0	6
1972			1	0		0	0	0	6
Career			3	0		0	0	0	18

Doug Wyatt

Year	Team	Lg	TD	1XP	2XP	FG	FGA	SAF	Pts
1971	NO	N	1	0		0	0	0	6
1972			1	0		0	0	0	6
Career			2	0		0	0	0	12

Sam Wyche

Year	Team	Lg	TD	1XP	2XP	FG	FGA	SAF	Pts
1969	CIN	A	1	0	0	0	0	0	6
1970	CIN	N	2	0		0	0	0	12
Career			3	0	0	0	0	0	18

Frank Wycheck

Year	Team	Lg	TD	1XP	2XP	FG	FGA	SAF	Pts
1994	WAS	N	1	0	0	0	0	0	6
1995	HOU	N	2	0	0	0	0	0	12

Frank Wycheck *continued*

Year	Team	Lg	TD	1XP	2XP	FG	FGA	SAF	Pts
1996			6	0	0	0	0	0	36
Career			9	0	0	0	0	0	54

Doug Wycoff

Year	Team	Lg	TD	1XP	2XP	FG	FGA	SAF	Pts
1926	NEW	A	1	1		0		0	7
1927	NYG	N	3	1		0		0	19
1929	SI	N	2	0		0		0	12
1930			4	0		0		0	24
1931	NYG	N	2	0		0		0	12
1932	SI	N	1	0		0		0	6
1934	BOS	N	1	0		0		0	6
Career			14	2		0		0	86

Arnie Wyman

Year	Team	Lg	TD	1XP	2XP	FG	FGA	SAF	Pts
1920	RI	A	**5**	0		0		0	30

Dave Wyman

Year	Team	Lg	TD	1XP	2XP	FG	FGA	SAF	Pts
1993	DEN	N	1	0		0	0	0	6

Will Wynn

Year	Team	Lg	TD	1XP	2XP	FG	FGA	SAF	Pts
1973	PHI	N	1	0		0	0	0	6
1974			1	0		0	0	0	6
Career			2	0		0	0	0	12

Vinnie Yablonski

Year	Team	Lg	TD	1XP	2XP	FG	FGA	SAF	Pts
1948	CHIC	N	0	0		1	4	0	3
1949			0	1		5	6	0	16
1950			1	7		2	3	0	19
1951			0	8		2	5	0	14
Career			1	16		10	18	0	52

Ron Yankowski

Year	Team	Lg	TD	1XP	2XP	FG	FGA	SAF	Pts
1974	STL	N	1	0		0	0	0	6

Ryan Yarborough

Year	Team	Lg	TD	1XP	2XP	FG	FGA	SAF	Pts
1994	NYJ	N	1	0	0	0	0	0	6
1995			2	0	0	0	0	0	12
Career			3	0	0	0	0	0	18

George Yarno

Year	Team	Lg	TD	1XP	2XP	FG	FGA	SAF	Pts
1983	TB	N	0	1		0	0	0	1

Howie Yeager

Year	Team	Lg	TD	1XP	2XP	FG	FGA	SAF	Pts
1941	NYG	N	4	0		0	0	0	24

Billy Yelverton

Year	Team	Lg	TD	1XP	2XP	FG	FGA	SAF	Pts
1960	DEN	A	1	0	0	0	0	0	6

Garo Yepremian

Year	Team	Lg	TD	1XP	2XP	FG	FGA	SAF	Pts
1966	DET	N	0	11		13	22	0	50
1967			0	22		2	6	0	28
1970	MIA	N	0	31		22	29	0	97
1971			0	33		28	40	0	**117**
1972			0	43		24	37	0	115
1973			0	38		25	37	0	113
1974			0	43		8	15	0	67
1975			0	40		13	16	0	79
1976			0	29		16	23	0	77
1977			0	37		10	22	0	67
1978			0	41		19	23	0	98
1979	NO	N	0	39		12	16	0	75
1980	TB	N	0	31		16	23	0	79
1981			0	6		2	4	0	12
Career			0	444		210	313	0	1074
Playoffs			0	28		12	20	0	64

Tom Yewcic

Year	Team	Lg	TD	1XP	2XP	FG	FGA	SAF	Pts
1961	BOS	A	1	0	0	0	0	0	6
1962			2	0	0	0	0	0	12
1963			1	0	0	0	0	0	6
Career			4	0	0	0	0	0	24

Mack Yoho

Year	Team	Lg	TD	1XP	2XP	FG	FGA	SAF	Pts
1960	BUF	A	1	0	0	2	5	0	12
1961			0	0	0	0	4	0	0
1962			0	20	0	1	3	0	23
1963			0	32	0	10	23	0	62
Career			1	52	0	13	35	0	97
Playoffs			0	0	0	0	1	0	0

John Yonakor

Year	Team	Lg	TD	1XP	2XP	FG	FGA	SAF	Pts
1946	CLE	AA	2	0		0	0	0	12

John Yonakor *continued*

Year	Team	Lg	TD	1XP	2XP	FG	FGA	SAF	Pts
1947			2	0		0	0	0	12
Career			4	0		0	0	0	24

Jim Youel

Year	Team	Lg	TD	1XP	2XP	FG	FGA	SAF	Pts
1946	WAS	N	1	0		0	0	0	6
1947			1	0		0	0	0	6
1948			1	0		0	0	0	6
Career			3	0		0	0	0	18

Len Younce

Year	Team	Lg	TD	1XP	2XP	FG	FGA	SAF	Pts
1943	NYG	N	1	0		0	1	0	6
1947			0	1		1	1	0	4
1948			0	36		1	7	0	39
Career			1	37		2	9	0	49

Al Young

Year	Team	Lg	TD	1XP	2XP	FG	FGA	SAF	Pts
Playoffs			1	0	0	0	0	0	6

Andre Young

Year	Team	Lg	TD	1XP	2XP	FG	FGA	SAF	Pts
1983	SD	N	1	0		0	0	0	6

Anthony Young

Year	Team	Lg	TD	1XP	2XP	FG	FGA	SAF	Pts
1985	IND	N	1	0		0	0	0	6

Ben Young

Year	Team	Lg	TD	1XP	2XP	FG	FGA	SAF	Pts
1983	ATL	N	1	0		0	0	0	6

Bill Young

Year	Team	Lg	TD	1XP	2XP	FG	FGA	SAF	Pts
1938	WAS	N	1	0		0	0	0	6

Bryant Young

Year	Team	Lg	TD	1XP	2XP	FG	FGA	SAF	Pts
1996	SF	N	0	0	0	0	0	2	4

Buddy Young

Year	Team	Lg	TD	1XP	2XP	FG	FGA	SAF	Pts
1947	NY	AA	7	0		0	0	0	42
1948			5	0		0	0	0	30
1949	B-NY	AA	8	0		0	0	0	48
1950	NYY	N	2	0		0	0	0	12
1951			6	0		0	0	0	36
1952	DAL	N	5	0		0	0	0	30
1953	BAL	N	4	0		0	0	0	24
1954			5	0		0	0	0	30
1955			2	0		0	0	0	12
Career			44	0		0	0	0	264

Charle Young

Year	Team	Lg	TD	1XP	2XP	FG	FGA	SAF	Pts
1973	PHI	N	7	0		0	0	0	42
1974			3	0		0	0	0	18
1975			3	0		0	0	0	18
1977	LA	N	1	0		0	0	0	6
1979			2	0		0	0	0	12
1980	SF	N	2	0		0	0	0	12
1981			5	0		0	0	0	30
1983	SEA	N	2	0		0	0	0	12
1984			1	0		0	0	0	6
1985			2	0		0	0	0	12
Career			28	0		0	0	0	168
Playoffs			2	0		0	0	0	12

Charley Young

Year	Team	Lg	TD	1XP	2XP	FG	FGA	SAF	Pts
1975	DAL	N	3	0		0	0	0	18
1976			1	0		0	0	0	6
Career			4	0		0	0	0	24

Dave Young

Year	Team	Lg	TD	1XP	2XP	FG	FGA	SAF	Pts
1981	NYG	N	1	0		0	0	0	6
1984	IND	N	2	0		0	0	0	12
Career			3	0		0	0	0	18

Dick Young

Year	Team	Lg	TD	1XP	2XP	FG	FGA	SAF	Pts
1957	PIT	N	2	0		0	0	0	12

Duane Young

Year	Team	Lg	TD	1XP	2XP	FG	FGA	SAF	Pts
1993	SD	N	2	0		0	0	0	12
1994			1	0	0	0	0	0	6
Career			3	0	0	0	0	0	18

Fredd Young

Year	Team	Lg	TD	1XP	2XP	FG	FGA	SAF	Pts
1987	SEA	N	1	0		0	0	0	6

George Young

Year	Team	Lg	TD	1XP	2XP	FG	FGA	SAF	Pts
1948	CLE	AA	1	0		0	0	0	6
1951	CLE	N	1	0		0	0	0	6

George Young *continued*

Year	Team		TD	1XP	2XP	FG	FGA	SAF	Pts
1952			0	0		0	0	1	2
Career			2	0		0	0	1	14
Playoffs			1	0		0	0	0	6

Glen Young

Year	Team		TD	1XP	2XP	FG	FGA	SAF	Pts
1983	PHI	N	1	0		0	0	0	6
1985	CLE	N	1	0		0	0	0	6
Career			2	0		0	0	0	12

Herm Young

Year	Team		TD	1XP	2XP	FG	FGA	SAF	Pts
1930	PRO	N	1	0		0		0	6

James Young

Year	Team		TD	1XP	2XP	FG	FGA	SAF	Pts
1977	HOU	N	0	0		0	0	2	4

Mike Young

Year	Team		TD	1XP	2XP	FG	FGA	SAF	Pts
1986	LARM	N	3	0		0	0	0	18
1987			1	0		0	0	0	6
1989	DEN	N	2	0		0	0	0	12
1990			4	0		0	0	0	24
1991			2	0		0	0	0	12
1993	PHI	N	2	0		0	0	0	12
Career			14	0		0	0	0	84
Playoffs			1	0		0	0	0	6

Rickey Young

Year	Team		TD	1XP	2XP	FG	FGA	SAF	Pts
1975	SD	N	6	0		0	0	0	36
1976			5	0		0	0	0	30
1977			4	0		0	0	0	24
1978	MIN	N	6	0		0	0	0	36
1979			7	0		0	0	0	42
1980			5	0		0	0	0	30
1981			2	0		0	0	0	12
1982			2	0		0	0	0	12
1983			2	0		0	0	0	12
Career			39	0		0	0	0	234

Steve Young

Year	Team		TD	1XP	2XP	FG	FGA	SAF	Pts
1985	TB	N	1	0		0	0	0	6
1986			5	0		0	0	0	30
1987	SF	N	1	0		0	0	0	6
1988			1	0		0	0	0	6
1989			2	0		0	0	0	12
1991			4	0		0	0	0	24
1992			4	0		0	0	0	24
1993			2	0		0	0	0	12
1994			7	0	0	0	0	0	42
1995			3	0	0	0	0	0	18
1996			4	0	1	0	0	0	26
Career			34	0	1	0	0	0	206
Playoffs			7	0	0	0	0	0	42

Tyrone Young

Year	Team		TD	1XP	2XP	FG	FGA	SAF	Pts
1983	NO	N	3	0		0	0	0	18
1984			3	0		0	0	0	18
Career			6	0		0	0	0	36

Wilbur Young

Year	Team		TD	1XP	2XP	FG	FGA	SAF	Pts
1974	KC	N	1	0		0	0	0	6
1979	SD	N	1	0		0	0	1	8
Career			2	0		0	0	1	14

George Youngblood

Year	Team		TD	1XP	2XP	FG	FGA	SAF	Pts
1969	CHI	N	1	0		0	0	0	6

Jack Youngblood

Year	Team		TD	1XP	2XP	FG	FGA	SAF	Pts
1975	LA	N	0	0		0	0	1	2
1983	LARM	N	0	0		0	0	1	2
Career			0	0		0	0	2	4
Playoffs			1	0		0	0	0	6

Jim Youngblood

Year	Team		TD	1XP	2XP	FG	FGA	SAF	Pts
1977	LA	N	1	0		0	0	0	6
1979			2	0		0	0	0	12
1980			1	0		0	0	0	6
Career			4	0		0	0	0	24

Tank Younger

Year	Team		TD	1XP	2XP	FG	FGA	SAF	Pts
1950	LA	N	2	0		0	0	0	12

Tank Younger *continued*

Year	Team		TD	1XP	2XP	FG	FGA	SAF	Pts
1951			1	0		0	0	0	6
1952			1	0		0	0	0	6
1953			9	0		0	0	0	54
1954			8	0		0	0	0	48
1955			5	0		0	0	0	30
1956			3	0		0	0	0	18
1957			3	0		0	0	0	18
1958	PIT	N	3	0		0	0	0	18
Career			35	0		0	0	0	210

Swede Youngstrom

Year	Team		TD	1XP	2XP	FG	FGA	SAF	Pts
1920	BUF	A	1	0		0		0	6
1921			1	0		0		0	6
1926	FRA	N	2	0		0		0	12
Career			4	0		0		0	24

Steve Zabel

Year	Team		TD	1XP	2XP	FG	FGA	SAF	Pts
1970	PHI	N	1	0		0	0	0	6
1971			2	0		0	0	0	12
1976	NE	N	0	1		0	0	0	1
Career			3	1		0	0	0	19

Bert Zagers

Year	Team		TD	1XP	2XP	FG	FGA	SAF	Pts
1955	WAS	N	3	0		0	0	0	18
1957			2	0		0	0	0	12
1958			1	0		0	0	0	6
Career			6	0		0	0	0	36

Ernie Zalejski

Year	Team		TD	1XP	2XP	FG	FGA	SAF	Pts
1950	BAL	N	2	0		0	0	0	12

Silvio Zaninelli

Year	Team		TD	1XP	2XP	FG	FGA	SAF	Pts
1936	PIT	N	1	0		0		0	6

Eric Zeier

Year	Team		TD	1XP	2XP	FG	FGA	SAF	Pts
1995	CLE	N	0	0	1	0	0	0	2

Ray Zellars

Year	Team		TD	1XP	2XP	FG	FGA	SAF	Pts
1995	NO	N	2	0	0	0	0	0	12
1996			4	0	0	0	0	0	24
Career			6	0	0	0	0	0	36

Jerry Zeller

Year	Team		TD	1XP	2XP	FG	FGA	SAF	Pts
1921	EVA	A	1	0		0		0	6

Joe Zeller

Year	Team		TD	1XP	2XP	FG	FGA	SAF	Pts
1933	CHIB	N	1	0		0		0	6
1938			1	0		0		0	6
Career			2	0		0		0	12

Bob Zeman

Year	Team		TD	1XP	2XP	FG	FGA	SAF	Pts
1961	SD	A	1	0	0	0	0	0	6
1962	DEN	A	1	0	0	0	0	0	6
Career			2	0	0	0	0	0	12

Joaquin Zendejas

Year	Team		TD	1XP	2XP	FG	FGA	SAF	Pts
1983	NE	N	0	3		0	1	0	3

Luis Zendejas

Year	Team		TD	1XP	2XP	FG	FGA	SAF	Pts
1987	DAL	N	0	10		3	4	0	19
1988	DAL-PHI	N	0	35		20	27	0	95
1989	PHI-DAL	N	0	33		14	24	0	75
Career			0	78		37	55	0	189
Playoffs			0	0		4	5	0	12

Max Zendejas

Year	Team		TD	1XP	2XP	FG	FGA	SAF	Pts
1986	WAS	N	0	23		9	14	0	50
1987	GB	N	0	13		16	19	0	61
1988			0	17		9	16	0	44
Career			0	53		34	49	0	155

Tony Zendejas

Year	Team		TD	1XP	2XP	FG	FGA	SAF	Pts
1985	HOU	N	0	29		21	27	0	92
1986			0	28		22	27	0	94
1987			0	32		20	26	0	92
1988			0	48		22	34	0	114
1989			0	40		25	37	0	115
1990			0	20		7	12	0	41
1991	LARM	N	0	25		17	17	0	76

Tony Zendejas *continued*

Year	Team		TD	1XP	2XP	FG	FGA	SAF	Pts
1992			0	38		15	20	0	83
1993			0	23		16	23	0	71
1994			0	28	0	18	23	0	82
1995	ATL-SF	N	0	5	0	3	6	0	14
Career			0	316	0	186	252	0	874
Playoffs			0	9	0	9	14	0	36

Frank Ziegler

Year	Team		TD	1XP	2XP	FG	FGA	SAF	Pts
1949	PHI	N	1	0		0	0	0	6
1950			3	0		0	0	0	18
1951			2	0		0	0	0	12
1952			4	0		0	0	0	24
1953			5	0		0	0	0	30
Career			15	0		0	0	0	90

Jack Zilly

Year	Team		TD	1XP	2XP	FG	FGA	SAF	Pts
1948	LA	N	4	0		0	0	0	24

Don Zimmerman

Year	Team		TD	1XP	2XP	FG	FGA	SAF	Pts
1973	PHI	N	3	0		0	0	0	18
1974			2	0		0	0	0	12
Career			5	0		0	0	0	30

Giff Zimmerman

Year	Team		TD	1XP	2XP	FG	FGA	SAF	Pts
1925	CAN	N	2	0		0		0	12

Roy Zimmerman

Year	Team		TD	1XP	2XP	FG	FGA	SAF	Pts
1940	WAS	N	0	0		0	0	0	0
1942			0	1		1	1	0	4
1943	P-P	N	1	26		1	6	0	35
1944	PHI		1	32		4	8	0	62
1945			1	29		4	8	0	47
1946			1	2		2	4	0	14
1947	DET	N	1	30		5	11	0	51
1948	BOS	N	0	13		1	4	0	16
Career			7	133		18	42	0	229

Mickey Zofko

Year	Team		TD	1XP	2XP	FG	FGA	SAF	Pts
1972	DET	N	0	1		0	0	0	1

Dick Zoll

Year	Team		TD	1XP	2XP	FG	FGA	SAF	Pts
1938	CLE	N	0	1		0	0	0	1

Lou Zontini

Year	Team		TD	1XP	2XP	FG	FGA	SAF	Pts
1940	CHIC	N	0	10		2	5	0	16
1941			0	5		0	4	0	5
1944	CLE	N	4	14		3	6	0	47
1946	BUF	AA	0	30		4	8	0	42
Career			4	59		9	23	0	110

John Zook

Year	Team		TD	1XP	2XP	FG	FGA	SAF	Pts
1971	ATL	N	0	0		0	0	1	2
1972			1	0		0	0	0	6
Career			1	0		0	0	1	8

Mike Zordich

Year	Team		TD	1XP	2XP	FG	FGA	SAF	Pts
1988	NYJ	N	1	0		0	0	0	6
1989	PHX	N	1	0		0	0	0	6
1994	PHI		1	0	0	0	0	0	6
1995			1	0		0	0	0	6
Career			4	0		0	0	0	24

Chris Zorich

Year	Team		TD	1XP	2XP	FG	FGA	SAF	Pts
1992	CHI	N	1	0		0	0	0	6

Jim Zorn

Year	Team		TD	1XP	2XP	FG	FGA	SAF	Pts
1976	SEA	N	4	0		0	0	0	24
1977			1	0		0	0	0	6
1978			6	0		0	0	0	36
1979			2	0		0	0	0	12
1980			1	0		0	0	0	6
1981			1	0		0	0	0	6
1982			1	0		0	0	0	6
1983			1	0		0	0	0	6
Career			17	0		0	0	0	102

Vic Zucco

Year	Team		TD	1XP	2XP	FG	FGA	SAF	Pts
1957	CHIB	N	1	0		0	0	0	6

RUSHING REGISTER

Year	Team		Att	Yds	Avg	Lg	TD
Walter Payton							
1975	CHI	N	196	679	3.5	54t	7
1976			**311**	1390	4.5	60	13
1977			**339**	**1852**	**5.5**	73	**14**
1978			**333**	1395	4.2	76	11
1979			**369**	1610	4.4	43t	14
1980			317	1460	4.6	69t	6
1981			339	1222	3.6	39	6
1982			148	596	4.0	26	1
1983			314	1421	4.5	49t	6
1984			381	1684	4.4	72t	11
1985			324	1551	4.8	40t	9
1986			321	1333	4.2	41	8
1987			146	533	3.7	17	4
Career			**3838**	**16726**	4.4	76	**110**
Playoffs			180	632	3.5		2

Key

Team   The team (and league) the player played for.
Att   Attempts
Yds   Yards
Avg   Average gain per attempt
Lg   Longest gain of the season
TD   Touchdowns

In addition, boldface numbers indicate that the player led the league in that category that season. For example, Payton's 1852 yards gained in 1977 are boldfaced, meaning that he led the league in rushing that year. Also, boldfaced career and playoff stats indicate all-time highs. Payton's 16726 yards gained indicate that he is the all-time career leader in this category.

Lou Abbruzzi

Year	Team		Att	Yds	Avg	Lg	TD
1946	BOS	N	6	26	4.3	10	0

Karim Abdul-Jabbar

Year	Team		Att	Yds	Avg	Lg	TD
1996	MIA	N	307	1116	3.6	29	11

Walter Abercrombie

Year	Team		Att	Yds	Avg	Lg	TD
1982	PIT	N	21	100	4.8	34	2
1983			112	446	4.0	50t	4
1984			145	610	4.2	31	1
1985			227	851	3.7	32t	7
1986			214	877	4.1	38t	6
1987			123	459	3.7	28t	2
1988	PHI	N	5	14	2.8	5	0
Career			847	3357	4.0	50t	22
Playoffs			38	179	4.7		0

Cliff Aberson

Year	Team		Att	Yds	Avg	Lg	TD
1946	GB	N	48	161	3.4	13	0

Danny Abramowicz

Year	Team		Att	Yds	Avg	Lg	TD
1968	NO	N	2	27	13.5	18	0
1969			3	61	20.3	28	0
1970			1	7	7.0	7	0
Career			6	95	15.8	28	0

Dick Abrell

Year	Team		Att	Yds	Avg	Lg	TD
1920	DAY	A					1

Mike Adamle

Year	Team		Att	Yds	Avg	Lg	TD
1971	KC	N	13	43	3.3	15	0
1972			73	303	4.2	19	1
1973	NYJ	N	67	264	3.9	36	0
1974			28	93	3.3	21	2
1975	CHI	N	94	353	3.8	21	1
1976			33	93	2.8	12	0
Career			308	1149	3.7	36	4

Tony Adamle

Year	Team		Att	Yds	Avg	Lg	TD
1947	CLE	AA	23	95	4.1		1
1948			17	88	5.2		1
1949			17	64	3.8		0
1950	CLE	N	3	8	2.7	3	0
Career			60	255	4.3	3	2
Playoffs			2	-1	-0.5		0

Bob Adams

Year	Team		Att	Yds	Avg	Lg	TD
1973	NE	N	2	7	3.5	4	0

Curtis Adams

Year	Team		Att	Yds	Avg	Lg	TD
1985	SD	N	16	49	3.1	14	1
1986			118	366	3.1	22	4
1987			90	343	3.8	24	1
1988			38	149	3.9	14	1
Career			262	907	3.5	24	7

David Adams

Year	Team		Att	Yds	Avg	Lg	TD
1987	DAL	N	7	49	7.0	27t	1

George Adams

Year	Team		Att	Yds	Avg	Lg	TD
1985	NYG	N	128	498	3.9	39	2
1987			61	169	2.8	14	1
1988			29	76	2.6	15	0
1989			9	29	3.2	8	0
1990	NE	N	28	111	4.0	13	0
1991			2	3	1.5	2	0
Career			257	886	3.4	39	3
Playoffs			4	13	3.3		0

John Adams

Year	Team		Att	Yds	Avg	Lg	TD
1959	CHIB	N	4	-13	-3.3	8	0
1960	CHI	N	23	114	5.0	62	0
1961			14	-2	-0.1	10t	1
Career			41	99	2.4	62	1

Tony Adams

Year	Team		Att	Yds	Avg	Lg	TD
1975	KC	N	8	42	5.3	16	0
1976			5	46	9.2	21	0
1977			5	21	4.2	8	0
1978			9	11	1.7	6	0
1987	MIN	N	11	31	2.8	12	0
Career			38	155	4.1	21	0

Willis Adams

Year	Team		Att	Yds	Avg	Lg	TD
1979	CLE	N	2	4	2.0	3	0
1980			2	7	3.5	15	0
1983			1	2	2.0	2	0
Career			5	13	2.6	15	0

Bob Adkins

Year	Team		Att	Yds	Avg	Lg	TD
1940	GB	N	1	5	5.0	5	0

Sam Adkins

Year	Team		Att	Yds	Avg	Lg	TD
1977	SEA	N	3	6	2.0	4	0
1979			2	11	5.5	9	0
1980			6	18	3.0	12	0
1981			3	28	9.3	13	0
Career			14	63	4.5	13	0

Sam Agee

Year	Team		Att	Yds	Avg	Lg	TD
1938	CHIC	N	48	178	3.7		1
1939			45	138	3.1		1
Career			93	316	3.4		2

Tommie Agee

Year	Team		Att	Yds	Avg	Lg	TD
1988	SEA	N	1	2	2.0	2	0
1989	KC	N	1	3	3.0	3	0
1990	DAL	N	53	213	4.0	28	0
1991			9	20	2.2	8	1
1992			16	54	3.4	10	0
1993			6	13	2.2	6	0
1994			5	4	0.8	3	0
Career			91	309	3.4	28	1
Playoffs			3	12	4.0		0

Bob Agler

Year	Team		Att	Yds	Avg	Lg	TD
1948	LA	N	8	41	5.1	12	0
1949			4	7	1.8	4	0
Career			12	48	4.0	12	0

Louie Aguiar

Year	Team		Att	Yds	Avg	Lg	TD
1991	NYJ	N	1	18	18.0	18	0
1993			3	-27	-9.0	5	0
Career			4	-9	-2.3	18	0

Joe Aguirre

Year	Team		Att	Yds	Avg	Lg	TD
1943	WAS	N	1	21	21.0	21	0
1946	LA	AA	2	-5	-2.5		0
Career			3	16	5.3	21	0

Tony Aiello

Year	Team		Att	Yds	Avg	Lg	TD
1944	DET	N	6	22	3.7	5	0

Carl Aikens

Year	Team		Att	Yds	Avg	Lg	TD
1987	LARI	N	1	1	1.0	1	0

Troy Aikman

Year	Team		Att	Yds	Avg	Lg	TD
1989	DAL	N	38	302	7.9	25	0
1990			40	172	4.3	20	1
1991			16	5	0.3	9	1
1992			37	105	2.8	19	1
1993			32	125	3.9	20	0
1994			30	62	2.1	13	1
1995			21	32	1.5	12	1
1996			35	42	1.2	10	1
Career			249	845	3.4	25	6
Playoffs			31	87	2.8		1

Al Akins

Year	Team		Att	Yds	Avg	Lg	TD
1946	CLE	AA	5	42	8.4		1
1947	BKN	AA	15	79	5.3		1
1948			4	-9	-2.3		0
Career			24	112	4.7		2

Frank Akins

Year	Team		Att	Yds	Avg	Lg	TD
1943	WAS	N	10	25	2.5	11	0
1944			46	154	3.3	15	1
1945			147	797	5.4	45	6
1946			41	166	4.0	16	0
Career			244	1142	4.7	45	7
Playoffs			12	22	1.8		0

Vannie Albanese

Year	Team		Att	Yds	Avg	Lg	TD
1937	BKN	N	21	53	2.5		0
1938			27	97	3.6		0
Career			48	150	3.1		0

Frankie Albert

Year	Team		Att	Yds	Avg	Lg	TD
1946	SF	AA	69	-10	-0.1		4
1947			46	179	3.9		5
1948			69	349	5.1		8
1949			35	249	7.1		3
1950	SF	N	53	272	5.1	42	3
1951			35	146	4.2	34	3
1952			22	87	4.0	20	1
Career			329	1272	3.9	42	27
Playoffs			14	92	6.6		0

Grady Alderman

Year	Team		Att	Yds	Avg	Lg	TD
1964	MIN	N	0	22		16L	0

Bennie Aldridge

Year	Team		Att	Yds	Avg	Lg	TD
1950	NYY	N	16	69	4.3	35	0
1952	SF	N	13	36	2.8	11	0
Career			29	105	3.6	35	0

Charles Alexander

Year	Team		Att	Yds	Avg	Lg	TD
1979	CIN	N	88	286	3.3	17	1
1980			169	702	4.2	37	2
1981			98	292	3.0	16	2
1982			64	207	3.2	18	1
1983			153	523	3.4	12	3
1984			132	479	3.6	22	2
1985			44	156	3.5	18	2
Career			748	2645	3.5	37	13
Playoffs			34	125	3.7		2

Derrick Alexander

Year	Team		Att	Yds	Avg	Lg	TD
1994	CLE	N	4	38	9.5	25	0
1995			1	29	29.0	29	0
1996	BAL	N	3	0	0.0	12	0
Career			8	67	8.4	29	0

Harold Alexander

Year	Team		Att	Yds	Avg	Lg	TD
1993	ATL	N	2	-7	-3.5	0	0
1994			1	0	0.0	0	0
Career			3	-7	-2.3	0	0

Jeff Alexander

Year	Team		Att	Yds	Avg	Lg	TD
1989	DEN	N	45	146	3.2	11	2

Robert Alexander

Year	Team		Att	Yds	Avg	Lg	TD
1982	LARM	N	1	3	3.0	3	0
1983			7	28	4.0	8	0
Career			8	31	3.9	8	0

Vincent Alexander

Year	Team		Att	Yds	Avg	Lg	TD
1987	NO	N	21	71	3.4	16	1

Julie Alfonse

Year	Team		Att	Yds	Avg	Lg	TD
1937	CLE	N	33	60	1.8		0
1938			16	16	1.0		0
Career			49	76	1.6		0

Gene Alford

Year	Team		Att	Yds	Avg	Lg	TD
1931	POR	N					1

Buddy Allen

Year	Team		Att	Yds	Avg	Lg	TD
1961	DEN	A	3	-4	-1.3	2	0

Carl Allen

Year	Team		Att	Yds	Avg	Lg	TD
1948	BKN	AA	1	9	9.0	9	0

Don Allen

Year	Team		Att	Yds	Avg	Lg	TD
1960	DEN	A	30	18	0.6	4	1

Eddie Allen

Year	Team		Att	Yds	Avg	Lg	TD
1947	CHIB	N	12	16	1.3	7	0

Ermal Allen

Year	Team		Att	Yds	Avg	Lg	TD
1947	CLE	AA	7	11	1.6		0

Gary Allen

Year	Team		Att	Yds	Avg	Lg	TD
1982	HOU	N	2	2	1.0	9	0
1983			1	5	5.0	5	0
Career			3	7	2.3	9	0

Greg Allen

Year	Team		Att	Yds	Avg	Lg	TD
1985	CLE	N	8	32	4.0	8	0
1986	TB	N	1	3	3.0		0
Career			9	35	3.9		0

Jerry Allen

Year	Team		Att	Yds	Avg	Lg	TD
1967	WAS	N	77	262	3.4	23	3
1968			123	399	3.2	20	4
1969			1	3	3.0	3	0
Career			201	664	3.3	23	7

Marcus Allen

Year	Team		Att	Yds	Avg	Lg	TD
1982	LARI	N	160	697	4.4	53	11
1983			266	1014	3.8	19	9
1984			275	1168	4.2	52t	13
1985			380	1759	4.6	61t	11
1986			208	759	3.6	28t	5
1987			200	754	3.8	44	5
1988			223	831	3.7	32	7
1989			69	293	4.2	15	2
1990			179	682	3.8	28	12
1991			63	287	4.6	26	2
1992			67	301	4.5	21	2
1993	KC	N	206	764	3.7	39	12
1994			189	709	3.8	36t	7
1995			207	890	4.3	38	5
1996			206	830	4.0	35	9
Career			2898	11738	4.1	61t	112
Playoffs			255	1310	5.1		11

Marvin Allen

Year	Team		Att	Yds	Avg	Lg	TD
1988	NE	N	7	40	5.7	12	0
1989			11	51	4.6	18	1
1990			63	237	3.8	29	1
1991			13	50	3.8	11	0
Career			94	378	4.0	29	2

Terry Allen

Year	Team		Att	Yds	Avg	Lg	TD
1991	MIN	N	120	563	4.7	55t	2
1992			266	1201	4.5	51	13
1994			255	1031	4.0	45	8
1995	WAS	N	338	1309	3.9	28	10
1996			347	1353	3.9	49t	21
Career			1326	5457	4.1	55t	54
Playoffs			22	75	3.4		1

Jim Allison

Year	Team		Att	Yds	Avg	Lg	TD
1965	SD	A	29	100	3.4	17	0
1966			31	213	6.9	61	2
1967			10	34	3.4	26	0
1968			23	31	1.3	6	0
Career			93	378	4.1	61	2

Mack Alston

Year	Team		Att	Yds	Avg	Lg	TD
1973	HOU	N	1	13	13.0	13	0
1974			1	-3	-3.0	-3	0
Career			2	10	5.0	13	0

Mike Alstott

Year	Team		Att	Yds	Avg	Lg	TD
1996	TB	N	96	377	3.9	39	3

Lance Alworth

Year	Team		Att	Yds	Avg	Lg	TD
1962	SD	A	1	17	17.0	17	0
1963			2	14	7.0	21	0
1964			3	60	20.0	35	2
1965			3	-12	-4.0	-1	0
1966			3	10	3.3	4	0
1967			1	5	5.0	5	0
1968			3	18	6.0	10	0
1969			5	25	5.0	16	0
1971	DAL	N	2	-10	-5.0	-4	0
1972			1	2	2.0	2	0
Career			24	129	5.4	35	2

John Amberg

Year	Team		Att	Yds	Avg	Lg	TD
1951	NYG	N	7	35	5.0	8	0
1952			7	27	3.9	9	0
Career			14	62	4.4	9	0

Alan Ameche

Year	Team		Att	Yds	Avg	Lg	TD
1955	BAL	N	213	961	4.5	79t	9
1956			178	858	4.8	43	8
1957			144	493	3.4	49	5
1958			171	791	4.6	28	8
1959			178	679	3.8	26	7
1960			80	263	3.3	16	3
Career			964	4045	4.2	79t	40
Playoffs			23	90	3.9		2

George Amundson

Year	Team		Att	Yds	Avg	Lg	TD
1973	HOU	N	15	56	3.7	10	0
1974			59	138	2.3	11	4
Career			74	194	2.6	11	4

Vito Ananis

Year	Team		Att	Yds	Avg	Lg	TD
1945	WAS	N	3	8	2.7	5	0

Kimble Anders

Year	Team		Att	Yds	Avg	Lg	TD
1992	KC	N	1	1	1.0	1	0
1993			75	291	3.9	18	0
1994			62	231	3.7	19	2
1995			58	398	6.9	44	2
1996			54	201	3.7	15t	2
Career			250	1122	4.5	44	6
Playoffs			18	61	3.4		0

Alfred Anderson

Year	Team		Att	Yds	Avg	Lg	TD
1984	MIN	N	201	773	3.8	23	2
1985			50	121	2.4	10	4
1986			83	347	4.2	29	2
1987			68	319	4.7	27	2
1988			87	300	3.4	18	7
1989			52	189	3.6	14	2
1990			59	207	3.5	14	2
1991			26	118	4.5	19	1
Career			626	2374	3.8	29	22
Playoffs			27	101	3.7		2

Anthony Anderson

Year	Team		Att	Yds	Avg	Lg	TD
1979	PIT	N	18	118	6.6	31	1
1980	ATL	N	6	5	0.8	8	0
Career			24	123	5.1	31	1
Playoffs			1	-4	-4.0		0

Art Anderson

Year	Team		Att	Yds	Avg	Lg	TD
1962	CHI	N	1	7	7.0	7	0

Bill Anderson

Year	Team		Att	Yds	Avg	Lg	TD
1960	WAS	N	1	6	6.0	6	0
1961			3	5	1.7	13	0
Career			4	11	2.8	13	0

Billy Anderson

Year	Team		Att	Yds	Avg	Lg	TD
1954	CHIB	N	3	8	2.7	6	0

Bob Anderson

Year	Team		Att	Yds	Avg	Lg	TD
1963	NYG	N	1	-2	-2.0	-2	0

Bobby Anderson

Year	Team		Att	Yds	Avg	Lg	TD
1970	DEN	N	83	368	4.4	27t	4
1971			139	533	3.8	36	3
1972			72	319	4.4	40	1
1973			19	61	3.2	11	1
1975	NE	N	1	1	1.0	1	0
Career			314	1282	4.1	40	9

Donny Anderson

Year	Team		Att	Yds	Avg	Lg	TD
1966	GB	N	25	104	4.2	15	2
1967			97	402	4.1	40	6
1968			170	761	4.5	42	5
1969			87	288	3.3	16t	1
1970			222	853	3.8	54	5
1971			186	757	4.1	31	5
1972	STL	N	153	536	3.5	19	4
1973			167	679	4.1	54	10
1974			90	316	3.5	16	3
Career			1197	4696	3.9	54	41
Playoffs			48	165	3.4		2

Ezzrett Anderson

Year	Team		Att	Yds	Avg	Lg	TD
1947	LA	AA	3	24	8.0		0

Flipper Anderson

Year	Team		Att	Yds	Avg	Lg	TD
1989	LARM	N	1	-1	-1.0	-1	0
1990			1	13	13.0	13	0
1994			1	11	11.0	11	0
Career			3	23	13	7.7	0

Gary Anderson

Year	Team		Att	Yds	Avg	Lg	TD
1985	SD	N	116	429	3.7	27	4
1986			127	442	3.5	17	1
1987			80	260	3.3	25	3
1988			225	1119	5.0	36	3

Gary Anderson *continued*

Year	Team		Att	Yds	Avg	Lg	TD
1990	TB	N	166	646	3.9	22	3
1991			72	263	3.7	64t	1
1992			55	194	3.5	18	1
1993			28	56	2.0	13	0
Career			869	3409	3.9	64t	16

Gary Anderson

Year	Team		Att	Yds	Avg	Lg	TD
1994	PIT	N	1	3	3.0	3	0

Jamal Anderson

Year	Team		Att	Yds	Avg	Lg	TD
1994	ATL	N	2	-1	-0.5	0	0
1995			39	161	4.1	13	1
1996			232	1055	4.5	32t	5
Career			273	1215	4.5	32t	6

Ken Anderson

Year	Team		Att	Yds	Avg	Lg	TD
1971	CIN	N	22	125	5.7	16	1
1972			22	94	4.3	18	3
1973			26	97	3.7	17	0
1974			43	314	7.3	20	2
1975			49	188	3.8	29	4
1976			31	134	4.3	25	1
1977			26	128	4.9	17t	2
1978			29	167	5.8	16	1
1979			28	235	8.4	21	2
1980			16	122	7.6	20	0
1981			46	320	7.0	25	1
1982			25	85	3.4	12t	4
1983			22	147	6.7	29	1
1984			11	64	5.8	14	0
1985			1	0	0.0	0	0
Career			397	2220	5.6	29	20
Playoffs			19	112	5.9		1

Kim Anderson

Year	Team		Att	Yds	Avg	Lg	TD
1981	BAL	N	1	0	0.0	0	0

Max Anderson

Year	Team		Att	Yds	Avg	Lg	TD
1968	BUF	A	147	525	3.6	45	2
1969			13	74	5.7	16	1
Career			160	599	3.7	45	3

Neal Anderson

Year	Team		Att	Yds	Avg	Lg	TD
1986	CHI	N	35	146	4.2	23	0
1987			129	586	4.5	38t	3
1988			249	1106	4.4	80t	12
1989			274	1275	4.7	73	11
1990			260	1078	4.1	52	10
1991			210	747	3.6	42t	6
1992			156	582	3.7	49t	5
1993			202	646	3.2	45	4
Career			1515	6166	4.1	80t	51
Playoffs			81	279	3.4		1

Ockie Anderson

Year	Team		Att	Yds	Avg	Lg	TD
1920	BUF	A					2
1921							6
Career							8

O.J. Anderson

Year	Team		Att	Yds	Avg	Lg	TD
1979	STL	N	331	1605	4.8	76t	8
1980			301	1352	4.5	52	9
1981			328	1376	4.2	28	9
1982			145	587	4.0	64	3
1983			296	1270	4.3	43	5
1984			289	1174	4.1	24	6
1985			117	479	4.1	38	4
1986	STL-NYG	N	75	237	3.2	16	3
1987	NYG	N	2	6	3.0	4	0
1988			65	208	3.2	11	8
1989			325	1023	3.1	36t	14
1990			225	784	3.5	28	11
1991			53	141	2.7	9	1
1992			10	31	3.1	6	0
Career			2562	10273	4.0	76t	81
Playoffs			101	433	4.3		3

Richie Anderson

Year	Team		Att	Yds	Avg	Lg	TD
1994	NYJ	N	43	207	4.8	55	1
1995			5	17	3.4	10	0
1996			47	150	3.2	11	1
Career			95	374	3.9	55	2

Rickey Anderson

Year	Team		Att	Yds	Avg	Lg	TD
1978	SD	N	3	11	3.7	6	0

Taz Anderson

Year	Team		Att	Yds	Avg	Lg	TD
1961	STL	N	15	39	2.6	19	1

Terry Anderson

Year	Team		Att	Yds	Avg	Lg	TD
1977	MIA	N	1	11	11.0	11	0

Vickey Ray Anderson

Year	Team		Att	Yds	Avg	Lg	TD
1980	GB	N	4	5	1.3	4	0

John Andrews

Year	Team		Att	Yds	Avg	Lg	TD
1974	BAL	N	5	6	1.2	4	0

William Andrews

Year	Team		Att	Yds	Avg	Lg	TD
1979	ATL	N	239	1023	4.3	23	3
1980			265	1308	4.9	33	4
1981			289	1301	4.5	29	10
1982			139	573	4.1	19t	5
1983			331	1567	4.7	27	7
1986			52	214	4.1	13	1
Career			1315	5986	4.6	33	30
Playoffs			25	91	3.6		0

Zenon Andrusyshyn

Year	Team		Att	Yds	Avg	Lg	TD
1978	KC	N	1	0	0.0	0	0

Charlie Ane

Year	Team		Att	Yds	Avg	Lg	TD
1959	DET	N	0	10		10L	0

Elmer Angsman

Year	Team		Att	Yds	Avg	Lg	TD
1946	CHIC	N	48	328	6.8	61t	2
1947			110	412	3.7	18	7
1948			131	638	4.9	72t	8
1949			125	674	5.4	82	6
1950			102	362	3.5	21	1
1951			121	380	3.1	28t	3
1952			46	114	2.5	9	0
Career			683	2908	4.3	82	27
Playoffs			20	192	9.6		2

Dunc Annan

Year	Team		Att	Yds	Avg	Lg	TD
1920	CHIT	A					1
1922	TOL	N					2
1925	AKR	N					1
Career							4

Tyrone Anthony

Year	Team		Att	Yds	Avg	Lg	TD
1984	NO	N	20	105	5.3	19	1
1985			17	65	3.8	13	0
Career			37	170	4.6	19	1

Jim Apple

Year	Team		Att	Yds	Avg	Lg	TD
1961	NY	A	7	2	0.3	7	0

Leo Araguz

Year	Team		Att	Yds	Avg	Lg	TD
1996	OAK	N	1	0	0.0	0	0

Fred Arbanas

Year	Team		Att	Yds	Avg	Lg	TD
1968	KC	A	3	14	4.7	8	0
1969			1	1	1.0	1	0
Career			4	15	3.8	8	0

David Archer

Year	Team		Att	Yds	Avg	Lg	TD
1984	ATL	N	6	38	6.3	12	0
1985			70	347	5.0	29t	2
1986			52	298	5.7	22	0
1987			2	8	4.0	7	0
1988	WAS	N	3	1	0.3	4	0
1989	SD	N	2	14	7.0	14	0
Career			135	706	5.2	29t	2

Joe Arenas

Year	Team		Att	Yds	Avg	Lg	TD
1951	SF	N	34	183	5.4	14	3
1952			44	183	4.2	14	0
1953			72	380	5.3	60t	6
1954			11	77	7.0	26	0
1955			37	150	4.1	30	0
1957			5	14	2.8	7t	1
Career			203	987	4.9	60t	10
Playoffs			1	2	2.0		0

Bob Argus

Year	Team		Att	Yds	Avg	Lg	TD
1922	ROC	N					1

Justin Armour

Year	Team		Att	Yds	Avg	Lg	TD
1995	BUF	N	4	-5	-1.3	6	0

Adger Armstrong

Year	Team		Att	Yds	Avg	Lg	TD
1981	HOU	N	31	146	4.7	18	0
1982			8	15	1.9	5	0
1983	TB	N	7	30	4.3	15	0
1984			10	34	3.4	9	2
1985			2	6	3.0	8	0
Career			58	231	4.0	18	2

Charlie Armstrong

Year	Team		Att	Yds	Avg	Lg	TD
1946	BKN	AA	22	78	3.5		0

Johnny Armstrong

Year	Team		Att	Yds	Avg	Lg	TD
1923	RI	N					2
1924							1
1926	RI	A					1
Career							4

Otis Armstrong

Year	Team		Att	Yds	Avg	Lg	TD
1973	DEN	N	26	90	3.5	24	0
1974			263	1407	5.3	43	9
1975			31	155	5.0	33	0
1976			247	1008	4.1	31	5
1977			130	489	3.8	35	4
1978			112	381	3.4	20	1
1979			108	453	4.2	26	2
1980			106	470	4.4	20	4
Career			1023	4453	4.4	43	25
Playoffs			38	141	3.7		1

Tyji Armstrong

Year	Team		Att	Yds	Avg	Lg	TD
1993	TB	N	2	5	2.5	4	0
1994			1	-1	-1.0	-1	0
Career			3	4	1.3	4	0

Jon Arnett

Year	Team		Att	Yds	Avg	Lg	TD
1957	LA	N	86	347	4.0	68t	2
1958			133	683	5.1	57	6
1959			73	371	5.1	80t	2
1960			104	436	4.2	31	2
1961			158	609	3.9	26	4
1962			76	238	3.1	40	2
1963			58	208	3.6	20	1
1964	CHI	N	119	400	3.4	21	1
1965			102	363	3.6	24t	5
1966			55	178	3.2	21	1
Career			964	3833	4.0	80t	26

Jahine Arnold

Year	Team		Att	Yds	Avg	Lg	TD
1996	PIT	N	1	-3	-3.0	-3	0

Jay Arnold

Year	Team		Att	Yds	Avg	Lg	TD
1937	PHI	N	5	7	1.4		0
1938			19	22	1.2		0
1939			8	1	0.1		0
1940			3	9	3.0		0
1941	PIT	N	2	4	2.0	4	0
Career			37	43	1.2	4	0

Jim Arnold

Year	Team		Att	Yds	Avg	Lg	TD
1984	KC	N	1	0	0.0	0	0
1991	DET	N	2	42	21.0	21	0
Career			3	42	14.0	21	0

Rick Arrington

Year	Team		Att	Yds	Avg	Lg	TD
1970	PHI	N	4	33	8.3	15	1
1971			5	23	4.6	11	0
1972			1	2	2.0	2	0
Career			10	58	5.8	15	1

Willie Asbury

Year	Team		Att	Yds	Avg	Lg	TD
1966	PIT	N	169	544	3.2	45	7
1967			80	315	3.9	73	4
1968			4	9	2.3	4	0
Career			253	868	3.4	73	11

Frank Aschenbrenner

Year	Team		Att	Yds	Avg	Lg	TD
1949	CHI	AA	8	14	1.8		0

Josh Ashton

Year	Team		Att	Yds	Avg	Lg	TD
1972	NE	N	128	546	4.3	35	3
1973			93	305	3.3	34	0
1974			26	99	3.8	22	0
1975	STL	N	10	44	4.4	9	0
Career			257	994	3.9	35	3

Joe Aska

Year	Team		Att	Yds	Avg	Lg	TD
1996	OAK	N	62	326	5.3	38	1

Pete Athas

Year	Team		Att	Yds	Avg	Lg	TD
1971	NYG	N	1	3	3.0	3	0

Dale Atkeson

Year	Team		Att	Yds	Avg	Lg	TD
1954	WAS	N	68	176	2.6	14	2
1955			77	300	3.9	45	1
1956			63	163	2.6	12	1
Career			208	639	3.1	45	4

Billy Atkins

Year	Team		Att	Yds	Avg	Lg	TD
1958	SF	N	1	5	5.0	5	0
1960	BUF	A	2	47	23.5		0
1961			2	87	43.5	56	1
Career			5	139	27.8	56	1

Dave Atkins

Year	Team		Att	Yds	Avg	Lg	TD
1973	SF	N	4	19	4.8	8	1
1975	SD	N	1	4	4.0	4	0
Career			5	23	4.6	8	1

Pervis Atkins

Year	Team		Att	Yds	Avg	Lg	TD
1961	LA	N	5	19	3.8	13	0
1962			7	19	2.7	16	0
1963			5	11	2.2	6	0
1964	WAS	N	25	98	3.9	17t	1
1965			18	44	2.4	16	0
1966	OAK	A	14	10	0.7	9	0
Career			74	201	2.7	17t	1

Steve Atkins

Year	Team		Att	Yds	Avg	Lg	TD
1979	GB	N	42	239	5.7	60	1
1980			67	216	3.2	16	1
1981	GB-PHI	N	12	33	2.8	21	0
Career			121	488	4.0	60	2

Jess Atkinson

Year	Team		Att	Yds	Avg	Lg	TD
1985	NYG	N	1	14	14.0	14t	1

John Atwood

Year	Team		Att	Yds	Avg	Lg	TD
1948	NYG	N	9	6	0.7	9	0

Joe Auer

Year	Team		Att	Yds	Avg	Lg	TD
1964	BUF	A	63	191	3.0	21	2
1965			3	19	6.3	14	0
1966	MIA	A	121	416	3.4	41	4
1967			44	128	2.9	23	1
1968	ATL	N	3	19	6.3	16	0
Career			234	773	3.3	41	7

Mike Augustyniak

Year	Team		Att	Yds	Avg	Lg	TD
1981	NYJ	N	85	339	4.0	12	1
1982			50	178	3.6	16	4
1983			18	50	2.8	16	2
Career			153	567	3.7	16	7
Playoffs			8	29	3.6		0

Cliff Austin

Year	Team		Att	Yds	Avg	Lg	TD
1983	NO	N	4	16	4.0	11	0
1984	ATL	N	4	7	1.8	3	0
1985			20	110	5.5	17	0
1986			62	280	4.5	22	1
1987	TB	N	19	32	1.7	8	1
Career			109	445	4.1	22	2

Kent Austin

Year	Team		Att	Yds	Avg	Lg	TD
1986	STL	N	1	0	0.0	0	0

Bob Avellini

Year	Team		Att	Yds	Avg	Lg	TD
1975	CHI	N	4	-3	-0.8	1t	1
1976			18	58	3.2	15	1
1977			37	109	2.9	21	1
1978			34	54	1.6	10	2
1979			3	10	3.3	5	0
1981			5	2	0.4	2	0

Bob Avellini *continued*

Year	Team		Att	Yds	Avg	Lg	TD
1984			3	-5	-1.7	0	0
Career			104	225	2.2	21	5
Playoffs			1	4	4.0		0

Steve Avery

Year	Team		Att	Yds	Avg	Lg	TD
1994	PIT	N	2	4	2.0	5	0
1995			1	3	3.0	3	0
Career			3	7	2.3	5	0

Clarence Avinger

Year	Team		Att	Yds	Avg	Lg	TD
1953	NYG	N	5	6	1.2	5	0

Rob Awalt

Year	Team		Att	Yds	Avg	Lg	TD
1987	STL	N	2	-9	-4.5	-1	0

Mike Baab

Year	Team		Att	Yds	Avg	Lg	TD
1985	CLE	N	1	0	0.0	0	0

Gene Babb

Year	Team		Att	Yds	Avg	Lg	TD
1957	SF	N	102	330	3.2	19	3
1958			7	9	1.3	4	0
1960	DAL	N	39	115	2.9	12	0
1962	HOU	A	3	0	0.0	1	0
1963			1	7	7.0	7	0
Career			152	461	3.0	19	3
Playoffs			2	3	1.5		0

Frank Bacon

Year	Team		Att	Yds	Avg	Lg	TD
1920	DAY	A					3
1921							5
1922	DAY	N					1
1923							1
Career							10

Rick Badanjek

Year	Team		Att	Yds	Avg	Lg	TD
1987	ATL	N	29	87	3.0	31	1

Steve Bagarus

Year	Team		Att	Yds	Avg	Lg	TD
1945	WAS	N	39	154	3.9	18t	1
1946			53	168	3.2	18	0
1947	LA	N	3	15	5.0	10	0
1948	WAS	N	3	6	2.0	3	0
Career			98	343	3.5	18t	1
Playoffs			5	-4	-0.8		0

Billy Baggett

Year	Team		Att	Yds	Avg	Lg	TD
1952	DAL	N	19	65	3.4	15	0

Ken Bahnsen

Year	Team		Att	Yds	Avg	Lg	TD
1953	SF	N	1	1	1.0	1	0

Matt Bahr

Year	Team		Att	Yds	Avg	Lg	TD
1988	CLE	N	1	-8	-8.0	-8	0

Aaron Bailey

Year	Team		Att	Yds	Avg	Lg	TD
1995	IND	N	1	34	34.0	34	0

By Bailey

Year	Team		Att	Yds	Avg	Lg	TD
1952	DET	N	19	74	3.9	11	2
1953	GB	N	13	29	2.2	13	0
Career			32	103	3.2	13	2

Clarence Bailey

Year	Team		Att	Yds	Avg	Lg	TD
1987	MIA	N	10	55	5.5	13	0

Harold Bailey

Year	Team		Att	Yds	Avg	Lg	TD
1982	HOU	N	1	13	13.0	13	0

Henry Bailey

Year	Team		Att	Yds	Avg	Lg	TD
1996	NYJ	N	1	-4	-4.0	-4	0

Johnny Bailey

Year	Team		Att	Yds	Avg	Lg	TD
1990	CHI	N	26	86	3.3	9	0
1991			15	43	2.9	11	1
1992	PHX	N	52	233	4.5	15	1
1993			49	253	5.2	31	1
1994	LARM	N	11	35	3.2	9	1
1995	STL	N	36	182	5.1	17	2
Career			189	832	4.4	31	6

Mark Bailey

Year	Team		Att	Yds	Avg	Lg	TD
1977	KC	N	66	266	4.0	37t	2

Mark Bailey *continued*

Year	Team		Att	Yds	Avg	Lg	TD
1978			83	298	3.6	17	0
Career			149	564	3.8	37t	2

Stacey Bailey

Year	Team		Att	Yds	Avg	Lg	TD
1983	ATL	N	2	-5	-2.5	0	0
1985			1	-3	-3.0	-3	0
1986			1	6	6.0	6	0
Career			4	-2	-0.5	6	0

Tom Bailey

Year	Team		Att	Yds	Avg	Lg	TD
1971	PHI	N	23	41	1.8	7	1
1972			7	22	3.1	5	0
1973			20	91	4.5	15	0
1974			10	32	3.2	11	0
Career			60	186	3.1	15	1

Bill Baird

Year	Team		Att	Yds	Avg	Lg	TD
1964	NY	A	1	8	8.0	8	0

Art Baker

Year	Team		Att	Yds	Avg	Lg	TD
1961	BUF	A	152	498	3.3	35	3
1962			2	9	4.5	7	0
Career			154	507	3.3	35	3

Bullet Baker

Year	Team		Att	Yds	Avg	Lg	TD
1927	NYY	N					1

Ed Baker

Year	Team		Att	Yds	Avg	Lg	TD
1972	HOU	N	1	9	9.0	9	0

Melvin Baker

Year	Team		Att	Yds	Avg	Lg	TD
1975	NO	N	1	21	21.0	21	0
1976	HOU	N	1	2	2.0	2	0
Career			2	23	11.5	21	0

Sam Baker

Year	Team		Att	Yds	Avg	Lg	TD
1953	WAS	N	17	72	4.2	31t	1
1956			25	117	4.7	32	0
1957			2	23	11.5	12	1
1959			2	3	1.5	5	0
1960	CLE	N	1	-11	-11.0	-11	0
1963	DAL	N	1	15	15.0	15	0
1966	PHI	N	1	15	15.0	15	0
Career			49	234	4.8	32	2

Stephen Baker

Year	Team		Att	Yds	Avg	Lg	TD
1987	NYG	N	1	18	18.0	8t	0
1990			1	3	3.0	3	0
Career			2	21	10.5	8t	0

Terry Baker

Year	Team		Att	Yds	Avg	Lg	TD
1963	LA	N	9	46	5.1	12	0
1964			24	82	3.4	18	0
1965			25	82	3.3	10	1
Career			58	210	3.6	18	1

Tony Baker

Year	Team		Att	Yds	Avg	Lg	TD
1968	NO	N	4	2	0.5	3	0
1969			134	642	**4.8**	54	1
1970			82	337	4.1	29	1
1971	NO-PHI	N	46	174	3.8	20	0
1972	PHI	N	90	322	3.6	14	0
1973	LA	N	85	344	4.0	17	7
1974			53	135	2.5	13	5
1975	SD	N	42	131	3.1	18	1
Career			536	2087	3.9	54	15
Playoffs			4	6	1.5		1

Tony Baker

Year	Team		Att	Yds	Avg	Lg	TD
1986	ATL	N	1	3	3.0	3	0
1988	CLE	N	3	19	6.3	13	0
1989	PHX	N	20	31	1.6	6	0
Career			24	53	2.2	13	0

Jim Bakken

Year	Team		Att	Yds	Avg	Lg	TD
1965	STL	N	1	28	28.0	28	0

Frank Balazs

Year	Team		Att	Yds	Avg	Lg	TD
1939	GB	N	11	41	3.7		0
1940			25	107	4.3		1
1941	CHIC-GB	N	23	81	3.5	30	0
1945	CHIC	N	1	-1	-1.0	-1	0
Career			60	228	3.8	30	1

Lou Baldacci

Year	Team		Att	Yds	Avg	Lg	TD
1956	PIT	N	31	140	4.5	29	0

Al Baldwin

Year	Team		Att	Yds	Avg	Lg	TD
1949	BUF	AA	2	1	0.5		0

Burr Baldwin

Year	Team		Att	Yds	Avg	Lg	TD
1949	LA	AA	1	1	1.0	1	0

Randy Baldwin

Year	Team		Att	Yds	Avg	Lg	TD
1992	CLE	N	10	31	3.1	11	0
1993			18	61	3.4	11	0
1994			23	78	3.4	16	0
1995	CAR	N	23	61	2.7	9	0
Career			74	231	3.1	16	0

Eric Ball

Year	Team		Att	Yds	Avg	Lg	TD
1989	CIN	N	98	391	4.0	27	3
1990			22	72	3.3	15	1
1991			10	21	2.1	10	1
1992			16	55	3.4	17	2
1993			8	37	4.6	18	1
1994			2	0	0.0	1	0
1995	OAK	N	2	10	5.0	10	0
Career			158	586	3.7	27	8
Playoffs			12	47	3.9		1

Gary Ballman

Year	Team		Att	Yds	Avg	Lg	TD
1962	PIT	N	3	7	2.3	3	0
1963			8	59	7.4	18	0
1964			11	43	3.9	11	0
1965			17	46	2.7	11	3
1967	PHI	N	1	17	17.0	17t	1
1968			1	30	30.0	30	0
Career			41	202	4.9	30	4

Pete Banaszak

Year	Team		Att	Yds	Avg	Lg	TD
1966	OAK	A	4	18	4.5	7	0
1967			68	376	5.5	47	1
1968			91	362	4.0	43t	4
1969			88	377	4.3	40	0
1970	OAK	N	21	75	3.6	16	2
1971			137	563	4.1	30	8
1972			30	138	4.6	15	1
1973			34	198	5.8	26	0
1974			80	272	3.4	20t	5
1975			187	672	3.6	27t	**16**
1976			114	370	3.2	15	5
1977			67	214	3.2	11	5
1978			43	137	3.2	10	0
Career			964	3772	3.9	47	47
Playoffs			115	427	3.7		5

Herb Banet

Year	Team		Att	Yds	Avg	Lg	TD
1937	GB	N	9	29	3.2		0

Emil Banjavic

Year	Team		Att	Yds	Avg	Lg	TD
1942	DET	N	11	67	6.1	45	0

Chuck Banks

Year	Team		Att	Yds	Avg	Lg	TD
1986	HOU	N	29	80	2.8	9	0
1987	IND	N	50	245	4.9	35	0
Career			79	325	4.1	35	0

Estes Banks

Year	Team		Att	Yds	Avg	Lg	TD
1967	OAK	A	10	26	2.6	13	0
1968	CIN	A	34	131	3.9	20	0
Career			44	157	3.6	20	0

Fred Banks

Year	Team		Att	Yds	Avg	Lg	TD
1990	MIA	N	1	3	3.0	3	0

Gordon Banks

Year	Team		Att	Yds	Avg	Lg	TD
1980	NO	N	1	-5	-5.0	-5	0
1985	DAL	N	1	-1	-1.0	-1	0
Career			2	-6	-3.0	-1	0

Tony Banks

Year	Team		Att	Yds	Avg	Lg	TD
1996	STL	N	61	212	3.5	22	0

Warren Bankston

Year	Team		Att	Yds	Avg	Lg	TD
1969	PIT	N	62	259	4.2	15	1
1970			26	122	4.7	31	2
1971			70	274	3.9	30	0

Warren Bankston *continued*

Year	Team		Att	Yds	Avg	Lg	TD
1972			7	20	2.9	11	0
1974	OAK	N	1	6	6.0	6	0
1976			1	3	3.0	3	0
Career			167	684	4.1	31	3

Jack Banta

Year	Team		Att	Yds	Avg	Lg	TD
1941	PHI-WAS	N	29	93	3.2	31	1
1944	PHI	N	38	198	5.2	60t	3
1945			15	49	3.3	22t	1
1946	LA	N	44	209	4.8	25	0
1947			40	193	4.8	23	1
1948			32	105	3.3	14	0
Career			198	847	4.3	60t	6

Marion Barber

Year	Team		Att	Yds	Avg	Lg	TD
1982	NYJ	N	8	24	3.0	4	0
1983			15	77	5.1	13	1
1984			31	148	4.8	18	2
1985			9	41	4.6	10	0
1986			11	27	2.5	8	0
Career			74	317	4.3	18	3

Mark Barber

Year	Team		Att	Yds	Avg	Lg	TD
1937	CLE	N	14	35	2.5		0

Mike Barber

Year	Team		Att	Yds	Avg	Lg	TD
1978	HOU	N	2	14	7.0	13	0
1979			2	4	2.0	6	0
1980			1	1	1.0	1	0
Career			5	19	3.8	13	0

Mike Barber

Year	Team		Att	Yds	Avg	Lg	TD
1990	CIN	N	1	-13	-13.0	-13	0

Bryan Barker

Year	Team		Att	Yds	Avg	Lg	TD
Playoffs			1	-16	-16.0		0

Hub Barker

Year	Team		Att	Yds	Avg	Lg	TD
1944	NYG	N	1	3	3.0	3	0

Jerome Barkum

Year	Team		Att	Yds	Avg	Lg	TD
1973	NYJ	N	1	2	2.0	2	0
1974			1	2	2.0	2	0
1975			1	-7	-7.0	-7	0
Career			3	-3	-1.0	2	0

Billy Ray Barnes

Year	Team		Att	Yds	Avg	Lg	TD
1957	PHI	N	143	529	3.7	41	1
1958			156	551	3.5	70t	7
1959			181	687	3.8	61t	7
1960			117	315	2.7	23t	4
1961			92	309	3.4	43	1
1962	WAS	N	159	492	3.1	32t	3
1963			93	374	4.0	19	5
1965	MIN	N	48	148	3.1	18	0
1966			5	16	3.2	4	1
Career			994	3421	3.4	70t	29
Playoffs			13	42	3.2		1

Ernie Barnes

Year	Team		Att	Yds	Avg	Lg	TD
1963	DEN	A	0	2		2L	0

Joe Barnes

Year	Team		Att	Yds	Avg	Lg	TD
1974	CHI	N	1	19	19.0	19	0

Larry Barnes

Year	Team		Att	Yds	Avg	Lg	TD
1957	SF	N	20	78	3.9	16	0

Larry Barnes

Year	Team		Att	Yds	Avg	Lg	TD
1977	SD	N	24	70	2.9	7	0
1978	SD-PHI	N	4	12	3.0	4t	1
1979	PHI	N	25	74	3.0	21	1
Career			53	156	2.9	21	2

Fred Barnett

Year	Team		Att	Yds	Avg	Lg	TD
1990	PHI	N	2	13	6.5	12	0
1991			1	0	0.0	0	0
1992			1	-15	-15.0	-15	0
Career			4	-2	-0.5	12	0

Tim Barnett

Year	Team		Att	Yds	Avg	Lg	TD
1993	KC	N	1	3	3.0	3	0

Tom Barnett

Year	Team		Att	Yds	Avg	Lg	TD
1959	PIT	N	75	238	3.2	19	1
1960			6	25	4.2	16	0
Career			81	263	3.2	19	1

Eppie Barney

Year	Team		Att	Yds	Avg	Lg	TD
1968	CLE	N	0	8		8tL	1

Lem Barney

Year	Team		Att	Yds	Avg	Lg	TD
1969	DET	N	3	36	12.0	27	0
1973			2	9	4.5	7	0
Career			5	45	9.0	27	0

Tommy Barnhardt

Year	Team		Att	Yds	Avg	Lg	TD
1987	NO	N	1	-13	-13.0	-13	0
1991			1	0	0.0	0	0
1992			4	-2	-0.5	12	0
1993			1	18	18.0	18	0
1994			1	21	21.0	21	0
1996	TB	N	2	27	13.5	25	0
Career			10	51	5.1	25	0

Len Barnum

Year	Team		Att	Yds	Avg	Lg	TD
1938	NYG	N	35	97	2.8		1
1939			91	237	2.6		2
1940			48	128	2.7		0
1941	PHI	N	35	64	1.8	20	0
1942			30	64	2.1	7	0
Career			239	590	2.5	20	3
Playoffs			7	12	1.7		0

Malcolm Barnwell

Year	Team		Att	Yds	Avg	Lg	TD
1982	LARI	N	2	18	9.0	14	0
1983			1	12	12.0	12	0
Career			3	30	10.0	14	0

Dave Barr

Year	Team		Att	Yds	Avg	Lg	TD
1995	STL	N	1	5	5.0	5	0

Shorty Barr

Year	Team		Att	Yds	Avg	Lg	TD
1923	RAC	N					1

Terry Barr

Year	Team		Att	Yds	Avg	Lg	TD
1959	DET	N	5	57	11.4	37	1
1960			17	74	4.4	19t	1
1961			6	-8	-1.3	9	0
1963			1	9	9.0	9	0
1964			2	31	15.5	19	0
1965			1	-12	-12.0	-12	0
Career			32	151	4.7	37	2

Jeff Barrett

Year	Team		Att	Yds	Avg	Lg	TD
1937	BKN	N	1	8	8.0	8	0
1938			2	3	1.5		0
Career			3	11	3.7	8	0

Tom Barrington

Year	Team		Att	Yds	Avg	Lg	TD
1966	WAS	N	10	37	3.7	21	0
1967	NO	N	34	121	3.6	22	0
1968			45	111	2.5	22	0
1969			7	33	4.7	17	1
1970			72	228	3.2	16	2
Career			168	530	3.2	22	3

Norm Barry

Year	Team		Att	Yds	Avg	Lg	TD
1921	GB	A					1

Odell Barry

Year	Team		Att	Yds	Avg	Lg	TD
1964	DEN	A	3	7	2.3	11	0
1965			2	19	9.5	11	0
Career			5	26	5.2	11	0

Paul Barry

Year	Team		Att	Yds	Avg	Lg	TD
1950	LA	N	50	231	4.6	28	2
1952			3	-1	-0.3	4	0
1953	WAS	N	56	218	3.9	22	0
1954	CHIC	N	50	156	3.1	26	0
Career			159	604	3.8	28	2
Playoffs			8	16	2.0		0

Steve Bartalo

Year	Team		Att	Yds	Avg	Lg	TD
1987	TB	N	9	30	3.3	6	1

Sam Bartholomew

Year	Team		Att	Yds	Avg	Lg	TD
1941	PHI	N	21	71	3.4	10	0

Steve Bartkowski

Year	Team		Att	Yds	Avg	Lg	TD
1975	ATL	N	14	15	1.1	5	2
1976			8	-10	-1.3	2	1
1977			18	13	0.7	8	0
1978			33	60	1.8	8	2
1979			14	36	2.6	18	2
1980			25	35	1.4	11	2
1981			11	2	0.2	5	0
1982			13	4	0.3	10	1
1983			16	38	2.4	13	1
1984			15	34	2.3	8	0
1985			5	9	1.8	5	0
1986	LARM	N	6	3	0.5	7	0
Career			178	239	1.3	18	11
Playoffs			2	3	1.5		0

Don Barton

Year	Team		Att	Yds	Avg	Lg	TD
1953	GB	N	7	40	5.7	14	0

Joe Bartos

Year	Team		Att	Yds	Avg	Lg	TD
1950	WAS	N	9	36	4.0	13	0

Mike Basca

Year	Team		Att	Yds	Avg	Lg	TD
1941	PHI	N	14	43	3.1	19	1

Brian Baschnagel

Year	Team		Att	Yds	Avg	Lg	TD
1976	CHI	N	1	-12	-12.0	-12	0
1977			1	0	0.0	0	0
1978			2	0	0.0	0	0
1981			1	10	10.0	10	0
1983			2	2	1.0	2	0
1984			1	0	0.0	0	0
Career			8	0	0.0	10	0

Myrt Basing

Year	Team		Att	Yds	Avg	Lg	TD
1923	GB	N					2
1925							4
1926							1
Career							7

Billy Bass

Year	Team		Att	Yds	Avg	Lg	TD
1947	CHI	AA	28	44	1.6		0

Dick Bass

Year	Team		Att	Yds	Avg	Lg	TD
1960	LA	N	31	153	4.9	33	0
1961			98	608	6.2	73t	4
1962			196	1033	5.3	57	6
1963			143	520	3.6	51	5
1964			72	342	4.8	59	2
1965			121	549	4.5	49t	2
1966			248	1090	4.4	50	8
1967			187	627	3.4	27	6
1968			121	494	4.1	20	1
1969			1	1	1.0	1	0
Career			1218	5417	4.4	73t	34
Playoffs			14	40	2.9		0

Don Bass

Year	Team		Att	Yds	Avg	Lg	TD
1978	CIN	N	1	-4	-4.0	-4	0
1979			4	35	8.8	14	0
1981			1	9	9.0	9	0
Career			6	40	6.7	14	0

Glenn Bass

Year	Team		Att	Yds	Avg	Lg	TD
1961	BUF	A	2	8	4.0	16	0
1963			14	59	4.2	9	0
Career			16	67	4.2	16	0
Playoffs			2	4			0

Mo Bassett

Year	Team		Att	Yds	Avg	Lg	TD
1954	CLE	N	144	588	4.1	22	6
1955			38	174	4.6	30t	3
1956			41	129	3.1	12	1
Career			223	891	4.0	30t	10
Playoffs			19	76	4.0		0

Reds Bassman

Year	Team		Att	Yds	Avg	Lg	TD
1936	PHI	N	4	19	4.8		0

Marv Bateman

Year	Team		Att	Yds	Avg	Lg	TD
1977	BUF	N	1	0	0.0		0

Year	Team		Att	Yds	Avg	Lg	TD

Bill Bates
1989	DAL	N	1	0	0.0	0	0
1990			1	4	4.0	4	0
Career			2	4	2.0	4	0
Playoffs			1	0	0.0		0

Mario Bates
1994	NO	N	151	579	3.8	40	6
1995			244	951	3.9	66t	7
1996			164	584	3.6	33	4
Career			559	2114	3.8	66t	17

Michael Bates
1993	SEA	N	2	12	6.0	6	0
1994			2	-4	-2.0	7	0
Career			4	8	2.0	7	0

Ron Battle
| 1982 | LARM | N | 1 | 1 | 1.0 | 1 | 0 |

Cliff Battles
1932	BOS	N	148	576	3.9		3
1933			146	737	5.0		3
1934			103	511	5.0		6
1935			84	310	3.7		1
1936			176	614	3.5		5
1937	WAS	N	216	874	4.0		5
Career			873	3622	4.1		23
Playoffs			21	61	2.9		1

Bobby Batton
| 1980 | NYJ | N | 3 | 4 | 1.3 | 3 | 0 |

Hank Bauer
1977	SD	N	4	4	1.0	3	0
1978			85	304	3.6	37t	8
1979			22	28	1.3	6	8
1980			10	34	3.4	7	1
1981			2	7	3.5	4	0
Career			123	377	3.1	37t	17

Sammy Baugh
1937	WAS	N	86	240	2.8		1
1938			15	35	2.3		0
1939			14	46	3.3		0
1940			20	16	0.8		0
1941			27	12	0.4	16	0
1942			20	61	3.0	28	1
1943			19	-42	-2.2	4	0
1944			19	-38	-2.0	17	0
1945			19	-71	-3.7	34	0
1946			18	-76	-4.2	13	0
1947			25	47	1.9	19	2
1948			4	4	1.0	7	1
1949			13	67	5.2	17	2
1950			7	27	3.9	11	1
1951			11	-5	-0.5	7	0
1952			1	1	1.0	1	0
Career			318	324	1.0	34	8
Playoffs			7	-4	-0.6		0

Brad Baxter
1990	NYJ	N	124	539	4.3	28t	6
1991			184	666	3.6	31	11
1992			152	698	4.6	30	6
1993			174	559	3.2	16	7
1994			60	170	2.8	13	4
1995			85	296	3.5	26	1
Career			779	2928	3.8	31	35
Playoffs			5	14	2.8		0

Craig Baynham
1967	DAL	N	3	6	2.0	3	1
1968			103	438	4.3	22t	5
1969			3	-2	-0.7	2	0
1970	CHI	N	26	68	2.6	9	0
1972	STL	N	17	43	2.5	11	0
Career			152	553	3.6	22t	6
Playoffs			24	55	2.3		2

Winnie Baze
| 1937 | PHI | N | 3 | 14 | 4.7 | | 0 |

Walter Beach
| 1960 | BOS | A | 6 | -4 | -0.7 | | 0 |

Alyn Beals
1946	SF	AA	2	-7	-3.5		0
1947			5	48	9.6		0
1949			4	32	8.0		0
Career			11	73	6.6		0

Bubba Bean
1976	ATL	N	124	428	3.5	30	2
1978			193	707	3.7	25t	3
1979			88	393	4.5	60t	1
Career			405	1528	3.8	60t	6
Playoffs			26	86	3.3		1

Terry Beasley
1974	SF	N	1	-3	-3.0	-3	0
1975			1	5	5.0	5	0
Career			2	2	1.0	5	0

Pete Beathard
1964	KC	A	4	43	10.8	41	0
1965			25	138	5.5	26	4
1966			20	152	7.6	52	1
1967	HOU	A	32	133	4.2	23	1
1968			18	79	4.4	20	2
1969			19	89	4.7	16	2
1970	STL	N	2	2	1.0	2	0
1971			4	29	7.3	15	0
1972	LA	N	1	-1	-1.0	-1	0
1973	KC	N	6	16	2.7	11	1
Career			131	680	5.2	52	11
Playoffs			5	7	1.4		0

Gary Beban
| 1968 | WAS | N | 5 | 18 | 3.6 | 5 | 0 |

Hub Bechtol
| 1947 | BAL | AA | 2 | -1 | -0.5 | | 0 |

Wayland Becker
| 1937 | GB | N | 2 | 4 | 2.0 | | 0 |

Don Beebe
1990	BUF	N	1	23	23.0	23	0
1992			1	-6	-6.0	-6	0
1994			2	11	5.5	6	0
Career			4	28	7.0	23	0

Keith Beebe
| 1944 | NYG | N | 8 | 12 | 1.5 | 7 | 0 |

Earl Beecham
| 1987 | NYG | N | 5 | 22 | 4.4 | 10 | 0 |

Jim Beirne
| 1968 | HOU | A | 1 | 3 | 3.0 | 3 | 0 |

Bunny Belden
1930	CHIC	N					1
1931							3
Career							4

Steve Belichick
| 1941 | DET | N | 28 | 118 | 4.2 | 11 | 2 |

Rocky Belk
| 1983 | CLE | N | 1 | -5 | -5.0 | -5 | 0 |

Bill Bell
| 1972 | ATL | N | 1 | -3 | -3.0 | -3 | 0 |

Eddie Bell
1970	NYJ	N	2	-7	-3.5	0	0
1972			1	-5	-5.0	-5	0
Career			3	-12	-4.0	0	0

Gordon Bell
1976	NYG	N	67	233	3.5	26	2
1977			16	63	3.9	13	0
1978	STL	N	7	23	3.3	9	0
Career			90	319	3.5	26	2

Greg Bell
1984	BUF	N	262	1100	4.2	85t	7
1985			223	883	4.0	77t	8
1986			90	377	4.2	42	4
1987	BUF-LARM	N	22	86	3.9	13	0
1988	LARM	N	288	1212	4.2	44	16
1989			272	1137	4.2	47	15
1990	LARI	N	47	164	3.5	21	1
Career			1204	4959	4.1	85t	51
Playoffs			76	358	4.7		1

Henry Bell
| 1960 | DEN | A | 43 | 238 | 5.5 | 69 | 0 |

Ken Bell
1986	DEN	N	9	17	1.9	12	0
1987			13	43	3.3	11	0
1988			9	36	4.0	6	0
Career			31	96	3.1	12	0
Playoffs			4	19	4.8		0

Kerwin Bell
| 1996 | IND | N | 1 | -1 | -1.0 | -1 | 0 |

Nick Bell
1991	LARI	N	78	307	3.9	15	3
1992			81	366	4.5	66t	3
1993			67	180	2.7	12	1
Career			226	853	3.8	66t	7
Playoffs			22	110	5.0		0

Richard Bell
| 1990 | PIT | N | 5 | 18 | 3.6 | 12 | 0 |

Ricky Bell
1977	TB	N	148	436	2.9	20	1
1978			185	679	3.7	56	6
1979			283	1263	4.5	49	7
1980			174	599	3.4	40	2
1981			30	80	2.7	8	0
1982	SD	N	2	6	3.0	4	0
Career			822	3063	3.7	56	16
Playoffs			58	201	3.5		2

Theo Bell
1976	PIT	N	1	5	5.0	5	0
1981	TB	N	1	7	7.0	7	0
Career			2	12	6.0	7	0

William Bell
| 1995 | WAS | N | 4 | 13 | 3.3 | 5 | 0 |

Joe Bellino
1965	BOS	A	24	49	2.0	10	0
1967			6	15	2.5	10	0
Career			30	64	2.1	10	0

Horace Belton
1978	KC	N	24	79	3.3	8	0
1979			44	134	3.0	12	1
1980			68	273	4.0	14	2
Career			136	486	3.6	14	3

Willie Belton
1971	ATL	N	56	237	4.2	16	1
1972			10	20	2.0	8	0
1974	STL	N	12	49	4.1	10	0
Career			78	306	3.9	16	1

Guy Benjamin
1978	MIA	N	1	-2	-2.0	-2	0
1981	SF	N	1	1	1.0	1	0
1983			1	1	1.0	1	0
Career			3	0	0.0	1	0

Ryan Benjamin
| 1993 | CIN | N | 3 | 5 | 1.7 | 2 | 0 |

Tony Benjamin
1977	SEA	N	13	48	3.7	10	0
1978			1	7	7.0	7	0
1979			5	13	2.6	8	0
Career			19	68	3.6	10	0

Fred Benners

Year	Team		Att	Yds	Avg	Lg	TD
1952	NYG	N	5	16	3.2	8	0

Ben Bennett

Year	Team		Att	Yds	Avg	Lg	TD
1987	CIN	N	2	17	8.5	9	0

Chuck Bennett

Year	Team		Att	Yds	Avg	Lg	TD
1930	POR	N					5

Donnell Bennett

Year	Team		Att	Yds	Avg	Lg	TD
1994	KC	N	46	178	3.9	17	2
1995			7	11	1.6	11	0
1996			36	166	4.6	34	0
Career			89	355	4.0	34	2

Edgar Bennett

Year	Team		Att	Yds	Avg	Lg	TD
1992	GB	N	61	214	3.5	18	0
1993			159	550	3.5	19	9
1994			178	623	3.5	39t	5
1995			316	1067	3.4	23	3
1996			222	899	4.0	23	2
Career			936	3353	3.6	39t	19
Playoffs			163	561	3.4		5

Woody Bennett

Year	Team		Att	Yds	Avg	Lg	TD
1979	NYJ	N	2	4	2.0	3	1
1980	NYJ-MIA	N	46	200	4.3	19	0
1981	MIA	N	28	104	3.7	12	0
1982			9	15	1.7	5	0
1983			49	197	4.0	25	2
1984			144	606	4.2	23	7
1985			54	256	4.7	17	0
1986			36	162	4.5	16	0
1987			25	102	4.1	18	0
1988			31	115	3.7	12	0
Career			424	1761	4.2	25	10
Playoffs			59	179	3.0		4

Cliff Benson

Year	Team		Att	Yds	Avg	Lg	TD
1984	ATL	N	3	8	2.7	6	0

George Benson

Year	Team		Att	Yds	Avg	Lg	TD
1947	BKN	AA	2	5	2.5		0

Albert Bentley

Year	Team		Att	Yds	Avg	Lg	TD
1985	IND	N	54	288	5.3	26t	2
1986			73	351	4.8	70t	3
1987			142	631	4.4	17t	7
1988			45	230	5.1	20	2
1989			75	299	4.0	22	1
1990			137	556	4.1	26t	4
Career			526	2355	4.5	70t	19
Playoffs			4	9	2.3		1

Jim Benton

Year	Team		Att	Yds	Avg	Lg	TD
1939	CLE	N	7	19	2.7		0
1940			1	0	0.0	0	0
Career			8	19	2.4	0	0

Dave Bernard

Year	Team		Att	Yds	Avg	Lg	TD
1944	CLE	N	1	6	6.0	6	0

Karl Bernard

Year	Team		Att	Yds	Avg	Lg	TD
1987	DET	N	45	187	4.2	14	2

Frank Bernardi

Year	Team		Att	Yds	Avg	Lg	TD
1955	CHIC	N	8	17	2.1	20	0
1956			14	4	0.3	7	0
1957			1	4	4.0	4	0
Career			23	25	1.1	20	0

Rick Berns

Year	Team		Att	Yds	Avg	Lg	TD
1979	TB	N	23	102	4.4	16	0
1980			39	131	3.4	17	0
1983	LARI	N	6	22	3.7	13	0
Career			68	255	3.8	17	0

Rod Bernstine

Year	Team		Att	Yds	Avg	Lg	TD
1987	SD	N	1	9	9.0	9	0
1988			2	7	3.5	5	0
1989			15	137	9.1	32t	1
1990			124	589	4.8	40t	4
1991			159	766	4.8	63t	3
1992			106	499	4.7	25t	4

Rod Bernstine continued

Year	Team		Att	Yds	Avg	Lg	TD
1993	DEN	N	223	816	3.7	24	4
1994			17	91	5.4	24	0
1995			23	76	3.3	18	1
Career			670	2990	4.5	63t	22
Playoffs			1	3	3.0		0

Bob Berry

Year	Team		Att	Yds	Avg	Lg	TD
1966	MIN	N	3	12	4.0	5	0
1968	ATL	N	26	139	5.3	45	2
1969			20	68	3.4	30	0
1970			13	60	4.6	16	0
1971			19	31	1.6	9	0
1972			24	86	3.6	16	2
1973	MIN	N	2	5	2.5	5	0
1974			1	8	8.0	8	0
1975			1	0	0.0	0	0
Career			109	409	3.8	45	4

Gil Berry

Year	Team		Att	Yds	Avg	Lg	TD
1935	CHIC	N	44	77	1.8		0

Rex Berry

Year	Team		Att	Yds	Avg	Lg	TD
1952	SF	N	1	7	7.0	7	0

Wayne Berry

Year	Team		Att	Yds	Avg	Lg	TD
1954	NYG	N	1	30	30.0	30	0

Angelo Bertelli

Year	Team		Att	Yds	Avg	Lg	TD
1946	LA	AA	11	-16	-1.5		1
1947	CHI	AA	1	2	2.0	2	0
1948			2	-1	-0.5		0
Career			14	-15	-1.1	2	1

Jim Bertelsen

Year	Team		Att	Yds	Avg	Lg	TD
1972	LA	N	123	581	4.7	42	5
1973			206	854	4.1	49	4
1974			127	419	3.3	20	2
1975			116	457	3.9	19	3
1976			42	155	3.7	18	2
Career			614	2466	4.0	49	16
Playoffs			32	136	4.3		0

Jim Bertoglio

Year	Team		Att	Yds	Avg	Lg	TD
1926	COL	N					1

Willie Berzinski

Year	Team		Att	Yds	Avg	Lg	TD
1956	PHI	N	15	72	4.8	20	0

Art Best

Year	Team		Att	Yds	Avg	Lg	TD
1977	CHI	N	6	20	3.3	6	0
1978			2	11	5.5	6	0
Career			8	31	3.9	6	0

James Betterson

Year	Team		Att	Yds	Avg	Lg	TD
1977	PHI	N	62	233	3.8	17	1
1978			11	32	2.9	5	0
Career			73	265	3.6	17	1

Jerome Bettis

Year	Team		Att	Yds	Avg	Lg	TD
1993	LARM	N	294	1429	4.9	71t	7
1994			319	1025	3.2	19	3
1995	STL	N	183	637	3.5	41	3
1996	PIT	N	320	1431	4.5	50t	11
Career			1116	4522	4.1	71t	24
Playoffs			38	145	3.8		2

John Bettridge

Year	Team		Att	Yds	Avg	Lg	TD
1937	CHIB-CLE	N	22	35	1.6		0

Steve Beuerlein

Year	Team		Att	Yds	Avg	Lg	TD
1988	LARI	N	30	35	1.2	20	0
1989			16	39	2.4	10	0
1991	DAL	N	7	-14	-2.0	-1	0
1992			4	-7	-1.8	-1	0
1993	PHX	N	22	45	2.0	20	0
1994	ARI	N	22	39	1.8	19	1
1995	JAC	N	5	32	6.4	13	0
1996	CAR	N	12	17	1.4	13	0
Career			118	186	1.6	20	1
Playoffs			6	5	0.8		0

David Beverly

Year	Team		Att	Yds	Avg	Lg	TD
1974	HOU	N	1	4	4.0	4	0

David Beverly continued

Year	Team		Att	Yds	Avg	Lg	TD
1977	GB	N	2	-3	-1.5	0	0
1978			1	0	0.0	0	0
1980			6	21	3.5	11	0
Career			10	22	2.2	11	0

Dwight Beverly

Year	Team		Att	Yds	Avg	Lg	TD
1987	NO	N	62	217	3.5	25	2

Tim Biakabutuka

Year	Team		Att	Yds	Avg	Lg	TD
1996	CAR	N	71	229	3.2	17	0

Johnny Biancone

Year	Team		Att	Yds	Avg	Lg	TD
1936	BKN	N	8	34	4.3		0

Dick Bielski

Year	Team		Att	Yds	Avg	Lg	TD
1955	PHI	N	28	67	2.4	8	1
1956			52	162	3.1	15	1
Career			80	229	2.9	15	2

Eric Bieniemy

Year	Team		Att	Yds	Avg	Lg	TD
1991	SD	N	3	17	5.7	15	0
1992			74	264	3.6	21	3
1993			33	135	4.1	12	1
1994			73	295	4.0	36	0
1995	CIN	N	98	381	3.9	27	3
1996			56	269	4.8	33t	2
Career			337	1361	4.0	36	9
Playoffs			22	100	4.5		0

Fred Biletnikoff

Year	Team		Att	Yds	Avg	Lg	TD
Playoffs			1	-10	-10.0		0

Don Bingham

Year	Team		Att	Yds	Avg	Lg	TD
1956	CHIB	N	7	36	5.1	12	0
Playoffs			1	1	1.0		0

John Binotto

Year	Team		Att	Yds	Avg	Lg	TD
1942	PIT-PHI	N	17	47	2.8	30	0

Carl Birdsong

Year	Team		Att	Yds	Avg	Lg	TD
1981	STL	N	1	-2	-2.0	-2	0

Charlie Bivins

Year	Team		Att	Yds	Avg	Lg	TD
1960	CHI	N	1	-11	-11.0	-11	0
1961			43	188	4.4	24	1
1962			14	44	3.1	15	1
1963			44	104	2.4	17	0
1964			29	92	3.2	17	0
1967	PIT N-BUF	A	22	81	3.7	43	1
Career			153	498	3.3	43	3

Hank Bjorklund

Year	Team		Att	Yds	Avg	Lg	TD
1972	NYJ	N	15	42	2.8	10	0
1973			22	72	3.3	14	0
1974			23	57	2.5	12	0
Career			60	171	2.9	14	0

Blondy Black

Year	Team		Att	Yds	Avg	Lg	TD
1946	BUF	AA	1	10	10.0	10	0
1947	BAL	AA	5	39	7.8		0
Career			6	49	8.2	10	0

Mike Black

Year	Team		Att	Yds	Avg	Lg	TD
1983	DET	N	2	-10	-5.0	0	0
1984			3	-6	-2.0	4	0
1985			1	0	0.0	0	0
1986			1	-8	-8.0	-8	0
1987			1	0	0.0	0	0
Career			8	-24	-3.0	4	0

Bill Blackburn

Year	Team		Att	Yds	Avg	Lg	TD
1946	CHIC	N	1	10	10.0	10	0

Todd Blackledge

Year	Team		Att	Yds	Avg	Lg	TD
1983	KC	N	1	0	0.0	0	0
1984			18	102	5.7	26	1
1985			17	97	5.7	25	0
1986			23	60	2.6	14	0
1987			5	21	4.2	11	0
1988	PIT	N	8	25	3.1	10	1
1989			9	20	2.2	11	0
Career			81	325	4.0	26	2
Playoffs			4	33	8.3		0

Alois Blackwell

Year	Team		Att	Yds	Avg	Lg	TD
1978	DAL	N	9	37	4.1	13	0

Brian Blades

Year	Team		Att	Yds	Avg	Lg	TD
1988	SEA	N	5	24	4.8	12	0
1989			1	3	3.0	3	0
1990			3	19	6.3	12	0
1991			2	17	8.5	11	0
1992			1	5	5.0	5	0
1993			5	52	10.4	26	0
1994			2	32	16.0	40	0
1995			2	4	2.0	4	0
Career			21	156	7.4	40	0

Russ Blailock

Year	Team		Att	Yds	Avg	Lg	TD
1923	MIL	N					1

Jeff Blake

Year	Team		Att	Yds	Avg	Lg	TD
1992	NYJ	N	2	-2	-1.0	1	0
1994	CIN	N	37	204	5.5	16	1
1995			53	309	5.8	30	2
1996			72	317	4.4	18	2
Career			164	828	5.0	30	5

Ricky Blake

Year	Team		Att	Yds	Avg	Lg	TD
1991	DAL	N	15	80	5.3	30t	1

Tom Blanchard

Year	Team		Att	Yds	Avg	Lg	TD
1972	NYG	N	1	17	17.0	17	0
1978	NO	N	2	0	0.0	0	0
1979	TB	N	1	0	0.0	0	0
1981			1	0	0.0	0	0
Career			5	17	3.4	17	0

Carl Bland

Year	Team		Att	Yds	Avg	Lg	TD
1988	DET	N	1	4	4.0	4	0

George Blanda

Year	Team		Att	Yds	Avg	Lg	TD
1949	CHIB	N	1	9	9.0	9	1
1952			20	104	5.2	16	1
1953			24	62	2.6	16	0
1954			19	41	2.2	19	0
1955			15	54	3.6	10	2
1956			6	47	7.8	17	0
1957			5	-5	-1.0	1t	1
1960	HOU	A	25	-60	-2.4	4	4
1961			7	12	1.7	7	0
1962			3	6	2.0	10	0
1963			4	1	0.3	19	7
0							
1964			4	-2	-0.5	6	0
1965			4	-6	-1.5	9	0
1966			3	1	0.3	1	0
1969	OAK	A	1	0	0.0	0	0
1970	OAK	N	2	4	2.0	4	0
Career			143	268	1.9	19	0
Playoffs			3	0	0.0		0

Ernie Blandin

Year	Team		Att	Yds	Avg	Lg	TD
1947	CLE	AA	1	-6	-6.0	-6	0

Sid Blanks

Year	Team		Att	Yds	Avg	Lg	TD
1964	HOU	A	145	756	5.2	91	6
1966			71	235	3.3	30	0
1967			66	206	3.1	16	1
1968			63	169	2.7	10	0
1969	BOS	A	7	30	4.3	12	0
1970	BOS	N	13	44	3.4	12	0
Career			365	1440	3.9	91	7
Playoffs			1	6	6.0		0

Curtis Bledsoe

Year	Team		Att	Yds	Avg	Lg	TD
1981	KC	N	20	65	3.3	13	0
1982			10	20	2.0	5	0
Career			30	85	2.8	13	0

Drew Bledsoe

Year	Team		Att	Yds	Avg	Lg	TD
1993	NE	N	32	82	2.6	15	0
1994			44	40	0.9	7	0
1995			20	28	1.4	15	0
1996			24	27	1.1	8	0
Career			120	177	1.5	15	0
Playoffs			5	6	1.2		

Mel Bleeker

Year	Team		Att	Yds	Avg	Lg	TD
1944	PHI	N	60	315	5.3	37	4
1945			50	167	3.3	20	2
1946			6	-7	-1.2	6	0
1947	LA	N	23	111	4.8	25	1
Career			139	586	4.2	37	7

Bob Bleier

Year	Team		Att	Yds	Avg	Lg	TD
1987	NE	N	5	-5	-1.0	1t	1

Rocky Bleier

Year	Team		Att	Yds	Avg	Lg	TD
1968	PIT	N	6	39	6.5	21	0
1972			1	17	17.0	17	0
1973			3	0	0.0	1	0
1974			88	373	4.2	18	2
1975			140	528	3.8	17	2
1976			220	1036	4.7	28	5
1977			135	465	3.4	16	4
1978			165	633	3.8	24	5
1979			92	434	4.7	70t	4
1980			78	340	4.4	19	1
Career			928	3865	4.2	70t	23
Playoffs			141	480	3.4		4

Dennis Bligen

Year	Team		Att	Yds	Avg	Lg	TD
1985	NYJ	N	22	107	4.9	28t	1
1986			20	65	3.3	10	1
1987			31	128	4.1	15	1
Career			73	300	4.1	28t	3

Johnny Blood

Year	Team		Att	Yds	Avg	Lg	TD
1926	DUL	N					1
1929	GB	N					2
1931							2
1935			42	115	2.7		0
1936			13	65	5.0		0
1937	PIT	N	9	37	4.1		0
1938			21	-5	-0.2		0
Career			85	212	2.5		5
Playoffs			2	8	4.0		0

Al Bloodgood

Year	Team		Att	Yds	Avg	Lg	TD
1926	KC	N					2
1927	CLE	N					4
Career							6

Alvin Blount

Year	Team		Att	Yds	Avg	Lg	TD
1987	DAL	N	46	125	2.7	15	3

Ed Blount

Year	Team		Att	Yds	Avg	Lg	TD
1987	SF	N	1	0	0.0	0	0

Eric Blount

Year	Team		Att	Yds	Avg	Lg	TD
1992	PHX	N	1	-1	-1.0	-1	0
1993			5	28	5.6	7	1
Career			6	27	4.5	7	1

Jeb Blount

Year	Team		Att	Yds	Avg	Lg	TD
1977	TB	N	5	26	5.2	12	0

Lamar Blount

Year	Team		Att	Yds	Avg	Lg	TD
1947	BUF-BAL	AA	4	5	1.3		0

Luther Blue

Year	Team		Att	Yds	Avg	Lg	TD
1977	DET	N	1	-6	-6.0	-6	0
1978			5	9	1.8	10	0
1979			1	-8	-8.0	-8	0
Career			7	-5	-0.7	10	0

Jimmy Blumenstock

Year	Team		Att	Yds	Avg	Lg	TD
1947	NYG	N	54	168	3.1	25	0

Ronnie Blye

Year	Team		Att	Yds	Avg	Lg	TD
1968	NYG	N	53	243	4.6	17	1
1969	PHI	N	8	25	3.1	11	0
Career			61	268	4.4	17	1

Tony Boddie

Year	Team		Att	Yds	Avg	Lg	TD
1986	DEN	N	1	2	2.0	2	0
1987			3	7	2.3	4	1
Career			4	9	2.3	4	1
Playoffs			1	8	8.0		0

Billy Boedecker

Year	Team		Att	Yds	Avg	Lg	TD
1946	CHI	AA	6	8	1.3		0
1947	CLE	AA	31	194	6.3		4
1948			78	254	3.3		3
1949			50	269	5.4		1
1950	GB	N	8	16	2.0	8	0
Career			173	741	4.3	8	8

Dewey Bohling

Year	Team		Att	Yds	Avg	Lg	TD
1960	NY	A	123	431	3.5		2
1961	NY-BUF	A	55	153	2.8	18	2
Career			178	584	3.3	18	4

George Bolan

Year	Team		Att	Yds	Avg	Lg	TD
1922	CHIB	N					2

Leroy Bolden

Year	Team		Att	Yds	Avg	Lg	TD
1958	CLE	N	15	55	3.7	15	0
1959			4	11	2.8	9	0
Career			19	66	3.5	15	0

Chase Boldt

Year	Team		Att	Yds	Avg	Lg	TD
1922	LOU	N					1

Andy Bolton

Year	Team		Att	Yds	Avg	Lg	TD
1976	SEA-DET	N	15	71	4.7	22	0
1977	DET	N	3	4	1.3	2	0
1978			2	5	2.5	3	0
Career			20	80	4.0	22	0

Rink Bond

Year	Team		Att	Yds	Avg	Lg	TD
1939	PIT	N	1	4	4.0	4	0

Ernie Bonelli

Year	Team		Att	Yds	Avg	Lg	TD
1945	CHIC	N	32	93	2.9	22	0
1946	PIT	N	6	7	1.2	4	0
Career			38	100	2.6	22	0

Glen Bonner

Year	Team		Att	Yds	Avg	Lg	TD
1974	SD	N	66	199	3.0	12	3
1975			28	120	4.3	12	0
Career			94	319	3.4	12	3

Steve Bono

Year	Team		Att	Yds	Avg	Lg	TD
1987	PIT	N	8	27	3.4	23	1
1991	SF	N	17	46	2.7	18	0
1992			15	23	1.5	19	0
1993			12	14	1.2	10	1
1994	KC	N	4	-1	-0.3	2	0
1995			28	113	4.0	76t	5
1996			26	27	1.0	17	0
Career			110	249	2.3	76t	7

Greg Boone

Year	Team		Att	Yds	Avg	Lg	TD
1987	TB	N	1	2	2.0	2	0

Jack Boone

Year	Team		Att	Yds	Avg	Lg	TD
1942	CLE	N	3	-1	-0.3	3	0

J.R. Boone

Year	Team		Att	Yds	Avg	Lg	TD
1948	CHIB	N	48	266	5.5	40	5
1949			35	111	3.2	22	0
1950			13	15	1.2	7	0
1951			3	9	3.0	6	0
1952	SF	N	24	72	3.0	12	0
1953	GB	N	7	24	3.4	24	0
Career			130	497	3.8	40	5

Dick Booth

Year	Team		Att	Yds	Avg	Lg	TD
1941	DET	N	29	79	2.7	17	1
1945			4	20	5.0	9	0
Career			33	99	3.0	17	1

Emerson Boozer

Year	Team		Att	Yds	Avg	Lg	TD
1966	NY	A	97	455	4.7	54	5
1967			119	442	3.7	48	10
1968			143	441	3.1	33	5
1969			130	604	4.6	50	4
1970	NYJ	N	139	581	4.2	27	5
1971			188	618	3.3	19	5
1972			120	549	4.6	37t	11
1973			182	831	4.6	52	3
1974			153	563	3.7	20	4

Year	Team		Att	Yds	Avg	Lg	TD

Emerson Boozer continued

Year	Team		Att	Yds	Avg	Lg	TD
1975			20	51	2.5	8	0
Career			1291	5135	4.0	54	52
Playoffs			24	84	3.5		1

Mike Boryla

1974	PHI	N	6	25	4.2	11	0
1975			8	33	4.1	11	0
1976			29	166	5.7	22	2
Career			43	224	5.2	22	2

Don Bosseler

1957	WAS	N	167	673	4.0	28	7
1958			109	475	4.4	23	4
1959			119	644	5.4	41t	3
1960			109	428	3.9	29	2
1961			77	220	2.9	16	2
1962			93	336	3.6	15	2
1963			79	290	3.7	18	2
1964			22	46	2.1	9	0
Career			775	3112	4.0	41t	22

Lee Bouggess

1970	PHI	N	159	401	2.5	20	2
1971			97	262	2.7	26	2
1973			15	34	2.3	11	1
Career			271	697	2.6	26	5

Matt Bouza

1986	IND	N	1	12	12.0	12	0

Tony Bova

1943	P-P	N	1	11	11.0	11	0
1944	C-P	N	14	-22	-1.6	3	0
1945	PIT	N	6	11	1.8	5	0
Career			21	0	0.0	11	0

Bill Bowman

1954	DET	N	96	397	4.1	61	2
1956			20	84	4.2	13	1
1957	PIT	N	28	76	2.7	13	0
Career			144	557	3.9	61	3
Playoffs			7	61	8.7		1

Arda Bowser

1922	CAN	N					2

Cloyce Box

1949	DET	N	30	62	2.1	11	0
1954			1	20	20.0	20	0
Career			31	82	2.6	20	0

Bill Boyd

1930	CHIC	N					1

Bob Boyd

1950	LA	N	1	-2	-2.0	-2	0
1956			1	-7	-7.0	-7	0
Career			2	-9	-4.5	-2	0

Bobby Boyd

1962	BAL	N	2	13	6.5	15	0
1964			1	25	25.0	25	0
Career			3	38	12.7	25	0
Playoffs			1	-9	-9.0		0

Greg Boykin

1977	NO	N	5	-9	-1.8	4	0
1978	SF	N	102	361	3.5	23	2
Career			107	352	3.3	23	2

Benny Boynton

1921	ROC-WAS	A					4
1924	BUF	N					1
Career							5

Bill Bradley

1969	PHI	N	1	5	5.0	5	0
1970			1	14	14.0	14	0
1973			1	0	0.0	0	0
Career			3	19	6.3	14	0

Freddie Bradley

1996	SD	N	32	109	3.4	17	0

Steve Bradley

1987	CHI	N	1	-3	-3.0	-3	0

Jim Bradshaw

1926	LA	A					1

Morris Bradshaw

1975	OAK	N	1	-5	-5.0	-5	0
1976			1	4	4.0	4	0
1978			1	5	5.0	5	0
Career			3	4	1.3	5	0

Terry Bradshaw

1970	PIT	N	32	233	7.3	22	1
1971			53	247	4.7	39	5
1972			58	346	6.0	20t	7
1973			34	145	4.3	21	3
1974			34	224	6.6	34	2
1975			35	210	6.0	27	3
1976			31	219	7.1	17	3
1977			31	171	5.5	26	3
1978			32	93	2.9	17	1
1979			21	83	4.0	28	0
1980			36	111	3.1	18	2
1981			38	162	4.3	16	2
1982			8	10	1.3	6	0
1983			1	3	3.0	3	0
Career			444	2257	5.1	39	32
Playoffs			51	288	5.6		3

Mike Bragg

1968	WAS	N	1	-3	-3.0	-3	0
1969			1	3	3.0	3	0
1970			2	25	12.5	40	0
Career			4	25	6.3	40	0

Mark Brammer

1980	BUF	N	1	8	8.0	8	0
1981			2	17	8.5	11	0
Career			3	25	8.3	11	0

George Brancato

1954	CHIC	N	2	26	13.0	18	0

Cliff Branch

1972	OAK	N	1	5	5.0	5	0
1975			2	18	9.0	15	0
1976			3	12	4.0	10	0
1979			1	4	4.0	4	0
1980			1	1	1.0	1	0
1982	LARI	N	2	10	5.0	7	0
1983			1	20	20.0	20	0
Career			11	70	6.4	20	0

Reggie Branch

1987	WAS	N	4	9	2.3	3	1

Jim Brandt

1953	PIT	N	42	106	2.5	9	3
1954			19	82	4.3	20	1
Career			61	188	3.1	20	4

Zeke Bratkowski

1954	CHIB	N	15	35	2.3	19	1
1957			12	83	6.9	14	0
1958			3	0	0.0	2	0
1959			7	86	12.3	41	0
1960	CHI	N	8	20	2.5	10	0
1961	LA	N	12	36	3.0	16	3
1962			7	14	2.0	11	0
1963	LA-GB	N	4	-3	-0.8	1	0
1964	GB	N	2	0	0.0	0	0
1965			4	-1	-0.3	-1	0
1966			4	7	1.8	4	0
1967			5	6	1.2	4	0
1968			8	24	3.0	13	0
1971			1	1	1.0	1t	1
Career			92	308	3.3	41	5

Jason Bratton

1996	BUF	N	4	8	2.0	5	0

Melvin Bratton

1989	DEN	N	30	108	3.6	9	1
1990			27	82	3.0	10	3
Career			57	190	3.3	10	4
Playoffs			5	7	1.4		2

Hez Braxton

1962	SD	A	17	35	2.1	15	1

Jim Braxton

1971	BUF	N	21	84	4.0	14	0
1972			116	453	3.9	21	5
1973			108	494	4.6	36	4
1974			146	543	3.7	21t	4
1975			186	823	4.4	29	9
1976			1	0	0.0	0	0
1977			113	372	3.3	12	1
1978	BUF-MIA	N	50	121	2.4	15	2
Career			741	2890	3.9	36	25
Playoffs			5	48	9.6		0

Carl Brazell

1938	CLE	N	4	14	3.5		0

Don Breaux

1963	DEN	A	10	51	5.1	15	0
1965	SD	A	1	-1	-1.0	-1	0
Career			11	50	4.5	15	80
Playoffs			1	-2	-2.0		0

Bill Bredde

1954	CHIC	N	13	57	4.4	14	1

Bill Breeden

1937	PIT	N	10	25	2.5		0

Adrian Breen

1987	CIN	N	6	18	3.0	9	0

Wayne Brenkert

1923	AKR	N					2
1924							3
Career							5

Matt Brennan

1926	BKN	N					1

Brooke Brewer

1922	AKR	N					1

Chris Brewer

1984	DEN	N	10	28	2.8	8	0
1987	CHI	N	24	55	2.3	16	2
Career			34	83	2.4	16	2

John Brewer

1952	PHI	N	50	188	3.8	71t	2
1953			17	85	5.0	19	1
Career			67	273	4.1	71t	3

Frank Briante

1929	SI	N					1

George Brickley

1920	CLE	A					1

Bob Briggs

1965	WAS	N	6	10	1.7	6	0

Walter Briggs

1987	NYJ	N	1	4	4.0	4	0

Leon Bright

1981	NYG	N	51	197	3.9	25	2
1982			1	5	5.0	5	0
1983			1	2	2.0	2	0
Career			53	204	3.8	25	2
Playoffs			1	5	5.0		0

Year	Team		Att	Yds	Avg	Lg	TD

James Brim
| 1987 | MIN | N | 2 | 36 | 18.0 | 38t | 1 |

Larry Brink
| 1948 | LA | N | 1 | -3 | -3.0 | -3 | 0 |

Dana Brinson
| 1989 | SD | N | 17 | 64 | 3.8 | 9 | 0 |

Larry Brinson
1977	DAL	N	8	28	3.5	20t	1
1978			18	96	5.3	39t	2
1979			14	48	3.4	10	0
1980	SEA	N	16	57	3.6	22t	1
Career			56	229	4.1	39t	4
Playoffs			3	3	1.0		0

Marlin Briscoe
1968	DEN	A	41	308	7.5	34	3
1970	BUF	N	3	19	6.3	11	0
1973	MIA	N	2	-5	-2.5	2	0
1974			1	17	17.0	17	0
1975	DET	N	2	-3	-1.5	6	0
Career			49	336	6.9	34	3

Bubby Brister
1986	PIT	N	6	10	1.7	9	1
1988			45	209	4.6	20	6
1989			27	25	0.9	15	0
1990			25	64	2.6	11	0
1991			11	17	1.5	8	0
1992			10	16	1.6	8	0
1993	PHI	N	20	39	2.0	13	0
1994			1	7	7.0	7	0
1995	NYJ	N	16	18	1.1	7	0
Career			161	405	2.5	20	7
Playoffs			3	5	1.7		0

Eddie Britt
1936	BOS	N	72	180	2.5		0
1937	WAS	N	7	21	3.0		0
Career			79	201	2.5		0
Playoffs			1	-2	-2.0		0

Jon Brittenum
| 1968 | SD | A | 2 | -4 | -2.0 | 0 | 0 |

Earl Britton
| 1926 | BKN | A | | | | | 1 |

Dieter Brock
| 1985 | LARM | N | 20 | 38 | 1.9 | 13 | 0 |
| Playoffs | | | 1 | 0 | 0.0 | | 0 |

Lou Brock
1940	GB	N	18	60	3.3		0
1941			14	44	3.1	14	0
1942			95	237	2.5	24	2
1943			45	67	1.5	9	2
1944			36	200	5.6	42t	3
1945			46	196	4.3	28	3
Career			254	804	3.2	42t	10

John Brockington
1971	GB	N	216	1105	5.1	52t	4
1972			274	1027	3.7	30t	8
1973			265	1144	4.3	53	3
1974			266	883	3.3	33	5
1975			144	434	3.0	19	7
1976			117	406	3.5	29	2
1977	GB-KC	N	65	186	2.9	12	1
Career			1347	5185	3.8	53	30
Playoffs			13	9	0.7		0

Bob Brodhead
| 1960 | BUF | A | 21 | 45 | 2.1 | | 0 |

John Brodie
1957	SF	N	2	0	0.0	0	0
1958			11	-12	-1.1	6	1
1959			5	6	1.2	6	0
1960			18	171	9.5	30	1
1961			28	90	3.2	29	2
1962			37	258	7.0	21	4

John Brodie *continued*
1963			7	63	9.0	24	0
1964			27	135	5.0	38	2
1965			15	60	4.0	13	1
1966			5	18	3.6	7	3
1967			20	147	7.3	15	1
1968			18	71	3.9	15	0
1969			11	62	5.6	15	0
1970			9	29	3.2	12t	2
1971			14	45	3.2	12	3
1972			3	8	2.7	4	1
1973			5	16	3.2	14	1
Career			235	1167	5.0	38	22
Playoffs			2	4	2.0		1

J.W. Brodnax
| 1960 | DEN | A | 15 | 18 | 1.2 | 7 | 0 |

Jeff Brohm
| 1996 | SF | N | 16 | 43 | 2.7 | 22 | 0 |

Mitchell Brookins
| 1984 | BUF | N | 2 | 27 | 13.5 | 16 | 0 |

Bill Brooks
1986	IND	N	4	5	1.3	12	0
1987			2	-2	-1.0	1	0
1988			5	62	12.4	38	0
1989			2	-3	-1.5	0	0
1992			2	14	7.0	8	0
1993	BUF	N	3	30	10.0	15	0
1995			3	7	2.3	9	0
Career			21	113	5.4	38	0
Playoffs			2	28	14.0		0

Billy Brooks
1976	CIN	N	1	-13	-13.0	-13	0
1977			2	-4	-2.0	4	0
Career			3	-17	-5.7	4	0

Bob Brooks
| 1961 | NY | A | 15 | 55 | 3.7 | 9 | 0 |

James Brooks
1981	SD	N	109	525	4.8	28t	3
1982			87	430	4.9	48t	6
1983			127	516	4.1	61	3
1984	CIN	N	103	396	3.8	33	2
1985			192	929	4.8	39	7
1986			205	1087	**5.3**	56t	5
1987			94	290	3.1	18	1
1988			182	931	5.1	51t	8
1989			221	1239	5.6	65t	7
1990			195	1004	5.1	56t	5
1991			152	571	3.8	25	2
1992	CLE-TB	N	18	44	2.4	13	0
Career			1685	7962	4.7	65t	49
Playoffs			58	216	3.7		1

Reggie Brooks
1993	WAS	N	223	1063	4.8	85t	3
1994			100	297	3.0	15	2
1995			2	-2	-1.0	-1	0
1996	TB	N	112	368	3.3	56	2
Career			437	1726	3.9	85t	7

Robert Brooks
1992	GB	N	2	14	7.0	8	0
1993			3	17	5.7	21	0
1994			1	0	0.0	0	0
1995			4	21	5.3	21	0
1996			4	2	0.5	6	0
Career			14	54	3.9	21	0
Playoffs			4	51	12.8		0

Walter Broughton
| 1986 | BUF | N | 1 | -6 | -6.0 | -6 | 0 |

Steve Broussard
1990	ATL	N	126	454	3.6	50t	4
1991			99	449	4.5	36	4
1992			84	363	4.3	27	1
1993			39	206	5.3	26	1
1994	CIN	N	94	403	4.3	37t	2

Steve Broussard *continued*
1995	SEA	N	46	222	4.8	21t	1
1996			15	106	7.1	26t	1
Career			503	2203	4.4	50t	14

Angie Brovelli
1933	PIT	N					2
1934							1
Career							3

A.B. Brown
1989	NYJ	N	12	63	5.3	17	0
1990			1	8	8.0	8	0
1991			3	4	1.3	2	1
1992			24	42	1.8	9	0
Career			40	117	2.9	17	1

Bill Brown
| 1944 | BKN | N | 4 | 10 | 2.5 | 3 | 0 |

Bill Brown
1961	CHI	N	22	81	3.7	20	0
1962	MIN	N	34	103	3.0	15	0
1963			128	445	3.5	21	5
1964			226	866	3.8	48	7
1965			160	699	4.4	40	6
1966			**251**	829	3.3	33t	6
1967			185	610	3.3	29	5
1968			222	805	3.6	32	11
1969			126	430	3.4	30	3
1970			101	324	3.2	18	0
1971			46	136	3.0	23t	2
1972			82	263	3.2	19	4
1973			47	206	4.4	21	3
1974			19	41	2.2	11	0
Career			1649	5838	3.5	48	52
Playoffs			42	139	3.3		2

Bob Brown
| 1970 | STL | N | 1 | 8 | 8.0 | 8 | 0 |

Carlos Brown
| 1976 | GB | N | 12 | 49 | 4.1 | 21 | 0 |

Charlie Brown
| 1968 | BUF | A | 3 | 39 | 13.0 | 27 | 0 |

Charlie Brown
| 1967 | NO | N | 8 | 16 | 2.0 | 7 | 2 |

Charlie Brown
| 1983 | WAS | N | 4 | 53 | 13.3 | 21 | 0 |

Curtis Brown
1977	BUF	N	8	34	4.3	9	0
1978			128	591	4.6	58t	4
1979			172	574	3.3	25	1
1980			153	559	3.7	34t	3
1981			62	226	3.6	13	0
1982			41	187	4.6	19	0
1983	HOU	N	3	0	0.0	1t	1
Career			567	2171	3.8	58t	9
Playoffs			10	19	1.9		0

Dave Brown
1943	NYG	N	32	131	4.1	14	0
1946			9	5	0.6	8	0
1947			6	5	0.8	3	0
Career			47	141	3.0	14	0

Dave Brown
1992	NYG	N	2	-1	-0.5	1	0
1993			3	-4	-1.3	-1	0
1994			60	196	3.3	21	2
1995			45	228	5.1	23	4
1996			50	170	3.4	18	0
Career			160	589	3.7	23	6
Playoffs			1	8	8.0		0

Derek Brown
1993	NO	N	180	705	3.9	60	2
1994			146	489	3.3	16	3
1995			49	159	3.2	35t	1

Derek Brown *continued*

Year	Team		Att	Yds	Avg	Lg	TD
1996			13	30	2.3	12	0
Career			388	1383	3.6	60	6

Ed Brown

Year	Team		Att	Yds	Avg	Lg	TD
1954	CHIB	N	9	36	4.0	18	0
1955			43	203	4.7	32t	2
1956			40	164	4.1	31	1
1957			31	129	4.2	31	1
1958			32	94	2.9	28	3
1959			33	108	3.3	48	1
1960	CHI	N	19	89	4.7	38	2
1961			13	18	1.4	13	0
1962	PIT	N	2	-8	-4.0	-2	0
1963			15	20	1.3	7	2
1964			26	110	4.2	22	2
1965	PIT-BAL	N	2	-3	-1.5	-1	0
Career			265	960	3.6	48	14
Playoffs			5	-3	-0.6		0

Eddie Brown

Year	Team		Att	Yds	Avg	Lg	TD
1985	CIN	N	14	129	9.2	35	0
1986			8	32	4.0	17	0
1987			1	0	0.0	0	0
1988			1	-5	-5.0	-5	0
1991			1	8	8.0	8	0
Career			25	164	6.6	35	0

Fred Brown

Year	Team		Att	Yds	Avg	Lg	TD
1961	BUF	A	53	192	3.6	13	1
1963			6	18	3.0	6	1
Career			59	210	3.6	13	2

Gary Brown

Year	Team		Att	Yds	Avg	Lg	TD
1991	HOU	N	8	85	10.6	39t	1
1992			19	87	4.6	26	1
1993			195	1002	5.1	26	6
1994			169	648	3.8	18	4
1995			86	293	3.4	21	0
Career			477	2115	4.4	39t	12
Playoffs			11	17	1.5		1

Gordon Brown

Year	Team		Att	Yds	Avg	Lg	TD
1987	IND	N	19	85	4.5	18t	1

Hardy Brown

Year	Team		Att	Yds	Avg	Lg	TD
1948	BKN	AA	6	23	3.8		1
1949	CHI	AA	1	2	2.0	2	0
Career			7	25	3.6	2	1

Ivory Lee Brown

Year	Team		Att	Yds	Avg	Lg	TD
1992	PHX	N	68	194	2.9	13	2

Jesse Brown

Year	Team		Att	Yds	Avg	Lg	TD
1926	POT	N					1

Jim Brown

Year	Team		Att	Yds	Avg	Lg	TD
1957	CLE	N	202	942	4.7	69t	9
1958			257	1527	5.9	65t	17
1959			290	1329	4.6	70t	14
1960			215	1257	5.8	71t	9
1961			305	1408	4.6	38	8
1962			230	996	4.3	31	13
1963			291	1863	6.4	80t	12
1964			280	1446	5.2	71	7
1965			289	1544	5.3	67	17
Career			2359	12312	5.2	80t	106
Playoffs			66	241	3.7		1

Ken Brown

Year	Team		Att	Yds	Avg	Lg	TD
1970	CLE	N	1	-8	-8.0	-8	0
1971			11	47	4.3	17	0
1972			32	114	3.6	14	2
1973			161	537	3.3	17	0
1974			125	458	3.7	27	4
1975			16	45	2.8	8	1
Career			346	1193	3.4	27	7
Playoffs			4	13	3.3		0

Kevin Brown

Year	Team		Att	Yds	Avg	Lg	TD
1987	CHI	N	1	0	0.0	0	0

Larry Brown

Year	Team		Att	Yds	Avg	Lg	TD
1969	WAS	N	202	888	4.4	57	4

Larry Brown *continued*

Year	Team		Att	Yds	Avg	Lg	TD
1970			237	1125	4.7	75t	5
1971			253	948	3.7	34	4
1972			285	1216	4.3	38t	8
1973			273	860	3.2	27	8
1974			163	430	2.6	16	3
1975			97	352	3.6	43	3
1976			20	56	2.8	11	0
Career			1530	5875	3.8	75t	35
Playoffs			151	499	3.3		1

Lomas Brown

Year	Team		Att	Yds	Avg	Lg	TD
1989	DET	N	1	3	3.0	3	0

Marv Brown

Year	Team		Att	Yds	Avg	Lg	TD
1957	DET	N	2	6	3.0	3	0

Pete Brown

Year	Team		Att	Yds	Avg	Lg	TD
1954	SF	N	1	-6	-6.0	-6	0

Ray Brown

Year	Team		Att	Yds	Avg	Lg	TD
1958	BAL	N	1	-9	-9.0	-9	0
1959			2	4	2.0	3	0
1960			2	25	12.5	23	0
Career			5	20	4.0	23	0

Reggie Brown

Year	Team		Att	Yds	Avg	Lg	TD
1987	PHI	N	39	136	3.5	23	0

Ron Brown

Year	Team		Att	Yds	Avg	Lg	TD
1984	LARM	N	2	25	12.5	16	0
1985			2	13	6.5	9	0
1986			4	5	1.3	11	0
1987			2	22	11.0	11	0
1988			3	24	8.0	13	0
1989			6	27	4.5	12	0
1991			2	11	5.5	11	0
Career			21	127	6.0	16	0

Ron Brown

Year	Team		Att	Yds	Avg	Lg	TD
1987	STL	N	1	9	9.0	9	0

Ted Brown

Year	Team		Att	Yds	Avg	Lg	TD
1979	MIN	N	130	551	4.2	34	1
1980			219	912	4.2	55t	8
1981			274	1063	3.9	34	6
1982			120	515	4.3	30	1
1983			120	476	4.0	43	10
1984			98	442	4.5	19	3
1985			93	336	3.6	30	7
1986			63	251	4.0	60	4
Career			1117	4546	4.1	60	40
Playoffs			42	160	3.8		3

Theotis Brown

Year	Team		Att	Yds	Avg	Lg	TD
1979	STL	N	73	318	4.4	30t	7
1980			40	186	4.7	19	1
1981	STL-SEA	N	156	583	3.7	43	8
1982	SEA	N	53	141	2.7	17	2
1983	SEA-KC	N	130	481	3.7	49t	8
1984	KC	N	97	337	3.5	25	4
Career			549	2046	3.7	49t	30

Tim Brown

Year	Team		Att	Yds	Avg	Lg	TD
1988	LARI	N	14	50	3.6	12	1
1991			5	16	3.2	9	0
1992			3	-4	-1.3	3	0
1993			2	7	3.5	14	0
1996	OAK	N	6	35	5.8	15	0
Career			30	104	3.5	15	1

Timmy Brown

Year	Team		Att	Yds	Avg	Lg	TD
1960	PHI	N	9	35	3.9	13	2
1961			50	338	6.8	47	1
1962			137	545	4.0	61t	5
1963			192	841	4.4	34	6
1964			90	356	4.0	36	5
1965			158	861	5.4	54t	6
1966			161	548	3.4	24	3
1967			53	179	3.4	13t	1
1968	BAL	N	39	159	4.1	10	2
Career			889	3862	4.3	61t	31

Tom Brown

Year	Team		Att	Yds	Avg	Lg	TD
1987	MIA	N	3	3	1.0	3	0
1989			13	26	2.0	6	0
Career			16	29	1.8	6	0

Willie Brown

Year	Team		Att	Yds	Avg	Lg	TD
1965	LA	N	44	133	3.0	19	0

Jim Browne

Year	Team		Att	Yds	Avg	Lg	TD
1987	LARI	N	2	1	0.5	2	0

Gail Bruce

Year	Team		Att	Yds	Avg	Lg	TD
1948	SF	AA	1	1	1.0	1	0

Isaac Bruce

Year	Team		Att	Yds	Avg	Lg	TD
1994	LARM	N	1	2	2.0	2	0
1995	STL	N	3	17	5.7	12	0
1996			1	4	4.0	4	0
Career			5	23	4.6	12	0

Hank Bruder

Year	Team		Att	Yds	Avg	Lg	TD
1931	GB	N					1
1932							2
1933							3
1934							1
1935			44	158	3.6		0
1936			4	-7	-1.8		0
1937			15	56	3.7		1
1938			2	6	3.0		0
Career			65	213	3.3		8
Playoffs			1	0	0.0		0

Woody Bruder

Year	Team		Att	Yds	Avg	Lg	TD
1925	BUF	N					1
1926	FRA	N					2
Career							3

Bob Bruer

Year	Team		Att	Yds	Avg	Lg	TD
1979	SF	N	5	-4	-0.8	6	0

Boyd Brumbaugh

Year	Team		Att	Yds	Avg	Lg	TD
1938	BKN	N	45	191	4.2		1
1939	BKN-PIT	N	111	343	3.1		2
1940	PIT	N	32	79	2.5		0
1941			68	114	1.7	8	2
Career			256	727	2.8		5

Carl Brumbaugh

Year	Team		Att	Yds	Avg	Lg	TD
1930	CHIB	N					2
1931							1
1933			20	39	2.0		0
1934			7	9	1.3		0
1936			9	-1	-0.1		0
1937	CLE-BKN	N	13	-3	-0.2		0
1938	CHIB	N	3	-15	-5.0		0
Career			52	29	0.6		3
Playoffs			1	1			0

Bob Brumley

Year	Team		Att	Yds	Avg	Lg	TD
1945	DET	N	5	18	3.6	4	0

Mark Brunell

Year	Team		Att	Yds	Avg	Lg	TD
1994	GB	N	6	7	1.2	5t	1
1995	JAC	N	67	480	7.2	27t	4
1996			80	396	5.0	33	3
Career			153	883	5.8	33	8
Playoffs			20	113	5.7		0

Bob Brunet

Year	Team		Att	Yds	Avg	Lg	TD
1968	WAS	N	71	227	3.2	15	0
1970			9	37	4.1	11	0
1971			10	27	2.7	5	0
1972			30	82	2.7	18	2
1973			2	4	2.0	3	0
1975			6	23	3.8	11	1
1977			3	6	2.0	3	0
Career			131	406	3.1	18	3

Scott Brunner

Year	Team		Att	Yds	Avg	Lg	TD
1980	NYG	N	10	18	1.8	12	0
1981			14	20	1.4	23	0
1982			19	27	1.4	10	1
1983			26	64	2.5	10	0

Year	Team		Att	Yds	Avg	Lg	TD

Scott Brunner *continued*

Year	Team		Att	Yds	Avg	Lg	TD
1985	STL	N	3	8	2.7	8	0
Career			72	137	1.9	23	1
Playoffs			8	9	1.1		0

Larry Brunson

Year	Team		Att	Yds	Avg	Lg	TD
1974	KC	N	5	-33	-6.6	0	0
1975			2	89	44.5	65	0
1976			3	-1	-0.3	5	0
1977			2	8	4.0	11	0
Career			12	63	5.3	65	0

Mike Brunson

Year	Team		Att	Yds	Avg	Lg	TD
1970	ATL	N	1	9	9.0	9	0

Johnny Bryan

Year	Team		Att	Yds	Avg	Lg	TD
1923	CHIB	N					4
1924							2
1926	MIL	N					1
Career							7

Beno Bryant

Year	Team		Att	Yds	Avg	Lg	TD
1994	SEA	N	1	6	6.0	6	0

Charlie Bryant

Year	Team		Att	Yds	Avg	Lg	TD
1966	STL	N	5	31	6.2	18	0
1967			3	16	5.3	8	0
1968	ATL	N	9	29	3.2	7	0
1969			50	246	4.9	41	0
Career			67	322	4.8	41	0

Cullen Bryant

Year	Team		Att	Yds	Avg	Lg	TD
1974	LA	N	10	24	2.4	7	0
1975			117	467	4.0	18	2
1976			21	64	3.0	12	2
1977			6	42	7.0	24	0
1978			178	658	3.7	26	7
1979			177	619	3.5	15	5
1980			183	807	4.4	20	3
1981			109	436	4.0	20	1
1983	SEA	N	27	87	3.2	9	0
1984			20	58	2.9	8	0
1987	LARM	N	1	2	2.0	2	0
Career			849	3264	3.8	26	20
Playoffs			113	447	4.0		

Hubie Bryant

Year	Team		Att	Yds	Avg	Lg	TD
1970	PIT	N	3	25	8.3	24	0
1971	NE	N	4	1	0.3	1	0
Career			7	26	3.7	24	

Kelvin Bryant

Year	Team		Att	Yds	Avg	Lg	TD
1986	WAS	N	69	258	3.7	22t	4
1987			77	406	5.3	28	1
1988			108	498	4.6	25	1
1990			6	24	4.0	12	0
Career			260	1186	4.6	28	6
Playoffs			32	137	4.3		0

Walter Bryant

Year	Team		Att	Yds	Avg	Lg	TD
1955	BAL	N	2	4	2.0	8	0

Mike Buck

Year	Team		Att	Yds	Avg	Lg	TD
1992	NO	N	3	-4	-1.3	-1	0
1993			1	0	0.0	0	0
1995	ARI	N	1	0	0.0	0	0
Career			5	-4	-0.8	0	0

Ted Bucklin

Year	Team		Att	Yds	Avg	Lg	TD
1927	CHIC	N					1

Doug Buffone

Year	Team		Att	Yds	Avg	Lg	TD
1971	CHI	N	1	19	19.0	19	0
1979			1	14	14.0	14	0
Career			2	33	16.5	19	0

Maury Buford

Year	Team		Att	Yds	Avg	Lg	TD
1986	CHI	N	1	-13	-13.0	-13	0
1989			1	6	6.0	6	0
1990			1	-9	-9.0	-9	0
Career			3	-16	-5.3	6	0

Danny Buggs

Year	Team		Att	Yds	Avg	Lg	TD
1975	NYG	N	1	0	0.0	0	0

Larry Buhler

Year	Team		Att	Yds	Avg	Lg	TD
1939	GB	N	5	3	0.6		0
1940			36	118	3.3		0
Career			41	121	3.0		0

Drew Buie

Year	Team		Att	Yds	Avg	Lg	TD
1971	OAK	N	2	32	16.0	24	0

Ray Buivid

Year	Team		Att	Yds	Avg	Lg	TD
1937	CHIB	N	19	24	1.3		0
1938			32	65	2.0		0
Career			51	89	1.7		0
Playoffs			3	-12	-4.0		0

Glenn Bujnoch

Year	Team		Att	Yds	Avg	Lg	TD
1977	CIN	N	1	4	4.0	4t	1

Joe Bukant

Year	Team		Att	Yds	Avg	Lg	TD
1938	PHI	N	48	119	2.5		0
1939			59	136	2.3		3
1940			18	50	2.8		1
1942	CHIC	N	17	34	2.0	15	0
1943			42	87	2.1	10	0
Career			184	426	2.3	15	4

Fred Bukaty

Year	Team		Att	Yds	Avg	Lg	TD
1961	DEN	A	76	187	2.5	54	5

Rudy Bukich

Year	Team		Att	Yds	Avg	Lg	TD
1953	LA	N	14	28	2.0	17	1
1956			1	8	8.0	8	0
1957	WAS	N	8	-2	-0.3	16	0
1958	WAS-CHIB	N	2	16	8.0	23	0
1959	CHIB	N	1	0	0.0	0	0
1960	PIT	N	3	-8	-2.7		0
1961			14	4	0.3	12	2
1963	CHI	N	7	1	0.1	2	1
1964			12	28	2.3	12	0
1965			28	33	1.2	24	3
1966			18	14	0.8	12t	2
1967			4	-13	-3.3	2	0
Career			112	109	1.0	24	9

George Buksar

Year	Team		Att	Yds	Avg	Lg	TD
1949	CHI	AA	13	16	1.2		1
1950	BAL	N	12	44	3.7	25	0
1952	WAS	N	3	3	1.0	3	0
Career			28	63	2.3	25	1

Norm Bulaich

Year	Team		Att	Yds	Avg	Lg	TD
1970	BAL	N	139	426	3.1	15	3
1971			152	741	4.9	67t	8
1972			27	109	4.0	18	1
1973	PHI	N	106	436	4.1	20	1
1974			50	152	3.0	13	0
1975	MIA	N	78	309	4.0	30	5
1976			122	540	4.4	35	4
1977			91	416	4.6	29	4
1978			40	196	4.9	63	2
1979			9	37	4.1	9	2
Career			814	3362	4.1	67t	30
Playoffs			67	215	3.2		2

Ronnie Bull

Year	Team		Att	Yds	Avg	Lg	TD
1962	CHI	N	113	363	3.2	24t	1
1963			117	404	3.5	18	1
1964			86	320	3.7	50	1
1965			91	417	4.6	33t	3
1966			100	318	3.2	13	0
1967			61	176	2.9	11	0
1968			107	472	4.4	24	3
1969			44	187	4.3	16	0
1970			68	214	3.1	28	0
1971	PHI	N	94	351	3.7	39	0
Career			881	3222	3.7	50	9
Playoffs			13	42	3.2		0

Scott Bull

Year	Team		Att	Yds	Avg	Lg	TD
1976	SF	N	15	66	4.4	18	2
1977			5	20	4.0	8	0
1978			29	100	3.4	5t	1
Career			49	186	3.8	18	3

Amos Bullocks

Year	Team		Att	Yds	Avg	Lg	TD
1962	DAL	N	33	196	5.9	73t	2
1963			96	341	3.6	17	2
1966	PIT	N	29	83	2.9	13	1
Career			158	620	3.9	73t	5

Rex Bumgardner

Year	Team		Att	Yds	Avg	Lg	TD
1948	BUF	AA	14	82	5.9		0
1949			101	391	3.9		1
1950	CLE	N	67	231	3.4	26	2
1951			45	126	2.8	20	1
1952			9	38	4.2	24	0
Career			236	868	3.7	26	4
Playoffs			39	112	2.9		1

Jarrod Bunch

Year	Team		Att	Yds	Avg	Lg	TD
1991	NYG	N	1	0	0.0	0	0
1992			104	501	4.8	37	3
1993			33	128	3.9	13	2
Career			138	629	4.6	37	5
Playoffs			3	6	2.0		0

Chris Burford

Year	Team		Att	Yds	Avg	Lg	TD
1961	DAL	A	1	-13	-13.0	-13	0
1962			1	13	13.0	13	0
1963	KC	A	1	10	10.0	10	0
Career			3	10	3.3	13	0

Adrian Burk

Year	Team		Att	Yds	Avg	Lg	TD
1950	BAL	N	11	19	1.7	10	1
1951	PHI	N	28	12	0.4	11	1
1952			7	28	4.0	12	0
1953			8	54	6.8	32t	3
1954			15	18	1.2	15	0
1955			36	132	3.7	30	2
1956			17	61	3.6	11	0
Career			122	324	2.7	32t	7

Chris Burkett

Year	Team		Att	Yds	Avg	Lg	TD
1989	NYJ	N	1	-4	-4.0	-4	0
1991			1	-2	-2.0	-2	0
Career			2	-6	-3.0	-2	0

Jeff Burkett

Year	Team		Att	Yds	Avg	Lg	TD
1947	CHIC	N	1	11	11.0	11	0

Ray Burks

Year	Team		Att	Yds	Avg	Lg	TD
1977	KC	N	1	51	51.0	51	0

Steve Burks

Year	Team		Att	Yds	Avg	Lg	TD
1976	NE	N	1	2	2.0	2	0

Alex Burl

Year	Team		Att	Yds	Avg	Lg	TD
1956	CHIC	N	1	2	2.0	2	0

Bobby Burnett

Year	Team		Att	Yds	Avg	Lg	TD
1966	BUF	A	187	766	4.1	32	4
1967			45	96	2.1	18	0
1969	DEN	A	5	9	1.8	5	0
Career			237	871	3.7	32	4
Playoffs			3	6	2.0		0

Dale Burnett

Year	Team		Att	Yds	Avg	Lg	TD
1930	NYG	N					4
1931							1
1933			17	36	2.1		0
1934			4	6	1.5		0
1936			10	0	0.0		0
1937			7	4	0.6		0
1938			6	13	2.2		0
1939			1	3	3.0	3	0
Career			45	62	1.4	3	5
Playoffs			2	3	1.5		0

Ray Burnett

Year	Team		Att	Yds	Avg	Lg	TD
1938	CHIC	N	1	-10	-10.0	-10	0

Tom Burnette

Year	Team		Att	Yds	Avg	Lg	TD
1938	PIT	N	1	0	0.0	0	0

Bob Burns

Year	Team		Att	Yds	Avg	Lg	TD
1974	NYJ	N	40	158	4.0	12	0

Jason Burns

Year	Team		Att	Yds	Avg	Lg	TD
1995	CIN	N	1	1	1.0	1	0

Leon Burns

Year	Team		Att	Yds	Avg	Lg	TD
1971	SD	N	61	223	3.7	25	1
1972	STL	N	26	69	2.7	9	2
Career			87	292	3.4	25	3

Johnny Burrell

Year	Team		Att	Yds	Avg	Lg	TD
1962	PIT	N	6	38	6.3	18	0

Ode Burrell

Year	Team		Att	Yds	Avg	Lg	TD
1964	HOU	A	8	10	1.3	5	0
1965			130	528	4.1	63	3
1966			122	406	3.3	45	0
1967			3	-3	-1.0	2	0
1969			41	147	3.6	19	0
Career			304	1088	3.6	63	3

Ken Burrough

Year	Team		Att	Yds	Avg	Lg	TD
1970	NO	N	1	4	4.0	4	0
1973	HOU	N	5	38	7.6	34	1
1974			1	0	0.0	0	0
1976			3	22	7.3	12	0
1977			4	10	2.5	28	0
1978			3	-11	-3.7	1	0
Career			17	63	3.7	34	1

Ken Burrow

Year	Team		Att	Yds	Avg	Lg	TD
1971	ATL	N	1	5	5.0	5	0
1972			3	3	1.0	8	0
1973			2	17	8.5	9	0
Career			6	25	4.2	9	0

Harry Burrus

Year	Team		Att	Yds	Avg	Lg	TD
1946	NY	AA	1	3	3.0	3	0
1947			1	5	5.0	5	0
1948	BKN	AA	1	-3	-3.0	-3	0
Career			3	5	1.7	5	0

Tony Burse

Year	Team		Att	Yds	Avg	Lg	TD
1987	SEA	N	7	36	5.1	16	0

Larry Burton

Year	Team		Att	Yds	Avg	Lg	TD
1975	NO	N	2	8	4.0	5	0
1976			3	-4	-1.3	4	0
Career			5	4	0.8	5	0

Leon Burton

Year	Team		Att	Yds	Avg	Lg	TD
1960	NY	A	16	119	7.4		1

Ron Burton

Year	Team		Att	Yds	Avg	Lg	TD
1960	BOS	A	66	280	4.2	77t	1
1961			82	260	3.2	43	2
1962			134	548	4.1	59	2
1964			102	340	3.3	33	3
1965			45	108	2.4	22	1
Career			429	1536	3.6	77t	9
Playoffs			9	15	1.7		0

Dexter Bussey

Year	Team		Att	Yds	Avg	Lg	TD
1974	DET	N	9	22	2.4	9	0
1975			157	696	4.4	32t	2
1976			196	858	4.4	46	3
1977			85	338	4.0	31	4
1978			225	924	4.1	36	5
1979			144	625	4.3	38	1
1980			145	720	5.0	40	3
1981			105	446	4.2	23	0
1982			48	136	2.8	10	0
1983			57	249	4.4	26	0
1984			32	91	2.8	18	0
Career			1203	5105	4.2	46	18
Playoffs			5	19	3.8		0

Young Bussey

Year	Team		Att	Yds	Avg	Lg	TD
1941	CHIB	N	13	9	0.7	16	0
Playoffs			1	-2	-2.0		0

Wendell Butcher

Year	Team		Att	Yds	Avg	Lg	TD
1938	BKN	N	39	99	2.5		1
1939			2	2	1.0		0
1941			1	2	2.0	2	0
Career			42	103	2.5	2	1

Dick Butkus

Year	Team		Att	Yds	Avg	Lg	TD
1972	CHI	N	1	28	28.0	28	0

Bill Butler

Year	Team		Att	Yds	Avg	Lg	TD
1959	GB	N	7	49	7.0	16	0
1963	MIN	N	17	48	2.8	11	0
1964			5	11	2.2	6	0
Career			29	108	3.7	16	0

Bill Butler

Year	Team		Att	Yds	Avg	Lg	TD
1972	NO	N	54	233	4.3	27	0
1973			87	348	4.0	19	1
1974			21	74	3.5	10	0
Career			162	655	4.0	27	1

Gary Butler

Year	Team		Att	Yds	Avg	Lg	TD
1973	KC	N	2	10	5.0	9	0

Jerry Butler

Year	Team		Att	Yds	Avg	Lg	TD
1979	BUF	N	2	13	6.5	12	0
1980			1	18	18.0	18	0
1981			1	1	1.0	1	0
Career			4	32	8.0	18	0

Jerry Butler

Year	Team		Att	Yds	Avg	Lg	TD
1987	ATL	N	1	1	1.0	1	0

Jim Butler

Year	Team		Att	Yds	Avg	Lg	TD
1965	PIT	N	46	108	2.3	12	0
1966			46	114	2.5	19	2
1967			90	293	3.3	24	0
1968	ATL		94	365	3.9	60t	2
1969			163	655	4.0	39	3
1970			166	636	3.8	33	0
1971			186	594	3.2	19	2
1972	STL		6	3	0.5	5	0
Career			797	2768	3.5	60t	9

Johnny Butler

Year	Team		Att	Yds	Avg	Lg	TD
1943	P-P	N	87	362	4.2	69	3
1944	C-P-BKN	N	60	94	1.6	14	0
1945	PHI	N	21	61	2.9	18	1
Career			168	517	3.1	69	4

Ray Butler

Year	Team		Att	Yds	Avg	Lg	TD
1982	BAL	N	3	10	3.3	10	0
1985	IND	N	1	-1	-1.0	-1	0
Career			4	9	2.3	10	0

Skip Butler

Year	Team		Att	Yds	Avg	Lg	TD
1976	HOU	N	1	0	0.0	0	0

Sol Butler

Year	Team		Att	Yds	Avg	Lg	TD
1924	HAM-AKR	N					2

Greg Buttle

Year	Team		Att	Yds	Avg	Lg	TD
1976	NYJ	N	1	26	26.0	26	0

Marion Butts

Year	Team		Att	Yds	Avg	Lg	TD
1989	SD	N	170	683	4.0	50t	9
1990			265	1225	4.6	52	8
1991			193	834	4.3	44	6
1992			218	809	3.7	22	4
1993			185	746	4.0	27	4
1994	NE	N	243	703	2.9	26	8
1995	HOU	N	71	185	2.6	9	4
Career			1345	5185	3.9	52	43
Playoffs			22	144	6.5		1

Keith Byars

Year	Team		Att	Yds	Avg	Lg	TD
1986	PHI	N	177	577	3.3	32	1
1987			116	426	3.7	30	3
1988			152	517	3.4	52	6
1989			133	452	3.4	16t	5
1990			37	141	3.8	23	0
1991			94	383	4.1	28	1
1992			41	176	4.3	23	1
1993	MIA	N	64	269	4.2	77t	3
1994			19	64	3.4	12	2
1995			15	44	2.9	15	1
1996	NE	N	2	2	1.0	3	0
Career			850	3051	3.6	77t	23
Playoffs			14	65	4.6		0

Earnest Byner

Year	Team		Att	Yds	Avg	Lg	TD
1984	CLE	N	72	426	5.9	54	2
1985			244	1002	4.1	36	8
1986			94	277	2.9	37	2
1987			105	432	4.1	21	8
1988			157	576	3.7	27t	3
1989	WAS	N	134	580	4.3	24	7
1990			297	1219	4.1	22	6
1991			274	1048	3.8	32	5
1992			262	998	3.8	23	6
1993			23	105	4.6	16	1
1994	CLE	N	75	219	2.9	15	2
1995			115	432	3.8	23	2
1996	BAL	N	159	634	4.0	42	4
Career			2011	7948	4.0	54	56
Playoffs			186	839	4.5		5

Carl Byrum

Year	Team		Att	Yds	Avg	Lg	TD
1986	BUF	N	38	156	4.1	18	0
1987			66	280	4.2	30	0
1988			28	91	3.3	11	0
Career			132	527	4.0	30	0
Playoffs			2	3	1.5		0

Larry Cabrelli

Year	Team		Att	Yds	Avg	Lg	TD
1944	PHI	N	1	-2	-2.0	-2	0

Ernie Caddel

Year	Team		Att	Yds	Avg	Lg	TD
1933	POR	N	74	286	3.9		3
1934	DET	N	101	428	4.2		4
1935			87	450	5.2		5
1936			91	580	6.4		4
1937			76	429	5.6		3
1938			14	38	2.7		1
Career			443	2211	5.0		20
Playoffs				62			1

George Cafego

Year	Team		Att	Yds	Avg	Lg	TD
1940	BKN	N	41	109	2.7		0
1943	BKN-WAS	N	34	-12	-0.4	20	0
1944	BOS	N	61	31	0.5	17	1
1945			19	-51	-2.7	3	0
Career			155	77	0.5	20	1
Playoffs			6	-11	-1.8		0

Chris Cagle

Year	Team		Att	Yds	Avg	Lg	TD
1931	NYG	N					1
1932							1
Career							2

Ronnie Cahill

Year	Team		Att	Yds	Avg	Lg	TD
1943	CHIC	N	62	-11	-0.2	25	0

Lynn Cain

Year	Team		Att	Yds	Avg	Lg	TD
1979	ATL	N	63	295	4.7	35t	2
1980			235	914	3.9	37	8
1981			156	542	3.5	35	4
1982			54	173	3.2	8	1
1983			19	63	3.3	48	0
1984			77	276	3.6	31t	3
1985	LARM	N	11	46	4.2	9	0
Career			615	2309	3.8	48	19
Playoffs			16	60	3.8		1

Pete Calac

Year	Team		Att	Yds	Avg	Lg	TD
1920	CAN	A					2
1921	CLE	A					3
1922	OOR	N					2
1924	BUF	N					2
Career							9

Bruce Caldwell

Year	Team		Att	Yds	Avg	Lg	TD
1928	NYG	N					1

Scotty Caldwell

Year	Team		Att	Yds	Avg	Lg	TD
1987	DEN	N	16	53	3.3	7	0

Jamie Caleb

Year	Team		Att	Yds	Avg	Lg	TD
1960	CLE	N	8	60	7.5	30	1
1961	MIN	N	3	11	3.7	4	0
Career			11	71	6.5	30	1

Don Calhoun

Year	Team		Att	Yds	Avg	Lg	TD
1974	BUF	N	21	88	4.2	15	0

Don Calhoun *continued*

Year	Team		Att	Yds	Avg	Lg	TD
1975	BUF-NE	N	42	184	4.4	38t	1
1976	NE	N	129	721	5.6	54	1
1977			198	727	3.7	25	4
1978			76	391	5.1	73	1
1979			137	456	3.3	29	5
1980			200	787	3.9	22t	9
1981			57	205	3.6	33	2
Career			860	3559	4.1	73	23
Playoffs			5	17	3.4		0

Rick Calhoun

Year	Team		Att	Yds	Avg	Lg	TD
1987	LARI	N	7	36	5.1	18	0

Jack Call

Year	Team		Att	Yds	Avg	Lg	TD
1957	BAL	N	33	145	4.4	24	0
1958			37	154	4.2	35	0
1959	PIT	N	3	9	3.0	4	0
Career			73	308	4.2	35	0

Jim Callahan

Year	Team		Att	Yds	Avg	Lg	TD
1946	DET	N	52	86	1.7	40	2

Ken Callicut

Year	Team		Att	Yds	Avg	Lg	TD
1979	DET	N	3	6	2.0	10	0

Len Calligaro

Year	Team		Att	Yds	Avg	Lg	TD
1944	NYG	N	3	4	1.3	3	1

Bill Callihan

Year	Team		Att	Yds	Avg	Lg	TD
1943	DET	N	5	17	3.4	6	1
1944			1	3	3.0	3	0
1945			27	85	3.1	16	0
Career			33	105	3.2	16	1

Chris Calloway

Year	Team		Att	Yds	Avg	Lg	TD
1994	NYG	N	8	77	9.6	20	0
1995			2	-9	-4.5	-3	0
1996			1	2	2.0	2	0
Career			11	70	6.4	20	0

Tom Calvin

Year	Team		Att	Yds	Avg	Lg	TD
1952	PIT	N	7	14	2.0	11	0
1953			13	65	5.0	15	0
1954			12	57	4.8	8	0
Career			32	136	4.3	15	0

Rich Camarillo

Year	Team		Att	Yds	Avg	Lg	TD
1987	NE	N	1	0	0.0	0	0
1990	PHX	N	1	-11	-11.0	-11	0
1993			1	0	0.0	0	0
Career			3	-11	-3.7	0	0

Jim Camp

Year	Team		Att	Yds	Avg	Lg	TD
1948	BKN	AA	8	43	5.4		

Al Campana

Year	Team		Att	Yds	Avg	Lg	TD
1950	CHIB	N	45	134	3.0	23	1
1951			2	3	1.5	3	0
1952			9	14	1.6	6	0
1953	CHIC	N	2	-5	-2.5		0
Career			58	146	2.5	23	1
Playoffs			4	29	7.3		1

Bob Campbell

Year	Team		Att	Yds	Avg	Lg	TD
1969	PIT	N	1	5	5.0	5	0

Earl Campbell

Year	Team		Att	Yds	Avg	Lg	TD
1978	HOU	N	302	1450	4.8	81t	13
1979			368	1697	4.6	61t	19
1980			373	1934	5.2	55t	13
1981			361	1376	3.8	43	10
1982			157	538	3.4	22	2
1983			322	1301	4.0	42	12
1984	HOU-NO	N	146	468	3.2	22	4
1985	NO	N	158	643	4.1	45	1
Career			2187	9407	4.3	81t	74
Playoffs			135	420	3.1		4

Jeff Campbell

Year	Team		Att	Yds	Avg	Lg	TD
1994	DEN	N	2	6	3.0	6	0

Leon Campbell

Year	Team		Att	Yds	Avg	Lg	TD
1950	BAL	N	20	93	4.7	14	0

Leon Campbell *continued*

Year	Team		Att	Yds	Avg	Lg	TD
1952	CHIB	N	24	76	3.2	18	0
1953			22	130	5.9	39	0
1954			18	38	2.1	24	0
1955	PIT	N	18	42	2.3	27	0
Career			102	379	3.7	39	0

Mike Campbell

Year	Team		Att	Yds	Avg	Lg	TD
1968	DET	N	7	24	3.4	5	0

Milt Campbell

Year	Team		Att	Yds	Avg	Lg	TD
1957	CLE	N	7	23	3.3	14	0

Rich Campbell

Year	Team		Att	Yds	Avg	Lg	TD
1984	GB	N	2	2	1.0	5	0

Scott Campbell

Year	Team		Att	Yds	Avg	Lg	TD
1984	PIT	N	3	-5	-1.7	0	0
1985			9	28	3.1	14	0
1986	ATL	N	1	7	7.0	7	0
1987			21	102	4.9	24	2
1990			9	38	4.2	20	0
Career			43	170	4.0	24	2

Sonny Campbell

Year	Team		Att	Yds	Avg	Lg	TD
1970	ATL	N	28	116	4.1	15	2
1971			29	79	2.7	8	0
Career			57	195	3.4	15	2

Woody Campbell

Year	Team		Att	Yds	Avg	Lg	TD
1967	HOU	A	110	511	4.6	42	4
1968			115	436	3.8	37	6
1969			28	98	3.5	10	1
1970	HOU	N	59	189	3.2	28	1
1971			96	259	2.7	18	1
Career			408	1493	3.7	42	13
Playoffs			7	15	2.1		0

Billy Campfield

Year	Team		Att	Yds	Avg	Lg	TD
1978	PHI	N	61	247	4.0	50	0
1979			30	165	5.5	40	3
1980			44	120	2.7	9	1
1981			31	115	3.7	13	1
1982			1	2	2.0	2	0
1983	NYG	N	2	21	10.5	0	0
Career			169	670	4.0	50	5
Playoffs			3	13	4.3		0

Bob Campiglio

Year	Team		Att	Yds	Avg	Lg	TD
1932	SI	N	104	504	4.8		2

Larry Canada

Year	Team		Att	Yds	Avg	Lg	TD
1978	DEN	N	79	365	4.6	47	3
1979			36	143	4.0	17	0
1981			33	113	3.4	11	3
Career			148	621	4.2	47	6
Playoffs			5	32	6.4		0

Tony Canadeo

Year	Team		Att	Yds	Avg	Lg	TD
1941	GB	N	43	137	3.2	16	3
1942			89	272	3.1	50	3
1943			94	489	5.2	35	3
1944			31	149	4.8	34	0
1946			122	476	3.9	27	0
1947			103	464	4.5	35	2
1948			123	589	4.8	49	4
1949			208	1052	5.1	54	4
1950			93	247	2.7	15	4
1951			54	131	2.4	15	1
1952			65	191	2.9	35	2
Career			1025	4197	4.1	54	26
Playoffs			5	7	1.4		0

Jim Canady

Year	Team		Att	Yds	Avg	Lg	TD
1948	CHIB	N	2	8	4.0	6	0
1949	CHIB-NYB	N	23	91	4.0	46	0
Career			25	99	4.0	46	0

Sheldon Canley

Year	Team		Att	Yds	Avg	Lg	TD
1992	NYJ	N	4	9	2.3	4	0

John Cannady

Year	Team		Att	Yds	Avg	Lg	TD
1947	NYG	N	1	14	14.0	14	0

Tony Cannava

Year	Team		Att	Yds	Avg	Lg	TD
1950	GB	N	1	2	2.0	2	0

Billy Cannon

Year	Team		Att	Yds	Avg	Lg	TD
1960	HOU	A	152	644	4.2	39	1
1961			200	948	4.7	61	6
1962			147	474	3.2	64	7
1963			13	45	3.5	12	0
1964	OAK	A	89	338	3.8	34	3
1970	KC	N	1	6	6.0	6	0
Career			602	2455	4.1	64	17
Playoffs			44	135	3.1		1

Leo Cantor

Year	Team		Att	Yds	Avg	Lg	TD
1942	NYG	N	67	124	1.9	18	2
1945	CHIC	N	83	291	3.5	18	5
Career			150	415	2.8	18	7

Wayne Capers

Year	Team		Att	Yds	Avg	Lg	TD
1984	PIT	N	1	-3	-3.0	-3	0
1985	IND	N	3	18	6.0	20t	0
1986			1	11	11.0	11	0
Career			5	26	5.2	20t	1

Bob Cappadona

Year	Team		Att	Yds	Avg	Lg	TD
1966	BOS	A	22	88	4.0	13	1
1967			28	100	3.6	11	0
1968	BUF	A	73	272	3.7	33t	1
Career			123	460	3.7	33t	2

Gino Cappelletti

Year	Team		Att	Yds	Avg	Lg	TD
1962	BOS	A	1	-5	-5.0	-5	0
1963			1	2	2.0	2	0
1964			1	7	7.0	7	0
1968			1	2	2.0	2	0
Career			4	6	1.5	7	0

John Cappelletti

Year	Team		Att	Yds	Avg	Lg	TD
1974	LA	N	55	198	3.6	20	0
1975			48	158	3.3	30t	1
1976			177	688	3.9	38	1
1977			178	598	3.4	15	5
1978			174	604	3.5	26	3
1980	SD	N	101	364	3.6	46	5
1981			68	254	3.7	30	4
1982			22	82	3.7	17	0
1983			1	5	5.0	5	0
Career			824	2951	3.6	46	24
Playoffs			63	211	3.3		1

Bill Cappelman

Year	Team		Att	Yds	Avg	Lg	TD
1973	DET	N	1	-2	-2.0	-2	0

Dom Cara

Year	Team		Att	Yds	Avg	Lg	TD
1938	PIT	N	1	-1	-1.0	-1	0

Glenn Carano

Year	Team		Att	Yds	Avg	Lg	TD
1980	DAL	N	4	6	1.5	5	0
1981			8	9	1.1	11	0
Career			12	15	1.3	11	0

Joe Caravello

Year	Team		Att	Yds	Avg	Lg	TD
1989	SD	N	1	0	0.0	0	0

Lloyd Cardwell

Year	Team		Att	Yds	Avg	Lg	TD
1937	DET	N	36	181	5.0		0
1938			73	294			4
1939			29	141	4.9		1
1940			48	186	3.9		0
1941			10	19	1.9	12	0
1942			6	78	13.0	80	1
1943			3	6	2.0	2	0
Career			205	905	4.4	80	8

Harland Carl

Year	Team		Att	Yds	Avg	Lg	TD
1956	CHIB	N	29	66	2.3	12	1

Cody Carlson

Year	Team		Att	Yds	Avg	Lg	TD
1988	HOU	N	12	36	3.0	10	1
1989			3	-3	-1.0	0	0
1990			11	52	4.7	16	0
1991			4	-3	-0.8	0	0
1992			27	77	2.9	13	1
1993			14	41	2.9	10t	1

Cody Carlson *continued*

Year	Team		Att	Yds	Avg	Lg	TD
1994			10	17	1.7	6	0
Career			81	217	2.7	16	4
Playoffs			4	22	5.5		0

Dean Carlson

Year	Team		Att	Yds	Avg	Lg	TD
1974	KC	N	2	17	8.5	11	0

Jeff Carlson

Year	Team		Att	Yds	Avg	Lg	TD
1990	TB	N	1	0	0.0	0	0
1991			5	25	5.0	11	0
1992	NE	N	11	32	2.9	7	0
Career			17	57	3.4	11	0

Wray Carlton

Year	Team		Att	Yds	Avg	Lg	TD
1960	BUF	A	137	533	3.9	54t	7
1961			101	311	3.1	27	4
1962			94	530	5.6	51	2
1963			29	125	4.3	19	0
1964			39	114	2.9	11	1
1965			156	592	3.8	80	6
1966			156	696	4.5	23	6
1967			107	467	4.4	21	3
Career			819	3368	4.1	80	29
Playoffs			43	164	3.8		1

Al Carmichael

Year	Team		Att	Yds	Avg	Lg	TD
1953	GB	N	49	199	4.1	41t	1
1954			33	130	3.9	23	0
1955			6	45	7.5	20	0
1956			32	199	6.2	35	0
1957			37	118	3.2	10	1
1958			9	21	2.3	8	0
1960	DEN	A	41	211	5.1	47	2
1961			15	24	1.6	8	0
Career			222	947	4.3	47	4

Harold Carmichael

Year	Team		Att	Yds	Avg	Lg	TD
1973	PHI	N	3	42	14.0	23	0
1974			2	-6	-3.0	-1	0
1975			1	6	6.0	6	0
1978			1	21	21.0	21	0
1979			1	0	0.0	0	0
1981			1	1	1.0	1	0
Career			9	64	7.1	23	0

Ray Carnelly

Year	Team		Att	Yds	Avg	Lg	TD
1939	BKN	N	15	64	4.3		0

J.C. Caroline

Year	Team		Att	Yds	Avg	Lg	TD
1956	CHIB	N	34	141	4.1	26	2
1957			1	1	1.0	1	0
1958			33	121	3.7	19	0
Career			68	263	3.9	26	2
Playoffs			7	10	1.4		0

Ken Carpenter

Year	Team		Att	Yds	Avg	Lg	TD
1950	CLE	N	35	181	5.2	61t	1
1951			85	402	4.7	30	4
1952			72	408	5.7	37	3
1953			46	195	4.2	30	3
1960	DEN	A	4	13	3.3	9	0
Career			242	1199	5.0	61t	11
Playoffs			10	41	4.1		1

Lew Carpenter

Year	Team		Att	Yds	Avg	Lg	TD
1953	DET	N	7	24	3.4	13	0
1954			104	476	4.6	60t	3
1955			137	543	4.0	49t	6
1957	CLE	N	83	315	3.8	55	4
1958			73	308	4.2	30	2
1959	GB	N	60	322	5.4	55t	3
1960			1	24	24.0	24	0
1961			1	5	5.0	5	0
1963			2	8	4.0	5	0
Career			468	2025	4.3	60t	16
Playoffs			25	149	6.0		1

Preston Carpenter

Year	Team		Att	Yds	Avg	Lg	TD
1956	CLE	N	188	756	4.0	30	0
1957			3	86	28.7	39	1
1958			3	2	0.7	22	0
1959			1	4	4.0	4	0
1960	PIT	N	17	36	2.1	20	0

Preston Carpenter *continued*

Year	Team		Att	Yds	Avg	Lg	TD
1961			7	9	1.3	13	0
1962			1	-3	-3.0	-3	0
1963			1	-3	-3.0	-3	0
1964	WAS	N	1	7	7.0	7	0
1966	MIN	N	1	-10	-10.0	-10	0
Career			223	884	4.0	39	1

Rob Carpenter

Year	Team		Att	Yds	Avg	Lg	TD
1977	HOU	N	144	652	4.5	77	1
1978			82	348	4.2	20	5
1979			92	355	3.9	13	3
1980			97	359	3.7	46	3
1981	HOU-NYG	N	208	822	4.0	35	5
1982	NYG	N	67	204	3.0	23	1
1983			170	624	3.7	37	4
1984			250	795	3.2	22	7
1985			60	201	3.4	46	0
1986	LARM	N	2	3	1.5	3	0
1992	NYJ	N	1	2	2.0	2	0
Career			1173	4365	3.7	77	29
Playoffs			109	406	3.7		1

Earl Carr

Year	Team		Att	Yds	Avg	Lg	TD
1978	SF	N	1	2	2.0	2	0
1979	PHI	N	1	-1	-1.0	-1	0
Career			2	1	0.5	2	0

Ed Carr

Year	Team		Att	Yds	Avg	Lg	TD
1947	SF	AA	11	42	3.8		0
1948			14	121	8.6	54	1
1949			19	120	6.3		2
Career			44	283	6.4	54	3

Harlan Carr

Year	Team		Att	Yds	Avg	Lg	TD
1927	BUF-POT	N					2

Jimmy Carr

Year	Team		Att	Yds	Avg	Lg	TD
1955	CHIC	N	30	115	3.8	41	0

Roger Carr

Year	Team		Att	Yds	Avg	Lg	TD
1980	BAL	N	1	-8	-8.0	-8	0
Playoffs			1	-13	-13.0		0

Duane Carrell

Year	Team		Att	Yds	Avg	Lg	TD
1976	NYJ	N	2	0	0.0	0	0
1977			2	-15	-7.5	0	0
Career			4	-15	-3.8	0	0

Mark Carrier

Year	Team		Att	Yds	Avg	Lg	TD
1993	CLE	N	4	26	6.5	15t	1
1994			1	14	14.0	14t	1
1995	CAR	N	3	-4	-1.3	4	0
Career			8	36	4.5	15t	2

Paul Ott Carruth

Year	Team		Att	Yds	Avg	Lg	TD
1986	GB	N	81	308	3.8	42	2
1987			64	192	3.0	23	3
1988			49	114	2.3	14	0
Career			194	614	3.2	42	5

Carlos Carson

Year	Team		Att	Yds	Avg	Lg	TD
1980	KC	N	2	41	20.5	37	0
1981			1	-1	-1.0	-1	0
1983			2	20	10.0	18	0
1984			1	-8	-8.0	-8	0
1985			3	25	8.3	13	0
1987			1	-7	-7.0	-7	0
1988			1	1	1.0	1	0
1989	PHI	N	1	-9	-9.0	-9	0
Career			12	62	5.2	37	0

Kern Carson

Year	Team		Att	Yds	Avg	Lg	TD
1965	NY	A	7	25	3.6	15	2

Allen Carter

Year	Team		Att	Yds	Avg	Lg	TD
1975	NE	N	22	95	4.3	19	0

Anthony Carter

Year	Team		Att	Yds	Avg	Lg	TD
1986	MIN	N	1	12	12.0	12	0
1988			4	41	10.3	21	0
1989			3	18	6.0	17	0
1990			3	16	5.3	11	0
1991			13	117	9.0	32	1

Anthony Carter *continued*

Year	Team		Att	Yds	Avg	Lg	TD
1992			16	66	4.1	14	1
1993			7	19	2.7	9	0
Career			47	289	6.1	32	2
Playoffs			2	34	17.0		0

Cris Carter

Year	Team		Att	Yds	Avg	Lg	TD
1988	PHI	N	1	1	1.0	1	0
1989			2	16	8.0	11	0
1990	MIN	N	2	6	3.0	8	0
1992			5	15	3.0	6	0
1995			1	0	0.0	0	0
Career			11	38	3.5	11	0

Dale Carter

Year	Team		Att	Yds	Avg	Lg	TD
1993	KC	N	1	2	2.0	2	0
1996			1	3	3.0	3	0
Career			2	5	2.5	3	0

Dexter Carter

Year	Team		Att	Yds	Avg	Lg	TD
1990	SF	N	114	460	4.0	74t	1
1991			85	379	4.5	53t	2
1992			4	9	2.3	6	0
1993			10	72	7.2	50t	1
1994			8	34	4.3	18	0
1995			7	22	3.1	15	0
1996			19	66	3.5	18	1
Career			247	1042	4.2	74t	5
Playoffs			4	21	5.3		0

Gerald Carter

Year	Team		Att	Yds	Avg	Lg	TD
1983	TB	N	1	0	0.0	0	0
1984			1	16	16.0	16	0
1985			1	13	13.0	13	0
1986			1	-5	-5.0	-5	0
Career			4	24	6.0	16	0

Joe Carter

Year	Team		Att	Yds	Avg	Lg	TD
1939	PHI	N	1	4	4.0	4	0
1940			1	-3	-3.0	-3	0
Career			2	1	0.5	4	0

Joe Carter

Year	Team		Att	Yds	Avg	Lg	TD
1984	MIA	N	100	495	5.0	35	1
1985			14	76	5.4	19	0
1986			4	18	4.5	9	0
Career			118	589	5.0	35	1
Playoffs			9	66	7.3		0

Ki-Jana Carter

Year	Team		Att	Yds	Avg	Lg	TD
1996	CIN	N	91	264	2.9	31t	8

Louis Carter

Year	Team		Att	Yds	Avg	Lg	TD
1975	OAK	N	11	27	2.5	11	0
1976	TB	N	171	521	3.0	26	1
1977			59	117	2.0	20	2
1978			81	275	3.4	17	1
Career			322	940	2.9	26	4

Mike Carter

Year	Team		Att	Yds	Avg	Lg	TD
1972	SD	N	1	25	25.0	25	0

Rodney Carter

Year	Team		Att	Yds	Avg	Lg	TD
1987	PIT	N	5	12	2.4	4	0
1988			36	216	6.0	64t	3
1989			11	16	1.5	7	1
Career			52	244	4.7	64t	4

Tony Carter

Year	Team		Att	Yds	Avg	Lg	TD
1995	CHI	N	10	34	3.4	7	0
1996			11	43	3.9	23	0
Career			21	77	3.7	23	0
Playoffs			1	0	0.0		0

Virgil Carter

Year	Team		Att	Yds	Avg	Lg	TD
1968	CHI	N	48	265	5.5	31	4
1969			4	19	4.8	11	0
1970	CIN	N	34	246	7.2	73	2
1971			8	42	5.3	19	0
1972			12	57	4.8	14	2
1975	SD	N	2	11	5.5	9	0
1976	CHI	N	1	0	0.0	0	0
Career			109	640	5.9	73	8
Playoffs			2	16	8.0		0

Willie Carter

Year	Team	Att	Yds	Avg	Lg	TD
1953	CHIC	N	2	-3	-1.5	2	0

Maurice Carthon

Year	Team		Att	Yds	Avg	Lg	TD
1985	NYG	N	27	70	2.6	12	0
1986			72	260	3.6	12	0
1987			26	60	2.3	10	0
1988			46	146	3.2	8	2
1989			57	153	2.7	18	0
1990			36	143	4.0	12	0
1991			32	109	3.4	10	0
1992	IND	N	4	9	2.3	5	0
Career			300	950	3.2	18	2
Playoffs			30	91	3.0		1

Mel Carver

Year	Team		Att	Yds	Avg	Lg	TD
1982	TB	N	70	229	3.3	13t	1
1983			114	348	3.1	16	0
1984			11	44	4.0	12	0
1987	IND	N	2	3	1.5	3	0
Career			197	624	3.2	16	1
Playoffs			7	12	1.7		0

Ken Casanega

Year	Team		Att	Yds	Avg	Lg	TD
1946	SF	AA	29	90	3.1		1

Tommy Casanova

Year	Team		Att	Yds	Avg	Lg	TD
1977	CIN	N	1	20	20.0	20	0

Rick Casares

Year	Team		Att	Yds	Avg	Lg	TD
1955	CHIB	N	125	672	5.4	81t	4
1956			234	1126	4.8	68t	12
1957			204	700	3.4	25t	6
1958			176	651	3.7	64t	2
1959			177	699	3.9	47	10
1960	CHI	N	160	566	3.5	35	5
1961			135	588	4.4	23	8
1962			75	255	3.4	18	2
1963			65	277	4.3	30	0
1964			35	123	3.5	28	0
1965	WAS	N	2	5	2.5	3	0
1966	MIA	A	43	135	3.1	10	0
Career			1431	5797	4.1	81t	49
Playoffs			14	43	3.1		1

Ernie Case

Year	Team		Att	Yds	Avg	Lg	TD
1947	BAL	AA	1	0	0.0	0	0

Pete Case

Year	Team		Att	Yds	Avg	Lg	TD
1967	NYG	N	0	16		16L	0

Stoney Case

Year	Team		Att	Yds	Avg	Lg	TD
1995	ARI	N	1	4	4.0	4	0

Bernie Casey

Year	Team		Att	Yds	Avg	Lg	TD
1966	SF	N	1	23	23.0	23	0

Tom Casey

Year	Team		Att	Yds	Avg	Lg	TD
1948	NY	AA	18	75	4.2		0

Keith Cash

Year	Team		Att	Yds	Avg	Lg	TD
1993	KC	N	1	0	0.0	0	0

Jim Cason

Year	Team		Att	Yds	Avg	Lg	TD
1948	SF	AA	20	146	7.3	59t	2
1949			21	70	3.3		1
1950	SF	N	38	129	3.4	24t	1
1951			1	5	5.0	5	0
1954			2	1	0.5	3	0
Career			82	351	4.3	59t	4

Cy Casper

Year	Team		Att	Yds	Avg	Lg	TD
1935	PIT	N	56	102	1.8		1

Dave Casper

Year	Team		Att	Yds	Avg	Lg	TD
1976	OAK	N	1	5	5.0	5	0
1978			1	5	5.0	5	0
1980	HOU	N	2	8	4.0	6	0
1982			2	9	4.5	8	0
Career			6	27	4.5	8	0
Playoffs			1	-13	-13.0		0

Howard Cassady

Year	Team		Att	Yds	Avg	Lg	TD
1956	DET	N	97	413	4.3	33	0

Howard Cassady continued

Year	Team		Att	Yds	Avg	Lg	TD
1957			73	250	3.4	57	3
1958			45	198	4.4	33	0
1959			52	203	3.9	13	1
1960			17	28	1.6	10	1
1961			31	131	4.2	14	1
1962	PHI	N	1	6	6.0	6	0
Career			316	1229	3.9	57	6
Playoffs			11	53	4.8		0

Frank Cassara

Year	Team		Att	Yds	Avg	Lg	TD
1954	SF	N	3	17	5.7	10	0

Tom Cassese

Year	Team		Att	Yds	Avg	Lg	TD
1967	DEN	A	1	5	5.0	5	0

Dick Cassiano

Year	Team		Att	Yds	Avg	Lg	TD
1940	BKN	N	35	84	2.4		0

Mike Casteel

Year	Team		Att	Yds	Avg	Lg	TD
1922	RI	N					1

Rich Caster

Year	Team		Att	Yds	Avg	Lg	TD
1971	NYJ	N	2	10	5.0	17	0
1972			2	6	3.0	6	0
1973			1	-9	-9.0	-9	0
1976			6	73	12.2	60	0
1977			2	-15	-7.5	-6	0
1978	HOU	N	5	32	6.4	11	0
1979			4	25	6.3	10	0
1981	NO	N	1	-3	-3.0	-3	0
Career			23	119	5.2	60	0
Playoffs			1	0	0.0		0

Jim Castiglia

Year	Team		Att	Yds	Avg	Lg	TD
1941	PHI	N	60	183	3.0	47	4
1945			13	39	3.0	6	0
1946			39	87	2.2	14	1
1947	BAL-WAS		113	444	3.9		5
1948	WAS	N	97	330	3.4	16	0
Career			322	1083	3.4	47	10

Greg Cater

Year	Team		Att	Yds	Avg	Lg	TD
1980	BUF	N	2	-10	-5.0	-1	0
1987	STL	N	2	3	1.5	11	0
Career			4	-7	-1.8	11	0

Royal Cathcart

Year	Team		Att	Yds	Avg	Lg	TD
1950	SF	N	3	5	1.7	3	0

Sam Cathcart

Year	Team		Att	Yds	Avg	Lg	TD
1949	SF	AA	69	412	6.0	57	1
1950	SF	N	33	76	2.3	17	0
1952			6	21	3.5	7	0
Career			108	509	4.7	57	1
Playoffs			13	22	1.7		0

Daryl Cato

Year	Team		Att	Yds	Avg	Lg	TD
1946	MIA	AA	0	3		3L	0

Matt Cavanaugh

Year	Team		Att	Yds	Avg	Lg	TD
1979	NE	N	1	-2	-2.0	-2	0
1980			19	97	5.1	22	0
1981			17	92	5.4	11	3
1982			2	3	1.5	3	0
1983	SF	N	1	8	8.0	8	0
1984			4	-11	-2.8	-1	0
1985			4	5	1.3	13	0
1986	PHI	N	9	26	2.9	11	0
1987			1	-2	-2.0	-2	0
1989			2	-3	-1.5	0	0
Career			60	213	3.5	22	3
Playoffs			1	2	2.0		0

John Cavosie

Year	Team		Att	Yds	Avg	Lg	TD
1932	POR	N					2

Bob Celeri

Year	Team		Att	Yds	Avg	Lg	TD
1951	NYY	N	36	107	3.0	17	0
1952	DAL	N	17	135	7.9	31	0
Career			53	242	4.6	31	0

Larry Centers

Year	Team		Att	Yds	Avg	Lg	TD
1991	PHX	N	14	44	3.1	8	0

Larry Centers continued

Year	Team		Att	Yds	Avg	Lg	TD
1992			37	139	3.8	28	0
1993			25	152	6.1	33	0
1994	ARI	N	115	336	2.9	17	5
1995			78	254	3.3	20	2
1996			116	425	3.7	24	2
Career			385	1350	3.5	33	9

Frank Cephous

Year	Team		Att	Yds	Avg	Lg	TD
1984	NYG	N	3	2	0.7	2	0

Jeff Chadwick

Year	Team		Att	Yds	Avg	Lg	TD
1984	DET	N	1	12	12.0	12t	1
1987			1	-6	-6.0	-6	0
1990	SEA	N	1	-3	-3.0	-3	0
Career			3	3	1.0	12t	1

Pat Chaffey

Year	Team		Att	Yds	Avg	Lg	TD
1991	ATL	N	29	127	4.4	27	1
1992	NYJ	N	27	186	6.9	32	1
1993			5	17	3.4	7	0
Career			61	330	5.4	32	2
Playoffs			3	8	2.7		0

Guy Chamberlin

Year	Team		Att	Yds	Avg	Lg	TD
1922	CAN	N					3

Bob Chandler

Year	Team		Att	Yds	Avg	Lg	TD
1972	BUF	N	3	27	9.0	16	0
1973			5	-14	-2.8	18	0
1975			2	5	2.5	5	0
1976			1	0	0.0	0	0
Career			11	18	1.6	18	0

Chris Chandler

Year	Team		Att	Yds	Avg	Lg	TD
1988	IND	N	46	139	3.0	29t	3
1989			7	57	8.1	23	1
1990	TB	N	13	71	5.5	18	1
1991	TB-PHX	N	26	111	4.3	12	0
1992	PHX	N	36	149	4.1	18	1
1993			3	2	0.7	1	0
1994	LARM	N	18	61	3.4	22	1
1995	HOU	N	28	58	2.1	9	2
1996			28	113	4.0	16	0
Career			205	761	3.7	29t	9

Don Chandler

Year	Team		Att	Yds	Avg	Lg	TD
1956	NYG	N	1	7	7.0	7	0
1957			1	2	2.0	2	0
1958			1	15	15.0	15	0
1959			1	24	24.0	24	0
1960			2	19	9.5	24	0
1961			3	30	10.0	30	0
1962			1	-11	-11.0	-11	0
1963			1	0	0.0	0	0
1965	GB	N	1	27	27.0	27	0
1966			1	33	33.0	33	0
Career			13	146	11.2	33	0

Wes Chandler

Year	Team		Att	Yds	Avg	Lg	TD
1978	NO	N	2	10	5.0	10	0
1980			1	9	9.0	9	0
1981	SD	N	5	-1	-0.2	9	0
1982			5	32	6.4	21	0
1983			2	25	12.5	23	0
1985			1	9	9.0	9	0
Career			16	84	5.3	23	0

Lynn Chandnois

Year	Team		Att	Yds	Avg	Lg	TD
1950	PIT	N	71	216	3.0	17	0
1951			108	332	3.1	34	2
1952			97	298	3.1	25	1
1953			123	470	3.8	38	3
1954			45	147	3.3	15	1
1955			105	353	3.4	23	5
1956			44	118	2.7	28	4
Career			593	1934	3.3	38	16

Dave Chapple

Year	Team		Att	Yds	Avg	Lg	TD
1973	LA	N	1	0	0.0	0	0

Bob Chappuis

Year	Team		Att	Yds	Avg	Lg	TD
1948	BKN	AA	52	310	6.0		1

Year	Team		Att	Yds	Avg	Lg	TD

Bob Chappuis *continued*

Year	Team		Att	Yds	Avg	Lg	TD
1949	CHI	AA	4	13	3.3		0
Career			56	323	5.8		1

Cliff Chatman

1982	NYG	N	22	80	3.6	13	2

Lloyd Cheatham

1942	CHIC	N	1	1	1.0	1	0
1946	NY	AA	3	2	0.7		0
1947			1	-2	-2.0	-2	0
1948			2	1	0.5		0
Career			7	2	0.3	1	0

Ed Cherry

1938	CHIC	N	6	18	3.0		0
1939			10	30	3.0		0
Career			16	48	3.0		0

Tony Cherry

1986	SF	N	11	42	3.8	10	0
1987			13	65	5.0	16	1
Career			24	107	4.5	16	1

George Chesser

1966	MIA	A	16	74	4.6	19	0
1967			2	3	1.5	2	0
Career			18	77	4.3	19	0

Wes Chesson

1971	ATL	N	1	-4	-4.0	-4	0

Raymond Chester

1971	OAK	N	3	5	1.7	6	0
1972			1	3	3.0	3	0
1973	BAL	N	1	1	1.0	1	0
Career			5	9	1.8	6	0

George Cheverko

1947	NYG	N	19	63	3.3	20	0
1948			3	10	3.3	6	0
Career			22	73	3.3	20	0

Fred Chicken

1920	RI	A					3

Joe Childress

1956	CHIC	N	43	203	4.7	30	0
1957			41	168	4.1	39t	1
1958			50	170	3.4	30	0
1959			30	59	2.0	9	0
1960	STL	N	34	240	7.1	28	0
1962			37	162	4.4	15	0
1963			174	701	4.0	28	2
1964			102	413	4.0	17	0
1965			19	94	4.9	13	0
Career			530	2210	4.2	39t	3

Clarence Childs

1964	NYG	N	40	102	2.5	19	0

Henry Childs

1976	NO	N	1	16	16.0	16t	1
1978			2	-4	-2.0	-1	0
1981	LA	N	1	0	0.0	0	0
Career			4	12	3.0	16t	1

Gene Chilton

1991	NE	N	1	0	0.0	0	0

Bill Chipley

1947	BOS	N	1	3	3.0	3	0

John Chirico

1987	NYJ	N	12	22	1.8	4	1

Max Choboian

1966	DEN	A	21	45	2.1	12	2

Wayne Chrebet

1995	NYJ	N	1	1	1.0	1	0

Frank Christensen

1934	DET	N					2

Frank Christensen *continued*

Year	Team		Att	Yds	Avg	Lg	TD
1935			11	6	0.5		0
1936			2	-2	-1.0		0
Career			13	4	0.3		2

Jeff Christensen

1983	CIN	N	1	-2	-2.0	-2	0
1987	CLE	N	11	41	3.7	15	0
Career			12	39	3.3	15	0

Todd Christensen

1982	LARI	N	1	-6	-6.0	-6	0

Bob Christian

1993	CHI	N	8	19	2.4	12	0
1994			7	29	4.1	8	0
1995	CAR		41	158	3.9	17	0
Career			56	206	3.7	17	0

Jack Christiansen

1952	DET	N	19	148	7.8	65t	2
1953			0	-5		-5L	0
Career			19	143	7.5	65t	2
Playoffs			4	9	2.3		

Marty Christiansen

1940	CHIC	N	32	71	2.2		1

Oscar Christianson

1921	MIN	A					1

Paul Christman

1945	CHIC	N	30	-34	-1.1	9	1
1946			28	-61	-2.2	6	3
1947			8	11	1.4	3	2
1948			8	6	0.8	5	1
1949			4	34	8.5	22	0
1950	GB	N	7	18	2.6	4	1
Career			85	-26	-0.3	22	8
Playoffs			8	2	0.3		0

Ryan Christopherson

1995	JAC	N	16	16	1.0	10	1

Dick Christy

1958	PIT	N	38	101	2.7	19	0
1960	BOS	A	78	363	4.7		4
1961	NY	A	81	180	2.2	16	2
1962			114	535	4.7	47	3
1963			26	88	3.4	13	1
Career			337	1267	3.8	47	10

Bob Cifers

1946	DET	N	8	18	2.3	6	0
1947	PIT	N	87	356	4.1	41	0
1948			112	361	3.2	21	1
1949	GB	N	23	52	2.3	19	0
Career			230	787	3.4	41	1
Playoffs			10	29	2.9		0

Ed Cifers

1948	CHIB	N	1	5	5.0	5	0

Larry Cipa

1974	NO	N	12	35	2.9	15	1
1975			6	2	0.3	3	0
Career			18	37	2.1	15	1

Darryl Clack

1986	DAL	N	4	19	4.8	8	0
1988			11	54	4.9	17	0
1989			14	40	2.9	17	2
Career			29	113	3.9	17	2

Rickey Claitt

1980	WAS	N	57	215	3.8	16	1
1981			3	19	6.3	11	0
Career			60	234	3.9	16	1

Jack Clancy

1967	MIA	A	3	-4	-1.3	2	0

Stu Clancy

1931	SI	N					1

Stu Clancy *continued*

Year	Team		Att	Yds	Avg	Lg	TD
1933	NYG	N	44	136	3.1		3
1934			17	60	3.5		0
1935							1
Career			61	196	3.2		5
Playoffs			3	7	2.3		0

Dennis Claridge

1965	GB	N	2	-3	-1.5	-3	0
1966	ATL	N	5	15	3.0	16	0
Career			7	12	1.7	16	0

Algy Clark

1931	CLE	N					2

Allan Clark

1979	NE	N	19	84	4.4	19	2
1980			9	56	6.2	15	1
Career			28	140	5.0	19	3

Beryl Clark

1940	CHIC	N	39	9	0.2		0

Boobie Clark

1973	CIN	N	254	988	3.9	26	8
1974			99	312	3.2	22	5
1975			167	594	3.6	17	4
1976			151	671	4.4	24	7
1977			68	226	3.3	10t	1
1978			40	187	4.7	20	0
1979	HOU	N	22	51	2.3	7	0
1980			1	3	3.0	3	0
Career			802	3032	3.8	26	25
Playoffs			24	116	4.8		1

Bret Clark

1986	ATL	N	2	8	4.0	6	0

Darryl Clark

1987	CHI	N	5	11	2.2	5	0

Derrick Clark

1994	DEN	N	56	168	3.0	12	3

Dutch Clark

1931	POR	N					9
1932			112	461	4.1		3
1934	DET	N	122	763	6.3		8
1935			120	412	3.4		4
1936			123	628	5.1		7
1937			96	468	4.9		5
1938			7	25	3.6		0
Career			580	2757	4.8		36
Playoffs				80			1

Dwight Clark

1981	SF	N	3	32	10.7	18	0
1983			3	18	6.0	8	0
Career			6	50	8.3	18	0
Playoffs			2	4	2.0		0

Gary Clark

1985	WAS	N	2	10	5.0	7	0
1987			1	0	0.0	0	0
1988			2	6	3.0	4	0
1989			2	19	9.5	11	0
1990			1	1	1.0	1	0
1991			1	0	0.0	0	0
1992			2	18	9.0	12	0
Career			11	54	4.9	12	0
Playoffs			3	24	8.0		0

Harry Clark

1940	CHIB	N	56	258	4.6		2
1941			28	122	4.4	15	0
1942			58	273	4.7	26	4
1943			120	556	4.6	20	2
1946	LA	AA	62	250	4.0		2
1947			44	173	3.9		2
1948	LA-CHI	AA	22	79	3.6		0
Career			390	1711	4.4	26	10
Playoffs			16	96	6.0		2

Year	Team		Att	Yds	Avg	Lg	TD

Jessie Clark

Year	Team		Att	Yds	Avg	Lg	TD
1983	GB	N	71	328	4.6	42	0
1984			87	375	4.3	43t	4
1985			147	633	4.3	80	5
1986			18	41	2.3	9	0
1987			56	211	3.8	57	0
1989	PHX-MIN	N	20	99	5.0	14	0
1990	MIN	N	16	49	3.1	11	0
Career			415	1736	4.2	80	9

Ken Clark

Year	Team		Att	Yds	Avg	Lg	TD
1979	LA	N	1	3	3.0	3	0

Ken Clark

Year	Team		Att	Yds	Avg	Lg	TD
1990	IND	N	7	10	1.4	11	0
1991			114	366	3.2	25	0
1992			40	134	3.4	13	0
Career			161	510	3.2	25	0

Wayne Clark

Year	Team		Att	Yds	Avg	Lg	TD
1972	SD	N	2	-8	-4.0	3	0
1973			13	86	6.6	16	0
1974	CIN	N	1	8	8.0	8t	1
Career			16	86	5.4	16	1

Frank Clarke

Year	Team		Att	Yds	Avg	Lg	TD
1960	DAL	N	1	-6	-6.0	-6	0
1963			1	12	12.0	12	0
1964			10	46	4.6	21	0
1965			8	58	7.3	21	0
1966			8	49	6.1	26	0
1967			4	72	18.0	56t	1
Career			32	231	7.2	56t	1
Playoffs			2	0	0.0		0

Leon Clarke

Year	Team		Att	Yds	Avg	Lg	TD
1957	LA	N	1	-4	-4.0	-4	0

Corwin Clatt

Year	Team		Att	Yds	Avg	Lg	TD
1948	CHIC	N	6	38	6.3	26	0
Playoffs			1	2	2.0		0

Bobby Clatterbuck

Year	Team		Att	Yds	Avg	Lg	TD
1954	NYG	N	19	-21	-1.1	3	1
1955			1	-3	-3.0	-3	0
1957			3	3	1.0	3	0
1960	LA	A	6	-6	-1.0		0
Career			29	-27	-0.9	3	1
Playoffs			1	0	0.0		0

Randy Clay

Year	Team		Att	Yds	Avg	Lg	TD
1950	NYG	N	74	254	3.4	56	2
1953			16	26	1.6	6	0
Career			90	280	3.1	56	2

Walt Clay

Year	Team		Att	Yds	Avg	Lg	TD
1946	CHI	AA	65	283	4.4		1
1947	LA	AA	9	42	4.7		0
1948			86	293	3.4		3
1949			9	34	3.8		0
Career			169	652	3.9		4

Mark Clayton

Year	Team		Att	Yds	Avg	Lg	TD
1983	MIA	N	2	9	4.5	9	0
1984			3	35	11.7	30	0
1985			1	10	10.0	10	0
1986			2	33	16.5	22	0
1987			2	8	4.0	4	0
1988			1	4	4.0	4	0
1989			3	9	3.0	11	0
Career			14	108	7.7	30	0
Playoffs			1	0	0.0		0

Bob Clemens

Year	Team		Att	Yds	Avg	Lg	TD
1962	BAL	N	2	9	4.5	6	0

Cal Clemens

Year	Team		Att	Yds	Avg	Lg	TD
1936	GB	N	3	-8	-2.7		0

Johnny Clement

Year	Team		Att	Yds	Avg	Lg	TD
1941	CHIC	N	61	94	1.5	25	1
1946	PIT	N	43	60	1.4	13	1
1947			129	670	5.2	43	4
1948			67	261	3.9	28t	2

Johnny Clement continued

Year	Team		Att	Yds	Avg	Lg	TD
1949	CHI	AA	106	388	3.7		5
Career			406	1473	3.6	43	13
Playoffs			14	59	4.2		0

Tom Clements

Year	Team		Att	Yds	Avg	Lg	TD
1980	KC	N	2	0	0.0	0	0

Vin Clements

Year	Team		Att	Yds	Avg	Lg	TD
1972	NYG	N	46	221	4.8	19	0
1973			57	214	3.8	11	1
Career			103	435	4.2	19	1

Michael Clemons

Year	Team		Att	Yds	Avg	Lg	TD
1987	KC	N	2	7	3.5	7	0

Topper Clemons

Year	Team		Att	Yds	Avg	Lg	TD
1987	PHI	N	3	0	0.0	3	0

Doug Cline

Year	Team		Att	Yds	Avg	Lg	TD
1960	HOU	A	37	105	2.8		2

Ollie Cline

Year	Team		Att	Yds	Avg	Lg	TD
1948	CLE	AA	29	129	4.4		0
1949	BUF	AA	125	518	4.1		3
1950	DET	N	69	227	3.3	41t	0
1951			3	15	5.0	10	0
1952			13	36	2.8	8	1
1953			42	169	4.0	31	0
Career			281	1094	3.9	41t	6
Playoffs			7	24	3.4		0

Jack Cloud

Year	Team		Att	Yds	Avg	Lg	TD
1950	GB	N	18	52	2.9	13	3
1951			29	61	2.1	19	1
1952	WAS	N	7	21	3.0	5	0
1953			3	7	2.3	5	0
Career			57	141	2.5	19	4

Bert Coan

Year	Team		Att	Yds	Avg	Lg	TD
1962	SD	A	12	10	0.8	8	0
1963	KC	A	17	100	5.9	51	0
1964			11	56	5.1	37	2
1965			45	137	3.0	21	1
1966			96	521	5.4	57	7
1967			63	275	4.4	38	4
1968			40	160	4.0	24	1
Career			284	1259	4.4	57	15
Playoffs			5	7	1.4		0

Ben Coates

Year	Team		Att	Yds	Avg	Lg	TD
1991	NE	N	1	-6	-6.0	-6	0
1992			1	2	2.0	2	0
1994			1	0	0.0	0	0
Career			3	-4	-1.3	2	0

Ray Coates

Year	Team		Att	Yds	Avg	Lg	TD
1948	NYG	N	50	176	3.5	18	1
1949			27	55	2.0	11	0
Career			77	231	3.0	18	1

Marvin Cobb

Year	Team		Att	Yds	Avg	Lg	TD
1977	CIN	N	1	0	0.0	0	0

Reggie Cobb

Year	Team		Att	Yds	Avg	Lg	TD
1990	TB	N	151	480	3.2	17	2
1991			196	752	3.8	59t	7
1992			310	1171	3.8	25	9
1993			221	658	3.0	16	3
1994	GB	N	153	579	3.8	30	3
1995	JAC	N	9	18	2.0	5	0
1996	NYJ	N	25	85	3.4	9	1
Career			1065	3743	3.5	59t	25
Playoffs			12	26	2.2		0

Eric Cobble

Year	Team		Att	Yds	Avg	Lg	TD
1987	HOU	N	9	23	2.6	12	0

Red Cochran

Year	Team		Att	Yds	Avg	Lg	TD
1947	CHIC	N	14	36	2.6	9	1
1948			3	15	5.0	9	0
1949			20	87	4.3	22	1
Career			37	138	3.7	22	2

Tom Cochran

Year	Team		Att	Yds	Avg	Lg	TD
1949	WAS	N	34	135	4.0	16	1

Don Cockroft

Year	Team		Att	Yds	Avg	Lg	TD
1971	CLE	N	1	12	12.0	12	0
1973			1	-3	-3.0	-3	0
Career			2	9	4.5	12	0
Playoffs			1	0	0.0		0

Ed Cody

Year	Team		Att	Yds	Avg	Lg	TD
1947	GB	N	56	263	4.7	32t	2
1948			26	58	2.2	10	0
1949	CHIB	N	11	25	2.3	11	0
Career			93	346	3.7	32t	2

Pat Coffee

Year	Team		Att	Yds	Avg	Lg	TD
1937	CHIC	N	55	157	2.9		1
1938			40	169	4.2		2
Career			95	326	3.4		3

Junior Coffey

Year	Team		Att	Yds	Avg	Lg	TD
1965	GB	N	3	12	4.0	10	0
1966	ATL	N	199	722	3.6	37	4
1967			180	722	4.0	20t	4
1969	ATL-NYG	N	131	511	3.9	20	2
1971	NYG	N	22	70	3.2	10	0
Career			535	2037	3.8	37	10

Paul Coffman

Year	Team		Att	Yds	Avg	Lg	TD
1980	GB	N	1	3	3.0	3	0

Gail Cogdill

Year	Team		Att	Yds	Avg	Lg	TD
1962	DET	N	1	2	2.0	2	0
1964			1	-4	-4.0	-4	0
Career			2	-2	-1.0	2	0

Angelo Coia

Year	Team		Att	Yds	Avg	Lg	TD
1960	CHI	N	3	-4	-1.3	25	0
1963			2	2	1.0	4	0
Career			5	-2	-0.4	25	0

Jim Colclough

Year	Team		Att	Yds	Avg	Lg	TD
1961	BOS	A	3	37	12.3	16	0
1962			1	14	14.0	14	0
Career			4	51	12.8	16	0

Emerson Cole

Year	Team		Att	Yds	Avg	Lg	TD
1950	CLE	N	26	105	4.0	16	0
1951			46	252	5.5	23	1
Career			72	357	5.0	23	1

John Cole

Year	Team		Att	Yds	Avg	Lg	TD
1938	PHI	N	1	4	4.0	4	0
1940			26	75	2.9		0
Career			27	79	2.9	4	0

Terry Cole

Year	Team		Att	Yds	Avg	Lg	TD
1968	BAL	N	104	418	4.0	21	3
1969			73	204	2.8	27	2
1970	PIT	N	9	8	0.9	6	0
1971	MIA	N	3	11	3.7	4	0
Career			189	641	3.4	27	5
Playoffs			3	14	4.7		0

Tom Colella

Year	Team		Att	Yds	Avg	Lg	TD
1942	DET	N	23	51	2.2	34	0
1943			15	25	1.7	18	0
1944	CLE	N	53	208	3.9	75t	2
1945			46	224	4.9	30	2
1946	CLE	AA	30	118	3.9	50t	2
1947			11	77	7.0		1
1948			14	60	4.3		1
1949	BUF	AA	7	-9	-1.3		0
Career			199	754	3.8	75t	8
Playoffs			6	21	3.5		0

Andre Coleman

Year	Team		Att	Yds	Avg	Lg	TD
1996	SD	N	2	0	0.0	7	0

Greg Coleman

Year	Team		Att	Yds	Avg	Lg	TD
1977	CLE	N	1	-3	-3.0	-3	0
1978	MIN	N	2	22	11.0	17	0
1982			1	15	15.0	15	0
1983			1	-9	-9.0	-9	0

Year	Team		Att	Yds	Avg	Lg	TD

Greg Coleman continued

1984			2	11	5.5	13	0
1985			2	0	0.0	0	0
1986	WAS	N	2	46	23.0	30	0
1988	WAS	N	2	-13	-6.5	0	0
Career			13	69	5.3	30	0

Lincoln Coleman

1993	DAL	N	34	132	3.9	16	2
1994			64	180	2.8	13	1
Career			98	312	3.2	16	3
Playoffs			6	16	2.7		0

Monte Coleman

| 1989 | WAS | N | 1 | -1 | -1.0 | -1 | 0 |

Pat Coleman

1993	HOU	N	1	1	1.0	1	0
1994			1	2	2.0	2	0
Career			2	3	1.5	2	0

Ronnie Coleman

1974	HOU	N	52	193	3.7	37	1
1975			175	790	4.5	46t	5
1976			171	684	4.0	39	2
1977			185	660	3.6	22	5
1978			61	188	3.1	16	1
1979			21	81	3.9	10	0
1980			14	82	5.9	27	1
1981			21	91	4.3	30	1
Career			700	2769	4.0	46t	16
Playoffs			11	21	1.9		0

Mike Collier

1975	PIT	N	21	124	5.9	23	3
1977	BUF	N	31	116	3.7	15	0
1979			34	130	3.8	22	2
Career			86	370	4.3	23	5
Playoffs			1	8	8.0		0

Reggie Collier

1986	DAL	N	6	53	8.8	21	0
1987	PIT	N	4	20	5.0	12	0
Career			10	73	7.3	21	0

Dwight Collins

| 1984 | MIN | N | 3 | -14 | -4.7 | 1 | 0 |

Gary Collins

1965	CLE	N	1	16	16.0	16	0
1966			2	38	19.0	36	0
1967			1	6	6.0	6	0
Career			4	60	15.0	36	0

Kerry Collins

1995	CAR	N	42	74	1.8	10	3
1996			32	38	1.2	14	0
Career			74	112	1.5	14	3
Playoffs			7	4	0.6		0

Larry Collins

| 1978 | CLE | N | 22 | 64 | 2.9 | 19 | 1 |

Patrick Collins

| 1988 | GB | N | 2 | 2 | 1.0 | 2 | 0 |

Paul Collins

| 1945 | CHIC | N | 10 | 13 | 1.3 | 6 | 0 |

Rip Collins

1949	CHI	AA	28	88	3.1		0
1950	BAL	N	69	101	1.5	12	0
1951	GB	N	5	4	0.8	6	0
Career			102	193	1.9	12	0

Sonny Collins

| 1976 | ATL | N | 91 | 319 | 3.5 | 47 | 0 |

Todd Collins

1995	BUF	N	9	23	2.6	10	0
1996			21	43	2.0	10	0
Career			30	66	2.2	10	0

Tony Collins

1981	NE	N	204	873	4.3	29	7
1982			164	632	3.9	54	1
1983			219	1049	4.8	50t	10
1984			138	550	4.0	21	5
1985			163	657	4.0	28	3
1986			156	412	2.6	17	3
1987			147	474	3.2	19	3
Career			1191	4647	3.9	54	32
Playoffs			47	200	4.3		0

Cris Collinsworth

1982	CIN	N	1	-11	-11.0	-11	0
1983			2	2	1.0	8	0
1984			1	7	7.0	7	0
1985			1	3	3.0	3	0
1986			2	-16	-8.0	-6	0
Career			7	-15	-2.1	8	0
Playoffs			1	2	2.0		0

Mickey Colmer

1946	BKN	AA	46	155	3.4		0
1947			152	578	3.8		9
1948			164	704	4.3		6
1949	B-NY	AA	36	100	2.8		0
Career			398	1537	3.9		15

Craig Colquitt

1980	PIT	N	1	17	17.0	17	0
1981			1	8	8.0	8	0
1984			1	0	0.0	0	0
Career			3	25	8.3	17	0

Irv Comp

1943	GB	N	77	182	2.4	27	3
1944			52	134	2.6	28	2
1945			57	75	1.3	18	1
1946			61	62	1.0	29	1
1947			5	46	9.2	34	0
1948			3	3	1.0	2	0
Career			255	502	2.0	34	7
Playoffs			9	21	2.3		0

Tony Compagno

1946	PIT	N	67	217	3.2	23	1
1947			34	126	3.7	13	4
1948			24	101	4.2	20	0
Career			125	444	3.6	23	5
Playoffs			4	9	2.3		0

Dick Compton

1962	DET	N	1	3	3.0	3	0
1964			3	2	0.7	4	0
1965	HOU	A	1	2	2.0	2	0
1967	PIT	N	1	1	1.0	1	0
Career			6	8	1.3	4	0

Ogden Compton

| 1955 | CHIC | N | 6 | -8 | -1.3 | 5 | 0 |

Jack Concannon

1964	PHI	N	16	134	8.4	29	1
1965			9	104	11.6	38	0
1966			25	195	7.8	29	2
1967	CHI	N	67	279	4.2	31	3
1968			28	104	3.7	16	2
1969			22	62	2.8	30	1
1970			42	136	3.2	16	2
1971			5	5	1.0	2	0
1974	GB	N	3	7	2.3	6	1
Career			217	1026	4.7	38	12

Merl Condit

1940	PIT	N	52	205	3.9		0
1941	BKN	N	91	357	3.9	41	4
1942			129	647	5.0	63	2
1943			67	190	2.8	25	1
1945	WAS	N	36	173	4.8	41	3
1946	PIT	N	46	141	3.1	23	1
Career			421	1713	4.1	63	11
Playoffs			9	18	2.0		0

Fred Cone

| 1951 | GB | N | 56 | 190 | 3.4 | 16 | 1 |

Fred Cone continued

1952			70	276	3.9	30t	2
1953			92	301	3.3	41t	5
1954			15	18	1.2	11	0
1955			12	25	2.1	14	0
1956			49	211	4.3	21	2
1957			53	135	2.5	26t	2
Career			347	1156	3.3	41t	12

Charlie Conerly

1948	NYG	N	40	160	4.0	40	5
1949			23	42	1.8	7	0
1950			23	22	1.0	14	1
1951			17	65	3.8	18	1
1952			27	115	4.3	33	0
1953			24	91	3.8	24	0
1954			24	107	4.5	24	1
1955			12	10	0.8	12	0
1956			11	11	1.0	8	0
1957			15	24	1.6	13	1
1958			12	-17	-1.4	11	0
1959			15	38	2.5	10	1
1960			14	1	0.1	17	0
1961			13	16	1.2	9	0
Career			270	685	2.5	40	10
Playoffs			4	15	3.8		1

Larry Conjar

1967	CLE	N	20	78	3.9	16	0
1968	PHI	N	8	21	2.6	6	0
1969	BAL	N	1	0	0.0	0	0
1970			1	3	3.0	3	0
Career			30	102	3.4	16	0

Cary Conklin

1992	WAS	N	3	-4	-1.3	-1	0
1993			2	-2	-1.0	-1	0
Career			5	-6	-1.2	-1	0

Steve Conley

| 1972 | CIN | N | 3 | 8 | 2.7 | 5 | 0 |

Mike Connell

| 1981 | WAS | N | 1 | 0 | 0.0 | 0 | 0 |

Harry Connolly

| 1946 | BKN | AA | 8 | 18 | 2.3 | | 0 |

Bobby Joe Conrad

1959	CHIC	N	74	328	4.4	56t	2
1960	STL	N	23	91	4.0	33	0
1961			20	22	1.1	7	0
1963			1	0	0.0	0	0
Career			118	441	3.7	56t	2

Enio Conti

| 1941 | PHI | N | 1 | -1 | -1.0 | -1 | 0 |

Curtis Conway

1993	CHI	N	5	44	8.8	18	0
1994			6	31	5.2	12	0
1995			5	77	15.4	20	0
1996			8	50	6.3	19	0
Career			24	202	8.4	20	0

Jimmy Conzelman

1920	DEC	A					1
1921	RI	A					1
1922	RI	N					7
1923	MIL	N					2
1924							1
1926	DET	N					1
1927	PRO	N					1
Career							14

Dave Cook

1935	CHIC	N	31	121	3.9		1
1936	CHIC-BKN	N	10	24	2.4		0
Career			41	145	3.5		1

Greg Cook

| 1969 | CIN | A | 25 | 148 | 5.9 | 30 | 1 |

Year	Team		Att	Yds	Avg	Lg	TD

Kelly Cook
| 1987 | GB | N | 2 | 3 | 1.5 | 2 | 0 |

Bill Cooper
| 1937 | CLE | N | 19 | 45 | 2.4 | | 0 |

Bill Cooper
1961	SF	N	8	17	2.1	6	1
1962			2	-2	-1.0	2	0
Career			10	15	1.5	6	1

Earl Cooper
1980	SF	N	171	720	4.2	47	5
1981			98	330	3.4	23	1
1982			24	77	3.2	9	0
1984			3	13	4.3	7	0
1985			2	12	6.0	14	0
Career			298	1152	3.9	47	6
Playoffs			25	125	5.0		0

Joe Cooper
| 1984 | HOU | N | 1 | -2 | -2.0 | -2 | 0 |

Horace Copeland
| 1993 | TB | N | 3 | 34 | 11.3 | 22 | 0 |

Russell Copeland
1994	BUF	N	1	-7	-7.0	-7	0
1995			1	-1	-1.0	-1	0
Career			2	-8	-4.0	-1	0
Playoffs			1	-4	-4.0		0

George Corbett
1933	CHIB	N	25	54	2.2		0
1934			30	119	4.0		0
1936			13	45	3.5		0
1938			7	29	4.1		0
Career			75	247	3.3		0
Playoffs			5	-9	-1.8		0

Jim Corbett
| 1977 | CIN | N | 1 | -1 | -1.0 | -1 | 0 |

King Corcoran
| 1968 | BOS | A | 1 | -1 | -1.0 | -1 | 0 |

Ollie Cordill
| 1940 | CLE | N | 24 | 73 | 3.0 | | 0 |

Chuck Corgan
| 1924 | KC | N | | | | | 2 |

Mike Corgan
| 1943 | DET | N | 5 | 14 | 2.8 | 8 | 0 |

Anthony Corley
| 1984 | PIT | N | 18 | 89 | 4.9 | 23 | 0 |

Joe Corn
| 1948 | LA | N | 11 | 27 | 2.5 | 6 | 0 |

Bo Cornell
1971	CLE	N	11	12	1.1	6	0
1972			7	8	1.1	7	0
1973	BUF	N	4	13	3.3	7	0
Career			22	33	1.5	7	0

Bobby Coronado
| 1961 | PIT | N | 1 | -7 | -7.0 | -7 | 0 |

Red Corzine
1933	CIN	N					1
1934	C-S	N					1
1935	NYG	N	32	105	3.3		0
1936			7	12	1.7		0
1937			8	23	2.9		0
Career			47	140	3.0		2

Doug Cosbie
1981	DAL	N	4	33	8.3	15	0
1982			1	-2	-2.0	-2	0
1986			1	9	9.0	9	0
1987			1	-5	-5.0	-5	0
Career			7	35	5.0	15	0
Playoffs			1	0	0.0		0

Bruce Coslet
| 1975 | CIN | N | 1 | 1 | 1.0 | 1 | 0 |

Paul Costa
1966	BUF	A	0	1		1L	0
1968			2	11	5.5	6t	1
Career			2	12	6.0	6t	1

Jeff Cothran
1994	CIN	N	26	85	3.3	13	0
1995			16	62	3.9	15	0
1996			15	44	2.9	9	1
Career			57	191	3.4	15	1

Johnny Counts
| 1962 | NYG | N | 14 | 55 | 3.9 | 23 | 0 |

Al Couppee
| 1946 | WAS | N | 3 | 22 | 7.3 | 11 | 0 |

Gerry Courtney
| 1942 | BKN | N | 8 | 12 | 1.5 | 11 | 1 |

Larry Coutre
1950	GB	N	41	283	6.9	53	1
1953			22	39	1.8	17	0
Career			63	322	5.1	53	1

Jamie Covington
| 1987 | NYG | N | 4 | 0 | 0.0 | 2 | 0 |

Bob Cowan
1947	CLE	AA	38	181	4.8		2
1948			33	99	3.0		1
1949	BAL	AA	1	0	0.0	0	0
Career			72	280	3.9	0	3

Larry Cowan
| 1982 | MIA | N | 1 | 3 | 3.0 | 3 | 0 |

Gerry Cowhig
1947	LA	N	25	104	4.2	21	0
1948			46	206	4.5	14	2
1949			10	32	3.2	8	1
Career			81	342	4.2	21	3

Billy Cox
1951	WAS	N	2	7	3.5	5	0
1952			3	-1	-0.3	14	0
Career			5	6	1.2	14	0

Norm Cox
1946	CHI	AA	1	12	12.0	12	0
1947			1	-3	-3.0	-3	0
Career			2	9	4.5	12	0

Steve Cox
| 1982 | CLE | N | 2 | -11 | -5.5 | 0 | 0 |

Clyde Crabtree
| 1930 | FRA | N | | | | | 1 |

Eric Crabtree
1967	DEN	A	2	2	1.0	6	0
1970	CIN	N	3	23	7.7	16	0
1971	CIN-NE	N	3	12	4.0	18	0
Career			8	37	4.6	18	0

Nat Craddock
| 1963 | BAL | N | 1 | 1 | 1.0 | 1 | 0 |

Donnie Craft
1982	HOU	N	18	42	2.3	10	3
1983			55	147	2.7	8	0
Career			73	189	2.6	10	3

Russ Craft
1946	PHI	N	27	108	4.0	24	0
1947			5	-1	-0.2	4	0
1948			13	67	5.2	23	0
1949			11	5	0.5	5	0
1950			8	52	6.5	19	0
Career			64	231	3.6	24	0
Playoffs			16	11	0.7		1

Dobie Craig
| 1962 | OAK | A | 1 | 8 | 8.0 | 8 | 0 |

Larry Craig
1939	GB	N	2	6	3.0		0
1940			3	9	3.0		0
1941			1	1	1.0	1	0
1942			2	0	0.0	4	0
1943			1	3	3.0	3	0
1946			1	-3	-3.0	-3	0
Career			10	16	1.6	4	0

Roger Craig
1983	SF	N	176	725	4.1	71	8
1984			155	649	4.2	28	7
1985			214	1050	4.9	62t	9
1986			204	830	4.1	25	7
1987			215	815	3.8	25	3
1988			310	1502	4.8	46t	7
1989			271	1054	3.9	27	6
1990			141	439	3.1	26	1
1991	LARI	N	162	590	3.6	15	1
1992	MIN	N	105	416	4.0	21	4
1993			38	119	3.1	11	1
Career			1991	8189	4.1	71	56
Playoffs			207	840	4.1		7

Milt Crain
| 1944 | BOS | N | 26 | 78 | 3.0 | 8 | 0 |

Carl Cramer
1921	AKR	A					4
1922	AKR	N					6
1924							1
Career							11

Jack Crangle
| 1923 | CHIC | N | | | | | 3 |

Bill Crass
| 1937 | CHIC | N | 5 | 8 | 1.6 | | 0 |

Aaron Craver
1991	MIA	N	20	58	2.9	7t	1
1992			3	9	3.0	8	0
1994			6	43	7.2	19	0
1995	DEN	N	73	333	4.6	23	5
1996			59	232	3.9	28	2
Career			161	675	4.2	28	8
Playoffs			12	98	8.2		1

Charles Crawford
| 1986 | PHI | N | 28 | 88 | 3.1 | 15 | 1 |

Jim Crawford
1960	BOS	A	51	238	4.7		2
1961			41	148	3.6	34	0
1962			139	459	3.3	22	2
1963			71	233	3.3	19	1
Career			302	1078	3.6	34	5

Rufus Crawford
| 1978 | SEA | N | 8 | 19 | 2.4 | 11 | 0 |

Dick Crayne
1936	BKN	N	64	203	3.2		1
1937			47	135	2.9		0
Career			111	338	3.0		1

Willis Crenshaw
1964	STL	N	60	297	5.0	49	1
1965			127	437	3.4	27	0
1966			94	360	3.8	33	0
1967			44	149	3.4	23	0
1968			203	813	4.0	66t	6
1969			55	172	3.1	26t	3
1970	DEN	N	69	200	2.9	25	5
Career			652	2428	3.7	66t	15

Joe Cribbs
1980	BUF	N	306	1185	3.9	48	11
1981			257	1097	4.3	35	3
1982			134	633	4.7	62t	3
1983			263	1131	4.3	45	3
1985			122	399	3.3	16	1

Joe Cribbs *continued*

Year	Team		Att	Yds	Avg	Lg	TD
1986	SF	N	152	590	3.9	19	5
1987			70	300	4.3	20	1
1988	MIA	N	5	21	4.2	11	0
Career			1309	5356	4.1	62t	27
Playoffs			60	224	3.7		3

Hal Crisler

Year	Team		Att	Yds	Avg	Lg	TD
1946	BOS	N	4	6	1.5	6	0

Ray Criswell

Year	Team		Att	Yds	Avg	Lg	TD
1987	TB	N	1	0	0.0	0	0
1988			2	0	0.0	0	0
Career			3	0	0.0	0	0

Ray Crittenden

Year	Team		Att	Yds	Avg	Lg	TD
1993	NE	N	1	-3	-3.0	-3	0

Jim Crocicchia

Year	Team		Att	Yds	Avg	Lg	TD
1987	NYG	N	4	5	1.3	7	0

Zack Crockett

Year	Team		Att	Yds	Avg	Lg	TD
1995	IND	N	1	0	0.0	0	0
1996			31	164	5.3	25	0
Career			32	164	5.1	25	0
Playoffs			20	161	8.1		2

Nolan Cromwell

Year	Team		Att	Yds	Avg	Lg	TD
1978	LA	N	1	16	16.0	16t	1
1979			1	5	5.0	5t	1
1980			2	0	0.0	0	0
1981			1	17	17.0	17	0
1982	LARM	N	1	17	17.0	17t	1
1983			1	0	0.0	0	0
Career			7	55	7.9	17t	3
Playoffs			1	7	7.0		0

Bill Cronin

Year	Team		Att	Yds	Avg	Lg	TD
1926	BOS	A					1
1927	PRO	N					1
Career							2

Jack Cronin

Year	Team		Att	Yds	Avg	Lg	TD
1928	PRO	N					3
1929							1
Career							4

Corey Croom

Year	Team		Att	Yds	Avg	Lg	TD
1993	NE	N	60	198	3.3	22	1
1995			13	54	4.2	12	0
Career			73	252	3.5	22	1
Playoffs			9	35	3.9		0

Ron Crosby

Year	Team		Att	Yds	Avg	Lg	TD
1983	NYJ	N	1	5	5.0	5	0

Steve Crosby

Year	Team		Att	Yds	Avg	Lg	TD
1974	NYG	N	14	55	3.9	10	0
1976			1	-1	-1.0	-1	0
Career			15	54	3.6	10	0

Billy Cross

Year	Team		Att	Yds	Avg	Lg	TD
1951	CHIC	N	53	283	5.3	39t	3
1952			71	347	4.9	45	2
1953			51	196	3.8	56	1
Career			175	826	4.7	56	

Leon Crosswhite

Year	Team		Att	Yds	Avg	Lg	TD
1973	DET	N	11	30	2.7	5	1
1974			12	49	4.1	9	1
Career			23	79	3.4	9	2

Ray Crouse

Year	Team		Att	Yds	Avg	Lg	TD
1984	GB	N	53	169	3.2	14	0

Jake Crouthamel

Year	Team		Att	Yds	Avg	Lg	TD
1960	BOS	A	4	16	4.0		0

John David Crow

Year	Team		Att	Yds	Avg	Lg	TD
1958	CHIC	N	52	221	4.3	83t	2
1959			140	666	4.8	73	3
1960	STL	N	183	1071	5.9	47	6
1961			48	192	4.0	17	1
1962			192	751	3.9	35	14
1963			9	34	3.8	9	0

John David Crow *continued*

Year	Team		Att	Yds	Avg	Lg	TD
1964			163	554	3.4	57	7
1965	SF	N	132	514	3.9	30	2
1966			121	477	3.9	3	1
1967			113	479	4.2	39	2
1968			4	4	1.0	3	0
Career			1157	4963	4.3	83t	38

Wayne Crow

Year	Team		Att	Yds	Avg	Lg	TD
1961	OAK	A	119	490	4.1	62	2
1962	BUF	A	110	589	5.4	52	1
1963			6	6	1.0	7	0
Career			235	1085	4.6	62	3

Earl Crowder

Year	Team		Att	Yds	Avg	Lg	TD
1939	CHIC	N	6	-5	-0.8		0

Larry Crowe

Year	Team		Att	Yds	Avg	Lg	TD
1972	PHI	N	1	2	2.0	2	0

Paul Crowe

Year	Team		Att	Yds	Avg	Lg	TD
1948	SF	AA	12	65	5.4		0
1949	SF-LA	AA	3	2	0.7	2	0
Career			15	67	4.5	2	0

Harry Crump

Year	Team		Att	Yds	Avg	Lg	TD
1963	BOS	A	49	120	2.4	21	5
Playoffs			12	27	2.3		0

Tommy Crutcher

Year	Team		Att	Yds	Avg	Lg	TD
1964	GB	N	1	5	5.0	5	0

Dwayne Crutchfield

Year	Team		Att	Yds	Avg	Lg	TD
1982	NYJ	N	22	78	3.5	8	1
1983	NYJ-HOU	N	140	578	4.1	17	3
1984	LARM	N	73	337	4.6	36	1
Career			235	993	4.2	36	5
Playoffs			3	-1	-0.3		1

Larry Csonka

Year	Team		Att	Yds	Avg	Lg	TD
1968	MIA	A	138	540	3.9	40	6
1969			131	566	4.3	54t	2
1970	MIA	N	193	874	4.5	53	6
1971			195	1051	5.4	28	7
1972			213	1117	5.2	45	6
1973			219	1003	4.6	25	5
1974			197	749	3.8	24	9
1976	NYG	N	160	569	3.6	13	4
1977			134	464	3.5	15	1
1978			91	311	3.4	12	6
1979	MIA	N	220	837	3.8	22	12
Career			1891	8081	4.3	54t	64
Playoffs			225	891	4.0		9

Ward Cuff

Year	Team		Att	Yds	Avg	Lg	TD
1937	NYG	N	4	32	8.0		2
1938			18	38	2.1		0
1939			23	102	4.4		0
1940			15	86	5.7		1
1941			28	157	5.6	37	0
1942			38	189	5.0	15	0
1943			80	523	6.5	65	3
1944			76	425	5.6	29	0
1945			48	214	4.5	25	0
1946	CHIC	N	13	78	6.0	26	1
1947	GB	N	1	7	7.0	7	0
Career			344	1851	5.4	65	7
Playoffs			28	99	3.5		1

Jim Culbreath

Year	Team		Att	Yds	Avg	Lg	TD
1977	GB	N	12	53	4.4	18	0
1978			30	92	3.1	15	0
1979			5	8	1.6	6	0
1980	PHI	N	1	3	3.0	3	0
Career			48	156	3.3	18	0

Rodney Culver

Year	Team		Att	Yds	Avg	Lg	TD
1992	IND	N	121	321	2.7	36t	7
1993			65	150	2.3	9	3
1994	SD	N	8	63	7.9	22	0
1995			47	155	3.3	17	3
Career			241	689	2.9	36t	13
Playoffs			6	14	2.3		0

Bennie Cunningham

Year	Team		Att	Yds	Avg	Lg	TD
Playoffs			1	0	0.0		0

Doug Cunningham

Year	Team		Att	Yds	Avg	Lg	TD
1967	SF	N	43	212	4.9	64t	2
1968			6	7	1.2	5	0
1969			147	541	3.7	33	3
1970			128	443	3.5	25	3
1971			25	98	3.9	14	1
1972			8	32	4.0	12	0
1973			44	165	3.8	12	1
1974	WAS	N	5	17	3.4	5	0
Career			406	1515	3.7	64t	10
Playoffs			6	14	2.3		0

Jim Cunningham

Year	Team		Att	Yds	Avg	Lg	TD
1961	WAS	N	69	160	2.3	19	1
1962			35	144	4.1	27	1
1963			16	33	2.1	7	1
Career			120	337	2.8	27	3

Leon Cunningham

Year	Team		Att	Yds	Avg	Lg	TD
1985	PHI	N	29	205	7.1	37	0
1994			65	288	4.4	22	3
Career			94	493	5.2	37	3

Randall Cunningham

Year	Team		Att	Yds	Avg	Lg	TD
1986	PHI	N	66	540	8.2	20	5
1987			76	505	6.6	45	3
1988			93	624	6.7	33t	6
1989			104	621	6.0	51	4
1990			118	942	8.0	52t	5
1992			87	549	6.3	30	5
1993			18	110	6.1	26	1
1995			21	98	4.7	20	0
Career			583	3989	6.8	52t	29
Playoffs			28	206	7.4		0

Sam Cunningham

Year	Team		Att	Yds	Avg	Lg	TD
1973	NE	N	155	516	3.3	25	4
1974			166	811	4.9	75t	9
1975			169	666	3.9	17	6
1976			172	824	4.8	24	3
1977			270	1015	3.8	31t	4
1978			199	768	3.9	52t	8
1979			159	563	3.5	27	5
1981			86	269	3.1	12	4
1982			9	21	2.3	4	0
Career			1385	5453	3.9	75t	43
Playoffs			30	110	3.7		0

Gary Cuozzo

Year	Team		Att	Yds	Avg	Lg	TD
1963	BAL	N	3	26	8.7	26	0
1964			7	-2	-0.3	10	0
1965			6	8	1.3	10	0
1966			1	9	9.0	9	0
1967	NO	N	19	43	2.3	10	1
1968	MIN	N	1	4	4.0	4	0
1969			3	-4	-1.3	2	0
1970			17	61	3.6	15	0
1971			15	24	1.6	9	0
1972	STL	N	4	7	1.8	9	0
Career			76	176	2.3	26	1
Playoffs			1	11	11.0		0

Tony Curcillo

Year	Team		Att	Yds	Avg	Lg	TD
1953	CHIC	N	8	29	3.6	12	0

Armand Cure

Year	Team		Att	Yds	Avg	Lg	TD
1947	BAL	AA	2	-1	-0.5		0

Will Cureton

Year	Team		Att	Yds	Avg	Lg	TD
1975	CLE	N	1	1	1.0	1	0

Pat Curran

Year	Team		Att	Yds	Avg	Lg	TD
1970	LA	N	25	92	3.7	11	0
1975	SD	N	3	21	7.0	12	0
1976			1	12	12.0	12	0
1977			1	2	2.0	2	0
Career			30	127	4.2	12	0

Don Currivan

Year	Team		Att	Yds	Avg	Lg	TD
1948	BOS-LA	N	1	-4	-4.0	-4	0

Isaac Curtis

Year	Team		Att	Yds	Avg	Lg	TD
1973	CIN	N	2	-11	-5.5	1	0
1974			8	62	7.8	20	0
1975			6	-9	-1.5	14	0
1976			3	29	9.7	19	0
1978			1	1	1.0	1	0
1979			2	-11	-5.5	-4	0
1982			3	15	5.0	8	0
Career			25	76	3.0	20	0
Playoffs			1	-1	-1.0		0

Mike Curtis

Year	Team		Att	Yds	Avg	Lg	TD
1965	BAL	N	6	1	0.2	4	0

Randy Cuthbert

Year	Team		Att	Yds	Avg	Lg	TD
1993	PIT	N	1	7	7.0	7	0

Dave D'Addio

Year	Team		Att	Yds	Avg	Lg	TD
1984	DET	N	7	46	6.6	14	0

Carroll Dale

Year	Team		Att	Yds	Avg	Lg	TD
1963	LA	N	1	12	12.0	12	0
1967	GB	N	1	9	9.0	9	0
1970			2	9	4.5	8	0
Career			4	30	7.5	12	0

Bill Daley

Year	Team		Att	Yds	Avg	Lg	TD
1946	BKN-MIA	AA	14	63	4.5		0
1947	CHI	AA	121	447	3.7	52	4
1948	NY	AA	40	102	2.5		1
Career			175	612	3.5	52	5

Pete D'Alonzo

Year	Team		Att	Yds	Avg	Lg	TD
1951	DET	N	2	11	5.5	7	0
1952			5	7	1.4	3	0
Career			7	18	2.6	7	0

Boley Dancewicz

Year	Team		Att	Yds	Avg	Lg	TD
1946	BOS	N	14	81	5.8	41	0
1947			47	145	3.1	41	1
1948			4	3	0.8	2	1
Career			65	229	3.5	41	2

Clem Daniels

Year	Team		Att	Yds	Avg	Lg	TD
1960	DAL	A	1	-2	-2.0	-2	0
1961	OAK	A	31	154	5.0	39	2
1962			161	766	4.8	72	7
1963			215	**1099**	5.1	74	3
1964			173	824	4.8	42	2
1965			219	884	4.0	57	5
1966			204	801	3.9	64	7
1967			130	575	4.4	52	4
1968	SF	N	12	37	3.1	11	0
Career			1146	5138	4.5	74	30

Gary Danielson

Year	Team		Att	Yds	Avg	Lg	TD
1977	DET	N	7	62	8.9	16	0
1978			22	93	4.2	25	0
1980			48	232	4.8	33	2
1981			9	23	2.6	11t	2
1982			23	92	4.0	16	0
1983			6	8	1.3	8	0
1984			41	218	5.3	40	3
1985	CLE	N	25	126	5.0	28	0
1987			1	0	0.0	0	0
1988			4	3	0.8	5	0
Career			186	857	4.6	40	7
Playoffs			4	17	4.3		0

Ed Danowski

Year	Team		Att	Yds	Avg	Lg	TD
1934	NYG	N	75	248	3.3		0
1935			130	335	2.6		2
1936			91	259	2.8		0
1937			66	95	1.4		1
1938			48	215	4.5		1
1939			25	21	0.8		0
Career			435	1173	2.7		4
Playoffs			21	63	3.0		1

Paul Darby

Year	Team		Att	Yds	Avg	Lg	TD
1980	NYJ	N	1	15	15.0	15	0

Dan Darragh

Year	Team		Att	Yds	Avg	Lg	TD
1968	BUF	A	13	11	0.8	8	0

Dan Darragh *continued*

Year	Team		Att	Yds	Avg	Lg	TD
1969			6	14	2.3	8	0
1970	BUF	N	1	26	26.0	26	0
Career			20	51	2.5	26	0

Ron Davenport

Year	Team		Att	Yds	Avg	Lg	TD
1985	MIA	N	98	370	3.8	33	11
1986			75	314	4.2	35	0
1987			32	114	3.6	27	1
1988			55	273	5.0	64	0
1989			14	56	4.0	9	1
Career			274	1127	4.1	64	13
Playoffs			9	54	6.0		2

Bill Davidson

Year	Team		Att	Yds	Avg	Lg	TD
1937	PIT	N	101	293	2.9		1
1938			33	52	1.6		0
1939			21	27	1.3		0
Career			155	372	2.4		1

Cotton Davidson

Year	Team		Att	Yds	Avg	Lg	TD
1954	BAL	N	11	31	2.8	15	0
1960	DAL	A	31	-122	-3.9	7	1
1961			21	123	5.9	40	1
1962	OAK	A	25	54	2.2	19	3
1963			26	115	4.4	18	4
1964			29	167	5.8	33	2
1966			6	-11	-1.8	5	0
Career			149	357	2.4	40	11

Al Davis

Year	Team		Att	Yds	Avg	Lg	TD
1971	PHI	N	47	163	3.5	21	1

Anthony Davis

Year	Team		Att	Yds	Avg	Lg	TD
1977	TB	N	95	297	3.1	35	1
1978	LA	N	3	7	2.3	4	0
Career			98	304	3.1	35	1
Playoffs			4	17	4.3		0

Art Davis

Year	Team		Att	Yds	Avg	Lg	TD
1956	PIT	N	5	6	1.2	9	0

Bob Davis

Year	Team		Att	Yds	Avg	Lg	TD
1938	CLE	N	22	100	4.5		0
1942	PHI	N	43	207	4.8	44	2
1944	BOS	N	95	363	3.8	80	1
1945			29	91	3.1	12	0
1946			41	143	3.5	21	0
Career			230	904	3.9	80	3

Bob Davis

Year	Team		Att	Yds	Avg	Lg	TD
1967	HOU	A	5	32	6.4	10	0
1968			15	91	6.1	20	1
1969			3	2	0.7	4	0
1970	NYJ	N	2	11	5.5	10	0
1971			18	154	8.6	24	1
1972			6	32	5.3	20	0
1973	NO		3	10	3.3	7	0
Career			52	332	6.4	24	2

Bruce Davis

Year	Team		Att	Yds	Avg	Lg	TD
1984	CLE	N	1	6	6.0	6	0

Charlie Davis

Year	Team		Att	Yds	Avg	Lg	TD
1974	CIN	N	72	375	5.2	29	0
1976	TB	N	41	107	2.6	13	1
Career			113	482	4.3	29	1

Clarence Davis

Year	Team		Att	Yds	Avg	Lg	TD
1971	OAK	N	54	321	5.9	39	2
1972			71	363	5.1	45t	6
1973			116	609	5.3	32t	4
1974			129	554	4.3	41	2
1975			112	486	4.3	41	4
1976			114	516	4.5	31	3
1977			194	787	4.1	37t	5
1978			14	4	0.3	7	0
Career			804	3640	4.5	45t	26
Playoffs			128	506	4.0		2

Corby Davis

Year	Team		Att	Yds	Avg	Lg	TD
1938	CLE	N	71	202	2.8		3
1939			13	15	1.2		1
1941			31	110	3.5	18	0

Corby Davis *continued*

Year	Team		Att	Yds	Avg	Lg	TD
1942			28	55	2.0	12	0
Career			143	382	2.7	18	4

Dave Davis

Year	Team		Att	Yds	Avg	Lg	TD
1972	GB	N	2	0	0.0	7	0

Dick Davis

Year	Team		Att	Yds	Avg	Lg	TD
1970	NO	N	27	94	3.5	25	0

Elgin Davis

Year	Team		Att	Yds	Avg	Lg	TD
1987	NE	N	9	43	4.8	27	0

Gary Davis

Year	Team		Att	Yds	Avg	Lg	TD
1976	MIA	N	31	160	5.2	57	1
1977			126	533	4.2	60t	2
1978			62	313	5.0	65t	3
1979			98	383	3.9	42	1
1980	TB	N	7	21	3.0	12	0
Career			324	1410	4.4	65t	7
Playoffs			2	12	6.0		0

Glenn Davis

Year	Team		Att	Yds	Avg	Lg	TD
1950	LA	N	88	416	4.7	55	3
1951			64	200	3.1	23	1
Career			152	616	4.1	55	4
Playoffs			20	15	0.8		0

Harper Davis

Year	Team		Att	Yds	Avg	Lg	TD
1949	LA	AA	13	33	2.5		1
1950	CHIB	N	10	57	5.7	36t	1
Career			23	90	3.9	36t	2

Harrison Davis

Year	Team		Att	Yds	Avg	Lg	TD
1974	SD	N	2	-7	-3.5	2	0

Jerry Davis

Year	Team		Att	Yds	Avg	Lg	TD
1948	CHIC	N	12	77	6.4	35	0
1951			1	-7	-7.0	-7	0
Career			13	70	5.4	35	0

Johnny Davis

Year	Team		Att	Yds	Avg	Lg	TD
1978	TB	N	97	370	3.8	8t	3
1979			59	221	3.7	18	2
1980			39	130	3.3	8	1
1981	SF	N	94	297	3.2	14	7
1982	CLE	N	4	3	0.8	2	1
1983			13	42	3.2	16	0
1984			3	15	5.0	8	1
1985			4	9	2.3	5	0
1987			1	7	7.0	7	0
Career			314	1094	3.5	18	15
Playoffs			9	21	2.3		1

Kenneth Davis

Year	Team		Att	Yds	Avg	Lg	TD
1986	GB	N	114	519	4.6	50	0
1987			109	413	3.8	39t	3
1988			39	121	3.1	27	1
1989	BUF	N	29	149	5.1	21	1
1990			64	302	4.7	47	4
1991			129	624	4.8	78t	4
1992			139	613	4.4	64t	6
1993			109	391	3.6	19	6
1994			91	381	4.2	60	2
Career			823	3513	4.3	78t	27
Playoffs			128	549	4.3		7

Lamar Davis

Year	Team		Att	Yds	Avg	Lg	TD
1946	MIA	AA	14	64	4.6	55t	0
1947	BAL	AA	3	14	4.7		0
Career			17	78	4.6	55t	0

Paul Davis

Year	Team		Att	Yds	Avg	Lg	TD
1947	PIT	N	4	5	1.3	6	0
1948			2	-1	-0.5	1	0
Career			6	4	0.7	6	0

Red Davis

Year	Team		Att	Yds	Avg	Lg	TD
1933	PHI	N					1

Russell Davis

Year	Team		Att	Yds	Avg	Lg	TD
1980	PIT	N	33	132	4.0	12	1
1981			47	270	5.7	28	1

Russell Davis continued

Year	Team	Att	Yds	Avg	Lg	TD
1982		24	72	3.0	9	0
Career		104	474	4.6	28	2

Stephen Davis

Year	Team	Att	Yds	Avg	Lg	TD
1996	WAS N	23	139	.6.0	39t	2

Steve Davis

Year	Team	Att	Yds	Avg	Lg	TD
1972	PIT N	20	85	4.3	28t	1
1973		67	266	4.0	27	2
1974		71	246	3.5	22	2
1975	NYJ N	70	290	4.1	24	1
1976		94	418	4.4	26	3
Career		322	1305	4.1	28t	9
Playoffs		5	32	6.4		0

Terrell Davis

Year	Team	Att	Yds	Avg	Lg	TD
1995	DEN N	237	1117	4.7	60t	7
1996		345	1538	4.5	71t	13
Career		582	2655	4.6	71t	20
Playoffs		14	91	6.5		1

Tommy Davis

Year	Team	Att	Yds	Avg	Lg	TD
1965	SF N	1	21	21.0	21	0
1966		3	43	14.3	22	0
1969		2	21	10.5	16	0
Career		6	85	14.2	22	0

Tony Davis

Year	Team	Att	Yds	Avg	Lg	TD
1976	CIN N	36	178	4.9	16	1
1977		27	81	3.0	13	2
1978		21	57	2.7	15	2
1980	TB N	5	24	4.8	8	0
1981		2	5	2.5	3	0
Career		91	345	3.8	16	5

Wendell Davis

Year	Team	Att	Yds	Avg	Lg	TD
1988	CHI N	1	3	3.0	3	0
1992		4	42	10.5	21	0
Career		5	45	9.0	21	0

Willie Davis

Year	Team	Att	Yds	Avg	Lg	TD
1992	KC N	1	-11	-11.0	-11	0
1996	HOU N	1	15	15.0	15	0
Career		2	4	2.0	15	0

Joe Dawkins

Year	Team	Att	Yds	Avg	Lg	TD
1970	HOU N	124	517	4.2	49	2
1971		42	135	3.2	21	2
1972	DEN N	56	243	4.3	19	2
1973		160	706	4.4	72t	2
1974	NYG N	156	561	3.6	16	2
1975		129	438	3.4	15	2
1976	HOU N	31	61	2.0	7	1
Career		698	2661	3.8	72t	13

Fred Dawley

Year	Team	Att	Yds	Avg	Lg	TD
1944	DET N	2	16	8.0	13	0

Lawrence Dawsey

Year	Team	Att	Yds	Avg	Lg	TD
1991	TB N	1	9	9.0	9t	1

Gib Dawson

Year	Team	Att	Yds	Avg	Lg	TD
1953	GB N	5	18	3.6	18	0

Lake Dawson

Year	Team	Att	Yds	Avg	Lg	TD
1994	KC N	3	24	8.0	13	0
1995		1	-9	-9.0	-9	0
Career		4	15	3.8	13	0

Len Dawson

Year	Team	Att	Yds	Avg	Lg	TD
1957	PIT N	3	31	10.3	27	0
1958		2	-1	-0.5	1	0
1959		4	20	5.0	10	0
1960	CLE N	1	0	0.0	0	0
1961		1	-10	-10.0	-10	0
1962	DAL A	38	252	6.6	22	3
1963	KC A	37	272	7.4	43	2
1964		40	89	2.2	18	2
1965		43	142	3.3	40	2
1966		24	167	7.0	18	2
1967		20	68	3.4	24	0
1968		20	40	2.0	22	0
1969		1	3	3.0	3	0

Len Dawson continued

Year	Team	Att	Yds	Avg	Lg	TD
1970	KC N	11	46	4.2	21	0
1971		12	24	2.0	8	0
1972		15	75	5.0	20	0
1973		6	40	6.7	13	0
1974		11	28	2.5	10	0
1975		5	7	1.4	9	0
Career		294	1293	4.4	43	9
Playoffs		21	103	4.9		1

Eagle Day

Year	Team	Att	Yds	Avg	Lg	TD
1959	WAS N	3	27	9.0	18	0
1960		3	1	0.3	5	0
Career		6	28	4.7	18	0

Harry Dayhoff

Year	Team	Att	Yds	Avg	Lg	TD
1924	FRA N					2

Tony Daykin

Year	Team	Att	Yds	Avg	Lg	TD
1978	DET N	1	8	8.0	8	0
1981	ATL N	1	2	2.0	2	0
Career		2	10	5.0	8	0

Rufus Deal

Year	Team	Att	Yds	Avg	Lg	TD
1942	WAS N	5	12	2.4	6	0

Randy Dean

Year	Team	Att	Yds	Avg	Lg	TD
1978	NYG N	14	94	6.7	19	0
1979		8	56	7.0	19	1
Career		22	150	6.8	19	1

Ted Dean

Year	Team	Att	Yds	Avg	Lg	TD
1960	PHI N	113	304	2.7	32	0
1961		66	321	4.9	44	2
1963		79	268	3.4	26	0
1964	MIN N	5	30	6.0	9	0
Career		263	923	3.5	44	2
Playoffs		13	54	4.2		1

Steve DeBerg

Year	Team	Att	Yds	Avg	Lg	TD
1978	SF N	15	20	1.3	7	1
1979		17	10	0.6	-8	0
1980		6	4	0.7	7	0
1981	DEN N	9	40	4.4	11	0
1982		8	27	3.4	6t	1
1983		13	28	2.2	11	1
1984	TB N	28	59	2.1	14	2
1985		9	28	3.1	13	0
1986		2	1	0.5	1t	1
1987		8	-8	-1.0	0	0
1988	KC N	18	30	1.7	13	1
1989		14	-8	-0.6	15	0
1990		21	-5	-0.2	6	0
1991		21	-15	-0.7	0	0
1992	TB N	3	3	1.0	4	0
1993	MIA N	4	-4	-1.0	-1	0
Career		196	210	1.1	15	7
Playoffs		3	-5	-1.7		0

Bill deCorrevont

Year	Team	Att	Yds	Avg	Lg	TD
1945	WAS N	22	91	4.1	18	0
1946	DET N	8	-32	-4.0	-5	0
1947	CHIC N	29	149	5.1	27	1
1948	CHIB N	16	23	1.4	7	0
Career		75	231	3.1	27	1
Playoffs		1	-2	-2.0		0

Bob DeFruiter

Year	Team	Att	Yds	Avg	Lg	TD
1945	WAS N	7	36	5.1	17	0
1946		2	-2	-1.0	0	0
1947	DET N	1	-2	-2.0	-2	0
1948	LA N	3	4	1.3	4	0
Career		13	36	2.8	17	0
Playoffs		1	15	15.0		0

Jack DeGrenier

Year	Team	Att	Yds	Avg	Lg	TD
1974	NO N	33	110	3.3	10	0

Al Dekdebrun

Year	Team	Att	Yds	Avg	Lg	TD
1946	BUF AA	25	-55	-2.2	0	0
1947	CHI AA	20	71	3.5	0	0
1948	NYY-BOS AA-N	9	38	4.2	13	0
Career		54	54	1.0	13	0

Joe Delaney

Year	Team	Att	Yds	Avg	Lg	TD
1981	KC N	234	1121	4.8	82t	3
1982		95	380	4.0	36	0
Career		329	1501	4.6	82t	3

Jack Del Bello

Year	Team	Att	Yds	Avg	Lg	TD
1953	BAL N	14	14	1.0	9	0

Jim Del Gaizo

Year	Team	Att	Yds	Avg	Lg	TD
1972	MIA N	1	0	0.0	0	0
1973	GB N	4	1	0.3	3	0
1974	NYG N	3	15	5.0	6	0
Career		8	16	2.0	6	0

Al Del Greco

Year	Team	Att	Yds	Avg	Lg	TD
1988	PHX N	1	8	8.0	8	0

Spiro Dellerba

Year	Team	Att	Yds	Avg	Lg	TD
1947	CLE AA	29	176	6.1		0
1948	BAL AA	2	0	0.0		0
Career		31	176	5.7		0

Jack Deloplaine

Year	Team	Att	Yds	Avg	Lg	TD
1976	PIT N	17	91	5.4	19	2
1977		2	7	3.5	5	0
1978		11	49	4.5	19	0
1979	CHI N	7	18	2.6	6	0
Career		37	165	4.5	19	2
Playoffs		4	32	8.0		0

Robert Delpino

Year	Team	Att	Yds	Avg	Lg	TD
1988	LARM N	34	147	4.3	13	0
1989		78	368	4.7	32t	1
1990		13	52	4.0	13	0
1991		214	688	3.2	36	9
1992		32	115	3.6	31	0
1993	DEN N	131	445	3.4	18	8
Career		502	1815	3.6	36	18
Playoffs		13	39	3.0		0

Jack Del Rio

Year	Team	Att	Yds	Avg	Lg	TD
1986	NO N	1	16	16.0	16	0

Bill Demory

Year	Team	Att	Yds	Avg	Lg	TD
1973	NYJ N	4	-1	-0.3	0	0

Bob DeMoss

Year	Team	Att	Yds	Avg	Lg	TD
1949	NYB N	5	1	0.2	4	0

Preston Dennard

Year	Team	Att	Yds	Avg	Lg	TD
1979	LA N	4	32	8.0	15	0
1980		2	20	10.0	21	0
1981		6	29	4.8	21	0
Career		12	81	6.8	21	0

Austin Denney

Year	Team	Att	Yds	Avg	Lg	TD
1968	CHI N	1	-1	-1.0	-1	0
1969		1	4	4.0	4	0
Career		2	3	1.5	4	0

Mike Dennis

Year	Team	Att	Yds	Avg	Lg	TD
1968	LA N	29	136	4.7	16	0

Doug Dennison

Year	Team	Att	Yds	Avg	Lg	TD
1974	DAL N	16	52	3.3	14	4
1975		111	383	3.5	27	7
1976		153	542	3.5	14	6
1977		12	60	5.0	17	1
1978		14	75	5.4	23	1
Career		306	1112	3.6	27	19
Playoffs		38	130	3.4		2

Glenn Dennison

Year	Team	Att	Yds	Avg	Lg	TD
1984	NYJ N	1	4	4.0	4	0

Earl Denny

Year	Team	Att	Yds	Avg	Lg	TD
1968	MIN N	2	9	4.5	9	0

Al Denson

Year	Team	Att	Yds	Avg	Lg	TD
1965	DEN A	1	-4	-4.0	-4	0
1967		1	-2	-2.0	-2	0
1969		1	9	9.0	9	0
1971	MIN N	1	0	0.0	0	0
Career		4	3	0.8	9	0

Moses Denson

Year	Team		Att	Yds	Avg	Lg	TD
1974	WAS	N	103	391	3.8	23	0
1975			56	195	3.5	4t	0
Career			159	586	3.7	23	0
Playoffs			7	5	0.7		1

Jerry DePoyster

Year	Team		Att	Yds	Avg	Lg	TD
1968	DET	N	1	20	20.0	20	0
1971	OAK	N	1	-14	-14.0	-14	0
Career			2	6	3.0	20	0

Lee DeRamus

Year	Team		Att	Yds	Avg	Lg	TD
1996	NO	N	1	2	2.0	2	0

Dean Derby

Year	Team		Att	Yds	Avg	Lg	TD
1957	PIT	N	18	49	2.7	7	2

Dan DeSantis

Year	Team		Att	Yds	Avg	Lg	TD
1941	PHI	N	45	125	2.8	26	0

Chuck DeShane

Year	Team		Att	Yds	Avg	Lg	TD
1946	DET	N	2	3	1.5	2	0

Darrell Dess

Year	Team		Att	Yds	Avg	Lg	TD
1967	NYG	N	0	1		Llt	1

Fred DeStefano

Year	Team		Att	Yds	Avg	Lg	TD
1924	CHIC	N					1

Ty Detmer

Year	Team		Att	Yds	Avg	Lg	TD
1993	GB	N	1	-2	-2.0	-2	0
1995			3	3	1.0	5	0
1996	PHI	N	31	59	1.9	9	1
Career			35	60	1.7	9	1

Jim Dewar

Year	Team		Att	Yds	Avg	Lg	TD
1947	CLE	AA	14	64	4.6		1

Billy Dewell

Year	Team		Att	Yds	Avg	Lg	TD
1941	CHIC	N	1	-1	-1.0	-1	0

Herb DeWitz

Year	Team		Att	Yds	Avg	Lg	TD
1927	CLE	N					1

Rufe DeWitz

Year	Team		Att	Yds	Avg	Lg	TD
1926	KC	N					1

Buddy Dial

Year	Team		Att	Yds	Avg	Lg	TD
1960	PIT	N	1	8	8.0	8	0
1961			3	6	2.0	15	0
Career			4	14	3.5	15	0

Rich Diana

Year	Team		Att	Yds	Avg	Lg	TD
1982	MIA	N	8	31	3.9	7	0

Dorne Dibble

Year	Team		Att	Yds	Avg	Lg	TD
1956	DET	N	1	8	8.0	8	0
1957			1	5	5.0	5	0
Career			2	13	6.5	8	0

Eric Dickerson

Year	Team		Att	Yds	Avg	Lg	TD
1983	LARM	N	390	1808	4.6	85t	18
1984			379	2105	5.6	66	14
1985			292	1234	4.2	43	12
1986			404	1821	4.5	42t	11
1987	LARM-IND	N	283	1288	4.6	57	6
1988	IND	N	388	1659	4.3	41t	14
1989			314	1311	4.2	21t	7
1990			166	677	4.1	43	4
1991			167	536	3.2	28	2
1992	LARI	N	187	729	3.9	40t	2
1993	ATL	N	26	91	3.5	10	0
Career			2996	13259	4.4	85t	90
Playoffs			148	724	4.9		3

Ron Dickerson

Year	Team		Att	Yds	Avg	Lg	TD
1994	KC	N	1	0	0.0	0	0

Curtis Dickey

Year	Team		Att	Yds	Avg	Lg	TD
1980	BAL	N	176	800	4.5	51t	11
1981			164	779	4.8	67t	7
1982			66	232	3.5	25	1
1983			254	1122	4.4	56	4
1984	IND	N	131	523	4.0	30	3

Curtis Dickey *continued*

Year	Team		Att	Yds	Avg	Lg	TD
1985	IND-CLE	N	11	40	3.6	11	0
1986	CLE	N	135	523	3.9	47	6
Career			937	4019	4.3	67t	32
Playoffs			9	32	3.6		0

Lynn Dickey

Year	Team		Att	Yds	Avg	Lg	TD
1971	HOU	N	1	4	4.0	4	0
1973			6	9	1.5	6	0
1974			3	7	2.3	7	0
1975			1	3	3.0	3	0
1976	GB	N	11	19	1.7	12	1
1977			5	24	4.8	10	0
1979			5	13	2.6	8	0
1980			19	11	0.6	7t	1
1981			19	6	0.3	13	0
1982			13	19	1.5	11	0
1983			21	12	0.6	4	3
1984			18	6	0.3	9	3
1985			18	-12	-0.7	3	1
Career			140	121	0.9	13	9
Playoffs			2	0	0.0	0	0

Bo Dickinson

Year	Team		Att	Yds	Avg	Lg	TD
1960	DAL	A	35	143	4.1	31	1
1961			71	263	3.7	65	3
1962	DEN	A	73	247	3.4	42	0
1963	DEN-HOU	A	6	33	5.5	13	1
1964	OAK	A	4	8	2.0	6	0
Career			189	694	3.7	65	5

Parnell Dickinson

Year	Team		Att	Yds	Avg	Lg	TD
1976	TB	N	13	103	7.9	46	0

Chuck Dicus

Year	Team		Att	Yds	Avg	Lg	TD
1971	SD	N	1	-2	-2.0	-2	0
1972			1	-11	-11.0	-11	0
Career			2	-13	-6.5	-2	0

Wally Diehl

Year	Team		Att	Yds	Avg	Lg	TD
1928	FRA	N					3
1929							6
Career							9

Scott Dierking

Year	Team		Att	Yds	Avg	Lg	TD
1977	NYJ	N	79	315	4.0	21	0
1978			170	681	4.0	26	4
1979			186	767	4.1	40	3
1980			156	567	3.6	15	6
1981			74	328	4.4	15t	1
1982			38	130	3.4	11	1
1983			28	113	4.0	31	3
1984	TB	N	3	14	4.7	9	0
Career			734	2915	4.0	40	18
Playoffs			6	16	2.7		1

Shelton Diggs

Year	Team		Att	Yds	Avg	Lg	TD
1977	NYJ	N	1	16	16.0	16	0

Trent Dilfer

Year	Team		Att	Yds	Avg	Lg	TD
1994	TB	N	2	27	13.5	15	0
1995			23	115	5.0	21t	2
1996			32	124	3.9	19	0
Career			57	266	4.7	21t	2

Steve Dils

Year	Team		Att	Yds	Avg	Lg	TD
1980	MIN	N	3	26	8.7	19	0
1981			4	14	3.5	7	0
1982			1	5	5.0	5	0
1983			16	28	1.8	5	0
1985	LARM	N	2	-4	-2.0	-2	0
1986			10	5	0.5	5	0
1987			7	-4	-0.6	5	0
1988	ATL	N	2	1	0.5	1t	1
Career			45	71	1.6	19	1

Bucky Dilts

Year	Team		Att	Yds	Avg	Lg	TD
1977	DEN	N	1	0	0.0	0	0
1979	BAL	N	1	-14	-14.0	-14	0
Career			2	-14	-7.0	0	0

Anthony Dilweg

Year	Team		Att	Yds	Avg	Lg	TD
1990	GB	N	21	114	5.4	22	0

Babe Dimancheff

Year	Team		Att	Yds	Avg	Lg	TD
1945	BOS	N	30	69	2.3	15	0
1946			57	238	4.2	24	0
1947	CHIC	N	30	116	3.9	14	0
1948			27	117	4.3	26t	1
1949			38	151	4.0	22	3
1950			8	5	0.6	5	0
1952	CHIB	N	17	106	6.2	77t	1
Career			207	802	3.9	77t	5

Tom Dimitroff

Year	Team		Att	Yds	Avg	Lg	TD
1960	BOS	A	2	-10	-5.0		0

Mike Dingle

Year	Team		Att	Yds	Avg	Lg	TD
1991	CIN	N	21	91	4.3	21	0

Tom Dinkel

Year	Team		Att	Yds	Avg	Lg	TD
1978	CIN	N	1	20	20.0	20	0
1979			2	14	7.0	9	0
Career			3	34	11.3	20	0

Fred DiRenzo

Year	Team		Att	Yds	Avg	Lg	TD
1987	NYG	N	1	5	5.0	5	0

Bob DiRico

Year	Team		Att	Yds	Avg	Lg	TD
1987	NYG	N	25	90	3.6	14	0

Mike Ditka

Year	Team		Att	Yds	Avg	Lg	TD
1971	DAL	N	2	2	1.0	11	0
Playoffs			1	17	17.0		0

Joe DiVito

Year	Team		Att	Yds	Avg	Lg	TD
1968	DEN	A	1	-1	-1.0	-1	0

Al Dixon

Year	Team		Att	Yds	Avg	Lg	TD
1981	KC	N	1	-5	-5.0	-5	0

Floyd Dixon

Year	Team		Att	Yds	Avg	Lg	TD
1986	ATL	N	11	67	6.1	23	0
1987			3	-3	-1.0	7	0
1988			7	69	9.9	24	0
1989			2	-23	-11.5	0	0
Career			23	110	4.8	24	0

Hewritt Dixon

Year	Team		Att	Yds	Avg	Lg	TD
1963	DEN	A	23	105	4.6	18	2
1964			18	25	1.4	17	0
1966	OAK	A	68	277	4.1	23	5
1967			153	559	3.7	40	5
1968			206	865	4.2	28	2
1969			107	398	3.7	19	0
1970	OAK	N	197	861	4.4	39t	1
Career			772	3090	4.0	40	15
Playoffs			94	419	4.5		1

James Dixon

Year	Team		Att	Yds	Avg	Lg	TD
1989	DAL	N	3	30	10.0	13	0
1990			11	43	3.9	18	0
Career			14	73	5.2	18	0

Zack Dixon

Year	Team		Att	Yds	Avg	Lg	TD
1979	DEN	N	3	9	3.0	7	0
1980	PHI	N	2	8	4.0	5	0
1981	BAL	N	73	285	3.9	41	0
1982			58	249	4.3	32	1
1983	BAL-SEA	N	9	32	3.6	7	0
1984	SEA	N	52	149	2.9	17	2
Career			197	732	3.7	41	3
Playoffs			6	28	4.7		0

Dinger Doane

Year	Team		Att	Yds	Avg	Lg	TD
1922	MIL	N					1
1923							2
1924							4
1925	DET	N					5
1926							2
Career							14

Glenn Dobbs

Year	Team		Att	Yds	Avg	Lg	TD
1946	BKN	AA	95	208	2.2	58t	4
1947	BKN-LA	AA	42	131	3.1		1
1948	LA	AA	91	539	5.9	50	4
1949			34	161	4.7		3
Career			262	1039	4.0	58t	12

Al Dodd

Year	Team		Att	Yds	Avg	Lg	TD
1969	NO	N	3	12	4.0	9	0
1970			5	31	6.2	16	0
1971			1	7	7.0	7	0
Career			9	50	5.6	16	0

Les Dodson

Year	Team		Att	Yds	Avg	Lg	TD
1941	PIT	N	2	-4	-2.0	6	0

John Doehring

Year	Team		Att	Yds	Avg	Lg	TD
1932	CHIB	N					1
1933			13	58	4.5		0
1934			8	6	0.8		0
1935	PIT	N	3	-6	-2.0		0
1936	CHIB	N	18	101	5.6		0
1937			9	33	3.7		0
Career			51	192	3.8		1

Jack Dolbin

Year	Team		Att	Yds	Avg	Lg	TD
1975	DEN	N	5	72	14.4	25	0
1976			2	5	2.5	8	0
1977			2	12	6.0	14	0
Career			9	89	9.9	25	0

Don Doll

Year	Team		Att	Yds	Avg	Lg	TD
1949	DET	N	8	25	3.1	10	1

Tony Dollinger

Year	Team		Att	Yds	Avg	Lg	TD
1987	DET	N	8	22	2.8	8	0

Dick Dolly

Year	Team		Att	Yds	Avg	Lg	TD
1941	PIT	N	1	2	2.0	2	0

Marty Domres

Year	Team		Att	Yds	Avg	Lg	TD
1969	SD	A	19	145	7.6	22	4
1970	SD	N	14	39	2.8	7	0
1971			1	0	0.0	0	0
1972	BAL	N	30	137	4.6	15t	1
1973			32	126	3.9	14	2
1974			22	145	6.6	21	2
1975			4	46	11.5	20t	1
1976	SF	N	4	18	4.5	8	0
1977	NYJ	N	4	23	5.8	11	0
Career			130	679	5.2	22	10
Playoffs			4	17	4.3		

Gene Donaldson

Year	Team		Att	Yds	Avg	Lg	TD
1967	BUF	A	3	-1	-0.3	-2	0

John Donaldson

Year	Team		Att	Yds	Avg	Lg	TD
1949	LA	AA	1	-2	-2.0	-2	0

Al Donelli

Year	Team		Att	Yds	Avg	Lg	TD
1941	PIT	N	15	32	2.1	7	0
1942			2	-4	-2.0		0
Career			17	28	1.6	7	0

Doug Donley

Year	Team		Att	Yds	Avg	Lg	TD
1984	DAL	N	2	5	2.5	6	0
Playoffs			1	25	25.0	25	0

Rick Donnelly

Year	Team		Att	Yds	Avg	Lg	TD
1985	ATL	N	2	-5	-2.5	0	0
1987			3	-6	-2.0	0	0
Career			5	-11	-2.2	0	0

Bill Donohue

Year	Team		Att	Yds	Avg	Lg	TD
1927	FRA	N					1

Jack Doolan

Year	Team		Att	Yds	Avg	Lg	TD
1945	NYG	N	10	26	2.6	10	0
1946			12	33	2.8	24	0
Career			22	59	2.7	24	0
Playoffs			1	4	4.0		

Jim Dooley

Year	Team		Att	Yds	Avg	Lg	TD
1952	CHIB	N	1	0	0.0	0	0

Dan Doornink

Year	Team		Att	Yds	Avg	Lg	TD
1978	NYG	N	60	306	5.1	24	1
1979	SEA	N	152	500	3.3	26t	8
1980			100	344	3.4	22	3
1981			65	194	3.0	11	1
1982			45	178	4.0	46	0

Dan Doornink continued

Year	Team		Att	Yds	Avg	Lg	TD
1983			40	99	2.5	9	2
1984			57	215	3.8	25	0
1985			4	0	0.0	3	0
Career			523	1836	3.5	46	15
Playoffs			39	161	4.1		0

Jim Doran

Year	Team		Att	Yds	Avg	Lg	TD
1951	DET	N	2	23	11.5	7	0
1952			1	36	36.0	36	0
Career			3	59	19.7	36	0

Al Dorow

Year	Team		Att	Yds	Avg	Lg	TD
1954	WAS	N	34	117	3.4	14	3
1955			8	49	6.1	19	0
1956			30	105	3.5	30	0
1957	PHI	N	17	52	3.1	14	2
1960	NY	A	124	167	1.3		7
1961			54	317	5.9	40	4
1962	BUF	A	15	57	3.8	15	0
Career			282	864	3.1	40	16

Tony Dorsett

Year	Team		Att	Yds	Avg	Lg	TD
1977	DAL	N	208	1007	4.8	84t	12
1978			290	1325	4.6	63	7
1979			250	1107	4.4	41	6
1980			278	1185	4.3	56	11
1981			342	1646	4.8	75t	4
1982			**177**	745	4.2	99t	5
1983			289	1321	4.6	77	8
1984			302	1189	3.9	31t	6
1985			305	1307	4.3	60t	7
1986			184	748	4.1	33	5
1987			130	456	3.5	24	1
1988	DEN	N	181	703	3.9	26	5
Career			2936	12739	4.3	99t	77
Playoffs			302	1383	4.6		9

Larry Dorsey

Year	Team		Att	Yds	Avg	Lg	TD
1976	SD	N	1	-12	-12.0	-12	0

Noble Doss

Year	Team		Att	Yds	Avg	Lg	TD
1947	PHI	N	11	45	4.1	20	0
1948			62	193	3.1	18	0
1949	B-NY	AA	5	15	3.0		0
Career			78	253	3.2	20	0

Kayo Dottley

Year	Team		Att	Yds	Avg	Lg	TD
1951	CHIB	N	127	670	5.3	38	3
1952			65	302	4.6	44t	3
1953			58	150	2.6	12	1
Career			250	1122	4.5	44t	7

Glenn Doughty

Year	Team		Att	Yds	Avg	Lg	TD
1972	BAL	N	2	33	16.5	17	0
1973			10	96	9.6	30	0
1974			7	51	7.3	17	0
1975			1	5	5.0	5	0
1976			3	7	2.3	3	0
1977			2	11	5.5	16	0
1978			1	-1	-1.0	-1	0
Career			26	202	7.8	30	0

Bob Douglas

Year	Team		Att	Yds	Avg	Lg	TD
1938	PIT	N	4	10	2.5		0

Merrill Douglas

Year	Team		Att	Yds	Avg	Lg	TD
1958	CHIB	N	10	53	5.3	18	0
1959			24	47	2.0	9	2
1960	CHI	N	11	82	7.5	20	0
1961	DAL	N	5	24	4.8	6	0
1962	PHI	N	4	7	1.8	6	0
Career			54	213	3.9	20	2

Bobby Douglass

Year	Team		Att	Yds	Avg	Lg	TD
1969	CHI	N	51	408	8.0	39t	2
1970			7	22	3.1	7	0
1971			39	284	7.3	30	3
1972			141	968	**6.9**	57t	8
1973			94	525	5.6	42	5
1974			36	229	6.4	17	1
1975	CHI-SD	N	15	76	5.1	18	1
1976	NO	N	21	92	4.4	19	2
1977			2	23	11.5	20	0

Bobby Douglass continued

Year	Team		Att	Yds	Avg	Lg	TD
1978	GB	N	4	27	6.8	17	0
Career			410	2654	6.5	57t	22

Bob Dove

Year	Team		Att	Yds	Avg	Lg	TD
1948	CHIC	N	1	-2	-2.0	-2	0

Woody Dow

Year	Team		Att	Yds	Avg	Lg	TD
1938	PHI	N	4	20	5.0		0
1939			1	-7	-7.0	-7	0
Career			5	13	2.6	-7	0

Harry Dowda

Year	Team		Att	Yds	Avg	Lg	TD
1949	WAS	N	65	239	3.7	21	2
1950			23	47	2.0	11	0
1951			29	111	3.8	32	0
1952			6	5	0.8	5	0
1953			1	3	3.0	3	0
Career			124	405	3.3	32	2

Mule Dowell

Year	Team		Att	Yds	Avg	Lg	TD
1936	CHIC	N	54	151	2.8		0

Boyd Dowler

Year	Team		Att	Yds	Avg	Lg	TD
1959	GB	N	1	20	20.0	20	0
1960			1	8	8.0	8	0
Career			2	28	14.0	20	0

Brian Dowling

Year	Team		Att	Yds	Avg	Lg	TD
1972	NE	N	7	35	5.0	11	3

Gary Downs

Year	Team		Att	Yds	Avg	Lg	TD
1994	NYG	N	15	51	3.4	8	0
1996			29	94	3.2	27	0
Career			44	145	3.3	27	0

D.J. Dozier

Year	Team		Att	Yds	Avg	Lg	TD
1987	MIN	N	69	257	3.7	19	5
1988			42	167	4.0	19t	2
1989			46	207	4.5	38	0
1990			6	12	2.0	4	0
1991	DET	N	9	48	5.3	29	0
Career			172	691	4.0	38	7
Playoffs			16	54	3.4		1

Oscar Dragon

Year	Team		Att	Yds	Avg	Lg	TD
1972	SD	N	9	30	3.3	7	0

Johnny Drake

Year	Team		Att	Yds	Avg	Lg	TD
1937	CLE	N	98	333	3.4		3
1938			74	188	2.5		1
1939			118	453	3.8		**9**
1940			134	480	3.6		**9**
1941			101	246	2.4	15	2
Career			525	1700	3.2	15	24

Troy Drayton

Year	Team		Att	Yds	Avg	Lg	TD
1993	LARM	N	1	7	7.0	7	0
1994			1	4	4.0	4	0
Career			2	11	5.5	7	0

Chuck Drazenovich

Year	Team		Att	Yds	Avg	Lg	TD
1950	WAS	N	35	155	4.4	28	1
1951			34	76	2.2	7	3
1952			29	66	2.3	15	3
1953			11	27	2.5	9	1
1954			8	6	0.8	3	0
Career			117	330	2.8	28	8

Chris Dressel

Year	Team		Att	Yds	Avg	Lg	TD
1983	HOU	N	1	3	3.0	3	0

Chuck Dressen

Year	Team		Att	Yds	Avg	Lg	TD
1922	RAC	N					2

Doug Dressler

Year	Team		Att	Yds	Avg	Lg	TD
1970	CIN	N	18	77	4.3	17	0
1971			54	204	3.8	13	1
1972			128	565	4.4	43t	6
1974			72	255	3.5	17	2
1975	NE-KC	N	6	24	4.0	11	0
Career			278	1125	4.0	43t	9

Willie Drewrey

Year	Team		Att	Yds	Avg	Lg	TD
1985	HOU	N	2	-4	-2.0	5	0

Wally Dreyer

Year	Team		Att	Yds	Avg	Lg	TD
1949	CHIB	N	45	172	3.8	38	0
1950	GB	N	1	0	0.0	0	0
Career			46	172	3.7	38	0

Paddy Driscoll

Year	Team		Att	Yds	Avg	Lg	TD
1920	CHIC	A					2
1921							2
1922	CHIC	N					1
1924							2
1925							3
1926	CHIB	N					4
1927							5
1928							2
1929							1
Career							22

Stacey Driver

Year	Team		Att	Yds	Avg	Lg	TD
1987	CLE	N	9	31	3.4	16	0

Al Drulis

Year	Team		Att	Yds	Avg	Lg	TD
1945	CHIC	N	12	49	4.1	13	0
1946			1	0	0.0	0	0
Career			13	49	3.8	13	0

Robert Drummond

Year	Team		Att	Yds	Avg	Lg	TD
1989	PHI	N	32	127	4.0	16	0
1990			8	33	4.1	9	1
1991			12	27	2.3	7	2
Career			52	187	3.6	16	3

Ron Drzewiecki

Year	Team		Att	Yds	Avg	Lg	TD
1955	CHIB	N	10	54	5.4	19	1
1957			5	11	2.2	6	0
Career			15	65	4.3	19	1

Elbert Dubenion

Year	Team		Att	Yds	Avg	Lg	TD
1960	BUF	A	16	94	5.9	66	1
1961			17	173	10.2	72	2
1962			7	40	5.7	43	0
1964			1	20	20.0	20	0
1966			3	16	5.3	17	0
1967			2	-17	-8.5	-1	0
Career			46	326	7.1	72	3
Playoffs			1	9	9.0		0

Tom Dublinski

Year	Team		Att	Yds	Avg	Lg	TD
1952	DET	N	1	3	3.0	3	0
1953			6	39	6.5	17	0
1954			21	76	3.6	15	1
Career			28	118	4.2	17	1
Playoffs			1	5	5.0		0

Doug DuBose

Year	Team		Att	Yds	Avg	Lg	TD
1987	SF	N	10	33	3.3	11	0
1988			24	116	4.8	37t	2
Career			34	149	4.4	37t	2

Jimmy DuBose

Year	Team		Att	Yds	Avg	Lg	TD
1976	TB	N	20	62	3.1	24	0
1977			71	284	4.0	13	0
1978			93	358	3.8	12	4
Career			184	704	3.8	24	4

Kenny Duckett

Year	Team		Att	Yds	Avg	Lg	TD
1983	NO	N	2	-16	-8.0	2	0
1984			1	-3	-3.0	-3	0
Career			3	-19	-6.3	2	0

Joe Dudek

Year	Team		Att	Yds	Avg	Lg	TD
1987	DEN	N	35	154	4.4	16	2

Andy Dudish

Year	Team		Att	Yds	Avg	Lg	TD
1946	BUF	AA	30	106	3.5		0
1947	BAL	AA	28	30	1.1		1
1948	DET	N	1	5	5.0	5	0
Career			59	141	2.4	5	1

Bill Dudley

Year	Team		Att	Yds	Avg	Lg	TD
1942	PIT	N	162	696	4.3	66	5
1945			57	204	3.6	32	3

Bill Dudley *continued*

Year	Team		Att	Yds	Avg	Lg	TD
1946			**146**	**604**	4.1	4	3
1947	DET	N	80	302	3.8	28	4
1948			33	97	2.9	11	0
1949			125	402	3.2	22	4
1950	WAS	N	66	339	5.1	27	1
1951			91	398	4.4	40	2
1953			5	15	3.0	7	0
Career			765	3057	4.0	40	22

Paul Dudley

Year	Team		Att	Yds	Avg	Lg	TD
1962	NYG	N	27	100	3.7	38	0
1963	PHI		11	21	1.9	6	0
Career			38	121	3.2	38	0

Joe Dufek

Year	Team		Att	Yds	Avg	Lg	TD
1984	BUF	N	9	22	2.4	13	1

Fred Dugan

Year	Team		Att	Yds	Avg	Lg	TD
1962	WAS	N	1	-9	-9.0	-9	0

Paul Duhart

Year	Team		Att	Yds	Avg	Lg	TD
1944	GB	N	51	183	3.6	16	2
1945	PIT-BOS	N	17	17	1.0	9	1
Career			68	200	2.9	16	3
Playoffs			7	15	2.1		

Bobby Duhon

Year	Team		Att	Yds	Avg	Lg	TD
1968	NYG	N	101	362	3.6	13	3
1970			18	111	6.2	38	0
1971			93	344	3.7	27	1
1972			9	23	2.6	7	0
Career			221	840	3.8	38	4

Dave Dunaway

Year	Team		Att	Yds	Avg	Lg	TD
1969	NYG	N	1	4	4.0	4	0

Jubilee Dunbar

Year	Team		Att	Yds	Avg	Lg	TD
1973	NO	N	3	3	1.0	13	0

Vaughn Dunbar

Year	Team		Att	Yds	Avg	Lg	TD
1992	NO	N	154	565	3.7	25	3
1994			3	9	3.0	3	0
1995	JAC	N	110	361	3.3	26	2
Career			267	935	3.5	26	5
Playoffs			4	28	7.0		0

Brian Duncan

Year	Team		Att	Yds	Avg	Lg	TD
1976	CLE	N	11	44	4.0	11	0
1977			5	16	3.2	10	0
1978	HOU	N	1	0	0.0	0	0
Career			17	60	3.5	11	0
Playoffs			2	7	3.5		

Curtis Duncan

Year	Team		Att	Yds	Avg	Lg	TD
1989	HOU	N	1	0	0.0	0	0

Maury Duncan

Year	Team		Att	Yds	Avg	Lg	TD
1955	SF	N	1	-5	-5.0	-5	0

Randy Duncan

Year	Team		Att	Yds	Avg	Lg	TD
1961	DAL	A	5	42	8.4	19	0

Tony Dungy

Year	Team		Att	Yds	Avg	Lg	TD
1977	PIT	N	3	8	2.7	6	0

David Dunn

Year	Team		Att	Yds	Avg	Lg	TD
1995	CIN	N	1	-13	-13.0	-13	0

Perry Lee Dunn

Year	Team		Att	Yds	Avg	Lg	TD
1964	DAL	N	26	103	4.0	14	1
1965			54	171	3.2	12	2
1966	ATL	N	22	52	2.4	10	0
1967			27	63	2.3	11	0
1968			72	219	3.0	15	3
1969	BAL	N	13	45	3.5	11	0
Career			214	653	3.1	15	6

Red Dunn

Year	Team		Att	Yds	Avg	Lg	TD
1924	MIL	N					2
1925	CHIC	N					3
Career							5

Elwyn Dunstan

Year	Team		Att	Yds	Avg	Lg	TD
1939	CHIC	N	3	2	0.7		0
1940	CLE	N	1	4	4.0	4	0
Career			4	6	1.5	4	0

Reggie Dupard

Year	Team		Att	Yds	Avg	Lg	TD
1986	NE	N	15	39	2.6	11	0
1987			94	318	3.4	49	3
1988			52	151	2.9	15	2
1989	NE-WAS	N	37	111	3.0	19	1
1990	WAS	N	19	85	4.5	11	0
Career			217	704	3.2	49	6
Playoffs			5	18	3.6		

Mark Duper

Year	Team		Att	Yds	Avg	Lg	TD
1986	MIA	N	1	-10	-10.0	-10	0

L.G. Dupre

Year	Team		Att	Yds	Avg	Lg	TD
1955	BAL	N	88	338	3.8	60	1
1956			49	182	3.7	21	2
1957			101	375	3.7	22	2
1958			95	390	4.1	39	3
1959			23	54	2.3	21	0
1960	DAL	N	104	362	3.5	18	3
1961			16	60	3.8	12	0
Career			476	1761	3.7	60	11
Playoffs			11	30	2.7		

Billy Joe Dupree

Year	Team		Att	Yds	Avg	Lg	TD
1973	DAL	N	2	2	1.0	6	0
1974			4	43	10.8	20	0
1975			1	3	3.0	3	0
1976			7	50	7.1	13	0
1977			3	9	3.0	7	0
1978			1	15	15.0	15	0
1979			2	19	9.5	20	0
1980			4	19	4.8	11	0
1981			1	12	12.0	12	0
1982			1	6	6.0	6t	0
Career			26	178	6.8	20	0
Playoffs			5	56	11.2		0

Marcus Dupree

Year	Team		Att	Yds	Avg	Lg	TD
1990	LARM	N	19	72	3.8	13	0
1991			49	179	3.7	24	1
Career			68	251	3.7	24	1

Don Durdan

Year	Team		Att	Yds	Avg	Lg	TD
1946	SF	AA	32	132	4.1	62	0
1947			1	2	2.0	2	0
Career			33	134	4.1	62	0

Sandy Durko

Year	Team		Att	Yds	Avg	Lg	TD
1971	CIN	N	1	7	7.0	7	0

Jeff Durkota

Year	Team		Att	Yds	Avg	Lg	TD
1948	LA	AA	14	66	4.7		0

Bill Dusenbery

Year	Team		Att	Yds	Avg	Lg	TD
1970	NO	N	4	6	1.5	3	0

Bill Dutton

Year	Team		Att	Yds	Avg	Lg	TD
1946	PIT	N	53	169	3.2	38t	0

Ben Dvorak

Year	Team		Att	Yds	Avg	Lg	TD
1921	MIN	A					2

Henry Dyer

Year	Team		Att	Yds	Avg	Lg	TD
1968	LA	N	55	136	2.5	15	1
1969	WAS	N	6	18	3.0	9	0
1970			21	102	4.9	12	0
Career			82	256	3.1	15	1

Eagle Feather

Year	Team		Att	Yds	Avg	Lg	TD
1922	OOR	N					1

Kay Eakin

Year	Team		Att	Yds	Avg	Lg	TD
1940	NYG	N	14	20	1.4	3	0
1941			27	17	0.6	17	0
1946	MIA	AA	15	-41	-2.7		0
Career			56	-4	-0.1	17	0
Playoffs			1	-1	-1.0		

Ralph Earhart

Year	Team		Att	Yds	Avg	Lg	TD
1948	GB	N	30	140	4.7	72t	1
1949			20	54	2.7	14	0
Career			50	194	3.9	72t	1

Robin Earl

Year	Team		Att	Yds	Avg	Lg	TD
1977	CHI	N	56	233	4.2	34	1
1978			3	17	5.7	9	0
1979			35	132	3.8	12	0
Career			94	382	4.1	34	1
Playoffs			2	6	3.0		0

Quinn Early

Year	Team		Att	Yds	Avg	Lg	TD
1988	SD	N	7	63	9.0	37	0
1989			1	19	19.0	19	0
1991	NO	N	3	13	4.3	6	0
1992			3	-1	-0.3	7	0
1993			2	32	16.0	26	0
1994			2	10	5.0	8	0
1995			2	-3	-1.5	9	0
1996	BUF	N	3	39	13.0	29	0
Career			23	172	7.5	37	0

Walt Easley

Year	Team		Att	Yds	Avg	Lg	TD
1981	SF	N	76	224	2.9	9	1
1982			5	11	2.2	5	0
Career			81	235	2.9	9	1
Playoffs			6	15	2.5		0

Tony Eason

Year	Team		Att	Yds	Avg	Lg	TD
1983	NE	N	19	39	2.1	12	0
1984			40	154	3.9	25t	5
1985			22	70	3.2	23	1
1986			35	170	4.9	26	0
1987			3	25	8.3	13	0
1988			5	18	3.6	10	0
1989	NE-NYJ	N	3	2	0.7	0	0
1990	NYJ	N	7	29	4.1	24	0
Career			134	507	3.8	26	6
Playoffs			14	26	1.9		0

Ox Eckhardt

Year	Team		Att	Yds	Avg	Lg	TD
1928	NYG	N					2

Jerry Eckwood

Year	Team		Att	Yds	Avg	Lg	TD
1979	TB	N	194	690	3.6	61t	2
1980			149	504	3.4	35t	2
1981			172	651	3.8	59	2
Career			515	1845	3.6	61t	6
Playoffs			14	26	1.9		0

Floyd Eddings

Year	Team		Att	Yds	Avg	Lg	TD
1982	NYG	N	2	12	6.0	16	0
1983			1	3	3.0	3	0
Career			3	15	5.0	16	0

Nick Eddy

Year	Team		Att	Yds	Avg	Lg	TD
1968	DET	N	48	176	3.7	20	0
1969			78	272	3.5	26	2
1970			18	47	2.6	9	1
1972			8	28	3.5	10	0
Career			152	523	3.4	26	3

Shayne Edge

Year	Team		Att	Yds	Avg	Lg	TD
1996	PIT	N	1	-16	-16.0	-16	0

Bob Edler

Year	Team		Att	Yds	Avg	Lg	TD
1923	CLE	N					1

Bobby Joe Edmonds

Year	Team		Att	Yds	Avg	Lg	TD
1986	SEA	N	1	-11	-11.0	-11	0
1995	TB	N	5	28	5.6	9	0
Career			6	17	2.8	9	0

Ferrell Edmunds

Year	Team		Att	Yds	Avg	Lg	TD
1988	MIA	N	1	-8	-8.0	-8	0
1990			1	-7	-7.0	-7	0
Career			2	-15	-7.5	-7	0

Al Edwards

Year	Team		Att	Yds	Avg	Lg	TD
1991	BUF	N	1	17	17.0	17	0
1992			1	8	8.0	8	0
Career			2	25	12.5	17	0

Anthony Edwards

Year	Team		Att	Yds	Avg	Lg	TD
1996	ARI	N	1	-8	-8.0	-8	0

Cid Edwards

Year	Team		Att	Yds	Avg	Lg	TD
1968	STL	N	31	214	6.9	42	1
1969			107	504	4.7	48	3
1970			70	350	5.0	22	1
1971			108	316	2.9	14	4
1972	SD	N	157	679	4.3	31t	5
1973			133	609	4.6	50	1
1974			65	261	4.0	30	0
1975	CHI	N	27	73	2.7	16	0
Career			698	3006	4.3	50	15

Emmett Edwards

Year	Team		Att	Yds	Avg	Lg	TD
1975	HOU	N	1	-4	-4.0	-4	0
1976	BUF	N	1	0	0.0	0	0
Career			2	-4	-2.0	0	0

Kelvin Edwards

Year	Team		Att	Yds	Avg	Lg	TD
1986	NO	N	1	6	6.0	6	0
1987	DAL	N	2	61	30.5	62t	1
Career			3	67	22.3	62t	1

Marshall Edwards

Year	Team		Att	Yds	Avg	Lg	TD
1943	BKN	N	1	5	5.0	5	0

Stan Edwards

Year	Team		Att	Yds	Avg	Lg	TD
1982	HOU	N	15	58	3.9	8	0
1983			16	40	2.5	9	0
1984			60	267	4.5	20	1
1985			25	96	3.8	19	1
1986			1	3	3.0	3	0
1987	DET	N	32	69	2.2	13	0
Career			149	533	3.6	20	2

Patrick Egu

Year	Team		Att	Yds	Avg	Lg	TD
1989	NE	N	3	20	6.7	15t	1

Charley Eikenberg

Year	Team		Att	Yds	Avg	Lg	TD
1948	CHIC	N	2	9	4.5	18	0

Mike Eischeid

Year	Team		Att	Yds	Avg	Lg	TD
1968	OAK	A	2	41	20.5	24	0
1969			1	10	10.0	10	0
1972	MIN	N	1	-13	-13.0	-13	0
Career			4	38	9.5	24	0

Alfred Eissler

Year	Team		Att	Yds	Avg	Lg	TD
1920	CHIT	A					1

Monroe Eley

Year	Team		Att	Yds	Avg	Lg	TD
1975	ATL	N	1	3	3.0	3	0
1977			97	273	2.8	16	1
Career			98	276	2.8	16	1

Bruce Elia

Year	Team		Att	Yds	Avg	Lg	TD
1978	SF	N	1	0	0.0	0	0

Keith Elias

Year	Team		Att	Yds	Avg	Lg	TD
1994	NYG	N	2	4	2.0	5	0
1995			10	44	4.4	8	0
1996			9	24	2.7	8	0
Career			21	72	3.4	8	0

Larry Elkins

Year	Team		Att	Yds	Avg	Lg	TD
1967	HOU	A	2	19	9.5	14	0

Henry Ellard

Year	Team		Att	Yds	Avg	Lg	TD
1983	LARM	N	3	7	2.3	12	0
1984			3	-5	-1.7	5	0
1985			3	8	2.7	16	0
1986			1	-15	-15.0	-15	0
1987			1	4	4.0	4	0
1988			1	7	7.0	7	0
1989			2	10	5.0	6	0
1990			2	21	10.5	13	0
1993			2	18	9.0	15	0
1994	WAS	N	1	-5	-5.0	-5	0
Career			19	50	2.6	16	0
Playoffs			1	2	2.0		0

Gary Ellerson

Year	Team		Att	Yds	Avg	Lg	TD
1985	GB	N	32	205	6.4	37t	2

Gary Ellerson continued

Year	Team		Att	Yds	Avg	Lg	TD
1986			90	287	3.2	18	3
1987	DET	N	47	196	4.2	33	3
Career			169	688	4.1	37t	8

Al Elliott

Year	Team		Att	Yds	Avg	Lg	TD
1922	RAC	N					2
1924							1
Career							3

Doc Elliott

Year	Team		Att	Yds	Avg	Lg	TD
1922	CAN	N					2
1923							6
1924	CLE	N					6
1925							2
1931							1
Career							17

Lenvil Elliott

Year	Team		Att	Yds	Avg	Lg	TD
1973	CIN	N	22	122	5.5	15	1
1974			68	345	5.1	26	1
1975			71	308	4.3	27	1
1976			69	276	4.0	24	0
1977			65	269	4.1	32	0
1978			29	75	2.6	12	0
1979	SF	N	33	135	4.1	13	3
1980			76	341	4.5	20	2
1981			7	29	4.1	9	0
Career			440	1900	4.3	32	8
Playoffs			21	88	4.2		1

Craig Ellis

Year	Team		Att	Yds	Avg	Lg	TD
1986	MIA	N	3	6	2.0	2	0
1987	LARI	N	33	138	4.2	14	2
Career			36	144	4.0	14	2

Drew Ellis

Year	Team		Att	Yds	Avg	Lg	TD
1939	PHI	N	6	1	0.2		0

Gerry Ellis

Year	Team		Att	Yds	Avg	Lg	TD
1980	GB	N	126	545	4.3	22	5
1981			196	860	4.4	29	4
1982			62	228	3.7	29	1
1983			141	696	4.9	71	4
1984			123	581	4.7	50	4
1985			104	571	5.5	39t	5
1986			84	345	4.1	24	2
Career			836	3826	4.6	71	25
Playoffs			9	48	5.3		0

Jerry Ellison

Year	Team		Att	Yds	Avg	Lg	TD
1995	TB	N	26	218	8.4	75	5
1996			35	106	3.0	13	0
Career			61	324	5.3	75	5

Willie Ellison

Year	Team		Att	Yds	Avg	Lg	TD
1967	LA	N	14	84	6.0	42	0
1968			151	616	4.1	52t	5
1969			20	56	2.8	15	1
1970			90	381	4.2	24	5
1971			211	1000	4.7	80t	4
1972			170	764	4.5	37	5
1973	KC	N	108	411	3.8	19	2
1974			37	114	3.1	11	2
Career			801	3426	4.3	80t	24
Playoffs			4	22	5.5		0

Swede Ellstrom

Year	Team		Att	Yds	Avg	Lg	TD
1934	PHI	N					1
1935	PIT	N	10	14	1.4		0
1936	CHIC	N	4	12	3.0		0
Career			14	26	1.9		1

Doug Elmore

Year	Team		Att	Yds	Avg	Lg	TD
1962	WAS	N	1	-14	-14.0	-14	0

Earl Elsey

Year	Team		Att	Yds	Avg	Lg	TD
1946	LA	AA	47	165	3.5		0

Art Elston

Year	Team		Att	Yds	Avg	Lg	TD
1942	CLE	N	1	15	15.0	15	0

Leo Elter

Year	Team		Att	Yds	Avg	Lg	TD
1953	PIT	N	26	81	3.1	10	0

Leo Elter continued

Year	Team		Att	Yds	Avg	Lg	TD
1954			13	54	4.2	12	0
1955	WAS	N	97	361	3.7	33t	3
1956			145	544	3.8	48	2
1957			45	211	4.7	22	2
1958	PIT	N	37	104	2.8	18	2
1959			8	25	3.1	9	0
Career			371	1380	3.7	48	9

John Elway

Year	Team		Att	Yds	Avg	Lg	TD
1983	DEN	N	28	146	5.2	23	1
1984			56	237	4.2	21	1
1985			51	253	5.0	22	0
1986			52	257	4.9	24	1
1987			66	304	4.6	29	4
1988			54	234	4.3	26	1
1989			48	244	5.1	31	3
1990			50	258	5.2	21	3
1991			55	255	4.6	17t	6
1992			34	94	2.8	9	2
1993			44	153	3.5	18	0
1994			58	235	4.1	22	4
1995			41	176	4.3	25	1
1996			50	249	5.0	22	4
Career			687	3095	4.5	31	31
Playoffs			76	402	5.3		4

Bert Emanuel

Year	Team		Att	Yds	Avg	Lg	TD
1994	ATL	N	2	4	2.0	2	0
1995			1	0	0.0	0	0
Career			3	4	1.3	2	0

Larry Emery

Year	Team		Att	Yds	Avg	Lg	TD
1987	ATL	N	1	5	5.0	5	0

Frank Emmons

Year	Team		Att	Yds	Avg	Lg	TD
1940	PHI	N	29	77	2.7		1

Wuert Engelmann

Year	Team		Att	Yds	Avg	Lg	TD
1930	GB	N					1
1931							1
Career							2

Rick Engels

Year	Team		Att	Yds	Avg	Lg	TD
1976	SEA	N	3	37	12.3	15	0
1978	PHI	N	1	16	16.0	16	0
Career			4	53	13.3	16	0

Keith English

Year	Team		Att	Yds	Avg	Lg	TD
1990	LARM	N	2	-19	-9.5	-8	0

Hunter Enis

Year	Team		Att	Yds	Avg	Lg	TD
1960	DAL	A	12	-12	-1.0	11	3
1961	SD	A	16	13	0.8	9	2
1962	OAK	A	2	24	12.0	13	0
Career			30	25	0.8	13	5

Fred Enke

Year	Team		Att	Yds	Avg	Lg	TD
1948	DET	N	74	365	4.9	41	0
1949			36	134	3.7	33	1
1950			9	16	1.8	16	0
1951			4	6	1.5	4	0
1952	PHI	N	14	25	1.8	12	0
1953	BAL	N	28	91	3.3	25	0
1954			5	3	0.6	5	0
Career			170	640	3.8	41	1

Rex Enright

Year	Team		Att	Yds	Avg	Lg	TD
1926	GB	N					1
1927							2
Career							3

Bill Enyart

Year	Team		Att	Yds	Avg	Lg	TD
1969	BUF	A	47	191	4.1	26	1
1970	BUF	N	58	196	3.4	17	0
Career			105	387	3.7	26	1

Bobby Epps

Year	Team		Att	Yds	Avg	Lg	TD
1954	NYG	N	30	110	3.7	11	0
1955			95	375	3.9	24	2
1957			63	286	4.5	55	0
Career			188	771	4.1	55	2

Phillip Epps

Year	Team		Att	Yds	Avg	Lg	TD
1985	GB	N	5	103	20.6	34	1
1986			4	18	4.5	20	0
1987			1	0	0.0	0	0
1989	NYJ	N	1	14	14.0	14	0
Career			11	135	12.3	34	1

Dick Erdlitz

Year	Team		Att	Yds	Avg	Lg	TD
1942	PHI	N	21	69	3.3	17	1
1945			6	24	4.0	16	0
1946	MIA	AA	26	38	1.5		1
Career			53	131	2.5	17	2

Rich Erenberg

Year	Team		Att	Yds	Avg	Lg	TD
1984	PIT	N	115	405	3.5	31t	2
1985			17	67	3.9	12	0
1986			42	170	4.0	17	1
Career			174	642	3.7	31t	3
Playoffs			6	27	4.5		1

Craig Erickson

Year	Team		Att	Yds	Avg	Lg	TD
1992	TB	N	1	-1	-1.0	-1	0
1993			26	96	3.7	15	0
1994			26	68	2.6	17	1
1995	IND	N	9	14	1.6	15	0
1996	MIA	N	11	16	1.5	12	0
Career			73	193	2.6	17	1

Hal Erickson

Year	Team		Att	Yds	Avg	Lg	TD
1923	MIL	N					1
1925	CHIC	N					2
Career							3

Jack Ernst

Year	Team		Att	Yds	Avg	Lg	TD
1925	POT	N					2

Mike Ernst

Year	Team		Att	Yds	Avg	Lg	TD
1972	DEN	N	1	4	4.0	4	0

Ricky Ervins

Year	Team		Att	Yds	Avg	Lg	TD
1991	WAS	N	145	680	4.7	65t	3
1992			151	495	3.3	25	2
1993			50	201	4.0	18	0
1994			185	650	3.5	49	3
1995	SF	N	23	88	3.8	13	0
Career			554	2114	3.8	65t	8
Playoffs			49	229	4.7		1

Terry Erwin

Year	Team		Att	Yds	Avg	Lg	TD
1968	DEN	A	24	76	3.2	9	0

Russell Erxleben

Year	Team		Att	Yds	Avg	Lg	TD
1981	NO	N	2	10	5.0	26	0
1983			2	-9	-4.5	1	0
Career			4	1	0.3	26	0

Len Eshmont

Year	Team		Att	Yds	Avg	Lg	TD
1941	NYG	N	50	164	3.3	25	0
1946	SF	AA	73	340	4.7		6
1947			84	381	4.5		0
1948			50	296	5.9		1
1949			25	164	6.6		0
Career			282	1345	4.8	25	7
Playoffs			2	2	1.0		

Boomer Esiason

Year	Team		Att	Yds	Avg	Lg	TD
1984	CIN	N	19	63	3.3	9	2
1985			33	79	2.4	20	1
1986			44	146	3.3	23	1
1987			52	241	4.6	19	0
1988			43	248	5.8	24	1
1989			47	278	5.9	24	0
1990			49	157	3.2	21	0
1991			24	66	2.8	16	0
1992			21	66	3.1	15	0
1993	NYJ	N	45	118	2.6	17	1
1994			28	59	2.1	15	0
1995			19	14	0.7	15	0
1996	ARI	N	15	52	3.5	13	1
Career			439	1587	3.6	24	7
Playoffs			19	105	5.5		1

Alex Espinoza

Year	Team		Att	Yds	Avg	Lg	TD
1987	KC	N	1	5	5.0	5	0

Mike Esposito

Year	Team		Att	Yds	Avg	Lg	TD
1976	ATL	N	60	317	5.3	36t	2
1977			34	101	3.0	23	0
1978			7	21	3.0	7	0
Career			101	439	4.3	36t	2
Playoffs			2	6	3.0		0

Sam Etcheverry

Year	Team		Att	Yds	Avg	Lg	TD
1961	STL	N	33	73	2.2	44	0
1962			8	5	0.6	13	0
Career			41	78	1.9	44	0

Charlie Evans

Year	Team		Att	Yds	Avg	Lg	TD
1971	NYG	N	48	171	3.6	17	5
1972			91	317	3.5	24t	4
1973			34	77	2.3	15	1
1974	WAS	N	32	79	2.5	9	2
Career			205	644	3.1	24t	12

Chuck Evans

Year	Team		Att	Yds	Avg	Lg	TD
1993	MIN	N	14	32	2.3	5	0
1994			6	20	3.3	8	0
1995			19	59	3.1	12	1
1996			13	29	2.2	9	0
Career			52	140	2.7	12	1

Donald Evans

Year	Team		Att	Yds	Avg	Lg	TD
1987	LARM	N	3	10	3.3	5	0

Fred Evans

Year	Team		Att	Yds	Avg	Lg	TD
1946	CLE	AA	8	27	3.4		0
1947	BUF-CHI	AA	31	124	4.0		1
1948	CHIB	N	10	15	1.5	7	0
Career			49	166	3.4	7	1

Johnny Evans

Year	Team		Att	Yds	Avg	Lg	TD
1978	CLE	N	2	12	6.0	12	0
1980			3	-6	-2.0	0	0
Career			5	6	1.2	12	0

Murray Evans

Year	Team		Att	Yds	Avg	Lg	TD
1942	DET	N	1	-1	-1.0	-1	0
1943			2	3	1.5	2	0
Career			3	2	0.7	2	0

Ray Evans

Year	Team		Att	Yds	Avg	Lg	TD
1948	PIT	N	99	343	3.5	24	2

Reggie Evans

Year	Team		Att	Yds	Avg	Lg	TD
1983	WAS	N	16	11	0.7	5	4
Playoffs			3	4	1.3		0

Vince Evans

Year	Team		Att	Yds	Avg	Lg	TD
1977	CHI	N	1	0	0.0	0	0
1978			6	23	3.8	13	0
1979			12	72	6.0	17	1
1980			60	306	5.1	58	8
1981			43	218	5.1	25	3
1982			2	0	0.0	6	0
1983			22	142	6.5	27	0
1987	LARI	N	11	144	13.1	24	1
1989			1	16	16.0	16	0
1990			1	-2	-2.0	-2	0
1991			8	20	2.5	11	0
1992			11	79	7.2	16	0
1993			14	51	3.6	17	0
1994			6	24	4.0	23	0
1995	OAK	N	14	36	2.6	11	0
Career			212	1129	5.3	58	14
Playoffs			4	33	8.3		0

Jim Everett

Year	Team		Att	Yds	Avg	Lg	TD
1986	LARM	N	16	46	2.9	14	1
1987			18	83	4.6	16	1
1988			34	104	3.1	19	0
1989			25	31	1.2	13t	0
1990			20	31	1.6	15	1
1991			27	44	1.6	10	0
1992			32	133	4.2	22	0
1993			19	38	2.0	14	0
1994	NO	N	15	35	2.3	14	0
1995			24	42	1.8	9	0

Year	Team		Att	Yds	Avg	Lg	TD

Jim Everett continued

Year	Team		Att	Yds	Avg	Lg	TD
1996			22	3	0.1	3	0
Career			252	590	2.3	22	4
Playoffs			12	47	3.9		0

Major Everett

Year	Team		Att	Yds	Avg	Lg	TD
1983	PHI	N	5	7	1.4	7	0
1985			4	13	3.3	8	0
1986	CLE	N	12	43	3.6	8	0
1987			34	95	2.8	16	0
Career			55	158	2.9	16	0

Vilnis Ezerins

Year	Team		Att	Yds	Avg	Lg	TD
1968	LA	N	2	2	1.0	1	0

Blake Ezor

Year	Team		Att	Yds	Avg	Lg	TD
1990	DEN	N	23	81	3.5	15	0

Nuu Faaola

Year	Team		Att	Yds	Avg	Lg	TD
1986	NYJ	N	3	5	1.7	2	0
1987			14	43	3.1	18	2
1988			1	13	13.0	13	0
1989	MIA	N	2	10	5.0	5	0
Career			20	71	3.5	18	2

Julian Fagan

Year	Team		Att	Yds	Avg	Lg	TD
1970	NO	N	1	-6	-6.0	-6	0
1971			1	-17	-17.0	-17	0
1973	NYJ	N	2	47	23.5	26	0
Career			4	24	6.0	26	0

Art Faircloth

Year	Team		Att	Yds	Avg	Lg	TD
1947	NYG	N	10	9	0.9	7	0
1948			1	-1	-1.0	-1	0
Career			11	8	0.7	7	0

Nello Falaschi

Year	Team		Att	Yds	Avg	Lg	TD
1938	NYG	N	1	6	6.0	6	0
1939			1	4	4.0	4	0
Career			2	10	5.0	6	0

Guil Falcon

Year	Team		Att	Yds	Avg	Lg	TD
1921	CAN	A					3
1922	TOL	N					1
1924	HAM	N					2
Career							6

Tony Falkenstein

Year	Team		Att	Yds	Avg	Lg	TD
1943	GB	N	58	198	3.4	59	1
1944	BKN-BOS	N	4	2	0.5	3	0
Career			62	200	3.2	59	1

Gary Famiglietti

Year	Team		Att	Yds	Avg	Lg	TD
1938	CHIB	N	33	129	3.9		0
1939			33	128	3.9		0
1940			93	320	3.4		4
1941			36	101	2.8	10	1
1942			118	503	4.3	21	7
1943			64	229	3.6	31	2
1944			63	282	4.5	16	2
1945			65	235	3.6	14	3
1946	BOS	N	23	54	2.3	13	4
Career			528	1981	3.8	31	23
Playoffs			14	50	3.6		1

Andy Farkas

Year	Team		Att	Yds	Avg	Lg	TD
1938	WAS	N	75	315	4.2		6
1939			139	547	3.9		5
1940			1	0	0.0	0	0
1941			85	224	2.6	10	2
1942			125	468	3.7	22	3
1943			110	327	3.0	36	5
1944			21	85	4.0	20	0
1945	DET	N	31	137	4.4	27	0
Career			587	2103	3.6	36	21
Playoffs			46	142	3.1		5

John Farley

Year	Team		Att	Yds	Avg	Lg	TD
1984	CIN	N	7	11	1.6	5	0

George Farmer

Year	Team		Att	Yds	Avg	Lg	TD
1971	CHI	N	1	11	11.0	11	0
1972			2	-13	-6.5	-2	0

George Farmer continued

Year	Team		Att	Yds	Avg	Lg	TD
1973			1	8	8.0	8	0
Career			4	6	1.5	11	0

George Farmer

Year	Team		Att	Yds	Avg	Lg	TD
1983	LARM	N	1	-9	-9.0	-9	0

Karl Farmer

Year	Team		Att	Yds	Avg	Lg	TD
1977	ATL	N	1	4	4.0	4	0

Teddy Farmer

Year	Team		Att	Yds	Avg	Lg	TD
1978	STL	N	1	4	4.0	4	0

Tom Farmer

Year	Team		Att	Yds	Avg	Lg	TD
1946	LA	N	28	90	3.2	17	1
1947	WAS	N	15	29	1.9	9	1
1948			52	188	3.6	17	1
Career			95	307	3.2	17	3

Mel Farr

Year	Team		Att	Yds	Avg	Lg	TD
1967	DET	N	206	860	4.2	57	3
1968			128	597	4.7	46	3
1969			58	245	4.2	52	4
1970			166	717	4.3	36	9
1971			22	64	2.9	14	0
1972			62	216	3.5	22	3
1973			97	373	3.8	32t	4
Career			739	3072	4.2	57	26
Playoffs			12	31	2.6		0

Scrapper Farrell

Year	Team		Att	Yds	Avg	Lg	TD
1938	PIT-BKN	N	109	425	3.9		3

Bo Farrington

Year	Team		Att	Yds	Avg	Lg	TD
1960	CHI	N	1	-2	-2.0	-2	0

Tom Farris

Year	Team		Att	Yds	Avg	Lg	TD
1946	CHIB	N	23	17	0.7	6	0
1947			1	-3	-3.0	-3	0
1948	CHI	AA	4	5	1.3		0
Career			28	19	0.7	6	0

Marshall Faulk

Year	Team		Att	Yds	Avg	Lg	TD
1994	IND	N	314	1282	4.1	52	11
1995			289	1078	3.7	40	11
1996			198	587	3.0	43	7
Career			801	2947	3.7	52	29
Playoffs			10	41	4.1		0

Frank Fausch

Year	Team		Att	Yds	Avg	Lg	TD
1921	EVA	A					3

George Faust

Year	Team		Att	Yds	Avg	Lg	TD
1939	CHIC	N	22	71	3.2		0

Brett Favre

Year	Team		Att	Yds	Avg	Lg	TD
1992	GB	N	47	198	4.2	19	1
1993			58	216	3.7	27	1
1994			42	202	4.8	36t	2
1995			39	181	4.6	40	3
1996			49	136	2.8	23	2
Career			235	933	4.0	40	9
Playoffs			29	67	2.3		1

Ricky Feacher

Year	Team		Att	Yds	Avg	Lg	TD
1979	CLE	N	1	-1	-1.0	-1	0
1981			1	-1	-1.0	-1	0
Career			2	-2	-1.0	-1	0

Jeff Feagles

Year	Team		Att	Yds	Avg	Lg	TD
1988	NE	N	1	0	0.0	0	0
1990	PHI	N	2	3	1.5	3	0
1991			3	-1	-0.3	11	0
1993			2	6	3.0	6	0
1994	ARI	N	2	8	4.0	12	0
1995			2	4	2.0	4	0
1996			1	0	0.0	0	0
Career			13	20	1.5	12	0

Tom Fears

Year	Team		Att	Yds	Avg	Lg	TD
1948	LA	N	1	8	8.0	8	0
1949			1	-3	-3.0	-3	0
1952			1	0	0.0	0	0

Tom Fears continued

Year	Team		Att	Yds	Avg	Lg	TD
1954			1	10	10.0	10	0
Career			4	15	3.8	10	0

Tiny Feather

Year	Team		Att	Yds	Avg	Lg	TD
1928	DET	N					6
1929	NYG	N					2
1930							1
1933			2	4	2.0		0
Career			2	4	2.0		9

Beattie Feathers

Year	Team		Att	Yds	Avg	Lg	TD
1934	CHIB	N	119	1004	8.4	82t	8
1935			56	281	5.0		3
1936			97	350	3.6		2
1937			66	211	3.2		1
1938	BKN	N	28	94	3.4		2
1939			8	21	2.6		0
1940	GB	N	4	19	4.8		0
Career			378	1980	5.2	82t	16

Walt Fedora

Year	Team		Att	Yds	Avg	Lg	TD
1942	BKN	N	16	34	2.1	12	0

Gene Fekete

Year	Team		Att	Yds	Avg	Lg	TD
1946	CLE	AA	26	106	4.1		1

John Fekete

Year	Team		Att	Yds	Avg	Lg	TD
1946	BUF	AA	1	-1	-1.0	-1	0

Ralph Felton

Year	Team		Att	Yds	Avg	Lg	TD
1954	WAS	N	3	8	2.7	5	0

Bobby Felts

Year	Team		Att	Yds	Avg	Lg	TD
1965	BAL-DET	N	22	58	2.6	6	0
1966	DET	N	34	83	2.4	14	2
1967			10	66	6.6	22	0
Career			66	207	3.1	22	2

Chuck Fenenbock

Year	Team		Att	Yds	Avg	Lg	TD
1943	DET	N	46	180	3.9	25	0
1945			72	143	2.0	37	2
1946	LA	AA	50	420	8.4	76t	3
1947			58	185	3.2		3
1948	CHI	AA	43	174	4.0		0
Career			269	1102	4.1	76t	8

Gill Fenerty

Year	Team		Att	Yds	Avg	Lg	TD
1990	NO	N	73	355	4.9	60t	2
1991			139	477	3.4	54	3
Career			212	832	3.9	60t	5
Playoffs			8	29	3.6		0

Bob Fenimore

Year	Team		Att	Yds	Avg	Lg	TD
1947	CHIB	N	53	189	3.6	13	1

Derrick Fenner

Year	Team		Att	Yds	Avg	Lg	TD
1989	SEA	N	11	41	3.7	9	1
1990			215	859	4.0	36	14
1991			91	267	2.9	15	4
1992	CIN	N	112	500	4.5	35t	7
1993			121	482	4.0	26	1
1994			141	468	3.3	21	1
1995	OAK	N	39	110	2.8	10	0
1996			67	245	3.7	17	4
Career			797	2972	3.7	36	32

Rick Fenney

Year	Team		Att	Yds	Avg	Lg	TD
1987	MIN	N	42	174	4.1	12	2
1988			55	271	4.9	28	3
1989			151	588	3.9	25	4
1990			87	376	4.3	27	2
1991			23	99	4.3	17	0
Career			358	1508	4.2	28	11
Playoffs			21	55	2.6		1

Bob Ferguson

Year	Team		Att	Yds	Avg	Lg	TD
1962	PIT	N	20	37	1.9	13	0
1963	PIT-MIN	N	46	172	3.7	19	1
Career			66	209	3.2	19	1

Howie Ferguson

Year	Team		Att	Yds	Avg	Lg	TD
1953	GB	N	52	134	2.6	12	0
1954			83	276	3.3	25	0

Howie Ferguson continued

Year	Team		Att	Yds	Avg	Lg	TD
1955			192	859	4.5	57	4
1956			99	367	3.7	24	0
1957			59	216	3.7	40t	1
1958			59	268	4.5	29	1
1960	LA	A	126	438	3.5		4
Career			670	2558	3.8	57	10
Playoffs			4	11	2.8		0

Joe Ferguson

Year	Team		Att	Yds	Avg	Lg	TD
1973	BUF	N	48	147	3.1	24	2
1974			54	111	2.1	15	2
1975			23	82	3.6	17	1
1976			18	81	4.5	19	0
1977			41	279	6.8	41	2
1978			27	76	2.8	12	0
1979			22	68	3.1	15	1
1980			31	65	2.1	15	0
1981			20	29	1.5	16	1
1982			16	46	2.9	13	1
1983			20	88	4.4	19	0
1984			19	102	5.4	20	0
1985	DET	N	4	12	3.0	15	1
1986			5	25	5.0	14	0
1988	TB	N	1	0	0.0	0	0
1989			4	6	1.5	7	0
Career			353	1217	3.4	41	11
Playoffs			3	-1	-0.3		0

Larry Ferguson

Year	Team		Att	Yds	Avg	Lg	TD
1963	DET	N	13	23	1.8	5	0

Vagas Ferguson

Year	Team		Att	Yds	Avg	Lg	TD
1980	NE	N	211	818	3.9	44	2
1981			78	340	4.4	19t	3
1982			1	5	5.0	5	0
Career			290	1163	4.0	44	5

Mervyn Fernandez

Year	Team		Att	Yds	Avg	Lg	TD
1988	LARI	N	1	9	9.0	9	0
1989			2	16	8.0	12	0
1990			3	10	3.3	9	0
Career			6	35	5.8	12	0

Vince Ferragamo

Year	Team		Att	Yds	Avg	Lg	TD
1977	LA	N	1	0	0.0	0	0
1978			2	10	5.0	12	0
1979			3	-2	-0.7	2	0
1980			15	34	2.3	15	1
1982	LARM	N	4	3	0.8	2	1
1983			22	17	0.8	5	0
1984			4	0	0.0	2	0
1985	BUF	N	8	15	1.9	5	1
1986	GB	N	1	0	0.0	0	0
Career			60	77	1.3	15	3
Playoffs			7	-5	-0.7		

Bobby Ferrell

Year	Team		Att	Yds	Avg	Lg	TD
1976	SF	N	9	28	3.1	11	1
1977			41	160	3.9	12	1
1978			125	471	3.8	20	1
1979			8	33	4.1	8	0
Career			183	692	3.8	20	3

Earl Ferrell

Year	Team		Att	Yds	Avg	Lg	TD
1983	STL	N	7	53	7.6	11	1
1984			44	203	4.6	25	1
1985			46	208	4.5	30	2
1986			124	548	4.4	25	0
1987			113	512	4.5	35t	7
1988	PHX	N	202	924	4.6	47	7
1989			149	502	3.4	44t	7
Career			685	2950	4.3	47	24

Neil Ferris

Year	Team		Att	Yds	Avg	Lg	TD
1952	WAS	N	11	22	2.0	11t	1

Gus Fetz

Year	Team		Att	Yds	Avg	Lg	TD
1923	CHIB	N					1

Frank Filchock

Year	Team		Att	Yds	Avg	Lg	TD
1938	PIT-WAS	N	69	198	2.9		1
1939	WAS	N	103	413	4.0		1
1940			50	126	2.5		2

Frank Filchock continued

Year	Team		Att	Yds	Avg	Lg	TD
1941			115	383	3.3	51	1
1944			33	-34	-1.0	9	0
1945			9	21	2.3	29	0
1946	NYG	N	98	371	3.8	70	2
Career			477	1478	3.1	70	7
Playoffs			16	-10	-0.6		0

Steve Filipowicz

Year	Team		Att	Yds	Avg	Lg	TD
1945	NYG	N	53	142	2.7	13	1
1946			2	3	1.5	2	1
Career			55	145	2.6	13	2
Playoffs			9	20	2.2		

Gene Filipski

Year	Team		Att	Yds	Avg	Lg	TD
1956	NYG	N	13	85	6.5	35t	1
1957			22	89	4.0	11	0
Career			35	174	5.0	35t	1
Playoffs			1	0	0.0		0

John Fina

Year	Team		Att	Yds	Avg	Lg	TD
1993	BUF	N	1	-2	-2.0	-2	0

Jim Finks

Year	Team		Att	Yds	Avg	Lg	TD
1949	PIT	N	35	135	3.9	38	1
1950			1	2	2.0	2	0
1951			3	27	9.0	22	0
1952			23	37	1.6	20t	5
1953			12	0	0.0	4t	2
1954			9	17	1.9	6	0
1955			35	76	2.2	9	4
Career			118	294	2.5	38	12

Jack Finn

Year	Team		Att	Yds	Avg	Lg	TD
1924	FRA	N					2

Dave Finzer

Year	Team		Att	Yds	Avg	Lg	TD
1984	CHI	N	2	0	0.0	5	0
1985	SEA	N	1	-2	-2.0	-2	0
Career			3	-2	-0.7	5	0
Playoffs			1	-7	-7.0		0

Clete Fischer

Year	Team		Att	Yds	Avg	Lg	TD
1949	NYG	N	26	72	2.8	10	0

Dick Fishel

Year	Team		Att	Yds	Avg	Lg	TD
1933	BKN	N					1

Ev Fisher

Year	Team		Att	Yds	Avg	Lg	TD
1939	CHIC	N	18	63	3.5		0

Alex Fishman

Year	Team		Att	Yds	Avg	Lg	TD
1921	EVA	A					1

Bill Fisk

Year	Team		Att	Yds	Avg	Lg	TD
1940	DET	N	2	0	0.0		0

Max Fiske

Year	Team		Att	Yds	Avg	Lg	TD
1936	PIT	N	58	92	1.6		0
1937			28	44	1.6		0
1938			29	83	2.9		0
Career			115	219	1.9		0

Paul Fitzgibbons

Year	Team		Att	Yds	Avg	Lg	TD
1926	DUL	N					1
1930	GB	N					1
Career							2

Bob Fitzke

Year	Team		Att	Yds	Avg	Lg	TD
1925	FRA	N					1

Scott Fitzkee

Year	Team		Att	Yds	Avg	Lg	TD
1980	PHI	N	1	15	15.0	15	0

Terrence Flagler

Year	Team		Att	Yds	Avg	Lg	TD
1987	SF	N	6	11	1.8	5	0
1988			3	5	1.7	4	0
1989			33	129	3.9	29t	1
1990	PHX	N	13	85	6.5	29t	1
1991			1	7	7.0	7	0
Career			56	237	4.2	29t	2
Playoffs			24	49	2.0		0

Dick Flanagan

Year	Team		Att	Yds	Avg	Lg	TD
1948	CHIB	N	5	14	2.8	6	0

Ed Flanagan

Year	Team		Att	Yds	Avg	Lg	TD
1967	DET	N	0	5		5L	0

Hoot Flanagan

Year	Team		Att	Yds	Avg	Lg	TD
1925	POT	N					5

Jim Flanigan

Year	Team		Att	Yds	Avg	Lg	TD
1995	CHI	N	1	0	0.0	0	0

Jack Flavin

Year	Team		Att	Yds	Avg	Lg	TD
1923	BUF	N					2

George Fleming

Year	Team		Att	Yds	Avg	Lg	TD
1961	OAK	A	31	112	3.6	23	1

Mack Flenniken

Year	Team		Att	Yds	Avg	Lg	TD
1930	CHIC	N					3
1931	NYG	N					1
Career							4

Terrell Fletcher

Year	Team		Att	Yds	Avg	Lg	TD
1995	SD	N	26	140	5.4	46	1
1996			77	282	3.7	19	0
Career			103	422	4.1	46	1
Playoffs			3	23	7.7		0

Tom Flick

Year	Team		Att	Yds	Avg	Lg	TD
1986	SD	N	6	5	0.8	7	1

Tom Flores

Year	Team		Att	Yds	Avg	Lg	TD
1960	OAK	A	39	-42	-1.1		3
1961			23	36	1.6	13	1
1963			11	2	0.2	7	0
1964			11	64	5.8	14	0
1965			11	32	2.9	15	0
1966			5	50	10.0	27	1
1969	KC	A	1	0	0.0	0	0
Career			101	142	1.4	27	5

Charlie Flowers

Year	Team		Att	Yds	Avg	Lg	TD
1960	LA	A	39	161	4.1		1
1961	SD	A	51	177	3.5	11	3
1962	NY	A	21	78	3.7	14	0
Career			111	416	3.7	14	4

Kenny Flowers

Year	Team		Att	Yds	Avg	Lg	TD
1987	ATL	N	14	61	4.4	14	0
1989			13	24	1.8	4	1
Career			27	85	3.1	14	1

Bobby Jack Floyd

Year	Team		Att	Yds	Avg	Lg	TD
1952	GB	N	61	236	3.9	17	1
1953	CHIB	N	16	70	4.4	16	0
Career			77	306	4.0	17	1

Victor Floyd

Year	Team		Att	Yds	Avg	Lg	TD
1989	SD	N	8	15	1.9	5	0

William Floyd

Year	Team		Att	Yds	Avg	Lg	TD
1994	SF	N	87	305	3.5	26	6
1995			64	237	3.7	23	2
1996			47	186	4.0	12	2
Career			198	728	3.7	26	10
Playoffs			36	103	2.9		4

Doug Flutie

Year	Team		Att	Yds	Avg	Lg	TD
1986	CHI	N	9	36	4.0	19	1
1987	NE	N	6	43	7.2	13	0
1988			38	179	4.7	16	1
1989			16	87	5.4	22	0
Career			69	345	5.0	22	2
Playoffs			2	12	6.0		0

Glenn Foley

Year	Team		Att	Yds	Avg	Lg	TD
1995	NYJ	N	1	9	9.0	9	0
1996			7	22	3.1	12	0
Career			8	31	3.9	12	0

Steve Foley

Year	Team		Att	Yds	Avg	Lg	TD
1978	DEN	N	1	14	14.0	14	0

Year	Team		Att	Yds	Avg	Lg	TD

Lee Folkins

Year	Team		Att	Yds	Avg	Lg	TD
1964	DAL	N	1	9	9.0	9	0

Art Folz

| 1925 | CHIC | N | | | | | 2 |

Herman Fontenot

1986	CLE	N	25	105	4.2	16	1
1987			15	33	2.2	14	0
1988			28	87	3.1	17	0
1989	GB	N	17	69	4.1	19	1
1990			17	76	4.5	18	0
Career			102	370	3.6	19	2
Playoffs			9	9	1.0		0

Adrian Ford

| 1927 | FRA | N | | | | | 2 |

Fred Ford

| 1960 | BUF-LA | A | 38 | 194 | 5.1 | | 2 |
| Playoffs | | | 2 | -5 | -2.5 | 0 | |

Garrett Ford

| 1968 | DEN | A | 41 | 186 | 4.5 | 23 | 1 |

Henry Ford

1955	CLE	N	2	1	0.5	1	0
1956	PIT	N	12	26	2.2	16	2
Career			14	27	1.9	16	2

Jim Ford

1971	NO	N	93	379	4.1	35	2
1972			11	28	2.5	9	0
Career			104	407	3.9	35	2

Jim Fordham

1944	CHIB	N	73	381	5.2	40	4
1945			45	153	3.4	11	1
Career			118	534	4.5	40	5

Chuck Foreman

1973	MIN	N	182	801	4.4	50t	4
1974			199	777	3.9	32	9
1975			280	1070	3.8	31t	13
1976			278	1155	4.2	46	13
1977			270	1112	4.1	51	6
1978			237	749	3.2	21	5
1979			87	223	2.6	16	2
1980	NE	N	23	63	2.7	7	1
Career			1556	5950	3.8	51	53
Playoffs			229	860	3.8		7

Nick Forkovitch

| 1948 | BKN | AA | 1 | 4 | 4.0 | 4 | 0 |

Bob Forte

1946	GB	N	17	73	4.3	20	0
1947			29	80	2.8	12	1
1948			12	30	2.5	9	0
1949			40	135	3.4	35	0
1950			9	13	1.4	11	0
Career			107	331	3.1	35	1

Ike Forte

1976	NE	N	25	100	4.0	26	1
1977			62	157	2.5	16	2
1978	WAS	N	4	4	1.0	2	0
1979			25	125	5.0	20t	1
1980			30	51	1.7	6	1
1981	NYG	N	19	74	3.9	15	0
Career			165	511	3.1	26	5

Joe Fortunato

| 1957 | CHIB | N | 2 | -9 | -4.5 | 1t | 1 |

Barry Foster

1990	PIT	N	36	203	5.6	38	1
1991			96	488	5.1	56t	1
1992			390	1690	4.3	69	11
1993			177	711	4.0	38	8
1994			216	851	3.9	29t	5
Career			915	3943	4.3	69	26
Playoffs			64	284	4.4		0

Bob Foster

| 1922 | RAC | N | | | | | 3 |

Derrick Foster

| 1987 | NYJ | N | 1 | 9 | 9.0 | 9 | 0 |

Geno Foster

1965	SD	A	121	469	3.9	22	2
1966			81	352	4.3	37	1
1967			38	78	2.1	18	0
1968			109	394	3.6	22	1
1969			64	236	3.7	24	0
1970	SD	N	32	84	2.6	15	0
Career			445	1613	3.6	37	4
Playoffs			2	9	4.5		0

John Fourcade

1987	NO	N	19	134	7.1	18	0
1989			14	91	6.5	14	1
1990			15	77	5.1	12	1
Career			48	302	6.3	18	2
Playoffs			2	13	6.5		0

Dan Fouts

1973	SD	N	7	32	4.6	16	0
1974			19	63	3.3	16	1
1975			23	170	7.4	32	2
1976			18	65	3.6	13	0
1977			6	13	2.2	11	0
1978			20	43	2.1	22	2
1979			26	49	1.9	26	2
1980			23	15	0.7	9	2
1981			22	56	2.5	13	0
1982			9	8	0.9	9	1
1983			12	-5	-0.4	3	1
1984			12	-29	-2.4	3	0
1985			11	-1	-0.1	7	0
1986			4	-3	-0.8	0	0
1987			12	0	0.0	2	2
Career			224	476	2.1	32	13
Playoffs			8	15	1.9		0

Aubrey Fowler

| 1948 | BAL | AA | 6 | 30 | 5.0 | | 0 |

Bobby Fowler

| 1962 | NY | A | 5 | 27 | 5.4 | 15 | 0 |

Bobby Fowler

| 1985 | NO | N | 2 | 4 | 2.0 | 3 | 0 |

Todd Fowler

1985	DAL	N	7	25	3.6	6	0
1986			6	5	0.8	2	0
1988			3	6	2.0	4	0
Career			16	36	2.3	6	0

Willmer Fowler

1960	BUF	A	93	370	4.0	76	1
1961			1	2	2.0	2	0
Career			94	372	4.0	76	1

Terry Fox

1941	PHI	N	21	97	4.6	13	0
1946	MIA	AA	12	26	2.2		0
Career			33	123	3.7	13	0

Pete Franceschi

| 1946 | SF | AA | 8 | -5 | -0.6 | | 1 |

Joe Francis

1958	GB	N	24	153	6.4	20	1
1959			2	5	2.5	8	0
Career			26	158	6.1	20	1

Jon Francis

| 1987 | LARM | N | 35 | 138 | 3.9 | 23 | 0 |

Phil Francis

1979	SF	N	31	118	3.8	16	1
1980			7	36	5.1	14	0
Career			38	154	4.1	16	1

Russ Francis

| 1976 | NE | N | 2 | 12 | 6.0 | 8 | 0 |

Sam Francis

1937	CHIB	N	48	129	2.7		0
1938			85	297	3.5		3
1939	PIT-BKN	N	76	230	3.0		1
1940	BKN	N	44	217	4.9		1
Career			253	873	3.5		5

Wallace Francis

1975	ATL	N	2	12	6.0	9	0
1977			4	6	1.5	11	0
1978			2	-11	-5.5	-5	0
1980			1	2	2.0	2	0
1981			1	8	8.0	8t	1
Career			10	17	1.7	11	1

George Franck

1941	NYG	N	48	101	2.1	17	3
1945			29	61	2.1	9	0
1946			43	270	6.3	46	0
1947			24	93	3.9	25	0
Career			144	525	3.6	46	3
Playoffs			8	85	10.6		0

Mike Franckowiak

1975	DEN	N	1	1	1.0	1	0
1976			12	25	2.1	7	0
1977	BUF	N	1	0	0.0	0	0
Career			14	26	1.9	7	0

John Frank

1986	SF	N	1	-3	-3.0	-3	0
1987			1	2	2.0	2	0
Career			2	-1	-0.5	2	0

Andra Franklin

1981	MIA	N	201	711	3.5	29	7
1982			177	701	4.0	25t	7
1983			224	746	3.3	18	8
1984			20	74	3.7	12	0
Career			622	2232	3.6	29	22
Playoffs			93	335	3.6		2

Bobby Franklin

1961	CLE	N	1	12	12.0	12t	1
1963			1	-10	-10.0	-10	0
1965			1	-11	-11.0	-11	0
Career			3	-9	-3.0	12t	1

Byron Franklin

1981	BUF	N	1	-11	-11.0	-11	0
1983			1	3	3.0	3	0
1984			1	-7	-7.0	-7	0
1985	SEA	N	1	5	5.0	5	0
1986			1	2	2.0	2	0
Career			5	-8	-1.6	5	0

Cleveland Franklin

1977	PHI	N	1	0	0.0	0	0
1978			60	167	2.8	9	0
1980	BAL	N	83	264	3.2	21	2
1981			21	52	2.5	8	1
1982			43	152	3.5	19	0
Career			208	635	3.1	21	3

George Franklin

| 1978 | ATL | N | 1 | -8 | -8.0 | -8 | 0 |
| Playoffs | | | 8 | 24 | 3.0 | 0 | |

Pat Franklin

| 1986 | TB | N | 7 | 7 | 1.0 | 4 | 0 |

Paul Franklin

| 1931 | CHIB | N | | | | | 1 |

Red Franklin

1935	BKN	N	100	284	2.8		3
1936			15	70	4.7		1
1937			4	12	3.0		0
Career			119	366	3.1		4

Tony Franklin

Year	Team		Att	Yds	Avg	Lg	TD
1985	NE	N	1	-5	-5.0	5	0

Al Frazier

Year	Team		Att	Yds	Avg	Lg	TD
1961	DEN	A	23	110	4.8	43	0
1962			39	168	4.3	35	2
Career			62	278	4.5	43	2

Charlie Frazier

Year	Team		Att	Yds	Avg	Lg	TD
1964	HOU	A	1	-4	-4.0	-4	0
1965			1	10	10.0	10	0
1969	BOS	A	2	-1	-0.5	9	0
Career			4	5	1.3	10	0

Paul Frazier

Year	Team		Att	Yds	Avg	Lg	TD
1989	NO	N	25	112	4.5	21	1

Willie Frazier

Year	Team		Att	Yds	Avg	Lg	TD
1970	SD	N	5	120	24.0	70	1
1971	KC	N	1	-2	-2.0	-2	0
Career			6	118	19.7	70	1

Tucker Frederickson

Year	Team		Att	Yds	Avg	Lg	TD
1965	NYG	N	195	659	3.4	41	5
1967			97	311	3.2	17	2
1968			142	486	3.4	19	1
1969			33	136	4.1	19	0
1970			120	375	3.1	15	1
1971			64	242	3.8	37	0
Career			651	2209	3.4	41	9

Bobby Freeman

Year	Team		Att	Yds	Avg	Lg	TD
1958	CLE	N	2	1	0.5	9	0

Phil Freeman

Year	Team		Att	Yds	Avg	Lg	TD
1987	TB	N	1	1	1.0	1	0

Jess Freitas

Year	Team		Att	Yds	Avg	Lg	TD
1946	SF	AA	6	-21	-3.5		0
1947			6	-9	-1.5		0
1948	CHI	AA	24	25	1.0		0
1949	BUF	AA	3	13	4.3		0
Career			39	8	0.2		0

Jesse Freitas

Year	Team		Att	Yds	Avg	Lg	TD
1974	SD	N	6	16	2.7	9	0
1975			11	56	5.1	17	0
Career			17	72	4.2	17	0

Walt French

Year	Team		Att	Yds	Avg	Lg	TD
1925	POT	N					3

Gus Frerotte

Year	Team		Att	Yds	Avg	Lg	TD
1994	WAS	N	4	1	0.3	2	0
1995			22	16	0.7	10	1
1996			28	16	0.6	17	0
Career			54	33	0.6	17	1

Glenn Frey

Year	Team		Att	Yds	Avg	Lg	TD
1936	PHI	N	7	8	1.1		0
1937			5	11	2.2		0
Career			12	19	1.6		0

Benny Friedman

Year	Team		Att	Yds	Avg	Lg	TD
1927	CLE	N					2
1928	DET	N					4
1929	NYG	N					2
1930							6
1931							2
Career							16

John Friesz

Year	Team		Att	Yds	Avg	Lg	TD
1990	SD	N	1	3	3.0	3	0
1991			10	18	1.8	11	0
1993			10	3	0.3	2	0
1994	WAS	N	1	1	1.0	1	0
1995	SEA	N	11	0	0.0	2	0
1996			12	1	0.1	3	0
Career			45	26	0.6	11	0

Ted Fritsch

Year	Team		Att	Yds	Avg	Lg	TD
1942	GB	N	74	223	3.0	55	0
1943			54	169	3.1	14	4
1944			94	322	3.4	18	4

Ted Fritsch *continued*

Year	Team		Att	Yds	Avg	Lg	TD
1945			88	282	3.2	21	7
1946			128	444	3.5	32	9
1947			68	247	3.6	48	6
1948			37	173	4.7	30	0
1949			69	227	3.3	27	1
1950			7	13	1.9	5	0
Career			619	2100	3.4	55	31
Playoffs			18	59	3.3		1

Stan Fritts

Year	Team		Att	Yds	Avg	Lg	TD
1975	CIN	N	94	375	4.0	22	8
1976			47	200	4.3	13	3
Career			141	575	4.1	22	11
Playoffs			6	14	2.3		1

Ed Frutig

Year	Team		Att	Yds	Avg	Lg	TD
1941	GB	N	1	11	11.0	11	0

Wes Fry

Year	Team		Att	Yds	Avg	Lg	TD
1927	NYY	N					3

Irving Fryar

Year	Team		Att	Yds	Avg	Lg	TD
1984	NE	N	2	-11	-5.5	0	0
1985			7	27	3.9	13	1
1986			4	80	20.0	31	0
1987			9	52	5.8	16	0
1988			6	12	2.0	6	0
1989			2	15	7.5	11	0
1990			2	-4	-2.0	-1	0
1991			2	11	5.5	9	0
1992			1	6	6.0	6	0
1993	MIA	N	3	-4	-1.3	2	0
1996	PHI	N	1	-4	-4.0	-4	0
Career			39	180	4.6	31	1
Playoffs			2	1	0.5		0

Phil Frye

Year	Team		Att	Yds	Avg	Lg	TD
1987	MIN	N	4	4	1.0	2	0

Kenny Fryer

Year	Team		Att	Yds	Avg	Lg	TD
1944	BKN	N	15	15	1.0	9	0

Jean Fugett

Year	Team		Att	Yds	Avg	Lg	TD
1972	DAL	N	3	2	0.7	9	0
1973			1	34	34.0	34	0
1975			1	2	2.0	2	0
1976	WAS	N	2	0	0.0	0	0
Career			7	38	5.4	34	0
Playoffs			3	10	3.3		0

Scott Fulhage

Year	Team		Att	Yds	Avg	Lg	TD
1989	ATL	N	1	0	0.0	0	0
1992			1	0	0.0	0	0
Career			2	0	0.0	0	0

Charley Fuller

Year	Team		Att	Yds	Avg	Lg	TD
1961	OAK	A	38	134	3.5	19	0

Eddie Fuller

Year	Team		Att	Yds	Avg	Lg	TD
1992	BUF	N	6	39	6.5	15	0

Larry Fuller

Year	Team		Att	Yds	Avg	Lg	TD
1944	WAS	N	4	10	2.5	6	0

Mike Fuller

Year	Team		Att	Yds	Avg	Lg	TD
1977	SD	N	1	7	7.0	7t	1
1979			1	0	0.0	0	0
1980			2	0	0.0	0	0
Career			4	7	1.8	7t	1

Steve Fuller

Year	Team		Att	Yds	Avg	Lg	TD
1979	KC	N	50	264	5.3	49	1
1980			60	274	4.6	38t	4
1981			19	118	6.2	27	0
1982			10	56	5.6	12	0
1984	CHI	N	15	89	5.9	26	1
1985			24	77	3.2	13	5
1986			8	30	3.8	10	0
Career			186	908	4.9	49	11
Playoffs			9	45	5.0		0

Brent Fullwood

Year	Team		Att	Yds	Avg	Lg	TD
1987	GB	N	84	274	3.3	18	5

Brent Fullwood *continued*

Year	Team		Att	Yds	Avg	Lg	TD
1988			101	483	4.8	33t	7
1989			204	821	4.0	38	5
1990			44	124	2.8	16	1
Career			433	1702	3.9	38	18

John Fuqua

Year	Team		Att	Yds	Avg	Lg	TD
1969	NYG	N	20	89	4.5	35	0
1970	PIT	N	138	691	5.0	85t	7
1971			155	625	4.0	30t	4
1972			150	665	4.4	47	4
1973			117	457	3.9	25	2
1974			50	156	3.1	14	2
1975			74	285	3.9	18	1
1976			15	63	4.2	12	1
Career			719	3031	4.2	85t	21
Playoffs			46	163	3.5		0

Will Furrer

Year	Team		Att	Yds	Avg	Lg	TD
1995	HOU	N	8	20	2.5	11	0

Chuck Fusina

Year	Team		Att	Yds	Avg	Lg	TD
1980	TB	N	1	14	14.0	14	0
1981			3	3	1.0	7	0
1986	GB	N	7	11	1.6	6	0
Career			11	28	2.5	14	0

Roman Gabriel

Year	Team		Att	Yds	Avg	Lg	TD
1962	LA	N	18	93	5.2	15	0
1963			39	132	3.4	16	3
1964			11	5	0.5	6	1
1965			23	79	3.4	17	2
1966			52	176	3.4	14	3
1967			43	198	4.6	23	6
1968			34	139	4.1	19t	4
1969			35	156	4.5	22	5
1970			28	104	3.7	15	1
1971			18	48	2.7	10	2
1972			14	16	1.1	11	1
1973	PHI	N	12	10	0.8	5	1
1974			14	76	5.4	11	0
1975			13	70	5.4	39	1
1976			4	2	0.5	1	0
Career			358	1304	3.6	39	30
Playoffs			7	32	4.6		0

Derrick Gaffney

Year	Team		Att	Yds	Avg	Lg	TD
1978	NYJ	N	2	-2	-1.0	1	0

Jim Gaffney

Year	Team		Att	Yds	Avg	Lg	TD
1945	WAS	N	1	-6	-6.0	-6	0
1946			25	96	3.8	12	0
Career			26	90	3.5	12	0

Monk Gafford

Year	Team		Att	Yds	Avg	Lg	TD
1946	MIA-BKN	AA	24	66	2.8		1
1947	BKN	AA	46	232	5.0	79t	1
1948			30	51	1.7		1
Career			100	349	3.5	79t	3

Bobby Gage

Year	Team		Att	Yds	Avg	Lg	TD
1949	PIT	N	46	228	5.0	97	3
1950			39	106	2.7	18	3
Career			85	334	3.9	97	6

Bob Gagliano

Year	Team		Att	Yds	Avg	Lg	TD
1989	DET	N	41	192	4.7	19	4
1990			46	145	3.2	22	0
1991	SD	N	3	19	6.3	16	0
1992			3	-4	-1.3	0	0
Career			93	352	3.8	22	4

Dave Gagnon

Year	Team		Att	Yds	Avg	Lg	TD
1974	CHI	N	1	15	15.0	15	0

Derrick Gainer

Year	Team		Att	Yds	Avg	Lg	TD
1990	CLE	N	30	81	2.7	9	1
1992	LARI	N	2	10	5.0	6	0
1993	DAL	N	9	29	3.2	8	0
Career			41	120	2.9	9	1
Playoffs			11	30	2.7		1

Clark Gaines

Year	Team		Att	Yds	Avg	Lg	TD
1976	NYJ	N	157	724	4.6	33	3

Clark Gaines *continued*

Year	Team		Att	Yds	Avg	Lg	TD
1977			158	595	3.8	19	3
1978			44	154	3.5	33	2
1979			186	905	4.9	52	0
1980			36	174	4.8	15	0
1982	KC	N	1	0	0.0	0	0
Career			582	2552	4.4	52	8

Lawrence Gaines

Year	Team		Att	Yds	Avg	Lg	TD
1976	DET	N	155	659	4.3	26t	4
1978			54	178	3.3	12	1
1979			23	55	2.4	6	0
Career			232	892	3.8	26t	5

Bob Gaiters

Year	Team		Att	Yds	Avg	Lg	TD
1961	NYG	N	116	460	4.0	29	6
1962	NYG-SF	N	43	193	4.5	53	0
1963	DEN	A	9	20	2.2	8	0
Career			168	673	4.0	53	6
Playoffs			1	2	2.0		0

Bill Gaiver

Year	Team		Att	Yds	Avg	Lg	TD
1923	RI	N					4

Hokie Gajan

Year	Team		Att	Yds	Avg	Lg	TD
1982	NO	N	19	77	4.1	12	0
1983			81	415	5.1	58	4
1984			102	615	6.0	62t	5
1985			50	251	5.0	26	2
Career			252	1358	5.4	62t	11

Tony Galbreath

Year	Team		Att	Yds	Avg	Lg	TD
1976	NO	N	136	570	4.2	74t	7
1977			168	644	3.8	26	3
1978			186	635	3.4	20t	5
1979			189	708	3.7	27	9
1980			81	308	3.8	26	3
1981	MIN	N	42	198	4.7	21	2
1982			39	116	3.0	12	1
1983			113	474	4.2	52t	4
1984	NYG	N	22	97	4.4	11	0
1985			29	187	6.4	18	0
1986			16	61	3.8	10	0
1987			10	74	7.4	17	0
Career			1031	4072	3.9	74t	34
Playoffs			17	73	4.3		0

Arnie Galiffa

Year	Team		Att	Yds	Avg	Lg	TD
1953	NYG	N	5	1	0.2	7	0
1954	SF	N	1	2	2.0	2	0
Career			6	3	0.5	7	0

Willie Galimore

Year	Team		Att	Yds	Avg	Lg	TD
1957	CHIB	N	127	538	4.2	67t	5
1958			130	619	4.8	36t	8
1959			58	199	3.4	36	1
1960	CHI	N	74	368	5.0	54	1
1961			153	707	4.6	50t	4
1962			43	233	5.4	77t	2
1963			85	321	3.8	51t	5
Career			670	2985	4.5	77t	26
Playoffs			7	12	1.7		0

Hugh Gallarneau

Year	Team		Att	Yds	Avg	Lg	TD
1941	CHIB	N	49	304	6.2	40	8
1942			68	292	4.3	20	4
1945			75	260	3.5	31	2
1946			112	476	4.3	52t	7
1947			39	89	2.3	9	6
Career			343	1421	4.1	52t	27
Playoffs			17	41	2.4		0

Chan Gallegos

Year	Team		Att	Yds	Avg	Lg	TD
1962	OAK	A	3	25	8.3	16	0

Tony Gallovich

Year	Team		Att	Yds	Avg	Lg	TD
1941	CLE	N	1	1	1.0	1	0

Joey Galloway

Year	Team		Att	Yds	Avg	Lg	TD
1995	SEA	N	11	154	14.0	86t	1
1996			15	127	8.5	51	0
Career			26	281	10.8	86t	1

John Galvin

Year	Team		Att	Yds	Avg	Lg	TD
1947	BAL	AA	1	-4	-4.0	-4	0

Lu Gambino

Year	Team		Att	Yds	Avg	Lg	TD
1948	BAL	AA	54	194	3.6		1
1949			56	208	3.7		0
Career			110	402	3.7		1
Playoffs			1	2	2.0		0

Kenny Gamble

Year	Team		Att	Yds	Avg	Lg	TD
1989	KC	N	6	24	4.0	20	1

R.C. Gamble

Year	Team		Att	Yds	Avg	Lg	TD
1968	BOS	A	78	311	4.0	45t	1
1969			16	35	2.2	9	0
Career			94	346	3.7	45t	1

Bob Gambold

Year	Team		Att	Yds	Avg	Lg	TD
1953	PHI	N	2	-2	-1.0	0	0

Billy Gambrell

Year	Team		Att	Yds	Avg	Lg	TD
1965	STL	N	4	15	3.8	11	0
1966			3	26	8.7	24	0
Career			7	41	5.9	24	0

Chris Gannon

Year	Team		Att	Yds	Avg	Lg	TD
1990	NE	N	1	0	0.0	0	0

Rich Gannon

Year	Team		Att	Yds	Avg	Lg	TD
1988	MIN	N	4	29	7.3	15	0
1990			52	268	5.2	27	1
1991			43	236	5.5	42	2
1992			45	187	4.2	14	0
1993	WAS	N	21	88	4.2	12	1
1995	KC	N	8	25	3.1	12t	1
1996			12	81	6.8	19	0
Career			185	914	4.9	42	5
Playoffs			7	29	4.1		0

Earl Gant

Year	Team		Att	Yds	Avg	Lg	TD
1979	KC	N	56	196	3.5	16	1
1980			9	32	3.6	11	0
Career			65	228	3.5	16	1

Reuben Gant

Year	Team		Att	Yds	Avg	Lg	TD
1978	BUF	N	1	14	14.0	14	0

Frank Garcia

Year	Team		Att	Yds	Avg	Lg	TD
1986	TB	N	1	-11	-11.0	-11	0

Carwell Gardner

Year	Team		Att	Yds	Avg	Lg	TD
1990	BUF	N	15	41	2.7	14	0
1991			42	146	3.5	18	4
1992			40	166	4.2	19	2
1993			20	56	2.8	8	0
1994			41	135	3.3	13	4
1995			20	77	3.9	17	0
1996	BAL	N	26	108	4.2	19	0
Career			204	729	3.6	19	10
Playoffs			13	52	4.0		1

Don Garlin

Year	Team		Att	Yds	Avg	Lg	TD
1949	SF	AA	21	113	5.4	60	1
1950	SF	N	3	3	1.0	2	0
Career			24	116	4.8	60	1
Playoffs			7	29	4.1		0

Charlie Garner

Year	Team		Att	Yds	Avg	Lg	TD
1994	PHI	N	109	399	3.7	28t	3
1995			108	588	5.4	55t	6
1996			66	346	5.2	46	1
Career			283	1333	4.7	55t	10
Playoffs			20	101	5.0		1

Alvin Garrett

Year	Team		Att	Yds	Avg	Lg	TD
1980	NYG	N	9	31	3.4	10	0
1981			1	2	2.0	2	0
1983	WAS	N	2	0	0.0	4	0
Career			12	33	2.8	10	0
Playoffs			3	46	15.3		1

Bobby Garrett

Year	Team		Att	Yds	Avg	Lg	TD
1954	GB	N	1	-3	-3.0	-3	0

Carl Garrett

Year	Team		Att	Yds	Avg	Lg	TD
1969	BOS	A	137	691	5.0	80t	5
1970	BOS	N	88	272	3.1	26	4
1971	NE	N	181	784	4.3	38	1
1972			131	488	3.7	41t	5
1973	CHI	N	175	655	3.7	35	5
1974			96	346	3.6	19	1
1975	NYJ	N	122	566	4.6	40	5
1976	OAK	N	48	220	4.6	17	1
1977			53	175	3.3	13	1
Career			1031	4197	4.1	80t	28
Playoffs			8	33	4.1		0

Jason Garrett

Year	Team		Att	Yds	Avg	Lg	TD
1993	DAL	N	8	-8	-1.0	0	0
1994			3	-2	-0.7	0	0
1995			1	-1	-1.0	-1	0
Career			12	-11	-0.9	0	0

J.D. Garrett

Year	Team		Att	Yds	Avg	Lg	TD
1964	BOS	A	56	259	4.6	58	2
1965			42	147	3.5	26	1
1966			13	21	1.6	5	0
1967			5	7	1.4	8	0
Career			116	434	3.7	58	3

Mike Garrett

Year	Team		Att	Yds	Avg	Lg	TD
1966	KC	A	147	801	5.4	77	6
1967			236	1087	4.6	38	9
1968			164	564	3.4	37	3
1969			168	732	4.4	34t	6
1970	KC-SD	N	67	208	3.1	22	1
1971	SD	N	140	591	4.2	36	4
1972			272	1031	3.8	41t	6
1973			114	467	4.1	68	0
Career			1308	5481	4.2	77	35
Playoffs			61	186	3.0		3

Mike Garrett

Year	Team		Att	Yds	Avg	Lg	TD
1981	BAL	N	2	4	2.0	3	0

Gary Garrison

Year	Team		Att	Yds	Avg	Lg	TD
1966	SD	A	1	-3	-3.0	-3	0
1967			1	1	1.0	1	0
1970	SD	N	4	7	1.8	10	0
1971			1	0	0.0	0	0
1972			2	-6	-3.0	0	0
1975			3	30	10.0	20	0
Career			12	29	2.4	20	0

Walt Garrison

Year	Team		Att	Yds	Avg	Lg	TD
1966	DAL	N	16	62	3.9	13	1
1967			24	146	6.1	26	1
1968			45	271	6.0	22	5
1969			176	818	4.6	21	2
1970			126	507	4.0	18t	3
1971			127	429	3.4	34	1
1972			167	784	4.7	41	7
1973			105	440	4.2	33	6
1974			113	429	3.8	18	5
Career			899	3886	4.3	41	30
Playoffs			126	493	3.9		1

Larry Garron

Year	Team		Att	Yds	Avg	Lg	TD
1960	BOS	A	8	27	3.4		0
1961			69	389	5.6	85	2
1962			67	392	5.9	41	2
1963			179	750	4.2	47	2
1964			183	585	3.2	16	2
1965			74	259	3.5	59	1
1966			101	319	3.2	54	4
1967			46	163	3.5	20	0
1968			36	97	2.7	18	1
Career			763	2981	3.9	85	14
Playoffs			22	59	2.7		1

Ben Garry

Year	Team		Att	Yds	Avg	Lg	TD
1979	BAL	N	13	41	3.2	14	0

Cleveland Gary

Year	Team		Att	Yds	Avg	Lg	TD
1989	LARM	N	37	163	4.4	18	1
1990			204	808	4.0	48	14
1991			68	245	3.6	14	1
1992			279	1125	4.0	63	7

Year	Team		Att	Yds	Avg	Lg	TD

Cleveland Gary continued

Year	Team		Att	Yds	Avg	Lg	TD
1993			79	293	3.7	15	1
1994	MIA	N	7	11	1.6	4	0
Career			674	2645	3.9	63	24
Playoffs			1	3	3.0		0

Sammy Garza

| 1987 | STL | N | 8 | 31 | 3.9 | 10 | 1 |

Sam Gash

1992	NE	N	5	7	1.4	4	1
1993			48	149	3.1	14	1
1994			30	86	2.9	10	0
1995			8	24	3.0	9	0
1996			8	15	1.9	3	0
Career			99	281	2.8	14	2

Joe Gasparella

| 1948 | PIT | N | 1 | 5 | 5.0 | 5 | 0 |

Bob Gaudio

1948	CLE	AA	1	2	2.0	2	0
1949			1	-2	-2.0	-2	0
Career			2	0	0.0	2	0

Charlie Gauer

| 1943 | P-P | | 12 | 69 | 5.8 | 25 | 0 |

Willie Gault

1983	CHI	N	4	31	7.8	22	0
1985			5	18	3.6	11	0
1986			8	79	9.9	33	0
1987			2	16	8.0	9	0
1988	LARI	N	1	4	4.0	4	0
1992			1	6	6.0	6	0
Career			21	154	7.3	33	0

Prentice Gautt

1960	CLE	N	28	159	5.7	23	1
1961	STL	N	129	523	4.1	54t	3
1962			114	470	4.1	34	2
1963			3	5	1.7	2	0
1964			59	191	3.2	30	1
1965			44	175	4.0	20	2
1966			110	370	3.4	23t	1
1967			142	573	4.0	30	1
Career			629	2466	3.9	54t	11

Pat Gavin

1922	RI-BUF	N					6
1924	RI	N					7
Career							13

Doug Gaynor

| 1986 | CIN | N | 1 | 4 | 4.0 | 4 | 0 |

Gene Gedman

1953	DET	N	83	255	3.1	27	3
1956			135	479	3.5	33	7
1957			67	278	4.1	59	3
1958			92	209	2.3	17	4
Career			377	1221	3.2	59	17
Playoffs			26	69	2.7		2

Fred Gehrke

1945	CLE	N	74	467	6.3	72t	7
1946	LA	N	71	371	5.2	53	3
1947			59	304	5.2	29	1
1948			56	246	4.4	24	1
1949			58	203	3.5	53	2
1950	SF-CHIC	N	25	73	2.9	12	1
Career			343	1664	4.9	72t	15
Playoffs			10	42	4.2		0

Jack Gehrke

| 1971 | DEN | N | 1 | 2 | 2.0 | 2 | 0 |

Stan Gelbaugh

1989	BUF	N	1	-3	-3.0	-3	0
1991	PHX	N	9	23	2.6	13	0
1992	SEA	N	16	79	4.9	22	0
1993			1	-1	-1.0	-1	0
1994			1	10	10.0	10	0
Career			28	108	3.9	22	0

Pete Gent

| 1968 | DAL | N | 2 | -5 | -2.5 | 0 | 0 |

Dale Gentry

| 1946 | LA | AA | 5 | 29 | 5.8 | | 1 |

Dennis Gentry

1982	CHI	N	4	21	5.3	9	0
1983			16	65	4.1	17	0
1984			21	79	3.8	28	1
1985			30	160	5.3	21	2
1986			11	103	9.4	29	1
1987			6	41	6.8	12	0
1988			7	86	12.3	58t	1
1989			17	106	6.2	29	0
1990			11	43	3.9	11	0
1991			9	58	6.4	17	0
1992			5	2	0.4	3	0
Career			137	764	5.6	58t	5
Playoffs			9	34	3.8		0

Lee Gentry

| 1941 | WAS | N | 5 | 13 | 2.6 | 7 | 0 |

Eddie George

| 1996 | HOU | N | 335 | 1368 | 4.1 | 76 | 8 |

Jeff George

1990	IND	N	11	2	0.2	6	1
1991			16	36	2.3	13	0
1992			14	26	1.9	13	1
1993			13	39	3.0	14	0
1994	ATL	N	30	66	2.2	10	0
1995			27	17	0.6	6	0
1996			5	10	2.0	5	0
Career			116	196	1.7	14	2
Playoffs			1	0	0.0		0

Tom Geredine

1973	ATL	N	1	-3	-3.0	-3	0
1976	LA	N	1	8	8.0	8	0
Career			2	5	2.5	8	0

Joe Geri

1949	PIT	N	133	543	4.1	25	5
1950			188	705	3.8	47	2
1951			90	252	2.8	17	3
1952	CHIC	N	20	50	2.5	21	0
Career			431	1550	3.6	47	10

Jimmy German

| 1939 | WAS | N | 20 | 58 | 2.9 | | 2 |

Bill Geyer

1942	CHIB	N	9	18	2.0	6	0
1943			16	36	2.3	15	2
Career			25	54	2.2	15	2

Lou Ghecas

| 1941 | PHI | N | 2 | 3 | 1.5 | 3 | 0 |

Milt Ghee

| 1921 | CLE | A | | | | | 2 |

Ralph Giacomarro

1983	ATL	N	2	13	6.5	13	0
1984			1	0	0.0	0	0
Career			3	13	4.3	13	0

Louie Giammona

1976	NYJ	N	39	150	3.8	35	1
1978	PHI	N	4	6	1.5	3	0
1979			15	38	2.5	9	0
1980			97	361	3.7	44	4
1981			35	98	2.8	9	1
1982			11	29	2.6	8	1
Career			201	682	3.4	44	7
Playoffs			8	18	2.3		0

Hal Giancanelli

1953	PHI	N	44	131	3.0	30	1
1954			33	47	1.4	11	0
1955			97	385	4.0	20	2

Hal Giancanelli continued

| 1956 | | | 42 | 148 | 3.5 | 21 | 1 |
| Career | | | 216 | 711 | 3.3 | 30 | 4 |

Nick Giaquinto

1980	MIA	N	5	16	3.2	5	0
1981	MIA-WAS	N	20	104	5.2	20	0
1982	WAS	N	1	5	5.0	5	0
1983			14	53	3.8	25	1
Career			40	178	4.5	25	1
Playoffs			4	9	2.3		0

Abe Gibron

| 1953 | CLE | N | 0 | -7 | | -7L | |

Frank Gifford

1952	NYG	N	38	116	3.1	15	0
1953			50	157	3.1	15	2
1954			66	368	5.6	30	2
1955			86	351	4.1	49	3
1956			159	819	5.2	69	5
1957			136	528	3.9	41	5
1958			115	468	4.1	53	8
1959			106	540	5.1	79	3
1960			77	232	3.0	15	4
1962			2	18	9.0	12	1
1963			4	10	2.5	12	0
1964			1	2	2.0	2t	1
Career			840	3609	4.3	79	34
Playoffs			49	235	4.8		1

Wayne Gift

| 1937 | CLE | N | 3 | 7 | 2.3 | | 0 |

Gale Gilbert

1985	SEA	N	7	4	0.6	8	0
1986			3	8	2.7	12	0
1994	SD	N	8	-3	-0.4	5	0
1995			6	11	1.8	8	0
Career			24	20	0.8	12	0
Playoffs			1	8	8.0		0

Wally Gilbert

| 1923 | DUL | N | | | | | 1 |

Tom Gilburg

| Playoffs | | | 1 | -5 | -5.0 | | 0 |

Cookie Gilchrist

1962	BUF	A	214	1096	5.1	44	13
1963			232	979	4.2	32	12
1964			230	981	4.3	67	6
1965	DEN	A	252	954	3.8	44	6
1966	MIA	A	72	262	3.6	22	0
1967	DEN	A	10	21	2.1	6	0
Career			1010	4293	4.3	67	37
Playoffs			24	129	5.4		1

Johnny Gildea

1935	PIT	N	49	1	0.0		0
1936			35	31	0.9		0
1937			49	65	1.3		1
1938	NYG	N	1	2	2.0	2	0
Career			134	99	0.7	2	1

Jimmie Giles

1977	HOU	N	1	-10	-10.0	-10	0
1978	TB	N	1	-1	-1.0	-1	0
1979			2	7	3.5	9	0
1982			1	1	1.0	1	0
Career			5	-3	-0.6	9	0

Owen Gill

1985	IND	N	45	262	5.8	67	2
1986			53	228	4.3	18	1
Career			98	490	5.0	67	3

Fernandars Gillespie

| 1984 | PIT | N | 7 | 18 | 2.6 | 9 | 0 |

Fred Gillett

| 1962 | SD | A | 2 | 8 | 4.0 | 5 | 0 |

Year	Team		Att	Yds	Avg	Lg	TD

Jim Gillette

Year	Team		Att	Yds	Avg	Lg	TD
1940	CLE	N	1	1	1.0	1	0
1944			26	131	5.0	58t	2
1945			63	390	6.2	52	1
1946	BOS	N	30	99	3.3	46t	1
1947	GB	N	50	207	4.1	26	0
1948	DET	N	2	3	1.5	2	0
Career			172	831	4.8	58t	4
Playoffs			17	101	5.9		0

Walker Gillette

Year	Team		Att	Yds	Avg	Lg	TD
1976	NYG	N	1	-4	-4.0	-4	0

Joe Gilliam

Year	Team		Att	Yds	Avg	Lg	TD
1972	PIT	N	2	0	0.0	0	0
1973			6	23	3.8	14	0
1974			14	41	2.9	13	1
Career			22	64	2.9	14	1
Playoffs			1	12	12.0		0

John Gilliam

Year	Team		Att	Yds	Avg	Lg	TD
1967	NO	N	7	41	5.9	19	0
1968			2	36	18.0	29	0
1969	STL	N	1	-4	-4.0	-4	0
1970			5	68	13.6	48t	1
1971			2	16	8.0	12	0
1972	MIN	N	8	14	1.8	14	0
1973			5	71	14.2	44t	1
1974			2	16	8.0	9	0
1975			3	35	11.7	22	0
Career			35	293	8.4	48t	2
Playoffs			1	16	16.0		0

Jon Gilliam

Year	Team		Att	Yds	Avg	Lg	TD
1961	DAL	A	1	-6	-6.0	-6	0

Hank Gillo

Year	Team		Att	Yds	Avg	Lg	TD
1922	RAC	N					5
1923							2
1924							3
Career							10

Horace Gillom

Year	Team		Att	Yds	Avg	Lg	TD
1949	CLE	AA	2	8	4.0		0
1955	CLE	N	1	-15	-15.0	-15	0
Career			3	-7	-2.3	-15	0

Harry Gilmer

Year	Team		Att	Yds	Avg	Lg	TD
1949	WAS	N	31	167	5.4	25	0
1950			22	145	6.6	20	1
1951			19	141	7.4	37	0
1952			100	365	3.6	30	0
1954			6	19	3.2	11	0
1955	DET	N	15	67	4.5	19	0
1956			8	19	2.4	6	0
Career			201	923	4.6	37	1

Hubie Ginn

Year	Team		Att	Yds	Avg	Lg	TD
1970	MIA	N	5	-1	-0.2	8	0
1971			22	97	4.4	46	0
1972			27	142	5.3	22	1
1973	BAL	N	16	47	2.9	8	0
1974	MIA	N	26	99	3.8	41t	2
1975			21	78	3.7	14	0
1976	OAK	N	10	53	5.3	16	0
1977			5	6	1.2	5	0
Career			132	521	3.9	46	3
Playoffs			2	9	4.5		0

Paul Gipson

Year	Team		Att	Yds	Avg	Lg	TD
1969	ATL	N	62	303	4.9	33	1
1970			52	177	3.4	16	0
1971	DET	N	4	12	3.0	5	0
1973	NE	N	5	-1	-0.2	4	0
Career			123	491	4.0	33	1

Earl Girard

Year	Team		Att	Yds	Avg	Lg	TD
1948	GB	N	13	26	2.0	7	0
1949			45	198	4.4	35	1
1950			14	39	2.8	11	0
1951			4	20	5.0	31	0
1952	DET	N	61	222	3.6	36	2
1953			19	73	3.8	17	0
1954			9	36	4.0	16	0

Year	Team		Att	Yds	Avg	Lg	TD

Earl Girard *continued*

Year	Team		Att	Yds	Avg	Lg	TD
1955			10	27	2.7	10	0
1956			17	67	3.9	11	0
1957	PIT	N	2	-5	-2.5	0	0
Career			194	703	3.6	36	3

Ernest Givins

Year	Team		Att	Yds	Avg	Lg	TD
1986	HOU	N	9	148	16.4	43t	1
1987			1	-13	-13.0	-13	0
1988			4	26	6.5	10	0
1990			3	65	21.7	31	0
1991			4	30	7.5	23	0
1992			7	75	10.7	44	0
1993			6	19	3.2	16	0
1994			1	-5	-5.0	-5	0
Career			35	345	9.9	44	1
Playoffs			2	-2	-1.0		0

Scotty Glacken

Year	Team		Att	Yds	Avg	Lg	TD
1966	DEN	A	2	-1	-0.5	5	0
1967			1	10	10.0	10	0
Career			3	9	3.0	10	0

Bob Gladieux

Year	Team		Att	Yds	Avg	Lg	TD
1970	BOS	N	4	8	2.0	8	0
1971	NE	N	37	175	4.7	31	0
1972			24	56	2.3	11	0
Career			65	239	3.7	31	0

Charles Gladman

Year	Team		Att	Yds	Avg	Lg	TD
1987	TB	N	12	29	2.4	6	0

Joe Glamp

Year	Team		Att	Yds	Avg	Lg	TD
1947	PIT	N	1	2	2.0	2	0
1948			28	107	3.8	55t	1
1949			3	-8	-2.7	2	0
Career			32	101	3.2	55t	1

Leland Glass

Year	Team		Att	Yds	Avg	Lg	TD
1972	GB	N	2	13	6.5	13	0

Bill Glassgow

Year	Team		Att	Yds	Avg	Lg	TD
1930	POR	N					4

Bill Glenn

Year	Team		Att	Yds	Avg	Lg	TD
1944	CHIB	N	1	1	1.0	1	0

Terry Glenn

Year	Team		Att	Yds	Avg	Lg	TD
1996	NE	N	5	42	8.4	26	0

Gary Glick

Year	Team		Att	Yds	Avg	Lg	TD
1960	WAS	N	1	15	15.0	15	0

Fred Gloden

Year	Team		Att	Yds	Avg	Lg	TD
1941	PHI	N	22	55	2.5	10	0
1946	MIA	AA	18	24	1.3		1
Career			40	79	2.0	10	1

Les Goble

Year	Team		Att	Yds	Avg	Lg	TD
1954	CHIC	N	30	42	1.4	8t	1
1955			7	11	1.6	5	0
Career			37	53	1.4	8t	1

Ed Goddard

Year	Team		Att	Yds	Avg	Lg	TD
1937	BKN-CLE	N	57	162	2.8		2
1938	CLE	N	40	-16	-0.4		0
Career			97	146	1.5		2

Brad Goebel

Year	Team		Att	Yds	Avg	Lg	TD
1991	PHI	N	1	2	2.0	2	0

Paul Goebel

Year	Team		Att	Yds	Avg	Lg	TD
1926	NY	A					1

Marshall Goldberg

Year	Team		Att	Yds	Avg	Lg	TD
1939	CHIC	N	56	152	2.7		2
1940			87	325	3.7		2
1941			117	427	3.6	35	3
1942			116	369	3.2	29	1
1943			6	6	1.0	5	0
1946			43	210	4.9	32t	3
1947			51	155	3.0	10	0
Career			476	1644	3.5	32t	11

Year	Team		Att	Yds	Avg	Lg	TD

Buckets Goldenberg

Year	Team		Att	Yds	Avg	Lg	TD
1933	GB	N					4
1934							2
1935			15	52	3.5		0
1936			6	9	1.5		0
1937			4	18	4.5		0
Career			25	79	3.2		6

Joe Golding

Year	Team		Att	Yds	Avg	Lg	TD
1947	BOS	N	26	71	2.7	15	1
1948			24	36	1.5	9	0
1949	NYB	N	63	249	4.0	39	0
1950	NYY	N	1	2	2.0	2	0
Career			114	358	3.1	39	1

Sam Goldman

Year	Team		Att	Yds	Avg	Lg	TD
1946	BOS	N	2	-3	-1.5	-1	0

Al Goldstein

Year	Team		Att	Yds	Avg	Lg	TD
1960	OAK	A	3	-2	-0.7		0

Ralph Goldston

Year	Team		Att	Yds	Avg	Lg	TD
1952	PHI	N	65	210	3.2	20	3
1955			14	-7	-0.5	7	0
Career			79	203	2.6	20	3

Jerry Golsteyn

Year	Team		Att	Yds	Avg	Lg	TD
1977	NYG	N	3	-4	-1.3	-1	0
1978			1	-3	-3.0	-3	0
1979	DET	N	1	0	0.0	0	0
1983	TB	N	5	3	0.6	2	0
Career			10	-4	-0.4	2	0

Bill Gompers

Year	Team		Att	Yds	Avg	Lg	TD
1948	BUF	AA	48	219	4.6		1

George Gonda

Year	Team		Att	Yds	Avg	Lg	TD
1942	PIT	N	17	147	8.6	68	2

Kelly Goodburn

Year	Team		Att	Yds	Avg	Lg	TD
1987	KC	N	1	16	16.0	16	0
1988			1	15	15.0	15	0
1990			1	5	5.0	5	0
1992	WAS	N	2	1	0.5	5	0
Career			5	37	7.4	16	0

Kerry Goode

Year	Team		Att	Yds	Avg	Lg	TD
1988	TB	N	63	231	3.7	22	0

Rob Goode

Year	Team		Att	Yds	Avg	Lg	TD
1949	WAS	N	61	261	4.3	54	2
1950			136	560	4.1	80t	5
1951			208	951	4.6	33	**9**
1954			108	462	4.3	44	0
1955	WAS-PHI	N	83	297	3.6	36	0
Career			596	2531	4.2	80t	16

Eugene Goodlow

Year	Team		Att	Yds	Avg	Lg	TD
1983	NO	N	1	3	3.0	3	0
1984			1	5	5.0	5	0
1985			1	3	3.0	3	0
Career			3	11	3.7	5	0

Les Goodman

Year	Team		Att	Yds	Avg	Lg	TD
1941	CLE	N	21	-8	-0.4	7	0
1973	GB	N	18	88	4.9	19	1
1974			20	101	5.0	47	0
Career			59	181	3.1	47	1

Clyde Goodnight

Year	Team		Att	Yds	Avg	Lg	TD
1945	GB	N	8	26	3.3	12	0
1947			1	-1	-1.0	-1	0
Career			9	25	2.8	12	0

Ronnie Goodwin

Year	Team		Att	Yds	Avg	Lg	TD
1964	PHI	N	1	-23	-23.0	-23	0
1967			1	1	1.0	1	0
Career			2	-22	-11.0	1	0

Tod Goodwin

Year	Team		Att	Yds	Avg	Lg	TD
1936	NYG	N	3	-1	-0.3		0

Johnny Goodyear

Year	Team		Att	Yds	Avg	Lg	TD
1942	WAS	N	2	1	0.5	1	0

Year	Team		Att	Yds	Avg	Lg	TD

Bobby Gordon
Year	Team		Att	Yds	Avg	Lg	TD
1958	CHIC	N	2	10	5.0	12	0

Dick Gordon
Year	Team		Att	Yds	Avg	Lg	TD
1965	CHI	N	2	10	5.0	6	0
1966			1	2	2.0	2	0
1967			3	-7	-2.3	9	0
1969			2	28	14.0	22	0
1970			4	17	4.3	7	0
1973	LA-GB	N	2	15	7.5	19	0
1974	SD	N	1	25	25.0	25	0
Career			15	90	6.0	25	0

Gordon Gore
Year	Team		Att	Yds	Avg	Lg	TD
1939	DET	N	8	7	0.9		0

Walt Gorinski
Year	Team		Att	Yds	Avg	Lg	TD
1946	PIT	N	1	3	3.0	3	0

Jeff Gossett
Year	Team		Att	Yds	Avg	Lg	TD
1992	LARI	N	1	-12	-12.0	-12	0
1993			1	-10	-10.0	-10	0
1996	OAK	N	3	28	9.3	18	0
Career			5	6	1.2	18	0

Paul Governali
Year	Team		Att	Yds	Avg	Lg	TD
1946	BOS	N	33	-187	-5.7	4t	2
1947	NYG	N	40	151	3.8	28	2
1948			6	-48	-8.0	10	0
Career			79	-84	-1.1	28	4

Casimir Gozdowski
Year	Team		Att	Yds	Avg	Lg	TD
1922	TOL	N					2

Jim Grabowski
Year	Team		Att	Yds	Avg	Lg	TD
1966	GB	N	29	127	4.4	36t	1
1967			120	466	3.9	24	2
1968			135	518	3.8	25	3
1969			73	261	3.6	22	1
1970			67	210	3.1	17	1
1971	CHI	N	51	149	2.9	16	0
Career			475	1731	3.6	36t	8
Playoffs			2	2	1.0		0

Neil Graff
Year	Team		Att	Yds	Avg	Lg	TD
1975	NE	N	2	2	1.0	2	0
1977	PIT	N	5	3	0.6	4	0
Career			7	5	0.7	4	0

Art Graham
Year	Team		Att	Yds	Avg	Lg	TD
1967	BOS	A	1	-5	-5.0	-5	0

Jeff Graham
Year	Team		Att	Yds	Avg	Lg	TD
Playoffs			1	3	3.0		

Kent Graham
Year	Team		Att	Yds	Avg	Lg	TD
1992	NYG	N	6	36	6.0	15	0
1993			2	-3	-1.5	-1	0
1994			2	11	5.5	9	0
1996	ARI	N	21	87	4.1	19	0
Career			31	131	4.2	19	0

Mike Graham
Year	Team		Att	Yds	Avg	Lg	TD
1948	LA	AA	19	69	3.6		1

Otto Graham
Year	Team		Att	Yds	Avg	Lg	TD
1946	CLE	AA	30	-125	-4.2		1
1947			19	72	3.8		1
1948			23	146	6.3		6
1949			27	107	4.0		3
1950	CLE	N	55	145	2.6	20	6
1951			35	29	0.8	12	4
1952			42	130	3.1	21	4
1953			43	143	3.3	21	6
1954			63	114	1.8	14	8
1955			68	121	1.8	36	6
Career			405	882	2.2	36	45
Playoffs			72	365	5.1		6

Scottie Graham
Year	Team		Att	Yds	Avg	Lg	TD
1992	NYJ	N	14	29	2.1	6	0
1993	MIN	N	118	488	4.1	31	3
1994			64	207	3.2	11	2
1995			110	406	3.7	26	2

Scottie Graham *continued*
Year	Team		Att	Yds	Avg	Lg	TD
1996			57	138	2.4	12	0
Career			363	1268	3.5	31	7
Playoffs			25	84	3.4		0

Ken Grandberry
Year	Team		Att	Yds	Avg	Lg	TD
1974	CHI	N	144	475	3.3	31	2

Sonny Grandelius
Year	Team		Att	Yds	Avg	Lg	TD
1953	NYG	N	108	278	2.6	31	1

Red Grange
Year	Team		Att	Yds	Avg	Lg	TD
1925	CHIB	N					2
1926	NY	A					4
1927	NYY	N					1
1929	CHIB	N					2
1930							6
1931							5
1932			77	232	3.0		3
1933			81	277	3.4		1
1934			32	136	4.3		1
Career			190	645	3.4		25
Playoffs			6	24	4.0		0

Hoyle Granger
Year	Team		Att	Yds	Avg	Lg	TD
1966	HOU	A	56	388	6.9	37	6
1967			236	1194	5.1	67	6
1968			202	848	4.2	47t	7
1969			186	740	4.0	23	3
1970	HOU	N	51	169	3.3	15	1
1971	NO	N	32	139	4.3	16	1
1972	HOU	N	42	175	4.2	14	0
Career			805	3653	4.5	67	19
Playoffs			28	48	1.7		0

Norm Granger
Year	Team		Att	Yds	Avg	Lg	TD
1987	ATL	N	6	12	2.0	6	0

Frank Grant
Year	Team		Att	Yds	Avg	Lg	TD
1974	WAS	N	1	-10	-10.0	-10	0
1975			3	46	15.3	25	0
1976			1	-9	-9.0	-9	0
Career			5	27	5.4	25	0

Otis Grant
Year	Team		Att	Yds	Avg	Lg	TD
1983	LARM	N	2	-10	-5.0	1	0
1987	PHI	N	1	20	20.0	20	0
Career			3	10	3.3	20	0

Earnest Gray
Year	Team		Att	Yds	Avg	Lg	TD
1979	NYG	N	2	2	1.0	9	0

Mel Gray
Year	Team		Att	Yds	Avg	Lg	TD
1971	STL	N	2	56	28.0	38	0
1975			1	6	6.0	6	0
1977			1	-1	-1.0	-1	0
1978			5	51	10.2	27t	1
1979			4	41	10.3	38	0
1980			1	-3	-3.0	-3	0
1981			1	4	4.0	4	0
Career			15	154	10.3	38	1

Mel Gray
Year	Team		Att	Yds	Avg	Lg	TD
1986	NO	N	6	29	4.8	11	0
1987			8	37	4.6	12	1
1989	DET	N	3	22	7.3	14	0
1991			2	11	5.5	6	0
Career			19	99	5.2	14	1

Oscar Gray
Year	Team		Att	Yds	Avg	Lg	TD
1996	SEA	N	2	4	2.0	2	0

Elvis Grbac
Year	Team		Att	Yds	Avg	Lg	TD
1994	SF	N	13	1	0.1	6	0
1995			20	33	1.6	11	2
1996			23	21	0.9	12	2
Career			56	55	1.0	12	4
Playoffs			9	27	3.0		1

Art Green
Year	Team		Att	Yds	Avg	Lg	TD
1972	NO	N	14	51	3.6	14	0

Bobby Joe Green
Year	Team		Att	Yds	Avg	Lg	TD
1961	PIT	N	2	37	18.5	33	0

Bobby Joe Green *continued*
Year	Team		Att	Yds	Avg	Lg	TD
1963	CHI	N	2	-10	-5.0	-6	0
1964			2	-2	-1.0	7	0
1968			1	4	4.0	4	0
1969			1	17	17.0	17	0
1970			1	7	7.0	7	0
Career			9	53	5.9	33	0

Boyce Green
Year	Team		Att	Yds	Avg	Lg	TD
1983	CLE	N	104	497	4.8	29	3
1984			202	673	3.3	29	0
1986	KC	N	90	314	3.5	27	3
1987	SEA	N	21	77	3.7	17	0
Career			417	1561	3.7	29	6
Playoffs			8	15	1.9		0

Darrell Green
Year	Team		Att	Yds	Avg	Lg	TD
1985	WAS	N	1	6	6.0	6	0

Dave Green
Year	Team		Att	Yds	Avg	Lg	TD
1976	TB	N	1	0	0.0	0	0
1977			1	0	0.0	0	0
1978			1	0	0.0	0	0
Career			3	0	0.0	0	0

Ernie Green
Year	Team		Att	Yds	Avg	Lg	TD
1962	CLE	N	31	139	4.5	45	0
1963			87	526	6.0	72	0
1964			109	491	4.5	37t	6
1965			111	436	3.9	41	2
1966			144	750	5.2	35	3
1967			145	710	4.9	59t	4
1968			41	152	3.7	14	0
Career			668	3204	4.8	72	15
Playoffs			27	90	3.3		1

Gaston Green
Year	Team		Att	Yds	Avg	Lg	TD
1988	LARM	N	35	117	3.3	13	0
1989			26	73	2.8	9	0
1990			68	261	3.8	31	0
1991	DEN	N	261	1037	4.0	63t	4
1992			161	648	4.0	67t	2
Career			551	2136	3.9	67t	6
Playoffs			36	112	3.1		0

Harold Green
Year	Team		Att	Yds	Avg	Lg	TD
1990	CIN	N	83	353	4.3	39	1
1991			158	731	4.6	75t	2
1992			265	1170	4.4	53	2
1993			215	589	2.7	25	0
1994			76	223	2.9	22	1
1995			171	661	3.9	23t	2
1996	STL	N	127	523	4.1	35t	4
Career			1095	4250	3.9	75t	12
Playoffs			11	55	5.0		0

Johnny Green
Year	Team		Att	Yds	Avg	Lg	TD
1960	BUF	A	46	-156	-3.4		2
1961			14	15	1.1	14	1
1962	NY	A	17	35	2.1	8	3
Career			77	-106	-1.4	14	6

Mark Green
Year	Team		Att	Yds	Avg	Lg	TD
1989	CHI	N	5	46	9.2	37t	1
1990			27	126	4.7	14	0
1991			61	217	3.6	18	3
1992			23	107	4.7	18	2
Career			116	496	4.3	37t	6
Playoffs			2	8	4.0		0

Robert Green
Year	Team		Att	Yds	Avg	Lg	TD
1992	WAS	N	8	46	5.8	23	0
1993	CHI	N	15	29	1.9	10	0
1994			25	122	4.9	14	0
1995			107	570	5.3	38	3
1996			60	249	4.2	19	0
Career			215	1016	4.7	38	3
Playoffs			7	25	3.6		0

Roy Green
Year	Team		Att	Yds	Avg	Lg	TD
1981	STL	N	3	60	20.0	44t	1
1982			6	8	1.3	13	0
1983			4	49	12.3	7t	0
1984			1	-10	-10.0	-10	0

Roy Green continued

Year	Team		Att	Yds	Avg	Lg	TD
1985			1	2	2.0	2	0
1986			2	-4	-2.0	1	0
1987			2	34	17.0	26	0
1988	PHX	N	4	1	0.3	18	0
Career			23	140	6.1	44t	1
Playoffs			1	4	4.0		0

Tony Green

Year	Team		Att	Yds	Avg	Lg	TD
1978	WAS	N	22	82	3.7	13	1

Willie Green

Year	Team		Att	Yds	Avg	Lg	TD
1996	CAR	N	1	1	1.0	1	0

Woody Green

Year	Team		Att	Yds	Avg	Lg	TD
1974	KC	N	135	509	3.8	43	3
1975			167	611	3.7	42	5
1976			73	322	4.4	27	1
Career			375	1442	3.8	43	9

Tom Greene

Year	Team		Att	Yds	Avg	Lg	TD
1960	BOS	A	16	-27	-1.7		0

Bobby Greenhalgh

Year	Team		Att	Yds	Avg	Lg	TD
1949	NYG	N	62	188	3.0	14	0

Don Greenwood

Year	Team		Att	Yds	Avg	Lg	TD
1945	CLE	N	101	376	3.7	35	4
1946	CLE	AA	77	274	3.6		6
1947			18	94	5.2		0
Career			196	744	3.8	35	10
Playoffs			14	33	2.4		0

Ben Gregory

Year	Team		Att	Yds	Avg	Lg	TD
1968	BUF	A	52	283	5.4	67	1

Bob Gresham

Year	Team		Att	Yds	Avg	Lg	TD
1971	NO	N	127	383	3.0	18	6
1972			121	381	3.1	23	3
1973	HOU	N	104	400	3.8	52	2
1974			3	6	2.0	3	0
1975	NYJ	N	25	98	3.9	16	1
1976			30	92	3.1	24	0
Career			410	1360	3.3	52	12

Marrio Grier

Year	Team		Att	Yds	Avg	Lg	TD
1996	NE	N	27	105	3.9	26	1
Playoffs			5	7	1.4		0

Bob Griese

Year	Team		Att	Yds	Avg	Lg	TD
1967	MIA	A	37	157	4.2	22	1
1968			42	230	5.5	35	1
1969			21	102	4.9	22	0
1970	MIA	N	26	89	3.4	16	2
1971			26	82	3.2	21	0
1972			3	11	3.7	5	1
1973			13	20	1.5	21	0
1974			16	66	4.1	22	1
1975			17	59	3.5	17	1
1976			23	108	4.7	26	0
1977			16	30	1.9	13	0
1978			9	10	1.1	9	0
1979			11	30	2.7	18	0
1980			1	0	0.0	0	0
Career			261	994	3.8	35	7
Playoffs			13	84	6.5		0

Archie Griffin

Year	Team		Att	Yds	Avg	Lg	TD
1976	CIN	N	138	625	4.5	77t	3
1977			137	549	4.0	31	0
1978			132	484	3.7	30	0
1979			140	688	4.9	63	0
1980			85	260	3.1	14	0
1981			47	163	3.5	23	3
1982			12	39	3.3	10t	1
Career			691	2808	4.1	77t	7
Playoffs			5	25	5.0		0

Don Griffin

Year	Team		Att	Yds	Avg	Lg	TD
1946	CHI	AA	28	13	0.5		0

Keith Griffin

Year	Team		Att	Yds	Avg	Lg	TD
1984	WAS	N	97	408	4.2	31	0
1985			102	473	4.6	66t	3

Keith Griffin continued

Year	Team		Att	Yds	Avg	Lg	TD
1986			62	197	3.2	12	0
1987			62	242	3.9	13	0
1988			6	23	3.8	9	0
Career			329	1343	4.1	66t	3
Playoffs			6	10	1.7		0

Steve Griffin

Year	Team		Att	Yds	Avg	Lg	TD
1987	ATL	N	1	-2	-2.0	-2	0

Glynn Griffing

Year	Team		Att	Yds	Avg	Lg	TD
1963	NYG	N	5	20	4.0	10	0

Forrest Griffith

Year	Team		Att	Yds	Avg	Lg	TD
1950	NYG	N	45	162	3.6	39	2
1951			54	115	2.1	27	0
Career			99	277	2.8	39	2

Howard Griffith

Year	Team		Att	Yds	Avg	Lg	TD
1994	LARM	N	9	30	3.3	7	0
1995	CAR	N	65	197	3.0	15	1
1996			12	7	0.6	3	1
Career			86	234	2.7	15	2

Russell Griffith

Year	Team		Att	Yds	Avg	Lg	TD
1987	SEA	N	1	0	0.0	0	0

Johnny Grigas

Year	Team		Att	Yds	Avg	Lg	TD
1943	CHIC	N	105	333	3.2	28	3
1944	C-P	N	185	610	3.3	29	3
1945	BOS	N	64	160	2.5	45	2
1946			84	426	5.1	59t	2
1947			27	52	1.9	13	0
Career			465	1581	3.4	59t	10

Tex Grigg

Year	Team		Att	Yds	Avg	Lg	TD
1920	CAN	A					1
1923	CAN	N					3
Career							4

Hal Griggs

Year	Team		Att	Yds	Avg	Lg	TD
1926	AKR	N					2

Frank Grigonis

Year	Team		Att	Yds	Avg	Lg	TD
1942	DET	N	37	131	3.5	12	1

Bob Grim

Year	Team		Att	Yds	Avg	Lg	TD
1967	MIN	N	1	20	20.0	20	0
1971			6	127	21.2	54	0
1973	NYG	N	1	-10	-10.0	-10	0
Career			8	137	17.1	54	0
Playoffs			1	2	2.0		0

Billy Joe Grimes

Year	Team		Att	Yds	Avg	Lg	TD
1949	LA	AA	83	429	5.2	51	4
1950	GB	N	84	480	5.7	73t	5
1951			44	123	2.8	18t	1
1952			17	59	3.5	31	0
Career			228	1091	4.8	73t	10

George Grimes

Year	Team		Att	Yds	Avg	Lg	TD
1948	DET	N	1	8	8.0	8	0

Clif Groce

Year	Team		Att	Yds	Avg	Lg	TD
1996	IND	N	46	184	4.0	24	0
Playoffs			2	11	5.5		0

Ron Groce

Year	Team		Att	Yds	Avg	Lg	TD
1976	MIN	N	3	18	6.0	13	0

Steve Grogan

Year	Team		Att	Yds	Avg	Lg	TD
1975	NE	N	30	110	3.7	14	1
1976			60	397	6.6	41t	12
1977			61	324	5.3	41	1
1978			81	539	6.7	31	5
1979			64	368	5.8	26	2
1980			30	112	3.7	19	1
1981			12	49	4.1	24t	2
1982			9	42	4.7	19	1
1983			23	108	4.7	17	2
1984			7	12	1.7	1	0
1985			20	29	1.5	12	2
1986			9	23	2.6	10	1
1987			20	37	1.9	8	2

Steve Grogan continued

Year	Team		Att	Yds	Avg	Lg	TD
1988			6	12	2.0	6	1
1989			9	19	2.1	7	0
1990			4	-5	-1.3	0	0
Career			445	2176	4.9	41t	35
Playoffs			9	54	6.0		0

Bill Groman

Year	Team		Att	Yds	Avg	Lg	TD
1961	HOU	A	1	2	2.0	2t	1

Mel Groomes

Year	Team		Att	Yds	Avg	Lg	TD
1948	DET	N	2	1	0.5	7	0
1949			1	1	1.0	1	0
Career			3	2	0.7	7	0

Earl Gros

Year	Team		Att	Yds	Avg	Lg	TD
1962	GB	N	29	155	5.3	56	2
1963			48	203	4.2	19t	2
1964	PHI	N	154	748	4.9	59t	2
1965			145	479	3.3	33	7
1966			102	396	3.9	26	7
1967	PIT	N	72	252	3.5	23	1
1968			151	579	3.8	55	3
1969			116	343	3.0	16t	4
1970	NO	N	4	2	0.5	4	0
Career			821	3157	3.8	59t	28

Lee Grosscup

Year	Team		Att	Yds	Avg	Lg	TD
1960	NYG	N	3	1	0.3	5	0
1961			2	10	5.0	10	0
1962	NY	A	8	62	7.8	18	0
Career			13	73	5.6	18	0

Jack Grossman

Year	Team		Att	Yds	Avg	Lg	TD
1932	BKN	N					2
1935			67	208	3.1		2
Career			67	208	3.1		4

Rex Grossman

Year	Team		Att	Yds	Avg	Lg	TD
1948	BAL	AA	8	-3	-0.4		0

George Grosvenor

Year	Team		Att	Yds	Avg	Lg	TD
1935	CHIB	N	55	234	4.3		0
1936	CHIB-CHIC	N	170	612	3.6		4
1937	CHIC	N	137	461	3.4		2
Career			362	1307	3.6		6

Jeff Groth

Year	Team		Att	Yds	Avg	Lg	TD
1981	NO	N	2	27	13.5	28	0
1982			1	1	1.0	1	0
1983			1	15	15.0	15	0
Career			4	43	10.8	28	0

Roger Grove

Year	Team		Att	Yds	Avg	Lg	TD
1934	GB	N					1

Bob Grupp

Year	Team		Att	Yds	Avg	Lg	TD
1980	KC	N	3	-14	-4.7	0	0
1981			1	-19	-19.0	-19	0
Career			4	-33	-8.3	0	0

Al Grygo

Year	Team		Att	Yds	Avg	Lg	TD
1944	CHIB	N	53	322	6.1	66t	2
1945			23	98	4.3	16	0
Career			76	420	5.5	66t	2

Scotty Gudmundson

Year	Team		Att	Yds	Avg	Lg	TD
1944	BOS	N	14	-21	-1.5	6	0
1945			23	4	0.2	20	0
Career			37	-17	-0.5	20	0

Terry Guess

Year	Team		Att	Yds	Avg	Lg	TD
1996	NO	N	2	-4	-2.0	-1	0

Ralph Guglielmi

Year	Team		Att	Yds	Avg	Lg	TD
1955	WAS	N	18	51	2.8	17	1
1958			17	74	4.4	17	0
1959			26	97	3.7	19	0
1960			79	247	3.1	16	0
1961	STL	N	22	101	4.6	23	1
1962	NYG	N	11	40	3.6	18	0
1963	NYG-PHI	N	4	23	5.8	20	0
Career			177	633	3.6	23	2

Year	Team		Att	Yds	Avg	Lg	TD

Eric Guliford

Year	Team		Att	Yds	Avg	Lg	TD
1995	CAR	N	2	2	1.0	1	0

George Gulyanics

Year	Team		Att	Yds	Avg	Lg	TD
1947	CHIB	N	35	212	6.1	46t	4
1948			119	439	3.7	24	4
1949			102	452	4.4	31	5
1950			146	571	3.9	31	2
1951			105	403	3.8	30	4
1952			2	4	2.0	3	0
Career			509	2081	4.1	46t	19
Playoffs			15	94	6.3		1

Mike Guman

Year	Team		Att	Yds	Avg	Lg	TD
1980	LA	N	100	410	4.1	17	4
1981			115	433	3.8	18	4
1982	LARM	N	69	266	3.9	15	2
1983			7	42	6.0	40	0
1984			1	2	2.0	2	0
1985			11	32	2.9	6	0
1986			2	2	1.0	3	0
1987			36	98	2.7	7	1
1988			1	1	1.0	1	0
Career			342	1286	3.8	40	11

Michael Gunter

Year	Team		Att	Yds	Avg	Lg	TD
1984	KC	N	15	12	0.8	4	0

Ed Gustafson

Year	Team		Att	Yds	Avg	Lg	TD
1948	BKN	AA	1	7	7.0	7	0

Jim Gustafson

Year	Team		Att	Yds	Avg	Lg	TD
1987	MIN	N	1	-2	-2.0	-2	0

Ace Gutowsky

Year	Team		Att	Yds	Avg	Lg	TD
1932	POR	N					3
1933			103	385	3.7		1
1934	DET	N	141	517	3.7		5
1935			102	295	2.9		2
1936			191	827	4.3		6
1937			126	361	2.9		1
1938			131	444	3.4		2
1939	BKN	N	58	202	3.5		0
Career			852	3031	3.6		20

Ray Guy

Year	Team		Att	Yds	Avg	Lg	TD
1973	OAK	N	1	21	21.0	21	0
1976			1	0	0.0	0	0
1980			3	38	12.7	24	0
1982	LARI	N	2	-3	-1.5	7	0
1983			2	-13	-6.5	-3	0
1985			1	0	0.0	0	0
1986			1	0	0.0	0	0
Career			11	43	3.9	24	0
Playoffs			1	2	2.0	2	0

Joe Guyon

Year	Team		Att	Yds	Avg	Lg	TD
1920	CAN	A					1
1921	CLE	A					2
1922	OOR	N					2
1923							1
Career							6

Elmer Hackney

Year	Team		Att	Yds	Avg	Lg	TD
1940	PHI	N	32	101	3.2		1
1941	PIT	N	63	253	4.0	31	1
1942	DET	N	34	208	6.1	78	2
1943			27	87	3.2	16	2
1944			58	184	3.2	16	4
1945			6	13	2.2	6	0
Career			220	846	3.8	78	10

Michael Haddix

Year	Team		Att	Yds	Avg	Lg	TD
1983	PHI	N	91	220	2.4	11	2
1984			48	130	2.7	21	1
1985			67	213	3.2	12	0
1986			79	276	3.5	18	0
1987			59	165	2.8	11	0
1988			57	185	3.2	15	0
1989	GB	N	44	135	3.1	10	0
1990			98	311	3.2	13	0
Career			543	1635	3.0	21	3
Playoffs			1	3	3.0		0

Year	Team		Att	Yds	Avg	Lg	TD

Al Haddon

Year	Team		Att	Yds	Avg	Lg	TD
1925	DET	N					1

Pat Haden

Year	Team		Att	Yds	Avg	Lg	TD
1976	LA	N	25	84	3.4	16	4
1977			29	106	3.7	23	2
1978			33	206	6.2	24	0
1979			16	97	6.1	17	0
1980			3	12	4.0	6	0
1981			18	104	5.8	16	0
Career			124	609	4.9	24	6
Playoffs			18	81	4.5		1

John Hadl

Year	Team		Att	Yds	Avg	Lg	TD
1962	SD	A	40	139	3.5	18	1
1963			8	26	3.3	33	0
1964			20	70	3.5	20	1
1965			28	91	3.3	23	1
1966			38	95	2.5	21	2
1967			37	107	2.9	26	3
1968			23	14	0.6	9	2
1969			26	109	4.2	17	2
1970	SD	N	28	188	6.7	34	1
1971			18	75	4.2	37	1
1972			22	99	4.5	17	1
1973	LA	N	14	5	0.4	6	0
1974	LA-GB	N	19	25	1.3	9	0
1975	GB	N	20	47	2.4	9	0
1976	HOU	N	7	11	1.6	8	0
1977			3	11	3.7	6t	1
Career			351	1112	3.2	37	16
Playoffs			12	48	4.0		1

James Hadnot

Year	Team		Att	Yds	Avg	Lg	TD
1980	KC	N	76	244	3.2	11	2
1981			140	603	4.3	30	3
1982			46	172	3.7	25	0
1983			4	10	2.5	7	0
Career			266	1029	3.9	30	5

Mike Haffner

Year	Team		Att	Yds	Avg	Lg	TD
1968	DEN	A	2	2	1.0	1	0
1970	DEN	N	1	1	1.0	1	0
Career			3	3	1.0	1	0

Roger Hagberg

Year	Team		Att	Yds	Avg	Lg	TD
1965	OAK	A	48	171	3.6	19	1
1966			62	282	4.5	30	0
1967			44	146	3.3	11	2
1968			39	164	4.2	16	1
1969			1	3	3.0	3	0
Career			194	766	3.9	30	4
Playoffs			8	20	2.5		

Mike Hagen

Year	Team		Att	Yds	Avg	Lg	TD
1987	SEA	N	2	3	1.5	4	0

Jack Hagerty

Year	Team		Att	Yds	Avg	Lg	TD
1926	NYG	N					1
1927							1
1930							2
Career							4

Isaac Hagins

Year	Team		Att	Yds	Avg	Lg	TD
1977	TB	N	1	2	2.0	2	0
1980			3	24	8.0	26	0
Career			4	26	6.5	26	0

Mac Haik

Year	Team		Att	Yds	Avg	Lg	TD
1968	HOU	A	2	7	3.5	5	0
1969			2	21	10.5	11	0
Career			4	28	7.0	11	0

By Haines

Year	Team		Att	Yds	Avg	Lg	TD
1937	PIT	N	24	29	1.2		0

Hinkey Haines

Year	Team		Att	Yds	Avg	Lg	TD
1925	NY	N					1
1926	NYG	N					5
1928							4
1929	SI	N					2
Career							12

Year	Team		Att	Yds	Avg	Lg	TD

Dick Haley

Year	Team		Att	Yds	Avg	Lg	TD
1959	WAS	N	14	51	3.6	15	1

Eddie Halicki

Year	Team		Att	Yds	Avg	Lg	TD
1929	FRA	N					3
1930							3
Career							6

Dino Hall

Year	Team		Att	Yds	Avg	Lg	TD
1979	CLE	N	22	152	6.9	52t	1
1980			2	26	13.0	19	0
1982			2	14	7.0	13	0
1983			1	2	2.0	2	0
Career			27	194	7.2	52t	1

Forrest Hall

Year	Team		Att	Yds	Avg	Lg	TD
1948	SF	AA	66	413	6.3	65t	2

Galen Hall

Year	Team		Att	Yds	Avg	Lg	TD
1962	WAS	N	2	2	1.0	1t	1
1963	NY	A	9	24	2.7	11	1
Career			11	26	2.4	11	2

Irv Hall

Year	Team		Att	Yds	Avg	Lg	TD
1942	PHI	N	8	14	1.8	11	1

Johnny Hall

Year	Team		Att	Yds	Avg	Lg	TD
1940	CHIC	N	39	88	2.3		1
1941			53	165	3.1	24	2
1942	DET	N	2	-8	-4.0		0
1943	CHIC	N	22	51	2.3	14	0
Career			116	296	2.6	24	3

Ken Hall

Year	Team		Att	Yds	Avg	Lg	TD
1959	CHIC	N	14	81	5.8	20	0
1960	HOU	A	30	118	3.9		0
1961			7	13	1.9	9	0
Career			51	212	4.2	20	0
Playoffs			3	5	1.7		0

Parker Hall

Year	Team		Att	Yds	Avg	Lg	TD
1939	CLE	N	120	458	3.8		2
1940			94	365	3.9		1
1941			57	232	4.1	60	2
1942			41	-3	-0.1	13	1
1946	SF	AA	17	31	1.8		0
Career			329	1083	3.3	60	6

Tim Hall

Year	Team		Att	Yds	Avg	Lg	TD
1996	OAK	N	3	7	2.3	4	0

Tom Hall

Year	Team		Att	Yds	Avg	Lg	TD
1964	MIN	N	4	-4	-1.0	5	0

Shawn Halloran

Year	Team		Att	Yds	Avg	Lg	TD
1987	STL	N	3	-9	-3.0	2	0

Tex Hamer

Year	Team		Att	Yds	Avg	Lg	TD
1924	FRA	N					12
1925							5
1926							2
Career							19

Mal Hammack

Year	Team		Att	Yds	Avg	Lg	TD
1955	CHIC	N	51	160	3.1	17	2
1957			30	158	5.3	17	0
1958			35	121	3.5	15	1
1959			49	237	4.8	19	0
1960	STL	N	96	347	3.6	24	2
1961			18	79	4.4	28t	1
1962			38	160	4.2	60t	1
1963			3	16	5.3	9	0
Career			320	1278	4.0	60t	7

Bobby Hammond

Year	Team		Att	Yds	Avg	Lg	TD
1977	NYG	N	154	577	3.7	30	3
1978			131	554	4.2	39	1
1979	WAS	N	2	5	2.5	3	0
1980			45	265	5.9	36	0
Career			332	1401	4.2	39	4

Gary Hammond

Year	Team		Att	Yds	Avg	Lg	TD
1973	STL	N	4	11	2.8	7	0

Year	Team		Att	Yds	Avg	Lg	TD

Gary Hammond *continued*

Year	Team		Att	Yds	Avg	Lg	TD
1975			3	13	4.3	6	0
Career			7	24	3.4	7	0

Kim Hammond

Year	Team		Att	Yds	Avg	Lg	TD
1968	MIA	A	1	0	0.0	0	0

Dave Hampton

Year	Team		Att	Yds	Avg	Lg	TD
1969	GB	N	80	365	4.6	53	4
1970			48	115	2.4	14	0
1971			67	307	4.6	41	3
1972	ATL	N	230	995	4.3	56t	6
1973			263	997	3.8	25	4
1974			127	464	3.7	34	2
1975			250	1002	4.0	22	5
1976	ATL-PHI	N	83	291	3.5	59	1
Career			1148	4536	4.0	59	25

Lorenzo Hampton

Year	Team		Att	Yds	Avg	Lg	TD
1985	MIA	N	105	369	3.5	15	3
1986			186	830	4.5	54t	9
1987			75	289	3.9	34	1
1988			117	414	3.5	33	9
1989			17	47	2.8	9	0
Career			500	1949	3.9	54t	22

Rodney Hampton

Year	Team		Att	Yds	Avg	Lg	TD
1990	NYG	N	109	455	4.2	41	2
1991			256	1059	4.1	44	10
1992			257	1141	4.4	63t	14
1993			292	1077	3.7	20	5
1994			327	1075	3.3	27t	6
1995			306	1182	3.9	32	10
1996			254	827	3.3	25	1
Career			1801	6816	3.8	63t	48
Playoffs			42	176	4.2		2

Bob Hanlon

Year	Team		Att	Yds	Avg	Lg	TD
1948	CHIC	N	6	11	1.8	5	0
1949	PIT	N	6	14	2.3	7	0
Career			12	25	2.1	7	0

Travis Hannah

Year	Team		Att	Yds	Avg	Lg	TD
1995	HOU	N	1	5	5.0	5	0

Chuck Hanneman

Year	Team		Att	Yds	Avg	Lg	TD
1937	DET	N	2	53	26.5		1
1938			1	6	6.0	6	0
Career			3	59	19.7	6	1

Terry Hanratty

Year	Team		Att	Yds	Avg	Lg	TD
1969	PIT	N	10	106	10.6	31	0
1970			4	-5	-1.3	0	0
1971			1	3	3.0	3t	1
1973			3	0	0.0	0	0
1974			1	-6	-6.0	-6	0
1975			1	0	0.0	0	0
1976	TB	N	1	1	1.0	0	0
Career			21	99	4.7	31	0

Brian Hansen

Year	Team		Att	Yds	Avg	Lg	TD
1984	NO	N	2	-27	-13.5	-12	0
1986			1	0	0.0	0	0
1987			2	-6	-3.0	-3	0
1988			1	10	10.0	10	0
1990	NE	N	1	0	0.0	0	0
1991	CLE	N	2	-3	-1.5	0	0
1996	NYJ	N	1	1	1.0	1	0
Career			10	-25	-2.5	10	0

Bruce Hansen

Year	Team		Att	Yds	Avg	Lg	TD
1987	NE	N	16	44	2.8	7	0

Tom Hanson

Year	Team		Att	Yds	Avg	Lg	TD
1932	SI	N					1
1933	PHI	N	133	494	3.7		3
1934			147	805	5.5		7
1935			77	209	2.7		0
1936			119	359	3.0		1
1937			18	59	3.3		1
1938	PIT	N	15	50	3.3		0
Career			509	1976	3.9		13

Chet Hanulak

Year	Team		Att	Yds	Avg	Lg	TD
1954	CLE	N	59	296	5.0	24	4
1957			125	375	3.0	64t	3
Career			184	671	3.6	64t	7
Playoffs			5	44	8.8		1

Merle Hapes

Year	Team		Att	Yds	Avg	Lg	TD
1942	NYG	N	95	363	3.8	52	2
1946			51	161	3.2	26	5
Career			146	524	3.6	52	7

Jim Harbaugh

Year	Team		Att	Yds	Avg	Lg	TD
1987	CHI	N	4	15	3.8	9	0
1988			19	110	5.8	19	1
1989			45	276	6.1	26t	3
1990			51	321	6.3	17	4
1991			70	338	4.8	20	2
1992			47	272	5.8	17	1
1993			60	277	4.6	25	4
1994	IND	N	39	223	5.7	41	0
1995			52	235	4.5	21	2
1996			48	192	4.0	21	1
Career			435	2259	5.2	41	18
Playoffs			30	119	4.0		1

Buddy Hardeman

Year	Team		Att	Yds	Avg	Lg	TD
1979	WAS	N	31	124	4.0	22	0
1980			40	132	3.3	13	0
Career			71	256	3.6	22	0

Don Hardeman

Year	Team		Att	Yds	Avg	Lg	TD
1975	HOU	N	166	648	3.9	39	5
1976			32	114	3.6	21	1
1977			42	162	3.9	18	2
1978	BAL	N	48	244	5.1	46	0
1979			109	292	2.7	16	3
Career			397	1460	3.7	46	11

Pat Harder

Year	Team		Att	Yds	Avg	Lg	TD
1946	CHIC	N	106	545	5.1	55	4
1947			113	371	3.3	45t	7
1948			126	534	4.2	71t	6
1949			106	447	4.2	42	7
1950			99	454	4.6	22	1
1951	DET	N	101	380	3.8	28	6
1952			81	244	3.0	22	2
1953			8	21	2.6	10	0
Career			740	2996	4.0	71t	33
Playoffs			37	167	4.5		2

Andre Hardy

Year	Team		Att	Yds	Avg	Lg	TD
1984	PHI	N	14	41	2.9	10	0
1985	SEA	N	5	5	1.0	4	0
1987	SF	N	7	48	6.9	14	0
Career			26	94	3.6	14	0

Bruce Hardy

Year	Team		Att	Yds	Avg	Lg	TD
1983	MIA	N	1	2	2.0	2	0

Carroll Hardy

Year	Team		Att	Yds	Avg	Lg	TD
1955	SF	N	15	37	2.5	24	0

Jim Hardy

Year	Team		Att	Yds	Avg	Lg	TD
1946	LA	N	10	-10	-1.0	6	0
1947			3	-6	-2.0	7	0
1948			5	14	2.8	9	0
1949	CHIC	N	7	6	0.9	4	1
1950			10	14	1.4	19	1
1951			12	38	3.2	16	0
1952	DET	N	5	16	3.2	9	0
Career			52	72	1.4	19	2

Cecil Hare

Year	Team		Att	Yds	Avg	Lg	TD
1941	WAS	N	6	22	3.7	6	0
1942			14	57	4.1	11	1
1945			3	0	0.0	0	0
Career			23	79	3.4	11	1

Eddie Hare

Year	Team		Att	Yds	Avg	Lg	TD
1979	NE	N	1	0	0.0	0	0

Ray Hare

Year	Team		Att	Yds	Avg	Lg	TD
1940	WAS	N	1	2	2.0	2	0
1941			11	48	4.4	12	1

Ray Hare *continued*

Year	Team		Att	Yds	Avg	Lg	TD
1942			27	197	7.3	47	1
1943			21	96	4.6	16	0
1944	BKN	N	72	196	2.7	36	0
Career			132	539	4.1	47	2
Playoffs			9	22	2.4		0

Edd Hargett

Year	Team		Att	Yds	Avg	Lg	TD
1969	NO	N	5	15	3.0	11	0
1970			4	7	1.8	7	0
1971			9	24	2.7	11	1
Career			18	46	2.6	11	1

Jimmy Hargrove

Year	Team		Att	Yds	Avg	Lg	TD
1981	CIN	N	16	66	4.1	27	1
1987	GB	N	11	38	3.5	7	1
Career			27	104	3.9	27	2

Lem Harkey

Year	Team		Att	Yds	Avg	Lg	TD
1955	SF	N	6	27	4.5	15	0

Steve Harkey

Year	Team		Att	Yds	Avg	Lg	TD
1971	NYJ	N	20	62	3.1	10	0
1972			45	129	2.9	10	0
Career			65	191	2.9	10	0

Clarence Harmon

Year	Team		Att	Yds	Avg	Lg	TD
1977	WAS	N	94	310	3.3	21	0
1978			34	141	4.1	47	0
1979			65	267	4.1	18	0
1980			128	484	3.8	23	4
1981			1	4	4.0	4	0
1982			38	168	4.4	20	1
Career			360	1374	3.8	47	5
Playoffs			9	40	4.4		0

Derrick Harmon

Year	Team		Att	Yds	Avg	Lg	TD
1984	SF	N	39	192	4.9	19	1
1985			28	92	3.3	17	0
1986			27	77	2.9	15	1
Career			94	361	3.8	19	2
Playoffs			10	37	3.7		0

Kevin Harmon

Year	Team		Att	Yds	Avg	Lg	TD
1988	SEA	N	2	13	6.5	8	0
1989			1	24	24.0	24	0
Career			3	37	12.3	24	0

Ronnie Harmon

Year	Team		Att	Yds	Avg	Lg	TD
1986	BUF	N	54	172	3.2	38	0
1987			116	485	4.2	21	2
1988			57	212	3.7	32	1
1989			17	99	5.8	24	0
1990	SD	N	66	363	5.5	41	0
1991			89	544	6.1	33	1
1992			55	235	4.3	33	3
1993			46	216	4.7	19	1
1994			25	94	3.8	15t	1
1995			51	187	3.7	48t	1
1996	HOU	N	29	131	4.5	25	1
Career			605	2738	4.5	48t	10
Playoffs			14	63	4.5		0

Tommy Harmon

Year	Team		Att	Yds	Avg	Lg	TD
1946	LA	N	47	236	5.0	84t	2
1947			60	306	5.1	32t	3
Career			107	542	5.1	84t	5

Alvin Harper

Year	Team		Att	Yds	Avg	Lg	TD
1992	DAL	N	1	15	15.0	15	0
Playoffs			1	3	3.0		0

Bruce Harper

Year	Team		Att	Yds	Avg	Lg	TD
1977	NYJ	N	44	198	4.5	18	0
1978			58	303	5.2	32	2
1979			65	282	4.3	31	0
1980			45	126	2.8	22	0
1981			81	393	4.9	29t	4
1982			20	125	6.3	40	0
1983			51	354	6.9	78t	1
1984			10	48	4.8	16	1
Career			374	1829	4.9	78t	8
Playoffs			2	9	4.5		0

Darrell Harper

Year	Team	Att	Yds	Avg	Lg	TD
1960	BUF A	1	3	3.0	3	0

Jack Harper

Year	Team	Att	Yds	Avg	Lg	TD
1967	MIA A	41	197	4.8	37t	1

Michael Harper

Year	Team	Att	Yds	Avg	Lg	TD
1989	NYJ N	1	3	3.0	3	0

Roland Harper

Year	Team	Att	Yds	Avg	Lg	TD
1975	CHI N	100	453	4.5	32	1
1976		147	625	4.3	28	2
1977		120	457	3.8	19	0
1978		240	992	4.1	31	6
1980		113	404	3.6	13	5
1981		34	106	3.1	11	1
1982		3	7	2.3	8	0
Career		757	3044	4.0	32	15
Playoffs		5	11	2.2		0

Charley Harraway

Year	Team	Att	Yds	Avg	Lg	TD
1966	CLE N	7	40	5.7	18	0
1967		5	-14	-2.8	2	0
1968		91	334	3.7	23	0
1969	WAS N	141	428	3.0	17	6
1970		146	577	4.0	57t	5
1971		156	635	4.1	57t	2
1972		148	567	3.8	24	6
1973		128	452	3.5	16	1
Career		822	3019	3.7	57t	20
Playoffs		65	196	3.0		1

Sam Harrell

Year	Team	Att	Yds	Avg	Lg	TD
1981	MIN N	1	7	7.0	7	0
1987		5	8	1.6	4	0
Career		6	15	2.5	7	0

Willard Harrell

Year	Team	Att	Yds	Avg	Lg	TD
1975	GB N	121	359	3.0	26t	1
1976		130	435	3.3	56	3
1977		60	140	2.3	9	1
1978	STL N	35	134	3.8	15	0
1979		19	100	5.3	19	0
1980		42	170	4.0	26	3
1981		5	6	1.2	4	1
1982		4	14	3.5	8	0
1983		4	13	3.3	8	0
1984		6	7	1.2	4	1
Career		426	1378	3.2	56	10

La Rue Harrington

Year	Team	Att	Yds	Avg	Lg	TD
1980	SD N	4	-7	-1.8	-1	0

Perry Harrington

Year	Team	Att	Yds	Avg	Lg	TD
1980	PHI N	32	166	5.2	19t	1
1981		34	140	4.1	16	2
1982		56	231	4.1	37	1
1983		23	98	4.3	35	1
1984	STL N	3	6	2.0	5	0
1985		7	42	6.0	22	1
Career		155	683	4.4	37	6
Playoffs		3	10	3.3		1

Bill Harris

Year	Team	Att	Yds	Avg	Lg	TD
1968	ATL N	53	144	2.7	11	0
1969	MIN N	6	13	2.2	5	0
1971	NO N	1	1	1.0	1	0
Career		60	158	2.6	11	0

Corey Harris

Year	Team	Att	Yds	Avg	Lg	TD
1992	GB N	2	10	5.0	7	0

Darryl Harris

Year	Team	Att	Yds	Avg	Lg	TD
1988	MIN N	34	151	4.4	34	1

Derrick Harris

Year	Team	Att	Yds	Avg	Lg	TD
1996	STL N	3	5	1.7	3	0

Duriel Harris

Year	Team	Att	Yds	Avg	Lg	TD
1979	MIA N	1	20	20.0	20	0
1982		1	13	13.0	13	0
1983		1	0	0.0	0	0
Career		3	33	11.0	20	0
Playoffs		1	1	1.0		0

Elmore Harris

Year	Team	Att	Yds	Avg	Lg	TD
1947	BKN AA	3	-2	-0.7		0

Elroy Harris

Year	Team	Att	Yds	Avg	Lg	TD
1989	SEA N	8	23	2.9	8	0

Franco Harris

Year	Team	Att	Yds	Avg	Lg	TD
1972	PIT N	188	1055	5.6	75t	10
1973		188	698	3.7	35	3
1974		208	1006	4.8	54	5
1975		262	1246	4.8	36	10
1976		289	1128	3.9	30	14
1977		300	1162	3.9	61t	11
1978		310	1082	3.5	37	8
1979		267	1186	4.4	71t	11
1980		208	789	3.8	26	4
1981		242	987	4.1	50	8
1982		140	604	4.3	21	2
1983		279	1007	3.6	19	5
1984	SEA N	68	170	2.5	16	0
Career		2949	12120	4.1	75t	91
Playoffs		400	1556	3.9		16

Frank Harris

Year	Team	Att	Yds	Avg	Lg	TD
1987	CHI N	6	23	3.8	18	0

Harry Harris

Year	Team	Att	Yds	Avg	Lg	TD
1920	AKR A					1

Ike Harris

Year	Team	Att	Yds	Avg	Lg	TD
1978	NO N	2	22	11.0	22	0
1979		2	9	4.5	16	0
Career		4	31	7.8	22	0

Jack Harris

Year	Team	Att	Yds	Avg	Lg	TD
1925	GB N					1
1926						2
Career						3

Jackie Harris

Year	Team	Att	Yds	Avg	Lg	TD
1991	GB N	1	1	1.0	1	0

James Harris

Year	Team	Att	Yds	Avg	Lg	TD
1969	BUF A	10	25	2.5	9	0
1970	BUF N	3	-8	-2.7	1	0
1971		6	42	7.0	13	0
1973	LA N	4	29	7.3	19	0
1974		42	112	2.7	15	5
1975		18	45	2.5	15	1
1976		12	76	6.3	20	2
1977	SD N	10	13	1.3	12	2
1978		10	7	0.7	9	0
1979		6	26	4.3	18	0
Career		121	367	3.0	20	10
Playoffs		9	34	3.8		0

Larry Harris

Year	Team	Att	Yds	Avg	Lg	TD
Playoffs		45	190	4.2		1

Leonard Harris

Year	Team	Att	Yds	Avg	Lg	TD
1987	HOU N	1	17	17.0	17	0
1992		1	8	8.0	8	0
Career		2	25	12.5	17	0

Leroy Harris

Year	Team	Att	Yds	Avg	Lg	TD
1977	MIA N	91	417	4.6	77t	4
1978		123	512	4.2	51	2
1979	PHI N	107	504	4.7	80	2
1980		104	341	3.3	22	3
1982		17	39	2.3	14	2
Career		442	1813	4.1	80	13

M.L. Harris

Year	Team	Att	Yds	Avg	Lg	TD
1980	CIN N	1	0	0.0	0	0
1982		2	-3	-1.5	5	0
1984		1	-2	-2.0	-2	0
Career		4	-5	-1.3	5	0

Raymont Harris

Year	Team	Att	Yds	Avg	Lg	TD
1994	CHI N	123	464	3.8	13	1
1996		194	748	3.9	23	4
Career		317	1212	3.8	23	5
Playoffs		21	93	4.4		1

Rudy Harris

Year	Team	Att	Yds	Avg	Lg	TD
1993	TB N	7	29	4.1	12	0
1994		2	0	0.0	3	0
Career		9	29	3.2	12	0

Steve Harris

Year	Team	Att	Yds	Avg	Lg	TD
1987	MIN N	4	3	0.8	2	0

Tim Harris

Year	Team	Att	Yds	Avg	Lg	TD
1983	PIT N	2	15	7.5	10	0
Playoffs		1	2	2.0		0

Dwight Harrison

Year	Team	Att	Yds	Avg	Lg	TD
1971	DEN N	5	36	7.2	16	0
1972		1	9	9.0	9	0
Career		6	45	7.5	16	0

Glynn Harrison

Year	Team	Att	Yds	Avg	Lg	TD
1976	KC N	16	41	2.6	7	0

James Harrison

Year	Team	Att	Yds	Avg	Lg	TD
1971	CHI N	5	13	2.6	12	0
1972		167	622	3.7	19	2
1973		100	370	3.7	17	1
1974		36	94	2.6	16	1
Career		308	1099	3.6	19	4

Kenny Harrison

Year	Team	Att	Yds	Avg	Lg	TD
1977	SF N	6	15	2.5	15	0
1980	WAS N	2	-11	-5.5	-3	0
Career		8	4	0.5	15	0

Marvin Harrison

Year	Team	Att	Yds	Avg	Lg	TD
1996	IND N	3	15	5.0	15	0

Reggie Harrison

Year	Team	Att	Yds	Avg	Lg	TD
1974	PIT N	6	30	5.0	15	1
1975		43	191	4.4	17	3
1976		54	235	4.4	27	4
1977		36	175	4.9	33	0
Career		139	631	4.5	33	8
Playoffs		21	84	4.0		3

Rob Harrison

Year	Team	Att	Yds	Avg	Lg	TD
1987	LARI N	9	49	5.4	13	0

Emile Harry

Year	Team	Att	Yds	Avg	Lg	TD
1989	KC N	1	9	9.0	9	0
1992		1	27	27.0	27	0
Career		2	36	18.0	27	0

Harold Hart

Year	Team	Att	Yds	Avg	Lg	TD
1974	OAK N	51	268	5.3	25t	2
1975		56	173	3.1	19	3
1978		7	44	6.3	16	0
Career		114	485	4.3	25t	5

Jim Hart

Year	Team	Att	Yds	Avg	Lg	TD
1967	STL N	13	36	2.8	23t	3
1968		19	20	1.1	3	6
1969		7	16	2.3	10	2
1970		18	18	1.0	4	0
1971		13	9	0.7	3	0
1972		9	17	1.9	8	0
1973		3	-3	-1.0	0	0
1974		10	21	2.1	16	2
1975		11	7	0.6	6	1
1976		8	7	0.9	10	0
1977		11	18	1.6	13	0
1978		11	11	1.0	9t	2
1979		6	11	1.8	12	0
1980		9	11	1.2	12	0
1981		3	2	0.7	4	0
1983		5	12	2.4	13	0
1984	WAS N	3	-6	-2.0	-2	0
Career		159	207	1.3	23t	16
Playoffs		1	10	10.0		0

Leo Hart

Year	Team	Att	Yds	Avg	Lg	TD
1972	BUF N	5	19	3.8	16	0

Leon Hart

Year	Team	Att	Yds	Avg	Lg	TD
1951	DET N	4	-6	-1.5	3	0
1952		3	10	3.3	11	0

Leon Hart continued

Year	Team	Att	Yds	Avg	Lg	TD
1953		1	2	2.0	2	0
1955		35	159	4.5	21	0
1956		76	348	4.6	40	5
1957		24	99	4.1	15	0
Career		143	612	4.3	40	5

Pete Hart

Year	Team	Att	Yds	Avg	Lg	TD
1960	NY A	25	113	4.5		0

Howard Hartley

Year	Team	Att	Yds	Avg	Lg	TD
1948	WAS N	5	40	8.0	26t	1

Bill Hartman

Year	Team	Att	Yds	Avg	Lg	TD
1938	WAS N	71	195	2.7		0

John Harvey

Year	Team	Att	Yds	Avg	Lg	TD
1990	TB N	27	113	4.2	14	0

Clint Haslerig

Year	Team	Att	Yds	Avg	Lg	TD
1975	BUF N	2	9	4.5	6	0

Wilbert Haslip

Year	Team	Att	Yds	Avg	Lg	TD
1979	KC N	2	1	0.5	1	0

Andre Hastings

Year	Team	Att	Yds	Avg	Lg	TD
1995	PIT N	1	14	14.0	14	0
1996		4	71	17.8	37	0
Career		5	85	17.0	37	0
Playoffs		2	7	3.5		0

Dale Hatcher

Year	Team	Att	Yds	Avg	Lg	TD
1989	LARM N	1	0	0.0	0	0

Sam Havrilak

Year	Team	Att	Yds	Avg	Lg	TD
1969	BAL N	5	49	9.8	29	1
1970		54	159	2.9	23	0
1972		12	72	6.0	32t	2
1973		2	9	4.5	8	0
Career		73	289	4.0	32t	3
Playoffs		5	5	1.0		0

Alex Hawkins

Year	Team	Att	Yds	Avg	Lg	TD
1959	BAL N	12	44	3.7	11	0
1960		76	267	3.5	17	2
1961		86	379	4.4	39	4
1962		29	87	3.0	13	4
1963		3	-2	-0.7	-1	0
1967		2	12	6.0	7	0
Career		208	787	3.8	39	10

Ben Hawkins

Year	Team	Att	Yds	Avg	Lg	TD
1969	PHI N	1	-3	-3.0	-3	0
1970		2	3	1.5	4	0
1971		4	8	2.0	10	0
1972		3	0	0.0	12	0
Career		10	8	0.8	12	0

Clarence Hawkins

Year	Team	Att	Yds	Avg	Lg	TD
1979	OAK N	21	72	3.4	34	0

Courtney Hawkins

Year	Team	Att	Yds	Avg	Lg	TD
1995	TB N	4	5	1.3	11	0
1996		1	-13	-13.0	-13	0
Career		5	-8	-1.6	11	0

Frank Hawkins

Year	Team	Att	Yds	Avg	Lg	TD
1981	OAK N	40	165	4.1	19	0
1982	LARI N	27	54	2.0	11	2
1983		110	526	4.8	32	6
1984		108	376	3.5	17	3
1985		84	269	3.2	21t	4
1986		58	245	4.2	15	0
1987		4	24	6.0	7	0
Career		431	1659	3.8	32	15
Playoffs		40	136	3.4		4

Les Haws

Year	Team	Att	Yds	Avg	Lg	TD
1924	FRA N					3
1925						1
Career						4

Greg Hawthorne

Year	Team	Att	Yds	Avg	Lg	TD
1979	PIT N	28	123	4.4	19	1

Greg Hawthorne continued

Year	Team	Att	Yds	Avg	Lg	TD
1980		63	226	3.6	15	4
1981		25	58	2.3	16	2
1982		15	68	4.5	11	0
1983		5	47	9.4	20	0
1986	NE N	1	5	5.0	5	0
Career		137	527	3.8	20	7
Playoffs		6	19	3.2		0

Aaron Hayden

Year	Team	Att	Yds	Avg	Lg	TD
1995	SD N	128	470	3.7	20	3
1996		55	166	3.0	13	0
Career		183	636	3.5	20	3
Playoffs		18	80	4.4		0

Leo Hayden

Year	Team	Att	Yds	Avg	Lg	TD
1972	STL N	8	11	1.4	5	1

Bob Hayes

Year	Team	Att	Yds	Avg	Lg	TD
1965	DAL N	4	-8	-2.0	11t	1
1966		1	-1	-1.0	-1	0
1968		4	2	0.5	6	0
1969		4	17	4.3	8	0
1970		4	34	8.5	13t	1
1971		3	18	6.0	11	0
1972		2	8	4.0	7	0
1975	SF N	2	-2	-1.0	-1	0
Career		24	68	2.8	13t	2
Playoffs		1	16	16.0		0

Jeff Hayes

Year	Team	Att	Yds	Avg	Lg	TD
1983	WAS N	2	63	31.5	17	0
1984		2	13	6.5	24	0
1986	CIN N	3	92	30.7	61t	1
Career		7	168	24.0	61t	1
Playoffs		1	14	14.0		0

Mercury Hayes

Year	Team	Att	Yds	Avg	Lg	TD
1996	NO N	2	7	3.5	5	0

Ray Hayes

Year	Team	Att	Yds	Avg	Lg	TD
1961	MIN N	73	319	4.4	22	2

Wendell Hayes

Year	Team	Att	Yds	Avg	Lg	TD
1965	DEN A	130	526	4.0	43	5
1966		105	417	4.0	56	1
1967		85	255	3.0	18	4
1968	KC A	85	340	4.0	25	4
1969		62	208	3.4	11	4
1970	KC N	109	381	3.5	22	5
1971		132	537	4.1	27	1
1972		128	536	4.2	28	0
1973		95	352	3.7	27	2
1974		57	206	3.6	19	2
Career		988	3758	3.8	56	28
Playoffs		51	208	4.1		1

Gary Hayman

Year	Team	Att	Yds	Avg	Lg	TD
1974	BUF N	7	31	4.4	8	0
1975		10	30	3.0	7	0
Career		17	61	3.6	8	0

Abner Haynes

Year	Team	Att	Yds	Avg	Lg	TD
1960	DAL A	**156**	**875**	5.6	67	**9**
1961		179	841	4.7	59	**9**
1962		221	1049	4.7	71	**13**
1963	KC A	99	352	3.6	46	4
1964		139	697	5.0	80	4
1965	DEN A	41	166	4.0	47	3
1966		129	304	2.4	20	2
1967	MIA-NY A	72	346	4.8	65t	2
Career		1036	4630	4.5	80	46
Playoffs		14	26	1.9		1

Hall Haynes

Year	Team	Att	Yds	Avg	Lg	TD
1950	WAS N	2	20	10.0	17	0
1953		2	0	0.0	4	0
Career		4	20	5.0	17	0

Michael Haynes

Year	Team	Att	Yds	Avg	Lg	TD
1989	ATL N	4	35	8.8	21	0
1994	NO N	4	43	10.8	15	0
Career		8	78	9.8	21	0

Reggie Haynes

Year	Team	Att	Yds	Avg	Lg	TD
1978	WAS N	1	13	13.0	13	0

Bob Hazelhurst

Year	Team	Att	Yds	Avg	Lg	TD
1948	BOS N	11	15	1.4	7	0

Joe Heap

Year	Team	Att	Yds	Avg	Lg	TD
1955	NYG N	8	29	3.6	16	0

Walt Heap

Year	Team	Att	Yds	Avg	Lg	TD
1947	LA AA	5	3	0.6		0
1948		3	12	4.0		0
Career		8	15	1.9		0

Herman Heard

Year	Team	Att	Yds	Avg	Lg	TD
1984	KC N	165	684	4.1	69t	4
1985		164	595	3.6	33	4
1986		71	295	4.2	40	2
1987		82	466	5.7	64t	3
1988		106	438	4.1	20	0
1989		63	216	3.4	28	0
Career		651	2694	4.1	69t	13
Playoffs		1	1	1.0		0

Garrison Hearst

Year	Team	Att	Yds	Avg	Lg	TD
1993	PHX N	76	264	3.5	57	1
1994	ARI N	37	169	4.6	36	1
1995		284	1070	3.8	38	0
1996	CIN N	225	847	3.8	24	0
Career		622	2350	3.8	57	2

Larry Heater

Year	Team	Att	Yds	Avg	Lg	TD
1980	NYG N	111	360	3.2	11	3
1982		3	13	4.3	8	0
Career		114	373	3.3	11	3

Clayton Heath

Year	Team	Att	Yds	Avg	Lg	TD
1976	MIA N	1	0	0.0	0	0

Leon Heath

Year	Team	Att	Yds	Avg	Lg	TD
1951	WAS N	64	159	2.5	16	0
1952		90	388	4.3	74	2
1953		76	266	3.5	43	4
Career		230	813	3.5	74	6

Stan Heath

Year	Team	Att	Yds	Avg	Lg	TD
1949	GB N	10	25	2.5	18	1

Bobby Hebert

Year	Team	Att	Yds	Avg	Lg	TD
1985	NO N	12	26	2.2	8	0
1986		5	14	2.8	7	0
1987		13	95	7.3	19	0
1988		37	79	2.1	16	0
1989		25	87	3.5	11	0
1991		18	56	3.1	16	0
1992		32	95	3.0	18	0
1993	ATL N	24	49	2.0	14	0
1994		9	43	4.8	20	0
1995		5	-1	-0.2	2	0
1996		15	59	3.9	25	1
Career		195	602	3.1	25	1
Playoffs		6	29	4.8		0

Vaughn Hebron

Year	Team	Att	Yds	Avg	Lg	TD
1993	PHI N	84	297	3.5	33	3
1994		82	325	4.0	19	2
1996	DEN N	49	262	5.3	47	0
Career		215	884	4.1	47	5
Playoffs		2	5	2.5		1

Johnny Hector

Year	Team	Att	Yds	Avg	Lg	TD
1983	NYJ N	16	85	5.3	42	0
1984		124	531	4.3	64	1
1985		145	572	3.9	22	6
1986		164	605	3.7	41	8
1987		111	435	3.9	20t	**11**
1988		137	561	4.1	19	10
1989		177	702	4.0	24	3
1990		91	377	4.1	22	0
1991		62	345	5.6	47	0
1992		24	67	2.8	14	0
Career		1051	4280	4.1	64	41
Playoffs		16	59	3.7		0

Year	Team		Att	Yds	Avg	Lg	TD

Randy Hedberg

1977	TB	N	9	35	3.9	12	0

Johnny Heimsch

1926	MIL	N					3

Lakei Heimuli

1987	CHI	N	34	128	3.8	12	0

Ken Heineman

1940	CLE	N	6	-5	-0.8		0
1943	BKN	N	49	126	2.6	43	0
Career			55	121	2.2	43	0

Don Heinrich

1954	NYG	N	1	0	0.0	0	0
1955			7	4	0.6	5t	2
1956			5	-4	-0.8	2	0
1957			4	10	2.5	7	2
1958			5	4	0.8	6	1
1959			2	3	1.5	9	0
1960	DAL	N	2	3	1.5	8	0
1962	OAK	A	1	4	4.0	4	0
Career			27	24	0.9	9	5

Paul Held

1954	PIT	N	3	3	1.0	3	0
1955	GB	N	1	8	8.0	8	0
Career			4	11	2.8	8	0

Warren Heller

1934	PIT	N	132	528	4.0		1
1935			37	112	3.0		0
1936			106	332	3.1		0
Career			275	972	3.5		1

Barry Helton

1988	SF	N	1	0	0.0	0	0
1989			1	0	0.0	0	0
Career			2	0	0.0	0	0

Herb Henderson

1921	EVA	A					4

Keith Henderson

1989	SF	N	7	30	4.3	11t	1
1990			6	14	2.3	9	0
1991			137	561	4.1	25	2
1992	SF-MIN	N	44	150	3.4	12	1
Career			194	755	3.9	25	4
Playoffs			1	1	1.0		0

William Henderson

1995	GB	N	7	35	5.0	17	0
1996			39	130	3.3	14	0
Career			46	165	3.6	17	0
Playoffs			5	8	1.6		0

John Hendren

1920	CAN	A					1
1921	CLE	A					1
Career							2

Dutch Hendrian

1923	CAN	N					1
1924	GB	N					3
Career							4

Steve Hendrickson

1991	SD	N	1	3	3.0	3t	1
1993			1	0	0.0	0	0
1994			1	3	3.0	3	0
Career			3	6	2.0	3t	1
Playoffs			1	5	5.0		1

Carey Henley

1962	BUF	A	3	2	0.7	4	0

Wally Henry

1977	PHI	N	1	-2	-2.0	-2	0
1981			1	-2	-2.0	-2	0
Career			2	-4	-2.0	-2	0

Harold Henson

1975	CIN	N	11	38	3.5	8	0

Craig Hentrich

Playoffs			1	-22	-22.0		0

Arnie Herber

1931	GB	N					1
1932							1
1935			19	0	0.0		0
1936			20	-32	-1.6		0
1937			5	9	1.8		0
1938			6	-1	-0.2		0
1939			18	-11	-0.6		1
1940			6	-23	-3.8		0
1944	NYG	N	7	-58	-8.3	-14	0
1945			6	-27	-4.5		0
Career			87	-143	-1.6	-14	3
Playoffs			11	3	0.3		0

George Herring

1960	DEN	A	5	-46	-9.2		0
1961			15	74	4.9	20	2
Career			20	28	1.4	20	2

Mark Herrmann

1982	DEN	N	3	7	2.3	6t	1
1983	BAL	N	1	0	0.0	0	0
1985	SD	N	18	-8	-0.4	11	0
1986			2	6	3.0	6	0
1987			4	-1	-0.3	0	0
1988	LARM	N	1	-1	-1.0	-1	0
1989			2	-1	-0.5	0	0
1991	IND	N	1	-1	-1.0	-1	0
1992			3	-2	-0.7	0	0
Career			35	-1	0.0	11	1

Don Herrmann

1972	NYG	N	3	9	3.0	11	0
1977	NO	N	1	-17	-17.0	-17	0
Career			4	-8	-2.0	11	0

Mack Herron

1973	NE	N	61	200	3.3	17	2
1974			231	824	3.6	28	7
1975	NE-ATL	N	62	274	4.4	53	0
Career			354	1298	3.7	53	9

Rob Hertel

1978	CIN	N	1	0	0.0	0	0

Jessie Hester

1985	LARI	N	1	13	13.0	13t	1
1988	ATL	N	1	3	3.0	3	0
1990	IND	N	4	9	2.3	10	0
1994	LARM	N	2	28	14.0	24	0
Career			8	53	6.6	24	1

Bill Hewitt

1932	CHIB	N					1
1934			1	14	14.0	14	0
1936			2	-9	-4.5		0
1939	PHI	N	1	1	1.0	1	0
Career			4	6	1.5	14	1

Craig Heyward

1988	NO	N	74	355	4.8	73t	1
1989			49	183	3.7	15	1
1990			129	599	4.6	47t	4
1991			76	260	3.4	15	4
1992			104	416	4.0	23	3
1993	CHI	N	68	206	3.0	11	0
1994	ATL	N	183	779	4.3	17	7
1995			236	1083	4.6	31	6
1996			72	321	4.5	34	3
Career			991	4202	4.2	73t	29
Playoffs			23	54	2.3		1

Ralph Heywood

1948	DET-BOS	N	1	11	11.0	11	0
1949	NYB	N	3	-6	-2.0	2	0
Career			4	5	1.3	11	0

Bo Hickey

1967	DEN	A	73	263	3.6	20	4

Red Hickey

1941	CLE	N	7	7	1.0	7	0

Larry Hickman

1959	CHIC	N	5	18	3.6	5	0
1960	GB	N	7	22	3.1	4	0
Career			12	40	3.3	5	0

Eddie Hicks

1980	NYG	N	19	50	2.6	9	0

Michael Hicks

1996	CHI	N	27	92	3.4	23	0

Victor Hicks

1980	LA	N	1	19	19.0	19	0

Mark Higgs

1989	PHI	N	49	184	3.8	13	0
1990	MIA	N	10	67	6.7	27	0
1991			231	905	3.9	24	4
1992			256	915	3.6	23	7
1993			186	693	3.7	31	3
1994	MIA-ARI	N	62	195	3.1	21	0
Career			794	2959	3.7	31	14

Alonzo Highsmith

1987	HOU	N	29	106	3.7	25	1
1988			94	466	5.0	42	2
1989			128	531	4.1	25	4
1990	DAL	N	19	48	2.5	7	0
1991	TB	N	5	21	4.2	10	0
1992			8	23	2.9	5	0
Career			283	1195	4.2	42	7
Playoffs			26	149	5.7		0

Don Highsmith

1970	OAK	N	2	2	1.0	4	0
1971			76	307	4.0	26	1
1972			9	11	1.2	12	1
1973	GB	N	7	7	1.0	4	0
Career			94	327	3.5	26	2

Ben Hightower

1943	DET	N	1	-5	-5.0	-5	0

Rusty Hilger

1985	LARI	N	3	8	2.7	4	0
1986			6	48	8.0	16	0
1987			8	8	1.0	6	0
1988	DET	N	18	27	1.5	11	0
Career			35	91	2.6	16	0

Bruce Hill

1987	TB	N	3	3	1.0	9	0
1988			2	-11	-5.5	3	0
1990			1	0	0.0	0	0
Career			6	-8	-1.3	9	0

Calvin Hill

1969	DAL	N	204	942	4.6	55	8
1970			153	577	3.8	20	4
1971			106	468	4.4	17	8
1972			245	1036	4.2	26	6
1973			273	1142	4.2	21	6
1974			185	844	4.6	27	7
1976	WAS	N	79	301	3.8	15	1
1977			69	257	3.7	34	0
1978	CLE	N	80	289	3.6	21	1
1979			53	193	3.6	33	1
1980			1	11	11.0	11	0
1981			4	23	5.8	9	0
Career			1452	6083	4.2	55	42
Playoffs			92	358	3.9		3

Charlie Hill

1925	KC	N					2
1926							1
Career							3

David Hill

1977	DET	N	4	10	2.5	14	0
1978			3	12	4.0	13	0
1979			1	15	15.0	15	0
Career			8	37	4.6	15	0

Drew Hill

1980	LA	N	1	4	4.0	4	0

Drew Hill continued

Year	Team		Att	Yds	Avg	Lg	TD
1981			1	14	14.0	14	0
1991	HOU	N	1	1	1.0	1	0
Career			3	19	6.3	14	0

Eddie Hill

Year	Team		Att	Yds	Avg	Lg	TD
1979	LA	N	29	114	3.9	27	1
1980			39	120	3.1	19	0
1981	MIA	N	37	146	3.9	24	1
1982			13	51	3.9	13	0
1983			2	12	6.0	10	0
Career			120	443	3.7	27	2
Playoffs			3	8	2.7		0

Fred Hill

Year	Team		Att	Yds	Avg	Lg	TD
1966	PHI	N	1	5	5.0	5	0

Greg Hill

Year	Team		Att	Yds	Avg	Lg	TD
1994	KC	N	141	574	4.1	20	1
1995			155	667	4.3	27	1
1996			135	645	4.8	28	4
Career			431	1886	4.4	28	6
Playoffs			2	14	7.0		0

Harlon Hill

Year	Team		Att	Yds	Avg	Lg	TD
1956	CHIB	N	2	24	12.0	12	0
1957			2	7	3.5	8	0
1959			1	0	0.0	0	0
1962	PIT	N	7	72	10.3	24	0
Career			12	103	8.6	24	0

Harry Hill

Year	Team		Att	Yds	Avg	Lg	TD
1923	TOL	N					3
1924	KC	N					1
1925							1
1926	NYG	N					2
Career							7

Ike Hill

Year	Team		Att	Yds	Avg	Lg	TD
1973	CHI	N	3	-14	-4.7	5	0

Irv Hill

Year	Team		Att	Yds	Avg	Lg	TD
1932	CHIC	N					3

J.D. Hill

Year	Team		Att	Yds	Avg	Lg	TD
1971	BUF	N	1	2	2.0	2	0
1972			1	11	11.0	11	0
1975			1	1	1.0	1	0
Career			3	14	4.7	11	0

Jeff Hill

Year	Team		Att	Yds	Avg	Lg	TD
1995	CIN	N	1	-3	-3.0	-3	0

Jerry Hill

Year	Team		Att	Yds	Avg	Lg	TD
1961	BAL	N	1	4	4.0	4	0
1963			100	440	4.4	20t	5
1964			88	384	4.4	50	5
1965			147	516	3.5	20	5
1966			104	395	3.8	14	0
1967			90	311	3.5	18	2
1968			91	360	4.0	2	1
1969			49	143	2.9	14	2
1970			36	115	3.2	15t	2
Career			706	2668	3.8	50	22
Playoffs			61	210	3.4		1

King Hill

Year	Team		Att	Yds	Avg	Lg	TD
1958	CHIC	N	1	0	0.0	0	0
1959			39	167	4.3	29	5
1960	STL	N	16	47	2.9	10	1
1961	PHI	N	2	9	4.5	7	0
1962			4	40	10.0	22	1
1963			3	-1	-0.3	6	0
1964			8	27	3.4	14	0
1965			7	20	2.9	7	2
1966			7	-2	-0.3	2	0
1968			1	1	1.0	1	0
Career			88	308	3.5	29	9

Lonzell Hill

Year	Team		Att	Yds	Avg	Lg	TD
1987	NO	N	1	-9	-9.0	-9	0
1988			2	7	3.5	5	0
1989			1	-7	-7.0	-7	0
Career			4	-9	-2.3	5	0

Mack Lee Hill

Year	Team		Att	Yds	Avg	Lg	TD
1964	KC	A	105	576	5.5	71	4
1965			125	627	5.0	66	2
Career			230	1203	5.2	71	6

Randal Hill

Year	Team		Att	Yds	Avg	Lg	TD
1992	PHX	N	1	4	4.0	4	0

Tony Hill

Year	Team		Att	Yds	Avg	Lg	TD
1978	DAL	N	3	17	5.7	14	0
1979			2	18	9.0	12	0
1980			4	27	6.8	15	0
1981			1	-3	-3.0	-3	0
1982			1	22	22.0	22	0
1983			1	2	2.0	2	0
1984			1	7	7.0	7	0
1985			1	-6	-6.0	-6	0
Career			14	84	6.0	22	0
Playoffs			1	-6	-6.0		0

Ira Hillary

Year	Team		Att	Yds	Avg	Lg	TD
1989	CIN	N	1	-2	-2.0	-2	0

Billy Hillenbrand

Year	Team		Att	Yds	Avg	Lg	TD
1946	CHI	AA	50	175	3.5		2
1947	BAL	AA	66	204	3.1		2
1948			100	510	5.1		7
Career			216	889	4.1		11
Playoffs			6	5	0.8		0

Dalton Hilliard

Year	Team		Att	Yds	Avg	Lg	TD
1986	NO	N	121	425	3.5	36	5
1987			123	508	4.1	30t	7
1988			204	823	4.0	36	5
1989			344	1262	3.7	40	13
1990			90	284	3.2	17	0
1991			79	252	3.2	65t	4
1992			115	445	3.9	22	3
1993			50	165	3.3	16	2
Career			1126	4164	3.7	65t	39
Playoffs			19	64	3.4		1

Bill Hillman

Year	Team		Att	Yds	Avg	Lg	TD
1947	DET	N	2	0	0.0	4	0

John Hilton

Year	Team		Att	Yds	Avg	Lg	TD
1967	PIT	N	1	15	15.0	15	0

Jimmy Hines

Year	Team		Att	Yds	Avg	Lg	TD
1969	MIA	A	1	7	7.0	7	0

Clarke Hinkle

Year	Team		Att	Yds	Avg	Lg	TD
1932	GB	N	95	331	3.5	27	3
1933			139	393	2.8	33	2
1934			142	384	2.7	32	1
1935			76	258	3.4	17	2
1936			100	476	4.8	57	5
1937			129	552	4.3	41	5
1938			114	299	2.6	46	3
1939			135	381	2.8	29	5
1940			109	383	3.5	31	2
1941			129	393	3.0	20	5
Career			1168	3850	3.3	57	33
Playoffs			59	161	2.7		2

Jack Hinkle

Year	Team		Att	Yds	Avg	Lg	TD
1943	P-P	N	116	571	4.9	56	3
1944	PHI	N	92	421	4.6	26	2
1945			11	40	3.6	40	0
1946			18	33	1.8	8	0
1947			1	2	2.0	2	0
Career			238	1067	4.5	56	5

Eddie Hinton

Year	Team		Att	Yds	Avg	Lg	TD
1969	BAL	N	1	-3	-3.0	-3	0
1970			5	58	11.6	21	2
1971			4	56	14.0	30	0
1973	HOU	N	1	-2	-2.0	-2	0
1974	NE	N	1	1	1.0	1	0
Career			12	110	9.2	30	2
Playoffs			1	-5	-5.0		0

J.W. Hinton

Year	Team		Att	Yds	Avg	Lg	TD
1932	SI	N					1

Eric Hipple

Year	Team		Att	Yds	Avg	Lg	TD
1981	DET	N	41	168	4.1	18	7
1982			10	57	5.7	20	0
1983			41	171	4.2	27	3
1984			2	3	1.5	2	0
1985			32	89	2.8	26	2
1986			16	46	2.9	13	0
1988			1	5	5.0	5	0
1989			2	11	5.5	10	1
Career			145	550	3.8	27	13
Playoffs			6	47	7.8		0

Ed Hirsch

Year	Team		Att	Yds	Avg	Lg	TD
1947	BUF	AA	4	7	1.8		0

Elroy Hirsch

Year	Team		Att	Yds	Avg	Lg	TD
1946	CHI	AA	87	226	2.6		1
1947			23	51	2.2		1
1948			23	93	4.0		0
1949	LA	N	68	287	4.2	51	1
1950			2	19	9.5	15	0
1951			1	3	3.0	3	0
1953			1	-6	-6.0	-6	0
1954			1	6	6.0	6	0
1957			1	8	8.0	8	0
Career			207	687	3.3	51	3
Playoffs			2	0	0.0		0

Joel Hitt

Year	Team		Att	Yds	Avg	Lg	TD
1939	CLE	N	1	3	3.0	3	0

Terry Hoage

Year	Team		Att	Yds	Avg	Lg	TD
1988	PHI	N	1	38	38.0	38t	0

Joe Hoague

Year	Team		Att	Yds	Avg	Lg	TD
1941	PIT	N	33	112	3.4	29	1
1942			65	168	2.6	42	1
1946	BOS	N	1	2	2.0	2	0
Career			99	282	2.8	42	3

Dick Hoak

Year	Team		Att	Yds	Avg	Lg	TD
1961	PIT	N	85	302	3.6	22	0
1962			117	442	3.8	38	4
1963			216	679	3.1	17	6
1964			84	258	3.1	17	2
1965			131	426	3.3	42t	5
1966			81	212	2.6	16	1
1967			52	142	2.7	11	1
1968			175	858	4.9	77t	3
1969			151	531	3.5	13	2
1970			40	115	2.9	13	1
Career			1132	3965	3.5	77t	25

Leroy Hoard

Year	Team		Att	Yds	Avg	Lg	TD
1990	CLE	N	58	149	2.6	42	3
1991			37	154	4.2	52	2
1992			54	236	4.4	37	0
1993			56	227	4.1	30	0
1994			209	890	4.3	39	5
1995			136	547	4.0	25	0
1996	BAL-CAR-MIN	N	125	492	3.9	25	3
Career			675	2695	4.0	52	13
Playoffs			23	95	4.1		1

Billy Joe Hobert

Year	Team		Att	Yds	Avg	Lg	TD
1995	OAK	N	3	5	1.7	6	0
1996			2	13	6.5	14	0
Career			5	18	3.6	14	0

Ben Hobson

Year	Team		Att	Yds	Avg	Lg	TD
1926	BUF	N					1

Merwin Hodel

Year	Team		Att	Yds	Avg	Lg	TD
1953	NYG	N	5	11	2.2	6	0

Floyd Hodge

Year	Team		Att	Yds	Avg	Lg	TD
1982	ATL	N	2	11	5.5	11	0
1984			2	17	8.5	9	0
Career			4	28	7.0	11	0

Norm Hodgins

Year	Team		Att	Yds	Avg	Lg	TD
1974	CHI	N	1	3	3.0	3	0

Tommy Hodson

Year	Team		Att	Yds	Avg	Lg	TD
1990	NE	N	12	79	6.6	23	0

Year	Team		Att	Yds	Avg	Lg	TD

Tommy Hodson *continued*

Year	Team		Att	Yds	Avg	Lg	TD
1991			4	0	0.0	1	0
1992			5	11	2.2	5	0
Career			21	90	4.3	23	0

Dick Hoerner

1947	LA	N	30	124	4.1	23	2
1948			76	354	4.7	23	4
1949			155	582	3.8	37	6
1950			95	381	4.0	64t	10
1951			94	569	6.1	43t	6
1952	DAL	N	56	162	2.9	14	2
Career			506	2172	4.3	64t	30
Playoffs			43	119	2.8		3

Bob Hoernschemeyer

1946	CHI	AA	111	375	3.4	57	0
1947	CHI-BKN	AA	152	704	4.6	84t	5
1948	BKN	AA	110	574	5.2	61	3
1949	CHI	AA	133	456	3.4		2
1950	DET	N	84	471	5.6	96t	1
1951			132	678	5.1	85t	2
1952			106	457	4.3	41	4
1953			101	482	4.8	49t	7
1954			94	242	2.6	35	2
1955			36	109	3.0	10	1
Career			1059	4548	4.3	96t	27
Playoffs			37	125	3.4		1

Paul Hofer

1976	SF	N	18	74	4.1	17	0
1977			34	106	3.1	10	0
1978			121	465	3.8	40	7
1979			123	615	5.0	47	7
1980			60	293	4.9	26t	1
1981			60	193	3.2	12	1
Career			416	1746	4.2	47	16

Bob Hoffman

1940	WAS	N	3	7	2.3		0
1941			1	2	2.0	2	0
1946	LA	N	42	162	3.9	19	3
1947			42	159	3.8	20	3
1948			22	68	3.1	8	4
Career			110	398	3.6	20	10

Dalton Hoffman

1964	HOU	A	2	3	1.5	2	1
1965			1	11	11.0	11	0
Career			3	14	4.7	11	1

John Hoffman

1949	CHIB	N	53	216	4.1	27	1
1950			42	154	3.7	25	1
1951			1	-3	-3.0	-3	0
1953			32	95	3.0	34t	3
1954			39	178	4.6	19t	1
1955			94	454	4.8	47	0
1956			56	272	4.9	39	2
Career			317	1366	4.3	47	8
Playoffs			6	19	3.2		0

Mike Hogan

1976	PHI	N	123	561	4.6	32	0
1977			155	546	3.5	19	0
1978			145	607	4.2	33	4
1979	SF	N	9	31	3.4	6	0
1980	NYG-PHI	N	34	90	2.6	12	2
Career			466	1835	3.9	33	6
Playoffs			14	31	2.2		0

Paul Hogan

| 1927 | CHIC | N | | | | | 1 |

Merril Hoge

1987	PIT	N	3	8	2.7	5	0
1988			170	705	4.1	20	3
1989			186	621	3.3	31	8
1990			203	772	3.8	41t	7
1991			165	610	3.7	24	2
1992			41	150	3.7	15	0
1993			51	249	4.9	30	1
1994	CHI	N	6	24	4.0	8	0
Career			825	3139	3.8	41t	21
Playoffs			39	247	6.3		2

Gary Hogeboom

1982	DAL	N	3	0	0.0	0	0
1983			6	-10	-1.7	-1	0
1984			15	19	1.3	11	0
1985			8	48	6.0	15	1
1986	IND	N	10	20	2.0	6	1
1987			3	3	1.0	2	0
1988			11	-8	-0.7	6	1
1989	PHX	N	27	89	3.3	15	1
Career			83	161	1.9	15	4

Mike Hohensee

| 1987 | CHI | N | 9 | 56 | 6.2 | 26 | 0 |

Mike Hold

| 1987 | TB | N | 7 | 69 | 9.9 | 35 | 0 |

Steve Holden

1974	CLE	N	1	6	6.0	6	0
1975			2	-4	-2.0	0	0
Career			3	2	0.7	6	0

Lew Holder

| 1949 | LA | AA | 1 | -1 | -1.0 | -1 | 0 |

John Holifield

| 1989 | CIN | N | 11 | 20 | 1.8 | 11 | 0 |

Jamie Holland

1987	SD	N	1	17	17.0	17	0
1988			3	19	6.3	10	0
1989			6	46	7.7	24	0
Career			10	82	8.2	24	0

John Hollar

1948	WAS	N	4	7	1.8	6	0
1949	DET-WAS	N	13	35	2.7	12	1
Career			17	42	2.5	12	1

Donald Hollas

1991	CIN	N	12	66	5.5	27	0
1992			20	109	5.5	24	0
Career			32	175	5.5	27	0

Ed Holler

| 1964 | PIT | N | 1 | 8 | 8.0 | 8 | 0 |

Tommy Holleran

| 1923 | BUF | N | | | | | 2 |

Ken Holley

| 1946 | MIA | AA | 2 | -22 | -11.0 | | 0 |

Ron Holliday

| 1973 | SD | N | 6 | 70 | 11.7 | 22 | 0 |

Joe Hollingsworth

1949	PIT	N	6	13	2.2	7	0
1950			1	2	2.0	2	0
1951			7	11	1.6	6	0
Career			14	26	1.9	7	0

Bob Holly

1983	WAS	N	4	13	3.3	13	0
1985	ATL	N	3	36	12.0	20t	1
Career			7	49	7.0	20t	1
Playoffs			1	-3	-3.0		0

Bernie Holm

| 1931 | POR | N | | | | | 1 |

Walter Holman

| 1987 | WAS | N | 2 | 7 | 3.5 | 5 | 0 |

Walt Holmer

1930	CHIB	N					2
1932	CHIC	N					1
1933	BOS	N					1
Career							4

Darick Holmes

1995	BUF	N	172	698	4.1	38t	4
1996			189	571	3.0	37	4
Career			361	1269	3.5	38t	8
Playoffs			28	111	4.0		1

Jack Holmes

1978	NO	N	2	4	2.0	4	0
1979			17	68	4.0	14	0
1980			38	119	3.1	20	2
1981			58	194	3.3	11	2
1982			2	8	4.0	5	0
Career			117	393	3.4	20	4

Mike Holmes

| 1975 | SF | N | 1 | -4 | -4.0 | -4 | 0 |

Robert Holmes

1968	KC	A	174	866	5.0	76t	7
1969			150	612	4.1	25	2
1970	KC	N	63	206	3.3	22	3
1971	KC-HOU	N	112	323	2.9	31	4
1972	HOU	N	43	172	4.0	18	0
1973	SD	N	78	289	3.7	24	7
1975	HOU	N	19	42	2.2	11	0
Career			639	2510	3.9	76t	23
Playoffs			37	67	1.8		1

Pete Holohan

| 1989 | LARM | N | 1 | 3 | 3.0 | 3 | 0 |

Mike Holovak

1946	LA	N	55	211	3.8	22	3
1947	CHIB	N	51	281	5.5	52	1
1948			30	228	7.6	47t	2
Career			136	720	5.3	52	6

Harry Holt

1983	CLE	N	3	8	2.7	4	0
1984			1	12	12.0	12	0
1986			1	16	16.0	16t	1
Career			5	36	7.2	16t	1

Robert Holt

| 1982 | BUF | N | 1 | 3 | 3.0 | 3 | 0 |

Dennis Homan

| 1970 | DAL | N | 2 | -3 | -1.5 | 0 | 0 |

Henry Homan

1926	FRA	N					1
1927							1
Career							2

Todd Hons

| 1987 | DET | N | 5 | 49 | 9.8 | 23 | 0 |

Jim Hooks

1973	DET	N	19	110	5.8	24	0
1974			44	143	3.3	17	0
1975			4	-8	-2.0	3	0
Career			67	245	3.7	24	0

Roland Hooks

1976	BUF	N	25	116	4.6	24	0
1977			128	497	3.9	66	0
1978			76	358	4.7	66	2
1979			89	320	3.6	32t	6
1980			25	118	4.7	25	1
1981			51	250	4.9	19	3
1982			5	23	4.6	9	0
Career			399	1682	4.2	66	12
Playoffs			9	30	3.3		0

Mitch Hoopes

1975	DAL	N	1	13	13.0	13	0
1976	SD	N	2	10	5.0	10	0
Career			3	23	7.7	13	0

Mel Hoover

| 1982 | PHI | N | 1 | 5 | 5.0 | 5 | 0 |

Andy Hopkins

| 1971 | HOU | N | 2 | 2 | 1.0 | 2 | 0 |

Roy Hopkins

1967	HOU	A	13	42	3.2	19	0
1968			31	104	3.4	18	0
1969			131	473	3.6	43t	4
1970	HOU	N	57	207	3.6	12	3
Career			232	826	3.6	43t	7

Harry Hopp

Year	Team		Att	Yds	Avg	Lg	TD
1941	DET	N	69	202	2.9	29	1
1942			66	230	3.5	44	0
1943			56	99	1.8	16	4
1946	BUF-MIA	AA	61	218	3.6	55t	3
1947	LA	AA	10	52	5.2		0
Career			262	801	3.1	55t	8

Mike Horan

Year	Team		Att	Yds	Avg	Lg	TD
1985	PHI	N	1	12	12.0	12	0
1986	DEN	N	1	0	0.0	0	0
1991			2	9	4.5	9	0
1995	NYG	N	1	0	0.0	0	0
Career			5	21	4.2	12	0
Playoffs			1	-12	-12.0		0

Don Horn

Year	Team		Att	Yds	Avg	Lg	TD
1967	GB	N	1	-2	-2.0	-2	0
1968			3	-7	-2.3	1	0
1969			3	-7	-2.3	2t	1
1970			5	4	0.8	4	0
1971	DEN	N	6	15	2.5	10	0
Career			18	3	0.2	10	1

Joe Horn

Year	Team		Att	Yds	Avg	Lg	TD
1996	KC	N	1	8	8.0	8	0

Marty Horn

Year	Team		Att	Yds	Avg	Lg	TD
1987	PHI	N	1	0	0.0	0	0

Greg Horne

Year	Team		Att	Yds	Avg	Lg	TD
1988	PHX	N	3	20	6.7	20	0

Sam Horner

Year	Team		Att	Yds	Avg	Lg	TD
1960	WAS	N	22	80	3.6	16	0
1961			96	275	2.9	32	0
Career			118	355	3.0	32	0

Paul Hornung

Year	Team		Att	Yds	Avg	Lg	TD
1957	GB	N	60	319	5.3	72	3
1958			69	310	4.5	55	2
1959			152	681	4.5	63	7
1960			160	671	4.2	37	13
1961			127	597	4.7	54t	8
1962			57	219	3.8	37	5
1964			103	415	4.0	40	5
1965			89	299	3.4	17	5
1966			76	200	2.6	9	2
Career			893	3711	4.2	72	50
Playoffs			67	323	4.8		3

Ethan Horton

Year	Team		Att	Yds	Avg	Lg	TD
1985	KC	N	48	146	3.0	19t	3
1987	LARI	N	31	95	3.1	14	0
Career			79	241	3.1	19t	3

Les Horvath

Year	Team		Att	Yds	Avg	Lg	TD
1947	LA	N	18	68	3.8	25	0
1948			30	118	3.9	19	0
1949	CLE	AA	10	35	3.5		1
Career			58	221	3.8	25	1

Arnie Horween

Year	Team		Att	Yds	Avg	Lg	TD
1922	CHIC	N					4

Jeff Hostetler

Year	Team		Att	Yds	Avg	Lg	TD
1986	NYG	N	1	1	1.0	1	0
1988			5	-3	-0.6	0	0
1989			11	71	6.5	19t	2
1990			39	190	4.9	30	2
1991			42	273	6.5	47t	2
1992			35	172	4.9	27	3
1993	LARI	N	55	202	3.7	19	5
1994			46	159	3.5	14	2
1995	OAK	N	31	119	3.8	18	0
1996			37	179	4.8	17	1
Career			302	1363	4.5	47t	17
Playoffs			24	98	4.1		1

Kevin House

Year	Team		Att	Yds	Avg	Lg	TD
1980	TB	N	1	32	32.0	32	0
1981			2	9	4.5	8	0
1982			1	-1	-1.0	-1	0
1983			1	-4	-4.0	-4	0

Kevin House *continued*

Year	Team		Att	Yds	Avg	Lg	TD
1986			2	5	2.5	4	0
Career			7	41	5.9	32	0

Rich Houston

Year	Team		Att	Yds	Avg	Lg	TD
1969	NYG	N	1	11	11.0	11	0
1971			2	2	1.0	2	0
Career			3	13	4.3	11	0

John Hovious

Year	Team		Att	Yds	Avg	Lg	TD
1945	NYG	N	22	-7	-0.3	7	0

Bobby Howard

Year	Team		Att	Yds	Avg	Lg	TD
1986	TB	N	30	110	3.7	16	1
1987			30	100	3.3	31	1
Career			60	210	3.5	31	2

Desmond Howard

Year	Team		Att	Yds	Avg	Lg	TD
1992	WAS	N	3	14	4.7	7	0
1993			2	17	8.5	9	0
1994			1	4	4.0	4	0
1995	JAC	N	1	8	8.0	8	0
Career			7	43	6.1	9	0

Lynn Howard

Year	Team		Att	Yds	Avg	Lg	TD
1921	GB	A					1

Ron Howard

Year	Team		Att	Yds	Avg	Lg	TD
1976	SEA	N	1	2	2.0	2	0

Sherman Howard

Year	Team		Att	Yds	Avg	Lg	TD
1949	B-NY	AA	117	459	3.9	79	3
1950	NYY	N	71	362	5.1	60t	3
1951			94	343	3.6	31	4
1952	CLE	N	34	95	2.8	22	0
1953			7	42	6.0	34	0
Career			323	1301	4.0	79	10
Playoffs			16	37	2.3		1

William Howard

Year	Team		Att	Yds	Avg	Lg	TD
1988	TB	N	115	452	3.9	29t	1
1989			108	357	3.3	5t	1
Career			223	809	3.6	29t	2

Dixie Howell

Year	Team		Att	Yds	Avg	Lg	TD
1937	WAS	N	5	9	1.8		

Earl Howell

Year	Team		Att	Yds	Avg	Lg	TD
1949	LA	AA	31	116	3.7		1

Johnny Howell

Year	Team		Att	Yds	Avg	Lg	TD
1938	GB	N	7	7	1.0		0

Steve Howell

Year	Team		Att	Yds	Avg	Lg	TD
1979	MIA	N	3	8	2.7	5	0
1980			60	206	3.4	23	1
1981			5	21	4.2	9	0
Career			68	235	3.5	23	1

Billy Howton

Year	Team		Att	Yds	Avg	Lg	TD
1957	GB	N	4	20	5.0	11	0
1961	DAL	N	1	9	9.0	9	0
Career			5	29	5.8	11	0

John Huarte

Year	Team		Att	Yds	Avg	Lg	TD
1966	BOS	A	7	40	5.7	13	0
1967			2	5	2.5	4	0
1968	PHI	N	2	9	4.5	11	0
1972	CHI	N	1	-2	-2.0	-2	0
Career			12	52	4.3	13	0

Mike Hubach

Year	Team		Att	Yds	Avg	Lg	TD
1980	NE	N	1	0	0.0	0	0

Marv Hubbard

Year	Team		Att	Yds	Avg	Lg	TD
1969	OAK	A	21	119	5.7	18	0
1970	OAK	N	51	246	4.8	15	1
1971			181	867	4.8	20	5
1972			219	1100	5.0	39	4
1973			193	903	4.7	50	6
1974			188	865	4.6	32	4
1975			60	294	4.9	53	2
1977	DET	N	38	150	3.9	16	1
Career			951	4544	4.8	50	23
Playoffs			114	402	3.5		3

Brad Hubbert

Year	Team		Att	Yds	Avg	Lg	TD
1967	SD	A	116	643	5.5	80t	2
1968			28	119	4.3	21	2
1969			94	333	3.5	24	4
1970	SD	N	49	175	3.6	11	1
Career			287	1270	4.4	80t	9

Pooley Hubert

Year	Team		Att	Yds	Avg	Lg	TD
1926	NY	A					1

Gene Hubka

Year	Team		Att	Yds	Avg	Lg	TD
1947	PIT	N	2	4	2.0	3	0

Harlan Huckleby

Year	Team		Att	Yds	Avg	Lg	TD
1980	GB	N	6	11	1.8	9	1
1981			139	381	2.7	22	5
1982			4	19	4.8	7	0
1983			50	182	3.6	20	4
1984			35	145	4.1	23	0
1985			8	41	5.1	15	0
Career			242	779	3.2	23	10
Playoffs			2	-1	-0.5		0

Dick Hudson

Year	Team		Att	Yds	Avg	Lg	TD
1964	BUF	A	1	1	1.0	1	0

Doug Hudson

Year	Team		Att	Yds	Avg	Lg	TD
1987	KC	N	1	0	0.0	0	0

Gary Huff

Year	Team		Att	Yds	Avg	Lg	TD
1973	CHI	N	11	22	2.0	8	0
1974			23	37	1.6	11	2
1975			5	7	1.4	10	0
1977	TB	N	8	10	1.3	2	0
1978			3	10	3.3	10	0
Career			50	86	1.7	11	2

Ken Huffine

Year	Team		Att	Yds	Avg	Lg	TD
1921	DEC	A					2
1922	DAY	N					3
Career							5

Darvell Huffman

Year	Team		Att	Yds	Avg	Lg	TD
1991	IND	N	1	-8	-8.0	-8	0

Vern Huffman

Year	Team		Att	Yds	Avg	Lg	TD
1937	DET	N	35	187	5.3		0
1938			69	181	2.6		1
Career			104	368	3.5		1

John Hufnagel

Year	Team		Att	Yds	Avg	Lg	TD
1974	DEN	N	2	22	11.0	18	0
1975			8	47	5.9	13	0
Career			10	69	6.9	18	0

Harry Hugasian

Year	Team		Att	Yds	Avg	Lg	TD
1955	BAL	N	12	34	2.8	15	0

Roy Huggins

Year	Team		Att	Yds	Avg	Lg	TD
1944	CLE	N	12	41	3.4	18	0

Danan Hughes

Year	Team		Att	Yds	Avg	Lg	TD
1995	KC	N	1	5	5.0	5	0

David Hughes

Year	Team		Att	Yds	Avg	Lg	TD
1981	SEA	N	47	135	2.9	15	0
1982			30	106	3.5	13	0
1983			83	313	3.8	26	1
1984			94	327	3.5	14	1
1985			40	128	3.2	9	0
1986	PIT	N	14	32	2.3	8	0
Career			308	1041	3.4	26	2
Playoffs			31	119	3.8		1

Dennis Hughes

Year	Team		Att	Yds	Avg	Lg	TD
1970	PIT	N	1	-8	-8.0	-8	0

Dick Hughes

Year	Team		Att	Yds	Avg	Lg	TD
1957	PIT	N	2	6	3.0	4	0

Tyrone Hughes

Year	Team		Att	Yds	Avg	Lg	TD
1994	NO	N	2	6	3.0	7	0

Tommy Hughitt

Year	Team		Att	Yds	Avg	Lg	TD
1920	BUF	A					1

Tommy Hughitt continued

Year	Team		Att	Yds	Avg	Lg	TD
1921							1
1922	BUF	N					2
1923							1
Career							5

George Hughley

Year	Team		Att	Yds	Avg	Lg	TD
1965	WAS	N	37	175	4.7	19	0

Mike Hull

Year	Team		Att	Yds	Avg	Lg	TD
1968	CHI	N	12	22	1.8	12	0
1969			29	81	2.8	14	1
1970			32	99	3.1	13	0
1971	WAS	N	2	8	4.0	6	0
1973			2	-3	-1.5	-1	0
Career			77	207	2.7	14	1

Dick Humbert

Year	Team		Att	Yds	Avg	Lg	TD
1946	PHI	N	1	2	2.0	2	0

Weldon Humble

Year	Team		Att	Yds	Avg	Lg	TD
1947	CLE	AA	1	0	0.0	0	0
1950	CLE	N	1	-10	-10.0	-10	0
Career			2	-10	-5.0	0	0

David Humm

Year	Team		Att	Yds	Avg	Lg	TD
1975	OAK	N	7	21	3.0	8	0
1978			5	-4	-0.8	4	0
1980	BUF	N	1	5	5.0	5	0
1983	LARI	N	1	-1	-1.0	-1	0
1984			2	7	3.5	9	0
Career			16	28	1.8	9	0

Bobby Humphery

Year	Team		Att	Yds	Avg	Lg	TD
1985	NYJ	N	1	10	10.0	10	0

Bobby Humphrey

Year	Team		Att	Yds	Avg	Lg	TD
1989	DEN	N	294	1151	3.9	40	7
1990			288	1202	4.2	37t	7
1991			11	33	3.0	7	0
1992	MIA	N	102	471	4.6	21	1
Career			695	2857	4.1	40	15
Playoffs			69	262	3.8		0

Buddy Humphrey

Year	Team		Att	Yds	Avg	Lg	TD
1960	LA	N	2	7	3.5	6	0
1965	STL	N	2	4	2.0	2	0
Career			4	11	2.8	6	0

Ronald Humphrey

Year	Team		Att	Yds	Avg	Lg	TD
1994	IND	N	18	85	4.7	27	0
1995			2	6	3.0	5	0
Career			20	91	4.5	27	0
Playoffs			5	10	2.0		0

Stan Humphries

Year	Team		Att	Yds	Avg	Lg	TD
1989	WAS	N	5	10	2.0	9	0
1990			23	106	4.6	17	2
1992	SD	N	28	79	2.8	25	4
1993			8	37	4.6	27	0
1994			19	19	1.0	8	0
1995			33	53	1.6	18	1
1996			21	28	1.3	7	0
Career			137	332	2.4	27	7
Playoffs			13	43	3.3		0

Chuck Hunsinger

Year	Team		Att	Yds	Avg	Lg	TD
1950	CHIB	N	61	326	5.3	45	2
1951			73	369	5.1	39	3
1952			58	139	2.4	30	0
Career			192	834	4.3	45	5
Playoffs			2	7	3.5		0

Bobby Hunt

Year	Team		Att	Yds	Avg	Lg	TD
1968	CIN	A	1	5	5.0	5t	1

Jackie Hunt

Year	Team		Att	Yds	Avg	Lg	TD
1945	CHIB	N	1	1	1.0	1	0

Al Hunter

Year	Team		Att	Yds	Avg	Lg	TD
1977	SEA	N	32	179	5.6	20	1
1978			105	348	3.3	55t	2
1979			34	174	5.1	67	1
1980			9	14	1.6	7	0
Career			180	715	4.0	67	4

Daniel Hunter

Year	Team		Att	Yds	Avg	Lg	TD
1996	BAL-NO	N	15	44	2.9	9	0

Earnest Hunter

Year	Team		Att	Yds	Avg	Lg	TD
1995	CLE	N	30	100	3.3	15	0
1996	BAL-NO	N	15	44	2.9	9	0
Career			45	144	3.2	15	0

Eddie Hunter

Year	Team		Att	Yds	Avg	Lg	TD
1987	NYJ-TB	N	56	210	3.8	23	0

Herman Hunter

Year	Team		Att	Yds	Avg	Lg	TD
1985	PHI	N	27	121	4.5	74t	1
1986	DET	N	3	22	7.3	18	0
1987	HOU	N	34	144	4.2	21	0
Career			64	287	4.5	74t	1

Ivy Joe Hunter

Year	Team		Att	Yds	Avg	Lg	TD
1989	IND	N	13	47	3.6	11	0
1991	NE	N	18	53	2.9	9	0
Career			31	100	3.2	11	0

Scott Hunter

Year	Team		Att	Yds	Avg	Lg	TD
1971	GB	N	21	50	2.4	16	4
1972			22	37	1.7	15	5
1973			8	3	0.4	6	1
1976	ATL	N	14	41	2.9	16	1
1977			28	70	2.5	18	1
1979	DET	N	2	3	1.5	2	1
Career			95	204	2.1	18	13
Playoffs			2	13	6.5		0

Tony Hunter

Year	Team		Att	Yds	Avg	Lg	TD
1983	BUF	N	2	28	14.0	24	0
1984			1	6	6.0	6	0
1986	LARM	N	1	-6	-6.0	-6	0
Career			4	28	7.0	24	0

Tony Hunter

Year	Team		Att	Yds	Avg	Lg	TD
1987	GB	N	1	0	0.0	0	0

Richard Huntley

Year	Team		Att	Yds	Avg	Lg	TD
1996	ATL	N	2	8	4.0	5	0

John Hurlburt

Year	Team		Att	Yds	Avg	Lg	TD
1924	CHIC	N					2

Bill Hutchinson

Year	Team		Att	Yds	Avg	Lg	TD
1942	NYG	N	7	27	3.9	15	0

Anthony Hutchison

Year	Team		Att	Yds	Avg	Lg	TD
1983	CHI	N	6	13	2.2	5	1
1984			14	39	2.8	6	1
1985	BUF	N	2	11	5.5	7	0
Career			22	63	2.9	7	2

Don Hutson

Year	Team		Att	Yds	Avg	Lg	TD
1936	GB	N	1	-3	-3.0	-3	0
1937			14	26	1.9		0
1938			3	-1	-0.3		0
1939			5	26	5.2		0
1941			4	22	5.5	18	2
1942			3	4	1.3	9	0
1943			6	41	6.8	16	0
1944			12	87	7.3	37	0
1945			8	60	7.5	18	1
Career			56	262	4.7	37	3
Playoffs			1	3	3.0		0

Tom Hutton

Year	Team		Att	Yds	Avg	Lg	TD
1995	PHI	N	1	0	0.0	0	0

John Huzvar

Year	Team		Att	Yds	Avg	Lg	TD
1952	PHI	N	105	349	3.3	26	2
1953	BAL	N	119	515	4.3	36t	4
1954			19	29	1.5	6	0
Career			243	893	3.7	36t	6

Henry Hynoski

Year	Team		Att	Yds	Avg	Lg	TD
1975	CLE	N	7	38	5.4	11	0

Ken Iman

Year	Team		Att	Yds	Avg	Lg	TD
1966	LA	N	1	2	2.0	2	0

Tut Imlay

Year	Team		Att	Yds	Avg	Lg	TD
1926	LA	N					3

Kevin Ingram

Year	Team		Att	Yds	Avg	Lg	TD
1987	NO	N	2	14	7.0	9	0

Mark Ingram

Year	Team		Att	Yds	Avg	Lg	TD
1989	NYG	N	1	1	1.0	1	0
1990			1	4	4.0	4	0
1995	GB	N	1	-3	-3.0	-3	0
Career			3	2	0.7	4	0

Michael Irvin

Year	Team		Att	Yds	Avg	Lg	TD
1988	DAL	N	1	2	2.0	2	0
1989			1	6	6.0	6	0
1992			1	-9	-9.0	-9	0
1993			2	6	3.0	9	0
Career			5	5	1.0	9	0

Don Irwin

Year	Team		Att	Yds	Avg	Lg	TD
1936	BOS	N	17	78	4.6		2
1937	WAS	N	89	315	3.5		2
1938			66	130	2.0		1
1939			10	63	6.3		1
Career			182	586	3.2		6
Playoffs			23	70	3.0		0

Wilmer Isabel

Year	Team		Att	Yds	Avg	Lg	TD
1923	COL	N					2

Cecil Isbell

Year	Team		Att	Yds	Avg	Lg	TD
1938	GB	N	85	445	5.2		2
1939			132	407	3.1		2
1940			97	270	2.8		4
1941			72	317	4.4	24	1
1942			36	83	2.3	32	1
Career			422	1522	3.6	32	10
Playoffs			36	40	1.1		0

John Isenbarger

Year	Team		Att	Yds	Avg	Lg	TD
1970	SF	N	18	43	2.4	27	0
1971			5	34	6.8	22	0
1972			3	9	3.0	7	0
1973			1	-6	-6.0	-6	0
Career			27	80	3.0	27	0

Qadry Ismail

Year	Team		Att	Yds	Avg	Lg	TD
1993	MIN	N	3	14	4.7	6	0
1995			1	7	7.0	7	0
1996	CAR	N	8	80	10.0	35t	1
Career			12	101	8.4	35t	1

Raghib Ismail

Year	Team		Att	Yds	Avg	Lg	TD
1993	LARI	N	4	-5	-1.3	10	0
1994			4	31	7.8	13	0
1995	OAK	N	6	29	4.8	13	0
Career			14	55	3.9	13	0
Playoffs			1	7	7.0		0

Rickey Isom

Year	Team		Att	Yds	Avg	Lg	TD
1987	MIA	N	9	41	4.6	8	1

Jack Itzel

Year	Team		Att	Yds	Avg	Lg	TD
1945	PIT	N	4	11	2.8	5	0

Duke Iverson

Year	Team		Att	Yds	Avg	Lg	TD
1949	B-NY	AA	6	50	8.3		0
Playoffs			1	4	4.0		0

Eddie Lee Ivery

Year	Team		Att	Yds	Avg	Lg	TD
1979	GB	N	3	24	8.0	11	0
1980			202	831	4.1	38t	3
1981			14	72	5.1	28	1
1982			127	453	3.6	32	9
1983			86	340	4.0	21	2
1984			99	552	5.6	49	6
1985			132	636	4.8	34	2
1986			4	25	6.3	15	0
Career			667	2933	4.4	49	23
Playoffs			20	91	4.5		1

Horace Ivory

Year	Team		Att	Yds	Avg	Lg	TD
1977	NE	N	3	10	3.3	9	0
1978			141	693	4.9	28	11
1979			143	522	3.7	52	1

Horace Ivory *continued*

Year	Team		Att	Yds	Avg	Lg	TD
1980			42	111	2.6	20t	2
1981	SEA	N	9	38	4.2	7	0
1982			13	51	3.9	27	1
Career			351	1425	4.1	52	15
Playoffs			3	11	3.7		0

George Izo

Year	Team		Att	Yds	Avg	Lg	TD
1961	WAS	N	3	-1	-0.3	4	0
1962			1	-3	-3.0	-3	0
1963			3	4	1.3	2	0
1965	DET	N	1	-5	-5.0	-5	0
1966	PIT	N	2	-18	-9.0	-4	0
Career			10	-23	-2.3	4	0

Larry Izzo

Year	Team		Att	Yds	Avg	Lg	TD
1996	MIA	N	1	26	26.0	26	0

Alfred Jackson

Year	Team		Att	Yds	Avg	Lg	TD
1981	ATL	N	2	5	2.5	5	0
1982			1	4	4.0	4	0
Career			3	9	3.0	5	0

Andrew Jackson

Year	Team		Att	Yds	Avg	Lg	TD
1987	HOU	N	60	232	3.9	16t	1

Billy Jackson

Year	Team		Att	Yds	Avg	Lg	TD
1981	KC	N	111	398	3.6	31	10
1982			86	243	2.8	18	3
1983			152	499	3.3	19	2
1984			50	225	4.5	16	1
Career			399	1365	3.4	31	16

Bo Jackson

Year	Team		Att	Yds	Avg	Lg	TD
1987	LARI	N	81	554	6.8	91t	4
1988			136	580	4.3	25	3
1989			173	950	5.5	92t	4
1990			125	698	5.6	88	5
Career			515	2782	5.4	92t	16
Playoffs			6	77	12.8		0

Bob Jackson

Year	Team		Att	Yds	Avg	Lg	TD
1950	NYG	N	12	113	9.4	57t	2
1951			5	9	1.8	6	0
Career			17	122	7.2	57t	2

Bob Jackson

Year	Team		Att	Yds	Avg	Lg	TD
1962	SD	A	106	411	3.9	19	5
1963			18	64	3.6	14	4
1964	HOU-OAK	A	23	64	2.8	27	3
1965	HOU	A	37	85	2.3	7	2
Career			184	624	3.4	27	14

Bobby Jackson

Year	Team		Att	Yds	Avg	Lg	TD
Playoffs			1	0	0.0		0

Cedric Jackson

Year	Team		Att	Yds	Avg	Lg	TD
1991	DET	N	17	55	3.2	10	0

Don Jackson

Year	Team		Att	Yds	Avg	Lg	TD
1936	PHI	N	46	76	1.7		0

Earnest Jackson

Year	Team		Att	Yds	Avg	Lg	TD
1983	SD	N	11	39	3.5	6	0
1984			296	1179	4.0	32t	8
1985	PHI	N	282	1028	3.6	59	5
1986	PIT	N	216	910	4.2	31	5
1987			180	696	3.9	39	1
1988			74	315	4.3	29t	3
Career			1059	4167	3.9	59	22

Frank Jackson

Year	Team		Att	Yds	Avg	Lg	TD
1961	DAL	A	65	386	5.9	49	3
1962			47	251	5.3	35	3
1963	KC	A	3	52	17.3	25	1
1964			2	5	2.5	12	0
1965			1	26	26.0	26	0
1966	MIA	A	2	22	11.0	24	0
1967			1	48	48.0	48	0
Career			121	790	6.5	49	7

Harold Jackson

Year	Team		Att	Yds	Avg	Lg	TD
1969	PHI	N	2	10	5.0	6	0
1970			1	-5	-5.0	-5	0
1971			5	41	8.2	18	0

Harold Jackson *continued*

Year	Team		Att	Yds	Avg	Lg	TD
1972			9	76	8.4	34	0
1973	LA	N	2	-8	-4.0	-3	0
1974			1	4	4.0	4	0
1976			1	15	15.0	15	0
1977			1	6	6.0	6	0
1978	NE	N	1	7	7.0	7	0
1979			3	12	4.0	12	0
1980			5	37	7.4	16	0
1981			2	-14	-7.0	-5	0
Career			33	181	5.5	34	0

Jazz Jackson

Year	Team		Att	Yds	Avg	Lg	TD
1974	NYJ	N	20	74	3.7	16	0
1975			6	11	1.8	7	0
1976			1	6	6.0	6	0
Career			27	91	3.4	16	0

Jim Jackson

Year	Team		Att	Yds	Avg	Lg	TD
1966	SF	N	4	7	1.8	4	0

Kenny Jackson

Year	Team		Att	Yds	Avg	Lg	TD
1986	PHI	N	1	6	6.0	6	0
1987			6	27	4.5	10	0
1991			1	18	18.0	18	0
Career			8	51	6.4	18	0

Leroy Jackson

Year	Team		Att	Yds	Avg	Lg	TD
1962	WAS	N	49	112	2.3	14	0
1963			3	30	10.0	17	0
Career			52	142	2.7	17	0

Louis Jackson

Year	Team		Att	Yds	Avg	Lg	TD
1981	NYG	N	27	68	2.5	9	1

Mark Jackson

Year	Team		Att	Yds	Avg	Lg	TD
1986	DEN	N	2	6	3.0	5	0
1988			1	5	5.0	5	0
1989			5	13	2.6	8	0
1990			5	28	5.6	16t	1
1991			2	18	9.0	21	0
1992			3	-1	-0.3	1	0
1993	NYG	N	3	25	8.3	20	0
Career			21	94	4.5	21	1
Playoffs			2	1	0.5		0

Michael Jackson

Year	Team		Att	Yds	Avg	Lg	TD
1992	CLE	N	1	21	21.0	21	0
1993			1	1	1.0	1	0
Career			2	22	11.0	21	0

Pete Jackson

Year	Team		Att	Yds	Avg	Lg	TD
1928	DET	N					2

Randy Jackson

Year	Team		Att	Yds	Avg	Lg	TD
1972	BUF	N	17	57	3.4	15	0
1973	SF	N	6	10	1.7	5	0
1974	PHI	N	7	3	0.4	2	0
Career			30	70	2.3	15	0

Rusty Jackson

Year	Team		Att	Yds	Avg	Lg	TD
1978	BUF	N	1	-13	-13.0	-13	0
Playoffs			1	-8	-8.0		0

Wilbur Jackson

Year	Team		Att	Yds	Avg	Lg	TD
1974	SF	N	174	705	4.1	64	0
1975			78	303	3.9	44	0
1976			200	792	4.0	24	1
1977			179	780	4.4	80	7
1979			114	375	3.3	16	2
1980	WAS	N	176	708	4.0	55t	3
1981			46	183	4.0	14	0
1982			4	6	1.5	2	0
Career			971	3852	4.0	80	13
Playoffs			8	27	3.4		0

Willie Jackson

Year	Team		Att	Yds	Avg	Lg	TD
1996	JAC	N	1	2	2.0	2	0

Allen Jacobs

Year	Team		Att	Yds	Avg	Lg	TD
1965	GB	N	3	5	1.7	2	0
1966	NYG	N	77	273	3.5	19	1
1967			11	23	2.1	5	0
Career			91	301	3.3	19	1

Jack Jacobs

Year	Team		Att	Yds	Avg	Lg	TD
1942	CLE	N	32	91	2.8	13	0
1945			2	0	0.0	0	0
1946	WAS	N	18	34	1.9	9	0
1947	GB	N	18	64	3.6	15	1
1948			24	73	3.0	23	1
Career			94	262	2.8	23	2

Harry Jacunski

Year	Team		Att	Yds	Avg	Lg	TD
Playoffs			1	11	11.0		0

Harry Jagade

Year	Team		Att	Yds	Avg	Lg	TD
1949	BAL	AA	33	174	5.3		2
1951	CLE	N	7	30	4.3	22	0
1952			57	373	6.5	30	2
1953			86	344	4.0	23	4
1954	CHIB	N	157	498	3.2	46	3
1955			72	309	4.3	51	2
Career			412	1728	4.2	51	13
Playoffs			30	208	6.9		2

Claudis James

Year	Team		Att	Yds	Avg	Lg	TD
1968	GB	N	1	15	15.0	15	0

Craig James

Year	Team		Att	Yds	Avg	Lg	TD
1984	NE	N	160	790	4.9	73	1
1985			263	1227	4.7	65t	5
1986			154	427	2.8	16	4
1987			4	10	2.5	5	0
1988			4	15	3.8	8t	1
Career			585	2469	4.2	73	11
Playoffs			82	290	3.5		1

Dick James

Year	Team		Att	Yds	Avg	Lg	TD
1956	WAS	N	58	280	4.8	41t	1
1957			7	19	2.7	8	0
1958			24	88	3.7	14	1
1959			100	384	3.8	39	3
1960			73	199	2.7	27t	4
1961			71	374	5.3	39t	3
1962			9	13	1.4	7	0
1963			105	384	3.7	15	4
1964	NYG	N	55	189	3.4	18	3
Career			502	1930	3.8	41t	19

Garry James

Year	Team		Att	Yds	Avg	Lg	TD
1986	DET	N	159	688	4.3	60t	3
1987			82	270	3.3	17	4
1988			182	552	3.0	35	5
Career			423	1510	3.6	60t	12

John James

Year	Team		Att	Yds	Avg	Lg	TD
1979	ATL	N	1	0	0.0	0	0
1980			1	13	13.0	13	0
1981			1	-7	-7.0	-7	0
1983	HOU	N	1	0	0.0	0	0
Career			4	6	1.5	13	0

Lionel James

Year	Team		Att	Yds	Avg	Lg	TD
1984	SD	N	25	115	4.6	20	0
1985			105	516	4.9	56t	2
1986			51	224	4.4	24	0
1987			27	102	3.8	15t	1
1988			23	105	4.6	23	0
Career			231	1062	4.6	56t	4

Lynn James

Year	Team		Att	Yds	Avg	Lg	TD
1990	CIN	N	1	11	11.0	11	0

Ron James

Year	Team		Att	Yds	Avg	Lg	TD
1972	PHI	N	182	565	3.1	22	0
1973			36	178	4.9	24	1
1974			67	276	4.1	15	2
1975			43	196	4.6	51	1
Career			328	1215	3.7	51	4

Tommy James

Year	Team		Att	Yds	Avg	Lg	TD
1947	DET	N	2	-1	-0.5	2	0
1948	CLE	AA	1	8	8.0	8	0
1949			10	28	2.8		0
1950	CLE	N	1	-1	-1.0	-1	0
1954			1	-6	-6.0	-6	0
1955			1	2	2.0	2	0
Career			16	30	1.9	8	0
Playoffs			2	7	3.5		

Year	Team		Att	Yds	Avg	Lg	TD

Dick Jamieson

Year	Team		Att	Yds	Avg	Lg	TD
1960	NY	A	8	-61	-7.6		0

Len Janiak

Year	Team		Att	Yds	Avg	Lg	TD
1939	BKN	N	18	56	3.1		0
1940	CLE	N	19	44	2.3		0
1941			14	20	1.4	12	0
1942			34	108	3.2	20	0
Career			85	228	2.7	20	0

Ed Jankowski

Year	Team		Att	Yds	Avg	Lg	TD
1937	GB	N	61	325	5.3		2
1938			42	124	3.0		2
1939			75	278	3.7		2
1940			48	211	4.4		2
1941			47	65	1.4	13	0
Career			273	1003	3.7	13	8
Playoffs			13	32	2.5		1

Vic Janowicz

Year	Team		Att	Yds	Avg	Lg	TD
1954	WAS	N	6	13	2.2	3	0
1955			93	397	4.3	33	4
Career			99	410	4.1	33	4

Val Jansante

Year	Team		Att	Yds	Avg	Lg	TD
1946	PIT	N	2	5	2.5	5	0
1948			1	-3	-3.0	-3	0
Career			3	2	0.7	5	0

Toimi Jarvi

Year	Team		Att	Yds	Avg	Lg	TD
1944	PHI	N	5	16	3.2	4	0
1945	PIT	N	9	24	2.7	11	0
Career			14	40	2.9	11	0

Ray Jarvis

Year	Team		Att	Yds	Avg	Lg	TD
1971	ATL	N	1	13	13.0	13	0
1975	DET	N	1	0	0.0	0	0
Career			2	13	6.5	13	0

Ron Jaworski

Year	Team		Att	Yds	Avg	Lg	TD
1974	LA	N	7	34	4.9	17	1
1975			12	33	2.8	21	2
1976			2	15	7.5	14	1
1977	PHI	N	40	127	3.2	44	5
1978			30	79	2.6	15	0
1979			43	119	2.8	21	2
1980			27	95	3.5	19	1
1981			22	128	5.8	26	0
1982			10	9	0.9	6	0
1983			25	129	5.2	29	1
1984			5	18	3.6	10	1
1985			17	35	2.1	31	2
1986			13	33	2.5	10	0
1989	KC	N	4	5	1.3	4	0
Career			257	859	3.3	44	16
Playoffs			21	49	2.3		1

Dave Jaynes

Year	Team		Att	Yds	Avg	Lg	TD
1974	KC	N	1	0	0.0	0	0

Garland Jean Batiste

Year	Team		Att	Yds	Avg	Lg	TD
1987	NO	N	8	18	2.3	7	0

Billy Jefferson

Year	Team		Att	Yds	Avg	Lg	TD
1941	DET	N	56	164	2.9	20	1
1942	PHI-BKN	N	12	58	4.8	13	0
Career			68	222	3.3	20	1

John Jefferson

Year	Team		Att	Yds	Avg	Lg	TD
1978	SD	N	1	7	7.0	7	0
1980			1	16	16.0	16	0
1981	GB	N	2	22	11.0	15	0
1982			2	16	8.0	11	0
Career			6	61	10.2	16	0

Roy Jefferson

Year	Team		Att	Yds	Avg	Lg	TD
1965	PIT	N	1	-1	-1.0	-1	0
1966			2	36	18.0	24	0
1967			5	-11	-2.2	20	0
1968			6	57	9.5	22	0
1969			4	46	11.5	22	0
1970	BAL	N	4	47	11.8	19	0
1971	WAS	N	2	13	6.5	13	0

Roy Jefferson continued

Year	Team		Att	Yds	Avg	Lg	TD
1973			1	1	1.0	1	0
Career			25	188	7.5	24	0
Playoffs			4	-8	-2.0		0

Shawn Jefferson

Year	Team		Att	Yds	Avg	Lg	TD
1991	SD	N	1	27	27.0	27	0
1993			5	53	10.6	33	0
1994			3	40	13.3	22	0
1995			2	1	0.5	11	0
1996	NE	N	1	6	6.0	6	0
Career			12	127	10.6	33	0
Playoffs			2	13	6.5		0

Tony Jeffery

Year	Team		Att	Yds	Avg	Lg	TD
1988	PHX	N	3	8	2.7	9	0

Neal Jeffrey

Year	Team		Att	Yds	Avg	Lg	TD
1976	SD	N	1	0	0.0	0	0

Alfred Jenkins

Year	Team		Att	Yds	Avg	Lg	TD
1977	ATL	N	2	7	3.5	9	0

Jack Jenkins

Year	Team		Att	Yds	Avg	Lg	TD
1943	WAS	N	4	20	5.0	8	0
1946			64	200	3.1	15	0
1947			16	54	3.4	9	0
Career			84	274	3.3	15	1

Ken Jenkins

Year	Team		Att	Yds	Avg	Lg	TD
1984	DET	N	78	358	4.6	25t	1
1985	WAS	N	2	39	19.5	37	0
Career			80	397	5.0	37	1

Keyvan Jenkins

Year	Team		Att	Yds	Avg	Lg	TD
1987	SD	N	22	88	4.0	9	0

Dave Jennings

Year	Team		Att	Yds	Avg	Lg	TD
1978	NYG	N	1	0	0.0	0	0
1979			2	11	5.5	9	0
1986	NYJ	N	1	0	0.0	0	0
1987			2	5	2.5	4	0
Career			6	16	2.7	9	0
Playoffs			1	-3	-3.0		0

Ricky Jennings

Year	Team		Att	Yds	Avg	Lg	TD
1976	OAK	N	10	22	2.2	10	0

Stanford Jennings

Year	Team		Att	Yds	Avg	Lg	TD
1984	CIN	N	79	379	4.8	20t	2
1985			31	92	3.0	19	1
1986			16	54	3.4	10	1
1987			70	314	4.5	18	1
1988			17	47	2.8	9	1
1989			83	293	3.5	17	2
1990			12	46	3.8	13	1
1992	TB	N	5	25	5.0	10	0
Career			313	1250	4.0	20t	9
Playoffs			9	31	3.4		0

Derrick Jensen

Year	Team		Att	Yds	Avg	Lg	TD
1979	OAK	N	73	251	3.4	15	0
1980			14	30	2.1	4	0
1981			117	456	3.9	33	4
1983	LARI	N	1	5	5.0	5	0
1984			3	3	1.0	2	1
1985			16	35	2.2	8	0
Career			224	780	3.5	33	5
Playoffs			9	23	2.6		0

Jim Jensen

Year	Team		Att	Yds	Avg	Lg	TD
1977	DEN	N	40	143	3.6	12	1
1979			106	400	3.8	30	1
1980			101	476	4.7	32	2
1981	GB	N	27	79	2.9	15	0
1982			9	28	3.1	10	0
Career			283	1126	4.0	32	4
Playoffs			13	46	3.5		0

Jim Jensen

Year	Team		Att	Yds	Avg	Lg	TD
1987	MIA	N	4	18	4.5	9	0
1988			10	68	6.8	23	0
1989			8	50	6.3	14	0

Jim Jensen continued

Year	Team		Att	Yds	Avg	Lg	TD
1990			4	6	1.5	2	0
Career			26	142	5.5	23	0
Playoffs			2	-6	-3.0		0

Travis Jervey

Year	Team		Att	Yds	Avg	Lg	TD
1996	GB	N	26	106	4.1	12	0

Ron Jessie

Year	Team		Att	Yds	Avg	Lg	TD
1971	DET	N	1	0	0.0	0	0
1973			5	31	6.2	17	1
1974			6	17	2.8	18t	1
1975	LA	N	2	15	7.5	9	0
1976			4	37	9.3	22	0
1980	BUF	N	1	-9	-9.0	-9	0
Career			19	91	4.8	22	2
Playoffs			1	3	3.0		0

Tim Jessie

Year	Team		Att	Yds	Avg	Lg	TD
1987	WAS	N	10	37	3.7	14t	1

Billy Jessup

Year	Team		Att	Yds	Avg	Lg	TD
1954	SF	N	1	-5	-5.0	-5	0

Perry Jeter

Year	Team		Att	Yds	Avg	Lg	TD
1956	CHIB	N	60	316	5.3	51	2
1957			10	11	1.1	7	0
Career			70	327	4.7	51	2

James Jett

Year	Team		Att	Yds	Avg	Lg	TD
1993	LARI	N	1	0	0.0	0	0

John Jett

Year	Team		Att	Yds	Avg	Lg	TD
1996	DAL	N	1	-23	-23.0	-23	0

Jim Jodat

Year	Team		Att	Yds	Avg	Lg	TD
1977	LA	N	5	15	3.0	5	1
1978			26	100	3.8	18	0
1979			6	6	1.0	4	0
1980	SEA	N	155	632	4.1	26	5
1981			31	106	3.4	15	1
1982	SD	N	3	7	2.3	3	0
Career			226	866	3.8	26	7
Playoffs			3	-2	-0.7		1

Billy Joe

Year	Team		Att	Yds	Avg	Lg	TD
1963	DEN	A	154	649	4.2	68	4
1964			112	415	3.7	51	2
1965	BUF	A	123	377	3.1	30	4
1966	MIA	A	71	232	3.3	14	0
1967	NY	A	37	154	4.2	26	2
1968			42	186	4.4	32t	3
Career			539	2013	3.7	68	15
Playoffs			16	35	2.2		0

Larry Joe

Year	Team		Att	Yds	Avg	Lg	TD
1949	BUF	AA	2	18	9.0		0

Herb Joesting

Year	Team		Att	Yds	Avg	Lg	TD
1929	MIN	N					2
1930	MIN-FRA	N					3
1931	FRA-CHIB	N					2
Career							7

Paul Johns

Year	Team		Att	Yds	Avg	Lg	TD
1982	SEA	N	1	-1	-1.0	-1	0
1983			2	12	6.0	26	0
Career			3	11	3.7	26	0

Al Johnson

Year	Team		Att	Yds	Avg	Lg	TD
1972	HOU	N	11	13	1.2	7	0
1973			1	-3	-3.0	-3	0
Career			12	10	0.8	7	0

Andy Johnson

Year	Team		Att	Yds	Avg	Lg	TD
1974	NE	N	2	-4	-2.0	-2	0
1975			117	488	4.2	66t	3
1976			169	699	4.1	69t	6
1978			147	675	4.6	52	3
1979			43	132	3.1	15	1
1980			11	26	2.4	11	0
1981			2	1	0.5	5	0
Career			491	2017	4.1	69t	13
Playoffs			20	46	2.3		1

Year	Team		Att	Yds	Avg	Lg	TD

Anthony Johnson

Year	Team		Att	Yds	Avg	Lg	TD
1991	IND	N	22	94	4.3	15	0
1992			178	592	3.3	19	0
1993			95	331	3.5	14	1
1994	NYJ	N	5	12	2.4	5	0
1995	CHI-CAR	N	30	140	4.7	23t	1
1996	CAR	N	300	1120	3.7	29	6
Career			630	2289	3.6	29	8
Playoffs			37	135	3.6		0

Bert Johnson

Year	Team		Att	Yds	Avg	Lg	TD
1937	BKN	N	41	59	1.4		0
1938	CHIB		37	138	3.7		2
1939	CHIB-CHIC	N	38	95	2.5		0
1940	CHIC	N	6	15	2.5		0
1941			3	7	2.3	6	0
1942	PHI	N	27	54	2.0	13	0
Career			152	368	2.4	13	2

Bill Johnson

Year	Team		Att	Yds	Avg	Lg	TD
1985	CIN	N	8	44	5.5	15	0
1986			39	226	5.8	34	0
1987			39	205	5.3	20	1
Career			86	475	5.5	34	1

Billy Johnson

Year	Team		Att	Yds	Avg	Lg	TD
1974	HOU	N	5	82	16.4	47t	1
1975			5	17	3.4	19	0
1976			6	6	1.0	10	0
1977			6	102	17.0	61	1
1980			2	1	0.5	4	0
1983	ATL	N	15	83	5.5	36	0
1984			3	8	2.7	11	0
1985			8	-8	-1.0	6	0
1986			6	25	4.2	10	0
Career			56	316	5.6	61	2

Bobby Lee Johnson

Year	Team		Att	Yds	Avg	Lg	TD
1986	NYG	N	2	28	14.0	22	0

Brad Johnson

Year	Team		Att	Yds	Avg	Lg	TD
1994	MIN	N	2	-2	-1.0	-1	0
1995			9	-9	-1.0	3	0
1996			34	90	2.6	13	1
Career			45	79	1.8	13	1
Playoffs			3	14	4.7		1

Butch Johnson

Year	Team		Att	Yds	Avg	Lg	TD
1977	DAL	N	1	-3	-3.0	-3	0
1979			1	13	13.0	13	0
1982			1	9	9.0	9	0
1983			1	0	0.0	0	0
1984	DEN	N	1	3	3.0	3	0
Career			5	22	4.4	13	0
Playoffs			2	-4	-2.0		0

Cecil Johnson

Year	Team		Att	Yds	Avg	Lg	TD
1943	BKN	N	26	38	1.5	19	0
1944			30	41	1.4	19	0
Career			56	79	1.4	19	0

Charles Johnson

Year	Team		Att	Yds	Avg	Lg	TD
1994	PIT	N	4	-1	-0.3	7	0
1995			1	-10	-10.0	-10	0
Career			5	-11	-2.2	7	0

Charley Johnson

Year	Team		Att	Yds	Avg	Lg	TD
1961	STL	N	1	-3	-3.0	-3	0
1962			25	138	5.5	19	3
1963			41	143	3.5	16	1
1964			31	93	3.0	19	2
1965			25	60	2.4	15	1
1966			20	39	2.0	9	2
1968			5	-1	-0.2	3	0
1969			17	51	3.0	15	1
1970	HOU	N	5	3	0.6	9	0
1971			2	0	0.0	0	0
1972	DEN	N	3	0	0.0	0	0
1973			7	-2	-0.3	0	0
1974			4	-3	-0.8	0	0
1975			10	21	2.1	13	0
Career			196	539	2.8	19	10

Curley Johnson

Year	Team		Att	Yds	Avg	Lg	TD
1960	DAL	A	23	43	1.9	8	1
1961	NY	A	1	3	3.0	3	0
1962			26	114	4.4	25	0
1963			2	6	3.0	5	0
1964			6	22	3.7	8	0
1965			2	3	1.5	2	0
1966			2	24	12.0	20	0
1968			2	-6	-3.0		0
Career			64	209	3.3	25	1

Dennis Johnson

Year	Team		Att	Yds	Avg	Lg	TD
1978	BUF	N	55	222	4.0	30	2
1979			3	5	1.7	2	0
Career			58	227	3.9	30	2

Don Johnson

Year	Team		Att	Yds	Avg	Lg	TD
1953	PHI	N	83	439	5.3	66t	5
1954			7	16	2.3	11	0
1955			3	1	0.3	4	0
Career			93	456	4.9	66t	5

Ellis Johnson

Year	Team		Att	Yds	Avg	Lg	TD
1965	BOS	A	19	29	1.5	9	0

Essex Johnson

Year	Team		Att	Yds	Avg	Lg	TD
1968	CIN	A	26	178	6.8	41t	3
1969			15	54	3.6	13	0
1970	CIN	N	65	273	4.2	26	2
1971			85	522	6.1	86t	4
1972			212	825	3.9	19	4
1973			195	997	5.1	46	4
1974			19	44	2.3	11	0
1975			58	177	3.1	15	1
1976	TB	N	47	166	3.5	27	1
Career			722	3236	4.5	86t	19
Playoffs			7	17	2.4		0

Gil Johnson

Year	Team		Att	Yds	Avg	Lg	TD
1949	B-NY	AA	3	21	7.0		0

Harvey Johnson

Year	Team		Att	Yds	Avg	Lg	TD
1946	NY	AA	16	63	3.9		0

Herb Johnson

Year	Team		Att	Yds	Avg	Lg	TD
1954	NYG	N	42	168	4.0	21	1

Jason Johnson

Year	Team		Att	Yds	Avg	Lg	TD
1988	DEN	N	1	3	3.0	3	0

Jerry Johnson

Year	Team		Att	Yds	Avg	Lg	TD
1922	RI	N					1

Joe Johnson

Year	Team		Att	Yds	Avg	Lg	TD
1954	GB	N	7	31	4.4	10	0
1955			49	210	4.3	21	0
1956			35	129	3.7	14	0
1957			2	6	3.0	3	0
Career			93	376	4.0	21	0

Joe Johnson

Year	Team		Att	Yds	Avg	Lg	TD
1992	MIN	N	4	26	6.5	9	0
Playoffs			1	2	2.0		0

John Henry Johnson

Year	Team		Att	Yds	Avg	Lg	TD
1954	SF	N	129	681	5.3	38t	9
1955			19	69	3.6	12	1
1956			80	301	3.8	54	2
1957	DET	N	129	621	4.8	62	5
1958			56	254	4.5	19	0
1959			82	270	3.3	39	2
1960	PIT	N	118	621	5.3	87t	2
1961			213	787	3.7	44	6
1962			251	1141	4.5	40	7
1963			186	773	4.2	45	4
1964			235	1048	4.5	45t	7
1965			3	11	3.7	7	0
1966	HOU	A	70	226	3.2	28	3
Career			1571	6803	4.3	87t	48
Playoffs			13	60	4.6		0

Johnny Johnson

Year	Team		Att	Yds	Avg	Lg	TD
1990	PHX	N	234	926	4.0	41	5
1991			196	666	3.4	21	4

Johnny Johnson *continued*

Year	Team		Att	Yds	Avg	Lg	TD
1992			178	734	4.1	42t	6
1993	NYJ	N	198	821	4.1	57t	3
1994			240	931	3.9	90	3
Career			1046	4078	3.9	90	21

Kenny Johnson

Year	Team		Att	Yds	Avg	Lg	TD
1979	NYG	N	62	168	2.7	12	0

Kermit Johnson

Year	Team		Att	Yds	Avg	Lg	TD
1975	SF	N	4	25	6.3	19	0
1976			32	99	3.1	16	1
Career			36	124	3.4	19	1

Lee Johnson

Year	Team		Att	Yds	Avg	Lg	TD
1985	HOU	N	1	0	0.0	0	0
1989	CIN	N	1	-7	-7.0	-7	0
1991			1	-2	-2.0	-2	0
1995			1	-16	-16.0	-16	0
Career			4	-25	-6.3	0	0

LeShon Johnson

Year	Team		Att	Yds	Avg	Lg	TD
1994	GB	N	26	99	3.8	43	0
1995			2	-2	-1.0	0	0
1996	ARI	N	141	634	4.5	70t	3
Career			169	731	4.3	70t	3

Mitch Johnson

Year	Team		Att	Yds	Avg	Lg	TD
1970	LA	N	1	1	1.0	1	0

Pete Johnson

Year	Team		Att	Yds	Avg	Lg	TD
1977	CIN	N	153	585	3.8	65	4
1978			180	762	4.2	50t	7
1979			243	865	3.6	35t	14
1980			186	747	4.0	57t	6
1981			274	1077	3.9	39t	12
1982			156	622	4.0	21	7
1983			210	763	3.6	16t	14
1984	SD-MIA	N	87	205	2.4	9	12
Career			1489	5626	3.8	65	76
Playoffs			77	248	3.2		2

Preston Johnson

Year	Team		Att	Yds	Avg	Lg	TD
1968	BOS	A	2	6	3.0	6	0

Randy Johnson

Year	Team		Att	Yds	Avg	Lg	TD
1966	ATL	N	35	142	4.1	21	4
1967			24	144	6.0	17t	1
1968			11	97	8.8	26	1
1969			11	55	5.0	13	1
1970			7	21	3.0	14	0
1971	NYG	N	6	29	4.8	17	0
1972			9	26	2.9	9	0
1973			4	24	6.0	11	1
1975	WAS	N	2	10	5.0	10	0
1976	GB	N	5	25	5.0	11	1
Career			114	573	5.0	26	10

Ray Johnson

Year	Team		Att	Yds	Avg	Lg	TD
1937	CLE	N	7	28	4.0		0

Reggie Johnson

Year	Team		Att	Yds	Avg	Lg	TD
1992	DEN	N	2	7	3.5	8	0

Richard Johnson

Year	Team		Att	Yds	Avg	Lg	TD
1969	HOU	A	11	42	3.8	9	0

Richard Johnson

Year	Team		Att	Yds	Avg	Lg	TD
1989	DET	N	12	38	3.2	14	0

Rob Johnson

Year	Team		Att	Yds	Avg	Lg	TD
1995	JAC	N	3	17	5.7	7	0

Ron Johnson

Year	Team		Att	Yds	Avg	Lg	TD
1989	PHI	N	1	3	3.0	3	0

Ron Johnson

Year	Team		Att	Yds	Avg	Lg	TD
1969	CLE	N	137	471	3.4	48t	7
1970	NYG	N	263	1027	3.9	68t	8
1971			32	156	4.9	17	1
1972			298	1182	4.0	35t	9
1973			260	902	3.5	29	6
1974			97	218	2.2	14	4

Ron Johnson *continued*

Year	Team		Att	Yds	Avg	Lg	TD
1975			116	351	3.0	23	5
Career			1203	4307	3.6	68t	40
Playoffs			2	-5	-2.5		0

Rudy Johnson

Year	Team		Att	Yds	Avg	Lg	TD
1964	SF	N	16	48	3.0	24	1
1965			6	9	1.5	4	0
1966	ATL	N	3	3	1.0	3	0
Career			25	60	2.4	24	1

Sammy Johnson

Year	Team		Att	Yds	Avg	Lg	TD
1974	SF	N	44	237	5.4	32	2
1975			55	185	3.4	26t	3
1976	SF-MIN	N	41	150	3.7	18	2
1977	MIN	N	55	217	3.9	26	2
1978			11	41	3.7	17	0
Career			206	830	4.0	32	9
Playoffs			10	35	3.5		2

Tracy Johnson

Year	Team		Att	Yds	Avg	Lg	TD
1989	HOU	N	4	16	4.0	8	0
1990	ATL	N	30	106	3.5	12	3
1991			8	26	3.3	6	0
1992	SEA	N	3	26	8.7	19	0
1993			2	8	4.0	5	0
1994			12	44	3.7	14	2
1995			1	2	2.0	2t	1
Career			60	228	3.8	19	6
Playoffs			8	33	4.1		1

Troy Johnson

Year	Team		Att	Yds	Avg	Lg	TD
1987	STL	N	1	9	9.0	9	0

Vance Johnson

Year	Team		Att	Yds	Avg	Lg	TD
1985	DEN	N	10	36	3.6	14	0
1986			5	15	3.0	6	0
1987			1	-8	-8.0	-8	0
1988			1	1	1.0	1	0
Career			17	44	2.6	14	0
Playoffs			2	-7	-3.5		0

Luke Johnsos

Year	Team		Att	Yds	Avg	Lg	TD
1935	CHIB	N	1	4	4.0	4	0

Chet Johnston

Year	Team		Att	Yds	Avg	Lg	TD
1934	C-S	N					1
1935	GB	N	52	176	3.4		0
1936			42	110	2.6		1
1939	PIT	N	59	220	3.7		2
1940			41	113	2.8		0
Career			194	619	3.2		4
Playoffs			2	4	2.0		0

Daryl Johnston

Year	Team		Att	Yds	Avg	Lg	TD
1989	DAL	N	67	212	3.2	13	0
1990			10	35	3.5	8	1
1991			17	54	3.2	10	0
1992			17	61	3.6	14	0
1993			24	74	3.1	11	3
1994			40	140	3.5	9t	2
1995			25	111	4.4	18	2
1996			22	48	2.2	7	0
Career			222	733	3.3	18	8
Playoffs			23	70	3.0		2

Jimmy Johnston

Year	Team		Att	Yds	Avg	Lg	TD
1939	WAS	N	7	47	6.7		0
1940			84	256	3.0		3
1946	CHIC	N	6	18	3.0	11	0
Career			97	321	3.3	11	3
Playoffs			4	14	3.5		0

Preston Johnston

Year	Team		Att	Yds	Avg	Lg	TD
1946	MIA-BUF	AA	45	218	4.8		2

Rex Johnston

Year	Team		Att	Yds	Avg	Lg	TD
1960	PIT	N	4	12	3.0	17	0

Charlie Joiner

Year	Team		Att	Yds	Avg	Lg	TD
1972	HOU-CIN	N	3	14	4.7	9	0
1974	CIN	N	4	20	5.0	8	0
1979	SD	N	1	-12	-12.0	-12	0
Career			8	22	2.8	9	0

Lewis Jolley

Year	Team		Att	Yds	Avg	Lg	TD
1973	HOU	N	7	6	0.9	3	0

A.J. Jones

Year	Team		Att	Yds	Avg	Lg	TD
1985	DET	N	1	2	2.0	2	0
Playoffs			4	28	7.0		0

Art Jones

Year	Team		Att	Yds	Avg	Lg	TD
1941	PIT	N	52	239	4.6	34	4
1945			15	64	4.3	20	0
Career			67	303	4.5	34	4

Ben Jones

Year	Team		Att	Yds	Avg	Lg	TD
1923	CAN	N					6
1924	CLE	N					4
1925	CAN-FRA	N					3
1926	FRA	N					7
1927	CHIC	N					2
Career							22

Bert Jones

Year	Team		Att	Yds	Avg	Lg	TD
1973	BAL	N	18	58	3.2	17	0
1974			39	279	7.2	39	4
1975			47	321	6.8	36	3
1976			38	214	5.6	17	2
1977			28	146	5.2	22	2
1978			9	38	4.2	14	0
1979			10	40	4.0	25	1
1980			27	175	6.5	19	2
1981			20	85	4.3	17	0
1982	LARM	N	11	73	6.6	17	0
Career			247	1429	5.8	39	14
Playoffs			10	39	3.9	0	

Bill Jones

Year	Team		Att	Yds	Avg	Lg	TD
1990	KC	N	10	47	4.7	14	0
Playoffs			1	9	9.0		0

Bobby Jones

Year	Team		Att	Yds	Avg	Lg	TD
1979	NYJ	N	1	4	4.0	4	0
1983	CLE	N	1	19	19.0	19	0
Career			2	23	11.5	19	0

Calvin Jones

Year	Team		Att	Yds	Avg	Lg	TD
1994	LARI	N	22	93	4.2	10	0
1995	OAK	N	5	19	3.8	15	0
Career			27	112	4.1	15	0

Cedric Jones

Year	Team		Att	Yds	Avg	Lg	TD
1986	NE	N	1	-7	-7.0	-7	0
1989			1	3	3.0	3	0
Career			2	-4	-2.0	3	0

Clint Jones

Year	Team		Att	Yds	Avg	Lg	TD
1967	MIN	N	13	23	1.8	9	0
1968			128	536	4.2	43	1
1969			54	241	4.5	80t	3
1970			120	369	3.1	23	9
1971			180	675	3.8	73t	4
1972			52	164	3.2	33	2
1973	SD	N	55	170	3.1	38	
Career			602	2178	3.6	80t	20
Playoffs			34	119	3.5		1

Drew Jones

Year	Team		Att	Yds	Avg	Lg	TD
1975	NO	N	42	108	2.6	18	1
1976			1	2	2.0	2	0
Career			43	110	2.6	18	1

Dub Jones

Year	Team		Att	Yds	Avg	Lg	TD
1946	BKN	AA	19	62	3.3		0
1947			43	136	3.2		1
1948	CLE	AA	33	149	4.5		1
1949			77	312	4.1		4
1950	CLE	N	83	384	4.6	61t	6
1951			104	492	4.7	43t	7
1952			65	270	4.2	35	2
1953			31	28	0.9	10	0
1954			54	234	4.3	26	2
1955			10	44	4.4	13	0
Career			519	2111	4.1	61t	23
Playoffs			44	127	2.9		1

Edgar Jones

Year	Team		Att	Yds	Avg	Lg	TD
1945	CHIB	N	8	41	5.1	12	0
1946	CLE	AA	77	539	7.0	56	4
1947			69	443	**6.4**		5
1948			100	400	4.0		5
1949			43	127	3.0		3
Career			297	1550	5.2	56	18
Playoffs			50	145	2.9		4

E.J. Jones

Year	Team		Att	Yds	Avg	Lg	TD
1985	KC	N	12	19	1.6	7	0
1987	DAL	N	2	7	3.5	5	0
Career			14	26	1.9	7	0

Ernie Jones

Year	Team		Att	Yds	Avg	Lg	TD
1989	PHX	N	1	18	18.0	18	0
1990			4	33	8.3	15	0
1991			5	24	4.8	9	0
1992			2	-3	-1.5	1	0
1993	LARM	N	1	4	4.0	4	0
Career			13	76	5.8	18	0

Fred Jones

Year	Team		Att	Yds	Avg	Lg	TD
1990	KC	N	1	-1	-1.0	-1	0
1993			5	34	6.8	13	0
Career			6	33	5.5	13	0

Gordon Jones

Year	Team		Att	Yds	Avg	Lg	TD
1979	TB	N	1	12	12.0	12	0
1980			1	-10	-10.0	-10	0
Career			2	2	1.0	12	0

Greg Jones

Year	Team		Att	Yds	Avg	Lg	TD
1970	BUF	N	31	113	3.6	17	1
1971			16	53	3.3	11	0
Career			47	166	3.5	17	1

Harry Jones

Year	Team		Att	Yds	Avg	Lg	TD
1967	PHI	N	8	17	2.1	6	0
1968			22	24	1.1	10	0
1969			1	0	0.0	0	0
1970			13	44	3.4	16	0
Career			44	85	1.9	16	0

Hassan Jones

Year	Team		Att	Yds	Avg	Lg	TD
1986	MIN	N	1	14	14.0	14	0
1988			1	7	7.0	7	0
1989			1	37	37.0	37	0
1990			1	-7	-7.0	-7	0
1992			1	1	1.0	1	0
Career			5	52	10.4	37	0

Harvey Jones

Year	Team		Att	Yds	Avg	Lg	TD
1944	CLE	N	38	133	3.5	36t	1
1945			8	15	1.9	5	0
Career			46	148	3.2	36t	1

Henry Jones

Year	Team		Att	Yds	Avg	Lg	TD
1969	DEN	A	1	3	3.0	3	0

Homer Jones

Year	Team		Att	Yds	Avg	Lg	TD
1965	NYG	N	1	17	17.0	17	0
1966			5	43	8.6	11	0
1967			5	60	12.0	46t	1
1968			3	18	6.0	11	0
1969			3	8	2.7	9	0
Career			17	146	8.6	46t	1

James Jones

Year	Team		Att	Yds	Avg	Lg	TD
1980	DAL	N	41	135	3.3	9	0
1981			34	183	5.4	59t	1
1984			8	13	1.6	6	0
1985			1	0	0.0	0	0
Career			84	331	3.9	59t	1
Playoffs			18	84	4.7		1

James Jones

Year	Team		Att	Yds	Avg	Lg	TD
1983	DET	N	135	475	3.5	18	6
1984			137	532	3.9	34	3
1985			244	886	3.6	29	6
1986			252	903	3.6	39	8
1987			96	342	3.6	19	0
1988			96	314	3.3	13	0
1990	SEA	N	5	20	4.0	5	0

James Jones *continued*

Year	Team		Att	Yds	Avg	Lg	TD
1991			45	154	3.4	22	3
Career			1010	3626	3.6	39	26
Playoffs			10	33	3.3		0

James Jones

Year	Team		Att	Yds	Avg	Lg	TD
1993	CLE	N	2	2	1.0	1t	1
1994			1	0	0.0	0	0
Career			3	2	0.7	1t	1

Jim Jones

Year	Team		Att	Yds	Avg	Lg	TD
1946	DET	N	3	3	1.0	4	0

Jimmie Lee Jones

Year	Team		Att	Yds	Avg	Lg	TD
1974	DET	N	32	147	4.6	21	1

Jimmy Jones

Year	Team		Att	Yds	Avg	Lg	TD
1965	CHI	N	2	13	6.5	7	0
1966			1	-7	-7.0	-7	0
1967			4	19	4.8	24	0
1968	DEN	A	1	-1	-1.0	-1	0
Career			8	24	3.0	24	0

J.J. Jones

Year	Team		Att	Yds	Avg	Lg	TD
1975	NYJ	N	9	59	6.6	19	0

Joey Jones

Year	Team		Att	Yds	Avg	Lg	TD
1986	ATL	N	1	7	7.0	7	0

Johnny Jones

Year	Team		Att	Yds	Avg	Lg	TD
1980	NYJ	N	2	5	2.5	7	0
1981			2	0	0.0	5	0
1982			1	2	2.0	2	0
1983			4	10	2.5	9	0
Career			9	17	1.9	9	0

June Jones

Year	Team		Att	Yds	Avg	Lg	TD
1978	ATL	N	10	-3	-0.3	17	0
1979			6	19	3.2	9	0
1981			1	-1	-1.0	-1	0
Career			17	15	0.9	17	0

Keith Jones

Year	Team		Att	Yds	Avg	Lg	TD
1989	CLE	N	43	160	3.7	15	1

Keith Jones

Year	Team		Att	Yds	Avg	Lg	TD
1989	ATL	N	52	202	3.9	19	6
1990			49	185	3.8	22	0
1991			35	126	3.6	14	0
1992			79	278	3.5	26	0
Career			215	791	3.7	26	6

Kim Jones

Year	Team		Att	Yds	Avg	Lg	TD
1976	NO	N	6	21	3.5	10	0
1977			8	23	2.9	8	0
1978			9	31	3.4	8	0
1979			3	5	1.7	3	0
Career			26	80	3.1	10	0

Larry Jones

Year	Team		Att	Yds	Avg	Lg	TD
1977	WAS	N	1	1	1.0	1	0
1978	SF	N	1	-9	-9.0	-9	0
Career			2	-8	-4.0	1	0

Mike Jones

Year	Team		Att	Yds	Avg	Lg	TD
1983	MIN	N	1	9	9.0	9	0
1984			4	45	11.3	36	0
1985			2	6	3.0	6	0
Career			7	60	8.6	36	0

Spike Jones

Year	Team		Att	Yds	Avg	Lg	TD
1972	BUF	N	2	18	9.0	10	0
1973			1	0	0.0	0	0
1975	PHI	N	1	-1	-1.0	-1	0
Career			4	17	4.3	10	0

Steve Jones

Year	Team		Att	Yds	Avg	Lg	TD
1973	BUF	N	3	9	3.0	7	0
1975	STL	N	54	275	5.1	23	2
1976			113	451	4.0	19	8
1977			24	77	3.2	18	3
1978			105	392	3.7	17	2
Career			299	1204	4.0	23	15
Playoffs			6	28	4.7		1

Thurman Jones

Year	Team		Att	Yds	Avg	Lg	TD
1941	BKN	N	1	3	3.0	3	0
1942			1	2	2.0	2	0
Career			2	5	2.5	3	0

Tony Jones

Year	Team		Att	Yds	Avg	Lg	TD
1990	HOU	N	1	-2	-2.0	-2	0

Victor Jones

Year	Team		Att	Yds	Avg	Lg	TD
1990	HOU	N	14	75	5.4	14	0

Willie Jones

Year	Team		Att	Yds	Avg	Lg	TD
1962	BUF	A	4	17	4.3	10	0

Buford Jordan

Year	Team		Att	Yds	Avg	Lg	TD
1986	NO	N	68	207	3.0	10	1
1987			12	36	3.0	8t	2
1988			19	115	6.1	44	0
1989			38	179	4.7	32	3
1991			47	150	3.2	25	2
Career			184	687	3.7	44	8
Playoffs			4	3	0.8		0

Charles Jordan

Year	Team		Att	Yds	Avg	Lg	TD
1994	GB	N	1	5	5.0	5	0

Donald Jordan

Year	Team		Att	Yds	Avg	Lg	TD
1984	CHI	N	11	70	6.4	29	0

Jeff Jordan

Year	Team		Att	Yds	Avg	Lg	TD
1970	LA	N	10	50	5.0	10	0

Randy Jordan

Year	Team		Att	Yds	Avg	Lg	TD
1993	LARI	N	12	33	2.8	12	0
1995	JAC	N	21	62	3.0	10	0
Career			33	95	2.9	12	0

Steve Jordan

Year	Team		Att	Yds	Avg	Lg	TD
1984	MIN	N	1	4	4.0	4t	1

Tony Jordan

Year	Team		Att	Yds	Avg	Lg	TD
1988	PHX	N	61	160	2.6	12	3
1989			83	211	2.5	15	2
Career			144	371	2.6	15	5

James Joseph

Year	Team		Att	Yds	Avg	Lg	TD
1991	PHI	N	135	440	3.3	24	3
1993			39	140	3.6	12	0
1994			60	203	3.4	34t	1
1995	CIN	N	16	40	2.5	8	0
Career			250	823	3.3	34t	4

Les Josephson

Year	Team		Att	Yds	Avg	Lg	TD
1964	LA	N	96	451	4.7	75	3
1965			71	225	3.2	18	0
1966			14	97	6.9	14	0
1967			178	800	4.5	27	4
1969			124	461	3.7	17	0
1970			150	640	4.3	23	5
1971			99	449	4.5	57	3
1972			18	75	4.2	13	0
1973			36	174	4.8	14	2
1974			11	35	3.2	8	0
Career			797	3407	4.3	75	17
Playoffs			19	32	1.7		0

Yonel Jourdain

Year	Team		Att	Yds	Avg	Lg	TD
1994	BUF	N	17	56	3.3	16	0
1995			8	31	3.9	19	0
Career			25	87	3.5	19	0

Terry Joyce

Year	Team		Att	Yds	Avg	Lg	TD
1976	STL	N	1	0	0.0	0	0
1977			1	-13	-13.0	-13	0
Career			2	-13	-6.5	0	0

Willie Joyner

Year	Team		Att	Yds	Avg	Lg	TD
1984	HOU	N	14	22	1.6	9	0

Sonny Jurgensen

Year	Team		Att	Yds	Avg	Lg	TD
1957	PHI	N	10	-3	-0.3	8	2
1958			1	1	1.0	1	0
1960			4	5	1.3	9	0
1961			20	27	1.4	14	0

Sonny Jurgensen *continued*

Year	Team		Att	Yds	Avg	Lg	TD
1962			17	44	2.6	30	2
1963			13	38	2.9	13	1
1964	WAS	N	27	57	2.1	24	3
1965			17	23	1.4	27t	2
1966			12	14	1.2	16	0
1967			15	46	3.1	21	2
1968			8	21	2.6	11	1
1969			17	156	9.2	33	1
1970			6	39	6.5	14	1
1971			3	29	9.7	11	0
1972			4	-5	-1.3	0	0
1973			3	7	2.3	7	0
1974			4	-6	-1.5	0	0
Career			181	493	2.7	33	15

Charlie Justice

Year	Team		Att	Yds	Avg	Lg	TD
1950	WAS	N	59	285	4.8	71	0
1952			36	129	3.6	26	0
1953			115	616	5.4	43	2
1954			56	254	4.5	50t	1
Career			266	1284	4.8	71	3

Ed Justice

Year	Team		Att	Yds	Avg	Lg	TD
1937	WAS	N	8	35	4.4		0
1938			10	11	1.1		0
1939			5	56	11.2		1
1940			3	34	11.3		0
1941			4	-8	-2.0	2	0
1942			3	-1	-0.3	2	0
Career			33	127	3.8	2	1
Playoffs			2	6	3.0		0

Paul Justin

Year	Team		Att	Yds	Avg	Lg	TD
1995	IND	N	3	1	0.3	2	0
1996			2	7	3.5	6	0
Career			5	8	1.6	6	0

Steve Juzwik

Year	Team		Att	Yds	Avg	Lg	TD
1942	WAS	N	15	75	5.0	39	2
1946	BUF	AA	71	455	6.4	68	3
1947			26	130	5.0		0
1948	CHI	AA	13	19	1.5		0
Career			125	679	5.4	68	5

Mike Kabealo

Year	Team		Att	Yds	Avg	Lg	TD
1944	CLE	N	47	152	3.2	11	1

Bob Kahler

Year	Team		Att	Yds	Avg	Lg	TD
1942	GB	N	8	4	0.5	13	0
1943			1	5	5.0	5	0
Career			9	9	1.0	13	0

George Kakasic

Year	Team		Att	Yds	Avg	Lg	TD
1936	PIT	N	1	-8	-8.0	-8	0

Tommy Kalmanir

Year	Team		Att	Yds	Avg	Lg	TD
1949	LA	N	29	218	7.5	51	1
1950			20	83	4.2	33	0
1951			16	61	3.8	23	0
1953	BAL	N	16	53	3.3	32	0
Career			81	415	5.1	51	1
Playoffs			2	0	0.0		0

Rick Kane

Year	Team		Att	Yds	Avg	Lg	TD
1977	DET	N	124	421	3.4	35	4
1978			44	153	3.5	19	2
1979			94	332	3.5	26t	4
1980			31	125	4.0	22	0
1981			77	332	4.3	20	2
1982			7	17	2.4	6	0
1983			4	19	4.8	9	0
1984	WAS	N	17	43	2.5	10	0
1985	DET	N	11	44	4.0	7	0
Career			409	1486	3.6	35	12

Danny Kanell

Year	Team		Att	Yds	Avg	Lg	TD
1996	NYG	N	7	6	0.9	13	0

Joe Kantor

Year	Team		Att	Yds	Avg	Lg	TD
1966	WAS	N	1	2	2.0	2	0

Sam Kaplan

Year	Team		Att	Yds	Avg	Lg	TD
1921	WAS	A					1

Joe Kapp

Year	Team		Att	Yds	Avg	Lg	TD
1967	MIN	N	27	167	6.2	24	2
1968			50	269	5.4	27	3
1969			22	104	4.7	18	0
1970	BOS	N	20	71	3.5	14	0
Career			119	611	5.1	27	5
Playoffs			27	160	5.9		2

George Karamatic

Year	Team		Att	Yds	Avg	Lg	TD
1938	WAS	N	50	185	3.7		0

Ken Karcher

Year	Team		Att	Yds	Avg	Lg	TD
1987	DEN	N	9	3	0.3	8	0

John Karcis

Year	Team		Att	Yds	Avg	Lg	TD
1932	BKN	N					1
1935			68	188	2.8		1
1936	PIT		89	272	3.1		2
1937			128	511	4.0		3
1938	PIT-NYG	N	89	212	2.4		4
1939	NYG	N	31	93	3.0		0
1943			12	25	2.1	7	0
Career			417	1301	3.1	7	11
Playoffs			3	3	1.0		0

Abe Karnofsky

Year	Team		Att	Yds	Avg	Lg	TD
1945	PHI	N	41	134	3.3	19t	2
1946	BOS	N	36	84	2.3	35t	2
Career			77	218	2.8	35t	4

Ed Karpowich

Year	Team		Att	Yds	Avg	Lg	TD
1937	PIT	N	1	15	15.0	15	0

Bill Karr

Year	Team		Att	Yds	Avg	Lg	TD
1936	CHIB	N	4	11	2.8		1
1937			1	10	10.0	10	0
1938			1	6	6.0	6	0
Career			6	27	4.5	10	1

Johnny Karras

Year	Team		Att	Yds	Avg	Lg	TD
1952	CHIC	N	24	42	1.8	17	0

John Karrs

Year	Team		Att	Yds	Avg	Lg	TD
1944	CLE	N	7	0	0.0	3	0

Tony Kaska

Year	Team		Att	Yds	Avg	Lg	TD
1936	BKN	N	9	29	3.2		1
1937			1	4	4.0	4	0
1938			2	1	0.5		0
Career			12	34	2.8	4	1

Mike Katolin

Year	Team		Att	Yds	Avg	Lg	TD
1987	CLE	N	1	0	0.0	0	0

Napoleon Kaufman

Year	Team		Att	Yds	Avg	Lg	TD
1995	OAK	N	108	490	4.5	28	1
1996			150	874	5.8	77	1
Career			258	1364	5.3	77	2

Tom Keane

Year	Team		Att	Yds	Avg	Lg	TD
1948	LA		7	16	2.3	3	0

Val Keckin

Year	Team		Att	Yds	Avg	Lg	TD
1962	SD	A	1	3	3.0	3	0

Joe Keeble

Year	Team		Att	Yds	Avg	Lg	TD
1937	CLE	N	12	40	3.3		0

Jack Keefer

Year	Team		Att	Yds	Avg	Lg	TD
1926	PRO	N					2

Rex Keeling

Year	Team		Att	Yds	Avg	Lg	TD
1968	CIN	A	1	10	10.0	10	0

Allen Keen

Year	Team		Att	Yds	Avg	Lg	TD
1937	PHI	N	34	154	4.5		0
1938			3	10	3.3		0
Career			37	164	4.4		0

Bob Keene

Year	Team		Att	Yds	Avg	Lg	TD
1943	DET	N	1	1	1.0	1	0
1944			9	26	2.9	7	0
1945			2	2	1.0	2	0
Career			12	29	2.4	7	0

Gary Keithley

Year	Team		Att	Yds	Avg	Lg	TD
1973	STL	N	8	29	3.6	18	0

Bill Kellagher

Year	Team		Att	Yds	Avg	Lg	TD
1946	CHI	AA	49	178	3.6	53t	3
1947			42	243	5.8		0
1948			33	97	2.9		1
Career			124	518	4.2	53t	4

Mark Kellar

Year	Team		Att	Yds	Avg	Lg	TD
1976	MIN	N	7	25	3.6	11	0
1977			7	15	2.1	9	0
1978			11	34	3.1	5	0
Career			25	74	3.0	11	0
Playoffs			2	7	3.5		0

Kenny Keller

Year	Team		Att	Yds	Avg	Lg	TD
1956	PHI	N	112	433	3.9	51t	4
1957			57	195	3.4	15	0
Career			169	628	3.7	51t	4

Larry Keller

Year	Team		Att	Yds	Avg	Lg	TD
1977	NYJ	N	1	25	25.0	25	0

Brian Kelley

Year	Team		Att	Yds	Avg	Lg	TD
1978	NYG	N	1	2	2.0		0

Ed Kelley

Year	Team		Att	Yds	Avg	Lg	TD
1949	LA	AA	1	-2	-2.0	-2	0

Frank Kelley

Year	Team		Att	Yds	Avg	Lg	TD
1927	CLE	N					2

Mike Kelley

Year	Team		Att	Yds	Avg	Lg	TD
1987	SD		4	17	4.3	10	0

Bill Kellogg

Year	Team		Att	Yds	Avg	Lg	TD
1924	FRA	N					3
1925	ROC	N					1
Career							4

Bobby Kellogg

Year	Team		Att	Yds	Avg	Lg	TD
1940	CHIC	N	9	31	3.4		0

Clarence Kellogg

Year	Team		Att	Yds	Avg	Lg	TD
1936	CHIC	N	66	164	2.5		0

Mike Kellogg

Year	Team		Att	Yds	Avg	Lg	TD
1966	DEN	A	6	3	0.5	5	0

Bill Kelly

Year	Team		Att	Yds	Avg	Lg	TD
1927	NYY	N					3
1928							1
1929	FRA	N					1
1930	BKN	N					1
Career							6

Bob Kelly

Year	Team		Att	Yds	Avg	Lg	TD
1947	LA	AA	51	205	4.0		2
1948			3	10	3.3	50	0
1949	BAL	AA	9	17	1.9		0
Career			63	232	3.7	50	2

Jim Kelly

Year	Team		Att	Yds	Avg	Lg	TD
1986	BUF	N	41	199	4.9	20	0
1987			29	133	4.6	24	0
1988			35	154	4.4	20	0
1989			29	137	4.7	19	2
1990			22	63	2.9	15	0
1991			20	45	2.3	12	1
1992			31	53	1.7	10	0
1993			36	102	2.8	17	0
1994			25	77	3.1	18	1
1995			17	20	1.2	17	0
1996			19	66	3.5	22	2
Career			304	1049	3.5	24	7
Playoffs			44	161	3.7		0

John Kelly

Year	Team		Att	Yds	Avg	Lg	TD
1933	BKN	N					2
1934							1
1937			16	29	1.8		0
Career			16	29	1.8		3

Leroy Kelly

Year	Team		Att	Yds	Avg	Lg	TD
1964	CLE	N	6	12	2.0	5	0
1965			37	139	3.8	16	0
1966			209	1141	5.5	70t	15
1967			235	1205	5.1	42t	11
1968			248	1239	5.0	65	16
1969			196	817	4.2	31	9
1970			206	656	3.2	33t	6
1971			234	865	3.7	35	10
1972			224	811	3.6	18	4
1973			132	389	2.9	19	3
Career			1727	7274	4.2	70t	74
Playoffs			100	417	4.2		2

Jack Kemp

Year	Team		Att	Yds	Avg	Lg	TD
1957	PIT	N	3	-1	-0.3	2	0
1960	LA	A	90	-103	-1.1		8
1961	SD	A	43	105	2.4	23	6
1962	SD-BUF	A	20	84	4.2	28	2
1963	BUF	A	52	226	4.3	26	8
1964			37	124	3.4	14	5
1965			36	49	1.4	12	4
1966			40	130	3.3	26	5
1967			36	58	1.6	14	2
1969			37	124	3.4	13	0
Career			394	796	2.0	28	40
Playoffs			18	11	0.6		1

Jeff Kemp

Year	Team		Att	Yds	Avg	Lg	TD
1981	LA	N	2	9	4.5	7	0
1983	LARM	N	3	-2	-0.7	0	0
1984			34	153	4.5	23	1
1985			5	0	0.0	3	0
1986	SF	N	15	49	3.3	12	0
1987	SEA	N	5	9	1.8	12	0
1988			6	51	8.5	21	0
1989			1	0	0.0	0	0
1991	SEA-PHI	N	38	179	4.7	18	0
Career			109	448	4.1	23	1
Playoffs			1	2	2.0		0

Perry Kemp

Year	Team		Att	Yds	Avg	Lg	TD
1989	GB	N	5	43	8.6	14	0
1990			1	-1	-1.0	-1	0
Career			6	42	7.0	14	0

Herb Kempton

Year	Team		Att	Yds	Avg	Lg	TD
1921	CAN	A					1

Jim Kendrick

Year	Team		Att	Yds	Avg	Lg	TD
1925	BUF	N					1
1926							2
Career							3

Vince Kendrick

Year	Team		Att	Yds	Avg	Lg	TD
1974	ATL	N	17	71	4.2	17	0
1976	TB	N	1	3	3.0	3	0
Career			18	74	4.1	17	0

Bob Kennedy

Year	Team		Att	Yds	Avg	Lg	TD
1949	LA	AA	2	14	7.0		0

Bob Kennedy

Year	Team		Att	Yds	Avg	Lg	TD
1946	NY	AA	58	179	3.1		2
1947			44	258	5.9	78t	1
1948			33	90	2.7		1
1949	B-NY	AA	118	490	4.2		5
Career			253	1017	4.0	78t	9
Playoffs			8	6	0.8		0

Tom Kennedy

Year	Team		Att	Yds	Avg	Lg	TD
1966	NYG	N	5	16	3.2	10	0

Bill Kenney

Year	Team		Att	Yds	Avg	Lg	TD
1980	KC	N	8	8	1.0	4	0
1981			24	89	3.7	21	1
1982			13	40	3.1	12	0
1983			23	59	2.6	11	3
1984			9	-8	-0.9	1	0
1985			14	1	0.1	5	1
1986			18	0	0.0	9	0
1987			12	-2	-0.2	6	0
1988			2	4	2.0	2	0
Career			123	191	1.6	21	5

Year	Team		Att	Yds	Avg	Lg	TD

Dick Kercher

Year	Team		Att	Yds	Avg	Lg	TD
1954	DET	N	3	1	0.3	2	0

Ralph Kercheval

Year	Team		Att	Yds	Avg	Lg	TD
1935	BKN	N	34	89	2.6		0
1936			66	261	4.0		2
1937			48	84	1.8		1
1938			51	86	1.7		1
1939			34	99	2.9		0
1940			11	19	1.7		0
Career			244	638	2.6		4

Gary Kerkorian

Year	Team		Att	Yds	Avg	Lg	TD
1952	PIT	N	2	20	10.0	20	0
1954	BAL	N	22	36	1.6	11	1
1955			6	20	3.3	12	1
Career			30	76	2.5	20	2

Bill Kerr

Year	Team		Att	Yds	Avg	Lg	TD
1946	LA	AA	1	10	10.0	10	0

Mike Kerrigan

Year	Team		Att	Yds	Avg	Lg	TD
1983	NE	N	1	14	14.0	14	0

Merritt Kersey

Year	Team		Att	Yds	Avg	Lg	TD
1974	PHI	N	1	2	2.0	2	0

Ken Keuper

Year	Team		Att	Yds	Avg	Lg	TD
1947	GB	N	6	14	2.3	8	0

Bob Keyes

Year	Team		Att	Yds	Avg	Lg	TD
1960	OAK	A	1	7	7.0	7	0

Leroy Keyes

Year	Team		Att	Yds	Avg	Lg	TD
1969	PHI	N	121	361	3.0	28	3
1970			2	7	3.5	5	0
1973	KC	N	2	1	0.5	2	0
Career			125	369	3.0	28	3

Brady Keys

Year	Team		Att	Yds	Avg	Lg	TD
1961	PIT	N	6	14	2.3	11	0

Jon Keyworth

Year	Team		Att	Yds	Avg	Lg	TD
1974	DEN	N	81	374	4.6	30t	10
1975			182	725	4.0	34	3
1976			122	349	2.9	13	3
1977			83	311	3.7	16	1
1978			112	444	4.0	30	3
1979			81	323	4.0	17	1
1980			38	127	3.3	14	1
Career			699	2653	3.8	34	22
Playoffs			24	60	2.5		1

John Kidd

Year	Team		Att	Yds	Avg	Lg	TD
1986	BUF	N	1	0	0.0	0	0
1992	SD	N	2	-13	-6.5	0	0
1993			3	-13	-4.3	2t	1
1996	MIA	N	1	3	3.0	3	0
Career			7	-23	-3.3	3	1
Playoffs			1	18	18.0		0

Blair Kiel

Year	Team		Att	Yds	Avg	Lg	TD
1946	PIT	N	2	-2	-1.0	1	0
1986	IND	N	3	20	6.7	9	0
1987			4	30	7.5	16	0
1990	GB	N	5	9	1.8	4	1
1991			4	46	11.5	26	0
Career			18	103	5.7	26	1

George Kiick

Year	Team		Att	Yds	Avg	Lg	TD
1940	PIT	N	66	212	3.2		0
1945			15	45	3.0	9	1
Career			81	257	3.2	9	1

Jim Kiick

Year	Team		Att	Yds	Avg	Lg	TD
1968	MIA	A	165	621	3.8	25	4
1969			180	575	3.2	27	9
1970	MIA	N	191	658	3.4	56	6
1971			162	738	4.6	34	3
1972			137	521	3.8	26	5
1973			76	257	3.4	32	0
1974			86	274	3.2	15	1
1976	DEN	N	31	114	3.7	19	1

Jim Kiick continued

Year	Team		Att	Yds	Avg	Lg	TD
1977			1	1	1.0	1	0
Career			1029	3759	3.7	56	29
Playoffs			115	401	3.5		6

Charlie Killett

Year	Team		Att	Yds	Avg	Lg	TD
1963	NYG	N	11	36	3.3	8	0

Billy Kilmer

Year	Team		Att	Yds	Avg	Lg	TD
1961	SF	N	96	509	5.3	31	10
1962			93	478	5.1	35	5
1964			36	113	3.1	14	0
1966			3	23	7.7	13	0
1967	NO	N	20	142	7.1	31	1
1968			21	97	4.6	22	2
1969			11	18	1.6	12	0
1970			12	42	3.5	15	0
1971	WAS	N	17	5	0.3	3t	2
1972			3	-3	-1.0	1	0
1973			9	10	1.1	5	0
1974			6	27	4.5	10	0
1975			11	34	3.1	11	1
1976			13	-7	-0.5	2	0
1977			10	20	2.0	12	0
1978			1	1	1.0	1	0
Career			362	1509	4.2	35	21
Playoffs			9	41	4.6		0

John Kimbrough

Year	Team		Att	Yds	Avg	Lg	TD
1946	LA	AA	122	473	3.9		6
1947			131	562	4.3		8
1948			76	189	2.5		3
Career			329	1224	3.7		17

Billy Kinard

Year	Team		Att	Yds	Avg	Lg	TD
1956	CLE	N	1	27	27.0	27t	1

Todd Kinchen

Year	Team		Att	Yds	Avg	Lg	TD
1993	LARM	N	2	10	5.0	8	0
1994			1	44	44.0	44t	1
1995	STL	N	4	16	4.0	15	0
Career			7	70	10.0	44t	1

Keith Kinderman

Year	Team		Att	Yds	Avg	Lg	TD
1964	SD	A	24	111	4.6	22	0
Playoffs			4	14	3.5		0

Don Kindt

Year	Team		Att	Yds	Avg	Lg	TD
1947	CHIB	N	61	266	4.4	48	2
1948			54	189	3.5	66t	2
1949			41	118	2.9	13	0
1950			1	4	4.0	4	0
1951			2	5	2.5	3	0
1952			3	13	4.3	6	0
1954			10	-9	-0.9	10	0
Career			172	586	3.4	66t	4

Andy King

Year	Team		Att	Yds	Avg	Lg	TD
1921	AKR	A					1
1922	AKR	N					2
Career							3

Bruce King

Year	Team		Att	Yds	Avg	Lg	TD
1985	KC	N	28	83	3.0	9	0
1986	BUF	N	4	10	2.5	7	0
1987			9	28	3.1	8	0
Career			41	121	3.0	9	0

Claude King

Year	Team		Att	Yds	Avg	Lg	TD
1961	HOU	A	12	50	4.2	17	2
1962	BOS	A	21	144	6.9	71	1
Career			33	194	5.9	71	3

Emmett King

Year	Team		Att	Yds	Avg	Lg	TD
1954	CHIC	N	57	167	2.9	17	0

Horace King

Year	Team		Att	Yds	Avg	Lg	TD
1975	DET	N	61	260	4.3	26	2
1976			93	325	3.5	22	0
1977			155	521	3.4	35	1
1978			155	660	4.3	75t	4
1979			39	160	4.1	23	1
1980			18	57	3.2	8	1
1981			7	25	3.6	7	0

Horace King continued

Year	Team		Att	Yds	Avg	Lg	TD
1982			18	67	3.7	25	0
1983			3	6	2.0	4	0
Career			549	2081	3.8	75t	9
Playoffs			4	10	2.5		0

Kenny King

Year	Team		Att	Yds	Avg	Lg	TD
1979	HOU	N	3	9	3.0	4	0
1980	OAK	N	172	761	4.4	89t	4
1981			170	828	4.9	60	0
1982	LARI	N	69	264	3.8	21	2
1983			82	294	3.6	16	1
1984			67	254	3.8	18	0
1985			16	67	4.2	19	0
Career			579	2477	4.3	89t	7
Playoffs			66	213	3.2		1

Phil King

Year	Team		Att	Yds	Avg	Lg	TD
1958	NYG	N	83	316	3.8	38	1
1959			72	232	3.2	24	0
1960			26	97	3.7	30	0
1961			4	7	1.8	4	0
1962			108	460	4.3	20	2
1963			161	613	3.8	50t	3
1964	PIT	N	26	71	2.7	12	1
1965	MIN	N	72	356	4.9	21	0
1966			17	40	2.4	12	0
Career			569	2192	3.9	50t	7
Playoffs			37	99	2.7		0

Wayne Kingery

Year	Team		Att	Yds	Avg	Lg	TD
1949	BAL	AA	3	3	1.0		0

Larry Kinnebrew

Year	Team		Att	Yds	Avg	Lg	TD
1983	CIN	N	39	156	4.0	17	3
1984			154	623	4.0	23	9
1985			170	714	4.2	29	9
1986			131	519	4.0	39	8
1987			145	570	3.9	52	8
1989	BUF	N	131	533	4.1	25	6
1990			9	18	2.0	4	1
Career			779	3133	4.0	52	44
Playoffs			7	17	2.4		0

Jeff Kinney

Year	Team		Att	Yds	Avg	Lg	TD
1972	KC	N	38	122	3.2	16	1
1973			50	128	2.6	8	1
1974			63	249	4.0	21	0
1975			85	304	3.6	20	2
1976	KC-BUF	N	117	482	4.1	22	1
Career			353	1285	3.6	22	5

Carl Kinscherf

Year	Team		Att	Yds	Avg	Lg	TD
1943	NYG	N	49	77	1.6	10	1
1944			9	21	2.3	4	0
Career			58	98	1.7	10	1

Jack Kirby

Year	Team		Att	Yds	Avg	Lg	TD
1949	GB	N	3	6	2.0	8	0

Terry Kirby

Year	Team		Att	Yds	Avg	Lg	TD
1993	MIA	N	119	390	3.3	20	3
1994			60	233	3.9	30	2
1995			108	414	3.8	38	4
1996	SF	N	134	559	4.2	31	3
Career			421	1596	3.8	38	12
Playoffs			24	65	2.7		1

Mike Kirkland

Year	Team		Att	Yds	Avg	Lg	TD
1978	BAL	N	8	35	4.4	18	0

Frank Kirkleski

Year	Team		Att	Yds	Avg	Lg	TD
1927	POT	N					1
1929	ORA	N					1
1930	NEW	N					1
Career							3

Ben Kish

Year	Team		Att	Yds	Avg	Lg	TD
1943	P-P	N	22	50	2.3	11	0
1944	PHI	N	22	96	4.4	20	0
1945			9	82	9.1	22	0
1946			6	13	2.2	4	0
1947			3	-1	-0.3	-1	0
1948			10	106	10.6	66t	

Year	Team		Att	Yds	Avg	Lg	TD

Ben Kish *continued*

Year	Team		Att	Yds	Avg	Lg	TD
1949			2	-2	-1.0	0	0
Career			74	344	4.6	66t	1
Playoffs			1	6	6.0		0

Adolph Kissell

| 1942 | CHIB | N | 2 | -1 | -0.5 | 11 | 0 |

Vito Kissell

1949	BUF	AA	10	19	1.9		0
1950	BAL	N	2	6	3.0	7	0
Career			12	25	2.1	7	0

Paul Kittredge

| 1929 | BOS | N | | | | | 1 |

John Kitzmiller

| 1931 | NYG | N | | | | | 4 |

Lee Kizzire

| 1937 | DET | N | 7 | 20 | 2.9 | | 0 |

Bob Klein

1971	LA	N	3	21	7.0	13	0
1972			1	-7	-7.0	-7	0
Career			4	14	3.5	13	0

Ed Klewicki

1937	DET	N	10	53	5.3		0
1938			10	76	7.6		0
Career			20	129	6.5		0

Harry Kline

| Playoffs | | | 1 | 1 | 1.0 | 0 | |

David Klingler

1992	CIN	N	11	53	4.8	12	0
1993			41	282	6.9	29	0
1994			17	85	5.0	15	0
1996	OAK	N	5	34	6.8	14	0
Career			74	454	6.1	29	0

Don Klosterman

| 1952 | LA | N | 1 | -9 | -9.0 | -9 | 0 |

Mike Klotovich

| 1945 | NYG | N | 5 | 26 | 5.2 | 15 | 0 |

Pete Kmetovic

1946	PHI	N	5	30	6.0	27	0
1947	DET	N	14	23	1.6	6	0
Career			19	53	2.8	27	0

Jeff Knapple

| 1980 | DEN | N | 6 | 0 | 0.0 | 9 | 0 |

Johnny Knolla

1942	CHIC	N	15	43	2.9	14	0
1945			15	36	2.4	8	0
Career			30	79	2.6	14	0

Oscar Knop

1923	CHIB	N					1
1924							1
1925							1
1926							1
Career							4

Mickey Kobrosky

| 1937 | NYG | N | 13 | 41 | 3.2 | | 0 |

George Koch

1945	CLE	N	12	101	8.4	32	0
1947	BUF	AA	37	149	4.0		1
Career			49	250	5.1	32	1
Playoffs			2	1	0.5		0

Roger Kochman

| 1963 | BUF | A | 47 | 232 | 4.9 | 48 | 0 |

Bob Koehler

1920	DEC	A					2
1921	CHIC	A					1
1922	CHIC	N					2
1924							1

Bob Koehler *continued*

| 1925 | | | | | | | 4 |
| Career | | | | | | | 10 |

Matt Kofler

1982	BUF	N	2	21	10.5	12	0
1983			4	25	6.3	11	0
1984			10	80	8.0	19	0
1985	IND	N	4	33	8.3	23	1
Career			20	159	8.0	23	1

Jeff Komlo

1979	DET	N	30	107	3.6	16	2
1981			6	3	0.5	5	0
1983	TB	N	2	11	5.5	11	0
Career			38	121	3.2	16	2

Mark Konecny

| 1987 | MIA | N | 6 | 46 | 7.7 | 19 | 0 |

Dave Kopay

1964	SF	N	75	271	3.6	18	0
1965			28	81	2.9	10	2
1966			47	204	4.3	32t	0
1967			6	21	3.5	10	0
1968	DET	N	53	207	3.9	22	0
1969	WAS	N	3	4	1.3	3	0
1970			13	49	3.8	14	0
1972	GB	N	10	39	3.9	20	0
Career			235	876	3.7	32t	3

Bernie Kosar

1985	CLE	N	26	-12	-0.5	10	1
1986			24	19	0.8	17	0
1987			15	22	1.5	7	1
1988			12	-1	-0.1	13	1
1989			30	70	2.3	23	1
1990			10	13	1.3	5	0
1991			26	74	2.8	14	0
1992			5	12	2.4	8	0
1993	CLE-DAL	N	23	26	1.1	10	0
1994	MIA	N	1	17	17.0	17	0
1995			7	19	2.7	14	1
1996			1	6	6.0	6	0
Career			180	265	1.5	23	5
Playoffs			16	31	1.9		0

Stan Kosel

1938	BKN	N	13	43	3.3		0
1939			2	6	3.0		0
Career			15	49	3.3		0

Gary Kosins

1972	CHI	N	3	5	1.7	3	0
1973			24	65	2.7	7	0
1974			8	30	3.8	12	1
Career			35	100	2.9	12	1

Stan Koslowski

| 1946 | MIA | AA | 18 | 61 | 3.4 | | 0 |

Stan Kostka

| 1935 | BKN | N | 63 | 249 | 4.0 | | 0 |

Eddie Kotal

1926	GB	N					1
1927							1
1928							2
Career							4

Doug Kotar

1974	NYG	N	106	396	3.7	53t	4
1975			122	378	3.1	46t	6
1976			185	731	4.0	24	3
1977			132	480	3.6	32	2
1978			149	625	4.2	46	1
1979			160	616	3.9	32	3
1981			46	154	3.3	18	1
Career			900	3380	3.8	53t	20

Ed Kovac

1960	BAL	N	4	1	0.3	5	0
1962	NY	A	3	5	1.7	3	0
Career			7	6	0.9	5	0

Walt Kowalczyk

1958	PHI	N	17	43	2.5	17	1
1959			26	37	1.4	6	0
1960	DAL	N	50	156	3.1	34	1
1961	OAK	A	10	28	2.8	18	0
Career			103	264	2.6	34	2

Nick Kowgios

| 1987 | DET | N | 1 | 2 | 2.0 | 2 | 0 |

Ernie Koy

1965	NYG	N	35	174	5.0	27	0
1966			66	146	2.2	13	0
1967			146	704	4.8	61	4
1968			89	394	4.4	26	3
1969			76	300	3.9	24	2
1970			2	5	2.5	7	0
Career			414	1723	4.2	61	9

Ted Koy

| 1972 | BUF | N | 1 | 9 | 9.0 | 9 | 0 |

Glen Kozlowski

| 1988 | CHI | N | 1 | 3 | 3.0 | 3 | 0 |

George Kracum

| 1941 | BKN | N | 52 | 169 | 3.3 | 17 | 3 |

Jerry Krall

| 1950 | DET | N | 3 | 0 | 0.0 | 6 | 0 |

Erik Kramer

1987	ATL	N	2	10	5.0	11	0
1991	DET	N	35	26	0.7	12	1
1992			12	34	2.8	11	0
1993			10	5	0.5	4	0
1994	CHI	N	6	-2	-0.3	2	0
1995			35	39	1.1	11	1
1996			8	4	0.5	3	0
Career			108	116	1.1	12	2
Playoffs			5	5	1.0		0

Ron Kramer

1961	GB	N	5	13	2.6	12	0
1962			1	-4	-4.0	-4	0
Career			6	9	1.5	12	0

Tommy Kramer

1977	MIN	N	10	3	0.3	8	0
1978			1	10	10.0	10	0
1979			32	138	4.3	20	1
1980			31	115	3.7	13	1
1981			10	13	1.3	8	0
1982			21	77	3.7	18t	3
1983			8	3	0.4	8	0
1984			15	9	0.6	14	0
1985			27	54	2.0	11	0
1986			23	48	2.1	13	1
1987			10	44	4.4	15	2
1988			14	8	0.6	5	0
1989			12	9	0.8	5	0
Career			214	531	2.5	20	8
Playoffs			11	18	1.6		0

Larry Krause

1970	GB	N	2	13	6.5	12	0
1971			3	-6	-2.0	2	0
1973			1	8	8.0	8	0
Career			6	15	2.5	12	0

Max Krause

1933	NYG	N	33	61	1.8		0
1934			26	69	2.7		0
1935			32	121	3.8		0
1936			11	37	3.4		0
1937	WAS	N	21	47	2.2		1
1938			25	214	8.6		2
1939			3	23	7.7		0
1940			4	21	5.3		0
Career			155	593	3.8		3
Playoffs			3	7	2.3		1

Paul Krause

| 1972 | MIN | N | 1 | 0 | 0.0 | 0 | 0 |

Year	Team		Att	Yds	Avg	Lg	TD

Barry Krauss
| 1983 | BAL | N | 1 | -1 | -1.0 | -1 | 0 |

Steve Kreider
1979	CIN	N	2	0	0.0	0	0
1981			1	21	21.0	21	0
1983			1	2	2.0	2	0
Career			4	23	5.8	21	0

Rich Kreitling
1960	CLE	N	2	-17	-8.5		0
1961			0	4		4L	0
Career			2	-13	-6.5	4L	0

Keith Krepfle
| 1980 | PHI | N | 1 | 2 | 2.0 | 2 | 0 |

Al Kreuz
| 1926 | PHI | A | | | | | 1 |

Dave Krieg
1981	SEA	N	11	56	5.1	29	1
1982			6	-3	-0.5	4	0
1983			16	55	3.4	10t	2
1984			46	186	4.0	37t	3
1985			35	121	3.5	17	1
1986			35	122	3.5	19	1
1987			36	155	4.3	17	2
1988			24	64	2.7	17	0
1989			40	160	4.0	18	0
1990			32	115	3.6	25	0
1991			13	59	4.5	24	0
1992	KC	N	37	74	2.0	17	2
1993			21	24	1.1	20	0
1994	DET	N	23	35	1.5	15	0
1995	ARI	N	19	29	1.5	17	0
1996	CHI	N	16	12	0.8	2	1
Career			410	1264	3.1	37t	13
Playoffs			17	20	1.2		1

Jim Krieg
| 1972 | DEN | N | 1 | 63 | 63.0 | 63 | 0 |

Mike Kruczek
1976	PIT	N	18	106	5.9	22t	2
1977			1	0	0.0	0	0
1978			5	7	1.4	8	0
1979			4	20	5.0	22	0
1980	WAS	N	9	5	0.6	5	0
Career			37	138	3.7	22t	2
Playoffs			1	-3	-3.0		0

Larry Krutko
1958	PIT	N	4	6	1.5	5	0
1959			75	226	3.0	12	4
1960			17	99	5.8	18	0
Career			96	331	3.4	18	4

Gary Kubiak
1983	DEN	N	4	17	4.3	8	1
1984			9	27	3.0	17	1
1985			1	6	6.0	6	0
1986			6	22	3.7	10	0
1987			1	3	3.0	3	0
1988			17	65	3.8	15	0
1989			15	35	2.3	10	0
1990			9	52	5.8	18	0
1991			3	11	3.7	12	0
Career			65	238	3.7	18	2
Playoffs			5	19	3.8		1

Waddy Kuehl
1920	RI	A					2
1921	DET	A					1
1922	BUF	N					2
1923	RI	N					2
Career							7

Joe Kulbacki
| 1960 | BUF | A | 41 | 108 | 2.6 | | 1 |

Vic Kulbitski
| 1946 | BUF | AA | 97 | 605 | 6.2 | 69 | 2 |
| 1947 | | | 56 | 249 | 4.4 | | 1 |

Vic Kulbitski *continued*
1948			40	152	3.8		0
Career			193	1006	5.2	69	3
Playoffs			2	1	0.5		0

Terry Kunz
| 1976 | OAK | N | 4 | 33 | 8.3 | 11 | 0 |

Craig Kupp
| 1991 | PHX | N | 1 | 5 | 5.0 | 5 | 0 |

Ralph Kurek
1965	CHI	N	1	0	0.0	0	0
1966			52	179	3.4	12	1
1967			37	112	3.0	13	0
1968			17	95	5.6	23t	1
1969			8	24	3.0	6	0
1970			6	24	4.0	11	0
Career			121	434	3.6	23t	2

Rod Kush
| 1981 | BUF | N | 1 | -6 | -6.0 | -6 | 0 |

Johnny Kusko
1936	PHI	N	49	209	4.3		1
1937			17	27	1.6		0
Career			66	236	3.6		1

Lou Kusserow
1949	B-NY	AA	39	136	3.5		0
1950	NYY	N	1	6	6.0	6	0
Career			40	142	3.5	6	0

Mal Kutner
1946	CHIC	N	1	-1	-1.0	-1	0
1948			5	50	10.0	32t	1
1949			5	10	2.0	4	0
Career			11	59	5.4	32t	1

Ted Kwalick
1970	SF		3	65	21.7	45	0
1971			6	62	10.3	28	0
1972			5	11	2.2	10	0
1973			5	37	7.4	20	0
Career			19	175	9.2	45	0
Playoffs			1	2	2.0		0

John Kyle
| 1923 | CLE | N | | | | | 1 |

Steve Lach
1942	CHIC	N	30	97	3.2	9	0
1946	PIT	N	42	111	2.6	14	5
1947			120	372	3.1	19	8
Career			192	580	3.0	19	13

Rick Lackman
| 1935 | PHI | N | 22 | 56 | 2.5 | | |

Ken Lacy
1984	KC	N	46	165	3.6	24t	2
1985			6	21	3.5	6	0
1987			14	49	3.5	17	0
Career			66	235	3.6	24t	2

Jeff Lageman
| 1989 | NYJ | N | 1 | -5 | -5.0 | -5 | 0 |

Morris LaGrand
| 1975 | KC | N | 13 | 38 | 2.9 | 11 | 1 |

Thomas Lahey
| 1946 | CHI | AA | 1 | -2 | -2.0 | -2 | 0 |

Warren Lahr
1949	CLE	AA	9	36	4.0		1
1954	CLE	N	3	18	6.0	14	0
Career			12	54	4.5	14	1
Playoffs			1	7	7.0		0

Scott Laidlaw
1975	DAL	N	3	10	3.3	10	0
1976			94	424	4.5	28	3
1977			9	15	1.7	8	0
1978			75	312	4.2	59	3

Scott Laidlaw *continued*
1979			69	236	3.4	15	3
1980	NYG	N	5	10	2.0	3	0
Career			255	1007	3.9	59	9
Playoffs			33	101	3.1		3

Jim Laird
1921	ROC-CAN	A					5
1922	BUF	N					3
1925	PRO	N					3
Career							11

Bill Lajousky
| 1936 | PIT | N | 1 | 1 | 1.0 | 1 | 0 |

Peter Lamana
| 1946 | CHI | AA | 6 | 21 | 3.5 | | 0 |

Brad Lamb
| **Playoffs** | | | 1 | 16 | 16.0 | | 0 |

Roddy Lamb
1925	RI	N					2
1926	CHIC	N					1
1927							1
Career							4

Ron Lamb
1968	DEN-CIN	A	39	107	2.7	17	0
1969	CIN	A	5	8	1.6	7	0
1970	CIN	N	6	35	5.8	16	0
1971			5	13	2.6	7	0
Career			55	163	3.0	17	0

Curly Lambeau
1921	GB	A					2
1922	GB	N					3
1923							1
1927							2
Career							8

Pete Lammons
| 1971 | NYJ | N | 0 | 3 | | 3L | 0 |

Daryle Lamonica
1963	BUF	A	9	8	0.9	7	0
1964			55	289	5.3	18	6
1965			10	30	3.0	10	1
1966			9	6	0.7	14	0
1967	OAK	A	22	110	5.0	26	4
1968			19	98	5.2	28	1
1969			13	36	2.8	12	1
1970	OAK	N	8	24	3.0	13	0
1971			4	16	4.0	13	0
1972			10	33	3.3	14	0
1973			5	-7	-1.4	6	0
1974			2	-3	-1.5	0	0
Career			166	640	3.9	28	14
Playoffs			9	25	2.8		1

Dan Land
| 1987 | TB | N | 9 | 20 | 2.2 | 6 | 0 |

Walt Landers
1978	GB	N	7	40	5.7	10	0
1979			17	41	2.4	14	0
Career			24	81	3.4	14	0

Sean Landeta
| 1996 | STL | N | 2 | 0 | 0.0 | 0 | 0 |

Greg Landry
1968	DET	N	7	39	5.6	14	1
1969			33	243	7.4	26	1
1970			35	350	10.0	76	1
1971			76	530	7.0	52	3
1972			81	524	6.5	38	9
1973			42	267	6.4	18	2
1974			22	95	4.3	19	1
1975			20	92	4.6	14	0
1976			43	234	5.4	28	1
1977			25	99	4.0	13	0
1978			5	29	5.8	19	0
1979	BAL	N	31	115	3.7	19	0
1980			7	26	3.7	14	1

Greg Landry *continued*

Year	Team		Att	Yds	Avg	Lg	TD
1981			1	11	11.0	11	0
1984	CHI	N	2	1	0.5	1t	1
Career			430	2655	6.2	76	21
Playoffs			3	15	5.0		0

Tom Landry

Year	Team		Att	Yds	Avg	Lg	TD
1949	B-NY	AA	19	91	4.8		0
1952	NYG	N	7	40	5.7	8	1
Career			26	131	5.0	8	1
Playoffs			3	-2	-0.7		0

Mort Landsberg

Year	Team		Att	Yds	Avg	Lg	TD
1941	PHI	N	23	69	3.0	33	0
1947	LA	AA	2	-11	-5.5		0
Career			25	58	2.3	33	0

Eric Lane

Year	Team		Att	Yds	Avg	Lg	TD
1981	SEA	N	8	22	2.8	5	0
1983			3	1	0.3	7	0
1984			80	299	3.7	40t	4
1985			14	32	2.3	12	0
1986			6	11	1.8	4	0
1987			13	40	3.1	7	0
Career			124	405	3.3	40t	4
Playoffs			4	17	4.3		0

Gary Lane

Year	Team		Att	Yds	Avg	Lg	TD
1967	CLE	N	2	21	10.5	12	0

MacArthur Lane

Year	Team		Att	Yds	Avg	Lg	TD
1968	STL	N	23	74	3.2	11	0
1969			25	93	3.7	13	1
1970			206	977	4.7	75	11
1971			150	592	3.9	40t	3
1972	GB	N	177	821	4.6	41	3
1973			170	528	3.1	20	1
1974			137	362	2.6	20	3
1975	KC	N	79	311	3.9	39	2
1976			162	542	3.3	20	5
1977			25	79	3.2	9	1
1978			52	277	5.3	30	0
Career			1206	4656	3.9	75	30
Playoffs			14	56	4.0		0

David Lang

Year	Team		Att	Yds	Avg	Lg	TD
1992	LARM	N	33	203	6.2	71	5
1993			9	29	3.2	28	0
1994			6	34	5.7	17	0
1995	DAL	N	1	7	7.0	7	0
Career			49	273	5.6	71	5

Gene Lang

Year	Team		Att	Yds	Avg	Lg	TD
1984	DEN	N	8	42	5.3	15	2
1985			84	318	3.8	26	5
1986			29	94	3.2	14	1
1987			89	303	3.4	28	2
1988	ATL	N	53	191	3.6	19	0
1989			47	176	3.7	22	1
1990			9	24	2.7	9	0
Career			319	1148	3.6	28	11
Playoffs			29	138	4.8		2

Izzy Lang

Year	Team		Att	Yds	Avg	Lg	TD
1964	PHI	N	12	37	3.1	30	0
1965			10	25	2.5	8	1
1966			52	239	4.6	39	1
1967			101	336	3.3	21	2
1968			69	235	3.4	17	0
1969	LA	N	1	1	1.0	1	0
Career			245	873	3.6	39	4

Irv Langhoff

Year	Team		Att	Yds	Avg	Lg	TD
1922	RAC	N					1

Reggie Langhorne

Year	Team		Att	Yds	Avg	Lg	TD
1986	CLE	N	1	-11	-11.0	-11	0
1988			2	26	13.0	20t	1
1989			5	19	3.8	18	0
1992	IND	N	1	-7	-7.0	-7	0
Career			9	27	3.0	20t	1
Playoffs			2	-1	-0.5		0

Jim Lankas

Year	Team		Att	Yds	Avg	Lg	TD
1943	GB	N	2	2	1.0	1	0

Grenny Lansdell

Year	Team		Att	Yds	Avg	Lg	TD
1940	NYG	N	7	9	1.3		0

Ralph Lanum

Year	Team		Att	Yds	Avg	Lg	TD
1920	DEC	A					1
1923	CHIB	N					1
Career							2

Bob Laraba

Year	Team		Att	Yds	Avg	Lg	TD
1960	LA	A	4	7	1.8		0
1961	SD	A	5	5	1.0	9	0
Career			9	12	1.3	9	0

Steve Largent

Year	Team		Att	Yds	Avg	Lg	TD
1976	SEA	N	4	-14	-3.5	7	0
1980			1	2	2.0	2	0
1981			6	47	7.8	15	1
1982			1	8	8.0	8	0
1984			2	10	5.0	6	0
1987			2	33	16.5	21	0
1988			1	-3	-3.0	-3	0
Career			17	83	4.9	21	1
Playoffs			1	-2	-2.0		0

Jack Larscheid

Year	Team		Att	Yds	Avg	Lg	TD
1960	OAK	A	94	397	4.2	87t	1
1961			6	3	0.5	7	0
Career			100	400	4.0	87t	1

Greg Larson

Year	Team		Att	Yds	Avg	Lg	TD
1966	NYG	N	0	-2		L-2	0

Paul Larson

Year	Team		Att	Yds	Avg	Lg	TD
1957	CHIC	N	8	12	1.5	8	0

Pete Larson

Year	Team		Att	Yds	Avg	Lg	TD
1967	WAS	N	25	84	3.4	34	1
1968			44	132	3.0	16	1
Career			69	216	3.1	34	2

Yale Lary

Year	Team		Att	Yds	Avg	Lg	TD
1953	DET	N	1	21	21.0	21	0
1956			1	10	10.0	10	0
1957			1	32	32.0	32	0
1958			1	2	2.0	2	0
1959			1	18	18.0	18	0
1960			1	19	19.0	19	0
1961			1	14	14.0	14	0
1963			1	26	26.0	26	0
1964			2	11	5.5	9	0
Career			10	153	15.3	32	0

Jim Lash

Year	Team		Att	Yds	Avg	Lg	TD
1976	SF	N	3	5	1.7	8	0

Derrick Lassic

Year	Team		Att	Yds	Avg	Lg	TD
1993	DAL	N	75	269	3.6	15	3
Playoffs			3	7	2.3		0

Kwamie Lassiter

Year	Team		Att	Yds	Avg	Lg	TD
1995	ARI	N	1	1	1.0	1	0

Jerry Latin

Year	Team		Att	Yds	Avg	Lg	TD
1975	STL	N	35	165	4.7	57t	1
1976			25	115	4.6	26	1
1977			56	208	3.7	17	2
1978	STL-LA	N	24	72	3.0	11	0
Career			140	560	4.0	57t	4
Playoffs			1	2	2.0		0

Tony Latone

Year	Team		Att	Yds	Avg	Lg	TD
1925	POT	N					7
1926							4
1928							3
1929	BOS	N					9
1930	PRO	N					3
Career							26

Chuck Latourette

Year	Team		Att	Yds	Avg	Lg	TD
1967	STL	N	2	23	11.5	27	0
1968			1	15	15.0	15	0
1970			2	38	19.0	33	0
1971			3	19	6.3	20	0
Career			8	95	11.9	33	0

Greg Latta

Year	Team		Att	Yds	Avg	Lg	TD
1976	CHI	N	2	-8	-4.0	-3	0

Johnny Lattner

Year	Team		Att	Yds	Avg	Lg	TD
1954	PIT	N	69	237	3.4	17	5

Hal Lauer

Year	Team		Att	Yds	Avg	Lg	TD
1922	RI	N					5

Babe Laufenberg

Year	Team		Att	Yds	Avg	Lg	TD
1988	SD	N	31	120	3.9	23	0
1990	DAL	N	2	6	3.0	5	0
Career			33	126	3.8	23	0

Henry Laughlin

Year	Team		Att	Yds	Avg	Lg	TD
1955	SF	N	20	58	2.9	14	0

Hank Lauricella

Year	Team		Att	Yds	Avg	Lg	TD
1952	DAL		19	55	2.9	13	0

Ted Laux

Year	Team		Att	Yds	Avg	Lg	TD
1943	P-P	N	9	23	2.6	12	0
1944	PHI	N	2	-1	-0.5	0	0
Career			11	22	2.0	12	0

Dante Lavelli

Year	Team		Att	Yds	Avg	Lg	TD
1946	CLE	AA	1	14	14.0	14	0
1948			1	9	9.0	9	0
Career			2	23	11.5	14	0
Playoffs			1	-5	-5.0		0

Robert Lavette

Year	Team		Att	Yds	Avg	Lg	TD
1985	DAL	N	13	34	2.6	10	0
1986			10	6	0.6	5	0
Career			23	40	1.7	10	0

Dennis Law

Year	Team		Att	Yds	Avg	Lg	TD
1978	CIN	N	1	-1	-1.0	-1	0

Hubbard Law

Year	Team		Att	Yds	Avg	Lg	TD
1942	PIT	N	1	6	6.0	6	0

Al Lawler

Year	Team		Att	Yds	Avg	Lg	TD
1948	CHIB	N	9	44	4.9	16	0

Amos Lawrence

Year	Team		Att	Yds	Avg	Lg	TD
1981	SF	N	13	48	3.7	14	1
1982			5	7	1.4	4	0
Career			18	55	3.1	14	1

Jimmy Lawrence

Year	Team		Att	Yds	Avg	Lg	TD
1936	CHIC	N	26	84	3.2		0
1937			19	60	3.2		1
1938			78	207	2.7		3
1939	CHIC-GB	N	7	6	0.9		0
Career			130	357	2.7		4

Larry Lawrence

Year	Team		Att	Yds	Avg	Lg	TD
1974	OAK	N	4	39	9.8	19	0
1975			2	-3	-1.5	-1	0
Career			6	36	6.0	19	0

Joe Laws

Year	Team		Att	Yds	Avg	Lg	TD
1934	GB	N					1
1935			24	63	2.6		1
1936			50	296	5.9		1
1937			74	310	4.2		1
1938			60	253	4.2		0
1939			55	162	2.9		2
1940			7	21	3.0		0
1941			21	58	2.8	10	0
1942			29	100	3.4	17	0
1943			43	232	5.4	31	0
1944			45	200	4.4	50	3
1945			16	82	5.1	20	0
Career			424	1777	4.2	50	9
Playoffs			21	112	5.3		0

Odell Lawson

Year	Team		Att	Yds	Avg	Lg	TD
1970	BOS	N	56	99	1.8	15	0
1971	NE	N	8	8	1.0	6	0
1973	NO	N	6	23	3.8	11	0
Career			70	130	1.9	15	0

Roger Lawson

Year	Team		Att	Yds	Avg	Lg	TD
1972	CHI	N	33	106	3.2	14	1
1973			24	70	2.9	12	0
Career			57	176	3.1	14	1

Pete Layden

Year	Team		Att	Yds	Avg	Lg	TD
1948	NY	AA	95	576	6.1		3
1949	B-NY	AA	19	96	5.1		0
Career			114	672	5.9		3
Playoffs			2	18	9.0		0

Bobby Layne

Year	Team		Att	Yds	Avg	Lg	TD
1948	CHIB	N	13	80	6.2	18	1
1949	NYB	N	54	196	3.6	27	3
1950	DET	N	56	250	4.5	30	4
1951			61	290	4.8	36	1
1952			94	411	4.4	29	1
1953			87	343	3.9	23	0
1954			30	119	4.0	34	2
1955			31	111	3.6	19	0
1956			46	169	3.7	20	5
1957			24	99	4.1	21	0
1958	DET-PIT	N	40	154	3.9	21	3
1959	PIT	N	33	181	5.5	21	2
1960			19	12	0.6	13	1
1961			8	11	1.4	9	0
1962			15	25	1.7	17	1
Career			611	2451	4.0	36	25
Playoffs			33	120	3.6		1

Bill Lazetich

Year	Team		Att	Yds	Avg	Lg	TD
1939	CLE	N	6	23	3.8		0
1942			3	19	6.3	18	1
Career			9	42	4.7	18	1

Pat Leahy

Year	Team		Att	Yds	Avg	Lg	TD
1988	NYJ	N	1	10	10.0	10	0

Robert Leahy

Year	Team		Att	Yds	Avg	Lg	TD
1971	PIT	N	1	-6	-6.0	-6	0

Roosevelt Leaks

Year	Team		Att	Yds	Avg	Lg	TD
1975	BAL	N	41	175	4.3	17	1
1976			118	445	3.8	42	7
1977			59	237	4.0	39	3
1978			83	266	3.2	11	2
1979			49	145	3.0	17	1
1980	BUF	N	67	219	3.3	15	2
1981			91	357	3.9	31	6
1982			97	405	4.2	17	5
1983			58	157	2.7	12	2
Career			663	2406	3.6	42	28
Playoffs			25	77	3.1		2

Eddie LeBaron

Year	Team		Att	Yds	Avg	Lg	TD
1952	WAS	N	43	164	3.8	32	2
1953			21	95	4.5	27	2
1955			37	190	5.1	25	4
1956			11	6	0.5	9	0
1957			20	-12	-0.6	11	0
1958			12	30	2.5	13	0
1959			13	7	0.5	15	0
1960	DAL	N	17	94	5.5	23	1
1961			20	72	3.6	21	0
1962			6	-1	-0.2	3	0
1963			2	5	2.5	4	0
Career			202	650	3.2	32	9

Mike LeBlanc

Year	Team		Att	Yds	Avg	Lg	TD
1987	NE	N	49	170	3.5	42	1

Bill Leckonby

Year	Team		Att	Yds	Avg	Lg	TD
1939	BKN	N	4	-1	-0.3		0
1940			19	53	2.8		0
1941			54	202	3.7	17	0
Career			77	254	3.3	17	0

Jim LeClair

Year	Team		Att	Yds	Avg	Lg	TD
1967	DEN	A	8	6	0.8	10	1
1968			12	40	3.3	12	0
Career			20	46	2.3	12	1

Terry LeCount

Year	Team		Att	Yds	Avg	Lg	TD
1981	MIN	N	3	51	17.0	38	0

Terry LeCount *continued*

Year	Team		Att	Yds	Avg	Lg	TD
1982			1	-3	-3.0	-3	0
1983			2	42	21.0	23	0
Career			6	90	15.0	38	0

Homer Ledbetter

Year	Team		Att	Yds	Avg	Lg	TD
1932	SI	N					2

Toy Ledbetter

Year	Team		Att	Yds	Avg	Lg	TD
1950	PHI	N	67	320	4.8	23	1
1953			41	120	2.9	32	1
1954			81	241	3.0	14	1
1955			21	48	2.3	7	0
Career			210	729	3.5	32	3

Hal Ledyard

Year	Team		Att	Yds	Avg	Lg	TD
1953	SF	N	1	3	3.0	3	0

Amp Lee

Year	Team		Att	Yds	Avg	Lg	TD
1992	SF	N	91	362	4.0	43	2
1993			72	230	3.2	13	1
1994	MIN		29	104	3.6	16	0
1995			69	371	5.4	66t	2
1996			51	161	3.2	12	0
Career			312	1228	3.9	66t	5
Playoffs			9	37	4.1		0

Bob Lee

Year	Team		Att	Yds	Avg	Lg	TD
1969	MIN	N	3	9	3.0	7	0
1970			10	20	2.0	10	1
1971			11	14	1.3	4t	1
1973	ATL	N	29	67	2.3	11	0
1974			19	99	5.2	17	1
1975	MIN	N	1	0	0.0	0	0
1976			2	2	1.0	2	0
1977			12	-8	-0.7	7	0
1979	LA	N	4	-5	-1.3	0	0
1980			1	-1	-1.0	-1	0
Career			92	197	2.1	17	3
Playoffs			8	22	2.8		0

David Lee

Year	Team		Att	Yds	Avg	Lg	TD
1968	BAL	N	3	12	4.0	21	0
1973			2	-16	-8.0	0	0
1976			1	-12	-12.0	-12	0
1977			2	-2	-1.0	0	0
Career			8	-18	-2.3	21	0

Dwight Lee

Year	Team		Att	Yds	Avg	Lg	TD
1968	SF-ATL	N	6	7	1.2	6	0

Jack Lee

Year	Team		Att	Yds	Avg	Lg	TD
1939	PIT	N	1	-11	-11.0	-11	0

Jacky Lee

Year	Team		Att	Yds	Avg	Lg	TD
1960	HOU	A	16	-57	-3.6		0
1961			8	36	4.5	9	0
1962			4	1	0.3	4	0
1963			2	9	4.5	8	0
1964	DEN	A	42	163	3.9	16	3
1965			2	1	0.5	2	0
1966	HOU	A	1	-3	-3.0	-3	0
1967	HOU-KC	A	6	-3	-0.5	7	0
1969	KC	A	1	3	3.0	3	0
Career			82	150	1.8	16	3

Kevin Lee

Year	Team		Att	Yds	Avg	Lg	TD
1995	NE	N	1	4	4.0	4	0

Ron Lee

Year	Team		Att	Yds	Avg	Lg	TD
1976	BAL	N	41	220	5.4	69t	1
1977			84	346	4.1	30	3
1978			81	374	4.6	24	1
Career			206	940	4.6	69t	5
Playoffs			11	46	4.2		2

Tuffy Leemans

Year	Team		Att	Yds	Avg	Lg	TD
1936	NYG	N	206	830	4.0		2
1937			144	429	3.0		0
1938			121	463	3.8		4
1939			128	429	3.4		3
1940			132	474	3.6		1
1941			100	332	3.3	26	4
1942			51	116	2.3	16	3

Tuffy Leemans *continued*

Year	Team		Att	Yds	Avg	Lg	TD
1943			37	69	1.9	13	0
Career			919	3142	3.4	26	17
Playoffs			41	93	2.3		1

Billy Lefear

Year	Team		Att	Yds	Avg	Lg	TD
1972	CLE	N	3	6	2.0	4	0
1973			26	135	5.2	43	0
1974			6	2	0.3	4	0
Career			35	143	4.1	43	0

Clyde LeForce

Year	Team		Att	Yds	Avg	Lg	TD
1947	DET	N	18	143	7.9	32	0
1948			28	86	3.1	18	1
1949			13	58	4.5	27	1
Career			59	287	4.9	32	2

Dick Leftridge

Year	Team		Att	Yds	Avg	Lg	TD
1966	PIT	N	8	17	2.1	5	2

Jake Leicht

Year	Team		Att	Yds	Avg	Lg	TD
1948	BAL	AA	20	88	4.4		1
1949			6	-7	-1.2		0
Career			26	81	3.1	5	1
Playoffs			6	31	5.2		0

Charlie Leigh

Year	Team		Att	Yds	Avg	Lg	TD
1968	CLE	N	23	144	6.3	20t	1
1971	MIA	N	5	15	3.0	7	0
1972			21	79	3.8	10	0
1973			22	134	6.1	34t	1
1974	GB	N	1	0	0.0	0	0
Career			72	372	5.2	34t	2
Playoffs			1	8	8.0		0

Walt LeJeune

Year	Team		Att	Yds	Avg	Lg	TD
1922	AKR	N					3

Frank LeMaster

Year	Team		Att	Yds	Avg	Lg	TD
1977	PHI	N	1	30	30.0	30	0
1978			2	29	14.5	23	0
1979			1	15	15.0	15	0
1980			2	21	10.5	11	0
1981			1	7	7.0	7	0
1982			1	-1	-1.0	-1	0
Career			8	101	12.6	30	0

Bruce Lemmerman

Year	Team		Att	Yds	Avg	Lg	TD
1968	ATL	N	1	0	0.0	0	0
1969			10	57	5.7	20	1
Career			11	57	5.2	20	1

Bobby Leo

Year	Team		Att	Yds	Avg	Lg	TD
1967	BOS	A	1	7	7.0	7	0

Jim Leonard

Year	Team		Att	Yds	Avg	Lg	TD
1934	PHI	N					1
1935			74	171	2.3		1
1936			33	72	2.2		0
Career			107	243	2.3		2

Jimmy Lesane

Year	Team		Att	Yds	Avg	Lg	TD
1952	CHIB	N	1	5	5.0	5	0

Darrell Lester

Year	Team		Att	Yds	Avg	Lg	TD
1964	MIN	N	4	18	4.5	7	0
1966	DEN	A	34	84	2.5	10	0
Career			38	102	2.7	10	0

Tim Lester

Year	Team		Att	Yds	Avg	Lg	TD
1993	LARM	N	11	74	6.7	26	0
1994			7	14	2.0	8	0
1995	PIT	N	5	9	1.8	3	1
1996			8	20	2.5	5t	1
Career			31	117	3.8	26	2
Playoffs			1	2	2.0		0

Dorsey Levens

Year	Team		Att	Yds	Avg	Lg	TD
1994	GB	N	5	15	3.0	5	0
1995			36	120	3.3	22	3
1996			121	566	4.7	24	5
Career			162	701	4.3	24	8
Playoffs			44	208	4.7		1

Mike Levenseller

Year	Team		Att	Yds	Avg	Lg	TD
1980	CIN	N	1	6	6.0	6	0

Jim Levey

Year	Team		Att	Yds	Avg	Lg	TD
1935	PIT	N	42	69	1.6		1
1936			4	3	0.8		0
Career			46	72	1.6		1

Jerry LeVias

Year	Team		Att	Yds	Avg	Lg	TD
1969	HOU	A	6	18	3.0	10	0
1970	HOU	N	7	37	5.3	24	0
1971	SD	N	4	73	18.3	38	0
1973			2	33	16.5	22	0
Career			19	161	8.5	38	0
Playoffs			1	4	4.0		0

Chuck Levy

Year	Team		Att	Yds	Avg	Lg	TD
1994	ARI	N	3	15	5.0	22	0

Verne Lewellen

Year	Team		Att	Yds	Avg	Lg	TD
1924	GB	N					2
1925							1
1926							3
1927							5
1928							6
1929							6
1930							8
1931							6
Career							37

Cliff Lewis

Year	Team		Att	Yds	Avg	Lg	TD
1946	CLE	AA	24	-34	-1.4		0
1947			11	66	6.0		0
1948			5	44	8.8		0
1949			9	-17	-1.9		1
1950	CLE	N	2	-1	-0.5	2	0
1951			3	-10	-3.3	1	0
Career			54	48	0.9	2	1
Playoffs			2	10	5.0		0

Danny Lewis

Year	Team		Att	Yds	Avg	Lg	TD
1958	DET	N	25	131	5.2	20	0
1959			49	199	4.1	20	2
1960			92	438	4.8	74t	1
1961			110	451	4.1	27	4
1962			120	488	4.1	64t	6
1963			133	528	4.0	27	2
1964			122	463	3.8	28	1
1965	WAS	N	117	343	2.9	23	2
1966	NYG	N	32	164	5.1	57	1
Career			800	3205	4.0	74t	19

Darren Lewis

Year	Team		Att	Yds	Avg	Lg	TD
1991	CHI	N	15	36	2.4	9	0
1992			90	382	4.2	33	4
1993			7	13	1.9	3	0
Career			112	431	3.8	33	4
Playoffs			9	65	7.2		0

Dave Lewis

Year	Team		Att	Yds	Avg	Lg	TD
1970	CIN	N	2	8	4.0	7	0
1971			6	6	1.0	9	0
1972			1	15	15.0	15	0
1973			3	-7	-2.3	5	0
Career			12	22	1.8	15	0
Playoffs			3	10	3.3		0

Ernie Lewis

Year	Team		Att	Yds	Avg	Lg	TD
1946	CHI	AA	57	164	2.9		1
1947			13	47	3.6		0
1948			13	54	4.2		0
1949			11	43	3.9		0
Career			94	308	3.3		2

Frank Lewis

Year	Team		Att	Yds	Avg	Lg	TD
1972	PIT	N	3	68	22.7	41	0
1973			1	-1	-1.0	-1	0
1974			2	25	12.5	22	0
1975			2	36	18.0	24	0
1976			2	24	12.0	16t	1
1979	BUF	N	2	-6	-3.0	-1	0
Career			12	146	12.2	41	1

Gary Lewis

Year	Team		Att	Yds	Avg	Lg	TD
1964	SF	N	43	115	2.7	17	1
1965			52	256	4.9	60t	3
1966			36	130	3.6	15	2
1967			67	342	5.1	52	6
1968			141	573	4.1	22	1
1969			4	5	1.3	4	0
Career			343	1421	4.1	60t	13

Gary Lewis

Year	Team		Att	Yds	Avg	Lg	TD
1983	GB	N	4	16	4.0	16	1

Greg Lewis

Year	Team		Att	Yds	Avg	Lg	TD
1991	DEN	N	99	376	3.8	27	4
1992			73	268	3.7	22	4
Career			172	644	3.7	27	8
Playoffs			3	2	0.7		2

Hal Lewis

Year	Team		Att	Yds	Avg	Lg	TD
1959	BAL	N	4	2	0.5	2	0
1962	OAK	A	9	18	2.0	14	0
Career			13	20	1.5	14	0

Jeff Lewis

Year	Team		Att	Yds	Avg	Lg	TD
1996	DEN	N	4	39	9.8	18	0

Jermaine Lewis

Year	Team		Att	Yds	Avg	Lg	TD
1996	BAL	N	1	-3	-3.0	-3	0

Kenny Lewis

Year	Team		Att	Yds	Avg	Lg	TD
1981	NYJ	N	6	18	3.0	7	0
1983			5	25	5.0	7	0
Career			11	43	3.9	7	0

Leo Lewis

Year	Team		Att	Yds	Avg	Lg	TD
1981	MIN	N	1	16	16.0	16	0
1983			1	2	2.0	2	0
1984			2	11	5.5	6	0
1985			1	2	2.0	2	0
1986			3	-16	-5.3	-2	0
1987			5	-7	-1.4	4	0
1989			1	11	11.0	11	0
Career			14	19	1.4	16	0

Nate Lewis

Year	Team		Att	Yds	Avg	Lg	TD
1990	SD	N	4	25	6.3	10t	1
1991			3	10	3.3	9	0
1992			2	7	3.5	4	0
1993			3	2	0.7	7	0
Career			12	44	3.7	10t	1

Tiny Lewis

Year	Team		Att	Yds	Avg	Lg	TD
1930	POR	N					2

Woodley Lewis

Year	Team		Att	Yds	Avg	Lg	TD
1952	LA	N	19	114	6.0	51	0
1953			2	2	1.0	5	0
1954			26	72	2.8	18	0
Career			47	188	4.0	51	0

Carl Lidberg

Year	Team		Att	Yds	Avg	Lg	TD
1926	GB	N					4
1929							2
1930							1
Career							7

Don Lieberum

Year	Team		Att	Yds	Avg	Lg	TD
1942	NYG	N	11	29	2.6	19	0

Joe Lillard

Year	Team		Att	Yds	Avg	Lg	TD
1933	CHIC	N					1

Verl Lillywhite

Year	Team		Att	Yds	Avg	Lg	TD
1948	SF	AA	53	340	6.4		3
1949			69	263	3.8		2
1950	SF	N	7	4	0.6	5	0
1951			67	397	5.9	60t	1
Career			196	1004	5.1	60t	6
Playoffs			5	41	8.2		1

Garrett Limbrick

Year	Team		Att	Yds	Avg	Lg	TD
1990	MIA	N	5	14	2.8	5	0

Keith Lincoln

Year	Team		Att	Yds	Avg	Lg	TD
1961	SD	A	41	150	3.7	17	0
1962			117	574	4.9	86	2
1963			128	826	6.5	76	5
1964			155	632	4.1	25	4
1965			75	302	4.0	24	3
1966			58	214	3.7	23	1
1967	BUF	A	159	601	3.8	28	4
1968			26	84	3.2	24	0
Career			759	3383	4.5	86	19
Playoffs			23	276	12.0		1

Mike Lind

Year	Team		Att	Yds	Avg	Lg	TD
1963	SF	N	8	26	3.3	7	0
1964			100	256	2.6	21	7
1965	PIT	N	111	375	3.4	20	1
1966			3	4	1.3	3	0
Career			222	661	3.0	21	8

Hub Lindsay

Year	Team		Att	Yds	Avg	Lg	TD
1968	DEN	A	4	17	4.3	7	0

Jim Lindsey

Year	Team		Att	Yds	Avg	Lg	TD
1966	MIN	N	57	146	2.6	14	1
1967			4	10	2.5	6	0
1968			53	152	2.9	9	4
1969			6	21	3.5	10	1
1970			11	47	4.3	9	0
1971			46	182	4.0	19	0
1972			1	8	8.0	8	0
Career			178	566	3.2	19	6
Playoffs			2	5	2.5		0

Menz Lindsey

Year	Team		Att	Yds	Avg	Lg	TD
1921	EVA	A					2

Louis Lipps

Year	Team		Att	Yds	Avg	Lg	TD
1984	PIT	N	3	71	23.7	36t	1
1985			2	16	8.0	15t	1
1986			4	-3	-0.8	8	0
1988			6	129	21.5	39t	1
1989			13	180	13.8	58t	1
1990			1	-5	-5.0	-5	0
Career			29	388	13.4	58t	4
Playoffs			2	1	0.5		0

Don Lisbon

Year	Team		Att	Yds	Avg	Lg	TD
1963	SF	N	109	399	3.7	25	0
1964			55	162	2.9	14	0
Career			164	561	3.4	25	0

Rusty Lisch

Year	Team		Att	Yds	Avg	Lg	TD
1983	STL	N	2	9	4.5	5	0
1984	CHI	N	18	121	6.7	31	0
Career			20	130	6.5	31	0

Pete Liske

Year	Team		Att	Yds	Avg	Lg	TD
1964	NY	A	1	0	0.0	0	0
1969	DEN	A	10	50	5.0	19	0
1970	DEN	N	7	42	6.0	14	1
1971	PHI	N	13	29	2.2	9	1
1972			7	20	2.9	9	0
Career			38	141	3.7	19	2

Floyd Little

Year	Team		Att	Yds	Avg	Lg	TD
1967	DEN	A	130	381	2.9	14	1
1968			158	584	3.7	55t	3
1969			146	729	5.0	48t	6
1970	DEN	N	209	901	4.3	80t	3
1971			284	1133	4.0	40	6
1972			216	859	4.0	55t	9
1973			256	979	3.8	47	12
1974			117	312	2.7	22	1
1975			125	445	3.6	19	2
Career			1641	6323	3.9	80t	43

Steve Little

Year	Team		Att	Yds	Avg	Lg	TD
1978	STL	N	1	0	0.0	0	0
1979			2	0	0.0	0	0
Career			3	0	0.0	0	0

Carl Littlefield

Year	Team		Att	Yds	Avg	Lg	TD
1938	CLE	N	19	69	3.6		0

Year	Team		Att	Yds	Avg	Lg	TD

Carl Littlefield *continued*

Year	Team		Att	Yds	Avg	Lg	TD
1939	PIT	N	39	141	3.6		0
Career			58	210	3.6		0

Andy Livingston

Year	Team		Att	Yds	Avg	Lg	TD
1964	CHI	N	2	-3	-1.5	5	0
1965			63	363	5.8	30	2
1967			28	41	1.5	6	0
1968			7	25	3.6	8	0
1969	NO	N	181	761	4.2	18	5
1970			10	29	2.9	10	0
Career			291	1216	4.2	30	7

Dale Livingston

Year	Team		Att	Yds	Avg	Lg	TD
1968	CIN	A	1	11	11.0	11	0
1969			1	18	18.0	18	0
1970	GB	N	1	1	1.0	1	0
Career			3	30	10.0	18	0

Howie Livingston

Year	Team		Att	Yds	Avg	Lg	TD
1944	NYG	N	84	313	3.7	43	2
1945			40	109	2.7	13	3
1946			19	38	2.0	18	1
1947			19	86	4.5	43	0
1949	WAS	N	1	1	1.0	1	1
1950			1	0	0.0	0	0
Career			164	547	3.3	43	7
Playoffs			16	41	2.6		0

Mike Livingston

Year	Team		Att	Yds	Avg	Lg	TD
1968	KC	A	2	2	1.0	3	0
1969			15	102	6.8	39	0
1970	KC	N	3	26	8.7	16	0
1971			5	11	2.2	5	0
1972			14	133	9.5	51	0
1973			19	94	4.9	28	2
1974			9	28	3.1	9	0
1975			13	68	5.2	28	1
1976			31	89	2.9	19	2
1977			19	78	4.1	13	1
1978			23	49	2.1	18	1
1979			3	2	0.7	5	0
Career			156	682	4.4	51	7

Walt Livingston

Year	Team		Att	Yds	Avg	Lg	TD
1960	BOS	A	10	16	1.6		1

Bob Livingstone

Year	Team		Att	Yds	Avg	Lg	TD
1948	CHI	AA	55	174	3.2		0
1949	BUF	AA	1	0	0.0	0	0
1950	BAL	N	1	-3	-3.0	-3	0
Career			57	171	3.0	0	0

J.W. Lockett

Year	Team		Att	Yds	Avg	Lg	TD
1961	SF-DAL	N	77	298	3.9	21	1
1962	DAL	N	8	24	3.0	7	1
1963	BAL	N	81	273	3.4	18	0
1964	WAS	N	63	175	2.8	13	1
Career			229	770	3.4	21	3

Scott Lockwood

Year	Team		Att	Yds	Avg	Lg	TD
1992	NE	N	35	162	4.6	23	0

James Lofton

Year	Team		Att	Yds	Avg	Lg	TD
1978	GB	N	3	13	4.3	15	0
1979			1	-1	-1.0	-1	0
1982			4	101	25.3	83t	1
1983			9	36	4.0	8	0
1984			10	82	8.2	26	0
1985			4	14	3.5	21	0
1987	LARI	N	1	1	1.0	1	0
Career			32	246	7.7	83t	1
Playoffs			3	55	18.3		1

Marc Logan

Year	Team		Att	Yds	Avg	Lg	TD
1987	CIN	N	37	203	5.5	51	1
1988			2	10	5.0	9	0
1989	MIA	N	57	201	3.5	14	0
1990			79	317	4.0	17	2
1991			4	5	1.3	2	0
1992	SF	N	8	44	5.5	26	1
1993			58	280	4.8	45	7
1994			33	143	4.3	22	1
1995	WAS	N	23	72	3.1	13	1

Marc Logan *continued*

Year	Team		Att	Yds	Avg	Lg	TD
1996			20	111	5.5	36t	2
Career			321	1386	4.3	51	15
Playoffs			21	63	3.0		1

Neil Lomax

Year	Team		Att	Yds	Avg	Lg	TD
1981	STL	N	19	104	5.5	22t	2
1982			28	119	4.3	19	1
1983			27	127	4.7	35	2
1984			35	184	5.3	20	3
1985			32	125	3.9	23	0
1986			35	148	4.2	18	1
1987			29	107	3.7	19	0
1988	PHX	N	17	55	3.2	13	1
Career			222	969	4.4	35	10
Playoffs			4	9	2.3		0

Bill Long

Year	Team		Att	Yds	Avg	Lg	TD
1949	PIT	N	2	6	3.0	10	0

Chuck Long

Year	Team		Att	Yds	Avg	Lg	TD
1986	DET	N	2	0	0.0	0	0
1987			22	64	2.9	15	0
1988			7	22	3.1	11	0
1989			3	2	0.7	6	0
Career			34	88	2.6	15	0
Playoffs			1	-1	-1.0		0

Cutter Long

Year	Team		Att	Yds	Avg	Lg	TD
1953	NYG	N	20	58	2.9	21	0
1954			32	106	3.3	11	1
Career			52	164	3.2	21	1

Johnny Long

Year	Team		Att	Yds	Avg	Lg	TD
1944	CHIB	N	24	2	0.1	12	0
1945			2	3	1.5	5	0
Career			26	5	0.2	12	0

Kevin Long

Year	Team		Att	Yds	Avg	Lg	TD
1977	NYJ	N	56	170	3.0	12	1
1978			214	954	4.5	27	10
1979			116	442	3.8	25	7
1980			115	355	3.1	18	6
1981			73	269	3.7	19	2
Career			574	2190	3.8	27	25
Playoffs			8	28	3.5		1

Clint Longley

Year	Team		Att	Yds	Avg	Lg	TD
1974	DAL	N	4	-13	-3.3	1	0
1975			3	12	4.0	7	0
1976	SD	N	4	22	5.5	9	0
Career			11	21	1.9	9	0

Dean Look

Year	Team		Att	Yds	Avg	Lg	TD
1962	NY	A	2	9	4.5	8	0

Don Looney

Year	Team		Att	Yds	Avg	Lg	TD
1940	PHI	N	2	-4	-2.0		0

Joe Don Looney

Year	Team		Att	Yds	Avg	Lg	TD
1964	BAL	N	23	127	5.5	58t	1
1965	DET	N	114	356	3.1	35	5
1966	DET-WAS	N	63	220	3.5	24t	4
1967	WAS	N	11	26	2.4	20	1
1969	NO	N	3	-5	-1.7	4	0
Career			214	724	3.4	58t	11

Tony Lorick

Year	Team		Att	Yds	Avg	Lg	TD
1964	BAL	N	100	513	5.1	60	4
1965			63	296	4.7	38	1
1966			143	524	3.7	41	3
1967			133	436	3.3	72	6
1968	NO	N	104	344	3.3	36	0
1969			5	11	2.2	6	0
Career			548	2124	3.9	72	14
Playoffs			1	1	1.0		0

Jack Losch

Year	Team		Att	Yds	Avg	Lg	TD
1956	GB	N	19	43	2.3	8	0

Billy Lothridge

Year	Team		Att	Yds	Avg	Lg	TD
1964	DAL	N	2	-6	-3.0	2t	1
1966	ATL	N	1	22	22.0	22	0
1967			1	16	16.0	16	0

Billy Lothridge *continued*

Year	Team		Att	Yds	Avg	Lg	TD
1968			1	-16	-16.0	-16	0
Career			5	16	3.2	22	1

Billy Lott

Year	Team		Att	Yds	Avg	Lg	TD
1958	NYG	N	4	30	7.5	12	0
1960	OAK	A	99	520	5.3		5
1961	BOS	A	100	461	4.6	38	5
1962			8	34	4.3	11	0
1963			35	78	2.2	7	3
Career			246	1123	4.6	38	13
Playoffs			5	17	3.4		0

Thomas Lott

Year	Team		Att	Yds	Avg	Lg	TD
1979	STL	N	11	50	4.5	13	0

Randy Love

Year	Team		Att	Yds	Avg	Lg	TD
1980	STL	N	1	3	3.0	3	0
1981			3	11	3.7	4	0
1983			35	103	2.9	16	2
1984			25	90	3.6	13	1
1985			1	4	4.0	4	0
Career			65	211	3.2	16	3

Edwin Lovelady

Year	Team		Att	Yds	Avg	Lg	TD
1987	NYG	N	2	11	5.5	8	0

Derek Loville

Year	Team		Att	Yds	Avg	Lg	TD
1990	SEA	N	7	12	1.7	4	0
1991			22	69	3.1	22	0
1994	SF	N	31	99	3.2	13	0
1995			218	723	3.3	27	10
1996			70	229	3.3	16	2
Career			348	1132	3.3	27	12
Playoffs			10	2	0.2		1

Paul Lowe

Year	Team		Att	Yds	Avg	Lg	TD
1960	LA	A	136	855	**6.3**	63	**9**
1961	SD	A	175	767	4.4	87	**9**
1963			177	1010	5.7	66	8
1964			130	496	3.8	50	3
1965			222	**1121**	5.0	59	**7**
1966			146	643	4.4	57	3
1967			28	71	2.5	21	1
1968	SD-KC	A	2	-1	-0.5	9	0
1969	KC	A	10	33	3.3	18	0
Career			1026	4995	4.9	87	40
Playoffs			57	380	6.7		2

Russ Lowther

Year	Team		Att	Yds	Avg	Lg	TD
1944	DET	N	9	18	2.0	11	0
1945	PIT	N	15	54	3.6	17	0
Career			24	72	3.0	17	0

Mike Loyd

Year	Team		Att	Yds	Avg	Lg	TD
1980	STL	N	6	2	0.3	3	0

Richie Lucas

Year	Team		Att	Yds	Avg	Lg	TD
1960	BUF	A	46	90	2.0		2
1961			10	15	1.5	9	0
Career			56	105	1.9	9	2

Lew Luce

Year	Team		Att	Yds	Avg	Lg	TD
1961	WAS	N	3	1	0.3	3	0

Johnny Lucente

Year	Team		Att	Yds	Avg	Lg	TD
1945	PIT	N	82	242	3.0	18	2

Oliver Luck

Year	Team		Att	Yds	Avg	Lg	TD
1983	HOU	N	17	55	3.2	17	0
1984			10	75	7.5	18	1
1985			15	95	6.3	17	0
1986			2	12	6.0	8	0
Career			44	237	5.4	18	1

Terry Luck

Year	Team		Att	Yds	Avg	Lg	TD
1977	CLE	N	3	-2	-0.7	1	0

Mick Luckhurst

Year	Team		Att	Yds	Avg	Lg	TD
Playoffs			1	17	17.0		1

Sid Luckman

Year	Team		Att	Yds	Avg	Lg	TD
1939	CHIB	N	24	42	1.8		0
1940			23	-65	-2.8		0

Sid Luckman *continued*

Year	Team			Att	Yds	Avg	Lg	TD
1941				18	18	1.0	20	1
1942				13	24	1.8	9	0
1943				22	-40	-1.8	8	1
1944				20	-96	-4.8	7	1
1945				36	-118	-3.3	22	0
1946				25	-76	-3.0	25	0
1947				10	86	8.6	40t	1
1948				8	11	1.4	18	0
1949				3	4	1.3	14	0
1950				2	1	0.5	1	0
Career				204	-209	-1.0	40t	4
Playoffs				18	31	1.7		2

Johnny Lujack

Year	Team			Att	Yds	Avg	Lg	TD
1948	CHIB	N		15	110	7.3	26	1
1949				8	64	8.0	20	2
1950				63	397	**6.3**	40	**11**
1951				47	171	3.6	22	7
Career				133	742	5.6	40	21
Playoffs				3	2	0.7		0

Roy Lumpkin

Year	Team			Att	Yds	Avg	Lg	TD
1930	POR	N						3
1931								1
1934	DET	N						1
1936	BKN	N		11	29	2.6		0
Career				11	29	2.6		5

Bobby Luna

Year	Team			Att	Yds	Avg	Lg	TD
1959	PIT	N		3	3	1.0	10	0

Bill Lund

Year	Team			Att	Yds	Avg	Lg	TD
1946	CLE	AA		23	72	3.1		1
1947				14	105	7.5	63t	1
Career				37	177	4.8	63t	2

Herb Lusk

Year	Team			Att	Yds	Avg	Lg	TD
1976	PHI	N		61	254	4.2	22	0
1977				52	229	4.4	70t	2
Career				113	483	4.3	70t	2

Ed Luther

Year	Team			Att	Yds	Avg	Lg	TD
1980	SD	N		3	5	1.7	9	0
1981				3	-8	-2.7	-1	0
1982				1	-13	-13.0	-13	0
1983				9	-14	-1.6	8	0
1984				4	11	2.8	7	0
Career				20	-19	-0.9	9	0

Garry Lyle

Year	Team			Att	Yds	Avg	Lg	TD
1968	CHI	N		4	28	7.0	26	0

Keith Lyle

Year	Team			Att	Yds	Avg	Lg	TD
1995	STL	N		1	4	4.0	4	0
1996				3	39	13.0	20	0
Career				4	43	10.8	20	0

Lenny Lyles

Year	Team			Att	Yds	Avg	Lg	TD
1958	BAL	N		22	41	1.9	27t	1
1959	SF	N		13	28	2.2	13t	1
Career				35	69	2.0	27t	2

Eric Lynch

Year	Team			Att	Yds	Avg	Lg	TD
1993	DET	N		53	207	3.9	15	2
1994				1	0	0.0	0	0
1996				2	2	1.0	2	0
Career				56	209	3.7	15	2

Fran Lynch

Year	Team			Att	Yds	Avg	Lg	TD
1967	DEN	A		2	7	3.5	7	0
1968				66	221	3.3	19	4
1969				96	407	4.2	54	2
1970	DEN	N		20	81	4.0	19	1
1971				26	162	6.2	23	0
1972				34	164	4.8	28	2
1974				3	-2	-0.7	1	0
1975				57	218	3.8	20	3
Career				304	1258	4.1	54	12

John Lynch

Year	Team			Att	Yds	Avg	Lg	TD
1996	TB	N		1	40	40.0	40	0

Anthony Lynn

Year	Team			Att	Yds	Avg	Lg	TD
1995	SF	N		2	11	5.5	6	0
1996				24	164	6.8	67	0
Career				26	175	6.7	67	0

Rob Lytle

Year	Team			Att	Yds	Avg	Lg	TD
1977	DEN	N		104	408	3.9	21	1
1978				81	341	4.2	25	2
1979				102	371	3.6	19	4
1980				57	223	3.9	35	1
1981				30	106	3.5	18	4
1982				2	2	1.0	2	0
Career				376	1451	3.9	35	12
Playoffs				34	93	2.7		2

Mike Machurek

Year	Team			Att	Yds	Avg	Lg	TD
1984	DET	N		1	9	9.0	9	0

Art Macioszczyk

Year	Team			Att	Yds	Avg	Lg	TD
1944	PHI	N		16	55	3.4	12	0
1947				30	104	3.5	11	0
Career				46	159	3.5	12	0

Bill Mack

Year	Team			Att	Yds	Avg	Lg	TD
1962	PIT	N		2	-2	-1.0	7	0
1963				2	1	0.5	1	0
Career				4	-1	-0.3	7	0

Kevin Mack

Year	Team			Att	Yds	Avg	Lg	TD
1985	CLE	N		222	1104	5.0	61	7
1986				174	665	3.8	20	10
1987				201	735	3.7	22t	5
1988				123	485	3.9	65	3
1989				37	130	3.5	12	1
1990				158	702	4.4	26	5
1991				197	726	3.7	51t	8
1992				169	543	3.2	37	6
1993				10	33	3.3	7	1
Career				1291	5123	4.0	65	46
Playoffs				107	424	4.0		1

John Mackey

Year	Team			Att	Yds	Avg	Lg	TD
1963	BAL	N		1	3	3.0	3	0
1964				1	-1	-1.0	-1	0
1965				1	7	7.0	7	0
1966				1	-6	-6.0	-6	0
1968				10	103	10.3	33	0
1969				2	3	1.5	7	0
1971				3	18	6.0	9	0
Career				19	127	6.7	33	0
Playoffs				3	13	4.3		0

Kyle Mackey

Year	Team			Att	Yds	Avg	Lg	TD
1987	MIA	N		17	98	5.8	17	2
1989	NYJ	N		2	3	1.5	5	0
Career				19	101	5.3	17	2

Jacque Mac Kinnon

Year	Team			Att	Yds	Avg	Lg	TD
1962	SD	A		59	240	4.1	24	0
1964				24	124	5.2	48	2
1965				3	17	5.7	9	0
Career				86	381	4.4	48	2
Playoffs				1	17	17.0		0

Bill Mackrides

Year	Team			Att	Yds	Avg	Lg	TD
1947	PHI	N		7	-15	-2.1	2	0
1948				7	4	0.6	9	0
1949				14	17	1.2	17	1
1950				21	82	3.9	18	0
1951				7	9	1.3	3	0
1953	NYG-PIT	N		14	27	1.9	4	1
Career				70	124	1.8	18	2

Bob Mac Leod

Year	Team			Att	Yds	Avg	Lg	TD
1939	CHIB	N		17	88	5.2		1

Eddie Macon

Year	Team			Att	Yds	Avg	Lg	TD
1952	CHIB	N		30	194	6.5	50t	1
1953				40	130	3.3	17	1
Career				70	324	4.6	50t	2

Elmer Madarik

Year	Team			Att	Yds	Avg	Lg	TD
1945	DET	N		2	5	2.5	4	0
1946				8	7	0.9	4	0

Elmer Madarik *continued*

Year	Team			Att	Yds	Avg	Lg	TD
1947				19	29	1.5	9	1
1948	WAS	N		2	7	3.5	5	0
Career				31	48	1.5	9	1

Lloyd Madden

Year	Team			Att	Yds	Avg	Lg	TD
1940	CHIC	N		29	186	6.4		2

Tommy Maddox

Year	Team			Att	Yds	Avg	Lg	TD
1992	DEN	N		9	20	2.2	11	0
1993				2	-2	-1.0	-1	0
1994	LARM	N		1	1	1.0	1	0
1995	NYG	N		1	4	4.0	4	0
Career				13	23	1.8	11	0
Playoffs				1	1	1.0		0

Archie Maggiolo

Year	Team			Att	Yds	Avg	Lg	TD
1948	BUF	AA		11	27	2.5		0

Dante Magnani

Year	Team			Att	Yds	Avg	Lg	TD
1940	CLE	N		7	19	2.7		0
1941				24	137	5.7	29	0
1942				59	344	5.8	71	2
1943	CHIB	N		51	310	6.1	79	2
1946				68	277	4.1	33	0
1947	LA			48	178	3.7	27	0
1948				38	144	3.8	15	0
1949	CHIB	N		33	59	1.8	9	0
1950	DET	N		3	7	2.3	5	0
Career				331	1475	4.5	79	4
Playoffs				2	6	3.0		0

Paul Maguire

Year	Team			Att	Yds	Avg	Lg	TD
1961	SD	A		1	-11	-11.0	-11	0
1965	BUF	A		1	21	21.0	21	0
1968				1	6	6.0	6	0
Career				3	16	5.3	21	0

George Magulick

Year	Team			Att	Yds	Avg	Lg	TD
1944	C-P	N		17	102	6.0	49	0

Bruce Maher

Year	Team			Att	Yds	Avg	Lg	TD
1962	DET	N		3	8	2.7	7	0

Frank Mahoney

Year	Team			Att	Yds	Avg	Lg	TD
1926	CHIC	N						1

Al Mahrt

Year	Team			Att	Yds	Avg	Lg	TD
1920	DAY							1

Armin Mahrt

Year	Team			Att	Yds	Avg	Lg	TD
1924	DAY	N						1
1925	POT	N						1
Career								2

Jack Maitland

Year	Team			Att	Yds	Avg	Lg	TD
1970	BAL	N		74	209	2.8	24	1
1971	NE	N		13	25	1.9	6	1
1972				13	33	2.5	6	0
Career				100	267	2.7	24	2

Don Majkowski

Year	Team			Att	Yds	Avg	Lg	TD
1987	GB	N		15	127	8.5	33	0
1988				47	225	4.8	24	1
1989				75	358	4.8	20	5
1990				29	186	6.4	24	1
1991				25	108	4.3	15	2
1992				8	33	4.1	8	0
1993	IND	N		2	4	2.0	4	0
1994				24	34	1.4	10	3
1995	DET	N		9	1	0.1	4	0
1996				14	38	2.7	12	0
Career				248	1114	4.5	33	12
Playoffs				3	16	5.3		0

Howie Maley

Year	Team			Att	Yds	Avg	Lg	TD
1946	BOS	N		13	67	5.2	42	0
1947				32	132	4.1	27	0
Career				45	199	4.4	42	0

Gene Malinowski

Year	Team			Att	Yds	Avg	Lg	TD
1948	BOS	N		11	21	1.9	9	0

Larry Mallory

Year	Team		Att	Yds	Avg	Lg	TD
1976	NYG	N	1	0	0.0	0	0

Ray Mallouf

Year	Team		Att	Yds	Avg	Lg	TD
1941	CHIC	N	43	104	2.4	15	0
1946			4	6	1.5	18	0
1947			5	13	2.6	17	0
1948			13	17	1.3	12	1
1949	NYG	N	1	-1	-1.0	-1	0
Career			66	139	2.1	18	1
Playoffs			2	5	2.5		0

Art Malone

Year	Team		Att	Yds	Avg	Lg	TD
1970	ATL	N	40	136	3.4	12	0
1971			120	438	3.6	19	6
1972			180	798	4.4	27	8
1973			76	336	4.4	14	2
1974			116	410	3.5	13	2
1975	PHI	N	101	325	3.2	18	0
1976			2	14	7.0	15t	1
Career			635	2457	3.9	27	19

Benny Malone

Year	Team		Att	Yds	Avg	Lg	TD
1974	MIA	N	117	479	4.1	23t	3
1975			65	220	3.4	21	3
1976			186	797	4.3	31	4
1977			129	615	4.8	66t	5
1978	MIA-WAS	N	33	110	3.3	31	1
1979	WAS	N	176	472	2.7	14	3
Career			706	2693	3.8	66t	19
Playoffs			14	83	5.9		1

Mark Malone

Year	Team		Att	Yds	Avg	Lg	TD
1981	PIT	N	16	68	4.3	19	2
1984			25	42	1.7	13t	3
1985			15	80	5.3	25	1
1986			31	107	3.5	45	5
1987			34	162	4.8	42t	3
1988	SD	N	37	169	4.6	36t	4
1989	NYJ	N	1	0	0.0	0	0
Career			159	628	3.9	45	18
Playoffs			5	-6	-1.2		0

Jack Manders

Year	Team		Att	Yds	Avg	Lg	TD
1933	CHIB	N	65	244	3.8		0
1934			57	184	3.2		2
1935			93	296	3.2		0
1936			63	207	3.3		3
1937			73	319	4.4		0
1938			67	263	3.9		2
1939			25	63	2.5		3
1940			8	20	2.5		0
Career			451	1596	3.5		10
Playoffs			19	84	4.4		1

Pug Manders

Year	Team		Att	Yds	Avg	Lg	TD
1939	BKN	N	114	**482**	4.2		2
1940			80	311	3.9		5
1941			111	486	4.4	46	
1942			93	316	3.4	23	6
1943			89	266	3.0	43	3
1944			127	430	3.4	13	5
1945	BOS	N	76	238	3.1	34	6
1946	NY	AA	49	168	3.4		3
1947	BUF	AA	3	15	5.0		
Career			742	2712	3.7	46	35

Pete Mandley

Year	Team		Att	Yds	Avg	Lg	TD
1987	DET	N	1	3	3.0	3	0
1988			6	44	7.3	21t	1
1989	KC	N	2	1	0.5	8	0
Career			9	48	5.3	21t	1

Joe Maniaci

Year	Team		Att	Yds	Avg	Lg	TD
1936	BKN	N	35	70	2.0		0
1937			92	433	4.7		2
1938	BKN-CHIB	N	88	345	3.9		3
1939	CHIB	N	77	544	**7.1**		4
1940			84	368	4.4		2
1941			28	95	3.4	14	3
Career			404	1855	4.6	14	14
Playoffs			11	68	6.2		1

Jim Mankins

Year	Team		Att	Yds	Avg	Lg	TD
1967	ATL	N	2	7	3.5	7	0

Bob Mann

Year	Team		Att	Yds	Avg	Lg	TD
1948	DET	N	6	46	7.7	23	0
1951	GB	N	2	9	4.5	9	0
Career			8	55	6.9	23	0

Dave Mann

Year	Team		Att	Yds	Avg	Lg	TD
1955	CHIC	N	87	336	3.9	65t	4
1956			45	116	2.6	15	0
1957			22	92	4.2	25	0
Career			154	544	3.5	65t	4

Archie Manning

Year	Team		Att	Yds	Avg	Lg	TD
1971	NO	N	33	172	5.2	17	4
1972			63	351	5.6	18	2
1973			63	293	4.7	23	2
1974			28	204	7.3	26	1
1975			33	186	5.6	16	1
1977			39	270	6.9	27	5
1978			38	202	5.3	19	1
1979			35	186	5.3	20	2
1980			23	166	7.2	24	0
1981			2	28	14.0	15	0
1982	HOU	N	13	85	6.5	24	0
1983	HOU-MIN	N	3	12	4.0	11	0
1984	MIN	N	11	42	3.8	16	0
Career			384	2197	5.7	27	18

Joe Manning

Year	Team		Att	Yds	Avg	Lg	TD
1926	HAR	N					2

Tim Manoa

Year	Team		Att	Yds	Avg	Lg	TD
1987	CLE	N	23	116	5.0	35	0
1988			99	389	3.9	34	2
1989			87	289	3.3	22	3
1991	IND	N	27	144	5.3	44	1
Career			236	938	4.0	44	6
Playoffs			9	21	2.3		1

Ed Manske

Year	Team		Att	Yds	Avg	Lg	TD
1938	PIT	N	5	29	5.8		

Tillie Manton

Year	Team		Att	Yds	Avg	Lg	TD
1936	NYG	N	30	86	2.9		0
1937			8	16	2.0		0
1938	WAS	N	2	3	1.5		0
1943	BKN	N	2	-7	-3.5	2	0
Career			42	98	2.3	2	0

Dan Manucci

Year	Team		Att	Yds	Avg	Lg	TD
1980	BUF	N	3	29	9.7	17	0
1987			4	6	1.5	9	0
Career			7	35	5.0	17	0
Playoffs			2	21	10.5		0

Lionel Manuel

Year	Team		Att	Yds	Avg	Lg	TD
1984	NYG	N	3	2	0.7	11	0
1986			1	25	25.0	25	0
1987			1	-10	-10.0	-10	0
1988			4	27	6.8	14	0
Career			9	44	4.9	25	0
Playoffs			1	-5	-5.0		0

Frank Manumaleuga

Year	Team		Att	Yds	Avg	Lg	TD
1979	KC	N	1	-3	-3.0	-3	0

Gary Marangi

Year	Team		Att	Yds	Avg	Lg	TD
1974	BUF	N	4	20	5.0	16	0
1975			7	78	11.1	30	0
1976			39	230	5.9	21	2
Career			50	328	6.6	30	2

Ted Marchibroda

Year	Team		Att	Yds	Avg	Lg	TD
1953	PIT	N	1	15	15.0	15	0
1955			6	-1	-0.2	8t	1
1956			39	152	3.9	26	2
1957	CHIC	N	4	10	2.5	7	0
Career			50	176	3.5	26	3

Hugo Marcolini

Year	Team		Att	Yds	Avg	Lg	TD
1948	BKN	AA	5	11	2.2		0

Joe Marconi

Year	Team		Att	Yds	Avg	Lg	TD
1956	LA	N	75	298	4.0	23	7
1957			104	481	4.6	31	3
1958			89	428	4.8	45	1
1959			52	176	3.4	21	4
1960			42	240	5.7	75t	3
1961			36	146	4.1	14	3
1962	CHI	N	89	406	4.6	57	5
1963			118	446	3.8	19t	2
1964			46	98	2.1	8	2
1965			19	47	2.5	10	0
1966			3	5	1.7	3	0
Career			673	2771	4.1	75t	30
Playoffs			3	5	1.7		0

Andrew Marefos

Year	Team		Att	Yds	Avg	Lg	TD
1941	NYG	N	60	153	2.5	11	2
1942			48	138	2.9	14	1
1946	LA	AA	30	93	3.1		4
Career			138	384	2.8	14	7
Playoffs			1	-5	-5.0		0

Jodie Marek

Year	Team		Att	Yds	Avg	Lg	TD
1943	BKN	N	6	9	1.5	7	0

Bob Margarita

Year	Team		Att	Yds	Avg	Lg	TD
1944	CHIB	N	88	463	5.3	47t	4
1945			112	497	4.4	38	3
1946			4	0	0.0	2	0
Career			204	960	4.7	47t	7

Ken Margerum

Year	Team		Att	Yds	Avg	Lg	TD
1981	CHI	N	1	11	11.0	11	0
1983			1	7	7.0	7	0
1985			1	-7	-7.0	-7	0
Career			3	11	3.7	11	0

Joe Margucci

Year	Team		Att	Yds	Avg	Lg	TD
1947	DET	N	26	97	3.7	26	1
1948			34	14	0.4	10	2
Career			60	111	1.9	26	3

Ed Marinaro

Year	Team		Att	Yds	Avg	Lg	TD
1972	MIN	N	66	223	3.4	19	0
1973			95	302	3.2	27	2
1974			44	124	2.8	8	1
1975			101	358	3.5	14	1
1976	NYJ	N	77	312	4.1	17	2
Career			383	1319	3.4	27	6
Playoffs			5	14	2.8		0

Dan Marino

Year	Team		Att	Yds	Avg	Lg	TD
1983	MIA	N	28	45	1.6	15	2
1984			28	-7	-0.3	10	0
1985			26	-24	-0.9	6	0
1986			12	-3	-0.3	13	0
1987			12	-5	-0.4	5t	1
1988			20	-17	-0.8	6	0
1989			14	-7	-0.5	2	0
1990			16	29	1.8	15	0
1991			27	32	1.2	11	1
1992			20	66	3.3	12	0
1993			9	-4	-0.4	4t	1
1994			22	-6	-0.3	10	1
1995			11	14	1.3	12	0
1996			11	-3	-0.3	7	0
Career			256	110	0.4	15	8
Playoffs			11	1	0.1		1

Todd Marinovich

Year	Team		Att	Yds	Avg	Lg	TD
1991	LARI	N	3	14	4.7	11	0
1992			9	30	3.3	11	0
Career			12	44	3.7	11	0

Phil Marion

Year	Team		Att	Yds	Avg	Lg	TD
1925	DET	N					4

Steve Marko

Year	Team		Att	Yds	Avg	Lg	TD
1944	BKN	N	6	10	1.7	9	0

Larry Marks

Year	Team		Att	Yds	Avg	Lg	TD
1926	NY	A					1

Year	Team		Att	Yds	Avg	Lg	TD

Aaron Marsh
Year	Team		Att	Yds	Avg	Lg	TD
1968	BOS	A	4	8	2.0	11	0

Amos Marsh
1961	DAL	N	84	379	4.5	71	1
1962			144	802	**5.6**	70	6
1963			99	483	4.9	41t	5
1964			100	401	4.0	28	2
1965	DET	N	131	495	3.8	62t	6
1966			134	433	3.2	27	3
1967			58	229	3.9	25	2
Career			750	3222	4.3	71	25

Doug Marsh
1984	STL	N	1	-5	-5.0	-5	0
1986			1	5	5.0	5	0
Career			2	0	0.0	5	0

Arthur Marshall
1992	DEN	N	11	56	5.1	16	0
1994	NYG	N	2	8	4.0	6	0
1995			1	1	1.0	1	0
Career			14	65	4.6	16	0

Henry Marshall
1976	KC	N	5	101	20.2	59t	1
1977			7	11	1.6	7	0
1978			1	-5	-5.0	-5	0
1979			2	34	17.0	23t	1
1980			3	22	7.3	9	0
1981			3	69	23.0	34	0
1982			3	25	8.3	16	0
Career			24	257	10.7	59t	2

Wilber Marshall
| 1987 | CHI | N | 1 | 1 | 1.0 | 1 | 0 |

Paul Martha
1964	PIT	N	4	12	3.0	10	0
1965			2	3	1.5	6	0
Career			6	15	2.5	10	0

Abe Martin
| 1932 | CHIC | N | | | | | 1 |

Billy Martin
| 1962 | CHI | N | 9 | 28 | 3.1 | 12t | 1 |

Blanche Martin
| 1960 | NY-LA | A | 18 | 58 | 3.2 | | 0 |

Curtis Martin
1995	NE	N	368	1487	4.0	49	14
1996			316	1152	3.6	57	14
Career			684	2639	3.9	57	28
Playoffs			49	267	5.4		5

Eric Martin
1985	NO	N	2	-1	-0.5	11	0
1988			2	12	6.0	9	0
Career			4	11	2.8	11	0

Frank Martin
1943	BKN	N	25	50	2.0	22	0
1944			11	18	1.6	10	0
1945	BOS-NYG	N	3	11	3.7	7	0
Career			39	79	2.0	22	0

Ike Martin
| 1920 | CAN | A | | | | | 1 |

Jamie Martin
| 1996 | STL | N | 7 | 14 | 2.0 | 11 | 0 |

John Martin
1941	CHIC	N	25	56	2.2	17	1
1942			30	10	0.3	27	0
1943			30	98	3.3	15	0
1944	C-P-BOS	N	19	7	0.4	11	0
1945	BOS	N	39	191	4.9	76	2
Career			143	362	2.5	76	3

Kelvin Martin
| 1988 | DAL | N | 4 | -4 | -1.0 | 11 | 0 |

Kelvin Martin *continued*
Year	Team		Att	Yds	Avg	Lg	TD
1990			4	-2	-0.5	3	0
1992			2	13	6.5	8	0
1993	SEA	N	1	0	0.0	0	0
Career			11	7	0.6	11	0

Mike Martin
1983	CIN	N	2	21	10.5	15	0
1984			1	3	3.0	3	0
Career			3	24	8.0	15	0

Robbie Martin
1984	DET	N	1	14	14.0	14	0
1985	IND	N	1	23	23.0	23	0
Career			2	37	18.5	23	0

Sammy Martin
| 1989 | NE | N | 2 | 20 | 10.0 | 13 | 0 |

Tony Martin
1990	MIA	N	1	8	8.0	8	0
1992			1	-2	-2.0	-2	0
1993			1	6	6.0	6	0
1994	SD	N	2	-9	-4.5	4	0
Career			5	3	0.6	8	0

Vern Martin
| 1942 | PIT | N | | | | | 1 |

Roy Martineau
| 1923 | BUF | N | | | | | 1 |

Len Masini
1947	SF	AA	38	167	4.4		2
1948	LA	AA	3	12	4.0		0
Career			41	179	4.4		2

Larry Mason
1987	CLE	N	56	207	3.7	22	2
1988	GB	N	48	194	4.0	17	0
Career			104	401	3.9	22	2

Tommy Mason
1961	MIN	N	60	226	3.8	21	3
1962			167	740	4.4	71	2
1963			166	763	4.6	70t	7
1964			169	691	4.1	51t	4
1965			141	597	4.2	26	10
1966			58	235	4.1	52t	2
1967	LA	N	63	213	3.4	16	0
1968			108	395	3.7	19	3
1969			33	135	4.1	17	1
1970			44	123	2.8	13	0
1971	WAS	N	31	85	2.7	11	0
Career			1040	4203	4.0	71	32
Playoffs			3	15	5.0		0

Billy Masters
1968	BUF	A	6	70	11.7	35	0
1969			1	-3	-3.0	-3	0
1971	DEN	N	7	71	10.1	37	0
1972			3	-15	-5.0		0
1973			1	-9	-9.0	-9	0
Career			18	114	6.3	37	0

Bob Masters
1937	PHI	N	9	32	3.6		0
1939	PIT	N	9	39	4.3		0
1942	PHI	N	1	3	3.0	3	0
1943	P-P-CHIB	N	4	16	4.0	10	0
1944	CHIB	N	11	9	0.8	6	0
Career			34	99	2.9	10	0

Walt Masters
1936	PHI	N	7	18	2.6		0
1943	CHIC	N	14	-17	-1.2	4	0
1944	C-P	N	1	-14	-14.0	-14	0
Career			22	-13	-0.6	4	0

Bernie Masterson
1934	CHIB	N	4	11	2.8		0
1935			21	2	0.1		1
1936			9	-7	-0.8		2
1937			30	21	0.7		1

Bernie Masterson *continued*
Year	Team		Att	Yds	Avg	Lg	TD
1938			13	-16	-1.2		0
1939			21	-31	-1.5		2
1940			10	-7	-0.7		1
Career			108	-27	-0.3		7
Playoffs			2	-9	-4.5		0

Bob Masterson
1938	WAS	N	3	89	29.7		0
1940			1	0	0.0	0	0
1941			1	3	3.0	3	0
1942			3	12	4.0	11	0
Career			8	104	13.0	11	0
Playoffs			1	-1	-1.0		0

Le'Shai Maston
1993	HOU	N	1	10	10.0	10	0
1995	JAC	N	41	186	4.5	21	0
1996			8	22	2.8	7	0
Career			50	218	4.4	21	0

Ed Matesic
1935	PHI	N	50	138	2.8		1
1936	PIT	N	46	58	1.3		0
Career			96	196	2.0		1

Ned Mathews
1941	DET	N	31	56	1.8	16	0
1942			21	79	3.8	14	0
1943			38	124	3.3	42	1
1945	BOS	N	27	146	5.4	49	0
1946	CHI-SF	AA	30	109	3.6		1
1947	SF	AA	39	238	6.1		2
Career			186	752	4.0	49	4

Ray Mathews
1951	PIT	N	21	37	1.8	15	0
1952			66	315	4.8	36	0
1953			65	260	4.0	31	2
1954			80	242	3.0	24	2
1955			57	187	3.3	23	1
1956			3	-11	-3.7	2	0
1957			3	-1	-0.3	6	0
1958			4	24	6.0	14	0
1959			1	4	4.0	4	0
Career			300	1057	3.5	36	5

Bill Mathis
1960	NY	A	92	307	3.3		2
1961			**202**	846	4.2	30	7
1962			71	245	3.5	41	3
1963			107	268	2.5	16	1
1964			105	305	2.9	31	4
1965			147	604	4.1	79	5
1966			72	208	2.9	23	2
1967			78	243	3.1	18	4
1968			74	208	2.8	16	5
1969			96	355	3.7	27	4
Career			1044	3589	3.4	79	37
Playoffs			12	21	1.8		0

Terance Mathis
1990	NYJ	N	2	9	4.5	10	0
1991			1	19	19.0	19	0
1992			3	25	8.3	10t	0
1993			2	20	10.0	17t	1
Career			8	73	9.1	19	2

Bruce Mathison
1983	SD	N	1	0	0.0	0	0
1985	BUF	N	27	231	8.6	22	1
1986	SD	N	1	-1	-1.0	-1	0
1987	SEA	N	5	15	3.0	10	0
Career			34	245	7.2	22	1

Charlie Mathys
1922	GB	N					1
1923							1
Career							2

Ollie Matson
1952	CHIC	N	96	344	3.6	25	3
1954			101	506	5.0	79t	4
1955			109	475	4.4	54	1

Ollie Matson *continued*

Year	Team		Att	Yds	Avg	Lg	TD
1956			192	924	4.8	79t	5
1957			134	577	4.3	56t	6
1958			129	505	3.9	55t	4
1959	LA	N	161	863	5.4	50	6
1960			61	170	2.8	27	1
1961			24	181	7.5	69t	2
1962			3	0	0.0	2	0
1963	DET	N	13	20	1.5	9	0
1964	PHI	N	96	404	4.2	63	4
1965			22	103	4.7	22	2
1966			29	101	3.5	28	1
Career			1170	5173	4.4	79t	39

Tom Matte

Year	Team		Att	Yds	Avg	Lg	TD
1961	BAL	N	13	54	4.2	11	0
1962			74	226	3.1	29	2
1963			133	541	4.1	81t	4
1964			42	215	5.1	80t	1
1965			69	235	3.4	20	1
1966			86	381	4.4	30	0
1967			147	636	4.3	30	9
1968			183	662	3.6	23	9
1969			235	909	3.9	26	11
1970			12	43	3.6	16	0
1971			173	607	3.5	26	8
1972			33	137	4.2	18	0
Career			1200	4646	3.9	81t	45
Playoffs			75	318	4.2		3

Aubrey Matthews

Year	Team		Att	Yds	Avg	Lg	TD
1986	ATL	N	1	12	12.0	12	0
1987			1	-4	-4.0	-4	0
1988	GB	N	3	3	1.0	4	0
1993	DET	N	2	7	3.5	9	0
Career			7	18	2.6	12	0

Bo Matthews

Year	Team		Att	Yds	Avg	Lg	TD
1974	SD	N	95	328	3.5	16	4
1975			71	254	3.6	24	3
1976			46	199	4.3	42t	3
1977			43	193	4.5	22	0
1978			71	286	4.0	28	0
1979			30	112	3.7	22	1
1980	NYG	N	64	180	2.8	18	0
1981			4	14	3.5	6	0
Career			424	1566	3.7	42t	11

Henry Matthews

Year	Team		Att	Yds	Avg	Lg	TD
1973	NO	N	4	4	1.0	3	0

Ira Matthews

Year	Team		Att	Yds	Avg	Lg	TD
1979	OAK	N	2	3	1.5	3	0
1980			5	11	2.2	5	0
Career			7	14	2.0	5	0

Shane Matthews

Year	Team		Att	Yds	Avg	Lg	TD
1996	CHI	N	1	2	2.0	2t	1

Harry Mattos

Year	Team		Att	Yds	Avg	Lg	TD
1936	GB	N	1	2	2.0	2	0
1937	CLE	N	26	16	0.6		1
Career			27	18	0.7	2	1

Tuffy Maul

Year	Team		Att	Yds	Avg	Lg	TD
1926	LA	N					2

Rich Mauti

Year	Team		Att	Yds	Avg	Lg	TD
1980	NO	N	1	2	2.0	2	0

Alvin Maxson

Year	Team		Att	Yds	Avg	Lg	TD
1974	NO	N	165	714	4.3	66t	2
1975			139	371	2.7	14	3
1976			34	120	3.5	16	1
1977	PIT	N	18	56	3.1	8	0
1978			4	9	2.3	7	0
Career			360	1270	3.5	66t	6

Bruce Maxwell

Year	Team		Att	Yds	Avg	Lg	TD
1970	DET	N	1	9	9.0	9	0

Bill May

Year	Team		Att	Yds	Avg	Lg	TD
1937	CHIC	N	4	16	4.0		0

Dean May

Year	Team		Att	Yds	Avg	Lg	TD
1987	DEN	N	2	-4	-2.0	-2	0

Sheriden May

Year	Team		Att	Yds	Avg	Lg	TD
1995	NYJ	N	2	5	2.5	3	0

Doug Mayberry

Year	Team		Att	Yds	Avg	Lg	TD
1961	MIN	N	13	40	3.1	13	0
1962			74	274	3.7	17	1
Career			87	314	3.6	17	1

James Mayberry

Year	Team		Att	Yds	Avg	Lg	TD
1979	ATL	N	45	193	4.3	21	1
1980			18	88	4.9	24	0
1981			18	66	3.7	11	0
Career			81	347	4.3	24	1

Carl Mayes

Year	Team		Att	Yds	Avg	Lg	TD
1952	LA	N	5	2	0.4	6	0

Rueben Mayes

Year	Team		Att	Yds	Avg	Lg	TD
1986	NO	N	286	1353	4.7	50	8
1987			243	917	3.8	38	5
1988			170	628	3.7	21	3
1990			138	510	3.7	18	7
1992	SEA	N	28	74	2.6	14	0
1993			1	2	2.0	2	0
Career			866	3484	4.0	50	23
Playoffs			3	11	3.7		0

Don Maynard

Year	Team		Att	Yds	Avg	Lg	TD
1958	NYG	N	12	45	3.8	14	0
1963	NY	A	2	6	3.0	8	0
1964			3	3	1.0	14	0
1965			1	2	2.0	2	0
1967			4	18	4.5	7	0
1969			1	-6	-6.0	-6	0
1971	NYJ	N	1	2	2.0	2	0
Career			24	70	2.9	14	0

Lew Mayne

Year	Team		Att	Yds	Avg	Lg	TD
1946	BKN	AA	70	191	2.7		1
1947	CLE	AA	41	75	1.8		0
1948	BAL	AA	14	26	1.9		0
Career			125	292	2.3		1
Playoffs			4	0	0.0		0

Dave Mays

Year	Team		Att	Yds	Avg	Lg	TD
1976	CLE	N	5	14	2.8	6	0
1977			4	2	0.5	2	0
Career			9	16	1.8	6	0

Frank Maznicki

Year	Team		Att	Yds	Avg	Lg	TD
1942	CHIB	N	54	343	6.4	42	1
1946			19	43	2.3	9	0
1947	BOS	N	34	77	2.3	17	2
Career			107	463	4.3	42	3
Playoffs			5	14	2.8		0

Gino Mazzanti

Year	Team		Att	Yds	Avg	Lg	TD
1950	BAL	N	7	22	3.1	7t	0

Dean McAdams

Year	Team		Att	Yds	Avg	Lg	TD
1941	BKN	N	38	99	2.6	39	0
1942			110	314	2.9	25	0
1943			41	-38	-0.9	14	0
Career			189	375	2.0	39	0

Derrick McAdoo

Year	Team		Att	Yds	Avg	Lg	TD
1987	STL	N	53	230	4.3	17	3

Fred McAfee

Year	Team		Att	Yds	Avg	Lg	TD
1991	NO	N	109	494	4.5	34	2
1992			39	114	2.9	19	1
1993			51	160	3.1	27	1
1994	ARI-PIT	N	18	51	2.8	13	2
1995	PIT	N	39	156	4.0	22t	1
1996			7	17	2.4	5	0
Career			263	992	3.8	34	7
Playoffs			24	100	4.2		0

George McAfee

Year	Team		Att	Yds	Avg	Lg	TD
1940	CHIB	N	47	253	5.4		2
1941			65	474	7.3	70	7

George McAfee *continued*

Year	Team		Att	Yds	Avg	Lg	TD
1945			16	139	8.7	38	3
1946			14	53	3.8	14	0
1947			63	209	3.3	39	3
1948			92	392	4.3	23	5
1949			42	161	3.8	23	3
1950			1	4	4.0	4	0
Career			340	1685	5.0	70	23
Playoffs			41	234	5.7		1

Wes McAfee

Year	Team		Att	Yds	Avg	Lg	TD
1941	PHI	N	9	6	0.7	3	0

James McAlister

Year	Team		Att	Yds	Avg	Lg	TD
1975	PHI	N	103	335	3.3	18	1
1976			68	265	3.9	20	0
1978	NE	N	19	77	4.1	16	2
Career			190	677	3.6	20	3

Charlie McBride

Year	Team		Att	Yds	Avg	Lg	TD
1936	CHIC	N	2	1	0.5		0

Jack McBride

Year	Team		Att	Yds	Avg	Lg	TD
1925	NY	N					2
1926	NYG	N					5
1927							6
1930	BKN	N					8
1931							3
1932	BKN-NY	N	84	302	3.6		1
1933	NYG	N	33	87	2.6		0
1934			4	14	3.5		0
Career			121	403	3.3		25
Playoffs			2	10	5.0		0

Ed McCaffrey

Year	Team		Att	Yds	Avg	Lg	TD
1995	DEN	N	1	-1	-1.0	-1	0

Bob McCall

Year	Team		Att	Yds	Avg	Lg	TD
1973	NE	N	10	15	1.5	14	0

Don McCall

Year	Team		Att	Yds	Avg	Lg	TD
1967	NO	N	21	86	4.1	49t	1
1968			155	637	4.1	48	4
1969	PIT	N	30	98	3.3	14	0
1970	NO	N	23	63	2.7	11	1
Career			229	884	3.9	49t	6

Joe McCall

Year	Team		Att	Yds	Avg	Lg	TD
1984	LARI	N	1	3	3.0	3	0

Napoleon McCallum

Year	Team		Att	Yds	Avg	Lg	TD
1986	LARI	N	142	536	3.8	18	1
1990			10	25	2.5	6	0
1991			31	110	3.5	9	1
1993			37	114	3.1	14	3
1994			3	5	1.7	3	1
Career			223	790	3.5	18	6
Playoffs			33	141	4.3	5	

Jim McCann

Year	Team		Att	Yds	Avg	Lg	TD
1971	SF	N	2	-15	-7.5	-6	0

Brendan McCarthy

Year	Team		Att	Yds	Avg	Lg	TD
1968	ATL-DEN	N	59	175	3.0	18	1

John McCarthy

Year	Team		Att	Yds	Avg	Lg	TD
1944	C-P	N	6	-49	-8.2	-8	0

Shawn McCarthy

Year	Team		Att	Yds	Avg	Lg	TD
1992	NE	N	3	-10	-3.3	0	0

Vince McCarthy

Year	Team		Att	Yds	Avg	Lg	TD
1924	RI	N					1
1925							1
Career							2

Don McCauley

Year	Team		Att	Yds	Avg	Lg	TD
1971	BAL	N	58	246	4.2	19	2
1972			178	675	3.8	36	2
1973			144	514	3.6	24	2
1974			30	90	3.0	15	0
1975			60	196	3.3	18	10
1976			69	227	3.3	16	9
1977			83	234	2.8	16	6

Year	Team		Att	Yds	Avg	Lg	TD

Don McCauley *continued*

Year	Team		Att	Yds	Avg	Lg	TD
1978			44	107	2.4	10	5
1979			59	168	2.8	13	3
1980			35	133	3.8	12	1
1981			10	37	3.7	8	0
Career			770	2627	3.4	36	40
Playoffs			24	72	3.0		0

Thomas McCauley

Year	Team		Att	Yds	Avg	Lg	TD
1969	ATL	N	2	49	24.5	32	0

Bob McChesney

Year	Team		Att	Yds	Avg	Lg	TD
1939	WAS	N	1	5	5.0	5	0
1942			2	22	11.0	23	0
Career			3	27	9.0	23	0

Bob McChesney

Year	Team		Att	Yds	Avg	Lg	TD
1952	NYG	N	2	2	1.0	2	0

Cliff McClain

Year	Team		Att	Yds	Avg	Lg	TD
1971	NYJ	N	12	108	9.0	63t	2
1972			59	305	5.2	30	0
1973			8	32	4.0	13	0
Career			79	445	5.6	63t	2

Clint McClain

Year	Team		Att	Yds	Avg	Lg	TD
1941	NYG	N	9	36	4.0	11	2

Brent McClanahan

Year	Team		Att	Yds	Avg	Lg	TD
1973	MIN	N	17	69	4.1	10	0
1974			9	41	4.6	14	1
1975			92	336	3.7	15	0
1976			130	382	2.9	19	4
1977			95	324	3.4	18	1
1978			10	26	2.6	22	0
1979			14	29	2.1	9	0
Career			367	1207	3.3	22	6
Playoffs			28	128	4.6		1

Willie McClendon

Year	Team		Att	Yds	Avg	Lg	TD
1979	CHI	N	37	160	4.3	33	1
1980			10	88	8.8	48	1
1981			30	74	2.5	17	0
1982			17	47	2.8	13	0
Career			94	369	3.9	48	2
Playoffs			2	6	3.0		0

Curtis McClinton

Year	Team		Att	Yds	Avg	Lg	TD
1962	DAL	A	111	604	5.4	69	2
1963	KC	A	142	568	4.0	36	3
1964			73	252	3.5	30	1
1965			175	661	3.8	48	6
1966			140	540	3.9	49	4
1967			97	392	4.0	34	2
1968			24	107	4.5	19	0
Career			762	3124	4.1	69	18
Playoffs			41	124	3.0		0

Brian McClure

Year	Team		Att	Yds	Avg	Lg	TD
1987	BUF	N	2	4	2.0	3	0

David McCluskey

Year	Team		Att	Yds	Avg	Lg	TD
1987	CIN	N	29	94	3.2	12	1

Mike McCormack

Year	Team		Att	Yds	Avg	Lg	TD
1957	CLE	N	0	4		4L	0
1961			0	4		4L	0
Career			0	8		4L	0

Frank McCormick

Year	Team		Att	Yds	Avg	Lg	TD
1920	AKR	A					1
1921							3
Career							4

John McCormick

Year	Team		Att	Yds	Avg	Lg	TD
1962	MIN	N	2	4	2.0	4	0
1963	DEN	A	3	-5	-1.7	-2	0
1965			1	-2	-2.0	-2	0
1966			4	2	0.5	3	0
Career			10	-1	-0.1	4	0

Tom McCormick

Year	Team		Att	Yds	Avg	Lg	TD
1953	LA	N	20	29	1.5	8	0
1954			48	173	3.6	16	0

Tom McCormick *continued*

Year	Team		Att	Yds	Avg	Lg	TD
1955			16	66	4.1	14	1
1956	SF	N	2	4	2.0	2	0
Career			86	272	3.2	16	1

Joel McCoy

Year	Team		Att	Yds	Avg	Lg	TD
1946	DET	N	19	-29	-1.5	15	0

Fred McCrary

Year	Team		Att	Yds	Avg	Lg	TD
1995	PHI	N	3	1	0.3	1t	1

Greg McCrary

Year	Team		Att	Yds	Avg	Lg	TD
1978	SD	N	2	18	9.0	16	0

Hurdis McCrary

Year	Team		Att	Yds	Avg	Lg	TD
1929	GB	N					1
1930							4
1931							1
1932							1
Career							7

Earl McCullouch

Year	Team		Att	Yds	Avg	Lg	TD
1968	DET	N	3	13	4.3	5	0
1969			1	4	4.0	4	0
1970			1	7	7.0	7	0
1971			1	-7	-7.0	-7	0
1973			2	12	6.0	13	0
Career			8	29	3.6	13	0

Hal McCullough

Year	Team		Att	Yds	Avg	Lg	TD
1942	BKN	N	21	11	0.5	14	0

Hugh McCullough

Year	Team		Att	Yds	Avg	Lg	TD
1939	PIT	N	60	96	1.6		1
1940	CHIC	N	52	278	5.3		3
1941			15	34	2.3	14	0
1945	BOS	N	2	1	0.5	2	0
Career			129	409	3.2	14	4

Lawrence McCutcheon

Year	Team		Att	Yds	Avg	Lg	TD
1973	LA	N	210	1097	5.2	37	2
1974			236	1109	4.7	23t	3
1975			213	911	4.3	43t	2
1976			291	1168	4.0	40	9
1977			294	1238	4.2	48	7
1978			118	420	3.6	18	0
1979			73	243	3.3	21	0
1980	DEN-SEA	N	52	254	4.9	32	3
1981	BUF	N	34	138	4.1	12	0
Career			1521	6578	4.3	48	26
Playoffs			173	687	4.0		2

Ed McDaniel

Year	Team		Att	Yds	Avg	Lg	TD
1965	NY	A	1	13	13.0	13	0

Johnny McDaniel

Year	Team		Att	Yds	Avg	Lg	TD
1974	CIN	N	1	5	5.0	5	0
1975			1	-2	-2.0	-2	0
1978	WAS	N	2	25	12.5	13	0
Career			4	28	7.0	13	0

Randall McDaniel

Year	Team		Att	Yds	Avg	Lg	TD
1996	MIN	N	2	1	0.5	1	0

Gary McDermott

Year	Team		Att	Yds	Avg	Lg	TD
1968	BUF	A	47	102	2.2	17	3
1969	ATL	N	7	6	0.9	3	0
Career			54	108	2.0	17	3

Ed McDonald

Year	Team		Att	Yds	Avg	Lg	TD
1936	PIT	N	9	18	2.0		0

Jim McDonald

Year	Team		Att	Yds	Avg	Lg	TD
1939	DET	N	25	80	3.2		0

Keith McDonald

Year	Team		Att	Yds	Avg	Lg	TD
1989	DET	N	1	-2	-2.0	-2	0

Les McDonald

Year	Team		Att	Yds	Avg	Lg	TD
1938	CHIB	N	1	0	0.0	0	0
1939			1	-2	-2.0	-2	0
1940	PHI	N	2	-2	-1.0		0
Career			4	-4	-1.0	0	0

Paul McDonald

Year	Team		Att	Yds	Avg	Lg	TD
1980	CLE	N	3	-2	-0.7	0	0
1981			2	0	0.0	2	0
1982			7	-13	-1.9	10	0
1983			3	17	5.7	10	0
1984			22	4	0.2	10	1
Career			37	6	0.2	10	1
Playoffs			2	-4	-2.0		0

Ray McDonald

Year	Team		Att	Yds	Avg	Lg	TD
1967	WAS	N	52	223	4.3	35t	4

Tommy McDonald

Year	Team		Att	Yds	Avg	Lg	TD
1957	PHI	N	12	36	3.0	22	0
1958			3	-4	-1.3	5	0
1959			2	-10	-5.0		0
Career			17	22	1.3	22	0

Walt McDonald

Year	Team		Att	Yds	Avg	Lg	TD
1946	MIA-BKN	AA	4	-11	-2.8		0
1947	BKN	AA	1	1	1.0	1	0
1948			6	15	2.5		0
1949	CHI	AA	1	0	0.0	0	0
Career			12	5	0.4	1	0

Mickey McDonnell

Year	Team		Att	Yds	Avg	Lg	TD
1926	CHIC	N					1

Coley McDonough

Year	Team		Att	Yds	Avg	Lg	TD
1939	CHIC-PIT	N	27	75	2.8		0
1940	PIT	N	15	33	2.2		1
1941			20	64	3.2	28	0
1944	C-P	N	3	7	2.3	4	0
Career			65	179	2.8	28	1

Paul McDonough

Year	Team		Att	Yds	Avg	Lg	TD
1940	CLE	N	2	5	2.5		0

Gerry McDougall

Year	Team		Att	Yds	Avg	Lg	TD
1962	SD	A	43	197	4.6	24	3
1963			38	199	5.2	22	1
1964			23	73	3.2	24	2
Career			104	469	4.5	24	6
Playoffs			1	2	2.0		0

Anthony McDowell

Year	Team		Att	Yds	Avg	Lg	TD
1992	TB	N	14	81	5.8	23	0
1993			2	6	3.0	3	0
1994			21	58	2.8	8	0
Career			37	145	3.9	23	0

O.J. McDuffie

Year	Team		Att	Yds	Avg	Lg	TD
1993	MIA	N	1	-4	-4.0	-4	0
1994			5	32	6.4	12	0
1995			3	6	2.0	11	0
1996			2	7	3.5	7	0
Career			11	41	3.7	12	0
Playoffs			2	28	14.0		0

Hugh McElhenny

Year	Team		Att	Yds	Avg	Lg	TD
1952	SF	N	98	684	7.0	89t	6
1953			112	503	4.5	33	3
1954			64	515	8.0	60t	6
1955			90	327	3.6	44	4
1956			185	916	5.0	86t	8
1957			102	478	4.7	61	1
1958			113	451	4.0	34	6
1959			18	67	3.7	18	1
1960			95	347	3.7	38	0
1961	MIN	N	120	570	4.8	41	3
1962			50	200	4.0	27	0
1963	NYG	N	55	175	3.2	23	0
1964	DET	N	22	48	2.2	14	0
Career			1124	5281	4.7	89t	38
Playoffs			21	101	4.8		0

Leeland McElroy

Year	Team		Att	Yds	Avg	Lg	TD
1996	ARI	N	89	305	3.4	32	1

Bill McElwain

Year	Team		Att	Yds	Avg	Lg	TD
1926	CHIC	N					1

Doug McEnulty

Year	Team		Att	Yds	Avg	Lg	TD
1943	CHIB	N	16	45	2.8	9	0

Year	Team		Att	Yds	Avg	Lg	TD

Doug McEnulty *continued*

Year	Team		Att	Yds	Avg	Lg	TD
1944			8	11	1.4	7	0
Career			24	56	2.3	9	0

Banks McFadden

Year	Team		Att	Yds	Avg	Lg	TD
1940	BKN	N	65	411	**6.3**		1

Nyle McFarlane

Year	Team		Att	Yds	Avg	Lg	TD
1960	OAK	A	4	52	13.0		0

Buford McGee

Year	Team		Att	Yds	Avg	Lg	TD
1984	SD	N	67	226	3.4	30	4
1985			42	181	4.3	44	3
1986			63	187	3.0	20	7
1987	LARM	N	3	6	2.0	2t	1
1988			22	69	3.1	12	0
1989			21	99	4.7	15	1
1990			44	234	5.3	19	1
1991			19	65	3.4	9	0
1992	GB	N	8	19	2.4	4	0
Career			289	1086	3.8	44	17
Playoffs			5	52	10.4		0

Max McGee

Year	Team		Att	Yds	Avg	Lg	TD
1954	GB	N	1	9	9.0	9	0
1957			5	40	8.0	24	0
1958			1	9	9.0	9	0
1960			2	11	5.5	16	0
1962			3	52	17.3	36	0
Career			12	121	10.1	36	0
Playoffs			1	35	35.0		0

Sylvester McGee

Year	Team		Att	Yds	Avg	Lg	TD
1974	ATL	N	7	30	4.3	10	0

Tim McGee

Year	Team		Att	Yds	Avg	Lg	TD
1986	CIN	N	4	10	2.5	8	0
1987			1	-10	-10.0	-10	0
1989			2	36	18.0	25	0
1994			1	-18	-18.0	-18	0
Career			8	18	2.3	25	0

Willie McGee

Year	Team		Att	Yds	Avg	Lg	TD
1976	SF	N	3	12	4.0	19	0
1977			1	-3	-3.0	-3	0
Career			4	9	2.3	19	0

Rich McGeorge

Year	Team		Att	Yds	Avg	Lg	TD
1970	GB	N	1	3	3.0	3	0

Charlie McGibbony

Year	Team		Att	Yds	Avg	Lg	TD
1944	BKN	N	26	81	3.1	37	0

Dan McGwire

Year	Team		Att	Yds	Avg	Lg	TD
1992	SEA	N	3	13	4.3	11	0
1993			1	-1	-1.0	-1	0
1994			10	-6	-0.6	2	0
Career			14	6	0.4	11	0

Lamar McHan

Year	Team		Att	Yds	Avg	Lg	TD
1954	CHIC	N	34	152	4.5	18	1
1955			56	194	3.5	38	2
1956			58	161	2.8	17	5
1957			25	82	3.3	18t	2
1958			17	65	3.8	32	1
1959	GB	N	16	64	4.0	19	0
1960			8	67	8.4	35t	1
1961	BAL	N	4	1	0.3	7	0
1962			4	4	1.0	5	0
1963	SF	N	17	59	3.5	16	0
Career			239	849	3.6	38	12

Pat McHugh

Year	Team		Att	Yds	Avg	Lg	TD
1947	PHI	N	22	171	7.8	41	2
1948			4	12	3.0	5	0
1949			2	5	2.5	5	0
1950			4	14	3.5	5	0
Career			32	202	6.3	41	2
Playoffs			1	-5	-5.0		0

Don McIlhenny

Year	Team		Att	Yds	Avg	Lg	TD
1956	DET	N	87	372	4.3	30	3
1957	GB	N	100	384	3.8	40t	1
1958			74	239	3.2	36	1

Don McIlhenny *continued*

Year	Team		Att	Yds	Avg	Lg	TD
1959			47	231	4.9	46	1
1960	DAL	N	96	321	3.3	21	1
1961	DAL-SF	N	10	24	2.4	15	0
Career			414	1571	3.8	46	7

Pat McInally

Year	Team		Att	Yds	Avg	Lg	TD
1977	CIN	N	1	4	4.0	4	0
1979			1	18	18.0	18	0
1980			1	0	0.0	0	0
1981			1	-27	-27.0	-27	0
1985			1	-2	-2.0	-2	0
Career			5	-7	-1.4	18	0

Hugh McInnis

Year	Team		Att	Yds	Avg	Lg	TD
1961	STL	N	4	30	7.5	16	0

Joe McIntosh

Year	Team		Att	Yds	Avg	Lg	TD
1987	ATL	N	5	11	2.2	5	0

Secedrik McIntyre

Year	Team		Att	Yds	Avg	Lg	TD
1977	ATL	N	13	65	5.0	11	0

Rick McIvor

Year	Team		Att	Yds	Avg	Lg	TD
1984	STL	N	3	5	1.7	6	0

Paul McJulien

Year	Team		Att	Yds	Avg	Lg	TD
1991	GB	N	1	0	0.0	0	0

Bill McKalip

Year	Team		Att	Yds	Avg	Lg	TD
1936	DET	N	7	39	5.6		0

Roy McKay

Year	Team		Att	Yds	Avg	Lg	TD
1944	GB	N	5	12	2.4	11	0
1945			71	231	3.3	41	2
1946			21	34	1.6	9t	1
1947			3	11	3.7	5	0
Career			100	288	2.9	41	3

Hugh McKinnis

Year	Team		Att	Yds	Avg	Lg	TD
1973	CLE	N	28	77	2.8	12	0
1974			124	519	4.2	44t	2
1975			71	259	3.6	14	4
1976	SEA	N	46	105	2.3	14	4
Career			269	960	3.6	44t	10

Dennis McKinnon

Year	Team		Att	Yds	Avg	Lg	TD
1984	CHI	N	2	12	6.0	21	0
1985			1	0	0.0	0	0
1988			3	25	8.3	12	1
1989			3	5	1.7	3	0
1990	DAL	N	1	-8	-8.0	-8	0
Career			10	34	3.4	21	1
Playoffs			2	-11	-5.5		0

Roland McKinnon

Year	Team		Att	Yds	Avg	Lg	TD
1996	ARI	N	1	-4	-4.0	-4	0

Ted McKnight

Year	Team		Att	Yds	Avg	Lg	TD
1977	KC	N	11	74	6.7	19	0
1978			104	627	**6.0**	41t	6
1979			153	755	4.9	64t	8
1980			206	693	3.4	25	3
1981			54	195	3.6	26	5
Career			528	2344	4.4	64t	22

Mayes McLain

Year	Team		Att	Yds	Avg	Lg	TD
1930	POR						4

Ray McLean

Year	Team		Att	Yds	Avg	Lg	TD
1940	CHIB	N	14	10	0.7		1
1941			13	78	6.0	21	1
1942			26	63	2.4	15	0
1943			35	127	3.6	34	2
1944			29	25	0.9	18	2
1945			9	22	2.4	15	0
1946			16	29	1.8	11	1
1947			10	58	5.8	24	0
Career			152	412	2.7	34	7
Playoffs			13	49	3.8		0

Chris McLemore

Year	Team		Att	Yds	Avg	Lg	TD
1987	IND	N	17	58	3.4	9	0

Bruce McLenna

Year	Team		Att	Yds	Avg	Lg	TD
1966	DET	N	16	51	3.2	19	0

Jim McMahon

Year	Team		Att	Yds	Avg	Lg	TD
1982	CHI	N	24	105	4.4	11	1
1983			55	307	5.6	32	2
1984			39	276	7.1	30	2
1985			47	252	5.4	19	3
1986			22	152	6.9	23	1
1987			22	88	4.0	13	2
1988			26	104	4.0	16	4
1989	SD	N	29	141	4.9	15	0
1990	PHI	N	3	1	0.3	3	0
1991			22	55	2.5	12	1
1992			6	23	3.8	12	0
1993	MIN	N	33	96	2.9	16	0
1994	ARI	N	6	32	5.3	17	0
1996	GB	N	4	-1	-0.3	2	0
Career			338	1631	4.8	32	16
Playoffs			24	77	3.2		3

John McMakin

Year	Team		Att	Yds	Avg	Lg	TD
1972	PIT	N	1	0	0.0	0	0

John McMichael

Year	Team		Att	Yds	Avg	Lg	TD
1944	BKN	N	3	1	0.3	2	0

Randy McMillan

Year	Team		Att	Yds	Avg	Lg	TD
1981	BAL	N	149	597	4.0	42	3
1982			101	305	3.0	13	1
1983			198	802	4.1	39t	5
1984	IND	N	163	705	4.3	31t	5
1985			190	858	4.5	38	7
1986			189	609	3.2	28	3
Career			990	3876	3.9	42	24

Greg McMurtry

Year	Team		Att	Yds	Avg	Lg	TD
1992	NE	N	2	3	1.5	2	0

Dexter McNabb

Year	Team		Att	Yds	Avg	Lg	TD
1992	GB	N	2	11	5.5	8	0

Steve McNair

Year	Team		Att	Yds	Avg	Lg	TD
1995	HOU	N	11	38	3.5	13	0
1996			31	169	5.5	24t	2
Career			42	207	4.9	24t	2

Todd McNair

Year	Team		Att	Yds	Avg	Lg	TD
1989	KC	N	23	121	5.3	25	0
1990			14	61	4.4	13	0
1991			10	51	5.1	11	0
1992			21	124	5.9	30	1
1993			51	278	5.5	47	2
1995	HOU	N	19	136	7.2	22	0
1996	KC	N	9	32	3.6	9	0
Career			147	803	5.5	47	3
Playoffs			8	37	4.6		0

Bob McNamara

Year	Team		Att	Yds	Avg	Lg	TD
1960	DEN	A	17	33	1.9	7	1

Travis McNeal

Year	Team		Att	Yds	Avg	Lg	TD
1990	SEA	N	1	2	2.0		0

Clifton McNeil

Year	Team		Att	Yds	Avg	Lg	TD
1968	SF	N	1	-1	-1.0	-1	0
1970	NYG	N	4	7	1.8	9	0
Career			5	6	1.2	9	0

Freeman McNeil

Year	Team		Att	Yds	Avg	Lg	TD
1981	NYJ	N	137	623	4.5	43	2
1982			151	**786**	5.2	48	6
1983			160	654	4.1	19	1
1984			229	1070	4.7	53	5
1985			294	1331	4.5	69	3
1986			214	856	4.0	40	5
1987			121	530	4.4	30	0
1988			219	944	4.3	28	6
1989			80	352	4.4	19t	2
1990			99	458	4.6	29	6
1991			51	300	5.9	58	2
1992			43	170	4.0	18	0
Career			1798	8074	4.5	69	38
Playoffs			149	633	4.2		3

Year	Team		Att	Yds	Avg	Lg	TD

Gerald McNeil

Year	Team		Att	Yds	Avg	Lg	TD
1986	CLE	N	1	12	12.0	12	0
1987			1	17	17.0	17	0
1989			2	32	16.0	18	0
Career			4	61	15.3	18	0

Pat McNeil

Year	Team		Att	Yds	Avg	Lg	TD
1976	KC	N	8	26	3.3	7	0

Rod McNeill

Year	Team		Att	Yds	Avg	Lg	TD
1974	NO	N	22	90	4.1	24	1
1975			61	206	3.4	17	2
1976	TB	N	27	135	5.0	17	0
Career			110	431	3.9	24	3

Tom McNeill

Year	Team		Att	Yds	Avg	Lg	TD
1967	NO	N	4	38	9.5	25	0
1968			2	1	0.5	15	0
Career			6	39	6.5	25	0

Buck McPhail

Year	Team		Att	Yds	Avg	Lg	TD
1953	BAL	N	53	138	2.6	30	0

Hal McPhail

Year	Team		Att	Yds	Avg	Lg	TD
1934	BOS	N					1
1935			45	105	2.3		0
Career			45	105	2.3		1

Jerris McPhail

Year	Team		Att	Yds	Avg	Lg	TD
1996	MIA	N	6	28	4.7	10	0

Leon McQuay

Year	Team		Att	Yds	Avg	Lg	TD
1974	NYG	N	55	240	4.4	21	1
1975	NE	N	33	47	1.4	9	0
Career			88	287	3.3	21	1

Kim McQuilken

Year	Team		Att	Yds	Avg	Lg	TD
1974	ATL	N	2	1	0.5	1	0
1975			4	26	6.5	14	0
1976			9	26	2.9	17	0
1977			2	-1	-0.5	-1	0
1979	WAS	N	2	-3	-1.5	-1	0
Career			19	49	2.6	17	0

Bill McRaven

Year	Team		Att	Yds	Avg	Lg	TD
1939	CLE	N	7	29	4.1		0

Chuck McSwain

Year	Team		Att	Yds	Avg	Lg	TD
1987	NE	N	9	23	2.6	9	0

Warren McVea

Year	Team		Att	Yds	Avg	Lg	TD
1968	CIN	A	9	133	14.8	80t	1
1969	KC	A	106	500	4.7	80t	7
1970	KC	N	61	260	4.3	34	0
1971			68	288	4.2	19	3
1973			4	5	1.3	2	0
Career			248	1186	4.8	80t	11
Playoffs			16	39	2.4		0

Bill McWatters

Year	Team		Att	Yds	Avg	Lg	TD
1964	MIN	N	14	60	4.3	16	1

Tom McWilliams

Year	Team		Att	Yds	Avg	Lg	TD
1949	LA	AA	3	15	5.0		0
1950	PIT	N	10	39	3.9	12	0
Career			13	54	4.2	12	0

Jim Meade

Year	Team		Att	Yds	Avg	Lg	TD
1939	WAS	N	13	34	2.6		0
1940			48	115	2.4		0
Career			61	149	2.4		0

Mike Meade

Year	Team		Att	Yds	Avg	Lg	TD
1982	GB	N	14	42	3.0	19	0
1983			55	201	3.7	15	1
1985	DET	N	3	18	6.0	9	0
Career			72	261	3.6	19	1

Eddie Meador

Year	Team		Att	Yds	Avg	Lg	TD
1963	LA	N	1	1	1.0	1	0
1965			2	35	17.5	24	1
1966			1	7	7.0	7	0
1968			1	11	11.0	11	0
1969			1	5	5.0	5	0
Career			6	59	9.8	24	1

Natrone Means

Year	Team		Att	Yds	Avg	Lg	TD
1993	SD	N	160	645	4.0	65t	8
1994			343	1350	3.9	25	12
1995			186	730	3.9	36	5
1996	JAC	N	152	507	3.3	35	2
Career			841	3232	3.8	65t	27
Playoffs			134	610	4.6		4

Curt Mecham

Year	Team		Att	Yds	Avg	Lg	TD
1942	BKN	N	3	0	0.0	5	0

Greg Meehan

Year	Team		Att	Yds	Avg	Lg	TD
1987	CIN	N	4	19	4.8	17	0

Dave Meggett

Year	Team		Att	Yds	Avg	Lg	TD
1989	NYG	N	28	117	4.2	18	0
1990			22	164	7.5	51	0
1991			29	153	5.3	30t	1
1992			32	167	5.2	30	0
1993			69	329	4.8	23	0
1994			91	298	3.3	26t	4
1995	NE	N	60	250	4.2	25	2
1996			40	122	3.0	12	0
Career			371	1600	4.3	51	7
Playoffs			30	141	4.7		0

Steve Meilinger

Year	Team		Att	Yds	Avg	Lg	TD
1961	PIT	N	1	6	6.0	6	0

Jim Mello

Year	Team		Att	Yds	Avg	Lg	TD
1947	BOS	N	33	62	1.9	9	0
1948	LAN-CHIAA		57	246	4.3	55	1
Career			90	308	3.4	55	1

Dan Melville

Year	Team		Att	Yds	Avg	Lg	TD
1979	SF	N	3	0	0.0	0	0

Chuck Mercein

Year	Team		Att	Yds	Avg	Lg	TD
1965	NYG	N	18	55	3.1	15	2
1966			94	327	3.5	22	0
1967	GB	N	14	56	4.0	15	1
1968			17	49	2.9	8	1
1970	NYJ	N	20	44	2.2	10	0
Career			163	531	3.3	22	4
Playoffs			19	33	1.7		1

Ken Mercer

Year	Team		Att	Yds	Avg	Lg	TD
1927	FRA	N					2
1928							5
Career							7

Mike Mercer

Year	Team		Att	Yds	Avg	Lg	TD
1961	MIN	N	1	-32	-32.0	-32	0
1963	OAK	A	1	-5	-5.0	-5	0
1965			1	-1	-1.0	-1	0
Career			3	-38	-12.7	-1	0

Don Meredith

Year	Team		Att	Yds	Avg	Lg	TD
1960	DAL	N	3	4	1.3	8	0
1961			22	176	8.0	28	1
1962			21	74	3.5	14	0
1963			41	185	4.5	26	3
1964			32	81	2.5	17	4
1965			35	247	7.1	22	1
1966			38	242	6.4	22	5
1967			28	84	3.0	16	0
1968			22	123	5.6	16	1
Career			242	1216	5.0	28	15
Playoffs			8	42	5.3		0

Guido Merkens

Year	Team		Att	Yds	Avg	Lg	TD
1981	NO	N	2	-1	-0.5	2	0
1982			9	30	3.3	19	0
1983			1	16	16.0	15	0
1985			1	-2	-2.0	-2	0
1987	PHI	N	3	-8	-2.7	1	0
Career			16	35	2.2	19	0

Bus Mertes

Year	Team		Att	Yds	Avg	Lg	TD
1945	CHIC	N	24	107	4.5	52	0
1946	LA	AA	40	111	2.8		0
1947	BAL	AA	95	321	3.4		2
1948			155	680	4.4		4

Bus Mertes continued

Year	Team		Att	Yds	Avg	Lg	TD
1949	BAL-NYG	AA-N	27	54	2.0		0
Career			341	1273	3.7	52	6
Playoffs			0	73	0.0		2

Dale Messer

Year	Team		Att	Yds	Avg	Lg	TD
1961	SF	N	3	13	4.3	6	0

Frank Mestnik

Year	Team		Att	Yds	Avg	Lg	TD
1960	STL	N	104	429	4.1	55	3
1961			95	334	3.5	26	1
1963	GB	N	1	4	4.0	4	0
Career			200	767	3.8	55	4

Eric Metcalf

Year	Team		Att	Yds	Avg	Lg	TD
1989	CLE	N	187	633	3.4	43	6
1990			80	248	3.1	17	1
1991			30	107	3.6	15	0
1992			73	301	4.1	31	1
1993			129	611	4.7	55	1
1994			93	329	3.5	37t	2
1995	ATL	N	28	133	4.8	23t	0
1996			3	8	2.7	4	0
Career			623	2370	3.8	55	12
Playoffs			14	20	1.4		0

Terry Metcalf

Year	Team		Att	Yds	Avg	Lg	TD
1973	STL	N	148	628	4.2	50	2
1974			152	718	4.7	75t	6
1975			165	816	4.9	52t	9
1976			134	537	4.0	36	3
1977			149	739	5.0	62t	4
1981	WAS	N	18	60	3.3	12	0
Career			766	3498	4.6	75t	24
Playoffs			23	82	3.6		1

Russ Method

Year	Team		Att	Yds	Avg	Lg	TD
1924	DUL						1

Fred Meyer

Year	Team		Att	Yds	Avg	Lg	TD
1942	PHI	N	2	13	6.5	10	0

Ron Meyer

Year	Team		Att	Yds	Avg	Lg	TD
1966	PIT	N	1	-2	-2.0	-2	0

Bob Meyers

Year	Team		Att	Yds	Avg	Lg	TD
1952	SF	N	1	2	2.0	2	0

Al Michaels

Year	Team		Att	Yds	Avg	Lg	TD
1924	AKR	N					1

Mike Michel

Year	Team		Att	Yds	Avg	Lg	TD
1977	MIA	N	1	-2	-2.0	-2	0
1978	PHI	N	1	0	0.0	0	0
Career			2	-2	-1.0	0	0

Tom Michel

Year	Team		Att	Yds	Avg	Lg	TD
1964	MIN	N	39	129	3.3	14	0

Bobby Micho

Year	Team		Att	Yds	Avg	Lg	TD
1987	DEN	N	4	8	2.0	5	0

Mike Micka

Year	Team		Att	Yds	Avg	Lg	TD
1944	WAS	N	25	94	3.8	14	0
1945	WAS-BOS	N	19	62	3.3	6	0
1946	BOS	N	20	76	3.8	19	0
1947			1	-4	-4.0	-4	0
1948			4	3	0.8	3	0
Career			69	231	3.3	19	0

Dave Middleton

Year	Team		Att	Yds	Avg	Lg	TD
1955	DET	N	59	201	3.4	16	2
1956			3	9	3.0	10	0
1958			2	1	0.5	2	0
1960			3	-1	-0.3	1	0
Career			67	210	3.1	16	2

Frank Middleton

Year	Team		Att	Yds	Avg	Lg	TD
1984	IND	N	92	275	3.0	20	1
1985			13	35	2.7	13	1
1987	SD	N	28	74	2.6	21	1
Career			133	384	2.9	21	3

Terdell Middleton

Year	Team		Att	Yds	Avg	Lg	TD
1977	GB	N	35	97	2.8	16	0

Terdell Middleton continued

Year	Team		Att	Yds	Avg	Lg	TD
1978			284	1116	3.9	76t	11
1979			131	495	3.8	28	2
1980			56	155	2.8	15	2
1981			53	181	3.4	34	0
1983	TB	N	2	4	2.0	2	0
Career			561	2048	3.7	76t	15

Nick Mike-Mayer

Year	Team		Att	Yds	Avg	Lg	TD
1979	BUF	N	1	4	4.0	4	0

Mike Mikulak

Year	Team		Att	Yds	Avg	Lg	TD
1934	CHIC	N					4
1935			68	82	1.2		1
1936			24	56	2.3		0
Career			92	138	1.5		5

Don Milano

Year	Team		Att	Yds	Avg	Lg	TD
1975	GB	N	4	41	10.3	15	0

Glyn Milburn

Year	Team		Att	Yds	Avg	Lg	TD
1993	DEN	N	52	231	4.4	26	0
1994			58	201	3.5	20	1
1995			49	266	5.4	29	0
Career			159	698	4.4	29	1
Playoffs			2	-2	-1.0		0

Jack Mildren

Year	Team		Att	Yds	Avg	Lg	TD
1972	BAL	N	3	8	2.7	5	0
1973			2	14	7.0	10	0
Career			5	22	4.4	10	0

Ostell Miles

Year	Team		Att	Yds	Avg	Lg	TD
1992	CIN	N	8	22	2.8	9	0
1993			22	56	2.5	15	1
Career			30	78	2.6	15	1

Hugh Millen

Year	Team		Att	Yds	Avg	Lg	TD
1988	ATL	N	1	7	7.0	7	0
1989			1	0	0.0	0	0
1990			7	-12	-1.7	2	0
1991	NE	N	31	92	3.0	14	1
1992			17	108	6.4	26	0
1994	DEN	N	5	57	11.4	24	0
1995			3	8	2.7	7	0
Career			65	260	4.0	26	1

Alan Miller

Year	Team		Att	Yds	Avg	Lg	TD
1960	BOS	A	101	416	4.1		1
1961	OAK	A	85	255	3.0	15	3
1962			65	182	2.8	11	1
1963			62	270	4.4	35	3
1965			73	272	3.7	26	1
Career			386	1395	3.6	35	9

Anthony Miller

Year	Team		Att	Yds	Avg	Lg	TD
1988	SD	N	7	45	6.4	20	0
1989			4	21	5.3	24	0
1990			3	13	4.3	10	0
1992			1	-1	-1.0	-1	0
1993			1	0	0.0	0	0
1994	DEN	N	3	3	3.0	3	0
1995			1	5	5.0	5	0
1996			3	39	13.0	26t	1
Career			21	125	6.0	26t	1

Candy Miller

Year	Team		Att	Yds	Avg	Lg	TD
1922	CAN	N					1

Chris Miller

Year	Team		Att	Yds	Avg	Lg	TD
1987	ATL	N	4	21	5.3	11	0
1988			31	138	4.5	29	1
1989			10	20	2.0	7	0
1990			26	99	3.8	18	1
1991			32	229	7.2	20	0
1992			23	89	3.9	16	0
1993			2	11	5.5	6	0
1994	LARM	N	20	100	5.0	16	0
1995	STL	N	22	67	3.0	13	0
Career			170	774	4.6	29	2
Playoffs			4	18	4.5		0

Cleo Miller

Year	Team		Att	Yds	Avg	Lg	TD
1974	KC	N	40	186	4.7	47	0
1975	KC-CLE	N	13	23	1.8	10	1

Cleo Miller continued

Year	Team		Att	Yds	Avg	Lg	TD
1976	CLE	N	153	613	4.0	21	4
1977			163	756	4.6	38	4
1978			89	336	3.8	18	1
1979			39	213	5.5	39t	1
1980			28	139	5.0	50	3
1981			52	165	3.2	13	2
1982			16	61	3.8	17	0
Career			593	2492	4.2	50	16
Playoffs			1	1	1.0		0

Eddie Miller

Year	Team		Att	Yds	Avg	Lg	TD
1939	NYG	N	30	99	3.3		1
1940			65	206			1
Career			95	305	3.2		2
Playoffs			3	10	3.3		0

Jim Miller

Year	Team		Att	Yds	Avg	Lg	TD
1980	SF	N	2	-12	-6.0	0	0

Jim Miller

Year	Team		Att	Yds	Avg	Lg	TD
1995	PIT	N	1	2	2.0	2	0
1996			2	4	-2.0	0	0
Career			3	-2	-0.7	2	0

Junior Miller

Year	Team		Att	Yds	Avg	Lg	TD
1980	ATL	N	2	-2	-1.0	0	0
1983			1	2	2.0	2	0
Career			3	0	0.0	2	0

Larry Miller

Year	Team		Att	Yds	Avg	Lg	TD
1987	MIN	N	1	-1	-1.0	-1	0

Mark Miller

Year	Team		Att	Yds	Avg	Lg	TD
1978	CLE	N	7	63	9.0	17	1
1979			1	-2	-2.0	-2	0
Career			8	61	7.6	17	1

Mike Miller

Year	Team		Att	Yds	Avg	Lg	TD
1983	NYG	N	1	2	2.0	2	0

Paul Miller

Year	Team		Att	Yds	Avg	Lg	TD
1936	GB	N	52	227	4.4		1
1937			71	265	3.7		0
1938			20	48	2.4		0
Career			143	540	3.8		1
Playoffs			2	-6	-3.0		0

Robert Miller

Year	Team		Att	Yds	Avg	Lg	TD
1975	MIN	N	30	93	3.1	10	1
1976			67	286	4.3	36	0
1977			46	152	3.3	14	0
1978			70	213	3.0	19	3
1979			35	109	3.1	20	2
1980			27	98	3.6	27t	1
Career			275	951	3.5	36	7
Playoffs			35	92	2.6		0

Ron Miller

Year	Team		Att	Yds	Avg	Lg	TD
1962	LA	N	3	27	9.0	13	0

Solomon Miller

Year	Team		Att	Yds	Avg	Lg	TD
1986	NYG	N	1	3	3.0	3	0

Terry Miller

Year	Team		Att	Yds	Avg	Lg	TD
1978	BUF	N	238	1060	4.5	60t	7
1979			139	484	3.5	75	1
1980			12	35	2.9	6	0
1981	SEA	N	2	4	2.0	2	0
Career			391	1583	4.0	75	8

Tom Miller

Year	Team		Att	Yds	Avg	Lg	TD
1944	PHI	N	1	-2	-2.0	-2	0

Willie Miller

Year	Team		Att	Yds	Avg	Lg	TD
1975	CLE	N	1	-2	-2.0	-2	0
1978	LA	N	1	-7	-7.0	-7	0
1979			1	4	4.0	4	0
1980			1	-2	-2.0	-2	0
1982	LARM	N	1	5	5.0	5	0
Career			5	-2	-0.4	5	0

Wayne Millner

Year	Team		Att	Yds	Avg	Lg	TD
1937	WAS	N	2	6	3.0		0
1938			3	5	1.7		0

Wayne Millner continued

Year	Team		Att	Yds	Avg	Lg	TD
1939			4	12	3.0		0
1940			3	31	10.3		0
1941			2	8	4.0	8	0
Career			14	62	4.4	8	0

Ernie Mills

Year	Team		Att	Yds	Avg	Lg	TD
1992	PIT	N	1	20	20.0	20	0
1993			3	12	4.0	19	0
1994			3	18	6.0	17	0
1995			5	39	7.8	20	0
1996			2	24	12.0	15	0
Career			14	113	8.1	20	0
Playoffs			3	12	4.0		0

Joe Mills

Year	Team		Att	Yds	Avg	Lg	TD
1922	AKR	N					1

Stan Mills

Year	Team		Att	Yds	Avg	Lg	TD
1923	GB	N					1

Brian Milne

Year	Team		Att	Yds	Avg	Lg	TD
1996	CIN	N	8	22	2.8	5	1

Charley Milstead

Year	Team		Att	Yds	Avg	Lg	TD
1960	HOU	A	6	-21	-3.5		0

Eugene Milton

Year	Team		Att	Yds	Avg	Lg	TD
1968	MIA	A	2	46	23.0	34	0
1969			7	62	8.9	27	0
Career			9	108	12.0	34	0

David Mims

Year	Team		Att	Yds	Avg	Lg	TD
1993	ATL	N	1	3	3.0	3	0

Gene Mingo

Year	Team		Att	Yds	Avg	Lg	TD
1960	DEN	A	83	323	3.9	39	4
1961			18	51	2.8	15	0
1962			54	287	5.3	82	4
1963			24	90	3.8	17	0
1964			6	26	4.3	9	0
Career			185	777	4.2	82	8

Frank Minini

Year	Team		Att	Yds	Avg	Lg	TD
1947	CHIB	N	26	132	5.1	33t	2
1948			24	79	3.3	18	2
1949	PIT	N	1	5	5.0	5	0
Career			51	216	4.2	33t	4

Tony Minisi

Year	Team		Att	Yds	Avg	Lg	TD
1948	NYG	N	36	160	4.4	19	1

Randy Minniear

Year	Team		Att	Yds	Avg	Lg	TD
1967	NYG	N	35	98	2.8	13	1
1968			14	38	2.7	9	2
1969			35	141	4.0	16	1
1970	CLE	N	12	39	3.3	9	1
Career			96	316	3.3	16	5

Lincoln Minor

Year	Team		Att	Yds	Avg	Lg	TD
1973	NO	N	3	10	3.3		0

Cedric Minter

Year	Team		Att	Yds	Avg	Lg	TD
1984	NYJ	N	34	136	4.0	14	1
1985			8	23	2.9	11	0
Career			42	159	3.8	14	1

Ed Mioduszewski

Year	Team		Att	Yds	Avg	Lg	TD
1953	BAL	N	3	33	11.0	25	0

George Mira

Year	Team		Att	Yds	Avg	Lg	TD
1964	SF	N	18	177	9.8	37	0
1965			5	64	12.8	25	0
1966			10	103	10.3	38	0
1967			7	23	3.3	9	0
1968			1	5	5.0	5	0
1969	PHI	N	3	16	5.3	6	0
1971	MIA	N	6	-9	-1.5	3	0
Career			50	379	7.6	38	0

Rick Mirer

Year	Team		Att	Yds	Avg	Lg	TD
1993	SEA	N	68	343	5.0	33	3
1994			34	153	4.5	14	0
1995			43	193	4.5	24	1

Rick Mirer continued

Year	Team	Att	Yds	Avg	Lg	TD
1996		33	191	5.8	33	2
Career		178	880	4.9	33	6

Bob Mitchell

Year	Team	Att	Yds	Avg	Lg	TD
1946	LA AA	8	-12	-1.5		0
1947		32	85	2.7		0
1948		2	-2	-1.0		0
Career		42	71	1.7		0

Bobby Mitchell

Year	Team	Att	Yds	Avg	Lg	TD
1958	CLE N	80	500	6.3	63t	1
1959		131	743	5.7	90t	5
1960		111	506	4.6	50	5
1961		101	548	5.4	56t	5
1962	WAS N	1	5	5.0	5	0
1963		3	24	8.0	21	0
1964		2	33	16.5	19	0
1966		13	141	10.8	48	1
1967		61	189	3.1	16	1
1968		10	46	4.6	13	0
Career		513	2735	5.3	90t	18

Brian Mitchell

Year	Team	Att	Yds	Avg	Lg	TD
1990	WAS N	15	81	5.4	21	1
1991		3	14	4.7	8	0
1992		6	70	11.7	33	0
1993		63	246	3.9	29t	3
1994		78	311	4.0	33	0
1995		46	301	6.5	36t	1
1996		39	193	4.9	32	0
Career		250	1216	4.9	36t	5
Playoffs		25	149	6.0		1

Charlie Mitchell

Year	Team	Att	Yds	Avg	Lg	TD
1963	DEN A	23	45	2.0	7	0
1964		177	590	3.3	33	5
1966		70	199	2.8	21	0
1967		82	308	3.8	35	0
Career		352	1142	3.2	35	5

Fondren Mitchell

Year	Team	Att	Yds	Avg	Lg	TD
1946	MIA AA	5	17	3.4		0

Gran Mitchell

Year	Team	Att	Yds	Avg	Lg	TD
1937	BKN N	2	4	2.0		0

Jim Mitchell

Year	Team	Att	Yds	Avg	Lg	TD
1969	ATL N	5	77	15.4	40	0
1970		5	23	4.6	12	1
1971		4	25	6.3	24	0
1972		2	19	9.5	18	0
1973		5	34	6.8	13	0
1974		3	21	7.0	15	0
1976		1	-6	-6.0	-6	0
1977		1	-6	-6.0	-6	0
Career		26	187	7.2	40	1

Lydell Mitchell

Year	Team	Att	Yds	Avg	Lg	TD
1972	BAL N	45	215	4.8	14	1
1973		253	963	3.8	36	2
1974		214	757	3.5	31t	5
1975		289	1193	4.1	70t	11
1976		289	1200	4.2	43	5
1977		301	1159	3.9	64t	3
1978	SD N	214	820	3.8	25	3
1979		63	211	3.3	15	0
1980	LA N	7	16	2.3	5	0
Career		1675	6534	3.9	70t	30
Playoffs		73	218	3.0		1

Scott Mitchell

Year	Team	Att	Yds	Avg	Lg	TD
1992	MIA N	8	10	1.3	8	0
1993		21	89	4.2	32	0
1994	DET N	15	24	1.6	7	1
1995		36	104	2.9	18	4
1996		37	83	2.2	9	4
Career		117	310	2.6	32	9
Playoffs		1	-1	-1.0		0

Stan Mitchell

Year	Team	Att	Yds	Avg	Lg	TD
1967	MIA A	83	269	3.2	22	3
1968		54	176	3.3	30	1
1969		28	80	2.9	12	0

Stan Mitchell continued

Year	Team	Att	Yds	Avg	Lg	TD
1970	MIA N	8	23	2.9	9	0
Career		173	548	3.2	30	4

Stump Mitchell

Year	Team	Att	Yds	Avg	Lg	TD
1981	STL N	31	175	5.6	43	0
1982		39	189	4.8	32t	1
1983		68	373	5.5	46	3
1984		81	434	5.4	39	9
1985		183	1006	5.5	64	7
1986		174	800	4.6	44	5
1987		203	781	3.8	42	3
1988	PHX N	164	726	4.4	47	4
1989		43	165	3.8	14	0
Career		986	4649	4.7	64	32
Playoffs		7	21	3.0		0

Tom Mitchell

Year	Team	Att	Yds	Avg	Lg	TD
1971	BAL N	2	9	4.5	13	0
1972		0	7		7L	0
1974	SF N	1	-2	-2.0	-2	0
Career		3	14	4.7	13	0

Billy Mixon

Year	Team	Att	Yds	Avg	Lg	TD
1953	SF	25	176	7.0	33	1
1954		7	19	2.7	7	0
Career		32	195	6.1	33	1

Kelly Moan

Year	Team	Att	Yds	Avg	Lg	TD
1939	CLE N	2	-15	-7.5		0

Orson Mobley

Year	Team	Att	Yds	Avg	Lg	TD
1986	DEN N	1	-1	-1.0	-1	0

Rudy Mobley

Year	Team	Att	Yds	Avg	Lg	TD
1947	BAL AA	26	90	3.5		1

Ed Modzelewski

Year	Team	Att	Yds	Avg	Lg	TD
1952	PIT N	82	195	2.4	14	3
1955	CLE N	185	619	3.3	25	6
1956		107	431	4.0	23	2
1957		10	21	2.1	5	0
1958		3	8	2.7	3	0
1959		6	18	3.0	18	0
Career		393	1292	3.3	25	11
Playoffs		13	61	4.7		0

Dicky Moegle

Year	Team	Att	Yds	Avg	Lg	TD
1955	SF N	41	235	5.7	39	5
1956		7	18	2.6	12	0
1957		9	48	5.3	18t	1
1959		3	9	3.0	4	0
Career		60	310	5.2	39	6

Tim Moffett

Year	Team	Att	Yds	Avg	Lg	TD
1987	SD N	1	1	1.0	1	0

Johnny Mohardt

Year	Team	Att	Yds	Avg	Lg	TD
1926	CHI A					4

Chris Mohr

Year	Team	Att	Yds	Avg	Lg	TD
1992	BUF N	1	11	11.0	11	0
1994		1	-9	-9.0	-9	0
Career		2	2	1.0	11	0
Playoffs		1	-14	-14.0		0

Ralf Mojsiejenko

Year	Team	Att	Yds	Avg	Lg	TD
1985	SD N	1	0	0.0	0	0
1990	WAS N	1	0	0.0	0	0
Career		2	0	0.0	0	0

Bo Molenda

Year	Team	Att	Yds	Avg	Lg	TD
1928	NYY N					1
1929	GB N					3
1930						3
1931						3
1933	NYG N	77	203	2.6		3
1934		28	99	3.5		0
Career		105	302	2.9		13
Playoffs		2	6	3.0		0

Keith Molesworth

Year	Team	Att	Yds	Avg	Lg	TD
1931	CHIB N					1

Keith Molesworth continued

Year	Team	Att	Yds	Avg	Lg	TD
1932						2
1933		60	145	2.4		0
1934		61	125	2.0		1
1935		81	293	3.6		4
1936		60	276	4.6		0
1937		20	53	2.6		0
Career		282	892	3.2		8
Playoffs		23	11	0.5		0

Lou Molinet

Year	Team	Att	Yds	Avg	Lg	TD
1927	FRA N					1

Jim Monachino

Year	Team	Att	Yds	Avg	Lg	TD
1951	SF N	21	74	3.5	7t	2
1953		4	10	2.5	5	0
1955	WAS N	46	207	4.5	24	2
Career		71	291	4.1	24	4

Avery Monfort

Year	Team	Att	Yds	Avg	Lg	TD
1941	CHIC N	3	8	2.7	11	0

Art Monk

Year	Team	Att	Yds	Avg	Lg	TD
1981	WAS N	1	-5	-5.0	-5	0
1982		7	21	3.0	14	0
1983		3	-19	-6.3	2	0
1984		2	18	9.0	18	0
1985		7	51	7.3	16	0
1986		4	27	6.8	21	0
1987		6	63	10.5	26	0
1988		7	46	6.6	23	0
1989		3	8	2.7	14	0
1990		7	59	8.4	26	0
1991		9	19	2.1	14	0
1992		6	45	7.5	16	0
1993		1	-1	-1.0	-1	0
Career		63	332	5.3	26	0
Playoffs		6	17	2.8		0

Bob Monnett

Year	Team	Att	Yds	Avg	Lg	TD
1933	GB N	108	412	3.8		4
1934						2
1935		68	336	4.9		1
1936		104	224	2.2		0
1937		87	161	1.9		1
1938		75	225	3.0		0
Career		442	1358	3.1		8
Playoffs		16	27	1.7		1

Carl Monroe

Year	Team	Att	Yds	Avg	Lg	TD
1983	SF N	10	23	2.3	13	0
1984		3	13	4.3	7	0
1987		2	26	13.0	17	0
Career		15	62	4.1	17	0
Playoffs		1	10	10.0		0

Tommy Mont

Year	Team	Att	Yds	Avg	Lg	TD
1947	WAS N	1	7	7.0	7	0
1948		11	103	9.4	33t	0
1949		14	75	5.4	27	0
Career		26	185	7.1	33t	1

Joe Montana

Year	Team	Att	Yds	Avg	Lg	TD
1979	SF N	3	22	7.3	13	0
1980		32	77	2.4	11	2
1981		25	95	3.8	20t	2
1982		30	118	3.9	21	1
1983		61	284	4.7	18	2
1984		39	118	3.0	15	2
1985		42	153	3.6	16	3
1986		17	38	2.2	17	0
1987		35	141	4.0	20	1
1988		38	132	3.5	15	3
1989		49	227	4.6	19	3
1990		40	162	4.0	20	1
1992		3	28	9.3	16	0
1993	KC N	25	64	2.6	17	0
1994		18	17	0.9	13	0
Career		457	1676	3.7	21	20
Playoffs		63	314	5.0		2

Bill Montgomery

Year	Team	Att	Yds	Avg	Lg	TD
1946	CHIC N	8	11	1.4	6	0

Year	Team		Att	Yds	Avg	Lg	TD

Cleo Montgomery

Year	Team		Att	Yds	Avg	Lg	TD
1980	CIN	N	1	12	12.0	12	0
1983	LARI	N	2	7	3.5	5	0
1984			1	1	1.0	1	0
Career			4	20	5.0	12	0
Playoffs			1	11	11.0		0

Greg Montgomery

Year	Team		Att	Yds	Avg	Lg	TD
1989	HOU	N	3	17	5.7	11	0
1992			2	-14	-7.0	0	0
1996	BAL	N	1	0	0.0	0	0
Career			6	3	0.5	11	0
Playoffs			1	0	0.0		0

Mike Montgomery

Year	Team		Att	Yds	Avg	Lg	TD
1971	SD	N	60	226	3.8	26	1
1972	DAL	N	35	81	2.3	10	1
1973			1	-10	-10.0	-10	0
Career			96	297	3.1	26	2

Ross Montgomery

Year	Team		Att	Yds	Avg	Lg	TD
1969	CHI	N	15	52	3.5	6	0
1970			62	229	3.7	38	0
Career			77	281	3.6	38	0

Tyrone Montgomery

Year	Team		Att	Yds	Avg	Lg	TD
1993	LARI	N	37	106	2.9	15	0
1994			36	97	2.7	15	0
Career			73	203	2.8	15	0
Playoffs			24	72	3.0		0

Wilbert Montgomery

Year	Team		Att	Yds	Avg	Lg	TD
1977	PHI	N	45	183	4.1	27t	2
1978			259	1220	4.7	47	9
1979			338	1512	4.5	62t	9
1980			193	778	4.0	72t	8
1981			286	1402	4.9	41	8
1982			114	515	4.5	90t	7
1983			29	139	4.8	32	0
1984			201	789	3.9	27	2
1985	DET	N	75	251	3.3	22	0
Career			1540	6789	4.4	90t	45
Playoffs			141	518	3.7		6

Warren Moon

Year	Team		Att	Yds	Avg	Lg	TD
1984	HOU	N	58	211	3.6	31	1
1985			39	130	3.3	17	0
1986			42	157	3.7	19	2
1987			34	112	3.3	20	3
1988			33	88	2.7	14	5
1989			70	268	3.8	19	4
1990			55	215	3.9	17	2
1991			33	68	2.1	12	2
1992			27	147	5.4	23	1
1993			48	145	3.0	35	1
1994	MIN	N	27	55	2.0	12	0
1995			33	82	2.5	16	0
1996			9	6	0.7	5	0
Career			508	1684	3.3	35	21
Playoffs			35	114	3.3		0

Tipp Mooney

Year	Team		Att	Yds	Avg	Lg	TD
1944	CHIB	N	29	88	3.0	14	0
1945			17	105	6.2	64	0
Career			46	193	4.2	64	0

Alex Moore

Year	Team		Att	Yds	Avg	Lg	TD
1968	DEN	A	4	22	5.5	10	0

Alvin Moore

Year	Team		Att	Yds	Avg	Lg	TD
1983	BAL	N	57	205	3.6	13	1
1984	IND	N	38	127	3.3	18	2
1985	DET	N	80	221	2.8	18	4
1986			19	73	3.8	18	0
1987	SEA	N	3	15	5.0	13	0
Career			197	641	3.3	18	7

Bill Moore

Year	Team		Att	Yds	Avg	Lg	TD
1932	CHIC	N					1

Bill Moore

Year	Team		Att	Yds	Avg	Lg	TD
1939	DET	N	1	7	7.0	7	0

Bob Moore

Year	Team		Att	Yds	Avg	Lg	TD
1976	TB	N	2	23	11.5	22	0
Playoffs			1	3	3.0		0

Booker Moore

Year	Team		Att	Yds	Avg	Lg	TD
1982	BUF	N	16	38	2.4	9	0
1983			60	275	4.6	21	0
1984			24	84	3.5	21	0
1985			15	23	1.5	4	1
Career			115	420	3.7	21	1

Dave Moore

Year	Team		Att	Yds	Avg	Lg	TD
1995	TB	N	1	4	4.0	4	0

Derrick Moore

Year	Team		Att	Yds	Avg	Lg	TD
1993	DET	N	88	405	4.6	48	3
1994			27	52	1.9	12	4
1995	CAR	N	195	740	3.8	53t	4
Career			310	1197	3.9	53t	11
Playoffs			1	5	5.0		1

Dinty Moore

Year	Team		Att	Yds	Avg	Lg	TD
1927	POT	N					1

Gene Moore

Year	Team		Att	Yds	Avg	Lg	TD
1969	SF	N	2	4	2.0	2	0

Henry Moore

Year	Team		Att	Yds	Avg	Lg	TD
1956	NYG	N	2	-2	-1.0	0	0
Playoffs			1	0	0.0		0

Jeff Moore

Year	Team		Att	Yds	Avg	Lg	TD
1979	SEA	N	44	168	3.8	18	2
1980			60	202	3.4	20	0
1981			1	15	15.0	15	0
1982	SF	N	85	281	3.3	19	4
1983			15	43	2.9	11	1
1984	WAS	N	3	13	4.3	5	0
Career			208	722	3.5	20	7

Jerald Moore

Year	Team		Att	Yds	Avg	Lg	TD
1996	STL	N	11	32	2.9	14	0

Joe Moore

Year	Team		Att	Yds	Avg	Lg	TD
1971	CHI	N	29	90	3.1	12	0
1973			58	191	3.3	25	0
Career			87	281	3.2	25	0

Lenny Moore

Year	Team		Att	Yds	Avg	Lg	TD
1956	BAL	N	86	649	7.5	79t	8
1957			98	488	5.0	55t	3
1958			82	598	7.3	73t	7
1959			92	422	4.6	31t	2
1960			91	374	4.1	57t	4
1961			92	648	7.0	54t	7
1962			106	470	4.4	25	2
1963			27	136	5.0	25t	2
1964			157	584	3.7	32t	16
1965			133	464	3.5	28t	5
1966			63	209	3.3	18	3
1967			42	132	3.1	21	4
Career			1069	5174	4.8	79t	63
Playoffs			34	104	3.1		0

Leonard Moore

Year	Team		Att	Yds	Avg	Lg	TD
1987	MIN	N	4	11	2.8	4	0

Manfred Moore

Year	Team		Att	Yds	Avg	Lg	TD
1974	SF	N	10	24	2.4	8	1
1975			3	10	3.3	4	0
1976	TB	N	7	4	0.6	7	0
Career			20	38	1.9	8	1

Nat Moore

Year	Team		Att	Yds	Avg	Lg	TD
1974	MIA	N	3	16	5.3	15	0
1975			8	69	8.6	36	0
1976			4	36	9.0	21	0
1977			14	89	6.4	24	1
1978			4	-3	-0.8	4	0
1979			3	22	7.3	18	0
1980			1	3	3.0	3	0
1981			1	3	3.0	3	0
1984			1	3	3.0	3	0

Nat Moore continued

Year	Team		Att	Yds	Avg	Lg	TD
1985			1	11	11.0	11	0
Career			40	249	6.2	36	1
Playoffs			1	7	7.0		0

Paul Moore

Year	Team		Att	Yds	Avg	Lg	TD
1940	DET	N	2	4	2.0		0

Ricky Moore

Year	Team		Att	Yds	Avg	Lg	TD
1986	BUF	N	33	104	3.2	14	1
1987	HOU	N	7	22	3.1	11	0
Career			40	126	3.1	14	1

Rob Moore

Year	Team		Att	Yds	Avg	Lg	TD
1990	NYJ	N	2	-4	-2.0	4	0
1992			1	21	21.0	21	0
1993			1	-6	-6.0	-6	0
1994			1	-3	-3.0	-3	0
Career			5	8	1.6	21	0

Ron Moore

Year	Team		Att	Yds	Avg	Lg	TD
1993	PHX	N	263	1018	3.9	20	9
1994	ARI	N	232	780	3.4	24	4
1995	NYJ	N	43	121	2.8	14	0
1996			1	1	1.0	1	0
Career			539	1920	3.6	24	13

Shawn Moore

Year	Team		Att	Yds	Avg	Lg	TD
1992	DEN	N	8	39	4.9	11	0

Tom Moore

Year	Team		Att	Yds	Avg	Lg	TD
1960	GB	N	45	237	5.3	58t	4
1961			61	302	5.0	69	1
1962			112	377	3.4	32t	7
1963			132	658	5.0	77t	6
1964			102	371	3.6	35	2
1965			51	124	2.4	13	0
1966	LA	N	104	272	2.6	18	1
1967	ATL	N	53	104	2.0	18	0
Career			660	2445	3.7	77t	21
Playoffs			22	79	3.6		0

Wilbur Moore

Year	Team		Att	Yds	Avg	Lg	TD
1939	WAS	N	27	100	3.7		0
1940			15	89	5.9		2
1941			10	48	4.8	42	1
1942			10	25	2.5	18	0
1943			40	231	5.8	47	2
1944			37	140	3.8	75t	2
1945			29	206	7.1	57t	1
1946			15	62	4.1	19	0
Career			183	901	4.9	75t	8
Playoffs			6	2	0.3		0

Emery Moorehead

Year	Team		Att	Yds	Avg	Lg	TD
1977	NYG	N	1	5	5.0	5	0
1979			36	95	2.6	11	0
1980	DEN	N	2	7	3.5	4	0
1982	CHI	N	2	3	1.5	6	0
1983			5	6	1.2	5	0
1984			1	-2	-2.0	-2	0
Career			47	114	2.4	11	0

Gonzalo Morales

Year	Team		Att	Yds	Avg	Lg	TD
1947	PIT	N	29	96	3.3	18	0
1948			13	20	1.5	8	0
Career			42	116	2.8	18	0

Fran Moran

Year	Team		Att	Yds	Avg	Lg	TD
1926	FRA	N					5
1927	FRA-CHIC	N					2
1930	NYG	N					4
1931							2
1932							1
1933			4	8	2.0		0
Career			4	8	2.0		14

Doug Moreau

Year	Team		Att	Yds	Avg	Lg	TD
1967	MIA	A	1	-2	-2.0	-2	0

Arnold Morgado

Year	Team		Att	Yds	Avg	Lg	TD
1977	KC	N	3	12	4.0	9	0
1978			160	593	3.7	18	7
1979			75	231	3.1	19	4

Arnold Morgado *continued*

Year	Team		Att	Yds	Avg	Lg	TD
1980			47	120	2.6	11	4
Career			285	956	3.4	19	15

Anthony Morgan

Year	Team		Att	Yds	Avg	Lg	TD
1991	CHI	N	3	18	6.0	13	0
1992			3	68	22.7	35	0
Career			6	86	14.3	35	0

Boyd Morgan

Year	Team		Att	Yds	Avg	Lg	TD
1939	WAS	N	1	0	0.0	0	0

Joe Morgan

Year	Team		Att	Yds	Avg	Lg	TD
1949	SF	AA	0	-1		-1L	0

Stanley Morgan

Year	Team		Att	Yds	Avg	Lg	TD
1977	NE	N	1	10	10.0	10	0
1978			2	11	5.5	6	0
1979			7	39	5.6	17	0
1980			4	36	9.0	16	0
1981			2	21	10.5	1t	0
1982			2	3	1.5	3	0
1983			1	13	13.0	13	0
1985			1	0	0.0	0	0
1988			1	-6	-6.0	-6	0
Career			21	127	6.0	17	0
Playoffs			1	-2	-2.0		0

Larry Moriarty

Year	Team		Att	Yds	Avg	Lg	TD
1983	HOU	N	65	321	4.9	80	3
1984			189	785	4.2	51t	6
1985			106	381	3.6	18	3
1986	HOU-KC	N	90	252	2.8	11	1
1987	KC	N	30	107	3.6	11	0
1988			20	62	3.1	9	0
Career			500	1908	3.8	80	13
Playoffs			2	7	3.5		0

Pat Moriarty

Year	Team		Att	Yds	Avg	Lg	TD
1979	CLE	N	14	11	0.8	8	2

Milt Morin

Year	Team		Att	Yds	Avg	Lg	TD
1968	CLE	N	1	8	8.0	8	0
1969			2	30	15.0	22	0
1970			1	2	2.0	2	0
1971			1	1	1.0	1	0
Career			5	41	8.2	22	0

Jack Morlock

Year	Team		Att	Yds	Avg	Lg	TD
1940	DET	N	1	0	0.0	0	0

Mike Moroski

Year	Team		Att	Yds	Avg	Lg	TD
1979	ATL	N	3	31	10.3	19	1
1981			3	17	5.7	14	0
1983			2	12	6.0	7	0
1984			21	98	4.7	17	0
1985	HOU	N	2	2	1.0	2	0
1986	SF	N	6	22	3.7	12	1
Career			37	182	4.9	19	2

Earl Morrall

Year	Team		Att	Yds	Avg	Lg	TD
1956	SF	N	6	10	1.7	8	0
1957	PIT	N	41	81	2.0	35	2
1958	PIT-DET	N	11	80	7.3	40	0
1959	DET	N	26	112	4.3	22	0
1960			10	37	3.7	17	1
1961			20	86	4.3	25	0
1962			17	65	3.8	29	1
1963			26	105	4.0	18	1
1964			10	70	7.0	25	0
1965	NYG	N	17	52	3.1	14	0
1966			5	12	2.4	9	0
1967			4	11	2.8	10	1
1968	BAL	N	11	18	1.6	11	1
1970			2	6	3.0	5	0
1971			6	13	2.2	16	0
1972	MIA	N	17	67	3.9	31t	1
1973			1	9	9.0	9	0
1974			1	11	11.0	11	0
1975			4	33	8.3	16	0
Career			235	878	3.7	40	8
Playoffs			8	2	0.3		0

Bam Morris

Year	Team		Att	Yds	Avg	Lg	TD
1994	PIT	N	198	836	4.2	20	7
1995			148	559	3.8	30t	9
1996	BAL	N	172	737	4.3	19	4
Career			518	2132	4.1	30t	20
Playoffs			75	250	3.3		4

Frank Morris

Year	Team		Att	Yds	Avg	Lg	TD
1942	CHIB	N	3	7	2.3	6	0

George Morris

Year	Team		Att	Yds	Avg	Lg	TD
1941	CLE	N	24	69	2.9	20	0
1942			22	65	3.0	28	0
Career			46	134	2.9	28	0

Jamie Morris

Year	Team		Att	Yds	Avg	Lg	TD
1988	WAS	N	126	437	3.5	27t	2
1989			124	336	2.7	12t	2
1990	NE	N	2	4	2.0	3	0
Career			252	777	3.1	27t	4

Joe Morris

Year	Team		Att	Yds	Avg	Lg	TD
1982	NYG	N	15	48	3.2	7	1
1983			35	145	4.1	16	0
1984			133	510	3.8	28	4
1985			294	1336	4.5	65t	21
1986			341	1516	4.4	54	14
1987			193	658	3.4	34	3
1988			307	1083	3.5	27	5
1991	CLE	N	93	289	3.1	15	2
Career			1411	5585	4.0	65t	50
Playoffs			140	553	4.0		4

Johnny Morris

Year	Team		Att	Yds	Avg	Lg	TD
1958	CHIB	N	52	239	4.6	32	2
1959			87	312	3.6	33	0
1960	CHI	N	73	417	5.7	61t	3
1961			8	49	6.1	21	0
1962			2	7	3.5	7	0
1963			1	10	10.0	10	0
1967			1	6	6.0	6	0
Career			224	1040	4.6	61t	5

Larry Morris

Year	Team		Att	Yds	Avg	Lg	TD
1955	LA	N	40	148	3.7	22	1

Larry Morris

Year	Team		Att	Yds	Avg	Lg	TD
1987	GB	N	8	18	2.3	10	0

Lee Morris

Year	Team		Att	Yds	Avg	Lg	TD
1987	GB	N	2	2	1.0	4	0

Max Morris

Year	Team		Att	Yds	Avg	Lg	TD
1946	CHI	AA	1	20	20.0	20	0

Mercury Morris

Year	Team		Att	Yds	Avg	Lg	TD
1969	MIA	A	23	110	4.8	37	1
1970	MIA	N	60	409	6.8	40	0
1971			57	315	5.5	51	1
1972			190	1000	5.3	33	12
1973			149	954	6.4	70t	10
1974			56	214	3.8	17t	1
1975			219	875	4.0	49	4
1976	SD	N	50	256	5.1	30	2
Career			804	4133	5.1	70t	31
Playoffs			95	440	4.6		1

Randall Morris

Year	Team		Att	Yds	Avg	Lg	TD
1984	SEA	N	58	189	3.3	16	0
1985			55	236	4.3	21	0
1986			19	149	7.8	49t	1
1987			21	71	3.4	13	0
1988			3	6	2.0	5	0
Career			156	651	4.2	49t	1
Playoffs			4	2	0.5		0

Ron Morris

Year	Team		Att	Yds	Avg	Lg	TD
1988	CHI	N	3	40	13.3	21	0
1989			1	-14	-14.0	-14	0
1990			2	26	13.0	16	0
Career			6	52	8.7	21	0

Wayne Morris

Year	Team		Att	Yds	Avg	Lg	TD
1976	STL	N	64	292	4.6	27	3

Wayne Morris *continued*

Year	Team		Att	Yds	Avg	Lg	TD
1977			165	661	4.0	35	8
1978			174	631	3.6	27	1
1979			106	387	3.7	16	8
1980			117	456	3.9	24	6
1981			109	417	3.8	14	5
1982			84	274	3.3	11	4
1983			75	257	3.4	17	2
1984	SD	N	5	12	2.4	5	1
Career			899	3387	3.8	35	38
Playoffs			3	14	4.7		0

Dennis Morrison

Year	Team		Att	Yds	Avg	Lg	TD
1974	SF	N	1	0	0.0	0	0

Duke Morrison

Year	Team		Att	Yds	Avg	Lg	TD
1926	LA	A					2

Fred Morrison

Year	Team		Att	Yds	Avg	Lg	TD
1950	CHIB	N	66	252	3.8	25	1
1951			29	96	3.3	26	0
1952			95	367	3.9	57	3
1953			95	307	3.2	17	2
1954	CLE	N	51	231	4.5	24	0
1955			156	824	5.3	56	3
1956			83	340	4.1	41	1
Career			575	2417	4.2	57	10
Playoffs			26	66	2.5		2

Joe Morrison

Year	Team		Att	Yds	Avg	Lg	TD
1959	NYG	N	62	165	2.7	14	1
1960			103	346	3.4	9	2
1961			33	48	1.5	14	1
1962			35	146	4.2	21	1
1963			119	568	4.8	70t	3
1964			45	138	3.1	15t	1
1965			3	20	6.7	11t	0
1966			67	275	4.1	20	2
1967			36	161	4.5	11	2
1968			9	28	3.1	11	0
1969			107	387	3.6	13	4
1970			11	25	2.3	7	0
1971			38	131	3.4	20	0
1972			9	36	4.0	45	0
Career			677	2474	3.7	70t	18
Playoffs			18	61	3.4		0

Reece Morrison

Year	Team		Att	Yds	Avg	Lg	TD
1968	CLE	N	18	39	2.2	11	1
1969			60	301	5.0	54	1
1970			73	175	2.4	18	0
1971			5	-2	-0.4	4	0
1972	CIN	N	1	2	2.0	2	0
1973			3	11	3.7	8	0
Career			160	526	3.3	54	2
Playoffs			2	3	1.5		0

Bob Morrow

Year	Team		Att	Yds	Avg	Lg	TD
1941	CHIC	N	37	128	3.5	15	1
1942			45	145	3.2	16	1
1943			38	129	3.4	9	2
1946	NY	AA	8	54	6.8		0
Career			128	456	3.6	16	4

Russ Morrow

Year	Team		Att	Yds	Avg	Lg	TD
1946	BKN	AA	0	22		22tL	1

Bobby Morse

Year	Team		Att	Yds	Avg	Lg	TD
1987	PHI	N	6	14	2.3	7	0
1989	NO	N	2	43	21.5	39	0
1991			3	7	2.3	8	0
Career			11	64	5.8	39	0

Ray Morse

Year	Team		Att	Yds	Avg	Lg	TD
1937	DET	N	1	-3	-3.0	-3	0

Steve Morse

Year	Team		Att	Yds	Avg	Lg	TD
1985	PIT	N	8	17	2.1	9	0

Emmett Mortell

Year	Team		Att	Yds	Avg	Lg	TD
1937	PHI	N	100	312	3.1		0
1938			110	296	2.7		0
1939			37	88	2.4		0
Career			247	696	2.8		0

Year	Team		Att	Yds	Avg	Lg	TD

Craig Morton

Year	Team		Att	Yds	Avg	Lg	TD
1965	DAL	N	3	-8	-2.7	5	0
1966			7	50	7.1	12	0
1967			15	42	2.8	11	0
1968			4	28	7.0	12	2
1969			16	62	3.9	15	1
1970			16	37	2.3	11	0
1971			4	9	2.3	4	1
1972			8	26	3.3	12t	2
1973			1	0	0.0	0	0
1974	NYG	N	4	5	1.3	2	0
1975			22	72	3.3	11	0
1976			15	48	3.2	10	0
1977	DEN	N	31	125	4.0	15	4
1978			17	71	4.2	12	0
1979			23	13	0.6	7	1
1980			21	29	1.4	9	1
1981			8	18	2.3	5	0
Career			215	627	2.9	15	12
Playoffs			20	28	1.4		1

Johnnie Morton

Year	Team		Att	Yds	Avg	Lg	TD
1995	DET	N	3	33	11.0	18	0
1996			9	35	3.9	18	0
Career			12	68	5.7	18	0

Michael Morton

Year	Team		Att	Yds	Avg	Lg	TD
1982	TB	N	2	3	1.5	2	0
1983			13	28	2.2	27	0
1984			16	27	1.7	9	0
1987	SEA	N	19	52	2.7	10	1
Career			50	110	2.2	27	1

Jim Moscrip

Year	Team		Att	Yds	Avg	Lg	TD
1939	DET	N	1	8	8.0	8	0

Dom Moselle

Year	Team		Att	Yds	Avg	Lg	TD
1950	CLE	N	5	39	7.8	15	0
1951	GB	N	12	23	1.9	7	1
1954	PHI	N	29	114	3.9	14	1
Career			46	176	3.8	15	2

Rick Moser

Year	Team		Att	Yds	Avg	Lg	TD
1978	PIT	N	42	153	3.6	15	0
1979			11	33	3.0	8	1
1981			1	4	4.0	4	0
Career			54	190	3.5	15	1
Playoffs			5	13	2.6		0

Haven Moses

Year	Team		Att	Yds	Avg	Lg	TD
1968	BUF	A	5	-4	-0.8	19	0
1972	DEN	N	2	11	5.5	14	0
1973			3	25	8.3	22t	1
1974			2	16	8.0	11	0
1976			1	-4	-4.0	-4	0
1977			5	-1	-0.2	8	0
Career			18	43	2.4	22t	1
Playoffs			1	-10	-10.0		0

Wayne Moseley

Year	Team		Att	Yds	Avg	Lg	TD
1974	BUF	N	2	6	3.0	4	0

John Mosier

Year	Team		Att	Yds	Avg	Lg	TD
1971	DEN	N	4	31	7.8	29	0

Anthony Mosley

Year	Team		Att	Yds	Avg	Lg	TD
1987	CHI	N	18	80	4.4	16	0

Henry Mosley

Year	Team		Att	Yds	Avg	Lg	TD
1955	CHIB	N	3	10	3.3	4	0

Norm Mosley

Year	Team		Att	Yds	Avg	Lg	TD
1948	PIT	N	13	39	3.0	8	1

Russ Mosley

Year	Team		Att	Yds	Avg	Lg	TD
1945	GB	N	16	49	3.1	9	0

Brent Moss

Year	Team		Att	Yds	Avg	Lg	TD
1995	STL	N	22	90	4.1	18	0

Eddie Moss

Year	Team		Att	Yds	Avg	Lg	TD
1973	STL	N	14	41	2.9	13	0
1974			4	13	3.3	5	0

Eddie Moss *continued*

Year	Team		Att	Yds	Avg	Lg	TD
1975			4	12	3.0	5t	1
Career			22	66	3.0	13	1

Perry Moss

Year	Team		Att	Yds	Avg	Lg	TD
1948	GB	N	5	2	0.4	3	0

Marion Motley

Year	Team		Att	Yds	Avg	Lg	TD
1946	CLE	AA	73	601	8.2	76t	5
1947			146	889	6.1	50t	8
1948			157	964	6.1		5
1949			113	570	5.0		8
1950	CLE	N	140	810	5.8	69t	3
1951			61	273	4.5	26	1
1952			104	444	4.3	59	1
1953			32	161	5.0	34	0
1955	PIT	N	2	8	4.0	8	0
Career			828	4720	5.7	76t	31
Playoffs			80	571	7.1		5

Eric Moulds

Year	Team		Att	Yds	Avg	Lg	TD
1996	BUF	N	12	44	3.7	11	0

Rudy Mucha

Year	Team		Att	Yds	Avg	Lg	TD
1941	CLE	N	1	0	0.0	0	0
1946	CHIB	N	1	-1	-1.0	-1	0
Career			2	-1	-0.5	0	0

Larry Mucker

Year	Team		Att	Yds	Avg	Lg	TD
1978	TB	N	5	35	7.0	13	0
1979			4	16	4.0	16	0
Career			9	51	5.7	16	0
Playoffs			1	24	24.0		0

Frank Muehlheuser

Year	Team		Att	Yds	Avg	Lg	TD
1948	BOS	N	38	169	4.4	35t	1
1949	NYB	N	9	10	1.1	3	1
Career			47	179	3.8	35t	2

Jamie Mueller

Year	Team		Att	Yds	Avg	Lg	TD
1987	BUF	N	82	354	4.3	20	2
1988			81	296	3.7	20	0
1989			16	44	2.8	9	0
1990			59	207	3.5	20	2
Career			238	901	3.8	20	4
Playoffs			19	54	2.8		0

Vance Mueller

Year	Team		Att	Yds	Avg	Lg	TD
1986	LARI	N	13	30	2.3	8	0
1987			37	175	4.7	35	1
1988			17	60	3.5	13	0
1989			48	161	3.4	19	2
1990			13	43	3.3	12	0
Career			128	469	3.7	35	3

Joe Muha

Year	Team		Att	Yds	Avg	Lg	TD
1946	PHI	N	12	41	3.4	16	0
1947			27	107	4.0	28t	2
1948			25	90	3.6	14	0
1949			3	19	6.3	13	0
Career			67	257	3.8	28t	2
Playoffs			17	49	2.9		0

Mushin Muhammad

Year	Team		Att	Yds	Avg	Lg	TD
1996	CAR	N	1	-1	-1.0	-1	0

Mike Mularkey

Year	Team		Att	Yds	Avg	Lg	TD
1988	MIN	N	1	-6	-6.0	-6	0

Herb Mul-Key

Year	Team		Att	Yds	Avg	Lg	TD
1972	WAS	N	33	155	4.7	35	1
1973			8	20	2.5	7	0
1974			1	3	3.0	3	0
Career			42	178	4.2	35	1

Eric Mullins

Year	Team		Att	Yds	Avg	Lg	TD
1984	HOU	N	1	0	0.0	0	0

Noah Mullins

Year	Team		Att	Yds	Avg	Lg	TD
1946	CHIB	N	20	117	5.8	45	0
1947			9	55	6.1	41	0
1948			36	208	5.8	74t	1
1949	NYG	N	2	-3	-1.5	-1	0
Career			67	377	5.6	74t	1

Chuck Muncie

Year	Team		Att	Yds	Avg	Lg	TD
1976	NO	N	149	659	4.4	51	2
1977			201	811	4.0	36	6
1978			160	557	3.5	28t	7
1979			238	1198	5.0	69t	11
1980	NO-SD	N	175	827	4.7	53	6
1981	SD	N	251	1144	4.6	73t	19
1982			138	569	4.1	27	8
1983			235	886	3.8	34t	12
1984			14	51	3.6	11	0
Career			1561	6702	4.3	73t	71
Playoffs			110	516	4.7		3

Bill Munson

Year	Team		Att	Yds	Avg	Lg	TD
1964	LA	N	19	150	7.9	83	0
1965			26	157	6.0	38	1
1966			4	3	0.8	2	0
1967			2	-22	-11.0	0	0
1968	DET	N	25	109	4.4	20	1
1969			7	31	4.4	13	0
1970			9	33	3.7	11	0
1971			3	9	3.0	6	0
1972			1	0	0.0	0	0
1973			10	33	3.3	11	0
1974			18	40	2.2	9	1
1975			4	-3	-0.8	2	0
1976	SEA	N	1	6	6.0	6	0
1977	SD	N	1	2	2.0	2	0
Career			130	548	4.2	83	3

George Murphy

Year	Team		Att	Yds	Avg	Lg	TD
1949	LA	AA	1	0	0.0	0	0

Calvin Murray

Year	Team		Att	Yds	Avg	Lg	TD
1981	PHI	N	23	134	5.8	20	0

Franny Murray

Year	Team		Att	Yds	Avg	Lg	TD
1939	PHI	N	49	137	2.8		1
1940			8	7	0.9		0
Career			57	144	2.5		1

Adrian Murrell

Year	Team		Att	Yds	Avg	Lg	TD
1993	NYJ	N	34	157	4.6	37t	1
1994			33	160	4.8	19	0
1995			192	795	4.1	30	1
1996	NYJ	N	301	1249	4.1	78	6
Career			560	2361	4.2	78	2

Bill Musgrave

Year	Team		Att	Yds	Avg	Lg	TD
1993	SF	N	3	-3	-1.0	-1	0
1995	DEN	N	4	-4	-1.0	0	0
1996			12	-4	-0.3	6	0
Career			19	-11	-0.6	6	0

Jim Musick

Year	Team		Att	Yds	Avg	Lg	TD
1932	BOS	N	77	343	4.5		1
1933			173	809	4.7		5
1935			60	174	2.9		2
1936			6	14	2.3		0
Career			316	1340	4.2		8

Johnny Musso

Year	Team		Att	Yds	Avg	Lg	TD
1975	CHI	N	6	33	5.5	16	0
1976			57	200	3.5	11	4
1977			37	132	3.6	13	2
Career			100	365	3.6	16	6

Brad Muster

Year	Team		Att	Yds	Avg	Lg	TD
1988	CHI	N	44	197	4.5	15	0
1989			82	327	4.0	20	5
1990			141	664	4.7	28	6
1991			90	412	4.6	24	6
1992			98	414	4.2	35	3
1993	NO	N	64	214	3.3	18	3
1994			1	3	3.0	3t	1
Career			520	2231	4.3	35	24
Playoffs			28	118	4.2		0

Chet Mutryn

Year	Team		Att	Yds	Avg	Lg	TD
1946	BUF	AA	57	289	5.1		1
1947			140	868	6.2	50	9
1948			147	823	5.6	68t	10
1949			131	696	5.3		8

Year	Team		Att	Yds	Avg	Lg	TD

Chet Mutryn continued

Year	Team		Att	Yds	Avg	Lg	TD
1950	BAL	N	108	355	3.3	34t	2
Career			583	3031	5.2	68t	30
Playoffs			16	32	2.0		

Steve Myer

1977	SEA	N	6	1	0.2	4	0
1978			2	10	5.0	5	0
1979			1	0	0.0	0	0
Career			9	11	1.2	5	0

Brad Myers

1953	LA	N	40	124	3.1	31t	3
1956			6	33	5.5	12	0
1958	PHI	N	9	23	2.6	15	0
Career			55	180	3.3	31t	3

Jack Myers

1948	PHI	N	21	118	5.6	29t	1
1949			48	182	3.8	12	1
1950			29	159	5.5	42	0
1952	LA	N	27	82	3.0	14	1
Career			125	541	4.3	42	3
Playoffs			5	16	3.2		0

Tommy Myers

1973	NO	N	1	8	8.0	8	0
1981			2	-3	-1.5	6	0
Career			3	5	1.7	8	0

Steve Myhra

| 1957 | BAL | N | 1 | 1 | 1.0 | 1 | 0 |

Jesse Myles

1983	DEN	N	8	52	6.5	16	0
1984			5	7	1.4	2	0
Career			13	59	4.5	16	0

Ray Nagel

| 1953 | CHIC | N | 4 | 8 | 2.0 | 6 | 0 |

Browning Nagle

1991	NYJ	N	1	-1	-1.0	-1	0
1992			24	57	2.4	20	0
1994	IND	N	1	12	12.0	12	0
Career			26	68	2.6	20	0

Bronko Nagurski

1930	CHIB	N					5
1931							2
1932			109	486	4.5		4
1933			128	533	4.2		1
1934			123	586	4.8		7
1935			50	170	3.4		1
1936			122	529	4.3		3
1937			73	343	4.7		1
1943			16	84	5.3	11	1
Career			621	2731	4.4	11	25
Playoffs			57	214	3.8		2

John Naioti

| 1945 | PIT | N | 1 | -17 | -17.0 | -17 | 0 |

Joe Namath

1965	NY	A	8	19	2.4	14	0
1966			6	42	7.0	39	2
1967			6	14	2.3	13	0
1968			5	11	2.2	4	2
1969			11	33	3.0	16	2
1970	NYJ	N	1	-1	-1.0	-1	0
1971			3	-1	-0.3	1	0
1972			6	8	1.3	2	0
1973			1	-2	-2.0	-2	0
1974			8	1	0.1	3t	1
1975			10	6	0.6	6	0
1976			2	5	2.5	5	0
1977	LA	N	4	5	1.3	7	0
Career			71	140	2.0	39	7
Playoffs			2	15	7.5		0

Jim Nance

1965	BOS	A	111	321	2.9	20	5
1966			**299**	**1458**	4.9	65	**11**
1967			269	1216	4.5	53	7

Jim Nance continued

Year	Team		Att	Yds	Avg	Lg	TD
1968			177	593	3.4	30t	4
1969			**193**	750	3.9	43	6
1970	BOS	N	145	522	3.6	21t	7
1971	NE	N	129	463	3.6	50t	5
1973	NYJ	N	18	78	4.3	18	0
Career			1341	5401	4.0	65	45

Bob Naponic

| 1970 | HOU | N | 3 | 12 | 4.0 | 11 | 0 |

Dick Nardi

1938	DET	N	20	109	5.5		0
1939	PIT-BKN	N	10	15	1.5		0
Career			30	124	4.1	0	

Tony Nathan

1979	MIA	N	16	68	4.3	18	0
1980			60	327	5.5	18	1
1981			147	782	**5.3**	46	5
1982			66	233	3.5	15	1
1983			151	685	4.5	40	3
1984			118	558	4.7	22	1
1985			143	667	4.7	22	5
1986			27	203	7.5	20	0
1987			4	20	5.0	8	0
Career			732	3543	4.8	46	16
Playoffs			118	454	3.8		3

Ricky Nattiel

1987	DEN	N	2	13	6.5	10	0
1988			5	51	10.2	29	0
Career			7	64	9.1	29	0

Johnny Naumu

| 1948 | LA | AA | 1 | 0 | 0.0 | 0 | 0 |

Dan Neal

| 1981 | CHI | N | 1 | -6 | -6.0 | -6 | 0 |

Frankie Neal

| 1987 | GB | N | 1 | 0 | 0.0 | 0 | 0 |

Lorenzo Neal

1993	NO	N	21	175	8.3	74t	1
1994			30	90	3.0	12	1
1995			5	3	0.6	3	0
1996			21	58	2.8	11	1
Career			77	326	4.2	74t	3

Louis Neal

| 1974 | ATL | N | 1 | -1 | -1.0 | -1 | 0 |

Speedy Neal

| 1984 | BUF | N | 49 | 175 | 3.6 | 10 | 1 |

Derrick Ned

1993	NO	N	9	71	7.9	35t	1
1994			11	36	3.3	15	0
1995			3	1	0.3	5	0
Career			23	108	4.7	35t	1

Ralph Neely

| 1972 | DAL | N | 1 | 10 | 10.0 | 10 | 0 |

Renaldo Nehemiah

| 1982 | SF | N | 1 | -1 | -1.0 | -1 | 0 |

Jim Neill

| 1937 | NYG | N | 7 | 55 | 7.9 | | 0 |

Bill Nelsen

1963	PIT	N	1	-6	-6.0	-6	0
1964			3	17	5.7	13	0
1965			26	84	3.2	21	1
1966			6	18	3.0	9	0
1967			9	-19	-2.1	11	0
1968	CLE	N	13	30	2.3	18	1
1969			5	-11	-2.2	11	0
1970			7	-4	-0.6	2	0
1971			13	-18	-1.4	1	0
1972			1	-2	-2.0	-2	0
Career			84	89	1.1	21	2
Playoffs			4	-7	-1.8		0

Bob Nelson

| 1948 | LA | AA | 1 | -7 | -7.0 | -7 | 0 |

Darrin Nelson

1982	MIN	N	44	136	3.1	18	0
1983			154	642	4.2	56t	1
1984			80	406	5.1	39	3
1985			200	893	4.5	37	5
1986			191	793	4.2	42	4
1987			131	642	**4.9**	72	2
1988			112	380	3.4	27	1
1989	MIN-SD	N	67	321	4.8	28	0
1990	SD	N	3	14	4.7	5	0
1991	MIN	N	28	210	7.5	29	2
1992			10	5	0.5	9	0
Career			1020	4442	4.4	72	18
Playoffs			46	170	3.7	0	

David Nelson

| 1984 | MIN | N | 1 | 3 | 3.0 | 3 | 0 |

Dennis Nelson

| 1973 | BAL | N | 0 | 3 | | 3L | 0 |

Frank Nelson

1948	BOS	N	18	60	3.3	19	0
1949	NYB	N	8	26	3.3	25	0
Career			26	86	3.3	25	0

Herb Nelson

| 1946 | BUF | AA | 1 | 1 | 1.0 | 1 | 0 |

Jimmy Nelson

| 1946 | MIA | AA | 39 | 163 | 4.2 | 75t | 2 |

Ralph Nelson

1975	WAS	N	31	139	4.5	16	0
1976	SEA	N	52	173	3.3	25	1
Career			83	312	3.8	25	1

Terry Nelson

1974	LA	N	1	3	3.0	3	0
1977			3	31	10.3	18	0
1978			6	67	11.2	17	1
1979			2	-16	-8.0	-6	0
Career			12	85	7.1	18	1
Playoffs			2	2	1.0		0

Steve Nemeth

1946	CHI	AA	4	10	2.5		0
1947	BAL	AA	1	1	1.0	1	0
Career			5	11	2.2	1	0

Dick Nesbitt

1930	CHIB	N					1
1931							1
1932							2
1933	CHIC	N					1
Career							5

Rick Neuheisel

| 1987 | SD | N | 6 | 41 | 6.8 | 18 | 1 |

Bob Neuman

| 1936 | CHIC | N | 1 | 3 | 3.0 | 3 | 0 |

Tom Neumann

| 1963 | BOS | A | 44 | 148 | 3.4 | 17 | 0 |
| Playoffs | | | 1 | 16 | 16.0 | 0 | |

Ernie Nevers

1926	DUL	N					8
1927							4
1929	CHIC	N					12
1930							6
1931							7
Career							37

Tom Neville

| 1971 | NE | N | 0 | -8 | | -8L | 0 |

Robert Newhouse

| 1972 | DAL | N | 28 | 116 | 4.1 | 19 | 1 |
| 1973 | | | 84 | 436 | 5.2 | 54 | 1 |

Year	Team	Att	Yds	Avg	Lg	TD

Robert Newhouse *continued*

Year	Team	Att	Yds	Avg	Lg	TD
1974		124	501	4.0	23	3
1975		209	930	4.4	29	2
1976		116	450	3.9	24t	3
1977		180	721	4.0	29	3
1978		140	584	4.2	24	8
1979		124	449	3.6	21	3
1980		118	451	3.8	29t	6
1981		14	33	2.4	6	0
1982		14	79	5.6	27	1
1983		9	34	3.8	22	0
Career		1160	4784	4.1	54	31
Playoffs		174	651	3.7		3

Bob Newland

Year	Team	Att	Yds	Avg	Lg	TD
1973	NO	N	1	6	6.0	6	0

Harry Newman

Year	Team	Att	Yds	Avg	Lg	TD
1933	NYG	N	130	437	3.4		3
1934		131	503	3.8		3
1935		65	166	2.6		0
Career		326	1106	3.4		6
Playoffs		5	11	2.2		0

Harry Newsome

Year	Team	Att	Yds	Avg	Lg	TD
1987	PIT	N	2	16	8.0	16	0
1988		2	0	0.0	0	0
1989		2	-8	-4.0	0	0
1990	MIN	N	2	-2	-1.0	0	0
Career		8	6	0.8	16	0

Ozzie Newsome

Year	Team	Att	Yds	Avg	Lg	TD
1978	CLE	N	13	96	7.4	33t	2
1979		1	6	6.0	6	0
1980		2	13	6.5	9	0
1981		2	20	10.0	14	0
Career		18	135	7.5	33t	2

Timmy Newsome

Year	Team	Att	Yds	Avg	Lg	TD
1980	DAL	N	25	79	3.2	23	2
1981		13	38	2.9	7	0
1982		15	98	6.5	25	1
1983		44	185	4.2	20	2
1984		66	268	4.1	30	5
1985		88	252	2.9	15	2
1986		34	110	3.2	13	2
1987		25	121	4.8	24t	2
1988		32	75	2.3	8	3
Career		342	1226	3.6	30	19
Playoffs		6	44	7.3		2

Chuck Newton

Year	Team	Att	Yds	Avg	Lg	TD
1939	PHI	N	1	0	0.0	0	0

Tom Newton

Year	Team	Att	Yds	Avg	Lg	TD
1977	NYJ	N	8	39	4.9	8	0
1978		11	45	4.1	7	2
1979		37	145	3.9	51t	6
1980		59	299	5.1	23	0
1981		73	244	3.3	13	1
Career		188	772	4.1	51t	9
Playoffs		2	6	3.0		0

Al Nichelini

Year	Team	Att	Yds	Avg	Lg	TD
1935	CHIC	N	94	234	2.5		4
1936		55	189	3.4		0
Career		149	423	2.8		4

Al Nichols

Year	Team	Att	Yds	Avg	Lg	TD
1945	PIT	N	10	5	0.5	9	0

Mark Nichols

Year	Team	Att	Yds	Avg	Lg	TD
1981	DET	N	3	50	16.7	30	0
1982		1	3	3.0	3	0
1983		1	13	13.0	13	0
1984		3	27	9.0	13	0
1985		1	15	15.0	15	0
Career		9	108	12.0	30	0

Mike Nichols

Year	Team	Att	Yds	Avg	Lg	TD
1960	DEN	A	0	3		3L	0

Sid Nichols

Year	Team	Att	Yds	Avg	Lg	TD
1920	RI	A					1

Sid Nichols *continued*

Year	Team	Att	Yds	Avg	Lg	TD
1921						1
Career						2

Frank Niehaus

Year	Team	Att	Yds	Avg	Lg	TD
1925	AKR	N					1

Gifford Nielsen

Year	Team	Att	Yds	Avg	Lg	TD
1979	HOU	N	5	7	1.4	7	0
1980		1	0	0.0	0	0
1981		6	2	0.3	4	0
1982		9	37	4.1	9	0
1983		8	43	5.4	20	0
Career		29	89	3.1	20	0
Playoffs		3	9	3.0		0

Walt Nielson

Year	Team	Att	Yds	Avg	Lg	TD
1940	NYG	N	73	269	3.7		1

Jerry Niles

Year	Team	Att	Yds	Avg	Lg	TD
1947	NYG	N	8	34	4.3	20	0

Jim Ninowski

Year	Team	Att	Yds	Avg	Lg	TD
1958	CLE	N	2	1	0.5	7	0
1959		1	11	11.0	11	0
1960	DET	N	32	81	2.5	14	5
1961		33	238	7.2	72t	5
1962	CLE		9	15	1.7	7	0
1963		5	-19	-3.8	2	0
1964		1	-8	-8.0	0	0
1965		4	46	11.5	17	0
1966		3	-11	-3.7	4	0
1968	WAS	N	2	13	6.5	8	0
Career		92	367	4.0	72t	10

Emery Nix

Year	Team	Att	Yds	Avg	Lg	TD
1943	NYG	N	19	26	1.4	25	0
1946		8	-25	-3.1	3	0
Career		27	1	0.0	25	0

Kent Nix

Year	Team	Att	Yds	Avg	Lg	TD
1967	PIT	N	15	45	3.0	15	2
1968		6	15	2.5	12	0
1969		10	70	7.0	20	0
1971	CHI	N	9	12	1.3	14	0
1972	HOU	N	3	3	1.0	5	0
Career		43	145	3.4	20	2

Dave Noble

Year	Team	Att	Yds	Avg	Lg	TD
1924	CLE	N					4
1925						3
1926	CLE	A					4
Career						11

George Nock

Year	Team	Att	Yds	Avg	Lg	TD
1969	NY	A	3	-5	-1.7	4	0
1970	NYJ	N	135	402	3.0	19	5
1971		48	137	2.9	17	3
1972	WAS	N	6	22	3.7	6	0
Career		192	556	2.9	19	8

Terry Nofsinger

Year	Team	Att	Yds	Avg	Lg	TD
1961	PIT	N	6	6	1.0	3	0
1965	STL	N	4	1	0.3	2	1
1966		18	25	1.4	12	2
1967	ATL	N	3	33	11.0	31	0
Career		31	65	2.1	31	3

Ray Nolting

Year	Team	Att	Yds	Avg	Lg	TD
1936	CHIB	N	76	352	4.6		0
1937		106	424	4.0		2
1938		62	297			2
1939		50	216	4.3		2
1940		78	373	4.8		1
1941		40	169	4.2	28	1
1942		57	245	4.3	39	2
1943		38	209	5.5	22	1
Career		508	2285	4.5	39	11
Playoffs		42	183	4.4		1

Leo Nomellini

Year	Team	Att	Yds	Avg	Lg	TD
1952	SF	N	1	5	5.0	5	0

Jerry Noonan

Year	Team	Att	Yds	Avg	Lg	TD
1924	ROC	N					1

Karl Noonan

Year	Team	Att	Yds	Avg	Lg	TD
1969	MIA	A	1	-11	-11.0	-11	0
1970	MIA	N	1	-9	-9.0	-9	0
Career		2	-20	-10.0	-9	0

John Noppenberg

Year	Team	Att	Yds	Avg	Lg	TD
1940	PIT	N	2	4	2.0		0
1941	DET-PIT	N	11	16	1.5	8	0
Career		13	20	1.5	8	0

Reino Nori

Year	Team	Att	Yds	Avg	Lg	TD
1937	BKN	N	26	81	3.1		0
1938	CHIB	N	1	1	1.0	1	0
Career		27	82	3.0	1	0

Chris Norman

Year	Team	Att	Yds	Avg	Lg	TD
1985	DEN	N	1	0	0.0	0	0
1986		1	-11	-11.0	-11	0
Career		2	-11	-5.5	0	0

Pettis Norman

Year	Team	Att	Yds	Avg	Lg	TD
1967	DAL	N	9	91	10.1	28	0
1968		4	51	12.8	26	0
1969		5	20	4.0	21	0
1970		2	16	8.0	22	0
1971	SD	N	1	1	1.0	1	0
1972		1	9	9.0	9	0
1973		1	10	10.0	10	0
Career		23	198	8.6	28	0
Playoffs		2	10	5.0		0

David Norrie

Year	Team	Att	Yds	Avg	Lg	TD
1987	NYJ	N	5	5	1.0	2	0

Mike Norseth

Year	Team	Att	Yds	Avg	Lg	TD
1988	CIN	N	1	5	5.0	5	0

Don Norton

Year	Team	Att	Yds	Avg	Lg	TD
1960	LA	A	1	2	2.0	2	0
1965	SD	A	1	-5	-5.0	-5	0
Career		2	-3	-1.5	2	0
Playoffs		1	-7	-7.0		0

Jerry Norton

Year	Team	Att	Yds	Avg	Lg	TD
1954	PHI	N	1	-3	-3.0	-3	0
1955		36	144	4.0	23t	1
1957		2	73	36.5	61	0
1959	CHIC	N	2	41	20.5	24	0
1960	STL	N	2	47	23.5	26	0
1961		1	15	15.0	15	0
1963	GB	N	2	0	0.0	4	0
1964		1	24	24.0	24	0
Career		47	341	7.3	61	1

Jim Norton

Year	Team	Att	Yds	Avg	Lg	TD
1963	HOU	A	1	15	15.0	15	0
1967		1	-7	-7.0	-7	0
1968		1	20	20.0	20	0
Career		3	28	9.3	20	0

Marty Norton

Year	Team	Att	Yds	Avg	Lg	TD
1922	MIN	N					2
1924						2
1925	GB	N					1
1926	RI	A					1
Career						6

Ray Norton

Year	Team	Att	Yds	Avg	Lg	TD
1960	SF	N	2	2	1.0	9	0
1961		2	-2	-1.0	2	0
Career		4	0	0.0	9	0

Rick Norton

Year	Team	Att	Yds	Avg	Lg	TD
1966	MIA	A	3	2	0.7	3	0
1967		7	14	2.0	13	0
1968		1	9	9.0	9	0
1969		8	16	2.0	9	0
Career		19	41	2.2	13	0

Doug Nott

Year	Team	Att	Yds	Avg	Lg	TD
1935	DET-BOS	N	48	98	2.0		0

Year	Team		Att	Yds	Avg	Lg	TD

Don Nottingham

Year	Team		Att	Yds	Avg	Lg	TD
1971	BAL	N	95	388	4.1	36	5
1972			123	466	3.8	25	3
1973	BAL-MIA	N	52	252	4.8	30	1
1974	MIA	N	66	273	4.1	24	8
1975			168	718	4.3	56	12
1976			63	185	2.9	13	3
1977			44	214	4.9	13	2
Career			611	2496	4.1	56	34
Playoffs			36	142	3.9		2

Jay Novacek

Year	Team		Att	Yds	Avg	Lg	TD
1988	PHX	N	1	10	10.0	10	0
1993	DAL	N	1	2	2.0	2t	1
Career			2	12	6.0	10	1

Eddie Novak

Year	Team		Att	Yds	Avg	Lg	TD
1925	RI	N					1

Ray Novotny

Year	Team		Att	Yds	Avg	Lg	TD
1930	POR	N					1

Bob Nowaskey

Year	Team		Att	Yds	Avg	Lg	TD
1940	CHIB	N	1	4	4.0	4	0
1941			3	5	1.7	3	0
1942			1	3	3.0	3	0
1946	LA	AA	3	14	4.7		0
Career			8	26	3.3	4	0
Playoffs			1	7	7.0		0

Tom Nowatzke

Year	Team		Att	Yds	Avg	Lg	TD
1965	DET	N	27	73	2.7	14	1
1966			151	512	3.4	21	6
1967			70	288	4.1	15	4
1968			36	116	3.2	11	1
1970	BAL	N	73	248	3.4	14	1
1971			1	1	1.0	1	0
1972			3	11	3.7	6	0
Career			361	1249	3.5	21	13
Playoffs			31	96	3.1		1

Terry Nugent

Year	Team		Att	Yds	Avg	Lg	TD
1987	IND	N	2	1	0.5	3	0

Bob Nussbaumer

Year	Team		Att	Yds	Avg	Lg	TD
1946	GB	N	29	43	1.5	16	0
1947	WAS	N	43	136	3.2	47	0
1948			23	59	2.6	18	0
Career			95	238	2.5	47	0

Doug Nussmeier

Year	Team		Att	Yds	Avg	Lg	TD
1996	NO	N	3	6	2.0	6	0

Jerry Nuzum

Year	Team		Att	Yds	Avg	Lg	TD
1948	PIT	N	26	109	4.2	20	0
1949			139	611	4.4	64	5
1950			57	154	2.7	32	1
1951			27	56	2.1	9	1
Career			249	930	3.7	64	7

Mally Nydahl

Year	Team		Att	Yds	Avg	Lg	TD
1929	MIN	N					2
1930	FRA	N					2
Career							4

Dick Nyers

Year	Team		Att	Yds	Avg	Lg	TD
1957	BAL	N	1	-4	-4.0	-4	0

Bernie Nygren

Year	Team		Att	Yds	Avg	Lg	TD
1946	LA	AA	26	111	4.3		0

Vic Nyvall

Year	Team		Att	Yds	Avg	Lg	TD
1970	NO	N	5	6	1.2		0

Harry O'Boyle

Year	Team		Att	Yds	Avg	Lg	TD
1928	GB	N					1

Bill O'Brien

Year	Team		Att	Yds	Avg	Lg	TD
1947	DET	N	1	2	2.0	2	0

Davey O'Brien

Year	Team		Att	Yds	Avg	Lg	TD
1939	PHI	N	108	-14	-0.1		1
1940			100	-180	-1.8		1
Career			208	-194	-0.9		2

Jim O'Brien

Year	Team		Att	Yds	Avg	Lg	TD
1972	BAL	N	3	9	3.0	7	0

Ken O'Brien

Year	Team		Att	Yds	Avg	Lg	TD
1984	NYJ	N	16	29	1.8	7	0
1985			25	58	2.3	22	0
1986			17	46	2.7	11	0
1987			30	61	2.0	11	0
1988			21	25	1.2	17	0
1989			9	18	2.0	5	0
1990			21	72	3.4	15	0
1991			23	60	2.6	13	0
1992			8	8	1.0	7	0
1993	PHI	N	4	17	4.3	11	0
Career			174	394	2.3	22	0
Playoffs			6	36	6.0		0

Tommy O'Connell

Year	Team		Att	Yds	Avg	Lg	TD
1953	CHIB	N	7	16	2.3	17	0
1956	CLE	N	24	40	1.7	11	2
1957			14	-5	-0.4	7	1
1960	BUF	A	22	-24	-1.1		0
Career			67	27	0.4	17	3

Curly Oden

Year	Team		Att	Yds	Avg	Lg	TD
1926	PRO	N					5
1927							1
1928							1
Career							7

Henry Odom

Year	Team		Att	Yds	Avg	Lg	TD
1983	PIT	N	2	7	3.5	4	0
Playoffs			1	4	4.0		0

Steve Odom

Year	Team		Att	Yds	Avg	Lg	TD
1974	GB	N	6	66	11.0	28	1
1975			5	55	11.0	27	0
1976			4	78	19.5	28	0
1977			1	6	6.0	6	0
Career			16	205	12.8	28	1

Riley Odoms

Year	Team		Att	Yds	Avg	Lg	TD
1972	DEN	N	5	72	14.4	27	0
1973			5	53	10.6	21	0
1974			4	25	6.3	31	0
1975			5	27	5.4	12	0
1976			3	36	12.0	15t	2
1978			2	5	2.5	7	0
1979			1	-7	-7.0	-7	0
Career			25	211	8.4	31	2

Neil O'Donnell

Year	Team		Att	Yds	Avg	Lg	TD
1991	PIT	N	18	82	4.6	22	1
1992			27	5	0.2	-9	1
1993			26	111	4.3	27	0
1994			31	80	2.6	18	1
1995			24	45	1.9	14	0
1996	NYJ	N	6	30	5.0	17	0
Career			132	353	2.7	27	3
Playoffs			12	25	2.1		0

John Oelerich

Year	Team		Att	Yds	Avg	Lg	TD
1938	CHIB-PIT	N	14	23	1.6		0

Ray Ogden

Year	Team		Att	Yds	Avg	Lg	TD
1968	ATL	N	1	12	12.0	12	0

Christian Okoye

Year	Team		Att	Yds	Avg	Lg	TD
1987	KC	N	157	660	4.2	43t	3
1988			105	473	4.5	48	3
1989			370	1480	4.0	59	12
1990			245	805	3.3	32	7
1991			225	1031	4.6	48	9
1992			144	448	3.1	22	6
Career			1246	4897	3.9	59	40
Playoffs			14	85	6.1		0

Cliff Olander

Year	Team		Att	Yds	Avg	Lg	TD
1977	SD	N	7	30	4.3	17	0
1978			1	-3	-3.0	-3	0
Career			8	27	3.4	17	0

Bill Olds

Year	Team		Att	Yds	Avg	Lg	TD
1973	BAL	N	26	100	3.8	17	2

Bill Olds *continued*

Year	Team		Att	Yds	Avg	Lg	TD
1974			129	475	3.7	34	1
1975			94	281	3.0	14	2
1976	SEA-PHI	N	38	129	3.4	11	1
Career			287	985	3.4	34	6
Playoffs			5	6	1.2		0

Elmer Oliphant

Year	Team		Att	Yds	Avg	Lg	TD
1921	BUF	A					1

Mike Oliphant

Year	Team		Att	Yds	Avg	Lg	TD
1988	WAS	N	8	30	3.8	20	0
1989	CLE	N	15	97	6.5	21t	1
Career			23	127	5.5	21t	1

Darryl Oliver

Year	Team		Att	Yds	Avg	Lg	TD
1987	ATL	N	1	0	0.0	0	0

Greg Oliver

Year	Team		Att	Yds	Avg	Lg	TD
1973	PHI	N	1	6	6.0	6	0
1974			7	19	2.7	7	0
Career			8	25	3.1	7	0

Hubie Oliver

Year	Team		Att	Yds	Avg	Lg	TD
1981	PHI	N	75	329	4.4	39	1
1983			121	434	3.6	24	1
1984			72	263	3.7	17	0
1985			1	3	3.0	3	0
1986	HOU	N	1	1	1.0	1	0
Career			270	1030	3.8	39	2
Playoffs			5	12	2.4		0

Vince Oliver

Year	Team		Att	Yds	Avg	Lg	TD
1945	CHIC	N	11	-3	-0.3	15	0

Winslow Oliver

Year	Team		Att	Yds	Avg	Lg	TD
1996	CAR	N	47	183	3.9	16	0
Playoffs			5	26	5.2		0

Johnny Olszewski

Year	Team		Att	Yds	Avg	Lg	TD
1953	CHIC	N	106	386	3.6	34	4
1954			106	352	3.3	23	1
1955			84	326	3.9	41t	1
1956			157	598	3.8	34	2
1957			83	271	3.3	38	2
1958	WAS	N	98	505	5.2	45t	1
1959			65	432	6.6	65	1
1960			75	227	3.0	15	3
1961	DET	N	30	109	3.6	15	0
1962	DEN	A	33	114	3.5	46	0
Career			837	3320	4.0	65	16

Tom O'Malley

Year	Team		Att	Yds	Avg	Lg	TD
1950	GB	N	1	-9	-9.0	-9	0

Steve O'Neal

Year	Team		Att	Yds	Avg	Lg	TD
1970	NYJ	N	1	16	16.0	16	0
1973	NO	N	2	-1	-0.5	6	0
Career			3	15	5.0	16	0

Ed O'Neil

Year	Team		Att	Yds	Avg	Lg	TD
1978	DET	N	1	25	25.0	25	0
1979			1	0	0.0	0	0
Career			2	25	12.5	25	0

Bill O'Neill

Year	Team		Att	Yds	Avg	Lg	TD
1937	CLE	N	4	12	3.0		0

Tip O'Neill

Year	Team		Att	Yds	Avg	Lg	TD
1922	DAY	N					1

Joe Orduna

Year	Team		Att	Yds	Avg	Lg	TD
1972	NYG	N	36	129	3.6	17	1
1973			36	104	2.9	25	1
1974	BAL	N	2	3	1.5	2t	1
Career			74	236	3.2	25	3

Elliott Ormsbee

Year	Team		Att	Yds	Avg	Lg	TD
1946	PHI	N	4	12	3.0	11	0

Tom Orosz

Year	Team		Att	Yds	Avg	Lg	TD
1981	MIA	N	1	13	13.0	13	0

Tom Orosz continued

Year	Team		Att	Yds	Avg	Lg	TD
1983	SF	N	2	39	19.5	10	0
Career			3	52	17.3	13	0
Playoffs			1	11	11.0		0

Charlie O'Rourke

Year	Team		Att	Yds	Avg	Lg	TD
1942	CHIB	N	18	-17	-0.9	17	1
1946	LA	AA	47	50	1.1		1
1947			24	55	2.3		1
1948	BAL	AA	7	15	2.1		1
Career			96	103	1.1	17	4

Jimmy Orr

Year	Team		Att	Yds	Avg	Lg	TD
1958	PIT	N	1	8	8.0	8	0
1959			5	43	8.6	20	0
1960			8	57	7.3	19	0
1962	BAL	N	1	14	14.0	14	0
Career			15	122	8.1	20	0

Chuck Ortmann

Year	Team		Att	Yds	Avg	Lg	TD
1951	PIT	N	59	327	5.5	32	0
1952	DAL	N	8	24	3.0	15	0
Career			67	351	5.2	32	0

Dave Osborn

Year	Team		Att	Yds	Avg	Lg	TD
1965	MIN	N	20	106	5.3	12	2
1966			87	344	4.0	25	1
1967			215	972	4.5	73	2
1968			42	140	3.3	23	0
1969			186	643	3.5	58t	7
1970			207	681	3.3	16	5
1971			123	349	2.8	15	5
1972			82	261	3.2	14t	2
1973			48	216	4.5	14	0
1974			131	514	3.9	17	4
1975			32	94	2.9	9	1
1976	GB	N	6	16	2.7	6	0
Career			1179	4336	3.7	73	29
Playoffs			109	380	3.5		5

Sandy Osiecki

Year	Team		Att	Yds	Avg	Lg	TD
1984	KC	N	1	-2	-2.0	-2	0

Bill Osmanski

Year	Team		Att	Yds	Avg	Lg	TD
1939	CHIB	N	121	699	5.8		7
1940			50	192	3.8		3
1941			76	361	4.8	23	4
1942			2	9	4.5	14	0
1943			37	102	2.8	9	1
1946			78	343	4.4	20t	5
1947			10	37	3.7	15	0
Career			374	1743	4.7	23	20
Playoffs			39	191	4.9		1

Joe Osmanski

Year	Team		Att	Yds	Avg	Lg	TD
1946	CHIB	N	55	202	3.7	19	2
1947			64	328	5.1	24t	1
1948			74	341	4.6	32	1
1949	CHIB-NYB	N	81	312	3.9	48	2
Career			274	1183	4.3	48	6
Playoffs			8	20	2.5		0

Jimmy Ostendarp

Year	Team		Att	Yds	Avg	Lg	TD
1950	NYG	N	18	144	8.0	55	2

Jim Otis

Year	Team		Att	Yds	Avg	Lg	TD
1970	NO	N	71	211	3.0	15	0
1971	KC	N	49	184	3.8	14	0
1972			29	92	3.2	12	0
1973	STL	N	55	234	4.3	19	1
1974			158	664	4.2	23	1
1975			269	1076	4.0	30	5
1976			233	891	3.8	23	2
1977			99	334	3.4	25t	2
1978			197	664	3.4	17	8
Career			1160	4350	3.8	30	19
Playoffs			23	86	3.7		2

Dick Ottele

Year	Team		Att	Yds	Avg	Lg	TD
1948	LA	AA	2	11	5.5		0

David Overstreet

Year	Team		Att	Yds	Avg	Lg	TD
1983	MIA	N	85	392	4.6	44	1
Playoffs			9	50	5.6		0

Don Overton

Year	Team		Att	Yds	Avg	Lg	TD
1990	NE	N	5	8	1.6	6	0
1991	DET	N	14	59	4.2	9	0
Career			19	67	3.5	9	0
Playoffs			3	17	5.7		0

Al Owen

Year	Team		Att	Yds	Avg	Lg	TD
1939	NYG	N	8	11	1.4		0
1940			2	10	5.0		0
1942			8	27	3.4	6	0
Career			18	48	2.7	6	0
Playoffs			1	-2	-2.0		0

Tom Owen

Year	Team		Att	Yds	Avg	Lg	TD
1974	SF	N	16	36	2.3	7	1
1975			1	1	1.0	1	0
1979	NE	N	2	-1	-0.5	0	0
Career			19	36	1.9	7	1

Artie Owens

Year	Team		Att	Yds	Avg	Lg	TD
1977	SD	N	1	3	3.0	3	0
1979			40	151	3.8	23	1
Career			41	154	3.8	23	1

James Owens

Year	Team		Att	Yds	Avg	Lg	TD
1979	SF	N	7	33	4.7	11	0
1981	TB	N	91	406	4.5	35t	3
1982			76	238	3.1	14	0
1983			96	266	2.8	15	5
1984			1	1	1.0	1	0
Career			271	944	3.5	35t	8
Playoffs			12	40	3.3		0

Morris Owens

Year	Team		Att	Yds	Avg	Lg	TD
1976	TB	N	2	2	1.0	18	0
1977			2	-2	-1.0	5	0
Career			4	0	0.0	18	0

R.C. Owens

Year	Team		Att	Yds	Avg	Lg	TD
1959	SF	N	1	0	0.0	0	0
1961			0	23		23tL	1
Career			1	23	23.0	23tL	1

Steve Owens

Year	Team		Att	Yds	Avg	Lg	TD
1970	DET	N	36	122	3.4	23	2
1971			246	1035	4.2	23	8
1972			143	519	3.6	18	4
1973			113	401	3.5	-16	3
1974			97	374	3.9	27	3
Career			635	2451	3.9	27	20
Playoffs			2	9	4.5		0

Jim Pace

Year	Team		Att	Yds	Avg	Lg	TD
1958	SF	N	52	161	3.1	34	2

Bob Paffrath

Year	Team		Att	Yds	Avg	Lg	TD
1946	BKN-MIA	AA	31	100	3.2		2

Fred Pagac

Year	Team		Att	Yds	Avg	Lg	TD
1974	CHI	N	1	-1	-1.0	-1	0
1976	TB	N	1	4	4.0	4	0
Career			2	3	1.5	4	0

Paul Page

Year	Team		Att	Yds	Avg	Lg	TD
1949	BAL	AA	25	81	3.2		0

Mike Pagel

Year	Team		Att	Yds	Avg	Lg	TD
1982	BAL	N	19	82	4.3	32	1
1983			54	441	8.2	33	0
1984	IND	N	26	149	5.7	23	1
1985			25	160	6.4	29	2
1986	CLE	N	2	0	0.0	0	0
1988			4	1	0.3	5	0
1989			2	-1	-0.5	4	0
1990			3	-1	-0.3	0	0
1992	LARM	N	1	0	0.0	0	0
Career			136	831	6.1	33	4
Playoffs			1	-1	-1.0		0

Joe Pagliei

Year	Team		Att	Yds	Avg	Lg	TD
1959	PHI	N	2	-5	-2.5	1	0
1960	NY	A	17	69	4.1		1
Career			19	64	3.4	1	1

Louie Pahl

Year	Team		Att	Yds	Avg	Lg	TD
1923	MIN	N					1

Stephone Paige

Year	Team		Att	Yds	Avg	Lg	TD
1984	KC	N	3	19	6.3	9	0
1985			1	15	15.0	15	0
1986			2	-2	-1.0	12	0
Career			6	32	5.3	15	0
Playoffs			1	-1	-1.0		0

Tony Paige

Year	Team		Att	Yds	Avg	Lg	TD
1984	NYJ	N	35	130	3.7	24	7
1985			55	158	2.9	30	8
1986			47	109	2.3	9	2
1987	DET	N	4	13	3.3	6	0
1988			52	207	4.0	20	0
1989			30	105	3.5	16	0
1990	MIA	N	32	95	3.0	11	2
1991			10	25	2.5	6	0
1992			7	11	1.6	6	1
Career			272	853	3.1	30	20
Playoffs			6	16	2.7		0

Carl Painter

Year	Team		Att	Yds	Avg	Lg	TD
1988	DET	N	17	42	2.5	13	0
1989			15	64	4.3	9	0
Career			32	106	3.3	13	0

Mike Palm

Year	Team		Att	Yds	Avg	Lg	TD
1926	NYG	N					1

David Palmer

Year	Team		Att	Yds	Avg	Lg	TD
1994	MIN	N	1	1	1.0	1	0
1995			7	15	2.1	9	0
1996			2	9	4.5	8	0
Career			10	25	2.5	9	0

Paul Palmer

Year	Team		Att	Yds	Avg	Lg	TD
1987	KC	N	24	155	6.5	35	0
1988			134	452	3.4	26t	2
1989	DAL	N	112	446	4.0	63t	2
Career			270	1053	3.9	63t	4

Don Panciera

Year	Team		Att	Yds	Avg	Lg	TD
1949	B-NY	AA	10	-4	-0.4		0
1952	CHIC	N	4	6	1.5	8	0
Career			14	2	0.1	8	0

John Panelli

Year	Team		Att	Yds	Avg	Lg	TD
1949	DET	N	10	37	3.7	9	0
1950			32	82	2.6	14	0
1951	CHIC	N	13	38	2.9	18	0
Career			55	157	2.9	18	0

Hal Pangle

Year	Team		Att	Yds	Avg	Lg	TD
1935	CHIC	N	18	48	2.7		0
1936			38	101	2.7		1
1937			61	203	3.3		2
1938			2	3	1.5		0
Career			119	355	3.0		3

Nick Papac

Year	Team		Att	Yds	Avg	Lg	TD
1961	OAK	A	6	28	4.7	11	0

George Papach

Year	Team		Att	Yds	Avg	Lg	TD
1948	PIT	N	60	324	5.4	42	2
1949			99	407	4.1	25	0
Career			159	731	4.6	42	2

Oran Pape

Year	Team		Att	Yds	Avg	Lg	TD
1930	MIN	N					2
1931	PRO	N					1
Career							3

Johnny Papit

Year	Team		Att	Yds	Avg	Lg	TD
1951	WAS	N	44	175	4.0	33	0
1952			34	102	3.0	13	0
1953	WAS-GB	N	17	102	6.0	21	1
Career			95	379	4.0	33	1

Bob Paremore

Year	Team		Att	Yds	Avg	Lg	TD
1963	STL	N	36	107	3.0	14	0

Babe Parilli

Year	Team		Att	Yds	Avg	Lg	TD
1952	GB	N	32	106	3.3	19	1
1953			42	171	4.1	19	4
1956	CLE	N	18	65	3.6	19	0
1957	GB	N	24	83	3.5	20	2
1958			8	15	1.9	5	0
1960	OAK	A	32	25	0.8		1
1961	BOS	A	38	183	4.8	24	5
1962			28	169	6.0	33	2
1963			36	126	3.5	19	5
1964			34	168	4.9	32	2
1965			50	200	4.0	17	0
1966			28	42	1.5	17	1
1967			14	61	4.4	18	0
1968	NY	A	7	-2	-0.3	10	1
1969			3	4	1.3	2	0
Career			394	1416	3.6	33	24
Playoffs			2	10	5.0		0

Kaulana Park

Year	Team		Att	Yds	Avg	Lg	TD
1987	NYG	N	6	11	1.8	4	0

Ace Parker

Year	Team		Att	Yds	Avg	Lg	TD
1937	BKN	N	34	26	0.8		1
1938			93	253	2.7		2
1939			104	271	2.6		5
1940			89	306	3.4		2
1941			85	301	3.5	60	0
1945	BOS	N	18	-49	-2.7	7	0
1946	NY	AA	75	184	2.5		3
Career			498	1292	2.6	60	13
Playoffs			9	5	0.6		0

Buddy Parker

Year	Team		Att	Yds	Avg	Lg	TD
1935	DET	N	59	156	2.6		0
1936			6	21	3.5		0
1937	CHIC	N	50	115	2.3		1
1938			45	144	3.2		2
1939			12	37	3.1		0
1940			6	8	1.3		1
1941			1	-1	-1.0	-1	0
1942			1	9	9.0	9	0
Career			180	489	2.7	9	4
Playoffs				70			1

Freddie Parker

Year	Team		Att	Yds	Avg	Lg	TD
1987	GB	N	8	33	4.1	17	0

Joel Parker

Year	Team		Att	Yds	Avg	Lg	TD
1974	NO	N	2	2	1.0	6	0

Robert Parker

Year	Team		Att	Yds	Avg	Lg	TD
1987	KC	N	47	150	3.2	10	1

Rodney Parker

Year	Team		Att	Yds	Avg	Lg	TD
Playoffs			1	12	12.0		0

Billy Parks

Year	Team		Att	Yds	Avg	Lg	TD
1971	SD	N	5	77	15.4	54	0

Dave Parks

Year	Team		Att	Yds	Avg	Lg	TD
1966	SF	N	1	-1	-1.0	-1	0
1971	NO	N	2	-2	-1.0	10	0
1972			1	-7	-7.0	-7	0
Career			4	-10	-2.5	10	0

Bernie Parmalee

Year	Team		Att	Yds	Avg	Lg	TD
1992	MIA	N	6	38	6.3	20	0
1993			4	16	4.0	12	0
1994			216	868	4.0	47t	6
1995			236	878	3.7	40	9
1996			25	80	3.2	17	0
Career			487	1880	3.9	47t	15
Playoffs			35	104	3.0		1

Jim Parmer

Year	Team		Att	Yds	Avg	Lg	TD
1948	PHI	N	30	167	5.6	42t	3
1949			66	234	3.5	34	5
1950			60	203	3.4	27	7
1951			92	316	3.4	15t	2
1952			12	23	1.9	8	0
1953			38	158	4.2	15	2
1954			119	408	3.4	24	0
1955			34	129	3.8	36	1

Jim Parmer continued

Year	Team		Att	Yds	Avg	Lg	TD
1956			1	-2	-2.0	-2	0
Career			452	1636	3.6	42t	20
Playoffs			15	41	2.7		0

Rick Parros

Year	Team		Att	Yds	Avg	Lg	TD
1981	DEN	N	176	749	4.3	25	2
1982			77	277	3.6	14	1
1983			30	96	3.2	13	1
1984			46	208	4.5	25	2
1985	SEA	N	8	19	2.4	6	0
1987			13	32	2.5	7	1
Career			350	1381	3.9	25	7
Playoffs			1	0	0.0		0

Ara Parseghian

Year	Team		Att	Yds	Avg	Lg	TD
1948	CLE	AA	32	135	4.2		1
1949			12	31	2.6		0
Career			44	166	3.8		1
Playoffs			4	14	3.5		0

Bob Parsons

Year	Team		Att	Yds	Avg	Lg	TD
1972	CHI	N	1	0	0.0	0	0
1973			2	2	1.0	5	0
1976			1	2	2.0	2	0
1978			1	0	0.0	0	0
1980			2	4	2.0	4	0
1981			1	-6	-6.0	-6	0
1983			1	27	27.0	27	0
Career			9	29	3.2	27	0

Earle Parsons

Year	Team		Att	Yds	Avg	Lg	TD
1946	SF	AA	74	362	4.9	65t	2
1947			33	125	3.8		0
Career			107	487	4.6	65t	2

Lloyd Parsons

Year	Team		Att	Yds	Avg	Lg	TD
1941	DET	N	5	9	1.8	4	0

Dennis Partee

Year	Team		Att	Yds	Avg	Lg	TD
1971	SD	N	1	7	7.0	7	0

Lou Partlow

Year	Team		Att	Yds	Avg	Lg	TD
1920	DAY	A					3
1921							1
1922	DAY	N					1
1924							1
Career							6

Rick Partridge

Year	Team		Att	Yds	Avg	Lg	TD
1980	SD	N	3	0	0.0	0	0
1987	BUF	N	1	13	13.0	13	0
Career			4	13	3.3	13	0

Bill Paschal

Year	Team		Att	Yds	Avg	Lg	TD
1943	NYG	N	147	572	3.9	54	10
1944			196	737	3.8	68t	9
1945			59	247	4.2	77t	2
1946			117	362	3.1	30t	4
1947	BOS	N	78	263	3.4	23	2
1948			80	249	3.1	20	1
Career			677	2430	3.6	77t	28
Playoffs			18	60	3.3		0

Doug Paschal

Year	Team		Att	Yds	Avg	Lg	TD
1980	MIN	N	15	53	3.5	10t	1
Playoffs			4	26	6.5		0

Gordon Paschka

Year	Team		Att	Yds	Avg	Lg	TD
1947	NYG	N	48	143	3.0	15	2

George Paskvan

Year	Team		Att	Yds	Avg	Lg	TD
1941	GB	N	38	116	3.1	12	0
Playoffs			2	7	3.5		0

Ralph Pasquariello

Year	Team		Att	Yds	Avg	Lg	TD
1950	LA	N	7	31	4.4	14	1
1951	CHIC	N	53	251	4.7	28	1
1952			48	129	2.7	13	0
Career			108	411	3.8	28	2
Playoffs			2	4	2.0		0

Dan Pastorini

Year	Team		Att	Yds	Avg	Lg	TD
1971	HOU	N	26	140	5.4	27	3

Dan Pastorini continued

Year	Team		Att	Yds	Avg	Lg	TD
1972			38	205	5.4	17	2
1973			31	102	3.3	17	0
1974			24	-6	-0.3	7	0
1975			23	97	4.2	19	1
1976			11	45	4.1	11	0
1977			18	39	2.2	15	2
1978			18	11	0.6	11	0
1979			15	23	1.5	14	0
1980	OAK	N	4	24	6.0	10	0
1981	LA	N	7	5	0.7	13	0
1983	PHI	N	1	0	0.0	0	0
Career			216	685	3.2	27	8
Playoffs			3	-9	-3.0		0

Alan Pastrana

Year	Team		Att	Yds	Avg	Lg	TD
1970	DEN	N	14	89	6.4	14	1

Loyd Pate

Year	Team		Att	Yds	Avg	Lg	TD
1970	BUF	N	46	162	3.5	18	1

Greg Paterra

Year	Team		Att	Yds	Avg	Lg	TD
1989	ATL	N	9	32	3.6	8	0

Frank Patrick

Year	Team		Att	Yds	Avg	Lg	TD
1938	CHIC	N	1	1	1.0	1	0
1939			30	84	2.8		1
Career			31	85	2.7	1	1

Frank Patrick

Year	Team		Att	Yds	Avg	Lg	TD
1970	GB	N	2	5	2.5	3	0

Mike Patrick

Year	Team		Att	Yds	Avg	Lg	TD
1976	NE	N	1	-16	-16.0	-16	0

Wayne Patrick

Year	Team		Att	Yds	Avg	Lg	TD
1968	BUF	A	1	2	2.0	2	0
1969			83	361	4.3	72	3
1970	BUF	N	66	259	3.9	20	1
1971			79	332	4.2	41	1
1972			35	130	3.7	9	0
Career			264	1084	4.1	72	5

Maury Patt

Year	Team		Att	Yds	Avg	Lg	TD
1938	DET	N	3	30	10.0		0
1939	CLE	N	6	20	3.3		0
1940			1	0	0.0	0	0
1941			5	16	3.2	11	0
Career			15	66	4.4	11	0

Billy Patterson

Year	Team		Att	Yds	Avg	Lg	TD
1939	CHIB	N	14	34	2.4		0
1940	PIT	N	87	171	2.0		0
Career			101	205	2.0		0

Paul Patterson

Year	Team		Att	Yds	Avg	Lg	TD
1949	CHI	AA	2	0	0.0		0

Jimmy Patton

Year	Team		Att	Yds	Avg	Lg	TD
1956	NYG	N	2	-1	-0.5	0	0

Ricky Patton

Year	Team		Att	Yds	Avg	Lg	TD
1978	ATL	N	68	206	3.0	15	1
1979	ATL-GB	N	40	135	3.4	14	0
1980	SF	N	1	1	1.0	1	0
1981			152	543	3.6	28	4
Career			261	885	3.4	28	5
Playoffs			24	87	3.6		1

Don Paul

Year	Team		Att	Yds	Avg	Lg	TD
1950	CHIC	N	14	80	5.7	18	0
1951			37	247	6.7	68t	3
1952			6	28	4.7	12	0
1953			16	114	7.1	36	0
Career			73	469	6.4	68t	3

Ken Payne

Year	Team		Att	Yds	Avg	Lg	TD
1975	GB	N	1	-2	-2.0	-2	0
1978	PHI	N	1	17	17.0	17	0
Career			2	15	7.5	17	0

Eddie Payton

Year	Team		Att	Yds	Avg	Lg	TD
1977	DET	N	4	13	3.3	14	0

Eddie Payton *continued*

Year	Team		Att	Yds	Avg	Lg	TD
1980	MIN	N	2	15	7.5	8	0
Career			6	28	4.7	14	0

Sean Payton

Year	Team		Att	Yds	Avg	Lg	TD
1987	CHI	N	1	28	28.0	28	0

Walter Payton

Year	Team		Att	Yds	Avg	Lg	TD
1975	CHI	N	196	679	3.5	54t	7
1976			311	1390	4.5	60	13
1977			339	1852	5.5	73	14
1978			333	1395	4.2	76	11
1979			369	1610	4.4	43t	14
1980			317	1460	4.6	69t	6
1981			339	1222	3.6	39	6
1982			148	596	4.0	26	1
1983			314	1421	4.5	49t	6
1984			381	1684	4.4	72t	11
1985			324	1551	4.8	40t	9
1986			321	1333	4.2	41	8
1987			146	533	3.7	17	4
Career			3838	16726	4.4	76	110
Playoffs			180	632	3.5		2

Larry Peace

Year	Team		Att	Yds	Avg	Lg	TD
1941	BKN	N	4	2	0.5	2	0

Elvis Peacock

Year	Team		Att	Yds	Avg	Lg	TD
1979	LA	N	52	224	4.3	15	0
1980			164	777	4.7	36	7
Career			216	1001	4.6	36	7

Clarence Peaks

Year	Team		Att	Yds	Avg	Lg	TD
1957	PHI	N	125	495	4.0	35	1
1958			115	386	3.4	23	3
1959			124	451	3.6	34	3
1960			86	465	5.4	57	3
1961			135	471	3.5	33	5
1962			137	447	3.3	48	3
1963			64	212	3.3	26	1
1964	PIT	N	118	503	4.3	70t	2
1965			47	230	4.9	36	0
Career			951	3660	3.8	70t	21

Harley Pearce

Year	Team		Att	Yds	Avg	Lg	TD
1926	COL	N					1

Walt Pearce

Year	Team		Att	Yds	Avg	Lg	TD
1920	DEC	A					1
1921							1
Career							2

Barry Pearson

Year	Team		Att	Yds	Avg	Lg	TD
1974	KC	N	1	1	1.0	1	0

Dennis Pearson

Year	Team		Att	Yds	Avg	Lg	TD
1978	ATL	N	1	1	1.0	1	0

Drew Pearson

Year	Team		Att	Yds	Avg	Lg	TD
1974	DAL	N	3	6	2.0	22	0
1975			1	11	11.0	11	0
1976			2	20	10.0	11	0
1977			2	22	11.0	11	0
1978			3	29	9.7	33	0
1979			3	27	9.0	16	0
1980			2	30	15.0	32	0
1981			3	31	10.3	25	0
1983			2	13	6.5	10	0
Career			21	189	9.0	33	0
Playoffs			4	16	4.0		0

Lindy Pearson

Year	Team		Att	Yds	Avg	Lg	TD
1950	DET	N	31	82	2.6	11	2
1951			22	88	4.0	25	0
1952	DET-GB	N	5	2	0.4	2	0
Career			58	172	3.0	25	2

Preston Pearson

Year	Team		Att	Yds	Avg	Lg	TD
1968	BAL	N	19	78	4.1	13	0
1969			24	81	3.4	10	0
1970	PIT	N	173	503	2.9	30	2
1971			131	605	4.6	29	0
1972			67	264	3.9	21	0
1973			132	554	4.2	47	2

Preston Pearson *continued*

Year	Team		Att	Yds	Avg	Lg	TD
1974			70	317	4.5	53	4
1975	DAL	N	133	509	3.8	32	2
1976			68	233	3.4	21	1
1977			89	341	3.8	22	1
1978			25	104	4.2	18	0
1979			7	14	2.0	11	1
1980			3	6	2.0	2	0
Career			941	3609	3.8	53	13
Playoffs			51	149	2.9		0

Brent Pease

Year	Team		Att	Yds	Avg	Lg	TD
1987	HOU	N	15	33	2.2	8	1
1988			8	-2	-0.3	4t	1
Career			23	31	1.3	8	2

George Pease

Year	Team		Att	Yds	Avg	Lg	TD
1926	NY	A					1

Doug Pederson

Year	Team		Att	Yds	Avg	Lg	TD
1993	MIA	N	2	-1	-0.5	0	0

Danny Peebles

Year	Team		Att	Yds	Avg	Lg	TD
1989	TB	N	2	-6	-3.0	1	0

Jim Peebles

Year	Team		Att	Yds	Avg	Lg	TD
1949	WAS	N	1	-3	-3.0	-3	0

Rodney Peete

Year	Team		Att	Yds	Avg	Lg	TD
1989	DET	N	33	148	4.5	14t	4
1990			47	363	7.7	37	6
1991			25	125	5.0	26	2
1992			21	83	4.0	12	0
1993			45	165	3.7	28	1
1994	DAL	N	9	-2	-0.2	2	0
1995	PHI	N	32	147	4.6	18	1
1996			20	31	1.6	11	1
Career			232	1060	4.6	37	15
Playoffs			3	20	6.7		0

Erric Pegram

Year	Team		Att	Yds	Avg	Lg	TD
1991	ATL	N	101	349	3.5	34	1
1992			21	89	4.2	15	0
1993			292	1185	4.1	29	3
1994			103	358	3.5	25	1
1995	PIT	N	213	813	3.8	38	5
1996			97	509	5.2	27	1
Career			827	3303	4.0	38	11
Playoffs			38	122	3.2		0

Ray Pelfrey

Year	Team		Att	Yds	Avg	Lg	TD
1951	GB	N	3	44	14.7	24	0

Steve Pelluer

Year	Team		Att	Yds	Avg	Lg	TD
1985	DAL	N	3	-2	-0.7	1	0
1986			41	255	6.2	21	1
1987			25	142	5.7	21	1
1988			51	314	6.2	27	2
1989	KC	N	17	143	8.4	27	2
1990			5	6	1.2	5	0
Career			142	858	6.0	27	6

Carlos Pennywell

Year	Team		Att	Yds	Avg	Lg	TD
1981	NE	N	1	3	3.0	3	0

Craig Penrose

Year	Team		Att	Yds	Avg	Lg	TD
1976	DEN	N	2	-3	-1.5	-1	0
1977			4	24	6.0	17	0
1978			1	0	0.0	0	0
Career			7	21	3.0	17	0

Leon Pense

Year	Team		Att	Yds	Avg	Lg	TD
1945	PIT	N	6	1	0.2	1	0

George Peoples

Year	Team		Att	Yds	Avg	Lg	TD
1982	DAL	N	7	22	3.1	7	0
1984	TB	N	1	2	2.0	2	0
Career			8	24	3.0	7	0

Bob Perina

Year	Team		Att	Yds	Avg	Lg	TD
1946	NY	AA	45	135	3.0		1
1947	BKN	AA	67	116	1.7		3
1948	CHI	AA	6	1	0.2		0

Bob Perina *continued*

Year	Team		Att	Yds	Avg	Lg	TD
1949	CHIB	N	4	4	1.0	2	0
Career			122	256	2.1	2	4

Pete Perini

Year	Team		Att	Yds	Avg	Lg	TD
1954	CHIB	N	4	11	2.8	4	0
1955			2	0	0.0	1	0
Career			6	11	1.8	4	0

Art Perkins

Year	Team		Att	Yds	Avg	Lg	TD
1962	LA	N	48	181	3.8	20	2
1963			37	70	1.9	8	4
Career			85	251	3.0	20	6

Bill Perkins

Year	Team		Att	Yds	Avg	Lg	TD
1963	NY	A	3	8	2.7	8	0

Bruce Perkins

Year	Team		Att	Yds	Avg	Lg	TD
1990	TB	N	13	36	2.8	9	0
1991	IND	N	4	11	2.8	4	0
Career			17	47	2.8	9	0

Don Perkins

Year	Team		Att	Yds	Avg	Lg	TD
1961	DAL	N	200	815	4.1	47	4
1962			222	945	4.3	35	7
1963			149	614	4.1	19t	7
1964			174	768	4.4	59	6
1965			177	690	3.9	43	0
1966			186	726	3.9	24	8
1967			201	823	4.1	30	6
1968			191	836	4.4	28t	4
Career			1500	6217	4.1	59	42
Playoffs			66	284	4.3		3

Don Perkins

Year	Team		Att	Yds	Avg	Lg	TD
1944	GB	N	58	207	3.6	26	0
1945	GB-CHIB	N	46	273	5.9	49	2
1946	CHIB	N	34	105	3.1	36	0
Career			138	585	4.2	49	2
Playoffs			6	14	2.3		0

Johnny Perkins

Year	Team		Att	Yds	Avg	Lg	TD
1978	NYG	N	1	3	3.0	3	0
1981			2	-1	-0.5	10	0
Career			3	2	0.7	10	0

Ray Perkins

Year	Team		Att	Yds	Avg	Lg	TD
1969	BAL	N	3	36	12.0	18	0
1970			2	6	3.0	4	0
1971			5	35	7.0	18	0
Career			10	77	7.7	18	0

John Perko

Year	Team		Att	Yds	Avg	Lg	TD
1937	PIT	N	1	5	5.0	5	0

Brett Perriman

Year	Team		Att	Yds	Avg	Lg	TD
1988	NO	N	3	17	5.7	17	0
1989			1	-10	-10.0	-10	0
1991	DET	N	4	10	2.5	6	0
1993			4	16	4.0	16	0
1994			9	86	9.6	25	0
1995			5	48	9.6	16	0
1996			1	13	13.0	13	0
Career			27	180	6.7	25	0
Playoffs			1	-4	-4.0		0

Benny Perrin

Year	Team		Att	Yds	Avg	Lg	TD
1983	STL	N	1	0	0.0	0	0

Lonnie Perrin

Year	Team		Att	Yds	Avg	Lg	TD
1976	DEN	N	37	118	3.2	14	2
1977			110	456	4.1	62	3
1978			108	455	4.2	28	4
1979	WAS-CHI	N	7	18	2.6	5	0
Career			262	1047	4.0	62	9
Playoffs			20	56	2.8		0

Joe Perry

Year	Team		Att	Yds	Avg	Lg	TD
1948	SF	AA	77	562	7.3	57t	10
1949			115	783	6.8	59t	8
1950	SF	N	124	647	5.2	78t	5
1951			136	677	5.0	58t	3
1952			158	725	4.6	78t	8
1953			192	1018	5.3	51t	10

Year	Team		Att	Yds	Avg	Lg	TD

Joe Perry *continued*

Year	Team		Att	Yds	Avg	Lg	TD
1954			**173**	**1049**	6.1	58	8
1955			156	701	4.5	42	2
1956			115	520	4.5	39	3
1957			97	454	4.7	34	3
1958			125	758	6.1	73t	4
1959			139	602	4.3	40	3
1960			36	95	2.6	21	1
1961	BAL	N	168	675	4.0	27	3
1962			94	359	3.8	21	0
1963	SF	N	24	98	4.1	16	0
Career			1929	9723	5.0	78t	71
Playoffs			23	85	3.7		0

Leon Perry

Year	Team		Att	Yds	Avg	Lg	TD
1980	NYG	N	59	272	4.6	17	1
1981			72	257	3.6	23	0
1982			3	14	4.7	15	0
Career			134	543	4.1	23	1
Playoffs			5	12	2.4		0

Lowell Perry

Year	Team		Att	Yds	Avg	Lg	TD
1956	PIT	N	2	37	18.5	23	0

William Perry

Year	Team		Att	Yds	Avg	Lg	TD
1985	CHI	N	5	7	1.4	2	2
1986			1	-1	-1.0	-1	0
1987			1	0	0.0	0	0
1990			1	-1	-1.0	-1	0
Career			8	5	0.6	2	2
Playoffs			1	1	1.0		1

Bob Perryman

Year	Team		Att	Yds	Avg	Lg	TD
1987	NE	N	41	187	4.6	48	0
1988			146	448	3.1	16	6
1989			150	562	3.7	18	2
1990			32	97	3.0	13	1
1991	DEN	N	21	45	2.1	6	0
1992			3	-1	-0.3	1	0
Career			393	1338	3.4	48	9

John Petchel

Year	Team		Att	Yds	Avg	Lg	TD
1942	CLE	N	1	-2	-2.0	-2	0
1944			5	11	2.2	6	0
1945	PIT	N	2	2	1.0	15	0
Career			8	11	1.4	15	0

Forest Peters

Year	Team		Att	Yds	Avg	Lg	TD
1930	PRO	N					1

Volney Peters

Year	Team		Att	Yds	Avg	Lg	TD
1952	CHIC	N	1	-7	-7.0	-7	0

Ken Peterson

Year	Team		Att	Yds	Avg	Lg	TD
1935	CHIC	N	85	225	2.6		0
1936	DET	N	42	278	6.6		3
Career			127	503	4.0		3

Nelson Peterson

Year	Team		Att	Yds	Avg	Lg	TD
1938	CLE	N	21	70	3.3		1

Johnny Petitbon

Year	Team		Att	Yds	Avg	Lg	TD
1955	CLE	N	3	10	3.3	7	0

Richie Petitbon

Year	Team		Att	Yds	Avg	Lg	TD
1970	LA	N	1	3	3.0	3	0
1971	WAS	N	1	-2	-2.0	-2	0
Career			2	1	0.5	3	0

John Petrella

Year	Team		Att	Yds	Avg	Lg	TD
1945	PIT	N	15	33	2.2	11	0

Elmer Petrie

Year	Team		Att	Yds	Avg	Lg	TD
1922	TOL	N					2

Bill Petrilas

Year	Team		Att	Yds	Avg	Lg	TD
1944	NYG	N	12	29	2.4	12	0

John Petty

Year	Team		Att	Yds	Avg	Lg	TD
1942	CHIB	N	41	149	3.6	14	2
Playoffs			3	-1	-0.3		0

Bob Pfohl

Year	Team		Att	Yds	Avg	Lg	TD
1948	BAL	AA	107	455	4.3		4

Bob Pfohl *continued*

Year	Team		Att	Yds	Avg	Lg	TD
1949			67	205	3.1		2
Career			174	660	3.8		6
Playoffs			16	63	3.9		0

Art Pharmer

Year	Team		Att	Yds	Avg	Lg	TD
1930	MIN	N					1

Bob Phelan

Year	Team		Att	Yds	Avg	Lg	TD
1922	TOL	N					2

Don Phelps

Year	Team		Att	Yds	Avg	Lg	TD
1950	CLE	N	39	198	5.1	33	2
1951			16	65	4.1	10	1
Career			55	263	4.8	33	3

Todd Philcox

Year	Team		Att	Yds	Avg	Lg	TD
1991	CLE	N	1	-1	-1.0	-1	0
1993			2	3	1.5	3t	1
Career			3	2	0.7	3t	1

Bobby Phillips

Year	Team		Att	Yds	Avg	Lg	TD
1995	MIN	N	14	26	1.9	7	0

Jess Phillips

Year	Team		Att	Yds	Avg	Lg	TD
1968	CIN	A	1	7	7.0	7	0
1969			118	578	4.9	83	3
1970	CIN	N	163	648	4.0	76t	4
1971			94	420	4.5	31	0
1972			48	207	4.3	20	1
1973	NO	N	198	663	3.3	20	0
1974			174	556	3.2	14	2
1975	OAK	N	63	298	4.7	66	1
1976	NE	N	24	164	6.8	46	1
1977			5	27	5.4	13	1
Career			888	3568	4.0	83	13
Playoffs			17	41	2.4		1

Lawrence Phillips

Year	Team		Att	Yds	Avg	Lg	TD
1996	STL	N	193	632	3.3	38	4

Rod Phillips

Year	Team		Att	Yds	Avg	Lg	TD
1975	LA	N	17	69	4.1	20	0
1976			34	206	6.1	33	1
1977			37	183	4.9	25	1
1978			28	81	2.9	11	0
1979	STL	N	3	50	16.7	17	1
1980			2	6	3.0	4	0
Career			121	595	4.9	33	3
Playoffs			6	21	3.5		0

Dean Philpott

Year	Team		Att	Yds	Avg	Lg	TD
1958	CHIC	N	12	44	3.7	7	0

Dino Philyaw

Year	Team		Att	Yds	Avg	Lg	TD
1996	CAR	N	12	38	3.2	8	1

Mike Phipps

Year	Team		Att	Yds	Avg	Lg	TD
1970	CLE	N	11	94	8.5	26	0
1971			6	35	5.8	15	0
1972			60	256	4.3	18	5
1973			60	395	6.6	27	5
1974			39	279	7.2	19	1
1975			18	70	3.9	12	0
1976			4	26	6.5	24	0
1978	CHI	N	13	34	2.6	10	0
1979			27	51	1.9	12	0
1980			15	38	2.5	9	2
1981			1	0	0.0	0	0
Career			254	1278	5.0	27	13
Playoffs			9	50	5.6		1

Brian Piccolo

Year	Team		Att	Yds	Avg	Lg	TD
1966	CHI	N	3	12	4.0	5	0
1967			87	317	3.6	73	0
1968			123	450	3.7	19	2
1969			45	148	3.3	14	2
Career			258	927	3.6	73	4

Lou Piccone

Year	Team		Att	Yds	Avg	Lg	TD
1976	NYJ	N	1	11	11.0	11	0
1977	BUF	N	1	6	6.0	6	0
Career			2	17	8.5	11	0

Bob Pickard

Year	Team		Att	Yds	Avg	Lg	TD
1974	DET	N	1	5	5.0	5	0

Carl Pickens

Year	Team		Att	Yds	Avg	Lg	TD
1995	CIN	N	1	6	6.0	6	0
1996			2	2	1.0	2	0
Career			3	8	2.7	6	0

Milt Piepul

Year	Team		Att	Yds	Avg	Lg	TD
1941	DET	N	20	56	2.8	13	0

Aaron Pierce

Year	Team		Att	Yds	Avg	Lg	TD
1995	NYG	N	1	6	6.0	6	0
1996			1	1	1.0	1t	1
Career			2	7	3.5	6	1

Danny Pierce

Year	Team		Att	Yds	Avg	Lg	TD
1970	WAS	N	5	6	1.2	8	0

Nick Pietrosante

Year	Team		Att	Yds	Avg	Lg	TD
1959	DET	N	76	447	5.9	37	3
1960			161	872	5.4	57	8
1961			201	841	4.2	42	5
1962			134	445	3.3	22t	5
1963			112	418	3.7	22	5
1964			147	536	3.6	21	4
1965			107	374	3.5	12	1
1966	CLE	N	7	20	2.9	8	0
1967			10	73	7.3	31	0
Career			955	4026	4.2	57	28

Bert Piggott

Year	Team		Att	Yds	Avg	Lg	TD
1947	LA	AA	46	161	3.5		0

Pete Pihos

Year	Team		Att	Yds	Avg	Lg	TD
1948	PHI	N	8	-3	-0.4	5	0
1954			1	-1	-1.0	-1	0
Career			9	-4	-0.4	5	0

Joe Pilconis

Year	Team		Att	Yds	Avg	Lg	TD
1937	PHI	N	2	21	10.5		0

Erny Pinckert

Year	Team		Att	Yds	Avg	Lg	TD
1934	BOS	N					1
1936			18	80	4.4		0
1937	WAS	N	2	10	5.0		0
1938			3	7	2.3		0
1939			5	17	3.4		0
Career			28	114	4.1		1

Stan Pincura

Year	Team		Att	Yds	Avg	Lg	TD
1937	CLE	N	5	-22	-4.4		0
1938			2	-6	-3.0		0
Career			7	-28	-4.0		0

Cyril Pinder

Year	Team		Att	Yds	Avg	Lg	TD
1968	PHI	N	40	117	2.9	21	0
1969			60	309	5.2	50	1
1970			166	657	4.0	40t	2
1971	CHI	N	63	311	4.9	40t	1
1972			87	300	3.4	19	3
1973	DAL	N	12	15	1.3	5	0
Career			428	1709	4.0	50	7

Johnny Pingel

Year	Team		Att	Yds	Avg	Lg	TD
1939	DET	N	72	301	4.2		1

Allen Pinkett

Year	Team		Att	Yds	Avg	Lg	TD
1986	HOU	N	77	225	2.9	14	2
1987			31	149	4.8	22	2
1988			122	513	4.2	27	7
1989			94	449	4.8	60	1
1990			66	268	4.1	19	0
1991			171	720	4.2	32	9
Career			561	2324	4.1	60	21
Playoffs			47	213	4.5		1

Woody Pippens

Year	Team		Att	Yds	Avg	Lg	TD
1987	KC	N	3	16	5.3	11	0

Rocco Pirro

Year	Team		Att	Yds	Avg	Lg	TD
1941	PIT	N	1	1	1.0	1	0

Year	Team		Att	Yds	Avg	Lg	TD

Joe Pisarcik

Year	Team		Att	Yds	Avg	Lg	TD
1977	NYG	N	27	57	2.1	14	2
1978			17	68	4.0	11	1
1979			1	6	6.0	6	0
1980	PHI	N	3	-3	-1.0	0	0
1981			7	1	0.1	10	0
1983			3	-1	-0.3	0	0
1984			7	19	2.7	16	2
Career			65	147	2.3	16	5

Steve Pisarkiewicz

Year	Team		Att	Yds	Avg	Lg	TD
1978	STL	N	5	-1	-0.2	2	0
1979			11	20	1.8	12	0
Career			16	19	1.2	12	0

Charlie Pittman

Year	Team		Att	Yds	Avg	Lg	TD
1970	STL	N	2	4	2.0	2	0
1971	BAL	N	2	3	1.5	3	0
Career			4	7	1.8	3	0

Danny Pittman

Year	Team		Att	Yds	Avg	Lg	TD
1980	NYG	N	1	-7	-7.0	-7	0

Elijah Pitts

Year	Team		Att	Yds	Avg	Lg	TD
1961	GB	N	23	75	3.3	17t	1
1962			22	110	5.0	26t	2
1963			54	212	3.9	34t	5
1964			27	127	4.7	27	1
1965			54	122	2.3	12	4
1966			115	393	3.4	20	7
1967			77	247	3.2	30	6
1968			72	264	3.7	14	2
1969			35	134	3.8	13	0
1970	LA-NO	N	35	104	3.0	11	0
Career			514	1788	3.5	34t	28
Playoffs			29	127	4.4		2

Frank Pitts

Year	Team		Att	Yds	Avg	Lg	TD
1967	KC	A	3	19	6.3	15t	1
1968			11	107	9.7	28	0
1969			5	28	5.6	11	0
1970	KC	N	5	84	16.8	42	0
1972	CLE	N	3	29	9.7	13	0
1974	OAK	N	1	-10	-10.0	-10	0
Career			28	257	9.2	42	1
Playoffs			3	37	12.3		0

Tony Plansky

Year	Team		Att	Yds	Avg	Lg	TD
1928	NYG	N					1
1929							8
Career							9

Jerry Planutis

Year	Team		Att	Yds	Avg	Lg	TD
1956	WAS	N	2	6	3.0	3	0

Dick Plasman

Year	Team		Att	Yds	Avg	Lg	TD
1941	CHIB	N	1	1	1.0	1	0

George Platukas

Year	Team		Att	Yds	Avg	Lg	TD
1938	PIT	N	3	6	2.0		0

Milt Plum

Year	Team		Att	Yds	Avg	Lg	TD
1957	CLE	N	26	118	4.5	30	0
1958			37	107	2.9	22	4
1959			21	20	1.0	17	1
1960			17	-24	-1.4	7	2
1961			24	-17	-0.7	14	1
1962	DET	N	29	170	5.9	45t	1
1963			9	26	2.9	13	0
1964			12	28	2.3	18	1
1965			21	37	1.8	15	3
1966			12	59	4.9	15	0
1967			6	5	0.8	10	0
1968	LA	N	2	3	1.5	2	0
1969	NYG	N	1	-1	-1.0	-1	0
Career			217	531	2.4	45t	13
Playoffs			6	59	9.8		0

Gary Plummer

Year	Team		Att	Yds	Avg	Lg	TD
1989	SD	N	1	6	6.0	6	0
1990			2	3	1.5	2	1
Career			3	9	3.0	6	1

Jim Plunkett

Year	Team		Att	Yds	Avg	Lg	TD
1971	NE	N	45	210	4.7	16	0
1972			36	230	6.4	21	1
1973			44	209	4.8	20	5
1974			30	161	5.4	37	2
1975			4	7	1.8	5	1
1976	SF	N	19	95	5.0	12	0
1977			28	71	2.5	9	1
1979	OAK	N	3	18	6.0	15	0
1980			28	141	5.0	17	2
1981			12	38	3.2	13t	1
1982	LARI	N	15	6	0.4	10	0
1983			26	78	3.0	20	0
1984			16	14	0.9	9	1
1985			5	12	2.4	7	0
1986			12	47	3.9	11	0
Career			323	1337	4.1	37	14
Playoffs			28	97	3.5		1

Ray Poage

Year	Team		Att	Yds	Avg	Lg	TD
1968	NO	N	1	22	22.0	22	0
1969			1	-3	-3.0	-3	0
1970			1	13	13.0	13	0
Career			3	32	10.7	22	0

Ed Podolak

Year	Team		Att	Yds	Avg	Lg	TD
1970	KC	N	168	749	4.5	65t	3
1971			184	708	3.8	25	9
1972			171	615	3.6	30	4
1973			210	721	3.4	25	3
1974			101	386	3.8	14	2
1975			102	351	3.4	25	3
1976			88	371	4.2	22t	5
1977			133	550	4.1	41	5
Career			1157	4451	3.8	65t	34
Playoffs			17	85	5.0		1

Jim Podoley

Year	Team		Att	Yds	Avg	Lg	TD
1957	WAS	N	114	442	3.9	33	2
1958			48	169	3.5	9	0
1959			18	83	4.6	25	0
1960			29	52	1.8	9	0
Career			209	746	3.6	33	2

Dick Poillon

Year	Team		Att	Yds	Avg	Lg	TD
1942	WAS	N	55	148	2.7	13	0
1946			25	45	1.8	8	1
1947			28	104	3.7	21	2
1948			71	233	3.3	14	1
1949			7	5	0.7	5	0
Career			186	535	2.9	21	4

John Polanski

Year	Team		Att	Yds	Avg	Lg	TD
1942	DET	N	17	67	3.9	13	0
1946	LA	AA	28	77	2.8		1
Career			45	144	3.2	13	1

Al Pollard

Year	Team		Att	Yds	Avg	Lg	TD
1951	NYY-PHI	N	26	121	4.7	28	0
1952	PHI	N	55	186	3.4	23	1
1953			23	44	1.9	11	0
Career			104	351	3.4	28	1

Frank Pollard

Year	Team		Att	Yds	Avg	Lg	TD
1980	PIT	N	4	16	4.0	12	0
1981			123	570	4.6	29	2
1982			62	238	3.8	18	2
1983			135	608	4.5	32	4
1984			213	851	4.0	52	6
1985			233	991	4.3	56	3
1986			24	86	3.6	12	0
1987			128	536	4.2	33	3
1988			31	93	3.0	7	0
Career			953	3989	4.2	56	20
Playoffs			45	231	5.1		2

Fritz Pollard

Year	Team		Att	Yds	Avg	Lg	TD
1920	AKR	A					2
1921							6
1922	MIL	N					3
1925	AKR	N					2
Career							13

Red Pollock

Year	Team		Att	Yds	Avg	Lg	TD
1935	CHIB	N	45	254	5.6		3

Larry Poole

Year	Team		Att	Yds	Avg	Lg	TD
1975	CLE	N	17	114	6.7	26	0
1976			78	356	4.6	26	1
1977			38	118	3.1	12t	1
Career			133	588	4.4	26	2
Playoffs			4	19	4.8		0

Nathan Poole

Year	Team		Att	Yds	Avg	Lg	TD
1979	CIN	N	1	-3	-3.0	-3	0
1980			5	6	1.2	7	0
1982	DEN	N	7	36	5.1	20	0
1983			81	246	3.0	19	4
1985			4	12	3.0	6	0
1987			28	126	4.5	15	1
Career			126	423	3.4	20	5
Playoffs			7	25	3.6		0

Bucky Pope

Year	Team		Att	Yds	Avg	Lg	TD
1964	LA	N	2	11	5.5	17	0

Lew Pope

Year	Team		Att	Yds	Avg	Lg	TD
1933	CIN	N					1

Johnny Popovich

Year	Team		Att	Yds	Avg	Lg	TD
1944	C-P	N	8	29	3.6	9	0
1945	PIT	N	4	-8	-2.0	4	0
Career			12	21	1.8	9	0

Milt Popovich

Year	Team		Att	Yds	Avg	Lg	TD
1938	CHIC	N	6	13	2.2		0
1939			26	78	3.0		0
1940			41	138	3.4		0
1941			5	4	0.8	4	0
Career			78	233	3.0	4	0

Kerry Porter

Year	Team		Att	Yds	Avg	Lg	TD
1987	BUF	N	2	0	0.0	1	0
1989	LARI	N	13	54	4.2	23	0
1990	DEN	N	1	3	3.0	3	0
Career			16	57	3.6	23	0

Lewis Porter

Year	Team		Att	Yds	Avg	Lg	TD
1970	KC	N	2	21	10.5	14	0

Ricky Porter

Year	Team		Att	Yds	Avg	Lg	TD
1987	BUF	N	47	177	3.8	13	0

Dickie Post

Year	Team		Att	Yds	Avg	Lg	TD
1967	SD	A	161	663	4.1	67t	7
1968			151	758	5.0	62t	3
1969			182	873	4.8	60	6
1970	SD	N	74	225	3.0	18	1
1971	DEN-HOU	N	40	86	2.1	16	0
Career			608	2605	4.3	67t	17

Al Postus

Year	Team		Att	Yds	Avg	Lg	TD
1945	PIT	N	2	4	2.0	12	0

Johnny Poto

Year	Team		Att	Yds	Avg	Lg	TD
1947	BOS	N	6	27	4.5	11	1
1948			13	32	2.5	12	0
Career			19	59	3.1	12	1

Roosevelt Potts

Year	Team		Att	Yds	Avg	Lg	TD
1993	IND	N	179	711	4.0	34	0
1994			77	336	4.4	52	1
1995			65	309	4.8	37	0
Career			321	1356	4.2	52	1

Ernie Pough

Year	Team		Att	Yds	Avg	Lg	TD
1976	PIT	N	2	8	4.0	6	0
1978	NYG	N	3	33	11.0	25	0
Career			5	41	8.2	25	0

Darnell Powell

Year	Team		Att	Yds	Avg	Lg	TD
1976	BUF	N	11	40	3.6	20	0
1978	NYJ	N	20	77	3.9	17	1
Career			31	117	3.8	20	1

Preston Powell

Year	Team		Att	Yds	Avg	Lg	TD
1961	CLE	N	1	5	5.0	5	0

Year	Team		Att	Yds	Avg	Lg	TD

Steve Powell
| 1979 | BUF | N | 10 | 29 | 2.9 | 9 | 0 |

Jim Powers
1950	SF	N	3	4	1.3	3	0
1953			3	-10	-3.3		0
Career			6	-6	-1.0	3	0

John Powers
| 1964 | PIT | N | 2 | 10 | 5.0 | 9 | 0 |

Ricky Powers
| 1995 | CLE | N | 14 | 51 | 3.6 | 15 | 0 |

Guy Prather
| 1985 | GB | N | 1 | 0 | 0.0 | 0 | 0 |

Steve Preece
1973	LA	N	1	11	11.0	11t	1
1974			1	-4	-4.0	-4	0
1976			1	0	0.0	0	0
Career			3	7	2.3	11t	1

Glenn Presnell
1931	POR	N					3
1932							1
1933			118	522	4.4		6
1934	DET	N	117	413	3.5		7
1935			72	206	2.9		0
1936			48	201	4.2		1
Career			355	1342	3.8		18

Leo Pressley
| 1945 | WAS | N | 1 | 1 | 1.0 | 1 | 0 |

Dave Preston
1978	DEN	N	66	296	4.5	16	1
1979			43	169	3.9	18	1
1980			111	385	3.5	19	4
1981			183	640	3.5	23	3
1982			19	81	4.3	13	0
1983			57	222	3.9	28	1
Career			479	1793	3.7	28	10
Playoffs			13	38	2.9		1

Luke Prestridge
1979	DEN	N	1	29	29.0	29	0
1983			1	7	7.0	7	0
Career			2	36	18.0	29	0

Charley Price
1940	DET	N	42	122	2.9		2
1941			16	36	2.3	13	0
1945			24	71	3.0	14	0
1946	MIA	AA	15	-55	-3.7		0
Career			97	174	1.8	14	2

Eddie Price
1950	NYG	N	126	703	5.6	74	4
1951			271	971	3.6	80t	7
1952			183	748	4.1	75t	5
1953			101	206	2.0	15	2
1954			135	555	4.1	47	2
1955			30	109	3.6	29	0
Career			846	3292	3.9	80t	20
Playoffs			21	65	3.1		0

Sam Price
1966	MIA	A	31	107	3.5	14	0
1967			46	179	3.9	38	1
1968			5	27	5.4	15	0
Career			82	313	3.8	38	1

Billy Pricer
1957	BAL	N	2	18	9.0	14	0
1958			10	26	2.6	4	1
1959			34	128	3.8	16	0
1960			46	131	2.8	11	0
1961	DAL	A	5	13	2.6	5	0
Career			97	316	3.3	16	2
Playoffs			4	14	3.5		0

Tom Pridemore
| 1984 | ATL | N | 1 | 7 | 7.0 | 7 | 0 |

Tom Pridemore continued
| 1985 | | | 1 | 48 | 48.0 | 48 | 0 |
| Career | | | 2 | 55 | 27.5 | 48 | 0 |

James Primus
| 1988 | ATL | N | 35 | 95 | 2.7 | 29t | 1 |

Dom Principe
1940	NYG	N	11	8	0.7		0
1941			1	5	5.0	5	0
1946	BKN	AA	39	139	3.6		2
Career			51	152	3.0	5	2

Mike Pringle
| 1990 | ATL | N | 2 | 9 | 4.5 | 9 | 0 |

Bill Pritchard
| 1927 | PRO | N | | | | | 1 |

Bosh Pritchard
1942	CLE-PHI	N	38	166	4.4	36	0
1946	PHI	N	42	218	5.2	68t	3
1947			69	294	4.3	31	1
1948			117	517	4.4	65t	4
1949			84	506	6.0	77	3
1951	PHI-NYG	N	42	29	0.7	9	0
Career			392	1730	4.4	68t	11
Playoffs			21	71	3.4		0

Mike Pritchard
1992	ATL	N	5	37	7.4	22	0
1993			2	4	2.0	4	0
1995	DEN	N	6	17	2.8	9	0
1996	SEA	N	2	13	6.5	7	0
Career			15	71	4.7	22	0

Billy Pritchett
1975	CLE	N	75	199	2.7	19	0
1976	ATL	N	14	74	5.3	16	1
1977			3	7	2.3	6	0
Career			92	280	3.0	19	1

Stanley Pritchett
| 1996 | MIA | N | 7 | 27 | 3.9 | 16 | 0 |

Dewey Proctor
1946	NY	AA	23	76	3.3		1
1947			15	15	1.0		0
1948	CHI	AA	47	190	4.0	54	1
1949	B-NY	AA	1	-1	-1.0	-1	0
Career			86	280	3.3	54	3

Ricky Proehl
1990	PHX	N	1	4	4.0	4	0
1991			3	21	7.0	17	0
1992			3	23	7.7	10	0
1993			8	47	5.9	17	0
Career			15	95	6.3	17	0

Joe Profit
1971	ATL	N	3	10	3.3	4t	1
1972			40	132	3.3	14	0
1973	ATL-NO	N	90	329	3.7	22	2
Career			133	471	3.5	22	3

Eddie Prokop
1946	NY	AA	65	236	3.6		1
1947			76	324	4.3	52t	4
1948	CHI	AA	54	266	4.9		1
1949	B-NY	AA	31	109	3.5		2
Career			226	935	4.1	52t	8
Playoffs			10	19	1.9		0

Joe Prokop
1989	NYJ	N	1	17	17.0	17t	1
1990			3	2	0.7	8	0
1991	SF	N	1	-10	-10.0	-10	0
Career			5	9	1.8	17t	1

Fred Provo
| 1948 | GB | N | 29 | 90 | 3.1 | 28 | 0 |

Greg Pruitt
| 1973 | CLE | N | 61 | 369 | 6.0 | 65t | 4 |

Greg Pruitt continued
1974			126	540	4.3	54	3
1975			217	1067	4.9	50	8
1976			209	1000	4.8	64	4
1977			236	1086	4.6	78t	3
1978			176	960	5.5	70t	3
1979			62	233	3.8	27	0
1980			40	117	2.9	19	0
1981			31	124	4.0	15	0
1982	LARI	N	4	22	5.5	13	0
1983			26	154	5.9	18	2
1984			8	0	0.0	3	0
Career			1196	5672	4.7	78t	27
Playoffs			15	57	3.8		

Mike Pruitt
1976	CLE	N	52	138	2.7	18	0
1977			47	205	4.4	21	1
1978			135	560	4.1	71t	5
1979			264	1294	4.9	77t	9
1980			249	1034	4.2	56t	6
1981			247	1103	4.5	21	7
1982			143	516	3.6	17	3
1983			293	1184	4.0	27	10
1984			163	506	3.1	14	6
1985	BUF-KC	N	112	390	3.5	54	2
1986	KC	N	139	448	3.2	16	2
Career			1844	7378	4.0	77t	51
Playoffs			21	67	3.2		0

Barry Pryor
| 1970 | MIA | N | 2 | 0 | 0.0 | 5 | 0 |

Bob Ptacek
| 1959 | CLE | N | 3 | 13 | 4.3 | 6 | 0 |

Marion Pugh
1941	NYG	N	24	50	2.1	45	0
1945			24	-52	-2.2	8	0
1946	MIA	AA	29	-125	-4.3		2
Career			77	-127	-1.6	45	2

Cal Purdin
1943	CHIC	N	9	20	2.2	13	0
1946	BKN-MIA	AA	10	12	1.2		0
Career			19	32	1.7	13	0

Mike Purdy
| 1922 | MIL | N | | | | | 1 |

Pid Purdy
| 1927 | GB | N | | | | | 1 |

Frank Purnell
| 1957 | GB | N | 5 | 22 | 4.4 | 7 | 0 |

Bernard Quarles
| 1987 | LARM | N | 1 | 8 | 8.0 | 8 | 0 |

Frank Quayle
| 1969 | DEN | A | 57 | 183 | 3.2 | 17 | 0 |

Jeff Queen
1970	SD	N	77	261	3.4	19	1
1971			95	318	3.3	41	4
1972	OAK	N	4	10	2.5	10	0
1974	HOU	N	2	7	3.5	4	0
Career			178	596	3.3	41	5

Jeff Query
1990	GB	N	3	39	13.0	18	0
1992	CIN	N	1	1	1.0	1	0
1993			2	13	6.5	8	0
Career			6	53	8.8	18	0

Mike Quick
| 1984 | PHI | N | 1 | -5 | -5.0 | -5 | 0 |

Skeets Quinlan
1952	LA	N	52	224	4.3	36t	1
1953			97	705	7.3	74t	2
1954			82	490	6.0	35	4
1955			15	70	4.7	8	1

Year	Team		Att	Yds	Avg	Lg	TD

Skeets Quinlan continued

Year	Team		Att	Yds	Avg	Lg	TD
1956	LA-CLE	N	12	25	2.1	9	0
Career			258	1514	5.9	74t	9
Playoffs			6	60	10.0		0

Ed Quirk

Year	Team		Att	Yds	Avg	Lg	TD
1948	WAS	N	77	328	4.3	24	4
1949			40	139	3.5	13	1
Career			117	467	4.0	24	5

Warren Rabb

Year	Team		Att	Yds	Avg	Lg	TD
1961	BUF	A	13	47	3.6	19	0
1962			37	77	2.1	14	3
Career			50	124	2.5	19	3

Bill Rademacher

Year	Team		Att	Yds	Avg	Lg	TD
1968	NY	A	1	-13	-13.0	-13	0

Mike Rae

Year	Team		Att	Yds	Avg	Lg	TD
1976	OAK	N	10	37	3.7	12	1
1977			13	75	5.8	21	1
1978	TB	N	20	186	9.3	42	0
1979			1	2	2.0	2	0
Career			44	300	6.8	42	2
Playoffs			3	9	3.0		0

George Ragsdale

Year	Team		Att	Yds	Avg	Lg	TD
1977	TB	N	3	21	7.0	15	0
1978			25	121	4.8	18	1
1979			6	5	0.8	3	0
Career			34	147	4.3	18	1

Steve Raible

Year	Team		Att	Yds	Avg	Lg	TD
1976	SEA	N	1	2	2.0	2	0
1978			2	13	6.5	13	0
Career			3	15	5.0	13	0

Ben Raimondi

Year	Team		Att	Yds	Avg	Lg	TD
1947	NY	AA	6	11	1.8		0

Larry Rakestraw

Year	Team		Att	Yds	Avg	Lg	TD
1966	CHI	N	1	-5	-5.0	-5	0
1967			11	42	3.8	20	2
1968			9	12	1.3	7	0
Career			21	49	2.3	20	2

Chuck Ramsey

Year	Team		Att	Yds	Avg	Lg	TD
1979	NYJ	N	2	0	0.0	0	0
1980			1	-15	-15.0	-15	0
1981			3	0	0.0	0	0
Career			6	-15	-2.5	0	0

Garrard Ramsey

Year	Team		Att	Yds	Avg	Lg	TD
1946	CHIC	N	1	5	5.0	5	0

Ray Ramsey

Year	Team		Att	Yds	Avg	Lg	TD
1947	CHI	AA	70	433	6.2		2
1948	CHI-BKN	AA	22	48	2.2		0
1949	CHI	AA	32	43	1.3		0
Career			124	524	4.2		2

Steve Ramsey

Year	Team		Att	Yds	Avg	Lg	TD
1971	DEN	N	3	6	2.0	6	0
1972			6	15	2.5	18	2
1974			5	-2	-0.4	1	0
1975			6	38	6.3	17	0
1976			13	51	3.9	15	0
Career			33	108	3.3	18	2

Tom Ramsey

Year	Team		Att	Yds	Avg	Lg	TD
1986	NE	N	1	-6	-6.0	-6	0
1987			13	75	5.8	19	1
1988			3	8	2.7	9	0
1989	IND	N	4	5	1.3	3	0
Career			21	82	3.9	19	1

Eason Ramson

Year	Team		Att	Yds	Avg	Lg	TD
1978	STL	N	2	8	4.0	5	0
1980	SF	N	2	-2	-1.0	1	0
1983			1	3	3.0	3	0
Career			5	9	1.8	5	0

Walt Rankin

Year	Team		Att	Yds	Avg	Lg	TD
1943	CHIC	N	2	1	0.5	1	0

Walt Rankin continued

Year	Team		Att	Yds	Avg	Lg	TD
1944	C-P	N	3	13	4.3	6	0
1945	CHIC	N	7	11	1.6	5	0
1946			5	1	0.2	5	0
1947			3	4	1.3	2	0
Career			20	30	1.5	6	0

Bob Rapp

Year	Team		Att	Yds	Avg	Lg	TD
1922	COL	N					1
1923							2
1924							1
1925							1
Career							5

Ahmad Rashad

Year	Team		Att	Yds	Avg	Lg	TD
1972	STL	N	9	44	4.9	15	0
1980	MIN	N	1	8	8.0	8	0
Career			10	52	5.2	15	0

Kenyon Rasheed

Year	Team		Att	Yds	Avg	Lg	TD
1993	NYG	N	9	42	4.7	23t	1
1994			17	44	2.6	6	0
1995	NYJ	N	1	3	3.0	3	0
Career			27	89	3.3	23t	1

Bo Rather

Year	Team		Att	Yds	Avg	Lg	TD
1974	CHI	N	2	10	5.0	14	0
1975			4	24	6.0	18	0
1976			1	4	4.0	4	0
1977			2	8	4.0	10	0
Career			9	46	5.1	18	0

Tom Rathman

Year	Team		Att	Yds	Avg	Lg	TD
1986	SF	N	33	138	4.2	29t	1
1987			62	257	4.1	35	1
1988			102	427	4.2	26	2
1989			79	305	3.9	13	1
1990			101	318	3.1	22	7
1991			63	183	2.9	16	6
1992			57	194	3.4	17	5
1993			19	80	4.2	19	3
1994	LARI	N	28	118	4.2	14	0
Career			544	2020	3.7	35	26
Playoffs			64	287	4.5		4

George Ratterman

Year	Team		Att	Yds	Avg	Lg	TD
1947	BUF	AA	17	-49	-2.9		1
1948			12	-18	-1.5		3
1949			36	85	2.4		4
1950	NYY	N	11	0	0.0	3	3
1951			3	9	3.0	7	0
1952	CLE	N	1	2	2.0	2	0
1953			2	6	3.0	3	0
1954			8	-13	-1.6	2	1
1955			6	8	1.3	10	1
1956			10	19	1.9	11	1
Career			106	49	0.5	11	14
Playoffs			1	2	2.0		0

John Rauch

Year	Team		Att	Yds	Avg	Lg	TD
1949	NYB	N	3	46	15.3	17	1
1950	NYY	N	2	12	6.0	7	0
1951	PHI	N	6	21	3.5	11	0
1951	NYY-PHI	N	7	26	3.7	11	0
Career			18	105	5.8	17	1

Bob Ravensburg

Year	Team		Att	Yds	Avg	Lg	TD
1949	CHIC	N	2	8	4.0	6	0

Eddie Ray

Year	Team		Att	Yds	Avg	Lg	TD
1970	BOS	N	5	13	2.6	4	0
1971	SD	N	2	15	7.5	8	0
1972	ATL	N	8	34	4.3	9	0
1973			96	434	4.5	17	9
1974			46	139	3.0	17	0
1976	BUF	N	24	56	2.3	7	0
Career			181	691	3.8	17	9

Frank Reagan

Year	Team		Att	Yds	Avg	Lg	TD
1941	NYG	N	35	146	4.2	21	4
1946			62	246	4.0	52t	2
1947			14	22	1.6	20	0

Frank Reagan continued

Year	Team		Att	Yds	Avg	Lg	TD
1950	PHI	N	3	55	18.3	40	0
Career			114	469	4.1	52t	6
Playoffs			3	3	1.0		0

Tommy Reamon

Year	Team		Att	Yds	Avg	Lg	TD
1976	KC	N	103	314	3.0	14	4

Gary Reasons

Year	Team		Att	Yds	Avg	Lg	TD
1989	NYG	N	1	2	2.0	2	0
Playoffs			1	30	30.0		0

John Reaves

Year	Team		Att	Yds	Avg	Lg	TD
1972	PHI	N	18	109	6.1	16	1
1973			2	2	1.0	3	0
1974			1	8	8.0	8	0
1975	CIN	N	6	13	2.2	9	2
1977			5	0	0.0	0	0
1978			6	50	8.3	20	0
1981	HOU	N	6	13	2.2	13	0
Career			44	195	4.4	20	3

Willard Reaves

Year	Team		Att	Yds	Avg	Lg	TD
1989	WAS	N	1	-1	-1.0	-1	0

Bert Rechichar

Year	Team		Att	Yds	Avg	Lg	TD
1956	BAL	N	1	1	1.0	1	0

Ron Rector

Year	Team		Att	Yds	Avg	Lg	TD
1966	WAS-ATL	N	9	40	4.4	20	0
1967	ATL	N	24	127	5.3	16	0
Career			33	167	5.1	20	0

Barry Redden

Year	Team		Att	Yds	Avg	Lg	TD
1982	LARM	N	8	24	3.0	7	0
1983			75	372	5.0	40t	2
1984			45	247	5.5	35	0
1985			87	380	4.4	41	0
1986			110	467	4.2	41t	4
1987	SD	N	11	36	3.3	7	0
1988			19	30	1.6	5t	3
1989	CLE	N	40	180	4.5	38t	1
1990			1	-1	-1.0	-1	0
Career			396	1735	4.4	41t	10
Playoffs			33	114	3.5		0

Gus Redman

Year	Team		Att	Yds	Avg	Lg	TD
1922	DAY	N					1

Rick Redman

Year	Team		Att	Yds	Avg	Lg	TD
1966	SD	A	2	14	7.0	32	0
1967			1	-13	-13.0	-13	0
Career			3	1	0.3	32	0

Jarvis Redwine

Year	Team		Att	Yds	Avg	Lg	TD
1981	MIN	N	5	20	4.0	8	0
1982			2	2	1.0	2	0
1983			10	48	4.8	14	0
Career			17	70	4.1	14	0

Don Reece

Year	Team		Att	Yds	Avg	Lg	TD
1946	MIA	AA	30	109	3.6		2

Andre Reed

Year	Team		Att	Yds	Avg	Lg	TD
1985	BUF	N	3	-1	-0.3	14t	1
1986			3	-8	-2.7	4	0
1987			1	1	1.0	1	0
1988			6	64	10.7	36	0
1989			2	31	15.5	23	0
1990			3	23	7.7	26	0
1991			12	136	11.3	46	0
1992			8	65	8.1	24	0
1993			9	21	2.3	15	0
1994			10	87	8.7	20	0
1995			7	48	6.9	14	0
1996			8	22	2.8	13	0
Career			72	489	6.8	46	1
Playoffs			7	27	3.9		0

Bob Reed

Year	Team		Att	Yds	Avg	Lg	TD
1962	MIN	N	6	22	3.7	11	0
1963			21	88	4.2	16	0
Career			27	110	4.1	16	0

Joe Reed

Year	Team		Att	Yds	Avg	Lg	TD
1972	SF	N	4	22	5.5	22	0
1973			15	85	5.7	20	0
1974			16	107	6.7	27	0
1975	DET	N	34	193	5.7	22	1
1976			11	63	5.7	14	1
1977			1	3	3.0	3	0
1978			1	0	0.0	0	0
1979			2	11	5.5	11	0
Career			84	484	5.8	27	2

J.T. Reed

Year	Team		Att	Yds	Avg	Lg	TD
1937	CHIC	N	10	33	3.3		0
1939			5	-6	-1.2		0
Career			15	27	1.8		0

Mark Reed

Year	Team		Att	Yds	Avg	Lg	TD
1983	BAL	N	2	27	13.5	18	0

Oscar Reed

Year	Team		Att	Yds	Avg	Lg	TD
1968	MIN	N	2	6	3.0	5	0
1969			83	393	4.7	23	1
1970			42	132	3.1	21	1
1971			50	182	3.6	18	1
1972			151	639	4.2	43	2
1973			100	401	4.0	30	3
1974			62	215	3.5	15	0
1975	ATL	N	14	40	2.9	7	0
Career			504	2008	4.0	43	8
Playoffs			56	229	4.1		0

Smith Reed

Year	Team		Att	Yds	Avg	Lg	TD
1965	NYG	N	19	70	3.7	17	0

Tony Reed

Year	Team		Att	Yds	Avg	Lg	TD
1977	KC	N	126	505	4.0	59	2
1978			206	1053	5.1	62t	5
1979			113	446	3.9	23	1
1980			68	180	2.6	24	0
1981	DEN	N	68	156	2.3	10	0
Career			581	2340	4.0	62t	8

Dan Reeder

Year	Team		Att	Yds	Avg	Lg	TD
1986	PIT	N	6	20	3.3	6	0
1987			2	8	4.0	4	0
Career			8	28	3.5	6	0

Ken Reese

Year	Team		Att	Yds	Avg	Lg	TD
1947	DET	N	3	1	0.3	5	0

Lloyd Reese

Year	Team		Att	Yds	Avg	Lg	TD
1946	CHIB	N	18	84	4.7	16	2

Bryan Reeves

Year	Team		Att	Yds	Avg	Lg	TD
1994	ARI	N	1	-1	-1.0	-1	0

Dan Reeves

Year	Team		Att	Yds	Avg	Lg	TD
1965	DAL	N	33	102	3.1	13	2
1966			175	757	4.3	67t	8
1967			173	603	3.5	32	5
1968			40	178	4.5	25	4
1969			59	173	2.9	14	4
1970			35	84	2.4	8	2
1971			17	79	4.6	22	0
1972			3	14	4.7	14	0
Career			535	1990	3.7	67t	25
Playoffs			36	91	2.5		1

Frank Reich

Year	Team		Att	Yds	Avg	Lg	TD
1986	BUF	N	1	0	0.0	0	0
1988			3	-3	-1.0	-1	0
1989			9	30	3.3	9	0
1990			15	24	1.6	9	0
1991			13	6	0.5	8	0
1992			9	-9	-1.0	0	0
1993			6	-6	-1.0	-1	0
1994			6	3	0.5	5	0
1995	CAR	N	1	3	3.0	3	0
1996	NYJ	N	18	31	1.7	10	0
Career			81	79	1.0	10	0
Playoffs			10	-8	-0.8		0

Bill Reichardt

Year	Team		Att	Yds	Avg	Lg	TD
1952	GB	N	39	121	3.1	14	1

Mike Reichenbach

Year	Team		Att	Yds	Avg	Lg	TD
1989	PHI	N	1	30	30.0	30	0

Jerry Reichow

Year	Team		Att	Yds	Avg	Lg	TD
1956	DET	N	1	1	1.0	1	0
1957			2	9	4.5	7	0
1959			13	98	7.5	46	0
1961	MIN	N	3	9	3.0	21	0
1963			1	-12	-12.0	-12	0
Career			20	105	5.3	46	0
Playoffs			1	0	0.0		0

Floyd Reid

Year	Team		Att	Yds	Avg	Lg	TD
1950	GB	N	87	394	4.5	57	1
1951			23	73	3.2	33	0
1952			58	156	2.7	14	2
1953			95	492	5.2	43	3
1954			99	507	5.1	69t	5
1955			83	303	3.7	28	2
1956			14	39	2.8	11	0
Career			459	1964	4.3	69t	13

Billy Reinhard

Year	Team		Att	Yds	Avg	Lg	TD
1947	LA	AA	1	2	2.0	2t	1
1948			6	31	5.2		0
Career			7	33	4.7	2t	1

Bob Reinhard

Year	Team		Att	Yds	Avg	Lg	TD
1946	LA	AA	1	-30	-30.0	-30	0
1947			41	150	3.7		0
1948			1	21	21.0	21	0
Career			43	141	3.3	21	0

Albie Reisz

Year	Team		Att	Yds	Avg	Lg	TD
1944	CLE	N	69	134	1.9	46t	2
1945			12	-2	-0.2	16	0
1947	BUF	AA	2	32	16.0		0
Career			83	164	2.0	46t	2
Playoffs			3	14	4.7		0

Dean Renfro

Year	Team		Att	Yds	Avg	Lg	TD
1955	BAL	N	4	13	3.3	5	0

Dick Renfro

Year	Team		Att	Yds	Avg	Lg	TD
1946	SF	AA	18	85	4.7		3

Mel Renfro

Year	Team		Att	Yds	Avg	Lg	TD
1966	DAL	N	8	52	6.5	27	0

Mike Renfro

Year	Team		Att	Yds	Avg	Lg	TD
1978	HOU	N	1	9	9.0	9	0
1980			1	12	12.0	12	0
1983			1	3	3.0	3	0
Career			3	24	8.0	12	0

Ray Renfro

Year	Team		Att	Yds	Avg	Lg	TD
1952	CLE	N	10	26	2.6	11	0
1953			60	352	5.9	58t	4
1954			29	151	5.2	35	0
1955			29	90	3.1	14	0
1956			4	24	6.0	14	0
1957			2	22	11.0	16	0
1958			3	17	5.7	12	0
Career			137	682	5.0	58t	4
Playoffs			11	47	4.3		0

Bobby Renn

Year	Team		Att	Yds	Avg	Lg	TD
1961	NY	A	1	14	14.0	14	0

Bill Renner

Year	Team		Att	Yds	Avg	Lg	TD
1986	GB	N	1	0	0.0	0	0

Pug Rentner

Year	Team		Att	Yds	Avg	Lg	TD
1935	BOS	N	81	243	3.0		1
1936			95	404	4.3		1
1937	CHIB	N	21	70	3.3		0
Career			197	717	3.6		2
Playoffs			14	13	0.9		1

Lance Rentzel

Year	Team		Att	Yds	Avg	Lg	TD
1965	MIN	N	1	-1	-1.0	-1	0
1969	DAL	N	2	11	5.5	14	0
1970			1	11	11.0	11	0
1971	LA	N	14	113	8.1	50t	1

Lance Rentzel continued

Year	Team		Att	Yds	Avg	Lg	TD
1972			7	71	10.1	18	1
1974			1	-9	-9.0	-9	0
Career			26	196	7.5	50t	2

Palmer Retzlaff

Year	Team		Att	Yds	Avg	Lg	TD
1958	PHI	N	1	-4	-4.0	-4	0
1959			2	-11	-5.5		0
1960			2	3	1.5	7	0
1961			1	8	8.0	8	0
Career			6	-4	-0.7	8	0

Bill Reynolds

Year	Team		Att	Yds	Avg	Lg	TD
1944	BKN	N	11	71	6.5	29	1
1945	CHIC	N	7	10	1.4	4	0
Career			18	81	4.5	29	1

Billy Reynolds

Year	Team		Att	Yds	Avg	Lg	TD
1953	CLE	N	72	313	4.3	16	3
1954			64	180	2.8	33	2
1957			29	57	2.0	8	1
1958	PIT	N	10	29	2.9	11	1
1960	OAK	A	1	6	6.0	6	0
Career			176	585	3.3	33	7
Playoffs			12	32	2.7		0

Jim Reynolds

Year	Team		Att	Yds	Avg	Lg	TD
1946	MIA	AA	32	96	3.0		0

M.C. Reynolds

Year	Team		Att	Yds	Avg	Lg	TD
1958	CHIC	N	48	252	5.3	50	0
1959			5	-4	-0.8	11	0
1960	WAS	N	4	20	5.0	12	0
1961	BUF	A	30	142	4.7	20	4
1962	OAK	A	1	9	9.0	9	0
Career			88	419	4.8	50	4

Errict Rhett

Year	Team		Att	Yds	Avg	Lg	TD
1994	TB	N	284	1011	3.6	27	7
1995			332	1207	3.6	21	11
1996			176	539	3.1	35	3
Career			792	2757	3.5	35	21

Ray Rhodes

Year	Team		Att	Yds	Avg	Lg	TD
1974	NYG	N	1	-6	-6.0	-6	0
1975			3	-4	-1.3	14	0
1976			2	10	5.0	16	0
Career			6	0		-16	0

Jerry Rhome

Year	Team		Att	Yds	Avg	Lg	TD
1965	DAL	N	4	11	2.8	16	0
1966			7	37	5.3	11	0
1967			2	-11	-5.5	-2	0
1969	CLE	N	1	0	0.0		0
1970	HOU	N	9	54	6.0	11	1
1971	LA	N	3	0	0.0	0	0
Career			26	91	3.5	16	1

Paul Riblett

Year	Team		Att	Yds	Avg	Lg	TD
1936	BKN	N	2	4	2.0		0

Allen Rice

Year	Team		Att	Yds	Avg	Lg	TD
1984	MIN	N	14	58	4.1	16	1
1985			31	104	3.4	15	3
1986			73	220	3.0	19	2
1987			51	131	2.6	13	1
1988			110	322	2.9	24	6
1989			6	25	4.2	10	0
1990			22	74	3.4	13	0
1991	GB	N	30	100	3.3	21	0
Career			337	1034	3.1	24	13
Playoffs			33	125	3.8		1

Daniel Rice

Year	Team		Att	Yds	Avg	Lg	TD
1987	CIN	N	18	59	3.3	8	0

Jerry Rice

Year	Team		Att	Yds	Avg	Lg	TD
1985	SF	N	6	26	4.3	15t	1
1986			10	72	7.2	18	1
1987			8	51	6.4	17	1
1988			13	107	8.2	29	1
1989			5	33	6.6	17	0
1990			2	0	0.0	2	0
1991			1	2	2.0	2	0

Jerry Rice continued

Year	Team		Att	Yds	Avg	Lg	TD
1992			9	58	6.4	26t	1
1993			3	69	23.0	43t	1
1994			7	93	13.3	28t	2
1995			5	36	7.2	20t	1
1996			11	77	7.0	38	1
Career			80	624	7.8	43t	10
Playoffs			7	44	6.3		0

Herb Rich

Year	Team		Att	Yds	Avg	Lg	TD
1950	BAL	N	2	6	3.0	5	0

Curvin Richards

Year	Team		Att	Yds	Avg	Lg	TD
1991	DAL	N	2	4	2.0	3	0
1992			49	176	3.6	15	1
1993	DET	N	4	1	0.3	1	0
Career			55	181	3.3	15	1

Golden Richards

Year	Team		Att	Yds	Avg	Lg	TD
1973	DAL	N	1	2	2.0	2	0
1974			1	-5	-5.0	-5	0
1975			3	18	6.0	11	0
Career			5	15	3.0	11	0

Kink Richards

Year	Team		Att	Yds	Avg	Lg	TD
1933	NYG	N	41	277	6.8		4
1934			48	178	3.7		1
1935			149	449	3.0		4
1936			114	421	3.7		1
1937			87	329	3.8		2
1938			25	111	4.4		0
1939			40	117	2.9		1
Career			504	1882	3.7		13
Playoffs			16	56	3.5		0

Bucky Richardson

Year	Team		Att	Yds	Avg	Lg	TD
1992	HOU	N	1	-1	-1.0	-1	0
1993			2	9	4.5	11	0
1994			30	217	7.2	18	1
Career			33	225	6.8	18	1

Gloster Richardson

Year	Team		Att	Yds	Avg	Lg	TD
1968	KC	A	1	-3	-3.0	-3	0
1970	KC	N	1	4	4.0	4	0
1973	CLE	N	3	-10	-3.3	4	0
Career			5	-9	-1.8	4	0

Mike Richardson

Year	Team		Att	Yds	Avg	Lg	TD
1969	HOU	A	5	51	10.2	28	0
1970	HOU	N	103	368	3.6	34	2
1971			17	33	1.9	13	0
Career			125	452	3.6	34	2

Terry Richardson

Year	Team		Att	Yds	Avg	Lg	TD
1996	PIT	N	5	17	3.4	8	0

Tony Richardson

Year	Team		Att	Yds	Avg	Lg	TD
1995	KC	N	8	18	2.3	5	0
1996			4	10	2.5	4	0
Career			12	28	2.3	5	0

Willie Richardson

Year	Team		Att	Yds	Avg	Lg	TD
1971	BAL	N	2	27	13.5	24	0

Les Richter

Year	Team		Att	Yds	Avg	Lg	TD
1962	LA	N	0	8		8L	0

Pat Richter

Year	Team		Att	Yds	Avg	Lg	TD
1964	WAS	N	1	-9	-9.0	-9	0

Paul Rickards

Year	Team		Att	Yds	Avg	Lg	TD
1948	LA	N	2	21	10.5	11	0

Harold Ricks

Year	Team		Att	Yds	Avg	Lg	TD
1987	TB	N	24	76	3.2	14	1

Lawrence Ricks

Year	Team		Att	Yds	Avg	Lg	TD
1983	KC	N	21	28	1.3	10	0
1984			2	1	0.5	1	0
Career			23	29	1.3	10	0

Robb Riddick

Year	Team		Att	Yds	Avg	Lg	TD
1981	BUF	N	3	29	9.7	12	0
1983			4	18	4.5	12	0

Robb Riddick continued

Year	Team		Att	Yds	Avg	Lg	TD
1984			3	3	1.0	6	0
1986			150	632	4.2	41t	4
1987			59	221	3.7	25	5
1988			111	438	3.9	21	12
Career			330	1341	4.1	41t	21
Playoffs			10	16	1.6		1

Preston Ridlehuber

Year	Team		Att	Yds	Avg	Lg	TD
1966	ATL	N	4	23	5.8	12	0
1968	OAK	A	4	7	1.8	10	0
1969	BUF	A	4	25	6.3	11	0
Career			12	55	4.6	12	0

Dick Riffle

Year	Team		Att	Yds	Avg	Lg	TD
1938	PHI	N	65	227	3.5		1
1939			18	61	3.4		0
1940			81	238	2.9		3
1941	PIT	N	109	388	3.6		4
1942			115	467		44	4
Career			388	1381	3.6	54	9

John Riggins

Year	Team		Att	Yds	Avg	Lg	TD
1971	NYJ	N	180	769	4.3	25	1
1972			207	944	4.6	40	7
1973			134	482	3.6	15	4
1974			169	680	4.0	34	5
1975			238	1005	4.2	42	8
1976	WAS	N	162	572	3.5	15	3
1977			68	203	3.0	12	0
1978			248	1014	4.1	31	5
1979			260	1153	4.4	66t	9
1981			195	714	3.7	24	13
1982			177	553	3.1	19	3
1983			375	1347	3.6	44	24
1984			327	1239	3.8	24	14
1985			176	677	3.8	51	8
Career			2916	11352	3.9	66t	104
Playoffs			251	996	4.0		12

Gerald Riggs

Year	Team		Att	Yds	Avg	Lg	TD
1982	ATL	N	78	299	3.8	37	5
1983			100	437	4.4	40t	8
1984			353	1486	4.2	57	13
1985			397	1719	4.3	50	10
1986			343	1327	3.9	31	9
1987			203	875	4.3	44	2
1988			113	488	4.3	34	1
1989	WAS	N	201	834	4.1	58	4
1990			123	475	3.9	20	6
1991			78	248	3.2	32	11
Career			1989	8188	4.1	58	69
Playoffs			44	120	2.7		6

Bill Ring

Year	Team		Att	Yds	Avg	Lg	TD
1981	SF	N	22	106	4.8	16	0
1982			48	183	3.8	11	1
1983			64	254	4.0	25	2
1984			38	162	4.3	34	3
1985			8	23	2.9	9t	1
1986			3	4	1.3	4	0
Career			183	732	4.0	34	7
Playoffs			23	78	3.4		1

Jim Ringo

Year	Team		Att	Yds	Avg	Lg	TD
1958	GB	N	0	13		13L	0

Tim Riordan

Year	Team		Att	Yds	Avg	Lg	TD
1987	NO	N	1	3	3.0	3	0

Alan Risher

Year	Team		Att	Yds	Avg	Lg	TD
1985	TB	N	1	10	10.0	10	0
1987	GB	N	11	64	5.8	15	1
Career			12	74	6.2	15	1

Andre Rison

Year	Team		Att	Yds	Avg	Lg	TD
1989	IND	N	3	18	6.0	18	0
1991	ATL	N	1	-9	-9.0	-9	0
1995	CLE	N	2	0	0.0	5	0
Career			6	9	1.5	18	0

Reggie Rivers

Year	Team		Att	Yds	Avg	Lg	TD
1991	DEN	N	2	5	2.5	3	0
1992			74	282	3.8	48	3

Reggie Rivers continued

Year	Team		Att	Yds	Avg	Lg	TD
1993			15	50	3.3	14	1
1994			43	83	1.9	11	2
1995			2	2	1.0	1	0
1996			2	6	3.0	3	0
Career			138	428	3.1	48	6
Playoffs			2	5	2.5		0

Ron Rivers

Year	Team		Att	Yds	Avg	Lg	TD
1995	DET	N	18	73	4.1	19	1
1996			19	86	4.5	26	0
Career			37	159	4.3	26	1
Playoffs			3	16	5.3		1

Don Rives

Year	Team		Att	Yds	Avg	Lg	TD
1974	CHI	N	1	2	2.0	2	0

Jack Rizzo

Year	Team		Att	Yds	Avg	Lg	TD
1973	NYG	N	1	3	3.0	3	0

John Roach

Year	Team		Att	Yds	Avg	Lg	TD
1959	CHIC	N	9	20	2.2	7	0
1960	STL	N	19	39	2.1	19	1
1961	GB	N	2	-5	-2.5	1t	0
1962			1	5	5.0	5	0
1963			3	31	10.3	22	0
1964	DAL	N	8	9	1.1	11	0
Career			42	99	2.4	22	2
Playoffs			1	0	0.0		0

Rollin Roach

Year	Team		Att	Yds	Avg	Lg	TD
1927	CHIC	N					1

Harry Robb

Year	Team		Att	Yds	Avg	Lg	TD
1922	CAN	N					3
1923							1
1926							2
Career							6

Jack Robbins

Year	Team		Att	Yds	Avg	Lg	TD
1938	CHIC	N	63	213	3.4		0
1939			38	97	2.6		0
Career			101	310	3.1		0

Bo Roberson

Year	Team		Att	Yds	Avg	Lg	TD
1961	SD	A	58	275	4.7	59	3
1962	OAK	A	89	270	3.0	63	3
1963			19	47	2.5	11	0
1964			1	-4	-4.0	-4	0
1965			1	-4	-4.0	-4	0
Career			168	584	3.5	63	6
Playoffs			8	37	4.6		0

C.R. Roberts

Year	Team		Att	Yds	Avg	Lg	TD
1959	SF	N	10	67	6.7	19	1
1960			73	213	2.9	30	2
1961			63	338	5.4	54	1
1962			9	19	2.1	12	0
Career			155	637	4.1	54	4

Gene Roberts

Year	Team		Att	Yds	Avg	Lg	TD
1947	NYG	N	86	296	3.4	46	1
1948			145	491	3.4	27	0
1949			152	634	4.2	63	9
1950			116	483	4.2	62t	4
Career			499	1904	3.8	63	14
Playoffs			12	76	6.3		0

George Roberts

Year	Team		Att	Yds	Avg	Lg	TD
1978	MIA	N	1	-7	-7.0	-7	0
1981	SD	N	1	2	2.0	2	0
Career			2	-5	-2.5	2	0
Playoffs			1	-9	-9.0		0

Jack Roberts

Year	Team		Att	Yds	Avg	Lg	TD
1933	PHI	N					1

Walt Roberts

Year	Team		Att	Yds	Avg	Lg	TD
1965	CLE	N	3	30	10.0	14	0
1970	WAS	N	2	15	7.5	21	0
Career			5	45	9.0	21	0

Wooky Roberts

Year	Team		Att	Yds	Avg	Lg	TD
1922	CAN	N					1

Wooky Roberts continued

Year	Team		Att	Yds	Avg	Lg	TD
1923							1
Career							2

Bobbie Robertson

Year	Team		Att	Yds	Avg	Lg	TD
1942	BKN	N	46	132	2.9	34	0

Jimmy Robertson

Year	Team		Att	Yds	Avg	Lg	TD
1925	AKR	N					1

Bill Robinson

Year	Team		Att	Yds	Avg	Lg	TD
1952	GB	N	3	4	1.3	4	0

Bo Robinson

Year	Team		Att	Yds	Avg	Lg	TD
1979	DET	N	87	302	3.5	29	2
1980			3	2	0.7	4	0
1981	ATL	N	9	24	2.7	5	0
1982			19	108	5.7	16	0
1983			3	9	3.0	7	0
Career			121	445	3.7	29	2

Greg Robinson

Year	Team		Att	Yds	Avg	Lg	TD
1993	LARI	N	156	591	3.8	16	1
1995	STL	N	40	165	4.1	37	0
1996			32	134	4.2	24	1
Career			228	890	3.9	24	2

Jacque Robinson

Year	Team		Att	Yds	Avg	Lg	TD
1987	PHI	N	24	114	4.8	18	0

Jerry Robinson

Year	Team		Att	Yds	Avg	Lg	TD
1962	SD	A	2	10	5.0	7	0
1964			1	10	10.0	10	0
Career			3	20	6.7	10	0

Johnny Robinson

Year	Team		Att	Yds	Avg	Lg	TD
1960	DAL	A	98	458	4.7	49	4
1961			52	200	3.8	45	2
Career			150	658	4.4	49	6

Larry Robinson

Year	Team		Att	Yds	Avg	Lg	TD
1973	DAL	N	2	17	8.5	11	0

Matt Robinson

Year	Team		Att	Yds	Avg	Lg	TD
1977	NYJ	N	5	45	9.0	19	0
1978			28	23	0.8	15	0
1979			3	4	1.3	10	1
1980	DEN	N	21	47	2.2	22	3
1981	BUF	N	1	-2	-2.0	-2	0
Career			58	117	2.0	22	4

Patrick Robinson

Year	Team		Att	Yds	Avg	Lg	TD
1993	CIN	N	1	6	6.0	6	0

Paul Robinson

Year	Team		Att	Yds	Avg	Lg	TD
1968	CIN	A	**238**	**1023**	4.3	87t	**8**
1969			160	489	3.1	24	4
1970	CIN	N	149	622	4.2	26t	6
1971			49	213	4.3	17	1
1972	CIN-HOU	N	107	449	4.2	30t	3
1973	HOU	N	34	151	4.4	22	2
Career			737	2947	4.0	87t	24
Playoffs			5	25	5.0		0

Tony Robinson

Year	Team		Att	Yds	Avg	Lg	TD
1987	WAS	N	2	0	0.0	2	0

Virgil Robinson

Year	Team		Att	Yds	Avg	Lg	TD
1971	NO	N	29	96	3.3	12	1
1972			5	1	0.2	5	0
Career			34	97	2.9	12	1

Terry Robiskie

Year	Team		Att	Yds	Avg	Lg	TD
1977	OAK	N	22	100	4.5	10	1
1978			49	189	3.9	18	2
1979			10	14	1.4	16	0
1980	MIA	N	78	250	3.2	36	2
Career			159	553	3.5	36	5

Ed Robnett

Year	Team		Att	Yds	Avg	Lg	TD
1947	SF	AA	7	18	2.6		0

Reggie Roby

Year	Team		Att	Yds	Avg	Lg	TD
1986	MIA	N	2	-8	-4.0	0	0

Reggie Roby continued

Year	Team		Att	Yds	Avg	Lg	TD
1987			1	0	0.0	0	0
1989			2	0	0.0	0	0
1993	WAS	N	1	0	0.0	0	0
1995	TB	N	1	0	0.0	0	0
Career			7	-8	-1.1	0	0

Hank Rockwell

Year	Team		Att	Yds	Avg	Lg	TD
1940	CLE	N	1	5	5.0	5	0

Mike Rodak

Year	Team		Att	Yds	Avg	Lg	TD
1939	CLE	N	1	-1	-1.0	-1	0
1940			1	4	4.0	4	0
Career			2	3	1.5	4	0

Jeff Rodenberger

Year	Team		Att	Yds	Avg	Lg	TD
1987	NO	N	17	35	2.1	5	0

Del Rodgers

Year	Team		Att	Yds	Avg	Lg	TD
1982	GB	N	46	175	3.8	13	1
1984			25	94	3.8	15	0
1987	SF	N	11	46	4.2	15	1
Career			82	315	3.8	15	2
Playoffs			10	60	6.0		0

Hosea Rodgers

Year	Team		Att	Yds	Avg	Lg	TD
1949	LA	AA	131	494	3.8		5

Johnny Rodgers

Year	Team		Att	Yds	Avg	Lg	TD
1977	SD	N	3	44	14.7	33	0
1978			1	5	5.0	5	0
Career			4	49	12.3	33	0

Willie Rodgers

Year	Team		Att	Yds	Avg	Lg	TD
1972	HOU	N	71	204	2.9	14	2
1974			122	413	3.4	20t	5
1975			18	55	3.1	8	1
Career			211	672	3.2	20t	8

Ruben Rodriguez

Year	Team		Att	Yds	Avg	Lg	TD
1987	SEA	N	1	0	0.0	0	0
1988			1	0	0.0	0	0
1989			1	0	0.0	0	0
Career			3	0	0.0	0	0

Johnny Roepke

Year	Team		Att	Yds	Avg	Lg	TD
1928	FRA	N					1

John Rogalla

Year	Team		Att	Yds	Avg	Lg	TD
1945	PHI	N	2	2	1.0	6	0

Fran Rogel

Year	Team		Att	Yds	Avg	Lg	TD
1950	PIT	N	92	418	4.5	40t	3
1951			109	385	3.5	51	3
1952			84	230	2.7	14	3
1953			137	527	3.8	58	2
1954			111	415	3.7	16	1
1955			168	588	3.5	19	2
1956			131	476	3.6	40	2
1957			68	232	3.4	23	1
Career			900	3271	3.6	58	17

Charley Rogers

Year	Team		Att	Yds	Avg	Lg	TD
1927	FRA	N					3
1928							1
Career							4

Cullen Rogers

Year	Team		Att	Yds	Avg	Lg	TD
1946	PIT	N	6	-8	-1.3	4	0

George Rogers

Year	Team		Att	Yds	Avg	Lg	TD
1981	NO	N	378	1674	4.4	79t	13
1982			122	535	4.4	38	3
1983			256	1144	4.5	76t	5
1984			239	914	3.8	28	2
1985	WAS	N	231	1093	4.7	35	7
1986			303	1203	4.0	42	**18**
1987			163	613	3.8	29	6
Career			1692	7176	4.2	79t	54
Playoffs			89	278	3.1		2

Jimmy Rogers

Year	Team		Att	Yds	Avg	Lg	TD
1980	NO	N	80	366	4.6	24	1
1981			9	37	4.1	15	0

Jimmy Rogers continued

Year	Team		Att	Yds	Avg	Lg	TD
1982			60	178	3.0	32	2
1983			26	80	3.1	13	0
Career			175	661	3.8	32	3

Steve Rogers

Year	Team		Att	Yds	Avg	Lg	TD
1975	NO	N	17	62	3.6	22	0

Herm Rohrig

Year	Team		Att	Yds	Avg	Lg	TD
1941	GB	N	21	2	0.1	18	0
1946			15	-23	-1.5	15	0
1947			7	22	3.1	6	0
Career			43	1	0.0	18	0

Johnny Roland

Year	Team		Att	Yds	Avg	Lg	TD
1966	STL	N	192	695	3.6	50	5
1967			234	876	3.7	70	10
1968			121	455	3.8	45	2
1969			138	498	3.6	21	5
1970			94	392	4.2	20	3
1971			78	278	3.6	16	0
1972			105	414	3.9	18	2
1973	NYG	N	53	142	2.7	10	1
Career			1015	3750	3.7	70	28

Dave Rolle

Year	Team		Att	Yds	Avg	Lg	TD
1960	DEN	A	130	501	3.9	57	2

Steve Romanik

Year	Team		Att	Yds	Avg	Lg	TD
1951	CHIB	N	12	23	1.9	10	1
1952			6	9	1.5	7	0
1953	CHIC		1	1	1.0	1t	1
1953	CHIB-CHIC		2	1	0.5	1t	1
1954	CHIC		7	2	0.3	4	1
Career			28	36	1.3	10	4

Rudy Romboli

Year	Team		Att	Yds	Avg	Lg	TD
1946	BOS	N	1	-3	-3.0	-3	0
1947			23	50	2.2	15	0
1948			25	90	3.6	15	1
Career			49	137	2.8	15	1

Stan Rome

Year	Team		Att	Yds	Avg	Lg	TD
1979	KC	N	1	-5	-5.0	-5	0

Al Romine

Year	Team		Att	Yds	Avg	Lg	TD
1958	GB	N	1	0	0.0	0	0

Milt Romney

Year	Team		Att	Yds	Avg	Lg	TD
1926	CHIB	N					3
1927							1
1928							1
Career							5

Gene Ronzani

Year	Team		Att	Yds	Avg	Lg	TD
1933	CHIB	N	26	91	3.5		0
1934			84	485	5.8		0
1935			79	356	4.5		0
1936			37	186	5.0		0
1937			12	17	1.4		0
1938			7	12	1.7		0
1944			12	26	2.2	14	0
1945			3	-20	-6.7	5	0
Career			260	1153	4.4	14	1
Playoffs			16	69	4.3		0

Bill Rooney

Year	Team		Att	Yds	Avg	Lg	TD
1925	NY	N					1

Cobb Rooney

Year	Team		Att	Yds	Avg	Lg	TD
1926	DUL	N					1
1927							1
1929	CHIC	N					1
Career							3

Jim Root

Year	Team		Att	Yds	Avg	Lg	TD
1953	CHIC	N	26	12	0.5	19	1
1956			17	45	2.6	18	2
Career			43	57	1.3	19	3

Sal Rosato

Year	Team		Att	Yds	Avg	Lg	TD
1945	WAS	N	23	85	3.7	15	2
1946			62	238	3.8	21	2

Year	Team		Att	Yds	Avg	Lg	TD

Sal Rosato *continued*

Year	Team		Att	Yds	Avg	Lg	TD
1947			74	297	4.0	20	0
Career			159	620	3.9	21	4
Playoffs			6	17	2.8		0

Al Rose

Year	Team		Att	Yds	Avg	Lg	TD
1936	NYG	N	2	13	6.5		0

Gene Rose

Year	Team		Att	Yds	Avg	Lg	TD
1929	CHIC	N					1
1930							4
Career							5

Timm Rosenbach

Year	Team		Att	Yds	Avg	Lg	TD
1989	PHX	N	6	26	4.3	8	0
1990			86	470	5.5	25	3
1992			9	11	1.2	10	0
Career			101	507	5.0	25	3

Ken Roskie

Year	Team		Att	Yds	Avg	Lg	TD
1946	SF	AA	9	16	1.8		0
1948	GB-DET	N	6	29	4.8	9	1
Career			15	45	3.0	9	1

Alvin Ross

Year	Team		Att	Yds	Avg	Lg	TD
1987	PHI	N	14	54	3.9	12	1

Jermaine Ross

Year	Team		Att	Yds	Avg	Lg	TD
1996	STL	N	1	3	3.0	3t	1

Oliver Ross

Year	Team		Att	Yds	Avg	Lg	TD
1973	DEN	N	5	21	4.2	8	0
1974			3	8	2.7	7	0
1975			42	121	2.9	21	0
1976	SEA	N	13	23	1.8	11	0
Career			63	173	2.7	21	0

Willie Ross

Year	Team		Att	Yds	Avg	Lg	TD
1964	BUF	A	4	14	3.5	12	1

Kyle Rote

Year	Team		Att	Yds	Avg	Lg	TD
1951	NYG	N	21	114	5.4	31	1
1952			103	421	4.1	52t	2
1953			63	213	3.4	18	1
1954			30	59	2.0	14	0
1955			10	46	4.6	14	0
1956			3	5	1.7	3	0
1957			1	13	13.0	13	0
Career			231	871	3.8	52t	4

Tobin Rote

Year	Team		Att	Yds	Avg	Lg	TD
1950	GB	N	27	158	5.9	29	0
1951			76	523	6.9	55t	3
1952			58	313	5.4	30	2
1953			33	180	5.5	21	0
1954			67	301	4.5	30	8
1955			74	332	4.5	49	5
1956			84	398	4.7	39	11
1957	DET		70	366	5.2	23	1
1958			77	351	4.6	27	3
1959			35	156	4.5	21	2
1963	SD	A	24	62	2.6	15	2
1964			10	-12	-1.2	9	0
Career			635	3128	4.9	55t	37
Playoffs			16	53	3.3		2

Pete Roth

Year	Team		Att	Yds	Avg	Lg	TD
1987	MIA	N	3	10	3.3	9	0

George Roudebush

Year	Team		Att	Yds	Avg	Lg	TD
1921	DAY	A					1

Tom Rouen

Year	Team		Att	Yds	Avg	Lg	TD
1993	DEN	N	1	0	0.0	0	0

James Rouse

Year	Team		Att	Yds	Avg	Lg	TD
1990	CHI	N	16	56	3.5	10	0
1991			27	74	2.7	10	0
Career			43	130	3.0	10	0

Stillman Rouse

Year	Team		Att	Yds	Avg	Lg	TD
1940	DET	N	2	0	0.0		

Lee Rouson

Year	Team		Att	Yds	Avg	Lg	TD
1985	NYG	N	1	1	1.0	1	0
1986			54	179	3.3	21t	2
1987			41	155	3.8	14	0
1988			1	1	1.0	1	0
1989			11	51	4.6	9	0
1990			3	14	4.7	6	0
1991	CLE	N	3	14	4.7	9	0
Career			114	415	3.6	21t	2
Playoffs			12	52	4.3		0

Harmon Rowe

Year	Team		Att	Yds	Avg	Lg	TD
1947	NY	AA	2	-3	-1.5		0
1949	B-NY	AA	6	21	3.5		0
Career			8	18	2.3		0

Brad Rowland

Year	Team		Att	Yds	Avg	Lg	TD
1951	CHIB	N	10	50	5.0	20	0

Mark Royals

Year	Team		Att	Yds	Avg	Lg	TD
1994	PIT	N	1	-13	-13.0	-13	0
1995	DET	N	1	-7	-7.0	-7	0
Career			2	-20	-10.0	-7	0
Playoffs			1	0	0.0		0

Mazio Royster

Year	Team		Att	Yds	Avg	Lg	TD
1993	TB	N	33	115	3.5	19	1
1994			9	7	0.8	6	0
Career			42	122	2.9	19	1

Mike Rozier

Year	Team		Att	Yds	Avg	Lg	TD
1985	HOU	N	133	462	3.5	30	8
1986			199	662	3.3	19t	4
1987			229	957	4.2	41	3
1988			251	1002	4.0	28	10
1989			88	301	3.4	17	2
1990	HOU-ATL	N	163	717	4.4	67	3
1991	ATL	N	96	361	3.8	19	0
Career			1159	4462	3.8	67	30
Playoffs			55	182	3.3		2

Ed Rubbert

Year	Team		Att	Yds	Avg	Lg	TD
1987	WAS	N	9	31	3.4	14	0

Rob Rubick

Year	Team		Att	Yds	Avg	Lg	TD
1982	DET	N	1	1	1.0	1t	1

T.J. Rubley

Year	Team		Att	Yds	Avg	Lg	TD
1993	LARM	N	29	102	3.5	13	0
1995	GB	N	2	6	3.0	6	0
Career			31	108	3.5	13	0

Eddie Rucinski

Year	Team		Att	Yds	Avg	Lg	TD
1941	BKN	N	2	13	6.5	7	0
1944	C-P	N	16	72	4.5	22	0
Career			18	85	4.7	22	0

Reggie Rucker

Year	Team		Att	Yds	Avg	Lg	TD
1971	NYG	N	1	14	14.0	14	0
1972	NE	N	3	5	1.7	8	0
1973			2	-1	-0.5	0	0
1976	CLE	N	2	30	15.0	27	0
1977			2	6	3.0	3	0
1978			2	14	7.0	9	0
Career			12	68	5.7	27	0

Emmett Ruh

Year	Team		Att	Yds	Avg	Lg	TD
1922	COL	N					1

Max Runager

Year	Team		Att	Yds	Avg	Lg	TD
1983	PHI	N	1	6	6.0	6	0
1984	SF	N	1	-5	-5.0	-5	0
1988	CLE	N	1	0	0.0	0	0
1989	PHI	N	2	5	2.5	5	0
Career			5	6	1.2	6	0

Tommy Runnels

Year	Team		Att	Yds	Avg	Lg	TD
1956	WAS	N	96	334	3.5	17	0
1957			20	52	2.6	16	0
Career			116	386	3.3	17	0

Clive Rush

Year	Team		Att	Yds	Avg	Lg	TD
1953	GB	N	1	-6	-6.0	-6	0

Booker Russell

Year	Team		Att	Yds	Avg	Lg	TD
1978	OAK	N	11	65	5.9	15	0
1979			33	190	5.8	72	4
1980	SD	N	8	41	5.1	10	0
1981	PHI	N	38	123	3.2	17	4
Career			90	419	4.7	72	8

Derek Russell

Year	Team		Att	Yds	Avg	Lg	TD
1994	DEN	N	1	6	6.0	6	0

Doug Russell

Year	Team		Att	Yds	Avg	Lg	TD
1934	CHIC	N					1
1935			140	499	3.6		0
1936			3	11	3.7		0
1937			23	76	3.3		0
1938			31	60	1.9		1
1939	CHIC-CLE	N	9	21	2.3		0
Career			206	667	3.2		2

Leonard Russell

Year	Team		Att	Yds	Avg	Lg	TD
1991	NE	N	266	959	3.6	24	4
1992			123	390	3.2	23	2
1993			300	1088	3.6	21	7
1994	DEN	N	190	620	3.3	22t	9
1995	STL	N	66	203	3.1	18	0
1996	SD	N	219	713	3.3	21	7
Career			1164	3973	3.4	24	29

Ralph Ruthstrom

Year	Team		Att	Yds	Avg	Lg	TD
1945	CLE	N	10	74	7.4	34	0
1946	LA	N	2	-4	-2.0	1	0
1947	WAS	N	2	5	2.5	4	0
Career			14	75	5.4	34	0

Ed Rutkowski

Year	Team		Att	Yds	Avg	Lg	TD
1963	BUF	A	48	144	3.0	45	0
1966			1	10	10.0	10	0
1968			20	96	4.8	33	1
Career			69	250	3.6	45	1

Jeff Rutledge

Year	Team		Att	Yds	Avg	Lg	TD
1979	LA	N	5	27	5.4	14	0
1981			5	-3	-0.6	4	0
1983	NYG	N	7	27	3.9	10	0
1985			2	-6	-3.0	-2	0
1986			3	19	6.3	18	0
1987			15	31	2.1	20	0
1988			3	-1	-0.3	0	0
1990	WAS	N	4	12	3.0	12t	1
1991			8	-13	-1.6	-1	0
Career			52	93	1.8	20	1
Playoffs			7	-3	-0.4		0

Dave Ryan

Year	Team		Att	Yds	Avg	Lg	TD
1945	DET	N	36	93	2.6	8	1
1946			71	65	0.9	27	1
1948	BOS	N	3	1	0.3	3	0
Career			110	159	1.4	27	2

Frank Ryan

Year	Team		Att	Yds	Avg	Lg	TD
1958	LA	N	5	45	9.0	14	0
1959			19	57	3.0	13	1
1960			19	85	4.5	24	1
1961			38	139	3.7	28	0
1962	CLE	N	42	242	5.8	27	1
1963			62	224	3.6	25	2
1964			37	217	5.9	19	1
1965			19	72	3.8	18	0
1966			36	156	4.3	17	0
1967			22	57	2.6	12	0
1968			11	64	5.8	19	0
Career			310	1358	4.4	28	6
Playoffs			10	25	2.5		0

Kent Ryan

Year	Team		Att	Yds	Avg	Lg	TD
1938	DET	N	24	180	7.5		0
1939			8	41	5.1		1
1940			22	42	1.9		1
Career			54	263	4.9		1

Pat Ryan

Year	Team		Att	Yds	Avg	Lg	TD
1981	NYJ	N	3	-5	-1.7	-1	0
1982			1	-1	-1.0	-1	0
1983			4	23	5.8	25	0

Year	Team		Att	Yds	Avg	Lg	TD

Pat Ryan *continued*

Year	Team		Att	Yds	Avg	Lg	TD
1984			23	92	4.0	16	0
1985			3	-5	-1.7	-1	0
1986			8	28	3.5	18	0
1987			4	5	1.3	8t	1
1988			5	22	4.4	15	0
1989			1	-1	-1.0	-1	0
1991	PHI	N	1	-2	-2.0	-2	0
Career			53	156	2.9	25	1
Playoffs			2	30	15.0		0

Tom Rychlec

Year	Team		Att	Yds	Avg	Lg	TD
1961	BUF	A	1	-18	-18.0	-18	0

Nick Ryder

Year	Team		Att	Yds	Avg	Lg	TD
1963	DET	N	10	23	2.3	12	1
1964			11	11	1.0	7	0
Career			21	34	1.6	12	1

Julie Rykovich

Year	Team		Att	Yds	Avg	Lg	TD
1947	BUF	AA	92	414	4.5		4
1948	BUF-CHI	AA	96	425	4.4		6
1949	CHIB	N	88	340	3.9	18	5
1950			122	394	3.2	18	7
1951			83	399	4.8	56t	4
1952	WAS	N	94	361	3.8	21	1
1953			73	251	3.4	19	0
Career			648	2584	4.0	56t	27
Playoffs			14	67	4.8		0

Mark Rypien

Year	Team		Att	Yds	Avg	Lg	TD
1988	WAS	N	9	31	3.4	19t	1
1989			26	56	2.2	15	1
1990			15	4	0.3	8	0
1991			15	6	0.4	11	1
1992			36	50	1.4	11	3
1993			9	4	0.4	5	3
1994	CLE	N	7	4	0.6	2	0
1995	STL	N	9	10	1.1	5	0
Career			126	165	1.3	19t	8
Playoffs			17	-8	-0.5		1

Lou Saban

Year	Team		Att	Yds	Avg	Lg	TD
1946	CLE	AA	4	-4	-1.0		0

Lenny Sachs

Year	Team		Att	Yds	Avg	Lg	TD
1923	MIL	N					2

Frankie Sachse

Year	Team		Att	Yds	Avg	Lg	TD
1943	BKN	N	8	14	1.8	7	0
1944			9	13	1.4	5	0
1945	BOS	N	5	9	1.8	29	0
Career			22	36	1.6	29	0

Norb Sacksteder

Year	Team		Att	Yds	Avg	Lg	TD
1922	CAN	N					2

Nick Sacrinty

Year	Team		Att	Yds	Avg	Lg	TD
1947	CHIB	N	4	4	1.0	5	0

Steve Sader

Year	Team		Att	Yds	Avg	Lg	TD
1943	P-P	N	3	5	1.7	16	0

Eddie Saenz

Year	Team		Att	Yds	Avg	Lg	TD
1946	WAS	N	55	213	3.9	12	1
1947			51	143	2.8	18	2
1948			8	21	2.6	5	0
1949			53	170	3.2	14	0
1950			20	64	3.2	13	1
1951			3	8	2.7	6	0
Career			190	619	3.3	18	4

Saint Saffold

Year	Team		Att	Yds	Avg	Lg	TD
1968	CIN	A	1	21	21.0	21	0

George Saimes

Year	Team		Att	Yds	Avg	Lg	TD
1963	BUF	A	12	41	3.4	7	0

Rashaan Salaam

Year	Team		Att	Yds	Avg	Lg	TD
1995	CHI	N	296	1074	3.6	42	10
1996			143	496	3.5	32	3
Career			439	1570	3.6	42	13

Jay Saldi

Year	Team		Att	Yds	Avg	Lg	TD
1976	DAL	N	1	19	19.0	19	0
1979			1	-1	-1.0	-1	0
Career			2	18	9.0	19	0

Sean Salisbury

Year	Team		Att	Yds	Avg	Lg	TD
1992	MIN	N	11	0	0.0	4	0
1993			10	-1	-0.1	6	0
1994			3	2	0.7	5	0
1996	SD	N	6	14	2.3	11	0
Career			30	15	0.5	11	0
Playoffs			1	0	0.0		0

Jim Salsbury

Year	Team		Att	Yds	Avg	Lg	TD
1958	GB	N	0	3		3L	0

Jack Salschneider

Year	Team		Att	Yds	Avg	Lg	TD
1949	NYG	N	26	105	4.0	43	0

Chuck Sample

Year	Team		Att	Yds	Avg	Lg	TD
1942	GB	N	57	255	4.5	31	4
1945			2	2	1.0	3	0
Career			59	257	4.4	31	4

Johnny Sample

Year	Team		Att	Yds	Avg	Lg	TD
1960	BAL	N	1	7	7.0	7	0

Clint Sampson

Year	Team		Att	Yds	Avg	Lg	TD
Playoffs			1	8	8.0		0

Eber Sampson

Year	Team		Att	Yds	Avg	Lg	TD
1921	MIN	A					2
1923	MIN	N					1
Career							3

Don Samuel

Year	Team		Att	Yds	Avg	Lg	TD
1949	PIT	N	39	163	4.2	31	1

Chris Samuels

Year	Team		Att	Yds	Avg	Lg	TD
1991	SD	N	2	10	5.0	6	0

Terry Samuels

Year	Team		Att	Yds	Avg	Lg	TD
1994	ARI	N	1	1	1.0	1	0

Dick Sandefur

Year	Team		Att	Yds	Avg	Lg	TD
1936	PIT	N	7	13	1.9		0

Barry Sanders

Year	Team		Att	Yds	Avg	Lg	TD
1989	DET	N	280	1470	5.3	34	14
1990			255	**1304**	5.1	45t	13
1991			342	1548	4.5	69t	**16**
1992			312	1352	4.3	55t	9
1993			243	1115	4.6	42	3
1994			331	**1883**	**5.7**	85	7
1995			314	1500	4.8	75t	11
1996			307	**1553**	5.1	54t	11
Career			2384	11725	4.9	85	84
Playoffs			73	321	4.4		1

Charlie Sanders

Year	Team		Att	Yds	Avg	Lg	TD
1968	DET	N	2	3	1.5	2	0
1969			1	-8	-8.0	-8	0
1973			1	-1	-1.0	-1	0
Career			4	-6	-1.5	2	0

Chris Sanders

Year	Team		Att	Yds	Avg	Lg	TD
1995	HOU	N	2	-19	-9.5	-6	0

Chuck Sanders

Year	Team		Att	Yds	Avg	Lg	TD
1986	PIT	N	4	12	3.0	13	0
1987			11	65	5.9	14	1
Career			15	77	5.1	14	1

Daryl Sanders

Year	Team		Att	Yds	Avg	Lg	TD
1965	DET	N	1	2	2.0	2	0

Deion Sanders

Year	Team		Att	Yds	Avg	Lg	TD
1992	ATL	N	1	-4	-4.0	-4	0
1995	DAL	N	2	9	4.5	8	0
1996			3	2	0.7	3	0
Career			6	7	1.2	8	0
Playoffs			4	39	9.8		1

Frank Sanders

Year	Team		Att	Yds	Avg	Lg	TD
1995	ARI	N	1	1	1.0	1	0
1996			2	-4	-2.0	1	0
Career			3	-3	-1.0	1	0

Paul Sanders

Year	Team		Att	Yds	Avg	Lg	TD
1944	BOS	N	6	4	0.7	8	0

Ricky Sanders

Year	Team		Att	Yds	Avg	Lg	TD
1987	WAS	N	1	-4	-4.0	-4	0
1988			2	14	7.0	7	0
1989			4	19	4.8	13	0
1990			4	17	4.3	12	0
1991			7	47	6.7	17	1
1992			4	-6	-1.5	3	0
1993			1	7	7.0	7	0
Career			23	94	4.1	17	1
Playoffs			4	28	7.0		0

Spec Sanders

Year	Team		Att	Yds	Avg	Lg	TD
1946	NY	AA	140	**709**	5.1	75t	**6**
1947			231	**1432**	6.2	70t	**18**
1948			169	759	4.5	60t	9
Career			540	2900	5.4	75t	33
Playoffs			26	95	3.7		1

Thomas Sanders

Year	Team		Att	Yds	Avg	Lg	TD
1985	CHI	N	25	104	4.2	28	1
1986			27	224	8.3	75t	5
1987			23	122	5.3	17	1
1988			95	332	3.5	20t	3
1989			41	127	3.1	19	0
1990	PHI	N	56	208	3.7	39	1
1991			54	122	2.3	16	1
Career			321	1239	3.9	75t	12
Playoffs			23	147	6.4		0

Reggie Sanderson

Year	Team		Att	Yds	Avg	Lg	TD
1973	CHI	N	3	8	2.7	6	0

Dan Sandifer

Year	Team		Att	Yds	Avg	Lg	TD
1948	WAS	N	18	67	3.7	13	0
1949			20	64	3.2	21	0
1950	DET	N	1	3	3.0	3	0
1951	PHI	N	35	113	3.2	13	1
Career			74	247	3.3	21	1

Curt Sandig

Year	Team		Att	Yds	Avg	Lg	TD
1942	PIT	N	50	116		39	3
1946	BUF	AA	22	52	2.4		1
Career			72	168	2.3	39	4

Ollie Sansen

Year	Team		Att	Yds	Avg	Lg	TD
1932	BKN	N					1
1933							1
Career							2

Dom Sanzotta

Year	Team		Att	Yds	Avg	Lg	TD
1942	DET	N	71	268	3.8	18	0
1946			6	72	12.0	51	0
Career			77	340	4.4	51	0

Theron Sapp

Year	Team		Att	Yds	Avg	Lg	TD
1959	PHI	N	41	145	3.5	17	1
1960			9	20	2.2	7	0
1961			7	24	3.4	8	1
1962			23	53	2.3	17	2
1963	PHI-PIT	N	104	452	4.3	27	1
1964	PIT	N	4	15	3.8	5	0
1965			14	54	3.9	24	0
Career			202	763	3.8	27	5

Tony Sarausky

Year	Team		Att	Yds	Avg	Lg	TD
1935	NYG	N					1
1936			32	150	4.7		1
1937			4	18	4.5		0
1938	BKN	N	8	42	5.3		0
Career			44	210	4.8		2

Phil Sarboe

Year	Team		Att	Yds	Avg	Lg	TD
1935	CHIC	N	38	129	3.4		0
1936	CHIC-BKN	N	83	103	1.2		0
Career			121	232	1.9		0

Broderick Sargent

Year	Team	Att	Yds	Avg	Lg	TD
1987	STL N	18	90	5.0	16	0
1989	DAL N	20	87	4.3	43	1
Career		38	177	4.7	43	1

Charley Sarratt

Year	Team	Att	Yds	Avg	Lg	TD
1948	DET N	3	3	1.0	3	0

Paul Sarringhaus

Year	Team	Att	Yds	Avg	Lg	TD
1946	CHIC N	2	1	0.5	1	0
1948	DET N	19	38	2.0	7	0
Career		21	39	1.9	7	0

Martin Sartin

Year	Team	Att	Yds	Avg	Lg	TD
1987	SD N	19	52	2.7	10	1

George Sauer

Year	Team	Att	Yds	Avg	Lg	TD
1935	GB N	89	334	3.8		3
1936		94	305	3.2		3
1937		7	17	2.4		0
Career		190	656	3.5		6
Playoffs		4	8	2.0		0

George Sauer

Year	Team	Att	Yds	Avg	Lg	TD
1967	NY A	1	-3	-3.0	-3	0
1968		2	21	10.5	15	0
1969		1	5	5.0	5	0
Career		4	23	5.8	15	0

Todd Sauerbrun

Year	Team	Att	Yds	Avg	Lg	TD
1996	CHI N	1	3	3.0	3	0

Syl Saumer

Year	Team	Att	Yds	Avg	Lg	TD
1934	C-S N					1

Russ Saunders

Year	Team	Att	Yds	Avg	Lg	TD
1931	GB N					1

Joe Savoldi

Year	Team	Att	Yds	Avg	Lg	TD
1930	CHIB N					1

James Saxon

Year	Team	Att	Yds	Avg	Lg	TD
1988	KC N	60	236	3.9	14	2
1989		58	233	4.0	19	3
1990		3	15	5.0	8	0
1991		6	13	2.2	8	0
1992	MIA N	4	7	1.8	4	0
1993		5	13	2.6	9	0
1994		8	16	2.0	7	0
1995	PHI N	1	0	0.0	0	0
Career		145	533	3.7	19	5
Playoffs		6	6	1.0		0

Mike Saxon

Year	Team	Att	Yds	Avg	Lg	TD
1989	DAL N	1	1	1.0	1	0
1990		1	20	20.0	20	0
1993	NE	2	2	1.0	2	0
1994	MIN N	1	0	0.0	0	0
Career		5	23	4.6	20	0

Jimmy Saxton

Year	Team	Att	Yds	Avg	Lg	TD
1962	DAL A	3	1	0.3	9	0

Gale Sayers

Year	Team	Att	Yds	Avg	Lg	TD
1965	CHI N	166	867	5.2	61t	14
1966		229	**1231**	5.4	58t	8
1967		186	880	4.7	70	7
1968		138	856	**6.2**	63	2
1969		**236**	**1032**	4.4	28	8
1970		23	52	2.3	15	0
1971		13	38	2.9	9	0
Career		991	4956	5.0	70	39

Ron Sayers

Year	Team	Att	Yds	Avg	Lg	TD
1969	SD A	14	53	3.8	8	0

Ralph Sazio

Year	Team	Att	Yds	Avg	Lg	TD
1948	BKN AA	0	5		5L	

Charley Scales

Year	Team	Att	Yds	Avg	Lg	TD
1960	PIT N	26	81	3.1	9	0
1961		50	184	3.7	27	0
1962	CLE N	56	239	4.3	27	3
1963		2	-3	-1.5	2t	1

Charley Scales continued

Year	Team	Att	Yds	Avg	Lg	TD
1964		2	5	2.5	3	0
1965		11	59	5.4	20	0
1966	ATL N	10	38	3.8	10	0
Career		157	603	3.8	27	4

Ted Scalissi

Year	Team	Att	Yds	Avg	Lg	TD
1947	CHI AA	35	37	1.1		0

John Scanlon

Year	Team	Att	Yds	Avg	Lg	TD
1921	CHIC A					1

Jack Scarbath

Year	Team	Att	Yds	Avg	Lg	TD
1953	WAS N	22	98	4.5	40	0
1954		17	36	2.1	6	0
1956	PIT N	4	19	4.8	21	0
Career		43	153	3.6	40	0

Sam Scarber

Year	Team	Att	Yds	Avg	Lg	TD
1975	SD N	15	68	4.5	18	1
1976		61	236	3.9	14	1
Career		76	304	4.0	18	2

Joe Scarpati

Year	Team	Att	Yds	Avg	Lg	TD
1965	PHI N	1	6	6.0	6	0

Bob Scarpitto

Year	Team	Att	Yds	Avg	Lg	TD
1964	DEN A	1	5	5.0	5	0
1965		4	94	23.5	44	0
1966		4	110	27.5	63	1
1967		1	5	5.0	5	0
Career		10	214	21.4	63	1

Elmer Schaake

Year	Team	Att	Yds	Avg	Lg	TD
1933	POR N	125	412	3.3		0

Pete Schabarum

Year	Team	Att	Yds	Avg	Lg	TD
1951	SF N	76	311	4.1	67	2
1953		18	104	5.8	23	0
1954		21	79	3.8	16	1
Career		115	494	4.3	67	3

Don Schaefer

Year	Team	Att	Yds	Avg	Lg	TD
1956	PHI N	102	320	3.1	11	2

Eddie Scharer

Year	Team	Att	Yds	Avg	Lg	TD
1926	DET N					1

Herb Schell

Year	Team	Att	Yds	Avg	Lg	TD
1924	COL N					1

Cory Schlesinger

Year	Team	Att	Yds	Avg	Lg	TD
1995	DET N	1	1	1.0	1	0

Art Schlichter

Year	Team	Att	Yds	Avg	Lg	TD
1982	BAL N	1	3	3.0	3	0
1984	IND N	19	145	7.6	22	1
1985		2	13	6.5	9	0
Career		22	161	7.3	22	1

Walt Schlinkman

Year	Team	Att	Yds	Avg	Lg	TD
1946	GB N	97	379	3.9	44	1
1947		115	439	3.8	20	2
1948		106	441	4.2	19	4
1949		47	196	4.2	37	0
Career		365	1455	4.0	44	7

Art Schmaehl

Year	Team	Att	Yds	Avg	Lg	TD
1921	GB A					2

Ted Schmitt

Year	Team	Att	Yds	Avg	Lg	TD
1940	PHI N	1	6	6.0	6	0

Don Schneider

Year	Team	Att	Yds	Avg	Lg	TD
1948	BUF AA	15	70	4.7		0

Herm Schneidman

Year	Team	Att	Yds	Avg	Lg	TD
1937	GB N	5	17	3.4		0
1938		4	8	2.0		0
Career		9	25	2.8		0

Turk Schonert

Year	Team	Att	Yds	Avg	Lg	TD
1981	CIN N	7	41	5.9	19	0
1982		3	-8	-2.7	-3	0

Turk Schonert continued

Year	Team	Att	Yds	Avg	Lg	TD
1983		29	117	4.0	15	2
1984		13	77	5.9	17	1
1985		8	39	4.9	17	0
1986	ATL N	11	12	1.1	7	1
1988	CIN N	2	10	5.0	7	0
Career		73	288	3.9	19	4

Ivan Schottel

Year	Team	Att	Yds	Avg	Lg	TD
1946	DET N	4	12	3.0	5	0

Larry Schreiber

Year	Team	Att	Yds	Avg	Lg	TD
1971	SF N	34	180	5.3	23	0
1972		118	420	3.6	20	2
1973		42	163	3.9	13	0
1974		174	634	3.6	21	3
1975		134	337	2.5	15	5
1976	CHI N	4	15	3.8	11	0
Career		506	1749	3.5	23	10
Playoffs		30	59	2.0		3

Bill Schroeder

Year	Team	Att	Yds	Avg	Lg	TD
1946	CHI AA	12	42	3.5		0
1947		11	45	4.1		0
Career		23	87	3.8		0

Gene Schroeder

Year	Team	Att	Yds	Avg	Lg	TD
1951	CHIB N	1	4	4.0	4	0

Jay Schroeder

Year	Team	Att	Yds	Avg	Lg	TD
1985	WAS N	17	30	1.8	14	0
1986		36	47	1.3	20	1
1987		26	120	4.6	31	3
1988	LARI N	29	109	3.8	12	1
1989		15	38	2.5	19	0
1990		37	81	2.2	17	0
1991		28	76	2.7	15	0
1992		28	160	5.7	19	0
1993	CIN N	10	41	4.1	20	0
1994	ARI N	16	59	3.7	16	0
Career		242	761	3.1	31	5
Playoffs		12	39	3.3		0

Bill Schroll

Year	Team	Att	Yds	Avg	Lg	TD
1950	DET N	1	1	1.0	1	0

Karl Schuelke

Year	Team	Att	Yds	Avg	Lg	TD
1939	PIT N	2	2	1.0		0

Randy Schultz

Year	Team	Att	Yds	Avg	Lg	TD
1966	CLE N	7	32	4.6	20	0
1967	NO N	32	117	3.7	22t	2
1968		43	152	3.5	22t	2
Career		82	301	3.7	22t	2

Vic Schwall

Year	Team	Att	Yds	Avg	Lg	TD
1947	CHIC N	12	33	2.8	16	0
1948		15	107	7.1	23	1
1949		12	47	3.9	18	0
1950		17	114	6.7	26	0
Career		56	301	5.4	26	1
Playoffs		1	0	0.0		0

Elmer Schwartz

Year	Team	Att	Yds	Avg	Lg	TD
1931	POR N					2

Perry Schwartz

Year	Team	Att	Yds	Avg	Lg	TD
1938	BKN N	2	-3	-1.5		0
1941		1	7	7.0	7	0
1942		2	20	10.0	17	0
Career		5	24	4.8	17	0

Ger Schwedes

Year	Team	Att	Yds	Avg	Lg	TD
1961	BOS A	10	14	1.4	5	0

Bob Schweickert

Year	Team	Att	Yds	Avg	Lg	TD
1967	NY A	1	1	1.0	1	0

Dick Schweidler

Year	Team	Att	Yds	Avg	Lg	TD
1938	CHIB N	16	57	3.6		0
1939		5	15	3.0		0
1946		20	94	4.7	27t	3
Career		41	166	4.0	27t	3

Year	Team		Att	Yds	Avg	Lg	TD

Wilson Schwenk

Year	Team		Att	Yds	Avg	Lg	TD
1942	CHIC	N	111	313	2.8	28	2
1946	CLE	AA	6	-1	-0.2		1
1947	BAL	AA	25	58	2.3		1
1948	NY	AA	3	6	2.0		0
Career			145	376	2.6	28	4

John Sciarra

Year	Team		Att	Yds	Avg	Lg	TD
1978	PHI	N	8	11	1.4	4	2
1980			3	11	3.7	9	0
1981			1	0	0.0	0	0
Career			12	22	1.8	9	2

Bo Scott

Year	Team		Att	Yds	Avg	Lg	TD
1969	CLE	N	44	157	3.6	20	0
1970			151	625	4.1	63t	7
1971			179	606	3.4	35	9
1972			123	571	4.6	27t	2
1973			34	79	2.3	20	0
1974			23	86	3.7	20	0
Career			554	2124	3.8	63t	18
Playoffs			41	169	4.1		2

Bobby Scott

Year	Team		Att	Yds	Avg	Lg	TD
1973	NO	N	9	18	2.0	4	0
1974			1	1	1.0	1	0
1976			12	48	4.0	13	1
1977			4	11	2.8	9	0
1978			1	0	0.0	0	0
1981			3	-4	-1.3	-1	0
Career			30	74	2.5	13	1

Clyde Scott

Year	Team		Att	Yds	Avg	Lg	TD
1949	PHI	N	40	195	4.9	39	1
1950			13	46	3.5	22	0
1951			45	161	3.6	40	1
1952	DET	N	2	-2	-1.0	4	0
Career			100	400	4.0	40	2
Playoffs			6	23	3.8		0

Darnay Scott

Year	Team		Att	Yds	Avg	Lg	TD
1994	CIN	N	10	106	10.6	23	0
1995			5	11	2.2	9	0
1996			3	4	1.3	8	0
Career			18	121	6.7	23	0

Freddie Scott

Year	Team		Att	Yds	Avg	Lg	TD
1974	BAL	N	2	12	6.0	9	0
1978	DET	N	4	53	13.3	36	0
1979			6	21	3.5	18	0
1980			5	86	17.2	48t	1
1981			7	25	3.6	10	0
1982			1	-6	-6.0	-6	0
Career			25	191	7.6	48t	1

James Scott

Year	Team		Att	Yds	Avg	Lg	TD
1976	CHI	N	2	-4	-2.0	3	0

Joe Scott

Year	Team		Att	Yds	Avg	Lg	TD
1948	NYG	N	48	198	4.1	20	2
1949			70	224	3.2	13	4
1950			72	322	4.5	48	2
1951			94	367	3.9	37	1
1952			38	107	2.8	30t	3
Career			322	1218	3.8	48	12
Playoffs			3	-2	-0.7		0

Johnny Scott

Year	Team		Att	Yds	Avg	Lg	TD
1921	BUF	A					2

Kevin Scott

Year	Team		Att	Yds	Avg	Lg	TD
1989	DAL	N	2	-4	-2.0	-1	0

Lindsay Scott

Year	Team		Att	Yds	Avg	Lg	TD
1982	NO	N	1	-4	-4.0	-4	0

Patrick Scott

Year	Team		Att	Yds	Avg	Lg	TD
1987	GB	N	1	2	2.0	2	0

Ronald Scott

Year	Team		Att	Yds	Avg	Lg	TD
1987	MIA	N	47	199	4.2	24	3

Tom Scott

Year	Team		Att	Yds	Avg	Lg	TD
1959	NYG	N	2	10	5.0	10	0

Willie Scott

Year	Team		Att	Yds	Avg	Lg	TD
1983	KC	N	1	1	1.0	1	0

Bob Scrabis

Year	Team		Att	Yds	Avg	Lg	TD
1961	NY	A	1	1	1.0	1t	1

Bucky Scribner

Year	Team		Att	Yds	Avg	Lg	TD
1987	MIN	N	1	-7	-7.0	-7	0
1988			1	0	0.0	0	0
Career			2	-7	-3.5	0	0

Rob Scribner

Year	Team		Att	Yds	Avg	Lg	TD
1973	LA	N	20	109	5.5	17	0
1974			9	24	2.7	5	0
1975			42	216	5.1	34	2
1976			2	12	6.0	11	1
Career			73	361	4.9	34	3
Playoffs			6	19	3.2		0

Joe Scudero

Year	Team		Att	Yds	Avg	Lg	TD
1954	WAS	N	21	19	0.9	12	0
1955			6	27	4.5	13	0
1956			2	3	1.5	2	0
1957			9	60	6.7	43	0
1958			5	30	6.0	9	0
Career			43	139	3.2	43	0

Charlie Seabright

Year	Team		Att	Yds	Avg	Lg	TD
1947	PIT	N	1	4	4.0	4t	1

Paul Seal

Year	Team		Att	Yds	Avg	Lg	TD
1974	NO	N	2	7	3.5	6t	1
1975			1	10	10.0	10	0
1976			2	-7	-3.5	-1	0
Career			5	10	2.0	10	1

Jimmy Sears

Year	Team		Att	Yds	Avg	Lg	TD
1957	CHIC	N	17	68	4.0	49t	1
1958			17	51	3.0	13	0
Career			34	119	3.5	49t	1

George Seasholtz

Year	Team		Att	Yds	Avg	Lg	TD
1924	KEN	N					1

Mike Sebastian

Year	Team		Att	Yds	Avg	Lg	TD
1935	PHI-PIT	N	18	76	4.2		0
1937	CLE	N	6	4	0.7		0
Career			24	80	3.3		0

Scott Secules

Year	Team		Att	Yds	Avg	Lg	TD
1989	MIA	N	4	39	9.8	17	0
1990			8	34	4.3	17	0
1991			4	30	7.5	12	1
1993	NE	N	8	33	4.1	13	0
Career			24	136	5.7	17	1

Len Sedbrook

Year	Team		Att	Yds	Avg	Lg	TD
1928	DET	N					1
1929	NYG	N					4
1930							5
1931							2
Career							12

Larry Seiple

Year	Team		Att	Yds	Avg	Lg	TD
1967	MIA	A	3	58	19.3	34	0
1968			5	42	8.4	32	0
1969			1	6	6.0	6	0
1970	MIA	N	2	21	10.5	24	0
1971			1	14	14.0	14	0
1975			1	4	4.0	4	0
1976			3	14	4.7	7	0
Career			16	159	9.9	34	0
Playoffs			1	37	37.0		0

Warren Seitz

Year	Team		Att	Yds	Avg	Lg	TD
1986	PIT	N	3	2	0.7	2	0

Clarence Self

Year	Team		Att	Yds	Avg	Lg	TD
1949	CHIC	N	4	16	4.0	6	0
1950	DET	N	3	9	3.0	6	0
1952	GB	N	0	21		21L	0
Career			7	46	6.6	21L	0

Harry Seltzer

Year	Team		Att	Yds	Avg	Lg	TD
1942	DET	N	14	44	3.1	24	0

Bernie Semes

Year	Team		Att	Yds	Avg	Lg	TD
1944	C-P	N	17	38	2.2	3	0

Bill Senn

Year	Team		Att	Yds	Avg	Lg	TD
1926	CHIB	N					7
1927							5
1928							1
1929							1
1930							1
1931							1
Career							16

Frank Seno

Year	Team		Att	Yds	Avg	Lg	TD
1943	WAS	N	26	152	5.8	52	0
1944			43	140	3.3	14	0
1945	CHIC	N	93	355	3.8	47t	2
1946			62	191	3.1	27	0
1947	BOS	N	69	212	3.1	22	1
1948			71	242	3.4	21	0
Career			364	1292	3.5	52	3
Playoffs			5	23	4.6		0

Dean Sensenbaugher

Year	Team		Att	Yds	Avg	Lg	TD
1948	CLE	AA	18	59	3.3		1
1949	NYB	N	20	36	1.8	7	1
Career			38	95	2.5	7	2
Playoffs			2	2	1.0		0

Joe Senser

Year	Team		Att	Yds	Avg	Lg	TD
1980	MIN	N	1	-1	-1.0	-1	0
1981			1	2	2.0	2	0
Career			2	1	0.5	2	0

Joe Setcavage

Year	Team		Att	Yds	Avg	Lg	TD
1943	BKN	N	1	3	3.0	3	0

John Settle

Year	Team		Att	Yds	Avg	Lg	TD
1987	ATL	N	19	72	3.8	12	0
1988			232	1024	4.4	62	7
1989			179	689	3.8	20	3
1990			9	16	1.8	4	0
Career			439	1801	4.1	62	10

Frank Seurer

Year	Team		Att	Yds	Avg	Lg	TD
1987	KC	N	9	33	3.7	11	0

Steve Sewell

Year	Team		Att	Yds	Avg	Lg	TD
1985	DEN	N	81	275	3.4	16	4
1986			23	123	5.3	15	1
1987			19	83	4.4	17	2
1988			32	135	4.2	26	1
1989			7	44	6.3	10	0
1990			17	46	2.7	8	1
1991			50	211	4.2	26	2
Career			229	917	4.0	26	13
Playoffs			26	94	3.6		1

Lin Sexton

Year	Team		Att	Yds	Avg	Lg	TD
1948	LA	AA	7	39	5.6		0

Bob Seymour

Year	Team		Att	Yds	Avg	Lg	TD
1940	WAS	N	57	170	3.0		4
1941			62	137	2.2	17	1
1942			54	190	3.5	18	1
1943			65	232	3.6	40	0
1944			92	315	3.4	35	3
1945			30	102	3.4	23	2
1946	LA	AA	37	165	4.5		0
Career			397	1311	3.3	40	11
Playoffs			25	59	2.4		0

Jim Seymour

Year	Team		Att	Yds	Avg	Lg	TD
1972	CHI	N	1	-9	-9.0	-9	0

Leland Shaffer

Year	Team		Att	Yds	Avg	Lg	TD
1936	NYG	N	3	10	3.3		0
1937			8	35	4.4		0
1938			1	4	4.0	4	0
1939			3	6	2.0		0
1940			7	20	2.9		1
1942			1	3	3.0	3	0
1943			1	3	3.0	3	0
Career			24	81	3.4	4	1

Ron Shanklin

Year	Team		Att	Yds	Avg	Lg	TD
1971	PIT	N	2	1	0.5	2	0
1973			3	1	0.3	10	0
Career			5	2	0.4	10	0

Jim Shanley

Year	Team		Att	Yds	Avg	Lg	TD
1958	GB	N	23	30	1.3	5	0

Carver Shannon

Year	Team		Att	Yds	Avg	Lg	TD
1964	LA	N	17	35	2.1	8	0

Luis Sharpe

Year	Team		Att	Yds	Avg	Lg	TD
1983	STL	N	1	11	11.0	11	0

Shannon Sharpe

Year	Team		Att	Yds	Avg	Lg	TD
1991	DEN	N	1	15	15.0	15	0
1992			2	-6	-3.0	-3	0
Career			3	9	3.0	15	0

Sterling Sharpe

Year	Team		Att	Yds	Avg	Lg	TD
1988	GB	N	4	-2	-0.5	5	0
1989			2	25	12.5	26	0
1990			2	14	7.0	10	0
1991			4	4	1.0	12	0
1992			4	8	2.0	14	0
1993			4	8	2.0	5	0
1994			3	15	5.0	8	0
Career			23	72	3.1	26	0

Dennis Shaw

Year	Team		Att	Yds	Avg	Lg	TD
1970	BUF	N	39	210	5.4	20	0
1971			14	82	5.9	12	0
1972			35	138	3.9	16	0
1973			4	2	0.5	1	0
1975	STL	N	3	-12	-4.0	-2	0
Career			95	420	4.4	20	0

Ed Shaw

Year	Team		Att	Yds	Avg	Lg	TD
1922	CAN	N					5

George Shaw

Year	Team		Att	Yds	Avg	Lg	TD
1955	BAL	N	68	301	4.4	37	3
1956			20	63	3.1	19	0
1957			5	30	6.0	11	1
1958			5	-3	-0.6	3	1
1959	NYG	N	3	3	1.0	1	0
1960			15	-12	-0.8	15	0
1961	MIN	N	10	39	3.9	19	0
1962	DEN	A	4	10	2.5	9	1
Career			130	431	3.3	37	6

Glenn Shaw

Year	Team		Att	Yds	Avg	Lg	TD
1962	LA	N	18	76	4.2	38	0
1963	OAK	N	20	46	2.3	15	1
1964			9	26	2.9	9	2
Career			47	148	3.1	38	3

Pat Shea

Year	Team		Att	Yds	Avg	Lg	TD
1965	SD	A	1	-5	-5.0	-5	0

Ed Shedlosky

Year	Team		Att	Yds	Avg	Lg	TD
1945	NYG	N	9	11	1.2	4	0

Willie Shelby

Year	Team		Att	Yds	Avg	Lg	TD
1976	CIN	N	5	9	1.8	3	0
1978	STL	N	2	5	2.5	4	0
Career			7	14	2.0	4	0

Charley Shepard

Year	Team		Att	Yds	Avg	Lg	TD
1956	PIT	N	30	91	3.0	14	0

Derrick Shepard

Year	Team		Att	Yds	Avg	Lg	TD
1989	DAL	N	3	12	4.0	12	0

Bill Shepherd

Year	Team		Att	Yds	Avg	Lg	TD
1935	BOS-DET	N	143	425	3.0		4
1936	DET	N	74	292	3.9		1
1937			93	325	3.5		2
1938			100	455	4.5		3
1939			85	420	4.9		2
1940			24	67	2.8		4
Career			519	1984	3.8		16

Johnny Shepherd

Year	Team		Att	Yds	Avg	Lg	TD
1987	BUF	N	12	42	3.5	19	0

Leslie Shepherd

Year	Team		Att	Yds	Avg	Lg	TD
1995	WAS	N	7	63	9.0	26	1
1996			6	96	16.0	32t	2
Career			13	159	12.2	32t	3

Allie Sherman

Year	Team		Att	Yds	Avg	Lg	TD
1943	P-P	N	17	-20	-1.2	5	1
1944	PHI	N	22	-42	-1.9	17	0
1945			16	-7	-0.4	8	1
1946			21	8	0.4	12	0
1947			17	17	1.0	16	0
Career			93	-44	-0.5	17	2
Playoffs			2	12	6.0		0

Heath Sherman

Year	Team		Att	Yds	Avg	Lg	TD
1989	PHI	N	40	177	4.4	37	2
1990			164	685	4.2	36	1
1991			106	279	2.6	12	0
1992			112	583	5.2	34	5
1993			115	406	3.5	19	2
Career			537	2130	4.0	37	10
Playoffs			53	214	4.0		1

Rod Sherman

Year	Team		Att	Yds	Avg	Lg	TD
1967	OAK	A	1	13	13.0	13t	1
1968	CIN	A	1	3	3.0	3	0
1970	OAK	N	1	2	2.0	2	0
1972	DEN	N	1	2	2.0	2	0
Career			4	20	5.0	13t	1

Solly Sherman

Year	Team		Att	Yds	Avg	Lg	TD
1939	CHIB	N	3	-5	-1.7		0
1940			8	10	1.3		0
Career			11	5	0.5		0

Tom Sherman

Year	Team		Att	Yds	Avg	Lg	TD
1968	BOS	A	25	80	3.2	17	0
1969	BUF	A	2	14	7.0	10	0
Career			27	94	3.5	17	0

Mike Sherrard

Year	Team		Att	Yds	Avg	Lg	TD
1986	DAL	N	2	11	5.5	8	0
1994	NYG	N	1	-10	-10.0	-10	0
Career			3	1	0.3	8	0

Rhoten Shetley

Year	Team		Att	Yds	Avg	Lg	TD
1940	BKN	N	7	30	4.3		0
1941			1	7	7.0	7t	1
1946	BKN	AA	9	21	2.3		0
Career			17	58	3.4	7t	1

Burrell Shields

Year	Team		Att	Yds	Avg	Lg	TD
1954	PIT	N	7	28	4.0	13	0
1955	BAL	N	10	34	3.4	14	0
Career			17	62	3.6	14	0

Dick Shiner

Year	Team		Att	Yds	Avg	Lg	TD
1964	WAS	N	2	8	4.0	5	0
1965			12	35	2.9	29	0
1966			1	10	10.0	10	0
1967	CLE	N	2	-7	-3.5	-3	0
1968	PIT	N	14	53	3.8	12	0
1969			14	55	3.9	18t	1
1971	ATL	N	10	9	0.9	4t	1
1973			3	-2	-0.7	3	0
Career			58	161	2.8	29	2

Jerry Shipkey

Year	Team		Att	Yds	Avg	Lg	TD
1948	PIT	N	64	129	2.0	16	8
1949			26	93	3.6	14	4
1950			18	17	0.9	11	3
1952			1	1	1.0	1	0
Career			109	240	2.2	16	15

Roy Shivers

Year	Team		Att	Yds	Avg	Lg	TD
1966	STL	N	1	5	5.0	5	0
1967			20	64	3.2	12	1
1968			44	184	4.2	42t	4
1969			27	115	4.3	17	2
1970			24	98	4.1	29t	2
1971			55	202	3.7	10	1
1972			5	12	2.4	9	0
Career			176	680	3.9	42t	10

Bill Shockley

Year	Team		Att	Yds	Avg	Lg	TD
1960	NY	A	37	156	4.2		0
1961			5	9	1.8	9	0
Career			42	165	3.9	9	0

Hal Shoener

Year	Team		Att	Yds	Avg	Lg	TD
1950	SF	N	1	1	1.0	1	0

Del Shofner

Year	Team		Att	Yds	Avg	Lg	TD
1959	LA	N	1	6	6.0	6	0
1960			1	-15	-15.0	-15	0
1961	NYG	N	1	6	6.0	6	0
1962			1	4	4.0	4	0
Career			4	1	0.3	6	0

Paul Shoults

Year	Team		Att	Yds	Avg	Lg	TD
1949	NYB	N	46	124	2.7	17	0

Don Shula

Year	Team		Att	Yds	Avg	Lg	TD
1954	BAL	N	2	3	1.5	3	0

Heath Shuler

Year	Team		Att	Yds	Avg	Lg	TD
1994	WAS	N	26	103	4.0	26	0
1995			18	57	3.2	13	0
1996			1	0	0.0	0	0
Career			45	160	3.6	26	0

Mike Shumann

Year	Team		Att	Yds	Avg	Lg	TD
1979	SF	N	1	19	19.0	19	0

Don Shy

Year	Team		Att	Yds	Avg	Lg	TD
1967	PIT	N	99	341	3.4	33t	4
1968			35	106	3.0	39	1
1969	NO	N	21	75	3.6	22	1
1970	CHI	N	79	227	2.9	45	1
1971			116	420	3.6	21t	2
1972			91	342	3.8	22	1
1973	STL	N	16	66	4.1	18	0
Career			457	1577	3.5	45	10

Les Shy

Year	Team		Att	Yds	Avg	Lg	TD
1966	DAL	N	17	118	6.9	18	1
1967			17	59	3.5	13	0
1968			64	179	2.8	17t	1
1969			42	154	3.7	23	1
1970	NYG	N	4	13	3.3	6	0
Career			144	523	3.6	68	3
Playoffs			3	3	1.0		0

Jimmy Sidle

Year	Team		Att	Yds	Avg	Lg	TD
1966	ATL	N	1	12	12.0	12	0

Wallie Sieb

Year	Team		Att	Yds	Avg	Lg	TD
1922	RAC	N					2

Jules Siegle

Year	Team		Att	Yds	Avg	Lg	TD
1948	NYG	N	2	6	3.0	8	0

Jeff Siemon

Year	Team		Att	Yds	Avg	Lg	TD
1981	MIN	N	1	0	0.0	0	0

Eric Sievers

Year	Team		Att	Yds	Avg	Lg	TD
1983	SD	N	1	-7	-7.0	-7	0

Vai Sikahema

Year	Team		Att	Yds	Avg	Lg	TD
1986	STL	N	16	62	3.9	23	0
1989	PHX	N	38	145	3.8	27	0
1990			3	8	2.7	4	0
1992	PHI	N	2	2	1.0	1	0
Career			59	217	3.7	27	0

Frank Sillin

Year	Team		Att	Yds	Avg	Lg	TD
1928	DAY	N					1

Floyd Simmons

Year	Team		Att	Yds	Avg	Lg	TD
1948	CHI	AA	36	121	3.4		1

Jerry Simmons

Year	Team		Att	Yds	Avg	Lg	TD
1968	ATL	N	1	-6	-6.0	-6	0
1971	DEN	N	1	7	7.0	7	0
1973			1	-4	-4.0	-4	0
Career			3	-3	-1.0	7	0

Jim Simmons

Year	Team		Att	Yds	Avg	Lg	TD
1927	CLE	N					5

Year	Team		Att	Yds	Avg	Lg	TD

Phil Simms

Year	Team		Att	Yds	Avg	Lg	TD
1979	NYG	N	29	166	5.7	27	1
1980			36	190	5.3	20	1
1981			19	42	2.2	24	0
1984			42	162	3.9	21	0
1985			37	132	3.6	28	0
1986			43	72	1.7	18	1
1987			14	44	3.1	20	0
1988			33	152	4.6	17	0
1989			32	141	4.4	15	1
1990			21	61	2.9	20	1
1991			9	42	4.7	19	1
1992			6	17	2.8	7	0
1993			28	31	1.1	9	0
Career			349	1252	3.6	28	6
Playoffs			30	68	2.3		0

Nate Simpson

Year	Team		Att	Yds	Avg	Lg	TD
1977	GB	N	60	204	3.4	40	0
1978			27	58	2.1	11	0
1979			66	235	3.6	22	1
Career			153	497	3.2	40	1

O.J. Simpson

Year	Team		Att	Yds	Avg	Lg	TD
1969	BUF	A	181	697	3.9	32t	2
1970	BUF	N	120	488	4.1	56t	5
1971			183	742	4.1	46t	5
1972			292	1251	4.3	94t	6
1973			332	2003	6.0	80t	12
1974			270	1125	4.2	41t	3
1975			329	1817	5.5	88t	16
1976			290	1503	5.2	75t	8
1977			126	557	4.4	39	0
1978	SF	N	161	593	3.7	34	1
1979			120	460	3.8	22	3
Career			2404	11236	4.7	94t	61
Playoffs			15	49	3.3		0

Willie Simpson

Year	Team		Att	Yds	Avg	Lg	TD
1962	OAK	A	10	32	3.2	11	0

Billy Sims

Year	Team		Att	Yds	Avg	Lg	TD
1980	DET	N	313	1303	4.2	52	13
1981			296	1437	4.9	51	13
1982			172	639	3.7	29	4
1983			220	1040	4.7	41	7
1984			130	687	5.3	81	5
Career			1131	5106	4.5	81	42
Playoffs			26	133	5.1		2

David Sims

Year	Team		Att	Yds	Avg	Lg	TD
1977	SEA	N	99	369	3.7	17t	5
1978			174	752	4.3	44t	14
1979			20	53	2.6	8	0
Career			293	1174	4.0	44t	19

Marvin Sims

Year	Team		Att	Yds	Avg	Lg	TD
1980	BAL	N	54	186	3.4	13	2

Frankie Sinkwich

Year	Team		Att	Yds	Avg	Lg	TD
1943	DET	N	93	266	2.9	17	1
1944			150	563	3.8	72t	6
1946	NY	AA	7	20	2.9		0
1947	NY-BAL	AA	71	241	3.4		0
Career			321	1090	3.4	72t	7

Brian Sipe

Year	Team		Att	Yds	Avg	Lg	TD
1974	CLE	N	16	44	2.8	17	4
1975			9	60	6.7	21	0
1976			18	71	3.9	17	0
1977			10	14	1.4	9	0
1978			28	87	3.1	35	3
1979			45	178	4.0	34	2
1980			20	55	2.8	24	1
1981			38	153	4.0	22	1
1982			13	44	3.4	12	0
1983			26	56	2.2	9	0
Career			223	762	3.4	35	11
Playoffs			6	13	2.2		0

Johnny Sisk

Year	Team		Att	Yds	Avg	Lg	TD
1933	CHIB	N	52	219	4.2		1
1934			41	156	3.8		1
1935			38	222	5.8		1

Johnny Sisk continued

Year	Team		Att	Yds	Avg	Lg	TD
1936			41	163	4.0		0
Career			172	760	4.4		3
Playoffs			1	0	0.0		0

Emil Sitko

Year	Team		Att	Yds	Avg	Lg	TD
1950	SF	N	23	105	4.6	15	1
1951	CHIC	N	52	183	3.5	61	0
1952			88	348	4.0	46	1
Career			163	636	3.9	61	2

John Skibinski

Year	Team		Att	Yds	Avg	Lg	TD
1979	CHI	N	3	10	3.3	4	0
1980			13	54	4.2	8	0
Career			16	64	4.0	8	0

Stan Skoczen

Year	Team		Att	Yds	Avg	Lg	TD
1944	CLE	N	1	0	0.0	0	0

Fritz Slackford

Year	Team		Att	Yds	Avg	Lg	TD
1921	CAN	A					1

Walt Slater

Year	Team		Att	Yds	Avg	Lg	TD
1947	PIT	N	46	167	3.6	19	0

Mickey Slaughter

Year	Team		Att	Yds	Avg	Lg	TD
1963	DEN	A	32	124	3.9	19	1
1964			20	54	2.7	18	0
1965			20	75	3.8	13	0
1966			1	10	10.0	10	0
Career			73	263	3.6	19	1

Webster Slaughter

Year	Team		Att	Yds	Avg	Lg	TD
1986	CLE	N	1	1	1.0	1	0
1990			5	29	5.8	17	0
1992	HOU	N	3	20	6.7	10	0
Career			9	50	5.6	17	0

Leroy Sledge

Year	Team		Att	Yds	Avg	Lg	TD
1971	HOU	N	24	74	3.1	19	0

Dwight Sloan

Year	Team		Att	Yds	Avg	Lg	TD
1938	CHIC	N	56	126	2.3		0
1939	DET	N	79	225	2.8		4
1940			58	225	3.9		0
Career			193	576	3.0		4

Steve Sloan

Year	Team		Att	Yds	Avg	Lg	TD
1967	ATL	N	1	2	2.0	2	0

Phil Slosburg

Year	Team		Att	Yds	Avg	Lg	TD
1948	BOS	N	32	89	2.8	16	0
1949	NYB	N	37	121	3.3	23	1
Career			69	210	3.0	23	1

Marty Slovak

Year	Team		Att	Yds	Avg	Lg	TD
1939	CLE	N	42	135	3.2		0
1940			53	129	2.4		1
1941			46	132	2.9	14	0
Career			141	396	2.8	14	1

Torrance Small

Year	Team		Att	Yds	Avg	Lg	TD
1995	NO	N	6	75	12.5	44t	1
1996			4	51	12.8	22	1
Career			10	126	12.6	44t	2

Bronko Smilanich

Year	Team		Att	Yds	Avg	Lg	TD
1939	CLE	N	1	-3	-3.0	-3	0

Tommie Smiley

Year	Team		Att	Yds	Avg	Lg	TD
1968	CIN	A	63	146	2.3	11	1
1969	DEN	A	56	166	3.0	26	3
1970	HOU	N	1	0	0.0	0	0
Career			120	312	2.6	26	4

Allen Smith

Year	Team		Att	Yds	Avg	Lg	TD
1966	BUF	A	31	148	4.8	20	0

Barry Smith

Year	Team		Att	Yds	Avg	Lg	TD
1973	GB	N	1	5	5.0	5	0

Barty Smith

Year	Team		Att	Yds	Avg	Lg	TD
1974	GB	N	9	19	2.1	4	0
1975			60	243	4.0	17	4

Barty Smith continued

Year	Team		Att	Yds	Avg	Lg	TD
1976			97	355	3.7	16	5
1977			166	554	3.3	11	2
1978			154	567	3.7	33	4
1979			57	201	3.5	23	3
1980			1	3	3.0	3	0
Career			544	1942	3.6	33	18

Bill Smith

Year	Team		Att	Yds	Avg	Lg	TD
1934	CHIC	N					2
1936			2	13	6.5		0
1939			1	3	3.0	3	0
Career			3	16	5.3	3	2

Bob Smith

Year	Team		Att	Yds	Avg	Lg	TD
1953	DET	N	6	51	8.5	30	0
1954			3	1	0.3	1	0
Career			9	52	5.8	30	0

Bob Smith

Year	Team		Att	Yds	Avg	Lg	TD
1955	CLE	N	37	142	3.8	31t	1
1956	CLE-PHI	N	11	18	1.6	7	0
Career			48	160	3.3	31t	1
Playoffs			3	2	0.7		0

Bobby Smith

Year	Team		Att	Yds	Avg	Lg	TD
1964	BUF	A	62	306	4.9	37	4
1965			43	137	3.2	13	1
1966	PIT	N	24	93	3.9	21	0
Career			129	536	4.2	37	5
Playoffs			1	5	5.0		0

Bruce Smith

Year	Team		Att	Yds	Avg	Lg	TD
1945	GB	N	21	94	4.5	27	0
1946			22	119	5.4	36	0
1947			47	288	6.1	37	1
1948	GB-LA	N	18	59	3.3	20	0
Career			108	560	5.2	37	1

Bruce Smith

Year	Team		Att	Yds	Avg	Lg	TD
1985	BUF	N	1	0	0.0	0	0

Carl Smith

Year	Team		Att	Yds	Avg	Lg	TD
1960	BUF	A	19	61	3.2		0

Cedric Smith

Year	Team		Att	Yds	Avg	Lg	TD
1920	BUF	A					4
1921							3
Career							7

Cedric Smith

Year	Team		Att	Yds	Avg	Lg	TD
1990	MIN	N	9	19	2.1	7	0
1994	WAS	N	10	48	4.8	13	0
1995			3	13	4.3	5	0
1996	ARI	N	14	15	1.1	3	1
Career			36	95	2.6	13	1

Charlie Smith

Year	Team		Att	Yds	Avg	Lg	TD
1947	CHIC	N	9	23	2.6	12	0

Charlie Smith

Year	Team		Att	Yds	Avg	Lg	TD
1968	OAK	A	95	504	5.3	65t	5
1969			177	600	3.4	26	2
1970	OAK	N	168	681	4.1	24	3
1971			11	4	0.4	8	1
1972			170	686	4.0	28	8
1973			173	682	3.9	19	4
1974			64	194	3.0	22	1
Career			858	3351	3.9	65t	24
Playoffs			97	355	3.7		1

Charlie Smith

Year	Team		Att	Yds	Avg	Lg	TD
1975	PHI	N	9	85	9.4	36	0
1976			9	25	2.8	14	1
1977			2	13	6.5	8	0
1980			5	33	6.6	16	0
1981			2	5	2.5	5	0
Career			27	161	6.0	36	1

Chris Smith

Year	Team		Att	Yds	Avg	Lg	TD
1987	KC	N	26	114	4.4	11	0

Dave Smith

Year	Team		Att	Yds	Avg	Lg	TD
1960	HOU	A	154	643	4.2	65	5

Year	Team		Att	Yds	Avg	Lg	TD

Dave Smith *continued*

Year	Team		Att	Yds	Avg	Lg	TD
1961			60	258	4.3	21	2
1962			56	249	4.4	41	1
1963			50	202	4.0	16	3
1964			8	16	2.0	8	0
Career			328	1368	4.2	65	11
Playoffs			21	48	2.3		0

Dave Smith

Year	Team		Att	Yds	Avg	Lg	TD
1970	PIT	N	1	6	6.0	6	0
1971			1	-10	-10.0	-10	0
Career			2	-4	-2.0	6	0

Dave Smith

Year	Team		Att	Yds	Avg	Lg	TD
1970	SD	N	14	42	3.0	15	0

Dick Smith

Year	Team		Att	Yds	Avg	Lg	TD
1968	WAS	N	3	5	1.7	3	0

Don Smith

Year	Team		Att	Yds	Avg	Lg	TD
1988	TB	N	13	46	3.5	15	1
1989			7	37	5.3	17	0
1990	BUF	N	20	82	4.1	13	2
Career			40	165	4.1	17	3
Playoffs			4	4	1.0		1

Ed Smith

Year	Team		Att	Yds	Avg	Lg	TD
1936	BOS	N	7	39	5.6		0

Ed Smith

Year	Team		Att	Yds	Avg	Lg	TD
1948	GB	N	27	85	3.1	10	0
1949	GB-NYB	N	16	24	1.5	11	0
Career			43	109	2.5	11	0

Emmitt Smith

Year	Team		Att	Yds	Avg	Lg	TD
1990	DAL	N	241	937	3.9	48t	11
1991			365	1563	4.3	75t	12
1992			373	1713	4.6	68t	18
1993			283	1486	5.3	62t	9
1994			368	1484	4.0	46	21
1995			377	1773	4.7	60t	25
1996			327	1204	3.7	42	12
Career			2334	10160	4.4	75t	108
Playoffs			318	1413	4.4		18

Gaylon Smith

Year	Team		Att	Yds	Avg	Lg	TD
1939	CLE	N	58	98	1.7		2
1940			19	18	0.9		0
1941			11	22	2.0	12	0
1942			83	332	4.0	50	2
1946	CLE	AA	62	240	3.9		5
Career			233	710	3.0	50	9

George Smith

Year	Team		Att	Yds	Avg	Lg	TD
1943	CHIC	N	4	12	3.0	4	0

Gordon Smith

Year	Team		Att	Yds	Avg	Lg	TD
1964	MIN	N	1	2	2.0	2	0

Jackie Smith

Year	Team		Att	Yds	Avg	Lg	TD
1966	STL	N	1	8	8.0	8	0
1967			9	86	9.6	18	0
1968			12	163	13.6	37	3
1969			4	0	0.0	9	0
1970			5	43	8.6	26	0
1971			1	10	10.0	10	0
1972			5	31	6.2	17	0
1973			1	-14	-14.0	-14	0
Career			38	327	8.6	37	3
Playoffs			1	-9	-9.0		0

J.D. Smith

Year	Team		Att	Yds	Avg	Lg	TD
1958	SF	N	26	209	8.0	80t	3
1959			207	1036	5.0	73t	10
1960			174	780	4.5	41	5
1961			167	823	4.9	33	8
1962			258	907	3.5	28	6
1963			162	560	3.5	52t	5
1964			13	55	4.2	16	0
1965	DAL	N	86	295	3.4	24	2
1966			7	7	1.0	2	1
Career			1100	4672	4.2	80t	40

J.D. Smith

Year	Team		Att	Yds	Avg	Lg	TD
1960	OAK	A	63	214	3.4		6
1961	CHI	N	3	6	2.0	5	0
Career			66	220	3.3	5	6

Jeff Smith

Year	Team		Att	Yds	Avg	Lg	TD
1985	KC	N	30	118	3.9	27	0
1986			54	238	4.4	32t	3
1987	TB	N	100	309	3.1	46	2
1988			20	87	4.3	23	0
Career			204	752	3.7	46	5
Playoffs			4	12	3.0		1

Jerry Smith

Year	Team		Att	Yds	Avg	Lg	TD
1969	WAS	N	3	8	2.7	6	0
1970			2	29	14.5	20	0
1971			1	5	5.0	5	0
1972			1	9	9.0	9	0
1974			1	5	5.0	5	0
Career			8	56	7.0	20	0
Playoffs			1	6	6.0		0

Jim Smith

Year	Team		Att	Yds	Avg	Lg	TD
1948	BUF	AA	1	7	7.0	7	0
1949	DET	N	33	162	4.9	20	0
1952			3	12	4.0	10	0
Career			37	181	4.9	20	0

Jim Smith

Year	Team		Att	Yds	Avg	Lg	TD
1979	PIT	N	1	12	12.0	12	0
1980			1	-1	-1.0	-1	0
1981			1	15	15.0	15	0
Career			3	26	8.7	15	0
Playoffs			1	4	4.0		0

Jimmy Smith

Year	Team		Att	Yds	Avg	Lg	TD
1987	MIN	N	7	13	1.9	5	0

Joe Smith

Year	Team		Att	Yds	Avg	Lg	TD
1948	BAL	AA	1	1	1.0	1	0

J.T. Smith

Year	Team		Att	Yds	Avg	Lg	TD
1985	STL	N	3	36	12.0	30	0
1988	PHX	N	1	15	15.0	15	0
1989			2	21	10.5	11	0
1990			1	4	4.0	4	0
Career			7	76	10.9	30	0

Kevin Smith

Year	Team		Att	Yds	Avg	Lg	TD
1994	LARI	N	1	2	2.0	2	0

Lamar Smith

Year	Team		Att	Yds	Avg	Lg	TD
1994	SEA	N	2	-1	-0.5	0	0
1995			36	215	6.0	68	0
1996			153	680	4.4	29	8
Career			191	894	4.7	68	8

Larry Smith

Year	Team		Att	Yds	Avg	Lg	TD
1969	LA	N	166	599	3.6	46	1
1970			77	338	4.4	19	1
1971			91	404	4.4	64t	5
1972			60	276	4.6	68	2
1973			79	291	3.7	16	2
1974	WAS	N	55	149	2.7	13	0
Career			528	2057	3.9	68	11
Playoffs			13	53	4.1		0

Laverne Smith

Year	Team		Att	Yds	Avg	Lg	TD
1977	PIT	N	14	55	3.9	16	0

Noland Smith

Year	Team		Att	Yds	Avg	Lg	TD
1967	KC	A	1	8	8.0	8	0
1968			2	-2	-1.0	1	0
Career			3	6	2.0	8	0

Ollie Smith

Year	Team		Att	Yds	Avg	Lg	TD
1973	BAL	N	1	-3	-3.0	-3	0

Phil Smith

Year	Team		Att	Yds	Avg	Lg	TD
1984	IND	N	2	-10	-5.0	-3	0

Ralph Smith

Year	Team		Att	Yds	Avg	Lg	TD
1962	PHI	N	1	13	13.0	13	0

Ralph Smith *continued*

Year	Team		Att	Yds	Avg	Lg	TD
1968	CLE	N	1	13	13.0	13	0
Career			2	26	13.0	13	0

Ray Gene Smith

Year	Team		Att	Yds	Avg	Lg	TD
1957	CHIB	N	1	8	8.0	8	0

Red Smith

Year	Team		Att	Yds	Avg	Lg	TD
1928	NYY	N					3

Riley Smith

Year	Team		Att	Yds	Avg	Lg	TD
1936	BOS	N	30	26	0.9		0
1937	WAS	N	12	39	3.3		2
1938			3	-7	-2.3		0
Career			45	58	1.3		2
Playoffs			5	0	0.0		0

Robert Smith

Year	Team		Att	Yds	Avg	Lg	TD
1993	MIN	N	82	399	4.9	26t	2
1994			31	106	3.4	14t	0
1995			139	632	4.5	58t	5
1996			162	692	4.3	57	3
Career			414	1829	4.4	58t	11
Playoffs			1	0	0.0		0

Rod Smith

Year	Team		Att	Yds	Avg	Lg	TD
1996	DEN	N	1	1	1.0	1	0

Ron Smith

Year	Team		Att	Yds	Avg	Lg	TD
1966	PIT	N	4	-9	-2.3	2	0

Ron Smith

Year	Team		Att	Yds	Avg	Lg	TD
1967	ATL	N	8	42	5.3	12	0

Ronnie Smith

Year	Team		Att	Yds	Avg	Lg	TD
1981	PHI	N	1	7	7.0	7	0
Playoffs			1	-1	-1.0		0

Russ Smith

Year	Team		Att	Yds	Avg	Lg	TD
1967	SD	A	22	115	5.2	16	1
1968			88	426	4.8	37t	4
1969			51	211	4.1	16	2
1970	SD	N	52	163	3.1	21	3
Career			213	915	4.3	37t	10

Sammie Smith

Year	Team		Att	Yds	Avg	Lg	TD
1989	MIA	N	200	659	3.3	25	6
1990			226	831	3.7	33	8
1991			83	297	3.6	18	1
1992	DEN	N	23	94	4.1	15	0
Career			532	1881	3.5	33	15
Playoffs			41	181	4.4		0

Sherman Smith

Year	Team		Att	Yds	Avg	Lg	TD
1976	SEA	N	119	537	4.5	53t	4
1977			163	763	4.7	39	4
1978			165	805	4.9	67	6
1979			194	775	4.0	31	11
1980			23	94	4.1	23	0
1981			83	253	3.0	21	3
1982			63	202	3.2	19	0
1983	SD	N	24	91	3.8	20	0
Career			834	3520	4.2	67	28

Steve Smith

Year	Team		Att	Yds	Avg	Lg	TD
1987	LARI	N	5	18	3.6	15	0
1988			38	162	4.3	21	3
1989			117	471	4.0	21	1
1990			81	327	4.0	17	2
1991			62	265	4.3	19	1
1992			44	129	2.9	15	0
1993			47	156	3.3	13	0
1994	SEA	N	26	80	3.1	12	2
1995			9	19	2.1	4	0
Career			429	1627	3.8	21	9
Playoffs			12	43	3.6		0

Stu Smith

Year	Team		Att	Yds	Avg	Lg	TD
1937	PIT	N	65	211	3.2		0
1938			80	241	3.0		0
Career			145	452	3.1		0

Tim Smith

Year	Team		Att	Yds	Avg	Lg	TD
1983	HOU	N	2	16	8.0	9	0

Year	Team		Att	Yds	Avg	Lg	TD

Timmy Smith

Year	Team		Att	Yds	Avg	Lg	TD
1987	WAS	N	29	126	4.3	15	0
1988			155	470	3.0	29	3
1990	DAL	N	6	6	1.0	3	0
Career			190	602	3.2	29	3
Playoffs			51	342	6.7		2

Tony Smith

Year	Team		Att	Yds	Avg	Lg	TD
1992	ATL	N	87	329	3.8	32	2

Truett Smith

Year	Team		Att	Yds	Avg	Lg	TD
1951	PIT	N	1	1	1.0	1	0

Vitamin Smith

Year	Team		Att	Yds	Avg	Lg	TD
1949	LA	N	40	112	2.8	26	2
1950			51	250	4.9	25	1
1951			52	143	2.8	31t	1
1952			57	133	2.3	20t	3
1953			8	26	3.3	21	0
Career			208	664	3.2	31t	7
Playoffs			26	41	1.6		0

Waddell Smith

Year	Team		Att	Yds	Avg	Lg	TD
1984	DAL	N	1	-5	-5.0	-5	0

Willis Smith

Year	Team		Att	Yds	Avg	Lg	TD
1934	NYG	N	80	323	4.0		2

Mark Smolinski

Year	Team		Att	Yds	Avg	Lg	TD
1961	BAL	N	31	98	3.2	14	0
1962			85	265	3.1	11	1
1963	NY	A	150	561	3.7	36	4
1964			34	117	3.4	19	1
1965			24	59	2.5	14	0
1966			21	69	3.3	21	2
1967			64	139	2.2	10	1
1968			12	15	1.3	5	0
Career			421	1323	3.1	36	9

Dave Smukler

Year	Team		Att	Yds	Avg	Lg	TD
1936	PHI	N	99	321	3.2		0
1937			92	247	2.7		1
1938			96	313	3.3		1
1939			45	218	4.8		0
1944	BOS	N	2	7	3.5	6	0
Career			334	1106	3.3	6	2

Lou Smythe

Year	Team		Att	Yds	Avg	Lg	TD
1921	CAN	A					1
1923	CAN	N					7
1925	FRA	N					2
1926	HAR	N					1
Career							11

Norm Snead

Year	Team		Att	Yds	Avg	Lg	TD
1961	WAS	N	34	47	1.4	9	3
1962			20	10	0.5	9	3
1963			23	100	4.3	16	2
1964	PHI	N	16	59	3.7	19	2
1965			24	81	3.4	20	3
1966			15	32	2.1	17	1
1967			9	30	3.3	21	2
1968			9	27	3.0	9	0
1969			8	2	0.3	5t	2
1970			18	35	1.9	16	3
1971	MIN	N	6	6	1.0	5	1
1972	NYG	N	10	21	2.1	15	0
1973			4	13	3.3	14	0
1974	NYG-SF	N	4	29	7.3	25	0
1975	SF	N	9	30	3.3	10	1
1976	NYG	N	3	-1	-0.3	0	0
Career			212	521	2.5	25	23

Bob Sneddon

Year	Team		Att	Yds	Avg	Lg	TD
1944	WAS	N	14	30	2.1	19	0
1946	LA	AA	3	6	2.0		0
Career			17	36	2.1	19	0

George Snell

Year	Team		Att	Yds	Avg	Lg	TD
1926	BKN	N					1

Matt Snell

Year	Team		Att	Yds	Avg	Lg	TD
1964	NY	A	215	948	4.4	42	5
1965			169	763	4.5	44	4

Matt Snell *continued*

Year	Team		Att	Yds	Avg	Lg	TD
1966			178	644	3.6	25	4
1967			61	207	3.4	13	0
1968			179	747	4.2	60	6
1969			191	695	3.6	34	4
1970	NYJ	N	64	281	4.4	19	1
Career			1057	4285	4.1	60	24
Playoffs			61	253	4.1		1

Ken Snelling

Year	Team		Att	Yds	Avg	Lg	TD
1945	GB	N	3	10	3.3	8	0

Lee Snoots

Year	Team		Att	Yds	Avg	Lg	TD
1922	COL	N					1
1923							1
Career							2

Jack Snow

Year	Team		Att	Yds	Avg	Lg	TD
1971	LA	N	1	-10	-10.0	10	0
1974			1	13	13.0	13	0
Career			2	3	1.5	13	0

Bob Snyder

Year	Team		Att	Yds	Avg	Lg	TD
1937	CLE	N	82	232	2.8		1
1938			44	78	1.8		0
1939	CHIB	N	15	56	3.7		0
1940			7	12	1.7		0
1941			7	-10	-1.4	13	0
1943			6	-20	-3.3	3	0
Career			161	348	2.2	13	1
Playoffs			5	-7	-1.4		0

Gerry Snyder

Year	Team		Att	Yds	Avg	Lg	TD
1929	NYG	N					2

Loren Snyder

Year	Team		Att	Yds	Avg	Lg	TD
1987	DAL	N	2	0	0.0	0	0

Hank Soar

Year	Team		Att	Yds	Avg	Lg	TD
1937	NYG	N	120	442	3.7		0
1938			122	401	3.3		2
1939			66	158	2.4		2
1940			80	246	3.1		1
1941			29	90	3.1	19	0
1942			49	187	3.8	49	1
1943			2	8	4.0	5	0
1944			9	10	1.1	10	0
1946			1	3	3.0	3	0
Career			478	1545	3.2	49	6
Playoffs			32	81	2.5		0

Kurt Sohn

Year	Team		Att	Yds	Avg	Lg	TD
1985	NYJ	N	1	12	12.0	12	0
1986			2	-11	-5.5	-3	0
Career			3	1	0.3	12	0

Freddie Solomon

Year	Team		Att	Yds	Avg	Lg	TD
1975	MIA	N	4	87	21.8	35	0
1976			4	60	15.0	59t	1
1977			6	43	7.2	14	0
1978	SF	N	14	70	5.0	17	1
1979			6	85	14.2	56t	1
1980			8	56	7.0	11	0
1981			9	43	4.8	16	0
1982			1	-4	-4.0	-4	0
1983			1	3	3.0	3	0
1984			6	72	12.0	47	1
1985			2	4	2.0	6	0
Career			61	519	8.5	59t	4
Playoffs			3	31	10.3		0

Jesse Solomon

Year	Team		Att	Yds	Avg	Lg	TD
1992	ATL	N	2	12	6.0	12	0

Gordie Soltau

Year	Team		Att	Yds	Avg	Lg	TD
1951	SF	N	1	-4	-4.0	-4	0

Mike Sommer

Year	Team		Att	Yds	Avg	Lg	TD
1959	WAS-BAL	N	62	231	3.7	53t	2
1961	BAL-WAS	N	11	1	0.1	9	0
1963	OAK	A	5	21	4.2	13	0
Career			78	253	3.2	53t	2
Playoffs			6	15	2.5		0

Eddie Songin

Year	Team		Att	Yds	Avg	Lg	TD
1960	BOS	A	36	-140	-3.9		2
1961			8	39	4.9	11	0
1962	NY	A	4	11	2.8	10	0
Career			48	-90	-1.9	11	2

Gus Sonnenberg

Year	Team		Att	Yds	Avg	Lg	TD
1923	COL	N					1

Bill Sortet

Year	Team		Att	Yds	Avg	Lg	TD
1936	PIT	N	1	47	47.0	47	0
1938			1	-5	-5.0	-5	0
Career			2	42	21.0	47	0

Ronnie South

Year	Team		Att	Yds	Avg	Lg	TD
1968	NO	N	4	5	1.3	2	0

Vic Spadaccini

Year	Team		Att	Yds	Avg	Lg	TD
1938	CLE	N	9	46	5.1		0

Gene Spangler

Year	Team		Att	Yds	Avg	Lg	TD
1946	DET	N	1	1	1.0	1	0

Frank Spaniel

Year	Team		Att	Yds	Avg	Lg	TD
1950	BAL-WAS	N	15	22	1.5	15t	0

Jim Spavital

Year	Team		Att	Yds	Avg	Lg	TD
1949	LA	AA	15	44	2.9		0
1950	BAL	N	58	246	4.2	96t	2
Career			73	290	4.0	96t	2

Mac Speedie

Year	Team		Att	Yds	Avg	Lg	TD
1947	CLE	AA	1	-7	-7.0	-7	0
1948			1	7	7.0	7	0
Career			2	0	0.0	7	0

Tim Spencer

Year	Team		Att	Yds	Avg	Lg	TD
1985	SD	N	124	478	3.9	24	10
1986			99	350	3.5	23	6
1987			73	228	3.1	16	0
1988			44	215	4.9	24	0
1989			134	521	3.9	15	3
Career			474	1792	3.8	24	19

Todd Spencer

Year	Team		Att	Yds	Avg	Lg	TD
1984	PIT	N	1	0	0.0	0	0
1985			13	56	4.3	11	0
1987	SD	N	14	24	1.7	5	0
Career			28	80	2.9	11	0

Willie Spencer

Year	Team		Att	Yds	Avg	Lg	TD
1976	MIN	N	4	2	0.5	2	0
1977	NYG	N	62	184	3.0	9	3
1978			38	61	1.6	9	2
Career			104	247	2.4	9	5

Cotton Speyrer

Year	Team		Att	Yds	Avg	Lg	TD
1973	BAL	N	1	1	1.0	1	0

Irving Spikes

Year	Team		Att	Yds	Avg	Lg	TD
1994	MIA	N	70	312	4.5	40	6
1995			32	126	3.9	17t	1
1996			87	316	3.6	49	3
Career			189	754	4.0	49	6
Playoffs			9	49	5.4		0

Jack Spikes

Year	Team		Att	Yds	Avg	Lg	TD
1960	DAL	A	115	457	4.0	36	5
1961			39	334	8.6	74	5
1962			57	232	4.1	17	0
1963	KC	A	84	257	3.1	15	2
1964			34	112	3.3	13	0
1965	HOU	A	47	173	3.7	20	3
1966	BUF	A	28	119	4.3	36	3
1967			4	9	2.3	6	0
Career			408	1693	4.1	74	18
Playoffs			11	77	7.0		0

Jack Spinks

Year	Team		Att	Yds	Avg	Lg	TD
1952	PIT	N	22	94	4.3	42	0
1953	CHIC	N	6	0	0.0	7	0
Career			28	94	3.4	42	0

Johnny Spirida

Year	Team		Att	Yds	Avg	Lg	TD
1939	WAS	N	2	5	2.5		0

Ron Springs

Year	Team		Att	Yds	Avg	Lg	TD
1979	DAL	N	67	248	3.7	15	2
1980			89	326	3.7	20t	6
1981			172	625	3.6	16	10
1982			59	243	4.1	46t	2
1983			149	541	3.6	19t	7
1984			68	197	2.9	16	1
1985	TB	N	16	54	3.4	11	0
1986			74	285	3.9	40	0
Career			694	2519	3.6	46t	28
Playoffs			42	201	4.8		2

Ed Sprinkle

Year	Team		Att	Yds	Avg	Lg	TD
1948	CHIB	N	1	-2	-2.0	-2	0
1949			1	5	5.0	5	0
1950			1	-1	-1.0	-1	0
Career			3	2	0.7	5	0

Dennis Sproul

Year	Team		Att	Yds	Avg	Lg	TD
1978	GB	N	2	0	0.0	0	0

Steve Spurrier

Year	Team		Att	Yds	Avg	Lg	TD
1967	SF	N	5	18	3.6	9	0
1968			1	-15	-15.0	-15	0
1969			5	49	9.8	29	0
1970			2	-18	-9.0	-5	0
1971			1	2	2.0	2	0
1972			11	51	4.6	15	0
1973			9	32	3.6	12	2
1975			15	91	6.1	14	0
1976	TB	N	12	48	4.0	10	0
Career			61	258	4.2	29	2

Ken Stabler

Year	Team		Att	Yds	Avg	Lg	TD
1970	OAK	N	1	-4	-4.0	-4	0
1971			4	29	7.3	18	2
1972			6	27	4.5	15	0
1973			21	101	4.8	13	0
1974			12	-2	-0.2	6	1
1975			6	-5	-0.8	0	0
1976			7	-2	-0.3	5	1
1977			3	-3	-1.0	0	0
1978			4	0	0.0	0	0
1979			16	-4	-0.3	13	0
1980	HOU	N	15	-22	-1.5	0	0
1981			10	-3	-0.3	4	0
1982	NO	N	3	-4	-1.3	0	0
1983			9	-14	-1.6	0	0
1984			1	-1	-1.0	-1	0
Career			118	93	0.8	18	4
Playoffs			8	34	4.3		2

Ray Stachowicz

Year	Team		Att	Yds	Avg	Lg	TD
1982	GB	N	2	0	0.0	0	0

Jack Stackpool

Year	Team		Att	Yds	Avg	Lg	TD
1942	PHI	N	15	47	3.1	9	0

Harry Stafford

Year	Team		Att	Yds	Avg	Lg	TD
1934	NYG	N	4	4	1.0		0

Jon Staggers

Year	Team		Att	Yds	Avg	Lg	TD
1971	PIT	N	1	5	5.0	5	0
1972	GB	N	1	-8	-8.0	-8	0
1973			4	33	8.3	20t	1
1975	DET	N	2	26	13.0	14	0
Career			8	56	7.0	20t	1

John Stallworth

Year	Team		Att	Yds	Avg	Lg	TD
1974	PIT	N	1	-9	-9.0	-9	0
1976			0	47		47tL	1
1977			6	47	7.8	15	0
1981			1	17	17.0	17	0
1982			1	9	9.0	9	0
Career			9	111	12.3	47tL	1

Sylvester Stamps

Year	Team		Att	Yds	Avg	Lg	TD
1984	ATL	N	3	15	5.0	8	0
1986			30	220	7.3	48	0
1987			1	6	6.0	6	0
1988			3	0	0.0	3	0

Sylvester Stamps continued

Year	Team		Att	Yds	Avg	Lg	TD
1989	TB	N	29	141	4.9	21t	1
Career			66	382	5.8	48	1

Haskel Stanback

Year	Team		Att	Yds	Avg	Lg	TD
1974	ATL	N	57	235	4.1	23t	1
1975			105	440	4.2	26t	5
1976			95	324	3.4	30	3
1977			247	873	3.5	35	6
1978			188	588	3.1	26	5
1979			36	202	5.6	55t	5
Career			728	2662	3.7	55t	25
Playoffs			25	120	4.8		0

Jeff Stanciel

Year	Team		Att	Yds	Avg	Lg	TD
1969	ATL	N	4	-1	-0.3	4	0

Norm Standlee

Year	Team		Att	Yds	Avg	Lg	TD
1941	CHIB	N	81	414	5.1	46	5
1946	SF	AA	134	651	4.9		2
1947			145	585	4.0		8
1948			52	261	5.0	57t	3
1949			44	237	5.4		4
1950	SF	N	12	23	1.9	8	1
1951			16	65	4.1	13	0
1952			2	8	4.0	9	0
Career			486	2244	4.6	57t	23
Playoffs			46	218	4.7		4

Walter Stanley

Year	Team		Att	Yds	Avg	Lg	TD
1986	GB	N	1	19	19.0	19	0
1987			4	38	9.5	24	0
1988			1	1	1.0	1	0
Career			6	58	9.7	24	0

Rohn Stark

Year	Team		Att	Yds	Avg	Lg	TD
1982	BAL	N	1	8	8.0	8	0
1983			1	8	8.0	8	0
1984	IND	N	2	0	0.0	0	0
1989			1	-11	-11.0	-11	0
1991			1	-13	-13.0	-13	0
1993			1	11	11.0	11	0
Career			7	3	0.4	11	0
Playoffs			1	0	0.0		0

Paul Staroba

Year	Team		Att	Yds	Avg	Lg	TD
1973	GB	N	1	11	11.0	11	0

Bart Starr

Year	Team		Att	Yds	Avg	Lg	TD
1956	GB	N	5	35	7.0	14	0
1957			31	98	3.2	16	3
1958			25	113	4.5	20	1
1959			16	83	5.2	39	0
1960			7	12	1.7	13	0
1961			12	56	4.7	21t	1
1962			21	72	3.4	18	1
1963			13	116	8.9	20	0
1964			24	165	6.9	28	3
1965			18	169	9.4	38	1
1966			21	104	5.0	21	2
1967			21	90	4.3	23	0
1968			11	62	5.6	15	1
1969			7	60	8.6	18	0
1970			12	62	5.2	15	1
1971			3	11	3.7	9	1
Career			247	1308	5.3	39	15
Playoffs			8	26	3.3		1

Ben Starrett

Year	Team		Att	Yds	Avg	Lg	TD
1941	PIT	N	7	9	1.3	15	0
1943	GB	N	1	1	1.0	1	0
1944			10	21	2.1	8	2
1945			5	26	5.2	13	0
Career			23	57	2.5	15	2

Stephen Starring

Year	Team		Att	Yds	Avg	Lg	TD
1984	NE	N	2	-16	-8.0	0	0
1986			1	0	0.0	0	0
1987			2	13	6.5	10	0
Career			5	-3	-0.6	10	0

Leo Stasica

Year	Team		Att	Yds	Avg	Lg	TD
1941	BKN	N	3	17	5.7		0
1943	WAS	N	9	-10	-1.1	4	0

Leo Stasica continued

Year	Team		Att	Yds	Avg	Lg	TD
1944	BOS	N	23	-16	-0.7	10	0
Career			35	-9	-0.3	10	0

Roger Staubach

Year	Team		Att	Yds	Avg	Lg	TD
1969	DAL	N	15	60	4.0	19	1
1970			27	221	8.2	25	0
1971			41	343	8.4	31	2
1972			6	45	7.5	20	0
1973			46	250	5.4	18	3
1974			47	320	6.8	29	3
1975			55	316	5.7	17	4
1976			43	184	4.3	18	3
1977			51	171	3.4	33	3
1978			42	182	4.3	23	1
1979			37	172	4.6	20	0
Career			410	2264	5.5	33	20
Playoffs			76	432	5.7		0

Scott Stauch

Year	Team		Att	Yds	Avg	Lg	TD
1981	NO	N	2	6	3.0	5	0

Ernie Steele

Year	Team		Att	Yds	Avg	Lg	TD
1942	PHI	N	24	124	5.2	55	0
1943	P-P	N	85	409	4.8	47	4
1944	PHI	N	59	247	4.2	56t	5
1945			20	212	10.6	46	2
1946			31	108	3.5	43	1
1947			26	138	5.3	49	1
1948			13	99	7.6	56	1
Career			258	1337	5.2	56t	14
Playoffs			7	34	4.9		0

Anthony Steels

Year	Team		Att	Yds	Avg	Lg	TD
1985	SD-BUF	N	10	38	3.8	22	0
1987	SD	N	1	3	3.0	3	0
Career			11	41	3.7	22	0

Gil Steinke

Year	Team		Att	Yds	Avg	Lg	TD
1945	PHI	N	7	46	6.6	18	1
1946			38	154	4.1	40	1
1947			16	50	3.1	15	0
1948			5	17	3.4	8	0
Career			66	267	4.0	40	2

Ken Steinmetz

Year	Team		Att	Yds	Avg	Lg	TD
1944	BOS	N	11	24	2.2	8	0
1945			4	12	3.0	9	0
Career			15	36	2.4	9	0

Jan Stenerud

Year	Team		Att	Yds	Avg	Lg	TD
1976	KC	N	1	0	0.0	0	0

Harold Stephens

Year	Team		Att	Yds	Avg	Lg	TD
1962	NY	A	6	33	5.5	14	0

John Stephens

Year	Team		Att	Yds	Avg	Lg	TD
1988	NE	N	297	1168	3.9	52	4
1989			244	833	3.4	35t	7
1990			212	808	3.8	26	2
1991			63	163	2.6	13	2
1992			75	277	3.7	19	2
1993	GB-KC	N	54	191	3.5	22	1
Career			945	3440	3.6	52	18

Kay Stephenson

Year	Team		Att	Yds	Avg	Lg	TD
1967	SD	A	2	11	5.5	7	0
1968	BUF	A	4	30	7.5	12	0
Career			6	41	6.8	12	0

John Sterling

Year	Team		Att	Yds	Avg	Lg	TD
1987	GB	N	5	20	4.0	9	0

Ed Sternaman

Year	Team		Att	Yds	Avg	Lg	TD
1920	DEC	A					1
1921							2
1922	CHIB	N					2
1923							4
1924							3
1925							1
1926							1
Career							14

Year	Team		Att	Yds	Avg	Lg	TD

Joey Sternaman

Year	Team		Att	Yds	Avg	Lg	TD
1922	CHIB	N					5
1923							2
1924							4
1925							5
1926	CHI	A					3
1927	CHIB	N					1
1928							4
1930							1
Career							25

Bob Steuber

Year	Team		Att	Yds	Avg	Lg	TD
1943	CHIB	N	1	3	3.0	3	0
1946	CLE	AA	8	19	2.4		0
1947	LA	AA	1	2	2.0	2	0
1948	BUF	AA	69	437	6.3		3
Career			79	461	5.8	3	3

Don Stevens

Year	Team		Att	Yds	Avg	Lg	TD
1952	PHI	N	33	95	2.9	36	0

Howard Stevens

Year	Team		Att	Yds	Avg	Lg	TD
1973	NO	N	45	183	4.1	15	2
1974			43	190	4.4	25	1
1976	BAL	N	1	3	3.0	3t	1
Career			89	376	4.2	25	4

Mark Stevens

Year	Team		Att	Yds	Avg	Lg	TD
1987	SF	N	10	45	4.5	16	1

Matt Stevens

Year	Team		Att	Yds	Avg	Lg	TD
1987	KC	N	3	7	2.3	6	0

Dean Steward

Year	Team		Att	Yds	Avg	Lg	TD
1943	P-P	N	1	-6	-6.0	-6	0

James Stewart

Year	Team		Att	Yds	Avg	Lg	TD
1995	JAC	N	137	525	3.8	22	2
1996			190	723	3.8	34	8
Career			327	1248	3.8	34	10
Playoffs			16	59	3.7		0

James Stewart

Year	Team		Att	Yds	Avg	Lg	TD
1995	MIN	N	31	144	4.6	51	0

Kordell Stewart

Year	Team		Att	Yds	Avg	Lg	TD
1995	PIT	N	15	86	5.7	22t	1
1996			39	171	4.4	80t	5
Career			54	257	4.8	80t	6
Playoffs			22	99	4.5		2

Dave Stief

Year	Team		Att	Yds	Avg	Lg	TD
1978	STL	N	1	-8	-8.0	-8	0
1981			1	8	8.0	8	0
Career			2	0	0.0	8	0

Jim Stiger

Year	Team		Att	Yds	Avg	Lg	TD
1963	DAL	N	31	140	4.5	14	1
1964			68	280	4.1	64	1
1965	DAL-LA	N	14	62	4.4	16	0
1966	LA	N	24	95	4.0	19	0
1967			3	6	2.0	3	0
Career			140	583	4.2	64	2

Jim Still

Year	Team		Att	Yds	Avg	Lg	TD
1948	BUF	AA	5	-26	-5.2		0
1949			2	6	3.0		0
Career			7	-20	-2.9		0
Playoffs			1	0	0.0		0

Pete Stinchcomb

Year	Team		Att	Yds	Avg	Lg	TD
1921	DEC	A					4
1922	CHIB	N					3
Career							7

Darryl Stingley

Year	Team		Att	Yds	Avg	Lg	TD
1973	NE	N	6	64	10.7	19	0
1974			5	63	12.6	23t	1
1975			6	39	6.5	21	0
1976			8	45	5.6	27	0
1977			3	33	11.0	34t	1
Career			28	244	8.7	34t	2

Jim Stinnette

Year	Team		Att	Yds	Avg	Lg	TD
1961	DEN	A	19	8	0.4	9	0
1962			21	87	4.1	14	1
Career			40	95	2.4	14	1

Bill Stits

Year	Team		Att	Yds	Avg	Lg	TD
1955	DET	N	46	165	3.6	15	0
1956			3	0	0.0	6	0
Career			49	165	3.4	15	0

Ralph Stockemer

Year	Team		Att	Yds	Avg	Lg	TD
1987	KC	N	1	2	2.0	2	0

Hust Stockton

Year	Team		Att	Yds	Avg	Lg	TD
1926	FRA	N					2
1928							3
1929	BOS	N					1
Career							6

John Stofa

Year	Team		Att	Yds	Avg	Lg	TD
1966	MIA	A	3	17	5.7	14	0
1967			2	2	1.0	8t	1
1968	CIN	A	10	1	0.1	13	0
1970	MIA	N	2	5	2.5	4	0
Career			17	25	1.5	14	1

Ken Stofer

Year	Team		Att	Yds	Avg	Lg	TD
1946	BUF		16	36	2.3		0

Eddie Stofko

Year	Team		Att	Yds	Avg	Lg	TD
1945	PIT	N	13	-16	-1.2	6	0

Billy Stone

Year	Team		Att	Yds	Avg	Lg	TD
1949	BAL	AA	51	205	4.0		2
1950	BAL	N	14	113	8.1	72t	1
1951	CHIB	N	30	123	4.1	42t	1
1952			50	196	3.9	48	2
1953			72	169	2.3	28	2
1954			79	306	3.9	23	3
Career			296	1112	3.8	72t	11

Donnie Stone

Year	Team		Att	Yds	Avg	Lg	TD
1961	DEN	A	127	505	4.0	34	4
1962			94	360	3.8	27	3
1963			96	382	4.0	39	3
1964			12	26	2.2	5	0
1965	BUF	A	19	61	3.2	14	0
1966	HOU	A	6	18	3.0	12	0
Career			354	1352	3.8	39	10
Playoffs			3	5	1.7		0

Dwight Stone

Year	Team		Att	Yds	Avg	Lg	TD
1987	PIT	N	17	135	7.9	51	0
1988			40	127	3.2	11	0
1989			10	53	5.3	32	0
1990			2	-6	-3.0	10	0
1991			1	2	2.0	2	0
1992			12	118	9.8	30	0
1993			12	121	10.1	38t	1
1994			2	7	3.5	4	0
1995	CAR	N	1	3	3.0	3	0
1996			1	6	6.0	6	0
Career			98	566	5.8	51	1
Playoffs			5	29	5.8		0

Jack Storer

Year	Team		Att	Yds	Avg	Lg	TD
1924	FRA	N					7

Ed Storm

Year	Team		Att	Yds	Avg	Lg	TD
1934	PHI	N					2
1935			84	164	2.0		0
Career			84	164	2.0		2

Cliff Stoudt

Year	Team		Att	Yds	Avg	Lg	TD
1980	PIT	N	9	35	3.9	13	0
1981			3	11	3.7	10	0
1982			11	28	2.5	8	0
1983			77	479	6.2	23	4
1986	STL	N	7	53	7.6	17	0
1987			1	-2	-2.0	-2	0
1988	PHX	N	14	57	4.1	14	0
Career			122	661	5.4	23	4
Playoffs			9	50	5.6		0

Kelly Stouffer

Year	Team		Att	Yds	Avg	Lg	TD
1988	SEA	N	19	27	1.4	17	0
1989			2	11	5.5	9	0
1992			9	37	4.1	11	0
Career			30	75	2.5	17	0

Pete Stout

Year	Team		Att	Yds	Avg	Lg	TD
1949	WAS	N	62	245	4.0	74	4
1950			9	53	5.9	19	0
Career			71	298	4.2	74	4

Jerry Stovall

Year	Team		Att	Yds	Avg	Lg	TD
1963	STL	N	1	32	32.0	32	0
1966			1	17	17.0	17	0
Career			2	49	24.5	32	0

Otto Stowe

Year	Team		Att	Yds	Avg	Lg	TD
1973	DAL	N	3	28	9.3	14	0
1974	DEN	N	1	1	1.0	1	0
Career			4	29	7.3	14	0

Mike Strachan

Year	Team		Att	Yds	Avg	Lg	TD
1975	NO	N	161	668	4.1	21	2
1976			66	258	3.9	31	2
1977			55	271	4.9	18	0
1978			108	388	3.6	21	4
1979			62	276	4.5	23	6
1980			20	41	2.0	10	0
Career			472	1902	4.0	31	14

Steve Strachan

Year	Team		Att	Yds	Avg	Lg	TD
1985	LARI	N	2	1	0.5	1	0
1986			18	53	2.9	10	0
1987			28	108	3.9	20	0
1988			4	12	3.0	5	0
Career			52	174	3.3	20	0

Red Strader

Year	Team		Att	Yds	Avg	Lg	TD
1927	CHIC	N					1

Troy Stradford

Year	Team		Att	Yds	Avg	Lg	TD
1987	MIA	N	145	619	4.3	51	6
1988			95	335	3.5	18	2
1989			66	240	3.6	13	1
1990			37	138	3.7	15	1
1991	KC	N	1	7	7.0	7	0
1992	LARM-DET	N	12	41	3.4	11	0
Career			356	1380	3.9	51	10

Bob Stransky

Year	Team		Att	Yds	Avg	Lg	TD
1960	DEN	A	28	78	2.8	16	0

Jimmy Strausbaugh

Year	Team		Att	Yds	Avg	Lg	TD
1946	CHIC	N	37	183	4.9	29	3

Dutch Strauss

Year	Team		Att	Yds	Avg	Lg	TD
1924	KC	N					1

Les Strayhorn

Year	Team		Att	Yds	Avg	Lg	TD
1973	DAL	N	11	62	5.6	24	1
1974			11	66	6.0	24	0
Career			22	128	5.8	24	1

Eric Streater

Year	Team		Att	Yds	Avg	Lg	TD
1987	TB	N	1	5	5.0	5	0

Bishop Strickland

Year	Team		Att	Yds	Avg	Lg	TD
1951	SF	N	34	165	4.9	15	0

Bob Stringer

Year	Team		Att	Yds	Avg	Lg	TD
1952	PHI	N	2	5	2.5	3	0
1953			1	5	5.0	5	0
Career			3	10	3.3	5	0

Joe Stringfellow

Year	Team		Att	Yds	Avg	Lg	TD
1942	DET	N	16	41	2.6	11	0

Don Strock

Year	Team		Att	Yds	Avg	Lg	TD
1974	MIA	N	1	-7	-7.0	-7	0
1975			6	38	6.3	18	1
1976			2	13	6.5	11	1
1978			10	23	2.3	12	0
1979			3	18	6.0	11	0
1980			1	-3	-3.0	-3	0

Year	Team		Att	Yds	Avg	Lg	TD

Don Strock *continued*

Year	Team		Att	Yds	Avg	Lg	TD
1981			14	-26	-1.9	9	0
1982			3	-9	-3.0	0	0
1983			6	-16	-2.7	0	0
1984			2	-5	-2.5	0	0
1985			2	-6	-3.0	-3	0
1986			1	0	0.0	0	0
1988	CLE	N	6	-2	-0.3	5	0
Career			57	18	0.3	18	2
Playoffs			2	-2	-1.0		0

Rick Strom

Year	Team		Att	Yds	Avg	Lg	TD
1989	PIT	N	4	-3	-0.8	0	0
1990			4	10	2.5	10	0
Career			8	7	0.9	10	0

Jim Strong

Year	Team		Att	Yds	Avg	Lg	TD
1970	SF	N	2	3	1.5	3	0
1971	NO	N	95	404	4.3	39	3
1972			37	120	3.2	9	0
Career			134	527	3.9	39	3

Ken Strong

Year	Team		Att	Yds	Avg	Lg	TD
1929	SI	N					4
1930							2
1931							6
1932			96	375	3.9		2
1933	NYG	N	108	386	3.6		2
1934			110	410	3.7		6
1935			46	151	3.3		1
1939			1	1	1.0	1	0
1944			2	-2	-1.0	2	0
Career			363	1321	3.6	2	23
Playoffs			17	129	7.6		2

Mack Strong

Year	Team		Att	Yds	Avg	Lg	TD
1994	SEA	N	27	114	4.2	14	2
1995			8	23	2.9	9	1
1996			5	8	1.6	4	0
Career			40	145	3.6	14	3

Ray Strong

Year	Team		Att	Yds	Avg	Lg	TD
1978	ATL	N	30	99	3.3	14	2
1979			2	7	3.5	4	0
1980			6	42	7.0	21t	1
1981			3	6	2.0	3	0
1982			4	9	2.3	4	0
Career			45	163	3.6	21t	3

Art Strutt

Year	Team		Att	Yds	Avg	Lg	TD
1935	PIT	N	92	323	3.5		0
1936			84	180	2.1		1
Career			176	503	2.9		1

Dan Stryzinski

Year	Team		Att	Yds	Avg	Lg	TD
1990	PIT	N	3	17	5.7	9	0
1991			4	-11	-2.8	0	0
1992	TB	N	1	7	7.0	7	0
1995	ATL	N	1	0	0.0	0	0
Career			9	13	1.4	9	0

Johnny Strzykalski

Year	Team		Att	Yds	Avg	Lg	TD
1946	SF	AA	79	346	4.4	50	2
1947			143	906	6.3	50	5
1948			141	915	6.5		4
1949			66	287	4.3		3
1950	SF	N	136	612	4.5	38	2
1951			81	296	3.7	13	3
1952			16	53	3.3	11	0
Career			662	3415	5.2	50	19

Les Studdard

Year	Team		Att	Yds	Avg	Lg	TD
1982	KC	N	1	0	0.0	0	0

Pat Studstill

Year	Team		Att	Yds	Avg	Lg	TD
1962	DET	N	1	-11	-11.0	-11	0
1965			1	-4	-4.0	-4	0
1966			2	20	10.0	15	0
1970	LA	N	1	23	23.0	23	0
1972	NE	N	1	11	11.0	11	0
Career			6	39	6.5	23	0

Jerry Sturm

Year	Team		Att	Yds	Avg	Lg	TD
1961	DEN	A	8	31	3.9	9	0

Steve Sucic

Year	Team		Att	Yds	Avg	Lg	TD
1946	LA	N	7	18	2.6	9	0
1947	BOS-DET	N	3	3	1.0	2	0
1948	DET	N	6	20	3.3	8	0
Career			16	41	2.6	9	0

Matt Suhey

Year	Team		Att	Yds	Avg	Lg	TD
1980	CHI	N	22	45	2.0	10	0
1981			150	521	3.5	26	3
1982			70	206	2.9	15	3
1983			149	681	4.6	39	4
1984			124	424	3.4	21	4
1985			115	471	4.1	17	1
1986			84	270	3.2	17	2
1987			7	24	3.4	6	0
1988			87	253	2.9	19	2
1989			20	51	2.5	8	1
Career			828	2946	3.6	39	20
Playoffs			43	156	3.6		1

Joe Sulatis

Year	Team		Att	Yds	Avg	Lg	TD
1943	NYG	N	1	6	6.0	6	0
1944			9	38	4.2	16	0
1945			10	37	3.7	10	0
1948			5	18	3.6	10	0
1949			14	42	3.0	12	0
Career			39	141	3.6	16	1
Playoffs			1	-1	-1.0		0

Bob Sullivan

Year	Team		Att	Yds	Avg	Lg	TD
1947	PIT	N	21	61	2.9	14	1
1948	BKN	AA	2	-1	-0.5	0	0
Career			23	60	2.6	14	1

Bob Sullivan

Year	Team		Att	Yds	Avg	Lg	TD
1948	SF	AA	33	121	3.7		0

George Sullivan

Year	Team		Att	Yds	Avg	Lg	TD
1924	FRA	N					5
1925							2
Career							7

Pat Sullivan

Year	Team		Att	Yds	Avg	Lg	TD
1972	ATL	N	2	8	4.0	10	0
1973			3	19	6.3	9	0
1974			3	19	6.3	12	0
1975			6	9	1.5	4	0
Career			14	55	3.9	12	0

Tom Sullivan

Year	Team		Att	Yds	Avg	Lg	TD
1972	PHI	N	13	13	1.0	5	0
1973			217	968	4.5	37	4
1974			244	760	3.1	28t	11
1975			173	632	3.7	28	0
1976			99	399	4.0	26	2
1977			125	363	2.9	14	0
1978	CLE	N	5	7	1.4	5	0
Career			876	3142	3.6	37	17

Carl Summerell

Year	Team		Att	Yds	Avg	Lg	TD
1974	NYG	N	2	8	4.0	6	0
1975			3	4	1.3	4	0
Career			5	12	2.4	6	0

Bob Summerhays

Year	Team		Att	Yds	Avg	Lg	TD
1949	GB	N	29	101	3.5	14	0

Wilbur Summers

Year	Team		Att	Yds	Avg	Lg	TD
1977	DET	N	1	0	0.0	0	0

Len Supulski

Year	Team		Att	Yds	Avg	Lg	TD
1942	PHI	N	1	1	1.0	1	0

Ed Susteric

Year	Team		Att	Yds	Avg	Lg	TD
1949	CLE	AA	23	114	5.0		1

George Sutch

Year	Team		Att	Yds	Avg	Lg	TD
1946	CHIC	N	5	4	0.8	4	0

Ed Sutton

Year	Team		Att	Yds	Avg	Lg	TD
1957	WAS	N	108	407	3.8	31	5
1958			93	335	3.6	18	3
1959			61	232	3.8	30	1

Ed Sutton *continued*

Year	Team		Att	Yds	Avg	Lg	TD
1960	NYG	N	20	135	6.8	44	0
Career			282	1109	3.9	44	9

Joe Sutton

Year	Team		Att	Yds	Avg	Lg	TD
1949	BUF	AA	9	63	7.0		0
1950	PHI	N	1	1	1.0	1	0
Career			10	64	6.4	1	0

Bill Svoboda

Year	Team		Att	Yds	Avg	Lg	TD
1951	CHIC	N	5	15	3.0	6	0

Karl Swanke

Year	Team		Att	Yds	Avg	Lg	TD
1986	GB	N	1	0	0.0	0	0

Lynn Swann

Year	Team		Att	Yds	Avg	Lg	TD
1974	PIT	N	1	14	14.0	14	0
1975			3	13	4.3	11	0
1976			1	2	2.0	2	0
1977			2	6	3.0	14	0
1978			1	7	7.0	7	0
1979			1	9	9.0	9t	0
1980			1	-4	-4.0	-4	0
1982			1	25	25.0	25	0
Career			11	72	6.5	25	1
Playoffs			3	17	5.7		0

Calvin Sweeney

Year	Team		Att	Yds	Avg	Lg	TD
1983	PIT	N	1	-2	-2.0	-2	0

Kevin Sweeney

Year	Team		Att	Yds	Avg	Lg	TD
1987	DAL	N	5	8	1.6	5	0
1988			6	34	5.7	10	0
Career			11	42	3.8	10	0

Walt Sweeney

Year	Team		Att	Yds	Avg	Lg	TD
1965	SD	A	0	8		8L	0

Joe Sweet

Year	Team		Att	Yds	Avg	Lg	TD
1972	LA	N	1	1	1.0	1	0

Karl Sweetan

Year	Team		Att	Yds	Avg	Lg	TD
1966	DET	N	34	219	6.4	34	1
1967			17	93	5.5	18	1
1968	NO	N	4	-5	-1.3	2	0
1969	LA	N	1	-1	-1.0	-1	0
Career			56	306	5.5	34	2

Fred Sweetland

Year	Team		Att	Yds	Avg	Lg	TD
1920	AKR	A					1

Bob Sweiger

Year	Team		Att	Yds	Avg	Lg	TD
1946	NY	AA	7	22	3.1		0
1947			9	44	4.9		0
1948			3	4	1.3		0
1949	CHI	AA	3	17	5.7		0
Career			22	87	4.0		0

Larry Swider

Year	Team		Att	Yds	Avg	Lg	TD
1979	DET	N	1	0	0.0	0	0
1981	TB	N	1	-9	-9.0	-9	0
Career			2	-9	-4.5	0	0

Jim Swink

Year	Team		Att	Yds	Avg	Lg	TD
1960	DAL	A	10	16	1.6		0

Bob Swisher

Year	Team		Att	Yds	Avg	Lg	TD
1938	CHIB	N	22	133	6.0		0
1939			30	192	6.4		2
1940			15	70	4.7		0
1941			37	149	4.0	20	0
Career			104	544	5.2	20	2
Playoffs			5	38	7.6		1

Veryl Switzer

Year	Team		Att	Yds	Avg	Lg	TD
1954	GB	N	15	59	3.9	33	0
1955			16	101	6.3	38	0
Career			31	160	5.2	38	0

Harry Sydney

Year	Team		Att	Yds	Avg	Lg	TD
1987	SF	N	29	125	4.3	15	0
1988			9	50	5.6	13	0
1989			9	56	6.2	18	0
1990			35	166	4.7	19	2

Year	Team		Att	Yds	Avg	Lg	TD

Harry Sydney *continued*

Year	Team		Att	Yds	Avg	Lg	TD
1991			57	245	4.3	32	5
1992	GB	N	51	163	3.2	19	2
Career			190	805	4.2	32	9
Playoffs			11	34	3.1		0

Bob Sykes

Year	Team		Att	Yds	Avg	Lg	TD
1952	WAS	N	4	10	2.5	4	0

Johnny Sylvester

Year	Team		Att	Yds	Avg	Lg	TD
1947	NY	AA	17	101	5.9		0

Paul Szakash

Year	Team		Att	Yds	Avg	Lg	TD
1938	DET	N	20	55	2.8		0
1939			3	11	3.7		0
Career			23	66	2.9		0

Doyle Tackett

Year	Team		Att	Yds	Avg	Lg	TD
1946	BKN	AA	11	-6	-0.5		0

Jerry Tagge

Year	Team		Att	Yds	Avg	Lg	TD
1972	GB	N	8	-3	-0.4	2	1
1973			15	62	4.1	41t	2
1974			18	58	3.2	12	0
Career			41	117	2.9	41t	3

John Tagliaferri

Year	Team		Att	Yds	Avg	Lg	TD
1987	MIA	N	13	45	3.5	7	1

Bob Talamini

Year	Team		Att	Yds	Avg	Lg	TD
1960	HOU	A	0	14		14L	0

George Taliaferro

Year	Team		Att	Yds	Avg	Lg	TD
1949	LA	AA	95	472	5.0		5
1950	NYY	N	88	411	4.7	44	4
1951			62	330	5.3	65t	3
1952	DAL	N	100	410	4.1	38	1
1953	BAL	N	102	479	4.7	50	2
1954			48	157	3.3	29	0
1955	PHI	N	3	-2	-0.7	0	0
Career			498	2257	4.5	65t	15

Mike Taliaferro

Year	Team		Att	Yds	Avg	Lg	TD
1964	NY	A	9	45	5.0	14	0
1965			7	4	0.6	10	0
1967			2	20	10.0	12	0
1968	BOS	A	8	51	6.4	21	0
1969			12	-16	-1.3	4	0
1970	BOS	N	3	11	3.7	6	0
1972	BUF	N	5	19	3.8	14	0
Career			46	134	2.9	21	0

John Tanner

Year	Team		Att	Yds	Avg	Lg	TD
1924	CLE	N					2

Fran Tarkenton

Year	Team		Att	Yds	Avg	Lg	TD
1961	MIN	N	56	308	5.5	52t	5
1962			41	361	8.8	31	2
1963			28	162	5.8	24	1
1964			50	330	6.6	31	2
1965			56	356	6.4	36	1
1966			62	376	6.1	28	2
1967	NYG	N	44	306	7.0	22	2
1968			57	301	5.3	22t	3
1969			37	172	4.6	21	2
1970			43	236	5.5	20	2
1971			30	111	3.7	16	3
1972	MIN	N	27	180	6.7	21	0
1973			41	202	4.9	16	1
1974			21	120	5.7	15	2
1975			16	108	6.8	21t	1
1976			27	45	1.7	20	1
1977			15	6	0.4	8	0
1978			24	-6	-0.3	15	1
Career			675	3674	5.4	52t	32
Playoffs			25	70	2.8		1

Jim Tarrant

Year	Team		Att	Yds	Avg	Lg	TD
1946	MIA	AA	5	-46	-9.2		0

John Tarver

Year	Team		Att	Yds	Avg	Lg	TD
1972	NE	N	42	132	3.1	21	1
1973			72	321	4.5	28	4
1974			41	101	2.5	18	2

John Tarver *continued*

Year	Team		Att	Yds	Avg	Lg	TD
1975	PHI	N	7	20	2.9	9	0
Career			162	574	3.5	28	7

Carl Taseff

Year	Team		Att	Yds	Avg	Lg	TD
1951	CLE	N	13	49	3.8	15	2
1953	BAL	N	1	1	1.0	1t	1
1954			41	228	5.6	24	0
1956			1	2	2.0	2	0
1960			4	3	0.8	4	0
Career			60	283	4.7	24	3

Steve Tasker

Year	Team		Att	Yds	Avg	Lg	TD
1985	HOU	N	2	16	8.0	13	0
1992	BUF	N	1	9	9.0	9	0
1995			8	74	9.3	17	0
1996			9	31	3.4	11	0
Career			20	130	6.5	17	0
Playoffs			4	56	14.0		0

Lars Tate

Year	Team		Att	Yds	Avg	Lg	TD
1988	TB	N	122	467	3.8	47t	7
1989			167	589	3.5	48	8
1990	CHI	N	3	5	1.7	4	0
Career			292	1061	3.6	48	15

Rodney Tate

Year	Team		Att	Yds	Avg	Lg	TD
1982	CIN	N	2	2	1.0	2	0
1983			25	77	3.1	13	0
Career			27	79	2.9	13	0

Mosi Tatupu

Year	Team		Att	Yds	Avg	Lg	TD
1978	NE	N	3	6	2.0	3	0
1979			23	71	3.1	12	0
1980			33	97	2.9	11	3
1981			38	201	5.3	43	2
1982			30	168	5.6	26	0
1983			106	578	**5.5**	55	4
1984			133	553	4.2	20t	4
1985			47	152	3.2	11	2
1986			71	172	2.4	13	1
1987			79	248	3.1	19	0
1988			22	75	3.4	22	2
1989			11	38	3.5	20	0
1990			16	56	3.5	15	0
Career			612	2415	3.9	55	18
Playoffs			11	30	2.7		1

Biff Taugher

Year	Team		Att	Yds	Avg	Lg	TD
1922	GB	N					1

Junior Tautalatasi

Year	Team		Att	Yds	Avg	Lg	TD
1986	PHI	N	51	163	3.2	50	0
1987			26	69	2.7	17	0
1988			14	28	2.0	9	0
1989	DAL	N	6	15	2.5	6	0
Career			97	275	2.8	50	0

Altie Taylor

Year	Team		Att	Yds	Avg	Lg	TD
1969	DET	N	118	348	2.9	26	0
1970			198	666	3.4	34	2
1971			174	736	4.2	36t	4
1972			154	658	4.3	38t	4
1973			176	719	4.1	34	5
1974			150	532	3.5	27	5
1975			195	638	3.3	24	4
1976	HOU	N	5	11	2.2	8	0
Career			1170	4308	3.7	38t	24
Playoffs			9	16	1.8		0

Billy Taylor

Year	Team		Att	Yds	Avg	Lg	TD
1978	NYG	N	73	250	3.4	19	0
1979			198	700	3.5	31	7
1980			147	580	3.9	35	4
1981	NYG-NYJ	N	38	111	2.9	14	2
1982	LARI	N	4	3	0.8	2	0
Career			460	1644	3.6	35	13

Brian Taylor

Year	Team		Att	Yds	Avg	Lg	TD
1989	CHI	N	2	7	3.5	7	0

Charley Taylor

Year	Team		Att	Yds	Avg	Lg	TD
1964	WAS	N	199	755	3.8	50	5
1965			145	402	2.8	39	3

Charley Taylor *continued*

Year	Team		Att	Yds	Avg	Lg	TD
1966			87	262	3.0	24	3
1968			2	-3	-1.5	4	0
1969			3	24	8.0	18	0
1970			1	17	17.0	17	0
1972			3	39	13.0	17	0
1973			1	-7	-7.0	-7	0
1974			1	-1	-1.0	-1	0
Career			442	1488	3.4	50	11
Playoffs			1	8	8.0		0

Charlie Taylor

Year	Team		Att	Yds	Avg	Lg	TD
1944	BKN	N	7	19	2.7	8	0

Cliff Taylor

Year	Team		Att	Yds	Avg	Lg	TD
1974	CHI	N	9	18	2.0	9t	1
1976	GB	N	14	47	3.4	17	1
Career			23	65	2.8	17	2

Corky Taylor

Year	Team		Att	Yds	Avg	Lg	TD
1955	LA	N	26	95	3.7	13	0

Craig Taylor

Year	Team		Att	Yds	Avg	Lg	TD
1989	CIN	N	30	111	3.7	16	3
1990			51	216	4.2	24	2
1991			33	153	4.6	34t	2
Career			114	480	4.2	34t	7

Hugh Taylor

Year	Team		Att	Yds	Avg	Lg	TD
1947	WAS	N	1	7	7.0	7	0

Jesse Taylor

Year	Team		Att	Yds	Avg	Lg	TD
1972	SD	N	13	58	4.5	17	0

Jim Taylor

Year	Team		Att	Yds	Avg	Lg	TD
1958	GB	N	52	247	4.8	25	1
1959			120	452	3.8	21	6
1960			**230**	1101	4.8	32	11
1961			243	1307	5.4	53	**15**
1962			**272**	**1474**	5.4	51	**19**
1963			248	1018	4.1	40t	9
1964			235	1169	5.0	84t	12
1965			207	734	3.5	35	4
1966			204	705	3.5	19	4
1967	NO	N	130	390	3.0	16	2
Career			1941	8597	4.4	84t	83
Playoffs			145	505	3.5		2

John Taylor

Year	Team		Att	Yds	Avg	Lg	TD
1989	SF	N	1	6	6.0	6	0
1992			1	10	10.0	10	0
1993			2	17	8.5	12	0
1994			2	-2	-1.0	1	0
Career			6	31	5.2	12	0
Playoffs			1	15	15.0		0

Kitrick Taylor

Year	Team		Att	Yds	Avg	Lg	TD
1988	KC	N	1	2	2.0	2	0

Lenny Taylor

Year	Team		Att	Yds	Avg	Lg	TD
1987	ATL	N	1	-13	-13.0	-13	0

Lionel Taylor

Year	Team		Att	Yds	Avg	Lg	TD
1960	DEN	A	2	-6	-3.0		0
1962			2	26	13.0	18	0
Career			4	20	5.0	18	0

Otis Taylor

Year	Team		Att	Yds	Avg	Lg	TD
1965	KC	A	2	17	8.5	15	0
1966			2	33	16.5	19	0
1967			5	29	5.8	24t	1
1968			5	41	8.2	30	1
1969			2	-2	-1.0	10	0
1970	KC	N	3	13	4.3	7	0
1971			1	25	25.0	25t	1
1972			5	13	2.6	11	0
1973			4	-14	-3.5	5	0
1974			1	6	6.0	6	0
Career			30	161	5.4	30	3

Troy Taylor

Year	Team		Att	Yds	Avg	Lg	TD
1990	NYJ	N	2	20	10.0	15	1
1991			7	23	3.3	13	0
Career			9	43	4.8	15	1

Year	Team		Att	Yds	Avg	Lg	TD

John Teltschik

Year	Team		Att	Yds	Avg	Lg	TD
1986	PHI	N	1	0	0.0	0	0
1987			3	32	10.7	23	0
1988			2	36	18.0	23	0
1989			1	23	23.0	23	0
Career			7	91	13.0	23	0

Mark Temple

Year	Team		Att	Yds	Avg	Lg	TD
1936	BKN-BOS	N	5	4	0.8		1

Steve Tensi

Year	Team		Att	Yds	Avg	Lg	TD
1966	SD	A	1	-1	-1.0	-1	0
1967	DEN	A	24	4	0.2	13	0
1968			6	2	0.3	3	0
1969			12	63	5.3	17	0
1970	DEN	N	4	14	3.5	15	0
Career			47	82	1.7	17	0

Tony Teresa

Year	Team		Att	Yds	Avg	Lg	TD
1960	OAK	A	139	608	4.4	83	6

George Terlep

Year	Team		Att	Yds	Avg	Lg	TD
1946	BUF	AA	36	29	0.8		1
1947			4	11	2.8		0
1948	CLE	AA	1	4	4.0	4	0
Career			41	44	1.1	4	1
Playoffs			2	-5	-2.5		0

Ray Terrell

Year	Team		Att	Yds	Avg	Lg	TD
1946	CLE	AA	39	117	3.0		0
1947	CLE-BAL	AA	26	48	1.8		0
Career			65	165	2.5		0
Playoffs			1	-4	-4.0		0

Vinny Testaverde

Year	Team		Att	Yds	Avg	Lg	TD
1987	TB	N	13	50	3.8	17	1
1988			28	138	4.9	24	1
1989			25	139	5.6	16	0
1990			38	280	7.4	48t	1
1991			32	101	3.2	19	0
1992			36	197	5.5	18	2
1993	CLE	N	18	74	4.1	14	0
1994			21	37	1.8	12	2
1995			18	62	3.4	14	2
1996	BAL	N	34	188	5.5	22	2
Career			263	1266	4.8	48t	11
Playoffs			5	19	3.8		0

Don Testerman

Year	Team		Att	Yds	Avg	Lg	TD
1976	SEA	N	67	246	3.7	16	1
1977			119	459	3.9	20	1
1978			43	155	3.6	16	0
1980	MIA	N	1	5	5.0	5	0
Career			230	865	3.8	20	2

Lee Tevis

Year	Team		Att	Yds	Avg	Lg	TD
1947	BKN	AA	4	44	11.0		0

Lowell Tew

Year	Team		Att	Yds	Avg	Lg	TD
1948	NY	AA	24	95	4.0		5
1949	B-NY	AA	14	65	4.6		1
Career			38	160	4.2		6

James Thaxton

Year	Team		Att	Yds	Avg	Lg	TD
1974	CLE	N	1	-10	-10.0	-10	0
1977	NO	N	1	-3	-3.0	-3	0
Career			2	-13	-6.5	-3	0

Joe Theismann

Year	Team		Att	Yds	Avg	Lg	TD
1974	WAS	N	3	12	4.0	12	1
1975			3	34	11.3	21	0
1976			17	97	5.7	22	1
1977			29	149	5.1	14	1
1978			37	177	4.8	20	1
1979			46	181	3.9	22	4
1980			29	175	6.0	37t	3
1981			36	177	4.9	24	2
1982			31	150	4.8	16	2
1983			37	234	6.3	22	1
1984			62	314	5.1	27	1
1985			25	115	4.6	25	2
Career			355	1815	5.1	37t	17
Playoffs			19	95	5.0		0

Harry Theofiledes

Year	Team		Att	Yds	Avg	Lg	TD
1968	WAS	N	3	0	0.0	7	0

Jim Thibaut

Year	Team		Att	Yds	Avg	Lg	TD
1946	BUF	AA	10	48	4.8		1

Yancey Thigpen

Year	Team		Att	Yds	Avg	Lg	TD
1995	PIT	N	1	1	1.0	1	0

Aaron Thomas

Year	Team		Att	Yds	Avg	Lg	TD
1961	SF	N	1	-15	-15.0	-15	0
1968	NYG	N	2	14	7.0	23	0
Career			3	-1	-0.3	23	0

Andre Thomas

Year	Team		Att	Yds	Avg	Lg	TD
1987	MIN	N	6	4	0.7	5	0

Bill Thomas

Year	Team		Att	Yds	Avg	Lg	TD
1973	HOU	N	10	39	3.9	17	0
1974	KC	N	3	-3	-1.0	2	0
Career			13	36	2.8	17	0

Blair Thomas

Year	Team		Att	Yds	Avg	Lg	TD
1990	NYJ	N	123	620	5.0	41	1
1991			189	728	3.9	25	3
1992			97	440	4.5	19	0
1993			59	221	3.7	24	1
1994	NE-DAL	N	43	137	3.2	13	2
1995	CAR	N	22	90	4.1	13	0
Career			533	2236	4.2	41	7
Playoffs			23	70	3.0		2

Bob Thomas

Year	Team		Att	Yds	Avg	Lg	TD
1972	LA	N	77	433	5.6	49	3
1973	SD	N	22	48	2.2	12	0
1974			21	56	2.7	12	0
Career			120	537	4.5	49	3

Calvin Thomas

Year	Team		Att	Yds	Avg	Lg	TD
1982	CHI	N	5	4	0.8	3	0
1983			8	25	3.1	5	0
1984			40	186	4.7	37	1
1985			31	125	4.0	17	4
1986			56	224	4.0	23	0
1987			25	88	3.5	18	0
1988	CHI-DEN	N	6	20	3.3	8	0
Career			171	672	3.9	37	5
Playoffs			16	46	2.9		1

Clendon Thomas

Year	Team		Att	Yds	Avg	Lg	TD
1960	LA	N	16	63	3.9	33	0
1964	PIT	N	2	7	3.5	4	0
Career			18	70	3.9	33	0

Derrick Thomas

Year	Team		Att	Yds	Avg	Lg	TD
1987	TB	N	1	2	2.0	2	0

Doug Thomas

Year	Team		Att	Yds	Avg	Lg	TD
1992	SEA	N	3	7	2.3	8	0
1993			1	4	4.0	4	0
Career			4	11	2.8	8	0

Duane Thomas

Year	Team		Att	Yds	Avg	Lg	TD
1970	DAL	N	151	803	5.3	47t	5
1971			175	793	4.5	56t	11
1973	WAS	N	32	95	3.0	13	0
1974			95	347	3.7	66	5
Career			453	2038	4.5	66	21
Playoffs			130	518	4.0		4

Earl Thomas

Year	Team		Att	Yds	Avg	Lg	TD
1972	CHI	N	5	13	2.6	8	0
1973			1	5	5.0	5	0
Career			6	18	3.0	8	0

Gene Thomas

Year	Team		Att	Yds	Avg	Lg	TD
1966	KC	A	7	53	7.6	28	1
1967			35	133	3.8	19	1
1968	BOS	A	88	215	2.4	25	2
Career			130	401	3.1	28	4
Playoffs			2	2	1.0		0

George Thomas

Year	Team		Att	Yds	Avg	Lg	TD
1950	WAS	N	20	41	2.0	18	0

George Thomas continued

Year	Team		Att	Yds	Avg	Lg	TD
1951			42	130	3.1	17	0
1952	NYG	N	6	18	3.0	11	0
Career			68	189	2.8	18	0

Jewerl Thomas

Year	Team		Att	Yds	Avg	Lg	TD
1980	LA	N	65	427	6.6	61	2
1981			34	118	3.5	40	0
1982	LARM	N	16	80	5.0	11	0
1983	KC	N	44	115	2.6	11	0
1984	SD	N	14	43	3.1	9	2
Career			173	783	4.5	61	4
Playoffs			14	48	3.4		1

Jimmy Thomas

Year	Team		Att	Yds	Avg	Lg	TD
1969	SF	N	23	190	8.3	75t	1
1970			31	89	2.9	14	0
1971			3	36	12.0	25t	1
1972			52	250	4.8	22	1
1973			56	259	4.6	16	1
Career			165	824	5.0	75t	4
Playoffs			2	2	1.0		0

John Thomas

Year	Team		Att	Yds	Avg	Lg	TD
1962	SF	N	1	-9	-9.0	-9	0

J.T. Thomas

Year	Team		Att	Yds	Avg	Lg	TD
1996	STL	N	1	-1	-1.0	-1	0

Ken Thomas

Year	Team		Att	Yds	Avg	Lg	TD
1983	KC	N	15	55	3.7	28	0

Lamar Thomas

Year	Team		Att	Yds	Avg	Lg	TD
1995	TB	N	1	5	5.0	5	0

Lavale Thomas

Year	Team		Att	Yds	Avg	Lg	TD
1987	GB	N	5	19	3.8	5	0

Louis Thomas

Year	Team		Att	Yds	Avg	Lg	TD
1969	CIN	A	4	16	4.0	16t	1
1970	CIN	N	2	7	3.5	13	0
1971			2	-1	-0.5	0	0
Career			8	22	2.8	16t	1

Mike Thomas

Year	Team		Att	Yds	Avg	Lg	TD
1975	WAS	N	235	919	3.9	34	4
1976			254	1101	4.3	26	5
1977			228	806	3.5	31	3
1978			161	533	3.3	26	3
1979	SD	N	91	353	3.9	21	1
1980			118	484	4.1	18	3
Career			1087	4196	3.9	34	19
Playoffs			28	115	4.1		0

Rex Thomas

Year	Team		Att	Yds	Avg	Lg	TD
1926	BKN	N					2
1927	CLE	N					1
1928	DET	N					1
Career							4

Robb Thomas

Year	Team		Att	Yds	Avg	Lg	TD
1992	SEA	N	1	-1	-1.0	-1	0

Rodney Thomas

Year	Team		Att	Yds	Avg	Lg	TD
1995	HOU	N	251	947	3.8	74t	5
1996			49	151	3.1	24t	1
Career			300	1098	3.7	74t	6

Thurman Thomas

Year	Team		Att	Yds	Avg	Lg	TD
1988	BUF	N	207	881	4.3	37t	2
1989			298	1244	4.2	38	6
1990			271	1297	4.8	80t	11
1991			288	1407	4.9	33	7
1992			312	1487	4.8	44	9
1993			355	1315	3.7	27	6
1994			287	1093	3.8	29	7
1995			267	1005	3.8	49	6
1996			281	1033	3.7	36	8
Career			2566	10762	4.2	80t	62
Playoffs			327	1399	4.3		15

Bobby Thomason

Year	Team		Att	Yds	Avg	Lg	TD
1951	GB	N	5	-5	-1.0	10	0
1952	PHI	N	17	88	5.2	23	0

Year	Team		Att	Yds	Avg	Lg	TD

Bobby Thomason *continued*

Year	Team		Att	Yds	Avg	Lg	TD
1953			9	23	2.6	20	1
1954			10	45	4.5	19	0
1955			17	29	1.7	20	0
1956			21	48	2.3	19	2
1957			15	62	4.1	19	3
Career			94	290	3.1	23	6

Jim Thomason

Year	Team		Att	Yds	Avg	Lg	TD
1945	DET	N	9	9	1.0	10	0

John Thomason

Year	Team		Att	Yds	Avg	Lg	TD
1930	BKN	N					3
1936	PHI	N	109	333	3.1		0
Career			109	333	3.1		3

Anthony Thompson

Year	Team		Att	Yds	Avg	Lg	TD
1990	PHX	N	106	390	3.7	40	4
1991			126	376	3.0	22	1
1992	PHX-LARM		19	65	3.4	12	1
Career			251	831	3.3	40	6

Aundra Thompson

Year	Team		Att	Yds	Avg	Lg	TD
1978	GB	N	4	25	6.3	13	0
1979			2	-18	-9.0	-7	0
1980			5	5	1.0	16	0
1981			1	2	2.0	2	0
1982	NO	N	1	2	2.0	2	0
Career			13	16	1.2	16	0

Bobby Thompson

Year	Team		Att	Yds	Avg	Lg	TD
1975	DET	N	51	268	5.3	46t	1
1976			13	42	3.2	9	0
Career			64	310	4.8	46t	1

Darrell Thompson

Year	Team		Att	Yds	Avg	Lg	TD
1990	GB	N	76	264	3.5	37	1
1991			141	471	3.3	40t	1
1992			76	254	3.3	33	2
1993			169	654	3.9	60t	3
1994			2	-2	-1.0	2	0
Career			464	1641	3.5	60t	7
Playoffs			19	69	3.6		0

Del Thompson

Year	Team		Att	Yds	Avg	Lg	TD
1982	KC	N	4	7	1.8	4	0

Ernie Thompson

Year	Team		Att	Yds	Avg	Lg	TD
1991	LARM	N	2	9	4.5	9	0
1993	KC	N	11	28	2.5	14	0
Career			13	37	2.8	14	0

Hal Thompson

Year	Team		Att	Yds	Avg	Lg	TD
1947	BKN	AA	1	4	4.0	4	0

Jack Thompson

Year	Team		Att	Yds	Avg	Lg	TD
1979	CIN	N	21	116	5.5	21	5
1980			18	84	4.7	15t	1
1983	TB	N	26	27	1.0	9	0
1984			5	35	7.0	13	0
Career			70	262	3.7	21	6

Jesse Thompson

Year	Team		Att	Yds	Avg	Lg	TD
1978	DET	N	2	7	3.5	10	0
1980			1	-4	-4.0	-4	0
Career			3	3	1.0	10	0

Leonard Thompson

Year	Team		Att	Yds	Avg	Lg	TD
1975	DET	N	1	-12	-12.0	-12	0
1976			1	0	0.0	0	0
1977			31	91	2.9	16t	1
1978			1	7	7.0	7	0
1979			5	24	4.8	16	0
1980			6	61	10.2	30	0
1981			10	75	7.5	21	1
1982			2	16	8.0	13	0
1983			4	72	18.0	40t	1
1984			3	-7	-2.3	4	0
Career			64	327	5.1	40t	3
Playoffs			1	24	24.0		0

Leroy Thompson

Year	Team		Att	Yds	Avg	Lg	TD
1991	PIT	N	20	60	3.0	14	0
1992			35	157	4.5	25	1

Leroy Thompson *continued*

Year	Team		Att	Yds	Avg	Lg	TD
1993			205	763	3.7	36	3
1994	NE	N	102	312	3.1	13	2
1995	KC	N	28	73	2.6	10	0
1996	TB	N	14	25	1.8	10	0
Career			404	1390	3.4	36	6
Playoffs			30	79	2.6		0

Rocky Thompson

Year	Team		Att	Yds	Avg	Lg	TD
1971	NYG	N	54	177	3.3	23	1
1972			9	35	3.9	13	0
1973			5	5	1.0	4	0
Career			68	217	3.2	23	1

Tom Thompson

Year	Team		Att	Yds	Avg	Lg	TD
1974	SD	N	6	8	1.3	8	0

Tommy Thompson

Year	Team		Att	Yds	Avg	Lg	TD
1940	PIT	N	40	39	1.0		0
1941	PHI	N	54	28	0.5	14	0
1942			92	9	0.1	22	1
1945			8	-13	-1.6	7	0
1946			34	-116	-3.4	6	0
1947			23	52	2.3	16	2
1948			12	46	3.8	13	1
1949			15	17	1.1	3	2
1950			15	34	2.3	7	0
Career			293	96	0.3	22	6
Playoffs			22	64	2.9		0

Tuffy Thompson

Year	Team		Att	Yds	Avg	Lg	TD
1937	PIT	N	43	80	1.9		0
1938			39	139	3.6		1
1939	GB	N	6	9	1.5		0
Career			88	228	2.6		1

Vince Thompson

Year	Team		Att	Yds	Avg	Lg	TD
1981	DET	N	35	211	6.0	30	1
1983			40	138	3.5	10	1
Career			75	349	4.7	30	2

Woody Thompson

Year	Team		Att	Yds	Avg	Lg	TD
1975	ATL	N	68	247	3.6	18	0
1976			42	152	3.6	10	0
1977			132	478	3.6	22	1
Career			242	877	3.6	22	1

Bill Thornton

Year	Team		Att	Yds	Avg	Lg	TD
1963	STL	N	19	111	5.8	55t	1
1964			39	236	6.1	62	1
1965			31	188	6.1	38	0
1967			4	9	2.3	7	0
Career			93	544	5.8	62	2

James Thornton

Year	Team		Att	Yds	Avg	Lg	TD
1989	CHI	N	1	4	4.0	4	0

Sidney Thornton

Year	Team		Att	Yds	Avg	Lg	TD
1977	PIT	N	27	103	3.8	18	2
1978			71	264	3.7	27	2
1979			118	585	5.0	75	6
1980			78	325	4.2	28	3
1981			56	202	3.6	17t	4
1982			6	33	5.5	13	1
Career			356	1512	4.2	75	18
Playoffs			22	81	3.7		1

Jim Thorpe

Year	Team		Att	Yds	Avg	Lg	TD
1921	CLE	A					1
1922	OOR	N					3
1926	CAN	N					2
Career							6

Bob Thurbon

Year	Team		Att	Yds	Avg	Lg	TD
1943	P-P	N	71	291	4.1	25	5
1944	C-P	N	69	185	2.7	25t	4
1946	BUF	AA	3	2	0.7		0
Career			143	478	3.3	25t	9

Steve Thurlow

Year	Team		Att	Yds	Avg	Lg	TD
1964	NYG	N	64	210	3.3	13	0
1965			106	440	4.2	43	4
1966	NYG-WAS	N	80	260	3.3	20	0
1967	WAS	N	13	33	2.5	5	0

Steve Thurlow *continued*

Year	Team		Att	Yds	Avg	Lg	TD
1968			51	184	3.6	11	0
Career			314	1127	3.6	43	4

Billy Tidwell

Year	Team		Att	Yds	Avg	Lg	TD
1954	SF	N	1	1	1.0	1	0

Travis Tidwell

Year	Team		Att	Yds	Avg	Lg	TD
1950	NYG	N	29	133	4.6	54	2
1951			11	14	1.3	13	0
Career			40	147	3.7	54	2

Jim Tiller

Year	Team		Att	Yds	Avg	Lg	TD
1962	NY	A	31	43	1.4	25	0

Pat Tilley

Year	Team		Att	Yds	Avg	Lg	TD
1978	STL	N	1	32	32.0	32	0

Ed Tillison

Year	Team		Att	Yds	Avg	Lg	TD
1992	DET	N	4	22	5.5	10	0

Lawyer Tillman

Year	Team		Att	Yds	Avg	Lg	TD
1992	CLE	N	2	15	7.5	15	0
Playoffs			1	8	8.0		0

Lewis Tillman

Year	Team		Att	Yds	Avg	Lg	TD
1989	NYG	N	79	290	3.7	19	0
1990			84	231	2.8	17	1
1991			65	287	4.4	17	1
1992			6	13	2.2	6	0
1993			121	585	4.8	58	3
1994	CHI	N	275	899	3.3	25t	7
1995			29	78	2.7	9	0
Career			659	2383	3.6	58	12
Playoffs			39	87	2.2		2

Spencer Tillman

Year	Team		Att	Yds	Avg	Lg	TD
1987	HOU	N	12	29	2.4	13	1
1988			3	5	1.7	2	0
1991	SF	N	13	40	3.1	8	0
1992	HOU	N	1	1	1.0	1	0
1993			9	94	10.4	34	0
1994			2	12	6.0	9	0
Career			40	181	4.5	34	1

Charlie Timmons

Year	Team		Att	Yds	Avg	Lg	TD
1946	BKN	AA	23	65	2.8		0

Michael Timpson

Year	Team		Att	Yds	Avg	Lg	TD
1991	NE	N	1	-4	-4.0	-4	0
1994			2	14	7.0	10	0
1995	CHI	N	3	28	9.3	16	1
1996			3	21	7.0	13	0
Career			9	59	6.6	16	1

Tim Tindale

Year	Team		Att	Yds	Avg	Lg	TD
1995	BUF	N	5	16	3.2	6	0
1996			14	49	3.5	15	0
Career			19	65	3.4	15	0
Playoffs			5	73	14.6		1

Gerald Tinker

Year	Team		Att	Yds	Avg	Lg	TD
1974	ATL	N	2	5	2.5	9	0
1975	GB	N	1	5	5.0	5	0
Career			3	10	3.3	9	0

Gaynell Tinsley

Year	Team		Att	Yds	Avg	Lg	TD
1937	CHIC	N	1	2	2.0	2	1
1938			4	26	6.5		0
1940			1	17	17.0	17	0
Career			6	45	7.5	17	1

Scott Tinsley

Year	Team		Att	Yds	Avg	Lg	TD
1987	PHI	N	4	2	0.5	2	0

Sid Tinsley

Year	Team		Att	Yds	Avg	Lg	TD
1945	PIT	N	5	3	0.6	4	0

Howie Tipton

Year	Team		Att	Yds	Avg	Lg	TD
1937	CHIC	N	9	23	2.6		0

Bob Titchenal

Year	Team		Att	Yds	Avg	Lg	TD
1946	SF	AA	1	2	2.0	2	0

Bob Titchenal *continued*

Year	Team		Att	Yds	Avg	Lg	TD
1947	LA	AA	1	0	0.0	0	0
Career			2	2	1.0	2	0

Y.A. Tittle

Year	Team		Att	Yds	Avg	Lg	TD
1948	BAL	AA	52	157	3.0		4
1949			29	89	3.1		2
1950	BAL	N	20	77	3.9	33	2
1951	SF	N	13	18	1.4	5	1
1952			11	-11	-1.0	4	0
1953			14	41	2.9	14	6
1954			28	68	2.4	10	4
1955			23	114	5.0	35	0
1956			24	67	2.8	13	4
1957			40	220	5.5	45	6
1958			22	35	1.6	12	2
1959			11	24	2.2	22	0
1960			10	61	6.1	28	0
1961	NYG	N	25	85	3.4	17	3
1962			17	108	6.4	23	2
1963			18	99	5.5	18	2
1964			15	-7	-0.5	7t	1
Career			372	1245	3.3	45	39
Playoffs			6	-12	-2.0		0

Bill Tobin

Year	Team		Att	Yds	Avg	Lg	TD
1963	HOU	A	75	270	3.6	32	4

Dick Todd

Year	Team		Att	Yds	Avg	Lg	TD
1939	WAS	N	57	266	4.7		2
1940			76	408	5.4		4
1941			55	138	2.5	11	1
1942			65	195	3.0	22	0
1945			7	54	7.7	31	0
1946			41	266	6.5	29t	3
1947			10	45	4.5	12	0
1948			57	201	3.5	21	1
Career			368	1573	4.3	31	11
Playoffs			3	13	4.3		0

Jim Todd

Year	Team		Att	Yds	Avg	Lg	TD
1966	DET	N	2	6	3.0	3	0

Larry Todd

Year	Team		Att	Yds	Avg	Lg	TD
1965	OAK	A	32	183	5.7	57	0
1967			29	116	4.0	16	2
1968			13	89	6.8	31t	2
1969			47	198	4.2	51	1
1970	OAK	N	17	39	2.3	13	0
Career			138	625	4.5	57	5
Playoffs			16	64	4.0		0

Richard Todd

Year	Team		Att	Yds	Avg	Lg	TD
1976	NYJ	N	28	107	3.8	22	1
1977			24	46	1.9	13	2
1978			14	18	1.3	10	0
1979			36	93	2.6	21	5
1980			49	330	6.7	31t	5
1981			32	131	4.1	19	0
1982			13	-5	-0.4	7t	1
1983			35	101	2.9	17	0
1984	NO	N	28	111	4.0	15	0
Career			259	932	3.6	31t	14
Playoffs			14	32	2.3		0

Charley Tolar

Year	Team		Att	Yds	Avg	Lg	TD
1960	HOU	A	54	179	3.3	40	3
1961			157	577	3.7	38	4
1962			**244**	1012	4.1	25	7
1963			194	659	3.4	33	3
1964			139	515	3.7	40	4
1965			73	230	3.2	18	0
1966			46	105	2.3	17	0
Career			907	3277	3.6	40	21
Playoffs			33	110	3.3		1

Ken Toler

Year	Team		Att	Yds	Avg	Lg	TD
1982	NE	N	1	4	4.0	4	0

Billy Joe Tolliver

Year	Team		Att	Yds	Avg	Lg	TD
1989	SD	N	7	0	0.0	3	0
1990			14	22	1.6	14	0
1991	ATL	N	9	6	0.7	7	0
1992			4	15	3.8	15	0

Billy Joe Tolliver *continued*

Year	Team		Att	Yds	Avg	Lg	TD
1993			7	48	6.9	24	0
1994	HOU	N	12	37	3.1	10	2
Career			53	128	2.4	24	2

Lou Tomasetti

Year	Team		Att	Yds	Avg	Lg	TD
1939	PIT	N	49	86	1.8		1
1940			68	246	3.6		1
1941	DET-PHI	N	16	41	2.6	11	1
1942	PHI	N	45	102	2.3	14	0
1946	BUF	AA	43	139	3.2		1
1947			92	326	3.5		2
1948			134	716	5.3		7
1949			54	249	4.6		2
Career			501	1905	3.8	14	15
Playoffs			15	29	1.9		0

Andy Tomasic

Year	Team		Att	Yds	Avg	Lg	TD
1942	PIT	N	60	214	3.6	34	0

Pat Tomberlin

Year	Team		Att	Yds	Avg	Lg	TD
1992	CLE	N	24	39	1.6	16	0

Mike Tomczak

Year	Team		Att	Yds	Avg	Lg	TD
1985	CHI	N	2	3	1.5	3	0
1986			23	117	5.1	16	3
1987			18	54	3.0	10	1
1988			13	40	3.1	17	1
1989			24	71	3.0	18	1
1990			12	41	3.4	14	2
1991	GB	N	17	93	5.5	48	1
1993	PIT	N	5	-4	-0.8	2	0
1994			4	22	5.5	13	0
1995			11	25	2.3	11	0
1996			22	-7	-0.3	6	0
Career			151	455	3.0	48	9
Playoffs			9	29	3.2		0

Mario Tonelli

Year	Team		Att	Yds	Avg	Lg	TD
1940	CHIC	N	51	148	2.9		1

Ed Toner

Year	Team		Att	Yds	Avg	Lg	TD
1993	IND	N	2	6	3.0	6	0
1994			1	11	11.0	11	0
Career			3	17	5.7	11	0

Anthony Toney

Year	Team		Att	Yds	Avg	Lg	TD
1986	PHI	N	69	285	4.1	43	1
1987			127	473	3.7	36	5
1988			139	502	3.6	20	4
1989			172	582	3.4	44	3
1990			132	452	3.4	20	1
Career			639	2294	3.6	44	14
Playoffs			12	18	1.5		1

Al Toon

Year	Team		Att	Yds	Avg	Lg	TD
1985	NYJ	N	1	5	5.0	5	0
1986			2	-3	-1.5	2	0
1988			1	5	5.0	5	0
Career			4	7	1.8	5	0

Eric Torkelson

Year	Team		Att	Yds	Avg	Lg	TD
1974	GB	N	13	60	4.6	21	0
1975			42	226	5.4	29	2
1976			88	289	3.3	15	2
1977			103	309	3.0	29	1
1978			6	18	3.0	6	0
1979			98	401	4.1	15	3
1981			1	4	4.0	4	0
Career			351	1307	3.7	29	8

Gino Torretta

Year	Team		Att	Yds	Avg	Lg	TD
1996	SEA	N	2	12	6.0	13	0

Bob Torrey

Year	Team		Att	Yds	Avg	Lg	TD
1979	MIA	N	13	61	4.7	17	1

Zollie Toth

Year	Team		Att	Yds	Avg	Lg	TD
1950	NYY	N	131	636	4.9	51	5
1951			119	384	3.2	16	4
1952	DAL	N	82	266	3.2	18	4
1954	BAL	N	86	303	3.5	15	1
Career			418	1589	3.8	51	14

Willie Totten

Year	Team		Att	Yds	Avg	Lg	TD
1987	BUF	N	12	11	0.9	7	0

Dan Towler

Year	Team		Att	Yds	Avg	Lg	TD
1950	LA	N	46	130	2.8	34t	6
1951			126	854	6.8	79t	6
1952			156	**894**	5.7	44t	**10**
1953			152	879	5.8	73t	7
1954			149	599	4.0	24	**11**
1955			43	137	3.2	14	3
Career			672	3493	5.2	79t	43
Playoffs			45	156	3.5		2

JoJo Townsell

Year	Team		Att	Yds	Avg	Lg	TD
1986	NYJ	N	1	2	2.0	2	0
1987			1	-2	-2.0	-2	0
Career			2	0	0.0	2	0

Tom Tracy

Year	Team		Att	Yds	Avg	Lg	TD
1956	DET	N	12	32	2.7	9	0
1957			16	46	2.9	17	0
1958	PIT	N	169	714	4.2	64	5
1959			199	794	4.0	51	3
1960			192	680	3.5	28t	5
1961			147	402	2.7	26	2
1962			20	116	5.8	35	0
1963	PIT-WAS	N	29	61	2.1	9	1
1964	WAS	N	24	67	2.8	16t	1
Career			808	2912	3.6	64	17
Playoffs			11	86	7.8		2

Mike Trainor

Year	Team		Att	Yds	Avg	Lg	TD
1923	BUF	N					1

Jerry Traynham

Year	Team		Att	Yds	Avg	Lg	TD
1961	DEN	A	6	12	2.0	8	0

Ivan Trebotich

Year	Team		Att	Yds	Avg	Lg	TD
1944	DET	N	1	2	2.0	2	0
1945			3	3	1.0	4	0
1947	BAL	AA	3	-4	-1.3		0
Career			7	1	0.1	4	0

Frank Trigillo

Year	Team		Att	Yds	Avg	Lg	TD
1946	LA-MIA	AA	41	126	3.1		1

Bill Triplett

Year	Team		Att	Yds	Avg	Lg	TD
1962	STL	N	2	12	6.0	10	0
1963			134	652	4.9	63t	5
1965			174	617	3.5	59t	6
1966			13	25	1.9	5	0
1967	NYG	N	58	171	2.9	14	2
1968	DET	N	120	384	3.2	17	0
1969			111	377	3.4	33	3
1970			48	156	3.3	11t	1
1971			4	4	1.0	6	0
1972			17	48	2.8	9	0
Career			681	2446	3.6	63t	17

Mel Triplett

Year	Team		Att	Yds	Avg	Lg	TD
1955	NYG	N	34	138	4.1	19	0
1956			125	515	4.1	25	5
1957			61	216	3.5	16	0
1958			118	466	3.9	24	1
1959			91	381	4.2	20	1
1960			124	573	4.6	40	4
1961	MIN	N	80	407	5.1	37	1
1962			52	160	3.1	18	2
Career			685	2856	4.2	40	14
Playoffs			29	140	4.8		2

Wally Triplett

Year	Team		Att	Yds	Avg	Lg	TD
1949	DET	N	53	221	4.2	80	1
1950			14	92	6.6	14	1
1953	CHIC	N	3	8	2.7	16	0
Career			70	321	4.6	80	2

Charley Trippi

Year	Team		Att	Yds	Avg	Lg	TD
1947	CHIC	N	83	401	4.8	41	3
1948			128	690	**5.4**	50t	6
1949			112	553	4.9	55	3
1950			99	426	4.3	22	3
1951			78	501	6.4	32	4
1952			72	350	4.9	59t	4

Charley Trippi *continued*

Year	Team		Att	Yds	Avg	Lg	TD
1953			97	433	4.5	21	0
1954			18	152	8.4	57t	1
Career			687	3506	5.1	59t	24
Playoffs			20	110	5.5		1

Frank Tripucka

Year	Team		Att	Yds	Avg	Lg	TD
1949	**DET**	**N**	12	36	3.0	19	1
1950	**CHIC**	**N**	4	35	8.8	21	1
1951			1	14	14.0	14	0
1952	**CHIC-DAL**	**N**	10	25	2.5	15	3
1960	**DEN**	**A**	37	-226	-6.1		0
1961			4	-8	-2.0	0	0
1962			2	-1	-0.5	1	1
Career			70	-125	-1.8	21	6

Bob Trocolor

Year	Team		Att	Yds	Avg	Lg	TD
1942	**NYG**	**N**	26	18	0.7	19	0
1943			6	-4	-0.7	11	0
1944	**BKN**	**N**	3	8	2.7	5	0
Career			35	22	0.6	19	0

Bill Troup

Year	Team		Att	Yds	Avg	Lg	TD
1976	**BAL**	**N**	5	-1	-0.2	6t	1
1977			7	-8	-1.1	7	0
1978			18	25	1.4	10	1
Career			30	16	0.5	10	2

Jack Trudeau

Year	Team		Att	Yds	Avg	Lg	TD
1986	**IND**	**N**	13	21	1.6	8	1
1987			15	7	0.5	9	0
1989			35	91	2.6	17	2
1990			10	28	2.8	9	0
1992			13	6	0.5	5	0
1993			5	3	0.6	2	0
1994	**NYJ**	**N**	6	30	5.0	15	0
Career			97	186	1.9	17	3
Playoffs			2	4	2.0		0

Don Trull

Year	Team		Att	Yds	Avg	Lg	TD
1964	**HOU**	**A**	12	42	3.5	15	0
1965			29	145	5.0	18	2
1966			38	139	3.7	23	7
1967	**HOU-BOS**	**A**	22	30	1.4	10	3
1968	**HOU**	**A**	14	47	3.4	15	0
1969			8	25	3.1	7	2
Career			123	428	3.5	23	14

Bob Trumpy

Year	Team		Att	Yds	Avg	Lg	TD
1968	**CIN**	**A**	1	-1	-1.0	-1	0

Eddie Tryon

Year	Team		Att	Yds	Avg	Lg	TD
1926	**NY**	**A**					5
1927	**NYY**	**N**					2
Career							7

Bill Tucker

Year	Team		Att	Yds	Avg	Lg	TD
1967	**SF**	**N**	3	5	1.7	3	0
1968			30	135	4.5	18	3
1969			20	72	3.6	24t	2
1970			42	137	3.3	11	1
1971	**CHI**	**N**	32	82	2.6	11	0
Career			127	431	3.4	24t	6
Playoffs			7	5	0.7		0

Bob Tucker

Year	Team		Att	Yds	Avg	Lg	TD
1971	**NYG**	**N**	1	1	1.0	1	0
1972			3	6	2.0	13t	1
1973			1	4	4.0	4	0
1975			1	-5	-5.0	-5	0
Career			6	6	1.0	13t	1

Gary Tucker

Year	Team		Att	Yds	Avg	Lg	TD
1968	**MIA**	**A**	4	13	3.3	7	0

Dick Tuckey

Year	Team		Att	Yds	Avg	Lg	TD
1938	**WAS-CLE**	**N**	43	76	1.8		0

John Tuggle

Year	Team		Att	Yds	Avg	Lg	TD
1983	**NYG**	**N**	17	49	2.9	21	1

Darrell Tully

Year	Team		Att	Yds	Avg	Lg	TD
1939	**DET**	**N**	31	50	1.6		1

Emlen Tunnell

Year	Team		Att	Yds	Avg	Lg	TD
1948	**NYG**	**N**	17	43	2.5	15	0

Tom Tupa

Year	Team		Att	Yds	Avg	Lg	TD
1989	**PHX**	**N**	15	75	5.0	13	0
1990			1	0	0.0	0	0
1991			28	97	3.5	17	1
1992	**IND**	**N**	3	9	3.0	0	0
1995	**CLE**	**N**	1	9	9.0	9	0
Career			48	190	4.0	17	1

Frank Turbert

Year	Team		Att	Yds	Avg	Lg	TD
1944	**BOS**	**N**	14	-16	-1.1	9	0

Matt Turk

Year	Team		Att	Yds	Avg	Lg	TD
1996	**WAS**	**N**	1	0	0.0	0	0

John Turley

Year	Team		Att	Yds	Avg	Lg	TD
1935	**PIT**	**N**	4	7	1.8		0

Bake Turner

Year	Team		Att	Yds	Avg	Lg	TD
1962	**BAL**	**N**	1	17	17.0	17	0
1969	**NY**	**A**	1	-4	-4.0	-4	0
Career			2	13	6.5	17	0

Bulldog Turner

Year	Team		Att	Yds	Avg	Lg	TD
1944	**CHIB**	**N**	1	48	48.0	48t	1

Cecil Turner

Year	Team		Att	Yds	Avg	Lg	TD
1968	**CHI**	**N**	2	16	8.0	14	0
1969	**CIN**	**A**	23	105	4.6	34	0
1970	**CHI**	**N**	3	-3	-1.0	1	0
1972			3	0	0.0	11	0
Career			31	118	3.8	34	0

Clem Turner

Year	Team		Att	Yds	Avg	Lg	TD
1970	**DEN**	**N**	29	106	3.7	14	2
1971			17	43	2.5	9	0
1972			5	16	3.2	13	0
Career			51	165	3.2	14	2

Deacon Turner

Year	Team		Att	Yds	Avg	Lg	TD
1978	**CIN**	**N**	84	333	4.0	65	0
1979			28	86	3.1	10	1
1980			30	130	4.3	24	0
Career			142	549	3.9	65	1

Floyd Turner

Year	Team		Att	Yds	Avg	Lg	TD
1989	**NO**	**N**	2	8	4.0	6	0
1994	**IND**	**N**	3	-3	-1.0	5	0
1996	**BAL**	**N**	2	12	6.0	6	0
Career			7	17	2.4	6	0

Jay Turner

Year	Team		Att	Yds	Avg	Lg	TD
1938	**WAS**	**N**	5	25	5.0		0
1939			2	1	0.5		0
Career			7	26	3.7		0

Jim Turner

Year	Team		Att	Yds	Avg	Lg	TD
1964	**NY**	**A**	1	3	3.0	3	0
1970	**NYJ**	**N**	1	1	1.0	1	0
Career			2	4	2.0	3	0

Kevin Turner

Year	Team		Att	Yds	Avg	Lg	TD
1992	**NE**	**N**	10	40	4.0	11	0
1993			50	231	4.6	49	0
1994			36	111	3.1	13	1
1995	**PHI**	**N**	2	9	4.5	12	0
1996			18	39	2.2	7	0
Career			116	430	3.7	49	1
Playoffs			4	8	2.0		0

Nate Turner

Year	Team		Att	Yds	Avg	Lg	TD
1993	**BUF**	**N**	11	36	3.3	10	0
1994			2	4	2.0	4	0
Career			13	40	3.1	10	0

Odessa Turner

Year	Team		Att	Yds	Avg	Lg	TD
1989	**NYG**	**N**	2	11	5.5	14	0

Ricky Turner

Year	Team		Att	Yds	Avg	Lg	TD
1988	**IND**	**N**	16	42	2.6	14	2

Vernon Turner

Year	Team		Att	Yds	Avg	Lg	TD
1991	**LARM**	**N**	7	44	6.3	11	0
1992			2	14	7.0	9	0
1994	**TB**	**N**	4	13	3.3	9	0
Career			13	71	5.5	11	0

Rick Tuten

Year	Team		Att	Yds	Avg	Lg	TD
1992	**SEA**	**N**	1	0	0.0	0	0

Pete Tyler

Year	Team		Att	Yds	Avg	Lg	TD
1937	**CHIC**	**N**	5	-5	-1.0		0
1938			1	1	1.0	1	0
Career			6	-4	-0.7	1	0

Toussaint Tyler

Year	Team		Att	Yds	Avg	Lg	TD
1981	**NO**	**N**	36	183	5.1	42	0
1982			10	21	2.1	11	0
Career			46	204	4.4	42	0

Wendell Tyler

Year	Team		Att	Yds	Avg	Lg	TD
1977	**LA**	**N**	61	317	5.2	44t	3
1978			14	45	3.2	18	0
1979			218	1109	**5.1**	63t	9
1980			30	157	5.2	17	0
1981			260	1074	4.1	69t	12
1982	**LARM**	**N**	137	564	4.1	54	9
1983	**SF**	**N**	176	856	4.9	39	4
1984			246	1262	5.1	40	7
1985			171	867	5.1	30	6
1986			31	127	4.1	14	0
Career			1344	6378	4.7	69t	50
Playoffs			137	575	4.2		2

Layne Tynes

Year	Team		Att	Yds	Avg	Lg	TD
1924	**COL**	**N**					1
1925							1
Career							2

Tim Tyrrell

Year	Team		Att	Yds	Avg	Lg	TD
1987	**LARM**	**N**	11	44	4.0	13	0
1989	**PIT**	**N**	1	3	3.0	3	0
Career			12	47	3.9	13	0

Eddie Ulinski

Year	Team		Att	Yds	Avg	Lg	TD
1946	**CLE**	**AA**	1	2	2.0	2	0

Johnny Unitas

Year	Team		Att	Yds	Avg	Lg	TD
1956	**BAL**	**N**	28	155	5.5	34	1
1957			42	171	4.1	24	1
1958			33	139	4.2	28	3
1959			29	145	5.0	21	2
1960			36	195	5.4	27	0
1961			54	190	3.5	18	2
1962			50	137	2.7	25	0
1963			47	224	4.8	26	0
1964			37	162	4.4	20	2
1965			17	68	4.0	18t	1
1966			20	44	2.2	16	1
1967			22	89	4.0	13	0
1968			3	-1	-0.3	5	0
1969			11	23	2.1	13	0
1970			9	16	1.8	9	0
1971			9	5	0.6	3	0
1972			3	15	5.0	8	0
Career			450	1777	3.9	34	13
Playoffs			19	98	5.2		1

Rick Upchurch

Year	Team		Att	Yds	Avg	Lg	TD
1975	**DEN**	**N**	16	97	6.1	15	1
1976			6	71	11.8	25	1
1977			1	19	19.0	19t	1
1978			5	31	6.2	11	0
1979			3	17	5.7	18	0
1980			5	49	9.8	21	0
1981			5	56	11.2	37	0
1982			2	-10	-5.0	-3	0
1983			6	19	3.2	9	0
Career			49	349	7.1	37	3
Playoffs			1	3	3.0		0

Andy Uram

Year	Team		Att	Yds	Avg	Lg	TD
1938	**GB**	**N**	28	145	5.2		2
1939			52	272	5.2		1
1940			71	270	3.8		1

Year	Team		Att	Yds	Avg	Lg	TD

Andy Uram *continued*

Year	Team		Att	Yds	Avg	Lg	TD
1941			49	258	5.3	61	0
1942			24	75	3.1	8	0
1943			15	53	3.5	9	0
Career			239	1073	4.5	61	4
Playoffs			12	37	3.1		0

Alex Urban

1944	GB	N	1	2	2.0	2	0

Rube Ursella

1920	RI	A					1

Eddie Usher

1922	RI-GB	N					2

Sam Vacanti

1947	CHI	AA	11	-9	-0.8		1
1948			7	7	1.0		2
1949	BAL	AA	7	10	1.4		0
Career			25	8	0.3		3

Ira Valentine

1987	HOU	N	5	10	2.0	4	0

Norm Van Brocklin

1949	LA	N	4	-1	-0.3	2	0
1950			15	22	1.5	16	1
1951			7	2	0.3	4	2
1952			7	-10	-1.4	9	0
1953			8	11	1.4	6	0
1954			6	-10	-1.7	5	0
1955			11	24	2.2	9	0
1956			4	1	0.3	1t	1
1957			10	-4	-0.4	3	4
1958	PHI	N	8	5	0.6	2	1
1959			11	13	1.2	12	0
1960			11	-13	-1.2	1	0
Career			102	40	0.4	16	11
Playoffs			5	-10	-2.0		0

Ebert Van Buren

1951	PHI	N	16	60	3.8	11	0
1952			7	1	0.1	6	0
Career			23	61	2.7	11	0

Steve Van Buren

1944	PHI	N	80	444	5.5	70t	5
1945			143	832	5.8	69t	15
1946			116	529	4.6	58	5
1947			217	1008	4.6	45	13
1948			201	945	4.7	29	10
1949			263	1146	4.4	41	11
1950			188	629	3.3	41	4
1951			112	327	2.9	17	6
Career			1320	5860	4.4	70t	69
Playoffs			93	365	3.9		2

Joe Vance

1931	BKN	N					2

Ron Vander Kelen

1963	MIN	N	8	65	8.1	20	0
1964			1	10	10.0	10	0
1965			4	13	3.3	20	0
1966			4	19	4.8	15	0
1967			9	9	1.0	16	1
Career			26	116	4.5	20	1

Jimmy Van Dyke

1922	LOU	N					1

Mark van Eeghen

1974	OAK	N	28	139	5.0	17	0
1975			136	597	4.4	22	2
1976			233	1012	4.3	21	3
1977			324	1273	3.9	27	7
1978			270	1080	4.0	34	9
1979			223	818	3.7	19	7
1980			222	838	3.8	34	5
1981			39	150	3.8	11	2
1982	NE	N	82	386	4.7	17	0

Mark van Eeghen *continued*

1983			95	358	3.8	11	2
Career			1652	6651	4.0	34	37
Playoffs			172	619	3.6		4

Hal Van Every

1940	GB	N	38	154	4.1		0
1941			25	127	5.1	31	2
Career			63	281	4.5	31	2
Playoffs			6	6	1.0		0

Tim Van Galder

1972	STL	N	9	28	3.1	16	0

Billy Van Heusen

1968	DEN	A	1	6	6.0	6	0
1971	DEN	N	1	10	10.0	10	0
1972			3	76	25.3	66t	1
1973			4	34	8.5	32	0
1974			1	-1	-1.0	-1	0
1975			2	26	13.0	24	0
1976			1	20	20.0	20	0
Career			13	171	13.2	66t	1

Tamarick Vanover

1995	KC	N	6	31	5.2	13	0
1996			4	6	1.5	6	0
Career			10	37	3.7	13	0

Alex Van Pelt

1996	BUF	N	3	-5	-1.7	-1	0
Playoffs			2	8	4.0		0

Jeff Van Raaphorst

1987	ATL	N	1	6	6.0	6	0

Art Van Tone

1943	DET	N	2	1	0.5	2	0
1944			25	30	1.2	26	1
1945			3	14	4.7	7	0
1946	BKN	AA	4	10	2.5		0
Career			34	55	1.6	26	1

Pete Van Valkenberg

1973	BUF	N	2	20	10.0	12	0

Fred Vanzo

1939	DET	N	5	46	9.2		0
1940			1	-1	-1.0	-1	0
Career			6	45	7.5	-1	0

Mike Varajon

1987	SF	N	18	82	4.6	11	0

Tommy Vardell

1992	CLE	N	99	369	3.7	35	0
1993			171	644	3.8	54	3
1994			15	48	3.2	9	0
1995			4	9	2.3	6	0
1996	SF	N	58	192	3.3	17	2
Career			347	1262	3.6	54	5
Playoffs			2	6	3.0		0

Johnny Vardian

1946	MIA	AA	5	-8	-1.6		0
1947	BAL	AA	35	57	1.6		0
1948			6	13	2.2		0
Career			46	62	1.3		0

Frank Varrichione

1956	PIT	N	0	-2		-2L	0

Randy Vataha

1973	NE	N	2	-15	-7.5	-4	0
1974			3	21	7.0	24	0
1975			1	4	4.0	4	0
Career			6	10	1.7	24	0

Harp Vaughan

1933	PIT	N					1

Pug Vaughan

1935	DET	N	13	51	3.9		0

Pug Vaughan *continued*

1936	CHIC	N	67	79	1.2		0
Career			80	130	1.6		0

Jon Vaughn

1991	NE	N	31	146	4.7	23	2
1992			113	451	4.0	36	1
1993	SEA	N	36	153	4.3	37	0
1994			27	96	3.6	16	1
Career			207	846	4.1	37	4

Elton Veals

1984	PIT	N	31	87	2.8	9	0
Playoffs			1	1	1.0		0

Sam Venuto

1952	WAS	N	4	16	4.0	6	1

Clarence Verdin

1987	WAS	N	1	14	14.0	14	0
1988	IND	N	8	77	9.6	44	0
1989			4	39	9.8	26	0
1991			1	4	4.0	4	0
1993			3	33	11.0	29	0
Career			17	167	9.8	44	0

Ed Vereb

1960	WAS	N	19	38	2.0	15	0

David Verser

1981	CIN	N	2	11	5.5	9	0
1982			1	1	1.0	1	0
1983			2	31	15.5	29	0
1984			2	5	2.5	3	0
1987	CLE	N	1	9	9.0	9	0
Career			8	57	7.1	29	0

Billy Vessels

1956	BAL	N	44	215	4.9	31	2

Joe Vetrano

1946	SF	AA	23	69	3.0		1
1947			10	11	1.1		0
1948			12	71	5.9		1
1949			11	50	4.5		0
Career			56	201	3.6		2

Jack Vetter

1942	BKN	N	1	4	4.0		0

Roger Vick

1987	NYJ	N	77	257	3.3	14	0
1988			128	540	4.2	17	3
1989			112	434	3.9	39t	5
1990	PHI	N	16	58	3.6	17	1
Career			333	1289	3.9	39t	10

Tommy Vigorito

1981	MIA	N	35	116	3.3	30t	1
1982			19	99	5.2	33t	1
Career			54	215	4.0	33t	2
Playoffs			4	17	4.3		0

Danny Villanueva

1966	DAL	N	1	23	23.0	23	0
1967			1	-15	-15.0	-15	0
Career			2	8	4.0	23	0

Paul Vinnola

1946	LA	AA	23	36	1.6		0

Lionel Vital

1987	WAS	N	80	346	4.3	22t	2

Mark Vlasic

1988	SD	N	2	0	0.0	0	0
1990			1	0	0.0	0	0
1991	KC	N	1	-1	-1.0	-1	0
Career			4	-1	-0.3	0	0

Joe Vodicka

1945	CHIC	N	3	-1	-0.3	3	0
Playoffs			1	3	3.0		0

Year	Team		Att	Yds	Avg	Lg	TD

Mike Voight
| 1977 | HOU | N | 7 | 20 | 2.9 | 6 | 0 |

Stu Voigt
1972	MIN	N	1	1	1.0	1t	1
1973			1	2	2.0	2	0
Career			2	3	1.5	2	1

Otto Vokaty
| 1931 | CLE | N | | | | | 4 |

Jim Vollenweider
1962	SF	N	11	37	3.4	10	0
1963			47	124	2.6	12	2
Career			58	161	2.8	12	2

Wilbur Volz
| 1949 | BUF | AA | 4 | 7 | 1.8 | | 1 |

Tillie Voss
| 1923 | TOL | N | | | | | 1 |

Billy Waddy
1977	LA	N	2	34	17.0	30	0
1978			5	31	6.2	11	0
1980			1	-1	-1.0	-1	0
1982	LARM	N	2	-11	-5.5	5	0
1984	MIN	N	3	24	8.0	11	0
Career			13	77	5.9	30	0
Playoffs			3	5	1.7		0

Billy Wade
1954	LA	N	28	190	6.8	35	1
1955			11	43	3.9	14	0
1956			26	93	3.6	33	3
1957			1	5	5.0	5	0
1958			42	90	2.1	22	2
1959			25	95	3.8	17	2
1960			26	171	6.6	66t	2
1961	CHI	N	45	255	5.7	29	2
1962			40	146	3.6	21	5
1963			45	132	2.9	17	6
1964			24	96	4.0	31	1
1965			5	18	3.6	16	0
Career			318	1334	4.2	66t	24
Playoffs			9	38	4.2		2

Charlie Wade
| 1974 | CHI | N | 1 | -15 | -15.0 | -15 | 0 |

Jim Wade
| 1949 | NYB | N | 9 | 23 | 2.6 | 6 | 0 |

Tommy Wade
| 1965 | PIT | N | 8 | 43 | 5.4 | 41 | 0 |

Harmon Wages
1968	ATL	N	59	211	3.6	31	0
1969			72	375	5.2	66t	2
1970			119	422	3.5	40	1
1971			64	266	4.2	27	1
1973			18	47	2.6	13	1
Career			332	1321	4.0	66t	5

Bryan Wagner
| 1988 | CHI | N | 2 | 0 | 0.0 | 0 | 0 |

Lowell Wagner
1946	NY	AA	15	29	1.9		0
1949	SF	AA	3	17	5.7		0
1950	SF	N	2	5	2.5	3	0
1953			1	4	4.0	4	0
Career			21	55	2.6	4	0
Playoffs			3	17	5.7		0

Steve Wagner
| 1979 | GB | N | 1 | 16 | 16.0 | 16 | 0 |

Carl Waite
| 1929 | ORA | N | | | | | 1 |

Bobby Walden
| 1964 | MIN | N | 1 | 18 | 18.0 | 18 | 0 |
| 1966 | | | 5 | 82 | 16.4 | 45 | 0 |

Bobby Walden *continued*
1968	PIT	N	2	5	2.5	5	0
1971			1	14	14.0	14	0
1973			1	0	0.0	0	0
1976			3	7	2.3	7	0
1977			1	0	0.0	0	0
Career			14	126	9.0	45	0

Adam Walker
| 1987 | MIN | N | 5 | 24 | 4.8 | 11 | 0 |

Adam Walker
1993	SF	N	5	17	3.4	11	0
1994			13	54	4.2	14	1
1995			14	44	3.1	16	1
Career			32	115	3.6	16	2
Playoffs			3	3	1.0		1

Clarence Walker
| 1963 | DEN | A | 2 | 14 | 7.0 | 9 | 0 |

Doak Walker
1950	DET	N	83	386	4.7	30t	5
1951			79	356	4.5	34	2
1952			26	106	4.1	20	0
1953			66	337	5.1	50t	2
1954			32	240	7.5	31	1
1955			23	95	4.1	51	2
Career			309	1520	4.9	51	12
Playoffs			23	146	6.3		2

Dwight Walker
1983	CLE	N	19	100	5.3	15	0
1984			1	-8	-8.0	-8	0
Career			20	92	4.6	15	0

Herschel Walker
1986	DAL	N	151	737	4.9	84t	12
1987			209	891	4.3	60t	7
1988			361	1514	4.2	38	5
1989	DAL-MIN	N	250	915	3.7	47	7
1990	MIN	N	184	770	4.2	58t	5
1991			198	825	4.2	71t	10
1992	PHI	N	267	1070	4.0	38	8
1993			174	746	4.3	35	1
1994			113	528	4.7	91t	5
1995	NYG	N	31	126	4.1	36	0
1996	DAL	N	10	83	8.3	39t	1
Career			1948	8205	4.2	91t	61
Playoffs			28	132	4.7		0

Randy Walker
| 1974 | GB | N | 1 | 18 | 18.0 | 18 | 0 |

Rick Walker
1980	WAS	N	1	-8	-8.0	-8	0
1981			1	5	5.0	5	0
1982			2	11	5.5	6	0
1983			2	10	5.0	11	0
1984			1	2	2.0	2	0
1985			3	16	5.3	9	0
Career			10	36	3.6	11	0
Playoffs			3	20	6.7		0

Wayne Walker
| 1989 | SD | N | 1 | 9 | 9.0 | 9 | 0 |

Wesley Walker
1977	NYJ	N	3	25	8.3	11	0
1978			1	-3	-3.0	-3	0
1984			1	1	1.0	1	0
1988			1	12	12.0	12	0
Career			6	35	5.8	12	0

Willie Walker
| 1966 | DET | N | 1 | 4 | 4.0 | 4 | 0 |

Beverly Wallace
1948	SF	AA	3	2	0.7		0
1949			2	2	1.0		1
1951	NYY	N	1	-8	-8.0	-8	0
Career			6	-4	-0.7	-8	1

Bob Wallace
1968	CHI	N	3	29	9.7	18	0
1969			4	16	4.0	15	0
1971			1	0	0.0	0	0
Career			8	45	5.6	18	0

Ray Wallace
1986	HOU	N	52	218	4.2	19	3
1987			19	102	5.4	19	0
1989	PIT	N	5	10	2.0	5	1
Career			76	330	4.3	19	4
Playoffs			2	11	5.5		0

Ron Waller
1955	LA	N	151	716	4.7	55t	7
1956			83	543	6.5	46	1
1957			48	292	6.1	76	0
1958			3	13	4.3	2	0
1960	LA	A	9	5	0.6		0
Career			294	1569	5.3	76	8
Playoffs			11	48	4.4		1

Herkie Walls
1983	HOU	N	5	44	8.8	14	0
1984			4	20	5.0	20	0
Career			9	64	7.1	20	0

Laurie Walquist
1924	CHIB	N					1
1925							2
1926							1
1928							2
1929							3
Career							9

Jimmy Walsh
| 1980 | SEA | N | 2 | 4 | 2.0 | 2 | 0 |

Steve Walsh
1989	DAL	N	6	16	2.7	14	0
1990	DAL-NO	N	20	25	1.3	18	0
1991	NO	N	8	0	0.0	3	0
1993			4	-4	-1.0	-1	0
1994	CHI	N	30	4	0.1	12	1
1996	STL	N	6	10	1.7	13	0
Career			74	51	0.7	18	1
Playoffs			6	5	0.8		0

Ward Walsh
1971	HOU	N	38	129	3.4	19	0
1972			8	36	4.5	14	0
Career			46	165	3.6	19	0

Bobby Walston
1955	PHI	N	1	-3	-3.0	-3	0
1957			1	7	7.0	7	0
1959			2	8	4.0	7	0
Career			4	12	3.0	7	0

Dave Walter
| 1987 | CIN | N | 16 | 70 | 4.4 | 16 | 0 |

Chuck Walton
| 1969 | DET | N | 2 | 6 | 3.0 | 17 | 0 |

Johnnie Walton
1976	PHI	N	2	1	0.5	1	0
1978			2	0	0.0	0	0
1979			6	-5	-0.8	2	0
Career			10	-4	-0.4	2	0

Larry Walton
1970	DET	N	2	20	10.0	16	0
1971			1	-7	-7.0	-7	0
1973			5	100	20.0	57t	1
1974			2	3	1.5	10	0
1976			1	5	5.0	5	0
Career			11	121	11.0	57t	1
Playoffs			1	5	5.0		0

Jim Ward
| 1967 | BAL | N | 5 | 23 | 4.6 | 8 | 0 |

Andre Ware

Year	Team		Att	Yds	Avg	Lg	TD
1990	DET	N	7	64	9.1	30	0
1991			4	6	1.5	10	0
1992			20	124	6.2	32	0
1993			7	23	3.3	8	0
Career			38	217	5.7	32	0
Playoffs			3	23	7.7		0

Paul Warfield

Year	Team		Att	Yds	Avg	Lg	TD
1967	CLE	N	2	10	5.0	18	0
1969			2	23	11.5	16	0
1970	MIA	N	2	13	6.5	16	0
1971			9	115	12.8	39	0
1972			4	23	5.8	21	0
1973			1	15	15.0	15	0
1976	CLE	N	1	3	3.0	3	0
1977			1	2	2.0	2	0
Career			22	204	9.3	39	0
Playoffs			5	31	6.2		0

Charley Warner

Year	Team		Att	Yds	Avg	Lg	TD
1965	BUF	A	1	2	2.0	2	0

Curt Warner

Year	Team		Att	Yds	Avg	Lg	TD
1983	SEA	N	335	1449	4.3	60	13
1984			10	40	4.0	9	0
1985			291	1094	3.8	38	8
1986			319	1481	4.6	60t	13
1987			234	985	4.2	57t	8
1988			266	1025	3.9	29	10
1989			194	631	3.3	34	3
1990	LARM	N	49	139	2.8	9	1
Career			1698	6844	4.0	60t	56
Playoffs			71	249	3.5		2

Buist Warren

Year	Team		Att	Yds	Avg	Lg	TD
1945	PHI-PIT	N	96	285	3.0	75t	2

Chris Warren

Year	Team		Att	Yds	Avg	Lg	TD
1990	SEA	N	6	11	1.8	4	1
1991			11	13	1.2	7	0
1992			223	1017	4.6	52	3
1993			273	1072	3.9	45t	7
1994			333	1545	4.6	41	9
1995			310	1346	4.3	52	15
1996			203	855	4.2	51	5
Career			1359	5859	4.3	52	40

Dewey Warren

Year	Team		Att	Yds	Avg	Lg	TD
1968	CIN	A	4	17	4.3	12	0

Don Warren

Year	Team		Att	Yds	Avg	Lg	TD
1985	WAS	N	1	5	5.0	5	0

Lamont Warren

Year	Team		Att	Yds	Avg	Lg	TD
1994	IND	N	18	80	4.4	34	0
1995			47	152	3.2	42	1
1996			67	230	3.4	53	1
Career			132	462	3.5	53	2
Playoffs			46	133	2.9		0

Morrie Warren

Year	Team		Att	Yds	Avg	Lg	TD
1948	BKN	AA	1	1	1.0	1	0

Terrence Warren

Year	Team		Att	Yds	Avg	Lg	TD
1994	SEA	N	3	15	5.0	11	0

Clyde Washington

Year	Team		Att	Yds	Avg	Lg	TD
1960	BOS	A	2	10	5.0	3	0
1961			1	3	3.0	3	0
Career			3	13	4.3	3	0

Gene Washington

Year	Team		Att	Yds	Avg	Lg	TD
1969	SF	N	1	-4	-4.0	-4	0
1974			2	4	2.0	7	0
1975			1	-4	-4.0	-4	0
1976			1	3	3.0	3	0
1979	DET	N	1	24	24.0	24	0
Career			6	23	3.8	24	0

Joe Washington

Year	Team		Att	Yds	Avg	Lg	TD
1973	ATL	N	4	36	9.0	16	0

Joe Washington

Year	Team		Att	Yds	Avg	Lg	TD
1977	SD	N	62	217	3.5	19	0
1978	BAL	N	240	956	4.0	29	0
1979			242	884	3.7	26	4
1980			144	502	3.5	17	1
1981	WAS	N	210	916	4.4	32	4
1982			44	190	4.3	40	1
1983			145	772	5.3	41	0
1984			56	192	3.4	12	1
1985	ATL	N	52	210	4.0	14	1
Career			1195	4839	4.0	41	12
Playoffs			19	56	2.9		0

Kenny Washington

Year	Team		Att	Yds	Avg	Lg	TD
1946	LA	N	23	114	5.0	19	1
1947			60	444	7.4	92t	5
1948			57	301	5.3	31t	2
Career			140	859	6.1	92t	8

Teddy Washington

Year	Team		Att	Yds	Avg	Lg	TD
1968	CIN	A	1	4	4.0	4	0

Vic Washington

Year	Team		Att	Yds	Avg	Lg	TD
1971	SF	N	191	811	4.2	42	3
1972			141	468	3.3	33	3
1973			151	534	3.5	25	8
1974	HOU	N	74	281	3.8	23	2
1975	BUF	N	9	49	5.4	9	0
1976			22	65	3.0	10	0
Career			588	2208	3.8	42	16
Playoffs			36	173	4.8		0

Bob Waterfield

Year	Team		Att	Yds	Avg	Lg	TD
1945	CLE	N	18	18	1.0	16t	5
1946	LA	N	16	-60	-3.8	6	1
1947			3	6	2.0	4	1
1948			7	12	1.7	10	0
1949			5	-4	-0.8	5	1
1950			8	14	1.8	13t	1
1951			9	49	5.4	25	3
1952			9	-14	-1.6	19t	1
Career			75	21	0.3	25	13
Playoffs			10	14	1.4		0

Bobby Waters

Year	Team		Att	Yds	Avg	Lg	TD
1960	SF	N	1	8	8.0	8	0
1961			47	233	5.0	35	3
1962			12	42	3.5	14	0
1963			5	-2	-0.4	8	0
Career			65	281	4.3	35	3

Charlie Waters

Year	Team		Att	Yds	Avg	Lg	TD
1974	DAL	N	1	6	6.0	6	0

Mike Waters

Year	Team		Att	Yds	Avg	Lg	TD
1986	PHI	N	5	8	1.6	5	0

Bobby Watkins

Year	Team		Att	Yds	Avg	Lg	TD
1955	CHIB	N	110	553	5.0	33	8
1956			68	276	4.1	25	2
1957			57	212	3.7	19	1
1958	CHIC	N	3	17	5.7	9	0
Career			238	1058	4.4	33	11
Playoffs			3	9	3.0		0

Foster Watkins

Year	Team		Att	Yds	Avg	Lg	TD
1940	PHI	N	14	-76	-5.4		0
1941			15	11	0.7	8	0
Career			29	-65	-2.2	8	0

Larry Watkins

Year	Team		Att	Yds	Avg	Lg	TD
1969	DET	N	62	201	3.2	12	1
1970	PHI	N	32	96	3.0	11	1
1971			35	98	2.8	11t	1
1972			67	262	3.9	28	1
1973	BUF	N	98	414	4.2	17	2
1974			41	170	4.1	13	2
1975	NYG	N	68	303	4.5	12	3
1976			26	96	3.7	13	1
1977			19	71	3.7	9	0
Career			448	1711	3.8	28	12

Tommy Watkins

Year	Team		Att	Yds	Avg	Lg	TD
1961	CLE	N	43	209	4.9	21	0

Tommy Watkins *continued*

Year	Team		Att	Yds	Avg	Lg	TD
1962	DET	N	113	485	4.3	60	3
1963			97	423	4.4	32	2
1964			80	218	2.7	15	1
1965			29	95	3.3	12	0
1967			106	361	3.4	28	4
Career			468	1791	3.8	60	10

Sid Watson

Year	Team		Att	Yds	Avg	Lg	TD
1955	PIT	N	29	31	1.1	15	0
1956			112	298	2.7	18	4
1957			12	21	1.8	12	0
1958	WAS	N	46	166	3.6	23	0
Career			199	516	2.6	23	4

Steve Watson

Year	Team		Att	Yds	Avg	Lg	TD
1981	DEN	N	2	6	3.0	6	0
1982			1	-4	-4.0	-4	0
1983			3	17	5.7	10	0
Career			6	19	3.2	10	0
Playoffs			2	-2	-1.0		0

Joe Watt

Year	Team		Att	Yds	Avg	Lg	TD
1947	DET	N	11	7	0.6	7	0
1948			20	54	2.7	10	0
Career			31	61	2.0	10	0

Walt Watt

Year	Team		Att	Yds	Avg	Lg	TD
1945	CHIC	N	6	7	1.2	4	0

Frank Wattelet

Year	Team		Att	Yds	Avg	Lg	TD
1985	NO	N	2	42	21.0	23	0

Ricky Watters

Year	Team		Att	Yds	Avg	Lg	TD
1992	SF	N	206	1013	4.9	43	9
1993			208	950	4.6	39	10
1994			239	877	3.7	23	6
1995	PHI	N	337	1273	3.8	57	11
1996			353	1411	4.0	56t	13
Career			1343	5524	4.1	57	49
Playoffs			156	626	4.0		8

Rickey Watts

Year	Team		Att	Yds	Avg	Lg	TD
1979	CHI	N	1	-6	-6.0	-6	0
1980			1	-16	-16.0	-16	0
1982			1	-1	-1.0	-1	0
Career			3	-23	-7.7	-1	0

Charles Way

Year	Team		Att	Yds	Avg	Lg	TD
1995	NYG	N	2	6	3.0	6	0
1996			22	79	3.6	18	1
Career			24	85	3.5	18	1

Charlie Way

Year	Team		Att	Yds	Avg	Lg	TD
1924	FRA	N					4
1926	PHI	A					1
Career							5

Clarence Weathers

Year	Team		Att	Yds	Avg	Lg	TD
1983	NE	N	1	28	28.0	28	0
1985	CLE	N	1	18	18.0	18	0
Career			2	46	23.0	28	0

Robert Weathers

Year	Team		Att	Yds	Avg	Lg	TD
1982	NE	N	24	83	3.5	18	1
1983			73	418	5.7	77	1
1985			41	174	4.2	42t	1
1986			21	58	2.8	16t	1
Career			159	733	4.6	77	4
Playoffs			26	108	4.2		0

Herman Weaver

Year	Team		Att	Yds	Avg	Lg	TD
1973	DET	N	1	18	18.0	18	0
1976			1	0	0.0	0	0
1977	SEA	N	1	-2	-2.0	-2	0
1978			2	-5	-2.5	0	0
1979			2	-6	-3.0	0	0
Career			7	5	0.7	18	0

Larrye Weaver

Year	Team		Att	Yds	Avg	Lg	TD
1955	NYG	N	3	0	0.0	2	0

Allan Webb

Year	Team		Att	Yds	Avg	Lg	TD
1961	NYG	N	6	51	8.5	21	0

Year	Team		Att	Yds	Avg	Lg	TD

Ken Webb

Year	Team		Att	Yds	Avg	Lg	TD
1958	DET	N	56	172	3.1	22	2
1959			60	222	3.7	29	2
1960			59	166	2.8	17	2
1961			7	6	0.9	3	1
1962			70	267	3.8	25	1
1963	CLE	N	12	58	4.8	19	0
Career			264	891	3.4	29	8

Dick Weber

Year	Team		Att	Yds	Avg	Lg	TD
1945	DET	N	7	10	1.4	7	0

Alex Webster

Year	Team		Att	Yds	Avg	Lg	TD
1955	NYG	N	128	634	5.0	71	5
1956			178	694	3.9	34t	7
1957			135	478	3.5	34	5
1958			100	398	4.0	54	3
1959			79	250	3.2	16t	5
1960			22	48	2.2	10	0
1961			196	928	4.7	59	2
1962			207	743	3.6	55	5
1963			75	255	3.4	12	4
1964			76	210	2.8	14	3
Career			1196	4638	3.9	71	39
Playoffs			69	220	3.2		2

Herman Wedemeyer

Year	Team		Att	Yds	Avg	Lg	TD
1948	LA	AA	79	249	3.2		0
1949	BAL	AA	64	291	4.5		0
Career			143	540	3.8		0

Norris Weese

Year	Team		Att	Yds	Avg	Lg	TD
1976	DEN	N	23	142	6.2	20	0
1977			11	56	5.1	21	1
1978			17	48	2.8	8	1
1979			18	116	6.4	20	3
Career			69	362	5.2	21	5
Playoffs			7	69	9.9		0

Ted Wegert

Year	Team		Att	Yds	Avg	Lg	TD
1955	PHI	N	26	120	4.6	38	2
1956			47	127	2.7	19	1
1960	NY-BUF	A	36	161	4.5		1
Career			109	408	3.7	38	4

Roger Wehrli

Year	Team		Att	Yds	Avg	Lg	TD
1976	STL	N	2	8	4.0	8	0
1977			1	19	19.0	19	0
1978			1	0	0.0	0	0
1982			1	18	18.0	18t	1
Career			5	45	9.0	19	1

Lee Weigel

Year	Team		Att	Yds	Avg	Lg	TD
1987	GB	N	10	26	2.6	7	0

Chuck Weimer

Year	Team		Att	Yds	Avg	Lg	TD
1929	BUF	N					1

Izzy Weinstock

Year	Team		Att	Yds	Avg	Lg	TD
1935	PHI	N	58	176	3.0		0
1937	PIT	N	33	88	2.7		0
1938			1	0	0.0	0	0
Career			92	264	2.9	0	0

Heinie Weisenbaugh

Year	Team		Att	Yds	Avg	Lg	TD
1935	PIT-BOS	N	36	50	1.4		0
1936	BOS	N	3	9	3.0		0
Career			39	59	1.5		0

Dick Weisgerber

Year	Team		Att	Yds	Avg	Lg	TD
1938	GB	N	6	13	2.2		0
1942			5	21	4.2	6	0
Career			11	34	3.1	6	0

Howie Weiss

Year	Team		Att	Yds	Avg	Lg	TD
1939	DET	N	37	150	4.1		0
1940			79	298	3.8		3
Career			116	448	3.9		3

Claxton Welch

Year	Team		Att	Yds	Avg	Lg	TD
1969	DAL	N	6	21	3.5	6	0
1970			5	13	2.6	5t	1
1971			14	51	3.6	14	1

Claxton Welch continued

Year	Team		Att	Yds	Avg	Lg	TD
1973	NE	N	1	-2	-2.0	-2	0
Career			26	83	3.2	14	2
Playoffs			5	27	5.4		0

Gibby Welch

Year	Team		Att	Yds	Avg	Lg	TD
1929	PRO	N					2

Jim Welch

Year	Team		Att	Yds	Avg	Lg	TD
1960	BAL	N	5	23	4.6	7	0
1961			1	60	60.0	60t	1
1967			2	6	3.0	4	0
1968	DET	N	3	14	4.7	11	0
Career			11	103	9.4	60t	1

Casey Weldon

Year	Team		Att	Yds	Avg	Lg	TD
1995	TB	N	5	5	1.0	6	1
1996			2	-1	-0.5	0	0
Career			7	4	0.6	6	1

John Weldon

Year	Team		Att	Yds	Avg	Lg	TD
1920	BUF	A					1

Larry Weldon

Year	Team		Att	Yds	Avg	Lg	TD
1944	WAS	N	8	8	1.0	24	0

Louis Weller

Year	Team		Att	Yds	Avg	Lg	TD
1933	BOS	N					2

Gary Wellman

Year	Team		Att	Yds	Avg	Lg	TD
1993	HOU	N	2	6	3.0	4	0
1994			1	-3	-3.0	-3	0
Career			3	3	1.0	4	0

Billy Wells

Year	Team		Att	Yds	Avg	Lg	TD
1954	WAS	N	100	516	5.2	88t	3
1956			69	185	2.7	17	1
1957	PIT	N	154	532	3.5	51	0
1958	PHI	N	24	92	3.8	12	1
1960	BOS	A	14	59	4.2		0
Career			361	1384	3.8	88t	5

Joel Wells

Year	Team		Att	Yds	Avg	Lg	TD
1961	NYG	N	65	216	3.3	17	1
Playoffs			3	9	3.0		0

Terence Wells

Year	Team		Att	Yds	Avg	Lg	TD
1975	GB	N	33	139	4.2	25	0

Warren Wells

Year	Team		Att	Yds	Avg	Lg	TD
1967	OAK	A	1	7	7.0	7	0
1968			2	38	19.0	41t	1
1969			3	24	8.0	17	0
1970	OAK	N	3	34	11.3	14	0
Career			9	103	11.4	41t	1

Doug Wellsandt

Year	Team		Att	Yds	Avg	Lg	TD
1990	NYJ	N	1	-3	-3.0	-3	0

Cy Wentworth

Year	Team		Att	Yds	Avg	Lg	TD
1925	PRO	N					2

Barney Wentz

Year	Team		Att	Yds	Avg	Lg	TD
1925	POT	N					5
1926							9
1927							2
Career							16

Ed West

Year	Team		Att	Yds	Avg	Lg	TD
1984	GB	N	1	2	2.0	2t	1
1985			1	0	0.0	0	0
Career			2	2	1.0	2t	1

Jeff West

Year	Team		Att	Yds	Avg	Lg	TD
1976	SD	N	1	0	0.0	0	0
1978			1	0	0.0	0	0
1979			1	-2	-2.0	-2	0
1981	SEA	N	3	25	8.3	27	0
Career			6	23	3.8	27	0

Mel West

Year	Team		Att	Yds	Avg	Lg	TD
1961	BOS-NY	A	72	322	4.5	35	3
1962	NY	A	9	16	1.8	7	0
Career			81	338	4.2	35	3

Pat West

Year	Team		Att	Yds	Avg	Lg	TD
1945	CLE	N	19	45	2.4	9	0
1946	LA	N	40	226	5.7	72	1
1947			42	162	3.9	21	2
1948	LA-GB	N	4	24	6.0	16	0
Career			105	457	4.4	72	3
Playoffs			3	17	5.7		0

Robert West

Year	Team		Att	Yds	Avg	Lg	TD
1972	KC	N	2	2	1.0	10	0

Walt West

Year	Team		Att	Yds	Avg	Lg	TD
1944	CLE	N	66	220	3.3	31	0

Willie West

Year	Team		Att	Yds	Avg	Lg	TD
1960	STL	N	7	45	6.4	14	0

Don Westbrook

Year	Team		Att	Yds	Avg	Lg	TD
1978	NE	N	1	-2	-2.0	-2	0
1979			2	8	4.0	4	0
Career			3	6	2.0	4	0

Michael Westbrook

Year	Team		Att	Yds	Avg	Lg	TD
1995	WAS	N	6	114	19.0	58t	1
1996			2	2	1.0	2	0
Career			8	116	14.5	58t	1

Cleve Wester

Year	Team		Att	Yds	Avg	Lg	TD
1987	DET	N	33	113	3.4	14	0

Bob Westfall

Year	Team		Att	Yds	Avg	Lg	TD
1944	DET	N	65	277	4.3	75t	3
1945			82	234	2.9	19	6
1946			28	54	1.9	9	1
1947			34	132	3.9	18	1
Career			209	697	3.3	75t	11

Ed Westfall

Year	Team		Att	Yds	Avg	Lg	TD
1933	PIT	N					1

Chet Wetterlund

Year	Team		Att	Yds	Avg	Lg	TD
1942	DET	N	23	6	0.3	12	0

Damon Wetzel

Year	Team		Att	Yds	Avg	Lg	TD
1935	CHIB-PIT	N	22	41	1.9		1

Jim Whalen

Year	Team		Att	Yds	Avg	Lg	TD
1968	BOS	A	1	0	0.0	0	0

Tyrone Wheatley

Year	Team		Att	Yds	Avg	Lg	TD
1995	NYG	N	78	245	3.1	19t	3
1996			112	400	3.6	37	1
Career			190	645	3.4	37	4

Ernie Wheeler

Year	Team		Att	Yds	Avg	Lg	TD
1939	PIT-CHIC	N	17	0	0.0		0

Manch Wheeler

Year	Team		Att	Yds	Avg	Lg	TD
1962	BUF	A	3	7	2.3	7	0

Ernie Wheelwright

Year	Team		Att	Yds	Avg	Lg	TD
1964	NYG	N	100	402	4.0	26	0
1965			24	96	4.0	16	0
1966	ATL	N	121	458	3.8	63	3
1967	ATL-NO	N	80	241	3.0	13	1
1968	NO	N	21	99	4.7	15	1
1969			25	85	3.4	17	4
1970			16	45	2.8	9	0
Career			387	1426	3.7	63	9

Ken Whisenhunt

Year	Team		Att	Yds	Avg	Lg	TD
1985	ATL	N	1	3	3.0	3	0
1986			1	20	20.0	20	0
Career			2	23	11.5	20	0

Bob White

Year	Team		Att	Yds	Avg	Lg	TD
1951	SF	N	8	33	4.1	9	0
1952			24	33	1.4	17	1
Career			32	66	2.1	17	1

Charles White

Year	Team		Att	Yds	Avg	Lg	TD
1980	CLE	N	86	279	3.2	16	5
1981			97	342	3.5	26	1
1982			69	259	3.8	18t	3

Year	Team		Att	Yds	Avg	Lg	TD

Charles White *continued*

Year	Team		Att	Yds	Avg	Lg	TD
1984			24	62	2.6	8	0
1985	LARM	N	70	310	4.4	32	3
1986			22	126	5.7	19	0
1987	NYJ		324	1374	4.2	58	11
1988			88	323	3.7	13	0
Career			780	3075	3.9	58	23
Playoffs			10	32	3.2		0

Charlie White

Year	Team		Att	Yds	Avg	Lg	TD
1977	NYJ	N	50	151	3.0	27	1
1978	TB	N	11	42	3.8	8	0
Career			61	193	3.2	27	1

Danny White

Year	Team		Att	Yds	Avg	Lg	TD
1976	DAL	N	6	17	2.8	14	0
1977			1	-2	-2.0	-2	0
1978			5	7	1.4	4	0
1979			1	25	25.0	25	0
1980			27	114	4.2	48	1
1981			38	104	2.7	17	0
1982			17	91	5.4	21	0
1983			18	31	1.7	7	4
1984			6	21	3.5	8	0
1985			22	44	2.0	21	1
1986			8	16	2.0	10	1
1987			10	14	1.4	8	1
Career			159	482	3.0	48	8
Playoffs			19	19	1.0		0

Gerald White

Year	Team		Att	Yds	Avg	Lg	TD
1987	DAL	N	1	-4	-4.0	-4	0

Harvey White

Year	Team		Att	Yds	Avg	Lg	TD
1960	BOS	A	5	7	1.4		0

Lee White

Year	Team		Att	Yds	Avg	Lg	TD
1969	NY	A	28	88	3.1	10	0
1970	NYJ	N	70	215	3.1	16	0
1971	LA	N	2	11	5.5	6	0
1972	SD	N	23	75	3.3	12	0
Career			123	389	3.2	16	0

Lorenzo White

Year	Team		Att	Yds	Avg	Lg	TD
1988	HOU	N	31	115	3.7	16	0
1989			104	349	3.4	33	5
1990			168	702	4.2	22	8
1991			110	465	4.2	20	4
1992			265	1226	4.6	44	7
1993			131	465	3.5	14	2
1994			191	757	4.0	33	3
1995	CLE	N	62	163	2.6	11	1
Career			1062	4242	4.0	44	30
Playoffs			76	264	3.5		1

Marsh White

Year	Team		Att	Yds	Avg	Lg	TD
1975	NYG	N	17	90	5.3	14	1
1976			69	223	3.2	29	1
Career			86	313	3.6	29	2

Paul White

Year	Team		Att	Yds	Avg	Lg	TD
1947	PIT	N	22	85	3.9	52t	0
Playoffs			1	5	5.0		0

Paul White

Year	Team		Att	Yds	Avg	Lg	TD
1971	STL	N	1	3	3.0	3	0

Phil White

Year	Team		Att	Yds	Avg	Lg	TD
1925	NY	N					3
1927	NYG	N					3
Career							6

Roy White

Year	Team		Att	Yds	Avg	Lg	TD
1925	CHIB	N					3
1926	CHI	A					1
1927	CHIB	N					2
1928							3
1929							2
Career							11

Russell White

Year	Team		Att	Yds	Avg	Lg	TD
1993	LARM	N	2	10	5.0	5	0

Sammy White

Year	Team		Att	Yds	Avg	Lg	TD
1976	MIN	N	5	-10	-2.0	6	0
1978			5	30	6.0	16	0
1979			1	6	6.0	6	0
1980			4	65	16.3	45	0
1981			2	-1	-0.5	1	0
1983			1	7	7.0	7	0
Career			18	97	5.4	45	0
Playoffs			3	-2	-0.7		0

Stan White

Year	Team		Att	Yds	Avg	Lg	TD
1979	BAL	N	1	3	3.0	3	0

Walter White

Year	Team		Att	Yds	Avg	Lg	TD
1975	KC	N	3	-10	-3.3	0	0
1976			2	15	7.5	8	0
1977			2	-3	-1.5	3	0
Career			7	2	0.3	8	0

Whizzer White

Year	Team		Att	Yds	Avg	Lg	TD
1938	PIT	N	152	567	3.7		4
1940	DET	N	146	514	3.5		5
1941			89	238	2.7	20	2
Career			387	1319	3.4	20	11

Wilbur White

Year	Team		Att	Yds	Avg	Lg	TD
1936	DET	N	8	21	2.6		0

Wilford White

Year	Team		Att	Yds	Avg	Lg	TD
1951	CHIB	N	9	86	9.6	38	1
1952			19	-19	-1.0	18	0
Career			28	67	2.4	38	1

Marv Whited

Year	Team		Att	Yds	Avg	Lg	TD
1942	WAS	N	1	3	3.0	3	0

David Whitehurst

Year	Team		Att	Yds	Avg	Lg	TD
1977	GB	N	14	55	3.9	19	1
1978			28	67	2.4	18	1
1979			18	73	4.1	17	4
1981			15	51	3.4	15	1
1983			2	-4	-2.0	0	0
Career			77	242	3.1	19	7

A.D. Whitfield

Year	Team		Att	Yds	Avg	Lg	TD
1965	DAL	N	1	0	0.0	0	0
1966	WAS	N	93	472	5.1	63t	2
1967			91	384	4.2	44	1
1968			37	125	3.4	17	0
Career			222	981	4.4	63t	3

Dave Whitsell

Year	Team		Att	Yds	Avg	Lg	TD
1963	CHI	N	1	-8	-8.0	-8	0
1964			1	14	14.0	14	0
1968	NO	N	1	-1	-1.0	-1	0
Career			3	5	1.7	14	0

Todd Whitten

Year	Team		Att	Yds	Avg	Lg	TD
1987	NE	N	2	-6	-3.0	-2	0

Arthur Whittington

Year	Team		Att	Yds	Avg	Lg	TD
1978	OAK	N	172	661	3.8	26t	7
1979			109	397	3.6	22	2
1980			91	299	3.3	42t	3
1981			69	220	3.2	13	1
1982	BUF	N	7	15	2.1	4	0
Career			448	1592	3.6	42t	13
Playoffs			14	15	1.1		0

Ricky Whittle

Year	Team		Att	Yds	Avg	Lg	TD
1996	NO	N	20	52	2.6	15	0

Ossie Wiberg

Year	Team		Att	Yds	Avg	Lg	TD
1927	CLE	N					1
1928	DET	N					1
1930	NYG	N					4
Career							6

Bob Wiese

Year	Team		Att	Yds	Avg	Lg	TD
1947	DET	N	20	61	3.0	21	0

J.R. Wilburn

Year	Team		Att	Yds	Avg	Lg	TD
1969	PIT	N	2	29	14.5	35	0

J.R. Wilburn *continued*

Year	Team		Att	Yds	Avg	Lg	TD
1970			5	25	5.0	10	0
Career			7	54	7.7	35	0

Ned Wilcox

Year	Team		Att	Yds	Avg	Lg	TD
1926	FRA	N					2
1927							2
Career							4

George Wilde

Year	Team		Att	Yds	Avg	Lg	TD
1947	WAS	N	4	-1	-0.3	2	0

James Wilder

Year	Team		Att	Yds	Avg	Lg	TD
1981	TB	N	107	370	3.5	23t	4
1982			83	324	3.9	47	3
1983			161	640	4.0	75t	4
1984			407	1544	3.8	37	13
1985			365	1300	3.6	28	10
1986			190	704	3.7	45t	2
1987			106	488	4.6	21	0
1988			86	343	4.0	19	1
1989			70	244	3.5	14	0
1990	DET	N	11	51	4.6	13	0
Career			1586	6008	3.8	75t	37
Playoffs			18	116	6.4		0

Erik Wilhelm

Year	Team		Att	Yds	Avg	Lg	TD
1989	CIN	N	6	30	5.0	14	0
1990			6	6	1.0	4	0
1991			1	9	9.0	9	0
1996			6	24	4.0	18	0
Career			19	69	3.6	18	0
Playoffs			3	-2	-0.7		0

Dick Wilkins

Year	Team		Att	Yds	Avg	Lg	TD
1949	LA	AA	8	28	3.5		0

Gary Wilkins

Year	Team		Att	Yds	Avg	Lg	TD
1986	BUF	N	3	18	6.0	11	0

Bob Wilkinson

Year	Team		Att	Yds	Avg	Lg	TD
1952	NYG	N	26	26	1.0	7	0

Ken Willard

Year	Team		Att	Yds	Avg	Lg	TD
1965	SF	N	189	778	4.1	82	5
1966			191	763	4.0	49	5
1967			169	510	3.0	20	5
1968			227	967	4.3	69t	7
1969			171	557	3.3	18	7
1970			236	789	3.3	20	7
1971			216	855	4.0	49	4
1972			100	345	3.5	23	4
1973			83	366	4.4	33	1
1974	STL	N	40	175	4.4	12	0
Career			1622	6105	3.8	82	45
Playoffs			66	176	2.7		0

Gerald Willhite

Year	Team		Att	Yds	Avg	Lg	TD
1982	DEN	N	70	347	5.0	23	2
1983			43	188	4.4	24t	3
1984			77	371	4.8	52	3
1985			66	237	3.6	14	3
1986			85	365	4.3	42	5
1987			26	141	5.4	29	0
1988			13	39	3.0	7	2
Career			380	1688	4.4	52	17
Playoffs			16	40	2.5		1

Kevin Willhite

Year	Team		Att	Yds	Avg	Lg	TD
1987	GB	N	53	251	4.7	61	0

Al Williams

Year	Team		Att	Yds	Avg	Lg	TD
1987	SD	N	1	11	11.0	11	0

Alonzo Williams

Year	Team		Att	Yds	Avg	Lg	TD
1987	LARM	N	2	9	4.5	7	0

Art Williams

Year	Team		Att	Yds	Avg	Lg	TD
1928	PRO	N					3
1929							6
1930							2
Career							11

Year	Team		Att	Yds	Avg	Lg	TD

Bobby Williams

Year	Team		Att	Yds	Avg	Lg	TD
1951	CHIB	N	5	0	0.0	3	0
1952			11	33	3.0	12	0
1955			13	79	6.1	19	0
Career			29	112	3.9	19	0

Byron Williams

Year	Team		Att	Yds	Avg	Lg	TD
1985	NYG	N	2	18	9.0	17	0
Playoffs			1	-9	-9.0		0

Calvin Williams

Year	Team		Att	Yds	Avg	Lg	TD
1990	PHI	N	2	20	10.0	18	0
1994			2	11	5.5	6	0
1995			1	-2	-2.0	-2	0
Career			5	29	5.8	18	0

Clancy Williams

Year	Team		Att	Yds	Avg	Lg	TD
1965	LA	N	3	3	1.0	2	0

Clarence Williams

Year	Team		Att	Yds	Avg	Lg	TD
1977	SD	N	50	215	4.3	46	2
1978			27	76	2.8	12	0
1979			200	752	3.8	55t	12
1980			97	258	2.7	13	3
1981			20	26	1.3	6	0
Career			394	1327	3.4	55t	17
Playoffs			11	30	2.7		1

Dave Williams

Year	Team		Att	Yds	Avg	Lg	TD
1967	STL	N	1	7	7.0	7	0
1968			3	47	15.7	43	0
1969			1	1	1.0	1	0
1972	SD	N	1	14	14.0	14	0
Career			6	69	11.5	43	0

Dave Williams

Year	Team		Att	Yds	Avg	Lg	TD
1977	SF	N	2	6	3.0	6	0
1978			15	18	1.2	6	0
1979	CHI	N	127	401	3.2	16	1
1980			26	57	2.2	14	0
1981			2	19	9.5	15	0
Career			172	501	2.9	16	1
Playoffs			10	23	2.3		0

Delvin Williams

Year	Team		Att	Yds	Avg	Lg	TD
1974	SF	N	36	201	5.6	71t	3
1975			117	631	5.4	52	3
1976			248	1203	4.9	80t	7
1977			268	931	3.5	40	7
1978	MIA	N	272	1258	4.6	58	8
1979			184	703	3.8	39	3
1980			187	671	3.6	65	2
Career			1312	5598	4.3	80t	33
Playoffs			21	42	2.0		0

Dokie Wlliams

Year	Team		Att	Yds	Avg	Lg	TD
1986	LARI	N	3	27	9.0	19	0

Doug Williams

Year	Team		Att	Yds	Avg	Lg	TD
1978	TB	N	27	23	0.9	7	1
1979			35	119	3.4	16	2
1980			58	370	6.4	27	4
1981			48	209	4.4	29	4
1982			35	158	4.5	14	2
1987	WAS	N	7	9	1.3	7	1
1988			9	0	0.0	4	1
1989			1	-4	-4.0	-4	0
Career			220	884	4.0	29	15
Playoffs			16	32	2.0		0

Ed Williams

Year	Team		Att	Yds	Avg	Lg	TD
1974	CIN	N	58	238	4.1	18	3
1975			35	136	3.9	19	2
1976	TB	N	87	324	3.7	19	2
1977			63	198	3.1	14	0
Career			243	896	3.7	19	7
Playoffs			1	0	0.0		0

Eugene Williams

Year	Team		Att	Yds	Avg	Lg	TD
1985	SEA	N	1	2	2.0	2	0

Harvey Williams

Year	Team		Att	Yds	Avg	Lg	TD
1991	KC	N	97	447	4.6	21	1
1992			78	262	3.4	11	1

Harvey Williams *continued*

Year	Team		Att	Yds	Avg	Lg	TD
1993			42	149	3.5	19	0
1994	LARI	N	282	983	3.5	28	4
1995	OAK	N	255	1114	4.4	60	9
1996			121	431	3.6	44	0
Career			875	3386	3.9	60	15
Playoffs			22	63	2.9		0

Jeff Williams

Year	Team		Att	Yds	Avg	Lg	TD
1966	MIN	N	1	2	2.0	2	0

Jerry Williams

Year	Team		Att	Yds	Avg	Lg	TD
1949	LA	N	19	104	5.5	18	3
1950			13	108	8.3	88	1
1951			21	106	5.0	32	2
1952			11	65	5.9	26	0
1953	PHI	N	61	345	5.7	48t	3
1954			47	183	3.9	33	1
Career			172	911	5.3	88	10
Playoffs			1	6	6.0		0

Joe Williams

Year	Team		Att	Yds	Avg	Lg	TD
1925	NY	N					1

Joe Williams

Year	Team		Att	Yds	Avg	Lg	TD
1971	DAL	N	21	67	3.2	16	1
1972	NO	N	31	72	2.3	11	0
Career			52	139	2.7	16	1

Joel Williams

Year	Team		Att	Yds	Avg	Lg	TD
1950	BAL	N	0	50		50tL	1

John Williams

Year	Team		Att	Yds	Avg	Lg	TD
1985	DAL	N	13	40	3.1	9	0

John L. Williams

Year	Team		Att	Yds	Avg	Lg	TD
1986	SEA	N	129	538	4.2	36	0
1987			113	500	4.4	48	1
1988			189	877	4.6	44t	4
1989			146	499	3.4	21	1
1990			187	714	3.8	25	3
1991			188	741	3.9	42	4
1992			114	339	3.0	14	1
1993			82	371	4.5	38	3
1994	PIT	N	68	317	4.7	23	1
1995			29	110	3.8	31	0
Career			1245	5006	4.0	48	18
Playoffs			26	101	3.9		2

Johnny Williams

Year	Team		Att	Yds	Avg	Lg	TD
1952	WAS	N	2	3	1.5	2	0

Karl Williams

Year	Team		Att	Yds	Avg	Lg	TD
1996	TB	N	1	-3	-3.0	-3	0

Keith Williams

Year	Team		Att	Yds	Avg	Lg	TD
1986	ATL	N	3	18	6.0	8	0

Kevin Williams

Year	Team		Att	Yds	Avg	Lg	TD
1993	DAL	N	7	26	3.7	12	2
1994			6	20	3.3	8	0
1995			10	53	5.3	14	0
1996			4	11	2.8	9	0
Career			27	110	4.1	14	2
Playoffs			5	21	4.2		0

Lawrence Williams

Year	Team		Att	Yds	Avg	Lg	TD
1977	KC	N	2	30	15.0	17	1

Leonard Williams

Year	Team		Att	Yds	Avg	Lg	TD
1987	BUF	N	9	25	2.8	9	0

Mike Williams

Year	Team		Att	Yds	Avg	Lg	TD
1979	KC	N	69	261	3.8	22	1
1981			2	0	0.0	3	0
Career			71	261	3.7	22	1

Mike Williams

Year	Team		Att	Yds	Avg	Lg	TD
1983	PHI	N	103	385	3.7	32	0
1984			33	83	2.5	8	0
1987	ATL	N	14	49	3.5	9	0
Career			150	517	3.4	32	0

Newton Williams

Year	Team		Att	Yds	Avg	Lg	TD
1983	BAL	N	28	77	2.8	13	0

Perry Williams

Year	Team		Att	Yds	Avg	Lg	TD
1969	GB	N	18	55	3.1	13	0
1970			17	44	2.6	4	0
1971			3	4	1.3	3	0
1972			33	139	4.2	14	0
1973			32	87	2.7	9	1
1974	CHI	N	74	218	2.9	12	1
Career			177	547	3.1	14	2

Ray Williams

Year	Team		Att	Yds	Avg	Lg	TD
1980	DET	N	2	17	8.5	11t	1

Richard Williams

Year	Team		Att	Yds	Avg	Lg	TD
1983	ATL	N	1	5	5.0	5	0

Rollie Williams

Year	Team		Att	Yds	Avg	Lg	TD
1923	RAC	N					1

Scott Williams

Year	Team		Att	Yds	Avg	Lg	TD
1986	DET	N	13	22	1.7	5	2
1987			8	29	3.6	8	0
1988			9	22	2.4	5	1
Career			30	73	2.4	8	3

Sherman Williams

Year	Team		Att	Yds	Avg	Lg	TD
1995	DAL	N	48	205	4.3	44t	1
1996			69	269	3.9	27	0
Career			117	474	4.1	44t	1
Playoffs			28	100	3.6		0

Ted Williams

Year	Team		Att	Yds	Avg	Lg	TD
1942	PHI	N	50	183		33	2
1944	BOS	N	52	13	0.3	25t	1
Career			102	196	1.9	33	3

Travis Williams

Year	Team		Att	Yds	Avg	Lg	TD
1921	EVA	A					1

Travis Williams

Year	Team		Att	Yds	Avg	Lg	TD
1967	GB	N	35	188	5.4	37	1
1968			33	63	1.9	9	0
1969			129	536	4.2	39t	4
1970			74	276	3.7	37	1
1971	LA	N	18	103	5.7	36	0
Career			289	1166	4.0	39t	6
Playoffs			30	137	4.6		2

Van Williams

Year	Team		Att	Yds	Avg	Lg	TD
1983	BUF	N	3	11	3.7	5	0
1984			18	51	2.8	7	0
1987	NYG	N	29	108	3.7	17	0
Career			50	170	3.4	17	0

Vince Williams

Year	Team		Att	Yds	Avg	Lg	TD
1982	SF	N	20	68	3.4	2t	0

Walt Williams

Year	Team		Att	Yds	Avg	Lg	TD
1946	CHI	AA	21	19	0.9		1

Wandy Williams

Year	Team		Att	Yds	Avg	Lg	TD
1969	DEN	A	10	18	1.8	8	1

Warren Williams

Year	Team		Att	Yds	Avg	Lg	TD
1988	PIT	N	87	409	4.7	33	0
1989			37	131	3.5	13	1
1990			68	389	5.7	70t	3
1991			57	262	4.6	21	4
1992			2	0	0.0	2	0
Career			251	1191	4.7	70t	8

Chester Willis

Year	Team		Att	Yds	Avg	Lg	TD
1981	OAK	N	16	54	3.4	15t	1
1982	LARI	N	6	15	2.5	5	0
1983			5	0	0.0	4	0
1984			5	4	0.8	2	0
Career			32	73	2.3	15t	1
Playoffs			4	10	2.5		0

Fred Willis

Year	Team		Att	Yds	Avg	Lg	TD
1971	CIN	N	135	590	4.4	36	7
1972	CIN-HOU	N	134	461	3.4	43	0

Year	Team		Att	Yds	Avg	Lg	TD

Fred Willis continued

Year	Team		Att	Yds	Avg	Lg	TD
1973	HOU	N	171	579	3.4	25	4
1974			74	239	3.2	18	3
1975			118	420	3.6	23	2
1976			148	542	3.7	44	2
Career			780	2831	3.6	44	18

Jamal Willis

Year	Team		Att	Yds	Avg	Lg	TD
1995	SF	N	12	35	2.9	15	0

Peter Tom Willis

Year	Team		Att	Yds	Avg	Lg	TD
1991	CHI	N	2	6	3.0	8	0
1992			1	2	2.0	2	0
1993			2	6	3.0	6	0
Career			5	14	2.8	8	0

Klaus Wilmsmeyer

Year	Team		Att	Yds	Avg	Lg	TD
1992	SF	N	2	0	0.0	10	0
1993			2	0	0.0	0	0
Career			4	0	0.0	10	0

Ben Wilson

Year	Team		Att	Yds	Avg	Lg	TD
1963	LA	N	109	394	3.6	39	1
1964			159	553	3.5	27	5
1965			60	189	3.1	20	1
1967	GB	N	103	453	4.4	40	2
Career			431	1589	3.7	40	9
Playoffs			21	75	3.6		0

Bobby Wilson

Year	Team		Att	Yds	Avg	Lg	TD
1936	BKN	N	104	505	4.9		3

Brett Wilson

Year	Team		Att	Yds	Avg	Lg	TD
1987	MIN	N	5	16	3.2	6	0

Camp Wilson

Year	Team		Att	Yds	Avg	Lg	TD
1946	DET	N	64	207	3.2	15	3
1947			89	412	4.6	48	0
1948			157	612	3.9	38	2
1949			68	222	3.3	24	1
Career			378	1453	3.8	48	6

Charles Wilson

Year	Team		Att	Yds	Avg	Lg	TD
1991	GB	N	3	3	1.0	5	0
1993	TB	N	2	7	3.5	4	0
1994			2	15	7.5	11	0
Career			7	25	3.6	11	0

Dave Wilson

Year	Team		Att	Yds	Avg	Lg	TD
1981	NO	N	5	1	0.2	9	0
1983			5	3	0.6	5	1
1984			3	-7	-2.3	-2	0
1985			18	7	0.4	17	0
1986			14	19	1.4	14	1
Career			45	23	0.5	17	2

Eddie Wilson

Year	Team		Att	Yds	Avg	Lg	TD
1962	DAL	A	1	5	5.0	5	0
1963	KC	A	8	45	5.6	21	0
1964			6	5	0.8	8	1
1965	BOS	A	8	4	0.5	17	0
Career			23	59	2.6	21	1

Gene Wilson

Year	Team		Att	Yds	Avg	Lg	TD
1947	GB	N	1	-2	-2.0	-2	0

George Wilson

Year	Team		Att	Yds	Avg	Lg	TD
1926	LA	A					4
1927	PRO	N					4
1928							5
1929							1
Career							14

George Wilson

Year	Team		Att	Yds	Avg	Lg	TD
1966	MIA	A	27	137	5.1	37	0

Harry Wilson

Year	Team		Att	Yds	Avg	Lg	TD
1969	PHI	N	4	7	1.8	4	0

Jack Wilson

Year	Team		Att	Yds	Avg	Lg	TD
1946	LA	N	19	120	6.3	35	0
1947			3	3	1.0	4	0
Career			22	123	5.6	35	0

Jerrel Wilson

Year	Team		Att	Yds	Avg	Lg	TD
1963	KC	A	9	41	4.6	12	0
1964			1	-10	-10.0	-10	0
1965			2	4	2.0	3	0
1966			3	7	2.3	5	0
1967			1	10	10.0	10	0
1968			5	1	0.2	3	0
1978	NE	N	1	0	0.0	0	0
Career			22	53	2.4	12	0

Joe Wilson

Year	Team		Att	Yds	Avg	Lg	TD
1973	CIN	N	10	39	3.9	11	0
1974	NE	N	15	57	3.8	12	0
Career			25	96	3.8	12	0

Larry Wilson

Year	Team		Att	Yds	Avg	Lg	TD
1963	STL	N	2	38	19.0	35t	1
1964			2	-14	-7.0	4	0
1968			1	12	12.0	12	0
Career			5	36	7.2	35t	1

Marc Wilson

Year	Team		Att	Yds	Avg	Lg	TD
1980	OAK	N	1	3	3.0	3	0
1981			30	147	4.9	18	2
1983	LARI	N	13	122	9.4	23	0
1984			30	56	1.9	14t	1
1985			24	98	4.1	17	2
1986			14	45	3.2	13	0
1987			17	91	5.4	16	0
1989	NE	N	7	42	6.0	11	0
1990			5	7	1.4	6	0
1991	LARI	N	6	21	3.5	8	0
Career			147	632	4.3	23	5
Playoffs			3	3	1.0		0

Marcus Wilson

Year	Team		Att	Yds	Avg	Lg	TD
1993	GB	N	6	3	0.5	5	0

Mule Wilson

Year	Team		Att	Yds	Avg	Lg	TD
1927	NYG	N					3
1928							1
1929							1
1930							1
1931	GB	N					2
Career							8

Robert Wilson

Year	Team		Att	Yds	Avg	Lg	TD
1991	TB	N	42	179	4.3	20	0
1994	DAL	N	1	-1	-1.0	-1	0
1995	MIA	N	1	5	5.0	5	0
1996			1	0	0.0	0	0
Career			45	183	4.1	20	0

Stanley Wilson

Year	Team		Att	Yds	Avg	Lg	TD
1983	CIN	N	56	267	4.8	18	1
1984			17	74	4.4	9	0
1986			68	379	5.6	58t	8
1988			112	398	3.6	19	2
Career			253	1118	4.4	58t	11
Playoffs			12	74	6.2		2

Ted Wilson

Year	Team		Att	Yds	Avg	Lg	TD
1987	WAS	N	2	28	14.0	16t	1

Tim Wilson

Year	Team		Att	Yds	Avg	Lg	TD
1977	HOU	N	99	343	3.5	16	3
1978			126	431	3.4	24	0
1979			84	319	3.8	19	2
1980			66	257	3.9	15	1
1981			13	35	2.7	7	0
1983	NO	N	8	21	2.6	9	0
1984			2	8	4.0	5	0
Career			398	1414	3.6	24	6
Playoffs			54	174	3.2		1

Tommy Wilson

Year	Team		Att	Yds	Avg	Lg	TD
1956	LA	N	64	470	7.3	46	0
1957			127	616	4.9	46	3
1958			73	475	6.5	82t	9
1959			40	210	5.3	60	0
1960			41	139	3.4	35	0
1961			44	220	5.0	34	1
1962	CLE	N	46	141	3.1	17	1

Tommy Wilson continued

Year	Team		Att	Yds	Avg	Lg	TD
1963	MIN	N	73	282	3.9	30t	4
Career			508	2553	5.0	82t	18

Wade Wilson

Year	Team		Att	Yds	Avg	Lg	TD
1983	MIN	N	3	-3	-1.0	2	0
1984			9	30	3.3	12	0
1986			13	9	0.7	13	1
1987			41	263	6.4	38	5
1988			36	136	3.8	15	2
1989			32	132	4.1	23	1
1990			12	79	6.6	24	0
1991			13	33	2.5	15	0
1992	ATL	N	15	62	4.1	12	0
1993	NO	N	31	230	7.4	44	0
1994			7	15	2.1	9	0
1995	DAL	N	10	12	1.2	10	0
1996			4	5	1.3	8	0
Career			226	1003	4.4	44	9
Playoffs			25	93	3.7		0

Walter Wilson

Year	Team		Att	Yds	Avg	Lg	TD
1990	SD	N	1	0	0.0	0	0

Wayne Wilson

Year	Team		Att	Yds	Avg	Lg	TD
1979	NO	N	5	26	5.2	16	0
1980			63	188	3.0	15	1
1981			44	137	3.1	13	1
1982			103	413	4.0	20	3
1983			199	787	4.0	29	9
1984			74	261	3.5	36	0
1985			168	645	3.8	41t	5
1986	MIN-NO		10	19	1.9	6	0
1987	WAS	N	18	55	3.1	11	2
Career			684	2531	3.7	41t	18

Tydus Winans

Year	Team		Att	Yds	Avg	Lg	TD
1994	WAS	N	1	5	5.0	5	0

Sammy Winder

Year	Team		Att	Yds	Avg	Lg	TD
1982	DEN	N	67	259	3.9	18	1
1983			196	757	3.9	52	3
1984			296	1153	3.9	24	4
1985			199	714	3.6	42	8
1986			240	789	3.3	31	9
1987			196	741	3.8	19	6
1988			149	543	3.6	35	4
1989			110	351	3.2	16	2
1990			42	120	2.9	19	2
Career			1495	5427	3.6	52	39
Playoffs			144	461	3.2		1

Bob Windsor

Year	Team		Att	Yds	Avg	Lg	TD
1967	SF	N	1	7	7.0	7	0
1969			5	39	7.8	13	0
1971			1	21	21.0	21	0
1972	NE	N	1	-4	-4.0	-4	0
1973			1	-6	-6.0	-6	0
Career			9	57	6.3	21	0

Stan Winfrey

Year	Team		Att	Yds	Avg	Lg	TD
1975	MIA	N	3	10	3.3	5	0
1976			52	205	3.9	13	1
Career			55	215	3.9	13	1

Ben Winkleman

Year	Team		Att	Yds	Avg	Lg	TD
1923	MIL	N					1
1924							1
Career							2

George Winslow

Year	Team		Att	Yds	Avg	Lg	TD
1989	NO	N	1	0	0.0	0	0

Paul Winslow

Year	Team		Att	Yds	Avg	Lg	TD
1960	GB	N	2	-3	-1.5	3	0

Lloyd Winston

Year	Team		Att	Yds	Avg	Lg	TD
1962	SF	N	1	-15	-15.0	-15	0
1963			27	127	4.7	38	1
Career			28	112	4.0	38	1

Sonny Winters

Year	Team		Att	Yds	Avg	Lg	TD
1923	COL	N					2

Year	Team		Att	Yds	Avg	Lg	TD

Sonny Winters *continued*

Year	Team		Att	Yds	Avg	Lg	TD
1924							1
Career							3

Derrick Witherspoon

Year	Team		Att	Yds	Avg	Lg	TD
1995	PHI	N	2	7	3.5	5	0
Playoffs			5	21	4.2		0

John Witkowski

Year	Team		Att	Yds	Avg	Lg	TD
1984	DET	N	7	33	4.7	10	0
1988			1	0	0.0	0	0
Career			8	33	4.1	10	0

Jon Witman

Year	Team		Att	Yds	Avg	Lg	TD
1996	PIT	N	17	69	4.1	15	0
Playoffs			10	59	5.9		1

Tom Wittum

Year	Team		Att	Yds	Avg	Lg	TD
1973	SF	N	1	63	63.0	63	0
1974			1	13	13.0	13	0
1975			1	-10	-10.0	-10	0
Career			3	66	22.0	63	0

Alex Wizbicki

Year	Team		Att	Yds	Avg	Lg	TD
1947	BUF	AA	9	44	4.9		0
1949			5	-10	-2.0		0
Career			14	34	2.4		0

Al Wolden

Year	Team		Att	Yds	Avg	Lg	TD
1987	CHI	N	2	8	4.0	7	0

Dick Wolf

Year	Team		Att	Yds	Avg	Lg	TD
1923	CLE	N					1
1924							1
Career							2

Hugh Wolfe

Year	Team		Att	Yds	Avg	Lg	TD
1938	NYG	N	15	19	1.3		0

Ron Wolfley

Year	Team		Att	Yds	Avg	Lg	TD
1985	STL	N	24	64	2.7	11	0
1986			8	19	2.4	8	0
1987			26	87	3.3	8	1
1988	PHX	N	9	43	4.8	20	0
1989			13	36	2.8	5t	1
1990			2	3	1.5	2	0
1992	CLE	N	1	2	2.0	2	0
1995	STL	N	3	9	3.0	4	0
Career			86	263	3.1	20	2

Jeff Womack

Year	Team		Att	Yds	Avg	Lg	TD
1987	MIN	N	9	20	2.2	13	0

Joe Womack

Year	Team		Att	Yds	Avg	Lg	TD
1962	PIT	N	128	468	3.7	28	5

Royce Womble

Year	Team		Att	Yds	Avg	Lg	TD
1954	BAL	N	60	174	2.9	24	0
1955			4	2	0.5	4	0
1956			20	72	3.6	12	0
1957			7	18	2.6	7	0
Career			91	266	2.9	24	0

George Wonsley

Year	Team		Att	Yds	Avg	Lg	TD
1984	IND	N	37	111	3.0	13	0
1985			138	716	5.2	36	6
1986			60	214	3.6	46	1
1987			18	71	3.9	12	1
1988			26	48	1.8	4	1
1989	NE	N	2	-2	-1.0	0	0
Career			281	1158	4.1	46	9

Nathan Wonsley

Year	Team		Att	Yds	Avg	Lg	TD
1986	TB	N	73	339	4.6	59t	3

Otis Wonsley

Year	Team		Att	Yds	Avg	Lg	TD
1981	WAS	N	3	11	3.7	7	0
1982			11	36	3.3	7	0
1983			25	88	3.5	9	0
1984			18	38	2.1	7	4
1985			4	8	2.0	5	0
Career			61	181	3.0	9	4
Playoffs			2	3	1.5		0

Dick Wood

Year	Team		Att	Yds	Avg	Lg	TD
1962	SD	A	1	0	0.0	0	0
1963	NY	A	7	17	2.4	11	1
1964			9	6	0.7	6	1
1965	OAK	A	4	16	4.0	21	1
1966	MIA	A	5	6	1.2	7	1
Career			26	45	1.7	21	4

Gary Wood

Year	Team		Att	Yds	Avg	Lg	TD
1964	NYG	N	39	158	4.1	14	3
1965			5	68	13.6	25	0
1966			28	196	7.0	28	3
1968			2	0	0.0	2	0
1969			1	3	3.0	3	0
Career			75	425	5.7	28	6

Al Woodall

Year	Team		Att	Yds	Avg	Lg	TD
1969	NY	A	4	13	3.3	14	0
1970	NYJ	N	28	110	3.9	27	0
1971			13	26	2.0	7	0
1973			13	68	5.2	17	0
1974			2	-3	-1.5	-1	0
Career			60	214	3.6	27	0

Tom Woodeshick

Year	Team		Att	Yds	Avg	Lg	TD
1963	PHI	N	5	18	3.6	11	0
1964			37	180	4.9	13	2
1965			28	145	5.2	14	0
1966			85	330	3.9	21	0
1967			155	670	4.3	41	6
1968			217	947	4.4	54t	3
1969			186	831	4.5	21	4
1970			52	254	4.9	57t	2
1971			66	188	2.8	19	0
1972	STL	N	5	14	2.8	6	0
Career			836	3577	4.3	57t	21

David Woodley

Year	Team		Att	Yds	Avg	Lg	TD
1980	MIA	N	55	214	3.9	17	3
1981			63	272	4.3	26	4
1982			36	207	5.8	29	2
1983			19	78	4.1	15	0
1984	PIT	N	11	14	1.3	7	0
1985			17	71	4.2	13	2
Career			201	856	4.3	29	11
Playoffs			17	102	6.0		1

Lee Woodruff

Year	Team		Att	Yds	Avg	Lg	TD
1931	PRO	N					4
1933	PHI	N					1
Career							5

Carl Woods

Year	Team		Att	Yds	Avg	Lg	TD
1987	NE	N	4	20	5.0	13	1

Don Woods

Year	Team		Att	Yds	Avg	Lg	TD
1974	SD	N	227	1162	5.1	56t	7
1975			87	317	3.6	17	2
1976			126	450	3.6	24	3
1977			118	405	3.4	29t	1
1978			151	514	3.4	27	3
1980	SD-SF	N	54	239	4.4	23	0
Career			763	3087	4.0	56t	16

Ickey Woods

Year	Team		Att	Yds	Avg	Lg	TD
1988	CIN	N	203	1066	**5.3**	56	15
1989			29	94	3.2	12	2
1990			64	268	4.2	32	6
1991			36	97	2.7	12	4
Career			332	1525	4.6	56	27
Playoffs			89	391	4.4		4

Robert Woods

Year	Team		Att	Yds	Avg	Lg	TD
1978	HOU	N	2	4	2.0	5	0
Playoffs			1	9	9.0		0

Keith Woodside

Year	Team		Att	Yds	Avg	Lg	TD
1988	GB	N	83	195	2.3	10	3
1989			46	273	5.9	68t	1
1990			46	182	4.0	21	1
1991			84	326	3.9	29	1
Career			259	976	3.8	68t	6

Abe Woodson

Year	Team		Att	Yds	Avg	Lg	TD
1958	SF	N	2	12	6.0	9	0
1960			4	4	1.0	4	0
1961			14	23	1.6	14	0
Career			20	39	2.0	14	0

Rod Woodson

Year	Team		Att	Yds	Avg	Lg	TD
1993	PIT	N	1	0	0.0	0	0

Butch Woolfolk

Year	Team		Att	Yds	Avg	Lg	TD
1982	NYG	N	112	439	3.9	18	2
1983			246	857	3.5	22	4
1984			40	92	2.3	17	1
1985	HOU	N	103	392	3.8	43	1
1986			23	57	2.5	15	0
1987	DET	N	12	82	6.8	31	0
1988			1	4	4.0	4	0
Career			537	1923	3.6	43	8

Barry Word

Year	Team		Att	Yds	Avg	Lg	TD
1987	NO	N	36	133	3.7	20	2
1990	KC	N	204	1015	5.0	53t	4
1991			160	684	4.3	37	4
1992			163	607	3.7	44t	4
1993	MIN	N	142	458	3.2	14	2
Career			705	2897	4.1	53t	16
Playoffs			59	197	3.3		1

Jim Worden

Year	Team		Att	Yds	Avg	Lg	TD
1945	CLE	N	4	3	0.8	7	0

Neil Worden

Year	Team		Att	Yds	Avg	Lg	TD
1954	PHI	N	58	128	2.2	12	1
1957			42	133	3.2	17	0
Career			100	261	2.6	17	1

Vince Workman

Year	Team		Att	Yds	Avg	Lg	TD
1989	GB	N	4	8	2.0	3	1
1990			8	51	6.4	31	0
1991			71	237	3.3	30t	7
1992			159	631	4.0	44	2
1993	TB	N	78	284	3.6	21	2
1994			79	291	3.7	18	0
1995	CAR-IND	N	44	165	3.8	14	1
1996	IND	N	24	70	2.9	11	0
Career			467	1737	3.7	44	13

Tim Worley

Year	Team		Att	Yds	Avg	Lg	TD
1989	PIT	N	195	770	3.9	38	5
1990			109	418	3.8	38	0
1991			22	117	5.3	16	0
1993	PIT-CHI	N	120	470	3.9	28	2
1994	CHI	N	9	17	1.9	4	1
Career			455	1792	3.9	38	8
Playoffs			24	104	4.3		1

John Wozniak

Year	Team		Att	Yds	Avg	Lg	TD
1948	BKN	AA	0	13		13L	0

Adrian Wright

Year	Team		Att	Yds	Avg	Lg	TD
1987	TB	N	37	112	3.0	11	0

Alexander Wright

Year	Team		Att	Yds	Avg	Lg	TD
1990	DAL	N	3	26	8.7	14	0
1991			2	-1	-0.5	3	0
1995	STL	N	1	17	17.0	17	0
Career			6	42	7.0	17	0

Dana Wright

Year	Team		Att	Yds	Avg	Lg	TD
1987	CIN	N	24	74	3.1	10	0

Elmo Wright

Year	Team		Att	Yds	Avg	Lg	TD
1971	KC	N	1	-10	-10.0	-10	0
1972			1	24	24.0	24	0
1973			5	29	5.8	9	0
1974			3	26	8.7	12t	1
Career			10	69	6.9	24	1
Playoffs			2	15	7.5		0

James Wright

Year	Team		Att	Yds	Avg	Lg	TD
1981	DEN	N	1	11	11.0	11	0
1982			1	-4	-4.0	-4	0
1983			1	-11	-11.0	-11	0
Career			3	-4	-1.3	11	0

John Wright

Year	Team		Att	Yds	Avg	Lg	TD
1947	BAL	AA	38	113	3.0		0

Johnnie Wright

Year	Team		Att	Yds	Avg	Lg	TD
1982	BAL	N	1	3	3.0	3	0

Randy Wright

Year	Team		Att	Yds	Avg	Lg	TD
1984	GB	N	8	11	1.4	5	0
1985			8	8	1.0	8	0
1986			18	41	2.3	18	1
1987			13	70	5.4	27	0
1988			8	43	5.4	19	2
Career			55	173	3.1	27	3

Rayfield Wright

Year	Team		Att	Yds	Avg	Lg	TD
1968	DAL	N	1	-10	-10.0	-10	0

Ted Wright

Year	Team		Att	Yds	Avg	Lg	TD
1934	BOS	N					1
1935							0
1935	BOS-BKN	N	65	45	0.7		0
Career			65	45	0.7		1

Toby Wright

Year	Team		Att	Yds	Avg	Lg	TD
1995	STL	N	1	9	9.0	9	0

Sam Wyche

Year	Team		Att	Yds	Avg	Lg	TD
1968	CIN	A	12	74	6.2	21	0
1969			12	107	8.9	22	1
1970	CIN	N	19	118	6.2	23	2
1971	WAS	N	1	4	4.0	4	0
1974	DET	N	1	0	0.0	0	0
Career			45	303	6.7	23	3

Frank Wycheck

Year	Team		Att	Yds	Avg	Lg	TD
1995	HOU	N	1	1	1.0	1t	1
1996			2	3	1.5	3	0
Career			3	4	1.3	3	1

Doug Wycoff

Year	Team		Att	Yds	Avg	Lg	TD
1926	NEW	A					1
1927	NYG	N					2
1929	SI	N					2
1930							4
1931	NYG	N					1
1932	SI	N					1
1934	BOS	N					1
Career							12

Arnie Wyman

Year	Team		Att	Yds	Avg	Lg	TD
1920	RI	A					1

Vinnie Yablonski

Year	Team		Att	Yds	Avg	Lg	TD
1948	CHIC	N	48	233	4.9	47	0
1949			32	97	3.0	22	0
1950			30	110	3.7	39	1
1951			14	20	1.4	6	0
Career			124	460	3.7	47	1

Howie Yeager

Year	Team		Att	Yds	Avg	Lg	TD
1941	NYG	N	22	67	3.0	39	1
Playoffs			2	7	3.5		0

Tom Yewcic

Year	Team		Att	Yds	Avg	Lg	TD
1961	BOS	A	11	51	4.6	13	1
1962			33	215	6.5	27	2
1963			22	161	7.3	46	1
1964			5	2	0.4	2	0
1966			1	-5	-5.0	-5	0
Career			72	424	5.9	46	4
Playoffs			1	14	14.0		0

Wally Yonamine

Year	Team		Att	Yds	Avg	Lg	TD
1947	SF	AA	19	74	3.9		0

Jim Youel

Year	Team		Att	Yds	Avg	Lg	TD
1946	WAS	N	13	60	4.6	36t	1
1947			10	44	4.4	19	1
1948	BOS-WAS	N	19	79	4.2	20	1
Career			42	183	4.4	36t	3

Buddy Young

Year	Team		Att	Yds	Avg	Lg	TD
1947	NY	AA	116	712	6.1		3
1948			70	245	3.5		1

Buddy Young *continued*

Year	Team		Att	Yds	Avg	Lg	TD
1949	B-NY	AA	76	495	6.5	71t	5
1950	NYY	N	76	334	4.4	20	1
1951			46	165	3.6	17	1
1952	DAL	N	71	243	3.4	30	3
1953	BAL	N	40	135	3.4	24	0
1954			70	311	4.4	57t	2
1955			32	87	2.7	25	1
Career			597	2727	4.6	71t	17
Playoffs			19	80	4.2		0

Charle Young

Year	Team		Att	Yds	Avg	Lg	TD
1973	PHI	N	4	24	6.0	17t	1
1974			6	38	6.3	14	0
1975			2	1	0.5	3	0
1976			1	6	6.0	6	0
1978	LA	N	2	6	3.0	5	0
1984	SEA	N	1	5	5.0	5	0
Career			16	80	5.0	17t	1

Charley Young

Year	Team		Att	Yds	Avg	Lg	TD
1974	DAL	N	33	205	6.2	53	0
1975			50	225	4.5	29	2
1976			48	208	4.3	24	0
Career			131	638	4.9	53	2
Playoffs			6	17	2.8		0

Dick Young

Year	Team		Att	Yds	Avg	Lg	TD
1955	BAL	N	17	39	2.3	10	0
1956			5	7	1.4	3	0
1957	PIT	N	56	153	2.7	14	2
Career			78	199	2.6	14	2

Jim Young

Year	Team		Att	Yds	Avg	Lg	TD
1965	MIN	N	3	4	1.3	4	0

Rickey Young

Year	Team		Att	Yds	Avg	Lg	TD
1975	SD	N	138	577	4.2	48t	5
1976			162	802	5.0	46t	4
1977			157	543	3.5	15	4
1978	MIN	N	134	417	3.1	16	1
1979			188	708	3.8	26	3
1980			130	351	2.7	4t	3
1981			47	129	2.7	13	0
1982			16	49	3.1	11	1
1983			39	90	2.3	9	2
Career			1011	3666	3.6	48t	23
Playoffs			3	6	2.0		0

Steve Young

Year	Team		Att	Yds	Avg	Lg	TD
1985	TB	N	40	233	5.8	20	1
1986			74	425	5.7	31	5
1987	SF	N	26	190	7.3	29t	1
1988			27	184	6.8	49t	1
1989			38	126	3.3	22	2
1990			15	159	10.6	31	0
1991			66	415	6.3	21	4
1992			76	537	7.1	39t	4
1993			69	407	5.9	35	2
1994			58	293	5.1	27	7
1995			50	250	5.0	29	3
1996			52	310	6.0	33	4
Career			591	3529	6.0	49t	34
Playoffs			81	512	6.3		7

Waddy Young

Year	Team		Att	Yds	Avg	Lg	TD
1940	BKN	N	1	1	1.0	1	0

Willie Young

Year	Team		Att	Yds	Avg	Lg	TD
1967	NYG	N	0	2		2L	0
1968			2	-2	-1.0	5	0
Career			2	0	0.0	5	0

Sid Youngelman

Year	Team		Att	Yds	Avg	Lg	TD
1957	PHI	N	0	3		3L	0

Tank Younger

Year	Team		Att	Yds	Avg	Lg	TD
1949	LA	N	52	191	3.7	16	0
1950			8	28	3.5	6	2
1951			36	223	6.2	24	1
1952			63	331	5.3	38	1
1953			84	350	4.2	39t	8
1954			91	610	6.7	75t	8
1955			138	644	4.7	54	5

Tank Younger *continued*

Year	Team		Att	Yds	Avg	Lg	TD
1956			114	518	4.5	33	3
1957			96	401	4.2	29	3
1958	PIT	N	88	344	3.9	36	3
Career			770	3640	4.7	75t	34
Playoffs			8	34	4.3		0

Frank Youso

Year	Team		Att	Yds	Avg	Lg	TD
1964	OAK	A	0	4		4L	0

Steve Zabel

Year	Team		Att	Yds	Avg	Lg	TD
1971	PHI	N	1	-5	-5.0	-5	0

Kenny Zachary

Year	Team		Att	Yds	Avg	Lg	TD
1987	SD	N	1	3	3.0	3	0

Frank Zadworney

Year	Team		Att	Yds	Avg	Lg	TD
1940	BKN	N	2	5	2.5		0

Bert Zagers

Year	Team		Att	Yds	Avg	Lg	TD
1955	WAS	N	89	395	4.4	41	2
1958			27	82	3.0	16	1
Career			116	477	4.1	41	3

Ernie Zalejski

Year	Team		Att	Yds	Avg	Lg	TD
1950	BAL	N	7	-2	-0.3	6t	1

Silvio Zaninelli

Year	Team		Att	Yds	Avg	Lg	TD
1936	PIT	N	31	61	2.0		0
1937			4	14	3.5		0
Career			35	75	2.1		0

Eric Zeier

Year	Team		Att	Yds	Avg	Lg	TD
1995	CLE	N	15	80	5.3	17	0
1996	BAL	N	2	8	4.0	5	0
Career			17	88	5.2	17	0

Ray Zellars

Year	Team		Att	Yds	Avg	Lg	TD
1995	NO	N	50	162	3.2	11	2
1996			120	475	4.0	63	4
Career			170	637	3.7	63	6

Coleman Zeno

Year	Team		Att	Yds	Avg	Lg	TD
1971	NYG	N	2	10	5.0	7	0

Frank Ziegler

Year	Team		Att	Yds	Avg	Lg	TD
1949	PHI	N	84	283	3.4	41	1
1950			172	733	4.3	52	1
1951			113	418	3.7	34	2
1952			67	172	2.6	12	2
1953			83	320	3.9	52	5
Career			519	1926	3.7	52	11
Playoffs			3	4	1.3		0

Don Zimmerman

Year	Team		Att	Yds	Avg	Lg	TD
1976	GB	N	1	3	3.0	3	0

Giff Zimmerman

Year	Team		Att	Yds	Avg	Lg	TD
1925	CAN	N					1

Roy Zimmerman

Year	Team		Att	Yds	Avg	Lg	TD
1940	WAS	N	31	127	4.1		0
1941			20	54	2.7	12	0
1942			12	56	4.7	16	0
1943	P-P	N	33	-41	-1.2	12	1
1944	PHI	N	26	-84	-3.2	5	3
1945			29	-11	-0.4	9	1
1946			23	43	1.9	12	1
1947	DET	N	13	28	2.2	10	1
1948	BOS	N	13	72	5.5	18	0
Career			200	244	1.2	18	7
Playoffs			2	-15	-7.5		0

Walt Zirinsky

Year	Team		Att	Yds	Avg	Lg	TD
1945	CLE	N	3	3	1.0	2	0

Mickey Zofko

Year	Team		Att	Yds	Avg	Lg	TD
1972	DET	N	7	28	4.0	9	0
1973			11	33	3.0	8	0
1974			3	6	2.0	3	0
Career			21	67	3.2	9	0

Scott Zolak

Year	Team		Att	Yds	Avg	Lg	TD
1992	NE	N	18	71	3.9	19	0

Scott Zolak *continued*

Year	Team	Att	Yds	Avg	Lg	TD
1993		1	0	0.0	0	0
1994		1	-1	-1.0	-1	0
1995		4	19	4.8	12	0
1996		4	-3	-0.8	0	0
Career		28	86	3.1	19	0
Playoffs		3	-4	-1.3		0

Lou Zontini

Year	Team		Att	Yds	Avg	Lg	TD
1940	CHIC	N	1	1	1.0	1	0
1941			1	-9	-9.0	-9	0
1944	CLE	N	33	105	3.2	16	3
1946	BUF	AA	13	36	2.8		0
Career			48	133	2.8	16	3

Jim Zorn

Year	Team		Att	Yds	Avg	Lg	TD
1976	SEA	N	52	246	4.7	19	4
1977			25	141	5.6	15	1
1978			59	290	4.9	23t	6
1979			46	279	6.1	41	2
1980			44	214	4.9	25	1
1981			30	140	4.7	20	1
1982			15	113	7.5	35	1
1983			30	71	2.4	18t	1
1984			7	-3	-0.4	7	0
1985	GB	N	10	9	0.9	8	0
1987	TB	N	4	4	1.0	5	0
Career			322	1504	4.7	41	17
Playoffs			1	2	2.0		0

PASSING REGISTER

Year	Team		Att	Com	PC	Yds	Avg	TD	Int	Lg	Rtg
Steve Young											
1985	**TB**	**N**	138	72	52.2	935	6.8	3	8	59	56.9
1986			363	195	53.7	2282	6.3	8	13	46	65.5
1987	**SF**	**N**	69	37	53.6	570	8.3	10	0	50t	120.8
1988			101	54	53.5	680	6.7	3	3	73t	72.2
1989			92	64	69.6	1001	10.9	8	3	50t	120.8
1990			62	38	61.3	427	6.9	2	0	34t	92.6
1991			279	180	64.5	2517	**9.0**	17	8	97t	**101.8**
1992			402	268	**66.7**	3465	**8.6**	**25**	7	80t	**107.0**
1993			462	314	68.0	4023	**8.7**	**29**	16	80t	101.5
1994			461	324	**70.3**	3969	**8.6**	**35**	10	69t	**112.8**
1995			447	299	**66.9**	3200	7.2	20	11	57	92.3
1996			316	214	**67.7**	2410	7.6	14	6	52	**97.2**
Career			3192	2059	64.5	25479	8.0	174	85	97t	**96.2**
Playoffs			334	207	62.0	2381	7.1	15	7		89.7

Key

Team	The team (and league) the player played for.
Att	Attempts
Com	Completions
PC	Completion percentage
Yds	Yards
Avg	Average gain per attempt
TD	Touchdowns
Int	Interceptions
Lg	Long pass play
Rtg	Passer rating

In addition, boldface numbers indicate that the player led the league in that category that season. For example, Young's 25 touchdown passes in 1992 are boldfaced, meaning that he led the league in passing that year. Also, boldfaced career and playoff stats indicate all-time highs. Young's 96.2 passer rating indicates that he is the all-time career leader in this category.

Year	Team		Att	Com	PC	Yds	Avg	TD	Int	Lg	Rtg

Lou Abbruzzi
| 1946 | BOS | N | 1 | 1 | 100.0 | 11 | 11.0 | 0 | 0 | 1 | 112.5 |

Karim Abdul-Jabbar
| 1996 | MIA | N | 0 | 0 | | 0 | | 0 | 0 | 0 | |

Cliff Aberson
| 1946 | GB | N | 41 | 14 | 34.1 | 184 | 4.5 | 0 | 5 | 30 | 9.7 |

Danny Abramowicz
| 1974 | SF | N | 1 | 1 | 100.0 | 41 | 41.0 | 0 | 0 | 41 | 118.8 |

Mike Adamle
| 1975 | CHI | N | 2 | 2 | 100.0 | 57 | 28.5 | 0 | 0 | 44 | 118.8 |

George Adams
| 1985 | NYG | N | 1 | 0 | 0.0 | 0 | 0.0 | 0 | 0 | | 39.6 |

John Adams
| 1961 | CHI | N | 1 | 1 | 100.0 | 11 | 11.0 | 0 | 0 | 11 | 112.5 |

Tony Adams
1975	KC	N	77	36	46.8	445	5.8	2	4	32	52.1
1976			71	36	50.7	575	8.1	3	4	49t	68.7
1977			92	47	51.1	691	7.5	2	11	63	43.6
1978			79	44	55.7	415	5.3	2	3	26t	63.0
1987	MIN	N	89	49	55.1	607	6.8	3	5	63t	64.2
Career			408	212	52.0	2733	6.7	12	27	63t	55.5

Sam Adkins
1977	SEA	N	0	0		0		0	0		
1979			3	0	0.0	0	0.0	0	0		39.6
1980			23	10	43.5	136	5.9	1	3	22	37.9
1981			13	7	53.8	96	7.4	1	1	31t	71.3
Career			39	17	43.6	232	5.9	2	4	31t	40.7

Sam Agee
1938	CHIC	N	2	2	100.0	27	13.5	0	0		118.8
1939			3	0	0.0	0	0.0	0	0		39.6
Career			5	2	40.0	27	5.4	0	0		57.9

Tommie Agee
| 1988 | SEA | N | 1 | 0 | 0.0 | 0 | 0.0 | 0 | 1 | | 0.0 |

Louie Aguiar
| 1993 | NYJ | N | 2 | 0 | 0.0 | 0 | 0.0 | 0 | 1 | | 0.0 |

Joe Aguirre
| 1946 | LA | AA | 1 | 0 | 0.0 | 0 | 0.0 | 0 | 0 | | 39.6 |

Troy Aikman
1989	DAL	N	293	155	52.9	1749	6.0	9	18	75t	55.7
1990			399	226	56.6	2579	6.5	11	18	61t	66.6
1991			363	237	65.3	2754	7.6	11	10	61	86.7
1992			473	302	63.8	3445	7.3	23	14	87t	89.5
1993			392	271	69.1	3100	7.9	15	6	80t	99.0
1994			361	233	64.5	2676	7.4	13	12	90	84.9
1995			432	280	64.8	3304	7.6	16	7	50	93.6
1996			465	296	63.7	3126	6.7	12	13	61	80.1
Career			3178	2000	62.9	22733	7.2	110	98	90	83.0
Playoffs			415	276	66.5	3372	8.1	22	13		96.0

Vannie Albanese
1937	BKN	N	2	1	50.0	5	2.5	0	0	5	56.3
1938			1	0	0.0	0	0.0	0	0		39.6
Career			3	1	33.3	5	1.7	0	0	5	42.4

Frankie Albert
1946	SF	AA	197	104	52.8	1404	7.1	14	14	54t	69.8
1947			242	128	52.9	1692	7.0	18	15	60	74.3
1948			264	154	58.3	1990	7.5	29	10	59t	102.9
1949			260	129	49.6	1862	7.2	27	16	75t	82.2
1950	SF	N	306	155	50.7	1767	5.8	14	23	43	52.3
1951			166	90	54.2	1116	6.7	5	10	47	60.2
1952			129	71	55.0	964	7.5	8	10	60	67.5
Career			1564	831	53.1	10795	6.9	115	98	75t	73.5
Playoffs			41	17	41.5	204	5.0	2	2		53.3

Julie Alfonse
1937	CLE	N	10	4	40.0	48	4.8	0	0		55.4
1938			2	2	100.0	19	9.5	0	0		106.3
Career			12	6	50.0	67	5.6	0	0		67.0

Ermal Allen
| 1947 | CLE | AA | 13 | 4 | 30.8 | 88 | 6.8 | 0 | 0 | 62 | 55.9 |

Marcus Allen
1982	LARI	N	4	1	25.0	47	11.8	0	0	47	76.0
1983			7	4	57.1	111	15.9	3	0	43t	141.4
1984			4	1	25.0	38	9.5	0	0	38	66.7
1985			2	1	50.0	16	8.0	0	0	16	77.1
1987			2	1	50.0	23	11.5	0	0	23	91.7
1988			2	1	50.0	21	10.5	0	0	21	87.5
1990			1	0	0.0	0	0.0	0	1		0.0
1991			2	1	50.0	11	5.5	1	0	11t	106.3
1996	KC	N	1	0	0.0	0	0.0	0	0	0	39.6
Career			25	10	40.0	267	10.7	4	1	47	102.8

Jim Allison
| 1968 | SD | A | 1 | 1 | 100.0 | 23 | 23.0 | 1 | 0 | 23t | 158.3 |

Lance Alworth
1964	SD	A	1	1	100.0	-11	-11.0	0	0	-11	79.2
1967			1	0	0.0	0	0.0	0	0		39.6
Career			2	1	50.0	-11	-5.5	0	0	-11	56.3

George Amundson
| 1974 | HOU | N | 1 | 0 | 0.0 | 0 | 0.0 | 0 | 1 | | 0.0 |

Kimble Anders
| 1993 | KC | N | 0 | 0 | | 0 | | 0 | 0 | | |

Alfred Anderson
1984	MIN	N	7	3	42.9	95	13.6	2	1	43t	89.9
1986			2	1	50.0	17	8.5	0	0	17	79.2
Career			9	4	44.4	112	12.4	2	1	43t	91.0

Bill Anderson
| 1963 | WAS | N | 1 | 0 | 0.0 | 0 | 0.0 | 0 | 1 | | 0.0 |

Bobby Anderson
1970	DEN	N	7	4	57.1	59	8.4	0	0	25	84.8
1971			3	1	33.3	48	16.0	0	0	48	81.9
1972			3	1	33.3	14	4.7	1	0	14t	88.9
1973			3	2	66.7	47	15.7	0	0	28	109.7
1975	WAS	N	1	0	0.0	0	0.0	0	0		39.6
Career			17	8	47.1	168	9.9	1	0	48	102.1

Donny Anderson
1967	GB	N	2	1	50.0	19	9.5	0	0	19	83.3
1968			3	1	33.3	12	4.0	1	0	12t	86.1
1970			1	0	0.0	0	0.0	0	0		39.6
1971			4	2	50.0	9	2.3	1	0	5	95.8
1972	STL	N	3	2	66.7	71	23.7	0	0	38	109.7
Career			13	6	46.2	111	8.5	2	0	38	115.7

Gary Anderson
1985	SD	N	0	0		0		0	0		
1986			1	1	100.0	4	4.0	1	0	4t	122.9
Career			1	1	100.0	4	4.0	1	0	4t	122.9

Ken Anderson
1971	CIN	N	131	72	55.0	777	5.9	5	4	44	72.6
1972			301	171	56.8	1918	6.4	7	7	65t	74.0
1973			329	179	54.4	2428	7.4	18	12	78t	81.2
1974			328	213	64.9	2667	8.1	18	10	77t	95.7
1975			377	228	60.5	3169	8.4	21	11	55	93.9
1976			338	179	53.0	2367	7.0	19	14	85t	76.9
1977			323	166	51.4	2145	6.6	11	11	94t	69.7
1978			319	173	54.2	2219	7.0	10	22	57	58.0
1979			339	189	55.8	2340	6.9	16	10	73t	80.7
1980			275	166	60.4	1778	6.5	6	13	67t	66.9
1981			479	300	62.6	3754	7.8	29	10	74t	98.4
1982			309	218	70.6	2495	8.1	12	9	56t	95.3
1983			297	198	66.7	2333	7.9	12	13	80t	85.6
1984			275	175	63.6	2107	7.7	10	12	80t	81.0
1985			32	16	50.0	170	5.3	2	0	44t	86.7
1986			23	11	47.8	171	7.4	1	2	43	51.2
Career			4475	2654	59.3	32838	7.3	197	160	94t	81.9
Playoffs			166	110	66.3	1321	8.0	9	6		93.5

Max Anderson
| 1968 | BUF | A | 1 | 0 | 0.0 | 0 | 0.0 | 0 | 0 | | 39.6 |

Neal Anderson
| 1988 | CHI | N | 1 | 0 | 0.0 | 0 | 0.0 | 0 | 0 | | 39.6 |
| 1991 | | | 1 | 0 | 0.0 | 0 | 0.0 | 0 | 0 | | 39.6 |

Year	Team		Att	Com	PC	Yds	Avg	TD	Int	Lg	Rtg

Neal Anderson *continued*

Year	Team		Att	Com	PC	Yds	Avg	TD	Int	Lg	Rtg
1993			1	0	0.0	0	0.0	0	0		39.6
Career			3	0	0.0	0	0.0	0	0		39.6
Playoffs			1	1	100.0	22	22.0	0	0		118.8

Ockie Anderson

| 1921 | BUF | A | | | | | | | 1 | | |

O.J. Anderson

| 1979 | STL | N | 1 | 0 | 0.0 | 0 | 0.0 | 0 | 0 | | 39.6 |

Richie Anderson

| 1995 | NYJ | N | 1 | 0 | 0.0 | 0 | 0.0 | 0 | 0 | | 39.6 |

Roy Andrews

| 1924 | KC | N | | | | | | | 1 | | |

William Andrews

1982	ATL	N	0	0		0		0	0		
1983			1	0	0.0	0	0.0	0	0		39.6
Career			1	0	0.0	0	0.0	0	0		39.6

Elmer Angsman

1946	CHIC	N	1	0	0.0	0	0.0	0	0		39.6
1949			1	0	0.0	0	0.0	0	0		39.6
Career			2	0	0.0	0	0.0	0	0		39.6

Evan Arapostathis

| 1986 | STL | N | 1 | 0 | 0.0 | 0 | 0.0 | 0 | 0 | | 39.6 |

David Archer

1984	ATL	N	18	11	61.1	181	10.1	1	1	34	90.3
1985			312	161	51.6	1992	6.4	7	17	62t	56.5
1986			294	150	51.0	2007	6.8	10	9	65	71.6
1987			23	9	39.1	95	4.1	0	2	33	15.7
1988	WAS	N	2	0	0.0	0	0.0	0	0		39.6
1989	SD	N	12	5	41.7	62	5.2	0	1	17	23.6
Career			661	336	50.8	4337	6.6	18	30	65	61.9

Joe Arenas

1952	SF	N	1	0	0.0	0	0.0	0	0		39.6
1953			1	0	0.0	0	0.0	0	0		39.6
1955			1	0	0.0	0	0.0	0	0		39.6
1957			3	3	100.0	92	30.7	2	0	33t	158.3
Career			6	3	50.0	92	15.3	2	0	33t	135.4

Justin Armour

| 1995 | BUF | N | 1 | 0 | 0.0 | 0 | 0.0 | 0 | 0 | | 39.6 |

Charlie Armstrong

| 1946 | BKN | AA | 21 | 9 | 42.9 | 126 | 6.0 | 1 | 2 | 52t | 39.1 |

Johnny Armstrong

1923	RI	N						3			
1924								1			
1925								3			
Career								7			

Jon Arnett

1958	LA	N	1	0	0.0	0	0.0	0	0		39.6
1959			5	1	20.0	13	2.6	0	0	13	39.6
1960			1	0	0.0	0	0.0	0	0		39.6
1961			13	3	23.1	47	3.6	0	1	20	10.1
1962			5	3	60.0	28	5.6	1	0	15t	115.0
1963			1	0	0.0	0	0.0	0	1		0.0
1964	CHI	N	4	0	0.0	0	0.0	0	0		39.6
1965			2	1	50.0	59	29.5	1	0	59t	135.4
1966			1	0	0.0	0	0.0	0	0		39.6
Career			33	8	24.2	147	4.5	2	2	59t	40.6

Jim Arnold

| 1988 | DET | N | 1 | 0 | 0.0 | 0 | 0.0 | 0 | 0 | | 39.6 |

Rick Arrington

1970	PHI	N	73	37	50.7	328	4.5	1	3	23	50.5
1971			118	55	46.6	576	4.9	2	5	65	49.3
1972			13	5	38.5	46	3.5	0	1	16	16.8
Career			204	97	47.5	950	4.7	3	9	65	47.6

Willie Asbury

| 1966 | PIT | N | 1 | 0 | 0.0 | 0 | 0.0 | 0 | 0 | | 39.6 |

Reggie Attache

| 1922 | OOR | N | | | | | | | 1 | | |

Bob Avellini

1975	CHI	N	126	67	53.2	942	7.5	6	11	57	57.0
1976			271	118	43.5	1580	5.8	8	15	63t	49.4
1977			293	154	52.6	2004	6.8	11	18	75t	61.3
1978			264	141	53.4	1718	6.5	5	16	61	54.8
1979			51	27	52.9	310	6.1	2	3	54t	60.1
1981			32	15	46.9	185	5.8	1	3	72t	36.6
1982			20	8	40.0	84	4.2	0	0	21	52.9
1984			53	30	56.6	288	5.4	0	3	50	48.3
Career			1110	560	50.5	7111	6.4	33	69	75t	54.8
Playoffs			25	15	60.0	177	7.1	1	4		55.3

John Aveni

| 1961 | WAS | N | 1 | 0 | 0.0 | 0 | 0.0 | 0 | 0 | | 39.6 |

Rob Awalt

| 1989 | PHX | N | 1 | 0 | 0.0 | 0 | 0.0 | 0 | 1 | | 0.0 |

Frank Bacon

| 1922 | DAY | N | | | | | | | 1 | | |

Red Badgro

| 1930 | NYG | N | | | | | | | 1 | | |

Pete Bahan

| 1923 | CLE | N | | | | | | | 1 | | |

Johnny Bailey

| 1990 | CHI | N | 1 | 1 | 100.0 | 22 | 22.0 | 0 | 0 | 22 | 118.8 |

Bullet Baker

1926	NY	A							1		
1927	NYY	N							1		
1931	SI	N							1		
Career									3		

Ed Baker

| 1972 | HOU | N | 10 | 4 | 40.0 | 47 | 4.7 | 0 | 4 | 18 | 15.4 |

Sam Baker

1962	DAL	N	1	0	0.0	0	0.0	0	0		39.6
1968	PHI	N	1	1	100.0	58	58.0	1	0	58t	158.3
Career			2	1	50.0	58	29.0	1	0	58t	135.4

Terry Baker

1963	LA	N	19	11	57.9	140	7.4	0	4	49	41.4
1964			1	0	0.0	0	0.0	0	0		39.6
1965			1	1	100.0	14	14.0	0	0	14	118.8
Career			21	12	57.1	154	7.3	0	4	49	40.7

Jim Bakken

| 1975 | STL | N | 0 | 0 | | 0 | | 0 | 0 | | |

Frank Balazs

1940	GB	N	1	0	0.0	0	0.0	0	1		0.0
1941	CHIC	N	4	0	0.0	0	0.0	0	2		0.0
Career			5	0	0.0	0	0.0	0	3		0.0

Lou Baldacci

| 1956 | PIT | N | 1 | 0 | 0.0 | 0 | 0.0 | 0 | 0 | | 39.6 |

Gary Ballman

1964	PIT	N	1	0	0.0	0	0.0	0	1		0.0
1970	PHI	N	1	0	0.0	0	0.0	0	0		39.6
Career			2	0	0.0	0	0.0	0	1		0.0

Pete Banaszak

| 1968 | OAK | A | 1 | 0 | 0.0 | 0 | 0.0 | 0 | 1 | | 0.0 |

Herb Banet

| 1937 | GB | N | 7 | 1 | 14.3 | 2 | 0.3 | 0 | 2 | 2 | 0.0 |

Tony Banks

| 1996 | STL | N | 368 | 192 | 52.2 | 2544 | 6.9 | 15 | 15 | 77t | 71.0 |

Mark Barber

| 1937 | CLE | N | 3 | 1 | 33.3 | 7 | 2.3 | 0 | 0 | 7 | 42.4 |

Mike Barber

| Playoffs | | | 1 | 0 | 0.0 | 0 | 0.0 | 0 | 0 | | 39.6 |

Billy Ray Barnes

Year	Team		Att	Com	PC	Yds	Avg	TD	Int	Lg	Rtg
1957	PHI	N	1	0	0.0	0	0.0	0	0		39.6
1958			6	4	66.7	104	17.3	3	0	71t	149.3
1959			7	0	0.0	0	0.0	0	2		0.0
1960			3	0	0.0	0	0.0	0	2		0.0
1962	WAS	N	4	3	75.0	48	12.0	0	0	22	114.6
1963			4	3	75.0	81	20.3	1	0	32	156.3
Career			25	10	40.0	233	9.3	4	4	71t	74.3

Joe Barnes

Year	Team		Att	Com	PC	Yds	Avg	TD	Int	Lg	Rtg
1974	CHI	N	9	2	22.2	29	3.2	0	1	24	0.9

Larry Barnes

Year	Team		Att	Com	PC	Yds	Avg	TD	Int	Lg	Rtg
1957	SF	N	1	1	100.0	-2	-2.0	0	0	-2	79.2

Tommy Barnhardt

Year	Team		Att	Com	PC	Yds	Avg	TD	Int	Lg	Rtg
1993	NO	N	1	1	100.0	7	7.0	0	0	7	95.8
1994			1	0	0.0	0	0.0	0	0		39.6
Career			2	1	50.0	7	3.5	0	0	7	58.3

Dan Barnhart

Year	Team		Att	Com	PC	Yds	Avg	TD	Int	Lg	Rtg
1934	PHI	N						1			

Len Barnum

Year	Team		Att	Com	PC	Yds	Avg	TD	Int	Lg	Rtg
1938	NYG	N	6	1	16.7	45	7.5	0	1	45	18.8
1939			27	8	29.6	141	5.2	3	1		70.4
1940			23	9	39.1	150	6.5	3	2		65.2
1941	PHI	N	55	19	34.5	260	4.7	0	10	33	11.0
1942			9	1	11.1	6	0.7	0	1	6	0.0
Career			120	38	31.7	602	5.0	6	15	45	26.5
Playoffs			4	0	0.0	0	0.0	0	1		0.0

Dave Barr

Year	Team		Att	Com	PC	Yds	Avg	TD	Int	Lg	Rtg
1995	STL	N	9	5	55.6	42	4.7	0	0	18	67.8

Shorty Barr

Year	Team		Att	Com	PC	Yds	Avg	TD	Int	Lg	Rtg
1923	RAC	N						5			
1926								1			
Career								6	18		

Terry Barr

Year	Team		Att	Com	PC	Yds	Avg	TD	Int	Lg	Rtg
1959	DET	N	1	0	0.0	0	0.0	0	0		39.6
1960			1	0	0.0	0	0.0	0	0		39.6
1964			1	0	0.0	0	0.0	0	0		39.6
Career			3	0	0.0	0	0.0	0	0		39.6

Tom Barrington

Year	Team		Att	Com	PC	Yds	Avg	TD	Int	Lg	Rtg
1966	WAS	N	1	0	0.0	0	0.0	0	0		39.6
1967	NO	N	2	0	0.0	0	0.0	0	0		39.6
1968			6	2	33.3	42	7.0	0	0	23	59.0
1969			2	1	50.0	15	7.5	0	0	15	75.0
Career			11	3	27.3	57	5.2	0	0	23	48.7

Steve Bartalo

Year	Team		Att	Com	PC	Yds	Avg	TD	Int	Lg	Rtg
1987	TB	N	1	0	0.0	0	0.0	0	1		0.0

Steve Bartkowski

Year	Team		Att	Com	PC	Yds	Avg	TD	Int	Lg	Rtg
1975	ATL	N	255	115	45.1	1662	6.5	13	15	68	59.3
1976			120	57	47.5	677	5.6	2	9	50t	39.5
1977			136	64	47.1	796	5.9	5	13	73t	38.4
1978			369	187	50.7	2489	6.7	10	18	71	61.1
1979			380	204	53.7	2505	6.6	17	20	65	67.3
1980			463	257	55.5	3544	7.7	31	16	81t	88.2
1981			533	297	55.7	3829	7.2	30	23	70t	79.2
1982			262	166	63.4	1905	7.3	8	11	86t	77.9
1983			432	274	63.4	3167	7.3	22	5	76t	97.6
1984			269	181	67.3	2158	8.0	11	10	61	89.7
1985			111	69	62.2	738	6.6	5	1	62t	92.8
1986	LARM	N	126	61	48.4	654	5.2	2	3	42	59.4
Career			3456	1932	55.9	24124	7.0	156	144	86t	75.4
Playoffs			111	53	47.7	792	7.1	5	8		56.6

Greg Barton

Year	Team		Att	Com	PC	Yds	Avg	TD	Int	Lg	Rtg
1969	DET	N	1	0	0.0	0	0.0	0	0		39.6

Mike Basca

Year	Team		Att	Com	PC	Yds	Avg	TD	Int	Lg	Rtg
1941	PHI	N	4	0	0.0	0	0.0	0	1		0.0

Brian Baschnagel

Year	Team		Att	Com	PC	Yds	Avg	TD	Int	Lg	Rtg
1977	CHI	N	1	0	0.0	0	0.0	0	0		39.6
1979			1	0	0.0	0	0.0	0	0		39.6
1981			1	1	100.0	18	18.0	0	0	18	118.8
1982			1	0	0.0	0	0.0	0	0		39.6

Brian Baschnagel *continued*

Year	Team		Att	Com	PC	Yds	Avg	TD	Int	Lg	Rtg
1984			2	1	50.0	7	3.5	0	0	7	58.3
Career			6	2	33.3	25	4.2	0	0	18	47.2

Billy Bass

Year	Team		Att	Com	PC	Yds	Avg	TD	Int	Lg	Rtg
1947	CHI	AA	1	1	100.0	14	14.0	0	0	14	118.8

Dick Bass

Year	Team		Att	Com	PC	Yds	Avg	TD	Int	Lg	Rtg
1962	LA	N	3	1	33.3	22	7.3	0	0	22	60.4
1963			1	0	0.0	0	0.0	0	0		39.6
Career			4	1	25.0	22	5.5	0	0	22	50.0

Reds Bassman

Year	Team		Att	Com	PC	Yds	Avg	TD	Int	Lg	Rtg
1936	PHI	N	3	1	33.3	3	1.0	0	1	3	2.8

Cliff Battles

Year	Team		Att	Com	PC	Yds	Avg	TD	Int	Lg	Rtg
1936	BOS	N	52	18	34.6	242	4.7	1	6		17.1
1937	WAS	N	33	13	39.4	142	4.3	0	3		15.0
Career			85	31	36.5	384	4.5	1	9	3	15.6
Playoffs			5	3	60.0	21	4.2	0	1		30.0

Hank Bauer

Year	Team		Att	Com	PC	Yds	Avg	TD	Int	Lg	Rtg
1979	SD	N	0	0		0		0	0		

Sammy Baugh

Year	Team		Att	Com	PC	Yds	Avg	TD	Int	Lg	Rtg
1937	WAS	N	171	81	47.4	1127	6.6	8	14	59	50.5
1938			128	63	49.2	853	6.7	5	11	60	48.1
1939			96	53	55.2	518	5.4	6	9	44	52.3
1940			177	111	62.7	1367	7.7	12	10	81	85.6
1941			193	106	54.9	1236	6.4	10	19	55	52.2
1942			225	132	58.7	1524	6.8	16	11	53	82.5
1943			239	133	55.6	1754	7.3	23	19	72	78.0
1944			146	82	56.2	849	5.8	4	8	71	59.4
1945			182	128	70.3	1669	9.2	11	4	70	109.9
1946			161	87	54.0	1163	7.2	8	17	51	54.2
1947			354	210	59.3	2938	8.3	25	15	74	92.0
1948			315	185	58.7	2599	8.3	22	23	86	78.3
1949			255	145	56.9	1903	7.5	18	14	76	81.2
1950			166	90	54.2	1130	6.8	10	11	56t	68.1
1951			154	67	43.5	1104	7.2	7	17	53t	43.8
1952			33	20	60.6	152	4.6	2	1	20	79.4
Career			2995	1693	56.5	21886	7.3	187	203	86	72.2
Playoffs			101	57	56.4	840	8.3	7	8		73.9

Craig Baynham

Year	Team		Att	Com	PC	Yds	Avg	TD	Int	Lg	Rtg
1968	DAL	N	1	0	0.0	0	0.0	0	0		39.6

Winnie Baze

Year	Team		Att	Com	PC	Yds	Avg	TD	Int	Lg	Rtg
1937	PHI	N	3	0	0.0	0	0.0	0	0		39.6

Bubba Bean

Year	Team		Att	Com	PC	Yds	Avg	TD	Int	Lg	Rtg
1976	ATL	N	1	1	100.0	49	49.0	1	0	49t	158.3
1978			1	0	0.0	0	0.0	0	1		0.0
Career			2	1	50.0	49	24.5	1	1	49t	95.8

Pete Beathard

Year	Team		Att	Com	PC	Yds	Avg	TD	Int	Lg	Rtg
1964	KC	A	9	4	44.4	50	5.6	1	2		59.7
1965			89	36	40.4	632	7.1	1	6	73	41.0
1966			90	39	43.3	578	6.4	4	4	77	61.3
1967	KC-HOU	A	231	94	40.7	1114	4.8	9	14	43t	43.8
1968	HOU	A	223	105	47.1	1559	7.0	7	16	66t	51.0
1969			370	180	48.6	2455	6.6	10	21	86t	55.6
1970	STL	N	17	7	41.2	114	6.7	2	1	58t	79.0
1971			141	60	42.6	1030	7.3	6	12	80t	46.7
1972	LA	N	48	19	39.6	255	5.3	1	7	33	24.6
1973	KC	N	64	31	48.4	389	6.1	2	1	44	71.7
Career			1282	575	44.9	8176	6.4	43	84	86t	49.9
Playoffs			86	34	39.5	368	4.3	2	5		36.4

Gary Beban

Year	Team		Att	Com	PC	Yds	Avg	TD	Int	Lg	Rtg
1968	WAS	N	1	0	0.0	0	0.0	0	0		39.6

Keith Beebe

Year	Team		Att	Com	PC	Yds	Avg	TD	Int	Lg	Rtg
1944	NY	N	3	1	33.3	9	3.0	0	1	9	2.8

Eddie Bell

Year	Team		Att	Com	PC	Yds	Avg	TD	Int	Lg	Rtg
1970	NYJ	N	1	0	0.0	0	0.0	0	0		0.0

Greg Bell

Year	Team		Att	Com	PC	Yds	Avg	TD	Int	Lg	Rtg
1985	BUF	N	1	0	0.0	0	0.0	0	0		39.6

Kerwin Bell

Year	Team		Att	Com	PC	Yds	Avg	TD	Int	Lg	Rtg
1996	IND	N	5	5	100.0	75	15.0	1	0	30	158.3

Guy Benjamin

Year	Team		Att	Com	PC	Yds	Avg	TD	Int	Lg	Rtg
1978	MIA	N	8	6	75.0	91	11.4	1	1	43	112.0
1979			4	3	75.0	28	7.0	0	0	17	93.8
1980	NO	N	17	7	41.2	28	1.6	0	1	17	24.4
1981	SF	N	26	15	57.7	171	6.6	1	1	27t	74.4
1982			1	1	100.0	10	10.0	0	0	10	108.3
1983			12	7	58.3	111	9.3	1	0	73t	117.0
Career			68	39	57.4	439	6.5	3	3	73t	73.1

Fred Benners

Year	Team		Att	Com	PC	Yds	Avg	TD	Int	Lg	Rtg
1952	NYG	N	58	25	43.1	320	5.5	0	5	35	25.1

Ben Bennett

Year	Team		Att	Com	PC	Yds	Avg	TD	Int	Lg	Rtg
1987	CIN	N	6	2	33.3	25	4.2	0	1	18	7.6

Albert Bentley

Year	Team		Att	Com	PC	Yds	Avg	TD	Int	Lg	Rtg
1985	IND	N	1	1	100.0	6	6.0	0	0	6	91.7
1986			0	0		0		0	0		
1988			1	0	0.0	0	0.0	0	0		39.6
1989			1	0	0.0	0	0.0	0	0		39.6
Career			3	1	33.3	6	2.0	0	0	6	42.4

Dave Bernard

Year	Team		Att	Com	PC	Yds	Avg	TD	Int	Lg	Rtg
1944	CLE	N	4	0	0.0	0	0.0	0	2		0.0

Frank Bernardi

Year	Team		Att	Com	PC	Yds	Avg	TD	Int	Lg	Rtg
1957	CHIC	N	1	0	0.0	0	0.0	0	0		39.6

Rod Bernstine

Year	Team		Att	Com	PC	Yds	Avg	TD	Int	Lg	Rtg
1991	SD	N	1	1	100.0	11	11.0	1	0	11t	152.1

Bob Berry

Year	Team		Att	Com	PC	Yds	Avg	TD	Int	Lg	Rtg
1965	MIN	N	2	0	0.0	0	0.0	0	0		39.6
1966			37	13	35.1	215	5.8	1	5	52t	25.0
1967			7	3	42.9	43	6.1	0	0	21	63.4
1968	ATL	N	153	81	52.9	1433	9.4	7	13	66	65.1
1969			124	71	57.3	1087	8.8	10	2	88t	106.5
1970			269	156	58.0	1806	6.7	16	13	51t	78.1
1971			226	136	60.2	2005	8.9	11	16	84	75.9
1972			277	154	55.6	2158	7.8	13	12	57t	78.5
1973	MIN	N	24	10	41.7	121	5.0	1	2	30t	37.0
1974			48	34	70.8	305	6.4	5	1	21	113.6
1975			6	3	50.0	24	4.0	0	0	17	60.4
Career			1173	661	56.4	9197	7.8	64	64	88t	77.2

Angelo Bertelli

Year	Team		Att	Com	PC	Yds	Avg	TD	Int	Lg	Rtg
1946	LA	AA	127	67	52.8	917	7.2	7	14	71t	54.9
1947	CHI	AA	7	2	28.6	-5	-0.7	0	2		0.0
1948			32	7	21.9	60	1.9	1	3		10.9
Career			166	76	45.8	972	5.9	8	19	71t	41.1

Steve Beuerlein

Year	Team		Att	Com	PC	Yds	Avg	TD	Int	Lg	Rtg
1988	LARI	N	238	105	44.1	1643	6.9	8	7	57	66.6
1989			217	108	49.8	1677	7.7	13	9	67t	78.4
1991	DAL	N	137	68	49.6	909	6.6	5	2	66t	77.2
1992			18	12	66.7	152	8.4	0	1	27	69.7
1993	PHX	N	418	258	61.7	3164	7.6	18	17	65t	82.5
1994	ARI	N	255	130	51.0	1545	6.1	5	9	63	61.6
1995	JAC	N	142	71	50.0	952	6.7	4	7	71t	60.5
1996	CAR	N	123	69	56.1	879	7.1	8	2	40t	93.5
Career			1548	821	53.0	10921	7.1	61	54	71t	74.3
Playoffs			31	16	51.6	271	8.7	1	1		78.8

David Beverly

Year	Team		Att	Com	PC	Yds	Avg	TD	Int	Lg	Rtg
1976	GB	N	1	1	100.0	18	18.0	0	0	18	118.8
1978			2	2	100.0	88	44.0	0	0	57	118.8
1979			2	1	50.0	23	11.5	0	0	23	91.7
1980			1	0	0.0	0	0.0	0	0		39.6
Career			6	4	66.7	129	21.5	0	0	57	109.7

Johnny Biancone

Year	Team		Att	Com	PC	Yds	Avg	TD	Int	Lg	Rtg
1936	BKN	N	3	1	33.3	29	9.7	0	0	29	70.1

Eric Bieniemy

Year	Team		Att	Com	PC	Yds	Avg	TD	Int	Lg	Rtg
1995	CIN	N	2	0	0.0	0	0.0	0	0		39.6

Dick Bilda

Year	Team		Att	Com	PC	Yds	Avg	TD	Int	Lg	Rtg
1944	GB	N	1	0	0.0	0	0.0	0	0		39.6

Carl Birdsong

Year	Team		Att	Com	PC	Yds	Avg	TD	Int	Lg	Rtg
1983	STL	N	1	1	100.0	11	11.0	0	0	11	112.5
1985			1	0	0.0	0	0.0	0	0		39.6
Career			2	1	50.0	11	5.5	0	0	11	66.7

Don Bishop

Year	Team		Att	Com	PC	Yds	Avg	TD	Int	Lg	Rtg
1958	PIT	N	0	0		0		0	0		

Mike Black

Year	Team		Att	Com	PC	Yds	Avg	TD	Int	Lg	Rtg
1983	DET	N	1	0	0.0	0	0.0	0	1		0.0

Todd Blackledge

Year	Team		Att	Com	PC	Yds	Avg	TD	Int	Lg	Rtg
1983	KC	N	34	20	58.8	259	7.6	3	0	43	112.3
1984			294	147	50.0	1707	5.8	6	11	46t	59.2
1985			172	86	50.0	1190	6.9	6	14	70t	50.3
1986			211	96	45.5	1200	5.7	10	6	70t	67.6
1987			31	15	48.4	154	5.0	1	1	19	60.4
1988	PIT	N	79	38	48.1	494	6.3	2	3	34	60.8
1989			60	22	36.7	282	4.7	1	3	30	36.9
Career			881	424	48.1	5286	6.0	29	38	70t	60.2
Playoffs			21	12	57.1	80	3.8	1	2		41.9

Brian Blades

Year	Team		Att	Com	PC	Yds	Avg	TD	Int	Lg	Rtg
1988	SEA	N	0	0		0		0	0		

Jeff Blake

Year	Team		Att	Com	PC	Yds	Avg	TD	Int	Lg	Rtg
1992	NYJ	N	9	4	44.4	40	4.4	0	1	19	18.1
1994	CIN	N	306	156	51.0	2154	7.0	14	9	76	76.9
1995			567	326	57.5	3822	6.7	28	17	88t	82.1
1996			549	308	56.1	3624	6.6	24	14	61t	80.3
Career			1431	794	55.5	9640	6.7	66	41	88t	79.8

Tom Blanchard

Year	Team		Att	Com	PC	Yds	Avg	TD	Int	Lg	Rtg
1971	NYG	N	1	1	100.0	18	18.0	0	0	18	118.8
1972			1	0	0.0	0		0	0		39.6
1976	NO	N	0	0		0		0	0		
1977			3	1	33.3	3	1.0	1	1	3t	42.4
Career			5	2	40.0	21	4.2	1	1	18	52.9

George Blanda

Year	Team		Att	Com	PC	Yds	Avg	TD	Int	Lg	Rtg
1949	CHIB	N	21	9	42.9	197	9.4	0	5	44	37.3
1950			1	0	0.0	0		0	0		39.6
1952			131	47	35.9	664	5.1	8	11	59t	38.5
1953			362	169	46.7	2164	6.0	14	23	72	52.3
1954			281	131	46.6	1929	6.9	15	17	76t	62.1
1955			97	42	43.3	459	4.7	4	7	51t	41.6
1956			69	37	53.6	439	6.4	7	4	69t	82.9
1957			19	8	42.1	65	3.4	0	3	13	11.8
1958			7	2	28.6	19	2.7	0	0	12	39.6
1960	HOU	A	363	169	46.6	2413	6.6	24	22	88t	65.4
1961			362	187	51.7	3330	9.2	36	22	88t	91.3
1962			418	197	47.1	2810	6.7	27	42		51.3
1963			423	224	53.0	3003	7.1	24	25	80t	70.1
1964			505	262	51.9	3287	6.5	17	27	80t	61.4
1965			442	186	42.1	2542	5.8	20	30	95	47.9
1966			271	122	45.0	1764	6.5	17	21	79	55.3
1967	OAK	A	38	15	39.5	285	7.5	3	3	50t	59.6
1968			49	30	61.2	522	10.7	6	2	94t	120.1
1969			13	6	46.2	73	5.6	2	1	20	71.5
1970	OAK	N	55	29	52.7	461	8.4	6	5	44t	79.4
1971			58	32	55.2	378	6.5	4	6	37	58.6
1972			15	5	33.3	77	5.1	1	0	26t	73.5
1974			4	1	25.0	28	7.0	1	0	28t	95.8
1975			3	1	33.3	11	3.7	0	1	11	5.6
Career			4007	1911	47.7	26920	6.7	236	277	95	60.6
Playoffs			189	89	47.1	1190	6.3	7	17		42.4

Sid Blanks

Year	Team		Att	Com	PC	Yds	Avg	TD	Int	Lg	Rtg
1964	HOU	A	1	1	100.0	8	8.0	1	0	8t	139.6

Drew Bledsoe

Year	Team		Att	Com	PC	Yds	Avg	TD	Int	Lg	Rtg
1993	NE	N	429	214	49.9	2494	5.8	15	15	54t	65.0
1994			691	400	57.9	4555	6.6	25	27	62t	73.6
1995			636	323	50.8	3507	5.5	13	16	47t	63.7
1996			623	373	59.9	4086	6.6	27	15	84t	83.7
Career			2379	1310	55.1	14642	6.2	80	73	84t	72.0
Playoffs			155	80	51.6	830	5.4	4	10		49.1

Bob Bleier

Year	Team		Att	Com	PC	Yds	Avg	TD	Int	Lg	Rtg
1987	NE	N	39	14	35.9	181	4.6	1	1	35	49.2

Johnny Blood

Year	Team		Att	Com	PC	Yds	Avg	TD	Int	Lg	Rtg
1929	GB	N							1		
1931									1		
1935			33	11	33.3	165	5.0	0	3		12.8
1936			6	3	50.0	20	3.3	1	0		97.2
1937	PIT	N	25	10	40.0	115	4.6	1	2		34.6
Career			64	24	37.5	300	4.7	4	5	35	30.7

Year	Team		Att	Com	PC	Yds	Avg	TD	Int	Lg	Rtg
Jeb Blount											
1977	TB	N	89	37	41.6	522	5.9	0	7	56	28.4
Jimmy Blumenstock											
1947	NYG	N	8	4	50.0	48	6.0	0	1	19	29.2
Matt Blundin											
1993	KC	N	3	1	33.3	2	0.7	0	0	2	42.4
1994			5	1	20.0	13	2.6	0	1	13	0.0
Career			8	2	25.0	15	1.9	0	1	13	0.0
Dewey Bohling											
1960	NY	A	5	0	0.0	0	0.0	0	0		39.6
1961	BUF	A	1	0	0.0	0	0.0	0	0		39.6
Career			6	0	0.0	0	0.0	0	0		39.6
Steve Bono											
1985	MIN	N	10	1	10.0	5	0.5	0	0	5	39.6
1986			1	1	100.0	3	3.0	0	0	3	79.2
1987	PIT	N	74	34	45.9	438	5.9	5	2	57	76.3
1988			35	10	28.6	110	3.1	1	2	15	25.9
1989	SF	N	5	4	80.0	62	12.4	1	0	45t	157.9
1991			237	141	59.5	1617	6.8	11	4	78	88.5
1992			56	36	64.3	463	8.3	2	2	36	87.1
1993			61	39	63.9	416	6.8	0	1	33	76.9
1994	KC	N	117	66	56.4	796	6.8	4	4	62t	74.6
1995			520	293	56.3	3121	6.0	21	10	60t	79.5
1996			438	235	53.7	2572	5.9	12	13	69	68.0
Career			1554	860	55.3	9603	6.2	57	38	78	76.0
Playoffs			27	13	48.1	137	5.1	1	3		36.1
J.R. Boone											
1948	CHIB	N	1	1	100.0	4	4.0	0	0	4	83.3
1953	GB	N	1	1	100.0	-2	-2.0	0	0	-2	79.2
Career			2	2	100.0	2	1.0	0	0	4	79.2
Dick Booth											
1941	DET	N	8	5	62.5	135	16.9	2	1	71	106.3
John Borton											
1957	CLE	N	6	3	50.0	22	3.7	0	1	8	19.4
Mike Boryla											
1974	PHI	N	102	60	58.8	580	5.7	5	3	29	78.9
1975			166	87	52.4	996	6.0	6	12	46	52.7
1976			246	123	50.0	1247	5.1	9	14	48t	53.4
1978	TB	N	5	2	40.0	15	3.0	0	0	18	47.9
Career			519	272	52.4	2838	5.5	20	29	48t	58.1
Don Bosseler											
1959	WAS	N	1	0	0.0	0	0.0	0	0		39.6
Lee Bouggess											
1970	PHI	N	1	0	0.0	0	0.0	0	0		39.6
Tony Bova											
1944	C-P	N	30	6	20.0	96	3.2	0	1	34	26.5
1945	PIT	N	1	0	0.0	0	0.0	0	0		39.6
Career			31	6	19.4	96	3.1	0	1	34	26.5
Bobby Boyd											
1961	BAL	N	1	0	0.0	0	0.0	0	0		39.6
Mike Boyda											
1949	NYB	N	1	0	0.0	0	0.0	0	0		39.6
Benny Boynton											
1921	ROC-WAS	A						5			
1924	BUF	N						6			
Career								11			
Charlie Brackins											
1955	GB	N	2	0	0.0	0	0.0	0	0		39.6
Bill Bradley											
1969	PHI	N	1	0	0.0	0	0.0	0	0		39.6
Steve Bradley											
1987	CHI	N	18	6	33.3	77	4.3	2	3	18t	45.1
Terry Bradshaw											
1970	PIT	N	218	83	38.1	1410	6.5	6	24	87t	30.4
1971			373	203	54.4	2259	6.1	13	22	49	59.7

Year	Team		Att	Com	PC	Yds	Avg	TD	Int	Lg	Rtg
Terry Bradshaw *continued*											
1972			308	147	47.7	1887	6.1	12	12	78t	64.1
1973			180	89	49.4	1183	6.6	10	15	67	54.5
1974			148	67	45.3	785	5.3	7	8	56	55.2
1975			286	165	57.7	2055	7.2	18	9	59	88.0
1976			192	92	47.9	1177	6.1	10	9	50	65.4
1977			314	162	51.6	2523	**8.0**	17	19	65t	71.4
1978			368	207	56.3	2915	**7.9**	**28**	20	70	84.7
1979			472	259	54.9	3724	7.9	26	25	65t	77.0
1980			424	218	51.4	3339	7.9	24	22	68t	75.0
1981			370	201	54.3	2887	7.8	22	14	90t	83.9
1982			240	127	52.9	1768	7.4	**17**	11	74t	81.4
1983			8	5	62.5	77	9.6	2	0	24	133.9
Career			3901	2025	51.9	27989	7.2	212	210	90t	70.9
Playoffs			456	261	57.2	3833	8.4	30	26		83.0
Pat Brady											
1952	PIT	N	3	1	33.3	14	4.7	0	0	14	49.3
1953			1	0	0.0	0	0.0	0	0		39.6
Career			4	1	25.0	14	3.5	0	0	14	41.7
Mike Bragg											
1970	WAS	N	1	0	0.0	0	0.0	0	0		39.6
1978			2	2	100.0	69	34.5	0	0	56	118.8
Career			3	2	66.7	69	23.0	0	0	56	109.7
Jim Brandt											
1953	PIT	N	1	0	0.0	0	0.0	0	0		39.6
Zeke Bratkowski											
1954	CHIB	N	130	67	51.5	1087	8.4	8	17	71t	60.8
1957			80	37	46.3	527	6.6	1	9	44	32.7
1958			90	41	45.6	571	6.3	7	6	67t	64.6
1959			62	31	50.0	403	6.5	2	5	6	48.0
1960	CHI	N	175	87	49.7	1051	6.0	6	21	59	40.4
1961	LA	N	230	124	53.9	1547	6.7	8	13	84t	63.1
1962			219	110	50.2	1541	7.0	9	16	80t	56.5
1963	LA-GB	N	93	49	52.7	567	6.1	4	9	64	46.1
1964	GB	N	36	19	52.8	277	7.7	1	1	33t	75.8
1965			48	21	43.8	348	7.3	3	4	80t	54.9
1966			64	36	56.3	569	8.9	4	2	74	93.8
1967			94	53	56.4	724	7.7	5	9	86t	59.3
1968			126	68	54.0	835	6.6	3	7	72t	59.5
1971			37	19	51.4	298	8.1	4	3	50	80.7
Career			1484	762	51.3	10345	7.0	65	122	86t	54.3
Playoffs			40	22	55.0	248	6.2	0	2		52.9
Jim Braxton											
1971	BUF	N	3	1	33.3	49	16.3	0	0	49	81.9
Don Breaux											
1963	DEN	A	138	70	50.7	935	6.8	7	6		71.4
1965	SD	A	43	22	51.2	404	9.4	2	4	66	60.6
Career			181	92	50.8	1339	7.4	9	10	66	68.8
Playoffs			2	1	50.0	24	12.0	0	0		93.8
Jim Breech											
1992	CIN	N	1	1	100.0	12	12.0	0	0	12	116.7
Adrian Breen											
1987	CIN	N	8	3	37.5	9	1.1	1	0	6	85.4
Brian Brennan											
1985	CLE	N	1	1	100.0	33	33.0	1	0	33t	158.3
1986			1	1	100.0	35	35.0	0	0	35	118.8
Career			2	2	100.0	68	34.0	1	0	35	158.3
Playoffs			1	1	100.0	5	5.0	0	0		87.5
Matt Brennan											
1926	BKN	N						1			
Walter Briggs											
1987	NYJ	N	2	0	0.0	0	0.0	0	1		0.0
Marlin Briscoe											
1968	DEN	A	224	93	41.5	1589	7.1	14	13	66t	62.9
1969	BUF	A	1	0	0.0	0	0.0	0	1		0.0
1971	BUF	N	2	1	50.0	36	18.0	0	0	36	95.8
1972	MIA	N	3	3	100.0	72	24.0	0	0	26	118.8
1974			1	0	0.0	0	0.0	0	0		39.6
1975	DET	N	2	0	0.0	0	0.0	0	0		39.6
1976	NE	N	0	0		0					
Career			233	97	41.6	1697	7.3	14	14	66t	62.1
Playoffs			1	0	0.0	0	0.0	0	1		0.0

Bubby Brister

Year	Team		Att	Com	PC	Yds	Avg	TD	Int	Lg	Rtg
1986	PIT	N	60	21	35.0	291	4.8	0	2	58	37.6
1987			12	4	33.3	20	1.7	0	3	10	2.8
1988			370	175	47.3	2634	7.1	11	14	89t	65.3
1989			342	187	54.7	2365	6.9	9	10	79t	73.1
1990			387	223	57.6	2725	7.0	20	14	90	81.6
1991			190	103	54.2	1350	7.1	9	9	65t	72.9
1992			116	63	54.3	719	6.2	2	5	42	61.0
1993	PHI	N	309	181	58.6	1905	6.2	14	5	58	84.9
1994			76	51	67.1	507	6.7	2	1	53	89.1
1995	NYJ	N	170	93	54.7	726	4.3	4	8	32	53.7
Career			2032	1101	54.2	13242	6.5	71	71	90	71.5
Playoffs			62	34	54.8	356	5.7	1	0		77.1

Obie Bristow

Year	Team		Att	Com	PC	Yds	Avg	TD	Int	Lg	Rtg
1925	KC	N							2		

Eddie Britt

Year	Team		Att	Com	PC	Yds	Avg	TD	Int	Lg	Rtg
1936	BOS	N	44	18	40.9	294	6.7	3	5		47.2
Playoffs			1	0	0.0	0	0.0	0	0		39.6

Jon Brittenum

Year	Team		Att	Com	PC	Yds	Avg	TD	Int	Lg	Rtg
1968	SD	A	17	9	52.9	125	7.4	1	1	22	71.9

Earl Britton

Year	Team		Att	Com	PC	Yds	Avg	TD	Int	Lg	Rtg
1926	BKN	A						1			

Dieter Brock

Year	Team		Att	Com	PC	Yds	Avg	TD	Int	Lg	Rtg
1985	LARM	N	365	218	59.7	2658	7.3	16	13	64t	82.0
Playoffs			53	16	30.2	116	2.2	0	2		24.0

Lou Brock

Year	Team		Att	Com	PC	Yds	Avg	TD	Int	Lg	Rtg
1940	GB	N	2	0	0.0	0	0.0	0	0		39.6
1943			22	9	40.9	274	12.5	3	1	86	108.7
1944			21	5	23.8	94	4.5	2	0	48	77.5
1945			22	5	22.7	151	6.9	2	3	50	46.4
Career			67	19	28.4	519	7.7	7	4	86	69.3
Playoffs			1	0	0.0	0	0.0	0	0		39.6

John Brockington

Year	Team		Att	Com	PC	Yds	Avg	TD	Int	Lg	Rtg
1973	GB	N	1	0	0.0	0	0.0	0	0		39.6

Bob Brodhead

Year	Team		Att	Com	PC	Yds	Avg	TD	Int	Lg	Rtg
1960	BUF	A	25	7	28.0	75	3.0	0	3		0.0

John Brodie

Year	Team		Att	Com	PC	Yds	Avg	TD	Int	Lg	Rtg
1957	SF	N	21	11	52.4	160	7.6	2	3	28	69.6
1958			172	103	**59.9**	1224	7.1	6	13	61	61.8
1959			64	30	46.9	354	5.5	2	7	34	35.0
1960			207	103	49.8	1111	5.4	6	9	65t	57.5
1961			283	155	54.8	2588	**9.1**	14	12	70t	84.7
1962			304	175	57.6	2272	7.5	18	16	80t	79.0
1963			61	30	49.2	367	6.0	3	4	44t	57.2
1964			392	193	49.2	2498	6.4	14	16	83t	64.6
1965			391	242	**61.9**	3112	8.0	**30**	16	65t	95.3
1966			427	232	54.3	2810	6.6	16	22	65t	65.8
1967			349	168	48.1	2013	5.8	11	16	63t	57.6
1968			**404**	234	57.9	3020	7.5	22	21	65t	70.0
1969			347	194	55.9	2405	6.9	16	15	80t	74.9
1970			378	**223**	59.0	**2941**	7.8	**24**	10	79t	**93.8**
1971			387	208	53.7	2642	6.8	18	24	71t	65.0
1972			110	70	63.6	905	8.2	9	8	53	86.4
1973			194	98	50.5	1126	5.8	3	12	66	47.7
Career			4491	2469	55.0	31548	7.0	214	224	83t	72.3
Playoffs			143	71	49.7	973	6.8	4	7		60.7

Jeff Brohm

Year	Team		Att	Com	PC	Yds	Avg	TD	Int	Lg	Rtg
1996	SF	N	34	21	61.8	189	5.6	1	0	49	86.5

James Brooks

Year	Team		Att	Com	PC	Yds	Avg	TD	Int	Lg	Rtg
1985	CIN	N	1	1	100.0	8	8.0	1	0	8t	139.6
1986			1	0	0.0	0	0.0	0	0		39.6
Career			2	1	50.0	8	4.0	1	0	8t	100.0

Steve Broussard

Year	Team		Att	Com	PC	Yds	Avg	TD	Int	Lg	Rtg
1994	CIN	N	1	0	0.0	0	0.0	0	0		39.6

Bill Brown

Year	Team		Att	Com	PC	Yds	Avg	TD	Int	Lg	Rtg
1944	BKN	N	3	1	33.3	11	3.7	0	0	11	45.1

Bill Brown

Year	Team		Att	Com	PC	Yds	Avg	TD	Int	Lg	Rtg
1966	MIN	N	1	0	0.0	0	0.0	0	0		39.6
1968			1	1	100.0	3	3.0	0	0	3	79.2
Career			2	1	50.0	3	1.5	0	0	3	56.3

Carlos Brown

Year	Team		Att	Com	PC	Yds	Avg	TD	Int	Lg	Rtg
1975	GB	N	4	3	75.0	63	15.8	1	0	27	156.3
1976			74	26	35.1	333	4.5	2	6	47	25.3
Career			78	29	37.2	396	5.1	3	6	47	35.0

Dave Brown

Year	Team		Att	Com	PC	Yds	Avg	TD	Int	Lg	Rtg
1992	NYG	N	7	4	57.1	21	3.0	0	0	8	62.2
1994			350	201	57.4	2536	7.2	12	16	53	72.5
1995			456	254	55.7	2814	6.2	11	10	57t	73.1
1996			398	214	53.8	2412	6.1	12	20	37t	61.3
Career			1211	673	55.6	7783	6.4	35	46	57t	69.0
Playoffs			10	6	60.0	56	5.6	0	1		35.8

Ed Brown

Year	Team		Att	Com	PC	Yds	Avg	TD	Int	Lg	Rtg
1954	CHIB	N	17	10	58.8	283	16.6	3	1	69t	118.3
1955			164	85	51.8	1307	8.0	9	10	86t	71.4
1956			168	96	**57.1**	1667	**9.9**	11	12	70t	**83.1**
1957			185	84	45.4	1321	7.1	6	16	74t	44.4
1958			218	102	46.8	1418	6.5	10	17	79t	51.0
1959			247	125	50.6	1881	7.6	13	10	88t	76.7
1960	CHI	N	149	59	39.6	1079	7.2	7	11	91t	50.2
1961			98	46	46.9	742	7.6	4	11	84t	46.8
1962	PIT	N	84	43	51.2	726	8.6	5	6	50	70.8
1963			362	168	46.4	2982	8.2	21	20	85t	71.4
1964			272	121	44.5	1990	7.3	12	19	54	55.2
1965	PIT-BAL	N	23	10	43.5	204	8.9	1	5	68t	50.2
Career			1987	949	47.8	15600	7.9	102	138	91t	62.8
Playoffs			20	8	40.0	97	4.8	0	1		34.8

Eddie Brown

Year	Team		Att	Com	PC	Yds	Avg	TD	Int	Lg	Rtg
1985	CIN	N	0	0		0		0	0		

Hardy Brown

Year	Team		Att	Com	PC	Yds	Avg	TD	Int	Lg	Rtg
1954	SF	N	1	1	100.0	19	19.0	0	0	19	118.8

Jesse Brown

Year	Team		Att	Com	PC	Yds	Avg	TD	Int	Lg	Rtg
1926	POT	N						3			

Jim Brown

Year	Team		Att	Com	PC	Yds	Avg	TD	Int	Lg	Rtg
1961	CLE	N	3	1	33.3	37	12.3	1	0	37t	120.8
1962			2	1	50.0	28	14.0	0	0	28	95.8
1963			4	0	0.0	0	0.0	0	0		39.6
1964			1	1	100.0	13	13.0	1	0	13t	158.3
1965			2	1	50.0	39	19.5	1	0	39t	135.4
Career			12	4	33.3	117	9.8	3	0	39t	110.1

Larry Brown

Year	Team		Att	Com	PC	Yds	Avg	TD	Int	Lg	Rtg
1974	WAS	N	1	1	100.0	16	16.0	0	0	16	118.8

Ray Brown

Year	Team		Att	Com	PC	Yds	Avg	TD	Int	Lg	Rtg
1958	BAL	N	2	1	50.0	-1	-0.5	0	0	-1	56.3
1959			4	1	25.0	14	3.5	0	0	14	41.7
1960			13	6	46.2	65	5.0	1	0	21	87.0
Career			19	8	42.1	78	4.1	1	0	21	71.8

Ted Brown

Year	Team		Att	Com	PC	Yds	Avg	TD	Int	Lg	Rtg
1981	MIN	N	1	0	0.0	0	0.0	0	1		0.0

Theotis Brown

Year	Team		Att	Com	PC	Yds	Avg	TD	Int	Lg	Rtg
1983	KC	N	1	1	100.0	11	11.0	0	0	11	112.5

Timmy Brown

Year	Team		Att	Com	PC	Yds	Avg	TD	Int	Lg	Rtg
1963	PHI	N	3	1	33.3	11	3.7	1	1	11t	45.1
1964			2	0	0.0	0	0.0	0	1		0.0
1965			1	0	0.0	0	0.0	0	0		39.6
Career			6	1	16.7	11	1.8	1	2	11t	39.6

Isaac Bruce

Year	Team		Att	Com	PC	Yds	Avg	TD	Int	Lg	Rtg
1996	STL	N	2	1	50.0	15	7.5	0	1	15	35.4

Hank Bruder

Year	Team		Att	Com	PC	Yds	Avg	TD	Int	Lg	Rtg
1931	GB	N						1			
1935			1	1	100.0	17	17.0	0	0	17	118.8
1937			6	0	0.0	0	0.0	0	2		0.0
Career			7	1	14.3	17	2.4	1	2	17	0.0

Boyd Brumbaugh

Year	Team		Att	Com	PC	Yds	Avg	TD	Int	Lg	Rtg
1939	BKN-PIT	N	10	3	30.0	121	12.1	2	1		77.5
1940	PIT	N	7	2	28.6	46	6.6	0	1		14.9
1941			41	13	31.7	260	6.3	2	8	72	31.6
Career			58	18	31.0	427	7.4	4	10	72	42.0

Carl Brumbaugh

Year	Team		Att	Com	PC	Yds	Avg	TD	Int	Lg	Rtg
1931	CHIB	N						3			

Year	Team		Att	Com	PC	Yds	Avg	TD	Int	Lg	Rtg

Carl Brumbaugh *continued*

Year	Team		Att	Com	PC	Yds	Avg	TD	Int	Lg	Rtg
1933								1			
1934			33	8	24.2	232	7.0	4	2		70.7
1936			28	8	28.6	140	5.0	5	3		47.9
1937	CLE-BKN	N	18	5	27.8	87	4.8	0	3		7.6
1938	CHIB	N	4	2	50.0	25	6.3	0	0		69.8
Career			83	23	27.7	484	5.8	13	8		27.9
Playoffs			5	0	0.0	0	0.0	0	2		0.0

Mark Brunell

Year	Team		Att	Com	PC	Yds	Avg	TD	Int	Lg	Rtg
1994	GB	N	27	12	44.4	95	3.5	0	0	25	53.8
1995	JAC	N	346	201	58.1	2168	6.3	15	7	45	82.6
1996			557	353	63.4	**4367**	**7.8**	19	20	62	84.0
Career			930	566	60.9	6630	7.1	34	27	62	82.6
Playoffs			111	59	53.2	699	6.3	3	4		66.6

Scott Brunner

Year	Team		Att	Com	PC	Yds	Avg	TD	Int	Lg	Rtg
1980	NYG	N	112	52	46.4	610	5.4	4	6	50t	53.1
1981			190	79	41.6	978	5.1	5	11	43	42.8
1982			298	161	54.0	2017	6.8	10	9	47	73.9
1983			386	190	49.2	2516	6.5	9	22	62	54.3
1985	STL	N	60	30	50.0	336	5.6	1	6	40t	33.1
Career			1046	512	48.9	6457	6.2	29	54	62	56.3
Playoffs			51	25	49.0	386	7.6	6	3		89.2

Johnny Bryan

Year	Team		Att	Com	PC	Yds	Avg	TD	Int	Lg	Rtg
1923	CHIB	N						2			

Kelvin Bryant

Year	Team		Att	Com	PC	Yds	Avg	TD	Int	Lg	Rtg
1987	WAS	N	1	0	0.0	0	0.0	0	0		39.6

Steve Bryant

Year	Team		Att	Com	PC	Yds	Avg	TD	Int	Lg	Rtg
1983	HOU	N	1	1	100.0	24	24.0	1	0	24t	158.3

Howard Buck

Year	Team		Att	Com	PC	Yds	Avg	TD	Int	Lg	Rtg
1924	GB	N						1			

Mike Buck

Year	Team		Att	Com	PC	Yds	Avg	TD	Int	Lg	Rtg
1991	NO	N	2	1	50.0	61	30.5	0	1	61	56.3
1992			4	2	50.0	10	2.5	0	0	10	56.3
1993			54	32	59.3	448	8.3	4	3	63t	87.6
1995	ARI	N	32	20	62.5	271	8.5	1	0	28	99.9
Career			92	55	59.8	790	8.6	5	4	63t	87.7

Maury Buford

Year	Team		Att	Com	PC	Yds	Avg	TD	Int	Lg	Rtg
1983	SD	N	1	0	0.0	0	0.0	0	0		39.6
1985	CHI	N	1	1	100.0	5	5.0	0	0	5	87.5
Career			2	1	50.0	5	2.5	0	0	5	56.3
Playoffs			1	1	100.0	15	15.0	0	0		118.8

Ray Buivid

Year	Team		Att	Com	PC	Yds	Avg	TD	Int	Lg	Rtg
1937	CHIB	N	35	17	48.6	215	6.1	6	2		**83.9**
1938			48	17	35.4	295	6.1	5	2		74.6
Career			83	34	41.0	510	6.1	11	4		81.3
Playoffs			11	3	27.3	41	3.7	0	1		4.7

Joe Bukant

Year	Team		Att	Com	PC	Yds	Avg	TD	Int	Lg	Rtg
1938	PHI	N	1	1	100.0	14	14.0	0	0	14	118.8
1939			1	0	0.0	0	0.0	0	0		39.6
1942	CHIC	N	15	4	26.7	56	3.7	0	2	20	3.1
1943			40	14	35.0	109	2.7	1	5	15	12.5
Career			57	19	33.3	179	3.1	1	7	20	9.2

Rudy Bukich

Year	Team		Att	Com	PC	Yds	Avg	TD	Int	Lg	Rtg
1953	LA	N	32	14	43.8	169	5.3	0	3	30	21.5
1956			23	10	43.5	130	5.7	1	3	34	36.8
1957	WAS	N	28	6	21.4	103	3.7	0	3	35	2.8
1958	WAS-CHIB	N	23	8	34.8	166	7.2	1	1	37	57.5
1960	PIT	N	51	25	49.0	358	7.0	2	3	51	60.7
1961			156	89	57.1	1253	8.0	11	16	88t	67.0
1962	CHI	N	13	3	23.1	79	6.1	1	4	65t	38.5
1963			43	29	67.4	369	8.6	3	2	44t	97.9
1964			160	99	**61.9**	1099	6.9	12	7	63t	89.0
1965			312	176	56.4	2641	8.5	20	9	80t	93.7
1966			309	147	47.6	1858	6.0	10	21	80t	49.3
1967			33	18	54.5	185	5.6	0	2	30	45.6
1968			7	2	28.6	23	3.3	0	0	13	40.8
Career			1190	626	52.6	8433	7.1	61	74	88t	66.6

George Buksar

Year	Team		Att	Com	PC	Yds	Avg	TD	Int	Lg	Rtg
1949	CHI	AA	1	0	0.0	0	0.0	0	0		39.6

Ronnie Bull

Year	Team		Att	Com	PC	Yds	Avg	TD	Int	Lg	Rtg
1962	CHI	N	3	0	0.0	0	0.0	0	0		39.6

Ronnie Bull *continued*

Year	Team		Att	Com	PC	Yds	Avg	TD	Int	Lg	Rtg
1963			3	0	0.0	0	0.0	0	0		39.6
1964			3	1	33.3	13	4.3	0	0	13	47.9
1965			3	2	66.7	63	21.0	0	0	54	109.7
1966			1	1	100.0	21	21.0	0	0	21	118.8
1968			1	0	0.0	0	0.0	0	0		39.6
1969			1	0	0.0	0	0.0	0	0		39.6
1970			4	2	50.0	46	11.5	1	1	34	91.7
1971	PHI	N	1	1	100.0	15	15.0	0	0	15	118.8
Career			20	7	35.0	158	7.9	1	1	54	60.0

Scott Bull

Year	Team		Att	Com	PC	Yds	Avg	TD	Int	Lg	Rtg
1976	SF	N	48	21	43.8	252	5.3	2	4	30	39.6
1977			24	7	29.2	89	3.7	0	2	26	7.8
1978			121	48	39.7	651	5.4	1	11	48	22.4
Career			193	76	39.4	992	5.1	3	17	48	24.8

Amos Bullocks

Year	Team		Att	Com	PC	Yds	Avg	TD	Int	Lg	Rtg
1966	PIT	N	1	0	0.0	0	0.0	0	0		39.6

Adrian Burk

Year	Team		Att	Com	PC	Yds	Avg	TD	Int	Lg	Rtg
1950	BAL	N	119	43	36.1	798	6.7	6	12	69t	37.4
1951	PHI	N	218	92	42.2	1329	6.1	14	23	53t	44.5
1952			82	37	45.1	561	6.8	4	5	84t	59.0
1953			119	56	47.1	788	6.6	4	9	61	48.6
1954			231	123	53.2	1740	7.5	**23**	17	84t	**80.4**
1955			228	110	48.2	1359	6.0	9	17	59	49.2
1956			82	39	47.6	426	5.2	1	6	40	36.9
Career			1079	500	46.3	7001	6.5	61	89	84t	52.2

Mike Burke

Year	Team		Att	Com	PC	Yds	Avg	TD	Int	Lg	Rtg
1974	LA	N	1	0	0.0	0	0.0	0	0		39.6

Ray Burnett

Year	Team		Att	Com	PC	Yds	Avg	TD	Int	Lg	Rtg
1938	CHIC	N	2	1	50.0	19	9.5	0	0	19	83.3

Tom Burnette

Year	Team		Att	Com	PC	Yds	Avg	TD	Int	Lg	Rtg
1938	PIT	N	1	0	0.0	0	0.0	0	0		39.6

Ode Burrell

Year	Team		Att	Com	PC	Yds	Avg	TD	Int	Lg	Rtg
1966	HOU	A	1	1	100.0	9	9.0	0	0	9	104.2

Ken Burrough

Year	Team		Att	Com	PC	Yds	Avg	TD	Int	Lg	Rtg
1977	HOU	N	1	0	0.0	0	0.0	0	0		39.6
1978			1	0	0.0	0	0.0	0	0		39.6
1979			1	0	0.0	0	0.0	0	0		39.6
Career			3	0	0.0	0	0.0	0	0	19	39.6

Ron Burton

Year	Team		Att	Com	PC	Yds	Avg	TD	Int	Lg	Rtg
1961	BOS	A	1	0	0.0	0	0.0	0	1		0.0

Mike Busch

Year	Team		Att	Com	PC	Yds	Avg	TD	Int	Lg	Rtg
1987	NYG	N	47	17	36.2	278	5.9	3	2	63t	60.4

Young Bussey

Year	Team		Att	Com	PC	Yds	Avg	TD	Int	Lg	Rtg
1941	CHIB	N	40	13	32.5	353	8.8	5	3	48	74.3
Playoffs			1	1	100.0	8	8.0	0	0		100.0

Johnny Butler

Year	Team		Att	Com	PC	Yds	Avg	TD	Int	Lg	Rtg
1943	P-P	N	13	6	46.2	84	6.5	0	1	26	35.4
1944	BKN	N	23	8	34.8	107	4.7	0	1	30	32.3
Career			36	14	38.9	191	5.3	0	2	30	33.4

Keith Byars

Year	Team		Att	Com	PC	Yds	Avg	TD	Int	Lg	Rtg
1986	PHI	N	2	1	50.0	55	27.5	1	0	55t	135.4
1988			2	0	0.0	0	0.0	0	0		39.6
1990			4	4	100.0	53	13.3	4	0	18t	158.3
1991			2	0	0.0	0	0.0	0	1		0.0
1992			1	0	0.0	0	0.0	0	0		39.6
1993	MIA	N	2	1	50.0	11	5.5	1	0	11t	106.3
Career			13	6	46.2	119	9.2	6	1	55t	86.2

Earnest Byner

Year	Team		Att	Com	PC	Yds	Avg	TD	Int	Lg	Rtg
1989	WAS	N	1	0	0.0	0	0.0	0	0		39.6
1990			2	1	50.0	31	15.5	1	0	31t	135.4
1991			4	1	25.0	18	4.5	1	0	18t	135.4
1992			3	1	33.3	41	13.7	1	0	41t	121.5
Career			10	3	30.0	90	9.0	3	0	41t	104.2
Playoffs			1	0	0.0	0	0.0	0	0		39.6

Ernie Caddel

Year	Team		Att	Com	PC	Yds	Avg	TD	Int	Lg	Rtg
1934	DET	N						1			
1935								2			
1936			4	1	25.0	30	7.5	0	2	30	18.8

Ernie Caddel *continued*

Year	Team		Att	Com	PC	Yds	Avg	TD	Int	Lg	Rtg
1937			4	0	0.0	0	0.0	0	0		39.6
1938			2	2	100.0	45	22.5	0	0		118.8
Career			10	3	30.0	75	7.5	3	2	30	18.8

George Cafego

Year	Team		Att	Com	PC	Yds	Avg	TD	Int	Lg	Rtg
1940	**BKN**	**N**	17	7	41.2	105	6.2	1	2		42.2
1943	**BKN-WAS**	**N**	45	22	48.9	258	5.7	1	3	36	46.3
1944	**BOS**	**N**	73	35	47.9	454	6.2	3	7	50	42.1
1945			26	13	50.0	149	5.7	0	3	29	28.0
Career			161	77	47.8	966	6.0	5	15	50	38.5
Playoffs			12	3	25.0	76	6.3	0	3		13.9

Chris Cagle

Year	Team		Att	Com	PC	Yds	Avg	TD	Int	Lg	Rtg
1933	**BKN**	**N**	74	31	41.9	385	5.2	2	9		28.1
1934								3			
Career			74	31	41.9	385	5.2	5	9		28.1

Ronnie Cahill

Year	Team		Att	Com	PC	Yds	Avg	TD	Int	Lg	Rtg
1943	**CHIC**	**N**	109	50	45.9	608	5.6	3	21	67	33.1

Jamie Caleb

Year	Team		Att	Com	PC	Yds	Avg	TD	Int	Lg	Rtg
1961	**MIN**	**N**	1	0	0.0	0	0.0	0	0		39.6

Jim Callahan

Year	Team		Att	Com	PC	Yds	Avg	TD	Int	Lg	Rtg
1946	**DET**	**N**	68	22	32.4	359	5.3	2	7	56	21.3

Bill Callihan

Year	Team		Att	Com	PC	Yds	Avg	TD	Int	Lg	Rtg
1942	**DET**	**N**	1	0	0.0	0	0.0	0	1		0.0
1943			2	0	0.0	0	0.0	0	1		0.0
1945			5	3	60.0	34	6.8	1	2	15	80.4
Career			8	3	37.5	34	4.3	1	4	15	51.0

Rich Camarillo

Year	Team		Att	Com	PC	Yds	Avg	TD	Int	Lg	Rtg
1989	**PHX**	**N**	1	1	100.0	0	0.0	0	0	0	79.2
1991			1	0	0.0	0	0.0	0	0		39.6
1994	**HOU**	**N**	1	0	0.0	0	0.0	0	0		39.6
1995			1	0	0.0	0	0.0	0	0		39.6
Career			4	1	25.0	0	0.0	0	0	0	39.6

Earl Campbell

Year	Team		Att	Com	PC	Yds	Avg	TD	Int	Lg	Rtg
1980	**HOU**	**N**	2	1	50.0	57	28.5	1	0	57t	135.4
1982			1	0	0.0	0	0.0	0	1		0.0
Career			3	1	33.3	57	19.0	1	1	57t	81.9
Playoffs			1	0	0.0	0	0.0	0	0		39.6

Milt Campbell

Year	Team		Att	Com	PC	Yds	Avg	TD	Int	Lg	Rtg
1957	**CLE**	**N**	1	0	0.0	0	0.0	0	0		39.6

Rich Campbell

Year	Team		Att	Com	PC	Yds	Avg	TD	Int	Lg	Rtg
1981	**GB**	**N**	30	15	50.0	168	5.6	0	4	27	27.5
1984			38	16	42.1	218	5.7	3	5	43t	47.8
Career			68	31	45.6	386	5.7	3	9	43t	38.8
Playoffs			2	1	50.0	15	7.5	0	0		75.0

Scott Campbell

Year	Team		Att	Com	PC	Yds	Avg	TD	Int	Lg	Rtg
1984	**PIT**	**N**	15	8	53.3	109	7.3	1	1	25t	71.2
1985			96	43	44.8	612	6.4	4	6	51	53.8
1986	**PIT-ATL**	**N**	7	1	14.3	7	1.0	0	0	7	39.6
1987	**ATL**	**N**	260	136	52.3	1728	6.6	11	14	44t	65.0
1990			76	36	47.4	527	6.9	3	4	70	61.7
Career			454	224	49.3	2983	6.6	19	25	70	61.6

Woody Campbell

Year	Team		Att	Com	PC	Yds	Avg	TD	Int	Lg	Rtg
1967	**HOU**	**A**	1	0	0.0	0	0.0	0	0		39.6
1971	**HOU**	**N**	2	2	100.0	34	17.0	2	0	20t	158.3
Career			3	2	66.7	34	11.3	2	0	20t	144.4

Tony Canadeo

Year	Team		Att	Com	PC	Yds	Avg	TD	Int	Lg	Rtg
1941	**GB**	**N**	16	4	25.0	54	3.4	2	0	18	80.7
1942			59	24	40.7	310	5.3	3	4	36	46.6
1943			129	56	43.4	875	6.8	9	12	51	51.0
1944			20	9	45.0	89	4.5	0	0	17	58.1
1946			27	7	25.9	189	7.0	1	3	51	29.0
1947			8	3	37.5	101	12.6	1	1	38	85.4
1948			8	2	25.0	24	3.0	0	0	15	39.6
1952			1	0	0.0	0	0.0	0	0		39.6
Career			268	105	39.2	1642	6.1	16	20	51	49.1
Playoffs			2	1	50.0	40	20.0	0	1		56.3

Billy Cannon

Year	Team		Att	Com	PC	Yds	Avg	TD	Int	Lg	Rtg
1960	**HOU**	**A**	3	0	0.0	0	0.0	0	0		39.6
1961			5	0	0.0	0	0.0	0	1		0.0
1962			3	2	66.7	46	15.3	1	0		149.3

Billy Cannon *continued*

Year	Team		Att	Com	PC	Yds	Avg	TD	Int	Lg	Rtg
1963			1	0	0.0	0	0.0	0	0		39.6
Career			12	2	16.7	46	3.8	1	1		36.1
Playoffs			1	0	0.0	0	0.0	0	0		39.6

Leo Cantor

Year	Team		Att	Com	PC	Yds	Avg	TD	Int	Lg	Rtg
1942	**NYG**	**N**	29	12	41.4	155	5.3	1	1	35	56.0
1945	**CHIC**	**N**	18	3	16.7	116	6.4	0	4	62	14.4
Career			47	15	31.9	271	5.8	1	5	62	20.2

Gino Cappelletti

Year	Team		Att	Com	PC	Yds	Avg	TD	Int	Lg	Rtg
1961	**BOS**	**A**	1	1	100.0	27	27.0	1	0	27t	158.3

Bill Cappelman

Year	Team		Att	Com	PC	Yds	Avg	TD	Int	Lg	Rtg
1970	**MIN**	**N**	7	4	57.1	49	7.0	0	0	26	78.9
1973	**DET**	**N**	11	5	45.5	33	3.0	0	1	8	14.6
Career			18	9	50.0	82	4.6	0	1	26	39.6

Glenn Carano

Year	Team		Att	Com	PC	Yds	Avg	TD	Int	Lg	Rtg
1980	**DAL**	**N**	12	5	41.7	69	5.8	2	0	25	100.3
1981			45	16	35.6	235	5.2	1	1	55	51.6
Career			57	21	36.8	304	5.3	3	1	55	65.2

Lloyd Cardwell

Year	Team		Att	Com	PC	Yds	Avg	TD	Int	Lg	Rtg
1938	**DET**	**N**	1	1	100.0	35	35.0	0	0	35	118.8
1940			1	0	0.0	0	0.0	0	0		39.6
Career			2	1	50.0	35	17.5	0	0	35	95.8

Cody Carlson

Year	Team		Att	Com	PC	Yds	Avg	TD	Int	Lg	Rtg
1988	**HOU**	**N**	112	52	46.4	775	6.9	4	6	51t	59.2
1989			31	15	48.4	155	5.0	0	1	23	49.8
1990			55	37	67.3	383	7.0	4	2	53t	96.3
1991			12	7	58.3	114	9.5	1	0	68t	118.1
1992			227	149	65.6	1710	7.5	9	11	65	81.2
1993			90	51	56.7	605	6.7	2	4	47	66.2
1994			132	59	44.7	727	5.5	1	4	81	52.2
Career			659	370	56.1	4469	6.8	21	28	81	70.0
Playoffs			33	16	48.5	165	5.0	2	1		70.9

Dean Carlson

Year	Team		Att	Com	PC	Yds	Avg	TD	Int	Lg	Rtg
1974	**KC**	**N**	15	7	46.7	116	7.7	0	1	34	45.4

Jeff Carlson

Year	Team		Att	Com	PC	Yds	Avg	TD	Int	Lg	Rtg
1991	**TB**	**N**	65	31	47.7	404	6.2	1	6	36	34.4
1992	**NE**	**N**	49	18	36.7	232	4.7	1	3	40	33.7
Career			114	49	43.0	636	5.6	2	9	40	34.1

Wray Carlton

Year	Team		Att	Com	PC	Yds	Avg	TD	Int	Lg	Rtg
1961	**BUF**	**A**	2	0	0.0	0	0.0	0	0		39.6

Al Carmichael

Year	Team		Att	Com	PC	Yds	Avg	TD	Int	Lg	Rtg
1960	**DEN**	**A**	1	1	100.0	26	26.0	0	0	26	118.8

Harold Carmichael

Year	Team		Att	Com	PC	Yds	Avg	TD	Int	Lg	Rtg
1974	**PHI**	**N**	1	0	0.0	0	0.0	0	0		39.6
1976			2	0	0.0	0	0.0	0	0		39.6
1983			1	1	100.0	45	45.0	1	0	45t	158.3
Career			4	1	25.0	45	11.3	1	0	45t	113.5

Ray Carnelly

Year	Team		Att	Com	PC	Yds	Avg	TD	Int	Lg	Rtg
1939	**BKN**	**N**	14	3	21.4	35	2.5	0	3		0.0

Ken Carpenter

Year	Team		Att	Com	PC	Yds	Avg	TD	Int	Lg	Rtg
1950	**CLE**	**N**	1	0	0.0	0	0.0	0	1		0.0
Playoffs			1	0	0.0	0	0.0	0	0		39.6

Preston Carpenter

Year	Team		Att	Com	PC	Yds	Avg	TD	Int	Lg	Rtg
1960	**PIT**	**N**	2	1	50.0	2	1.0	0	0	2	56.3
1964	**WAS**	**N**	1	0	0.0	0	0.0	0	0		39.6
Career			3	1	33.3	2	0.7	0	0	2	42.4

Rob Carpenter

Year	Team		Att	Com	PC	Yds	Avg	TD	Int	Lg	Rtg
1992	**NYJ**	**N**	1	0	0.0	0	0.0	0	0		39.6

Duane Carrell

Year	Team		Att	Com	PC	Yds	Avg	TD	Int	Lg	Rtg
1974	**DAL**	**N**	1	1	100.0	37	37.0	0	0	37	118.8

Paul Ott Carruth

Year	Team		Att	Com	PC	Yds	Avg	TD	Int	Lg	Rtg
1987	**GB**	**N**	1	1	100.0	3	3.0	1	0	3t	118.8
1988			2	0	0.0	0	0.0	0	0		39.6
Career			3	1	33.3	3	1.0	1	0	3t	81.9

Carlos Carson

Year	Team		Att	Com	PC	Yds	Avg	TD	Int	Lg	Rtg
1983	**KC**	**N**	1	1	100.0	48	48.0	1	0	48t	158.3

Anthony Carter

Year	Team		Att	Com	PC	Yds	Avg	TD	Int	Lg	Rtg
1992	MIN	N	1	0	0.0	0	0.0	0	0		39.6

Cris Carter

Year	Team		Att	Com	PC	Yds	Avg	TD	Int	Lg	Rtg
1987	PHI	N	1	0	0.0	0	0.0	0	0		39.6
Playoffs			1	0	0.0	0	0.0	0	0		39.6

Louis Carter

Year	Team		Att	Com	PC	Yds	Avg	TD	Int	Lg	Rtg
1976	TB	N	5	2	40.0	24	4.8	1	0	23	95.0
1977			2	0	0.0	0	0.0	0	0		39.6
1978			5	2	40.0	87	17.4	0	0	66	87.5
Career			12	4	33.3	111	9.3	1	0	66	96.2

Rodney Carter

Year	Team		Att	Com	PC	Yds	Avg	TD	Int	Lg	Rtg
1988	PIT	N	3	2	66.7	56	18.7	0	0	40	109.7
1989			1	1	100.0	15	15.0	0	0	15	118.8
Career			4	3	75.0	71	17.8	0	0	40	116.7

Virgil Carter

Year	Team		Att	Com	PC	Yds	Avg	TD	Int	Lg	Rtg
1968	CHI	N	122	55	45.1	769	6.3	4	5	50t	59.8
1969			71	36	50.7	343	4.8	2	5	41t	44.5
1970	CIN	N	278	143	51.4	1647	5.9	9	9	56t	66.9
1971			222	138	**62.2**	1624	7.3	10	7	90t	86.2
1972			82	47	57.3	579	7.1	3	4	36	71.1
1975	SD	N	5	3	60.0	24	4.8	0	1	11	32.5
1976	CHI	N	5	3	60.0	77	15.4	1	0	55t	143.8
Career			785	425	54.1	5063	6.4	29	31	90t	69.9
Playoffs			20	7	35.0	64	3.2	0	1		23.8

Rick Casares

Year	Team		Att	Com	PC	Yds	Avg	TD	Int	Lg	Rtg
1955	CHIB	N	3	2	66.7	27	9.0	1	1	23	95.1
1956			3	0	0.0	0	0.0	0	1		0.0
1957			2	1	50.0	32	16.0	0	0	32	95.8
1958			4	1	25.0	13	3.3	1	0	13t	80.2
1959			1	0	0.0	0	0.0	0	1		0.0
1962	CHI	N	2	1	50.0	35	17.5	1	0	35t	135.4
Career			15	5	33.3	107	7.1	3	3	32	59.6

Ernie Case

Year	Team		Att	Com	PC	Yds	Avg	TD	Int	Lg	Rtg
1947	BAL	AA	11	4	36.4	49	4.5	0	1		13.1

Stoney Case

Year	Team		Att	Com	PC	Yds	Avg	TD	Int	Lg	Rtg
1995	ARI	N	2	1	50.0	19	9.5	0	1	19	43.8

Tom Casey

Year	Team		Att	Com	PC	Yds	Avg	TD	Int	Lg	Rtg
1948	NY	AA	5	2	40.0	31	6.2	1	0		100.8

Jim Cason

Year	Team		Att	Com	PC	Yds	Avg	TD	Int	Lg	Rtg
1949	SF	AA	2	1	50.0	38	19.0	1	0	38	135.4
1954	SF	N	13	7	53.8	40	3.1	0	1	25	27.7
Career			15	8	53.3	78	5.2	1	1	38	62.6

Dave Casper

Year	Team		Att	Com	PC	Yds	Avg	TD	Int	Lg	Rtg
1978	OAK	N	1	0	0.0	0	0.0	0	0		39.6

Howard Cassady

Year	Team		Att	Com	PC	Yds	Avg	TD	Int	Lg	Rtg
1956	DET	N	2	0	0.0	0	0.0	0	1		0.0
1961			1	0	0.0	0	0.0	0	0		39.6
Career			3	0	0.0	0	0.0	0	1		0.0

Dick Cassiano

Year	Team		Att	Com	PC	Yds	Avg	TD	Int	Lg	Rtg
1940	BKN	N	30	9	30.0	128	4.3	1	2		28.2

Jim Castiglia

Year	Team		Att	Com	PC	Yds	Avg	TD	Int	Lg	Rtg
1941	PHI	N	7	0	0.0	0	0.0	0	1		0.0

Greg Cater

Year	Team		Att	Com	PC	Yds	Avg	TD	Int	Lg	Rtg
1980	BUF	N	1	1	100.0	15	15.0	0	0	15	118.8

Sam Cathcart

Year	Team		Att	Com	PC	Yds	Avg	TD	Int	Lg	Rtg
1952	SF	N	1	0	0.0	0	0.0	0	1		0.0

Matt Cavanaugh

Year	Team		Att	Com	PC	Yds	Avg	TD	Int	Lg	Rtg
1979	NE	N	1	1	100.0	10	10.0	0	0	10	108.3
1980			105	63	60.0	885	8.4	9	5	40	95.9
1981			219	115	52.5	1633	7.5	5	13	65	59.8
1982			60	27	45.0	490	8.2	5	5	75t	66.7
1984	SF	N	61	33	54.1	449	7.4	4	0	51t	99.7
1985			54	28	51.9	334	6.2	1	1	41	69.5
1986	PHI	N	58	28	48.3	397	6.8	2	4	49	53.6
1988			16	7	43.8	101	6.3	1	1	42	59.6
1989			5	3	60.0	33	6.6	1	1	13t	79.6
Career			579	305	52.7	4332	7.5	28	30	75t	71.7
Playoffs			2	1	50.0	3	1.5	0	0		56.3

John Cavosie

Year	Team		Att	Com	PC	Yds	Avg	TD	Int	Lg	Rtg
1932	POR	N						1			

Bob Celeri

Year	Team		Att	Com	PC	Yds	Avg	TD	Int	Lg	Rtg
1951	NYY	N	238	102	42.9	1797	7.6	12	15	75t	59.8
1952	DAL	N	75	31	41.3	490	6.5	3	3	78t	60.4
Career			313	133	42.5	2287	7.3	15	18	78t	60.0

Larry Centers

Year	Team		Att	Com	PC	Yds	Avg	TD	Int	Lg	Rtg
1995	ARI	N	1	0	0.0	0	0.0	0	1		0.0

Bob Chandler

Year	Team		Att	Com	PC	Yds	Avg	TD	Int	Lg	Rtg
1973	BUF	N	1	0	0.0	0	0.0	0	0		39.6

Chris Chandler

Year	Team		Att	Com	PC	Yds	Avg	TD	Int	Lg	Rtg
1988	IND	N	233	129	55.4	1619	6.9	8	12	54	67.2
1989			80	39	48.8	537	6.7	2	3	82t	63.4
1990	TB	N	83	42	50.6	464	5.6	1	6	68t	41.4
1991	TB-PHI	N	154	78	50.6	846	5.5	5	10	45t	50.9
1992	PHX	N	413	245	59.3	2832	6.9	15	15	72t	77.1
1993			103	52	50.5	471	4.6	3	2	27t	64.8
1994	LARM	N	176	108	61.4	1352	7.7	7	2	72t	93.8
1995	HOU	N	356	225	63.2	2460	6.9	17	10	76t	87.8
1996			320	184	57.5	2099	6.6	16	11	63t	79.7
Career			1918	1102	57.5	12680	6.6	74	71	82t	74.9

Don Chandler

Year	Team		Att	Com	PC	Yds	Avg	TD	Int	Lg	Rtg
1957	NYG	N	2	2	100.0	40	20.0	0	0	27	118.8
1958			1	1	100.0	27	27.0	0	0	27	118.8
Career			3	3	100.0	67	22.3	0	0	27	118.8

Wes Chandler

Year	Team		Att	Com	PC	Yds	Avg	TD	Int	Lg	Rtg
1980	NO	N	1	1	100.0	43	43.0	0	0	43	118.8
1981	SD	N	2	0	0.0	0	0.0	0	0		39.6
1983			0	0		0		0	0	0	
Career			3	1	33.3	43	14.3	0	0	43	81.9

Lynn Chandnois

Year	Team		Att	Com	PC	Yds	Avg	TD	Int	Lg	Rtg
1950	PIT	N	6	1	16.7	5	0.8	0	2	5	0.0
1951			43	16	37.2	256	6.0	2	4	49t	34.6
1952			2	0	0.0	0	0.0	0	0		39.6
1953			3	1	33.3	11	3.7	0	0	11	45.1
1954			3	1	33.3	13	4.3	0	0	13	47.9
1955			1	0	0.0	0	0.0	0	1		0.0
1956			1	0	0.0	0	0.0	0	0		39.6
Career			59	19	32.2	285	4.8	2	7	49t	20.8

Bob Chappuis

Year	Team		Att	Com	PC	Yds	Avg	TD	Int	Lg	Rtg
1948	BKN	AA	213	100	46.9	1402	6.6	8	15	78t	51.8
1949	CHI	AA	14	2	14.3	40	2.9	0	4		0.0
Career			227	102	44.9	1442	6.4	8	19	78t	42.9

Joe Childress

Year	Team		Att	Com	PC	Yds	Avg	TD	Int	Lg	Rtg
1957	CHIC	N	2	1	50.0	43	21.5	0	1	43	56.3
1958			1	0	0.0	0	0.0	0	0		39.6
Career			3	1	33.3	43	14.3	0	1	43	42.4

Ed Chlebek

Year	Team		Att	Com	PC	Yds	Avg	TD	Int	Lg	Rtg
1963	NY	A	4	2	50.0	5	1.3	0	0		56.3

Max Choboian

Year	Team		Att	Com	PC	Yds	Avg	TD	Int	Lg	Rtg
1966	DEN	A	163	82	50.3	1110	6.8	4	12	79	49.9

Frank Christensen

Year	Team		Att	Com	PC	Yds	Avg	TD	Int	Lg	Rtg
1936	DET	N	6	2	33.3	22	3.7	0	1		5.6

Jeff Christensen

Year	Team		Att	Com	PC	Yds	Avg	TD	Int	Lg	Rtg
1987	CLE	N	58	24	41.4	297	5.1	1	3	34	42.1

Todd Christensen

Year	Team		Att	Com	PC	Yds	Avg	TD	Int	Lg	Rtg
1980	OAK	N	0	0		0		0	0		

Paul Christman

Year	Team		Att	Com	PC	Yds	Avg	TD	Int	Lg	Rtg
1945	CHIC	N	**219**	89	40.6	1147	5.2	5	12	70	42.6
1946			229	100	43.7	1656	7.2	13	18	82	54.8
1947			301	138	45.8	2191	7.3	17	22	80	59.0
1948			114	51	44.7	740	6.5	5	4	71	66.4
1949			151	75	49.7	1015	6.7	11	13	50	59.9
1950	GB	N	126	51	40.5	545	4.3	7	7	44t	49.2
Career			1140	504	44.2	7294	6.4	58	76	82	54.8
Playoffs			14	3	21.4	54	3.9	0	2		3.6

Dick Christy

Year	Team		Att	Com	PC	Yds	Avg	TD	Int	Lg	Rtg
1960	BOS	A	11	6	54.5	94	8.5	2	2		83.1

Year	Team		Att	Com	PC	Yds	Avg	TD	Int	Lg	Rtg

Dick Christy *continued*

Year	Team		Att	Com	PC	Yds	Avg	TD	Int	Lg	Rtg
1961	NY	A	1	0	0.0	0	0.0	0	0		39.6
1962			6	0	0.0	0	0.0	0	0		39.6
Career			18	6	33.3	94	5.2	2	2		49.1

Bob Cifers

Year	Team		Att	Com	PC	Yds	Avg	TD	Int	Lg	Rtg
1946	DET	N	6	2	33.3	24	4.0	0	1	26	6.9
1947	PIT	N	3	2	66.7	28	9.3	0	0	22	96.5
1948			4	0	0.0	0	0.0	0	1		0.0
Career			13	4	30.8	52	4.0	0	2	26	4.8
Playoffs			2	0	0.0	0	0.0	0	0		39.6

Larry Cipa

Year	Team		Att	Com	PC	Yds	Avg	TD	Int	Lg	Rtg
1974	NO	N	55	20	36.4	242	4.4	0	0	30	50.7
1975			37	14	37.8	182	4.9	1	3	28	29.3
Career			92	34	37.0	424	4.6	1	3	30	42.1

Jack Clancy

Year	Team		Att	Com	PC	Yds	Avg	TD	Int	Lg	Rtg
1967	MIA	A	1	1	100.0	17	17.0	0	0	17	118.8

Dennis Claridge

Year	Team		Att	Com	PC	Yds	Avg	TD	Int	Lg	Rtg
1965	GB	N	1	1	100.0	13	13.0	0	0	13	118.8
1966	ATL	N	70	40	57.1	471	6.7	2	2	62t	75.4
Career			71	41	57.7	484	6.8	2	2	62t	76.3

Beryl Clark

Year	Team		Att	Com	PC	Yds	Avg	TD	Int	Lg	Rtg
1940	CHIC	N	58	25	43.1	316	5.4	2	6		32.6

Dutch Clark

Year	Team		Att	Com	PC	Yds	Avg	TD	Int	Lg	Rtg
1931	POR	N							1		
1932			52	17	32.7	272	5.2	2			
1934	DET	N	49	23	46.9	383	7.8	0	3		48.3
1935			26	11	42.3	133	5.1	3			
1936			71	38	**53.5**	467	6.6	4	6		57.7
1937			39	19	48.7	202	5.2	1	3		40.8
1938			12	6	50.0	50	4.2	1	2		49.3
Career			249	114	45.8	1507	6.1	12	14		48.4

Dwight Clark

Year	Team		Att	Com	PC	Yds	Avg	TD	Int	Lg	Rtg
1981	SF	N	1	0	0.0	0	0.0	0	0		39.6
1983			1	0	0.0	0	0.0	0	0		39.6
1984			1	0	0.0	0	0.0	0	0		39.6
Career			3	0	0.0	0	0.0	0	0		39.6

Harry Clark

Year	Team		Att	Com	PC	Yds	Avg	TD	Int	Lg	Rtg
1940	CHIB	N	3	0	0.0	0	0.0	0	2		0.0
1943			1	0	0.0	0	0.0	0	1		0.0
Career			4	0	0.0	0	0.0	0	3		0.0

Ken Clark

Year	Team		Att	Com	PC	Yds	Avg	TD	Int	Lg	Rtg
1979	LA	N	2	2	100.0	32	16.0	0	0	30	118.8

Mike Clark

Year	Team		Att	Com	PC	Yds	Avg	TD	Int	Lg	Rtg
1967	PIT	N	1	0	0.0	0	0.0	0	0		39.6

Wayne Clark

Year	Team		Att	Com	PC	Yds	Avg	TD	Int	Lg	Rtg
1970	SD	N	2	1	50.0	48	24.0	0	0	48	95.8
1972			6	2	33.3	67	11.2	0	2	62	36.8
1973			90	40	44.4	532	5.9	0	9	54	24.2
1974	CIN	N	22	9	40.9	98	4.5	0	3	19	15.2
Career			120	52	43.3	745	6.2	0	14	62	24.5

Frank Clarke

Year	Team		Att	Com	PC	Yds	Avg	TD	Int	Lg	Rtg
1964	DAL	N	1	0	0.0	0	0.0	0	0		39.6

Bobby Clatterbuck

Year	Team		Att	Com	PC	Yds	Avg	TD	Int	Lg	Rtg
1954	NYG	N	101	50	49.5	781	7.7	6	7	72t	66.5
1955			16	6	37.5	46	2.9	0	0	14	45.8
1956			7	4	57.1	54	7.7	0	1	21	42.3
1957			2	2	100.0	39	19.5	1	0	28	158.3
1960	LA	A	23	15	65.2	112	4.9	1	1	19	73.1
Career			149	77	51.7	1032	6.9	8	9	72t	66.7
Playoffs			3	1	33.3	12	4.0	0	0		46.5

Walt Clay

Year	Team		Att	Com	PC	Yds	Avg	TD	Int	Lg	Rtg
1946	CHI	AA	27	12	44.4	140	5.2	2	3		45.8
1949	LA	AA	1	1	100.0	8	8.0	0	0	8	100.0
Career			28	13	46.4	148	5.3	2	3	8	47.0

Mark Clayton

Year	Team		Att	Com	PC	Yds	Avg	TD	Int	Lg	Rtg
1983	MIA	N	1	1	100.0	48	48.0	1	0	48t	158.3
1984			1	0	0.0	0	0.0	0	1		0.0
1985			0	0		0		0	0		
Career			2	1	50.0	48	24.0	1	1	48t	95.8
Playoffs			1	0	0.0	0	0.0	0	0		39.6

Cal Clemens

Year	Team		Att	Com	PC	Yds	Avg	TD	Int	Lg	Rtg
1936	GB	N	1	0	0.0	0	0.0	0	0		39.6

Johnny Clement

Year	Team		Att	Com	PC	Yds	Avg	TD	Int	Lg	Rtg
1941	CHIC	N	100	48	48.0	690	6.9	3	7	76	51.7
1946	PIT	N	47	16	34.0	345	7.3	1	3	52	41.5
1947			123	52	42.3	1004	8.2	7	9	68	59.8
1948			58	18	31.0	281	4.8	3	7	39	25.8
1949	CHI	AA	114	58	50.9	906	7.9	6	13		55.6
Career			442	192	43.4	3226	7.3	20	39	76	47.0
Playoffs			16	4	25.0	52	3.3	0	0		40.6

Tom Clements

Year	Team		Att	Com	PC	Yds	Avg	TD	Int	Lg	Rtg
1980	KC	N	12	7	58.3	77	6.4	0	0	18	77.4

Bert Coan

Year	Team		Att	Com	PC	Yds	Avg	TD	Int	Lg	Rtg
1966	KC	A	1	1	100.0	18	18.0	1	0	18t	158.3

Ray Coates

Year	Team		Att	Com	PC	Yds	Avg	TD	Int	Lg	Rtg
1948	NYG	N	2	1	50.0	26	13.0	1	0	26	135.4

Marvin Cobb

Year	Team		Att	Com	PC	Yds	Avg	TD	Int	Lg	Rtg
1977	CIN	N	1	0	0.0	0	0.0	0	0		39.6

Red Cochran

Year	Team		Att	Com	PC	Yds	Avg	TD	Int	Lg	Rtg
1947	CHIC	N	1	0	0.0	0	0.0	0	0		39.6
1949			1	0	0.0	0	0.0	0	0		39.6
Career			2	0	0.0	0	0.0	0	0		39.6

Don Cockroft

Year	Team		Att	Com	PC	Yds	Avg	TD	Int	Lg	Rtg
1974	CLE	N	1	1	100.0	27	27.0	0	0	27	118.8
1975			2	2	100.0	0	0.0	0	0	1	79.2
1976			1	0	0.0	0	0.0	0	0		39.6
Career			4	3	75.0	27	6.8	0	0	27	92.7

Pat Coffee

Year	Team		Att	Com	PC	Yds	Avg	TD	Int	Lg	Rtg
1937	CHIC	N	119	52	43.7	804	6.8	5	11	95t	42.1
1938			39	16	41.0	200	5.1	0	4		18.1
Career			158	68	43.0	1004	6.4	5	15	95t	35.4

Tom Colella

Year	Team		Att	Com	PC	Yds	Avg	TD	Int	Lg	Rtg
1942	DET	N	41	18	43.9	178	4.3	0	4	23	17.2
1943			31	11	35.5	103	3.3	0	4	21	5.9
1944	CLE	N	76	27	35.5	336	4.4	4	10	25	28.1
1945			1	0	0.0	0	0.0	0	0		39.6
Career			149	56	37.6	617	4.1	4	18	25	20.0

Greg Coleman

Year	Team		Att	Com	PC	Yds	Avg	TD	Int	Lg	Rtg
1984	MIN	N	1	0	0.0	0	0.0	0	0		39.6
1988	WAS	N	1	0	0.0	0	0.0	0	0		39.6
Career			2	0	0.0	0	0.0	0	0		39.6

Ronnie Coleman

Year	Team		Att	Com	PC	Yds	Avg	TD	Int	Lg	Rtg
1974	HOU	N	2	0	0.0	0	0.0	0	0		39.6
1975			1	0	0.0	0	0.0	0	0		39.6
1976			1	0	0.0	0	0.0	0	1		0.0
1977			3	1	33.3	44	14.7	1	0	44t	121.5
Career			7	1	14.3	44	6.3	1	1	44t	53.3

Reggie Collier

Year	Team		Att	Com	PC	Yds	Avg	TD	Int	Lg	Rtg
1986	DAL	N	15	8	53.3	96	6.4	1	2	27	55.8
1987	PIT	N	7	4	57.1	110	15.7	2	1	49	101.8
Career			22	12	54.5	206	9.4	3	3	49	86.6

Kerry Collins

Year	Team		Att	Com	PC	Yds	Avg	TD	Int	Lg	Rtg
1995	CAR	N	433	214	49.4	2717	6.3	14	19	89t	61.9
1996			364	204	56.0	2454	6.7	14	9	55	79.4
Career			797	418	52.4	5171	6.5	28	28	89t	69.9
Playoffs			59	31	52.5	315	5.3	3	3		63.9

Paul Collins

Year	Team		Att	Com	PC	Yds	Avg	TD	Int	Lg	Rtg
1945	CHIC	N	17	3	17.6	43	2.5	0	2	26	0.0

Rip Collins

Year	Team		Att	Com	PC	Yds	Avg	TD	Int	Lg	Rtg
1949	CHI	AA	1	0	0.0	0	0.0	0	0		39.6

Todd Collins

Year	Team		Att	Com	PC	Yds	Avg	TD	Int	Lg	Rtg
1995	BUF	N	29	14	48.3	112	3.9	0	1	18	44.0
1996			99	55	55.6	739	7.5	4	5	95t	71.9
Career			128	69	53.9	851	6.6	4	6	95t	65.6
Playoffs			4	1	25.0	7	1.8	0	0		39.6

Tony Collins

Year	Team		Att	Com	PC	Yds	Avg	TD	Int	Lg	Rtg
1981	NE	N	1	0	0.0	0	0.0	0	0		39.6

Year	Team		Att	Com	PC	Yds	Avg	TD	Int	Lg	Rtg

Cris Collinsworth

Year	Team		Att	Com	PC	Yds	Avg	TD	Int	Lg	Rtg
1985	CIN	N	1	0	0.0	0	0.0	0	1		0.0

Mickey Colmer

Year	Team		Att	Com	PC	Yds	Avg	TD	Int	Lg	Rtg
1947	BKN	AA	3	1	33.3	20	6.7	0	0	20	57.6
1948			1	0	0.0	0	0.0	0	0		39.6
1949	B-NY	AA	1	0	0.0	0	0.0	0	0		39.6
Career			5	1	20.0	20	4.0	0	0	20	43.8

Irv Comp

Year	Team		Att	Com	PC	Yds	Avg	TD	Int	Lg	Rtg
1943	GB	N	92	46	50.0	662	7.2	7	4	79	81.0
1944			177	80	45.2	1159	6.5	12	21	55	50.0
1945			106	44	41.5	865	8.2	7	11	75	53.1
1946			94	27	28.7	333	3.5	1	8	35	9.9
1947			1	0	0.0	0	0.0	0	1		0.0
1948			49	16	32.7	335	6.8	1	7	50	25.0
Career			519	213	41.0	3354	6.5	28	52	79	41.6
Playoffs			10	3	30.0	74	7.4	1	3		51.7

Ogden Compton

Year	Team		Att	Com	PC	Yds	Avg	TD	Int	Lg	Rtg
1955	CHIC	N	61	22	36.1	339	5.6	1	6	98t	21.2

Jack Concannon

Year	Team		Att	Com	PC	Yds	Avg	TD	Int	Lg	Rtg
1964	PHI	N	23	12	52.2	199	8.7	2	1	38	92.5
1965			29	12	41.4	176	6.1	1	3	34	33.8
1966			51	21	41.2	262	5.1	1	4	44	31.7
1967	CHI	N	186	92	49.5	1260	6.8	6	14	93t	50.9
1968			143	71	49.7	715	5.0	5	9	51t	49.7
1969			160	87	54.4	783	4.9	4	8	38	55.3
1970			385	194	50.4	2130	5.5	16	18	69t	61.5
1971			77	42	54.5	334	4.3	0	3	28	49.4
1974	GB	N	54	28	51.9	381	7.1	1	3	56t	57.7
1975	DET	N	2	1	50.0	30	15.0	0	0	30	95.8
Career			1110	560	50.5	6270	5.6	36	63	93t	54.8

Merl Condit

Year	Team		Att	Com	PC	Yds	Avg	TD	Int	Lg	Rtg
1940	PIT	N	15	2	13.3	33	2.2	0	2		0.0
1941	BKN	N	6	1	16.7	3	0.5	0	1	3	0.0
1942			17	5	29.4	27	1.6	0	3	14	0.0
1943			6	0	0.0	0	0.0	0	0		39.6
1946	PIT	N	4	2	50.0	89	22.3	1	0	80	135.4
Career			48	10	20.8	152	3.2	1	6	80	7.6

Charlie Conerly

Year	Team		Att	Com	PC	Yds	Avg	TD	Int	Lg	Rtg
1948	NYG	N	299	162	54.2	2175	7.3	22	13	65	84.0
1949			305	152	49.8	2138	7.0	17	20	85	64.1
1950			132	56	42.4	1000	7.6	8	7	43	67.1
1951			189	93	49.2	1277	6.8	10	22	69t	49.3
1952			169	82	48.5	1090	6.4	13	10	70t	70.4
1953			303	143	47.2	1711	5.6	13	25	60t	44.9
1954			210	103	49.0	1439	6.9	17	11	68t	76.7
1955			202	98	48.5	1310	6.5	13	13	71t	64.2
1956			174	90	51.7	1143	6.6	10	7	48	75.0
1957			232	128	55.2	1712	7.4	11	11	70	74.9
1958			184	88	47.8	1199	6.5	10	9	44	66.8
1959			194	113	58.2	1706	8.8	14	4	77t	102.7
1960			134	66	49.3	954	7.1	8	7	70t	70.9
1961			106	44	41.5	634	6.0	7	8	37t	52.2
Career			2833	1418	50.1	19488	6.9	173	167	85	68.2
Playoffs			90	47	52.2	791	8.8	4	4		78.5

Cary Conklin

Year	Team		Att	Com	PC	Yds	Avg	TD	Int	Lg	Rtg
1992	WAS	N	2	2	100.0	16	8.0	1	0	10t	139.6
1993			87	46	52.9	496	5.7	4	3	34t	70.9
1995	SF	N	12	4	33.3	48	4.0	0	0	28	46.5
Career			101	52	51.5	560	5.5	5	3	34t	72.2

Harry Connolly

Year	Team		Att	Com	PC	Yds	Avg	TD	Int	Lg	Rtg
1946	BKN	AA	8	2	25.0	29	3.6	0	1		2.6

Bobby Joe Conrad

Year	Team		Att	Com	PC	Yds	Avg	TD	Int	Lg	Rtg
1959	CHIC	N	3	2	66.7	82	27.3	1	1	52	109.7
1961	STL	N	1	1	100.0	5	5.0	0	0	5	87.5
Career			4	3	75.0	87	21.8	1	1	52	116.7

Curtis Conway

Year	Team		Att	Com	PC	Yds	Avg	TD	Int	Lg	Rtg
1994	CHI	N	1	1	100.0	23	23.0	1	0	23t	158.3
1995			1	0	0.0	0	0.0	0	0		39.6
1996			1	1	100.0	33	33.0	1	0	33t	158.3
Career			3	2	66.7	56	18.7	2	0	33t	149.3

Jimmy Conzelman

Year	Team		Att	Com	PC	Yds	Avg	TD	Int	Lg	Rtg
1920	DEC	A							2		
1921	RI	A							2		
1922	RI-MIL	N							2		

Jimmy Conzelman continued

Year	Team		Att	Com	PC	Yds	Avg	TD	Int	Lg	Rtg
1923	MIL	N							1		
1924									3		
Career									10		

Dave Cook

Year	Team		Att	Com	PC	Yds	Avg	TD	Int	Lg	Rtg
1935	CHIC	N	1	1	100.0	7	7.0	0	0	7	95.8

Greg Cook

Year	Team		Att	Com	PC	Yds	Avg	TD	Int	Lg	Rtg
1969	CIN	A	197	106	53.8	1854	9.4	15	11	78t	88.3
1973	CIN	N	3	1	33.3	11	3.7	0	0	11	45.1
Career			200	107	53.5	1865	9.3	15	11	78t	87.6

Bill Cooper

Year	Team		Att	Com	PC	Yds	Avg	TD	Int	Lg	Rtg
1937	CLE	N	5	2	40.0	21	4.2	0	0		13.3

George Corbett

Year	Team		Att	Com	PC	Yds	Avg	TD	Int	Lg	Rtg
1934	CHIB	N	3	1	33.3	36	12.0	1	0	36t	119.4
1935			7	1	14.3	9	1.3	0	0	9	39.6
1936			13	5	38.5	64	4.9	0	1		22.6
1938			9	3	33.3	32	3.6	0	3		5.1
Career			32	10	31.3	141	4.4	1	4	36t	17.3
Playoffs			3	2	66.7	79	26.3	0	0		109.7

Art Corcoran

Year	Team		Att	Com	PC	Yds	Avg	TD	Int	Lg	Rtg
1922	AKR	N							1		

King Corcoran

Year	Team		Att	Com	PC	Yds	Avg	TD	Int	Lg	Rtg
1968	BOS	A	7	3	42.9	33	4.7	0	2	14	17.9

Frank Corral

Year	Team		Att	Com	PC	Yds	Avg	TD	Int	Lg	Rtg
1981	LA	N	1	0	0.0	0	0.0	0	0		39.6

Red Corzine

Year	Team		Att	Com	PC	Yds	Avg	TD	Int	Lg	Rtg
1937	NYG	N	1	0	0.0	0	0.0	0	0		39.6

Gerry Courtney

Year	Team		Att	Com	PC	Yds	Avg	TD	Int	Lg	Rtg
1942	BKN	N	4	1	25.0	14	3.5	0	2	14	2.1

Fred Cox

Year	Team		Att	Com	PC	Yds	Avg	TD	Int	Lg	Rtg
1970	MIN	N	1	1	100.0	-1	-1.0	0	0	-1	79.2

Norm Cox

Year	Team		Att	Com	PC	Yds	Avg	TD	Int	Lg	Rtg
1947	CHI	AA	2	1	50.0	9	4.5	0	0	9	62.5

Steve Cox

Year	Team		Att	Com	PC	Yds	Avg	TD	Int	Lg	Rtg
1984	CLE	N	1	1	100.0	16	16.0	0	0	16	118.8
1985	WAS	N	1	1	100.0	11	11.0	0	0	11	112.5
Career			2	2	100.0	27	13.5	0	0	16	118.0

Bill Crass

Year	Team		Att	Com	PC	Yds	Avg	TD	Int	Lg	Rtg
1937	CHIC	N	1	0	0.0	0	0.0	0	0		39.6

Aaron Craver

Year	Team		Att	Com	PC	Yds	Avg	TD	Int	Lg	Rtg
1996	DEN	N	1	0	0.0	0	0.0	0	0	0	39.6

Jim Crawford

Year	Team		Att	Com	PC	Yds	Avg	TD	Int	Lg	Rtg
1963	BOS	A	2	2	100.0	27	13.5	0	0		118.8

Dick Crayne

Year	Team		Att	Com	PC	Yds	Avg	TD	Int	Lg	Rtg
1936	BKN	N	2	1	50.0	52	26.0	0	0	52	95.8
1937			4	2	50.0	20	5.0	0	0		64.6
Career			6	3	50.0	72	12.0	0	0	52	93.8

Joe Cribbs

Year	Team		Att	Com	PC	Yds	Avg	TD	Int	Lg	Rtg
1980	BUF	N	1	1	100.0	13	13.0	0	0	13	118.8
1981			1	1	100.0	9	9.0	1	0	9t	143.8
1982			1	0	0.0	0	0.0	0	1		0.0
1983			2	1	50.0	3	1.5	0	0	3	56.3
Career			5	3	60.0	25	5.0	1	1	13	72.9

Jim Crocicchia

Year	Team		Att	Com	PC	Yds	Avg	TD	Int	Lg	Rtg
1987	NYG	N	15	6	40.0	89	5.9	1	0	46t	82.4

Nolan Cromwell

Year	Team		Att	Com	PC	Yds	Avg	TD	Int	Lg	Rtg
1980	LA	N	1	0	0.0	0	0.0	0	0		39.6

John David Crow

Year	Team		Att	Com	PC	Yds	Avg	TD	Int	Lg	Rtg
1958	CHIC	N	1	0	0.0	0	0.0	0	1		0.0
1960	STL	N	18	9	50.0	247	13.7	2	1	52t	109.7
1961			14	4	28.6	76	5.4	1	1	32t	43.8
1962			20	12	60.0	241	12.1	0	0	57	102.3
1963			3	2	66.7	27	9.0	1	0	17	134.7
1964			1	0	0.0	0	0.0	0	0		39.6

Year	Team		Att	Com	PC	Yds	Avg	TD	Int	Lg	Rtg

John David Crow *continued*

Year	Team		Att	Com	PC	Yds	Avg	TD	Int	Lg	Rtg
1965	SF	N	4	2	50.0	61	15.3	1	1	45t	95.8
1966			4	2	50.0	61	15.3	0	1	46	56.3
1967			5	2	40.0	46	9.2	0	0	25	73.8
Career			70	33	47.1	759	10.8	5	5	57	80.6

Wayne Crow

Year	Team		Att	Com	PC	Yds	Avg	TD	Int	Lg	Rtg
1961	OAK	A	10	6	60.0	165	16.5	0	0		104.2
1962	BUF	A	4	2	50.0	16	4.0	0	1		20.8
Career			14	8	57.1	181	12.9	0	1		72.0

Earl Crowder

Year	Team		Att	Com	PC	Yds	Avg	TD	Int	Lg	Rtg
1939	CHIC	N	7	2	28.6	6	0.9	0	0		39.6

Ward Cuff

Year	Team		Att	Com	PC	Yds	Avg	TD	Int	Lg	Rtg
1943	NY	N	1	0	0.0	0	0.0	0	0		39.6

Doug Cunningham

Year	Team		Att	Com	PC	Yds	Avg	TD	Int	Lg	Rtg
1969	SF	N	3	3	100.0	48	16.0	1	0	31	158.3

Randall Cunningham

Year	Team		Att	Com	PC	Yds	Avg	TD	Int	Lg	Rtg
1985	PHI	N	81	34	42.0	548	6.8	1	8	69	29.8
1986			209	111	53.1	1391	6.7	8	7	75t	72.9
1987			406	223	54.9	2786	6.9	23	12	70t	83.0
1988			560	301	53.8	3808	6.8	24	16	80t	77.6
1989			532	290	54.5	3400	6.4	21	15	66t	75.5
1990			465	271	58.3	3466	7.5	30	13	95t	91.6
1991			4	1	25.0	19	4.8	0	0	19	46.9
1992			384	233	60.7	2775	7.2	19	11	75t	87.3
1993			110	76	69.1	850	7.7	5	5	80t	88.1
1994			490	265	54.1	3229	6.6	16	13	93	74.4
1995			121	69	57.0	605	5.0	3	5	33	61.5
Career			3362	1874	55.7	22877	6.8	150	105	95t	78.7
Playoffs			214	113	52.8	1390	6.5	3	6		66.1

Gary Cuozzo

Year	Team		Att	Com	PC	Yds	Avg	TD	Int	Lg	Rtg
1963	BAL	N	17	10	58.8	104	6.1	0	0	23	76.6
1964			36	15	41.7	163	4.5	2	3	22	39.5
1965			105	54	51.4	700	6.7	7	4	44	79.1
1966			50	26	52.0	424	8.5	4	2	69	90.8
1967	NO	N	260	134	51.5	1562	6.0	7	12	49t	59.8
1968	MIN	N	33	24	72.7	297	9.0	1	0	31	110.3
1969			98	49	50.0	693	7.1	4	5	50	65.6
1970			257	128	49.8	1720	6.7	7	10	72	64.3
1971			168	75	44.6	842	5.0	6	8	52t	52.2
1972	STL	N	158	69	43.7	897	5.7	5	11	68t	43.7
Career			1182	584	49.4	7402	6.3	43	55	72	62.1
Playoffs			52	22	42.3	286	5.5	2	5		33.5

Will Cureton

Year	Team		Att	Com	PC	Yds	Avg	TD	Int	Lg	Rtg
1975	CLE	N	32	10	31.3	95	3.0	1	1	16	38.0

Pat Curran

Year	Team		Att	Com	PC	Yds	Avg	TD	Int	Lg	Rtg
1970	LA	N	2	0	0.0	0	0.0	0	1		0.0

Harry Curzon

Year	Team		Att	Com	PC	Yds	Avg	TD	Int	Lg	Rtg
1925	HAM	N							1		

Bill Daley

Year	Team		Att	Com	PC	Yds	Avg	TD	Int	Lg	Rtg
1947	CHI	AA	6	3	50.0	70	11.7	1	1		92.4

Boley Dancewicz

Year	Team		Att	Com	PC	Yds	Avg	TD	Int	Lg	Rtg
1946	BOS	N	34	13	38.2	162	4.8	1	5	45	24.0
1947			169	66	39.1	1203	7.1	11	18	69	46.4
1948			35	17	48.6	186	5.3	0	5	33	25.1
Career			238	96	40.3	1551	6.5	12	28	69	40.1

Clem Daniels

Year	Team		Att	Com	PC	Yds	Avg	TD	Int	Lg	Rtg
1962	OAK	A	1	0	0.0	0	0.0	0	0		39.6
1963			1	1	100.0	10	10.0	0	0	10	108.3
1964			1	0	0.0	0	0.0	0	0		39.6
1965			2	2	100.0	95	47.5	0	0	53	118.8
1966			3	0	0.0	0	0.0	0	1		0.0
1967			1	1	100.0	28	28.0	0	0	28	118.8
Career			9	4	44.4	133	14.8	0	1	53	51.6

Gary Danielson

Year	Team		Att	Com	PC	Yds	Avg	TD	Int	Lg	Rtg
1977	DET	N	100	42	42.0	445	4.5	1	5	61	38.1
1978			351	199	56.7	2294	6.5	18	17	47	73.5
1980			417	244	58.5	3223	7.7	13	11	87t	82.4
1981			96	56	58.3	784	8.2	3	5	45	73.4
1982			197	100	50.8	1343	6.8	10	14	70t	60.1
1983			113	59	52.2	720	6.4	7	4	54	78.0
1984			410	252	61.5	3076	7.5	17	15	77t	83.1

Gary Danielson *continued*

Year	Team		Att	Com	PC	Yds	Avg	TD	Int	Lg	Rtg
1985	CLE	N	163	97	59.5	1274	7.8	8	6	72t	85.3
1987			33	25	75.8	281	8.5	4	0	23	140.3
1988			52	31	59.6	324	6.2	0	1	26	69.7
Career			1932	1105	57.2	13764	7.1	81	78	87t	76.6
Playoffs			38	24	63.2	236	6.2	0	5		41.0

Ed Danowski

Year	Team		Att	Com	PC	Yds	Avg	TD	Int	Lg	Rtg
1934	NYG	N	32	15	46.9	230	7.2	2	3		52.9
1935			113	57	50.4	794	7.0	11	9		72.7
1936			104	47	45.2	515	5.0	6	10		40.0
1937			134	66	49.3	814	6.1	7	5		70.3
1938			129	70	54.3	848	6.6	7	8		66.9
1939			101	42	41.6	437	4.3	3	6		39.9
1941			24	12	50.0	179	7.5	2	2	65	67.9
Career			637	309	48.5	3817	6.0	38	43	65	59.2
Playoffs			46	21	45.7	296	6.4	4	6		56.3

Dan Darragh

Year	Team		Att	Com	PC	Yds	Avg	TD	Int	Lg	Rtg
1968	BUF	A	215	92	42.8	917	4.3	3	14	41	33.0
1969			52	24	46.2	365	7.0	1	6	53	36.6
1970	BUF	N	29	11	37.9	71	2.4	0	2	19	17.5
Career			296	127	42.9	1353	4.6	4	22	53	30.4

Red Daum

Year	Team		Att	Com	PC	Yds	Avg	TD	Int	Lg	Rtg
1922	AKR								1		

Bill Davidson

Year	Team		Att	Com	PC	Yds	Avg	TD	Int	Lg	Rtg
1937	PIT	N	24	8	33.3	81	3.4	0	5		4.3
1938			2	2	100.0	10	5.0	0	0		87.5
1939			7	1	14.3	8	1.1	0	0	8	39.6
Career			33	11	33.3	99	3.0	0	5	8	2.8

Cotton Davidson

Year	Team		Att	Com	PC	Yds	Avg	TD	Int	Lg	Rtg
1954	BAL	N	63	28	44.4	309	4.9	0	5	29	26.5
1957			2	0	0.0	0	0.0	0	1		0.0
1960	DAL	A	379	179	47.2	2474	6.5	15	16	74t	64.2
1961			330	151	45.8	2445	7.4	17	23	71	59.2
1962	OAK	A	321	119	37.1	1977	6.2	7	23	90t	36.1
1963			194	77	39.7	1276	6.6	11	10	73	60.0
1964			320	155	48.4	2497	7.8	21	19		72.1
1965			1	1	100.0	8	8.0	0	0	8	100.0
1966			139	59	42.4	770	5.5	2	11	51	32.4
1968			2	1	50.0	4	2.0	0	0	4	56.3
Career			1751	770	44.0	11760	6.7	73	108	90t	54.9

Al Davis

Year	Team		Att	Com	PC	Yds	Avg	TD	Int	Lg	Rtg
1971	PHI	N	1	0	0.0	0	0.0	0	0		39.6

Bob Davis

Year	Team		Att	Com	PC	Yds	Avg	TD	Int	Lg	Rtg
1938	CLE	N	26	6	23.1	49	1.9	0	2		7.5
1944	BOS	N	18	8	44.4	88	4.9	1	2	25	38.4
1945			10	5	50.0	73	7.3	3	0	23	113.8
1946			1	1	100.0	7	7.0	0	0	7	95.8
Career			55	20	36.4	217	3.9	4	4	25	42.8

Bob Davis

Year	Team		Att	Com	PC	Yds	Avg	TD	Int	Lg	Rtg
1967	HOU	A	19	9	47.4	71	3.7	0	2	17	17.5
1968			86	33	38.4	441	5.1	0	6	53	26.4
1969			42	25	59.5	223	5.3	2	4	22	50.1
1970	NYJ	N	17	6	35.3	66	3.9	0	0	16	47.7
1971			121	49	40.5	624	5.2	10	8	44	57.3
1972			22	10	45.5	114	5.2	2	1	35	72.9
1973	NO	N	17	5	29.4	14	0.8	0	2	14	0.0
Career			324	137	42.3	1553	4.8	14	23	53	42.1

Corby Davis

Year	Team		Att	Com	PC	Yds	Avg	TD	Int	Lg	Rtg
1938	CLE	N	1	0	0.0	0	0.0	0	0		39.6
1942			2	1	50.0	22	11.0	0	1	22	50.0
Career			3	1	33.3	22	7.3	0	1	22	20.8

Glenn Davis

Year	Team		Att	Com	PC	Yds	Avg	TD	Int	Lg	Rtg
1950	LA	N	5	3	60.0	97	19.4	2	0	58t	149.8
1951			2	1	50.0	5	2.5	0	0	5	56.3
Career			7	4	57.1	102	14.6	2	0	58t	141.4

Lamar Davis

Year	Team		Att	Com	PC	Yds	Avg	TD	Int	Lg	Rtg
1947	BAL	AA	1	0	0.0	0	0.0	0	0		39.6

Red Davis

Year	Team		Att	Com	PC	Yds	Avg	TD	Int	Lg	Rtg
1933	PHI	N							1		

Ricky Davis

Year	Team		Att	Com	PC	Yds	Avg	TD	Int	Lg	Rtg
1976	TB	N	1	1	100.0	-7	-7.0	0	0	-7	79.2

Tommy Davis

Year	Team		Att	Com	PC	Yds	Avg	TD	Int	Lg	Rtg
1963	SF	N	1	0	0.0	0	0.0	0	0		39.6

Len Dawson

Year	Team		Att	Com	PC	Yds	Avg	TD	Int	Lg	Rtg
1957	PIT	N	4	2	50.0	25	6.3	0	0	15	69.8
1958			6	1	16.7	11	1.8	0	2	11	0.0
1959			7	3	42.9	60	8.6	1	0	82	113.1
1960	CLE	N	13	8	61.5	23	1.8	0	0	23	65.9
1961			15	7	46.7	85	5.7	1	3	17t	47.2
1962	DAL	A	310	189	**61.0**	2759	**8.9**	**29**	17	92t	**98.3**
1963	KC	A	352	190	54.0	2389	6.8	**26**	19	82t	77.5
1964			354	199	**56.2**	2879	8.1	30	18	72t	**89.9**
1965			305	163	**53.4**	2262	7.4	**21**	14	67	**81.3**
1966			284	159	**56.0**	2527	**8.9**	**26**	10	89t	**101.7**
1967			357	206	**57.7**	2651	7.4	24	17	71t	**83.7**
1968			224	131	**58.5**	2109	**9.4**	17	9	92t	**98.6**
1969			166	98	**59.0**	1323	8.0	9	13	55t	69.9
1970	KC	N	262	141	53.8	1876	7.2	13	14	61t	71.0
1971			301	167	55.5	2504	8.3	15	13	82	81.6
1972			305	175	57.4	1835	6.0	13	12	44	72.8
1973			101	66	65.3	725	7.2	2	5	48	72.4
1974			235	138	58.7	1573	6.7	7	13	84t	61.8
1975			140	93	**66.4**	1095	7.8	5	4	51	90.0
Career			3741	2136	57.1	28711	7.7	239	183	92t	82.6
Playoffs			188	107	56.9	1497	8.0	7	8		77.4

Eagle Day

Year	Team		Att	Com	PC	Yds	Avg	TD	Int	Lg	Rtg
1959	WAS	N	13	6	46.2	79	6.1	0	1	20	33.8
1960			19	9	47.4	115	6.1	0	1	27	44.8
Career			32	15	46.9	194	6.1	0	2	27	40.4

Randy Dean

Year	Team		Att	Com	PC	Yds	Avg	TD	Int	Lg	Rtg
1978	NYG	N	39	19	48.7	188	4.8	1	3	48	39.3
1979			26	11	42.3	91	3.5	0	2	20	19.9
Career			65	30	46.2	279	4.3	1	5	48	31.5

Steve DeBerg

Year	Team		Att	Com	PC	Yds	Avg	TD	Int	Lg	Rtg
1978	SF	N	302	137	45.4	1570	5.2	8	22	58t	40.0
1979			**578**	**347**	60.0	3652	6.3	17	21	50	73.1
1980			321	186	57.9	1998	6.2	12	17	93t	66.7
1981	DEN	N	108	64	59.3	797	7.4	6	6	44	77.6
1982			223	131	58.7	1405	6.3	7	11	51t	67.2
1983			215	119	55.3	1617	7.5	9	7	54	79.9
1984	TB	N	509	308	60.5	3554	7.0	19	18	55	79.3
1985			370	197	53.2	2488	6.7	19	18	57	71.3
1986			96	50	52.1	610	6.4	5	12	45	49.7
1987			275	159	57.8	1891	6.9	14	7	64t	85.3
1988	KC	N	414	224	54.1	2935	7.1	16	16	80t	73.5
1989			324	196	60.5	2529	7.8	11	16	50	75.8
1990			444	258	58.1	3444	7.8	23	4	90t	96.3
1991			434	256	59.0	2965	6.8	17	14	63	79.3
1992	TB	N	125	76	60.8	710	5.7	3	4	28t	71.1
1993	TB-MIA	N	227	136	59.9	1707	7.5	7	10	47	75.3
Career			4965	2844	57.3	33872	6.8	193	203	93t	74.2
Playoffs			72	45	62.5	511	7.1	3	3		80.3

Bill deCorrevont

Year	Team		Att	Com	PC	Yds	Avg	TD	Int	Lg	Rtg
1946	DET	N	19	8	42.1	155	8.2	2	2	70	66.7

Al Dekdebrun

Year	Team		Att	Com	PC	Yds	Avg	TD	Int	Lg	Rtg
1946	BUF	AA	66	28	42.4	517	7.8	8	8	53	70.1
1947	CHI	AA	75	45	60.0	556	7.4	5	7	61t	66.3
1948	NYY-BOS	N-A	23	11	47.8	151	6.6	0	3		29.7
Career			164	84	51.2	1224	7.5	13	18	61t	62.7

Jack Del Bello

Year	Team		Att	Com	PC	Yds	Avg	TD	Int	Lg	Rtg
1953	BAL	N	61	27	44.3	229	3.8	1	5	66t	25.9

Jim Del Gaizo

Year	Team		Att	Com	PC	Yds	Avg	TD	Int	Lg	Rtg
1972	MIA	N	9	5	55.6	165	18.3	2	1	51t	100.5
1973	GB	N	62	27	43.5	318	5.1	2	6	28	30.9
1974	NYG	N	32	12	37.5	165	5.2	0	3	44	15.8
Career			103	44	42.7	648	6.3	4	10	51t	37.3

Bill Demory

Year	Team		Att	Com	PC	Yds	Avg	TD	Int	Lg	Rtg
1973	NYJ	N	39	12	30.8	159	4.1	2	8	31t	22.2

Bob DeMoss

Year	Team		Att	Com	PC	Yds	Avg	TD	Int	Lg	Rtg
1949	NYB	N	18	6	33.3	60	3.3	0	2	20	4.2

Mike Dennis

Year	Team		Att	Com	PC	Yds	Avg	TD	Int	Lg	Rtg
1968	LA	N	2	0	0.0	0	0.0	0	0		39.6

Dan DeSantis

Year	Team		Att	Com	PC	Yds	Avg	TD	Int	Lg	Rtg
1941	PHI	N	7	3	42.9	78	11.1	1	1	40	84.2

Chuck DeShane

Year	Team		Att	Com	PC	Yds	Avg	TD	Int	Lg	Rtg
1946	DET	N	1	0	0.0	0	0.0	0	0		39.6

Ty Detmer

Year	Team		Att	Com	PC	Yds	Avg	TD	Int	Lg	Rtg
1993	GB	N	5	3	60.0	26	5.2	0	0	25	73.8
1995			16	8	50.0	81	5.1	1	1	25	59.6
1996	PHI	N	401	238	59.4	2911	7.3	15	13	42	80.8
Career			422	249	59.0	3018	7.2	16	14	42	79.9
Playoffs			21	14	66.7	148	7.0	0	2		47.4

Mark Devlin

Year	Team		Att	Com	PC	Yds	Avg	TD	Int	Lg	Rtg
1920	CLE	A							1		

Benjy Dial

Year	Team		Att	Com	PC	Yds	Avg	TD	Int	Lg	Rtg
1967	PHI	N	3	1	33.3	5	1.7	0	0	5	42.4

Eric Dickerson

Year	Team		Att	Com	PC	Yds	Avg	TD	Int	Lg	Rtg
1984	LARM	N	1	0	0.0	0	0.0	0	1		0.0
1986			1	1	100.0	15	15.0	1	0	15t	158.3
1989	IND	N	0	0		0		0	0		
Career			2	1	50.0	15	7.5	1	1	15t	75.0
Playoffs			1	1	100.0	1	1.0	0	0		79.2

Curtis Dickey

Year	Team		Att	Com	PC	Yds	Avg	TD	Int	Lg	Rtg
1984	IND	N	1	1	100.0	63	63.0	1	0	63t	158.3

Lynn Dickey

Year	Team		Att	Com	PC	Yds	Avg	TD	Int	Lg	Rtg
1971	HOU	N	57	19	33.3	315	5.5	0	9	42	13.3
1973			120	71	59.2	888	7.4	6	10	66t	64.2
1974			113	63	55.8	704	6.2	2	8	59	50.9
1975			4	2	50.0	46	11.5	0	1	28	52.1
1976	GB	N	243	115	47.3	1465	6.0	7	14	69t	52.2
1977			220	113	51.4	1346	6.1	5	14	95t	51.4
1979			119	60	50.4	787	6.6	5	4	52t	71.7
1980			478	278	58.2	3529	7.4	15	25	69t	70.0
1981			354	204	57.6	2593	7.3	17	15	75t	79.0
1982			218	124	56.9	1790	8.2	12	14	80t	75.3
1983			484	289	59.7	**4458**	**9.2**	**32**	29	75t	87.3
1984			401	237	59.1	3195	8.0	25	19	79t	85.6
1985			314	172	54.8	2206	7.0	15	17	63	70.4
Career			3125	1747	55.9	23322	7.5	141	179	95t	70.9
Playoffs			59	36	61.0	592	10.0	5	3		101.8

Parnell Dickinson

Year	Team		Att	Com	PC	Yds	Avg	TD	Int	Lg	Rtg
1976	TB	N	39	15	38.5	210	5.4	1	5	49	25.5

Wally Diehl

Year	Team		Att	Com	PC	Yds	Avg	TD	Int	Lg	Rtg
1928	FRA	N							3		
1929									1		
1930									1		
Career									5	49	

Scott Dierking

Year	Team		Att	Com	PC	Yds	Avg	TD	Int	Lg	Rtg
1978	NYJ	N	1	0	0.0	0	0.0	0	0		39.6

Trent Dilfer

Year	Team		Att	Com	PC	Yds	Avg	TD	Int	Lg	Rtg
1994	TB	N	82	38	46.3	433	5.3	1	6	42	36.3
1995			415	224	54.0	2774	6.7	4	18	64t	60.1
1996			482	267	55.4	2859	5.9	12	19	45	64.8
Career			979	529	54.0	6066	6.2	17	43	64t	60.4

Steve Dils

Year	Team		Att	Com	PC	Yds	Avg	TD	Int	Lg	Rtg
1980	MIN	N	51	32	62.7	352	6.9	3	0	58t	102.7
1981			102	54	52.9	607	6.0	1	2	44	66.1
1982			26	11	42.3	68	2.6	0	0	12	49.8
1983			444	239	53.8	2840	6.4	11	16	68	66.8
1984	LARM	N	7	4	57.1	44	6.3	1	1	14t	75.9
1986			129	59	45.7	693	5.4	4	4	65t	60.0
1987			114	56	49.1	646	5.7	5	4	51	66.6
1988	ATL	N	99	49	49.5	566	5.7	2	5	50	52.8
Career			972	504	51.9	5816	6.0	27	32	68	65.8

Bucky Dilts

Year	Team		Att	Com	PC	Yds	Avg	TD	Int	Lg	Rtg
Playoffs			1	1	100.0	16	16.0	0	0		118.8

Anthony Dilweg

Year	Team		Att	Com	PC	Yds	Avg	TD	Int	Lg	Rtg
1989	GB	N	1	1	100.0	7	7.0	0	0	7	95.8
1990			192	101	52.6	1267	6.6	8	7	59	72.1
Career			193	102	52.8	1274	6.6	8	7	59	72.3

Year	Team		Att	Com	PC	Yds	Avg		TD	Int	Lg	Rtg

Tom Dimitroff
| 1960 | BOS | A | 2 | 0 | 0.0 | 0 | 0.0 | | 0 | 0 | | 39.6 |

Bob Dinsmore
| 1926 | PHI | A | | | | | | | 2 | | | |

Joe DiVito
| 1968 | DEN | A | 6 | 1 | 16.7 | 16 | 2.7 | | 0 | 0 | 16 | 39.6 |

Glenn Dobbs
1946	BKN	AA	**269**	**135**	50.2	**1886**	7.0		13	15	65t	66.0
1947	BKN-LA	AA	143	61	42.7	762	5.3		7	8		52.8
1948	LA	AA	**369**	**185**	50.1	2403	6.5		21	20	67	67.4
1949			153	65	42.5	825	5.4		4	9		44.2
Career			934	446	47.8	5876	6.3		45	52	67	61.0

Al Dodd
| 1970 | NO | N | 1 | 0 | 0.0 | 0 | 0.0 | | 0 | 0 | | 39.6 |

Les Dodson
| 1941 | PIT | N | 8 | 1 | 12.5 | 7 | 0.9 | | 0 | 3 | 7 | 0.0 |

John Doehring
1932	CHIB	N							2			
1933									1			
1934			11	3	27.3	48	4.4		1	0		75.6
1935	PIT	N							1			
1936	CHIB	N	12	5	41.7	145	12.1		1	0		114.9
1937			3	2	66.7	25	8.3		0	0		92.4
Career			26	10	38.5	218	8.4		6	0		94.7

Marty Domres
1969	SD	A	112	47	42.0	631	5.6		2	10	55	29.3
1970	SD	N	55	28	50.9	491	8.9		2	4	80t	63.5
1971			12	7	58.3	97	8.1		1	3	25t	72.6
1972	BAL	N	222	115	51.8	1392	6.3		11	6	62t	76.6
1973			191	93	48.7	1153	6.0		9	13	66t	55.2
1974			153	77	50.3	803	5.2		0	12	44	33.2
1975			10	8	80.0	123	12.3		1	0	32	151.2
1976	SF	N	14	7	50.0	101	7.2		0	1	44	44.0
1977	NYJ	N	40	17	42.5	113	2.8		1	1	18	47.9
Career			809	399	49.3	4904	6.1		27	50	80t	53.8
Playoffs			11	2	18.2	9	0.8		1	2		30.3

John Donaldson
| 1949 | LA | AA | 1 | 0 | 0.0 | 0 | 0.0 | | 0 | 0 | | 39.6 |

Billy Donckers
1976	STL	N	1	1	100.0	16	16.0		0	0	16	118.8
1977			5	5	100.0	38	7.6		0	0	16	98.3
Career			6	6	100.0	54	9.0		0	0	16	104.2

Al Donelli
| 1941 | PIT | N | 8 | 2 | 25.0 | 13 | 1.6 | | 1 | 3 | 10 | 39.6 |

Al Dorow
1954	WAS	N	138	70	50.7	997	7.2		8	17	80t	54.2
1955			12	2	16.7	37	3.1		0	1	19	5.2
1956			112	55	49.1	730	6.5		8	8	51t	64.2
1957	PHI	N	36	17	47.2	212	5.9		1	4	49	35.6
1960	NY	A	396	201	50.8	2748	6.9		**26**	26		67.8
1961			**438**	**197**	45.0	2651	6.1		19	30		50.7
1962	BUF	A	75	30	40.0	333	4.4		2	7		23.9
Career			1207	572	47.4	7708	6.4		64	93	80t	53.8

Tony Dorsett
1977	DAL	N	1	1	100.0	34	34.0		0	0	34	118.8
1978			1	0	0.0	0	0.0		0	0		39.6
1980			1	0	0.0	0	0.0		0	0		39.6
1982			1	0	0.0	0	0.0		0	0		39.6
1983			1	0	0.0	0	0.0		0	0		39.6
1984			1	0	0.0	0	0.0		0	1		39.6
1988	DEN	N	2	1	50.0	7	3.5		1	0	7t	97.9
Career			8	2	25.0	41	5.1		1	1	34	48.4

Bobby Douglass
1969	CHI	N	148	68	45.9	773	5.2		5	8	48	50.9
1970			30	12	40.0	218	7.3		4	3	53t	65.7
1971			225	91	40.4	1164	5.2		5	15	64	37.0
1972			198	75	37.9	1246	6.3		9	12	85t	49.8
1973			174	81	46.6	1057	6.1		5	7	63	59.0
1974			100	41	41.0	387	3.9		2	4	40	42.4
1975	CHI-SD	N	47	15	31.9	140	3.0		0	3	34	14.6
1976	NO	N	213	103	48.4	1288	6.0		4	8	74	58.2

Bobby Douglass *continued*
1977			31	16	51.6	130	4.2		1	3	31	33.7
1978	GB	N	12	5	41.7	90	7.5		1	1	30	61.1
Career			1178	507	43.0	6493	5.5		36	64	85t	48.5

Mule Dowell
| 1936 | CHIC | N | 2 | 1 | 50.0 | 6 | 3.0 | | 0 | 0 | 6 | 56.3 |

Brian Dowling
1972	NE	N	54	29	53.7	383	7.1		2	1	42	81.0
1977	GB	N	1	0	0.0	0	0.0		0	0		39.6
Career			55	29	52.7	383	7.0		2	1	42	79.6

D.J. Dozier
| 1989 | MIN | N | 1 | 1 | 100.0 | 19 | 19.0 | | 1 | 0 | 19t | 158.3 |

Johnny Drake
1937	CLE	N	1	0	0.0	0	0.0		0	0		39.6
1938			3	1	33.3	8	2.7		0	0	8	42.4
1940			4	2	50.0	16	4.0		2	0		100.0
1941			2	0	0.0	0	0.0		0	0		39.6
Career			10	3	30.0	24	2.4		2	0	8	79.2

Chuck Dressen
| 1922 | RAC | N | | | | | | | 1 | | | |

Paddy Driscoll
1921	CHIC	A							1			
1922	CHIC	N							1			
1924									2			
1925									1			
1926	CHIB	N							**6**			
1927									3			
1928									3			
1929									2			
Career									19			

Tom Dublinski
1952	DET	N	6	1	16.7	39	6.5		0	1	39	14.6
1953			30	14	46.7	174	5.8		0	5	26	25.6
1954			138	77	55.8	1073	7.8		8	7	66t	79.2
1958	NYG	N	3	1	33.3	14	4.7		0	0	14	49.3
Career			177	93	52.5	1300	7.3		8	13	66t	60.9
Playoffs			2	1	50.0	18	9.0		0	0		81.3

Bill Dudley
1942	PIT	N	94	35	37.2	438	4.7		2	5	38	37.5
1945			32	10	31.3	58	1.8		0	2	32	14.6
1946			90	32	35.6	452	5.0		2	9	37	20.5
1947	DET	N	4	3	75.0	24	6.0		0	0	11	129.2
1948			1	0	0.0	0	0.0		0	1		0.0
1951	WAS	N	1	1	100.0	13	13.0		0	0	13	118.8
Career			222	81	36.5	985	4.4		6	17	38	28.1

Paul Dudley
1962	NYG	N	1	0	0.0	0	0.0		0	1		0.0
1963	PHI	N	0	0		0			0	0		
Career			1	0	0.0	0	0.0		0	1		0.0

Joe Dufek
| 1984 | BUF | N | 150 | 74 | 49.3 | 829 | 5.5 | | 4 | 8 | 64t | 52.9 |

Paul Duhart
1944	GB	N	13	4	30.8	42	3.2		0	0	12	41.2
1945	PIT-BOS	N	9	3	33.3	27	3.0		0	2	21	2.8
Career			22	7	31.8	69	3.1		0	2	21	3.8

Bobby Duhon
1968	NYG	N	2	2	100.0	24	12.0		0	0	19	116.7
1970			2	2	100.0	28	14.0		0	1	15	118.8
1971			1	0	0.0	0	0.0		0	0		0.0
Career			5	4	80.0	52	10.4		0	1	19	70.4

Maury Duncan
1954	SF	N	14	4	28.6	82	5.9		0	2	29	11.9
1955			12	4	33.3	40	3.3		0	0	27	43.8
Career			26	8	30.8	122	4.7		0	2	29	15.2

Randy Duncan
| 1961 | DAL | A | 67 | 25 | 37.3 | 361 | 5.4 | | 1 | 3 | | 41.9 |

Tony Dungy
| 1977 | PIT | N | 8 | 3 | 37.5 | 43 | 5.4 | | 0 | 2 | 18 | 16.1 |

Bob Dunlap

Year	Team		Att	Com	PC	Yds	Avg	TD	Int	Lg	Rtg
1935	CHIB	N	37	11	29.7	111	3.0	1	2		26.1

David Dunn

Year	Team		Att	Com	PC	Yds	Avg	TD	Int	Lg	Rtg
1995	CIN	N	1	0	0.0	0	0.0	0	0		39.6

Perry Lee Dunn

Year	Team		Att	Com	PC	Yds	Avg	TD	Int	Lg	Rtg
1964	DAL	N	2	0	0.0	0	0.0	0	0		39.6
1966	ATL	N	2	0	0.0	0	0.0	0	2		39.6
1967			2	1	50.0	32	16.0	1	0	32t	135.4
Career			6	1	16.7	32	5.3	1	2	32t	49.3

Red Dunn

Year	Team		Att	Com	PC	Yds	Avg	TD	Int	Lg	Rtg
1924	MIL	N						6			
1925	CHIC	N						8			
1926								2			
1927	GB	N						3			
1928								4			
1929								5			
1930								12			
1931								8			
Career								48			

L.G. Dupre

Year	Team		Att	Com	PC	Yds	Avg	TD	Int	Lg	Rtg
1959	BAL	N	1	0	0.0	0	0.0	0	0		39.6

Bill Dutton

Year	Team		Att	Com	PC	Yds	Avg	TD	Int	Lg	Rtg
1946	PIT	N	6	4	66.7	31	5.2	0	0	11	79.2

Kay Eakin

Year	Team		Att	Com	PC	Yds	Avg	TD	Int	Lg	Rtg
1940	NYG	N	43	17	39.5	199	4.6	0	3		25.2
1941			19	5	26.3	71	3.7	1	4	41	20.6
1946	MIA	AA	45	19	42.2	331	7.4	2	5		43.1
Career			107	41	38.3	601	5.6	3	12	41	27.2

Walt Easley

Year	Team		Att	Com	PC	Yds	Avg	TD	Int	Lg	Rtg
1981	SF	N	1	1	100.0	5	5.0	0	0	5	87.5

Tony Eason

Year	Team		Att	Com	PC	Yds	Avg	TD	Int	Lg	Rtg
1983	NE	N	95	46	48.4	557	5.9	1	5	35	48.4
1984			431	259	60.1	3228	7.5	23	8	76t	93.4
1985			299	168	56.2	2156	7.2	11	17	90t	67.5
1986			448	276	61.6	3328	7.4	19	10	49	89.2
1987			79	42	53.2	453	5.7	3	2	45	72.4
1988			43	28	65.1	249	5.8	0	2	26	61.1
1989	NE-NYJ	N	141	79	56.0	1016	7.2	4	6	63t	70.5
1990	NYJ	N	28	13	46.4	155	5.5	0	1	31	49.0
Career			1564	911	58.2	11142	7.1	61	51	90t	79.7
Playoffs			72	42	58.3	561	7.8	7	0		115.6

Vic Eaton

Year	Team		Att	Com	PC	Yds	Avg	TD	Int	Lg	Rtg
1955	PIT	N	2	0	0.0	0	0.0	0	0		39.6

Byron Eby

Year	Team		Att	Com	PC	Yds	Avg	TD	Int	Lg	Rtg
1930	POR	N						1			

Jerry Eckwood

Year	Team		Att	Com	PC	Yds	Avg	TD	Int	Lg	Rtg
1979	TB	N	1	0	0.0	0	0.0	0	0		39.6
1980			4	0	0.0	0	0.0	0	0		39.6
1981			0	0		0		0	0		
Career			5	0	0.0	0	0.0	0	0		39.6
Playoffs			1	1	100.0	42	42.0	0	0		118.8

Charley Eikenberg

Year	Team		Att	Com	PC	Yds	Avg	TD	Int	Lg	Rtg
1948	CHIC	N	19	6	31.6	116	6.1	3	2	52	53.8
Playoffs			2	0	0.0	0	0.0	0	1		0.0

Mike Eischeid

Year	Team		Att	Com	PC	Yds	Avg	TD	Int	Lg	Rtg
1974	MIN	N	1	1	100.0	6	6.0	0	0	6	91.7

Mike Elkins

Year	Team		Att	Com	PC	Yds	Avg	TD	Int	Lg	Rtg
1989	KC	N	2	1	50.0	5	2.5	0	1	5	16.7

Al Elliott

Year	Team		Att	Com	PC	Yds	Avg	TD	Int	Lg	Rtg
1924	RAC	N						1			

Doc Elliott

Year	Team		Att	Com	PC	Yds	Avg	TD	Int	Lg	Rtg
1925	CLE	N						2			

Lenvil Elliott

Year	Team		Att	Com	PC	Yds	Avg	TD	Int	Lg	Rtg
1974	CIN	N	1	1	100.0	17	17.0	0	0	17	118.8

Gerry Ellis

Year	Team		Att	Com	PC	Yds	Avg	TD	Int	Lg	Rtg
1981	GB	N	2	1	50.0	23	11.5	0	0	23	91.7

Gerry Ellis *continued*

Year	Team		Att	Com	PC	Yds	Avg	TD	Int	Lg	Rtg
1983			5	2	40.0	31	6.2	1	1	20	61.3
1984			4	1	25.0	17	4.3	0	0	17	44.8
1985			1	0	0.0	0	0.0	0	0		39.6
Career			12	4	33.3	71	5.9	1	1	23	47.6
Playoffs			1	1	100.0	11	11.0	0	0		112.5

Willie Ellison

Year	Team		Att	Com	PC	Yds	Avg	TD	Int	Lg	Rtg
1968	LA	N	1	0	0.0	0	0.0	0	0		39.6
1969			2	0	0.0	0	0.0	0	0		39.6
Career			3	0	0.0	0	0.0	0	0		39.6

Swede Ellstrom

Year	Team		Att	Com	PC	Yds	Avg	TD	Int	Lg	Rtg
1934	PHI	N						1			

Doug Elmore

Year	Team		Att	Com	PC	Yds	Avg	TD	Int	Lg	Rtg
1962	WAS	N	1	0	0.0	0	0.0	0	0		39.6

John Elway

Year	Team		Att	Com	PC	Yds	Avg	TD	Int	Lg	Rtg
1983	DEN	N	259	123	47.5	1663	6.4	7	14	49t	54.9
1984			380	214	56.3	2598	6.8	18	15	73	76.8
1985			605	327	54.0	3891	6.4	22	23	65t	70.2
1986			504	280	55.6	3485	6.9	19	13	53	79.0
1987			410	224	54.6	3198	7.8	19	12	72t	83.4
1988			496	274	55.2	3309	6.7	17	19	86	71.4
1989			416	223	53.6	3051	7.3	18	18	69	73.7
1990			502	294	58.6	3526	7.0	15	14	66	78.5
1991			451	242	53.7	3253	7.2	13	12	71	75.4
1992			316	174	55.1	2242	7.1	10	17	80t	65.7
1993			551	348	63.2	4030	7.3	25	10	63	92.8
1994			494	307	62.1	3490	7.1	16	10	63	85.7
1995			542	316	58.3	3970	7.3	26	14	62t	86.4
1996			466	287	61.6	3328	7.1	26	14	51	89.2
Career			6392	3633	56.8	45034	7.0	251	205	86	78.5
Playoffs			469	254	54.2	3547	7.6	21	18		77.7

Bert Emanuel

Year	Team		Att	Com	PC	Yds	Avg	TD	Int	Lg	Rtg
1994	ATL	N	1	0	0.0	0	0.0	0	1		0.0

Rick Engels

Year	Team		Att	Com	PC	Yds	Avg	TD	Int	Lg	Rtg
1976	SEA	N	1	1	100.0	8	8.0	0	0	8	100.0
1978	PHI	N	1	1	100.0	-2	-2.0	0	0	-2	79.2
Career			2	2	100.0	6	3.0	0	0	8	79.2

Hunter Enis

Year	Team		Att	Com	PC	Yds	Avg	TD	Int	Lg	Rtg
1960	DAL	A	54	30	55.6	357	6.6	1	2	39	66.7
1961	SD	A	55	23	41.8	365	6.6	2	3	45	54.0
1962	DEN-OAK	A	51	27	52.9	225	4.4	1	1		62.9
Career			160	80	50.0	947	5.9	4	6	45	61.1

Fred Enke

Year	Team		Att	Com	PC	Yds	Avg	TD	Int	Lg	Rtg
1948	DET	N	221	100	45.2	1328	6.0	11	17	51	49.4
1949			142	63	44.4	793	5.6	6	5	58	61.7
1950			53	22	41.5	424	8.0	5	7	46t	61.9
1951			9	2	22.2	22	2.4	0	1	12	0.0
1952	PHI	N	67	22	32.8	377	5.6	1	5	65	26.8
1953	BAL	N	169	71	42.0	1054	6.2	8	15	55t	41.9
1954			28	17	60.7	171	6.1	0	3	42	38.5
Career			689	297	43.1	4169	6.1	31	53	65	46.2

Bobby Epps

Year	Team		Att	Com	PC	Yds	Avg	TD	Int	Lg	Rtg
1957	NYG	N	1	0	0.0	0	0.0	0	0		39.6

Dick Erdlitz

Year	Team		Att	Com	PC	Yds	Avg	TD	Int	Lg	Rtg
1946	MIA	AA	1	1	100.0	10	10.0	0	0	10	108.3

Craig Erickson

Year	Team		Att	Com	PC	Yds	Avg	TD	Int	Lg	Rtg
1992	TB	N	26	15	57.7	121	4.7	0	0	24	69.6
1993			457	233	51.0	3054	6.7	18	21	67t	66.4
1994			399	225	56.4	2919	7.3	16	10	71t	82.5
1995	IND	N	83	50	60.2	586	7.1	3	4	39	73.7
1996	MIA	N	99	55	55.6	780	7.9	4	2	61	86.3
Career			1064	578	54.3	7460	7.0	41	37	71t	74.9

Jack Ernst

Year	Team		Att	Com	PC	Yds	Avg	TD	Int	Lg	Rtg
1925	POT	N						8			
1926								1			
1927								3			
1928								1			
1930	FRA	N						1			
Career								14			

Mike Ernst

Year	Team		Att	Com	PC	Yds	Avg	TD	Int	Lg	Rtg
1972	DEN	N	4	1	25.0	10	2.5	0	0	10	39.6

Russell Erxleben

Year	Team		Att	Com	PC	Yds	Avg	TD	Int	Lg	Rtg
1979	NO	N	1	0	0.0	0	0.0	0	1		0.0
1980			1	0	0.0	0	0.0	0	0		39.6
1982			2	1	50.0	39	19.5	1	0	39t	135.4
1983			1	1	100.0	24	24.0	0	0	24	118.8
Career			5	2	40.0	63	12.6	1	1	39t	87.5

Len Eshmont

Year	Team		Att	Com	PC	Yds	Avg	TD	Int	Lg	Rtg
1941	NYG	N	3	2	66.7	32	10.7	1	0	16	141.7
1946	SF	AA	2	1	50.0	42	21.0	1	0	42t	135.4
Career			5	3	60.0	74	14.8	2	0	42t	143.8
Playoffs			1	0	0.0	0	0.0	0	0		39.6

Boomer Esiason

Year	Team		Att	Com	PC	Yds	Avg	TD	Int	Lg	Rtg
1984	CIN	N	102	51	50.0	530	5.2	3	3	36	62.9
1985			431	251	58.2	3443	8.0	27	12	68t	93.2
1986			469	273	58.2	3959	**8.4**	24	17	57	87.7
1987			440	240	54.5	3321	7.5	16	19	61t	73.1
1988			388	223	57.5	3572	**9.2**	28	14	86t	**97.4**
1989			455	258	56.7	3525	7.7	28	11	74t	92.1
1990			402	224	55.7	3031	7.5	24	22	53	77.0
1991			413	233	56.4	2883	7.0	13	16	53	72.5
1992			278	144	51.8	1407	5.1	11	15	38	57.0
1993	NYJ	N	473	288	60.9	3421	7.2	16	11	77	84.5
1994			440	255	58.0	2782	6.3	17	13	69	77.3
1995			389	221	56.8	2275	5.8	16	15	43t	71.4
1996	ARI	N	339	190	56.0	2293	6.8	11	14	64t	70.6
Career			5019	2851	56.8	36442	7.3	234	182	86t	80.1
Playoffs			99	51	51.5	600	6.1	4	3		71.1

Alex Espinoza

Year	Team		Att	Com	PC	Yds	Avg	TD	Int	Lg	Rtg
1987	KC	N	14	9	64.3	69	4.9	0	2	16	36.6

Mike Esposito

Year	Team		Att	Com	PC	Yds	Avg	TD	Int	Lg	Rtg
1976	ATL	N	1	0	0.0	0	0.0	0	0		39.6
1977			1	0	0.0	0	0.0	0	0		39.6
Career			2	0	0.0	0	0.0	0	0	16	39.6

Sam Etcheverry

Year	Team		Att	Com	PC	Yds	Avg	TD	Int	Lg	Rtg
1961	STL	N	196	96	49.0	1275	6.5	14	11	78	70.4
1962			106	58	54.7	707	6.7	2	10	68t	42.5
Career			302	154	51.0	1982	6.6	16	21	78	60.6

Fred Evans

Year	Team		Att	Com	PC	Yds	Avg	TD	Int	Lg	Rtg
1947	CHI	AA	2	0	0.0	0	0.0	0	0		39.6

Johnny Evans

Year	Team		Att	Com	PC	Yds	Avg	TD	Int	Lg	Rtg
1978	CLE	N	1	1	100.0	19	19.0	0	0	19	118.8
1979			2	1	50.0	14	7.0	0	0	14	72.9
Career			3	2	66.7	33	11.0	0	0	19	103.5

Murray Evans

Year	Team		Att	Com	PC	Yds	Avg	TD	Int	Lg	Rtg
1942	DET	N	17	7	41.2	64	3.8	0	1	15	27.6
1943			5	1	20.0	8	1.6	0	2	8	0.0
Career			22	8	36.4	72	3.3	0	3	15	6.4

Ray Evans

Year	Team		Att	Com	PC	Yds	Avg	TD	Int	Lg	Rtg
1948	PIT	N	137	64	46.7	924	6.7	5	17	66	41.7

Vince Evans

Year	Team		Att	Com	PC	Yds	Avg	TD	Int	Lg	Rtg
1978	CHI	N	3	1	33.3	38	12.7	0	1	38	42.4
1979			63	32	50.8	508	8.1	4	5	65t	66.1
1980			278	148	53.2	2039	7.3	11	16	89t	66.2
1981			436	195	44.7	2354	5.4	11	20	85t	51.1
1982			28	12	42.9	125	4.5	0	4	19	16.8
1983			145	76	52.4	1108	7.6	5	7	72t	69.0
1987	LARI	N	83	39	47.0	630	7.6	5	4	47	72.9
1989			2	2	100.0	50	25.0	0	0	40	118.8
1990			1	1	100.0	36	36.0	0	0	36	118.8
1991			14	6	42.9	127	9.1	1	2	80t	59.8
1992			53	29	54.7	372	7.0	4	3	50	78.5
1993			76	45	59.2	640	8.4	3	4	68t	77.7
1994			33	18	54.5	222	6.7	2	0	65t	95.8
1995	OAK	N	175	100	57.1	1236	7.1	6	8	73t	71.5
Career			1390	704	50.6	9485	6.8	52	74	89t	63.0
Playoffs			8	2	25.0	26	3.3	0	1		1.0

Jim Everett

Year	Team		Att	Com	PC	Yds	Avg	TD	Int	Lg	Rtg
1986	LARM	N	147	73	49.7	1018	6.9	8	8	60t	67.8
1987			302	162	53.6	2064	6.8	10	13	81t	68.4
1988			517	308	59.6	3964	7.7	**31**	18	69t	89.2
1989			518	304	58.7	4310	8.3	**29**	17	78t	90.6
1990			554	307	55.4	3989	7.2	23	17	55t	79.3
1991			490	277	56.5	3438	7.0	11	20	78	68.9

Jim Everett *continued*

Year	Team		Att	Com	PC	Yds	Avg	TD	Int	Lg	Rtg
1992			475	281	59.2	3323	7.0	22	18	67t	80.2
1993			274	135	49.3	1652	6.0	8	12	60t	59.7
1994	NO	N	540	346	64.1	3855	7.1	22	18	78t	84.9
1995			567	345	60.8	3970	7.0	26	14	70t	87.0
1996			464	267	57.5	2797	6.0	12	16	51	69.4
Career			4848	2805	57.9	34380	7.1	202	171	81t	79.0
Playoffs			176	87	49.4	1120	6.4	7	11		57.0

Art Faircloth

Year	Team		Att	Com	PC	Yds	Avg	TD	Int	Lg	Rtg
1947	NYG	N	5	3	60.0	30	6.0	1	0	14	116.7

Gary Famiglietti

Year	Team		Att	Com	PC	Yds	Avg	TD	Int	Lg	Rtg
1946	BOS	N	1	1	100.0	6	6.0	0	0	6	91.7

Andy Farkas

Year	Team		Att	Com	PC	Yds	Avg	TD	Int	Lg	Rtg
Playoffs			1	1	100.0	14	14.0	0	0		118.8

Tom Farmer

Year	Team		Att	Com	PC	Yds	Avg	TD	Int	Lg	Rtg
1946	LA	N	2	0	0.0	0	0.0	0	0		39.6

Mel Farr

Year	Team		Att	Com	PC	Yds	Avg	TD	Int	Lg	Rtg
1967	DET	N	2	0	0.0	0	0.0	0	0		39.6
1969			1	0	0.0	0	0.0	0	0		39.6
Career			3	0	0.0	0	0.0	0	0		39.6

Tom Farris

Year	Team		Att	Com	PC	Yds	Avg	TD	Int	Lg	Rtg
1946	CHIB	N	21	8	38.1	108	5.1	1	3	20	31.5
1947			2	0	0.0	0	0.0	0	0		39.6
1948	CHI	AA	9	3	33.3	24	2.7	0	3		2.8
Career			32	11	34.4	132	4.1	1	6	20	18.8

Frank Fausch

Year	Team		Att	Com	PC	Yds	Avg	TD	Int	Lg	Rtg
1922	EVA	N							1		

George Faust

Year	Team		Att	Com	PC	Yds	Avg	TD	Int	Lg	Rtg
1939	CHIC	N	5	0	0.0	0	0.0	0	1		0.0

Brett Favre

Year	Team		Att	Com	PC	Yds	Avg	TD	Int	Lg	Rtg
1991	ATL	N	5	0	0.0	0	0.0	0	2		0.0
1992	GB	N	471	302	64.1	3227	6.9	18	13	76t	85.3
1993			522	318	60.9	3303	6.3	19	24	66t	72.2
1994			582	363	62.4	3882	6.7	33	14	49	90.7
1995			570	359	63.0	**4413**	7.7	**38**	13	99t	99.5
1996			543	325	59.9	3899	7.2	**39**	13	80t	95.8
Career			2693	1667	61.9	18724	7.0	147	79	99t	88.6
Playoffs			317	194	61.2	2430	7.7	18	7		94.7

Jeff Feagles

Year	Team		Att	Com	PC	Yds	Avg	TD	Int	Lg	Rtg
1989	NE	N	2	0	0.0	0	0.0	0	0		39.6
1990	PHI	N	1	0	0.0	0	0.0	0	0		39.6
Career			3	0	0.0	0	0.0	0	0		39.6

Tiny Feather

Year	Team		Att	Com	PC	Yds	Avg	TD	Int	Lg	Rtg
1931	NYG	N							1		

Beattie Feathers

Year	Team		Att	Com	PC	Yds	Avg	TD	Int	Lg	Rtg
1934	CHIB	N	12	4	33.3	41	3.4	1	1		37.2
1935			14	5	35.7	53	3.8	0	2		8.0
1936			11	1	9.1	10	0.9	0	2	10	0.0
1937			6	2	33.3	12	2.0	0	0		42.4
Career			43	12	27.9	116	2.7	1	5	10	7.8

Bobby Felts

Year	Team		Att	Com	PC	Yds	Avg	TD	Int	Lg	Rtg
1965	DET	N	1	0	0.0	0	0.0	0	0		39.6

Chuck Fenenbock

Year	Team		Att	Com	PC	Yds	Avg	TD	Int	Lg	Rtg
1943	DET	N	58	20	34.5	338	5.8	3	9	72	32.8
1945			110	45	40.9	752	6.8	7	11	56	46.3
1946	LA	AA	1	0	0.0	0	0.0	0	0		39.6
1947			7	1	14.3	7	1.0	0	2	7	0.0
1948	CHI	AA	15	4	26.7	136	9.1	2	1	60t	76.7
Career			191	70	36.6	1233	6.5	12	23	72	40.9

Bob Fenimore

Year	Team		Att	Com	PC	Yds	Avg	TD	Int	Lg	Rtg
1947	CHIB	N	3	2	66.7	27	9.0	0	0	15	95.1

Howie Ferguson

Year	Team		Att	Com	PC	Yds	Avg	TD	Int	Lg	Rtg
1957	GB	N	1	0	0.0	0	0.0	0	0		39.6
1958			1	0	0.0	0	0.0	0	0		39.6
Career			2	0	0.0	0	0.0	0	0		39.6

Joe Ferguson

Year	Team		Att	Com	PC	Yds	Avg	TD	Int	Lg	Rtg
1973	BUF	N	164	73	44.5	939	5.7	4	10	42	45.8

Joe Ferguson *continued*

Year	Team		Att	Com	PC	Yds	Avg	TD	Int	Lg	Rtg
1974			232	119	51.3	1588	6.8	12	12	55t	69.0
1975			321	169	52.6	2426	7.6	**25**	17	77t	81.3
1976			151	74	49.0	1086	7.2	9	1	58t	90.0
1977			**457**	221	48.4	**2803**	6.1	12	24	42	54.8
1978			330	175	53.0	2136	6.5	16	15	92t	70.5
1979			458	238	52.0	3572	7.8	14	15	84t	74.4
1980			439	251	57.2	2805	6.4	20	18	69	74.5
1981			498	252	50.6	3652	7.3	24	20	67t	74.1
1982			264	144	54.5	1597	6.0	7	16	47	56.3
1983			508	281	55.3	2995	5.9	26	25	43t	69.3
1984			344	191	55.5	1991	5.8	12	17	68t	63.5
1985	DET	N	54	31	57.4	364	6.7	2	3	38	67.2
1986			155	73	47.1	941	6.1	7	7	73	62.9
1988	TB	N	46	31	67.4	368	8.0	3	1	34	104.3
1989			90	44	48.9	533	5.9	3	6	69t	50.8
1990	IND	N	8	2	25.0	21	2.6	0	2	13	0.0
Career			4519	2369	52.4	29817	6.6	196	209	92t	68.4
Playoffs			120	58	48.3	814	6.8	6	9		56.0

Vince Ferragamo

Year	Team		Att	Com	PC	Yds	Avg	TD	Int	Lg	Rtg
1977	LA	N	15	9	60.0	83	5.5	2	0	17t	114.7
1978			20	7	35.0	114	5.7	0	2	28	15.4
1979			110	53	48.2	778	7.1	5	10	71t	49.0
1980			404	240	59.4	3199	7.9	30	19	74t	89.7
1982	LARM	N	209	118	56.5	1609	7.7	9	9	85t	77.6
1983			464	274	59.1	3276	7.1	22	23	61t	75.9
1984			66	29	43.9	317	4.8	2	8	68	29.2
1985	BUF	N	287	149	51.9	1677	5.8	5	17	48	50.8
1986	GB	N	40	23	57.5	283	7.1	1	3	50	56.6
Career			1615	902	55.9	11336	7.0	76	91	85t	70.1
Playoffs			188	92	48.9	1228	6.5	8	11		59.9

Frank Filchock

Year	Team		Att	Com	PC	Yds	Avg	TD	Int	Lg	Rtg
1938	PIT-WAS	N	101	41	40.6	469	4.6	3	11		25.6
1939	WAS	N	89	55	**61.8**	1094	12.3	**11**	7	99t	**111.6**
1940			54	28	51.9	460	8.5	6	9		78.2
1941			68	28	41.2	327	4.8	1	11	35	21.8
1944			147	**84**	**57.1**	1139	7.7	**13**	9	61	**86.0**
1945			46	18	39.1	169	3.7	1	6	27	17.7
1946	NY	N	169	87	51.5	1262	7.5	12	25	57	60.2
1950	BAL	N	3	1	33.3	1	0.3	0	0	1	42.4
Career			677	342	50.5	4921	7.3	47	78	99t	58.0
Playoffs			63	25	39.7	401	6.4	4	12		43.3

Steve Filipowicz

Year	Team		Att	Com	PC	Yds	Avg	TD	Int	Lg	Rtg
1945	NY	N	2	0	0.0	0	0.0	0	0		39.6

Jim Finks

Year	Team		Att	Com	PC	Yds	Avg	TD	Int	Lg	Rtg
1949	PIT	N	71	24	33.8	322	4.5	2	8	35	19.0
1950			9	5	55.6	35	3.9	0	1	19	25.0
1951			24	14	58.3	201	8.4	1	1	40t	82.1
1952			336	158	47.0	2307	6.9	**20**	19	60t	66.2
1953			292	131	44.9	1484	5.1	8	14	77t	49.8
1954			306	164	53.6	2003	6.5	14	19	78t	63.4
1955			**344**	**165**	48.0	**2270**	6.6	10	26	62t	47.7
Career			1382	661	47.8	8622	6.2	55	88	78t	54.7

Dave Finzer

Year	Team		Att	Com	PC	Yds	Avg	TD	Int	Lg	Rtg
1985	SEA	N	1	0	0.0	0	0.0	0	1		0.0

Max Fiske

Year	Team		Att	Com	PC	Yds	Avg	TD	Int	Lg	Rtg
1936	PIT	N	15	6	40.0	64	4.3	0	3		13.6
1937			43	17	39.5	318	7.4	4	4		58.1
1938			37	11	29.7	121	3.3	0	4		1.1
Career			95	34	35.8	503	5.3	4	11		28.4

Paul Fitzgibbons

Year	Team		Att	Com	PC	Yds	Avg	TD	Int	Lg	Rtg
1931	GB	N						3			

Hoot Flanagan

Year	Team		Att	Com	PC	Yds	Avg	TD	Int	Lg	Rtg
1925	POT	N						1			

George Fleming

Year	Team		Att	Com	PC	Yds	Avg	TD	Int	Lg	Rtg
1961	OAK	A	1	0	0.0	0	0.0	0	1		0.0

Mack Flenniken

Year	Team		Att	Com	PC	Yds	Avg	TD	Int	Lg	Rtg
1931	NYG	N						2			

Tom Flick

Year	Team		Att	Com	PC	Yds	Avg	TD	Int	Lg	Rtg
1981	WAS	N	27	13	48.1	143	5.3	0	2	33	33.4
1982	NE	N	5	0	0.0	0	0.0	0	0		39.6
1984	CLE	N	1	1	100.0	2	2.0	0	0	2	79.2

Tom Flick *continued*

Year	Team		Att	Com	PC	Yds	Avg	TD	Int	Lg	Rtg
1986	SD	N	73	33	45.2	361	4.9	2	8	26	29.9
Career			106	47	44.3	506	4.8	2	10	33	25.9

Tom Flores

Year	Team		Att	Com	PC	Yds	Avg	TD	Int	Lg	Rtg
1960	OAK	A	252	136	**54.0**	1738	6.9	12	12		**71.8**
1961			366	190	51.9	2176	5.9	15	19		62.1
1963			247	113	45.7	2101	8.5	20	13	93t	80.7
1964			200	98	49.0	1389	6.9	7	14		54.4
1965			269	122	45.4	1593	5.9	14	11	69	64.9
1966			306	151	49.3	2638	8.6	24	14	78	86.2
1967	BUF	A	64	22	34.4	260	4.1	0	8	59	8.1
1968			5	3	60.0	15	3.0	0	1	12	25.0
1969	BUF-KC	A	6	3	50.0	49	8.2	1	0	33t	117.4
Career			1715	838	48.9	11959	7.0	93	92	93t	67.6

Dick Flowers

Year	Team		Att	Com	PC	Yds	Avg	TD	Int	Lg	Rtg
1953	BAL	N	4	2	50.0	18	4.5	0	0	12	62.5

Doug Flutie

Year	Team		Att	Com	PC	Yds	Avg	TD	Int	Lg	Rtg
1986	CHI	N	46	23	50.0	361	7.8	3	2	58t	80.1
1987	NE	N	25	15	60.0	199	8.0	1	0	30	98.6
1988			179	92	51.4	1150	6.4	8	10	80t	63.3
1989			91	36	39.6	493	5.4	2	4	36	46.6
Career			341	166	48.7	2203	6.5	14	16	80t	63.7
Playoffs			31	11	35.5	134	4.3	1	2		33.5

Glenn Foley

Year	Team		Att	Com	PC	Yds	Avg	TD	Int	Lg	Rtg
1994	NYJ	N	8	5	62.5	45	5.6	0	1	16	38.0
1995			29	16	55.2	128	4.4	0	1	32	52.1
1996			110	54	49.1	559	5.1	3	7	46t	46.7
Career			147	75	51.0	732	5.0	3	9	46t	46.6

Herman Fontenot

Year	Team		Att	Com	PC	Yds	Avg	TD	Int	Lg	Rtg
1985	CLE	N	1	0	0.0	0	0.0	0	0		39.6
1986			1	1	100.0	46	46.0	1	0	46t	158.3
1987			1	1	100.0	14	14.0	0	0	14	118.8
1988			1	0	0.0	0	0.0	0	0		39.6
1989	GB	N	0	0		0		0	0		
Career			4	2	50.0	60	15.0	1	0	46t	135.4

Fred Ford

Year	Team		Att	Com	PC	Yds	Avg	TD	Int	Lg	Rtg
1960	LA	A	1	0	0.0	0	0.0	0	0		39.6

Chuck Foreman

Year	Team		Att	Com	PC	Yds	Avg	TD	Int	Lg	Rtg
Playoffs			1	0	0.0	0	0.0	0	0		39.6

Bob Forte

Year	Team		Att	Com	PC	Yds	Avg	TD	Int	Lg	Rtg
1946	GB	N	7	3	42.9	28	4.0	1	1	15	54.5
1947			2	1	50.0	8	4.0	0	0	8	60.4
1949			1	0	0.0	0	0.0	0	0		39.6
1950			2	2	100.0	24	12.0	0	0	14	116.7
1952			2	2	100.0	4	2.0	0	0	5	79.2
Career			14	8	57.1	64	4.6	1	1	15	62.8

Barry Foster

Year	Team		Att	Com	PC	Yds	Avg	TD	Int	Lg	Rtg
1992	PIT	N	1	0	0.0	0	0.0	0	0		39.6

Geno Foster

Year	Team		Att	Com	PC	Yds	Avg	TD	Int	Lg	Rtg
1965	SD	A	3	2	66.7	31	10.3	0	0	21	100.7
1967			1	0	0.0	0	0.0	0	0		39.6
1968			7	6	85.7	169	24.1	0	0	50	118.8
1969			5	2	40.0	39	7.8	1	0	30t	107.5
1970	SD	N	3	1	33.3	9	3.0	0	0	9	42.4
Career			19	11	57.9	248	13.1	1	0	50	120.0

Wally Foster

Year	Team		Att	Com	PC	Yds	Avg	TD	Int	Lg	Rtg
1925	BUF	N						1			

John Fourcade

Year	Team		Att	Com	PC	Yds	Avg	TD	Int	Lg	Rtg
1987	NO	N	89	48	53.9	597	6.7	4	3	82t	75.9
1988			1	0	0.0	0	0.0	0	0		39.6
1989			107	61	57.0	930	8.7	7	4	54t	92.0
1990			116	50	43.1	785	6.8	3	8	68t	46.1
Career			313	159	50.8	2312	7.4	14	15	82t	70.1
Playoffs			16	5	31.3	79	4.9	0	2		9.1

Dan Fouts

Year	Team		Att	Com	PC	Yds	Avg	TD	Int	Lg	Rtg
1973	SD	N	194	87	44.8	1126	5.8	6	13	69t	46.0
1974			237	115	48.5	1732	7.3	8	13	75t	61.4
1975			195	106	54.4	1396	7.2	2	10	57	59.3
1976			359	208	57.9	2535	7.1	14	15	81t	75.4
1977			109	69	63.3	869	8.0	4	6	67t	77.4
1978			381	224	58.8	2999	7.9	24	20	55t	83.0

Dan Fouts *continued*

Year	Team		Att	Com	PC	Yds	Avg		TD	Int	Lg	Rtg
1979			530	332	62.6	4082	7.7		24	24	65t	82.6
1980			589	348	59.1	4715	8.0		30	24	65	84.7
1981			609	360	59.1	4802	7.9		33	17	67t	90.6
1982			330	204	61.8	2883	8.7		17	11	44t	93.3
1983			340	215	63.2	2975	8.8		20	15	59t	92.5
1984			507	317	62.5	3740	7.4		19	17	61t	83.4
1985			430	254	59.1	3638	8.5		27	20	75t	88.1
1986			430	252	58.6	3031	7.0		16	22	65t	71.4
1987			364	206	56.6	2517	6.9		10	15	46	70.0
Career			5604	3297	58.8	43040	7.7		254	242	81t	80.2
Playoffs			286	159	55.6	2125	7.4		12	16		70.0

Jeff Francis

Year	Team		Att	Com	PC	Yds	Avg		TD	Int	Lg	Rtg
1990	CLE	N	2	2	100.0	26	13.0		0	0	17	118.8

Joe Francis

Year	Team		Att	Com	PC	Yds	Avg		TD	Int	Lg	Rtg
1958	GB	N	31	15	48.4	175	5.6		2	2	50t	60.6
1959			18	5	27.8	91	5.1		0	1		25.0
Career			49	20	40.8	266	5.4		2	3	50t	46.8

Russ Francis

Year	Team		Att	Com	PC	Yds	Avg		TD	Int	Lg	Rtg
1982	SF	N	1	1	100.0	45	45.0		0	0	45	118.8
Playoffs			1	0	0.0	0	0.0		0	1		0.0

Sam Francis

Year	Team		Att	Com	PC	Yds	Avg		TD	Int	Lg	Rtg
1937	CHIB	N	6	3	50.0	34	5.7		1	2		67.4
1938			3	1	33.3	0	0.0		0	0	0	42.4
Career			9	4	44.4	34	3.8		1	2	0	52.3

George Franck

Year	Team		Att	Com	PC	Yds	Avg		TD	Int	Lg	Rtg
1941	NYG	N	1	0	0.0	0	0.0		0	0		39.6
1945	NY	N	1	1	100.0	4	4.0		0	0	4	83.3
Career			2	1	50.0	4	2.0		0	0	4	56.3
Playoffs			1	0	0.0	0	0.0		0	0		39.6

Red Franklin

Year	Team		Att	Com	PC	Yds	Avg		TD	Int	Lg	Rtg
1935	BKN	N								2		
1936			7	1	14.3	17	2.4		0	0	17	39.6
1937			4	0	0.0	0	0.0		0	0		39.6
Career			11	1	9.1	17	1.5		2	0	17	39.6

Al Frazier

Year	Team		Att	Com	PC	Yds	Avg		TD	Int	Lg	Rtg
1961	DEN	A	1	0	0.0	0	0.0		0	1		0.0

Tucker Frederickson

Year	Team		Att	Com	PC	Yds	Avg		TD	Int	Lg	Rtg
1965	NYG	N	1	0	0.0	0	0.0		0	1		0.0

Jess Freitas

Year	Team		Att	Com	PC	Yds	Avg		TD	Int	Lg	Rtg
1946	SF	AA	44	22	50.0	234	5.3		3	7		49.1
1947			33	13	39.4	215	6.5		4	2		76.4
1948	CHI	AA	167	84	50.3	1425	8.5		14	16	74t	67.9
1949	BUF	AA	9	4	44.4	10	1.1		0	2		12.0
Career			253	123	48.6	1884	7.4		21	27	74t	61.7

Jesse Freitas

Year	Team		Att	Com	PC	Yds	Avg		TD	Int	Lg	Rtg
1974	SD	N	109	49	45.0	719	6.6		3	8	71t	45.6
1975			110	49	44.5	525	4.8		5	5	42	55.3
Career			219	98	44.7	1244	5.7		8	13	71t	50.5

Gus Frerotte

Year	Team		Att	Com	PC	Yds	Avg		TD	Int	Lg	Rtg
1994	WAS	N	100	46	46.0	600	6.0		5	5	51	61.3
1995			396	199	50.3	2751	6.9		13	13	73t	70.2
1996			470	270	57.4	3453	7.3		12	11	52t	79.3
Career			966	515	53.3	6804	7.0		30	29	73t	73.7

Glenn Frey

Year	Team		Att	Com	PC	Yds	Avg		TD	Int	Lg	Rtg
1937	PHI	N	1	0	0.0	0	0.0		0	0		39.6

Benny Friedman

Year	Team		Att	Com	PC	Yds	Avg		TD	Int	Lg	Rtg
1927	CLE	N							11			
1928	DET	N							10			
1929	NYG	N							20			
1930									13			
1931									3			
1932	BKN	N							5			
1933			80	42	52.5	597	7.5		5	7		61.3
Career			80	42	52.5	597	7.5		67	7		61.3

John Friesz

Year	Team		Att	Com	PC	Yds	Avg		TD	Int	Lg	Rtg
1990	SD	N	22	11	50.0	98	4.5		1	1	17	58.5
1991			487	262	53.8	2896	5.9		12	15	58	67.1
1993			238	128	53.8	1402	5.9		6	4	66t	72.8
1994	WAS	N	180	105	58.3	1266	7.0		10	9	73t	77.7

John Friesz *continued*

Year	Team		Att	Com	PC	Yds	Avg		TD	Int	Lg	Rtg
1995	SEA	N	120	64	53.3	795	6.6		6	3	43t	80.4
1996			211	120	56.9	1629	7.7		8	4	80t	86.4
Career			1258	690	54.8	8086	6.4		43	36	80t	74.0

Ted Fritsch

Year	Team		Att	Com	PC	Yds	Avg		TD	Int	Lg	Rtg
1949	GB	N	1	0	0.0	0	0.0		0	0		39.6

Stan Fritts

Year	Team		Att	Com	PC	Yds	Avg		TD	Int	Lg	Rtg
1975	CIN	N	4	2	50.0	31	7.8		0	0	16	76.0

Wes Fry

Year	Team		Att	Com	PC	Yds	Avg		TD	Int	Lg	Rtg
1927	NYY	N								1		

Irving Fryar

Year	Team		Att	Com	PC	Yds	Avg		TD	Int	Lg	Rtg
1991	NE	N	1	0	0.0	0	0.0		0	0		39.6

Kenny Fryer

Year	Team		Att	Com	PC	Yds	Avg		TD	Int	Lg	Rtg
1944	BKN	N	24	9	37.5	91	3.8		0	2	25	14.4

Scott Fulhage

Year	Team		Att	Com	PC	Yds	Avg		TD	Int	Lg	Rtg
1989	ATL	N	1	1	100.0	12	12.0		0	0	12	116.7

Charley Fuller

Year	Team		Att	Com	PC	Yds	Avg		TD	Int	Lg	Rtg
1961	OAK	A	1	0	0.0	0	0.0		0	0		39.6

Mike Fuller

Year	Team		Att	Com	PC	Yds	Avg		TD	Int	Lg	Rtg
1979	SD	N	1	0	0.0	0	0.0		0	0		39.6

Steve Fuller

Year	Team		Att	Com	PC	Yds	Avg		TD	Int	Lg	Rtg
1979	KC	N	270	146	54.1	1484	5.5		6	14	40	55.8
1980			320	193	60.3	2250	7.0		10	12	77	76.4
1981			134	77	57.5	934	7.0		3	4	53	74.0
1982			93	49	52.7	665	7.2		3	2	51	77.6
1984	CHI	N	78	53	67.9	595	7.6		3	0	31	103.3
1985			107	53	49.5	777	7.3		1	5	69	57.3
1986			64	34	53.1	451	7.0		2	4	50t	60.1
Career			1066	605	56.8	7156	6.7		28	41	77	70.1
Playoffs			41	22	53.7	298	7.3		2			83.2

Will Furrer

Year	Team		Att	Com	PC	Yds	Avg		TD	Int	Lg	Rtg
1992	CHI	N	25	9	36.0	89	3.6		0	3	16	7.3
1995	HOU	N	99	48	48.5	483	4.9		2	7	48	40.1
Career			124	57	46.0	572	4.6		2	10	48	31.4

Chuck Fusina

Year	Team		Att	Com	PC	Yds	Avg		TD	Int	Lg	Rtg
1980	TB	N	4	2	50.0	18	4.5		0	1	13	22.9
1981			1	1	100.0	2	2.0		1	0	2t	118.8
1986	GB	N	32	19	59.4	178	5.6		0	1	42	61.7
Career			37	22	59.5	198	5.4		1	2	42	60.4

Roman Gabriel

Year	Team		Att	Com	PC	Yds	Avg		TD	Int	Lg	Rtg
1962	LA	N	101	57	56.4	670	6.6		3	2	65t	78.4
1963			281	130	46.3	1947	6.9		8	11	77t	62.7
1964			143	65	45.5	1236	8.6		9	5	70t	82.4
1965			173	83	48.0	1321	7.6		11	5	60t	83.0
1966			397	217	54.7	2540	6.4		10	16	84t	65.9
1967			371	196	52.8	2779	7.5		25	13	80t	85.2
1968			366	184	50.3	2364	6.5		19	16	60t	70.0
1969			399	217	54.4	2549	6.4		24	7	93t	86.8
1970			407	211	51.8	2552	6.3		16	12	71	72.2
1971			352	180	51.1	2238	6.4		17	10	68	75.4
1972			323	165	51.1	2027	6.3		12	15	57t	63.8
1973	PHI	N	460	270	58.7	3219	7.0		23	12	80t	86.0
1974			338	193	57.1	1867	5.5		9	12	64t	66.8
1975			292	151	51.7	1644	5.6		13	11	62t	67.8
1976			92	46	50.0	476	5.2		2	2	34	63.5
1977			3	1	33.3	15	5.0		0	0	15	50.7
Career			4498	2366	52.6	29444	6.5		201	149	93t	74.3
Playoffs			63	33	52.4	336	5.3		3	2		70.6

Monk Gafford

Year	Team		Att	Com	PC	Yds	Avg		TD	Int	Lg	Rtg
1946	MIA	AA	5	1	20.0	-3	-0.6		0	2	-3	0.0
1948	BKN	AA	39	17	43.6	268	6.9		4	2	60t	79.9
Career			44	18	40.9	265	6.0		4	4	60t	53.7

Bobby Gage

Year	Team		Att	Com	PC	Yds	Avg		TD	Int	Lg	Rtg
1949	PIT	N	36	17	47.2	329	9.1		2	4	52	58.4
1950			58	21	36.2	294	5.1		1	5	42t	23.2
Career			94	38	40.4	623	6.6		3	9	52	34.4

Bob Gagliano

Year	Team		Att	Com	PC	Yds	Avg		TD	Int	Lg	Rtg
1982	KC	N	1	1	100.0	7	7.0		0	0	7	95.8
1987	SF	N	29	16	55.2	229	7.9		1	1	50	78.1

Bob Gagliano *continued*

Year	Team		Att	Com	PC	Yds	Avg	TD	Int	Lg	Rtg
1989	DET	N	232	117	50.4	1671	7.2	6	12	75t	61.2
1990			159	87	54.7	1190	7.5	10	10	47t	73.6
1991	SD	N	23	9	39.1	76	3.3	0	1	17	30.3
1992			42	19	45.2	258	6.1	0	3	55	35.6
Career			486	249	51.2	3431	7.1	17	27	75t	62.7

Bob Gaiters

Year	Team		Att	Com	PC	Yds	Avg	TD	Int	Lg	Rtg
1961	NYG	N	3	3	100.0	42	14.0	2	0	27	158.3
1962			2	0	0.0	0	0.0	0	0		39.6
Career			5	3	60.0	42	8.4	2	0	27	126.7
Playoffs			1	0	0.0	0	0.0	0	0		39.6

Hokie Gajan

Year	Team		Att	Com	PC	Yds	Avg	TD	Int	Lg	Rtg
1983	NO	N	1	0	0.0	0	0.0	0	0		39.6
1984			1	1	100.0	34	34.0	1	0	34t	158.3
Career			2	1	50.0	34	17.0	1	0	34t	135.4

Tony Galbreath

Year	Team		Att	Com	PC	Yds	Avg	TD	Int	Lg	Rtg
1979	NO	N	3	2	66.7	70	23.3	0	1	48	70.1
1980			2	0	0.0	0	0.0	0	0		39.6
1984	NYG	N	1	1	100.0	13	13.0	0	0	13	118.8
1986			1	0	0.0	0	0.0	0	0		39.6
Career			7	3	42.9	83	11.9	0	1	48	47.6

Arnie Galiffa

Year	Team		Att	Com	PC	Yds	Avg	TD	Int	Lg	Rtg
1953	NYG	N	13	4	30.8	129	9.9	1	5	75t	55.1
1954	SF	N	12	3	25.0	54	4.5	0	0	25	45.8
Career			25	7	28.0	183	7.3	1	5	75t	31.3

Willie Galimore

Year	Team		Att	Com	PC	Yds	Avg	TD	Int	Lg	Rtg
1958	CHIB	N	1	0	0.0	0	0.0	0	1		0.0

Chan Gallegos

Year	Team		Att	Com	PC	Yds	Avg	TD	Int	Lg	Rtg
1962	OAK	A	35	18	51.4	298	8.5	2	3	35	63.8

John Galvin

Year	Team		Att	Com	PC	Yds	Avg	TD	Int	Lg	Rtg
1947	BAL	AA	6	3	50.0	34	5.7	0	0		67.4

Bob Gambold

Year	Team		Att	Com	PC	Yds	Avg	TD	Int	Lg	Rtg
1953	PHI	N	14	6	42.9	107	7.6	0	2	41	30.1

Rich Gannon

Year	Team		Att	Com	PC	Yds	Avg	TD	Int	Lg	Rtg
1987	MIN	N	6	2	33.3	18	3.0	0	1	12	2.8
1988			15	7	46.7	90	6.0	0	0	19	66.0
1990			349	182	52.1	2278	6.5	16	16	78t	68.9
1991			354	211	59.6	2166	6.1	12	6	50	81.5
1992			279	159	57.0	1905	6.8	12	13	60t	72.9
1993	WAS	N	125	74	59.2	704	5.6	3	7	54	59.6
1995	KC	N	11	7	63.6	57	5.2	0	0	18	76.7
1996			90	54	60.0	491	5.5	6	1	25	92.4
Career			1229	696	56.6	7709	6.3	49	44	78t	73.8
Playoffs			26	18	69.2	174	6.7	0	1		71.6

Greg Gantt

Year	Team		Att	Com	PC	Yds	Avg	TD	Int	Lg	Rtg
1975	NYJ	N	1	1	100.0	1	1.0	0	0	1	79.2

Frank Garcia

Year	Team		Att	Com	PC	Yds	Avg	TD	Int	Lg	Rtg
1984	TB	N	1	0	0.0	0	0.0	0	0		39.6

Chris Gardocki

Year	Team		Att	Com	PC	Yds	Avg	TD	Int	Lg	Rtg
1992	CHI	N	3	1	33.3	43	14.3	0	0	43	81.9
1993			2	0	0.0	0	0.0	0	0		39.6
1995	IND	N	1	0	0.0	0	0.0	0	0		39.6
Career			6	1	16.7	43	7.2	0	0	43	56.9

Bobby Garrett

Year	Team		Att	Com	PC	Yds	Avg	TD	Int	Lg	Rtg
1954	GB	N	30	15	50.0	143	4.8	0	1	16	49.7

Carl Garrett

Year	Team		Att	Com	PC	Yds	Avg	TD	Int	Lg	Rtg
1969	BOS	A	1	0	0.0	0	0.0	0	0		39.6
1972	NE	N	1	0	0.0	0	0.0	0	1		0.0
1973	CHI	N	1	0	0.0	0	0.0	0	0		39.6
Career			3	0	0.0	0	0.0	0	1		0.0

Jason Garrett

Year	Team		Att	Com	PC	Yds	Avg	TD	Int	Lg	Rtg
1993	DAL	N	19	9	47.4	61	3.2	0	0	16	54.9
1994			31	16	51.6	315	10.2	2	1	68	95.5
1995			5	4	80.0	46	9.2	1	0	24	144.6
1996			3	3	100.0	44	14.7	0	0	32	118.8
Career			58	32	55.2	466	8.0	3	1	68	91.6
Playoffs			2	2	100.0	14	7.0	0	0		95.8

Mike Garrett

Year	Team		Att	Com	PC	Yds	Avg	TD	Int	Lg	Rtg
1966	KC	A	1	0	0.0	0	0.0	0	0		39.6
1967			4	1	25.0	17	4.3	1	0	17t	84.4
1968			1	0	0.0	0	0.0	0	1		0.0
1970	SD	N	0	0		0		0	0		
1971			1	1	100.0	53	53.0	0	0	53	118.8
1972			1	0	0.0	0	0.0	0	0		39.6
1973			1	0	0.0	0	0.0	0	0	0	39.6
Career			9	2	22.2	70	7.8	1	1	53	56.9

Walt Garrison

Year	Team		Att	Com	PC	Yds	Avg	TD	Int	Lg	Rtg
1973	DAL	N	1	0	0.0	0	0.0	0	0	0	39.6

Larry Garron

Year	Team		Att	Com	PC	Yds	Avg	TD	Int	Lg	Rtg
1962	BOS	A	3	1	33.3	39	13.0	0	0	39	81.9
1963			1	0	0.0	0	0.0	0	0		39.6
1964			2	0	0.0	0	0.0	0	0		39.6
Career			6	1	16.7	39	6.5	0	0	39	54.2

Cleveland Gary

Year	Team		Att	Com	PC	Yds	Avg	TD	Int	Lg	Rtg
1993	LARM	N	1	1	100.0	8	8.0	0	0	8	100.0

Sammy Garza

Year	Team		Att	Com	PC	Yds	Avg	TD	Int	Lg	Rtg
1987	STL	N	20	11	55.0	183	9.2	1	2	38t	63.1

Joe Gasparella

Year	Team		Att	Com	PC	Yds	Avg	TD	Int	Lg	Rtg
1948	PIT	N	57	23	40.4	294	5.2	0	4	43	28.0
1950			54	23	42.6	383	7.1	3	5	51	47.1
1951			2	0	0.0	0	0.0	0	1		0.0
Career			113	46	40.7	677	6.0	3	10	51	32.9

Don Gault

Year	Team		Att	Com	PC	Yds	Avg	TD	Int	Lg	Rtg
1970	CLE	N	19	2	10.5	67	3.5	0	3	44	2.2

Prentice Gautt

Year	Team		Att	Com	PC	Yds	Avg	TD	Int	Lg	Rtg
1961	STL	N	11	6	54.5	100	9.1	1	1	22	77.8
1963			1	0	0.0	0	0.0	0	0		39.6
1965			1	0	0.0	0	0.0	0	0		39.6
Career			13	6	46.2	100	7.7	1	1	22	66.2

Doug Gaynor

Year	Team		Att	Com	PC	Yds	Avg	TD	Int	Lg	Rtg
1986	CIN	N	3	3	100.0	30	10.0	0	0	16	108.3

Gene Gedman

Year	Team		Att	Com	PC	Yds	Avg	TD	Int	Lg	Rtg
1957	DET	N	2	0	0.0	0	0.0	0	0		39.6
1958			3	2	66.7	111	37.0	1	0	81t	149.3
Career			5	2	40.0	111	22.2	1	0	81t	127.1

Fred Gehrke

Year	Team		Att	Com	PC	Yds	Avg	TD	Int	Lg	Rtg
1940	CLE	N	1	0	0.0	0	0.0	0	0		39.6
1946	LA	N	1	1	100.0	29	29.0	0	0	29	118.8
1948			1	0	0.0	0	0.0	0	0		39.6
Career			3	1	33.3	29	9.7	0	0	29	70.1

Jack Gehrke

Year	Team		Att	Com	PC	Yds	Avg	TD	Int	Lg	Rtg
1969	CIN	A	1	1	100.0	13	13.0	0	0	13	118.8
1971	DEN	N	2	1	50.0	19	9.5	0	0	19	83.3
Career			3	2	66.7	32	10.7	0	0	19	102.1

Stan Gelbaugh

Year	Team		Att	Com	PC	Yds	Avg	TD	Int	Lg	Rtg
1991	PHX	N	118	61	51.7	674	5.7	3	10	34t	42.1
1992	SEA	N	255	121	47.5	1307	5.1	6	11	57	52.9
1993			5	3	60.0	39	7.8	0	1	22	45.0
1994			11	7	63.6	80	7.3	1	0	25t	115.7
1996			2	0	0.0	0	0.0	0	0		39.6
Career			391	192	49.1	2100	5.4	10	22	57	50.5

Jeff George

Year	Team		Att	Com	PC	Yds	Avg	TD	Int	Lg	Rtg
1990	IND	N	334	181	54.2	2152	6.4	16	13	75	73.8
1991			485	292	60.2	2910	6.0	10	12	49t	73.8
1992			306	167	54.6	1963	6.4	7	15	57t	61.5
1993			407	234	57.5	2526	6.2	8	6	72t	76.3
1994	ATL	N	524	322	61.5	3734	7.1	23	18	85t	83.3
1995			557	336	60.3	4143	7.4	24	11	62t	89.5
1996			99	56	56.6	698	7.1	3	3	67	76.1
Career			2712	1588	58.6	18126	6.7	91	78	85t	77.9
Playoffs			54	30	55.6	366	6.8	2	2		73.5

Joe Geri

Year	Team		Att	Com	PC	Yds	Avg	TD	Int	Lg	Rtg
1949	PIT	N	77	31	40.3	554	7.2	5	5	63	60.2
1950			113	41	36.3	866	7.7	6	15	78t	42.4
1951			90	29	32.2	506	5.6	2	7	77t	27.4
Career			280	101	36.1	1926	6.9	13	27	78t	36.7

Year	Team		Att	Com	PC	Yds	Avg	TD	Int	Lg	Rtg

Jimmy German

| 1939 | WAS | N | 12 | 6 | 50.0 | 97 | 8.1 | 1 | 2 | | 65.6 |

Milt Ghee

| 1921 | CLE | A | | | | | | | 1 | | |

Ralph Giacomarro

| 1983 | ATL | N | 1 | 1 | 100.0 | 23 | 23.0 | 0 | 0 | 23 | 118.8 |

Louie Giammona

1980	PHI	N	3	3	100.0	55	18.3	1	0	27	158.3
1982			1	0	0.0	0	0.0	0	1		0.0
Career			4	3	75.0	55	13.8	1	1	27	116.7

Sonny Gibbs

| 1964 | DET | N | 3 | 1 | 33.3 | 3 | 1.0 | 0 | 1 | 3 | 2.8 |

Frank Gifford

1952	NYG	N	2	1	50.0	18	9.0	1	0	18t	120.8
1953			6	3	50.0	47	7.8	1	0	21	116.0
1954			8	4	50.0	155	19.4	3	1	83t	95.8
1955			6	2	33.3	96	16.0	2	0	71t	121.5
1956			5	2	40.0	35	7.0	2	1	29t	64.6
1957			6	4	66.7	143	23.8	2	0	68t	149.3
1958			10	3	30.0	109	10.9	1	1	63	66.3
1959			11	5	45.5	151	13.7	2	2	43	92.0
1960			6	3	50.0	24	4.0	0	1	13	20.8
1962			2	1	50.0	12	6.0	0	0	12	68.8
1964			1	1	100.0	33	33.0	0	0	33	118.8
Career			63	29	46.0	823	13.1	14	6	83t	92.5
Playoffs			2	1	50.0	18	9.0	0	1		41.7

Wayne Gift

| 1937 | CLE | N | 3 | 0 | 0.0 | 0 | 0.0 | 0 | 0 | | 39.6 |

Gale Gilbert

1985	SEA	N	40	19	47.5	218	5.5	1	2	37t	51.9
1986			76	42	55.3	485	6.4	3	3	38t	71.4
1990	BUF	N	15	8	53.3	106	7.1	2	2	23	76.0
1994	SD	N	67	41	61.2	410	6.1	3	1	26	87.3
1995			61	36	59.0	325	5.3	0	4	41	46.1
Career			259	146	56.4	1544	6.0	9	12	41	66.2
Playoffs			6	3	50.0	30	5.0	0	1		25.0

Wally Gilbert

1924	DUL	N							1		
1925									1		
Career									2		

Cookie Gilchrist

| 1963 | BUF | A | 1 | 1 | 100.0 | 35 | 35.0 | 0 | 0 | 35 | 118.8 |

Johnny Gildea

1935	PIT	N	95	28	29.5	529	5.6	3	20		21.2
1936			29	9	31.0	147	5.1	1	5		21.0
1937			47	14	29.8	288	6.1	2	9		27.2
Career			171	51	29.8	964	5.6	6	34		22.7

Jim Gillette

| 1940 | CLE | N | 4 | 0 | 0.0 | 0 | 0.0 | 0 | 2 | | 0.0 |

Joe Gilliam

1972	PIT	N	11	7	63.6	48	4.4	0	0	9	73.3
1973			60	20	33.3	331	5.5	2	6	46t	24.4
1974			212	96	45.3	1274	6.0	4	8	61t	55.4
1975			48	24	50.0	450	9.4	3	3	53	77.6
Career			331	147	44.4	2103	6.4	9	17	61t	53.2
Playoffs			2	0	0.0	0	0.0	0	0		39.6

Horace Gillom

| 1950 | CLE | N | 1 | 1 | 100.0 | 3 | 3.0 | 0 | 0 | 3 | 79.2 |

Willie Gillus

| 1987 | GB | N | 5 | 2 | 40.0 | 28 | 5.6 | 0 | 0 | 15 | 58.8 |

Harry Gilmer

1948	WAS	N	5	2	40.0	69	13.8	0	0	45	87.5
1949			132	49	37.1	869	6.6	4	15	61	31.0
1950			141	63	44.7	948	6.7	8	12	74t	50.8
1951			68	31	45.6	391	5.8	1	6	47	32.2
1952			58	31	53.4	555	9.6	4	4	61	80.7
1954			7	2	28.6	18	2.6	0	1	10	0.0
1955	DET	N	122	58	47.5	633	5.2	2	4	34t	55.1

Harry Gilmer continued

| 1956 | | | 46 | 27 | 58.7 | 303 | 6.6 | 4 | 3 | 41t | 80.3 |
| Career | | | 579 | 263 | 45.4 | 3786 | 6.5 | 23 | 45 | 74t | 48.0 |

Paul Gipson

| 1969 | ATL | N | 1 | 0 | 0.0 | 0 | 0.0 | 0 | 1 | | 0.0 |

Earl Girard

1948	GB	N	14	4	28.6	117	8.4	1	1	40	56.0
1949			175	62	35.4	881	5.0	4	12	50	31.6
1952	DET	N	4	0	0.0	0	0.0	0	0		39.6
1953			1	0	0.0	0	0.0	0	0		39.6
1955			1	0	0.0	0	0.0	0	0		39.6
1956			1	1	100.0	19	19.0	0	0	19	118.8
1957	PIT	N	1	0	0.0	0	0.0	0	0		39.6
Career			197	67	34.0	1017	5.2	5	13	50	32.9

Ernest Givins

| 1986 | HOU | N | 2 | 0 | 0.0 | 0 | 0.0 | 0 | 0 | | 39.6 |

Scotty Glacken

1966	DEN	A	11	6	54.5	84	7.6	1	0	22	109.7
1967			4	0	0.0	0	0.0	0	0		39.6
Career			15	6	40.0	84	5.6	1	0	22	81.0

Bob Gladieux

1971	NE	N	2	1	50.0	48	24.0	0	0	48	95.8
1972			1	0	0.0	0	0.0	0	1		0.0
Career			3	1	33.3	48	16.0	0	1	48	42.4

Joe Glamp

| 1948 | PIT | N | 1 | 0 | 0.0 | 0 | 0.0 | 0 | 0 | | 39.6 |

Bill Glenn

| 1944 | CHIB | N | 4 | 1 | 25.0 | 22 | 5.5 | 0 | 0 | 22 | 50.0 |

Ed Goddard

1937	BKN-CLE	N	41	13	31.7	180	4.4	2	8		23.5
1938	CLE	N	43	19	44.2	238	5.5	0	6		22.4
Career			84	32	38.1	418	5.0	2	14		22.9

Brad Goebel

1991	PHI	N	56	30	53.6	267	4.8	0	6	26	27.0
1992	CLE	N	3	2	66.7	32	10.7	0	0	22	102.1
Career			59	32	54.2	299	5.1	0	6	26	28.8

Paul Goebel

| 1923 | COL | N | | | | | | | 1 | | |

Marshall Goldberg

1939	CHIC	N	7	1	14.3	4	0.6	0	1	4	0.0
1940			2	0	0.0	0	0.0	0	0		39.6
1941			19	7	36.8	110	5.8	1	1	44	52.5
Career			28	8	28.6	114	4.1	1	2	44	26.2

Jerry Golsteyn

1977	NYG	N	70	31	44.3	416	5.9	2	8	47	33.7
1978			40	12	30.0	110	2.8	0	1	20	29.2
1979	DET	N	9	2	22.2	16	1.8	0	2	15	0.0
1982	TB	N	1	0	0.0	0	0.0	0	0		39.6
1983			97	47	48.5	535	5.5	0	2	52	56.9
Career			217	92	42.4	1077	5.0	2	13	52	36.2

Kelly Goodburn

| Playoffs | | | 1 | 1 | 100.0 | 10 | 10.0 | 0 | 0 | | 108.3 |

Owen Goodnight

| 1941 | CLE | N | 36 | 12 | 33.3 | 182 | 5.1 | 1 | 5 | 61 | 20.6 |

Gordon Gore

| 1939 | DET | N | 1 | 0 | 0.0 | 0 | 0.0 | 0 | 0 | | 39.6 |

Jeff Gossett

1985	CLE	N	1	0	0.0	0	0.0	0	0		39.6
1986			2	1	50.0	30	15.0	0	1	30	56.3
1989	LARI	N	1	0	0.0	0	0.0	0	0		39.6
1991			1	1	100.0	34	34.0	0	0	34	118.8
Career			5	2	40.0	64	12.8	0	1	61	47.9

Paul Governali

1946	BOS	N	192	83	43.2	1293	6.7	13	10	62	67.0
1947	BOS-NYG	N	252	108	42.9	1775	7.0	17	22	78	53.3
1948	NYG	N	56	27	48.2	280	5.0	1	1	21	61.6
Career			500	218	43.6	3348	6.7	31	33	78	59.5

Year	Team		Att	Com	PC	Yds	Avg	TD	Int	Lg	Rtg

Neil Graff

Year	Team		Att	Com	PC	Yds	Avg	TD	Int	Lg	Rtg
1974	NE	N	1	1	100.0	20	20.0	0	0	20	118.8
1975			35	18	51.4	221	6.3	2	3	31t	54.6
1977	PIT	N	12	6	50.0	47	3.9	0	0	21	60.1
Career			48	25	52.1	288	6.0	2	3	31t	58.3

Kent Graham

Year	Team		Att	Com	PC	Yds	Avg	TD	Int	Lg	Rtg
1992	NYG	N	97	42	43.3	470	4.8	1	4	44	44.6
1993			22	8	36.4	79	3.6	0	0	18	47.3
1994			53	24	45.3	295	5.6	3	2	55	66.2
1996	ARI	N	274	146	53.3	1624	5.9	12	7	69	75.1
Career			446	220	49.3	2468	5.5	16	13	69	66.1

Otto Graham

Year	Team		Att	Com	PC	Yds	Avg	TD	Int	Lg	Rtg
1946	CLE	AA	174	95	54.6	1834	10.5	17	5	79t	112.1
1947			269	163	60.6	2753	10.2	25	11	99t	109.2
1948			333	173	52.0	2713	8.1	25	15	78t	85.6
1949			285	161	56.5	2785	9.8	19	10	74t	97.5
1950	CLE	N	253	137	54.2	1943	7.7	14	20	80t	64.7
1951			265	147	55.5	2205	8.3	17	16	81t	79.2
1952			364	181	49.7	2816	7.7	20	24	68t	66.6
1953			258	167	64.7	2722	10.6	11	9	70	99.7
1954			240	142	59.2	2092	8.7	11	17	64t	73.5
1955			185	98	53.0	1721	9.3	15	8	61t	94.0
Career			2626	1464	55.8	23584	9.0	174	135	99t	86.6
Playoffs			301	159	52.8	2101	7.0	14	17		67.2

Red Grange

Year	Team		Att	Com	PC	Yds	Avg	TD	Int	Lg	Rtg
1925	CHIB	N							1		
1926	NY	A							1		
1929	CHIB	N							3		
1930									3		
1933									2		
1934			25	6	24.0	81	3.2	1	7		14.3
Career			25	6	24.0	81	3.2	11	7		14.3

Otis Grant

Year	Team		Att	Com	PC	Yds	Avg	TD	Int	Lg	Rtg
1987	PHI	N	1	0	0.0	0	0.0	0	0		39.6

Elvis Grbac

Year	Team		Att	Com	PC	Yds	Avg	TD	Int	Lg	Rtg
1994	SF	N	50	35	70.0	393	7.9	2	1	42	98.2
1995			183	127	69.4	1469	8.0	8	5	81t	96.6
1996			197	122	61.9	1236	6.3	8	10	40	72.2
Career			430	284	66.0	3098	7.2	18	16	81t	85.6
Playoffs			41	21	51.2	172	4.2	1	3		39.9

Bobby Joe Green

Year	Team		Att	Com	PC	Yds	Avg	TD	Int	Lg	Rtg
1961	PIT	N	1	0	0.0	0	0.0	0	0		39.6
1963	CHI	N	1	0	0.0	0	0.0	0	0		39.6
1969			2	2	100.0	30	15.0	0	0	19	118.8
1970			2	2	100.0	37	18.5	0	0	34	118.8
1971			2	1	50.0	13	6.5	0	0	13	70.8
1972			2	1	50.0	23	11.5	0	1	23	52.1
Career			10	6	60.0	103	10.3	0	1	34	55.4

Boyce Green

Year	Team		Att	Com	PC	Yds	Avg	TD	Int	Lg	Rtg
1986	KC	N	1	0	0.0	0	0.0	0	1		0.0

Charlie Green

Year	Team		Att	Com	PC	Yds	Avg	TD	Int	Lg	Rtg
1966	OAK	A	2	2	100.0	17	8.5	0	0	11	102.1

Dave Green

Year	Team		Att	Com	PC	Yds	Avg	TD	Int	Lg	Rtg
1974	CIN	N	2	1	50.0	22	11.0	0	0	22	89.6
1975			1	0	0.0	0	0.0	0	0		39.6
1977	TB	N	2	2	100.0	59	29.5	0	0	45	118.8
1978			3	2	66.7	25	8.3	0	0	25	92.4
Career			8	5	62.5	106	13.3	0	0	45	106.3

Johnny Green

Year	Team		Att	Com	PC	Yds	Avg	TD	Int	Lg	Rtg
1960	BUF	A	228	89	39.0	1267	5.6	10	10	70t	54.1
1961			126	56	44.4	903	7.2	6	5		68.3
1962	NY	A	258	128	49.6	1741	6.7	10	18		55.4
1963			6	2	33.3	10	1.7	0	1		2.8
Career			618	275	44.5	3921	6.3	26	34	70t	56.7

Roy Green

Year	Team		Att	Com	PC	Yds	Avg	TD	Int	Lg	Rtg
1982	STL	N	1	0	0.0	0	0.0	0	0		39.6
1990	PHX	N	1	1	100.0	20	20.0	0	0	20	118.8
Career			2	1	50.0	20	10.0	0	0	20	85.4

Tom Greene

Year	Team		Att	Com	PC	Yds	Avg	TD	Int	Lg	Rtg
1960	BOS	A	63	27	42.9	251	4.0	1	6		20.1

Don Greenwood

Year	Team		Att	Com	PC	Yds	Avg	TD	Int	Lg	Rtg
1946	CLE	AA	1	1	100.0	27	27.0	0	0	27	118.8

Bob Gresham

Year	Team		Att	Com	PC	Yds	Avg	TD	Int	Lg	Rtg
1972	NO	N	1	0	0.0	0	0.0	0	0		39.6
1976	NYJ	N	1	1	100.0	29	29.0	0	0	29	118.8
Career			2	1	50.0	29	14.5	0	0	29	95.8

Marrio Grier

Year	Team		Att	Com	PC	Yds	Avg	TD	Int	Lg	Rtg
1996	NE	N	1	0	0.0	0	0.0	0	0	0	39.6

Bob Griese

Year	Team		Att	Com	PC	Yds	Avg	TD	Int	Lg	Rtg
1967	MIA	A	331	166	50.2	2005	6.1	15	18	68t	61.6
1968			355	186	52.4	2473	7.0	21	16	50t	75.7
1969			252	121	48.0	1695	6.7	10	16	53t	56.9
1970	MIA	N	245	142	58.0	2019	8.2	12	17	54	72.1
1971			263	145	55.1	2089	7.9	19	9	86t	90.9
1972			97	53	54.6	638	6.6	4	4	39	71.6
1973			218	116	53.2	1422	6.5	17	8	46	84.3
1974			253	152	60.1	1968	7.8	16	15	54	80.9
1975			191	118	61.8	1693	8.9	14	13	79t	86.6
1976			272	162	59.6	2097	7.7	11	12	47t	78.9
1977			307	180	58.6	2252	7.3	22	13	73t	87.8
1978			235	148	63.0	1791	7.6	11	11	63t	82.4
1979			310	176	56.8	2160	7.0	14	16	51	72.0
1980			100	61	61.0	790	7.9	6	4	54	89.2
Career			3429	1926	56.2	25092	7.3	192	172	86t	77.1
Playoffs			208	112	53.8	1467	7.1	10	12		68.3

Archie Griffin

Year	Team		Att	Com	PC	Yds	Avg	TD	Int	Lg	Rtg
1977	CIN	N	1	1	100.0	18	18.0	1	0	18t	158.3
1978			3	2	66.7	21	7.0	1	0	18	126.4
Career			4	3	75.0	39	9.8	2	0	18t	144.8

Don Griffin

Year	Team		Att	Com	PC	Yds	Avg	TD	Int	Lg	Rtg
1946	CHI	AA	1	0	0.0	0	0.0	0	1		0.0

Glynn Griffing

Year	Team		Att	Com	PC	Yds	Avg	TD	Int	Lg	Rtg
1963	NYG	N	40	16	40.0	306	7.7	3	4	64	52.7
Playoffs			1	0	0.0	0	0.0	0	0		39.6

Johnny Grigas

Year	Team		Att	Com	PC	Yds	Avg	TD	Int	Lg	Rtg
1943	CHIC	N	19	4	21.1	98	5.2	0	4	50	9.0
1944	C-P	N	131	50	38.2	690	5.3	6	21	72	31.5
1945	BOS	N	14	5	35.7	85	6.1	0	1	30	27.4
1946			2	1	50.0	16	8.0	0	1	16	37.5
Career			166	60	36.1	889	5.4	6	27	72	27.0

Cecil Grigg

Year	Team		Att	Com	PC	Yds	Avg	TD	Int	Lg	Rtg
1921	CAN	A						2			
1923	CAN	N						1			
Career								3			

Bob Grim

Year	Team		Att	Com	PC	Yds	Avg	TD	Int	Lg	Rtg
1971	MIN	N	1	0	0.0	0	0.0	0	0		39.6
1975	CHI	N	1	0	0.0	0	0.0	0	0		39.6
Career			2	0	0.0	0	0.0	0	0		39.6

Billy Joe Grimes

Year	Team		Att	Com	PC	Yds	Avg	TD	Int	Lg	Rtg
1949	LA	AA	3	3	100.0	105	35.0	1	0		158.3

Steve Grogan

Year	Team		Att	Com	PC	Yds	Avg	TD	Int	Lg	Rtg
1975	NE	N	274	139	50.7	1976	7.2	11	18	62t	60.4
1976			302	145	48.0	1903	6.3	18	20	58t	60.6
1977			305	160	52.5	2162	7.1	17	21	68	65.2
1978			362	181	50.0	2824	7.8	15	23	75t	63.6
1979			423	206	48.7	3286	7.8	28	20	63t	77.4
1980			306	175	57.2	2475	8.1	18	22	71	73.1
1981			216	117	54.2	1859	8.6	7	16	76t	63.0
1982			122	66	54.1	930	7.6	7	4	62t	84.4
1983			303	168	55.4	2411	8.0	15	12	76t	81.4
1984			68	32	47.1	444	6.5	3	6	65t	46.4
1985			156	85	54.5	1311	8.4	7	5	56	84.1
1986			102	62	60.8	976	9.6	9	2	69t	113.8
1987			161	93	57.8	1183	7.3	10	9	40	78.2
1988			140	67	47.9	834	6.0	4	13	41t	37.6
1989			261	133	51.0	1697	6.5	9	14	55t	60.8
1990			92	50	54.3	615	6.7	4	3	48	76.1
Career			3593	1879	52.3	26886	7.5	182	208	76t	69.6
Playoffs			95	48	50.5	571	6.0	3	7		49.1

Bill Groman

Year	Team		Att	Com	PC	Yds	Avg	TD	Int	Lg	Rtg
1960	HOU	A	1	1	100.0	3	3.0	1	0	3	118.8

Year Team	Att	Com	PC	Yds	Avg	TD	Int	Lg	Rtg

Bill Groman *continued*

Year Team	Att	Com	PC	Yds	Avg	TD	Int	Lg	Rtg
1961	1	0	0.0	0	0.0	0	0		39.6
Career	2	1	50.0	3	1.5	1	0	3	95.8
Playoffs	1	0	0.0	0	0.0	0	1		0.0

Earl Gros

Year Team	Att	Com	PC	Yds	Avg	TD	Int	Lg	Rtg
1964 PHI N	1	0	0.0	0	0.0	0	0		39.6
1965	2	1	50.0	63	31.5	1	0	63t	135.4
1966	1	0	0.0	0	0.0	0	0		39.6
Career	4	1	25.0	63	15.8	1	0	63t	118.8

Lee Grosscup

Year Team	Att	Com	PC	Yds	Avg	TD	Int	Lg	Rtg
1960 NYG N	25	11	44.0	144	5.8	1	1	26t	59.4
1961	22	5	22.7	87	4.0	1	3	32t	19.1
1962 NY A	126	57	45.2	855	6.8	8	8	86t	62.8
Career	173	73	42.2	1086	6.3	10	12	86t	53.8

Jack Grossman

Year Team	Att	Com	PC	Yds	Avg	TD	Int	Lg	Rtg
1934 BKN N							1		

Rex Grossman

Year Team	Att	Com	PC	Yds	Avg	TD	Int	Lg	Rtg
1949 BAL AA	1	0	0.0	0	0.0	0	1		0.0

George Grosvenor

Year Team	Att	Com	PC	Yds	Avg	TD	Int	Lg	Rtg
1935 CHIB N	15	6	40.0	69	4.6	0	1		26.8
1936 CHIC N	34	12	35.3	173	5.1	0	6		13.1
1937	50	21	42.0	325	6.5	3	7		44.6
Career	99	39	39.4	567	5.7	3	14		29.3

Roger Grove

Year Team	Att	Com	PC	Yds	Avg	TD	Int	Lg	Rtg
1931 GB N							2		

Lou Groza

Year Team	Att	Com	PC	Yds	Avg	TD	Int	Lg	Rtg
1950 CLE N	1	0	0.0	0	0.0	0	0		39.6
1963	1	0	0.0	0	0.0	0	0		0.0
1965	1	0	0.0	0	0.0	0	0		39.6
1966	1	1	100.0	-7	-7.0	0	0	-7	79.2
Career	4	1	25.0	-7	-1.8	0	1	-7	0.0

Bob Grupp

Year Team	Att	Com	PC	Yds	Avg	TD	Int	Lg	Rtg
1979 KC N	1	0	0.0	0	0.0	0	0		39.6

Al Grygo

Year Team	Att	Com	PC	Yds	Avg	TD	Int	Lg	Rtg
1945 CHIB N	1	1	100.0	11	11.0	0	0	11	112.5

Albert Guarnieri

Year Team	Att	Com	PC	Yds	Avg	TD	Int	Lg	Rtg
1924 BUF N							1		

Scotty Gudmundson

Year Team	Att	Com	PC	Yds	Avg	TD	Int	Lg	Rtg
1944 BOS N	38	16	42.1	226	5.9	1	4	38	31.1
1945	43	17	39.5	299	7.0	1	5	43	32.2
Career	81	33	40.7	525	6.5	2	9	43	31.7

Ralph Guglielmi

Year Team	Att	Com	PC	Yds	Avg	TD	Int	Lg	Rtg
1955 WAS N	62	20	32.3	242	3.9	2	4	43	29.1
1958	81	34	42.0	458	5.7	2	6	64t	38.0
1959	89	36	40.4	617	6.9	4	11	70	40.1
1960	223	125	56.1	1547	6.9	9	19	50	55.7
1961 STL N	116	56	48.3	927	8.0	5	8	80t	61.2
1962 NYG N	31	14	45.2	210	6.8	2	1	41t	76.0
1963 NYG-PHI N	24	7	29.2	118	4.9	0	3	32	8.0
Career	626	292	46.6	4119	6.6	24	52	80t	46.5

Eric Guliford

Year Team	Att	Com	PC	Yds	Avg	TD	Int	Lg	Rtg
1995 CAR N	2	1	50.0	46	23.0	0	1	46	56.3

George Gulyanics

Year Team	Att	Com	PC	Yds	Avg	TD	Int	Lg	Rtg
1947 CHIB N	2	1	50.0	55	27.5	0	1	55	56.3
1949	1	0	0.0	0	0.0	0	0		39.6
1950	1	1	100.0	16	16.0	0	0	16	118.8
Career	4	2	50.0	71	17.8	0	1	55	56.3

Mike Guman

Year Team	Att	Com	PC	Yds	Avg	TD	Int	Lg	Rtg
1980 LA N	1	1	100.0	31	31.0	1	0	31t	158.3
1981	1	1	100.0	7	7.0	1	0	7t	135.4
1982 LARM N	1	0	0.0	0	0.0	0	1		0.0
Career	3	2	66.7	38	12.7	2	1	31t	109.7

Ace Gutowsky

Year Team	Att	Com	PC	Yds	Avg	TD	Int	Lg	Rtg
1933 POR N							1		
1935 DET N							2		
1936	13	2	15.4	21	1.6	0	4		0.0
1937	8	1	12.5	30	3.8	0	2	30	3.1
1938	7	3	42.9	41	5.9	0	0		62.2

Ace Gutowsky *continued*

Year Team	Att	Com	PC	Yds	Avg	TD	Int	Lg	Rtg
1939 BKN N	1	1	100.0	5	5.0	0	0	5	87.5
Career	29	7	24.1	97	3.3	3	6	30	1.4

Ray Guy

Year Team	Att	Com	PC	Yds	Avg	TD	Int	Lg	Rtg
1974 OAK N	1	0	0.0	0	0.0	0	1		0.0
1975	1	1	100.0	22	22.0	0	0	22	118.8
1980	1	1	100.0	32	32.0	0	0	32	118.8
1981	0	0		0		0	0		
Career	3	2	66.7	54	18.0	0	1	32	70.1

Joe Guyon

Year Team	Att	Com	PC	Yds	Avg	TD	Int	Lg	Rtg
1921 CLE A							1		
1923 OOR N							1		
Career							2		

Elmer Hackney

Year Team	Att	Com	PC	Yds	Avg	TD	Int	Lg	Rtg
1941 PIT N	1	0	0.0	0	0.0	0	0		39.6
1943 DET N	3	1	33.3	-1	-0.3	0	0	-1	42.4
1944	1	1	100.0	19	19.0	0	0	19	118.8
Career	5	2	40.0	18	3.6	0	0	19	50.4

Al Haddon

Year Team	Att	Com	PC	Yds	Avg	TD	Int	Lg	Rtg
1926 DET N							1		

Pat Haden

Year Team	Att	Com	PC	Yds	Avg	TD	Int	Lg	Rtg
1976 LA N	105	60	57.1	896	8.5	8	4	65t	94.8
1977	216	122	56.5	1551	7.2	11	6	58	84.5
1978	444	229	51.6	2995	6.7	13	19	68t	65.1
1979	290	163	56.2	1854	6.4	11	14	50	68.1
1980	41	19	46.3	185	4.5	0	4	24	19.9
1981	267	138	51.7	1815	6.8	9	13	67t	64.4
Career	1363	731	53.6	9296	6.8	52	60	68t	69.6
Playoffs	123	55	44.7	728	5.9	4	12		35.3

John Hadl

Year Team	Att	Com	PC	Yds	Avg	TD	Int	Lg	Rtg
1962 SD A	260	107	41.2	1632	6.3	15	24	72t	43.3
1963	65	28	43.1	502	7.7	6	6	69	62.5
1964	274	147	53.6	2157	7.9	18	15	76t	78.7
1965	348	174	50.0	2798	8.0	20	21	85t	71.3
1966	375	200	53.3	2846	7.6	23	14	78t	83.0
1967	427	217	50.8	3365	7.9	24	22	72t	74.5
1968	440	208	47.3	3473	7.9	27	32	84t	64.5
1969	324	158	48.8	2253	7.0	10	11	76t	67.8
1970 SD N	327	162	49.5	2388	7.3	22	15	67	77.1
1971	431	233	54.1	3075	7.1	21	25	77t	68.9
1972	370	190	51.4	2449	6.6	15	26	61	56.7
1973 LA N	258	135	52.3	2008	7.8	22	11	69t	88.8
1974 LA-GB N	299	142	47.5	1752	5.9	8	14	68t	55.5
1975 GB N	353	191	54.1	2095	5.9	6	21	54	52.8
1976 HOU N	113	60	53.1	634	5.6	7	8	69t	60.9
1977	24	11	45.8	76	3.2	0	3	18	13.9
Career	4688	2363	50.4	33503	7.1	244	268	85	67.4
Playoffs	66	27	40.9	416	6.3	1	4		42.2

James Hadnot

Year Team	Att	Com	PC	Yds	Avg	TD	Int	Lg	Rtg
1981 KC N	1	0	0.0	0	0.0	0	1		0.0

Mike Haffner

Year Team	Att	Com	PC	Yds	Avg	TD	Int	Lg	Rtg
1968 DEN A	1	1	100.0	18	18.0	0	0	18	118.8

Jack Hagerty

Year Team	Att	Com	PC	Yds	Avg	TD	Int	Lg	Rtg
1929 NYG N							1		
1932							2		
Career							3		

By Haines

Year Team	Att	Com	PC	Yds	Avg	TD	Int	Lg	Rtg
1937 PIT N	6	1	16.7	14	2.3	0	0	14	0.0

Hinkey Haines

Year Team	Att	Com	PC	Yds	Avg	TD	Int	Lg	Rtg
1926 NYG N							1		
1929 SI N							1		
Career							2		

Eddie Halicki

Year Team	Att	Com	PC	Yds	Avg	TD	Int	Lg	Rtg
1930 FRA N							1		

Galen Hall

Year Team	Att	Com	PC	Yds	Avg	TD	Int	Lg	Rtg
1962 WAS N	32	19	59.4	274	8.6	2	1	48t	95.1
1963 NY A	118	45	38.1	611	5.2	3	9		32.1
Career	150	64	42.7	885	5.9	5	10	48t	45.6

Johnny Hall

Year Team	Att	Com	PC	Yds	Avg	TD	Int	Lg	Rtg
1940 CHIC N	3	0	0.0	0	0.0	0	2		0.0

Johnny Hall *continued*

Year	Team	Att	Com	PC	Yds	Avg	TD	Int	Lg	Rtg
1941		1	0	0.0	0	0.0	0	0		39.6
1942	DET N	1	0	0.0	0	0.0	0	0		39.6
1943	CHIC N	4	2	50.0	24	6.0	0	2	15	29.2
Career		9	2	22.2	24	2.7	0	4	15	0.0

Parker Hall

Year	Team	Att	Com	PC	Yds	Avg	TD	Int	Lg	Rtg
1939	CLE N	208	106	51.0	1227	5.9	9	13		57.5
1940		183	77	42.1	1108	6.1	6	16		36.9
1941		190	84	44.2	863	4.5	7	19	39	30.5
1942		140	62	44.3	815	5.8	7	19	59	40.3
1946	SF AA	8	2	25.0	15	1.9	0	0		39.6
Career		729	331	45.4	4028	5.5	29	67	59	37.9

Shawn Halloran

Year	Team	Att	Com	PC	Yds	Avg	TD	Int	Lg	Rtg
1987	STL N	42	18	42.9	263	6.3	0	1	49	54.0

Jim Haluska

Year	Team	Att	Com	PC	Yds	Avg	TD	Int	Lg	Rtg
1956	CHIB N	4	1	25.0	8	2.0	0	0	8	39.6

Tex Hamer

Year	Team	Att	Com	PC	Yds	Avg	TD	Int	Lg	Rtg
1924	FRA N						4			

Gary Hammond

Year	Team	Att	Com	PC	Yds	Avg	TD	Int	Lg	Rtg
1973	STL N	1	0	0.0	0	0.0	0	0		39.6
1974		1	1	100.0	81	81.0	0	0	81	118.8
Career		2	1	50.0	81	40.5	0	0	81	95.8

Kim Hammond

Year	Team	Att	Com	PC	Yds	Avg	TD	Int	Lg	Rtg
1968	MIA A	26	13	50.0	116	4.5	0	2	25	30.3
1969	BOS A	6	2	33.3	31	5.2	0	0	18	51.4
Career		32	15	46.9	147	4.6	0	2	25	34.2

Charley Hannah

Year	Team	Att	Com	PC	Yds	Avg	TD	Int	Lg	Rtg
1980	TB N	1	0	0.0	0	0.0	0	0		39.6

Terry Hanratty

Year	Team	Att	Com	PC	Yds	Avg	TD	Int	Lg	Rtg
1969	PIT N	126	52	41.3	716	5.7	8	13	41	41.7
1970		163	64	39.3	842	5.2	5	8	72t	46.1
1971		29	7	24.1	159	5.5	2	3	40	33.3
1972		4	2	50.0	23	5.8	0	0	14	67.7
1973		69	31	44.9	643	9.3	8	5	53t	86.8
1974		26	3	11.5	95	3.7	1	5	35	15.5
1976	TB N	14	6	42.9	32	2.3	0	1	12	20.5
Career		431	165	38.3	2510	5.8	24	35	72t	43.0
Playoffs		10	5	50.0	57	5.7	0	0		67.5

Brian Hansen

Year	Team	Att	Com	PC	Yds	Avg	TD	Int	Lg	Rtg
1985	NO N	1	1	100.0	8	8.0	0	0	8	100.0
1991	CLE N	1	1	100.0	11	11.0	1	0	11t	152.1
Career		2	2	100.0	19	9.5	1	0	11t	145.8

Tom Hanson

Year	Team	Att	Com	PC	Yds	Avg	TD	Int	Lg	Rtg
1935	PHI N	1	1	100.0	23	23.0	0	0	23	118.8
1936		15	0	0.0	0	0.0	0	3		39.6
1937		2	0	0.0	0	0.0	0	0		39.6
Career		18	1	5.6	23	1.3	0	3	23	0.0

Chet Hanulak

Year	Team	Att	Com	PC	Yds	Avg	TD	Int	Lg	Rtg
1957	CLE N	2	1	50.0	32	16.0	1	0	32t	135.4
Playoffs		1	0	0.0	0	0.0	0	1		0.0

Merle Hapes

Year	Team	Att	Com	PC	Yds	Avg	TD	Int	Lg	Rtg
1942	NYG N	2	2	100.0	-12	-6.0	0	0	-2	79.2

Jim Harbaugh

Year	Team	Att	Com	PC	Yds	Avg	TD	Int	Lg	Rtg
1987	CHI N	11	8	72.7	62	5.6	0	0	21	86.2
1988		97	47	48.5	514	5.3	0	2	56	55.9
1989		178	111	62.4	1204	6.8	5	9	49t	70.5
1990		312	180	57.7	2178	7.0	10	6	80t	81.9
1991		478	275	57.5	3121	6.5	15	16	84t	73.7
1992		358	202	56.4	2486	6.9	13	12	83t	76.2
1993		325	200	61.5	2002	6.2	7	11	48	72.1
1994	IND N	202	125	61.9	1440	7.1	9	6	85t	85.8
1995		314	200	63.7	2575	**8.2**	17	5	52	**100.7**
1996		405	232	57.3	2630	6.5	13	11	51	76.3
Career		2680	1580	59.0	18212	6.8	89	78	85t	78.5
Playoffs		163	83	50.9	906	5.6	6	5		67.2

Buddy Hardeman

Year	Team	Att	Com	PC	Yds	Avg	TD	Int	Lg	Rtg
1979	WAS N	2	1	50.0	30	15.0	0	1	30	56.3
1980		1	0	0.0	0	0.0	0	0		39.6
Career		3	1	33.3	30	10.0	0	1	30	31.9

Pat Harder

Year	Team	Att	Com	PC	Yds	Avg	TD	Int	Lg	Rtg
1951	DET N	1	0	0.0	0	0.0	0	0		39.6

Bruce Hardy

Year	Team	Att	Com	PC	Yds	Avg	TD	Int	Lg	Rtg
1979	MIA N	1	0	0.0	0	0.0	0	0		39.6

Jim Hardy

Year	Team	Att	Com	PC	Yds	Avg	TD	Int	Lg	Rtg
1946	LA N	64	24	37.5	285	4.5	2	7	60	22.7
1947		57	23	40.4	388	6.8	5	7	64	53.7
1948		211	112	53.1	1390	6.6	14	7	69	82.1
1949	CHIC N	150	63	42.0	748	5.0	10	13	48	44.0
1950		257	117	45.5	1636	6.4	17	24	58t	49.7
1951		114	56	49.1	809	7.1	3	10	80t	44.8
1952	DET N	59	28	47.5	434	7.4	3	5	49	53.9
Career		912	423	46.4	5690	6.2	54	73	80t	53.1

Eddie Hare

Year	Team	Att	Com	PC	Yds	Avg	TD	Int	Lg	Rtg
1979	NE N	1	1	100.0	4	4.0	0	0	4	83.3

Ray Hare

Year	Team	Att	Com	PC	Yds	Avg	TD	Int	Lg	Rtg
1944	BKN N	1	0	0.0	0	0.0	0	0		39.6

Edd Hargett

Year	Team	Att	Com	PC	Yds	Avg	TD	Int	Lg	Rtg
1969	NO N	52	31	59.6	403	7.8	0	0	32	84.1
1970		175	78	44.6	1133	6.5	5	5	49t	63.8
1971		210	96	45.7	1191	5.7	6	5	49	63.4
Career		437	205	46.9	2727	6.2	11	10	49	66.0

Chic Harley

Year	Team	Att	Com	PC	Yds	Avg	TD	Int	Lg	Rtg
1921	DEC A						3			

Derrick Harmon

Year	Team	Att	Com	PC	Yds	Avg	TD	Int	Lg	Rtg
1984	SF N	2	0	0.0	0	0.0	0	0		39.6
1985		1	0	0.0	0	0.0	0	0		39.6
Career		3	0	0.0	0	0.0	0	0		39.6

Tommy Harmon

Year	Team	Att	Com	PC	Yds	Avg	TD	Int	Lg	Rtg
1947	LA N	3	1	33.3	31	10.3	0	0	31	72.9

Alvin Harper

Year	Team	Att	Com	PC	Yds	Avg	TD	Int	Lg	Rtg
1993	DAL N	1	1	100.0	46	46.0	0	0	46	118.8
Playoffs		1	0	0.0	0	0.0	0	0		39.6

Bruce Harper

Year	Team	Att	Com	PC	Yds	Avg	TD	Int	Lg	Rtg
1977	NYJ N	1	0	0.0	0	0.0	0	0		39.6

Roland Harper

Year	Team	Att	Com	PC	Yds	Avg	TD	Int	Lg	Rtg
1977	CHI N	2	0	0.0	0	0.0	0	0		39.6
1978		1	0	0.0	0	0.0	0	1		0.0
Career		3	0	0.0	0	0.0	0	1		0.0

Willard Harrell

Year	Team	Att	Com	PC	Yds	Avg	TD	Int	Lg	Rtg
1975	GB N	5	3	60.0	61	12.2	3	0	24t	142.5
1976		4	1	25.0	40	10.0	1	1	40t	68.8
1977		1	1	100.0	33	33.0	0	0	33	118.8
1979	STL N	1	0	0.0	0	0.0	0	0		39.6
1982		1	1	100.0	10	10.0	0	0	10	108.3
Career		12	6	50.0	144	12.0	4	1	40t	98.6

Franco Harris

Year	Team	Att	Com	PC	Yds	Avg	TD	Int	Lg	Rtg
1978	PIT N	1	0	0.0	0	0.0	0	0		39.6

Ike Harris

Year	Team	Att	Com	PC	Yds	Avg	TD	Int	Lg	Rtg
1978	NO N	1	0	0.0	0	0.0	0	0		39.6

James Harris

Year	Team	Att	Com	PC	Yds	Avg	TD	Int	Lg	Rtg
1969	BUF A	36	15	41.7	270	7.5	1	1	55	65.7
1970	BUF N	50	24	48.0	338	6.8	3	4	32	56.9
1971		103	51	49.5	512	5.0	1	6	62	43.0
1973	LA N	11	7	63.6	68	6.2	0	0	27	80.9
1974		198	106	53.5	1544	7.8	11	6	50t	85.1
1975		285	157	55.1	2148	7.5	14	15	54t	73.8
1976		158	91	57.6	1460	9.2	8	6	80t	89.6
1977	SD N	211	109	51.7	1240	5.9	5	11	78	55.8
1978		88	42	47.7	518	5.9	2	9	34t	34.4
1979		9	5	55.6	38	4.2	0	1	10	26.4
Career		1149	607	52.8	8136	7.1	45	59	80t	67.3
Playoffs		49	21	42.9	343	7.0	2	5		41.0

Ken Harris

Year	Team	Att	Com	PC	Yds	Avg	TD	Int	Lg	Rtg
1923	DUL N						2			

Kenny Harrison

Year	Team	Att	Com	PC	Yds	Avg	TD	Int	Lg	Rtg
1977	SF N	1	0	0.0	0	0.0	0	0		39.6

Year	Team		Att	Com	PC	Yds	Avg	TD	Int	Lg	Rtg

Jim Hart

Year	Team		Att	Com	PC	Yds	Avg	TD	Int	Lg	Rtg
1966	STL	N	11	4	36.4	29	2.6	0	0	15	44.9
1967			397	192	48.4	3008	7.6	19	30	76t	58.4
1968			316	140	44.3	2059	6.5	15	18	80t	58.2
1969			169	84	49.7	1086	6.4	6	12	60t	52.5
1970			373	171	45.8	2575	6.9	14	18	79	61.5
1971			243	110	45.3	1626	6.7	8	14	57t	54.7
1972			119	60	50.4	857	7.2	5	5	98	70.6
1973			320	178	55.6	2223	6.9	15	10	69t	80.0
1974			**388**	200	51.5	2411	6.2	20	8	80t	79.5
1975			345	182	52.8	2507	7.3	19	19	80	71.7
1976			388	218	56.2	2946	7.6	18	13	77t	82.0
1977			355	186	52.4	2542	7.2	13	20	69t	64.3
1978			477	240	50.3	3121	6.5	16	18	74	66.7
1979			378	194	51.3	2218	5.9	9	20	51t	55.2
1980			425	228	53.6	2946	6.9	16	20	69t	68.6
1981			241	134	55.6	1694	7.0	11	14	58t	68.7
1982			33	19	57.6	199	6.0	1	0	22	85.3
1983			91	50	54.9	592	6.5	4	8	39t	53.0
1984	WAS	N	7	3	42.9	26	3.7	0	0	13	53.3
Career			5076	2593	51.1	34665	6.8	209	247	98	66.6
Playoffs			81	40	49.4	491	6.1	2	4		56.1

Leo Hart

Year	Team		Att	Com	PC	Yds	Avg	TD	Int	Lg	Rtg
1971	ATL	N	1	0	0.0	0	0.0	0	0		39.6
1972	BUF	N	15	6	40.0	53	3.5	0	3	13	10.6
Career			16	6	37.5	53	3.3	0	3	13	7.6

Bill Hartman

Year	Team		Att	Com	PC	Yds	Avg	TD	Int	Lg	Rtg
1938	WAS	N	77	38	49.4	558	7.2	4	10		51.1

Sam Havrilak

Year	Team		Att	Com	PC	Yds	Avg	TD	Int	Lg	Rtg
1970	BAL	N	2	2	100.0	82	41.0	0	0	54	118.8
1972			1	0	0.0	0	0.0	0	0		39.6
Career			3	2	66.7	82	27.3	0	0	54	109.7
Playoffs			1	1	100.0	25	25.0	0	0		118.8

Alex Hawkins

Year	Team		Att	Com	PC	Yds	Avg	TD	Int	Lg	Rtg
1962	BAL	N	1	0	0.0	0	0.0	0	0		39.6

Wendell Hayes

Year	Team		Att	Com	PC	Yds	Avg	TD	Int	Lg	Rtg
1965	DEN	A	1	0	0.0	0	0.0	0	1		0.0

Abner Haynes

Year	Team		Att	Com	PC	Yds	Avg	TD	Int	Lg	Rtg
1960	DAL	A	1	0	0.0	0	0.0	0	0		39.6
1962			1	0	0.0	0	0.0	0	0		39.6
1963	KC	A	2	1	50.0	24	12.0	0	0	24	93.8
1964			1	0	0.0	0	0.0	0	0		39.6
1965	DEN	A	1	0	0.0	0	0.0	0	0		39.6
1966			2	0	0.0	0	0.0	0	2		0.0
Career			8	1	12.5	24	3.0	0	2	24	0.0

Garrison Hearst

Year	Team		Att	Com	PC	Yds	Avg	TD	Int	Lg	Rtg
1993	PHX	N	1	0	0.0	0	0.0	0	1		0.0
1994	ARI	N	1	1	100.0	10	10.0	1	0	10t	147.9
1995			2	1	50.0	16	8.0	0	0	16	77.1
Career			4	2	50.0	26	6.5	1	1	16	70.8

Stan Heath

Year	Team		Att	Com	PC	Yds	Avg	TD	Int	Lg	Rtg
1949	GB	N	106	26	24.5	355	3.3	1	14	42	4.6

Bobby Hebert

Year	Team		Att	Com	PC	Yds	Avg	TD	Int	Lg	Rtg
1985	NO	N	181	97	53.6	1208	6.7	5	4	76t	74.6
1986			79	41	51.9	498	6.3	2	8	84	40.5
1987			294	164	55.8	2119	7.2	15	9	67	82.9
1988			478	280	58.6	3156	6.6	20	15	40t	79.3
1989			353	222	62.9	2686	7.6	15	15	54t	82.7
1991			248	149	60.1	1676	6.8	9	8	65t	79.0
1992			422	249	59.0	3287	7.8	19	16	72t	82.9
1993	ATL	N	430	263	61.2	2978	6.9	24	17	98t	84.0
1994			103	52	50.5	610	5.9	2	6	40	51.0
1995			45	28	62.2	313	7.0	2	1	37t	88.5
1996			489	295	60.3	3162	6.5	22	25	57	73.0
Career			3122	1840	58.9	21693	6.9	135	124	98t	78.0
Playoffs			102	58	56.9	648	6.4	3	7		57.1

Johnny Hector

Year	Team		Att	Com	PC	Yds	Avg	TD	Int	Lg	Rtg
1988	NYJ	N	1	0	0.0	0	0.0	0	0		39.6

Randy Hedberg

Year	Team		Att	Com	PC	Yds	Avg	TD	Int	Lg	Rtg
1977	TB	N	90	25	27.8	244	2.7	0	10	19	0.0

Mel Hein

Year	Team		Att	Com	PC	Yds	Avg	TD	Int	Lg	Rtg
1943	NY	N	1	0	0.0	0	0.0	0	0		39.6

Ken Heineman

Year	Team		Att	Com	PC	Yds	Avg	TD	Int	Lg	Rtg
1940	CLE	N	8	3	37.5	74	9.3	1	1		71.9
1943	BKN	N	57	19	33.3	285	5.0	3	8	65	28.7
Career			65	22	33.8	359	5.5	4	9	65	34.2

Don Heinrich

Year	Team		Att	Com	PC	Yds	Avg	TD	Int	Lg	Rtg
1954	NYG	N	9	4	44.4	56	6.2	0	2	31	25.5
1955			67	31	46.3	413	6.2	2	2	37t	63.8
1956			88	37	42.0	369	4.2	5	5	43t	49.9
1957			26	11	42.3	224	8.6	1	1	63	70.0
1958			68	26	38.2	369	5.4	4	2	41t	63.9
1959			58	22	37.9	329	5.7	1	6	49	23.5
1960	DAL	N	61	23	37.7	371	6.1	3	3	64t	54.7
1962	OAK	A	29	10	34.5	156	5.4	1	2		36.0
Career			406	164	40.4	2287	5.6	17	23	64t	49.6
Playoffs			17	6	35.3	65	3.8	0	2		7.8

Paul Held

Year	Team		Att	Com	PC	Yds	Avg	TD	Int	Lg	Rtg
1954	PIT	N	73	24	32.9	305	4.2	1	6	37	17.2
1955	GB	N	4	2	50.0	27	6.8	0	0	18	71.9
Career			77	26	33.8	332	4.3	1	6	37	20.0

Warren Heller

Year	Team		Att	Com	PC	Yds	Avg	TD	Int	Lg	Rtg
1934	PIT	N	112	31	27.7	511	4.6	2	15		12.5
1936			5	0	0.0	0	0.0	0	1		0.0
Career			117	31	26.5	511	4.4	2	16		11.4

Barry Helton

Year	Team		Att	Com	PC	Yds	Avg	TD	Int	Lg	Rtg
1990	SF	N	1	1	100.0	0	0.0	0	0	0	79.2
1991	LARM	N	1	1	100.0	22	22.0	0	0	22	118.8
Career			2	2	100.0	22	11.0	0	0	22	112.5

Keith Henderson

Year	Team		Att	Com	PC	Yds	Avg	TD	Int	Lg	Rtg
1992	MIN	N	1	1	100.0	36	36.0	1	0	36t	158.3

Pete Henry

Year	Team		Att	Com	PC	Yds	Avg	TD	Int	Lg	Rtg
1925	CAN	N							1		

Craig Hentrich

Year	Team		Att	Com	PC	Yds	Avg	TD	Int	Lg	Rtg
1996	GB	N	1	0	0.0	0	0.0	0	0	0	39.6

Arnie Herber

Year	Team		Att	Com	PC	Yds	Avg	TD	Int	Lg	Rtg
1930	GB	N							3		
1932			**101**	37	36.6	**639**	6.3	9	9		51.5
1933			126	50	39.7	656	5.2	4	12		27.8
1934			**115**	42	36.5	**799**	6.9	8	12		45.1
1935			106	40	37.7	729	6.9	8	6		63.8
1936			**173**	**77**	44.5	**1239**	7.2	11	13		58.9
1937			104	47	45.2	676	6.5	7	10		49.7
1938			55	22	40.0	336	6.1	4	4		54.8
1939			139	57	41.0	1107	8.0	8	9		61.6
1940			89	38	42.7	560	6.3	5	7		49.8
1944	NY	N	86	36	41.9	651	7.6	6	8	58	53.0
1945			80	35	43.8	641	8.0	9	8	54t	69.8
Career			1174	481	41.0	8033	6.8	82	98	58	53.2
Playoffs			59	24	40.7	436	7.4	4	8		49.8

George Herring

Year	Team		Att	Com	PC	Yds	Avg	TD	Int	Lg	Rtg
1960	DEN	A	22	9	40.9	137	6.2	0	1	21	43.2
1961			211	93	44.1	1160	5.5	5	22	54	30.0
Career			233	102	43.8	1297	5.6	5	23	54	29.3

Mark Herrmann

Year	Team		Att	Com	PC	Yds	Avg	TD	Int	Lg	Rtg
1982	DEN	N	60	32	53.3	421	7.0	1	4	39	53.5
1983	BAL	N	36	18	50.0	256	7.1	0	3	35	38.7
1984	IND	N	56	29	51.8	352	6.3	1	6	74t	37.8
1985	SD	N	201	132	65.7	1537	7.6	10	10	59	84.5
1986			97	51	52.6	627	6.5	2	3	28	66.8
1987			57	37	64.9	405	7.1	1	5	34	55.1
1988	LARM	N	5	4	80.0	38	7.6	0	0	15	98.3
1989			5	4	80.0	59	11.8	0	1	23	76.3
1990	IND	N	1	1	100.0	6	6.0	0	0	6	91.7
1991			19	11	57.9	137	7.2	0	3	26	40.8
1992			24	15	62.5	177	7.4	1	1	27	81.4
Career			561	334	59.5	4015	7.2	16	36	74t	64.3

Rob Hertel

Year	Team		Att	Com	PC	Yds	Avg	TD	Int	Lg	Rtg
1978	CIN	N	4	1	25.0	9	2.3	0	0	9	39.6

Wally Hess

Year	Team		Att	Com	PC	Yds	Avg	TD	Int	Lg	Rtg
1925	HAM	N							1		

Bill Hewitt

Year	Team		Att	Com	PC	Yds	Avg	TD	Int	Lg	Rtg
1933	CHIB	N							3		

Year	Team		Att	Com	PC	Yds	Avg	TD	Int	Lg	Rtg

Bill Hewitt continued

Year	Team		Att	Com	PC	Yds	Avg	TD	Int	Lg	Rtg
1934			2	1	50.0	4	2.0	0	0	4	56.3
1935			1	0	0.0	0	0.0	0	0		39.6
Career			3	1	33.3	4	1.3	3	0	4	42.4

Craig Heyward

1990	NO	N	1	0	0.0	0	0.0	0	1		0.0
1991			1	1	100.0	44	44.0	0	0	44	118.8
Career			2	1	50.0	44	22.0	0	1	44	56.3

Rusty Hilger

1985	LARI	N	13	4	30.8	54	4.2	1	0	29	70.7
1986			38	19	50.0	266	7.0	1	1	54	70.7
1987			106	55	51.9	706	6.7	2	6	49	55.8
1988	DET	N	306	126	41.2	1558	5.1	7	12	56	48.9
1991	IND	N	1	0	0.0	0	0.0	0	0		39.6
Career			464	204	44.0	2584	5.6	11	19	56	52.8

Calvin Hill

1969	DAL	N	3	3	100.0	137	45.7	2	0	59t	158.3
1970			4	1	25.0	12	3.0	0	0	12	39.6
1971			1	0	0.0	0	0.0	0	1		0.0
1972			3	1	33.3	55	18.3	1	0	55t	121.5
1973			1	0	0.0	0	0.0	0	0		39.6
1976	WAS	N	1	0	0.0	0	0.0	0	0		39.6
Career			13	5	38.5	204	15.7	3	1	59t	93.8
Playoffs			1	0	0.0	0	0.0	0	0		39.6

Charlie Hill

| 1926 | KC | N | | 1 | | | | | | | |

David Hill

1976	DET	N	1	0	0.0	0	0.0	0	1		0.0
1977			1	0	0.0	0	0.0	0	0		39.6
Career			2	0	0.0	0	0.0	0	1		0.0

Drew Hill

| 1987 | HOU | N | 1 | 0 | 0.0 | 0 | 0.0 | 0 | 0 | | 39.6 |

Eddie Hill

1981	MIA	N	1	1	100.0	14	14.0	0	0	14	118.8
1982			1	0	0.0	0	0.0	0	0		39.6
Career			2	1	50.0	14	7.0	0	0	14	72.9

Harlon Hill

| 1956 | CHIB | N | 1 | 0 | 0.0 | 0 | 0.0 | 0 | 0 | | 39.6 |

Ike Hill

1973	CHI	N	1	1	100.0	35	35.0	0	0	35	118.8
1974			1	0	0.0	0	0.0	0	0		39.6
Career			2	1	50.0	35	17.5	0	0	35	95.8

King Hill

1958	CHIC	N	9	1	11.1	18	2.0	0	2	18	0.0
1959			181	82	45.3	1015	5.6	7	13	31	46.2
1960	STL	N	55	20	36.4	205	3.7	1	5	25	16.1
1961	PHI	N	12	6	50.0	101	8.4	2	2	23	78.8
1962			61	31	50.8	361	5.9	0	5	37	34.9
1963			186	91	48.9	1213	6.5	10	17	80t	49.9
1964			88	49	55.7	641	7.3	3	4	38t	71.3
1965			113	60	53.1	857	7.6	5	10	55	55.8
1966			97	53	54.6	571	5.9	5	7	30	59.3
1967			7	2	28.6	33	4.7	1	0	18	86.3
1968			71	33	46.5	531	7.5	3	6	92t	50.9
1969	STL	N	1	1	100.0	7	7.0	0	0	7	95.8
Career			881	429	48.7	5553	6.3	37	71	92t	49.3

Lonzell Hill

1988	NO	N	1	0	0.0	0	0.0	0	0		39.6
1989			0	0		0		0	0		
Career			1	0	0.0	0	0.0	0	0		39.6

Tony Hill

1978	DAL	N	1	0	0.0	0	0.0	0	0		39.6
1985			1	1	100.0	42	42.0	0	0	42	118.8
Career			2	1	50.0	42	21.0	0	0	42	95.8

Ira Hillary

| 1987 | CIN | N | 0 | 0 | | 0 | | 0 | 0 | | |

Billy Hillenbrand

1946	CHI	AA	3	0	0.0	0	0.0	0	2		0.0
1947	BAL	AA	1	0	0.0	0	0.0	0	1		0.0
Career			4	0	0.0	0	0.0	0	3		0.0

Dalton Hilliard

1986	NO	N	3	1	33.3	29	9.7	1	0	29t	109.7
1987			1	1	100.0	23	23.0	1	0	23t	158.3
1988			2	1	50.0	27	13.5	1	0	27t	135.4
1989			1	1	100.0	35	35.0	1	0	35t	158.3
Career			7	4	57.1	114	16.3	4	0	35t	141.4

Clarke Hinkle

1935	GB	N	1	1	100.0	12	12.0	0	0	12	116.7
1936			2	1	50.0	10	5.0	0	0	10	64.6
1937			3	2	66.7	43	14.3	0	0		109.7
1938			2	1	50.0	6	3.0	0	0	6	56.3
Career			8	5	62.5	71	8.9	0	0	12	91.1

Eric Hipple

1981	DET	N	279	140	50.2	2358	8.5	14	15	94t	73.4
1982			86	36	41.9	411	4.8	2	4	52	45.3
1983			387	204	52.7	2577	6.7	12	18	80t	64.7
1984			38	16	42.1	246	6.5	1	1	40	62.0
1985			406	223	54.9	2952	7.3	17	18	56	73.6
1986			305	192	63.0	1919	6.3	9	11	46	75.6
1988			27	12	44.4	158	5.9	0	0	31	63.5
1989			18	7	38.9	90	5.0	0	3	15	15.7
Career			1546	830	53.7	10711	6.9	55	70	94t	68.7
Playoffs			38	22	57.9	298	7.8	1	2		69.8

Elroy Hirsch

1946	CHI	AA	20	12	60.0	156	7.8	1	2		61.7
1947			1	0	0.0	0	0.0	0	0		39.6
1950	LA	N	1	0	0.0	0	0.0	0	0		39.6
Career			22	12	54.5	156	7.1	1	2		54.4

Joe Hoague

1941	PIT	N	1	0	0.0	0	0.0	0	0		39.6
1942			1	0	0.0	0	0.0	0	0		39.6
Career			2	0	0.0	0	0.0	0	0		39.6

Dick Hoak

1961	PIT	N	3	1	33.3	13	4.3	1	1	13t	47.9
1962			1	0	0.0	0	0.0	0	0		39.6
1964			1	0	0.0	0	0.0	0	0		39.6
1966			6	4	66.7	87	14.5	1	0	42t	149.3
1967			8	4	50.0	69	8.6	1	1	21	79.7
1968			16	7	43.8	188	11.8	0	1	62	61.5
1969			3	2	66.7	30	10.0	0	0	16	99.3
1970			2	2	100.0	40	20.0	1	0	27t	158.3
Career			40	20	50.0	427	10.7	4	3	62	90.3

Leroy Hoard

| 1993 | CLE | N | 1 | 0 | 0.0 | 0 | 0.0 | 0 | 0 | | 39.6 |

Daryl Hobbs

1995	OAK	N	1	0	0.0	0	0.0	0	0		39.6
1996			1	1	100.0	7	7.0	0	0	7	95.8
Career			2	1	50.0	7	3.5	0	0	7	58.3

Billy Joe Hobert

1995	OAK	N	80	44	55.0	540	6.8	6	4	80t	80.2
1996			104	57	54.8	667	6.4	4	5	51	67.3
Career			184	101	54.9	1207	6.6	10	9	80t	72.9

Floyd Hodge

| 1983 | ATL | N | 2 | 1 | 50.0 | 28 | 14.0 | 0 | 1 | 28 | 56.3 |

Norm Hodgins

| 1974 | CHI | N | 1 | 0 | 0.0 | 0 | 0.0 | 0 | 0 | | 39.6 |

Tommy Hodson

1990	NE	N	156	85	54.5	968	6.2	4	5	56	68.5
1991			68	36	52.9	345	5.1	1	4	32	47.7
1992			91	50	54.9	496	5.5	2	2	54t	68.8
1995	NO	N	5	3	60.0	14	2.8	0	0	9	64.6
Career			320	174	54.4	1823	5.7	7	11	56	64.1

Bob Hoernschemeyer

1946	CHI	AA	193	95	49.2	1266	6.6	14	14	68t	64.4
1947	CHI-BKN	AA	173	73	42.2	926	5.4	4	11	73t	40.8
1948	BKN	AA	155	71	45.8	854	5.5	8	15		40.8
1949	CHI	AA	167	69	41.3	1063	6.4	6	11	77t	47.6
1950	DET	N	4	1	25.0	19	4.8	1	1	19t	46.9
1951			4	2	50.0	46	11.5	2	0	30t	131.3
1952			4	2	50.0	14	3.5	2	1	10t	58.3
1953			5	2	40.0	16	3.2	1	1	8t	48.8
1954			7	3	42.9	81	11.6	3	1	66t	86.0

Bob Hoernschemeyer *continued*

Year	Team		Att	Com	PC	Yds	Avg	TD	Int	Lg	Rtg
1955			2	1	50.0	17	8.5	1	1	17t	79.2
Career			714	319	44.7	4302	6.0	42	56	77t	51.3
Playoffs			1	1	100.0	24	24.0	0	0		118.8

Paul Hogan

Year	Team		Att	Com	PC	Yds	Avg	TD	Int	Lg	Rtg
1925	CAN	N							3		

Gary Hogeboom

Year	Team		Att	Com	PC	Yds	Avg	TD	Int	Lg	Rtg
1982	DAL	N	8	3	37.5	45	5.6	0	1	26	17.2
1983			17	11	64.7	161	9.5	1	1	24	90.6
1984			367	195	53.1	2366	6.4	7	14	68t	63.7
1985			126	70	55.6	978	7.8	5	7	58t	70.8
1986	IND	N	144	85	59.0	1154	8.0	6	6	60	81.2
1987			168	99	58.9	1145	6.8	9	5	72t	85.0
1988			131	76	58.0	996	7.6	7	7	58	77.7
1989	PHX	N	364	204	56.0	2591	7.1	14	19	59t	69.5
Career			1325	743	56.1	9436	7.1	49	60	72t	71.9
Playoffs			29	14	48.3	162	5.6	2	2		59.8

Mike Hohensee

Year	Team		Att	Com	PC	Yds	Avg	TD	Int	Lg	Rtg
1987	CHI	N	52	28	53.8	343	6.6	4	1	28	92.1

Steve Hokuf

Year	Team		Att	Com	PC	Yds	Avg	TD	Int	Lg	Rtg
1934	BOS	N	51	13	25.5	203	4.0	3	10		23.7

Mike Hold

Year	Team		Att	Com	PC	Yds	Avg	TD	Int	Lg	Rtg
1987	TB	N	24	8	33.3	123	5.1	2	1	61t	61.6

Donald Hollas

Year	Team		Att	Com	PC	Yds	Avg	TD	Int	Lg	Rtg
1991	CIN	N	55	32	58.2	310	5.6	1	4	23t	49.8
1992			58	35	60.3	335	5.8	2	0	24t	87.9
1994			2	0	0.0	0	0.0	0	1		0.0
Career			115	67	58.3	645	5.6	3	5	24t	64.6

Tommy Holleran

Year	Team		Att	Com	PC	Yds	Avg	TD	Int	Lg	Rtg
1922	TOL	N							1		

Ken Holley

Year	Team		Att	Com	PC	Yds	Avg	TD	Int	Lg	Rtg
1946	MIA	AA	11	3	27.3	36	3.3	0	4		1.1

Ron Holliday

Year	Team		Att	Com	PC	Yds	Avg	TD	Int	Lg	Rtg
1973	SD	N	2	0	0.0	0	0.0	0	1		0.0

Joe Hollingsworth

Year	Team		Att	Com	PC	Yds	Avg	TD	Int	Lg	Rtg
1949	PIT	N	1	0	0.0	0	0.0	0	0		39.6

Bob Holly

Year	Team		Att	Com	PC	Yds	Avg	TD	Int	Lg	Rtg
1983	WAS	N	1	1	100.0	5	5.0	0	0	5	87.5
1985	ATL	N	39	24	61.5	295	7.6	1	2	44	72.1
Career			40	25	62.5	300	7.5	1	2	44	72.9
Playoffs			2	2	100.0	13	6.5	0	0		93.8

Bernie Holm

Year	Team		Att	Com	PC	Yds	Avg	TD	Int	Lg	Rtg
1933	PIT	N	52	16	30.8	406	7.8	2	13		33.5

Walt Holmer

Year	Team		Att	Com	PC	Yds	Avg	TD	Int	Lg	Rtg
1929	CHIB	N						2			
1931	CHIC	N						1			
1932								2			
Career								5			

Jack Holmes

Year	Team		Att	Com	PC	Yds	Avg	TD	Int	Lg	Rtg
1980	NO	N	3	1	33.3	23	7.7	1	0	23t	101.4
1982			1	0	0.0	0	0.0	0	0		39.6
Career			4	1	25.0	23	5.8	1	0	23t	90.6

Pete Holohan

Year	Team		Att	Com	PC	Yds	Avg	TD	Int	Lg	Rtg
1983	SD	N	1	0	0.0	0	0.0	0	0		39.6
1984			2	1	50.0	25	12.5	1	0	25t	135.4
1985			1	0	0.0	0	0.0	0	0		39.6
1986			2	1	50.0	21	10.5	0	0	21	87.5
Career			6	2	33.3	46	7.7	1	0	25t	101.4

Henry Homan

Year	Team		Att	Com	PC	Yds	Avg	TD	Int	Lg	Rtg
1925	FRA	N							1		

Todd Hons

Year	Team		Att	Com	PC	Yds	Avg	TD	Int	Lg	Rtg
1987	DET	N	92	43	46.7	552	6.0	5	5	53t	61.5

Mitch Hoopes

Year	Team		Att	Com	PC	Yds	Avg	TD	Int	Lg	Rtg
1975	DAL	N	3	1	33.3	21	7.0	0	0	21	59.0

Harry Hopp

Year	Team		Att	Com	PC	Yds	Avg	TD	Int	Lg	Rtg
1941	DET	N	3	0	0.0	0	0.0	0	1		0.0
1942			68	20	29.4	258	3.8	0	13	50	3.3
1943			8	5	62.5	60	7.5	0	0	36	85.4
1946	BUF	AA	22	11	50.0	190	8.6	0	0		79.7
Career			101	36	35.6	508	5.0	0	14	50	13.2

Don Horn

Year	Team		Att	Com	PC	Yds	Avg	TD	Int	Lg	Rtg
1967	GB	N	24	12	50.0	171	7.1	1	1	29t	70.0
1968			16	10	62.5	187	11.7	2	0	67t	142.4
1969			168	89	53.0	1505	**9.0**	11	11	60t	78.1
1970			76	28	36.8	428	5.6	2	10	89t	25.4
1971	DEN	N	173	89	51.4	1056	6.1	3	14	74	42.4
1973	CLE	N	8	4	50.0	22	2.8	1	0	12	95.8
Career			465	232	49.9	3369	7.2	20	36	89t	55.9

Marty Horn

Year	Team		Att	Com	PC	Yds	Avg	TD	Int	Lg	Rtg
1987	PHI	N	11	5	45.5	68	6.2	0	0	23	65.7

Paul Hornung

Year	Team		Att	Com	PC	Yds	Avg	TD	Int	Lg	Rtg
1957	GB	N	6	1	16.7	1	0.2	0	0		39.6
1958			1	0	0.0	0	0.0	0	0		39.6
1959			8	5	62.5	95	11.9	2	0	30	143.2
1960			16	6	37.5	118	7.4	2	0	40t	103.6
1961			5	3	60.0	42	8.4	1	0	20	126.7
1962			6	4	66.7	80	13.3	0	2	41	70.1
1964			10	3	30.0	25	2.5	0	1	10	0.0
1965			2	1	50.0	19	9.5	0	1	19	43.8
1966			1	1	100.0	5	5.0	0	0	5	87.5
Career			55	24	43.6	385	7.0	5	4	41	67.6
Playoffs			6	1	16.7	21	3.5	0	0		41.7

Ethan Horton

Year	Team		Att	Com	PC	Yds	Avg	TD	Int	Lg	Rtg
1985	KC	N	1	0	0.0	0	0.0	0	0		39.6

Arnie Horween

Year	Team		Att	Com	PC	Yds	Avg	TD	Int	Lg	Rtg
1923	CHIC	N							1		

Jeff Hostetler

Year	Team		Att	Com	PC	Yds	Avg	TD	Int	Lg	Rtg
1988	NYG	N	29	16	55.2	244	8.4	1	2	85t	65.9
1989			39	20	51.3	294	7.5	3	2	35t	80.5
1990			87	47	54.0	614	7.1	3	1	44t	83.2
1991			285	179	62.8	2032	7.1	5	4	55	84.1
1992			192	103	53.6	1225	6.4	8	3	46	80.8
1993	LARI	N	419	236	56.3	3242	7.7	14	10	74t	82.5
1994			455	263	57.8	3334	7.3	20	16	77t	80.8
1995	OAK	N	286	172	60.1	1998	7.0	12	9	80t	82.2
1996			402	242	60.2	2548	6.3	23	14	62t	83.2
Career			2194	1278	58.2	15531	7.1	89	61	85t	82.1
Playoffs			115	72	62.6	1034	9.0	7	0		112.0

Kevin House

Year	Team		Att	Com	PC	Yds	Avg	TD	Int	Lg	Rtg
1981	TB	N	1	0	0.0	0	0.0	0	0		39.6
1986	LARM	N	0	0		0		0	0		
Career			1	0	0.0	0	0.0	0	0		39.6

John Hovious

Year	Team		Att	Com	PC	Yds	Avg	TD	Int	Lg	Rtg
1945	NY	N	46	22	47.8	373	8.1	4	5	53	65.1

Dixie Howell

Year	Team		Att	Com	PC	Yds	Avg	TD	Int	Lg	Rtg
1937	WAS	N	6	1	16.7	14	2.3	0	3	14	0.0

Bobby Hoying

Year	Team		Att	Com	PC	Yds	Avg	TD	Int	Lg	Rtg
1996	PHI	N	0	0		0		0	0		

John Huarte

Year	Team		Att	Com	PC	Yds	Avg	TD	Int	Lg	Rtg
1966	BOS	A	11	5	45.5	63	5.7	0	1	17	25.9
1967			9	3	33.3	25	2.8	0	1	15	2.8
1968	PHI	N	15	7	46.7	110	7.3	0	2	48	54.2
1970	KC	N	2	0	0.0	0	0.0	0	1		0.0
1971			6	2	33.3	18	3.0	0	0	26	42.4
1972	CHI	N	5	2	40.0	14	2.8	0	0	8	47.9
Career			48	19	39.6	230	4.8	0	5	48	22.4

Brad Hubbert

Year	Team		Att	Com	PC	Yds	Avg	TD	Int	Lg	Rtg
1969	SD	A	1	0	0.0	0	0.0	0	0		39.6

Pooley Hubert

Year	Team		Att	Com	PC	Yds	Avg	TD	Int	Lg	Rtg
1926	NY	A							1		

Doug Hudson

Year	Team		Att	Com	PC	Yds	Avg	TD	Int	Lg	Rtg
1987	KC	N	1	0	0.0	0	0.0	0	0		39.6

Year	Team		Att	Com	PC	Yds	Avg	TD	Int	Lg	Rtg

Jim Hudson

Year	Team		Att	Com	PC	Yds	Avg	TD	Int	Lg	Rtg
1966	NY	A	1	0	0.0	0	0.0	0	0		39.6

Gary Huff

Year	Team		Att	Com	PC	Yds	Avg	TD	Int	Lg	Rtg
1973	CHI	N	126	54	42.9	525	4.2	3	8	29t	36.6
1974			283	142	50.2	1663	5.9	6	17	73	50.4
1975			205	114	55.6	1083	5.3	3	9	49	57.0
1977	TB	N	138	67	48.6	889	6.4	3	13	67t	37.4
1978			36	15	41.7	169	4.7	1	3	31t	30.9
Career			788	392	49.7	4329	5.5	16	50	73	46.8

Ken Huffine

Year	Team		Att	Com	PC	Yds	Avg	TD	Int	Lg	Rtg
1921	DEC	A							1		

Vern Huffman

Year	Team		Att	Com	PC	Yds	Avg	TD	Int	Lg	Rtg
1937	DET	N	23	5	21.7	102	4.4	2	6		35.0
1938			85	27	31.8	382	4.5	2	8		15.9
Career			108	32	29.6	484	4.5	4	14		18.5

John Hufnagel

Year	Team		Att	Com	PC	Yds	Avg	TD	Int	Lg	Rtg
1974	DEN	N	10	6	60.0	70	7.0	0	1	28	41.7
1975			51	16	31.4	287	5.6	1	8	80t	18.6
Career			61	22	36.1	357	5.9	1	9	80t	22.4

Bernie Hughes

Year	Team		Att	Com	PC	Yds	Avg	TD	Int	Lg	Rtg
1932	BOS	N	10	2	20.0	47	4.7	1	0		80.0

Danan Hughes

Year	Team		Att	Com	PC	Yds	Avg	TD	Int	Lg	Rtg
1996	KC	N	1	1	100.0	30	30.0	0	0	30	118.8

Tommy Hughitt

Year	Team		Att	Com	PC	Yds	Avg	TD	Int	Lg	Rtg
1921	BUF	A							2		
1922	BUF	N							2		
1923									1		
Career									5	30	

David Humm

Year	Team		Att	Com	PC	Yds	Avg	TD	Int	Lg	Rtg
1975	OAK	N	38	18	47.4	246	6.5	3	2	43	72.9
1976			5	3	60.0	41	8.2	0	0	29	86.3
1978			26	14	53.8	151	5.8	0	1	23	55.1
1980	BUF	N	14	4	28.6	39	2.8	0	1	19	9.8
1981	BAL	N	24	7	29.2	90	3.8	0	2	20	8.0
1982			23	13	56.5	130	5.7	0	1	23	54.6
1984	LARI	N	7	4	57.1	56	8.0	0	1	21	43.5
Career			137	63	46.0	753	5.5	3	8	43	46.3

Bobby Humphrey

Year	Team		Att	Com	PC	Yds	Avg	TD	Int	Lg	Rtg
1989	DEN	N	2	1	50.0	17	8.5	1	0	17t	118.8
1990			2	0	0.0	0	0.0	0	0		39.6
Career			4	1	25.0	17	4.3	1	0	17t	84.4

Buddy Humphrey

Year	Team		Att	Com	PC	Yds	Avg	TD	Int	Lg	Rtg
1960	LA	N	24	9	37.5	78	3.3	0	2	16	12.2
1961	DAL	N	2	1	50.0	16	8.0	0	0	16	77.1
1963	STL	N	11	4	36.4	96	8.7	1	0	33	99.1
1964			1	0	0.0	0	0.0	0	0		39.6
1965			105	58	55.2	736	7.0	1	9	53t	44.8
1966	HOU	A	32	15	46.9	168	5.3	2	1	32	70.8
Career			175	87	49.7	1094	6.3	4	12	53t	48.6

Stan Humphries

Year	Team		Att	Com	PC	Yds	Avg	TD	Int	Lg	Rtg
1989	WAS	N	10	5	50.0	91	9.1	1	1	39	75.4
1990			156	91	58.3	1015	6.5	3	10	44	57.5
1992	SD	N	454	263	57.9	3356	7.4	16	18	67t	76.4
1993			324	173	53.4	1981	6.1	12	10	48t	71.5
1994			453	264	58.3	3209	7.1	17	12	99t	81.6
1995			478	282	59.0	3381	7.1	17	14	51t	80.4
1996			416	232	55.8	2670	6.4	18	13	63t	76.7
Career			2291	1310	57.2	15703	6.9	84	78	99t	76.3
Playoffs			228	118	51.8	1347	5.9	6	13		54.8

Earnest Hunter

Year	Team		Att	Com	PC	Yds	Avg	TD	Int	Lg	Rtg
1996	NO	N	1	0	0.0	0	0.0	0	0	0	39.6

Herman Hunter

Year	Team		Att	Com	PC	Yds	Avg	TD	Int	Lg	Rtg
1985	PHI	N	2	1	50.0	38	19.0	1	0	38t	135.4

Scott Hunter

Year	Team		Att	Com	PC	Yds	Avg	TD	Int	Lg	Rtg
1971	GB	N	163	75	46.0	1210	7.4	7	17	77t	46.1
1972			199	86	43.2	1252	6.3	6	9	44	55.5
1973			84	35	41.7	442	5.3	2	4	30	46.8
1976	ATL	N	110	51	46.4	633	5.8	5	4	34t	64.7
1977			151	70	46.4	898	5.9	2	3	49t	61.6

Scott Hunter *continued*

Year	Team		Att	Com	PC	Yds	Avg	TD	Int	Lg	Rtg
1979	DET	N	41	18	43.9	321	7.8	1	1	82	69.3
Career			748	335	44.8	4756	6.4	23	38	82	55.0
Playoffs			24	12	50.0	150	6.3	0	1		52.4

Bill Hutchinson

Year	Team		Att	Com	PC	Yds	Avg	TD	Int	Lg	Rtg
1942	NYG	N	4	1	25.0	-3	-0.8	0	2	-3	0.0

Don Hutson

Year	Team		Att	Com	PC	Yds	Avg	TD	Int	Lg	Rtg
1937	GB	N	4	0	0.0	0	0.0	0	1		0.0
1943			4	1	25.0	38	9.5	1	1	38	66.7
1944			3	0	0.0	0	0.0	0	0		39.6
Career			11	1	9.1	38	3.5	1	2	38	32.2

Henry Hynoski

Year	Team		Att	Com	PC	Yds	Avg	TD	Int	Lg	Rtg
1975	CLE	N	1	0	0.0	0	0.0	0	0		39.6

Tut Imlay

Year	Team		Att	Com	PC	Yds	Avg	TD	Int	Lg	Rtg
1926	LA	N							1		

Kevin Ingram

Year	Team		Att	Com	PC	Yds	Avg	TD	Int	Lg	Rtg
1987	NO	N	2	1	50.0	5	2.5	1	0	5t	95.8

Mark Ingram

Year	Team		Att	Com	PC	Yds	Avg	TD	Int	Lg	Rtg
1991	NYG	N	1	0	0.0	0	0.0	0	0		39.6

Einar Irgens

Year	Team		Att	Com	PC	Yds	Avg	TD	Int	Lg	Rtg
1922	MIN	N							1		
1923									1		
Career									2	5t	

Don Irwin

Year	Team		Att	Com	PC	Yds	Avg	TD	Int	Lg	Rtg
1936	BOS	N	5	0	0.0	0	0.0	0	0		0.0
1937	WAS	N	3	0	0.0	0	0.0	0	0		39.6
1938			6	0	0.0	0	0.0	0	2		0.0
Career			14	0	0.0	0	0.0	0	3		0.0

Wilmer Isabel

Year	Team		Att	Com	PC	Yds	Avg	TD	Int	Lg	Rtg
1923	COL	N							1		

Cecil Isbell

Year	Team		Att	Com	PC	Yds	Avg	TD	Int	Lg	Rtg
1938	GB	N	91	37	40.7	659	7.2	7	10		52.2
1939			103	43	41.7	749	7.3	6	5		66.4
1940			150	68	45.3	1037	6.9	9	12		55.3
1941			**206**	**117**	56.8	**1479**	7.2	**15**	11	56	81.4
1942			268	**146**	54.5	**2021**	7.5	**24**	14	73	87.0
Career			818	411	50.2	5945	7.3	61	52	73	72.6
Playoffs			26	13	50.0	235	9.0	2	1		91.0

John Isenbarger

Year	Team		Att	Com	PC	Yds	Avg	TD	Int	Lg	Rtg
1970	SF	N	1	0	0.0	0	0.0	0	0		39.6
1972			1	0	0.0	0	0.0	0	0		39.6
1973			1	1	100.0	48	48.0	0	0	48	118.8
Career			3	1	33.3	48	16.0	0	0	48	81.9

Eddie Lee Ivery

Year	Team		Att	Com	PC	Yds	Avg	TD	Int	Lg	Rtg
1982	GB	N	1	0	0.0	0	0.0	0	0		39.6
1983			2	2	100.0	50	25.0	0	0	35	118.8
1985			1	0	0.0	0	0.0	0	0		39.6
Career			4	2	50.0	50	12.5	0	0	35	95.8

George Izo

Year	Team		Att	Com	PC	Yds	Avg	TD	Int	Lg	Rtg
1960	STL	N	24	10	41.7	115	4.8	0	0	24	56.8
1961	WAS	N	40	16	40.0	214	5.3	1	6	33	26.5
1962			37	17	45.9	284	7.7	3	4	49t	59.8
1963			58	25	43.1	378	6.5	3	6	99t	42.8
1964			18	5	27.8	83	4.6	1	2	29t	25.2
1965	DET	N	59	24	40.7	357	6.1	2	6	61t	32.9
1966	PIT	N	81	35	43.2	360	4.4	2	8	37t	25.3
Career			317	132	41.6	1791	5.6	12	32	99t	33.4

Don Jackson

Year	Team		Att	Com	PC	Yds	Avg	TD	Int	Lg	Rtg
1936	PHI	N	35	7	20.0	80	2.3	0	11		0.0

Frank Jackson

Year	Team		Att	Com	PC	Yds	Avg	TD	Int	Lg	Rtg
1961	DAL	A	2	1	50.0	9	4.5	0	1	9	22.9

Harold Jackson

Year	Team		Att	Com	PC	Yds	Avg	TD	Int	Lg	Rtg
1979	NE	N	1	0	0.0	0	0.0	0	0		39.6
1980			2	2	100.0	35	17.5	0	0	23	118.8
1981			1	0	0.0	0	0.0	0	0		39.6
Career			4	2	50.0	35	8.8	0	0	23	80.2

Michael Jackson

Year	Team		Att	Com	PC	Yds	Avg	TD	Int	Lg	Rtg
1993	CLE	N	1	1	100.0	25	25.0	0	0	25	118.8
1994			2	0	0.0	0	0.0	0	0		39.6
1995			1	0	0.0	0	0.0	0	1		0.0
Career			4	1	25.0	25	6.3	0	1	25	13.5

Jack Jacobs

Year	Team		Att	Com	PC	Yds	Avg	TD	Int	Lg	Rtg
1942	CLE	N	93	43	46.2	640	6.9	6	6	67	63.9
1945			5	3	60.0	12	2.4	0	0	11	64.6
1946	WAS	N	12	5	41.7	98	8.2	0	2	35	31.3
1947	GB	N	242	108	44.6	1615	6.7	16	17	69	59.8
1948			184	82	44.6	848	4.6	5	21	64	27.9
1949			16	3	18.8	55	3.4	0	3	39	1.8
Career			552	244	44.2	3268	5.9	27	49	69	42.9

Jeff Jaeger

Year	Team		Att	Com	PC	Yds	Avg	TD	Int	Lg	Rtg
1987	CLE	N	1	0	0.0	0	0.0	0	0		39.6

Craig James

Year	Team		Att	Com	PC	Yds	Avg	TD	Int	Lg	Rtg
1985	NE	N	2	2	100.0	16	8.0	2	0	11t	139.6
1986			4	1	25.0	10	2.5	1	1	10t	39.6
Career			6	3	50.0	26	4.3	3	1	11t	61.8
Playoffs			1	1	100.0	8	8.0	0	0		100.0

Dick James

Year	Team		Att	Com	PC	Yds	Avg	TD	Int	Lg	Rtg
1960	WAS	N	1	0	0.0	0	0.0	0	0		39.6
1961			4	1	25.0	15	3.8	0	0	15	42.7
1963			1	0	0.0	0	0.0	0	0		39.6
1964	NYG	N	1	0	0.0	0	0.0	0	1		0.0
Career			7	1	14.3	15	2.1	0	1	15	0.0

John James

Year	Team		Att	Com	PC	Yds	Avg	TD	Int	Lg	Rtg
1975	ATL	N	1	1	100.0	25	25.0	0	0	25	118.8
1977			1	0	0.0	0	0.0	0	0		39.6
1979			1	1	100.0	20	20.0	0	0	20	118.8
1980			1	0	0.0	0	0.0	0	1		0.0
1981			1	0	0.0	0	0.0	0	0		39.6
1983	HOU	N	1	1	100.0	7	7.0	0	0	7	95.8
Career			6	3	50.0	52	8.7	0	1	25	40.3

Lionel James

Year	Team		Att	Com	PC	Yds	Avg	TD	Int	Lg	Rtg
1984	SD	N	2	0	0.0	0	0.0	0	1		0.0
1988			0	0		0		0	0		
Career			2	0	0.0	0	0.0	0	1		0.0

Lynn James

Year	Team		Att	Com	PC	Yds	Avg	TD	Int	Lg	Rtg
1990	CIN	N	1	0	0.0	0	0.0	0	0		39.6

Dick Jamieson

Year	Team		Att	Com	PC	Yds	Avg	TD	Int	Lg	Rtg
1960	NY	A	70	35	50.0	586	8.4	6	2		95.3

Len Janiak

Year	Team		Att	Com	PC	Yds	Avg	TD	Int	Lg	Rtg
1942	CLE	N	1	1	100.0	11	11.0	0	0	11	112.5

Vic Janowicz

Year	Team		Att	Com	PC	Yds	Avg	TD	Int	Lg	Rtg
1954	WAS	N	1	0	0.0	0	0.0	0	0		39.6
1955			5	0	0.0	0	0.0	0	1		0.0
Career			6	0	0.0	0	0.0	0	1		0.0

Toimi Jarvi

Year	Team		Att	Com	PC	Yds	Avg	TD	Int	Lg	Rtg
1945	PIT	N	10	4	40.0	50	5.0	0	3	21	16.7

Ron Jaworski

Year	Team		Att	Com	PC	Yds	Avg	TD	Int	Lg	Rtg
1974	LA	N	24	10	41.7	144	6.0	0	1	22	44.4
1975			48	24	50.0	302	6.3	0	2	25	52.6
1976			52	20	38.5	273	5.3	1	5	42	22.8
1977	PHI	N	346	166	48.0	2183	6.3	18	21	55t	60.4
1978			398	206	51.8	2487	6.2	16	16	56t	67.9
1979			374	190	50.8	2669	7.1	18	12	53t	76.8
1980			451	257	57.0	3529	7.8	27	12	56t	91.0
1981			461	250	54.2	3095	6.7	23	20	85t	73.8
1982			286	167	58.4	2076	7.3	12	12	57	77.5
1983			446	235	52.7	3315	7.4	20	18	83t	75.1
1984			427	234	54.8	2754	6.4	16	14	90t	73.5
1985			484	255	52.7	3450	7.1	17	20	99t	70.2
1986			245	128	52.2	1405	5.7	8	6	56	70.2
1988	MIA	N	14	9	64.3	123	8.8	1	0	22	116.1
1989	KC	N	61	36	59.0	385	6.3	2	5	32	54.3
Career			4117	2187	53.1	28190	6.8	179	164	99t	72.8
Playoffs			270	126	46.7	1669	6.2	10	10		63.6

Dave Jaynes

Year	Team		Att	Com	PC	Yds	Avg	TD	Int	Lg	Rtg
1974	KC	N	2	0	0.0	0	0.0	0	1		0.0

Billy Jefferson

Year	Team		Att	Com	PC	Yds	Avg	TD	Int	Lg	Rtg
1941	DET	N	72	18	25.0	181	2.5	0	9	32	0.0
1942	PHI-BKN	N	4	1	25.0	11	2.8	0	0	11	39.6
Career			76	19	25.0	192	2.5	0	9	32	0.0

Neal Jeffrey

Year	Team		Att	Com	PC	Yds	Avg	TD	Int	Lg	Rtg
1976	SD	N	2	2	100.0	11	5.5	0	0	7	89.6

Alfred Jenkins

Year	Team		Att	Com	PC	Yds	Avg	TD	Int	Lg	Rtg
1976	ATL	N	1	0	0.0	0	0.0	0	1		0.0

Ken Jenkins

Year	Team		Att	Com	PC	Yds	Avg	TD	Int	Lg	Rtg
1984	DET	N	1	0	0.0	0	0.0	0	0		39.6

Dave Jennings

Year	Team		Att	Com	PC	Yds	Avg	TD	Int	Lg	Rtg
1978	NYG	N	1	1	100.0	-1	-1.0	0	0	-1	79.2
1979			2	2	100.0	48	24.0	0	0	28	118.8
1980			0	0		0		0	0		
1983			1	0	0.0	0	0.0	0	0		39.6
1987	NYJ	N	1	1	100.0	16	16.0	0	0	16	118.8
Career			5	4	80.0	63	12.6	0	0	28	118.8

Jim Jensen

Year	Team		Att	Com	PC	Yds	Avg	TD	Int	Lg	Rtg
1982	MIA	N	1	0	0.0	0	0.0	0	0		39.6
1984			1	1	100.0	35	35.0	1	0	35t	158.3
1986			2	0	0.0	0	0.0	0	0		39.6
1989			1	1	100.0	19	19.0	1	0	19t	158.3
1990			1	1	100.0	31	31.0	0	0	31	118.8
1991			1	1	100.0	17	17.0	0	0	17	118.8
Career			7	4	57.1	102	14.6	2	0	35t	141.4

Ron Jessie

Year	Team		Att	Com	PC	Yds	Avg	TD	Int	Lg	Rtg
1972	DET	N	1	0	0.0	0	0.0	0	0		39.6

Billy Jessup

Year	Team		Att	Com	PC	Yds	Avg	TD	Int	Lg	Rtg
1958	SF	N	1	0	0.0	0	0.0	0	1		0.0

Perry Jeter

Year	Team		Att	Com	PC	Yds	Avg	TD	Int	Lg	Rtg
1956	CHIB	N	1	0	0.0	0	0.0	0	0		39.6

Herb Joesting

Year	Team		Att	Com	PC	Yds	Avg	TD	Int	Lg	Rtg
1929	MIN	N						2			

Andy Johnson

Year	Team		Att	Com	PC	Yds	Avg	TD	Int	Lg	Rtg
1976	NE	N	2	0	0.0	0	0.0	0	0		39.6
1978			2	0	0.0	0	0.0	0	0		39.6
1981			9	7	77.8	194	21.6	4	1	66t	118.8
Career			13	7	53.8	194	14.9	4	1	66t	106.6
Playoffs			1	1	100.0	24	24.0	1	0		158.3

Anthony Johnson

Year	Team		Att	Com	PC	Yds	Avg	TD	Int	Lg	Rtg
1992	IND	N	1	0	0.0	0	0.0	0	0		39.6
1993			1	0	0.0	0	0.0	0	1		0.0
Career			2	0	0.0	0	0.0	0	1		0.0

Bert Johnson

Year	Team		Att	Com	PC	Yds	Avg	TD	Int	Lg	Rtg
1937	BKN	N	11	0	0.0	0	0.0	0	1		1.7
1938	CHIB	N	2	1	50.0	4	2.0	0	0	4	56.3
1939	CHIC	N	40	14	35.0	208	5.2	0	5		13.3
1940			1	1	100.0	25	25.0	0	0	25	118.8
Career			54	16	29.6	237	4.4	0	6	25	5.8

Billy Johnson

Year	Team		Att	Com	PC	Yds	Avg	TD	Int	Lg	Rtg
1977	HOU	N	0	0		0		0	0		
1983	ATL	N	1	0	0.0	0	0.0	0	0		39.6
Career			1	0	0.0	0	0.0	0	0		39.6

Brad Johnson

Year	Team		Att	Com	PC	Yds	Avg	TD	Int	Lg	Rtg
1994	MIN	N	37	22	59.5	150	4.1	0	0	15	68.5
1995			36	25	69.4	272	7.6	0	2	39	68.3
1996			311	195	62.7	2258	7.3	17	10	82t	89.4
Career			384	242	63.0	2680	7.0	17	12	82t	85.4
Playoffs			27	15	55.6	208	7.7	1	2		62.0

Cecil Johnson

Year	Team		Att	Com	PC	Yds	Avg	TD	Int	Lg	Rtg
1943	BKN	N	8	4	50.0	16	2.0	0	1	10	16.7
1944			25	10	40.0	193	7.7	2	4	58	54.7
Career			33	14	42.4	209	6.3	2	5	58	44.4

Charley Johnson

Year	Team		Att	Com	PC	Yds	Avg	TD	Int	Lg	Rtg
1961	STL	N	13	5	38.5	51	3.9	0	2	16	10.9
1962			308	150	48.7	2440	7.9	16	20	86t	65.9
1963			**423**	222	52.5	3280	7.8	28	21	78t	79.5
1964			**420**	**223**	53.1	**3045**	7.3	21	24	78t	69.4

Charley Johnson *continued*

Year	Team	Att	Com	PC	Yds	Avg	TD	Int	Lg	Rtg
1965		322	155	48.1	2439	7.6	18	15	78t	73.0
1966		205	103	50.2	1334	6.5	10	11	69t	65.0
1967		29	12	41.4	162	5.6	1	3	36t	31.8
1968		67	29	43.3	330	4.9	1	1	30	57.4
1969		260	131	50.4	1847	7.1	13	13	84t	69.5
1970	HOU N	281	144	51.2	1652	5.9	7	12	63t	59.8
1971		94	46	48.9	592	6.3	3	7	70t	48.7
1972	DEN N	238	132	55.5	1783	7.5	14	14	60	74.6
1973		346	184	53.2	2465	7.1	20	17	62t	74.9
1974		244	136	55.7	1969	8.1	13	9	73t	84.5
1975		142	65	45.8	1021	7.2	5	12	90t	46.7
Career		3392	1737	51.2	24410	7.2	170	181	90t	69.2

Curley Johnson

Year	Team	Att	Com	PC	Yds	Avg	TD	Int	Lg	Rtg
1964	NY A	1	0	0.0	0	0.0	0	0		39.6

Flip Johnson

Year	Team	Att	Com	PC	Yds	Avg	TD	Int	Lg	Rtg
1989	BUF N	0	0		0		0	0		

Gil Johnson

Year	Team	Att	Com	PC	Yds	Avg	TD	Int	Lg	Rtg
1949	B-NY AA	36	12	33.3	179	5.0	0	5		11.0

John Henry Johnson

Year	Team	Att	Com	PC	Yds	Avg	TD	Int	Lg	Rtg
1954	SF N	2	1	50.0	10	5.0	1	0	10t	104.2
1960	PIT N	1	1	100.0	15	15.0	1	0	15t	158.3
1961		2	0	0.0	0	0.0	0	1		39.6
Career		5	2	40.0	25	5.0	2	1	15t	56.3

Johnny Johnson

Year	Team	Att	Com	PC	Yds	Avg	TD	Int	Lg	Rtg
1990	PHX N	1	0	0.0	0	0.0	0	1		0.0

Lee Johnson

Year	Team	Att	Com	PC	Yds	Avg	TD	Int	Lg	Rtg
1990	CIN N	1	1	100.0	4	4.0	1	0	4t	122.9
1991		1	1	100.0	3	3.0	0	0	3	79.2
1993		1	0	0.0	0	0.0	0	0		39.6
1994		1	1	100.0	7	7.0	1	0	7t	135.4
1995		1	1	100.0	5	5.0	0	0	5	87.5
Career		5	4	80.0	19	3.8	2	0	7t	122.1

Norm Johnson

Year	Team	Att	Com	PC	Yds	Avg	TD	Int	Lg	Rtg
1982	SEA N	1	1	100.0	27	27.0	0	0	27	118.8

Randy Johnson

Year	Team	Att	Com	PC	Yds	Avg	TD	Int	Lg	Rtg
1966	ATL N	295	129	43.7	1795	6.1	12	21	53t	47.8
1967		288	142	49.3	1620	5.6	10	21	82t	47.8
1968		156	73	46.8	892	5.7	2	10	71t	42.5
1969		93	51	54.8	788	8.5	8	5	65t	89.4
1970		72	40	55.6	443	6.2	2	8	34	43.7
1972	NYG N	17	10	58.8	230	13.5	3	3	63t	103.2
1973		177	99	55.9	1279	7.2	7	8	48	73.2
1975	WAS N	79	41	51.9	556	7.0	4	10	36t	52.0
1976	GB N	35	21	60.0	249	7.1	0	1	45	69.8
Career		1212	606	50.0	7852	6.5	48	87	82t	54.0

Ray Johnson

Year	Team	Att	Com	PC	Yds	Avg	TD	Int	Lg	Rtg
1938	CLE N	5	3	60.0	45	9.0	0	1		50.0

Rob Johnson

Year	Team	Att	Com	PC	Yds	Avg	TD	Int	Lg	Rtg
1995	JAC N	7	3	42.9	24	3.4	0	1	19	12.5

Ron Johnson

Year	Team	Att	Com	PC	Yds	Avg	TD	Int	Lg	Rtg
1969	CLE N	1	0	0.0	0	0.0	0	0		39.6
1971	NYG N	74	41	55.4	477	6.4	3	3	45t	71.7
1972		1	0	0.0	0	0.0	0	0		39.6
Career		76	41	53.9	477	6.3	3	3	45t	69.9

Sammy Johnson

Year	Team	Att	Com	PC	Yds	Avg	TD	Int	Lg	Rtg
1975	SF N	2	0	0.0	0	0.0	0	0		39.6

Vance Johnson

Year	Team	Att	Com	PC	Yds	Avg	TD	Int	Lg	Rtg
1985	DEN N	1	0	0.0	0	0.0	0	0		39.6
1986		1	0	0.0	0	0.0	0	0		39.6
1987		1	0	0.0	0	0.0	0	0		39.6
1989		1	0	0.0	0	0.0	0	0		39.6
Career		4	0	0.0	0	0.0	0	0		39.6

Preston Johnston

Year	Team	Att	Com	PC	Yds	Avg	TD	Int	Lg	Rtg
1946	MIA AA	1	1	100.0	9	9.0	0	0	9	104.2

Charlie Joiner

Year	Team	Att	Com	PC	Yds	Avg	TD	Int	Lg	Rtg
1976	SD N	1	0	0.0	0	0.0	0	0		39.6

Art Jones

Year	Team	Att	Com	PC	Yds	Avg	TD	Int	Lg	Rtg
1941	PIT N	23	6	26.1	86	3.7	0	3	19	3.1

Bert Jones

Year	Team	Att	Com	PC	Yds	Avg	TD	Int	Lg	Rtg
1973	BAL N	108	43	39.8	539	5.0	4	12	51	28.8
1974		270	143	53.0	1610	6.0	8	12	57	62.4
1975		344	203	59.0	2483	7.2	18	8	90t	89.1
1976		343	207	60.3	**3104**	9.0	24	9	79t	102.5
1977		393	**224**	57.0	2686	6.8	17	11	78t	80.8
1978		42	27	64.3	370	8.8	4	1	78t	114.2
1979		92	43	46.7	643	7.0	3	3	59	67.4
1980		446	248	55.6	3134	7.0	23	21	47	75.3
1981		426	244	57.3	3094	7.3	21	20	67	76.9
1982	LARM N	87	48	55.2	527	6.1	2	4	51t	61.8
Career		2551	1430	56.1	18190	7.1	124	101	90t	78.2
Playoffs		62	29	46.8	399	6.4	1	2		59.8

Cedric Jones

Year	Team	Att	Com	PC	Yds	Avg	TD	Int	Lg	Rtg
1987	NE N	1	0	0.0	0	0.0	0	0		39.6

Dub Jones

Year	Team	Att	Com	PC	Yds	Avg	TD	Int	Lg	Rtg
1946	BKN AA	2	1	50.0	0	0.0	0	1	0	16.7
1947		15	3	20.0	37	2.5	0	2		0.0
1952	CLE N	2	1	50.0	3	1.5	1	0	3t	95.8
1953		1	0	0.0	0	0.0	0	0		39.6
Career		20	5	25.0	40	2.0	1	3	3t	16.7

Edgar Jones

Year	Team	Att	Com	PC	Yds	Avg	TD	Int	Lg	Rtg
1945	CHIB N	1	0	0.0	0	0.0	0	0		39.6
1946	CLE AA	4	1	25.0	4	1.0	0	0	4	39.6
1947		3	2	66.7	79	26.3	0	0	58	109.7
1949		1	0	0.0	0	0.0	0	0		39.6
Career		9	3	33.3	83	9.2	0	0	58	68.3
Playoffs		2	0	0.0	0	0.0	0	0		39.6

Hassan Jones

Year	Team	Att	Com	PC	Yds	Avg	TD	Int	Lg	Rtg
1991	MIN N	0	0		0		0	0		
1992		1	1	100.0	18	18.0	0	0	18	118.8
Career		1	1	100.0	18	18.0	0	0	18	118.8

James Jones

Year	Team	Att	Com	PC	Yds	Avg	TD	Int	Lg	Rtg
1985	DAL N	2	1	50.0	12	6.0	1	1	12t	68.8

James Jones

Year	Team	Att	Com	PC	Yds	Avg	TD	Int	Lg	Rtg
1983	DET N	2	0	0.0	0	0.0	0	0		39.6
1984		5	3	60.0	62	12.4	1	0	27	143.3
1985		1	0	0.0	0	0.0	0	0		39.6
1987		1	0	0.0	0	0.0	0	1		0.0
1988		1	0	0.0	0	0.0	0	0		39.6
Career		10	3	30.0	62	6.2	1	1	27	46.7

Jim Jones

Year	Team	Att	Com	PC	Yds	Avg	TD	Int	Lg	Rtg
1946	DET N	4	0	0.0	0	0.0	0	1		0.0

J.J. Jones

Year	Team	Att	Com	PC	Yds	Avg	TD	Int	Lg	Rtg
1975	NYJ N	57	16	28.1	181	3.2	1	5	20	9.6

June Jones

Year	Team	Att	Com	PC	Yds	Avg	TD	Int	Lg	Rtg
1977	ATL N	1	1	100.0	-1	-1.0	0	0	-1	79.2
1978		79	34	43.0	394	5.0	1	4	38t	41.9
1979		83	38	45.8	505	6.1	2	3	49	58.6
1981		3	2	66.7	25	8.3	0	0	14	92.4
Career		166	75	45.2	923	5.6	3	7	49	51.4

Keith Jones

Year	Team	Att	Com	PC	Yds	Avg	TD	Int	Lg	Rtg
1989	ATL N	1	0	0.0	0	0.0	0	0		39.6
1990		1	1	100.0	37	37.0	0	0	37	118.8
1992		1	0	0.0	0	0.0	0	0		39.6
Career		3	1	33.3	37	12.3	0	0	37	81.3

Spike Jones

Year	Team	Att	Com	PC	Yds	Avg	TD	Int	Lg	Rtg
1972	BUF N	2	1	50.0	4	2.0	0	0	4	56.3
1976	PHI N	1	1	100.0	-4	-4.0	0	0	-4	79.2
Career		3	2	66.7	0	0.0	0	0	4	70.1

Les Josephson

Year	Team	Att	Com	PC	Yds	Avg	TD	Int	Lg	Rtg
1965	LA N	2	1	50.0	15	7.5	1	0	15t	114.6
1967		5	2	40.0	47	9.4	0	1	24	35.0
1970		1	1	100.0	25	25.0	0	0	25	118.8
Career		8	4	50.0	87	10.9	1	1	25	89.1

Terry Joyce

Year	Team	Att	Com	PC	Yds	Avg	TD	Int	Lg	Rtg
1977	STL N	1	1	100.0	1	1.0	0	0		79.2

Year	Team		Att	Com	PC	Yds	Avg	TD	Int	Lg	Rtg

Sonny Jurgensen

Year	Team		Att	Com	PC	Yds	Avg	TD	Int	Lg	Rtg
1957	PHI	N	70	33	47.1	470	6.7	5	8	61t	53.6
1958			22	12	54.5	259	11.8	0	1	61	77.7
1959			5	3	60.0	27	5.4	1	0	19	114.2
1960			44	24	54.5	486	11.0	5	1	71	122.0
1961			416	235	56.5	3723	8.9	32	24	69	88.1
1962			366	196	53.6	3261	8.9	22	26	84	74.3
1963			184	99	53.8	1413	7.7	11	13	75t	69.4
1964	WAS	N	385	207	53.8	2934	7.6	24	13	80t	85.4
1965			356	190	53.4	2367	6.6	15	16	55t	69.6
1966			436	254	58.3	3209	7.4	28	19	86t	84.5
1967			508	288	56.7	3747	7.4	31	16	86t	87.3
1968			292	167	57.2	1980	6.8	17	11	99t	81.7
1969			442	274	62.0	3102	7.0	22	15	88t	85.4
1970			337	202	59.9	2354	7.0	23	10	66t	91.5
1971			28	16	57.1	170	6.1	0	2	30	45.2
1972			59	39	66.1	633	10.7	2	4	36t	84.9
1973			145	87	60.0	904	6.2	6	5	36	77.5
1974			167	107	64.1	1185	7.1	11	5	44	94.5
Career			4262	2433	57.1	32224	7.6	255	189	99t	82.6
Playoffs			12	6	50.0	78	6.5	0	3		31.3

Charlie Justice

Year	Team		Att	Com	PC	Yds	Avg	TD	Int	Lg	Rtg
1950	WAS	N	4	1	25.0	15	3.8	0	0	15	42.7
1952			1	0	0.0	0	0.0	0	1		0.0
1954			2	0	0.0	0	0.0	0	1		0.0
Career			7	1	14.3	15	2.1	0	2	15	0.0

Paul Justin

Year	Team		Att	Com	PC	Yds	Avg	TD	Int	Lg	Rtg
1995	IND	N	36	20	55.6	212	5.9	0	2	20	49.8
1996			127	74	58.3	839	6.6	2	0	38	83.4
Career			163	94	57.7	1051	6.4	2	2	38	76.0
Playoffs			1	1	100.0	6	6.0	0	0		91.7

Mike Kabealo

Year	Team		Att	Com	PC	Yds	Avg	TD	Int	Lg	Rtg
1944	CLE	N	1	1	100.0	54	54.0	1	0	54	158.3

Danny Kanell

Year	Team		Att	Com	PC	Yds	Avg	TD	Int	Lg	Rtg
1996	NYG	N	60	23	38.3	227	3.8	1	1	25	48.4

Ave Kaplan

Year	Team		Att	Com	PC	Yds	Avg	TD	Int	Lg	Rtg
1923	MIN	N						2			
1926	RI	A						1			
Career								3		54	

Joe Kapp

Year	Team		Att	Com	PC	Yds	Avg	TD	Int	Lg	Rtg
1967	MIN	N	214	102	47.7	1386	6.5	8	17	85t	48.2
1968			248	129	52.0	1695	6.8	10	17	61t	58.8
1969			237	120	50.6	1726	7.3	19	13	83t	78.5
1970	BOS	N	219	98	44.7	1104	5.0	3	17	48	32.6
Career			918	449	48.9	5911	6.4	40	64	85t	55.1
Playoffs			101	61	60.4	835	8.3	3	6		72.0

Ken Karcher

Year	Team		Att	Com	PC	Yds	Avg	TD	Int	Lg	Rtg
1987	DEN	N	102	56	54.9	628	6.2	5	4	49	73.5
1988			12	6	50.0	128	10.7	1	0	74t	116.0
Career			114	62	54.4	756	6.6	6	4	74t	78.0

John Karcis

Year	Team		Att	Com	PC	Yds	Avg	TD	Int	Lg	Rtg
1936	PIT	N	4	0	0.0	0	0.0	0	2		0.0
1937			3	1	33.3	2	0.7	1	1	2t	42.4
Career			7	1	14.3	2	0.3	1	3	2t	39.6

John Karrs

Year	Team		Att	Com	PC	Yds	Avg	TD	Int	Lg	Rtg
1944	CLE	N	10	4	40.0	49	4.9	0	4	23	16.3

Tony Kaska

Year	Team		Att	Com	PC	Yds	Avg	TD	Int	Lg	Rtg
1936	BKN	N	1	0	0.0	0	0.0	0	1		0.0

Eddie Kaw

Year	Team		Att	Com	PC	Yds	Avg	TD	Int	Lg	Rtg
1924	BUF	N						4			

Tom Keane

Year	Team		Att	Com	PC	Yds	Avg	TD	Int	Lg	Rtg
1951	LA	N	1	0	0.0	0	0.0	0	1		0.0
1954	BAL	N	1	1	100.0	0	0.0	0	0	0	79.2
Career			2	1	50.0	0	0.0	0	1	0	16.7

Val Keckin

Year	Team		Att	Com	PC	Yds	Avg	TD	Int	Lg	Rtg
1962	SD	A	9	5	55.6	64	7.1	0	4	25	38.4

Joe Keeble

Year	Team		Att	Com	PC	Yds	Avg	TD	Int	Lg	Rtg
1937	CLE	N	9	2	22.2	25	2.8	0	3		0.0

Jack Keefer

Year	Team		Att	Com	PC	Yds	Avg	TD	Int	Lg	Rtg
1926	PRO	N							1		

Rex Keeling

Year	Team		Att	Com	PC	Yds	Avg	TD	Int	Lg	Rtg
1968	CIN	A	1	0	0.0	0	0.0	0	0		39.6

Allen Keen

Year	Team		Att	Com	PC	Yds	Avg	TD	Int	Lg	Rtg
1937	PHI	N	6	1	16.7	86	14.3	1	0	86t	118.8

Gary Keithley

Year	Team		Att	Com	PC	Yds	Avg	TD	Int	Lg	Rtg
1973	STL	N	73	32	43.8	369	5.1	1	5	80t	35.7

Bill Kellagher

Year	Team		Att	Com	PC	Yds	Avg	TD	Int	Lg	Rtg
1946	CHI	AA	3	2	66.7	15	5.0	0	1		38.9

Mike Kelley

Year	Team		Att	Com	PC	Yds	Avg	TD	Int	Lg	Rtg
1987	SD	N	29	17	58.6	305	10.5	1	0	67	106.3

Bobby Kellogg

Year	Team		Att	Com	PC	Yds	Avg	TD	Int	Lg	Rtg
1940	CHIC	N	18	6	33.3	42	2.3	0	4		2.8

Bill Kelly

Year	Team		Att	Com	PC	Yds	Avg	TD	Int	Lg	Rtg
1927	NYY	N						6			
1928								7			
1929	FRA	N						3			
1930	BKN	N						6			
Career								22		86t	

Jim Kelly

Year	Team		Att	Com	PC	Yds	Avg	TD	Int	Lg	Rtg
1986	BUF	N	480	285	59.4	3593	7.5	22	17	84t	83.3
1987			419	250	59.7	2798	6.7	19	11	47	83.8
1988			452	269	59.5	3380	7.5	15	17	66t	78.2
1989			391	228	58.3	3130	8.0	25	18	78t	86.2
1990			346	219	63.3	2829	8.2	24	9	71	101.2
1991			474	304	64.1	3844	8.1	33	17	77t	97.6
1992			462	269	58.2	3457	7.5	23	19	65t	81.2
1993			470	288	61.3	3382	7.2	18	18	65t	79.9
1994			448	285	63.6	3114	7.0	22	17	83t	84.6
1995			458	255	55.7	3130	6.8	22	13	77t	81.1
1996			379	222	58.6	2810	7.4	14	19	67t	73.2
Career			4779	2874	60.1	35467	7.4	237	175	84t	84.4
Playoffs			545	322	59.1	3863	7.1	21	28		72.3

John Kelly

Year	Team		Att	Com	PC	Yds	Avg	TD	Int	Lg	Rtg
1937	BKN	N	12	2	16.7	21	1.8	0	3		0.0

Leroy Kelly

Year	Team		Att	Com	PC	Yds	Avg	TD	Int	Lg	Rtg
1966	CLE	N	1	0	0.0	0	0.0	0	0		39.6
1967			1	0	0.0	0	0.0	0	0		39.6
1968			4	1	25.0	34	8.5	1	0	34t	102.1
1969			5	1	20.0	36	7.2	1	0	36t	96.7
1971			4	1	25.0	23	5.8	0	0	23	51.0
1972			1	0	0.0	0	0.0	0	0		39.6
Career			16	3	18.8	93	5.8	2	0	36t	90.9

Jack Kemp

Year	Team		Att	Com	PC	Yds	Avg	TD	Int	Lg	Rtg
1957	PIT	N	18	8	44.4	88	4.9	0	2	21	19.9
1960	LA	A	406	211	52.0	3018	7.4	20	25	69	67.1
1961	SD	A	364	165	45.3	2686	7.4	15	22	91t	59.2
1962	SD-BUF	A	139	64	46.0	928	6.7	5	6		62.3
1963	BUF	A	384	194	50.5	2914	7.6	13	20	89t	65.4
1964			269	119	44.2	2285	8.5	13	26	94t	50.9
1965			391	179	45.8	2368	6.1	10	18	78	54.8
1966			389	166	42.7	2451	6.3	11	16	55	56.2
1967			369	161	43.6	2503	6.8	14	26	63t	56.0
1969			344	170	49.4	1981	5.8	13	22	55t	53.2
Career			3073	1437	46.8	21222	6.9	114	183	94t	57.4
Playoffs			160	78	48.8	1126	7.0	2	10		50.2

Jeff Kemp

Year	Team		Att	Com	PC	Yds	Avg	TD	Int	Lg	Rtg
1981	LA	N	6	2	33.3	25	4.2	0	1	19	7.6
1983	LARM	N	25	12	48.0	135	5.4	1	0	21	77.9
1984			284	143	50.4	2021	7.1	13	7	63t	78.7
1985			38	16	42.1	214	5.6	0	1	35	49.7
1986	SF	N	200	119	59.5	1554	7.8	11	8	66t	85.7
1987	SEA	N	33	23	69.7	396	12.0	5	1	55	137.1
1988			35	13	37.1	132	3.8	0	5	19	9.2
1991	SEA-PHI	N	295	151	51.2	1753	5.9	9	17	57	55.7
Career			916	479	52.3	6230	6.8	39	40	66t	70.0
Playoffs			37	18	48.6	173	4.7	0	1		50.8

Jim Kendrick

Year	Team		Att	Com	PC	Yds	Avg	TD	Int	Lg	Rtg
1925	BUF	N							1		

Jim Kendrick continued

Year	Team		Att	Com	PC	Yds	Avg	TD	Int	Lg	Rtg
1926								5			
Career								6			

Bob Kennedy

Year	Team		Att	Com	PC	Yds	Avg	TD	Int	Lg	Rtg
1946	NY	AA	6	2	33.3	45	7.5	0	3		21.5
1947			3	2	66.7	56	18.7	0	0		109.7
1948			1	0	0.0	0	0.0	0	0		39.6
1949	B-NY	AA	1	1	100.0	27	27.0	0	0		118.8
Career			11	5	45.5	128	11.6	0	3		48.9

Tom Kennedy

Year	Team		Att	Com	PC	Yds	Avg	TD	Int	Lg	Rtg
1966	NYG	N	100	55	55.0	748	7.5	7	6	82t	77.4

Bill Kenney

Year	Team		Att	Com	PC	Yds	Avg	TD	Int	Lg	Rtg
1980	KC	N	69	37	53.6	542	7.9	5	2	75t	91.6
1981			274	147	53.6	1983	7.2	9	16	64t	63.6
1982			169	95	56.2	1192	7.1	7	6	51	77.3
1983			603	346	57.4	4348	7.2	24	18	53	80.8
1984			282	151	53.5	2098	7.4	15	10	65t	80.7
1985			338	181	53.6	2536	7.5	17	9	84t	83.6
1986			308	161	52.3	1922	6.2	13	11	53	70.8
1987			273	154	56.4	2107	7.7	15	9	81t	85.8
1988			114	58	50.9	549	4.8	0	5	25	46.3
Career			2430	1330	54.7	17277	7.1	105	86	84t	77.0
Playoffs			16	8	50.0	97	6.1	0	0		69.0

Ralph Kercheval

Year	Team		Att	Com	PC	Yds	Avg	TD	Int	Lg	Rtg
1936	BKN	N	25	6	24.0	92	3.7	0	3		2.8
1937			19	11	57.9	154	8.1	1	1		79.7
1938			9	3	33.3	98	10.9	0	1		35.6
1939			1	1	100.0	7	7.0	0	0	7	95.8
1940			7	4	57.1	38	5.4	1	0		111.9
Career			61	25	41.0	389	6.4	2	5	7	39.6

Gary Kerkorian

Year	Team		Att	Com	PC	Yds	Avg	TD	Int	Lg	Rtg
1952	PIT	N	11	5	45.5	79	7.2	1	3	27	60.6
1954	BAL	N	217	117	53.9	1515	7.0	9	12	78t	66.9
1955			29	15	51.7	209	7.2	1	3	48	47.1
1956			2	2	100.0	59	29.5	1	0	40	158.3
Career			259	139	53.7	1862	7.2	12	18	78t	63.2

Mike Kerrigan

Year	Team		Att	Com	PC	Yds	Avg	TD	Int	Lg	Rtg
1983	NE	N	14	6	42.9	72	5.1	0	1	19	29.5
1984			1	1	100.0	13	13.0	0	0	13	118.8
Career			15	7	46.7	85	5.7	0	1	19	36.8

Leroy Keyes

Year	Team		Att	Com	PC	Yds	Avg	TD	Int	Lg	Rtg
1969	PHI	N	2	1	50.0	14	7.0	0	0	14	72.9
1973	KC	N	1	0	0.0	0	0.0	0	0		39.6
Career			3	1	33.3	14	4.7	0	0	14	49.3

Jon Keyworth

Year	Team		Att	Com	PC	Yds	Avg	TD	Int	Lg	Rtg
1979	DEN	N	1	1	100.0	32	32.0	1	0	32t	158.3

John Kidd

Year	Team		Att	Com	PC	Yds	Avg	TD	Int	Lg	Rtg
1985	BUF	N	0	0		0		0	0		
1987			1	0	0.0	0	0.0	0	0		39.6
Career			1	0	0.0	0	0.0	0	0		39.6
Playoffs			1	0	0.0	0	0.0	0	0		39.6

Blair Kiel

Year	Team		Att	Com	PC	Yds	Avg	TD	Int	Lg	Rtg
1986	IND	N	25	11	44.0	236	9.4	2	0	50	104.8
1987			33	17	51.5	195	5.9	1	3	21	41.9
1990	GB	N	85	51	60.0	504	5.9	2	2	22	74.8
1991			50	29	58.0	361	7.2	3	2	35	83.8
Career			193	108	56.0	1296	6.7	8	7	50	75.4

George Kiick

Year	Team		Att	Com	PC	Yds	Avg	TD	Int	Lg	Rtg
1940	PIT	N	2	0		0		0	1		0.0

Jim Kiick

Year	Team		Att	Com	PC	Yds	Avg	TD	Int	Lg	Rtg
1968	MIA	A	1	0	0.0	0	0.0	0	0		39.6
1970	MIA	N	1	1	100.0	25	25.0	0	0	25	118.8
1974			1	1	100.0	13	13.0	0	0	13	118.8
Career			3	2	66.7	38	12.7	0	0	25	109.7

Jon Kilgore

Year	Team		Att	Com	PC	Yds	Avg	TD	Int	Lg	Rtg
1966	LA	N	1	1	100.0	47	47.0	0	0	47	118.8
1968	CHI	N	1	0	0.0	0	0.0	0	0		39.6
Career			2	1	50.0	47	23.5	0	0	47	95.8

Billy Kilmer

Year	Team		Att	Com	PC	Yds	Avg	TD	Int	Lg	Rtg
1961	SF	N	34	19	55.9	286	8.4	0	4	28	44.1

Billy Kilmer continued

Year	Team		Att	Com	PC	Yds	Avg	TD	Int	Lg	Rtg
1962			13	8	61.5	191	14.7	1	3	73	91.5
1964			14	8	57.1	92	6.6	1	1	24	71.1
1966			16	5	31.3	84	5.3	0	1	26	24.0
1967	NO	N	204	97	47.5	1341	6.6	6	11	96	56.4
1968			315	167	53.0	2060	6.5	15	17	51	66.9
1969			360	193	53.6	2532	7.0	20	17	52	74.9
1970			237	135	57.0	1557	6.6	6	17	46t	55.5
1971	WAS	N	306	166	54.2	2221	7.3	13	13	71t	74.0
1972			225	120	53.3	1648	7.3	19	11	89t	84.8
1973			227	122	53.7	1656	7.3	14	9	64t	81.3
1974			234	137	58.5	1632	7.0	10	6	51	83.5
1975			346	178	51.4	2440	7.1	23	16	96t	77.2
1976			206	108	52.4	1252	6.1	12	10	53t	70.3
1977			201	99	49.3	1187	5.9	8	7	59t	66.5
1978			46	23	50.0	316	6.9	4	3	50t	74.2
Career			2984	1585	53.1	20495	6.9	152	146	96t	71.6
Playoffs			178	92	51.7	1060	6.0	8	7		68.6

Todd Kinchen

Year	Team		Att	Com	PC	Yds	Avg	TD	Int	Lg	Rtg
1995	STL	N	1	0	0.0	0	0.0	0	0		39.6

Keith Kinderman

Year	Team		Att	Com	PC	Yds	Avg	TD	Int	Lg	Rtg
1964	SD	A	1	0	0.0	0	0.0	0	0		39.6

Andy King

Year	Team		Att	Com	PC	Yds	Avg	TD	Int	Lg	Rtg
1920	AKR	A							3		
1921									4		
1922	AKR	N							2		
Career									9		

Horace King

Year	Team		Att	Com	PC	Yds	Avg	TD	Int	Lg	Rtg
1975	DET	N	1	0	0.0	0	0.0	0	0		39.6
1978			0	0		0		0	0		
Career			1	0	0.0	0	0.0	0	0		39.6

Phil King

Year	Team		Att	Com	PC	Yds	Avg	TD	Int	Lg	Rtg
1966	MIN	N	1	1	100.0	9	9.0	0	0	9	104.2
Playoffs			1	0	0.0	0	0.0	0	0		39.6

Terry Kirby

Year	Team		Att	Com	PC	Yds	Avg	TD	Int	Lg	Rtg
1995	MIA	N	1	1	100.0	31	31.0	1	0	31t	158.3
1996	SF	N	2	1	50.0	24	12.0	1	0	24t	133.3
Career			3	2	66.7	55	18.3	2	0	31t	149.3

Mike Kirkland

Year	Team		Att	Com	PC	Yds	Avg	TD	Int	Lg	Rtg
1978	BAL	N	41	19	46.3	211	5.1	1	8	34	30.7

Frank Kirkleski

Year	Team		Att	Com	PC	Yds	Avg	TD	Int	Lg	Rtg
1927	POT	N							3		
1929	ORA	N							1		
1930	NEW	N							3		
Career									7	34	

Roger Kirkman

Year	Team		Att	Com	PC	Yds	Avg	TD	Int	Lg	Rtg
1933	PHI	N	73	22	30.1	354	4.8	3	13		21.5
1934									1		
1935									1		
Career			73	22	30.1	354	4.8	5	13		21.5

Perry Klein

Year	Team		Att	Com	PC	Yds	Avg	TD	Int	Lg	Rtg
1994	ATL	N	1	0	0.0	0	0.0	0	0		39.6

David Klingler

Year	Team		Att	Com	PC	Yds	Avg	TD	Int	Lg	Rtg
1992	CIN	N	98	47	48.0	530	5.4	3	2	83t	66.3
1993			343	190	55.4	1935	5.6	6	9	51	66.6
1994			231	131	56.7	1327	5.7	6	9	56	65.7
1995			15	7	46.7	88	5.9	1	1	33	59.9
1996	OAK	N	24	10	41.7	87	3.6	0	0	20	51.9
Career			711	385	54.1	3967	5.6	16	21	83t	65.6

Don Klosterman

Year	Team		Att	Com	PC	Yds	Avg	TD	Int	Lg	Rtg
1952	LA	N	10	3	30.0	47	4.7	0	3	30	7.1

Jeff Knapple

Year	Team		Att	Com	PC	Yds	Avg	TD	Int	Lg	Rtg
1980	DEN	N	4	1	25.0	15	3.8	0	0	15	42.7

Curt Knight

Year	Team		Att	Com	PC	Yds	Avg	TD	Int	Lg	Rtg
1969	WAS	N	1	0	0.0	0	0.0	0	1		0.0

Johnny Knolla

Year	Team		Att	Com	PC	Yds	Avg	TD	Int	Lg	Rtg
1942	CHIC	N	6	1	16.7	16	2.7	0	0	16	39.6

Johnny Knolla continued

Year	Team		Att	Com	PC	Yds	Avg	TD	Int	Lg	Rtg
1945			1	0	0.0	0	0.0	0	0		39.6
Career			7	1	14.3	16	2.3	0	0	16	39.6

Mickey Kobrosky

Year	Team		Att	Com	PC	Yds	Avg	TD	Int	Lg	Rtg
1937	NYG	N	13	2	15.4	18	1.4	0	2		0.0

Bob Koehler

Year	Team		Att	Com	PC	Yds	Avg	TD	Int	Lg	Rtg
1922	CHIC	N							1		

Matt Kofler

Year	Team		Att	Com	PC	Yds	Avg	TD	Int	Lg	Rtg
1983	BUF	N	61	35	57.4	440	7.2	4	3	28t	81.3
1984			93	33	35.5	432	4.6	2	5	70t	35.8
1985	IND	N	48	23	47.9	284	5.9	1	3	33t	47.6
Career			202	91	45.0	1156	5.7	7	11	70t	52.3

Mike Koken

Year	Team		Att	Com	PC	Yds	Avg	TD	Int	Lg	Rtg
1933	CHIC	N							1		

Jeff Komlo

Year	Team		Att	Com	PC	Yds	Avg	TD	Int	Lg	Rtg
1979	DET	N	368	183	49.7	2238	6.1	11	23	40	52.8
1980			4	2	50.0	26	6.5	0	1	20	31.3
1981			57	29	50.9	290	5.1	1	3	46	49.6
1983	TB	N	8	4	50.0	49	6.1	0	1	17	29.7
Career			437	218	49.9	2603	6.0	12	28	46	50.9

Dave Kopay

Year	Team		Att	Com	PC	Yds	Avg	TD	Int	Lg	Rtg
1964	SF	N	1	0	0.0	0	0.0	0	0		39.6

Joe Kopcha

Year	Team		Att	Com	PC	Yds	Avg	TD	Int	Lg	Rtg
1935	CHIB	N	1	0	0.0	0	0.0	0	0		39.6

Walt Koppisch

Year	Team		Att	Com	PC	Yds	Avg	TD	Int	Lg	Rtg
1926	NYG	N							1		

Bernie Kosar

Year	Team		Att	Com	PC	Yds	Avg	TD	Int	Lg	Rtg
1985	CLE	N	248	124	50.0	1578	6.4	8	7	68t	69.3
1986			531	310	58.4	3854	7.3	17	10	72t	83.8
1987			389	241	62.0	3033	7.8	22	9	54t	95.4
1988			259	156	60.2	1890	7.3	10	7	77t	84.3
1989			513	303	59.1	3533	6.9	18	14	97t	80.3
1990			423	230	54.4	2562	6.1	10	15	50	65.7
1991			494	307	62.1	3487	7.1	18	9	71t	87.8
1992			155	103	66.5	1160	7.5	8	7	69t	87.0
1993	CLE-DAL	N	201	115	57.2	1217	6.1	8	3	86	82.0
1994	MIA	N	12	7	58.3	80	6.7	1	1	22	71.5
1995			108	74	68.5	699	6.5	3	5	31t	76.1
1996			32	24	75.0	208	6.5	1	0	20	102.1
Career			3365	1994	59.3	23301	6.9	124	87	97t	81.8
Playoffs			270	152	56.3	1953	7.2	16	10		83.5

Stan Kosel

Year	Team		Att	Com	PC	Yds	Avg	TD	Int	Lg	Rtg
1938	BKN	N	1	0	0.0	0	0.0	0	0		39.6

Stan Kostka

Year	Team		Att	Com	PC	Yds	Avg	TD	Int	Lg	Rtg
1935	BKN	N							1		

Eddie Kotal

Year	Team		Att	Com	PC	Yds	Avg	TD	Int	Lg	Rtg
1926	GB	N							1		
1928									1		
Career									2		

Ernie Koy

Year	Team		Att	Com	PC	Yds	Avg	TD	Int	Lg	Rtg
1965	NYG	N	2	0	0.0	0	0.0	0	1		0.0
1966			2	0	0.0	0	0.0	0	0		39.6
1967			4	3	75.0	101	25.3	1	0	68t	156.3
1968			3	2	66.7	13	4.3	0	0	11	75.7
1969	NY	N	1	1	100.0	15	15.0	0	0	15	118.8
Career			12	6	50.0	129	10.8	1	1	68t	81.6

Erik Kramer

Year	Team		Att	Com	PC	Yds	Avg	TD	Int	Lg	Rtg
1987	ATL	N	92	45	48.9	559	6.1	4	5	33	60.0
1991	DET	N	265	136	51.3	1635	6.2	11	8	73t	71.8
1992			106	58	54.7	771	7.3	4	8	77t	59.1
1993			138	87	63.0	1002	7.3	8	3	48	95.1
1994	CHI	N	158	99	62.7	1129	7.1	8	8	85t	79.9
1995			522	315	60.3	3838	7.4	29	10	76t	93.5
1996			150	73	48.7	781	5.2	3	6	58t	54.3
Career			1431	813	56.8	9715	6.8	67	48	85t	79.3
Playoffs			130	91	70.0	999	7.7	6	3		98.2

Ron Kramer

Year	Team		Att	Com	PC	Yds	Avg	TD	Int	Lg	Rtg
1957	GB	N	1	0	0.0	0	0.0	0	1		0.0

Tommy Kramer

Year	Team		Att	Com	PC	Yds	Avg	TD	Int	Lg	Rtg
1977	MIN	N	57	30	52.6	425	7.5	5	4	69t	77.0
1978			16	5	31.3	50	3.1	0	1	19	15.1
1979			566	315	55.7	3397	6.0	23	24	55t	69.3
1980			522	299	57.3	3582	6.9	19	23	76t	72.2
1981			593	322	54.3	3912	6.6	26	24	63	72.6
1982			308	176	57.1	2037	6.6	15	12	65	77.3
1983			82	55	67.1	550	6.7	3	4	49	77.8
1984			236	124	52.5	1678	7.1	9	10	70t	70.6
1985			506	277	54.7	3522	7.0	19	26	57t	67.8
1986			372	208	55.9	3000	8.1	24	10	76t	92.6
1987			81	40	49.4	452	5.6	4	3	40t	67.5
1988			173	83	48.0	1264	7.3	5	9	47	60.5
1989			136	77	56.6	906	6.7	7	7	39	72.7
1990	NO	N	3	1	33.3	2	0.7	0	1	2	2.8
Career			3651	2012	55.1	24777	6.8	159	158	76t	72.8
Playoffs			140	71	50.7	874	6.2	3	7		56.7

Paul Krause

Year	Team		Att	Com	PC	Yds	Avg	TD	Int	Lg	Rtg
1972	MIN	N	1	0	0.0	0	0.0	0	0		39.6
1977			1	1	100.0	11	11.0	1	0	11t	152.1
Career			2	1	50.0	11	5.5	1	0	11t	106.3

Steve Kreider

Year	Team		Att	Com	PC	Yds	Avg	TD	Int	Lg	Rtg
1979	CIN	N	0	0		0		0	0		
1980			1	0	0.0	0	0.0	0	0		39.6
1981			3	1	33.3	13	4.3	0	0	13	47.9
1983			1	0	0.0	0	0.0	0	0		39.6
1985			1	1	100.0	1	1.0	0	0	1	79.2
1986			1	0	0.0	0	0.0	0	1		0.0
Career			7	2	28.6	14	2.0	0	1	13	0.0

Dave Krieg

Year	Team		Att	Com	PC	Yds	Avg	TD	Int	Lg	Rtg
1980	SEA	N	2	0	0.0	0	0.0	0	0		39.6
1981			112	64	57.1	843	7.5	7	5	57t	83.3
1982			78	49	62.8	501	6.4	2	2	44	79.1
1983			243	147	60.5	2139	8.8	18	11	50t	95.0
1984			480	276	57.5	3671	7.6	32	24	80t	83.3
1985			532	285	53.6	3602	6.8	27	20	54	76.2
1986			375	225	60.0	2921	7.8	21	11	72	91.0
1987			294	178	60.5	2131	7.2	23	15	75t	87.6
1988			228	134	58.8	1741	7.6	18	8	75t	94.6
1989			499	286	57.3	3309	6.6	21	20	60t	74.8
1990			448	265	59.2	3194	7.1	15	20	63t	73.6
1991			285	187	65.6	2080	7.3	11	12	60	82.5
1992	KC	N	413	230	55.7	3115	7.5	15	12	77t	79.9
1993			189	105	55.6	1238	6.6	7	3	66t	81.4
1994	DET	N	212	131	61.8	1629	7.7	14	3	51t	101.7
1995	ARI	N	521	304	58.3	3554	6.8	16	21	48	72.6
1996	CHI	N	377	226	59.9	2278	6.0	14	12	53t	76.3
Career			5288	3092	58.5	37946	7.2	261	199	80t	81.5
Playoffs			282	144	51.1	1895	6.7	11	9		72.3

Mike Kruczek

Year	Team		Att	Com	PC	Yds	Avg	TD	Int	Lg	Rtg
1976	PIT	N	85	51	60.0	758	8.9	0	3	64	74.5
1977			7	2	28.6	19	2.7	0	0	13	39.6
1978			11	5	45.5	46	4.2	0	2	21	17.8
1979			20	13	65.0	153	7.7	0	1	31	67.3
1980	WAS	N	31	22	71.0	209	6.7	0	2	41	62.4
Career			154	93	60.4	1185	7.7	0	8	64	62.8
Playoffs			6	5	83.3	44	7.3	0	0		97.2

Johnny Ksionzyk

Year	Team		Att	Com	PC	Yds	Avg	TD	Int	Lg	Rtg
1947	LA	N	7	1	14.3	17	2.4	0	2	17	0.0

Gary Kubiak

Year	Team		Att	Com	PC	Yds	Avg	TD	Int	Lg	Rtg
1983	DEN	N	22	12	54.5	186	8.5	1	1	78t	79.0
1984			75	44	58.7	440	5.9	4	1	41	87.6
1985			5	2	40.0	61	12.2	1	0	54t	125.8
1986			38	23	60.5	249	6.6	1	3	26	55.7
1987			7	3	42.9	25	3.6	0	2	17	13.1
1988			69	43	62.3	497	7.2	5	3	68t	90.1
1989			55	32	58.2	284	5.2	2	2	22	69.1
1990			22	11	50.0	145	6.6	0	4	36	31.6
1991			5	3	60.0	33	6.6	0	0	14	79.6
Career			298	173	58.1	1920	6.4	14	16	78t	70.6
Playoffs			19	16	84.2	212	11.2	0	0		113.2

Waddy Kuehl

Year	Team		Att	Com	PC	Yds	Avg	TD	Int	Lg	Rtg
1922	BUF	N							1		

Craig Kupp

Year	Team		Att	Com	PC	Yds	Avg	TD	Int	Lg	Rtg
1991	PHX	N	7	3	42.9	23	3.3	0	0	11	51.5

Year	Team		Att	Com	PC	Yds	Avg	TD	Int	Lg	Rtg

Johnny Kusko

Year	Team		Att	Com	PC	Yds	Avg	TD	Int	Lg	Rtg
1936	PHI	N	27	6	22.2	108	4.0	0	9		4.2
1937			7	2	28.6	11	1.6	0	2		0.0
Career			34	8	23.5	119	3.5	0	11	11	2.1

Lou Kusserow

Year	Team		Att	Com	PC	Yds	Avg	TD	Int	Lg	Rtg
1949	B-NY	AA	1	0	0.0	0	0.0	0	0		39.6

Steve Lach

Year	Team		Att	Com	PC	Yds	Avg	TD	Int	Lg	Rtg
1946	PIT	N	1	0	0.0	0	0.0	0	0	..	39.6
1947			5	2	40.0	12	2.4	1	0	6	87.5
Career			6	2	33.3	12	2.0	1	0	6	81.9

Rick Lackman

Year	Team		Att	Com	PC	Yds	Avg	TD	Int	Lg	Rtg
1935	PHI	N	1	1	100.0	8	8.0	0	0	8	100.0

Warren Lahr

Year	Team		Att	Com	PC	Yds	Avg	TD	Int	Lg	Rtg
1954	CLE	N	1	0	0.0	0	0.0	0	1		0.0

Roddy Lamb

Year	Team		Att	Com	PC	Yds	Avg	TD	Int	Lg	Rtg
1925	RI	N						3			

Curly Lambeau

Year	Team		Att	Com	PC	Yds	Avg	TD	Int	Lg	Rtg
1921	GB	A						1			
1922	GB	N						2			
1923								3			
1924								8			
1925								5			
1926								3			
1927								1			
1928								1			
Career								24			

Daryle Lamonica

Year	Team		Att	Com	PC	Yds	Avg	TD	Int	Lg	Rtg
1963	BUF	A	71	33	46.5	437	6.2	3	4		57.1
1964			128	55	43.0	1137	8.9	6	8		64.5
1965			70	29	41.4	376	5.4	3	6	74	37.6
1966			84	33	39.3	549	6.5	4	5	55	53.1
1967	OAK	A	425	220	51.8	3228	7.6	30	20	72	80.8
1968			416	206	49.5	3245	7.8	25	15	82	80.9
1969			426	221	51.9	3302	7.8	34	25	80t	79.8
1970	OAK	N	356	179	50.3	2516	7.1	22	15	60t	76.5
1971			242	118	48.8	1717	7.1	16	16	67t	66.8
1972			281	149	53.0	1998	7.1	18	12	70t	79.5
1973			93	42	45.2	614	6.6	2	8	48	38.6
1974			9	3	33.3	35	3.9	1	4	13	43.5
Career			2601	1288	49.5	19154	7.4	164	138	82	72.9
Playoffs			263	117	44.5	1928	7.3	19	10		77.9

Sean Landeta

Year	Team		Att	Com	PC	Yds	Avg	TD	Int	Lg	Rtg
1985	NYG	N	1	0	0.0	0	0.0	0	0		39.6

Greg Landry

Year	Team		Att	Com	PC	Yds	Avg	TD	Int	Lg	Rtg
1968	DET	N	48	23	47.9	338	7.0	2	7	80t	45.7
1969			160	80	50.0	853	5.3	4	10	43	48.3
1970			136	83	61.0	1072	7.9	9	5	58	92.5
1971			261	136	52.1	2237	8.6	16	13	76t	80.9
1972			268	134	50.0	2066	7.7	18	17	82t	71.8
1973			128	70	54.7	908	7.1	3	10	84t	52.5
1974			82	49	59.8	572	7.0	3	3	45	77.9
1975			56	31	55.4	403	7.2	1	0	36	84.2
1976			291	168	57.7	2191	7.5	17	8	74t	89.6
1977			240	135	56.3	1359	5.7	6	7	39	68.7
1978			77	48	62.3	452	5.9	1	1	20	77.4
1979	BAL	N	457	270	59.1	2932	6.4	15	15	67t	75.3
1980			47	24	51.1	275	5.9	2	3	32	56.6
1981			29	14	48.3	195	6.7	0	1	34	56.0
1984	CHI	N	20	11	55.0	199	9.9	1	3	55t	66.5
Career			2300	1276	55.5	16052	7.0	98	103	84t	72.9
Playoffs			12	5	41.7	48	4.0	0	0		53.5

Tom Landry

Year	Team		Att	Com	PC	Yds	Avg	TD	Int	Lg	Rtg
1952	NYG	N	47	11	23.4	172	3.7	1	7	70t	9.8

Eric Lane

Year	Team		Att	Com	PC	Yds	Avg	TD	Int	Lg	Rtg
1982	SEA	N	1	0	0.0	0	0.0	0	0		39.6

Gary Lane

Year	Team		Att	Com	PC	Yds	Avg	TD	Int	Lg	Rtg
1967	CLE	N	43	21	48.8	254	5.9	2	1	23	73.2

MacArthur Lane

Year	Team		Att	Com	PC	Yds	Avg	TD	Int	Lg	Rtg
1972	GB	N	2	2	100.0	19	9.5	0	0	10	106.3
1973			2	1	50.0	23	11.5	1	0	23t	131.3
1974			1	0	0.0	0	0.0	0	0		39.6

MacArthur Lane *continued*

Year	Team		Att	Com	PC	Yds	Avg	TD	Int	Lg	Rtg
1976	KC	N	0	0		0		0	0		
Career			5	3	60.0	42	8.4	1	0	23t	126.7

Gene Lang

Year	Team		Att	Com	PC	Yds	Avg	TD	Int	Lg	Rtg
1987	DEN	N	1	0	0.0	0	0.0	0	0		39.6

Izzy Lang

Year	Team		Att	Com	PC	Yds	Avg	TD	Int	Lg	Rtg
1966	PHI	N	3	2	66.7	51	17.0	0	0	36	109.7
1967			1	1	100.0	26	26.0	0	0	26	118.8
Career			4	3	75.0	77	19.3	0	0	36	116.7

Grenny Lansdell

Year	Team		Att	Com	PC	Yds	Avg	TD	Int	Lg	Rtg
1940	NYG	N	3	2	66.7	23	7.7	1	0		129.2

Bob Laraba

Year	Team		Att	Com	PC	Yds	Avg	TD	Int	Lg	Rtg
1960	LA	A	7	2	28.6	23	3.3	0	2	16	1.2

Steve Largent

Year	Team		Att	Com	PC	Yds	Avg	TD	Int	Lg	Rtg
1976	SEA	N	1	0	0.0	0	0.0	0	0		39.6
1981			1	0	0.0	0	0.0	0	0		39.6
1983			1	1	100.0	11	11.0	0	0	11	112.5
1985			1	0	0.0	0	0.0	0	0		39.6
1986			1	1	100.0	18	18.0	0	0	18	118.8
1987			2	0	0.0	0	0.0	0	0		39.6
Career			7	2	28.6	29	4.1	0	0	18	44.3

Jack Larscheid

Year	Team		Att	Com	PC	Yds	Avg	TD	Int	Lg	Rtg
1960	OAK	A	6	3	50.0	71	11.8	0	2		53.5
1961			1	0	0.0	0	0.0	0	1		0.0
Career			7	3	42.9	71	10.1	0	3		40.5

Paul Larson

Year	Team		Att	Com	PC	Yds	Avg	TD	Int	Lg	Rtg
1957	CHIC	N	14	6	42.9	61	4.4	0	1	21	26.2

Yale Lary

Year	Team		Att	Com	PC	Yds	Avg	TD	Int	Lg	Rtg
1957	DET	N	1	0	0.0	0	0.0	0	0		39.6
1958			1	0	0.0	0	0.0	0	0		39.6
1959			1	0	0.0	0	0.0	0	0		39.6
1962			1	0	0.0	0	0.0	0	0		39.6
Career			4	0	0.0	0	0.0	0	0		39.6

Jim Lash

Year	Team		Att	Com	PC	Yds	Avg	TD	Int	Lg	Rtg
1975	MIN	N	1	0	0.0	0	0.0	0	0		39.6

Tony Latone

Year	Team		Att	Com	PC	Yds	Avg	TD	Int	Lg	Rtg
1928	POT	N							1		

Chuck Latourette

Year	Team		Att	Com	PC	Yds	Avg	TD	Int	Lg	Rtg
1968	STL	N	1	0	0.0	0	0.0	0	0		39.6

Hal Lauer

Year	Team		Att	Com	PC	Yds	Avg	TD	Int	Lg	Rtg
1923	TOL	N							1		

Babe Laufenberg

Year	Team		Att	Com	PC	Yds	Avg	TD	Int	Lg	Rtg
1988	SD	N	144	69	47.9	778	5.4	4	5	47t	59.3
1990	DAL	N	67	24	35.8	279	4.2	1	6	27t	16.9
Career			211	93	44.1	1057	5.0	5	11	47t	45.9

Hank Lauricella

Year	Team		Att	Com	PC	Yds	Avg	TD	Int	Lg	Rtg
1952	DAL	N	22	11	50.0	177	8.0	4	2	34t	79.0

Jimmy Lawrence

Year	Team		Att	Com	PC	Yds	Avg	TD	Int	Lg	Rtg
1936	CHIC	N	2	0	0.0	0	0.0	0	1		0.0
1937			3	0	0.0	0	0.0	0	0		39.6
1938			11	3	27.3	65	5.9	0	4		12.1
1939	GB	N	4	1	25.0	15	3.8	0	1	15	3.1
Career			20	4	20.0	80	4.0	0	6	15	4.2

Larry Lawrence

Year	Team		Att	Com	PC	Yds	Avg	TD	Int	Lg	Rtg
1974	OAK	N	11	4	36.4	29	2.6	0	1	17	7.0
1975			15	5	33.3	50	3.3	0	1	17	16.0
1976	TB	N	5	0	0.0	0	0.0	0	2		0.0
Career			31	9	29.0	79	2.5	0	4	17	0.0

Joe Laws

Year	Team		Att	Com	PC	Yds	Avg	TD	Int	Lg	Rtg
1935	GB	N	1	1	100.0	8	8.0	0	0	8	100.0
1936			4	1	25.0	22	5.5	1	0	22t	89.6
1937			11	5	45.5	42	3.8	1	2		46.6
1938			5	0	0.0	0	0.0	0	2		0.0
1939			1	0	0.0	0	0.0	0	0		39.6
1942			3	2	66.7	76	25.3	1	0	62	149.3
1944			4	1	25.0	15	3.8	0	1	15	3.1
Career			29	10	34.5	163	5.6	3	5	62	49.1

Year	Team		Att	Com	PC	Yds	Avg	TD	Int	Lg	Rtg

Pete Layden

Year	Team		Att	Com	PC	Yds	Avg	TD	Int	Lg	Rtg
1948	NY	AA	105	43	41.0	816	7.8	9	8	70t	65.4
1949	B-NY	AA	10	2	20.0	25	2.5	0	1		0.0
Career			115	45	39.1	841	7.3	9	9	70t	58.6

Bobby Layne

Year	Team		Att	Com	PC	Yds	Avg	TD	Int	Lg	Rtg
1948	CHIB	N	52	16	30.8	232	4.5	3	2	35	49.5
1949	NYB	N	299	155	51.8	1796	6.0	9	18	69	55.3
1950	DET	N	336	152	45.2	2323	6.9	16	18	82t	62.1
1951			332	152	45.8	2403	7.2	26	23	63	67.6
1952			287	139	48.4	1999	7.0	19	20	77t	64.5
1953			273	125	45.8	2088	7.6	16	21	97t	59.6
1954			246	135	54.9	1818	7.4	14	12	55	77.3
1955			270	143	53.0	1830	6.8	11	17	77t	61.8
1956			244	129	52.9	1909	7.8	9	17	70	62.0
1957			179	87	48.6	1169	6.5	6	12	65t	53.0
1958	DET-PIT	N	294	145	49.3	2510	8.5	14	12	78t	77.6
1959	PIT	N	297	142	47.8	1986	6.7	20	21	48	62.8
1960			209	103	49.3	1814	8.7	13	17	70	66.2
1961			149	75	50.3	1205	8.1	11	16	53	62.8
1962			233	116	49.8	1686	7.2	9	17	62	56.2
Career			3700	1814	49.0	26768	7.2	196	243	97t	63.4
Playoffs			97	46	47.4	568	5.9	1	12		29.9

Robert Leahy

Year	Team		Att	Com	PC	Yds	Avg	TD	Int	Lg	Rtg
1971	PIT		11	3	27.3	18	1.6	0	1	9	1.7

Roosevelt Leaks

Year	Team		Att	Com	PC	Yds	Avg	TD	Int	Lg	Rtg
1981	BUF	N	1	0	0.0	0	0.0	0	0		39.6

Eddie LeBaron

Year	Team		Att	Com	PC	Yds	Avg	TD	Int	Lg	Rtg
1952	WAS	N	194	95	49.0	1420	7.3	14	15	70t	65.2
1953			149	62	41.6	874	5.9	3	17	66	28.3
1955			178	79	44.4	1270	7.1	9	15	70	50.5
1956			98	47	48.0	554	5.7	3	10	33	36.2
1957			167	99	59.3	1508	9.0	11	10	82t	86.1
1958			145	79	54.5	1365	9.4	11	10	71t	83.3
1959			173	77	44.5	1077	6.2	8	11	49	54.0
1960	DAL	N	225	111	49.3	1736	7.7	12	25	76t	53.5
1961			236	120	50.8	1741	7.4	14	16	80t	66.7
1962			166	95	57.2	1436	8.7	16	9	85t	95.4
1963			65	33	50.8	418	6.4	3	3	75t	67.3
Career			1796	897	49.9	13399	7.5	104	141	85t	61.4

Bill Leckonby

Year	Team		Att	Com	PC	Yds	Avg	TD	Int	Lg	Rtg
1939	BKN	N	1	0	0.0	0	0.0	0	0		39.6
1940			13	7	53.8	74	5.7	0	0		70.7
1941			64	25	39.1	299	4.7	1	5	32	26.8
Career			78	32	41.0	373	4.8	1	5	32	33.8

Jim LeClair

Year	Team		Att	Com	PC	Yds	Avg	TD	Int	Lg	Rtg
1967	DEN	A	45	19	42.2	275	6.1	1	1	48	60.9
1968			54	27	50.0	401	7.4	1	5	50	42.3
Career			99	46	46.5	676	6.8	2	6	50	50.7

Roger LeClerc

Year	Team		Att	Com	PC	Yds	Avg	TD	Int	Lg	Rtg
1963	CHI	N	1	0	0.0	0	0.0	0	0		39.6

Terry LeCount

Year	Team		Att	Com	PC	Yds	Avg	TD	Int	Lg	Rtg
1979	MIN	N	0	0		0		0	0		
1983			1	0	0.0	0	0.0	0	0		39.6
Career			1	0	0.0	0	0.0	0	0		39.6

Hal Ledyard

Year	Team		Att	Com	PC	Yds	Avg	TD	Int	Lg	Rtg
1953	SF	N	9	0	0.0	0	0.0	0	1		0.0

Bob Lee

Year	Team		Att	Com	PC	Yds	Avg	TD	Int	Lg	Rtg
1969	MIN	N	11	7	63.6	79	7.2	1	0	30	115.3
1970			79	40	50.6	610	7.7	5	5	52	71.2
1971			90	45	50.0	598	6.6	2	4	51	60.3
1972			6	3	50.0	75	12.5	1	0	63	135.4
1973	ATL	N	230	120	52.2	1786	7.8	10	8	57	77.9
1974			172	78	45.3	852	5.0	3	14	52	32.4
1975	MIN	N	14	5	35.7	103	7.4	2	1	33t	72.3
1976			30	15	50.0	156	5.2	0	2	21	37.6
1977			72	42	58.3	522	7.3	4	4	48t	76.3
1978			4	2	50.0	10	2.5	0	1	6	16.7
1979	LA	N	22	11	50.0	243	11.0	2	1	41t	101.1
Career			730	368	50.4	5034	6.9	30	40	63	63.7
Playoffs			67	33	49.3	382	5.7	1	3		53.2

Jack Lee

Year	Team		Att	Com	PC	Yds	Avg	TD	Int	Lg	Rtg
1939	PIT	N	1	0	0.0	0	0.0	0	0		39.6

Jacky Lee

Year	Team		Att	Com	PC	Yds	Avg	TD	Int	Lg	Rtg
1960	HOU	A	77	41	53.2	842	10.9	5	6	92t	81.2
1961			127	66	52.0	1205	9.5	12	6	80t	96.7
1962			50	26	52.0	433	8.7	4	5	98t	68.6
1963			75	37	49.3	475	6.3	2	8		38.9
1964	DEN	A	265	133	50.2	1611	6.1	11	20		51.6
1965			80	44	55.0	692	8.7	5	3	66	89.2
1966	HOU	A	8	4	50.0	27	3.4	0	1	10	18.2
1967	HOU-KC	A	91	42	46.2	414	4.5	3	6	53	43.0
1968	KC	A	45	25	55.6	383	8.5	3	1	61t	96.8
1969			20	12	60.0	109	5.5	1	1	31	70.6
Career			838	430	51.3	6191	7.4	46	57	98t	65.6

Tuffy Leemans

Year	Team		Att	Com	PC	Yds	Avg	TD	Int	Lg	Rtg
1936	NYG	N	42	13	31.0	258	6.1	3	6		37.7
1937			20	5	25.0	64	3.2	1	1		36.2
1938			42	19	45.2	249	5.9	3	6		48.7
1939			26	12	46.2	198	7.6	0	2		40.2
1940			31	15	48.4	159	5.1	2	3		45.7
1941			66	31	47.0	475	7.2	4	5	44	59.8
1942			69	35	50.7	555	8.0	7	4	50	87.5
1943	NY	N	87	37	42.5	366	4.2	5	5	28	50.3
Career			383	167	43.6	2324	6.1	25	32	50	50.6
Playoffs			25	7	28.0	143	5.7	1	8		24.7

Clyde LeForce

Year	Team		Att	Com	PC	Yds	Avg	TD	Int	Lg	Rtg
1947	DET	N	175	94	53.7	1384	7.9	13	20	79	65.0
1948			101	50	49.5	912	9.0	9	8	83	77.7
1949			112	53	47.3	665	5.9	3	9	40	41.7
Career			388	197	50.8	2961	7.6	25	37	83	58.1

Dave Leggett

Year	Team		Att	Com	PC	Yds	Avg	TD	Int	Lg	Rtg
1955	CHIC	N	1	0	0.0	0	0.0	0	0		39.6

Bruce Lemmerman

Year	Team		Att	Com	PC	Yds	Avg	TD	Int	Lg	Rtg
1968	ATL	N	15	3	20.0	40	2.7	0	1	18	11.8
1969			62	25	40.3	330	5.3	1	4	57	36.4
Career			77	28	36.4	370	4.8	1	5	57	29.7

Jim Leonard

Year	Team		Att	Com	PC	Yds	Avg	TD	Int	Lg	Rtg
1936	PHI	N	6	2	33.3	45	7.5	0	2		21.5

Jimmy Lesane

Year	Team		Att	Com	PC	Yds	Avg	TD	Int	Lg	Rtg
1952	CHIB	N	1	0	0.0	0	0.0	0	0		39.6
1954	BAL	N	1	0	0.0	0	0.0	0	0		39.6
Career			2	0	0.0	0	0.0	0	0		39.6

Jerry LeVias

Year	Team		Att	Com	PC	Yds	Avg	TD	Int	Lg	Rtg
1969	HOU	A	2	0	0.0	0	0.0	0	0		39.6
1970	HOU		1	0	0.0	0	0.0	0	1		0.0
Career			3	0	0.0	0	0.0	0	1		0.0

Verne Lewellen

Year	Team		Att	Com	PC	Yds	Avg	TD	Int	Lg	Rtg
1928	GB	N						1			
1929								5			
1930								2			
Career								8			

Cliff Lewis

Year	Team		Att	Com	PC	Yds	Avg	TD	Int	Lg	Rtg
1946	CLE	AA	30	11	36.7	125	4.2	1	1		47.2
1947			11	5	45.5	70	6.4	1	1		58.9
1948			8	4	50.0	69	8.6	1	0		119.3
1949			10	5	50.0	144	14.4	2	2		95.8
1950	CLE	N	4	1	25.0	38	9.5	1	0	38t	106.3
1951			6	4	66.7	68	11.3	1	1	20	104.9
Career			69	30	43.5	514	7.4	7	5	38t	73.0

Danny Lewis

Year	Team		Att	Com	PC	Yds	Avg	TD	Int	Lg	Rtg
1962	DET	N	1	0	0.0	0	0.0	0	0		39.6
1964			1	0	0.0	0	0.0	0	0		39.6
1965	WAS	N	2	1	50.0	26	13.0	1	0	26t	135.4
1966	NYG	N	1	1	100.0	4	4.0	0	0	4	83.3
Career			5	2	40.0	30	6.0	1	0	26t	100.0

Dave Lewis

Year	Team		Att	Com	PC	Yds	Avg	TD	Int	Lg	Rtg
1970	CIN	N	4	3	75.0	39	9.8	0	0	18	105.2
1971			10	3	30.0	18	1.8	0	0	13	39.6
Career			14	6	42.9	57	4.1	0	0	18	54.8

Ernie Lewis

Year	Team		Att	Com	PC	Yds	Avg	TD	Int	Lg	Rtg
1946	CHI	AA	8	4	50.0	17	2.1	0	1		16.7

Greg Lewis

Year	Team		Att	Com	PC	Yds	Avg	TD	Int	Lg	Rtg
1992	DEN	N	1	0	0.0	0	0.0	0	0		39.6

Year	Team		Att	Com	PC	Yds	Avg	TD	Int	Lg	Rtg

Jeff Lewis

Year	Team		Att	Com	PC	Yds	Avg	TD	Int	Lg	Rtg
1996	DEN	N	17	9	52.9	58	3.4	0	1	11	35.9

Joe Lillard

| 1933 | CHIC | N | | | | | | | 2 | | |

Verl Lillywhite

| 1948 | SF | AA | 1 | 0 | 0.0 | 0 | 0.0 | 0 | 1 | | 0.0 |
| Playoffs | | | 1 | 0 | 0.0 | 0 | 0.0 | 0 | 0 | | 39.6 |

Keith Lincoln

1962	SD	A	5	2	40.0	43	8.6	2	0	23	110.8
1963			1	0	0.0	0	0.0	0	0		39.6
1964			4	2	50.0	61	15.3	1	0		135.4
1965			3	2	66.7	65	21.7	1	1	34	109.7
1966			4	2	50.0	71	17.8	1	0	36	135.4
Career			17	8	47.1	240	14.1	5	1	36	108.5
Playoffs			1	1	100.0	20	20.0	0	0		118.8

Mike Lind

| 1964 | SF | N | 1 | 1 | 100.0 | 69 | 69.0 | 1 | 0 | 69t | 158.3 |

Joe Lintzenich

| 1931 | CHIB | N | | | | | | | 2 | | |

Louis Lipps

| 1988 | PIT | N | 2 | 1 | 50.0 | 13 | 6.5 | 1 | 1 | 13t | 70.8 |

Don Lisbon

| 1963 | SF | N | 2 | 1 | 50.0 | 45 | 22.5 | 1 | 0 | 45t | 135.4 |

Rusty Lisch

1980	STL	N	17	6	35.3	68	4.0	0	3	23	8.6
1983			13	6	46.2	66	5.1	1	2	26	47.8
1984	CHI	N	85	43	50.6	413	4.9	0	6	23	35.1
Career			115	55	47.8	547	4.8	1	11	26	25.1

Pete Liske

1964	NY	A	18	9	50.0	55	3.1	0	2		16.9
1969	DEN	A	115	61	53.0	845	7.3	9	11	71	63.4
1970	DEN	N	238	112	47.1	1340	5.6	7	11	74	55.3
1971	PHI	N	269	143	53.2	1957	7.3	11	15	69t	67.1
1972			138	71	51.4	973	7.1	3	7	67t	60.4
Career			778	396	50.9	5170	6.6	30	46	74	60.4

Floyd Little

1968	DEN	A	2	0	0.0	0	0.0	0	0		39.6
1969			2	0	0.0	0	0.0	0	0		39.6
1970	DEN	N	2	0	0.0	0	0.0	0	0		39.6
1971			1	0	0.0	0	0.0	0	0		39.6
1972			2	2	100.0	43	21.5	1	0	35t	158.3
Career			9	2	22.2	43	4.8	1	0	35t	84.0

Steve Little

| 1979 | STL | N | 3 | 2 | 66.7 | 31 | 10.3 | 0 | 0 | 16 | 100.7 |

Carl Littlefield

| 1938 | CLE | N | 15 | 1 | 6.7 | 23 | 1.5 | 0 | 5 | 23 | 0.0 |

Andy Livingston

| 1969 | NO | N | 4 | 3 | 75.0 | 38 | 9.5 | 1 | 1 | 14 | 104.2 |

Dale Livingston

| 1969 | CIN | A | 2 | 2 | 100.0 | 15 | 7.5 | 0 | 0 | 17 | 97.9 |

Howie Livingston

| 1944 | NY | N | 1 | 0 | 0.0 | 0 | 0.0 | 0 | 1 | | 0.0 |

Mike Livingston

1969	KC	A	161	84	52.2	1123	7.0	4	6	93t	67.4
1970	KC	N	22	11	50.0	122	5.5	0	1	31	47.9
1971			28	12	42.9	130	4.6	0	0	36	57.1
1972			78	41	52.6	480	6.2	7	8	36t	61.9
1973			145	75	51.7	916	6.3	6	7	48	65.2
1974			141	66	46.8	732	5.2	4	10	48	42.6
1975			176	88	50.0	1245	7.1	8	6	69t	74.2
1976			338	189	55.9	2682	7.9	12	13	57	77.6
1977			282	143	50.7	1823	6.5	9	15	49	59.8
1978			290	159	54.8	1573	5.4	5	13	44	57.4
1979			90	44	48.9	469	5.2	1	4	38t	49.7
Career			1751	912	52.1	11295	6.5	56	83	93t	63.3

J.W. Lockett

| 1961 | DAL | N | 2 | 0 | 0.0 | 0 | 0.0 | 0 | 0 | | 39.6 |

J.W. Lockett *continued*

Year	Team		Att	Com	PC	Yds	Avg	TD	Int	Lg	Rtg
1962			1	0	0.0	0	0.0	0	0		39.6
Career			3	0	0.0	0	0.0	0	0		39.6

James Lofton

1978	GB	N	2	0	0.0	0	0.0	0	0		39.6
1979			1	0	0.0	0	0.0	0	0		39.6
1982			1	1	100.0	43	43.0	0	0	43	118.8
1986			1	0	0.0	0	0.0	0	0		39.6
Career			5	1	20.0	43	8.6	0	0	43	62.9

Dave Logan

| 1977 | CLE | N | 2 | 0 | 0.0 | 0 | 0.0 | 0 | 0 | | 39.6 |

Neil Lomax

1981	STL	N	236	119	50.4	1575	6.7	4	10	75	59.9
1982			205	109	53.2	1367	6.7	5	6	42	70.1
1983			354	209	59.0	2636	7.4	24	11	71t	92.0
1984			560	345	61.6	4614	8.2	28	16	83t	92.5
1985			471	265	56.3	3214	6.8	18	12	47	79.5
1986			421	240	57.0	2583	6.1	13	12	48t	73.6
1987			**463**	**275**	59.4	**3387**	7.3	24	12	57	88.5
1988	PHX	N	443	255	57.6	3395	7.7	20	11	93t	86.7
Career			3153	1817	57.6	22771	7.2	136	90	93t	82.7
Playoffs			51	32	62.7	385	7.5	2	2		82.6

Chuck Long

1986	DET	N	40	21	52.5	247	6.2	2	2	34t	67.4
1987			416	232	55.8	2598	6.2	11	20	53	63.4
1988			141	75	53.2	856	6.1	6	6	40	68.2
1989			5	2	40.0	42	8.4	0	0	37	70.4
1990	LARM	N	5	1	20.0	4	0.8	0	0	4	39.6
Career			607	331	54.5	3747	6.2	19	28	53	64.5

Johnny Long

| 1944 | CHIB | N | 14 | 9 | 64.3 | 128 | 9.1 | 1 | 1 | 51 | 87.8 |

Clint Longley

1974	DAL	N	21	12	57.1	209	10.0	2	0	50t	122.9
1975			23	7	30.4	102	4.4	1	1	23	42.3
1976	SD	N	24	12	50.0	130	5.4	2	3	28t	54.5
Career			68	31	45.6	441	6.5	5	4	50t	67.1
Playoffs			2	2	100.0	26	13.0	0	0		118.8

Dean Look

| 1962 | NY | A | 1 | 0 | 0.0 | 0 | 0.0 | 0 | 1 | | 0.0 |

Joe Don Looney

| 1969 | NO | N | 1 | 0 | 0.0 | 0 | 0.0 | 0 | 0 | | 39.6 |

Jack Losch

| 1956 | GB | N | 1 | 1 | 100.0 | 63 | 63.0 | 1 | 0 | 63t | 158.3 |

Billy Lothridge

1964	DAL	N	9	2	22.2	24	2.7	0	2	13	0.0
1966	ATL	N	1	0	0.0	0	0.0	0	0		39.6
1968			0	0		0		0	0		
1969			1	1	100.0	9	9.0	0	0	9	104.2
1971			1	1	100.0	27	27.0	0	0	27	118.8
Career			12	4	33.3	60	5.0	0	2	27	11.1

Gary Lowe

| 1964 | DET | N | 1 | 0 | 0.0 | 0 | 0.0 | 0 | 1 | | 0.0 |

Paul Lowe

1960	LA	A	3	1	33.3	24	8.0	0	0	24	63.2
1961	SD	A	4	2	50.0	70	17.5	0	0	36	95.8
1963			4	2	50.0	100	25.0	1	1	71	95.8
1964			2	0	0.0	0	0.0	0	0		39.6
1965			4	3	75.0	81	20.3	0	0	42	116.7
1966			3	1	33.3	25	8.3	0	0	25	64.6
1967			1	1	100.0	26	26.0	0	0	26	118.8
Career			21	10	47.6	326	15.5	1	1	71	89.9

Russ Lowther

1944	DET	N	10	7	70.0	54	5.4	0	2	13	43.3
1945	PIT	N	4	0	0.0	0	0.0	0	1		0.0
Career			14	7	50.0	54	3.9	0	3	13	20.2

Mike Loyd

| 1980 | STL | N | 28 | 5 | 17.9 | 49 | 1.8 | 0 | 1 | 20 | 24.7 |

Richie Lucas

| 1960 | BUF | A | 49 | 23 | 46.9 | 314 | 6.4 | 2 | 3 | | 56.0 |

Richie Lucas *continued*

Year	Team		Att	Com	PC	Yds	Avg	TD	Int	Lg	Rtg
1961			50	20	40.0	282	5.6	2	4		38.9
Career			99	43	43.4	596	6.0	4	7	20	47.4

Oliver Luck

Year	Team		Att	Com	PC	Yds	Avg	TD	Int	Lg	Rtg
1983	HOU	N	217	124	57.1	1375	6.3	8	13	66	63.4
1984			36	22	61.1	256	7.1	2	1	37	89.6
1985			100	56	56.0	572	5.7	2	2	46t	70.9
1986			60	31	51.7	341	5.7	1	5	27	39.7
Career			413	233	56.4	2544	6.2	13	21	66	64.1

Terry Luck

Year	Team		Att	Com	PC	Yds	Avg	TD	Int	Lg	Rtg
1977	CLE	N	50	25	50.0	316	6.3	1	7	33	37.2

Sid Luckman

Year	Team		Att	Com	PC	Yds	Avg	TD	Int	Lg	Rtg
1939	CHIB	N	51	23	45.1	636	**12.5**	5	4		91.6
1940			105	48	45.7	941	**9.0**	4	9		54.5
1941			119	68	**57.1**	1181	9.9	9	6	65	95.3
1942			105	57	54.3	1023	9.7	10	13	52	80.1
1943			202	110	54.5	**2194**	**10.9**	**28**	12	66	**107.5**
1944			143	71	49.7	1018	7.1	11	11	86	66.7
1945			217	117	53.9	**1725**	7.9	**14**	10	65	82.4
1946			229	110	48.0	**1826**	8.0	17	16	48	71.0
1947			323	176	54.5	2712	8.4	24	31	81	67.7
1948			163	89	54.6	1047	6.4	13	14	53	65.1
1949			50	22	44.0	200	4.0	1	3	34	37.1
1950			37	13	35.1	180	4.9	1	2	44t	38.1
Career			1744	904	51.8	14683	8.4	137	131	86	75.2
Playoffs			86	45	52.3	742	8.6	7	4		89.4

Johnny Lujack

Year	Team		Att	Com	PC	Yds	Avg	TD	Int	Lg	Rtg
1948	CHIB	N	66	36	54.5	611	**9.3**	6	3	64	97.5
1949			**312**	**162**	51.9	**2658**	8.5	**23**	22	81	76.0
1950			254	121	47.6	1731	6.8	4	21	70	41.0
1951			176	85	48.3	1295	7.4	8	8	78t	69.2
Career			808	404	50.0	6295	7.8	41	54	81	65.3
Playoffs			29	15	51.7	193	6.7	0	3		33.3

Roy Lumpkin

Year	Team		Att	Com	PC	Yds	Avg	TD	Int	Lg	Rtg
1930	POR	N						3			

Bobby Luna

Year	Team		Att	Com	PC	Yds	Avg	TD	Int	Lg	Rtg
1959	PIT	N	1	1	100.0	55	55.0	0	0	55	118.8

Booth Lusteg

Year	Team		Att	Com	PC	Yds	Avg	TD	Int	Lg	Rtg
1967	MIA	A	1	0	0.0	0	0.0	0	0		39.6

Ed Luther

Year	Team		Att	Com	PC	Yds	Avg	TD	Int	Lg	Rtg
1980	SD	N	3	2	66.7	26	8.7	0	1	13	54.2
1981			15	7	46.7	68	4.5	0	1	25	32.1
1982			4	2	50.0	55	13.8	0	1	55	56.3
1983			287	151	52.6	1875	6.5	7	17	46	56.6
1984			151	83	55.0	1163	7.7	5	3	88t	82.7
Career			460	245	53.3	3187	6.9	12	23	88t	63.2

Garry Lyle

Year	Team		Att	Com	PC	Yds	Avg	TD	Int	Lg	Rtg
1970	CHI	N	0	0		0		0	0		

Fran Lynch

Year	Team		Att	Com	PC	Yds	Avg	TD	Int	Lg	Rtg
1968	DEN	A	2	1	50.0	4	2.0	0	0	4	56.3

Mike Machurek

Year	Team		Att	Com	PC	Yds	Avg	TD	Int	Lg	Rtg
1984	DET	N	43	14	32.6	193	4.5	0	6	48	8.3

Kyle Mackey

Year	Team		Att	Com	PC	Yds	Avg	TD	Int	Lg	Rtg
1987	MIA	N	109	57	52.3	604	5.5	3	5	30	58.8
1989	NYJ	N	25	11	44.0	125	5.0	0	1	22	42.9
Career			134	68	50.7	729	5.4	3	6	30	55.8

Bill Mackrides

Year	Team		Att	Com	PC	Yds	Avg	TD	Int	Lg	Rtg
1947	PHI	N	17	8	47.1	58	3.4	2	3	15	55.1
1948			53	18	34.0	276	5.2	2	4	28	33.2
1949			36	14	38.9	182	5.1	2	2	37	50.9
1950			46	14	30.4	228	5.0	4	6	59	37.5
1951			54	23	42.6	333	6.2	3	5	43t	43.2
1953	NYG-PIT	N	109	54	49.5	506	4.6	2	8	36	38.2
Career			315	131	41.6	1583	5.0	15	28	59	36.5

Eddie Macon

Year	Team		Att	Com	PC	Yds	Avg	TD	Int	Lg	Rtg
1953	CHIB	N	1	0	0.0	0	0.0	0	0		39.6

Elmer Madarik

Year	Team		Att	Com	PC	Yds	Avg	TD	Int	Lg	Rtg
1946	DET	N	14	7	50.0	104	7.4	1	0	47	98.5

Tommy Maddox

Year	Team		Att	Com	PC	Yds	Avg	TD	Int	Lg	Rtg
1992	DEN	N	121	66	54.5	757	6.3	5	9	38	56.4
1993			1	1	100.0	1	1.0	1	0	1t	118.8
1994	LARM	N	19	10	52.6	141	7.4	0	2	39	37.3
1995	NYG	N	23	6	26.1	49	2.1	0	3	13	0.0
Career			164	83	50.6	948	5.8	6	14	39	45.0
Playoffs			7	3	42.9	34	4.9	0	0		58.0

Chet Maeda

Year	Team		Att	Com	PC	Yds	Avg	TD	Int	Lg	Rtg
1945	CHIC	N	1	0	0.0	0	0.0	0	0		39.6

Archie Maggiolo

Year	Team		Att	Com	PC	Yds	Avg	TD	Int	Lg	Rtg
1948	BUF	AA	1	1	100.0	0	0.0	0	0	0	79.2

Dante Magnani

Year	Team		Att	Com	PC	Yds	Avg	TD	Int	Lg	Rtg
1942	CLE	N	1	0	0.0	0	0.0	0	0		39.6

Paul Maguire

Year	Team		Att	Com	PC	Yds	Avg	TD	Int	Lg	Rtg
1969	BUF	A	1	1	100.0	19	19.0	0	0	19	118.8

Al Mahrt

Year	Team		Att	Com	PC	Yds	Avg	TD	Int	Lg	Rtg
1920	DAY	A						**7**			
1921								1			
1922	DAY	N						1			
Career								9			

Lou Mahrt

Year	Team		Att	Com	PC	Yds	Avg	TD	Int	Lg	Rtg
1926	DAY	N						2			

Don Majkowski

Year	Team		Att	Com	PC	Yds	Avg	TD	Int	Lg	Rtg
1987	GB	N	127	55	43.3	875	6.9	5	3	70t	70.2
1988			336	178	53.0	2119	6.3	9	11	56	67.8
1989			**599**	**353**	58.9	**4318**	7.2	27	20	79t	82.3
1990			264	150	56.8	1925	7.3	10	12	76t	73.5
1991			226	115	50.9	1362	6.0	3	8	39	59.3
1992			55	38	69.1	271	4.9	2	2	32	77.2
1993	IND	N	24	13	54.2	105	4.4	0	1	17	48.1
1994			152	84	55.3	1010	6.6	6	7	29	69.8
1995	DET	N	20	15	75.0	161	8.1	1	0	22	114.8
1996			102	55	53.9	554	5.4	3	3	27	67.2
Career			1905	1056	55.4	12700	6.7	66	67	79t	72.9
Playoffs			23	14	60.9	206	9.0	3	2		93.5

Howie Maley

Year	Team		Att	Com	PC	Yds	Avg	TD	Int	Lg	Rtg
1946	BOS	N	8	3	37.5	71	8.9	1	2	43	70.3
1947			12	6	50.0	144	12.0	1	1	63	86.8
Career			20	9	45.0	215	10.8	2	3	63	78.1

Gene Malinowski

Year	Team		Att	Com	PC	Yds	Avg	TD	Int	Lg	Rtg
1948	BOS	N	54	15	27.8	218	4.0	3	7	68	22.8

Larry Mallory

Year	Team		Att	Com	PC	Yds	Avg	TD	Int	Lg	Rtg
1978	NYG	N	1	1	100.0	35	35.0	0	0	35	118.8

Ray Mallouf

Year	Team		Att	Com	PC	Yds	Avg	TD	Int	Lg	Rtg
1941	CHIC	N	96	48	50.0	725	7.6	2	4	80	64.8
1946			34	14	41.2	260	7.6	4	2	59	83.0
1947			36	21	58.3	340	**9.4**	1	2	52	76.2
1948			143	73	51.0	1160	8.1	13	6	54	91.2
1949	NYG	N	16	3	18.8	19	1.2	0	2	11	0.0
Career			325	159	48.9	2504	7.7	20	16	80	75.0
Playoffs			7	3	42.9	35	5.0	0	0		58.6

Mark Malone

Year	Team		Att	Com	PC	Yds	Avg	TD	Int	Lg	Rtg
1981	PIT	N	88	45	51.1	553	6.3	3	5	30	58.6
1983			20	9	45.0	124	6.2	1	2	38	42.5
1984			272	147	54.0	2137	7.9	16	17	61t	73.4
1985			233	117	50.2	1428	6.1	13	7	45t	75.5
1986			425	216	50.8	2444	5.8	15	18	48	62.5
1987			336	156	46.4	1896	5.6	6	19	63	46.7
1988	SD	N	272	147	54.0	1580	5.8	6	13	59	58.8
1989	NYJ	N	2	2	100.0	13	6.5	0	0	11	93.8
Career			1648	839	50.9	10175	6.2	60	81	63	61.9
Playoffs			71	40	56.3	558	7.9	4	3		83.0

Jack Manders

Year	Team		Att	Com	PC	Yds	Avg	TD	Int	Lg	Rtg
1934	CHIB	N	3	2	66.7	14	4.7	0	0		77.1
1935			9	1	11.1	10	1.1	0	1	10	0.0
1936			3	2	66.7	52	17.3	0	0		109.7
1938			1	0	0.0	0	0.0	0	0		39.6
Career			16	5	31.3	76	4.8	0	1	10	21.9

Pug Manders

Year	Team		Att	Com	PC	Yds	Avg	TD	Int	Lg	Rtg
1940	BKN	N	1	0	0.0	0	0.0	0	0		39.6

Year	Team		Att	Com	PC	Yds	Avg	TD	Int	Lg	Rtg

Pug Manders *continued*

Year	Team		Att	Com	PC	Yds	Avg	TD	Int	Lg	Rtg
1942			1	0	0.0	0	0.0	0	0		39.6
1943			5	4	80.0	31	6.2	1	0	11	132.1
1944			34	9	26.5	96	2.8	0	4		0.0
1945	BOS	N	9	5	55.6	42	4.7	0	1	12	28.2
1946	NY	AA	3	2	66.7	14	4.7	0	0		77.1
Career			53	20	37.7	183	3.5	1	5	12	14.9

Joe Maniaci

Year	Team		Att	Com	PC	Yds	Avg	TD	Int	Lg	Rtg
1936	BKN	N	4	4	100.0	1	0.3	0	0	1	79.2
1937			4	1	25.0	0	0.0	0	2	0	0.0
1938			2	1	50.0	19	9.5	1	0	19t	122.9
1939	CHIB	N	2	1	50.0	10	5.0	0	0	10	64.6
Career			12	7	58.3	30	2.5	1	2	19t	51.4

Dave Mann

Year	Team		Att	Com	PC	Yds	Avg	TD	Int	Lg	Rtg
1955	CHIC	N	10	5	50.0	53	5.3	2	0	50	105.4
1956			2	0	0.0	0	0.0	0	1		0.0
1957			1	0	0.0	0	0.0	0	0		39.6
Career			13	5	38.5	53	4.1	2	1	50	58.7

Archie Manning

Year	Team		Att	Com	PC	Yds	Avg	TD	Int	Lg	Rtg
1971	NO	N	177	86	48.6	1164	6.6	6	9	63t	60.1
1972			448	230	51.3	2781	6.2	18	21	66t	64.6
1973			267	140	52.4	1642	6.1	10	12	65t	65.2
1974			261	134	51.3	1429	5.5	6	16	79t	49.8
1975			338	159	47.0	1683	5.0	7	20	71t	44.3
1977			205	113	55.1	1284	6.3	8	9	59t	68.8
1978			471	291	61.8	3416	7.3	17	16	71t	81.7
1979			420	252	60.0	3169	7.5	15	20	85	75.6
1980			509	309	60.7	3716	7.3	23	20	56	81.8
1981			232	134	57.8	1447	6.2	5	11	55	63.6
1982	NO-HOU	N	132	67	50.8	880	6.7	6	8	54t	62.1
1983	HOU	N	88	44	50.0	755	8.6	2	8	47t	49.2
1984	MIN	N	94	52	55.3	545	5.8	2	3	56	66.1
Career			3642	2011	55.2	23911	6.6	125	173	85	67.1

Tillie Manton

Year	Team		Att	Com	PC	Yds	Avg	TD	Int	Lg	Rtg
1936	NYG	N	5	3	60.0	27	5.4	0	0		74.6
1937			1	1	100.0	14	14.0	0	0	14	118.8
1943	BKN	N	4	2	50.0	26	6.5	0	0	17	70.8
Career			10	6	60.0	67	6.7	0	0	17	80.0

Dan Manucci

Year	Team		Att	Com	PC	Yds	Avg	TD	Int	Lg	Rtg
1980	BUF	N	6	5	83.3	64	10.7	0	0	22	111.1
1987			21	7	33.3	68	3.2	0	2	15	3.8
Career			27	12	44.4	132	4.9	0	2	22	28.6
Playoffs			1	0	0.0	0	0.0	0	0		39.6

Gary Marangi

Year	Team		Att	Com	PC	Yds	Avg	TD	Int	Lg	Rtg
1974	BUF	N	18	9	50.0	140	7.8	2	3	44t	73.6
1975			33	13	39.4	235	7.1	3	2	64t	69.6
1976			232	82	35.3	998	4.3	7	16	39	30.8
Career			283	104	36.7	1373	4.9	12	21	64t	36.1

Ted Marchibroda

Year	Team		Att	Com	PC	Yds	Avg	TD	Int	Lg	Rtg
1953	PIT	N	22	9	40.9	66	3.0	1	2	16	25.9
1955			43	24	55.8	280	6.5	2	3	47t	62.2
1956			275	124	45.1	1585	5.8	12	19	75t	49.4
1957	CHIC	N	45	15	33.3	238	5.3	1	5	75t	19.7
Career			385	172	44.7	2169	5.6	16	29	75t	45.3

Andrew Marefos

Year	Team		Att	Com	PC	Yds	Avg	TD	Int	Lg	Rtg
1941	NYG	N	8	2	25.0	79	9.9	1	1	75	68.2
1942			29	11	37.9	176	6.1	1	5	60	30.9
Career			37	13	35.1	255	6.9	2	6	75	38.5

Joe Margucci

Year	Team		Att	Com	PC	Yds	Avg	TD	Int	Lg	Rtg
1947	DET	N	31	13	41.9	171	5.5	1	5	39	31.2

Dan Marino

Year	Team		Att	Com	PC	Yds	Avg	TD	Int	Lg	Rtg
1983	MIA	N	296	173	58.4	2210	7.5	20	6	85t	96.0
1984			564	362	64.2	5084	9.0	48	17	80t	108.9
1985			567	336	59.3	4137	7.3	30	21	73	84.1
1986			623	378	60.7	4746	7.6	44	23	85t	92.5
1987			444	263	59.2	3245	7.3	26	13	59t	89.2
1988			606	354	58.4	4434	7.3	28	23	80t	80.8
1989			550	308	56.0	3997	7.3	24	22	78t	76.9
1990			531	306	57.6	3563	6.7	21	11	69t	82.6
1991			549	318	57.9	3970	7.2	25	13	54	85.8
1992			554	330	59.6	4116	7.4	24	16	62t	85.1
1993			150	91	60.7	1218	8.1	8	3	80t	95.9
1994			615	385	62.6	4453	7.2	30	17	64t	89.2

Dan Marino *continued*

Year	Team		Att	Com	PC	Yds	Avg	TD	Int	Lg	Rtg
1995			482	309	64.1	3668	7.6	24	15	67t	90.8
1996			373	221	59.2	2795	7.5	17	9	74t	87.8
Career			6904	4134	59.9	51636	7.5	369	209	85t	88.3
Playoffs			518	291	56.2	3600	6.9	29	17		82.8

Todd Marinovich

Year	Team		Att	Com	PC	Yds	Avg	TD	Int	Lg	Rtg
1991	LARI	N	40	23	57.5	243	6.1	3	0	26t	100.3
1992			165	81	49.1	1102	6.7	5	9	68t	58.2
Career			205	104	50.7	1345	6.6	8	9	68t	66.4
Playoffs			23	12	52.2	140	6.1	0	4		31.3

Steve Marko

Year	Team		Att	Com	PC	Yds	Avg	TD	Int	Lg	Rtg
1944	BKN	N	7	1	14.3	2	0.3	0	2	0	0.0

Larry Marks

Year	Team		Att	Com	PC	Yds	Avg	TD	Int	Lg	Rtg
1926	NY	A							1		
1927	NYY	N							1		
Career									2		

Amos Marsh

Year	Team		Att	Com	PC	Yds	Avg	TD	Int	Lg	Rtg
1965	DET	N	1	0	0.0	0	0.0	0	0		39.6

Arthur Marshall

Year	Team		Att	Com	PC	Yds	Avg	TD	Int	Lg	Rtg
1992	DEN	N	1	1	100.0	81	81.0	1	0	81t	158.3
1993			1	1	100.0	30	30.0	1	0	30t	158.3
1994	NYG	N	0	0		0		0	0		
Career			2	2	100.0	111	55.5	2	0	81t	158.3

Henry Marshall

Year	Team		Att	Com	PC	Yds	Avg	TD	Int	Lg	Rtg
1981	KC	N	1	0	0.0	0	0.0	0	1		0.0
1982			1	0	0.0	0	0.0	0	0		39.6
1983			0	0		0		0	0	0	
1986			1	0	0.0	0	0.0	0	0		39.6
Career			3	0	0.0	0	0.0	0	1		0.0

Frank Martin

Year	Team		Att	Com	PC	Yds	Avg	TD	Int	Lg	Rtg
1943	BKN	N	4	2	50.0	15	3.8	0	0	12	59.4
1944			1	1	100.0	7	7.0	0	0	7	95.8
Career			5	3	60.0	22	4.4	0	0	12	70.4

Jamie Martin

Year	Team		Att	Com	PC	Yds	Avg	TD	Int	Lg	Rtg
1996	STL	N	34	23	67.6	241	7.1	3	2	22t	92.9

Tony Martin

Year	Team		Att	Com	PC	Yds	Avg	TD	Int	Lg	Rtg
1992	MIA	N	1	0	0.0	0	0.0	0	0		39.6
1994	SD	N	1	0	0.0	0	0.0	0	1		0.0
1995			1	0	0.0	0	0.0	0	0		39.6
Career			3	0	0.0	0	0.0	0	1		0.0

Tommy Mason

Year	Team		Att	Com	PC	Yds	Avg	TD	Int	Lg	Rtg
1961	MIN	N	1	0	0.0	0	0.0	0	0		39.6
1962			1	0	0.0	0	0.0	0	1		0.0
1964			1	1	100.0	30	30.0	1	0	30t	158.3
1965			1	0	0.0	0	0.0	0	1		0.0
1967	LA	N	3	2	66.7	65	21.7	0	0	51t	149.3
1968			2	0	0.0	0	0.0	0	0		39.6
Career			9	3	33.3	95	10.6	2	2	51t	73.8

Bob Masters

Year	Team		Att	Com	PC	Yds	Avg	TD	Int	Lg	Rtg
1939	PIT	N	3	1	33.3	9	3.0	0	1	9	2.8

Walt Masters

Year	Team		Att	Com	PC	Yds	Avg	TD	Int	Lg	Rtg
1936	PHI	N	6	1	16.7	11	1.8	0	1	11	0.0
1943	CHIC	N	45	17	37.8	249	5.5	2	7	37	31.9
1944	C-P	N	7	1	14.3	13	1.9	0	2	13	0.0
Career			58	19	32.8	273	4.7	2	10	37	20.9

Bernie Masterson

Year	Team		Att	Com	PC	Yds	Avg	TD	Int	Lg	Rtg
1934	CHIB	N	2	2	100.0	35	17.5	0	0		118.8
1935			44	18	40.9	456	10.4	6	4		81.1
1936			42	10	23.8	292	7.0	3	6		40.3
1937			72	26	36.1	615	8.5	9	7		67.8
1938			112	46	41.1	848	7.6	7	9		55.2
1939			113	44	38.9	914	8.1	8	9		58.6
1940			23	9	39.1	212	9.2	2	3		62.5
Career			408	155	38.0	3372	8.3	35	38		58.0
Playoffs			17	4	23.5	131	7.7	2	2		58.8

Bob Masterson

Year	Team		Att	Com	PC	Yds	Avg	TD	Int	Lg	Rtg
1942	WAS	N	1	0	0.0	0	0.0	0	0		39.6
1944	BKN	N	1	1	100.0	1	1.0	0	0	1	79.2
Career			2	1	50.0	1	0.5	0	0	1	56.3

Year	Team		Att	Com	PC	Yds	Avg	TD	Int	Lg	Rtg

Ed Matesic

Year	Team		Att	Com	PC	Yds	Avg	TD	Int	Lg	Rtg
1934	PHI	N	60	20	33.3	272	4.5	2	5		25.1
1935								2			
1936	PIT	N	138	64	46.4	850	6.2	4	16		36.5
Career			198	84	42.4	1122	5.7	8	21		31.6

Ned Mathews

Year	Team		Att	Com	PC	Yds	Avg	TD	Int	Lg	Rtg
1941	DET	N	8	3	37.5	59	7.4	1	0	27	103.6
1942			22	6	27.3	43	2.0	1	2	18	16.9
1943			12	4	33.3	76	6.3	1	0	33	84.0
1945	BOS	N	1	0	0.0	0	0.0	0	0		39.6
1946	SF	AA	1	1	100.0	26	26.0	0	0	26	118.8
1947			2	0	0.0	0	0.0	0	0		39.6
Career			46	14	30.4	204	4.4	3	2	33	49.5

Ray Mathews

Year	Team		Att	Com	PC	Yds	Avg	TD	Int	Lg	Rtg
1951	PIT	N	31	15	48.4	208	6.7	2	0	39	91.9
1952			13	3	23.1	104	8.0	0	1	69	28.4
1953			2	0	0.0	0	0.0	0	0		39.6
1954			4	0	0.0	0	0.0	0	1		0.0
1959			1	1	100.0	38	38.0	0	0	38	118.8
Career			51	19	37.3	350	6.9	2	2	69	58.5

Bill Mathis

Year	Team		Att	Com	PC	Yds	Avg	TD	Int	Lg	Rtg
1963	NY	A	1	0	0.0	0	0.0	0	1		0.0

Bruce Mathison

Year	Team		Att	Com	PC	Yds	Avg	TD	Int	Lg	Rtg
1983	SD	N	5	3	60.0	41	8.2	0	1	25	46.7
1985	BUF	N	228	113	49.6	1635	7.2	4	14	60t	53.5
1987	SEA	N	76	36	47.4	501	6.6	3	5	47	54.8
Career			309	152	49.2	2177	7.0	7	20	60t	53.0

Charlie Mathys

Year	Team		Att	Com	PC	Yds	Avg	TD	Int	Lg	Rtg
1923	GB	N						2			
1925								6			
1926								2			
Career								10			

Ollie Matson

Year	Team		Att	Com	PC	Yds	Avg	TD	Int	Lg	Rtg
1954	CHIC	N	2	0	0.0	0	0.0	0	0		39.6
1955			1	1	100.0	43	43.0	0	0	43	118.8
1956			3	0	0.0	0	0.0	0	0		39.6
1957			5	2	40.0	59	11.8	0	0	82	84.6
1958			2	1	50.0	4	2.0	0	0	4	56.3
1959	LA	N	1	0	0.0	0	0.0	0	1		0.0
1962			1	1	100.0	13	13.0	0	0	13	118.8
Career			15	5	33.3	119	7.9	0	1	82	35.1

Tom Matte

Year	Team		Att	Com	PC	Yds	Avg	TD	Int	Lg	Rtg
1962	BAL	N	13	5	38.5	85	6.5	1	0	30	87.0
1963			5	1	20.0	20	4.0	0	0	20	43.8
1964			4	3	75.0	58	14.5	1	0	22	156.3
1965			7	1	14.3	19	2.7	0	1	19	0.0
1966			3	0	0.0	0	0.0	0	1		0.0
1967			5	1	20.0	18	3.6	0	0	18	42.1
1968			1	0	0.0	0	0.0	0	0		39.6
1969			3	1	33.3	46	15.3	0	0	46	81.9
1971			1	0	0.0	0	0.0	0	0		39.6
Career			42	12	28.6	246	5.9	2	2	46	47.5
Playoffs			12	5	41.7	40	3.3	0	0		50.7

Shane Matthews

Year	Team		Att	Com	PC	Yds	Avg	TD	Int	Lg	Rtg
1996	CHI	N	17	13	76.5	158	9.3	1	0	26	124.1

Harry Mattos

Year	Team		Att	Com	PC	Yds	Avg	TD	Int	Lg	Rtg
1936	GB	N	12	4	33.3	32	2.7	0	2		2.8
1937	CLE	N	22	5	22.7	94	4.3	1	4		20.5
Career			34	9	26.5	126	3.7	1	6		12.7

Tuffy Maul

Year	Team		Att	Com	PC	Yds	Avg	TD	Int	Lg	Rtg
1926	LA	N						1			

Dean May

Year	Team		Att	Com	PC	Yds	Avg	TD	Int	Lg	Rtg
1984	PHI	N	1	1	100.0	33	33.0	0	0	33	118.8
1987	DEN	N	5	0	0.0	0	0.0	0	1		0.0
Career			6	1	16.7	33	5.5	0	1	33	10.4

Lew Mayne

Year	Team		Att	Com	PC	Yds	Avg	TD	Int	Lg	Rtg
1946	BKN	AA	25	14	56.0	219	8.8	3	4		85.3

Dave Mays

Year	Team		Att	Com	PC	Yds	Avg	TD	Int	Lg	Rtg
1976	CLE	N	20	9	45.0	101	5.0	0	1	21	39.8
1977			121	67	55.4	797	6.6	6	10	60	57.8

Dave Mays *continued*

Year	Team		Att	Com	PC	Yds	Avg	TD	Int	Lg	Rtg
1978	BUF	N	15	4	26.7	39	2.6	1	0	19	61.8
Career			156	80	51.3	937	6.0	7	11	60	55.4

Frank Maznicki

Year	Team		Att	Com	PC	Yds	Avg	TD	Int	Lg	Rtg
1942	CHIB	N	1	0	0.0	0	0.0	0	0		39.6
1947	BOS	N	1	0	0.0	0	0.0	0	1		0.0
Career			2	0	0.0	0	0.0	0	1		0.0
Playoffs			1	0	0.0	0	0.0	0	1		0.0

Dean McAdams

Year	Team		Att	Com	PC	Yds	Avg	TD	Int	Lg	Rtg
1941	BKN	N	27	12	44.4	176	6.5	2	3	36	51.4
1942			89	35	39.3	441	5.0	2	15	56	23.4
1943			75	37	49.3	315	4.2	0	7	49	21.8
Career			191	84	44.0	932	4.9	4	25	56	26.5

George McAfee

Year	Team		Att	Com	PC	Yds	Avg	TD	Int	Lg	Rtg
1940	CHIB	N	11	4	36.4	50	4.5	2	0		90.9
1941			3	1	33.3	44	14.7	1	0	44	121.5
1945			1	0	0.0	0	0.0	0	0		39.6
1946			2	1	50.0	0	0.0	0	0	0	56.3
1948			4	0	0.0	0	0.0	0	0		39.6
1950			1	0	0.0	0	0.0	0	1		0.0
Career			22	6	27.3	94	4.3	3	1	44	65.5
Playoffs			1	0	0.0	0	0.0	0	0		39.6

Wes McAfee

Year	Team		Att	Com	PC	Yds	Avg	TD	Int	Lg	Rtg
1941	PHI	N	4	1	25.0	4	1.0	0	0	4	39.6

Jack McAuliffe

Year	Team		Att	Com	PC	Yds	Avg	TD	Int	Lg	Rtg
1926	GB	N							1		

Jack McBride

Year	Team		Att	Com	PC	Yds	Avg	TD	Int	Lg	Rtg
1925	NYG	N							7		
1926									2		
1927									7		
1929	PRO	N							2		
1930	BKN	N							4		
1931									2		
1932	BKN-NYG	N	74	36	48.6	463	6.3	6	9		56.6
1933	NYG	N							2		
1934			3	3	100.0	37	12.3	1	0		157.6
Career			77	39	50.6	500	6.5	33	9	4	62.1

Don McCall

Year	Team		Att	Com	PC	Yds	Avg	TD	Int	Lg	Rtg
1968	NO	N	1	0	0.0	0	0.0	0	0		39.6

Jim McCarthy

Year	Team		Att	Com	PC	Yds	Avg	TD	Int	Lg	Rtg
1947	BKN	AA	2	1	50.0	17	8.5	0	1	17	39.6

John McCarthy

Year	Team		Att	Com	PC	Yds	Avg	TD	Int	Lg	Rtg
1944	C-P	N	67	20	29.9	250	3.7	0	13	38	3.0

Shawn McCarthy

Year	Team		Att	Com	PC	Yds	Avg	TD	Int	Lg	Rtg
1991	NE	N	1	1	100.0	11	11.0	0	0	11	112.5

Vince McCarthy

Year	Team		Att	Com	PC	Yds	Avg	TD	Int	Lg	Rtg
1925	RI	N							1		

Don McCauley

Year	Team		Att	Com	PC	Yds	Avg	TD	Int	Lg	Rtg
1974	BAL	N	2	1	50.0	11	5.5	1	0	11t	106.3

Cliff McClain

Year	Team		Att	Com	PC	Yds	Avg	TD	Int	Lg	Rtg
1972	NYJ	N	1	0	0.0	0	0.0	0	0		39.6

Billy McClard

Year	Team		Att	Com	PC	Yds	Avg	TD	Int	Lg	Rtg
1974	NO	N	1	0	0.0	0	0.0	0	1		0.0

Curtis McClinton

Year	Team		Att	Com	PC	Yds	Avg	TD	Int	Lg	Rtg
1963	KC	A	2	1	50.0	33	16.5	1	0	33t	135.4
1965			1	0	0.0	0	0.0	0	0		39.6
Career			3	1	33.3	33	11.0	1	0	33t	115.3

Brian McClure

Year	Team		Att	Com	PC	Yds	Avg	TD	Int	Lg	Rtg
1987	BUF	N	38	20	52.6	181	4.8	0	3	30	32.9

Bill McColl

Year	Team		Att	Com	PC	Yds	Avg	TD	Int	Lg	Rtg
1955	CHIB	N	2	1	50.0	59	29.5	0	0	59	95.8
1956			4	1	25.0	79	19.8	1	2	79t	79.2
Career			6	2	33.3	138	23.0	1	2	79t	81.9

John McCormick

Year	Team		Att	Com	PC	Yds	Avg	TD	Int	Lg	Rtg
1962	MIN	N	18	7	38.9	104	5.8	0	5	53	19.0
1963	DEN	A	72	28	38.9	417	5.8	4	3		59.8

Year	Team		Att	Com	PC	Yds	Avg		TD	Int	Lg	Rtg

John McCormick *continued*

Year	Team		Att	Com	PC	Yds	Avg		TD	Int	Lg	Rtg
1965			253	103	40.7	1292	5.1		7	14	90	43.5
1966			193	68	35.2	993	5.1		6	15	64	30.9
1968			19	8	42.1	89	4.7		0	1	18	34.8
Career			555	214	38.6	2895	5.2		17	38	90	37.6

Joel McCoy

| 1946 | DET | N | 18 | 6 | 33.3 | 72 | 4.0 | | 0 | 4 | 34 | 6.9 |

Hurdis McCrary

| 1929 | GB | N | | | | | | | 1 | | | |

Earl McCullouch

| 1972 | DET | N | 1 | 1 | 100.0 | 23 | 23.0 | | 0 | 0 | 23 | 118.8 |

Hal McCullough

| 1942 | BKN | N | 38 | 12 | 31.6 | 211 | 5.6 | | 1 | 3 | 71 | 27.4 |

Hugh McCullough

1939	PIT	N	100	32	32.0	443	4.4		2	12		14.3
1940	CHIC	N	116	43	37.1	529	4.6		4	21		23.9
1941			32	12	37.5	133	4.2		0	5	35	11.1
1945	BOS	N	5	0		0	0.0		0	3		0.0
Career			253	87	34.4	1105	4.4		6	41	35	17.3

Lawrence McCutcheon

1975	LA	N	1	0	0.0	0	0.0		0	0		39.6
1978			1	0	0.0	0	0.0		0	0		39.6
1980	DEN-SEA	N	2	1	50.0	12	6.0		0	0	12	68.8
Career			4	1	25.0	12	3.0		0	0	12	39.6
Playoffs			2	1	50.0	24	12.0		1	0		133.3

Gary McDermott

| 1968 | BUF | A | 3 | 2 | 66.7 | 35 | 11.7 | | 0 | 0 | 27 | 106.3 |

Paul McDonald

1981	CLE	N	57	35	61.4	463	8.1		4	2	46	95.9
1982			149	73	49.0	993	6.7		5	8	56t	59.5
1983			68	32	47.1	341	5.0		1	4	27	42.6
1984			493	271	55.0	3472	7.0		14	23	64	67.3
Career			767	411	53.6	5269	6.9		24	37	64	65.7
Playoffs			37	18	48.6	281	7.6		1	0		83.3

Tommy McDonald

1957	PHI	N	1	1	100.0	11	11.0		0	0	11	112.5
1962			1	1	100.0	10	10.0		1	0	10t	147.9
Career			2	2	100.0	21	10.5		1	0	11	150.0

Walt McDonald

| 1946 | MIA | AA | 3 | 1 | 33.3 | 24 | 8.0 | | 0 | 1 | 24 | 23.6 |

Coley McDonough

1939	CHIC-PIT	N	47	17	36.2	365	7.8		2	8		39.2
1940	PIT	N	14	8	57.1	92	6.6		0	3		37.5
1941			41	12	29.3	200	4.9		1	5	59	16.0
1944	C-P	N	23	10	43.5	208	9.0		2	4	67	65.4
Career			125	47	37.6	865	6.9		5	20	67	36.0

Gerry McDougall

| 1963 | SD | A | 1 | 1 | 100.0 | 11 | 11.0 | | 0 | 0 | 11 | 152.1 |

O.J. McDuffie

| Playoffs | | | 1 | 0 | 0.0 | 0 | 0.0 | | 0 | 0 | | 39.6 |

Hugh McElhenny

1953	SF	N	3	2	66.7	13	4.3		1	0	11t	115.3
1956			1	0	0.0	0	0.0		0	1		0.0
1958			2	0	0.0	0	0.0		0	0		39.6
1961	MIN	N	1	0	0.0	0	0.0		0	0		39.6
Career			7	2	28.6	13	1.9		1	1	11t	39.6

Banks McFadden

| 1940 | BKN | N | 8 | 3 | 37.5 | 103 | 12.9 | | 1 | 1 | | 85.4 |

Buford McGee

1986	SD	N	1	1	100.0	1	1.0		0	0	1	79.2
1990	LARM	N	2	2	100.0	23	11.5		1	0	22t	154.2
Career			3	3	100.0	24	8.0		1	0	22t	139.6

Max McGee

| 1958 | GB | N | 1 | 0 | 0.0 | 0 | 0.0 | | 0 | 0 | | 39.6 |

Max McGee *continued*

Year	Team		Att	Com	PC	Yds	Avg		TD	Int	Lg	Rtg
1962			1	0	0.0	0	0.0		0	1		0.0
Career			2	0	0.0	0	0.0		0	1		0.0

Charlie McGibbony

| 1944 | BKN | N | 48 | 18 | 37.5 | 262 | 5.5 | | 1 | 10 | 65 | 23.4 |

Lee McGriff

| 1976 | TB | N | 1 | 1 | 100.0 | 39 | 39.0 | | 0 | 0 | 39 | 118.8 |

Monte McGuire

| 1987 | DEN | N | 3 | 2 | 66.7 | 23 | 7.7 | | 0 | 0 | 13 | 89.6 |

Dan McGwire

1991	SEA	N	7	3	42.9	27	3.9		0	1	13	14.3
1992			30	17	56.7	116	3.9		0	3	20	25.8
1993			5	3	60.0	24	4.8		1	0	17t	111.7
1994			105	51	48.6	578	5.5		1	2	36	60.7
1995	MIA	N	1	0	0.0	0	0.0		0	0		39.6
Career			148	74	50.0	745	5.0		2	6	65	52.3

Lamar McHan

1954	CHIC	N	255	105	41.2	1475	5.8		6	22	70	32.4
1955			207	78	37.7	1085	5.2		11	19	74t	34.8
1956			152	72	47.4	1159	7.6		10	8	75	73.3
1957			200	87	43.5	1568	7.8		10	15	83t	56.4
1958			198	91	46.0	1291	6.5		12	13	71t	60.4
1959	GB	N	108	48	44.4	805	7.5		8	9	81	60.1
1960			91	33	36.3	517	5.7		3	5	47	44.1
1961	BAL	N	15	3	20.0	28	1.9		1	4	17t	22.2
1962			20	10	50.0	278	13.9		3	2	74t	95.8
1963	BAL-SF	N	196	83	42.3	1243	6.3		8	11	68t	54.0
Career			1442	610	42.3	9449	6.6		72	108	83t	50.1

Don McIlhenny

| 1956 | DET | N | 1 | 0 | 0.0 | 0 | 0.0 | | 0 | 0 | | 39.6 |

Pat McInally

1977	CIN	N	1	1	100.0	4	4.0		0	0	4	83.3
1984			2	2	100.0	77	38.5		0	0	43	118.8
1985			1	0	0.0	0	0.0		0	0		39.6
Career			4	3	75.0	81	20.3		0	0	43	116.7

Rick McIvor

| 1984 | STL | N | 4 | 0 | 0.0 | 0 | 0.0 | | 0 | 0 | | 39.6 |

Paul McJulien

| 1992 | GB | N | 1 | 0 | 0.0 | 0 | 0.0 | | 0 | 0 | | 39.6 |

Roy McKay

1944	GB	N	14	6	42.9	72	5.1		1	2	26	43.5
1945			89	32	36.0	520	5.8		5	9	59	35.5
Career			103	38	36.9	592	5.7		6	11	59	36.6

Emmett McLemore

| 1923 | OOR | N | | | | | | | 1 | | | |

Jim McMahon

1982	CHI	N	210	120	57.1	1501	7.1		9	7	50t	79.9
1983			295	175	59.3	2184	7.4		12	13	87t	77.6
1984			143	85	59.4	1146	8.0		8	2	61t	97.8
1985			313	178	56.9	2392	7.6		15	11	70t	82.6
1986			150	77	51.3	995	6.6		5	8	58t	61.4
1987			210	125	59.5	1639	7.8		12	8	59t	87.4
1988			192	114	59.4	1346	7.0		6	7	63t	76.0
1989	SD	N	318	176	55.3	2132	6.7		10	10	69t	73.5
1990	PHI	N	9	6	66.7	63	7.0		0	0	21	86.8
1991			311	187	60.1	2239	7.2		12	11	75t	80.3
1992			43	22	51.2	279	6.5		1	2	42t	60.1
1993	MIN	N	331	200	60.4	1968	5.9		9	8	58	76.2
1994	ARI	N	43	23	53.5	219	5.1		1	3	33	46.6
1995	GB	N	1	1	100.0	6	6.0		0	0	6	91.7
1996			4	3	75.0	39	9.8		0	0	24	105.2
Career			2573	1492	58.0	18148	7.1		100	90	87t	78.2
Playoffs			155	82	52.9	1112	7.2		5	4		76.1

John McMichael

| 1944 | BKN | N | 1 | 0 | 0.0 | 0 | 0.0 | | 0 | 1 | | 0.0 |

Bo McMillin

| 1923 | MIL | N | | | | | | | 1 | | | |

Greg McMurtry

| 1992 | NE | N | 1 | 0 | 0.0 | 0 | 0.0 | | 0 | 0 | | 39.6 |

Steve McNair

Year	Team		Att	Com	PC	Yds	Avg	TD	Int	Lg	Rtg
1995	HOU	N	80	41	51.2	569	7.1	3	1	53	81.7
1996			143	88	61.5	1197	8.4	6	4	83t	90.6
Career			223	129	57.8	1766	7.9	9	5	83t	87.4

Clifton McNeil

Year	Team		Att	Com	PC	Yds	Avg	TD	Int	Lg	Rtg
1968	SF	N	2	1	50.0	43	21.5	1	1	43t	95.8

Freeman McNeil

Year	Team		Att	Com	PC	Yds	Avg	TD	Int	Lg	Rtg
1983	NYJ	N	1	1	100.0	5	5.0	1	0	5t	127.1
Playoffs			1	1	100.0	14	14.0	1	0		158.3

Tom McNeill

Year	Team		Att	Com	PC	Yds	Avg	TD	Int	Lg	Rtg
1967	NO	N	1	1	100.0	24	24.0	0	0	24	118.8

Kim McQuilken

Year	Team		Att	Com	PC	Yds	Avg	TD	Int	Lg	Rtg
1974	ATL	N	79	34	43.0	373	4.7	0	9	26	18.0
1975			61	20	32.8	253	4.1	1	9	31	12.6
1976			121	48	39.7	450	3.7	2	10	39	21.7
1977			7	5	71.4	47	6.7	1	0	14	129.2
1979	WAS	N	4	1	25.0	12	3.0	0	1	12	0.0
Career			272	108	39.7	1135	4.2	4	29	39	17.9

Warren McVea

Year	Team		Att	Com	PC	Yds	Avg	TD	Int	Lg	Rtg
1969	KC	A	3	1	33.3	50	16.7	1	0	50t	121.5
1970	KC	N	1	0	0.0	0	0.0	0	0		39.6
Career			4	1	25.0	50	12.5	1	0	50t	118.8

Tom McWilliams

Year	Team		Att	Com	PC	Yds	Avg	TD	Int	Lg	Rtg
1949	LA	AA	2	0	0.0	0	0.0	0	0		39.6
1950	PIT	N	8	5	62.5	113	14.1	0	1	63	66.7
Career			10	5	50.0	113	11.3	0	1	63	51.3

Eddie Meador

Year	Team		Att	Com	PC	Yds	Avg	TD	Int	Lg	Rtg
1964	LA	N	1	0	0.0	0	0.0	0	0		39.6
1965			1	0	0.0	0	0.0	0	0		39.6
1966			1	0	0.0	0	0.0	0	0		39.6
1967			1	1	100.0	18	18.0	1	0	18t	158.3
1969			1	0	0.0	0	0.0	0	0		39.6
Career			5	1	20.0	18	3.6	1	0	18t	81.7

Natrone Means

Year	Team		Att	Com	PC	Yds	Avg	TD	Int	Lg	Rtg
1993	SD	N	1	0	0.0	0	0.0	0	0		39.6
1994			1	0	0.0	0	0.0	0	0		39.6
Career			2	0	0.0	0	0.0	0	0		39.6

Curt Mecham

Year	Team		Att	Com	PC	Yds	Avg	TD	Int	Lg	Rtg
1942	BKN	N	4	1	25.0	9	2.3	0	1	9	0.0

Dave Meggett

Year	Team		Att	Com	PC	Yds	Avg	TD	Int	Lg	Rtg
1991	NYG	N	1	0	0.0	0	0.0	0	0		39.6
1993			2	2	100.0	63	31.5	2	0	42t	158.3
1994			2	1	50.0	16	8.0	1	0	16t	116.7
1995	NE	N	1	0	0.0	0	0.0	0	0		39.6
1996			1	0	0.0	0	0.0	0	0		39.6
Career			7	3	42.9	79	11.3	3	0	42t	124.4
Playoffs			2	0	0.0	0	0.0	0	0		39.6

Charlie Mehelich

Year	Team		Att	Com	PC	Yds	Avg	TD	Int	Lg	Rtg
1948	PIT	N	2	0	0.0	0	0.0	0	0		39.6

Ken Mercer

Year	Team		Att	Com	PC	Yds	Avg	TD	Int	Lg	Rtg
1927	FRA	N							4		
1928									5		
1929									3		
Career									12		

Mike Mercer

Year	Team		Att	Com	PC	Yds	Avg	TD	Int	Lg	Rtg
1965	OAK	A	1	1	100.0	14	14.0	0	0	14	118.8

Don Meredith

Year	Team		Att	Com	PC	Yds	Avg	TD	Int	Lg	Rtg
1960	DAL	N	68	29	42.6	281	4.1	2	5	23	34.0
1961			182	94	51.6	1161	6.4	9	11	56	63.0
1962			212	105	49.5	1679	7.9	15	8	69t	84.2
1963			310	167	53.9	2381	7.7	17	18	55	73.1
1964			323	158	48.9	2143	6.6	9	16	49	59.1
1965			305	141	46.2	2415	7.9	22	13	65t	79.9
1966			344	177	51.5	2805	8.2	24	12	95t	87.7
1967			255	128	50.2	1834	7.2	16	16	60t	68.7
1968			309	171	55.3	2500	8.1	21	12	65t	88.4
Career			2308	1170	50.7	17199	7.5	135	111	95t	74.8
Playoffs			77	38	49.4	551	7.2	3	5		59.0

Guido Merkens

Year	Team		Att	Com	PC	Yds	Avg	TD	Int	Lg	Rtg
1981	NO	N	2	1	50.0	20	10.0	0	0	20	85.4
1982			49	18	36.7	186	3.8	1	2	37	38.3
1985			1	1	100.0	7	7.0	1	0	7t	135.4
1987	PHI	N	14	7	50.0	70	5.0	0	0	17	64.6
Career			66	27	40.9	283	4.3	2	2	37	51.5

Eric Metcalf

Year	Team		Att	Com	PC	Yds	Avg	TD	Int	Lg	Rtg
1989	CLE	N	2	1	50.0	32	16.0	1	0	32t	135.4
1991			0	0		0		0	0	0	
1992			1	0	0.0	0	0.0	0	0		39.6
1994			1	0	0.0	0	0.0	0	0		39.6
1995	ATL	N	1	0	0.0	0	0.0	0	0		39.6
Career			5	1	20.0	32	6.4	1	0	32t	93.3

Terry Metcalf

Year	Team		Att	Com	PC	Yds	Avg	TD	Int	Lg	Rtg
1974	STL	N	2	0	0.0	0	0.0	0	0		39.6
1975			2	1	50.0	51	25.5	1	0	51t	135.4
1976			1	0	0.0	0	0.0	0	0		39.6
1977			5	3	60.0	27	5.4	1	1	11t	74.6
Career			10	4	40.0	78	7.8	2	1	51t	67.9

Ron Meyer

Year	Team		Att	Com	PC	Yds	Avg	TD	Int	Lg	Rtg
1966	PIT	N	19	7	36.8	59	3.1	0	1	19	23.8

Al Michaels

Year	Team		Att	Com	PC	Yds	Avg	TD	Int	Lg	Rtg
1925	CLE	N							2		
1926	CLE	A							3		
Career									5		

Nick Mike-Mayer

Year	Team		Att	Com	PC	Yds	Avg	TD	Int	Lg	Rtg
1981	BUF	N	1	0	0.0	0	0.0	0	0		39.6

Pete Mikolajewski

Year	Team		Att	Com	PC	Yds	Avg	TD	Int	Lg	Rtg
1969	SD	A	0	0		0		0	0		

Don Milano

Year	Team		Att	Com	PC	Yds	Avg	TD	Int	Lg	Rtg
1975	GB	N	32	15	46.9	181	5.7	1	1	56	62.1

Scott Milanovich

Year	Team		Att	Com	PC	Yds	Avg	TD	Int	Lg	Rtg
1996	TB	N	3	2	66.7	9	3.0	0	0	8	70.1

Jack Mildren

Year	Team		Att	Com	PC	Yds	Avg	TD	Int	Lg	Rtg
1972	BAL	N	1	0	0.0	0	0.0	0	0		39.6

Hugh Millen

Year	Team		Att	Com	PC	Yds	Avg	TD	Int	Lg	Rtg
1987	LARM	N	1	1	100.0	0	0.0	0	0	0	79.2
1988	ATL	N	31	17	54.8	215	6.9	0	2	38	49.8
1989			50	31	62.0	432	8.6	1	2	47	79.8
1990			63	34	54.0	427	6.8	1	0	53	80.6
1991	NE	N	409	246	60.1	3073	7.5	9	18	60t	72.5
1992			203	124	61.1	1203	5.9	8	10	39	70.3
1994	DEN	N	131	81	61.8	893	6.8	2	3	76	77.6
1995			40	26	65.0	197	4.9	1	0	18	85.1
Career			928	560	60.3	6440	6.9	22	35	76	73.5

Chris Miller

Year	Team		Att	Com	PC	Yds	Avg	TD	Int	Lg	Rtg
1987	ATL	N	92	39	42.4	552	6.0	1	9	57	26.4
1988			351	184	52.4	2133	6.1	11	12	68t	67.3
1989			526	280	53.2	3459	6.6	16	10	72t	76.1
1990			388	222	57.2	2735	7.0	17	14	75t	78.7
1991			413	220	53.3	3103	7.5	26	18	80t	80.6
1992			253	152	60.1	1739	6.9	15	6	89t	90.7
1993			66	32	48.5	345	5.2	1	3	32t	50.4
1994	LARM	N	317	173	54.6	2104	6.6	16	14	54	73.6
1995	STL	N	405	232	57.3	2623	6.5	18	15	72	76.2
Career			2811	1534	54.6	18793	6.7	121	101	89t	74.8
Playoffs			62	35	56.5	469	7.6	3	5		63.2

Eddie Miller

Year	Team		Att	Com	PC	Yds	Avg	TD	Int	Lg	Rtg
1939	NYG	N	23	13	56.5	195	8.5	2	2		77.3
1940			73	35	47.9	505	6.9	3	7		45.0
Career			96	48	50.0	700	7.3	5	9		52.4
Playoffs			6	3	50.0	40	6.7	0	1		31.9

Jim Miller

Year	Team		Att	Com	PC	Yds	Avg	TD	Int	Lg	Rtg
1995	PIT	N	56	32	57.1	397	7.1	2	5	42t	53.9
1996			25	13	52.0	123	4.9	0	0	17	65.9
Career			81	45	55.6	520	6.4	2	5	42t	57.6

Larry Miller

Year	Team		Att	Com	PC	Yds	Avg	TD	Int	Lg	Rtg
1987	MIN	N	6	1	16.7	2	0.3	0	1	2	0.0

Mark Miller

Year	Team		Att	Com	PC	Yds	Avg	TD	Int	Lg	Rtg
1978	CLE	N	39	13	33.3	212	5.4	1	4	44	21.5
1979			8	2	25.0	31	3.9	0	1	17	3.6
Career			47	15	31.9	243	5.2	1	5	44	17.7

Mark Miller

Year	Team		Att	Com	PC	Yds	Avg	TD	Int	Lg	Rtg
1987	BUF	N	3	1	33.3	9	3.0	0	1	9	2.8

Paul Miller

Year	Team		Att	Com	PC	Yds	Avg	TD	Int	Lg	Rtg
1936	GB	N	1	0	0.0	0	0.0	0	1		0.0

Ron Miller

Year	Team		Att	Com	PC	Yds	Avg	TD	Int	Lg	Rtg
1962	LA	N	43	17	39.5	250	5.8	1	1	55t	57.3

Willie Miller

Year	Team		Att	Com	PC	Yds	Avg	TD	Int	Lg	Rtg
1975	CLE	N	1	1	100.0	26	26.0	1	0	26t	158.3

Charley Milstead

Year	Team		Att	Com	PC	Yds	Avg	TD	Int	Lg	Rtg
1960	HOU	A	7	4	57.1	43	6.1	0	0		75.3

Gene Mingo

Year	Team		Att	Com	PC	Yds	Avg	TD	Int	Lg	Rtg
1960	DEN	A	7	1	14.3	46	6.6	0	0	46	54.5
1961			8	4	50.0	136	17.0	2	0	52	135.4
1962			2	1	50.0	18	9.0	0	1	18	41.7
1963			1	0	0.0	0	0.0	0	0		39.6
Career			18	6	33.3	200	11.1	2	1	52	90.0

Tony Minisi

Year	Team		Att	Com	PC	Yds	Avg	TD	Int	Lg	Rtg
1948	NYG	N	3	0	0.0	0	0.0	0	2		0.0

Ed Mioduszewski

Year	Team		Att	Com	PC	Yds	Avg	TD	Int	Lg	Rtg
1953	BAL	N	30	11	36.7	113	3.8	2	2	17	42.8

George Mira

Year	Team		Att	Com	PC	Yds	Avg	TD	Int	Lg	Rtg
1964	SF	N	53	23	43.4	331	6.2	2	5	79t	37.5
1965			58	28	48.3	460	7.9	4	3	46	76.8
1966			53	22	41.5	284	5.4	5	2	29	74.7
1967			65	35	53.8	592	9.1	5	3	58	91.3
1968			11	4	36.4	44	4.0	1	1	43t	41.5
1969	PHI	N	76	25	32.9	240	3.2	1	5	35	19.6
1971	MIA	N	30	11	36.7	159	5.3	1	1	43	51.9
Career			346	148	42.8	2110	6.1	19	20	79t	57.4

Rick Mirer

Year	Team		Att	Com	PC	Yds	Avg	TD	Int	Lg	Rtg
1993	SEA	N	486	274	56.4	2833	5.8	12	17	53t	67.0
1994			381	195	51.2	2151	5.6	11	7	51	70.2
1995			391	209	53.5	2564	6.6	13	20	59t	63.7
1996			265	136	51.3	1546	5.8	5	12	60	56.6
Career			1523	814	53.4	9094	6.0	41	56	60	65.2

John Mistler

Year	Team		Att	Com	PC	Yds	Avg	TD	Int	Lg	Rtg
1983	NYG	N	1	0	0.0	0	0.0	0	0		39.6

Bobby Mitchell

Year	Team		Att	Com	PC	Yds	Avg	TD	Int	Lg	Rtg
1960	CLE	N	1	1	100.0	23	23.0	1	0	23t	158.3
1966	WAS	N	1	1	100.0	21	21.0	0	0	21	118.8
1967			1	1	100.0	17	17.0	0	0	17	118.8
Career			3	3	100.0	61	20.3	1	0	23t	158.3

Brian Mitchell

Year	Team		Att	Com	PC	Yds	Avg	TD	Int	Lg	Rtg
1990	WAS	N	6	3	50.0	40	6.7	0	0	18	71.5
1992			1	0	0.0	0	0.0	0	0		39.6
1993			2	1	50.0	50	25.0	0	1	50	56.3
1994			1	0	0.0	0	0.0	0	1		0.0
1996			1	0	0.0	0	0.0	0	0		39.6
Career			11	4	36.4	90	8.2	0	2	50	26.9

Charlie Mitchell

Year	Team		Att	Com	PC	Yds	Avg	TD	Int	Lg	Rtg
1964	DEN	A	1	0	0.0	0	0.0	0	0		39.6

Paul Mitchell

Year	Team		Att	Com	PC	Yds	Avg	TD	Int	Lg	Rtg
1946	LA	AA	10	3	30.0	19	1.9	0	2		0.0
1948			2	1	50.0	15	7.5	0	1	15	35.4
Career			12	4	33.3	34	2.8	0	3	15	2.8

Scott Mitchell

Year	Team		Att	Com	PC	Yds	Avg	TD	Int	Lg	Rtg
1992	MIA	N	8	2	25.0	32	4.0	0	1	18	4.2
1993			233	133	57.1	1773	7.6	12	8	77t	84.2
1994	DET	N	246	119	48.4	1456	5.9	10	11	34	62.0
1995			583	346	59.3	4338	7.4	32	12	91t	92.3
1996			437	253	57.9	2917	6.7	17	17	62t	74.9
Career			1507	853	56.6	10516	7.0	71	49	91t	80.5
Playoffs			29	13	44.8	155	5.3	1	4		33.6

Stump Mitchell

Year	Team		Att	Com	PC	Yds	Avg	TD	Int	Lg	Rtg
1984	STL	N	1	1	100.0	20	20.0	0	0	20	118.8
1985			2	1	50.0	31	15.5	0	0	31	95.8
1986			3	1	33.3	15	5.0	1	0	15t	90.3
1987			3	1	33.3	17	5.7	0	0	17	53.5
Career			9	4	44.4	83	9.2	1	0	31	114.6

Kelly Moan

Year	Team		Att	Com	PC	Yds	Avg	TD	Int	Lg	Rtg
1939	CLE	N	9	3	33.3	77	8.6	1	2		63.0

Dicky Moegle

Year	Team		Att	Com	PC	Yds	Avg	TD	Int	Lg	Rtg
1955	SF	N	1	0	0.0	0	0.0	0	0		39.6
1959			1	0	0.0	0	0.0	0	0		39.6
Career			2	0	0.0	0	0.0	0	0		39.6

Johnny Mohardt

Year	Team		Att	Com	PC	Yds	Avg	TD	Int	Lg	Rtg
1923	CHIC	N							1		
1924	RAC	N							1		
1925	CHIB	N							1		
Career									3		

Chris Mohr

Year	Team		Att	Com	PC	Yds	Avg	TD	Int	Lg	Rtg
1991	BUF	N	1	1	100.0	-9	-9.0	0	0	-9	79.2

Bo Molenda

Year	Team		Att	Com	PC	Yds	Avg	TD	Int	Lg	Rtg
1928	NYY	N							1		
1931	GB	N							4		
Career									5		

Keith Molesworth

Year	Team		Att	Com	PC	Yds	Avg	TD	Int	Lg	Rtg
1931	CHIB	N							1		
1932			54	22	40.7	475	8.8	3	6		51.6
1933			50	19	38.0	421	8.4	4	4		62.2
1934			36	13	36.1	225	6.3	3	4		46.4
1935			36	13	36.1	266	7.4	3	3		56.0
1936			31	15	48.4	188	6.1	4	4		**67.7**
1937			6	1	16.7	4	0.7	0	0	4	39.6
Career			213	83	39.0	1579	7.4	18	21	4	52.5
Playoffs			15	7	46.7	119	7.9	0	1		46.3

Art Monk

Year	Team		Att	Com	PC	Yds	Avg	TD	Int	Lg	Rtg
1983	WAS	N	1	1	100.0	46	46.0	0	0	46	118.8
1988			1	0	0.0	0	0.0	0	0		39.6
Career			2	1	50.0	46	23.0	0	0	46	95.8

Bob Monnett

Year	Team		Att	Com	PC	Yds	Avg	TD	Int	Lg	Rtg
1933	GB	N	46	23	50.0	315	6.8	3	3		66.8
1934			47	16	34.0	223	4.7	2	4		28.9
1935			65	31	47.7	454	7.0	2	6		42.7
1936			52	20	38.5	280	5.4	4	2		66.2
1937			73	37	**50.7**	580	**7.9**	**9**	8		77.4
1938			57	31	**54.4**	465	**8.2**	**9**	4		**91.7**
Career			340	158	46.5	2317	6.8	29	27		64.5
Playoffs			8	3	37.5	21	2.6	0	1		6.3

Tommy Mont

Year	Team		Att	Com	PC	Yds	Avg	TD	Int	Lg	Rtg
1948	WAS	N	28	12	42.9	157	5.6	2	2	35	55.2
1949			7	3	42.9	44	6.3	0	0	31	64.0
Career			35	15	42.9	201	5.7	2	2	35	57.0

Joe Montana

Year	Team		Att	Com	PC	Yds	Avg	TD	Int	Lg	Rtg
1979	SF	N	23	13	56.5	96	4.2	1	0	18	81.1
1980			273	176	**64.5**	1795	6.6	15	9	71t	87.8
1981			488	311	**63.7**	3565	7.3	19	12	78t	88.4
1982			**346**	213	61.6	2613	7.6	**17**	11	55	88.0
1983			515	332	64.5	3910	7.6	26	12	77t	94.6
1984			432	279	64.6	3630	8.4	28	10	80t	102.9
1985			494	303	**61.3**	3653	7.4	27	13	73	91.3
1986			307	191	62.2	2236	7.3	8	9	48	80.7
1987			398	266	**66.8**	3054	7.7	**31**	13	57t	**102.1**
1988			397	238	59.9	2981	7.5	18	10	96t	87.9
1989			386	271	**70.2**	3521	**9.1**	26	8	95t	**112.4**
1990			520	321	61.7	3944	7.6	26	16	78t	89.0
1992			21	15	71.4	126	6.0	2	0	17	118.4
1993	KC	N	298	181	60.7	2144	7.2	13	7	50t	87.4
1994			493	299	60.6	3283	6.7	16	9	57t	83.6
Career			5391	3409	63.2	40551	7.5	273	139	96t	92.3
Playoffs			**734**	**460**	62.7	**5772**	7.9	**45**	21		95.6

Cliff Montgomery

Year	Team		Att	Com	PC	Yds	Avg	TD	Int	Lg	Rtg
1934	BKN	N							1		

Mike Montgomery

Year	Team		Att	Com	PC	Yds	Avg	TD	Int	Lg	Rtg
1971	SD	N	6	3	50.0	80	13.3	1	0	33	135.4

Mike Montgomery *continued*

Year	Team		Att	Com	PC	Yds	Avg	TD	Int	Lg	Rtg
1972	DAL	N	3	1	33.3	31	10.3	0	0	31	72.9
1973			1	0	0.0	0	0.0	0	0		39.6
Career			10	4	40.0	111	11.1	1	0	33	115.0

Wilbert Montgomery

Year	Team		Att	Com	PC	Yds	Avg	TD	Int	Lg	Rtg
1980	PHI	N	1	0	0.0	0	0.0	0	0		39.6
1984			2	0	0.0	0	0.0	0	0		39.6
Career			3	0	0.0	0	0.0	0	0		39.6

Warren Moon

Year	Team		Att	Com	PC	Yds	Avg	TD	Int	Lg	Rtg
1984	HOU	N	450	259	57.6	3338	7.4	12	14	76	76.9
1985			377	200	53.1	2709	7.2	15	19	80t	68.5
1986			488	256	52.5	3489	7.1	13	26	81t	62.3
1987			368	184	50.0	2806	7.6	21	18	83t	74.2
1988			294	160	54.4	2327	7.9	17	8	57t	88.4
1989			464	280	60.3	3631	7.8	23	14	55	88.9
1990			**584**	**362**	62.0	**4689**	8.0	**33**	13	87t	96.8
1991			**655**	404	61.7	**4690**	7.2	23	21	85t	81.7
1992			346	224	64.7	2521	7.3	18	12	72	89.3
1993			520	303	58.3	3485	6.7	21	21	80t	75.2
1994	MIN	N	601	371	61.7	4264	7.1	18	19	65t	79.9
1995			606	**377**	62.2	4228	7.0	33	14	85t	91.5
1996			247	134	54.3	1610	6.5	7	9	54t	68.7
Career			6000	3514	58.6	43787	7.3	254	208	87t	81.0
Playoffs			403	259	64.3	2870	7.1	17	14		84.9

Alvin Moore

Year	Team		Att	Com	PC	Yds	Avg	TD	Int	Lg	Rtg
1984	IND	N	1	0	0.0	0	0.0	0	0		39.6
1985	DET	N	1	0	0.0	0	0.0	0	0		39.6
Career			2	0	0.0	0	0.0	0	0		39.6

Dave Moore

Year	Team		Att	Com	PC	Yds	Avg	TD	Int	Lg	Rtg
1993	TB	N	1	0	0.0	0	0.0	0	0		39.6

Lenny Moore

Year	Team		Att	Com	PC	Yds	Avg	TD	Int	Lg	Rtg
1956	BAL	N	4	1	25.0	8	2.0	1	1	8t	39.6
1957			2	0	0.0	0	0.0	0	0		39.6
1959			3	2	66.7	25	8.3	1	0	13	131.9
1960			1	0	0.0	0	0.0	0	0		39.6
1961			2	0	0.0	0	0.0	0	1		0.0
1966			0	0		0		0	0		
Career			12	3	25.0	33	2.8	2	2	13	39.6

Nat Moore

Year	Team		Att	Com	PC	Yds	Avg	TD	Int	Lg	Rtg
1974	MIA	N	1	1	100.0	31	31.0	0	0	31	118.8
1980			1	0	0.0	0	0.0	0	0		39.6
Career			2	1	50.0	31	15.5	0	0	31	95.8

Rob Moore

Year	Team		Att	Com	PC	Yds	Avg	TD	Int	Lg	Rtg
1995	ARI	N	2	1	50.0	33	16.5	0	1	33	56.3

Ron Moore

Year	Team		Att	Com	PC	Yds	Avg	TD	Int	Lg	Rtg
1994	ARI	N	1	0	0.0	0	0.0	0	0		39.6

Shawn Moore

Year	Team		Att	Com	PC	Yds	Avg	TD	Int	Lg	Rtg
1992	DEN	N	34	17	50.0	232	6.8	0	3	40	35.4

Tom Moore

Year	Team		Att	Com	PC	Yds	Avg	TD	Int	Lg	Rtg
1961	GB	N	2	2	100.0	42	21.0	1	0	22t	158.3
1962			5	2	40.0	70	14.0	2	1	45t	87.5
1963			4	3	75.0	99	24.8	1	0	49	156.3
1964			3	1	33.3	28	9.3	0	0	28	68.8
1965			2	2	100.0	22	11.0	0	0	13	112.5
1966	LA	N	1	1	100.0	20	20.0	0	0	20	118.8
1967	ATL	N	2	2	100.0	102	51.0	1	0	75t	158.3
Career			19	13	68.4	383	20.2	5	1	75t	128.8

Gonzalo Morales

Year	Team		Att	Com	PC	Yds	Avg	TD	Int	Lg	Rtg
1947	PIT	N	27	8	29.6	78	2.9	1	4	23	12.3
1948			4	3	75.0	30	7.5	0	0	14	95.8
Career			31	11	35.5	108	3.5	1	4	23	17.3

Fran Moran

Year	Team		Att	Com	PC	Yds	Avg	TD	Int	Lg	Rtg
1928	POT	N							3		
1929	NYG	N							3		
1930									2		
1932									1		
Career									9		

Larry Moriarty

Year	Team		Att	Com	PC	Yds	Avg	TD	Int	Lg	Rtg
1984	HOU	N	1	1	100.0	16	16.0	0	0	16	118.8

Mike Moroski

Year	Team		Att	Com	PC	Yds	Avg	TD	Int	Lg	Rtg
1979	ATL	N	15	8	53.3	97	6.5	0	0	23	73.5
1980			3	2	66.7	24	8.0	0	0	18	91.0
1981			26	12	46.2	132	5.1	0	1	22	45.7
1982			13	10	76.9	87	6.7	1	0	15	119.7
1983			70	45	64.3	575	8.2	2	4	50t	75.6
1984			191	102	53.4	1207	6.3	2	9	48t	56.8
1985	HOU	N	34	20	58.8	249	7.3	1	1	46	79.2
1986	SF	N	73	42	57.5	493	6.8	2	3	52	70.2
Career			425	241	56.7	2864	6.7	8	18	52	66.0

Earl Morrall

Year	Team		Att	Com	PC	Yds	Avg	TD	Int	Lg	Rtg
1956	SF	N	78	38	48.7	621	8.0	1	6	37	48.1
1957	PIT	N	289	139	**48.1**	1900	6.6	11	12	64	64.9
1958	PIT-DET	N	78	25	32.1	463	5.9	5	9	66	35.3
1959	DET	N	137	65	47.4	1102	8.0	5	6	79t	69.1
1960			49	32	65.3	423	8.6	4	3	65t	94.2
1961			150	69	46.0	909	6.1	7	9	61t	56.2
1962			52	32	61.5	449	8.6	4	4	53	82.9
1963			328	174	53.0	2621	8.0	24	14	75t	86.2
1964			91	50	54.9	588	6.5	4	3	48	75.7
1965	NYG	N	302	155	51.3	2446	8.1	22	12	89t	86.3
1966			151	71	47.0	1105	7.3	7	12	98t	54.1
1967			24	13	54.2	181	7.5	3	1	27t	100.9
1968	BAL	N	317	182	57.4	2909	9.2	**26**	17	84	93.2
1969			99	46	46.5	755	7.6	5	7	42t	60.0
1970			93	51	54.8	792	8.5	9	4	44	97.6
1971			167	84	50.3	1210	7.2	7	12	64	58.2
1972	MIA	N	150	83	55.3	1360	**9.1**	11	7	49	**91.0**
1973			38	17	44.7	253	6.7	0	4	53	27.5
1974			27	17	63.0	301	11.1	2	3	46t	86.1
1975			43	26	60.5	273	6.3	3	2	31	82.8
1976			26	10	38.5	148	5.7	1	1	67t	54.6
Career			2689	1379	51.2	20809	7.7	161	148	98t	74.1
Playoffs			103	50	48.5	806	7.8	3	7		56.5

Randall Morris

Year	Team		Att	Com	PC	Yds	Avg	TD	Int	Lg	Rtg
1984	SEA	N	0	0		0		0	0		
1985			1	0	0.0	0	0.0	0	0		39.6
1986			1	0	0.0	0	0.0	0	0		39.6
Career			2	0	0.0	0	0.0	0	0		39.6

Dennis Morrison

Year	Team		Att	Com	PC	Yds	Avg	TD	Int	Lg	Rtg
1974	SF	N	51	21	41.2	227	4.5	1	5	26	21.9

Fred Morrison

Year	Team		Att	Com	PC	Yds	Avg	TD	Int	Lg	Rtg
1951	CHIB	N	1	1	100.0	7	7.0	0	0	7	95.8

Joe Morrison

Year	Team		Att	Com	PC	Yds	Avg	TD	Int	Lg	Rtg
1959	NYG	N	2	1	50.0	14	7.0	0	0	14	72.9
1960			1	0	0.0	0	0.0	0	1		0.0
1963			2	1	50.0	18	9.0	0	0	18	81.3
1967			1	1	100.0	12	12.0	0	0	12	116.7
Career			6	3	50.0	44	7.3	0	1	26	34.7

Reece Morrison

Year	Team		Att	Com	PC	Yds	Avg	TD	Int	Lg	Rtg
1969	CLE	N	1	1	100.0	16	16.0	0	0	16	118.8

Emmett Mortell

Year	Team		Att	Com	PC	Yds	Avg	TD	Int	Lg	Rtg
1937	PHI	N	71	18	25.4	320	4.5	1	8		11.0
1938			57	12	21.1	201	3.5	7	7		41.8
1939			41	12	29.3	134	3.3	1	0		48.8
Career			169	42	24.9	655	3.9	9	15	16	24.0

Craig Morton

Year	Team		Att	Com	PC	Yds	Avg	TD	Int	Lg	Rtg
1965	DAL	N	34	17	50.0	173	5.1	2	4	49t	45.0
1966			27	13	48.1	225	8.3	3	1	41t	98.5
1967			137	69	50.4	978	7.1	10	10	64t	67.7
1968			85	44	51.8	752	8.8	4	6	53	68.4
1969			302	162	53.6	2619	8.7	21	15	67t	85.4
1970			207	102	49.3	1819	**8.8**	15	7	89t	89.8
1971			143	78	54.5	1131	7.9	7	8	76t	73.5
1972			339	185	54.6	2396	7.1	15	21	46	65.9
1973			32	13	40.6	174	5.4	3	1	53t	76.8
1974	DAL-NYG	N	239	124	51.9	1522	6.4	9	13	72	61.7
1975	NYG	N	363	186	51.2	2359	6.5	11	16	56	63.6
1976			284	153	53.9	1865	6.6	9	20	63t	55.6
1977	DEN	N	254	131	51.6	1929	7.6	14	8	81t	82.0
1978			267	146	54.7	1802	6.7	11	8	42t	77.0
1979			370	204	55.1	2626	7.1	16	19	64t	70.6
1980			301	183	60.8	2150	7.1	12	13	41	77.8
1981			376	225	59.8	3195	8.5	21	14	95t	90.5

Year	Team		Att	Com	PC	Yds	Avg	TD	Int	Lg	Rtg

Craig Morton *continued*

Year	Team		Att	Com	PC	Yds	Avg	TD	Int	Lg	Rtg
1982			26	18	69.2	193	7.4	0	3	20	51.1
Career			3786	2053	54.2	27908	7.4	183	187	95t	73.5
Playoffs			227	91	40.1	1235	5.4	9	16		42.0

Mike Mosley

Year	Team		Att	Com	PC	Yds	Avg	TD	Int	Lg	Rtg
1984	BUF	N	1	0	0.0	0	0.0	0	0		39.6

Norm Mosley

Year	Team		Att	Com	PC	Yds	Avg	TD	Int	Lg	Rtg
1948	PIT	N	2	0	0.0	0	0.0	0	0		39.6

Russ Mosley

Year	Team		Att	Com	PC	Yds	Avg	TD	Int	Lg	Rtg
1945	GB	N	1	0	0.0	0	0.0	0	0		39.6

Perry Moss

Year	Team		Att	Com	PC	Yds	Avg	TD	Int	Lg	Rtg
1948	GB	N	17	4	23.5	20	1.2	0	0	10	39.6

Marion Motley

Year	Team		Att	Com	PC	Yds	Avg	TD	Int	Lg	Rtg
1948	CLE	AA	1	0	0.0	0	0.0	0	0		39.6
1952	CLE	N	2	0	0.0	0	0.0	0	0		39.6
Career			3	0	0.0	0	0.0	0	0		39.6
Playoffs			1	0	0.0	0	0.0	0	0		39.6

Noah Mullins

Year	Team		Att	Com	PC	Yds	Avg	TD	Int	Lg	Rtg
1946	CHIB	N	1	1	100.0	16	16.0	0	0	16	118.8
1948			1	0	0.0	0	0.0	0	0		39.6
Career			2	1	50.0	16	8.0	0	0	16	77.1

Chuck Muncie

Year	Team		Att	Com	PC	Yds	Avg	TD	Int	Lg	Rtg
1978	NO	N	1	0	0.0	0	0.0	0	0		39.6
1979			2	1	50.0	40	20.0	1	0	40t	135.4
1981	SD	N	1	1	100.0	3	3.0	1	0	3t	118.8
1982			3	2	66.7	83	27.7	2	0	66t	149.3
Career			7	4	57.1	126	18.0	4	0	66t	141.4
Playoffs			1	0	0.0	0	0.0	0	0		39.6

George Munns

Year	Team		Att	Com	PC	Yds	Avg	TD	Int	Lg	Rtg
1921	CIN	A							2		

Bill Munson

Year	Team		Att	Com	PC	Yds	Avg	TD	Int	Lg	Rtg
1964	LA	N	223	108	48.4	1533	6.9	9	15	95t	56.5
1965			267	144	53.9	1701	6.4	10	14	47t	64.2
1966			50	30	60.0	284	5.7	2	1	25	80.8
1967			10	5	50.0	38	3.8	1	2	18	53.3
1968	DET	N	329	181	55.0	2311	7.0	15	8	86t	82.3
1969			166	84	50.6	1062	6.4	7	8	62t	64.9
1970			158	84	53.2	1049	6.6	10	7	56	76.7
1971			38	21	55.3	216	5.7	1	1	34	69.6
1972			35	20	57.1	194	5.5	1	1	29t	70.4
1973			187	95	50.8	1129	6.0	9	8	54	67.8
1974			292	166	56.8	1874	6.4	8	7	56	75.3
1975			109	65	59.6	626	5.7	5	2	32	83.4
1976	SEA	N	37	20	54.1	295	8.0	1	3	44	55.6
1977	SD	N	31	20	64.5	225	7.3	1	1	28	83.4
1978	BUF	N	43	24	55.8	328	7.6	4	2	43	76.2
1979			7	3	42.9	31	4.4	0	0	16	56.3
Career			1982	1070	54.0	12896	6.5	84	80	95t	71.5
Playoffs			8	2	25.0	44	5.5	0	1		10.4

Bill Musgrave

Year	Team		Att	Com	PC	Yds	Avg	TD	Int	Lg	Rtg
1991	SF	N	5	4	80.0	33	6.6	1	0	15t	133.8
1995	DEN	N	12	8	66.7	93	7.8	0	0	23	89.9
1996			52	31	59.6	276	5.3	0	2	46	57.9
Career			69	43	62.3	402	5.8	1	2	46	71.0
Playoffs			1	1	100.0	6	6.0	0	0		91.7

Jim Musick

Year	Team		Att	Com	PC	Yds	Avg	TD	Int	Lg	Rtg
1936	BOS	N	1	1	100.0	9	9.0	0	0	9	104.2

Brad Muster

Year	Team		Att	Com	PC	Yds	Avg	TD	Int	Lg	Rtg
1992	CHI	N	1	0	0.0	0	0.0	0	1		0.0

Chet Mutryn

Year	Team		Att	Com	PC	Yds	Avg	TD	Int	Lg	Rtg
1948	BUF	AA	6	2	33.3	21	3.5	0	0		44.4
1950	BAL	N	1	1	100.0	4	4.0	0	0	4	83.3
Career			7	3	42.9	25	3.6	0	0	4	52.7

Steve Myer

Year	Team		Att	Com	PC	Yds	Avg	TD	Int	Lg	Rtg
1977	SEA	N	130	70	53.8	729	5.6	6	12	45t	47.2
1978			22	11	50.0	94	4.3	0	2	17	23.7
1979			8	2	25.0	28	3.5	0	0	18	41.7
Career			160	83	51.9	851	5.3	6	14	45t	43.5

Tom Myers

Year	Team		Att	Com	PC	Yds	Avg	TD	Int	Lg	Rtg
1965	DET	N	5	3	60.0	16	3.2	0	1	8	25.8
1966			1	0	0.0	0	0.0	0	1		0.0
Career			6	3	50.0	16	2.7	0	2	8	16.7

Tommy Myers

Year	Team		Att	Com	PC	Yds	Avg	TD	Int	Lg	Rtg
1981	NO	N	2	1	50.0	8	4.0	1	0	8t	100.0

Ray Nagel

Year	Team		Att	Com	PC	Yds	Avg	TD	Int	Lg	Rtg
1953	CHIC	N	62	30	48.4	192	3.1	0	5	27	21.7

Browning Nagle

Year	Team		Att	Com	PC	Yds	Avg	TD	Int	Lg	Rtg
1991	NYJ	N	2	1	50.0	10	5.0	0	0	10	64.6
1992			387	192	49.6	2280	5.9	7	17	51	55.7
1993			14	6	42.9	71	5.1	0	1	18	58.9
1994	IND	N	21	8	38.1	69	3.3	0	1	23	27.7
1996	ATL	N	13	6	46.2	59	4.5	1	2	17	45.5
Career			437	213	48.7	2489	5.7	8	20	51	53.5

Bronko Nagurski

Year	Team		Att	Com	PC	Yds	Avg	TD	Int	Lg	Rtg
1932	CHIB	N							3		
1934			8	5	62.5	48	6.0	2	1		79.2
1935			3	0	0.0	0	0.0	0	1		0.0
1936			5	1	20.0	8	1.6	1	2	8	39.6
1937			2	1	50.0	35	17.5	1	0	35t	135.4
Career			18	7	38.9	91	5.1	4	4	35t	55.6
Playoffs			4	3	75.0	50	12.5	2	0		156.3

Joe Namath

Year	Team		Att	Com	PC	Yds	Avg	TD	Int	Lg	Rtg
1965	NY	A	340	164	48.2	2220	6.5	18	15	62	68.8
1966			**471**	**232**	49.3	**3379**	7.2	19	27	77	62.6
1967			**491**	**258**	52.5	**4007**	**8.2**	26	28	75t	73.8
1968			380	187	49.2	3147	8.3	15	17	87t	72.1
1969			361	185	51.2	2734	7.6	19	17	60t	74.3
1970	NYJ	N	179	90	50.3	1259	7.0	5	12	72t	54.7
1971			59	28	47.5	537	9.1	5	6	74t	68.2
1972			324	162	50.0	**2816**	8.7	**19**	21	83t	72.5
1973			133	68	51.1	966	7.3	5	6	63	68.7
1974			361	191	52.9	2616	7.2	20	22	89t	69.4
1975			326	157	48.2	2286	7.0	15	28	91	51.0
1976			230	114	49.6	1090	4.7	4	16	35	39.9
1977	LA	N	107	50	46.7	606	5.7	3	5	42	54.5
Career			3762	1886	50.1	27663	7.4	173	220	91	65.5
Playoffs			117	50	42.7	636	5.4	3	4		54.6

Bob Naponic

Year	Team		Att	Com	PC	Yds	Avg	TD	Int	Lg	Rtg
1970	HOU	N	20	6	30.0	85	4.3	0	2	21	5.2

Dick Nardi

Year	Team		Att	Com	PC	Yds	Avg	TD	Int	Lg	Rtg
1939	PIT-BKN	N	5	2	40.0	12	2.4	0	1		8.3

Tony Nathan

Year	Team		Att	Com	PC	Yds	Avg	TD	Int	Lg	Rtg
1980	MIA	N	1	0	0.0	0	0.0	0	0		39.6
1981			1	0	0.0	0	0.0	0	0		39.6
1982			2	1	50.0	15	7.5	1	0	15t	114.6
1983			4	3	75.0	46	11.5	0	0	22	112.5
Career			8	4	50.0	61	7.6	1	0	22	115.1
Playoffs			2	2	100.0	34	17.0	0	0		118.8

Ricky Nattiel

Year	Team		Att	Com	PC	Yds	Avg	TD	Int	Lg	Rtg
1988	DEN	N	1	0	0.0	0	0.0	0	0		39.6

Frankie Neal

Year	Team		Att	Com	PC	Yds	Avg	TD	Int	Lg	Rtg
1987	GB	N	1	0	0.0	0	0.0	0	0		39.6

Jim Neill

Year	Team		Att	Com	PC	Yds	Avg	TD	Int	Lg	Rtg
1937	NYG	N	3	1	33.3	0	0.0	0	1	0	2.8

Bill Nelsen

Year	Team		Att	Com	PC	Yds	Avg	TD	Int	Lg	Rtg
1963	PIT	N	2	0	0.0	0	0.0	0	0		39.6
1964			42	16	38.1	276	6.6	2	3	44	47.3
1965			270	121	44.8	1917	7.1	8	17	87t	52.7
1966			112	63	56.3	1122	10.0	7	1	68t	107.8
1967			165	74	44.8	1125	6.8	10	9	58t	65.3
1968	CLE	N	293	152	51.9	2366	8.1	19	10	87	86.4
1969			352	190	54.0	2743	7.8	23	19	82t	78.8
1970			313	159	50.8	2156	6.9	16	16	78t	68.9
1971			325	174	53.5	2319	7.1	13	23	53t	60.3
1972			31	14	45.2	141	4.5	0	3	26	19.1
Career			1905	963	50.6	14165	7.4	98	101	87t	70.2
Playoffs			132	68	51.5	839	6.4	3	8		53.8

Darrin Nelson

Year	Team		Att	Com	PC	Yds	Avg	TD	Int	Lg	Rtg
1991	MIN	N	1	1	100.0	25	25.0	1	0	25t	158.3

Frank Nelson

Year	Team		Att	Com	PC	Yds	Avg	TD	Int	Lg	Rtg
1948	BOS	N	17	8	47.1	71	4.2	0	2	20	19.1

Jimmy Nelson

Year	Team		Att	Com	PC	Yds	Avg	TD	Int	Lg	Rtg
1946	MIA	AA	24	8	33.3	135	5.6	0	4		13.7

Steve Nemeth

Year	Team		Att	Com	PC	Yds	Avg	TD	Int	Lg	Rtg
1945	CLE	N	1	0	0.0	0	0.0	0	0		39.6
1946	CHI	AA	23	5	21.7	68	3.0	0	0		39.6
1947	BAL	AA	6	2	33.3	18	3.0	0	2		2.8
Career			30	7	23.3	86	2.9	0	2		11.8

Dick Nesbitt

Year	Team		Att	Com	PC	Yds	Avg	TD	Int	Lg	Rtg
1931	CHIB	N							1		

Frank Nesser

Year	Team		Att	Com	PC	Yds	Avg	TD	Int	Lg	Rtg
1920	COL	A							1		
1921									4		
Career									5		

Rick Neuheisel

Year	Team		Att	Com	PC	Yds	Avg	TD	Int	Lg	Rtg
1987	SD	N	59	40	67.8	367	6.2	1	1	32	83.1

Ernie Nevers

Year	Team		Att	Com	PC	Yds	Avg	TD	Int	Lg	Rtg
1926	DUL	N							2		
1927									5		
1929	CHIC	N							6		
1930									4		
1931									6		
Career									23		

Robert Newhouse

Year	Team		Att	Com	PC	Yds	Avg	TD	Int	Lg	Rtg
1975	DAL	N	2	1	50.0	46	23.0	1	0	46t	135.4
Playoffs			1	1	100.0	29	29.0	1	0		158.3

Harry Newman

Year	Team		Att	Com	PC	Yds	Avg	TD	Int	Lg	Rtg
1933	NYG	N	136	53	39.0	973	7.2	11	17		51.7
1934			91	35	38.5	366	4.0	1	5		31.7
1935			29	9	31.0	132	4.6	0	0		
Career			256	97	37.9	1105	4.3	12	22		37.0
Playoffs			20	13	65.0	209	10.4	2	2		93.5

Harry Newsome

Year	Team		Att	Com	PC	Yds	Avg	TD	Int	Lg	Rtg
1986	PIT	N	2	1	50.0	12	6.0	1	0	12t	108.3
1992	MIN	N	1	0	0.0	0	0.0	0	0		39.6
Career			3	1	33.3	12	4.0	1	0	12t	86.1

Al Nichelini

Year	Team		Att	Com	PC	Yds	Avg	TD	Int	Lg	Rtg
1935	CHIC	N	1	1	100.0	16	16.0	0	0	16	118.8

Sid Nichols

Year	Team		Att	Com	PC	Yds	Avg	TD	Int	Lg	Rtg
1920	RI	A							1		

Gifford Nielsen

Year	Team		Att	Com	PC	Yds	Avg	TD	Int	Lg	Rtg
1978	HOU	N	4	2	50.0	0	0.0	0	0	0	56.3
1979			61	32	52.5	404	6.6	3	3	41	69.3
1980			4	2	50.0	12	3.0	1	0	8t	95.8
1981			93	60	64.5	709	7.6	5	3	44	92.1
1982			161	87	54.0	1005	6.2	6	8	46	64.8
1983			175	90	51.4	1125	6.4	5	8	48	62.2
Career			498	273	54.8	3255	6.5	20	22	48	70.0
Playoffs			24	13	54.2	129	5.4	1	2		48.8

Walt Nielson

Year	Team		Att	Com	PC	Yds	Avg	TD	Int	Lg	Rtg
1940	NYG	N	1	0	0.0	0	0.0	0	0		39.6

Jerry Niles

Year	Team		Att	Com	PC	Yds	Avg	TD	Int	Lg	Rtg
1947	NYG	N	57	19	33.3	269	4.7	1	7	64	15.8

Jim Ninowski

Year	Team		Att	Com	PC	Yds	Avg	TD	Int	Lg	Rtg
1958	CLE	N	17	8	47.1	139	8.2	1	3	34	55.4
1959			10	3	30.0	41	4.1	0	1	20	4.6
1960	DET	N	283	134	47.3	1599	5.7	2	18	55	40.9
1961			247	117	47.4	1921	7.8	7	18	84t	53.0
1962	CLE	N	173	87	50.3	1178	6.8	7	8	53t	66.6
1963			61	29	47.5	423	6.9	2	6	70	41.9
1964			9	6	66.7	125	13.9	2	0	41	149.3
1965			83	40	48.2	549	6.6	4	3	32	70.8
1966			18	11	61.1	175	9.7	4	1	44t	110.0
1967	WAS	N	18	12	66.7	123	6.8	0	1	31	63.0
1968			95	49	51.6	633	6.7	4	6	56	60.5
1969	NO	N	34	17	50.0	227	6.7	1	2	70	56.9
Career			1048	513	49.0	7133	6.8	34	67	84t	55.4
Playoffs			15	3	20.0	31	2.1	0	1		11.8

Emery Nix

Year	Team		Att	Com	PC	Yds	Avg	TD	Int	Lg	Rtg
1943	NY	N	53	24	45.3	390	7.4	3	3	56	65.8
1946			19	10	52.6	156	8.2	2	0	35	115.2
Career			72	34	47.2	546	7.6	5	3	56	78.8
Playoffs			10	2	20.0	13	1.3	0	0		39.6

Kent Nix

Year	Team		Att	Com	PC	Yds	Avg	TD	Int	Lg	Rtg
1967	PIT	N	268	136	50.7	1587	5.9	8	19	66t	49.5
1968			130	56	43.1	720	5.5	4	8	61	45.7
1969			53	25	47.2	290	5.5	2	6	47t	37.2
1970	CHI	N	1	0	0.0	0	0.0	0	0		39.6
1971			137	51	37.2	760	5.5	6	10	45	40.4
1972	HOU	N	63	33	52.4	287	4.6	3	6	19	41.0
Career			652	301	46.2	3644	5.6	23	49	66t	44.3

Terry Nofsinger

Year	Team		Att	Com	PC	Yds	Avg	TD	Int	Lg	Rtg
1961	PIT	N	11	7	63.6	78	7.1	0	0	23	84.7
1963			3	2	66.7	46	15.3	0	0	27	109.7
1964			4	3	75.0	35	8.8	0	1	22	61.5
1965	STL	N	20	8	40.0	47	2.4	1	1	12	43.8
1966			162	68	42.0	799	4.9	2	8	49	41.2
1967	ATL	N	60	30	50.0	352	5.9	1	2	38	59.9
Career			260	118	45.4	1357	5.2	4	12	49	47.5

Ray Nolting

Year	Team		Att	Com	PC	Yds	Avg	TD	Int	Lg	Rtg
1936	CHIB	N	13	3	23.1	30	2.3	2	1		47.1
1937			4	0	0.0	0	0.0	0	1		0.0
1938			11	0	0.0	0	0.0	0	3		0.0
1940			2	1	50.0	38	19.0	0	0	38	95.8
1941			5	3	60.0	71	14.2	1	0	53	143.8
Career			35	7	20.0	139	4.0	3	5	53	32.6

Jerry Noonan

Year	Team		Att	Com	PC	Yds	Avg	TD	Int	Lg	Rtg
1921	ROC	A							1		

John Noppenberg

Year	Team		Att	Com	PC	Yds	Avg	TD	Int	Lg	Rtg
1941	PIT	N	3	0	0.0	0	0.0	0	0		39.6

Reino Nori

Year	Team		Att	Com	PC	Yds	Avg	TD	Int	Lg	Rtg
1937	BKN	N	23	11	47.8	168	7.3	1	3		47.3

Chris Norman

Year	Team		Att	Com	PC	Yds	Avg	TD	Int	Lg	Rtg
1985	DEN	N	1	0	0.0	0	0.0	0	0		39.6
1986			1	1	100.0	43	43.0	1	0	43t	158.3
Career			2	1	50.0	43	21.5	1	0	43t	135.4

David Norrie

Year	Team		Att	Com	PC	Yds	Avg	TD	Int	Lg	Rtg
1987	NYJ	N	68	35	51.5	376	5.5	1	4	41t	48.4

Don Norton

Year	Team		Att	Com	PC	Yds	Avg	TD	Int	Lg	Rtg
1963	SD	A	1	1	100.0	15	15.0	0	0	15	118.8

Jerry Norton

Year	Team		Att	Com	PC	Yds	Avg	TD	Int	Lg	Rtg
1955	PHI	N	1	0	0.0	0	0.0	0	0		39.6
1957			1	0	0.0	0	0.0	0	0		39.6
Career			2	0	0.0	0	0.0	0	0	41t	39.6

Rick Norton

Year	Team		Att	Com	PC	Yds	Avg	TD	Int	Lg	Rtg
1966	MIA	A	55	21	38.2	192	3.5	3	6	43	27.0
1967			133	53	39.8	596	4.5	1	9	32	28.3
1968			41	17	41.5	254	6.2	0	4	65	22.9
1969			148	65	43.9	709	4.8	2	11	29	32.2
1970	GB	N	5	3	60.0	64	12.8	1	0	29t	143.8
Career			382	159	41.6	1815	4.8	7	30	65	30.0

Doug Nott

Year	Team		Att	Com	PC	Yds	Avg	TD	Int	Lg	Rtg
1935	BOS	N							1		

Mike Nott

Year	Team		Att	Com	PC	Yds	Avg	TD	Int	Lg	Rtg
1976	KC	N	10	4	40.0	46	4.6	0	0	23	54.6

Eddie Novak

Year	Team		Att	Com	PC	Yds	Avg	TD	Int	Lg	Rtg
1921	RI	A							1		

Ray Novotny

Year	Team		Att	Com	PC	Yds	Avg	TD	Int	Lg	Rtg
1930	POR	N							1		

Terry Nugent

Year	Team		Att	Com	PC	Yds	Avg	TD	Int	Lg	Rtg
1987	IND	N	5	3	60.0	47	9.4	0	0	21	91.3

Bob Nussbaumer

Year	Team		Att	Com	PC	Yds	Avg	TD	Int	Lg	Rtg
1946	GB	N	1	1	100.0	10	10.0	0	0	10	108.3

Doug Nussmeier

Year	Team		Att	Com	PC	Yds	Avg		TD	Int	Lg	Rtg
1996	NO	N	50	28	56.0	272	5.4		1	1	57t	69.8

Jerry Nuzum

Year	Team		Att	Com	PC	Yds	Avg		TD	Int	Lg	Rtg
1949	PIT	N	1	1	100.0	21	21.0		0	0	21	118.8

Davey O'Brien

Year	Team		Att	Com	PC	Yds	Avg		TD	Int	Lg	Rtg
1939	PHI	N	201	99	49.3	**1324**	6.6		7	17		46.9
1940			**277**	**124**	44.8	1290	4.7		6	17		40.4
Career			478	223	46.7	2614	5.5		13	34	57t	43.2

Ken O'Brien

Year	Team		Att	Com	PC	Yds	Avg		TD	Int	Lg	Rtg
1984	NYJ	N	203	116	57.1	1402	6.9		6	7	49	74.0
1985			488	297	60.9	3888	8.0		25	8	96t	**96.2**
1986			482	300	62.2	3690	7.7		25	20	83t	85.8
1987			393	234	59.5	2696	6.9		13	8	59	82.8
1988			424	236	55.7	2567	6.1		15	7	50t	78.6
1989			477	288	60.4	3346	7.0		12	18	57	74.3
1990			411	226	55.0	2855	6.9		13	10	69t	77.3
1991			489	287	58.7	3300	6.7		10	11	53	76.6
1992			98	55	56.1	642	6.6		5	6	55t	67.6
1993	PHI	N	137	71	51.8	708	5.2		4	3	41	67.4
Career			3602	2110	58.6	25094	7.0		128	98	96t	80.4
Playoffs			67	45	67.2	504	7.5		2	4		74.5

Tommy O'Connell

Year	Team		Att	Com	PC	Yds	Avg		TD	Int	Lg	Rtg
1953	CHIB	N	67	33	49.3	437	6.5		1	4	40	50.4
1956	CLE	N	96	42	43.8	551	5.7		4	8	46t	41.6
1957			110	63	57.3	1229	**11.2**		9	8	65t	**93.3**
1960	BUF	A	145	65	44.8	1033	7.1		7	13	64	47.9
1961			5	1	20.0	11	2.2		0	1	11	0.0
Career			423	204	48.2	3261	7.7		21	34	65t	57.5
Playoffs			8	4	50.0	61	7.6		0	2		35.9

Curly Oden

Year	Team		Att	Com	PC	Yds	Avg		TD	Int	Lg	Rtg
1926	PRO	N							1			
1930									1			
1931									1			
Career									3			

Neil O'Donnell

Year	Team		Att	Com	PC	Yds	Avg		TD	Int	Lg	Rtg
1991	PIT	N	286	156	54.5	1963	6.9		11	7	89t	78.8
1992			313	185	59.1	2283	7.3		13	9	51	83.6
1993			486	270	55.6	3208	6.6		14	7	71t	79.5
1994			370	212	57.3	2443	6.6		13	9	60t	78.9
1995			416	246	59.1	2970	7.1		17	7	71t	87.7
1996	NYJ	N	188	110	58.5	1147	6.1		4	7	78t	67.8
Career			2059	1179	57.3	14014	6.8		72	46	89t	80.5
Playoffs			273	158	57.9	1690	6.2		9	8		74.9

John Oelerich

Year	Team		Att	Com	PC	Yds	Avg		TD	Int	Lg	Rtg
1938	CHIB	N	1	1	100.0	10	10.0		0	0	10	108.3

Cliff Olander

Year	Team		Att	Com	PC	Yds	Avg		TD	Int	Lg	Rtg
1977	SD	N	16	7	43.8	76	4.8		0	2	15	18.8
1978			8	5	62.5	49	6.1		0	1	22	40.1
Career			24	12	50.0	125	5.2		0	3	22	25.9

Elmer Oliphant

Year	Team		Att	Com	PC	Yds	Avg		TD	Int	Lg	Rtg
1921	BUF	A							**7**			

Vince Oliver

Year	Team		Att	Com	PC	Yds	Avg		TD	Int	Lg	Rtg
1945	CHIC	N	10	4	40.0	22	2.2		0	0	10	47.9

Johnny Olszewski

Year	Team		Att	Com	PC	Yds	Avg		TD	Int	Lg	Rtg
1953	CHIC	N	1	0	0.0	0	0.0		0	1		0.0

Tom O'Malley

Year	Team		Att	Com	PC	Yds	Avg		TD	Int	Lg	Rtg
1950	GB	N	15	4	26.7	31	2.1		0	6	20	0.0

Steve O'Neal

Year	Team		Att	Com	PC	Yds	Avg		TD	Int	Lg	Rtg
1970	NYJ	N	1	1	100.0	2	2.0		0	0	2	79.2
1971			1	0	0.0	0	0.0		0	0		39.6
Career			2	1	50.0	2	1.0		0	0	2	56.3

Chuck O'Neil

Year	Team		Att	Com	PC	Yds	Avg		TD	Int	Lg	Rtg
1921	EVA	A							1			

Bill O'Neill

Year	Team		Att	Com	PC	Yds	Avg		TD	Int	Lg	Rtg
1937	CLE	N	2	1	50.0	20	10.0		0	1	20	45.8

Pat O'Neill

Year	Team		Att	Com	PC	Yds	Avg		TD	Int	Lg	Rtg
Playoffs			1	1	100.0	21	21.0		0	0	21	118.8

Charlie O'Rourke

Year	Team		Att	Com	PC	Yds	Avg		TD	Int	Lg	Rtg
1942	CHIB	N	88	37	42.0	951	**10.8**		11	16	68	82.1
1946	LA	AA	182	105	**57.7**	1250	6.9		12	14	68t	68.7
1947			178	89	50.0	1449	8.1		13	16	54t	64.6
1948	BAL	AA	51	24	47.1	377	7.4		3	4		59.0
1949			7	1	14.3	12	1.7		0	0		0.0
Career			506	256	50.6	4039	8.0		39	51	68t	63.6
Playoffs			6	4	66.7	110	18.3		0	0		109.7

Jimmy Orr

Year	Team		Att	Com	PC	Yds	Avg		TD	Int	Lg	Rtg
1959	PIT	N	1	0	0.0	0	0.0		0	0		39.6

Chuck Ortmann

Year	Team		Att	Com	PC	Yds	Avg		TD	Int	Lg	Rtg
1951	PIT	N	139	56	40.3	671	4.8		3	13	37t	24.0
1952	DAL	N	15	5	33.3	73	4.9		0	1	54	22.4
Career			154	61	39.6	744	4.8		3	14	54	23.8

Sandy Osiecki

Year	Team		Att	Com	PC	Yds	Avg		TD	Int	Lg	Rtg
1984	KC	N	17	7	41.2	64	3.8		0	1	19	27.6

Bill Osmanski

Year	Team		Att	Com	PC	Yds	Avg		TD	Int	Lg	Rtg
1941	CHIB	N	1	0	0.0	0	0.0		0	0		39.6

Tom Owen

Year	Team		Att	Com	PC	Yds	Avg		TD	Int	Lg	Rtg
1974	SF	N	184	88	47.8	1327	7.2		10	15	68t	56.1
1975			51	24	47.1	318	6.2		1	2	24	57.5
1976	NE	N	5	1	20.0	7	1.4		0	0	7	39.6
1978			26	15	57.7	182	7.0		0	2	23	47.3
1979			47	27	57.4	248	5.3		2	3	32	59.5
1981			36	15	41.7	218	6.1		1	4	28	31.7
Career			349	170	48.7	2300	6.6		14	26	68t	52.5
Playoffs			22	12	54.5	144	6.5		1	1		71.0

Bob Paffrath

Year	Team		Att	Com	PC	Yds	Avg		TD	Int	Lg	Rtg
1946	BKN	AA	1	0	0.0	0	0.0		0	0		39.6

Mike Pagel

Year	Team		Att	Com	PC	Yds	Avg		TD	Int	Lg	Rtg
1982	BAL	N	221	111	50.2	1281	5.8		5	7	53t	62.4
1983			328	163	49.7	2353	7.2		12	17	72t	64.0
1984	IND	N	212	114	53.8	1426	6.7		8	8	54t	71.8
1985			393	199	50.6	2414	6.1		14	15	80t	65.8
1986	CLE	N	3	2	66.7	53	17.7		0	0	45	109.7
1988			134	71	53.0	736	5.5		3	4	28	64.1
1989			14	5	35.7	60	4.3		1	1	18	43.8
1990			148	69	46.6	819	5.5		3	8	32	48.2
1991	LARM	N	27	11	40.7	150	5.6		2	0	30	83.9
1992			20	8	40.0	99	5.0		1	2	22	33.1
1993			9	3	33.3	23	2.6		0	1	10	2.8
Career			1509	756	50.1	9414	6.2		49	63	80t	63.3
Playoffs			25	17	68.0	179	7.2		2	1		98.6

Paul Palmer

Year	Team		Att	Com	PC	Yds	Avg		TD	Int	Lg	Rtg
1987	KC	N	1	0	0.0	0	0.0		0	0		39.6

Don Panciera

Year	Team		Att	Com	PC	Yds	Avg		TD	Int	Lg	Rtg
1949	B-NY	AA	150	51	34.0	801	5.3		5	16		24.2
1952	CHIC	N	96	35	36.5	582	6.1		5	9	47t	36.0
Career			246	86	35.0	1383	5.6		10	25	47t	28.6

Hal Pangle

Year	Team		Att	Com	PC	Yds	Avg		TD	Int	Lg	Rtg
1936	CHIC	N	2	0	0.0	0	0.0		0	0		39.6
1937			2	0	0.0	0	0.0		0	1		0.0
Career			4	0	0.0	0	0.0		0	1		0.0

Nick Papac

Year	Team		Att	Com	PC	Yds	Avg		TD	Int	Lg	Rtg
1961	OAK	A	44	13	29.5	173	3.9		2	7		19.0

George Papach

Year	Team		Att	Com	PC	Yds	Avg		TD	Int	Lg	Rtg
1949	PIT	N	1	0	0.0	0	0.0		0	0		39.6

Oran Pape

Year	Team		Att	Com	PC	Yds	Avg		TD	Int	Lg	Rtg
1932	SI	N								1		

Babe Parilli

Year	Team		Att	Com	PC	Yds	Avg		TD	Int	Lg	Rtg
1952	GB	N	177	77	43.5	1416	8.0		13	17	90t	56.6
1953			166	74	44.6	830	5.0		4	19	45	28.5
1956	CLE	N	49	24	49.0	409	8.3		3	7	68t	58.5
1957	GB	N	102	39	38.2	669	6.6		4	12	75t	34.8
1958			157	68	43.3	1068	6.8		10	13	80t	53.3
1960	OAK	A	187	87	46.5	1003	5.4		5	11		47.6
1961	BOS	A	198	104	52.5	1314	6.6		13	9		76.5
1962			253	140	55.3	1988	7.9		18	8	67t	91.5
1963			337	153	45.4	2335	6.9		13	24	77t	52.0
1964			473	228	48.2	**3465**	7.3		**31**	27	80t	70.8

Year	Team		Att	Com	PC	Yds	Avg	TD	Int	Lg	Rtg

Babe Parilli *continued*

Year	Team		Att	Com	PC	Yds	Avg	TD	Int	Lg	Rtg
1965			426	173	40.6	2597	6.1	18	26	73t	50.0
1966			382	181	47.4	2721	7.1	20	20	63t	66.9
1967			344	161	46.8	2317	6.7	19	24	79t	58.5
1968	NY	A	55	29	52.7	401	7.3	5	2	40t	91.6
1969			24	14	58.3	138	5.8	2	1	29	85.1
Career			3330	1552	46.6	22671	6.8	178	220	90t	59.6
Playoffs			65	28	43.1	489	7.5	1	2		61.6

Ace Parker

Year	Team		Att	Com	PC	Yds	Avg	TD	Int	Lg	Rtg
1937	BKN	N	61	28	45.9	514	8.4	1	7		41.3
1938			**148**	63	42.6	**865**	5.8	4	7		51.2
1939			157	72	45.9	977	6.2	4	13		40.2
1940			111	49	44.1	817	7.4	10	7		73.3
1941			102	51	50.0	642	6.3	4	8	47	50.4
1945	BOS	N	24	10	41.7	123	5.1	0	5	41	18.6
1946	NY	AA	115	62	53.9	763	6.6	8	3	75	87.0
Career			718	335	46.7	4701	6.5	31	50	75	53.6
Playoffs			18	8	44.4	81	4.5	0	1		34.7

Buddy Parker

Year	Team		Att	Com	PC	Yds	Avg	TD	Int	Lg	Rtg
1937	CHIC	N	1	0	0.0	0	0.0	0	0		39.6
1938			2	2	100.0	21	10.5	0	0		110.4
1939			1	0	0.0	0	0.0	0	0		39.6
Career			4	2	50.0	21	5.3	0	0		65.6

Joel Parker

Year	Team		Att	Com	PC	Yds	Avg	TD	Int	Lg	Rtg
1974	NO	N	1	0	0.0	0	0.0	0	0		39.6

Dave Parks

Year	Team		Att	Com	PC	Yds	Avg	TD	Int	Lg	Rtg
1968	NO	N	1	0	0.0	0	0.0	0	0		39.6

Cliff Parsley

Year	Team		Att	Com	PC	Yds	Avg	TD	Int	Lg	Rtg
1981	HOU	N	2	2	100.0	43	21.5	0	0	31	118.8

Bob Parsons

Year	Team		Att	Com	PC	Yds	Avg	TD	Int	Lg	Rtg
1974	CHI	N	1	0	0.0	0	0.0	0	0		39.6
1975			1	0	0.0	0	0.0	0	0		39.6
1976			2	2	100.0	48	24.0	0	0	25	118.8
1977			4	4	100.0	61	15.3	0	0	32	118.8
1978			1	0	0.0	0	0.0	0	0		39.6
1979			2	1	50.0	22	11.0	0	0	22	89.6
1980			1	0	0.0	0	0.0	0	0		39.6
1981			1	0	0.0	0	0.0	0	0		39.6
Career			13	7	53.8	131	10.1	0	0	32	88.9

Lou Partlow

Year	Team		Att	Com	PC	Yds	Avg	TD	Int	Lg	Rtg
1921	DAY	A							1		

Bill Paschal

Year	Team		Att	Com	PC	Yds	Avg	TD	Int	Lg	Rtg
1944	NY	N	8	2	25.0	31	3.9	0	2	19	3.6
1945			1	0	0.0	0	0.0	0	0		39.6
1947	BOS	N	1	0	0.0	0	0.0	0	0		39.6
Career			10	2	20.0	31	3.1	0	2	19	0.4

Dan Pastorini

Year	Team		Att	Com	PC	Yds	Avg	TD	Int	Lg	Rtg
1971	HOU	N	270	127	47.0	1702	6.3	7	21	62t	43.8
1972			299	144	48.2	1711	5.7	7	12	82t	57.1
1973			290	154	53.1	1482	5.1	5	17	50	49.0
1974			247	140	56.7	1571	6.4	10	10	65	72.4
1975			342	163	47.7	2053	6.0	14	16	77t	61.0
1976			309	167	54.0	1795	5.8	10	10	67t	68.6
1977			319	169	53.0	1987	6.2	13	18	85t	62.3
1978			368	199	54.1	2473	6.7	16	17	80t	70.4
1979			324	163	50.3	2090	6.5	14	18	55t	62.1
1980	OAK	N	130	66	50.8	932	7.2	5	8	56	61.4
1981	LA	N	152	64	42.1	719	4.7	2	14	46	22.9
1983	PHI	N	5	0	0.0	0	0.0	0	0		39.6
Career			3055	1556	50.9	18515	6.1	103	161	85t	59.1
Playoffs			116	71	61.2	954	8.2	4	8		70.1

Alan Pastrana

Year	Team		Att	Com	PC	Yds	Avg	TD	Int	Lg	Rtg
1970	DEN	N	75	29	38.7	420	5.6	1	9	58t	22.5

Frank Patrick

Year	Team		Att	Com	PC	Yds	Avg	TD	Int	Lg	Rtg
1938	CHIC	N	1	0	0.0	0	0.0	0	0		39.6
1939			79	22	27.8	291	3.7	1	13		7.1
Career			80	22	27.5	291	3.6	1	13		6.8

Frank Patrick

Year	Team		Att	Com	PC	Yds	Avg	TD	Int	Lg	Rtg
1970	GB	N	14	6	42.9	59	4.2	0	1	16	25.6
1971			5	1	20.0	39	7.8	0	1	39	20.0
1972			4	1	25.0	9	2.3	0	0		39.6
Career			23	8	34.8	107	4.7	0	2	39	14.2

Billy Patterson

Year	Team		Att	Com	PC	Yds	Avg	TD	Int	Lg	Rtg
1939	CHIB	N	38	14	36.8	227	6.0	3	4		44.4
1940	PIT	N	117	34	29.1	529	4.5	3	15		14.9
Career			155	48	31.0	756	4.9	6	19		21.5

Don Paul

Year	Team		Att	Com	PC	Yds	Avg	TD	Int	Lg	Rtg
1953	CHIC	N	2	1	50.0	13	6.5	0	0	13	70.8

Eddie Payton

Year	Team		Att	Com	PC	Yds	Avg	TD	Int	Lg	Rtg
1977	DET	N	1	0	0.0	0	0.0	0	0		39.6

Sean Payton

Year	Team		Att	Com	PC	Yds	Avg	TD	Int	Lg	Rtg
1987	CHI	N	23	8	34.8	79	3.4	0	1	20	27.3

Walter Payton

Year	Team		Att	Com	PC	Yds	Avg	TD	Int	Lg	Rtg
1975	CHI	N	1	0	0.0	0	0.0	0	1		0.0
1979			1	1	100.0	54	54.0	1	0	54t	158.3
1980			3	0	0.0	0	0.0	0	0		39.6
1981			2	0	0.0	0	0.0	0	0		39.6
1982			3	1	33.3	39	13.0	1	0	39t	121.5
1983			6	3	50.0	95	15.8	3	2	56t	95.8
1984			8	3	37.5	47	5.9	2	1	42	57.8
1985			5	3	60.0	96	19.2	1	0	50	143.8
1986			4	0	0.0	0	0.0	0	1		0.0
1987			1	0	0.0	0	0.0	0	1		0.0
Career			34	11	32.4	331	9.7	8	6	56t	69.6
Playoffs			2	1	50.0	19	9.5	1	0		122.9

Clarence Peaks

Year	Team		Att	Com	PC	Yds	Avg	TD	Int	Lg	Rtg
1957	PHI	N	3	2	66.7	56	18.7	0	1	37	70.1
1961			1	0	0.0	0	0.0	0	0		39.6
Career			4	2	50.0	56	14.0	0	1	37	56.3

Drew Pearson

Year	Team		Att	Com	PC	Yds	Avg	TD	Int	Lg	Rtg
1974	DAL	N	1	1	100.0	46	46.0	1	0	46t	158.3
1976			1	1	100.0	39	39.0	1	0	39t	158.3
1981			2	2	100.0	81	40.5	1	0	59	158.3
1982			2	1	50.0	26	13.0	0	1	26	56.3
1983			1	0	0.0	0	0.0	0	1		0.0
Career			7	5	71.4	192	27.4	3	2	59	113.7
Playoffs			2	1	50.0	49	24.5	0	0		95.8

Lindy Pearson

Year	Team		Att	Com	PC	Yds	Avg	TD	Int	Lg	Rtg
1950	DET	N	3	0	0.0	0	0.0	0	3		0.0

Brent Pease

Year	Team		Att	Com	PC	Yds	Avg	TD	Int	Lg	Rtg
1987	HOU	N	113	56	49.6	728	6.4	3	5	51	60.6
1988			22	6	27.3	64	2.9	0	4	21	0.0
Career			135	62	45.9	792	5.9	3	9	51	44.4

George Pease

Year	Team		Att	Com	PC	Yds	Avg	TD	Int	Lg	Rtg
1926	NY	A						**9**			
1929	ORA	N						2			
Career								11			

Doug Pederson

Year	Team		Att	Com	PC	Yds	Avg	TD	Int	Lg	Rtg
1993	MIA	N	8	4	50.0	41	5.1	0	0	12	65.1

Rodney Peete

Year	Team		Att	Com	PC	Yds	Avg	TD	Int	Lg	Rtg
1989	DET	N	195	103	52.8	1479	7.6	5	9	69	67.0
1990			271	142	52.4	1974	7.3	13	8	68t	79.8
1991			194	116	59.8	1339	6.9	5	9	68t	69.9
1992			213	123	57.7	1702	8.0	9	9	78t	80.0
1993			252	157	62.3	1670	6.6	6	14	93t	66.4
1994	DAL	N	56	33	58.9	470	8.4	4	1	65t	102.5
1995	PHI	N	375	215	57.3	2326	6.2	8	14	37t	67.3
1996			134	80	59.7	992	7.4	3	5	62	74.6
Career			1690	969	57.3	11952	7.1	53	69	93t	72.8
Playoffs			32	20	62.5	298	9.3	3	0		124.2

Steve Pelluer

Year	Team		Att	Com	PC	Yds	Avg	TD	Int	Lg	Rtg
1985	DAL	N	8	5	62.5	47	5.9	0	0	28	78.6
1986			378	215	56.9	2727	7.2	8	17	84t	67.9
1987			101	55	54.5	642	6.4	3	2	44	75.6
1988			435	245	56.3	3139	7.2	17	19	61t	73.9
1989	KC	N	47	26	55.3	301	6.4	1	0	24	82.0
1990			5	2	40.0	14	2.8	0	1	11	8.3
Career			974	548	56.3	6870	7.1	29	39	84t	71.6

Craig Penrose

Year	Team		Att	Com	PC	Yds	Avg	TD	Int	Lg	Rtg
1976	DEN	N	36	16	44.4	265	7.4	3	3	41	62.8
1977			39	21	53.8	217	5.6	0	4	35	30.6
1978			37	16	43.2	185	5.0	2	4	29	37.4

Craig Penrose *continued*

Year	Team		Att	Com	PC	Yds	Avg	TD	Int	Lg	Rtg
1979			5	2	40.0	44	8.8	0	1	29	32.5
Career			117	55	47.0	711	6.1	5	12	41	41.2

Bob Perina

Year	Team		Att	Com	PC	Yds	Avg	TD	Int	Lg	Rtg
1946	NY	AA	48	21	43.8	279	5.8	1	4		35.0
1947	BKN	AA	24	11	45.8	91	3.8	0	2		21.4
Career			72	32	44.4	370	5.1	1	6		30.4

Brett Perriman

Year	Team		Att	Com	PC	Yds	Avg	TD	Int	Lg	Rtg
1994	DET	N	1	0	0.0	0	0.0	0	0		39.6

Benny Perrin

Year	Team		Att	Com	PC	Yds	Avg	TD	Int	Lg	Rtg
1983	STL	N	1	1	100.0	4	4.0	0	0	4	83.3
1984			1	1	100.0	0	0.0	0	0	0	79.2
Career			2	2	100.0	4	2.0	0	0	4	79.2

Joe Perry

Year	Team		Att	Com	PC	Yds	Avg	TD	Int	Lg	Rtg
1949	SF	AA	2	0	0.0	0	0.0	0	0		39.6
1951	SF	N	1	1	100.0	31	31.0	1	0	31t	158.3
1952			2	0	0.0	0	0.0	0	0		39.6
1953			1	1	100.0	14	14.0	0	0	14	118.8
1954			1	1	100.0	34	34.0	0	0	34	118.8
1955			2	0	0.0	0	0.0	0	0		39.6
1957			1	0	0.0	0	0.0	0	0		39.6
1963			1	0	0.0	0	0.0	0	0		39.6
Career			11	3	27.3	79	7.2	1	0	34	87.3

John Petchel

Year	Team		Att	Com	PC	Yds	Avg	TD	Int	Lg	Rtg
1944	CLE	N	3	2	66.7	27	9.0	0	0	14	95.1
1945	PIT	N	1	1	100.0	8	8.0	0	0	8	100.0
Career			4	3	75.0	35	8.8	0	0	14	101.0

Forest Peters

Year	Team		Att	Com	PC	Yds	Avg	TD	Int	Lg	Rtg
1930	PRO	N							2		
1931	BKN	N							1		
Career									3		

Ken Peterson

Year	Team		Att	Com	PC	Yds	Avg	TD	Int	Lg	Rtg
1935	CHIC	N						1			
1936	DET	N	6	0	0.0	0	0.0	0	1		0.0
Career			6	0	0.0	0	0.0	1	1		0.0

Nelson Peterson

Year	Team		Att	Com	PC	Yds	Avg	TD	Int	Lg	Rtg
1938	CLE	N	6	0	0.0	0	0.0	0	2		0.0

Ray Peterson

Year	Team		Att	Com	PC	Yds	Avg	TD	Int	Lg	Rtg
1937	GB	N	6	3	50.0	47	7.8	0	0		76.4

Richie Petitbon

Year	Team		Att	Com	PC	Yds	Avg	TD	Int	Lg	Rtg
1967	CHI	N	0	0	0.0	0		0	0		

Art Pharmer

Year	Team		Att	Com	PC	Yds	Avg	TD	Int	Lg	Rtg
1930	FRA	N							1		

Todd Philcox

Year	Team		Att	Com	PC	Yds	Avg	TD	Int	Lg	Rtg
1990	CIN	N	2	0	0.0	0	0.0	0	1		0.0
1991	CLE	N	8	4	50.0	49	6.1	0	1	28	29.7
1992			27	13	48.1	217	8.0	3	1	69t	97.3
1993			108	52	48.1	699	6.5	4	7	56	44.5
Career			145	69	47.6	965	6.7	7	10	69t	56.8

Lawrence Phillips

Year	Team		Att	Com	PC	Yds	Avg	TD	Int	Lg	Rtg
1996	STL	N	0	0		0		0	0	0	

Mike Phipps

Year	Team		Att	Com	PC	Yds	Avg	TD	Int	Lg	Rtg
1970	CLE	N	60	29	48.3	529	8.8	1	5	53t	49.9
1971			47	13	27.7	179	3.8	1	4	39	14.6
1972			305	144	47.2	1994	6.5	13	16	80t	61.0
1973			299	148	49.5	1719	5.7	9	20	51t	49.4
1974			256	117	45.7	1384	5.4	9	17	55	46.7
1975			313	162	51.8	1749	5.6	4	19	48	47.5
1976			37	20	54.1	146	3.9	3	0	23t	90.6
1977	CHI	N	5	3	60.0	5	1.0	0	0	10	64.6
1978			83	44	53.0	465	5.6	2	10	35t	38.1
1979			255	134	52.5	1535	6.0	9	8	68t	69.6
1980			122	61	50.0	630	5.2	2	9	54t	40.0
1981			17	11	64.7	171	10.1	2	0	43t	137.1
Career			1799	886	49.2	10506	5.8	55	108	80t	52.6
Playoffs			59	25	42.4	300	5.1	1	7		24.6

Carl Pickens

Year	Team		Att	Com	PC	Yds	Avg	TD	Int	Lg	Rtg
1993	CIN	N	1	0	0.0	0	0.0	0	0		39.6

Carl Pickens *continued*

Year	Team		Att	Com	PC	Yds	Avg	TD	Int	Lg	Rtg
1996			1	1	100.0	12	12.0	0	0	12	116.7
Career			2	1	50.0	12	6.0	0	0	12	68.8

Milt Piepul

Year	Team		Att	Com	PC	Yds	Avg	TD	Int	Lg	Rtg
1941	DET	N	1	1	100.0	23	23.0	0	0	23	118.8

Nick Pietrosante

Year	Team		Att	Com	PC	Yds	Avg	TD	Int	Lg	Rtg
1963	DET	N	1	1	100.0	37	37.0	0	0	37	118.8
1964			1	0	0.0	0	0.0	0	1		0.0
Career			2	1	50.0	37	18.5	0	1	37	56.3

Erny Pinckert

Year	Team		Att	Com	PC	Yds	Avg	TD	Int	Lg	Rtg
Playoffs			1	0	0.0	0	0.0	0	0		39.6

Stan Pincura

Year	Team		Att	Com	PC	Yds	Avg	TD	Int	Lg	Rtg
1937	CLE	N	27	9	33.3	92	3.4	0	3		4.5
1938			33	13	39.4	240	7.3	2	7		45.8
Career			60	22	36.7	332	5.5	2	10		27.2

Johnny Pingel

Year	Team		Att	Com	PC	Yds	Avg	TD	Int	Lg	Rtg
1939	DET	N	48	27	56.3	343	7.1	3	4		64.8

Joe Pisarcik

Year	Team		Att	Com	PC	Yds	Avg	TD	Int	Lg	Rtg
1977	NYG	N	241	103	42.7	1346	5.6	4	14	82	42.3
1978			301	143	47.5	2096	7.0	12	23	67t	52.1
1979			108	43	39.8	537	5.0	2	6	48	39.0
1980	PHI	N	22	15	68.2	187	8.5	0	0	46	94.3
1981			15	8	53.3	154	10.3	2	2	44t	89.3
1982			1	1	100.0	24	24.0	0	0	24	118.8
1983			34	16	47.1	172	5.1	1	0	33	72.2
1984			176	96	54.5	1036	5.9	3	3	40	70.6
Career			898	425	47.3	5552	6.2	24	48	82	53.9

Steve Pisarkiewicz

Year	Team		Att	Com	PC	Yds	Avg	TD	Int	Lg	Rtg
1978	STL	N	29	10	34.5	164	5.7	0	3	40	14.8
1979			109	52	47.7	621	5.7	3	4	78t	59.5
1980	GB	N	5	2	40.0	19	3.8	0	0	16	51.3
Career			143	64	44.8	804	5.6	3	7	78t	49.4

Elijah Pitts

Year	Team		Att	Com	PC	Yds	Avg	TD	Int	Lg	Rtg
1962	GB	N	2	0	0.0	0	0.0	0	0		39.6
1963			2	2	100.0	41	20.5	1	0	21t	158.3
1965			2	1	50.0	51	25.5	0	0	51	95.8
1966			2	0	0.0	0	0.0	0	0		39.6
1967			1	1	100.0	21	21.0	0	0	21	118.8
Career			9	4	44.4	113	12.6	1	0	51	128.2

Tony Plansky

Year	Team		Att	Com	PC	Yds	Avg	TD	Int	Lg	Rtg
1929	NYG	N							2		

Dick Plasman

Year	Team		Att	Com	PC	Yds	Avg	TD	Int	Lg	Rtg
1939	CHIB	N	1	0	0.0	0	0.0	0	0		39.6

Milt Plum

Year	Team		Att	Com	PC	Yds	Avg	TD	Int	Lg	Rtg
1957	CLE	N	76	41	53.9	590	7.8	2	5	58t	60.7
1958			189	102	54.0	1619	8.6	11	11	74	77.9
1959			266	156	58.6	1992	7.5	14	8	76	87.2
1960			250	151	60.4	2297	9.2	21	5	80t	110.4
1961			302	177	58.6	2416	8.0	18	10	77	90.3
1962	DET	N	325	179	55.1	2378	7.3	15	20	80t	68.2
1963			77	27	35.1	339	4.4	2	12	39	18.7
1964			287	154	53.7	2241	7.8	18	15	92t	78.5
1965			308	143	46.4	1710	5.6	12	19	55t	51.2
1966			146	82	56.2	943	6.5	4	13	63	47.8
1967			172	86	50.0	925	5.4	4	8	43	54.5
1968	LA	N	12	5	41.7	49	4.1	1	1	25	46.9
1969	NY	N	9	3	33.3	37	4.1	0	0	23	47.0
Career			2419	1306	54.0	17536	7.2	122	127	92t	72.2
Playoffs			25	12	48.0	134	5.4	0	4		24.8

Jim Plunkett

Year	Team		Att	Com	PC	Yds	Avg	TD	Int	Lg	Rtg
1971	NE	N	328	158	48.2	2158	6.6	19	16	88t	68.6
1972			355	169	47.6	2196	6.2	8	25	62	45.7
1973			376	193	51.3	2550	6.8	13	17	64	65.8
1974			352	173	49.1	2457	7.0	19	22	69t	64.1
1975			92	36	39.1	571	6.2	3	7	76	39.7
1976	SF	N	243	126	51.9	1592	6.6	13	16	85t	63.0
1977			248	128	51.6	1693	6.8	9	14	47t	62.1
1979	OAK	N	15	7	46.7	89	5.9	1	1	39	60.1
1980			320	165	51.6	2299	7.2	18	16	86t	72.9
1981			179	94	52.5	1045	5.8	4	9	42	56.7
1982	LARI	N	261	152	58.2	2035	7.8	14	15	52	77.0
1983			379	230	60.7	2935	7.7	20	18	99t	82.7

Jim Plunkett continued

Year	Team		Att	Com	PC	Yds	Avg	TD	Int	Lg	Rtg
1984			198	108	54.5	1473	7.4	6	10	73t	67.6
1985			103	71	68.9	803	7.8	3	3	41t	89.6
1986			252	133	52.8	1986	7.9	14	9	81t	82.5
Career			3701	1943	52.5	25882	7.0	164	198	99t	67.5
Playoffs			272	162	59.6	2293	8.4	11	12		81.9

Ray Poage

Year	Team		Att	Com	PC	Yds	Avg	TD	Int	Lg	Rtg
1965	PHI	N	1	0	0.0	0	0.0	0	0		39.6

Ed Podolak

Year	Team		Att	Com	PC	Yds	Avg	TD	Int	Lg	Rtg
1970	KC	N	2	2	100.0	40	20.0	0	0	24	118.8
1971			2	2	100.0	42	21.0	0	0	23	118.8
1973			1	0	0.0	0	0.0	0	0		39.6
1975			1	0	0.0	0	0.0	0	1		0.0
Career			6	4	66.7	82	13.7	0	1	24	70.1

Jim Podoley

Year	Team		Att	Com	PC	Yds	Avg	TD	Int	Lg	Rtg
1959	WAS	N	1	0	0.0	0	0.0	0	0		39.6

Dick Poillon

Year	Team		Att	Com	PC	Yds	Avg	TD	Int	Lg	Rtg
1942	WAS	N	15	2	13.3	52	3.5	0	3	33	1.9

Fritz Pollard

Year	Team		Att	Com	PC	Yds	Avg	TD	Int	Lg	Rtg
1925	AKR	N						3			
1926								1			
Career								4			

Red Pollock

Year	Team		Att	Com	PC	Yds	Avg	TD	Int	Lg	Rtg
1935	CHIB	N	12	1	8.3	18	1.5	0	2	18	0.0

Milt Popovich

Year	Team		Att	Com	PC	Yds	Avg	TD	Int	Lg	Rtg
1939	CHIC	N	6	5	83.3	52	8.7	0	0		102.8

Tracy Porter

Year	Team		Att	Com	PC	Yds	Avg	TD	Int	Lg	Rtg
1982	DET	N	1	0	0.0	0	0.0	0	0		39.6

Dickie Post

Year	Team		Att	Com	PC	Yds	Avg	TD	Int	Lg	Rtg
1967	SD	A	6	1	16.7	9	1.5	0	0	9	39.6
1968			4	1	25.0	23	5.8	0	0	23	51.0
1969			2	1	50.0	4	2.0	0	0	4	56.3
Career			12	3	25.0	36	3.0	0	0	23	39.6

Al Postus

Year	Team		Att	Com	PC	Yds	Avg	TD	Int	Lg	Rtg
1945	PIT	N	5	2	40.0	73	14.6	0	1	52	47.9

Jim Powers

Year	Team		Att	Com	PC	Yds	Avg	TD	Int	Lg	Rtg
1950	SF	N	20	9	45.0	108	5.4	0	2	50	22.5
1952			1	0	0.0	0	0.0	0	0		39.6
1953			49	22	44.9	259	5.3	1	2	28	51.3
Career			70	31	44.3	367	5.2	1	4	52	41.8

Steve Preece

Year	Team		Att	Com	PC	Yds	Avg	TD	Int	Lg	Rtg
1977	SEA	N	1	0	0.0	0	0.0	0	0		39.6

Glenn Presnell

Year	Team		Att	Com	PC	Yds	Avg	TD	Int	Lg	Rtg
1931	POR	N						5			
1932								3			
1933			125	47	37.6	774	6.2	5	12		33.0
1934	DET	N	57	13	22.8	236	4.1	2	9		16.4
1936			36	15	41.7	221	6.1	2	7		41.3
Career			218	75	34.4	1231	5.6	17	28		28.5

Dave Preston

Year	Team		Att	Com	PC	Yds	Avg	TD	Int	Lg	Rtg
1979	DEN	N	1	0	0.0	0	0.0	0	0		39.6

Luke Prestridge

Year	Team		Att	Com	PC	Yds	Avg	TD	Int	Lg	Rtg
1979	DEN	N	1	0	0.0	0	0.0	0	0		39.6

Charley Price

Year	Team		Att	Com	PC	Yds	Avg	TD	Int	Lg	Rtg
1940	DET	N	66	33	50.0	456	6.9	3	7		48.1
1941			33	9	27.3	112	3.4	0	4	19	1.6
1945			52	16	30.8	256	4.9	3	8	63	27.9
1946	MIA	AA	74	36	48.6	484	6.5	2	5		50.7
Career			225	94	41.8	1308	5.8	8	24	63	33.4

Bosh Pritchard

Year	Team		Att	Com	PC	Yds	Avg	TD	Int	Lg	Rtg
1946	PHI	N	1	0	0.0	0	0.0	0	0		39.6
1949			1	0	0.0	0	0.0	0	1		0.0
Career			2	0	0.0	0	0.0	0	1		0.0

Dewey Proctor

Year	Team		Att	Com	PC	Yds	Avg	TD	Int	Lg	Rtg
1947	NY	AA	1	0	0.0	0	0.0	0	0		39.6

Ricky Proehl

Year	Team		Att	Com	PC	Yds	Avg	TD	Int	Lg	Rtg
1992	PHX	N	1	0	0.0	0	0.0	0	1		0.0

Eddie Prokop

Year	Team		Att	Com	PC	Yds	Avg	TD	Int	Lg	Rtg
1946	NY	AA	11	4	36.4	72	6.5	0	0		59.7
1947			8	4	50.0	137	17.1	2	1	70t	95.8
1948	CHI	AA	1	0	0.0	0	0.0	0	0		39.6
Career			20	8	40.0	209	10.4	2	1	70t	91.5
Playoffs			1	0	0.0	0	0.0	0	0		39.6

Fred Provo

Year	Team		Att	Com	PC	Yds	Avg	TD	Int	Lg	Rtg
1948	GB	N	1	1	100.0	20	20.0	1	0	20	158.3

James Pruitt

Year	Team		Att	Com	PC	Yds	Avg	TD	Int	Lg	Rtg
1973	CLE	N	1	0	0.0	0	0.0	0	0		39.6
1974			2	2	100.0	115	57.5	2	0	60t	158.3
1976			3	2	66.7	39	13.0	1	0	29	149.3
1977			9	4	44.4	28	3.1	3	0	13	91.7
1978			3	0	0.0	0	0.0	0	2		0.0
1983	LARI	N	1	0	0.0	0	0.0	0	0		39.6
Career			19	8	42.1	182	9.6	6	2	60t	77.1

Marion Pugh

Year	Team		Att	Com	PC	Yds	Avg	TD	Int	Lg	Rtg
1941	NYG	N	24	12	50.0	161	6.7	1	0	53	85.6
1945	NY	N	58	27	46.6	390	6.7	3	3	47	64.6
1946	MIA	AA	118	55	46.6	608	5.2	5	12	63t	36.9
Career			200	94	47.0	1159	5.8	9	15	63t	49.1

Cal Purdin

Year	Team		Att	Com	PC	Yds	Avg	TD	Int	Lg	Rtg
1943	CHIC	N	2	1	50.0	7	3.5	0	0	7	58.3
1946	BKN	AA	1	1	100.0	-2	-2.0	0	0	-2	79.2
Career			3	2	66.7	5	1.7	0	0	7	70.1

Mike Purdy

Year	Team		Att	Com	PC	Yds	Avg	TD	Int	Lg	Rtg
1922	MIL	N							1		

Pid Purdy

Year	Team		Att	Com	PC	Yds	Avg	TD	Int	Lg	Rtg
1926	GB	N							1		

Bernard Quarles

Year	Team		Att	Com	PC	Yds	Avg	TD	Int	Lg	Rtg
1987	LARM	N	3	1	33.3	40	13.3	1	1	40t	81.9

Skeets Quinlan

Year	Team		Att	Com	PC	Yds	Avg	TD	Int	Lg	Rtg
1952	LA	N	4	0	0.0	0	0.0	0	0		39.6
1953			4	2	50.0	60	15.0	0	1	40	56.3
1954			2	1	50.0	34	17.0	0	1	34	56.3
Career			10	3	30.0	94	9.4	0	2	40	26.7

Warren Rabb

Year	Team		Att	Com	PC	Yds	Avg	TD	Int	Lg	Rtg
1961	BUF	A	74	34	45.9	586	7.9	5	2	76	84.6
1962			177	67	37.9	1196	6.8	10	14	76t	47.7
Career			251	101	40.2	1782	7.1	15	16	76t	58.6

Vic Radzevich

Year	Team		Att	Com	PC	Yds	Avg	TD	Int	Lg	Rtg
1926	HAR	N							1		

Mike Rae

Year	Team		Att	Com	PC	Yds	Avg	TD	Int	Lg	Rtg
1976	OAK	N	65	35	53.8	417	6.4	6	1	37t	98.0
1977			30	15	50.0	162	5.4	1	4	30	37.8
1978	TB	N	118	57	48.3	705	6.0	4	7	33t	53.8
1979			36	17	47.2	252	7.0	1	2	29	56.7
Career			249	124	49.8	1536	6.2	12	14	37t	61.9
Playoffs			13	2	15.4	42	3.2	0	0		40.5

Billy Rafter

Year	Team		Att	Com	PC	Yds	Avg	TD	Int	Lg	Rtg
1921	SYR	A							1		

Ben Raimondi

Year	Team		Att	Com	PC	Yds	Avg	TD	Int	Lg	Rtg
1947	NY	AA	15	3	20.0	54	3.6	0	0		42.1

Larry Rakestraw

Year	Team		Att	Com	PC	Yds	Avg	TD	Int	Lg	Rtg
1966	CHI	N	0	0		0		0	0		
1967			44	21	47.7	228	5.2	3	2	34	67.2
1968			67	30	44.8	361	5.4	1	7	80t	27.2
Career			111	51	45.9	589	5.3	4	9	80t	40.7

Chuck Ramsey

Year	Team		Att	Com	PC	Yds	Avg	TD	Int	Lg	Rtg
1980	NYJ	N	2	1	50.0	6	3.0	0	0	6	56.3

Ray Ramsey

Year	Team		Att	Com	PC	Yds	Avg	TD	Int	Lg	Rtg
1948	BKN	AA	1	0	0.0	0	0.0	0	0		39.6

Steve Ramsey

Year	Team		Att	Com	PC	Yds	Avg	TD	Int	Lg	Rtg
1970	NO	N	2	0	0.0	0	0.0	0	0		39.6

Steve Ramsey *continued*

Year	Team		Att	Com	PC	Yds	Avg	TD	Int	Lg	Rtg
1971	DEN	N	178	84	47.2	1120	6.3	5	13	47	46.6
1972			137	65	47.4	1050	7.7	3	9	55	53.5
1973			27	10	37.0	194	7.2	2	2	76t	56.7
1974			74	41	55.4	580	7.8	5	7	43t	64.0
1975			233	128	54.9	1562	6.7	9	14	66t	63.6
1976			270	128	47.4	1931	7.2	11	13	71t	64.9
Career			921	456	49.5	6437	7.0	35	58	76t	58.9

Tom Ramsey

Year	Team		Att	Com	PC	Yds	Avg	TD	Int	Lg	Rtg
1986	NE	N	3	1	33.3	7	2.3	0	0	7	42.4
1987			134	71	53.0	898	6.7	6	6	40	70.4
1988			27	12	44.4	100	3.7	0	3	22	15.0
1989	IND	N	50	24	48.0	280	5.6	1	1	47	63.8
Career			214	108	50.5	1285	6.0	7	10	47	60.6

Bob Rapp

Year	Team		Att	Com	PC	Yds	Avg	TD	Int	Lg	Rtg
1926	COL	N							1		

Manny Rapp

Year	Team		Att	Com	PC	Yds	Avg	TD	Int	Lg	Rtg
1934	C-S	N							1		

Bo Rather

Year	Team		Att	Com	PC	Yds	Avg	TD	Int	Lg	Rtg
1974	CHI	N	1	0	0.0	0	0.0	0	0		39.6

George Ratterman

Year	Team		Att	Com	PC	Yds	Avg	TD	Int	Lg	Rtg
1947	BUF	AA	244	124	50.8	1840	7.5	22	20	61t	71.8
1948			335	168	50.1	2577	7.7	16	22	71	64.5
1949			252	146	**57.9**	1777	7.1	14	13		76.8
1950	NYY	N	294	140	47.6	2251	7.7	**22**	24	69t	64.6
1951			67	31	46.3	340	5.1	2	6	36	34.4
1952	CLE	N	6	2	33.3	20	3.3	1	2	11t	43.8
1953			41	23	56.1	301	7.3	4	0	45	111.9
1954			53	32	60.4	465	8.8	3	3	48t	84.2
1955			47	32	68.1	504	10.7	6	3	35	116.5
1956			57	39	68.4	398	7.0	1	3	46t	72.1
Career			1396	737	52.8	10473	7.5	91	96	71	70.4
Playoffs			76	37	48.7	470	6.2	6	6		61.8

John Rauch

Year	Team		Att	Com	PC	Yds	Avg	TD	Int	Lg	Rtg
1949	NYB	N	25	11	44.0	169	6.8	1	3	61	40.7
1950	NYY	N	51	29	56.9	502	9.8	6	2	82t	113.4
1951	NYY-PHI	N	94	30	31.9	288	3.1	1	4	39t	27.3
Career			170	70	41.2	959	5.6	8	9	82t	53.5

Frank Reagan

Year	Team		Att	Com	PC	Yds	Avg	TD	Int	Lg	Rtg
1941	NYG	N	6	1	16.7	16	2.7	0	0	16	39.6
1946	NY	N	6	3	50.0	32	5.3	0	0	22	66.0
1947	NYG	N	25	12	48.0	191	7.6	1	2	88	53.9
Career			37	16	43.2	239	6.5	1	2	88	51.5

John Reaves

Year	Team		Att	Com	PC	Yds	Avg	TD	Int	Lg	Rtg
1972	PHI	N	224	108	48.2	1508	6.7	7	12	77t	58.4
1973			19	5	26.3	17	0.9	0	1	6	17.7
1974			20	5	25.0	84	4.2	0	2	29	5.0
1975	CIN	N	51	25	49.0	297	5.8	2	3	51	55.8
1976			22	8	36.4	76	3.5	2	1	19	58.1
1977			59	24	40.7	383	6.5	0	5	40	27.7
1978			144	74	51.4	790	5.5	3	8	51t	51.6
1981	HOU	N	61	31	50.8	379	6.2	2	2	51t	67.6
1987	TB	N	16	6	37.5	83	5.2	1	0	26t	75.8
Career			616	286	46.4	3617	5.9	17	34	77t	51.4

Gus Redman

Year	Team		Att	Com	PC	Yds	Avg	TD	Int	Lg	Rtg
1924	DAY	N							1		

Andre Reed

Year	Team		Att	Com	PC	Yds	Avg	TD	Int	Lg	Rtg
1994	BUF	N	1	1	100.0	32	32.0	0	0	32	118.8

Joe Reed

Year	Team		Att	Com	PC	Yds	Avg	TD	Int	Lg	Rtg
1973	SF	N	114	51	44.7	589	5.2	2	6	38	44.8
1974			74	29	39.2	316	4.3	2	7	58t	22.1
1975	DET	N	191	86	45.0	1181	6.2	9	10	65t	59.3
1976			62	32	51.6	425	6.9	3	3	57	69.6
1977			40	13	32.5	150	3.8	0	4	26	5.2
1979			32	14	43.8	164	5.1	2	1	50	67.7
Career			513	225	43.9	2825	5.5	18	31	65t	48.1

J.T. Reed

Year	Team		Att	Com	PC	Yds	Avg	TD	Int	Lg	Rtg
1937	CHIC	N	1	0	0.0	0	0.0	0	0		39.6
1939			1	1	100.0	2	2.0	0	0	2	79.2
Career			2	1	50.0	2	1.0	0	0	2	56.3

Mark Reed

Year	Team		Att	Com	PC	Yds	Avg	TD	Int	Lg	Rtg
1983	BAL	N	10	6	60.0	34	3.4	0	1	16	26.7

Tony Reed

Year	Team		Att	Com	PC	Yds	Avg	TD	Int	Lg	Rtg
1981	DEN	N	1	0	0.0	0	0.0	0	1		0.0

Dan Reeves

Year	Team		Att	Com	PC	Yds	Avg	TD	Int	Lg	Rtg
1965	DAL	N	2	1	50.0	11	5.5	0	0	11	66.7
1966			6	3	50.0	48	8.0	0	0	29	77.1
1967			7	4	57.1	195	27.9	2	1	74t	101.8
1968			4	2	50.0	43	10.8	0	0	24	88.5
1969			3	1	33.3	35	11.7	0	1	35	38.9
1970			3	1	33.3	14	4.7	0	1	14	9.7
1971			5	2	40.0	24	4.8	0	1	14	15.8
1972			2	0	0.0	0	0.0	0	0		39.6
Career			32	14	43.8	370	11.6	2	4	74t	68.0
Playoffs			1	1	100.0	50	50.0	1	0		158.3

Frank Reich

Year	Team		Att	Com	PC	Yds	Avg	TD	Int	Lg	Rtg
1985	BUF	N	1	1	100.0	19	19.0	0	0	19	118.8
1986			19	9	47.4	104	5.5	0	2	37	24.8
1989			87	53	60.9	701	8.1	7	2	63t	103.7
1990			63	36	57.1	469	7.4	2	0	43	91.3
1991			41	27	65.9	305	7.4	6	2	29	107.2
1992			47	24	51.1	221	4.7	0	2	21	46.5
1993			26	16	61.5	153	5.9	2	0	30t	103.5
1994			93	56	60.2	568	6.1	1	4	47	63.4
1995	CAR	N	84	37	44.0	441	5.3	2	2	46	58.7
1996	NYJ	N	331	175	52.9	2205	6.7	15	16	52t	68.9
Career			792	434	54.8	5186	6.5	35	30	63t	74.0
Playoffs			89	56	62.9	654	7.3	7	3		97.3

Jerry Reichow

Year	Team		Att	Com	PC	Yds	Avg	TD	Int	Lg	Rtg
1956	DET	N	6	3	50.0	19	3.2	0	1	14	17.4
1957			2	0	0.0	0	0.0	0	0		39.6
1959			27	9	33.3	168	6.2	0	2	41	24.9
1961	MIN	N	3	0	0.0	0	0.0	0	1		0.0
Career			38	12	31.6	187	4.9	0	4	41	9.3
Playoffs			3	1	33.3	16	5.3	1	0		91.7

Floyd Reid

Year	Team		Att	Com	PC	Yds	Avg	TD	Int	Lg	Rtg
1951	GB	N	1	0	0.0	0	0.0	0	0		39.6

Billy Reinhard

Year	Team		Att	Com	PC	Yds	Avg	TD	Int	Lg	Rtg
1947	LA	AA	2	0	0.0	0	0.0	0	0		39.6
1948			5	0	0.0	0	0.0	0	0		39.6
Career			7	0	0.0	0	0.0	0	0		39.6

Bob Reinhard

Year	Team		Att	Com	PC	Yds	Avg	TD	Int	Lg	Rtg
1946	LA	AA	1	1	100.0	7	7.0	0	0	7	95.8
1947			4	2	50.0	21	5.3	0	0		65.6
Career			5	3	60.0	28	5.6	0	0	7	75.4

Albie Reisz

Year	Team		Att	Com	PC	Yds	Avg	TD	Int	Lg	Rtg
1944	CLE	N	113	49	43.4	777	6.9	8	10	70	53.6
1945			21	8	38.1	146	7.0	2	3	44	55.0
Career			134	57	42.5	923	6.9	10	13	70	51.5

Mike Renfro

Year	Team		Att	Com	PC	Yds	Avg	TD	Int	Lg	Rtg
1984	DAL	N	2	1	50.0	49	24.5	1	0	49t	135.4
1986			1	1	100.0	23	23.0	0	0	23	118.8
Career			3	2	66.7	72	24.0	1	0	49t	149.3

Ray Renfro

Year	Team		Att	Com	PC	Yds	Avg	TD	Int	Lg	Rtg
1953	CLE	N	3	1	33.3	36	12.0	1	0	36t	119.4
1954			1	0	0.0	0	0.0	0	1		0.0
1955			2	0	0.0	0	0.0	0	0		39.6
Career			6	1	16.7	36	6.0	1	1	36t	52.1

Neil Rengel

Year	Team		Att	Com	PC	Yds	Avg	TD	Int	Lg	Rtg
1930	FRA	N							1		

Pug Rentner

Year	Team		Att	Com	PC	Yds	Avg	TD	Int	Lg	Rtg
1935	BOS	N						1			
1936			39	15	38.5	198	5.1	0	6		15.7
Career			39	15	38.5	198	5.1	1	6		15.7
Playoffs			6	4	66.7	60	10.0	0	0		99.3

Lance Rentzel

Year	Team		Att	Com	PC	Yds	Avg	TD	Int	Lg	Rtg
1970	DAL	N	1	1	100.0	58	58.0	1	0	58t	158.3

M.C. Reynolds

Year	Team		Att	Com	PC	Yds	Avg	TD	Int	Lg	Rtg
1958	CHIC	N	195	105	53.8	1422	7.3	11	11	91t	72.6
1959			39	19	48.7	329	8.4	4	1	85t	101.3

Year	Team		Att	Com	PC	Yds	Avg	TD	Int	Lg	Rtg

M.C. Reynolds *continued*

Year	Team		Att	Com	PC	Yds	Avg	TD	Int	Lg	Rtg
1960	WAS	N	30	13	43.3	154	5.1	0	3	31	20.0
1961	BUF	A	181	83	45.9	1004	5.5	2	13	52	37.2
1962	OAK	A	5	2	40.0	23	4.6	0	0		54.6
Career			450	222	49.3	2932	6.5	17	28	91t	57.0

Jerry Rhome

Year	Team		Att	Com	PC	Yds	Avg	TD	Int	Lg	Rtg
1965	DAL	N	21	9	42.9	157	7.5	1	1	82t	65.0
1966			36	21	58.3	253	7.0	0	1	47	68.4
1967			18	9	50.0	86	4.8	0	1	19	40.5
1969	CLE	N	19	7	36.8	35	1.8	0	2	22	5.7
1970	HOU	N	168	88	52.4	1031	6.1	5	8	87t	61.4
1971	LA	N	18	5	27.8	66	3.7	1	1	43	37.7
Career			280	139	49.6	1628	5.8	7	14	87t	55.2
Playoffs			2	2	100.0	35	17.5	0	0		118.8

Allen Rice

Year	Team		Att	Com	PC	Yds	Avg	TD	Int	Lg	Rtg
1986	MIN	N	1	0	0.0	0	0.0	0	0		39.6
1989			0	0		0		0	0		
Career			1	0	0.0	0	0.0	0	0		39.6
Playoffs			1	1	100.0	10	10.0	1	0		147.9

Jerry Rice

Year	Team		Att	Com	PC	Yds	Avg	TD	Int	Lg	Rtg
1986	SF	N	2	1	50.0	16	8.0	0	0	16	77.1
1988			3	1	33.3	14	4.7	0	1	14	9.7
1995			1	1	100.0	41	41.0	1	0	41t	158.3
1996			1	0	0.0	0	0.0	0	0	0	39.6
Career			7	3	42.9	71	10.1	1	1	41t	80.1
Playoffs			1	0	0.0	0	0.0	0	0		39.6

Kink Richards

Year	Team		Att	Com	PC	Yds	Avg	TD	Int	Lg	Rtg
1934	NYG	N	1	1	100.0	10	10.0	0	0	10	108.3
1938			1	0	0.0	0	0.0	0	1		0.0
Career			2	1	50.0	10	5.0	0	1	10	25.0

Bucky Richardson

Year	Team		Att	Com	PC	Yds	Avg	TD	Int	Lg	Rtg
1992	HOU	N	0	0		0		0	0		
1993			4	3	75.0	55	13.8	0	0	34	116.7
1994			181	94	51.9	1202	6.6	6	6	76t	70.3
Career			185	97	52.4	1257	6.8	6	6	76t	71.4

Paul Rickards

Year	Team		Att	Com	PC	Yds	Avg	TD	Int	Lg	Rtg
1948	LA	N	2	2	100.0	4	2.0	0	0	3	79.2

Robb Riddick

Year	Team		Att	Com	PC	Yds	Avg	TD	Int	Lg	Rtg
1987	BUF	N	1	1	100.0	35	35.0	0	0	35	118.8
1988			2	2	100.0	31	15.5	0	0	26	118.8
Career			3	3	100.0	66	22.0	0	0	35	118.8

Preston Ridlehuber

Year	Team		Att	Com	PC	Yds	Avg	TD	Int	Lg	Rtg
1969	BUF	A	1	1	100.0	45	45.0	1	0	45t	158.3

Dick Riffle

Year	Team		Att	Com	PC	Yds	Avg	TD	Int	Lg	Rtg
1938	PHI	N	31	9	29.0	178	5.7	1	4		22.2
1939			4	1	25.0	2	0.5	0	1	2	0.0
1941	PIT	N	39	8	20.5	88	2.3	1	9	22	8.5
1942			8	3	37.5	64	8.0	0	1	27	27.1
Career			82	21	25.6	332	4.0	2	15	27	12.5

John Riggins

Year	Team		Att	Com	PC	Yds	Avg	TD	Int	Lg	Rtg
1983	WAS	N	1	0	0.0	0	0.0	0	0		39.6
1985			1	0	0.0	0	0.0	0	0		39.6
Career			2	0	0.0	0	0.0	0	0		39.6
Playoffs			1	1	100.0	36	36.0	0	0		118.8

Gerald Riggs

Year	Team		Att	Com	PC	Yds	Avg	TD	Int	Lg	Rtg
1986	ATL	N	1	0	0.0	0	0.0	0	0		39.6

Tim Riordan

Year	Team		Att	Com	PC	Yds	Avg	TD	Int	Lg	Rtg
1987	NO	N	1	0	0.0	0	0.0	0	0		39.6

Alan Risher

Year	Team		Att	Com	PC	Yds	Avg	TD	Int	Lg	Rtg
1987	GB	N	74	44	59.5	564	7.6	3	3	46t	80.0

Reggie Rivers

Year	Team		Att	Com	PC	Yds	Avg	TD	Int	Lg	Rtg
1994	DEN	N	1	0	0.0	0	0.0	0	0		39.6

John Roach

Year	Team		Att	Com	PC	Yds	Avg	TD	Int	Lg	Rtg
1959	CHIC	N	57	22	38.6	340	6.0	2	4	62	41.6
1960	STL	N	188	87	46.3	1423	7.6	17	19	57t	62.7
1961	GB	N	4	0	0.0	0	0.0	0	0		39.6
1962			12	3	25.0	33	2.8	0	0	18	39.6
1963			84	38	45.2	620	7.4	4	8	45t	46.8

John Roach *continued*

Year	Team		Att	Com	PC	Yds	Avg	TD	Int	Lg	Rtg
1964	DAL	N	68	32	47.1	349	5.1	1	6	37	30.8
Career			413	182	44.1	2765	6.7	24	37	62	48.7

Harry Robb

Year	Team		Att	Com	PC	Yds	Avg	TD	Int	Lg	Rtg
1921	CAN	A							1		

Jack Robbins

Year	Team		Att	Com	PC	Yds	Avg	TD	Int	Lg	Rtg
1938	CHIC	N	97	52	53.6	577	5.9	2	9		39.8
1939			85	36	42.4	499	5.9	4	10		37.9
Career			182	88	48.4	1076	5.9	6	19		38.4

Bo Roberson

Year	Team		Att	Com	PC	Yds	Avg	TD	Int	Lg	Rtg
1962	OAK	A	6	0	0.0	0	0.0	0	0		39.6

Archie Roberts

Year	Team		Att	Com	PC	Yds	Avg	TD	Int	Lg	Rtg
1967	MIA	A	10	5	50.0	11	1.1	0	1	9	16.7

Gene Roberts

Year	Team		Att	Com	PC	Yds	Avg	TD	Int	Lg	Rtg
1949	NYG	N	1	0	0.0	0	0.0	0	1		0.0

Guy Roberts

Year	Team		Att	Com	PC	Yds	Avg	TD	Int	Lg	Rtg
1926	CLE	A							1		

Wooky Roberts

Year	Team		Att	Com	PC	Yds	Avg	TD	Int	Lg	Rtg
1922	CAN	N							1		
1923									1		
1924	CLE	N							2		
Career									4		

Bobbie Robertson

Year	Team		Att	Com	PC	Yds	Avg	TD	Int	Lg	Rtg
1942	BKN	N	3	1	33.3	1	0.3	0	1	1	2.8

Johnny Robinson

Year	Team		Att	Com	PC	Yds	Avg	TD	Int	Lg	Rtg
1960	DAL	A	1	0	0.0	0	0.0	0	1		0.0

Matt Robinson

Year	Team		Att	Com	PC	Yds	Avg	TD	Int	Lg	Rtg
1977	NYJ	N	54	20	37.0	310	5.7	2	8	58	29.6
1978			266	124	46.6	2002	7.5	13	16	77t	63.5
1979			31	17	54.8	191	6.2	0	2	33	46.6
1980	DEN	N	162	78	48.1	942	5.8	2	12	52	39.7
1981	BUF	N	2	0	0.0	0	0.0	0	0		39.6
1982			8	5	62.5	74	9.3	1	0	31	132.3
Career			523	244	46.7	3519	6.7	18	38	77t	50.2

Tony Robinson

Year	Team		Att	Com	PC	Yds	Avg	TD	Int	Lg	Rtg
1987	WAS	N	18	11	61.1	152	8.4	0	2	42	48.6

Doug Roby

Year	Team		Att	Com	PC	Yds	Avg	TD	Int	Lg	Rtg
1923	CLE	N							3		

Reggie Roby

Year	Team		Att	Com	PC	Yds	Avg	TD	Int	Lg	Rtg
1995	TB	N	1	1	100.0	48	48.0	0	0	48	118.8

Mike Rodak

Year	Team		Att	Com	PC	Yds	Avg	TD	Int	Lg	Rtg
1939	CLE	N	1	0	0.0	0	0.0	0	1		0.0

Hosea Rodgers

Year	Team		Att	Com	PC	Yds	Avg	TD	Int	Lg	Rtg
1949	LA	AA	1	0	0.0	0	0.0	0	0		39.6

Kelly Rodriguez

Year	Team		Att	Com	PC	Yds	Avg	TD	Int	Lg	Rtg
1930	FRA	N							1		

Ruben Rodriguez

Year	Team		Att	Com	PC	Yds	Avg	TD	Int	Lg	Rtg
1989	SEA	N	1	1	100.0	4	4.0	0	0	4	83.3

Johnny Roepke

Year	Team		Att	Com	PC	Yds	Avg	TD	Int	Lg	Rtg
1928	FRA	N							1		

Fran Rogel

Year	Team		Att	Com	PC	Yds	Avg	TD	Int	Lg	Rtg
1950	PIT	N	4	3	75.0	30	7.5	0	0	11	95.8
1951			1	0	0.0	0	0.0	0	0		39.6
1953			1	0	0.0	0	0.0	0	0		39.6
Career			6	3	50.0	30	5.0	0	0	11	64.6

Cullen Rogers

Year	Team		Att	Com	PC	Yds	Avg	TD	Int	Lg	Rtg
1946	PIT	N	1	0	0.0	0	0.0	0	0		39.6

Herm Rohrig

Year	Team		Att	Com	PC	Yds	Avg	TD	Int	Lg	Rtg
1941	GB	N	1	1	100.0	3	3.0	0	0	3	79.2
1946			8	2	25.0	97	12.1	1	1	65	77.6
Career			9	3	33.3	100	11.1	1	1	65	73.6

Johnny Roland

Year	Team		Att	Com	PC	Yds	Avg		TD	Int	Lg	Rtg
1966	STL	N	8	5	62.5	130	16.3		1	0	45	145.8
1967			4	0	0.0	0	0.0		0	1		0.0
1968			1	0	0.0	0	0.0		0	1		0.0
Career			13	5	38.5	130	10.0		1	2	45	61.9

Steve Romanik

Year	Team		Att	Com	PC	Yds	Avg		TD	Int	Lg	Rtg
1950	CHIB	N	2	0	0.0	0	0.0		0	0		39.6
1951			101	43	42.6	791	7.8		3	9	54t	43.0
1952			126	49	38.9	772	6.1		4	11	49	34.2
1953	CHIB-CHIC	N	125	51	40.8	650	5.2		4	11	42	31.8
1954	CHIC	N	79	36	45.6	343	4.3		2	5	38	40.2
Career			433	179	41.3	2556	5.9		13	36	54t	36.5

Milt Romney

Year	Team		Att	Com	PC	Yds	Avg		TD	Int	Lg	Rtg
1928	CHIB	N							1			

Gene Ronzani

Year	Team		Att	Com	PC	Yds	Avg		TD	Int	Lg	Rtg
1934	CHIB	N	32	15	46.9	150	4.7		3	0		91.9
1935			41	16	39.0	230	5.6		2	5		34.7
1936			12	8	66.7	170	14.2		1	2		97.9
1937			13	4	30.8	84	6.5		0	1		22.6
1938			1	0	0.0	0	0.0		0	0		39.6
1944			56	26	46.4	448	8.0		9	5	61	76.5
1945			24	10	41.7	119	5.0		0	2	29	22.7
Career			179	79	44.1	1201	6.7		15	15	61	59.8
Playoffs			6	2	33.3	13	2.2		0	1		2.8

Cobb Rooney

Year	Team		Att	Com	PC	Yds	Avg		TD	Int	Lg	Rtg
1924	DUL	N							3			

Jim Root

Year	Team		Att	Com	PC	Yds	Avg		TD	Int	Lg	Rtg
1953	CHIC	N	192	80	41.7	1149	6.0		8	11	77	51.8
1956			57	28	49.1	333	5.8		3	5	34t	48.4
Career			249	108	43.4	1482	6.0		11	16	77	51.0

Timm Rosenbach

Year	Team		Att	Com	PC	Yds	Avg		TD	Int	Lg	Rtg
1989	PHX	N	22	9	40.9	95	4.3		0	1	24	35.2
1990			437	237	54.2	3098	7.1		16	17	68t	72.8
1992			92	49	53.3	483	5.3		0	6	45	41.2
Career			551	295	53.5	3676	6.7		16	24	68t	66.0

Kyle Rote

Year	Team		Att	Com	PC	Yds	Avg		TD	Int	Lg	Rtg
1952	NYG	N	4	2	50.0	113	28.3		1	0	72t	135.4
1953			8	2	25.0	45	5.6		0	1	23	10.9
1954			6	2	33.3	36	6.0		1	1	18t	54.9
1955			1	0	0.0	0	0.0		0	0		39.6
1956			1	0	0.0	0	0.0		0	0		39.6
Career			20	6	30.0	194	9.7		2	2	72t	61.3

Tobin Rote

Year	Team		Att	Com	PC	Yds	Avg		TD	Int	Lg	Rtg
1950	GB	N	224	83	37.1	1231	5.5		7	24	96t	26.7
1951			256	106	41.4	1540	6.0		15	20	85	48.6
1952			157	82	52.2	1268	8.1		13	8	81t	85.6
1953			185	72	38.9	1005	5.4		5	15	80t	32.4
1954			382	180	47.1	2311	6.0		14	18	82t	59.1
1955			342	157	45.9	1977	5.8		17	19	60t	57.8
1956			308	146	47.4	2203	7.2		18	15	66t	70.6
1957	DET	N	177	76	42.9	1070	6.0		11	10	48	60.2
1958			257	118	45.9	1678	6.5		14	10	65t	69.5
1959			162	62	38.3	861	5.3		5	19	59	26.8
1963	SD	A	286	170	59.4	2510	8.8		20	17	85t	86.7
1964			163	74	45.4	1156	7.1		9	15	82t	49.5
1966	DEN	A	8	3	37.5	40	5.0		0	1	20	14.6
Career			2907	1329	45.7	18850	6.5		148	191	96t	56.8
Playoffs			90	48	53.3	785	8.7		8	3		83.2

George Roudebush

Year	Team		Att	Com	PC	Yds	Avg		TD	Int	Lg	Rtg
1920	DAY	A							1			
1921									2			
Career									3			

Mark Royals

Year	Team		Att	Com	PC	Yds	Avg		TD	Int	Lg	Rtg
1992	PIT	N	1	1	100.0	44	44.0		0	0	44	118.8
1996	DET	N	1	1	100.0	-8	-8.0		0	0	-8	79.2
Career			2	2	100.0	36	18.0		0	0	44	118.8

Mike Rozier

Year	Team		Att	Com	PC	Yds	Avg		TD	Int	Lg	Rtg
1986	HOU	N	1	1	100.0	13	13.0		0	0	13	118.8

Ed Rubbert

Year	Team		Att	Com	PC	Yds	Avg		TD	Int	Lg	Rtg
1987	WAS	N	49	26	53.1	532	10.9		4	1	88t	110.2

T.J. Rubley

Year	Team		Att	Com	PC	Yds	Avg		TD	Int	Lg	Rtg
1993	LARM	N	189	108	57.1	1338	7.1		8	6	54	80.1
1995	GB	N	6	4	66.7	39	6.5		0	1	17	45.1
Career			195	112	57.4	1377	7.1		8	7	54	78.1

Tommy Runnels

Year	Team		Att	Com	PC	Yds	Avg		TD	Int	Lg	Rtg
1956	WAS	N	3	1	33.3	34	11.3		0	0	34	77.1
1957			1	1	100.0	35	35.0		0	0	35	118.8
Career			4	2	50.0	69	17.3		0	0	35	95.8

Benny Russell

Year	Team		Att	Com	PC	Yds	Avg		TD	Int	Lg	Rtg
1968	BUF	A	2	1	50.0	3	1.5		0	0	3	56.3

Doug Russell

Year	Team		Att	Com	PC	Yds	Avg		TD	Int	Lg	Rtg
1935	CHIC	N							1			
1936			1	0	0.0	0	0.0		0	0		39.6
1937			11	4	36.4	94	8.5		1	2		58.7
1938			7	1	14.3	98	14.0		1	2	98t	79.2
1939	CLE	N	1	0	0.0	0	0.0		0	0		39.6
Career			20	5	25.0	192	9.6		3	4	98t	60.8

Ed Rutkowski

Year	Team		Att	Com	PC	Yds	Avg		TD	Int	Lg	Rtg
1963	BUF	A	1	0	0.0	0	0.0		0	0		39.6
1967			1	0	0.0	0	0.0		0	0		39.6
1968			100	41	41.0	380	3.8		0	6	37	27.1
Career			102	41	40.2	380	3.7		0	6	37	26.6

Jeff Rutledge

Year	Team		Att	Com	PC	Yds	Avg		TD	Int	Lg	Rtg
1979	LA	N	32	13	40.6	125	3.9		1	4	22	23.0
1980			4	1	25.0	26	6.5		0	0	26	54.2
1981			50	30	60.0	442	8.8		3	4	64	75.6
1983	NYG	N	174	87	50.0	1208	6.9		3	8	54	59.3
1984			1	1	100.0	9	9.0		0	0	9	104.2
1986			3	1	33.3	13	4.3		1	0	13t	87.5
1987			155	79	51.0	1048	6.8		5	11	50	53.9
1988			17	11	64.7	113	6.6		0	1	33	59.2
1990	WAS	N	68	40	58.8	455	6.7		2	1	40	82.7
1991			22	11	50.0	189	8.6		1	0	40t	94.7
Career			526	274	52.1	3628	6.9		16	29	64	61.4
Playoffs			1	1	100.0	23	23.0		0	0		118.8

Roger Ruzek

Year	Team		Att	Com	PC	Yds	Avg		TD	Int	Lg	Rtg
1989	PHI	N	1	1	100.0	22	22.0		1	0	22t	158.3

Dave Ryan

Year	Team		Att	Com	PC	Yds	Avg		TD	Int	Lg	Rtg
1945	DET	N	44	13	29.5	331	7.5		3	10	61	41.6
1946			154	73	47.4	965	6.3		6	17	88	41.1
Career			198	86	43.4	1296	6.5		9	27	88	41.1

Frank Ryan

Year	Team		Att	Com	PC	Yds	Avg		TD	Int	Lg	Rtg
1958	LA	N	14	5	35.7	34	2.4		1	3	14	28.6
1959			89	42	47.2	709	8.0		2	4	67	63.4
1960			128	62	48.4	816	6.4		7	9	61t	57.9
1961			142	72	50.7	1115	7.9		5	7	96t	68.3
1962	CLE	N	194	112	57.7	1541	7.9		10	7	65t	85.4
1963			256	135	52.7	2026	7.9		25	13	83t	90.4
1964			334	174	52.1	2404	7.2		25	19	62t	76.7
1965			243	119	49.0	1751	7.2		18	13	80t	75.3
1966			382	200	52.4	2974	7.8		29	14	54	88.2
1967			280	136	48.6	2026	7.2		20	16	49t	72.7
1968			66	31	47.0	639	9.7		7	6	57t	79.0
1969	WAS	N	1	1	100.0	4	4.0		0	0	4	83.3
1970			4	1	25.0	3	0.8		0	0	3	39.6
Career			2133	1090	51.1	16042	7.5		149	111	96t	77.6
Playoffs			72	35	48.6	534	7.4		6	4		78.1

Kent Ryan

Year	Team		Att	Com	PC	Yds	Avg		TD	Int	Lg	Rtg
1938	DET	N	9	2	22.2	27	3.0		0	0		39.6
1940			2	0	0.0	0	0.0		0	0		39.6
Career			11	2	18.2	27	2.5		0	0		39.6

Pat Ryan

Year	Team		Att	Com	PC	Yds	Avg		TD	Int	Lg	Rtg
1978	NYJ	N	14	9	64.3	106	7.6		0	2	18	47.6
1979			4	2	50.0	13	3.3		0	1	7	17.7
1981			10	4	40.0	48	4.8		1	1	18	49.2
1982			18	12	66.7	146	8.1		2	1	20t	105.3
1983			40	21	52.5	259	6.5		2	2	36	68.6
1984			285	156	54.7	1939	6.8		14	14	44t	72.0
1985			9	6	66.7	95	10.6		0	0	50	101.6
1986			55	34	61.8	342	6.2		2	1	36	84.1
1987			53	32	60.4	314	5.9		4	2	35t	86.5
1988			113	63	55.8	807	7.1		5	4	42t	78.3
1989			30	15	50.0	153	5.1		1	3	25	36.5

Year	Team		Att	Com	PC	Yds	Avg	TD	Int	Lg	Rtg
Pat Ryan *continued*											
1991	PHI	N	26	10	38.5	98	3.8	0	4	32	10.3
Career			657	364	55.4	4320	6.6	31	35	50	69.2
Playoffs			51	32	62.7	340	6.7	5	1		106.7
Julie Rykovich											
1948	CHI	AA	1	1	100.0	12	12.0	0	0	12	116.7
1951	CHIB	N	3	0	0.0	0	0.0	0	1		0.0
Career			4	1	25.0	12	3.0	0	1	12	0.0
Mark Rypien											
1988	WAS	N	208	114	54.8	1730	8.3	18	13	60t	85.2
1989			476	280	58.8	3768	7.9	22	13	80t	88.1
1990			304	166	54.6	2070	6.8	16	11	53t	78.4
1991			421	249	59.1	3564	8.5	28	11	82t	97.9
1992			479	269	56.2	3282	6.9	13	17	62t	71.7
1993			319	166	52.0	1514	4.7	4	10	43	56.3
1994	CLE	N	128	59	46.1	694	5.4	4	3	43	63.7
1995	STL	N	217	129	59.4	1448	6.7	9	8	50	77.9
1996	PHI	N	13	10	76.9	76	5.8	1	0	16	116.2
Career			2565	1442	56.2	18146	7.1	115	86	82t	79.4
Playoffs			234	126	53.8	1776	7.6	8	10		72.2
Lou Saban											
1946	CLE	AA	3	0	0.0	0	0.0	0	1		0.0
Tony Sacca											
1992	PHX	N	11	4	36.4	29	2.6	0	2	16	5.3
Frankie Sachse											
1943	BKN	N	9	5	55.6	72	8.0	1	1	57	79.2
1944			45	18	40.0	226	5.0	0	5	50	16.8
1945	BOS	N	21	9	42.9	203	9.7	2	0	80	109.8
Career			75	32	42.7	501	6.7	3	6	80	45.5
Norb Sacksteder											
1922	CAN	N							1		
Nick Sacrinty											
1947	CHIB	N	48	15	31.3	299	6.2	5	3	44	62.8
Eddie Salem											
1951	WAS	N	3	0	0.0	0	0.0	0	2		0.0
Sean Salisbury											
1987	IND	N	12	8	66.7	68	5.7	0	2	11	41.7
1992	MIN	N	175	97	55.4	1203	6.9	5	2	51	81.7
1993			195	115	59.0	1413	7.2	9	6	55	84.0
1994			34	16	47.1	156	4.6	0	1	38	48.2
1996	SD	N	161	82	50.9	984	6.1	5	8	56	59.6
Career			577	318	55.1	3824	6.6	19	19	56	72.9
Playoffs			44	14	31.8	234	5.3	0	3		22.3
Don Samuel											
1949	PIT	N	21	7	33.3	67	3.2	0	1	13	23.3
Barry Sanders											
1992	DET	N	1	0	0.0	0	0.0	0	0		39.6
1995			2	1	50.0	11	5.5	0	0	11	66.7
1996			1	0	0.0	0	0.0	0	1	0	0.0
Career			4	1	25.0	11	2.8	0	1	11	0.0
Deion Sanders											
1993	ATL	N	1	0	0.0	0	0.0	0	0		39.6
Ricky Sanders											
1989	WAS	N	1	1	100.0	32	32.0	0	0	32	118.8
Spec Sanders											
1946	NY	AA	79	33	41.8	411	5.2	4	9		35.9
1947			171	93	54.4	1442	8.4	14	17	55	70.2
1948			168	78	46.4	918	5.5	5	11	57	46.2
1950	NYY	N	3	2	66.7	58	19.3	0	0	29	109.7
Career			421	206	48.9	2829	6.7	23	37	57	52.4
Playoffs			19	7	36.8	89	4.7	0	1		30.4
Curt Sandig											
1942	PIT	N	4	2	50.0	10	2.5	0	0	8	56.3
Dom Sanzotta											
1942	DET	N	15	4	26.7	45	3.0	0	0	17	39.6
1946			1	0	0.0	0	0.0	0	0		39.6
Career			16	4	25.0	45	2.8	0	0	17	39.6

Year	Team		Att	Com	PC	Yds	Avg	TD	Int	Lg	Rtg
Tony Sarausky											
1936	NYG	N	27	6	22.2	87	3.2	1	1		37.4
1937			10	3	30.0	31	3.1	0	0		40.0
1938	BKN	N	8	2	25.0	10	1.3	0	0		39.6
Career			45	11	24.4	128	2.8	1	1		37.7
Phil Sarboe											
1934	CHIC	N							1		
1936	CHIC-BKN	N	114	47	41.2	680	6.0	3	13		30.5
Career			114	47	41.2	680	6.0	4	13		30.5
Charley Sarratt											
1948	DET	N	1	1	100.0	48	48.0	0	0	48	118.8
George Sauer											
1935	GB	N	27	10	37.0	184	6.8	1	3		34.1
1936			4	2	50.0	26	6.5	0	1		31.3
Career			31	12	38.7	210	6.8	1	4		33.7
Todd Sauerbrun											
1996	CHI	N	2	2	100.0	63	31.5	0	0	47	118.8
Russ Saunders											
1931	GB	N							1		
James Saxon											
1989	KC	N	1	0	0.0	0	0.0	0	1		0.0
Mike Saxon											
1989	DAL	N	1	1	100.0	4	4.0	0	0	4	83.3
1994	MIN	N	1	0	0.0	0	0.0	0	0		39.6
Career			2	1	50.0	4	2.0	0	0	4	56.3
Gale Sayers											
1965	CHI	N	3	2	66.7	53	17.7	1	1	27	109.7
1966			6	2	33.3	58	9.7	0	1	39	30.6
1967			5	0	0.0	0	0.0	0	0		39.6
1968			2	0	0.0	0	0.0	0	0		39.6
1969			2	0	0.0	0	0.0	0	0		39.6
Career			18	4	22.2	111	6.2	1	2	39	31.7
Charley Scales											
1962	CLE	N	1	0	0.0	0	0.0	0	1		0.0
Johnny Scalzi											
1931	BKN	N							1		
Jack Scarbath											
1953	WAS	N	129	45	34.9	862	6.7	9	12	71t	43.5
1954			109	44	40.4	798	7.3	7	13	60	48.1
1956	PIT	N	41	12	29.3	208	5.1	2	5	47t	24.9
Career			279	101	36.2	1868	6.7	18	30	71t	42.1
Joe Scarpati											
1968	PHI	N	2	1	50.0	3	1.5	0	0	3	56.3
Pete Schabarum											
1954	SF	N	1	0	0.0	0	0.0	0	0		39.6
Don Schaefer											
1956	PHI	N	3	1	33.3	11	3.7	1	0	11t	84.7
Eddie Scharer											
1926	DET	N							5		
Art Schlichter											
1982	BAL	N	37	17	45.9	197	5.3	0	2	24	40.0
1984	IND	N	140	62	44.3	702	5.0	3	7	54	46.2
1985			25	12	48.0	107	4.3	0	2	16	26.6
Career			202	91	45.0	1006	5.0	3	11	54	42.6
Turk Schonert											
1981	CIN	N	19	10	52.6	166	8.7	0	0	36	82.3
1982			1	1	100.0	6	6.0	0	0	6	91.7
1983			156	92	59.0	1159	7.4	2	5	54	73.1
1984			117	78	66.7	945	8.1	4	7	57t	77.8
1985			51	33	64.7	460	9.0	1	0	71	100.1
1986	ATL	N	154	95	61.7	1032	6.7	4	8	41	68.4
1988	CIN	N	4	2	50.0	20	5.0	0	0	17	64.6
1989			2	0	0.0	0	0.0	0	0		39.6
Career			504	311	61.7	3788	7.5	11	20	71	75.6
Playoffs			1	0	0.0	0	0.0	0	0		39.6

Year	Team		Att	Com	PC	Yds	Avg	TD	Int	Lg	Rtg

Bill Schroeder

Year	Team		Att	Com	PC	Yds	Avg	TD	Int	Lg	Rtg
1946	CHI	AA	2	1	50.0	10	5.0	0	0	10	64.6

Jay Schroeder

Year	Team		Att	Com	PC	Yds	Avg	TD	Int	Lg	Rtg
1985	WAS	N	209	112	53.6	1458	7.0	5	5	53	73.8
1986			541	276	51.0	4109	7.6	22	22	71t	72.9
1987			267	129	48.3	1878	7.0	12	10	84t	71.0
1988	LARI	N	256	113	44.1	1839	7.2	13	13	85t	64.6
1989			194	91	46.9	1550	8.0	8	13	84t	60.3
1990			334	182	54.5	2849	**8.5**	19	9	68t	90.8
1991			357	189	52.9	2562	7.2	15	16	78t	71.4
1992			253	123	48.6	1476	5.8	11	11	53	63.3
1993	CIN	N	159	78	49.1	832	5.2	5	2	37	70.0
1994	ARI	N	238	133	55.9	1510	6.3	4	7	48t	68.4
Career			2808	1426	50.8	20063	7.1	114	108	85t	71.7
Playoffs			158	72	45.6	791	5.0	5	8		50.4

Vic Schwall

Year	Team		Att	Com	PC	Yds	Avg	TD	Int	Lg	Rtg
1948	CHIC	N	1	0	0.0	0	0.0	0	0		39.6
1949			2	0	0.0	0	0.0	0	0		39.6
Career			3	0	0.0	0	0.0	0	0		39.6

Dick Schweidler

Year	Team		Att	Com	PC	Yds	Avg	TD	Int	Lg	Rtg
1938	CHIB	N	1	0	0.0	0	0.0	0	0		39.6

Wilson Schwenk

Year	Team		Att	Com	PC	Yds	Avg	TD	Int	Lg	Rtg
1942	CHIC	N	295	126	42.7	1350	4.6	6	27	69	25.4
1946	CLE	AA	23	15	65.2	276	12.0	4	0	63t	146.0
1947	BAL	AA	**327**	**168**	51.4	2236	6.8	13	20	72t	61.2
1948	NY	AA	17	6	35.3	52	3.1	0	3		4.7
Career			662	315	47.6	3914	5.9	23	50	72t	46.5

John Sciarra

Year	Team		Att	Com	PC	Yds	Avg	TD	Int	Lg	Rtg
1978	PHI	N	1	0	0.0	0	0.0	0	0		39.6

Bobby Scott

Year	Team		Att	Com	PC	Yds	Avg	TD	Int	Lg	Rtg
1973	NO	N	54	18	33.3	245	4.5	1	3	42	31.8
1974			71	31	43.7	366	5.2	4	4	36t	55.3
1975			17	8	47.1	96	5.6	0	1	33	40.3
1976			190	103	54.2	1065	5.6	4	6	60t	64.5
1977			82	36	43.9	516	6.3	3	8	53t	37.5
1978			5	3	60.0	36	7.2	0	0	23	82.1
1979			2	2	100.0	12	6.0	0	0	6	91.7
1980			33	16	48.5	200	6.1	2	1	40	75.3
1981			46	20	43.5	245	5.3	1	5	31	28.2
Career			500	237	47.4	2781	5.6	15	28	60t	51.4

Darnay Scott

Year	Team		Att	Com	PC	Yds	Avg	TD	Int	Lg	Rtg
1994	CIN	N	1	1	100.0	53	53.0	0	0	53	118.8

Freddie Scott

Year	Team		Att	Com	PC	Yds	Avg	TD	Int	Lg	Rtg
1981	DET	N	1	0	0.0	0	0.0	0	0		39.6

Johnny Scott

Year	Team		Att	Com	PC	Yds	Avg	TD	Int	Lg	Rtg
1921	BUF	A						1			
1926	PHI	A						3			
Career								4			

Bob Scrabis

Year	Team		Att	Com	PC	Yds	Avg	TD	Int	Lg	Rtg
1960	NY	A	3	0	0.0	0	0.0	0	0		39.6
1961			21	7	33.3	82	3.9	1	2		22.4
1962			2	0	0.0	0	0.0	0	1		0.0
Career			26	7	26.9	82	3.2	1	3		13.5

Bucky Scribner

Year	Team		Att	Com	PC	Yds	Avg	TD	Int	Lg	Rtg
1984	GB	N	1	0	0.0	0	0.0	0	0		39.6

Charlie Seabright

Year	Team		Att	Com	PC	Yds	Avg	TD	Int	Lg	Rtg
1941	CLE	N	1	0	0.0	0	0.0	0	1		0.0
1948	PIT	N	1	0	0.0	0	0.0	0	0		39.6
1949			1	1	100.0	17	17.0	1	0	17	158.3
1950			3	1	33.3	3	1.0	0	0	3	42.4
Career			6	2	33.3	20	3.3	1	1	17	43.8

Jimmy Sears

Year	Team		Att	Com	PC	Yds	Avg	TD	Int	Lg	Rtg
1957	CHIC	N	3	0	0.0	0	0.0	0	0		39.6
1958			1	0	0.0	0	0.0	0	0		39.6
Career			4	0	0.0	0	0.0	0	0		39.6

Nick Sebek

Year	Team		Att	Com	PC	Yds	Avg	TD	Int	Lg	Rtg
1950	WAS	N	3	0	0.0	0	0.0	0	2		0.0

Scott Secules

Year	Team		Att	Com	PC	Yds	Avg	TD	Int	Lg	Rtg
1989	MIA	N	50	22	44.0	286	5.7	1	3	44t	44.3
1990			7	3	42.9	17	2.4	0	1	8	10.7
1991			13	8	61.5	90	6.9	1	1	17	75.8
1993	NE	N	134	75	56.0	918	6.9	2	9	82	54.3
Career			204	108	52.9	1311	6.4	4	14	82	50.9

Larry Seiple

Year	Team		Att	Com	PC	Yds	Avg	TD	Int	Lg	Rtg
1967	MIA	A	2	2	100.0	61	30.5	0	0	42	118.8
1969			1	1	100.0	8	8.0	0	0	8	100.0
Career			3	3	100.0	69	23.0	0	0	42	118.8

Bill Senn

Year	Team		Att	Com	PC	Yds	Avg	TD	Int	Lg	Rtg
1928	CHIB	N							2		

Frank Seno

Year	Team		Att	Com	PC	Yds	Avg	TD	Int	Lg	Rtg
1945	CHIC	N	1	0	0.0	0	0.0	0	0		39.6
1946			1	0	0.0	0	0.0	0	0		39.6
Career			2	0	0.0	0	0.0	0	0		39.6

Joe Senser

Year	Team		Att	Com	PC	Yds	Avg	TD	Int	Lg	Rtg
1980	MIN	N	1	0	0.0	0	0.0	0	0		39.6

Joe Setcavage

Year	Team		Att	Com	PC	Yds	Avg	TD	Int	Lg	Rtg
1943	BKN	N	1	0	0.0	0	0.0	0	0		39.6

Frank Seurer

Year	Team		Att	Com	PC	Yds	Avg	TD	Int	Lg	Rtg
1987	KC	N	55	26	47.3	340	6.2	0	4	33	36.9

Steve Sewell

Year	Team		Att	Com	PC	Yds	Avg	TD	Int	Lg	Rtg
1985	DEN	N	1	0	0.0	0	0.0	0	0		39.6
1986			1	1	100.0	23	23.0	1	0	23t	158.3
1987			0	0		0		0	0		
1988			1	0	0.0	0	0.0	0	0		39.6
1990			1	0	0.0	0	0.0	0	0		39.6
1991			3	1	33.3	24	8.0	0	0	24	63.2
Career			7	2	28.6	47	6.7	1	0	24	94.6
Playoffs			2	2	100.0	33	16.5	0	0		118.8

Sterling Sharpe

Year	Team		Att	Com	PC	Yds	Avg	TD	Int	Lg	Rtg
1993	GB	N	1	1	100.0	1	1.0	0	0	1	79.2

Dennis Shaw

Year	Team		Att	Com	PC	Yds	Avg	TD	Int	Lg	Rtg
1970	BUF	N	321	178	55.5	2507	7.8	10	20	48	65.3
1971			291	149	51.2	1813	6.2	11	26	75t	46.1
1972			258	136	52.7	1666	6.5	14	17	58t	63.5
1973			46	22	47.8	300	6.5	0	4	40	32.9
1975	STL	N	8	4	50.0	61	7.6	0	1	21	35.9
Career			924	489	52.9	6347	6.9	35	68	75t	56.8

George Shaw

Year	Team		Att	Com	PC	Yds	Avg	TD	Int	Lg	Rtg
1955	BAL	N	237	119	50.2	1586	6.7	10	19	82t	52.5
1956			75	45	60.0	645	8.6	3	7	49t	62.4
1957			9	5	55.6	58	6.4	1	1	11	72.7
1958			89	41	46.1	531	6.0	7	4	57	72.8
1959	NYG	N	36	24	66.7	433	12.0	1	1	48	105.4
1960			155	76	49.0	1263	8.1	11	13	71t	65.6
1961	MIN	N	91	46	50.5	530	5.8	4	4	42t	64.8
1962	DEN	A	110	49	44.5	783	7.1	4	14	97t	41.4
Career			802	405	50.5	5829	7.3	41	63	97t	58.8

Al Sheard

Year	Team		Att	Com	PC	Yds	Avg	TD	Int	Lg	Rtg
1923	ROC	N							1		

Dexter Shelley

Year	Team		Att	Com	PC	Yds	Avg	TD	Int	Lg	Rtg
1931	PRO	N							4		

Bill Shepherd

Year	Team		Att	Com	PC	Yds	Avg	TD	Int	Lg	Rtg
1935	BOS-DET	N							2		
1936	DET	N	9	3	33.3	57	6.3	0	1		16.7
1937			46	19	41.3	297	6.5	1	7		31.1
1938			32	8	25.0	167	5.2	0	6		9.2
1939			1	0	0.0	0	0.0	0	0		39.6
Career			88	30	34.1	521	5.9	3	14		19.4

Allie Sherman

Year	Team		Att	Com	PC	Yds	Avg	TD	Int	Lg	Rtg
1943	P-P	N	37	16	43.2	208	5.6	2	1	49	68.3
1944	PHI	N	31	16	51.6	156	5.0	1	2	23	49.9
1945			29	15	51.7	172	5.9	2	3	20	53.3
1946			33	17	51.5	264	**8.0**	4	2	53	**92.7**
1947			5	2	40.0	23	4.6	0	1	13	15.0
Career			135	66	48.9	823	6.1	9	9	53	62.7
Playoffs			1	0	0.0	0	0.0	0	0		39.6

Year	Team		Att	Com	PC	Yds	Avg	TD	Int	Lg	Rtg

Solly Sherman

Year	Team		Att	Com	PC	Yds	Avg	TD	Int	Lg	Rtg
1939	CHIB	N	4	2	50.0	43	10.8	0	0		88.5
1940			4	1	25.0	15	3.8	1	0	15t	82.3
Career			8	3	37.5	58	7.3	1	0	15t	103.1

Tom Sherman

Year	Team		Att	Com	PC	Yds	Avg	TD	Int	Lg	Rtg
1968	BOS	A	226	90	39.8	1199	5.3	12	16	87t	45.6
1969	BUF	A	2	2	100.0	20	10.0	1	0	19t	147.9
Career			228	92	40.4	1219	5.3	13	16	87t	47.8

Rhoten Shetley

Year	Team		Att	Com	PC	Yds	Avg	TD	Int	Lg	Rtg
1940	BKN	N	4	1	25.0	2	0.5	0	1	2	0.0
1941			1	0	0.0	0	0.0	0	0		39.6
Career			5	1	20.0	2	0.4	0	1	2	0.0

Dick Shiner

Year	Team		Att	Com	PC	Yds	Avg	TD	Int	Lg	Rtg
1964	WAS	N	1	0	0.0	0	0.0	0	0		39.6
1965			65	28	43.1	470	7.2	3	4	80t	57.9
1966			5	0	0.0	0	0.0	0	1		0.0
1967	CLE	N	9	3	33.3	34	3.8	0	1	21	6.0
1968	PIT	N	304	148	48.7	1856	6.1	18	17	61t	64.5
1969			209	97	46.4	1422	6.8	7	10	63	60.3
1970	NYG	N	12	9	75.0	87	7.3	0	0	26	94.8
1971	ATL	N	57	30	52.6	463	8.1	5	5	47	72.5
1973	ATL-NE	N	68	36	52.9	432	6.4	3	4	34t	62.9
1974	NE	N	6	3	50.0	37	6.2	0	1	18	29.9
Career			736	354	48.1	4801	6.5	36	43	80t	61.3

Roy Shivers

Year	Team		Att	Com	PC	Yds	Avg	TD	Int	Lg	Rtg
1971	STL	N	1	0	0.0	0	0.0	0	0		39.6

Del Shofner

Year	Team		Att	Com	PC	Yds	Avg	TD	Int	Lg	Rtg
1958	LA	N	1	0	0.0	0	0.0	0	0		39.6

Heath Shuler

Year	Team		Att	Com	PC	Yds	Avg	TD	Int	Lg	Rtg
1994	WAS	N	265	120	45.3	1658	6.3	10	12	81t	59.6
1995			125	66	52.8	745	6.0	3	7	44	55.6
Career			390	186	47.7	2403	6.2	13	19	81t	58.3

Johnny Shultz

Year	Team		Att	Com	PC	Yds	Avg	TD	Int	Lg	Rtg
1930	FRA	N							1		

Don Shy

Year	Team		Att	Com	PC	Yds	Avg	TD	Int	Lg	Rtg
1971	CHI	N	1	1	100.0	23	23.0	1	0	23t	158.3

Vai Sikahema

Year	Team		Att	Com	PC	Yds	Avg	TD	Int	Lg	Rtg
1989	PHX	N	1	0	0.0	0	0.0	0	0		39.6

Phil Simms

Year	Team		Att	Com	PC	Yds	Avg	TD	Int	Lg	Rtg
1979	NYG	N	265	134	50.6	1743	6.6	13	14	61	66.0
1980			402	193	48.0	2321	5.8	15	19	58t	58.9
1981			316	172	54.4	2031	6.4	11	9	80	74.0
1983			13	7	53.8	130	10.0	0	1	36	56.6
1984			533	286	53.7	4044	7.6	22	18	65t	78.1
1985			495	275	55.6	3829	7.7	22	20	70t	78.6
1986			468	259	55.3	3487	7.5	21	22	49	74.6
1987			282	163	57.8	2230	7.9	17	9	50t	90.0
1988			479	263	54.9	3359	7.0	21	11	62t	82.1
1989			405	228	56.3	3061	7.6	14	14	62t	77.6
1990			311	184	59.2	2284	7.3	15	4	80t	92.7
1991			141	82	58.2	993	7.0	8	4	38	87.0
1992			137	83	60.6	912	6.7	5	3	38	83.3
1993			400	247	61.8	3038	7.6	15	9	62	88.3
Career			4647	2576	55.4	33462	7.2	199	157	80t	78.5
Playoffs			279	157	56.3	1679	6.0	10	6		77.0

Eber Simpson

Year	Team		Att	Com	PC	Yds	Avg	TD	Int	Lg	Rtg
1923	STL	N							1		

O.J. Simpson

Year	Team		Att	Com	PC	Yds	Avg	TD	Int	Lg	Rtg
1970	BUF	N	2	0	0.0	0	0.0	0	0		39.6
1971			2	0	0.0	0	0.0	0	0		39.6
1972			8	5	62.5	113	14.1	1	0	34	145.8
1973			2	1	50.0	-3	-1.5	0	0	-3	56.3
1974			1	0	0.0	0	0.0	0	0		39.6
1977			1	0	0.0	0	0.0	0	0		39.6
Career			16	6	37.5	110	6.9	1	0	34	82.8

David Sims

Year	Team		Att	Com	PC	Yds	Avg	TD	Int	Lg	Rtg
1977	SEA	N	4	1	25.0	43	10.8	1	1	43t	71.9
1978			1	1	100.0	15	15.0	0	0	15	118.8
1979			2	1	50.0	18	9.0	0	0	18	81.3
Career			7	3	42.9	76	10.9	1	1	43t	83.0

Frankie Sinkwich

Year	Team		Att	Com	PC	Yds	Avg	TD	Int	Lg	Rtg
1943	DET	N	126	50	39.7	699	5.5	7	20	67	37.2
1944			148	58	39.2	1060	7.2	12	20	57	52.0
1946	NY	AA	12	5	41.7	61	5.1	0	2		18.4
1947			15	8	53.3	93	6.2	0	0		72.4
Career			301	121	40.2	1913	6.4	19	42	67	43.5

Brian Sipe

Year	Team		Att	Com	PC	Yds	Avg	TD	Int	Lg	Rtg
1974	CLE	N	108	59	54.6	603	5.6	1	7	37	47.0
1975			88	45	51.1	427	4.9	1	3	22	54.5
1976			312	178	57.1	2113	6.8	17	14	52	77.3
1977			195	112	57.4	1233	6.3	9	14	52t	61.8
1978			399	222	55.6	2906	7.3	21	15	69t	80.7
1979			535	286	53.5	3793	7.1	28	26	74	73.4
1980			554	337	60.8	4132	7.5	30	14	65	91.4
1981			567	313	55.2	3876	6.8	17	25	62	68.2
1982			185	101	54.6	1064	5.8	4	8	40t	60.7
1983			496	291	58.7	3566	7.2	26	23	66t	79.1
Career			3439	1944	56.5	23713	6.9	154	149	74	74.8
Playoffs			40	13	32.5	183	4.6	0	3		17.0

Johnny Sisk

Year	Team		Att	Com	PC	Yds	Avg	TD	Int	Lg	Rtg
1934	CHIB	N	9	2	22.2	13	1.4	0	1		0.0
1935			1	1	100.0	-1	-1.0	0	0	-1	79.2
Career			10	3	30.0	12	1.2	0	1	-1	0.0

Tom Skladany

Year	Team		Att	Com	PC	Yds	Avg	TD	Int	Lg	Rtg
1978	DET	N	1	0	0.0	0	0.0	0	0		39.6
1979			1	0	0.0	0	0.0	0	0		39.6
1980			2	2	100.0	38	19.0	0	0	19	118.8
1981			3	3	100.0	43	14.3	0	0	19	118.8
1982			1	0	0.0	0	0.0	0	0		39.6
Career			8	5	62.5	81	10.1	0	0	19	96.4

Walt Slater

Year	Team		Att	Com	PC	Yds	Avg	TD	Int	Lg	Rtg
1947	PIT	N	39	18	46.2	215	5.5	1	5	37	32.5

Mickey Slaughter

Year	Team		Att	Com	PC	Yds	Avg	TD	Int	Lg	Rtg
1963	DEN	A	223	112	50.2	1689	7.6	12	14		67.3
1964			189	97	51.3	930	4.9	3	11		46.4
1965			147	75	51.0	864	5.9	6	12	51	48.7
1966			25	7	28.0	124	5.0	1	0	67	61.1
Career			584	291	49.8	3607	6.2	22	37	67	55.5

Dwight Sloan

Year	Team		Att	Com	PC	Yds	Avg	TD	Int	Lg	Rtg
1938	CHIC	N	79	37	46.8	333	4.2	1	7		26.0
1939	DET	N	102	45	44.1	658	6.5	2	3		60.0
1940			46	18	39.1	260	5.7	0	8		18.7
Career			227	100	44.1	1251	5.5	3	18		33.1

Steve Sloan

Year	Team		Att	Com	PC	Yds	Avg	TD	Int	Lg	Rtg
1966	ATL	N	13	6	46.2	96	7.4	0	2	32	31.7
1967			18	4	22.2	38	2.1	0	2	15	0.0
Career			31	10	32.3	134	4.3	0	4	32	7.4

Phil Slosburg

Year	Team		Att	Com	PC	Yds	Avg	TD	Int	Lg	Rtg
1948	BOS	A	20	8	40.0	119	6.0	1	3	68	37.3

Marty Slovak

Year	Team		Att	Com	PC	Yds	Avg	TD	Int	Lg	Rtg
1939	CLE	N	27	13	48.1	97	3.6	2	5		42.3
1940			28	17	60.7	234	8.4	1	4		59.8
1941			54	27	50.0	287	5.3	2	9	48	38.7
Career			109	57	52.3	618	5.7	5	18	48	45.0

Torrance Small

Year	Team		Att	Com	PC	Yds	Avg	TD	Int	Lg	Rtg
1995	NO	N	0	0		0		0	0		

Bronko Smilanich

Year	Team		Att	Com	PC	Yds	Avg	TD	Int	Lg	Rtg
1939	CLE	N	2	1	50.0	11	5.5	0	0	11	66.7

Bill Smith

Year	Team		Att	Com	PC	Yds	Avg	TD	Int	Lg	Rtg
1936	CHIC	N	1	0	0.0	0	0.0	0	1		0.0

Billy Ray Smith

Year	Team		Att	Com	PC	Yds	Avg	TD	Int	Lg	Rtg
1987	SD	N	1	0	0.0	0	0.0	0	1		0.0

Bruce Smith

Year	Team		Att	Com	PC	Yds	Avg	TD	Int	Lg	Rtg
1948	GB	N	1	0	0.0	0	0.0	0	0		39.6

Dave Smith

Year	Team		Att	Com	PC	Yds	Avg	TD	Int	Lg	Rtg
1960	HOU	A	5	3	60.0	70	14.0	1	0		143.8
1961			2	1	50.0	33	16.5	0	0	33	95.8
1962			3	2	66.7	34	11.3	0	0		104.9

Dave Smith continued

Year	Team		Att	Com	PC	Yds	Avg	TD	Int	Lg	Rtg
1963			2	0	0.0	0	0.0	0	0		39.6
Career			12	6	50.0	137	11.4	1	0	33	119.1

Don Smith

Year	Team		Att	Com	PC	Yds	Avg	TD	Int	Lg	Rtg
1990	BUF	N	1	0	0.0	0	0.0	0	0		39.6

Ed Smith

Year	Team		Att	Com	PC	Yds	Avg	TD	Int	Lg	Rtg
1936	BOS	N	40	11	27.5	120	3.0	1	2		27.1
1937	GB	N	2	0	0.0	0	0.0	0	1		0.0
Career			42	11	26.2	120	2.9	1	3		17.8
Playoffs			2	0	0.0	0	0.0	0	0		39.6

Gaylon Smith

Year	Team		Att	Com	PC	Yds	Avg	TD	Int	Lg	Rtg
1939	CLE	N	5	4	80.0	3	0.6	0	0		79.2
1940			18	10	55.6	150	8.3	2	2		80.6
1941			2	0	0.0	0	0.0	0	1		0.0
1942			12	2	16.7	49	4.1	0	1	19	9.4
Career			37	16	43.2	202	5.5	2	4	19	39.3

Jackie Smith

Year	Team		Att	Com	PC	Yds	Avg	TD	Int	Lg	Rtg
1967	STL	N	1	0	0.0	0	0.0	0	1		0.0
1972			2	0	0.0	0	0.0	0	0		39.6
Career			3	0	0.0	0	0.0	0	1		0.0

J.D. Smith

Year	Team		Att	Com	PC	Yds	Avg	TD	Int	Lg	Rtg
1961	SF	N	1	0	0.0	0	0.0	0	1		0.0

Larry Smith

Year	Team		Att	Com	PC	Yds	Avg	TD	Int	Lg	Rtg
1969	LA	N	1	0	0.0	0	0.0	0	0		39.6
1970			2	0	0.0	0	0.0	0	0		39.6
1973			2	2	100.0	31	15.5	0	0	21	118.8
Career			5	2	40.0	31	6.2	0	0	21	61.3

Red Smith

Year	Team		Att	Com	PC	Yds	Avg	TD	Int	Lg	Rtg
1931	NYG	N							1		

Riley Smith

Year	Team		Att	Com	PC	Yds	Avg	TD	Int	Lg	Rtg
1936	BOS	N	33	14	42.4	239	**7.2**	0	3		29.7
1937	WAS	N	9	4	44.4	33	3.7	3	0		94.0
1938			4	1	25.0	18	4.5	0	0	18	45.8
Career			46	19	41.3	290	6.3	3	3	18	57.3
Playoffs			15	3	20.0	38	2.5	0	2		0.0

Ron Smith

Year	Team		Att	Com	PC	Yds	Avg	TD	Int	Lg	Rtg
1966	PIT	N	181	79	43.6	1249	6.9	8	12	84t	54.3

Russ Smith

Year	Team		Att	Com	PC	Yds	Avg	TD	Int	Lg	Rtg
1968	SD	A	3	0	0.0	0	0.0	0	0		39.6

Sherman Smith

Year	Team		Att	Com	PC	Yds	Avg	TD	Int	Lg	Rtg
1976	SEA	N	2	0	0.0	0	0.0	0	0		39.6
1977			1	0	0.0	0	0.0	0	0		39.6
1979			1	1	100.0	11	11.0	0	0	11	112.5
1982			1	0	0.0	0	0.0	0	0		39.6
1983	SD	N	1	0	0.0	0	0.0	0	0		39.6
Career			6	1	16.7	11	1.8	0	0	11	39.6

Stu Smith

Year	Team		Att	Com	PC	Yds	Avg	TD	Int	Lg	Rtg
1937	PIT	N	2	0	0.0	0	0.0	0	1		0.0

Vitamin Smith

Year	Team		Att	Com	PC	Yds	Avg	TD	Int	Lg	Rtg
1950	LA	N	1	1	100.0	11	11.0	0	0	11	112.5
1952			1	0	0.0	0	0.0	0	0		39.6
1953			2	1	50.0	50	25.0	0	0	50	95.8
Career			4	2	50.0	61	15.3	0	0	50	95.8

Willis Smith

Year	Team		Att	Com	PC	Yds	Avg	TD	Int	Lg	Rtg
1934	NYG	N	5	2	40.0	47	9.4	1	1		74.6

Dave Smukler

Year	Team		Att	Com	PC	Yds	Avg	TD	Int	Lg	Rtg
1936	PHI	N	68	21	30.9	345	5.1	3	6		26.9
1937			118	42	35.6	432	3.7	6	11		25.1
1938			102	42	41.2	524	5.1	7	8		48.0
1939			20	7	35.0	56	2.8	0	4		4.2
Career			308	112	36.4	1357	4.4	16	29		28.8

Lou Smythe

Year	Team		Att	Com	PC	Yds	Avg	TD	Int	Lg	Rtg
1921	CAN	A							1		
1922	CAN	N							1		
1923									5		
1925	ROC	N							3		

Lou Smythe continued

Year	Team		Att	Com	PC	Yds	Avg	TD	Int	Lg	Rtg
1926	HAR	N							1		
Career									11		

Norm Snead

Year	Team		Att	Com	PC	Yds	Avg	TD	Int	Lg	Rtg
1961	WAS	N	375	172	45.9	2337	6.2	11	22	80t	51.6
1962			354	184	52.0	2926	8.3	22	22	85t	74.7
1963			363	175	48.2	3043	8.4	13	27	77	58.1
1964	PHI	N	283	138	48.8	1906	6.7	14	12	87t	69.6
1965			288	150	52.1	2346	8.1	15	13	78	78.0
1966			226	103	45.6	1275	5.6	8	11	48	55.1
1967			434	240	55.3	3399	7.8	29	24	87t	80.0
1968			291	152	52.2	1655	5.7	11	21	55t	51.8
1969			379	190	50.1	2768	7.3	19	23	80t	65.7
1970			335	181	54.0	2323	6.9	15	20	79t	66.1
1971	MIN	N	75	37	49.3	470	6.3	1	6	55t	40.4
1972	NYG	N	325	196	**60.3**	2307	7.1	17	12	94t	84.0
1973			235	131	55.7	1483	6.3	7	22	46	45.8
1974	NYG-SF	N	159	97	61.0	983	6.2	5	8	53	68.2
1975	SF	N	189	108	57.1	1337	7.1	9	10	60t	73.0
1976	NYG	N	42	22	52.4	239	5.7	0	4	31	29.9
Career			4353	2276	52.3	30797	7.1	196	257	94t	65.5

George Snell

Year	Team		Att	Com	PC	Yds	Avg	TD	Int	Lg	Rtg
1926	BKN	N							1		

Matt Snell

Year	Team		Att	Com	PC	Yds	Avg	TD	Int	Lg	Rtg
1964	NY	A	1	0	0.0	0	0.0	0	1		0.0
1966			1	0	0.0	0	0.0	0	0		39.6
1968			1	1	100.0	26	26.0	0	0	26	118.8
Career			3	1	33.3	26	8.7	0	1	26	26.4

Lee Snoots

Year	Team		Att	Com	PC	Yds	Avg	TD	Int	Lg	Rtg
1922	COL	N							1		

Bob Snyder

Year	Team		Att	Com	PC	Yds	Avg	TD	Int	Lg	Rtg
1937	CLE	N	66	25	37.9	378	5.7	2	6		29.7
1938			87	36	41.4	631	7.3	7	9		54.0
1939	CHIB	N	12	5	41.7	135	11.3	0	1		49.0
1940			22	5	22.7	145	6.6	1	1		50.8
1941			28	13	46.4	353	**12.6**	3	2	59	**98.8**
1943			26	7	26.9	116	4.5	0	4	55	6.1
Career			241	91	37.8	1758	7.3	13	23	59	42.3
Playoffs			13	5	38.5	57	4.4	0	0		52.4

Loren Snyder

Year	Team		Att	Com	PC	Yds	Avg	TD	Int	Lg	Rtg
1987	DAL	N	9	4	44.4	44	4.9	0	0	22	59.5

Hank Soar

Year	Team		Att	Com	PC	Yds	Avg	TD	Int	Lg	Rtg
1937	NYG	N	21	5	23.8	83	4.0	1	2		19.8
1938			7	1	14.3	0		0	3	0	0.0
1941			5	3	60.0	75	15.0	1	0	38	143.8
1942			10	3	30.0	34	3.4	0	1	20	1.7
1944	NY	N	10	4	40.0	113	11.3	2	1	35	82.5
Career			53	16	30.2	305	5.8	4	7	38	36.8
Playoffs			5	0	0.0	0	0.0	0	0		39.6

Freddie Solomon

Year	Team		Att	Com	PC	Yds	Avg	TD	Int	Lg	Rtg
1976	MIA	N	1	0	0.0	0	0.0	0	0		39.6
1978	SF	N	10	5	50.0	85	8.5	0	1	30	39.6
1979			1	1	100.0	12	12.0	0	0	12	116.7
1980			1	0	0.0	0	0.0	0	0		39.6
1981			1	1	100.0	25	25.0	0	0	25	118.8
1985			1	0	0.0	0	0.0	0	0		39.6
Career			15	7	46.7	122	8.1	0	1	30	47.1

Butch Songin

Year	Team		Att	Com	PC	Yds	Avg	TD	Int	Lg	Rtg
1960	BOS	A	392	187	47.7	2476	6.3	22	15	78	70.9
1961			212	98	46.2	1429	6.7	14	9	58t	73.0
1962	NY	A	90	42	46.7	442	4.9	2	7		36.4
Career			694	327	47.1	4347	6.3	38	31	78	67.1

Gus Sonnenberg

Year	Team		Att	Com	PC	Yds	Avg	TD	Int	Lg	Rtg
1928	PRO	N							1		

Ronnie South

Year	Team		Att	Com	PC	Yds	Avg	TD	Int	Lg	Rtg
1968	NO	N	38	14	36.8	129	3.4	1	3	19	22.8

Vic Spadaccini

Year	Team		Att	Com	PC	Yds	Avg	TD	Int	Lg	Rtg
1940	CLE	N	1	0	0.0	0	0.0	0	0		39.6

Emmett Specht

Year	Team		Att	Com	PC	Yds	Avg	TD	Int	Lg	Rtg
1920	HAM	A							1		

Year	Team		Att	Com	PC	Yds	Avg	TD	Int	Lg	Rtg

Cotton Speyrer

Year	Team		Att	Com	PC	Yds	Avg	TD	Int	Lg	Rtg
1973	BAL	N	1	1	100.0	54	54.0	1	0	54t	158.3

Jack Spikes

Year	Team		Att	Com	PC	Yds	Avg	TD	Int	Lg	Rtg
1963	KC	A	1	0	0.0	0	0.0	0	1		0.0
1964			1	0	0.0	0	0.0	0	0		39.6
Career			2	0	0.0	0	0.0	0	1		0.0

Ron Springs

Year	Team		Att	Com	PC	Yds	Avg	TD	Int	Lg	Rtg
1979	DAL	N	3	1	33.3	30	10.0	1	0	30t	111.1
1981			1	0	0.0	0	0.0	0	1		0.0
1983			2	1	50.0	15	7.5	1	0	15t	114.6
1984			1	0	0.0	0	0.0	0	0		39.6
Career			7	2	28.6	45	6.4	2	1	30t	53.9
Playoffs			2	0	0.0	0	0.0	0	0		39.6

Ed Sprinkle

Year	Team		Att	Com	PC	Yds	Avg	TD	Int	Lg	Rtg
1949	CHIB	N	1	0	0.0	0	0.0	0	0		39.6

Dennis Sproul

Year	Team		Att	Com	PC	Yds	Avg	TD	Int	Lg	Rtg
1978	GB	N	13	5	38.5	87	6.7	0	0	25	62.0

Steve Spurrier

Year	Team		Att	Com	PC	Yds	Avg	TD	Int	Lg	Rtg
1967	SF	N	50	23	46.0	211	4.2	0	7	21	18.4
1969			146	81	55.5	926	6.3	5	11	75t	54.8
1970			4	3	75.0	49	12.3	1	0	26	155.2
1971			4	1	25.0	46	11.5	0	0	46	75.0
1972			269	147	54.6	1983	7.4	18	16	81t	75.9
1973			157	83	52.9	882	5.6	4	7	58	59.5
1974			3	1	33.3	2	0.7	0	0	2	42.4
1975			207	102	49.3	1151	5.6	5	7	68t	60.3
1976	TB	N	311	156	50.2	1628	5.2	7	12	38	57.1
Career			1151	597	51.9	6878	6.0	40	60	81t	60.1

Ken Stabler

Year	Team		Att	Com	PC	Yds	Avg	TD	Int	Lg	Rtg
1970	OAK	N	7	2	28.6	52	7.4	0	1	33	18.5
1971			48	24	50.0	268	5.6	1	4	23	39.2
1972			74	44	59.5	524	7.1	4	3	22	82.3
1973			260	163	62.7	1997	7.7	14	10	80t	88.3
1974			310	178	57.4	2469	8.0	26	12	67t	94.9
1975			293	171	58.4	2296	7.8	16	24	53	67.4
1976			291	194	66.7	2737	9.4	27	17	88t	103.4
1977			294	169	57.5	2176	7.4	20	20	44t	75.2
1978			406	237	58.4	2944	7.3	16	30	49	63.3
1979			498	304	61.0	3615	7.3	26	22	66t	82.2
1980	HOU	N	457	293	64.1	3202	7.0	13	28	79t	68.7
1981			285	165	57.9	1988	7.0	14	18	71t	69.5
1982	NO	N	189	117	61.9	1343	7.1	6	10	48	71.8
1983			311	176	56.6	1988	6.4	9	18	48	61.4
1984			70	33	47.1	339	4.8	2	5	29	41.3
Career			3793	2270	59.8	27938	7.4	194	222	88t	75.3
Playoffs			351	203	57.8	2641	7.5	19	13		84.2

Jon Staggers

Year	Team		Att	Com	PC	Yds	Avg	TD	Int	Lg	Rtg
1972	GB	N	1	0	0.0	0	0.0	0	0		39.6

Haskel Stanback

Year	Team		Att	Com	PC	Yds	Avg	TD	Int	Lg	Rtg
1975	ATL	N	1	1	100.0	41	41.0	1	0	41t	158.3

Scott Stankavage

Year	Team		Att	Com	PC	Yds	Avg	TD	Int	Lg	Rtg
1984	DEN	N	18	4	22.2	58	3.2	0	1	16	17.4
1987	MIA	N	7	4	57.1	8	1.1	0	1	8	22.6
Career			25	8	32.0	66	2.6	0	2	16	7.9

Rohn Stark

Year	Team		Att	Com	PC	Yds	Avg	TD	Int	Lg	Rtg
1982	BAL	N	1	0	0.0	0	0.0	0	0		39.6
1983			1	0	0.0	0	0.0	0	0		39.6
1984	IND	N	1	0	0.0	0	0.0	0	1		0.0
1985			1	0	0.0	0	0.0	0	0		39.6
1990			1	1	100.0	40	40.0	0	0	40	118.8
1992			1	1	100.0	17	17.0	0	0	17	118.8
Career			6	2	33.3	57	9.5	0	1	40	29.9

Bart Starr

Year	Team		Att	Com	PC	Yds	Avg	TD	Int	Lg	Rtg
1956	GB	N	44	24	54.5	325	7.4	2	3	39t	65.1
1957			215	117	54.4	1489	6.9	8	10	77t	69.3
1958			157	78	49.7	875	5.6	3	12	55t	41.2
1959			134	70	52.2	972	7.3	6	7	44	69.0
1960			172	98	57.0	1358	7.9	4	8	91t	70.8
1961			295	172	58.3	2418	8.2	16	16	78t	80.3
1962			285	178	62.5	2438	8.6	12	9	83t	90.7
1963			244	132	54.1	1855	7.6	15	10	53t	82.3
1964			272	163	59.9	2144	7.9	15	4	73	97.1
1965			251	140	55.8	2055	8.2	16	9	77t	89.0

Bart Starr *continued*

Year	Team		Att	Com	PC	Yds	Avg	TD	Int	Lg	Rtg
1966			251	156	62.2	2257	9.0	14	3	83t	105.0
1967			210	115	54.8	1823	8.7	9	17	84	64.4
1968			171	109	63.7	1617	9.5	15	8	63t	104.3
1969			148	92	62.2	1161	7.8	9	6	51	89.9
1970			255	140	54.9	1645	6.5	8	13	65t	63.9
1971			45	24	53.3	286	6.4	0	3	31	45.2
Career			3149	1808	57.4	24718	7.8	152	138	91t	80.5
Playoffs			213	130	61.0	1753	8.2	15	4		102.9

Ben Starrett

Year	Team		Att	Com	PC	Yds	Avg	TD	Int	Lg	Rtg
1941	PIT	N	2	0	0.0	0	0.0	0	1		0.0

Leo Stasica

Year	Team		Att	Com	PC	Yds	Avg	TD	Int	Lg	Rtg
1941	BKN	N	2	1	50.0	14	7.0	0	0	14	72.9
1943	WAS	N	6	1	16.7	34	5.7	0	1	34	11.1
1944	BOS	N	47	21	44.7	225	4.8	1	7	42	26.8
Career			55	23	41.8	273	5.0	1	8	42	24.1

Roger Staubach

Year	Team		Att	Com	PC	Yds	Avg	TD	Int	Lg	Rtg
1969	DAL	N	47	23	48.9	421	9.0	1	2	75t	69.5
1970			82	44	53.7	542	6.6	2	8	43	42.9
1971			211	126	59.7	1882	8.9	15	4	85t	104.8
1972			20	9	45.0	98	4.9	0	2	21	20.4
1973			286	179	62.6	2428	8.5	23	15	53	94.6
1974			360	190	52.8	2552	7.1	11	15	58t	68.4
1975			348	198	56.9	2666	7.7	17	16	62	78.5
1976			369	208	56.4	2715	7.4	14	11	53	79.9
1977			361	210	58.2	2620	7.3	18	9	67	87.0
1978			413	231	55.9	3190	7.7	25	16	91t	84.9
1979			461	267	57.9	3586	7.8	27	11	75t	92.3
Career			2958	1685	57.0	22700	7.7	153	109	91t	83.4
Playoffs			410	223	54.4	2817	6.9	24	19		76.2

Ernie Steele

Year	Team		Att	Com	PC	Yds	Avg	TD	Int	Lg	Rtg
1943	P-P	N	1	0	0.0	0	0.0	0	1		0.0
1945	PHI	N	2	1	50.0	12	6.0	0	1	12	29.2
1948			1	0	0.0	0	0.0	0	1		0.0
Career			4	1	25.0	12	3.0	0	3	12	0.0

Ken Steinmetz

Year	Team		Att	Com	PC	Yds	Avg	TD	Int	Lg	Rtg
1944	BOS	N	1	0	0.0	0	0.0	0	0		39.6

Steve Stenstrom

Year	Team		Att	Com	PC	Yds	Avg	TD	Int	Lg	Rtg
1996	CHI	N	4	3	75.0	37	9.3	0	0	28	103.1

Harold Stephens

Year	Team		Att	Com	PC	Yds	Avg	TD	Int	Lg	Rtg
1962	NY	A	22	15	68.2	123	5.6	0	0		82.2

John Stephens

Year	Team		Att	Com	PC	Yds	Avg	TD	Int	Lg	Rtg
1990	NE	N	1	0	0.0	0	0.0	0	1		0.0

Kay Stephenson

Year	Team		Att	Com	PC	Yds	Avg	TD	Int	Lg	Rtg
1967	SD	A	26	11	42.3	117	4.5	2	2	21	49.7
1968	BUF	A	79	29	36.7	364	4.6	4	7	55t	31.8
Career			105	40	38.1	481	4.6	6	9	55t	36.2

Ed Sternaman

Year	Team		Att	Com	PC	Yds	Avg	TD	Int	Lg	Rtg
1921	DEC	A							1		

Joey Sternaman

Year	Team		Att	Com	PC	Yds	Avg	TD	Int	Lg	Rtg
1922	CHIB	N							1		
1924									1		
1925									2		
1926	CHI	A							1		
1927	CHIB	N							1		
1928									3		
1930									2		
Career									11		

Bob Steuber

Year	Team		Att	Com	PC	Yds	Avg	TD	Int	Lg	Rtg
1948	BUF	AA	2	1	50.0	-4	-2.0	0	0	4	56.3

Billy Stevens

Year	Team		Att	Com	PC	Yds	Avg	TD	Int	Lg	Rtg
1968	GB	N	2	0	0.0	0	0.0	0	0		39.6
1969			3	1	33.3	12	4.0	0	0	12	46.5
Career			5	1	20.0	12	2.4	0	0	12	39.6

Mark Stevens

Year	Team		Att	Com	PC	Yds	Avg	TD	Int	Lg	Rtg
1987	SF	N	4	2	50.0	52	13.0	1	0	39t	135.4

Matt Stevens

Year	Team		Att	Com	PC	Yds	Avg	TD	Int	Lg	Rtg
1987	KC	N	57	32	56.1	315	5.5	1	1	23	70.4

Year	Team		Att	Com	PC	Yds	Avg	TD	Int	Lg	Rtg

Kordell Stewart

Year	Team		Att	Com	PC	Yds	Avg	TD	Int	Lg	Rtg
1995	PIT	N	7	5	71.4	60	8.6	1	0	32	136.9
1996			30	11	36.7	100	3.3	0	2	15	18.8
Career			37	16	43.2	160	4.3	1	2	32	42.6
Playoffs			11	1	9.1	0	0.0	0	0		39.6

Dave Stief

Year	Team		Att	Com	PC	Yds	Avg	TD	Int	Lg	Rtg
1978	STL	N	1	1	100.0	43	43.0	0	0	43	118.8

Jim Stiger

Year	Team		Att	Com	PC	Yds	Avg	TD	Int	Lg	Rtg
1964	DAL	N	1	0	0.0	0	0.0	0	0		39.6

Jim Still

Year	Team		Att	Com	PC	Yds	Avg	TD	Int	Lg	Rtg
1948	BUF	AA	14	5	35.7	89	6.4	1	3		42.6
1949			12	6	50.0	86	7.2	1	1		66.7
Career			26	11	42.3	175	6.7	2	4		51.4
Playoffs			21	6	28.6	80	3.8	1	2		19.2

Bill Stits

Year	Team		Att	Com	PC	Yds	Avg	TD	Int	Lg	Rtg
1955	DET	N	2	2	100.0	62	31.0	1	0	41	158.3
1956			1	0	0.0	0	0.0	0	1		0.0
Career			3	2	66.7	62	20.7	1	1	41	109.7

Hust Stockton

Year	Team		Att	Com	PC	Yds	Avg	TD	Int	Lg	Rtg
1925	FRA	N						7			
1926								4			
1929	PRO-BOS	N						3			
Career								14			

John Stofa

Year	Team		Att	Com	PC	Yds	Avg	TD	Int	Lg	Rtg
1966	MIA	A	57	29	50.9	425	7.5	4	2	48	84.3
1967			2	2	100.0	51	25.5	0	0	45	118.8
1968	CIN	A	177	85	48.0	896	5.1	5	5	60	60.8
1969	MIA	A	23	14	60.9	146	6.3	0	2	42	43.0
1970	MIA	N	53	16	30.2	240	4.5	3	2	52t	49.3
Career			312	146	46.8	1758	5.6	12	11	60	62.7

Ken Stofer

Year	Team		Att	Com	PC	Yds	Avg	TD	Int	Lg	Rtg
1946	BUF	AA	26	9	34.6	86	3.3	1	1		41.5

Eddie Stofko

Year	Team		Att	Com	PC	Yds	Avg	TD	Int	Lg	Rtg
1945	PIT	N	17	7	41.2	94	5.5	0	4	26	19.9

Donnie Stone

Year	Team		Att	Com	PC	Yds	Avg	TD	Int	Lg	Rtg
1961	DEN	A	2	1	50.0	18	9.0	1	0	18t	120.8
1962			3	1	33.3	13	4.3	0	0	13	47.9
1963			3	0	0.0	0	0.0	0	0		39.6
Career			8	2	25.0	31	3.9	1	0	18t	82.8

Jack Storer

Year	Team		Att	Com	PC	Yds	Avg	TD	Int	Lg	Rtg
1924	FRA	N						1			

Ed Storm

Year	Team		Att	Com	PC	Yds	Avg	TD	Int	Lg	Rtg
1935	PHI	N						3			

Cliff Stoudt

Year	Team		Att	Com	PC	Yds	Avg	TD	Int	Lg	Rtg
1980	PIT	N	60	32	53.3	493	8.2	2	2	72	78.0
1981			3	1	33.3	17	5.7	0	0	17	53.5
1982			35	14	40.0	154	4.4	0	5	24	14.2
1983			381	197	51.7	2553	6.7	12	21	52	60.6
1986	STL	N	91	52	57.1	542	6.0	3	7	24t	53.5
1987			1	0	0.0	0	0.0	0	0		39.6
1988	PHX	N	113	63	55.8	747	6.6	6	8	52t	64.3
Career			684	359	52.5	4506	6.6	23	43	72	58.3
Playoffs			20	10	50.0	187	9.3	1	1		78.5

Kelly Stouffer

Year	Team		Att	Com	PC	Yds	Avg	TD	Int	Lg	Rtg
1988	SEA	N	173	98	56.6	1106	6.4	4	6	53	69.2
1989			59	29	49.2	270	4.6	0	3	29	40.9
1991			15	6	40.0	57	3.8	0	1	19	23.5
1992			190	92	48.4	900	4.7	3	9	33	47.7
Career			437	225	51.5	2333	5.3	7	19	53	54.5

Matt Stover

Year	Team		Att	Com	PC	Yds	Avg	TD	Int	Lg	Rtg
1992	CLE	N	1	0	0.0	0	0.0	0	1		0.0

Mike Strachan

Year	Team		Att	Com	PC	Yds	Avg	TD	Int	Lg	Rtg
1978	NO	N	1	0	0.0	0	0.0	0	0		39.6

Troy Stradford

Year	Team		Att	Com	PC	Yds	Avg	TD	Int	Lg	Rtg
1987	MIA	N	1	1	100.0	6	6.0	0	0	6	91.7
1988			1	0	0.0	0	0.0	0	0		39.6
Career			2	1	50.0	6	3.0	0	0	6	56.3

Jimmy Strausbaugh

Year	Team		Att	Com	PC	Yds	Avg	TD	Int	Lg	Rtg
1946	CHIC	N	1	1	100.0	35	35.0	0	0	35	118.8

Joe Stringfellow

Year	Team		Att	Com	PC	Yds	Avg	TD	Int	Lg	Rtg
1942	DET	N	13	5	38.5	67	5.2	0	2	21	16.0

Don Strock

Year	Team		Att	Com	PC	Yds	Avg	TD	Int	Lg	Rtg
1975	MIA	N	45	26	57.8	230	5.1	2	2	25	67.8
1976			47	21	44.7	359	7.6	3	2	53t	74.7
1977			4	2	50.0	12	3.0	0	1	9	16.7
1978			135	72	53.3	825	6.1	12	6	57	83.1
1979			100	56	56.0	830	8.3	6	6	53	78.3
1980			62	30	48.4	313	5.0	1	5	33	35.2
1981			130	79	60.8	901	6.9	6	8	52	71.3
1982			55	30	54.5	306	5.6	2	5	43	45.0
1983			52	34	65.4	403	7.8	4	1	47	106.5
1984			6	4	66.7	27	4.5	0	0	12	76.4
1985			9	7	77.8	141	15.7	1	0	67t	155.8
1986			20	14	70.0	152	7.6	2	0	21	125.4
1987			23	13	56.5	114	5.0	0	1	26	51.7
1988	CLE	N	91	55	60.4	736	8.1	6	5	41	85.2
Career			779	443	56.9	5349	6.9	45	42	67t	74.9
Playoffs			65	40	61.5	564	8.7	4	3		90.8

Rick Strom

Year	Team		Att	Com	PC	Yds	Avg	TD	Int	Lg	Rtg
1989	PIT	N	1	0	0.0	0	0.0	0	0		39.6
1990			21	14	66.7	162	7.7	0	1	22	69.9
Career			22	14	63.6	162	7.4	0	1	22	66.9

Ken Strong

Year	Team		Att	Com	PC	Yds	Avg	TD	Int	Lg	Rtg
1929	SI	N						1			
1930								2			
1931								1			
1932								1			
1933	NYG	N						2			
1934			15	8	53.3	112	7.5	0	2		38.1
Career			15	8	53.3	112	7.5	7	2		38.1
Playoffs			2	2	100.0	19	9.5	0	0		106.3

Art Strutt

Year	Team		Att	Com	PC	Yds	Avg	TD	Int	Lg	Rtg
1936	PIT	N	1	1	100.0	15	15.0	0	0	15	118.8

Dan Stryzinski

Year	Team		Att	Com	PC	Yds	Avg	TD	Int	Lg	Rtg
1992	TB	N	2	2	100.0	14	7.0	0	0	12	95.8
1994			1	1	100.0	21	21.0	0	0	21	118.8
Career			3	3	100.0	35	11.7	0	0	21	115.3

Johnny Strzykalski

Year	Team		Att	Com	PC	Yds	Avg	TD	Int	Lg	Rtg
1947	SF	AA	4	1	25.0	38	9.5	0	0	38	66.7
1948			1	0	0.0	0	0.0	0	0		39.6
Career			5	1	20.0	38	7.6	0	0	38	58.8

Pat Studstill

Year	Team		Att	Com	PC	Yds	Avg	TD	Int	Lg	Rtg
1968	LA	N	1	0	0.0	0	0.0	0	0		39.6
1970			1	0	0.0	0	0.0	0	0		39.6
1972	NE	N	1	0	0.0	0	0.0	0	0		39.6
Career			3	0	0.0	0	0.0	0	0		39.6

Harry Stuhldreher

Year	Team		Att	Com	PC	Yds	Avg	TD	Int	Lg	Rtg
1926	BKN	A							2		

Dick Sturtridge

Year	Team		Att	Com	PC	Yds	Avg	TD	Int	Lg	Rtg
1928	CHIB	N							2		

Matt Suhey

Year	Team		Att	Com	PC	Yds	Avg	TD	Int	Lg	Rtg
1983	CHI	N	1	1	100.0	74	74.0	1	0	74t	158.3
1984			1	0	0.0	0	0.0	0	0		39.6
Career			2	1	50.0	74	37.0	1	0	74t	135.4

Joe Sulatis

Year	Team		Att	Com	PC	Yds	Avg	TD	Int	Lg	Rtg
1944	NY	N	17	4	23.5	53	3.1	1	4	22	20.1
1945			13	7	53.8	126	9.7	0	0	38	87.3
1948	NYG	N	1	0	0.0	0	0.0	0	0		39.6
Career			31	11	35.5	179	5.8	1	4	38	26.9

Bob Sullivan

Year	Team		Att	Com	PC	Yds	Avg	TD	Int	Lg	Rtg
1947	PIT	N	9	3	33.3	52	5.8	0	1	24	14.4

Jack Sullivan

Year	Team		Att	Com	PC	Yds	Avg	TD	Int	Lg	Rtg
1921	WAS	A							1		

Pat Sullivan

Year	Team		Att	Com	PC	Yds	Avg	TD	Int	Lg	Rtg
1972	ATL	N	19	3	15.8	44	2.3	0	3	18	0.0
1973			26	14	53.8	175	6.7	1	0	21t	87.8

Pat Sullivan *continued*

Year	Team		Att	Com	PC	Yds	Avg	TD	Int	Lg	Rtg
1974			105	48	45.7	556	5.3	1	8	48	33.7
1975			70	28	40.0	380	5.4	3	5	49	42.6
Career			220	93	42.3	1155	5.3	5	16	49	36.5

Pat Summerall

Year	Team		Att	Com	PC	Yds	Avg	TD	Int	Lg	Rtg
1960	NYG	N	1	0	0.0	0	0.0	0	0		39.6

Carl Summerell

Year	Team		Att	Com	PC	Yds	Avg	TD	Int	Lg	Rtg
1974	NYG	N	13	6	46.2	59	4.5	0	3	26	19.9
1975			16	7	43.8	98	6.1	0	2	41	24.5
Career			29	13	44.8	157	5.4	0	5	41	22.4

Wilbur Summers

Year	Team		Att	Com	PC	Yds	Avg	TD	Int	Lg	Rtg
1977	DET	N	1	1	100.0	5	5.0	0	0	5	87.5

Ed Sutton

Year	Team		Att	Com	PC	Yds	Avg	TD	Int	Lg	Rtg
1957	WAS	N	5	3	60.0	95	19.0	0	0	51	104.2
1958			3	0	0.0	0	0.0	0	0		39.6
1959			7	2	28.6	51	7.3	1	0	29	97.0
Career			15	5	33.3	146	9.7	1	0	51	92.6

Evar Swanson

Year	Team		Att	Com	PC	Yds	Avg	TD	Int	Lg	Rtg
1927	CHIC	N						1			

Kevin Sweeney

Year	Team		Att	Com	PC	Yds	Avg	TD	Int	Lg	Rtg
1987	DAL	N	28	14	50.0	291	10.4	4	1	77t	111.8
1988			78	33	42.3	314	4.0	3	5	28	40.2
Career			106	47	44.3	605	5.7	7	6	77t	61.2

Karl Sweetan

Year	Team		Att	Com	PC	Yds	Avg	TD	Int	Lg	Rtg
1966	DET	N	309	157	50.8	1809	5.9	4	14	99t	54.3
1967			177	74	41.8	901	5.1	10	11	52t	51.1
1968	NO	N	78	27	34.6	318	4.1	1	9	42	12.6
1969	LA	N	13	5	38.5	101	7.8	1	0	67t	92.1
1970			13	6	46.2	81	6.2	1	0	22	92.1
Career			590	269	45.6	3210	5.4	17	34	99t	48.3

Larry Swider

Year	Team		Att	Com	PC	Yds	Avg	TD	Int	Lg	Rtg
1979	DET	N	1	1	100.0	36	36.0	0	0	36	118.8

Bob Swisher

Year	Team		Att	Com	PC	Yds	Avg	TD	Int	Lg	Rtg
1938	CHIB	N	4	1	25.0	8	2.0	0	1	8	0.0
1940			1	0	0.0	0	0.0	0	0		39.6
Career			5	1	20.0	8	1.6	0	1	8	0.0

Harry Sydney

Year	Team		Att	Com	PC	Yds	Avg	TD	Int	Lg	Rtg
1987	SF	N	1	1	100.0	50	50.0	1	0	50t	158.3
1988			1	0	0.0	0	0.0	0	0		39.6
1991			1	0	0.0	0	0.0	0	0		39.6
Career			3	1	33.3	50	16.7	1	0	50t	121.5
Playoffs			2	1	50.0	28	14.0	0	0		95.8

Johnny Sylvester

Year	Team		Att	Com	PC	Yds	Avg	TD	Int	Lg	Rtg
1947	NY	AA	1	0	0.0	0	0.0	0	0		39.6

Jerry Tagge

Year	Team		Att	Com	PC	Yds	Avg	TD	Int	Lg	Rtg
1972	GB	N	29	10	34.5	154	5.3	0	0	31	52.9
1973			106	56	52.8	720	6.8	2	7	50	53.2
1974			146	70	47.9	709	4.9	1	10	30	36.0
Career			281	136	48.4	1583	5.6	3	17	50	44.2

George Taliaferro

Year	Team		Att	Com	PC	Yds	Avg	TD	Int	Lg	Rtg
1949	LA	AA	124	45	36.3	790	6.4	4	14		30.0
1950	NYY	N	7	3	42.9	83	11.9	1	0	50t	126.8
1951			33	13	39.4	251	7.6	1	3	51	38.8
1952	DAL	N	63	16	25.4	298	4.7	2	6	48	17.8
1953	BAL	N	55	15	27.3	211	3.8	2	5	45	17.3
1954			2	0	0.0	0	0.0	0	1		0.0
Career			284	92	32.4	1633	5.8	10	29	51	25.2

Mike Taliaferro

Year	Team		Att	Com	PC	Yds	Avg	TD	Int	Lg	Rtg
1964	NY	A	73	23	31.5	341	4.7	2	5		28.4
1965			119	45	37.8	531	4.5	3	7	37	36.1
1966			41	19	46.3	177	4.3	2	2	21	54.6
1967			20	11	55.0	96	4.8	1	1	20t	63.8
1968	BOS	A	176	67	38.1	889	5.1	4	15	70t	26.9
1969			331	160	48.3	2160	6.5	19	18	77	66.0
1970	BOS	N	173	78	45.1	871	5.0	4	11	45	41.8
1972	BUF	N	33	16	48.5	176	5.3	1	4	24	35.2
Career			966	419	43.4	5241	5.4	36	63	77	46.1

James Tanguay

Year	Team		Att	Com	PC	Yds	Avg	TD	Int	Lg	Rtg
1933	PIT	N						1			

Fran Tarkenton

Year	Team		Att	Com	PC	Yds	Avg	TD	Int	Lg	Rtg
1961	MIN	N	280	157	56.1	1997	7.1	18	17	71t	74.7
1962			329	163	49.5	2595	7.9	22	25	89t	66.9
1963			297	170	57.2	2311	7.8	15	15	67t	78.0
1964			306	171	55.9	2506	8.2	22	11	64	91.8
1965			329	171	52.0	2609	7.9	19	11	72t	83.8
1966			358	192	53.6	2561	7.2	17	16	68t	73.8
1967	NYG	N	377	204	54.1	3088	8.2	29	19	70t	85.9
1968			337	182	54.0	2555	7.6	21	12	84	84.6
1969			409	220	53.8	2918	7.1	23	8	65	87.2
1970			389	219	56.3	2777	7.1	19	12	59	82.2
1971			386	226	58.5	2567	6.7	11	21	81t	65.4
1972	MIN	N	378	215	56.9	2651	7.0	18	13	76t	80.2
1973			274	169	61.7	2113	7.7	15	7	54t	93.2
1974			351	199	56.7	2598	7.4	17	12	80t	82.1
1975			**425**	**273**	64.2	2994	7.0	**25**	13	46	91.8
1976			412	**255**	61.9	2961	7.2	17	8	56t	89.3
1977			258	155	60.1	1734	6.7	9	14	59t	69.2
1978			**572**	**345**	60.3	**3468**	6.1	25	32	58t	68.9
Career			6467	3686	57.0	47003	7.3	342	266	89t	80.4
Playoffs			292	149	51.0	1803	6.2	11	17		58.6

Jim Tarrant

Year	Team		Att	Com	PC	Yds	Avg	TD	Int	Lg	Rtg
1946	MIA	AA	12	5	41.7	95	7.9	1	0	56	97.6

Carl Taseff

Year	Team		Att	Com	PC	Yds	Avg	TD	Int	Lg	Rtg
1962	BUF	A	1	0	0.0	0	0.0	0	0		39.6

Mosi Tatupu

Year	Team		Att	Com	PC	Yds	Avg	TD	Int	Lg	Rtg
1987	NE	N	1	1	100.0	15	15.0	1	0	15t	158.3
1989			1	1	100.0	15	15.0	0	0	15	118.8
Career			2	2	100.0	30	15.0	1	0	15t	158.3

Charley Taylor

Year	Team		Att	Com	PC	Yds	Avg	TD	Int	Lg	Rtg
1964	WAS	N	10	2	20.0	54	5.4	0	1	41	10.0
1965			4	1	25.0	45	11.3	1	0	45t	113.5
Career			14	3	21.4	99	7.1	1	1	45t	50.6

Hugh Taylor

Year	Team		Att	Com	PC	Yds	Avg	TD	Int	Lg	Rtg
1948	WAS	N	1	0	0.0	0	0.0	0	0		39.6

Jim Bob Taylor

Year	Team		Att	Com	PC	Yds	Avg	TD	Int	Lg	Rtg
1983	BAL	N	2	1	50.0	20	10.0	0	1	20	45.8

John Taylor

Year	Team		Att	Com	PC	Yds	Avg	TD	Int	Lg	Rtg
1993	SF	N	1	1	100.0	41	41.0	0	0	41	118.8
1995			1	1	100.0	21	21.0	0	0	21	118.8
Career			2	2	100.0	62	31.0	0	0	41	118.8

Lionel Taylor

Year	Team		Att	Com	PC	Yds	Avg	TD	Int	Lg	Rtg
1961	DEN	A	2	0	0.0	0	0.0	0	1		0.0
1962			2	0	0.0	0	0.0	0	0		39.6
1963			1	0	0.0	0	0.0	0	0		39.6
1964			1	0	0.0	0	0.0	0	1		0.0
Career			6	0	0.0	0	0.0	0	2		0.0

Otis Taylor

Year	Team		Att	Com	PC	Yds	Avg	TD	Int	Lg	Rtg
1966	KC	A	1	0	0.0	0	0.0	0	1		0.0

Troy Taylor

Year	Team		Att	Com	PC	Yds	Avg	TD	Int	Lg	Rtg
1990	NYJ	N	10	7	70.0	49	4.9	1	0	15	114.2
1991			10	5	50.0	76	7.6	1	1	51	69.2
Career			20	12	60.0	125	6.3	2	1	51	90.6

John Teltschik

Year	Team		Att	Com	PC	Yds	Avg	TD	Int	Lg	Rtg
1987	PHI	N	0	0		0		0	0		
1988			3	1	33.3	18	6.0	0	0	18	54.9
Career			3	1	33.3	18	6.0	0	0	18	54.9

Mark Temple

Year	Team		Att	Com	PC	Yds	Avg	TD	Int	Lg	Rtg
1936	BKN	N	7	0	0.0	0	0.0	0	5		0.0

Steve Tensi

Year	Team		Att	Com	PC	Yds	Avg	TD	Int	Lg	Rtg
1966	SD	A	52	21	40.4	405	7.8	5	1	63	92.2
1967	DEN	A	325	131	40.3	1915	5.9	16	17	76t	54.8
1968			119	48	40.3	709	6.0	5	8	72t	46.5
1969			286	131	45.8	1990	7.0	14	12	79t	68.1
1970	DEN	N	80	38	47.5	539	6.7	3	8	42	42.7
Career			862	369	42.8	5558	6.4	43	46	79t	59.0

Tony Teresa

Year	Team		Att	Com	PC	Yds	Avg	TD	Int	Lg	Rtg
1960	OAK	A	18	9	50.0	111	6.2	1	3		48.4

George Terlep

Year	Team		Att	Com	PC	Yds	Avg	TD	Int	Lg	Rtg
1946	BUF	AA	123	48	39.0	574	4.7	7	14		33.4
1947			23	5	21.7	51	2.2	2	3		29.0
1948	BUF-CLE	AA	4	1	25.0	27	6.8	0	2	27	15.6
Career			150	54	36.0	652	4.3	9	19	27	30.6

Ray Terrell

Year	Team		Att	Com	PC	Yds	Avg	TD	Int	Lg	Rtg
1946	CLE	AA	2	0	0.0	0	0.0	0	0		39.6

Vinny Testaverde

Year	Team		Att	Com	PC	Yds	Avg	TD	Int	Lg	Rtg
1987	TB	N	165	71	43.0	1081	6.6	5	6	40	60.2
1988			466	222	47.6	3240	7.0	13	35	59t	48.8
1989			480	258	53.8	3133	6.5	20	22	78t	68.9
1990			365	203	55.6	2818	7.7	17	18	89t	75.6
1991			326	166	50.9	1994	6.1	8	15	87t	59.0
1992			358	206	57.5	2554	7.1	14	16	81t	74.2
1993	CLE	N	230	130	56.5	1797	7.8	14	9	62t	85.7
1994			376	207	55.1	2575	6.8	16	18	81t	70.7
1995			392	241	61.5	2883	7.4	17	10	70t	87.8
1996	BAL	N	549	325	59.2	4177	7.6	33	19	86t	88.7
Career			3707	2029	54.7	26252	7.1	157	168	89t	72.4
Playoffs			61	33	54.1	412	6.8	2	2		72.6

Lee Tevis

Year	Team		Att	Com	PC	Yds	Avg	TD	Int	Lg	Rtg
1947	BKN	AA	3	0	0.0	0	0.0	0	0		39.6
1948			1	0	0.0	0	0.0	0	0		39.6
Career			4	0	0.0	0	0.0	0	0		39.6

Joe Theismann

Year	Team		Att	Com	PC	Yds	Avg	TD	Int	Lg	Rtg
1974	WAS	N	11	9	81.8	145	13.2	1	0	69	149.1
1975			22	10	45.5	96	4.4	1	3	30t	33.7
1976			163	79	48.5	1036	6.4	8	10	44	59.8
1977			182	84	46.2	1097	6.0	7	9	52	57.9
1978			390	187	47.9	2593	6.6	13	18	63	61.6
1979			395	233	59.0	2797	7.1	20	13	62	83.9
1980			454	262	57.7	2962	6.5	17	16	54t	75.2
1981			496	293	59.1	3568	7.2	19	20	79t	77.3
1982			252	161	63.9	2033	8.1	13	9	78t	91.3
1983			459	276	60.1	3714	8.1	29	11	84	97.0
1984			477	283	59.3	3391	7.1	24	13	80t	86.6
1985			301	167	55.5	1774	5.9	8	16	55	59.6
Career			3602	2044	56.7	25206	7.0	160	138	84	77.4
Playoffs			211	128	60.7	1782	8.4	11	7		91.4

Harry Theofiledes

Year	Team		Att	Com	PC	Yds	Avg	TD	Int	Lg	Rtg
1968	WAS	N	20	11	55.0	211	10.6	2	1	39t	104.4

Blair Thomas

Year	Team		Att	Com	PC	Yds	Avg	TD	Int	Lg	Rtg
1991	NYJ	N	1	1	100.0	16	16.0	1	0	16t	158.3

Duane Thomas

Year	Team		Att	Com	PC	Yds	Avg	TD	Int	Lg	Rtg
1971	DAL	N	1	0	0.0	0	0.0	0	0		39.6

Earl Thomas

Year	Team		Att	Com	PC	Yds	Avg	TD	Int	Lg	Rtg
1973	CHI	N	1	0	0.0	0	0.0	0	1		0.0

Jewerl Thomas

Year	Team		Att	Com	PC	Yds	Avg	TD	Int	Lg	Rtg
1983	KC	N	2	1	50.0	18	9.0	1	1	18t	81.3

Mike Thomas

Year	Team		Att	Com	PC	Yds	Avg	TD	Int	Lg	Rtg
1976	WAS	N	0	0		0		0	0		
1979	SD	N	1	1	100.0	18	18.0	0	0	18	118.8
1980			2	0	0.0	0	0.0	0	1		0.0
Career			3	1	33.3	18	6.0	0	1	18	15.3

Rex Thomas

Year	Team		Att	Com	PC	Yds	Avg	TD	Int	Lg	Rtg
1926	BKN	N							1		
1928	DET	N							2		
Career									3		

Thurman Thomas

Year	Team		Att	Com	PC	Yds	Avg	TD	Int	Lg	Rtg
1993	BUF	N	1	0	0.0	0	0.0	0	0		39.6

Bobby Thomason

Year	Team		Att	Com	PC	Yds	Avg	TD	Int	Lg	Rtg
1949	LA	N	12	6	50.0	50	4.2	0	1	15	26.4
1951	GB	N	221	125	**56.6**	1306	5.9	11	9	75t	73.5
1952	PHI	N	212	95	44.8	1334	6.3	8	9	44	60.5
1953			304	162	53.3	2462	8.1	**21**	20	62t	75.8
1954			170	83	48.8	1242	7.3	10	13	63	61.0
1955			171	88	51.5	1337	7.8	10	7	63t	80.0
1956			164	82	50.0	1119	6.8	4	21	52	40.7
1957			92	46	50.0	630	6.8	4	10	67t	47.2
Career			1346	687	51.0	9480	7.0	68	90	75t	62.9

John Thomason

Year	Team		Att	Com	PC	Yds	Avg	TD	Int	Lg	Rtg
1936	PHI	N	10	1	10.0	11	1.1	0	2	11	0.0

Anthony Thompson

Year	Team		Att	Com	PC	Yds	Avg	TD	Int	Lg	Rtg
1991	PHX	N	1	0	0.0	0	0.0	0	0		39.6

Jack Thompson

Year	Team		Att	Com	PC	Yds	Avg	TD	Int	Lg	Rtg
1979	CIN	N	87	39	44.8	481	5.5	1	5	50	42.4
1980			234	115	49.1	1324	5.7	11	12	59t	60.9
1981			49	21	42.9	267	5.4	1	2	21	50.3
1983	TB	N	423	249	58.9	2906	6.9	18	21	80	73.3
1984			52	25	48.1	337	6.5	2	5	74t	42.4
Career			845	449	53.1	5315	6.3	33	45	80	63.4
Playoffs			1	1	100.0	14	14.0	0	0		118.8

Leonard Thompson

Year	Team		Att	Com	PC	Yds	Avg	TD	Int	Lg	Rtg
1977	DET	N	1	0	0.0	0	0.0	0	0		39.6

Tommy Thompson

Year	Team		Att	Com	PC	Yds	Avg	TD	Int	Lg	Rtg
1940	PIT	N	28	9	32.1	145	5.2	1	3		22.8
1941	PHI	N	162	86	53.1	974	6.0	8	14	50	51.8
1942			203	95	46.8	1410	6.9	8	16	65	50.3
1945			28	15	53.6	146	5.2	0	2	27	38.7
1946			103	57	**55.3**	745	7.2	6	9	45	61.3
1947			201	106	52.7	1680	8.4	16	15	69	76.3
1948			246	141	57.3	1965	8.0	**25**	11	70	**98.4**
1949			214	116	54.2	1727	8.1	16	11	75	84.4
1950			239	107	44.8	1608	6.7	11	22	75	44.4
Career			1424	732	51.4	10400	7.3	91	103	75	66.5
Playoffs			82	45	54.9	503	6.1	4	7		54.1

Tuffy Thompson

Year	Team		Att	Com	PC	Yds	Avg	TD	Int	Lg	Rtg
1937	PIT	N	14	6	42.9	100	7.1	1	4		51.8
1938			7	0	0.0	0	0.0	0	3		0.0
Career			21	6	28.6	100	4.8	1	7		23.2

Jim Thorpe

Year	Team		Att	Com	PC	Yds	Avg	TD	Int	Lg	Rtg
1921	CLE	A							1		
1922	OOR	N							1		
1923									1		
1924	RI	N							1		
Career									4		

Bruce Threadgill

Year	Team		Att	Com	PC	Yds	Avg	TD	Int	Lg	Rtg
1978	SF	N	2	0	0.0	0	0.0	0	2		0.0

Willie Thrower

Year	Team		Att	Com	PC	Yds	Avg	TD	Int	Lg	Rtg
1953	CHIB	N	8	3	37.5	27	3.4	0	1	12	7.8

Steve Thurlow

Year	Team		Att	Com	PC	Yds	Avg	TD	Int	Lg	Rtg
1964	NYG	N	5	3	60.0	65	13.0	0	0	33	104.2
1965			1	1	100.0	49	49.0	0	0	49	118.8
Career			6	4	66.7	114	19.0	0	0	49	109.7

Billy Tidwell

Year	Team		Att	Com	PC	Yds	Avg	TD	Int	Lg	Rtg
1954	SF	N	1	0	0.0	0	0.0	0	0		39.6

Travis Tidwell

Year	Team		Att	Com	PC	Yds	Avg	TD	Int	Lg	Rtg
1950	NYG	N	55	25	45.5	338	6.1	4	3	47	67.1
1951			21	8	38.1	155	7.4	1	4	56t	40.9
Career			76	33	43.4	493	6.5	5	7	56t	48.8
Playoffs			3	0	0.0	0	0.0	0	0		39.6

Scott Tinsley

Year	Team		Att	Com	PC	Yds	Avg	TD	Int	Lg	Rtg
1987	PHI	N	86	48	55.8	637	7.4	3	4	62t	71.7

Y.A. Tittle

Year	Team		Att	Com	PC	Yds	Avg	TD	Int	Lg	Rtg
1948	BAL	AA	289	161	55.7	2522	**8.7**	16	9	80t	90.3
1949			**289**	148	51.2	2209	7.6	14	18	80t	66.8
1950	BAL	N	315	**161**	51.1	1884	6.0	8	19	62	52.9
1951	SF	N	114	63	55.3	808	7.1	8	9	48t	68.2
1952			208	106	51.0	1407	6.8	11	12	77	66.3
1953			259	149	57.5	2121	8.2	20	16	71	84.1
1954			295	170	57.6	2205	7.5	9	9	70	78.7
1955			287	147	51.2	2185	7.6	**17**	28	78t	56.6
1956			218	124	56.9	1641	7.5	7	12	77t	68.6
1957			279	**176**	63.1	2157	7.7	13	15	46	80.0
1958			208	120	57.7	1467	7.1	9	15	64t	63.9
1959			199	102	51.3	1331	6.7	10	15	75	58.0
1960			127	69	54.3	694	5.5	4	3	45	70.8
1961	NYG	N	285	163	57.2	2272	8.0	17	12	62	85.3
1962			375	200	53.3	3224	8.6	**33**	20	69t	89.5
1963			367	221	**60.2**	3145	**8.6**	**36**	14	70t	**104.8**

Year	Team		Att	Com	PC	Yds	Avg	TD	Int	Lg	Rtg

Y.A. Tittle *continued*

Year	Team		Att	Com	PC	Yds	Avg	TD	Int	Lg	Rtg
1964			281	147	52.3	1798	6.4	10	22	54	51.6
Career			4395	2427	55.2	33070	7.5	242	248	80t	74.3
Playoffs			157	70	44.6	874	5.6	4	14		33.8

Elgie Tobin

Year	Team		Att	Com	PC	Yds	Avg	TD	Int	Lg	Rtg
1921	AKR	A							1		

Dick Todd

Year	Team		Att	Com	PC	Yds	Avg	TD	Int	Lg	Rtg
1939	WAS	N	4	3	75.0	86	21.5	0	0		116.7
1940			1	1	100.0	7	7.0	0	0	7	95.8
1942			6	1	16.7	11	1.8	0	1	11	0.0
Career			11	5	45.5	104	9.5	0	1	11	41.5

Larry Todd

Year	Team		Att	Com	PC	Yds	Avg	TD	Int	Lg	Rtg
1965	OAK	A	1	0	0.0	0	0.0	0	0		39.6

Richard Todd

Year	Team		Att	Com	PC	Yds	Avg	TD	Int	Lg	Rtg
1976	NYJ	N	162	65	40.1	870	5.4	3	12	44t	33.2
1977			265	133	50.2	1863	7.0	11	17	87t	60.3
1978			107	60	56.1	849	7.9	6	10	49	61.6
1979			334	171	51.2	2660	**8.0**	16	22	72t	66.5
1980			479	264	55.1	3329	6.9	17	30	55	62.7
1981			497	279	56.1	3231	6.5	25	13	49	81.8
1982			261	153	58.6	1961	7.5	14	8	56t	87.3
1983			518	308	59.5	3478	6.7	18	26	64t	70.3
1984	NO	N	312	161	51.6	2178	7.0	11	19	74	60.6
1985			32	16	50.0	191	6.0	3	4	56t	60.3
Career			2967	1610	54.3	20610	6.9	124	161	87t	67.6
Playoffs			139	78	56.1	1026	7.4	4	12		53.2

Charley Tolar

Year	Team		Att	Com	PC	Yds	Avg	TD	Int	Lg	Rtg
1961	HOU	A	1	0	0.0	0	0.0	0	0		39.6
1962			1	0	0.0	0	0.0	0	1		0.0
1965			1	0	0.0	0	0.0	0	0		39.6
1966			1	0	0.0	0	0.0	0	0		39.6
Career			4	0	0.0	0	0.0	0	1		0.0

Billy Joe Tolliver

Year	Team		Att	Com	PC	Yds	Avg	TD	Int	Lg	Rtg
1989	SD	N	185	89	48.1	1097	5.9	5	8	49	57.9
1990			410	216	52.7	2574	6.3	16	16	45t	68.9
1991	ATL	N	82	40	48.8	531	6.5	4	2	75t	75.8
1992			131	73	55.7	787	6.0	5	5	30t	70.4
1993			76	39	51.3	464	6.1	3	5	42t	56.0
1994	HOU	N	240	121	50.4	1287	5.4	6	7	44	62.6
Career			1124	578	51.4	6740	6.0	39	43	75t	65.5

Lou Tomasetti

Year	Team		Att	Com	PC	Yds	Avg	TD	Int	Lg	Rtg
1939	PIT	N	47	13	27.7	140	3.0	1	7		7.1
1940			6	3	50.0	30	5.0	0	2		25.0
Career			53	16	30.2	170	3.2	1	9		7.3

Andy Tomasic

Year	Team		Att	Com	PC	Yds	Avg	TD	Int	Lg	Rtg
1942	PIT	N	54	11	20.4	174	3.2	0	5	41	1.9
1946			12	4	33.3	53	4.4	0	1	20	13.5
Career			66	15	22.7	227	3.4	0	6	41	3.5

Mike Tomczak

Year	Team		Att	Com	PC	Yds	Avg	TD	Int	Lg	Rtg
1985	CHI	N	6	2	33.3	33	5.5	0	0	24	52.8
1986			151	74	49.0	1105	7.3	2	10	85	50.2
1987			178	97	54.5	1220	6.9	5	10	56t	62.0
1988			170	86	50.6	1310	7.7	7	6	76t	75.4
1989			306	156	51.0	2058	6.7	16	16	79t	68.2
1990			104	39	37.5	521	5.0	3	5	48	43.8
1991	GB	N	238	128	53.8	1490	6.3	11	9	75t	72.6
1992	CLE	N	211	120	56.9	1693	8.0	7	7	52	80.1
1993	PIT	N	54	29	53.7	398	7.4	2	5	39t	51.3
1994			93	54	58.1	804	8.6	4	0	84t	100.8
1995			113	65	57.5	666	5.9	1	9	29	44.3
1996			401	222	55.4	2767	6.9	15	17	70t	71.8
Career			2025	1072	52.9	14065	6.9	73	94	85	67.8
Playoffs			143	74	51.7	884	6.2	2	9		49.4

Anthony Toney

Year	Team		Att	Com	PC	Yds	Avg	TD	Int	Lg	Rtg
1987	PHI	N	1	0	0.0	0	0.0	0	0		39.6

Al Toon

Year	Team		Att	Com	PC	Yds	Avg	TD	Int	Lg	Rtg
1990	NYJ	N	2	0	0.0	0	0.0	0	0		39.6
1991			1	1	100.0	27	27.0	0	0	27	118.8
Career			3	1	33.3	27	9.0	0	0	27	67.4

Gino Torretta

Year	Team		Att	Com	PC	Yds	Avg	TD	Int	Lg	Rtg
1996	SEA	N	16	5	31.3	41	2.6	1	1	32t	35.4

Zollie Toth

Year	Team		Att	Com	PC	Yds	Avg	TD	Int	Lg	Rtg
1954	BAL	N	1	0	0.0	0	0.0	0	1		0.0

Willie Totten

Year	Team		Att	Com	PC	Yds	Avg	TD	Int	Lg	Rtg
1987	BUF	N	33	13	39.4	155	4.7	2	2	37	49.4

Tom Tracy

Year	Team		Att	Com	PC	Yds	Avg	TD	Int	Lg	Rtg
1958	PIT	N	16	6	37.5	270	16.9	2	2	72t	85.4
1959			12	3	25.0	159	13.3	0	2	68	39.6
1960			22	9	40.9	322	14.6	4	1	70t	108.9
1961			12	4	33.3	73	6.1	0	0	38	55.2
1962			1	1	100.0	7	7.0	0	0	7	95.8
1963	PIT-WAS	N	4	1	25.0	23	5.8	0	0	23	51.0
Career			67	24	35.8	854	12.7	6	5	72t	82.8

Ivan Trebotich

Year	Team		Att	Com	PC	Yds	Avg	TD	Int	Lg	Rtg
1945	DET	N	1	1	100.0	8	8.0	0	0	8	100.0

Mel Triplett

Year	Team		Att	Com	PC	Yds	Avg	TD	Int	Lg	Rtg
Playoffs			1	0	0.0	0	0.0	0	0		39.6

Charley Trippi

Year	Team		Att	Com	PC	Yds	Avg	TD	Int	Lg	Rtg
1947	CHIC	N	2	1	50.0	49	24.5	0	1	49	56.3
1948			8	4	50.0	118	14.8	1	0	64	135.4
1949			2	0	0.0	0	0.0	0	0		39.6
1950			3	1	33.3	19	6.3	0	0	19	56.3
1951			191	88	46.1	1191	6.2	8	13	80t	52.1
1952			181	84	46.4	890	4.9	5	13	56t	40.5
1953			34	20	58.8	195	5.7	2	1	21	82.4
1954			13	7	53.8	85	6.5	0	3	22	34.6
Career			434	205	47.2	2547	5.9	16	31	80t	48.4
Playoffs			2	0	0.0	0	0.0	0	0		39.6

Frank Tripucka

Year	Team		Att	Com	PC	Yds	Avg	TD	Int	Lg	Rtg
1949	DET	N	145	62	42.8	833	5.7	9	14	64	42.8
1950	CHIC	N	108	47	43.5	720	6.7	4	7	81t	51.5
1951			29	17	58.6	244	8.4	2	1	48	94.6
1952	CHIC-DAL	N	186	91	48.9	809	4.3	3	17	42t	28.3
1960	DEN	A	**478**	**248**	51.9	**3038**	6.4	24	34	80	58.9
1961			344	167	48.5	1690	4.9	10	21	87	47.3
1962			**440**	**240**	54.5	**2917**	6.6	17	25	96t	64.4
1963			15	7	46.7	31	2.1	0	5		13.9
Career			1745	879	50.4	10282	5.9	69	124	96t	52.2

Bob Trocolor

Year	Team		Att	Com	PC	Yds	Avg	TD	Int	Lg	Rtg
1942	NYG	N	5	3	60.0	52	10.4	1	1	29	95.4
1943			7	2	28.6	4	0.6	0	1	3	0.0
Career			12	5	41.7	56	4.7	1	2	29	44.4

Bill Troup

Year	Team		Att	Com	PC	Yds	Avg	TD	Int	Lg	Rtg
1976	BAL	N	18	8	44.4	117	6.5	0	1	32	43.1
1977			2	0	0.0	0	0.0	0	1		0.0
1978			296	154	52.0	1882	6.4	10	21	67t	53.6
1980	GB	N	12	4	33.3	48	4.0	0	3	24	6.9
Career			328	166	50.6	2047	6.2	10	26	67t	47.4

Jack Trudeau

Year	Team		Att	Com	PC	Yds	Avg	TD	Int	Lg	Rtg
1986	IND	N	417	204	48.9	2225	5.3	8	18	84t	53.5
1987			229	128	55.9	1587	6.9	6	6	55	75.4
1988			34	14	41.2	158	4.6	0	3	48	19.0
1989			362	190	52.5	2317	6.4	15	13	71	71.3
1990			144	84	58.3	1078	7.5	6	6	73	78.4
1991			7	2	28.6	19	2.7	0	1	11	0.0
1992			181	105	58.0	1271	7.0	4	8	81	68.6
1993			162	85	52.5	992	6.1	2	7	68	57.4
1994	NYJ	N	91	50	54.9	496	5.5	1	4	24t	55.9
1995	CAR	N	17	11	64.7	100	5.9	0	3	19	40.9
Career			1644	873	53.1	10243	6.2	42	69	84t	63.3
Playoffs			33	21	63.6	251	7.6	2	1		94.4

Don Trull

Year	Team		Att	Com	PC	Yds	Avg	TD	Int	Lg	Rtg
1964	HOU	A	86	36	41.9	439	5.1	1	2		52.4
1965			107	38	35.5	528	4.9	5	5	57	48.3
1966			172	84	48.8	1200	7.0	10	5	62	79.1
1967	HOU-BOS	A	92	31	33.7	480	5.2	1	7	52	23.8
1968	HOU	A	105	53	50.5	864	8.2	10	3	60	98.3
1969			75	34	45.3	469	6.3	3	6	57	45.9
Career			637	276	43.3	3980	6.2	30	28	62	61.6

Dick Tuckey

Year	Team		Att	Com	PC	Yds	Avg	TD	Int	Lg	Rtg
1938	WAS-CLE	N	32	8	25.0	140	4.4	1	3		16.7

Darrell Tully

Year	Team		Att	Com	PC	Yds	Avg	TD	Int	Lg	Rtg
1939	DET		69	20	29.0	356	5.2	2	13		18.7

Emlen Tunnell

Year	Team		Att	Com	PC	Yds	Avg	TD	Int	Lg	Rtg
1948	NYG	N	2	1	50.0	23	11.5	0	0	23	91.7

Tom Tupa

Year	Team		Att	Com	PC	Yds	Avg	TD	Int	Lg	Rtg
1988	PHX	N	6	4	66.7	49	8.2	0	0	22	91.7
1989			134	65	48.5	973	7.3	3	9	77t	52.2
1991			315	165	52.4	2053	6.5	6	13	62t	62.0
1992	IND	N	33	17	51.5	156	4.7	1	2	19	49.6
1995	CLE	N	1	1	100.0	25	25.0	0	0	25	118.8
1996	NE	N	2	0	0.0	0	0.0	0	0	0	39.6
Career			491	252	51.3	3256	6.6	10	24	77t	58.9

Frank Turbert

Year	Team		Att	Com	PC	Yds	Avg	TD	Int	Lg	Rtg
1944	BOS	N	14	5	35.7	37	2.6	0	0	21	44.3

John Turley

Year	Team		Att	Com	PC	Yds	Avg	TD	Int	Lg	Rtg
1935	PIT	N						1			

Jim Turner

Year	Team		Att	Com	PC	Yds	Avg	TD	Int	Lg	Rtg
1967	NY	A	4	2	50.0	25	6.3	0	0	13	69.8
1973	DEN	N	1	0	0.0	0	0.0	0	1		0.0
Career			5	2	40.0	25	5.0	0	1	13	16.7

Kevin Turner

Year	Team		Att	Com	PC	Yds	Avg	TD	Int	Lg	Rtg
1993	NE	N	1	0	0.0	0	0.0	0	0		39.6

Ricky Turner

Year	Team		Att	Com	PC	Yds	Avg	TD	Int	Lg	Rtg
1988	IND	N	4	3	75.0	92	23.0	0	0	37	116.7

Rick Tuten

Year	Team		Att	Com	PC	Yds	Avg	TD	Int	Lg	Rtg
1992	SEA	N	1	0	0.0	0	0.0	0	0		39.6
1993			1	0	0.0	0	0.0	0	0		39.6
1994			1	0	0.0	0	0.0	0	0		39.6
Career			3	0	0.0	0	0.0	0	0		39.6

Pete Tyler

Year	Team		Att	Com	PC	Yds	Avg	TD	Int	Lg	Rtg
1937	CHIC	N	1	0	0.0	0	0.0	0	0		39.6

Layne Tynes

Year	Team		Att	Com	PC	Yds	Avg	TD	Int	Lg	Rtg
1925	COL	N						1			

Johnny Unitas

Year	Team		Att	Com	PC	Yds	Avg	TD	Int	Lg	Rtg
1956	BAL	N	198	110	55.6	1498	7.6	9	10	54	74.0
1957			**301**	172	57.1	**2550**	8.5	**24**	17	82t	88.0
1958			263	136	51.7	2007	7.6	**19**	7	77t	**90.0**
1959			**367**	**193**	52.6	**2899**	7.9	**32**	14	71	92.0
1960			**378**	**190**	50.3	**3099**	8.2	**25**	24	80t	73.7
1961			**420**	229	54.5	2990	7.1	16	24	72t	66.1
1962			389	222	57.1	2967	7.6	23	23	80t	76.5
1963			410	**237**	57.8	**3481**	8.5	20	12	64t	89.7
1964			305	158	51.8	2824	**9.3**	19	6	74t	96.4
1965			282	164	58.2	2530	**9.0**	23	12	61	**97.4**
1966			348	195	56.0	2748	7.9	22	24	89t	74.0
1967			436	255	**58.5**	3428	7.9	20	16	88t	83.6
1968			32	11	34.4	139	4.3	2	4	37	30.1
1969			327	178	54.4	2342	7.2	12	20	52t	64.0
1970			321	166	51.7	2213	6.9	14	18	55t	65.1
1971			176	92	52.3	942	5.4	3	9	35	52.3
1972			157	88	56.1	1111	7.1	4	6	63t	70.8
1973	SD	N	76	34	44.7	471	6.2	3	7	51	40.0
Career			5186	2830	54.6	40239	7.8	290	253	89t	78.2
Playoffs			226	120	53.1	1676	7.4	7	10		69.1

Rick Upchurch

Year	Team		Att	Com	PC	Yds	Avg	TD	Int	Lg	Rtg
1975	DEN	N	0	0		0		0	0		
1979			1	0	0.0	0	0.0	0	0		39.6
1982			0	0		0		0	0		
1983			2	0	0.0	0	0.0	0	0		39.6
Career			3	0	0.0	0	0.0	0	0		39.6

Andy Uram

Year	Team		Att	Com	PC	Yds	Avg	TD	Int	Lg	Rtg
1939	GB	N	1	0	0.0	0	0.0	0	0		39.6
1943			6	2	33.3	60	10.0	1	1	48	71.5
Career			7	2	28.6	60	8.6	1	1	48	62.8

Sam Vacanti

Year	Team		Att	Com	PC	Yds	Avg	TD	Int	Lg	Rtg
1947	CHI	AA	225	96	42.7	1571	7.0	16	16	80t	60.8
1948			116	47	40.5	633	5.5	2	15		24.7
1949	BAL	AA	27	11	40.7	134	5.0	0	1		41.3
Career			368	154	41.8	2338	6.4	18	32	80t	43.5

Norm Van Brocklin

Year	Team		Att	Com	PC	Yds	Avg	TD	Int	Lg	Rtg
1949	LA	N	58	32	55.2	601	**10.4**	6	2	51	**111.4**
1950			233	127	54.5	2061	**8.8**	18	14	58	**85.1**

Norm Van Brocklin *continued*

Year	Team		Att	Com	PC	Yds	Avg	TD	Int	Lg	Rtg
1951			194	100	51.5	1725	8.9	13	11	81t	80.8
1952			205	113	**55.1**	1736	**8.5**	14	17	84t	71.5
1953			286	156	54.5	2393	8.4	19	14	70t	84.1
1954			260	139	53.5	**2637**	10.1	13	21	80t	71.9
1955			272	144	52.9	1890	**6.9**	8	15	74t	62.0
1956			124	68	54.8	966	7.8	7	12	58t	59.5
1957			265	132	49.8	2105	7.9	20	21	70t	68.8
1958	PHI	N	**374**	**198**	52.9	2409	6.4	15	20	91t	64.1
1959			340	191	56.2	2617	7.7	16	14	71	79.5
1960			284	153	53.9	2471	8.7	24	17	64t	86.5
Career			2895	1553	53.6	23611	8.2	173	178	91t	75.1
Playoffs			95	46	48.4	736	7.7	4	8		53.7

Steve Van Buren

Year	Team		Att	Com	PC	Yds	Avg	TD	Int	Lg	Rtg
1945	PHI	N	1	0	0.0	0	0.0	0	0		39.6
1946			1	1	100.0	35	35.0	0	0	35	118.8
1948			1	0	0.0	0	0.0	0	0		39.6
Career			3	1	33.3	35	11.7	0	0	35	78.5

Ron Vander Kelen

Year	Team		Att	Com	PC	Yds	Avg	TD	Int	Lg	Rtg
1963	MIN	N	58	27	46.6	376	6.5	1	2	53t	59.3
1964			19	7	36.8	78	4.1	0	1	18	28.0
1965			40	18	45.0	252	6.3	2	0	38	82.5
1966			20	10	50.0	147	7.3	0	1	43	53.5
1967			115	45	39.1	522	4.5	3	7	42	36.9
Career			252	107	42.5	1375	5.5	6	11	53t	50.0

Hal Van Every

Year	Team		Att	Com	PC	Yds	Avg	TD	Int	Lg	Rtg
1940	GB	N	41	12	29.3	199	4.9	4	6		40.2
1941			30	11	36.7	195	6.5	0	2	44	31.9
Career			71	23	32.4	394	5.5	4	8	44	31.4
Playoffs			6	2	33.3	75	12.5	0	1		42.4

Tim Van Galder

Year	Team		Att	Com	PC	Yds	Avg	TD	Int	Lg	Rtg
1972	STL	N	79	40	50.6	434	5.5	1	7	71	34.5

Billy Van Heusen

Year	Team		Att	Com	PC	Yds	Avg	TD	Int	Lg	Rtg
1970	DEN	N	1	0	0.0	0	0.0	0	0		39.6
1971			1	0	0.0	0	0.0	0	0		39.6
1973			1	0	0.0	0	0.0	0	0		39.6
1974			1	1	100.0	41	41.0	0	0	41	118.8
1975			1	1	100.0	30	30.0	0	0	30	118.8
Career			5	2	40.0	71	14.2	0	0	71	87.5

Alex Van Pelt

Year	Team		Att	Com	PC	Yds	Avg	TD	Int	Lg	Rtg
1995	BUF	N	18	10	55.6	106	5.9	2	0	19t	110.0
1996			5	2	40.0	9	1.8	0	0	5	47.9
Career			23	12	52.2	115	5.0	2	0	19t	95.4
Playoffs			10	4	40.0	27	2.7	1	0		81.3

Jeff Van Raaphorst

Year	Team		Att	Com	PC	Yds	Avg	TD	Int	Lg	Rtg
1987	ATL	N	34	18	52.9	174	5.1	1	2	24	52.8

Art Van Tone

Year	Team		Att	Com	PC	Yds	Avg	TD	Int	Lg	Rtg
1943	DET	N	3	1	33.3	7	2.3	0	1	7	2.8
1944			1	0	0.0	0	0.0	0	0		39.6
Career			4	1	25.0	7	1.8	0	1	7	0.0

Johnny Vardian

Year	Team		Att	Com	PC	Yds	Avg	TD	Int	Lg	Rtg
1946	MIA	AA	1	1	100.0	-4	-4.0	0	0	-4	79.2

Harp Vaughan

Year	Team		Att	Com	PC	Yds	Avg	TD	Int	Lg	Rtg
1934	PIT	N	39	14	35.9	272	7.0	2	5		38.6

Pug Vaughan

Year	Team		Att	Com	PC	Yds	Avg	TD	Int	Lg	Rtg
1935	DET	N						2			
1936	CHIC	N	79	30	38.0	545	6.9	3	10		35.5
Career			79	30	38.0	545	6.9	5	10		35.5

Jon Vaughn

Year	Team		Att	Com	PC	Yds	Avg	TD	Int	Lg	Rtg
1991	NE	N	2	1	50.0	13	6.5	1	0	13t	110.4

Ed Vereb

Year	Team		Att	Com	PC	Yds	Avg	TD	Int	Lg	Rtg
1960	WAS	N	1	0	0.0	0	0.0	0	0		39.6

Dick Vick

Year	Team		Att	Com	PC	Yds	Avg	TD	Int	Lg	Rtg
1924	KEN	N						1			
1925	DET	N						7			
Career								8			

Danny Villanueva

Year	Team		Att	Com	PC	Yds	Avg	TD	Int	Lg	Rtg
1961	LA	N	1	0	0.0	0	0.0	0	0		39.6

Mark Vlasic

Year	Team		Att	Com	PC	Yds	Avg	TD	Int	Lg	Rtg
1987	SD	N	6	3	50.0	8	1.3	0	1	7	16.7
1988			52	25	48.1	270	5.2	1	2	57	54.2
1990			40	19	47.5	168	4.2	1	2	27	46.7
1991	KC	N	44	28	63.6	316	7.2	2	0	30	100.2
Career			142	75	52.8	762	5.4	4	5	57	63.2
Playoffs			20	9	45.0	124	6.2	1	4		42.5

Jim Vollenweider

Year	Team		Att	Com	PC	Yds	Avg	TD	Int	Lg	Rtg
1963	SF	N	1	0	0.0	0	0.0	0	1		0.0

Billy Wade

Year	Team		Att	Com	PC	Yds	Avg	TD	Int	Lg	Rtg
1954	LA	N	59	31	52.5	509	8.6	2	1	48	86.1
1955			71	31	43.7	316	4.5	1	3	25	44.1
1956			178	91	51.1	1461	8.2	10	13	76t	67.2
1957			24	10	41.7	116	4.8	1	1	35t	53.5
1958			341	181	53.1	2875	8.4	18	22	93t	72.2
1959			261	153	58.6	2001	7.7	12	17	72t	71.1
1960			182	106	58.2	1294	7.1	12	11	63	77.0
1961	CHI	N	250	139	55.6	2258	9.0	22	13	98t	93.7
1962			412	225	54.6	3172	7.7	18	24	73t	70.0
1963			356	192	53.9	2301	6.5	15	12	63	74.0
1964			327	182	55.7	1944	5.9	13	14	68	68.6
1965			41	20	48.8	204	5.0	0	2	29	43.1
1966			21	9	42.9	79	3.8	0	1	14	33.6
Career			2523	1370	54.3	18530	7.3	124	134	98t	72.2
Playoffs			31	10	32.3	138	4.5	0	1		34.1

Tommy Wade

Year	Team		Att	Com	PC	Yds	Avg	TD	Int	Lg	Rtg
1964	PIT	N	3	1	33.3	7	2.3	0	0	7	42.4
1965			66	33	50.0	463	7.0	2	13	49	43.5
Career			69	34	49.3	470	6.8	2	13	49	41.6

Harmon Wages

Year	Team		Att	Com	PC	Yds	Avg	TD	Int	Lg	Rtg
1968	ATL	N	2	1	50.0	21	10.5	0	0	21	87.5
1969			1	1	100.0	16	16.0	1	0	16t	158.3
1970			1	1	100.0	13	13.0	0	0	13	118.8
Career			4	3	75.0	50	12.5	1	0	21	156.3

Bryan Wagner

Year	Team		Att	Com	PC	Yds	Avg	TD	Int	Lg	Rtg
1988	CHI	N	1	1	100.0	3	3.0	0	0	3	79.2

Bobby Walden

Year	Team		Att	Com	PC	Yds	Avg	TD	Int	Lg	Rtg
1968	PIT	N	1	0	0.0	0	0.0	0	0		39.6
1970			1	1	100.0	20	20.0	0	0	20	118.8
1971			1	1	100.0	10	10.0	0	0	10	108.3
1972			1	0	0.0	0	0.0	0	0		39.6
1975			3	2	66.7	39	13.0	0	0	20	109.7
Career			7	4	57.1	69	9.9	0	0	20	90.8

Doak Walker

Year	Team		Att	Com	PC	Yds	Avg	TD	Int	Lg	Rtg
1950	DET	N	7	1	14.3	6	0.9	0	0	6	39.6
1951			5	2	40.0	29	5.8	1	0	22t	99.2
1952			2	1	50.0	9	4.5	0	1	9	22.9
1953			7	3	42.9	31	4.4	1	0	23t	95.8
1954			4	0	0.0	0	0.0	0	1		0.0
1955			3	0	0.0	0	0.0	0	0		39.6
Career			28	7	25.0	75	2.7	2	2	23t	33.6
Playoffs			3	1	33.3	24	8.0	1	0		102.8

Dwight Walker

Year	Team		Att	Com	PC	Yds	Avg	TD	Int	Lg	Rtg
1983	CLE	N	3	1	33.3	25	8.3	0	1	25	25.0

Glen Walker

Year	Team		Att	Com	PC	Yds	Avg	TD	Int	Lg	Rtg
1977	LA	N	1	1	100.0	13	13.0	0	0	13	118.8
1978			1	0	0.0	0	0.0	0	1		0.0
Career			2	1	50.0	13	6.5	0	1	25	31.3

Herschel Walker

Year	Team		Att	Com	PC	Yds	Avg	TD	Int	Lg	Rtg
1990	MIN	N	2	1	50.0	12	6.0	0	0	12	68.8
1992	PHI	N	1	0	0.0	0	0.0	0	0		39.6
1993			0	0		0		0	0		
Career			3	1	33.3	12	4.0	0	0	12	46.5

Jay Walker

Year	Team		Att	Com	PC	Yds	Avg	TD	Int	Lg	Rtg
1996	MIN	N	2	2	100.0	31	15.5	0	0	19	118.8

Beverly Wallace

Year	Team		Att	Com	PC	Yds	Avg	TD	Int	Lg	Rtg
1947	SF	AA	16	5	31.3	48	3.0	0	2		1.0
1948			22	8	36.4	114	5.2	1	3		29.5
1949			23	9	39.1	95	4.1	0	4		12.3
1951	NYY	N	8	1	12.5	9	1.1	0	0	9	39.6
Career			69	23	33.3	266	3.9	1	9	19	11.2

Bob Wallace

Year	Team		Att	Com	PC	Yds	Avg	TD	Int	Lg	Rtg
1971	CHI	N	1	0	0.0	0	0.0	0	0		39.6

Ron Waller

Year	Team		Att	Com	PC	Yds	Avg	TD	Int	Lg	Rtg
1955	LA	N	1	0	0.0	0	0.0	0	0		39.6
1956			3	1	33.3	44	14.7	0	0	44	81.9
1957			6	2	33.3	35	5.8	0	0	30	54.2
1960	LA	A	1	0	0.0	0	0.0	0	1		0.0
Career			11	3	27.3	79	7.2	0	1	44	19.1

Laurie Walquist

Year	Team		Att	Com	PC	Yds	Avg	TD	Int	Lg	Rtg
1922	CHIB	N						1			
1924								1			
1925								1			
1926								2			
1927								1			
1930								1			
Career								7			

Chris Walsh

Year	Team		Att	Com	PC	Yds	Avg	TD	Int	Lg	Rtg
1996	MIN	N	1	0	0.0	0	0.0	0	0	0	39.6

Steve Walsh

Year	Team		Att	Com	PC	Yds	Avg	TD	Int	Lg	Rtg
1989	DAL	N	219	110	50.2	1371	6.3	5	9	46	60.5
1990	DAL-NO	N	336	179	53.3	2010	6.0	12	13	58	67.2
1991	NO	N	255	141	55.3	1638	6.4	11	6	41	79.5
1993			38	20	52.6	271	7.1	2	3	54t	60.3
1994	CHI	N	343	208	60.6	2078	6.1	10	8	50	77.9
1996	STL	N	77	33	42.9	344	4.5	0	5	32	29.4
Career			1268	691	54.5	7712	6.1	40	44	58	68.9
Playoffs			58	31	53.4	373	6.4	2	4		56.2

Dave Walter

Year	Team		Att	Com	PC	Yds	Avg	TD	Int	Lg	Rtg
1987	CIN	N	21	10	47.6	113	5.4	0	0	35	64.2

Johnnie Walton

Year	Team		Att	Com	PC	Yds	Avg	TD	Int	Lg	Rtg
1976	PHI	N	28	12	42.9	125	4.5	0	2	33	26.6
1978			1	0	0.0	0	0.0	0	0		39.6
1979			36	19	52.8	213	5.9	3	1	31	86.9
Career			65	31	47.7	338	5.2	3	3	33	59.6

Larry Walton

Year	Team		Att	Com	PC	Yds	Avg	TD	Int	Lg	Rtg
1969	DET	N	1	1	100.0	43	43.0	1	0	43t	158.3
1971			0	0		0		0	0		
1974			2	1	50.0	29	14.5	0	0	29	95.8
Career			3	2	66.7	72	24.0	1	0	43t	149.3

Jim Ward

Year	Team		Att	Com	PC	Yds	Avg	TD	Int	Lg	Rtg
1967	BAL	N	16	9	56.3	115	7.2	2	1	21t	92.4
1968			9	3	33.3	46	5.1	0	1	22	11.6
1971	PHI	N	1	1	100.0	4	4.0	0	0	4	83.3
Career			26	13	50.0	165	6.3	2	2	22	63.8

Andre Ware

Year	Team		Att	Com	PC	Yds	Avg	TD	Int	Lg	Rtg
1990	DET	N	30	13	43.3	164	5.5	1	2	33	44.3
1992			86	50	58.1	677	7.9	3	4	59	75.6
1993			45	20	44.4	271	6.0	1	2	47	53.1
Career			161	83	51.6	1112	6.9	5	8	59	63.5
Playoffs			9	4	44.4	15	1.7	0	1		12.0

Buist Warren

Year	Team		Att	Com	PC	Yds	Avg	TD	Int	Lg	Rtg
1945	PIT	N	92	36	39.1	368	4.0	0	10	47	11.8

Dewey Warren

Year	Team		Att	Com	PC	Yds	Avg	TD	Int	Lg	Rtg
1968	CIN	A	80	47	58.8	506	6.3	1	4	45t	60.7

Lamont Warren

Year	Team		Att	Com	PC	Yds	Avg	TD	Int	Lg	Rtg
1994	IND	N	1	0	0.0	0	0.0	0	0		39.6
Playoffs			1	0	0.0	0	0.0	0	0		39.6

Gene Washington

Year	Team		Att	Com	PC	Yds	Avg	TD	Int	Lg	Rtg
1975	SF	N	1	0	0.0	0	0.0	0	0		39.6

Joe Washington

Year	Team		Att	Com	PC	Yds	Avg	TD	Int	Lg	Rtg
1977	SD	N	1	1	100.0	32	32.0	1	0	32t	158.3
1978	BAL	N	4	2	50.0	80	20.0	2	0	54t	135.4
1979			1	0	0.0	0	0.0	0	1		0.0
1981	WAS	N	2	1	50.0	32	16.0	0	0	32	95.8
1982			1	1	100.0	35	35.0	0	0	35	118.8
1983			1	0	0.0	0	0.0	0	0		39.6
1984			1	0	0.0	0	0.0	0	0		39.6
Career			11	5	45.5	179	16.3	3	1	54t	93.8

Year	Team		Att	Com	PC	Yds	Avg	TD	Int	Lg	Rtg

Kenny Washington

Year	Team		Att	Com	PC	Yds	Avg	TD	Int	Lg	Rtg
1946	LA	N	8	1	12.5	19	2.4	0	0	19	39.6
1947			5	2	40.0	14	2.8	0	1	18	8.3
1948			1	0	0.0	0	0.0	0	0		39.6
Career			14	3	21.4	33	2.4	0	1	19	9.8

Bob Waterfield

Year	Team		Att	Com	PC	Yds	Avg	TD	Int	Lg	Rtg
1945	CLE	N	171	88	51.5	1609	**9.4**	**14**	16	84t	72.5
1946	LA	N	251	127	50.6	1747	7.0	**18**	17	57	68.9
1947			221	96	43.4	1210	5.5	8	18	45	39.2
1948			180	87	48.3	1354	7.5	14	18	80	60.0
1949			296	154	52.0	2168	7.3	17	24	71	61.3
1950			213	122	**57.3**	1540	7.2	11	13	72t	71.7
1951			176	88	50.0	1566	**8.9**	13	10	91t	**81.8**
1952			109	51	46.8	655	6.0	3	11	63t	35.7
Career			1617	813	50.3	11849	7.3	98	127	91t	62.0
Playoffs			125	63	50.4	965	7.7	6	11		55.6

Bobby Waters

Year	Team		Att	Com	PC	Yds	Avg	TD	Int	Lg	Rtg
1960	SF	N	2	2	100.0	61	30.5	1	0	41t	158.3
1961			28	13	46.4	183	6.5	1	2	26t	50.1
1962			6	2	33.3	28	4.7	0	0	15	49.3
1963			88	42	47.7	435	4.9	1	6	42	37.8
Career			124	59	47.6	707	5.7	3	8	42	46.7

Charlie Waters

Year	Team		Att	Com	PC	Yds	Avg	TD	Int	Lg	Rtg
1977	DAL	N	0	0		0		0	0		

Foster Watkins

Year	Team		Att	Com	PC	Yds	Avg	TD	Int	Lg	Rtg
1940	PHI	N	85	28	32.9	565	6.6	1	3		46.4
1941			10	6	60.0	62	6.2	1	0	15	111.3
Career			95	34	35.8	627	6.6	2	3	15	53.3

Tommy Watkins

Year	Team		Att	Com	PC	Yds	Avg	TD	Int	Lg	Rtg
1964	DET	N	1	1	100.0	58	58.0	1	0	58t	158.3

Rat Watson

Year	Team		Att	Com	PC	Yds	Avg	TD	Int	Lg	Rtg
1922	TOL	N							2		

Sid Watson

Year	Team		Att	Com	PC	Yds	Avg	TD	Int	Lg	Rtg
1955	PIT	N	0	0		0		0	0		

Frank Wattelet

Year	Team		Att	Com	PC	Yds	Avg	TD	Int	Lg	Rtg
1986	NO	N	1	1	100.0	13	13.0	0	0	13	118.8

Ricky Watters

Year	Team		Att	Com	PC	Yds	Avg	TD	Int	Lg	Rtg
1992	SF	N	1	0	0.0	0	0.0	0	0		39.6

Herman Weaver

Year	Team		Att	Com	PC	Yds	Avg	TD	Int	Lg	Rtg
1975	DET	N	1	0	0.0	0	0.0	0	0		39.6
1976			2	1	50.0	14	7.0	0	0	14	72.9
1978	SEA	N	1	1	100.0	9	9.0	0	0	9	104.2
1979			4	3	75.0	73	18.3	0	0	39	116.7
1980			2	0	0.0	0	0.0	0	0		39.6
Career			10	5	50.0	96	9.6	0	0	39	83.8

Dick Weber

Year	Team		Att	Com	PC	Yds	Avg	TD	Int	Lg	Rtg
1945	DET	N	22	6	27.3	70	3.2	0	5	27	0.8

Alex Webster

Year	Team		Att	Com	PC	Yds	Avg	TD	Int	Lg	Rtg
1959	NYG	N	1	0	0.0	0	0.0	0	0		39.6

Herman Wedemeyer

Year	Team		Att	Com	PC	Yds	Avg	TD	Int	Lg	Rtg
1948	LA	AA	30	9	30.0	79	2.6	0	3		0.0
1949	BAL	AA	1	0	0.0	0	0.0	0	1		0.0
Career			31	9	29.0	79	2.5	0	4		0.0

Norris Weese

Year	Team		Att	Com	PC	Yds	Avg	TD	Int	Lg	Rtg
1976	DEN	N	47	24	51.1	314	6.7	1	6	43	40.0
1977			20	11	55.0	119	6.0	1	0	31	89.4
1978			87	55	63.2	723	8.3	4	5	31	80.8
1979			97	53	54.6	731	7.5	1	3	50	69.6
Career			251	143	57.0	1887	7.5	7	14	50	66.9
Playoffs			26	12	46.2	140	5.4	0	0		63.0

Roger Wehrli

Year	Team		Att	Com	PC	Yds	Avg	TD	Int	Lg	Rtg
1976	STL	N	1	0	0.0	0	0.0	0	0		39.6
1980			0	0		0		0	0		
Career			1	0	0.0	0	0.0	0	0		39.6

Chuck Weimer

Year	Team		Att	Com	PC	Yds	Avg	TD	Int	Lg	Rtg
1929	BUF	N							3		

Year	Team		Att	Com	PC	Yds	Avg	TD	Int	Lg	Rtg

Al Weiner

Year	Team		Att	Com	PC	Yds	Avg	TD	Int	Lg	Rtg
1934	PHI	N							2		

Gibby Welch

Year	Team		Att	Com	PC	Yds	Avg	TD	Int	Lg	Rtg
1928	NYY	N							1		

Casey Weldon

Year	Team		Att	Com	PC	Yds	Avg	TD	Int	Lg	Rtg
1993	TB	N	11	6	54.5	55	5.0	0	1	20	30.5
1994			9	7	77.8	63	7.0	0	0	27	95.8
1995			91	42	46.2	519	5.7	1	2	40	58.8
1996			9	5	55.6	76	8.4	0	1	42	44.0
Career			120	60	50.0	713	5.9	1	4	42	57.4

Larry Weldon

Year	Team		Att	Com	PC	Yds	Avg	TD	Int	Lg	Rtg
1944	WAS	N	6	4	66.7	33	5.5	0	0	14	80.6

Larry Weltman

Year	Team		Att	Com	PC	Yds	Avg	TD	Int	Lg	Rtg
1922	ROC	N							1		

Cy Wentworth

Year	Team		Att	Com	PC	Yds	Avg	TD	Int	Lg	Rtg
1926	PRO	N							1		

Jeff West

Year	Team		Att	Com	PC	Yds	Avg	TD	Int	Lg	Rtg
1981	SEA	N	1	0	0.0	0	0.0	0	0		39.6

Don Westbrook

Year	Team		Att	Com	PC	Yds	Avg	TD	Int	Lg	Rtg
1979	NE	N	2	2	100.0	52	26.0	0	0	28	118.8

Bob Westfall

Year	Team		Att	Com	PC	Yds	Avg	TD	Int	Lg	Rtg
1944	DET	N	47	23	48.9	342	7.3	4	6	46	62.0
1945			4	3	75.0	91	22.8	1	0	63	156.3
1946			2	1	50.0	-5	-2.5	0	1	-5	16.7
Career			53	27	50.9	428	8.1	5	7	63	70.0

Ed Westfall

Year	Team		Att	Com	PC	Yds	Avg	TD	Int	Lg	Rtg
1933	BOS	N							1		

Chet Wetterlund

Year	Team		Att	Com	PC	Yds	Avg	TD	Int	Lg	Rtg
1942	DET	N	44	13	29.5	230	5.2	0	10	51	9.3

Tyrone Wheatley

Year	Team		Att	Com	PC	Yds	Avg	TD	Int	Lg	Rtg
1996	NYG	N	1	1	100.0	24	24.0	1	0	24t	158.3

Ernie Wheeler

Year	Team		Att	Com	PC	Yds	Avg	TD	Int	Lg	Rtg
1939	PIT-CHIC	N	17	5	29.4	94	5.5	1	7		30.1

Danny White

Year	Team		Att	Com	PC	Yds	Avg	TD	Int	Lg	Rtg
1976	DAL	N	20	13	65.0	213	10.7	2	2	56	94.4
1977			10	4	40.0	35	3.5	0	1	12	10.4
1978			34	20	58.8	215	6.3	0	1	35	65.2
1979			39	19	48.7	267	6.8	1	2	45	58.4
1980			436	260	59.6	3287	7.5	28	25	58t	80.7
1981			391	223	57.0	3098	7.9	22	13	73t	87.5
1982			247	156	63.2	2079	8.4	16	12	49	91.1
1983			533	334	62.7	3980	7.5	29	23	80t	85.6
1984			233	126	54.1	1580	6.8	11	11	66t	71.5
1985			450	267	59.3	3157	7.0	21	17	56t	80.6
1986			153	95	62.1	1157	7.6	12	5	63	97.9
1987			362	215	59.4	2617	7.2	12	17	43	73.2
1988			42	29	69.0	274	6.5	1	3	24	65.0
Career			2950	1761	59.7	21959	7.4	155	132	80t	81.7
Playoffs			360	206	57.2	2284	6.3	15	16		71.6

Harvey White

Year	Team		Att	Com	PC	Yds	Avg	TD	Int	Lg	Rtg
1960	BOS	A	7	3	42.9	44	6.3	0	0		64.0

Paul White

Year	Team		Att	Com	PC	Yds	Avg	TD	Int	Lg	Rtg
1947	PIT	N	3	1	33.3	21	7.0	0	0	21	59.0

Phil White

Year	Team		Att	Com	PC	Yds	Avg	TD	Int	Lg	Rtg
1925	KC	N							2		

Walter White

Year	Team		Att	Com	PC	Yds	Avg	TD	Int	Lg	Rtg
1975	KC	N	1	0	0.0	0	0.0	0	1		0.0
1978			1	1	100.0	44	44.0	0	0	44	118.8
Career			2	1	50.0	44	22.0	0	1	44	56.3

Whizzer White

Year	Team		Att	Com	PC	Yds	Avg	TD	Int	Lg	Rtg
1938	PIT	N	73	29	39.7	393	5.4	2	18		27.2
1940	DET	N	80	35	43.8	461	5.8	0	11		23.0
1941			62	22	35.5	338	5.5	2	5	47	31.5
Career			215	86	40.0	1192	5.5	4	34	47	25.1

Year	Team		Att	Com	PC	Yds	Avg	TD	Int	Lg	Rtg

Wilbur White

1935	BKN	N						2			
1936	DET	N	1	0	0.0	0	0.0	0	0		39.6
Career			1	0	0.0	0	0.0	2	0		39.6

Wilford White

1951	CHIB	N	1	0	0.0	0	0.0	0	0		39.6
1952			2	0	0.0	0	0.0	0	0		39.6
Career			3	0	0.0	0	0.0	0	0		39.6

Bud Whitehead

| 1967 | SD | A | 1 | 0 | 0.0 | 0 | 0.0 | 0 | 0 | | 39.6 |

David Whitehurst

1977	GB	N	105	50	47.6	634	6.0	1	7	48	42.3
1978			328	168	51.2	2093	6.4	10	17	58t	59.9
1979			322	179	55.6	2247	7.0	10	18	78t	64.5
1980			15	5	33.3	55	3.7	0	1	24	17.4
1981			128	66	51.6	792	6.2	7	5	46t	72.8
1982			47	18	38.3	235	5.0	0	1	22	46.0
1983			35	18	51.4	149	4.3	0	2	19	38.9
Career			980	504	51.4	6205	6.3	28	51	78t	59.2

Ron Widby

| 1972 | GB | N | 2 | 2 | 100.0 | 102 | 51.0 | 1 | 0 | 68t | 158.3 |

James Wilder

| 1984 | TB | N | 1 | 1 | 100.0 | 16 | 16.0 | 1 | 0 | 16t | 158.3 |

Erik Wilhelm

1989	CIN	N	56	30	53.6	425	7.6	4	2	46t	87.3
1990			19	12	63.2	117	6.2	0	0	19	80.4
1991			42	24	57.1	217	5.2	0	2	29	51.4
1993			6	4	66.7	63	10.5	0	0	27	101.4
1996			13	7	53.8	90	6.9	1	2	38	61.9
Career			136	77	56.6	912	6.7	5	6	46t	71.1
Playoffs			5	1	20.0	12	2.4	0	0		39.6

Dick Wilkins

| 1949 | LA | AA | 1 | 0 | 0.0 | 0 | 0.0 | 0 | 0 | | 39.6 |

Ken Willard

| 1965 | SF | N | 1 | 0 | 0.0 | 0 | 0.0 | 0 | 1 | | 0.0 |

Gerald Willhite

1982	DEN	N	2	0	0.0	0	0.0	0	1		0.0
1983			1	0	0.0	0	0.0	0	0		39.6
1984			2	1	50.0	20	10.0	0	0	20	85.4
1985			3	0	0.0	0	0.0	0	0		39.6
1986			4	1	25.0	11	2.8	0	0	11	39.6
1987			1	0	0.0	0	0.0	0	0		39.6
Career			13	2	15.4	31	2.4	0	1	20	7.5
Playoffs			1	1	100.0	52	52.0	0	0		118.8

Bobby Williams

1951	CHIB	N	33	14	42.4	146	4.4	1	2	19t	40.7
1952			87	45	51.7	579	6.7	6	5	56	72.0
1955			40	15	37.5	256	6.4	3	5	37t	45.4
Career			160	74	46.3	981	6.1	10	12	56	55.8

Delvin Williams

1976	SF	N	1	1	100.0	18	18.0	0	0	18	118.8
1977			1	0	0.0	0	0.0	0	1		0.0
1978	MIA	N	1	0	0.0	0	0.0	0	0		39.6
1979			1	0	0.0	0	0.0	0	0		39.6
1980			1	0	0.0	0	0.0	0	0		39.6
Career			5	1	20.0	18	3.6	0	1	18	2.5

Doug Williams

1978	TB	N	194	73	37.6	1170	6.0	7	8	56t	53.4
1979			397	166	41.8	2448	6.2	18	24	66t	52.5
1980			521	254	48.8	3396	6.5	20	16	61	69.9
1981			471	238	50.5	3563	7.6	19	14	84t	76.8
1982			307	164	53.4	2071	6.7	9	11	62t	69.6
1986	WAS	N	1	0	0.0	0	0.0	0	0		39.6
1987			143	81	56.6	1156	8.1	11	5	62	94.0
1988			380	213	56.1	2609	6.9	15	12	58	77.4
1989			93	51	54.8	585	6.3	1	3	46	64.1
Career			2507	1240	49.5	16998	6.8	100	93	84t	69.4
Playoffs			169	68	40.2	1110	6.6	9	11		53.6

Harvey Williams

| 1993 | SEA | N | 1 | 0 | 0.0 | 0 | 0.0 | 0 | 0 | | 39.6 |
| 1995 | OAK | N | 1 | 1 | 100.0 | 13 | 13.0 | 1 | 0 | 13t | 158.3 |

Harvey Williams *continued*

| 1996 | | | 2 | 1 | 50.0 | 18 | 9.0 | 1 | 0 | 18t | 120.8 |
| **Career** | | | 4 | 2 | 50.0 | 31 | 7.8 | 2 | 0 | 18t | 115.6 |

John L. Williams

| 1991 | KC | N | 1 | 0 | 0.0 | 0 | 0.0 | 0 | 0 | | 39.6 |
| **Playoffs** | | | 1 | 0 | 0.0 | 0 | 0.0 | 0 | 0 | | 39.6 |

Ray Williams

| 1980 | DET | N | 0 | 0 | | 0 | | 0 | 0 | | |

Sherman Williams

| 1996 | DAL | N | 1 | 0 | 0.0 | 0 | 0.0 | 0 | 0 | | 39.6 |

Ted Williams

| 1944 | BOS | N | 6 | 0 | 0.0 | 0 | 0.0 | 0 | 2 | | 0.0 |

Walt Williams

1946	CHI	AA	30	13	43.3	226	7.5	1	5	50	41.1
1947	BOS	N	1	0	0.0	0	0.0	0	1		0.0
Career			31	13	41.9	226	7.3	1	6	50	38.6

Fred Willis

1971	CIN	N	2	1	50.0	8	4.0	0	0	8	60.4
1972	CIN-HOU	N	4	1	25.0	16	4.0	0	1	16	4.2
1973	HOU	N	1	0	0.0	0	0.0	0	0		39.6
Career			7	2	28.6	24	3.4	0	1	16	1.8

Peter Tom Willis

1990	CHI	N	13	9	69.2	106	8.2	1	1	18	87.3
1991			18	11	61.1	171	9.5	1	1	42	88.0
1992			92	54	58.7	716	7.8	4	8	68t	61.7
1993			60	30	50.0	268	4.5	0	5	29	27.6
Career			183	104	56.8	1261	6.9	6	15	68t	54.9

Klaus Wilmsmeyer

| 1995 | NO | N | 1 | 1 | 100.0 | 18 | 18.0 | 0 | 0 | 18 | 118.8 |

Ben Wilson

| 1965 | LA | N | 1 | 1 | 100.0 | 8 | 8.0 | 0 | 0 | 8 | 100.0 |

Bobby Wilson

| 1936 | BKN | N | 40 | 11 | 27.5 | 148 | 3.7 | 0 | 9 | | 2.9 |

Dave Wilson

1981	NO	N	159	82	51.6	1058	6.7	1	11	50	46.1
1983			112	66	58.9	770	6.9	5	7	42	68.7
1984			93	51	54.8	647	7.0	7	4	54t	83.9
1985			293	145	49.5	1843	6.3	11	15	50	60.7
1986			342	189	55.3	2353	6.9	10	17	63t	65.8
1987			24	13	54.2	243	10.1	2	0	38	117.2
1988			16	5	31.3	73	4.6	0	1	25	21.1
Career			1039	551	53.0	6987	6.7	36	55	63t	63.8
Playoffs			12	2	16.7	20	1.7	0	2		0.0

Eddie Wilson

1962	DAL	A	11	6	54.5	65	5.9	0	0		72.2
1963	KC	A	82	39	47.6	537	6.5	3	2		71.0
1964			47	25	53.2	392	8.3	1	1		79.4
1965	BOS	A	46	20	43.5	257	5.6	1	3	30	41.7
Career			186	90	48.4	1251	6.7	5	6	30	65.9

George Wilson

1926	LA	A							5		
1927	PRO	N							4		
1928									5		
1929									3		
Career									17		

George Wilson

| 1966 | MIA | A | 112 | 46 | 41.1 | 764 | 6.8 | 5 | 10 | 80 | 42.4 |

Jerrel Wilson

1972	KC	N	1	1	100.0	20	20.0	0	0	20	118.8
1973			1	1	100.0	9	9.0	0	0	9	104.2
1974			2	0	0.0	0	0.0	0	0		39.6
Career			4	2	50.0	29	7.3	0	0	20	74.0

Larry Wilson

| 1972 | STL | N | 2 | 0 | 0.0 | 0 | 0.0 | 0 | 0 | | 39.6 |

Marc Wilson

| 1980 | OAK | N | 5 | 3 | 60.0 | 31 | 6.2 | 0 | 0 | 12 | 77.9 |
| 1981 | | | 366 | 173 | 47.3 | 2311 | 6.3 | 14 | 19 | 66t | 58.9 |

Year	Team		Att	Com	PC	Yds	Avg	TD	Int	Lg	Rtg

Marc Wilson *continued*

Year	Team		Att	Com	PC	Yds	Avg	TD	Int	Lg	Rtg
1982	LARI	N	2	1	50.0	4	2.0	0	0	4	56.3
1983			117	67	57.3	864	7.4	8	6	50t	82.0
1984			282	153	54.3	2151	7.6	15	17	92	71.7
1985			388	193	49.7	2608	6.7	16	21	59	62.7
1986			240	129	53.8	1721	7.2	12	15	57t	67.4
1987			266	152	57.1	2070	7.8	12	8	47t	84.6
1989	NE	N	150	75	50.0	1006	6.7	3	5	65t	64.5
1990			265	139	52.5	1625	6.1	6	11	36t	61.6
Career			2081	1085	52.1	14391	6.9	86	102	92	67.7
Playoffs			27	11	40.7	135	5.0	1	3		29.6

Mike Wilson

| 1929 | FRA | N | | | | | | | 1 | | |

Mule Wilson

| 1931 | GB | N | | | | | | | 1 | | |

Tommy Wilson

Year	Team		Att	Com	PC	Yds	Avg	TD	Int	Lg	Rtg
1956	LA	N	1	0	0.0	0	0.0	0	0	0	39.6
1958			1	0	0.0	0	0.0	0	1	0	0.0
Career			2	0	0.0	0	0.0	0	1	0	0.0

Wade Wilson

Year	Team		Att	Com	PC	Yds	Avg	TD	Int	Lg	Rtg
1981	MIN	N	13	6	46.2	48	3.7	0	2	22	16.3
1983			28	16	57.1	124	4.4	1	2	36	50.3
1984			195	102	52.3	1019	5.2	5	11	38	52.5
1985			60	33	55.0	404	6.7	3	3	42t	71.8
1986			143	80	55.9	1165	8.1	7	5	39	84.4
1987			264	140	53.0	2106	**8.0**	14	13	73t	76.7
1988			332	204	**61.4**	2746	8.3	15	9	48t	91.5
1989			362	194	53.6	2543	7.0	9	12	50	70.5
1990			146	82	56.2	1155	7.9	9	8	75t	79.6
1991			122	72	59.0	825	6.8	3	10	46t	53.5
1992	ATL	N	163	111	68.1	1366	8.4	13	4	60t	110.1
1993	NO	N	388	221	57.0	2457	6.3	12	15	42t	70.1
1994			28	20	71.4	172	6.1	0	0	16	87.2
1995	DAL	N	57	38	66.7	391	6.9	1	3	38	70.1
1996			18	8	44.4	79	4.4	0	1	20	34.3
Career			2319	1327	57.2	16600	7.2	92	98	75t	75.2
Playoffs			185	99	53.5	1322	7.1	7	6		75.6

Sammy Winder

| 1985 | DEN | N | 1 | 0 | 0.0 | 0 | 0.0 | 0 | 0 | | 39.6 |

Kellen Winslow

Year	Team		Att	Com	PC	Yds	Avg	TD	Int	Lg	Rtg
1981	SD	N	2	0	0.0	0	0.0	0	0		39.6
1982			1	0	0.0	0	0.0	0	0		39.6
Career			3	0	0.0	0	0.0	0	0		39.6
Playoffs			1	1	100.0	28	28.0	0	0		118.8

Sonny Winters

1923	COL	N						5			
1924								7			
Career								12			

John Witkowski

Year	Team		Att	Com	PC	Yds	Avg	TD	Int	Lg	Rtg
1984	DET	N	34	13	38.2	210	6.2	0	0	39	59.7
1988			1	0	0.0	0	0.0	0	0		39.6
Career			35	13	37.1	210	6.0	0	0	39	58.0

Tom Wittum

| 1977 | SF | N | 3 | 1 | 33.3 | 15 | 5.0 | 0 | 0 | 15 | 50.7 |

Dick Wood

Year	Team		Att	Com	PC	Yds	Avg	TD	Int	Lg	Rtg
1962	SD	A	97	41	42.3	655	6.8	4	7	47	49.1
1963	NY	A	351	160	45.6	2202	6.3	18	18		61.9
1964			358	169	47.2	2298	6.4	17	25		54.9
1965	OAK	A	157	69	43.9	1003	6.4	8	6	57	66.4
1966	MIA	A	230	83	36.1	993	4.3	4	14	71	30.6
Career			1193	522	43.8	7151	6.0	51	70	71	53.3

Gary Wood

Year	Team		Att	Com	PC	Yds	Avg	TD	Int	Lg	Rtg
1964	NYG	N	143	66	46.2	952	6.7	6	3	70	73.5
1965			36	15	41.7	190	5.3	1	2	28t	44.9
1966	NO	N	170	81	47.6	1142	6.7	6	13	58	49.7
1967	NO	N	11	5	45.5	62	5.6	0	0	27	63.4
1968	NYG	N	24	9	37.5	123	5.1	0	5	43	15.1
1969	NY	N	16	10	62.5	106	6.6	1	0	25	102.6
Career			400	186	46.5	2575	6.4	14	23	70	55.4

Mike Wood

| 1978 | STL | N | 1 | 1 | 100.0 | 29 | 29.0 | 0 | 0 | 29 | 118.8 |

Mike Wood *continued*

Year	Team		Att	Com	PC	Yds	Avg	TD	Int	Lg	Rtg
1982	BAL	N	1	1	100.0	5	5.0	1	0	5t	127.1
Career			2	2	100.0	34	17.0	1	0	29	158.3

Al Woodall

Year	Team		Att	Com	PC	Yds	Avg	TD	Int	Lg	Rtg
1969	NY	A	9	4	44.4	67	7.4	0	2	35	30.6
1970	NYJ	N	188	96	51.1	1265	6.7	9	9	67	68.7
1971			97	42	43.3	395	4.1	0	2	26	46.5
1973			201	101	50.2	1228	6.1	9	8	56t	67.8
1974			8	3	37.5	15	1.9	0	2	8	6.3
Career			503	246	48.9	2970	5.9	18	23	67	60.3

David Woodley

Year	Team		Att	Com	PC	Yds	Avg	TD	Int	Lg	Rtg
1980	MIA	N	327	176	53.8	1850	5.7	14	17	61	63.1
1981			366	191	52.2	2470	6.7	12	13	69t	69.8
1982			179	98	54.7	1080	6.0	5	8	46	63.5
1983			89	43	48.3	528	5.9	3	4	64t	59.6
1984	PIT	N	156	85	54.5	1273	8.2	8	7	80t	79.9
1985			183	94	51.4	1357	7.4	6	14	69	54.8
Career			1300	687	52.8	8558	6.6	48	63	80t	65.7
Playoffs			81	48	59.3	645	8.0	5	6		74.4

Jim Woodruff

| 1929 | BUF | N | | | | | | | 1 | | |

Don Woods

Year	Team		Att	Com	PC	Yds	Avg	TD	Int	Lg	Rtg
1974	SD	N	3	1	33.3	28	9.3	1	1	28t	68.8
1976			2	1	50.0	11	5.5	1	0	11t	106.3
1977			1	0	0.0	0	0.0	0	0		39.6
1980	SF	N	2	1	50.0	6	3.0	0	0	6	56.3
Career			8	3	37.5	45	5.6	2	1	28t	56.8

Harry Workman

| 1924 | CLE | N | | | | | | | 9 | | |

Vince Workman

| 1995 | CAR | N | 1 | 0 | 0.0 | 0 | 0.0 | 0 | 0 | | 39.6 |

Ab Wright

| 1930 | FRA | N | | | | | | | 1 | | |

Randy Wright

Year	Team		Att	Com	PC	Yds	Avg	TD	Int	Lg	Rtg
1984	GB	N	62	27	43.5	310	5.0	2	6	56	30.4
1985			74	39	52.7	552	7.5	2	4	38	63.6
1986			492	263	53.5	3247	6.6	17	23	62	66.2
1987			247	132	53.4	1507	6.1	6	11	66	61.6
1988			244	141	57.8	1490	6.1	4	13	51	58.9
Career			1119	602	53.8	7106	6.4	31	57	66	61.4

Freddy Wyant

| 1956 | WAS | N | 2 | 1 | 50.0 | 17 | 8.5 | 0 | 0 | 17 | 79.2 |

Sam Wyche

Year	Team		Att	Com	PC	Yds	Avg	TD	Int	Lg	Rtg
1968	CIN	A	55	35	63.6	494	9.0	2	2	80t	89.5
1969			108	54	50.0	838	7.8	7	4	80t	82.3
1970	CIN	N	57	26	45.6	411	7.2	3	2	51t	73.1
1974	DET	N	1	0	0.0	0	0.0	0	1		0.0
1976	STL	N	1	1	100.0	5	5.0	0	0	5	87.5
Career			222	116	52.3	1748	7.9	12	9	80t	79.6
Playoffs			1	1	100.0	29	29.0	0	0		118.8

Doug Wycoff

1929	SI	N							1		
1930									5		
1934	BOS	N							1		
Career									7		

Arnie Wyman

| 1920 | RI | A | | | | | | | 2 | | |

Tom Yewcic

Year	Team		Att	Com	PC	Yds	Avg	TD	Int	Lg	Rtg
1961	BOS	A	8	3	37.5	25	3.1	1	2		46.4
1962			126	54	42.9	903	7.2	7	5	78	69.6
1963			70	29	41.4	444	6.3	4	5		52.3
1964			1	1	100.0	2	2.0	0	0		79.2
1965			1	0	0.0	0	0.0	0	0		39.6
Career			206	87	42.2	1374	6.7	12	12	78	60.2
Playoffs			8	3	37.5	39	4.9	0	1		14.1

Jim Youel

Year	Team		Att	Com	PC	Yds	Avg	TD	Int	Lg	Rtg
1946	WAS	N	48	20	41.7	352	7.3	2	3	66	55.2
1947			62	21	33.9	398	6.4	3	3	55	53.0
1948	BOS-WAS	N	36	9	25.0	99	2.8	2	4	16	18.5
Career			146	50	34.2	849	5.8	7	10	66	42.3

Year	Team		Att	Com	PC	Yds	Avg	TD	Int	Lg	Rtg

Buddy Young

Year	Team		Att	Com	PC	Yds	Avg	TD	Int	Lg	Rtg
1947	NY	AA	2	1	50.0	13	6.5	0	0	13	70.8
1952	DAL	N	3	0	0.0	0	0.0	0	1		0.0
Career			5	1	20.0	13	2.6	0	1	13	0.0

Steve Young

Year	Team		Att	Com	PC	Yds	Avg	TD	Int	Lg	Rtg
1985	TB	N	138	72	52.2	935	6.8	3	8	59	56.9
1986			363	195	53.7	2282	6.3	8	13	46	65.5
1987	SF	N	69	37	53.6	570	8.3	10	0	50t	120.8
1988			101	54	53.5	680	6.7	3	3	73t	72.2
1989			92	64	69.6	1001	10.9	8	3	50t	120.8
1990			62	38	61.3	427	6.9	2	0	34t	92.6
1991			279	180	64.5	2517	9.0	17	8	97t	101.8
1992			402	268	66.7	3465	8.6	25	7	80t	107.0
1993			462	314	68.0	4023	8.7	29	16	80t	101.5
1994			461	324	70.3	3969	8.6	35	10	69t	112.8
1995			447	299	66.9	3200	7.2	20	11	57	92.3
1996			316	214	67.7	2410	7.6	14	6	52	97.2
Career			3192	2059	64.5	25479	8.0	174	85	97t	96.2
Playoffs			334	207	62.0	2381	7.1	15	7		89.7

Tank Younger

Year	Team		Att	Com	PC	Yds	Avg	TD	Int	Lg	Rtg
1957	LA	N	1	0	0.0	0	0.0	0	1		0.0

Silvio Zaninelli

Year	Team		Att	Com	PC	Yds	Avg	TD	Int	Lg	Rtg
1935	PIT	N						1			
1936			6	1	16.7	2	0.3	0	1	2	0.0
Career			6	1	16.7	2	0.3	1	1	2	0.0

Eric Zeier

Year	Team		Att	Com	PC	Yds	Avg	TD	Int	Lg	Rtg
1995	CLE	N	161	82	50.9	864	5.4	4	9	59	51.9
1996	BAL	N	21	10	47.6	97	4.6	1	1	15	57.0
Career			182	92	50.5	961	5.3	5	10	59	52.5

Tony Zendejas

Year	Team		Att	Com	PC	Yds	Avg	TD	Int	Lg	Rtg
1985	HOU	N	1	1	100.0	-7	-7.0	0	0	-7	79.2
1989			1	0	0.0	0	0.0	0	1		0.0
Career			2	1	50.0	-7	-3.5	0	1	-7	16.7

Frank Ziegler

Year	Team		Att	Com	PC	Yds	Avg	TD	Int	Lg	Rtg
1953	PHI	N	1	0	0.0	0	0.0	0	0		39.6

Roy Zimmerman

Year	Team		Att	Com	PC	Yds	Avg	TD	Int	Lg	Rtg
1940	WAS	N	12	4	33.3	53	4.4	0	3		8.7
1941			1	0	0.0	0	0.0	0	0		39.6

Roy Zimmerman *continued*

Year	Team		Att	Com	PC	Yds	Avg	TD	Int	Lg	Rtg
1942			10	2	20.0	13	1.3	0	2	9	0.0
1943	P-P	N	124	43	34.7	846	6.8	9	17	60	44.0
1944	PHI	N	105	39	37.1	785	7.5	8	10	75	50.0
1945			132	67	50.8	991	7.5	9	8	74t	73.1
1946			79	41	51.9	597	7.6	4	8	59	54.1
1947	DET	N	138	57	41.3	867	6.3	7	9	53	52.4
1948	BOS	N	107	46	43.0	649	6.1	7	13	69	45.4
Career			708	299	42.2	4801	6.8	44	70	75	46.7
Playoffs			12	3	25.0	34	2.8	0	2		0.0

Mickey Zofko

Year	Team		Att	Com	PC	Yds	Avg	TD	Int	Lg	Rtg
1973	DET	N	1	1	100.0	35	35.0	0	0	35	118.8

Scott Zolak

Year	Team		Att	Com	PC	Yds	Avg	TD	Int	Lg	Rtg
1992	NE	N	100	52	52.0	561	5.6	2	4	65t	58.8
1993			2	0	0.0	0	0.0	0	0		39.6
1994			8	5	62.5	28	3.5	0	0	13	68.8
1995			49	28	57.1	282	5.8	1	0	72	80.5
1996			1	1	100.0	5	5.0	0	0	5	87.5
Career			160	86	53.8	876	5.5	3	4	72	65.5
Playoffs			2	1	50.0	3	1.5	0	0		56.3

Lou Zontini

Year	Team		Att	Com	PC	Yds	Avg	TD	Int	Lg	Rtg
1944	CLE	N	2	2	100.0	18	9.0	0	0	18	104.2
1946	BUF	AA	1	0	0.0	0	0.0	0	0		39.6
Career			3	2	66.7	18	6.0	0	0	18	82.6

Frank Zoppetti

Year	Team		Att	Com	PC	Yds	Avg	TD	Int	Lg	Rtg
1941	PIT	N	1	0	0.0	0	0.0	0	0		39.6

Jim Zorn

Year	Team		Att	Com	PC	Yds	Avg	TD	Int	Lg	Rtg
1976	SEA	N	439	208	47.4	2571	5.9	12	27	80t	49.5
1977			251	104	41.4	1687	6.7	16	19	82t	54.3
1978			443	248	56.0	3283	7.4	15	20	64	72.1
1979			505	285	56.4	3661	7.2	20	18	65t	77.7
1980			488	276	56.6	3346	6.9	17	20	67t	72.3
1981			397	236	59.4	2788	7.0	13	9	80t	82.4
1982			245	126	51.4	1540	6.3	7	11	50	61.9
1983			205	103	50.2	1166	5.7	7	7	43	64.8
1984			17	7	41.2	80	4.7	0	2	21	16.4
1985	GB	N	123	56	45.5	794	6.5	4	6	56t	57.4
1987	TB	N	36	20	55.6	199	5.5	0	2	26	48.3
Career			3149	1669	53.0	21115	6.7	111	141	82t	67.3
Playoffs			28	14	50.0	134	4.8	2	2		57.7

Receiving Register

Year	Team		No	Yds	Avg	Lg	TD
Jerry Rice							
1985	**SF**	**N**	49	927	18.9	66t	3
1986			86	**1570**	18.3	66t	**15**
1987			65	1078	16.6	57t	**22**
1988			64	1306	20.4	98t	9
1989			82	**1483**	18.1	68t	**17**
1990			**100**	**1502**	15.0	64t	**13**
1991			80	1206	15.1	73t	**14**
1992			84	1201	14.3	80t	10
1993			98	**1503**	15.3	80t	**15**
1994			112	**1499**	13.4	69t	13
1995			122	**1848**	15.1	81t	15
1996			**108**	1254	11.6	39	8
Career			**1050**	**16377**	15.6	98t	**154**
Playoffs			**120**	**1742**	14.5		**18**

Key

Team	The team (and league) the player played for.
No	Number of receptions
Yds	Yards
Avg	Average gain per reception
Lg	Longest pass receptionof the season
TD	Touchdowns

In addition, boldface numbers indicate that the player led the league in that category that season. For example, Rice's 22 touchdown catches in 1987 are boldfaced, meaning that he led the league in receptions that year. Also, boldfaced career and playoff stats indicate all-time highs. Rice's 1050 receptions indicate that he is the all-time career leader in this category.

Joe Abbey

Year	Team		No	Yds	Avg	Lg	TD
1948	CHIB	N	5	67	13.4	35	0
1949	CHIB-NYB	N	8	110	13.8	48	0
Career			13	177	13.6	48	0

Fay Abbott

Year	Team		No	Yds	Avg	Lg	TD
1921	DAY	A					1

Lou Abbruzzi

Year	Team		No	Yds	Avg	Lg	TD
1946	BOS	N	2	55	27.5	38	0

Karim Abdul-Jabbar

Year	Team		No	Yds	Avg	Lg	TD
1996	MIA	N	23	139	6.0	23	0

Walter Abercrombie

Year	Team		No	Yds	Avg	Lg	TD
1982	PIT	N	1	14	14.0	14	0
1983			26	391	15.0	51t	3
1984			16	135	8.4	59	0
1985			24	209	8.7	27	2
1986			47	395	8.4	27	2
1987			24	209	8.7	24	0
1988	PHI	N	1	-2	-2.0	-2	0
Career			139	1351	9.7	59	7
Playoffs			5	35	7.0		0

Danny Abramowicz

Year	Team		No	Yds	Avg	Lg	TD
1967	NO	N	50	721	14.4	80t	6
1968			54	890	16.5	47t	7
1969			73	1015	13.9	49t	7
1970			55	906	16.5	48	5
1971			37	657	17.8	63t	5
1972			38	668	17.6	51	7
1973	NO-SF	N	37	460	12.4	54	1
1974	SF	N	25	369	14.8	30	1
Career			369	5686	15.4	80t	39

Mike Adamle

Year	Team		No	Yds	Avg	Lg	TD
1971	KC	N	1	6	6.0	6t	1
1972			15	76	5.1	11	0
1973	NYJ	N	9	63	7.0	13	0
1974			9	84	9.3	16	0
1975	CHI	N	15	111	7.4	25	0
1976			4	28	7.0	12	1
Career			53	368	6.9	25	2

Tony Adamle

Year	Team		No	Yds	Avg	Lg	TD
1947	CLE	AA	1	22	22.0	22	0
1949			1	13	13.0	13	0
Career			2	35	17.5	22	0

Bob Adams

Year	Team		No	Yds	Avg	Lg	TD
1969	PIT	N	6	80	13.3	19	0
1970			3	36	12.0	17	0
1971			20	160	8.0	21	0
1973	NE	N	14	197	14.1	30	0
1974			17	244	14.4	29.	0
1976	ATL	N	1	15	15.0	15	0
Career			61	732	12.0	30	0

Chet Adams

Year	Team		No	Yds	Avg	Lg	TD
1940	CLE	N	2	28	14.0		0

Curtis Adams

Year	Team		No	Yds	Avg	Lg	TD
1985	SD	N	1	12	12.0	12	0
1986			4	26	6.5	10	0
1987			4	38	9.5	21	0
Career			9	76	8.4	21	0

David Adams

Year	Team		No	Yds	Avg	Lg	TD
1987	DAL	N	1	8	8.0	8	0

George Adams

Year	Team		No	Yds	Avg	Lg	TD
1985	NYG	N	31	389	12.5	70t	2
1987			35	298	8.5	25	1
1988			27	174	6.4	19	0
1989			2	7	3.5	10	0
1990	NE	N	16	146	9.1	28	0
Career			111	1014	9.1	70t	4
Playoffs			4	70	17.5		0

John Adams

Year	Team		No	Yds	Avg	Lg	TD
1960	CHI	N	2	-20	-10.0	0	0
1961			5	80	16.0	36	0
1962			5	111	22.2	59t	3

John Adams *continued*

Year	Team		No	Yds	Avg	Lg	TD
1963	LA	N	9	93	10.3	19	0
Career			21	264	12.6	59t	3

O'Neal Adams

Year	Team		No	Yds	Avg	Lg	TD
1942	NYG	N	6	87	14.5	24	3
1943			8	65	8.1	17	1
1944			13	342	26.3	39	1
1946	BKN	AA	15	225	15.0		2
Career			42	719	17.1	39	7

Tom Adams

Year	Team		No	Yds	Avg	Lg	TD
1962	MIN	N	3	51	17.0	22	0

Tony Adams

Year	Team		No	Yds	Avg	Lg	TD
1975	KC	N	1	-7	-7.0	-7	0

Verlin Adams

Year	Team		No	Yds	Avg	Lg	TD
1944	NYG	N	1	12	12.0	12	0

Willis Adams

Year	Team		No	Yds	Avg	Lg	TD
1979	CLE	N	1	6	6.0	6	0
1980			8	165	20.6	39	0
1981			1	24	24.0	24	0
1983			20	374	18.7	59	2
1984			21	261	12.4	24	0
1985			10	132	13.2	22	0
Career			61	962	15.8	59	2

Mark Adickes

Year	Team		No	Yds	Avg	Lg	TD
1987	KC	N	1	3	3.0	3t	1

Bob Adkins

Year	Team		No	Yds	Avg	Lg	TD
1940	GB	N	4	73	18.3		1

Margene Adkins

Year	Team		No	Yds	Avg	Lg	TD
1971	DAL	N	4	53	13.3	23	0
1972	NO	N	9	96	10.7	38	0
1973	NYJ	N	6	109	18.2	29	0
Career			19	258	13.6	38	0

Erik Affholter

Year	Team		No	Yds	Avg	Lg	TD
1991	GB	N	7	68	9.7	20	0

Sam Agee

Year	Team		No	Yds	Avg	Lg	TD
1938	CHIC	N	2	5	2.5		0
1939			1	6	6.0	6	0
Career			3	11	3.7	6	0

Tommie Agee

Year	Team		No	Yds	Avg	Lg	TD
1988	SEA	N	3	31	10.3	13	0
1990	DAL	N	30	272	9.1	30	1
1991			7	43	6.1	9	0
1992			3	18	6.0	8	0
1994			1	2	2.0	2	0
Career			44	366	8.3	30	1
Playoffs			1	-4	-4.0		0

Joe Aguirre

Year	Team		No	Yds	Avg	Lg	TD
1941	WAS	N	10	103	10.3	17	2
1943			37	420	11.4	44	7
1944			34	410	12.1	58t	4
1945			16	289	18.1	28	0
1946	LA	AA	14	246	17.6	68t	2
1947			8	158	19.8	51t	4
1948			38	599	15.8	67	9
1949			3	37	12.3		1
Career			160	2262	14.1	58t	29
Playoffs			3	46	15.3		1

Dave Ahrens

Year	Team		No	Yds	Avg	Lg	TD
1983	STL	N	1	4	4.0	4	0

Carl Aikens

Year	Team		No	Yds	Avg	Lg	TD
1987	LARI	N	8	134	16.8	32t	3

Troy Aikman

Year	Team		No	Yds	Avg	Lg	TD
1989	DAL	N	1	-13	-13.0	-13	0
1991			1	-6	-6.0	-6	0
Career			2	-19	-9.5	-6	0

Al Akins

Year	Team		No	Yds	Avg	Lg	TD
1947	BKN	AA	6	101	16.8	60t	1

Al Akins *continued*

Year	Team		No	Yds	Avg	Lg	TD
1948	BKN-BUF	AA	3	12	4.0		0
Career			9	113	12.6	60t	1

Frank Akins

Year	Team		No	Yds	Avg	Lg	TD
1943	WAS	N	1	52	52.0	52	0
1944			5	27	5.4	9	0
1945			8	57	7.1	18	0
1946			2	15	7.5	8	0
Career			16	151	9.4	51	0

Mike Akiu

Year	Team		No	Yds	Avg	Lg	TD
1985	HOU	N	2	32	16.0	24	0
1986			4	67	16.8	27	0
Career			6	99	16.5	27	0

Frankie Albert

Year	Team		No	Yds	Avg	Lg	TD
1948	SF	AA	1	1	1.0	1	0

Bennie Aldridge

Year	Team		No	Yds	Avg	Lg	TD
1950	NYY	N	4	56	14.0	28	0
1952	SF	N	4	22	5.5	16t	1
Career			8	78	9.8	28	1

Charles Alexander

Year	Team		No	Yds	Avg	Lg	TD
1979	CIN	N	11	91	8.3	13	0
1980			36	192	5.3	23	0
1981			28	262	9.4	65t	1
1982			14	85	6.1	14	1
1983			32	187	5.8	14	0
1984			29	203	7.0	22	0
1985			15	110	7.3	19	0
Career			165	1130	6.8	65t	2
Playoffs			6	38	6.3		0

Dan Alexander

Year	Team		No	Yds	Avg	Lg	TD
Playoffs			1	-1	-1.0		0

David Alexander

Year	Team		No	Yds	Avg	Lg	TD
1994	PHI	N	2	1	0.5	1	0

Derrick Alexander

Year	Team		No	Yds	Avg	Lg	TD
1994	CLE	N	48	828	17.3	81t	2
1995			15	216	14.4	40	0
1996	BAL	N	62	1099	17.7	64t	9
Career			125	2143	17.1	81t	11
Playoffs			5	69	13.8		0

Glenn Alexander

Year	Team		No	Yds	Avg	Lg	TD
1970	BUF	N	4	51	12.8	16	0

Jeff Alexander

Year	Team		No	Yds	Avg	Lg	TD
1989	DEN	N	8	84	10.5	28	0

Kevin Alexander

Year	Team		No	Yds	Avg	Lg	TD
1996	NYG	N	4	88	22.0	35	0

Mike Alexander

Year	Team		No	Yds	Avg	Lg	TD
1989	LARI	N	15	295	19.7	61	1
1991	BUF	N	1	7	7.0	7	0
Career			16	302	18.9	61	1

Ray Alexander

Year	Team		No	Yds	Avg	Lg	TD
1984	DEN	N	8	132	16.5	41	1
1988	DAL	N	54	788	14.6	50t	6
1989			1	16	16.0	16	0
Career			63	936	14.9	50t	7
Playoffs			1	9	9.0		0

Robert Alexander

Year	Team		No	Yds	Avg	Lg	TD
1982	LARM	N	1	-7	-7.0	-7	0
1983			1	10	10.0	10	0
Career			2	3	1.5	10	0

Vincent Alexander

Year	Team		No	Yds	Avg	Lg	TD
1987	NO	N	2	15	7.5	10	0

Julie Alfonse

Year	Team		No	Yds	Avg	Lg	TD
1937	CLE	N	5	113	22.6		0
1938			2	47	23.5		0
Career			7	160	22.9		0

Bruce Alford

Year	Team		No	Yds	Avg	Lg	TD
1946	NY	AA	13	173	13.3		0

Bruce Alford (continued)

Year	Team		No	Yds	Avg	Lg	TD
1947			20	298	14.9	52t	5
1948			32	578	18.1	57	3
1949	B-NY	AA	11	213	19.4		1
1950	NYY	N	1	14	14.0	14	0
1951			4	65	16.3	59	0
Career			81	1341	16.6	59	9

Gene Alford

Year	Team		No	Yds	Avg	Lg	TD
1931	POR	N					1
1933							1
Career							2

Anthony Allen

Year	Team		No	Yds	Avg	Lg	TD
1985	ATL	N	14	207	14.8	37t	2
1986			10	156	15.6	32	2
1987	WAS	N	13	337	25.9	88t	3
1988			5	48	9.6	18	1
1989	SD	N	2	19	9.5	11	0
Career			44	767	17.4	88t	8
Playoffs			1	9	9.0		0

Don Allen

Year	Team		No	Yds	Avg	Lg	TD
1960	DEN	A	5	34	6.8	17	0

Duane Allen

Year	Team		No	Yds	Avg	Lg	TD
1961	LA	N	2	80	40.0	48t	2
1962			3	90	30.0	43t	2
1964			2	29	14.5	19	1
1966	CHI	N	3	28	9.3	14	0
Career			10	227	22.7	48t	5

Gary Allen

Year	Team		No	Yds	Avg	Lg	TD
1982	HOU	N	2	35	17.5	23t	1

Jerry Allen

Year	Team		No	Yds	Avg	Lg	TD
1967	WAS	N	11	101	9.2	21	1
1968			21	294	14.0	99t	1
1969			1	5	5.0	5	0
Career			33	400	12.1	99t	2

Marcus Allen

Year	Team		No	Yds	Avg	Lg	TD
1982	LARI	N	38	401	10.6	51t	3
1983			68	590	8.7	36	2
1984			64	758	11.8	92	5
1985			67	555	8.3	44	3
1986			46	453	9.8	36	2
1987			51	410	8.0	39	0
1988			34	303	8.9	30t	1
1989			20	191	9.6	26	0
1990			15	189	12.6	30	1
1991			15	131	8.7	25	0
1992			28	277	9.9	40	1
1993	KC	N	34	238	7.0	18t	3
1994			42	349	8.3	38	0
1995			27	210	7.8	20	0
1996			27	270	10.0	59	0
Career			576	5325	9.2	92	21
Playoffs			52	522	10.0		2

Marvin Allen

Year	Team		No	Yds	Avg	Lg	TD
1990	NE	N	6	48	8.0	19	0
1991			1	9	9.0	9	0
Career			7	57	8.1	19	0

Nate Allen

Year	Team		No	Yds	Avg	Lg	TD
1972	KC	N	1	20	20.0	20	0

Terry Allen

Year	Team		No	Yds	Avg	Lg	TD
1991	MIN	N	6	49	8.2	21	1
1992			49	478	9.8	36t	2
1994			17	148	8.7	31	0
1995	WAS	N	31	232	7.5	24	1
1996			32	194	6.1	28	0
Career			135	1101	8.2	36t	4
Playoffs			3	12	4.0		0

Don Alley

Year	Team		No	Yds	Avg	Lg	TD
1967	BAL	N	1	11	11.0	11	0
1969	PIT	N	1	16	16.0	16	0
Career			2	27	13.5	16	0

Jim Allison

Year	Team		No	Yds	Avg	Lg	TD
1965	SD	A	8	109	13.6	44	0

Jim Allison (continued)

Year	Team		No	Yds	Avg	Lg	TD
1966			12	99	8.3	20	0
1968			2	22	11.0	12	0
Career			22	230	10.5	44	0

Neely Allison

Year	Team		No	Yds	Avg	Lg	TD
1926	BUF	N					1

Gerald Alphin

Year	Team		No	Yds	Avg	Lg	TD
1990	NO	N	4	57	14.3	17	0

Lyneal Alston

Year	Team		No	Yds	Avg	Lg	TD
1987	PIT	N	3	84	28.0	42t	2

Mack Alston

Year	Team		No	Yds	Avg	Lg	TD
1971	WAS	N	5	87	17.4	21	0
1972			2	53	26.5	36	0
1973	HOU	N	19	195	10.3	39t	4
1974			17	249	14.6	33	3
1975			18	165	9.2	26	4
1976			19	174	9.2	29	1
1978	BAL	N	18	210	11.7	23	2
1979			10	114	11.4	26	1
Career			108	1247	11.5	39t	15

Mike Alstott

Year	Team		No	Yds	Avg	Lg	TD
1996	TB	N	65	557	8.6	29	3

Lance Alworth

Year	Team		No	Yds	Avg	Lg	TD
1962	SD	A	10	226	22.6	67	3
1963			61	1206	19.8	85	11
1964			61	1235	20.2	82	**13**
1965			69	**1602**	**23.2**	85	**14**
1966			**73**	**1383**	18.9	78	**13**
1967			52	1010	19.4	71t	9
1968			**68**	**1312**	19.3	80t	10
1969			**64**	1003	15.7	76t	4
1970	SD	N	35	608	17.4	80t	4
1971	DAL	N	34	487	14.3	26	2
1972			15	195	13.0	30	2
Career			542	10267	18.9	85	85
Playoffs			16	292	18.3		2

John Amberg

Year	Team		No	Yds	Avg	Lg	TD
1952	NYG	N	3	40	13.3	18	0

Alan Ameche

Year	Team		No	Yds	Avg	Lg	TD
1955	BAL	N	27	141	5.2	18	0
1956			26	189	7.3	22	0
1957			15	137	9.1	40	2
1958			13	81	6.2	18	1
1959			13	129	9.9	30	1
1960			7	56	8.0	19	0
Career			101	733	7.3	40	4
Playoffs			4	26	6.5		0

Dave Ames

Year	Team		No	Yds	Avg	Lg	TD
1961	DEN	A	6	20	3.3	9	0

George Amundson

Year	Team		No	Yds	Avg	Lg	TD
1973	HOU	N	7	60	8.6	18	0
1974			18	152	8.4	29	1
Career			25	212	8.5	29	1

Kimble Anders

Year	Team		No	Yds	Avg	Lg	TD
1991	KC	N	2	30	15.0	23	0
1992			5	65	13.0	28	0
1993			40	326	8.2	27	1
1994			67	525	7.8	30	1
1995			55	349	6.3	28	1
1996			60	529	8.8	45	2
Career			229	1824	8.0	45	5
Playoffs			17	184	10.8		1

Stan Andersen

Year	Team		No	Yds	Avg	Lg	TD
1941	DET-CLE	N	7	79	11.3	24	0

Alfred Anderson

Year	Team		No	Yds	Avg	Lg	TD
1984	MIN	N	17	102	6.0	28t	1
1985			16	175	10.9	54t	1
1986			17	179	10.5	37t	2
1987			7	69	9.9	22	0
1988			23	242	10.5	19	1
1989			20	193	9.7	18	0

Alfred Anderson (continued)

Year	Team		No	Yds	Avg	Lg	TD
1990			13	80	6.2	17	0
1991			1	2	2.0	2	0
Career			114	1042	9.1	54t	5
Playoffs			11	67	6.1		0

Bill Anderson

Year	Team		No	Yds	Avg	Lg	TD
1958	WAS	N	18	396	22.0	71t	2
1959			35	734	21.0	70t	6
1960			38	488	12.8	48	3
1961			40	637	15.9	42	0
1962			23	386	16.8	46t	2
1963			14	288	20.6	49	1
1966	GB	N	2	14	7.0	8	0
Career			170	2943	17.3	71t	14
Playoffs			8	78	9.8		0

Billy Anderson

Year	Team		No	Yds	Avg	Lg	TD
1953	CHIB	N	3	33	11.0	16	0

Bobby Anderson

Year	Team		No	Yds	Avg	Lg	TD
1970	DEN	N	9	140	15.6	37	0
1971			37	353	9.5	31	1
1972			23	215	9.3	40	1
1973			15	153	10.2	29	0
Career			84	861	10.3	40	2

Brad Anderson

Year	Team		No	Yds	Avg	Lg	TD
1984	CHI	N	3	77	25.7	49t	1
1985			1	6	6.0	6	0
Career			4	83	20.8	49t	1

Chet Anderson

Year	Team		No	Yds	Avg	Lg	TD
1967	PIT	N	8	141	17.6	48	2

Cliff Anderson

Year	Team		No	Yds	Avg	Lg	TD
1952	CHIC	N	11	191	17.4	30	2
1953	CHIC-NYG	N	17	266	15.6	32	0
Career			28	457	16.3	32	2

Dick Anderson

Year	Team		No	Yds	Avg	Lg	TD
1969	MIA	A	1	8	8.0	8	0

Donny Anderson

Year	Team		No	Yds	Avg	Lg	TD
1960	LA	A	44	614	14.0	46	5
1965	GB	N	8	105	13.1	27t	1
1966			2	33	16.5	22	0
1967			22	331	15.0	37	3
1968			25	333	13.3	47t	1
1969			14	308	22.0	51	1
1970			36	414	11.5	34	0
1971			26	306	11.8	39	1
1972	STL	N	28	298	10.6	56	2
1973			41	409	10.0	44	3
1974			15	116	7.7	25	3
Career			261	3267	12.5	56	20
Playoffs			8	92	11.5		0

Eddie Anderson

Year	Team		No	Yds	Avg	Lg	TD
1925	CHIC	N					1

Ezz Anderson

Year	Team		No	Yds	Avg	Lg	TD
1947	LA	AA	11	126	11.5		1

Flipper Anderson

Year	Team		No	Yds	Avg	Lg	TD
1988	LARM	N	11	319	29.0	56	0
1989			44	1146	**26.0**	78t	5
1990			51	1097	**21.5**	55t	4
1991			32	530	16.6	54	1
1992			38	657	17.3	51	7
1993			37	552	14.9	56t	4
1994			46	945	20.5	72t	5
1995	IND	N	8	111	13.9	28	2
Career			267	5357	20.1	78t	28
Playoffs			7	170	24.3		2

Gary Anderson

Year	Team		No	Yds	Avg	Lg	TD
1985	SD	N	35	422	12.1	52t	2
1986			80	871	10.9	65t	8
1987			47	503	10.7	38	2
1988			32	182	5.7	20	0
1990	TB	N	38	464	12.2	74	2
1991			25	184	7.4	21	0

Gary Anderson *continued*

Year	Team		No	Yds	Avg	Lg	TD
1992			34	284	8.4	34	0
1993			11	89	8.1	28	1
Career			302	2999	9.9	74	15

Jamal Anderson

Year	Team		No	Yds	Avg	Lg	TD
1995	ATL	N	4	42	10.5	17	0
1996			49	473	9.7	34	1
Career			53	515	9.7	34	1

Jesse Anderson

Year	Team		No	Yds	Avg	Lg	TD
1990	TB	N	5	77	15.4	52	0
1991			6	73	12.2	34	2
Career			11	150	13.6	52	2

Marcus Anderson

Year	Team		No	Yds	Avg	Lg	TD
1981	CHI	N	9	243	27.0	85t	2

Max Anderson

Year	Team		No	Yds	Avg	Lg	TD
1968	BUF	A	22	140	6.4	23	0
1969			7	65	9.3	22	0
Career			29	205	7.1	23	0

Neal Anderson

Year	Team		No	Yds	Avg	Lg	TD
1986	CHI	N	4	80	20.0	58t	1
1987			47	467	9.9	59t	3
1988			39	371	9.5	36	0
1989			50	434	8.7	49t	4
1990			42	484	11.5	50t	3
1991			47	368	7.8	26t	3
1992			42	399	9.5	30t	6
1993			31	160	5.2	35	0
Career			302	2763	9.1	59t	20
Playoffs			17	107	6.3		0

Ockie Anderson

Year	Team		No	Yds	Avg	Lg	TD
1921	BUF	A					1
1922	BUF	N					1
Career							2

O.J. Anderson

Year	Team		No	Yds	Avg	Lg	TD
1979	STL	N	41	308	7.5	28	2
1980			36	308	8.6	35	0
1981			51	387	7.6	27	0
1982			14	106	7.6	19	0
1983			54	459	8.5	40	1
1984			70	611	8.7	57	2
1985			23	225	9.8	43	0
1986	STL-NYG	N	19	137	7.2	19	0
1987	NYG	N	2	16	8.0	9	0
1988			9	57	6.3	13	0
1989			28	268	9.6	26	0
1990			18	139	7.7	18	0
1991			11	41	3.7	13	0
Career			376	3062	8.1	57	5
Playoffs			6	14	2.3		0

Ralph Anderson

Year	Team		No	Yds	Avg	Lg	TD
1958	CHIB	N	11	177	16.1	30t	1

Richie Anderson

Year	Team		No	Yds	Avg	Lg	TD
1994	NYJ	N	25	212	8.5	27t	1
1995			5	26	5.2	9	0
1996			44	385	8.8	48	0
Career			74	623	8.4	48	1

Rickey Anderson

Year	Team		No	Yds	Avg	Lg	TD
1978	SD	N	1	-3	-3.0	-3	0

Stevie Anderson

Year	Team		No	Yds	Avg	Lg	TD
1994	NYJ	N	9	90	10.0	17	0
1995	ARI	N	3	34	11.3	18	1
1996			4	64	16.0	19	0
Career			16	188	11.8	19	1

Taz Anderson

Year	Team		No	Yds	Avg	Lg	TD
1961	STL	N	22	399	18.1	78	2
1962			35	535	15.3	51	3
1963			5	47	9.4	16	0
1964			7	60	8.6	13	0
1966	ATL	N	10	195	19.5	62t	3
1967			8	99	12.4	21t	1
Career			87	1335	15.3	78	9

Terry Anderson

Year	Team		No	Yds	Avg	Lg	TD
1978	WAS	N	1	56	56.0	56	0

Vickey Ray Anderson

Year	Team		No	Yds	Avg	Lg	TD
1980	GB	N	2	2	1.0	2	0

Winnie Anderson

Year	Team		No	Yds	Avg	Lg	TD
1936	NYG	N	7	74	10.6		0

George Andrews

Year	Team		No	Yds	Avg	Lg	TD
1979	LA	N	1	2	2.0	2	0

John Andrews

Year	Team		No	Yds	Avg	Lg	TD
1973	BAL	N	1	1	1.0	1t	1

Mitch Andrews

Year	Team		No	Yds	Avg	Lg	TD
1987	DEN	N	4	53	13.3	20	0

William Andrews

Year	Team		No	Yds	Avg	Lg	TD
1979	ATL	N	39	309	7.9	34	2
1980			51	456	8.9	26	1
1981			81	735	9.1	70t	2
1982			42	503	12.0	86t	2
1983			59	609	10.3	40	4
1986			5	35	7.0	14	0
Career			277	2647	9.6	86t	11
Playoffs			2	19	9.5		1

Teddy Andrulewicz

Year	Team		No	Yds	Avg	Lg	TD
1930	NEW	N					1

Elmer Angsman

Year	Team		No	Yds	Avg	Lg	TD
1946	CHIC	N	2	44	22.0	38	0
1947			5	138	27.6	52	1
1948			9	142	15.8	38t	1
1949			5	57	11.4	32	0
1950			7	56	8.0	20	1
1951			9	195	21.7	80t	1
1952			4	22	5.5	9	1
Career			41	654	16.0	80t	5
Playoffs			1	-4	-4.0		0

Dunc Annan

Year	Team		No	Yds	Avg	Lg	TD
1922	TOL	N					2

Terry Anthony

Year	Team		No	Yds	Avg	Lg	TD
1991	TB	N	4	51	12.8	14	0

Tyrone Anthony

Year	Team		No	Yds	Avg	Lg	TD
1984	NO	N	12	113	9.4	32	0
1985			28	185	6.6	36	0
Career			40	298	7.5	36	0

Fred Arbanas

Year	Team		No	Yds	Avg	Lg	TD
1962	DAL	A	29	469	16.2	47	6
1963	KC	A	34	373	11.0	40	6
1964			34	686	20.2	59	8
1965			24	418	17.4	67	4
1966			22	305	13.9	36	4
1967			20	295	14.8	43	5
1968			11	189	17.2	48	0
1969			16	258	16.1	44	0
1970	KC	N	8	108	13.5	26t	1
Career			198	3101	15.7	67	34
Playoffs			9	144	16.0		1

Charles Arbuckle

Year	Team		No	Yds	Avg	Lg	TD
1992	IND	N	13	152	11.7	23t	1
1993			15	90	6.0	23	0
1994			1	7	7.0	7	0
1995			4	33	8.3	12	0
Career			33	282	8.5	23t	1

Joe Arenas

Year	Team		No	Yds	Avg	Lg	TD
1951	SF	N	1	12	12.0	12	1
1952			5	47	9.4	14	1
1953			10	113	11.3	38	1
1954			2	12	6.0	12	0
1955			13	255	19.6	53t	2
1956			14	226	16.1	50	1
1957			1	10	10.0	10	0
Career			46	675	14.7	53t	6

Justin Armour

Year	Team		No	Yds	Avg	Lg	TD
1995	BUF	N	26	300	11.5	28t	3

Adger Armstrong

Year	Team		No	Yds	Avg	Lg	TD
1981	HOU	N	29	278	9.6	48	1
1982			12	75	6.3	14	0
1983	TB	N	15	173	11.5	41	2
1984			22	180	8.2	18	3
1985			2	4	2.0	3	1
Career			80	710	8.9	48	7

Graham Armstrong

Year	Team		No	Yds	Avg	Lg	TD
1948	BUF	AA	1	0	0.0	0	0

Johnny Armstrong

Year	Team		No	Yds	Avg	Lg	TD
1925	RI	N					3

Neill Armstrong

Year	Team		No	Yds	Avg	Lg	TD
1947	PHI	N	17	197	11.6	46	2
1948			24	325	13.5	33	3
1949			24	271	11.3	45	5
1950			8	124	15.5	36	1
1951			3	44	14.7	18	0
Career			76	961	12.6	46	11
Playoffs			2	16	8.0		0

Otis Armstrong

Year	Team		No	Yds	Avg	Lg	TD
1973	DEN	N	2	43	21.5	36t	1
1974			38	405	10.7	48t	3
1975			1	10	10.0	10	0
1976			39	457	11.7	36t	1
1977			18	128	7.1	20	0
1978			12	98	8.2	19	1
1979			14	138	9.9	17	1
1980			7	23	3.3	8	0
Career			131	1302	9.9	48t	7
Playoffs			3	31	10.3		0

Tyji Armstrong

Year	Team		No	Yds	Avg	Lg	TD
1992	TB	N	7	138	19.7	81t	1
1993			9	86	9.6	29	1
1994			22	265	12.0	29	1
1995			7	68	9.7	29	0
1996	DAL	N	2	10	5.0	6	0
Career			47	567	12.1	81t	3

Jon Arnett

Year	Team		No	Yds	Avg	Lg	TD
1957	LA	N	18	322	17.9	66t	3
1958			35	494	14.1	75t	1
1959			38	419	11.0	38t	1
1960			29	226	7.8	24t	2
1961			28	194	6.9	29	0
1962			12	137	11.4	40	1
1963			15	119	7.9	41	1
1964	CHI	N	25	223	8.9	27	2
1965			12	114	9.5	30	0
1966			10	42	4.2	10	0
Career			222	2290	10.3	75t	10

Jahine Arnold

Year	Team		No	Yds	Avg	Lg	TD
1996	PIT	N	6	76	12.7	26	0
Playoffs			2	16	8.0		0

Jay Arnold

Year	Team		No	Yds	Avg	Lg	TD
1937	PHI	N	8	142	17.8		0
1938			6	74	12.3		2
1939			13	207	15.9		1
1940			7	145	20.7		0
1941	PIT	N	1	5	5.0	5	0
Career			35	573	16.4	5	3

Walt Arnold

Year	Team		No	Yds	Avg	Lg	TD
1980	LA	N	5	75	15.0	33	1
1981			20	212	10.6	24	2
1983	HOU	N	12	137	11.4	37	1
1984	KC	N	11	95	8.6	15	1
1985			28	339	12.1	38	1
1986			20	169	8.4	27	1
1987			3	26	8.7	10	0
Career			99	1053	10.6	38	7

Arrowhead

Year	Team		No	Yds	Avg	Lg	TD
1923	OOR	N					2

Year	Team		No	Yds	Avg	Lg	TD

Gary Arthur

Year	Team		No	Yds	Avg	Lg	TD
1971	NYJ	N	1	12	12.0	12	0

Herman Arvie

1996	BAL	N	1	1	1.0	1t	1

Doug Asad

1960	OAK	A	14	197	14.1		1
1961			36	501	13.9	51	2
Career			50	698	14.0	51	3

Willie Asbury

1966	PIT	N	19	228	12.0	37t	2
1967			3	52	17.3	21	0
1968			3	27	9.0	16	0
Career			25	307	12.3	37t	2

Frank Aschenbrenner

1949	CHI	AA	2	-4	-2.0		0

Jamie Asher

1995	WAS	N	14	172	12.3	20	0
1996			42	481	11.5	34	4
Career			56	653	11.7	34	4

Josh Ashton

1972	NE	N	22	207	9.4	24t	1
1973			11	113	10.3	51	0
Career			33	320	9.7	51	1

Joe Aska

1996	OAK	N	8	63	7.9	22	0

Bert Askson

1975	GB	N	2	25	12.5	18	0
1976			1	2	2.0	2t	1
1977			2	51	25.5	34	0
Career			5	78	15.6	34	1

Jack Atchason

1960	BOS-HOU	A	5	48	9.6		1

Dale Atkeson

1954	WAS	N	4	75	18.8	45	0
1955			9	81	9.0	15	1
1956			6	28	4.7	26	0
Career			19	184	9.7	45	1

Dave Atkins

1973	SF	N	1	-3	-3.0	-3	0

Pervis Atkins

1961	LA	N	5	67	13.4	28	0
1962			35	393	11.2	48t	0
1963			14	174	12.4	21	1
1964	WAS	N	8	35	4.4	10	0
1965	WAS-OAK	N-A	2	6	3.0	6	0
Career			64	675	10.5	48t	2

Steve Atkins

1979	GB	N	10	89	8.9	19	0
1980			7	47	6.7	16	1
1981			1	2	2.0	2	0
Career			18	138	7.7	19	1

John Atwood

1948	NYG	N	10	141	14.1	54	1

Joe Auer

1964	BUF	A	11	166	15.1	43	0
1966	MIA	A	22	263	12.0	27	4
1967			18	218	12.1	68t	2
Career			51	647	12.7	68t	6

Steve August

1981	SEA	N	1	9	9.0	9	0

Mike Augustyniak

1981	NYJ	N	18	144	8.0	15	0
1982			24	189	7.9	15	0
1983			10	71	7.1	17	1
Career			52	404	7.8	17	1
Playoffs			5	34	6.8		0

Cliff Austin

1983	NO	N	2	25	12.5	18	0
1985	ATL	N	1	21	21.0	21	0
1986			3	21	7.0	9	0
1987	TB	N	5	51	10.2	20	0
Career			11	118	10.7	21	0

Jim Austin

1937	BKN	N	13	185	14.2		0
1938			14	180	12.9		1
1939	DET	N	5	102	20.4		0
Career			32	467	14.6		1

John Aveni

1961	WAS	N	6	84	14.0	4t	1

Steve Avery

1994	PIT	N	1	2	2.0	2	0
1995			11	82	7.5	18t	1
Career			12	84	7.0	18t	1

Clarence Avinger

1953	NYG	N	2	8	4.0	4	0

Rob Awalt

1987	STL	N	42	526	12.5	35	6
1988	PHX	N	39	454	11.6	52t	4
1989			33	360	10.9	28	0
1990	DAL	N	13	133	10.2	25	0
1991			5	57	11.4	20	0
1992	BUF	N	4	34	8.5	10	0
1993			2	19	9.5	10	0
Career			138	1583	11.5	52t	10
Playoffs			1	2	2.0		0

Gene Babb

1957	SF	N	20	141	7.0	17	0
1960	DAL	N	13	140	10.8	27t	1
Career			33	281	8.5	27t	1
Playoffs			1	1	1.0		0

Harry Babcock

1953	SF	N	7	59	8.4	13	0
1954			6	91	15.2	33	0
1955			3	31	10.3	16	0
Career			16	181	11.3	33	0

Carl Bacchus

1927	CLE	N					3
1928	DET	N					4
Career							7

Frank Bacon

1920	DAY	A					1
1921							1
Career							2

Rick Badanjek

1987	ATL	N	6	35	5.8	16	0

Red Badgro

1927	NYY	N					1
1930	NYG	N					3
1933			9	176	19.6		2
1934			16	206	12.9		1
1936	BKN	N	3	59	19.7		0
Career			28	441	15.8		7
Playoffs			2	38	19.0		1

Steve Bagarus

1945	WAS	N	35	623	17.8	70t	5
1946			31	438	14.1	51t	3
1948			15	100	6.7	14t	1
Career			81	1161	14.3	70t	9
Playoffs			3	95	31.7		1

Herm Bagby

1926	BKN	N					1

Eddie Bagdon

1950	CHIC	N	1	19	19.0	19	0

Billy Baggett

1952	DAL	N	3	41	13.7	27t	1

Aaron Bailey

1994	IND	N	2	30	15.0	23	0
1995			21	379	18.0	45	3
1996			18	302	16.8	40	0
Career			41	711	17.3	45	3
Playoffs			4	55	13.8		1

Bill Bailey

1940	BKN	N	1	12	12.0	12	0
1941			1	14	14.0	14	0
Career			2	26	13.0	14	0

By Bailey

1952	DET	N	2	28	14.0	24	0
1953	GB	N	8	119	14.9	50	0
Career			10	147	14.7	50	0

Edwin Bailey

1986	SEA	N	1	3	3.0	3	0

Elmer Bailey

1980	MIA	N	4	105	26.3	39	0

Eric Bailey

1987	PHI	N	8	69	8.6	19	0

Harold Bailey

1982	HOU	N	26	367	14.1	27	0

Henry Bailey

1996	NYJ	N	5	65	13.0	28	0

Johnny Bailey

1992	PHX	N	33	331	10.0	34	1
1993			32	243	7.6	30	0
1994	LARM	N	58	516	8.9	28	0
1995	STL	N	38	265	7.0	25	0
Career			161	1355	8.4	34	1

Mark Bailey

1977	KC	N	17	206	12.1	47t	0
1978			5	13	2.6	15	0
Career			22	219	10.0	47t	0

Stacey Bailey

1982	ATL	N	2	24	12.0	15	1
1983			55	881	16.0	53	6
1984			67	1138	17.0	61	6
1985			30	364	12.1	31	0
1986			3	39	13.0	21	0
1987			20	325	16.3	35	3
1988			17	437	25.7	68t	2
1989			8	170	21.3	41	0
1990			4	44	11.0	13	0
Career			206	3422	16.6	68t	18

Tom Bailey

1971	PHI	N	7	55	7.9	24	0
1972			5	32	6.4	9	0
1973			10	80	8.0	19	1
1974			6	27	4.5	15	0
Career			28	194	6.9	24	1

Victor Bailey

1993	PHI	N	41	545	13.3	58	0
1994			20	311	15.6	61	1
1996	KC	N	1	12	12.0	12	0
Career			62	868	14.0	61	2

Art Baker

1961	BUF	A	6	73	12.2	29	0
1962			3	12	4.0	9	0
Career			9	85	9.4	29	0

Bullet Baker

1926	NY	A					1

Frank Baker

1931	GB	N					1

Johnny Baker

1964	HOU	A	2	18	9.0	10	0

Keith Baker

Year	Team		No	Yds	Avg	Lg	TD
1985	PHI	N	2	25	12.5	20	0

Melvin Baker

Year	Team		No	Yds	Avg	Lg	TD
1974	MIA	N	4	121	30.3	46t	2
1975	NO	N	2	26	13.0	17	0
1976	HOU	N	3	32	10.7	14	0
Career			9	179	19.9	46t	2

Sam Baker

Year	Team		No	Yds	Avg	Lg	TD
1953	WAS	N	2	21	10.5	11	0
1956			4	35	8.8	17	0
1968	PHI	N	1	3	3.0	3	0
Career			7	59	8.4	17	0

Shannon Baker

Year	Team		No	Yds	Avg	Lg	TD
1994	IND	N	2	15	7.5	10	0

Stephen Baker

Year	Team		No	Yds	Avg	Lg	TD
1987	NYG	N	15	277	18.5	50	2
1988			40	656	16.4	85t	7
1989			13	255	19.6	39t	2
1990			26	541	20.8	80t	4
1991			30	525	17.5	52	4
1992			17	333	19.6	46	2
Career			141	2587	18.3	85t	21
Playoffs			9	157	17.4		2

Terry Baker

Year	Team		No	Yds	Avg	Lg	TD
1964	LA	N	8	92	11.5	31	0
1965			22	210	9.5	38t	2
Career			30	302	10.1	38t	2

Tony Baker

Year	Team		No	Yds	Avg	Lg	TD
1969	NO	N	34	352	10.4	35	1
1970			12	47	3.9	11	0
1971	NO-PHI	N	10	80	8.0	29t	1
1972	PHI	N	16	114	7.1	14	0
1974	LA	N	4	65	16.3	42	0
1975	SD	N	6	27	4.5	7	0
Career			82	685	8.4	42	2

Tony Baker

Year	Team		No	Yds	Avg	Lg	TD
1989	PHX	N	2	18	9.0	9	0

Ed Balatti

Year	Team		No	Yds	Avg	Lg	TD
1946	SF	AA	4	15	3.8		0
1947			8	98	12.3		1
Career			12	113	9.4		1

Frank Balazs

Year	Team		No	Yds	Avg	Lg	TD
1939	GB	N	1	11	11.0	11	0
1940			1	7	7.0	7	0
1941	GB-CHIC	N	2	17	8.5	9	0
1945	CHIC	N	1	15	15.0	15	0
Career			5	50	10.0	15	0

Lou Baldacci

Year	Team		No	Yds	Avg	Lg	TD
1956	PIT	N	5	62	12.4	22	0

Brian Baldinger

Year	Team		No	Yds	Avg	Lg	TD
1988	IND	N	1	37	37.0	37	0

Al Baldwin

Year	Team		No	Yds	Avg	Lg	TD
1947	BUF	AA	25	468	18.7	59t	7
1948			54	916	17.0	58t	8
1949			53	719	13.6		7
1950	GB	N	28	555	19.8	85t	3
Career			160	2658	16.6	85t	25
Playoffs			3	64	21.3		2

Burr Baldwin

Year	Team		No	Yds	Avg	Lg	TD
1947	LA	AA	12	275	22.9		1
1948			10	96	9.6		0
1949			2	26	13.0		0
Career			24	397	16.5		1

Randy Baldwin

Year	Team		No	Yds	Avg	Lg	TD
1992	CLE	N	2	30	15.0	20	0
1993			1	5	5.0	5t	0
1994			3	15	5.0	15	0
Career			6	50	8.3	20	1

Eric Ball

Year	Team		No	Yds	Avg	Lg	TD
1989	CIN	N	6	44	7.3	15	0
1990			2	46	23.0	48t	1
1991			3	17	5.7	9	0
1992			6	66	11.0	35t	2
1993			4	39	9.8	24	0
1994			1	4	4.0	4	0
Career			22	216	9.8	48t	3

Gary Ballman

Year	Team		No	Yds	Avg	Lg	TD
1963	PIT	N	26	492	18.9	67t	5
1964			47	935	19.9	47t	7
1965			40	859	21.5	87t	5
1966			41	663	16.2	79t	5
1967	PHI	N	36	524	14.6	67t	6
1968			30	341	11.4	55t	4
1969			31	492	15.9	80t	2
1970			47	601	12.8	26	3
1971			13	238	18.3	57	0
1972			9	183	20.3	43	0
1973	NYG-MIN	N	3	38	12.7	16	0
Career			323	5366	16.6	87t	37

Pete Banaszak

Year	Team		No	Yds	Avg	Lg	TD
1966	OAK	A	1	11	11.0	11	0
1967			16	192	12.0	72	1
1968			15	182	12.1	49t	1
1969			17	119	7.0	19	3
1970	OAK	N	1	2	2.0	2	0
1971			13	128	9.8	28	0
1972			9	63	7.0	16	0
1973			6	31	5.2	9	0
1974			9	64	7.1	12	0
1975			10	64	6.4	11	0
1976			15	74	4.9	20	0
1977			2	14	7.0	8	0
1978			1	78	11.1	20	0
Career			121	1022	8.4	72	5
Playoffs			15	133	8.9		1

Bruno Banducci

Year	Team		No	Yds	Avg	Lg	TD
1950	SF	N	0	11		11tL	1
1952			1	-4	-4.0	-4	0
Career			1	7	7.0	11tL	1

Herb Banet

Year	Team		No	Yds	Avg	Lg	TD
1937	GB	N	1	6	6.0	6	0

Emil Banjavic

Year	Team		No	Yds	Avg	Lg	TD
1942	DET	N	5	50	10.0	18	1

Carl Banks

Year	Team		No	Yds	Avg	Lg	TD
1989	NYG	N	1	22	22.0	22t	1

Chuck Banks

Year	Team		No	Yds	Avg	Lg	TD
1986	HOU	N	7	71	10.1	17	0
1987	IND	N	9	50	5.6	18	0
Career			16	121	7.6	18	0

Estes Banks

Year	Team		No	Yds	Avg	Lg	TD
1968	CIN	A	4	15	3.8	13	1

Fred Banks

Year	Team		No	Yds	Avg	Lg	TD
1985	CLE	N	5	62	12.4	17t	2
1987	MIA	N	1	10	10.0	10t	1
1988			23	430	18.7	55	2
1989			30	520	17.3	61	1
1990			13	131	10.1	23	0
1991			9	119	13.2	25	1
1992			22	319	14.5	39t	3
1993	MIA-CHI	N	2	45	22.5	26	0
Career			105	1636	15.6	61	10
Playoffs			2	18	9.0		0

Gordon Banks

Year	Team		No	Yds	Avg	Lg	TD
1980	NO	N	1	7	7.0	7	0
1981			2	18	9.0	12	0
1986	DAL	N	17	202	11.9	23	0
1987			15	231	15.4	34	1
Career			35	458	13.1	34	1

Warren Bankston

Year	Team		No	Yds	Avg	Lg	TD
1969	PIT	N	6	6	1.0	8	0
1970			7	30	4.3	20	0

Warren Bankston continued

Year	Team		No	Yds	Avg	Lg	TD
1971			17	148	8.7	31	0
1972			1	5	5.0	5	0
1975	OAK	N	2	21	10.5	13	1
1976			5	73	14.6	29	1
Career			38	283	7.4	31	2
Playoffs			2	11	5.5		1

Bradford Banta

Year	Team		No	Yds	Avg	Lg	TD
1995	IND	N	1	6	6.0	6	0

Jack Banta

Year	Team		No	Yds	Avg	Lg	TD
1941	PHI-WAS	N	2	42	21.0	37	0
1944	PHI	N	1	8	8.0	8	0
1945			1	10	10.0	10	0
1946	LA	N	8	81	10.1	32	1
1947			14	198	14.1	64	0
1948			4	34	8.5	14	0
Career			30	373	12.4	64	1

Marion Barber

Year	Team		No	Yds	Avg	Lg	TD
1983	NYJ	N	7	48	6.9	12	1
1984			10	79	7.9	17	0
1985			3	46	15.3	22	0
1986			5	36	7.2	16	0
Career			25	209	8.4	22	1

Mike Barber

Year	Team		No	Yds	Avg	Lg	TD
1977	HOU	N	9	94	10.4	23	1
1978			32	513	16.0	72t	3
1979			27	377	14.0	37t	3
1980			59	712	12.1	79t	5
1981			13	190	14.6	35	1
1982	LARM	N	18	166	9.2	21	1
1983			55	657	11.9	42t	3
1984			7	42	6.0	11	0
1985	LARM-DEN	N	2	37	18.5	29	0
Career			222	2788	12.6	79t	17
Playoffs			24	422	17.6		2

Mike Barber

Year	Team		No	Yds	Avg	Lg	TD
1990	CIN	N	14	196	14.0	28	1
1991			23	255	11.1	42t	1
1992	TB	N	1	32	32.0	32	0
Career			38	483	12.7	42t	2
Playoffs			1	12	12.0		0

Ed Barker

Year	Team		No	Yds	Avg	Lg	TD
1953	PIT	N	17	172	10.1	22	1
1954	WAS	N	23	353	15.3	32t	3
Career			40	525	13.1	32t	4

Hub Barker

Year	Team		No	Yds	Avg	Lg	TD
1944	NYG	N	3	34	11.3	16	0
Playoffs			1	0	0.0		0

Rod Barksdale

Year	Team		No	Yds	Avg	Lg	TD
1986	LARI	N	18	434	24.1	57t	2
1987	DAL	N	12	165	13.8	22	1
Career			30	599	20.0	57t	3

Jerome Barkum

Year	Team		No	Yds	Avg	Lg	TD
1972	NYJ	N	16	304	19.0	52	2
1973			44	810	18.4	63	6
1974			41	524	12.8	39	3
1975			36	549	15.3	56	5
1976			5	54	10.8	25	1
1977			26	450	17.3	40t	6
1978			28	391	14.0	27	3
1979			27	401	14.9	40	4
1980			13	244	18.8	28	1
1981			39	495	12.7	40t	7
1982			19	182	9.6	29	1
1983			32	385	12.0	34	1
Career			326	4789	14.7	63	40
Playoffs			6	81	13.5		0

Lou Barle

Year	Team		No	Yds	Avg	Lg	TD
1939	CLE	N	2	16	8.0		0

Reggie Barlow

Year	Team		No	Yds	Avg	Lg	TD
Playoffs			1	2	2.0		0

Year	Team		No	Yds	Avg	Lg	TD

Hap Barnard

Year	Team		No	Yds	Avg	Lg	TD
1938	NYG	N	1	33	33.0	33	0
Playoffs			1	20	20.0		1

Al Barnes

Year	Team		No	Yds	Avg	Lg	TD
1972	DET	N	4	58	14.5	17	1
1973			3	43	14.3	23t	1
Career			7	101	14.4	23t	2

Benny Barnes

Year	Team		No	Yds	Avg	Lg	TD
1974	DAL	N	1	37	37.0	37	0
1976			1	43	43.0	43	0
Career			2	80	40.0	43	0

Billy Ray Barnes

Year	Team		No	Yds	Avg	Lg	TD
1957	PHI	N	19	212	11.2	67t	1
1958			35	423	12.1	33	0
1959			32	314	9.8	47t	2
1960			19	132	6.9	16	2
1961			15	194	12.9	59t	3
1962	WAS	N	14	220	15.7	56	0
1963			15	256	17.1	54	1
1965	MIN	N	3	15	5.0	7	0
1966			1	20	20.0	20	0
Career			153	1786	11.7	67t	9
Playoffs			1	13	13.0		0

Charlie Barnes

Year	Team		No	Yds	Avg	Lg	TD
1961	DAL	A	1	13	13.0	13	0

Erich Barnes

Year	Team		No	Yds	Avg	Lg	TD
1961	NYG	N	2	74	37.0	62t	1

Gary Barnes

Year	Team		No	Yds	Avg	Lg	TD
1963	DAL	N	15	195	13.0	27	0
1964	CHI	N	4	61	15.3	33	0
1966	ATL	N	12	173	14.4	53t	1
1967			10	154	15.4	44	1
Career			41	583	14.2	53t	2

Johnnie Barnes

Year	Team		No	Yds	Avg	Lg	TD
1993	SD	N	10	137	13.7	21	0
1994			1	6	6.0	6	0
1995	PIT	N	3	48	16.0	25	0
Career			14	191	13.6	25	0

Larry Barnes

Year	Team		No	Yds	Avg	Lg	TD
1957	SF	N	1	1	1.0	1	0

Larry Barnes

Year	Team		No	Yds	Avg	Lg	TD
1977	SD	N	1	10	10.0	10	0
1978			2	13	6.5	7	0
1979	PHI	N	1	6	6.0	6	0
Career			4	29	7.3	10	0

Lew Barnes

Year	Team		No	Yds	Avg	Lg	TD
1986	CHI	N	4	54	13.5	14	0

Buster Barnett

Year	Team		No	Yds	Avg	Lg	TD
1981	BUF	N	4	36	9.0	16	1
1982			4	39	9.8	22	0
1983			10	94	9.4	14	0
1984			8	67	8.4	18	0
Career			26	236	9.1	22	1

Fred Barnett

Year	Team		No	Yds	Avg	Lg	TD
1990	PHI	N	36	721	20.0	95t	8
1991			62	948	15.3	75t	4
1992			67	1083	16.2	71t	6
1993			17	170	10.0	21	0
1994			78	1127	14.4	54	5
1995			48	585	12.2	33	5
1996	MIA	N	36	562	15.6	66	3
Career			344	5196	15.1	95t	31
Playoffs			18	283	15.7		3

Tim Barnett

Year	Team		No	Yds	Avg	Lg	TD
1991	KC	N	41	564	13.8	63	5
1992			24	442	18.4	77t	4
1993			17	182	10.7	25	1
Career			82	1188	14.5	77t	10
Playoffs			6	74	12.3		1

Tom Barnett

Year	Team		No	Yds	Avg	Lg	TD
1959	PIT	N	7	52	7.4	14	1

Eppie Barney

Year	Team		No	Yds	Avg	Lg	TD
1967	CLE	N	1	3	3.0	3	0
1968			18	189	10.5	18	1
Career			19	192	10.1	18	1

Milton Barney

Year	Team		No	Yds	Avg	Lg	TD
1987	ATL	N	10	175	17.5	32	2

Len Barnum

Year	Team		No	Yds	Avg	Lg	TD
1938	NYG	N	3	37	12.3		0
1939			3	50	16.7		0
1940			1	15	15.0	15	0
1941	PHI	N	1	11	11.0	11	0
1942			3	54	18.0	32	0
Career			11	167	15.2	32	0
Playoffs			2	26	13.0		0

Malcolm Barnwell

Year	Team		No	Yds	Avg	Lg	TD
1981	OAK	N	9	190	21.1	61t	1
1982	LARI	N	23	387	16.8	52	0
1983			35	513	14.7	41	1
1984			45	851	18.9	51t	2
1985	WAS	N	3	28	9.3	13	0
Career			115	1969	17.1	61t	4
Playoffs			15	301	20.1		1

Terry Barr

Year	Team		No	Yds	Avg	Lg	TD
1959	DET	N	10	180	18.0	45	0
1960			5	26	5.2	11	1
1961			40	630	15.8	61t	6
1962			25	425	17.0	80t	3
1963			66	1086	16.5	75t	13
1964			57	1030	18.1	58t	9
1965			24	433	18.0	61t	3
Career			227	3810	16.8	80t	35

Jan Barrett

Year	Team		No	Yds	Avg	Lg	TD
1963	OAK	A	1	9	9.0	9	0
1964			12	212	17.7	41	2
Career			13	221	17.0	41	2

Jeff Barrett

Year	Team		No	Yds	Avg	Lg	TD
1936	BKN	N	14	268	19.1		1
1937			20	461	23.1		3
1938			13	205	15.8		2
Career			47	934	19.9		6

Reggie Barrett

Year	Team		No	Yds	Avg	Lg	TD
1992	DET	N	4	67	16.8	24	1

Tom Barrington

Year	Team		No	Yds	Avg	Lg	TD
1966	WAS	N	2	23	11.5	12	0
1967	NO	N	4	50	12.5	29	0
1968			9	33	3.7	10	1
1969			4	42	10.5	15	0
1970			22	130	5.9	20	0
Career			41	278	6.8	29	1

Odell Barry

Year	Team		No	Yds	Avg	Lg	TD
1964	DEN	A	4	31	7.8	13	0
1965			2	11	5.5	9	0
Career			6	42	7.0	13	0

Paul Barry

Year	Team		No	Yds	Avg	Lg	TD
1950	LA	N	7	122	17.4	39	0
1952			2	43	21.5	25t	1
1953	WAS	N	8	70	8.8	18	0
1954	CHIC	N	7	29	4.1	26	0
Career			24	264	11.0	39	1

Steve Bartalo

Year	Team		No	Yds	Avg	Lg	TD
1987	TB	N	1	5	5.0	5	0

Sam Bartholomew

Year	Team		No	Yds	Avg	Lg	TD
1941	PHI	N	3	15	5.0	7	0

Don Barton

Year	Team		No	Yds	Avg	Lg	TD
1953	GB	N	2	51	25.5	42t	1

Mike Bartrum

Year	Team		No	Yds	Avg	Lg	TD
1996	NE	N	1	1	1.0	1t	1

Mike Basca

Year	Team		No	Yds	Avg	Lg	TD
1941	PHI	N	2	45	22.5	25	0

Brian Baschnagel

Year	Team		No	Yds	Avg	Lg	TD
1976	CHI	N	13	226	17.4	58	0
1977			4	50	12.5	25	0
1978			2	29	14.5	22	0
1979			30	452	15.1	54t	2
1980			28	396	14.1	37	2
1981			34	554	16.3	72t	3
1982			12	194	16.2	39t	2
1983			5	70	14.0	24	0
1984			6	53	8.8	17	0
Career			134	2024	15.1	72t	9
Playoffs			3	38	12.7		0

Myrt Basing

Year	Team		No	Yds	Avg	Lg	TD
1925	GB	N					2

Billy Bass

Year	Team		No	Yds	Avg	Lg	TD
1947	CHI	AA	8	79	9.9		1

Dick Bass

Year	Team		No	Yds	Avg	Lg	TD
1960	LA	N	13	92	7.1	26	0
1961			16	145	9.1	37	0
1962			30	262	8.7	33t	2
1963			30	348	11.6	53	0
1964			9	83	9.2	24	0
1965			21	230	11.0	36	2
1966			31	274	8.8	40	0
1967			27	212	7.9	30	1
1968			27	195	7.2	28t	2
Career			204	1841	9.0	53	7

Don Bass

Year	Team		No	Yds	Avg	Lg	TD
1978	CIN	N	27	447	16.6	51t	4
1979			58	724	12.5	50	3
1980			32	409	12.8	55t	6
Career			117	1580	13.5	55t	13
Playoffs			1	3	3.0		1

Glenn Bass

Year	Team		No	Yds	Avg	Lg	TD
1961	BUF	A	50	765	15.3	76	3
1962			32	555	17.3	76	4
1963			9	153	17.0	74	1
1964			43	897	20.9	94	7
1965			18	299	16.6	38	1
1966			10	130	13.0	19	0
1967	HOU	A	5	42	8.4	15	1
Career			167	2841	17.0	94	17
Playoffs			8	141	17.6		0

Mo Bassett

Year	Team		No	Yds	Avg	Lg	TD
1954	CLE	N	20	205	10.3	33	0
1955			9	83	9.2	25	0
1956			4	29	7.3	31t	1
Career			33	317	9.6	33	1
Playoffs			2	14	7.0		0

Dick Bassi

Year	Team		No	Yds	Avg	Lg	TD
1941	PIT	N	1	6	6.0	6	0

Reds Bassman

Year	Team		No	Yds	Avg	Lg	TD
1936	PHI	N	2	38	19.0		0

Mario Bates

Year	Team		No	Yds	Avg	Lg	TD
1994	NO	N	8	62	7.8	14	0
1995			18	114	6.3	26	0
1996			13	44	3.4	15	0
Career			39	220	5.6	26	0

Michael Bates

Year	Team		No	Yds	Avg	Lg	TD
1993	SEA	N	1	6	6.0	6	0
1994			5	112	22.4	40t	1
Career			6	118	19.7	40t	1

John Batorski

Year	Team		No	Yds	Avg	Lg	TD
1946	BUF	AA	2	27	13.5		0

Marco Battaglia

Year	Team		No	Yds	Avg	Lg	TD
1996	CIN	N	8	79	9.9	17	0

Mike Battle

Year	Team		No	Yds	Avg	Lg	TD
1970	NYJ	N	1	2	2.0	2	0

Year	Team		No	Yds	Avg	Lg	TD

Ron Battle
| 1982 | LARM | N | 2 | 62 | 31.0 | 51t | 1 |

Cliff Battles
1932	BOS	N	4	70	17.5		1
1933			11	185	16.8		0
1934			5	95	19.0		1
1935			2	22	11.0		0
1936			6	103	17.2		1
1937	WAS	N	9	81	9.0		1
Career			37	556	15.0		4
Playoffs			3	80	26.7		0

Greg Baty
1986	NE	N	37	331	8.9	22	2
1987	NE-LARM	N	18	175	9.7	22	2
1991	MIA	N	20	269	13.4	30	1
1992			3	19	6.3	12	1
1993			5	78	15.6	32	1
1994			2	11	5.5	8	1
Career			85	883	10.4	32	8
Playoffs			3	31	10.3		0

Hank Bauer
1977	SD	N	1	15	15.0	15t	1
1978			10	78	7.8	14t	1
1981			1	4	4.0	4t	1
Career			12	97	8.1	15t	3

Sammy Baugh
| 1944 | WAS | N | 1 | 0 | 0.0 | 0 | 0 |

Mark Bavaro
1985	NYG	N	37	511	13.8	32	4
1986			66	1001	15.2	41	4
1987			55	867	15.8	38	8
1988			53	672	12.7	36	4
1989			22	278	12.6	29	3
1990			33	393	11.9	61	5
1992	CLE	N	25	315	12.6	39	2
1993	PHI	N	43	481	11.2	27	6
1994			17	215	12.6	27t	3
Career			351	4733	13.5	61	39
Playoffs			30	366	12.2		3

Bibbles Bawel
1952	PHI	N	2	60	30.0	52	0
1955			1	6	6.0	6	0
Career			3	66	22.0	52	0

Brad Baxter
1990	NYJ	N	8	73	9.1	22	0
1991			12	124	10.3	34	0
1992			4	32	8.0	12	0
1993			20	158	7.9	24	0
1994			10	40	4.0	7	0
1995			26	160	6.2	20	0
Career			80	587	7.3	34	0

Fred Baxter
1993	NYJ	N	3	48	16.0	25	1
1994			3	11	3.7	6	1
1995			18	222	12.3	32	1
1996			7	114	16.3	23	0
Career			31	395	12.7	32	3

Craig Baynham
1967	DAL	N	3	13	4.3	17	0
1968			29	380	13.1	40	3
1970	CHI	N	12	43	3.6	13	0
1972	STL	N	1	10	10.0	10	0
Career			45	446	9.9	40	3
Playoffs			3	34	11.3		1

Winnie Baze
| 1937 | PHI | N | 1 | 2 | 2.0 | 2 | 0 |

Pat Beach
1982	BAL	N	4	45	11.3	17	1
1983			5	56	11.2	16	1
1985	IND	N	36	376	10.4	30	6
1986			25	265	10.6	26	1
1987			28	239	8.5	16	0

Year	Team		No	Yds	Avg	Lg	TD

Pat Beach *continued*
1988			26	235	9.0	23	0
1989			14	87	6.2	17	2
1990			12	124	10.3	21	1
1991			5	56	11.2	26	0
1992	PHI	N	8	75	9.4	16	2
Career			163	1558	9.6	30	14
Playoffs			2	6	3.0		1

Sanjay Beach
1991	SF	N	4	43	10.8	20	0
1992	GB	N	17	122	7.2	20	1
1993	SF	N	5	59	11.8	20t	1
Career			26	224	8.6	20t	2

Walter Beach
| 1960 | BOS | A | 9 | 132 | 14.7 | | 1 |

Alyn Beals
1946	SF	AA	40	586	14.7		10
1947			47	655	13.9	54	10
1948			46	591	12.8		14
1949			44	678	15.4		12
1950	SF	N	22	315	14.3	38	3
1951			12	126	10.5	22	0
Career			211	2951	14.0	54	49
Playoffs			3	26	8.7		0

Bubba Bean
1976	ATL	N	16	148	9.3	50t	1
1978			31	209	6.7	38t	1
1979			12	137	11.4	49	0
Career			59	494	8.4	50t	2
Playoffs			4	44	11.0		0

John Beasley
1967	MIN	N	13	120	9.2	16	4
1968			23	289	12.6	20	0
1969			33	361	10.9	32	4
1970			17	237	13.9	40	2
1972			28	232	8.3	18	1
1973	MIN-NO	N	32	283	8.8	15	2
1974	NO	N	5	85	17.0	30	0
Career			151	1607	10.6	40	13
Playoffs			8	122	15.3		0

Terry Beasley
1972	SF	N	1	20	20.0	20	0
1974			17	253	14.9	68t	3
1975			20	297	14.9	28	0
Career			38	570	15.0	68t	3

Gary Beban
| 1968 | WAS | N | 1 | 12 | 12.0 | 12 | 0 |

Hub Bechtol
1947	BAL	AA	17	167	9.8		1
1948			2	25	12.5		0
Career			19	192	10.1		1

Wayland Becker
1934	CHIB	N	1	18	18.0	18	0
1935	BKN	N	10	131	13.1		1
1936	GB	N	5	66	13.2		1
1937			2	13	6.5		0
1938			7	166	23.7		0
Career			25	394	15.8	18	2
Playoffs			2	79	39.5		0

Brad Beckman
| 1989 | ATL | N | 11 | 102 | 9.3 | 21 | 1 |

Ed Beckman
1977	KC	N	1	3	3.0	3	0
1979			2	21	10.5	12	0
1983			13	130	10.0	20	0
1984			7	44	6.3	9	1
Career			23	198	8.6	20	1

Hal Bedsole
1964	MIN	N	18	295	16.4	43t	5
1965			8	123	15.4	36t	3
Career			26	418	16.1	43t	8

Year	Team		No	Yds	Avg	Lg	TD

Don Beebe
1989	BUF	N	17	317	18.6	63t	2
1990			11	221	20.1	49	1
1991			32	414	12.9	34t	6
1992			33	554	16.8	65t	2
1993			31	504	16.3	65t	3
1994			40	527	13.2	72t	4
1995	CAR	N	14	152	10.9	24	1
1996	GB	N	39	699	17.9	80t	4
Career			217	3388	15.6	72t	23
Playoffs			35	466	13.3		3

Tom Beer
1967	DEN	A	11	155	14.1	29	0
1968			20	276	13.8	31	1
1969			9	200	22.2	48	0
1970	BOS	N	11	150	13.6	25	0
1971	NE	N	12	191	15.9	31t	3
1972			2	40	20.0	21	0
Career			65	1012	15.6	48	4

Charlie Behan
| 1942 | DET | N | 4 | 63 | 15.8 | 25 | 0 |

Tom Beier
| 1967 | MIA | A | 1 | 19 | 19.0 | 19 | 0 |

Jim Beirne
1968	HOU	A	31	474	15.3	6t	4
1969			42	540	12.9	37t	4
1970	HOU	N	16	216	13.5	25	1
1971			38	550	14.5	40	1
1972			7	95	13.6	19	1
1974	SD	N	7	121	17.3	26	0
1975	HOU	N	1	15	15.0	15	0
Career			142	2011	14.2	40	11
Playoffs			5	48	9.6		0

Kevin Belcher
| 1984 | NYG | N | 1 | 4 | 4.0 | 4 | 0 |

Bunny Belden
| 1930 | CHIC | N | | | | | 2 |

Steve Belichick
| 1941 | DET | N | 1 | 13 | 13.0 | 13 | 0 |

Rocky Belk
| 1983 | CLE | N | 5 | 141 | 28.2 | 64t | 2 |

Veno Belk
| 1987 | BUF | N | 1 | 7 | 7.0 | 7 | 0 |

Coleman Bell
| 1995 | WAS | N | 14 | 166 | 11.9 | 29t | 1 |

Eddie Bell
1970	NYJ	N	21	246	11.7	26	2
1971			5	110	22.0	31	1
1972			35	629	18.0	83t	2
1973			24	319	13.3	38t	2
1974			13	126	9.7	22	1
1975			20	344	17.2	38	4
Career			118	1774	15.0	83t	12

Gordon Bell
1976	NYG	N	25	198	7.9	20	0
1977			4	33	8.3	12	0
1978	STL	N	3	28	9.3	17	0
Career			32	259	8.1	20	0

Greg Bell
1984	BUF	N	34	277	8.1	37	1
1985			58	576	9.9	49	1
1986			12	142	11.8	40t	2
1987	BUF-LARM	N	9	96	10.7	32t	1
1988	LARM	N	24	124	5.2	20	2
1989			19	85	4.5	14	0
1990	LARI	N	1	7	7.0	7	0
Career			157	1307	8.3	49	7
Playoffs			8	95	11.9		0

Henry Bell
| 1960 | DEN | A | 2 | 13 | 6.5 | 11 | 0 |

Jerry Bell

Year	Team		No	Yds	Avg	Lg	TD
1982	TB	N	1	5	5.0	5	0
1983			18	200	11.1	33	1
1984			29	397	13.7	27	4
1985			43	496	11.5	27	2
1986			10	120	12.0	25	0
Career			101	1218	12.1	33	7

Ken Bell

Year	Team		No	Yds	Avg	Lg	TD
1986	DEN	N	2	10	5.0	7	0
1987			1	8	8.0	8	0
Career			3	18	6.0	8	0

Mark Bell

Year	Team		No	Yds	Avg	Lg	TD
1979	SEA	N	2	20	10.0	16	0
1980			1	13	13.0	13	0
Career			3	33	11.0	16	0

Mark Bell

Year	Team		No	Yds	Avg	Lg	TD
1980	STL	N	8	123	15.4	34	0

Nick Bell

Year	Team		No	Yds	Avg	Lg	TD
1991	LARI	N	6	62	10.3	24	0
1992			4	40	10.0	16	0
1993			11	111	10.1	18	0
Career			21	213	10.1	24	0

Richard Bell

Year	Team		No	Yds	Avg	Lg	TD
1990	PIT	N	12	137	11.4	43	1

Ricky Bell

Year	Team		No	Yds	Avg	Lg	TD
1977	TB	N	11	88	8.0	23	0
1978			15	122	8.1	22	0
1979			25	248	9.9	26	2
1980			38	292	7.7	22	1
1981			8	92	11.5	22	0
Career			97	842	8.7	26	3
Playoffs			2	12	6.0		0

Theo Bell

Year	Team		No	Yds	Avg	Lg	TD
1976	PIT	N	3	43	14.3	19	1
1978			6	53	8.8	15t	1
1979			3	61	20.3	31	0
1980			29	748	25.8	72	2
1981	TB	N	21	318	15.1	58t	2
1982			15	203	13.5	25	0
1983			25	410	16.4	52	2
1984			22	350	15.9	29	0
1985			12	189	15.8	24	0
Career			136	2375	17.5	72	8
Playoffs			7	82	11.7		0

William Bell

Year	Team		No	Yds	Avg	Lg	TD
1996	WAS	N	3	23	7.7	12	0

Mark Bellini

Year	Team		No	Yds	Avg	Lg	TD
1987	IND	N	5	69	13.8	19	0
1988			5	64	12.8	25	0
Career			10	133	13.3	25	0
Playoffs			1	21	21.0		

Joe Bellino

Year	Team		No	Yds	Avg	Lg	TD
1965	BOS	A	5	74	14.8	20	0
1966			6	77	12.8	25	1
Career			11	151	13.7	25	1

Horace Belton

Year	Team		No	Yds	Avg	Lg	TD
1978	KC	N	11	88	8.0	22	0
1979			4	44	11.0	23	0
1980			5	94	18.8	55	0
Career			20	226	11.3	55	0

Willie Belton

Year	Team		No	Yds	Avg	Lg	TD
1971	ATL	N	3	22	7.3	10	0
1972			1	-1	-1.0	-1	0
Career			4	21	5.3	10	0

Al Bemiller

Year	Team		No	Yds	Avg	Lg	TD
1968	BUF	A	1	0	0.0	0	0

Wes Bender

Year	Team		No	Yds	Avg	Lg	TD
1994	LARI	N	2	14	7.0	7	0

Jesse Bendross

Year	Team		No	Yds	Avg	Lg	TD
1984	SD	N	16	213	13.3	29	0
1985			11	156	14.2	54t	2
Career			27	369	13.7	54t	2

Brant Bengen

Year	Team		No	Yds	Avg	Lg	TD
1987	SEA	N	2	33	16.5	24	0

Ryan Benjamin

Year	Team		No	Yds	Avg	Lg	TD
1993	CIN	N	1	16	16.0	16	0

Tony Benjamin

Year	Team		No	Yds	Avg	Lg	TD
1977	SEA	N	4	27	6.8	9	0
1978			1	9	9.0	9	0
1979			1	6	6.0	6	0
Career			6	42	7.0	9	0

Donnell Bennett

Year	Team		No	Yds	Avg	Lg	TD
1994	KC	N	7	53	7.6	15	0
1995			1	12	12.0	12	0
1996			8	21	2.6	10	0
Career			16	86	5.4	15	0

Edgar Bennett

Year	Team		No	Yds	Avg	Lg	TD
1992	GB	N	13	93	7.2	22	0
1993			59	457	7.7	39t	1
1994			78	546	7.0	40	4
1995			61	648	10.6	35	4
1996			31	176	5.7	25t	1
Career			242	1920	7.9	40	10
Playoffs			31	170	5.5		0

Lewis Bennett

Year	Team		No	Yds	Avg	Lg	TD
1987	NYG	N	10	184	18.4	46t	1

Woody Bennett

Year	Team		No	Yds	Avg	Lg	TD
1979	NYJ	N	1	9	9.0	9	0
1980	MIA	N	3	26	8.7	19t	1
1981			4	22	5.5	10	0
1983			6	35	5.8	9	0
1984			6	44	7.3	20	1
1985			10	101	10.1	27t	1
1986			4	33	8.3	13	0
1987			4	18	4.5	6	0
1988			2	16	8.0	12	0
Career			40	304	7.6	27t	3
Playoffs			2	26	13.0		

Cliff Benson

Year	Team		No	Yds	Avg	Lg	TD
1984	ATL	N	26	244	9.4	30	0
1985			10	37	3.7	6	0
1987	NO	N	2	11	5.5	6	0
1988			1	5	5.0	5	0
Career			39	297	7.6	30	0

Albert Bentley

Year	Team		No	Yds	Avg	Lg	TD
1985	IND	N	11	85	7.7	16	0
1986			25	230	9.2	38	0
1987			34	447	13.1	72t	2
1988			26	252	9.7	21	1
1989			52	525	10.1	61	3
1990			71	664	9.4	73	2
1991			7	42	6.0	11	0
Career			226	2245	9.9	73	8
Playoffs			4	47	11.8		

Jim Benton

Year	Team		No	Yds	Avg	Lg	TD
1938	CLE	N	21	418	19.9		5
1939			27	388	14.4		7
1940			22	351	16.0		3
1942			23	345	15.0	45	1
1943	CHIB	N	13	235	18.1	55	3
1944	CLE	N	39	505	12.9	36	6
1945			45	1067	23.7	84t	8
1946	LA	N	63	981	15.6	57	6
1947			35	511	14.6	43	6
Career			288	4801	16.7	84t	45
Playoffs			10	154	15.4		2

Karl Bernard

Year	Team		No	Yds	Avg	Lg	TD
1987	DET	N	13	91	7.0	12	0

Frank Bernardi

Year	Team		No	Yds	Avg	Lg	TD
1955	CHIC	N	4	77	19.3	39t	1

Frank Bernardi *continued*

Year	Team		No	Yds	Avg	Lg	TD
1956			4	56	14.0	19	0
1957			1	13	13.0	13	0
Career			9	146	16.2	39t	1

Ed Bernet

Year	Team		No	Yds	Avg	Lg	TD
1955	PIT	N	22	276	12.5	38	1
1960	DAL	A	4	49	12.3	15	0
Career			26	325	12.5	38	1

Rick Berns

Year	Team		No	Yds	Avg	Lg	TD
1979	TB	N	5	40	8.0	12	0
1980			1	6	6.0	6	0
Career			6	46	7.7	12	0

Rod Bernstine

Year	Team		No	Yds	Avg	Lg	TD
1987	SD	N	10	76	7.6	15	1
1988			29	340	11.7	59	0
1989			21	222	10.6	36	1
1990			8	40	5.0	11	0
1991			11	124	11.3	25	0
1992			12	86	7.2	16	0
1993	DEN	N	44	372	8.5	41	0
1994			9	70	7.8	16	0
1995			5	54	10.8	38	0
Career			149	1384	9.3	59	2

Eddie Berrang

Year	Team		No	Yds	Avg	Lg	TD
1949	WAS	N	1	5	5.0	5	0
1950			1	14	14.0	14	0
Career			2	19	9.5	14	0

Bob Berry

Year	Team		No	Yds	Avg	Lg	TD
1972	ATL	N	1	-9	-9.0	-9	0

Charlie Berry

Year	Team		No	Yds	Avg	Lg	TD
1925	POT	N					4
1926							2
Career							6

Connie Mack Berry

Year	Team		No	Yds	Avg	Lg	TD
1942	CHIB	N	4	29	7.3	16	0
1943			4	99	24.8	54	2
1944			21	378	18.0	51t	6
1945			12	202	16.8	51	0
1946			4	58	14.5	21	0
Career			45	766	17.0	54	8

Howard Berry

Year	Team		No	Yds	Avg	Lg	TD
1921	ROC	A					1

Raymond Berry

Year	Team		No	Yds	Avg	Lg	TD
1955	BAL	N	13	205	15.8	45	0
1956			37	601	16.2	54	6
1957			47	800	17.0	67t	6
1958			56	794	14.2	54	9
1959			66	959	14.5	55t	14
1960			74	1298	17.5	70t	10
1961			75	873	11.6	44	0
1962			51	687	13.5	37	3
1963			44	703	16.0	64t	6
1964			43	663	15.4	46	6
1965			58	739	12.7	40	7
1966			56	786	14.0	40t	7
1967			11	167	15.2	40	1
Career			631	9275	14.7	70t	68
Playoffs			20	284	14.2		1

Rex Berry

Year	Team		No	Yds	Avg	Lg	TD
1951	SF	N	1	12	12.0	12t	1

Jim Bertelsen

Year	Team		No	Yds	Avg	Lg	TD
1972	LA	N	29	331	11.4	22	1
1973			19	267	14.1	44	1
1974			20	175	8.8	19	0
1975			14	208	14.9	22	0
1976			6	33	5.5	10	0
Career			88	1014	11.5	44	2
Playoffs			6	58	9.7		0

Willie Berzinski

Year	Team		No	Yds	Avg	Lg	TD
1956	PHI	N	3	35	11.7	17	0

James Betterson

Year	Team		No	Yds	Avg	Lg	TD
1977	PHI	N	4	41	10.3	15	0
1978			2	8	4.0	5	0
Career			6	49	8.2	15	0

Jerome Bettis

Year	Team		No	Yds	Avg	Lg	TD
1993	LARM	N	26	244	9.4	28	0
1994			31	293	9.5	34	1
1995	STL	N	18	106	5.9	19	0
1996	PIT	N	22	122	5.5	16	0
Career			97	765	7.9	34	1
Playoffs			3	3	1.0		0

John Bettridge

Year	Team		No	Yds	Avg	Lg	TD
1937	CLE	N	1	17	17.0	17	0

Steve Beuerlein

Year	Team		No	Yds	Avg	Lg	TD
1988	LARI	N	1	21	21.0	21	0

Dwight Beverly

Year	Team		No	Yds	Avg	Lg	TD
1987	NO	N	1	8	8.0	8	0

Dick Bielski

Year	Team		No	Yds	Avg	Lg	TD
1955	PHI	N	8	48	6.0	19	0
1956			8	63	7.9	17	0
1957			8	81	10.1	19	2
1958			23	234	10.2	30	1
1959			15	264	17.6	57	1
1960	DAL	N	4	38	9.5	15	1
1961			26	377	14.5	28	3
1962	BAL	N	15	200	13.3	22	2
Career			107	1305	12.2	57	10

Tom Bienemann

Year	Team		No	Yds	Avg	Lg	TD
1951	CHIC	N	1	8	8.0	8	0

Eric Bieniemy

Year	Team		No	Yds	Avg	Lg	TD
1992	SD	N	5	49	9.8	25	0
1993			1	0	0.0	0	0
1994			5	48	9.6	25	0
1995	CIN	N	43	424	9.9	33	0
1996			32	272	8.5	42	0
Career			86	793	9.2	42	0
Playoffs			2	29	14.5		0

Scotty Bierce

Year	Team		No	Yds	Avg	Lg	TD
1921	AKR	A					1
1922	AKR	N					2
1923	CLE	N					2
Career							7

Jack Bighead

Year	Team		No	Yds	Avg	Lg	TD
1954	BAL	N	6	89	14.8	25	0

Fred Biletnikoff

Year	Team		No	Yds	Avg	Lg	TD
1965	OAK	A	24	331	13.8	53	0
1966			17	272	16.0	78	3
1967			40	876	21.9	72	5
1968			61	1037	17.0	82	6
1969			54	837	15.5	53t	12
1970	OAK	N	45	768	17.1	51	7
1971			61	929	15.2	49	9
1972			58	802	13.8	39t	7
1973			48	660	13.8	32	4
1974			42	593	14.1	46	7
1975			43	587	13.7	26	2
1976			43	551	12.8	32t	7
1977			33	446	13.5	44t	5
1978			20	285	14.3	49	2
Career			589	8974	15.2	82	76
Playoffs			70	1167	16.7		10

Don Bingham

Year	Team		No	Yds	Avg	Lg	TD
1956	CHIB	N	1	7	7.0	7	0

J.J. Birden

Year	Team		No	Yds	Avg	Lg	TD
1990	KC	N	15	352	23.5	90t	3
1991			27	465	17.2	57t	2
1992			42	644	15.3	72t	3
1993			51	721	14.1	50t	2
1994			48	637	13.3	44	4
1995	ATL	N	31	303	9.8	24	1

J.J. Birden *continued*

Year	Team		No	Yds	Avg	Lg	TD
1996			30	319	10.6	57	2
Career			244	3441	14.1	90t	17
Playoffs			33	427	12.9		3

Keith Birlem

Year	Team		No	Yds	Avg	Lg	TD
1939	CHIC	N	2	17	8.5		0

Joe Biscaha

Year	Team		No	Yds	Avg	Lg	TD
1959	NYG	N	1	5	5.0	5	0

Don Bishop

Year	Team		No	Yds	Avg	Lg	TD
1958	PIT	N	3	57	19.0	29	0

Harold Bishop

Year	Team		No	Yds	Avg	Lg	TD
1995	CLE	N	16	135	8.4	21	0
1996	BAL	N	2	22	11.0	13	0
Career			18	157	8.7	21	0

Sonny Bishop

Year	Team		No	Yds	Avg	Lg	TD
1964	HOU	A	1	0	0.0	0	0
Playoffs			1	-6	-6.0		0

Charlie Bivins

Year	Team		No	Yds	Avg	Lg	TD
1961	CHI	N	4	-9	-2.3	4	0
1962			3	52	17.3	28	0
1963			3	22	7.3	19	0
1964			11	59	5.4	21t	0
1965			4	108	27.0	52t	2
1966			2	6	3.0	4	0
1967	PIT	N	1	24	24.0	24	0
Career			28	262	9.4	52t	3

Hank Bjorklund

Year	Team		No	Yds	Avg	Lg	TD
1972	NYJ	N	4	54	13.5	35	0
1973			2	15	7.5	11	0
1974			2	15	7.5	8	0
Career			8	84	10.5	35	0

Eric Bjornson

Year	Team		No	Yds	Avg	Lg	TD
1995	DAL	N	7	53	7.6	16	0
1996			48	388	8.1	25	3
Career			55	441	8.0	25	3
Playoffs			4	23	5.8		0

Blondy Black

Year	Team		No	Yds	Avg	Lg	TD
1946	BUF	AA	1	21	21.0	21	0
1947	BAL	AA	1	7	7.0	7	0
Career			2	28	14.0	21	0

Kelly Blackwell

Year	Team		No	Yds	Avg	Lg	TD
1992	CHI	N	5	54	10.8	18	0

Lyle Blackwood

Year	Team		No	Yds	Avg	Lg	TD
1976	SEA	N	1	8	8.0	8	0

Brian Blades

Year	Team		No	Yds	Avg	Lg	TD
1988	SEA	N	40	682	17.1	55	8
1989			77	1063	13.8	60t	5
1990			49	525	10.7	24	3
1991			70	1003	14.3	52	2
1992			19	256	13.5	37	1
1993			80	945	11.8	41	3
1994			81	1086	13.4	49	4
1995			77	1001	13.0	49	4
1996			43	556	12.9	80t	2
Career			536	7117	13.3	80t	32
Playoffs			5	78	15.6		0

Brian Blados

Year	Team		No	Yds	Avg	Lg	TD
1985	CIN	N	1	4	4.0	4	0

Ricky Blake

Year	Team		No	Yds	Avg	Lg	TD
1991	DAL	N	1	5	5.0	5	0

Carl Bland

Year	Team		No	Yds	Avg	Lg	TD
1985	DET	N	12	157	13.1	24	0
1986			44	511	11.6	34	2
1987			2	14	7.0	11t	1
1988			21	307	14.6	35	2
1989	GB	N	11	164	14.9	46t	1
Career			90	1153	12.8	46t	6

George Blanda

Year	Team		No	Yds	Avg	Lg	TD
1953	CHIB	N	0	7		7L	0
1961	HOU	A	1	-16	-16.0	-16	0
1964			0	-7		-7L	0
Career			1	-16	-16.0	7L	0

Ernie Blandin

Year	Team		No	Yds	Avg	Lg	TD
1950	BAL	N	1	16	16.0	16	0

Sid Blanks

Year	Team		No	Yds	Avg	Lg	TD
1964	HOU	A	56	497	8.9	45	1
1966			19	234	12.3	42	2
1967			11	93	8.5	39t	1
1968			13	184	14.2	61	0
1969	BOS	A	2	16	8.0	13	0
1970	BOS	N	5	49	9.8	18	0
Career			106	1073	10.1	61	4

Tony Blazine

Year	Team		No	Yds	Avg	Lg	TD
1937	CHIC	N	1	2	2.0	2	0

Curtis Bledsoe

Year	Team		No	Yds	Avg	Lg	TD
1981	KC	N	3	27	9.0	17	0
1982			1	5	5.0	5	0
Career			4	32	8.0	17	0

Drew Bledsoe

Year	Team		No	Yds	Avg	Lg	TD
1995	NE	N	1	-9	-9.0	-9	0

Mel Bleeker

Year	Team		No	Yds	Avg	Lg	TD
1944	PHI	N	8	299	**37.4**	75t	4
1945			3	32	10.7	15	0
1946			3	29	9.7	20	0
Career			14	360	25.7	75t	4

Rocky Bleier

Year	Team		No	Yds	Avg	Lg	TD
1968	PIT	N	3	68	22.7	54	0
1974			7	87	12.4	24	0
1975			15	65	4.3	13	0
1976			24	294	12.3	32	0
1977			18	161	8.9	30	0
1978			17	168	9.9	32	1
1979			31	277	8.9	28	0
1980			21	174	8.3	17	1
Career			136	1294	9.5	54	2
Playoffs			19	202	10.6		2

Dennis Bligen

Year	Team		No	Yds	Avg	Lg	TD
1985	NYJ	N	5	43	8.6	14	0
1986			2	6	3.0	4	0
1987			11	81	7.4	19	0
Career			18	130	7.2	19	0

Johnny Blood

Year	Team		No	Yds	Avg	Lg	TD
1926	DUL	N					1
1927							1
1928	POT	N					2
1929	GB	N					2
1930							**5**
1931							**10**
1932			19	326	17.2		**3**
1933			7	214	30.6		3
1935			25	404	16.2		3
1936			7	147	21.0		2
1937	PIT	N	10	168	16.8		4
1938			2	5	2.5		0
Career			70	1264	18.1		36
Playoffs			1	64	32.0		0

Al Bloodgood

Year	Team		No	Yds	Avg	Lg	TD
1926	KC	N					1
1927	CLE	N					1
Career							2

Alvin Blount

Year	Team		No	Yds	Avg	Lg	TD
1987	DAL	N	1	5	5.0	5	0

Eric Blount

Year	Team		No	Yds	Avg	Lg	TD
1992	PHX	N	3	18	6.0	18	0
1993			5	36	7.2	9	0
Career			8	54	6.8	18	0

Lamar Blount

Year	Team		No	Yds	Avg	Lg	TD
1946	MIA	AA	13	218	16.8		1

Lamar Blount *continued*

Year	Team		No	Yds	Avg	Lg	TD
1947	BAL	AA	8	148	18.5		0
Career			21	366	17.4		1

Al Blozis

Year	Team		No	Yds	Avg	Lg	TD
1943	NYG	N	1	15	15.0	15	0
Playoffs			1	8	8.0		0

Luther Blue

Year	Team		No	Yds	Avg	Lg	TD
1977	DET	N	8	90	11.3	21	1
1978			31	350	11.3	26	2
1979			8	102	12.8	26	1
Career			47	542	11.5	26	4

Jimmy Blumenstock

Year	Team		No	Yds	Avg	Lg	TD
1947	NYG	N	4	15	3.8	24	0

Herb Blumer

Year	Team		No	Yds	Avg	Lg	TD
1925	CHIC	N					2

Ronnie Blye

Year	Team		No	Yds	Avg	Lg	TD
1968	NYG	N	10	91	9.1	23	0
1969	PHI	N	2	-6	-3.0	1	0
Career			12	85	7.1	23	0

Tony Boddie

Year	Team		No	Yds	Avg	Lg	TD
1987	DEN	N	9	85	9.4	26	0
Playoffs			1	15	15.0		0

Billy Boedecker

Year	Team		No	Yds	Avg	Lg	TD
1946	CHI	AA	5	82	16.4		1
1947	CLE	AA	8	175	21.9	69	1
1948			13	237	18.2	51	2
1949			11	371	33.7	74t	2
1950	GB	N	1	10	10.0	10	0
Career			38	875	23.0	74t	6

Dewey Bohling

Year	Team		No	Yds	Avg	Lg	TD
1960	NY	A	30	268	8.9		4
1961	NY-BUF	A	13	217	16.7	41	1
Career			43	485	11.3	41	5

Rickey Bolden

Year	Team		No	Yds	Avg	Lg	TD
1984	CLE	N	1	19	19.0	19	0
1988			1	3	3.0	3t	1
Career			2	22	11.0	19	1

Jim Bolger

Year	Team		No	Yds	Avg	Lg	TD
1926	BKN	A					1

Russ Bolinger

Year	Team		No	Yds	Avg	Lg	TD
1979	DET	N	1	-1	-1.0	-1	0

Andy Bolton

Year	Team		No	Yds	Avg	Lg	TD
1977	DET	N	1	6	6.0	6	0

Scott Bolton

Year	Team		No	Yds	Avg	Lg	TD
1988	GB	N	2	33	16.5	18	0

Lynn Bomar

Year	Team		No	Yds	Avg	Lg	TD
1925	NY	N					3
1926	NYG	N					2
Career							5

Ernie Bonelli

Year	Team		No	Yds	Avg	Lg	TD
1945	CHIC	N	3	9	3.0	7	0
1946	PIT	N	1	26	26.0	26	0
Career			4	35	8.8	26	0

Glen Bonner

Year	Team		No	Yds	Avg	Lg	TD
1974	SD	N	11	101	9.2	22	1
1975			2	8	4.0	5	0
Career			13	109	8.4	22	1

Steve Bono

Year	Team		No	Yds	Avg	Lg	TD
1987	PIT	N	1	2	2.0	2	0

Jack Boone

Year	Team		No	Yds	Avg	Lg	TD
1942	CLE	N	2	58	29.0	43	1

J.R. Boone

Year	Team		No	Yds	Avg	Lg	TD
1948	CHIB	N	10	143	14.3	38	3
1949			14	326	23.3	43	3
1950			8	139	17.4	31	0

J.R. Boone *continued*

Year	Team		No	Yds	Avg	Lg	TD
1951			6	117	19.5	24	0
1952	SF	N	25	461	18.4	53	1
1953	GB	N	6	55	9.2	18	1
Career			69	1241	18.0	53	8
Playoffs			1	13	13.0		0

Dick Booth

Year	Team		No	Yds	Avg	Lg	TD
1941	DET	N	7	103	14.7	36	1
1945			3	90	30.0	54t	1
Career			10	193	19.3	54t	2

John Booty

Year	Team		No	Yds	Avg	Lg	TD
1995	TB	N	1	48	48.0	48	0

Emerson Boozer

Year	Team		No	Yds	Avg	Lg	TD
1966	NY	A	8	133	16.6	26	0
1967			12	205	17.1	49t	3
1968			12	101	8.4	23	0
1969			20	222	11.1	29	0
1970	NYJ	N	28	258	9.2	33	0
1971			11	120	10.9	36	1
1972			11	142	12.9	49t	3
1973			22	130	5.9	15t	3
1974			14	161	11.5	29	1
1975			1	16	16.0	16t	1
Career			139	1488	10.7	49t	12
Playoffs			2	21	10.5		0

Mark Bortz

Year	Team		No	Yds	Avg	Lg	TD
1986	CHI	N	1	8	8.0	8	0

Cap Boso

Year	Team		No	Yds	Avg	Lg	TD
1987	CHI	N	17	188	11.1	31	2
1988			6	50	8.3	15	0
1989			17	182	10.7	43	1
1990			11	135	12.3	25	1
1991			3	36	12.0	22	0
Career			54	591	10.9	43	4
Playoffs			5	35	7.0		0

Don Bosseler

Year	Team		No	Yds	Avg	Lg	TD
1957	WAS	N	19	152	8.0	25	0
1958			14	101	7.2	18	0
1959			11	47	4.3	10	0
1960			13	86	6.6	50	0
1961			16	94	5.9	18	1
1962			32	258	8.1	35	0
1963			25	289	11.6	61	0
1964			6	56	9.3	18	0
Career			136	1083	8.0	61	1

Jeff Bostic

Year	Team		No	Yds	Avg	Lg	TD
1981	WAS	N	1	-4	-4.0	-4	0

Kirk Botkin

Year	Team		No	Yds	Avg	Lg	TD
1995	NO	N	1	8	8.0	8	0
1996	PIT	N	4	36	9.0	17	0
Career			5	44	8.8	17	0
Playoffs			4	46	11.5		0

Lee Bouggess

Year	Team		No	Yds	Avg	Lg	TD
1970	PHI	N	50	401	8.0	34	2
1971			24	170	7.1	27	1
1973			4	18	4.5	6	0
Career			78	589	7.6	34	3

Gil Bouley

Year	Team		No	Yds	Avg	Lg	TD
1947	LA	N	1	15	15.0	15	0
1948			1	15	15.0	15	0
1950			1	11	11.0	11	0
Career			3	41	13.7	15	0

Tommy Boutwell

Year	Team		No	Yds	Avg	Lg	TD
1969	MIA	A	4	29	7.3	12	0

Willie Bouyer

Year	Team		No	Yds	Avg	Lg	TD
1989	SEA	N	1	9	9.0	9	0

Matt Bouza

Year	Team		No	Yds	Avg	Lg	TD
1982	BAL	N	22	287	13.0	34	2
1983			25	385	15.4	26	0
1984	IND	N	22	270	12.3	22	0
1985			27	381	14.1	40	2

Matt Bouza *continued*

Year	Team		No	Yds	Avg	Lg	TD
1986			71	830	11.7	33	5
1987			42	569	13.5	44t	4
1988			25	342	13.7	28	4
Career			234	3064	13.1	44t	17
Playoffs			2	24	12.0		0

Tony Bova

Year	Team		No	Yds	Avg	Lg	TD
1942	PIT	N	3	37	12.3	17	0
1943	P-P	N	17	419	24.6	51	5
1944	C-P	N	19	287	15.1	46t	2
1945	PIT	N	15	220	14.7	52	0
1946			6	171	28.5	37	0
Career			60	1134	18.9	52	7

Gordon Bowdell

Year	Team		No	Yds	Avg	Lg	TD
1971	DEN	N	1	19	19.0	19	0

Sam Bowers

Year	Team		No	Yds	Avg	Lg	TD
1987	CHI	N	1	6	6.0	6	0

Larry Bowie

Year	Team		No	Yds	Avg	Lg	TD
1996	WAS	N	3	17	5.7	8	0

Bill Bowman

Year	Team		No	Yds	Avg	Lg	TD
1954	DET	N	34	288	8.5	66t	3
1956			5	34	6.8	18t	1
1957	PIT	N	11	107	9.7	21	0
Career			50	429	8.6	66t	3
Playoffs			1	0	0.0		0

Kevin Bowman

Year	Team		No	Yds	Avg	Lg	TD
1987	PHI	N	6	127	21.2	62t	1

Cloyce Box

Year	Team		No	Yds	Avg	Lg	TD
1949	DET	N	15	276	18.4	43	4
1950			50	1009	20.2	82t	11
1952			42	924	22.0	77t	15
1953			16	403	25.2	97t	2
1954			6	53	8.8	14	0
Career			129	2665	20.7	97t	32
Playoffs			7	84	12.0		0

Bill Boyd

Year	Team		No	Yds	Avg	Lg	TD
1930	CHIC	N					1

Bob Boyd

Year	Team		No	Yds	Avg	Lg	TD
1950	LA	N	9	220	24.4	72t	1
1951			9	128	14.2	28t	1
1953			24	548	22.8	70t	4
1954			53	1212	22.9	80t	6
1955			22	383	17.4	74t	3
1956			30	586	19.5	61t	7
1957			29	534	18.4	51	3
Career			176	3611	20.5	80t	28
Playoffs			1	-4	-4.0		0

Dennis Boyd

Year	Team		No	Yds	Avg	Lg	TD
1981	SEA	N	1	3	3.0	3t	1

Elmo Boyd

Year	Team		No	Yds	Avg	Lg	TD
1978	SF	N	9	115	12.8	32	1

Sam Boyd

Year	Team		No	Yds	Avg	Lg	TD
1939	PIT	N	21	423	20.1		2

Max Boydston

Year	Team		No	Yds	Avg	Lg	TD
1955	CHIC	N	3	79	26.3	67t	1
1956			6	116	19.3	39t	2
1957			14	193	13.8	33	0
1958			3	42	14.0	25	1
1960	DAL	A	29	357	12.3	25	3
1961			12	167	13.9	24	1
1962	OAK	A	30	374	12.5	58	0
Career			97	1328	13.7	67t	8

Mark Boyer

Year	Team		No	Yds	Avg	Lg	TD
1985	IND	N	25	274	11.0	33	1
1986			22	237	10.8	38	1
1987			10	73	7.3	15	0
1988			27	256	9.5	24t	2
1989			11	58	5.3	15	2
1990	NYJ	N	40	334	8.3	25	1
1991			16	153	9.6	22	0

Mark Boyer *continued*

Year	Team		No	Yds	Avg	Lg	TD
1992			19	149	7.8	23	0
Career			170	1534	9.0	38	6
Playoffs			3	20	6.7		0

Greg Boykin

Year	Team		No	Yds	Avg	Lg	TD
1977	NO	N	3	21	7.0	9	0
1978	SF	N	19	112	5.9	22	0
Career			22	133	6.0	22	0

Jim Boylan

Year	Team		No	Yds	Avg	Lg	TD
1963	MIN	N	6	78	13.0	19	1

Jim Boyle

Year	Team		No	Yds	Avg	Lg	TD
1987	PIT	N	1	0	0.0	0	0

Benny Boynton

Year	Team		No	Yds	Avg	Lg	TD
1924	BUF	N					4

Tom Braatz

Year	Team		No	Yds	Avg	Lg	TD
1957	WAS	N	2	52	26.0	37	0

Chuck Bradley

Year	Team		No	Yds	Avg	Lg	TD
1975	SD	N	1	42	42.0	42	0
1976			1	7	7.0	7	0
Career			2	49	24.5	42	0

Danny Bradley

Year	Team		No	Yds	Avg	Lg	TD
1987	DET	N	7	50	7.1	14	2

Freddie Bradley

Year	Team		No	Yds	Avg	Lg	TD
1996	SD	N	1	20	20.0	20	0

Hal Bradley

Year	Team		No	Yds	Avg	Lg	TD
1938	WAS	N	1	14	14.0	14	0
1939	CHIC	N	3	29	9.7		0
Career			4	43	10.8	14	0

Morris Bradshaw

Year	Team		No	Yds	Avg	Lg	TD
1975	OAK	N	7	180	25.7	48t	4
1976			1	25	25.0	25t	1
1977			5	90	18.0	28	0
1978			40	552	13.8	44t	2
1979			3	28	9.3	12	0
1980			6	132	22.0	45t	1
1981			22	298	13.5	29t	3
1982	NE	N	6	111	18.5	48	1
Career			90	1416	15.7	48t	12
Playoffs			1	25	25.0		0

Terry Bradshaw

Year	Team		No	Yds	Avg	Lg	TD
1978	PIT	N	0	1		1L	0

Wes Bradshaw

Year	Team		No	Yds	Avg	Lg	TD
1926	RI	A					1

Kyle Brady

Year	Team		No	Yds	Avg	Lg	TD
1995	NYJ	N	26	252	9.7	29	2
1996			15	144	9.6	25	1
Career			41	396	9.7	29	3

Mark Brammer

Year	Team		No	Yds	Avg	Lg	TD
1980	BUF	N	26	283	10.9	36	4
1981			33	365	11.1	24	2
1982			25	225	9.0	22	2
1983			25	215	8.6	21	2
1984			7	49	7.0	12	0
Career			116	1137	9.8	36	10
Playoffs			9	102	11.3		0

George Brancato

Year	Team		No	Yds	Avg	Lg	TD
1954	CHIC	N	3	28	9.3	22	0

Cliff Branch

Year	Team		No	Yds	Avg	Lg	TD
1972	OAK	N	3	41	13.7	19	0
1973			19	290	15.3	54t	3
1974			60	1092	18.2	67t	13
1975			51	893	17.5	53	9
1976			46	1111	24.2	88t	12
1977			33	540	16.4	43	6
1978			49	709	14.5	41	1
1979			59	844	14.3	66t	6
1980			44	858	19.5	86t	7
1981			41	635	15.5	53	1

Cliff Branch *continued*

Year	Team		No	Yds	Avg	Lg	TD
1982	LARI	N	30	575	19.2	51	4
1983			39	696	17.8	99t	5
1984			27	401	14.9	47	0
Career			501	8685	17.3	99t	67
Playoffs			73	1289	17.7		5

John Brandes

Year	Team		No	Yds	Avg	Lg	TD
1987	IND	N	5	35	7.0	13	0

Jim Brandt

Year	Team		No	Yds	Avg	Lg	TD
1953	PIT	N	2	15	7.5	11	0
1954			1	9	9.0	9	0
Career			3	24	8.0	11	0

Chris Brantley

Year	Team		No	Yds	Avg	Lg	TD
1994	LARM	N	4	29	7.3	10	0
1996	BUF	N	5	47	9.4	22t	1
Career			9	76	8.4	22t	1

Melvin Bratton

Year	Team		No	Yds	Avg	Lg	TD
1989	DEN	N	10	69	6.9	17t	3
1990			29	276	9.5	63	1
Career			39	345	8.8	63	4
Playoffs			2	21	10.5		0

Hez Braxton

Year	Team		No	Yds	Avg	Lg	TD
1962	SD	A	4	17	4.3	6	0

Jim Braxton

Year	Team		No	Yds	Avg	Lg	TD
1971	BUF	N	18	141	7.8	25	0
1972			24	232	9.7	25	1
1973			6	101	16.8	37	0
1974			18	171	9.5	15	0
1975			26	282	10.8	32	4
1977			43	461	10.7	27	1
1978	BUF-MIA	N	9	85	9.4	19	0
Career			144	1473	10.2	37	6
Playoffs			1	8	8.0		0

Carl Brazell

Year	Team		No	Yds	Avg	Lg	TD
1938	CLE	N	7	100	14.3		0

Bill Bredde

Year	Team		No	Yds	Avg	Lg	TD
1954	CHIC	N	3	44	14.7	27	0

John Bredice

Year	Team		No	Yds	Avg	Lg	TD
1956	PHI	N	10	146	14.6	40	1

Bill Breeden

Year	Team		No	Yds	Avg	Lg	TD
1937	PIT	N	6	59	9.8		0

Brian Brennan

Year	Team		No	Yds	Avg	Lg	TD
1984	CLE	N	35	455	13.0	52	3
1985			32	487	15.2	57	0
1986			55	838	15.2	57t	6
1987			43	607	14.1	53t	6
1988			46	579	12.6	33	0
1989			28	289	10.3	38	0
1990			45	568	12.6	28	2
1991			31	325	10.5	30	1
1992	CIN-SD	N	19	188	9.9	21	1
Career			334	4336	13.0	57t	20
Playoffs			24	329	13.7		4

Hoby Brenner

Year	Team		No	Yds	Avg	Lg	TD
1981	NO	N	7	143	20.4	34	0
1982			16	171	10.7	25	0
1983			41	574	14.0	38t	3
1984			28	554	19.8	57	6
1985			42	652	15.5	30	3
1986			18	286	15.9	34	0
1987			20	280	14.0	29	2
1988			5	67	13.4	24	0
1989			34	398	11.7	30t	4
1990			17	213	12.5	31t	2
1991			16	179	11.2	21	0
1992			12	161	13.4	23	0
1993			11	171	15.5	27	1
Career			267	3849	14.4	57t	21
Playoffs			5	74	14.8		0

Monte Brethauer

Year	Team		No	Yds	Avg	Lg	TD
1953	BAL	N	10	133	13.3	25	0

Jeep Brett

Year	Team		No	Yds	Avg	Lg	TD
1936	PIT	N	7	139	19.9		0
1937			8	135	16.9		1
Career			15	274	18.3		1

Bob Breunig

Year	Team		No	Yds	Avg	Lg	TD
1975	DAL	N	1	21	21.0	21	0

Chris Brewer

Year	Team		No	Yds	Avg	Lg	TD
1984	DEN	N	2	20	10.0	16	0
1987	CHI	N	5	56	11.2	19	1
Career			7	76	10.9	19	1

John Brewer

Year	Team		No	Yds	Avg	Lg	TD
1952	PHI	N	5	19	3.8	12	0
1953			4	43	10.8	16	0
Career			9	62	6.9	16	0

Johnny Brewer

Year	Team		No	Yds	Avg	Lg	TD
1962	CLE	N	22	290	13.2	37	2
1963			29	454	15.7	55	0
1964			25	338	13.5	41	3
1965			13	174	13.4	25t	1
Career			89	1256	14.1	55	6
Playoffs			2	26	13.0		0

Darrell Brewster

Year	Team		No	Yds	Avg	Lg	TD
1952	CLE	N	4	117	29.3	47t	1
1953			32	632	19.8	45	4
1954			42	676	16.1	57	4
1955			34	622	18.3	41t	6
1956			28	417	14.9	41	1
1957			30	614	20.5	56	2
1958			16	294	18.4	38	1
1959	PIT	N	22	360	16.4	42	2
1960			2	26	13.0	18	0
Career			210	3758	17.9	57	21
Playoffs			11	223	20.3		1

Greg Brezina

Year	Team		No	Yds	Avg	Lg	TD
1969	ATL	N	1	9	9.0	9	0
1971			1	3	3.0	3	0
Career			2	12	6.0	9	0

Harry Brian

Year	Team		No	Yds	Avg	Lg	TD
1926	HAR	N					1

Bob Briggs

Year	Team		No	Yds	Avg	Lg	TD
1965	WAS	N	3	40	13.3	31	0

Leon Bright

Year	Team		No	Yds	Avg	Lg	TD
1981	NYG	N	28	291	10.4	36	0
1982			2	19	9.5	13	0
1983			2	33	16.5	19	0
Career			32	343	10.7	36	0
Playoffs			1	9	9.0		0

James Brim

Year	Team		No	Yds	Avg	Lg	TD
1987	MIN	N	18	282	15.7	63t	2

Larry Brink

Year	Team		No	Yds	Avg	Lg	TD
1948	LA	N	4	36	9.0	18	0

Dana Brinson

Year	Team		No	Yds	Avg	Lg	TD
1989	SD	N	12	71	5.9	11	0

Larry Brinson

Year	Team		No	Yds	Avg	Lg	TD
1980	SEA	N	1	9	9.0	9	0
Playoffs			1	6	6.0		0

Vincent Brisby

Year	Team		No	Yds	Avg	Lg	TD
1993	NE	N	45	626	13.9	39	2
1994			58	904	15.6	43	5
1995			66	974	14.8	72	3
Career			169	2504	14.8	72	10
Playoffs			8	95	11.9		0

Marlin Briscoe

Year	Team		No	Yds	Avg	Lg	TD
1969	BUF	A	32	532	16.6	50t	5
1970	BUF	N	57	1036	18.2	48	8
1971			44	603	13.7	75t	4
1972	MIA	N	16	279	17.4	51t	5
1973			30	447	14.9	53	2
1974			11	132	12.0	20	1

Year	Team		No	Yds	Avg	Lg	TD

Marlin Briscoe *continued*

Year	Team		No	Yds	Avg	Lg	TD
1975	SD-DET	N	24	372	15.5	59t	4
1976	NE	N	10	136	13.6	21	1
Career			224	3537	15.8	75t	30
Playoffs			5	49	9.8		0

Bubby Brister

1989	PIT	N	1	-10	-10.0	-10	0
1995	NYJ	N	1	2	2.0	2	0
Career			2	-8	-4.0	2	0

Willie Brister

1974	NYJ	N	5	90	18.0	32	0
1975			1	3	3.0	3	0
Career			6	93	15.5	32	0

Gene Brito

1951	WAS	N	24	313	13.0	38	0
1952			21	270	12.9	28t	2
1953			2	35	17.5	24	0
Career			47	618	13.1	38	2

Eddie Britt

| 1936 | BOS | N | 6 | 106 | 17.7 | | 0 |

Maury Britt

| 1941 | DET | N | 1 | 45 | 45.0 | 45 | 1 |

Jerry Broadnax

| 1974 | HOU | N | 3 | 69 | 23.0 | 42 | 0 |

Lou Brock

1940	GB	N	5	97	19.4		0
1941			22	307	14.0	36	2
1942			20	139	7.0	29	1
1943			4	57	14.3	32	1
1944			4	74	18.5	52t	2
1945			4	87	21.8	46	0
Career			59	761	12.9	52t	6

Pete Brock

| 1976 | NE | N | 1 | 6 | 6.0 | 6t | 1 |

John Brockington

1971	GB	N	14	98	7.0	29	1
1972			19	243	12.8	48t	1
1973			16	128	8.0	37	0
1974			43	314	7.3	29	0
1975			33	242	7.3	21	1
1976			11	49	4.5	20	0
1977	GB-KC	N	21	223	10.6	48	1
Career			157	1297	8.3	48t4	
Playoffs			2	17	8.5		0

J.W. Brodnax

| 1960 | DEN | A | 5 | 39 | 7.8 | 19 | 1 |

Tommy Brooker

1962	DAL	A	4	138	34.5	92	3
1963	KC	A	2	32	16.0	16	0
Career			6	170	28.3	92	3

Mitchell Brookins

1984	BUF	N	18	318	17.7	70t	1
1985			3	71	23.7	46	0
Career			21	389	18.5	70t	1

Bill Brooks

1986	IND	N	65	1131	17.4	84t	8
1987			51	722	14.2	52t	3
1988			54	867	16.1	53t	3
1989			63	919	14.6	55t	4
1990			62	823	13.3	75	5
1991			72	888	12.3	46	4
1992			44	468	10.6	26	1
1993	BUF	N	60	714	11.9	32	5
1994			42	482	11.5	32	2
1995			53	763	14.4	51t	11
1996	WAS	N	17	224	13.2	31	0
Career			583	8001	13.7	84t	46
Playoffs			27	312	11.6		2

Billy Brooks

| 1976 | CIN | N | 16 | 191 | 11.9 | 25 | 0 |

Year	Team		No	Yds	Avg	Lg	TD

Billy Brooks *continued*

1977			39	772	19.8	94t	4
1978			30	506	16.9	45	2
1979			8	214	26.8	73t	1
1981	SD-HOU	N	3	37	12.3	21	0
Career			96	1720	17.9	94t	7

James Brooks

1981	SD	N	46	329	7.2	29t	3
1982			13	66	5.1	12	0
1983			25	215	8.6	36	0
1984	CIN	N	34	268	7.9	27t	2
1985			55	576	10.5	57t	5
1986			54	686	12.7	54	4
1987			22	272	12.4	46	2
1988			29	287	9.9	28t	6
1989			37	306	8.3	25	2
1990			26	269	10.3	35	4
1991			40	348	8.7	40	2
1992	CLE	N	2	-1	-0.5	4	0
Career			383	3621	9.5	57t	30
Playoffs			14	137	9.8		3

Reggie Brooks

1993	WAS	N	21	186	8.9	43	0
1994			13	68	5.2	16	0
1996	TB	N	3	13	4.3	9	0
Career			37	267	7.2	43	0

Robert Brooks

1992	GB	N	12	126	10.5	18	1
1993			20	180	9.0	25	0
1994			58	648	11.2	35	4
1995			102	1497	14.7	99t	13
1996			23	344	15.0	38	4
Career			215	2795	13.0	99t	22
Playoffs			36	547	15.2		4

Mal Bross

| 1926 | LA | A | | | | | 2 |

Walter Broughton

1986	BUF	N	3	71	23.7	57	0
1987			5	90	18.0	39	1
Career			8	161	20.1	57	1

Steve Broussard

1990	ATL	N	24	160	6.7	18	0
1991			12	120	10.0	25t	1
1992			11	96	8.7	24	1
1993			1	4	4.0	4	0
1994	CIN	N	34	218	6.4	25	0
1995	SEA	N	10	94	9.4	25	0
1996			6	26	4.3	9	0
Career			98	718	7.3	25t	2

A.B. Brown

1989	NYJ	N	4	10	2.5	6	0
1992			4	30	7.5	20	0
Career			8	40	5.0	20	0

Allen Brown

| 1967 | GB | N | 3 | 43 | 14.3 | 17 | 0 |

Andre Brown

1989	MIA	N	24	410	17.1	48t	5
1990			3	49	16.3	24	0
Career			27	459	17.0	48t	5

Barry Brown

1969	BOS	A	6	69	11.5	15	0
1970	BOS	N	15	145	9.7	22	0
Career			21	214	10.2	22	0

Bill Brown

1943	BKN	N	4	42	10.5	19	0
1944			2	10	5.0	8	0
Career			6	52	8.7	19	0

Bill Brown

1961	CHI	N	2	6	3.0	13	0
1962	MIN	N	10	124	12.4	29	1
1963			17	109	6.4	30	2
1964			48	703	14.6	64	9

Year	Team		No	Yds	Avg	Lg	TD

Bill Brown *continued*

1965			41	503	12.3	47	1
1966			37	359	9.7	56	0
1967			22	26	1.2	43	0
1968			31	329	10.6	57t	3
1969			21	183	8.7	27	0
1970			15	149	9.9	17t	2
1971			10	94	9.4	36	0
1972			22	298	13.5	76t	4
1973			5	22	4.4	7	1
1974			5	41	8.2	21	0
Career			286	2946	10.3	76t	23
Playoffs			15	142	9.5		1

Bob Brown

1971	MIN	N	6	141	23.5	48	0
1972	NO	N	11	175	15.9	34	1
1973			11	132	12.0	26	0
Career			28	448	16.0	48	1

Boyd Brown

| 1975 | DEN | N | 1 | 14 | 14.0 | 14 | 0 |

Charlie Brown

| 1967 | NO | N | 3 | 23 | 7.7 | 9 | 0 |

Charlie Brown

1982	WAS	N	32	690	21.6	78t	8
1983			78	1225	15.7	75t	8
1984			18	200	11.1	36	3
1985	ATL	N	24	412	17.2	48	2
1986			63	918	14.6	42	4
1987			5	103	20.6	23	0
Career			220	3548	16.1	78t	25
Playoffs			31	643	20.7		3

Charlie Brown

| 1970 | DET | N | 2 | 38 | 19.0 | 23 | 0 |

Corwin Brown

| Playoffs | | | 1 | 21 | 21.0 | | 0 |

Curtis Brown

1977	BUF	N	5	20	4.0	12t	1
1978			18	130	7.2	31	0
1979			39	401	10.3	84t	3
1980			27	137	5.1	20	0
1981			7	46	6.6	10	1
1982			6	38	6.3	28	0
Career			102	772	7.6	84t	5

Dave Brown

1943	NYG	N	5	29	5.8	12	1
1947			1	5	5.0	5	0
Career			6	34	5.7	12	1

Derek Brown

1992	NYG	N	4	31	7.8	9	0
1993			7	56	8.0	14	0
1996	JAC	N	17	141	8.3	16	0
Career			28	228	8.1	16	0
Playoffs			2	18	9.0		0

Derek Brown

1993	NO	N	21	170	8.1	19	1
1994			44	428	9.7	37	1
1995			35	266	7.6	19	1
1996			8	54	6.8	18	0
Career			108	918	8.5	37	3

Ed Brown

| 1960 | CHI | N | 1 | -6 | -6.0 | -6 | 0 |

Eddie Brown

1985	CIN	N	53	942	17.8	68t	8
1986			58	964	16.6	57	4
1987			44	608	13.8	47t	3
1988			53	1273	24.0	86t	9
1989			52	814	15.7	46	6
1990			44	706	16.0	50t	9
1991			59	827	14.0	53	2
Career			363	6134	16.9	86t	41
Playoffs			9	99	11.0		0

Year	Team		No	Yds	Avg	Lg	TD

Eric Brown
Year	Team		No	Yds	Avg	Lg	TD
1987	KC	N	5	69	13.8	23	0

Fred Brown
Year	Team		No	Yds	Avg	Lg	TD
1961	BUF	A	1	11	11.0	11	0
1963			2	7	3.5	7	0
Career			3	18	6.0	11	0

Fred Brown
Year	Team		No	Yds	Avg	Lg	TD
1969	PHI	N	1	20	20.0	20	0

Gary Brown
Year	Team		No	Yds	Avg	Lg	TD
1991	HOU	N	2	1	0.5	4	0
1992			1	5	5.0	5	0
1993			21	240	11.4	38t	2
1994			18	194	10.8	24	1
1995			6	16	2.7	7	0
Career			48	456	9.5	38t	3
Playoffs			4	26	6.5		0

Hardy Brown
Year	Team		No	Yds	Avg	Lg	TD
1948	BKN	AA	3	36	12.0		1
1949	CHI	AA	1	10	10.0	10	0
Career			4	46	11.5	10	1

Ivory Lee Brown
Year	Team		No	Yds	Avg	Lg	TD
1992	PHX	N	7	54	7.7	18	0

Jim Brown
Year	Team		No	Yds	Avg	Lg	TD
1957	CLE	N	16	55	3.4	12	1
1958			16	138	8.6	46	1
1959			24	190	7.9	25	0
1960			19	204	10.7	37t	2
1961			46	459	10.0	77t	2
1962			47	517	11.0	53t	5
1963			24	268	11.2	83t	3
1964			36	340	9.4	40t	2
1965			34	328	9.6	32t	4
Career			262	2499	9.5	83t	20
Playoffs			8	99	12.4		0

Ken Brown
Year	Team		No	Yds	Avg	Lg	TD
1972	CLE	N	5	64	12.8	19	0
1973			22	187	8.5	46	0
1974			29	194	6.7	19	2
1975			2	23	11.5	17	0
Career			58	468	8.1	46	2

Laron Brown
Year	Team		No	Yds	Avg	Lg	TD
1987	DEN	N	4	40	10.0	18	0

Larry Brown
Year	Team		No	Yds	Avg	Lg	TD
1969	WAS	N	34	302	8.9	31	0
1970			37	341	9.2	66	2
1971			16	176	11.0	36t	2
1972			32	473	14.8	89t	4
1973			40	482	12.1	64t	4
1974			37	388	10.5	34	4
1975			25	225	9.0	39	2
1976			17	98	5.8	15	0
Career			238	2485	10.4	89t	20
Playoffs			16	117	7.3		1

Larry Brown
Year	Team		No	Yds	Avg	Lg	TD
1971	PIT	N	1	3	3.0	3t	1
1972			1	13	13.0	13t	1
1973			5	88	17.6	45	0
1974			17	190	11.2	35	1
1975			16	244	15.3	27	1
1976			7	97	13.9	35	0
1979			1	1	1.0	1t	1
Career			48	636	13.3	45	5
Playoffs			12	186	15.5		2

Marc Brown
Year	Team		No	Yds	Avg	Lg	TD
1987	BUF	N	9	120	13.3	30	1

Preston Brown
Year	Team		No	Yds	Avg	Lg	TD
1982	NE	N	4	114	28.5	41	1
Playoffs			1	8	8.0		0

Reggie Brown
Year	Team		No	Yds	Avg	Lg	TD
1987	PHI	N	8	53	6.6	14	0

Reggie Brown
Year	Team		No	Yds	Avg	Lg	TD
1993	HOU	N	2	30	15.0	26	0
1994			4	34	8.5	11	0
Career			6	64	10.7	26	0

Ron Brown
Year	Team		No	Yds	Avg	Lg	TD
1984	LARM	N	23	478	20.8	54	4
1985			14	215	15.4	43t	3
1986			25	396	15.8	65t	3
1987			26	521	20.0	52	2
1988			2	16	8.0	10	0
1989			5	113	22.6	39t	1
1991			3	52	17.3	21	0
Career			98	1791	18.3	65t	13
Playoffs			9	107	11.9		0

Ron Brown
Year	Team		No	Yds	Avg	Lg	TD
1987	STL	N	2	16	8.0	9	0

Ted Brown
Year	Team		No	Yds	Avg	Lg	TD
1979	MIN	N	31	197	6.4	35	0
1980			62	623	10.0	67t	2
1981			83	694	8.4	63	2
1982			31	207	6.7	29	2
1983			41	357	8.7	25	1
1984			46	349	7.6	35	3
1985			30	291	9.7	54t	3
1986			15	132	8.8	20	0
Career			339	2850	8.4	67t	13
Playoffs			12	96	8.0		0

Terry Brown
Year	Team		No	Yds	Avg	Lg	TD
1969	STL	N	1	7	7.0	7	0

Theotis Brown
Year	Team		No	Yds	Avg	Lg	TD
1979	STL	N	25	191	7.6	19	0
1980			21	190	9.0	38	1
1981	STL-SEA	N	29	328	11.3	51	0
1982	SEA	N	12	95	7.9	18	0
1983	KC	N	47	418	8.9	53	2
1984			38	236	6.2	17	0
Career			172	1558	9.1	63	3

Tim Brown
Year	Team		No	Yds	Avg	Lg	TD
1988	LARI	N	43	725	16.9	65t	5
1989			1	8	8.0	8	0
1990			18	265	14.7	51	3
1991			36	554	15.4	78t	5
1992			49	693	14.1	68t	7
1993			80	1180	14.8	71t	7
1994			89	1309	14.7	77t	9
1995	OAK	N	89	1342	15.1	80t	10
1996			90	1104	12.3	42t	9
Career			495	7180	14.5	80t	55
Playoffs			17	317	18.6		2

Timmy Brown
Year	Team		No	Yds	Avg	Lg	TD
1960	PHI	N	9	247	27.4	71	2
1961			14	264	18.9	65	2
1962			52	849	16.3	82t	6
1963			36	487	13.5	80t	4
1964			15	244	16.3	87t	5
1965			50	682	13.6	45t	3
1966			33	371	11.2	39	3
1967			22	202	9.2	41	1
1968	BAL	N	4	53	13.3	18	0
Career			235	3399	14.5	87t	26

Tom Brown
Year	Team		No	Yds	Avg	Lg	TD
1942	PIT	N	4	69	17.3	30	0

Tom Brown
Year	Team		No	Yds	Avg	Lg	TD
1987	MIA	N	1	6	6.0	6	0
1989			13	117	9.0	23	0
Career			14	123	8.8	23	0

Troy Brown
Year	Team		No	Yds	Avg	Lg	TD
1993	NE	N	2	22	11.0	14	0
1995			14	159	11.4	31	0
1996			21	222	10.6	38	0
Career			37	403	10.9	38	0

Tyrone Brown
Year	Team		No	Yds	Avg	Lg	TD
1995	ATL	N	17	198	11.6	26	0

Tyrone Brown continued
Year	Team		No	Yds	Avg	Lg	TD
1996			28	325	11.6	38	1
Career			45	523	11.6	38	1
Playoffs			1	14	14.0		0

Willie Brown
Year	Team		No	Yds	Avg	Lg	TD
1964	LA	N	1	19	19.0	19	0
1965			4	91	22.8	37	1
Career			5	110	22.0	37	1

Jim Browne
Year	Team		No	Yds	Avg	Lg	TD
1987	LARI	N	2	8	4.0	5	0

Greg Browning
Year	Team		No	Yds	Avg	Lg	TD
1947	NYG	N	1	12	12.0	12	0

Dick Brubaker
Year	Team		No	Yds	Avg	Lg	TD
1955	CHIC	N	6	125	20.8	43	0
1960	BUF	A	7	75	10.7		1
Career			13	200	15.4	43	1

Aundray Bruce
Year	Team		No	Yds	Avg	Lg	TD
1991	ATL	N	1	11	11.0	11	0

Gail Bruce
Year	Team		No	Yds	Avg	Lg	TD
1948	SF	AA	5	49	9.8		0
1949			1	9	9.0	9	0
1950	SF	N	1	10	10.0	10	0
Career			7	68	9.7	10	0

Isaac Bruce
Year	Team		No	Yds	Avg	Lg	TD
1994	LARM	N	21	272	13.0	34t	3
1995	STL	N	119	1781	15.0	72	13
1996			84	**1338**	15.9	70	7
Career			224	3391	15.1	72	23

Nick Bruckner
Year	Team		No	Yds	Avg	Lg	TD
1984	NYJ	N	1	11	11.0	11	0

Hank Bruder
Year	Team		No	Yds	Avg	Lg	TD
1931	GB	N					2
1932							2
1934							1
1935			4	71	17.8		0
1936			2	25	12.5		0
1938			2	14	7.0		0
1939			4	65	16.3		0
1940	PIT	N	5	49	9.8		0
Career			17	224	13.2		6

Mark Bruener
Year	Team		No	Yds	Avg	Lg	TD
1995	PIT	N	26	238	9.2	29	3
1996			12	141	11.8	36	0
Career			38	379	10.0	36	3
Playoffs			1	6	6.0		0

Bob Bruer
Year	Team		No	Yds	Avg	Lg	TD
1979	SF	N	26	254	9.8	19	1
1981	MIN	N	7	38	5.4	10	3
1982			8	102	12.8	24	2
1983			31	315	10.2	26	2
Career			72	709	9.8	26	8
Playoffs			1	8	8.0		0

Boyd Brumbaugh
Year	Team		No	Yds	Avg	Lg	TD
1938	BKN	N	1	5	5.0	5	1
1939	BKN-PIT	N	5	95	19.0		2
1940	PIT	N	1	0	0.0	0	0
1941			1	1	1.0	1	0
Career			8	101	12.6	5	2

Carl Brumbaugh
Year	Team		No	Yds	Avg	Lg	TD
1934	CHIB	N	5	84	16.8		2
1936			5	39	7.8		2
1938			1	23	23.0	23	0
Career			11	146	13.3	23	4
Playoffs			4	96	24.0		0

Bob Brumley
Year	Team		No	Yds	Avg	Lg	TD
1945	DET	N	2	27	13.5	29	0

Bob Brunet
Year	Team		No	Yds	Avg	Lg	TD
1968	WAS	N	18	160	8.9	39t	0
1970			3	28	9.3	14	0

Year	Team		No	Yds	Avg	Lg	TD

Bob Brunet continued

Year	Team		No	Yds	Avg	Lg	TD
1971			2	4	2.0	5	0
1972			1	8	8.0	8	0
Career			24	200	8.3	39t	1

Larry Brunson

Year	Team		No	Yds	Avg	Lg	TD
1974	KC	N	22	374	17.0	84t	2
1975			23	398	17.3	36	2
1976			33	656	19.9	57	1
1977			20	295	14.8	63	0
1979	OAK	N	5	49	9.8	17	1
1980	DEN	N	1	15	15.0	15	0
Career			104	1787	17.2	84t	6

Johnny Bryan

Year	Team		No	Yds	Avg	Lg	TD
1924	CHIB	N					1
1925							1
Career							2

Bob Bryant

Year	Team		No	Yds	Avg	Lg	TD
1960	DAL	A	5	43	8.6		0

Charlie Bryant

Year	Team		No	Yds	Avg	Lg	TD
1968	ATL	N	1	11	11.0	11	0
1969			2	15	7.5	9	0
Career			3	26	8.7	11	0

Cullen Bryant

Year	Team		No	Yds	Avg	Lg	TD
1974	LA	N	2	14	7.0	8	0
1975			20	229	11.4	31	0
1976			2	28	14.0	25	0
1977			4	28	7.0	14	0
1978			8	76	9.5	37	0
1979			31	227	7.3	24	0
1980			53	386	7.3	25	3
1981			22	160	7.3	39	0
1983	SEA	N	3	8	2.7	3	0
1984			3	20	6.7	11	0
Career			148	1176	7.9	39	3
Playoffs			19	151	7.9		1

Hubie Bryant

Year	Team		No	Yds	Avg	Lg	TD
1970	PIT	N	8	154	19.3	63	0
1971	NE	N	14	212	15.1	48	1
Career			22	366	16.6	63	1

Kelvin Bryant

Year	Team		No	Yds	Avg	Lg	TD
1986	WAS	N	43	449	10.4	40	3
1987			43	490	11.4	39	5
1988			42	447	10.6	47	5
1990			26	248	9.5	37	1
Career			154	1634	10.6	47	14
Playoffs			18	191	10.6		2

Steve Bryant

Year	Team		No	Yds	Avg	Lg	TD
1983	HOU	N	16	211	13.2	26	0
1984			19	278	14.6	28	0
1987	IND	N	1	12	12.0	12	0
Career			36	501	13.9	28	0

Richard Buchanan

Year	Team		No	Yds	Avg	Lg	TD
1994	LARM	N	5	60	12.0	18	0

Frank Bucher

Year	Team		No	Yds	Avg	Lg	TD
1925	POT	N					2

Don Buckey

Year	Team		No	Yds	Avg	Lg	TD
1976	NYJ	N	5	36	7.2	14	0

Phil Bucklew

Year	Team		No	Yds	Avg	Lg	TD
1937	CLE	N	3	51	17.0	14	0
1938			1	14	14.0	14	0
Career			4	65	16.3	14	0

Ralph Buckley

Year	Team		No	Yds	Avg	Lg	TD
1930	SI	N					1

Tom Buckman

Year	Team		No	Yds	Avg	Lg	TD
1969	DEN	A	4	48	12.0	20	1

Frank Budd

Year	Team		No	Yds	Avg	Lg	TD
1962	PHI	N	5	130	26.0	49t	1
1963	WAS	N	5	106	21.2	50	0
Career			10	236	23.6	50	1

Doug Buffone

Year	Team		No	Yds	Avg	Lg	TD
1979	CHI	N	1	22	22.0	22	0

Danny Buggs

Year	Team		No	Yds	Avg	Lg	TD
1976	WAS	N	2	25	12.5	13	0
1977			26	341	13.1	45	1
1978			36	575	16.0	63	2
1979			46	631	13.7	45	1
Career			110	1572	14.3	63	4

Larry Buhler

Year	Team		No	Yds	Avg	Lg	TD
Playoffs			1	8	8.0		0

Drew Buie

Year	Team		No	Yds	Avg	Lg	TD
1969	OAK	A	1	37	37.0	37	0
1970	OAK	N	2	52	26.0	33	0
1971			5	133	26.6	63t	2
1972	CIN	N	1	5	5.0	5	0
Career			9	227	25.2	63t	2

Ray Buivid

Year	Team		No	Yds	Avg	Lg	TD
1937	CHIB	N	1	4	4.0	4	0
1938			1	8	8.0	8	0
Career			2	12	6.0	8	0

Joe Bukant

Year	Team		No	Yds	Avg	Lg	TD
1940	PHI	N	1	13	13.0	13	0
1943	CHIC	N	1	0	0.0	0	0
Career			2	13	6.5	13	0

Fred Bukaty

Year	Team		No	Yds	Avg	Lg	TD
1961	DEN	A	14	94	6.7	13	0

George Buksar

Year	Team		No	Yds	Avg	Lg	TD
1950	BAL	N	2	2	1.0	2	0
1952	WAS	N	2	3	1.5	3	0
Career			4	5	1.3	3	0

Norm Bulaich

Year	Team		No	Yds	Avg	Lg	TD
1970	BAL	N	11	123	11.2	20	0
1971			25	229	9.2	30t	2
1972			9	55	6.1	10	0
1973	PHI	N	42	403	9.6	80t	3
1974			28	204	7.3	26	0
1975	MIA	N	32	276	8.6	59t	5
1976			28	151	5.4	25	0
1977			25	180	7.2	14	0
1978			16	92	5.8	22	0
1979			8	53	6.6	13	1
Career			224	1766	7.9	80t	11
Playoffs			3	19	6.3		0

Ronnie Bull

Year	Team		No	Yds	Avg	Lg	TD
1962	CHI	N	31	331	10.7	52	0
1963			19	132	6.9	44t	2
1964			15	35	2.3	9	0
1965			16	186	11.6	41	1
1966			20	174	8.7	28	0
1967			18	250	13.9	63	1
1968			17	145	8.5	24	0
1969			14	91	6.5	17	0
1970			13	60	4.6	17	0
1971	PHI	N	9	75	8.3	15	1
Career			172	1479	8.6	63	5
Playoffs			1	-5	-5.0		0

Amos Bullocks

Year	Team		No	Yds	Avg	Lg	TD
1962	DAL	N	3	46	15.3	22t	1
1963			7	70	10.0	22	0
1966	PIT	N	5	64	12.8	18	1
Career			15	180	12.0	22t	2

Rex Bumgardner

Year	Team		No	Yds	Avg	Lg	TD
1948	BUF	AA	1	63	63.0	63	0
1949			7	168	24.0		4
1950	CLE	N	9	112	12.4	25t	1
1951			5	61	12.2	19	1
Career			22	404	18.4	63	6
Playoffs			14	202	14.4		1

Jarrod Bunch

Year	Team		No	Yds	Avg	Lg	TD
1991	NYG	N	2	8	4.0	6	0
1992			11	50	4.5	13	0

Jarrod Bunch continued

Year	Team		No	Yds	Avg	Lg	TD
1993			13	98	7.5	15	1
Career			26	156	6.0	15	2

Cornell Burbage

Year	Team		No	Yds	Avg	Lg	TD
1987	DAL	N	7	168	24.0	77t	2
1988			2	50	25.0	41	0
1989			17	134	7.9	15	0
Career			26	352	13.5	77t	2

Jerry Burch

Year	Team		No	Yds	Avg	Lg	TD
1961	OAK	A	18	235	13.1	54	1

Don Burchfield

Year	Team		No	Yds	Avg	Lg	TD
1971	NO	N	3	36	12.0	16	0

Chris Burford

Year	Team		No	Yds	Avg	Lg	TD
1960	DAL	A	46	789	17.2	57	5
1961			51	850	16.7	54	4
1962			45	645	14.3	49	12
1963	KC	A	68	824	12.1	69	9
1964			51	675	13.2	55	7
1965			47	575	12.2	57	6
1966			58	758	13.1	38	8
1967			25	389	15.6	55	3
Career			391	5505	14.1	69	54
Playoffs			8	143	17.9		0

John Burke

Year	Team		No	Yds	Avg	Lg	TD
1994	NE	N	9	86	9.6	17	0
1995			15	136	9.1	21	0
1996			1	19	19.0	19	0
Career			25	241	9.6	21	0
Playoffs			1	8	8.0		0

Randy Burke

Year	Team		No	Yds	Avg	Lg	TD
1979	BAL	N	6	151	25.2	59	0
1980			14	185	13.2	19t	3
1981			10	153	15.3	24	0
Career			30	489	16.3	59	3

Vern Burke

Year	Team		No	Yds	Avg	Lg	TD
1965	SF	N	2	38	19.0	27t	1
1966	ATL	N	28	348	12.4	45	1
1967	NO	N	8	84	10.5	21	0
Career			38	470	12.4	45	2

Chris Burkett

Year	Team		No	Yds	Avg	Lg	TD
1985	BUF	N	21	371	17.7	38	0
1986			34	778	22.9	84t	4
1987			56	765	13.7	47	4
1988			23	354	15.4	34	1
1989	BUF-NYJ	N	24	298	12.4	30	1
1990	NYJ	N	14	204	14.6	46	0
1991			23	327	14.2	50t	4
1992			57	724	12.7	37t	1
1993			40	531	13.3	77	4
Career			292	4352	14.9	84t	19
Playoffs			3	55	18.3		1

Jeff Burkett

Year	Team		No	Yds	Avg	Lg	TD
1947	CHIC	N	2	44	22.0	27	1

Randy Burks

Year	Team		No	Yds	Avg	Lg	TD
1976	CHI	N	1	55	55.0	55t	1

Steve Burks

Year	Team		No	Yds	Avg	Lg	TD
1975	NE	N	6	158	26.3	76	0
1976			2	27	13.5	17	0
1977			5	79	15.8	22	0
Career			13	264	20.3	76	0

Alex Burl

Year	Team		No	Yds	Avg	Lg	TD
1956	CHIC	N	2	24	12.0	19t	1

Bobby Burnett

Year	Team		No	Yds	Avg	Lg	TD
1966	BUF	A	34	419	12.3	48	4
1967			11	114	10.4	38	0
Career			45	533	11.8	48	4
Playoffs			6	127	21.2		0

Dale Burnett

Year	Team		No	Yds	Avg	Lg	TD
1930	NYG	N					2
1931							2

Year	Team		No	Yds	Avg	Lg	TD

Dale Burnett continued

Year	Team		No	Yds	Avg	Lg	TD
1932							1
1933			12	211	17.6		**3**
1934			9	152	16.9		2
1935			12	199	16.6		**6**
1936			16	246	15.4		3
1937			10	121	12.1		1
1938			13	145	11.2		1
1939			8	86	10.8		0
Career			80	1160	14.5		21
Playoffs			7	124	17.7		0

Tom Burnette

Year	Team		No	Yds	Avg	Lg	TD
1938	PIT	N	1	3	3.0	3	0

Hank Burnine

Year	Team		No	Yds	Avg	Lg	TD
1956	PHI	N	10	208	20.8	52	2
1957			7	63	9.0	16	0
Career			17	271	15.9	52	2

Bob Burns

Year	Team		No	Yds	Avg	Lg	TD
1974	NYJ	N	11	83	7.5	18	1

Leon Burns

Year	Team		No	Yds	Avg	Lg	TD
1971	SD	N	3	22	7.3	10	0
1972	STL	N	6	24	4.0	12	0
Career			9	46	5.1	12	0

Johnny Burrell

Year	Team		No	Yds	Avg	Lg	TD
1962	PIT	N	8	193	24.1	42	0
1963			2	27	13.5	14	0
1964			6	113	18.8	43	0
1966	WAS	N	1	9	9.0	9	0
1967			9	95	10.6	23	0
Career			26	437	16.8	43	0

Ode Burrell

Year	Team		No	Yds	Avg	Lg	TD
1964	HOU	A	5	73	14.6	36	0
1965			55	650	11.8	52	4
1966			33	400	12.1	34	5
1967			12	193	16.1	39	0
1968			2	35	17.5	33	0
1969			5	28	5.6	9	0
Career			112	1379	12.3	52	9

Ken Burrough

Year	Team		No	Yds	Avg	Lg	TD
1970	NO	N	13	196	15.1	35	2
1971	HOU	N	25	370	14.8	62t	1
1972			26	521	20.0	80t	4
1973			43	577	13.4	49t	2
1974			36	492	13.7	51	2
1975			53	**1063**	20.1	77t	8
1976			51	932	18.3	69t	7
1977			43	816	19.0	85t	8
1978			47	624	13.3	44	2
1979			40	752	18.8	55t	6
1980			4	91	22.8	54	0
1981			40	668	16.7	71t	7
Career			421	7102	16.9	85t	49
Playoffs			9	194	21.6		1

Ken Burrow

Year	Team		No	Yds	Avg	Lg	TD
1971	ATL	N	33	741	22.5	84	6
1972			29	492	17.0	40	5
1973			31	567	18.3	57	7
1974			34	545	16.0	48	1
1975			25	323	12.9	23	2
Career			152	2668	17.6	84	21

Harry Burrus

Year	Team		No	Yds	Avg	Lg	TD
1946	NY	AA	10	251	25.1	75	1
1947			8	192	24.0		2
1948	BKN	AA	10	227	22.7	60t	1
Career			28	670	23.9	75	4

Russ Burt

Year	Team		No	Yds	Avg	Lg	TD
1924	BUF	N					1

Larry Burton

Year	Team		No	Yds	Avg	Lg	TD
1975	NO	N	16	305	19.1	71t	2
1976			18	297	16.5	69t	2
1977			1	13	13.0	13	0
1978	SD	N	5	127	25.4	55t	3

Larry Burton continued

Year	Team		No	Yds	Avg	Lg	TD
1979			4	62	15.5	23	0
Career			44	804	18.3	71t	7

Leon Burton

Year	Team		No	Yds	Avg	Lg	TD
1960	NY	A	3	8	2.7		0

Ron Burton

Year	Team		No	Yds	Avg	Lg	TD
1960	BOS	A	21	196	9.3		0
1961			13	115	8.8	45	0
1962			40	462	11.6	69	4
1964			27	306	11.3	59	2
1965			10	127	12.7	73	2
Career			111	1206	10.9	73	8
Playoffs			7	34	4.9		0

Sam Busich

Year	Team		No	Yds	Avg	Lg	TD
1936	BOS	N	6	57	9.5		1
1937	CLE	N	13	136	10.5		0
Career			19	193	10.2		1

Dexter Bussey

Year	Team		No	Yds	Avg	Lg	TD
1974	DET	N	4	24	6.0	8	0
1975			14	175	12.5	65t	2
1976			28	218	7.8	27	0
1977			11	116	10.5	39	1
1978			31	275	8.9	18t	0
1979			15	102	6.8	22	0
1980			39	364	9.3	30	0
1981			18	92	5.1	16	0
1982			16	138	8.6	21	0
1983			8	49	6.1	14t	1
1984			9	63	7.0	19	0
Career			193	1616	8.4	65t	5
Playoffs			1	-2	-2.0		0

Wendell Butcher

Year	Team		No	Yds	Avg	Lg	TD
1938	BKN	N	3	44	14.7		0
1939			9	73	8.1		0
1940			2	21	10.5		0
1942			1	16	16.0	16	0
Career			15	154	10.3	16	0

Bill Butler

Year	Team		No	Yds	Avg	Lg	TD
1959	GB	N	1	-2	-2.0	-2	0
1963	MIN	N	4	39	9.8	19	0
1964			1	58	58.0	58	0
Career			6	95	15.8	58	0

Bill Butler

Year	Team		No	Yds	Avg	Lg	TD
1972	NO	N	25	226	9.0	21	2
1973			19	125	6.6	16	2
1974			2	3	1.5	2	0
Career			46	354	7.7	21	4

Gary Butler

Year	Team		No	Yds	Avg	Lg	TD
1973	KC	N	8	124	15.5	48	2
1977	TB	N	1	21	21.0	21	0
Career			9	145	16.1	48	2

Jack Butler

Year	Team		No	Yds	Avg	Lg	TD
1952	PIT	N	3	37	12.3	20t	2
1953			2	43	21.5	33t	1
1954			1	12	12.0	12	0
1956			1	10	10.0	10t	1
Career			7	102	14.6	33t	4

Jerry Butler

Year	Team		No	Yds	Avg	Lg	TD
1979	BUF	N	48	834	17.4	75t	4
1980			57	832	14.6	69	6
1981			55	842	15.3	67t	8
1982			26	336	12.9	47	4
1983			36	385	10.7	25	3
1985			41	770	18.8	60t	2
1986			15	302	20.1	53	2
Career			278	4301	15.5	75t	29
Playoffs			7	123	17.6		1

Jerry Butler

Year	Team		No	Yds	Avg	Lg	TD
1987	ATL	N	2	7	3.5	4	0

Jim Butler

Year	Team		No	Yds	Avg	Lg	TD
1965	PIT	N	9	117	13.0	43t	1

Jim Butler continued

Year	Team		No	Yds	Avg	Lg	TD
1966			4	93	23.3	66t	1
1967			4	23	5.8	13	0
1968	ATL	N	15	127	8.5	31	0
1969			17	297	17.5	65t	2
1970			24	151	6.3	25	1
1971			15	143	9.5	27t	2
1972	STL	N	1	8	8.0	8	0
Career			89	959	10.8	66t	7

Johnny Butler

Year	Team		No	Yds	Avg	Lg	TD
1943	P-P	N	3	63	21.0	37	0
1944	C-P	N	3	109	36.3	67t	2
1945	PHI	N	2	14	7.0	9	0
Career			8	186	23.3	67t	2

Ray Butler

Year	Team		No	Yds	Avg	Lg	TD
1980	BAL	N	34	574	16.9	42	2
1981			46	832	18.1	67t	9
1982			17	268	15.8	53t	2
1983			10	207	20.7	60	3
1984	IND	N	43	664	15.4	74t	6
1985			19	345	18.2	72t	2
1986	SEA	N	19	351	18.5	67t	4
1987			33	465	14.1	40t	5
1988			18	242	13.4	46t	4
Career			239	3948	16.5	74t	37
Playoffs			5	113	22.6		0

Marion Butts

Year	Team		No	Yds	Avg	Lg	TD
1989	SD	N	7	21	3.0	8	0
1990			16	117	7.3	26	0
1991			10	91	9.1	46	1
1992			9	73	8.1	22	0
1993			15	105	7.0	23	0
1994	NE	N	9	54	6.0	15	0
1995	HOU	N	2	10	5.0	10	0
Career			68	471	6.9	46	1
Playoffs			3	17	5.7		0

Keith Byars

Year	Team		No	Yds	Avg	Lg	TD
1986	PHI	N	11	44	4.0	17	0
1987			21	177	8.4	30	1
1988			72	705	9.8	37t	4
1989			68	721	10.6	60	0
1990			81	819	10.1	54	3
1991			62	564	9.1	37	3
1992			56	502	9.0	46	2
1993	MIA	N	61	613	10.0	27	3
1994			49	418	8.5	34	5
1995			51	362	7.1	26	2
1996	MIA-NE	N	32	289	9.0	27	2
Career			564	5214	9.2	60	25
Playoffs			45	398	8.8		2

Earnest Byner

Year	Team		No	Yds	Avg	Lg	TD
1984	CLE	N	11	118	10.7	26	0
1985			45	460	10.2	31	2
1986			37	328	8.9	40	2
1987			52	552	10.6	37	2
1988			59	576	9.8	39t	2
1989	WAS	N	54	458	8.5	27	2
1990			31	279	9.0	19	1
1991			34	308	9.1	31	0
1992			39	338	8.7	29	1
1993			27	194	7.2	20	0
1994	CLE	N	11	102	9.3	30	0
1995			61	494	8.1	29t	2
1996	BAL	N	30	270	9.0	40	1
Career			491	4477	9.1	40	15
Playoffs			39	388	9.9		3

Reggie Bynum

Year	Team		No	Yds	Avg	Lg	TD
1987	BUF	N	2	24	12.0	17	0

Sylvester Byrd

Year	Team		No	Yds	Avg	Lg	TD
1987	ATL	N	7	125	17.9	33	0

Carl Byrum

Year	Team		No	Yds	Avg	Lg	TD
1986	BUF	N	13	104	8.0	17	1
1987			3	23	7.7	20	0
1988			2	0	0.0	3	0
Career			18	127	7.1	20	1

Year	Team		No	Yds	Avg	Lg	TD

Brian Cabral
| 1984 | CHI | N | 1 | 7 | 7.0 | 7 | 0 |

Larry Cabrelli
1941	PHI	N	4	90	22.5	50	1
1942			15	249	16.6	29	1
1943	P-P	N	12	199	16.6	49	1
1944	PHI		13	152	11.7	30t	1
1945			15	140	9.3	19	0
1946			8	98	12.3	38t	1
Career			67	928	13.9	50	5

Ernie Caddel
1933	POR	N					2
1934	DET	N	9	125	13.9		1
1935			10	171	17.1		1
1936			19	150	7.9		1
1937			9	80	8.9		0
1938			1	6	6.0	6	0
Career			48	532	11.1	6	5

George Cafego
1940	BKN	N	9	105	11.7		0
1944	BOS	N	2	8	4.0	5	0
1945			2	20	10.0	15	0
Career			13	133	10.2	15	0

Chris Cagle
| 1932 | NYG | N | | | | | 2 |

Jim Cain
| 1950 | DET | N | 1 | 8 | 8.0 | 8 | 0 |

J.V. Cain
1974	STL	N	13	152	11.7	40t	1
1975			12	134	11.2	18	1
1976			26	400	15.4	34	5
1977			25	328	13.1	38	2
Career			76	1014	13.3	40t	9
Playoffs			2	17	8.5		

Lynn Cain
1979	ATL	N	15	181	12.1	28	2
1980			24	223	9.3	30	1
1981			55	421	7.7	28	2
1982			13	101	7.8	17t	1
1983			3	24	8.0	11	0
1984			12	87	7.3	18	0
1985	LARM	N	5	24	4.8	13	0
Career			127	1061	8.4	30	6
Playoffs			3	34	11.3		

Mike Caldwell
| 1996 | SF | N | 2 | 9 | 4.5 | 8 | 0 |

Scotty Caldwell
| 1987 | DEN | N | 4 | 34 | 8.5 | 14 | 0 |

Jamie Caleb
1960	CLE	N	5	-18	-3.6	2	0
1961	MIN	N	2	-8	-4.0	5	0
Career			7	-26	-3.7	5	0

Don Calhoun
1974	BUF	N	2	10	5.0	7	0
1975	NE	N	5	111	22.2	62t	1
1976			12	56	4.7	12	0
1977			13	152	11.7	47	0
1978			3	29	9.7	15	0
1979			15	66	4.4	14	1
1980			27	129	4.8	12	0
1981			7	71	10.1	20	0
Career			84	624	7.4	62t	2

Rick Calhoun
| 1987 | LARI | N | 1 | 17 | 17.0 | 17 | 0 |

Jack Call
1957	BAL	N	4	18	4.5	8	0
1958			4	28	7.0	12	0
1959	PIT	N	1	0	0.0	0	0
Career			9	46	5.1	12	0

Ken Callicut
1979	DET	N	2	16	8.0	11	0
1980			1	19	19.0	19	0
1981			2	24	12.0	16	0
Career			5	59	11.8	19	0

Len Calligaro
| 1944 | NYG | N | 2 | 11 | 5.5 | 10 | 0 |

Bill Callihan
1940	DET	N	4	38	9.5		0
1941			4	34	8.5	22	0
1942			4	48	12.0	17	0
1943			8	108	13.5	40	3
1944			8	67	8.4	21	0
1945			4	88	22.0	29t	1
Career			32	383	12.0	40	4

Chris Calloway
1990	PIT	N	10	124	12.4	20t	1
1991			15	254	16.9	33t	1
1992	NYG	N	27	335	12.4	28	1
1993			35	513	14.7	47	3
1994			43	666	15.5	51t	2
1995			56	796	14.2	49	3
1996			53	739	13.9	36	4
Career			239	3427	14.3	51t	15
Playoffs			4	54	13.5		0

Tom Calvin
1952	PIT	N	2	4	2.0	6	0
1953			4	28	7.0	16	0
1954			1	19	19.0	19	0
Career			7	51	7.3	19	0

Jack Cameron
| 1984 | CHI | N | 1 | 13 | 13.0 | 13 | 0 |

Jim Camp
| 1948 | BKN | AA | 1 | 43 | 43.0 | 43 | 0 |

Al Campana
1950	CHIB	N	5	58	11.6	30	0
1952			1	3	3.0	3	0
Career			6	61	10.2	30	0

Bob Campbell
| 1969 | PIT | N | 1 | 32 | 32.0 | 32 | 0 |

Earl Campbell
1978	HOU	N	12	48	4.0	20	0
1979			16	94	5.9	46	0
1980			11	47	4.3	10	0
1981			36	156	4.3	17	0
1982			18	130	7.2	46	0
1983			19	216	11.4	66	0
1984			3	27	9.0	15	0
1985	NO	N	6	88	14.7	39	0
Career			121	806	6.7	66	0
Playoffs			5	45	9.0		0

Glenn Campbell
1929	NYG	N					1
1930							2
1931							2
1933							1
Career							6
Playoffs			1	12	12.0		0

Jeff Campbell
1990	DET	N	19	236	12.4	51	2
1991			2	49	24.5	28	0
1992			8	155	19.4	78t	1
1993			7	55	7.9	12	0
1994	DEN	N	1	22	22.0	22t	1
Career			37	517	14.0	78t	4

Leon Campbell
1950	BAL	N	1	5	5.0	5	0
1952	CHIB	N	2	1	0.5	3	0
1953			5	74	14.8	47	0
1954			3	0	0.0	2	0
1955	PIT	N	9	76	8.4	36	0
Career			20	156	7.8	47	0

Matthew Campbell
| 1995 | CAR | N | 3 | 32 | 10.7 | 12 | 0 |

Mike Campbell
| 1968 | DET | N | 2 | 15 | 7.5 | 9 | 0 |

Milt Campbell
| 1957 | CLE | N | 1 | 25 | 25.0 | 25t | 1 |

Sonny Campbell
1970	ATL	N	7	92	13.1	27	0
1971			3	40	13.3	29	0
Career			10	132	13.2	29	0

Woody Campbell
1967	HOU	A	17	136	8.0	32	2
1968			21	234	11.1	39	0
1969			7	82	11.7	37	0
1970	HOU	N	15	78	5.2	10	0
1971			20	179	8.9	24	0
Career			80	709	8.9	39	2
Playoffs			2	5	2.5		0

Billy Campfield
1978	PHI	N	15	101	6.7	25	0
1979			16	115	7.2	17	0
1980			26	275	10.6	50	2
1981			36	326	9.1	29t	3
1982			14	141	10.1	24	1
1983	NYG	N	1	12	12.0	12	0
Career			108	970	9.0	50	6
Playoffs			6	106	17.7		1

Bob Campiglio
| 1932 | SI | N | | | | | 1 |

Larry Canada
1978	DEN	N	6	37	6.2	12	0
1979			3	36	12.0	15	0
1981			3	37	12.3	20	1
Career			12	110	9.2	20	1
Playoffs			1	4	4.0		0

Tony Canadeo
1942	GB	N	10	66	6.6	15	0
1943			3	31	10.3	13	2
1944			1	12	12.0	12	0
1946			2	25	12.5	15	0
1948			9	81	9.0	32	0
1949			3	-2	-0.7	3	0
1950			10	54	5.4	20	0
1951			22	226	10.3	46	2
1952			9	86	9.6	21t	1
Career			69	579	8.4	46	5

Jim Canady
| 1949 | CHIB-NYB | N | 5 | 80 | 16.0 | 26 | 0 |

Whit Canale
| 1968 | BOS | A | 1 | 0 | 0.0 | 0 | 0 |

Tony Cannava
| 1950 | GB | N | 1 | 28 | 28.0 | 28 | 0 |

Billy Cannon
1960	HOU	A	15	187	12.5	88	5
1961			43	586	13.6	78	9
1962			32	451	14.1	60	6
1963			5	39	7.8	12	0
1964	OAK	A	37	454	12.3	40	5
1965			7	127	18.1	36	0
1966			14	436	31.1	75	2
1967			32	629	19.7	64t	10
1968			23	360	15.7	48t	6
1969			21	262	12.5	53t	2
1970	KC	N	7	125	17.9	45	2
Career			236	3656	15.5	88	47
Playoffs			27	400	14.8		3

Leo Cantor
| 1945 | CHIC | N | 15 | 159 | 10.6 | 33 | 0 |

Wayne Capers
| 1983 | PIT | N | 10 | 185 | 18.5 | 36 | 1 |

Year	Team		No	Yds	Avg	Lg	TD

Wayne Capers *continued*

Year	Team		No	Yds	Avg	Lg	TD
1984			7	81	11.6	19	0
1985	IND	N	25	438	17.5	80t	4
1986			9	118	13.1	27	0
Career			51	822	16.1	80t	5
Playoffs			3	83	27.7		1

Bob Cappadona

Year	Team		No	Yds	Avg	Lg	TD
1967	BOS	A	6	104	17.3	42	1
1968	BUF	A	18	92	5.1	21t	2
Career			24	196	8.2	42	3

Gino Cappelletti

Year	Team		No	Yds	Avg	Lg	TD
1960	BOS	A	1	28	28.0	28	0
1961			45	768	17.1	53	8
1962			34	479	14.1	40	5
1963			34	493	14.5	38	2
1964			49	865	17.7	58	7
1965			37	680	18.4	57	9
1966			43	676	15.7	63	6
1967			35	397	11.3	35	3
1968			13	182	14.0	30	2
1969			1	21	21.0	21	0
Career			292	4589	15.7	63	42
Playoffs			6	181	30.2		0

John Cappelletti

Year	Team		No	Yds	Avg	Lg	TD
1974	LA	N	6	35	5.8	9	0
1976			30	302	10.1	32t	1
1977			28	228	8.1	25t	1
1978			41	382	9.3	37	1
1980	SD	N	13	112	8.6	12	0
1981			10	126	12.6	25	1
1982			7	48	6.9	22	0
Career			135	1233	9.1	37	4
Playoffs			8	56	7.0		0

Dom Cara

Year	Team		No	Yds	Avg	Lg	TD
1937	PIT	N	2	36	18.0		0
1938			4	18	4.5		0
Career			6	54	9.0		0

Joe Caravello

Year	Team		No	Yds	Avg	Lg	TD
1987	WAS	N	2	29	14.5	22	0
1988			2	15	7.5	8	0
1989	SD	N	10	95	9.5	37	0
1990			2	21	10.5	17t	1
Career			16	160	10.0	37	1

Lloyd Cardwell

Year	Team		No	Yds	Avg	Lg	TD
1937	DET	N	3	51	17.0		1
1938			9	138	15.3		1
1939			13	350	26.9		2
1940			20	349	17.4		1
1942			5	35	7.0	51	0
1943			1	9	9.0	9	0
Career			51	932	18.3	51	5

Bob Carey

Year	Team		No	Yds	Avg	Lg	TD
1952	LA	N	36	539	15.0	61t	1
1954			5	49	9.8	13	0
1956			5	60	12.0	18	1
1958	CHIB	N	1	15	15.0	15	0
Career			47	663	14.1	61t	2
Playoffs			3	30	10.0		0

Harland Carl

Year	Team		No	Yds	Avg	Lg	TD
1956	CHIB	N	2	31	15.5	20	0

Roy Carlson

Year	Team		No	Yds	Avg	Lg	TD
1928	CHIB	N					1

Wray Carlton

Year	Team		No	Yds	Avg	Lg	TD
1960	BUF	A	29	477	16.4		4
1961			17	193	11.4	22	0
1962			7	54	7.7	25	0
1963			1	9	9.0	9	0
1964			2	23	11.5	17	0
1965			24	196	8.2	23	1
1966			21	280	13.3	55	0
1967			9	97	10.8	24	0
Career			110	1329	12.1	55	5
Playoffs			1	5	5.0		0

Al Carmichael

Year	Team		No	Yds	Avg	Lg	TD
1953	GB	N	12	131	10.9	52	0
1954			18	251	13.9	45	0
1955			16	222	13.9	32	1
1956			13	180	13.8	63	1
1957			13	184	14.2	39	0
1958			3	26	8.7	14t	1
1960	DEN	A	32	616	19.3	59	5
1961			5	23	4.6	14	0
Career			112	1633	14.6	63	8

Harold Carmichael

Year	Team		No	Yds	Avg	Lg	TD
1971	PHI	N	20	288	14.4	50	0
1972			20	276	13.8	54	2
1973			**67**	**1116**	16.7	73	9
1974			56	649	11.6	39	8
1975			49	639	13.0	62t	7
1976			42	503	12.0	24	5
1977			46	665	14.5	50t	7
1978			55	1072	19.5	56t	8
1979			52	872	16.8	50	11
1980			48	815	17.0	56t	9
1981			61	1028	16.9	85t	6
1982			35	540	15.4	46	4
1983			38	515	13.6	35	3
1984	DAL	N	1	7	7.0	7	0
Career			590	8985	15.2	85t	79
Playoffs			29	465	16.0		6

Ray Carnelly

Year	Team		No	Yds	Avg	Lg	TD
1939	BKN	N	1	5	5.0	5	0

Brett Carolan

Year	Team		No	Yds	Avg	Lg	TD
1994	SF	N	2	10	5.0	6	0
1995			1	3	3.0	3	0
1996	MIA	N	4	48	12.0	21	1
Career			7	61	8.7	21	1

Reg Carolan

Year	Team		No	Yds	Avg	Lg	TD
1962	SD	A	3	39	13.0	18	1
1964	KC	A	3	54	18.0	25	1
1965			6	65	10.8	14	0
1966			7	154	22.0	45	3
1967			2	26	13.0	23	0
1968			2	26	13.0	19	0
Career			23	364	15.8	45	5
Playoffs			1	7	7.0		0

J.C. Caroline

Year	Team		No	Yds	Avg	Lg	TD
1957	CHIB	N	1	33	33.0	33	0
1958			5	78	15.6	58t	1
Career			6	111	18.5	58t	1
Playoffs			1	8	8.0		0

Don Carothers

Year	Team		No	Yds	Avg	Lg	TD
1960	DEN	A	2	25	12.5	20	0

Jack Carpenter

Year	Team		No	Yds	Avg	Lg	TD
1949	BUF	AA	2	20	10.0		0

Ken Carpenter

Year	Team		No	Yds	Avg	Lg	TD
1950	CLE	N	5	45	9.0	16	0
1951			12	183	15.3	45t	2
1952			16	136	8.5	41t	1
1953			9	109	12.1	32	2
1960	DEN	A	29	350	12.1	36	1
Career			71	823	11.6	45t	6
Playoffs			5	55	11.0		0

Lew Carpenter

Year	Team		No	Yds	Avg	Lg	TD
1954	DET	N	16	145	9.1	23	2
1955			44	312	7.1	34t	2
1957	CLE	N	5	65	13.0	21	0
1958			5	47	9.4	18	0
1959	GB	N	5	47	9.4	23	0
1960			1	21	21.0	21	0
1961			3	29	9.7	16	0
1962			7	104	14.9	22	0
1963			1	12	12.0	12	0
Career			87	782	9.0	34t	4
Playoffs			9	30	3.3		0

Preston Carpenter

Year	Team		No	Yds	Avg	Lg	TD
1956	CLE	N	16	124	7.8	34	0

Preston Carpenter *continued*

Year	Team		No	Yds	Avg	Lg	TD
1957			27	398	14.7	33	2
1958			29	474	16.3	74	1
1959			24	372	15.5	43t	2
1960	PIT	N	29	495	17.1	70	2
1961			33	460	13.9	40t	4
1962			36	492	13.7	43t	4
1963			17	233	13.7	28t	1
1964	WAS	N	31	466	15.0	39	3
1965			23	298	13.0	36	0
1966	WAS-MIN	N	30	518	17.3	52t	4
1967	MIA	A	10	127	12.7	42	0
Career			305	4457	14.6	74	23
Playoffs			6	61	10.2		0

Rob Carpenter

Year	Team		No	Yds	Avg	Lg	TD
1977	HOU	N	23	156	6.8	27	0
1978			17	150	8.8	37	0
1979			16	116	7.3	22	1
1980			43	346	8.0	25	0
1981	HOU-NYG	N	37	281	7.6	37	1
1982	NYG	N	7	29	4.1	11	0
1983			26	258	9.9	38	2
1984			26	209	8.0	19	1
1985			20	162	8.1	23	0
Career			215	1707	7.9	38	5
Playoffs			40	253	6.3		0

Rob Carpenter

Year	Team		No	Yds	Avg	Lg	TD
1991	NE	N	3	45	15.0	23	0
1992	NYJ	N	13	161	12.4	51	1
1993			6	83	13.8	18	0
1995	PHI	N	29	318	11.0	29	0
Career			51	607	11.9	51	1
Playoffs			4	88	22.0		1

Earl Carr

Year	Team		No	Yds	Avg	Lg	TD
1979	PHI	N	1	2	2.0	2	0

Ed Carr

Year	Team		No	Yds	Avg	Lg	TD
1947	SF	AA	4	41	10.3		0
1948			3	40	13.3		0
1949			7	165	23.6	75t	3
Career			14	246	17.6	75t	3

Harlan Carr

Year	Team		No	Yds	Avg	Lg	TD
1927	POT	N					1

Jimmy Carr

Year	Team		No	Yds	Avg	Lg	TD
1955	CHIC	N	9	157	17.4	59	0

Roger Carr

Year	Team		No	Yds	Avg	Lg	TD
1974	BAL	N	21	405	19.3	57	0
1975			23	517	22.5	90t	2
1976			43	**1112**	25.9	79t	11
1977			11	199	18.1	45	1
1978			30	629	21.0	78t	6
1979			27	400	14.8	37	1
1980			61	924	15.1	43	5
1981			38	584	15.4	43	3
1982	SEA	N	15	265	17.7	50	2
1983	SD	N	2	36	18.0	23	0
Career			271	5071	18.7	90t	31
Playoffs			2	35	17.5		1

Mark Carrier

Year	Team		No	Yds	Avg	Lg	TD
1987	TB	N	26	423	16.3	38	3
1988			57	970	17.0	59t	5
1989			86	1422	16.5	78t	9
1990			49	813	16.6	68t	4
1991			47	698	14.9	35	2
1992			56	692	12.4	40	4
1993	CLE	N	43	746	17.3	55	3
1994			29	452	15.6	43	5
1995	CAR	N	66	1002	15.2	66t	6
1996			58	808	13.9	39	6
Career			517	8026	15.5	78t	44
Playoffs			9	93	10.3		1

Bird Carroll

Year	Team		No	Yds	Avg	Lg	TD
1921	CAN	A					1
1922	CAN	N					1
1923							1
Career							3

Jay Carroll

Year	Team		No	Yds	Avg	Lg	TD
1984	TB	N	5	50	10.0	17	1
1985	MIN	N	1	8	8.0	8	0
Career			6	58	9.7	17	1

Vic Carroll

Year	Team		No	Yds	Avg	Lg	TD
1941	WAS	N	1	31	31.0	31	0
1947	NYG	N	7	123	17.6	29	2
Career			8	154	19.3	31	2

Wesley Carroll

Year	Team		No	Yds	Avg	Lg	TD
1991	NO	N	18	184	10.2	31t	1
1992			18	292	16.2	72t	2
1993	CIN	N	6	81	13.5	28	0
Career			42	557	13.3	72t	3
Playoffs			2	23	11.5		0

Paul Ott Carruth

Year	Team		No	Yds	Avg	Lg	TD
1986	GB	N	24	134	5.6	19	2
1987			10	78	7.8	19	1
1988			24	211	8.8	31	0
1989	KC	N	1	3	3.0	3	0
Career			59	426	7.2	31	3

Carlos Carson

Year	Team		No	Yds	Avg	Lg	TD
1980	KC	N	5	68	13.6	32	0
1981			7	179	25.6	53t	1
1982			27	494	18.3	51	2
1983			80	1351	16.9	50t	7
1984			57	1078	18.9	57	4
1985			47	843	17.9	37t	4
1986			21	497	23.7	70t	4
1987			55	1044	19.0	81t	7
1988			46	711	15.5	80t	3
1989	KC-PHI	N	8	107	13.4	28	1
Career			353	6372	18.1	81t	33
Playoffs			2	43	21.5		0

Harry Carson

Year	Team		No	Yds	Avg	Lg	TD
1986	NYG	N	1	13	13.0	13t	1

Johnny Carson

Year	Team		No	Yds	Avg	Lg	TD
1954	WAS	N	12	139	11.6	42	0
1955			23	443	19.3	51	3
1956			39	504	12.9	26t	3
1957			34	583	17.1	38	3
1958			14	244	17.4	28t	2
1959			6	74	12.3	17	0
1960	HOU	A	45	604	13.4	51	4
Career			173	2591	15.0	51	15
Playoffs			1	13	13.0		0

Dwayne Carswell

Year	Team		No	Yds	Avg	Lg	TD
1995	DEN	N	3	37	12.3	23	0
1996			15	85	5.7	11	0
Career			18	122	6.8	23	0
Playoffs			2	18	9.0		0

Allen Carter

Year	Team		No	Yds	Avg	Lg	TD
1975	NE	N	2	39	19.5	26	0

Anthony Carter

Year	Team		No	Yds	Avg	Lg	TD
1985	MIN	N	43	821	19.1	57t	8
1986			38	686	18.1	60t	7
1987			38	922	**24.3**	73t	7
1988			72	1225	17.0	67t	6
1989			65	1066	16.4	50	4
1990			70	1008	14.4	56t	8
1991			51	553	10.8	46t	5
1992			41	580	14.1	54	2
1993			60	775	12.9	39	5
1994	DET	N	8	97	12.1	18	3
Career			486	7733	15.9	73t	55
Playoffs			37	644	17.4		1

Cris Carter

Year	Team		No	Yds	Avg	Lg	TD
1987	PHI	N	5	84	16.8	25	2
1988			39	761	19.5	80t	6
1989			45	605	13.4	42	11
1990	MIN	N	27	413	15.3	78t	3
1991			72	962	13.4	50	5
1992			53	681	12.8	44	6
1993			86	1071	12.5	58	9
1994			**122**	1256	10.3	65t	7

Cris Carter *continued*

Year	Team		No	Yds	Avg	Lg	TD
1995			122	1371	11.2	60t	**17**
1996			96	1163	12.1	43t	10
Career			667	8367	12.5	80t	76
Playoffs			21	290	13.8		3

Dale Carter

Year	Team		No	Yds	Avg	Lg	TD
1996	KC	N	6	89	14.8	46t	1

Dexter Carter

Year	Team		No	Yds	Avg	Lg	TD
1990	SF	N	25	217	8.7	26	0
1991			23	253	11.0	26	1
1992			1	43	43.0	43t	1
1993			3	40	13.3	14	0
1994			7	99	14.1	44	0
1995	NYJ-SF	N	2	4	2.0	4	0
Career			61	656	10.8	44	2
Playoffs			2	45	22.5		0

Gerald Carter

Year	Team		No	Yds	Avg	Lg	TD
1981	TB	N	1	10	10.0	10	0
1982			10	140	14.0	27	0
1983			48	694	14.5	56t	2
1984			60	816	13.6	74t	5
1985			40	557	13.9	40	3
1986			42	640	15.2	46	2
1987			38	586	15.4	57	5
Career			239	3443	14.4	74t	17

Joe Carter

Year	Team		No	Yds	Avg	Lg	TD
1933	PHI	N					2
1934			**16**	238	14.9		4
1935			11	260	23.6		2
1936			4	42	10.5		1
1937			15	282	18.8		3
1938			27	386	14.3		7
1939			24	292	12.2		2
1940			12	201	16.8		0
1942	GB	N	2	19	9.5	10	1
1944	BKN	N	13	143	11.0	45	0
1945	CHIC	N	3	17	5.7	10	1
Career			127	1880	14.8	45	22

Joe Carter

Year	Team		No	Yds	Avg	Lg	TD
1984	MIA	N	8	53	6.6	15	0
1985			2	7	3.5	4	0
1986			1	6	6.0	6	0
Career			11	66	6.0	15	0
Playoffs			1	2	2.0		0

Ki-Jana Carter

Year	Team		No	Yds	Avg	Lg	TD
1996	CIN	N	22	169	7.7	20	1

Louis Carter

Year	Team		No	Yds	Avg	Lg	TD
1975	OAK	N	2	39	19.5	22	0
1976	TB	N	20	135	6.8	19	0
1977			10	65	6.5	19	0
1978			19	139	7.3	17	0
Career			51	378	7.4	22	0

Marty Carter

Year	Team		No	Yds	Avg	Lg	TD
1994	TB	N	1	21	21.0	21	0

Mike Carter

Year	Team		No	Yds	Avg	Lg	TD
1972	SD	N	2	24	12.0	14	0

Pat Carter

Year	Team		No	Yds	Avg	Lg	TD
1988	DET	N	13	145	11.2	31	0
1990	LARM	N	8	58	7.3	16	0
1991			8	69	8.6	18t	2
1992			20	232	11.6	25	3
1993			14	166	11.9	38	1
1994	HOU	N	11	74	6.7	19	1
1996	ARI	N	26	329	12.7	36	1
Career			100	1073	10.7	38	8

Rodney Carter

Year	Team		No	Yds	Avg	Lg	TD
1987	PIT	N	16	180	11.3	26t	3
1988			32	363	11.3	33	2
1989			38	267	7.0	22t	3
Career			86	810	9.4	33	8

Steve Carter

Year	Team		No	Yds	Avg	Lg	TD
1987	TB	N	1	12	12.0	12	0

Tony Carter

Year	Team		No	Yds	Avg	Lg	TD
1994	CHI	N	1	24	24.0	24	0
1995			40	329	8.2	27	1
1996			41	233	5.7	29	0
Career			82	586	7.1	29	1
Playoffs			1	16	16.0		0

Maurice Carthon

Year	Team		No	Yds	Avg	Lg	TD
1985	NYG	N	8	81	10.1	22	0
1986			16	67	4.2	10	0
1987			8	71	8.9	25	0
1988			19	194	10.2	24	1
1989			15	132	8.8	18	0
1990			14	151	10.8	63	0
1991			7	39	5.6	9	0
1992	IND	N	3	10	3.3	6	0
Career			90	745	8.3	63	1
Playoffs			10	49	4.9		0

Charlie Cartin

Year	Team		No	Yds	Avg	Lg	TD
1925	FRA	N					1

Mel Carver

Year	Team		No	Yds	Avg	Lg	TD
1982	TB	N	4	46	11.5	24	1
1983			32	262	8.2	20	1
1984			3	27	9.0	12	0
Career			39	335	8.6	24	2

Ken Casanega

Year	Team		No	Yds	Avg	Lg	TD
1946	SF	AA	5	102	20.4		1

Rick Casares

Year	Team		No	Yds	Avg	Lg	TD
1955	CHIB	N	16	136	8.5	29	1
1956			23	203	8.8	33	2
1957			25	225	9.0	43	0
1958			32	290	9.1	50	1
1959			27	273	10.1	43t	2
1960	CHI	N	8	64	8.0	21	0
1961			8	69	8.6	31	0
1962			10	71	7.1	24	1
1963			19	94	4.9	25	1
1964			14	113	8.1	51t	2
1965	WAS	N	1	5	5.0	5	0
1966	MIA	A	8	45	5.6	20	1
Career			191	1588	8.3	51t	11
Playoffs			4	41	10.3		0

Al Casey

Year	Team		No	Yds	Avg	Lg	TD
1923	STL	N					1

Bernie Casey

Year	Team		No	Yds	Avg	Lg	TD
1961	SF	N	10	185	18.5	51t	1
1962			53	819	15.5	48t	6
1963			47	762	16.2	68t	7
1964			58	808	13.9	63t	4
1965			59	765	13.0	59t	8
1966			50	669	13.4	32	1
1967	LA	N	53	871	16.4	57t	8
1968			29	565	19.5	55t	5
Career			359	5444	15.2	68t	40
Playoffs			5	82	16.4		1

Keith Cash

Year	Team		No	Yds	Avg	Lg	TD
1991	PIT	N	7	90	12.9	20	1
1992	KC	N	12	113	9.4	19	2
1993			24	242	10.1	24	4
1994			19	192	10.1	31	2
1995			42	419	10.0	38t	2
1996			14	80	5.7	20	0
Career			118	1136	9.6	38t	10
Playoffs			21	266	12.7		1

Kerry Cash

Year	Team		No	Yds	Avg	Lg	TD
1991	IND	N	1	18	18.0	18	0
1992			43	521	12.1	41	3
1993			43	402	9.3	37	3
1994			16	190	11.9	24	1
1995	OAK	N	25	254	10.2	23	2
1996	CHI	N	4	42	10.5	14	0
Career			132	1427	10.8	41	9

Jim Cason

Year	Team		No	Yds	Avg	Lg	TD
1948	SF	AA	4	99	24.8		1
1949			5	38	7.6		0

Year	Team		No	Yds	Avg	Lg	TD

Jim Cason *continued*

Year	Team		No	Yds	Avg	Lg	TD
1950	SF	N	30	374	12.5	43	3
1951			1	8	8.0	8	0
Career			40	519	13.0	43	4

Cy Casper

1935	PIT	N	5	94	18.8		2

Dave Casper

1974	OAK	N	4	26	6.5	17	3
1975			5	71	14.2	20	1
1976			53	691	13.0	30t	10
1977			48	584	12.2	27	6
1978			62	852	13.7	44	9
1979			57	771	13.5	42	3
1980	OAK-HOU	N	56	796	14.2	43	4
1981	HOU		33	572	17.3	52t	8
1982			36	573	15.9	38	6
1983	HOU-MIN	N	20	251	12.6	34	0
1984	LARI	N	4	29	7.3	13	2
Career			378	5216	13.8	52t	52
Playoffs			27	363	13.4		7

Howard Cassady

1956	DET	N	9	83	9.2	21	0
1957			25	325	13.0	48	3
1958			23	406	17.7	81t	7
1959			15	316	21.1	59t	4
1960			20	238	11.9	40t	1
1961			5	45	9.0	76	1
1962	PHI	N	14	188	13.4	47t	2
Career			111	1601	14.4	81t	18
Playoffs			5	59	11.8		1

Frank Cassara

1954	SF	N	1	12	12.0	12	0

Dick Cassiano

1940	BKN	N	2	67	33.5		2

Ron Cassidy

1979	GB	N	6	102	17.0	23	0
1980			5	109	21.8	43	0
1981			1	6	6.0	6	0
1984			2	16	8.0	10	0
Career			14	233	16.6	43	0

Rich Caster

1970	NYJ	N	19	393	20.7	72t	3
1971			26	454	17.5	57t	6
1972			39	833	21.4	80t	10
1973			35	593	16.9	49	4
1974			38	745	19.6	89t	7
1975			47	820	17.4	91	4
1976			31	391	12.6	41	1
1977			10	205	20.5	58	1
1978	HOU	N	20	316	15.8	47t	5
1979			18	239	13.3	36	1
1980			27	341	12.6	68t	3
1981	NO-WAS	N	12	185	15.4	31	0
Career			322	5515	17.1	91	45
Playoffs			8	67	8.4		0

Jim Castiglia

1941	PHI	N	4	24	6.0	11	0
1946			11	51	4.6	23	0
1947	BAL-WAS	AA-N	12	98	8.2	21	0
1948	WAS	N	7	73	10.4	32t	2
Career			34	246	7.2	32t	2

Chris Castor

1984	SEA	N	8	89	11.1	21	0

Mike Caterbone

1987	MIA	N	2	46	23.0	30	0

Sam Cathcart

1949	SF	AA	12	182	15.2	72	0
1950	SF	N	7	99	14.1	24	0
1952			2	15	7.5	13	0
Career			21	296	14.1	72	0

Matt Cavanaugh

1981	NE	N	1	9	9.0	9	0

John Cavosie

1933	POR	N					1

Jimmy Cefalo

1978	MIA	N	6	145	24.2	43	3
1979			12	223	18.6	30	3
1980			11	199	18.1	52	1
1981			29	631	21.8	69t	3
1982			17	356	20.9	46	1
1984			18	185	10.3	25t	2
Career			93	1739	18.7	69t	13
Playoffs			12	297	24.8		2

Bob Celeri

1951	NYY	N	2	71	35.5	51	1
1952	DAL	N	4	37	9.3	13t	1
Career			6	108	18.0		2

Larry Centers

1991	PHX	N	19	176	9.3	23	0
1992			50	417	8.3	26	2
1993			66	603	9.1	29	3
1994	ARI	N	77	647	8.4	36	2
1995			101	962	9.5	32	2
1996			99	766	7.7	39	7
Career			412	3571	8.7	39	16

Jeff Chadwick

1983	DET	N	40	617	15.4	45	4
1984			37	540	14.6	46	2
1985			25	478	19.1	56	3
1986			53	995	18.8	73	5
1987			30	416	13.9	38	0
1988			20	304	15.2	32	3
1989	DET-SEA	N	9	104	11.6	19	0
1990	SEA	N	27	478	17.7	54t	4
1991			22	255	11.6	29	3
1992	LARM	N	29	362	12.5	27t	3
Career			292	4549	15.6	73	27
Playoffs			5	58	11.6		0

Pat Chaffey

1992	NYJ	N	7	56	8.0	14	0
1993			4	55	13.8	20t	1
Career			11	111	10.1	20t	1

Byron Chamberlain

1995	DEN	N	1	11	11.0	11	0
1996			12	129	10.8	17	0
Career			13	140	10.8	17	0

Dan Chamberlain

1960	BUF	A	17	279	16.4		4
1961			1	16	16.0	16	0
Career			18	295	16.4	16	4

Guy Chamberlin

1921	DEC	A					2
1922	CAN	N					1
1923							2
1924	CLE	N					2
1925	FRA	N					1
Career							8

Ed Champagne

1950	LA	N	4	52	13.0	2	1

Al Chandler

1974	CIN	N	1	9	9.0	9	0
1976	NE	N	5	49	9.8	29	3
1977			7	68	9.7	16	0
1978	STL	N	16	190	11.9	47	4
1979	STL-NE	N	6	51	8.5	28t	2
Career			35	367	10.5	47	9
Playoffs			1	1	1.0		0

Bob Chandler

1971	BUF	N	5	60	12.0	20	0
1972			33	528	16.0	43t	5
1973			30	427	14.2	37t	3
1974			7	88	12.6	21	1
1975			55	746	13.6	35	6
1976			61	824	13.5	58t	10

Bob Chandler *continued*

1977			60	745	12.4	31	4
1978			44	581	13.2	44	5
1980	OAK	N	49	786	16.0	56	10
1981			26	458	17.6	45	4
Career			370	5243	14.2	58t	48
Playoffs			7	119	17.0		0

Don Chandler

1956	NYG	N	1	5	5.0	5	0
Playoffs			1	12	12.0		0

Thornton Chandler

1986	DAL	N	6	57	9.5	15	2
1987			5	25	5.0	9	1
1988			18	186	10.3	29	1
Career			29	268	9.2	29	4

Wes Chandler

1978	NO	N	35	472	13.5	58t	2
1979			65	1069	16.4	85	6
1980			65	975	15.0	50	6
1981	NO-SD	N	69	1142	16.6	51t	6
1982	SD	N	49	1032	21.1	66t	9
1983			58	845	14.6	44t	5
1984			52	708	13.6	63t	6
1985			67	1199	17.9	75t	10
1986			56	874	15.6	40	4
1987			39	617	15.8	27	2
1988	SF	N	4	33	8.3	9	0
Career			559	8966	16.0	85	56
Playoffs			23	347	15.1		0

Lynn Chandnois

1950	PIT	N	7	158	22.6	51	0
1951			29	490	16.9	55	5
1952			28	370	13.2	48t	2
1953			43	412	9.6	55	0
1954			22	176	8.0	23	0
1955			27	385	14.3	55	0
1956			7	71	10.1	17t	1
Career			163	2062	12.7	55	8

Gil Chapman

1975	NO	N	1	7	7.0	7	0

Cliff Chatman

1982	NYG	N	1	13	13.0	13	0

Eddie Chavis

1987	MIA	N	7	108	15.4	27	0

Lloyd Cheatham

1942	CHIC	N	6	29	4.8	11	1
1946	NY	AA	4	54	13.5		1
1947			4	124	31.0	70t	2
1948			7	76	10.9	50	0
Career			21	283	13.5	70t	4

Raphel Cherry

1985	WAS	N	1	11	11.0	11	0

George Chesser

1966	MIA	A	1	4	4.0	4	0

Wes Chesson

1971	ATL	N	20	224	11.2	24	0
1972			18	338	18.8	46	1
1973			2	36	18.0	20	1
Career			40	598	14.9	46	2

Raymond Chester

1970	OAK	N	42	556	13.2	43t	7
1971			28	442	15.8	67t	7
1972			34	576	16.9	68t	8
1973	BAL		18	181	10.1	40	1
1974			37	461	12.5	45	1
1975			38	457	12.0	32	3
1976			24	467	19.5	40	3
1977			31	556	17.9	78t	3
1978	OAK	N	13	146	11.2	27	2
1979			58	712	12.3	39	8
1980			28	366	13.1	47	4

Year	Team		No	Yds	Avg	Lg	TD

Raymond Chester *continued*

Year	Team		No	Yds	Avg	Lg	TD
1981			13	93	7.2	15	1
Career			364	5013	13.8	78t	48
Playoffs			23	397	17.3		1

Joe Chetti

Year	Team		No	Yds	Avg	Lg	TD
1987	BUF	N	1	9	9.0	9	0

George Cheverko

Year	Team		No	Yds	Avg	Lg	TD
1947	NYG	N	17	300	17.6	62	3
1948			1	41	41.0	41	0
Career			18	341	18.9	62	3

Joe Childress

Year	Team		No	Yds	Avg	Lg	TD
1956	CHIC	N	6	82	13.7	34t	1
1957			10	146	14.6	28	0
1958			35	406	11.6	26	4
1959			4	73	18.3	52t	1
1960	STL	N	11	202	18.4	52t	3
1962			15	207	13.8	42	1
1963			25	354	14.2	78t	2
1964			12	203	16.9	46t	2
1965			3	27	9.0	10	0
Career			121	1700	14.0	78t	14

Clarence Childs

Year	Team		No	Yds	Avg	Lg	TD
1964	NYG	N	11	97	8.8	24	0

Henry Childs

Year	Team		No	Yds	Avg	Lg	TD
1975	NO	N	10	179	17.9	38	0
1976			26	349	13.4	46t	3
1977			33	518	15.7	59t	9
1978			53	869	16.4	52	4
1979			51	846	16.6	51	5
1980			34	463	13.6	30	6
1981	LA	N	12	145	12.1	39	1
1984	GB	N	4	32	8.0	17	0
Career			223	3401	15.3	59t	28

Jimmy Childs

Year	Team		No	Yds	Avg	Lg	TD
1978	STL	N	4	50	12.5	23	1
1979			8	93	11.6	22	0
Career			12	143	11.9	23	1

Bill Chipley

Year	Team		No	Yds	Avg	Lg	TD
1947	BOS	N	5	105	21.0	40	1
1948			13	131	10.1	22	1
1949	NYB	N	57	631	11.1	69	2
Career			75	867	11.6	69	4

John Chirico

Year	Team		No	Yds	Avg	Lg	TD
1987	NYJ	N	4	18	4.5	8	0

Mark Chmura

Year	Team		No	Yds	Avg	Lg	TD
1993	GB	N	2	13	6.5	7	0
1994			14	165	11.8	27	0
1995			54	679	12.6	33	7
1996			28	370	13.2	29	0
Career			98	1227	12.5	33	7
Playoffs			16	166	10.4		2

Wayne Chrebet

Year	Team		No	Yds	Avg	Lg	TD
1995	NYJ	N	66	726	11.0	32	4
1996			84	909	10.8	44	3
Career			150	1635	10.9	44	7

Frank Christensen

Year	Team		No	Yds	Avg	Lg	TD
1935	DET	N	5	57	11.4		1
1936			2	58	29.0		1
Career			7	115	16.4		2
Playoffs			1	26	26.0		0

Todd Christensen

Year	Team		No	Yds	Avg	Lg	TD
1981	OAK	N	8	115	14.4	30	2
1982	LARI	N	42	510	12.1	50	4
1983			92	1247	13.6	45	12
1984			80	1007	12.6	38	7
1985			82	987	12.0	48	6
1986			95	1153	12.1	35	8
1987			47	663	14.1	33	2
1988			15	190	12.7	22	0
Career			461	5872	12.7	50	41
Playoffs			31	358	11.5		1

Bob Christian

Year	Team		No	Yds	Avg	Lg	TD
1993	CHI	N	16	160	10.0	36	0
1994			2	30	15.0	21	0
1995	CAR	N	29	255	8.8	23	1
Career			47	445	9.5	36	1

Jack Christiansen

Year	Team		No	Yds	Avg	Lg	TD
1952	DET	N	3	32	10.7	11	0
Playoffs			1	5	5.0		0

Floyd Christman

Year	Team		No	Yds	Avg	Lg	TD
1925	BUF	N					1

Ryan Christopherson

Year	Team		No	Yds	Avg	Lg	TD
1995	JAC	N	1	-1	-1.0	-1	0

Dick Christy

Year	Team		No	Yds	Avg	Lg	TD
1958	PIT	N	7	73	10.4	26	0
1960	BOS	A	26	268	10.3		2
1961	NY	A	29	521	18.0	68	1
1962			62	538	8.7	41	3
1963			8	73	9.1	13	0
Career			132	1473	11.2	68	6

Bob Cifers

Year	Team		No	Yds	Avg	Lg	TD
1946	DET	N	4	178	44.5	70t	4
1947	PIT	N	3	58	19.3	37	0
1948			4	55	13.8	29	0
1949	GB	N	1	5	5.0	5	0
Career			12	296	24.7	70t	4
Playoffs			1	18	18.0		0

Ed Cifers

Year	Team		No	Yds	Avg	Lg	TD
1941	WAS	N	10	94	9.4	19	1
1942			18	196	10.9	19	1
1946			6	61	10.2	14	0
1947	CHIB	N	3	48	16.0	22	1
Career			37	399	10.8	22	3
Playoffs			1	8	8.0		0

Darryl Clack

Year	Team		No	Yds	Avg	Lg	TD
1986	DAL	N	1	18	18.0	18	0
1988			17	126	7.4	18	1
1989			4	69	17.3	44	0
Career			22	213	9.7	44	1

Robert Claiborne

Year	Team		No	Yds	Avg	Lg	TD
1992	SD	N	1	15	15.0	15	0
1993	TB	N	5	61	12.2	16	0
Career			6	76	12.7	16	0

Frank Clair

Year	Team		No	Yds	Avg	Lg	TD
1941	WAS	N	2	12	6.0	3	0

Rickey Claitt

Year	Team		No	Yds	Avg	Lg	TD
1980	WAS	N	3	34	11.3	26	1

Jack Clancy

Year	Team		No	Yds	Avg	Lg	TD
1967	MIA	A	67	868	13.0	44t	2
1969			21	289	13.8	50	1
1970	GB	N	16	244	15.3	33t	2
Career			104	1401	13.5	50	5

Stu Clancy

Year	Team		No	Yds	Avg	Lg	TD
1932	NYG	N					1

Allan Clark

Year	Team		No	Yds	Avg	Lg	TD
1979	NE	N	2	35	17.5	20	0

Beryl Clark

Year	Team		No	Yds	Avg	Lg	TD
1940	CHIC	N	1	20	20.0	20	0

Boobie Clark

Year	Team		No	Yds	Avg	Lg	TD
1973	CIN	N	45	347	7.7	39	0
1974			23	194	8.4	23	1
1975			42	334	8.0	27	0
1976			23	158	6.9	19	1
1977			7	33	4.7	11	0
1978			11	73	6.6	26	0
1979	HOU	N	6	58	9.7	38	0
Career			157	1197	7.6	39	2
Playoffs			6	56	9.3		0

Derrick Clark

Year	Team		No	Yds	Avg	Lg	TD
1994	DEN	N	9	47	5.2	10	0

Dutch Clark

Year	Team		No	Yds	Avg	Lg	TD
1932	POR	N	10	107	10.7		3
1934	DET	N	7	72	10.3		1
1935			9	124	13.8		2
1936			1	5	5.0	5	0
1937			2	33	16.5		1
Career			29	341	11.8	5	6

Dwight Clark

Year	Team		No	Yds	Avg	Lg	TD
1979	SF	N	18	232	12.9	30	0
1980			82	991	12.1	71t	8
1981			85	1105	13.0	78t	4
1982			60	913	15.2	51	5
1983			70	840	12.0	46t	8
1984			52	880	16.9	80t	6
1985			54	705	13.1	49t	10
1986			61	794	13.0	45t	2
1987			24	290	12.1	40t	5
Career			506	6750	13.3	80t	48
Playoffs			48	726	15.1		3

Gary Clark

Year	Team		No	Yds	Avg	Lg	TD
1985	WAS	N	72	926	12.9	55	5
1986			74	1265	17.1	55	7
1987			56	1066	19.0	84t	7
1988			59	892	15.1	60t	7
1989			79	1229	15.6	80t	9
1990			75	1112	14.8	53t	8
1991			70	1340	19.1	82t	10
1992			64	912	14.3	47	5
1993	PHX	N	63	818	13.0	55	4
1994	ARI	N	50	771	15.4	45	1
1995	MIA	N	37	525	14.2	42t	2
Career			699	10856	15.5	84t	65
Playoffs			58	826	14.2		6

Hal Clark

Year	Team		No	Yds	Avg	Lg	TD
1923	ROC	N					1

Harry Clark

Year	Team		No	Yds	Avg	Lg	TD
1940	CHIB	N	3	80	26.7		0
1941			2	61	30.5	38	0
1942			6	131	21.8	49	2
1943			23	535	23.3	52	7
1946	LA	AA	10	123	12.3	71t	1
1947			3	54	18.0		0
1948	LA-CHI	AA	4	38	9.5		0
Career			51	1022	20.0	71t	11
Playoffs			3	47	15.7		2

Howard Clark

Year	Team		No	Yds	Avg	Lg	TD
1960	LA	A	27	431	16.0	50	0
1961	SD	A	11	132	12.0	33	0
Career			38	563	14.8	50	0

Jessie Clark

Year	Team		No	Yds	Avg	Lg	TD
1983	GB	N	18	279	15.5	75t	1
1984			29	234	8.1	20	2
1985			24	252	10.5	55t	2
1986			6	41	6.8	12	0
1987			22	119	5.4	19	1
1989	MIN	N	2	14	7.0	12	0
1990			1	4	4.0	4	0
Career			102	943	9.2	75t	6

Jimmy Clark

Year	Team		No	Yds	Avg	Lg	TD
1934	PIT	N					1

Ken Clark

Year	Team		No	Yds	Avg	Lg	TD
1990	IND	N	5	23	4.6	11	0
1991			33	245	7.4	23	0
1992			5	46	9.2	17	0
Career			43	314	7.3	23	0

Louis Clark

Year	Team		No	Yds	Avg	Lg	TD
1988	SEA	N	1	20	20.0	20t	1
1989			25	260	10.4	28	1
1991			21	228	10.9	24t	2
1992			20	290	14.5	33	1
Career			67	798	11.9	33	5
Playoffs			1	8	8.0		0

Year	Team	No	Yds	Avg	Lg	TD

Robert Clark

Year	Team	No	Yds	Avg	Lg	TD
1987	NO	N	3	38	12.7	14	0
1988			19	245	12.9	21t	2
1989	DET	N	41	748	18.2	69	2
1990			52	914	17.6	57	8
1991			47	640	13.6	68t	6
1992	MIA	N	3	59	19.7	45	0
Career			165	2644	16.0	69	18
Playoffs			2	29	14.5		0

Wayne Clark

Year	Team	No	Yds	Avg	Lg	TD
1944	DET	N	2	27	13.5	19	0

Frank Clarke

Year	Team	No	Yds	Avg	Lg	TD
1957	CLE	N	4	77	19.3	43	0
1958			3	91	30.3	34	0
1959			3	44	14.7	20	0
1960	DAL	N	9	290	32.2	76t	3
1961			41	919	22.4	80t	9
1962			47	1043	22.2	66t	14
1963			43	833	19.4	75t	10
1964			65	973	15.0	49	5
1965			41	682	16.6	53t	4
1966			26	355	13.7	33	4
1967			9	119	13.2	2	1
Career			291	5426	18.6	80t	50
Playoffs			5	126	25.2		1

Leon Clarke

Year	Team	No	Yds	Avg	Lg	TD
1956	LA	N	36	650	18.1	60t	4
1957			23	442	19.2	70t	4
1958			18	135	7.5	17t	4
1959			29	453	15.6	60	0
1960	CLE	N	11	184	16.7	86t	4
1961			11	211	19.2	41t	2
1962			10	106	10.6	22	0
1963	MIN	N	3	34	11.3	14	0
Career			141	2215	15.7	86t	18

Hayward Clay

Year	Team	No	Yds	Avg	Lg	TD
1996	STL	N	4	51	12.8	34	0

Randy Clay

Year	Team	No	Yds	Avg	Lg	TD
1950	NYG	N	7	69	9.9	16	0
1953			5	51	10.2	33	1
Career			12	120	10.0	33	1

Walt Clay

Year	Team	No	Yds	Avg	Lg	TD
1946	CHI	AA	4	48	12.0		0
1947	LA	AA	1	52	52.0	52	0
1948			10	118	11.8		1
Career			15	218	14.5		1

Mark Clayton

Year	Team	No	Yds	Avg	Lg	TD
1983	MIA	N	6	114	19.0	39	1
1984			73	1389	19.0	65t	18
1985			70	996	14.2	45	4
1986			60	1150	19.2	68t	10
1987			46	776	16.9	43	7
1988			86	1129	13.1	45t	14
1989			64	1011	15.8	78t	9
1990			32	406	12.7	43	3
1991			70	1053	15.0	43t	12
1992			43	619	14.4	44t	3
1993	GB	N	32	331	10.3	32	3
Career			582	8974	15.4	78t	84
Playoffs			32	507	15.8		3

Paul Cleary

Year	Team	No	Yds	Avg	Lg	TD
1948	NY	AA	4	37	9.3		0

Cal Clemens

Year	Team	No	Yds	Avg	Lg	TD
1936	GB	N	1	18	18.0	18	0

Johnny Clement

Year	Team	No	Yds	Avg	Lg	TD
1946	PIT	N	1	22	22.0	22	0
1947			1	6	6.0	6	0
Career			2	28	14.0	22	0

Skip Clement

Year	Team	No	Yds	Avg	Lg	TD
1961	PIT	N	5	65	13.0	19	0

Vin Clements

Year	Team	No	Yds	Avg	Lg	TD
1972	NYG	N	9	118	13.1	39	0

Vin Clements continued

Year	Team	No	Yds	Avg	Lg	TD
1973			15	129	8.6	16	1
Career			24	247	10.3	39	1

Ray Clemons

Year	Team	No	Yds	Avg	Lg	TD
1939	DET	N	1	5	5.0	5	0

Topper Clemons

Year	Team	No	Yds	Avg	Lg	TD
1987	PHI	N	1	13	13.0	13t	1

Einar Cleve

Year	Team	No	Yds	Avg	Lg	TD
1922	MIN	N					1
1923							1
Career							2

Greg Clifton

Year	Team	No	Yds	Avg	Lg	TD
1993	WAS	N	2	15	7.5	10	0

Doug Cline

Year	Team	No	Yds	Avg	Lg	TD
1960	HOU	A	4	15	3.8		0

Ollie Cline

Year	Team	No	Yds	Avg	Lg	TD
1949	BUF	AA	15	110	7.3		0
1950	DET	N	7	18	2.6	25	0
1952			2	45	22.5	30	0
1953			10	126	12.6	28	1
Career			34	299	8.8	30	1
Playoffs			2	9	4.5		0

Tony Cline

Year	Team	No	Yds	Avg	Lg	TD
1977	SF	N	1	15	15.0	15	0

Tony Cline

Year	Team	No	Yds	Avg	Lg	TD
1995	BUF	N	8	64	8.0	17	0
1996			19	117	6.2	15	1
Career			27	181	6.7	17	1
Playoffs			5	68	13.6		1

Joey Clinkscales

Year	Team	No	Yds	Avg	Lg	TD
1987	PIT	N	13	240	18.5	57	1

Jack Cloud

Year	Team	No	Yds	Avg	Lg	TD
1950	GB	N	3	19	6.3	13	0
1951			3	16	5.3	6t	1
Career			6	35	5.8	13	1

Don Clune

Year	Team	No	Yds	Avg	Lg	TD
1975	NYG	N	5	97	19.4	41	0
1976	SEA	N	4	67	16.8	27	0
Career			9	164	18.2	41	0

Rich Coady

Year	Team	No	Yds	Avg	Lg	TD
1970	CHI	N	6	44	7.3	14	1

Bert Coan

Year	Team	No	Yds	Avg	Lg	TD
1962	SD	A	1	52	52.0	52	0
1963	KC	A	2	35	17.5	31	0
1964			2	8	4.0	4	0
1965			9	85	9.4	23	2
1966			18	131	7.3	20	2
1967			5	41	8.2	24	0
1968			2	15	7.5	12	0
Career			39	367	9.4	52	4
Playoffs			1	5	5.0		0

Ben Coates

Year	Team	No	Yds	Avg	Lg	TD
1991	NE	N	10	95	9.5	17	1
1992			20	171	8.6	22t	3
1993			53	659	12.4	54t	8
1994			96	1174	12.2	62t	7
1995			84	915	10.9	35	6
1996			62	682	11.0	84t	9
Career			325	3696	11.4	84t	34
Playoffs			16	169	10.6		1

Ray Coates

Year	Team	No	Yds	Avg	Lg	TD
1949	NYG	N	8	152	19.0	51	1

Garry Cobb

Year	Team	No	Yds	Avg	Lg	TD
1981	DET	N	1	19	19.0	19	0
1982			1	25	25.0	25	0
Career			2	44	22.0	25	0

Mike Cobb

Year	Team	No	Yds	Avg	Lg	TD
1978	CHI	N	1	7	7.0	7	0
1979			6	91	15.2	38	0
1980			2	16	8.0	9	0
1981			2	20	10.0	11	0
Career			11	134	12.2	38	0

Reggie Cobb

Year	Team	No	Yds	Avg	Lg	TD
1990	TB	N	39	299	7.7	17	0
1991			15	111	7.4	21	0
1992			21	156	7.4	27	0
1993			9	61	6.8	19	1
1994	GB	N	35	299	8.5	37t	1
1996	NYJ	N	4	23	5.8	12	0
Career			123	949	7.7	37t	2
Playoffs			2	30	15.0		0

Red Cochran

Year	Team	No	Yds	Avg	Lg	TD
1947	CHIC	N	1	7	7.0	7t	1
1949			7	107	15.3	33	1
Career			8	114	14.3	33	2

Tom Cochran

Year	Team	No	Yds	Avg	Lg	TD
1949	WAS	N	7	82	11.7	22	0

Ed Cody

Year	Team	No	Yds	Avg	Lg	TD
1947	GB	N	1	2	2.0	2	0

Junior Coffey

Year	Team	No	Yds	Avg	Lg	TD
1966	ATL	N	15	182	12.1	46	1
1967			30	196	6.5	22	1
1969	ATL-NYG	N	14	89	6.4	28	3
1971	NYG	N	5	20	4.0	11	0
Career			64	487	7.6	46	5

Wayne Coffey

Year	Team	No	Yds	Avg	Lg	TD
1987	NE	N	3	66	22.0	35	0

Paul Coffman

Year	Team	No	Yds	Avg	Lg	TD
1979	GB	N	56	711	12.7	78t	4
1980			42	496	11.8	25	3
1981			55	687	12.5	29	4
1982			23	287	12.5	42	2
1983			54	814	15.1	74	11
1984			43	562	13.1	44t	9
1985			49	666	13.6	32	6
1986	KC	N	12	75	6.3	10	2
1987			5	42	8.4	13t	1
Career			339	4340	12.8	78t	42
Playoffs			12	123	10.3		0

Gail Cogdill

Year	Team	No	Yds	Avg	Lg	TD
1960	DET	N	43	642	14.9	63	1
1961			45	956	21.2	84t	6
1962			53	991	18.7	72	7
1963			48	945	19.7	70t	10
1964			45	665	14.8	57	2
1965			20	247	12.4	33	0
1966			47	411	8.7	21	1
1967			21	322	15.3	52t	1
1968			3	42	14.0	20	0
1969	ATL	N	24	374	15.6	52	2
1970			7	101	14.4	30	1
Career			356	5696	16.0	84t	34

Angelo Coia

Year	Team	No	Yds	Avg	Lg	TD
1960	CHI	N	25	478	19.1	59	4
1961			12	249	20.8	64t	3
1962			22	361	16.4	71t	4
1963			11	116	10.5	18t	1
1964	WAS	N	29	500	17.2	80t	5
1965			18	240	13.3	45t	3
1966	ATL	N	4	93	23.3	39	0
Career			121	2037	16.8	80t	20
Playoffs			1	22	22.0		0

Darrell Colbert

Year	Team	No	Yds	Avg	Lg	TD
1987	KC	N	3	21	7.0	9	0
1988			1	-3	-3.0	-3	0
Career			4	18	4.5	9	0

Jim Colclough

Year	Team	No	Yds	Avg	Lg	TD
1960	BOS	A	49	666	13.6	61	9
1961			42	757	18.0	58	9

Year	Team		No	Yds	Avg	Lg	TD

Jim Colclough *continued*

Year	Team		No	Yds	Avg	Lg	TD
1962			40	868	**21.7**	78	10
1963			42	793	18.9	56	3
1964			32	657	20.5	59	5
1965			40	677	16.9	41	3
1966			16	284	17.8	32	0
1967			14	263	18.8	52	0
1968			8	136	17.0	44	0
Career			283	5101	18.0	78	39
Playoffs			4	35	8.8		0

Emerson Cole

Year	Team		No	Yds	Avg	Lg	TD
1951	CLE	N	4	30	7.5	17	0

John Cole

Year	Team		No	Yds	Avg	Lg	TD
1938	PHI	N	2	9	4.5		0
1940			2	11	5.5		0
Career			4	20	5.0		0

Linzy Cole

Year	Team		No	Yds	Avg	Lg	TD
1970	CHI	N	3	47	15.7	34	0

Terry Cole

Year	Team		No	Yds	Avg	Lg	TD
1968	BAL	N	13	75	5.8	18	0
1969			9	65	7.2	18t	1
1970	PIT	N	3	31	10.3	20	0
Career			25	171	6.8	20	1
Playoffs			1	2	2.0		0

Tom Colella

Year	Team		No	Yds	Avg	Lg	TD
1943	DET	N	1	-1	-1.0	-1	0
1944	CLE	N	2	64	32.0	54t	1
1945			7	64	9.1	20	2
1946	CLE	AA	1	12	12.0	12t	1
1947			4	63	15.8		1
1948			1	7	7.0	7	0
1949	BUF	AA	2	6	3.0		0
Career			18	215	11.9	54t	5
Playoffs			2	7	3.5		0

Andre Coleman

Year	Team		No	Yds	Avg	Lg	TD
1995	SD	N	3	67	22.3	41	0
1996			36	486	13.5	50	2
Career			39	553	14.2	50	2

Charles Coleman

Year	Team		No	Yds	Avg	Lg	TD
1987	NYG	N	1	5	5.0	5	0

Lincoln Coleman

Year	Team		No	Yds	Avg	Lg	TD
1993	DAL	N	4	24	6.0	10	0
1994			8	46	5.8	14	0
Career			12	70	5.8	14	0
Playoffs			2	6	3.0		0

Monte Coleman

Year	Team		No	Yds	Avg	Lg	TD
1980	WAS	N	1	12	12.0	12	0

Pat Coleman

Year	Team		No	Yds	Avg	Lg	TD
1991	HOU	N	11	138	12.5	26	1
1992			2	10	5.0	6	0
1993			9	129	14.3	25	0
1994			20	298	14.9	81	1
Career			42	575	13.7	81	2

Ronnie Coleman

Year	Team		No	Yds	Avg	Lg	TD
1974	HOU	N	4	9	2.3	7	0
1975			18	129	7.2	24	0
1976			40	247	6.2	19	3
1977			22	115	5.2	21	1
1978			19	246	12.9	33	1
1979			12	114	9.5	17	1
1980			16	168	10.5	27	0
1981			19	211	11.1	24	0
Career			150	1239	8.3	33	6
Playoffs			7	143	20.4		0

James Coley

Year	Team		No	Yds	Avg	Lg	TD
1990	CHI	N	1	7	7.0	7	0
1991	IND	N	1	13	13.0	13	0
Career			2	20	10.0	13	0

Jimmy Collier

Year	Team		No	Yds	Avg	Lg	TD
1962	NYG	N	1	27	27.0	27	0

Mike Collier

Year	Team		No	Yds	Avg	Lg	TD
1975	PIT	N	1	7	7.0	7	0
1977	BUF	N	3	23	7.7	11	0
1979			7	43	6.1	19	0
Career			11	73	6.6	19	0

Dwight Collins

Year	Team		No	Yds	Avg	Lg	TD
1984	MIN	N	11	143	13.0	43t	1

Gary Collins

Year	Team		No	Yds	Avg	Lg	TD
1962	CLE	N	11	153	13.9	29	2
1963			43	674	15.7	49t	**13**
1964			35	544	15.5	43	8
1965			50	884	17.7	67	10
1966			56	946	16.9	54	12
1967			32	500	15.6	33	7
1968			9	230	25.6	39	0
1969			54	786	14.6	48t	11
1970			26	351	13.5	28	4
1971			15	231	15.4	29	3
Career			331	5299	16.0	67	70
Playoffs			19	275	14.5		5

Larry Collins

Year	Team		No	Yds	Avg	Lg	TD
1978	CLE	N	1	4	4.0	4	0

Patrick Collins

Year	Team		No	Yds	Avg	Lg	TD
1988	GB	N	2	17	8.5	9	0

Rip Collins

Year	Team		No	Yds	Avg	Lg	TD
1949	CHI	AA	6	161	26.8		0
1950	BAL	N	19	295	15.5	63	0
1951	GB	N	1	5	5.0	5	0
Career			26	461	17.7	63	0

Shawn Collins

Year	Team		No	Yds	Avg	Lg	TD
1989	ATL	N	58	862	14.9	47	3
1990			34	503	14.8	61	2
1991			3	37	12.3	21	0
1992	CLE	N	3	31	10.3	11	0
Career			98	1433	14.6	61	5

Sonny Collins

Year	Team		No	Yds	Avg	Lg	TD
1976	ATL	N	4	37	9.3	20	0

Tony Collins

Year	Team		No	Yds	Avg	Lg	TD
1981	NE	N	26	232	8.9	22	0
1982			19	187	9.8	33	2
1983			27	257	9.5	20	0
1984			16	100	6.3	19	0
1985			52	549	10.6	49	2
1986			77	684	8.9	49	5
1987			44	347	7.9	29	3
Career			261	2356	9.0	49	12
Playoffs			13	119	9.2		1

Cris Collinsworth

Year	Team		No	Yds	Avg	Lg	TD
1981	CIN	N	67	1009	15.1	74t	8
1982			49	700	14.3	50	1
1983			66	1130	17.1	63	5
1984			64	989	15.5	57t	6
1985			65	1125	17.3	71	5
1986			62	1024	16.5	46t	10
1987			31	494	15.9	53	0
1988			13	227	17.5	36	1
Career			417	6698	16.1	74t	36
Playoffs			21	354	16.9		1

Mickey Colmer

Year	Team		No	Yds	Avg	Lg	TD
1946	BKN	AA	22	327	14.9		1
1947			18	190	10.6		1
1948			21	372	17.7	78t	4
1949	B-NY	AA	2	10	5.0		0
Career			63	899	14.3	78t	6

Lloyd Colteryahn

Year	Team		No	Yds	Avg	Lg	TD
1954	BAL	N	30	384	12.8	21	0
1955			21	251	12.0	22	3
1956			3	29	9.7	16	0
Career			54	664	12.3	22	3

Bill Combs

Year	Team		No	Yds	Avg	Lg	TD
1942	PHI	N	4	44	11.0	19	1

Chris Combs

Year	Team		No	Yds	Avg	Lg	TD
1980	STL	N	2	52	26.0	38t	1
1981			5	54	10.8	13	0
Career			7	106	15.1	38t	1

Marty Comer

Year	Team		No	Yds	Avg	Lg	TD
1946	MIA-BUF	AA	2	17	8.5		0
1947	BUF	AA	2	75	37.5	56t	1
1948			5	66	13.2		1
Career			9	158	17.6	56t	2

Irv Comp

Year	Team		No	Yds	Avg	Lg	TD
1944	GB	N	2	16	8.0	11t	1
1945			1	50	50.0	50t	0
Career			3	66	22.0	50t	1

Tony Compagno

Year	Team		No	Yds	Avg	Lg	TD
1946	PIT	N	7	77	11.0	36	0
1947			9	190	21.1	39t	1
1948			1	4	4.0	4	0
Career			17	271	15.9	39t	1

Dick Compton

Year	Team		No	Yds	Avg	Lg	TD
1963	DET	N	2	41	20.5	22	0
1965	HOU	A	3	140	46.7	95	2
1967	PIT	N	42	597	14.2	40	1
1968			5	45	9.0	14	1
Career			52	823	15.8	95	4

Jack Concannon

Year	Team		No	Yds	Avg	Lg	TD
1966	PHI	N	1	7	7.0	7	0

Merl Condit

Year	Team		No	Yds	Avg	Lg	TD
1940	PIT	N	4	30	7.5		1
1941	BKN	N	5	32	6.4	21	0
1942			9	111	12.3	56	0
1943			7	101	14.4	65	1
1945	WAS	N	3	16	5.3	12	0
1946	PIT	N	4	33	8.3	23	0
Career			32	323	10.1	65	2
Playoffs			1	1	1.0		0

Fred Cone

Year	Team		No	Yds	Avg	Lg	TD
1951	GB	N	28	315	11.3	49	0
1952			8	98	12.3	37t	1
1953			18	165	9.2	30	1
1954			4	19	4.8	13	0
1955			1	7	7.0	7	0
1956			12	218	18.2	69t	2
1957			4	30	7.5	10	0
Career			75	852	11.4	69t	4

Mel Conger

Year	Team		No	Yds	Avg	Lg	TD
1946	NY	AA	3	61	20.3		0

Larry Conjar

Year	Team		No	Yds	Avg	Lg	TD
1967	CLE	N	6	68	11.3	27	0

Bill Conkright

Year	Team		No	Yds	Avg	Lg	TD
1938	CHIB	N	1	2	2.0	2	1

George Conn

Year	Team		No	Yds	Avg	Lg	TD
1920	CLE	A					1

Clyde Conner

Year	Team		No	Yds	Avg	Lg	TD
1956	SF	N	22	362	16.5	49	1
1957			30	412	13.7	41	4
1958			49	512	10.4	26	5
1959			13	162	12.5	37t	1
1960			38	531	14.0	65t	2
1961			11	177	16.1	45	1
1962			24	240	10.0	18	4
1963			16	247	15.4	42	0
Career			203	2643	13.0	65t	18
Playoffs			1	10	10.0		0

George Connor

Year	Team		No	Yds	Avg	Lg	TD
1949	CHIB	N	3	51	17.0	25	0
1950			1	21	21.0	21	0
1953			1	17	17.0	17	0
Career			5	89	17.8	25	0

Scott Conover

Year	Team		No	Yds	Avg	Lg	TD
1994	DET	N	1	1	1.0	1t	1

Bobby Joe Conrad

Year	Team		No	Yds	Avg	Lg	TD
1959	CHIC	N	14	142	10.1	25	3
1960	STL	N	7	103	14.7	24	0
1961			30	499	16.6	50	2
1962			62	954	15.4	72t	4
1963			73	967	13.2	48	10
1964			61	780	12.8	53	6
1965			58	909	15.7	71t	5
1966			34	388	11.4	40t	2
1967			47	637	13.6	53	2
1968			32	449	14.0	80t	4
1969	DAL	N	4	74	18.5	34	0
Career			422	5902	14.0	80t	38

Curtis Conway

Year	Team		No	Yds	Avg	Lg	TD
1993	CHI	N	19	231	12.2	38t	2
1994			39	546	14.0	85t	2
1995			62	1037	16.7	76t	12
1996			81	1049	13.0	58t	7
Career			201	2863	14.2	85t	23
Playoffs			7	81	11.6		0

Ernie Conwell

Year	Team		No	Yds	Avg	Lg	TD
1996	STL	N	15	164	10.9	26	0

Jimmy Conzelman

Year	Team		No	Yds	Avg	Lg	TD
1923	MIL	N					1
1925	DET	N					3
1926							1
1927	PRO	N					3
1928							2
1929							1
Career							11

Dave Cook

Year	Team		No	Yds	Avg	Lg	TD
1936	CHIC-BKN	N	1	2	2.0	2	0

Gene Cook

Year	Team		No	Yds	Avg	Lg	TD
1959	DET	N	1	43	43.0	43	0

Marv Cook

Year	Team		No	Yds	Avg	Lg	TD
1989	NE	N	3	13	4.3	5	0
1990			51	455	8.9	35t	5
1991			82	808	9.9	49	3
1992			52	413	7.9	27	2
1993			22	154	7.0	17	1
1994	CHI	N	21	212	10.1	34	1
1995	STL	N	26	135	5.2	16	1
Career			257	2190	8.5	49	13

Ted Cook

Year	Team		No	Yds	Avg	Lg	TD
1947	DET	N	7	111	15.9	29	1
1948	GB	N	13	156	12.0	23	0
1949			25	442	17.7	50	1
1950			16	182	11.4	21t	3
Career			61	891	14.6	50	5

Toi Cook

Year	Team		No	Yds	Avg	Lg	TD
1989	NO	N	1	8	8.0	8	0

Bob Coolbaugh

Year	Team		No	Yds	Avg	Lg	TD
1961	OAK	A	32	435	13.6	46	4

Tom Coombs

Year	Team		No	Yds	Avg	Lg	TD
1983	NYJ	N	1	1	1.0	1	0

Rob Coons

Year	Team		No	Yds	Avg	Lg	TD
1995	BUF	N	3	28	9.3	13	0
1996			1	12	12.0	12	0
Career			4	40	10.0	13	0

Adrian Cooper

Year	Team		No	Yds	Avg	Lg	TD
1991	PIT	N	11	147	13.4	47t	2
1992			16	197	12.3	27	3
1993			9	112	12.4	38	0
1994	MIN	N	32	363	11.3	34	0
1995			18	207	11.5	41	0
1996	SF	N	1	11	11.0	11	0
Career			87	1037	11.9	47t	5
Playoffs			2	27	13.5		1

Earl Cooper

Year	Team		No	Yds	Avg	Lg	TD
1980	SF	N	83	567	6.8	66t	4
1981			51	477	9.4	50	0

Earl Cooper *continued*

Year	Team		No	Yds	Avg	Lg	TD
1982			19	153	8.1	20	1
1983			15	207	13.8	73t	3
1984			41	459	11.2	26	4
1985			4	45	11.3	20	0
Career			213	1908	9.0	73t	12
Playoffs			7	37	5.3		1

Mark Cooper

Year	Team		No	Yds	Avg	Lg	TD
1985	DEN	N	1	13	13.0	13	0

Norm Cooper

Year	Team		No	Yds	Avg	Lg	TD
1937	BKN	N	1	14	14.0	14	0

Richard Cooper

Year	Team		No	Yds	Avg	Lg	TD
1992	NO	N	0	20		20L	0

Thurlow Cooper

Year	Team		No	Yds	Avg	Lg	TD
1960	NY	A	9	161	17.9		3
1961			15	208	13.9	31	4
1962			12	122	10.2	25	1
Career			36	491	13.6	31	8

Horace Copeland

Year	Team		No	Yds	Avg	Lg	TD
1993	TB	N	30	633	21.1	67t	4
1994			17	308	18.1	65	0
1995			35	605	17.3	64t	2
Career			82	1546	18.9	67t	6

Russell Copeland

Year	Team		No	Yds	Avg	Lg	TD
1993	BUF	N	13	242	18.6	60	0
1994			21	255	12.1	35	1
1995			42	646	15.4	77t	1
1996			7	85	12.1	31	0
Career			83	1228	14.8	77t	2

Al Coppage

Year	Team		No	Yds	Avg	Lg	TD
1940	CHIC	N	15	163	10.9		1
1941			8	117	14.6	40	0
1942			30	196	6.5	32	0
1946	CLE	AA	2	34	17.0		0
1947	BUF	AA	20	226	11.3		2
Career			75	736	9.8	40	3

George Corbett

Year	Team		No	Yds	Avg	Lg	TD
1932	CHIB	N					1
1934			1	2	2.0	2	0
1935			2	5	2.5		0
1936			3	69	23.0		1
1938			1	10	10.0	10	0
Career			7	86	12.3	10	2

Jim Corbett

Year	Team		No	Yds	Avg	Lg	TD
1977	CIN	N	7	127	18.1	47t	1
1978			12	187	15.6	51	0
1979			3	34	11.3	15	0
1980			3	28	9.3	12	0
Career			25	376	15.0	51	1

Art Corcoran

Year	Team		No	Yds	Avg	Lg	TD
1921	CLE	A					1

Ollie Cordill

Year	Team		No	Yds	Avg	Lg	TD
1940	CLE	N	14	158	11.3		2

Chuck Corgan

Year	Team		No	Yds	Avg	Lg	TD
1924	KC	N					1
1925							1
Career							2

Mike Corgan

Year	Team		No	Yds	Avg	Lg	TD
1943	DET	N	1	9	9.0	9	0

Bo Cornell

Year	Team		No	Yds	Avg	Lg	TD
1971	CLE	N	1	18	18.0	18	0
1972			2	7	3.5	5	0
Career			3	25	8.3	18	0

Fred Cornwell

Year	Team		No	Yds	Avg	Lg	TD
1984	DAL	N	2	23	11.5	13	1
1985			6	77	12.8	32	1
Career			8	100	12.5	32	2

Bobby Coronado

Year	Team		No	Yds	Avg	Lg	TD
1961	PIT	N	3	32	10.7	14	0

Red Corzine

Year	Team		No	Yds	Avg	Lg	TD
1936	NYG	N	1	36	36.0	36t	1
1937			9	75	8.3		1
Career			10	111	11.1	36t	2

Doug Cosbie

Year	Team		No	Yds	Avg	Lg	TD
1979	DAL	N	5	36	7.2	12	0
1980			2	11	5.5	6	1
1981			17	225	13.2	28	5
1982			30	441	14.7	45	4
1983			46	588	12.8	61t	6
1984			60	789	13.2	36	4
1985			64	793	12.4	42	6
1986			28	312	11.1	22t	1
1987			36	421	11.7	30	3
1988			12	112	9.3	21	0
Career			300	3728	12.4	61t	30
Playoffs			22	243	11.0		3

Bruce Coslet

Year	Team		No	Yds	Avg	Lg	TD
1969	CIN	A	1	39	39.0	39t	1
1970	CIN	N	8	98	12.3	24	1
1971			21	356	17.0	71t	4
1972			5	48	9.6	17	1
1973			9	123	13.7	18	0
1974			2	24	12.0	18	0
1975			10	117	11.7	18	0
1976			5	73	14.6	32	2
Career			61	878	14.4	71t	9
Playoffs			2	14	7.0		0

Paul Costa

Year	Team		No	Yds	Avg	Lg	TD
1965	BUF	A	21	401	19.1	46	0
1966			27	400	14.8	50	3
1967			39	726	18.6	63t	2
1968			15	172	11.5	27	1
Career			102	1699	16.7	63t	6
Playoffs			2	32	16.0		0

Vince Costello

Year	Team		No	Yds	Avg	Lg	TD
1966	CLE	N	1	-7	-7.0	-7	0

Jeff Cothran

Year	Team		No	Yds	Avg	Lg	TD
1994	CIN	N	4	24	6.0	8	1
1995			8	44	5.5	15	0
1996			7	49	7.0	14	0
Career			19	117	6.2	15	1

Craig Cotton

Year	Team		No	Yds	Avg	Lg	TD
1970	DET	N	1	6	6.0	6	0
1971			6	88	14.7	34	0
1972			8	129	16.1	35	1
1973	CHI	N	13	186	14.3	63	0
Career			28	409	14.6	63	1

Russ Cotton

Year	Team		No	Yds	Avg	Lg	TD
1942	PIT	N	2	58	29.0	41	0

Tex Coulter

Year	Team		No	Yds	Avg	Lg	TD
1947	NYG	N	8	107	13.4	47	1
1952			1	9	9.0	9	0
Career			9	116	12.9	47	1

Johnny Counts

Year	Team		No	Yds	Avg	Lg	TD
1962	NYG	N	4	62	15.5	24	0

Gerry Courtney

Year	Team		No	Yds	Avg	Lg	TD
1942	BKN	N	1	1	1.0	1	0

Larry Coutre

Year	Team		No	Yds	Avg	Lg	TD
1950	GB	N	17	206	12.1	77t	2
1953			1	-4	-4.0	-4	0
Career			18	202	11.2	77t	2

Jamie Covington

Year	Team		No	Yds	Avg	Lg	TD
1987	NYG	N	1	9	9.0	9	0

Bob Cowan

Year	Team		No	Yds	Avg	Lg	TD
1947	CLE	AA	5	60	12.0		1
1948			15	265	17.7	63t	4

Year	Team		No	Yds	Avg	Lg	TD

Bob Cowan *continued*

Year	Team		No	Yds	Avg	Lg	TD
1949	BAL	AA	1	26	26.0	26	0
Career			21	351	16.7	63t	5

Charlie Cowan

Year	Team		No	Yds	Avg	Lg	TD
1975	LA	N	1	1	1.0	1	0

Gerry Cowhig

1948	LA	N	3	18	6.0	9	0

Aaron Cox

Year	Team		No	Yds	Avg	Lg	TD
1988	LARM	N	28	590	21.1	69t	5
1989			20	340	17.0	51t	3
1990			17	266	15.6	32	0
1991			15	216	14.4	39	0
1992			18	261	14.5	26	0
1993	IND	N	4	59	14.8	24	0
Career			102	1732	17.0	69t	8

Arthur Cox

Year	Team		No	Yds	Avg	Lg	TD
1983	ATL	N	9	83	9.2	19	1
1984			34	329	9.7	23t	1
1985			33	454	13.8	62t	2
1986			24	301	12.5	49	1
1987			11	101	9.2	19	0
1988	SD	N	18	144	8.0	20	0
1989			22	200	9.1	24	2
1990			14	93	6.6	12	1
1991			5	53	10.6	19	0
Career			170	1758	10.3	62t	10

Billy Cox

1952	WAS	N	2	19	9.5	13	0
1955			5	71	14.2	28	0
Career			7	90	12.9	28	0

Jim Cox

1968	MIA	A	11	147	13.4	30	0

Claude Crabb

1964	PHI	N	1	14	14.0	14	0
1965			2	41	20.5	27	0
1966	LA	N	1	47	47.0	47	0
Career			4	102	25.5	47	0

Clyde Crabtree

1930	FRA	N					1

Eric Crabtree

1966	DEN	A	1	38	38.0	38	0
1967			46	716	15.6	76t	5
1968			35	601	17.2	72t	5
1969	CIN	A	40	855	21.4	73t	7
1970	CIN	N	19	231	12.2	29	2
1971	CIN-NE	N	23	222	9.7	31t	3
Career			164	2663	16.2	76t	22

Donnie Craft

1982	HOU	N	23	230	10.0	49	1
1983			12	99	8.3	14	0
Career			35	329	9.4	49	1

Russ Craft

1946	PHI	N	4	48	12.0	35	0
1947			2	66	33.0	34	1
1948			4	138	34.5	70t	2
1949			1	37	37.0	37	0
1950			1	14	14.0	14	0
Career			12	303	25.3	70t	3
Playoffs			5	41	8.2		0

Dobie Craig

1962	OAK	A	27	492	18.2	46	4
1963			7	205	29.3	93	2
1964	HOU	A	4	46	11.5	25	1
Career			38	743	19.6	93	7

Larry Craig

1939	GB	N	3	44	14.7		0
1940			6	67	11.2		0
1941			2	13	6.5	12	0
1944			2	17	8.5	9	0

Larry Craig *continued*

Year	Team		No	Yds	Avg	Lg	TD
1947			1	14	14.0	14	0
Career			14	155	11.1	14	0
Playoffs			2	6	3.0		0

Neal Craig

1975	CLE	N	1	1	1.0	1	0

Paco Craig

1988	DET	N	2	29	14.5	18	0

Reggie Craig

1975	KC	N	1	10	10.0	10	0
1977	CLE	N	1	5	5.0	5	0
Career			2	15	7.5	10	0

Roger Craig

1983	SF	N	48	427	8.9	23	4
1984			71	675	9.5	64t	3
1985			92	1016	11.0	73	6
1986			81	624	7.7	48	0
1987			66	492	7.5	35t	1
1988			76	534	7.0	22	0
1989			49	473	9.7	44	1
1990			25	201	8.0	31	0
1991	LARI	N	17	136	8.0	20	0
1992	MIN	N	22	164	7.5	22	0
1993			19	169	8.9	31	1
Career			566	4911	8.7	73	17
Playoffs			63	606	9.6		2

Steve Craig

1974	MIN	N	4	26	6.5	10t	1
1975			6	68	11.3	17	0
1976			3	33	11.0	17	0
1977			1	14	14.0	14	0
1978			4	31	7.8	9	0
Career			18	172	9.6	17	1

Milt Crain

1944	BOS	N	1	16	16.0	16	0

Carl Cramer

1921	AKR	A					2

Aaron Craver

1991	MIA	N	8	67	8.4	25	0
1994			24	237	9.9	28	0
1995	DEN	N	43	369	8.6	32	1
1996			39	297	7.6	39t	1
Career			114	970	8.5	39t	2
Playoffs			12	88	7.3		0

Derrick Crawford

1986	SF	N	5	70	14.0	42	0

Eddie Crawford

1957	NYG	N	2	40	20.0	27	0

Fred Crawford

1935	CHIB	N	1	10	10.0	10	0

Jim Crawford

1960	BOS	A	10	92	9.2		0
1961			9	85	9.4	25	0
1962			22	224	10.2	44	2
1963			10	84	8.4	28	0
1964			1	11	11.0	11	0
Career			52	496	9.5	44	2

Keith Crawford

1993	NYG	N	1	6	6.0	6	0

Rufus Crawford

1978	SEA	N	4	25	6.3	8	0

Dick Crayne

1936	BKN	N	1	32	32.0	32	0
1937			1	4	4.0	4	0
Career			2	36	18.0	32	0

Milan Creighton

1931	CHIC	N					1

Ted Cremer

Year	Team		No	Yds	Avg	Lg	TD
1946	DET	N	15	179	11.9	39	0
1947			13	117	9.0	32	1
Career			28	296	10.6	39	1

Willis Crenshaw

1964	STL	N	8	58	7.3	19	0
1965			23	232	10.1	78t	1
1966			15	46	3.1	19	0
1967			6	30	5.0	12	0
1968			23	232	10.1	42	1
1969			11	94	8.5	31	0
1970	DEN	N	18	105	5.8	35	1
Career			104	797	7.7	78t	3

Bobby Crespino

1961	CLE	N	2	62	31.0	49	1
1962			2	13	6.5	9	0
1963			2	22	11.0	18	1
1964	NYG	N	12	165	13.8	27	0
1965			7	57	8.1	15	4
1966			16	167	10.4	19t	2
1967			10	125	12.5	24	1
1968			7	130	18.6	43	0
Career			58	741	12.8	49	9

Joe Cribbs

1980	BUF	N	52	415	8.0	21t	4
1981			40	603	15.1	65t	7
1982			13	99	7.6	31	0
1983			57	524	9.2	33t	7
1985			18	142	7.9	23	0
1986	SF	N	35	346	9.9	33	0
1987			9	70	7.8	16	0
Career			224	2199	9.8	65t	15
Playoffs			10	109	10.9		0

Hal Crisler

1946	BOS	N	32	385	12.0	62	5
1947			25	363	14.5	49	2
1948	WAS	N	33	599	18.2	79t	6
1949			26	388	14.9	47	4
1950	BAL	N	19	307	16.2	62	5
Career			135	2042	15.1	79t	22

Ray Crittenden

1993	NE	N	16	293	18.3	44	1
1994			28	379	13.5	32	3
Career			44	672	15.3	44	4

Jack Crittendon

1954	CHIC	N	5	43	8.6	15	0

Bobby Crockett

1966	BUF	A	31	533	17.2	53	3
1968			6	76	12.7	23	0
1969			4	50	12.5	19	0
Career			41	659	16.1	53	3
Playoffs			1	16	16.0		0

Monte Crockett

1960	BUF	A	14	173	12.4		1
1961			20	325	16.3	51	0
1962			1	14	14.0	14	0
Career			35	512	14.6	51	1

Zack Crockett

1995	IND	N	2	35	17.5	19	0
1996			11	96	8.7	32	1
Career			13	131	10.1	32	1
Playoffs			6	37	6.2		0

Abe Croft

1944	CHIB	N	9	140	15.6	67t	1
1945			2	12	6.0	10	0
Career			11	152	13.8	67t	2

Bill Cronin

1966	MIA	A	7	83	11.9	25	1

Tommy Cronin

1922	GB	N					1

Year	Team		No	Yds	Avg	Lg	TD

Corey Croom

Year	Team		No	Yds	Avg	Lg	TD
1993	NE	N	8	92	11.5	21	0
1995			1	8	8.0	8	0
Career			9	100	11.1	21	0
Playoffs			1	5	5.0		0

Marshall Cropper

Year	Team		No	Yds	Avg	Lg	TD
1967	PIT	N	1	11	11.0	11	0
1968			4	54	13.5	17	0
1969			9	116	12.9	19	0
Career			14	181	12.9	19	0

Steve Crosby

Year	Team		No	Yds	Avg	Lg	TD
1974	NYG	N	2	44	22.0	44	0

Billy Cross

Year	Team		No	Yds	Avg	Lg	TD
1951	CHIC	N	18	322	17.9	80t	3
1952			17	234	13.8	56t	2
1953			17	285	16.8	51t	1
Career			52	841	16.2	80t	6

Howard Cross

Year	Team		No	Yds	Avg	Lg	TD
1989	NYG	N	6	107	17.8	27	1
1990			8	106	13.3	21	0
1991			20	283	14.2	30	2
1992			27	357	13.2	29	2
1993			21	272	13.0	32	5
1994			31	364	11.7	40	4
1995			18	197	10.9	26	0
1996			22	178	8.1	19	1
Career			153	1864	12.2	40	15
Playoffs			9	87	9.7		1

Leon Crosswhite

Year	Team		No	Yds	Avg	Lg	TD
1973	DET	N	1	4	4.0	4	0
1974			3	31	10.3	13	0
Career			4	35	8.8	13	0

Ray Crouse

Year	Team		No	Yds	Avg	Lg	TD
1984	GB	N	9	93	10.3	25	1

John David Crow

Year	Team		No	Yds	Avg	Lg	TD
1958	CHIC	N	20	362	18.1	91t	3
1959			27	328	12.1	36t	4
1960	STL		25	462	18.5	52t	2
1961			20	306	15.3	35	3
1962			23	246	10.7	53	3
1964			23	257	11.2	22t	1
1965	SF		28	493	17.6	54	7
1966			30	341	11.4	54	3
1967			31	373	12.0	59t	3
1968			31	531	17.1	54t	5
Career			258	3699	14.3	91t	34

Wayne Crow

Year	Team		No	Yds	Avg	Lg	TD
1961	OAK	A	23	196	8.5	22	0
1962	BUF	A	8	80	10.0	25	1
1963			5	69	13.8	28	0
Career			36	345	9.6	28	1

Earl Crowder

Year	Team		No	Yds	Avg	Lg	TD
1939	CHIC	N	2	59	29.5		0
1940	CLE	N	2	33	16.5		0
Career			4	92	23.0		0

Paul Crowe

Year	Team		No	Yds	Avg	Lg	TD
1948	SF	AA	0	16		16L	1
1951	NYY	N	3	20	6.7	10	0
Career			3	36	12.0	16L	1

Jim Crowley

Year	Team		No	Yds	Avg	Lg	TD
1925	GB	N					1

Joe Crowley

Year	Team		No	Yds	Avg	Lg	TD
1944	BOS	N	13	279	21.5	67	3
1945			1	12	12.0	12	0
Career			14	291	20.8	67	3

Rae Crowther

Year	Team		No	Yds	Avg	Lg	TD
1925	FRA	N					3

Harry Crump

Year	Team		No	Yds	Avg	Lg	TD
1963	BOS	A	6	46	7.7	12	0
Playoffs			2	28	14.0		0

Carlester Crumpler

Year	Team		No	Yds	Avg	Lg	TD
1994	SEA	N	2	19	9.5	12	0
1995			23	254	11.0	24	1
1996			26	258	9.9	26	0
Career			51	531	10.4	26	1

Dwayne Crutchfield

Year	Team		No	Yds	Avg	Lg	TD
1983	NYJ	N	19	133	7.0	15	0
1984	LARM	N	2	11	5.5	7	1
Career			21	144	6.9	15	1

Larry Csonka

Year	Team		No	Yds	Avg	Lg	TD
1968	MIA	A	11	118	10.7	65	1
1969			21	183	8.7	42	1
1970	MIA	N	11	94	8.5	54	0
1971			13	113	8.7	25	1
1972			5	48	9.6	14	0
1973			7	22	3.1	9	0
1974			7	35	5.0	11	0
1976	NYG	N	6	39	6.5	14	0
1977			2	20	10.0	12	0
1978			7	73	10.4	23	0
1979	MIA	N	16	75	4.7	18	1
Career			106	820	7.7	65	4
Playoffs			4	26	6.5		1

Walt Cudzik

Year	Team		No	Yds	Avg	Lg	TD
1960	BOS	A	1	11	11.0	11	0

Ward Cuff

Year	Team		No	Yds	Avg	Lg	TD
1937	NYG	N	5	117	23.4		2
1938			8	114	14.3		1
1939			10	83	8.3		2
1940			13	220	16.9		1
1941			19	317	16.7	41	2
1942			16	267	16.7	35	2
1943			7	52	7.4	17	0
1944			11	135	12.3	23	2
1945			12	172	14.3	34	0
1946	CHIC	N	5	82	16.4	39	1
Career			106	1559	14.7	41	13
Playoffs			7	116	16.6		0

Jim Culbreath

Year	Team		No	Yds	Avg	Lg	TD
1977	GB	N	2	6	3.0	5	0
1978			7	78	11.1	19	0
Career			9	84	9.3	19	0

Rodney Culver

Year	Team		No	Yds	Avg	Lg	TD
1992	IND	N	26	210	8.1	27	2
1993			11	112	10.2	26	1
1995	SD	N	5	21	4.2	12	0
Career			42	343	8.2	27	3
Playoffs			2	23	11.5		0

Frank Cumiskey

Year	Team		No	Yds	Avg	Lg	TD
1937	BKN	N	5	50	10.0		0

Bennie Cunningham

Year	Team		No	Yds	Avg	Lg	TD
1976	PIT	N	5	49	9.8	20	1
1977			20	347	17.4	43t	2
1978			16	321	20.1	48	2
1979			36	512	14.2	28t	4
1980			18	232	12.9	35	2
1981			41	574	14.0	30	3
1982			21	277	13.2	31	2
1983			35	442	12.6	29	3
1984			4	64	16.0	29	1
1985			6	61	10.2	17	0
Career			202	2879	14.3	48	20
Playoffs			19	219	11.5		2

Cookie Cunningham

Year	Team		No	Yds	Avg	Lg	TD
1926	CLE	A					2

Doug Cunningham

Year	Team		No	Yds	Avg	Lg	TD
1967	SF	N	13	121	9.3	29	0
1968			2	25	12.5	16	0
1969			51	484	9.5	58	0
1970			35	209	6.0	29	0
1971			19	188	9.9	28	0
1973			15	118	7.9	23	0

Doug Cunningham continued

Year	Team		No	Yds	Avg	Lg	TD
1974	WAS	N	2	26	13.0	18	0
Career			137	1171	8.5	58	0
Playoffs			5	38	7.6		0

Doug Cunningham

Year	Team		No	Yds	Avg	Lg	TD
1979	MIN	N	5	50	10.0	15	0

Jim Cunningham

Year	Team		No	Yds	Avg	Lg	TD
1961	WAS	N	12	90	7.5	17	1
1962			6	43	7.2	33	1
1963			8	86	10.8	19	0
Career			26	219	8.4	33	2

Randall Cunningham

Year	Team		No	Yds	Avg	Lg	TD
1987	PHI	N	1	-3	-3.0	-3	0

Rick Cunningham

Year	Team		No	Yds	Avg	Lg	TD
1996	OAK	N	1	3	3.0	3t	1

Sam Cunningham

Year	Team		No	Yds	Avg	Lg	TD
1973	NE	N	15	144	9.6	34t	1
1974			22	214	9.7	37	2
1975			32	253	7.9	24	0
1976			27	299	11.1	41	0
1977			42	370	8.8	35	1
1978			31	297	9.6	31	0
1979			29	236	8.1	20	0
1981			12	92	7.7	12	0
Career			210	1905	9.1	41	6
Playoffs			5	42	8.4		0

Pat Curran

Year	Team		No	Yds	Avg	Lg	TD
1970	LA	N	3	25	8.3	14	0
1971			1	2	2.0	2t	1
1973			5	56	11.2	27	1
1975	SD	N	45	619	13.8	39	0
1976			33	349	10.6	29	1
1977			10	123	12.3	20	0
1978			9	92	10.2	20	2
Career			106	1266	11.9	39	5
Playoffs			1	12	12.0		0

Willie Curran

Year	Team		No	Yds	Avg	Lg	TD
1983	ATL	N	1	15	15.0	15	0
1984			1	7	7.0	7	0
Career			2	22	11.0	15	0

Don Currivan

Year	Team		No	Yds	Avg	Lg	TD
1943	CHIB	N	5	79	15.8	34	1
1944	C-P	N	7	163	23.3	72t	2
1945	BOS	N	16	397	24.8	80t	4
1946			11	262	23.8	60t	4
1947			24	782	32.6	78t	9
1948	BOS-LA	N	12	218	18.2	58t	3
1949	LA	N	3	78	26.0	40	1
Career			78	1979	25.4	80t	24

Roy Curry

Year	Team		No	Yds	Avg	Lg	TD
1963	PIT	N	1	31	31.0	31t	1

Isaac Curtis

Year	Team		No	Yds	Avg	Lg	TD
1973	CIN	N	45	843	18.7	77t	9
1974			30	633	21.1	77t	10
1975			44	934	21.2	55	7
1976			41	766	18.7	85t	6
1977			20	338	16.9	54	2
1978			47	737	15.7	57	3
1979			32	605	18.9	67t	8
1980			43	610	14.2	67t	3
1981			37	609	16.5	68	2
1982			23	320	13.9	45	1
1983			42	571	13.6	80t	2
1984			12	135	11.3	22	0
Career			416	7101	17.1	85t	53
Playoffs			13	184	14.2		2

Mike Curtis

Year	Team		No	Yds	Avg	Lg	TD
1965	BAL	N	1	5	5.0	5	0

Harry Curzon

Year	Team		No	Yds	Avg	Lg	TD
1925	BUF	N					1

Year	Team		No	Yds	Avg	Lg	TD

Randy Cuthbert

Year	Team		No	Yds	Avg	Lg	TD
1993	PIT	N	1	3	3.0	3	0

Jerry Daanen

Year	Team		No	Yds	Avg	Lg	TD
1968	STL	N	4	35	8.8	15	0
1969			2	12	6.0	7	0
1970			2	31	15.5	22	0
Career			8	78	9.8	22	0

Bill Daddio

Year	Team		No	Yds	Avg	Lg	TD
1941	CHIC	N	5	39	7.8	14	0
1942			11	108	9.8	23	1
Career			16	147	9.2	23	1

Dave D'Addio

Year	Team		No	Yds	Avg	Lg	TD
1984	DET	N	1	12	12.0	12	0

Dave Dalby

Year	Team		No	Yds	Avg	Lg	TD
1979	OAK	N	1	1	1.0	1	0

Carroll Dale

Year	Team		No	Yds	Avg	Lg	TD
1960	LA	N	19	336	17.7	63	3
1961			35	561	16.0	68t	2
1962			29	584	20.1	80t	3
1963			34	638	18.8	66t	7
1964			32	544	17.0	44	2
1965	GB	N	20	382	19.1	77t	2
1966			37	876	23.7	83t	7
1967			35	738	21.1	86t	5
1968			42	818	19.5	63t	8
1969			45	879	19.5	48	6
1970			49	814	16.6	89t	2
1971			31	598	19.3	77t	4
1972			16	317	19.8	48	1
1973	MIN	N	14	192	13.7	40	0
Career			438	8277	18.9	89t	52
Playoffs			31	565	18.2		3

Bill Daley

Year	Team		No	Yds	Avg	Lg	TD
1946	BKN	AA	2	-5	-2.5		0
1947	CHI	AA	12	116	9.7	52	0
1948	NY	AA	4	31	7.8		0
Career			18	142	7.9	52	0

Chris Dalman

Year	Team		No	Yds	Avg	Lg	TD
1995	SF	N	1	-1	-1.0	-1	0

Pete D'Alonzo

Year	Team		No	Yds	Avg	Lg	TD
1952	DET	N	2	4	2.0	10	0

Dick Danehe

Year	Team		No	Yds	Avg	Lg	TD
1947	LA	AA	0	8		8L	0

Joe Danelo

Year	Team		No	Yds	Avg	Lg	TD
1979	NYG	N	1	1	1.0	1	0

Clem Daniels

Year	Team		No	Yds	Avg	Lg	TD
1961	OAK	A	13	150	11.5	30	0
1962			24	318	13.3	74	1
1963			30	685	**22.8**	73	5
1964			42	696	16.6	60	6
1965			36	568	15.8	69	7
1966			40	652	16.3	68	3
1967			16	222	13.9	40t	2
1968	SF	N	2	23	11.5	16	0
Career			203	3314	16.3	74	24

David Daniels

Year	Team		No	Yds	Avg	Lg	TD
1991	SEA	N	4	38	9.5	19	0
1992			5	99	19.8	57	0
Career			9	137	15.2	57	0

Gary Danielson

Year	Team		No	Yds	Avg	Lg	TD
1984	DET	N	1	22	22.0	22t	1

Ed Danowski

Year	Team		No	Yds	Avg	Lg	TD
1941	NYG	N	1	12	12.0	12	0

Byron Darby

Year	Team		No	Yds	Avg	Lg	TD
1986	PHI	N	2	16	8.0	13	0

Paul Darby

Year	Team		No	Yds	Avg	Lg	TD
1980	NYJ	N	3	48	16.0	20	1

Bill Darnall

Year	Team		No	Yds	Avg	Lg	TD
1968	MIA	A	2	25	12.5	13	0
1969			1	13	13.0	13	0
Career			3	38	12.7	13	0

Chris Darrington

Year	Team		No	Yds	Avg	Lg	TD
1987	HOU	N	1	38	38.0	38	0

Ron Daugherty

Year	Team		No	Yds	Avg	Lg	TD
1987	MIN	N	2	21	10.5	13	0

Nick Daukas

Year	Team		No	Yds	Avg	Lg	TD
1946	BKN	AA	2	19	9.5		0

Red Daum

Year	Team		No	Yds	Avg	Lg	TD
1922	AKR	N					1
1925							1
Career							2

Charles Davenport

Year	Team		No	Yds	Avg	Lg	TD
1992	PIT	N	9	136	15.1	31	0
1993			4	51	12.8	19	0
Career			13	187	14.4	31	0
Playoffs			3	54	18.0		0

Ron Davenport

Year	Team		No	Yds	Avg	Lg	TD
1985	MIA	N	13	74	5.7	17t	2
1986			20	177	8.8	27	1
1987			27	249	9.2	29	1
1988			30	282	9.4	27	0
1989			3	19	6.3	9	0
Career			93	801	8.6	29	4
Playoffs			3	23	7.7		0

Bill Davidson

Year	Team		No	Yds	Avg	Lg	TD
1937	PIT	N	4	169	42.3		2
1938			12	229	19.1		0
1939			6	27	4.5		0
Career			22	425	19.3		2

Cotton Davidson

Year	Team		No	Yds	Avg	Lg	TD
1960	DAL	A	1	-1	-1.0	-1	0

Al Davis

Year	Team		No	Yds	Avg	Lg	TD
1971	PHI	N	11	46	4.2	12	0

Anthony Davis

Year	Team		No	Yds	Avg	Lg	TD
1977	TB	N	8	91	11.4	30	0

Art Davis

Year	Team		No	Yds	Avg	Lg	TD
1956	PIT	N	1	9	9.0	9	0

Bob Davis

Year	Team		No	Yds	Avg	Lg	TD
1938	CLE	N	3	31	10.3		0
1942	PHI	N	6	93	15.5	48	1
1944	BOS	N	19	97	5.1	23	0
1945			9	56	6.2	29	0
1946			10	150	15.0	37	1
Career			47	427	9.1	48	2

Bob Davis

Year	Team		No	Yds	Avg	Lg	TD
1946	PIT	N	1	13	13.0	13	0
1947			5	145	29.0	44	0
1948			2	14	7.0	11	0
Career			8	172	21.5	44	0

Bruce Davis

Year	Team		No	Yds	Avg	Lg	TD
1984	CLE	N	7	119	17.0	43t	2

Charlie Davis

Year	Team		No	Yds	Avg	Lg	TD
1974	CIN	N	19	171	9.0	32	0
1976	TB	N	3	32	10.7	23	0
Career			22	203	9.2	32	0

Clarence Davis

Year	Team		No	Yds	Avg	Lg	TD
1971	OAK	N	15	97	6.5	18	0
1972			8	82	10.3	26	0
1973			7	76	10.9	19	0
1974			11	145	13.2	45t	1
1975			11	126	11.5	31t	1
1976			27	191	7.1	17	0
1977			16	124	7.8	38	0

Clarence Davis continued

Year	Team		No	Yds	Avg	Lg	TD
1978			4	24	6.0	13	0
Career			99	865	8.7	45t	2
Playoffs			13	96	7.4		1

Corby Davis

Year	Team		No	Yds	Avg	Lg	TD
1938	CLE	N	1	2	2.0	2	0
1939			3	49	16.3		0
1941			13	64	4.9	12	0
1942			2	18	9.0	14	0
Career			19	133	7.0	14	0

Dave Davis

Year	Team		No	Yds	Avg	Lg	TD
1971	GB	N	6	59	9.8	20	0
1972			4	119	29.8	68t	1
1973	PIT	N	1	14	14.0	14	0
Career			11	192	17.5	68t	1

Dick Davis

Year	Team		No	Yds	Avg	Lg	TD
1970	NO	N	4	29	7.3	13	0

Donnie Davis

Year	Team		No	Yds	Avg	Lg	TD
1962	DAL	N	2	31	15.5	24	0

Gary Davis

Year	Team		No	Yds	Avg	Lg	TD
1976	MIA	N	2	8	4.0	6	0
1977			14	151	10.8	32	1
1978			24	218	9.1	34	0
1979			34	215	6.3	18	0
1980	TB	N	9	79	8.8	15	0
Career			83	671	8.1	34	1
Playoffs			2	24	12.0		0

Glenn Davis

Year	Team		No	Yds	Avg	Lg	TD
1950	LA	N	42	592	14.1	50	4
1951			8	90	11.3	21	1
Career			50	682	13.6	50	5
Playoffs			8	104	13.0		1

Glenn Davis

Year	Team		No	Yds	Avg	Lg	TD
1960	DET	N	1	17	17.0	17	0
1961			9	115	12.8	19	0
Career			10	132	13.2	19	0

Harper Davis

Year	Team		No	Yds	Avg	Lg	TD
1949	LA	AA	2	13	6.5		0
1950	CHIB	N	2	15	7.5	8	0
1951	GB	N	1	15	15.0	15	0
Career			5	43	8.6	15	0
Playoffs			1	5	5.0		0

Harrison Davis

Year	Team		No	Yds	Avg	Lg	TD
1974	SD	N	18	432	24.0	70t	2

Jerry Davis

Year	Team		No	Yds	Avg	Lg	TD
1951	CHIC	N	4	24	6.0	15	0

Joe Davis

Year	Team		No	Yds	Avg	Lg	TD
1946	BKN	AA	22	337	15.3	61	1

Johnny Davis

Year	Team		No	Yds	Avg	Lg	TD
1978	TB	N	5	13	2.6	7	0
1979			5	57	11.4	24	0
1980			4	17	4.3	9	0
1981	SF	N	3	-1	-0.3	3	0
1983	CLE	N	5	20	4.0	10	0
Career			22	106	4.8	24	0

Kenneth Davis

Year	Team		No	Yds	Avg	Lg	TD
1986	GB	N	21	142	6.8	18	1
1987			14	110	7.9	35	0
1988			11	81	7.4	11	0
1989	BUF	N	6	92	15.3	29	2
1990			9	78	8.7	16	1
1991			20	118	5.9	14t	1
1992			15	80	5.3	22	0
1993			21	95	4.5	28	0
1994			18	82	4.6	12	0
Career			135	878	6.5	35	5
Playoffs			22	181	8.2		0

Lamar Davis

Year	Team		No	Yds	Avg	Lg	TD
1946	MIA	AA	22	275	12.5		2

Year	Team		No	Yds	Avg	Lg	TD

Lamar Davis *continued*

Year	Team		No	Yds	Avg	Lg	TD
1947	BAL	AA	46	515	11.2	54	2
1948			41	765	18.7	80t	7
1949			38	548	14.4		1
Career			147	2103	14.3	80t	12
Playoffs			5	73	14.6		0

Ray Davis

Year	Team		No	Yds	Avg	Lg	TD
1936	CHIC	N	1	36	36.0	36	0

Russell Davis

Year	Team		No	Yds	Avg	Lg	TD
1981	PIT	N	4	34	8.5	19	0
1982			1	11	11.0	11	0
Career			5	45	9.0	19	0

Stan Davis

Year	Team		No	Yds	Avg	Lg	TD
1973	PHI	N	1	6	6.0	6	0

Steve Davis

Year	Team		No	Yds	Avg	Lg	TD
1972	PIT	N	1	5	5.0	5	0
1973			7	31	4.4	9	1
1974			11	152	13.8	61t	1
1975	NYJ	N	6	56	9.3	21	0
1976			8	57	7.1	21	0
Career			33	301	9.1	61t	2

Terrell Davis

Year	Team		No	Yds	Avg	Lg	TD
1995	DEN	N	49	367	7.5	31	1
1996			36	310	8.6	23	2
Career			85	677	8.0	31	3
Playoffs			7	24	3.4		0

Tony Davis

Year	Team		No	Yds	Avg	Lg	TD
1976	CIN	N	4	29	7.3	11	0
1977			9	83	9.2	28	0
1978			2	23	11.5	14	0
1980	TB	N	12	115	9.6	18	1
Career			27	250	9.3	28	1

Tyrone Davis

Year	Team		No	Yds	Avg	Lg	TD
1995	NYJ	N	1	9	9.0	9	0
1996			1	6	6.0	6	0
Career			2	15	7.5	9	0

Van Davis

Year	Team		No	Yds	Avg	Lg	TD
1947	NY	AA	8	179	22.4	55	0
1948			4	49	12.3		0
1949	B-NY	AA	2	26	13.0		0
Career			14	254	18.1	55	1
Playoffs			1	18	18.0		0

Wendell Davis

Year	Team		No	Yds	Avg	Lg	TD
1988	CHI	N	15	220	14.7	36	0
1989			26	397	15.3	52t	3
1990			39	572	14.7	51	3
1991			61	945	15.5	75t	6
1992			54	734	13.6	40	2
1993			12	132	11.0	17	0
Career			207	3000	14.5	75t	14
Playoffs			12	179	14.9		0

Willie Davis

Year	Team		No	Yds	Avg	Lg	TD
1992	KC	N	36	756	21.0	74t	3
1993			52	909	17.5	66t	7
1994			51	822	16.1	62t	5
1995			33	527	16.0	60t	5
1996	HOU	N	39	464	11.9	49	6
Career			211	3478	16.5	74t	26
Playoffs			16	239	14.9		1

Jerone Davison

Year	Team		No	Yds	Avg	Lg	TD
1996	OAK	N	4	21	5.3	8	0

Dale Dawkins

Year	Team		No	Yds	Avg	Lg	TD
1990	NYJ	N	5	68	13.6	31	0
1991			3	38	12.7	24	0
Career			8	106	13.3	31	0

Joe Dawkins

Year	Team		No	Yds	Avg	Lg	TD
1970	HOU	N	15	94	6.3	17	0
1971			9	53	5.9	13	0
1972	DEN	N	18	242	13.4	60	0
1973			30	329	11.0	42	0

Joe Dawkins *continued*

Year	Team		No	Yds	Avg	Lg	TD
1974	NYG	N	46	332	7.2	51t	3
1975			24	245	10.2	39	0
1976	HOU	N	3	21	7.0	14	0
Career			145	1316	9.1	60	3

Julius Dawkins

Year	Team		No	Yds	Avg	Lg	TD
1983	BUF	N	11	123	11.2	28t	1
1984			21	295	14.0	37t	2
Career			32	418	13.1	37t	3

Sean Dawkins

Year	Team		No	Yds	Avg	Lg	TD
1993	IND	N	26	430	16.5	68	1
1994			51	742	14.5	49	5
1995			52	784	15.1	52	3
1996			54	751	13.9	42	1
Career			183	2707	14.8	68	10
Playoffs			15	200	13.3		1

Lawrence Dawsey

Year	Team		No	Yds	Avg	Lg	TD
1991	TB	N	55	818	14.9	65t	3
1992			60	776	12.9	41	1
1993			15	203	13.5	24	0
1994			46	673	14.6	46	1
1995			30	372	12.4	26	0
1996	NYG	N	18	233	12.9	28	0
Career			224	3075	13.7	65t	5

Stacey Dawsey

Year	Team		No	Yds	Avg	Lg	TD
1987	NO	N	13	142	10.9	29	0

Lake Dawson

Year	Team		No	Yds	Avg	Lg	TD
1994	KC	N	37	537	14.5	50	2
1995			40	513	12.8	45t	5
1996			5	83	16.6	25	1
Career			82	1133	13.8	50	8
Playoffs			7	91	13.0		1

Lin Dawson

Year	Team		No	Yds	Avg	Lg	TD
1981	NE	N	7	126	18.0	42	0
1982			13	160	12.3	26	1
1983			9	84	9.3	14	1
1984			39	427	10.9	27	4
1985			17	148	8.7	26	0
1987			12	81	6.8	14	0
1988			8	106	13.3	38	2
1989			12	101	8.4	17	0
Career			117	1233	10.5	42	8
Playoffs			7	82	11.7		1

Rhett Dawson

Year	Team		No	Yds	Avg	Lg	TD
1972	HOU	N	6	78	13.0	20	1
1973	MIN	N	2	24	12.0	19	0
Career			8	102	12.8	20	1

Ted Dean

Year	Team		No	Yds	Avg	Lg	TD
1960	PHI	N	15	218	14.5	49t	3
1961			21	335	16.0	60t	1
1963			14	108	7.7	20	0
1964	MIN	N	1	23	23.0	23	0
Career			51	684	13.4	60t	4
Playoffs			1	22	22.0		0

Art DeCarlo

Year	Team		No	Yds	Avg	Lg	TD
1958	BAL	N	1	10	10.0	10	0
1960			8	116	14.5	22	0
Career			9	126	14.0	22	0

Bill deCorrevont

Year	Team		No	Yds	Avg	Lg	TD
1945	WAS	N	4	36	9.0	27	0
1946	DET	N	10	278	27.8	72t	2
1947	CHIC	N	4	52	13.0	19	0
1948	CHIB	N	2	7	3.5	6	0
1949			1	44	44.0	44	0
Career			21	417	19.9	72t	2

Bob DeFruiter

Year	Team		No	Yds	Avg	Lg	TD
1945	WAS	N	1	19	19.0	19	0
1946			1	9	9.0	9	0
Career			2	28	14.0	19	0

Jack DeGrenier

Year	Team		No	Yds	Avg	Lg	TD
1974	NO	N	4	13	3.3	8	0

Paul Dekker

Year	Team		No	Yds	Avg	Lg	TD
1953	WAS	N	14	182	13.0	34t	1

Joe Delaney

Year	Team		No	Yds	Avg	Lg	TD
1981	KC	N	22	246	11.2	61	0
1982			11	53	4.8	13	0
Career			33	299	9.1	61	0

Spiro Dellerba

Year	Team		No	Yds	Avg	Lg	TD
1947	CLE	AA	1	14	14.0	14	0

Greg DeLong

Year	Team		No	Yds	Avg	Lg	TD
1995	MIN	N	6	38	6.3	9	0
1996			8	34	4.3	9	0
Career			14	72	5.1	9	0

Jack Deloplaine

Year	Team		No	Yds	Avg	Lg	TD
1976	PIT	N	1	3	3.0	3	0
1979	CHI	N	2	13	6.5	15	0
Career			3	16	5.3	15	0

Robert Delpino

Year	Team		No	Yds	Avg	Lg	TD
1988	LARM	N	30	312	10.4	38	2
1989			34	334	9.8	25	1
1990			15	172	11.5	42t	4
1991			55	617	11.2	78	1
1992			18	139	7.7	12t	1
1993	DEN	N	26	195	7.5	25	0
Career			178	1769	9.9	78	9
Playoffs			5	64	12.8		0

Al DeMao

Year	Team		No	Yds	Avg	Lg	TD
1950	WAS	N	1	4	4.0	4	0

Vern Den Herder

Year	Team		No	Yds	Avg	Lg	TD
1978	MIA	N	1	7	7.0	7t	1

Preston Dennard

Year	Team		No	Yds	Avg	Lg	TD
1978	LA	N	3	35	11.7	15	0
1979			43	766	17.8	50	4
1980			36	596	16.6	44	6
1981			49	821	16.8	64	4
1982	LARM	N	25	383	15.3	39	2
1983			33	465	14.1	61t	5
1984	BUF	N	30	417	13.9	68t	7
1985	GB	N	13	182	14.0	34	2
Career			232	3665	15.8	68t	30
Playoffs			18	314	17.4		3

Vince Dennery

Year	Team		No	Yds	Avg	Lg	TD
1941	NYG	N	1	65	65.0	65	1

Austin Denney

Year	Team		No	Yds	Avg	Lg	TD
1967	CHI	N	12	113	9.4	19	0
1968			23	247	10.7	46t	2
1969			22	203	9.2	29	1
1970	BUF	N	14	201	14.4	31	0
Career			71	764	10.8	46t	3

Mark Dennis

Year	Team		No	Yds	Avg	Lg	TD
1995	CAR	N	1	3	3.0	3	0

Mike Dennis

Year	Team		No	Yds	Avg	Lg	TD
1968	LA	N	8	53	6.6	17	0

Doug Dennison

Year	Team		No	Yds	Avg	Lg	TD
1974	DAL	N	2	23	11.5	13	0
1975			2	5	2.5	4	0
1976			8	67	8.4	33	0
1977			1	9	9.0	9	0
1978			1	6	6.0	6	0
Career			14	110	7.9	33	0
Playoffs			3	20	6.7		0

Glenn Dennison

Year	Team		No	Yds	Avg	Lg	TD
1984	NYJ	N	16	141	8.8	20	1
1987	WAS	N	2	8	4.0	5	0
Career			18	149	8.3	20	1

Al Denson

Year	Team		No	Yds	Avg	Lg	TD
1964	DEN	A	25	383	15.3	82	1
1965			9	102	11.3	19	0
1966			36	725	20.1	65	3

Year	Team		No	Yds	Avg	Lg	TD

Al Denson *continued*

Year	Team		No	Yds	Avg	Lg	TD
1967			46	899	19.5	68t	**11**
1968			34	586	17.2	44t	5
1969			53	809	15.3	62t	10
1970	DEN	N	47	646	13.7	42	2
1971	MIN	N	10	125	12.5	17	0
Career			260	4275	16.4	82	32

Moses Denson

Year	Team		No	Yds	Avg	Lg	TD
1974	WAS	N	26	174	6.7	27	2
1975			13	81	6.2	14	0
Career			39	255	6.5	27	2
Playoffs			2	17	8.5		0

Lee DeRamus

Year	Team		No	Yds	Avg	Lg	TD
1995	NO	N	6	76	12.7	27	0
1996			15	182	12.1	28t	1
Career			21	258	12.3	28r	1

Dean Derby

Year	Team		No	Yds	Avg	Lg	TD
1957	PIT	N	4	79	19.8	36	0

Brian DeRoo

Year	Team		No	Yds	Avg	Lg	TD
1979	BAL	N	4	82	20.5	67t	1
1980			2	34	17.0	18	0
1981			1	38	38.0	38	0
Career			7	154	22.0	67t	1

Dan DeSantis

Year	Team		No	Yds	Avg	Lg	TD
1941	PHI	N	4	53	13.3	19	0

Chuck DeShane

Year	Team		No	Yds	Avg	Lg	TD
1945	DET	N	2	29	14.5	17	0
1946			2	13	6.5	13	0
Career			4	42	10.5	17	0

Versil Deskin

Year	Team		No	Yds	Avg	Lg	TD
1936	CHIC	N	3	60	20.0		1
1937			3	48	16.0		1
1938			6	57	9.5		0
1939			4	84	21.0		0
Career			16	249	15.6		2

Darrell Dess

Year	Team		No	Yds	Avg	Lg	TD
1960	NYG	N	1	3	3.0	3	0

Billy Dewell

Year	Team		No	Yds	Avg	Lg	TD
1940	CHIC	N	2	29	14.5		0
1941			28	262	9.4	30	1
1945			26	370	14.2	70	1
1946			27	643	**23.8**	82t	**7**
1947			42	576	13.7	46t	4
1948			33	442	13.4	48	2
1949			20	235	11.8	25	2
Career			178	2557	14.4	82t	17
Playoffs			2	54	27.0		0

Herb DeWitz

Year	Team		No	Yds	Avg	Lg	TD
1927	CLE	N					1

Willard Dewveall

Year	Team		No	Yds	Avg	Lg	TD
1959	CHIB	N	20	420	21.0	76t	3
1960	CHI	N	43	804	18.7	91t	5
1961	HOU	A	12	200	16.7	66	3
1962			33	576	17.5	98	5
1963			58	752	13.0	35	7
1964			38	552	14.5	60	4
Career			204	3304	16.2	91t	27
Playoffs			8	105	13.1		1

Buddy Dial

Year	Team		No	Yds	Avg	Lg	TD
1959	PIT	N	16	428	26.8	68	6
1960			40	972	24.3	70t	9
1961			53	1047	**19.8**	88t	12
1962			50	981	19.6	62	6
1963			60	1295	**21.6**	83t	9
1964	DAL	N	11	178	16.2	41	0
1965			17	283	16.6	46	1
1966			14	252	18.0	39	1
Career			261	5436	20.8	88t	44

Rich Diana

Year	Team		No	Yds	Avg	Lg	TD
1982	MIA	N	2	21	10.5	13	0
Playoffs			1	5	5.0		0

Dorne Dibble

Year	Team		No	Yds	Avg	Lg	TD
1951	DET	N	30	613	20.4	47	6
1953			16	274	17.1	47t	3
1954			46	768	16.7	45t	6
1955			14	179	12.8	44t	2
1956			32	597	18.7	56t	2
1957			8	121	15.1	23	0
Career			146	2552	17.5	56t	19
Playoffs			5	85	17.0		0

Eric Dickerson

Year	Team		No	Yds	Avg	Lg	TD
1983	LARM	N	51	404	7.9	37t	2
1984			21	139	6.6	19	0
1985			20	126	6.3	33	0
1986			26	205	7.9	28	0
1987	LARM-IND		18	171	9.5	28	0
1988	IND	N	36	377	10.5	50t	1
1989			30	211	7.0	22	1
1990			18	92	5.1	17	0
1991			41	269	6.6	26	1
1992	LARI	N	14	85	6.1	15	1
1993	ATL	N	6	58	9.7	30	0
Career			281	2137	7.6	50t	6
Playoffs			19	91	4.8		1

Ron Dickerson

Year	Team		No	Yds	Avg	Lg	TD
1994	KC	N	2	11	5.5	6	0

Charlie Dickey

Year	Team		No	Yds	Avg	Lg	TD
Playoffs			1	2	2.0		0

Curtis Dickey

Year	Team		No	Yds	Avg	Lg	TD
1980	BAL	N	25	204	8.2	32	2
1981			37	419	11.3	50	3
1982			21	228	10.9	34	0
1983			24	483	20.1	72t	3
1984	IND	N	14	135	9.6	33	0
1985			3	30	10.0	11	0
1986	CLE	N	10	78	7.8	12	0
Career			134	1577	11.8	72t	8

Eldridge Dickey

Year	Team		No	Yds	Avg	Lg	TD
1968	OAK	A	1	34	34.0	34	0
1971	OAK	N	4	78	19.5	31	1
Career			5	112	22.4	34	1

Bo Dickinson

Year	Team		No	Yds	Avg	Lg	TD
1960	DAL	A	3	38	12.7	21	0
1961			14	209	14.9	48	2
1962	DEN	N	60	554	9.2	33	4
1963	DEN-HOU	A	6	57	9.5	18	0
1964	OAK	A	3	28	9.3	18	0
Career			86	886	10.3	48	6

Chuck Dicus

Year	Team		No	Yds	Avg	Lg	TD
1971	SD	N	6	89	14.8	29	1
1972			18	227	12.6	46t	2
Career			24	316	13.2	46t	3

Clint Didier

Year	Team		No	Yds	Avg	Lg	TD
1982	WAS	N	2	10	5.0	8	1
1983			9	153	17.0	40t	4
1984			30	350	11.7	44	5
1985			41	433	10.6	29	4
1986			34	691	20.3	71t	4
1987			13	178	13.7	25	1
1988	GB	N	5	37	7.4	15	1
1989			7	71	10.1	24t	1
Career			141	1923	13.6	71t	21
Playoffs			18	269	14.9		2

Mark Didio

Year	Team		No	Yds	Avg	Lg	TD
1992	PIT	N	3	39	13.0	18	0

Dave Diehl

Year	Team		No	Yds	Avg	Lg	TD
1939	DET	N	1	12	12.0	12	0
1940			12	131	10.9		0
1944			18	426	23.7	57t	4
1945			1	9	9.0	9	0
Career			32	578	18.1	57t	4

Wally Diehl

Year	Team		No	Yds	Avg	Lg	TD
1928	FRA	N					1

Doug Dieken

Year	Team		No	Yds	Avg	Lg	TD
1983	CLE	N	1	14	14.0	14t	1

Scott Dierking

Year	Team		No	Yds	Avg	Lg	TD
1977	NYJ	N	4	29	7.3	15	1
1978			19	152	8.0	17	0
1979			10	121	12.1	27	0
1980			19	138	7.3	22	1
1981			26	228	8.8	23	1
1982			12	80	6.7	13t	1
1983			33	275	8.3	19	0
1984	TB	N	1	5	5.0	5t	1
Career			124	1028	8.3	27	5
Playoffs			11	74	6.7		0

Ken Dilger

Year	Team		No	Yds	Avg	Lg	TD
1995	IND	N	42	635	15.1	42	4
1996			42	503	12.0	51	4
Career			84	1138	13.5	51	8
Playoffs			4	43	10.8		1

Lavern Dilweg

Year	Team		No	Yds	Avg	Lg	TD
1927	GB	N					1
1929							3
1930							2
1931							4
1933			14	225	16.1		0
1934							2
Career			14	225	16.1		12

Babe Dimancheff

Year	Team		No	Yds	Avg	Lg	TD
1945	BOS	N	1	15	15.0	15	0
1946			5	121	24.2	45	1
1947	CHIC	N	22	438	19.9	80t	4
1948			13	260	20.0	52t	3
1949			10	130	13.0	50	1
1950			5	53	10.6	17	0
1952	CHIB	N	5	69	13.8	41t	1
Career			61	1086	17.8	80t	10

Mike Dingle

Year	Team		No	Yds	Avg	Lg	TD
1991	CIN	N	5	23	4.6	12	1

Bob DiRico

Year	Team		No	Yds	Avg	Lg	TD
1987	NYG	N	2	22	11.0	15	0

Mike Ditka

Year	Team		No	Yds	Avg	Lg	TD
1961	CHI	N	56	1076	19.2	76t	12
1962			58	904	15.6	69t	5
1963			59	794	13.5	63	8
1964			75	897	12.0	34	5
1965			36	454	12.6	44	2
1966			32	378	11.8	30	2
1967	PHI	N	26	274	10.5	25	2
1968			13	111	8.5	18	2
1969	DAL	N	17	268	15.8	51	3
1970			8	98	12.3	26	0
1971			30	360	12.0	29	1
1972			17	198	11.6	26	1
Career			427	5812	13.6	76t	43
Playoffs			11	107	9.7		1

Al Dixon

Year	Team		No	Yds	Avg	Lg	TD
1977	NYG	N	6	78	13.0	21	0
1978			18	376	20.9	47	3
1979			2	18	9.0	11	0
1980	KC	N	7	115	16.4	32	1
1981			29	356	12.3	48	2
1982			18	251	13.9	37	2
1983	PHI	N	4	54	13.5	22	0
Career			84	1248	14.9	48	8

Dwayne Dixon

Year	Team		No	Yds	Avg	Lg	TD
1984	TB	N	5	69	13.8	21	0
1987			1	18	18.0	18	0
Career			6	87	14.5	21	0

Floyd Dixon

Year	Team		No	Yds	Avg	Lg	TD
1986	ATL	N	42	617	14.7	65	2
1987			36	600	16.7	51t	5
1988			28	368	13.1	36	2
1989			25	357	14.3	53	2
1990			38	399	10.5	34	4
1991			12	146	12.2	23	1

Floyd Dixon *continued*

Year	Team		No	Yds	Avg	Lg	TD
1992	PHI	N	3	36	12.0	19	0
Career			184	2523	13.7	65	16
Playoffs			3	23	7.7		0

Hewritt Dixon

Year	Team		No	Yds	Avg	Lg	TD
1963	DEN	A	10	132	13.2	30	0
1964			38	585	15.4	62	1
1965			25	354	14.2	59	2
1966	OAK	A	29	345	11.9	76	4
1967			59	563	9.5	48	2
1968			38	360	9.5	41	2
1969			33	275	8.3	37t	1
1970	OAK	N	31	207	6.7	46t	1
Career			263	2821	10.7	76	13
Playoffs			13	85	6.5		0

James Dixon

Year	Team		No	Yds	Avg	Lg	TD
1989	DAL	N	24	477	19.9	75t	2
1990			2	26	13.0	21	0
Career			26	503	19.3	75t	2

Zack Dixon

Year	Team		No	Yds	Avg	Lg	TD
1980	PHI	N	1	5	5.0	5	0
1981	BAL	N	17	169	9.9	41	1
1982			20	185	9.3	24	0
1983			1	2	2.0	2	0
1984	SEA	N	2	6	3.0	6	0
Career			41	367	9.0	41	1

Glenn Dobbs

Year	Team		No	Yds	Avg	Lg	TD
1946	BKN	AA	1	-5	-5.0	-5	0
1947	LA	AA	2	21	10.5		0
1948			2	11	5.5		0
Career			5	27	5.4	-5	0

John Dockery

Year	Team		No	Yds	Avg	Lg	TD
1969	NY	A	1	6	6.0	6	0

Al Dodd

Year	Team		No	Yds	Avg	Lg	TD
1969	NO	N	37	600	16.2	52	1
1970			28	484	17.3	45t	1
1971			15	298	19.9	49	0
1973	ATL	N	19	291	15.3	25	0
1974			12	130	10.8	17	1
Career			111	1803	16.2	52	3

John Doehring

Year	Team		No	Yds	Avg	Lg	TD
1934	CHIB	N	1	14	14.0	14	0
1936			1	19	19.0	19	0
Career			2	33	16.5	19	0

Chris Doering

Year	Team		No	Yds	Avg	Lg	TD
1996	IND	N	1	10	10.0	10	0

Jack Dolbin

Year	Team		No	Yds	Avg	Lg	TD
1975	DEN	N	22	421	19.1	41	3
1976			19	354	18.6	40	1
1977			26	443	17.0	81t	3
1978			24	284	11.8	21	0
1979			3	74	24.7	45	0
Career			94	1576	16.8	81t	7
Playoffs			7	135	19.3		

Don Doll

Year	Team		No	Yds	Avg	Lg	TD
1949	DET	N	1	-5	-5.0	-5	0

Tony Dollinger

Year	Team		No	Yds	Avg	Lg	TD
1987	DET	N	3	25	8.3	15	0

Dick Dolly

Year	Team		No	Yds	Avg	Lg	TD
1945	PIT	N	8	122	15.3	47	0

Oscar Donahue

Year	Team		No	Yds	Avg	Lg	TD
1962	MIN	N	16	285	17.8	53	1

Gene Donaldson

Year	Team		No	Yds	Avg	Lg	TD
1967	BUF	A	1	20	20.0	20	0

Ray Donaldson

Year	Team		No	Yds	Avg	Lg	TD
1988	IND	N	1	-3	-3.0	-3	0

Al Donelli

Year	Team		No	Yds	Avg	Lg	TD
1941	PIT	N	2	25	12.5	14	0

Doug Donley

Year	Team		No	Yds	Avg	Lg	TD
1981	DAL	N	3	32	10.7	17	0
1982			2	23	11.5	12	0
1983			18	370	20.6	47	2
1984			32	473	14.8	49t	2
Career			55	898	16.3	49t	4
Playoffs			2	18	9.0		0

Mike Donohoe

Year	Team		No	Yds	Avg	Lg	TD
1968	ATL	N	6	52	8.7	14	1
1970			2	36	18.0	22	1
1973	GB	N	1	10	10.0	10	0
1974			1	8	8.0	8	0
Career			10	106	10.6	22	2

Bill Donohue

Year	Team		No	Yds	Avg	Lg	TD
1927	FRA	N					1

Jack Doolan

Year	Team		No	Yds	Avg	Lg	TD
1945	NYG	N	6	50	8.3	23	0
1946			3	28	9.3	13	0
1947	CHIC	N	1	17	17.0	17	0
Career			10	95	9.5	23	0
Playoffs			1	11	11.0		

Jim Dooley

Year	Team		No	Yds	Avg	Lg	TD
1953	CHIB	N	53	841	15.9	72	4
1954			34	658	19.4	69t	7
1956			4	47	11.8	15	0
1957			37	530	14.3	32	1
1959			41	580	14.1	41	3
1960	CHI	N	36	426	11.8	28	1
1961			6	90	15.0	25	0
Career			211	3172	15.0	72	16
Playoffs			6	66	11.0		

Dan Doornink

Year	Team		No	Yds	Avg	Lg	TD
1978	NYG	N	12	66	5.5	24	0
1979	SEA	N	54	432	8.0	41	1
1980			31	237	7.6	16	2
1981			27	350	13.0	80t	4
1982			22	176	8.0	44	0
1983			24	328	13.7	47	2
1984			31	365	11.8	32	2
1985			8	52	6.5	19	0
Career			209	2006	9.6	80t	11
Playoffs			15	111	7.4		1

Jim Doran

Year	Team		No	Yds	Avg	Lg	TD
1951	DET	N	10	225	22.5	48	2
1952			10	147	14.7	31	1
1953			6	75	12.5	30	0
1954			10	203	20.3	49	4
1955			38	552	14.5	38t	2
1956			25	448	17.9	31	0
1957			33	624	18.9	65t	5
1958			22	495	22.5	65t	4
1959			14	191	13.6	23	1
1960	DAL	N	31	554	17.9	75t	3
1961			13	153	11.8	29	2
Career			212	3667	17.3	75t	24
Playoffs			9	247	27.4		2

Tony Dorsett

Year	Team		No	Yds	Avg	Lg	TD
1977	DAL	N	29	273	9.4	23	1
1978			37	378	10.2	91t	2
1979			45	375	8.3	32	1
1980			34	263	7.7	27	0
1981			32	325	10.2	73t	2
1982			24	179	7.5	18	0
1983			40	287	7.2	24	1
1984			51	459	9.0	68t	1
1985			46	449	9.8	56t	3
1986			25	267	10.7	36t	1
1987			19	177	9.3	33	1
1988	DEN	N	16	122	7.6	16	0
Career			398	3554	8.9	91t	13
Playoffs			46	403	8.8		1

Dick Dorsey

Year	Team		No	Yds	Avg	Lg	TD
1962	OAK	A	21	344	16.4	90	2

Larry Dorsey

Year	Team		No	Yds	Avg	Lg	TD
1976	SD	N	8	108	13.5	19	0

Larry Dorsey *continued*

Year	Team		No	Yds	Avg	Lg	TD
1977			10	198	19.8	67t	2
1978	KC	N	9	169	18.8	33	2
Career			27	475	17.6	67t	4

Noble Doss

Year	Team		No	Yds	Avg	Lg	TD
1947	PHI	N	2	17	8.5	19	0
1948			8	96	12.0	30	0
Career			10	113	11.3	30	0

Kayo Dottley

Year	Team		No	Yds	Avg	Lg	TD
1951	CHIB	N	14	225	16.1	77t	1
1952			9	113	12.6	25t	1
1953			5	21	4.2	8	0
Career			28	359	12.8	77t	2

Glenn Doughty

Year	Team		No	Yds	Avg	Lg	TD
1972	BAL	N	3	31	10.3	19	0
1973			25	587	23.5	66t	4
1974			24	300	12.5	27	2
1975			39	666	17.1	63	4
1976			40	628	15.7	41	5
1977			28	435	15.5	57	4
1978			25	390	15.6	46	3
1979			35	510	14.6	54	2
Career			219	3547	16.2	66t	24
Playoffs			4	108	27.0		1

Ben Douglas

Year	Team		No	Yds	Avg	Lg	TD
1933	BKN	N					1

Leland Douglas

Year	Team		No	Yds	Avg	Lg	TD
1987	MIA	N	9	92	10.2	17	1

Merrill Douglas

Year	Team		No	Yds	Avg	Lg	TD
1959	CHIB	N	1	17	17.0	17	0
1960	CHI	N	2	11	5.5	9	0
1961	DAL	N	1	-2	-2.0	-2	0
Career			4	26	6.5	17	0

Omar Douglas

Year	Team		No	Yds	Avg	Lg	TD
1995	NYG	N	2	15	7.5	11	0
1996			1	8	8.0	8	0
Career			3	23	7.7	11	0

Bobby Douglass

Year	Team		No	Yds	Avg	Lg	TD
1976	NO	N	1	-2	-2.0	-2	0

Freddie Douglass

Year	Team		No	Yds	Avg	Lg	TD
1976	TB	N	3	58	19.3	35	0

Bob Dove

Year	Team		No	Yds	Avg	Lg	TD
1946	CHI	AA	7	67	9.6		1
1947			6	61	10.2		1
Career			13	128	9.8		2

Woody Dow

Year	Team		No	Yds	Avg	Lg	TD
1938	PHI	N	5	88	17.6		1
1939			5	58	11.6		0
Career			10	146	14.6		1

Harry Dowda

Year	Team		No	Yds	Avg	Lg	TD
1949	WAS	N	11	187	17.0	67	1
1950			2	16	8.0	10	0
1951			2	54	27.0	48	0
1952			3	20	6.7	12	1
Career			18	277	15.4	67	2

Marcus Dowdell

Year	Team		No	Yds	Avg	Lg	TD
1992	NO	N	1	6	6.0	6	0
1993			6	46	7.7	11	1
1995	ARI	N	10	96	9.6	23	0
1996			20	318	15.9	64t	2
Career			37	466	12.6	64t	3

Boyd Dowler

Year	Team		No	Yds	Avg	Lg	TD
1959	GB	N	32	549	17.2	35	4
1960			30	505	16.8	91t	2
1961			36	633	17.6	78t	3
1962			49	724	14.8	41	2
1963			53	901	17.0	53t	6
1964			45	623	13.8	50t	5
1965			44	610	13.9	47t	4
1966			29	392	13.5	40	0

Boyd Dowler *continued*

Year	Team		No	Yds	Avg	Lg	TD
1967			54	836	15.5	57t	4
1968			45	668	14.8	72t	6
1969			31	477	15.4	45	4
1971	WAS	N	26	352	13.5	30	0
Career			474	7270	15.3	91t	40
Playoffs			30	440	14.7		5

Gary Downs

Year	Team		No	Yds	Avg	Lg	TD
1994	NYG	N	2	15	7.5	10	0
1996			3	20	6.7	13	0
Career			5	35	7.0	13	0

Eddie Doyle

Year	Team		No	Yds	Avg	Lg	TD
1924	FRA	N					2
1925	POT	N					1
Career							3

D.J. Dozier

Year	Team		No	Yds	Avg	Lg	TD
1987	MIN	N	12	89	7.4	20t	2
1988			5	49	9.8	20	0
1989			14	148	10.6	30	0
1990			1	12	12.0	12	0
1991	DET	N	1	3	3.0	3	0
Career			33	301	9.1	30	2
Playoffs			3	15	5.0		0

Johnny Drake

Year	Team		No	Yds	Avg	Lg	TD
1937	CLE	N	10	172	17.2		2
1938			2	13	6.5		0
1939			5	53	10.6		0
1940			8	81	10.1		0
1941			16	211	13.2	48	1
Career			41	530	12.9	48	3

Troy Drayton

Year	Team		No	Yds	Avg	Lg	TD
1993	LARM	N	27	319	11.8	27	4
1994			32	276	8.6	22t	6
1995	STL	N	47	458	9.7	31	4
1996	STL-MIA	N	28	331	11.8	51	0
Career			134	1384	10.3	51	14

Chuck Drazenovich

Year	Team		No	Yds	Avg	Lg	TD
1950	WAS	N	3	38	12.7	23	0
1951			1	27	27.0	27	0
1952			4	62	15.5	20	0
1954			1	15	15.0	15	0
1955			1	-3	-3.0	-3	0
Career			10	139	13.9	27	0

Fred Dreher

Year	Team		No	Yds	Avg	Lg	TD
1938	CHIB	N	3	69	23.0		1

Chris Dressel

Year	Team		No	Yds	Avg	Lg	TD
1983	HOU	N	32	316	9.9	35t	4
1984			40	378	9.4	42	2
1985			3	17	5.7	12	1
1987	SF	N	1	8	8.0	8	0
1989	KC-NYJ	N	12	191	15.9	49t	1
1990	NYJ	N	6	66	11.0	21	0
1991			17	122	7.2	22	0
Career			111	1098	9.9	49t	8

Doug Dressler

Year	Team		No	Yds	Avg	Lg	TD
1971	CIN	N	19	145	7.6	26	0
1972			39	348	8.9	33	1
1974			29	196	6.8	23	0
1975	NE-KC	N	3	6	2.0	4	1
Career			90	695	7.7	33	2

Willie Drewrey

Year	Team		No	Yds	Avg	Lg	TD
1985	HOU	N	2	28	14.0	19	0
1986			18	299	16.6	31	0
1987			11	148	13.5	35	0
1988			11	172	15.6	55	1
1989	TB	N	14	157	11.2	18	1
1990			7	182	26.0	89t	1
1991			26	375	14.4	87t	2
1992			16	237	14.8	32	2
1993	HOU	N	1	3	3.0	3	0
Career			106	1601	15.1	89t	7
Playoffs			5	79	15.8		1

Wally Dreyer

Year	Team		No	Yds	Avg	Lg	TD
1949	CHIB	N	7	94	13.4	24	0

Paddy Driscoll

Year	Team		No	Yds	Avg	Lg	TD
1922	CHIC	N					1
1926	CHIB	N					1
Career							2

Al Drulis

Year	Team		No	Yds	Avg	Lg	TD
1945	CHIC	N	6	49	8.2	17	0

Robert Drummond

Year	Team		No	Yds	Avg	Lg	TD
1989	PHI	N	17	180	10.6	21	1
1990			5	39	7.8	29	0
Career			22	219	10.0	29	1

Hoot Drury

Year	Team		No	Yds	Avg	Lg	TD
1931	CHIB	N					1

John Druze

Year	Team		No	Yds	Avg	Lg	TD
1938	BKN	N	4	29	7.3		0

Ron Drzewiecki

Year	Team		No	Yds	Avg	Lg	TD
1955	CHIB	N	1	1	1.0	1	0
1957			1	7	7.0	7	0
Career			2	8	4.0	7	0

Elbert Dubenion

Year	Team		No	Yds	Avg	Lg	TD
1960	BUF	A	42	752	17.9	64	7
1961			31	461	14.9	61	6
1962			33	571	17.3	75	5
1963			55	974	17.7	89	4
1964			42	1139	**27.1**	72	10
1965			18	281	15.6	46	1
1966			50	747	14.9	44	2
1967			25	384	15.4	42	0
Career			296	5309	17.9	89	35
Playoffs			8	230	28.8		2

Phil DuBois

Year	Team		No	Yds	Avg	Lg	TD
1980	WAS	N	1	16	16.0	16	0

Doug DuBose

Year	Team		No	Yds	Avg	Lg	TD
1987	SF	N	4	37	9.3	14	0
1988			6	57	9.5	13	0
Career			10	94	9.4	14	0

Jimmy DuBose

Year	Team		No	Yds	Avg	Lg	TD
1976	TB	N	5	26	5.2	18	0
1977			11	89	8.1	17	0
1978			1	3	3.0	3	0
Career			17	118	6.9	18	0

Kenny Duckett

Year	Team		No	Yds	Avg	Lg	TD
1982	NO	N	12	196	16.3	31	2
1983			19	283	14.9	48	2
1984			3	24	8.0	11	0
Career			34	503	14.8	48	4

Bobby Duckworth

Year	Team		No	Yds	Avg	Lg	TD
1982	SD	N	2	77	38.5	55	0
1983			20	422	21.1	59t	5
1984			25	715	28.6	88t	4
1985	LARM	N	25	422	16.9	42	3
1986	LARM-PHI	N	10	148	14.8	32	1
Career			82	1784	21.8	88t	13
Playoffs			1	8	8.0		0

Joe Duckworth

Year	Team		No	Yds	Avg	Lg	TD
1947	WAS	N	14	250	17.9	55	3

Joe Dudek

Year	Team		No	Yds	Avg	Lg	TD
1987	DEN	N	7	41	5.9	19	0

Dick Duden

Year	Team		No	Yds	Avg	Lg	TD
1949	NYG	N	2	15	7.5	10	0

Andy Dudish

Year	Team		No	Yds	Avg	Lg	TD
1946	BUF	AA	2	33	16.5		0
1947	BAL	AA	7	130	18.6	70t	1
Career			9	163	18.1	70t	1

Bill Dudley

Year	Team		No	Yds	Avg	Lg	TD
1942	PIT	N	1	24	24.0	24	0

Bill Dudley *continued*

Year	Team		No	Yds	Avg	Lg	TD
1946			4	109	27.3	80t	1
1947	DET	N	27	375	13.9	64t	7
1948			20	210	10.5	22	6
1949			27	190	7.0	18	2
1950	WAS	N	22	172	7.8	17	1
1951			22	303	13.8	40	1
Career			123	1383	11.2	80t	18

Paul Dudley

Year	Team		No	Yds	Avg	Lg	TD
1962	NYG	N	9	112	12.4	88	1
1963	PHI	N	1	8	8.0	8	0
Career			10	120	12.0	88	1

Rickey Dudley

Year	Team		No	Yds	Avg	Lg	TD
1996	OAK	N	34	386	11.4	62t	4

John Duff

Year	Team		No	Yds	Avg	Lg	TD
Playoffs			1	5	5.0		0

Fred Dugan

Year	Team		No	Yds	Avg	Lg	TD
1958	SF	N	9	122	13.6	23	0
1959			6	72	12.0	13	0
1960	DAL	N	29	461	15.9	49	1
1961	WAS	N	53	817	15.4	80t	4
1962			36	466	12.9	27	5
1963			20	288	14.4	41t	3
Career			153	2226	14.5	80t	13

Jack Dugger

Year	Team		No	Yds	Avg	Lg	TD
1946	BUF	AA	1	15	15.0	15	0
1949	CHIB	N	1	11	11.0	11	0
Career			2	26	13.0	15	0

Paul Duhart

Year	Team		No	Yds	Avg	Lg	TD
1944	GB	N	9	176	19.6	32	2

Bobby Duhon

Year	Team		No	Yds	Avg	Lg	TD
1968	NYG	N	37	373	10.1	51	1
1970			4	58	14.5	22	0
1971			25	266	10.6	26	0
1972			2	20	10.0	12	0
Career			68	717	10.5	51	1

Billy DuMoe

Year	Team		No	Yds	Avg	Lg	TD
1921	GB	A					1

Dave Dunaway

Year	Team		No	Yds	Avg	Lg	TD
1969	NYG	N	2	37	18.5	25	0

Jubilee Dunbar

Year	Team		No	Yds	Avg	Lg	TD
1973	NO	N	23	447	19.4	65t	4
1974	CLE	N	6	74	12.3	25	0
Career			29	521	18.0	65t	4

Vaughn Dunbar

Year	Team		No	Yds	Avg	Lg	TD
1992	NO	N	9	62	6.9	13	0
1995	JAC	N	2	11	5.5	8	0
Career			11	73	6.6	13	0
Playoffs			4	49	12.3		0

Brian Duncan

Year	Team		No	Yds	Avg	Lg	TD
1976	CLE	N	6	49	8.2	17	1
1977			1	5	5.0	5t	1
1978	HOU	N	2	0	0.0	0	0
Career			9	54	6.0	17	2

Clyde Duncan

Year	Team		No	Yds	Avg	Lg	TD
1985	STL	N	4	39	9.8	14	1

Curtis Duncan

Year	Team		No	Yds	Avg	Lg	TD
1987	HOU	N	13	237	18.2	48	5
1988			22	302	13.7	36	1
1989			43	613	14.3	55	5
1990			66	785	11.9	37t	1
1991			55	588	10.7	42	4
1992			82	954	11.6	72	1
1993			41	456	11.1	47	3
Career			322	3935	12.2	72	20
Playoffs			34	274	8.1		2

Bob Dunlap

Year	Team		No	Yds	Avg	Lg	TD
1935	CHIB	N	1	10	10.0	10	0

Year	Team		No	Yds	Avg	Lg	TD

David Dunn

Year	Team		No	Yds	Avg	Lg	TD
1995	CIN	N	17	209	12.3	37	1
1996			32	509	15.9	40	1
Career			49	718	14.7	40	2

Jason Dunn

Year	Team		No	Yds	Avg	Lg	TD
1996	PHI	N	15	332	22.1	58	2

K.D. Dunn

Year	Team		No	Yds	Avg	Lg	TD
1986	TB	N	3	83	27.7	38	0
1988	NYJ	N	6	67	11.2	26	0
1989			2	13	6.5	8	0
Career			11	163	14.8	38	0

Perry Lee Dunn

Year	Team		No	Yds	Avg	Lg	TD
1964	DAL	N	2	30	15.0	18	0
1965			8	74	9.3	22	1
1966	ATL	N	5	45	9.0	16	0
1967			13	111	8.5	21	0
1968			9	118	13.1	43	0
1969	BAL	N	5	30	6.0	10	0
Career			42	408	9.7	43	1

Red Dunn

Year	Team		No	Yds	Avg	Lg	TD
1927	GB	N					1

Pat Dunsmore

Year	Team		No	Yds	Avg	Lg	TD
1983	CHI	N	8	102	12.8	24	0
1984			9	106	11.8	25	1
Career			17	208	12.2	25	1
Playoffs			2	22	11.0		1

Reggie Dupard

Year	Team		No	Yds	Avg	Lg	TD
1987	NE	N	3	1	0.3	2	0
1988			34	232	6.8	15	0
1989			6	70	11.7	45	0
Career			43	303	7.0	45	0

Mark Duper

Year	Team		No	Yds	Avg	Lg	TD
1983	MIA	N	51	1003	19.7	85t	10
1984			71	1306	18.4	80t	8
1985			35	650	18.6	67t	3
1986			67	1313	19.6	65t	11
1987			33	597	18.1	59t	8
1988			39	626	16.1	56	1
1989			49	717	14.6	41	1
1990			52	810	15.6	69t	5
1991			70	1085	15.5	43t	5
1992			44	762	17.3	62t	7
Career			511	8869	17.4	85t	59
Playoffs			32	595	18.6		5

L.G. Dupre

Year	Team		No	Yds	Avg	Lg	TD
1955	BAL	N	10	153	15.3	30	0
1956			16	216	13.5	49t	2
1957			32	339	10.6	43	2
1958			13	111	8.5	22	0
1959			6	47	7.8	18	1
1960	DAL	N	21	216	10.3	36	2
1961			6	49	8.2	17	0
Career			104	1131	10.9	49t	7
Playoffs			2	7	3.5		0

Billy Joe Dupree

Year	Team		No	Yds	Avg	Lg	TD
1973	DAL	N	29	392	13.5	40	5
1974			29	466	16.1	42t	4
1975			9	138	15.3	28	1
1976			42	680	16.2	38t	2
1977			28	347	12.4	23	3
1978			34	509	15.0	38	9
1979			29	324	11.2	33	5
1980			29	312	10.8	39	7
1981			19	214	11.3	33t	2
1982			7	41	5.9	12	2
1983			12	142	11.8	28	1
Career			267	3565	13.4	42t	41
Playoffs			39	447	11.5		4

Marcus Dupree

Year	Team		No	Yds	Avg	Lg	TD
1991	LARM	N	6	46	7.7	21	0

Don Durdan

Year	Team		No	Yds	Avg	Lg	TD
1946	SF	AA	2	27	13.5		1

John Durko

Year	Team		No	Yds	Avg	Lg	TD
1944	PHI	N	2	31	15.5	23t	1

Jeff Durkota

Year	Team		No	Yds	Avg	Lg	TD
1948	LA	AA	2	12	6.0		0

Bill Dutton

Year	Team		No	Yds	Avg	Lg	TD
1946	PIT	N	2	68	34.0	52	0

Mike Dyal

Year	Team		No	Yds	Avg	Lg	TD
1989	LARI	N	27	499	18.5	67t	2
1990			3	51	17.0	29	0
1992	KC	N	1	7	7.0	7	0
1993			7	83	11.9	31	0
Career			38	640	16.8	67t	2

Les Dye

Year	Team		No	Yds	Avg	Lg	TD
1944	WAS	N	24	281	11.7	61t	2
1945			7	84	12.0	25t	2
Career			31	365	11.8	61t	4
Playoffs			1	44	44.0		0

Henry Dyer

Year	Team		No	Yds	Avg	Lg	TD
1968	LA	N	8	37	4.6	15	0
1969	WAS	N	2	86	43.0	69t	1
1970			4	37	9.3	20	0
Career			14	160	11.4	69t	1

Ken Dyer

Year	Team		No	Yds	Avg	Lg	TD
1968	SD	A	1	22	22.0	22	0

Hart Lee Dykes

Year	Team		No	Yds	Avg	Lg	TD
1989	NE	N	49	795	16.2	42	5
1990			34	549	16.1	35t	2
Career			83	1344	16.2	42	7

Kay Eakin

Year	Team		No	Yds	Avg	Lg	TD
1941	NYG	N	5	81	16.2	38	1
1946	MIA	AA	6	67	11.2		0
Career			11	148	13.5	38	1

Ralph Earhart

Year	Team		No	Yds	Avg	Lg	TD
1948	GB	N	17	194	11.4	64t	2
1949			5	109	21.8	50	0
Career			22	303	13.8	64t	2

Robin Earl

Year	Team		No	Yds	Avg	Lg	TD
1977	CHI	N	6	32	5.3	20	0
1978			1	1	1.0	1	0
1979			8	56	7.0	19	0
1980			18	223	12.4	28	3
1981			10	118	11.8	24	1
1982			4	56	14.0	18	0
Career			47	486	10.3	28	4
Playoffs			1	15	15.0		0

Quinn Early

Year	Team		No	Yds	Avg	Lg	TD
1988	SD	N	29	375	12.9	38t	4
1989			11	126	11.5	21	0
1990			15	238	15.9	45t	1
1991	NO	N	32	541	16.9	52	2
1992			30	566	18.9	59t	5
1993			45	670	14.9	63t	6
1994			82	894	10.9	33	4
1995			81	1087	13.4	70t	8
1996	BUF	N	50	798	16.0	95t	4
Career			375	5295	14.1	95t	34
Playoffs			21	256	12.2		1

Walt Easley

Year	Team		No	Yds	Avg	Lg	TD
1981	SF	N	9	62	6.9	21	0

Scott Eaton

Year	Team		No	Yds	Avg	Lg	TD
1967	NYG	N	1	18	18.0	18	0

Harry Ebding

Year	Team		No	Yds	Avg	Lg	TD
1932	POR	N					1
1934	DET	N	9	257	28.6		2
1935			8	128	16.0		1
1936			10	194	19.4		3
1937			5	89	17.8		1
Career			32	668	20.9		8

Rick Eber

Year	Team		No	Yds	Avg	Lg	TD
1969	SD	A	9	141	15.7	43	1
1970	SD	N	2	43	21.5	31	0
Career			11	184	16.7	43	1

Ray Ebli

Year	Team		No	Yds	Avg	Lg	TD
1942	CHIC	N	6	83	13.8	31	0
1946	BUF	AA	2	15	7.5		1
1947	CHI	AA	4	38	9.5		1
Career			12	136	11.3	31	2

Byron Eby

Year	Team		No	Yds	Avg	Lg	TD
1930	POR	N					1

Jerry Eckwood

Year	Team		No	Yds	Avg	Lg	TD
1979	TB	N	22	268	12.2	31	0
1980			47	475	10.1	40	1
1981			24	213	8.9	33	0
Career			93	956	10.3	40	1

Floyd Eddings

Year	Team		No	Yds	Avg	Lg	TD
1982	NYG	N	14	275	19.6	47	0
1983			14	231	16.5	33	0
Career			28	506	18.1	47	0

Nick Eddy

Year	Team		No	Yds	Avg	Lg	TD
1968	DET	N	8	91	11.4	28	1
1969			10	78	7.8	14t	1
1970			4	22	5.5	9	0
1972			2	46	23.0	36t	1
Career			24	237	9.9	36t	2

Bobby Joe Edmonds

Year	Team		No	Yds	Avg	Lg	TD
1995	TB	N	1	8	8.0	8	0

Ferrell Edmunds

Year	Team		No	Yds	Avg	Lg	TD
1988	MIA	N	33	575	17.4	80t	3
1989			32	382	11.9	30	3
1990			31	446	14.4	35	1
1991			11	118	10.7	22	2
1992			10	91	9.1	15	1
1993	SEA	N	24	239	10.0	32	2
1994			7	43	6.1	8	0
Career			148	1894	12.8	80t	12
Playoffs			5	70	14.0		0

Al Edwards

Year	Team		No	Yds	Avg	Lg	TD
1990	BUF	N	2	11	5.5	6	0
1991			22	228	10.4	33t	1
1992			2	25	12.5	20	0
Career			26	264	10.2	33t	1
Playoffs			3	30	10.0		0

Anthony Edwards

Year	Team		No	Yds	Avg	Lg	TD
1989	PHI	N	2	74	37.0	66	0
1992	PHX	N	14	147	10.5	25t	1
1993			13	326	25.1	65t	1
1995	ARI	N	29	417	14.4	28t	2
1996			29	311	10.7	31	1
Career			87	1275	14.7	66	5

Bud Edwards

Year	Team		No	Yds	Avg	Lg	TD
1930	PRO	N					1

Cid Edwards

Year	Team		No	Yds	Avg	Lg	TD
1968	STL	N	1	2	2.0	2	0
1969			23	309	13.4	37	0
1970			19	150	7.9	39	1
1971			12	122	10.2	38	0
1972	SD	N	40	557	13.9	61	2
1973			25	164	6.6	28	0
1974			13	102	7.8	16	0
1975	CHI	N	11	86	7.8	14	1
Career			144	1492	10.4	61	4

Danny Edwards

Year	Team		No	Yds	Avg	Lg	TD
1948	BKN	AA	23	176	7.7		0
1949	CHI	AA	42	573	13.6	66	3
1950	NYY	N	52	775	14.9	82t	6
1951			39	509	13.1	53t	3
1952	DAL	N	3	22	7.3	13	0
1953	BAL	N	35	312	8.9	32t	3
1954			40	531	13.3	42	1
Career			234	2898	12.4	82t	16

Earl Edwards

Year	Team		No	Yds	Avg	Lg	TD
1969	SF	N	1	1	1.0	1	0

Emmett Edwards

Year	Team		No	Yds	Avg	Lg	TD
1975	HOU	N	2	22	11.0	18	0
1976	BUF	N	2	53	26.5	46	0
Career			4	75	18.8	46	0

Jimmy Edwards

Year	Team		No	Yds	Avg	Lg	TD
1979	MIN	N	1	2	2.0	2	0

Kelvin Edwards

Year	Team		No	Yds	Avg	Lg	TD
1986	NO	N	10	132	13.2	24	0
1987	DAL	N	34	521	15.3	38t	3
1988			5	93	18.6	27	0
Career			49	746	15.2	38t	3

Marshall Edwards

Year	Team		No	Yds	Avg	Lg	TD
1943	BKN	N	1	-4	-4.0	-4	0

Stan Edwards

Year	Team		No	Yds	Avg	Lg	TD
1982	HOU	N	9	53	5.9	21	0
1983			9	79	8.8	20	1
1984			20	151	7.5	20	0
1985			7	71	10.1	31	0
1987	DET	N	7	82	11.7	21	0
Career			52	436	8.4	31	1

Ron Egloff

Year	Team		No	Yds	Avg	Lg	TD
1977	DEN	N	2	27	13.5	20	0
1978			4	33	8.3	15	1
1979			5	70	14.0	22	0
1980			6	85	14.2	24	0
1981			17	231	13.6	40	1
1982			10	96	9.6	17	0
1983			20	205	10.3	32	2
1984	SD	N	11	92	8.4	17	0
Career			75	839	11.2	40	4
Playoffs			2	33	16.5		0

Monroe Eley

Year	Team		No	Yds	Avg	Lg	TD
1977	ATL	N	9	60	6.7	14	0

Keith Elias

Year	Team		No	Yds	Avg	Lg	TD
1995	NYG	N	9	69	7.7	18	0
1996			8	51	6.4	11	0
Career			17	120	7.1	18	0

Don Eliason

Year	Team		No	Yds	Avg	Lg	TD
1942	BKN	N	1	36	36.0	36	0
1946	BOS	N	1	9	9.0	9	0
Career			2	45	22.5	36	0

Larry Elkins

Year	Team		No	Yds	Avg	Lg	TD
1966	HOU	A	21	283	13.5	62	3
1967			3	32	10.7	16	0
Career			24	315	13.1	62	3

Henry Ellard

Year	Team		No	Yds	Avg	Lg	TD
1983	LARM	N	16	268	16.8	44	0
1984			34	622	18.3	63t	6
1985			54	811	15.0	64t	5
1986			34	447	13.1	34t	4
1987			51	799	15.7	81t	3
1988			86	**1414**	16.4	68	10
1989			70	1382	19.7	53	8
1990			76	1294	17.0	50t	4
1991			64	1052	16.4	38	3
1992			47	727	15.5	33t	3
1993			61	945	15.5	54	2
1994	WAS	N	74	1397	18.9	73t	6
1995			56	1005	17.9	59	5
1996			52	1014	**19.5**	51	2
Career			775	13177	17.0	81t	61
Playoffs			28	419	15.0		1

Rich Ellender

Year	Team		No	Yds	Avg	Lg	TD
1979	HOU	N	1	15	15.0	15	0

Gary Ellerson

Year	Team		No	Yds	Avg	Lg	TD
1985	GB	N	2	15	7.5	11	0
1986			12	130	10.8	32	0
1987	DET	N	5	48	9.6	23	1
Career			19	193	10.2	32	1

Al Elliott

Year	Team		No	Yds	Avg	Lg	TD
1923	RAC	N					2

Carl Elliott

Year	Team		No	Yds	Avg	Lg	TD
1951	GB	N	35	317	9.1	33t	5
1952			12	114	9.5	15	1
1953			13	150	11.5	19	0
Career			60	581	9.7	33t	6

Lenvil Elliott

Year	Team		No	Yds	Avg	Lg	TD
1973	CIN	N	1	12	12.0	12t	1
1974			18	187	10.4	28t	1
1975			20	196	9.8	31	3
1976			22	188	8.5	29t	3
1977			29	238	8.2	33	1
1978			12	100	8.3	18	0
1979	SF	N	23	197	8.6	30	0
1980			27	285	10.6	45t	1
1981			7	81	11.6	19	0
Career			159	1484	9.3	45t	10
Playoffs			12	91	7.6		0

Craig Ellis

Year	Team		No	Yds	Avg	Lg	TD
1987	LARI	N	5	39	7.8	15	0

Gerry Ellis

Year	Team		No	Yds	Avg	Lg	TD
1980	GB	N	48	496	10.3	69t	3
1981			65	499	7.7	46t	3
1982			18	140	7.8	20	0
1983			52	603	11.6	56	2
1984			36	312	8.7	22	2
1985			24	206	8.6	35	0
1986			24	258	10.8	29	0
Career			267	2514	9.4	69t	10
Playoffs			8	99	12.4		1

Jerry Ellison

Year	Team		No	Yds	Avg	Lg	TD
1995	TB	N	7	44	6.3	14	0
1996			18	208	11.6	42	0
Career			25	252	10.1	42	0

'OMar Ellison

Year	Team		No	Yds	Avg	Lg	TD
1995	SD	N	1	6	6.0	6	0
1996			3	15	5.0	6	0
Career			4	21	5.3	6	0

Willie Ellison

Year	Team		No	Yds	Avg	Lg	TD
1967	LA	N	1	18	18.0	18	0
1968			20	248	12.4	36t	2
1969			4	31	7.8	1t	1
1970			10	84	8.4	20	2
1971			32	238	7.4	49	0
1972			23	141	6.1	39t	1
1973	KC	N	9	64	7.1	17	0
1974			5	64	12.8	26	0
Career			104	888	8.5	49	6

Earl Elsey

Year	Team		No	Yds	Avg	Lg	TD
1946	LA	AA	14	179	12.8	50	0

Art Elston

Year	Team		No	Yds	Avg	Lg	TD
1942	CLE	N	4	58	14.5	18	0

Leo Elter

Year	Team		No	Yds	Avg	Lg	TD
1953	PIT	N	3	29	9.7	15	0
1954			4	16	4.0	26	0
1955	WAS	N	13	219	16.8	70	1
1956			11	99	9.0	17	0
1957			6	94	15.7	49t	1
1958	PIT	N	6	68	11.3	22	0
1959			3	31	10.3	28	0
Career			46	556	12.1	70	2

John Elway

Year	Team		No	Yds	Avg	Lg	TD
1986	DEN	N	1	23	23.0	23t	1
1991			1	24	24.0	24	0
Career			2	47	23.5	24	1
Playoffs			1	23	23.0		0

Jack Elwell

Year	Team		No	Yds	Avg	Lg	TD
1962	STL	N	1	11	11.0	11	0

Bert Emanuel

Year	Team		No	Yds	Avg	Lg	TD
1994	ATL	N	46	649	14.1	85t	4

Bert Emanuel *continued*

Year	Team		No	Yds	Avg	Lg	TD
1995			74	1039	14.0	52	5
1996			76	931	12.3	53	6
Career			196	2619	13.4	85t	15
Playoffs			6	62	10.3		0

John Embree

Year	Team		No	Yds	Avg	Lg	TD
1969	DEN	A	29	469	16.2	79t	5
1970	DEN	N	4	50	12.5	20	0
Career			33	519	15.7	79t	5

Mel Embree

Year	Team		No	Yds	Avg	Lg	TD
1953	BAL	N	23	272	11.8	24	1
1954	CHIC	N	2	20	10.0	15	0
Career			25	292	11.7	24	1

Larry Emery

Year	Team		No	Yds	Avg	Lg	TD
1987	ATL	N	5	31	6.2	13	0

Frank Emmons

Year	Team		No	Yds	Avg	Lg	TD
1940	PHI	N	3	19	6.3		1

Wuert Engelmann

Year	Team		No	Yds	Avg	Lg	TD
1930	GB	N					2
1931							2
1933							1
Career							5

Bobby Engram

Year	Team		No	Yds	Avg	Lg	TD
1996	CHI	N	33	389	11.8	24	6

Fred Enke

Year	Team		No	Yds	Avg	Lg	TD
1948	DET	N	1	6	6.0	6	0
1949			1	14	14.0	14	0
1952	PHI	N	2	19	9.5	18	0
Career			4	39	9.8	18	0

Rex Enright

Year	Team		No	Yds	Avg	Lg	TD
1927	GB	N					2

Bill Enyart

Year	Team		No	Yds	Avg	Lg	TD
1969	BUF	A	19	186	9.8	32t	2
1970	BUF	N	35	235	6.7	37t	1
Career			54	421	7.8	37t	3

Pat Epperson

Year	Team		No	Yds	Avg	Lg	TD
1960	DEN	A	11	99	9.0	16	0

Bobby Epps

Year	Team		No	Yds	Avg	Lg	TD
1954	NYG	N	5	20	4.0	10	0
1955			5	8	1.6	5	0
1957			8	81	10.1	34	0
Career			18	109	6.1	34	0

Phillip Epps

Year	Team		No	Yds	Avg	Lg	TD
1982	GB	N	10	226	22.6	50	2
1983			18	313	17.4	45	0
1984			26	435	16.7	56	3
1985			44	683	15.5	63	3
1986			49	612	12.5	53t	4
1987			34	516	15.2	40	2
1988			11	99	9.0	25	0
1989	NYJ	N	8	108	13.5	21	0
Career			200	2992	15.0	63	14
Playoffs			1	16	16.0		0

Dick Erdlitz

Year	Team		No	Yds	Avg	Lg	TD
1942	PHI	N	5	78	15.6	42	0
1946	MIA	AA	7	31	4.4		0
Career			12	109	9.1	42	0

Rich Erenberg

Year	Team		No	Yds	Avg	Lg	TD
1984	PIT	N	38	358	9.4	25	1
1985			33	326	9.9	35	3
1986			27	217	8.0	19	3
Career			98	901	9.2	35	7
Playoffs			5	59	11.8		0

Hal Erickson

Year	Team		No	Yds	Avg	Lg	TD
1924	MIL	N					3
1925	CHIC	N					3
1926							1
Career							7

Year	Team		No	Yds	Avg	Lg	TD

Jack Ernst
1926	POT	N					1
1928							2
1930	FRA	N					1
Career							4

Ricky Ervins
1991	WAS	N	16	181	11.3	28	1
1992			32	252	7.9	19	0
1993			16	123	7.7	20	0
1994			51	293	5.7	21	1
1995	SF	N	2	21	10.5	11	0
Career			117	870	7.4	28	2
Playoffs			3	24	8.0		0

Terry Erwin
1968	DEN	A	2	21	10.5	17	0

Len Eshmont
1941	NYG	N	1	4	4.0	4	0
1946	SF	AA	17	287	16.9		2
1947			19	303	15.9	60	2
1948			14	214	15.3		0
1949			3	107	35.7		2
Career			54	915	16.9	60	6

Boomer Esiason
1993	NYJ	N	1	-8	-8.0	-8	0

Mike Esposito
1976	ATL	N	17	88	5.2	13	0
1977			1	-1	-1.0	-1	0
1978			3	10	3.3	4	0
Career			21	97	4.6	13	0
Playoffs			1	7	7.0		0

Ron Essink
1980	SEA	N	1	2	2.0	2t	1

Richard Estell
1987	KC	N	3	24	8.0	11	0

Carlos Etheredge
1994	IND	N	1	6	6.0	6	0

Ray Ethridge
1996	BAL	N	2	24	12.0	15	0

Charlie Evans
1971	NYG	N	13	144	11.1	25	0
1972			26	182	7.0	18	1
1973			13	100	7.7	20	0
1974	WAS	N	2	44	22.0	44	0
Career			54	470	8.7	44	1
Playoffs			4	31	7.8		0

Chuck Evans
1993	MIN	N	4	39	9.8	21	0
1994			1	2	2.0	2	0
1995			18	119	6.6	24	1
1996			22	135	6.1	16	0
Career			45	295	6.6	24	1
Playoffs			3	9	3.0		0

Dick Evans
1940	GB	N	2	40	20.0		0
1941	CHIC	N	3	34	11.3	22	0
1943	GB	N	8	71	8.9	13	0
Career			13	145	11.2	22	0

Earl Evans
1925	CHIC	N					1

Fred Evans
1946	CLE	AA	1	7	7.0	7	0
1947	BUF-CHI	AA	5	84	16.8		1
1948	CHIB	N	1	-2	-2.0	-2	0
Career			7	89	12.7	7	1

Jerry Evans
1994	DEN	N	13	127	9.8	20t	2
1995			12	124	10.3	22	1
Career			25	251	10.0	22	3
Playoffs			1	7	7.0		0

Jimmy Evans
1964	NY	A	7	56	8.0	17	0
1965			2	24	12.0	17	0
Career			9	80	8.9	17	0

John Evans
1987	ATL	N	1	8	8.0	8	0

Murray Evans
1942	DET	N	2	32	16.0	19	0
1943			3	31	10.3	16	0
Career			5	63	12.6	19	0

Ray Evans
1948	PIT	N	7	93	13.3	36	0

Major Everett
1983	PHI	N	2	18	9.0	11	0
1985			4	25	6.3	11	0
1987	CLE	N	8	41	5.1	10	0
Career			14	84	6.0	11	0

Nuu Faaola
1987	NYJ	N	1	16	16.0	16	0
1989	MIA	N	1	8	8.0	8	0
Career			2	24	12.0	16	0

Keith Fahnhorst
1975	SF	N	1	1	1.0	1	0

Derrick Faison
1990	LARM	N	3	27	9.0	12	1

Nello Falaschi
1939	NYG	N	4	27	6.8		0
1940			2	9	4.5		0
1941			1	3	3.0	3	0
Career			7	39	5.6	3	0
Playoffs			2	6	3.0		0

Tony Falkenstein
1943	GB	N	3	39	13.0	18	0
1944	BKN-BOS	N	1	21	21.0	21	0
Career			4	60	15.0	21	0

Gary Famiglietti
1939	CHIB	N	3	72	24.0		0
1940			1	11	11.0	11	0
1942			1	12	12.0	12	0
1943			1	10	10.0	10	1
1944			1	23	23.0	23t	1
1945			4	42	10.5	13	0
1946	BOS	N	1	17	17.0	17	0
Career			12	187	15.6	23t	2

Chad Fann
1994	ARI	N	12	96	8.0	16	0
1995			5	41	8.2	13	0
Career			17	137	8.1	16	0

Andy Farkas
1938	WAS	N	9	66	7.3		0
1939			16	437	27.3	99t	5
1941			12	77	6.4	44	0
1942			11	143	13.0	35	2
1943			19	202	10.6	55	4
1944			4	29	7.3	12	0
1945	DET	N	9	132	14.7	29	2
Career			80	1086	13.6	99t	13
Playoffs			2	36	18.0		1

John Farley
1984	CIN	N	2	11	5.5	10	0

George Farmer
1970	CHI	N	31	496	16.0	60	2
1971			46	737	16.0	64	5
1972			14	380	27.1	85t	2
1973			15	219	14.6	25	1
1974			5	45	9.0	17	0
1975	CHI-DET	N	8	118	14.8	22	0
Career			119	1995	16.8	85t	10

George Farmer
1982	LARM	N	17	344	20.2	42t	2
1983			40	556	13.9	46t	5
1984			7	75	10.7	23	0
1987	MIA	N	1	5	5.0	5	0
Career			65	980	15.1	46t	7
Playoffs			5	47	9.4		1

Karl Farmer
1977	ATL	N	2	39	19.5	23	0

Tom Farmer
1946	LA	N	6	17	2.8	13	0
1947	WAS	N	8	137	17.1	31	0
1948			12	148	12.3	48	2
Career			26	302	11.6	48	2

Mel Farr
1967	DET	N	39	317	8.1	31	3
1968			24	375	15.6	86t	4
1969			13	94	7.2	24	0
1970			29	213	7.3	58	2
1971			5	60	12.0	39	1
1972			10	132	13.2	42	0
1973			26	183	7.0	27	0
Career			146	1374	9.4	86t	10

Mike Farr
1990	DET	N	12	170	14.2	44	0
1991			42	431	10.3	34t	1
1992			15	115	7.7	14	0
Career			69	716	10.4	44	1
Playoffs			11	135	12.3		0

Miller Farr
Playoffs			1	24	24.0		0

Sean Farrell
1988	NE	N	1	4	4.0	4	0

Bo Farrington
1961	CHI	N	21	349	16.6	98t	4
1962			13	197	15.2	51	1
1963			21	335	16.0	58	2
Career			55	881	16.0	98t	7

Tom Farris
1946	CHIB	N	1	16	16.0	16	0

Marshall Faulk
1994	IND	N	52	522	10.0	85t	1
1995			56	475	8.5	34	3
1996			56	428	7.6	30	0
Career			164	1425	8.7	85t	4
Playoffs			3	10	3.3		0

Mike Faulkerson
1995	CHI	N	2	22	11.0	12	0
1996			1	1	1.0	1t	1
Career			3	23	7.7	12	1

Chris Faulkner
1984	LARM	N	1	6	6.0	6	0
1985	SD	N	1	12	12.0	12	0
Career			2	18	9.0	12	0

Christian Fauria
1995	SEA	N	17	181	10.6	20t	1
1996			18	214	11.9	23t	1
Career			35	395	11.3	23t	2

George Faust
1939	CHIC	N	4	85	21.3		0

Brett Favre
1992	GB	N	1	-7	-7.0	-7	0

Jake Fawcett
1944	CLE	N	1	9	9.0	9	0

Ricky Feacher
1976	NE	N	2	38	19.0	21	0
1978	CLE	N	4	76	19.0	42	0
1979			7	103	14.7	25	1

Ricky Feacher *continued*

Year	Team		No	Yds	Avg	Lg	TD
1980			10	244	24.4	55t	4
1981			29	654	22.6	48	3
1982			28	408	14.6	46	3
1983			13	217	16.7	42t	3
1984			22	382	17.4	64	1
Career			115	2122	18.5	64	15
Playoffs			4	124	31.0		1

Tom Fears

Year	Team		No	Yds	Avg	Lg	TD
1948	**LA**	**N**	**51**	698	13.7	80t	4
1949			**77**	1013	13.2	51	**9**
1950			84	**1116**	13.3	53t	7
1951			32	528	16.5	54	3
1952			48	600	12.5	36	6
1953			23	278	12.1	31	4
1954			36	546	15.2	43	3
1955			44	569	12.9	31	2
1956			5	49	9.8	18	0
Career			400	5397	13.5	80t	38
Playoffs			30	587	19.6		5

Grant Feasel

Year	Team		No	Yds	Avg	Lg	TD
1989	**SEA**	**N**	1	5	5.0	5	0

Tiny Feather

Year	Team		No	Yds	Avg	Lg	TD
1928	**DET**	**N**					1
1929	**NYG**	**N**					1
Career							2

Beattie Feathers

Year	Team		No	Yds	Avg	Lg	TD
1934	**CHIB**	**N**	5	174	34.8		1
1935			3	18	6.0		0
1936			2	5	2.5		0
1938	**BKN**	**N**	3	34	11.3		0
1939			1	12	12.0	12	0
Career			14	243	17.4	12	1

Gene Fekete

Year	Team		No	Yds	Avg	Lg	TD
1946	**CLE**	**AA**	1	2	2.0	2	0

Gene Felker

Year	Team		No	Yds	Avg	Lg	TD
1952	**DAL**	**N**	6	63	10.5	17t	1

Bobby Felts

Year	Team		No	Yds	Avg	Lg	TD
1965	**DET**	**N**	3	28	9.3	17	0
1966			2	1	0.5	1	0
Career			5	29	5.8	17	0

Chuck Fenenbock

Year	Team		No	Yds	Avg	Lg	TD
1943	**DET**	**N**	5	45	9.0	33	1
1945			1	24	24.0	24	0
1946	**LA**	**AA**	11	67	6.1		0
1947			20	276	13.8	70t	2
1948	**CHI**	**AA**	8	111	13.9	53t	1
Career			45	523	11.6	70t	4

Gill Fenerty

Year	Team		No	Yds	Avg	Lg	TD
1990	**NO**	**N**	18	209	11.6	28	0
1991			26	235	9.0	50t	2
Career			44	444	10.1	50t	2
Playoffs			4	22	5.5		0

Bob Fenimore

Year	Team		No	Yds	Avg	Lg	TD
1947	**CHIB**	**N**	15	219	14.6	29t	2

Derrick Fenner

Year	Team		No	Yds	Avg	Lg	TD
1989	**SEA**	**N**	3	23	7.7	9	0
1990			17	143	8.4	50	1
1991			11	72	6.5	15	0
1992	**CIN**	**N**	7	41	5.9	15	1
1993			48	427	8.9	40	0
1994			36	276	7.7	29	1
1995	**OAK**	**N**	35	252	7.2	23	3
1996			31	252	8.1	23t	4
Career			188	1486	7.9	50	10

Lee Fenner

Year	Team		No	Yds	Avg	Lg	TD
1924	**DAY**	**N**					1

Rick Fenney

Year	Team		No	Yds	Avg	Lg	TD
1987	**MIN**	**N**	7	27	3.9	18	0
1988			15	224	14.9	42	0
1989			30	254	8.5	26	2

Rick Fenney *continued*

Year	Team		No	Yds	Avg	Lg	TD
1990			17	112	6.6	17	0
1991			2	11	5.5	8	0
Career			71	628	8.8	42	2
Playoffs			8	30	3.8		0

Duke Fergersen

Year	Team		No	Yds	Avg	Lg	TD
1977	**SEA**	**N**	19	374	19.7	45t	2
1978			11	116	10.5	17	0
1979			2	12	6.0	10	0
1980	**BUF**	**N**	3	41	13.7	19	0
Career			35	543	15.5	45t	2

Bob Ferguson

Year	Team		No	Yds	Avg	Lg	TD
1962	**PIT**	**N**	1	6	6.0	6	0
1963			3	7	2.3	9	0
Career			4	13	3.3	9	0

Charley Ferguson

Year	Team		No	Yds	Avg	Lg	TD
1961	**CLE**	**N**	2	68	34.0	60t	1
1962	**MIN**	**N**	14	364	26.0	89t	6
1963	**BUF**	**A**	9	181	20.1	72	3
1965			21	262	12.5	30	2
1966			16	293	18.3	32	1
Career			62	1168	18.8	89t	13
Playoffs			4	47	11.8		0

Howie Ferguson

Year	Team		No	Yds	Avg	Lg	TD
1953	**GB**	**N**	15	86	5.7	23	0
1954			41	398	9.7	49	0
1955			22	153	7.0	16	0
1956			22	214	9.7	25	0
1957			15	107	7.1	17	1
1958			12	121	10.1	27	0
1960	**LA**	**A**	21	206	9.8	26	2
Career			148	1285	8.7	49	3
Playoffs			2	19	9.5		0

Joe Ferguson

Year	Team		No	Yds	Avg	Lg	TD
1973	**BUF**	**N**	1	-3	-3.0	-3	0
1978			1	-6	-6.0	-6	0
Career			2	-9	-4.5	-3	0

Larry Ferguson

Year	Team		No	Yds	Avg	Lg	TD
1963	**DET**	**N**	2	8	4.0	7	0

Vagas Ferguson

Year	Team		No	Yds	Avg	Lg	TD
1980	**NE**	**N**	22	173	7.9	18	0
1981			4	39	9.8	20	0
Career			26	212	8.2	20	0

Mervyn Fernandez

Year	Team		No	Yds	Avg	Lg	TD
1987	**LARI**	**N**	14	236	16.9	47	0
1988			31	805	26.0	85t	4
1989			57	1069	18.8	75t	9
1990			52	839	16.1	66t	5
1991			46	694	15.1	59	1
1992			9	121	13.4	21	0
Career			209	3764	18.0	85t	19
Playoffs			8	93	11.6		1

Jack Ferrante

Year	Team		No	Yds	Avg	Lg	TD
1941	**PHI**	**N**	2	22	11.0	12	0
1944			3	66	22.0	45t	1
1945			21	474	22.6	74t	7
1946			28	451	16.1	48	4
1947			18	341	18.9	54t	4
1948			28	444	15.9	66t	7
1949			34	508	14.9	64	5
1950			35	588	16.8	58t	3
Career			169	2894	17.1	74t	31
Playoffs			16	180	11.3		1

Bobby Ferrell

Year	Team		No	Yds	Avg	Lg	TD
1976	**SF**	**N**	1	9	9.0	9	0
1977			2	12	6.0	7	0
1978			16	123	7.7	14	0
1979			2	4	2.0	3	0
Career			21	148	7.0	14	0

Earl Ferrell

Year	Team		No	Yds	Avg	Lg	TD
1984	**STL**	**N**	26	218	8.4	21	1
1985			25	277	11.1	30	2
1986			56	434	7.8	30t	3

Earl Ferrell *continued*

Year	Team		No	Yds	Avg	Lg	TD
1987			23	262	11.4	36	0
1988	**PHX**	**N**	38	315	8.3	30	2
1989			18	122	6.8	25	0
Career			186	1628	8.8	36	8

Neil Ferris

Year	Team		No	Yds	Avg	Lg	TD
1952	**WAS**	**N**	1	8	8.0	8	0

Frank Filchock

Year	Team		No	Yds	Avg	Lg	TD
1938	**PIT-WAS**	**N**	2	4	2.0		0
1944	**WAS**	**N**	3	51	17.0	28	0
1945			3	33	11.0	17	0
1946	**NYG**	**N**	1	-6	-6.0	-6	0
Career			9	82	9.1	28	0

Steve Filipowicz

Year	Team		No	Yds	Avg	Lg	TD
1945	**NYG**	**N**	4	49	12.3	26t	1
1946			7	84	12.0	29	1
Career			11	133	12.1	29	2
Playoffs			2	41	20.5		1

Gene Filipski

Year	Team		No	Yds	Avg	Lg	TD
1956	**NYG**	**N**	3	37	12.3	21	0
1957			1	7	7.0	7	0
Career			4	44	11.0	21	0

John Fina

Year	Team		No	Yds	Avg	Lg	TD
1992	**BUF**	**N**	1	1	1.0	1t	1

Steve Finch

Year	Team		No	Yds	Avg	Lg	TD
1987	**MIN**	**N**	3	54	18.0	20	0

Jim Finks

Year	Team		No	Yds	Avg	Lg	TD
1949	**PIT**	**N**	1	17	17.0	17t	1

Clete Fischer

Year	Team		No	Yds	Avg	Lg	TD
1949	**NYG**	**N**	3	45	15.0	36	1

Pat Fischer

Year	Team		No	Yds	Avg	Lg	TD
1961	**STL**	**N**	1	22	22.0	22	0

Bob Fisher

Year	Team		No	Yds	Avg	Lg	TD
1980	**CHI**	**N**	12	203	16.9	56t	2

Ev Fisher

Year	Team		No	Yds	Avg	Lg	TD
1938	**CHIC**	**N**	3	48	16.0		0
1939			6	62	10.3		0
1940	**PIT**	**N**	2	12	6.0		0
Career			11	122	11.1		0

Bill Fisk

Year	Team		No	Yds	Avg	Lg	TD
1940	**DET**	**N**	1	10	10.0	10	0
1941			9	140	15.6	32	2
1942			15	177	11.8	27	0
1943			11	137	12.5	28	0
1946	**SF**	**AA**	19	186	9.8		1
1947			5	39	7.8		0
1948	**LA**	**AA**	9	102	11.3		0
Career			69	791	11.5	32	3

Max Fiske

Year	Team		No	Yds	Avg	Lg	TD
1936	**PIT**	**N**	7	96	13.7		0
1937			1	0	0.0	0	0
Career			8	96	12.0	0	0

Paul Fitzgibbons

Year	Team		No	Yds	Avg	Lg	TD
1930	**GB**	**N**					2

Scott Fitzkee

Year	Team		No	Yds	Avg	Lg	TD
1979	**PHI**	**N**	8	105	13.1	19	1
1980			6	169	28.2	49	2
1982	**SD**	**N**	3	47	15.7	18t	1
Career			17	321	18.9	49	4
Playoffs			3	27	9.0		0

Jack Flagerman

Year	Team		No	Yds	Avg	Lg	TD
1948	**LA**	**AA**	0	6		6L	0

Terrence Flagler

Year	Team		No	Yds	Avg	Lg	TD
1987	**SF**	**N**	2	28	14.0	24	0
1988			4	72	18.0	57	0
1989			6	51	8.5	30	0
1990	**PHX**	**N**	13	130	10.0	21	1

Year	Team		No	Yds	Avg	Lg	TD

Terrence Flagler *continued*

Year	Team		No	Yds	Avg	Lg	TD
1991			8	85	10.6	17	0
Career			33	366	11.1	57	1

Dick Flaherty

Year	Team		No	Yds	Avg	Lg	TD
1926	GB	N					2

Pat Flaherty

Year	Team		No	Yds	Avg	Lg	TD
1926	BKN	A					1

Ray Flaherty

Year	Team		No	Yds	Avg	Lg	TD
1927	NYY	N					4
1928							1
1929	NYG	N					8
1931							1
1932			21	350	16.7		5
1933			11	187	17.0		0
1934			8	79	9.9		1
Career			40	616	15.4		20
Playoffs			4	56	14.0		0

Jim Flanigan

Year	Team		No	Yds	Avg	Lg	TD
1995	CHI	N	2	6	3.0	4t	2
1996			1	1	1.0	1t	1
Career			3	7	2.3	4t	3
Playoffs			1	2	2.0		1

Paul Flatley

Year	Team		No	Yds	Avg	Lg	TD
1963	MIN	N	51	867	17.0	62	4
1964			28	450	16.1	48	3
1965			50	896	17.9	58t	7
1966			50	777	15.5	41	3
1967			23	232	10.1	27	0
1968	ATL	N	20	305	15.3	66	0
1969			45	834	18.5	71t	6
1970			39	544	13.9	35	1
Career			306	4905	16.0	71t	24

Cory Fleming

Year	Team		No	Yds	Avg	Lg	TD
1995	DAL	N	6	83	13.8	16	0

George Fleming

Year	Team		No	Yds	Avg	Lg	TD
1961	OAK	A	10	49	4.9	22	0

Marv Fleming

Year	Team		No	Yds	Avg	Lg	TD
1963	GB	N	7	132	18.9	33	2
1964			4	36	9.0	10	0
1965			14	141	10.1	31t	2
1966			31	361	11.6	53t	2
1967			10	126	12.6	19	1
1968			25	278	11.1	32t	3
1969			18	226	12.6	23	2
1970	MIA	N	18	205	11.4	36	0
1971			13	137	10.5	23	2
1972			13	156	12.0	31	1
1973			3	22	7.3	15	0
1974			1	3	3.0	3t	1
Career			157	1823	11.6	53t	16
Playoffs			22	251	11.4		1

Ollie Fletcher

Year	Team		No	Yds	Avg	Lg	TD
1950	BAL	N	2	18	9.0	10	0

Terrell Fletcher

Year	Team		No	Yds	Avg	Lg	TD
1995	SD	N	3	26	8.7	15	0
1996			61	476	7.8	41	2
Career			64	502	7.8	41	2
Playoffs			2	42	21.0		0

Charlie Flowers

Year	Team		No	Yds	Avg	Lg	TD
1960	LA	A	12	115	9.6	55	1
1961	SD	A	16	175	10.9	31	0
1962	NY	A	7	55	7.9	14	0
Career			35	345	9.9	55	1
Playoffs			3	23	7.7		0

Kenny Flowers

Year	Team		No	Yds	Avg	Lg	TD
1987	ATL	N	7	50	7.1	24	0

Bobby Jack Floyd

Year	Team		No	Yds	Avg	Lg	TD
1952	GB	N	11	129	11.7	44	0
1953	CHIB	N	9	63	7.0	16	0
Career			20	192	9.6	44	0

John Floyd

Year	Team		No	Yds	Avg	Lg	TD
1979	SD	N	10	152	15.2	40	1
1980			1	31	31.0	31t	1
1981	STL	N	3	32	10.7	16	0
Career			14	215	15.4	40	2
Playoffs			3	51	17.0		0

Malcolm Floyd

Year	Team		No	Yds	Avg	Lg	TD
1996	HOU	N	10	145	14.5	63t	1

Victor Floyd

Year	Team		No	Yds	Avg	Lg	TD
1989	SD	N	1	6	6.0	6	0

William Floyd

Year	Team		No	Yds	Avg	Lg	TD
1994	SF	N	19	145	7.6	15	0
1995			47	348	7.4	23	1
1996			26	197	7.6	24	1
Career			92	690	7.5	24	2
Playoffs			17	113	6.6		1

Darren Flutie

Year	Team		No	Yds	Avg	Lg	TD
1988	SD	N	18	208	11.6	28	2

Hank Foldberg

Year	Team		No	Yds	Avg	Lg	TD
1948	BKN	AA	16	129	8.1		0
1949	CHI	AA	15	202	13.5		0
Career			31	331	10.7		0

Glenn Foley

Year	Team		No	Yds	Avg	Lg	TD
1995	NYJ	N	1	-9	-9.0	-9	0

Lee Folkins

Year	Team		No	Yds	Avg	Lg	TD
1962	DAL	N	39	536	13.7	52	6
1963			31	407	13.1	35t	4
1964			5	41	8.2	11	0
1965	PIT	N	5	58	11.6	16	0
Career			80	1042	13.0	52	10

Steve Folsom

Year	Team		No	Yds	Avg	Lg	TD
1988	DAL	N	9	84	9.3	20	2
1989			28	265	9.5	26	2
Career			37	349	9.4	26	4

Art Folz

Year	Team		No	Yds	Avg	Lg	TD
1925	CHIC	N					1

Herman Fontenot

Year	Team		No	Yds	Avg	Lg	TD
1985	CLE	N	2	19	9.5	17	0
1986			47	559	11.9	72t	1
1987			4	40	10.0	25	0
1988			19	170	8.9	15	1
1989	GB	N	40	372	9.3	38t	3
1990			31	293	9.5	59	1
Career			143	1453	10.2	72t	6
Playoffs			15	153	10.2		2

Adrian Ford

Year	Team		No	Yds	Avg	Lg	TD
1926	PHI	A					2

Bernard Ford

Year	Team		No	Yds	Avg	Lg	TD
1989	DAL	N	7	78	11.1	21	1
1990	HOU	N	10	98	9.8	24	1
Career			17	176	10.4	24	2

Fred Ford

Year	Team		No	Yds	Avg	Lg	TD
1960	BUF	A	1	5	5.0	5	0

Garrett Ford

Year	Team		No	Yds	Avg	Lg	TD
1968	DEN	A	6	40	6.7	12	0

Henry Ford

Year	Team		No	Yds	Avg	Lg	TD
1956	PIT	N	3	7	2.3	8	0

Jim Ford

Year	Team		No	Yds	Avg	Lg	TD
1971	NO	N	7	54	7.7	10	0
1972			1	9	9.0	9	0
Career			8	63	7.9	10	0

John Ford

Year	Team		No	Yds	Avg	Lg	TD
1989	DET	N	5	56	11.2	37	0

Len Ford

Year	Team		No	Yds	Avg	Lg	TD
1948	LA	AA	31	598	19.3	51	7

Len Ford *continued*

Year	Team		No	Yds	Avg	Lg	TD
1949			36	577	16.0		1
Career			67	1175	17.5	51	8

Jim Fordham

Year	Team		No	Yds	Avg	Lg	TD
1944	CHIB	N	1	13	13.0	13	0
1945			4	34	8.5	19	0
Career			5	47	9.4	19	0

Chuck Foreman

Year	Team		No	Yds	Avg	Lg	TD
1973	MIN	N	37	362	9.8	35	2
1974			53	586	11.1	66t	6
1975			73	691	9.5	33	9
1976			55	567	10.3	41t	1
1977			38	308	8.1	31t	3
1978			61	396	6.5	20	2
1979			19	147	7.7	22	0
1980	NE	N	14	99	7.1	18	0
Career			350	3156	9.0	66t	23
Playoffs			45	447	9.9		0

Bob Forte

Year	Team		No	Yds	Avg	Lg	TD
1946	GB	N	2	5	2.5	4	0
1947			7	80	11.4	22t	2
1948			6	63	10.5	19	1
1949			7	85	12.1	28	0
1950			2	9	4.5	10	0
Career			24	242	10.1	28	3

Ike Forte

Year	Team		No	Yds	Avg	Lg	TD
1976	NE	N	3	9	3.0	6t	1
1977			8	88	11.0	22	0
1979	WAS	N	10	105	10.5	22	0
1980			15	174	11.6	28	1
1981	NYG	N	3	11	3.7	6	0
Career			39	387	9.9	28	2

Roman Fortin

Year	Team		No	Yds	Avg	Lg	TD
1991	DET	N	1	4	4.0	4	0

Barry Foster

Year	Team		No	Yds	Avg	Lg	TD
1990	PIT	N	1	2	2.0	2	0
1991			9	117	13.0	31	1
1992			36	344	9.6	42	0
1993			27	217	8.0	21	1
1994			20	124	6.2	27	0
Career			93	804	8.6	42	2
Playoffs			6	19	3.2		0

Derrick Foster

Year	Team		No	Yds	Avg	Lg	TD
1987	NYJ	N	1	9	9.0	9	0

Eddie Foster

Year	Team		No	Yds	Avg	Lg	TD
1977	HOU	N	15	208	13.9	56	0

Geno Foster

Year	Team		No	Yds	Avg	Lg	TD
1965	SD	A	17	199	11.7	23	0
1966			26	260	10.0	63	2
1967			9	46	5.1	11	0
1968			23	224	9.7	48	0
1969			14	83	5.9	28	1
1970	SD	N	10	92	9.2	48	0
Career			99	904	9.1	63	3

Roy Foster

Year	Team		No	Yds	Avg	Lg	TD
Playoffs			1	2	2.0		1

Dan Fouts

Year	Team		No	Yds	Avg	Lg	TD
1984	SD	N	1	0	0.0	0	0

Bobby Fowler

Year	Team		No	Yds	Avg	Lg	TD
1985	NO	N	5	43	8.6	11	0

Todd Fowler

Year	Team		No	Yds	Avg	Lg	TD
1985	DAL	N	5	24	4.8	10	0
1986			1	19	19.0	19	0
1987			1	6	6.0	6	0
1988			10	64	6.4	13	0
Career			17	113	6.6	19	0

Willmer Fowler

Year	Team		No	Yds	Avg	Lg	TD
1960	BUF	A	10	99	9.9		0

Year	Team		No	Yds	Avg	Lg	TD

Chas Fox
| 1986 | STL | N | 5 | 59 | 11.8 | 38t | 1 |

Sam Fox
| 1945 | NYG | N | 10 | 120 | 12.0 | 28 | 2 |

Terry Fox
1941	PHI	N	6	71	11.8	21	0
1946	MIA	AA	3	27	9.0		0
Career			9	98	10.9	21	0

Todd Frain
| 1987 | NE | N | 2 | 22 | 11.0 | 11 | 0 |

Bill Fralic
| 1993 | DET | N | 1 | -4 | -4.0 | -4 | 0 |

Pete Franceschi
| 1946 | SF | AA | 3 | 35 | 11.7 | | 1 |

Jason Franci
| 1966 | DEN | A | 1 | 8 | 8.0 | 8 | 0 |

Jon Francis
| 1987 | LARM | N | 8 | 38 | 4.8 | 7 | 2 |

Phil Francis
1979	SF	N	32	198	6.2	19	0
1980			3	23	7.7	15	0
Career			35	221	6.3	19	0

Russ Francis
1975	NE	N	35	636	18.2	48	4
1976			26	367	14.1	48	3
1977			16	229	14.3	31t	4
1978			39	543	13.9	53	4
1979			39	557	14.3	44	5
1980			41	664	16.2	39t	8
1982	SF	N	23	278	12.1	26	2
1983			33	357	10.8	25	4
1984			23	285	12.4	32	2
1985			44	478	10.9	25	3
1986			41	505	12.3	52	1
1987			22	202	9.2	19	0
1988	NE	N	11	161	14.6	51	0
Career			393	5262	13.4	53	40
Playoffs			35	474	13.5		3

Sam Francis
1937	CHIB	N	1	9	9.0	9	0
1938			1	8	8.0	8	0
1939	PIT	N	2	5	2.5	5	0
Career			4	22	5.5	9	0

Wallace Francis
1975	ATL	N	13	270	20.8	67t	4
1976			2	24	12.0	12	0
1977			26	390	15.0	32	1
1978			45	695	15.4	54t	3
1979			74	1013	13.7	42	8
1980			54	862	16.0	81t	7
1981			30	441	14.7	36	4
Career			244	3695	15.1	81t	27
Playoffs			18	267	14.8		2

George Franck
1941	NYG	N	8	95	11.9	44	1
1945			3	39	13.0	18	0
1946			6	137	22.8	50	1
1947			10	265	26.5	88t	3
Career			27	536	19.9	88t	5
Playoffs			1	31	31.0		1

Mike Franckowiak
| 1976 | DEN | N | 4 | 42 | 10.5 | 11 | 0 |

John Frank
1984	SF	N	7	60	8.6	21	1
1985			7	50	7.1	14	1
1986			9	61	6.8	17	2
1987			26	296	11.4	27	3
1988			16	195	12.2	38	3
Career			65	662	10.2	38	10
Playoffs			8	76	9.5		2

Ike Frankian
1933	BOS	N					1
1934	NYG	N	2	10	5.0		0
1935			7	79	11.3		0
Career			9	89	9.9		1
Playoffs			1	28	28.0		1

Andra Franklin
1981	MIA	N	3	6	2.0	3t	1
1982			3	9	3.0	6	0
Career			6	15	2.5	6	1

Byron Franklin
1981	BUF	N	2	29	14.5	16	0
1983			30	452	15.1	43t	4
1984			69	862	12.5	64t	4
1985	SEA	N	10	119	11.9	28	0
1986			33	547	16.6	49	2
1987			1	7	7.0	7	0
Career			145	2016	13.9	64t	10

Cleveland Franklin
1978	PHI	N	7	46	6.6	15	0
1980	BAL	N	14	112	8.0	16	0
1981			6	39	6.5	10	0
1982			9	61	6.8	15	0
Career			36	258	7.2	16	0

Dennis Franklin
1975	DET	N	5	109	21.8	36	0
1976			1	16	16.0	16	0
Career			6	125	20.8	36	0

George Franklin
| 1978 | ATL | N | 1 | 19 | 19.0 | 19 | 0 |

Pat Franklin
| 1986 | TB | N | 7 | 29 | 4.1 | 9 | 1 |

Nolan Franz
| 1986 | GB | N | 1 | 7 | 7.0 | 7 | 0 |

Al Frazier
1961	DEN	A	47	799	17.0	87	6
1962			11	211	19.2	96	1
Career			58	1010	17.4	96	7

Charlie Frazier
1962	HOU	A	7	155	22.1	73	1
1963			16	269	16.8	80	1
1964			31	423	13.6	46	2
1965			38	717	18.9	64	6
1966			57	1129	19.8	79	12
1967			23	253	11.0	53	1
1968			9	123	13.7	19	0
1969	BOS	A	19	306	16.1	50t	7
1970	BOS	N	9	86	9.6	16	0
Career			209	3461	16.6	80	30
Playoffs			7	81	11.6		1

Paul Frazier
| 1989 | NO | N | 3 | 25 | 8.3 | 22 | 0 |

Willie Frazier
1964	HOU	A	9	208	23.1	80	1
1965			37	521	14.1	57	8
1966	SD	A	9	144	16.0	30	2
1967			57	922	16.2	72t	10
1968			16	237	14.8	48t	3
1969			17	205	12.1	50	0
1970	SD	N	38	497	13.1	51	6
1971	HOU-KC	N	10	154	15.4	33	0
1972	KC	N	13	172	13.2	35	5
1975	HOU	N	1	9	9.0	9	0
Career			207	3069	14.8	80	35
Playoffs			1	14	14.0		0

Tucker Frederickson
1965	NYG	N	24	177	7.4	31	1
1967			19	153	8.1	29	0
1968			10	64	6.4	14	2
1969			14	95	6.8	16	1
1970			40	408	10.2	57t	3

Tucker Frederickson *continued*
| 1971 | | | 21 | 114 | 5.4 | 20t | 1 |
| Career | | | 128 | 1011 | 7.9 | 57t | 8 |

Antonio Freeman
1995	GB	N	8	106	13.3	28	1
1996			56	933	16.7	51t	9
Career			64	1039	16.2	51t	10
Playoffs			13	217	16.7		2

Phil Freeman
1986	TB	N	14	229	16.4	33t	2
1987			8	141	17.6	64t	2
Career			22	370	16.8	64t	4

Rocky Freitas
| 1970 | DET | N | 1 | -8 | -8.0 | -8 | 0 |

Walt French
| 1925 | POT | N | | | | | 2 |

Mitch Frerotte
| 1992 | BUF | N | 2 | 4 | 2.0 | 2t | 2 |
| Playoffs | | | 1 | 1 | 1.0 | | 1 |

Glenn Frey
1936	PHI	N	3	65	21.7		0
1937			4	19	4.8		0
Career			7	84	12.0		0

Mike Friede
1980	DET-NYG	N	22	371	16.9	48	0
1981	NYG	N	18	250	13.9	43	1
Career			40	621	15.5	48	1

Andy Friedman
| 1921 | SYR | A | | | | | 1 |

David Frisch
1993	CIN	N	6	43	7.2	12	0
1996	MIN	N	3	27	9.0	21	1
Career			9	70	7.8	21	1

Ted Fritsch
1942	GB	N	9	60	6.7	21	0
1943			2	55	27.5	32	0
1944			3	5	1.7	13	0
1945			3	13	4.3	9	0
1946			2	13	6.5	12t	1
1949			6	81	13.5	35	0
Career			25	227	9.1	35	1
Playoffs			1	28	28.0		1

Stan Fritts
1975	CIN	N	6	63	10.5	17t	2
1976			9	75	8.3	19	0
Career			15	138	9.2	19	2

Ed Frutig
1941	GB	N	2	40	20.0	34	0
1945	DET	N	2	5	2.5	3t	1
1946			8	72	9.0	17	2
Career			12	117	9.8	34	3
Playoffs			3	75	25.0		0

Irving Fryar
1984	NE	N	11	164	14.9	26	1
1985			39	670	17.2	56	7
1986			43	737	17.1	69t	6
1987			31	467	15.1	40	5
1988			33	490	14.8	80t	5
1989			29	537	18.5	52	3
1990			54	856	15.9	56	4
1991			68	1014	14.9	56t	3
1992			55	791	14.4	54t	4
1993	MIA	N	64	1010	15.8	65t	5
1994			73	1270	17.4	54t	7
1995			62	910	14.7	67t	8
1996	PHI	N	88	1195	13.6	42	11
Career			650	10111	15.6	80t	69
Playoffs			25	314	12.6		2

Phil Frye
| 1987 | MIN | N | 3 | 25 | 8.3 | 12 | 0 |

Jean Fugett

Year	Team		No	Yds	Avg	Lg	TD
1972	DAL	N	7	94	13.4	29	0
1973			9	168	18.7	48t	3
1974			4	60	15.0	24t	1
1975			38	488	12.8	54t	3
1976	WAS	N	27	334	12.4	33t	6
1977			36	631	17.5	52	5
1978			25	367	14.7	49t	7
1979			10	128	12.8	30t	3
Career			156	2270	14.6	54t	28
Playoffs			11	125	11.4		0

Charley Fuller

Year	Team		No	Yds	Avg	Lg	TD
1961	OAK	A	12	277	23.1	85	2
1962			5	67	13.4	25	0
Career			17	344	20.2	85	2

Eddie Fuller

Year	Team		No	Yds	Avg	Lg	TD
1992	BUF	N	2	17	8.5	17	0

Larry Fuller

Year	Team		No	Yds	Avg	Lg	TD
1944	WAS	N	5	82	16.4	47t	1

Darrell Fullington

Year	Team		No	Yds	Avg	Lg	TD
1992	TB	N	1	12	12.0	12	0

Brent Fullwood

Year	Team		No	Yds	Avg	Lg	TD
1987	GB	N	2	11	5.5	12	0
1988			20	128	6.4	30t	1
1989			19	214	11.3	67	0
1990			3	17	5.7	10	0
Career			44	370	8.4	67	1

Danny Fulton

Year	Team		No	Yds	Avg	Lg	TD
1979	BUF	N	2	34	17.0	18	0
1981	CLE	N	2	38	19.0	27	0
1982			1	9	9.0	9	0
Career			5	81	16.2	27	0

John Fuqua

Year	Team		No	Yds	Avg	Lg	TD
1969	NYG	N	3	11	3.7	6	0
1970	PIT	N	23	289	12.6	57t	2
1971			49	427	8.7	40t	1
1972			18	152	8.4	28	0
1973			17	150	8.8	22	0
1974			6	68	11.3	18	0
1975			18	146	8.1	21	0
1976			1	4	4.0	4	0
Career			135	1247	9.2	57t	3
Playoffs			9	108	12.0		0

Ray Fuqua

Year	Team		No	Yds	Avg	Lg	TD
1935	BKN	N	8	82	10.3		1
1936			1	2	2.0	2	0
Career			9	84	9.3	2	1

Roman Gabriel

Year	Team		No	Yds	Avg	Lg	TD
1968	LA	N	1	-5	-5.0	-5	0

Dennis Gadbois

Year	Team		No	Yds	Avg	Lg	TD
1987	NE	N	3	51	17.0	20	0

Derrick Gaffney

Year	Team		No	Yds	Avg	Lg	TD
1978	NYJ	N	38	691	18.2	50	3
1979			32	534	16.7	43	1
1980			24	397	16.5	36	2
1981			14	246	17.6	39	0
1982			11	207	18.8	45t	1
1983			17	243	14.3	35	0
1984			19	285	15.0	29	0
1987			1	10	10.0	10	0
Career			156	2613	16.8	50	7
Playoffs			9	121	13.4		1

Jim Gaffney

Year	Team		No	Yds	Avg	Lg	TD
1946	WAS	N	7	85	12.1	41t	1

Monk Gafford

Year	Team		No	Yds	Avg	Lg	TD
1946	MIA	AA	14	270	19.3	63t	4
1947	BKN	AA	8	113	14.1		0
1948			15	274	18.3	60t	4
Career			37	657	17.8	63t	8

Bobby Gage

Year	Team		No	Yds	Avg	Lg	TD
1949	PIT	N	1	8	8.0	8	0
1950			6	127	21.2	48t	2
Career			7	135	19.3	48t	2

Dave Gagnon

Year	Team		No	Yds	Avg	Lg	TD
1974	CHI	N	4	20	5.0	16	0

Derrick Gainer

Year	Team		No	Yds	Avg	Lg	TD
1990	CLE	N	7	85	12.1	20	0
1993	DAL	N	6	37	6.2	8	0
Career			13	122	9.4	20	0

Clark Gaines

Year	Team		No	Yds	Avg	Lg	TD
1976	NYJ	N	41	400	9.8	27	2
1977			55	469	8.5	31	1
1978			3	23	7.7	13	0
1979			29	219	7.6	15	0
1980			36	310	8.6	16t	3
1982	KC	N	2	17	8.5	10	0
Career			166	1438	8.7	31	6

Lawrence Gaines

Year	Team		No	Yds	Avg	Lg	TD
1976	DET	N	23	130	5.7	24	1
1978			2	16	8.0	9	0
Career			25	146	5.8	24	1

Sheldon Gaines

Year	Team		No	Yds	Avg	Lg	TD
1987	BUF	N	9	115	12.8	37	0

Wendall Gaines

Year	Team		No	Yds	Avg	Lg	TD
1995	ARI	N	14	117	8.4	22t	2

Bob Gaiters

Year	Team		No	Yds	Avg	Lg	TD
1961	NYG	N	11	54	4.9	14	1
1962	NYG-SF	N	5	47	9.4	15	0
1963	DEN	A	1	74	74.0	74t	1
Career			17	175	10.3	74t	2

Hokie Gajan

Year	Team		No	Yds	Avg	Lg	TD
1982	NO	N	3	10	3.3	9	0
1983			17	130	7.6	26	0
1984			35	288	8.2	51	2
1985			8	87	10.9	22	0
Career			63	515	8.2	51	2

Scott Galbraith

Year	Team		No	Yds	Avg	Lg	TD
1990	CLE	N	4	62	15.5	28	0
1991			27	328	12.1	42	0
1992			4	63	15.8	28	1
1993	DAL	N	1	1	1.0	1t	1
1994			4	31	7.8	15	0
1995	WAS	N	10	80	8.0	25	2
1996			8	89	11.1	30t	2
Career			58	654	11.3	42	6
Playoffs			1	1	1.0		1

Tony Galbreath

Year	Team		No	Yds	Avg	Lg	TD
1976	NO	N	54	420	7.8	35	1
1977			41	265	6.5	30	0
1978			74	582	7.9	35	2
1979			58	484	8.3	38	1
1980			57	470	8.2	21	2
1981	MIN	N	18	144	8.0	23	0
1982			17	153	9.0	32	0
1983			45	348	7.7	23	2
1984	NYG	N	37	357	9.6	37	0
1985			30	327	10.9	49	1
1986			33	268	8.1	19	0
1987			26	248	9.5	21	0
Career			490	4066	8.3	49	9
Playoffs			11	71	6.5		0

Willie Galimore

Year	Team		No	Yds	Avg	Lg	TD
1957	CHIB	N	15	201	13.4	56t	2
1958			8	151	18.9	79t	3
1959			10	125	12.5	34t	2
1960	CHI	N	3	35	11.7	33	0
1961			33	502	15.2	84t	3
1962			5	56	11.2	29	0
1963			13	131	10.1	44	0
Career			87	1201	13.8	84t	10

Hugh Gallarneau

Year	Team		No	Yds	Avg	Lg	TD
1941	CHIB	N	11	204	18.5	46	2
1942			14	291	20.8	60	3
1945			7	58	8.3	36t	1
1946			12	185	15.4	36t	1
1947			7	56	8.0	28	0
Career			51	794	15.6	60	7

Joey Galloway

Year	Team		No	Yds	Avg	Lg	TD
1995	SEA	N	67	1039	15.5	59t	7
1996			57	987	17.3	65t	7
Career			124	2026	16.3	65t	14

Lu Gambino

Year	Team		No	Yds	Avg	Lg	TD
1948	BAL	AA	6	28	4.7		0
1949			10	67	6.7		1
Career			16	95	5.9		1

Kenny Gamble

Year	Team		No	Yds	Avg	Lg	TD
1988	KC	N	1	-7	-7.0	-7	0
1989			2	2	1.0	6	0
Career			3	-5	-1.7	6	0

R.C. Gamble

Year	Team		No	Yds	Avg	Lg	TD
1968	BOS	A	11	55	5.0	16	1
1969			7	74	10.6	20	0
Career			18	129	7.2	20	1

Billy Gambrell

Year	Team		No	Yds	Avg	Lg	TD
1963	STL	N	3	63	21.0	33	0
1964			24	398	16.6	47	2
1965			9	171	19.0	59t	2
1966			24	409	17.0	49	5
1967			28	398	14.2	48t	2
1968	DET	N	28	492	17.6	50	7
Career			116	1931	16.6	59t	18

Rich Gannon

Year	Team		No	Yds	Avg	Lg	TD
1991	MIN	N	1	0	0.0	0	0

Earl Gant

Year	Team		No	Yds	Avg	Lg	TD
1979	KC	N	15	101	6.7	26	0
1980			9	68	7.6	33	0
Career			24	169	7.0	33	0

Reuben Gant

Year	Team		No	Yds	Avg	Lg	TD
1975	BUF	N	9	107	11.9	19t	2
1976			12	263	21.9	39	3
1977			41	646	15.8	39	2
1978			34	408	12.0	25	5
1979			19	245	12.9	22	2
1980			12	181	15.1	48	1
Career			127	1850	14.6	39	15

Milt Gantenbein

Year	Team		No	Yds	Avg	Lg	TD
1931	GB	N					1
1933							1
1934			10	165	16.5		1
1935			12	165	13.8		1
1936			15	221	14.7		1
1937			12	237	19.8		2
1938			12	164	13.7		1
1939			7	127	18.1		1
1940			1	12	12.0	12	0
Career			69	1091	15.8	12	8
Playoffs			4	34	8.5		2

Bob Gaona

Year	Team		No	Yds	Avg	Lg	TD
1954	PIT	N	0	25		25L	0
1957	PHI	N	1	-9	-9.0	-9	0
Career			1	16	16.0	25L	0

Bubba Garcia

Year	Team		No	Yds	Avg	Lg	TD
1980	KC	N	3	27	9.0	10	1

Carwell Gardner

Year	Team		No	Yds	Avg	Lg	TD
1991	BUF	N	3	20	6.7	11	0
1992			7	67	9.6	17	0
1993			4	50	12.5	22	1
1994			11	89	8.1	21	0
1995			2	17	8.5	13	0
1996	BAL	N	7	28	4.0	7	0
Career			34	271	8.0	22	1
Playoffs			2	-5	-2.5		0

Year	Team		No	Yds	Avg	Lg	TD

Don Garlin

Year	Team		No	Yds	Avg	Lg	TD
1949	SF	AA	6	64	10.7		0
Playoffs			1	10	10.0		1

Bill Garnaas

Year	Team		No	Yds	Avg	Lg	TD
1946	PIT	N	3	56	18.7	30t	1
1947			5	144	28.8	68t	2
Career			8	200	25.0	68t	3

Charlie Garner

Year	Team		No	Yds	Avg	Lg	TD
1994	PHI	N	8	74	9.3	28	0
1995			10	61	6.1	29	0
1996			14	92	6.6	13	0
Career			32	227	7.1	29	0

Alvin Garrett

Year	Team		No	Yds	Avg	Lg	TD
1980	NYG	N	5	69	13.8	32t	1
1982	WAS	N	1	6	6.0	6	0
1983			25	332	13.3	84	1
1984			1	5	5.0	5	0
Career			32	412	12.9	84	2
Playoffs			18	274	15.2		5

Carl Garrett

Year	Team		No	Yds	Avg	Lg	TD
1969	BOS	A	29	267	9.2	34	2
1970	BOS	N	26	216	8.3	29	0
1971	NE	N	22	265	12.0	80t	1
1972			30	410	13.7	43	0
1973	CHI	N	23	292	12.7	39	0
1974			16	132	8.3	20	1
1975	NYJ	N	19	180	9.5	20	1
1976	OAK	N	9	108	12.0	26	0
1977			8	61	7.6	13	2
Career			182	1931	10.6	80t	7
Playoffs			2	15	7.5		0

J.D. Garrett

Year	Team		No	Yds	Avg	Lg	TD
1964	BOS	A	8	101	12.6	57	0
1965			7	49	7.0	15	2
1966			1	7	7.0	7	0
1967			1	12	12.0	12	0
Career			17	169	9.9	57	2

John Garrett

Year	Team		No	Yds	Avg	Lg	TD
1989	CIN	N	2	29	14.5	18	0

Len Garrett

Year	Team		No	Yds	Avg	Lg	TD
1972	GB	N	4	66	16.5	21	0
1973	NO	N	2	30	15.0	22	0
Career			6	96	16.0	22	0
Playoffs			1	17	17.0		0

Mike Garrett

Year	Team		No	Yds	Avg	Lg	TD
1966	KC	A	15	175	11.7	36	1
1967			46	261	5.7	34t	1
1968			33	359	10.9	43t	3
1969			43	432	10.0	41	2
1970	KC-SD	N	14	131	9.4	44t	1
1971	SD	N	41	283	6.9	40	3
1972			31	245	7.9	27t	1
1973			15	124	8.3	30	1
Career			238	2010	8.4	44t	13
Playoffs			13	100	7.7		0

Reggie Garrett

Year	Team		No	Yds	Avg	Lg	TD
1975	PIT	N	13	178	13.7	45t	1

Shane Garrett

Year	Team		No	Yds	Avg	Lg	TD
1991	CIN	N	3	32	10.7	13	0

Gary Garrison

Year	Team		No	Yds	Avg	Lg	TD
1966	SD	A	46	642	14.0	36	4
1967			44	772	17.5	62	2
1968			52	1103	21.2	84t	10
1969			40	804	20.1	50	7
1970	SD	N	44	1006	22.9	67	12
1971			42	889	21.2	77t	6
1972			52	744	14.3	52t	2
1973			14	292	20.9	51	2
1974			41	785	19.1	71t	5
1975			27	438	16.2	42	2
1976			2	58	29.0	36	1
1977	HOU	N	1	5	5.0	5	0
Career			405	7538	18.6	84t	58

Walt Garrison

Year	Team		No	Yds	Avg	Lg	TD
1966	DAL	N	2	18	9.0	17	0
1967			2	17	8.5	14	0
1968			7	111	15.9	53	0
1969			13	131	10.1	25	0
1970			21	205	9.8	36	2
1971			40	396	9.9	36	1
1972			37	390	10.5	26t	3
1973			26	273	10.5	53	2
1974			34	253	7.4	30	1
Career			182	1794	9.9	53	9
Playoffs			21	159	7.6		2

Gregg Garrity

Year	Team		No	Yds	Avg	Lg	TD
1983	PIT	N	19	279	14.7	38	1
1984			2	22	11.0	12	0
1985	PHI	N	7	142	20.3	34	0
1986			12	227	18.9	34	0
1987			12	242	20.2	41	2
1988			17	208	12.2	20	1
1989			13	209	16.1	31	2
Career			82	1329	16.2	41	6
Playoffs			2	16	8.0		0

Larry Garron

Year	Team		No	Yds	Avg	Lg	TD
1960	BOS	A	1	8	8.0	8	0
1961			24	341	14.2	51	3
1962			18	236	13.1	63	3
1963			26	418	16.1	92	2
1964			40	350	8.8	52	7
1965			15	222	14.8	52	1
1966			30	416	13.9	61	5
1967			30	507	16.9	66	5
1968			1	4	4.0	4	0
Career			185	2502	13.5	92	26
Playoffs			6	126	21.0		2

Ben Garry

Year	Team		No	Yds	Avg	Lg	TD
1979	BAL	N	3	9	3.0	12	0
1980			1	9	9.0	9	0
Career			4	18	4.5	12	0

Cleveland Gary

Year	Team		No	Yds	Avg	Lg	TD
1989	LARM	N	2	13	6.5	8	0
1990			30	150	5.0	22t	1
1991			13	110	8.5	22	3
1992			52	293	5.6	22	3
1993			36	289	8.0	60t	1
1994	MIA	N	2	19	9.5	11	0
Career			135	874	6.5	60t	5

Dan Garza

Year	Team		No	Yds	Avg	Lg	TD
1949	B-NY	AA	9	193	21.4		0
1951	NYY	N	31	470	15.2	69t	4
Career			40	663	16.6	69t	4

Sam Gash

Year	Team		No	Yds	Avg	Lg	TD
1993	NE	N	14	93	6.6	15	0
1994			9	61	6.8	19	0
1995			26	242	9.3	30	1
1996			33	276	8.4	28	2
Career			82	672	8.2	30	3

Joe Gasparella

Year	Team		No	Yds	Avg	Lg	TD
1950	PIT	N	1	3	3.0	3	0

Charlie Gauer

Year	Team		No	Yds	Avg	Lg	TD
1943	P-P	N	2	18	9.0	14	0
1944	PHI	N	2	35	17.5	18	0
Career			4	53	13.3	18	0

Willie Gault

Year	Team		No	Yds	Avg	Lg	TD
1983	CHI	N	40	836	20.9	87t	8
1984			34	587	17.3	61t	6
1985			33	704	21.3	70t	1
1986			42	818	19.5	53t	5
1987			35	705	20.1	56t	7
1988	LARI	N	16	392	24.5	57	2
1989			28	690	24.6	84t	4
1990			50	985	19.7	68t	3
1991			20	346	17.3	59t	4
1992			27	508	18.8	53	4
1993			8	64	8.0	12	0
Career			333	6635	19.9	87t	44
Playoffs			21	497	23.7		3

Steve Gaunty

Year	Team		No	Yds	Avg	Lg	TD
1979	KC	N	5	87	17.4	23	1

Prentice Gautt

Year	Team		No	Yds	Avg	Lg	TD
1960	CLE	N	1	10	10.0	10	0
1961	STL	N	12	132	11.0	45	3
1962			16	240	15.0	39	0
1963			1	3	3.0	3	0
1964			9	72	8.0	15	1
1965			9	128	14.2	54	0
1966			16	114	7.1	22	1
1967			15	202	13.5	32	1
Career			79	901	11.4	54	6

Everett Gay

Year	Team		No	Yds	Avg	Lg	TD
1988	DAL	N	15	205	13.7	25	1

Gene Gedman

Year	Team		No	Yds	Avg	Lg	TD
1953	DET	N	14	121	8.6	25	0
1956			15	142	9.5	43	1
1957			10	135	13.5	47	0
1958			14	106	7.6	24t	3
Career			53	504	9.5	47	4

Chris Gedney

Year	Team		No	Yds	Avg	Lg	TD
1993	CHI	N	10	98	9.8	24	0
1994			13	157	12.1	37t	3
1995			5	52	10.4	15	0
Career			28	307	11.0	37t	3

Mark Gehring

Year	Team		No	Yds	Avg	Lg	TD
1987	HOU	N	5	64	12.8	31t	1

Bruce Gehrke

Year	Team		No	Yds	Avg	Lg	TD
1948	NYG	N	9	109	12.1	27	1

Fred Gehrke

Year	Team		No	Yds	Avg	Lg	TD
1940	CLE	N	1	-2	-2.0	-2	0
1945			8	90	11.3	23	1
1946	LA	N	11	83	7.5	21t	2
1947			6	19	3.2	11	0
1948			16	173	10.8	34	1
1949			9	140	15.6	42	2
1950	SF-CHIC		5	26	5.2	13	1
Career			56	529	9.4	42	7

Jack Gehrke

Year	Team		No	Yds	Avg	Lg	TD
1971	DEN	N	14	254	18.1	48	0

Chuck Gelatka

Year	Team		No	Yds	Avg	Lg	TD
1937	NYG	N	1	17	17.0	17	0
1938			7	106	15.1		1
1939			6	71	11.8		0
1940			6	56	9.3		0
Career			20	250	12.5	17	1
Playoffs			1	24	24.0		0

Pete Gent

Year	Team		No	Yds	Avg	Lg	TD
1965	DAL	N	16	233	14.6	20t	2
1966			27	474	17.6	84t	2
1967			9	88	9.8	16t	1
1968			16	194	12.1	22	0
Career			68	989	14.5	84t	4
Playoffs			3	28	9.3		0

Dale Gentry

Year	Team		No	Yds	Avg	Lg	TD
1946	LA	AA	24	341	14.2		3
1947			22	352	16.0	54t	2
1948			28	309	11.0		0
Career			74	1002	13.5	54t	5

Dennis Gentry

Year	Team		No	Yds	Avg	Lg	TD
1982	CHI	N	1	9	9.0	9	0
1983			2	8	4.0	6	0
1984			4	29	7.3	13	0
1985			5	77	15.4	30	0
1986			19	238	12.5	41	0
1987			17	183	10.8	38t	1
1988			33	486	14.7	45	3
1989			39	463	11.9	79t	2
1990			23	320	13.9	80t	2
1991			16	149	9.3	18	0
1992			12	114	9.5	18	0
Career			171	2076	12.1	80t	7
Playoffs			13	205	15.8		0

Year	Team		No	Yds	Avg	Lg	TD

Eddie George

Year	Team		No	Yds	Avg	Lg	TD
1996	HOU	N	23	182	7.9	17	0

Tim George

| 1973 | CIN | N | 2 | 28 | 14.0 | 19 | 0 |

John Gerak

| 1995 | MIN | N | 1 | 3 | 3.0 | 3 | 0 |

Tom Geredine

1973	ATL	N	12	231	19.3	46	1
1974			4	69	17.3	24	0
1976	LA	N	1	23	23.0	23t	1
Career			17	323	19.0	46	2

Joe Geri

1950	PIT	N	1	33	33.0	33t	1
1951			2	9	4.5	8	0
Career			3	42	14.0	33t	1

John Gesek

| 1992 | DAL | N | 1 | 4 | 4.0 | 4 | 0 |

Gorham Getchell

| 1947 | BAL | AA | 2 | 17 | 8.5 | | 0 |

Charlie Getty

| 1976 | KC | N | 1 | -5 | -5.0 | -5 | 0 |

Bill Geyer

1942	CHIB	N	1	22	22.0	22	0
1943			5	123	24.6	64	2
Career			6	145	24.2	64	2

Louie Giammona

1976	NYJ	N	15	145	9.7	28	0
1980	PHI	N	17	178	10.5	30	1
1981			6	54	9.0	19	1
1982			8	67	8.4	16	0
Career			46	444	9.7	30	2

Hal Giancanelli

1953	PHI	N	20	346	17.3	47t	2
1954			14	195	13.9	49t	4
1955			25	379	15.2	59	1
1956			10	104	10.4	18	0
Career			69	1024	14.8	59	10

Nick Giaquinto

1980	MIA	N	24	192	8.0	25	1
1981	MIA-WAS	N	12	93	7.8	25	2
1982	WAS	N	2	65	32.5	36	0
1983			27	372	13.8	35	0
Career			65	722	11.1	36	3
Playoffs			6	77	12.8		0

Jim Gibbons

1958	DET	N	25	367	14.7	35t	2
1959			31	431	13.9	38	1
1960			51	604	11.8	65t	2
1961			45	566	12.6	36	1
1962			33	318	9.6	22	2
1963			32	412	12.9	32t	1
1964			45	605	13.4	82t	8
1965			12	111	9.3	24	2
1966			1	2	2.0	2t	1
1967			10	107	10.7	21	0
1968			2	38	19.0	20	0
Career			287	3561	12.4	82t	20

Abe Gibron

| 1949 | BUF | AA | 0 | 3 | | 3L | 0 |

Joe Gibson

| 1942 | CLE | N | 6 | 79 | 13.2 | 19 | 0 |

Paul Gibson

1947	BUF	AA	8	154	19.3		0
1948			11	216	19.6		0
1949			3	32	10.7		0
Career			22	402	18.3		0
Playoffs			1	7	7.0		0

Frank Gifford

| 1952 | NYG | N | 5 | 36 | 7.2 | 11 | 0 |

Frank Gifford *continued*

1953			18	292	16.2	49t	4
1954			14	154	11.0	35t	1
1955			33	437	13.2	54	4
1956			51	603	11.8	48	4
1957			41	588	14.3	63	4
1958			29	330	11.4	41	2
1959			42	768	18.3	77t	4
1960			24	344	14.3	44t	3
1962			39	796	20.4	63t	7
1963			42	657	15.6	64	7
1964			29	429	14.8	40t	3
Career			367	5434	14.8	77t	43
Playoffs			16	242	15.1		3

Wayne Gift

| 1937 | CLE | N | 3 | 20 | 6.7 | | 0 |

Lewis Gilbert

| 1980 | PHI | N | 1 | 7 | 7.0 | 7 | 0 |

Cookie Gilchrist

1962	BUF	A	24	319	13.3	86	2
1963			24	211	8.8	42	2
1964			30	345	11.5	37	0
1965	DEN	A	18	154	8.6	29	1
1966	MIA	A	13	110	8.5	22	1
1967	DEN	A	1	-4	-4.0	-4	0
Career			110	1135	10.3	86	6
Playoffs			3	33	11.0		0

Johnny Gildea

1936	PIT	N	5	70	14.0		0
1937			3	47	15.7		0
1938	NYG	N	1	3	3.0	3	0
Career			9	120	13.3	3	0

Jimmie Giles

1977	HOU	N	17	147	8.6	17	0
1978	TB	N	23	324	14.1	38	2
1979			40	579	14.5	66t	7
1980			33	602	18.2	51	4
1981			45	786	17.5	81t	6
1982			28	499	17.8	48	3
1983			25	349	14.0	80	1
1984			24	310	12.9	38	2
1985			43	673	15.7	44	8
1986	TB-DET	N	37	376	10.2	30	4
1987	DET-PHI	N	13	157	12.1	40t	1
1988	PHI	N	6	57	9.5	17	1
1989			16	225	14.1	68t	2
Career			350	5084	14.5	81t	41
Playoffs			6	148	24.7		1

Owen Gill

1985	IND	N	5	52	10.4	20	0
1986			16	137	8.6	15	0
Career			21	189	9.0	20	0

Roger Gill

1964	PHI	N	4	58	14.5	29	0
1965			1	27	27.0	27	0
Career			5	85	17.0	29	0

Fernandars Gillespie

| 1984 | PIT | N | 1 | 12 | 12.0 | 12 | 0 |

Willie Gillespie

1986	TB	N	1	18	18.0	18	0
1987	MIN	N	2	28	14.0	14	0
Career			3	46	15.3	18	0

Jim Gillette

1945	CLE	N	6	48	8.0	15	0
1946	BOS	N	5	96	19.2	60t	1
1947	GB	N	12	224	18.7	50	1
1948	DET	N	1	8	8.0	8	0
Career			24	376	15.7	60t	2
Playoffs			2	45	22.5		1

Walker Gillette

1970	SD	N	2	21	10.5	12	0
1971			10	147	14.7	25t	2
1972	STL	N	33	550	16.7	65t	2
1973			20	244	12.2	48t	1

Walker Gillette *continued*

1974	NYG	N	29	466	16.1	72	3
1975			43	600	14.0	50	2
1976			16	263	16.4	62t	2
Career			153	2291	15.0	72	12

John Gilliam

1967	NO	N	22	264	12.0	35	1
1968			24	284	11.8	39	0
1969	STL	N	52	997	19.2	84t	9
1970			45	952	21.2	79	5
1971			42	837	19.9	54	3
1972	MIN	N	47	1035	**22.0**	66t	7
1973			42	907	21.6	54t	8
1974			26	578	22.2	80t	5
1975			50	777	15.5	46	7
1976	ATL	N	21	292	13.9	49t	2
1977	NO	N	11	133	12.1	23	1
Career			382	7056	18.5	84t	48
Playoffs			14	261	18.6		5

Horace Gillom

1947	CLE	AA	2	24	12.0		0
1948			20	295	14.8		1
1949			23	359	15.6		0
1950	CLE	N	2	54	27.0	38t	1
1951			11	164	14.9	24	0
1952			4	45	11.3	21	1
1953			7	80	11.4	23	0
1954			5	62	12.4	24	0
Career			74	1083	14.6	38t	3
Playoffs			3	52	17.3		0

Harry Gilmer

1949	WAS	N	5	37	7.4	13	0
1952			15	143	9.5	37	1
Career			20	180	9.0	37	1

Hubie Ginn

1972	MIA	N	1	23	23.0	23	0
1974			2	3	1.5	3	0
1975			3	21	7.0	8	0
Career			6	47	7.8	23	0

Paul Gipson

1969	ATL	N	4	33	8.3	18	0
1970			16	186	11.6	51t	3
1971	DET	N	1	21	21.0	21	0
Career			21	240	11.4	51t	3

Earl Girard

1948	GB	N	1	2	2.0	2	0
1949			1	13	13.0	13	0
1950			4	89	22.3	55	0
1951			10	220	22.0	75t	2
1952	DET	N	17	316	18.6	39t	2
1953			2	24	12.0	15	0
1954			27	421	15.6	41t	7
1955			23	301	13.1	34	0
1956			3	33	11.0	16	0
1957	PIT	N	21	419	20.0	46	4
Career			109	1838	16.9	75t	15
Playoffs			5	57	11.4		0

Andy Gissinger

| 1984 | SD | N | 1 | 3 | 3.0 | 3 | 0 |

Ernest Givins

1986	HOU	N	61	1062	17.4	60	3
1987			53	933	17.6	83t	6
1988			60	976	16.3	46	5
1989			55	794	14.4	48	3
1990			72	979	13.6	80t	9
1991			70	996	14.2	49	5
1992			67	787	11.7	41	10
1993			68	887	13.0	80t	4
1994			36	521	14.5	76t	1
1995	JAC	N	29	280	9.7	18	3
Career			571	8215	14.4	83t	49
Playoffs			60	774	12.9		8

Bob Gladieux

1971	NE	N	6	60	10.0	25	0
1972			19	192	10.1	31	0
Career			25	252	10.1	31	0

Year	Team		No	Yds	Avg	Lg	TD

Charles Gladman

Year	Team		No	Yds	Avg	Lg	TD
1987	TB	N	2	8	4.0	5	0

Tony Gladney

| 1987 | SF | N | 4 | 60 | 15.0 | 19 | 0 |

Joe Glamp

1948	PIT	N	9	138	15.3	39t	2
1949			1	14	14.0	14	0
Career			10	152	15.2	39t	2

Brian Glasgow

| 1987 | CHI | N | 2 | 16 | 8.0 | 11 | 0 |

Nesby Glasgow

| 1989 | SEA | N | 1 | 4 | 4.0 | 4 | 0 |

Chip Glass

1969	CLE	N	4	91	22.8	40	2
1970			19	403	21.2	78t	2
1971			1	4	4.0	4t	1
1972			5	61	12.2	24	0
1973			2	60	30.0	47	0
1974	NYG	N	3	23	7.7	11	0
Career			34	642	18.9	78t	5
Playoffs			1	11	11.0		0

Glen Glass

| 1965 | PHI | N | 15 | 201 | 13.4 | 41 | 0 |

Leland Glass

1972	GB	N	15	261	17.4	31	1
1973			11	119	10.8	23	0
Career			26	380	14.6	31	1
Playoffs			2	23	11.5		0

Bill Glassgow

| 1931 | CHIC | N | | | | | 1 |

Bob Glazebrook

| 1979 | ATL | N | 1 | 20 | 20.0 | 20 | 0 |

Terry Glenn

| 1996 | NE | N | 90 | 1132 | 12.6 | 37t | 6 |
| Playoffs | | | 12 | 164 | 13.7 | | 0 |

Fred Gloden

| 1941 | PHI | N | 2 | 13 | 6.5 | 11 | 0 |

Clyde Glosson

| 1970 | BUF | N | 2 | 16 | 8.0 | 14 | 0 |

Andrew Glover

1991	LARI	N	5	45	9.0	18	3
1992			15	178	11.9	30	1
1993			4	55	13.8	26	1
1994			33	371	11.2	27t	2
1995	OAK	N	26	220	8.5	25	3
1996			9	101	11.2	25	1
Career			92	970	10.5	30	11

Les Goble

| 1954 | CHIC | N | 1 | -1 | -1.0 | -1 | 0 |

Ed Goddard

1937	CLE-BKN	N	6	61	10.2		0
1938	CLE	N	6	128	21.3		1
Career			12	189	15.8		1

Paul Goebel

1923	COL	N					1
1924							2
Career							3

Buckets Goldberg

1939	CHIC	N	5	90	18.0		1
1940			2	29	14.5		1
1941			16	313	19.6	76	1
1942			9	108	12.0	27	0
1943			4	31	7.8	11	1
1946			17	152	8.9	22	1
1947			7	52	7.4	19	0
Career			60	775	12.9	76	5

Charles Goldenberg

1933	GB	N					1
1935			3	42	14.0		0
Career			3	42	14.0		1

Joe Golding

1947	BOS	N	6	52	8.7	24t	2
1948			9	159	17.7	34t	4
1949	NYB	N	12	78	6.5	16	2
Career			27	289	10.7	34t	8

Sam Goldman

1944	BOS	N	2	21	10.5	11	0
1946			15	154	10.3	27	0
1947			1	9	9.0	9	0
Career			18	184	10.2	27	0

Al Goldstein

| 1960 | OAK | A | 27 | 354 | 13.1 | | 1 |

Ralph Goldston

1952	PHI	N	2	12	6.0	8	0
1955			2	8	4.0	9	0
Career			4	20	5.0	9	0

Archie Golembeski

| 1926 | PRO | N | | | | | 1 |

Bill Gompers

| Playoffs | | | | 66 | | | 1 |

George Gonda

| 1942 | PIT | N | 1 | 7 | 7.0 | 7 | 0 |

Bob Gonya

| 1934 | PHI | N | | | | | 1 |

Leon Gonzalez

1985	DAL	N	3	28	9.3	13	0
1987	ATL	N	3	40	13.3	22	0
Career			6	68	11.3	22	0

Royce Goodbread

| 1930 | FRA | N | | | | | 1 |

John Goode

| 1984 | STL | N | 3 | 23 | 7.7 | 10 | 0 |

Kerry Goode

| 1988 | TB | N | 7 | 68 | 9.7 | 22 | 0 |

Rob Goode

1949	WAS	N	16	279	17.4	54	0
1950			19	160	8.4	56t	0
1951			3	45	15.0	26	0
1954			4	4	1.0	10	0
1955	WAS-PHI	N	11	152	13.8	50	0
Career			53	640	12.1	56t	1

Eugene Goodlow

1983	NO	N	41	487	11.9	26	2
1984			22	281	12.8	23	3
1985			32	603	18.8	76t	3
1986			20	306	15.3	29t	2
Career			115	1677	14.6	76t	10

Les Goodman

1973	GB	N	2	19	9.5	12	0
1974			5	19	3.8	12	0
Career			7	38	5.4	12	0

Clyde Goodnight

1945	GB	N	7	283	40.4	75t	4
1946			16	308	19.3	51t	1
1947			38	593	15.6	69t	6
1948			28	448	16.0	57	3
1949	WAS	N	11	150	13.6	30	0
1950			12	185	15.4	33	2
Career			112	1967	17.6	75t	16

Robert Goodridge

| 1968 | MIN | N | 1 | 5 | 5.0 | 5 | 0 |

Hunter Goodwin

| 1996 | MIN | N | 1 | 24 | 24.0 | 24 | 0 |

Ronnie Goodwin

1963	PHI	N	15	215	14.3	35t	4
1964			23	335	14.6	44t	3
1965			18	252	14.0	35	1
1966			16	212	13.3	30	1
1967			6	65	10.8	23	0
Career			78	1079	13.8	44t	9

Tod Goodwin

1935	NYG	N	26	432	16.6		4
1936			7	79	11.3		2
Career			33	511	15.5		6
Playoffs			2	29	14.5		0

Dick Gordon

1965	CHI	N	13	279	21.5	51	3
1966			15	210	14.0	40	1
1967			31	534	17.2	93t	5
1968			29	477	16.4	51t	4
1969			36	414	11.5	41t	4
1970			71	1026	14.5	69t	13
1971			43	610	14.2	45	5
1972	LA	N	3	29	9.7	17	1
1974	SD	N	2	15	7.5	17	0
Career			243	3594	14.8	93t	36

Gordon Gore

| 1939 | DET | N | 1 | 20 | 20.0 | 20 | 0 |

Pete Gorgone

| Playoffs | | | 1 | -2 | -2.0 | | 0 |

Paul Gorrill

| 1926 | COL | N | | | | | 1 |

Preston Gothard

1985	PIT	N	6	83	13.8	24	0
1986			21	246	11.7	34	1
1987			2	9	4.5	7	1
1988			12	121	10.1	26	1
Career			41	459	11.2	34	3

Jim Grabowski

1966	GB	N	4	13	3.3	7	0
1967			12	171	14.3	53	1
1968			18	210	11.7	67t	1
1969			12	98	8.2	25	1
1970			19	83	4.4	19	0
1971	CHI	N	17	100	5.9	25	0
Career			82	675	8.2	67t	3

Sam Graddy

1988	DEN	N	1	30	30.0	30	0
1990	LARI	N	1	47	47.0	47t	1
1991			6	195	32.5	80t	1
1992			10	205	20.5	48	1
Career			18	477	26.5	80t	3

Art Graham

1963	BOS	A	21	559	26.6	77	5
1964			45	720	16.0	80	6
1965			25	316	12.6	33	0
1966			51	673	13.2	42	4
1967			41	606	14.8	79t	4
1968			16	242	15.1	34	1
Career			199	3116	15.7	80	20
Playoffs			3	90	30.0		0

Hason Graham

1995	NE	N	10	156	15.6	37t	2
1996			5	64	12.8	23	0
Career			15	220	14.7	37t	2

Jeff Graham

1991	PIT	N	2	21	10.5	15	0
1992			49	711	14.5	51	1
1993			38	579	15.2	51	0
1994	CHI	N	68	944	13.9	76t	4
1995			82	1301	15.9	51	4

Jeff Graham *continued*

Year	Team		No	Yds	Avg	Lg	TD
1996	NYJ	N	50	788	15.8	78t	6
Career			289	4344	15.0	78t	15
Playoffs			15	237	15.8		1

Scottie Graham

Year	Team		No	Yds	Avg	Lg	TD
1993	MIN	N	7	46	6.6	11	0
1994			1	1	1.0	1	0
1995			4	30	7.5	11	0
1996			7	48	6.9	18	0
Career			19	125	6.6	18	0
Playoffs			3	18	6.0		0

Ken Grandberry

Year	Team		No	Yds	Avg	Lg	TD
1974	CHI	N	30	212	7.1	40	0

Sonny Grandelius

Year	Team		No	Yds	Avg	Lg	TD
1953	NYG	N	15	80	5.3	26	0

Garland Grange

Year	Team		No	Yds	Avg	Lg	TD
1929	CHIB	N					2
1931							1
Career							3

Red Grange

Year	Team		No	Yds	Avg	Lg	TD
1926	NY	A					3
1930	CHIB	N					2
1931							2
1932			15	228	15.2		4
1933			3	74	24.7		0
1934			2	46	23.0		2
Career			20	348	17.4		13

Hoyle Granger

Year	Team		No	Yds	Avg	Lg	TD
1966	HOU	A	12	104	8.7	26	1
1967			31	300	9.7	43t	3
1968			26	361	13.9	55	0
1969			27	330	12.2	53	1
1970	HOU	N	11	118	10.7	22	0
1971	NO	N	12	52	4.3	11	0
1972	HOU	N	15	74	4.9	20	0
Career			134	1339	10.0	55	5
Playoffs			4	21	5.3		0

Norm Granger

Year	Team		No	Yds	Avg	Lg	TD
1987	ATL	N	2	34	17.0	26	0

Dave Grannell

Year	Team		No	Yds	Avg	Lg	TD
1974	SD	N	3	51	17.0	22	0

Bud Grant

Year	Team		No	Yds	Avg	Lg	TD
1952	PHI	N	56	997	17.8	84t	7

Frank Grant

Year	Team		No	Yds	Avg	Lg	TD
1973	WAS	N	1	12	12.0	12t	1
1974			9	196	21.8	69	1
1975			41	776	18.9	96t	8
1976			50	818	16.4	53t	5
1977			34	480	14.1	59t	3
1978	WAS-TB	N	14	204	14.6	23	0
Career			149	2486	16.7	96t	18
Playoffs			7	85	12.1		1

Otis Grant

Year	Team		No	Yds	Avg	Lg	TD
1983	LARM	N	12	221	18.4	57	1
1984			9	64	7.1	15	0
1987	PHI	N	16	280	17.5	41	0
Career			37	565	15.3	57	1

Rupert Grant

Year	Team		No	Yds	Avg	Lg	TD
1995	NE	N	1	4	4.0	4	0

Willie Grate

Year	Team		No	Yds	Avg	Lg	TD
1969	BUF	A	1	19	19.0	19t	1
1970	BUF	N	7	147	21.0	32	2
Career			8	166	20.8	32	3

Earnest Gray

Year	Team		No	Yds	Avg	Lg	TD
1979	NYG	N	28	537	19.2	53t	4
1980			52	777	14.9	50t	10
1981			22	360	16.4	45	2
1982			25	426	17.0	47	4
1983			78	1139	14.6	62	5
1984			38	529	13.9	31	2

Earnest Gray *continued*

Year	Team		No	Yds	Avg	Lg	TD
1985	STL	N	3	22	7.3	12	0
Career			246	3790	15.4	62	27
Playoffs			6	150	25.0		1

Mel Gray

Year	Team		No	Yds	Avg	Lg	TD
1971	STL	N	18	534	29.7	80t	4
1972			3	62	20.7	33	0
1973			29	513	17.7	80t	7
1974			39	770	19.7	80t	6
1975			48	926	19.3	74t	**11**
1976			36	686	19.1	77t	5
1977			38	782	20.6	69t	5
1978			44	871	19.8	74	1
1979			25	447	17.9	78t	1
1980			40	709	17.7	69t	3
1981			27	310	11.5	41t	2
1982			4	34	8.5	13	0
Career			351	6644	18.9	80t	45
Playoffs			8	129	16.1		1

Mel Gray

Year	Team		No	Yds	Avg	Lg	TD
1986	NO	N	2	45	22.5	38	0
1987			6	30	5.0	12	0
1989	DET	N	2	47	23.5	30	0
1991			3	42	14.0	31	0
Career			13	164	12.6	38	0

Oscar Gray

Year	Team		No	Yds	Avg	Lg	TD
1996	SEA	N	1	5	5.0	5	0

Sam Gray

Year	Team		No	Yds	Avg	Lg	TD
1946	PIT	N	1	20	20.0	20	0

Art Green

Year	Team		No	Yds	Avg	Lg	TD
1972	NO	N	7	49	7.0	15	0

Boyce Green

Year	Team		No	Yds	Avg	Lg	TD
1983	CLE	N	25	167	6.7	33	1
1984			12	124	10.3	44t	1
1986	KC	N	19	137	7.2	17	0
Career			56	428	7.6	44t	2
Playoffs			5	7	1.4		0

Dave Green

Year	Team		No	Yds	Avg	Lg	TD
1976	TB	N	1	9	9.0	9	0

Donnie Green

Year	Team		No	Yds	Avg	Lg	TD
1974	BUF	N	1	0	0.0	0	0

Eric Green

Year	Team		No	Yds	Avg	Lg	TD
1990	PIT	N	34	387	11.4	46	7
1991			41	582	14.2	49	6
1992			14	152	10.9	24	2
1993			63	942	15.0	71t	5
1994			46	618	13.4	46	4
1995	MIA	N	43	499	11.6	31t	5
1996	BAL	N	15	150	10.0	23	1
Career			256	3330	13.0	71t	28
Playoffs			9	138	15.3		2

Ernie Green

Year	Team		No	Yds	Avg	Lg	TD
1962	CLE	N	17	194	11.4	65	1
1963			28	305	10.9	35	3
1964			25	283	11.3	32	4
1965			25	298	11.9	69	2
1966			45	445	9.9	31t	6
1967			39	369	9.5	41t	2
1968			16	142	8.9	62t	2
Career			195	2036	10.4	69	20
Playoffs			3	18	6.0		0

Gaston Green

Year	Team		No	Yds	Avg	Lg	TD
1988	LARM	N	6	57	9.5	19	0
1989			1	-5	-5.0	-5	0
1990			2	23	11.5	16t	1
1991	DEN	N	13	78	6.0	13	0
1992			10	79	7.9	33	0
Career			32	232	7.3	33	1
Playoffs			1	1	1.0		0

Harold Green

Year	Team		No	Yds	Avg	Lg	TD
1990	CIN	N	12	90	7.5	22	1
1991			16	136	8.5	18	0

Harold Green *continued*

Year	Team		No	Yds	Avg	Lg	TD
1992			41	214	5.2	19	0
1993			22	115	5.2	16	0
1994			27	267	9.9	34	1
1995			27	182	6.7	24	1
1996	STL	N	37	246	6.6	19	1
Career			182	1250	6.9	34	4
Playoffs			2	15	7.5		1

Jerry Green

Year	Team		No	Yds	Avg	Lg	TD
1960	BOS	A	3	52	17.3		0

Jessie Green

Year	Team		No	Yds	Avg	Lg	TD
1979	SEA	N	1	9	9.0	9	0
1980			4	47	11.8	19	0
Career			5	56	11.2	19	0

Johnny Green

Year	Team		No	Yds	Avg	Lg	TD
1960	BUF	A	1	0	0.0	0	0

Mark Green

Year	Team		No	Yds	Avg	Lg	TD
1989	CHI	N	5	48	9.6	21	0
1990			4	26	6.5	10t	1
1991			6	54	9.0	15	0
1992			7	85	12.1	43	0
Career			22	213	9.7	43	1

Paul Green

Year	Team		No	Yds	Avg	Lg	TD
1992	SEA	N	9	67	7.4	15	1
1993			23	178	7.7	20	1
1994			30	208	6.9	20	1
1996	NO	N	7	91	13.0	23	0
Career			69	544	7.9	23	3

Robert Green

Year	Team		No	Yds	Avg	Lg	TD
1992	WAS	N	1	5	5.0	5	0
1993	CHI	N	13	63	4.8	9	0
1994			24	199	8.3	39t	2
1995			28	246	8.8	28	0
1996			13	78	6.0	18	0
Career			79	591	7.5	39t	2
Playoffs			6	48	8.0		0

Roy Green

Year	Team		No	Yds	Avg	Lg	TD
1979	STL	N	1	15	15.0	15	0
1981			33	708	21.5	60	4
1982			32	453	14.2	42	3
1983			78	1227	15.7	71t	14
1984			78	**1555**	19.9	83t	12
1985			50	693	13.9	47	5
1986			42	517	12.3	48t	6
1987			43	731	17.0	57	4
1988	PHX	N	68	1097	16.1	52	7
1989			44	703	16.0	59t	7
1990			53	797	15.0	54	4
1991	PHI	N	29	364	12.6	42	0
1992			8	105	13.1	21	0
Career			559	8965	16.0	83t	66
Playoffs			10	127	12.7		0

Tony Green

Year	Team		No	Yds	Avg	Lg	TD
1978	WAS	N	4	89	22.3	34	0

Van Green

Year	Team		No	Yds	Avg	Lg	TD
1974	CLE	N	1	27	27.0	27	0
1975			1	-1	-1.0	-1	0
Career			2	26	13.0	27	0

Willie Green

Year	Team		No	Yds	Avg	Lg	TD
1991	DET	N	39	592	15.2	73t	7
1992			33	586	17.8	73t	5
1993			28	462	16.5	47	2
1994	TB	N	9	150	16.7	28	0
1995	CAR	N	47	882	18.8	89t	7
1996			46	614	13.3	50	3
Career			202	3286	16.3	89t	23
Playoffs			24	306	12.8		4

Woody Green

Year	Team		No	Yds	Avg	Lg	TD
1974	KC	N	26	247	9.5	69t	1
1975			23	215	9.3	28	1
1976			9	100	11.1	31	0
Career			58	562	9.7	69t	2

Danny Greene

Year	Team		No	Yds	Avg	Lg	TD
1985	SEA	N	2	10	5.0	7	1

John Greene

Year	Team		No	Yds	Avg	Lg	TD
1945	DET	N	26	550	21.2	63t	5
1946			20	289	14.4	88t	2
1947			38	621	16.3	47	5
1948			25	595	23.8	83	5
1949			42	542	12.9	28	7
1950			22	368	16.7	46t	2
Career			173	2965	17.1	88t	26

Scott Greene

Year	Team		No	Yds	Avg	Lg	TD
1996	CAR	N	2	7	3.5	6	1

Tracy Greene

Year	Team		No	Yds	Avg	Lg	TD
1994	KC	N	6	69	11.5	20	1

Bobby Greenhalgh

Year	Team		No	Yds	Avg	Lg	TD
1949	NYG	N	3	23	7.7	14	0

Don Greenwood

Year	Team		No	Yds	Avg	Lg	TD
1945	CLE	N	3	72	24.0	42	0
1946	CLE	AA	4	0	0.0		0
1947			5	49	9.8		0
Career			12	121	10.1	42	0
Playoffs			0	2	0.0		0

Jim Greer

Year	Team		No	Yds	Avg	Lg	TD
1960	DEN	A	22	284	12.9	33	1

Terry Greer

Year	Team		No	Yds	Avg	Lg	TD
1986	CLE	N	3	51	17.0	22	0
1987	SF	N	6	111	18.5	50	1
1988			8	120	15.0	31	0
1989			1	26	26.0	26	0
1990	DET	N	20	332	16.6	68t	3
Career			38	640	16.8	68t	4

Ben Gregory

Year	Team		No	Yds	Avg	Lg	TD
1968	BUF	A	5	21	4.2	8	0

Bruce Gregory

Year	Team		No	Yds	Avg	Lg	TD
1926	DET	N					2

Glynn Gregory

Year	Team		No	Yds	Avg	Lg	TD
1961	DAL	N	3	30	10.0	13	0
1962			3	70	23.3	44	0
Career			6	100	16.7	44	0

Ken Gregory

Year	Team		No	Yds	Avg	Lg	TD
1963	NY	A	9	90	10.0	16	0

Bob Gresham

Year	Team		No	Yds	Avg	Lg	TD
1971	NO	N	17	203	11.9	37	0
1972			29	192	6.6	54	0
1973	HOU	N	28	244	8.7	62t	1
1974			3	19	6.3	9	0
1975	NYJ	N	2	4	2.0	6	0
1976			11	66	6.0	13	0
Career			90	728	8.1	62t	1

Marrio Grier

Year	Team		No	Yds	Avg	Lg	TD
1996	NE	N	1	8	8.0	8	0

Archie Griffin

Year	Team		No	Yds	Avg	Lg	TD
1976	CIN	N	16	138	8.6	23	0
1977			28	240	8.6	24	0
1978			35	284	8.1	27	3
1979			43	417	9.7	52t	2
1980			28	196	7.0	19	0
1981			20	160	8.0	17	1
1982			22	172	7.8	22	0
Career			192	1607	8.4	52t	6
Playoffs			3	14	4.7		1

Don Griffin

Year	Team		No	Yds	Avg	Lg	TD
1946	CHI	AA	5	28	5.6		0

Keith Griffin

Year	Team		No	Yds	Avg	Lg	TD
1984	WAS	N	8	43	5.4	8	0
1985			37	285	7.7	28	0
1986			11	110	10.0	28	0
1987			3	13	4.3	6t	1

Keith Griffin *continued*

Year	Team		No	Yds	Avg	Lg	TD
1988			2	9	4.5	5	1
Career			61	460	7.5	28	2
Playoffs			1	8	8.0		0

Forrest Griffith

Year	Team		No	Yds	Avg	Lg	TD
1950	NYG	N	1	26	26.0	26	0
1951			2	19	9.5	22	0
Career			3	45	15.0	26	0

Howard Griffith

Year	Team		No	Yds	Avg	Lg	TD
1994	LARM	N	16	113	7.1	13	1
1995	CAR	N	11	63	5.7	15	1
1996			27	223	8.3	21	1
Career			54	399	7.4	21	3
Playoffs			5	24	4.8		1

Rich Griffith

Year	Team		No	Yds	Avg	Lg	TD
1995	JAC	N	16	243	15.2	39	0
1996			5	53	10.6	18	0
Career			21	296	14.1	39	0

Johnny Grigas

Year	Team		No	Yds	Avg	Lg	TD
1943	CHIC	N	19	225	11.8	39	0
1944	C-P	N	2	33	16.5	36	0
1945	BOS	N	5	59	11.8	29	0
1946			3	61	20.3	44t	1
1947			1	1	1.0	1	0
Career			30	379	12.6	44t	1

Forrest Grigg

Year	Team		No	Yds	Avg	Lg	TD
1949	CLE	AA	0	2		2L	0

Tex Grigg

Year	Team		No	Yds	Avg	Lg	TD
1923	CAN	N					1

Billy Griggs

Year	Team		No	Yds	Avg	Lg	TD
1987	NYJ	N	2	17	8.5	13	1
1988			14	133	9.5	21	0
1989			9	112	12.4	23	0
Career			25	262	10.5	23	1
Playoffs			1	6	6.0		1

Hal Griggs

Year	Team		No	Yds	Avg	Lg	TD
1926	AKR	N					1

Frank Grigonis

Year	Team		No	Yds	Avg	Lg	TD
1942	DET	N	1	17	17.0	17	0

Bob Grim

Year	Team		No	Yds	Avg	Lg	TD
1967	MIN	N	6	108	18.0	26	1
1969			10	155	15.5	44	1
1970			23	287	12.5	35	0
1971			45	691	15.4	55t	7
1972	NYG	N	5	67	13.4	17	1
1973			37	593	16.0	48	2
1974			28	466	16.6	53	2
1975	CHI	N	28	374	13.4	57	2
1976	MIN	N	9	108	12.0	27	0
1977			3	65	21.7	23	0
Career			194	2914	15.0	55t	16
Playoffs			7	121	17.3		1

Billy Joe Grimes

Year	Team		No	Yds	Avg	Lg	TD
1949	LA	AA	13	189	14.5		2
1950	GB	N	17	261	15.4	96t	1
1951			15	170	11.3	38t	1
Career			45	620	13.8	96t	4

George Grimes

Year	Team		No	Yds	Avg	Lg	TD
1948	DET	N	1	17	17.0	17t	1

Clif Groce

Year	Team		No	Yds	Avg	Lg	TD
1996	IND	N	13	106	8.2	24	0

Steve Grogan

Year	Team		No	Yds	Avg	Lg	TD
1981	NE	N	2	27	13.5	16	0
1983			1	-8	-8.0	-8	0
Career			3	19	6.3	16	0

Bill Groman

Year	Team		No	Yds	Avg	Lg	TD
1960	HOU	A	72	**1473**	**20.5**	92t	12
1961			50	1175	**23.5**	80	**17**
1962			21	328	15.6	54	3

Bill Groman *continued*

Year	Team		No	Yds	Avg	Lg	TD
1963	DEN	A	27	437	16.2	74	3
1964	BUF	A	4	68	17.0	22	1
Career			174	3481	20.0	92t	36
Playoffs			6	69	11.5		1

Mel Groomes

Year	Team		No	Yds	Avg	Lg	TD
1948	DET	N	2	18	9.0	10	0
1949			3	33	11.0	20	1
Career			5	51	10.2	20	1

Elois Grooms

Year	Team		No	Yds	Avg	Lg	TD
1977	NO	N	1	3	3.0	3t	1

Earl Gros

Year	Team		No	Yds	Avg	Lg	TD
1963	GB	N	1	19	19.0	19	0
1964	PHI	N	29	234	8.1	29	0
1965			29	271	9.3	37	2
1966			18	214	11.9	48	2
1967	PIT	N	19	175	9.2	22	0
1968			27	211	7.8	21t	3
1969			17	131	7.7	20	3
1970	NO	N	2	0	0.0	1	0
Career			142	1255	8.8	48	10

Jack Grossman

Year	Team		No	Yds	Avg	Lg	TD
1932	BKN	N					3
1934			10	158	15.8		1
Career			10	158	15.8		4

Randy Grossman

Year	Team		No	Yds	Avg	Lg	TD
1974	PIT	N	13	164	12.6	32	0
1975			11	135	12.3	21	1
1976			15	181	12.1	35	1
1977			5	57	11.4	20	0
1978			37	448	12.1	26	1
1979			12	217	18.1	54	1
1980			23	293	12.7	35	0
1981			3	19	6.3	14t	1
Career			119	1514	12.7	54	5

Rex Grossman

Year	Team		No	Yds	Avg	Lg	TD
1950	BAL	N	1	4	4.0	4	0
Playoffs			15	186	12.4		1

George Grosvenor

Year	Team		No	Yds	Avg	Lg	TD
1936	CHIB-CHIC	N	1	6	6.0		0

Jeff Groth

Year	Team		No	Yds	Avg	Lg	TD
1979	HOU	N	1	6	6.0	6	0
1980			4	47	11.8	18	0
1981	NO	N	20	380	19.0	54	1
1982			30	383	12.8	39	1
1983			49	585	11.9	42	1
1984			33	487	14.8	31	0
1985			15	238	15.9	56t	2
Career			152	2126	14.0	56t	5

Roger Grove

Year	Team		No	Yds	Avg	Lg	TD
1931	GB	N					1
1932							3
1933			15	217	14.5		0
1934							3
Career			15	217	14.5		7

Lou Groza

Year	Team		No	Yds	Avg	Lg	TD
1950	CLE	N	1	23	23.0	23t	1

Al Grygo

Year	Team		No	Yds	Avg	Lg	TD
1944	CHIB	N	5	42	8.4	15	0
1945			5	68	13.6	33t	1
Career			10	110	11.0	33t	1

Darrell Grymes

Year	Team		No	Yds	Avg	Lg	TD
1987	DET	N	9	140	15.6	36t	2

Albert Guarnieri

Year	Team		No	Yds	Avg	Lg	TD
1924	BUF	N					2

Scotty Gudmundson

Year	Team		No	Yds	Avg	Lg	TD
1945	BOS	N	1	-8	-8.0	-8	0

Jim Gueno

Year	Team		No	Yds	Avg	Lg	TD
1979	GB	N	1	23	23.0	23	0

Year	Team		No	Yds	Avg	Lg	TD

Terry Guess

Year	Team		No	Yds	Avg	Lg	TD
1996	NO	N	2	69	34.5	57t	1

Roy Guffey

| 1926 | BUF | N | | | | | 1 |

Eric Guliford

1993	MIN	N	1	45	45.0	45	0
1995	CAR	N	29	444	15.3	49	1
Career			30	489	16.3	49	1

George Gulyanics

1947	CHIB	N	3	22	7.3	16	0
1948			8	130	16.3	36t	1
1949			16	165	10.3	34	1
1950			12	137	11.4	42	0
1951			13	146	11.2	32	0
Career			52	600	11.5	42	2
Playoffs			6	67	11.2		0

Mike Guman

1980	LA	N	14	131	9.4	41	0
1981			18	130	7.2	14	0
1982	LARM		31	310	10.0	46	0
1983			34	347	10.2	60	4
1984			19	161	8.5	29	0
1985			3	23	7.7	11	0
1986			9	68	7.6	13	0
1987			22	263	12.0	33	0
Career			150	1433	9.6	60	4
Playoffs			6	34	5.7		0

Mike Gussie

| 1940 | BKN | N | 1 | 9 | 9.0 | 9 | 1 |

Jim Gustafson

1986	MIN	N	5	61	12.2	18	2
1987			4	55	13.8	23	0
1988			15	231	15.4	47	1
1989			14	144	10.3	22	2
Career			38	491	12.9	47	5
Playoffs			6	128	21.3		0

Ace Gutowsky

1936	DET	N	1	30	30.0	30	0
1938			1	25	25.0	25	0
Career			2	55	27.5	30	0

Joe Guyon

| 1922 | OOR | N | | | | | 2 |

Bruno Haas

| 1921 | CLE | A | | | | | 1 |

Joey Hackett

1986	DEN	N	3	48	16.0	19	0
1988	GB	N	1	2	2.0	2t	1
Career			4	50	12.5	19	1

Elmer Hackney

1940	PHI	N	2	4	2.0		0
1941	PIT	N	1	10	10.0	10	0
1942	DET	N	3	22	7.3	12	0
1943			5	51	10.2	16	0
1944			7	163	23.3	10t	1
Career			18	250	13.9	16	1

Michael Haddix

1983	PHI	N	23	254	11.0	34	0
1984			33	231	7.0	22	0
1985			43	330	7.7	17	0
1986			26	150	5.8	29	0
1987			7	58	8.3	23	0
1988			12	82	6.8	14	0
1989	GB	N	15	111	7.4	23	1
1990			13	94	7.2	28	2
Career			172	1310	7.6	34	3
Playoffs			2	23	11.5		0

Al Haddon

1925	DET	N					3
1926							1
Career							4

John Hadl

1966	SD	A	2	-13	-6.5	4	0
1972	SD	N	1	4	4.0	4	0
Career			3	-9	-3.0		0

James Hadnot

1980	KC	N	15	97	6.5	18	0
1981			23	215	9.3	20	0
1982			14	96	6.9	28	0
1983			2	18	9.0	16	0
Career			54	426	7.9	28	0

Bernie Hafen

| 1949 | DET | N | 1 | 10 | 10.0 | 10 | 0 |

Mike Haffner

1968	DEN	A	12	232	19.3	52	1
1969			35	563	16.1	46	5
1970	DEN	N	12	196	16.3	28t	1
Career			59	991	16.8	52	7

Roger Hagberg

1965	OAK	A	12	121	10.1	18	0
1966			21	248	11.8	37	1
1967			11	114	10.4	25	1
1968			8	78	9.8	22	1
1969			6	84	14.0	20	1
Career			58	645	11.1	37	4

Rudy Hagberg

| 1929 | BUF | N | | | | | 3 |

Jack Hagerty

1926	NYG	N					1
1927							1
1929							2
1930							3
Career							7

Isaac Hagins

1977	TB	N	15	196	13.1	56	0
1978			6	65	10.8	21	0
1979			39	692	17.7	57	3
1980			23	364	15.8	48	2
Career			83	1317	15.9	57	5
Playoffs			4	76	19.0		0

Mac Haik

1968	HOU	A	32	584	18.3	59t	8
1969			27	375	13.9	42	1
1970	HOU	N	17	190	11.2	35	0
Career			76	1149	15.1	59t	9
Playoffs			2	42	21.0		0

By Haines

| 1937 | PIT | N | 2 | 17 | 8.5 | | 0 |

Hinkey Haines

1925	NY	N					2
1926	NYG	N					1
1927							4
Career							7

Kris Haines

| 1980 | CHI | N | 4 | 83 | 20.8 | 35 | 0 |

Russell Hairston

| 1987 | PIT | N | 2 | 16 | 8.0 | 11 | 1 |

George Halas

1920	DEC	A					2
1921							3
1922	CHIB	N					1
1927							1
1928							1
Career							8

Dick Haley

1959	WAS	N	2	14	7.0	8	0
1960			3	21	7.0	11	0
1961	MIN	N	3	43	14.3	22	0
Career			8	78	9.8	22	0

Eddie Halicki

1929	FRA	N					3
1930							1
Career							4

Charlie Hall

| 1976 | GB | N | 1 | 18 | 18.0 | 18 | 0 |

Dino Hall

1979	CLE	N	2	14	7.0	8	0
1982			5	78	15.6	31	1
1983			4	33	8.3	18	0
Career			11	125	11.4	31	1

Forrest Hall

| 1948 | SF | AA | 4 | 87 | 21.8 | | 0 |

Irv Hall

| 1942 | PHI | N | 2 | 18 | 9.0 | 14 | 0 |

Johnny Hall

1940	CHIC	N	4	111	27.8		2
1941			16	302	18.9	80	2
1942	DET	N	1	42	42.0	42	0
1943	CHIC	N	7	82	11.7	67	1
Career			28	537	19.2	80	5

Ken Hall

1959	CHIC	N	4	60	15.0	31t	1
1961	HOU-STL	A-N	4	58	14.5	20t	1
Career			8	118	14.8	31t	2

Parker Hall

1939	CLE	N	1	-16	-16.0	-16	0
1946	SF	AA	2	25	12.5		0
Career			3	9	3.0	-16	0

Pete Hall

| 1961 | NYG | N | 2 | 22 | 11.0 | 20 | 0 |

Ron Hall

1987	TB	N	16	169	10.6	29	1
1988			39	555	14.2	37	0
1989			30	331	11.0	32	2
1990			31	464	15.0	54t	2
1991			31	284	9.2	24	0
1992			39	351	9.0	32	4
1993			23	268	11.7	37t	1
1994	DET	N	10	106	10.6	18	0
1995			11	81	7.4	15	0
Career			230	2609	11.3	54t	10

Tom Hall

1963	DET	N	3	29	9.7	23t	0
1964	MIN	N	23	325	14.1	32	2
1965			15	287	19.1	69	2
1966			23	271	11.8	30	2
1967	NO	N	19	249	13.1	21	0
1968	MIN	N	19	298	15.7	37	1
1969			1	12	12.0	12	0
Career			103	1471	14.3	69	8

Death Halladay

1923	RAC	N					1
1924							1
Career							2

Paul Halleck

| 1937 | CLE | N | 3 | 57 | 19.0 | | 0 |

Ty Hallock

1993	DET	N	8	88	11.0	24	2
1994			7	75	10.7	21	0
1996	JAC	N	1	5	5.0	5	0
Career			16	168	10.5	24	2
Playoffs			1	15	15.0		0

Johnny Haman

| 1940 | CLE | N | 1 | 5 | 5.0 | 5 | 0 |

Andy Hamilton

| 1973 | KC | N | 2 | 35 | 17.5 | 20 | 0 |
| 1974 | | | 2 | 25 | 12.5 | 19 | 0 |

Andy Hamilton *continued*

Year	Team		No	Yds	Avg	Lg	TD
1975	NO	N	12	210	17.5	44	0
Career			16	270	16.9	44	0

Ray Hamilton

Year	Team		No	Yds	Avg	Lg	TD
1938	CLE	N	10	187	18.7		0
1939	DET	N	3	53	17.7		0
1944	CLE	N	3	113	37.7	70t	1
1945			4	50	12.5	14	0
1946	LA	N	8	92	11.5	16	0
1947			12	193	16.1	39	1
Career			40	688	17.2	70t	2

Mal Hammack

Year	Team		No	Yds	Avg	Lg	TD
1955	CHIC	N	5	13	2.6	10	0
1957			1	14	14.0	14	0
1958			3	11	3.7	13	0
1959			4	69	17.3	20	0
1960	STL	N	4	36	9.0	26	0
1961			5	70	14.0	26	0
1962			4	27	6.8	15	0
1963			1	15	15.0	15	0
Career			27	255	9.4	26	0

Bobby Hammond

Year	Team		No	Yds	Avg	Lg	TD
1977	NYG	N	19	136	7.2	28	0
1978			20	173	8.7	26	2
1979	WAS	N	2	16	8.0	12	0
1980			24	203	8.5	38	1
Career			65	528	8.1	38	3

Gary Hammond

Year	Team		No	Yds	Avg	Lg	TD
1973	STL	N	4	39	9.8	23	0
1974			2	14	7.0	9	0
1975			2	6	3.0	10	0
1976			1	5	5.0	5	0
Career			9	64	7.1	23	0
Playoffs			1	10	10.0		0

Dave Hampton

Year	Team		No	Yds	Avg	Lg	TD
1969	GB	N	15	216	14.4	50	2
1970			7	23	3.3	12	0
1971			3	37	12.3	19t	1
1972	ATL	N	23	244	10.6	43	1
1973			25	273	10.9	22	1
1974			13	111	8.5	21	0
1975			21	195	9.3	24	1
1976	PHI	N	12	57	4.8	19	0
Career			119	1156	9.7	50	6

Lorenzo Hampton

Year	Team		No	Yds	Avg	Lg	TD
1985	MIA	N	8	56	7.0	15	0
1986			61	446	7.3	19	3
1987			23	223	9.7	24	0
1988			23	204	8.9	39t	3
1989			8	25	3.1	12	0
Career			123	954	7.8	39t	6

Rodney Hampton

Year	Team		No	Yds	Avg	Lg	TD
1990	NYG	N	32	274	8.6	27t	2
1991			43	283	6.6	19	0
1992			28	215	7.7	31	0
1993			18	210	11.7	62	0
1994			14	103	7.4	17	0
1995			24	142	5.9	18	0
1996			15	82	5.5	16	0
Career			174	1309	7.5	62	2
Playoffs			8	35	4.4		0

Chris Hanburger

Year	Team		No	Yds	Avg	Lg	TD
1967	WAS	N	1	1	1.0	1	0

Anthony Hancock

Year	Team		No	Yds	Avg	Lg	TD
1982	KC	N	7	116	16.6	41t	1
1983			37	584	15.8	50	1
1984			10	217	21.7	46t	1
1985			15	286	19.1	48	2
1986			4	63	15.8	25	0
Career			73	1266	17.3	50	5

Mike Hancock

Year	Team		No	Yds	Avg	Lg	TD
1973	WAS	N	2	3	1.5	2t	2

Carl Hanke

Year	Team		No	Yds	Avg	Lg	TD
1924	CHIC	N					1

Ray Hanken

Year	Team		No	Yds	Avg	Lg	TD
1937	NYG	N	4	51	12.8		0
1938			5	73	14.6		2
Career			9	124	13.8		2

Bob Hanlon

Year	Team		No	Yds	Avg	Lg	TD
1949	PIT	N	1	4	4.0	4	0

Herb Hannah

Year	Team		No	Yds	Avg	Lg	TD
1951	NYG	N	0	8		8L	0

Travis Hannah

Year	Team		No	Yds	Avg	Lg	TD
1994	HOU	N	3	24	8.0	11	0
1995			10	142	14.2	42	0
Career			13	166	12.8	42	0

Chuck Hanneman

Year	Team		No	Yds	Avg	Lg	TD
1937	DET	N	1	9	9.0	9	0
1938			4	80	20.0		1
1939			12	257	21.4		2
1940			14	228	16.3		0
1941	CLE-DET		4	48	12.0	46	1
Career			35	622	17.8	46	4

Frank Hanny

Year	Team		No	Yds	Avg	Lg	TD
1923	CHIB	N					1
1926							4
Career							5

Bruce Hansen

Year	Team		No	Yds	Avg	Lg	TD
1987	NE	N	1	22	22.0	22	0

Tom Hanson

Year	Team		No	Yds	Avg	Lg	TD
1933	PHI	N	9	140	15.6		1
1934							1
1936			3	33	11.0		0
1938	PIT	N	1	2	2.0	2	0
Career			13	175	13.5	2	2

Chet Hanulak

Year	Team		No	Yds	Avg	Lg	TD
1954	CLE	N	6	80	13.3	22	0
1957			3	38	12.7	19	0
Career			9	118	13.1	22	0

Merle Hapes

Year	Team		No	Yds	Avg	Lg	TD
1942	NYG	N	10	79	7.9	16	2
1946			3	40	13.3	33	0
Career			13	119	9.2	33	2

Jim Harbaugh

Year	Team		No	Yds	Avg	Lg	TD
1993	CHI	N	1	1	1.0	1	0
1995	IND	N	1	-9	-9.0	-9	0
Career			2	-8	-4.0	1	0

James Harbour

Year	Team		No	Yds	Avg	Lg	TD
1986	IND	N	4	46	11.5	28	0

Buddy Hardeman

Year	Team		No	Yds	Avg	Lg	TD
1979	WAS	N	21	197	9.4	41t	1
1980			16	178	11.1	46	0
Career			37	375	10.1	46	1

Don Hardeman

Year	Team		No	Yds	Avg	Lg	TD
1975	HOU	N	5	10	2.0	9	0
1976			7	25	3.6	11	0
1977			11	47	4.3	9	1
1978	BAL	N	10	88	8.8	19	0
1979			25	115	4.6	14	1
Career			58	285	4.9	19	2

Derrick Harden

Year	Team		No	Yds	Avg	Lg	TD
1987	GB	N	2	29	14.5	15	0

Pat Harder

Year	Team		No	Yds	Avg	Lg	TD
1946	CHIC	N	11	128	11.6	24	1
1947			9	78	8.7	21	0
1948			13	93	7.2	26	0
1949			12	100	8.3	44	1
1950			15	111	7.4	35	0
1951	DET	N	17	193	11.4	26	2
1952			14	142	10.1	22	1

Pat Harder *continued*

Year	Team		No	Yds	Avg	Lg	TD
1953			1	19	19.0	19	0
Career			92	864	9.4	44	5
Playoffs			3	24	8.0		0

Andre Hardy

Year	Team		No	Yds	Avg	Lg	TD
1984	PHI	N	2	22	11.0	13	0
1985	SEA	N	3	7	2.3	3	0
1987	SF	N	1	7	7.0	7	0
Career			6	36	6.0	13	0

Bruce Hardy

Year	Team		No	Yds	Avg	Lg	TD
1978	MIA	N	4	32	8.0	15	2
1979			30	386	12.9	28	3
1980			19	159	8.4	19	2
1981			15	174	11.6	21	0
1982			12	66	5.5	19	2
1983			22	202	9.2	25	0
1984			28	257	9.2	19	5
1985			39	409	10.5	31	4
1986			54	430	8.0	18t	5
1987			28	292	10.4	31	2
1988			4	46	11.5	19	0
1989			1	2	2.0	2	0
Career			256	2455	9.6	31	25
Playoffs			26	336	12.9		4

Carroll Hardy

Year	Team		No	Yds	Avg	Lg	TD
1955	SF	N	12	338	28.2	78t	4

Charley Hardy

Year	Team		No	Yds	Avg	Lg	TD
1960	OAK	A	24	423	17.6		3
1961			24	337	14.0	55	4
1962			6	80	13.3	16	0
Career			54	840	15.6	55	7

Larry Hardy

Year	Team		No	Yds	Avg	Lg	TD
1978	NO	N	5	131	26.2	71t	1
1979			1	3	3.0	3t	1
1980			13	197	15.2	44	0
1981			23	275	12.0	27	1
1982			8	67	8.4	31	1
1983			2	29	14.5	22	0
1984			4	50	12.5	28t	1
1985			15	208	13.9	31	2
Career			71	960	13.5	71t	7

Cecil Hare

Year	Team		No	Yds	Avg	Lg	TD
1941	WAS	N	1	25	25.0	25	0
1942			3	35	11.7	33	1
1945			3	83	27.7	66	0
1946	NYG	N	2	30	15.0	20	0
Career			9	173	19.2	66	1
Playoffs			2	20	10.0		0

Ray Hare

Year	Team		No	Yds	Avg	Lg	TD
1941	WAS	N	12	87	7.3	18	0
1942			5	57	11.4	27	0
1943			2	9	4.5	8	0
1944	BKN	N	9	206	22.9	65t	1
Career			28	359	12.8	65t	1

Tony Hargain

Year	Team		No	Yds	Avg	Lg	TD
1992	KC	N	17	205	12.1	25	0
Playoffs			2	46	23.0		0

Jimmy Hargrove

Year	Team		No	Yds	Avg	Lg	TD
1981	CIN	N	1	0	0.0	0	0
1987	GB	N	1	6	6.0	6	0
Career			2	6	3.0	6	0

Marvin Hargrove

Year	Team		No	Yds	Avg	Lg	TD
1990	PHI	N	1	34	34.0	34t	1

Steve Harkey

Year	Team		No	Yds	Avg	Lg	TD
1971	NYJ	N	5	28	5.6	10	0
1972			9	114	12.7	24	0
Career			14	142	10.1	24	0

Clarence Harmon

Year	Team		No	Yds	Avg	Lg	TD
1977	WAS	N	14	119	8.5	22	1
1978			11	112	10.2	22	1
1979			32	434	13.6	40	5
1980			54	534	9.9	45	4

Clarence Harmon *continued*

Year	Team		No	Yds	Avg	Lg	TD
1981			11	98	8.9	23	0
1982			11	86	7.8	28	0
Career			133	1383	10.4	45	11
Playoffs			1	4	4.0		0

Derrick Harmon

Year	Team		No	Yds	Avg	Lg	TD
1984	SF	N	1	2	2.0	2	0
1985			14	123	8.8	42	0
1986			8	78	9.8	15	0
Career			23	203	8.8	42	0
Playoffs			2	19	9.5		0

Mike Harmon

Year	Team		No	Yds	Avg	Lg	TD
1983	NYJ	N	1	4	4.0	4	0

Ronnie Harmon

Year	Team		No	Yds	Avg	Lg	TD
1986	BUF	N	22	185	8.4	27	1
1987			56	477	8.5	42	2
1988			37	427	11.5	36	3
1989			29	363	12.5	42t	4
1990	SD	N	46	511	11.1	36t	2
1991			59	555	9.4	36	1
1992			79	914	11.6	55	1
1993			73	671	9.2	37	2
1994			58	615	10.6	35	1
1995			63	673	10.7	44	5
1996	HOU	N	42	488	11.6	43	2
Career			564	5879	10.4	55	24
Playoffs			51	470	9.2		0

Tommy Harmon

Year	Team		No	Yds	Avg	Lg	TD
1946	LA	N	10	199	19.9	45t	2
1947			5	89	17.8	33	1
Career			15	288	19.2	45t	3

Alvin Harper

Year	Team		No	Yds	Avg	Lg	TD
1991	DAL	N	20	326	16.3	39	1
1992			35	562	16.1	52	4
1993			36	777	21.6	80t	5
1994			33	821	**24.9**	90	8
1995	TB	N	46	633	13.8	49	2
1996			19	289	15.2	40t	1
Career			189	3408	18.0	90	21
Playoffs			24	655	**27.3**		4

Bruce Harper

Year	Team		No	Yds	Avg	Lg	TD
1977	NYJ	N	21	209	10.0	55	1
1978			13	196	15.1	44	2
1979			17	250	14.7	72t	2
1980			50	634	12.7	52	3
1981			52	459	8.8	24	1
1982			14	177	12.6	39t	1
1983			48	413	8.6	33	2
1984			5	71	14.2	28	0
Career			220	2409	10.9	72t	12
Playoffs			7	53	7.6		0

Jack Harper

Year	Team		No	Yds	Avg	Lg	TD
1967	MIA	A	11	212	19.3	40t	3

Michael Harper

Year	Team		No	Yds	Avg	Lg	TD
1987	NYJ	N	18	225	12.5	35t	1
1989			7	127	18.1	48	0
Career			25	352	14.1	48	1

Roland Harper

Year	Team		No	Yds	Avg	Lg	TD
1975	CHI	N	27	191	7.1	27	0
1976			29	291	10.0	39	1
1977			19	142	7.5	34	0
1978			43	340	7.9	33t	2
1980			7	31	4.4	16	0
1981			2	10	5.0	8	0
1982			1	8	8.0	8	0
Career			128	1013	7.9	39	3
Playoffs			1	6	6.0		0

Dennis Harrah

Year	Team		No	Yds	Avg	Lg	TD
1976	LA	N	0	3		3L	0

Charley Harraway

Year	Team		No	Yds	Avg	Lg	TD
1968	CLE	N	12	162	13.5	63	1
1969	WAS	N	55	489	8.9	64t	3
1970			24	136	5.7	29	0

Charley Harraway *continued*

Year	Team		No	Yds	Avg	Lg	TD
1971			20	121	6.0	20	0
1972			15	105	7.0	24	0
1973			32	291	9.1	31	3
Career			158	1304	8.3	64t	7
Playoffs			11	58	5.3		0

Sam Harrell

Year	Team		No	Yds	Avg	Lg	TD
1981	MIN	N	2	23	11.5	17	0
1987			3	20	6.7	8	0
Career			5	43	8.6	17	0

Willard Harrell

Year	Team		No	Yds	Avg	Lg	TD
1975	GB	N	34	261	7.7	36t	2
1976			17	201	11.8	69t	1
1977			19	194	10.2	48	0
1978	STL	N	3	5	1.7	2	0
1979			3	33	11.0	15	0
1980			9	52	5.8	14	0
1981			14	131	9.4	62t	1
1982			11	127	11.5	36	0
1983			3	25	8.3	13	0
1984			14	106	7.6	15	0
Career			127	1135	8.9	69t	4
Playoffs			2	10	5.0		0

John Harrington

Year	Team		No	Yds	Avg	Lg	TD
1946	CLE	AA	8	136	17.0	55	0
1947	CHI	AA	17	233	13.7		3
Career			25	369	14.8	55	3

Perry Harrington

Year	Team		No	Yds	Avg	Lg	TD
1980	PHI	N	3	24	8.0	17	0
1981			9	27	3.0	12	0
1982			13	74	5.7	18	0
1983			1	19	19.0	19	0
Career			26	144	5.5	19	0

Al Harris

Year	Team		No	Yds	Avg	Lg	TD
1981	CHI	N	1	18		18.0	18	0

Bill Harris

Year	Team		No	Yds	Avg	Lg	TD
1968	ATL	N	3	118	39.3	55t	1
1969	MIN	N	2	13	6.5	10	0
Career			5	131	26.2	55t	1

Corey Harris

Year	Team		No	Yds	Avg	Lg	TD
1993	GB	N	2	11	5.5	6	0

Darryl Harris

Year	Team		No	Yds	Avg	Lg	TD
1988	MIN	N	6	30	5.0	7.	0
1996	STL	N	4	17	4.3	8	0
Career			10	47	4.7	8	0

Duriel Harris

Year	Team		No	Yds	Avg	Lg	TD
1976	MIA	N	22	372	16.9	44	1
1977			34	601	17.7	47	5
1978			45	654	14.5	63t	3
1979			42	798	19.0	51	3
1980			33	583	17.7	54	2
1981			53	911	17.2	55	2
1982			22	331	15.0	45	1
1983			15	260	17.3	64t	1
1984	CLE-DAL	N	33	521	15.8	43	2
1985	MIA	N	3	24	8.0	11	0
Career			302	5055	16.7	64t	20
Playoffs			19	303	15.9		0

Elroy Harris

Year	Team		No	Yds	Avg	Lg	TD
1989	SEA	N	3	26	8.7	11	0

Franco Harris

Year	Team		No	Yds	Avg	Lg	TD
1972	PIT	N	21	180	8.6	29	1
1973			10	69	6.9	19	0
1974			23	200	8.7	31t	1
1975			28	214	7.6	44t	1
1976			23	151	6.6	39	0
1977			11	62	5.6	15	0
1978			22	144	6.5	15	0
1979			36	291	8.1	21	1
1980			30	196	6.5	31	2
1981			37	250	6.8	26	1
1982			31	249	8.0	20	0
1983			34	278	8.2	29t	2

Franco Harris *continued*

Year	Team		No	Yds	Avg	Lg	TD
1984	SEA	N	1	3	3.0	3	0
Career			307	2287	7.4	44t	9
Playoffs			51	504	9.9		2

Herbert Harris

Year	Team		No	Yds	Avg	Lg	TD
1986	NO	N	11	148	13.5	27	0

Ike Harris

Year	Team		No	Yds	Avg	Lg	TD
1975	STL	N	15	266	17.7	36	0
1976			52	782	15.0	40	1
1977			40	547	13.7	38t	3
1978	NO	N	40	590	14.8	45	4
1979			25	395	15.8	42	2
1980			37	692	18.7	44t	6
1981			2	33	16.5	20	0
Career			211	3305	15.7	45	16
Playoffs			2	33	16.5		0

Jackie Harris

Year	Team		No	Yds	Avg	Lg	TD
1990	GB	N	12	157	13.1	26	0
1991			24	264	11.0	35	3
1992			55	595	10.8	40	2
1993			42	604	14.4	66t	3
1994	TB	N	26	337	13.0	48t	3
1995			62	751	12.1	33	1
1996			30	349	11.6	36	1
Career			251	3057	12.2	66t	14

Leonard Harris

Year	Team		No	Yds	Avg	Lg	TD
1986	TB	N	3	52	17.3	23	0
1987	HOU	N	10	164	16.4	39	0
1988			10	136	13.6	42	0
1989			13	202	15.5	36	2
1990			13	172	13.2	42t	3
1991			8	101	12.6	29	0
1992			35	435	12.4	47	2
1993			4	53	13.3	17t	1
1994	ATL	N	9	113	12.6	26	0
Career			105	1428	13.6	47	8
Playoffs			9	103	11.4		0

Leroy Harris

Year	Team		No	Yds	Avg	Lg	TD
1977	MIA	N	7	29	4.1	11	0
1978			25	211	8.4	57	0
1979	PHI	N	22	107	4.9	15	0
1980			15	207	13.8	51t	1
1982			3	17	5.7	9	0
Career			72	571	7.9	57	1
Playoffs			6	52	8.7		0

M.L. Harris

Year	Team		No	Yds	Avg	Lg	TD
1980	CIN	N	10	137	13.7	26	0
1981			13	181	13.9	42	2
1982			10	103	10.3	17t	3
1983			8	66	8.3	14	2
1984			48	759	15.8	80t	2
1985			10	123	12.3	22t	1
Career			99	1369	13.8	80t	10
Playoffs			2	28	14.0		1

Raymont Harris

Year	Team		No	Yds	Avg	Lg	TD
1994	CHI	N	39	236	6.1	18	0
1995			1	4	4.0	4	0
1996			32	296	9.3	47	1
Career			72	536	7.4	47	1
Playoffs			8	44	5.5		0

Rod Harris

Year	Team		No	Yds	Avg	Lg	TD
1991	PHI	N	2	28	14.0	22	0

Ronnie Harris

Year	Team		No	Yds	Avg	Lg	TD
1994	NE	N	1	11	11.0	11	0
1996	SEA	N	2	26	13.0	21	0
Career			3	37	12.3	21	0

Rudy Harris

Year	Team		No	Yds	Avg	Lg	TD
1993	TB	N	4	48	12.0	25	0
1994			2	11	5.5	8	0
Career			6	59	9.8	25	0

Steve Harris

Year	Team		No	Yds	Avg	Lg	TD
1987	MIN	N	2	17	8.5	16	0

William Harris

Year	Team		No	Yds	Avg	Lg	TD
1987	STL	N	1	8	8.0	8	0
1989	TB	N	11	102	9.3	21	1
Career			12	110	9.2	21	1

Dick Harrison

Year	Team		No	Yds	Avg	Lg	TD
1944	BOS	N	1	9	9.0	9	0

Dwight Harrison

Year	Team		No	Yds	Avg	Lg	TD
1971	DEN	N	19	265	13.9	43t	2
1972	BUF	N	1	16	16.0	16	0
Career			20	281	14.1	43t	2

Ed Harrison

Year	Team		No	Yds	Avg	Lg	TD
1926	BKN	A					1

Glynn Harrison

Year	Team		No	Yds	Avg	Lg	TD
1976	KC	N	1	12	12.0	12	0

Gran Harrison

Year	Team		No	Yds	Avg	Lg	TD
1942	DET	N	3	21	7.0	9	0

James Harrison

Year	Team		No	Yds	Avg	Lg	TD
1971	CHI	N	2	18	9.0	12	0
1972			8	30	3.8	20	1
1973			21	200	9.5	44t	2
1974			5	38	7.6	14	0
Career			36	286	7.9	44t	3

Kenny Harrison

Year	Team		No	Yds	Avg	Lg	TD
1976	SF	N	3	65	21.7	41	0
1977			15	217	14.5	46	1
1978			16	320	20.0	50	0
1980	WAS	N	8	66	8.3	12	0
Career			42	668	15.9	50	1

Marvin Harrison

Year	Team		No	Yds	Avg	Lg	TD
1996	IND	N	64	836	13.1	41	8
Playoffs			3	71	23.7		0

Max Harrison

Year	Team		No	Yds	Avg	Lg	TD
1940	NYG	N	4	96	24.0		0

Reggie Harrison

Year	Team		No	Yds	Avg	Lg	TD
1974	PIT	N	1	2	2.0	2	0
1975			1	4	4.0	4	0
1976			2	19	9.5	10	0
1977			3	11	3.7	7	0
Career			7	36	5.1	10	0
Playoffs			6	47	7.8		0

Rob Harrison

Year	Team		No	Yds	Avg	Lg	TD
1987	LARI	N	2	18	9.0	15	0

Emile Harry

Year	Team		No	Yds	Avg	Lg	TD
1986	KC	N	9	211	23.4	53	1
1988			26	362	13.9	38	1
1989			33	430	13.0	25	2
1990			41	519	12.7	60	2
1991			35	431	12.3	36	3
1992	KC-LARM	N	6	58	9.7	13	0
Career			150	2011	13.4	60	9
Playoffs			2	59	29.5		0

Harold Hart

Year	Team		No	Yds	Avg	Lg	TD
1974	OAK	N	1	4	4.0	4	0
1975			6	27	4.5	15	0
1978			1	1	1.0	1	0
Career			8	32	4.0	15	0
Playoffs			1	16	16.0		0

Jim Hart

Year	Team		No	Yds	Avg	Lg	TD
1979	STL	N	1	-4	-4.0	-4	0

Leon Hart

Year	Team		No	Yds	Avg	Lg	TD
1950	DET	N	31	505	16.3	66t	1
1951			35	544	15.5	33t	12
1952			32	376	11.8	24	4
1953			25	472	18.9	49t	7
1954			24	377	15.7	40	0
1955			9	54	6.0	14	1
1956			14	116	8.3	29	1
1957			4	55	13.8	22	0
Career			174	2499	14.4	66t	26
Playoffs			7	120	17.1		1

Pete Hart

Year	Team		No	Yds	Avg	Lg	TD
1960	NY	A	3	19	6.3		0

Frank Hartley

Year	Team		No	Yds	Avg	Lg	TD
1994	CLE	N	3	13	4.3	8	1
1995			11	137	12.5	23	1
Career			14	150	10.7	23	2
Playoffs			2	17	8.5		0

Howard Hartley

Year	Team		No	Yds	Avg	Lg	TD
1948	WAS	N	1	10	10.0	10	0
1950	PIT	N	2	27	13.5	24	0
Career			3	37	12.3	24	0

Bill Hartman

Year	Team		No	Yds	Avg	Lg	TD
1938	WAS	N	1	6	6.0	6	0

John Harvey

Year	Team		No	Yds	Avg	Lg	TD
1990	TB	N	11	86	7.8	18	1

Clint Haslerig

Year	Team		No	Yds	Avg	Lg	TD
1975	MIN	N	2	28	14.0	17	0

Jim Haslett

Year	Team		No	Yds	Avg	Lg	TD
1982	BUF	N	1	4	4.0	4	0

Don Hasselbeck

Year	Team		No	Yds	Avg	Lg	TD
1977	NE	N	9	76	8.4	21	4
1978			7	107	15.3	24	0
1979			13	158	12.2	41	0
1980			8	130	16.3	35t	4
1981			46	808	17.6	51	6
1982			15	158	10.5	41	1
1983	NE-LARI	N	3	24	8.0	13t	2
1984	MIN	N	1	10	10.0	10	0
1985	NYG	N	5	71	14.2	30	1
Career			107	1542	14.4	51	18
Playoffs			8	90	11.3		2

Andre Hastings

Year	Team		No	Yds	Avg	Lg	TD
1993	PIT	N	3	44	14.7	18	0
1994			20	281	14.1	46	2
1995			48	502	10.5	36	1
1996			72	739	10.3	38	6
Career			143	1566	11.0	46	9
Playoffs			31	316	10.2		0

Earl Hauser

Year	Team		No	Yds	Avg	Lg	TD
1921	CIN	A					1

Sam Havrilak

Year	Team		No	Yds	Avg	Lg	TD
1969	BAL	N	1	5	5.0	5	0
1970			14	141	10.1	33	0
1971			1	12	12.0	12	0
1972			33	571	17.3	62t	4
1973			1	9	9.0	9	0
1974	NO	N	2	23	23.0	23	0
Career			51	761	14.9	62t	4
Playoffs			5	61	12.2		0

Alex Hawkins

Year	Team		No	Yds	Avg	Lg	TD
1960	BAL	N	25	280	11.2	49	3
1961			20	158	7.9	22	1
1962			4	37	9.3	14	0
1963			3	41	13.7	19	0
1964			2	42	21.0	27t	1
1965			2	32	16.0	27	1
1966	ATL	N	44	661	15.0	42	2
1967	BAL	N	27	469	17.4	54	4
1968			2	31	15.5	18	0
Career			129	1751	13.6	54	12

Ben Hawkins

Year	Team		No	Yds	Avg	Lg	TD
1966	PHI	N	14	143	10.2	23	0
1967			59	1265	21.4	87t	10
1968			42	707	16.8	92t	5
1969			43	761	17.7	58	8
1970			30	612	20.4	78t	4
1971			37	650	17.6	65	4
1972			30	512	17.1	67t	1
1973			6	114	19.0	37	0
Career			261	4764	18.3	92t	32

Clarence Hawkins

Year	Team		No	Yds	Avg	Lg	TD
1979	OAK	N	2	24	12.0	20t	1

Courtney Hawkins

Year	Team		No	Yds	Avg	Lg	TD
1992	TB	N	20	336	16.8	49	2
1993			62	933	15.0	67	5
1994			37	438	11.8	32	5
1995			41	493	12.0	47	0
1996			46	544	11.8	45	1
Career			206	2744	13.3	67	13

Frank Hawkins

Year	Team		No	Yds	Avg	Lg	TD
1981	OAK	N	10	109	10.9	35	0
1982	LARI	N	7	35	5.0	9	1
1983			20	150	7.5	28	2
1984			7	51	7.3	15	0
1985			27	174	6.4	20	0
1986			25	166	6.6	16	0
1987			1	6	6.0	6	0
Career			97	691	7.1	35	3
Playoffs			8	71	8.9		0

Nate Hawkins

Year	Team		No	Yds	Avg	Lg	TD
1975	HOU	N	1	32	32.0	32	0

Steve Hawkins

Year	Team		No	Yds	Avg	Lg	TD
1994	NE	N	2	22	11.0	14	0

Les Haws

Year	Team		No	Yds	Avg	Lg	TD
1924	FRA	N					1

Greg Hawthorne

Year	Team		No	Yds	Avg	Lg	TD
1979	PIT	N	8	47	5.9	17	0
1980			12	158	13.2	33	0
1981			4	23	5.8	12	0
1982			12	182	15.2	46t	3
1983			19	300	15.8	52	0
1984	NE	N	7	127	18.1	26	0
1985			3	42	14.0	28t	1
1986			24	192	8.0	17	0
1987	IND	N	3	41	13.7	21	0
Career			92	1112	12.1	52	4
Playoffs			1	6	6.0		0

Ken Haycraft

Year	Team		No	Yds	Avg	Lg	TD
1929	MIN	N					2

Aaron Hayden

Year	Team		No	Yds	Avg	Lg	TD
1995	SD	N	5	53	10.6	16	0
1996			1	10	10.0	10	0
Career			6	63	10.5	16	0

Leo Hayden

Year	Team		No	Yds	Avg	Lg	TD
1972	STL	N	1	17	17.0	17	0

Bob Hayes

Year	Team		No	Yds	Avg	Lg	TD
1965	DAL	N	46	1003	**21.8**	82t	**12**
1966			64	1232	19.3	95t	**13**
1967			49	998	20.4	64t	10
1968			53	909	17.2	54t	10
1969			40	746	18.6	67t	4
1970			34	889	26.1	89t	10
1971			35	840	**24.0**	85t	8
1972			15	200	13.3	29	0
1973			22	360	16.4	47	3
1974			7	118	16.9	35t	1
1975	SF	N	6	119	19.8	36	0
Career			371	7414	20.0	95t	71
Playoffs			31	492	15.9		2

Dave Hayes

Year	Team		No	Yds	Avg	Lg	TD
1921	RI	A					1

Jonathan Hayes

Year	Team		No	Yds	Avg	Lg	TD
1985	KC	N	5	39	7.8	12	1
1986			8	69	8.6	16	0
1987			21	272	13.0	23	2
1988			22	233	10.6	25	4
1989			18	229	12.7	23	2
1990			9	83	9.2	21	1
1991			19	208	10.9	23	2
1992			9	77	8.6	21	2
1993			24	331	13.8	49	1
1994	PIT	N	5	50	10.0	17	1
1995			11	113	10.3	32	1
1996			2	14	7.0	7	0
Career			153	1718	11.2	49	13
Playoffs			9	93	10.3		0

Year	Team		No	Yds	Avg	Lg	TD

Luther Hayes
| 1961 | SD | A | 14 | 280 | 20.0 | 39 | 3 |
| Playoffs | | | 1 | 5 | 5.0 | | 0 |

Mercury Hayes
| 1996 | NO | N | 4 | 101 | 25.3 | 50 | 0 |

Ray Hayes
| 1961 | MIN | N | 16 | 121 | 7.6 | 22 | 0 |

Wendell Hayes
1965	DEN	A	24	294	12.3	66	2
1966			8	49	6.1	29	0
1967			13	125	9.6	24	0
1968	KC	A	12	108	9.0	22	1
1969			9	64	7.1	17	0
1970	KC	N	26	219	8.4	28	0
1971			16	150	9.4	26t	1
1972			31	295	9.5	29t	3
1973			18	134	7.4	27	0
1974			4	23	5.8	9	0
Career			161	1461	9.1	66	7
Playoffs			9	55	6.1		0

Abner Haynes
1960	DAL	A	55	576	10.5	34	3
1961			34	558	16.4	69	3
1962			39	573	14.7	78	6
1963	KC	A	33	470	14.2	73	2
1964			38	562	14.8	68	3
1965	DEN	A	26	216	8.3	71	2
1966			46	480	10.4	52	1
1967	MIA	A	16	100	6.3	22	0
Career			287	3535	12.3	78	20
Playoffs			3	45	15.0		1

James Haynes
| 1985 | NO | N | 1 | 8 | 8.0 | 8 | 0 |

Michael Haynes
1988	ATL	N	13	232	17.8	49t	4
1989			40	681	17.0	72t	4
1990			31	445	14.4	60	0
1991			50	1122	22.4	80t	11
1992			48	808	16.8	89t	10
1993			72	778	10.8	98t	4
1994	NO	N	77	985	12.8	78t	5
1995			41	597	14.6	48	4
1996			44	786	17.9	51	4
Career			416	6434	15.5	98t	46
Playoffs			7	159	22.7		2

Reggie Haynes
| 1978 | WAS | N | 2 | 32 | 16.0 | 21 | 0 |

Walt Heap
1947	LA	AA	2	0	0.0		1
1948			2	9	4.5		0
Career			4	9	2.3		1

Herman Heard
1984	KC	N	25	223	8.9	17	0
1985			31	257	8.3	27	2
1986			17	83	4.9	13	0
1987			14	118	8.4	15	0
1988			20	198	9.9	32	0
1989			25	246	9.8	27	1
Career			132	1125	8.5	32	3
Playoffs			1	15	15.0		0

Les Hearden
| 1924 | GB | N | | | | | 1 |

Garrison Hearst
1993	PHX	N	6	18	3.0	9	0
1994	ARI	N	6	49	8.2	29	0
1995			29	243	8.4	39	1
1996	CIN	N	12	131	10.9	40	1
Career			53	441	8.3	40	2

Larry Heater
1980	NYG	N	10	139	13.9	43	0
1982			2	15	7.5	12	0
Career			12	154	12.8	43	0

Leon Heath
1951	WAS	N	1	3	3.0	3	0
1952			23	146	6.3	27	1
1953			5	45	9.0	17	0
Career			29	194	6.7	27	1

Bobby Hebert
1985	NO	N	1	7	7.0	7t	1
1986			1	1	1.0	1	0
1988			2	0	0.0	2	0
Career			4	8	2.0	7t	1

Vaughn Hebron
1993	PHI	N	11	82	7.5	12	0
1994			18	137	7.6	29	0
1996	DEN	N	7	43	6.1	11	0
Career			36	262	7.3	29	0

Steve Heckard
1965	LA	N	1	4	4.0	4	0
1966			5	102	20.4	50	0
Career			6	106	17.7	50	0

Norb Hecker
1951	LA	N	4	35	8.8	20t	1
1953			2	25	12.5	16	0
1955	WAS	N	3	31	10.3	13	1
Career			9	91	10.1	20t	2

Johnny Hector
1983	NYJ	N	5	61	12.2	22t	1
1984			20	182	9.1	26	0
1985			17	164	9.6	28	0
1986			33	302	9.2	23	0
1987			32	249	7.8	27	0
1988			26	237	9.1	30	0
1989			38	330	8.7	32	2
1990			8	72	9.0	25	0
1991			7	51	7.3	16	0
1992			2	13	6.5	9	0
Career			188	1661	8.8	32	3
Playoffs			1	11	11.0		1

Gene Heeter
1963	NY	A	8	160	20.0	40	1
1964			13	153	11.8	21	1
1965			1	14	14.0	14	0
Career			22	327	14.9	40	2

Vince Heflin
1985	MIA	N	6	98	16.3	46t	1
1986	TB	N	3	42	14.0	15	0
Career			9	140	15.6	46t	1

Lakei Heimuli
| 1987 | CHI | N | 5 | 51 | 10.2 | 17 | 1 |

Bob Hein
| 1947 | BKN | AA | 1 | 7 | 7.0 | 7 | 0 |

Mel Hein
1934	NYG	N	2	15	7.5		0
1937			1	7	7.0	7	0
Career			3	22	7.3	7	0

Carl Heldt
| 1936 | BKN | N | 2 | 39 | 19.5 | | 0 |

Ron Heller
| 1986 | TB | N | 1 | 1 | 1.0 | 1t | 1 |

Ron Heller
1987	SF	N	12	165	13.8	39t	3
1988			14	140	10.0	22	0
1989	ATL	N	33	324	9.8	30	1
1990	SEA	N	13	157	12.1	23	1
1992			12	85	7.1	17	0
Career			84	871	10.4	39t	5

Warren Heller
| 1936 | PIT | N | 12 | 160 | 13.3 | | 3 |

John Henderson
| 1965 | DET | N | 8 | 140 | 17.5 | 31t | 1 |
| 1966 | | | 6 | 121 | 20.2 | 53 | 0 |

John Henderson *continued*
1967			13	144	11.1	41	0
1968	MIN	N	4	42	10.5	12	0
1969			34	553	16.3	47t	5
1970			31	527	17.0	52	2
1971			2	18	9.0	12	0
1972			10	190	19.0	70t	2
Career			108	1735	16.1	70t	10
Playoffs			23	309	13.4		0

Jon Henderson
1968	PIT	N	3	26	8.7	13	0
1969			12	188	15.7	45	3
1970	WAS	N	13	176	13.5	56t	3
Career			28	390	13.9	56t	6

Keith Henderson
1989	SF	N	3	130	43.3	78	0
1990			4	35	8.8	9	0
1991			30	303	10.1	23	0
1992	MIN	N	4	60	15.0	23	0
1992	SF-MIN	N	5	64	12.8	23	0
Career			46	592	12.9	78	0
Playoffs			2	24	12.0		0

William Henderson
1995	GB	N	3	21	7.0	9	0
1996			27	203	7.5	27	1
Career			30	224	7.5	27	1
Playoffs			4	22	5.5		0

Dutch Hendrian
| 1925 | NY | N | | | | | 2 |

Steve Hendrickson
1990	SD	N	1	12	12.0	12	0
1991			4	36	9.0	20	1
Career			5	48	9.6	20	1

Ed Henke
1949	LA	AA	1	15	15.0	15	0
1952	SF	N	1	13	13.0	13	0
Career			2	28	14.0	15	0

Charley Hennigan
1960	HOU	A	44	722	16.4	73	6
1961			82	1746	21.3	80	12
1962			54	867	16.1	76	8
1963			61	1051	17.2	83	10
1964			101	1546	15.3	53	8
1965			41	578	14.1	53	4
1966			27	313	11.6	23	3
Career			410	6823	16.6	83	51
Playoffs			12	151	12.6		0

Bernard Henry
1982	BAL	N	7	110	15.7	23	0
1983			30	416	13.9	40t	2
1984	IND	N	11	139	12.6	19t	2
1985			2	31	15.5	16	0
1987	LARM	N	1	13	13.0	13	0
Career			51	709	13.9	40t	6

Charles Henry
| 1991 | MIA | N | 2 | 17 | 8.5 | 9 | 0 |

Pete Henry
| 1923 | CAN | N | | | | | 1 |

Wally Henry
1977	PHI	N	2	16	8.0	14	0
1980			4	68	17.0	22	0
1981			9	145	16.1	44t	2
Career			15	229	15.3	44t	2

Dick Hensley
1949	NYG	N	3	24	8.0	10	0
1952	PIT	N	12	217	18.1	60t	2
1953	CHIB	N	4	117	29.3	50	0
Career			19	358	18.8	60t	2

Harold Henson
| 1975 | CIN | N | 1 | -2 | -2.0 | -2 | 0 |

Arnie Herber

Year	Team		No	Yds	Avg	Lg	TD
1930	GB	N					1
1935			2	35	17.5		0
1938			5	84	16.8		2
1939			1	18	18.0	18	0
Career			8	137	17.1	18	3

Joe Hernandez

Year	Team		No	Yds	Avg	Lg	TD
1964	WAS	N	1	18	18.0	18	0

Don Herndon

Year	Team		No	Yds	Avg	Lg	TD
1960	NY	A	5	57	11.4		1

Ken Herock

Year	Team		No	Yds	Avg	Lg	TD
1963	OAK	A	15	269	17.9	38	2
1964			23	360	15.7	50	2
1965			18	221	12.3	22	0
1967			1	-1	-1.0	-1	0
1968	CIN	A	6	75	12.5	22	0
Career			63	924	14.7	50	4

Efren Herrera

Year	Team		No	Yds	Avg	Lg	TD
1979	SEA	N	1	20	20.0	20	0
1980			1	9	9.0	9	0
Career			2	29	14.5	20	0

Don Herrmann

Year	Team		No	Yds	Avg	Lg	TD
1969	NYG	N	33	423	12.8	62	5
1970			24	290	12.1	2	2
1971			27	297	11.0	22	1
1972			28	422	15.1	63t	5
1973			43	520	12.1	46	2
1974			10	97	9.7	16	0
1975	NO	N	3	47	15.7	28	1
1976			34	535	15.7	57	0
1977			32	408	12.8	39	0
Career			234	3039	13.0	63t	16

Mack Herron

Year	Team		No	Yds	Avg	Lg	TD
1973	NE	N	18	265	14.7	29	1
1974			38	474	12.5	48	5
1975			5	50	10.0	19	0
Career			61	789	12.9	48	6

Kirk Hershey

Year	Team		No	Yds	Avg	Lg	TD
1941	PHI	N	1	11	11.0	11	0

Wally Hess

Year	Team		No	Yds	Avg	Lg	TD
1920	HAM	A					1
1925	HAM	N					1
Career							2

Jessie Hester

Year	Team		No	Yds	Avg	Lg	TD
1985	LARI	N	32	665	20.8	59	4
1986			23	632	27.5	81t	6
1987			1	30	30.0	30	0
1988	ATL	N	12	176	14.7	41	0
1990	IND	N	54	924	17.1	64t	6
1991			60	753	12.6	49t	5
1992			52	792	15.2	81	1
1993			64	835	13.0	58	1
1994	LARM	N	45	644	14.3	41	3
1995	STL	N	30	399	13.3	38t	3
Career			373	5850	15.7	81t	29
Playoffs			1	16	16.0		1

Jim Hester

Year	Team		No	Yds	Avg	Lg	TD
1967	NO	N	2	10	5.0	7	0
1968			17	300	17.6	51	2
1969			3	44	14.7	22	1
1970	CHI	N	7	54	7.7	16	0
Career			29	408	14.1	51	3

Bill Hewitt

Year	Team		No	Yds	Avg	Lg	TD
1932	CHIB	N	4	44	11.0		0
1933			16	274	17.1		2
1934			10	151	15.1		5
1935			5	80	16.0		0
1936			15	358	23.9		6
1937	PHI	N	16	197	12.3		5
1938			18	327	18.2		4
1939			15	243	16.2		1
1943	P-P	N	2	22	11.0	11	0
Career			101	1696	16.8	11	23
Playoffs			3	33	11.0		0

Craig Heyward

Year	Team		No	Yds	Avg	Lg	TD
1988	NO	N	13	105	8.1	18	0
1989			13	69	5.3	12	0
1990			18	121	6.7	12	0
1991			4	34	8.5	22t	1
1992			19	159	8.4	21	0
1993	CHI	N	16	132	8.3	20	0
1994	ATL	N	32	335	10.5	34	1
1995			37	350	9.5	25	2
1996			16	168	10.5	25	0
Career			168	1473	8.8	34	4
Playoffs			6	65	10.8		

Ralph Heywood

Year	Team		No	Yds	Avg	Lg	TD
1946	CHI	AA	20	287	14.4		4
1947	DET	N	13	198	15.2	39t	2
1948	DET-BOS	N	14	208	14.9	42t	1
1949	NYB	N	37	499	13.5	61	3
Career			84	1192	14.2	61	10

Bo Hickey

Year	Team		No	Yds	Avg	Lg	TD
1967	DEN	A	7	36	5.1	22t	1

Red Hickey

Year	Team		No	Yds	Avg	Lg	TD
1941	CLE	N	21	294	14.0	39	4
1945			4	76	19.0	33	0
1946	LA	N	8	213	26.6	60	3
1947			12	196	16.3	42	2
1948			30	599	20.0	69t	7
Career			75	1378	18.4	69t	16

Larry Hickman

Year	Team		No	Yds	Avg	Lg	TD
1959	CHIC	N	1	11	11.0	11	0

Eddie Hicks

Year	Team		No	Yds	Avg	Lg	TD
1980	NYG	N	1	4	4.0	4	0

John Hicks

Year	Team		No	Yds	Avg	Lg	TD
1975	NYG	N	1	5	5.0	5	0

Michael Hicks

Year	Team		No	Yds	Avg	Lg	TD
1996	CHI	N	1	-1	-1.0	-1	0

Victor Hicks

Year	Team		No	Yds	Avg	Lg	TD
1980	LA	N	23	318	13.8	32t	3

Alex Higdon

Year	Team		No	Yds	Avg	Lg	TD
1988	ATL	N	3	60	20.0	34t	2

Bob Higgins

Year	Team		No	Yds	Avg	Lg	TD
1921	CAN	A					1

Mark Higgs

Year	Team		No	Yds	Avg	Lg	TD
1989	PHI	N	3	9	3.0	8	0
1991	MIA	N	11	80	7.3	13	0
1992			16	142	8.9	21	0
1993			10	72	7.2	15	0
Career			40	303	7.6	21	0

Alonzo Highsmith

Year	Team		No	Yds	Avg	Lg	TD
1987	HOU	N	4	55	13.8	33t	1
1988			12	131	10.9	28	0
1989			18	201	11.2	32	2
1990	DAL	N	3	13	4.3	7	0
1992	TB	N	5	28	5.6	11	0
Career			42	428	10.2	33t	3
Playoffs			12	69	5.8		0

Don Highsmith

Year	Team		No	Yds	Avg	Lg	TD
1971	OAK	N	10	109	10.9	47	0
1972			2	34	17.0	22	0
Career			12	143	11.9	47	0

Ben Hightower

Year	Team		No	Yds	Avg	Lg	TD
1942	CLE	N	19	317	16.7	59	3
1943	DET	N	10	172	17.2	46	1
Career			29	489	16.9	59	4

Joel Hilgenberg

Year	Team		No	Yds	Avg	Lg	TD
1990	NO	N	1	9	9.0	9	0

Bruce Hill

Year	Team		No	Yds	Avg	Lg	TD
1987	TB	N	23	403	17.5	40	2
1988			58	1040	17.9	42t	9
1989			50	673	13.5	53	5

Bruce Hill *continued*

Year	Team		No	Yds	Avg	Lg	TD
1990			42	641	15.3	48t	5
1991			17	185	10.9	18	2
Career			190	2942	15.5	53	23

Calvin Hill

Year	Team		No	Yds	Avg	Lg	TD
1969	DAL	N	20	232	11.6	28	0
1970			13	95	7.3	21	0
1971			19	244	12.8	27t	3
1972			43	364	8.5	33t	0
1973			32	290	9.1	29	0
1974			12	134	11.2	39	0
1976	WAS	N	7	100	14.3	23	0
1977			18	154	8.6	23	1
1978	CLE	N	25	334	13.4	53t	6
1979			38	381	10.0	31	2
1980			27	383	14.2	50	6
1981			17	150	8.8	23	2
Career			271	2861	10.6	53t	23
Playoffs			15	106	7.1		0

Charlie Hill

Year	Team		No	Yds	Avg	Lg	TD
1925	KC	N					2

David Hill

Year	Team		No	Yds	Avg	Lg	TD
1976	DET	N	19	249	13.1	24t	5
1977			32	465	14.5	61	2
1978			53	633	11.9	32	4
1979			47	569	12.1	40	3
1980			39	424	10.9	29	1
1981			33	462	14.0	34	4
1982			22	252	11.5	27	4
1983	LARM	N	28	280	10.0	34	2
1984			31	300	9.7	26	1
1985			29	271	9.3	37	1
1986			14	202	14.4	33	1
1987			11	105	9.5	24	0
Career			358	4212	11.8	61	28
Playoffs			11	90	8.2		2

Derek Hill

Year	Team		No	Yds	Avg	Lg	TD
1989	PIT	N	28	455	16.3	53	1
1990			25	391	15.6	66	0
Career			53	846	16.0	66	1
Playoffs			1	7	7.0		0

Don Hill

Year	Team		No	Yds	Avg	Lg	TD
1929	CHIC	N					1

Drew Hill

Year	Team		No	Yds	Avg	Lg	TD
1979	LA	N	4	94	23.5	43	1
1980			19	416	21.9	74t	2
1981			16	355	22.2	45	3
1982	LARM	N	7	92	13.1	23	0
1984			14	390	27.9	68	4
1985	HOU	N	64	1169	18.3	57t	9
1986			65	1112	17.1	81t	5
1987			49	989	20.2	52t	6
1988			72	1141	15.8	57t	10
1989			66	938	14.2	50	8
1990			74	1019	13.8	57	5
1991			90	1109	12.3	61t	4
1992	ATL	N	60	623	10.4	43	3
1993			34	384	11.3	30	0
Career			634	9831	15.5	81t	60
Playoffs			39	541	13.9		1

Eddie Hill

Year	Team		No	Yds	Avg	Lg	TD
1979	LA	N	4	36	9.0	21t	0
1980			4	29	7.3	11	0
1981	MIA	N	12	73	6.1	16	1
1982			6	33	5.5	10	0
Career			26	171	6.6	21t	2
Playoffs			2	3	1.5		0

Fred Hill

Year	Team		No	Yds	Avg	Lg	TD
1965	PHI	N	1	21	21.0	21	0
1966			29	304	10.5	36	0
1967			9	144	16.0	57	0
1968			30	370	12.3	31t	3
1969			6	64	10.7	23	1
1970			3	10	3.3	9	1
1971			7	92	13.1	35	0
Career			85	1005	11.8	57	5

Greg Hill

Year	Team		No	Yds	Avg	Lg	TD
1994	KC	N	16	92	5.8	21	0
1995			7	45	6.4	13	0
1996			3	60	20.0	34t	1
Career			26	197	7.6	34t	1
Playoffs			1	11	11.0		0

Harlon Hill

Year	Team		No	Yds	Avg	Lg	TD
1954	CHIB	N	45	1124	**25.0**	76t	**12**
1955			42	789	18.8	86t	**9**
1956			47	1128	**24.0**	79t	11
1957			21	483	23.0	53	2
1958			27	365	13.5	40	3
1959			36	573	15.9	88t	3
1960	CHI	N	5	98	19.6	45	0
1961			3	51	17.0	23	0
1962	PIT	N	7	101	14.4	25	0
1963	BAL	N	22	304	13.8	55	1
1965			20	112	5.6	20	0
1966			5	18	3.6	7	0
1967			19	156	8.2	33	0
1968			18	161	8.9	19	1
Career			317	5463	17.2	88t	42
Playoffs			6	87	14.5		

Harold Hill

Year	Team		No	Yds	Avg	Lg	TD
1938	BKN	N	3	61	20.3		0
1939			7	150	21.4		0
1940			1	9	9.0	9	0
Career			11	220	20.0	9	0

Ike Hill

Year	Team		No	Yds	Avg	Lg	TD
1971	BUF	N	5	55	11.0	26t	1
1973	CHI	N	10	119	11.9	18	0
1974			7	109	15.6	28	1
Career			22	283	12.9	28	2

Jack Hill

Year	Team		No	Yds	Avg	Lg	TD
1961	DEN	A	4	33	8.3	15	0

J.D. Hill

Year	Team		No	Yds	Avg	Lg	TD
1971	BUF	N	11	216	19.6	47t	2
1972			52	754	14.5	58t	5
1973			29	422	14.6	42	0
1974			32	572	17.9	55t	6
1975			36	667	18.5	77t	7
1976	DET	N	1	2	2.0	2	0
1977			24	247	10.3	23t	1
Career			185	2880	15.6	77t	21
Playoffs			4	59	14.8		0

Jeff Hill

Year	Team		No	Yds	Avg	Lg	TD
1995	CIN	N	4	44	11.0	18	0

Jerry Hill

Year	Team		No	Yds	Avg	Lg	TD
1964	BAL	N	14	113	8.1	27t	1
1969			11	44	4.0	12	0
1970			8	62	7.8	13	0
Career			33	219	6.6	27t	1
Playoffs			3	3	1.0		0

Lonzell Hill

Year	Team		No	Yds	Avg	Lg	TD
1987	NO	N	19	322	16.9	36	2
1988			66	703	10.7	35	7
1989			48	636	13.3	46	4
1990			3	35	11.7	13	0
Career			136	1696	12.5	46	13
Playoffs			2	15	7.5		0

Mack Lee Hill

Year	Team		No	Yds	Avg	Lg	TD
1964	KC	A	19	144	7.6	34	2
1965			21	264	12.6	46	1
Career			40	408	10.2	46	3

Randal Hill

Year	Team		No	Yds	Avg	Lg	TD
1991	PHX	N	43	495	11.5	31t	1
1992			58	861	14.8	49	3
1993			35	519	14.8	58t	4
1994	ARI	N	38	544	14.3	51	0
1995	MIA	N	12	260	21.7	58	0
1996			21	409	19.5	61	4
Career			207	3088	14.9	61	12
Playoffs			2	59	29.5		1

Tony Hill

Year	Team		No	Yds	Avg	Lg	TD
1977	DAL	N	2	21	10.5	12	0
1978			46	823	17.9	54	6
1979			60	1062	17.7	75t	10
1980			60	1055	17.6	58t	8
1981			46	953	20.7	63t	4
1982			35	526	15.0	47	1
1983			49	801	16.3	75t	7
1984			58	864	14.9	66t	5
1985			74	1113	15.0	53t	7
1986			49	770	15.7	63	3
Career			479	7988	16.7	75t	51
Playoffs			46	618	13.4		4

Ira Hillary

Year	Team		No	Yds	Avg	Lg	TD
1987	CIN	N	5	65	13.0	23	0
1988			5	76	15.2	31	1
1989			17	162	9.5	17	1
Career			27	303	11.2	31	2
Playoffs			1	17	17.0		0

Jerry Hillebrand

Year	Team		No	Yds	Avg	Lg	TD
1968	PIT	N	1	27	27.0	27	0

Billy Hillenbrand

Year	Team		No	Yds	Avg	Lg	TD
1946	CHI	AA	21	315	15.0	62t	4
1947	BAL	AA	39	702	18.0	58t	7
1948			50	**970**	19.4	78t	6
Career			110	1987	18.1	78t	17
Playoffs			7	75	10.7		0

Dalton Hilliard

Year	Team		No	Yds	Avg	Lg	TD
1986	NO	N	17	107	6.3	17	0
1987			23	264	11.5	38t	1
1988			34	335	9.9	26	1
1989			52	514	9.9	54t	5
1990			14	125	8.9	20	1
1991			21	127	6.0	14t	1
1992			48	465	9.7	41	4
1993			40	296	7.4	34	1
Career			249	2233	9.0	54t	14
Playoffs			8	58	7.3		0

Bill Hillman

Year	Team		No	Yds	Avg	Lg	TD
1947	DET	N	1	25	25.0	25	0

Carl Hilton

Year	Team		No	Yds	Avg	Lg	TD
1987	MIN	N	2	16	8.0	8t	2
1988			1	1	1.0	1t	1
Career			3	17	5.7	8t	3
Playoffs			2	12	6.0		2

John Hilton

Year	Team		No	Yds	Avg	Lg	TD
1965	PIT	N	4	32	8.0	12	0
1966			46	603	13.1	32t	4
1967			26	343	13.2	43t	5
1968			20	285	14.3	37t	1
1969			12	231	19.3	34	0
1970	GB	N	25	350	14.0	65t	4
1972	DET	N	5	133	26.6	66t	1
1973			6	70	11.7	31	1
Career			144	2047	14.2	66t	16

Jimmy Hines

Year	Team		No	Yds	Avg	Lg	TD
1969	MIA	A	2	23	11.5	22	0

Clarke Hinkle

Year	Team		No	Yds	Avg	Lg	TD
1933	GB	N	6	48	8.0		0
1934			10	110	11.0		1
1935			1	-2	-2.0	-2	0
1937			8	116	14.5		2
1938			7	98	14.0		4
1939			4	70	17.5		0
1940			4	28	7.0		1
1941			8	78	9.8	28	1
Career			48	546	11.4	28	9

Jack Hinkle

Year	Team		No	Yds	Avg	Lg	TD
1940	NYG	N	3	23	7.7		0
1943	P-P	N	1	3	3.0	3	0
1944	PHI	N	2	34	17.0	22	0
1945			1	8	8.0	8	0
Career			7	68	9.7	22	0

Mike Hinnant

Year	Team		No	Yds	Avg	Lg	TD
1988	PIT	N	1	23	23.0	23	0
1992	DET	N	3	28	9.3	13	0
Career			4	51	12.8	23	0

Chris Hinton

Year	Team		No	Yds	Avg	Lg	TD
1988	IND	N	1	1	1.0	1	0
1992	ATL	N	1	-2	-2.0	-2	0
1993			1	-8	-8.0	-8	0
Career			3	-9	-3.0	1	0

Eddie Hinton

Year	Team		No	Yds	Avg	Lg	TD
1969	BAL	N	13	269	20.7	46	1
1970			47	733	15.6	40	5
1971			25	436	17.4	33	2
1972			11	146	13.3	63t	1
1973	HOU	N	13	202	15.5	34t	1
1974	NE	N	2	36	18.0	20	0
Career			111	1822	16.4	63t	10
Playoffs			18	380	21.1		1

Elroy Hirsch

Year	Team		No	Yds	Avg	Lg	TD
1946	CHI	AA	27	347	12.9	68t	3
1947			10	282	**28.2**	76t	3
1948			7	101	14.4		1
1949	LA	N	22	326	14.8	48	4
1950			42	687	16.4	58t	7
1951			66	**1495**	22.7	91t	**17**
1952			25	590	23.6	84t	4
1953			61	941	15.4	70	4
1954			35	720	20.6	66	3
1955			25	460	18.4	72t	6
1956			35	603	17.2	76t	6
1957			32	477	14.9	45	6
Career			387	7029	18.2	91t	60
Playoffs			16	209	13.1		0

Joel Hitt

Year	Team		No	Yds	Avg	Lg	TD
1939	CLE	N	4	51	12.8		0

Billy Hix

Year	Team		No	Yds	Avg	Lg	TD
1950	PHI	N	2	25	12.5	20	0

Joe Hoague

Year	Team		No	Yds	Avg	Lg	TD
1941	PIT	N	2	21	10.5	14	1
1946	BOS	N	1	1	1.0	4	0
Career			3	22	7.3	14	1

Dick Hoak

Year	Team		No	Yds	Avg	Lg	TD
1961	PIT	N	3	18	6.0	7	0
1962			9	133	14.8	23	0
1963			11	118	10.7	23	1
1964			12	137	11.4	22t	3
1965			19	228	12.0	48	1
1966			23	239	10.4	31	0
1967			17	111	6.5	20	1
1968			28	253	9.0	30t	1
1969			20	190	9.5	26	1
1970			4	25	6.3	18	0
Career			146	1452	9.9	48	8

Leroy Hoard

Year	Team		No	Yds	Avg	Lg	TD
1990	CLE	N	10	73	7.3	17	0
1991			48	567	11.8	71t	9
1992			26	310	11.9	46t	1
1993			35	351	10.0	41	0
1994			45	445	9.9	65t	4
1995			13	103	7.9	24	0
1996	BAL-MIN	N	11	133	12.1	37	0
Career			188	1982	10.5	71t	14
Playoffs			3	37	12.3		0

Daryl Hobbs

Year	Team		No	Yds	Avg	Lg	TD
1994	LARI	N	5	52	10.4	14	0
1995	OAK	N	38	612	16.1	54t	3
1996			44	423	9.6	29	3
Career			87	1087	12.5	54t	6

Stephen Hobbs

Year	Team		No	Yds	Avg	Lg	TD
1990	WAS	N	1	18	18.0	18t	1
1991			3	24	8.0	10	0
Career			4	42	10.5	18t	1
Playoffs			1	13	13.0		0

Year	Team		No	Yds	Avg	Lg	TD

Merwin Hodel

Year	Team		No	Yds	Avg	Lg	TD
1953	NYG	N	2	-15	-7.5	0	0

Floyd Hodge

Year	Team		No	Yds	Avg	Lg	TD
1982	ATL	N	14	160	11.4	23	0
1983			25	280	11.2	76t	4
1984			24	234	9.8	26	0
Career			63	674	10.7	76t	4
Playoffs			2	29	14.5		

Herman Hodges

Year	Team		No	Yds	Avg	Lg	TD
1939	BKN	N	4	45	11.3		0
1940			3	38	12.7		0
1941			12	128	10.7	32	0
1942			4	74	18.5	40	0
Career			23	285	12.4	40	0

Tommy Hodson

Year	Team		No	Yds	Avg	Lg	TD
1992	NE	N	1	-6	-6.0	-6	0

Dick Hoerner

Year	Team		No	Yds	Avg	Lg	TD
1947	LA	N	1	20	20.0	20	0
1948			18	227	12.6	45	2
1949			17	213	12.5	39	0
1950			26	446	17.2	48	1
1951			8	102	12.8	21	1
1952	DAL	N	10	172	17.2	54	0
Career			80	1180	14.8	54	4
Playoffs			3	41	13.7		0

Bob Hoernschemeyer

Year	Team		No	Yds	Avg	Lg	TD
1946	CHI	AA	1	11	11.0	11	0
1947			1	4	4.0	4	0
1948	BKN	AA	11	173	15.7		3
1950	DET	N	8	78	9.8	41t	1
1951			23	263	11.4	48	3
1952			17	139	8.2	28	0
1953			23	282	12.3	35	2
1954			20	153	7.7	26	1
1955			5	36	7.2	15	0
Career			109	1139	10.4	48	10
Playoffs			2	-2	-1.0		0

Paul Hofer

Year	Team		No	Yds	Avg	Lg	TD
1976	SF	N	4	45	11.3	13t	1
1977			5	46	9.2	16	0
1978			12	170	14.2	46	0
1979			58	662	11.4	44	2
1980			41	467	11.4	28	2
1981			27	244	9.0	22	0
Career			147	1634	11.1	46	5

Bob Hoffman

Year	Team		No	Yds	Avg	Lg	TD
1947	LA	N	2	22	11.0	12	0
1948			3	28	9.3	13	1
1949	LA	AA	2	21	10.5		0
Career			7	71	10.1	13	1
Playoffs			2	8	4.0		1

Dalton Hoffman

Year	Team		No	Yds	Avg	Lg	TD
1964	HOU	A	1	1	1.0	1	0

Jack Hoffman

Year	Team		No	Yds	Avg	Lg	TD
1955	CHIB	N	6	86	14.3	32	0

John Hoffman

Year	Team		No	Yds	Avg	Lg	TD
1949	CHIB	N	25	373	14.9	64	2
1950			8	161	20.1	44t	2
1951			28	394	14.1	78t	2
1952			1	9	9.0	9	0
1953			28	341	12.2	40	1
1954			28	354	12.6	54	1
1955			11	153	13.9	37	1
1956			7	85	12.1	35	0
Career			136	1870	13.8	78t	9

Mike Hogan

Year	Team		No	Yds	Avg	Lg	TD
1976	PHI	N	15	89	5.9	18	0
1977			19	118	6.2	51t	1
1978			31	164	5.3	16	1
1979	SF	N	9	65	7.2	27	0
1980	NYG	N	5	46	9.2	12	0
Career			79	482	6.1	51t	2
Playoffs			1	6	6.0		0

Merril Hoge

Year	Team		No	Yds	Avg	Lg	TD
1987	PIT	N	7	97	13.9	27	1
1988			50	487	9.7	40	3
1989			34	271	8.0	22	0
1990			40	342	8.6	27	3
1991			49	379	7.7	25	1
1992			28	231	8.3	20	1
1993			33	247	7.5	18	4
1994	CHI	N	13	79	6.1	11	0
Career			254	2133	8.4	40	13
Playoffs			14	129	9.2		0

Doug Hogland

Year	Team		No	Yds	Avg	Lg	TD
1953	SF	N	1	-2	-2.0	-2	0

Al Hoisington

Year	Team		No	Yds	Avg	Lg	TD
1960	OAK-BUF	A	8	141	17.6		2

Steve Holden

Year	Team		No	Yds	Avg	Lg	TD
1973	CLE	N	3	27	9.0	17	0
1974			30	452	15.1	53	3
1975			21	320	15.2	28	0
1976			8	128	16.0	26t	1
Career			62	927	15.0	53	4

Lew Holder

Year	Team		No	Yds	Avg	Lg	TD
1949	LA	AA	5	71	14.2		0

John Holifield

Year	Team		No	Yds	Avg	Lg	TD
1989	CIN	N	2	18	9.0	14	0

Jamie Holland

Year	Team		No	Yds	Avg	Lg	TD
1987	SD	N	6	138	23.0	45	0
1988			39	536	13.7	45	1
1989			26	336	12.9	37	0
1992	CLE	N	2	27	13.5	16	0
Career			73	1037	14.2	45	1

John Holland

Year	Team		No	Yds	Avg	Lg	TD
1974	MIN	N	5	84	16.8	20	0
1975	BUF	N	7	144	20.6	63	1
1976			15	299	19.9	58t	2
1977			8	107	13.4	27	0
Career			35	634	18.1	63	3

John Hollar

Year	Team		No	Yds	Avg	Lg	TD
1949	WAS	N	4	38	9.5	15	1

Corey Holliday

Year	Team		No	Yds	Avg	Lg	TD
1996	PIT	N	1	7	7.0	7	0
Playoffs			3	27	9.0		0

Ron Holliday

Year	Team		No	Yds	Avg	Lg	TD
1973	SD	N	14	182	13.0	36	0

Brian Holloway

Year	Team		No	Yds	Avg	Lg	TD
1986	NE	N	1	5	5.0	5	0

Derek Holloway

Year	Team		No	Yds	Avg	Lg	TD
1986	WAS	N	1	7	7.0	7	0

Steve Holloway

Year	Team		No	Yds	Avg	Lg	TD
1987	TB	N	10	127	12.7	26	0

Bernie Holm

Year	Team		No	Yds	Avg	Lg	TD
1931	POR	N					1

Rodney Holman

Year	Team		No	Yds	Avg	Lg	TD
1982	CIN	N	3	18	6.0	10	1
1983			2	15	7.5	10	0
1984			21	239	11.4	27	1
1985			38	479	12.6	64t	7
1986			40	570	14.3	34t	2
1987			28	438	15.6	61t	2
1988			39	527	13.5	33	3
1989			50	736	14.7	73t	9
1990			40	596	14.9	53	5
1991			31	445	14.4	39	2
1992			26	266	10.2	26t	2
1993	DET	N	25	244	9.8	28t	2
1994			17	163	9.6	18	0
1995			5	35	7.0	9	0
Career			365	4771	13.1	73t	36
Playoffs			18	245	13.6		0

Scott Holman

Year	Team		No	Yds	Avg	Lg	TD
1986	STL	N	3	41	13.7	18	0
1987	NYJ	N	15	155	10.3	30	0
Career			18	196	10.9	30	0

Darick Holmes

Year	Team		No	Yds	Avg	Lg	TD
1995	BUF	N	24	214	8.9	47	0
1996			16	102	6.4	20	1
Career			40	316	7.9	47	1
Playoffs			1	11	11.0		0

Don Holmes

Year	Team		No	Yds	Avg	Lg	TD
1987	STL	N	11	132	12.0	23	0
1988	PHX	N	1	10	10.0	10	0
1989			13	271	20.8	77t	1
Career			25	413	16.5	77t	1

Jack Holmes

Year	Team		No	Yds	Avg	Lg	TD
1979	NO	N	3	19	6.3	13	0
1980			29	226	7.8	16	1
1981			38	206	5.4	19	0
1982			1	2	2.0	2	0
Career			71	453	6.4	19	1

Mike Holmes

Year	Team		No	Yds	Avg	Lg	TD
1975	SF	N	16	220	13.8	25	1
1976	MIA	N	1	11	11.0	11	0
Career			17	231	13.6	25	1

Robert Holmes

Year	Team		No	Yds	Avg	Lg	TD
1968	KC	A	19	201	10.6	43	0
1969			26	266	10.2	33t	3
1970	KC	N	23	173	7.5	31	1
1971	KC-HOU	N	19	154	8.1	22	0
1972	HOU	N	6	32	5.3	13	0
1973	SD	N	19	151	7.9	30	0
1975	HOU	N	1	5	5.0	5	0
Career			113	982	8.7	43	4
Playoffs			4	37	9.3		0

Pete Holohan

Year	Team		No	Yds	Avg	Lg	TD
1981	SD	N	1	14	14.0	14	0
1983			23	272	11.8	35	2
1984			56	734	13.1	51	1
1985			42	458	10.9	23	3
1986			29	356	12.3	34	1
1987			20	239	11.9	18	0
1988	LARM	N	59	640	10.8	20	3
1989			51	510	10.0	31	2
1990			49	475	9.7	28	2
1991	KC	N	13	113	8.7	26	2
1992	CLE	N	20	170	8.5	24	0
Career			363	3981	11.0	51	16
Playoffs			16	163	10.2		1

Mike Holovak

Year	Team		No	Yds	Avg	Lg	TD
1946	LA	N	2	6	3.0	8	0
1947	CHIB	N	7	119	17.0	60	0
1948			4	30	7.5	15	0
Career			13	155	11.9	60	0

Mike Holston

Year	Team		No	Yds	Avg	Lg	TD
1981	HOU	N	27	427	15.8	50t	2
1982			5	116	23.2	38t	1
1983			14	205	14.6	43	0
1984			22	287	13.0	28	1
1985	HOU-KC		6	76	12.7	25	0
Career			74	1111	15.0	50t	4

Harry Holt

Year	Team		No	Yds	Avg	Lg	TD
1983	CLE	N	29	420	14.5	48t	3
1984			20	261	13.1	36	0
1985			10	95	9.5	23	1
1986			4	61	15.3	34	1
1987	SD	N	7	56	8.0	17	0
Career			70	893	12.8	48t	5
Playoffs			4	44	11.0		0

Robert Holt

Year	Team		No	Yds	Avg	Lg	TD
1982	BUF	N	4	45	11.3	23	0

Dennis Homan

Year	Team		No	Yds	Avg	Lg	TD
1968	DAL	N	4	92	23.0	36t	1
1969			12	240	20.0	66	0

Dennis Homan continued

Year	Team		No	Yds	Avg	Lg	TD
1970			7	105	15.0	43	0
1971	KC	N	2	47	23.5	29	0
1972			12	135	11.3	38	1
Career			37	619	16.7	66	2

Henry Homan

Year	Team		No	Yds	Avg	Lg	TD
1925	FRA	N					1
1926							2
1927							1
1928							1
1929							2
Career							7

Fair Hooker

Year	Team		No	Yds	Avg	Lg	TD
1969	CLE	N	2	21	10.5	12	0
1970			28	490	17.5	69	2
1971			45	649	14.4	48	1
1972			32	441	13.8	43	2
1973			18	196	10.9	26	2
1974			4	48	12.0	17	1
Career			129	1845	14.3	69	8
Playoffs			4	92	23.0		1

Jim Hooks

Year	Team		No	Yds	Avg	Lg	TD
1973	DET	N	1	6	6.0	6	0
1974			9	53	5.9	19	0
1975			1	5	5.0	5	0
Career			11	64	5.8	19	0

Roland Hooks

Year	Team		No	Yds	Avg	Lg	TD
1976	BUF	N	6	72	12.0	28	0
1977			16	195	12.2	33	0
1978			15	110	7.3	21	1
1979			26	254	9.8	42	0
1980			23	179	7.8	26	0
1981			10	140	14.0	37	2
Career			96	950	9.9	42	3
Playoffs			3	16	5.3		0

Mel Hoover

Year	Team		No	Yds	Avg	Lg	TD
1983	PHI	N	10	221	22.1	68	0
1984			6	143	23.8	44	2
Career			16	364	22.8	68	2

Roy Hopkins

Year	Team		No	Yds	Avg	Lg	TD
1967	HOU	A	3	9	3.0	7	0
1968			4	40	10.0	26	0
1969			29	338	11.7	56	1
1970	HOU	N	14	142	10.1	43	0
Career			50	529	10.6	56	1

Harry Hopp

Year	Team		No	Yds	Avg	Lg	TD
1941	DET	N	2	7	3.5	5	0
1943			17	229	13.5	67	3
1946	BUF	AA	2	-1	-0.5		0
1947	LA	AA	3	59	19.7		0
Career			24	294	12.3	67	3

Joe Horn

Year	Team		No	Yds	Avg	Lg	TD
1996	KC	N	2	30	15.0	21	0

Dick Horne

Year	Team		No	Yds	Avg	Lg	TD
1946	MIA	AA	5	48	9.6		0
1947	SF	AA	3	69	23.0		0
Career			8	117	14.6		0

Sam Horner

Year	Team		No	Yds	Avg	Lg	TD
1960	WAS	N	7	106	15.1	35	0
1961			10	113	11.3	20	1
Career			17	219	12.9	35	1

Clarence Horning

Year	Team		No	Yds	Avg	Lg	TD
1922	TOL	N					1

Paul Hornung

Year	Team		No	Yds	Avg	Lg	TD
1957	GB	N	6	34	5.7	16	0
1958			15	137	9.1	39	0
1959			15	113	7.5	19	0
1960			28	257	9.2	33	2
1961			15	145	9.7	34t	2
1962			9	168	18.7	83t	2
1964			9	98	10.9	40	0
1965			19	336	17.7	65t	3

Paul Hornung continued

Year	Team		No	Yds	Avg	Lg	TD
1966			14	192	13.7	44t	3
Career			130	1480	11.4	83t	12
Playoffs			12	111	9.3		0

Roy Horstmann

Year	Team		No	Yds	Avg	Lg	TD
1933	BOS	N	11	185	16.8		0

Ethan Horton

Year	Team		No	Yds	Avg	Lg	TD
1985	KC	N	28	185	6.6	22	1
1987	LARI	N	3	44	14.7	32t	1
1989			4	44	11.0	20	1
1990			33	404	12.2	36	3
1991			53	650	12.3	52	5
1992			33	409	12.4	30	2
1993			43	467	10.9	32	1
1994	WAS	N	15	157	10.5	20	3
Career			212	2360	11.1	52	17
Playoffs			15	248	16.5		2

Les Horvath

Year	Team		No	Yds	Avg	Lg	TD
1947	LA	N	3	29	9.7	14	0
1948			4	42	10.5	19	0
1949	CLE	AA	2	71	35.5		1
Career			9	142	15.8	19	1

Jeff Hostetler

Year	Team		No	Yds	Avg	Lg	TD
1988	NYG	N	1	10	10.0	10	0

Kevin House

Year	Team		No	Yds	Avg	Lg	TD
1980	TB	N	24	531	22.1	61	5
1981			56	1176	21.0	84t	9
1982			28	438	15.6	62t	2
1983			47	769	16.4	74t	5
1984			76	1005	13.2	55	5
1985			44	803	18.3	59	5
1986	TB-LARM	N	18	384	21.3	60t	2
1987	LARM	N	6	63	10.5	15t	1
Career			299	5169	17.3	84t	34
Playoffs			8	132	16.5		1

Bill Houston

Year	Team		No	Yds	Avg	Lg	TD
1974	DAL	N	6	72	12.0	19	0

Jim Houston

Year	Team		No	Yds	Avg	Lg	TD
1966	CLE	N	1	10	10.0	10t	0

Lin Houston

Year	Team		No	Yds	Avg	Lg	TD
1949	CLE	AA	0	19		19L	0

Rich Houston

Year	Team		No	Yds	Avg	Lg	TD
1969	NYG	N	2	69	34.5	46	0
1970			4	68	17.0	35	0
1971			24	426	17.8	81t	4
1972			27	468	17.3	94t	3
1973			8	90	11.3	20	0
Career			65	1121	17.2	94t	7

Bob Howard

Year	Team		No	Yds	Avg	Lg	TD
1930	NYG	N					1

Bobby Howard

Year	Team		No	Yds	Avg	Lg	TD
1986	TB	N	5	60	12.0	29	0
1987			10	123	12.3	45	0
Career			15	183	12.2	45	0

Desmond Howard

Year	Team		No	Yds	Avg	Lg	TD
1992	WAS	N	3	20	6.7	8	0
1993			23	286	12.4	27	0
1994			40	727	18.2	81t	5
1995	JAC	N	26	276	10.6	24	1
1996	GB	N	13	95	7.3	12	0
Career			105	1404	13.4	81t	6

Percy Howard

Year	Team		No	Yds	Avg	Lg	TD
Playoffs			1	34	34.0		1

Ron Howard

Year	Team		No	Yds	Avg	Lg	TD
1976	SEA	N	37	422	11.4	30	0
1977			17	177	10.4	24	1
1978			18	251	13.9	42	1
Career			72	850	11.8	42	2

Sherman Howard

Year	Team		No	Yds	Avg	Lg	TD
1949	B-NY	AA	1	24	24.0	24	0
1950	NYY	N	12	278	23.2	40	5
1951			21	447	21.3	75t	3
1952	CLE	N	11	219	19.9	57t	3
Career			45	968	21.5	75t	11

William Howard

Year	Team		No	Yds	Avg	Lg	TD
1988	TB	N	11	97	8.8	16	0
1989			30	188	6.3	18	1
Career			41	285	7.0	18	1

Clarence Howell

Year	Team		No	Yds	Avg	Lg	TD
1948	SF	AA	1	9	9.0	9	0

Earl Howell

Year	Team		No	Yds	Avg	Lg	TD
1949	LA	AA	5	11	2.2		1

Jim Lee Howell

Year	Team		No	Yds	Avg	Lg	TD
1937	NYG	N	4	32	8.0		0
1938			12	163	13.6		2
1939			5	112	22.4		2
1940			14	255	18.2		2
1941			4	62	15.5	42	1
1942			10	115	11.5	23	0
1946			9	141	15.7	33	0
1947			3	41	13.7	21	0
Career			61	921	15.1	42	7
Playoffs			2	3	1.5		0

Steve Howell

Year	Team		No	Yds	Avg	Lg	TD
1979	MIA	N	3	23	7.7	11	0
1980			5	38	7.6	13	0
1981			2	9	4.5	5	0
Career			10	70	7.0	13	0

Billy Howton

Year	Team		No	Yds	Avg	Lg	TD
1952	GB	N	53	**1231**	23.2	90t	13
1953			25	463	18.5	80t	4
1954			52	768	14.8	59	2
1955			44	697	15.8	60	5
1956			55	**1188**	21.6	66t	**12**
1957			38	727	19.1	77t	5
1958			36	507	14.1	50	2
1959	CLE	N	39	510	13.1	36t	1
1960	DAL	N	23	363	15.8	41t	4
1961			56	785	14.0	53	4
1962			49	706	14.4	69t	6
1963			33	514	15.6	44t	3
Career			503	8459	16.8	90t	61

Frank Hrabetin

Year	Team		No	Yds	Avg	Lg	TD
1946	BKN	AA	1	17	17.0	17	0

Cal Hubbard

Year	Team		No	Yds	Avg	Lg	TD
1930	GB	N					1

Marv Hubbard

Year	Team		No	Yds	Avg	Lg	TD
1969	OAK	A	2	30	15.0	20	0
1971	OAK	N	22	167	7.6	31	1
1972			22	103	4.7	21	0
1973			15	116	7.7	25	0
1974			11	95	8.6	15	0
1975			7	81	11.6	16	0
1977	DET	N	6	36	6.0	9	0
Career			85	628	7.4	31	1
Playoffs			7	77	11.0		0

Wes Hubbard

Year	Team		No	Yds	Avg	Lg	TD
1935	BKN	N					1

Frank Hubbell

Year	Team		No	Yds	Avg	Lg	TD
1947	LA	N	2	60	30.0	45t	2
1948			10	134	13.4	48	1
1949			3	32	10.7	13	0
Career			15	226	15.1	48	3

Brad Hubbert

Year	Team		No	Yds	Avg	Lg	TD
1967	SD	A	19	214	11.3	48	2
1968			5	11	2.2	10	0
1969			11	43	3.9	18	0
1970	SD	N	7	44	6.3	11	0
Career			42	312	7.4	48	2

Year	Team		No	Yds	Avg	Lg	TD

Pooley Hubert
| 1926 | NY | A | | | | | 1 |

Harlan Huckleby
1980	GB	N	3	11	3.7	8	0
1981			27	221	8.2	39t	3
1983			10	87	8.7	14	0
1984			8	65	8.1	13	0
1985			5	27	5.4	8	0
Career			53	411	7.8	39t	3

Bob Hudson
1951	NYG	N	4	122	30.5	50	0
1952			4	40	10.0	19	0
Career			8	162	20.3	50	0

Bob Hudson
| 1973 | OAK | N | 1 | 9 | 9.0 | 9 | 0 |

Gordon Hudson
| 1986 | SEA | N | 13 | 131 | 10.1 | 30 | 1 |

Johnnie Hudson
| 1921 | WAS | A | | | | | 1 |

Ken Huff
| 1981 | BAL | N | 1 | -1 | -1.0 | -1 | 0 |

Darvell Huffman
| 1991 | IND | N | 3 | 14 | 4.7 | 7 | 0 |

Dick Huffman
| 1949 | LA | N | 2 | 36 | 18.0 | 23 | 0 |
| Playoffs | | | 2 | 26 | 13.0 | | 0 |

Vern Huffman
1937	DET	N	8	104	13.0		0
1938			1	17	17.0	17	0
Career			9	121	13.4	17	0

Harry Hugasian
| 1955 | BAL | N | 3 | 32 | 10.7 | 13 | 0 |

Roy Huggins
| 1944 | CLE | N | 1 | 0 | 0.0 | 0 | 0 |

Chuck Hughes
1968	PHI	N	3	39	13.0	18	0
1969			3	29	9.7	15	0
1970	DET	N	8	162	20.3	42	0
1971			1	32	32.0	32	0
Career			15	262	17.5	42	0

Danan Hughes
1994	KC	N	7	80	11.4	22	0
1995			14	103	7.4	16	1
1996			17	167	9.8	26	1
Career			38	350	9.2	26	2
Playoffs			2	26	13.0		0

David Hughes
1981	SEA	N	35	263	7.5	22	2
1982			11	98	8.9	29t	1
1983			10	100	10.0	33t	1
1984			22	121	5.5	25	1
1985			19	184	9.7	26	0
1986	PIT	N	10	98	9.8	22	0
Career			107	864	8.1	33t	5
Playoffs			2	18	9.0		0

Dennis Hughes
| 1970 | PIT | N | 24 | 332 | 13.8 | 72t | 3 |

George Hughes
| 1952 | PIT | N | 0 | 2 | | 2L | 0 |

Tommy Hughitt
| 1921 | BUF | A | | | | | 2 |

George Hughley
| 1965 | WAS | N | 9 | 93 | 10.3 | 27 | 1 |

Mike Hull
| 1968 | CHI | N | 4 | 20 | 5.0 | 9 | 0 |

Mike Hull continued
1969			12	63	5.3	29	0
1970			13	44	3.4	17	0
Career			29	127	4.4	29	0

Vivian Hultman
1925	DET	N					1
1926							1
1927	POT	N					1
Career							3

Dick Humbert
1941	PHI	N	29	332	11.4	33	3
1945			6	53	8.8	12	0
1946			18	191	10.6	22	3
1947			13	139	10.7	19	0
1948			1	2	2.0	2	0
1949			1	14	14.0	14	0
Career			68	731	10.8	33	6
Playoffs			2	30	15.0		0

Bobby Humphery
| 1984 | NYJ | N | 14 | 206 | 14.7 | 44t | 1 |

Bobby Humphrey
1989	DEN	N	22	156	7.1	13	1
1990			24	152	6.3	26	0
1992	MIA	N	54	507	9.4	26	1
Career			100	815	8.2	44t	2
Playoffs			14	138	9.9		0

Ronald Humphrey
1994	IND	N	3	19	6.3	12	0
1995			2	11	5.5	6	0
Career			5	30	6.0	12	0
Playoffs			1	-2	-2.0		0

Stan Humphries
| 1995 | SD | N | 1 | -4 | -4.0 | -4 | 0 |

James Hundon
| 1996 | CIN | N | 1 | 14 | 14.0 | 14t | 1 |

Chuck Hunsinger
1950	CHIB	N	1	20	20.0	20	0
1951			6	59	9.8	19t	1
1952			16	170	10.6	30t	2
Career			23	249	10.8	30t	3

Al Hunter
1977	SEA	N	5	42	8.4	20	0
1978			12	172	14.3	21	0
1979			7	77	11.0	18	0
1980			3	40	13.3	18	0
Career			27	331	12.3	21	0

Earnest Hunter
1995	CLE	N	5	42	8.4	17	0
1996	BAL-NO	N	18	163	9.1	25	0
Career			23	205	8.9	25	0

Eddie Hunter
| 1987 | NYJ-TB | N | 7 | 28 | 4.0 | 8t | 2 |

George Hunter
| 1965 | WAS | N | 1 | 29 | 29.0 | 29t | 1 |

Herman Hunter
1985	PHI	N	28	405	14.5	43	1
1986	DET	N	25	218	8.7	18t	1
1987	HOU	N	3	17	5.7	11	0
Career			56	640	11.4	43	2

Ivy Joe Hunter
| 1991 | NE | N | 11 | 97 | 8.8 | 25 | 0 |

Stan Hunter
| 1987 | NYJ | N | 6 | 50 | 8.3 | 12 | 1 |

Tony Hunter
1983	BUF	N	36	402	11.2	40t	3
1984			33	331	10.0	30	2
1985	LARM	N	50	562	11.2	47t	4

Tony Hunter continued
1986			15	206	13.7	42	0
Career			134	1501	11.2	47t	9
Playoffs			4	32	8.0		0

Richard Huntley
| 1996 | ATL | N | 1 | 14 | 14.0 | 14 | 0 |

John Hurlburt
| 1924 | CHIC | N | | | | | 1 |

Bill Hurley
| 1982 | NO | N | 1 | 39 | 39.0 | 39t | 1 |

Al Hust
| 1946 | CHIC | N | 1 | 9 | 9.0 | 9 | 0 |

Tom Hutchinson
1963	CLE	N	9	244	27.1	70	0
1964			3	24	8.0	12	0
1965			6	113	18.8	24t	2
1966	ATL	N	1	28	28.0	8	0
Career			19	409	21.5	70	2

Anthony Hutchison
| 1984 | CHI | N | 1 | 7 | 7.0 | 7 | 0 |

Don Hutson
1935	GB	N	18	420	23.3	83t	6
1936			**34**	**526**	15.5	87	9
1937			**41**	**552**	13.5	78	**7**
1938			32	**548**	17.1	54	9
1939			**34**	**846**	24.9	92	6
1940			45	664	14.8	36	**7**
1941			**58**	**738**	12.7	45	**10**
1942			**74**	**1211**	16.4	73	**17**
1943			**47**	**776**	16.5	79	**11**
1944			**58**	**866**	14.9	55t	9
1945			47	834	17.7	75t	9
Career			488	7981	16.4	92	100
Playoffs			10	172	17.2		1

John Huzvar
1952	PHI	N	13	37	2.8	12	0
1953	BAL	N	6	55	9.2	30t	1
Career			19	92	4.8	30t	1

Freddie Hyatt
1971	STL	N	4	58	14.5	30	0
1972			2	32	16.0	25	0
Career			6	90	15.0	30	0

Bob Hyland
| 1973 | NYG | N | 1 | 16 | 16.0 | 16 | 0 |

Henry Hynoski
| 1975 | CLE | N | 4 | 31 | 7.8 | 15 | 0 |

Ted Illman
| 1926 | LA | A | | | | | 1 |

Tut Imlay
| 1926 | LA | N | | | | | 1 |

Darryl Ingram
| 1989 | MIN | N | 5 | 47 | 9.4 | 21 | 1 |
| Playoffs | | | 2 | 9 | 4.5 | | 0 |

Mark Ingram
1987	NYG	N	2	32	16.0	18	0
1988			13	158	12.2	32	1
1989			17	290	17.1	41t	1
1990			26	499	19.2	57t	5
1991			51	824	16.2	41	3
1992			27	408	15.1	34	1
1993	MIA	N	44	707	16.1	77t	6
1994			44	506	11.5	64t	0
1995	GB	N	39	469	12.0	29	3
1996	PHI	N	2	33	16.5	20	0
Career			265	3926	14.8	77t	26
Playoffs			16	190	11.9		0

Michael Irvin
| 1988 | DAL | N | 32 | 654 | 20.4 | 61t | 5 |

Michael Irvin continued

Year	Team		No	Yds	Avg	Lg	TD
1989			26	378	14.5	65t	2
1990			20	413	20.6	61t	5
1991			93	**1523**	16.4	66t	8
1992			78	1396	17.9	87t	7
1993			88	1330	15.1	61t	7
1994			79	1241	15.7	65t	6
1995			111	1603	14.4	50	10
1996			64	962	15.0	61	2
Career			591	9500	16.1	87t	52
Playoffs			83	1283	15.5		8

Tex Irvin

Year	Team		No	Yds	Avg	Lg	TD
1933	NYG	N					1

Don Irwin

Year	Team		No	Yds	Avg	Lg	TD
1936	BOS	N	2	31	15.5		0
1937	WAS	N	8	112	14.0		0
1938			16	138	8.6		0
1939			1	8	8.0	8	0
Career			27	289	10.7	8	0
Playoffs			2	9	4.5		0

Cecil Isbell

Year	Team		No	Yds	Avg	Lg	TD
1938	GB	N	5	104	20.8		0
1939			9	71	7.9		0
1941			1	-1	-1.0	-1	0
Career			15	174	11.6	-1	0
Playoffs			1	22	22.0		0

John Isenbarger

Year	Team		No	Yds	Avg	Lg	TD
1970	SF	N	8	158	19.8	61t	1
1972			3	66	22.0	33	1
1973			10	67	6.7	18	0
Career			21	291	13.9	61t	2

Qadry Ismail

Year	Team		No	Yds	Avg	Lg	TD
1993	MIN	N	19	212	11.2	37	1
1994			45	696	15.5	65t	5
1995			32	597	18.7	85t	3
1996			22	351	16.0	54t	3
Career			118	1856	15.7	85t	12
Playoffs			7	113	16.1		0

Raghib Ismail

Year	Team		No	Yds	Avg	Lg	TD
1993	LARI	N	26	353	13.6	43t	1
1994			34	513	15.1	42	5
1995	OAK	N	28	491	17.5	73t	3
1996	CAR	N	12	214	17.8	51	0
Career			100	1571	15.7	73t	9
Playoffs			1	24	24.0		0

Rickey Isom

Year	Team		No	Yds	Avg	Lg	TD
1987	MIA	N	1	11	11.0	11	0

Jack Itzel

Year	Team		No	Yds	Avg	Lg	TD
1945	PIT	N	1	4	4.0	4	0

Duke Iverson

Year	Team		No	Yds	Avg	Lg	TD
1947	NYG	N	1	11	11.0	11	0
1948	NY	AA	4	30	7.5		0
Career			5	41	8.2	11	0

Eddie Lee Ivery

Year	Team		No	Yds	Avg	Lg	TD
1980	GB	N	50	481	9.6	46t	1
1981			2	10	5.0	8	0
1982			16	186	11.6	62	1
1983			16	139	8.7	17	1
1984			19	141	7.4	18	1
1985			28	270	9.6	24	2
1986			31	385	12.4	42	1
Career			162	1612	10.0	62	7
Playoffs			2	29	14.5		1

Horace Ivory

Year	Team		No	Yds	Avg	Lg	TD
1978	NE	N	14	122	8.7	18	0
1979			23	216	9.4	24	2
1980			12	95	7.9	19	0
1982	SEA	N	5	38	7.6	12	0
Career			54	471	8.7	24	2

Pop Ivy

Year	Team		No	Yds	Avg	Lg	TD
1940	CHIC	N	2	32	16.0		0
1941			20	183	9.2	16	0

Pop Ivy continued

Year	Team		No	Yds	Avg	Lg	TD
1942			27	259	9.6	19	0
1946			4	39	9.8	19	1
Career			53	513	9.7	19	1

Alfred Jackson

Year	Team		No	Yds	Avg	Lg	TD
1978	ATL	N	26	526	20.2	71	2
1979			11	156	14.2	23	0
1980			23	412	17.9	54t	7
1981			37	604	16.3	49	6
1982			26	361	13.9	40	1
1983			13	220	16.9	54t	3
1984			52	731	14.1	50t	2
Career			188	3010	16.0	71	21
Playoffs			3	21	7.0		0

Andrew Jackson

Year	Team		No	Yds	Avg	Lg	TD
1987	HOU	N	10	44	4.4	16	0

Bernie Jackson

Year	Team		No	Yds	Avg	Lg	TD
1974	CIN	N	1	22	22.0	22	0

Billy Jackson

Year	Team		No	Yds	Avg	Lg	TD
1981	KC	N	6	31	5.2	10	1
1982			5	41	8.2	13	0
1983			32	243	7.6	29	0
1984			15	101	6.7	11	1
Career			58	416	7.2	29	2

Bo Jackson

Year	Team		No	Yds	Avg	Lg	TD
1987	LARI	N	16	136	8.5	23	2
1988			9	79	8.8	27	0
1989			9	69	7.7	20	0
1990			6	68	11.3	18	0
Career			40	352	8.8	27	2

Bob Jackson

Year	Team		No	Yds	Avg	Lg	TD
1962	SD	A	13	136	10.5	33	2
1963			8	85	10.6	26	0
1964	OAK	A	10	81	8.1	14	0
1965	HOU	A	1	31	31.0	31	0
Career			32	333	10.4	33	2

Cedric Jackson

Year	Team		No	Yds	Avg	Lg	TD
1991	DET	N	1	-2	-2.0	-2	0

Cleveland Jackson

Year	Team		No	Yds	Avg	Lg	TD
1979	NYG	N	1	7	7.0	7	0

Earnest Jackson

Year	Team		No	Yds	Avg	Lg	TD
1983	SD	N	5	42	8.4	10	0
1984			39	222	5.7	21	1
1985	PHI	N	10	126	12.6	25	1
1986	PIT	N	17	169	9.9	28	0
1987			7	52	7.4	23	0
1988			9	84	9.3	24	0
Career			87	695	8.0	28	2

Frank Jackson

Year	Team		No	Yds	Avg	Lg	TD
1961	DAL	A	13	171	13.2	52	2
1962			10	177	17.7	62	1
1963	KC	A	50	785	15.7	82	8
1964			62	943	15.2	72	9
1965			28	440	15.7	73	1
1966	MIA	A	16	317	19.8	48	2
1967			9	122	13.6	26	1
Career			188	2955	15.7	82	24

Harold Jackson

Year	Team		No	Yds	Avg	Lg	TD
1969	PHI	N	65	**1116**	17.2	65t	9
1970			41	613	15.0	79t	5
1971			47	716	15.2	69t	3
1972			62	1048	16.9	77t	4
1973	LA	N	40	874	21.9	69t	13
1974			30	514	17.1	44t	5
1975			43	786	18.3	54t	7
1976			39	751	19.3	65t	5
1977			48	666	13.9	58	6
1978	NE	N	37	743	20.1	57	6
1979			45	1013	22.5	59	7
1980			35	737	21.1	40	5
1981			39	669	17.2	45	3

Harold Jackson continued

Year	Team		No	Yds	Avg	Lg	TD
1983	SEA	N	8	126	15.8	29	1
Career			579	10372	17.9	79t	76
Playoffs			24	548	22.8		5

Jack Jackson

Year	Team		No	Yds	Avg	Lg	TD
1996	CHI	N	4	39	9.8	14	0

Jazz Jackson

Year	Team		No	Yds	Avg	Lg	TD
1974	NYJ	N	2	44	22.0	24	1
1975			5	54	10.8	14	0
1976			2	3	1.5	6	0
Career			9	101	11.2	24	1

Jim Jackson

Year	Team		No	Yds	Avg	Lg	TD
1966	SF	N	1	63	63.0	63t	1

John Jackson

Year	Team		No	Yds	Avg	Lg	TD
1991	PHX	N	8	108	13.5	30	0
1992			1	5	5.0	5t	1
Career			9	113	12.6	30	1

Keith Jackson

Year	Team		No	Yds	Avg	Lg	TD
1988	PHI	N	81	869	10.7	41	6
1989			63	648	10.3	33	3
1990			50	670	13.4	37t	6
1991			48	569	11.9	73t	5
1992	MIA	N	48	594	12.4	42	5
1993			39	613	15.7	57t	6
1994			59	673	11.4	35	7
1995	GB	N	13	142	10.9	22	1
1996			40	505	12.6	51t	10
Career			441	5283	12.0	73t	49
Playoffs			51	834	16.4		6

Kenny Jackson

Year	Team		No	Yds	Avg	Lg	TD
1984	PHI	N	26	398	15.3	83t	1
1985			40	692	17.3	54	1
1986			30	506	16.9	49	6
1987			21	471	22.4	70t	3
1989	HOU	N	4	31	7.8	18	0
1990	PHI	N	1	43	43.0	43	0
1991			4	29	7.3	9	0
Career			126	2170	17.2	83t	11

Larron Jackson

Year	Team		No	Yds	Avg	Lg	TD
1973	DEN	N	1	-2	-2.0	-2	0

Leroy Jackson

Year	Team		No	Yds	Avg	Lg	TD
1962	WAS	N	10	253	25.3	85t	1

Louis Jackson

Year	Team		No	Yds	Avg	Lg	TD
1981	NYG	N	3	25	8.3	19	0

Mark Jackson

Year	Team		No	Yds	Avg	Lg	TD
1986	DEN	N	38	738	19.4	53	1
1987			26	436	16.8	52	2
1988			46	852	18.5	63	6
1989			28	446	15.9	49	2
1990			57	926	16.2	66	4
1991			33	603	18.3	71	1
1992			48	745	15.5	51t	8
1993	NYG	N	58	708	12.2	40t	4
1994	IND	N	8	97	12.1	22	1
Career			342	5551	16.2	71	29
Playoffs			25	451	18.0		2

Mel Jackson

Year	Team		No	Yds	Avg	Lg	TD
1976	GB	N	1	8	8.0	8	0

Michael Jackson

Year	Team		No	Yds	Avg	Lg	TD
1991	CLE	N	17	268	15.8	65t	2
1992			47	755	16.1	69t	7
1993			41	756	18.4	62t	8
1994			21	304	14.5	30	2
1995			44	714	16.2	70t	9
1996	BAL	N	76	1201	15.8	86t	14
Career			246	3998	16.3	86t	42
Playoffs			10	169	16.9		0

Noah Jackson

Year	Team		No	Yds	Avg	Lg	TD
1975	CHI	N	1	17	17.0	17	0

Randy Jackson

Year	Team		No	Yds	Avg	Lg	TD
1972	BUF	N	2	21	10.5	13t	1
1973	SF	N	1	20	20.0	20	0
1974	PHI	N	2	17	8.5	9	0
Career			5	58	11.6	20	1

Wilbur Jackson

Year	Team		No	Yds	Avg	Lg	TD
1974	SF	N	23	190	8.3	31	2
1975			17	128	7.5	20	0
1976			33	324	9.8	32	1
1977			22	169	7.7	24	0
1979			53	422	8.0	34	0
1980	WAS	N	27	279	10.3	27	1
1981			7	51	7.3	16	0
1982			1	9	9.0	9	0
Career			183	1572	8.6	34	4

Willie Jackson

Year	Team		No	Yds	Avg	Lg	TD
1995	JAC	N	53	589	11.1	45	5
1996			33	486	14.7	58	3
Career			86	1075	12.5	58	8
Playoffs			4	46	11.5		0

Allen Jacobs

Year	Team		No	Yds	Avg	Lg	TD
1966	NYG	N	10	69	6.9	29	0

Jack Jacobs

Year	Team		No	Yds	Avg	Lg	TD
1946	WAS	N	4	53	13.3	21	0

Harry Jacunski

Year	Team		No	Yds	Avg	Lg	TD
1939	GB	N	5	104	20.8		2
1940			2	29	14.5		0
1941			4	48	12.0	27	0
1942			8	125	15.6	49	1
1943			24	528	22.0	86	3
1944			9	151	16.8	48	0
Career			52	985	18.9	86	6
Playoffs			1	31	31.0		0

Harry Jagade

Year	Team		No	Yds	Avg	Lg	TD
1949	BAL	AA	8	44	5.5		0
1952	CLE	N	9	203	22.6	47t	1
1953			20	193	9.7	37	0
1954	CHIB	N	24	172	7.2	26	0
1955			7	16	2.3	15	0
Career			68	628	9.2	47t	1
Playoffs			1	18	18.0		0

Arrike James

Year	Team		No	Yds	Avg	Lg	TD
1987	HOU	N	1	14	14.0	14	0

Claudis James

Year	Team		No	Yds	Avg	Lg	TD
1968	GB	N	8	148	18.5	24	2

Craig James

Year	Team		No	Yds	Avg	Lg	TD
1984	NE	N	22	159	7.2	16	0
1985			27	360	13.3	90t	2
1986			18	129	7.2	17	0
1988			14	171	12.2	32	0
Career			81	819	10.1	90t	2
Playoffs			6	90	15.0		0

Dick James

Year	Team		No	Yds	Avg	Lg	TD
1956	WAS	N	7	127	18.1	34t	2
1958			2	33	16.5	18	0
1959			13	192	14.8	41t	1
1960			16	243	15.2	49t	2
1961			20	298	14.9	44	2
1962			19	373	19.6	49t	5
1963			15	302	20.1	77	2
1964	NYG	N	12	101	8.4	34	1
Career			104	1669	16.0	77	15

Garry James

Year	Team		No	Yds	Avg	Lg	TD
1986	DET	N	34	219	6.4	26	0
1987			16	215	13.4	46	0
1988			39	382	9.8	39t	2
Career			89	816	9.2	46	2

Lionel James

Year	Team		No	Yds	Avg	Lg	TD
1984	SD	N	23	206	9.0	31	0
1985			86	1027	11.9	67t	6
1986			23	173	7.5	18	0
1987			41	593	14.5	46	3

Lionel James *continued*

Year	Team		No	Yds	Avg	Lg	TD
1988			36	279	7.8	31	1
Career			209	2278	10.9	67t	10

Lynn James

Year	Team		No	Yds	Avg	Lg	TD
1990	CIN	N	3	36	12.0	16	0
1991			7	103	14.7	22	1
Career			10	139	13.9	22	1

Robert James

Year	Team		No	Yds	Avg	Lg	TD
1969	BUF	A	1	19	19.0	19	0

Ron James

Year	Team		No	Yds	Avg	Lg	TD
1972	PHI	N	20	156	7.8	35	1
1973			17	94	5.5	13	0
1974			33	230	7.0	34	0
1975			32	267	8.3	47t	1
Career			102	747	7.3	47t	2

Tommy James

Year	Team		No	Yds	Avg	Lg	TD
1948	CLE	AA	1	44	44.0	44	0

Al Jamison

Year	Team		No	Yds	Avg	Lg	TD
Playoffs			1	-9	-9.0		0

Bobby Jancik

Year	Team		No	Yds	Avg	Lg	TD
1964	HOU	A	1	14	14.0	14	0

Len Janiak

Year	Team		No	Yds	Avg	Lg	TD
1939	BKN	N	2	6	3.0		0
1940	CLE	N	1	3	3.0	3	0
1941			2	5	2.5	3	0
1942			6	51	8.5	19	1
Career			11	65	5.9	19	1

Bruce Jankowski

Year	Team		No	Yds	Avg	Lg	TD
1972	KC	N	2	24	12.0	18	0

Ed Jankowski

Year	Team		No	Yds	Avg	Lg	TD
1937	GB	N	1	60	60.0	60	1
1939			1	5	5.0	5	0
Career			2	65	32.5	60	1
Playoffs			1	19	19.0		0

Vic Janowicz

Year	Team		No	Yds	Avg	Lg	TD
1954	WAS	N	1	-1	-1.0	-1	0
1955			11	149	13.5	48t	3
Career			12	148	12.3	48t	3

Val Jansante

Year	Team		No	Yds	Avg	Lg	TD
1946	PIT	N	10	136	13.6	34	1
1947			35	599	17.1	46	5
1948			39	623	16.0	66t	3
1949			29	445	15.3	47	4
1950			26	353	13.6	40	0
1951	GB	N	1	6	6.0	6	0
1951	PIT-GB	N	16	200	12.5	46t	1
Career			156	2362	15.1	66t	14

Mike Jarmoluk

Year	Team		No	Yds	Avg	Lg	TD
1947	CHIB	N	2	33	16.5	24t	1

Toimi Jarvi

Year	Team		No	Yds	Avg	Lg	TD
1944	PHI	N	1	9	9.0	9	0

Ray Jarvis

Year	Team		No	Yds	Avg	Lg	TD
1972	ATL	N	1	18	18.0	18	0
1973	BUF	N	1	12	12.0	12	0
1974	DET	N	3	87	29.0	56	0
1975			29	501	17.3	62	4
1976			39	822	21.1	74t	5
1977			28	353	12.6	28	1
1978			1	9	9.0	9	0
1979	NE	N	2	30	15.0	15t	1
Career			104	1832	17.6	74t	11

Billy Jefferson

Year	Team		No	Yds	Avg	Lg	TD
1941	DET	N	2	14	7.0	11	0

John Jefferson

Year	Team		No	Yds	Avg	Lg	TD
1978	SD	N	56	1001	17.9	46t	**13**
1979			61	1090	17.9	65t	10
1980			82	**1340**	16.3	58t	**13**

John Jefferson *continued*

Year	Team		No	Yds	Avg	Lg	TD
1981	GB	N	39	632	16.2	41	4
1982			27	452	16.7	50	0
1983			57	830	14.6	36	7
1984			26	339	13.0	33	0
1985	CLE	N	3	30	10.0	17	0
Career			351	5714	16.3	65t	47
Playoffs			23	431	18.7		2

Roy Jefferson

Year	Team		No	Yds	Avg	Lg	TD
1965	PIT	N	13	287	22.1	50t	1
1966			32	772	24.1	84t	4
1967			29	459	15.8	58t	4
1968			58	**1074**	18.5	62	11
1969			67	1079	16.1	63	9
1970	BAL	N	44	749	17.0	55t	7
1971	WAS	N	47	701	14.9	70t	4
1972			35	550	15.7	45t	3
1973			41	595	14.5	36	1
1974			43	654	15.2	43	4
1975			15	255	17.0	36	2
1976			27	364	13.5	27	2
Career			451	7539	16.7	84t	52
Playoffs			30	434	14.5		4

Shawn Jefferson

Year	Team		No	Yds	Avg	Lg	TD
1991	SD	N	12	125	10.4	29	1
1992			29	377	13.0	51	2
1993			30	391	13.0	39t	2
1994			43	627	14.6	52t	3
1995			48	621	12.9	45	2
1996	NE	N	50	771	15.4	42	4
Career			212	2912	13.7	52t	14
Playoffs			21	261	12.4		1

Haywood Jeffires

Year	Team		No	Yds	Avg	Lg	TD
1987	HOU	N	7	89	12.7	23	0
1988			2	49	24.5	42	1
1989			47	619	13.2	45t	2
1990			74	1048	14.2	87t	8
1991			100	1181	11.8	44	7
1992			90	913	10.1	47	9
1993			66	753	11.4	66t	6
1994			68	783	11.5	50	6
1995			61	684	11.2	35t	8
1996	NO	N	20	215	10.8	27t	3
Career			535	6334	11.8	87t	50
Playoffs			41	513	12.5		3

Tom Jelley

Year	Team		No	Yds	Avg	Lg	TD
1951	PIT	N	1	8	8.0	8	0

Dietrich Jells

Year	Team		No	Yds	Avg	Lg	TD
1996	NE	N	1	5	5.0	5	0

Bob Jencks

Year	Team		No	Yds	Avg	Lg	TD
1963	CHI	N	1	6	6.0	6	0
1965	WAS	N	2	20	10.0	12	0
Career			3	26	8.7	12	0

Alfred Jenkins

Year	Team		No	Yds	Avg	Lg	TD
1975	ATL	N	38	767	20.2	68	6
1976			41	710	17.3	34t	6
1977			39	677	17.4	73t	4
1978			2	28	14.0	22	0
1979			50	858	17.2	57	3
1980			57	1026	18.0	57	6
1981			70	**1358**	19.4	67	**13**
1982			24	347	14.5	43t	1
1983			38	487	12.8	26	1
Career			359	6258	17.4	73t	40
Playoffs			6	207	34.5		1

Eddie Jenkins

Year	Team		No	Yds	Avg	Lg	TD
1974	BUF	N	1	12	12.0	12	0

Jack Jenkins

Year	Team		No	Yds	Avg	Lg	TD
1946	WAS	N	2	27	13.5	14	0
1947			5	96	19.2	37	0
Career			7	123	17.6	37	0

James Jenkins

Year	Team		No	Yds	Avg	Lg	TD
1994	WAS	N	8	32	4.0	9	4
1995			1	2	2.0	2	0

James Jenkins *continued*

Year	Team		No	Yds	Avg	Lg	TD
1996			1	7	7.0	7	0
Career			10	41	4.1	9	4

Ken Jenkins

Year	Team		No	Yds	Avg	Lg	TD
1984	DET	N	21	246	11.7	68	0

Keyvan Jenkins

Year	Team		No	Yds	Avg	Lg	TD
1987	SD	N	8	40	5.0	7	0

Keith Jennings

Year	Team		No	Yds	Avg	Lg	TD
1989	DAL	N	6	47	7.8	14	0
1991	CHI	N	8	109	13.6	19	0
1992			23	264	11.5	23	1
1993			14	150	10.7	29	0
1994			11	75	6.8	23t	3
1995			25	217	8.7	20	6
1996			6	56	9.3	20	0
Career			93	918	9.9	29	10
Playoffs			3	29	9.7		1

Ricky Jennings

Year	Team		No	Yds	Avg	Lg	TD
1976	OAK	N	1	10	10.0	10	0

Stanford Jennings

Year	Team		No	Yds	Avg	Lg	TD
1984	CIN	N	35	346	9.9	43	3
1985			12	101	8.4	24	3
1986			6	86	14.3	34	0
1987			35	277	7.9	24	2
1988			5	75	15.0	31	0
1989			10	119	11.9	43t	1
1990			4	23	5.8	13	0
1992	TB	N	9	69	7.7	20t	1
Career			116	1096	9.4	43t	10
Playoffs			3	23	7.7		1

Bob Jensen

Year	Team		No	Yds	Avg	Lg	TD
1948	CHI	AA	20	276	13.8		1
1949			2	14	7.0		0
Career			22	290	13.2		1

Derrick Jensen

Year	Team		No	Yds	Avg	Lg	TD
1979	OAK	N	7	23	3.3	7	1
1980			7	87	12.4	32	0
1981			28	271	9.7	21	0
1983	LARI	N	1	2	2.0	2t	1
1984			1	1	1.0	1t	1
Career			44	384	8.7	32	3

Jim Jensen

Year	Team		No	Yds	Avg	Lg	TD
1977	DEN	N	4	63	15.8	34	0
1979			19	144	7.6	25t	1
1980			49	377	7.7	28	1
1981	GB	N	5	49	9.8	16	0
1982			3	18	6.0	11	1
Career			80	651	8.1	34	3
Playoffs			6	73	12.2		1

Jim Jensen

Year	Team		No	Yds	Avg	Lg	TD
1984	MIA	N	13	139	10.7	20	2
1985			1	4	4.0	4t	1
1986			5	50	10.0	20t	1
1987			26	221	8.5	20	1
1988			58	652	11.2	31	5
1989			61	557	9.1	20	6
1990			44	365	8.3	18	1
1991			21	183	8.7	19	2
Career			229	2171	9.5	31	19
Playoffs			5	49	9.8		0

Ron Jessie

Year	Team		No	Yds	Avg	Lg	TD
1971	DET	N	4	87	21.8	51	0
1972			24	424	17.7	82t	4
1973			20	364	18.2	84t	3
1974			54	761	14.1	46	3
1975	LA	N	41	547	13.3	34	3
1976			34	779	22.9	58t	6
1977			9	139	15.4	21	0
1978			49	752	15.3	49	4
1979			11	169	15.4	39t	2
1980	BUF	N	4	56	14.0	20	1
1981			15	200	13.3	44	0
Career			265	4278	16.1	84t	26
Playoffs			21	326	15.5		1

Tim Jessie

Year	Team		No	Yds	Avg	Lg	TD
1987	WAS	N	1	8	8.0	8	0

Billy Jessup

Year	Team		No	Yds	Avg	Lg	TD
1951	SF	N	7	99	14.1	31	1
1952			6	108	18.0	58	1
1954			30	565	18.8	68t	3
1956			2	7	3.5	10	0
1957			2	29	14.5	22	0
1958			5	66	13.2	26t	1
1960	DEN	A	9	120	13.3	26	1
Career			61	994	16.3	68t	7

Bob Jeter

Year	Team		No	Yds	Avg	Lg	TD
1963	GB	N	1	2	2.0	2	0
1964			1	23	23.0	23	0
Career			2	25	12.5	23	0

Perry Jeter

Year	Team		No	Yds	Avg	Lg	TD
1956	CHIB	N	5	52	10.4	23	0
1957			2	9	4.5	11	0
Career			7	61	8.7	23	0

Tony Jeter

Year	Team		No	Yds	Avg	Lg	TD
1966	PIT	N	2	18	9.0	11	0
1968			1	9	9.0	9	0
Career			3	27	9.0	11	0

James Jett

Year	Team		No	Yds	Avg	Lg	TD
1993	LARI	N	33	771	**23.4**	74t	3
1994			15	253	16.9	54	0
1995	OAK	N	13	179	13.8	26t	1
1996			43	601	14.0	58t	4
Career			104	1804	17.3	74t	8
Playoffs			4	114	28.5		1

John Jett

Year	Team		No	Yds	Avg	Lg	TD
1941	DET	N	4	50	12.5	18	0

Bob Jewett

Year	Team		No	Yds	Avg	Lg	TD
1958	CHIB	N	15	192	12.8	26	1

Art Jocher

Year	Team		No	Yds	Avg	Lg	TD
1940	BKN	N	1	2	2.0	2	1

Jim Jodat

Year	Team		No	Yds	Avg	Lg	TD
1977	LA	N	1	2	2.0	2t	1
1978			3	21	7.0	10	0
1980	SEA	N	26	190	7.3	14	1
1981			4	52	13.0	26	0
1982	SD	N	1	0	0.0	0	0
Career			35	265	7.6	26	2

Billy Joe

Year	Team		No	Yds	Avg	Lg	TD
1963	DEN	A	15	90	6.0	34	1
1964			12	16	1.3	15	0
1965	BUF	A	27	271	10.0	78	2
1966	MIA	A	13	116	8.9	67	1
1967	NY	A	8	85	10.6	17	0
1968			2	11	5.5	11	0
Career			77	589	7.6	78	4

Larry Joe

Year	Team		No	Yds	Avg	Lg	TD
1949	BUF	AA	2	52	26.0		0

Herb Joesting

Year	Team		No	Yds	Avg	Lg	TD
1930	FRA	N					1

Paul Johns

Year	Team		No	Yds	Avg	Lg	TD
1981	SEA	N	8	131	16.4	34	1
1982			15	234	15.6	35	1
1983			34	486	14.3	30t	4
1984			17	207	12.2	32	1
Career			74	1058	14.3	35	7
Playoffs			11	168	15.3		1

Al Johnson

Year	Team		No	Yds	Avg	Lg	TD
1972	HOU	N	6	24	4.0	16	0

Andy Johnson

Year	Team		No	Yds	Avg	Lg	TD
1974	NE	N	8	147	18.4	34	0
1975			26	294	11.3	29	1
1976			29	343	11.8	53	4
1978			26	267	10.3	31	0

Andy Johnson *continued*

Year	Team		No	Yds	Avg	Lg	TD
1979			9	68	7.6	11	0
1980			24	259	10.8	22	3
1981			39	429	11.0	36	1
Career			161	1807	11.2	53	9
Playoffs			5	36	7.2		0

Anthony Johnson

Year	Team		No	Yds	Avg	Lg	TD
1990	IND	N	5	32	6.4	15t	2
1991			42	344	8.2	24	0
1992			49	517	10.6	57t	3
1993			55	443	8.1	36	0
1994	NYJ	N	5	31	6.2	9	0
1995	CHI-CAR	N	29	207	7.1	37	0
1996	CAR	N	26	192	7.4	55	0
Career			211	1766	8.4	57t	5
Playoffs			2	23	11.5		0

Barry Johnson

Year	Team		No	Yds	Avg	Lg	TD
1991	DEN	N	1	13	13.0	13	0

Bert Johnson

Year	Team		No	Yds	Avg	Lg	TD
1937	BKN	N	1	3	3.0	3	0
1940	CHIC	N	2	52	26.0		0
1941			4	90	22.5	29	0
1942	PHI	N	9	123	13.7	65	2
Career			16	268	16.8	65	3

Bill Johnson

Year	Team		No	Yds	Avg	Lg	TD
1951	SF	N	0	3		3L	0

Bill Johnson

Year	Team		No	Yds	Avg	Lg	TD
1986	CIN	N	13	103	7.9	17	0
1987			3	19	6.3	9	0
Career			16	122	7.6	17	0

Billy Johnson

Year	Team		No	Yds	Avg	Lg	TD
1974	HOU	N	29	388	13.4	44	2
1975			37	393	10.6	30	1
1976			47	495	10.5	40t	4
1977			20	412	20.6	71t	3
1978			1	10	10.0	10	0
1979			6	108	18.0	29	1
1980			31	343	11.1	57t	2
1982	ATL	N	2	11	5.5	6	0
1983			64	709	11.1	47t	4
1984			24	371	15.5	45t	3
1985			62	830	13.4	62t	5
1986			6	57	9.5	27	0
1987			8	84	10.5	19	0
Career			337	4211	12.5	71t	25
Playoffs			1	11	11.0		0

Bob Johnson

Year	Team		No	Yds	Avg	Lg	TD
1974	CIN	N	1	3	3.0	3	0

Bobby Lee Johnson

Year	Team		No	Yds	Avg	Lg	TD
1984	NYG	N	48	795	16.6	45	7
1985			33	533	16.2	42	8
1986			31	534	17.2	44t	5
Career			112	1862	16.6	45	20
Playoffs			6	61	10.2		1

Butch Johnson

Year	Team		No	Yds	Avg	Lg	TD
1976	DAL	N	5	84	16.8	43t	2
1977			12	135	11.3	22t	1
1978			12	155	12.9	23	0
1979			6	105	17.5	28	1
1980			19	263	13.8	29t	4
1981			25	552	22.1	55	5
1982			12	269	22.4	49	3
1983			41	561	13.7	46	3
1984	DEN	N	42	560	13.3	40	4
1985			19	380	20.0	65t	3
Career			193	3091	16.0	65t	28
Playoffs			25	394	15.8		4

Cecil Johnson

Year	Team		No	Yds	Avg	Lg	TD
1943	BKN	N	9	136	15.1	57	2

Charles Johnson

Year	Team		No	Yds	Avg	Lg	TD
1994	PIT	N	38	577	15.2	84t	3
1995			38	432	11.4	33	0

Year	Team		No	Yds	Avg	Lg	TD

Charles Johnson continued

Year	Team		No	Yds	Avg	Lg	TD
1996			60	1008	16.8	70t	3
Career			136	2017	14.8	84t	6
Playoffs			5	109	21.8		0

Curley Johnson

Year	Team		No	Yds	Avg	Lg	TD
1960	DAL	A	10	174	17.4	36	1
1961	NY	A	1	32	32.0	32	0
1962			14	62	4.4	12	0
1965			1	6	6.0	6	1
1966			1	18	18.0	18t	1
1968			5	78	15.6	18	0
Career			32	370	11.6	36	3

Damone Johnson

Year	Team		No	Yds	Avg	Lg	TD
1987	LARM	N	21	198	9.4	20	2
1988			42	350	8.3	23	6
1989			25	148	5.9	22	5
1990			12	66	5.5	11	3
1991			32	253	7.9	27	2
Career			132	1015	7.7	27	18
Playoffs			8	53	6.6		2

Dan Johnson

Year	Team		No	Yds	Avg	Lg	TD
1983	MIA	N	24	189	7.9	33	4
1984			34	426	12.5	42	3
1985			13	192	14.8	61t	3
1986			19	170	8.9	20	4
1987			4	35	8.8	22	2
Career			94	1012	10.8	61t	16
Playoffs			8	84	10.5		3

Dennis Johnson

Year	Team		No	Yds	Avg	Lg	TD
1978	BUF	N	10	83	8.3	28	0

Dick Johnson

Year	Team		No	Yds	Avg	Lg	TD
1963	KC	A	2	17	8.5	11	1

Don Johnson

Year	Team		No	Yds	Avg	Lg	TD
1953	PHI	N	12	227	18.9	41	2
1954			1	20	20.0	20	0
Career			13	247	19.0	41	2

Ellis Johnson

Year	Team		No	Yds	Avg	Lg	TD
1965	BOS	A	4	29	7.3	23	0

Essex Johnson

Year	Team		No	Yds	Avg	Lg	TD
1968	CIN	A	1	33	33.0	33	0
1969			1	3	3.0	3	0
1970	CIN	N	15	190	12.7	51t	2
1971			14	258	18.4	67t	2
1972			29	420	14.5	65t	2
1973			28	356	12.7	78t	3
1974			8	85	10.6	27t	1
1975			25	196	7.8	30	1
1976	TB	N	25	201	8.0	38	1
Career			146	1742	11.9	78t	12
Playoffs			1	6	6.0		0

Flip Johnson

Year	Team		No	Yds	Avg	Lg	TD
1988	BUF	N	9	170	18.9	66t	1
1989			25	303	12.1	36	1
Career			34	473	13.9	66t	2

Harvey Johnson

Year	Team		No	Yds	Avg	Lg	TD
1946	NY	AA	2	19	9.5		0
1948			1	6	6.0	6	0
Career			3	25	8.3	6	0

Herb Johnson

Year	Team		No	Yds	Avg	Lg	TD
1954	NYG	N	10	89	8.9	24	0

Jack Johnson

Year	Team		No	Yds	Avg	Lg	TD
1940	DET	N	1	48	48.0	48	1

Jason Johnson

Year	Team		No	Yds	Avg	Lg	TD
1988	DEN	N	1	6	6.0	6	0

Jimmie Johnson

Year	Team		No	Yds	Avg	Lg	TD
1989	WAS	N	4	84	21.0	39	0
1990			15	218	14.5	35	2
1991			3	7	2.3	4t	2
1992	DET	N	6	34	5.7	9	0
1993			2	18	9.0	9	0

Jimmie Johnson continued

Year	Team		No	Yds	Avg	Lg	TD
1994	KC	N	2	7	3.5	5	0
1995	PHI	N	6	37	6.2	9	0
1996			7	127	18.1	31	0
Career			45	532	11.8	39	4
Playoffs			3	37	12.3		0

Jimmy Johnson

Year	Team		No	Yds	Avg	Lg	TD
1962	SF	N	34	627	18.4	80t	4
1963			6	63	10.5	15	0
Career			40	690	17.3	80t	4

Joe Johnson

Year	Team		No	Yds	Avg	Lg	TD
1948	NYG	N	19	217	11.4	23	2

Joe Johnson

Year	Team		No	Yds	Avg	Lg	TD
1954	GB	N	10	72	7.2	17	1
1955			9	71	7.9	30t	1
1956			28	258	9.2	20	0
1957			7	75	10.7	14	1
1958			10	176	17.6	61	1
1960	BOS	A	11	186	16.9		3
1961			9	82	9.1	21	1
Career			84	920	11.0	61	8

Joe Johnson

Year	Team		No	Yds	Avg	Lg	TD
1990	WAS	N	3	36	12.0	17	0
1992	MIN	N	21	211	10.0	37	1
Career			24	247	10.3	37	1

John Henry Johnson

Year	Team		No	Yds	Avg	Lg	TD
1954	SF	N	28	183	6.5	34	0
1955			2	6	3.0	11	0
1956			8	90	11.3	28	0
1957	DET	N	20	141	7.0	16	0
1958			7	60	8.6	18	0
1959			7	34	4.9	18	1
1960	PIT	N	12	112	9.3	26	1
1961			24	262	10.9	51	1
1962			32	226	7.1	18	2
1963			21	145	6.9	26	1
1964			17	69	4.1	21	1
1966	HOU	A	8	150	18.8	53	0
Career			186	1478	7.9	53	7
Playoffs			1	16	16.0		0

Johnny Johnson

Year	Team		No	Yds	Avg	Lg	TD
1990	PHX	N	25	241	9.6	35	0
1991			29	225	7.8	51t	2
1992			14	103	7.4	26	0
1993	NYJ	N	67	641	9.6	48	1
1994			42	303	7.2	24	2
Career			177	1513	8.5	51t	5

Kelley Johnson

Year	Team		No	Yds	Avg	Lg	TD
1987	IND	N	1	15	15.0	15	0

Kenny Johnson

Year	Team		No	Yds	Avg	Lg	TD
1979	NYG	N	16	108	6.8	15	1

Kermit Johnson

Year	Team		No	Yds	Avg	Lg	TD
1976	SF	N	1	11	11.0	11	0

Keyshawn Johnson

Year	Team		No	Yds	Avg	Lg	TD
1996	NYJ	N	63	844	13.4	50	8

Leo Johnson

Year	Team		No	Yds	Avg	Lg	TD
1969	SF	N	4	42	10.5	14	0

LeShon Johnson

Year	Team		No	Yds	Avg	Lg	TD
1994	GB	N	13	168	12.9	33	0
1996	ARI	N	15	176	11.7	35	1
Career			28	344	12.3	35	1
Playoffs			1	9	9.0		0

Lonnie Johnson

Year	Team		No	Yds	Avg	Lg	TD
1994	BUF	N	3	42	14.0	21	0
1995			49	504	10.3	52	1
1996			46	457	9.9	33	0
Career			98	1003	10.2	52	1
Playoffs			8	55	6.9		0

Marshall Johnson

Year	Team		No	Yds	Avg	Lg	TD
1975	BAL	N	4	115	28.8	68t	2

Marshall Johnson continued

Year	Team		No	Yds	Avg	Lg	TD
1978			1	22	22.0	22	0
Career			5	137	27.4	68t	2

Marv Johnson

Year	Team		No	Yds	Avg	Lg	TD
1951	LA	N	2	38	19.0	28	0

Maurice Johnson

Year	Team		No	Yds	Avg	Lg	TD
1991	PHI	N	6	70	11.7	31t	2
1992			2	16	8.0	13	0
1993			10	81	8.1	17	0
1994			21	204	9.7	22	2
Career			39	371	9.5	31t	4

Mitch Johnson

Year	Team		No	Yds	Avg	Lg	TD
1966	WAS	N	1	1	1.0	1	0

Pete Johnson

Year	Team		No	Yds	Avg	Lg	TD
1977	CIN	N	5	49	9.8	21	0
1978			31	236	7.6	34	0
1979			24	154	6.4	15t	1
1980			21	172	8.2	28t	1
1981			46	320	7.0	33	4
1982			31	267	8.6	25	0
1983			15	129	8.6	18	0
1984	SD	N	2	7	3.5	7	0
Career			175	1334	7.6	34	6
Playoffs			9	52	5.8		0

Reggie Johnson

Year	Team		No	Yds	Avg	Lg	TD
1991	DEN	N	6	73	12.2	31	1
1992			10	139	13.9	48	1
1993			20	243	12.2	38	1
1994	GB	N	7	79	11.3	24	0
1995	PHI	N	5	68	13.6	33	2
1996	KC	N	18	189	10.5	26	1
Career			66	791	12.0	48	6
Playoffs			3	41	13.7		1

Richard Johnson

Year	Team		No	Yds	Avg	Lg	TD
1969	HOU	A	2	17	8.5	16	1

Richard Johnson

Year	Team		No	Yds	Avg	Lg	TD
1987	WAS	N	1	5	5.0	5	0
1989	DET	N	70	1091	15.6	75t	8
1990			64	727	11.4	44t	6
Career			135	1823	13.5	75t	14

Ron Johnson

Year	Team		No	Yds	Avg	Lg	TD
1985	PHI	N	11	186	16.9	37	0
1986			11	207	18.8	39	1
1988			19	417	21.9	54	2
1989			20	295	14.8	34	1
Career			61	1105	18.1	54	4
Playoffs			3	69	23.0		0

Ron Johnson

Year	Team		No	Yds	Avg	Lg	TD
1969	CLE	N	24	164	6.8	18	0
1970	NYG	N	48	487	10.1	50	4
1971			6	47	7.8	30	0
1972			45	451	10.0	39	5
1973			32	377	11.8	45t	3
1974			24	171	7.1	21t	2
1975			34	280	8.2	36t	1
Career			213	1977	9.3	50	15

Rudy Johnson

Year	Team		No	Yds	Avg	Lg	TD
1964	SF	N	5	21	4.2	12	0
1965			3	49	16.3	28	0
Career			8	70	8.8	28	0

Sammy Johnson

Year	Team		No	Yds	Avg	Lg	TD
1974	SF	N	11	106	9.6	23	0
1975			23	177	7.7	20	0
1976	SF-MIN	N	7	74	10.6	24	0
1977	MIN	N	4	21	5.3	8	0
Career			45	378	8.4	24	0
Playoffs			3	26	8.7		0

Steve Johnson

Year	Team		No	Yds	Avg	Lg	TD
1988	NE	N	1	5	5.0	5	0

Tony Johnson

Year	Team		No	Yds	Avg	Lg	TD
1996	NO	N	7	76	10.9	17	1

Tracy Johnson

Year	Team		No	Yds	Avg	Lg	TD
1989	HOU	N	1	8	8.0	8	0
1990	ATL	N	10	79	7.9	16	1
1991			3	27	9.0	13	0
1993	SEA	N	3	15	5.0	8	1
1994			10	91	9.1	17	0
1995			1	-2	-2.0	-2	0
Career			28	218	7.8	17	2

Troy Johnson

Year	Team		No	Yds	Avg	Lg	TD
1986	STL	N	14	203	14.5	39	0
1987			15	308	20.5	49t	2
1988	PIT	N	10	237	23.7	60	0
1989	DET	N	2	29	14.5	22	0
Career			41	777	19.0	60	2

Trumaine Johnson

Year	Team		No	Yds	Avg	Lg	TD
1985	SD	N	4	51	12.8	20t	1
1986			30	399	13.3	30	1
1987	BUF	N	15	186	12.4	26t	2
1988			37	514	13.9	49	0
Career			86	1150	13.4	49	4
Playoffs			5	79	15.8		0

Vance Johnson

Year	Team		No	Yds	Avg	Lg	TD
1985	DEN	N	51	721	14.1	63t	3
1986			31	363	11.7	34t	2
1987			42	684	16.3	59t	7
1988			68	896	13.2	86	5
1989			76	1095	14.4	69	7
1990			54	747	13.8	49	3
1991			21	208	9.9	22	3
1992			24	294	12.3	40	2
1993			36	517	14.4	56	5
1995			12	170	14.2	23	0
Career			415	5695	13.7	86	37
Playoffs			40	715	17.9		4

Luke Johnsos

Year	Team		No	Yds	Avg	Lg	TD
1929	CHIB	N					3
1930							4
1931							1
1932			19	321	16.9		2
1933			8	151	18.9		3
1934			4	57	14.3		1
1935			19	298	15.7		4
1936			5	121	24.2		2
Career			55	948	17.2		20

Chet Johnston

Year	Team		No	Yds	Avg	Lg	TD
1935	GB	N	6	59	9.8		1
1936			2	11	5.5		0
Career			8	70	8.8		1

Daryl Johnston

Year	Team		No	Yds	Avg	Lg	TD
1989	DAL	N	16	133	8.3	28	3
1990			14	148	10.6	26	1
1991			28	244	8.7	22	1
1992			32	249	7.8	18	2
1993			50	372	7.4	20	1
1994			44	325	7.4	24	2
1995			30	248	8.3	24	1
1996			43	278	6.5	23	1
Career			257	1997	7.8	28	12
Playoffs			36	242	6.7		1

Jimmy Johnston

Year	Team		No	Yds	Avg	Lg	TD
1939	WAS	N	11	111	10.1		1
1940			29	350	12.1		3
Career			40	461	11.5		4
Playoffs			3	9	3.0		0

Preston Johnston

Year	Team		No	Yds	Avg	Lg	TD
1946	MIA-BUF	AA	6	54	9.0		1

Charlie Joiner

Year	Team		No	Yds	Avg	Lg	TD
1969	HOU	A	7	77	11.0	16	0
1970	HOU		28	416	14.9	87t	3
1971			31	681	22.0	70t	7
1972	HOU-CIN	N	24	439	18.3	82t	2
1973	CIN		13	214	16.5	26	0
1974			24	390	16.3	65t	1
1975			37	726	19.6	51	5
1976	SD	N	50	1056	21.1	81t	7

Charlie Joiner continued

Year	Team		No	Yds	Avg	Lg	TD
1977			35	542	15.5	32t	6
1978			33	607	18.4	46	1
1979			72	1008	14.0	39	4
1980			71	1132	15.9	51	4
1981			70	1188	17.0	57	7
1982			36	545	15.1	43	0
1983			65	960	14.8	33t	3
1984			61	793	13.0	41	6
1985			59	932	15.8	39t	7
1986			34	440	12.9	33	2
Career			750	12146	16.2	87t	65
Playoffs			35	632	18.1		5

Vernon Joines

Year	Team		No	Yds	Avg	Lg	TD
1990	CLE	N	6	86	14.3	24	0

Lewis Jolley

Year	Team		No	Yds	Avg	Lg	TD
1973	HOU	N	3	56	18.7	48	0

Anthony Jones

Year	Team		No	Yds	Avg	Lg	TD
1984	WAS	N	1	6	6.0	6	0
1988	SD	N	1	11	11.0	11	0
1988	WAS-SD	N	3	21	7.0	11	0
Career			5	38	7.6	11	0

Art Jones

Year	Team		No	Yds	Avg	Lg	TD
1941	PIT	N	4	121	30.3	59	1
1945			5	8	1.6	6	0
Career			9	129	14.3	59	1

Ben Jones

Year	Team		No	Yds	Avg	Lg	TD
1924	CLE	N					1
1925	FRA	N					1
1926							1
Career							4

Bill Jones

Year	Team		No	Yds	Avg	Lg	TD
1990	KC	N	19	137	7.2	19	5
1991			14	97	6.9	14	1
1992			2	6	3.0	5	0
Career			35	240	6.9	19	6
Playoffs			3	27	9.0		0

Bob Jones

Year	Team		No	Yds	Avg	Lg	TD
1967	CHI	N	3	80	26.7	51t	1

Bob Jones

Year	Team		No	Yds	Avg	Lg	TD
1975	ATL	N	1	25	25.0	25	0

Bobby Jones

Year	Team		No	Yds	Avg	Lg	TD
1978	NYJ	N	1	18	18.0	18	0
1979			19	379	19.9	51	1
1980			14	193	13.8	25	0
1981			16	239	14.9	56t	1
1982			3	32	10.7	17	0
1983	CLE	N	36	507	14.1	32t	4
Career			89	1368	15.4	56t	6
Playoffs			4	64	16.0		0

Brent Jones

Year	Team		No	Yds	Avg	Lg	TD
1987	SF	N	2	35	17.5	22	0
1988			8	57	7.1	18t	2
1989			40	500	12.5	36t	4
1990			56	747	13.3	67t	5
1991			27	417	15.4	41	0
1992			45	628	14.0	43	4
1993			68	735	10.8	29	3
1994			49	670	13.7	69t	9
1995			60	595	9.9	39	3
1996			33	428	13.0	39	1
Career			388	4812	12.4	69t	31
Playoffs			56	689	12.3		5

Calvin Jones

Year	Team		No	Yds	Avg	Lg	TD
1994	LARI	N	2	6	3.0	4	0

Cedric Jones

Year	Team		No	Yds	Avg	Lg	TD
1982	NE	N	1	5	5.0	5	0
1983			20	323	16.1	30	1
1984			19	244	12.8	22	2
1985			21	237	11.3	29t	2
1986			14	222	15.9	28	1
1987			25	388	15.5	29	3

Cedric Jones continued

Year	Team		No	Yds	Avg	Lg	TD
1988			22	313	14.2	41t	1
1989			48	670	14.0	65t	6
1990			21	301	14.3	26	0
Career			191	2703	14.2	65t	16
Playoffs			1	19	19.0		0

Charlie Jones

Year	Team		No	Yds	Avg	Lg	TD
1955	WAS	N	4	58	14.5	21	0

Charlie Jones

Year	Team		No	Yds	Avg	Lg	TD
1996	SD	N	41	524	12.8	63t	4

Chris T. Jones

Year	Team		No	Yds	Avg	Lg	TD
1995	PHI	N	5	61	12.2	17	0
1996			70	859	12.3	38	5
Career			75	920	12.3	38	5
Playoffs			3	40	13.3		0

Clint Jones

Year	Team		No	Yds	Avg	Lg	TD
1968	MIN	N	4	26	6.5	14	0
1969			3	23	7.7	9	0
1970			9	117	13.0	72	0
1971			9	98	10.9	18	0
1972			6	42	7.0	10	0
1973	SD	N	7	125	17.9	37	0
Career			38	431	11.3	72	0
Playoffs			1	5	5.0		0

Dave Jones

Year	Team		No	Yds	Avg	Lg	TD
1969	CLE	N	2	33	16.5	22	0
1971			4	66	16.5	21	0
Career			6	99	16.5	22	0
Playoffs			1	17	17.0		0

David Jones

Year	Team		No	Yds	Avg	Lg	TD
1992	LARI	N	2	29	14.5	25	0

Drew Jones

Year	Team		No	Yds	Avg	Lg	TD
1975	NO	N	10	52	5.2	12	0

Dub Jones

Year	Team		No	Yds	Avg	Lg	TD
1948	CLE	AA	9	119	13.2		2
1949			12	241	20.1		1
1950	CLE	N	31	458	14.8	80t	5
1951			30	570	19.0	81t	5
1952			43	651	15.1	63t	4
1953			24	373	15.5	58	0
1954			19	347	18.3	48t	2
1955			3	115	38.3	46	1
Career			171	2874	16.8	81t	20
Playoffs			13	240	18.5		3

Edgar Jones

Year	Team		No	Yds	Avg	Lg	TD
1945	CHIB	N	1	0	0.0	0	0
1946	CLE	AA	4	120	30.0		1
1947			5	92	18.4	51	1
1948			14	293	20.9		5
1949			9	130	14.4		3
Career			33	635	19.2	51	10
Playoffs			16	194	12.1		1

E.J. Jones

Year	Team		No	Yds	Avg	Lg	TD
1985	KC	N	3	31	10.3	15	0
1987	DAL	N	3	16	5.3	10	0
Career			6	47	7.8	15	0

Ernie Jones

Year	Team		No	Yds	Avg	Lg	TD
1988	PHX	N	23	496	21.6	93t	3
1989			45	838	18.6	72t	3
1990			43	724	16.8	68t	4
1991			61	957	15.7	53	4
1992			38	559	14.7	72t	4
1993	LARM	N	5	56	11.2	21t	2
Career			215	3630	16.9	93t	20

Fred Jones

Year	Team		No	Yds	Avg	Lg	TD
1990	KC	N	1	5	5.0	5	0
1991			8	85	10.6	23	0
1992			18	265	14.7	56	0
1993			9	111	12.3	19	0
Career			36	466	12.9	56	0
Playoffs			6	60	10.0		2

Gordon Jones

Year	Team		No	Yds	Avg	Lg	TD
1979	TB	N	4	80	20.0	37t	1
1980			48	669	13.9	41t	5
1981			20	276	13.8	44	1
1982			14	205	14.6	26	1
1983	LARM	N	11	172	15.6	46	0
Career			97	1402	14.5	46	8
Playoffs			1	49	49.0		1

Greg Jones

Year	Team		No	Yds	Avg	Lg	TD
1970	BUF	N	8	98	12.3	24	0
1971			16	113	7.1	21	1
Career			24	211	8.8	24	1

Harry Jones

Year	Team		No	Yds	Avg	Lg	TD
1967	PHI	N	3	32	10.7	23	0
1968			5	87	17.4	48	0
1970			1	12	12.0	12	0
Career			9	131	14.6	48	0

Hassan Jones

Year	Team		No	Yds	Avg	Lg	TD
1986	MIN	N	28	570	20.4	5t	4
1987			7	189	27.0	58t	2
1988			40	778	19.4	68t	5
1989			42	694	16.5	50	1
1990			51	810	15.9	75t	7
1991			32	384	12.0	43	1
1992			22	308	14.0	43t	4
1993	KC	N	7	91	13.0	22	0
Career			229	3824	16.7	75t	24
Playoffs			13	166	12.8		3

Harvey Jones

Year	Team		No	Yds	Avg	Lg	TD
1944	CLE	N	6	59	9.8	19	0
1945			2	36	18.0	44t	1
Career			8	95	11.9	44t	1

Homer Jones

Year	Team		No	Yds	Avg	Lg	TD
1964	NYG	N	4	82	20.5	30	0
1965			26	709	27.3	89t	6
1966			48	1044	**21.8**	98t	8
1967			49	1209	**24.7**	70t	**13**
1968			45	1057	**23.5**	84	7
1969			42	744	17.7	54t	1
1970	CLE	N	10	141	14.1	43t	1
Career			224	4986	**22.3**	98t	36

James Jones

Year	Team		No	Yds	Avg	Lg	TD
1980	DAL	N	5	39	7.8	16	0
1981			6	37	6.2	16	0
1984			7	57	8.1	19	1
1985			24	179	7.5	35	0
Career			42	312	7.4	35	1
Playoffs			6	38	6.3		0

James Jones

Year	Team		No	Yds	Avg	Lg	TD
1983	DET	N	46	467	10.2	46	1
1984			77	662	8.6	39	5
1985			45	334	7.4	36	3
1986			54	334	6.2	21	1
1987			34	262	7.7	35	0
1988			29	259	8.9	40	0
1989	SEA	N	1	8	8.0	8	0
1990			1	22	22.0	22	0
1991			10	103	10.3	29	0
1992			21	190	9.0	30	0
Career			318	2641	8.3	46	10
Playoffs			5	44	8.8		0

James Jones

Year	Team		No	Yds	Avg	Lg	TD
1992	CLE	N	1	1	1.0	1t	1
1994			1	1	1.0	1	0
1996	BAL	N	1	2	2.0	2t	1
Career			3	4	1.3	2t	2

Jimmie Lee Jones

Year	Team		No	Yds	Avg	Lg	TD
1974	DET	N	4	35	8.8	15	0

Jimmy Jones

Year	Team		No	Yds	Avg	Lg	TD
1965	CHI	N	21	350	16.7	54	4
1966			28	504	18.0	80t	5
1967			7	138	19.7	34	0
1968	DEN	A	13	190	14.6	60t	2
Career			69	1182	17.1	80t	11

Joe Jones

Year	Team		No	Yds	Avg	Lg	TD
1987	IND	N	3	25	8.3	13	1

Joey Jones

Year	Team		No	Yds	Avg	Lg	TD
1986	ATL	N	7	141	20.1	41	0

Johnny Jones

Year	Team		No	Yds	Avg	Lg	TD
1980	NYJ	N	25	482	19.3	55	3
1981			20	342	17.1	47t	3
1982			18	294	16.3	51	2
1983			43	734	17.1	50t	4
1984			32	470	14.7	37	1
Career			138	2322	16.8	55	13
Playoffs			7	109	15.6		0

Keith Jones

Year	Team		No	Yds	Avg	Lg	TD
1989	CLE	N	15	126	8.4	36	0

Keith Jones

Year	Team		No	Yds	Avg	Lg	TD
1989	ATL	N	41	396	9.7	46	0
1990			13	103	7.9	16	0
1991			6	58	9.7	15	0
1992			12	94	7.8	15	0
Career			72	651	9.0	46	0

Kim Jones

Year	Team		No	Yds	Avg	Lg	TD
1976	NO	N	1	14	14.0	14	0
1977			1	9	9.0	9	0
1978			2	10	5.0	6	0
Career			4	33	8.3	14	0

Larry Jones

Year	Team		No	Yds	Avg	Lg	TD
1975	WAS	N	2	33	16.5	21	0
1977			5	55	11.0	15	0
1978	SF	N	1	21	21.0	21	0
Career			8	109	13.6	21	0

Mike Jones

Year	Team		No	Yds	Avg	Lg	TD
1983	MIN	N	6	95	15.8	47	0
1984			38	591	15.6	70t	1
1985			46	641	13.9	44t	4
1986	NO	N	48	625	13.0	45	3
1987			27	420	15.6	43t	3
Career			165	2372	14.4	70t	11

Mike Jones

Year	Team		No	Yds	Avg	Lg	TD
1991	MIN	N	2	8	4.0	5t	2
1992	SEA	N	3	18	6.0	7	0
Career			5	26	5.2	7	2

Ralph Jones

Year	Team		No	Yds	Avg	Lg	TD
1946	DET	N	4	84	21.0	29	0
1947	BAL	AA	3	23	7.7		0
Career			7	107	15.3	29	0

Rod Jones

Year	Team		No	Yds	Avg	Lg	TD
1987	KC	N	8	76	9.5	16	1

Steve Jones

Year	Team		No	Yds	Avg	Lg	TD
1975	STL	N	19	194	10.2	21	1
1976			29	152	5.2	15	1
1977			12	66	5.5	16	0
1978			27	217	8.0	38	0
Career			87	629	7.2	38	2
Playoffs			2	19	9.5		0

Tony Jones

Year	Team		No	Yds	Avg	Lg	TD
1990	HOU	N	30	409	13.6	47	6
1991			19	251	13.2	68t	2
1992	ATL	N	14	138	9.9	24	1
Career			63	798	12.7	68t	9
Playoffs			1	19	19.0		0

Victor Jones

Year	Team		No	Yds	Avg	Lg	TD
1992	DEN	N	3	17	5.7	16	0

Andrew Jordan

Year	Team		No	Yds	Avg	Lg	TD
1994	MIN	N	35	336	9.6	25	0
1995			27	185	6.9	17	2
1996			19	128	6.7	15	0
Career			81	649	8.0	25	2
Playoffs			1	10	10.0		0

Buford Jordan

Year	Team		No	Yds	Avg	Lg	TD
1986	NO	N	11	127	11.5	37	0
1987			2	13	6.5	11	0
1988			5	70	14.0	25	0
1989			4	53	13.3	17	0
1991			15	92	6.1	19	1
Career			37	355	9.6	37	1
Playoffs			1	5	5.0		0

Charles Jordan

Year	Team		No	Yds	Avg	Lg	TD
1995	GB	N	7	117	16.7	35	2
1996	MIA	N	7	152	21.7	43	0
Career			14	269	19.2	43	2

Donald Jordan

Year	Team		No	Yds	Avg	Lg	TD
1984	CHI	N	1	6	6.0	6	0

Jeff Jordan

Year	Team		No	Yds	Avg	Lg	TD
1970	LA	N	1	-5	-5.0	-5	0

Randy Jordan

Year	Team		No	Yds	Avg	Lg	TD
1993	LARI	N	4	42	10.5	33	0
1995	JAC	N	5	89	17.8	71t	1
Career			9	131	14.6	71t	1

Steve Jordan

Year	Team		No	Yds	Avg	Lg	TD
1982	MIN	N	3	42	14.0	29	0
1983			15	212	14.1	28	2
1984			38	414	10.9	26	2
1985			68	795	11.7	32	0
1986			58	859	14.8	68t	6
1987			35	490	14.0	38	2
1988			57	756	13.3	38	5
1989			35	506	14.5	34	3
1990			45	636	14.1	38	3
1991			57	638	11.2	25	2
1992			28	394	14.1	60t	2
1993			56	542	9.7	53	1
1994			3	23	7.7	10	0
Career			498	6307	12.7	68t	28
Playoffs			30	378	12.6		1

Tony Jordan

Year	Team		No	Yds	Avg	Lg	TD
1988	PHX	N	4	24	6.0	12	0
1989			6	20	3.3	8	0
Career			10	44	4.4	12	0

Tim Jorden

Year	Team		No	Yds	Avg	Lg	TD
1990	PHX	N	2	10	5.0	6	0
1991			15	127	8.5	19	0
1992	PIT	N	6	28	4.7	8	2
1993			1	12	12.0	12	0
Career			24	177	7.4	19	2

James Joseph

Year	Team		No	Yds	Avg	Lg	TD
1991	PHI	N	10	64	6.4	13	0
1993			29	291	10.0	48	1
1994			43	344	8.0	35t	2
1995	CIN	N	20	118	5.9	13	0
Career			102	817	8.0	48	3

Red Joseph

Year	Team		No	Yds	Avg	Lg	TD
1930	POR	N					1

Les Josephson

Year	Team		No	Yds	Avg	Lg	TD
1964	LA	N	21	269	12.8	58	1
1965			18	169	9.4	30	0
1966			2	10	5.0	6	1
1967			37	400	10.8	48	4
1969			32	295	9.2	51t	2
1970			44	427	9.7	30	0
1971			26	230	8.8	29t	2
1972			14	170	12.1	34	1
Career			194	1970	10.2	58	11
Playoffs			9	71	7.9		0

Yonel Jourdain

Year	Team		No	Yds	Avg	Lg	TD
1994	BUF	N	10	56	5.6	18	0
1995			1	7	7.0	7	0
Career			11	63	5.7	18	0

Saxon Judd

Year	Team		No	Yds	Avg	Lg	TD
1946	BKN	AA	34	443	13.0	52t	4
1947			18	204	11.3		1

Year	Team		No	Yds	Avg	Lg	TD

Saxon Judd continued

Year	Team		No	Yds	Avg	Lg	TD
1948			32	250	7.8		2
Career			84	897	10.7	52t	7

Kevin Juma

Year	Team		No	Yds	Avg	Lg	TD
1987	SEA	N	7	95	13.6	26	0

Steve Junker

Year	Team		No	Yds	Avg	Lg	TD
1957	DET	N	22	305	13.9	32	4
1960			6	55	9.2	14	0
1961	WAS	N	9	130	14.4	38	0
1962			11	149	13.5	35t	2
Career			48	639	13.3	38	6
Playoffs			13	201	15.5		3

Trey Junkin

Year	Team		No	Yds	Avg	Lg	TD
1985	LARI	N	2	8	4.0	5	1
1986			2	38	19.0	19	0
1987			2	15	7.5	8	0
1988			4	25	6.3	9	2
1989			3	32	10.7	28	2
1992	SEA	N	3	25	8.3	13	1
1994			1	1	1.0	1t	1
Career			17	144	8.5	28	7

Sonny Jurgensen

Year	Team		No	Yds	Avg	Lg	TD
1973	WAS	N	1	-3	-3.0	-3	0

Charlie Justice

Year	Team		No	Yds	Avg	Lg	TD
1950	WAS	N	19	180	9.5	37	2
1952			11	106	9.6	15	1
1953			22	434	19.7	54	2
1954			11	242	22.0	80t	2
Career			63	962	15.3	80t	7

Ed Justice

Year	Team		No	Yds	Avg	Lg	TD
1936	BOS	N	8	132	16.5		0
1937	WAS	N	9	150	16.7		3
1938			14	173	12.4		1
1939			7	124	17.7		1
1940			15	170	11.3		2
1941			9	149	16.6	36	1
1942			9	108	12.0	35	1
Career			71	1006	14.2	36	9
Playoffs			5	99	19.8		1

Steve Juzwik

Year	Team		No	Yds	Avg	Lg	TD
1946	BUF	AA	23	357	15.5	53	3
1947			5	35	7.0		1
1948	CHI	AA	1	5	5.0	5	0
Career			29	397	13.7	53	4

Vyto Kab

Year	Team		No	Yds	Avg	Lg	TD
1982	PHI	N	4	35	8.8	13	1
1983			18	195	10.8	25	1
1984			9	102	11.3	26	3
1987	DET	N	5	54	10.8	28	0
Career			36	386	10.7	28	5

Mike Kabealo

Year	Team		No	Yds	Avg	Lg	TD
1944	CLE	N	2	20	10.0	12	0

Bob Kahler

Year	Team		No	Yds	Avg	Lg	TD
1942	GB	N	2	21	10.5	12	0

Tommy Kalmanir

Year	Team		No	Yds	Avg	Lg	TD
1949	LA	N	2	36	18.0	23	0
1950			5	58	11.6	41t	1
1951			6	91	15.2	38t	1
1953	BAL	N	3	31	10.3	22t	1
Career			16	216	13.5	41t	3

John Kamana

Year	Team		No	Yds	Avg	Lg	TD
1987	ATL	N	7	51	7.3	15	1

Rick Kane

Year	Team		No	Yds	Avg	Lg	TD
1977	DET	N	18	186	10.3	20	0
1978			16	161	10.1	26	0
1979			9	104	11.6	36	1
1980			5	26	5.2	9	0
1981			18	187	10.4	40	1
1982			3	25	8.3	12	0
1983			2	15	7.5	9	0
1984	WAS	N	1	7	7.0	7	0

Rick Kane continued

Year	Team		No	Yds	Avg	Lg	TD
1985	DET	N	5	56	11.2	18	0
Career			77	767	10.0	40	2

Tommy Kane

Year	Team		No	Yds	Avg	Lg	TD
1988	SEA	N	6	32	5.3	9	0
1989			7	94	13.4	20	0
1990			52	776	14.9	63t	4
1991			50	763	15.3	60	2
1992			27	369	13.7	31	3
Career			142	2034	14.3	63t	9

Ave Kaplan

Year	Team		No	Yds	Avg	Lg	TD
1923	MIN	N					1

George Karamatic

Year	Team		No	Yds	Avg	Lg	TD
1938	WAS	N	4	99	24.8		1

John Karcis

Year	Team		No	Yds	Avg	Lg	TD
1935	BKN	N	5	58	11.6		0
1936	PIT	N	8	71	8.9		0
1937			2	18	9.0		0
1943	NYG	N	1	1	1.0	1	0
Career			16	148	9.3	1	0

Abe Karnofsky

Year	Team		No	Yds	Avg	Lg	TD
1945	PHI	N	5	113	22.6	38	0
1946	BOS	N	8	139	17.4	56t	1
Career			13	252	19.4	56t	1

Ed Karpowich

Year	Team		No	Yds	Avg	Lg	TD
1936	PIT	N	1	-6	-6.0	-6	0

Bill Karr

Year	Team		No	Yds	Avg	Lg	TD
1933	CHIB	N	8	184	23.0		3
1934			3	68	22.7		1
1935			9	220	24.4		6
1936			6	121	20.2		2
1937			7	188	26.9		2
1938			14	253	18.1		4
Career			47	1034	22.0		18
Playoffs			2	47	23.5		2

Johnny Karras

Year	Team		No	Yds	Avg	Lg	TD
1952	CHIC	N	5	63	12.6	29	1

Lou Karras

Year	Team		No	Yds	Avg	Lg	TD
1952	WAS	N	1	-2	-2.0	-2	0

Tony Kaska

Year	Team		No	Yds	Avg	Lg	TD
1936	BKN	N	1	5	5.0	5	0
1937			4	84	21.0		0
1938			2	77	38.5		0
Career			7	166	23.7	5	0

Chuck Kassel

Year	Team		No	Yds	Avg	Lg	TD
1927	FRA	N					1
1928							1
1929	CHIC	N					2
1931							1
1932							1
Career							6

Eric Kattus

Year	Team		No	Yds	Avg	Lg	TD
1986	CIN	N	11	99	9.0	28	1
1987			18	217	12.1	57	2
1988			2	8	4.0	11	0
1989			12	93	7.8	16	0
1990			11	145	13.2	31	2
1991			12	136	11.3	24	0
Career			66	698	10.6	57	5
Playoffs			2	19	9.5		1

Napoleon Kaufman

Year	Team		No	Yds	Avg	Lg	TD
1995	OAK	N	9	62	6.9	18	0
1996			22	143	6.5	19	1
Career			31	205	6.6	19	1

Jerry Kauric

Year	Team		No	Yds	Avg	Lg	TD
1990	CLE	N	1	21	21.0	21	0

Ken Kavanaugh

Year	Team		No	Yds	Avg	Lg	TD
1940	CHIB	N	12	276	23.0		3
1941			11	314	28.5	48	6

Ken Kavanaugh continued

Year	Team		No	Yds	Avg	Lg	TD
1945			25	539	21.6	64t	6
1946			18	337	18.7	38t	5
1947			32	818	25.6	81t	13
1948			18	352	19.6	64t	6
1949			29	655	22.6	81	9
1950			17	331	19.5	67t	2
Career			162	3622	22.4	81t	50
Playoffs			6	105	17.5		2

Eddie Kaw

Year	Team		No	Yds	Avg	Lg	TD
1924	BUF	N					2

Eddie Kawal

Year	Team		No	Yds	Avg	Lg	TD
1935	CHIB	N	1	11	11.0	11	0

Clarence Kay

Year	Team		No	Yds	Avg	Lg	TD
1984	DEN	N	16	136	8.5	21	3
1985			29	339	11.7	27	3
1986			15	195	13.0	34	1
1987			31	440	14.2	30	0
1988			34	352	10.4	27	4
1989			21	197	9.4	20t	2
1990			29	282	9.7	22	0
1991			11	139	12.6	32	0
1992			7	56	8.0	15	0
Career			193	2136	11.1	34	13
Playoffs			9	132	14.7		2

Jim Keane

Year	Team		No	Yds	Avg	Lg	TD
1946	CHIB	N	14	331	23.6	42t	3
1947			64	910	14.2	50	10
1948			30	414	13.8	53	3
1949			47	696	14.8	39	6
1950			36	433	12.0	70	0
1951			15	247	16.5	37	1
1952	GB	N	18	191	10.6	29t	1
Career			224	3222	14.4	70	24
Playoffs			5	75	15.0		0

Tom Keane

Year	Team		No	Yds	Avg	Lg	TD
1948	LA	N	11	195	17.7	57	2
1949			4	70	17.5	44	0
1950			1	19	19.0	19	0
1951			12	133	11.1	21	0
1952	DAL	N	3	73	24.3	47	0
1953	BAL	N	3	61	20.3	37	0
Career			34	551	16.2	57	2

Tim Kearse

Year	Team		No	Yds	Avg	Lg	TD
1987	IND	N	3	56	18.7	21	0

Joe Keeble

Year	Team		No	Yds	Avg	Lg	TD
1937	CLE	N	1	42	42.0	42	1

Jack Keefer

Year	Team		No	Yds	Avg	Lg	TD
1926	PRO	N					1

Mark Keel

Year	Team		No	Yds	Avg	Lg	TD
1987	SEA-KC	N	8	97	12.1	24t	1

Allen Keen

Year	Team		No	Yds	Avg	Lg	TD
1937	PHI	N	5	45	9.0		0

Bob Keene

Year	Team		No	Yds	Avg	Lg	TD
1943	DET	N	1	27	27.0	27	0
1944			5	91	18.2	46t	2
Career			6	118	19.7	46t	2

Craig Keith

Year	Team		No	Yds	Avg	Lg	TD
1994	PIT	N	1	2	2.0	2	0
1995	JAC	N	3	20	6.7	9	0
Career			4	22	5.5	9	0

Bill Kellagher

Year	Team		No	Yds	Avg	Lg	TD
1946	CHI	AA	2	36	18.0		0
1947			3	22	7.3		0
Career			5	58	11.6		0

Mark Kellar

Year	Team		No	Yds	Avg	Lg	TD
1976	MIN	N	2	22	11.0	19	0
1978			3	-5	-1.7	8	0
Career			5	17	3.4	19	0

Year	Team		No	Yds	Avg	Lg	TD

Kenny Keller
Year	Team		No	Yds	Avg	Lg	TD
1956	PHI	N	7	36	5.1	13	0
1957			4	31	7.8	30	0
Career			11	67	6.1	30	0

Billy Kelley
Year	Team		No	Yds	Avg	Lg	TD
1949	GB	N	17	222	13.1	32	1

Brian Kelley
Year	Team		No	Yds	Avg	Lg	TD
1978	NYG	N	1	-1	-1.0	-1	0

Frank Kelley
Year	Team		No	Yds	Avg	Lg	TD
1927	CLE	N					1

Bill Kellogg
Year	Team		No	Yds	Avg	Lg	TD
1925	ROC	N					1

Clarence Kellogg
Year	Team		No	Yds	Avg	Lg	TD
1936	CHIC	N	4	11	2.8		

Mike Kellogg
Year	Team		No	Yds	Avg	Lg	TD
1966	DEN	A	1	5	5.0	5	0

Bob Kelly
Year	Team		No	Yds	Avg	Lg	TD
1947	LA	AA	9	68	7.6		1
1949	BAL	AA	2	25	12.5		0
Career			11	93	8.5		1

Jim Kelly
Year	Team		No	Yds	Avg	Lg	TD
1964	PIT	N	10	186	18.6	27	1
1967	PHI	N	21	345	16.4	59	4
Career			31	531	17.1	59	5

Jim Kelly
Year	Team		No	Yds	Avg	Lg	TD
1974	CHI	N	8	100	12.5	24	0

Jim Kelly
Year	Team		No	Yds	Avg	Lg	TD
1987	BUF	N	1	35	35.0	35	0
1988			1	5	5.0	5	0
Career			2	40	20.0	35	0
Playoffs			1	-8	-8.0		0

John Kelly
Year	Team		No	Yds	Avg	Lg	TD
1933	BKN	N	22	246	11.2		3
1937			1	7	7.0	7	0
Career			23	253	11.0	7	3

Leroy Kelly
Year	Team		No	Yds	Avg	Lg	TD
1965	CLE	N	9	122	13.6	52	0
1966			32	366	11.4	40	1
1967			20	282	14.1	48	2
1968			22	297	13.5	68t	4
1969			20	267	13.4	36	1
1970			24	311	13.0	55	2
1971			25	252	10.1	29	2
1972			23	204	8.9	28	1
1973			15	180	12.0	36	0
Career			190	2281	12.0	68t	13
Playoffs			18	190	10.6		1

Mike Kelly
Year	Team		No	Yds	Avg	Lg	TD
1971	CIN	N	1	9	9.0	9	0

Pat Kelly
Year	Team		No	Yds	Avg	Lg	TD
1988	DEN	N	1	4	4.0	4	0
1989			3	13	4.3	6	0
Career			4	17	4.3	6	0

Jack Kemp
Year	Team		No	Yds	Avg	Lg	TD
1965	BUF	A	1	-9	-9.0	-9	0

Perry Kemp
Year	Team		No	Yds	Avg	Lg	TD
1987	CLE	N	12	224	18.7	34	2
1988	GB	N	48	620	12.9	36	0
1989			48	611	12.7	39	2
1990			44	527	12.0	29	2
1991			42	583	13.9	39	2
Career			194	2565	13.2	39	8

Florian Kempf
Year	Team		No	Yds	Avg	Lg	TD
1983	HOU	N	1	7	7.0	7	0

Vince Kendrick
Year	Team		No	Yds	Avg	Lg	TD
1974	ATL	N	12	86	7.2	12	1

Derek Kennard
Year	Team		No	Yds	Avg	Lg	TD
1994	DAL	N	1	-3	-3.0	-3	0

George Kenneally
Year	Team		No	Yds	Avg	Lg	TD
1927	POT	N					1
1928							1
Career							2

Bob Kennedy
Year	Team		No	Yds	Avg	Lg	TD
1946	NY	AA	11	59	5.4		0
1948			5	23	4.6		0
1949	B-NY	AA	7	55	7.9		1
Career			23	137	6.0		

Jimmie Kennedy
Year	Team		No	Yds	Avg	Lg	TD
1975	BAL	N	2	15	7.5	12	1
1976			1	32	32.0	32	0
Career			3	47	15.7	32	1
Playoffs			1	8	8.0		0

Bill Kenney
Year	Team		No	Yds	Avg	Lg	TD
1983	KC	N	1	0	0.0	0	0
1986			1	0	0.0	0	0
Career			2	0	0.0	0	0

Eddie Kennison
Year	Team		No	Yds	Avg	Lg	TD
1996	STL	N	54	924	17.1	77t	9

Randy Kerbow
Year	Team		No	Yds	Avg	Lg	TD
1963	HOU	A	5	61	12.2	30	1

Ralph Kercheval
Year	Team		No	Yds	Avg	Lg	TD
1934	BKN	N					3
1935			7	130	18.6		2
1936			7	63	9.0		0
1937			5	57	11.4		0
1938			11	136	12.4		0
1939			3	8	2.7		0
1940			1	17	17.0	17	0
Career			34	411	12.1	17	5

Don Kern
Year	Team		No	Yds	Avg	Lg	TD
1984	CIN	N	2	14	7.0	9	0

Bill Kerr
Year	Team		No	Yds	Avg	Lg	TD
1946	LA	AA	7	122	17.4		0

Ken Keuper
Year	Team		No	Yds	Avg	Lg	TD
1947	GB	N	2	37	18.5	26	1

Bob Keyes
Year	Team		No	Yds	Avg	Lg	TD
1960	OAK	A	1	19	19.0	19	0

Leroy Keyes
Year	Team		No	Yds	Avg	Lg	TD
1969	PHI	N	29	276	9.5	35	0
1973	KC	N	1	-6	-6.0	-6	0
Career			30	270	9.0	35	0

Jon Keyworth
Year	Team		No	Yds	Avg	Lg	TD
1974	DEN	N	12	109	9.1	18	0
1975			42	314	7.5	19t	1
1976			22	201	9.1	31	1
1977			11	48	4.4	14	0
1978			21	166	7.9	20	1
1979			18	132	7.3	18	0
1980			15	87	5.8	22	0
Career			141	1057	7.5	31	3
Playoffs			1	3	3.0		0

Walt Kichefski
Year	Team		No	Yds	Avg	Lg	TD
1940	PIT	N	4	26	6.5		0
1941			5	111	22.2	72	1
1942			15	189	12.6	26	0
1944	C-P		6	85	14.2	34	0
Career			30	411	13.7	72	1

George Kiick
Year	Team		No	Yds	Avg	Lg	TD
1940	PIT	N	3	22	7.3		0
1945			1	-2	-2.0	-2	0
Career			4	20	5.0	-2	0

Jim Kiick
Year	Team		No	Yds	Avg	Lg	TD
1968	MIA	A	44	422	9.6	38	0
1969			29	443	15.3	53t	1

Jim Kiick *continued*
Year	Team		No	Yds	Avg	Lg	TD
1970	MIA	N	42	497	11.8	47	0
1971			40	338	8.4	27	0
1972			21	147	7.0	15	1
1973			27	208	7.7	22	0
1974			18	155	8.6	19	1
1976	DEN	N	10	78	7.8	19	1
1977			2	14	7.0	11	0
Career			233	2302	9.9	53t	4
Playoffs			18	115	6.4		0

Glenn Killinger
Year	Team		No	Yds	Avg	Lg	TD
1926	PHI	A					1

Billy Kilmer
Year	Team		No	Yds	Avg	Lg	TD
1962	SF	N	16	152	9.5	34	1
1964			11	136	12.4	35	0
Career			27	288	10.7	35	1

Bill Kimber
Year	Team		No	Yds	Avg	Lg	TD
1960	NYG	N	2	48	24.0	41	0

Frank Kimble
Year	Team		No	Yds	Avg	Lg	TD
1945	PIT	N	2	16	8.0		0

John Kimbrough
Year	Team		No	Yds	Avg	Lg	TD
1946	LA	AA	9	162	18.0		1
1947			16	281	17.6		3
1948			10	131	13.1		2
Career			35	574	16.4		6

John Kimbrough
Year	Team		No	Yds	Avg	Lg	TD
1977	BUF	N	10	207	20.7	42	2

Tony Kimbrough
Year	Team		No	Yds	Avg	Lg	TD
1993	DEN	N	8	79	9.9	16	0
1994			2	20	10.0	12	0
Career			10	99	9.9	16	0

Frank Kinard
Year	Team		No	Yds	Avg	Lg	TD
1943	BKN	N	5	62	12.4	30	1

Brian Kinchen
Year	Team		No	Yds	Avg	Lg	TD
1988	MIA	N	1	3	3.0	3	0
1989			1	12	12.0	12	0
1993	CLE	N	29	347	12.0	40	2
1994			24	232	9.7	38	1
1995			20	216	10.8	41	0
1996	BAL	N	55	581	10.6	29	1
Career			130	1391	10.7	41	4
Playoffs			2	11	5.5		0

Todd Kinchen
Year	Team		No	Yds	Avg	Lg	TD
1993	LARM	N	8	137	17.1	35t	1
1994			23	352	15.3	43	3
1995	STL	N	36	419	11.6	35	4
1996	DEN	N	1	27	27.0	27	0
Career			68	935	13.8	43	8

Keith Kinderman
Year	Team		No	Yds	Avg	Lg	TD
1964	SD	A	3	21	7.0	18	0
Playoffs			4	52	13.0		0

Don Kindt
Year	Team		No	Yds	Avg	Lg	TD
1947	CHIB	N	2	24	12.0	14	0
1948			11	137	12.5	49	0
1949			12	118	9.8	38	0
1950			3	72	24.0	42t	0
1951			4	39	9.8	12	1
1954			9	101	11.2	21	0
1955			2	15	7.5	10	1
Career			43	506	11.8	49	2

Don Kindt
Year	Team		No	Yds	Avg	Lg	TD
1987	CHI	N	5	34	6.8	11	1

Steve Kiner
Year	Team		No	Yds	Avg	Lg	TD
1970	DAL	N	1	14	14.0	14	0

Bruce King
Year	Team		No	Yds	Avg	Lg	TD
1985	KC	N	7	45	6.4	8	0
1987	BUF	N	1	3	3.0	3	0
Career			8	48	6.0	8	0

Year	Team		No	Yds	Avg	Lg	TD

Claude King

Year	Team		No	Yds	Avg	Lg	TD
1961	HOU	A	3	83	27.7	44	1
1962	BOS	A	5	42	8.4	33	0
Career			8	125	15.6	44	1

Emmett King

| 1954 | CHIC | N | 6 | 43 | 7.2 | 17t | 1 |

Fay King

1946	BUF	AA	30	466	15.5	52t	6
1947			26	382	14.7	61t	6
1948	CHI	AA	50	647	12.9		7
1949			9	88	9.8		1
Career			115	1583	13.8	61t	20

Horace King

1975	DET	N	13	81	6.2	22	0
1976			21	163	7.8	19	0
1977			40	238	6.0	30	0
1978			48	396	8.3	34	2
1979			18	150	8.3	30	0
1980			19	184	9.7	29	1
1981			20	211	10.6	41	1
1982			9	74	8.2	14	1
1983			9	76	8.4	14	0
Career			197	1573	8.0	41	5
Playoffs			2	8	4.0		

Kenny King

1980	OAK	N	22	145	6.6	18	0
1981			27	216	8.0	30	0
1982	LARI	N	9	57	6.3	20	0
1983			14	149	10.6	34t	1
1984			14	99	7.1	15	0
1985			3	49	16.3	37	0
Career			89	715	8.0	37	1
Playoffs			14	222	15.9		2

Phil King

1958	NYG	N	11	132	12.0	35	0
1959			7	98	14.0	35	1
1960			3	6	2.0	4	0
1962			15	186	12.4	37	0
1963			32	377	11.8	46t	5
1964	PIT	N	4	32	8.0	13	1
1965	MIN	N	12	96	8.0	25	1
1966			2	24	12.0	18	1
Career			86	951	11.1	46t	9
Playoffs			7	37	5.3		0

Wayne Kingery

| 1949 | BAL | AA | 1 | -2 | -2.0 | -2 | 0 |

Doug Kingsriter

1973	MIN	N	2	27	13.5	14	0
1974			5	89	17.8	21	0
Career			7	116	16.6	21	0
Playoffs			1	9	9.0		0

Larry Kinnebrew

1983	CIN	N	2	4	2.0	2	0
1984			19	159	8.4	22	1
1985			22	187	8.5	29t	1
1986			13	136	10.5	31	1
1987			9	114	12.7	25	0
1989	BUF	N	5	60	12.0	18	0
Career			70	660	9.4	31	3
Playoffs			1	7	7.0		0

Jeff Kinney

1972	KC	N	4	45	11.3	19	0
1973			11	126	11.5	25	0
1974			18	105	5.8	16	1
1975			21	148	7.0	18	0
1976	BUF	N	14	78	5.6	15	0
Career			68	502	7.4	25	1

Vince Kinney

| 1978 | DEN | N | 1 | 23 | 23.0 | 23 | 0 |

Carl Kinscherf

1943	BKN	N	2	4	2.0		0
1944	NYG	N	1	9	9.0	9	0
Career			3	13	4.3	9	0

Terry Kirby

1993	MIA	N	75	874	11.7	47	3
1994			14	154	11.0	26	0
1995			66	618	9.4	46	3
1996	SF	N	52	439	8.4	52	1
Career			207	2085	10.1	52	7
Playoffs			16	127	7.9		1

Frank Kirkleski

| 1929 | ORA | N | | | | | 1 |

Roger Kirkman

1933	PHI	N					1
1934							1
Career							2

Ben Kish

1940	BKN	N	9	124	13.8		0
1941			4	50	12.5	27	0
1943	P-P	N	8	67	8.4	17	1
1944	PHI	N	5	73	14.6	45t	1
1945			8	78	9.8	18	0
1946			3	16	5.3	7	0
1947			1	12	12.0	12	0
Career			38	420	11.1	45t	2

George Kisiday

| 1948 | BUF | AA | 1 | 20 | 20.0 | 20 | 0 |

Vito Kissell

| 1949 | BUF | AA | 3 | 37 | 12.3 | | 0 |

Syd Kitson

| 1983 | GB | N | 1 | 9 | 9.0 | 9 | 0 |

Bob Klein

1969	LA	N	2	17	8.5	16	1
1970			2	20	10.0	12	0
1971			14	160	11.4	33t	4
1972			29	330	11.4	26t	1
1973			21	277	13.2	23t	2
1974			24	336	14.0	32	4
1975			16	237	14.8	44t	2
1976			20	229	11.4	26	1
1977	SD	N	20	244	12.2	41	1
1978			34	413	12.1	24	2
1979			37	424	11.5	54t	5
Career			219	2687	12.3	54t	23
Playoffs			10	89	8.9		2

Rocky Klever

1984	NYJ	N	3	29	9.7	13	1
1985			14	183	13.1	23	2
1986			15	150	10.0	21	0
1987			14	152	10.9	30	0
Career			46	514	11.2	30	3
Playoffs			1	9	9.0		0

Ed Klewicki

1935	DET	N					2
1936			4	90	22.5		0
1937			8	134	16.8		0
1938			3	57	19.0		0
Career			15	281	18.7		2
Playoffs			1	25	25.0		0

Harry Kline

| 1939 | NYG | N | 4 | 44 | 11.0 | | 1 |

David Klingler

| 1994 | CIN | N | 1 | -6 | -6.0 | -6 | 0 |

Mike Klotovich

| 1945 | NYG | N | 1 | 7 | 7.0 | 6 | 0 |

Jack Klotz

| 1960 | NY | A | 0 | 5 | | 5L | 0 |

John Klumb

1939	CHIC	N	4	21	5.3		0
1940	PIT	N	3	76	25.3		0
Career			7	97	13.9		0

Nick Klutka

| 1946 | BUF | AA | 1 | 9 | 9.0 | 9 | 0 |

Pete Kmetovic

1946	PHI	N	4	68	17.0	38	0
1947	DET	N	6	143	23.8	53t	2
Career			10	211	21.1	53t	2

Gary Knafelc

1954	CHIC-GB	N	5	48	9.6	15	0
1955	GB	N	40	613	15.3	48	8
1956			30	418	13.9	38	6
1957			9	164	18.2	53	2
1958			8	118	14.8	40	1
1959			27	384	14.2	33	4
1960			14	164	11.7	23	0
1961			3	32	10.7	13	0
1963	SF	N	18	221	12.3	45t	2
Career			154	2162	14.0	53	23
Playoffs			6	76	12.7		0

Ken Knapcyzk

| 1987 | CHI | N | 4 | 62 | 15.5 | 22 | 0 |

Gayle Knief

| 1970 | BOS | N | 3 | 39 | 13.0 | 22t | 1 |

David Knight

1973	NYJ	N	6	78	13.0	19	1
1974			40	579	14.5	42t	4
1976			20	403	20.1	44t	2
1977			7	129	18.4	49	0
Career			73	1189	16.3	49	7

Johnny Knolla

1942	CHIC	N	8	48	6.0	15	0
1945			1	15	15.0	15	0
Career			9	63	7.0	15	0

Oscar Knop

1925	CHIB	N					1
1927							1
Career							2

Larry Knorr

| 1942 | DET | N | 2 | 18 | 9.0 | 10 | 0 |

George Koch

| 1947 | BUF | AA | 1 | 10 | 10.0 | | 0 |

Roger Kochman

| 1963 | BUF | A | 4 | 148 | 37.0 | 68 | 1 |

Dave Kocourek

1960	LA	A	40	662	16.6	52	1
1961	SD	A	55	1055	19.2	76	4
1962			39	688	17.6	45	4
1963			23	359	15.6	35	5
1964			33	593	18.0	49	5
1965			28	363	13.0	29	2
1966	MIA	A	27	320	11.9	43	2
1967	OAK	A	1	4	4.0	4	0
1968			3	46	15.3	18	1
Career			249	4090	16.4	76	24
Playoffs			15	257	17.1		3

Elmer Kolberg

1939	PHI	N	3	33	11.0		0
1940			6	43	7.2		0
1941	PIT	N	1	2	2.0	2	0
Career			10	78	7.8		0

Chris Kolodziejski

| 1984 | PIT | N | 5 | 59 | 11.8 | 22 | 0 |

Mark Konecny

1987	MIA	N	6	26	4.3	10	0
1988	PHI	N	1	18	18.0	18	0
Career			7	44	6.3	18	0

Dave Kopay

1964	SF	N	20	135	6.8	30	2
1965			11	147	13.4	44	1
1966			10	67	6.7	26	1

Year	Team		No	Yds	Avg	Lg	TD

Dave Kopay continued

Year	Team		No	Yds	Avg	Lg	TD
1967			2	11	5.5	11	0
1968	DET	N	18	130	7.2	21	0
1969	WAS	N	6	60	10.0	18	0
1970			7	24	3.4	9	0
1972	GB	N	3	19	6.3	9	0
Career			77	593	7.7	44	4

Joe Kopcha

1934	CHIB	N	2	24	12.0		0

Bernie Kosar

1986	CLE	N	1	1	1.0	1	0
1989			1	-7	-7.0	-7	0
1991			1	1	1.0	1	0
Career			3	-5	-1.7	1	0

Stan Kosel

1939	BKN	N	2	40	20.0		1

Gary Kosins

1972	CHI	N	2	15	7.5	8	1
1973			4	8	2.0	10	0
1974			1	3	3.0	3	0
Career			7	26	3.7	10	1

Stan Koslowski

1946	MIA	AA	2	27	13.5		0

Stein Koss

1987	KC	N	2	25	12.5	14	0

Tony Kostos

1929	FRA	N					1
1930							1
Career							2

Eddie Kotal

1926	GB	N					1
1928							1
1929							3
Career							5

Doug Kotar

1974	NYG	N	10	57	5.7	18	0
1975			9	86	9.6	17	0
1976			36	319	8.9	30	0
1977			15	73	4.9	13	0
1978			22	225	10.2	31	1
1979			25	230	9.2	37	0
1981			9	32	3.6	11	0
Career			126	1022	8.1	37	1

Rich Kotite

1968	PIT	N	6	65	10.8	20t	2
1969	NYG	N	1	2	2.0	2t	1
1971			10	146	14.6	43t	2
Career			17	213	12.5	43t	5

Ed Kovac

1960	BAL	N	2	27	13.5	25	0
1962	NY	A	1	3	3.0	3	0
Career			3	30	10.0	25	0

Johnny Kovatch

1938	CLE	N	8	97	12.1		1

Johnny Kovatch

1942	WAS	N	12	90	7.5	15	0
1946			6	67	11.2	23	0
Career			18	157	8.7	23	1

Walt Kowalczyk

1958	PHI	N	8	72	9.0	15	0
1959			9	33	3.7	13	0
1960	DAL	N	14	143	10.2	23	1
1961	OAK	A	3	8	2.7	4	0
Career			34	256	7.5	23	1

Andy Kowalski

1943	BKN	N	11	145	13.2	35	0
1944			9	155	17.2	58t	1
Career			20	300	15.0	58t	1

Nick Kowgios

1987	DET	N	1	3	3.0	3	0

Ernie Koy

1965	NYG	N	4	22	5.5	9	0
1966			8	43	5.4	26	0
1967			32	212	6.6	24	1
1968			12	59	4.9	20	1
1969			19	152	8.0	41	4
1970			1	10	10.0	10	0
Career			76	498	6.6	26	6

Ted Koy

1971	BUF	N	10	133	13.3	22	1
1972			1	9	9.0	9	0
Career			11	142	12.9	22	1

Brian Kozlowski

1994	NYG	N	1	5	5.0	5	0
1995			2	17	8.5	12	0
1996			1	4	4.0	4t	1
Career			4	26	6.5	12	1

Glen Kozlowski

1987	CHI	N	15	199	13.3	28	3
1988			3	92	30.7	50	0
1989			3	74	24.7	55	0
1990			7	83	11.9	32	0
1991			2	16	8.0	11	0
1992			1	7	7.0	7	0
Career			31	471	15.2	55	3
Playoffs			1	10	10.0		

George Kracum

1941	BKN	N	2	17	8.5	13	0

Jerry Krall

1950	DET	N	2	61	30.5	41	0

Kent Kramer

1966	SF	N	5	81	16.2	24t	3
1967	NO	N	20	207	10.4	17	2
1969	MIN	N	2	37	18.5	24	1
1970			1	10	10.0	10	0
1971	PHI	N	6	65	10.8	17	1
1972			11	176	16.0	29	1
Career			45	576	12.8	29	8

Ron Kramer

1957	GB	N	28	337	12.0	31	0
1960			4	55	13.8	18	0
1961			35	559	16.0	53t	4
1962			37	555	15.0	54t	7
1963			32	537	16.8	49	4
1964			34	551	16.2	55	0
1965	DET	N	18	206	11.4	23	1
1966			37	432	11.7	68	0
1967			4	40	10.0	16	0
Career			229	3272	14.3	68	16
Playoffs			6	105	17.5		2

Tommy Kramer

1979	MIN	N	0	3		3L	
1984			1	20	20.0	20t	1
Career			1	23	23.0	20t	1

Larry Krause

1970	GB	N	2	22	11.0	11	0

Max Krause

1933	NYG	N					1
1934			1	4	4.0	4	0
1936			5	47	9.4		1
1937	WAS	N	2	13	6.5		0
1938			2	62	31.0		1
Career			10	126	12.6	4	3
Playoffs			1	13	13.0		

Paul Krause

1965	WAS	N	2	17	8.5	13	0

Barry Krauss

1982	BAL	N	1	5	5.0	5t	1

Steve Kreider

1979	CIN	N	3	20	6.7	8	0
1980			17	272	16.0	30	0
1981			37	520	14.1	46	5
1982			16	230	14.4	28	1
1983			42	554	13.2	54	1
1984			20	243	12.2	27	1
1985			10	184	18.4	56	1
1986			5	96	19.2	23	0
Career			150	2119	14.1	56	9
Playoffs			6	119	19.8		0

Rich Kreitling

1960	CLE	N	16	316	19.8	69t	3
1961			21	229	10.9	19	3
1962			44	659	15.0	53	3
1963			22	386	17.5	45	6
1964	CHI	N	20	185	9.3	22	2
Career			123	1775	14.4	69t	17

Mitch Krenk

1984	CHI	N	2	31	15.5	24	0

Keith Krepfle

1975	PHI	N	1	16	16.0	16	0
1976			6	80	13.3	30	1
1977			27	530	19.6	55t	3
1978			26	374	14.4	34t	3
1979			41	760	18.5	45	3
1980			30	450	15.0	27	4
1981			20	210	10.5	26	5
1982	ATL	N	1	5	5.0	5	0
Career			152	2425	16.0	55t	19
Playoffs			11	124	11.3		1

Dave Krieg

1983	SEA	N	1	11	11.0	11	0
1990			1	-6	-6.0	-6	0
1996	CHI	N	1	5	5.0	5	0
Career			3	10	3.3	11	0
Playoffs			1	1	1.0		

Jim Krieg

1972	DEN	N	4	99	24.8	37	0

Bob Krieger

1941	PHI	N	19	232	12.2	33	2
1946			2	47	23.5	35	0
Career			21	279	13.3	35	2

Al Krueger

1941	WAS	N	7	123	17.6	35	1
1942			9	65	7.2	19	0
1946	LA	AA	19	213	11.2		1
Career			35	401	11.5	35	2

Larry Krutko

1959	PIT	N	13	100	7.7	27	0
1960			1	8	8.0	8	0
Career			14	108	7.7	27	0

Gary Kubiak

1984	DEN	N	1	20	20.0	20	0

Bert Kuczynski

1943	DET	N	1	4	4.0	4	0
1946	PHI	N	1	9	9.0	9t	1
Career			2	13	6.5	9t	1

Waddy Kuehl

1920	RI	A					1
1921	BUF	A					1
1922	BUF	N					1
1923	RI	N					2
Career							6

Ray Kuffel

1947	BUF	AA	3	37	12.3		0
1948	CHI	AA	19	365	19.2	70t	3
Career			22	402	18.3	70t	3

Joe Kulbacki

1960	BUF	A	2	9	4.5		

Vic Kulbitski

Year	Team		No	Yds	Avg	Lg	TD
1946	BUF	AA	1	0	0.0	0	0
1947			9	117	13.0		4
1948			3	37	12.3		0
Career			13	154	11.8	0	4
Playoffs			1	14	14.0		0

George Kunz

Year	Team		No	Yds	Avg	Lg	TD
1971	ATL	N	1	2	2.0	2	0

Jake Kupp

Year	Team		No	Yds	Avg	Lg	TD
1966	WAS	N	4	28	7.0	13	0

Ralph Kurek

Year	Team		No	Yds	Avg	Lg	TD
1966	CHI	N	10	178	17.8	49	0
1967			5	30	6.0	8	0
1968			4	50	12.5	23	0
1969			4	30	7.5	13	0
1970			3	11	3.7	5	0
Career			26	299	11.5	49	0

Jamie Kurisko

Year	Team		No	Yds	Avg	Lg	TD
1987	NYJ	N	1	41	41.0	41t	1

Roy Kurrasch

Year	Team		No	Yds	Avg	Lg	TD
1947	NY	AA	2	53	26.5		0
Playoffs			1	20	20.0		0

Johnny Kusko

Year	Team		No	Yds	Avg	Lg	TD
1937	PHI	N	2	47	23.5		0

Mal Kutner

Year	Team		No	Yds	Avg	Lg	TD
1946	CHIC	N	27	634	23.5	63	5
1947			43	944	22.0	70t	7
1948			41	943	23.0	71t	14
1949			30	465	15.5	49	5
1950			4	74	18.5	51	0
Career			145	3060	21.1	71t	31
Playoffs			2	19	9.5		0

Ted Kwalick

Year	Team		No	Yds	Avg	Lg	TD
1969	SF	N	2	32	16.0	31	1
1970			10	148	14.8	26t	1
1971			52	664	12.8	42t	5
1972			40	751	18.8	81t	9
1973			47	729	15.5	48	5
1974			13	231	17.8	36	2
1976	OAK	N	4	15	3.8	6	0
Career			168	2570	15.3	81t	23
Playoffs			12	135	11.3		0

Troy Kyles

Year	Team		No	Yds	Avg	Lg	TD
1990	NYG	N	4	77	19.3	35	0

Steve Lach

Year	Team		No	Yds	Avg	Lg	TD
1942	CHIC	N	18	261	14.5	53	4
1946	PIT	N	2	11	5.5	7	0
1947			11	77	7.0	2	1
Career			31	349	11.3	53	5
Playoffs			1	2	2.0		0

Sean LaChapelle

Year	Team		No	Yds	Avg	Lg	TD
1993	LARM	N	2	23	11.5	14	0
1996	KC	N	27	422	15.6	69	2
Career			29	445	15.3	69	2

Rick Lackman

Year	Team		No	Yds	Avg	Lg	TD
1935	PHI	N	5	49	9.8		0

Ken Lacy

Year	Team		No	Yds	Avg	Lg	TD
1984	KC	N	13	87	6.7	20	2

Jim Ladd

Year	Team		No	Yds	Avg	Lg	TD
1954	CHIC	N	22	254	11.5	22	0

Dave Lafary

Year	Team		No	Yds	Avg	Lg	TD
1981	NO	N	1	5	5.0	5	0

Bill LaFitte

Year	Team		No	Yds	Avg	Lg	TD
1944	BKN	N	1	15	15.0	15	0

Greg LaFleur

Year	Team		No	Yds	Avg	Lg	TD
1981	STL	N	14	190	13.6	27t	2
1982			5	67	13.4	20	1

Greg LaFleur continued

Year	Team		No	Yds	Avg	Lg	TD
1983			12	99	8.3	21	0
1984			17	198	11.6	23	0
1985			9	119	13.2	24	0
1986	IND	N	7	56	8.0	11	0
Career			64	729	11.4	27t	3

Morris LaGrand

Year	Team		No	Yds	Avg	Lg	TD
1975	KC	N	1	-1	-1.0	-1	0

Thomas Lahey

Year	Team		No	Yds	Avg	Lg	TD
1946	CHI	AA	17	203	11.9		0
1947			13	148	11.4		0
Career			30	351	11.7		0

Warren Lahr

Year	Team		No	Yds	Avg	Lg	TD
1949	CLE	AA	1	20	20.0	20	0

Scott Laidlaw

Year	Team		No	Yds	Avg	Lg	TD
1975	DAL	N	11	100	9.1	25	0
1976			38	325	8.6	26	1
1977			5	60	12.0	18t	1
1978			6	108	18.0	44t	1
1979			12	59	4.9	12	0
1980	NYG	N	2	16	8.0	10	0
Career			74	668	9.0	44t	3
Playoffs			2	19	9.5		1

Aaron Laing

Year	Team		No	Yds	Avg	Lg	TD
1996	STL	N	13	116	8.9	22	0

Jim Laird

Year	Team		No	Yds	Avg	Lg	TD
1921	ROC	A					1
1922	BUF	N					1
Career							3

Brad Lamb

Year	Team		No	Yds	Avg	Lg	TD
1992	BUF	N	7	139	19.9	53	0

Roddy Lamb

Year	Team		No	Yds	Avg	Lg	TD
1925	RI	N					1

Ron Lamb

Year	Team		No	Yds	Avg	Lg	TD
1968	DEN-CIN	A	7	87	12.4	60	0
1972	ATL	N	1	10	10.0	10	0
Career			8	97	12.1	60	0

Walt Lamb

Year	Team		No	Yds	Avg	Lg	TD
1946	CHIB	N	1	10	10.0	10	0

Curly Lambeau

Year	Team		No	Yds	Avg	Lg	TD
1923	GB	N					2
1924							1
Career							3

Pete Lammons

Year	Team		No	Yds	Avg	Lg	TD
1966	NY	A	41	565	13.8	60	4
1967			45	515	11.4	61	2
1968			32	400	12.5	27t	3
1969			33	400	12.1	25	2
1970	NYJ	N	25	316	12.6	30	2
1971			8	149	18.6	27	1
1972	GB	N	1	19	19.0	19	0
Career			185	2364	12.8	61	14
Playoffs			9	102	11.3		1

Walt Landers

Year	Team		No	Yds	Avg	Lg	TD
1979	GB	N	5	60	12.0	55t	1

Mike Landrum

Year	Team		No	Yds	Avg	Lg	TD
1984	ATL	N	6	66	11.0	30	1

Tom Landry

Year	Team		No	Yds	Avg	Lg	TD
1949	B-NY	AA	6	109	18.2		0

Mort Landsberg

Year	Team		No	Yds	Avg	Lg	TD
1941	PHI	N	5	51	10.2	19	0
1947	LA	AA	1	0	0.0	0	0
Career			6	51	8.5	19	0

Dick Lane

Year	Team		No	Yds	Avg	Lg	TD
1954	CHIC	N	4	58	14.5	16	0
1955			2	110	55.0	93t	1
1956			1	75	75.0	75	0

Dick Lane continued

Year	Team		No	Yds	Avg	Lg	TD
1958			1	10	10.0	10	0
Career			8	253	31.6	93t	1

Eric Lane

Year	Team		No	Yds	Avg	Lg	TD
1981	SEA	N	7	58	8.3	22	0
1983			2	9	4.5	7	0
1984			11	101	9.2	55t	1
1985			15	153	10.2	20	0
1986			3	6	2.0	4	1
1987			4	30	7.5	12	0
Career			42	357	8.5	55t	2

MacArthur Lane

Year	Team		No	Yds	Avg	Lg	TD
1969	STL	N	9	61	6.8	14	0
1970			32	365	11.4	78t	2
1971			29	298	10.3	34	0
1972	GB	N	26	285	11.0	49	0
1973			27	255	9.4	30	1
1974			34	315	9.3	68t	3
1975	KC	N	25	202	8.1	31	0
1976			66	686	10.4	44	1
1977			3	40	13.3	21	0
1978			36	279	7.8	44	0
Career			287	2786	9.7	78t	7
Playoffs			4	42	10.5		0

David Lang

Year	Team		No	Yds	Avg	Lg	TD
1992	LARM	N	18	283	15.7	67t	1
1993			4	45	11.3	21	0
1994			8	60	7.5	12	0
Career			30	388	12.9	67t	1

Gene Lang

Year	Team		No	Yds	Avg	Lg	TD
1984	DEN	N	4	24	6.0	9t	1
1985			23	180	7.8	24	2
1986			13	105	8.1	26	2
1987			17	130	7.6	29	2
1988	ATL	N	37	398	10.8	50	1
1989			39	436	11.2	32	1
1990			1	7	7.0	7	0
Career			134	1280	9.6	50	9
Playoffs			5	38	7.6		0

Izzy Lang

Year	Team		No	Yds	Avg	Lg	TD
1964	PHI	N	6	69	11.5	23	0
1965			2	30	15.0	24	0
1966			12	107	8.9	24	0
1967			26	201	7.7	19	3
1968			17	147	8.6	25	1
Career			63	554	8.8	25	4

Reggie Langhorne

Year	Team		No	Yds	Avg	Lg	TD
1985	CLE	N	1	12	12.0	12	0
1986			39	678	17.4	66	1
1987			20	288	14.4	25	1
1988			57	780	13.7	77t	7
1989			60	749	12.5	62t	2
1990			45	585	13.0	39	2
1991			39	505	12.9	40t	2
1992	IND	N	65	811	12.5	34	1
1993			85	1038	12.2	72t	3
Career			411	5446	13.3	77t	19
Playoffs			26	370	14.2		2

Ken Lanier

Year	Team		No	Yds	Avg	Lg	TD
1990	DEN	N	1	-4	-4.0	-4	0

Ted Lapka

Year	Team		No	Yds	Avg	Lg	TD
1943	WAS	N	2	30	15.0	32	0
1944			4	61	15.3	42t	1
1946			3	28	9.3	11	0
Career			9	119	13.2	42t	1
Playoffs			3	41	13.7		1

Steve Largent

Year	Team		No	Yds	Avg	Lg	TD
1976	SEA	N	54	705	13.1	45	4
1977			33	643	19.5	74t	10
1978			71	1168	16.5	57t	8
1979			66	1237	18.7	55t	9
1980			66	1064	16.1	67t	6
1981			75	1224	16.3	57t	9
1982			34	493	14.5	45	3
1983			72	1074	14.9	46t	11

Year	Team		No	Yds	Avg	Lg	TD

Steve Largent *continued*

1984			74	1164	15.7	65	12
1985			79	**1287**	16.3	43	6
1986			70	1070	15.3	38t	9
1987			58	912	15.7	55	8
1988			39	645	16.5	46	2
1989			28	403	14.4	33	3
Career			819	13089	16.0	74t	100
Playoffs			23	434	18.9		4

Gordon Laro

| 1995 | JAC | N | 1 | 6 | 6.0 | 6 | 0 |

Jack Larscheid

1960	OAK	A	22	187	8.5		1
1961			2	11	5.5	6	0
Career			24	198	8.3	6	1

Bill Larson

1975	SF	N	5	64	12.8	24	0
1980	DEN-GB	N	5	44	8.8	21	1
Career			10	108	10.8	24	1

Greg Larson

| 1968 | NYG | N | 0 | 1 | | 1L | 0 |

Pete Larson

1967	WAS	N	8	45	5.6	13	0
1968			12	146	12.2	25	1
Career			20	191	9.6	25	1

Johnny Lascari

| 1942 | NYG | N | 3 | 38 | 12.7 | 15 | 1 |

Jim Lash

1973	MIN	N	2	34	17.0	18	0
1974			32	631	19.7	57	0
1975			37	535	14.5	45t	3
1976	MIN-SF	N	17	242	14.2	43	0
1977	SF	N	3	22	7.3	16	0
Career			91	1464	16.1	57	3
Playoffs			6	92	15.3		1

Derrick Lassic

| 1993 | DAL | N | 9 | 37 | 4.1 | 9 | 0 |
| Playoffs | | | 1 | 8 | 8.0 | | 0 |

Greg Lathan

| 1987 | LARI | N | 5 | 98 | 19.6 | 33 | 0 |

Jerry Latin

1975	STL	N	2	25	12.5	16	0
1976			4	35	8.8	15	0
1977			9	89	9.9	20	0
1978			1	3	3.0	3	0
Career			16	152	9.5	20	0
Playoffs			2	23	11.5		0

Greg Latta

1975	CHI	N	16	202	12.6	34	3
1976			18	254	14.1	56	0
1977			26	335	12.9	37t	4
1978			15	159	10.6	21	0
1979			15	131	8.7	25	0
Career			90	1081	12.0	56	7
Playoffs			4	31	7.8		0

Johnny Lattner

| 1954 | PIT | N | 25 | 305 | 12.2 | 43 | 2 |

Hal Lauer

| 1926 | DET | N | | | | | 1 |

Henry Laughlin

| 1955 | SF | N | 8 | 54 | 6.8 | 27 | 0 |

Ted Laux

1943	P-P	N	2	19	9.5	15	0
1944	PHI	N	1	6	6.0	6	0
Career			3	25	8.3	15	0

Dante Lavelli

| 1946 | CLE | AA | 40 | 843 | 21.1 | 63t | 8 |
| 1947 | | | 49 | 799 | 16.3 | 72t | 9 |

Dante Lavelli *continued*

1948			25	463	18.5	54t	5
1949			28	475	17.0	67t	7
1950	CLE	N	37	565	15.3	43	5
1951			43	586	13.6	47	6
1952			21	336	16.0	41	4
1953			45	783	17.4	55t	6
1954			47	802	17.1	64	7
1955			31	492	15.9	49	4
1956			20	344	17.2	68t	1
Career			386	6488	16.8	72t	62
Playoffs			46	668	14.5		5

Robert Lavette

1985	DAL	N	1	8	8.0	8	0
1986			5	31	6.2	9	1
1987			1	6	6.0	6	0
Career			7	45	6.4	9	1

Dennis Law

| 1978 | CIN | N | 5 | 81 | 16.2 | 20 | 0 |

Al Lawler

| 1948 | CHIB | N | 3 | 40 | 13.3 | 26 | 0 |

Amos Lawrence

1981	SF	N	3	10	3.3	5	0
1982			2	12	6.0	6	0
Career			5	22	4.4	6	0

Jimmy Lawrence

1936	CHIC	N	8	98	12.3		0
1937			3	32	10.7		0
1938			14	105	7.5		0
1939	CHIC-GB	N	3	39	13.0		0
Career			28	274	9.8		0

Kent Lawrence

| 1969 | PHI | N | 1 | 10 | 10.0 | 10 | 0 |

Reggie Lawrence

| 1993 | PHI | N | 1 | 5 | 5.0 | 5 | 0 |

Joe Laws

1934	GB	N					1
1935			4	82	20.5		0
1936			10	132	13.2		2
1937			10	121	12.1		0
1938			6	55	9.2		1
1939			11	177	16.1		1
1940			5	60	12.0		1
1941			4	48	12.0	18	1
1942			6	96	16.0	28	1
1943			5	33	6.6	22	0
1944			7	61	8.7	29t	1
1945			2	11	5.5	7	0
Career			70	876	12.5	29t	9
Playoffs			1	31	31.0		1

Odell Lawson

1970	BOS	N	11	113	10.3	19	0
1973	NO	N	2	-5	-2.5	4	0
Career			13	108	8.3	19	0

Roger Lawson

1972	CHI	N	8	120	15.0	40	0
1973			9	60	6.7	21	0
Career			17	180	10.6	40	0

Pete Layden

| 1949 | B-NY | AA | 1 | 0 | 0.0 | 0 | 0 |

Bill Lazetich

1939	CLE	N	8	44	5.5		1
1942			6	65	10.8	49	1
Career			14	109	7.8	49	2

Roosevelt Leaks

1975	BAL	N	1	5	5.0	5	0
1976			8	43	5.4	10	0
1977			3	39	13.0	26t	2
1978			9	111	12.3	27	2
1979			14	119	8.5	15	0
1980	BUF	N	8	57	7.1	18	1

Roosevelt Leaks *continued*

1981			7	51	7.3	13	0
1982			13	91	7.0	11	0
1983			8	74	9.3	12	0
Career			71	590	8.3	27	4
Playoffs			6	56	9.3		0

Tom Leary

| 1929 | SI | N | | | | | 2 |

Harper LeBel

| 1990 | PHI | N | 1 | 9 | 9.0 | 9 | 0 |

Mike LeBlanc

| 1987 | NE | N | 2 | 3 | 1.5 | 3 | 0 |

Bill Leckonby

1940	BKN	N	1	8	8.0	8	1
1941			1	9	9.0	9	1
Career			2	17	8.5	9	2

Terry LeCount

1978	SF	N	10	131	13.1	30	0
1979	MIN	N	6	119	19.8	36t	2
1980			13	168	12.9	21	0
1981			24	425	17.7	43t	2
1982			14	179	12.8	28	1
1983			21	318	15.1	49	2
1984			1	14	14.0	14	0
Career			89	1354	15.2	49	7
Playoffs			5	81	16.2		0

Monte Ledbetter

1967	HOU-BUF	A	13	204	15.7	60t	2
1968	BUF	A	4	94	23.5	43	1
1969	ATL	N	1	16	16.0	16	0
Career			18	314	17.4	60t	3

Toy Ledbetter

1950	PHI	N	4	81	20.3	29	2
1953			13	137	10.5	34t	2
1954			15	192	12.8	48t	3
1955			7	88	12.6	37t	1
Career			39	498	12.8	48t	8

Amp Lee

1992	SF	N	20	102	5.1	17	2
1993			16	115	7.2	22	2
1994	MIN	N	45	368	8.2	35	2
1995			71	558	7.9	33	1
1996			54	422	7.8	21	2
Career			206	1565	7.6	35	9
Playoffs			15	233	15.5		1

Danzell Lee

| 1987 | PIT | N | 12 | 124 | 10.3 | 24 | 0 |

Gary Lee

1987	DET	N	19	308	16.2	53	0
1988			22	261	11.9	18	1
Career			41	569	13.9	53	1

Herman Lee

| 1960 | CHI | N | 1 | 16 | 16.0 | 16 | 0 |

Jacky Lee

| 1967 | HOU | A | 1 | -1 | -1.0 | -1 | 0 |

Jeff Lee

| 1980 | STL | N | 2 | 19 | 9.5 | 12 | 0 |

Kevin Lee

| 1995 | NE | N | 8 | 107 | 13.4 | 33 | 0 |

Ron Lee

1976	BAL	N	1	-9	-9.0	-9	0
1977			10	60	6.0	15	0
1978			13	109	8.4	24	1
Career			24	160	6.7	24	1
Playoffs			2	22	11.0		0

Ronnie Lee

| 1979 | MIA | N | 2 | 14 | 7.0 | 10 | 0 |
| 1980 | | | 7 | 83 | 11.9 | 41 | 2 |

Year	Team		No	Yds	Avg	Lg	TD

Ronnie Lee *continued*

Year	Team		No	Yds	Avg	Lg	TD
1981			14	64	4.6	11	1
1982			2	6	3.0	5	0
Career			25	167	6.7	41	3
Playoffs			2	12	6.0		1

Tuffy Leemans

Year	Team		No	Yds	Avg	Lg	TD
1936	NYG	N	4	22	5.5		0
1937			11	157	14.3		1
1938			4	68	17.0		0
1939			8	185	23.1		2
1942			1	-10	-10.0	-10	0
Career			28	422	15.1	-10	3
Playoffs			2	42	21.0		0

Billy Lefear

Year	Team		No	Yds	Avg	Lg	TD
1973	CLE	N	5	38	7.6	13	0
1974			4	21	5.3	8	0
1975			1	14	14.0	14	0
Career			10	73	7.3	14	0

Clyde LeForce

Year	Team		No	Yds	Avg	Lg	TD
1948	DET	N	8	122	15.3	44	3

Jake Leicht

Year	Team		No	Yds	Avg	Lg	TD
1948	BAL	AA	12	134	11.2		1
1949			1	12	12.0	12	0
Career			13	146	11.2	12	1
Playoffs			2	32	16.0		0

Charlie Leigh

Year	Team		No	Yds	Avg	Lg	TD
1968	CLE	N	3	-4	-1.3	4	0
1969			2	-9	-4.5	-4	0
1973	MIA	N	4	9	2.3	7	0
Career			9	-4	-0.4	7	0

Walt LeJeune

Year	Team		No	Yds	Avg	Lg	TD
1922	AKR	N					1

Frank LeMaster

Year	Team		No	Yds	Avg	Lg	TD
1976	PHI	N	1	-4	-4.0	-4	0

Bobby Leo

Year	Team		No	Yds	Avg	Lg	TD
1967	BOS	A	1	25	25.0	25t	1

Jim Leonard

Year	Team		No	Yds	Avg	Lg	TD
1936	PHI	N	5	46	9.2		1

Darrell Lester

Year	Team		No	Yds	Avg	Lg	TD
1966	DEN	A	2	26	13.0	21	1

Tim Lester

Year	Team		No	Yds	Avg	Lg	TD
1993	LARM	N	18	154	8.6	21	0
1994			1	1	1.0	1	0
1996	PIT	N	7	70	10.0	19	0
Career			26	225	8.7	21	0
Playoffs			2	7	3.5		0

Dorsey Levens

Year	Team		No	Yds	Avg	Lg	TD
1994	GB	N	1	9	9.0	9	0
1995			48	434	9.0	27	4
1996			31	226	7.3	49	5
Career			80	669	8.4	49	9
Playoffs			18	204	11.3		2

Mike Levenseller

Year	Team		No	Yds	Avg	Lg	TD
1980	CIN	N	2	30	15.0	22	0

Jim Levey

Year	Team		No	Yds	Avg	Lg	TD
1935	PIT	N	11	112	10.2		3

Jerry LeVias

Year	Team		No	Yds	Avg	Lg	TD
1969	HOU	A	42	696	16.6	18	5
1970	HOU	N	41	529	12.9	63t	5
1971	SD	N	21	265	12.6	37t	1
1972			1	8	8.0	8	0
1973			30	536	17.9	69t	3
1974			9	105	11.7	18	0
Career			144	2139	14.9	69t	14
Playoffs			1	7	7.0		0

Chuck Levy

Year	Team		No	Yds	Avg	Lg	TD
1994	ARI	N	4	35	8.8	15	0

Verne Lewellen

Year	Team		No	Yds	Avg	Lg	TD
1925	GB	N					3
1926							3
1928							3
1929							1
1930							1
1932							1
Career							12

Cliff Lewis

Year	Team		No	Yds	Avg	Lg	TD
Playoffs			1	4	4.0		0

Danny Lewis

Year	Team		No	Yds	Avg	Lg	TD
1958	DET	N	1	12	12.0	12	0
1959			5	75	15.0	30	0
1960			12	192	16.0	55t	1
1961			8	118	14.8	22	0
1962			16	158	9.9	34	1
1963			15	115	7.7	30	0
1964			11	129	11.7	92t	1
1965	WAS	N	25	276	11.0	37	2
1966	NYG	N	6	87	14.5	25	0
Career			99	1162	11.7	92t	5

Darren Lewis

Year	Team		No	Yds	Avg	Lg	TD
1992	CHI	N	18	175	9.7	30	0
1993			4	26	6.5	18	0
Career			22	201	9.1	30	0
Playoffs			2	18	9.0		0

David Lewis

Year	Team		No	Yds	Avg	Lg	TD
1984	DET	N	16	236	14.8	58	3
1985			28	354	12.6	40	3
1986			10	88	8.8	16	1
1987	MIA	N	6	53	8.8	22	1
Career			60	731	12.2	58	8

Ernie Lewis

Year	Team		No	Yds	Avg	Lg	TD
1946	CHI	AA	2	26	13.0		0
1948			1	6	6.0	6	0
Career			3	32	10.7	6	0

Frank Lewis

Year	Team		No	Yds	Avg	Lg	TD
1971	PIT	N	3	44	14.7	22	5
1972			27	391	14.5	52	5
1973			23	409	17.8	53t	3
1974			30	365	12.2	31t	4
1975			17	308	18.1	40t	2
1976			17	306	18.0	64	1
1977			11	263	23.9	65t	1
1978	BUF	N	41	735	17.9	92t	7
1979			54	1082	20.0	55	2
1980			40	648	16.2	31t	6
1981			70	1244	17.8	33	4
1982			28	443	15.8	39	2
1983			36	486	13.5	27t	3
Career			397	6724	16.9	92t	40
Playoffs			27	553	20.5		5

Gary Lewis

Year	Team		No	Yds	Avg	Lg	TD
1964	SF	N	7	73	10.4	47	0
1965			10	25	2.5	12	0
1966			7	44	6.3	18t	1
1967			21	218	10.4	32t	1
1968			27	244	9.0	33	3
Career			72	604	8.4	47	5

Gary Lewis

Year	Team		No	Yds	Avg	Lg	TD
1981	GB	N	3	31	10.3	15	0
1982			3	21	7.0	12	0
1983			11	204	18.5	49	1
1984			4	29	7.3	15	0
Career			21	285	13.6	49	1

Greg Lewis

Year	Team		No	Yds	Avg	Lg	TD
1991	DEN	N	2	9	4.5	7	0
1992			4	30	7.5	16	0
Career			6	39	6.5	16	0

Hal Lewis

Year	Team		No	Yds	Avg	Lg	TD
1959	BAL	N	3	54	18.0	25	0
1962	OAK	A	7	53	7.6	13	0
Career			10	107	10.7	25	0

Jermaine Lewis

Year	Team		No	Yds	Avg	Lg	TD
1996	BAL	N	5	78	15.6	24	1

Kenny Lewis

Year	Team		No	Yds	Avg	Lg	TD
1980	NYJ	N	1	6	6.0	6	0
1981			2	14	7.0	8	0
1983			6	62	10.3	23	0
Career			9	82	9.1	23	0

Leo Lewis

Year	Team		No	Yds	Avg	Lg	TD
1981	MIN	N	2	58	29.0	52	0
1982			8	150	18.8	39t	3
1983			12	127	10.6	18	0
1984			47	830	17.7	56	4
1985			29	442	15.2	43t	3
1986			32	600	18.8	76t	2
1987			24	383	16.0	36	2
1988			11	141	12.8	46t	1
1989			12	148	12.3	28t	1
1990			1	9	9.0	9	0
1991			4	36	9.0	11	0
Career			182	2924	16.1	76t	16
Playoffs			10	124	12.4		1

Mark Lewis

Year	Team		No	Yds	Avg	Lg	TD
1986	GB	N	2	7	3.5	4t	2
1988	DET	N	3	32	10.7	23	1
Career			5	39	7.8	23	3

Nate Lewis

Year	Team		No	Yds	Avg	Lg	TD
1990	SD	N	14	192	13.7	40	1
1991			42	554	13.2	49t	3
1992			34	580	17.1	62	4
1993			38	463	12.2	47	4
1994	CHI	N	2	13	6.5	8	1
Career			130	1802	13.9	62	13
Playoffs			3	51	17.0		0

Rod Lewis

Year	Team		No	Yds	Avg	Lg	TD
1994	HOU	N	4	48	12.0	19	0
1995			16	116	7.3	16	0
1996			7	50	7.1	18	0
Career			27	214	7.9	19	0

Ron Lewis

Year	Team		No	Yds	Avg	Lg	TD
1990	SF	N	5	44	8.8	14	0
1992	GB	N	13	152	11.7	27	0
1993			2	21	10.5	17	0
1994			7	108	15.4	38	0
Career			27	325	12.0	38	0
Playoffs			1	7	7.0		0

Thomas Lewis

Year	Team		No	Yds	Avg	Lg	TD
1994	NYG	N	4	46	11.5	23	0
1995			12	208	17.3	46t	1
1996			53	694	13.1	34	4
Career			69	948	13.7	46t	5

Woodley Lewis

Year	Team		No	Yds	Avg	Lg	TD
1954	LA	N	2	19	9.5	12	0
1955			19	199	10.5	19	0
1957	CHIC	N	21	424	20.2	53t	5
1958			46	690	15.0	64	4
1959			34	534	15.7	85t	3
1960	DAL	N	1	19	19.0	19	0
Career			123	1885	15.3	85t	12

Frank Liebel

Year	Team		No	Yds	Avg	Lg	TD
1942	NYG	N	2	53	26.5	29	0
1943			11	199	18.1	56	3
1944			13	293	22.5	58t	5
1945			22	593	**27.0**	54t	**10**
1946			18	360	20.0	57t	4
1947			16	258	16.1	38	1
Career			82	1756	21.4	58t	23
Playoffs			4	108	27.0		1

Don Lieberum

Year	Team		No	Yds	Avg	Lg	TD
1942	NYG	N	6	65	10.8	30	0

Verl Lillywhite

Year	Team		No	Yds	Avg	Lg	TD
1948	SF	AA	1	-1	-1.0	-1	0
1949			8	82	10.3		2
1950	SF	N	1	6	6.0		0

Verl Lillywhite *continued*

Year	Team		No	Yds	Avg	Lg	TD
1951			11	125	11.4	29	1
Career			21	212	10.1	29	3

Garrett Limbrick

Year	Team		No	Yds	Avg	Lg	TD
1990	MIA	N	4	23	5.8	9	0

Keith Lincoln

Year	Team		No	Yds	Avg	Lg	TD
1961	SD	A	12	208	17.3	91	2
1962			16	214	13.4	29	1
1963			24	325	13.5	39	3
1964			34	302	8.9	37	2
1965			23	376	16.3	66	4
1966			14	264	18.9	67	2
1967	BUF	A	41	558	13.6	60t	5
1968			1	3	3.0	9	0
Career			165	2250	13.6	91	19
Playoffs			10	144	14.4		1

Mike Lind

Year	Team		No	Yds	Avg	Lg	TD
1963	SF	N	2	13	6.5	8	0
1964			25	178	7.1	26	0
1965	PIT	N	25	236	9.4	39	1
Career			52	427	8.2	39	1

Virgil Lindahl

Year	Team		No	Yds	Avg	Lg	TD
1945	NYG	N	1	32	32.0	32	0

Jim Lindsey

Year	Team		No	Yds	Avg	Lg	TD
1966	MIN	N	20	250	12.5	46	2
1967			4	36	9.0	21	0
1968			15	148	9.9	22	0
1969			2	45	22.5	30	1
1970			4	94	23.5	49	1
1971			8	31	3.9	9	0
1972			3	28	9.3	13	0
Career			56	632	11.3	49	4
Playoffs			2	34	17.0		0

Vic Lindskog

Year	Team		No	Yds	Avg	Lg	TD
1951	PHI	N	0	21		21L	0

Larry Linne

Year	Team		No	Yds	Avg	Lg	TD
1987	NE	N	11	158	14.4	30	2

Joe Lintzenich

Year	Team		No	Yds	Avg	Lg	TD
1931	CHIB	N					2

Louis Lipps

Year	Team		No	Yds	Avg	Lg	TD
1984	PIT	N	45	860	19.1	80t	9
1985			59	1134	19.2	51	12
1986			38	590	15.5	48	3
1987			11	164	14.9	27	0
1988			50	973	19.5	89t	5
1989			50	944	18.9	79t	5
1990			50	682	13.6	37	3
1991			55	671	12.2	35	2
1992	NO	N	1	1	1.0	1	0
Career			359	6019	16.8	89t	39
Playoffs			14	184	13.1		2

Don Lisbon

Year	Team		No	Yds	Avg	Lg	TD
1963	SF	N	21	259	12.3	51	2
1964			13	104	8.0	39t	1
Career			34	363	10.7	51	3

David Little

Year	Team		No	Yds	Avg	Lg	TD
1984	KC	N	1	13	13.0	13	0
1985	PHI	N	7	82	11.7	28	0
1986			14	132	9.4	26	0
1987			1	8	8.0	8	0
1989			2	8	4.0	7	1
Career			25	243	9.7	28	1

Floyd Little

Year	Team		No	Yds	Avg	Lg	TD
1967	DEN	A	7	11	1.6	15	0
1968			19	331	17.4	66t	1
1969			19	218	11.5	67t	1
1970	DEN	N	17	161	9.5	39	0
1971			26	255	9.8	74	0
1972			28	367	13.1	40	4
1973			41	423	10.3	50t	1
1974			29	344	11.9	72	0

Floyd Little *continued*

Year	Team		No	Yds	Avg	Lg	TD
1975			29	308	10.6	66t	2
Career			215	2418	11.2	74	9

Carl Littlefield

Year	Team		No	Yds	Avg	Lg	TD
1938	CLE	N	1	9	9.0	9	0
1939	PIT	N	1	18	18.0	18	0
Career			2	27	13.5	18	0

Joe Little Twig

Year	Team		No	Yds	Avg	Lg	TD
1925	RI	N					1

Andy Livingston

Year	Team		No	Yds	Avg	Lg	TD
1964	CHI	N	1	0	0.0	0	0
1965			12	134	11.2	80	0
1967			5	62	12.4	38	0
1969	NO	N	28	278	9.9	51t	3
Career			46	474	10.3	80	3

Howie Livingston

Year	Team		No	Yds	Avg	Lg	TD
1944	NYG	N	1	12	12.0	12t	1
1945			14	250	17.9	47	2
1946			2	36	18.0	34t	1
1947			12	273	22.8	65t	3
1949	WAS	N	3	41	13.7	29	0
1950			5	156	31.2	74t	2
Career			37	768	20.8	74t	9
Playoffs			2	21	10.5		0

Walt Livingston

Year	Team		No	Yds	Avg	Lg	TD
1960	BOS	A	1	0	0.0	0	0

Bob Livingstone

Year	Team		No	Yds	Avg	Lg	TD
1948	CHI	AA	15	240	16.0	55t	2
1949			3	80	26.7		0
Career			18	320	17.8	55t	2

Charles Lockett

Year	Team		No	Yds	Avg	Lg	TD
1987	PIT	N	7	116	16.6	25	1
1988			22	365	16.6	44	1
Career			29	481	16.6	44	2

J.W. Lockett

Year	Team		No	Yds	Avg	Lg	TD
1961	SF-DAL	N	19	149	7.8	26	2
1962	DAL	N	7	78	11.1	29t	2
1963	BAL	N	16	158	9.9	27	1
1964	WAS	N	20	204	10.2	29t	2
Career			62	589	9.5	29t	7

James Lofton

Year	Team		No	Yds	Avg	Lg	TD
1978	GB	N	46	818	17.8	58t	6
1979			54	968	17.9	52	4
1980			71	1226	17.3	47	4
1981			71	1294	18.2	75t	8
1982			35	696	19.9	80t	4
1983			58	1300	**22.4**	74t	8
1984			62	1361	**22.0**	79t	7
1985			69	1153	16.7	56t	4
1986			64	840	13.1	36	4
1987	LARI	N	41	880	21.5	49	5
1988			28	549	19.6	57	0
1989	BUF	N	8	166	20.8	47	3
1990			35	712	20.3	71	4
1991			57	1072	18.8	77t	8
1992			51	786	15.4	50	6
1993	LARM-PHI	N	14	183	13.1	32	0
Career			764	14004	18.3	80t	75
Playoffs			41	759	18.5		8

Oscar Lofton

Year	Team		No	Yds	Avg	Lg	TD
1960	BOS	A	19	360	18.9		4

Chuck Logan

Year	Team		No	Yds	Avg	Lg	TD
1964	PIT	N	1	7	7.0	7	0

Dave Logan

Year	Team		No	Yds	Avg	Lg	TD
Playoffs			3	63	21.0		0

Dave Logan

Year	Team		No	Yds	Avg	Lg	TD
1976	CLE	N	5	104	20.8	52	0
1977			19	284	14.9	42	1
1978			37	585	15.8	44	4
1979			59	982	16.6	46	7
1980			51	822	16.1	65	4

Dave Logan *continued*

Year	Team		No	Yds	Avg	Lg	TD
1981			31	497	16.0	40t	4
1982			23	346	15.0	55t	2
1983			37	627	16.9	34	2
1984	DEN	N	1	3	3.0	3	0
Career			263	4250	16.2	65	24

Marc Logan

Year	Team		No	Yds	Avg	Lg	TD
1987	CIN	N	3	14	4.7	18	0
1988			2	20	10.0	17	0
1989	MIA	N	5	34	6.8	11	0
1990			7	54	7.7	12	0
1992	SF	N	2	17	8.5	13	0
1993			37	348	9.4	24	0
1994			16	97	6.1	15	1
1995	WAS	N	25	276	11.0	32	2
1996			23	269	11.7	26	0
Career			120	1129	9.4	32	3
Playoffs			6	37	6.2		0

Joe Lokanc

Year	Team		No	Yds	Avg	Lg	TD
1941	CHIC	N	1	2	2.0	2	0

Neil Lomax

Year	Team		No	Yds	Avg	Lg	TD
1982	STL	N	1	10	10.0	10	0

Bill Long

Year	Team		No	Yds	Avg	Lg	TD
1949	PIT	N	2	21	10.5	13	0

Bob Long

Year	Team		No	Yds	Avg	Lg	TD
1964	GB	N	1	19	19.0	19	0
1965			13	304	23.4	62t	4
1966			3	68	22.7	42	0
1967			8	96	12.0	21	0
1968	ATL	N	22	484	22.0	71t	4
1969	WAS	N	48	533	11.1	52	1
1970	LA	N	3	35	11.7	15t	1
Career			98	1539	15.7	71t	10
Playoffs			1	9	9.0		0

Cutter Long

Year	Team		No	Yds	Avg	Lg	TD
1953	NYG	N	14	220	15.7	55t	2
1954			13	178	13.7	36t	1
1955			6	64	10.7	34t	1
Career			33	462	14.0	55t	4

Darren Long

Year	Team		No	Yds	Avg	Lg	TD
1986	LARM	N	5	47	9.4	13	0
Playoffs			1	5	5.0		0

Kevin Long

Year	Team		No	Yds	Avg	Lg	TD
1977	NYJ	N	5	17	3.4	7	0
1978			26	304	11.7	30	0
1979			10	115	11.5	27	0
1980			20	137	6.8	16	0
1981			13	66	5.1	18	3
Career			74	539	7.3	27	3

Mike Long

Year	Team		No	Yds	Avg	Lg	TD
1960	BOS	A	2	10	5.0		0

Paul Longua

Year	Team		No	Yds	Avg	Lg	TD
1929	ORA	N					1

Jack Lookabaugh

Year	Team		No	Yds	Avg	Lg	TD
1946	WAS	N	6	67	11.2	19	0
1947			6	78	13.0	31	1
Career			12	145	12.1	31	1

Ace Loomis

Year	Team		No	Yds	Avg	Lg	TD
1951	GB	N	1	9	9.0	9	0

Don Looney

Year	Team		No	Yds	Avg	Lg	TD
1940	PHI	N	**58**	**707**	12.2		4
1941	PIT	N	10	186	18.6	66	1
1942			7	59	8.4	14	1
Career			75	952	12.7	66	6

Joe Don Looney

Year	Team		No	Yds	Avg	Lg	TD
1964	BAL	N	1	1	1.0	1t	1
1965	DET	N	12	109	9.1	47t	1
1966	DET-WAS	N	12	49	4.1	18	0
1967	WAS	N	1	12	12.0	12	0
Career			26	171	6.6	47t	2

Tony Lorick

Year	Team		No	Yds	Avg	Lg	TD
1964	BAL	N	11	164	14.9	59	0
1965			15	184	12.3	49t	2
1966			12	81	6.8	19	0
1967			22	189	8.6	34	0
1968	NO	N	26	272	10.5	29	3
Career			86	890	10.3	59	5
Playoffs			3	18	6.0		0

Jack Losch

Year	Team		No	Yds	Avg	Lg	TD
1956	GB	N	7	85	12.1	43	0

Billy Lott

Year	Team		No	Yds	Avg	Lg	TD
1960	OAK	A	49	524	10.7	28	1
1961	BOS	A	32	333	10.4	47	6
1962			1	1	1.0	1	0
1963			3	61	20.3	55	1
Career			85	919	10.8	55	8
Playoffs			3	34	11.3		0

Thomas Lott

Year	Team		No	Yds	Avg	Lg	TD
1979	STL	N	2	8	4.0	5	0

Corey Louchiey

Year	Team		No	Yds	Avg	Lg	TD
1996	BUF	N	1	0	0.0	0	0

John Love

Year	Team		No	Yds	Avg	Lg	TD
1967	WAS	N	17	248	14.6	35	1
1972	LA	N	1	19	19.0	1t	1
Career			18	267	14.8	35	2

Randy Love

Year	Team		No	Yds	Avg	Lg	TD
1983	STL	N	6	58	9.7	16	1
1984			7	33	4.7	16	1
1985			2	4	2.0	3	0
Career			15	95	6.3	16	2

Edwin Lovelady

Year	Team		No	Yds	Avg	Lg	TD
1987	NYG	N	10	125	12.5	23t	2

Derek Loville

Year	Team		No	Yds	Avg	Lg	TD
1994	SF	N	2	26	13.0	19	0
1995			87	662	7.6	31	3
1996			16	138	8.6	44t	2
Career			105	826	7.9	44t	5
Playoffs			7	70	10.0		0

Frank LoVuolo

Year	Team		No	Yds	Avg	Lg	TD
1949	NYG	N	2	37	18.5	22	0

Lloyd Lowe

Year	Team		No	Yds	Avg	Lg	TD
1953	CHIB	N	4	34	8.5	11	0

Paul Lowe

Year	Team		No	Yds	Avg	Lg	TD
1960	LA	A	23	277	12.0	63	2
1961	SD	A	17	103	6.1	17	0
1963			26	191	7.3	31	2
1964			14	182	13.0	41	2
1965			17	126	7.4	45	1
1966			12	41	3.4	11	0
1967			2	25	12.5	13	0
Career			111	945	8.5	63	7
Playoffs			9	27	3.0		0

Alex Loyd

Year	Team		No	Yds	Avg	Lg	TD
1950	SF	N	32	402	12.6	38	0

Dick Lucas

Year	Team		No	Yds	Avg	Lg	TD
1958	PIT	N	4	47	11.8	17	0
1960	PHI	N	3	34	11.3	19	0
1961			8	67	8.4	18	5
1962			19	236	12.4	24	1
Career			34	384	11.3	24	6

Richie Lucas

Year	Team		No	Yds	Avg	Lg	TD
1960	BUF	A	5	58	11.6		1
1961			6	69	11.5	19	0
Career			11	127	11.5	19	1

Johnny Lucente

Year	Team		No	Yds	Avg	Lg	TD
1945	PIT	N	11	45	4.1	23	0

Terry Luck

Year	Team		No	Yds	Avg	Lg	TD
1977	CLE	N	1	4	4.0	4t	1

Sid Luckman

Year	Team		No	Yds	Avg	Lg	TD
1947	CHIB	N	1	15	15.0	15	0

Don Luft

Year	Team		No	Yds	Avg	Lg	TD
1954	PHI	N	3	59	19.7	30	0

Nolan Luhn

Year	Team		No	Yds	Avg	Lg	TD
1945	GB	N	10	151	15.1	44t	1
1946			16	224	14.0	36t	2
1947			42	696	16.6	44	7
1948			17	285	16.8	40	2
1949			15	169	11.3	30	1
Career			100	1525	15.3	44t	13

Johnny Lujack

Year	Team		No	Yds	Avg	Lg	TD
1950	CHIB	N	1	16	16.0	16	0

Jim Lukens

Year	Team		No	Yds	Avg	Lg	TD
1949	BUF	AA	24	249	10.4		2
Playoffs			4	32	8.0		0

Jack Lummus

Year	Team		No	Yds	Avg	Lg	TD
1941	NYG	N	1	5	5.0	5	0

Roy Lumpkin

Year	Team		No	Yds	Avg	Lg	TD
1932	POR	N					1
1933							1
1936	BKN	N	6	34	5.7		0
Career			6	34	5.7		2

Bill Lund

Year	Team		No	Yds	Avg	Lg	TD
1946	CLE	AA	4	64	16.0		2
1947			6	110	18.3	62	1
Career			10	174	17.4	62	3

Dennis Lundy

Year	Team		No	Yds	Avg	Lg	TD
1995	HOU	N	1	11	11.0	11	0

Lamar Lundy

Year	Team		No	Yds	Avg	Lg	TD
1957	LA	N	6	114	19.0	34t	3
1958			25	396	15.8	32	3
1959			4	74	18.5	26	0
Career			35	584	16.7	34t	6

Henry Lusk

Year	Team		No	Yds	Avg	Lg	TD
1996	NO	N	27	210	7.8	24	0

Herb Lusk

Year	Team		No	Yds	Avg	Lg	TD
1976	PHI	N	13	119	9.2	42	0
1977			5	102	20.4	36t	1
Career			18	221	12.3	42	1

Garry Lyle

Year	Team		No	Yds	Avg	Lg	TD
1968	CHI	N	5	32	6.4	13	0
1969			1	11	11.0	11	0
1970			1	5	5.0	5	0
Career			7	48	6.9	13	0

Lenny Lyles

Year	Team		No	Yds	Avg	Lg	TD
1958	BAL	N	5	24	4.8	11	1
1959	SF	N	3	33	11.0	18	0
Career			8	57	7.1	18	1

Link Lyman

Year	Team		No	Yds	Avg	Lg	TD
1923	CAN	N					1
1924	CLE	N					1
Career							2

Eddie Lynch

Year	Team		No	Yds	Avg	Lg	TD
1927	PRO	N					1

Eric Lynch

Year	Team		No	Yds	Avg	Lg	TD
1993	DET	N	13	82	6.3	11	0
1994			2	18	9.0	12	0
Career			15	100	6.7	12	0

Fran Lynch

Year	Team		No	Yds	Avg	Lg	TD
1968	DEN	A	4	52	13.0	22	0
1969			9	86	9.6	19	0
1970	DEN	N	7	69	9.9	36	0
1971			2	42	21.0	40t	1
1972			7	75	10.7	17	0
1975			6	33	5.5	19	1
Career			35	357	10.2	40t	2

Anthony Lynn

Year	Team		No	Yds	Avg	Lg	TD
1996	SF	N	2	14	7.0	8	0

Mitch Lyons

Year	Team		No	Yds	Avg	Lg	TD
1993	ATL	N	8	63	7.9	14	0
1994			7	54	7.7	10	0
1995			5	83	16.6	34	0
1996			4	16	4.0	5	1
Career			24	216	9.0	34	1
Playoffs			1	-1	-1.0		0

Tommy Lyons

Year	Team		No	Yds	Avg	Lg	TD
1976	DEN	N	1	-1	-1.0	-1	0

Rob Lytle

Year	Team		No	Yds	Avg	Lg	TD
1977	DEN	N	17	198	11.6	47t	1
1978			6	37	6.2	10	0
1979			13	93	7.2	12	0
1980			18	177	9.8	37	0
1981			6	47	7.8	14t	1
1982			1	10	10.0	10	0
Career			61	562	9.2	47t	2
Playoffs			1	-1	-1.0		0

Ken Mac Afee

Year	Team		No	Yds	Avg	Lg	TD
1954	NYG	N	24	438	18.3	72t	8
1955			11	170	15.5	40	1
1956			14	184	13.1	29t	4
1957			16	229	14.3	41	2
1958			5	52	10.4	22	2
1959	PHI-WAS	N	9	87	9.7	19	1
Career			79	1160	14.7	72t	18
Playoffs			1	15	15.0		0

Ken Mac Afee

Year	Team		No	Yds	Avg	Lg	TD
1978	SF	N	22	205	9.3	22	1
1979			24	266	11.1	50	4
Career			46	471	10.2	50	5

Jay Mac Dowell

Year	Team		No	Yds	Avg	Lg	TD
1946	PHI	N	1	28	28.0	28	0

Art Macioszczyk

Year	Team		No	Yds	Avg	Lg	TD
1944	PHI	N	3	28	9.3	21	0
1947			3	20	6.7	8	0
Career			6	48	8.0	21	0

Bill Mack

Year	Team		No	Yds	Avg	Lg	TD
1961	PIT	N	8	128	16.0	39	2
1962			8	203	25.4	40	2
1963			25	618	24.7	85t	3
1964	PHI	N	8	169	21.1	53t	1
1965	PIT	N	3	41	13.7	17	0
Career			52	1159	22.3	85t	8

Cedric Mack

Year	Team		No	Yds	Avg	Lg	TD
1984	STL	N	5	61	12.2	22	0
1985			1	16	16.0	16	0
Career			6	77	12.8	22	0

Kevin Mack

Year	Team		No	Yds	Avg	Lg	TD
1985	CLE	N	29	297	10.2	43	3
1986			28	292	10.4	44	0
1987			32	223	7.0	17	1
1988			11	87	7.9	25	0
1989			2	7	3.5	4	0
1990			42	360	8.6	30	2
1991			40	255	6.4	22	2
1992			13	81	6.2	23	0
Career			197	1602	8.1	44	8
Playoffs			19	149	7.8		1

Dee Mackey

Year	Team		No	Yds	Avg	Lg	TD
1960	SF	N	12	159	13.3	25	0
1961	BAL	N	4	66	16.5	19	0
1962			25	396	15.8	57	4
1963	NY	A	23	263	11.4	31	3
1964			14	213	15.2	35	0
1965			16	255	15.9	47	1
Career			94	1352	14.4	57	8

John Mackey

Year	Team		No	Yds	Avg	Lg	TD
1963	BAL	N	35	726	20.7	61t	7
1964			22	406	18.5	62	2

Year	Team		No	Yds	Avg	Lg	TD

John Mackey continued

Year	Team		No	Yds	Avg	Lg	TD
1965			40	814	20.4	68t	7
1966			50	829	16.6	89t	9
1967			55	686	12.5	34t	3
1968			45	644	14.3	72t	6
1969			34	443	13.0	52t	2
1970			28	435	15.5	54t	3
1971			11	143	13.0	28	0
1972	SD	N	11	110	10.0	21	0
Career			331	5236	15.8	89t	39
Playoffs			17	297	17.5		2

Jacque MacKinnon

Year	Team		No	Yds	Avg	Lg	TD
1961	SD	A	3	58	19.3	45	0
1962			9	125	13.9	32	2
1963			11	262	23.8	69	4
1964			10	177	17.7	37	0
1965			6	106	17.7	38	0
1966			26	477	18.3	46	6
1967			7	176	25.1	71	2
1968			33	646	19.6	62t	6
1969			7	82	11.7	23	0
Career			112	2109	18.8	71	20
Playoffs			6	74	12.3		0

Bob MacLeod

Year	Team		No	Yds	Avg	Lg	TD
1939	CHIB	N	10	231	23.1		3

Eddie Macon

Year	Team		No	Yds	Avg	Lg	TD
1952	CHIB	N	8	25	3.1	20	0
1953			6	24	4.0	10t	2
Career			14	49	3.5	20	2

Elmer Madar

Year	Team		No	Yds	Avg	Lg	TD
1947	BAL	AA	8	53	6.6		0

Elmer Madarik

Year	Team		No	Yds	Avg	Lg	TD
1946	DET	N	6	38	6.3	20	0
1947			4	75	18.8	26	0
Career			10	113	11.3	26	0

Lloyd Madden

Year	Team		No	Yds	Avg	Lg	TD
1940	CHIC	N	4	90	22.5		1

Calvin Magee

Year	Team		No	Yds	Avg	Lg	TD
1985	TB	N	26	288	11.1	35	3
1986			45	564	12.5	45	5
1987			34	424	12.5	37	3
1988			9	103	11.4	25	0
Career			114	1379	12.1	45	11

John Magee

Year	Team		No	Yds	Avg	Lg	TD
1951	PHI	N	0	7		7L	0

Archie Maggiolo

Year	Team		No	Yds	Avg	Lg	TD
1948	BUF	AA	3	23	7.7		0
1949	DET	N	1	9	9.0	9	0
Career			4	32	8.0	9	0

Dante Magnani

Year	Team		No	Yds	Avg	Lg	TD
1940	CLE	N	11	119	10.8		1
1941			14	189	13.5	61	1
1942			24	276	11.5	67	4
1943	CHIB	N	6	88	14.7	51	1
1946			14	156	11.1	38	1
1947	LA	N	4	57	14.3	40t	1
1948			3	28	9.3	16t	1
1949	CHIB	N	3	29	9.7	15	0
Career			79	942	11.9	67	10
Playoffs			4	122	30.5		2

George Magulick

Year	Team		No	Yds	Avg	Lg	TD
1944	C-P	N	6	50	8.3	21	0

Frank Mahoney

Year	Team		No	Yds	Avg	Lg	TD
1925	CHIC	N					1

Al Mahrt

Year	Team		No	Yds	Avg	Lg	TD
1921	DAY	A					1
1922	DAY	N					1
Career							2

Jack Maitland

Year	Team		No	Yds	Avg	Lg	TD
1970	BAL	N	9	67	7.4	13	1

Jack Maitland continued

Year	Team		No	Yds	Avg	Lg	TD
1971	NE	N	1	6	6.0	6	0
1972			4	33	8.3	9	0
Career			14	106	7.6	13	1

Howie Maley

Year	Team		No	Yds	Avg	Lg	TD
1946	BOS	N	2	35	17.5	33	0

Bill Malinchak

Year	Team		No	Yds	Avg	Lg	TD
1966	DET	N	5	34	6.8	13	0
1967			26	397	15.3	43	4
1968			1	41	41.0	41	0
1969			2	24	12.0	21	0
1976	WAS	N	1	12	12.0	12	0
Career			35	508	14.5	43	4

Gene Malinowski

Year	Team		No	Yds	Avg	Lg	TD
1948	BOS	N	3	-10	-3.3	1	0

John Mallory

Year	Team		No	Yds	Avg	Lg	TD
1968	PHI	N	1	58	58.0	58t	1
1971	ATL	N	1	27	27.0	27	0
Career			2	85	42.5	58t	1

Rick Mallory

Year	Team		No	Yds	Avg	Lg	TD
1986	TB	N	1	9	9.0	9	0

Les Malloy

Year	Team		No	Yds	Avg	Lg	TD
1931	CHIC	N					2

Art Malone

Year	Team		No	Yds	Avg	Lg	TD
1970	ATL	N	9	38	4.2	9	1
1971			34	380	11.2	46t	2
1972			50	585	11.7	57t	2
1973			19	177	9.3	33	1
1974			28	168	6.0	13	0
1975	PHI	N	20	120	6.0	15	0
1976			1	-3	-3.0	-3	0
Career			161	1465	9.1	57t	6

Benny Malone

Year	Team		No	Yds	Avg	Lg	TD
1974	MIA	N	2	26	13.0	13	0
1975			2	47	23.5	43	0
1976			9	103	11.4	36	0
1977			4	58	14.5	35	0
1978	WAS	N	3	29	9.7	19	0
1979			13	137	10.5	55t	1
Career			33	400	12.1	55t	1

Charley Malone

Year	Team		No	Yds	Avg	Lg	TD
1934	BOS	N	11	121	11.0		2
1935			22	**433**	19.7		2
1936			11	167	15.2		1
1937	WAS	N	28	419	15.0		4
1938			24	257	10.7		1
1939			18	274	15.2		3
1940			20	222	11.1		0
1942			3	29	9.7	10	0
Career			137	1922	14.0	10	13
Playoffs			6	95	15.8		0

Mark Malone

Year	Team		No	Yds	Avg	Lg	TD
1981	PIT	N	1	90	90.0	90t	0

Norm Maloney

Year	Team		No	Yds	Avg	Lg	TD
1948	SF	AA	1	29	29.0	29t	1

Red Maloney

Year	Team		No	Yds	Avg	Lg	TD
1926	NY	A					2
1927	NYY	N					1
Career							3

Jack Manders

Year	Team		No	Yds	Avg	Lg	TD
1934	CHIB	N	1	12	12.0	12	0
1935			2	16	8.0		0
1936			1	4	4.0	4t	1
1937			7	163	23.3		4
1938			2	27	13.5		1
1939			1	29	29.0	29	1
Career			14	251	17.9	27	7
Playoffs			1	37	37.0		1

Pug Manders

Year	Team		No	Yds	Avg	Lg	TD
1939	BKN	N	3	22	7.3		0

Pug Manders continued

Year	Team		No	Yds	Avg	Lg	TD
1940			1	38	38.0	38	1
1941			6	67	11.2	27	0
1942			4	53	13.3	22	0
1943			5	68	13.6	48	1
1944			6	78	13.0	30	0
1946	NY	AA	3	49	16.3		0
Career			28	375	13.4	48	2

Jim Mandich

Year	Team		No	Yds	Avg	Lg	TD
1970	MIA	N	1	3	3.0	3t	1
1971			3	19	6.3	10t	1
1972			11	168	15.3	39	3
1973			24	302	12.6	28t	4
1974			33	374	11.3	44	6
1975			21	217	10.3	32t	4
1976			22	260	11.8	31	4
1977			6	63	10.5	15	0
Career			121	1406	11.6	44	23
Playoffs			9	86	9.6		1

Pete Mandley

Year	Team		No	Yds	Avg	Lg	TD
1984	DET	N	3	38	12.7	19	0
1985			18	316	17.6	37	0
1986			7	106	15.1	51	0
1987			58	720	12.4	41	7
1988			44	617	14.0	56	4
1989	KC	N	35	476	13.6	44	1
1990			7	97	13.9	24	0
Career			172	2370	13.8	56	12

James Maness

Year	Team		No	Yds	Avg	Lg	TD
1985	CHI	N	1	34	34.0	34	0

Joe Maniaci

Year	Team		No	Yds	Avg	Lg	TD
1936	BKN	N	1	30	30.0	30	0
1937			3	11	3.7		0
1938	BKN-CHIB	N	9	127	14.1		0
1940	CHIB	N	1	-5	-5.0	-5	0
1941			2	21	10.5	19	0
Career			16	184	11.5	30	0
Playoffs			3	52	17.3		0

Jim Mankins

Year	Team		No	Yds	Avg	Lg	TD
1967	ATL	N	1	11	11.0	11	0

Willie Manley

Year	Team		No	Yds	Avg	Lg	TD
1950	GB	N	5	66	13.2	18	0

Bob Mann

Year	Team		No	Yds	Avg	Lg	TD
1948	DET	N	33	560	17.0	45	3
1949			66	**1014**	15.4	64	4
1950	GB	N	6	89	14.8	40	1
1951			50	696	13.9	52	8
1952			30	517	17.2	42	6
1953			23	327	14.2	45	2
Career			208	3203	15.4	64	24

Dave Mann

Year	Team		No	Yds	Avg	Lg	TD
1955	CHIC	N	16	137	8.6	42	1
1956			13	170	13.1	23	1
1957			8	137	17.1	32	0
Career			37	444	12.0	42	2

Archie Manning

Year	Team		No	Yds	Avg	Lg	TD
1971	NO	N	1	-7	-7.0	-7	0

Joe Manning

Year	Team		No	Yds	Avg	Lg	TD
1926	HAR	N					1

Wade Manning

Year	Team		No	Yds	Avg	Lg	TD
1981	DEN	N	3	49	16.3	34	0
1982			3	46	15.3	30	0
Career			6	95	15.8	34	0

Tim Manoa

Year	Team		No	Yds	Avg	Lg	TD
1987	CLE	N	1	8	8.0	8	0
1988			10	54	5.4	9	0
1989			27	241	8.9	32	2
1991	IND	N	2	5	2.5	5	0
Career			40	308	7.7	32	2
Playoffs			1	8	8.0		0

Year	Team		No	Yds	Avg	Lg	TD

Jerry Mansfield
| 1920 | RI | A | | | | | 1 |

Ed Manske
1935	PHI	N	9	205	22.8		4
1936			17	325	19.1		0
1937	CHIB	N	9	225	25.0		3
1938	PIT-CHIB	N	19	310	16.3		2
1939	CHIB	N	10	321	32.1		2
1940			6	81	13.5		0
Career			70	1467	21.0		11
Playoffs			2	55	27.5		1

Tillie Manton
1936	NYG	N	5	81	16.2		1
1937			3	15	5.0		1
1943	BKN	N	6	26	4.3	8	0
Career			14	122	8.7	8	2

Lionel Manuel
1984	NYG	N	33	619	18.8	53	4
1985			49	859	17.5	51t	5
1986			11	181	16.5	35	3
1987			30	545	18.2	50t	6
1988			65	1029	15.8	46	4
1989			33	539	16.3	49	1
1990			11	169	15.4	19	0
Career			232	3941	17.0	53	23
Playoffs			14	243	17.4		1

Sean Manuel
| 1996 | SF | N | 3 | 18 | 6.0 | 7 | 0 |

Gino Marchetti
1952	DAL	N	1	17	17.0	17t	1
1953	BAL	N	0	19		19L	0
Career			1	36	36.0	19L	1

Frank Marchlewski
| 1966 | ATL | N | 0 | 1 | | 1L | 0 |

Hugo Marcolini
| 1948 | BKN | AA | 2 | 38 | 19.0 | | 0 |

Joe Marconi
1956	LA	N	12	70	5.8	31	0
1957			16	171	10.7	61t	1
1958			10	87	8.7	15	0
1959			10	81	8.1	80	1
1960			9	32	3.6	17	0
1961			4	20	5.0	8t	1
1962	CHI	N	23	306	13.3	63	1
1963			28	335	12.0	63	2
1964			20	181	9.1	29	3
1965			4	43	10.8	29	0
Career			136	1326	9.8	80	9
Playoffs			3	64	21.3		0

Andrew Marefos
1941	NYG	N	1	5	5.0	5	0
1946	LA	AA	1	13	13.0	13	0
Career			2	18	9.0	13	0

Bob Margarita
1944	CHIB	N	15	130	8.7	22	0
1945			23	394	17.1	47	2
Career			38	524	13.8	47	2

Ken Margerum
1981	CHI	N	39	584	15.0	41	1
1982			14	207	14.8	28	3
1983			21	336	16.0	60	2
1985			17	190	11.2	20	2
1986	SF	N	2	12	6.0	6	0
1987			1	7	7.0	7	0
Career			94	1336	14.2	60	8
Playoffs			3	48	16.0		0

Joe Margucci
1947	DET	N	10	125	12.5	79t	1
1948			36	450	12.5	55t	2
Career			46	575	12.5	79t	3

Ed Marinaro
1972	MIN	N	28	218	7.8	18t	1
1973			26	196	7.5	17	2
1974			17	132	7.8	20	1
1975			54	462	8.6	25	3
1976	NYJ	N	21	168	8.0	35	0
Career			146	1176	8.1	35	7
Playoffs			8	109	13.6		0

Dan Marino
| 1995 | MIA | N | 1 | -6 | -6.0 | -6 | 0 |

Jerry Marion
| 1967 | PIT | N | 1 | 16 | 16.0 | 16 | 0 |

Larry Marks
1926	NY	A					1
1928	GB	N					2
Career							3

John Marquart
| 1921 | CHIC | A | | | | | 1 |

Vince Marrow
| 1994 | BUF | N | 5 | 44 | 8.8 | 14 | 0 |

Aaron Marsh
1968	BOS	A	19	331	17.4	70t	4
1969			8	108	13.5	21	0
Career			27	439	16.3	70t	4

Amos Marsh
1961	DAL	N	21	189	9.0	46	2
1962			35	467	13.3	85t	2
1963			26	224	8.6	35	0
1964			15	131	8.7	32	0
1965	DET	N	17	159	9.4	48t	2
1966			12	111	9.3	20	0
1967			7	103	14.7	35t	1
Career			133	1384	10.4	85t	7

Curtis Marsh
| 1995 | JAC | N | 7 | 127 | 18.1 | 34 | 0 |

Doug Marsh
1980	STL	N	22	269	12.2	29	4
1981			6	80	13.3	20	1
1982			5	83	16.6	21	0
1983			32	421	13.2	38	8
1984			39	608	15.6	47	5
1985			37	355	9.6	23	1
1986			25	313	12.5	27	0
Career			166	2129	12.8	47	19
Playoffs			2	18	9.0		0

Al Marshall
| 1974 | NE | N | 1 | 17 | 17.0 | 17t | 1 |

Arthur Marshall
1992	DEN	N	26	493	19.0	80t	1
1993			28	360	12.9	40	2
1994	NYG	N	16	219	13.7	34	0
1995			17	195	11.5	27	1
Career			87	1267	14.6	80t	4
Playoffs			5	69	13.8		0

Ed Marshall
1971	CIN	N	2	18	9.0	10	0
1976	NYG	N	8	166	20.8	52	3
1977			7	178	25.4	82	0
Career			17	362	21.3	82	3

Henry Marshall
1976	KC	N	28	443	15.8	31t	2
1977			23	445	19.3	49	4
1978			26	433	16.7	40	2
1979			21	332	15.8	38t	1
1980			47	799	17.0	75t	6
1981			38	620	16.3	54t	4
1982			40	549	13.7	44t	3
1983			50	788	15.8	52	6
1984			62	912	14.7	37	4
1985			25	446	17.8	50	0
1986			46	652	14.2	31	1

Henry Marshall continued
1987			10	126	12.6	19	0
Career			416	6545	15.7	75t	33
Playoffs			6	72	12.0		0

Marvin Marshall
| 1996 | TB | N | 2 | 27 | 13.5 | 20 | 0 |

Paul Martha
1964	PIT	N	6	145	24.2	54	0
1965			11	171	15.5	39	0
Career			17	316	18.6	54	0

Abe Martin
| 1932 | CHIC | N | | | | | 1 |

Billy Martin
1962	CHI	N	1	8	8.0	8	0
1964			1	9	9.0	9	0
Career			2	17	8.5	9	0

Billy Martin
1964	CHI	N	3	93	31.0	68	0
1965			1	-1	-1.0	-1	0
1966	ATL	N	29	330	11.4	35	0
1967			15	182	12.1	36	3
1968	MIN	N	10	101	10.1	15t	1
Career			58	705	12.2	68	4
Playoffs			1	1	1.0		1

Blanche Martin
| 1960 | LA | A | 2 | 18 | 9.0 | 11 | 1 |

Curtis Martin
1995	NE	N	30	261	8.7	27	1
1996			46	333	7.2	41	3
Career			76	594	7.8	41	4
Playoffs			8	55	6.9		0

Eric Martin
1985	NO	N	35	522	14.9	50	4
1986			37	675	18.2	84	5
1987			44	778	17.7	67	7
1988			85	1083	12.7	40t	7
1989			68	1090	16.0	53t	8
1990			63	912	14.5	58	5
1991			66	803	12.2	30	4
1992			68	1041	15.3	52t	5
1993			66	950	14.4	54t	3
1994	KC	N	21	307	14.6	61	1
Career			553	8161	14.8	84	49
Playoffs			15	204	13.6		0

Frank Martin
1943	BKN	N	13	152	11.7	34	0
1944			3	15	5.0	12	0
1945	BOS-NYG	N	4	67	16.8	53t	1
Career			20	234	11.7	53t	1

George Martin
| 1980 | NYG | N | 1 | 4 | 4.0 | 4t | 1 |

Jim Martin
| 1951 | DET | N | 0 | 10 | | 10L | 0 |

John Martin
1941	CHIC	N	4	53	13.3	27	1
1942			22	312	14.2	69	0
1943			7	138	19.7	50	0
1944	BOS	N	6	56	9.3	16	0
1945			2	20	10.0	17	0
Career			41	579	14.1	69	1

Kelvin Martin
1987	DAL	N	5	103	20.6	33	0
1988			49	622	12.7	35t	3
1989			46	644	14.0	46	2
1990			64	732	11.4	45	0
1991			16	243	15.2	27	0
1992			32	359	11.2	27	3
1993	SEA	N	57	798	14.0	53t	5
1994			56	681	12.2	32	1

Year	Team		No	Yds	Avg	Lg	TD

Kelvin Martin *continued*

Year	Team		No	Yds	Avg	Lg	TD
1995	PHI	N	17	206	12.1	22	0
1996	DAL	N	25	380	15.2	60t	1
Career			367	4768	13.0	60t	15
Playoffs			9	94	10.4		1

Mike Martin

Year	Team		No	Yds	Avg	Lg	TD
1983	CIN	N	2	22	11.0	12	0
1984			11	164	14.9	42	0
1985			14	187	13.4	28	0
1986			3	68	22.7	51	0
1987			20	394	19.7	54t	3
1988			2	22	11.0	15t	1
1989			15	160	10.7	21	2
Career			67	1017	15.2	54t	6

Robbie Martin

Year	Team		No	Yds	Avg	Lg	TD
1982	DET	N	1	18	18.0	18	0
1984			1	9	9.0	9	0
1985	IND	N	10	128	12.8	22	0
1986			1	41	41.0	41	0
Career			13	196	15.1	41	0

Sammy Martin

Year	Team		No	Yds	Avg	Lg	TD
1988	NE	N	4	51	12.8	21	0
1989			13	229	17.6	37	0
1990			4	65	16.3	19t	1
1991	IND	N	5	79	15.8	25	0
Career			26	424	16.3	37	1

Tony Martin

Year	Team		No	Yds	Avg	Lg	TD
1990	MIA	N	29	388	13.4	45	2
1991			27	434	16.1	64	2
1992			33	553	16.8	55t	2
1993			20	347	17.4	80t	3
1994	SD	N	50	885	17.7	99t	7
1995			90	1224	13.6	51t	6
1996			85	1171	13.8	55	14
Career			334	5002	15.0	99t	36
Playoffs			20	309	15.4		3

Vern Martin

Year	Team		No	Yds	Avg	Lg	TD
1942	PIT	N	7	64	9.1	24	1

Rich Martini

Year	Team		No	Yds	Avg	Lg	TD
1979	OAK	N	24	259	10.8	22t	2
1980			1	36	36.0	36	0
1981	NO	N	8	72	9.0	15	0
Career			33	367	11.1	36	2

Len Masini

Year	Team		No	Yds	Avg	Lg	TD
1948	LA	AA	1	-1	-1.0	-1	0

Matt Maslowski

Year	Team		No	Yds	Avg	Lg	TD
1971	LA	N	3	82	27.3	36t	1

Joel Mason

Year	Team		No	Yds	Avg	Lg	TD
1939	CHIC	N	18	188	10.4		0
1942	GB	N	7	86	12.3	19	0
1943			8	107	13.4	21	2
1944			1	9	9.0	9	0
Career			34	390	11.5	21	2

Larry Mason

Year	Team		No	Yds	Avg	Lg	TD
1987	CLE	N	5	26	5.2	15	1
1988	GB	N	8	84	10.5	39	1
Career			13	110	8.5	39	2

Tommy Mason

Year	Team		No	Yds	Avg	Lg	TD
1961	MIN	N	20	122	6.1	18	0
1962			36	603	16.8	74t	6
1963			40	365	9.1	41t	2
1964			26	239	9.2	29	1
1965			22	321	14.6	72t	1
1966			7	39	5.6	17	1
1967	LA	N	13	70	5.4	24	0
1968			15	144	9.6	31	0
1969			11	185	16.8	67t	1
1970			12	127	10.6	32	1
1971	WAS	N	12	109	9.1	18	0
Career			214	2324	10.9	74t	13
Playoffs			1	8	8.0		0

Rick Massie

Year	Team		No	Yds	Avg	Lg	TD
1987	DEN	N	13	244	18.8	39t	4
1988			3	39	13.0	21	0
Career			16	283	17.7	39t	4

Billy Masters

Year	Team		No	Yds	Avg	Lg	TD
1967	BUF	A	20	274	13.7	28	2
1968			8	101	12.6	21	0
1969			33	387	11.7	31	1
1970	DEN	N	9	83	9.2	18	2
1971			27	382	14.1	25	1
1972			25	393	15.7	27	3
1973			5	65	13.0	28	0
1975	KC	N	24	314	13.1	32	3
1976			18	269	14.9	30	3
Career			169	2268	13.4	32	15

Bob Masters

Year	Team		No	Yds	Avg	Lg	TD
1937	PHI	N	4	60	15.0		0
1939	PIT	N	2	12	6.0		0
Career			6	72	12.0		0

Bernie Masterson

Year	Team		No	Yds	Avg	Lg	TD
1934	CHIB	N	5	89	17.8		1
1935			7	99	14.1		0
1936			1	28	28.0	28	0
1938			1	4	4.0	4	0
1939			2	37	18.5		0
Career			16	257	16.1	28	1

Bob Masterson

Year	Team		No	Yds	Avg	Lg	TD
1938	WAS	N	10	213	21.3		1
1939			10	114	11.4		1
1940			18	283	15.7		4
1941			11	135	12.3	25	1
1942			22	308	14.0	33	2
1943			16	200	12.5	22	3
1944	BKN	N	24	258	10.8	30	1
1945	BOS	N	15	191	12.7	21	0
1946	NY	AA	10	119	11.9		0
Career			136	1821	13.4	33	13
Playoffs			11	135	12.3		

Le'Shai Maston

Year	Team		No	Yds	Avg	Lg	TD
1993	HOU	N	1	14	14.0	14	0
1994			2	12	6.0	10	0
1995	JAC	N	18	131	7.3	19	0
1996			6	54	9.0	17	0
Career			27	211	7.8	19	0
Playoffs			2	21	10.5		0

Ed Matesic

Year	Team		No	Yds	Avg	Lg	TD
1936	PIT	N	1	13	13.0	13	0

Jack Matheson

Year	Team		No	Yds	Avg	Lg	TD
1943	DET	N	13	156	12.0	46	1
1944			23	361	15.7	44	3
1945			19	341	17.9	34t	1
1946			17	178	10.5	33	0
1947	CHIB	N	1	8	8.0	8	0
Career			73	1044	14.3	46	5

Ned Mathews

Year	Team		No	Yds	Avg	Lg	TD
1941	DET	N	6	56	9.3	18	0
1942			3	38	12.7	20	0
1943			9	193	21.4	36	1
1945	BOS	N	4	56	14.0	23t	1
1946	CHI	AA	6	100	16.7		2
1947	SF	AA	6	51	8.5		2
Career			34	494	14.5	36	6

Ray Mathews

Year	Team		No	Yds	Avg	Lg	TD
1952	PIT	N	33	543	16.5	50	5
1953			27	346	12.8	77t	4
1954			44	652	14.8	78t	6
1955			42	762	18.1	61t	6
1956			31	540	17.4	64t	5
1957			15	369	24.6	64	4
1958			25	525	21.0	65	4
1959			13	182	14.0	56	0
1960	DAL	N	3	44	14.7	20	0
Career			233	3963	17.0	78t	34

Bill Mathis

Year	Team		No	Yds	Avg	Lg	TD
1960	NY	A	18	103	5.7		0
1961			12	42	3.5	14	1
1962			6	32	5.3	14	0
1963			18	177	9.8	33	1
1964			4	39	9.8	15	0
1965			17	242	14.2	32	1
1966			22	379	17.2	70	1
1967			25	429	17.2	38	3
1968			9	149	16.6	31	1
1969			18	183	10.2	35	1
Career			149	1775	11.9	70	9
Playoffs			4	24	6.0		0

Terance Mathis

Year	Team		No	Yds	Avg	Lg	TD
1990	NYJ	N	19	245	12.9	23	0
1991			28	329	11.8	39	1
1992			22	316	14.4	55t	3
1993			24	352	14.7	46	0
1994	ATL	N	111	1342	12.1	81	11
1995			78	1039	13.3	54t	9
1996			69	771	11.2	55	7
Career			351	4394	12.5	81	31
Playoffs			7	105	15.0		0

Charlie Mathys

Year	Team		No	Yds	Avg	Lg	TD
1922	GB	N					1
1924							2
Career							3

Trevor Matich

Year	Team		No	Yds	Avg	Lg	TD
1991	NYJ	N	3	23	7.7	14	1

Ollie Matson

Year	Team		No	Yds	Avg	Lg	TD
1952	CHIC	N	11	187	17.0	47t	3
1954			34	611	18.0	70	3
1955			17	237	13.9	70t	2
1956			15	199	13.3	45t	2
1957			20	451	22.6	75t	3
1958			33	465	14.1	59	3
1959	LA	N	18	130	7.2	49	0
1960			15	98	6.5	24	0
1961			29	537	18.5	96t	3
1962			3	49	16.3	20t	1
1963	DET	N	2	20	10.0	17	0
1964	PHI	N	17	242	14.2	32	1
1965			2	29	14.5	20	1
1966			6	30	5.0	11	1
Career			222	3285	14.8	96t	23

Tom Matte

Year	Team		No	Yds	Avg	Lg	TD
1961	BAL	N	1	8	8.0	8	0
1962			8	81	10.1	22	1
1963			48	466	9.7	49	1
1964			10	169	16.9	30	0
1965			12	131	10.9	15	0
1966			23	307	13.3	35	3
1967			35	496	14.2	88t	3
1968			25	275	11.0	50	1
1969			43	513	11.9	49	2
1970			1	2	2.0	2	0
1971			29	239	8.2	34	0
1972			14	182	13.0	43	1
Career			249	2869	11.5	88t	12
Playoffs			8	73	9.1		0

Allama Matthews

Year	Team		No	Yds	Avg	Lg	TD
1983	ATL	N	3	37	12.3	23	0
1984			1	7	7.0	7	0
1985			7	57	8.1	15	1
Career			11	101	9.2	23	1

Aubrey Matthews

Year	Team		No	Yds	Avg	Lg	TD
1986	ATL	N	1	25	25.0	25	0
1987			32	537	16.8	57	3
1988	ATL-GB	N	20	231	11.6	25	2
1989	GB	N	18	200	11.1	25	0
1990	DET	N	30	349	11.6	52	1
1991			3	21	7.0	11	0
1992			9	137	15.2	24	0
1993			11	171	15.5	40	0
1994			29	359	12.4	33	3
1995			4	41	10.3	12	0

Year	Team		No	Yds	Avg	Lg	TD

Aubrey Matthews *continued*

Year	Team		No	Yds	Avg	Lg	TD
1996			3	41	13.7	21	0
Career			160	2112	13.2	57	9
Playoffs			10	109	10.9		0

Bo Matthews

Year	Team		No	Yds	Avg	Lg	TD
1973	NO	N	2	19	9.5	12	0
1974	SD	N	12	90	7.5	23	0
1975			9	59	6.6	22	0
1976			12	81	6.8	15	0
1977			3	41	13.7	23	0
1978			11	78	7.1	13	0
1979			7	40	5.7	13	0
1980	NYG	N	19	86	4.5	12	0
1981			2	13	6.5	11	0
Career			77	507	6.6	23	0

Ira Matthews

Year	Team		No	Yds	Avg	Lg	TD
1980	OAK	N	3	33	11.0	20	0

Wes Matthews

Year	Team		No	Yds	Avg	Lg	TD
1966	MIA	A	1	20	20.0	20	0

Jack Mattiford

Year	Team		No	Yds	Avg	Lg	TD
1941	DET	N	1	21	21.0	21	0

Rich Mauti

Year	Team		No	Yds	Avg	Lg	TD
1977	NO	N	4	71	17.8	23	0
1978			8	69	8.6	16t	2
1979			2	64	32.0	61	0
1980			1	10	10.0	10	0
1982			4	70	17.5	37	0
1983			2	30	15.0	23	0
Career			21	314	15.0	61	2

Alvin Maxson

Year	Team		No	Yds	Avg	Lg	TD
1974	NO	N	42	294	7.0	22	1
1975			41	234	5.7	33	0
1976			7	21	3.0	14	0
1977	PIT	N	5	70	14.0	34	0
Career			95	619	6.5	34	1
Playoffs			3	11	3.7		0

Bill May

Year	Team		No	Yds	Avg	Lg	TD
1938	CHIC	N	1	16	16.0	16	0

Deems May

Year	Team		No	Yds	Avg	Lg	TD
1994	SD	N	2	22	11.0	18	0
1996			19	188	9.9	39	0
Career			21	210	10.0	39	0

Marc May

Year	Team		No	Yds	Avg	Lg	TD
1987	MIN	N	1	22	22.0	22	0

Doug Mayberry

Year	Team		No	Yds	Avg	Lg	TD
1961	MIN	N	2	18	9.0	13	0
1962			11	100	9.1	21	1
Career			13	118	9.1	21	1

James Mayberry

Year	Team		No	Yds	Avg	Lg	TD
1979	ATL	N	7	48	6.9	19	0
1980			3	1	0.3	6	0
1981			3	4	1.3	6	0
Career			13	53	4.1	19	0

Derrick Mayes

Year	Team		No	Yds	Avg	Lg	TD
1996	GB	N	6	46	7.7	12	2

Rueben Mayes

Year	Team		No	Yds	Avg	Lg	TD
1986	NO	N	17	96	5.6	18	0
1987			15	68	4.5	16	0
1988			11	103	9.4	25	0
1990			12	121	10.1	66	0
1992	SEA	N	2	13	6.5	7	0
Career			57	401	7.0	66	0

Gene Mayl

Year	Team		No	Yds	Avg	Lg	TD
1926	DAY	N					2

Don Maynard

Year	Team		No	Yds	Avg	Lg	TD
1958	NYG	N	5	84	16.8	31	0
1960	NY	A	72	1265	17.6	65	6
1961			43	629	14.6	45	8

Don Maynard *continued*

Year	Team		No	Yds	Avg	Lg	TD
1962			56	1041	18.6	86	8
1963			38	780	20.5	73	9
1964			46	847	18.4	68	8
1965			68	1218	17.9	56	14
1966			48	840	17.5	55	5
1967			71	1434	20.2	75t	10
1968			57	1297	22.8	87t	10
1969			47	938	20.0	60t	6
1970	NYJ	N	31	525	16.9	47	0
1971			21	408	19.4	74t	2
1972			29	510	17.6	41	2
1973	STL	N	1	18	18.0	18	0
Career			633	11834	18.7	87t	88
Playoffs			7	136	19.4		2

Lew Mayne

Year	Team		No	Yds	Avg	Lg	TD
1946	BKN	AA	5	9	1.8		0
1947	CLE	AA	6	238	39.7	69t	3
1948	BAL	AA	2	33	16.5		0
Career			13	280	21.5	69t	3
Playoffs			1	8	8.0		0

Frank Maznicki

Year	Team		No	Yds	Avg	Lg	TD
1942	CHIB	N	2	17	8.5	16	1
1946			2	38	19.0	22	0
1947	BOS	N	6	76	12.7	26	0
Career			10	131	13.1	26	1
Playoffs			1	39	39.0		0

Fred Mazurek

Year	Team		No	Yds	Avg	Lg	TD
1966	WAS	N	2	28	14.0	15	0

Vince Mazza

Year	Team		No	Yds	Avg	Lg	TD
1947	BUF	AA	2	11	5.5		0

Gino Mazzanti

Year	Team		No	Yds	Avg	Lg	TD
1950	BAL	N	1	11	11.0	11	0

Dean McAdams

Year	Team		No	Yds	Avg	Lg	TD
1941	BKN	N	7	94	13.4	47	0
1942			3	11	3.7	8	0
1943			2	6	3.0	8	0
Career			12	111	9.3	47	0

Derrick McAdoo

Year	Team		No	Yds	Avg	Lg	TD
1987	STL	N	2	12	6.0	6	0

Fred McAfee

Year	Team		No	Yds	Avg	Lg	TD
1991	NO	N	1	8	8.0	8	0
1992			1	16	16.0	16	0
1993			1	3	3.0	3	0
1994	ARI	N	1	4	4.0	4	0
1995	PIT	N	15	88	5.9	18	0
1996			5	21	4.2	9	0
Career			24	140	5.8	18	0
Playoffs			3	7	2.3		0

George McAfee

Year	Team		No	Yds	Avg	Lg	TD
1940	CHIB	N	7	117	16.7		0
1941			7	144	20.6	39	3
1945			3	85	28.3	65t	1
1946			10	137	13.7	25t	3
1947			32	490	15.3	53	1
1948			17	227	13.4	50	1
1949			9	157	17.4	52	1
Career			85	1357	16.0	65t	10
Playoffs			8	126	15.8		0

Wes McAfee

Year	Team		No	Yds	Avg	Lg	TD
1941	PHI	N	3	30	10.0	13	1

James McAlister

Year	Team		No	Yds	Avg	Lg	TD
1975	PHI	N	17	134	7.9	39t	2
1976			12	72	6.0	25	0
1978	NE	N	1	12	12.0	12	0
Career			30	218	7.3	39t	2

Charlie McBride

Year	Team		No	Yds	Avg	Lg	TD
1936	CHIC	N	1	38	38.0	38t	1

Oscar McBride

Year	Team		No	Yds	Avg	Lg	TD
1995	ARI	N	13	112	8.6	24	2

Don McCafferty

Year	Team		No	Yds	Avg	Lg	TD
1946	NYG	N	3	38	12.7	17	1

Ed McCaffrey

Year	Team		No	Yds	Avg	Lg	TD
1991	NYG	N	16	146	9.1	26	0
1992			49	610	12.4	44	5
1993			27	335	12.4	31	2
1994	SF	N	11	131	11.9	32	2
1995	DEN	N	39	477	12.2	35	2
1996			48	553	11.5	39t	7
Career			190	2252	11.9	44	18
Playoffs			11	118	10.7		1

Bob McCain

Year	Team		No	Yds	Avg	Lg	TD
1946	BKN	AA	3	27	9.0		0

Bob McCall

Year	Team		No	Yds	Avg	Lg	TD
1973	NE	N	3	18	6.0	14	0

Don McCall

Year	Team		No	Yds	Avg	Lg	TD
1967	NO	N	4	75	18.8	34	1
1968			26	270	10.4	25t	2
1969	PIT	N	2	2	1.0	5	0
1970	NO	N	5	43	8.6	17	0
Career			37	390	10.5	34	3

Reese McCall

Year	Team		No	Yds	Avg	Lg	TD
1978	BAL	N	11	160	14.5	34	1
1979			37	536	14.5	36	4
1980			18	322	17.9	47	5
1981			21	314	15.0	65t	2
1982			2	6	3.0	4	0
1983	DET	N	1	6	6.0	6	0
1984			3	15	5.0	7	0
1985			1	7	7.0	7	0
Career			94	1366	14.5	65t	12

Napoleon McCallum

Year	Team		No	Yds	Avg	Lg	TD
1986	LARI	N	13	103	7.9	22	0
1992			2	13	6.5	7	0
1993			2	5	2.5	3	0
Career			17	121	7.1	22	0
Playoffs			1	15	15.0		0

Keenan McCardell

Year	Team		No	Yds	Avg	Lg	TD
1992	CLE	N	1	8	8.0	8	0
1993			13	234	18.0	43	4
1994			10	182	18.2	34	0
1995			56	709	12.7	36	4
1996	JAC	N	85	1129	13.3	52	3
Career			165	2262	13.7	52	11
Playoffs			18	244	13.6		2

Brendan McCarthy

Year	Team		No	Yds	Avg	Lg	TD
1968	ATL-DEN	N-A	20	188	9.4	40t	2

Jim McCarthy

Year	Team		No	Yds	Avg	Lg	TD
1946	BKN	AA	11	296	26.9	65t	3
1947			10	147	14.7		0
1948	CHI	AA	3	30	10.0		0
1949			4	58	14.5		0
Career			28	531	19.0	65t	3

Vince McCarthy

Year	Team		No	Yds	Avg	Lg	TD
1925	RI	N					1

Don McCauley

Year	Team		No	Yds	Avg	Lg	TD
1971	BAL	N	3	6	2.0	8	0
1972			30	256	8.5	34	2
1973			25	186	7.4	34	0
1974			17	112	6.6	14	1
1975			14	93	6.6	32	1
1976			34	347	10.2	44	2
1977			51	495	9.7	34t	2
1978			34	296	8.7	21	0
1979			55	575	10.5	35	3
1980			34	314	9.2	19	4
1981			36	347	9.6	31	2
Career			333	3026	9.1	44	17
Playoffs			5	44	8.8		0

Bob McChesney

Year	Team		No	Yds	Avg	Lg	TD
1936	BOS	N	5	62	12.4		0

Bob McChesney continued

Year	Team		No	Yds	Avg	Lg	TD
1937	WAS	N	6	60	10.0		0
1938			3	49	16.3		1
1939			9	91	10.1		1
1940			9	119	13.2		1
1941			19	213	11.2	26	2
1942			8	100	12.5	33	2
Career			59	694	11.8	33	7
Playoffs			2	8	4.0		

Bob McChesney

Year	Team		No	Yds	Avg	Lg	TD
1950	NYG	N	19	380	20.0	43	6
1951			14	230	16.4	40	2
1952			21	430	20.5	72t	6
Career			54	1040	19.3	72t	14
Playoffs			1	19	19.0		0

Cliff McClain

Year	Team		No	Yds	Avg	Lg	TD
1970	NYJ	N	1	11	11.0	11	0
1972			6	88	14.7	44	0
1973			6	52	8.7	14	0
Career			13	151	11.6	44	0

Jack McClairen

Year	Team		No	Yds	Avg	Lg	TD
1955	PIT	N	1	13	13.0	13	0
1956			5	56	11.2	18	0
1957			46	630	13.7	48t	2
1958			29	491	16.9	35	1
1959			3	46	15.3	20	0
1960			1	17	17.0	17	0
Career			85	1253	14.7	48t	3

Brent McClanahan

Year	Team		No	Yds	Avg	Lg	TD
1974	MIN	N	3	35	11.7	17	0
1975			18	141	7.8	38	1
1976			40	252	6.3	23	1
1977			34	276	8.1	23	2
1978			2	11	5.5	7	0
1979			10	57	5.7	9	0
Career			107	772	7.2	38	4
Playoffs			3	29	9.7		0

Willie McClendon

Year	Team		No	Yds	Avg	Lg	TD
1979	CHI	N	6	27	4.5	13	0
1981			2	4	2.0	4	0
1982			1	7	7.0	7	0
Career			9	38	4.2	13	0

Curtis McClinton

Year	Team		No	Yds	Avg	Lg	TD
1962	DAL	A	29	333	11.5	28	0
1963	KC	A	27	301	11.1	46	3
1964			13	221	17.0	66	2
1965			37	590	15.9	69	3
1966			19	285	15.0	68	5
1967			26	219	8.4	25	1
1968			3	-4	-1.3	5	0
Career			154	1945	12.6	69	14
Playoffs			4	51	12.8		1

Mike McCloskey

Year	Team		No	Yds	Avg	Lg	TD
1983	HOU	N	16	137	8.6	20	1
1984			9	152	16.9	51	1
1985			4	29	7.3	24t	1
Career			29	318	11.0	51	3

David McCluskey

Year	Team		No	Yds	Avg	Lg	TD
1987	CIN	N	1	8	8.0	8	0

Bill McColl

Year	Team		No	Yds	Avg	Lg	TD
1952	CHIB	N	20	277	13.9	30	2
1953			36	453	12.6	55t	4
1954			24	368	15.3	45	2
1955			35	502	14.3	42	4
1956			24	322	13.4	69t	4
1957			19	282	14.8	30	1
1958			35	517	14.8	67t	8
1959			8	94	11.8	26	0
Career			201	2815	14.0	69t	25
Playoffs			3	35	11.7		

Phil McConkey

Year	Team		No	Yds	Avg	Lg	TD
1984	NYG	N	8	154	19.3	39	0
1985			25	404	16.2	48	1
1986			16	279	17.4	46	1

Phil McConkey continued

Year	Team		No	Yds	Avg	Lg	TD
1987			11	186	16.9	31	0
1988			5	72	14.4	28	0
1989	PHX	N	2	18	9.0	10	0
Career			67	1113	16.6	48	2
Playoffs			4	101	25.3		2

Dewey McConnell

Year	Team		No	Yds	Avg	Lg	TD
1954	PIT	N	1	2	2.0	2	0

Frank McCormick

Year	Team		No	Yds	Avg	Lg	TD
1920	AKR	A					1

Tom McCormick

Year	Team		No	Yds	Avg	Lg	TD
1953	LA	N	5	72	14.4	20	0
1954			3	58	19.3	31	0
1955			3	-1	-0.3	4	0
Career			11	129	11.7	31	0

Fred McCrary

Year	Team		No	Yds	Avg	Lg	TD
1995	PHI	N	9	60	6.7	11	0

Greg McCrary

Year	Team		No	Yds	Avg	Lg	TD
1977	ATL	N	2	48	24.0	49t	1
1978	SD	N	1	29	29.0	29t	1
1979			5	32	6.4	19	0
1980			11	106	9.6	28t	2
1981	WAS	N	3	13	4.3	12	0
Career			22	228	10.4	49t	4
Playoffs			3	53	17.7		

Hurdis McCrary

Year	Team		No	Yds	Avg	Lg	TD
1929	GB	N					2
1930							2
Career							4

Loaird McCreary

Year	Team		No	Yds	Avg	Lg	TD
1976	MIA	N	2	51	25.5	30	0
1977			2	10	5.0	9	1
1978			3	27	9.0	12	2
1979	NYG	N	1	7	7.0	7	0
Career			8	95	11.9	30	3

Earl McCullouch

Year	Team		No	Yds	Avg	Lg	TD
1968	DET	N	40	680	17.0	80t	5
1969			33	529	16.0	45	5
1970			15	278	18.5	44	4
1971			21	552	26.3	76t	3
1972			5	96	19.2	33	1
1973			9	179	19.9	42	1
1974	NO	N	1	5	5.0	5	0
Career			124	2319	18.7	80t	19
Playoffs			1	39	39.0		0

Bob McCullough

Year	Team		No	Yds	Avg	Lg	TD
1965	DEN	A	1	1	1.0	1	0

Hugh McCullough

Year	Team		No	Yds	Avg	Lg	TD
1939	PIT	N	4	57	14.3		0
1945	BOS	N	1	17	17.0	17	0
Career			5	74	14.8		0

Sam McCullum

Year	Team		No	Yds	Avg	Lg	TD
1974	MIN	N	7	138	19.7	34t	3
1975			2	25	12.5	20	0
1976	SEA	N	32	506	15.8	72t	4
1977			9	198	22.0	65t	1
1978			37	525	14.2	44t	3
1979			46	739	16.1	65t	4
1980			62	874	14.1	58	6
1981			46	567	12.3	36t	3
1982	MIN	N	12	131	10.9	21	0
1983			21	314	15.0	49t	2
Career			274	4017	14.7	72t	26
Playoffs			7	114	16.3		1

Lawrence McCutcheon

Year	Team		No	Yds	Avg	Lg	TD
1973	LA	N	30	289	9.6	31t	3
1974			39	408	10.5	50t	2
1975			31	230	7.4	24	1
1976			28	305	10.9	42	2
1977			25	274	11.0	30	2
1978			12	76	6.3	33	2
1979			19	101	5.3	11	0

Lawrence McCutcheon continued

Year	Team		No	Yds	Avg	Lg	TD
1980	DEN-SEA	N	9	76	8.4	17	1
1981	BUF	N	5	40	8.0	17	0
Career			198	1799	9.1	50t	13
Playoffs			17	150	8.8		0

Johnny McDaniel

Year	Team		No	Yds	Avg	Lg	TD
1974	CIN	N	2	79	39.5	60	0
1976			12	232	19.3	46	1
1977			12	148	12.3	31	0
1978	WAS	N	34	577	17.0	52	4
1979			25	357	14.3	62	2
1980			14	154	11.0	18	0
Career			99	1547	15.6	62	7

Gary McDermott

Year	Team		No	Yds	Avg	Lg	TD
1968	BUF	A	20	115	5.8	37	1

Mardye McDole

Year	Team		No	Yds	Avg	Lg	TD
1983	MIN	N	3	29	9.7	10	0

Don McDonald

Year	Team		No	Yds	Avg	Lg	TD
1944	PHI	N	4	26	6.5	9	1
1945			8	75	9.4	21t	1
1948	NY	AA	3	30	10.0		0
Career			15	131	8.7	21t	2

Dwight McDonald

Year	Team		No	Yds	Avg	Lg	TD
1975	SD	N	19	298	15.7	57	3
1976			11	161	14.6	44t	4
1977			13	174	13.4	22	0
1978			3	84	28.0	37t	1
Career			46	717	15.6	57	8

Ed McDonald

Year	Team		No	Yds	Avg	Lg	TD
1936	PIT	N	1	8	8.0	8	0

James McDonald

Year	Team		No	Yds	Avg	Lg	TD
1983	LARM	N	1	1	1.0	1t	1
1984			4	55	13.8	22	0
1985	DET-LARM	N	5	81	16.2	35	0
1987	LARM	N	4	31	7.8	13	2
Career			14	168	12.0	35	3
Playoffs			2	18	9.0		0

Jim McDonald

Year	Team		No	Yds	Avg	Lg	TD
1938	DET	N	2	41	20.5		0
1939			5	71	14.2		0
Career			7	112	16.0		0

Keith McDonald

Year	Team		No	Yds	Avg	Lg	TD
1987	HOU	N	4	56	14.0	24	1
1989	DET	N	12	138	11.5	24	0
Career			16	194	12.1	24	1

Les McDonald

Year	Team		No	Yds	Avg	Lg	TD
1937	CHIB	N	11	179	16.3		4
1938			9	175	19.4		1
1939			16	261	16.3		3
1940	PHI	N	15	309	20.6		0
Career			51	924	18.1		8
Playoffs			2	39	19.5		0

Paul McDonald

Year	Team		No	Yds	Avg	Lg	TD
1984	CLE	N	1	-4	-4.0	-4	0

Ray McDonald

Year	Team		No	Yds	Avg	Lg	TD
1967	WAS	N	10	60	6.0	18	0

Tommy McDonald

Year	Team		No	Yds	Avg	Lg	TD
1957	PHI	N	9	228	25.3	61t	3
1958			29	603	20.8	91t	9
1959			47	846	18.0	71	10
1960			39	801	20.5	64t	13
1961			64	1144	17.9	66	13
1962			58	1146	19.8	60t	10
1963			41	731	17.8	75t	8
1964	DAL	N	46	612	13.3	48t	2
1965	LA	N	67	1036	15.5	51	9
1966			55	714	13.0	62	2
1967	ATL	N	33	436	13.2	75t	4
1968	CLE	N	7	113	16.1	42	1
Career			495	8410	17.0	91t	84
Playoffs			3	90	30.0		1

Year	Team		No	Yds	Avg	Lg	TD

Walt McDonald

Year	Team		No	Yds	Avg	Lg	TD
1946	MIA-BKN	AA	12	126	10.5		0
1947	BKN	AA	3	30	10.0		0
1948			7	41	5.9		1
Career			22	197	9.0		1

Mickey McDonnell

Year	Team		No	Yds	Avg	Lg	TD
1925	DUL	N					1
1926	CHIC	N					1
1929							1
Career							3

Coley McDonough

Year	Team		No	Yds	Avg	Lg	TD
1939	PIT	N	1	3	3.0	3	1

Paul McDonough

Year	Team		No	Yds	Avg	Lg	TD
1938	PIT	N	6	86	14.3		0
1939	CLE	N	8	73	9.1		1
1940			12	315	26.3		1
1941			14	198	14.1	26	2
Career			40	672	16.8	26	4

Gerry McDougall

Year	Team		No	Yds	Avg	Lg	TD
1962	SD	A	4	27	6.8	10	0
1963			10	115	11.5	26	0
1964			8	106	13.3	24	0
Career			22	248	11.3	26	0
Playoffs			1	4	4.0		0

Anthony McDowell

Year	Team		No	Yds	Avg	Lg	TD
1992	TB	N	27	258	9.6	51t	2
1993			8	26	3.3	9	1
1994			29	193	6.7	19	1
Career			64	477	7.5	51t	4

O.J. Mc Duffie

Year	Team		No	Yds	Avg	Lg	TD
1993	MIA	N	19	197	10.4	18	0
1994			37	488	13.2	30	3
1995			62	819	13.2	48	8
1996			74	918	12.4	36	8
Career			192	2422	12.6	48	19
Playoffs			18	225	12.5		1

Hugh McElhenny

Year	Team		No	Yds	Avg	Lg	TD
1952	SF	N	26	367	14.1	77	3
1953			30	474	15.8	71	2
1954			8	162	20.3	53	0
1955			11	203	18.5	55t	2
1956			16	193	12.1	22	0
1957			37	458	12.4	43	2
1958			31	366	11.8	59t	2
1959			22	329	15.0	62t	3
1960			14	114	8.1	45	1
1961	MIN	N	37	283	7.6	26	3
1962			16	191	11.9	41	0
1963	NYG	N	11	91	8.3	24	2
1964	DET	N	5	16	3.2	27	0
Career			264	3247	12.3	77	20
Playoffs			8	116	14.5		1

Leeland McElroy

Year	Team		No	Yds	Avg	Lg	TD
1996	ARI	N	5	41	8.2	22t	1

Doug McEnulty

Year	Team		No	Yds	Avg	Lg	TD
1943	CHIB	N	1	10	10.0	10	0
1944			2	10	5.0	5	1
Career			3	20	6.7	10	1

Craig McEwen

Year	Team		No	Yds	Avg	Lg	TD
1987	WAS	N	12	164	13.7	42	0
1988			23	323	14.0	46	0
1989	SD	N	7	99	14.1	29	0
1990			29	325	11.2	32	3
1991			37	399	10.8	30	3
Career			108	1310	12.1	46	6

Banks McFadden

Year	Team		No	Yds	Avg	Lg	TD
1940	BKN	N	9	97	10.8		2

Thad McFadden

Year	Team		No	Yds	Avg	Lg	TD
1987	BUF	N	4	41	10.3	13t	1

Jim McFarland

Year	Team		No	Yds	Avg	Lg	TD
1971	STL	N	5	54	10.8	21	2

Jim McFarland continued

Year	Team		No	Yds	Avg	Lg	TD
1973			2	10	5.0	7	0
Career			7	64	9.1	21	2

Kay McFarland

Year	Team		No	Yds	Avg	Lg	TD
1962	SF	N	3	24	8.0	16	0
1963			11	126	11.5	33	1
1964			5	67	13.4	33	0
1965			8	106	13.3	35t	1
1966			13	219	16.8	43	1
1968			5	140	28.0	65	1
Career			45	682	15.2	65	4

Nyle McFarlane

Year	Team		No	Yds	Avg	Lg	TD
1960	OAK	A	5	89	17.8		2

Buford McGee

Year	Team		No	Yds	Avg	Lg	TD
1984	SD	N	9	76	8.4	43	2
1985			3	15	5.0	7	0
1986			10	105	10.5	18	0
1987	LARM	N	7	40	5.7	12	0
1988			16	117	7.3	16	3
1989			37	303	8.2	25	4
1990			47	388	8.3	25	4
1991			20	160	8.0	20	0
1992	GB	N	6	60	10.0	15	0
Career			155	1264	8.2	43	13
Playoffs			16	140	8.8		0

Max McGee

Year	Team		No	Yds	Avg	Lg	TD
1954	GB	N	36	614	17.1	82	9
1957			17	273	16.1	49	1
1958			37	655	17.7	80t	7
1959			30	695	23.2	81t	5
1960			38	787	20.7	57t	4
1961			51	883	17.3	53	7
1962			49	820	16.7	64	3
1963			39	749	19.2	63	6
1964			31	592	19.1	55	6
1965			10	154	15.4	37t	1
1966			4	91	22.8	39	1
1967			3	33	11.0	13	0
Career			345	6346	18.4	82	50
Playoffs			12	233	19.4		4

Tim McGee

Year	Team		No	Yds	Avg	Lg	TD
1986	CIN	N	16	276	17.3	51	1
1987			23	408	17.7	49	1
1988			36	686	19.1	78t	6
1989			65	1211	18.6	74t	8
1990			43	737	17.1	52	1
1991			51	802	15.7	52t	4
1992			35	408	11.7	36	3
1993	WAS	N	39	500	12.8	54	3
1994	CIN	N	13	175	13.5	25	1
Career			321	5203	16.2	78t	28
Playoffs			7	60	8.6		0

Tony McGee

Year	Team		No	Yds	Avg	Lg	TD
1993	CIN	N	44	525	11.9	37	0
1994			40	492	12.3	54	1
1995			55	754	13.7	41	4
1996			38	446	11.7	22	4
Career			177	2217	12.5	54	9

Willie McGee

Year	Team		No	Yds	Avg	Lg	TD
1973	SD	N	3	67	22.3	50	0
1975	LA	N	6	83	13.8	22	0
1976	SF	N	13	269	20.7	52t	4
1977			2	27	13.5	14	0
Career			24	446	18.6	52t	4

Rich McGeorge

Year	Team		No	Yds	Avg	Lg	TD
1970	GB	N	2	32	16.0	16t	2
1971			27	463	17.1	50	4
1972			4	50	12.5	23t	2
1973			16	260	16.3	44	1
1974			30	440	14.7	51	0
1975			32	458	14.3	43	1
1976			24	278	11.6	28	1
1977			17	142	8.4	18	1
1978			23	247	10.7	25	1
Career			175	2370	13.5	51	13

Eddie McGill

Year	Team		No	Yds	Avg	Lg	TD
1983	STL	N	1	11	11.0	11	0

Reggie McGowan

Year	Team		No	Yds	Avg	Lg	TD
1987	NYG	N	4	111	27.8	63t	1

Mark McGrath

Year	Team		No	Yds	Avg	Lg	TD
1981	SEA	N	4	47	11.8	16	0
1983	WAS	N	1	6	6.0	6	0
1984			10	118	11.8	24	1
Career			15	171	11.4	24	1

Lamar McHan

Year	Team		No	Yds	Avg	Lg	TD
1958	CHIC	N	0	1		1L	0

Pat McHugh

Year	Team		No	Yds	Avg	Lg	TD
1947	PHI	N	2	16	8.0	10	0
Playoffs			2	55	27.5		1

Don McIlhenny

Year	Team		No	Yds	Avg	Lg	TD
1956	DET	N	8	70	8.8	21	2
1957	GB	N	18	210	11.7	28t	2
1958			20	154	7.7	55t	1
1959			8	95	11.9	30	1
1960	DAL	N	15	120	8.0	64t	1
1961			1	6	6.0	6	0
Career			70	655	9.4	64t	7

Pat McInally

Year	Team		No	Yds	Avg	Lg	TD
1977	CIN	N	17	258	15.2	43t	3
1978			15	189	12.6	49	0
1979			1	24	24.0	24	0
1980			18	269	14.9	59t	2
1981			6	68	11.3	20	0
Career			57	808	14.2	59t	5

Hugh McInnis

Year	Team		No	Yds	Avg	Lg	TD
1960	STL	N	13	260	20.0	51	0
1961			7	107	15.3	22	0
1962			1	10	10.0	10	0
1964	DET	N	1	15	15.0	15	0
Career			22	392	17.8	51	0

Joe McIntosh

Year	Team		No	Yds	Avg	Lg	TD
1987	ATL	N	3	15	5.0	9	1

Guy McIntyre

Year	Team		No	Yds	Avg	Lg	TD
1988	SF	N	1	17	17.0	17t	1
1996	PHI	N	1	4	4.0	4	0
Career			2	21	10.5	17t	1

Secedrik McIntyre

Year	Team		No	Yds	Avg	Lg	TD
1977	ATL	N	1	27	27.0	27t	1

Bill McKalip

Year	Team		No	Yds	Avg	Lg	TD
1931	POR	N					4
1936	DET	N	1	10	10.0	10	0
Career			1	10	10.0	10	4

John McKay

Year	Team		No	Yds	Avg	Lg	TD
1976	TB	N	20	302	15.1	49	1
1977			12	164	13.7	26	0
1978			9	166	18.4	28	1
Career			41	632	15.4	49	2

Paul McKee

Year	Team		No	Yds	Avg	Lg	TD
1947	WAS	N	16	242	15.1	29	2
1948			14	171	12.2	22	0
Career			30	413	13.8	29	2

Marlin McKeever

Year	Team		No	Yds	Avg	Lg	TD
1963	LA	N	11	152	13.8	29	0
1964			41	582	14.2	46	1
1965			44	542	12.3	47t	4
1966			23	277	12.0	31	1
1967	MIN	N	14	184	13.1	42	0
Career			133	1737	13.1	47t	6

Keith McKeller

Year	Team		No	Yds	Avg	Lg	TD
1987	BUF	N	9	80	8.9	22	0
1989			20	341	17.1	39t	2
1990			34	464	13.6	43	5
1991			44	434	9.9	29t	3
1992			14	110	7.9	26	0

Year	Team		No	Yds	Avg	Lg	TD

Keith McKeller *continued*

Year	Team		No	Yds	Avg	Lg	TD
1993			3	35	11.7	13t	1
Career			124	1464	11.8	43	11
Playoffs			27	246	9.1		0

Hugh McKinnis

Year	Team		No	Yds	Avg	Lg	TD
1973	CLE	N	3	11	3.7	12	0
1974			32	258	8.1	55	0
1975			17	155	9.1	20	0
1976	SEA	N	13	148	11.4	22	0
Career			65	572	8.8	55	0

Dennis McKinnon

Year	Team		No	Yds	Avg	Lg	TD
Playoffs			20	345	17.3		4

Don McKinnon

Year	Team		No	Yds	Avg	Lg	TD
1983	CHI	N	20	326	16.3	49t	4
1984			29	431	14.9	32t	3
1985			31	555	17.9	48	7
1987			27	406	15.0	33	1
1988			45	704	15.6	76t	3
1989			28	418	14.9	41	3
1990	DAL	N	14	172	12.3	28t	1
Career			194	3012	15.5	76t	22

James McKnight

Year	Team		No	Yds	Avg	Lg	TD
1994	SEA	N	1	25	25.0	25t	1
1995			6	91	15.2	24	0
1996			1	73	73.0	73	0
Career			8	189	23.6	73	1

Ted McKnight

Year	Team		No	Yds	Avg	Lg	TD
1977	KC	N	1	11	11.0	11	0
1978			14	83	5.9	19	1
1979			38	226	5.9	24	0
1980			38	320	8.4	26	0
1981			8	77	9.6	23	0
Career			99	717	7.2	26	1

Mayes McLain

Year	Team		No	Yds	Avg	Lg	TD
1930	POR	N					3
1931	SI	N					2
Career							5

John McLaughry

Year	Team		No	Yds	Avg	Lg	TD
1940	NYG	N	1	-1	-1.0	-1	0

Ray McLean

Year	Team		No	Yds	Avg	Lg	TD
1940	CHIB	N	6	138	23.0		2
1941			5	84	16.8	40	1
1942			19	571	30.1	68	8
1943			18	435	24.2	66	2
1944			19	414	21.8	86t	5
1945			8	107	13.4	43	0
1946			17	348	20.5	48t	2
1947			11	125	11.4	19t	1
Career			103	2222	21.6	86t	21
Playoffs			5	60	12.0		0

Chris McLemore

Year	Team		No	Yds	Avg	Lg	TD
1987	IND	N	2	9	4.5	5	0

Emmett McLemore

Year	Team		No	Yds	Avg	Lg	TD
1923	OOR	N					1

Tom McLemore

Year	Team		No	Yds	Avg	Lg	TD
1992	DET	N	2	12	6.0	6	0

Bruce McLenna

Year	Team		No	Yds	Avg	Lg	TD
1966	DET	N	3	13	4.3	8	0

Bob McLeod

Year	Team		No	Yds	Avg	Lg	TD
1961	HOU	A	14	172	12.3	18	2
1962			33	578	17.5	55	6
1963			33	530	16.1	38	5
1964			8	81	10.1	20	2
1965			15	226	15.1	49	1
1966			23	339	14.7	41	3
Career			126	1926	15.3	55	19
Playoffs			6	80	13.3		0

Jim McMahon

Year	Team		No	Yds	Avg	Lg	TD
1983	CHI	N	1	18	18.0	18t	1
1984			1	42	42.0	42	0

Jim McMahon *continued*

Year	Team		No	Yds	Avg	Lg	TD
1985			1	13	13.0	13t	1
1989	SD	N	1	4	4.0	4	0
1991	PHI	N	1	-5	-5.0	-5	0
Career			5	72	14.4	42	2

John McMakin

Year	Team		No	Yds	Avg	Lg	TD
1972	PIT	N	21	277	13.2	78t	1
1973			13	195	15.0	44	1
1975	DET	N	2	43	21.5	30	0
1976	SEA	N	9	158	17.6	37	2
Career			45	673	15.0	78t	4
Playoffs			3	57	19.0		0

Randy McMillan

Year	Team		No	Yds	Avg	Lg	TD
1981	BAL	N	50	466	9.3	31	1
1982			15	90	6.0	17	0
1983			24	195	8.1	27	1
1984	IND	N	19	201	10.6	44	0
1985			22	115	5.2	17	0
1986			34	289	8.5	45	0
Career			164	1356	8.3	45	2

Bo McMillin

Year	Team		No	Yds	Avg	Lg	TD
1922	MIL	N					1

Greg McMurtry

Year	Team		No	Yds	Avg	Lg	TD
1990	NE	N	22	240	10.9	26	0
1991			41	614	15.0	40	2
1992			35	424	12.1	65t	1
1993			22	241	11.0	20	1
1994	CHI	N	8	112	14.0	30	1
Career			128	1631	12.7	65t	5

Todd McNair

Year	Team		No	Yds	Avg	Lg	TD
1989	KC	N	34	372	10.9	24	1
1990			40	507	12.7	65	2
1991			37	342	9.2	36	1
1992			44	380	8.6	36	1
1993			10	74	7.4	24	0
1994	HOU	N	8	78	9.8	21	0
1995			60	501	8.3	25	1
1996	KC	N	21	181	8.6	29	1
Career			254	2435	9.6	65	7
Playoffs			17	160	9.4		0

Bob McNamara

Year	Team		No	Yds	Avg	Lg	TD
1960	DEN	A	7	143	20.4	55	1

Travis McNeal

Year	Team		No	Yds	Avg	Lg	TD
1989	SEA	N	9	147	16.3	48	0
1990			10	143	14.3	30	0
1991			17	208	12.2	36	1
1992	LARM	N	4	79	19.8	38	0
1993			8	75	9.4	22t	1
Career			48	652	13.6	48	2

Clifton McNeil

Year	Team		No	Yds	Avg	Lg	TD
1964	CLE	N	4	69	17.3	28	1
1965			3	69	23.0	32	0
1966			2	94	47.0	50t	2
1967			3	33	11.0	23	2
1968	SF	N	71	994	14.0	65t	7
1969			17	255	15.0	80t	3
1970	NYG	N	50	764	15.3	59	4
1971	NYG-WAS	N	30	453	15.1	32t	3
1973	HOU	N	1	3	3.0	3	0
Career			181	2734	15.1	80t	22

Freeman McNeil

Year	Team		No	Yds	Avg	Lg	TD
1981	NYJ	N	18	171	9.5	18	1
1982			16	187	11.7	32t	1
1983			21	172	8.2	21	3
1984			25	294	11.8	32	1
1985			38	427	11.2	25	2
1986			49	410	8.4	26	1
1987			24	262	10.9	57	1
1988			34	288	8.5	25	1
1989			31	310	10.0	25t	1
1990			16	230	14.4	59	0
1991			7	56	8.0	13	0
1992			16	154	9.6	32	0
Career			295	2961	10.0	59	12
Playoffs			17	116	6.8		1

Gerald McNeil

Year	Team		No	Yds	Avg	Lg	TD
1986	CLE	N	1	9	9.0	9	0
1987			8	120	15.0	39t	2
1988			5	74	14.8	23	0
1989			10	114	11.4	32	0
1990	HOU	N	5	63	12.6	16	0
Career			29	380	13.1	39t	2
Playoffs			1	8	8.0		0

Pat McNeil

Year	Team		No	Yds	Avg	Lg	TD
1976	KC	N	2	33	16.5	18	0

Rod McNeill

Year	Team		No	Yds	Avg	Lg	TD
1974	NO	N	5	64	12.8	30	1
1975			18	138	7.7	17	2
1976	TB	N	7	33	4.7	9	0
Career			30	235	7.8	30	2

Buck McPhail

Year	Team		No	Yds	Avg	Lg	TD
1953	BAL	N	10	38	3.8	45	0

Jerris McPhail

Year	Team		No	Yds	Avg	Lg	TD
1996	MIA	N	20	282	14.1	52	0

Leon McQuay

Year	Team		No	Yds	Avg	Lg	TD
1974	NYG	N	5	59	11.8	25	0
1975	NE	N	4	27	6.8	16	0
Career			9	86	9.6	25	0

Jerrold McRae

Year	Team		No	Yds	Avg	Lg	TD
1979	PHI	N	1	-2	-2.0	-2	0

Bill McRaven

Year	Team		No	Yds	Avg	Lg	TD
1939	CLE	N	2	14	7.0		0

Warren McVea

Year	Team		No	Yds	Avg	Lg	TD
1968	CIN	A	21	264	12.6	55t	2
1969	KC	A	7	71	10.1	22	0
1970	KC	N	5	26	5.2	15	0
1971			5	-3	-0.6	10	0
Career			38	358	9.4	55t	2

Bill McWatters

Year	Team		No	Yds	Avg	Lg	TD
1964	MIN	N	2	-1	-0.5	1	0

Johnny McWilliams

Year	Team		No	Yds	Avg	Lg	TD
1996	ARI	N	6	59	9.8	13t	0

Jack Mead

Year	Team		No	Yds	Avg	Lg	TD
1946	NYG	N	3	36	12.0	19	0
1947			6	91	15.2	41	0
Career			9	127	14.1	41	0

Jim Meade

Year	Team		No	Yds	Avg	Lg	TD
1939	WAS	N	1	1	1.0	1	0
1940			4	39	9.8		0
Career			5	40	8.0	1	0

Mike Meade

Year	Team		No	Yds	Avg	Lg	TD
1982	GB	N	3	-5	-1.7	-1	0
1983			16	110	6.9	31t	2
1985	DET	N	2	21	10.5	14	0
Career			21	126	6.0	31t	2

Natrone Means

Year	Team		No	Yds	Avg	Lg	TD
1993	SD	N	10	59	5.9	11	0
1994			39	235	6.0	22	0
1995			7	46	6.6	14	0
1996	JAC	N	7	45	6.4	11t	1
Career			63	385	6.1	22	1
Playoffs			11	81	7.4		0

Greg Meehan

Year	Team		No	Yds	Avg	Lg	TD
1987	CIN	N	3	25	8.3	12	0

Herb Meeker

Year	Team		No	Yds	Avg	Lg	TD
1930	PRO	N					1

Dave Meggett

Year	Team		No	Yds	Avg	Lg	TD
1989	NYG	N	34	531	15.6	62t	4
1990			39	410	10.5	38	1
1991			50	412	8.2	22	3
1992			38	229	6.0	24	2
1993			38	319	8.4	50	0

Year	Team		No	Yds	Avg	Lg	TD

Dave Meggett *continued*

Year	Team		No	Yds	Avg	Lg	TD
1994			32	293	9.2	34	0
1995	NE	N	52	334	6.4	19	0
1996			33	292	8.8	26	0
Career			316	2820	8.9	62t	10
Playoffs			21	137	6.5		

Charlie Mehelich

Year	Team		No	Yds	Avg	Lg	TD
1946	PIT	N	10	116	11.6	35	0
1947			3	38	12.7	13	0
1950			2	18	9.0	10	0
Career			15	172	11.5	35	0

Steve Meilinger

Year	Team		No	Yds	Avg	Lg	TD
1956	WAS	N	24	395	16.5	51t	5
1957			13	183	14.1	34t	2
1958	GB	N	13	139	10.7	19	1
1960			2	43	21.5	23	0
1961	PIT	N	8	103	12.9	17	0
Career			60	863	14.4	51t	8

Jim Mello

Year	Team		No	Yds	Avg	Lg	TD
1947	BOS	N	2	26	13.0	23	0
1948	LA-CHI	N-AA	4	55	13.8	17	0
Career			6	81	13.5	23	0

John Mellus

Year	Team		No	Yds	Avg	Lg	TD
1947	BAL	AA	0	5		5L	0

Melvin

Year	Team		No	Yds	Avg	Lg	TD
1921	CIN	A					1

Hartwell Menefee

Year	Team		No	Yds	Avg	Lg	TD
1966	NYG	N	1	11	11.0	11	0

Chuck Mercein

Year	Team		No	Yds	Avg	Lg	TD
1965	NYG	N	3	14	4.7	5	0
1966			27	152	5.6	20	0
1967	GB	N	1	6	6.0	6	0
1968			3	6	2.0	9	0
1970	NYJ	N	3	27	9.0	15t	1
Career			37	205	5.5	20	1
Playoffs			4	32	8.0		0

Ken Mercer

Year	Team		No	Yds	Avg	Lg	TD
1928	FRA	N					1
1929							1
Career							2

Guido Merkens

Year	Team		No	Yds	Avg	Lg	TD
1978	HOU	N	1	6	6.0	6	0
1979			3	44	14.7	20	1
1981	NO	N	29	458	15.8	50	1
1985			3	61	20.3	39t	1
Career			36	569	15.8	50	3
Playoffs			1	12	12.0		0

Jim Mertens

Year	Team		No	Yds	Avg	Lg	TD
1969	MIA	A	2	26	13.0	15	0

Bus Mertes

Year	Team		No	Yds	Avg	Lg	TD
1945	CHIC	N	2	1	0.5	1	0
1946	LA	AA	5	61	12.2		1
1947	BAL	AA	2	28	14.0		0
1948			6	56	9.3		0
1949	BAL-NYG	AA-N	4	36	9.0	13	1
Career			19	182	9.6	13	2
Playoffs			1	12	12.0		0

Dale Messer

Year	Team		No	Yds	Avg	Lg	TD
1961	SF	N	3	33	11.0	14	0
1962			3	30	10.0	15	0
1964			4	72	18.0	28	0
1965			2	41	20.5	37	0
Career			12	176	14.7	37	0

Frank Mestnik

Year	Team		No	Yds	Avg	Lg	TD
1960	STL	N	3	24	8.0	15	0
1961			12	29	2.4	15	1
Career			15	53	3.5	15	1

Eric Metcalf

Year	Team		No	Yds	Avg	Lg	TD
1989	CLE	N	54	397	7.4	68t	4
1990			57	452	7.9	35	1

Eric Metcalf *continued*

Year	Team		No	Yds	Avg	Lg	TD
1991			29	294	10.1	45	0
1992			47	614	13.1	69t	5
1993			63	539	8.6	49t	2
1994			47	436	9.3	57t	3
1995	ATL	N	104	1189	11.4	62t	8
1996			54	599	11.1	67	6
Career			455	4520	9.9	69t	29
Playoffs			13	147	11.3		1

Terry Metcalf

Year	Team		No	Yds	Avg	Lg	TD
1973	STL	N	37	316	8.5	35	0
1974			50	377	7.5	22t	1
1975			43	378	8.8	30t	2
1976			33	388	11.8	48t	4
1977			34	403	11.9	68t	2
1981	WAS	N	48	595	12.4	52	0
Career			245	2457	10.0	68t	9
Playoffs			10	137	13.7		0

Russ Method

Year	Team		No	Yds	Avg	Lg	TD
1927	DUL	N					1

Pete Metzelaars

Year	Team		No	Yds	Avg	Lg	TD
1982	SEA	N	15	152	10.1	26	0
1983			7	72	10.3	17t	1
1984			5	80	16.0	25	0
1985	BUF	N	12	80	6.7	13	1
1986			49	485	9.9	44t	3
1987			28	290	10.4	34	0
1988			33	438	13.3	35	1
1989			18	179	9.9	23	2
1990			10	60	6.0	12	1
1991			5	54	10.8	51t	2
1992			30	298	9.9	53t	6
1993			68	609	9.0	51	4
1994			49	428	8.7	35t	5
1995	CAR	N	20	171	8.6	27	3
1996	DET	N	17	146	8.6	20	1
Career			366	3542	9.7	53t	29
Playoffs			23	194	8.4		2

Fred Meyer

Year	Team		No	Yds	Avg	Lg	TD
1942	PHI	N	16	323	20.2	60	1
1945			11	125	11.4	27t	1
Career			27	448	16.6	60	2

Gil Meyer

Year	Team		No	Yds	Avg	Lg	TD
1947	BAL	AA	1	3	3.0	3	0

Paul Meyers

Year	Team		No	Yds	Avg	Lg	TD
1923	RAC	N					1

Larry Mialik

Year	Team		No	Yds	Avg	Lg	TD
1973	ATL	N	2	30	15.0	17	0

Tom Michel

Year	Team		No	Yds	Avg	Lg	TD
1964	MIN	N	1	14	14.0	14	0

Bobby Micho

Year	Team		No	Yds	Avg	Lg	TD
1987	DEN	N	25	242	9.7	26t	2
Playoffs			1	20	20.0		0

Mike Micka

Year	Team		No	Yds	Avg	Lg	TD
1944	WAS	N	2	16	8.0	10	0
1945			2	74	37.0	64	0
1947	BOS	N	2	11	5.5	6	0
Career			6	101	16.8	64	0

Terry Mickens

Year	Team		No	Yds	Avg	Lg	TD
1994	GB	N	4	31	7.8	11	0
1995			3	50	16.7	24	0
1996			18	161	8.9	19	2
Career			25	242	9.7	24	2
Playoffs			3	55	18.3		0

Oren Middlebrook

Year	Team		No	Yds	Avg	Lg	TD
Playoffs			1	11	11.0		0

Dave Middleton

Year	Team		No	Yds	Avg	Lg	TD
1955	DET	N	44	663	15.1	77t	3
1956			39	606	15.5	56t	5
1957			18	294	16.3	56	2

Dave Middleton *continued*

Year	Team		No	Yds	Avg	Lg	TD
1958			29	506	17.4	46	3
1959			18	402	22.3	79t	2
1960			5	51	10.2	20	0
1961	MIN	N	30	444	14.8	57t	2
Career			183	2966	16.2	79t	17
Playoffs			3	59	19.7		1

Frank Middleton

Year	Team		No	Yds	Avg	Lg	TD
1984	IND	N	15	112	7.5	16	1
1985			5	54	10.8	34	0
1987	SD	N	8	43	5.4	17	0
Career			28	209	7.5	34	1

Ron Middleton

Year	Team		No	Yds	Avg	Lg	TD
1986	ATL	N	6	31	5.2	8	0
1987			1	1	1.0	1	0
1989	CLE	N	1	5	5.0	5t	1
1991	WAS	N	3	25	8.3	11	0
1992			7	50	7.1	16	0
1993			24	154	6.4	18	2
Career			42	266	6.3	18	3
Playoffs			5	40	8.0		1

Terdell Middleton

Year	Team		No	Yds	Avg	Lg	TD
1977	GB	N	1	27	27.0	27	0
1978			34	332	9.8	50	1
1979			18	155	8.6	29	1
1980			13	59	4.5	17	0
1981			12	86	7.2	27	1
Career			78	659	8.4	50	3

Lou Mihajlovich

Year	Team		No	Yds	Avg	Lg	TD
1948	LA	AA	4	42	10.5		0

Joe Mihal

Year	Team		No	Yds	Avg	Lg	TD
Playoffs			1	14	14.0		0

Russ Mikeska

Year	Team		No	Yds	Avg	Lg	TD
1979	ATL	N	1	14	14.0	14	0
1980			1	4	4.0	4	0
1981			2	16	8.0	11	0
1982			2	19	9.5	12	0
Career			6	53	8.8	14	0

Bill Miklich

Year	Team		No	Yds	Avg	Lg	TD
1947	NYG	N	1	-5	-5.0	-5	0

Mike Mikulak

Year	Team		No	Yds	Avg	Lg	TD
1935	CHIC	N	8	93	11.6		0
1936			6	62	10.3		0
Career			14	155	11.1		0

Glyn Milburn

Year	Team		No	Yds	Avg	Lg	TD
1993	DEN	N	38	300	7.9	50	3
1994			77	549	7.1	33	3
1995			22	191	8.7	23	0
Career			137	1040	7.6	50	6
Playoffs			5	8	1.6		0

Ostell Miles

Year	Team		No	Yds	Avg	Lg	TD
1993	CIN	N	6	89	14.8	27	0

Bryan Millard

Year	Team		No	Yds	Avg	Lg	TD
1987	SEA	N	1	-5	-5.0	-5	0

Alan Miller

Year	Team		No	Yds	Avg	Lg	TD
1960	BOS	A	29	284	9.8		2
1961	OAK	A	36	315	8.8	55	4
1962			20	259	12.9	71	0
1963			34	404	11.9	44	2
1965			21	208	9.9	39	3
Career			140	1470	10.5	71	11

Anthony Miller

Year	Team		No	Yds	Avg	Lg	TD
1988	SD	N	36	526	14.6	49	3
1989			75	1252	16.7	69t	10
1990			63	933	14.8	31t	7
1991			44	649	14.8	58	3
1992			72	1060	14.7	67t	7
1993			84	1162	13.8	66t	7
1994	DEN	N	60	1107	18.4	76	5
1995			59	1079	18.3	62t	14

Anthony Miller continued

Year	Team		No	Yds	Avg	Lg	TD
1996			56	735	13.1	46	3
Career			549	8503	15.5	76	59
Playoffs			9	137	15.2		0

Bill Miller

Year	Team		No	Yds	Avg	Lg	TD
1962	DAL	A	23	277	12.0	39	0
1963	BUF	A	69	860	12.5	36	3
1964	OAK	A	2	29	14.5	16	0
1967			38	537	14.1	38	6
1968			9	176	19.6	42	1
Career			141	1879	13.3	42	10
Playoffs			9	121	13.4		3

Cleo Miller

Year	Team		No	Yds	Avg	Lg	TD
1974	KC	N	14	149	10.6	34	0
1975	CLE	N	2	20	10.0	10	0
1976			16	145	9.1	38	0
1977			41	291	7.1	28	1
1978			20	152	7.6	23	0
1979			26	251	9.7	33	0
1980			2	8	4.0	7	0
1981			16	139	8.7	17	0
1982			3	20	6.7	11	0
Career			140	1175	8.4	38	1

Heinie Miller

Year	Team		No	Yds	Avg	Lg	TD
1921	BUF	A					3

Jim Miller

Year	Team		No	Yds	Avg	Lg	TD
1930	BKN	N					1

Junior Miller

Year	Team		No	Yds	Avg	Lg	TD
1980	ATL	N	46	584	12.7	36	9
1981			32	398	12.4	37	3
1982			20	221	11.1	39	1
1983			16	125	7.8	19	0
1984	NO	N	8	81	10.1	22	1
Career			122	1409	11.5	39	14
Playoffs			3	48	16.0		0

Kevin Miller

Year	Team		No	Yds	Avg	Lg	TD
1978	MIN	N	1	35	35.0	35t	1

Mike Miller

Year	Team		No	Yds	Avg	Lg	TD
1983	NYG	N	7	170	24.3	54	0

Paul Miller

Year	Team		No	Yds	Avg	Lg	TD
1936	GB	N	8	113	14.1		2
1937			6	66	11.0		1
1938			4	36	9.0		0
Career			18	215	11.9		3

Paul Miller

Year	Team		No	Yds	Avg	Lg	TD
1956	LA	N	11	129	11.7	21	0

Robert Miller

Year	Team		No	Yds	Avg	Lg	TD
1975	MIN	N	4	35	8.8	32	0
1976			23	181	7.9	19	1
1977			27	246	9.1	25	0
1978			22	230	10.5	29	0
1979			9	60	6.7	14	0
1980			10	19	1.9	13	0
Career			95	771	8.1	32	1
Playoffs			11	96	8.7		0

Scott Miller

Year	Team		No	Yds	Avg	Lg	TD
1991	MIA	N	4	49	12.3	15	0
1993			2	15	7.5	8	0
1994			6	94	15.7	27	1
1996			9	116	12.9	22	0
Career			21	274	13.0	27	1
Playoffs			1	10	10.0		0

Solomon Miller

Year	Team		No	Yds	Avg	Lg	TD
1986	NYG	N	9	144	16.0	32t	2
1987	TB	N	5	97	19.4	33	0
Career			14	241	17.2	33	2

Terry Miller

Year	Team		No	Yds	Avg	Lg	TD
1978	BUF	N	22	246	11.2	52	0
1979			10	111	11.1	52	0
1980			3	25	8.3	15	0
Career			35	382	10.9	52	0

Tom Miller

Year	Team		No	Yds	Avg	Lg	TD
1943	P-P	N	3	60	20.0	32	1
1944	PHI	N	8	135	16.9	49	0
1945	WAS	N	11	84	7.6	11	0
Career			22	279	12.7	49	1

Willie Miller

Year	Team		No	Yds	Avg	Lg	TD
1975	CLE	N	7	57	8.1	17	0
1978	LA	N	50	767	15.3	52	5
1979			8	111	13.9	23	1
1980			22	358	16.3	45	8
1981			10	147	14.7	20	0
1982	LARM	N	15	346	23.1	85t	1
Career			112	1786	15.9	85t	15
Playoffs			5	125	25.0		1

James Milling

Year	Team		No	Yds	Avg	Lg	TD
1988	ATL	N	5	66	13.2	34	0
1990			18	161	8.9	24	1
1992			3	25	8.3	15	0
Career			26	252	9.7	34	1

Bob Millman

Year	Team		No	Yds	Avg	Lg	TD
1926	POT	N					1

Wayne Millner

Year	Team		No	Yds	Avg	Lg	TD
1936	BOS	N	18	211	11.7		0
1937	WAS	N	14	216	15.4		2
1938			18	232	12.9		1
1939			19	294	15.5		4
1940			22	233	10.6		3
1941			20	262	13.1	55	0
1945			13	130	10.0	27	2
Career			124	1578	12.7	55	12
Playoffs			17	293	17.2		2

Ernie Mills

Year	Team		No	Yds	Avg	Lg	TD
1991	PIT	N	3	79	26.3	35t	1
1992			30	383	12.8	22	3
1993			29	386	13.3	30	1
1994			19	384	20.2	43	0
1995			39	679	17.4	62t	8
1996			7	92	13.1	22	1
Career			127	2003	15.8	62t	15
Playoffs			43	587	13.7		2

John Henry Mills

Year	Team		No	Yds	Avg	Lg	TD
1994	HOU	N	1	4	4.0	4	0

Stan Mills

Year	Team		No	Yds	Avg	Lg	TD
1923	GB	N					2

Sullivan Mills

Year	Team		No	Yds	Avg	Lg	TD
1965	BUF	A	1	43	43.0	43	0

Brian Milne

Year	Team		No	Yds	Avg	Lg	TD
1996	CIN	N	3	29	9.7	15	0

Eugene Milton

Year	Team		No	Yds	Avg	Lg	TD
1968	MIA	A	9	143	15.9	38t	1
1969			12	179	14.9	49	0
Career			21	322	15.3	49	1

David Mims

Year	Team		No	Yds	Avg	Lg	TD
1993	ATL	N	12	107	8.9	19	1
1994			3	14	4.7	6	0
Career			15	121	8.1	19	1

Hank Minarik

Year	Team		No	Yds	Avg	Lg	TD
1951	PIT	N	35	450	12.9	37	1

Gene Mingo

Year	Team		No	Yds	Avg	Lg	TD
1960	DEN	A	19	156	8.2	18	1
1961			8	110	13.8	69	2
1962			14	107	7.6	34	0
1963			3	11	3.7	27	0
1964	DEN-OAK	A	4	25	6.3	10	1
1965	OAK	A	1	5	5.0	5	0
1966	MIA	A	3	40	13.3	21	0
Career			52	454	8.7	69	4

Frank Minini

Year	Team		No	Yds	Avg	Lg	TD
1947	CHIB	N	2	23	11.5	12	

Frank Minini continued

Year	Team		No	Yds	Avg	Lg	TD
1948			1	14	14.0	14t	1
Career			3	37	12.3	14t	1

Tony Minisi

Year	Team		No	Yds	Avg	Lg	TD
1948	NYG	N	13	123	9.5	23	1

Randy Minniear

Year	Team		No	Yds	Avg	Lg	TD
1967	NYG	N	8	49	6.1	21	1
1968			4	32	8.0	18	0
1969			6	68	11.3	21	0
1970	CLE	N	1	-1	-1.0	-1	0
Career			19	148	7.8	21	1

Lincoln Minor

Year	Team		No	Yds	Avg	Lg	TD
1973	NO	N	1	5	5.0	5	0

Cedric Minter

Year	Team		No	Yds	Avg	Lg	TD
1984	NYJ	N	10	109	10.9	39t	1
1985			1	13	13.0	13	0
Career			11	122	11.1	39t	1

Bob Mischak

Year	Team		No	Yds	Avg	Lg	TD
1958	NYG	N	1	27	27.0	27	0
1963	OAK	A	2	25	12.5	15	0
Career			3	52	17.3	27	0

John Mistler

Year	Team		No	Yds	Avg	Lg	TD
1981	NYG	N	8	119	14.9	31	1
1982			18	191	10.6	24	2
1983			45	422	9.4	24	0
1984			1	5	5.0	5	0
Career			72	737	10.2	31	3
Playoffs			2	28	14.0		1

Gene Mitcham

Year	Team		No	Yds	Avg	Lg	TD
1958	PHI	N	3	39	13.0	20	1

Alvin Mitchell

Year	Team		No	Yds	Avg	Lg	TD
1989	TB	N	1	11	11.0	11	0

Bob Mitchell

Year	Team		No	Yds	Avg	Lg	TD
1946	LA	AA	1	1	1.0	1	0
1947			3	36	12.0		1
Career			4	37	9.3	1	1

Bobby Mitchell

Year	Team		No	Yds	Avg	Lg	TD
1958	CLE	N	16	131	8.2	25	3
1959			35	351	10.0	76t	4
1960			45	612	13.6	69t	6
1961			32	368	11.5	52t	3
1962	WAS	N	72	1384	19.2	81t	11
1963			69	1436	20.8	99t	7
1964			60	904	15.1	60	10
1965			60	867	14.4	80t	6
1966			58	905	15.6	70t	9
1967			60	866	14.4	65t	6
1968			14	130	9.3	18	0
Career			521	7954	15.3	99t	65

Brian Mitchell

Year	Team		No	Yds	Avg	Lg	TD
1990	WAS	N	2	5	2.5	5	0
1992			3	30	10.0	17	0
1993			20	157	7.8	18	0
1994			26	236	9.1	46t	1
1995			38	324	8.5	22t	1
1996			32	286	8.9	20	0
Career			121	1038	8.6	46t	2
Playoffs			9	80	8.9		0

Charlie Mitchell

Year	Team		No	Yds	Avg	Lg	TD
1963	DEN	A	8	71	8.9	20	0
1964			33	225	6.8	58	1
1966			14	239	17.1	79	2
1967			7	15	2.1	15	0
Career			62	550	8.9	79	3

Derrell Mitchell

Year	Team		No	Yds	Avg	Lg	TD
1994	NO	N	1	13	13.0	13	0

Fondren Mitchell

Year	Team		No	Yds	Avg	Lg	TD
1946	MIA	AA	8	131	16.4		0

Year	Team		No	Yds	Avg	Lg	TD

Gran Mitchell

Year	Team		No	Yds	Avg	Lg	TD
1936	NYG	N	2	10	5.0		0
1937	BKN	N	8	115	14.4		1
Career			10	125	12.5		1

Jim Mitchell

Year	Team		No	Yds	Avg	Lg	TD
1969	ATL	N	22	339	15.4	42t	4
1970			44	650	14.8	51	6
1971			33	593	18.0	43	5
1972			28	470	16.8	40t	4
1973			32	420	13.1	50	0
1974			30	479	16.0	52	1
1975			34	536	15.8	32	4
1976			17	209	12.3	39	0
1977			17	178	10.5	17	0
1978			32	366	11.4	24	2
1979			16	118	7.4	14	2
Career			305	4358	14.3	52	28
Playoffs			3	35	11.7		1

Johnny Mitchell

Year	Team		No	Yds	Avg	Lg	TD
1992	NYJ	N	16	210	13.1	37t	1
1993			39	630	16.2	65t	6
1994			58	749	12.9	55	4
1995			45	497	11.0	43t	5
1996	DAL	N	1	17	17.0	17	0
Career			159	2103	13.2	65t	16

Lydell Mitchell

Year	Team		No	Yds	Avg	Lg	TD
1972	BAL	N	18	147	8.2	26	1
1973			17	113	6.6	14	0
1974			72	544	7.6	24	2
1975			60	544	9.1	35t	4
1976			60	555	9.3	40t	3
1977			71	620	8.7	38	4
1978	SD	N	57	500	8.8	55t	2
1979			19	159	8.4	24	1
1980	LA	N	2	21	10.5	13	0
Career			376	3203	8.5	55t	17
Playoffs			16	127	7.9		0

Pete Mitchell

Year	Team		No	Yds	Avg	Lg	TD
1995	JAC	N	41	527	12.9	35	2
1996			52	575	11.1	30	1
Career			93	1102	11.8	35	3
Playoffs			12	136	11.3		0

Shannon Mitchell

Year	Team		No	Yds	Avg	Lg	TD
1994	SD	N	11	105	9.5	36	0
1995			3	31	10.3	24	1
1996			10	57	5.7	25	0
Career			24	193	8.0	36	1
Playoffs			1	19	19.0		0

Stan Mitchell

Year	Team		No	Yds	Avg	Lg	TD
1967	MIA	A	18	133	7.4	38	1
1968			8	190	23.8	48t	3
1969			10	125	12.5	34	0
1970	MIA	N	6	85	14.2	36t	1
Career			42	533	12.7	48t	5

Stump Mitchell

Year	Team		No	Yds	Avg	Lg	TD
1981	STL	N	6	35	5.8	16	1
1982			11	149	13.5	30	0
1983			7	54	7.7	17	0
1984			26	318	12.2	44t	2
1985			47	502	10.7	46	3
1986			41	276	6.7	24	0
1987			45	397	8.8	39	2
1988	PHX	N	25	214	8.6	28	1
1989			1	10	10.0	10	0
Career			209	1955	9.4	46	9
Playoffs			4	57	14.3		0

Tom Mitchell

Year	Team		No	Yds	Avg	Lg	TD
1966	OAK	A	23	301	13.1	24	1
1968	BAL	N	6	117	19.5	41t	4
1969			9	199	22.1	51t	4
1970			20	261	13.1	44	4
1971			33	402	12.2	35	0
1972			40	494	12.4	34	4
1973			25	313	12.5	33	4
1974	SF	N	19	262	13.8	25	0
1975			25	366	14.6	60t	3

Tom Mitchell *continued*

Year	Team		No	Yds	Avg	Lg	TD
1976			20	240	12.0	27	1
1977			19	226	11.9	31	0
Career			239	3181	13.3	60t	24
Playoffs			9	112	12.4		1

Billy Mixon

Year	Team		No	Yds	Avg	Lg	TD
1953	SF	N	1	7	7.0	7	0

Orson Mobley

Year	Team		No	Yds	Avg	Lg	TD
1986	DEN	N	22	332	15.1	32	1
1987			16	228	14.3	28	1
1988			21	218	10.4	28	2
1989			17	200	11.8	36	0
1990			8	41	5.1	9	0
Career			84	1019	12.1	36	4
Playoffs			11	161	14.6		1

Rudy Mobley

Year	Team		No	Yds	Avg	Lg	TD
1947	BAL	AA	11	121	11.0		1

Stacey Mobley

Year	Team		No	Yds	Avg	Lg	TD
1987	LARM	N	8	107	13.4	40t	1
1989	DET	N	13	158	12.2	30	0
Career			21	265	12.6	40t	1

Ed Modzelewski

Year	Team		No	Yds	Avg	Lg	TD
1952	PIT	N	11	109	9.9	23	0
1955	CLE	N	13	113	8.7	28	2
1956			10	27	2.7	6	0
1958			1	10	10.0	10	0
1959			3	18	6.0	13	1
Career			38	277	7.3	28	3
Playoffs			5	34	6.8		0

Hal Moe

Year	Team		No	Yds	Avg	Lg	TD
1933	CHIC	N					2

Dicky Moegle

Year	Team		No	Yds	Avg	Lg	TD
1955	SF	N	4	94	23.5	53	0
1956			3	79	26.3	37	0
1959			1	12	12.0	12	0
Career			8	185	23.1	53	0

Tim Moffett

Year	Team		No	Yds	Avg	Lg	TD
1985	LARI	N	5	90	18.0	34	0
1986			6	77	12.8	17	0
1987	SD	N	5	80	16.0	25	1
Career			16	247	15.4	34	1

Mike Moffitt

Year	Team		No	Yds	Avg	Lg	TD
1986	GB	N	4	87	21.8	34	0

Johnny Mohardt

Year	Team		No	Yds	Avg	Lg	TD
1922	CHIC	N					1
1925	CHIB	N					1
Career							2

Louie Mohs

Year	Team		No	Yds	Avg	Lg	TD
1923	MIN	N					1

Dick Moje

Year	Team		No	Yds	Avg	Lg	TD
1951	GB	N	1	11	11.0	11	0

Bo Molenda

Year	Team		No	Yds	Avg	Lg	TD
1927	NYY	N					1
1934	NYG	N	3	55	18.3		0
Career			3	55	18.3		1

Keith Molesworth

Year	Team		No	Yds	Avg	Lg	TD
1933	CHIB	N					1
1934			1	6	6.0	6	0
1935			7	154	22.0		0
1936			9	146	16.2		0
1937			4	21	5.3		0
Career			21	327	15.6	6	1
Playoffs			1	5	5.0		0

Jim Monachino

Year	Team		No	Yds	Avg	Lg	TD
1951	SF	N	1	6	6.0	6	0
1953			2	9	4.5	9	0
1955	WAS	N	8	74	9.3	24	0
Career			11	89	8.1	24	0

Art Monk

Year	Team		No	Yds	Avg	Lg	TD
1980	WAS	N	58	797	13.7	54t	3
1981			56	894	16.0	79t	6
1982			35	447	12.8	43	1
1983			47	746	15.9	43t	5
1984			106	1372	12.9	72	7
1985			91	1226	13.5	53	2
1986			73	1068	14.6	69	4
1987			38	483	12.7	62	6
1988			72	946	13.1	46t	5
1989			86	1186	13.8	60t	8
1990			68	770	11.3	44	5
1991			71	1049	14.8	64t	8
1992			46	644	14.0	49t	3
1993			41	398	9.7	29	2
1994	NYJ	N	46	581	12.6	69	3
1995	PHI	N	6	114	19.0	36	0
Career			940	12721	13.5	79t	68
Playoffs			69	1062	15.4		7

Bob Monnett

Year	Team		No	Yds	Avg	Lg	TD
1935	GB	N	1	8	8.0	8	0
1936			13	169	13.0		0
1937			4	32	8.0		0
1938			1	23	23.0	23	0
Career			19	232	12.2	23	0

Carl Monroe

Year	Team		No	Yds	Avg	Lg	TD
1983	SF	N	2	61	30.5	50	0
1984			11	139	12.6	47	1
1985			10	51	5.1	9	0
1986			2	6	3.0	5	0
1987			3	66	22.0	39t	1
Career			28	323	11.5	50	2
Playoffs			1	33	33.0		1

Tommy Mont

Year	Team		No	Yds	Avg	Lg	TD
1947	WAS	N	2	14	7.0	7	0
1949			8	105	13.1	30	2
Career			10	119	11.9	30	2

Dave Montagne

Year	Team		No	Yds	Avg	Lg	TD
1987	KC	N	5	47	9.4	16	0

Cleo Montgomery

Year	Team		No	Yds	Avg	Lg	TD
1983	LARI	N	2	29	14.5	15	0

Mike Montgomery

Year	Team		No	Yds	Avg	Lg	TD
1971	SD	N	28	361	12.9	39t	2
1972	DAL	N	8	131	16.4	46	1
1973			14	164	11.7	32t	3
1974	HOU	N	9	179	19.9	65	1
Career			59	835	14.2	65	7
Playoffs			4	34	8.5		0

Ross Montgomery

Year	Team		No	Yds	Avg	Lg	TD
1969	CHI	N	2	8	4.0	6	0
1970			14	75	5.4	17	0
Career			16	83	5.2	17	0

Tyrone Montgomery

Year	Team		No	Yds	Avg	Lg	TD
1993	LARI	N	10	43	4.3	9	0
1994			8	126	15.8	65t	1
Career			18	169	9.4	65t	1
Playoffs			6	55	9.2		0

Wilbert Montgomery

Year	Team		No	Yds	Avg	Lg	TD
1977	PHI	N	3	18	6.0	8	0
1978			34	195	5.7	23	1
1979			41	494	12.0	53t	5
1980			50	407	8.1	31	2
1981			49	521	10.6	35	2
1982			20	258	12.9	42t	2
1983			9	53	5.9	13	0
1984			60	501	8.3	28	0
1985	DET	N	7	55	7.9	28	0
Career			273	2502	9.2	53t	12
Playoffs			19	193	10.2		0

Mike Montler

Year	Team		No	Yds	Avg	Lg	TD
1976	BUF	N	1	6	6.0	6	0

Tipp Mooney

Year	Team		No	Yds	Avg	Lg	TD
1944	CHIB	N	2	74	37.0	61t	1

Tipp Mooney *continued*

Year	Team		No	Yds	Avg	Lg	TD
1945			2	10	5.0	6	0
Career			4	84	21.0	61t	1

Alex Moore

Year	Team		No	Yds	Avg	Lg	TD
1968	**DEN**	**A**	3	35	11.7	16	0

Alvin Moore

Year	Team		No	Yds	Avg	Lg	TD
1983	**BAL**	**N**	6	38	6.3	16	0
1984	**IND**	**N**	9	52	5.8	12	0
1985	**DET**	**N**	19	154	8.1	14	1
1986			8	47	5.9	8	0
Career			42	291	6.9	16	1

Bill Moore

Year	Team		No	Yds	Avg	Lg	TD
1939	**DET**	**N**	6	82	13.7		1

Blake Moore

Year	Team		No	Yds	Avg	Lg	TD
1984	**GB**	**N**	1	3	3.0	3t	1
1985			1	3	3.0	3t	1
Career			2	6	3.0	3t	2

Bob Moore

Year	Team		No	Yds	Avg	Lg	TD
1971	**OAK**	**N**	2	26	13.0	14	0
1972			6	49	8.2	17	1
1973			34	375	11.0	33	4
1974			30	356	11.9	32	2
1975			19	175	9.2	21	0
1976	**TB**	**N**	24	289	12.0	31	0
Career			115	1270	11.0	33	7
Playoffs			20	158	7.9		1

Booker Moore

Year	Team		No	Yds	Avg	Lg	TD
1982	**BUF**	**N**	1	8	8.0	8	0
1983			34	199	5.9	21	1
1984			33	172	5.2	14	0
1985			7	44	6.3	19	0
Career			75	423	5.6	21	1

Dave Moore

Year	Team		No	Yds	Avg	Lg	TD
1992	**TB**	**N**	1	10	10.0	10	0
1993			4	47	11.8	19t	1
1994			4	57	14.3	18	0
1995			13	102	7.8	21	0
1996			27	237	8.8	23	3
Career			49	453	9.2	23	4

Derrick Moore

Year	Team		No	Yds	Avg	Lg	TD
1993	**DET**	**N**	21	169	8.0	20	1
1994			1	10	10.0	10	0
1995	**CAR**	**N**	4	12	3.0	5	0
Career			26	191	7.3	20	1
Playoffs			4	14	3.5		0

Dinty Moore

Year	Team		No	Yds	Avg	Lg	TD
1927	**POT**	**N**					1

Gene Moore

Year	Team		No	Yds	Avg	Lg	TD
1969	**SF**	**N**	2	28	14.0	24	0

Herman Moore

Year	Team		No	Yds	Avg	Lg	TD
1991	**DET**	**N**	11	135	12.3	21	0
1992			51	966	18.9	77t	4
1993			61	935	15.3	93t	6
1994			72	1173	16.3	51t	11
1995			**123**	1686	13.7	69t	14
1996			106	1296	12.2	50t	9
Career			424	6191	14.6	93t	44
Playoffs			20	361	18.1		2

Jeff Moore

Year	Team		No	Yds	Avg	Lg	TD
1979	**SEA**	**N**	14	128	9.1	24	0
1980			25	231	9.2	34	0
1981			3	18	6.0	10	0
1982	**SF**	**N**	37	405	10.9	55	4
1983			19	206	10.8	34	0
1984	**WAS**	**N**	17	115	6.8	18	2
Career			115	1103	9.6	55	6
Playoffs			1	4	4.0		0

Jeff Moore

Year	Team		No	Yds	Avg	Lg	TD
1980	**LA**	**N**	10	168	16.8	37	1
1981			7	105	15.0	35	0
Career			17	273	16.1	37	1

Jerald Moore

Year	Team		No	Yds	Avg	Lg	TD
1996	**STL**	**N**	3	13	4.3	7	0

Joe Moore

Year	Team		No	Yds	Avg	Lg	TD
1971	**CHI**	**N**	2	22	11.0	18	0
1973			3	17	5.7	6	0
Career			5	39	7.8	18	0

Lenny Moore

Year	Team		No	Yds	Avg	Lg	TD
1956	**BAL**	**N**	11	102	9.3	27	1
1957			40	687	17.2	82t	7
1958			50	938	18.8	77t	7
1959			47	846	18.0	71	6
1960			45	936	20.8	80t	9
1961			49	728	14.9	72t	8
1962			18	215	11.9	80t	2
1963			21	288	13.7	34	2
1964			21	472	22.5	74t	3
1965			27	414	15.3	52t	3
1966			21	260	12.4	36	0
1967			13	153	11.8	37	0
Career			363	6039	16.6	82t	48
Playoffs			12	244	20.3		1

Leonard Moore

Year	Team		No	Yds	Avg	Lg	TD
1987	**MIN**	**N**	1	8	8.0	8	0

Malcolm Moore

Year	Team		No	Yds	Avg	Lg	TD
1987	**LARM**	**N**	6	107	17.8	26	1

Manfred Moore

Year	Team		No	Yds	Avg	Lg	TD
1974	**SF**	**N**	2	29	14.5	26	0
1975			1	11	11.0	11	0
1976	**TB**	**N**	5	46	9.2	23	0
Career			8	86	10.8	26	0

Nat Moore

Year	Team		No	Yds	Avg	Lg	TD
1974	**MIA**	**N**	37	605	16.4	48	2
1975			40	705	17.6	79t	4
1976			33	625	18.9	67t	4
1977			52	765	14.7	73t	**12**
1978			48	645	13.4	47	10
1979			48	840	17.5	53	6
1980			47	564	12.0	33	7
1981			26	452	17.4	52	2
1982			8	82	10.3	23	1
1983			39	558	14.3	66t	6
1984			43	573	13.3	37t	6
1985			51	701	13.7	69t	7
1986			38	431	11.3	38t	7
Career			510	7546	14.8	79t	74
Playoffs			23	291	12.7		3

Paul Moore

Year	Team		No	Yds	Avg	Lg	TD
1940	**DET**	**N**	4	29	7.3		1

Ricky Moore

Year	Team		No	Yds	Avg	Lg	TD
1986	**BUF**	**N**	23	184	8.0	27	0
1987	**HOU**	**N**	3	21	7.0	10	0
1988	**PHX**	**N**	1	15	15.0	15	0
Career			27	220	8.1	27	0

Rob Moore

Year	Team		No	Yds	Avg	Lg	TD
1990	**NYJ**	**N**	44	692	15.7	69t	6
1991			70	987	14.1	53	5
1992			50	726	14.5	48t	4
1993			64	843	13.2	51	1
1994			78	1010	12.9	41t	6
1995	**ARI**	**N**	63	907	14.4	45	5
1996			58	1016	17.5	69	4
Career			427	6181	14.5	69t	31
Playoffs			4	70	17.5		0

Ron Moore

Year	Team		No	Yds	Avg	Lg	TD
1993	**PHX**	**N**	3	16	5.3	6	0
1994	**ARI**	**N**	8	52	6.5	18	1
1995	**NYJ**	**N**	8	50	6.3	13	0
Career			19	118	6.2	18	1

Tom Moore

Year	Team		No	Yds	Avg	Lg	TD
1960	**GB**	**N**	5	40	8.0	12t	1
1961			8	41	5.1	11	1
1962			11	100	9.1	34	0
1963			23	237	10.3	45t	2

Tom Moore *continued*

Year	Team		No	Yds	Avg	Lg	TD
1964			17	140	8.2	33t	2
1965			7	87	12.4	31t	1
1966	**LA**	**N**	60	433	7.2	30t	3
1967	**ATL**	**N**	10	74	7.4	21	0
Career			141	1152	8.2	45t	10
Playoffs			3	5	1.7		0

Wilbur Moore

Year	Team		No	Yds	Avg	Lg	TD
1939	**WAS**	**N**	1	2	2.0	2	0
1940			2	26	13.0		1
1941			2	6	3.0	5	0
1942			10	114	11.4	30	2
1943			30	537	17.9	72	7
1944			33	424	12.8	59t	5
1945			13	115	8.8	32	1
Career			91	1224	13.5	72	16
Playoffs			11	206	18.7		1

Will Moore

Year	Team		No	Yds	Avg	Lg	TD
1995	**NE**	**N**	43	502	11.7	33	1
1996			3	37	12.3	16	0
Career			46	539	11.7	33	1

Emery Moorehead

Year	Team		No	Yds	Avg	Lg	TD
1977	**NYG**	**N**	12	143	11.9	20	1
1978			3	45	15.0	25	0
1979			9	62	6.9	19	0
1982	**CHI**	**N**	30	363	12.1	50t	5
1983			42	597	14.2	36	3
1984			29	497	17.1	50	1
1985			35	481	13.7	25	1
1986			26	390	15.0	85	1
1987			24	269	11.2	27	1
1988			14	133	9.5	28	2
Career			224	2980	13.3	85	15
Playoffs			7	70	10.0		0

Mo Moorman

Year	Team		No	Yds	Avg	Lg	TD
1973	**KC**	**N**	1	-1	-1.0	-1	0

Fran Moran

Year	Team		No	Yds	Avg	Lg	TD
1929	**NYG**	**N**					5
1931							2
1933							1
Career							8

Doug Moreau

Year	Team		No	Yds	Avg	Lg	TD
1966	**MIA**	**A**	2	15	7.5	9	0
1967			34	410	12.1	43	3
1968			27	365	13.5	28	3
1969			10	136	13.6	35	0
Career			73	926	12.7	43	6

Arnold Morgado

Year	Team		No	Yds	Avg	Lg	TD
1977	**KC**	**N**	2	21	10.5	12	0
1978			7	47	6.7	15	0
1979			5	55	11.0	22	0
1980			5	27	5.4	10	1
Career			19	150	7.9	22	1

Anthony Morgan

Year	Team		No	Yds	Avg	Lg	TD
1991	**CHI**	**N**	13	211	16.2	84t	2
1992			14	323	23.1	83t	2
1993	**GB**	**N**	1	8	8.0	8	0
1994			28	397	14.2	47t	4
1995			31	344	11.1	29t	4
Career			87	1283	14.7	84t	12
Playoffs			14	151	10.8		0

Boyd Morgan

Year	Team		No	Yds	Avg	Lg	TD
1939	**WAS**	**N**	1	4	4.0	4	0

Stanley Morgan

Year	Team		No	Yds	Avg	Lg	TD
1977	**NE**	**N**	21	443	21.1	64t	3
1978			34	820	24.1	75t	5
1979			44	1002	**22.8**	63t	**12**
1980			45	991	**22.0**	71	6
1981			44	1029	**23.4**	76t	6
1982			28	584	20.9	75t	3
1983			58	863	14.9	50t	2
1984			38	709	18.7	76t	5
1985			39	760	19.5	50t	5

Year	Team		No	Yds	Avg	Lg	TD

Stanley Morgan *continued*

Year	Team		No	Yds	Avg	Lg	TD
1986			84	1491	17.8	44t	10
1987			40	672	16.8	45	3
1988			31	502	16.2	32	4
1989			28	486	17.4	55t	3
1990	IND	N	23	364	15.8	42t	5
Career			557	10716	19.2	76t	72
Playoffs			18	302	16.8		3

Larry Moriarty

Year	Team		No	Yds	Avg	Lg	TD
1983	HOU	N	4	32	8.0	12	0
1984			31	206	6.6	24	1
1985			17	112	6.6	16	0
1986	HOU-KC	N	9	67	7.4	19	0
1987	KC	N	10	37	3.7	8	1
1988			6	40	6.7	12	0
Career			77	494	6.4	24	2
Playoffs			1	16	16.0		0

Pat Moriarty

Year	Team		No	Yds	Avg	Lg	TD
1979	CLE	N	1	17	17.0	17	0

Milt Morin

Year	Team		No	Yds	Avg	Lg	TD
1966	CLE	N	23	333	14.5	32	3
1967			7	90	12.9	21	0
1968			43	792	18.4	87	5
1969			37	495	13.4	35	0
1970			37	611	16.5	36	1
1971			40	581	14.5	31	2
1972			30	540	18.0	36	1
1973			26	417	16.0	51t	1
1974			27	330	12.2	32	3
1975			1	19	19.0	19	0
Career			271	4208	15.5	87	16
Playoffs			17	230	13.5		2

Bam Morris

Year	Team		No	Yds	Avg	Lg	TD
1994	PIT	N	22	204	9.3	49	0
1995			8	36	4.5	13	0
1996	BAL	N	25	242	9.7	52t	1
Career			55	482	8.8	52t	1
Playoffs			10	36	3.6		0

Frank Morris

Year	Team		No	Yds	Avg	Lg	TD
1942	CHIB	N	3	24	8.0	17	0

George Morris

Year	Team		No	Yds	Avg	Lg	TD
1941	CLE	N	9	17	1.9	6	0

Jamie Morris

Year	Team		No	Yds	Avg	Lg	TD
1988	WAS	N	1	3	3.0	3	0
1989			8	65	8.1	17	0
Career			9	68	7.6	17	0

Joe Morris

Year	Team		No	Yds	Avg	Lg	TD
1982	NYG	N	8	34	4.3	13	0
1983			2	1	0.5	6t	1
1984			12	124	10.3	26	0
1985			22	212	9.6	17	0
1986			21	233	11.1	23	1
1987			11	114	10.4	25	0
1988			22	166	7.5	24	0
1991	CLE	N	13	76	5.8	13	0
Career			111	960	8.6	26	2
Playoffs			11	74	6.7		0

Johnny Morris

Year	Team		No	Yds	Avg	Lg	TD
1958	CHIB	N	11	170	15.5	51	0
1959			13	197	15.2	51t	2
1960	CHI	N	20	224	11.2	66t	3
1961			36	548	15.2	80t	4
1962			58	889	15.3	73t	5
1963			47	705	15.0	51t	2
1964			**93**	**1200**	12.9	63t	**10**
1965			53	846	16.0	80t	4
1966			5	49	9.8	15	0
1967			20	231	11.6	31	1
Career			356	5059	14.2	80t	31
Playoffs			2	19	9.5		0

Lee Morris

Year	Team		No	Yds	Avg	Lg	TD
1987	GB	N	16	259	16.2	46t	1

Max Morris

Year	Team		No	Yds	Avg	Lg	TD
1946	CHI	AA	3	66	22.0		0
1947			22	239	10.9		1
1948	BKN	AA	28	372	13.3		1
Career			53	677	12.8		2

Mercury Morris

Year	Team		No	Yds	Avg	Lg	TD
1969	MIA	A	6	65	10.8	29	0
1970	MIA	N	12	149	12.4	50	0
1971			5	16	3.2	11	0
1972			15	168	11.2	34	0
1973			4	51	12.8	36	0
1974			2	27	13.5	23	1
1975			2	15	7.5	10	0
1976	SD	N	8	52	6.5	20	0
Career			54	543	10.1	50	1
Playoffs			3	9	3.0		0

Randall Morris

Year	Team		No	Yds	Avg	Lg	TD
1984	SEA	N	9	61	6.8	18	0
1985			6	14	2.3	6	0
Career			15	75	5.0	18	0
Playoffs			1	6	6.0		0

Ron Morris

Year	Team		No	Yds	Avg	Lg	TD
1987	CHI	N	20	379	18.9	42t	1
1988			28	498	17.8	63t	4
1989			30	486	16.2	58t	1
1990			31	437	14.1	67t	3
1991			8	147	18.4	33	0
1992			4	44	11.0	26	0
Career			121	1991	16.5	67t	9
Playoffs			8	151	18.9		1

Wayne Morris

Year	Team		No	Yds	Avg	Lg	TD
1976	STL	N	8	75	9.4	19	1
1977			24	222	9.3	34	1
1978			33	298	9.0	33	1
1979			35	237	6.8	20	1
1980			15	110	7.3	24	1
1981			19	165	8.7	21	0
1982			4	19	4.8	11	0
1983			14	55	3.9	11	0
1984	SD	N	5	20	4.0	9	0
Career			157	1201	7.6	34	5
Playoffs			3	32	10.7		0

Fred Morrison

Year	Team		No	Yds	Avg	Lg	TD
1950	CHIB	N	13	86	6.6	15	0
1951			1	-3	-3.0	-3	0
1952			10	129	12.9	39	1
1953			16	214	13.4	44	0
1954	CLE	N	12	81	6.8	16	0
1955			9	185	20.6	49	0
1956			6	29	4.8	10	1
Career			67	721	10.8	49	2
Playoffs			3	51	17.0		0

Joe Morrison

Year	Team		No	Yds	Avg	Lg	TD
1959	NYG	N	17	183	10.8	37	1
1960			29	367	12.7	51t	3
1961			11	67	6.1	16	1
1962			6	107	17.8	86	2
1963			31	284	9.2	57t	7
1964			40	505	12.6	70	2
1965			41	574	14.0	46t	4
1966			46	724	15.7	49	6
1967			37	524	14.2	59t	7
1968			37	425	11.5	68t	6
1969			44	647	14.7	65	7
1970			11	136	12.4	25	0
1971			40	411	10.3	45t	1
1972			5	39	7.8	13	0
Career			395	4993	12.6	86	47
Playoffs			4	18	4.5		0

Ram Morrison

Year	Team		No	Yds	Avg	Lg	TD
1926	LA	A					1

Reece Morrison

Year	Team		No	Yds	Avg	Lg	TD
1968	CLE	N	2	40	20.0	29	1
1969			6	71	11.8	26	0
1970			5	95	19.0	53t	1

Reece Morrison *continued*

Year	Team		No	Yds	Avg	Lg	TD
1973	CIN	N	1	4	4.0	4	0
Career			14	210	15.0	53t	2
Playoffs			1	18	18.0		0

Bob Morrow

Year	Team		No	Yds	Avg	Lg	TD
1943	CHIC	N	3	20	6.7	14	0
1946	NY	AA	1	6	6.0	6	0
Career			4	26	6.5	14	0

Russ Morrow

Year	Team		No	Yds	Avg	Lg	TD
1946	BKN	AA	1	8	8.0	8t	1

Bobby Morse

Year	Team		No	Yds	Avg	Lg	TD
1987	PHI	N	1	8	8.0	8	0

Ray Morse

Year	Team		No	Yds	Avg	Lg	TD
1935	DET	N	6	63	10.5		0
1936			5	83	16.6		0
1937			8	131	16.4		1
1938			3	55	18.3		0
1940			1	13	13.0	13	0
Career			23	345	15.0	13	1

Emmett Mortell

Year	Team		No	Yds	Avg	Lg	TD
1937	PHI	N	1	0	0.0	0	0

Jack Morton

Year	Team		No	Yds	Avg	Lg	TD
1945	CHIB	N	1	18	18.0	18	0
1946	LA	AA	4	44	11.0		1
Career			5	62	12.4	18	1

Johnnie Morton

Year	Team		No	Yds	Avg	Lg	TD
1994	DET	N	3	39	13.0	18t	1
1995			44	590	13.4	32t	8
1996			55	714	13.0	62t	6
Career			102	1343	13.2	62t	15
Playoffs			1	7	7.0		1

Michael Morton

Year	Team		No	Yds	Avg	Lg	TD
1982	TB	N	1	5	5.0	5	0
1983			1	9	9.0	9	0
Career			2	14	7.0	9	0

Jim Moscrip

Year	Team		No	Yds	Avg	Lg	TD
1938	DET	N	6	118	19.7		1
1939			14	176	12.6		0
Career			20	294	14.7		1

Dom Moselle

Year	Team		No	Yds	Avg	Lg	TD
1951	GB	N	14	233	16.6	85	2
1954	PHI	N	17	242	14.2	38t	2
Career			31	475	15.3	85	4

Rick Moser

Year	Team		No	Yds	Avg	Lg	TD
1978	PIT	N	1	-1	-1.0	-1	0
1979			1	6	6.0	6	0
1981			1	5	5.0	5t	1
Career			3	10	3.3	6	1

Haven Moses

Year	Team		No	Yds	Avg	Lg	TD
1968	BUF	A	42	633	15.1	55t	2
1969			39	752	19.3	55t	5
1970	BUF	N	39	726	18.6	45	2
1971			23	470	20.4	73t	2
1972	BUF-DEN	N	18	284	15.8	33	6
1973	DEN	N	28	518	18.5	76t	8
1974			34	559	16.4	42	2
1975			29	505	17.4	42	2
1976			25	498	19.9	71t	7
1977			27	539	20.0	35	4
1978			37	744	20.1	42	5
1979			54	943	17.5	64t	6
1980			38	674	17.7	33	4
1981			15	246	16.4	30	1
Career			448	8091	18.1	76t	56
Playoffs			13	314	24.2		2

John Mosier

Year	Team		No	Yds	Avg	Lg	TD
1971	DEN	N	3	36	12.0	19	0
1972	BAL	N	1	53	53.0	53	0
Career			4	89	22.3	53	0

Year	Team		No	Yds	Avg	Lg	TD

Anthony Mosley

Year	Team		No	Yds	Avg	Lg	TD
1987	CHI	N	2	16	8.0	16	0

Mike Mosley

1982	BUF	N	9	96	10.7	31	0
1983			14	180	12.9	35	3
1984			4	38	9.5	17	0
Career			27	314	11.6	35	3

Russ Mosley

| 1945 | GB | N | 1 | 10 | 10.0 | 10 | 0 |

Brent Moss

| 1995 | STL | N | 1 | -3 | -3.0 | -3 | 0 |

Paul Moss

1933	PIT	N	18	**383**	21.3		2
1934	C-S	N					1
Career			18	383	21.3		3

Roland Moss

1970	BUF	N	2	31	15.5	22	0
1971	NE	N	9	124	13.8	20t	1
Career			11	155	14.1	22	1

Kelley Mote

1947	DET	N	16	180	11.3	46t	1
1948			13	212	16.3	28	0
1949			4	58	14.5	22	0
1950	NYG	N	4	72	18.0	41	1
1951			11	187	17.0	39t	4
1952			4	45	11.3	19	0
Career			52	754	14.5	46t	6

Bob Motl

| 1946 | CHI | AA | 9 | 124 | 13.8 | | 1 |

Marion Motley

1946	CLE	AA	10	188	18.8	63	1
1947			7	73	10.4		0
1948			13	192	14.8	78t	2
1949			15	191	12.7		0
1950	CLE	N	11	151	13.7	41	1
1951			10	52	5.2	34	0
1952			13	213	16.4	68t	2
1953			6	47	7.8	23	0
Career			85	1107	13.0	78t	7
Playoffs			9	54	6.0		

Eric Moulds

| 1996 | BUF | N | 20 | 279 | 13.9 | 47 | 2 |

Zeke Mowatt

1983	NYG	N	21	280	13.3	46t	1
1984			48	698	14.5	34	6
1986			10	119	11.9	30	2
1987			3	39	13.0	29	1
1988			15	196	13.1	38t	1
1989			27	288	10.7	31	0
1990	NE	N	6	67	11.2	16	0
1991	NYG	N	5	78	15.6	33	1
Career			135	1765	13.1	46t	12
Playoffs			17	209	12.3		2

Bob Mrosko

1989	HOU	N	3	28	9.3	14	0
1990	NYG	N	3	27	9.0	16	1
1991	IND	N	8	90	11.3	20	0
Career			14	145	10.4	20	1
Playoffs			1	6	6.0		0

Rudy Mucha

| 1941 | CLE | N | 1 | 3 | 3.0 | 3 | 0 |

Larry Mucker

1977	TB	N	4	59	14.8	23	0
1978			13	271	20.8	48	0
1979			14	268	19.1	42t	5
1980			2	37	18.5	19	0
Career			33	635	19.2	48	5
Playoffs			2	76	38.0		0

Frank Muehlheuser

| 1948 | BOS | N | 3 | 19 | 6.3 | 12 | 0 |

Frank Muehlheuser *continued*

| 1949 | NYB | N | 2 | 26 | 13.0 | 10 | 0 |
| Career | | | 5 | 45 | 9.0 | 12 | 0 |

Jamie Mueller

1987	BUF	N	3	13	4.3	11	0
1988			8	42	5.3	17	0
1989			1	8	8.0	8	0
1990			16	106	6.6	30	1
Career			28	169	6.0	30	1
Playoffs			1	2	2.0		0

Vance Mueller

1986	LARI	N	6	54	9.0	20	0
1987			11	95	8.6	14	0
1988			5	63	12.6	28	0
1989			18	240	13.3	29	2
Career			40	452	11.3	29	2

Joe Muha

1947	PHI	N	1	10	10.0	10	0
1948			2	22	11.0	20t	1
1949			1	10	10.0	10	0
Career			4	42	10.5	20t	1
Playoffs			2	18	9.0		0

Calvin Muhammad

1982	LARI	N	3	92	30.7	43	1
1983			13	252	19.4	45	2
1984	WAS	N	42	729	17.4	80t	4
1985			9	116	12.9	32	1
1987	SD	N	2	87	43.5	67	0
Career			69	1276	18.5	80t	8
Playoffs			5	62	12.4		0

Mushin Muhammad

| 1996 | CAR | N | 25 | 407 | 16.3 | 54t | 1 |

Mike Mularkey

1984	MIN	N	14	134	9.6	26	2
1985			13	196	15.1	51t	1
1986			11	89	8.1	20	2
1987			1	6	6.0	6	0
1988			3	39	13.0	19	0
1989	PIT	N	22	326	14.8	34	1
1990			32	365	11.4	28	3
1991			6	67	11.2	21	0
Career			102	1222	12.0	51t	9
Playoffs			5	76	15.2		0

Joe Mulbarger

| 1921 | COL | A | | | | | 1 |

Herb Mulkey

| 1972 | WAS | N | 4 | 66 | 16.5 | 28 | 0 |

Tom Mullady

1980	NYG	N	28	391	14.0	42	2
1981			14	136	9.7	21	1
1982			27	287	10.6	32	0
1983			13	184	14.2	35	1
1984			2	35	17.5	22	0
Career			84	1033	12.3	42	4
Playoffs			3	44	14.7		1

Gary Mullen

| 1987 | CHI | N | 2 | 33 | 16.5 | 20 | 0 |

Verne Mullen

| 1926 | CHIB | N | | | | | 1 |

Carl Mulleneaux

1938	GB	N	4	97	24.3		2
1939			12	218	18.2		1
1940			16	288	18.0		6
1941			9	216	24.0	56	2
1945			3	31	10.3	13	0
Career			44	850	19.3	56	11
Playoffs			3	84	28.0		1

Brick Muller

| 1926 | LA | N | | | | | 1 |

George Mulligan

| 1936 | PHI | N | 1 | 3 | 3.0 | 3 | 0 |

Eric Mullins

| 1984 | HOU | N | 6 | 85 | 14.2 | 25 | 1 |

Gerry Mullins

1972	PIT	N	1	3	3.0	3t	1
1974			1	7	7.0	7t	1
Career			2	10	5.0	7t	2

Noah Mullins

1947	CHIB	N	1	4	4.0	4	0
1948			9	127	14.1	26	4
1949	NYG	N	2	45	22.5	24	1
Career			12	176	14.7	26	5

Jerry Mulready

| 1947 | CHI | AA | 7 | 108 | 15.4 | | 0 |

Chuck Muncie

1976	NO	N	31	272	8.8	33	0
1977			21	248	11.8	35t	0
1978			26	233	9.0	34	0
1979			40	308	7.7	28	0
1980	NO-SD	N	31	259	8.4	19	0
1981	SD	N	43	362	8.4	32	0
1982			25	207	8.3	39	1
1983			42	396	9.4	27	1
1984			4	38	9.5	20	0
Career			263	2323	8.8	39	3
Playoffs			17	128	7.5		0

Anthony Munoz

1980	CIN	N	1	-6	-6.0	-6	0
1984			1	1	1.0	1t	1
1985			1	1	1.0	1	0
1986			2	7	3.5	5t	2
1987			2	15	7.5	12	1
Career			7	18	2.6	12	4

Bill Munson

| 1974 | DET | N | 1 | -6 | -6.0 | -6 | 0 |

Bill Murphy

| 1968 | BOS | A | 18 | 268 | 14.9 | 26 | 0 |

Fred Murphy

| 1960 | CLE | N | 2 | 36 | 18.0 | 23 | 0 |

George Murphy

| 1949 | LA | AA | 1 | 17 | 17.0 | 17 | 0 |

James Murphy

| 1981 | KC | N | 2 | 36 | 18.0 | 22 | 0 |

Mark Muprhy

| 1978 | WAS | N | 1 | 13 | 13.0 | 13 | 0 |

Calvin Murray

| 1981 | PHI | N | 1 | 7 | 7.0 | 7 | 0 |

Earl Murray

| 1951 | NYG | N | 1 | -4 | -4.0 | -4 | 0 |

Franny Murray

1939	PHI	N	13	144	11.1		1
1940			12	125	10.4		0
Career			25	269	10.8		1

Walter Murray

1986	IND	N	2	34	17.0	24	0
1987			20	339	16.9	43	3
Career			22	373	17.0	43	3
Playoffs			1	25	25.0		0

Adrian Murrell

1993	NYJ	N	5	12	2.4	8	0
1994			7	76	10.9	20	0
1995			71	465	6.5	43	1
1996			17	81	4.8	30	1
Career			100	634	6.3	43	3

Year	Team		No	Yds	Avg	Lg	TD

Bill Murrell
1979	STL	N	2	20	10.0	14	0

George Murtagh
1929	NYG	N					1

Johnny Musso
1976	CHI	N	4	26	6.5	9	0
1977			3	13	4.3	21	0
Career			7	39	5.6	21	0

Brad Muster
1988	CHI	N	21	236	11.2	40t	1
1989			32	259	8.1	25	3
1990			47	452	9.6	48	0
1991			35	287	8.2	21	1
1992			34	389	11.4	44t	2
1993	NO	N	23	195	8.5	31	0
1994			10	88	8.8	21	0
Career			202	1906	9.4	48	7
Playoffs			6	51	8.5		0

Chet Mutryn
1946	BUF	AA	7	168	24.0		3
1947			10	176	17.6	58t	2
1948			39	794	20.4	71	5
1949			29	333	11.5		0
1950	BAL	N	36	379	10.5	30	2
Career			121	1850	15.3	71	12
Playoffs			8	86	10.8		2

Jim Mutscheller
1954	BAL	N	1	49	49.0	49	0
1955			33	518	15.7	48	7
1956			44	715	16.3	53t	6
1957			32	558	17.4	66t	8
1958			28	504	18.0	54t	7
1959			44	699	15.9	40t	8
1960			18	271	15.1	43t	2
1961			20	370	18.5	45	2
Career			220	3684	16.7	66t	40
Playoffs			9	103	11.4		0

Brad Myers
1953	LA	N	4	13	3.3	9	0
1958	PHI	N	4	25	6.3	13	0
Career			8	38	4.8	13	0

Chip Myers
1967	SF	N	2	13	6.5	8	0
1969	CIN	A	10	205	20.5	50	2
1970	CIN	N	32	542	16.9	56t	1
1971			27	286	10.6	20	1
1972			57	792	13.9	42	3
1973			7	77	11.0	18	0
1974			32	383	12.0	22	1
1975			36	527	14.6	34t	3
1976			17	267	15.7	63	1
Career			220	3092	14.1	63	12
Playoffs			7	133	19.0		0

Jack Myers
1948	PHI	N	7	57	8.1	31	0
1949			7	98	14.0	26	0
1950			12	204	17.0	39	0
1952	LA	N	2	1	0.5	3	0
Career			28	360	12.9	39	0
Playoffs			2	6	3.0		0

Jesse Myles
1983	DEN	N	7	119	17.0	33	1
1984			2	22	11.0	12	0
Career			9	141	15.7	33	1
Playoffs			7	73	10.4		1

Chip Myrtle
1968	DEN	A	1	18	18.0	18	0

Andy Nacrelli
1958	PHI	N	2	15	7.5	11	0

Dana Nafziger
1977	TB	N	9	119	13.2	38	0

Gern Nagler
1953	CHIC	N	43	610	14.2	41t	6
1955			7	218	31.1	74t	3
1956			14	268	19.1	49	4
1957			27	475	17.6	83t	4
1958			36	469	13.0	47	5
1959	PIT	N	14	222	15.9	35	2
1960	CLE	N	36	616	17.1	53t	3
1961			19	241	12.7	21t	1
Career			196	3119	15.9	83t	28

Bronko Nagurski
1932	CHIB	N	6	67	11.2		0
1934			3	32	10.7		0
1936			1	12	12.0	12	0
Career			10	111	11.1	12	0
Playoffs			2	16	8.0		0

John Naioti
1945	PIT	N	2	14	7.0	8	0

Jim Nance
1965	BOS	A	12	83	6.9	22	0
1966			8	103	12.9	45	0
1967			22	196	8.9	36	1
1968			14	51	3.6	13	0
1969			29	168	5.8	27	0
1970	BOS	N	26	148	5.7	16	0
1971	NE	N	18	95	5.3	12	0
1973	NYJ	N	4	26	6.5	9	0
Career			133	870	6.5	45	1

Dick Nardi
1939	BKN	N	1	3	3.0	3	0

Bob Nash
1920	AKR	A					1

Kenny Nash
1987	KC	N	2	22	11.0	14	0

Tom Nash
1929	GB	N					1
1930							1
1933	BKN	N					2
Career							4

Tony Nathan
1979	MIA	N	17	213	12.5	35	2
1980			57	588	10.3	61	5
1981			50	452	9.0	31	3
1982			16	114	7.1	16	0
1983			52	461	8.9	25	1
1984			61	579	9.5	26	2
1985			72	651	9.0	73	1
1986			48	457	9.5	23t	2
1987			10	77	7.7	14	0
Career			383	3592	9.4	73	16
Playoffs			65	649	10.0		2

Ricky Nattiel
1987	DEN	N	31	630	20.3	54	2
1988			46	574	12.5	74t	1
1989			10	183	18.3	43	1
1990			18	297	16.5	52t	2
1991			16	288	18.0	70t	2
Career			121	1972	16.3	74t	8
Playoffs			13	251	19.3		2

Clem Neacy
1924	MIL	N					2

Frankie Neal
1987	GB	N	36	420	11.7	38	3

Lorenzo Neal
1994	NO	N	2	9	4.5	5	0
1995			12	123	10.3	69t	1
1996			31	194	6.3	23	1
Career			45	326	7.2	69t	2

Louis Neal
1973	ATL	N	5	131	26.2	50	1

Louis Neal continued
1974			8	99	12.4	21	0
Career			13	230	17.7	50	1

Speedy Neal
1984	BUF	N	9	76	8.4	18	0

Derrick Ned
1993	NO	N	9	54	6.0	14	0
1994			13	86	6.6	19	0
1995			3	9	3.0	9	0
Career			25	149	6.0	19	0

Bobby Neely
1996	CHI	N	9	92	10.2	21	0

Renaldo Nehemiah
1982	SF	N	8	161	20.1	55	1
1983			17	236	13.9	27	1
1984			18	357	19.8	59t	2
Career			43	754	17.5	59t	4
Playoffs			4	56	14.0		0

Bill Nelsen
1965	PIT	N	1	-5	-5.0	-5	0

Bob Nelson
1947	LA	AA	3	61	20.3		1

Darrell Nelson
1984	PIT	N	2	31	15.5	19	0

Darrin Nelson
1982	MIN	N	9	100	11.1	22	0
1983			51	618	12.1	68	0
1984			27	162	6.0	17	1
1985			43	301	7.0	25t	1
1986			53	593	11.2	34	3
1987			26	129	5.0	13	0
1988			16	105	6.6	27	0
1989	MIN-SD	N	38	380	10.0	49	0
1990	SD	N	4	29	7.3	10	0
1991	MIN	N	19	142	7.5	13	0
Career			286	2559	8.9	68	5
Playoffs			8	104	13.0		0

Frank Nelson
1948	BOS	N	1	10	10.0	10	0

Herb Nelson
1946	BUF	AA	4	47	11.8		0
1947	BKN	AA	2	17	8.5		0
Career			6	64	10.7		0

Jimmy Nelson
1946	MIA	AA	4	20	5.0		0

Ralph Nelson
1975	WAS	N	5	58	11.6	27t	1
1976	SEA	N	12	96	8.0	18	0
Career			17	154	9.1	27t	1

Terry Nelson
1975	LA	N	1	5	5.0	5	0
1976			4	48	12.0	16	0
1977			31	401	12.9	46	3
1978			23	344	15.0	52	0
1979			25	293	11.7	26	3
1980			3	22	7.3	12	0
Career			87	1113	12.8	52	6
Playoffs			15	216	14.4		0

Jerry Nemecek
1931	BKN	N					1

Frank Nesser
1922	COL	N					1

Fred Nesser
1921	COL	A					1

Keith Neubert
1989	NYJ	N	28	302	10.8	35t	1

Year	Team		No	Yds	Avg	Lg	TD

Bob Neuman

| 1936 | CHIC | N | 3 | 41 | 13.7 | | 0 |

Tom Neumann

| 1963 | BOS | A | 10 | 48 | 4.8 | 16 | 1 |

Ernie Nevers

| 1931 | CHIC | N | | | | | 1 |

Steve Newall

| 1967 | SD | A | 7 | 68 | 9.7 | 14 | 0 |

Robert Newhouse

1972	DAL	N	1	8	8.0	8	0
1973			9	87	9.7	38	1
1974			9	67	7.4	21	0
1975			34	275	8.1	23	0
1976			15	86	5.7	16	0
1977			16	106	6.6	41	1
1978			20	176	8.8	24	2
1979			7	55	7.9	21t	1
1980			8	75	9.4	18	0
1981			1	21	21.0	21	0
Career			120	956	8.0	41	5
Playoffs			14	80	5.7		0

Bob Newland

1971	NO	N	21	319	15.2	44	0
1972			47	579	12.3	42t	2
1973			29	489	16.9	42	4
1974			27	490	18.1	79t	2
Career			124	1877	15.1	79t	8

Anthony Newman

| 1995 | NO | N | 1 | 18 | 18.0 | 18 | 0 |

Harry Newman

| Playoffs | | | 1 | -1 | -1.0 | | 0 |

Harry Newman

1933	NYG	N					1
1934			4	55	13.8		0
Career			4	55	13.8		1

Olin Newman

| 1925 | AKR | N | | | | | 1 |

Pat Newman

1991	NO	N	3	33	11.0	14	0
1992			3	21	7.0	8	0
1993			8	121	15.1	32	1
Career			14	175	12.5	32	1

Ozzie Newsome

1978	CLE	N	38	589	15.5	47	2
1979			55	781	14.2	74	9
1980			51	594	11.6	44	3
1981			69	1002	14.5	62	6
1982			49	633	12.9	54	3
1983			89	970	10.9	66t	6
1984			89	1001	11.2	52	5
1985			62	711	11.5	38	5
1986			39	417	10.7	31	3
1987			34	375	11.0	25	0
1988			35	343	9.8	28	2
1989			29	324	11.2	31	1
1990			23	240	10.4	38	2
Career			662	7980	12.1	74	47
Playoffs			27	373	13.8		1

Timmy Newsome

1980	DAL	N	4	43	10.8	16	0
1982			6	118	19.7	46t	1
1983			18	250	13.9	52t	4
1984			26	263	10.1	29	0
1985			46	361	7.8	24	1
1986			48	421	8.8	30	3
1987			34	274	8.1	30	2
1988			30	236	7.9	32	0
Career			212	1966	9.3	52t	11
Playoffs			17	143	8.4		1

Chuck Newton

| 1939 | PHI | N | 9 | 123 | 13.7 | | 1 |

Chuck Newton continued

| 1940 | | | 1 | 22 | 22.0 | 22 | 0 |
| Career | | | 10 | 145 | 14.5 | 22 | 1 |

Nate Newton

| 1988 | DAL | N | 1 | 2 | 2.0 | 2 | 0 |

Tom Newton

1977	NYJ	N	5	33	6.6	9	0
1978			5	48	9.6	14	0
1979			4	33	8.3	11	0
1980			20	144	7.2	18	0
1981			17	104	6.1	13	0
1982			1	7	7.0	7	0
Career			52	369	7.1	18	0
Playoffs			1	12	12.0		0

Al Nichelini

| 1936 | CHIC | N | 9 | 133 | 14.8 | | 1 |

Calvin Nicholas

| 1988 | SF | N | 1 | 14 | 14.0 | 14 | 0 |

Bobby Nichols

| 1967 | BOS | A | 1 | 19 | 19.0 | 19 | 0 |

Mark Nichols

1981	DET	N	10	222	22.2	59	1
1982			8	146	18.3	48t	2
1983			29	437	15.1	46t	1
1984			34	744	21.9	77t	1
1985			36	592	16.4	43	4
1987			7	87	12.4	23	0
Career			124	2228	18.0	77t	9

Elbie Nickel

1947	PIT	N	1	10	10.0	10	0
1948			23	324	14.1	35	1
1949			26	633	24.3	52	3
1950			22	527	24.0	65t	4
1951			28	447	16.0	77t	3
1952			55	884	16.1	54t	9
1953			62	743	12.0	40	4
1954			40	584	14.6	52t	5
1955			36	488	13.6	30t	2
1956			27	376	13.9	47t	5
1957			10	115	11.5	31	1
Career			330	5131	15.5	77t	37
Playoffs			2	32	16.0		0

Walt Nielson

| 1940 | NYG | N | 2 | 17 | 8.5 | | 0 |

Ray Nitschke

| 1972 | GB | N | 1 | 34 | 34.0 | 34 | 0 |

Jack Nix

| 1950 | SF | N | 9 | 114 | 12.7 | 50 | 0 |

Fred Nixon

1980	GB	N	4	78	19.5	32	0
1981			2	27	13.5	19	0
Career			6	105	17.5	32	0

Dave Noble

1924	CLE	N					2
1925							3
1926	CLE	A					1
Career							6

James Noble

| 1987 | IND | N | 10 | 78 | 7.8 | 18t | 2 |

George Nock

1970	NYJ	N	18	146	8.1	21	1
1971			6	44	7.3	19t	2
Career			24	190	7.9	21	3

Ray Nolting

1936	CHIB	N	2	50	25.0		1
1937			4	64	16.0		0
1938			4	90	22.5		1
1939			6	87	14.5		1
1940			3	36	12.0		0

Ray Nolting continued

1941			4	68	17.0	25	0
1942			2	23	11.5	15	0
1943			5	90	18.0	48	0
Career			30	508	16.9	48	3
Playoffs			2	23	11.5		0

Jerry Noonan

| 1921 | ROC | A | | | | | 2 |

Karl Noonan

1966	MIA	A	17	224	13.2	35	1
1967			12	141	11.8	32	1
1968			58	760	13.1	50t	11
1969			29	307	10.6	27	3
1970	MIA	N	10	186	18.6	51t	1
1971			10	180	18.0	43	0
Career			136	1798	13.2	51t	17

John Noppenberg

| 1940 | PIT | N | 4 | 74 | 18.5 | | 0 |

Hank Norberg

1946	SF	AA	3	29	9.7		0
1947			2	31	15.5		0
1948	CHIB	N	1	4	4.0	4	0
Career			6	64	10.7	4	0

John Norby

| 1934 | NYG | N | 1 | 6 | 6.0 | 6 | 0 |

Erik Norgard

1993	HOU	N	1	13	13.0	13	0
1996			1	1	1.0	1t	1
Career			2	14	7.0	13	1

Pettis Norman

1962	DAL	N	2	34	17.0	29	0
1963			18	341	18.9	49	3
1964			24	311	13.0	37	2
1965			11	110	10.0	21	3
1966			12	144	12.0	31	0
1967			20	220	11.0	39	2
1968			18	204	11.3	34	1
1969			13	238	18.3	31t	1
1970			6	70	11.7	23	0
1971	SD	N	27	358	13.3	30	1
1972			19	262	13.8	30	0
1973			13	200	15.4	24	0
Career			183	2492	13.6	49	15
Playoffs			7	71	10.1		0

Will Norman

| 1928 | POT | N | | | | | 1 |

Ulysses Norris

1979	DET	N	4	43	10.8	34	1
1981			8	132	16.5	34	0
1982			3	51	17.0	30	0
1983			26	291	11.2	41	7
1985	BUF	N	2	30	15.0	18	0
Career			43	547	12.7	41	8
Playoffs			1	5	5.0		0

John North

1948	BAL	AA	8	204	**25.5**	80t	1
1949			25	490	19.6	80t	4
1950	BAL	N	5	90	18.0	39	0
Career			38	784	20.6	80t	5

Don Norton

1960	LA	A	25	414	16.6	69	5
1961	SD	A	47	816	17.4	52	6
1962			48	771	16.1	47	7
1963			21	281	13.4	36	1
1964			49	669	13.7	58	6
1965			34	485	14.3	61	2
1966			4	50	12.5	18	0
Career			228	3486	15.3	69	27
Playoffs			13	195	15.0		1

Jerry Norton

| 1955 | PHI | N | 11 | 125 | 11.4 | 36t | 1 |

Jim Norton

Year	Team		No	Yds	Avg	Lg	TD
1960	HOU	A	1	5	5.0	5	0

Marty Norton

Year	Team		No	Yds	Avg	Lg	TD
1925	GB	N					4

Don Nottingham

Year	Team		No	Yds	Avg	Lg	TD
1971	BAL	N	15	88	5.9	35	0
1972			25	191	7.6	27	0
1973	BAL-MIA	N	3	26	8.7	16	0
1974	MIA	N	3	40	13.3	20	0
1975			9	66	7.3	18	0
1976			4	33	8.3	29	0
1977			8	58	7.3	16	0
Career			67	502	7.5	35	0
Playoffs			6	40	6.7		0

Jay Novacek

Year	Team		No	Yds	Avg	Lg	TD
1985	STL	N	1	4	4.0	4	0
1986			1	2	2.0	2	0
1987			20	254	12.7	25	3
1988	PHX	N	38	569	15.0	42t	4
1989			23	225	9.8	30	1
1990	DAL	N	59	657	11.1	41	4
1991			59	664	11.3	49	4
1992			68	630	9.3	34	6
1993			44	445	10.1	30	1
1994			47	475	10.1	27	2
1995			62	705	11.4	33t	5
Career			422	4630	11.0	49	30
Playoffs			62	645	10.4		6

Jack Novak

Year	Team		No	Yds	Avg	Lg	TD
1975	CIN	N	2	34	17.0	19	0
1976	TB	N	8	130	16.3	30t	1
1977			2	24	12.0	15	0
Career			12	188	15.7	30t	1

Brent Novoselsky

Year	Team		No	Yds	Avg	Lg	TD
1989	MIN	N	4	11	2.8	6	2
1991			4	27	6.8	8	0
1992			4	63	15.8	34	0
1994			2	7	3.5	4	0
Career			14	108	7.7	34	2

Bob Nowaskey

Year	Team		No	Yds	Avg	Lg	TD
1940	CHIB	N	5	105	21.0		2
1941			12	199	16.6	40	1
1942			6	128	21.3	29	0
1946	LA	AA	19	198	10.4		3
1947			8	106	13.3		0
1948	BAL	AA	1	31	31.0	31	0
Career			51	767	15.0	40	6
Playoffs			3	44	14.7		0

Tom Nowatzke

Year	Team		No	Yds	Avg	Lg	TD
1965	DET	N	5	45	9.0	22t	1
1966			54	316	5.9	25	1
1967			21	145	6.9	25t	2
1968			4	6	1.5	5	0
1970	BAL	N	16	93	5.8	17	0
Career			100	605	6.0	25t	4
Playoffs			1	45	45.0		0

Bob Nussbaumer

Year	Team		No	Yds	Avg	Lg	TD
1946	GB	N	10	143	14.3	35	0
1947	WAS	N	47	597	12.7	55t	4
1948			19	252	13.3	37	1
Career			76	992	13.1	55t	5

Jerry Nuzum

Year	Team		No	Yds	Avg	Lg	TD
1948	PIT	N	2	37	18.5	32	0
1949			4	81	20.3	63	2
1950			6	142	23.7	68	1
1951			2	43	21.5	39	0
Career			14	303	21.6	68	3

Bernie Nygren

Year	Team		No	Yds	Avg	Lg	TD
1946	LA	AA	13	170	13.1		1

Vic Nyvall

Year	Team		No	Yds	Avg	Lg	TD
1970	NO	N	2	-1	-0.5	1	0

Victor Oatis

Year	Team		No	Yds	Avg	Lg	TD
1983	BAL	N	6	93	15.5	25	0

Terry Obee

Year	Team		No	Yds	Avg	Lg	TD
1993	CHI	N	26	351	13.5	48	3

Jim Obradovich

Year	Team		No	Yds	Avg	Lg	TD
1975	NYG	N	7	65	9.3	28	1
1976	SF	N	1	11	11.0	11	0
1977			2	16	8.0	11	0
1978	TB	N	14	219	15.6	28t	3
1979			6	63	10.5	19	1
1980			11	152	13.8	24	0
1981			4	42	10.5	16	1
1982			2	22	11.0	15	0
1983			9	71	7.9	19	1
Career			56	661	11.8	28t	7

Jack O'Brien

Year	Team		No	Yds	Avg	Lg	TD
1954	PIT	N	1	9	9.0	9	0
1955			9	105	11.7	38	2
1956			6	71	11.8	25	0
Career			16	185	11.6	38	2

Jim O'Brien

Year	Team		No	Yds	Avg	Lg	TD
1970	BAL	N	1	28	28.0	28	0
1972			11	263	23.9	44	2
1973	DET	N	2	14	7.0	9	0
Career			14	305	21.8	44	2

Ken O'Brien

Year	Team		No	Yds	Avg	Lg	TD
1991	NYJ	N	1	27	27.0	27	0

Milt O'Connell

Year	Team		No	Yds	Avg	Lg	TD
1924	FRA	N					1

Bill O'Connor

Year	Team		No	Yds	Avg	Lg	TD
1948	BUF	AA	31	301	9.7		2
1951	NYY	N	14	192	13.7	33	0
Career			45	493	11.0	33	2
Playoffs			3	41	13.7		1

Curly Oden

Year	Team		No	Yds	Avg	Lg	TD
1926	PRO	N					1
1928							3
Career							4

McDonald Oden

Year	Team		No	Yds	Avg	Lg	TD
1980	CLE	N	3	18	6.0	8	0
1981			1	6	6.0	6	0
1982			1	4	4.0	4	0
Career			5	28	5.6	8	0

Phil Odle

Year	Team		No	Yds	Avg	Lg	TD
1968	DET	N	6	71	11.8	18	0
1969			2	24	12.0	14	0
Career			8	95	11.9	18	0

Henry Odom

Year	Team		No	Yds	Avg	Lg	TD
Playoffs			1	6	6.0		0

Steve Odom

Year	Team		No	Yds	Avg	Lg	TD
1974	GB	N	15	249	16.6	57	1
1975			15	299	19.9	56	4
1976			23	456	19.8	66t	2
1977			27	549	20.3	95t	3
1978			4	60	15.0	18t	1
Career			84	1613	19.2	95t	11

Riley Odoms

Year	Team		No	Yds	Avg	Lg	TD
1972	DEN	N	21	320	15.2	48	1
1973			43	629	14.6	47t	7
1974			42	639	15.2	41	6
1975			40	544	13.6	43	3
1976			30	477	15.9	47	3
1977			37	429	11.6	33	3
1978			54	829	15.4	42t	6
1979			40	638	15.9	45	1
1980			39	590	15.1	30	6
1981			38	516	13.6	28	5
1982			8	82	10.3	18	0
1983			2	42	15.5	21	0
Career			396	5755	14.5	48	41
Playoffs			11	92	8.4		1

Dicky O'Donnell

Year	Team		No	Yds	Avg	Lg	TD
1923	DUL	N					1
1925	GB	N					1
1926							2
1928							1
1931	BKN	N					1
Career							6

Joe O'Donnell

Year	Team		No	Yds	Avg	Lg	TD
1966	BUF	A	1	2	2.0	2	0

Arnie Oehlrich

Year	Team		No	Yds	Avg	Lg	TD
1928	FRA	N					2
1929							1
Career							3

John Oelerich

Year	Team		No	Yds	Avg	Lg	TD
1938	PIT	N	2	23	11.5		0

Jonathan Ogden

Year	Team		No	Yds	Avg	Lg	TD
1996	BAL	N	1	1	1.0	1	0

Ray Ogden

Year	Team		No	Yds	Avg	Lg	TD
1967	NO-ATL	N	20	327	16.4	82t	1
1968	ATL	N	25	452	18.1	60	2
1969	CHI	N	7	100	14.3	21	0
1970			1	6	6.0	6t	1
Career			53	885	16.7	82t	4

Christian Okoye

Year	Team		No	Yds	Avg	Lg	TD
1987	KC	N	24	169	7.0	22	0
1988			8	51	6.4	12	0
1989			2	12	6.0	8	0
1990			4	23	5.8	8	0
1991			3	34	11.3	13	0
1992			1	5	5.0	5	0
Career			42	294	7.0	22	0

Jim Oldham

Year	Team		No	Yds	Avg	Lg	TD
1926	RAC	N					1

Bill Olds

Year	Team		No	Yds	Avg	Lg	TD
1973	BAL	N	2	-4	-2.0	-1	0
1974			21	153	7.3	18	2
1975			30	194	6.5	28t	2
1976	PHI	N	9	29	3.2	14	0
Career			62	372	6.0	28t	4

Dave Olerich

Year	Team		No	Yds	Avg	Lg	TD
1967	SF	N	1	2	2.0	2	0

Mike Oliphant

Year	Team		No	Yds	Avg	Lg	TD
1988	WAS	N	15	111	7.4	16	0
1989	CLE	N	3	22	7.3	9	0
Career			18	133	7.4	16	0

Darryl Oliver

Year	Team		No	Yds	Avg	Lg	TD
1987	ATL	N	1	2	2.0	2	0

Greg Oliver

Year	Team		No	Yds	Avg	Lg	TD
1973	PHI	N	1	9	9.0	9	0

Hubie Oliver

Year	Team		No	Yds	Avg	Lg	TD
1981	PHI	N	10	37	3.7	16	0
1983			49	421	8.6	25	2
1984			32	142	4.4	21	0
1985			1	4	4.0	4	0
1986	HOU	N	1	-2	-2.0	-2	0
Career			93	602	6.5	27	2
Playoffs			1	7	7.0		0

Winslow Oliver

Year	Team		No	Yds	Avg	Lg	TD
1996	CAR	N	15	144	9.6	29	0
Playoffs			2	10	5.0		0

Al Olszewski

Year	Team		No	Yds	Avg	Lg	TD
1945	PIT	N	2	28	14.0	22	0

Johnny Olszewski

Year	Team		No	Yds	Avg	Lg	TD
1953	CHIC	N	21	210	10.0	77	1
1954			12	133	11.1	25	1
1955			9	37	4.1	9	0
1956			17	182	10.7	31	0
1957			3	36	12.0	24	0

Johnny Olszewski *continued*

Year	Team		No	Yds	Avg	Lg	TD
1958	WAS	N	11	102	9.3	36	0
1959	.		7	62	8.9	15	0
1960			10	62	6.2	31	0
1961	DET	N	1	14	14.0	14	0
1962	DEN	A	13	150	11.5	26	1
Career			104	988	9.5	77	3

Ken O'Neal

Year	Team		No	Yds	Avg	Lg	TD
1987	NO	N	3	10	3.3	5	1

Bob O'Neil

Year	Team		No	Yds	Avg	Lg	TD
1961	NY	A	1	-13	-13.0	-13	0

Ed O'Neil

Year	Team		No	Yds	Avg	Lg	TD
1976	DET	N	1	32	32.0	32t	1

Johnny O'Quinn

Year	Team		No	Yds	Avg	Lg	TD
1951	PHI	N	3	58	19.3	34	0

Joe Orduna

Year	Team		No	Yds	Avg	Lg	TD
1972	NYG	N	4	6	1.5	6	1
1973			6	44	7.3	17	0
1974	BAL	N	1	8	8.0	8	0
Career			11	58	5.3	17	1

Bob Oristaglio

Year	Team		No	Yds	Avg	Lg	TD
1949	BUF	AA	1	14	14.0	14	0
1950	BAL	N	14	134	9.6	16	0
1951	CLE	N	1	20	20.0	20t	1
Career			16	168	10.5	20t	1

Dan Orlich

Year	Team		No	Yds	Avg	Lg	TD
1949	GB	N	4	39	9.8	12	0
1951			1	9	9.0	9	0
Career			5	48	9.6	12	0

Jimmy Orr

Year	Team		No	Yds	Avg	Lg	TD
1958	PIT	N	33	910	**27.6**	78t	7
1959			35	604	17.3	43	5
1960			29	541	18.7	51t	4
1961	BAL	N	18	357	19.8	64	4
1962			55	974	17.7	80t	11
1963			41	708	17.3	60t	5
1964			40	867	21.7	69	6
1965			45	847	18.8	57	10
1966			37	618	16.7	61t	3
1967			3	72	24.0	55t	1
1968			29	743	25.6	84	6
1969			25	474	19.0	47	2
1970			10	199	19.9	29	2
Career			400	7914	19.8	84	66
Playoffs			9	142	15.8		0

Terry Orr

Year	Team		No	Yds	Avg	Lg	TD
1986	WAS	N	3	45	15.0	22t	1
1987			3	35	11.7	23	0
1988			11	222	20.2	58	2
1989			3	80	26.7	48	0
1991			10	201	20.1	47t	4
1992			22	356	16.2	58	3
Career			52	939	18.1	58	10
Playoffs			1	45	45.0		0

Keith Ortego

Year	Team		No	Yds	Avg	Lg	TD
1986	CHI	N	23	430	18.7	58t	2
Playoffs			2	36	18.0		0

Chuck Ortmann

Year	Team		No	Yds	Avg	Lg	TD
1951	PIT	N	4	62	15.5	22	0

Dave Osborn

Year	Team		No	Yds	Avg	Lg	TD
1965	MIN	N	1	4	4.0	4	0
1966			15	141	9.4	38t	2
1967			34	272	8.0	29	1
1969			22	236	10.7	31	1
1970			23	202	8.8	28t	1
1971			25	195	7.8	25	1
1972			20	166	8.3	18	1
1973			3	4	1.3	5	0
1974			29	196	6.8	25	0
1975			1	-4	-4.0	4	0
Career			173	1412	8.2	38t	7
Playoffs			10	53	5.3		0

Richard Osborne

Year	Team		No	Yds	Avg	Lg	TD
1976	NYJ	N	2	9	4.5	7	1
1977	PHI	N	1	6	6.0	6	0
1978			13	145	11.2	48	0
1979	STL	N	7	37	5.3	10	0
Career			23	197	8.6	48	1
Playoffs			3	15	5.0		0

Tom Osborne

Year	Team		No	Yds	Avg	Lg	TD
1960	WAS	N	7	46	6.6	10	0
1961			22	297	13.5	60t	2
Career			29	343	11.8	60t	2

Terry O'Shea

Year	Team		No	Yds	Avg	Lg	TD
1989	PIT	N	1	8	8.0	8	0
1990			1	13	13.0	13	0
Career			2	21	10.5	13	0

Bill Osmanski

Year	Team		No	Yds	Avg	Lg	TD
1939	CHIB	N	3	65	21.7		1
1940			1	13	13.0	13	0
1941			4	52	13.0	27	0
1946			4	40	10.0	28	0
Career			12	170	14.2	28	1

Joe Osmanski

Year	Team		No	Yds	Avg	Lg	TD
1946	CHIB	N	2	14	7.0	14	0
1947			7	134	19.1	39	0
1948			9	43	4.8	19	0
1949	CHIB-NYB	N	18	138	7.7	42	0
Career			36	329	9.1	42	0

Jim Otis

Year	Team		No	Yds	Avg	Lg	TD
1970	NO	N	20	124	6.2	22	0
1971	KC	N	13	81	6.2	26	2
1972			12	76	6.3	13	0
1973	STL	N	2	19	9.5	14	0
1974			19	109	5.7	13	0
1975			12	69	5.8	12	1
1976			2	15	7.5	8	0
1977			2	18	9.0	9	0
1978			8	38	4.8	12	0
Career			90	549	6.1	26	3
Playoffs			5	51	10.2		0

Lowell Otte

Year	Team		No	Yds	Avg	Lg	TD
1926	NY	A					1

Jim Otto

Year	Team		No	Yds	Avg	Lg	TD
Playoffs			1	5	5.0		0

David Overstreet

Year	Team		No	Yds	Avg	Lg	TD
1983	MIA	N	8	55	6.9	20	2

Don Overton

Year	Team		No	Yds	Avg	Lg	TD
1990	NE	N	2	19	9.5	15	0
1991	DET	N	4	38	9.5	14	0
Career			6	57	9.5	15	0
Playoffs			2	10	5.0		0

Al Owen

Year	Team		No	Yds	Avg	Lg	TD
1939	NYG	N	2	45	22.5		1
1940			1	5	5.0	5	0
1942			1	20	20.0	20	0
Career			4	70	17.5	20	1

Artie Owens

Year	Team		No	Yds	Avg	Lg	TD
1976	SD	N	3	54	18.0	28t	1
1978			9	188	20.9	41	0
1979			15	176	11.7	32t	1
Career			27	418	15.5	41	1

James Owens

Year	Team		No	Yds	Avg	Lg	TD
1979	SF	N	10	121	12.1	17	0
1980			9	133	14.8	29	0
1981	TB	N	12	145	12.1	35	0
1982			8	42	5.3	12	1
1983			15	81	5.4	11	1
1984			2	13	6.5	9	1
Career			56	535	9.6	35	3

Jim Owens

Year	Team		No	Yds	Avg	Lg	TD
1950	BAL	N	19	188	9.9	43	0

Morris Owens

Year	Team		No	Yds	Avg	Lg	TD
1976	TB	N	30	390	13.0	27t	6
1977			34	655	19.3	67t	3
1978			32	640	20.0	66	5
1979			20	377	18.9	64	0
Career			116	2062	17.8	67t	14
Playoffs			4	53	13.3		0

R.C. Owens

Year	Team		No	Yds	Avg	Lg	TD
1957	SF	N	27	395	14.6	46t	5
1958			40	620	15.5	48	1
1959			17	347	20.4	75t	3
1960			37	532	14.4	42	6
1961			55	1032	18.8	54	5
1962	BAL	N	25	307	12.3	26	2
1963			1	7	7.0	7	0
1964	NYG	N	4	45	11.3	14	0
Career			206	3285	15.9	75t	22
Playoffs			1	34	34.0		1

Steve Owens

Year	Team		No	Yds	Avg	Lg	TD
1970	DET	N	4	21	5.3	11	0
1971			32	350	10.9	74t	2
1972			15	100	6.7	15	0
1973			24	232	9.7	30	0
1974			24	158	6.6	13	0
Career			99	861	8.7	74t	2
Playoffs			1	7	7.0		0

Terrell Owens

Year	Team		No	Yds	Avg	Lg	TD
1996	SF	N	35	520	14.9	46t	4
Playoffs			1	7	7.0		0

Tinker Owens

Year	Team		No	Yds	Avg	Lg	TD
1976	NO	N	12	241	20.1	74	1
1978			40	446	11.2	47t	2
1979			7	72	10.3	21	1
1980			1	26	26.0	26	0
Career			60	785	13.1	74	4

Jim Pace

Year	Team		No	Yds	Avg	Lg	TD
1958	SF	N	10	59	5.9	24	0

Vince Pacewicz

Year	Team		No	Yds	Avg	Lg	TD
1947	WAS	N	5	42	8.4	15	0

Bob Paffrath

Year	Team		No	Yds	Avg	Lg	TD
1946	BKN-MIA	AA	4	-6	-1.5		0

Fred Pagac

Year	Team		No	Yds	Avg	Lg	TD
1974	CHI	N	6	79	13.2	24	0
1976	TB	N	2	15	7.5	10	0
Career			8	94	11.8	24	0

Paul Page

Year	Team		No	Yds	Avg	Lg	TD
1949	BAL	AA	4	62	15.5		0

Mike Pagel

Year	Team		No	Yds	Avg	Lg	TD
1985	IND	N	1	6	6.0	6	0

Joe Pagliei

Year	Team		No	Yds	Avg	Lg	TD
1959	PHI	N	2	9	4.5	11	0
1960	NY	A	1	13	13.0	13	0
Career			3	22	7.3	13	0

Stephone Paige

Year	Team		No	Yds	Avg	Lg	TD
1983	KC	N	30	528	17.6	43	6
1984			30	541	18.0	65t	4
1985			43	943	**21.9**	84t	10
1986			52	829	15.9	51	11
1987			43	707	16.4	51	4
1988			61	902	14.8	49	7
1989			44	759	17.3	50	2
1990			65	1021	15.7	86t	5
1991			9	111	12.3	26	0
Career			377	6341	16.8	86t	49
Playoffs			8	142	17.8		1

Tony Paige

Year	Team		No	Yds	Avg	Lg	TD
1984	NYJ	N	6	31	5.2	10	1
1985			18	120	6.7	19	2
1986			18	121	6.7	18	0
1987	DET	N	2	1	0.5	9	0
1988			11	100	9.1	15	0

Tony Paige continued

Year	Team		No	Yds	Avg	Lg	TD
1989			2	27	13.5	15	0
1990	MIA	N	35	247	7.1	17t	4
1991			57	469	8.2	26	1
1992			48	399	8.3	30	1
Career			197	1515	7.7	30	9
Playoffs			12	60	5.0		2

Carl Painter

Year	Team		No	Yds	Avg	Lg	TD
1988	DET	N	1	1	1.0	1	0
1989			3	41	13.7	27	0
Career			4	42	10.5	27	0

David Palmer

Year	Team		No	Yds	Avg	Lg	TD
1994	MIN	N	6	90	15.0	39	0
1995			12	100	8.3	19	0
1996			6	40	6.7	20	0
Career			24	230	9.6	39	0
Playoffs			1	11	11.0		0

Paul Palmer

Year	Team		No	Yds	Avg	Lg	TD
1987	KC	N	4	27	6.8	10	0
1988			53	611	11.5	71t	4
1989	DAL	N	17	93	5.5	13	0
Career			74	731	9.9	71t	4

John Panelli

Year	Team		No	Yds	Avg	Lg	TD
1949	DET	N	1	13	13.0	13	0
1950			2	9	4.5	7	0
1951	CHIC	N	1	5	5.0	5	0
Career			4	27	6.8	13	0

Hal Pangle

Year	Team		No	Yds	Avg	Lg	TD
1936	CHIC	N	9	195	21.7		0
1937			5	58	11.6		0
1938			2	14	7.0		0
Career			16	267	16.7		0

George Papach

Year	Team		No	Yds	Avg	Lg	TD
1948	PIT	N	4	72	18.0	31	1
1949			6	18	3.0	11	0
Career			10	90	9.0	31	1

Vince Papale

Year	Team		No	Yds	Avg	Lg	TD
1977	PHI	N	1	15	15.0	15	0

Oran Pape

Year	Team		No	Yds	Avg	Lg	TD
1931	PRO	N					2

Johnny Papit

Year	Team		No	Yds	Avg	Lg	TD
1951	WAS	N	3	43	14.3	24	0
1952			3	71	23.7	39	1
1953			1	9	9.0	9	0
Career			7	123	17.6	39	1

Curt Pardridge

Year	Team		No	Yds	Avg	Lg	TD
1987	SEA	N	8	145	18.1	47	1

Bob Paremore

Year	Team		No	Yds	Avg	Lg	TD
1963	STL	N	6	89	14.8	32	0

Babe Parilli

Year	Team		No	Yds	Avg	Lg	TD
1960	OAK	A	1	0	0.0	0	0

Kaulana Park

Year	Team		No	Yds	Avg	Lg	TD
1987	NYG	N	1	6	6.0	6	0

Ace Parker

Year	Team		No	Yds	Avg	Lg	TD
1938	BKN	N	1	19	19.0	19	1
1939			1	5	5.0	5	0
1940			3	139	46.3		2
1941			3	66	22.0	36	0
Career			8	229	28.6	36	3

Andy Parker

Year	Team		No	Yds	Avg	Lg	TD
1986	LARI	N	2	8	4.0	6	1
1988			4	33	8.3	12	0
1989	SD	N	2	5	2.5	4	1
Career			8	46	5.8	12	2

Buddy Parker

Year	Team		No	Yds	Avg	Lg	TD
1936	DET	N	1	15	15.0	15	0
1937	CHIC	N	2	14	7.0		0
1938			16	142	8.9		0
1939			5	33	6.6		0
1940			6	45	7.5		0
1941			8	122	15.3	44	0
1942			2	7	3.5	4	0
Career			40	378	9.4	44	0

Carl Parker

Year	Team		No	Yds	Avg	Lg	TD
1989	CIN	N	1	45	45.0	45	0

Dave Parker

Year	Team		No	Yds	Avg	Lg	TD
1941	BKN	N	1	10	10.0	10	0

Freddie Parker

Year	Team		No	Yds	Avg	Lg	TD
1987	GB	N	3	22	7.3	13	0

Howie Parker

Year	Team		No	Yds	Avg	Lg	TD
1948	NY	AA	1	17	17.0	17	0

Jeff Parker

Year	Team		No	Yds	Avg	Lg	TD
1992	TB	N	1	12	12.0	12	0

Joe Parker

Year	Team		No	Yds	Avg	Lg	TD
1946	CHIC	N	2	17	8.5	11	0

Joel Parker

Year	Team		No	Yds	Avg	Lg	TD
1974	NO	N	41	455	11.1	58	4
1975			9	123	13.7	32t	2
1977			1	7	7.0	7	0
Career			51	585	11.5	58	6

Orlando Parker

Year	Team		No	Yds	Avg	Lg	TD
1994	NYJ	N	1	7	7.0	7	0

Robert Parker

Year	Team		No	Yds	Avg	Lg	TD
1987	KC	N	7	44	6.3	14	0

Rodney Parker

Year	Team		No	Yds	Avg	Lg	TD
1980	PHI	N	9	148	16.4	30t	1
1981			8	168	21.0	55t	2
Career			17	316	18.6	55t	3
Playoffs			5	50	10.0		1

Billy Parks

Year	Team		No	Yds	Avg	Lg	TD
1971	SD	N	41	609	14.9	56t	4
1972	DAL	N	18	298	16.6	38t	1
1973	HOU	N	43	581	13.5	66t	1
1974			20	330	16.5	59	1
1975			1	8	8.0	8	0
Career			123	1826	14.8	66t	7
Playoffs			8	157	19.6		1

Dave Parks

Year	Team		No	Yds	Avg	Lg	TD
1964	SF	N	36	703	19.5	83t	8
1965			80	1344	16.8	53t	12
1966			66	974	14.8	65t	5
1967			26	313	12.0	43	2
1968	NO	N	25	258	10.3	41	0
1969			31	439	14.2	40	3
1970			26	447	17.2	38	2
1971			35	568	16.2	42	5
1972			32	542	16.9	66t	6
1973	HOU	N	3	31	10.3	12	1
Career			360	5619	15.6	83t	44

Jeff Parks

Year	Team		No	Yds	Avg	Lg	TD
1988	TB	N	1	22	22.0	22	0

Rickey Parks

Year	Team		No	Yds	Avg	Lg	TD
1987	MIN	N	3	46	15.3	19	0

Bernie Parmalee

Year	Team		No	Yds	Avg	Lg	TD
1993	MIA	N	1	1	1.0	1	0
1994			34	249	7.3	22	1
1995			39	345	8.8	35	1
1996			21	189	9.0	17	0
Career			95	784	8.3	35	2
Playoffs			8	93	11.6		0

Jim Parmer

Year	Team		No	Yds	Avg	Lg	TD
1949	PHI	N	5	33	6.6	30	0
1950			6	103	17.2	59	1
1951			13	80	6.2	16	0
1952			2	10	5.0	8	0
1953			14	89	6.4	15	0
1954			12	40	3.3	16	0
1955			1	-4	-4.0	-4	0
Career			53	351	6.6	59	1

Gary Parris

Year	Team		No	Yds	Avg	Lg	TD
1974	SD	N	3	36	12.0	17	0
1975	CLE	N	1	12	12.0	12	0
1976			5	73	14.6	20	0
1977			21	213	10.1	26t	5
1978			1	4	4.0	4	0
1979	STL	N	14	174	12.4	39	0
Career			45	512	11.4	39	5

Rick Parros

Year	Team		No	Yds	Avg	Lg	TD
1981	DEN	N	25	216	8.6	26	1
1982			37	259	7.0	24	2
1983			12	126	10.5	33t	2
1984			6	25	4.2	9	0
1985	SEA	N	1	27	27.0	27	0
1987			1	7	7.0	7	0
Career			82	660	8.0	33t	5

Owen Parry

Year	Team		No	Yds	Avg	Lg	TD
Playoffs			0	8			0

Ara Parseghian

Year	Team		No	Yds	Avg	Lg	TD
1948	CLE	AA	2	31	15.5		1
1949			1	2	2.0	2	0
Career			3	33	11.0	2	1

Bob Parsons

Year	Team		No	Yds	Avg	Lg	TD
1972	CHI	N	1	6	6.0	6t	1
1973			2	23	11.5	17	1
1974			2	9	4.5	5	1
1975			13	184	14.2	38	1
1976			1	9	9.0	9	0
Career			19	231	12.2	38	4

Earle Parsons

Year	Team		No	Yds	Avg	Lg	TD
1946	SF	AA	8	52	6.5		0
1947			9	163	18.1		2
Career			17	215	12.6		2

Lloyd Parsons

Year	Team		No	Yds	Avg	Lg	TD
1941	DET	N	1	3	3.0	3	0

Bill Paschal

Year	Team		No	Yds	Avg	Lg	TD
1943	NYG	N	9	74	8.2	24	2
1945			2	11	5.5	6	0
1946			9	78	8.7	35t	2
1947	BOS	N	4	70	17.5	30	0
1948			8	93	11.6	22t	4
Career			32	326	10.2	35t	8

Doug Paschal

Year	Team		No	Yds	Avg	Lg	TD
1980	MIN	N	2	18	9.0	11	0
Playoffs			1	19	19.0		0

Gordon Paschka

Year	Team		No	Yds	Avg	Lg	TD
1947	NYG	N	1	-6	-6.0	-6	0

Keith Paskett

Year	Team		No	Yds	Avg	Lg	TD
1987	GB	N	12	188	15.7	47t	1

Ralph Pasquariello

Year	Team		No	Yds	Avg	Lg	TD
1950	LA	N	1	2	2.0	2	0
1951	CHIC	N	2	-9	-4.5	-4	0
1952			7	46	6.6	10	0
Career			10	39	3.9	10	0

Alan Pastrana

Year	Team		No	Yds	Avg	Lg	TD
1969	DEN	A	1	15	15.0	15	0

Loyd Pate

Year	Team		No	Yds	Avg	Lg	TD
1970	BUF	N	19	103	5.4	21	0

Greg Paterra

Year	Team		No	Yds	Avg	Lg	TD
1989	ATL	N	5	42	8.4	20	0

Frank Patrick

Year	Team		No	Yds	Avg	Lg	TD
1938	CHIC	N	1	21	21.0	21	1

John Patrick

Year	Team		No	Yds	Avg	Lg	TD
1941	PIT	N	1	12	12.0	12	0

Wayne Patrick

Year	Team		No	Yds	Avg	Lg	TD
1968	BUF	A	1	5	5.0	5	0
1969			35	229	6.5	19	0
1970	BUF	N	16	142	8.9	38	0
1971			36	327	9.1	62	0
1972			8	42	5.3	10	1
Career			96	745	7.8	62	1

Maury Patt

Year	Team		No	Yds	Avg	Lg	TD
1938	DET	N	7	80	11.4		0
1939	CLE	N	15	165	11.0		0
1940			2	52	26.0		1
1941			17	163	9.6	25	1
Career			41	460	11.2	25	2

Elvis Patterson

Year	Team		No	Yds	Avg	Lg	TD
1991	LARI	N	1	34	34.0	34	0

Paul Patterson

Year	Team		No	Yds	Avg	Lg	TD
1949	CHI	AA	16	304	19.0	68t	4

Mark Pattison

Year	Team		No	Yds	Avg	Lg	TD
1986	LARI	N	2	12	6.0	6	0
1987	NO		9	132	14.7	36	0
1988			1	8	8.0	8	0
Career			12	152	12.7	36	0
Playoffs			2	18	9.0		0

Ricky Patton

Year	Team		No	Yds	Avg	Lg	TD
1978	ATL	N	10	90	9.0	32	1
1979	GB	N	6	41	6.8	9	0
1981	SF	N	27	195	7.2	31t	1
Career			43	326	7.6	32	2
Playoffs			3	44	14.7		0

Don Paul

Year	Team		No	Yds	Avg	Lg	TD
1950	CHIC	N	5	93	18.6	35t	0
1951			23	398	17.3	53	3
1952			4	32	8.0	11	1
1953			16	167	10.4	27	2
Career			48	690	14.4	53	7

Ken Payne

Year	Team		No	Yds	Avg	Lg	TD
1974	GB	N	5	63	12.6	18	0
1975			58	766	13.2	54	0
1976			33	467	14.2	57t	4
1977			7	99	14.1	45	1
1978	PHI	N	13	238	18.3	50	1
Career			116	1633	14.1	57t	6
Playoffs			1	10	10.0		0

Russell Payne

Year	Team		No	Yds	Avg	Lg	TD
1987	DEN	N	1	8	8.0	8	0

Eddie Payton

Year	Team		No	Yds	Avg	Lg	TD
1977	DET	N	2	10	5.0	14	0

Walter Payton

Year	Team		No	Yds	Avg	Lg	TD
1975	CHI	N	33	213	6.5	40	0
1976			15	149	9.9	34	0
1977			27	269	10.0	75t	2
1978			50	480	9.6	61	0
1979			31	313	10.1	65t	2
1980			46	367	8.0	54t	1
1981			41	379	9.2	30	2
1982			32	311	9.7	40	0
1983			53	607	11.5	74t	2
1984			45	368	8.2	31	0
1985			49	483	9.9	65	2
1986			37	382	10.3	57	3
1987			33	217	6.6	16	1
Career			492	4538	9.2	75t	15
Playoffs			22	178	8.1		0

Elvis Peacock

Year	Team		No	Yds	Avg	Lg	TD
1979	LA	N	21	261	12.4	49	0
1980			25	213	8.5	59t	2
Career			46	474	10.3	59t	2

Clarence Peaks

Year	Team		No	Yds	Avg	Lg	TD
1957	PHI	N	11	99	9.0	53	0
1958			29	248	8.6	33t	2

Clarence Peaks continued

Year	Team		No	Yds	Avg	Lg	TD
1959			28	209	7.5	23	0
1960			14	116	8.3	34	0
1961			32	472	14.8	48	0
1962			39	347	8.9	27	0
1963			22	167	7.6	23	1
1964	PIT	N	12	113	9.4	41	0
1965			3	22	7.3	21	0
Career			190	1793	9.4	53	3

Barry Pearson

Year	Team		No	Yds	Avg	Lg	TD
1973	PIT	N	23	317	13.8	46t	3
1974	KC	N	27	387	14.3	48	1
1975			36	608	16.9	45	3
Career			86	1312	15.3	48	7
Playoffs			2	7	3.5		1

Dennis Pearson

Year	Team		No	Yds	Avg	Lg	TD
1978	ATL	N	5	71	14.2	23	0
1979			7	119	17.0	40	0
Career			12	190	15.8	40	0
Playoffs			1	13	13.0		0

Drew Pearson

Year	Team		No	Yds	Avg	Lg	TD
1973	DAL	N	22	388	17.6	40	2
1974			62	1087	17.5	50t	2
1975			46	822	17.9	46t	8
1976			58	806	13.9	40t	6
1977			48	870	18.1	67	2
1978			44	714	16.2	53t	3
1979			55	1026	18.7	56t	8
1980			43	568	13.2	30	6
1981			38	614	16.2	42t	3
1982			26	382	14.7	48	3
1983			47	545	11.6	32	5
Career			489	7822	16.0	67	48
Playoffs			69	1131	16.4		8

Lindy Pearson

Year	Team		No	Yds	Avg	Lg	TD
1950	DET	N	1	4	4.0	4	0
1951			5	43	8.6	14	0
1952	GB	N	1	16	16.0	16	0
Career			7	63	9.0	16	0

Preston Pearson

Year	Team		No	Yds	Avg	Lg	TD
1968	BAL	N	2	70	35.0	61t	2
1969			4	64	16.0	37	0
1970	PIT	N	6	71	11.8	18	0
1971			20	246	12.3	41	2
1972			11	79	7.2	15	0
1973			11	173	15.7	36	2
1974			11	118	10.7	31	0
1975	DAL	N	27	351	13.0	49	2
1976			23	316	13.7	30	2
1977			46	535	11.6	36t	4
1978			47	526	11.2	34	0
1979			26	333	12.8	26t	1
1980			20	213	10.7	20	2
Career			254	3095	12.2	61t	17
Playoffs			45	529	11.8		3

George Pease

Year	Team		No	Yds	Avg	Lg	TD
1926	NY	A					1
1929	ORA	N					1
Career							2

Danny Peebles

Year	Team		No	Yds	Avg	Lg	TD
1989	TB	N	11	180	16.4	32	0
1990			6	50	8.3	18	1
Career			17	230	13.5	32	1

Jim Peebles

Year	Team		No	Yds	Avg	Lg	TD
1946	WAS	N	9	164	18.2	35	1
1947			4	26	6.5	11	0
Career			13	190	14.6	35	1

Brian Peets

Year	Team		No	Yds	Avg	Lg	TD
1978	SEA	N	1	14	14.0	14	0
1979			25	293	11.7	28	1
1981	SF	N	1	5	5.0	5	0
Career			27	312	11.6	28	1

Erric Pegram

Year	Team		No	Yds	Avg	Lg	TD
1991	ATL	N	1	-1	-1.0	-1	0
1992			2	25	12.5	19	0

Erric Pegram continued

Year	Team		No	Yds	Avg	Lg	TD
1993			33	302	9.2	30	0
1994			16	99	6.2	28	0
1995	PIT	N	26	206	7.9	22	1
1996			17	112	6.6	14	0
Career			95	743	7.8	30	1
Playoffs			4	29	7.3		0

Ray Pelfrey

Year	Team		No	Yds	Avg	Lg	TD
1951	GB	N	38	462	12.2	49t	5
1952	DAL-CHIC	N	20	264	13.2	48	2
1953	NYG	N	17	233	13.7	60t	3
Career			75	959	12.8	60t	10

Bill Pellington

Year	Team		No	Yds	Avg	Lg	TD
1955	BAL	N	1	10	10.0	10	0
1958			1	-1	-1.0	-1	0
Career			2	9	4.5	10	0

Chris Penn

Year	Team		No	Yds	Avg	Lg	TD
1994	KC	N	3	24	8.0	13	0
1995			1	12	12.0	12	0
1996			49	628	12.8	22	5
Career			53	664	12.5	22	5

Carlos Pennywell

Year	Team		No	Yds	Avg	Lg	TD
1978	NE	N	1	28	28.0	28	0
1979			4	35	8.8	13t	1
1980			4	31	7.8	16	1
1981			3	49	16.3	22t	1
Career			12	143	11.9	28	3

Leon Pense

Year	Team		No	Yds	Avg	Lg	TD
1945	PIT	N	1	32	32.0	32	0

Mac Percival

Year	Team		No	Yds	Avg	Lg	TD
1970	CHI	N	1	19	19.0	19	0

Willard Perdue

Year	Team		No	Yds	Avg	Lg	TD
1940	NYG	N	2	28	14.0		0

John Pergine

Year	Team		No	Yds	Avg	Lg	TD
1975	WAS	N	2	41	20.5	30t	1

Bob Perina

Year	Team		No	Yds	Avg	Lg	TD
1947	BKN	AA	9	67	7.4		1
1948	CHI	AA	2	13	6.5		0
1949	CHIB	N	3	33	11.0	14	0
Career			14	113	8.1	14	1

Pete Perini

Year	Team		No	Yds	Avg	Lg	TD
1954	CHIB	N	5	56	11.2	20	0
1955			1	3	3.0	3	0
Career			6	59	9.8	20	0

Art Perkins

Year	Team		No	Yds	Avg	Lg	TD
1962	LA	N	14	83	5.9	13	0
1963			8	61	7.6	17	0
Career			22	144	6.5	17	0

Bruce Perkins

Year	Team		No	Yds	Avg	Lg	TD
1990	TB	N	8	85	10.6	34	2
1991	IND	N	3	-2	-0.7	3	0
Career			11	83	7.5	34	2

Don Perkins

Year	Team		No	Yds	Avg	Lg	TD
1961	DAL	N	32	298	9.3	38	1
1962			13	104	8.0	21	0
1963			14	84	6.0	19	0
1964			15	155	10.3	37	0
1965			14	142	10.1	27	0
1966			23	231	10.0	39	0
1967			18	116	6.4	15	0
1968			17	180	10.6	24	2
Career			146	1310	9.0	39	3
Playoffs			1	4	4.0		0

Don Perkins

Year	Team		No	Yds	Avg	Lg	TD
1944	GB	N	1	1	1.0	1	0
1945	GB-CHIB	N	2	11	5.5	10	0
1946	CHIB	N	2	41	20.5	21	0
Career			5	53	10.6	21	0

Johnny Perkins

Year	Team		No	Yds	Avg	Lg	TD
1977	NYG	N	20	279	13.9	54	0

Year	Team		No	Yds	Avg	Lg	TD

Johnny Perkins *continued*

Year	Team		No	Yds	Avg	Lg	TD
1978			32	514	16.1	67t	3
1979			20	337	16.9	38t	4
1980			14	193	13.8	58t	3
1981			51	858	16.8	80	6
1982			26	430	16.5	35	2
Career			163	2611	16.0	80	18
Playoffs			8	132	16.5		2

Ray Perkins

Year	Team		No	Yds	Avg	Lg	TD
1967	BAL	N	16	302	18.9	57	2
1968			15	227	15.1	29	1
1969			28	391	14.0	47t	3
1970			10	194	19.4	41t	1
1971			24	424	17.7	64	4
Career			93	1538	16.5	64	11
Playoffs			6	109	18.2		1

Brett Perriman

Year	Team		No	Yds	Avg	Lg	TD
1988	NO	N	16	215	13.4	33	2
1989			20	356	17.8	47	0
1990			36	382	10.6	29	2
1991	DET	N	52	668	12.8	42	1
1992			69	810	11.7	40t	4
1993			49	496	10.1	34	2
1994			56	761	13.6	39	4
1995			108	1488	13.8	91t	9
1996			94	1021	10.9	44	5
Career			500	6197	12.4	91t	29
Playoffs			26	310	11.9		2

Lonnie Perrin

Year	Team		No	Yds	Avg	Lg	TD
1976	DEN	N	4	35	8.8	15	0
1977			6	106	17.7	41t	1
1978			10	54	5.4	13	1
1979	CHI	N	1	27	27.0	27	0
Career			21	222	10.6	41t	2
Playoffs			5	29	5.8		0

Mike Perrotti

Year	Team		No	Yds	Avg	Lg	TD
1948	LA	AA	0	7		7L	0

Joe Perry

Year	Team		No	Yds	Avg	Lg	TD
1948	SF	AA	8	79	9.9		1
1949			11	146	13.3		3
1950	SF	N	13	69	5.3	16	1
1951			18	167	9.3	35	1
1952			15	81	5.4	17	0
1953			19	191	10.1	60t	3
1954			26	203	7.8	70	0
1955			19	55	2.9	19	1
1956			18	104	5.8	20	0
1957			15	130	8.7	17	0
1958			23	218	9.5	64t	1
1959			12	53	4.4	15	0
1960			3	-3	-1.0	3	0
1961	BAL	N	34	322	9.5	27	1
1962			22	194	8.8	32	0
1963	SF	N	4	12	3.0	8	0
Career			260	2021	7.8	70	12

Leon Perry

Year	Team		No	Yds	Avg	Lg	TD
1980	NYG	N	8	84	10.5	25	1
1981			13	140	10.8	24	1
1982			1	-1	-1.0	-1	0
Career			22	223	10.1	25	2

Lowell Perry

Year	Team		No	Yds	Avg	Lg	TD
1956	PIT	N	14	334	23.9	75t	2

Mario Perry

Year	Team		No	Yds	Avg	Lg	TD
1987	LARI	N	1	3	3.0	3t	1

William Perry

Year	Team		No	Yds	Avg	Lg	TD
1985	CHI	N	1	4	4.0	4t	1

Bob Perryman

Year	Team		No	Yds	Avg	Lg	TD
1987	NE	N	3	13	4.3	7	0
1988			17	134	7.9	18	0
1989			29	195	6.7	16	0
1990			15	88	5.9	15	0
1991	DEN	N	17	171	10.1	24	0
1992			2	15	7.5	9	0
Career			83	616	7.4	24	0

John Petchel

Year	Team		No	Yds	Avg	Lg	TD
1942	CLE	N	1	16	16.0	16	0
1944			1	43	43.0	43t	1
1945	PIT	N	2	25	12.5	21	0
Career			4	84	21.0	43t	1

Bill Peterson

Year	Team		No	Yds	Avg	Lg	TD
1968	CIN	A	1	10	10.0	10	0

Ken Peterson

Year	Team		No	Yds	Avg	Lg	TD
1936	DET	N	8	38	4.8		0

Les Peterson

Year	Team		No	Yds	Avg	Lg	TD
1933	BKN	N	13	170	13.1		0

Nelson Peterson

Year	Team		No	Yds	Avg	Lg	TD
1938	CLE	N	4	43	10.8		1

Johnny Petitbon

Year	Team		No	Yds	Avg	Lg	TD
1952	DAL	N	1	11	11.0	11	0

Neal Petties

Year	Team		No	Yds	Avg	Lg	TD
1964	BAL	N	2	20	10.0	15t	1

John Petty

Year	Team		No	Yds	Avg	Lg	TD
1942	CHIB	N	4	53	13.3	16	0

Bob Pfohl

Year	Team		No	Yds	Avg	Lg	TD
1948	BAL	AA	13	134	10.3		1
1949			7	62	8.9		0
Career			20	196	9.8		1

Don Phelps

Year	Team		No	Yds	Avg	Lg	TD
1950	CLE	N	1	28	28.0	28	0

Ewell Phillips

Year	Team		No	Yds	Avg	Lg	TD
1936	NYG	N	1	5	5.0	5	0

Jason Phillips

Year	Team		No	Yds	Avg	Lg	TD
1989	DET	N	30	352	11.7	55t	1
1990			8	112	14.0	29	0
1991	ATL	N	6	73	12.2	24	0
1992			4	26	6.5	8	1
1993			1	15	15.0	15	0
Career			49	578	11.8	55t	2
Playoffs			1	11	11.0		0

Jess Phillips

Year	Team		No	Yds	Avg	Lg	TD
1969	CIN	A	13	128	9.8	31	0
1970	CIN	N	31	124	4.0	17	1
1971			22	125	5.7	19	1
1972			10	50	5.0	15	0
1973	NO	N	22	169	7.7	34	0
1974			11	55	5.0	17	0
1975	OAK	N	4	25	6.3	22	0
1976	NE	N	1	18	18.0	18	0
Career			114	694	6.1	34	2
Playoffs			2	12	6.0		0

Jim Phillips

Year	Team		No	Yds	Avg	Lg	TD
1958	LA	N	35	524	15.0	93t	2
1959			37	541	14.6	64	4
1960			52	883	17.0	61t	8
1961			78	1092	14.0	69t	5
1962			60	875	14.6	65t	5
1963			54	793	14.7	52	1
1964			17	245	14.4	33	2
1965	MIN	N	15	185	12.3	43	1
1966			32	554	17.3	68t	3
1967			21	352	16.8	42	3
Career			401	6044	15.1	93t	34

Kirk Phillips

Year	Team		No	Yds	Avg	Lg	TD
1984	DAL	N	1	6	6.0	6	0

Lawrence Phillips

Year	Team		No	Yds	Avg	Lg	TD
1996	STL	N	8	28	3.5	11t	1

Rod Phillips

Year	Team		No	Yds	Avg	Lg	TD
1975	LA	N	2	10	5.0	8	0
1976			4	23	5.8	15	0
1977			1	5	5.0	5	0
1978			7	48	6.9	16	0
Career			14	86	6.1	16	0
Playoffs			2	0	0.0		0

Dean Phillpot

Year	Team		No	Yds	Avg	Lg	TD
1958	CHIC	N	4	30	7.5	12	0

Alex Piasecky

Year	Team		No	Yds	Avg	Lg	TD
1943	WAS	N	3	17	5.7	7	1
1944			8	77	9.6	18	0
1945			1	18	18.0	18	0
Career			12	112	9.3	18	1
Playoffs			1	22	22.0		0

Brian Piccolo

Year	Team		No	Yds	Avg	Lg	TD
1967	CHI	N	13	103	7.9	25	0
1968			28	291	10.4	44	0
1969			17	143	8.4	25t	1
Career			58	537	9.3	44	1

Lou Piccone

Year	Team		No	Yds	Avg	Lg	TD
1975	NYJ	N	7	79	11.3	21	0
1976			12	147	12.3	23	0
1977	BUF	N	17	240	14.1	25	2
1978			7	71	10.1	15	2
1979			33	556	16.8	49	2
1980			7	82	11.7	16	0
1981			5	65	13.0	16	0
1982			12	140	11.7	29	0
Career			100	1380	13.8	49	6

Bob Pickard

Year	Team		No	Yds	Avg	Lg	TD
1974	DET	N	8	88	11.0	18	1

Carl Pickens

Year	Team		No	Yds	Avg	Lg	TD
1992	CIN	N	26	326	12.5	38	1
1993			43	565	13.1	36	6
1994			71	1127	15.9	70t	11
1995			99	1234	12.5	68t	17
1996			100	1180	11.8	61t	12
Career			339	4432	13.1	70t	47

Clay Pickering

Year	Team		No	Yds	Avg	Lg	TD
1987	NE	N	1	10	10.0	10	0

Aaron Pierce

Year	Team		No	Yds	Avg	Lg	TD
1993	NYG	N	12	212	17.7	54	0
1994			20	214	10.7	29	4
1995			33	310	9.4	26	0
1996			11	144	13.1	30	1
Career			76	880	11.6	54	5
Playoffs			2	15	7.5		0

Danny Pierce

Year	Team		No	Yds	Avg	Lg	TD
1970	WAS	N	1	6	6.0	6	0

Steve Pierce

Year	Team		No	Yds	Avg	Lg	TD
1987	CLE	N	2	21	10.5	13	0

Nick Pietrosante

Year	Team		No	Yds	Avg	Lg	TD
1959	DET	N	16	140	8.8	20	0
1960			13	129	9.9	28	0
1961			26	315	12.1	76	0
1962			26	251	9.7	26	2
1963			16	173	10.8	24	0
1964			19	152	8.0	20	0
1965			18	163	9.1	54	0
1966	CLE	N	1	12	12.0	12	0
1967			6	56	9.3	23	0
Career			141	1391	9.9	76	2

Bert Piggott

Year	Team		No	Yds	Avg	Lg	TD
1947	LA	AA	7	63	9.0		1

Pete Pihos

Year	Team		No	Yds	Avg	Lg	TD
1947	PHI	N	23	382	16.6	66t	7
1948			46	766	16.7	48	11
1949			34	484	14.2	49	4
1950			38	447	11.8	43	6
1951			35	536	15.3	38t	5
1952			12	219	18.3	47	1
1953			63	1049	16.7	59	10
1954			60	872	14.5	34	10
1955			62	864	13.9	49t	7
Career			373	5619	15.1	66t	61
Playoffs			6	76	12.7		1

Joe Pilconis

Year	Team		No	Yds	Avg	Lg	TD
1936	PHI	N	4	51	12.8		1

Year	Team		No	Yds	Avg	Lg	TD

Joe Pilconis *continued*
| 1937 | | | 6 | 59 | 9.8 | | 0 |
| Career | | | 10 | 110 | 11.0 | | 1 |

Frank Pillow
1988	TB	N	15	206	13.7	34	1
1990			8	118	14.8	23	0
Career			23	324	14.1	34	1

Erny Pinckert
1935	BOS	N	5	60	12.0		0
1936			1	17	17.0	17	0
1937	WAS	N	10	145	14.5		1
1938			3	20	6.7		0
1940			2	27	13.5		0
Career			21	269	12.8		1
Playoffs			1	18	18.0		0

Stan Pincura
1937	CLE	N	12	139	11.6		0
1938			6	72	12.0		1
Career			18	211	11.7		1

Cyril Pinder
1968	PHI	N	16	166	10.4	48	0
1969			12	77	6.4	20t	0
1970			28	249	8.9	27	0
1971	CHI	N	10	51	5.1	14	0
1972			1	13	13.0	13	0
Career			67	556	8.3	48	0

Allen Pinkett
1986	HOU	N	35	248	7.1	20	1
1987			1	7	7.0	7	0
1988			12	114	9.5	51t	2
1989			31	239	7.7	23	1
1990			11	85	7.7	38	0
1991			29	228	7.9	36t	1
Career			119	921	7.7	51t	5
Playoffs			10	87	8.7		1

Lovell Pinkney
| 1995 | STL | N | 1 | 13 | 13.0 | 13 | 0 |

Ray Pinney
1981	PIT	N	1	1	1.0	1t	1
1982			1	3	3.0	3t	1
Career			2	4	2.0	3t	2

Joyce Pipkin
| 1948 | NYG | N | 2 | 28 | 14.0 | 17 | 0 |

Woody Pippens
| 1987 | KC | N | 2 | 12 | 6.0 | 7 | 0 |

Hank Piro
| 1941 | PHI | N | 10 | 141 | 14.1 | 26 | 1 |

Rocco Pirro
| 1941 | PIT | N | 2 | 31 | 15.5 | 19 | 0 |

Danny Pittman
1980	NYG	N	25	308	12.3	22	0
1981			1	8	8.0	8	0
1982			1	21	21.0	21	0
1983	NYG-STL	N	9	175	19.4	40t	1
1984	STL	N	10	145	14.5	50	0
Career			46	657	14.3	50	1

Elijah Pitts
1961	GB	N	1	5	5.0	5	0
1962			3	44	14.7	29	0
1963			9	54	6.0	21	1
1964			6	38	6.3	22	0
1965			11	182	16.5	80t	1
1966			26	460	17.7	80	3
1967			15	210	14.0	84	0
1968			17	142	8.4	19	0
1969			9	47	5.2	21t	1
1970	NO	N	7	63	9.0	12	0
Career			104	1245	12.0	84	6
Playoffs			3	49	16.3		1

Frank Pitts
1965	KC	A	1	11	11.0	11	0
1966			1	11	11.0	11	0
1967			4	131	32.8	59t	1
1968			30	655	21.8	90t	6
1969			31	470	15.2	51	2
1970	KC	N	11	172	15.6	54t	2
1971	CLE	N	27	487	18.0	53t	4
1972			36	620	17.2	80t	8
1973			31	317	10.2	26t	4
1974	OAK	N	3	23	7.7	11	0
Career			175	2897	16.6	90t	27
Playoffs			11	129	11.7		0

Dave Pivec
1967	LA	N	2	2	1.0	2t	1
1968			3	27	9.0	12	0
1969	DEN	A	9	117	13.0	18	0
Career			14	146	10.4	18	1

Tony Plansky
| 1929 | NYG | N | | | | | 1 |

Jerry Planutis
| 1956 | WAS | N | 1 | 5 | 5.0 | 5 | 0 |

Dick Plasman
1937	CHIB	N	3	18	6.0		1
1938			8	117	14.6		1
1939			19	403	21.2		3
1940			11	245	22.3		2
1941			14	283	20.2	42	0
1944			1	17	17.0	17	0
Career			56	1083	19.3	42	7
Playoffs			4	92	23.0		0

George Platukas
1938	PIT	N	4	82	20.5		0
1939			7	170	24.3		3
1940			15	290	19.3		2
1941			2	15	7.5	11	0
1942	CLE	N	5	64	12.8	22	1
Career			33	621	18.8	22	6

Marquis Pleasant
| 1987 | CIN | N | 2 | 45 | 22.5 | 35 | 0 |

Milt Plum
| 1959 | CLE | N | 1 | 20 | 20.0 | 20 | 0 |

Gary Plummer
| 1990 | SD | N | 1 | 2 | 2.0 | 2t | 1 |

Warren Plunkett
| 1942 | CLE | N | 2 | 16 | 8.0 | 18 | 0 |

Ray Poage
1963	MIN	N	15	354	23.6	67t	2
1964	PHI	N	37	479	12.9	42t	1
1965			31	612	19.7	63t	5
1967	NO	N	24	380	15.8	65	0
1968			1	11	11.0	11	0
1969			18	236	13.1	29	0
1970			15	166	11.1	36t	1
1971	ATL	N	4	71	17.8	31	0
Career			145	2309	15.9	67t	13

Ed Podolak
1970	KC	N	26	307	11.8	59t	1
1971			36	252	7.0	23	0
1972			46	345	7.5	27t	2
1973			55	445	8.1	25	0
1974			43	306	7.1	26	1
1975			37	332	9.0	21	2
1976			13	156	12.0	23	0
1977			32	313	9.8	23	0
Career			288	2456	8.5	59t	6
Playoffs			8	110	13.8		1

Jim Podoley
1957	WAS	N	27	554	20.5	82t	4
1958			16	381	23.8	66	4
1959			18	282	15.7	48	2

Jim Podoley *continued*
| 1960 | | | 17 | 244 | 14.4 | 41 | 1 |
| Career | | | 78 | 1461 | 18.7 | 82t | 11 |

Dick Poillon
1946	WAS	N	7	114	16.3	33	0
1947			20	250	12.5	30	4
1948			9	105	11.7	21	1
1949			1	8	8.0	8	0
Career			37	477	12.9	33	5

John Polanski
| 1946 | LA | AA | 2 | 15 | 7.5 | | 1 |

Al Pollard
1951	NYY-PHI	N	3	35	11.7	18	0
1952	PHI	N	8	59	7.4	14	0
1953			7	33	4.7	24	0
Career			18	127	7.1	24	0

Frank Pollard
1981	PIT	N	19	156	8.2	26	0
1982			6	39	6.5	11	0
1983			16	127	7.9	17	0
1984			21	186	8.9	18	0
1985			24	250	10.4	20	0
1986			2	15	7.5	10	0
1987			14	77	5.5	17	0
1988			2	22	11.0	19	0
Career			104	872	8.4	26	0
Playoffs			9	90	10.0		0

Fritz Pollard
1920	AKR	A					1
1921							1
Career							2

Marcus Pollard
| 1996 | IND | N | 6 | 86 | 14.3 | 48t | 1 |

Red Pollock
1935	CHIB	N	7	135	19.3		1
1936			1	15	15.0	15	0
Career			8	150	18.8	15	1

Fran Polsfoot
1950	CHIC	N	38	653	17.2	81t	6
1951			57	796	14.0	80t	4
1953	WAS	N	11	164	14.9	66	0
Career			106	1613	15.2	81t	10

Hamp Pool
1940	CHIB	N	2	55	27.5		0
1941			5	101	20.2	56	1
1942			10	321	32.1	64	5
1943			18	363	20.2	42	5
1946	MIA	AA	3	63	21.0		0
Career			38	903	23.8	64	11
Playoffs			2	21	10.5		0

Barney Poole
1949	B-NY	AA	6	83	13.8		0
1952	DAL	N	2	23	11.5	15	0
Career			8	106	13.3	15	0

Bob Poole
1964	SF	N	1	8	8.0	8	0
1965			2	29	14.5	15	0
1966	HOU	A	12	131	10.9	19	0
1967			4	55	13.8	18	0
Career			19	223	11.7	19	0

Jim Poole
1937	NYG	N	5	79	15.8		2
1938			7	98	14.0		1
1939			7	99	14.1		0
1940			10	156	15.6		3
1941			6	74	12.3	16	2
1945	CHIC	N	6	82	13.7	29t	2
1946	NYG	N	24	307	12.8	31t	3
Career			65	895	13.8	31t	13
Playoffs			4	40	10.0		0

Year	Team		No	Yds	Avg	Lg	TD

Larry Poole

Year	Team		No	Yds	Avg	Lg	TD
1975	CLE	N	1	5	5.0	5	0
1976			14	70	5.0	21	0
1977			17	137	8.1	21	3
Career			32	212	6.6	21	3

Nathan Poole

Year	Team		No	Yds	Avg	Lg	TD
1979	CIN	N	1	-10	-10.0	-10	0
1980			2	-4	-2.0	3	0
1983	DEN	N	20	184	9.2	23	0
1987			1	9	9.0	9	0
Career			24	179	7.5	23	0
Playoffs			4	17	4.3		

Ollie Poole

Year	Team		No	Yds	Avg	Lg	TD
1947	NY	AA	1	19	19.0	19	0
1948	BAL	AA	1	2	2.0	2	0
Career			2	21	10.5	19	0

Ray Poole

Year	Team		No	Yds	Avg	Lg	TD
1947	NYG	N	23	395	17.2	61	4
1948			35	492	14.1	51	3
1949			25	277	11.1	40	1
1950	NYY	N	4	82	20.5	52t	1
Career			87	1246	14.3	61	9

Bucky Pope

Year	Team		No	Yds	Avg	Lg	TD
1964	LA	N	25	786	31.4	95t	10
1966			1	14	14.0	14t	1
1967			8	152	19.0	48t	2
Career			34	952	28.0	95t	13
Playoffs			1	12	12.0		0

Johnny Popovich

Year	Team		No	Yds	Avg	Lg	TD
1944	C-P	N	3	1	0.3	1	0

Milt Popovich

Year	Team		No	Yds	Avg	Lg	TD
1938	CHIC	N	1	8	8.0	8	0
1939			2	10	5.0		0
1940			5	32	6.4		0
1942			2	21	10.5	12	0
Career			10	71	7.1	12	0

Ted Popson

Year	Team		No	Yds	Avg	Lg	TD
1994	SF	N	13	141	10.8	24	0
1995			16	128	8.0	16	0
1996			26	301	11.6	39t	6
Career			55	570	10.4	39t	6
Playoffs			4	15	3.8		

Kerry Porter

Year	Team		No	Yds	Avg	Lg	TD
1990	DEN	N	4	44	11.0	16	0

Lewis Porter

Year	Team		No	Yds	Avg	Lg	TD
1970	KC	N	1	29	29.0	29	0

Ricky Porter

Year	Team		No	Yds	Avg	Lg	TD
1987	BUF	N	9	70	7.8	26	0
Playoffs			2	31	15.5		

Tracy Porter

Year	Team		No	Yds	Avg	Lg	TD
1981	DET	N	3	63	21.0	27t	1
1982			9	124	13.8	23	0
1983	BAL	N	28	384	13.7	38	0
1984	IND	N	39	590	15.1	63t	2
Career			79	1161	14.7	63t	3

Dickie Post

Year	Team		No	Yds	Avg	Lg	TD
1967	SD	A	32	278	8.7	66t	1
1968			18	165	9.2	23	0
1969			24	235	9.8	46	0
1970	SD	N	13	113	8.7	30	0
1971	DEN-HOU	N	9	112	12.4	28	1
Career			96	903	9.4	66t	2

Johnny Poto

Year	Team		No	Yds	Avg	Lg	TD
1948	BOS	N	10	101	10.1	19	0

Roosevelt Potts

Year	Team		No	Yds	Avg	Lg	TD
1993	IND	N	26	189	7.3	24	0
1994			26	251	9.7	30	1
1995			21	228	10.9	52	1
Career			73	668	9.2	52	2

Ernie Pough

Year	Team		No	Yds	Avg	Lg	TD
1976	PIT	N	8	161	20.1	50	1
1977			1	3	3.0	3	0
1978	NYG	N	1	2	2.0	2	0
Career			10	166	16.6	50	1

Karl Powe

Year	Team		No	Yds	Avg	Lg	TD
1985	DAL	N	14	237	16.9	34	0
Playoffs			1	19	19.0		0

Art Powell

Year	Team		No	Yds	Avg	Lg	TD
1960	NY	A	69	1167	16.9		14
1961			71	881	12.4	48	5
1962			64	1130	17.7	80	8
1963	OAK	A	73	1304	17.9	85	16
1964			76	1361	17.9	77	11
1965			52	800	15.4	66	12
1966			53	1026	19.4	46	11
1967	BUF	A	20	346	17.3	37t	4
1968	MIN	N	1	31	31.0	31	0
Career			479	8046	16.8	85	81

Charley Powell

Year	Team		No	Yds	Avg	Lg	TD
1957	SF	N	1	27	27.0	27	0

Darnell Powell

Year	Team		No	Yds	Avg	Lg	TD
1976	BUF	N	1	6	6.0	6	0

John Powers

Year	Team		No	Yds	Avg	Lg	TD
1962	PIT	N	1	16	16.0	16	0
1964			8	193	24.1	42	0
Career			9	209	23.2	42	0

Ricky Powers

Year	Team		No	Yds	Avg	Lg	TD
1995	CLE	N	1	6	6.0	6	0

Phil Pozderac

Year	Team		No	Yds	Avg	Lg	TD
1984	DAL	N	1	1	1.0	1	0

Bob Pratt

Year	Team		No	Yds	Avg	Lg	TD
1984	SEA	N	1	30	30.0	30	0
Playoffs			1	-3	-3.0		0

Gene Prebola

Year	Team		No	Yds	Avg	Lg	TD
1960	OAK	A	33	404	12.2		2
1961	DEN	A	29	349	12.0	54	1
1962			41	599	14.6	55	1
1963			30	471	15.7	57	2
Career			133	1823	13.7	57	6

Hal Prescott

Year	Team		No	Yds	Avg	Lg	TD
1946	GB	N	1	8	8.0	8	0
1947	PHI	N	1	15	15.0	15	0
1949	NYB	N	10	162	16.2	41	1
Career			12	185	15.4	41	1

Glenn Presnell

Year	Team		No	Yds	Avg	Lg	TD
1932	POR	N					1
1935	DET	N					1
Career							2

Dave Preston

Year	Team		No	Yds	Avg	Lg	TD
1978	DEN	N	24	199	8.3	21	1
1979			19	137	7.2	19	1
1980			35	309	8.8	36	0
1981			52	507	9.8	37	0
1982			14	134	9.6	20	0
1983			17	137	8.1	25	1
Career			161	1423	8.8	37	3
Playoffs			6	59	9.8		1

Roell Preston

Year	Team		No	Yds	Avg	Lg	TD
1995	ATL	N	7	129	18.4	61t	1
1996			21	208	9.9	17t	1
Career			28	337	12.0	61t	2

Charley Price

Year	Team		No	Yds	Avg	Lg	TD
1941	DET	N	1	6	6.0	6	0
1946	MIA	AA	2	17	8.5		0
Career			3	23	7.7	6	0

Derek Price

Year	Team		No	Yds	Avg	Lg	TD
1996	DET	N	1	14	14.0	14	0

Eddie Price

Year	Team		No	Yds	Avg	Lg	TD
1950	NYG	N	4	30	7.5	21	0
1951			5	19	3.8	8	0
1952			11	36	3.3	14	0
1953			26	233	9.0	31t	1
1954			28	352	12.6	83t	3
1955			1	2	2.0	2	0
Career			75	672	9.0	83t	4

Jim Price

Year	Team		No	Yds	Avg	Lg	TD
1991	LARM	N	35	410	11.7	27	2
1992			34	324	9.5	25	2
1993	DAL	N	1	4	4.0	4	0
1995	STL	N	4	29	7.3	24	0
Career			74	767	10.4	27	4

Sam Price

Year	Team		No	Yds	Avg	Lg	TD
1966	MIA	A	2	14	7.0	9	0
1967			8	56	7.0	27t	1
Career			10	70	7.0	27t	1

Billy Pricer

Year	Team		No	Yds	Avg	Lg	TD
1958	BAL	N	3	14	4.7	6	0
1959			2	3	1.5	4	0
1960			8	77	9.6	21	1
1961	DAL	A	2	21	10.5	11	0
Career			15	115	7.7	21	1
Playoffs			2	7	3.5		0

Bob Priestley

Year	Team		No	Yds	Avg	Lg	TD
1942	PHI	N	4	47	11.8	15	0

Greg Primus

Year	Team		No	Yds	Avg	Lg	TD
1994	CHI	N	3	25	8.3	12	0

James Primus

Year	Team		No	Yds	Avg	Lg	TD
1988	ATL	N	8	42	5.3	9	0

Dom Principe

Year	Team		No	Yds	Avg	Lg	TD
1941	NYG	N	4	54	13.5	28	0
1942			2	33	16.5	17	0
1946	BKN	AA	3	25	8.3		0
Career			9	112	12.4	28	0

Mike Prior

Year	Team		No	Yds	Avg	Lg	TD
1990	IND	N	1	40	40.0	40	0
1992			1	17	17.0	17	0
Career			2	57	28.5	40	0

Bill Pritchard

Year	Team		No	Yds	Avg	Lg	TD
1928	NYY	N					1

Bosh Pritchard

Year	Team		No	Yds	Avg	Lg	TD
1942	CLE-PHI	N	2	4	2.0	4	0
1946	PHI	N	14	309	22.1	59t	3
1947			16	315	19.7	69t	3
1948			27	252	9.3	34t	2
1949			8	185	23.1	75	2
1951			8	103	12.9	38	0
Career			75	1168	15.6	69t	10
Playoffs			4	48	12.0		0

Mike Pritchard

Year	Team		No	Yds	Avg	Lg	TD
1991	ATL	N	50	624	12.5	29	2
1992			77	827	10.7	38t	5
1993			74	736	9.9	34	7
1994	DEN	N	19	271	14.3	50t	1
1995			33	441	13.4	45t	2
1996	SEA	N	21	328	15.6	44	1
Career			274	3227	11.8	50t	19
Playoffs			10	119	11.9		0

Billy Pritchett

Year	Team		No	Yds	Avg	Lg	TD
1975	CLE	N	16	109	6.8	18	0
1976	ATL	N	1	1	1.0	1	0
Career			17	110	6.5	18	0

Stanley Pritchett

Year	Team		No	Yds	Avg	Lg	TD
1996	MIA	N	33	354	10.7	74t	2

Steve Pritko

Year	Team		No	Yds	Avg	Lg	TD
1943	NYG	N	1	12	12.0	12	0
1944	CLE	N	18	296	16.4	53t	3
1945			19	255	13.4	35	4

Steve Pritko *continued*

Year	Team		No	Yds	Avg	Lg	TD
1946	LA	N	18	185	10.3	29	2
1947			10	101	10.1	20	0
1948	BOS	N	3	42	14.0	29	0
1949	NYB-GB	N	7	98	14.0	24	2
1950	GB	N	17	125	7.4	14	2
Career			93	1114	12.0	53t	13
Playoffs			2	17	8.5		0

Ray Prochaska

Year	Team		No	Yds	Avg	Lg	TD
1941	CLE	N	4	29	7.3	11	0

Dewey Proctor

Year	Team		No	Yds	Avg	Lg	TD
1946	NY	AA	3	32	10.7		1
1947			1	4	4.0	4	0
1948	CHI	AA	2	18	9.0		0
Career			6	54	9.0	4	1

Ricky Proehl

Year	Team		No	Yds	Avg	Lg	TD
1990	PHX	N	56	802	14.3	45t	4
1991			55	766	13.9	62t	2
1992			60	744	12.4	63t	3
1993			65	877	13.5	51t	7
1994	ARI	N	51	651	12.8	63	5
1995	SEA	N	5	29	5.8	9	0
1996			23	309	13.4	56	2
Career			315	4178	13.3	63t	23

Joe Profit

Year	Team		No	Yds	Avg	Lg	TD
1972	ATL	N	3	22	7.3	14	0
1973	NO	N	11	108	9.8	26	0
Career			14	130	9.3	26	0

Eddie Prokop

Year	Team		No	Yds	Avg	Lg	TD
1946	NY	AA	5	52	10.4		1
1947			3	79	26.3		1
1948	CHI	AA	7	223	31.9	74t	3
1949	B-NY	AA	1	7	7.0	7	0
Career			16	361	22.6	74t	5
Playoffs			1	4	4.0		0

Fred Provo

Year	Team		No	Yds	Avg	Lg	TD
1948	GB	N	4	-9	-2.3	3	0

Greg Pruitt

Year	Team		No	Yds	Avg	Lg	TD
1973	CLE	N	9	110	12.2	42	1
1974			21	274	13.0	43	1
1975			44	299	6.8	48	1
1976			45	341	7.6	27	1
1977			37	471	12.7	60	1
1978			38	292	7.7	26t	2
1979			14	155	11.1	27	1
1980			50	444	8.9	43	5
1981			65	636	9.8	33	4
1982	LARI	N	2	29	14.5	23	1
1983			1	6	6.0	6	0
1984			2	12	6.0	8	0
Career			328	3069	9.4	60	18
Playoffs			5	68	13.6		0

James Pruitt

Year	Team		No	Yds	Avg	Lg	TD
1986	MIA	N	15	235	15.7	27	2
1987			26	404	15.5	37	3
1988			2	38	19.0	19	0
1989	IND	N	5	71	14.2	40	1
1990	MIA	N	13	235	18.1	35t	3
1991			2	30	15.0	24	0
Career			63	1013	16.1	40	9

Mike Pruitt

Year	Team		No	Yds	Avg	Lg	TD
1976	CLE	N	8	26	3.3	15	0
1977			3	12	4.0	6	0
1978			20	112	5.6	15	0
1979			41	372	9.1	50t	2
1980			63	471	7.5	28	0
1981			63	442	7.0	21	1
1982			22	140	6.4	13	0
1983			30	157	5.2	21	2
1984			5	29	5.8	9	0
1985	KC	N	7	43	6.1	9	0
1986			8	56	7.0	13	0
Career			270	1860	6.9	50t	5
Playoffs			3	17	5.7		0

Barry Pryor

Year	Team		No	Yds	Avg	Lg	TD
1969	MIA	A	2	-3	-1.5	0	0

Marion Pugh

Year	Team		No	Yds	Avg	Lg	TD
1946	MIA	AA	4	43	10.8		0

Alfred Pupunu

Year	Team		No	Yds	Avg	Lg	TD
1993	SD	N	13	142	10.9	28	0
1994			21	214	10.2	25	2
1995			35	315	9.0	26	0
1996			24	271	11.3	41	1
Career			93	942	10.1	41	3
Playoffs			13	163	12.5		2

Cal Purdin

Year	Team		No	Yds	Avg	Lg	TD
1943	CHIC	N	3	35	11.7	20	0
1946	BKN-MIA	AA	12	108	9.0		0
Career			15	143	9.5	20	0

Frank Purnell

Year	Team		No	Yds	Avg	Lg	TD
1957	GB	N	2	16	8.0	15	0

Bob Pylman

Year	Team		No	Yds	Avg	Lg	TD
1938	PHI	N	1	1	1.0	1	0

Frank Quayle

Year	Team		No	Yds	Avg	Lg	TD
1969	DEN	A	11	167	15.2	71	0

Jeff Queen

Year	Team		No	Yds	Avg	Lg	TD
1969	SD	A	10	148	14.8	42	0
1970	SD	N	20	236	11.8	65t	1
1971			23	270	11.7	54	3
1974	HOU	N	1	4	4.0	4t	1
Career			54	658	12.2	65t	5

Jeff Query

Year	Team		No	Yds	Avg	Lg	TD
1989	GB	N	23	350	15.2	45	2
1990			34	458	13.5	47t	2
1991			7	94	13.4	26	0
1992	CIN	N	16	265	16.6	83t	3
1993			56	654	11.7	51	4
1994			5	44	8.8	14	0
Career			141	1865	13.2	83t	11

Mike Quick

Year	Team		No	Yds	Avg	Lg	TD
1982	PHI	N	10	156	15.6	49t	1
1983			69	**1409**	20.4	83t	13
1984			61	1052	17.2	90t	9
1985			73	1247	17.1	99t	11
1986			60	939	15.7	75t	9
1987			46	790	17.2	61t	11
1988			22	508	23.1	55t	4
1989			13	228	17.5	40	2
1990			9	135	15.0	39	1
Career			363	6464	17.8	99t	61
Playoffs			5	82	16.4		0

Frank Quillen

Year	Team		No	Yds	Avg	Lg	TD
1946	CHI	AA	13	143	11.0		2
1947			7	113	16.1		1
Career			20	256	12.8		3

Skeets Quinlan

Year	Team		No	Yds	Avg	Lg	TD
1952	LA	N	14	265	18.9	80t	2
1953			17	260	15.3	59t	2
1954			18	324	18.0	80t	2
1955			19	245	12.9	46	0
1956	LA-CLE	N	7	87	12.4	31	0
Career			75	1181	15.7	80t	6
Playoffs			5	116	23.2		1

Ed Quirk

Year	Team		No	Yds	Avg	Lg	TD
1948	WAS	N	9	40	4.4	11	0
1949			5	33	6.6	15	0
Career			14	73	5.2	15	0

Bob Raba

Year	Team		No	Yds	Avg	Lg	TD
1979	NYJ	N	2	9	4.5	6	0

Bill Rademacher

Year	Team		No	Yds	Avg	Lg	TD
1966	NY	A	1	3	3.0	3	0
1968			2	11	5.5	6	0
1969	BOS	A	17	217	12.8	40	3

Bill Rademacher *continued*

Year	Team		No	Yds	Avg	Lg	TD
1970	BOS	N	4	51	12.8	16	0
Career			24	282	11.8	40	3

Tom Rafferty

Year	Team		No	Yds	Avg	Lg	TD
1983	DAL	N	1	8	8.0	8	0

George Ragsdale

Year	Team		No	Yds	Avg	Lg	TD
1977	TB	N	2	17	8.5	10	0
1978			3	41	13.7	31t	1
1979			3	28	9.3	19	0
Career			8	86	10.8	31t	1

Steve Raible

Year	Team		No	Yds	Avg	Lg	TD
1976	SEA	N	4	126	31.5	80t	1
1977			5	79	15.8	22	0
1978			22	316	14.4	38t	1
1979			20	252	12.6	41	1
1980			16	232	14.5	40	0
1981			1	12	12.0	12	0
Career			68	1017	15.0	80t	3

Derrick Ramsey

Year	Team		No	Yds	Avg	Lg	TD
1979	OAK	N	13	161	12.4	40	3
1980			5	117	23.4	58	0
1981			52	674	13.0	66t	4
1983	NE	N	24	335	14.0	39	6
1984			66	792	12.0	34	7
1985			28	285	10.2	26	1
Career			188	2364	12.6	66t	21
Playoffs			9	107	11.9		1

Herschel Ramsey

Year	Team		No	Yds	Avg	Lg	TD
1938	PHI	N	5	122	24.4		1
1939			31	359	11.6		1
1940			17	143	8.4		0
Career			53	624	11.8		2

Ray Ramsey

Year	Team		No	Yds	Avg	Lg	TD
1947	CHI	AA	35	768	21.9	80t	9
1948	CHI-BKN	AA	13	315	24.2	50t	2
1949	CHI	AA	17	366	21.5	77t	4
1951	CHIC	N	8	135	16.9	35	0
1952			3	27	9.0	13	0
1953			12	118	9.8	20	0
Career			88	1729	19.6	80t	15

Eason Ramson

Year	Team		No	Yds	Avg	Lg	TD
1978	STL	N	23	238	10.3	26	1
1980	SF	N	21	179	8.5	22	2
1981			4	45	11.3	16	0
1982			2	27	13.5	21	0
1983			17	125	7.4	16	1
1985	BUF	N	37	369	10.0	43	1
Career			104	983	9.5	43	5
Playoffs			5	62	12.4		0

Proc Randels

Year	Team		No	Yds	Avg	Lg	TD
1927	CLE	N					1
1928	DET	N					1
Career							2

Sonny Randle

Year	Team		No	Yds	Avg	Lg	TD
1959	CHIC	N	15	202	13.5	31	1
1960	STL	N	62	893	14.4	57t	**15**
1961			44	591	13.4	41	9
1962			63	1158	18.4	86t	7
1963			51	1014	19.9	68t	12
1964			25	517	20.7	50t	5
1965			51	845	16.6	72	9
1966			17	218	12.8	45	2
1967	SF	N	33	502	15.2	58	4
1968	SF-DAL	N	4	56	14.0	29t	1
Career			365	5996	16.4	86t	65

Walt Rankin

Year	Team		No	Yds	Avg	Lg	TD
1943	CHIC	N	10	44	4.4	17	0
1944	C-P	N	4	18	4.5	8	0
1945	CHIC	N	3	25	8.3	9	0
Career			17	87	5.1	17	0

Keith Ranspot

Year	Team		No	Yds	Avg	Lg	TD
1942	GB	N	1	25	25.0	25	1
1943	BKN	N	7	80	11.4	28	0

Year	Team		No	Yds	Avg	Lg	TD

Keith Ranspot *continued*

Year	Team		No	Yds	Avg	Lg	TD
1944	BOS	N	19	269	14.2	40	3
1945			8	117	14.6	30	0
Career			35	491	14.0	40	4

Bob Rapp

1923	COL	N					3
1924							4
1925							1
Career							8

Walter Rasby

1995	CAR	N	5	47	9.4	15	0

Ahmad Rashad

1972	STL	N	29	500	17.2	98	3
1973			30	409	13.6	65t	3
1974	BUF	N	36	433	12.0	29	4
1976	MIN	N	53	671	12.7	47	3
1977			51	681	13.4	48t	2
1978			66	769	11.7	58t	8
1979			80	1156	14.4	52t	9
1980			69	1095	15.9	76t	5
1981			58	884	15.2	53	7
1982			23	233	10.1	21	0
Career			495	6831	13.8	98	44
Playoffs			21	303	14.4		1

Kenyon Rasheed

1993	NYG	N	1	3	3.0	3	0
1994			10	97	9.7	22	0
1995	NYJ	N	2	15	7.5	9	0
Career			13	115	8.8	22	0

Bo Rather

1974	CHI	N	29	400	13.8	59t	3
1975			39	685	17.6	54	2
1976			5	33	6.6	7	0
1977			17	294	17.3	42t	2
1978	CHI-MIA	N	2	55	27.5	39	0
Career			92	1467	15.9	59t	7

Tom Rathman

1986	SF	N	13	121	9.3	14	0
1987			30	329	11.0	29	3
1988			42	382	9.1	24	0
1989			73	616	8.4	36	1
1990			48	327	6.8	28	0
1991			34	286	8.4	32	0
1992			44	343	7.8	27t	4
1993			10	86	8.6	17	0
1994	LARI	N	26	194	7.5	18	0
Career			320	2684	8.4	36	8
Playoffs			38	327	8.6		1

Bob Ravensburg

1949	CHIC	N	10	203	20.3	48	3

David Ray

1970	LA	N	1	11	11.0	11	0

Eddie Ray

1972	ATL	N	1	14	14.0	14	0
1973			19	192	10.1	39t	2
1974			10	43	4.3	10	0
1976	BUF	N	3	26	8.7	15	0
Career			33	275	8.3	39t	2

Jimmy Raye

1991	LARM	N	1	19	19.0	19	0

Frank Reagan

1946	NYG	N	4	71	17.8	36	0

Tommy Reamon

1976	KC	N	10	136	13.6	49t	1

Bert Rechichar

1953	BAL	N	3	151	50.3	66t	2
1958			4	34	8.5	12	1
Career			7	185	26.4	66t	3

Ron Rector

1966	WAS	N	2	9	4.5	6	0

Ron Rector *continued*

Year	Team		No	Yds	Avg	Lg	TD
1967	ATL	N	4	13	3.3	9	0
Career			6	22	3.7	9	0

Barry Redden

1982	LARM	N	4	16	4.0	11	0
1983			4	30	7.5	9	0
1984			4	39	9.8	6	0
1985			16	162	10.1	32	0
1986			28	217	7.8	24t	1
1987	SD	N	7	46	6.6	13	0
1988			1	11	11.0	11	0
1989	CLE	N	6	34	5.7	8	0
Career			70	555	7.9	32	1
Playoffs			2	35	17.5		0

Cornelius Redick

1987	GB	N	1	18	18.0	18	0

Jarvis Redwine

1983	MIN	N	1	4	4.0	4	0

Beasley Reece

1976	DAL	N	1	6	6.0	6	0

Danny Reece

1977	TB	N	2	59	29.5	45	0
1978			1	25	25.0	25	0
Career			3	84	28.0	45	0

Don Reece

1946	MIA	AA	1	5	5.0	5	0

Alvin Reed

1967	HOU	A	11	144	13.1	20	1
1968			46	747	16.2	60	5
1969			51	664	13.0	43t	2
1970	HOU	N	47	604	12.9	34	2
1971			25	408	16.3	36	1
1972			19	251	13.2	29	0
1973	WAS	N	9	124	13.8	34	0
1974			4	36	9.0	11t	1
1975			2	5	2.5	4t	2
Career			214	2983	13.9	60	14
Playoffs			11	141	12.8		1

Andre Reed

1985	BUF	N	48	637	13.3	32	4
1986			53	739	13.9	65t	7
1987			57	752	13.2	40	5
1988			71	968	13.6	65t	6
1989			88	1312	14.9	78t	9
1990			71	945	13.3	56t	8
1991			81	1113	13.7	55	10
1992			65	913	14.0	51	3
1993			52	854	16.4	65t	6
1994			90	1303	14.5	83t	8
1995			24	312	13.0	41t	3
1996			66	1036	15.7	67t	6
Career			766	10884	14.2	83t	75
Playoffs			80	1169	14.6		9

Bob Reed

1962	MIN	N	4	37	9.3	37t	1
1963			13	137	10.5	45	0
Career			17	174	10.2	45	1

Jake Reed

1992	MIN	N	6	142	23.7	51	0
1993			5	65	13.0	18	0
1994			85	1175	13.8	59	4
1995			72	1167	16.2	55t	9
1996			72	1320	18.3	82t	7
Career			240	3869	16.1	82t	20
Playoffs			6	65	10.8		0

J.T. Reed

1937	CHIC	N	2	26	13.0		0
1939			3	67	22.3		0
Career			5	93	18.6		0

Oscar Reed

1969	MIN	N	7	59	8.4	16	2
1970			6	53	8.8	19	0

Oscar Reed *continued*

Year	Team		No	Yds	Avg	Lg	TD
1971			15	138	9.2	26	0
1972			30	205	6.8	37	0
1973			19	122	6.4	13	0
1974			15	99	6.6	12	1
1975	ATL	N	2	1	0.5	1	0
Career			94	677	7.2	37	3
Playoffs			16	112	7.0		0

Smith Reed

1965	NYG	N	6	42	7.0	16	0

Tony Reed

1977	KC	N	12	125	10.4	20	0
1978			48	483	10.1	44	1
1979			34	352	10.4	40	0
1980			44	422	9.6	34	1
1981	DEN	N	34	317	9.3	33	0
Career			172	1699	9.9	44	2

Dan Reeder

1986	PIT	N	2	4	2.0	3	0

Dave Reese

1920	DAY	A					3

Bryan Reeves

1994	ARI	N	14	202	14.4	33	1
1995			6	62	10.3	22	0
Career			20	264	13.2	33	1

Dan Reeves

1965	DAL	N	9	210	23.3	47	1
1966			41	557	13.6	51t	8
1967			39	490	12.6	60t	6
1968			7	84	12.0	21	1
1969			18	187	10.4	29	1
1970			12	140	11.7	23	0
1971			3	25	8.3	11	0
Career			129	1693	13.1	60t	17
Playoffs			15	163	10.9		0

Walter Reeves

1989	PHX	N	1	5	5.0	5	0
1990			18	126	7.0	16	0
1991			8	45	5.6	13	0
1992			6	28	4.7	12	0
1993			9	67	7.4	18	1
1994	CLE	N	6	61	10.2	22	1
1995			6	12	2.0	3	1
1996	SD	N	1	3	3.0	3	0
Career			55	347	6.3	22	3

Bill Reichardt

1952	GB	N	5	18	3.6	12	0

Jerry Reichow

1956	DET	N	4	63	15.8	41t	1
1957			17	215	12.6	32t	3
1959			7	118	16.9	32	1
1961	MIN	N	50	859	17.2	51t	11
1962			39	561	14.4	41	3
1963			35	479	13.7	57t	3
1964			20	284	14.2	51	2
Career			172	2579	15.0	57t	24

Floyd Reid

1950	GB	N	11	120	10.9	44t	2
1951			9	115	12.8	29	0
1952			12	250	20.8	81t	2
1953			10	100	10.0	26	0
1954			14	129	9.2	25	0
1955			13	138	10.6	60t	1
1956			3	16	5.3	12	0
Career			72	868	12.1	81t	5

Dameon Reilly

1987	MIA	N	5	70	14.0	20	0

Billy Reinhard

1948	LA	AA	5	48	9.6		0

Bob Reinhard

1947	LA	AA	3	34	11.3		1

Bob Reinhard *continued*

Year	Team		No	Yds	Avg	Lg	TD
1949			1	2	2.0	2	0
1950	LA	N	1	11	11.0	11t	1
Career			5	47	9.4	11t	2

Albie Reisz

Year	Team		No	Yds	Avg	Lg	TD
1945	CLE	N	1	11	11.0	11	0

Reggie Rembert

Year	Team		No	Yds	Avg	Lg	TD
1991	CIN	N	9	117	13.0	23t	1
1992			19	219	11.5	27	0
1993			8	101	12.6	21	0
Career			36	437	12.1	27	1

Mel Renfro

Year	Team		No	Yds	Avg	Lg	TD
1966	DAL	N	4	65	16.3	42	0

Mike Renfro

Year	Team		No	Yds	Avg	Lg	TD
1978	HOU	N	26	339	13.0	58t	1
1979			16	323	20.2	49	2
1980			35	459	13.1	42	1
1981			39	451	11.6	43	1
1982			21	295	14.0	54t	3
1983			23	316	13.7	38t	2
1984	DAL	N	35	583	16.7	60t	4
1985			60	955	15.9	58t	8
1986			22	325	14.8	30t	3
1987			46	662	14.4	43	4
Career			323	4708	14.6	60t	28
Playoffs			7	168	24.0		1

Ray Renfro

Year	Team		No	Yds	Avg	Lg	TD
1952	CLE	N	1	8	8.0	8	0
1953			39	722	18.5	70	4
1954			13	228	17.5	64t	1
1955			29	603	**20.8**	61t	8
1956			17	325	19.1	46t	4
1957			21	589	**28.0**	65t	6
1958			24	573	23.9	52	6
1959			30	528	17.6	70t	6
1960			24	378	15.8	66t	4
1961			48	834	17.4	57	6
1962			31	638	20.6	65t	4
1963			4	82	20.5	39t	1
Career			281	5508	19.6	70t	50
Playoffs			13	195	15.0		3

Bobby Renn

Year	Team		No	Yds	Avg	Lg	TD
1961	NY	A	18	268	14.9	67	1

Pug Rentner

Year	Team		No	Yds	Avg	Lg	TD
1934	BOS	N					1
1936			4	33	8.3		0
1937	CHIB	N	6	101	16.8		1
Career			10	134	13.4		2
Playoffs			1	32	32.0		0

Lance Rentzel

Year	Team		No	Yds	Avg	Lg	TD
1966	MIN	N	2	10	5.0	8	0
1967	DAL		58	996	17.2	74t	8
1968			54	1009	18.7	65t	6
1969			43	960	**22.3**	75t	**12**
1970			28	556	19.9	86t	5
1971	LA	N	38	534	14.1	41	5
1972			27	365	13.5	40	1
1974			18	396	22.0	38	1
Career			268	4826	18.0	86t	38
Playoffs			11	242	22.0		2

Jay Repko

Year	Team		No	Yds	Avg	Lg	TD
1987	PHI	N	5	46	9.2	12	0

Pete Retzlaff

Year	Team		No	Yds	Avg	Lg	TD
1956	PHI	N	12	159	13.3	20	0
1957			10	120	12.0	28	0
1958			**56**	766	13.7	49	2
1959			34	595	17.5	45	1
1960			46	826	18.0	57t	5
1961			50	769	15.4	61t	8
1962			30	584	19.5	84	3
1963			57	895	15.7	46	4
1964			51	855	16.8	44	8
1965			66	1190	18.0	78	10

Pete Retzlaff *continued*

Year	Team		No	Yds	Avg	Lg	TD
1966			40	653	16.3	40	6
Career			452	7412	16.4	84	47
Playoffs			1	41	41.0		0

Freeman Rexer

Year	Team		No	Yds	Avg	Lg	TD
1943	CHIC	N	1	14	14.0	14	0

Billy Reynolds

Year	Team		No	Yds	Avg	Lg	TD
1953	CLE	N	9	120	13.3	55	0
1954			10	76	7.6	22	0
1957			1	12	12.0	12	0
1958	PIT	N	1	1	1.0	1	0
1960	OAK	A	3	43	14.3		0
Career			24	252	10.5	55	0
Playoffs			1	7	7.0		0

Bob Reynolds

Year	Team		No	Yds	Avg	Lg	TD
1971	STL	N	1	-4	-4.0	-4	0

Jim Reynolds

Year	Team		No	Yds	Avg	Lg	TD
1946	MIA	AA	1	32	32.0	32	0

Tom Reynolds

Year	Team		No	Yds	Avg	Lg	TD
1972	NE	N	8	152	19.0	36t	2
1973	CHI	N	7	127	18.1	30	0
Career			15	279	18.6	36t	2

Steve Rhem

Year	Team		No	Yds	Avg	Lg	TD
1995	NO	N	4	50	12.5	20	0

Errict Rhett

Year	Team		No	Yds	Avg	Lg	TD
1994	TB	N	22	119	5.4	12	0
1995			14	110	7.9	18	0
1996			4	11	2.8	5t	1
Career			40	240	6.0	18	1

Ray Rhodes

Year	Team		No	Yds	Avg	Lg	TD
1974	NYG	N	9	138	15.3	25	0
1975			26	537	20.7	56	6
1976			16	305	19.1	63t	1
Career			51	980	19.2	63t	7

Buster Rhymes

Year	Team		No	Yds	Avg	Lg	TD
1985	MIN	N	5	124	24.8	36	0
1986			3	25	8.3	12	0
Career			8	149	18.6	36	0

Paul Riblett

Year	Team		No	Yds	Avg	Lg	TD
1932	BKN	N					1
1933			12	172	14.3		1
1934							1
1935			6	86	14.3		0
1936			4	49	12.3		0
Career			22	307	14.0		3

Allen Rice

Year	Team		No	Yds	Avg	Lg	TD
1984	MIN	N	4	59	14.8	24	1
1985			9	61	6.8	13	1
1986			30	391	13.0	32t	3
1987			19	201	10.6	24	1
1988			30	279	9.3	38	0
1989			4	29	7.3	14	0
1990			4	46	11.5	24	0
1991	GB	N	2	10	5.0	7	0
Career			102	1076	10.5	38	6
Playoffs			12	109	9.1		0

Jerry Rice

Year	Team		No	Yds	Avg	Lg	TD
1985	SF	N	49	927	18.9	66t	3
1986			86	**1570**	18.3	66t	**15**
1987			65	1078	16.6	57t	**22**
1988			64	1306	20.4	98t	9
1989			82	**1483**	18.1	68t	**17**
1990			**100**	**1502**	15.0	64t	13
1991			80	1206	15.1	73t	14
1992			84	1201	14.3	80t	10
1993			98	**1503**	15.3	80t	15
1994			112	**1499**	13.4	69t	13
1995			**122**	**1848**	15.1	81t	15
1996			**108**	1254	11.6	39	8
Career			**1050**	**16377**	15.6	98t	**154**
Playoffs			**120**	**1742**	14.5		**18**

Curvin Richards

Year	Team		No	Yds	Avg	Lg	TD
1992	DAL	N	3	8	2.7	6	0

Elvin Richards

Year	Team		No	Yds	Avg	Lg	TD
1933	NYG	N					3
1934			6	60	10.0		1
1935			8	41	5.1		0
1936			7	146	20.9		1
1937			10	149	14.9		2
1938			1	8	8.0	8	1
1939			2	8	4.0		0
Career			34	412	12.1	8	7
Playoffs			1	16	16.0		0

Golden Richards

Year	Team		No	Yds	Avg	Lg	TD
1973	DAL	N	6	91	15.2	53t	1
1974			26	467	18.0	58t	5
1975			21	451	21.5	62	4
1976			19	414	21.8	56	3
1977			17	225	13.2	50t	3
1978	DAL-CHI	N	28	381	13.6	52	0
1979	CHI	N	5	107	21.4	52t	1
Career			122	2136	17.5	62	17
Playoffs			9	150	16.7		3

Perry Richards

Year	Team		No	Yds	Avg	Lg	TD
1957	PIT	N	1	15	15.0	15	0
1958	DET	N	7	90	12.9	30	0
1959	CHIC	N	5	89	17.8	25t	1
1960	STL	N	1	10	10.0	10	0
1961	BUF	A	19	285	15.0	43	3
1962	NY	A	6	69	11.5	22	0
Career			39	558	14.3	43	4

Eric Richardson

Year	Team		No	Yds	Avg	Lg	TD
1985	BUF	N	12	201	16.8	27	0
1986			3	49	16.3	32	0
Career			15	250	16.7	32	0

Gloster Richardson

Year	Team		No	Yds	Avg	Lg	TD
1967	KC	A	12	312	26.0	56t	2
1968			22	494	22.5	92t	6
1969			23	381	16.6	39	2
1970	KC	N	5	171	34.2	61t	2
1971	DAL	N	8	170	21.3	45t	3
1972	CLE	N	1	7	7.0	7	0
1973			12	175	14.6	32	1
1974			9	266	29.6	60t	2
Career			92	1976	21.5	92t	18
Playoffs			4	76	19.0		1

Jerry Richardson

Year	Team		No	Yds	Avg	Lg	TD
1959	BAL	N	7	81	11.6	15	3
1960			8	90	11.3	23	1
Career			15	171	11.4	23	4
Playoffs			1	12	12.0		1

Mike Richardson

Year	Team		No	Yds	Avg	Lg	TD
1970	HOU	N	34	381	11.2	67	1
1971			4	17	4.3	9	0
Career			38	398	10.5	67	1

Thomas Richardson

Year	Team		No	Yds	Avg	Lg	TD
1969	BOS	A	1	5	5.0	5	0

Tony Richardson

Year	Team		No	Yds	Avg	Lg	TD
1996	KC	N	2	18	9.0	17	0

Willie Richardson

Year	Team		No	Yds	Avg	Lg	TD
1963	BAL	N	17	204	12.0	22	0
1964			3	42	14.0	16	0
1965			1	14	14.0	14t	1
1966			14	246	17.6	69	2
1967			63	860	13.7	31t	8
1968			37	698	18.9	79t	8
1969			43	646	15.0	39	3
1970	MIA	N	7	67	9.6	27	1
1971	BAL	N	10	173	17.3	49t	2
Career			195	2950	15.1	79t	25
Playoffs			17	314	18.5		1

Pat Richter

Year	Team		No	Yds	Avg	Lg	TD
1963	WAS	N	27	383	14.2	34	3
1964			4	49	12.3	16	0

Pat Richter *continued*

Year	Team		No	Yds	Avg	Lg	TD
1965			16	189	11.8	35	2
1966			7	100	14.3	20	0
1967			1	31	31.0	31	0
1968			42	533	12.7	40	9
1970			2	30	15.0	26	0
Career			99	1315	13.3	40	14

Harold Ricks

Year	Team		No	Yds	Avg	Lg	TD
1987	TB	N	1	12	12.0	12	0

Lawrence Ricks

Year	Team		No	Yds	Avg	Lg	TD
1983	KC	N	3	5	1.7	7	0

Louis Riddick

Year	Team		No	Yds	Avg	Lg	TD
1995	CLE	N	1	25	25.0	25	0

Ray Riddick

Year	Team		No	Yds	Avg	Lg	TD
1940	GB	N	11	148	13.5		0
1941			4	78	19.5	45	0
1942			6	104	17.3	24	1
Career			21	330	15.7	45	1
Playoffs			1	45	45.0		0

Robb Riddick

Year	Team		No	Yds	Avg	Lg	TD
1983	BUF	N	3	43	14.3	24	0
1984			23	276	12.0	38	0
1986			49	468	9.6	31t	1
1987			15	96	6.4	17t	3
1988			30	282	9.4	26	1
Career			120	1165	9.7	38	5
Playoffs			3	28	9.3		0

Preston Ridlehuber

Year	Team		No	Yds	Avg	Lg	TD
1966	ATL	N	4	84	21.0	53t	2

Dick Rifenburg

Year	Team		No	Yds	Avg	Lg	TD
1950	DET	N	10	96	9.6	19t	1

Dick Riffle

Year	Team		No	Yds	Avg	Lg	TD
1939	PHI	N	6	57	9.5		0
1940			8	58	7.3		1
1941	PIT	N	2	24	12.0	14	1
1942			3	50	16.7	31	0
Career			19	189	9.9	31	2

John Riggins

Year	Team		No	Yds	Avg	Lg	TD
1971	NYJ	N	36	231	6.4	32t	2
1972			21	230	11.0	67t	1
1973			23	158	6.9	19	0
1974			19	180	9.5	32	2
1975			30	363	12.1	34	1
1976	WAS	N	21	172	8.2	18	1
1977			7	95	13.6	53t	2
1978			31	299	9.6	33	0
1979			28	163	5.8	23	3
1981			6	59	9.8	22	0
1982			10	50	5.0	11	0
1983			5	29	5.8	14	0
1984			7	43	6.1	11	0
1985			6	18	3.0	8	0
Career			250	2090	8.4	67t	12
Playoffs			6	45	7.5		0

Gerald Riggs

Year	Team		No	Yds	Avg	Lg	TD
1982	ATL	N	23	185	8.0	15	0
1983			17	149	8.8	25	0
1984			42	277	6.6	21	0
1985			33	267	8.1	44	0
1986			24	136	5.7	11	0
1987			25	199	8.0	48	0
1988			22	171	7.8	30	0
1989	WAS	N	7	67	9.6	13	0
1990			7	60	8.6	18	0
1991			1	5	5.0	5	0
Career			201	1516	7.5	48	0
Playoffs			3	24	8.0		0

Jim Riggs

Year	Team		No	Yds	Avg	Lg	TD
1988	CIN	N	9	82	9.1	16	0
1989			5	29	5.8	9	0
1990			8	79	9.9	21	0
1991			4	14	3.5	7	0

Jim Riggs *continued*

Year	Team		No	Yds	Avg	Lg	TD
1992			11	70	6.4	17	0
Career			37	274	7.4	21	0
Playoffs			3	18	6.0		0

Eric Riley

Year	Team		No	Yds	Avg	Lg	TD
1987	NYJ	N	4	42	10.5	16	0

Eugene Riley

Year	Team		No	Yds	Avg	Lg	TD
1991	DET	N	1	3	3.0	3	0

Ken Riley

Year	Team		No	Yds	Avg	Lg	TD
1969	CIN	A	2	15	7.5	17	0

Lee Riley

Year	Team		No	Yds	Avg	Lg	TD
1956	PHI	N	1	10	10.0	10	0

Preston Riley

Year	Team		No	Yds	Avg	Lg	TD
1970	SF	N	7	136	19.4	68	0
1971			3	39	13.0	24	0
1972			11	156	14.2	28t	1
Career			21	331	15.8	68	1
Playoffs			4	41	10.3		0

Bill Ring

Year	Team		No	Yds	Avg	Lg	TD
1981	SF	N	3	28	9.3	21	1
1982			13	94	7.2	15	0
1983			23	182	7.9	24	0
1984			3	10	3.3	15	0
1985			2	14	7.0	8	0
1986			1	8	8.0	8	0
Career			45	336	7.5	24	1
Playoffs			5	18	3.6		0

Andre Rison

Year	Team		No	Yds	Avg	Lg	TD
1989	IND	N	52	820	15.8	61	4
1990	ATL	N	82	1208	14.7	75t	10
1991			81	976	12.0	39t	12
1992			93	1119	12.0	71t	11
1993			86	1242	14.4	53t	15
1994			81	1088	13.4	69t	8
1995	CLE	N	47	701	14.9	59	3
1996	JAC-GB	N	47	593	12.6	61t	3
Career			569	7747	13.6	75t	66
Playoffs			18	261	14.5		3

Ron Rivera

Year	Team		No	Yds	Avg	Lg	TD
Playoffs			1	15	15.0		0

Steve Rivera

Year	Team		No	Yds	Avg	Lg	TD
1976	SF	N	1	7	7.0	7	0
1977	CHI	N	1	7	7.0	7	0
Career			2	14	7.0	7	0

Reggie Rivers

Year	Team		No	Yds	Avg	Lg	TD
1992	DEN	N	45	449	10.0	37	1
1993			6	59	9.8	17	1
1994			20	136	6.8	25	0
1995			3	32	10.7	23	0
1996			1	-1	-1.0	-1	0
Career			75	675	9.0	37	2
Playoffs			1	8	8.0		0

Ron Rivers

Year	Team		No	Yds	Avg	Lg	TD
1995	DET	N	1	5	5.0	5	0
1996			2	28	14.0	19	0
Career			3	33	11.0	19	0
Playoffs			2	36	18.0		0

Jack Rizzo

Year	Team		No	Yds	Avg	Lg	TD
1973	NYG	N	1	11	11.0	11	0

Carl Roaches

Year	Team		No	Yds	Avg	Lg	TD
1984	HOU	N	4	69	17.3	24	0

Michael Roan

Year	Team		No	Yds	Avg	Lg	TD
1995	HOU	N	8	46	5.8	11	0

Oscar Roan

Year	Team		No	Yds	Avg	Lg	TD
1975	CLE	N	41	463	11.3	31	3
1976			15	174	11.6	23t	4
1977			13	136	10.5	27	2
Career			69	773	11.2	31	9

Harry Robb

Year	Team		No	Yds	Avg	Lg	TD
1921	CAN	A					1
1925	CAN	N					3
Career							4

Jack Robbins

Year	Team		No	Yds	Avg	Lg	TD
1939	CHIC	N	2	12	6.0		0

Bo Roberson

Year	Team		No	Yds	Avg	Lg	TD
1961	SD	A	6	81	13.5	24	0
1962	OAK	A	29	583	20.1	72	3
1963			25	407	16.3	52	3
1964			44	624	14.2	54	1
1965	OAK-BUF	A	46	703	15.3	74	3
1966	MIA	A	26	519	20.0	80	2
Career			176	2917	16.6	80	12
Playoffs			4	99	24.8		0

Alfredo Roberts

Year	Team		No	Yds	Avg	Lg	TD
1988	KC	N	10	104	10.4	20	0
1989			8	55	6.9	25	1
1990			11	119	10.8	27	0
1991	DAL	N	16	136	8.5	21	1
1992			3	36	12.0	18	0
Career			48	450	9.4	27	2
Playoffs			2	26	13.0		0

Bill Roberts

Year	Team		No	Yds	Avg	Lg	TD
1956	GB	N	1	14	14.0	14	0

C.R. Roberts

Year	Team		No	Yds	Avg	Lg	TD
1960	SF	N	9	49	5.4	27	0
1961			10	83	8.3	19	0
1962			2	0	0.0	1	0
Career			21	132	6.3	27	0

Gene Roberts

Year	Team		No	Yds	Avg	Lg	TD
1947	NYG	N	4	58	14.5	30	0
1948			14	222	15.9	49t	3
1949			35	711	20.3	85	8
1950			11	144	13.1	47	1
Career			64	1135	17.7	85	12
Playoffs			1	17	17.0		0

Ray Roberts

Year	Team		No	Yds	Avg	Lg	TD
1993	SEA	N	1	4	4.0	4	0
1996	DET	N	0	5		5L	0
Career			1	9	9.0	5L	0

Walt Roberts

Year	Team		No	Yds	Avg	Lg	TD
1964	CLE	N	1	24	24.0	24t	1
1965			16	314	19.6	80t	4
1966			2	19	9.5	10	0
1967	NO	N	17	384	22.6	96	3
1969	WAS	N	4	66	16.5	22	0
1970			27	411	15.2	66t	1
Career			67	1218	18.2	96	9

Wooky Roberts

Year	Team		No	Yds	Avg	Lg	TD
1923	CAN	N					1
1924	CLE	N					3
1926	FRA	N					1
Career							5

Bobbie Robertson

Year	Team		No	Yds	Avg	Lg	TD
1942	BKN	N	5	61	12.2	26	0

Jimmy Robertson

Year	Team		No	Yds	Avg	Lg	TD
1925	AKR	N					1

Paul Robeson

Year	Team		No	Yds	Avg	Lg	TD
1922	MIL	N					1

Bo Robinson

Year	Team		No	Yds	Avg	Lg	TD
1979	DET	N	14	118	8.4	14	0
1982	ATL	N	7	55	7.9	29	2
1983			12	100	8.3	15	0
1984	NE	N	4	32	8.0	17	1
Career			37	305	8.2	29	3

Eddie Robinson

Year	Team		No	Yds	Avg	Lg	TD
1925	HAM	N					1

Year	Team		No	Yds	Avg	Lg	TD

Greg Robinson

Year	Team		No	Yds	Avg	Lg	TD
1993	LARI	N	15	142	9.5	58	0
1995	STL	N	2	12	6.0	6	0
1996			1	6	6.0	6	0
Career			18	160	8.9	58	0

Jacque Robinson

Year	Team		No	Yds	Avg	Lg	TD
1987	PHI	N	2	9	4.5	5	0

Jerry Robinson

Year	Team		No	Yds	Avg	Lg	TD
1962	SD	A	21	391	18.6	72	3
1963			18	315	17.5	36	2
1964			10	93	9.3	21	0
Career			49	799	16.3	72	5

Jimmy Robinson

Year	Team		No	Yds	Avg	Lg	TD
1976	NYG	N	18	249	13.8	30t	1
1977			22	422	19.2	80t	3
1978			32	620	19.4	52t	2
1979			13	146	11.2	31	0
Career			85	1437	16.9	80t	6

Johnny Robinson

Year	Team		No	Yds	Avg	Lg	TD
1960	DAL	A	41	611	14.9	74	4
1961			35	601	17.2	71	5
1962			1	16	16.0	16	0
Career			77	1228	15.9	74	9

Patrick Robinson

Year	Team		No	Yds	Avg	Lg	TD
1993	CIN	N	8	72	9.0	14	0
1994	ARI	N	1	5	5.0	5	0
Career			9	77	8.6	14	0

Paul Robinson

Year	Team		No	Yds	Avg	Lg	TD
1968	CIN	A	24	128	5.3	68t	1
1969			20	104	5.2	25	0
1970	CIN	N	17	175	10.3	27	1
1971			8	47	5.9	16	0
1972	HOU	N	14	112	8.0	24	0
1973			7	46	6.6	19	0
Career			90	612	6.8	68t	2

Stacy Robinson

Year	Team		No	Yds	Avg	Lg	TD
1986	NYG	N	29	494	17.0	49	2
1987			6	58	9.7	14	2
1988			7	143	20.4	62t	3
1989			4	41	10.3	16	0
1990			2	13	6.5	7	0
Career			48	749	15.6	62t	7
Playoffs			3	62	20.7		0

Virgil Robinson

Year	Team		No	Yds	Avg	Lg	TD
1971	NO	N	12	53	4.4	17	1

Terry Robiskie

Year	Team		No	Yds	Avg	Lg	TD
1978	OAK	N	5	51	10.2	21	0
1979			5	36	7.2	11	0
1980	MIA	N	13	60	4.6	15	0
Career			23	147	6.4	21	0

Andy Robustelli

Year	Team		No	Yds	Avg	Lg	TD
1954	LA	N	1	49	49.0	49t	1
1962	NYG	N	1	26	26.0	26	0
Career			2	75	37.5	49t	1

Doug Roby

Year	Team		No	Yds	Avg	Lg	TD
1923	CLE	N					1

Brian Roche

Year	Team		No	Yds	Avg	Lg	TD
1996	SD	N	13	111	8.5	19	0

Hank Rockwell

Year	Team		No	Yds	Avg	Lg	TD
1940	CLE	N	1	5	5.0	5	1
1948	LA	AA	0	6		6L	0
Career			1	11	11.0	6L	1

Mike Rodak

Year	Team		No	Yds	Avg	Lg	TD
1939	CLE	N	4	54	13.5		0

Jeff Rodenberger

Year	Team		No	Yds	Avg	Lg	TD
1987	NO	N	2	17	8.5	11	0

John Roderick

Year	Team		No	Yds	Avg	Lg	TD
1966	MIA	A	11	156	14.2	64	1

Del Rodgers

Year	Team		No	Yds	Avg	Lg	TD
1982	GB	N	3	23	7.7	16	0
1984			5	56	11.2	22	0
1987	SF	N	2	45	22.5	24	0
Career			10	124	12.4	24	0
Playoffs			1	10	10.0		0

Hosea Rodgers

Year	Team		No	Yds	Avg	Lg	TD
1949	LA	AA	7	97	13.9		0

John Rodgers

Year	Team		No	Yds	Avg	Lg	TD
1983	PIT	N	2	36	18.0	25	0

Johnny Rodgers

Year	Team		No	Yds	Avg	Lg	TD
1977	SD	N	12	187	15.6	43	0
1978			5	47	9.4	12	0
Career			17	234	13.8	43	0

Willie Rodgers

Year	Team		No	Yds	Avg	Lg	TD
1972	HOU	N	6	61	10.2	15	0
1974			24	153	6.4	24	0
Career			30	214	7.1	24	0

Fritz Roessler

Year	Team		No	Yds	Avg	Lg	TD
1922	RAC	N					1

John Rogalla

Year	Team		No	Yds	Avg	Lg	TD
1945	PHI	N	2	22	11.0	17	0

Fran Rogel

Year	Team		No	Yds	Avg	Lg	TD
1950	PIT	N	24	304	12.7	64t	1
1951			10	59	5.9	24	0
1952			12	140	11.7	26	0
1953			19	95	5.0	19	0
1954			18	51	2.8	16	1
1955			24	222	9.3	28	0
1956			23	88	3.8	13	0
1957			20	128	6.4	18	0
Career			150	1087	7.2	64t	2

Charley Rogers

Year	Team		No	Yds	Avg	Lg	TD
1927	FRA	N					1
1928							2
Career							3

George Rogers

Year	Team		No	Yds	Avg	Lg	TD
1981	NO	N	16	126	7.9	25	0
1982			4	21	5.3	10	0
1983			12	69	5.8	22	0
1984			12	76	6.3	15	0
1985	WAS	N	4	29	7.3	23	0
1986			3	24	8.0	13	0
1987			4	23	5.8	8	0
Career			55	368	6.7	25	0
Playoffs			2	15	7.5		0

Jimmy Rogers

Year	Team		No	Yds	Avg	Lg	TD
1980	NO	N	27	267	9.9	43	2
1981			2	12	6.0	9	0
1982			4	17	4.3	6	0
Career			33	296	9.0	43	2

Steve Rogers

Year	Team		No	Yds	Avg	Lg	TD
1975	NO	N	1	2	2.0	2	0

George Rogge

Year	Team		No	Yds	Avg	Lg	TD
1931	CHIC	N					1

Herm Rohrig

Year	Team		No	Yds	Avg	Lg	TD
1941	GB	N	11	58	5.3	19	0
1946			2	30	15.0	21	0
Career			13	88	6.8	21	0
Playoffs			1	2	2.0		0

John Rokisky

Year	Team		No	Yds	Avg	Lg	TD
1946	CLE	AA	1	13	13.0	13	0
1947	CHI	AA	1	8	8.0	8	0
Career			2	21	10.5	13	0

Johnny Roland

Year	Team		No	Yds	Avg	Lg	TD
1966	STL	N	21	213	10.1	37	0
1967			20	269	13.4	41	1
1968			8	97	12.1	40	0
1969			12	136	11.3	23	1

Johnny Roland continued

Year	Team		No	Yds	Avg	Lg	TD
1970			17	96	5.6	20	1
1971			15	108	7.2	15	0
1972			38	321	8.4	27	2
1973	NYG	N	22	190	8.6	30	1
Career			153	1430	9.3	41	6

Butch Rolle

Year	Team		No	Yds	Avg	Lg	TD
1986	BUF	N	4	56	14.0	20	0
1987			2	6	3.0	3t	2
1988			2	3	1.5	2t	2
1989			1	1	1.0	1t	1
1990			3	6	2.0	3t	3
1991			3	10	3.3	5	2
1992	PHX	N	13	64	4.9	12	0
1993			10	67	6.7	22	1
Career			38	213	5.6	22	11

Dave Rolle

Year	Team		No	Yds	Avg	Lg	TD
1960	DEN	A	21	122	5.8	33	1

John Roman

Year	Team		No	Yds	Avg	Lg	TD
1978	NYJ	N	1	-2	-2.0	-2	0

Rudy Romboli

Year	Team		No	Yds	Avg	Lg	TD
1947	BOS	N	4	30	7.5	27	0
1948			8	77	9.6	33	0
Career			12	107	8.9	33	0

Stan Rome

Year	Team		No	Yds	Avg	Lg	TD
1980	KC	N	3	58	19.3	33	0
1981			17	203	11.9	23	1
1982			2	25	12.5	16	0
Career			22	286	13.0	33	1

Tag Rome

Year	Team		No	Yds	Avg	Lg	TD
1987	SD	N	6	49	8.2	13	0

Tony Romeo

Year	Team		No	Yds	Avg	Lg	TD
1961	DAL	A	7	89	12.7	20	0
1962	BOS	A	34	608	17.9	62	1
1963			32	418	13.1	39	3
1964			26	445	17.1	38	4
1965			15	203	13.5	36	2
1966			2	46	23.0	29	0
1967			1	4	4.0	4	0
Career			117	1813	15.5	62	10

Dick Romey

Year	Team		No	Yds	Avg	Lg	TD
1926	CHI	A					1

Milt Romney

Year	Team		No	Yds	Avg	Lg	TD
1923	RAC	N					1
1924							1
1926	CHIB	N					1
1928							1
Career							4

Gene Ronzani

Year	Team		No	Yds	Avg	Lg	TD
1933	CHIB	N					1
1934			6	114	19.0		3
1935			8	122	15.3		1
1936			4	58	14.5		2
1937			2	40	20.0		1
Career			20	334	16.7		8
Playoffs			2	38	19.0		0

Bill Rooney

Year	Team		No	Yds	Avg	Lg	TD
1924	DUL	N					2

Cobb Rooney

Year	Team		No	Yds	Avg	Lg	TD
1929	CHIC	N					2
1930							1
Career							3

Joe Rooney

Year	Team		No	Yds	Avg	Lg	TD
1923	DUL	N					1
1925	RI	N					1
1926	DUL	N					1
1927							3
1928	POT	N					1
Career							7

Sal Rosato

Year	Team		No	Yds	Avg	Lg	TD
1945	WAS	N	1	7	7.0	7	0
1946			1	17	17.0	17	0
1947			7	107	15.3	26	1
Career			9	131	14.6	26	1

Al Rose

Year	Team		No	Yds	Avg	Lg	TD
1931	PRO	N					2
1933	GB	N					1
1934							2
1935			8	91	11.4		0
Career			8	91	11.4		5

Joe Rose

Year	Team		No	Yds	Avg	Lg	TD
1980	MIA	N	13	149	11.5	50	0
1981			23	316	13.7	50	2
1982			16	182	11.4	44	2
1983			29	345	11.9	37	3
1984			12	195	16.3	34t	2
1985			19	306	16.1	42	4
Career			112	1493	13.3	50	13
Playoffs			18	260	14.4		2

Roy Rose

Year	Team		No	Yds	Avg	Lg	TD
1936	NYG	N	6	73	12.2		0

Ted Rosequist

Year	Team		No	Yds	Avg	Lg	TD
1934	CHIB	N	2	20	10.0		0
1936			1	15	15.0	15	0
Career			3	35	11.7	15	0

Ken Roskie

Year	Team		No	Yds	Avg	Lg	TD
1946	SF	AA	0	7		7L	0

Alvin Ross

Year	Team		No	Yds	Avg	Lg	TD
1987	PHI	N	5	41	8.2	17	0

Dan Ross

Year	Team		No	Yds	Avg	Lg	TD
1979	CIN	N	41	516	12.6	41	1
1980			56	724	12.9	37	4
1981			71	910	12.8	37	5
1982			47	508	10.8	28	3
1983			42	483	11.5	30	3
1985	CIN-SEA	N	16	135	8.4	20	2
1986	GB	N	17	143	8.4	16	1
Career			290	3419	11.8	41	19
Playoffs			28	333	11.9		3

Dave Ross

Year	Team		No	Yds	Avg	Lg	TD
1960	NY	A	10	122	12.2		1

Jermaine Ross

Year	Team		No	Yds	Avg	Lg	TD
1994	LARM	N	1	36	36.0	36t	1
1996	STL	N	15	160	10.7	28	0
Career			16	196	12.3	36t	1

Oliver Ross

Year	Team		No	Yds	Avg	Lg	TD
1974	DEN	N	1	13	13.0	13	0
1975			7	69	9.9	30	0
1976	SEA	N	2	22	11.0	21	0
Career			10	104	10.4	30	0

Willie Ross

Year	Team		No	Yds	Avg	Lg	TD
Playoffs			1	-1	-1.0		0

Kyle Rote

Year	Team		No	Yds	Avg	Lg	TD
1951	NYG	N	8	62	7.8	18	0
1952			21	240	11.4	26	2
1953			26	440	16.9	75t	5
1954			29	551	19.0	63	2
1955			31	580	18.7	71t	8
1956			28	405	14.5	31	4
1957			25	358	14.3	33t	3
1958			12	244	20.3	44	3
1959			25	362	14.5	34	4
1960			42	750	17.9	71t	10
1961			53	805	15.2	57	7
Career			300	4797	16.0	75t	48
Playoffs			9	191	21.2		1

Tobin Rote

Year	Team		No	Yds	Avg	Lg	TD
1951	GB	N	0	11		11L	0
1952			1	28	28.0	28t	1

Tobin Rote continued

Year	Team		No	Yds	Avg	Lg	TD
1964	SD	A	1	-11	-11.0	-11	0
Career			2	28	14.0	28t	1

George Roudebush

Year	Team		No	Yds	Avg	Lg	TD
1920	DAY	A					1

James Rouse

Year	Team		No	Yds	Avg	Lg	TD
1991	CHI	N	15	93	6.2	14	0

Stillman Rouse

Year	Team		No	Yds	Avg	Lg	TD
1940	DET	N	2	17	8.5		0

Lee Rouson

Year	Team		No	Yds	Avg	Lg	TD
1986	NYG	N	8	121	15.1	37t	1
1987			11	129	11.7	26t	1
1988			4	61	15.3	31	0
1989			7	121	17.3	39	0
1990			1	12	12.0	12	0
1991	CLE	N	2	9	4.5	6	0
Career			33	453	13.7	39	2
Playoffs			3	45	15.0		0

Patrick Rowe

Year	Team		No	Yds	Avg	Lg	TD
1993	CLE	N	3	37	12.3	16	0

Brad Rowland

Year	Team		No	Yds	Avg	Lg	TD
1951	CHIB	N	1	-2	-2.0	-2	0

Mazio Royster

Year	Team		No	Yds	Avg	Lg	TD
1992	TB	N	1	8	8.0	8	0
1993			5	18	3.6	10	0
1994			7	36	5.1	12	0
Career			13	62	4.8	12	0

Mike Rozier

Year	Team		No	Yds	Avg	Lg	TD
1985	HOU	N	9	96	10.7	52	0
1986			24	180	7.5	23	0
1987			27	192	7.1	27	0
1988			11	99	9.0	18	1
1989			4	28	7.0	8	0
1990	HOU-ATL	N	13	105	8.1	24	0
1991	ATL	N	2	15	7.5	9	0
Career			90	715	7.9	52	1
Playoffs			3	18	6.0		0

Rob Rubick

Year	Team		No	Yds	Avg	Lg	TD
1983	DET	N	10	81	8.1	15	1
1984			14	188	13.4	29	1
1985			2	33	16.5	18	0
1986			5	62	12.4	27	0
1987			13	147	11.3	22	1
Career			44	511	11.6	29	3

Martin Ruby

Year	Team		No	Yds	Avg	Lg	TD
1946	BKN	AA	1	3	3.0	3	0

Eddie Rucinski

Year	Team		No	Yds	Avg	Lg	TD
1941	BKN	N	17	204	12.0	33	1
1942			9	99	11.0	24	1
1943	CHIC	N	26	398	15.3	47	3
1944	C-P	N	22	284	12.9	40t	1
1945	CHIC	N	23	400	17.4	62	2
1946			2	23	11.5	12	0
Career			99	1408	14.2	62	8

Conrad Rucker

Year	Team		No	Yds	Avg	Lg	TD
1978	HOU	N	2	38	19.0	22	0
1979			4	40	10.0	16	0
Career			6	78	13.0	22	0

Reggie Rucker

Year	Team		No	Yds	Avg	Lg	TD
1970	DAL	N	9	200	22.2	52t	1
1971	DAL-NYG-NE	N	4	52	13.0	19t	1
1972	NE	N	44	681	15.5	62	3
1973			53	743	14.0	64	3
1974			27	436	16.1	69t	4
1975	CLE	N	60	770	12.8	40t	3
1976			49	676	13.8	45	8
1977			36	565	15.7	40	2
1978			43	893	20.8	69t	8
1979			43	749	17.4	54	6
1980			52	768	14.8	45	4

Reggie Rucker continued

Year	Team		No	Yds	Avg	Lg	TD
1981			27	532	19.7	49	1
Career			447	7065	15.8	69t	44
Playoffs			3	59	19.7		0

Mike Ruether

Year	Team		No	Yds	Avg	Lg	TD
1991	ATL	N	1	22	22.0	22	0

Emmett Ruh

Year	Team		No	Yds	Avg	Lg	TD
1921	COL	A					1

Homer Ruh

Year	Team		No	Yds	Avg	Lg	TD
1920	COL	A					1
1921							1
Career							2

Tommy Runnels

Year	Team		No	Yds	Avg	Lg	TD
1956	WAS	N	6	56	9.3	22	1
1957			1	4	4.0	4	0
Career			7	60	8.6	22	1

Clive Rush

Year	Team		No	Yds	Avg	Lg	TD
1953	GB	N	14	190	13.6	24	0

Booker Russell

Year	Team		No	Yds	Avg	Lg	TD
1979	OAK	N	6	79	13.2	26	0
1981	PHI	N	1	-5	-5.0	-5	0
Career			7	74	10.6	26	0
Playoffs			1	4	4.0		0

Derek Russell

Year	Team		No	Yds	Avg	Lg	TD
1991	DEN	N	21	317	15.1	40	1
1992			12	140	11.7	22	0
1993			44	719	16.3	43	3
1994			25	342	13.7	43	1
1995	HOU	N	24	321	13.4	57	0
1996			34	421	12.4	29	2
Career			160	2260	14.1	57	7
Playoffs			3	51	17.0		1

Doug Russell

Year	Team		No	Yds	Avg	Lg	TD
1937	CHIC	N	12	263	21.9		1
1938			6	36	6.0		0
1939	CLE	N	5	67	13.4		1
Career			23	366	15.9		2

Jack Russell

Year	Team		No	Yds	Avg	Lg	TD
1946	NY	AA	23	223	9.7		4
1947			20	368	18.4		2
1948			23	433	18.8	70t	6
1949	B-NY	AA	7	130	18.6		1
1950	NYY	N	10	177	17.7	49t	2
Career			83	1331	16.0	70t	15
Playoffs			6	72	12.0		0

Leonard Russell

Year	Team		No	Yds	Avg	Lg	TD
1991	NE	N	18	81	4.5	18	0
1992			11	24	2.2	12	0
1993			26	245	9.4	69	0
1994	DEN	N	38	227	6.0	19	0
1995	STL	N	16	89	5.6	17	0
1996	SD	N	13	180	13.8	35	0
Career			122	846	6.9	69	0

Wade Russell

Year	Team		No	Yds	Avg	Lg	TD
1987	CIN	N	2	27	13.5	23	1

Ralph Ruthstrom

Year	Team		No	Yds	Avg	Lg	TD
1946	LA	N	1	9	9.0	9	0

Ed Rutkowski

Year	Team		No	Yds	Avg	Lg	TD
1963	BUF	A	19	264	13.9	58	1
1964			13	234	18.0	46	1
1965			18	247	13.7	47	1
1966			6	150	25.0	55	1
1967			6	59	9.8	17	0
1968			1	27	27.0	27	0
Career			63	981	15.6	58	4
Playoffs			3	45	15.0		0

Roger Ruzek

Year	Team		No	Yds	Avg	Lg	TD
1989	DAL	N	1	4	4.0	4	0

Year	Team		No	Yds	Avg	Lg	TD

Clarence Ryan
Year	Team		No	Yds	Avg	Lg	TD
1929	BUF	N					1

Dave Ryan
Year	Team		No	Yds	Avg	Lg	TD
1945	DET	N	2	67	33.5	63t	1
1946			1	-5	-5.0	-5	0
Career			3	62	20.7	63t	1

Frank Ryan
Year	Team		No	Yds	Avg	Lg	TD
1960	LA	N	0	32		32tL	1
1963	CLE	N	0	-1		-1L	0
Career			0	31		32tL	1

John Ryan
Year	Team		No	Yds	Avg	Lg	TD
1956	PHI	N	1	31	31.0	31	0
1957			4	91	22.8	46t	2
1958	CHIB		1	66	66.0	66	0
Career			6	188	31.3	66	2

Kent Ryan
Year	Team		No	Yds	Avg	Lg	TD
1938	DET	N	7	78	11.1		0
1939			7	46	6.6		1
1940			9	96	10.7		0
Career			23	220	9.6		1

Tom Rychlec
Year	Team		No	Yds	Avg	Lg	TD
1958	DET	N	2	21	10.5	23	0
1960	BUF	A	44	581	13.2	36	0
1961			33	405	12.3	27	2
1962			6	66	11.0	18	1
1963	DEN	A	1	7	7.0	7	0
Career			86	1080	12.6	36	3

Billy Ryckman
Year	Team		No	Yds	Avg	Lg	TD
1977	ATL	N	1	5	5.0	5t	1
1978			45	679	15.1	59t	2
1979			4	59	14.8	20t	2
Career			50	743	14.9	59t	5
Playoffs			2	27	13.5		0

Danny Ryczek
Year	Team		No	Yds	Avg	Lg	TD
1976	TB	N	1	6	6.0	6	0

Nick Ryder
Year	Team		No	Yds	Avg	Lg	TD
1964	DET	N	4	30	7.5	23t	1

Julie Rykovoch
Year	Team		No	Yds	Avg	Lg	TD
1947	BUF	AA	4	44	11.0		0
1948	BUF-CHI	AA	5	71	14.2		0
1949	CHIB	N	16	210	13.1	45	2
1950			21	344	16.4	39	0
1951			6	133	22.2	51	0
1952	WAS	N	16	283	17.7	42	1
1953			7	73	10.4	39	1
Career			75	1158	15.4	51	4
Playoffs			1	8	8.0		0

Lou Saban
Year	Team		No	Yds	Avg	Lg	TD
1946	CLE	AA	1	45	45.0	45	0

Frankie Sachse
Year	Team		No	Yds	Avg	Lg	TD
1943	BKN	N	3	26	8.7	14	0

Norb Sacksteder
Year	Team		No	Yds	Avg	Lg	TD
1920	DAY	A					3
1922	CAN	N					1
Career							4

Troy Sadowski
Year	Team		No	Yds	Avg	Lg	TD
1992	NYJ	N	1	20	20.0	20	0
1993			2	14	7.0	11	0
1994	CIN	N	11	54	4.9	11	0
1995			5	37	7.4	12	0
1996			3	15	5.0	8	0
Career			22	140	6.4	20	0

Eddie Saenz
Year	Team		No	Yds	Avg	Lg	TD
1946	WAS	N	12	242	20.2	66	3
1947			34	598	17.6	74t	4
1948			4	62	15.5	28	0
1949			23	251	10.9	31	0
1950			10	165	16.5	36	1
1951			1	9	9.0	9	0
Career			84	1327	15.8	74t	8

Saint Saffold
Year	Team		No	Yds	Avg	Lg	TD
1968	CIN	A	16	172	10.8	25	0

George Saimes
Year	Team		No	Yds	Avg	Lg	TD
1963	BUF	A	6	12	2.0	9	0

Rashaan Salaam
Year	Team		No	Yds	Avg	Lg	TD
1995	CHI	N	7	56	8.0	18	0
1996			7	44	6.3	11t	1
Career			14	100	7.1	18	1

Paul Salata
Year	Team		No	Yds	Avg	Lg	TD
1949	SF	AA	24	289	12.0		4
1950	SF-BAL	N	50	618	12.4	57t	4
Career			74	907	12.3	57t	8
Playoffs			3	47	15.7		1

Jay Saldi
Year	Team		No	Yds	Avg	Lg	TD
1976	DAL	N	1	6	6.0	6	0
1977			11	108	9.8	23	2
1978			3	8	2.7	5	2
1979			14	181	12.9	23t	1
1980			25	311	12.4	43	1
1981			8	82	10.3	18	1
1982			1	8	8.0	8	0
1983	CHI	N	12	119	9.9	16	0
1984			9	90	10.0	20	0
Career			84	913	10.9	43	7
Playoffs			6	106	17.7		1

Sam Salemi
Year	Team		No	Yds	Avg	Lg	TD
1928	NYY	N					1

Jack Salschneider
Year	Team		No	Yds	Avg	Lg	TD
1949	NYG	N	4	9	2.3	13	0

Chuck Sample
Year	Team		No	Yds	Avg	Lg	TD
1942	GB	N	6	35	5.8	10	1

Lawrence Sampleton
Year	Team		No	Yds	Avg	Lg	TD
1982	PHI	N	1	24	24.0	24	0
1983			2	28	14.0	19	0
1987	MIA	N	8	64	8.0	19	0
Career			11	116	10.5	24	0

Clint Sampson
Year	Team		No	Yds	Avg	Lg	TD
1978	HOU	N	1	-4	-4.0	-4	0
1983	DEN	N	10	200	20.0	49t	3
1984			9	123	13.7	25	1
1985			26	432	16.6	46	4
1986			21	259	12.3	43	0
Career			67	1010	15.1	49t	8
Playoffs			6	82	13.7		0

Don Samuel
Year	Team		No	Yds	Avg	Lg	TD
1949	PIT	N	1	2	2.0	2	0

Chris Samuels
Year	Team		No	Yds	Avg	Lg	TD
1991	SD	N	2	33	16.5	29	0

Terry Samuels
Year	Team		No	Yds	Avg	Lg	TD
1994	ARI	N	8	57	7.1	17	0
1995			2	19	9.5	12	0
Career			10	76	7.6	17	0

Tony Samuels
Year	Team		No	Yds	Avg	Lg	TD
1977	KC	N	5	65	13.0	32	0
1978			6	97	16.2	38	0
1979			14	147	10.5	30	0
1980			8	110	13.8	34	2
Career			33	419	12.7	38	2

Barry Sanders
Year	Team		No	Yds	Avg	Lg	TD
1989	DET	N	24	282	11.8	46	0
1990			36	480	13.3	47t	3
1991			41	307	7.5	34	1
1992			29	225	7.8	48	1
1993			36	205	5.7	17	0
1994			44	283	6.4	22	1
1995			48	398	8.3	40	1
1996			24	147	6.1	28	0
Career			282	2327	8.3	48	7
Playoffs			16	68	4.3		0

Charlie Sanders
Year	Team		No	Yds	Avg	Lg	TD
1968	DET	N	40	533	13.3	25	1
1969			42	656	15.6	47	3
1970			40	544	13.6	34	6
1971			31	502	16.2	49t	5
1972			27	416	15.4	38	2
1973			28	433	15.5	54	2
1974			42	532	12.7	47	3
1975			37	486	13.1	32	3
1976			35	545	15.6	36	5
1977			14	170	12.1	24	1
Career			336	4817	14.3	54	31

Chris Sanders
Year	Team		No	Yds	Avg	Lg	TD
1995	HOU	N	35	823	23.5	76t	9
1996			48	882	18.4	83t	4
Career			83	1705	20.5	83t	13

Chuck Sanders
Year	Team		No	Yds	Avg	Lg	TD
1986	PIT	N	2	19	9.5	10	0
1987			1	11	11.0	11	0
Career			3	30	10.0	11	0

Deion Sanders
Year	Team		No	Yds	Avg	Lg	TD
1989	ATL	N	1	-8	-8.0	-8	0
1991			1	17	17.0	17	0
1992			3	45	15.0	37t	1
1993			6	106	17.7	70t	1
1995	DAL	N	2	25	12.5	19	0
1996			36	475	13.2	41	1
Career			49	660	13.5	70t	3
Playoffs			3	95	31.7		0

Frank Sanders
Year	Team		No	Yds	Avg	Lg	TD
1995	ARI	N	52	883	17.0	48	2
1996			69	813	11.8	34	4
Career			121	1696	14.0	48	6

Paul Sanders
Year	Team		No	Yds	Avg	Lg	TD
1944	BOS	N	4	5	1.3	5	0

Ricky Sanders
Year	Team		No	Yds	Avg	Lg	TD
1986	WAS	N	14	286	20.4	71	2
1987			37	630	17.0	57	3
1988			73	1148	15.7	55t	12
1989			80	1138	14.2	68	4
1990			56	727	13.0	38	3
1991			45	580	12.9	45	5
1992			51	707	13.9	62t	3
1993			58	638	11.0	50	4
1994	ATL	N	67	599	8.9	28	1
1995			2	24	12.0	21	0
Career			483	6477	13.4	71	37
Playoffs			31	517	16.7		0

Spec Sanders
Year	Team		No	Yds	Avg	Lg	TD
1946	NY	AA	17	259	15.2		3
1947			1	13	13.0	13	0
Career			18	272	15.1	13	3

Thomas Sanders
Year	Team		No	Yds	Avg	Lg	TD
1985	CHI	N	1	9	9.0	9	0
1986			2	18	9.0	18	0
1987			3	53	17.7	25	0
1988			9	94	10.4	39	0
1989			3	28	9.3	16t	1
1990	PHI	N	2	20	10.0	12	0
1991			8	62	7.8	14	0
Career			28	284	10.1	39	1
Playoffs			8	69	8.6		0

Reggie Sanderson
Year	Team		No	Yds	Avg	Lg	TD
1973	CHI	N	5	23	4.6	9	0

Dan Sandifer
Year	Team		No	Yds	Avg	Lg	TD
1948	WAS	N	9	181	20.1	86t	1
1949			19	293	15.4	35	3
1951	PHI	N	2	36	18.0	30t	1
Career			30	510	17.0	86t	5

Curt Sandig
Year	Team		No	Yds	Avg	Lg	TD
1942	PIT	N	6	103	17.2	38	0
1946	BUF	AA	2	15	7.5		0
Career			8	118	14.8	38	0

Year	Team		No	Yds	Avg	Lg	TD

Sandy Sanford

| 1940 | WAS | N | 1 | 13 | 13.0 | 13 | 0 |

Dom Sanzotta

1942	DET	N	5	16	3.2	12	0
1946			2	19	9.5	14	0
Career			7	35	5.0	14	0

Rick Sapienza

| 1960 | NY | A | 1 | 4 | 4.0 | 4 | 0 |

Theron Sapp

1959	PHI	N	6	47	7.8	13	0
1960			2	20	10.0	14	0
1961			3	10	3.3	8	0
1962			6	80	13.3	34	0
1963	PHI-PIT	N	4	36	9.0	22	0
1964	PIT	N	1	44	44.0	44	0
1965			1	10	10.0	10	0
Career			23	247	10.7	44	0

Phil Sarboe

| 1936 | CHIC-BKN | N | 1 | 18 | 18.0 | 18 | 0 |

Broderick Sargent

1986	STL	N	1	8	8.0	8	0
1987			2	19	9.5	10	0
1989	DAL	N	6	50	8.3	21	0
Career			9	77	8.6	21	0

Charley Sarratt

| 1948 | DET | N | 1 | 3 | 3.0 | 3 | 0 |

Paul Sarringhaus

| 1948 | DET | N | 1 | -1 | -1.0 | -1 | 0 |

Martin Sartin

| 1987 | SD | N | 6 | 19 | 3.2 | 8 | 0 |

Howard Satterwhite

| 1976 | NYJ | N | 7 | 110 | 15.7 | 31 | 0 |

George Sauer

1935	GB	N	1	11	11.0	11	0
1936			6	110	18.3		0
Career			7	121	17.3	11	0

George Sauer

1965	NY	A	29	301	10.4	33	2
1966			63	1079	17.1	77	5
1967			75	1189	15.9	61t	6
1968			66	1141	17.3	43	3
1969			45	745	16.6	40t	8
1970	NYJ	N	31	510	16.5	67	4
Career			309	4965	16.1	77	28
Playoffs			20	264	13.2		0

John Sawyer

1975	HOU	N	7	144	20.6	51	1
1976			18	208	11.6	53	1
1977	SEA	N	10	105	10.5	27	0
1978			9	101	11.2	20	0
1980			36	410	11.4	32	0
1981			21	272	13.0	30	0
1982			8	92	11.5	17	0
1983	DEN	N	3	42	14.0	17	0
1984			17	122	7.2	25	0
Career			129	1496	11.6	53	2

James Saxon

1988	KC	N	19	177	9.3	22	0
1989			11	86	7.8	18	0
1990			1	5	5.0	5	0
1991			6	55	9.2	22	0
1992	MIA	N	5	41	8.2	14	0
1994			27	151	5.6	25	0
Career			69	515	7.5	25	0
Playoffs			3	29	9.7		0

Brian Saxton

| 1996 | NYG | N | 4 | 31 | 7.8 | 14 | 0 |

Jimmy Saxton

| 1962 | DAL | A | 5 | 64 | 12.8 | 33 | 0 |

Year	Team		No	Yds	Avg	Lg	TD

Gale Sayers

1965	CHI	N	29	507	17.5	80t	6
1966			34	447	13.1	80t	2
1967			16	126	7.9	32t	1
1968			15	117	7.8	21	0
1969			17	116	6.8	25	0
1970			1	-6	-6.0	-6	0
Career			112	1307	11.7	80t	9

Charley Scales

1960	PIT	N	1	-2	-2.0	-2	0
1961			7	43	6.1	16	0
1962	CLE	N	8	67	8.4	22	0
1963			1	13	13.0	13	0
1965			1	7	7.0	7	0
1966	ATL	N	3	16	5.3	15	0
Career			21	144	6.9	22	0

Dwight Scales

1976	LA	N	3	105	35.0	80t	1
1977			5	104	20.8	32	1
1978			5	105	21.0	38	0
1979	NYG	N	14	222	15.9	55	0
1981	SD	N	19	429	22.6	60t	1
1982			6	105	17.5	29t	1
1983			2	28	14.0	14	0
1984	SEA	N	2	22	11.0	11	0
Career			56	1120	20.0	80t	4
Playoffs			2	35	17.5		0

Greg Scales

1988	NO	N	2	20	10.0	14	1
1989			8	89	11.1	26	0
1990			8	64	8.0	20	1
1991			3	23	7.7	14	0
Career			21	196	9.3	26	2
Playoffs			1	31	31.0		0

Ted Scalissi

| 1947 | CHI | AA | 5 | 67 | 13.4 | | 2 |

Sam Scarber

1975	SD	N	12	68	5.7	12	1
1976			14	96	6.9	13	1
Career			26	164	6.3	13	2

Bob Scarpitto

1961	SD	A	9	163	18.1	69	2
1962	DEN	A	35	667	19.1	67	6
1963			21	463	22.0	66	5
1964			35	375	10.7	37	4
1965			32	585	18.3	90	5
1966			21	335	16.0	62	4
1967			1	14	14.0	14	0
1968	BOS	A	2	49	24.5	33t	1
Career			156	2651	17.0	90	27
Playoffs			1	9	9.0		0

Elmer Schaake

| 1933 | POR | N | | | | | 1 |

Pete Schabarum

1951	SF	N	10	162	16.2	47	0
1953			10	96	9.6	31	0
1954			4	70	17.5	42	0
Career			24	328	13.7	47	0

Don Schaefer

| 1956 | PHI | N | 13 | 117 | 9.0 | 27 | 0 |

Ed Schenk

| 1987 | MIN | N | 1 | 10 | 10.0 | 10 | 0 |

Bernie Scherer

1936	GB	N	2	18	9.0		0
1937			7	148	21.1		2
1938			2	31	15.5		1
1939	PIT	N	2	49	24.5		0
Career			13	246	18.9		3
Playoffs			1	19	19.0		0

Ralph Schilling

| 1946 | WAS | N | 1 | 14 | 14.0 | 14 | 0 |

Year	Team		No	Yds	Avg	Lg	TD

Cory Schlesinger

| 1995 | DET | N | 1 | 2 | 2.0 | 2 | 0 |

Walt Schlinkman

1946	GB	N	1	5	5.0	5	0
1947			2	-6	-3.0	-1	0
Career			3	-1	-0.3	5	0

Ted Schmitt

| 1940 | PHI | N | 1 | 8 | 8.0 | 8 | 0 |

Don Schneider

| 1948 | BUF | AA | 1 | 14 | 14.0 | 14 | 0 |
| Playoffs | | | 1 | 4 | 4.0 | | 0 |

Herm Schneidman

1935	GB	N	2	18	9.0		0
1936			3	68	22.7		1
1937			2	35	17.5		1
Career			7	121	17.3		2

Bob Schnelker

1953	PHI	N	4	34	8.5	12	0
1954	NYG	N	30	550	18.3	68t	5
1955			25	326	13.0	31	2
1956			9	122	13.6	19	1
1957			20	450	22.5	70	5
1958			24	460	19.2	63	5
1959			37	714	19.3	66t	6
1960			38	610	16.1	70t	2
1961	MIN-PIT	N	24	401	16.7	59	4
Career			211	3667	17.4	70t	33
Playoffs			13	284	21.8		1

Otto Schnellbacher

1948	NY	AA	5	72	14.4		0
1949	B-NY	AA	1	11	11.0	11	0
Career			6	83	13.8	11	0

John Schneller

1935	DET	N	7	149	21.3		2
1936			7	124	17.7		1
Career			14	273	19.5		3

Mike Schnitker

| 1971 | DEN | N | 1 | -11 | -11.0 | -11 | 0 |

Ivan Schottel

| 1946 | DET | N | 4 | 146 | 36.5 | 70t | 1 |

Larry Schreiber

1971	SF	N	3	79	26.3	46	1
1972			31	283	9.1	64t	1
1973			12	98	8.2	31	0
1974			30	217	7.2	16	1
1975			40	289	7.2	20	1
1976	CHI	N	1	16	16.0	16	0
Career			117	982	8.4	64t	4
Playoffs			4	42	10.5		0

Bill Schroeder

1946	CHI	AA	1	9	9.0	9	0
1947			2	19	9.5		1
Career			3	28	9.3	9	1

Gene Schroeder

1951	CHIB	N	24	461	19.2	75t	3
1952			39	660	16.9	56	6
1954			1	71	71.0	71t	1
1955			17	315	18.5	51t	2
1956			20	315	15.8	32	1
1957			3	48	16.0	18	0
Career			104	1870	18.0	75t	13

Steve Schubert

1974	NE	N	1	21	21.0	21t	1
1975	CHI	N	5	68	13.6	16	0
1976			4	74	18.5	25	0
1977			8	119	14.9	32	0
1978			4	51	12.8	19	0
1979			2	29	14.5	15	0
Career			24	362	15.1	32	1
Playoffs			5	69	13.8		1

Year	Team	No	Yds	Avg	Lg	TD

Bill Schultz
| 1992 | IND N | 1 | 3 | 3.0 | 3t | 1 |

John Schultz
| 1976 | DEN N | 2 | 29 | 14.5 | 16 | 0 |

Randy Schultz
1967	NO N	14	186	13.3	25	0
1968		12	34	2.8	14	0
Career		26	220	8.5	25	0

Vic Schwall
1948	CHIC N	2	13	6.5	7	0
1949		3	8	2.7	18	2
1950		1	7	7.0	7	0
Career		6	28	4.7	18	2

Perry Schwartz
1938	BKN N	8	132	16.5		1
1939		33	550	16.7		3
1940		21	370	17.6		3
1941		25	362	14.5	36	2
1942		13	299	23.0	71	1
1946	NY AA	5	82	16.4		0
Career		105	1795	17.1	71	10
Playoffs		1	12	12.0		0

Ger Schwedes
| 1961 | BOS A | 1 | 21 | 21.0 | 21 | 0 |

Scott Schwedes
1988	MIA N	6	130	21.7	42	0
1989		7	174	24.9	65t	1
1990		6	66	11.0	19	1
Career		19	370	19.5	65t	2

Dick Schweidler
1938	CHIB N	1	21	21.0	21	0
1939		2	43	21.5		0
1946		1	11	11.0	11	0
Career		4	75	18.8	21	0

Joe Scibelli
| 1961 | LA N | 1 | 1 | 1.0 | 1 | 0 |

Nick Scollard
1946	BOS N	7	78	11.1	19t	1
1947		2	18	9.0	11	0
1948		2	23	11.5	13	0
1949	NYB N	3	81	27.0	40	2
Career		14	200	14.3	40	3

Bo Scott
1969	CLE N	6	25	4.2	14	0
1970		40	351	8.8	24	4
1971		30	233	7.8	35	1
1972		23	172	7.5	30	0
1973		6	23	3.8	9	1
1974		7	22	3.1	13	0
Career		112	826	7.4	35	6
Playoffs		16	166	10.4		0

Chuck Scott
1986	LARM N	5	76	15.2	21	0
1987	DAL N	1	11	11.0	11	0
Career		6	87	14.5	21	0

Clyde Scott
1949	PHI N	8	148	18.5	70	1
1951		10	212	21.2	53t	3
1952	DET N	1	21	21.0	21	0
Career		19	381	20.1	70	4
Playoffs		1	17	17.0		0

Darnay Scott
1994	CIN N	46	866	18.8	76	5
1995		52	821	15.8	88t	5
1996		58	833	14.4	50t	5
Career		156	2520	16.2	88t	15

Freddie Scott
1974	BAL N	18	317	17.6	45	0
1976		3	35	11.7	18	0
1977		18	267	14.8	33	2

Freddie Scott continued
1978	DET N	37	564	15.2	47	2
1979		62	929	15.0	50	5
1980		53	834	15.7	43t	4
1981		53	1022	19.3	48	5
1982		13	231	17.8	36	1
1983		5	71	14.2	25	1
Career		262	4270	16.3	50	20
Playoffs		6	88	14.7		0

Freddie Scott
| 1996 | ATL N | 7 | 80 | 11.4 | 27 | 0 |

George Scott
| 1959 | NYG N | 1 | 12 | 12.0 | 12 | 0 |

James Scott
1976	CHI N	26	512	19.7	63t	6
1977		50	809	16.2	72t	3
1978		42	759	18.1	59	5
1979		21	382	18.2	64	3
1980		36	696	19.3	64t	3
1982		2	44	22.0	27	0
Career		177	3202	18.1	72t	20
Playoffs		3	29	9.7		0

Joe Scott
1948	NYG N	17	235	13.8	43	2
1949		15	111	7.4	24	1
1950		9	240	26.7	61	0
1951		23	356	15.5	57t	2
1952		14	251	17.9	35	1
1953		1	10	10.0	10	1
Career		79	1203	15.2	61	7

Johnny Scott
| 1921 | BUF A | | | | | 2 |

Kevin Scott
| 1989 | DAL N | 9 | 63 | 7.0 | 12 | 0 |

Lindsay Scott
1982	NO N	17	251	14.8	36	0
1983		24	274	11.4	35	0
1984		21	278	13.2	37	1
1985		7	61	8.7	15	0
Career		69	864	12.5	37	1

Malcom Scott
1983	NYG N	17	206	12.1	24	0
1987	NO N	6	35	5.8	11	0
Career		23	241	10.5	24	0

Patrick Scott
1987	GB N	8	79	9.9	16	0
1988		20	275	13.8	41	1
Career		28	354	12.6	41	1

Perry Scott
| 1942 | DET N | 1 | 7 | 7.0 | 7 | 0 |

Prince Scott
| 1946 | MIA AA | 13 | 180 | 13.8 | | 2 |

Ronald Scott
| 1987 | MIA N | 2 | 7 | 3.5 | 5 | 0 |

Willie Scott
1981	KC N	5	72	14.4	26	1
1982		8	49	6.1	13	1
1983		29	247	8.5	22	6
1984		28	253	9.0	27	3
1985		5	61	12.2	21	0
1986	NE N	8	41	5.1	8t	3
1987		5	35	7.0	15	1
1988		1	8	8.0	8	0
Career		89	766	8.6	27	15

Rob Scribner
1973	LA N	2	19	9.5	13	0
1974		2	28	14.0	14t	1
1975		2	28	14.0	25	0
Career		6	75	12.5	25	1

Ed Scruggs
1947	BKN AA	2	9	4.5		0
1948		1	8	8.0	8	0
Career		3	17	5.7	8	0

Joe Scudero
1954	WAS N	4	32	8.0	13t	1
1957		2	30	15.0	18	0
Career		6	62	10.3	18	1

Charlie Seabright
1941	CLE N	5	44	8.8	14	0
1946	PIT N	4	77	19.3	33	1
1947		7	16	2.3	10	0
1948		8	63	7.9	16	1
1949		4	4	1.0	5	0
1950		3	37	12.3	13t	1
Career		31	241	7.8	33	3

Malcolm Seabron
| 1995 | HOU N | 12 | 167 | 13.9 | 34 | 1 |

Paul Seal
1974	NO N	32	466	14.6	42	3
1975		28	414	14.8	38	1
1976		9	72	8.0	15	0
1977	SF N	13	230	17.7	47t	1
1978		21	370	17.6	41t	2
1979		3	34	11.3	14	0
Career		106	1586	15.0	47t	7

Jimmy Sears
1957	CHIC N	5	66	13.2	27	0
1958		13	187	14.4	55	2
Career		18	253	14.1	55	2

George Seasholtz
| 1924 | KEN N | | | | | 1 |

Mark Seay
1994	SD N	58	645	11.1	49t	6
1995		45	537	11.9	38t	3
1996	PHI N	19	260	13.7	35	0
Career		122	1442	11.8	49t	9
Playoffs		15	155	10.3		1

Virgil Seay
1981	WAS N	26	472	18.2	50	3
1982		6	154	25.7	37	0
1983		2	55	27.5	39t	1
1984		9	111	12.3	19	1
Career		43	792	18.4	50	5

Len Sedbrook
1928	DET N					2
1929	NYG N					6
1930						2
Career						10

Larry Seiple
1967	MIA A	1	21	21.0	21	0
1968		7	69	9.9	20	1
1969		41	577	14.1	41t	5
1970	MIA N	2	14	7.0	7	0
1971		1	32	32.0	32	0
1975		10	84	8.4	15	0
1976		10	138	13.8	25	1
1977		1	-1	-1.0	-1	0
Career		73	934	12.8	41t	7

Clarence Self
| 1950 | DET N | 1 | 12 | 12.0 | 12 | 0 |

Ron Sellers
1969	BOS A	27	705	26.1	77	6
1970	BOS N	38	550	14.5	48	4
1971	NE N	14	222	15.9	49	3
1972	DAL N	31	653	21.1	55t	5
1973	MIA N	2	54	27.0	42	0
Career		112	2184	19.5	77	18
Playoffs		4	50	12.5		1

Harry Seltzer
| 1942 | DET N | 2 | 23 | 11.5 | 16 | 0 |

Year	Team		No	Yds	Avg	Lg	TD

Bernie Semes

Year	Team		No	Yds	Avg	Lg	TD
1944	C-P	N	3	22	7.3	10	0

Bill Senn

Year	Team		No	Yds	Avg	Lg	TD
1927	CHIB	N					1
1928							3
1929							2
Career							6

Frank Seno

Year	Team		No	Yds	Avg	Lg	TD
1943	WAS	N	12	195	16.3	36	0
1944			17	146	8.6	47	0
1945	CHIC	N	7	129	18.4	36	0
1946			12	124	10.3	27t	1
1947	BOS	N	12	118	9.8	30	1
1948			13	322	24.8	69	3
Career			73	1034	14.2	69	5
Playoffs			4	21	5.3		0

Joe Senser

Year	Team		No	Yds	Avg	Lg	TD
1980	MIN	N	42	447	10.6	58t	7
1981			79	1004	12.7	53	8
1982			29	261	9.0	22	1
1984			15	110	7.3	26	0
Career			165	1822	11.0	58t	16
Playoffs			11	138	12.5		0

Joe Setcavage

Year	Team		No	Yds	Avg	Lg	TD
1943	BKN	N	5	26	5.2	17	0

John Settle

Year	Team		No	Yds	Avg	Lg	TD
1987	ATL	N	11	153	13.9	36	0
1988			68	570	8.4	27	1
1989			39	316	8.1	33	2
Career			118	1039	8.8	36	3

Jeff Sevy

Year	Team		No	Yds	Avg	Lg	TD
1975	CHI	N	1	6	6.0	6	0

Steve Sewell

Year	Team		No	Yds	Avg	Lg	TD
1985	DEN	N	24	224	9.3	54t	1
1986			23	294	12.8	40	1
1987			13	209	16.1	72t	1
1988			38	507	13.3	68t	5
1989			25	416	16.6	56	3
1990			26	268	10.3	36	0
1991			38	436	11.5	60	2
Career			187	2354	12.6	72t	13
Playoffs			31	375	12.1		0

Frank Seyfrit

Year	Team		No	Yds	Avg	Lg	TD
1923	TOL	N					1

Bob Seymour

Year	Team		No	Yds	Avg	Lg	TD
1940	WAS	N	2	3	1.5		0
1941			6	85	14.2	41	2
1942			3	20	6.7	12	0
1943			17	167	9.8	32	2
1944			19	263	13.8	71t	3
1945			8	91	11.4	27t	1
1946	LA	AA	17	188	11.1		3
Career			72	817	11.3	71t	11
Playoffs			3	29	9.7		1

Jim Seymour

Year	Team		No	Yds	Avg	Lg	TD
1970	CHI	N	6	145	24.2	53t	4
1971			5	75	15.0	21	0
1972			10	165	16.5	35t	1
Career			21	385	18.3		5

Paul Seymour

Year	Team		No	Yds	Avg	Lg	TD
1973	BUF	N	10	114	11.4	22	0
1974			15	246	16.4	40t	2
1975			19	268	14.1	32	1
1976			16	169	10.6	22	0
1977			2	21	10.5	11	0
Career			62	818	13.2	40t	3
Playoffs			2	35	17.5		1

Leland Shaffer

Year	Team		No	Yds	Avg	Lg	TD
1935	NYG	N	7	123	17.6		0
1936			2	30	15.0		1
1937			7	72	10.3		0
1938			12	86	7.2		2

Leland Shaffer *continued*

Year	Team		No	Yds	Avg	Lg	TD
1939			2	8	4.0		0
1940			15	121	8.1		2
1941			1	5	5.0	5	0
1942			3	20	6.7	10	0
1943			3	66	22.0	40	0
Career			52	531	10.2	40	5
Playoffs			2	16	8.0		0

Ron Shanklin

Year	Team		No	Yds	Avg	Lg	TD
1970	PIT	N	30	691	23.0	81t	4
1971			49	652	13.3	42	6
1972			38	669	17.6	57	3
1973			30	711	23.7	67	10
1974			19	324	17.1	35	1
1976	CHI	N	2	32	16.0	35	0
Career			168	3079	18.3	81t	24
Playoffs			6	119	19.8		0

Jim Shanley

Year	Team		No	Yds	Avg	Lg	TD
1958	GB	N	3	13	4.3	7	0

Carver Shannon

Year	Team		No	Yds	Avg	Lg	TD
1963	LA	N	2	7	3.5	6	0
1964			2	4	2.0	10	0
Career			4	11	2.8	10	0

Dan Sharp

Year	Team		No	Yds	Avg	Lg	TD
1987	ATL	N	2	6	3.0	5	0

Luis Sharpe

Year	Team		No	Yds	Avg	Lg	TD
1990	PHX	N	1	1	1.0	1t	1

Shannon Sharpe

Year	Team		No	Yds	Avg	Lg	TD
1990	DEN	N	7	99	14.1	33	1
1991			22	322	14.6	37	1
1992			53	640	12.1	55	2
1993			81	995	12.3	63	9
1994			87	1010	11.6	44	4
1995			63	756	12.0	49	4
1996			80	1062	13.3	51	10
Career			393	4884	12.4	63	31
Playoffs			21	247	11.8		2

Sterling Sharpe

Year	Team		No	Yds	Avg	Lg	TD
1988	GB	N	55	791	14.4	51	1
1989			90	1423	15.8	79t	12
1990			67	1105	16.5	76t	6
1991			69	961	13.9	58t	4
1992			108	1461	13.5	76t	13
1993			112	1274	11.4	54	11
1994			94	1119	11.9	49	18
Career			595	8134	13.7	79t	65
Playoffs			11	229	20.8		4

Bob Shaw

Year	Team		No	Yds	Avg	Lg	TD
1946	LA	N	4	63	15.8	28t	1
1949			29	535	18.4	71	6
1950	CHIC	N	48	971	20.2	65t	12
Career			81	1569	19.4	71	20
Playoffs			2	21	10.5		0

Bob Shaw

Year	Team		No	Yds	Avg	Lg	TD
1970	NO	N	1	49	49.0	49	0

Glenn Shaw

Year	Team		No	Yds	Avg	Lg	TD
1962	LA	N	3	51	17.0	30	0
1963	OAK	A	2	64	32.0	55	1
1964			3	31	10.3	15	0
Career			8	146	18.3	55	1

Al Sheard

Year	Team		No	Yds	Avg	Lg	TD
1925	ROC	N					2

Kenny Shedd

Year	Team		No	Yds	Avg	Lg	TD
1996	OAK	N	3	87	29.0	51	1

Ed Shedlosky

Year	Team		No	Yds	Avg	Lg	TD
1945	NYG	N	2	15	7.5	9	0

Paul Sheeks

Year	Team		No	Yds	Avg	Lg	TD
1921	AKR	A					1

Willie Shelby

Year	Team		No	Yds	Avg	Lg	TD
1976	CIN	N	1	3	3.0	3	0
1978	STL	N	1	11	11.0	11	0
Career			2	14	7.0	11	0

Donnie Shell

Year	Team		No	Yds	Avg	Lg	TD
1975	PIT	N	2	39	19.5	20	0

Charley Shepard

Year	Team		No	Yds	Avg	Lg	TD
1956	PIT	N	1	31	31.0	31	0

Derrick Shepard

Year	Team		No	Yds	Avg	Lg	TD
1989	NO-DAL	N	20	304	15.2	37t	1

Bill Shepherd

Year	Team		No	Yds	Avg	Lg	TD
1939	DET	N	14	143	10.2		1
1940			2	12	6.0		0
Career			16	155	9.7		1

Johnny Shepherd

Year	Team		No	Yds	Avg	Lg	TD
1987	BUF	N	1	2	2.0	2	0

Leslie Shepherd

Year	Team		No	Yds	Avg	Lg	TD
1994	WAS	N	1	8	8.0	8	0
1995			29	486	16.8	73t	2
1996			23	344	15.0	52t	3
Career			53	838	15.8	73t	5

Dave Sherer

Year	Team		No	Yds	Avg	Lg	TD
1959	BAL	N	1	9	9.0	9	0

Bob Sherlag

Year	Team		No	Yds	Avg	Lg	TD
1966	ATL	N	4	53	13.3	30t	1

Heath Sherman

Year	Team		No	Yds	Avg	Lg	TD
1989	PHI	N	8	85	10.6	17	0
1990			23	167	7.3	26	3
1991			14	59	4.2	11	0
1992			18	219	12.2	7t	1
1993			12	78	6.5	21	0
Career			75	608	8.1	26	4
Playoffs			7	62	8.9		0

Rod Sherman

Year	Team		No	Yds	Avg	Lg	TD
1967	OAK	A	5	61	12.2	22	0
1970	OAK	N	18	285	15.8	32	0
1971			12	187	15.6	32t	1
1972	DEN	N	38	661	17.4	55	3
1973	LA	N	1	8	8.0	8	0
Career			74	1202	16.2	55	4
Playoffs			8	187	23.4		3

Solly Sherman

Year	Team		No	Yds	Avg	Lg	TD
1939	CHIB	N	1	42	42.0	42	0

Tom Sherman

Year	Team		No	Yds	Avg	Lg	TD
1968	CIN	A	31	374	12.1	27t	1

Will Sherman

Year	Team		No	Yds	Avg	Lg	TD
1961	MIN	N	2	40	20.0	32	0

Mike Sherrard

Year	Team		No	Yds	Avg	Lg	TD
1986	DAL	N	41	744	18.1	68t	5
1990	SF	N	17	264	15.5	43	2
1991			24	296	12.3	31	2
1992			38	607	16.0	56	0
1993	NYG	N	24	433	18.0	55t	2
1994			53	825	15.6	55	6
1995			44	577	13.1	57t	4
1996	DEN	N	16	185	11.6	25t	1
Career			257	3931	15.3	68t	22
Playoffs			9	73	8.1		1

Tim Sherwin

Year	Team		No	Yds	Avg	Lg	TD
1981	BAL	N	2	19	9.5	11	0
1982			21	280	13.3	33	0
1983			25	358	14.3	30	0
1984	IND	N	11	169	15.4	26	0
1985			5	64	12.8	29	0
1986			3	26	8.7	15	1
1987			9	86	9.6	32	1
Career			76	1002	13.2	33	2

Rhoten Shetley

Year	Team		No	Yds	Avg	Lg	TD
1940	BKN	N	8	126	15.8		1
1941			5	63	12.6	22	0
1942			3	19	6.3	9	1
1946	BKN	AA	1	10	10.0	10	0
Career			17	218	12.8	22	2

Burrell Shields

Year	Team		No	Yds	Avg	Lg	TD
1954	PIT	N	1	22	22.0	22	0
1955	BAL	N	3	27	9.0	19	0
Career			4	49	12.3	22	0

Jerry Shipkey

Year	Team		No	Yds	Avg	Lg	TD
1948	PIT	N	10	106	10.6	43	0
1949			2	32	16.0	21	0
Career			12	138	11.5	43	0

Joe Shipp

Year	Team		No	Yds	Avg	Lg	TD
1979	BUF	N	3	43	14.3	27	1

Gary Shirk

Year	Team		No	Yds	Avg	Lg	TD
1976	NYG	N	4	52	13.0	31	1
1977			16	280	17.5	64	2
1978			10	127	12.7	45	2
1979			31	471	15.2	61	2
1980			21	211	10.0	21	1
1981			42	445	10.6	46	3
1982			6	54	9.0	19	0
Career			130	1640	12.6	64	11

John Shirk

Year	Team		No	Yds	Avg	Lg	TD
1940	CHIC	N	11	91	8.3		0

Roy Shivers

Year	Team		No	Yds	Avg	Lg	TD
1966	STL	N	5	81	16.2	40	0
1967			3	15	5.0	14	0
1968			9	103	11.4	40t	3
1969			7	61	8.7	26	1
1970			3	44	14.7	22	0
1971			10	76	7.6	19	0
1972			1	20	20.0	20	0
Career			38	400	10.5	40t	4

Bill Shockley

Year	Team		No	Yds	Avg	Lg	TD
1960	NY	A	8	69	8.6		2
1961			3	27	9.0	13	0
Career			11	96	8.7	13	2

Hal Shoener

Year	Team		No	Yds	Avg	Lg	TD
1948	SF	AA	15	76	5.1		3
1949			7	84	12.0		0
Career			22	160	7.3		3
Playoffs			2	25	12.5		0

Del Shofner

Year	Team		No	Yds	Avg	Lg	TD
1958	LA	N	51	**1097**	21.5	92t	8
1959			47	936	19.9	72t	7
1960			12	122	10.2	17t	1
1961	NYG	N	68	1125	16.5	46t	11
1962			53	1133	21.4	69t	12
1963			64	1181	18.5	70t	9
1964			22	323	14.7	54	0
1965			22	388	17.6	49	2
1966			3	19	6.3	9	0
1967			7	146	20.9	33t	1
Career			349	6470	18.5	92t	51
Playoffs			8	110	13.8		0

John Shonk

Year	Team		No	Yds	Avg	Lg	TD
1941	PHI	N	4	43	10.8	14	0

Chuck Shonta

Year	Team		No	Yds	Avg	Lg	TD
1961	BOS	A	1	9	9.0	9	0

Paul Shoults

Year	Team		No	Yds	Avg	Lg	TD
1949	NYB	N	10	124	12.4	23	0

Don Shula

Year	Team		No	Yds	Avg	Lg	TD
1953	BAL	N	1	6	6.0	6	0

Mickey Shuler

Year	Team		No	Yds	Avg	Lg	TD
1978	NYJ	N	11	67	6.1	15	0
1979			16	225	14.1	46	3
1980			22	226	10.3	26	2

Mickey Shuler *continued*

Year	Team		No	Yds	Avg	Lg	TD
1982			8	132	16.5	51	3
1983			26	272	10.5	28	1
1984			68	782	11.5	49	6
1985			76	879	11.6	35	7
1986			69	675	9.8	36t	4
1987			43	434	10.1	32t	3
1988			70	805	11.5	42t	5
1989			29	322	11.1	22	0
1990	PHI	N	18	190	10.6	25	0
1991			6	91	15.2	21	0
Career			462	5100	11.0	51	37
Playoffs			20	249	12.4		2

Mike Shumann

Year	Team		No	Yds	Avg	Lg	TD
1979	SF	N	39	452	11.6	39	4
1980	TB	N	4	75	18.8	25	1
1981	SF	N	3	21	7.0	8	0
1982	STL	N	5	58	11.6	23	0
1983			11	154	14.0	33	0
Career			62	760	12.3	39	5
Playoffs			5	70	14.0		1

Marshall Shurnas

Year	Team		No	Yds	Avg	Lg	TD
1947	CLE	AA	2	30	15.0		0

Don Shy

Year	Team		No	Yds	Avg	Lg	TD
1967	PIT	N	12	152	12.7	55	1
1968			13	106	8.2	21	0
1969	NO	N	9	141	15.7	70	1
1970	CHI	N	10	149	14.9	64	0
1971			19	163	8.6	25	0
1972			10	109	10.9	28	0
1973	STL	N	3	15	5.0	6	1
Career			76	835	11.0	70	3

Les Shy

Year	Team		No	Yds	Avg	Lg	TD
1967	DAL	N	3	36	12.0	19	0
1968			10	105	10.5	41	0
1969			8	124	15.5	49t	1
1970	NYG	N	2	8	4.0	6	0
Career			23	273	11.9	49t	1

Mike Siani

Year	Team		No	Yds	Avg	Lg	TD
1972	OAK	N	28	496	17.7	70t	5
1973			45	742	16.5	80t	3
1974			3	30	10.0	13	1
1975			17	294	17.3	44	0
1976			11	173	15.7	37t	2
1977			24	344	14.3	39	2
1978	BAL	N	6	151	25.2	49	1
1979			15	214	14.3	31t	2
1980			9	174	19.3	38t	1
Career			158	2618	16.6	80t	17
Playoffs			18	247	13.7		3

Mike Siano

Year	Team		No	Yds	Avg	Lg	TD
1987	PHI	N	9	137	15.2	34	1

Jimmy Sidle

Year	Team		No	Yds	Avg	Lg	TD
1966	ATL	N	1	16	16.0	16	0

Johnny Siegal

Year	Team		No	Yds	Avg	Lg	TD
1939	CHIB	N	3	71	23.7		0
1940			4	53	13.3		0
1941			9	220	24.4	65	3
1942			13	264	20.3	32	2
1943			2	29	14.5	18	0
Career			31	637	20.5	65	5
Playoffs			4	36	9.0		0

Eric Sievers

Year	Team		No	Yds	Avg	Lg	TD
1981	SD	N	22	276	12.5	32	3
1982			12	173	14.4	26	1
1983			33	452	13.7	28	3
1984			41	438	10.7	32	3
1985			41	438	10.7	30t	6
1986			2	14	7.0	9	0
1988			1	2	2.0	2	0
1989	NE	N	54	615	11.4	46	0
1990			8	77	9.6	25	0
Career			214	2485	11.6	46	16
Playoffs			5	51	10.2		1

Sig Sigurdson

Year	Team		No	Yds	Avg	Lg	TD
1947	BAL	AA	8	104	13.0		0

Vai Sikahema

Year	Team		No	Yds	Avg	Lg	TD
1986	STL	N	10	99	9.9	27	1
1989	PHX	N	23	245	10.7	37	0
1990			7	51	7.3	13	0
1992	PHI	N	13	142	10.9	22	0
Career			53	537	10.1	37	1

Floyd Simmons

Year	Team		No	Yds	Avg	Lg	TD
1948	CHI	AA	2	60	30.0		0

Jerry Simmons

Year	Team		No	Yds	Avg	Lg	TD
1965	PIT	N	2	16	8.0	9	0
1966			6	68	11.3	21t	1
1967	NO-ATL	N	23	312	13.6	30	2
1968	ATL	N	28	479	17.1	61	0
1969	ATL-CHI	N	14	182	13.0	48	0
1971	DEN	N	25	403	16.1	47	1
1972			17	235	13.8	35t	2
1973			13	249	19.2	53	1
1974			10	161	16.1	36	2
Career			138	2105	15.3	61	9

Stacey Simmons

Year	Team		No	Yds	Avg	Lg	TD
1990	IND	N	4	33	8.3	12	0

Bob Simms

Year	Team		No	Yds	Avg	Lg	TD
1960	NYG	N	1	58	58.0	58	0

Phil Simms

Year	Team		No	Yds	Avg	Lg	TD
1984	NYG	N	1	13	13.0	13	0
1993			1	-6	-6.0	-6	0
Career			2	7	3.5	13	0

Nate Simpson

Year	Team		No	Yds	Avg	Lg	TD
1977	GB	N	5	19	3.8	14	0
1978			1	4	4.0	4	0
1979			11	46	4.2	10	0
Career			17	69	4.1	14	0

O.J. Simpson

Year	Team		No	Yds	Avg	Lg	TD
1969	BUF	N	30	343	11.4	55t	3
1970			10	139	13.9	36	0
1971			21	162	7.7	38	0
1972			27	198	7.3	25	0
1973			6	70	11.7	24	0
1974			15	189	12.6	29t	1
1975			28	426	15.2	64t	7
1976			22	259	11.8	43	1
1977			16	138	8.6	18	0
1978	SF	N	21	172	8.2	19	2
1979			7	46	6.6	14	0
Career			203	2142	10.6	64t	14
Playoffs			3	37	12.3		0

Billy Sims

Year	Team		No	Yds	Avg	Lg	TD
1980	DET	N	51	621	12.2	87t	3
1981			28	451	16.1	81t	2
1982			34	342	10.1	52	0
1983			42	419	10.0	54	0
1984			31	239	7.7	20	0
Career			186	2072	11.1	87t	5
Playoffs			10	94	9.4		0

David Sims

Year	Team		No	Yds	Avg	Lg	TD
1977	SEA	N	12	176	14.7	82t	3
1978			30	195	6.5	25	1
1979			4	28	7.0	13	0
Career			46	399	8.7	82t	4

Keith Sims

Year	Team		No	Yds	Avg	Lg	TD
1991	MIA	N	1	9	9.0	9	0

Marvin Sims

Year	Team		No	Yds	Avg	Lg	TD
1980	BAL	N	9	64	7.1	13	0

Walt Singer

Year	Team		No	Yds	Avg	Lg	TD
1935	NYG	N					1
1936			6	38	6.3		0
Career			6	38	6.3		1
Playoffs			1	17	17.0		0

Reggie Singletary

Year	Team		No	Yds	Avg	Lg	TD
1987	PHI	N	1	-11	-11.0	-11	0

Nate Singleton

Year	Team		No	Yds	Avg	Lg	TD
1993	SF	N	8	126	15.8	33	1
1994			21	294	14.0	43t	2
1995			8	108	13.5	23	1
1996			1	11	11.0	11	0
Career			38	539	14.2	43t	4

Frankie Sinkwich

Year	Team		No	Yds	Avg	Lg	TD
1943	DET	N	1	8	8.0	8	0
1947	NY-BAL	AA	1	3	3.0	3	0
Career			2	11	5.5	8	0

Johnny Sisk

Year	Team		No	Yds	Avg	Lg	TD
1934	CHIB	N	1	14	14.0	14	0
1935			1	44	44.0	44	0
1936			1	39	39.0	39	0
Career			3	97	32.3	44	0

Vince Sites

Year	Team		No	Yds	Avg	Lg	TD
1936	PIT	N	2	22	11.0		1
1937			2	10	5.0		0
Career			4	32	8.0		1

Emil Sitko

Year	Team		No	Yds	Avg	Lg	TD
1950	SF	N	3	43	14.3	28t	1
1951	CHIC	N	4	28	7.0	15	0
1952			2	16	8.0	10	0
Career			9	87	9.7	28t	1

Paul Skansi

Year	Team		No	Yds	Avg	Lg	TD
1983	PIT	N	3	39	13.0	21	0
1984	SEA	N	7	85	12.1	27	0
1985			21	269	12.8	32	1
1986			22	271	12.3	30	0
1987			19	207	10.9	25	1
1988			24	238	9.9	21	1
1989			39	488	12.5	26	5
1990			22	257	11.7	25t	2
1991			9	96	10.7	21	0
Career			166	1950	11.7	32	10
Playoffs			5	55	11.0		0

John Skibinski

Year	Team		No	Yds	Avg	Lg	TD
1979	CHI	N	1	4	4.0	4	0
1980			5	18	3.6	8	0
Career			6	22	3.7	8	0

Joe Skladany

Year	Team		No	Yds	Avg	Lg	TD
1934	PIT	N	10	222	22.2		2

Ed Skoronski

Year	Team		No	Yds	Avg	Lg	TD
1936	PIT	N	8	95	11.9		1

Webster Slaughter

Year	Team		No	Yds	Avg	Lg	TD
1986	CLE	N	40	577	14.4	47t	4
1987			47	806	17.1	54t	7
1988			30	462	15.4	41	3
1989			65	1236	19.0	97t	6
1990			59	847	14.4	50	4
1991			64	906	14.2	62t	3
1992	HOU	N	39	486	12.5	36t	4
1993			77	904	11.7	41	5
1994			68	846	12.4	57	2
1995	KC	N	34	514	15.1	38	4
1996	NYJ	N	32	434	13.6	53	2
Career			555	8018	14.4	97t	44
Playoffs			33	464	14.1		6

Leroy Sledge

Year	Team		No	Yds	Avg	Lg	TD
1971	HOU	N	6	32	5.3	10	1

David Sloan

Year	Team		No	Yds	Avg	Lg	TD
1995	DET	N	17	184	10.8	24	1
1996			7	51	7.3	18	0
Career			24	235	9.8	24	1
Playoffs			5	67	13.4		2

Dwight Sloan

Year	Team		No	Yds	Avg	Lg	TD
1938	CHIC	N	1	10	10.0	10	0

Phil Slosburg

Year	Team		No	Yds	Avg	Lg	TD
1948	BOS	N	2	29	14.5	16	0
1949	NYB	N	4	11	2.8	9	0
Career			6	40	6.7	16	0

Elmer Slough

Year	Team		No	Yds	Avg	Lg	TD
1926	BUF	N					2

Bill Slyker

Year	Team		No	Yds	Avg	Lg	TD
1922	EVA	N					1

Torrance Small

Year	Team		No	Yds	Avg	Lg	TD
1992	NO	N	23	278	12.1	33	3
1993			16	164	10.3	17	1
1994			49	719	14.7	75t	5
1995			38	461	12.1	32t	5
1996			50	558	11.2	41	2
Career			176	2180	12.4	75t	16
Playoffs			1	6	6.0		0

Rudy Smeja

Year	Team		No	Yds	Avg	Lg	TD
1944	CHIB	N	7	110	15.7	19	1
1945			1	11	11.0	11	0
1946	PHI	N	3	45	15.0	17	0
Career			11	166	15.1	19	1

Tommie Smiley

Year	Team		No	Yds	Avg	Lg	TD
1968	CIN	A	19	86	4.5	17	0
1969	DEN	A	5	23	4.6	17t	1
Career			24	109	4.5	17t	1

Allen Smith

Year	Team		No	Yds	Avg	Lg	TD
1948	CHIB	N	3	29	9.7	18	0

Allen Smith

Year	Team		No	Yds	Avg	Lg	TD
1966	BUF	A	1	1	1.0	1	0

Barry Smith

Year	Team		No	Yds	Avg	Lg	TD
1973	GB	N	15	233	15.5	24	2
1975			6	77	12.8	20	1
1976	TB	N	4	88	22.0	39	0
Career			25	398	15.9	39	3

Barty Smith

Year	Team		No	Yds	Avg	Lg	TD
1974	GB	N	20	294	14.7	27t	1
1975			16	140	8.8	33	1
1976			11	88	8.0	35	0
1977			37	340	9.2	42	1
1978			37	256	6.9	24	0
1979			19	155	8.2	22	1
Career			140	1273	9.1	42	4

Ben Smith

Year	Team		No	Yds	Avg	Lg	TD
1934	PIT	N	12	190	15.8		0
1935			9	166	18.4		0
1937	WAS	N	2	37	18.5		0
Career			23	393	17.1		0

Bill Smith

Year	Team		No	Yds	Avg	Lg	TD
1934	CHIC	N					1
1935			24	318	13.3		2
1936			20	414	20.7		1
1937			3	52	17.3		0
1938			18	338	18.8		1
1939			21	387	18.4		4
Career			86	1509	17.5		9

Bob Smith

Year	Team		No	Yds	Avg	Lg	TD
1955	CLE	N	2	12	6.0	10	0

Bobby Smith

Year	Team		No	Yds	Avg	Lg	TD
1964	BUF	A	6	72	12.0	25	0
1965			12	116	9.7	21	0
1966	PIT	N	3	26	8.7	21	0
Career			21	214	10.2	25	0

Bruce Smith

Year	Team		No	Yds	Avg	Lg	TD
1947	GB	N	4	50	12.5	36t	1
1948	LA	N	4	29	7.3	10	0
Career			8	79	9.9	36t	1

Carl Smith

Year	Team		No	Yds	Avg	Lg	TD
1960	BUF	A	7	127	18.1		1

Cedric Smith

Year	Team		No	Yds	Avg	Lg	TD
1994	WAS	N	15	118	7.9	28	1
1996	ARI	N	3	3	1.0	2	1
Career			18	121	6.7	28	2

Charlie Smith

Year	Team		No	Yds	Avg	Lg	TD
1947	CHIC	N	1	-6	-6.0	-6	0

Charlie Smith

Year	Team		No	Yds	Avg	Lg	TD
1968	OAK	A	22	321	14.6	43t	2
1969			30	322	10.7	32	2
1970	OAK	N	23	173	7.5	27t	2
1971			2	67	33.5	44	0
1972			28	353	12.6	43	2
1973			28	260	9.3	20	1
1974			8	100	12.5	30	1
Career			141	1596	11.3	44	10
Playoffs			31	367	11.8		2

Charlie Smith

Year	Team		No	Yds	Avg	Lg	TD
1974	PHI	N	1	28	28.0	28	0
1975			37	515	13.9	46	6
1976			27	412	15.3	48t	4
1977			33	464	14.1	32	4
1978			11	142	12.9	27t	2
1979			24	399	16.6	39	1
1980			47	825	17.6	46	3
1981			38	564	14.8	45	4
Career			218	3349	15.4	48t	24
Playoffs			15	243	16.2		1

Chris Smith

Year	Team		No	Yds	Avg	Lg	TD
1987	KC	N	2	21	10.5	16	0

Dave Smith

Year	Team		No	Yds	Avg	Lg	TD
1960	HOU	A	22	216	9.8		2
1961			10	131	13.1	37	1
1962			17	117	6.9	20	2
1963			24	270	11.3	36	2
1964			7	38	5.4	15	0
Career			80	772	9.7	37	7
Playoffs			6	58	9.7		1

Dave Smith

Year	Team		No	Yds	Avg	Lg	TD
1970	PIT	N	30	458	15.3	87t	2
1971			47	663	14.1	49	5
1972	PIT-HOU	N	30	316	10.5	25	0
1973	KC	N	2	20	10.0	17	0
Career			109	1457	13.4	87t	7

Dave Smith

Year	Team		No	Yds	Avg	Lg	TD
1970	SD	N	4	65	16.3	42	0

Dick Smith

Year	Team		No	Yds	Avg	Lg	TD
1968	WAS	N	1	15	15.0	15	0

Don Smith

Year	Team		No	Yds	Avg	Lg	TD
1988	TB	N	12	138	11.5	25	0
1989			7	110	15.7	44	0
1990	BUF	N	21	225	10.7	39	0
Career			40	473	11.8	44	0

Ed Smith

Year	Team		No	Yds	Avg	Lg	TD
1948	GB	N	12	121	10.1	49	0

Emmitt Smith

Year	Team		No	Yds	Avg	Lg	TD
1990	DAL	N	24	228	9.5	57	0
1991			49	258	5.3	14	1
1992			59	335	5.7	26t	1
1993			57	414	7.3	86	1
1994			50	341	6.8	68	1
1995			62	375	6.0	40	0
1996			47	249	5.3	21	3
Career			348	2200	6.3	86	7
Playoffs			44	318	7.2		2

Gaylon Smith

Year	Team		No	Yds	Avg	Lg	TD
1939	CLE	N	3	57	19.0		0
1940			3	65	21.7		0
1942			3	66	22.0	33	0
1946	CLE	AA	7	73	10.4		0
Career			16	261	16.3	33	0

George Smith

Year	Team		No	Yds	Avg	Lg	TD
1943	CHIC	N	1	18	18.0	18	0

Gordon Smith

Year	Team		No	Yds	Avg	Lg	TD
1961	MIN	N	12	320	26.7	71t	4
1962			7	138	19.7	40	1
1963			6	177	29.5	54t	2
1964			10	211	21.1	44	1
1965			22	431	19.6	49	5
Career			57	1277	22.4	71t	13

Hank Smith

Year	Team		No	Yds	Avg	Lg	TD
1922	ROC	N					1

Holden Smith

Year	Team		No	Yds	Avg	Lg	TD
1982	BAL	N	2	36	18.0	23	0

Irv Smith

Year	Team		No	Yds	Avg	Lg	TD
1993	NO	N	16	180	11.3	23	2
1994			41	330	8.0	19	3
1995			45	466	10.4	43	3
1996			15	144	9.6	37	0
Career			117	1120	9.6	43	8

Jackie Smith

Year	Team		No	Yds	Avg	Lg	TD
1963	STL	N	28	445	15.9	55t	2
1964			47	657	14.0	78t	4
1965			41	648	15.8	70t	2
1966			45	810	18.0	69t	4
1967			56	1205	21.5	76t	9
1968			49	789	16.1	65t	2
1969			43	561	13.0	34	1
1970			37	687	18.6	59t	4
1971			21	379	18.0	61t	4
1972			26	407	15.7	71	2
1973			41	600	14.6	42	1
1974			25	413	16.5	81	3
1975			13	246	18.9	45	2
1976			3	22	7.3	16	0
1977			5	49	9.8	13	1
Career			480	7918	16.5	81	40
Playoffs			5	46	9.2		1

J.D. Smith

Year	Team		No	Yds	Avg	Lg	TD
1956	SF	N	1	13	13.0	13	0
1958			6	59	9.8	23	0
1959			13	133	10.2	21t	1
1960			36	181	5.0	21	1
1961			28	343	12.3	57	1
1962			21	197	9.4	47	1
1963			17	196	11.5	40	1
1965	DAL	N	5	10	2.0	5	1
1966			1	3	3.0	3	0
Career			128	1135	8.9	57	6

J.D. Smith

Year	Team		No	Yds	Avg	Lg	TD
1960	OAK	A	17	194	11.4		1

Jeff Smith

Year	Team		No	Yds	Avg	Lg	TD
1985	KC	N	18	157	8.7	45t	2
1986			33	230	7.0	18	3
1987	TB	N	20	197	9.8	34t	2
1988			16	134	8.4	22	0
Career			87	718	8.3	45t	7
Playoffs			2	12	6.0		0

Jeff Smith

Year	Team		No	Yds	Avg	Lg	TD
1987	NYG	N	6	72	12.0	19	0

Jerry Smith

Year	Team		No	Yds	Avg	Lg	TD
1965	WAS	N	19	257	13.5	54	2
1966			54	686	12.7	35	6
1967			67	849	12.7	43	12
1968			45	626	13.9	56	6
1969			54	682	12.6	28	9
1970			43	575	13.4	41	9
1971			16	227	14.2	31t	1
1972			21	353	16.8	34	7
1973			19	215	11.3	25	0
1974			44	554	12.6	30	3
1975			31	391	12.6	27	3
1976			7	75	10.7	20	2
1977			1	6	6.0	6	0
Career			421	5496	13.1	56	60
Playoffs			7	108	15.4		1

Jim Smith

Year	Team		No	Yds	Avg	Lg	TD
1949	CHI-DET	AA-N	3	47	15.7	31	0
1952	DET	N	1	18	18.0	18	0
1953			1	11	11.0	11	0
Career			5	76	15.2	31	0

Jim Smith

Year	Team		No	Yds	Avg	Lg	TD
1977	PIT	N	4	80	20.0	26	0
1978			6	83	13.8	29t	2
1979			17	243	14.3	25	2
1980			37	711	19.2	45t	9
1981			29	571	19.7	46t	7
1982			17	387	22.8	51	4
1985	LARI	N	3	28	9.3	14	1
Career			113	2103	18.6	51	25
Playoffs			5	81	16.2		0

Jimmy Smith

Year	Team		No	Yds	Avg	Lg	TD
1995	JAC	N	22	288	13.1	33	3
1996			83	1244	15.0	62	7
Career			105	1532	14.6	62	10
Playoffs			11	174	15.8		2

Joe Smith

Year	Team		No	Yds	Avg	Lg	TD
1948	BAL	AA	8	131	16.4		1

Joey Smith

Year	Team		No	Yds	Avg	Lg	TD
1992	NYG	N	3	45	15.0	22	0

J.T. Smith

Year	Team		No	Yds	Avg	Lg	TD
1979	KC	N	33	444	13.5	34	3
1980			46	655	14.2	77	2
1981			63	852	13.5	42	2
1982			10	168	16.8	51	1
1983			7	85	12.1	18	0
1984			8	69	8.6	16	0
1985	STL	N	43	581	13.5	34	1
1986			80	1014	12.7	45	6
1987			91	1117	12.3	38	8
1988	PHX	N	83	986	11.9	29	5
1989			62	778	12.5	31	5
1990			18	225	12.5	45t	2
Career			544	6974	12.8	77	35

Kendal Smith

Year	Team		No	Yds	Avg	Lg	TD
1989	CIN	N	10	140	14.0	41t	1
1990			7	45	6.4	11	0
Career			17	185	10.9	41t	1

Kevin Smith

Year	Team		No	Yds	Avg	Lg	TD
1994	LARI	N	1	8	8.0	8	0

Lamar Smith

Year	Team		No	Yds	Avg	Lg	TD
1995	SEA	N	1	10	10.0	10	0
1996			9	58	6.4	22	0
Career			10	68	6.8	22	0

Larry Smith

Year	Team		No	Yds	Avg	Lg	TD
1969	LA	N	46	300	6.5	38	2
1970			24	164	6.8	17t	0
1971			31	324	10.5	34	0
1972			15	186	12.4	47	1
1973			10	65	6.5	11	0
1974	WAS	N	23	137	6.0	14	1
Career			149	1176	7.9	47	5
Playoffs			8	49	6.1		0

Michael Smith

Year	Team		No	Yds	Avg	Lg	TD
Playoffs			1	28	28.0		0

Noland Smith

Year	Team		No	Yds	Avg	Lg	TD
1967	KC	A	1	42	42.0	42	0
1968			1	15	15.0	15	0
Career			2	57	28.5	42	0

Ollie Smith

Year	Team		No	Yds	Avg	Lg	TD
1973	BAL	N	1	37	37.0	37	0
1974			1	14	14.0	14	0
1976	GB	N	20	364	18.2	47	1
1977			22	357	16.2	41	0
Career			44	772	17.5	47	1

Phil Smith

Year	Team		No	Yds	Avg	Lg	TD
1986	PHI	N	6	94	15.7	36	0

Phil Smith *continued*

Year	Team		No	Yds	Avg	Lg	TD
1987	LARM	N	3	95	31.7	51	0
Career			9	189	21.0	51	0

Quintin Smith

Year	Team		No	Yds	Avg	Lg	TD
1990	CHI	N	2	20	10.0	12	0

Ralph Smith

Year	Team		No	Yds	Avg	Lg	TD
1962	PHI	N	1	29	29.0	29	0
1963			5	63	12.6	16	1
1964			4	35	8.8	12	0
1966	CLE	N	13	183	14.1	28	3
1967			14	211	15.1	49t	1
1968			2	11	5.5	7	0
1969	ATL	N	2	17	8.5	10	0
Career			41	549	13.4	49t	5

Ray Gene Smith

Year	Team		No	Yds	Avg	Lg	TD
1955	CHIB	N	1	13	13.0	13	0
1957			3	37	12.3	21	0
Career			4	50	12.5	21	0

Rico Smith

Year	Team		No	Yds	Avg	Lg	TD
1992	CLE	N	5	64	12.8	21	0
1993			4	55	13.8	17	0
1994			2	61	30.5	50	0
1995			13	173	13.3	29t	1
Career			24	353	14.7	50	1

Riley Smith

Year	Team		No	Yds	Avg	Lg	TD
1936	BOS	N	3	76	25.3		2
1937	WAS	N	11	93	8.5		1
1938			4	131	32.8		1
Career			18	300	16.7		3
Playoffs			2	20	10.0		0

Robert Smith

Year	Team		No	Yds	Avg	Lg	TD
1993	MIN	N	24	111	4.6	12	0
1994			15	105	7.0	15	0
1995			7	35	5.0	11	0
1996			7	39	5.6	16	0
Career			53	290	5.5	16	0

Rod Smith

Year	Team		No	Yds	Avg	Lg	TD
1995	DEN	N	6	152	25.3	43t	1
1996			16	237	14.8	49t	1
Career			22	389	17.7	49t	3
Playoffs			1	15	15.0		0

Ron Smith

Year	Team		No	Yds	Avg	Lg	TD
1967	ATL	N	11	227	20.6	60	0

Ronnie Smith

Year	Team		No	Yds	Avg	Lg	TD
1978	LA	N	1	15	15.0	15	0
1979			16	300	18.8	38	1
1980	SD	N	4	48	12.0	24	0
1981	SD-PHI	N	7	168	24.0	42	2
1982	PHI	N	34	475	14.0	41t	1
1983			1	8	8.0	8	0
Career			63	1014	16.1	42	4
Playoffs			10	236	23.6		3

Russ Smith

Year	Team		No	Yds	Avg	Lg	TD
1967	SD	A	1	6	6.0	6	0
1968			7	71	10.1	24	0
1969			10	144	14.4	55	0
1970	SD	N	5	44	8.8	11	0
Career			23	265	11.5	55	0

Sammie Smith

Year	Team		No	Yds	Avg	Lg	TD
1989	MIA	N	7	81	11.6	34	0
1990			11	134	12.2	53t	1
1991			14	95	6.8	12	0
Career			32	310	9.7	53t	1
Playoffs			3	31	10.3		0

Sherman Smith

Year	Team		No	Yds	Avg	Lg	TD
1976	SEA	N	36	384	10.7	34	1
1977			30	419	14.0	44t	2
1978			28	366	13.1	64t	4
1979			48	499	10.4	35	4
1980			6	72	12.0	19t	1
1981			44	406	9.2	28	1
1982			19	196	10.3	39	0

Sherman Smith *continued*

Year	Team		No	Yds	Avg	Lg	TD
1983	SD	N	6	51	8.5	21	0
Career			217	2393	11.0	64t	10

Sid Smith

Year	Team		No	Yds	Avg	Lg	TD
1971	KC	N	1	12	12.0	12	0

Steve Smith

Year	Team		No	Yds	Avg	Lg	TD
1987	LARI	N	3	46	15.3	32	0
1988			26	299	11.5	45t	6
1989			19	140	7.4	14	0
1990			4	30	7.5	17t	3
1991			15	130	8.7	37t	1
1992			28	217	7.8	19	1
1993			18	187	10.4	22	0
1994	SEA	N	11	142	12.9	25	1
1995			7	59	8.4	17	1
Career			131	1250	9.5	45t	13
Playoffs			2	14	7.0		0

Stu Smith

Year	Team		No	Yds	Avg	Lg	TD
1938	PIT	N	3	30	10.0		0

Tim Smith

Year	Team		No	Yds	Avg	Lg	TD
1980	HOU	N	2	21	10.5	13	0
1981			2	37	18.5	25	0
1983			83	1176	14.2	47t	6
1984			69	1141	16.5	75t	4
1985			46	660	14.3	33	2
1986			4	72	18.0	25	0
Career			206	3107	15.1	75t	12

Timmy Smith

Year	Team		No	Yds	Avg	Lg	TD
1987	WAS	N	1	-2	-2.0	-2	0
1988			8	53	6.6	16	0
Career			9	51	5.7	16	0
Playoffs			1	9	9.0		0

Tommie Smith

Year	Team		No	Yds	Avg	Lg	TD
1969	CIN	A	1	41	41.0	41	0

Tony Smith

Year	Team		No	Yds	Avg	Lg	TD
1992	ATL	N	2	14	7.0	8	0

Truett Smith

Year	Team		No	Yds	Avg	Lg	TD
1951	PIT	N	4	71	17.8	24	0

Vitamin Smith

Year	Team		No	Yds	Avg	Lg	TD
1949	LA	N	5	63	12.6	24	1
1950			16	279	17.4	67t	4
1951			16	278	17.4	67t	1
1952			16	254	15.9	56t	3
1953			6	151	25.2	54t	3
Career			59	1025	17.4	67t	12
Playoffs			7	110	15.7		0

Waddell Smith

Year	Team		No	Yds	Avg	Lg	TD
1984	DAL	N	1	7	7.0	7	0

Willie Smith

Year	Team		No	Yds	Avg	Lg	TD
1987	MIA	N	2	13	6.5	8	1

Willis Smith

Year	Team		No	Yds	Avg	Lg	TD
1934	NYG	N	2	32	16.0		0

Mark Smolinski

Year	Team		No	Yds	Avg	Lg	TD
1961	BAL	N	9	100	11.1	25	1
1962			13	128	9.8	33t	1
1963	NY	A	34	278	8.2	49	1
1964			3	19	6.3	12	0
1965			6	25	4.2	12	0
1966			11	74	6.7	24	1
1967			21	177	8.4	22	3
1968			6	40	6.7	19	0
Career			103	841	8.2	49	7

Dave Smukler

Year	Team		No	Yds	Avg	Lg	TD
1937	PHI	N	1	-4	-4.0	-4	0

Bill Smyth

Year	Team		No	Yds	Avg	Lg	TD
1947	LA	N	3	26	8.7	11	0
1948			6	66	11.0	21	1
1949			2	21	10.5	14	0

Bill Smyth *continued*

Year	Team		No	Yds	Avg	Lg	TD
1950			2	10	5.0	6	0
Career			13	123	9.5	21	1

Bob Sneddon

Year	Team		No	Yds	Avg	Lg	TD
1944	WAS	N	3	42	14.0	30	0
1946	LA	AA	2	11	5.5		0
Career			5	53	10.6	30	0

Matt Snell

Year	Team		No	Yds	Avg	Lg	TD
1964	NY	A	56	393	7.0	41	1
1965			38	264	6.9	35	0
1966			48	346	7.2	25	4
1967			11	54	4.9	21	0
1968			16	105	6.6	39	1
1969			22	187	8.5	54	1
1970	NYJ	N	2	26	13.0	27	0
Career			193	1375	7.1	54	7
Playoffs			6	64	10.7		0

Jack Snow

Year	Team		No	Yds	Avg	Lg	TD
1965	LA	N	38	559	14.7	60t	3
1966			34	634	18.6	84t	3
1967			28	735	26.3	80t	8
1968			29	500	17.2	54	3
1969			49	734	15.0	74t	6
1970			51	859	16.8	71	7
1971			37	666	18.0	68	5
1972			30	590	19.7	57t	4
1973			16	252	15.8	38t	2
1974			24	397	16.5	44t	3
1975			4	86	21.5	42t	1
Career			340	6012	17.7	84t	45
Playoffs			5	113	22.6		0

Al Snyder

Year	Team		No	Yds	Avg	Lg	TD
1964	BOS	A	1	12	12.0	12	0

Bob Snyder

Year	Team		No	Yds	Avg	Lg	TD
1937	CLE	N	3	20	6.7		0
1938			1	16	16.0	16	0
Career			4	36	9.0	16	0

Gerry Snyder

Year	Team		No	Yds	Avg	Lg	TD
1929	NYG	N					1

Todd Snyder

Year	Team		No	Yds	Avg	Lg	TD
1970	ATL	N	23	311	13.5	43	2
1972			1	19	19.0	19	0
Career			24	330	13.8	43	2

Hank Soar

Year	Team		No	Yds	Avg	Lg	TD
1937	NYG	N	6	77	12.8		1
1938			13	164	12.6		0
1939			12	134	11.2		0
1940			4	36	9.0		1
Career			35	411	11.7		2
Playoffs			3	41	13.7		1

Kurt Sohn

Year	Team		No	Yds	Avg	Lg	TD
1984	NYJ	N	2	28	14.0	16	0
1985			39	534	13.7	39t	4
1986			8	129	16.1	24t	2
1987			23	261	11.3	31	2
1988			7	66	9.4	17	2
Career			79	1018	12.9	39t	10
Playoffs			2	18	9.0		0

Freddie Solomon

Year	Team		No	Yds	Avg	Lg	TD
1975	MIA	N	22	339	15.4	58t	2
1976			27	453	16.8	53t	2
1977			12	181	15.1	54t	1
1978	SF	N	31	458	14.8	58t	2
1979			57	807	14.2	44t	7
1980			48	658	13.7	93t	8
1981			59	969	16.4	60t	8
1982			19	323	17.0	46t	3
1983			31	662	21.4	77t	4
1984			40	737	18.4	64t	10
1985			25	259	10.4	39	1
Career			371	5846	15.8	93t	48
Playoffs			34	537	15.8		6

Freddie Solomon

Year	Team		No	Yds	Avg	Lg	TD
1996	PHI	N	8	125	15.6	23	0

Gordie Soltau

Year	Team		No	Yds	Avg	Lg	TD
1950	SF	N	14	170	12.1	28	1
1951			59	826	14.0	48t	7
1952			55	774	14.1	49t	7
1953			43	620	14.4	54t	6
1954			22	316	14.4	42	2
1955			26	358	13.8	36	1
1956			18	299	16.6	33	1
1957			5	47	9.4	18	0
1958			7	77	11.0	22	0
Career			249	3487	14.0	54t	25

Mike Sommer

Year	Team		No	Yds	Avg	Lg	TD
1959	BAL	N	7	111	15.9	56	0
1961			1	31	31.0	31	0
1963	OAK	A	1	24	24.0	24	0
Career			9	166	18.4	56	0
Playoffs			1	-1	-1.0		0

Bill Sortet

Year	Team		No	Yds	Avg	Lg	TD
1935	PIT	N	6	136	22.7		0
1936			14	197	14.1		1
1937			9	121	13.4		1
1938			11	166	15.1		4
1939			16	196	12.3		1
1940			7	112	16.0		0
Career			63	928	14.7		7

Rick Sortun

Year	Team		No	Yds	Avg	Lg	TD
1966	STL	N	1	7	7.0	7	0

Frank Souchak

Year	Team		No	Yds	Avg	Lg	TD
1939	PIT	N	1	12	12.0	12	0

Cecil Souders

Year	Team		No	Yds	Avg	Lg	TD
1947	DET	N	15	184	12.3	34	1
1948			2	19	9.5	11	0
Career			17	203	11.9	34	1

Vic Spadaccini

Year	Team		No	Yds	Avg	Lg	TD
1938	CLE	N	8	101	12.6		0
1939			32	292	9.1		1
1940			22	276	12.5		2
Career			62	669	10.8		3

John Spagnola

Year	Team		No	Yds	Avg	Lg	TD
1979	PHI	N	2	24	12.0	14	0
1980			18	193	10.7	20	3
1981			6	83	13.8	28	0
1982			26	313	12.0	57	2
1984			65	701	10.8	34	1
1985			64	772	12.1	35	5
1986			39	397	10.2	38	1
1987			36	350	9.7	22	2
1988	SEA	N	5	40	8.0	16	1
1989	GB	N	2	13	6.5	14	0
Career			263	2886	11.0	57	15
Playoffs			2	29	14.5		0

Frank Spaniel

Year	Team		No	Yds	Avg	Lg	TD
1950	BAL	N	5	84	16.8	35	0

Jim Spavital

Year	Team		No	Yds	Avg	Lg	TD
1949	LA	AA	1	-1	-1.0	-1	0
1950	BAL	N	21	238	11.3	45t	1
Career			22	237	10.8	45t	1

Marcus Spears

Year	Team		No	Yds	Avg	Lg	TD
1996	CHI	N	1	1	1.0	1t	1

Mac Speedie

Year	Team		No	Yds	Avg	Lg	TD
1946	CLE	AA	24	564	23.5	79t	7
1947			**67**	**1146**	17.1	99t	6
1948			**58**	816	14.1	56	4
1949			**62**	**1028**	16.6		7
1950	CLE	N	42	548	13.0	45	1
1951			34	589	17.3	51	3
1952			**62**	911	14.7	50	5
Career			349	5602	16.1	99t	33
Playoffs			28	366	13.1		0

Julian Spence

Year	Team		No	Yds	Avg	Lg	TD
1961	HOU	A	1	14	14.0	14	0

Darryl Spencer

Year	Team		No	Yds	Avg	Lg	TD
1994	ATL	N	2	51	25.5	40	0
1995			5	60	12.0	22	0
Career			7	111	15.9	40	0

Tim Spencer

Year	Team		No	Yds	Avg	Lg	TD
1985	SD	N	11	135	12.3	43	0
1986			6	48	8.0	15	0
1987			17	123	7.2	18	0
1988			1	14	14.0	14	0
1989			18	112	6.2	23	0
Career			53	432	8.2	43	0

Todd Spencer

Year	Team		No	Yds	Avg	Lg	TD
1985	PIT	N	3	25	8.3	13	0
1987	SD	N	2	47	23.5	45	0
Career			5	72	14.4	45	0

Willie Spencer

Year	Team		No	Yds	Avg	Lg	TD
1977	NYG	N	4	20	5.0	15	0
1978			2	25	12.5	22	0
Career			6	45	7.5	22	0

Cotton Speyrer

Year	Team		No	Yds	Avg	Lg	TD
1972	BAL	N	8	114	14.3	21	0
1973			17	311	18.3	47	4
1974			9	110	12.2	27	1
Career			34	535	15.7	47	5

Irving Spikes

Year	Team		No	Yds	Avg	Lg	TD
1994	MIA	N	4	16	4.0	9	0
1995			5	18	3.6	13	1
1996			8	81	10.1	19	1
Career			17	115	6.8	19	2

Jack Spikes

Year	Team		No	Yds	Avg	Lg	TD
1960	DAL	A	11	158	14.4	25	0
1961			8	136	17.0	46	0
1962			10	132	13.2	35	1
1963	KC	A	11	125	11.4	30	1
1964			5	17	3.4	12	0
1965	HOU	A	8	57	7.1	17	0
1966	BUF	A	2	45	22.5	27	1
1967			1	9	9.0	9	0
Career			56	679	12.1	46	3
Playoffs			2	24	12.0		0

John Spilis

Year	Team		No	Yds	Avg	Lg	TD
1969	GB	N	7	89	12.7	16	0
1970			6	76	12.7	18	0
1971			14	281	20.1	39	1
Career			27	446	16.5	39	1

Jack Spinks

Year	Team		No	Yds	Avg	Lg	TD
1952	PIT	N	2	22	11.0	23	0
1953	CHIC	N	1	6	6.0	6	0
Career			3	28	9.3	23	0

Art Spinney

Year	Team		No	Yds	Avg	Lg	TD
1950	BAL	N	2	19	9.5	12	0

Johnny Spirida

Year	Team		No	Yds	Avg	Lg	TD
1939	WAS	N	2	95	47.5		0

Sebron Spivey

Year	Team		No	Yds	Avg	Lg	TD
1987	DAL	N	2	34	17.0	25	0

Bob Sponaugle

Year	Team		No	Yds	Avg	Lg	TD
1949	NYB	N	2	26	13.0	14	0

Hal Springer

Year	Team		No	Yds	Avg	Lg	TD
1945	NYG	N	4	63	15.8	36	0

Ron Springs

Year	Team		No	Yds	Avg	Lg	TD
1979	DAL	N	25	251	10.0	27	1
1980			15	212	14.1	58t	1
1981			46	359	7.8	32t	2
1982			17	163	9.6	34	2
1983			73	589	8.1	80t	1
1984			46	454	9.9	57t	3
1985	TB	N	3	44	14.7	22	0

Ron Springs *continued*

Year	Team		No	Yds	Avg	Lg	TD
1986			24	187	7.8	46	0
Career			249	2259	9.1	80t	10
Playoffs			18	106	5.9		1

Ed Sprinkle

Year	Team		No	Yds	Avg	Lg	TD
1946	CHIB	N	7	124	17.7	34t	2
1947			4	43	10.8	13	0
1948			10	132	13.2	34t	3
1949			4	69	17.3	47	0
1950			4	70	17.5	27	0
1951			2	11	5.5	7	1
1952			1	2	2.0	2t	1
Career			32	451	14.1	47	7
Playoffs			1	9	9.0		0

Brian Stablein

Year	Team		No	Yds	Avg	Lg	TD
1995	IND	N	8	95	11.9	16	0
1996			18	192	10.7	30t	1
Career			26	287	11.0	30t	1
Playoffs			4	46	11.5		0

Jack Stackpool

Year	Team		No	Yds	Avg	Lg	TD
1942	PHI	N	2	59	29.5	39	0

Billy Stacy

Year	Team		No	Yds	Avg	Lg	TD
1961	STL	N	12	241	20.1	80t	1

Harry Stafford

Year	Team		No	Yds	Avg	Lg	TD
1934	NYG	N	3	43	14.3		0

Jon Staggers

Year	Team		No	Yds	Avg	Lg	TD
1970	PIT	N	6	118	19.7	31	1
1971			8	103	12.9	20	0
1972	GB	N	8	123	15.4	48t	1
1973			25	412	16.5	50	3
1974			32	450	14.1	63	0
1975	DET	N	14	174	12.4	23	2
Career			93	1380	14.8	63	7
Playoffs			1	23	23.0		0

John Stallworth

Year	Team		No	Yds	Avg	Lg	TD
1974	PIT	N	16	269	16.8	56	1
1975			20	423	21.1	59	4
1976			9	111	12.3	25	2
1977			44	784	17.8	49	7
1978			41	798	19.5	70	9
1979			70	1183	16.9	65t	8
1980			9	197	21.9	50t	1
1981			63	1098	17.4	55	5
1982			27	441	16.3	74t	7
1983			8	100	12.5	20	0
1984			80	1395	17.4	51	11
1985			75	937	12.5	41	5
1986			34	466	13.7	40t	1
1987			41	521	12.7	45	2
Career			537	8723	16.2	74t	63
Playoffs			57	1054	18.5		12

Sylvester Stamps

Year	Team		No	Yds	Avg	Lg	TD
1984	ATL	N	4	48	12.0	31	0
1986			20	221	11.1	39t	1
1987			4	40	10.0	19	0
1988			5	22	4.4	7	0
1989	TB	N	15	82	5.5	21	0
Career			48	413	8.6	39t	1

Haskel Stanback

Year	Team		No	Yds	Avg	Lg	TD
1974	ATL	N	8	39	4.9	18	0
1975			14	115	8.2	14	0
1976			21	174	8.3	28	1
1977			30	261	8.7	36	0
1978			12	108	9.0	20	0
1979			13	89	6.8	22	0
Career			98	786	8.0	36	1
Playoffs			2	7	3.5		0

Norm Standlee

Year	Team		No	Yds	Avg	Lg	TD
1941	CHIB	N	2	-3	-1.5	3	0
1946	SF	AA	2	-5	-2.5		0
1947			2	22	11.0		0
1948			1	1	1.0	1	0
Career			7	15	2.1	3	0
Playoffs			2	34	17.0		0

Walter Stanley

Year	Team		No	Yds	Avg	Lg	TD
1986	GB	N	35	723	20.7	62	2
1987			38	672	17.7	70t	3
1988			28	436	15.6	56	0
1989	DET	N	24	304	12.7	37	0
1990	WAS	N	2	15	7.5	12	0
1992	NE	N	3	63	21.0	36	0
Career			130	2213	17.0	70t	5

Hank Stanton

Year	Team		No	Yds	Avg	Lg	TD
1946	NY	AA	2	25	12.5		0

Paul Staroba

Year	Team		No	Yds	Avg	Lg	TD
1972	CLE	N	1	19	19.0	19t	1
1973	GB	N	1	23	23.0	23	0
Career			2	42	21.0	23	1

Ben Starrett

Year	Team		No	Yds	Avg	Lg	TD
1944	GB	N	1	6	6.0	6	0

Stephen Starring

Year	Team		No	Yds	Avg	Lg	TD
1983	NE	N	17	389	22.9	76t	2
1984			46	657	14.3	65t	4
1985			16	235	14.7	40	0
1986			16	295	18.4	47	2
1987			17	289	17.0	34t	3
1988	TB-DET	N	8	164	20.5	53	0
Career			120	2029	16.9	76t	11
Playoffs			2	39	19.5		0

Art Statuto

Year	Team		No	Yds	Avg	Lg	TD
1948	BUF	AA	0	2		2L	0

Roger Staubach

Year	Team		No	Yds	Avg	Lg	TD
1974	DAL	N	1	-13	-13.0	-13	0

Scott Stauch

Year	Team		No	Yds	Avg	Lg	TD
1981	NO	N	1	7	7.0	7	0

Ernie Steele

Year	Team		No	Yds	Avg	Lg	TD
1942	PHI	N	7	114	16.3	36	1
1943	P-P	N	9	168	18.7	60	2
1944	PHI	N	1	22	22.0	22	0
1945			3	42	14.0	31	0
1946			5	69	13.8	24	0
1947			4	62	15.5	44	0
1948			2	43	21.5	32t	1
Career			31	520	16.8	60	4

Robert Steele

Year	Team		No	Yds	Avg	Lg	TD
1979	MIN	N	1	10	10.0	10	0

Anthony Steels

Year	Team		No	Yds	Avg	Lg	TD
1985	BUF	N	2	9	4.5	6	0
1987	SD	N	1	4	4.0	4	0
Career			3	13	4.3	6	0

Milt Stegall

Year	Team		No	Yds	Avg	Lg	TD
1992	CIN	N	3	35	11.7	13	1
1993			1	8	8.0	8	0
Career			4	43	10.8	13	1

Larry Stegent

Year	Team		No	Yds	Avg	Lg	TD
1971	STL	N	1	12	12.0	12	0

Sammy Stein

Year	Team		No	Yds	Avg	Lg	TD
1929	SI	N					1
1930							1
Career							2

Gil Steinke

Year	Team		No	Yds	Avg	Lg	TD
1945	PHI	N	2	12	6.0	9	0
1946			5	107	21.4	32	2
1947			4	90	22.5	60t	1
Career			11	209	19.0	60t	3

Greg Stemrick

Year	Team		No	Yds	Avg	Lg	TD
1976	HOU	N	1	10	10.0	10	0

Paul Stenn

Year	Team		No	Yds	Avg	Lg	TD
1949	CHIB	N	2	11	5.5	11	0

John Stephens

Year	Team		No	Yds	Avg	Lg	TD
1988	NE	N	14	98	7.0	17	0

Year	Team		No	Yds	Avg	Lg	TD

John Stephens *continued*

Year	Team		No	Yds	Avg	Lg	TD
1989			21	207	9.9	37	0
1990			28	196	7.0	43	1
1991			16	119	7.4	24	0
1992			21	161	7.7	32	0
1993	GB	N	5	31	6.2	10	0
Career			105	812	7.7	43	1

Johnny Stephens

Year	Team		No	Yds	Avg	Lg	TD
1938	CLE	N	6	75	12.5		0

Tom Stephens

Year	Team		No	Yds	Avg	Lg	TD
1960	BOS	A	22	320	14.5		3
1961			19	186	9.8	31	2
Career			41	506	12.3	31	5

Jack Steptoe

Year	Team		No	Yds	Avg	Lg	TD
1978	SF	N	2	46	23.0	35t	1

Ed Sternaman

Year	Team		No	Yds	Avg	Lg	TD
1923	CHIB	N					1

Joey Sternaman

Year	Team		No	Yds	Avg	Lg	TD
1922	CHIB	N					1
1924							1
1925							1
1927							1
1928							1
Career							5

Bob Steuber

Year	Team		No	Yds	Avg	Lg	TD
1946	CLE	AA	1	9	9.0	9	0
1948	BUF	AA	2	14	7.0		0
Career			3	23	7.7	9	0

Don Stevens

Year	Team		No	Yds	Avg	Lg	TD
1952	PHI	N	13	174	13.4	39	0

Howard Stevens

Year	Team		No	Yds	Avg	Lg	TD
1973	NO	N	4	39	9.8	14	0
1974			13	81	6.2	20	0
Career			17	120	7.1	20	0

James Stewart

Year	Team		No	Yds	Avg	Lg	TD
1995	JAC	N	21	190	9.0	38	1
1996			30	177	5.9	21t	2
Career			51	367	7.2	38	3
Playoffs			4	38	9.5		0

James Stewart

Year	Team		No	Yds	Avg	Lg	TD
1995	MIN	N	1	3	3.0	3	0

Joe Stewart

Year	Team		No	Yds	Avg	Lg	TD
1979	OAK	N	1	3	3.0	3	0

Kordell Stewart

Year	Team		No	Yds	Avg	Lg	TD
1995	PIT	N	14	235	16.8	71t	1
1996			17	293	17.2	48	3
Career			31	528	17.0	71t	4
Playoffs			4	45	11.3		1

Wayne Stewart

Year	Team		No	Yds	Avg	Lg	TD
1969	NY	A	5	39	7.8	9	0
1970	NYJ	N	1	7	7.0	7	0
1972			2	26	13.0	22	1
1974	SD	N	19	283	14.9	29	1
Career			27	355	13.1	29	2

Monty Stickles

Year	Team		No	Yds	Avg	Lg	TD
1960	SF	N	22	252	11.5	28	0
1961			43	794	18.5	54	5
1962			22	366	16.6	48	3
1963			11	152	13.8	31	0
1964			40	685	17.1	53t	3
1965			35	343	9.8	22	1
1966			27	315	11.7	38	2
1967			7	86	12.3	19	0
1968	NO	N	15	206	13.7	35	2
Career			222	3199	14.4	54	16

Dave Stief

Year	Team		No	Yds	Avg	Lg	TD
1978	STL	N	24	477	19.9	55t	4
1979			22	324	14.7	32	0
1980			16	165	10.3	23	0

Dave Stief *continued*

Year	Team		No	Yds	Avg	Lg	TD
1981			5	77	15.4	29	1
Career			67	1043	15.6	55t	5

Jim Stiger

Year	Team		No	Yds	Avg	Lg	TD
1963	DAL	N	13	131	10.1	42	0
1964			9	85	9.4	31t	1
1965			1	9	9.0	9	0
1966	LA	N	8	72	9.0	18	1
Career			31	297	9.6	42	2

Bryan Still

Year	Team		No	Yds	Avg	Lg	TD
1996	SD	N	6	142	23.7	56	0

Darryl Stingley

Year	Team		No	Yds	Avg	Lg	TD
1973	NE	N	23	339	14.7	25	2
1974			10	139	13.9	20t	1
1975			21	378	18.0	45	2
1976			17	370	21.8	58t	4
1977			39	657	16.8	68	5
Career			110	1883	17.1	68	14
Playoffs			2	36	18.0		0

Jim Stinnette

Year	Team		No	Yds	Avg	Lg	TD
1961	DEN	A	11	58	5.3	15	1
1962			13	109	8.4	32	0
Career			24	167	7.0	32	1

Bill Stits

Year	Team		No	Yds	Avg	Lg	TD
1955	DET	N	5	17	3.4	14	0
1956			3	52	17.3	27	0
Career			8	69	8.6	27	0

Mark Stock

Year	Team		No	Yds	Avg	Lg	TD
1989	PIT	N	4	74	18.5	27	0
1996	IND	N	2	24	12.0	13	0
Career			6	98	16.3	27	0
Playoffs			2	37	18.5		0

Ralph Stockemer

Year	Team		No	Yds	Avg	Lg	TD
1987	KC	N	1	4	4.0	4	0

Terry Stoepel

Year	Team		No	Yds	Avg	Lg	TD
1967	CHI	N	1	6	6.0	6	0

Ken Stofer

Year	Team		No	Yds	Avg	Lg	TD
1946	BUF	AA	1	14	14.0	14	0

J.J. Stokes

Year	Team		No	Yds	Avg	Lg	TD
1995	SF	N	38	517	13.6	41t	4
1996			18	249	13.8	40	0
Career			56	766	13.7	41t	4
Playoffs			3	24	8.0		0

Billy Stone

Year	Team		No	Yds	Avg	Lg	TD
1949	BAL	AA	31	621	20.0	66t	6
1950	BAL	N	12	324	27.0	69t	4
1951	CHIB	N	18	320	17.8	62t	1
1952			13	283	21.8	59t	2
1953			34	376	11.1	51	4
1954			35	395	11.3	42	3
Career			143	2319	16.2	69t	20

Donnie Stone

Year	Team		No	Yds	Avg	Lg	TD
1961	DEN	A	38	344	9.1	37	4
1962			20	223	11.2	56	2
1963			22	208	9.5	55	1
1964			4	38	9.5	16	0
1965	BUF	A	6	29	4.8	9	0
1966	HOU	A	1	17	17.0	17	0
Career			91	859	9.4	56	7

Dwight Stone

Year	Team		No	Yds	Avg	Lg	TD
1987	PIT	N	1	22	22.0	22	0
1988			11	196	17.8	72t	1
1989			7	92	13.1	16	0
1990			19	332	17.5	90	1
1991			32	649	20.3	89t	5
1992			34	501	14.7	49	3
1993			41	587	14.3	44	2
1994			7	81	11.6	25	0
1996	CAR	N	1	11	11.0	11	0
Career			153	2471	16.2	90	12
Playoffs			7	63	9.0		0

Ken Stone

Year	Team		No	Yds	Avg	Lg	TD
1977	STL	N	1	40	40.0	40	0

Steve Stonebreaker

Year	Team		No	Yds	Avg	Lg	TD
1962	MIN	N	12	227	18.9	56	1

Don Stonesifer

Year	Team		No	Yds	Avg	Lg	TD
1951	CHIC	N	27	343	12.7	49	2
1952			54	617	11.4	26	0
1953			56	684	12.2	46	2
1954			44	607	13.8	39t	3
1955			28	330	11.8	28t	5
1956			22	320	14.5	58t	2
Career			231	2901	12.6	58t	14

Jack Storer

Year	Team		No	Yds	Avg	Lg	TD
1924	FRA	N					1

Pete Stout

Year	Team		No	Yds	Avg	Lg	TD
1949	WAS	N	8	102	12.8	39	2
1950			2	15	7.5	8	0
Career			10	117	11.7	39	2

Otto Stowe

Year	Team		No	Yds	Avg	Lg	TD
1971	MIA	N	5	68	13.6	21	1
1972			13	276	21.2	49	2
1973	DAL	N	23	389	16.9	45	6
1974	DEN	N	2	9	4.5	5	1
Career			43	742	17.3	49	10

Tommie Stowers

Year	Team		No	Yds	Avg	Lg	TD
1992	NO	N	4	23	5.8	8	0

Mike Strachan

Year	Team		No	Yds	Avg	Lg	TD
1975	NO	N	30	224	7.5	27	0
1976			6	22	3.7	14	0
1977			3	26	8.7	10	0
1978			10	51	5.1	15	0
1979			3	9	3.0	5	0
1980			5	60	12.0	23	0
Career			57	392	6.9	27	0

Steve Strachan

Year	Team		No	Yds	Avg	Lg	TD
1987	LARI	N	4	42	10.5	14	0
1988			3	19	6.3	13t	1
Career			7	61	8.7	14	1

Tim Stracka

Year	Team		No	Yds	Avg	Lg	TD
1983	CLE	N	1	12	12.0	12	0
1984			1	15	15.0	15	0
Career			2	27	13.5	15	0

John Strada

Year	Team		No	Yds	Avg	Lg	TD
1974	KC	N	1	16	16.0	16	0

Troy Stradford

Year	Team		No	Yds	Avg	Lg	TD
1987	MIA	N	48	457	9.5	34	1
1988			56	426	7.6	36	1
1989			25	233	9.3	32	0
1990			30	257	8.6	23	0
1991	KC	N	9	91	10.1	17	0
1992	DET	N	2	15	7.5	12	0
Career			170	1479	8.7	36	2

Mike Stramiello

Year	Team		No	Yds	Avg	Lg	TD
1930	BKN	N					1

Bob Stransky

Year	Team		No	Yds	Avg	Lg	TD
1960	DEN	A	3	11	3.7	11	0

Mike Stratton

Year	Team		No	Yds	Avg	Lg	TD
1963	BUF	A	1	19	19.0	19	0

Jimmy Strausbaugh

Year	Team		No	Yds	Avg	Lg	TD
1946	CHIC	N	5	56	11.2	21	0

Les Strayhorn

Year	Team		No	Yds	Avg	Lg	TD
1974	DAL	N	2	12	6.0	10	0

Eric Streater

Year	Team		No	Yds	Avg	Lg	TD
1987	TB	N	5	117	23.4	61t	2

Bill Stribling

Year	Team		No	Yds	Avg	Lg	TD
1951	NYG	N	18	226	12.6	42	2

Year	Team	No	Yds	Avg	Lg	TD

Bill Stribling *continued*

Year	Team	No	Yds	Avg	Lg	TD
1952		26	399	15.3	55t	5
1953		16	175	10.9	19	0
1955	PHI N	38	568	14.9	56	6
1956		2	11	5.5	7	0
1957		14	194	13.9	58t	1
Career		114	1573	13.8	58t	14

Bob Stringer

Year	Team	No	Yds	Avg	Lg	TD
1952	PHI N	1	4	4.0	4	0

Korey Stringer

| 1995 | MIN N | 1 | -1 | -1.0 | -1 | 0 |

Joe Stringfellow

| 1942 | DET N | 8 | 89 | 11.1 | 20 | 0 |

Woody Strode

| 1946 | LA N | 4 | 37 | 9.3 | 19 | 0 |

Jim Strong

1971	NO N	16	78	4.9	14	0
1972		14	123	8.8	16	0
Career		30	201	6.7	16	0

Ken Strong

Year	Team	No	Yds	Avg	Lg	TD
1930	SI N					5
1932		5	56	11.2		0
1933	NYG N	7	146	20.9		2
1934		7	51	7.3		0
Career		19	253	13.3		7
Playoffs		4	67	16.8		2

Mack Strong

1994	SEA N	3	3	1.0	5	0
1995		12	117	9.8	25	3
1996		9	78	8.7	20	0
Career		24	198	8.3	25	3

Ray Strong

1978	ATL N	7	56	8.0	21	0
1979		1	6	6.0	6	0
1981		1	9	9.0	9	0
Career		9	71	7.9	21	0

Morris Stroud

1970	KC N	4	86	21.5	50t	1
1971		22	454	20.6	54	1
1972		4	80	20.0	44	1
1973		12	216	18.0	48	2
1974		12	141	11.8	25	2
Career		54	977	18.1	54	7

Art Strozier

1970	SD N	2	40	20.0	28	0
1971		1	6	6.0	6	0
Career		3	46	15.3	28	0

Art Strutt

1935	PIT N	7	112	16.0		0
1936		11	166	15.1		0
Career		18	278	15.4		0

Johnny Strzykalski

1946	SF AA	9	80	8.9		0
1947		15	258	17.2		3
1948		26	485	18.7	59t	7
1949		6	99	16.5		1
1950	SF N	24	187	7.8	28t	1
1951		12	105	8.8	13	0
1952		1	4	4.0	4	0
Career		93	1218	13.1	59t	12

Dave Studdard

1979	DEN N	1	2	2.0	2t	1
1981		1	10	10.0	10	0
1984		1	-4	-4.0	-4	0
1986		1	2	2.0	2t	1
Career		4	10	2.5	10	2

Pat Studstill

1961	DET N	5	54	10.8	25	0
1962		36	479	13.3	51	4
1964		7	102	14.6	27	1

Pat Studstill *continued*

Year	Team	No	Yds	Avg	Lg	TD
1965		28	389	13.9	55	3
1966		67	**1266**	18.9	99t	5
1967		10	162	16.2	37t	2
1968	LA N	7	108	15.4	25	1
1969		3	28	9.3	11	0
1970		18	252	14.0	40t	2
Career		181	2840	15.7	99t	18

Jerry Sturm

| 1961 | DEN A | 2 | -1 | -0.5 | | 0 |

Dick Sturtridge

| 1928 | CHIB N | | | | | 2 |

Joe Stydahar

| 1939 | CHIB N | 1 | 9 | 9.0 | 9 | 0 |

Steve Sucic

1946	LA N	1	1	1.0	1	0
1947	DET N	1	20	20.0	20	0
Career		2	21	10.5	20	0

Leo Sugar

| 1957 | CHIC N | 1 | 14 | 14.0 | 14 | 0 |

Matt Suhey

1980	CHI N	7	60	8.6	21	0
1981		33	168	5.1	15	0
1982		36	333	9.3	45	0
1983		49	429	8.8	52	1
1984		42	312	7.4	23	2
1985		33	295	8.9	35	1
1986		24	235	9.8	58	0
1987		7	54	7.7	12	0
1988		20	154	7.7	29	0
1989		9	73	8.1	22	1
Career		260	2113	8.1	58	5
Playoffs		13	96	7.4		0

Joe Sulatis

1943	NYG N	1	12	12.0	12	0
1945		2	12	6.0	6	0
1947		7	53	7.6	16	0
1948		26	298	11.5	26	1
1949		3	35	11.7	18	0
1950		1	3	3.0	3	0
1951		4	25	6.3	10	0
1952		4	31	7.8	16	0
Career		48	469	9.8	26	1
Playoffs		1	12	12.0		0

George Sulima

1952	PIT N	9	176	19.6	69	1
1953		10	131	13.1	17	0
1954		30	439	14.6	37	1
Career		49	746	15.2	69	2

Bob Sullivan

| 1947 | PIT N | 4 | 72 | 18.0 | 30t | 1 |

Bob Sullivan

| 1948 | SF AA | 4 | 58 | 14.5 | | 1 |

Dave Sullivan

| 1974 | CLE N | 5 | 92 | 18.4 | 37 | 0 |

George Sullivan

| 1925 | FRA N | | | | | 1 |

Tom Sullivan

1972	PHI N	4	17	4.3	7	0
1973		50	322	6.4	29	1
1974		39	312	8.0	23	1
1975		28	276	9.9	35	0
1976		14	116	8.3	20t	1
1977		26	223	8.6	30	2
1978	CLE N	1	20	20.0	20	0
Career		162	1286	7.9	35	5

Pat Summerall

1959	NYG N	2	32	16.0	21	0
1960		1	15	15.0	15	0
Career		3	47	15.7	21	0

Bob Summerhays

Year	Team	No	Yds	Avg	Lg	TD
1949	GB N	1	34	34.0	34	0

Don Summers

1984	DEN N	3	32	10.7	16	0
1987	GB N	7	83	11.9	17	1
Career		10	115	11.5	17	1

Len Supulski

| 1942 | PHI N | 8 | 149 | 18.6 | 41 | 1 |

Nick Susoeff

1946	SF AA	5	98	19.6		0
1947		24	223	9.3		2
1948		27	237	8.8		1
1949		5	52	10.4		1
Career		61	610	10.0		4

Ed Susteric

| 1949 | CLE AA | 1 | 7 | 7.0 | 7 | 0 |

Ed Sutton

1957	WAS N	2	32	16.0	17t	1
1958		6	112	18.7	26	0
1959		4	63	15.8	26	0
1960	NYG N	2	30	15.0	16	0
Career		14	237	16.9	26	1

Joe Sutton

| 1949 | BUF AA | 5 | 63 | 12.6 | | 1 |

George Svendsen

| 1937 | GB N | 1 | 11 | 11.0 | 11 | 0 |

Bill Svoboda

| 1951 | CHIC N | 6 | -9 | -1.5 | 3 | 0 |

Alton Swain

| 1926 | BUF N | | | | | 1 |

Karl Swanke

| 1981 | GB N | 1 | 2 | 2.0 | 2t | 1 |

Lynn Swann

1974	PIT N	11	208	18.9	54	2
1975		49	781	15.9	43t	11
1976		28	516	18.4	47	1
1977		50	789	15.8	46	7
1978		61	880	14.4	62	11
1979		41	808	19.7	65	5
1980		44	710	16.1	68t	7
1981		34	505	14.9	44	5
1982		18	265	14.7	60	0
Career		336	5462	16.3	68t	51
Playoffs		48	907	18.9		9

Evar Swanson

| 1924 | MIL N | | | | | 3 |

Shane Swanson

| 1987 | DEN N | 6 | 87 | 14.5 | 35t | 1 |

Calvin Sweeney

1980	PIT N	12	282	23.5	34	1
1981		2	53	26.5	32	0
1982		5	50	10.0	17	0
1983		39	577	14.8	42	5
1984		2	25	12.5	16	0
1985		16	234	14.6	69	0
1986		21	337	16.0	58	1
1987		16	217	13.6	34	0
Career		113	1775	15.7	69	7
Playoffs		5	66	13.2		0

Neal Sweeney

| 1967 | DEN A | 6 | 136 | 22.7 | 48 | 0 |

Steve Sweeney

| 1973 | OAK N | 2 | 52 | 26.0 | 34t | 1 |

Joe Sweet

1972	LA N	2	26	13.0	17t	1
1975	SD N	8	147	18.4	52	0
Career		10	173	17.3	52	1

Year	Team		No	Yds	Avg	Lg	TD

Tony Sweet

1987	NYJ	N	3	45	15.0	22	0

Bob Sweiger

1946	NY	AA	8	55	6.9		1
1947			11	108	9.8		1
1948			12	129	10.8		0
1949	CHI	AA	11	126	11.5		0
Career			42	418	10.0		2
Playoffs			2	12	6.0		0

Bill Swiacki

1948	NYG	N	39	550	14.1	65t	10
1949			47	652	13.9	42	4
1950			20	280	14.0	38t	3
1951	DET	N	16	188	11.8	24	0
1952			17	213	12.5	26	1
Career			139	1883	13.5	65t	18
Playoffs			1	14	14.0		0

Jim Swink

1960	DAL	A	4	37	9.3		0

Bob Swisher

1938	CHIB	N	4	65	16.3		0
1939			7	228	32.6		1
1940			2	106	53.0		0
1941			6	179	29.8	53	2
1945			2	4	2.0	4	0
Career			21	582	27.7	53	3
Playoffs			1	36	36.0		0

Veryl Switzer

1954	GB	N	17	166	9.8	28	2
1955			14	103	7.4	22	1
Career			31	269	8.7	28	3

Jeff Sydner

1993	PHI	N	2	42	21.0	31	0
1994			1	10	10.0	10	0
Career			3	52	17.3	31	0

Harry Sydney

1987	SF	N	1	3	3.0	3	0
1988			2	18	9.0	9	0
1989			9	71	7.9	13	0
1990			10	116	11.6	23t	1
1991			13	90	6.9	19	2
1992	GB	N	49	384	7.8	20	1
Career			84	682	8.1	23t	4
Playoffs			6	16	2.7		0

Al Sykes

1971	NE	N	1	15	15.0	15	0

Bob Sykes

1952	WAS	N	1	5	5.0	5	0

Johnny Sylvester

1947	NY	AA	1	5	5.0	5	0

Paul Szakash

1938	DET	N	1	0	0.0	0	0
1941			3	77	25.7	47	0
1942			5	53	10.6	21	0
Career			9	130	14.4	47	0

Dave Szott

Playoffs			1	6	6.0		0

Dick Szymanski

1961	BAL	N	1	5	5.0	5	0

Doyle Tackett

1946	BKN	AA	10	191	19.1		2
1947			0	25		25L	0
Career			10	216	21.6	25L	2

Charles Tackwell

1930	FRA	N					1

John Tagliaferri

1987	MIA	N	12	117	9.8	27	0

George Taliaferro

1949	LA	AA	0	42		42tL	1
1950	NYY	N	21	299	14.2	43	5
1951			16	230	14.4	47	2
1952	DAL	N	21	244	11.6	78t	1
1953	BAL	N	20	346	17.3	54	2
1954			14	122	8.7	29t	1
1955	PHI	N	3	17	5.7	14	0
Career			95	1300	13.7	78t	12

John Talley

1990	CLE	N	2	28	14.0	19	0
1991			1	13	13.0	13	0
Career			3	41	13.7	19	0

Bob Tanner

1930	FRA	N					1

John Tanner

1923	CLE	N					1

John Tanner

1971	SD	N	1	6	6.0	6	0
1974	NE	N	2	23	11.5	21	1
Career			3	29	9.7	21	1

Fran Tarkenton

1962	MIN	N	0	-12		-12L	0

Jerry Tarr

1962	DEN	A	8	211	26.4	97	2

John Tarver

1972	NE	N	11	112	10.2	22	1
1973			9	51	5.7	13	0
1974			9	37	4.1	12	0
1975	PHI	N	5	14	2.8	8	0
Career			34	214	6.3	22	1

Carl Taseff

1951	CLE	N	1	18	18.0	18	0
1954	BAL	N	16	159	9.9	30	1
1955			1	3	3.0	3	0
1960			1	13	13.0	13	0
Career			19	193	10.2	30	1

Steve Tasker

1985	HOU	N	2	19	9.5	14	0
1990	BUF	N	2	44	22.0	24t	2
1991			2	39	19.5	20t	1
1992			2	24	12.0	17	0
1993			2	26	13.0	22	0
1995			20	255	12.8	43	3
1996			21	372	17.7	62	3
Career			51	779	15.3	62	9
Playoffs			14	259	18.5		1

Lars Tate

1988	TB	N	5	23	4.6	9	1
1989			11	75	6.8	19	1
Career			16	98	6.1	19	2

Rodney Tate

1983	CIN	N	18	142	7.9	25	0

Jess Tatum

1938	PIT	N	1	16	16.0	16	0

Mosi Tatupu

1979	NE	N	2	9	4.5	5	0
1980			4	27	6.8	11	0
1981			12	132	11.0	41	1
1983			10	97	9.7	17	1
1984			16	159	9.9	24	0
1985			2	16	8.0	15	0
1986			15	145	9.7	25	0
1987			15	136	9.1	23	0
1988			8	58	7.3	17	0
1989			10	54	5.4	11	0
1990			2	10	5.0	6	0
Career			96	843	8.8	41	2
Playoffs			1	6	6.0		0

Junior Tautalatasi

1986	PHI	N	41	325	7.9	56	2
1987			25	176	7.0	22	0
1988			5	48	9.6	21	0
1989	DAL	N	17	157	9.2	23	0
Career			88	706	8.0	56	2

Altie Taylor

1969	DET	N	13	86	6.6	20	0
1970			27	261	9.7	42	2
1971			26	270	10.4	64	1
1972			29	250	8.6	40t	2
1973			27	252	9.3	35	0
1974			30	293	9.8	34	1
1975			21	111	5.3	17	0
1976	HOU	N	2	15	7.5	8	0
Career			175	1538	8.8	64	6
Playoffs			2	7	3.5		0

Billy Taylor

1978	NYG	N	9	70	7.8	18	0
1979			28	253	9.0	43	4
1980			33	253	7.7	42	0
1981			8	71	8.9	39	0
Career			78	647	8.3	43	4

Charley Taylor

1964	WAS	N	53	814	15.4	80t	5
1965			40	577	14.4	69	3
1966			72	1119	15.5	86t	12
1967			70	990	14.1	86t	9
1968			48	650	13.5	47	5
1969			71	883	12.4	88t	8
1970			42	593	14.1	41	0
1971			24	370	15.4	71t	4
1972			49	673	13.7	70t	7
1973			59	801	13.6	53	7
1974			54	738	13.7	51	5
1975			53	744	14.0	64	6
1977			14	158	11.3	19	0
Career			649	9110	14.0	88t	79
Playoffs			19	317	16.7		2

Charlie Taylor

1944	BKN	N	2	22	11.0	18	0

Cliff Taylor

1974	CHI	N	3	23	7.7	8	0
1976	GB	N	2	21	10.5	18	0
Career			5	44	8.8	18	0

Corky Taylor

1955	LA	N	7	47	6.7	17t	1

Craig Taylor

1989	CIN	N	4	44	11.0	18t	2
1990			3	22	7.3	20	1
1991			21	122	5.8	16	0
Career			28	188	6.7	20	3

Gene Taylor

1987	TB	N	2	21	10.5	11	0
1988			5	53	10.6	14	0
Career			7	74	10.6	14	0

Hugh Taylor

1947	WAS	N	26	511	19.7	62t	6
1948			20	341	17.1	66t	3
1949			45	781	17.4	76	9
1950			39	833	21.4	70t	9
1951			29	444	15.3	47	3
1952			41	961	23.4	70t	12
1953			35	703	20.1	71t	8
1954			37	659	17.8	60	8
Career			272	5233	19.2	76	58

Jim Taylor

1958	GB	N	4	72	18.0	31t	1
1959			9	71	7.9	20t	2
1960			15	121	8.1	27	0
1961			25	175	7.0	18	1
1962			22	106	4.8	25	0
1963			13	68	5.2	27t	1
1964			38	354	9.3	35t	3

Year	Team		No	Yds	Avg	Lg	TD

Jim Taylor *continued*

Year	Team		No	Yds	Avg	Lg	TD
1965			20	207	10.4	41	0
1966			41	331	8.1	21	2
1967	NO	N	38	251	6.6	27	0
Career			225	1756	7.8	41	10
Playoffs			19	137	7.2		0

John Taylor

Year	Team		No	Yds	Avg	Lg	TD
1987	SF	N	9	151	16.8	34	0
1988			14	325	23.2	73t	2
1989			60	1077	17.9	95t	10
1990			49	748	15.3	78t	7
1991			64	1011	15.8	97t	9
1992			25	428	17.1	54t	3
1993			56	940	16.8	76t	5
1994			41	531	13.0	35	5
1995			29	387	13.3	40	2
Career			347	5598	16.1	97t	43
Playoffs			46	734	16.0		6

Kitrick Taylor

Year	Team		No	Yds	Avg	Lg	TD
1988	KC	N	9	105	11.7	36	0
1991	SD	N	24	218	9.1	27	0
1992	GB	N	2	63	31.5	35t	1
1993	DEN	N	1	28	28.0	28	0
Career			36	414	11.5	36	1
Playoffs			1	13	13.0		0

Lenny Taylor

Year	Team		No	Yds	Avg	Lg	TD
1984	GB	N	1	8	8.0	8	0
1987	ATL	N	12	171	14.3	28	1
Career			13	179	13.8	28	1

Lionel Taylor

Year	Team		No	Yds	Avg	Lg	TD
1960	DEN	A	92	1235	13.4	80	12
1961			100	1176	11.8	52	4
1962			77	908	11.8	45	4
1963			78	1104	14.2	72	10
1964			76	873	11.5	57	5
1965			85	1131	13.3	63	7
1966			35	448	12.8	29	1
1967	HOU	A	18	233	12.9	23	1
1968			6	90	15.0	35	0
Career			567	7198	12.7	80	44
Playoffs			1	6	6.0		0

Otis Taylor

Year	Team		No	Yds	Avg	Lg	TD
1965	KC	A	26	446	17.2	48	5
1966			58	1297	22.4	89	8
1967			59	958	16.2	71t	11
1968			20	420	21.0	67t	4
1969			41	696	17.0	79	7
1970	KC	N	34	618	18.2	59t	3
1971			57	1110	19.5	82	7
1972			57	821	14.4	44	4
1973			34	565	16.6	46	4
1974			24	375	15.6	64	2
Career			410	7306	17.8	89	57
Playoffs			27	481	17.8		2

Sammy Taylor

Year	Team		No	Yds	Avg	Lg	TD
1965	SD	A	1	13	13.0	13	0

Jimmy Teal

Year	Team		No	Yds	Avg	Lg	TD
1985	BUF	N	1	24	24.0	24	0
1986			6	60	10.0	20	1
1987	SEA	N	14	198	14.1	47	2
Career			21	282	13.4	47	3

Gus Tebell

Year	Team		No	Yds	Avg	Lg	TD
1923	COL	N					2

Mark Temple

Year	Team		No	Yds	Avg	Lg	TD
1936	BKN-DET	N	1	10	10.0	10	0

Derek Tennell

Year	Team		No	Yds	Avg	Lg	TD
1987	CLE	N	9	102	11.3	24	3
1988			9	88	9.8	26	1
1989			1	4	4.0	4t	1
1991	DET	N	4	43	10.8	18	0
1992	MIN	N	2	12	6.0	8	0
1993			15	122	8.1	17	0
Career			40	371	9.3	26	5
Playoffs			2	6	3.0		1

Bob Tenner

Year	Team		No	Yds	Avg	Lg	TD
1935	GB	N	4	40	10.0		0

Tony Teresa

Year	Team		No	Yds	Avg	Lg	TD
1960	OAK	A	35	393	11.2		4

Joe Tereshinski

Year	Team		No	Yds	Avg	Lg	TD
1947	WAS	N	10	76	7.6	20t	1
1948			4	98	24.5	76t	1
1949			4	36	9.0	12	0
1950			17	148	8.7	17	0
1951			6	74	12.3	21	2
1952			2	19	9.5	11	0
Career			43	451	10.5	76t	4

Ray Terrell

Year	Team		No	Yds	Avg	Lg	TD
1946	CLE	AA	4	21	5.3		0
1947	BAL	AA	6	21	3.5		0
Career			10	42	4.2		0

Ryan Terry

Year	Team		No	Yds	Avg	Lg	TD
1996	ARI	N	1	0	0.0	0	0

Ray Tesser

Year	Team		No	Yds	Avg	Lg	TD
1933	PIT	N	14	274	19.6		0

Vinny Testaverde

Year	Team		No	Yds	Avg	Lg	TD
1990	TB	N	1	3	3.0	3	0
1995	CLE	N	1	7	7.0	7	0
Career			2	10	5.0	7	0

Don Testerman

Year	Team		No	Yds	Avg	Lg	TD
1976	SEA	N	25	232	9.3	25	1
1977			31	219	7.1	25	4
1978			17	143	8.4	21	0
Career			73	594	8.1	25	5

Lee Tevis

Year	Team		No	Yds	Avg	Lg	TD
1948	BKN	AA	1	-8	-8.0	-8	0

Lowell Tew

Year	Team		No	Yds	Avg	Lg	TD
1948	NY	AA	7	97	13.9		0

James Thaxton

Year	Team		No	Yds	Avg	Lg	TD
1973	SD	N	7	119	17.0	31	2
1974	CLE	N	4	71	17.8	34	0
1976	NO	N	7	112	16.0	25t	1
1977			14	211	15.1	41	1
1978	STL	N	3	31	10.3	16	1
Career			35	544	15.5	41	5

Carl Thiele

Year	Team		No	Yds	Avg	Lg	TD
1921	DAY	A					1
1922	DAY	N					1
Career							2

Yancey Thigpen

Year	Team		No	Yds	Avg	Lg	TD
1992	PIT	N	1	2	2.0	2	0
1993			9	154	17.1	39t	3
1994			36	546	15.2	60t	4
1995			85	1307	15.4	43	5
1996			12	244	20.3	39	2
Career			143	2253	15.8	60t	14
Playoffs			17	206	12.1		2

Aaron Thomas

Year	Team		No	Yds	Avg	Lg	TD
1961	SF	N	15	301	20.1	70t	2
1962	NYG	N	4	80	20.0	37	0
1963			22	469	21.3	55	3
1964			43	624	14.5	42t	6
1965			27	631	23.4	71t	5
1966			43	683	15.9	50	4
1967			51	877	17.2	48t	9
1968			29	449	15.5	49	4
1969			22	348	15.8	37	3
1970			6	92	15.3	29	1
Career			262	4554	17.4	71t	37
Playoffs			2	46	23.0		0

Andre Thomas

Year	Team		No	Yds	Avg	Lg	TD
1987	MIN	N	2	13	6.5	10	0

Bill Thomas

Year	Team		No	Yds	Avg	Lg	TD
1973	HOU	N	1	4	4.0	4	0

Blair Thomas

Year	Team		No	Yds	Avg	Lg	TD
1990	NYJ	N	20	204	10.2	55	1
1991			30	195	6.5	18	1
1992			7	49	7.0	10	0
1993			7	25	3.6	7	0
1994	NE-DAL	N	4	16	4.0	9	0
1995	CAR	N	3	24	8.0	14	0
Career			71	513	7.2	55	2
Playoffs			1	2	2.0		0

Bob Thomas

Year	Team		No	Yds	Avg	Lg	TD
1972	LA	N	11	95	8.6	19	0
1973	SD	N	7	51	7.3	37	1
1974			1	9	9.0	9	0
Career			19	155	8.2	37	1

Calvin Thomas

Year	Team		No	Yds	Avg	Lg	TD
1983	CHI	N	2	13	6.5	7	0
1984			9	39	4.3	9	0
1985			5	45	9.0	15	0
1986			4	18	4.5	18	0
Career			20	115	5.8	18	0
Playoffs			2	17	8.5		0

Chris Thomas

Year	Team		No	Yds	Avg	Lg	TD
1995	SF	N	6	73	12.2	23	0

Clendon Thomas

Year	Team		No	Yds	Avg	Lg	TD
1959	LA	N	1	6	6.0	6	0
1960			17	275	16.2	58	2
1964	PIT	N	17	334	19.6	49	1
1965			25	431	17.2	80t	1
Career			60	1046	17.4	80t	4

Curtland Thomas

Year	Team		No	Yds	Avg	Lg	TD
1987	NO	N	1	14	14.0	14	0

Damon Thomas

Year	Team		No	Yds	Avg	Lg	TD
1994	BUF	N	2	31	15.5	17	0
1995			1	18	18.0	18	0
Career			3	49	16.3	18	0

Doug Thomas

Year	Team		No	Yds	Avg	Lg	TD
1991	SEA	N	3	27	9.0	11	0
1992			8	85	10.6	19	0
1993			11	95	8.6	20	0
Career			22	207	9.4	20	0

Duane Thomas

Year	Team		No	Yds	Avg	Lg	TD
1970	DAL	N	10	73	7.3	17	0
1971			13	153	11.8	34t	2
1973	WAS	N	5	40	8.0	13	0
1974			10	31	3.1	9t	1
Career			38	297	7.8	34t	3
Playoffs			11	72	6.5		1

Earl Thomas

Year	Team		No	Yds	Avg	Lg	TD
1971	CHI	N	3	40	13.3	28	0
1972			20	365	18.3	44	3
1973			24	343	14.3	38	4
1974	STL	N	34	513	15.1	52t	5
1975			21	375	17.9	80t	2
1976	HOU	N	4	15	3.8	14	0
Career			106	1651	15.6	80t	14
Playoffs			6	64	10.7		1

Ed Thomas

Year	Team		No	Yds	Avg	Lg	TD
1991	TB	N	4	55	13.8	19	0

Gene Thomas

Year	Team		No	Yds	Avg	Lg	TD
1967	KC	A	13	99	7.6	27	2
1968	BOS	A	10	85	8.5	32	0
Career			23	184	8.0	32	2

George Thomas

Year	Team		No	Yds	Avg	Lg	TD
1950	WAS	N	2	7	3.5	4	0
1951			7	193	27.6	53	2
1952	NYG	N	1	8	8.0	8	0
Career			10	208	20.8	53	2

George Thomas

Year	Team		No	Yds	Avg	Lg	TD
1989	ATL	N	4	46	11.5	16	0
1990			18	383	21.3	72	1
1991			28	365	13.0	37	2

George Thomas *continued*

Year	Team		No	Yds	Avg	Lg	TD
1992			6	54	9.0	18	0
Career			56	848	15.1	72	3
Playoffs			2	34	17.0		0

Jewerl Thomas

Year	Team		No	Yds	Avg	Lg	TD
1980	LA	N	5	30	6.0	11	0
1981			5	37	7.4	13	0
1982	LARM	N	8	49	6.1	11	0
1983	KC	N	10	51	5.1	9	0
Career			28	167	6.0	13	0
Playoffs			3	26	8.7		0

Jimmy Thomas

Year	Team		No	Yds	Avg	Lg	TD
1969	SF	N	18	364	20.2	75t	5
1970			12	221	18.4	61t	3
1971			3	33	11.0	14	0
1972			15	148	9.9	29	0
1973			19	157	8.3	66	0
Career			67	923	13.8	75t	8

Johnny Thomas

Year	Team		No	Yds	Avg	Lg	TD
Playoffs			1	10	10.0		0

J.T. Thomas

Year	Team		No	Yds	Avg	Lg	TD
1995	STL	N	5	42	8.4	12	0
1996			7	46	6.6	11	0
Career			12	88	7.3	12	0

Ken Thomas

Year	Team		No	Yds	Avg	Lg	TD
1983	KC	N	28	236	8.4	25	1

Lamar Thomas

Year	Team		No	Yds	Avg	Lg	TD
1993	TB	N	8	186	23.3	62t	2
1994			7	94	13.4	27	0
1995			10	107	10.7	24	0
1996	MIA	N	10	166	16.6	34	1
Career			35	553	15.8	62t	3

Lavale Thomas

Year	Team		No	Yds	Avg	Lg	TD
1987	GB	N	2	52	26.0	30t	1

Louis Thomas

Year	Team		No	Yds	Avg	Lg	TD
1969	CIN	A	33	481	14.6	62	3
1970	CIN	N	21	257	12.2	27	2
1971			22	327	14.9	90t	2
1972			17	171	10.1	18	1
1974	NO	N	1	3	3.0	3	0
Career			94	1239	13.2	90t	8
Playoffs			1	9	9.0		0

Mike Thomas

Year	Team		No	Yds	Avg	Lg	TD
1975	WAS	N	40	483	12.1	33	3
1976			28	290	10.4	34	4
1977			28	245	8.8	25	2
1978			35	387	11.1	35	2
1979	SD	N	32	388	12.1	32	0
1980			29	218	7.5	27	0
Career			192	2011	10.5	35	11
Playoffs			8	60	7.5		0

Ralph Thomas

Year	Team		No	Yds	Avg	Lg	TD
1955	WAS	N	9	105	11.7	25	2

Rex Thomas

Year	Team		No	Yds	Avg	Lg	TD
1926	BKN	N					2
1927	CLE	N					2
1928	DET	N					2
1930	BKN	N					5
1931							1
Career							12

Robb Thomas

Year	Team		No	Yds	Avg	Lg	TD
1989	KC	N	8	58	7.3	12	2
1990			41	545	13.3	47t	4
1991			43	495	11.5	39	1
1992	SEA	N	11	136	12.4	31	0
1993			7	67	9.6	16	0
1994			4	70	17.5	35	0
1995			12	239	19.9	50t	1
1996	TB	N	33	427	12.9	31t	2
Career			159	2037	12.8	50t	10
Playoffs			5	34	6.8		0

Rodney Thomas

Year	Team		No	Yds	Avg	Lg	TD
1995	HOU	N	39	204	5.2	19	2
1996			13	128	9.8	33	0
Career			52	332	6.4	33	2

Thurman Thomas

Year	Team		No	Yds	Avg	Lg	TD
1988	BUF	N	18	208	11.6	34	0
1989			60	669	11.2	74t	6
1990			49	532	10.9	63	2
1991			62	631	10.2	50t	5
1992			58	626	10.8	43	3
1993			48	387	8.1	37	0
1994			50	349	7.0	28	2
1995			26	220	8.5	60	2
1996			26	254	9.8	69	0
Career			397	3876	9.8	74t	20
Playoffs			75	669	8.9		5

Zack Thomas

Year	Team		No	Yds	Avg	Lg	TD
1983	DEN	N	12	182	15.2	44	0
Playoffs			1	19	19.0		0

Rick Thomaselli

Year	Team		No	Yds	Avg	Lg	TD
1982	HOU	N	1	8	8.0	8	0

Jeff Thomason

Year	Team		No	Yds	Avg	Lg	TD
1992	CIN	N	2	14	7.0	10	0
1993			2	8	4.0	5	0
1995	GB	N	3	32	10.7	15	0
1996			3	45	15.0	24	0
Career			10	99	9.9	24	0

Jim Thomason

Year	Team		No	Yds	Avg	Lg	TD
1945	DET	N	1	6	6.0	6	0

John Thomason

Year	Team		No	Yds	Avg	Lg	TD
1930	BKN	N					1
1931							1
1932							1
Career							3

Anthony Thompson

Year	Team		No	Yds	Avg	Lg	TD
1990	PHX	N	2	11	5.5	6	0
1991			7	52	7.4	14	0
1992	LARM	N	5	11	2.2	7	0
Career			14	74	5.3	14	0

Aundra Thompson

Year	Team		No	Yds	Avg	Lg	TD
1977	GB	N	2	12	6.0	14	0
1978			26	527	20.3	57	2
1979			25	395	15.8	50	3
1980			40	609	15.2	55	2
1981	GB-NO	N	8	111	13.9	25	0
1982	NO	N	8	138	17.3	48	1
Career			109	1792	16.4	57	8

Bobby Thompson

Year	Team		No	Yds	Avg	Lg	TD
1975	DET	N	19	122	6.4	22	0
1976			10	108	10.8	38	0
Career			29	230	7.9	38	0

Craig Thompson

Year	Team		No	Yds	Avg	Lg	TD
1992	CIN	N	19	194	10.2	32	2
1993			17	87	5.1	10	1
Career			36	281	7.8	32	3

Darrell Thompson

Year	Team		No	Yds	Avg	Lg	TD
1990	GB	N	3	1	0.3	1	0
1991			7	71	10.1	18	0
1992			13	129	9.9	43	1
1993			18	129	7.2	34	0
Career			41	330	8.0	43	1
Playoffs			6	86	14.3		0

Ernie Thompson

Year	Team		No	Yds	Avg	Lg	TD
1991	LARM	N	2	35	17.5	22	1
1993	KC	N	4	33	8.3	13	0
Career			6	68	11.3	22	1
Playoffs			1	12	12.0		0

Hal Thompson

Year	Team		No	Yds	Avg	Lg	TD
1947	BKN	AA	15	148	9.9		0
1948			4	37	9.3		1
Career			19	185	9.7		1

James Thompson

Year	Team		No	Yds	Avg	Lg	TD
1978	NYG	N	7	113	16.1	46	0

Jesse Thompson

Year	Team		No	Yds	Avg	Lg	TD
1978	DET	N	18	175	9.7	21	4
1980			11	137	12.5	19	0
Career			29	312	10.8		4

John Thompson

Year	Team		No	Yds	Avg	Lg	TD
1982	GB	N	2	24	12.0	23t	2

Kenny Thompson

Year	Team		No	Yds	Avg	Lg	TD
1982	STL	N	1	5	5.0	5	0
1983			2	31	15.5	22	0
Career			3	36	12.0	22	0
Playoffs			3	41	13.7		0

Leonard Thompson

Year	Team		No	Yds	Avg	Lg	TD
1976	DET	N	3	52	17.3	21	0
1977			7	42	6.0	18	0
1978			10	167	16.7	45t	4
1979			24	451	18.8	82	2
1980			19	511	26.9	79t	3
1981			30	550	18.3	94t	3
1982			17	328	19.3	70t	4
1983			41	752	18.3	80t	3
1984			50	773	15.5	66t	6
1985			51	736	14.4	48	5
1986			25	320	12.8	38t	5
Career			277	4682	16.9	94t	35
Playoffs			13	224	17.2		0

Leroy Thompson

Year	Team		No	Yds	Avg	Lg	TD
1991	PIT	N	14	118	8.4	32	0
1992			22	278	12.6	29	0
1993			38	259	6.8	28	0
1994	NE	N	65	465	7.2	27t	5
1995	KC	N	9	37	4.1	7	0
1996	TB	N	5	36	7.2	12	0
Career			153	1193	7.8	32	5
Playoffs			7	37	5.3		1

Marty Thompson

Year	Team		No	Yds	Avg	Lg	TD
1993	DET	N	1	15	15.0	15	0

Ricky Thompson

Year	Team		No	Yds	Avg	Lg	TD
1976	BAL	N	1	11	11.0	11	0
1977			1	15	15.0	15	0
1978	WAS	N	23	350	15.2	49	1
1979			22	368	16.7	35	4
1980			22	313	14.2	54t	5
1981			28	423	15.1	57	4
Career			97	1480	15.3	57	14

Rocky Thompson

Year	Team		No	Yds	Avg	Lg	TD
1971	NYG	N	16	85	5.3	12	0

Tommy Thompson

Year	Team		No	Yds	Avg	Lg	TD
1940	PIT	N	4	55	13.8		0
1941	PHI	N	2	10	5.0	6	1
Career			6	65	10.8	6	1
Playoffs			1	-7	-7.0		0

Tuffy Thompson

Year	Team		No	Yds	Avg	Lg	TD
1937	PIT	N	6	126	21.0		1
1938			9	55	6.1		0
1939	GB	N	1	1	1.0	1	0
Career			16	182	11.4	1	1

Vince Thompson

Year	Team		No	Yds	Avg	Lg	TD
1981	DET	N	4	40	10.0	17	0
1983			4	16	4.0	8	0
Career			8	56	7.0	17	0

Weegie Thompson

Year	Team		No	Yds	Avg	Lg	TD
1984	PIT	N	17	291	17.1	59	3
1985			8	138	17.3	42	1
1986			17	191	11.2	20	5
1987			17	313	18.4	63	1
1988			16	370	23.1	50	1
1989			4	74	18.5	28	0
Career			79	1377	17.4	63	11
Playoffs			2	38	19.0		0

Year	Team		No	Yds	Avg	Lg	TD

Woody Thompson

Year	Team		No	Yds	Avg	Lg	TD
1975	ATL	N	14	92	6.6	14	0
1976			16	111	6.9	26	0
1977			12	56	4.7	9	0
Career			42	259	6.2	26	0

Bill Thornton

1963	STL	N	4	10	2.5	8	0
1964			7	43	6.1	19	0
1965			1	6	6.0	6	0
1967			1	9	9.0	9	0
Career			13	68	5.2	19	0

Bubba Thornton

1969	BUF	A	14	134	9.6	21	0

James Thornton

1988	CHI	N	15	135	9.0	19	0
1989			24	392	16.3	36t	3
1990			19	254	13.4	32	1
1991			17	278	16.4	33	1
1993	NYJ	N	12	108	9.0	22	2
1994			20	171	8.6	25	0
Career			107	1338	12.5	36t	7
Playoffs			10	135	13.5		1

Reggie Thornton

1991	IND	N	1	38	38.0	38	0

Sidney Thornton

1977	PIT	N	1	5	5.0	5	0
1978			5	66	13.2	24	1
1979			16	231	14.4	32	4
1980			15	131	8.7	29t	1
1981			8	78	9.8	30	0
1982			1	4	4.0	4	0
Career			46	515	11.2	32	6
Playoffs			4	56	14.0		0

Bob Thurbon

1943	P-P	N	6	100	16.7	43	1
1944	C-P	N	7	134	19.1	37t	1
1946	BUF	AA	1	-3	-3.0	-3	0
Career			14	231	16.5	43	2

Steve Thurlow

1964	NYG	N	7	74	10.6	17	1
1965			9	54	6.0	30	1
1966	WAS	N	23	165	7.2	22	0
1967			10	95	9.5	25	0
1968			12	151	12.6	56	0
Career			61	539	8.8	56	2

John Tice

1983	NO	N	7	33	4.7	12t	1
1984			6	55	9.2	17	1
1985			24	266	11.1	39t	1
1986			37	330	8.9	29t	3
1987			16	181	11.3	27t	6
1988			26	297	11.4	40	1
1989			9	98	10.9	23	1
1990			11	113	10.3	19	0
1991			22	230	10.5	22	1
Career			158	1603	10.1	40	15
Playoffs			4	45	11.3		0

Mike Tice

1981	SEA	N	5	47	9.4	14	0
1982			9	46	5.1	12	0
1984			8	90	11.3	30	3
1985			2	13	6.5	7	0
1986			15	150	10.0	25	0
1987			14	106	7.6	27	2
1988			29	244	8.4	26	0
1989	WAS	N	1	2	2.0	2	0
1991	SEA	N	10	70	7.0	16	4
1992	MIN	N	5	65	13.0	34t	1
1993			6	39	6.5	21	1
1995			3	22	7.3	9	0
Career			107	894	8.4	34t	11
Playoffs			2	28	14.0		0

Jim Tiller

1962	NY	A	13	108	8.3	19	0

Morgan Tiller

1945	PIT	N	10	146	14.6	35	0

Pat Tilley

1976	STL	N	26	407	15.7	45	1
1977			5	64	12.8	31	0
1978			62	900	14.5	43	3
1979			57	938	16.5	51t	6
1980			68	966	14.2	60t	6
1981			66	1040	15.8	75	3
1982			36	465	12.9	34	2
1983			44	690	15.7	71t	5
1984			52	758	14.6	42	5
1985			49	726	14.8	46t	6
1986			3	51	17.0	18	0
Career			468	7005	15.0	75	37
Playoffs			5	55	11.0		1

Andre Tillman

1975	MIA	N	5	60	12.0	16	0
1976			13	130	10.0	16	1
1977			17	169	9.9	37t	2
1978			31	398	12.8	33	3
Career			66	757	11.5	37t	6
Playoffs			2	24	12.0		0

Cedric Tillman

1992	DEN	N	12	211	17.6	81t	1
1993			17	193	11.4	30	2
1994			28	455	16.3	63	1
1995	JAC	N	30	368	12.3	28	3
Career			87	1227	14.1	81t	7
Playoffs			2	25	12.5		0

Lawyer Tillman

1989	CLE	N	6	70	11.7	19	2
1992			25	498	19.9	52	0
1993			5	68	13.6	18	1
1995	CAR	N	2	22	11.0	12	0
Career			38	658	17.3	52	3
Playoffs			1	15	15.0		0

Lewis Tillman

1989	NYG	N	1	9	9.0	9	0
1990			8	18	2.3	16	0
1991			5	30	6.0	12	0
1992			1	15	15.0	15	0
1993			1	21	21.0	21	0
1994	CHI	N	27	222	8.2	39	0
Career			43	315	7.3	39	0
Playoffs			3	25	8.3		0

Spencer Tillman

1991	SF	N	2	3	1.5	3	0
1993	HOU	N	1	4	4.0	4t	1
Career			3	7	2.3	4t	1

Charlie Timmons

1946	BKN	AA	1	4	4.0	4	0

Michael Timpson

1990	NE	N	5	91	18.2	42	0
1991			25	471	18.8	60t	2
1992			26	315	12.1	25	1
1993			42	654	15.6	48	2
1994			74	941	12.7	37	3
1995	CHI	N	24	289	12.0	36	1
1996			62	802	12.9	49	0
Career			258	3563	13.8	60t	10
Playoffs			2	20	10.0		0

Tim Tindale

1996	BUF	N	1	-1	-1.0	-1	0

Gerald Tinker

1974	ATL	N	1	12	12.0	12	0
1975	GB	N	4	84	21.0	35t	1
1975	ATL-GB	N	7	121	17.3	35t	2
Career			12	217	18.1	35t	3

Gaynell Tinsley

1937	CHIC	N	36	675	18.8	95t	5
1938			41	516	12.6	98t	1

Gaynell Tinsley *continued*

1940			16	165	10.3		1
Career			93	1356	14.6	98t	7

Keith Tinsley

1987	CLE	N	1	17	17.0	17	0

Howie Tipton

1933	CHIC	N					1
1936			1	15	15.0	15	0
1937			1	2	2.0	2	0
Career			2	17	8.5	15	1

Bob Titchenal

1942	WAS	N	1	7	7.0	7	0
1946	SF	AA	7	160	22.9	54t	2
1947	LA	AA	7	97	13.9		0
Career			15	264	17.6	54t	2

Herb Titmas

1931	PRO	N					1

Y.A. Tittle

1959	SF	N	1	4	4.0	4	0

Robbie Tobeck

1996	ATL	N	2	15	7.5	14	1

Bill Tobin

1963	HOU	A	13	272	20.9	33	1

Dick Todd

1939	WAS	N	19	230	12.1		3
1940			20	402	20.1		4
1941			8	125	15.6	25	1
1942			23	328	14.3	53	4
1946			8	107	13.4	23t	2
1947			4	84	21.0	38	0
1948			37	550	14.9	78t	6
Career			119	1826	15.3	78t	20
Playoffs			1	9	9.0		0

Larry Todd

1965	OAK	A	8	106	13.3	43	0
1966			14	134	9.6	17	1
1967			4	42	10.5	17	0
1968			4	40	10.0	18	0
1969			16	149	9.3	48t	1
1970	OAK	A	5	51	10.2	23	0
Career			51	522	10.2	48t	2
Playoffs			1	40	40.0		0

Richard Todd

1981	NYJ	N	1	1	1.0	1	0

Joe Tofil

1942	BKN	N	3	33	11.0	17	0

Charley Tolar

1960	HOU	A	7	71	10.1		0
1961			24	219	9.1	32	1
1962			30	251	8.4	35	1
1963			41	275	6.7	33	0
1964			35	244	7.0	52	0
1965			25	138	5.5	21	0
1966			13	68	5.2	14	0
Career			175	1266	7.2	52	2
Playoffs			3	10	3.3		0

Ken Toler

1981	NE	N	5	70	14.0	23	0
1982			2	63	31.5	33t	2
Career			7	133	19.0	33t	2
Playoffs			1	16	16.0		0

Johnny Tomaini

1930	NEW	N					1

Lou Tomasetti

1939	PIT	N	4	22	5.5		0
1940			6	129	21.5		1
1941	PHI-DET	N	2	40	20.0	40	1
1942	PHI	N	4	22	5.5	8	0
1946	BUF	AA	6	81	13.5		1

Lou Tomasetti *continued*

Year	Team		No	Yds	Avg	Lg	TD
1947			13	125	9.6		0
1948			22	213	9.7		1
1949			9	56	6.2		1
Career			66	688	10.4	40	5
Playoffs			4	35	8.8		1

Andy Tomasic

Year	Team		No	Yds	Avg	Lg	TD
1942	PIT	N	1	27	27.0	27	0

Mike Tomczak

Year	Team		No	Yds	Avg	Lg	TD
1990	CHI	N	1	5	5.0	5	0

Mario Tonelli

Year	Team		No	Yds	Avg	Lg	TD
1940	CHIC	N	5	53	10.6		0

Ed Toner

Year	Team		No	Yds	Avg	Lg	TD
1993	IND	N	1	5	5.0	5	0

Anthony Toney

Year	Team		No	Yds	Avg	Lg	TD
1986	PHI	N	13	177	13.6	47	0
1987			39	341	8.7	33	1
1988			34	256	7.5	24	1
1989			19	124	6.5	15	0
1990			17	133	7.8	32	3
Career			122	1031	8.5	47	5
Playoffs			6	44	7.3		0

Amani Toomer

Year	Team		No	Yds	Avg	Lg	TD
1996	NYG	N	1	12	12.0	12	0

Al Toon

Year	Team		No	Yds	Avg	Lg	TD
1985	NYJ	N	46	662	14.4	78t	3
1986			85	1176	13.8	62t	8
1987			68	976	14.4	58t	5
1988			93	1067	11.5	42	5
1989			63	693	11.0	37t	2
1990			57	757	13.3	46t	6
1991			74	963	13.0	32	1
1992			31	311	10.0	32	2
Career			517	6605	12.8	78t	31
Playoffs			26	330	12.7		2

Bob Topp

Year	Team		No	Yds	Avg	Lg	TD
1954	NYG	N	6	90	15.0	31	3

LaVerne Torczon

Year	Team		No	Yds	Avg	Lg	TD
1960	BUF	A	1	9	9.0	9	0

Eric Torkelson

Year	Team		No	Yds	Avg	Lg	TD
1974	GB	N	2	10	5.0	8	0
1975			6	37	6.2	12	0
1976			19	140	7.4	31	0
1977			11	107	9.7	14	0
1978			2	36	18.0	31	0
1979			19	139	7.3	14	0
Career			59	469	7.9	31	0

Bob Torrey

Year	Team		No	Yds	Avg	Lg	TD
1979	MIA	N	2	3	1.5	8	0
Playoffs			1	0	0.0		0

Flavio Tosi

Year	Team		No	Yds	Avg	Lg	TD
1935	BOS	N	10	169	16.9		1
1936			4	70	17.5		0
Career			14	239	17.1		1

Zollie Toth

Year	Team		No	Yds	Avg	Lg	TD
1950	NYY	N	15	189	12.6	60	3
1951			10	100	10.0	23	0
1952	DAL	N	13	54	4.2	20	0
1954	BAL	N	11	51	4.6	13	0
Career			49	394	8.0	60	3

Dan Towler

Year	Team		No	Yds	Avg	Lg	TD
1950	LA	N	8	63	7.9	17	0
1951			16	257	16.1	46	0
1952			11	68	6.2	13	0
1953			11	125	11.4	49	1
1954			10	127	12.7	36	0
1955			6	25	4.2	11	0
Career			62	665	10.7	49	1
Playoffs			3	35	11.7		0

JoJo Townsell

Year	Team		No	Yds	Avg	Lg	TD
1985	NYJ	N	12	187	15.6	36	0
1986			1	11	11.0	11	0
1987			4	37	9.3	11	0
1988			4	40	10.0	19	0
1989			45	787	17.5	63t	5
1990			4	57	14.3	18	0
Career			70	1119	16.0	63t	5

John Tracey

Year	Team		No	Yds	Avg	Lg	TD
1959	CHIC	N	17	258	15.2	51	0
1962	BUF	A	1	28	28.0	28	0
1965			1	2	2.0	2	0
1967			1	15	15.0	15	0
Career			20	303	15.2	51	0
Playoffs			1	12	12.0		0

Tom Tracy

Year	Team		No	Yds	Avg	Lg	TD
1956	DET	N	3	6	2.0	5	0
1957			6	24	4.0	7	0
1958	PIT	N	32	535	16.7	56	4
1959			23	273	11.9	45t	5
1960			24	349	14.5	65t	4
1961			14	133	9.5	38	1
1962			2	11	5.5	6	0
1963	PIT-WAS	N	7	112	16.0	34	0
1964	WAS	N	2	25	12.5	24	0
Career			113	1468	13.0	65t	14
Playoffs			2	23	11.5		0

John Trahan

Year	Team		No	Yds	Avg	Lg	TD
1987	KC	N	4	40	10.0	14	0

Mike Trainor

Year	Team		No	Yds	Avg	Lg	TD
1923	BUF	N					1
1924							1
Career							2

Richard Trapp

Year	Team		No	Yds	Avg	Lg	TD
1968	BUF	A	24	235	9.8	27	0
1969	SD	A	2	39	19.5	24	0
Career			26	274	10.5	27	0

Jerry Traynham

Year	Team		No	Yds	Avg	Lg	TD
1961	DEN	A	1	-1	-1.0	-1	0

Bill Triplett

Year	Team		No	Yds	Avg	Lg	TD
1963	STL	N	31	396	12.8	38	3
1965			26	256	9.8	37	1
1966			2	6	3.0	11	0
1967	NYG	N	7	69	9.9	16	0
1968	DET	N	28	135	4.8	25	0
1969			13	141	10.8	62t	1
1970			6	52	8.7	15	0
Career			113	1055	9.3	62t	5

Mel Triplett

Year	Team		No	Yds	Avg	Lg	TD
1955	NYG	N	3	9	3.0	12	0
1956			6	48	8.0	35t	1
1957			4	75	18.8	33	0
1958			7	110	15.7	32	0
1959			6	78	13.0	25	0
1960			5	48	9.6	24t	2
1961	MIN	N	10	41	4.1	15	0
1962			2	30	15.0	27	1
Career			43	439	10.2	35t	4
Playoffs			3	13	4.3		0

Wally Triplett

Year	Team		No	Yds	Avg	Lg	TD
1949	DET	N	8	90	11.3	32	0
1950			6	70	11.7	18	0
1953	CHIC	N	3	15	5.0	6	0
Career			17	175	10.3	32	0

Charley Trippi

Year	Team		No	Yds	Avg	Lg	TD
1947	CHIC	N	23	240	10.4	62	0
1948			22	228	10.4	33t	2
1949			34	412	12.1	44	6
1950			32	270	8.4	28	1
1952			5	66	13.2	21	0
1953			11	87	7.9	21	2
1954			3	18	6.0	7	0
Career			130	1321	10.2	62	11
Playoffs			1	20	20.0		0

Billy Truax

Year	Team		No	Yds	Avg	Lg	TD
1965	LA	N	6	108	18.0	59t	1
1966			29	314	10.8	21	0
1967			37	487	13.2	41	4
1968			35	417	11.9	23	3
1969			37	431	11.6	49	5
1970			36	420	11.7	34	3
1971	DAL	N	15	232	15.5	25	1
1972			4	49	12.3	18	0
Career			199	2458	12.4	59t	17
Playoffs			10	137	13.7		1

Olanda Truitt

Year	Team		No	Yds	Avg	Lg	TD
1993	MIN	N	4	40	10.0	13	0
1994	WAS	N	2	89	44.5	77t	1
1995			9	154	17.1	47	1
Career			15	283	18.9	77t	2

Bob Trumpy

Year	Team		No	Yds	Avg	Lg	TD
1968	CIN	A	37	639	17.3	80t	3
1969			37	835	22.6	80t	9
1970	CIN	N	29	480	16.6	53t	2
1971			40	531	13.3	44	3
1972			44	500	11.4	38	2
1973			29	435	15.0	53	5
1974			21	330	15.7	41	2
1975			22	276	12.5	35t	1
1976			21	323	15.4	48t	7
1977			18	251	13.9	32	1
Career			298	4600	15.4	80t	35
Playoffs			1	-7	-7.0		0

Eric Truvillion

Year	Team		No	Yds	Avg	Lg	TD
1987	DET	N	12	207	17.3	53t	1

Eddie Tryon

Year	Team		No	Yds	Avg	Lg	TD
1926	NY	A					3
1927	NYY	N					2
Career							5

Bill Tucker

Year	Team		No	Yds	Avg	Lg	TD
1967	SF	N	2	22	11.0	12	0
1968			15	197	13.1	43t	4
1969			14	104	7.4	18t	2
1970			17	108	6.4	28t	1
1971	CHI	N	11	65	5.9	21	0
Career			59	496	8.4	43t	7
Playoffs			6	48	8.0		0

Bob Tucker

Year	Team		No	Yds	Avg	Lg	TD
1970	NYG	N	40	571	14.3	41t	5
1971			59	791	13.4	63t	4
1972			55	764	13.9	39	4
1973			50	681	13.6	33	5
1974			41	496	12.1	29t	2
1975			34	484	14.2	47t	1
1976			42	498	11.9	39	1
1977	NYG-MIN	N	15	200	13.3	29	2
1978	MIN	N	47	540	11.5	35	0
1979			24	223	9.3	21	2
1980			15	173	11.5	25	1
Career			422	5421	12.8	63t	27
Playoffs			4	48	12.0		0

Travis Tucker

Year	Team		No	Yds	Avg	Lg	TD
1985	CLE	N	2	20	10.0	10	0
1986			2	29	14.5	16	0
Career			4	49	12.3	16	0

Wendell Tucker

Year	Team		No	Yds	Avg	Lg	TD
1968	LA	N	7	124	17.7	60t	4
1969			38	629	16.6	93t	7
1970			12	230	19.2	51	0
Career			57	983	17.2	93t	11
Playoffs			3	23	7.7		0

Dick Tuckey

Year	Team		No	Yds	Avg	Lg	TD
1938	CLE	N	1	10	10.0	10	0

John Tuggle

Year	Team		No	Yds	Avg	Lg	TD
1983	NYG	N	3	50	16.7	27	0

Walter Tullis

Year	Team		No	Yds	Avg	Lg	TD
1979	GB	N	10	173	17.3	52t	1

Year	Team		No	Yds	Avg	Lg	TD

George Tully
| 1926 | PHI | A | | | | | 1 |

Emlen Tunnell
1948	NYG	N	4	32	8.0	14	0
1949			1	7	7.0	7	0
Career			5	39	7.8	14	0

Frank Turbert
| 1944 | BOS | N | 1 | 16 | 16.0 | 16 | 0 |

Doug Turley
1944	WAS	N	8	112	14.0	35t	1
1945			17	185	10.9	29	1
1946			6	105	17.5	25	0
1947			6	95	15.8	24	1
1948			8	111	13.9	33	0
Career			45	608	13.5	35t	3
Playoffs			1	11	11.0		0

Bake Turner
1962	BAL	N	1	111	111.0	74t	1
1963	NY	A	71	1007	14.2	53	6
1964			58	974	16.8	71	9
1965			31	402	13.0	62	2
1966			7	115	16.4	42	0
1967			3	40	13.3	22	0
1968			10	241	24.1	71	2
1969			11	221	20.1	54t	3
1970	BOS	N	28	428	15.3	43	2
Career			220	3539	16.1	74t	25
Playoffs			2	25	12.5		0

Bulldog Turner
| 1952 | CHIB | N | 1 | 2 | 2.0 | 2 | 0 |

Cecil Turner
1968	CHI	N	14	208	14.9	80t	2
1969			1	19	19.0	19	0
1970			2	53	26.5	34	0
1971			1	13	13.0	13	0
1972			3	71	23.7	36	0
Career			21	364	17.3	80t	2

Clem Turner
1969	CIN	A	5	14	2.8	8	0
1970	DEN	N	8	23	2.9	11	0
1971			7	65	9.3	17	1
1972			1	10	10.0	10	0
Career			21	112	5.3	17	1

Daryl Turner
1984	SEA	N	35	715	20.4	80t	10
1985			34	670	19.7	54	13
1986			18	334	18.6	72t	7
1987			14	153	10.9	20t	6
Career			101	1872	18.5	80t	36
Playoffs			4	64	16.0		1

Deacon Turner
1978	CIN	N	11	50	4.5	8	0
1979			2	18	9.0	10	0
1980			12	73	6.1	15	1
Career			25	141	5.6	15	1

Floyd Turner
1989	NO	N	22	279	12.7	54t	1
1990			21	396	18.9	68t	4
1991			64	927	14.5	65t	8
1992			5	43	8.6	18	0
1993			12	163	13.6	52	1
1994	IND	N	52	593	11.4	28	6
1995			35	431	12.3	47t	4
1996	BAL	N	38	461	12.1	27t	2
Career			249	3293	13.2	68t	26
Playoffs			15	215	14.3		3

Jay Turner
1938	WAS	N	2	10	5.0		0
1939			2	15	7.5		0
Career			4	25	6.3		0

Jim Turner
| 1977 | DEN | N | 1 | 25 | 25.0 | 25t | 0 |

Jim Turner continued
1978			1	-4	-4.0	-4	0
1979			1	6	6.0	6	0
Career			3	27	9.0	25t	1

Kevin Turner
1992	NE	N	7	52	7.4	19t	2
1993			39	333	8.5	26	2
1994			52	471	9.1	32	2
1995	PHI	N	4	29	7.3	11	0
1996			43	409	9.5	41	1
Career			145	1294	8.9	41	7
Playoffs			3	25	8.3		0

Nate Turner
| 1994 | BUF | N | 1 | 26 | 26.0 | 26t | 1 |

Odessa Turner
1987	NYG	N	10	195	19.5	36	1
1988			10	128	12.8	28t	1
1989			38	467	12.3	44	4
1990			6	69	11.5	18	0
1991			21	356	17.0	55	0
1992	SF	N	9	200	22.2	57	2
1993			3	64	21.3	32	0
Career			97	1479	15.2	57	8
Playoffs			1	12	12.0		0

Vernon Turner
1991	LARM	N	3	41	13.7	19t	1
1992			5	42	8.4	16	0
1993	DET	N	1	7	7.0	7	0
Career			9	90	10.0	19t	1

Melvin Tuten
| 1995 | CIN | N | 2 | 12 | 6.0 | 9 | 1 |

Orville Tuttle
| 1938 | NYG | N | 1 | -2 | -2.0 | -2 | 0 |

Perry Tuttle
1982	BUF	N	7	107	15.3	26	0
1983			17	261	15.4	38	3
1984	ATL	N	1	7	7.0	7	0
Career			25	375	15.0	38	3

Howard Twilley
1966	MIA	A	10	128	12.8	20	0
1967			24	314	13.1	42	2
1968			39	604	15.5	40	1
1969			10	158	15.8	33	1
1970	MIA	N	22	281	12.8	23t	5
1971			23	349	15.2	41	4
1972			20	364	18.2	44	3
1973			2	30	15.0	29	0
1974			24	256	10.7	21	2
1975			24	366	15.3	32	4
1976			14	214	15.3	39	1
Career			212	3064	14.5	44	23
Playoffs			13	186	14.3		1

Andre Tyler
| 1983 | TB | N | 6 | 77 | 12.8 | 21 | 0 |

Pete Tyler
1937	CHIC	N	7	60	8.6		1
1938			2	24	12.0		1
Career			9	84	9.3		2

Rob Tyler
| 1989 | SEA | N | 14 | 148 | 10.6 | 27 | 0 |

Toussaint Tyler
1981	NO	N	23	135	5.9	18	0
1982			4	31	7.8	12	0
Career			27	166	6.1	18	0

Wendell Tyler
1977	LA	N	1	3	3.0	3	0
1978			2	17	8.5	16	0
1979			32	308	9.6	71t	1
1980			2	8	4.0	5	0
1981			45	436	9.7	67t	5
1982	LARM	N	38	375	9.9	40	4

Wendell Tyler continued
1983	SF	N	34	285	8.4	26	2
1984			28	230	8.2	26t	2
1985			20	154	7.7	16	2
Career			202	1816	9.0	71t	16
Playoffs			17	224	13.2		1

Layne Tynes
| 1924 | COL | N | | | | | 1 |

Jim Tyree
| 1948 | BOS | N | 13 | 106 | 8.2 | 52 | 0 |

Tim Tyrrell
1986	LARM	N	1	9	9.0	9	0
1987			6	59	9.8	16	0
Career			7	68	9.7	16	0

Rocky Ugoccioni
| 1944 | BKN | N | 7 | 94 | 13.4 | 26 | 0 |

Hub Ulrich
| 1946 | MIA | AA | 4 | 75 | 18.8 | | 1 |

Jack Underwood
| 1924 | DUL | N | | | | | 2 |

Johnny Unitas
| 1956 | BAL | N | 1 | 1 | 1.0 | 1 | 0 |

Rick Upchurch
1975	DEN	N	18	436	24.2	90t	2
1976			12	340	28.3	59t	1
1977			12	245	20.4	45	2
1978			17	210	12.4	29t	1
1979			64	937	14.6	47	7
1980			46	605	13.2	35	3
1981			32	550	17.2	63	3
1982			26	407	15.7	51t	3
1983			40	639	16.0	40	2
Career			267	4369	16.4	90t	24
Playoffs			1	9	9.0		0

Andy Uram
1938	GB	N	4	46	11.5		0
1939			7	93	13.3		2
1940			10	188	18.8		2
1941			6	124	20.7	44	0
1942			21	420	20.0	64	4
1943			10	212	21.2	51	2
Career			58	1083	18.7	64	10
Playoffs			1	24	24.0		0

Alex Urban
1941	GB	N	2	26	13.0	14	1
1944			1	10	10.0	10	0
1945			1	55	55.0	55	0
Career			4	91	22.8	55	1

Luke Urban
| 1921 | BUF | A | | | | | 1 |

Rube Ursella
| 1924 | RI | N | | | | | 1 |

Darryl Usher
| 1989 | PHX | N | 1 | 8 | 8.0 | 8 | 0 |

Ben Utt
| 1987 | IND | N | 1 | -4 | -4.0 | -4 | 0 |

Iheanyi Uwaezuoke
| 1996 | SF | N | 7 | 91 | 13.0 | 29t | 1 |

Walt Uzdavinis
| 1937 | CLE | N | 1 | 15 | 15.0 | 15 | 0 |

Ira Valentine
| 1987 | HOU | N | 2 | 10 | 5.0 | 7 | 0 |

Joe Valerio
| 1993 | KC | N | 1 | 1 | 1.0 | 1t | 1 |
| 1994 | | | 2 | 5 | 2.5 | 4t | 2 |

Year	Team	No	Yds	Avg	Lg	TD

Joe Valerio *continued*

Year	Team	No	Yds	Avg	Lg	TD
1995		1	1	1.0	1t	1
Career		4	7	1.8	4t	4

Ebert Van Buren

Year	Team		No	Yds	Avg	Lg	TD
1952	PHI	N	4	73	18.3	38	0

Steve Van Buren

Year	Team		No	Yds	Avg	Lg	TD
1945	PHI	N	10	123	12.3	44t	2
1946			6	75	12.5	33	0
1947			9	79	8.8	35	0
1948			10	96	9.6	34	0
1949			4	88	22.0	50	1
1950			2	34	17.0	29	0
1951			4	28	7.0	18	0
Career			45	523	11.6	50	3
Playoffs			4	29	7.3		1

Al Vandeweghe

Year	Team		No	Yds	Avg	Lg	TD
1946	BUF	AA	6	67	11.2		1

Alex Van Dyke

Year	Team		No	Yds	Avg	Lg	TD
1996	NYJ	N	17	118	6.9	12	1

Mark van Eeghen

Year	Team		No	Yds	Avg	Lg	TD
1974	OAK	N	4	33	8.3	12	0
1975			12	42	3.5	18t	1
1976			17	173	10.2	21	0
1977			15	135	9.0	30	0
1978			27	291	10.8	33	0
1979			51	474	9.3	36	2
1980			29	259	8.9	37	0
1981			7	60	8.6	13	0
1982	NE	N	2	14	7.0	9	1
1983			10	102	10.2	23	0
Career			174	1583	9.1	37	4
Playoffs			11	118	10.7		0

Hal Van Every

Year	Team		No	Yds	Avg	Lg	TD
1940	GB	N	4	41	10.3		0
1941			1	3	3.0	3	0
Career			5	44	8.8	3	0
Playoffs			2	24	12.0		1

Billy Van Heusen

Year	Team		No	Yds	Avg	Lg	TD
1968	DEN	A	19	353	18.6	50t	3
1969			3	64	21.3	36	0
1970	DEN	N	16	382	23.9	74	2
1971			1	10	10.0	10	0
1972			4	59	14.8	25	0
1973			8	149	18.6	62t	1
1974			16	421	26.3	73t	4
1975			15	246	16.4	28	1
Career			82	1684	20.5	74	11

Tamarick Vanover

Year	Team		No	Yds	Avg	Lg	TD
1995	KC	N	11	231	21.0	57	2
1996			21	241	11.5	24	1
Career			32	472	14.8	57	3

Brad Van Pelt

Year	Team		No	Yds	Avg	Lg	TD
1979	NYG	N	1	20	20.0	20	0

Art Van Tone

Year	Team		No	Yds	Avg	Lg	TD
1943	DET	N	6	112	18.7	72	1
1944			9	237	26.3	43t	4
1945			3	67	22.3	41	0
1946	BKN	AA	7	152	21.7	51t	3
Career			25	568	22.7	72	8

Pete Van Valkenberg

Year	Team		No	Yds	Avg	Lg	TD
1973	BUF	N	1	7	7.0	7	0

James Van Wagner

Year	Team		No	Yds	Avg	Lg	TD
1978	NO	N	1	-1	-1.0	-1	0

Fred Vanzo

Year	Team		No	Yds	Avg	Lg	TD
1938	DET	N	4	52	13.0		0
1939			4	110	27.5		0
1940			7	85	12.1		0
1941	DET-CHIC	N	2	20	10.0	12	0
Career			17	267	15.7	12	0

Mike Varajon

Year	Team		No	Yds	Avg	Lg	TD
1987	SF	N	3	25	8.3	12	0

Tommy Vardell

Year	Team		No	Yds	Avg	Lg	TD
1992	CLE	N	13	128	9.8	23	0
1993			19	151	7.9	28t	1
1994			16	137	8.6	19	1
1995			6	18	3.0	7	0
1996	SF	N	28	179	6.4	22	0
Career			82	613	7.5	28t	2

Johnny Vardian

Year	Team		No	Yds	Avg	Lg	TD
1946	MIA	AA	7	108	15.4		0
1947	BAL	AA	16	280	17.5	72t	1
1948			3	26	8.7		0
Career			26	414	15.9	72t	1

Larry Vargo

Year	Team		No	Yds	Avg	Lg	TD
1964	MIN	N	1	13	13.0	13	0

Frank Varrichione

Year	Team		No	Yds	Avg	Lg	TD
1960	PIT	N	0	-7		-7L	0

Vic Vasicek

Year	Team		No	Yds	Avg	Lg	TD
1949	BUF	AA	0	5		5L	0

Randy Vataha

Year	Team		No	Yds	Avg	Lg	TD
1971	NE	N	51	872	17.1	88t	9
1972			25	369	14.8	44	2
1973			20	341	17.1	48	2
1974			25	561	22.4	59t	3
1975			46	720	15.7	47	6
1976			11	192	17.5	44	1
1977	GB	N	10	109	10.9	20	0
Career			188	3164	16.8	88t	23

Jon Vaughn

Year	Team		No	Yds	Avg	Lg	TD
1991	NE	N	9	89	9.9	32	0
1992			13	84	6.5	28	0
1994	SEA	N	1	5	5.0	5t	1
Career			23	178	7.7	32	1

Clarence Verdin

Year	Team		No	Yds	Avg	Lg	TD
1987	WAS	N	2	62	31.0	55	0
1988	IND	N	20	437	21.9	54	4
1989			20	381	19.1	82t	1
1990			14	178	12.7	45	1
1991			21	214	10.2	28	0
1992			3	37	12.3	21	0
1993			2	20	10.0	19	1
Career			82	1329	16.2	82t	7

Ed Vereb

Year	Team		No	Yds	Avg	Lg	TD
1960	WAS	N	9	119	13.2	26	0

Chris Verhulst

Year	Team		No	Yds	Avg	Lg	TD
1989	HOU	N	4	48	12.0	21	0
1990	DEN	N	3	13	4.3	6	0
Career			7	61	8.7	21	0

David Verser

Year	Team		No	Yds	Avg	Lg	TD
1981	CIN	N	6	161	26.8	73t	2
1982			4	98	24.5	56t	1
1983			7	82	11.7	22	0
1984			6	113	18.8	28	0
Career			23	454	19.7	73t	3

Billy Vessels

Year	Team		No	Yds	Avg	Lg	TD
1956	BAL	N	11	177	16.1	30	1

John Vesser

Year	Team		No	Yds	Avg	Lg	TD
1926	LA	A					1
1927	CHIC	N					1
Career							2

Joe Vetrano

Year	Team		No	Yds	Avg	Lg	TD
1946	SF	AA	4	37	9.3		0
1948			1	34	34.0	34	0
Career			5	71	14.2	34	0

Roger Vick

Year	Team		No	Yds	Avg	Lg	TD
1987	NYJ	N	13	108	8.3	23	0
1988			19	120	6.3	17	0

Roger Vick *continued*

Year	Team		No	Yds	Avg	Lg	TD
1989			34	241	7.1	21	2
Career			66	469	7.1	23	2

Vic Vidoni

Year	Team		No	Yds	Avg	Lg	TD
1935	PIT	N	11	111	10.1		0
1936			2	35	17.5		0
Career			13	146	11.2		0

Tommy Vigorito

Year	Team		No	Yds	Avg	Lg	TD
1981	MIA	N	33	237	7.2	31t	2
1982			24	186	7.8	26	0
1983			1	7	7.0	7	0
1985			1	9	9.0	9	0
Career			59	439	7.4	31t	2
Playoffs			9	103	11.4		0

Paul Vinnola

Year	Team		No	Yds	Avg	Lg	TD
1946	LA	AA	4	39	9.8		0

Lionel Vital

Year	Team		No	Yds	Avg	Lg	TD
1987	WAS	N	1	13	13.0	13	0

Joe Vodicka

Year	Team		No	Yds	Avg	Lg	TD
1945	CHIC	N	1	3	3.0	1	0

Stu Voigt

Year	Team		No	Yds	Avg	Lg	TD
1971	MIN	N	15	214	14.3	25	1
1972			6	50	8.3	14	1
1973			23	318	13.8	43	2
1974			32	268	8.4	22	5
1975			34	363	10.7	22	4
1976			28	303	10.8	44	1
1977			20	212	10.6	24	1
1978			4	52	13.0	27	0
1979			15	139	9.3	18	2
Career			177	1919	10.8	44	17
Playoffs			30	362	12.1		3

Jim Vollenweider

Year	Team		No	Yds	Avg	Lg	TD
1962	SF	N	4	21	5.3	10	0
1963			1	26	26.0	26	0
Career			5	47	9.4	26	0

Bill Volok

Year	Team		No	Yds	Avg	Lg	TD
1937	CHIC	N	1	9	9.0	9	0

Wilbur Volz

Year	Team		No	Yds	Avg	Lg	TD
1949	BUF	AA	1	6	6.0		0

Tillie Voss

Year	Team		No	Yds	Avg	Lg	TD
1922	RI	N					1
1924	GB	N					5
1928	CHIB	N					1
Career							7

Tom Waddle

Year	Team		No	Yds	Avg	Lg	TD
1989	CHI	N	1	8	8.0	8	0
1990			2	32	16.0	23	0
1991			55	599	10.9	37t	3
1992			46	674	14.7	68t	4
1993			44	552	12.5	38	1
1994			25	244	9.8	22	1
Career			173	2109	12.2	68t	9
Playoffs			12	153	12.8		1

Billy Waddy

Year	Team		No	Yds	Avg	Lg	TD
1977	LA	N	23	355	15.4	42	1
1978			14	258	18.4	68t	1
1979			14	220	15.7	40t	3
1980			38	670	17.6	44t	5
1981			31	460	14.8	46	0
Career			120	1963	16.4	68t	10
Playoffs			11	219	19.9		1

Billy Wade

Year	Team		No	Yds	Avg	Lg	TD
1960	LA	N	0	10		10L	0

Charlie Wade

Year	Team		No	Yds	Avg	Lg	TD
1974	CHI	N	39	683	17.5	73	1

Jim Wade

Year	Team		No	Yds	Avg	Lg	TD
1949	NYB	N	4	58	14.5	33	0

Year	Team		No	Yds	Avg	Lg	TD

Clint Wager
Year	Team		No	Yds	Avg	Lg	TD
1943	CHIC	N	1	11	11.0	11	0
1944	C-P	N	5	73	14.6	38	0
1945	CHIC	N	1	32	32.0	32	0
Career			7	116	16.6	38	0

Harmon Wages
Year	Team		No	Yds	Avg	Lg	TD
1968	ATL	N	16	121	7.6	55t	1
1969			22	228	10.4	88t	1
1970			26	153	5.9	24	2
1971			19	249	13.1	47	1
1973			2	14	7.0	14	0
Career			85	765	9.0	88t	5

Barry Wagner
Year	Team		No	Yds	Avg	Lg	TD
1992	CHI	N	1	16	16.0	16	0

Lowell Wagner
Year	Team		No	Yds	Avg	Lg	TD
1946	NY	AA	9	126	14.0		1
1947			4	50	12.5		1
1948			6	99	16.5	54t	1
1952	SF	N	1	6	6.0	6	0
Career			20	281	14.1	54t	3

Frank Wainright
Year	Team		No	Yds	Avg	Lg	TD
1991	NO	N	1	3	3.0	3	0
1992			9	143	15.9	29	0
1996	MIA	N	1	2	2.0	2t	1
Career			11	148	13.5	29	1

Carl Waite
Year	Team		No	Yds	Avg	Lg	TD
1928	FRA	N					1
1930	NEW	N					1
Career							2

Van Waiters
Year	Team		No	Yds	Avg	Lg	TD
1989	CLE	N	1	14	14.0	14t	1

Billy Walik
Year	Team		No	Yds	Avg	Lg	TD
1970	PHI	N	1	0	0.0	0	0
1972			1	15	15.0	15t	1
Career			2	15	7.5	15t	1

Adam Walker
Year	Team		No	Yds	Avg	Lg	TD
1987	MIN	N	2	3	1.5	2	0

Adam Walker
Year	Team		No	Yds	Avg	Lg	TD
1993	SF	N	1	4	4.0	4	0
1995			11	78	7.1	15	0
Career			12	82	6.8	15	0
Playoffs			1	-3	-3.0		0

Byron Walker
Year	Team		No	Yds	Avg	Lg	TD
1982	SEA	N	10	156	15.6	40t	2
1983			12	248	20.7	50t	2
1984			13	236	18.2	41	1
1985			19	285	15.0	28t	2
Career			54	925	17.1	50t	7

Derrick Walker
Year	Team		No	Yds	Avg	Lg	TD
1990	SD	N	23	240	10.4	23	1
1991			20	134	6.7	14	0
1992			34	393	11.6	59	2
1993			21	212	10.1	25t	1
1994	KC	N	36	382	10.6	57t	2
1995			25	205	8.2	18t	1
1996			9	73	8.1	24	1
Career			168	1639	9.8	59	8
Playoffs			10	127	12.7		1

Doak Walker
Year	Team		No	Yds	Avg	Lg	TD
1950	DET	N	35	534	15.3	43	6
1951			22	421	19.1	63	4
1952			11	90	8.2	18	0
1953			30	502	16.7	83t	3
1954			32	564	17.6	66t	3
1955			22	428	19.5	70t	5
Career			152	2539	16.7	83t	21
Playoffs			7	135	19.3		4

Dwight Walker
Year	Team		No	Yds	Avg	Lg	TD
1982	CLE	N	8	136	17.0	46	0
1983			29	273	9.4	35	1
1984			10	122	12.2	25	0

Dwight Walker *continued*
Year	Team		No	Yds	Avg	Lg	TD
1987	NO	N	2	15	7.5	8	0
Career			49	546	11.1	46	1
Playoffs			4	47	11.8		0

Herschel Walker
Year	Team		No	Yds	Avg	Lg	TD
1986	DAL	N	76	837	11.0	84t	2
1987			60	715	11.9	44	1
1988			53	505	9.5	50	2
1989	DAL-MIN	N	40	423	10.6	52	2
1990	MIN	N	35	315	9.0	32	4
1991			33	204	6.2	19	0
1992	PHI	N	38	278	7.3	41	2
1993			75	610	8.1	55	3
1994			50	500	10.0	93	2
1995	NYG	N	31	234	7.5	34	1
1996	DAL	N	7	89	12.7	24	0
Career			498	4710	9.5	93	19
Playoffs			10	60	6.0		0

Paul Walker
Year	Team		No	Yds	Avg	Lg	TD
1948	NYG	N	1	11	11.0	11	0

Rick Walker
Year	Team		No	Yds	Avg	Lg	TD
1977	CIN	N	1	13	13.0	13	0
1978			12	126	10.5	28	2
1979			1	14	14.0	14t	1
1980	WAS	N	10	88	8.8	15t	1
1981			11	112	10.2	24	1
1982			12	92	7.7	25t	1
1983			17	168	9.9	29	2
1984			5	52	10.4	19	1
1985			1	8	8.0	8	0
Career			70	673	9.6	29	9
Playoffs			10	92	9.2		0

Wayne Walker
Year	Team		No	Yds	Avg	Lg	TD
1989	SD	N	24	395	16.5	49	1

Wesley Walker
Year	Team		No	Yds	Avg	Lg	TD
1977	NYJ	N	35	740	**21.1**	87t	3
1978			48	**1169**	**24.4**	77t	8
1979			23	569	24.7	71t	5
1980			18	376	20.9	47	1
1981			47	770	16.4	49	9
1982			39	620	15.9	56t	6
1983			61	868	14.2	64t	7
1984			41	623	15.2	44t	7
1985			34	725	21.3	96t	5
1986			49	1016	20.7	83t	12
1987			9	190	21.1	59	1
1988			26	551	21.2	50t	7
1989			8	89	11.1	31	0
Career			438	8306	19.0	96t	71
Playoffs			27	486	18.0		3

Willie Walker
Year	Team		No	Yds	Avg	Lg	TD
1966	DET	N	1	21	21.0	21	0

Bob Wallace
Year	Team		No	Yds	Avg	Lg	TD
1968	CHI	N	19	281	14.8	27	2
1969			47	553	11.8	45	5
1970			15	160	10.7	33	0
1971			27	400	14.8	58	2
1972			1	9	9.0	9	0
Career			109	1403	12.9	58	9

Jackie Wallace
Year	Team		No	Yds	Avg	Lg	TD
1977	LA	N	1	13	13.0	13	0

John Wallace
Year	Team		No	Yds	Avg	Lg	TD
1928	CHIB	N					1

Ray Wallace
Year	Team		No	Yds	Avg	Lg	TD
1986	HOU	N	17	177	10.4	35t	2
1987			7	34	4.9	7	0
Career			24	211	8.8	35t	2
Playoffs			1	11	11.0		0

Bill Waller
Year	Team		No	Yds	Avg	Lg	TD
1938	BKN	N	3	15	5.0		0

Ron Waller
Year	Team		No	Yds	Avg	Lg	TD
1955	LA	N	24	228	9.5	30	1

Ron Waller *continued*
Year	Team		No	Yds	Avg	Lg	TD
1956			9	76	8.4	16	0
1957			5	40	8.0	17	0
1958			3	75	25.0	63	0
1960	LA	A	2	24	12.0	23	0
Career			43	443	10.3	63	1
Playoffs			3	18	6.0		0

Herkie Walls
Year	Team		No	Yds	Avg	Lg	TD
1983	HOU	N	12	276	23.0	48	1
1984			18	291	16.2	76	1
1985			1	7	7.0	7	0
1987	TB	N	1	13	13.0	13	0
Career			32	587	18.3	76	2

Wesley Walls
Year	Team		No	Yds	Avg	Lg	TD
1989	SF	N	4	16	4.0	9	1
1990			5	27	5.4	11	0
1991			2	24	12.0	21	0
1994	NO	N	38	406	10.7	31	4
1995			57	694	12.2	29	4
1996	CAR	N	61	713	11.7	40t	10
Career			167	1880	11.3	40t	19
Playoffs			7	67	9.6		1

Will Walls
Year	Team		No	Yds	Avg	Lg	TD
1938	NYG	N	1	23	23.0	23	0
1939			2	19	9.5		0
1941			4	69	17.3	36	0
1942			7	192	27.4	60	2
1943			14	231	16.5	39	2
Career			28	534	19.1	60	4
Playoffs			1	3	3.0		0

Laurie Walquist
Year	Team		No	Yds	Avg	Lg	TD
1925	CHIB	N					1
1926							1
1927							1
Career							3

Chris Walsh
Year	Team		No	Yds	Avg	Lg	TD
1995	MIN	N	7	66	9.4	16	0
1996			4	39	9.8	17	1
Career			11	105	9.5	17	1

Ward Walsh
Year	Team		No	Yds	Avg	Lg	TD
1971	HOU	N	6	36	6.0	16	1
1972			4	22	5.5	16	0
Career			10	58	5.8	16	1

Bullets Walson
Year	Team		No	Yds	Avg	Lg	TD
1921	WAS	A					2

Bobby Walston
Year	Team		No	Yds	Avg	Lg	TD
1951	PHI	N	31	512	16.5	43t	8
1952			26	469	18.0	65	3
1953			41	750	18.3	62t	5
1954			31	581	18.7	75t	11
1955			27	443	16.4	63t	3
1956			39	590	15.1	51t	3
1957			11	266	24.2	49	1
1958			21	298	14.2	71t	3
1959			16	279	17.4	40	3
1960			30	564	18.8	49t	4
1961			34	569	16.7	68	2
1962			4	43	10.8	16	0
Career			311	5363	17.2	75t	46
Playoffs			3	38	12.7		0

Joey Walters
Year	Team		No	Yds	Avg	Lg	TD
1987	HOU	N	5	99	19.8	51	0

Chuck Walton
Year	Team		No	Yds	Avg	Lg	TD
1967	DET	N	1	-4	-4.0	-4	0

Joe Walton
Year	Team		No	Yds	Avg	Lg	TD
1957	WAS	N	3	57	19.0	24	0
1958			32	532	16.6	41	5
1959			21	317	15.1	41	3
1960			27	401	14.9	35t	3
1961	NYG	N	36	544	15.1	37	2
1962			33	406	12.3	37t	9

Joe Walton *continued*

Year	Team		No	Yds	Avg	Lg	TD
1963			26	371	14.3	43t	6
Career			178	2628	14.8	43t	28
Playoffs			6	94	15.7		0

Larry Walton

Year	Team		No	Yds	Avg	Lg	TD
1969	DET	N	12	109	9.1	16	0
1970			30	532	17.7	56	5
1971			30	491	16.4	60t	5
1972			24	485	20.2	48t	6
1973			22	309	14.0	49t	4
1974			31	404	13.0	48	3
1976			20	293	14.7	28t	3
1978	BUF	N	4	66	16.5	32t	1
Career			173	2689	15.5	60t	27
Playoffs			3	39	13.0		0

John Ward

Year	Team		No	Yds	Avg	Lg	TD
1973	MIN	N	1	1	1.0	1	0

Derek Ware

Year	Team		No	Yds	Avg	Lg	TD
1992	PHX	N	1	13	13.0	13	0
1993			3	45	15.0	27	0
1994	ARI	N	17	171	10.1	33	1
1995	CIN	N	2	36	18.0	21	0
1996	DAL	N	1	5	5.0	5	0
Career			24	270	11.3	33	1

Timmie Ware

Year	Team		No	Yds	Avg	Lg	TD
1986	SD	N	1	11	11.0	11	0
1987			2	38	19.0	23	0
Career			3	49	16.3	23	0

Paul Warfield

Year	Team		No	Yds	Avg	Lg	TD
1964	CLE	N	52	920	17.7	62t	9
1965			3	30	10.0	13	0
1966			36	741	20.6	51	5
1967			32	702	21.9	49t	8
1968			50	1067	21.3	65t	12
1969			42	886	21.1	82t	10
1970	MIA	N	28	703	25.1	54	6
1971			43	996	23.2	86t	11
1972			29	606	20.9	47	3
1973			29	514	17.7	45t	11
1974			27	536	19.9	54	2
1976	CLE	N	38	613	16.1	37t	6
1977			18	251	13.9	52t	2
Career			427	8565	20.1	86t	85
Playoffs			58	1121	19.3		5

Ernie Warlick

Year	Team		No	Yds	Avg	Lg	TD
1962	BUF	A	35	482	13.8	25	2
1963			24	479	20.0	55	1
1964			23	478	20.8	45	0
1965			8	112	14.0	27	1
Career			90	1551	17.2	55	4
Playoffs			8	109	13.6		1

Charley Warner

Year	Team		No	Yds	Avg	Lg	TD
1965	BUF	A	1	11	11.0	11t	1

Curt Warner

Year	Team		No	Yds	Avg	Lg	TD
1983	SEA	N	42	325	7.7	28	1
1984			1	19	19.0	19	0
1985			47	307	6.5	27t	1
1986			41	342	8.3	26	0
1987			17	167	9.8	30t	2
1988			22	154	7.0	17	2
1989			23	153	6.7	24	1
Career			193	1467	7.6	30t	7
Playoffs			11	69	6.3		0

Buist Warren

Year	Team		No	Yds	Avg	Lg	TD
1945	PIT	N	1	-1	-1.0	-1	0

Chris Warren

Year	Team		No	Yds	Avg	Lg	TD
1991	SEA	N	2	9	4.5	12	0
1992			16	134	8.4	33	0
1993			15	99	6.6	21	0
1994			41	323	7.9	51	2
1995			35	247	7.1	20t	1
1996			40	273	6.8	33	0
Career			149	1085	7.3	51	3

Don Warren

Year	Team		No	Yds	Avg	Lg	TD
1979	WAS	N	26	303	11.7	23	0
1980			31	323	10.4	35	0
1981			29	335	11.6	32	1
1982			27	310	11.5	29	0
1983			20	225	11.3	33	2
1984			18	192	10.7	26	0
1985			15	163	10.9	19	1
1986			20	164	8.2	20	1
1987			7	43	6.1	9	0
1988			12	112	9.3	32	0
1989			15	167	11.1	25	1
1990			15	123	8.2	18	1
1991			5	51	10.2	17	0
1992			4	25	6.3	11	0
Career			244	2536	10.4	35	7
Playoffs			25	175	7.0		1

Lamont Warren

Year	Team		No	Yds	Avg	Lg	TD
1994	IND	N	3	47	15.7	29	0
1995			17	159	9.4	18	0
1996			22	174	7.9	17	0
Career			42	380	9.0	29	0
Playoffs			13	100	7.7		0

Caleb Warrington

Year	Team		No	Yds	Avg	Lg	TD
1947	BKN	AA	0	2		2L	

Dave Washington

Year	Team		No	Yds	Avg	Lg	TD
1968	DEN	A	1	12	12.0	12	0

Dave Washington

Year	Team		No	Yds	Avg	Lg	TD
1971	DEN	N	1	0	0.0	0	0
1972	BUF	N	1	4	4.0	4	0
Career			2	4	2.0	4	0

Gene Washington

Year	Team		No	Yds	Avg	Lg	TD
1967	MIN	N	13	384	29.5	85t	2
1968			46	756	16.4	61t	6
1969			39	821	21.1	83t	9
1970			44	702	16.0	49t	4
1971			12	165	13.8	51	0
1972			18	259	14.4	39	2
1973	DEN	N	10	150	15.0	28	3
Career			182	3237	17.8	85t	26
Playoffs			19	408	21.5		2

Gene Washington

Year	Team		No	Yds	Avg	Lg	TD
1969	SF	N	51	711	13.9	52	3
1970			53	1100	20.8	79t	12
1971			46	884	19.2	71t	4
1972			46	918	20.0	62t	12
1973			37	606	16.4	58	2
1974			29	615	21.2	58t	6
1975			44	735	16.7	68t	9
1976			33	457	13.8	55	6
1977			32	638	19.9	47t	5
1979	DET	N	14	192	13.7	29t	1
Career			385	6856	17.8	79t	60
Playoffs			16	375	23.4		1

Harry Washington

Year	Team		No	Yds	Avg	Lg	TD
1978	MIN	N	1	24	24.0	24	0

Joe Washington

Year	Team		No	Yds	Avg	Lg	TD
1977	SD	N	31	244	7.9	29	0
1978	BAL	N	45	377	8.4	33	1
1979			82	750	9.1	43t	3
1980			51	494	9.7	33	3
1981	WAS	N	70	558	8.0	32	3
1982			19	134	7.1	17	1
1983			47	454	9.7	67	6
1984			13	74	5.7	12	0
1985	ATL	N	37	328	8.9	34	1
Career			395	3413	8.6	67	18
Playoffs			12	96	8.0		0

Kenny Washington

Year	Team		No	Yds	Avg	Lg	TD
1946	LA	N	6	83	13.8	20	0
1947			3	40	13.3	21	0
1948			6	104	17.3	43	1
Career			15	227	15.1	43	1

Vic Washington

Year	Team		No	Yds	Avg	Lg	TD
1971	SF	N	36	317	8.8	40	4
1972			43	393	9.1	33	1
1973			33	238	7.2	20	0
1974	HOU	N	13	92	7.1	15	0
1975	BUF	N	2	21	10.5	15	0
1976			3	29	9.7	11	0
Career			130	1090	8.4	40	5
Playoffs			5	46	9.2		0

Bob Waterfield

Year	Team		No	Yds	Avg	Lg	TD
1947	LA	N	2	14	7.0	18	0
1952			1	5	5.0	5	0
Career			3	19	6.3	18	0

Mike Waters

Year	Team		No	Yds	Avg	Lg	TD
1986	PHI	N	2	27	13.5	19	0
1987	NO	N	5	140	28.0	82t	1
Career			7	167	23.9	82t	1

Bobby Watkins

Year	Team		No	Yds	Avg	Lg	TD
1955	CHIB	N	6	79	13.2	34	0
1956			2	3	1.5	6t	1
1957			3	90	30.0	74t	1
1958	CHIC	N	4	62	15.5	48t	1
Career			15	234	15.6	74t	3

Foster Watkins

Year	Team		No	Yds	Avg	Lg	TD
1941	PHI	N	3	27	9.0	16	0

Kendell Watkins

Year	Team		No	Yds	Avg	Lg	TD
1995	DAL	N	1	8	8.0	8	0

Larry Watkins

Year	Team		No	Yds	Avg	Lg	TD
1969	DET	N	13	87	6.7	20	0
1970	PHI	N	3	6	2.0	5	0
1971			6	40	6.7	9	0
1972			6	-2	-0.3	4	0
1973	BUF	N	12	86	7.2	28	1
1974			1	7	7.0	7	0
1975	NYG	N	7	43	6.1	12	0
1976			2	8	4.0	12	0
1977			1	9	9.0	9	0
Career			51	284	5.6	28	1

Tommy Watkins

Year	Team		No	Yds	Avg	Lg	TD
1961	CLE	N	4	66	16.5	35	1
1962	DET	N	12	85	7.1	29	0
1963			16	168	10.5	32`	1
1964			10	125	12.5	37	1
1965			5	53	10.6	28	0
1967			8	93	11.6	27	1
Career			55	590	10.7	37	4

Louis Watson

Year	Team		No	Yds	Avg	Lg	TD
1987	CLE	N	1	9	9.0	9	0

Remi Watson

Year	Team		No	Yds	Avg	Lg	TD
1987	CLE	N	1	13	13.0	13	0

Sid Watson

Year	Team		No	Yds	Avg	Lg	TD
1955	PIT	N	19	223	11.7	62t	1
1956			12	138	11.5	37	0
1957			3	24	8.0	11	0
1958	WAS	N	5	38	7.6	24	1
Career			39	423	10.8	62t	2

Steve Watson

Year	Team		No	Yds	Avg	Lg	TD
1979	DEN	N	6	83	13.8	22	0
1980			6	146	24.3	52	0
1981			60	1244	20.7	65t	13
1982			36	555	15.4	41	2
1983			59	1133	19.2	78t	5
1984			69	1170	17.0	73	7
1985			61	915	15.0	60	5
1986			45	699	15.5	46	3
1987			11	167	15.2	49	1
Career			353	6112	17.3	78t	36
Playoffs			21	358	17.0		1

Joe Watt

Year	Team		No	Yds	Avg	Lg	TD
1947	DET	N	4	104	26.0	75t	2
1948			2	29	14.5	24	0
Career			6	133	22.2	75t	2

Year	Team		No	Yds	Avg	Lg	TD

Walt Watt
| 1945 | CHIC | N | 1 | 22 | 22.0 | 22 | 0 |

Len Watters
| 1924 | BUF | N | | | | | 1 |

Ricky Watters
1992	SF	N	43	405	9.4	35	2
1993			31	326	10.5	48t	1
1994			66	719	10.9	65t	5
1995	PHI	N	62	434	7.0	24	1
1996			51	444	8.7	36	0
Career			253	2328	9.2	65t	9
Playoffs			39	429	11.0		4

Rickey Watts
1979	CHI	N	24	421	17.5	68t	3
1980			22	444	20.2	89t	2
1981			27	465	17.2	42t	3
1982			8	217	27.1	40	0
Career			81	1547	19.1	89t	8
Playoffs			3	42	14.0		0

Charles Way
1995	NYG	N	7	76	10.9	34	1
1996			32	328	10.3	37t	1
Career			39	404	10.4	37t	2

Charlie Way
1921	CAN	A					1
1926	PHI	A					1
Career							2

Dave Waymer
| 1986 | NO | N | 1 | 13 | 13.0 | 13 | 0 |

Clarence Weathers
1983	NE	N	19	379	19.9	58t	3
1984			8	115	14.4	29	2
1985	CLE	N	16	449	28.1	72t	3
1986			9	100	11.1	16	0
1987			11	153	13.9	37t	2
1988			29	436	15.0	49	1
1989	IND-KC	N	23	254	11.0	27	0
1990	GB	N	33	390	11.8	29	1
1991			12	150	12.5	22	0
Career			160	2426	15.2	72t	12
Playoffs			7	108	15.4		0

Curtis Weathers
| 1979 | CLE | N | 1 | 14 | 14.0 | 14 | 0 |

Guy Weathers
| 1984 | GB | N | 6 | 54 | 9.0 | 29t | 4 |

Robert Weathers
1982	NE	N	3	24	8.0	22	0
1983			23	212	9.2	19	0
1985			2	18	9.0	13	0
1986			1	14	14.0	14	0
Career			29	268	9.2	22	0
Playoffs			2	5	2.5		1

Don Webb
| 1962 | BOS | A | 1 | 11 | 11.0 | 11 | 0 |

George Webb
| 1943 | BKN | N | 7 | 60 | 8.6 | 15 | 0 |

Ken Webb
1958	DET	N	11	85	7.7	34	1
1959			12	201	16.8	67	0
1960			10	68	6.8	25	0
1961			1	7	7.0	7	0
1962			10	120	12.0	53	0
1963	CLE	N	2	2	1.0	5	0
Career			46	483	10.5	67	1

Alex Webster
1955	NYG	N	22	269	12.2	48	1
1956			21	197	9.4	43t	3
1957			30	330	11.0	41	1
1958			25	279	11.2	37	3
1959			27	381	14.1	41	2

Alex Webster *continued*
1960			8	106	13.3	27	0
1961			26	313	12.0	59t	3
1962			47	477	10.1	58t	4
1963			15	128	8.5	19	0
1964			19	199	10.5	40	0
Career			240	2679	11.2	59t	17
Playoffs			15	166	11.1		0

Cornell Webster
| 1979 | SEA | N | 1 | 39 | 39.0 | 39 | 0 |

Herman Wedemeyer
1948	LA	AA	36	330	9.2	66	2
1949	BAL	AA	10	112	11.2		0
Career			46	442	9.6	66	2

Ted Wegert
1955	PHI	N	3	17	5.7	12	0
1956			6	46	7.7	19	0
1960	NY	A	5	68	13.6		1
Career			14	131	9.4	19	1

Ray Wehba
1943	BKN	N	4	43	10.8	19	0
1944	GB	N	6	67	11.2	17	0
Career			10	110	11.0	19	0

Lee Weigel
| 1987 | GB | N | 1 | 17 | 17.0 | 17 | 0 |

Chuck Weimer
| 1930 | BKN | N | | | | | 2 |

Art Weiner
| 1950 | NYY | N | 35 | 722 | 20.6 | 58t | 6 |

Arnie Weinmeister
| 1950 | NYG | N | 1 | 16 | 16.0 | 16 | 0 |

Izzy Weinstock
| 1935 | PHI | N | 8 | 107 | 13.4 | | 0 |

Sammy Weir
1965	HOU	A	1	12	12.0	12	0
1966	NY	A	1	4	4.0	4	0
Career			2	16	8.0	12	0

Heinie Weisenbaugh
1935	PIT-BOS	N	7	73	10.4		2
1936	BOS	N	3	37	12.3		0
Career			10	110	11.0		2

Dick Weisgerber
| 1940 | GB | N | 1 | 37 | 37.0 | 37 | 0 |

Howie Weiss
1939	DET	N	4	25	6.3		0
1940			4	56	14.0		0
Career			8	81	10.1		0

Johnny Weiss
1944	NYG	N	1	10	10.0	10	0
1945			4	82	20.5	39t	1
1946			4	70	17.5	35t	1
Career			9	162	18.0	39t	2

Claxton Welch
1971	DAL	N	1	-1	-1.0	-1	0
1973	NE	N	6	22	3.7	8	0
Career			7	21	3.0	8	0

Gibby Welch
1928	NYY	N					6
1929	PRO	N					4
Career							10

Gary Wellman
1993	HOU	N	31	430	13.9	44	1
1994			10	112	11.2	25	0
Career			41	542	13.2	44	1
Playoffs			6	80	13.3		0

Billy Wells
1954	WAS	N	19	295	15.5	48t	1
1956			6	86	14.3	34	0
1957	PIT	N	14	89	6.4	17	0
1958	PHI	N	4	49	12.3	21	0
1960	BOS	A	14	206	14.7		1
Career			57	725	12.7	48t	2

Don Wells
| 1946 | GB | N | 2 | 74 | 37.0 | 65 | 0 |

Joel Wells
| 1961 | NYG | N | 6 | 31 | 5.2 | 19 | 1 |

Terence Wells
1974	HOU	N	1	9	9.0	9	0
1975	GB	N	6	11	1.8	4	0
Career			7	20	2.9	9	0

Warren Wells
1964	DET	N	2	21	10.5	13	0
1967	OAK	A	13	302	23.2	50t	6
1968			53	1137	21.5	94t	11
1969			47	1260	26.8	80t	14
1970	OAK	A	43	935	21.7	60t	11
Career			158	3655	23.1	94t	42
Playoffs			14	325	23.2		3

Doug Wellsandt
| 1990 | NYJ | N | 5 | 57 | 11.4 | 20 | 0 |

Don Wemple
| 1941 | BKN | N | 2 | 37 | 18.5 | 29 | 1 |

Joe Wendlick
1940	PHI	N	8	67	8.4		0
1941	PIT	N	7	84	12.0	19	0
Career			15	151	10.1	19	0

Obe Wenig
| 1921 | RI | A | | | | | 2 |

Cy Wentworth
| 1929 | BOS | N | | | | | 2 |

Greg Werner
| 1989 | NYJ | N | 8 | 115 | 14.4 | 36 | 0 |

Ed West
1985	GB	N	8	95	11.9	30	1
1986			15	199	13.3	46t	1
1987			19	261	13.7	40	1
1988			30	276	9.2	35	3
1989			22	269	12.2	31	5
1990			27	356	13.2	50	5
1991			15	151	10.1	21	3
1992			4	30	7.5	10	0
1993			25	253	10.1	24	0
1994			31	377	12.2	26	2
1995	PHI	N	20	190	9.5	26	1
1996			8	91	11.4	29	0
Career			224	2548	11.4	50	22
Playoffs			9	100	11.1		0

Jeff West
| 1977 | SD | N | 1 | 3 | 3.0 | 3 | 0 |

Mel West
1961	BOS-NY	A	13	146	11.2	37	0
1962	NY	A	1	1	1.0	1	0
Career			14	147	10.5	37	0

Pat West
1945	CLE	N	1	-2	-2.0	-2	0
1948	LA	N	3	37	12.3	17	0
Career			4	35	8.8	17	0
Playoffs			1	5	5.0		0

Robert West
1972	KC	N	9	165	18.3	42t	2
1973			4	65	16.3	23	0
Career			13	230	17.7	42t	2

Year	Team		No	Yds	Avg	Lg	TD

Walt West
| 1944 | CLE | N | 9 | 64 | 7.1 | 18 | 0 |

Don Westbrook
1978	NE	N	3	38	12.7	19	0
1979			9	173	19.2	38	1
1980			4	60	15.0	21	0
1981			7	122	17.4	32	2
1995	WAS	N	34	522	15.4	45	1
Career			57	915	16.1	45	4

Michael Westbrook
| 1996 | WAS | N | 34 | 505 | 14.9 | 45 | 1 |

Bob Westfall
1944	DET	N	16	218	13.6	45	2
1945			12	209	17.4	43t	3
1946			17	142	8.4	24	0
1947			2	19	9.5	14	0
Career			47	588	12.5	45	5

Ed Westfall
| 1933 | PIT | N | | | | | 1 |

Ryan Wetnight
1993	CHI	N	9	93	10.3	25t	1
1994			11	104	9.5	19	1
1995			24	193	8.0	22	2
1996			21	223	10.6	38	1
Career			65	613	9.4	38	5
Playoffs			5	39	7.8		0

Jim Whalen
1965	BOS	A	22	381	17.3	67	0
1966			29	502	17.3	45	4
1967			39	651	16.7	41t	5
1968			47	718	15.3	87t	7
1969			16	235	14.7	47	1
1970	DEN	N	36	503	14.0	34	3
1971	DEN-PHI	N	8	165	20.6	41	0
Career			197	3155	16.0	87t	20

Tom Wham
| 1949 | CHIC | N | 1 | 11 | 11.0 | 11 | 0 |

Tyrone Wheatley
1995	NYG	N	5	27	5.4	16	0
1996			12	51	4.3	13	2
Career			17	78	4.6	16	2

Kyle Wheeler
| 1923 | GB | N | | | | | 1 |

Mark Wheeler
| 1987 | DET | N | 2 | 17 | 8.5 | 9 | 0 |

Ron Wheeler
| 1987 | LARI | N | 3 | 61 | 20.3 | 29 | 0 |

Wayne Wheeler
| 1974 | CHI | N | 5 | 59 | 11.8 | 19t | 1 |

Ernie Wheelwright
1964	NYG	N	14	204	14.6	33	3
1965			2	17	8.5	12	0
1966	ATL	N	15	137	9.1	35	3
1967	ATL-NO	N	13	107	8.2	30	0
1968	NO	N	1	-9	-9.0	-9	0
1969			8	68	8.5	20t	1
1970			1	7	7.0	7	0
Career			54	531	9.8	35	7

Tom Whelan
| 1921 | CLE | A | | | | | 1 |

Ken Whisenhunt
1985	ATL	N	3	48	16.0	29	0
1986			20	184	9.2	23t	3
1987			17	145	8.5	26	1
1988			16	174	10.9	25	1
1991	NYJ	N	4	34	8.5	16	0
1992			2	11	5.5	10	0
Career			62	596	9.6	29	5

Creston Whitaker
| 1972 | NO | N | 1 | 6 | 6.0 | 6 | 0 |

Danta Whitaker
1990	KC	N	2	17	8.5	16	1
1992	MIN	N	1	4	4.0	4	0
1993	CHI	N	6	53	8.8	18	0
Career			9	74	8.2	18	1

Andre White
1967	DEN	A	5	87	17.4	40	0
1968	CIN	A	2	18	9.0	11	0
Career			7	105	15.0	40	0

Bob White
1951	SF	N	3	36	12.0	22	0
1952			12	173	14.4	60t	2
Career			15	209	13.9	60t	2

Charles White
1980	CLE	N	17	153	9.0	31t	1
1981			27	219	8.1	21	0
1982			34	283	8.3	36	0
1984			5	29	5.8	17	0
1985	LARM	N	1	12	12.0	12	0
1986			1	7	7.0	7	0
1987			23	121	5.3	20	0
1988			6	36	6.0	18	0
Career			114	860	7.5	36	1
Playoffs			2	15	7.5		0

Charlie White
1977	NYJ	N	2	5	2.5	3t	1
1978	TB	N	2	31	15.5	18	0
Career			4	36	9.0	18	1

Craig White
| 1984 | BUF | N | 4 | 28 | 7.0 | 11 | 0 |

Danny White
1980	DAL	N	1	-9	-9.0	-9	0
1983			1	15	15.0	15t	1
1985			1	12	12.0	12t	1
Career			3	18	6.0	15t	2

Ed White
| 1972 | MIN | N | 0 | 3 | | 3L | 0 |
| Playoffs | | | 1 | -2 | -2.0 | | 0 |

Freeman White
| 1969 | NYG | N | 29 | 315 | 10.9 | 23t | 1 |

Gene White
| 1962 | OAK | A | 6 | 101 | 16.8 | 47 | 1 |

Gerald White
| 1987 | DAL | N | 5 | 46 | 9.2 | 14 | 0 |

Harvey White
| 1960 | BOS | A | 2 | 24 | 12.0 | | 0 |

Jan White
1971	BUF	N	13	130	10.0	21	0
1972			12	148	12.3	18	2
Career			25	278	11.1	21	2

John White
1960	HOU	A	1	18	18.0	18	0
1961			13	238	18.3	49	1
Career			14	256	18.3	49	1

Lee White
1969	NY	A	1	-2	-2.0	-2	0
1970	NYJ	N	12	125	10.4	19	1
1972	SD	N	3	20	6.7	8	0
Career			16	143	8.9	19	1

Lorenzo White
1989	HOU	N	6	37	6.2	11	0
1990			39	368	9.4	29	4
1991			27	211	7.8	20	0
1992			57	641	11.2	69t	2
1993			34	229	6.7	20	0
1994			21	188	9.0	41	1

Lorenzo White continued
1995	CLE	N	8	64	8.0	28	0
Career			192	1738	9.1	69t	6
Playoffs			12	83	6.9		0

Marsh White
1975	NYG	N	3	15	5.0	15	0
1976			2	7	3.5	4	0
Career			5	22	4.4	15	0

Paul White
| 1947 | PIT | N | 2 | 55 | 27.5 | 53 | 0 |

Phil White
| 1925 | KC | N | | | | | 1 |

Sammy White
1976	MIN	N	51	906	17.8	56t	10
1977			41	760	18.5	69t	9
1978			53	741	14.0	33t	9
1979			42	715	17.0	55t	4
1980			53	887	16.7	50	5
1981			66	1001	15.2	53	3
1982			29	503	17.3	65	5
1983			29	412	14.2	43t	4
1984			21	399	19.0	47	1
1985			8	76	9.5	15	0
Career			393	6400	16.3	69t	50
Playoffs			17	313	18.4		5

Walter White
1975	KC	N	23	559	24.3	69t	3
1976			47	808	17.2	41	7
1977			48	674	14.0	48t	5
1978			42	340	8.1	24	1
1979			3	15	5.0	12	0
Career			163	2396	14.7	69t	16

Whizzer White
1938	PIT	N	7	88	12.6		0
1940	DET	N	4	55	13.8		0
1941			5	158	31.6	71	1
Career			16	301	18.8	71	1

Wilbur White
| 1936 | DET | N | 2 | 21 | 10.5 | | 0 |

Wilford White
1951	CHIB	N	4	45	11.3	22	1
1952			8	152	19.0	49	0
Career			12	197	16.4	49	1

Bud Whitehead
| 1964 | SD | A | 1 | -4 | -4.0 | -4 | 0 |

A.D. Whitfield
1966	WAS	N	18	101	5.6	29	1
1967			36	494	13.7	53	2
1968			13	107	8.2	18	0
Career			67	702	10.5	53	3

Arthur Whittington
1978	OAK	N	23	106	4.6	20	0
1979			19	240	12.6	39	0
1980			19	205	10.8	55	0
1981			23	213	9.3	22	2
Career			84	764	9.1	55	2
Playoffs			5	85	17.0		1

Ricky Whittle
| 1996 | NO | N | 26 | 162 | 6.2 | 28 | 0 |

Ossie Wiberg
1927	CLE	N					2
1928	DET	N					2
Career							4

Bob Wicks
| 1972 | STL | N | 1 | 8 | 8.0 | 8 | 0 |

Doug Widell
| 1992 | DEN | N | 1 | -7 | -7.0 | -7 | 0 |

Bob Wiese

Year	Team		No	Yds	Avg	Lg	TD
1947	DET	N	5	53	10.6	24	0

John Wiethe

Year	Team		No	Yds	Avg	Lg	TD
1939	DET	N	2	5	2.5		0

Bill Wightkin

Year	Team		No	Yds	Avg	Lg	TD
1950	CHIB	N	3	24	8.0	17	0
1951			1	47	47.0	47	0
1952			7	120	17.1	29t	2
1953			2	22	11.0	13	0
Career			13	213	16.4	47	2

J.R. Wilburn

Year	Team		No	Yds	Avg	Lg	TD
1966	PIT	N	7	103	14.7	42	0
1967			51	767	15.0	66t	5
1968			39	514	13.2	41	3
1969			20	373	18.6	53	0
1970			6	77	12.8	15	0
Career			123	1834	14.9	66t	8

George Wilde

Year	Team		No	Yds	Avg	Lg	TD
1947	WAS	N	6	45	7.5	13	1

James Wilder

Year	Team		No	Yds	Avg	Lg	TD
1981	TB	N	48	507	10.6	38	1
1982			53	466	8.8	32	1
1983			57	380	6.7	31	2
1984			85	685	8.1	50	0
1985			53	341	6.4	20	0
1986			43	326	7.6	25	1
1987			40	328	8.2	32	1
1988			15	124	8.3	24	0
1989			36	335	9.3	27	3
1990	DET	N	1	8	8.0	8t	1
Career			431	3500	8.1	50	10
Playoffs			3	16	5.3		0

Jack Wiley

Year	Team		No	Yds	Avg	Lg	TD
1949	PIT	N	1	10	10.0	10	0

Willie Wilkin

Year	Team		No	Yds	Avg	Lg	TD
1946	CHI	AA	0	3		3L	0

Dick Wilkins

Year	Team		No	Yds	Avg	Lg	TD
1949	LA	AA	32	589	18.4		3
1952	DAL	N	32	416	13.0	42t	3
1954	NYG	N	4	45	11.3	18	1
Career			68	1050	15.4	42t	7

Gary Wilkins

Year	Team		No	Yds	Avg	Lg	TD
1986	BUF	N	8	74	9.3	26	0
1988	ATL	N	11	134	12.2	33	0
1989			8	179	22.4	36	3
1990			12	175	14.6	37	2
1991			3	22	7.3	12	1
Career			42	584	13.9	37	6

Bob Wilkinson

Year	Team		No	Yds	Avg	Lg	TD
1951	NYG	N	11	182	16.5	69t	1
1952			6	148	24.7	70t	2
Career			17	330	19.4	70t	3

Ken Willard

Year	Team		No	Yds	Avg	Lg	TD
1965	SF	N	32	253	7.9	29t	4
1966			42	351	8.4	62	2
1967			23	242	10.5	25	1
1968			36	232	6.4	20	0
1969			36	326	9.1	36	3
1970			31	259	8.4	32	3
1971			27	202	7.5	33	1
1972			24	131	5.5	15	1
1973			22	160	7.3	26	1
1974	STL	N	4	28	7.0	17	1
Career			277	2184	7.9	62	17
Playoffs			5	56	11.2		0

Norm Willey

Year	Team		No	Yds	Avg	Lg	TD
1954	PHI	N	2	50	25.0	37	0

Gerald Willhite

Year	Team		No	Yds	Avg	Lg	TD
1982	DEN	N	26	227	8.7	27	0
1983			14	153	10.9	26t	1
1984			27	298	11.0	63	0

Gerald Willhite *continued*

Year	Team		No	Yds	Avg	Lg	TD
1985			35	297	8.5	21	1
1986			64	529	8.3	31	3
1987			9	25	2.8	6	0
1988			32	238	7.4	15	0
Career			207	1767	8.5	63	5
Playoffs			10	72	7.2		0

Kevin Willhite

Year	Team		No	Yds	Avg	Lg	TD
1987	GB	N	6	37	6.2	12	0

A.D. Williams

Year	Team		No	Yds	Avg	Lg	TD
1959	GB	N	1	11	11.0	11	0
1960	CLE	N	1	5	5.0	5	0
1961	MIN	N	13	174	13.4	49	1
Career			15	190	12.7	49	1

Aeneas Williams

Year	Team		No	Yds	Avg	Lg	TD
1996	ARI	N	1	21	21.0	21	0

Al Williams

Year	Team		No	Yds	Avg	Lg	TD
1987	SD	N	12	247	20.6	57	1

Art Williams

Year	Team		No	Yds	Avg	Lg	TD
1928	PRO	N					1
1929							1
Career							2

Brooks Williams

Year	Team		No	Yds	Avg	Lg	TD
1979	NO	N	2	22	11.0	14	0
1980			26	351	13.5	56	2
1981	NO-CHI	N	8	82	10.3	16	0
1983	NE	N	1	0	0.0	0	0
Career			37	455	12.3	56	2

Byron Williams

Year	Team		No	Yds	Avg	Lg	TD
1983	NYG	N	20	346	17.3	43t	1
1984			24	471	19.6	65t	2
1985			15	280	18.7	45	0
Career			59	1097	18.6	65t	3
Playoffs			1	33	33.0		0

Calvin Williams

Year	Team		No	Yds	Avg	Lg	TD
1990	PHI	N	37	602	16.3	45t	9
1991			33	326	9.9	30	3
1992			42	598	14.2	49t	7
1993			60	725	12.1	80t	10
1994			58	813	14.0	53	3
1995			63	768	12.2	37t	2
1996	PHI-BAL	N	15	93	6.2	19	1
Career			308	3925	12.7	80t	35
Playoffs			17	200	11.8		1

Clarence Williams

Year	Team		No	Yds	Avg	Lg	TD
1977	SD	N	3	20	6.7	9	0
1978			1	17	17.0	17	0
1979			51	352	6.9	14	0
1980			26	230	8.8	26	1
1981			12	108	9.0	15	1
Career			93	727	7.8	26	2
Playoffs			4	30	7.5		0

Clarence Williams

Year	Team		No	Yds	Avg	Lg	TD
1993	CLE	N	1	14	14.0	14	0

Dave Williams

Year	Team		No	Yds	Avg	Lg	TD
1967	STL	N	28	405	14.5	49t	5
1968			43	682	15.9	71t	6
1969			56	702	12.5	61	7
1970			23	364	15.8	58t	3
1971			12	182	15.2	37	1
1972	SD	N	14	315	22.5	62	3
1973			7	118	16.9	30	0
Career			183	2768	15.1	71t	25
Playoffs			1	14	14.0		0

Dave Williams

Year	Team		No	Yds	Avg	Lg	TD
1978	SF	N	10	63	6.3	13	0
1979	CHI	N	42	354	8.4	54t	5
1980			22	132	6.0	18	0
1981			18	126	7.0	18t	2
Career			92	675	7.3	54t	7
Playoffs			2	4	2.0		0

David Williams

Year	Team		No	Yds	Avg	Lg	TD
1986	TB	N	6	91	15.2	25	0
1987	LARI	N	4	104	26.0	44	0
Career			10	195	19.5	44	0

Delvin Williams

Year	Team		No	Yds	Avg	Lg	TD
1974	SF	N	1	9	9.0	9	0
1975			34	370	10.9	30	1
1976			27	283	10.5	85t	2
1977			20	179	8.9	17	2
1978	MIA	N	18	192	10.7	42	0
1979			21	175	8.3	38	1
1980			31	207	6.7	19	0
Career			152	1415	9.3	85t	6
Playoffs			7	34	4.9		0

Derwin Williams

Year	Team		No	Yds	Avg	Lg	TD
1985	NE	N	9	163	18.1	30	0
1986			2	35	17.5	26	0
1987			3	30	10.0	12	0
Career			14	228	16.3	30	0

Dokie Williams

Year	Team		No	Yds	Avg	Lg	TD
1983	LARI	N	14	259	18.5	50t	3
1984			22	509	23.1	75t	4
1985			48	925	19.3	55	5
1986			43	843	19.6	53	8
1987			21	330	15.7	33	5
Career			148	2866	19.4	75t	25
Playoffs			3	33	11.0		0

Donnie Williams

Year	Team		No	Yds	Avg	Lg	TD
1970	LA	N	1	9	9.0	9	0

Ed Williams

Year	Team		No	Yds	Avg	Lg	TD
1974	CIN	N	13	98	7.5	19t	1
1975			10	96	9.6	20	1
1976	TB	N	23	166	7.2	18	0
1977			10	67	6.7	15	0
Career			56	427	7.6	20	2

Ellery Williams

Year	Team		No	Yds	Avg	Lg	TD
1950	NYG	N	4	78	19.5	34	0

Erwin Williams

Year	Team		No	Yds	Avg	Lg	TD
1969	PIT	N	3	14	4.7	6t	1

Frank Williams

Year	Team		No	Yds	Avg	Lg	TD
1948	NYG	N	1	5	5.0	5	0

Harvey Williams

Year	Team		No	Yds	Avg	Lg	TD
1991	KC	N	16	147	9.2	17	2
1992			5	24	4.8	12	0
1993			7	42	6.0	14	0
1994	LARI	N	47	391	8.3	27t	3
1995	OAK	N	54	375	6.9	28	0
1996			22	143	6.5	20	0
Career			151	1122	7.4	28	5
Playoffs			1	11	11.0		0

Henry Williams

Year	Team		No	Yds	Avg	Lg	TD
1989	PHI	N	4	32	8.0	11	0

Jamie Williams

Year	Team		No	Yds	Avg	Lg	TD
1984	HOU	N	41	545	13.3	32	3
1985			39	444	11.4	29	1
1986			22	227	10.3	33	1
1987			13	158	12.2	25	3
1988			6	46	7.7	10	0
1989	SF	N	3	38	12.7	17	0
1990			9	54	6.0	9	0
1991			22	235	10.7	21	1
1992			7	76	10.9	21	1
1993			16	132	8.3	15	1
1994	LARI	N	3	25	8.3	16	0
Career			181	1980	10.9	33	11

Jerry Williams

Year	Team		No	Yds	Avg	Lg	TD
1949	LA	N	7	102	14.6	42	0
1950			4	21	5.3	11	1
1951			5	49	9.8	13	0
1953	PHI	N	31	438	14.1	40	1
1954			44	668	15.2	84t	3
Career			91	1278	14.0	84t	5

Joe Williams

Year	Team		No	Yds	Avg	Lg	TD
1971	DAL	N	3	59	19.7	35	0
1972	NO	N	16	116	7.3	32	0
Career			19	175	9.2	35	0

John Williams

Year	Team		No	Yds	Avg	Lg	TD
1986	NO	N	1	5	5.0	5	0

John L. Williams

Year	Team		No	Yds	Avg	Lg	TD
1986	SEA	N	33	219	6.6	23	0
1987			38	420	11.1	75t	3
1988			58	651	11.2	75t	3
1989			76	657	8.6	51t	6
1990			73	699	9.6	60	0
1991			61	499	8.2	35	1
1992			74	556	7.5	27	2
1993			58	450	7.8	25	1
1994	PIT	N	51	378	7.4	23	2
1995			24	127	5.3	20	1
Career			546	4656	8.5	75t	19
Playoffs			31	243	7.8		2

Johnny Williams

Year	Team		No	Yds	Avg	Lg	TD
1952	WAS	N	1	13	13.0	13	0

Karl Williams

Year	Team		No	Yds	Avg	Lg	TD
1996	TB	N	22	246	11.2	25	0

Keith Williams

Year	Team		No	Yds	Avg	Lg	TD
1986	ATL	N	12	164	13.7	32t	1

Kevin Williams

Year	Team		No	Yds	Avg	Lg	TD
1993	DAL	N	20	151	7.5	33	2
1994			13	181	13.9	29	0
1995			38	613	16.1	48t	2
1996			27	323	12.0	31	1
Career			98	1268	12.9	48t	5
Playoffs			23	352	15.3		0

Lawrence Williams

Year	Team		No	Yds	Avg	Lg	TD
1976	KC	N	1	9	9.0	9	0
1977			7	94	13.4	24	0
Career			8	103	12.9	24	0

Leonard Williams

Year	Team		No	Yds	Avg	Lg	TD
1987	BUF	N	1	5	5.0	5	0

Mike Williams

Year	Team		No	Yds	Avg	Lg	TD
1979	KC	N	16	129	8.1	25	2
1980			2	9	4.5	6	1
1981			1	3	3.0	3	0
Career			19	141	7.4	25	3

Mike Williams

Year	Team		No	Yds	Avg	Lg	TD
1982	WAS	N	3	14	4.7	6	0

Mike Williams

Year	Team		No	Yds	Avg	Lg	TD
1983	PHI	N	17	142	8.4	29	0
1984			7	47	6.7	15	0
1987	ATL	N	9	70	7.8	15	0
Career			33	259	7.8	29	0

Mike Williams

Year	Team		No	Yds	Avg	Lg	TD
1992	MIA	N	3	43	14.3	18	0
1993			1	11	11.0	11	0
1994			15	221	14.7	29	0
1995			2	17	8.5	15	0
Career			21	292	13.9	29	0
Playoffs			3	44	14.7		1

Newton Williams

Year	Team		No	Yds	Avg	Lg	TD
1983	BAL	N	4	46	11.5	19	0

Oliver Williams

Year	Team		No	Yds	Avg	Lg	TD
1985	IND	N	9	175	19.4	30	1
1987	HOU	N	11	165	15.0	36t	1
Career			20	340	17.0	36t	2

Perry Williams

Year	Team		No	Yds	Avg	Lg	TD
1969	GB	N	4	63	15.8	24	0
1970			3	11	3.7	6	0
1973			5	44	8.8	14	0
1974	CHI	N	25	167	6.7	13	0
Career			37	285	7.7	24	0

Ray Williams

Year	Team		No	Yds	Avg	Lg	TD
1980	DET	N	10	146	14.6	22t	1

Ronnie Williams

Year	Team		No	Yds	Avg	Lg	TD
1994	MIA	N	2	26	13.0	17	0
1995			3	28	9.3	13	0
1996	SEA	N	5	25	5.0	11	1
Career			10	79	7.9	17	1
Playoffs			1	1	1.0		1

Sam Williams

Year	Team		No	Yds	Avg	Lg	TD
1961	DET	N	1	10	10.0	10	0

Scott Williams

Year	Team		No	Yds	Avg	Lg	TD
1986	DET	N	2	9	4.5	6	0
1987			4	16	4.0	7	1
1988			3	46	15.3	32	0
Career			9	71	7.9	32	1

Sherman Williams

Year	Team		No	Yds	Avg	Lg	TD
1995	DAL	N	3	28	9.3	24	0
1996			5	41	8.2	13	0
Career			8	69	8.6	24	0
Playoffs			1	2	2.0		0

Stan Williams

Year	Team		No	Yds	Avg	Lg	TD
1952	DAL	N	9	123	13.7	32	0

Stepfret Williams

Year	Team		No	Yds	Avg	Lg	TD
1996	DAL	N	1	32	32.0	32	0

Ted Williams

Year	Team		No	Yds	Avg	Lg	TD
1942	PHI	N	9	58	6.4	15	0
1944	BOS	N	6	28	4.7	16	0
Career			15	86	5.7	16	0

Travis Williams

Year	Team		No	Yds	Avg	Lg	TD
1967	GB	N	5	80	16.0	29t	1
1968			5	48	9.6	17	0
1969			27	275	10.2	60t	3
1970			12	127	10.6	55t	1
1971	LA	N	3	68	22.7	43	0
Career			52	598	11.5	60t	5
Playoffs			2	12	6.0		0

Tyrone Williams

Year	Team		No	Yds	Avg	Lg	TD
1993	DAL	N	1	25	25.0	25	0

Van Williams

Year	Team		No	Yds	Avg	Lg	TD
1984	BUF	N	5	46	9.2	32	1
1985			1	7	7.0	7	0
1987	NYG	N	5	36	7.2	12	0
Career			11	89	8.1	32	1

Vince Williams

Year	Team		No	Yds	Avg	Lg	TD
1982	SF	N	4	33	8.3	13	0

Walt Williams

Year	Team		No	Yds	Avg	Lg	TD
1946	CHI	AA	1	3	3.0	3	0
1947	BOS	N	1	2	2.0	2	0
Career			2	5	2.5	3	0

Wandy Williams

Year	Team		No	Yds	Avg	Lg	TD
1969	DEN	A	5	56	11.2	14	0

Warren Williams

Year	Team		No	Yds	Avg	Lg	TD
1988	PIT	N	11	66	6.0	21	1
1989			6	48	8.0	16	0
1990			5	42	8.4	13	1
1991			15	139	9.3	29	0
1992			1	44	44.0	44	0
Career			38	339	8.9	44	2

Willie Williams

Year	Team		No	Yds	Avg	Lg	TD
1991	PHX	N	1	3	3.0	3t	1
1994	NO	N	1	7	7.0	7	0
Career			2	10	5.0	7	1

Win Williams

Year	Team		No	Yds	Avg	Lg	TD
1948	BAL	AA	32	360	11.3		2
1949			20	266	13.3		1
Career			52	626	12.0		3
Playoffs			2	25	12.5		0

Chester Willis

Year	Team		No	Yds	Avg	Lg	TD
1981	OAK	N	1	24	24.0	24	0

Fred Willis

Year	Team		No	Yds	Avg	Lg	TD
1971	CIN	N	24	223	9.3	29	0
1972	CIN-HOU	N	45	297	6.6	27	2
1973	HOU	N	57	371	6.5	50	1
1974			25	130	5.2	21	1
1975			20	104	5.2	20	0
1976			32	255	8.0	42	1
Career			203	1380	6.8	50	5

Jamal Willis

Year	Team		No	Yds	Avg	Lg	TD
1995	SF	N	3	8	2.7	5	0

Len Willis

Year	Team		No	Yds	Avg	Lg	TD
1978	BUF	N	2	41	20.5	23	0

Jeff Wilner

Year	Team		No	Yds	Avg	Lg	TD
1994	GB	N	5	31	6.2	9	0

Ben Wilson

Year	Team		No	Yds	Avg	Lg	TD
1963	LA	N	9	173	19.2	77t	1
1964			15	116	7.7	30	1
1965			9	110	12.2	38	0
1967	GB	N	14	88	6.3	21	0
Career			47	487	10.4	77t	2

Billy Wilson

Year	Team		No	Yds	Avg	Lg	TD
1936	CHIC	N	1	12	12.0	12	0
1937			1	2	2.0	2	0
Career			2	14	7.0	12	0

Billy Wilson

Year	Team		No	Yds	Avg	Lg	TD
1951	SF	N	18	268	14.9	38	3
1952			23	304	13.2	40	3
1953			51	840	16.5	61t	10
1954			60	830	13.8	43	5
1955			53	831	15.7	72t	7
1956			60	889	14.8	77t	5
1957			52	757	14.6	40	6
1958			43	592	13.8	44t	5
1959			44	540	12.3	57t	4
1960			3	51	17.0	19t	1
Career			407	5902	14.5	77t	49
Playoffs			9	107	11.9		1

Bobby Wilson

Year	Team		No	Yds	Avg	Lg	TD
1936	BKN	N	1	12	12.0	12t	1

Brett Wilson

Year	Team		No	Yds	Avg	Lg	TD
1987	MIN	N	2	14	7.0	9	0

Butch Wilson

Year	Team		No	Yds	Avg	Lg	TD
1964	BAL	N	7	86	12.3	20	1
1965			1	38	38.0	38	0
1966			3	27	9.0	11	2
1968	NYG	N	4	34	8.5	13	0
1969			10	132	13.2	33	0
Career			25	317	12.7	38	3

Camp Wilson

Year	Team		No	Yds	Avg	Lg	TD
1946	DET	N	7	62	8.9	26	0
1947			5	96	19.2	38	0
1948			2	9	4.5	6	0
1949			6	31	5.2	19	0
Career			20	198	9.9	38	0

Charles Wilson

Year	Team		No	Yds	Avg	Lg	TD
1990	GB	N	7	84	12.0	18	0
1991			19	305	16.1	75t	1
1993	TB	N	15	225	15.0	24	0
1994			31	652	21.0	71t	6
1995	NYJ	N	41	484	11.8	24	4
Career			113	1750	15.5	75t	11

Gene Wilson

Year	Team		No	Yds	Avg	Lg	TD
1947	GB	N	3	34	11.3	15	0
1948			2	23	11.5	14	0
Career			5	57	11.4	15	0

George Wilson

Year	Team		No	Yds	Avg	Lg	TD
1937	CHIB	N	1	20	20.0	20	0
1938			4	81	20.3		1

George Wilson continued

Year	Team		No	Yds	Avg	Lg	TD
1939			5	66	13.2		0
1940			4	90	22.5		1
1941			4	75	18.8	21	0
1942			9	89	9.9	16	0
1943			21	293	14.0	28	5
1944			24	265	11.0	24t	4
1945			28	250	8.9	18	3
1946			11	104	9.5	17	1
Career			111	1333	12.0	28	15
Playoffs			4	44	11.0		0

Harry Wilson

Year	Team		No	Yds	Avg	Lg	TD
1967	PHI	N	2	20	10.0	12	0
1969			1	6	6.0	6	0
Career			3	26	8.7	12	0

Jack Wilson

Year	Team		No	Yds	Avg	Lg	TD
1946	LA	N	3	30	10.0	15	1
1947			1	-5	-5.0	-5	0
Career			4	25	6.3	15	1

Jerrel Wilson

Year	Team		No	Yds	Avg	Lg	TD
1963	KC	A	2	21	10.5	15	0
1964			1	11	11.0	11	0
1966			1	7	7.0	7	0
1968			1	14	14.0	14	0
Career			5	53	10.6	15	0

Joe Wilson

Year	Team		No	Yds	Avg	Lg	TD
1974	NE	N	3	38	12.7	23	0

Johnny Wilson

Year	Team		No	Yds	Avg	Lg	TD
1939	CLE	N	8	108	13.5		1
1940			7	93	13.3		1
1941			5	115	23.0	57	1
1942			6	113	18.8	45	1
Career			26	429	16.5	57	4

Marcus Wilson

Year	Team		No	Yds	Avg	Lg	TD
1993	GB	N	2	18	9.0	11	0

Mike Wilson

Year	Team		No	Yds	Avg	Lg	TD
1923	RI	N					1
1924							1
Career							2

Mike Wilson

Year	Team		No	Yds	Avg	Lg	TD
1981	SF	N	9	125	13.9	27t	1
1982			6	80	13.3	27	1
1983			30	433	14.4	49	0
1984			17	245	14.4	44	1
1985			10	165	16.5	52t	1
1986			9	104	11.6	18	1
1987			29	450	15.5	46t	5
1988			33	405	12.3	31	3
1989			9	103	11.4	19	1
1990			7	89	12.7	34	0
Career			159	2199	13.8	52t	15
Playoffs			24	271	11.3		2

Mule Wilson

Year	Team		No	Yds	Avg	Lg	TD
1927	NYG	N					2
1930							3
Career							5

Robert Wilson

Year	Team		No	Yds	Avg	Lg	TD
1991	TB	N	20	121	6.0	15	2
1995	MIA	N	1	3	3.0	3	0
1996			2	5	2.5	3t	1
Career			23	129	5.6	15	3

Sheddrick Wilson

Year	Team		No	Yds	Avg	Lg	TD
1996	HOU	N	2	24	12.0	14	0

Stanley Wilson

Year	Team		No	Yds	Avg	Lg	TD
1983	CIN	N	12	107	8.9	19	1
1984			2	15	7.5	11	0
1986			4	45	11.3	34	0
1988			9	110	12.2	28	1
Career			27	277	10.3	34	2

Steve Wilson

Year	Team		No	Yds	Avg	Lg	TD
1979	DAL	N	3	76	25.3	45	0

Steve Wilson continued

Year	Team		No	Yds	Avg	Lg	TD
1986	DEN	N	1	43	43.0	43t	1
Career			4	119	29.8	45	1
Playoffs			1	12	12.0		0

Stu Wilson

Year	Team		No	Yds	Avg	Lg	TD
1932	SI	N					1

Ted Wilson

Year	Team		No	Yds	Avg	Lg	TD
1987	WAS	N	5	112	22.4	64t	1

Tim Wilson

Year	Team		No	Yds	Avg	Lg	TD
1977	HOU	N	20	107	5.3	17	0
1978			15	91	6.1	14	1
1979			29	208	7.2	24t	1
1980			30	170	5.7	13	1
1981			5	33	6.6	11	0
Career			99	609	6.2	24t	3
Playoffs			24	202	8.4		1

Tommy Wilson

Year	Team		No	Yds	Avg	Lg	TD
1956	LA	N	6	86	14.3	34	0
1957			7	95	13.6	19	1
1958			9	101	11.2	38t	1
1959			12	83	6.9	20	1
1960			11	82	7.5	40t	0
1961			1	12	12.0	12	0
1962	CLE	N	8	110	13.8	42	0
1963	MIN	N	7	48	6.9	21	0
Career			61	617	10.1	42	5

Walter Wilson

Year	Team		No	Yds	Avg	Lg	TD
1990	SD	N	10	87	8.7	20	0

Wayne Wilson

Year	Team		No	Yds	Avg	Lg	TD
1980	NO	N	31	241	7.8	42	1
1981			31	384	12.4	55	4
1982			25	175	7.0	34	2
1983			20	178	8.9	24	2
1984			33	314	9.5	34t	3
1985			38	228	6.0	21	2
1986			1	-3	-3.0	-3	0
1987	WAS	N	2	16	8.0	9	0
Career			181	1533	8.5	55	14

Ab Wimberly

Year	Team		No	Yds	Avg	Lg	TD
1949	LA	AA	3	22	7.3		0
1950	GB	N	2	18	9.0	10	0
1951			1	10	10.0	10	0
Career			6	50	8.3	10	0

Tydus Winans

Year	Team		No	Yds	Avg	Lg	TD
1994	WAS	N	19	344	18.1	51	2
1995			4	77	19.3	32	0
Career			23	421	18.3	51	2

Sammy Winder

Year	Team		No	Yds	Avg	Lg	TD
1982	DEN	N	11	83	7.5	22	0
1983			23	150	6.5	17	0
1984			44	288	6.5	21	2
1985			31	197	6.4	24	0
1986			26	171	6.6	20t	5
1987			14	74	5.3	13	1
1988			17	103	6.1	14	1
1989			14	91	6.5	19	0
1990			17	145	8.5	17	0
Career			197	1302	6.6	24	9
Playoffs			20	193	9.7		2

Bob Windsor

Year	Team		No	Yds	Avg	Lg	TD
1967	SF	N	21	254	12.1	55t	2
1968			8	146	18.3	62	2
1969			49	597	12.2	32	2
1970			31	363	11.7	35	2
1971			2	32	16.0	30	0
1972	NE	N	33	383	11.6	24	1
1973			23	348	15.1	36	4
1974			12	127	10.6	20	1
1975			6	57	9.5	12	0
Career			185	2307	12.5	62	14
Playoffs			4	72	18.0		1

Stan Winfrey

Year	Team		No	Yds	Avg	Lg	TD
1976	MIA	N	6	55	9.2	16	1

Ben Winkleman

Year	Team		No	Yds	Avg	Lg	TD
1923	MIL	N					1
1924							1
Career							2

Doug Winslow

Year	Team		No	Yds	Avg	Lg	TD
1973	NO	N	4	45	11.3	14	0

Kellen Winslow

Year	Team		No	Yds	Avg	Lg	TD
1979	SD	N	25	255	10.2	30	2
1980			89	1290	14.5	65	9
1981			88	1075	12.2	67t	10
1982			54	721	13.4	40	6
1983			88	1172	13.3	46	8
1984			55	663	12.1	33	2
1985			25	318	12.7	26	0
1986			64	728	11.4	28t	5
1987			53	519	9.8	30	3
Career			541	6741	12.5	67t	45
Playoffs			28	380	13.6		4

Lloyd Winston

Year	Team		No	Yds	Avg	Lg	TD
1962	SF	N	1	2	2.0	2	0
1963			2	13	6.5	10	0
Career			3	15	5.0	10	0

Sonny Winters

Year	Team		No	Yds	Avg	Lg	TD
1923	COL	N					1

Al Witcher

Year	Team		No	Yds	Avg	Lg	TD
1960	HOU	A	4	34	8.5		1

Dick Witcher

Year	Team		No	Yds	Avg	Lg	TD
1966	SF	N	10	115	11.5	24	1
1967			46	705	15.3	63t	3
1968			39	531	13.6	59t	3
1969			33	435	13.2	49	3
1970			22	288	13.1	28	2
1971			18	250	13.9	50t	3
1972			3	22	7.3	17	1
1973			1	13	13.0	13	0
Career			172	2359	13.7	63t	14
Playoffs			10	120	12.0		2

Jon Witman

Year	Team		No	Yds	Avg	Lg	TD
1996	PIT	N	2	15	7.5	11	0
Playoffs			1	-2	-2.0		0

Mark Witte

Year	Team		No	Yds	Avg	Lg	TD
1983	TB	N	2	15	7.5	10	0
1985			3	28	9.3	13	0
1987	DET	N	1	19	19.0	19	0
Career			6	62	10.3	19	0

John Wittenborn

Year	Team		No	Yds	Avg	Lg	TD
1968	HOU	A	1	-8	-8.0	-8	0

Tom Wittum

Year	Team		No	Yds	Avg	Lg	TD
1975	SF	N	2	29	14.5	18	0

Alex Wojciechowicz

Year	Team		No	Yds	Avg	Lg	TD
1942	DET	N	4	44	11.0	13	0

Al Wolden

Year	Team		No	Yds	Avg	Lg	TD
1987	CHI	N	1	26	26.0	26	0

Dick Wolf

Year	Team		No	Yds	Avg	Lg	TD
1924	CLE	N					1
1925							1
1926	CLE	A					1
Career							3

Hugh Wolfe

Year	Team		No	Yds	Avg	Lg	TD
1938	NYG	N	2	23	11.5		0

Ron Wolfley

Year	Team		No	Yds	Avg	Lg	TD
1985	STL	N	2	18	9.0	17	0
1986			2	32	16.0	28	0
1987			8	68	8.5	16	0
1988	PHX	N	2	11	5.5	8	0
1989			5	38	7.6	22	0
1992	CLE	N	2	8	4.0	6	0
1993			5	25	5.0	9	1
Career			26	200	7.7	28	2

Year	Team		No	Yds	Avg	Lg	TD

Jeff Womack

Year	Team		No	Yds	Avg	Lg	TD
1987	MIN	N	5	46	9.2	23t	1

Joe Womack

| 1962 | PIT | N | 6 | 57 | 9.5 | 33 | 0 |

Royce Womble

1954	BAL	N	30	338	11.3	78t	3
1955			1	14	14.0	14	0
1956			9	180	20.0	43t	0
1957			7	69	9.9	37	0
1960	LA	A	32	316	9.9	34	4
Career			79	917	11.6	78t	9
Playoffs			6	29	4.8		0

George Wonsley

1984	IND	N	9	47	5.2	17	0
1985			30	257	8.6	26	0
1986			16	175	10.9	60	0
1987			5	48	9.6	16	0
Career			60	527	8.8	60	0

Nathan Wonsley

| 1986 | TB | N | 8 | 57 | 7.1 | 11 | 0 |

Otis Wonsley

1981	WAS	N	1	5	5.0	5	0
1982			1	1	1.0	1t	1
Career			2	6	3.0	5	1

Tom Woodeshick

1963	PHI	N	1	-3	-3.0	-3	0
1964			4	12	3.0	8	0
1965			6	86	14.3	60	0
1966			10	118	11.8	44t	1
1967			34	391	11.5	43t	4
1968			36	328	9.1	55	0
1969			22	177	8.0	15	0
1970			6	28	4.7	10	0
1971			6	36	6.0	11	1
1972	STL	N	1	2	2.0	2	0
Career			126	1175	9.3	60	6

David Woodley

1982	MIA	N	1	15	15.0	15t	1
1983			1	6	6.0	6	0
Career			2	21	10.5	15t	1

Tony Woodruff

1983	PHI	N	6	70	11.7	29t	2
1984			30	484	16.1	38	3
Career			36	554	15.4	29t	5

Chris Woods

| 1987 | LARI | N | 1 | 14 | 14.0 | 14 | 0 |

Don Woods

1974	SD	N	26	349	13.4	75t	3
1975			13	101	7.8	22	0
1976			34	224	6.6	34	1
1977			18	218	12.1	78	1
1978			34	295	8.7	29	0
1980	SF	N	20	171	8.6	23	0
Career			145	1358	9.4	78	5

Ickey Woods

1988	CIN	N	21	199	9.5	25	0
1990			20	162	8.1	22	0
1991			6	36	6.0	16	0
Career			47	397	8.4	25	0
Playoffs			3	18	6.0		0

Robert Woods

| 1978 | HOU | N | 6 | 96 | 16.0 | 80t | 2 |
| Playoffs | | | 3 | 26 | 8.7 | | 0 |

Keith Woodside

1988	GB	N	39	352	9.0	49t	2
1989			59	527	8.9	33	0
1990			24	184	7.7	25	0
1991			22	185	8.4	28	0
Career			144	1248	8.7	49t	2

Abe Woodson

| 1961 | SF | N | 8 | 74 | 9.3 | 28 | 0 |

Butch Woolfolk

1982	NYG	N	23	224	9.7	40t	2
1983			28	368	13.1	44	0
1984			9	53	5.9	13	0
1985	HOU	N	80	814	10.2	80t	4
1986			28	314	11.2	30	2
1987	DET	N	19	166	8.7	13	0
Career			187	1939	10.4	80t	8

Barry Word

1987	NO	N	6	54	9.0	17	0
1990	KC	N	4	28	7.0	10	0
1991			2	13	6.5	8	0
1992			9	80	8.9	22	0
1993	MIN	N	9	105	11.7	27	0
Career			30	280	9.3	27	0
Playoffs			1	8	8.0		0

Neil Worden

1954	PHI	N	7	63	9.0	23	0
1957			1	3	3.0	3	0
Career			8	66	8.3	23	0

Joe Work

| 1924 | CLE | N | | | | | 1 |

Vince Workman

1990	GB	N	4	30	7.5	9	1
1991			46	371	8.1	25	4
1992			47	290	6.2	21	0
1993	TB	N	54	411	7.6	42t	2
1994			11	82	7.5	23	0
1995	CAR	N	13	74	5.7	14	0
1996	IND	N	4	36	9.0	18	0
Career			179	1294	7.2	42t	7

Tim Worley

1989	PIT	N	15	113	7.5	19	0
1990			8	70	8.8	27	0
1993	PIT-CHI	N	11	62	5.6	15	0
1994	CHI	N	1	8	8.0	8	0
Career			35	253	7.2	27	0
Playoffs			5	56	11.2		0

Naz Worthen

| 1989 | KC | N | 5 | 69 | 13.8 | 21 | 0 |

John Woudenberg

| 1942 | PIT | N | 1 | -1 | -1.0 | -1 | 0 |

John Wozniak

1951	NYY	N	1	4	4.0	4	0
1952	DAL	N	1	-1	-1.0	-1	0
Career			2	3	1.5	4	0

Adrian Wright

| 1987 | TB | N | 13 | 98 | 7.5 | 15t | 1 |

Alexander Wright

1990	DAL	N	11	104	9.5	20	0
1991			10	170	17.0	53	0
1992	LARI	N	12	175	14.6	41t	2
1993			27	462	17.1	68t	4
1994			16	294	18.4	76t	2
1995	STL	N	23	368	16.0	50	2
1996			2	24	12.0	13	0
Career			101	1597	15.8	76t	10
Playoffs			2	30	15.0		0

Dana Wright

| 1987 | CIN | N | 4 | 28 | 7.0 | 11 | 0 |

Elmo Wright

1971	KC	N	26	528	20.3	69t	3
1972			11	81	7.4	14	0
1973			16	252	15.8	44	2
1974			13	209	16.1	51	1
1975	NE	N	4	46	11.5	20	0
Career			70	1116	15.9	69t	6
Playoffs			3	104	34.7		0

Eric Wright

| 1992 | CHI | N | 5 | 56 | 11.2 | 24 | 0 |

James Wright

1978	ATL	N	2	26	13.0	18	0
1981	DEN	N	3	22	7.3	14	1
1982			9	120	13.3	39	1
1983			13	134	10.3	23	0
1984			11	118	10.7	21	1
1985			28	246	8.8	30	1
Career			66	666	10.1	39	4
Playoffs			2	16	8.0		1

John Wright

| 1969 | DET | N | 12 | 130 | 10.8 | 26t | 2 |

Johnnie Wright

| 1982 | BAL | N | 1 | 12 | 12.0 | 12 | 0 |

Keith Wright

1978	CLE	N	8	76	9.5	20	0
1979			1	13	13.0	13	0
1980			3	62	20.7	39t	3
Career			12	151	12.6	39t	3

Lonnie Wright

| 1966 | DEN | A | 1 | -2 | -2.0 | -2 | 0 |

Nate Wright

| 1974 | MIN | N | 1 | 6 | 6.0 | 6 | 0 |

Rayfield Wright

1968	DAL	N	1	15	15.0	15t	1
1969			1	12	12.0	12	0
Career			2	27	13.5	15t	1

Tim Wrightman

1985	CHI	N	24	407	17.0	49	1
1986			22	241	11.0	29	0
Career			46	648	14.1	49	1
Playoffs			4	70	17.5		0

Jim Wulff

| 1961 | WAS | N | 1 | 6 | 6.0 | 6 | 0 |

Sam Wyche

| 1968 | CIN | A | 1 | 5 | 5.0 | 5 | 0 |

Frank Wycheck

1993	WAS	N	16	113	7.1	20	1
1994			7	55	7.9	20	1
1995	HOU	N	40	471	11.8	36t	1
1996			53	511	9.6	29	6
Career			116	1150	9.9	36t	8

Frank Wydo

| 1949 | PIT | N | 2 | 21 | 10.5 | 12 | 0 |

Arnie Wyman

| 1920 | RI | A | | | | | 1 |

Dave Wyman

| 1993 | DEN | N | 1 | 1 | 1.0 | 1t | 1 |

Harry Wynne

1944	BOS	N	10	205	20.5	42	0
1945	NYG	N	2	25	12.5	20	0
Career			12	230	19.2	42	0

Vinnie Yablonski

1948	CHIC	N	1	13	13.0	13	0
1949			6	35	5.8	15	0
1950			7	71	10.1	31	0
1951			1	8	8.0	8	0
Career			15	127	8.5	31	0

Eric Yarber

| 1987 | WAS | N | 1 | 5 | 5.0 | 5 | 0 |

Ryan Yarborough

1994	NYJ	N	6	42	7.0	12	1
1995			18	230	12.8	38	2
Career			24	272	11.3	38	3

Year	Team		No	Yds	Avg	Lg	TD

Ron Yary

Year	Team		No	Yds	Avg	Lg	TD
1980	MIN	N	1	5	5.0	5	0

Howie Yeager

| 1941 | NYG | N | 11 | 220 | 20.0 | 65 | 3 |

Tom Yewcic

1961	BOS	A	6	56	9.3	46	0
1965			1	13	13.0	13	0
Career			7	69	9.9	46	0

John Yonakor

1946	CLE	AA	7	98	14.0	52t	2
1947			6	95	15.8		2
1948			5	27	5.4		0
Career			18	220	12.2	52t	4
Playoffs			1	8	8.0		0

Wally Yonamine

| 1947 | SF | AA | 3 | 40 | 13.3 | | 0 |

Jim Youel

| 1948 | WAS | N | 1 | 20 | 20.0 | 20 | 0 |

Al Young

| 1972 | PIT | N | 6 | 86 | 14.3 | 33 | 0 |
| Playoffs | | | 5 | 58 | 11.6 | | 1 |

Ben Young

| 1983 | ATL | N | 6 | 74 | 12.3 | 19 | 1 |

Bill Young

| 1938 | WAS | N | 1 | 62 | 62.0 | 62 | 1 |

Buddy Young

1947	NY	AA	27	303	11.2	50t	2
1948			21	259	12.3		4
1949	B-NY	AA	12	171	14.3		2
1950	NYY	N	20	302	15.1	69t	1
1951			31	508	16.4		3
1952	DAL	N	22	269	12.2	45t	2
1953	BAL	N	12	201	16.8	49t	3
1954			15	272	18.1	78t	3
1955			19	426	22.4	82t	1
Career			179	2711	15.1	82t	21

Charle Young

1973	PHI	N	55	854	15.5	80t	6
1974			63	696	11.0	29	3
1975			49	659	13.4	47	3
1976			30	374	12.5	29	0
1977	LA	N	5	35	7.0	17	1
1978			18	213	11.8	19	0
1979			13	144	11.1	23	2
1980	SF	N	29	325	11.2	41	2
1981			37	400	10.8	29	5
1982			22	189	8.6	30	0
1983	SEA	N	36	529	14.7	47	2
1984			33	337	10.2	31	1
1985			28	351	12.5	32t	2
Career			418	5106	12.2	80t	27
Playoffs			16	202	12.6		2

Charley Young

1974	DAL	N	11	73	6.6	14	0
1975			18	184	10.2	42t	1
1976			11	134	12.2	25t	1
Career			40	391	9.8	42t	2
Playoffs			4	46	11.5		0

Dave Young

1981	NYG	N	5	49	9.8	15	1
1984	IND	N	14	164	11.7	28	2
Career			19	213	11.2	28	3
Playoffs			2	15	7.5		0

Dick Young

1955	BAL	N	2	15	7.5	11	0
1957	PIT	N	4	38	9.5	12	0
Career			6	53	8.8	12	0

Duane Young

1991	SD	N	2	12	6.0	6	0
1992			4	45	11.3	14	0
1993			6	41	6.8	12t	2
1994			17	217	12.8	31	1
1995			9	90	10.0	22	0
Career			38	405	10.7	31	3
Playoffs			1	3	3.0		0

George Young

1946	CLE	AA	3	37	12.3		0
1948			2	20	10.0		0
Career			5	57	11.4		0

Glen Young

1983	PHI	N	3	125	41.7	71t	1
1984	CLE	N	1	47	47.0	47	0
1985			5	111	22.2	45t	1
1988			2	34	17.0	25	0
Career			11	317	28.8	71t	2

Herm Young

| 1930 | PRO | N | | | | | 1 |

Mike Young

1985	LARM	N	14	157	11.2	23	0
1986			15	181	12.1	21	3
1987			4	56	14.0	26	1
1988			2	27	13.5	18	0
1989	DEN	N	22	402	18.3	47	2
1990			28	385	13.8	42	4
1991			44	629	14.3	52t	2
1992			1	11	11.0	11	0
1993	PHI	N	14	186	13.3	49t	2
Career			144	2034	14.1	52t	14
Playoffs			11	255	23.2		0

Rickey Young

1975	SD	N	21	166	7.9	16	1
1976			47	441	9.4	33	1
1977			48	423	8.8	28	0
1978	MIN	N	88	704	8.0	48	5
1979			72	519	7.2	18	4
1980			64	499	7.8	22	2
1981			43	296	6.9	22	2
1982			4	44	11.0	25	1
1983			21	193	9.2	48	0
Career			408	3285	8.1	48	16
Playoffs			12	119	9.9		0

Steve Young

| 1993 | SF | N | 2 | 2 | 1.0 | 6 | 0 |
| Playoffs | | | 0 | 2 | 0.0 | | 0 |

Theo Young

| 1987 | PIT | N | 2 | 10 | 5.0 | 6 | 0 |

Tyrone Young

1983	NO	N	7	85	12.1	32	3
1984			29	597	20.6	74	3
Career			36	682	18.9	74	6

Waddy Young

1939	BKN	N	8	100	12.5		0
1940			7	85	12.1		0
Career			15	185	12.3		0

Willie Young

1969	NYG	N	1	8	8.0	8	0
1973			1	-5	-5.0	-5	0
Career			2	3	1.5	8	0

Tank Younger

1949	LA	N	7	119	17.0	33	0
1951			5	72	14.4	52	0
1952			12	73	6.1	12	0
1953			20	259	12.9	48	1
1954			8	76	9.5	21	0
1955			6	51	8.5	13	0
1956			18	268	14.9	54	0
1957			8	61	7.6	16	0

Tank Younger continued

1958	PIT	N	16	188	11.8	51	0
Career			100	1167	11.7	54	1
Playoffs			1	6	6.0		0

Swede Youngstrom

| 1921 | BUF | A | | | | | 1 |

Steve Zabel

1970	PHI	N	8	119	14.9	25	1
1971			2	4	2.0	3t	2
Career			10	123	12.3	25	3

Bert Zagers

1955	WAS	N	14	306	21.9	57	0
1958			3	50	16.7	19	0
Career			17	356	20.9	57	0

Ernie Zalejski

| 1950 | BAL | N | 1 | 1 | 1.0 | 1 | 0 |

Emanuel Zanders

| 1981 | CHI | N | 1 | 7 | 7.0 | 7 | 0 |

Silvio Zaninelli

1936	PIT	N	2	12	6.0		0
1937			2	12	6.0		0
Career			4	24	6.0		0

Ray Zellars

1995	NO	N	7	33	4.7	9	0
1996			9	45	5.0	12	0
Career			16	78	4.9	12	0

Jerry Zeller

| 1921 | EVA | A | | | | | 1 |

Joe Zeller

| 1933 | CHIB | N | | | | | 1 |

Coleman Zeno

| 1971 | NYG | N | 5 | 97 | 19.4 | 53 | 0 |

Frank Ziegler

1949	PHI	N	3	33	11.0	24	0
1950			13	216	16.6	48t	0
1951			8	59	7.4	19	0
1952			8	120	15.0	57	2
1953			15	211	14.1	43	0
Career			47	639	13.6	57	4

Jack Zilly

1947	LA	N	7	75	10.7	19	0
1948			13	160	12.3	30	4
1949			3	35	11.7	14	0
Career			23	270	11.7	30	4

Don Zimmerman

1973	PHI	N	22	220	10.0	30t	3
1974			30	368	12.3	64t	2
1976	GB	N	1	13	13.0	13	0
Career			53	601	11.3	64t	5

Giff Zimmerman

| 1925 | CAN | N | | | | | 1 |

Roy Zimmerman

| 1941 | WAS | N | 5 | 36 | 7.2 | 11 | 0 |

Mickey Zofko

1972	DET	N	2	14	7.0	17	0
1973			2	16	8.0	9	0
1974			3	15	5.0	8	0
Career			7	45	6.4	17	0

Lou Zontini

1941	CHIC	N	1	22	22.0	22	0
1944	CLE	N	3	88	29.3	53t	1
Career			4	110	27.5	53t	1

Jim Zorn

| 1982 | SEA | N | 1 | 27 | 27.0 | 27 | 0 |

INTERCEPTIONS REGISTER

Year	Team		No	Yds	Avg	Lg	TD
Paul Krause							
1964	**WAS**	**N**	**12**	140	11.7	35t	1
1965			6	118	19.7	43	0
1966			2	0	0.0	0	0
1967			8	75	9.4	32	0
1968	**MIN**	**N**	7	82	11.7	29	0
1969			5	82	16.4	77t	1
1970			6	90	15.0	40	0
1971			6	112	18.7	31	0
1972			6	109	18.2	35	1
1973			4	28	7.0	24	0
1974			2	53	26.5	45	0
1975			10	**201**	20.1	81	0
1976			2	21	10.5	19	0
1977			2	25	12.5	25	0
1979			3	49	16.3	18	0
Career			**81**	1185	14.6	81	3
Playoffs			3	14	4.7		0

Key

Team	The team (and league) the player played for.
No	Number of interceptions
Yds	Yards
Avg	Average gain per interception
Lg	Longest interception return of the season
TD	Touchdowns

In addition, boldface numbers indicate that the player led the league in that category that season. For example, Krause's 12 interceptions in 1964 are boldfaced, meaning that he led the league in interceptions that year. Also, boldfaced career and playoff stats indicate all-time highs. Krause's 81 interceptions indicate that he is the all-time career leader in this category.

Bud Abell
Year	Team		No	Yds	Avg	Lg	TD
1968	KC	A	2	14	7.0	12	0

Cliff Aberson
Year	Team		No	Yds	Avg	Lg	TD
1946	GB	N	3	53	17.7	33	0

Clifton Abraham
Year	Team		No	Yds	Avg	Lg	TD
1996	TB	N	5	27	5.4	21	0

Robert Abraham
Year	Team		No	Yds	Avg	Lg	TD
1983	HOU	N	1	0	0.0	0	0
1984			1	1	1.0	1	0
Career			2	1	0.5	1	0

Nate Abrams
Year	Team		No	Yds	Avg	Lg	TD
1921	GB	A					1

Ray Abruzzese
Year	Team		No	Yds	Avg	Lg	TD
1962	BUF	A	3	44	14.7	26	0
1963			3	9	3.0	9	0
1965	NY	A	2	13	6.5	13	0
1966			2	9	4.5	9	0
Career			10	75	7.5	26	0
Playoffs			1	9	9.0		0

Dick Absher
Year	Team		No	Yds	Avg	Lg	TD
1969	NO	N	1	7	7.0	7	0
1971			1	21	21.0	21	0
1972	PHI	N	1	7	7.0	7	0
Career			3	35	11.7	21	0

Ron Acks
Year	Team		No	Yds	Avg	Lg	TD
1969	ATL	N	0	15		L15	0
1971			1	0	0.0	0	0
1973	NE	N	1	11	11.0	11	0
Career			2	26	13.0	L15	0

Fred Acorn
Year	Team		No	Yds	Avg	Lg	TD
1984	TB	N	1	14	14.0	14	0

Tony Adamle
Year	Team		No	Yds	Avg	Lg	TD
1947	CLE	AA	1	25	25.0	25	0
1949			4	42	10.5		0
1950	CLE		1	17	17.0	13	0
1951			1	12	12.0	8	0
Career			7	96	13.7	25	0
Playoffs			1	4	4.0		0

Chet Adams
Year	Team		No	Yds	Avg	Lg	TD
1946	CLE	AA	1	4	4.0	4t	1

Doug Adams
Year	Team		No	Yds	Avg	Lg	TD
1972	CIN	N	3	44	14.7	19	0

O'Neal Adams
Year	Team		No	Yds	Avg	Lg	TD
1942	NYG	N	1	66	66.0	66t	1

Stefon Adams
Year	Team		No	Yds	Avg	Lg	TD
1986	LARI	N	1	32	32.0	32	0
1987			1	8	8.0	8	0
Career			2	40	20.0	32	0

Vashone Adams
Year	Team		No	Yds	Avg	Lg	TD
1996	BAL	N	1	16	16.0	16	0

Verlin Adams
Year	Team		No	Yds	Avg	Lg	TD
1945	NYG	N	1	3	3.0	3	0

Herb Adderley
Year	Team		No	Yds	Avg	Lg	TD
1961	GB	N	1	9	9.0	9	0
1962			7	132	18.9	50t	1
1963			5	86	17.2	39	0
1964			4	56	14.0	35	0
1965			6	175	29.2	44	3
1966			4	125	31.3	68t	1
1967			4	16	4.0	12t	1
1968			3	27	9.0	17	0
1969			5	169	33.8	80t	1
1970	DAL	N	3	69	23.0	30	0
1971			6	182	30.3	46	0
Career			48	1046	21.8	80t	7
Playoffs			5	97	19.4		1

Tom Addison
Year	Team		No	Yds	Avg	Lg	TD
1961	BOS	A	4	17	4.3	10	0
1962			5	42	8.4	16	1
1963			4	27	6.8	16	0
1964			2	4	2.0	4	0
1965			1	13	13.0	13	0
Career			16	103	6.4	16	1

Bob Adkins
Year	Team		No	Yds	Avg	Lg	TD
1940	GB	N					1
1941			2	79	39.5	54	0
Career			2	79	39.5	54	1

Dick Afflis
Year	Team		No	Yds	Avg	Lg	TD
1954	GB	N	1	3	3.0	3	0

Alex Agase
Year	Team		No	Yds	Avg	Lg	TD
1947	CHI	AA	1	4	4.0	4	0
1949	CLE	AA	3	31	10.3		0
1950	CLE	N	1	14	14.0	14	0
1951			2	7	3.5	6	0
1953	BAL	N	1	5	5.0	5	0
Career			8	61	7.6	14	0

Ray Agnew
Year	Team		No	Yds	Avg	Lg	TD
1996	NYG	N	1	34	34.0	34t	1

Dave Ahrens
Year	Team		No	Yds	Avg	Lg	TD
1981	STL	N	1	14	14.0	14t	1

Len Akin
Year	Team		No	Yds	Avg	Lg	TD
1942	CHIB	N	1	0	0.0	0	0

Al Akins
Year	Team		No	Yds	Avg	Lg	TD
1946	CLE	AA	1	7	7.0	7	0
1947	BKN	AA	1	31	31.0	31	0
Career			2	38	19.0	31	0

Dick Alban
Year	Team		No	Yds	Avg	Lg	TD
1952	WAS	N	1	27	27.0	27	0
1953			4	13	3.3	11	0
1954			9	81	9.0	27	0
1955			2	48	24.0	25	0
1956	PIT	N	2	21	10.5	21	0
1957			1	35	35.0	35	0
1958			5	25	5.0	16	0
1959			6	119	19.8	46	0
Career			30	369	12.3	46	0

Trev Alberts
Year	Team		No	Yds	Avg	Lg	TD
1996	IND	N	1	19	19.0	19	0

Vince Albritton
Year	Team		No	Yds	Avg	Lg	TD
1989	DAL	N	1	3	3.0	3	0

Ki Aldrich
Year	Team		No	Yds	Avg	Lg	TD
1941	WAS	N	2	46	23.0	40	0
1946			3	31	10.3	31t	1
1947			2	9	4.5	7	0
Career			7	86	12.3	40	1
Playoffs			2	11	5.5		0

Bennie Aldridge
Year	Team		No	Yds	Avg	Lg	TD
1950	NYY	N	1	0	0.0	0	0
1951			5	57	11.4	36	0
1953	GB	N	5	85	17.0	34	0
Career			11	142	12.9	36	0

Brent Alexander
Year	Team		No	Yds	Avg	Lg	TD
1995	ARI	N	2	14	7.0	14	0
1996			2	3	1.5	3	0
Career			4	17	4.3	14	0

Bruce Alexander
Year	Team		No	Yds	Avg	Lg	TD
1991	DET	N	1	0	0.0	0	0
1992	MIA	N	1	0	0.0	0	0
Career			2	0	0.0	0	0

Elijah Alexander
Year	Team		No	Yds	Avg	Lg	TD
1994	DEN	N	1	2	2.0	2	0
1995			2	5	2.5	4	0
Career			3	7	2.3	4	0

Joe Alexander
Year	Team		No	Yds	Avg	Lg	TD
1925	NYG	N					1

Joe Alexander continued
Year	Team		No	Yds	Avg	Lg	TD
1926							1
Career							2

Kermit Alexander
Year	Team		No	Yds	Avg	Lg	TD
1963	SF	N	5	72	14.4	38	0
1964			5	65	13.0	24	0
1965			3	23	7.7	15	0
1966			4	73	18.3	55	0
1967			5	72	14.4	48	0
1968			9	155	17.2	68t	1
1969			5	39	7.8	22	0
1970	LA	N	4	47	11.8	25t	1
1971			3	122	40.7	82t	1
Career			43	668	15.5	82t	3

Willie Alexander
Year	Team		No	Yds	Avg	Lg	TD
1971	HOU	N	4	74	18.5	36	0
1972			1	16	16.0	16	0
1973			3	3	1.0	3	0
1974			2	56	28.0	29	0
1975			3	41	13.7	32	0
1977			3	111	37.0	95t	1
1978			5	51	10.2	29	0
1979			2	27	13.5	19	0
Career			23	379	16.5	95t	1
Playoffs			1	0	0.0		0

Bruce Alford
Year	Team		No	Yds	Avg	Lg	TD
1947	NY	AA	1	1	1.0	1	0

Warren Alfson
Year	Team		No	Yds	Avg	Lg	TD
1941	BKN	N	2	49	24.5	45	0

Carl Allen
Year	Team		No	Yds	Avg	Lg	TD
1948	BKN	AA	2	45	22.5		1

Carl Allen
Year	Team		No	Yds	Avg	Lg	TD
1977	STL	N	1	22	22.0	22	0
1978			6	54	9.0	21	0
1979			5	126	25.2	78	0
1980			3	104	34.7	70t	0
1982			1	0	0.0	0	0
Career			16	306	19.1	78	1

Chuck Allen
Year	Team		No	Yds	Avg	Lg	TD
1961	SD	A	5	111	22.2	59	1
1962			1	7	7.0	7	0
1963			5	37	7.4	26	0
1964			4	75	18.8	33	0
1965			1	0	0.0	0	0
1966			1	8	8.0	8	0
1967			2	2	1.0	2	0
1968			1	4	4.0	4	0
1970	PIT	N	4	48	12.0	30	0
1971			3	45	15.0	29	0
1972	PHI	N	1	15	15.0	15	0
Career			28	352	12.6	59	1

Dalva Allen
Year	Team		No	Yds	Avg	Lg	TD
1960	HOU	A	1	0	0.0	0	0

Doug Allen
Year	Team		No	Yds	Avg	Lg	TD
1974	BUF	N	1	16	16.0	16	0

Eric Allen
Year	Team		No	Yds	Avg	Lg	TD
1988	PHI	N	5	76	15.2	21	0
1989			8	38	4.8	18	0
1990			3	37	12.3	35t	1
1991			5	20	4.0	8	0
1992			4	49	12.3	36	0
1993			6	**201**	33.5	94t	4
1994			3	61	20.3	33	0
1995	NO	N	2	28	14.0	28	0
1996			1	33	33.0	33	0
Career			37	543	14.7	94t	5
Playoffs			3	25	8.3		1

Ermal Allen
Year	Team		No	Yds	Avg	Lg	TD
1947	CLE	AA	4	63	15.8		

Grady Allen
Year	Team		No	Yds	Avg	Lg	TD
1969	ATL	N	1	6	6.0	6	0

Grady Allen *continued*

Year	Team		No	Yds	Avg	Lg	TD
1970			1	0	0.0	0	0
Career			2	6	3.0	6	0

Jeff Allen

Year	Team		No	Yds	Avg	Lg	TD
1982	SD	N	1	0	0.0	0	0
Playoffs			1	8	8.0		0

Jimmy Allen

Year	Team		No	Yds	Avg	Lg	TD
1975	PIT	N	2	0	0.0	0	0
1977			5	76	15.2	48	0
1978	DET	N	5	70	14.0	27	0
1979			4	0	0.0	0	0
1980			6	38	6.3	23	0
1981			9	123	13.7	34	0
Career			31	307	9.9	48	0

Nate Allen

Year	Team		No	Yds	Avg	Lg	TD
1972	KC	N	1	4	4.0	4	0
1973			1	8	8.0	8	0
1974			1	52	52.0	52	0
1975	SF	N	1	37	37.0	37t	1
1976	MIN	N	3	44	14.7	30	0
1977			1	0	0.0	0	0
1979			1	0	0.0	0	0
Career			9	145	16.1	52	1
Playoffs			1	0	0.0		0

Patrick Allen

Year	Team		No	Yds	Avg	Lg	TD
1984	HOU	N	1	2	2.0	2	0
1986			3	20	6.7	18	0
1987			1	37	37.0	37	0
1988			1	23	23.0	23	0
1990			1	27	27.0	27	0
Career			7	109	15.6	37	0
Playoffs			1	2	2.0		0

Vaughn Alliston

Year	Team		No	Yds	Avg	Lg	TD
1960	DEN	A	1	65	65.0	65	0

Joe Allton

Year	Team		No	Yds	Avg	Lg	TD
1942	CHIC	N	1	24	24.0	24	0

John Amberg

Year	Team		No	Yds	Avg	Lg	TD
1951	NYG	N	3	38	12.7	23	0
1952			2	18	9.0	11	0
Career			5	56	11.2	23	0

Ashley Ambrose

Year	Team		No	Yds	Avg	Lg	TD
1994	IND	N	2	50	25.0	42	0
1995			3	12	4.0	7	0
1996	CIN	N	8	63	7.9	31t	1
Career			13	125	9.6	42	1
Playoffs			1	2	2.0		0

Dick Ambrose

Year	Team		No	Yds	Avg	Lg	TD
1978	CLE	N	2	46	23.0	39	0
1979			1	0	0.0	0	0
1981			1	0	0.0	0	0
1982			1	0	0.0	0	0
Career			5	46	9.2	39	0

Dave Ames

Year	Team		No	Yds	Avg	Lg	TD
1961	NY	A	1	0	0.0	0	0

Marty Amsler

Year	Team		No	Yds	Avg	Lg	TD
1967	CHI	N	1	0	0.0	0	0

Darren Anderson

Year	Team		No	Yds	Avg	Lg	TD
1993	TB	N	1	6	6.0	6	0

Dick Anderson

Year	Team		No	Yds	Avg	Lg	TD
1968	MIA	A	8	230	28.8	96t	1
1969			3	106	35.3	40	0
1970	MIA	N	8	191	23.9	86	0
1971			2	33	16.5	33	0
1972			3	34	11.3	22	0
1973			8	163	20.4	38t	2
1974			1	3	3.0	3	0
1976			1	32	32.0	32	0
Career			34	792	23.3	96t	3
Playoffs			5	107	21.4		1

Don Anderson

Year	Team		No	Yds	Avg	Lg	TD
1985	IND	N	1	1	1.0	1	0

Eddie Anderson

Year	Team		No	Yds	Avg	Lg	TD
1987	LARI	N	1	58	58.0	58	0
1988			2	-6	-3.0	2	0
1989			5	233	46.6	87t	2
1990			3	49	16.3	31	0
1991			2	14	7.0	14	0
1992			3	131	43.7	102t	1
1993			2	52	26.0	27	0
1995	OAK	N	1	0	0.0	0	0
Career			19	531	27.9	102t	3

John Anderson

Year	Team		No	Yds	Avg	Lg	TD
1978	GB	N	5	27	5.4	12	0
1981			3	12	4.0	8	0
1982			3	22	7.3	9	0
1983			5	54	10.8	27t	0
1984			3	24	8.0	22	0
1985			2	2	1.0	2	0
1986			1	3	3.0	3	0
1987			2	22	11.0	13	0
1989			1	1	1.0	1	0
Career			25	167	6.7	27t	1

Kim Anderson

Year	Team		No	Yds	Avg	Lg	TD
1980	BAL	N	2	35	17.5	18	0
1981			1	49	49.0	49	0
1982			2	25	12.5	25	0
1983			2	81	40.5	71t	1
Career			7	190	27.1	71t	1

Larry Anderson

Year	Team		No	Yds	Avg	Lg	TD
1979	PIT	N	1	19	19.0	19	0
1983	BAL	N	1	0	0.0	0	0
Career			2	19	9.5	19	0

Ralph Anderson

Year	Team		No	Yds	Avg	Lg	TD
1971	PIT	N	1	14	14.0	14	0
1972			3	68	22.7	41	0
1973	NE	N	2	3	1.5	3	0
Career			6	85	14.2	41	0

Roger Anderson

Year	Team		No	Yds	Avg	Lg	TD
1968	NYG	N	1	0	0.0	0	0

Al Andrews

Year	Team		No	Yds	Avg	Lg	TD
1971	BUF	N	1	0	0.0	0	0

Billy Andrews

Year	Team		No	Yds	Avg	Lg	TD
1970	CLE	N	1	25	25.0	25t	1
1971			3	34	11.3	19	0
1972			1	4	4.0	4	0
1974			1	18	18.0	18	0
1976	KC	N	1	11	11.0	11	0
Career			7	92	13.1	25t	1

George Andrews

Year	Team		No	Yds	Avg	Lg	TD
1983	LARM	N	1	22	22.0	22	0

George Andrie

Year	Team		No	Yds	Avg	Lg	TD
1966	DAL	N	1	6	6.0	6t	1
Playoffs			1	7	7.0		0

Dunc Annan

Year	Team		No	Yds	Avg	Lg	TD
1922	TOL	N					1

Charles Anthony

Year	Team		No	Yds	Avg	Lg	TD
1974	SD	N	1	23	23.0	23	0

Houston Antwine

Year	Team		No	Yds	Avg	Lg	TD
1965	BOS	A	1	2	2.0	2	0

Chuck Apolskis

Year	Team		No	Yds	Avg	Lg	TD
1941	CHIC	N	1	4	4.0	4	0
1942			2	15	7.5	9	0
1946			1	20	20.0	20	0
1949			1	16	16.0	16	0
1950			1	6	6.0	6	0
Career			6	61	10.2	20	0

Scott Appleton

Year	Team		No	Yds	Avg	Lg	TD
1964	HOU	A	2	11	5.5	11	0

Joe Arenas

Year	Team		No	Yds	Avg	Lg	TD
1953	SF	N	2	29	14.5	17	0
1954			3	26	8.7	26	0
1955			1	0	0.0	0	0
Career			6	55	9.2	26	0

Jessie Armstead

Year	Team		No	Yds	Avg	Lg	TD
1993	NYG	N	1	0	0.0	0	0
1994			1	0	0.0	0	0
1995			1	58	58.0	58t	1
1996			2	23	11.5	23	0
Career			5	81	16.2	58t	1

Charlie Armstrong

Year	Team		No	Yds	Avg	Lg	TD
1946	BKN	AA	2	54	27.0		0

Harvey Armstrong

Year	Team		No	Yds	Avg	Lg	TD
1986	IND	N	1	4	4.0	4	0

Johnny Armstrong

Year	Team		No	Yds	Avg	Lg	TD
1925	RI	N					1

Neill Armstrong

Year	Team		No	Yds	Avg	Lg	TD
1948	PHI	N	2	30	15.0	19	0
1950			3	4	1.3	4	0
1951			4	18	4.5	18	0
Career			9	52	5.8	19	0

Mark Arneson

Year	Team		No	Yds	Avg	Lg	TD
1973	STL	N	1	13	13.0	13	0
1975			1	6	6.0	6	0
1976			1	0	0.0	0	0
1977			2	23	11.5	15	0
Career			5	42	8.4	15	0
Playoffs			1	7	7.0		0

Jay Arnold

Year	Team		No	Yds	Avg	Lg	TD
1938	PHI	N					1
1941	PIT	N	1	0	0.0	0	0
Career			1	0	0.0	0	1

Walker Lee Ashley

Year	Team		No	Yds	Avg	Lg	TD
1988	MIN	N	1	94	94.0	94t	1
1989	KC	N	1	0	0.0	0	0
Career			2	94	47.0	94t	1

Pete Athas

Year	Team		No	Yds	Avg	Lg	TD
1971	NYG	N	2	52	26.0	37t	1
1972			4	11	2.8	9	0
1973			5	52	10.4	26	0
1974			2	0	0.0	0	0
1975	MIN	N	1	0	0.0	0	0
1976	NO	N	2	22	11.0	22	0
Career			16	137	8.6	37t	1

Billy Atkins

Year	Team		No	Yds	Avg	Lg	TD
1958	SF	N	1	6	6.0	6	0
1960	BUF	A	5	23	4.6		0
1961			10	158	15.8	29	0
1962	NY	A	4	30	7.5	17	0
Career			20	217	10.9	29	0

Bob Atkins

Year	Team		No	Yds	Avg	Lg	TD
1968	STL	N	2	0	0.0	0	0
1969			3	74	24.7	42	0
1970	HOU	N	1	7	7.0	7	0
1971			1	25	25.0	25t	1
1972			2	37	18.5	34	0
1974			6	85	14.2	36	0
1975			4	133	33.3	70	0
Career			19	361	19.0	70	0

Doug Atkins

Year	Team		No	Yds	Avg	Lg	TD
1963	CHI	N	1	0	0.0	0	0
1965			1	0	0.0	0	0
1966			1	3	3.0	3	0
Career			3	3	1.0	3	0

Gene Atkins

Year	Team		No	Yds	Avg	Lg	TD
1987	NO	N	3	12	4.0	8	0
1988			4	42	10.5	40	0
1989			1	-2	-2.0	-2	0
1990			2	15	7.5	15	0
1991			5	198	39.6	79	0

Year	Team		No	Yds	Avg	Lg	TD

Gene Atkins *continued*

Year	Team		No	Yds	Avg	Lg	TD
1992			3	0	0.0	0	0
1993			3	59	19.7	37	0
1994	MIA	N	3	24	8.0	18	0
1995			1	0	0.0	0	0
Career			25	348	13.9	79	0
Playoffs			1	26	26.0		0

Al Atkinson

Year	Team		No	Yds	Avg	Lg	TD
1965	NY	A	1	2	2.0	2	0
1966			4	48	12.0	26	0
1967			5	59	11.8	36	0
1968			2	24	12.0	22	0
1969			2	4	2.0	4	0
1970	NYJ	N	3	50	16.7	32	0
1971			2	19	9.5	17	0
1972			1	7	7.0	7	0
1973			1	11	11.0	11	0
Career			21	224	10.7	36	0

George Atkinson

Year	Team		No	Yds	Avg	Lg	TD
1968	OAK	A	4	66	16.5	33t	1
1969			2	38	19.0	22t	1
1970	OAK	N	3	35	11.7	22	0
1971			4	70	17.5	41	0
1972			4	37	9.3	23	0
1973			3	48	16.0	36	0
1974			4	39	9.8	26	0
1975			4	77	19.3	26	0
1977			2	38	19.0	24	0
Career			30	448	14.9	41	2
Playoffs			3	97	32.3		1

Steve Atwater

Year	Team		No	Yds	Avg	Lg	TD
1989	DEN	N	3	34	11.3	30	0
1990			2	32	16.0	27	0
1991			5	104	20.8	49	0
1992			2	22	11.0	22	0
1993			2	81	40.5	68	0
1994			1	24	24.0	24	0
1995			3	54	18.0	25	0
1996			3	11	3.7	11	0
Career			21	362	17.2	68	0
Playoffs			1	0	0.0		0

John Atwood

Year	Team		No	Yds	Avg	Lg	TD
1948	NYG	N	1	0	0.0	0	0

Bill Austin

Year	Team		No	Yds	Avg	Lg	TD
1949	NYG	N	1	0	0.0	0	0

Ocie Austin

Year	Team		No	Yds	Avg	Lg	TD
1969	BAL	N	2	10	5.0	10	0
1970	PIT	N	1	22	22.0	22	0
Career			3	32	10.7	22	0

Chuck Avedisian

Year	Team		No	Yds	Avg	Lg	TD
1944	NYG	N	1	48	48.0	48t	1

Ken Avery

Year	Team		No	Yds	Avg	Lg	TD
1970	CIN	N	1	5	5.0	5	0
1973			1	15	15.0	15	0
Career			2	20	10.0	15	0

Charlie Babb

Year	Team		No	Yds	Avg	Lg	TD
1972	MIA	N	1	24	24.0	24	0
1975			4	18	4.5	18	0
1976			2	20	10.0	20	0
1977			1	15	15.0	15	0
1978			3	61	20.3	36	0
1979			1	3	3.0	3	0
Career			12	141	11.8	36	0

Gene Babb

Year	Team		No	Yds	Avg	Lg	TD
1962	HOU	A	2	31	15.5	31	1
1963			2	24	12.0	18	0
Career			4	55	13.8	31	1

Bob Babich

Year	Team		No	Yds	Avg	Lg	TD
1972	SD	N	2	9	4.5	9	0
1973	CLE	N	1	48	48.0	48	0
1974			1	4	4.0	4	0

Bob Babich *continued*

Year	Team		No	Yds	Avg	Lg	TD
1976			2	29	14.5	21	0
Career			6	90	15.0	48	0

John Babinecz

Year	Team		No	Yds	Avg	Lg	TD
1975	CHI	N	1	15	15.0	15	0

Coy Bacon

Year	Team		No	Yds	Avg	Lg	TD
1971	LA	N	1	0	0.0	0	0
1973	SD	N	1	80	80.0	80t	1
Career			2	80	40.0	80t	1

Steve Bagarus

Year	Team		No	Yds	Avg	Lg	TD
1946	WAS	N	4	66	16.5	41	0
1947	LA	N	1	31	31.0	31	0
Career			5	97	19.4	41	0

Herm Bagby

Year	Team		No	Yds	Avg	Lg	TD
1926	BKN	N					1

Billy Baggett

Year	Team		No	Yds	Avg	Lg	TD
1952	DAL	N	1	10	10.0	10	0

Carlton Bailey

Year	Team		No	Yds	Avg	Lg	TD
1989	BUF	N	1	16	16.0	16	0
Playoffs			1	11	11.0		1

Jim Bailey

Year	Team		No	Yds	Avg	Lg	TD
1975	NYJ	N	1	8	8.0	8	0

Robert Bailey

Year	Team		No	Yds	Avg	Lg	TD
1992	LARM	N	3	61	20.3	37	1
1993			2	41	20.5	41	0
Career			5	102	20.4	41	1

Bill Baird

Year	Team		No	Yds	Avg	Lg	TD
1963	NY	A	6	31	5.2	26	0
1964			8	130	16.3	54	1
1965			3	9	3.0	9	0
1966			5	76	15.2	39	1
1967			3	27	9.0	17	0
1968			4	74	18.5	36	0
1969			5	10	2.0	7	0
Career			34	357	10.5	54	2

Bubba Baker

Year	Team		No	Yds	Avg	Lg	TD
1980	DET	N	1	0	0.0	0	0
1981			1	9	9.0	9	0
1983	STL	N	2	24	12.0	19	0
Career			4	33	8.3	19	0

Dave Baker

Year	Team		No	Yds	Avg	Lg	TD
1959	SF	N	5	75	15.0	29	0
1960			10	96	9.6	28	0
1961			6	123	20.5	40	0
Career			21	294	14.0	40	0

John Baker

Year	Team		No	Yds	Avg	Lg	TD
1960	LA	N	1	62	62.0	62	0
1967	PIT	N	1	0	0.0	0	0
Career			2	62	31.0	62	0

Johnny Baker

Year	Team		No	Yds	Avg	Lg	TD
1964	HOU	A	1	17	17.0	17t	1
1966			1	0	0.0	0	0
Career			2	17	8.5	17t	1

Ralph Baker

Year	Team		No	Yds	Avg	Lg	TD
1964	NY	A	2	17	8.5	11	0
1965			2	24	12.0	14	0
1967			1	0	0.0	0	0
1968			3	31	10.3	20	0
1969			1	0	0.0	0	0
1970	NYJ	N	2	8	4.0	8	0
1972			2	0	0.0	0	0
1973			4	51	12.8	22t	1
1974			2	87	43.5	67t	1
Career			19	218	11.5	67t	2

Ed Balatti

Year	Team		No	Yds	Avg	Lg	TD
1946	SF	AA	0	22			1

Al Baldwin

Year	Team		No	Yds	Avg	Lg	TD
1947	BUF	AA	2	90	45.0		0
1950	GB	N	5	35	7.0	22	0
Career			7	125	17.9	22	0

Burr Baldwin

Year	Team		No	Yds	Avg	Lg	TD
1949	LA	AA	2	4	2.0		0

Jerry Ball

Year	Team		No	Yds	Avg	Lg	TD
1996	OAK	N	1	66	66.0	66t	1

Larry Ball

Year	Team		No	Yds	Avg	Lg	TD
1973	MIA	N	1	2	2.0	2	0
1976	TB	N	1	2	2.0	2	0
Career			2	4	2.0	2	0

Michael Ball

Year	Team		No	Yds	Avg	Lg	TD
1989	IND	N	1	5	5.0	5	0

John Banaszak

Year	Team		No	Yds	Avg	Lg	TD
1979	PIT	N	1	3	3.0	3	0

Tony Banfield

Year	Team		No	Yds	Avg	Lg	TD
1960	HOU	A	3	22	7.3		0
1961			8	136	17.0	58	0
1962			6	17	2.8	11	0
1963			7	21	3.0	14	0
1965			3	28	9.3	28	0
Career			27	224	8.3	58	0

Emil Banjavic

Year	Team		No	Yds	Avg	Lg	TD
1942	DET	N	1	15	15.0	15	0

Carl Banks

Year	Team		No	Yds	Avg	Lg	TD
1987	NYG	N	1	0	0.0	0	0
1988			1	15	15.0	15t	1
1989			1	6	6.0	6	0
Career			3	21	7.0	15t	1

Chip Banks

Year	Team		No	Yds	Avg	Lg	TD
1982	CLE	N	1	14	14.0	14	0
1983			3	95	31.7	65t	1
1984			1	8	8.0	8	0
1987	SD	N	1	20	20.0	20	0
1989	IND	N	2	13	6.5	11	0
1992			1	3	3.0	3	0
Career			9	153	17.0	65t	1

Michael Bankston

Year	Team		No	Yds	Avg	Lg	TD
1995	ARI	N	1	28	28.0	28	0

Vincent Banonis

Year	Team		No	Yds	Avg	Lg	TD
1942	CHIC	N	2	22	11.0	12	0
1946			2	1	0.5	1	0
1947			3	55	18.3	41	0
1948			2	32	16.0	22	0
1949			4	66	16.5	28t	1
1951	DET	N	1	12	12.0	12	0
Career			14	188	13.4	41	1

Jack Banta

Year	Team		No	Yds	Avg	Lg	TD
1944	PHI	N	1	34	34.0	34	0
1946	LA	N	2	44	22.0	39	0
1947			2	13	6.5	13	0
Career			5	91	18.2	39	0

Gary Barbaro

Year	Team		No	Yds	Avg	Lg	TD
1976	KC	N	3	27	9.0	16	0
1977			8	165	20.6	102t	1
1978			3	92	30.7	35	0
1979			7	142	20.3	70t	1
1980			10	163	16.3	39	0
1981			5	134	26.8	34	0
1982			3	48	16.0	43t	1
Career			39	771	19.8	102t	3

Stew Barber

Year	Team		No	Yds	Avg	Lg	TD
1961	BUF	A	3	30	10.0	21	1

Leo Barker

Year	Team		No	Yds	Avg	Lg	TD
1986	CIN	N	2	7	3.5	7	0
1991			1	29	29.0	29	0
Career			3	36	12.0	29	0

Roy Barker

Year	Team		No	Yds	Avg	Lg	TD
1995	**MIN**	**N**	1	-2	-2.0	-2	0
Playoffs			1	5	5.0		0

George Barna

Year	Team		No	Yds	Avg	Lg	TD
1929	**FRA**	**N**					1

Benny Barnes

Year	Team		No	Yds	Avg	Lg	TD
1973	**DAL**	**N**	1	1	1.0	1	0
1976			1	23	23.0	23	0
1978			5	72	14.4	38	0
1979			2	20	10.0	11	0
1980			1	30	30.0	30	0
1981			1	24	24.0	24	0
Career			11	170	15.5	38	0
Playoffs			3	0	0.0		0

Erich Barnes

Year	Team		No	Yds	Avg	Lg	TD
1958	**CHIB**	**N**	4	90	22.5	30	1
1959			5	67	13.4	29	0
1961	**NYG**	**N**	7	**195**	27.9	102t	2
1962			6	61	10.2	22	0
1963			3	0	0.0	0	0
1964			2	26	13.0	26t	1
1965	**CLE**	**N**	1	35	35.0	35	0
1966			4	128	32.0	54	0
1967			4	47	11.8	40	0
1968			3	64	21.3	40t	1
1969			1	55	55.0	55t	1
1970			5	85	17.0	38t	1
Career			45	853	19.0	102t	7
Playoffs			1	2	2.0		0

Jeff Barnes

Year	Team		No	Yds	Avg	Lg	TD
1979	**OAK**	**N**	1	8	8.0	8	0
1984	**LARI**	**N**	1	15	15.0	15	0
1985			1	0	0.0	0	0
1986			2	7	3.5	7	0
Career			5	30	6.0	15	0

Pete Barnes

Year	Team		No	Yds	Avg	Lg	TD
1969	**SD**	**A**	5	64	12.8	25	0
1970	**SD**	**N**	3	22	7.3	15	0
1971			2	57	28.5	36t	1
1972			1	9	9.0	9	0
1973	**STL**	**N**	1	0	0.0	0	0
1975			2	26	13.0	23	0
1977	**NE**	**N**	1	13	13.0	13	0
Career			15	191	12.7	36t	1

Roosevelt Barnes

Year	Team		No	Yds	Avg	Lg	TD
1983	**DET**	**N**	2	70	35.0	70	0
1985			1	-1	-1.0	-1	0
Career			3	69	23.0	70	0

Tomur Barnes

Year	Team		No	Yds	Avg	Lg	TD
1995	**HOU**	**N**	2	6	3.0	6	0

Harlon Barnett

Year	Team		No	Yds	Avg	Lg	TD
1993	**NE**	**N**	1	40	40.0	40	0
1994			3	51	17.0	24	0
Career			4	91	22.8	40	0

Lem Barney

Year	Team		No	Yds	Avg	Lg	TD
1967	**DET**	**N**	**10**	**232**	23.2	71t	3
1968			7	82	11.7	62	0
1969			8	126	15.8	32	0
1970			7	168	24.0	49t	2
1971			3	78	26.0	28t	1
1972			3	88	29.3	64	0
1973			4	130	32.5	38	0
1974			4	61	15.3	39	0
1975			5	23	4.6	13	0
1976			2	62	31.0	26	1
1977			3	27	9.0	22	0
Career			56	1077	19.2	71t	7

Roy Barni

Year	Team		No	Yds	Avg	Lg	TD
1952	**CHIC**	**N**	6	70	11.7	38	0
1954	**PHI**	**N**	2	0	0.0	0	0
1955	**WAS**	**N**	1	0	0.0	0	0
1956			2	47	23.5	33	0
Career			11	117	10.6	38	0

Len Barnum

Year	Team		No	Yds	Avg	Lg	TD
1941	**PHI**	**N**	2	20	10.0	20	0
1942			1	11	11.0	11	0
Career			3	31	10.3	20	0
Playoffs			1	0	0.0		0

Pete Barnum

Year	Team		No	Yds	Avg	Lg	TD
1926	**COL**	**N**					1

Terry Barr

Year	Team		No	Yds	Avg	Lg	TD
1957	**DET**	**N**	1	0	0.0	0	0
1958			3	62	20.7	40	0
1959			1	29	29.0	29	0
Career			5	91	18.2	40	0
Playoffs			1	19	19.0		1

Jim Barron

Year	Team		No	Yds	Avg	Lg	TD
1921	**ROC**	**A**					1

Sam Bartholomew

Year	Team		No	Yds	Avg	Lg	TD
1941	**PHI**	**N**	1	5	5.0	5	0

Dick Barwegan

Year	Team		No	Yds	Avg	Lg	TD
1948	**BAL**	**AA**	1	0	0.0	0	0

Carl Barzilauskas

Year	Team		No	Yds	Avg	Lg	TD
1978	**GB**	**N**	1	5	5.0	5	0

Mike Basca

Year	Team		No	Yds	Avg	Lg	TD
1941	**PHI**	**N**	3	27	9.0	12	0

Billy Bass

Year	Team		No	Yds	Avg	Lg	TD
1947	**CHI**	**AA**	2	104	52.0	82t	1

Mike Bass

Year	Team		No	Yds	Avg	Lg	TD
1969	**WAS**	**N**	3	31	10.3	31	0
1970			4	37	9.3	22	0
1971			8	78	9.8	38t	1
1972			3	53	17.7	29	0
1973			5	161	32.2	68t	1
1974			3	33	11.0	28t	1
1975			4	85	21.3	30	0
Career			30	478	15.9	68t	3
Playoffs			1	28	28.0		0

Dick Bassi

Year	Team		No	Yds	Avg	Lg	TD
1946	**SF**	**AA**	1	2	2.0	2	0

Bill Bates

Year	Team		No	Yds	Avg	Lg	TD
1983	**DAL**	**N**	1	29	29.0	29	0
1984			1	3	3.0	3	0
1985			4	15	3.8	8	0
1987			3	28	9.3	28	0
1988			1	0	0.0	0	0
1989			1	18	18.0	18	0
1990			1	4	4.0	4	0
1993			2	25	12.5	22	0
Career			14	122	8.7	29	0
Playoffs			1	7	7.0		0

Patrick Bates

Year	Team		No	Yds	Avg	Lg	TD
1993	**LARI**	**N**	1	0	0.0	0	0

Mike Battle

Year	Team		No	Yds	Avg	Lg	TD
1969	**NY**	**A**	1	25	25.0	25	0

Cliff Battles

Year	Team		No	Yds	Avg	Lg	TD
1937	**WAS**	**N**					1
Playoffs			1	0	0.0		0

Sammy Baugh

Year	Team		No	Yds	Avg	Lg	TD
1940	**WAS**	**N**	3	84	28.0	44	0
1941			4	83	20.8	35	0
1942			5	77	15.4	29	0
1943			**11**	112	10.2	23	0
1944			4	21	5.3	18	0
1945			4	114	28.5	74	0
Career			31	491	15.8	74	0
Playoffs			3	48	16.0		0

Maxie Baughan

Year	Team		No	Yds	Avg	Lg	TD
1960	**PHI**	**N**	3	50	16.7	18	0
1961			1	22	22.0	22	0
1962			1	0	0.0	0	0

Maxie Baughan *continued*

Year	Team		No	Yds	Avg	Lg	TD
1963			1	9	9.0	9	0
1965			1	33	33.0	33	1
1966	**LA**	**N**	2	3	1.5	3	0
1967			4	69	17.3	31	0
1968			4	29	7.3	16	0
1970			1	3	3.0	3	0
Career			18	218	12.1	33	1

Bob Baumhower

Year	Team		No	Yds	Avg	Lg	TD
1978	**MIA**	**N**	1	0	0.0	0	0

Bibbles Bawel

Year	Team		No	Yds	Avg	Lg	TD
1952	**PHI**	**N**	8	121	15.1	35	0
1955			9	**168**	18.7	42t	2
1956			1	33	33.0	33	0
Career			18	322	17.9	42t	2

Martin Bayless

Year	Team		No	Yds	Avg	Lg	TD
1985	**BUF**	**N**	2	10	5.0	10	0
1986			1	0	0.0	0	0
1989	**SD**	**N**	1	0	0.0	0	0
1990			1	0	0.0	0	0
1991			1	0	0.0	0	0
1992	**KC**	**N**	1	0	0.0	0	0
1993			2	14	7.0	16	0
1994	**WAS**	**N**	3	38	12.7	19	0
Career			12	62	5.2	19	0

John Baylor

Year	Team		No	Yds	Avg	Lg	TD
1991	**IND**	**N**	4	50	12.5	32	0
1992			1	1	1.0	1	0
1993			3	11	3.7	7	0
Career			8	62	7.8	32	0

Walter Beach

Year	Team		No	Yds	Avg	Lg	TD
1961	**BOS**	**A**	1	37	37.0	37	0
1964	**CLE**	**N**	4	81	20.3	65t	1
1965			0	2		2	0
1966			1	0	0.0	0	0
Career			6	120	20.0	65t	1
Playoffs			2	9	4.5		0

Alyn Beals

Year	Team		No	Yds	Avg	Lg	TD
1947	**SF**	**AA**	1	0	0.0	0	0

Autry Beamon

Year	Team		No	Yds	Avg	Lg	TD
1975	**MIN**	**N**	1	0	0.0	0	0
1976			1	41	41.0	41	0
1977	**SEA**	**N**	6	36	6.0	20	0
1978			4	17	4.3	15	0
1979			1	38	38.0	38	0
Career			13	132	10.2	41	0

Willie Beamon

Year	Team		No	Yds	Avg	Lg	TD
1993	**NYG**	**N**	1	0	0.0	0	0
1996			1	20	20.0	20	0
Career			2	20	10.0	20	0

Ed Beard

Year	Team		No	Yds	Avg	Lg	TD
1968	**SF**	**N**	2	93	46.5	69	0
1972			1	10	10.0	10	0
Career			3	103	34.3	69	0

Aaron Beasley

Year	Team		No	Yds	Avg	Lg	TD
1996	**JAC**	**N**	1	0	0.0	0	0
Playoffs			1	15	15.0		0

Chuck Beatty

Year	Team		No	Yds	Avg	Lg	TD
1970	**PIT**	**N**	2	49	24.5	30t	1
1972			2	16	8.0	16	0
Career			4	65	16.3	30t	1

Al Beauchamp

Year	Team		No	Yds	Avg	Lg	TD
1968	**CIN**	**A**	2	35	17.5	18	1
1969			1	8	8.0	8	0
1970	**CIN**	**N**	1	2	2.0	2	0
1971			6	53	8.8	18t	1
1972			1	8	8.0	8	0
1973			3	4	1.3	4	0
1974			1	34	34.0	34	0
Career			15	144	9.6	34	2

Joe Beauchamp

Year	Team		No	Yds	Avg	Lg	TD
1966	SD	A	2	24	12.0	21	0
1967			3	44	14.7	28	0
1968			5	114	22.8	35t	2
1970	SD	N	1	25	25.0	25	0
1971			4	95	23.8	52	0
1972			6	96	16.0	47t	1
1974			1	35	35.0	35	0
1975			1	0	0.0	0	0
Career			23	433	18.8	52	3

Doug Beaudoin

Year	Team		No	Yds	Avg	Lg	TD
1978	NE	N	3	25	8.3	13	0
1979			1	30	30.0	30	0
Career			4	55	13.8	30	0

Aubrey Beavers

Year	Team		No	Yds	Avg	Lg	TD
1994	MIA	N	2	0	0.0	0	0
1995			1	8	8.0	8	0
Career			3	8	2.7	8	0

Hub Bechtol

Year	Team		No	Yds	Avg	Lg	TD
1947	BAL	AA	1	7	7.0	7	0
1949			1	6	6.0	6	0
Career			2	13	6.5	7	0

Ray Beck

Year	Team		No	Yds	Avg	Lg	TD
1956	NYG	N	1	2	2.0	2	0

Chuck Bednarik

Year	Team		No	Yds	Avg	Lg	TD
1950	PHI	N	1	9	9.0	9	0
1952			2	14	7.0	12	0
1953			6	116	19.3	41	1
1954			1	9	9.0	9	0
1955			1	36	36.0	36	0
1956			2	0	0.0	0	0
1957			3	51	17.0	37	0
1960			2	0	0.0	0	0
1961			2	33	16.5	3	0
Career			20	268	13.4	41	1

Keith Beebe

Year	Team		No	Yds	Avg	Lg	TD
1944	NYG	N	3	26	8.7	12	0

Terry Beeson

Year	Team		No	Yds	Avg	Lg	TD
1979	SEA	N	1	3	3.0	3	0

Bull Behman

Year	Team		No	Yds	Avg	Lg	TD
1925	FRA	N					1

Tom Beier

Year	Team		No	Yds	Avg	Lg	TD
1967	MIA	A	1	7	7.0	7	0
1969			1	7	7.0	7	0
Career			2	14	7.0	7	0

Randy Beisler

Year	Team		No	Yds	Avg	Lg	TD
1968	PHI	N	1	12	12.0	12	0

Steve Belichick

Year	Team		No	Yds	Avg	Lg	TD
1941	DET	N	1	10	10.0	10	0

Bill Belk

Year	Team		No	Yds	Avg	Lg	TD
1968	SF	N	1	6	6.0	6t	1

Anthony Bell

Year	Team		No	Yds	Avg	Lg	TD
1987	STL	N	1	13	13.0	13	0
1990	PHX	N	1	0	0.0	0	0
Career			2	13	6.5	13	0

Billy Bell

Year	Team		No	Yds	Avg	Lg	TD
1991	KC	N	1	4	4.0	4	0

Bobby Bell

Year	Team		No	Yds	Avg	Lg	TD
1963	KC	A	1	20	20.0	20	0
1964			1	4	4.0	4	0
1965			4	73	18.3	38	1
1966			2	14	7.0	13	0
1967			4	82	20.5	32t	1
1968			5	95	19.0	50	0
1970	KC	N	3	57	19.0	45t	1
1971			1	26	26.0	26t	1
1972			3	56	18.7	61t	1
1973			1	24	24.0	24	0

Bobby Bell *continued*

Year	Team		No	Yds	Avg	Lg	TD
1974			1	28	28.0	28t	1
Career			26	479	18.4	61t	6

Eddie Bell

Year	Team		No	Yds	Avg	Lg	TD
1955	PHI	N	1	30	30.0	30	0
1956			4	61	15.3	33	1
1957			2	38	19.0	38	0
1958			2	33	16.5	33	0
1960	NY	A	2	20	10.0		0
Career			11	182	16.5	38	1

Myron Bell

Year	Team		No	Yds	Avg	Lg	TD
1995	PIT	N	2	4	2.0	4	0

Todd Bell

Year	Team		No	Yds	Avg	Lg	TD
1981	CHI	N	1	92	92.0	92t	1
1984			4	46	11.5	36t	1
1986			1	-1	-1.0	-1	0
1988	PHI	N	0	24		24	0
1989			1	13	13.0	13	0
Career			7	174	24.9	92t	2
Playoffs			1	4	4.0		0

Jay Bellamy

Year	Team		No	Yds	Avg	Lg	TD
1996	SEA	N	3	18	6.0	16	0

Rodney Bellinger

Year	Team		No	Yds	Avg	Lg	TD
1984	BUF		1	0	0.0	0	0
1985			2	64	32.0	41	0
1986			1	14	14.0	14	0
Career			4	78	19.5	41	0

Jason Belser

Year	Team		No	Yds	Avg	Lg	TD
1992	IND	N	3	27	9.0	21	0
1993			1	14	14.0	14	0
1994			1	31	31.0	31	0
1995			1	0	0.0	0	0
1996			4	81	20.3	44t	2
Career			10	153	15.3	44t	2
Playoffs			2	68	34.0		0

Chuck Bennett

Year	Team		No	Yds	Avg	Lg	TD
1930	POR	N					1

Cornelius Bennett

Year	Team		No	Yds	Avg	Lg	TD
1988	BUF	N	2	30	15.0	30	0
1989			2	5	2.5	6	0
1993			1	5	5.0	5	0
1995			1	69	69.0	69t	1
1996	ATL	N	1	3	3.0	3	0
Career			7	112	16.0	69t	1

Roy Bennett

Year	Team		No	Yds	Avg	Lg	TD
1988	SD	N	1	21	21.0	21	0
1989			3	4	1.3	4	0
Career			4	25	6.3	21	0

Charles Benson

Year	Team		No	Yds	Avg	Lg	TD
1987	DET	N	1	2	2.0	2	0

Duane Benson

Year	Team		No	Yds	Avg	Lg	TD
1970	OAK	N	1	14	14.0	14	0
1974	HOU	N	2	0	0.0	5	0
Career			3	14	4.7	14	0

Tom Benson

Year	Team		No	Yds	Avg	Lg	TD
1989	LARI	N	2	36	18.0	19	0
1991			1	25	25.0	25	0
Career			3	61	20.3	25	0

Troy Benson

Year	Team		No	Yds	Avg	Lg	TD
1988	NYJ	N	1	2	2.0	2	0

Ray Bentley

Year	Team		No	Yds	Avg	Lg	TD
1988	BUF	N	1	0	0.0	0	0
1990			1	13	13.0	13	0
1991			1	58	58.0	58	0
Career			3	71	23.7	58	0
Playoffs			2	32	16.0		0

Larry Benz

Year	Team		No	Yds	Avg	Lg	TD
1963	CLE	N	7	114	16.3	38	0

Larry Benz *continued*

Year	Team		No	Yds	Avg	Lg	TD
1964			4	67	16.8	45	0
1965			5	78	15.6	31	0
Career			16	259	16.2	45	0

Bob Bercich

Year	Team		No	Yds	Avg	Lg	TD
1960	DAL	N	2	27	13.5	23	0
1961			3	48	16.0	28	0
Career			5	75	15.0	28	0

Bill Bergey

Year	Team		No	Yds	Avg	Lg	TD
1969	CIN	A	2	62	31.0	58	0
1970	CIN	N	3	35	11.7	26	0
1971			1	16	16.0	16	0
1973			3	50	16.7	22	0
1974	PHI	N	5	57	11.4	27	0
1975			3	48	16.0	20	0
1976			2	48	24.0	37	0
1977			2	4	2.0	4	0
1978			4	70	17.5	50	0
1979			1	0	0.0	0	0
1980			1	7	7.0	7	0
Career			27	397	14.7	58	0

Frank Bernardi

Year	Team		No	Yds	Avg	Lg	TD
1955	CHIC	N	1	18	18.0	18	0
1956			1	2	2.0	2	0
1957			2	40	20.0	23	0
Career			4	60	15.0	23	0

Eddie Berrang

Year	Team		No	Yds	Avg	Lg	TD
1951	DET	N	1	14	14.0	14	0
1952	WAS	N	2	4	2.0	4	0
Career			3	18	6.0	14	0

George Berry

Year	Team		No	Yds	Avg	Lg	TD
1925	AKR	N					1

Howard Berry

Year	Team		No	Yds	Avg	Lg	TD
1921	ROC	A					1

Ray Berry

Year	Team		No	Yds	Avg	Lg	TD
1991	MIN	N	1	11	11.0	11	0

Rex Berry

Year	Team		No	Yds	Avg	Lg	TD
1951	SF	N	4	77	19.3	38	0
1952			2	27	13.5	23	0
1953			7	142	20.3	29	1
1954			3	69	23.0	34t	1
1955			3	69	23.0	44t	1
1956			3	20	6.7	20	0
Career			22	404	18.4	44t	3

Rufus Bess

Year	Team		No	Yds	Avg	Lg	TD
1979	OAK	N	1	0	0.0	0	0
1981	BUF	N	1	12	12.0	12	0
1983	MIN	N	3	38	12.7	19	0
1984			3	7	2.3	7	0
1985			2	27	13.5	27	0
1986			1	12	12.0	12	0
Career			11	96	8.7	27	0
Playoffs			1	49	49.0		0

Don Bessillieu

Year	Team		No	Yds	Avg	Lg	TD
1980	MIA	N	4	13	3.3	12	0
1981			1	0	0.0	0	0
Career			5	13	2.6	12	0

Bobby Bethune

Year	Team		No	Yds	Avg	Lg	TD
1962	SD	A	3	6	2.0	4	0

Tom Bettis

Year	Team		No	Yds	Avg	Lg	TD
1959	GB	N	1	0	0.0	0	0

Randy Beverly

Year	Team		No	Yds	Avg	Lg	TD
1967	NY	A	4	54	13.5	28	0
1968			4	127	31.8	68t	1
1969			2	37	18.5	37	0
1971	NE	N	2	19	9.5	19	0
Career			12	237	19.8	68t	1
Playoffs			2	0	0.0		0

Year	Team		No	Yds	Avg	Lg	TD

Duane Bickett

Year	Team		No	Yds	Avg	Lg	TD
1985	IND	N	1	0	0.0	0	0
1986			2	10	5.0	10	0
1988			3	7	2.3	7	0
1989			1	6	6.0	6	0
1990			1	9	9.0	9	0
1992			1	14	14.0	14	0
Career			9	46	5.1	14	0

Greg Biekert

Year	Team		No	Yds	Avg	Lg	TD
1994	LARI	N	1	11	11.0	11	0
1996	OAK	N	0	0		L0	0
Career			1	11	11.0	11	0

Tom Bienemann

Year	Team		No	Yds	Avg	Lg	TD
1951	CHIC	N	1	5	5.0	5	0
1955			2	8	4.0	8	0
1956			1	2	2.0	2	0
Career			4	15	3.8	8	0

Verlon Biggs

Year	Team		No	Yds	Avg	Lg	TD
1965	NY	A	1	44	44.0	44	0

Dick Bilda

Year	Team		No	Yds	Avg	Lg	TD
1944	GB	N	1	25	25.0	25	0

Lewis Billups

Year	Team		No	Yds	Avg	Lg	TD
1988	CIN	N	4	47	11.8	29	0
1989			2	0	0.0	0	0
1990			3	39	13.0	29	0
Career			9	86	9.6	29	0
Playoffs			1	-3	-3.0		0

Les Bingaman

Year	Team		No	Yds	Avg	Lg	TD
1952	DET	N	1	8	8.0	8	0
1953			1	1	1.0	1	0
Career			2	9	4.5	8	0

Gregg Bingham

Year	Team		No	Yds	Avg	Lg	TD
1973	HOU	N	2	22	11.0	18	0
1974			4	36	9.0	18	0
1975			4	57	14.3	26	0
1976			2	18	9.0	15	0
1977			2	36	18.0	30	0
1979			3	78	26.0	54	0
1981			2	20	10.0	17	0
1982			1	8	8.0	8	0
1983			1	4	4.0	4	0
Career			21	279	13.3	54	0
Playoffs			3	38	12.7		0

Rodger Bird

Year	Team		No	Yds	Avg	Lg	TD
1966	OAK	A	4	48	12.0	23	0
1967			1	0	0.0	0	0
1968			3	62	20.7	33	1
Career			8	110	13.8	33	1

Danny Birdwell

Year	Team		No	Yds	Avg	Lg	TD
1964	OAK	A	2	21	10.5	16	0
1966			1	2	2.0	2	0
Career			3	23	7.7	16	0

Bill Bishop

Year	Team		No	Yds	Avg	Lg	TD
1953	CHIB	N	1	30	30.0	30	0
1955			1	5	5.0	5	0
Career			2	35	17.5	30	0

Blaine Bishop

Year	Team		No	Yds	Avg	Lg	TD
1993	HOU	N	1	1	1.0	1	0
1994			1	21	21.0	21	0
1995			1	62	62.0	62t	1
1996			1	6	6.0	6	0
Career			4	90	22.5	62t	1

Don Bishop

Year	Team		No	Yds	Avg	Lg	TD
1960	DAL	N	3	13	4.3	13	0
1961			8	172	21.5	57	0
1962			6	134	22.3	44	0
1963			5	45	9.0	31	0
Career			22	364	16.5	57	0

Blondy Black

Year	Team		No	Yds	Avg	Lg	TD
1946	BUF	AA	1	18	18.0	18	0

Bill Blackburn

Year	Team		No	Yds	Avg	Lg	TD
1946	CHIC	N	3	56	18.7	25	0
1947			3	35	11.7	20	0
1948			2	58	29.0	31t	2
1949			3	34	11.3	21	1
Career			11	183	16.6	31t	3

Don Blackmon

Year	Team		No	Yds	Avg	Lg	TD
1982	NE	N	2	7	3.5	7	0
1983			1	39	39.0	39	0
1984			1	3	3.0	3	0
1985			1	14	14.0	14	0
Career			5	63	12.6	39	0

Robert Blackmon

Year	Team		No	Yds	Avg	Lg	TD
1991	SEA	N	3	59	19.7	29	0
1992			1	69	69.0	69	0
1993			2	0	0.0	0	0
1994			1	24	24.0	24	0
1995			5	46	9.2	21	0
1996			3	48	16.0	38	0
Career			15	246	16.4	69	0

Richard Blackmore

Year	Team		No	Yds	Avg	Lg	TD
1980	PHI	N	2	0	0.0	0	0
1981			2	43	21.5	25	0
1982			1	20	20.0	20t	1
Career			5	63	12.6	25	1

Glenn Blackwood

Year	Team		No	Yds	Avg	Lg	TD
1980	MIA	N	3	0	0.0	0	0
1981			4	124	31.0	39	0
1982			2	42	21.0	35t	0
1983			3	0	0.0	0	0
1984			6	169	28.2	50	0
1985			6	36	6.0	17	0
1986			2	10	5.0	7	0
1987			3	17	5.7	17	0
Career			29	398	13.7	50	1
Playoffs			4	27	6.8		0

Lyle Blackwood

Year	Team		No	Yds	Avg	Lg	TD
1975	CIN	N	2	44	22.0	40	0
1977	BAL	N	10	163	16.3	37	0
1978			4	146	36.5	79t	2
1979			4	63	15.8	27	0
1980			1	0	0.0	0	0
1981	MIA	N	3	12	4.0	11	0
1982			2	41	20.5	21	0
1983			4	77	19.3	45	0
1984			3	29	9.7	15	0
1985			1	0	0.0	0	0
1986			1	14	14.0	14	0
Career			35	589	16.8	79t	2
Playoffs			4	11	2.8		0

Bennie Blades

Year	Team		No	Yds	Avg	Lg	TD
1988	DET	N	2	12	6.0	7	0
1990			2	25	12.5	21	0
1991			1	14	14.0	14	0
1992			3	56	18.7	34	0
1994			1	0	0.0	0	0
1995			1	0	0.0	0	0
1996			2	112	56.0	98t	1
Career			12	219	18.3	98t	1

Joe Blahak

Year	Team		No	Yds	Avg	Lg	TD
1973	HOU	N	2	120	60.0	87	0
1975	MIN	N	1	16	16.0	16	0
Career			3	136	45.3	87	0

George Blair

Year	Team		No	Yds	Avg	Lg	TD
1961	SD	A	2	4	2.0	4	0
1962			2	36	18.0	19	0
1963			1	40	40.0	40	0
Career			5	80	16.0	40	0

Matt Blair

Year	Team		No	Yds	Avg	Lg	TD
1974	MIN	N	1	-3	-3.0	-3	0
1975			1	18	18.0	18	0
1976			2	25	12.5	20	0
1977			1	18	18.0	18	0
1978			3	28	9.3	20	0
1979			3	32	10.7	16	0

Matt Blair *continued*

Year	Team		No	Yds	Avg	Lg	TD
1980			3	0	0.0	0	0
1981			1	1	1.0	1	0
1983			1	0	0.0	0	0
Career			16	119	7.4	20	0

Dick Blanchard

Year	Team		No	Yds	Avg	Lg	TD
1972	NE	N	1	20	20.0	20	0

George Blanda

Year	Team		No	Yds	Avg	Lg	TD
1951	CHIB	N	1	13	13.0	13	0

Jerry Blanton

Year	Team		No	Yds	Avg	Lg	TD
1984	KC	N	1	14	14.0	14	0

Anthony Blaylock

Year	Team		No	Yds	Avg	Lg	TD
1990	CLE	N	2	45	22.5	45	0
1992	SD	N	2	0	0.0	0	0
1993	CHI	N	2	3	1.5	3	0
Career			6	48	8.0	45	0

Mel Bleeker

Year	Team		No	Yds	Avg	Lg	TD
1944	PHI	N	1	0	0.0	0	0
1947	LA	N	1	0	0.0	0	0
Career			2	0	0.0	0	0

Stan Blinka

Year	Team		No	Yds	Avg	Lg	TD
1979	NYJ	N	2	12	6.0	8	0
1981			1	15	15.0	15	0
Career			3	27	9.0	15	0

Johnny Blood

Year	Team		No	Yds	Avg	Lg	TD
1928	POT	N					1
1931	GB	N					1
1932							1
1935							1
1936							1
Career							5

Mel Blount

Year	Team		No	Yds	Avg	Lg	TD
1970	PIT	N	1	4	4.0	4	0
1971			2	16	8.0	16	0
1972			3	75	25.0	34	0
1973			4	82	20.5	24	0
1974			2	74	37.0	52t	1
1975			11	121	11.0	47	0
1976			6	75	12.5	28	0
1977			6	65	10.8	37	0
1978			4	55	13.8	35	0
1979			3	0.3		1	0
1980			4	28	7.0	17	0
1981			6	106	17.7	50t	1
1982			1	2	2.0	2	0
1983			4	32	8.0	21	0
Career			57	736	12.9	52t	2
Playoffs			4	59	14.8		0

Hubert Bobo

Year	Team		No	Yds	Avg	Lg	TD
1961	NY	A	4	57	14.3	26	0
1962			1	14	14.0	14	0
Career			5	71	14.2	26	0

Billy Boedecker

Year	Team		No	Yds	Avg	Lg	TD
1946	CHI	AA	1	26	26.0	26	0

Fred Boensch

Year	Team		No	Yds	Avg	Lg	TD
1947	WAS	N	1	0	0.0	0	0

Kim Bokamper

Year	Team		No	Yds	Avg	Lg	TD
1978	MIA	N	1	2	2.0	2	0
1979			1	3	3.0	3	0
1980			1	6	6.0	6	0
1982			1	1	1.0	1	0
1983			2	43	21.5	24t	1
Career			6	55	9.2	24t	1

Ned Bolcar

Year	Team		No	Yds	Avg	Lg	TD
1990	SEA	N	1	0	0.0	0	0

Ron Bolton

Year	Team		No	Yds	Avg	Lg	TD
1973	NE	N	6	65	10.8	56	0
1974			7	18	2.6	10	0
1975			5	33	6.6	15	0

Ron Bolton *continued*

Year	Team		No	Yds	Avg	Lg	TD
1976	CLE	N	3	76	25.3	39	1
1977			3	50	16.7	43	0
1979			3	20	6.7	13	0
1980			6	62	10.3	29	0
1981			1	3	3.0	3	0
1982			1	0	0.0	0	0
Career			35	327	9.3	56	1
Playoffs			2	42	21.0		1

Ernie Bonelli

Year	Team		No	Yds	Avg	Lg	TD
1945	CHIC	N	1	23	23.0	23	0

Johnny Bookman

Year	Team		No	Yds	Avg	Lg	TD
1957	NYG	N	3	54	18.0	31t	1
1960	DAL	A	4	0	0.0		0
1961	NY	A	6	33	5.5	17	0
Career			13	87	6.7	31t	1

Billy Bookout

Year	Team		No	Yds	Avg	Lg	TD
1955	GB	N	2	39	19.5	27	0
1956			1	4	4.0	4	0
Career			3	43	14.3	27	0

Jack Boone

Year	Team		No	Yds	Avg	Lg	TD
1942	CLE	N	1	4	4.0	4	0

J.R. Boone

Year	Team		No	Yds	Avg	Lg	TD
1948	CHIB	N	1	12	12.0	12	0
1949			1	21	21.0	21	0
Career			2	33	16.5	21	0

Dick Booth

Year	Team		No	Yds	Avg	Lg	TD
1941	DET	N	1	18	18.0	18	0

Isaac Booth

Year	Team		No	Yds	Avg	Lg	TD
1994	CLE	N	1	4	4.0	4	0
1995			1	11	11.0	11	0
Career			2	15	7.5	11	0

John Booty

Year	Team		No	Yds	Avg	Lg	TD
1988	NYJ	N	3	0	0.0	0	0
1989			1	13	13.0	13	0
1991	PHI	N	1	24	24.0	24	0
1992			3	22	7.3	22	0
1993	PHX	N	2	24	12.0	19	0
1994	NYG	N	3	95	31.7	36	0
1995	TB	N	1	21	21.0	21	0
Career			14	199	14.2	36	0

Kenny Bordelon

Year	Team		No	Yds	Avg	Lg	TD
1979	NO	N	2	24	12.0	19t	1
1981			1	3	3.0	3	0
Career			3	27	9.0	19t	1

John Bostic

Year	Team		No	Yds	Avg	Lg	TD
1986	DET	N	1	8	8.0	8	0

Keith Bostic

Year	Team		No	Yds	Avg	Lg	TD
1983	HOU	N	2	0	0.0	0	0
1985			3	28	9.3	26	0
1986			1	0	0.0	0	0
1987			6	-14	-2.3	7	0
1988			1	7	7.0	7	0
Career			13	21	1.6	26	0

Ron Botchan

Year	Team		No	Yds	Avg	Lg	TD
1960	LA	A	2	8	4.0		0

Tony Bouie

Year	Team		No	Yds	Avg	Lg	TD
1995	TB	N	1	19	19.0	19	0

Marc Boutte

Year	Team		No	Yds	Avg	Lg	TD
1996	WAS	N	1	0	0.0	0	0

Tony Bova

Year	Team		No	Yds	Avg	Lg	TD
1942	PIT	N	1	16	16.0	16	0

Todd Bowles

Year	Team		No	Yds	Avg	Lg	TD
1986	WAS	N	2	0	0.0	0	0
1987			4	24	6.0	24	0
1988			1	20	20.0	20	0
1989			3	25	8.3	25	0

Todd Bowles *continued*

Year	Team		No	Yds	Avg	Lg	TD
1990			3	74	24.7	43	0
1991	SF	N	1	0	0.0	0	0
1992	WAS	N	1	65	65.0	65	0
Career			15	208	13.9	65	0

Jim Bowman

Year	Team		No	Yds	Avg	Lg	TD
1987	NE	N	2	3	1.5	3	0
1988			1	0	0.0	0	0
Career			3	3	1.0	3	0

Walt Bowyer

Year	Team		No	Yds	Avg	Lg	TD
1988	DEN	N	1	1	1.0	1	0

Bob Boyd

Year	Team		No	Yds	Avg	Lg	TD
1951	LA	N	2	3	1.5	3	0
1953			1	35	35.0	35	0
Career			3	38	12.7	35	0

Bobby Boyd

Year	Team		No	Yds	Avg	Lg	TD
1960	BAL	N	7	132	18.9	74	0
1961			2	0	0.0	0	0
1962			7	163	23.3	28	0
1963			3	17	5.7	9	0
1964			9	185	20.6	47	0
1965			9	78	8.7	24	1
1966			6	114	19.0	37t	1
1967			6	145	24.2	41	1
1968			8	160	20.0	49	1
Career			57	994	17.4	74	4
Playoffs			2	26	13.0		0

Malik Boyd

Year	Team		No	Yds	Avg	Lg	TD
1994	MIN	N	1	22	22.0	22	0

Mike Boyda

Year	Team		No	Yds	Avg	Lg	TD
1949	NYB	N	1	25	25.0	25	0

Garland Boyette

Year	Team		No	Yds	Avg	Lg	TD
1968	HOU	A	1	0	0.0	0	0
1970	HOU	N	1	18	18.0	18	0
Career			2	18	9.0	18	0

Tom Braatz

Year	Team		No	Yds	Avg	Lg	TD
1959	WAS	N	1	17	17.0	17	0
1960	DAL	N	1	4	4.0	4	0
Career			2	21	10.5	17	0

Danny Brabham

Year	Team		No	Yds	Avg	Lg	TD
1963	HOU	A	1	1	1.0	1	0

Greg Bracelin

Year	Team		No	Yds	Avg	Lg	TD
1982	BAL	N	1	31	31.0	31	0
1983			2	19	9.5	19	0
Career			3	50	16.7	31	0

Tony Brackens

Year	Team		No	Yds	Avg	Lg	TD
1996	JAC	N	1	27	27.0	27	0

M.L. Brackett

Year	Team		No	Yds	Avg	Lg	TD
1956	CHIB	N	1	24	24.0	24	0

Ronnie Bradford

Year	Team		No	Yds	Avg	Lg	TD
1993	DEN	N	1	0	0.0	0	0
1996	ARI	N	1	0	0.0	0	0
Career			2	0	0.0	0	0

Bill Bradley

Year	Team		No	Yds	Avg	Lg	TD
1969	PHI	N	1	56	56.0	56t	1
1971			11	248	22.5	51	0
1972			9	73	8.1	21	0
1973			4	21	5.3	18	0
1974			2	19	9.5	10	0
1975			5	56	11.2	20	0
1976			2	63	31.5	52	0
Career			34	536	15.8	56t	1

Carlos Bradley

Year	Team		No	Yds	Avg	Lg	TD
1985	SD	N	2	36	18.0	18	0

Ed Bradley

Year	Team		No	Yds	Avg	Lg	TD
1976	SEA	N	1	29	29.0	29	0

Luther Bradley

Year	Team		No	Yds	Avg	Lg	TD
1978	DET	N	3	85	28.3	76t	1
1979			4	11	2.8	11	0
1980			1	0	0.0	0	0
1981			1	0	0.0	0	0
Career			9	96	10.7	76t	1

Jim Bradshaw

Year	Team		No	Yds	Avg	Lg	TD
1963	PIT	N	1	0	0.0	0	0
1964			1	39	39.0	39	0
1965			5	117	23.4	82t	1
1966			4	82	20.5	28	1
Career			11	238	21.6	82t	2

Jeff Brady

Year	Team		No	Yds	Avg	Lg	TD
1995	MIN	N	2	7	3.5	9	0
1996			3	20	6.7	8	0
Career			5	27	5.4	9	0

Stephen Braggs

Year	Team		No	Yds	Avg	Lg	TD
1990	CLE	N	2	13	6.5	11	0
1991			3	15	5.0	15	0
Career			5	28	5.6	15	0

Larry Brahm

Year	Team		No	Yds	Avg	Lg	TD
1942	CLE	N	1	15	15.0	15	0

John Bramlett

Year	Team		No	Yds	Avg	Lg	TD
1965	DEN	A	1	25	25.0	25t	1
1966			1	12	12.0	12	0
1967	MIA	A	4	35	8.8	22	0
1968			2	14	7.0	14	0
1969	BOS	N	1	26	26.0	26	0
1970	BOS	N	1	16	16.0	16	0
Career			10	128	12.8	26	1

David Brandon

Year	Team		No	Yds	Avg	Lg	TD
1991	CLE	N	2	70	35.0	40	1
1992			2	123	61.5	92t	1
Career			4	193	48.3	92t	2

Scot Brantley

Year	Team		No	Yds	Avg	Lg	TD
1980	TB	N	1	6	6.0	6	0
1981			1	2	2.0	2	0
1983			1	0	0.0	0	0
1984			3	55	18.3	38	0
1986			2	65	32.5	57	0
Career			8	128	16.0	57	0

Alex Bravo

Year	Team		No	Yds	Avg	Lg	TD
1960	OAK	A	4	64	16.0		0
1961			2	0	0.0	0	0
Career			6	64	10.7		0

Tyrone Braxton

Year	Team		No	Yds	Avg	Lg	TD
1988	DEN	N	2	6	3.0	6	0
1989			6	103	17.2	34t	0
1990			1	10	10.0	10	0
1991			4	55	13.8	52t	1
1992			2	54	27.0	40	0
1993			3	37	12.3	25	0
1994	MIA	N	2	3	1.5	3	0
1995	DEN	N	2	36	18.0	36	0
1996			9	128	14.2	69t	1
Career			31	432	13.9	69t	3
Playoffs			1	5	5.0		0

Larry Braziel

Year	Team		No	Yds	Avg	Lg	TD
1979	BAL	N	4	49	12.3	31t	0
1980			2	87	43.5	60	0
1981			3	35	11.7	27	0
1985	CLE	N	2	40	20.0	40	0
Career			11	211	19.2	60	1

Robert Brazile

Year	Team		No	Yds	Avg	Lg	TD
1976	HOU	N	1	8	8.0	8	0
1977			3	40	13.3	16	0
1978			1	30	30.0	30	0
1979			2	45	22.5	26	0
1980			2	38	19.0	33	0
1981			2	7	3.5	7	0
1982			1	31	31.0	31	0
1984			1	2	2.0	2	0
Career			13	201	15.5	33	0

Year	Team		No	Yds	Avg	Lg	TD

Sam Brazinsky
| 1946 | BUF | AA | 2 | 7 | 3.5 | | 0 |

Carl Brazley
| 1987 | SD | N | 1 | 0 | 0.0 | 0 | 0 |

Bill Bredde
| 1954 | CHIC | N | 2 | 44 | 22.0 | 41 | 0 |

Louis Breeden
1978	CIN	N	3	25	8.3	18	0
1980			7	91	13.0	29	0
1981			4	145	36.3	102t	1
1982			2	9	4.5	9	0
1983			2	47	23.5	39	0
1984			4	96	24.0	70	0
1985			2	24	12.0	30	0
1986			7	72	10.3	36t	1
1987			2	49	24.5	44	0
Career			33	558	16.9	102t	2
Playoffs			1	0	0.0		0

Rod Breedlove
1960	WAS	N	3	67	22.3	32	0
1961			2	31	15.5	27	0
1962			3	27	9.0	12	0
1963			1	0	0.0	0	0
1966	PIT	N	2	10	5.0	9	0
Career			11	135	12.3	32	0

Monte Brethauer
| 1953 | BAL | N | 1 | 17 | 17.0 | 17 | 0 |

Carl Brettschneider
1959	CHIC	N	1	2	2.0	2	0
1962	DET	N	2	15	7.5	11	0
Career			3	17	5.7	11	0

Bob Breunig
1977	DAL	N	1	15	15.0	15	0
1978			1	2	2.0	2	0
1980			3	34	11.3	15	0
1981			2	8	4.0	8	0
1982			1	1	1.0	1	0
1983			1	0	0.0	0	0
Career			9	60	6.7	15	0

Johnny Brewer
1966	CLE	N	1	0	0.0	0	0
1967			2	75	37.5	70t	1
Career			3	75	25.0	70t	1

Greg Brezina
1969	ATL	N	1	2	2.0	2	0
1971			3	22	7.3	11	0
1973			3	51	17.0	36	0
1974			1	9	9.0	9	0
1975			4	11	2.8	8	0
Career			12	95	7.9	36	0

Frank Briante
| 1930 | NEW | N | | | | | 1 |

Alundis Brice
| 1995 | DAL | N | 1 | 2 | 2.0 | 2 | 0 |

Bob Briggs
| 1972 | CLE | N | 1 | 16 | 16.0 | 16 | 0 |

Greg Bright
| 1980 | CIN | N | 1 | 5 | 5.0 | 5 | 0 |

Mike Brim
1990	MIN	N	2	11	5.5	11	0
1991	NYJ	N	4	52	13.0	24	0
1992			6	139	23.2	77t	1
1993	CIN	N	3	74	24.7	30	1
1994			2	72	36.0	49	0
Career			17	348	20.5	77t	2

Larry Brink
| 1952 | LA | N | 1 | 0 | 0.0 | 0 | 0 |

Gene Brito
| 1956 | WAS | N | 1 | 6 | 6.0 | 6 | 0 |

Charley Britt
1960	LA	N	5	117	23.4	73	1
1961			5	29	5.8	13	0
1962			3	50	16.7	28	0
1963			1	45	45.0	45	0
Career			14	241	17.2	73	1

James Britt
1984	ATL	N	1	10	10.0	10	0
1985			1	8	8.0	8	0
1987			1	-1	-1.0	-1	0
Career			3	17	5.7	10	0

Charley Brock
1939	GB	N					1
1942			6	25	4.2	16	0
1943			4	60	15.0	41	0
1944			1	1	1.0	0	0
1945			4	122	30.5	38t	2
1947			2	14	7.0	7	0
Career			17	222	13.1	41	3
Playoffs			2	9	4.5		0

Lou Brock
1941	GB	N	2	3	1.5	3	0
1942			2	32	16.0	19	0
1943			1	9	9.0	9	0
1945			3	33	11.0	33	0
Career			8	77	9.6	33	0

Matt Brock
1993	GB	N	1	0	0.0	0	0
1995	NYJ	N	1	9	9.0	9	0
Career			2	9	4.5	9	0

Bobby Brooks
1975	NYG	N	4	38	9.5	38	0
1976			1	9	9.0	9	0
Career			5	47	9.4	38	0

Chet Brooks
| 1989 | SF | N | 3 | 31 | 10.3 | 19 | 0 |
| Playoffs | | | 2 | 66 | 33.0 | | 0 |

Derrick Brooks
| 1996 | TB | N | 1 | 6 | 6.0 | 6 | 0 |

Leo Brooks
| 1971 | HOU | N | 1 | 14 | 14.0 | 14 | 0 |

Michael Brooks
1991	DEN	N	2	7	3.5	9	0
1992			1	17	17.0	17	0
1994	NYG	N	1	10	10.0	10	0
Career			4	34	8.5	17	0

Tom Brookshier
1953	PHI	N	8	41	5.1	22	0
1956			1	31	31.0	31	0
1957			4	74	18.5	40	0
1958			1	0	0.0	0	0
1959			3	13	4.3	8	0
1960			1	14	14.0	14	0
1961			2	20	10.0	20	0
Career			20	193	9.7	40	0

Jay Brophy
| 1985 | MIA | N | 1 | 41 | 41.0 | 41 | 0 |

Al Brosky
| 1954 | CHIC | N | 2 | 11 | 5.5 | 11 | 0 |

Aaron Brown
| 1971 | KC | N | 1 | 68 | 68.0 | 68t | 1 |

Aaron Brown
| 1978 | TB | N | 1 | 10 | 10.0 | 10 | 0 |

Barry Brown
| 1966 | BAL | N | 1 | 7 | 7.0 | 7 | 0 |

Bill Brown
| 1944 | BKN | N | 1 | 6 | 6.0 | 6 | 0 |

Bill Brown
| 1960 | BOS | A | 1 | 8 | 8.0 | 8 | 0 |

Bud Brown
1984	MIA	N	1	53	53.0	53	0
1985			2	40	20.0	26	0
1986			1	3	3.0	3	0
1987			1	0	0.0	0	0
Career			5	96	19.2	53	0

Cedric Brown
1977	TB	N	2	66	33.0	27	0
1978			6	110	18.3	29	0
1979			3	79	26.3	72	0
1980			1	0	0.0	0	0
1981			9	215	23.9	81t	2
1982			3	31	10.3	24	0
1983			4	78	19.5	36	0
1984			1	14	14.0	14	0
Career			29	593	20.4	81t	2

Cedrick Brown
| 1987 | PHI | N | 1 | 9 | 9.0 | 9 | 0 |

Chad Brown
1994	PIT	N	1	9	9.0	9	0
1996			2	20	10.0	16	0
Career			3	29	9.7	16	0
Playoffs			1	0	0.0		0

Charlie Brown
| 1967 | CHI | N | 1 | 23 | 23.0 | 23 | 0 |

Chris Brown
| 1984 | PIT | N | 1 | 31 | 31.0 | 31 | 0 |

Dave Brown
| 1943 | NYG | N | 6 | 64 | 10.7 | 31 | 0 |
| Playoffs | | | 1 | 0 | 0.0 | | 0 |

Dave Brown
1976	SEA	N	4	70	17.5	33	0
1977			4	68	17.0	29	1
1978			3	44	14.7	44	0
1979			5	46	9.2	23	0
1980			6	32	5.3	24	0
1981			2	2	1.0	2	0
1982			1	3	3.0	3	0
1983			6	83	13.8	37	0
1984			8	179	22.4	90t	2
1985			6	58	9.7	28t	1
1986			5	58	11.6	24	1
1987	GB	N	3	16	5.3	11	0
1988			3	27	9.0	15	0
1989			6	12	2.0	12	0
Career			62	698	11.3	90t	5

Dean Brown
| 1970 | MIA | N | 1 | 32 | 32.0 | 32 | 0 |

Dennis Brown
1992	SF	N	1	0	0.0	0	0
1994			1	0	0.0	0	0
Career			2	0	0.0	0	0

Don Brown
1986	SD	N	1	23	23.0	23	0
1987	NYG	N	1	4	4.0	4	0
Career			2	27	13.5	23	0

Ed Brown
| 1954 | CHIB | N | 1 | 18 | 18.0 | 18 | 0 |

Eddie Brown
1974	CLE	N	2	24	12.0	24	0
1975	WAS	N	1	33	33.0	33	0
1976			1	8	8.0	8	0
1977			1	0	0.0	0	0
1979	LA	N	3	32	10.7	25	0
Career			8	97	12.1	33	0
Playoffs			2	27	13.5		0

Fred Brown

Year	Team		No	Yds	Avg	Lg	TD
1967	PHI	N	2	29	14.5	17	0

Guy Brown

Year	Team		No	Yds	Avg	Lg	TD
1981	DAL	N	1	28	28.0	28	0

Hardy Brown

Year	Team		No	Yds	Avg	Lg	TD
1948	BKN	AA	1	0	0.0	0	0
1949	CHI	AA	3	59	19.7	55	0
1950	BAL	N	1	16	16.0	16	0
1951	SF	N	1	5	5.0	5	0
1952			1	16	16.0	16	0
1953			1	7	7.0	7	0
1954			3	42	14.0	41t	1
1955			2	28	14.0	18	0
Career			13	173	13.3	55	1

J.B. Brown

Year	Team		No	Yds	Avg	Lg	TD
1991	MIA	N	1	0	0.0	0	0
1992			4	119	29.8	48	1
1993			5	43	8.6	29	0
1994			3	82	27.3	38	0
1995			2	20	10.0	20	0
1996			1	29	29.0	29	0
Career			16	293	18.3	48	1
Playoffs			2	56	28.0		0

Jerome Brown

Year	Team		No	Yds	Avg	Lg	TD
1987	PHI	N	2	7	3.5	6	0
1988			1	-5	-5.0	-5	0
Career			3	2	0.7	6	0

John Brown

Year	Team		No	Yds	Avg	Lg	TD
1947	LA	AA	1	4	4.0	4	0
1948			1	1	1.0	1	0
1949			3	46	15.3		0
Career			5	51	10.2	4	0

Larry Brown

Year	Team		No	Yds	Avg	Lg	TD
1991	DAL	N	2	31	15.5	20	0
1992			1	30	30.0	30	0
1994			4	21	5.3	14	0
1995			6	124	20.7	65t	2
1996	OAK	N	1	4	4.0	4	0
Career			14	210	15.0	65t	2
Playoffs			5	105	21.0		0

Mark Brown

Year	Team		No	Yds	Avg	Lg	TD
1983	MIA	N	1	0	0.0	0	0
1985			1	5	5.0	5	0
1988			2	13	6.5	13	0
Career			4	18	4.5	13	0

Otto Brown

Year	Team		No	Yds	Avg	Lg	TD
1969	DAL	N	1	31	31.0	31	0
1972	NYG	N	1	2	2.0	2	0
Career			2	33	16.5	31	0

Pete Brown

Year	Team		No	Yds	Avg	Lg	TD
1954	SF	N	1	47	47.0	47	0

Ray Brown

Year	Team		No	Yds	Avg	Lg	TD
1958	BAL	N	8	149	18.6	30	0
1959			5	89	17.8	44	0
Career			13	238	18.3	44	0

Ray Brown

Year	Team		No	Yds	Avg	Lg	TD
1971	ATL	N	3	32	10.7	23	0
1972			2	46	23.0	46	0
1973			6	99	16.5	24	0
1974			8	164	20.5	59t	1
1975			4	119	29.8	41t	1
1976			3	58	19.3	21	0
1977			5	56	11.2	24	0
1978	NO	N	4	50	12.5	19	0
1979			1	2	2.0	2	0
1980			2	31	15.5	29	0
Career			38	657	17.3	59t	2

Richard Brown

Year	Team		No	Yds	Avg	Lg	TD
1991	CLE	N	1	19	19.0	19	0

Robert Brown

Year	Team		No	Yds	Avg	Lg	TD
1984	GB	N	1	5	5.0	5t	1

Robert Brown *continued*

Year	Team		No	Yds	Avg	Lg	TD
1991			1	37	37.0	37	0
Career			2	42	21.0	37	1

Roger Brown

Year	Team		No	Yds	Avg	Lg	TD
1961	DET	N	1	10	10.0	10	0
1963			1	20	20.0	20	0
Career			2	30	15.0	20	0

Rush Brown

Year	Team		No	Yds	Avg	Lg	TD
1980	STL	N	1	9	9.0	9	0

Steve Brown

Year	Team		No	Yds	Avg	Lg	TD
1983	HOU	N	1	16	16.0	16	0
1984			1	26	26.0	26	0
1985			5	41	8.2	22	0
1986			2	34	17.0	38	0
1987			2	45	22.5	35	0
1988			2	48	24.0	44t	1
1989			5	54	10.8	41	0
Career			18	264	14.7	44t	1

Terry Brown

Year	Team		No	Yds	Avg	Lg	TD
1969	STL	N	1	21	21.0	21	0
1973	MIN	N	1	63	63.0	63t	1
1974			2	15	7.5	11	0
1975			2	33	16.5	18	0
1976	CLE	N	1	24	24.0	24	0
Career			7	156	22.3	63t	1

Tom Brown

Year	Team		No	Yds	Avg	Lg	TD
1964	GB	N	1	30	30.0	30	0
1965			3	42	14.0	27	0
1966			4	21	5.3	15	0
1967			1	51	51.0	51	0
1968			4	66	16.5	25	0
Career			13	210	16.2	51	0
Playoffs			2	20	10.0		0

Vincent Brown

Year	Team		No	Yds	Avg	Lg	TD
1989	NE	N	1	-1	-1.0	-1	0
1992			1	49	49.0	49t	1
1993			1	24	24.0	24	0
1994			3	22	7.3	12	0
1995			4	1	0.3	1	0
Career			10	95	9.5	49t	1

Willie Brown

Year	Team		No	Yds	Avg	Lg	TD
1963	DEN	A	1	0	0.0	0	0
1964			9	140	15.6	45	0
1965			2	18	9.0	18	0
1966			3	37	12.3	31	0
1967	OAK	A	7	33	4.7	25t	1
1968			2	27	13.5	27t	1
1969			5	111	22.2	30	0
1970	OAK	N	3	0	0.0	0	0
1971			2	2	1.0	2	0
1972			4	26	6.5	13	0
1973			3	-1	-0.3	0	0
1974			1	31	31.0	31	0
1975			4	-1	-0.3	0	0
1976			3	25	8.3	22	0
1977			4	24	6.0	18	0
1978			1	0	0.0	0	0
Career			54	472	8.7	45	2
Playoffs			7	196	28.0		3

Jim Browner

Year	Team		No	Yds	Avg	Lg	TD
1979	CIN	N	1	15	15.0	15	0

Joey Browner

Year	Team		No	Yds	Avg	Lg	TD
1983	MIN	N	2	0	0.0	0	0
1984			1	20	20.0	20	0
1985			2	17	8.5	15t	1
1986			4	62	15.5	39t	1
1987			6	67	11.2	23	0
1988			5	29	5.8	18	0
1989			5	70	14.0	34	0
1990			7	103	14.7	31	1
1991			5	97	19.4	45	0
Career			37	465	12.6	39t	3
Playoffs			3	40	13.3		0

Keith Browner

Year	Team		No	Yds	Avg	Lg	TD
1985	TB	N	1	25	25.0	25	0
1986			1	16	16.0	16	0
1988	SD	N	2	65	32.5	55t	1
Career			4	106	26.5	55t	1

Ross Browner

Year	Team		No	Yds	Avg	Lg	TD
1982	CIN	N	1	29	29.0	29	0

Dave Browning

Year	Team		No	Yds	Avg	Lg	TD
1981	OAK	N	1	8	8.0	8	0

Aundray Bruce

Year	Team		No	Yds	Avg	Lg	TD
1988	ATL	N	2	10	5.0	10	0
1989			1	0	0.0	0	0
1995	OAK	N	1	1	1.0	1t	1
Career			4	11	2.8	10	1

Gail Bruce

Year	Team		No	Yds	Avg	Lg	TD
1949	SF	AA	1	5	5.0	5	0
1950	SF	N	1	4	4.0	4	0
Career			2	9	4.5	5	0

Hank Bruder

Year	Team		No	Yds	Avg	Lg	TD
1934	GB	N					1
1935							1
Career							2
Playoffs			1	0	0.0		0

Bob Brudzinski

Year	Team		No	Yds	Avg	Lg	TD
1977	LA	N	2	24	12.0	23	0
1978			1	31	31.0	31t	1
1979			1	26	26.0	26	0
1981	MIA	N	2	35	17.5	19	0
1982			1	5	5.0	5	0
1984			1	0	0.0	0	0
1985			1	6	6.0	6	0
Career			9	127	14.1	31t	1

Bob Bruggers

Year	Team		No	Yds	Avg	Lg	TD
1967	MIA	A	1	20	20.0	20	0
1969	SD	A	1	5	5.0	5	0
Career			2	25	12.5	20	0

Larry Brune

Year	Team		No	Yds	Avg	Lg	TD
1980	MIN	N	2	68	34.0	52	0

Fred Bruney

Year	Team		No	Yds	Avg	Lg	TD
1953	SF	N	5	59	11.8	23	0
1956	PIT	N	1	39	39.0	39	0
1957			1	0	0.0	0	0
1960	BOS	A	3	35	11.7		0
1961			2	20	10.0	12	0
1962			3	70	23.3	33	1
Career			15	223	14.9	39	1

Ross Brupbacher

Year	Team		No	Yds	Avg	Lg	TD
1970	CHI	N	2	17	8.5	10	0
1971			2	34	17.0	34	0
1972			1	11	11.0	11	0
1976			7	49	7.0	25	0
Career			12	111	9.3	34	0

Tedy Bruschi

Year	Team		No	Yds	Avg	Lg	TD
Playoffs			1	12	12.0		0

Bill Bryant

Year	Team		No	Yds	Avg	Lg	TD
1977	NYG	N	3	54	18.0	54t	1

Bobby Bryant

Year	Team		No	Yds	Avg	Lg	TD
1968	MIN	N	2	60	30.0	51t	1
1969			8	97	12.1	56	0
1970			3	40	13.3	39t	1
1971			3	51	17.0	19	0
1972			4	82	20.5	34	0
1973			7	105	15.0	46t	0
1975			6	111	18.5	41	0
1976			2	30	15.0	25	0
1977			4	44	11.0	41	0
1978			7	69	9.9	23	0
1979			2	50	25.0	29	0
1980			3	10	3.3	7	0
Career			51	749	14.7	56	3
Playoffs			6	80	13.3		1

Year	Team		No	Yds	Avg	Lg	TD

Domingo Bryant

Year	Team		No	Yds	Avg	Lg	TD
1987	HOU	N	4	75	18.8	29	0
1988			3	56	18.7	36t	1
Career			7	131	18.7	36t	1

Jeff Bryant

1984	SEA	N	1	1	1.0	1	0

Trent Bryant

1983	KC	N	1	19	19.0	19	0
1987			1	0	0.0	0	0
Career			2	19	9.5	19	0

Walter Bryant

1955	BAL	N	1	4	4.0	4	0

Waymond Bryant

1974	CHI	N	2	11	5.5	11	0
1976			2	6	3.0	3	0
Career			4	17	4.3	11	0

Mark Buben

1981	NE	N	1	49	49.0	49	0

Buck Buchanan

1968	KC	A	1	11	11.0	11	0
1971	KC	N	1	9	9.0	9	0
1973			1	17	17.0	17	0
Career			3	37	12.3	17	0

Ray Buchanan

1993	IND	N	4	45	11.3	28	0
1994			8	221	27.6	90t	3
1995			2	60	30.0	60	0
1996			2	32	16.0	32	0
Career			16	358	22.4	90t	3

Willie Buchanon

1972	GB	N	4	62	15.5	26	0
1974			4	10	2.5	8	0
1976			2	28	14.0	22	0
1977			2	41	20.5	29t	1
1978			9	93	10.3	77t	1
1980	SD	N	2	13	6.5	7	0
1981			5	31	6.2	18	0
Career			28	278	9.9	77t	2
Playoffs			1	0	0.0		0

Vince Buck

1991	NO	N	5	12	2.4	12	0
1992			2	51	25.5	34t	1
1993			2	28	14.0	28	0
1994			1	0	0.0	0	0
Career			10	91	9.1	34t	1

Terrell Buckley

1992	GB	N	3	33	11.0	33t	1
1993			2	31	15.5	31	0
1994			5	38	7.6	26	0
1995	MIA	N	1	0	0.0	0	0
1996			6	164	27.3	91t	1
Career			17	266	15.6	91t	2
Playoffs			2	0	0.0		0

Frank Budka

1964	LA	N	2	18	9.0	18	0

Bill Budness

1964	OAK	A	2	29	14.5	23	0
1965			1	0	0.0	0	0
Career			3	29	9.7	23	0

Harry Buffington

1942	NYG	N	1	10	10.0	10	0

Doug Buffone

1967	CHI	N	3	39	13.0	22	0
1968			1	21	21.0	21	0
1969			2	12	6.0	12	0
1970			4	33	8.3	16	0
1971			2	27	13.5	18	0
1972			1	0	0.0	0	0
1973			3	22	7.3	22	0
1974			1	0	0.0	0	0

Doug Buffone continued

1975			1	12	12.0	12	0
1977			1	12	12.0	12	0
1978			3	22	7.3	16	0
1979			2	11	5.5	11	0
Career			24	211	8.8	22	0

George Buksar

1950	BAL	N	6	79	13.2	28	0
1951	WAS	N	1	20	20.0	20	0
Career			7	99	14.1	28	0

Rex Bumgardner

1948	BUF	AA	2	7	3.5		0
1952	CLE	N	2	33	16.5	33	0
Career			4	40	10.0	33	0

Frank Buncom

1962	SD	A	4	49	12.3	26	0
1964			1	11	11.0	11	0
Career			5	60	12.0	26	0

John Bunting

1972	PHI	N	1	45	45.0	45	0
1974			2	23	11.5	12	0
1975			1	6	6.0	6	0
1978			1	9	9.0	9	0
1979			2	13	6.5	13	0
1982			1	0	0.0	0	0
Career			8	96	12.0	45	0

Dan Bunz

1978	SF	N	1	13	13.0	13	0
1979			1	2	2.0	2	0
1984			1	2	2.0	2	0
1985	DET		1	17	17.0	17	0
Career			4	34	8.5	17	0

Nick Buoniconti

1962	BOS	A	2	3	1.5	3	0
1963			3	42	14.0	26	0
1964			5	75	15.0	26	0
1965			3	31	10.3	26	0
1966			4	43	10.8	41	0
1967			4	7	1.8	7	0
1968			3	22	7.3	14	0
1969	MIA	A	3	27	9.0	24	0
1971	MIA	N	1	16	16.0	16	0
1972			2	17	8.5	10	0
1974			2	29	14.5	16	0
Career			32	312	9.8	41	0
Playoffs			2	38	19.0		0

Don Burke

1952	SF	N	1	35	35.0	35t	1

Jackie Burkett

1961	BAL	N	1	23	23.0	23	0
1962			2	21	10.5	12	0
1967	NO	N	3	57	19.0	23	0
1970			4	36	9.0	16	0
Career			10	137	13.7	23	0

Jeff Burkett

1947	CHIC	N	1	25	25.0	25	0

Dale Burnett

1933	NYG	N					1

Mike Burns

1978	DET	N	1	0	0.0	0	0

Clinton Burrell

1980	CLE	N	5	51	10.2	29	0
1982			1	14	14.0	14t	1
1983			2	0	0.0	0	0
Career			8	65	8.1	29	1

George Burrell

1969	DEN	A	2	65	32.5	38t	1

Bo Burris

1968	NO	N	3	129	43.0	94t	1

Bo Burris continued

1969			1	24	24.0	24	0
Career			4	153	38.3	94t	1

Buddy Burris

1949	GB	N	1	0	0.0	0	0

Jeff Burris

1994	BUF	N	2	24	12.0	24	0
1995			1	19	19.0	19	0
1996			1	28	28.0	28	0
Career			4	71	17.8	28	0
Playoffs			1	38	38.0		1

Derrick Burroughs

1985	BUF	N	2	7	3.5	7	0
1986			2	49	24.5	41	0
1987			2	11	5.5	14	0
Career			6	67	11.2	41	0

Don Burroughs

1955	LA	N	9	103	11.4	34	0
1956			2	9	4.5	9	0
1957			3	29	9.7	24	0
1958			7	72	10.3	46	0
1960	PHI	N	9	124	13.8	46	0
1961			7	90	12.9	42	0
1962			7	96	13.7	28	0
1963			4	36	9.0	21	0
1964			2	5	2.5	3	0
Career			50	564	11.3	46	0
Playoffs			1	24	24.0		0

Jim Burroughs

1982	BAL	N	1	94	94.0	94t	1
1983			2	8	4.0	8	0
1984	IND	N	3	9	3.0	6	0
Career			6	111	18.5	94t	1

Harry Burrus

1946	NY	AA	2	37	18.5		0
1947			1	11	11.0	11	0
1948	BKN	AA	3	82	27.3		0
Career			6	130	21.7	11	0

Lloyd Burruss

1981	KC	N	4	75	18.8	46t	1
1982			1	25	25.0	25	0
1983			4	46	11.5	27	0
1984			2	16	8.0	16	0
1985			1	0	0.0	0	0
1986			5	193	38.6	72t	3
1988			2	57	28.5	32	0
1989			1	0	0.0	0	0
1990			1	14	14.0	14	0
1991			1	83	83.0	83	0
Career			22	509	23.1	72t	4

Jimmy Burson

1964	STL	N	3	53	17.7	40	0
1965			5	113	22.6	42	0
1966			2	20	10.0	15	0
1967			2	0	0.0	0	0
1968	ATL	N	4	100	25.0	73t	1
Career			16	286	17.9	73t	1

James Burton

1996	CHI	N	1	11	11.0	11	0

Ron Burton

1989	DAL	N	1	0	0.0	0	0

Devin Bush

1995	ATL	N	1	0	0.0	0	0
1996			1	2	2.0	2	0
Career			2	2	1.0	2	0

Lewis Bush

1995	SD	N	1	0	0.0	0	0

Steve Busick

1984	DEN	N	2	21	10.5	16	0

Year	Team		No	Yds	Avg	Lg	TD

Barney Bussey
Year	Team		No	Yds	Avg	Lg	TD
1986	CIN	N	1	19	19.0	19	0
1987			1	0	0.0	0	0
1989			1	0	0.0	0	0
1990			4	37	9.3	18	0
1991			2	18	9.0	18	0
1992			1	3	3.0	3	0
Career			10	77	7.7	19	0

Young Bussey
Year	Team		No	Yds	Avg	Lg	TD
1941	CHIB	N	2	5	2.5	5	0

Dick Butkus
Year	Team		No	Yds	Avg	Lg	TD
1965	CHI	N	5	84	16.8	38	0
1966			1	3	3.0	3	0
1967			1	24	24.0	24	0
1968			3	14	4.7	14	0
1969			2	13	6.5	11	0
1970			3	0	0.0	0	0
1971			4	9	2.3	9	0
1972			2	19	9.5	14	0
1973			1	0	0.0	0	0
Career			22	166	7.5	38	0

Bill Butler
Year	Team		No	Yds	Avg	Lg	TD
1960	DAL	N	1	0	0.0	0	0
1961	PIT	N	3	103	34.3	71t	1
1962	MIN	N	5	80	16.0	39t	1
1964			2	15	7.5	15	0
Career			11	198	18.0	71t	2

Bobby Butler
Year	Team		No	Yds	Avg	Lg	TD
1981	ATL	N	5	86	17.2	41	0
1982			2	0	0.0	0	0
1983			4	12	3.0	12	0
1984			2	25	12.5	25	0
1985			5	-4	-0.8	0	0
1986			1	33	33.0	33t	1
1987			4	48	12.0	31	0
1988			1	22	22.0	22	0
1990			3	0	0.0	0	0
Career			27	222	8.2	41	1

Jack Butler
Year	Team		No	Yds	Avg	Lg	TD
1951	PIT	N	5	142	28.4	52t	1
1952			7	168	24.0	41	0
1953			9	147	16.3	28	1
1954			4	75	18.8	41t	1
1956			6	113	18.8	34	0
1957			10	85	8.5	20	0
1958			9	81	9.0	19	0
1959			2	16	8.0	16	0
Career			52	827	15.9	52t	3

Johnny Butler
Year	Team		No	Yds	Avg	Lg	TD
1944	C-P-BKN	N	3	16	5.3	9	0
1945	PHI	N	1	32	32.0	32	0
Career			4	48	12.0	32	0

Keith Butler
Year	Team		No	Yds	Avg	Lg	TD
1979	SEA	N	1	4	4.0	4	0
1980			2	11	5.5	9	0
1981			2	0	0.0	0	0
1983			1	0	0.0	0	0
1985			2	31	15.5	31	0
Career			8	46	5.8	31	0

Le Roy Butler
Year	Team		No	Yds	Avg	Lg	TD
1990	GB	N	3	42	14.0	28	0
1991			3	6	2.0	6	0
1992			1	0	0.0	0	0
1993			6	131	21.8	39	0
1994			3	68	22.7	51	0
1995			5	105	21.0	76	0
1996			5	149	29.8	90t	1
Career			26	501	19.3	90t	1
Playoffs			1	14	14.0		0

Greg Buttle
Year	Team		No	Yds	Avg	Lg	TD
1976	NYJ	N	2	20	10.0	14	0
1977			2	54	27.0	44t	1
1978			2	34	17.0	29	0
1979			2	27	13.5	27	0
1980			1	15	15.0	15	0

Greg Buttle *continued*
Year	Team		No	Yds	Avg	Lg	TD
1981			2	34	17.0	22	0
1982			1	9	9.0	9	0
1983			1	17	17.0	17	0
1984			2	5	2.5	5	0
Career			15	215	14.3	44t	1
Playoffs			3	40	13.3		0

Dave Butz
Year	Team		No	Yds	Avg	Lg	TD
1978	WAS	N	1	3	3.0	3	0
1981			1	26	26.0	26	0
Career			2	29	14.5	26	0

Bernie Buzyniski
Year	Team		No	Yds	Avg	Lg	TD
1960	BUF	A	1	5	5.0	5	0

Rick Byas
Year	Team		No	Yds	Avg	Lg	TD
1977	ATL	N	3	122	40.7	72t	1
1978			2	37	18.5	32	0
1979			1	34	34.0	34	0
Career			6	193	32.2	72t	1

Butch Byrd
Year	Team		No	Yds	Avg	Lg	TD
1964	BUF	A	7	178	25.4	75	1
1965			5	119	23.8	62	0
1966			6	110	18.3	60	1
1967			5	25	5.0	12	0
1968			6	76	12.7	53t	1
1969			7	95	13.6	32	1
1970	BUF	N	4	63	15.8	33	1
Career			40	666	16.6	75	5
Playoffs			2	24	12.0		0

Gill Byrd
Year	Team		No	Yds	Avg	Lg	TD
1983	SD	N	1	0	0.0	0	0
1984			4	157	39.3	99t	2
1985			1	25	25.0	25	0
1986			5	45	9.0	18	0
1988			7	82	11.7	42	0
1989			7	38	5.4	22	0
1990			7	63	9.0	24	0
1991			6	48	8.0	22	0
1992			4	88	22.0	44	0
Career			42	546	13.0	99t	2

Richard Byrd
Year	Team		No	Yds	Avg	Lg	TD
1988	HOU	N	1	1	1.0	1	0

Larry Cabrelli
Year	Team		No	Yds	Avg	Lg	TD
1943	P-P	N	1	24	24.0	24t	1
1945	PHI	N	1	1	1.0	1	0
Career			2	25	12.5	24t	1

Ernie Caddel
Year	Team		No	Yds	Avg	Lg	TD
1934	DET	N					1

Mossy Cade
Year	Team		No	Yds	Avg	Lg	TD
1985	GB	N	1	0	0.0	0	0
1986			4	26	6.5	18	0
Career			5	26	5.2	18	0

George Cafego
Year	Team		No	Yds	Avg	Lg	TD
1944	BOS	N	1	39	39.0	39	0
1945			1	2	2.0	2	0
Career			2	41	20.5	39	0

Lee Roy Caffey
Year	Team		No	Yds	Avg	Lg	TD
1963	PHI	N	1	87	87.0	87t	1
1964	GB	N	1	44	44.0	44	0
1965			1	42	42.0	42t	1
1966			3	62	20.7	52t	1
1967			2	28	14.0	24	0
1969			2	1	0.5	1	0
1972	SD	N	1	4	4.0	4	0
Career			11	268	24.4	87t	3

Joe Cain
Year	Team		No	Yds	Avg	Lg	TD
1991	SEA	N	1	5	5.0	5	0
1992			2	3	1.5	3	0
Career			3	8	2.7	5	0

Alan Caldwell
Year	Team		No	Yds	Avg	Lg	TD
1979	NYG	N	2	2	1.0	2	0

Mike Caldwell
Year	Team		No	Yds	Avg	Lg	TD
1994	CLE	N	1	0	0.0	0	0
1995			2	24	12.0	24t	1
1996	BAL	N	1	45	45.0	45t	1
Career			4	69	17.3	45t	2

Ravin Caldwell
Year	Team		No	Yds	Avg	Lg	TD
Playoffs			1	13	13.0		0

Tony Caldwell
Year	Team		No	Yds	Avg	Lg	TD
1987	SEA	N	1	4	4.0	4	0

Jim Callahan
Year	Team		No	Yds	Avg	Lg	TD
1946	DET	N	2	8	4.0	8	0

Lee Calland
Year	Team		No	Yds	Avg	Lg	TD
1966	ATL	N	3	6	2.0	6	0
1967			3	106	35.3	77t	1
1968			2	34	17.0	21	0
1969	PIT	N	2	0	0.0	0	0
1970			7	38	5.4	21	0
1971			2	0	0.0	0	0
Career			19	184	9.7	77t	1

Bill Callihan
Year	Team		No	Yds	Avg	Lg	TD
1942	DET	N	3	29	9.7	20	0
1943			1	7	7.0	7	0
1945			2	8	4.0	6	0
Career			6	44	7.3	20	0

Tony Calvelli
Year	Team		No	Yds	Avg	Lg	TD
1940	DET	N					1
1947	SF	AA	1	2	2.0	2	0
Career			1	2	2.0	2	1

Glenn Cameron
Year	Team		No	Yds	Avg	Lg	TD
1980	CIN	N	3	43	14.3	27	0
1981			1	0	0.0	0	0
1984			1	15	15.0	15	0
Career			5	58	11.6	27	0

Paul Cameron
Year	Team		No	Yds	Avg	Lg	TD
1954	PIT	N	7	118	16.9	33	0

Jim Camp
Year	Team		No	Yds	Avg	Lg	TD
1948	BKN	AA	1	69	69.0	69	0

Al Campana
Year	Team		No	Yds	Avg	Lg	TD
1950	CHIB	N	1	0	0.0	0	0

Joe Campanella
Year	Team		No	Yds	Avg	Lg	TD
1954	BAL	N	1	0	0.0	0	0
1955			2	35	17.5	23	0
Career			3	35	11.7	23	0

Dick Campbell
Year	Team		No	Yds	Avg	Lg	TD
1958	PIT	N	1	58	58.0	58	0
1959			1	6	6.0	6	0
1960			1	5	5.0	5	0
Career			3	69	23.0	58	0

Gary Campbell
Year	Team		No	Yds	Avg	Lg	TD
1979	CHI	N	1	32	32.0	32	0
1980			3	36	12.0	15	0
Career			4	68	17.0	32	0

Jesse Campbell
Year	Team		No	Yds	Avg	Lg	TD
1993	NYG	N	1	0	0.0	0	0
1994			2	3	1.5	2	0
1996			2	14	7.0	14	0
Career			5	17	3.4	14	0

Jimmy Campbell
Year	Team		No	Yds	Avg	Lg	TD
1969	SD	A	1	0	0.0	0	0

John Campbell
Year	Team		No	Yds	Avg	Lg	TD
1966	PIT	N	2	6	3.0	6	0
1967			2	52	26.0	30	0
1968			1	20	20.0	20	0
Career			5	78	15.6	30	0

Marion Campbell
Year	Team		No	Yds	Avg	Lg	TD
1955	SF	N	1	0	0.0	0	0
1956	PHI	N	1	1	1.0	1	0

Marion Campbell *continued*

Year	Team		No	Yds	Avg	Lg	TD
1959			1	0	0.0	0	0
Career			3	1	0.3	1	0

Tony Canadeo

Year	Team		No	Yds	Avg	Lg	TD
1941	GB	N	2	30	15.0	22	0
1942			1	35	35.0	35	0
1943			2	15	7.5	15	0
1946			1	23	23.0	23	0
1948			3	26	8.7	25	0
Career			9	129	14.3	35	0

Jim Canady

Year	Team		No	Yds	Avg	Lg	TD
1949	CHIB-NYB	N	5	58	11.6	36	0

John Cannady

Year	Team		No	Yds	Avg	Lg	TD
1947	NYG	N	1	0	0.0	0	0
1948			2	22	11.0	22	0
1949			1	15	15.0	15	0
1950			2	23	11.5	16	0
1951			3	52	17.3	29	0
1952			2	2	1.0	2	0
1953			1	33	33.0	33	0
1954			2	16	8.0	14	0
Career			14	163	11.6	33	0

Joe Cannavino

Year	Team		No	Yds	Avg	Lg	TD
1960	OAK	A	4	45	11.3		0
1961			5	14	2.8	9	0
1962	BUF	A	1	19	19.0	19	0
Career			10	78	7.8	19	0

John Cannon

Year	Team		No	Yds	Avg	Lg	TD
1984	TB	N	1	0	0.0	0	0

Leo Cantor

Year	Team		No	Yds	Avg	Lg	TD
1942	NYG	N	2	46	23.0	26	0
1945	CHIC	N	5	70	14.0	26	0
Career			7	116	16.6	26	0

Gino Cappelletti

Year	Team		No	Yds	Avg	Lg	TD
1960	BOS	A	4	68	17.0	24	0

Jim Capuzzi

Year	Team		No	Yds	Avg	Lg	TD
1956	GB	N	2	65	32.5	65	0

Al Carapella

Year	Team		No	Yds	Avg	Lg	TD
1951	SF	N	1	11	11.0	11	0
1954			2	40	20.0	27	0
Career			3	51	17.0	27	0

Lloyd Cardwell

Year	Team		No	Yds	Avg	Lg	TD
1942	DET	N	2	40	20.0	40	0

Richard Carey

Year	Team		No	Yds	Avg	Lg	TD
1989	CIN	N	1	5	5.0	5	0

J.C. Caroline

Year	Team		No	Yds	Avg	Lg	TD
1956	CHIB	N	6	182	30.3	59t	2
1957			2	22	11.0	20	0
1959			5	14	2.8	8	0
1960	CHI	N	3	31	10.3	31	0
1961			3	48	16.0	28	0
1962			2	21	10.5	21	0
1963			1	3	3.0	3	0
1964			2	84	42.0	79	0
Career			24	405	16.9	79	2

Brian Carpenter

Year	Team		No	Yds	Avg	Lg	TD
1983	WAS	N	1	2	2.0	2	0
1984	BUF	N	3	11	3.7	11	0
Career			4	13	3.3	11	0

Lew Carpenter

Year	Team		No	Yds	Avg	Lg	TD
1953	DET	N	1	73	73.0	73t	1

Ronnie Carpenter

Year	Team		No	Yds	Avg	Lg	TD
1964	SD	A	1	29	29.0	29	0

Ed Carr

Year	Team		No	Yds	Avg	Lg	TD
1947	SF	AA	2	59	29.5		0
1948			7	144	20.6	56	1
1949			7	87	12.4		1
Career			16	290	18.1	56	2

Freddie Carr

Year	Team		No	Yds	Avg	Lg	TD
1970	GB	N	2	45	22.5	28	0
1974			1	0	0.0	0	0
1975			3	28	9.3	21	0
1976			1	10	10.0	10t	1
1977			1	15	15.0	15	0
Career			8	98	12.3	28	1

Gregg Carr

Year	Team		No	Yds	Avg	Lg	TD
1988	PIT	N	1	27	27.0	27	0

Henry Carr

Year	Team		No	Yds	Avg	Lg	TD
1965	NYG	N	2	19	9.5	19	0
1966			4	110	27.5	101t	1
1967			1	13	13.0	13	0
Career			7	142	20.3	101t	1

Jimmy Carr

Year	Team		No	Yds	Avg	Lg	TD
1959	PHI	N	5	65	13.0	12	0
1960			2	4	2.0	4	0
1961			2	20	10.0	20	0
1962			3	59	19.7	25	0
1963			1	25	25.0	25	0
1964	WAS	N	2	13	6.5	13	0
Career			15	186	12.4	25	0

Paul Carr

Year	Team		No	Yds	Avg	Lg	TD
1955	SF	N	1	11	11.0	11	0
1956			2	18	9.0	11	0
Career			3	29	9.7	11	0

Alphonso Carreker

Year	Team		No	Yds	Avg	Lg	TD
1987	GB	N	1	6	6.0	6	0

Mark Carrier

Year	Team		No	Yds	Avg	Lg	TD
1990	CHI	N	10	39	3.9	14	0
1991			2	54	27.0	39	0
1993			4	94	23.5	34t	1
1994			2	10	5.0	7	0
1996			2	0	0.0	0	0
Career			20	197	9.8	39	1
Playoffs			1	0	0.0		0

Darren Carrington

Year	Team		No	Yds	Avg	Lg	TD
1989	DEN	N	1	2	2.0	2	0
1991	SD	N	3	30	10.0	19	0
1992			6	152	25.3	69	1
1993			7	104	14.9	28	0
1994			3	51	17.0	32	0
1995	JAC	N	1	17	17.0	17	0
1996	OAK	N	1	21	21.0	21	0
Career			22	377	17.1	69	1
Playoffs			1	40	40.0		0

Russ Carroccio

Year	Team		No	Yds	Avg	Lg	TD
1955	NYG	N	1	7	7.0	7	0

Jim Carroll

Year	Team		No	Yds	Avg	Lg	TD
1965	NYG	N	1	3	3.0	3	0
1966	WAS	N	1	36	36.0	36	0
1967			1	0	0.0	0	0
Career			3	39	13.0	36	0

Vic Carroll

Year	Team		No	Yds	Avg	Lg	TD
1936	BOS	N					1
1941	WAS	N	2	38	19.0	30	1
1944	NYG	N	1	8	8.0	8	0
1947			1	31	31.0	31	0
Career			4	77	19.3	31	2

Harry Carson

Year	Team		No	Yds	Avg	Lg	TD
1978	NYG	N	3	86	28.7	42	0
1979			3	28	9.3	14	0
1982			1	6	6.0	6	0
1984			1	6	6.0	6	0
1986			1	20	20.0	20	0
1988			2	66	33.0	66	0
Career			11	212	19.3	66	0
Playoffs			1	14	14.0		1

Carl Carter

Year	Team		No	Yds	Avg	Lg	TD
1986	STL	N	2	12	6.0	11	0
1987			1	0	0.0	0	0
1988	PHX	N	3	0	0.0	0	0
1989			1	0	0.0	0	0

Carl Carter *continued*

Year	Team		No	Yds	Avg	Lg	TD
1991	TB	N	1	4	4.0	4	0
Career			8	16	2.0	11	0

Dale Carter

Year	Team		No	Yds	Avg	Lg	TD
1992	KC	N	7	65	9.3	36t	1
1993			1	0	0.0	0	0
1994			2	24	12.0	24	0
1995			4	45	11.3	29	0
1996			3	17	5.7	17	0
Career			17	151	8.9	36t	1

Jim Carter

Year	Team		No	Yds	Avg	Lg	TD
1971	GB	N	1	16	16.0	16	0
1972			1	0	0.0	0	0
1973			3	44	14.7	42t	1
1974			1	0	0.0	0	0
Career			6	60	10.0	42t	1

Marty Carter

Year	Team		No	Yds	Avg	Lg	TD
1991	TB	N	1	5	5.0	5	0
1992			3	1	0.3	1	0
1993			1	0	0.0	0	0
1995	CHI	N	2	20	10.0	15	0
1996			3	34	11.3	29	0
Career			10	60	6.0	29	0

Michael Carter

Year	Team		No	Yds	Avg	Lg	TD
1988	SF	N	1	0	0.0	0	0
Playoffs			1	61	61.0		1

M.L. Carter

Year	Team		No	Yds	Avg	Lg	TD
1979	KC	N	3	33	11.0	20	0

Russell Carter

Year	Team		No	Yds	Avg	Lg	TD
1984	NYJ	N	4	26	6.5	19	0
Playoffs			2	12	6.0		0

Tom Carter

Year	Team		No	Yds	Avg	Lg	TD
1993	WAS	N	6	54	9.0	29	0
1994			3	58	19.3	40	0
1995			4	116	29.0	51t	1
1996			5	24	4.8	24	0
Career			18	252	14.0	51t	1

Larry Carwell

Year	Team		No	Yds	Avg	Lg	TD
1967	HOU	A	0	31		L31	0
1968			4	81	20.3	41	1
1969	BOS	A	4	114	28.5	38	0
1971	NE	N	5	72	14.4	53t	1
1972			1	0	0.0	0	0
Career			14	298	21.3	53t	2

Ken Casanega

Year	Team		No	Yds	Avg	Lg	TD
1946	SF	AA	8	146	18.3		0

Tommy Casanova

Year	Team		No	Yds	Avg	Lg	TD
1972	CIN	N	5	108	21.6	33	0
1973			4	33	8.3	16	0
1974			2	26	13.0	26	0
1976			5	109	21.8	33t	2
1977			1	0	0.0	0	0
Career			17	276	16.2	33t	2
Playoffs			1	0	0.0		0

Ernie Case

Year	Team		No	Yds	Avg	Lg	TD
1947	BAL	AA	2	56	28.0		0

Scott Case

Year	Team		No	Yds	Avg	Lg	TD
1985	ATL	N	4	78	19.5	47	0
1986			4	41	10.3	41	0
1987			1	12	12.0	12	0
1988			10	47	4.7	12	0
1989			2	13	6.5	13	0
1990			3	38	12.7	36t	0
1991			2	23	11.5	17	0
1992			2	0	0.0	0	0
1993			0	3		L3	0
1994			2	12	6.0	12	0
Career			30	267	8.9	47	1

John Cash

Year	Team		No	Yds	Avg	Lg	TD
1962	DEN	A	1	5	5.0	5	0

Year	Team		No	Yds	Avg	Lg	TD

Jim Cason

Year	Team		No	Yds	Avg	Lg	TD
1948	SF	AA	5	46	9.2		0
1949			9	152	16.9		0
1950	SF	N	1	22	22.0	22	0
1951			8	147	18.4	65t	1
1952			2	4	2.0	4	0
1955	LA	N	5	41	8.2	25t	1
1956			4	63	15.8	29	0
Career			34	475	14.0	65t	2

Wendell Cason

Year	Team		No	Yds	Avg	Lg	TD
1985	ATL	N	3	30	10.0	22	0
1986			1	10	10.0	10	0
Career			4	40	10.0	22	0

Tom Cassese

Year	Team		No	Yds	Avg	Lg	TD
1967	DEN	A	1	24	24.0	24	0

Jesse Castete

Year	Team		No	Yds	Avg	Lg	TD
1956	CHIB	N	2	26	13.0	26	0

Jim Castiglia

Year	Team		No	Yds	Avg	Lg	TD
1941	PHI	N	1	0	0.0	0	0

Jeremiah Castille

Year	Team		No	Yds	Avg	Lg	TD
1983	TB	N	1	69	69.0	69t	1
1984			3	38	12.7	30	0
1985			7	49	7.0	20	0
1988	DEN	N	3	51	17.0	33	0
Career			14	207	14.8	69t	1
Playoffs			1	0	0.0		0

Sam Cathcart

Year	Team		No	Yds	Avg	Lg	TD
1949	SF	AA	1	0	0.0	0	0
1950	SF	N	3	58	19.3	19	0
1952			3	64	21.3	30	0
Career			7	122	17.4	30	0

Tom Catlin

Year	Team		No	Yds	Avg	Lg	TD
1953	CLE	N	1	16	16.0	16	0
1954			1	6	6.0	6	0
Career			2	22	11.0	16	0

Daryl Cato

Year	Team		No	Yds	Avg	Lg	TD
1946	MIA	AA	1	29	29.0	29	0

Ronnie Caveness

Year	Team		No	Yds	Avg	Lg	TD
1966	HOU	A	1	6	6.0	6	0

Grady Cavness

Year	Team		No	Yds	Avg	Lg	TD
1969	DEN	A	2	30	15.0	29	0

John Cavosie

Year	Team		No	Yds	Avg	Lg	TD
1932	POR	N					1

Les Caywood

Year	Team		No	Yds	Avg	Lg	TD
1930	NYG	N					1

Chuck Cecil

Year	Team		No	Yds	Avg	Lg	TD
1988	GB	N	4	56	14.0	33	0
1989			1	16	16.0	16	0
1990			1	0	0.0	0	0
1991			3	76	25.3	32	0
1992			4	52	13.0	29	0
1995	HOU	N	3	35	11.7	20t	1
Career			16	235	14.7	33	1

Tony Cemore

Year	Team		No	Yds	Avg	Lg	TD
1941	PHI	N	1	6	6.0	6	0

Guy Chamberlin

Year	Team		No	Yds	Avg	Lg	TD
1922	CAN	N					2

Rusty Chambers

Year	Team		No	Yds	Avg	Lg	TD
1978	MIA	N	1	49	49.0	49	0
1979			1	4	4.0	4	0
Career			2	53	26.5	49	0

Wally Chambers

Year	Team		No	Yds	Avg	Lg	TD
1976	CHI	N	1	8	8.0	8	0

Edgar Chandler

Year	Team		No	Yds	Avg	Lg	TD
1970	BUF	N	1	59	59.0	59t	1
1971			1	13	13.0	13	0
Career			2	72	36.0	59t	1

Clarence Chapman

Year	Team		No	Yds	Avg	Lg	TD
1977	NO	N	1	16	16.0	16	0
1978			2	-4	-2.0	0	0
1979			2	12	6.0	12	0
Career			5	24	4.8	16	0

John Charles

Year	Team		No	Yds	Avg	Lg	TD
1967	BOS	A	1	35	35.0	35t	1
1968			1	29	29.0	29	0
1969			4	46	11.5	25t	1
1970	MIN	N	1	25	25.0	25	0
1971	HOU	N	5	94	18.8	51	0
1972			2	6	3.0	6	0
1973			2	74	37.0	39	0
Career			16	309	19.3	51	2

Mike Charles

Year	Team		No	Yds	Avg	Lg	TD
1986	MIA	N	1	2	2.0	2	0

Carl Charon

Year	Team		No	Yds	Avg	Lg	TD
1962	BUF	A	7	131	18.7	25	1

Lloyd Cheatham

Year	Team		No	Yds	Avg	Lg	TD
1942	CHIC	N	1	4	4.0	4	0
1946	NY	AA	1	3	3.0	3	0
Career			2	7	3.5	4	0

Deron Cherry

Year	Team		No	Yds	Avg	Lg	TD
1981	KC	N	1	4	4.0	4	0
1983			7	100	14.3	41	0
1984			7	140	20.0	67	0
1985			7	87	12.4	47t	1
1986			9	150	16.7	49	0
1987			3	58	19.3	30	0
1988			7	51	7.3	24	0
1989			2	27	13.5	27	0
1990			3	40	13.3	21	0
1991			4	31	7.8	16	0
Career			50	688	13.8	67	1
Playoffs			3	47	15.7		0

Raphel Cherry

Year	Team		No	Yds	Avg	Lg	TD
1985	WAS	N	2	29	14.5	22	0
1987	DET	N	1	2	2.0	2	0
1988			2	0	0.0	0	0
Career			5	31	6.2	22	0

Chuck Cherundolo

Year	Team		No	Yds	Avg	Lg	TD
1941	PIT	N	1	13	13.0	13	0
1942			1	3	3.0	3	0
1945			1	17	17.0	17	0
1946			1	0	0.0	0	0
Career			4	33	8.3	17	0

Al Chesley

Year	Team		No	Yds	Avg	Lg	TD
1979	PHI	N	2	39	19.5	25	0
1981			2	66	33.0	35	0
Career			4	105	26.3	35	0

George Cheverko

Year	Team		No	Yds	Avg	Lg	TD
1947	NYG	N	3	54	18.0	27	0
1948	WAS-NYG	N	6	168	28.0	61	0
Career			9	222	24.7	61	0

Jim Cheyunski

Year	Team		No	Yds	Avg	Lg	TD
1968	BOS	A	1	21	21.0	21	0
1969			1	37	37.0	37	0
1971	NE	N	1	24	24.0	24	0
1973	BUF	N	3	31	10.3	31	0
1974			1	6	6.0	6	0
1975	BAL	N	2	8	4.0	6	0
Career			9	127	14.1	37	0

John Chickerneo

Year	Team		No	Yds	Avg	Lg	TD
1942	NYG	N	1	2	2.0	2	0

Clarence Childs

Year	Team		No	Yds	Avg	Lg	TD
1966	NYG	N	2	32	16.0	29	0

Bill Chipley

Year	Team		No	Yds	Avg	Lg	TD
1948	BOS	N	3	52	17.3	38t	1

Andy Chisick

Year	Team		No	Yds	Avg	Lg	TD
1941	CHIC	N	1	7	7.0	7	0

Frank Christensen

Year	Team		No	Yds	Avg	Lg	TD
Playoffs			1	28	28.0		0

Jack Christiansen

Year	Team		No	Yds	Avg	Lg	TD
1951	DET	N	2	53	26.5	53	0
1952			2	47	23.5	32	0
1953			12	238	19.8	92t	1
1954			8	84	10.5	30t	1
1955			3	49	16.3	29	0
1956			8	109	13.6	33	0
1957			10	137	13.7	52	1
1958			1	0	0.0	0	0
Career			46	717	15.6	92t	3
Playoffs			1	0	0.0		0

Herb Christopher

Year	Team		No	Yds	Avg	Lg	TD
1979	KC	N	2	1	0.5	1	0
1980			2	25	12.5	25	0
Career			4	26	6.5	25	0

Jim Christopherson

Year	Team		No	Yds	Avg	Lg	TD
1962	MIN	N	1	32	32.0	32	0

Earl Christy

Year	Team		No	Yds	Avg	Lg	TD
1968	NY	A	1	16	16.0	16	0

Ricky Churchman

Year	Team		No	Yds	Avg	Lg	TD
1980	SF	N	4	7	1.8	7	0

Mike Ciccolella

Year	Team		No	Yds	Avg	Lg	TD
1968	NYG	N	1	7	7.0	7	0

Bob Cifers

Year	Team		No	Yds	Avg	Lg	TD
1947	PIT	N	1	32	32.0	32	0

Ed Cifers

Year	Team		No	Yds	Avg	Lg	TD
1947	CHIB	N	1	20	20.0	20t	1

Al Clark

Year	Team		No	Yds	Avg	Lg	TD
1972	LA	N	1	18	18.0	18	0
1973			1	5	5.0	5	0
1976	PHI	N	1	0	0.0	0	0
Career			3	23	7.7	18	0

Bret Clark

Year	Team		No	Yds	Avg	Lg	TD
1986	ATL	N	5	94	18.8	34	0
1988			4	40	10.0	21	0
Career			9	134	14.9	34	0

Bruce Clark

Year	Team		No	Yds	Avg	Lg	TD
1984	NO	N	1	9	9.0	9	0

Don Clark

Year	Team		No	Yds	Avg	Lg	TD
1948	SF	AA	1	12	12.0	12	0
1949			1	16	16.0	16	0
Career			2	28	14.0	16	0

Ernie Clark

Year	Team		No	Yds	Avg	Lg	TD
1965	DET	N	1	7	7.0	7	0
1966			1	7	7.0	7	0
1967			1	0	0.0	0	0
1968	STL	N	1	15	15.0	15	0
Career			4	29	7.3	15	0

Harry Clark

Year	Team		No	Yds	Avg	Lg	TD
1940	CHIB	N	4	62	15.5		1
1941			2	62	31.0	35	0
1943			5	32	6.4	22	0
1946	LA	AA	2	7	3.5		0
Career			13	163	12.5	35	1

Herman Clark

Year	Team		No	Yds	Avg	Lg	TD
1952	CHIB	N	1	8	8.0	8	0

Kevin Clark

Year	Team		No	Yds	Avg	Lg	TD
1987	DEN	N	3	105	35.0	50	0

Mario Clark

Year	Team		No	Yds	Avg	Lg	TD
1976	BUF	N	2	21	10.5	21	0
1977			7	151	21.6	43	0
1978			5	29	5.8	29	0
1979			5	95	19.0	36	0
1980			1	0	0.0	0	0
1981			5	142	28.4	53	0

Mario Clark *continued*

Year	Team		No	Yds	Avg	Lg	TD
1984	SF	N	1	0	0.0	0	0
Career			26	438	16.8	53	0

Phil Clark

Year	Team		No	Yds	Avg	Lg	TD
1967	DAL	N	1	6	6.0	6	0
1969			2	2	1.0	2	0
1970	CHI	N	1	32	32.0	32	0
Career			4	40	10.0	32	0

Steve Clark

Year	Team		No	Yds	Avg	Lg	TD
1987	BUF	N	1	23	23.0	23	0

Vinnie Clark

Year	Team		No	Yds	Avg	Lg	TD
1991	GB	N	2	42	21.0	22	0
1992			2	70	35.0	43	0
1993	ATL	N	2	59	29.5	38	0
1994	ATL-NO	N	5	149	29.8	74	0
1995	JAC	N	1	0	0.0	0	0
1996			1	15	15.0	15	0
Career			13	335	25.8	74	0

Willie Clark

Year	Team		No	Yds	Avg	Lg	TD
1995	SD	N	2	14	7.0	13	0
1996			2	83	41.5	83t	1
Career			4	97	24.3	83t	1

Hagood Clarke

Year	Team		No	Yds	Avg	Lg	TD
1965	BUF	A	7	60	8.6	40	0
1966			5	118	23.6	66	1
Career			12	178	14.8	66	1

Stu Clarkson

Year	Team		No	Yds	Avg	Lg	TD
1946	CHIB	N	3	79	26.3	60t	1
1947			2	10	5.0	10	0
1948			2	14	7.0	13	0
1949			2	9	4.5	11	0
1951			1	0	0.0	0	0
Career			10	112	11.2	60t	1

Bob Clasby

Year	Team		No	Yds	Avg	Lg	TD
1988	PHX	N	1	7	7.0	7	0

Corwin Clatt

Year	Team		No	Yds	Avg	Lg	TD
1948	CHIC	N	1	20	20.0	20	0
1949			2	39	19.5	39	0
Career			3	59	19.7	39	0

Billy Clay

Year	Team		No	Yds	Avg	Lg	TD
1966	WAS	N	1	0	0.0	0	0

Randy Clay

Year	Team		No	Yds	Avg	Lg	TD
1950	NYG	N	2	42	21.0	32	0
1953			2	22	11.0	22	0
Career			4	64	16.0	32	0

Walt Clay

Year	Team		No	Yds	Avg	Lg	TD
1946	CHI	AA	6	72	12.0		0
1947	LA	AA	1	20	20.0	20	0
1948			2	33	16.5		0
Career			9	125	13.9	20	0

Willie Clay

Year	Team		No	Yds	Avg	Lg	TD
1994	DET	N	3	54	18.0	28t	1
1995			8	**173**	21.6	39	0
1996	NE	N	4	50	12.5	35	0
Career			15	277	18.5	39	1
Playoffs			2	14	7.0		0

Raymond Clayborn

Year	Team		No	Yds	Avg	Lg	TD
1978	NE	N	4	72	18.0	44	0
1979			5	56	11.2	27	0
1980			5	87	17.4	29	0
1981			2	39	19.5	39	0
1982			1	26	26.0	26	0
1984			3	102	34.0	85	0
1985			6	80	13.3	38	1
1986			3	4	1.3	4	0
1987			2	24	12.0	24	0
1988			4	65	16.3	31	0
1989			1	0	0.0	0	0
Career			36	555	15.4	85	1
Playoffs			1	0	0.0		0

Harvey Clayton

Year	Team		No	Yds	Avg	Lg	TD
1983	PIT	N	1	70	70.0	70t	1
1984			1	0	0.0	0	0
1986			3	18	6.0	14	0
Career			5	88	17.6	70t	1

Craig Clemons

Year	Team		No	Yds	Avg	Lg	TD
1973	CHI	N	2	30	15.0	30	0
1974			4	84	21.0	37	0
1975			2	109	54.5	76t	1
1976			1	28	28.0	28	0
Career			9	251	27.9	76t	1

Kyle Clifton

Year	Team		No	Yds	Avg	Lg	TD
1984	NYJ	N	1	0	0.0	0	0
1985			3	10	3.3	10	0
1986			2	8	4.0	7	0
1990			3	49	16.3	39	0
1991			1	3	3.0	3	0
1992			1	1	1.0	1	0
1993			1	3	3.0	3	0
Career			12	74	6.2	39	0

Doug Cline

Year	Team		No	Yds	Avg	Lg	TD
1961	HOU	A	1	24	24.0	24	0
1962			2	14	7.0	14	0
1963			3	16	5.3	9	0
1966			1	23	23.0	23	0
Career			7	77	11.0	24	0
Playoffs			1	7	7.0		0

Tony Cline

Year	Team		No	Yds	Avg	Lg	TD
1970	OAK	N	1	0	0.0	0	0
1971			1	0	0.0	0	0
1972			1	11	11.0	11	0
Career			3	11	3.7	11	0

Dextor Clinkscale

Year	Team		No	Yds	Avg	Lg	TD
1982	DAL	N	1	0	0.0	0	0
1983			2	68	34.0	68t	1
1984			3	32	10.7	23	0
1985			3	16	5.3	11	0
Career			9	116	12.9	68t	1
Playoffs			2	13	6.5		0

Jack Cloud

Year	Team		No	Yds	Avg	Lg	TD
1953	WAS	N	2	39	19.5	28t	1

Ray Coates

Year	Team		No	Yds	Avg	Lg	TD
1949	NYG	N	1	11	11.0	11	0

Garry Cobb

Year	Team		No	Yds	Avg	Lg	TD
1981	DET	N	3	32	10.7	17	0
1982			2	12	6.0	12	0
1983			4	19	4.8	13	0
1986	PHI	N	1	3	3.0	3	0
Career			10	66	6.6	17	0

Marvin Cobb

Year	Team		No	Yds	Avg	Lg	TD
1975	CIN	N	4	116	29.0	52t	1
1976			3	55	18.3	28	0
1977			2	37	18.5	34	0
1978			1	13	13.0	13	0
1979			3	19	6.3	14	0
Career			13	240	18.5	52t	1

Red Cochran

Year	Team		No	Yds	Avg	Lg	TD
1947	CHIC	N	8	122	15.3	39	0
1948			7	111	15.9	32	0
Career			15	233	15.5	39	0
Playoffs			2	20	10.0		0

Sherman Cocroft

Year	Team		No	Yds	Avg	Lg	TD
1985	KC	N	3	27	9.0	27	0
1986			3	32	10.7	13	0
1988	BUF	N	1	17	17.0	17	0
Career			7	76	10.9	27	0

Ed Cody

Year	Team		No	Yds	Avg	Lg	TD
1949	CHIB	N	2	50	25.0	38t	1

Mike Cofer

Year	Team		No	Yds	Avg	Lg	TD
1990	DET	N	1	0	0.0	0	0

Ken Coffey

Year	Team		No	Yds	Avg	Lg	TD
1983	WAS	N	4	62	15.5	29	0
1984			1	15	15.0	15	0
1986			2	0	0.0	0	0
Career			7	77	11.0	29	0
Playoffs			1	0	0.0		0

Tim Cofield

Year	Team		No	Yds	Avg	Lg	TD
1988	KC	N	1	0	0.0	0	0

Will Cokeley

Year	Team		No	Yds	Avg	Lg	TD
1987	BUF	N	1	4	4.0	4	0

Danny Colbert

Year	Team		No	Yds	Avg	Lg	TD
1975	SD	N	2	10	5.0	10	0

Larry Cole

Year	Team		No	Yds	Avg	Lg	TD
1968	DAL	N	1	5	5.0	5t	1
1969			1	41	41.0	41t	1
1978			1	13	13.0	13	0
1980			1	43	43.0	43t	1
Career			4	102	25.5	43t	3

Robin Cole

Year	Team		No	Yds	Avg	Lg	TD
1980	PIT	N	1	34	34.0	34	0
1981			1	29	29.0	29	0
1984			1	12	12.0	12	0
1985			1	4	4.0	4	0
1987			1	0	0.0	0	0
Career			5	79	15.8	34	0

Tom Colella

Year	Team		No	Yds	Avg	Lg	TD
1942	DET	N	1	10	10.0	10	0
1944	CLE	N	4	53	13.3	19	0
1946	CLE	AA	10	110	11.0		0
1947			6	130	21.7		1
1948			2	34	17.0		0
1949	BUF	AA	3	49	16.3		0
Career			26	386	14.8	19	1
Playoffs			2	14	7.0		0

Al Coleman

Year	Team		No	Yds	Avg	Lg	TD
1971	CIN	N	1	15	15.0	15	0

Eric Coleman

Year	Team		No	Yds	Avg	Lg	TD
1989	NE	N	1	1	1.0	1	0

Herb Coleman

Year	Team		No	Yds	Avg	Lg	TD
1946	CHI	AA	1	25	25.0	25	0

Leonard Coleman

Year	Team		No	Yds	Avg	Lg	TD
1986	IND	N	4	36	9.0	31	0
1988	SD	N	2	0	0.0	0	0
Career			6	36	6.0	31	0

Marcus Coleman

Year	Team		No	Yds	Avg	Lg	TD
1996	NYJ	N	1	23	23.0	23	0

Monte Coleman

Year	Team		No	Yds	Avg	Lg	TD
1979	WAS	N	1	13	13.0	13	0
1980			3	92	30.7	41	0
1981			3	52	17.3	52t	1
1984			1	49	49.0	49t	1
1987			2	53	26.5	28	0
1988			1	11	11.0	11	0
1989			2	24	12.0	24t	0
1990			1	0	0.0	0	0
1991			1	0	0.0	0	0
1993			2	27	13.5	14	0
Career			17	321	18.9	52t	3
Playoffs			2	15	7.5		0

Tim Collier

Year	Team		No	Yds	Avg	Lg	TD
1976	KC	N	2	10	5.0	10	0
1977			2	134	67.0	100t	0
1978			3	38	12.7	23	0
1979			2	45	22.5	40	0
1980	STL	N	2	22	11.0	22	0
1981			1	17	17.0	17	0
1983	SF	N	3	32	10.7	32t	1
Career			15	298	19.9	100t	2

Andre Collins

Year	Team		No	Yds	Avg	Lg	TD
1991	WAS	N	2	33	16.5	18	1

Year	Team		No	Yds	Avg	Lg	TD

Andre Collins *continued*

Year	Team		No	Yds	Avg	Lg	TD
1992			1	59	59.0	59	0
1993			1	5	5.0	5	0
1994			4	150	37.5	92t	2
1995	CIN	N	2	3	1.5	3	0
Career			10	250	25.0	92t	3

Jim Collins

Year	Team		No	Yds	Avg	Lg	TD
1983	LARM	N	2	46	23.0	29	0
1984			2	43	21.5	40	0
1985			2	8	4.0	4	0
Career			6	97	16.2	40	0

Kirk Collins

Year	Team		No	Yds	Avg	Lg	TD
1983	LARM	N	5	113	22.6	58	0
Playoffs			1	12	12.0		0

Mark Collins

Year	Team		No	Yds	Avg	Lg	TD
1986	NYG	N	1	0	0.0	0	0
1987			2	28	14.0	28	0
1988			1	13	13.0	13	0
1989			2	12	6.0	12	0
1990			2	0	0.0	0	0
1991			4	77	19.3	41	0
1992			1	0	0.0	0	0
1993			4	77	19.3	50t	1
1994	KC	N	2	83	41.5	78t	1
1995			1	8	8.0	8	0
1996			6	45	7.5	23	0
Career			26	343	13.2	78t	2
Playoffs			3	11	3.7		0

Rip Collins

Year	Team		No	Yds	Avg	Lg	TD
1949	CHI	AA	1	0	0.0	0	0
1950	BAL	N	1	7	7.0	7	0
1951	GB	N	2	0	0.0	0	0
Career			4	7	1.8	7	0

Todd Collins

Year	Team		No	Yds	Avg	Lg	TD
1993	NE	N	1	8	8.0	8	0
1996			1	7	7.0	7	0
Career			2	15	7.5	8	0

Wayne Colman

Year	Team		No	Yds	Avg	Lg	TD
1969	PHI	N	1	11	11.0	11	0
1971	NO	N	1	0	0.0	0	0
1974			1	17	17.0	17	0
Career			3	28	9.3	17	0

Mickey Colmer

Year	Team		No	Yds	Avg	Lg	TD
1946	BKN	AA	1	0	0.0	0	0

Don Colo

Year	Team		No	Yds	Avg	Lg	TD
1952	DAL	N	1	11	11.0	11	0
1956	CLE	N	1	0	0.0	0	0
Career			2	11	5.5	11	0

Harry Colon

Year	Team		No	Yds	Avg	Lg	TD
1993	DET	N	2	28	14.0	27	0
1994			1	3	3.0	3	0
1995	JAC	N	3	46	15.3	41	0
Career			6	77	12.8	41	0

Neal Colzie

Year	Team		No	Yds	Avg	Lg	TD
1975	OAK	N	4	38	9.5	38	0
1977			3	13	4.3	13	0
1978			3	62	20.7	28	0
1979	MIA	N	5	86	17.2	56	0
1980	TB	N	1	39	39.0	39	0
1981			6	110	18.3	82t	1
1982			3	64	21.3	51	0
Career			25	412	16.5	82t	1

Darren Comeaux

Year	Team		No	Yds	Avg	Lg	TD
1984	DEN	N	1	5	5.0	5	0
1988	SEA	N	1	18	18.0	18	0
1989			1	0	0.0	0	0
Career			3	23	7.7	18	0

Irv Comp

Year	Team		No	Yds	Avg	Lg	TD
1943	GB	N	10	149	14.9	35	1
1944			6	54	9.0	43	0
1945			2	67	33.5	54t	1

Irv Comp *continued*

Year	Team		No	Yds	Avg	Lg	TD
1946			2	38	19.0	21	0
1947			6	65	10.8	30	0
1948			5	86	17.2	28	0
1949			3	24	8.0	14	0
Career			34	483	14.2	54t	2

Tony Compagno

Year	Team		No	Yds	Avg	Lg	TD
1946	PIT	N	1	40	40.0	40	0
1947			4	163	40.8	64t	2
1948			7	179	25.6	82t	1
Career			12	382	31.8	82t	3

Dick Compton

Year	Team		No	Yds	Avg	Lg	TD
1963	DET	N	1	23	23.0	23	0

Merl Condit

Year	Team		No	Yds	Avg	Lg	TD
1941	BKN	N	3	15	5.0	5	0
1942			6	**117**	19.5	40	1
1943			1	0	0.0	0	0
Career			10	132	13.2	40	1

Bill Conkright

Year	Team		No	Yds	Avg	Lg	TD
1941	CLE	N	1	0	0.0	0	0
1942			2	10	5.0	9	0
1943	BKN	N	1	12	12.0	12	0
Career			4	22	5.5	12	0

Shane Conlan

Year	Team		No	Yds	Avg	Lg	TD
1988	BUF	N	1	0	0.0	0	0
1989			1	0	0.0	0	0
1992			1	7	7.0	7	0
1993	LARM	N	1	28	28.0	28	0
1995	STL	N	1	1	1.0	1	0
Career			5	36	7.2	28	0

Gerry Conlee

Year	Team		No	Yds	Avg	Lg	TD
1943	DET	N	1	2	2.0	2	0

Dick Conn

Year	Team		No	Yds	Avg	Lg	TD
1978	NE	N	1	24	24.0	24	0

Darion Conner

Year	Team		No	Yds	Avg	Lg	TD
1994	NO	N	1	56	56.0	56	0

Dan Conners

Year	Team		No	Yds	Avg	Lg	TD
1966	OAK	A	2	55	27.5	32	1
1967			3	42	14.0	30t	1
1968			2	5	2.5	5	0
1969			1	75	75.0	75t	1
1971	OAK	N	3	36	12.0	18	0
1972			1	0	0.0	0	0
1974			3	19	6.3	18	0
Career			15	232	15.5	75t	3
Playoffs			1	5	5.0		0

George Connor

Year	Team		No	Yds	Avg	Lg	TD
1950	CHIB	N	1	8	8.0	8	0
1951			2	21	10.5	11	0
1952			2	31	15.5	22	0
1954			1	6	6.0	6	0
1955			1	0	0.0	0	0
Career			7	66	9.4	22	0

Bobby JoeConrad

Year	Team		No	Yds	Avg	Lg	TD
1958	CHIC	N	4	46	11.5	31	0

Enio Conti

Year	Team		No	Yds	Avg	Lg	TD
1943	P-P	N	1	0	0.0	0	0

Fred Cook

Year	Team		No	Yds	Avg	Lg	TD
1975	BAL	N	1	8	8.0	8	0
1976			1	1	1.0	1	0
Career			2	9	4.5	8	0

Ted Cook

Year	Team		No	Yds	Avg	Lg	TD
1947	DET	N	2	0	0.0	0	0
1948	GB	N	6	81	13.5	27	0
1949			5	52	10.4	30	0
Career			13	133	10.2	30	0

Toi Cook

Year	Team		No	Yds	Avg	Lg	TD
1988	NO	N	1	0	0.0	0	0

Toi Cook *continued*

Year	Team		No	Yds	Avg	Lg	TD
1989			3	81	27.0	63t	1
1990			2	55	27.5	50	0
1991			3	54	18.0	22	0
1992			6	90	15.0	48t	1
1993			1	0	0.0	0	0
1994	SF	N	1	18	18.0	18	0
1996	CAR	N	3	28	9.3	22	0
Career			20	326	16.3	63t	2
Playoffs			1	1	1.0		0

Ed Cooke

Year	Team		No	Yds	Avg	Lg	TD
1961	NY	A	3	46	15.3	43	0
1962			1	20	20.0	20	0
1965	DEN	A	3	36	12.0	28	0
Career			7	102	14.6	43	0

Johnie Cooks

Year	Team		No	Yds	Avg	Lg	TD
1983	BAL	N	1	15	15.0	15	0
1985	IND	N	1	7	7.0	7	0
1986			1	1	1.0	1	0
1987			1	2	2.0	2	0
Career			4	25	6.3	15	0

Evan Cooper

Year	Team		No	Yds	Avg	Lg	TD
1985	PHI	N	2	13	6.5	13	0
1986			3	20	6.7	20	0
1987			2	0	0.0	0	0
1989	ATL	N	4	54	13.5	38	0
Career			11	87	7.9	38	0

Louis Cooper

Year	Team		No	Yds	Avg	Lg	TD
1987	KC	N	1	0	0.0	0	0

Danny Copeland

Year	Team		No	Yds	Avg	Lg	TD
1991	WAS	N	1	0	0.0	0	0
1993			1	0	0.0	0	0
Career			2	0	0.0	0	0
Playoffs			1	19	19.0		0

George Corbett

Year	Team		No	Yds	Avg	Lg	TD
1938	CHIB	N					1

Tom Corbo

Year	Team		No	Yds	Avg	Lg	TD
1944	CLE	N	1	0	0.0	0	0

Lou Cordileone

Year	Team		No	Yds	Avg	Lg	TD
1968	NO	N	1	7	7.0	7	0

Walt Corey

Year	Team		No	Yds	Avg	Lg	TD
1960	DAL	A	3	20	6.7		0
1964	KC	A	1	17	17.0	17	0
Career			4	37	9.3	17	0

Bert Corley

Year	Team		No	Yds	Avg	Lg	TD
1947	BUF	AA	1	41	41.0	41	0

Charles Cornelius

Year	Team		No	Yds	Avg	Lg	TD
1978	MIA	N	1	21	21.0	21	0
1979	SF	N	3	54	18.0	54	0
Career			4	75	18.8	54	0

Frank Cornish

Year	Team		No	Yds	Avg	Lg	TD
1967	CHI	N	2	10	5.0	6	0

Kip Corrington

Year	Team		No	Yds	Avg	Lg	TD
1989	DEN	N	1	8	8.0	8	0
Playoffs			1	1	1.0		0

Quentin Coryatt

Year	Team		No	Yds	Avg	Lg	TD
1995	IND	N	1	6	6.0	6	0
Playoffs			1	10	10.0		0

Vince Costello

Year	Team		No	Yds	Avg	Lg	TD
1957	CLE	N	2	19	9.5	12	0
1959			0	14		L14	0
1962			3	40	13.3	22	0
1963			7	118	16.9	31	0
1964			2	21	10.5	20	0
1965			3	33	11.0	23	0
1966			1	0	0.0	0	0
1967	NYG	N	4	54	13.5	26	0
Career			22	299	13.6	31	0
Playoffs			2	11	5.5		0

Year	Team		No	Yds	Avg	Lg	TD

Ray Costict
| 1979 | NE | N | 1 | 22 | 22.0 | 22 | 0 |

Chad Cota
| 1996 | CAR | N | 5 | 63 | 12.6 | 35 | 0 |
| Playoffs | | | 1 | 49 | 49.0 | | 0 |

Mark Cotney
1976	TB	N	3	25	8.3	25	0
1977			1	0	0.0	0	0
1978			2	28	14.0	28	0
1979			1	0	0.0	0	0
1980			3	28	9.3	21	0
1983			2	1	0.5	1	0
1984			5	123	24.6	29	0
Career			17	205	12.1	29	0
Playoffs			1	50	50.0		0

Russ Cotton
| 1942 | PIT | N | 1 | 0 | 0.0 | 0 | 0 |

Gerry Courtney
| 1942 | BKN | N | 1 | 32 | 32.0 | 32 | 0 |

Matt Courtney
| 1987 | SF | N | 1 | 30 | 30.0 | 30 | 0 |

Tom Cousineau
1982	CLE	N	1	6	6.0	6	0
1983			4	47	11.8	15	0
1984			2	9	4.5	9	0
1985			1	0	0.0	0	0
1986	SF	N	1	18	18.0	18	0
1987			1	11	11.0	11	0
Career			10	91	9.1	18	0

Tony Covington
1991	TB	N	3	21	7.0	18	0
1994			1	38	38.0	38	0
Career			4	59	14.8	38	0

Bob Cowan
| 1949 | BAL | AA | 3 | 17 | 5.7 | | 0 |

Gerry Cowhig
1947	LA	N	1	0	0.0	0	0
1948			1	9	9.0	9	0
1949			4	62	15.5	26	1
Career			6	71	11.8	26	1

Billy Cox
1951	WAS	N	2	0	0.0	0	0
1952			3	43	14.3	36	0
Career			5	43	8.6	36	0

Bryan Cox
1992	MIA	N	1	0	0.0	0	0
1993			1	26	26.0	26	0
1995			1	12	12.0	12	0
Career			3	38	12.7	26	0
Playoffs			1	7	7.0		0

Ron Cox
| 1995 | CHI | N | 1 | 1 | 1.0 | 1 | 0 |

Claude Crabb
1962	WAS	N	6	30	5.0	13	0
1963			3	82	27.3	58t	1
1967	LA	N	1	23	23.0	23	0
Career			10	135	13.5	58t	1

Bob Crable
1983	NYJ	N	1	0	0.0	0	0
1986			1	26	26.0	26	0
1987			1	8	8.0	8	0
Career			3	34	11.3	26	0

Russ Craft
1946	PHI	N	3	105	35.0	49	0
1947			1	0	0.0	0	0
1949			1	17	17.0	17	0
1950			7	70	10.0	29	0
1951			2	61	30.5	26	0
1952			1	32	32.0	32t	1

Russ Craft *continued*
1953			4	46	11.5	27	0
1954	PIT	N	3	120	40.0	81t	2
Career			22	451	20.5	81t	3

Larry Craig
| 1944 | GB | N | 1 | 20 | 20.0 | 20 | 0 |

Neal Craig
1971	CIN	N	1	0	0.0	0	0
1972			2	76	38.0	63t	1
1973			2	52	26.0	30	0
1974	BUF	N	1	55	55.0	55t	1
1975	CLE	N	1	0	0.0	0	0
1976			1	8	8.0	8	0
Career			8	191	23.9	63t	2
Playoffs			1	45	45.0		1

Milt Crain
| 1944 | BOS | N | 1 | 0 | 0.0 | 0 | 0 |

Paul Crane
1969	NY	A	3	63	21.0	27	1
1971	NYJ	N	1	23	23.0	23	0
1972			1	4	4.0	4	0
Career			5	90	18.0	27	1

Eddie Crawford
| 1957 | NYG | N | 1 | 3 | 3.0 | 3 | 0 |

Bernie Crimmins
| 1945 | GB | N | 1 | 12 | 12.0 | 12 | 0 |

Hal Crisler
| 1948 | WAS | N | 2 | 52 | 26.0 | 26 | 0 |

Chuck Crist
1972	NYG	N	1	14	14.0	14	0
1973			2	6	3.0	6	0
1974			3	20	6.7	20	0
1975	NO	N	3	69	23.0	42	0
1976			1	20	20.0	20	0
1977			4	6	1.5	6	0
1978	SF	N	6	159	26.5	32	0
Career			20	294	14.7	42	0

Ray Crockett
1989	DET	N	1	5	5.0	5	0
1990			3	17	5.7	9	0
1991			6	141	23.5	96t	1
1992			4	50	12.5	35	0
1993			2	31	15.5	31	0
1994	DEN	N	2	6	3.0	6	0
1996			2	34	17.0	34	0
Career			20	284	14.2	96t	1

Mike Croel
1993	DEN	N	1	22	22.0	22t	1
1996	BAL	N	1	16	16.0	16	0
Career			2	38	19.0	22t	1

Abe Croft
| 1944 | CHIB | N | 1 | 19 | 19.0 | 19 | 0 |

Nolan Cromwell
1978	LA	N	1	31	31.0	31	0
1979			5	109	21.8	34	0
1980			8	140	17.5	34	1
1981			5	94	18.8	94	0
1982	LARM	N	3	33	11.0	21	0
1983			3	76	25.3	43t	1
1984			3	54	18.0	33t	1
1985			2	5	2.5	5	0
1986			5	101	20.2	80t	1
1987			2	28	14.0	28	0
Career			37	671	18.1	94	4
Playoffs			2	44	22.0		0

Pete Cronan
| 1978 | SEA | N | 2 | 15 | 7.5 | 12 | 0 |

Gene Cronin
| 1960 | DAL | N | 1 | 2 | 2.0 | 2 | 0 |

Ron Crosby
| 1980 | NYJ | N | 2 | 47 | 23.5 | 42 | 0 |

Irv Cross
1961	PHI	N	2	36	18.0	33	0
1962			5	46	9.2	22	0
1963			2	6	3.0	3	0
1964			3	109	36.3	94t	1
1965			3	1	0.3	1	0
1966	LA	N	1	60	60.0	60t	1
1967			2	0	0.0	0	0
1968			3	0	0.0	0	0
1969	PHI	N	1	0	0.0	0	0
Career			22	258	11.7	94t	2

Jeff Cross
| 1994 | MIA | N | 1 | 0 | 0.0 | 0 | 0 |

Jim Crotty
1960	WAS	N	1	0	0.0	0	0
1961	BUF	A	2	0	0.0	0	0
Career			3	0	0.0	0	0

David Croudip
1986	ATL	N	2	35	17.5	29	0
1987			2	40	20.0	40	0
Career			4	75	18.8	40	0

Lindon Crow
1955	CHIC	N	3	11	3.7	7	0
1956			11	170	15.5	42	0
1957			1	0	0.0	0	0
1958	NYG	N	3	40	13.3	34	0
1959			5	54	10.8	30t	0
1960			3	3	1.0	3	0
1961	LA	N	6	117	19.5	31	0
1962			5	100	20.0	65t	1
1964			1	23	23.0	23	0
Career			38	518	13.6	65t	2
Playoffs			3				

Wayne Crow
| 1960 | OAK | A | 4 | 50 | 12.5 | | 0 |

Paul Crowe
1948	SF	AA	5	69	13.8		1
1949	LA	AA	1	25	25.0	25	0
1951	NYY	N	3	15	5.0	9	0
Career			9	109	12.1	25	1

Joe Crowley
1944	BOS	N	1	5	5.0	5	0
1945			1	45	45.0	45	0
Career			2	50	25.0	45	0

Dwayne Crump
| 1974 | STL | N | 1 | 10 | 10.0 | 10 | 0 |

Tommy Crutcher
1965	GB	N	1	4	4.0	4	0
1966			1	15	15.0	15	0
1969	NYG	N	1	0	0.0	0	0
Career			3	19	6.3	15	0

Ward Cuff
1938	NYG	N					1
1941			4	152	38.0	43	0
1942			1	43	43.0	43	0
1943			3	6	2.0	4	0
1944			2	31	15.5	20	0
1945			1	13	13.0	13	0
Career			11	245	22.3	43	1
Playoffs			1	0	0.0		0

Curley Culp
| 1977 | HOU | N | 1 | 25 | 25.0 | 25 | 0 |

George Cumby
1981	GB	N	3	22	7.3	17	0
1982			1	4	4.0	4	0
1984			1	7	7.0	7	0
Career			5	33	6.6	17	0

Year	Team		No	Yds	Avg	Lg	TD

Ed Cummings

Year	Team		No	Yds	Avg	Lg	TD
1964	NY	A	1	2	2.0	2	0

Carl Cunningham

Year	Team		No	Yds	Avg	Lg	TD
1967	DEN	A	1	16	16.0	16	0
1968			1	3	3.0	3	0
1969			2	10	5.0	5	0
Career			4	29	7.3	16	0

Jay Cunningham

Year	Team		No	Yds	Avg	Lg	TD
1965	BOS	A	2	16	8.0	10	0
1967			1	54	54.0	54t	1
Career			3	70	23.3	54t	1

Tony Curcillo

Year	Team		No	Yds	Avg	Lg	TD
1953	CHIC	N	2	16	8.0	13	0

Dan Currie

Year	Team		No	Yds	Avg	Lg	TD
1959	GB	N	1	25	25.0	25	0
1960			4	75	18.8	33	0
1961			3	59	19.7	21t	1
1963			1	23	23.0	23	0
1964			2	11	5.5	10	0
Career			11	193	17.5	33	1
Playoffs			1	30	30.0		0

Bill Currier

Year	Team		No	Yds	Avg	Lg	TD
1977	HOU	N	2	0	0.0	0	0
1978			1	8	8.0	8	0
1981	NYG	N	3	2	0.7	2	0
1982			1	0	0.0	0	0
1983			2	37	18.5	30t	1
1984			1	7	7.0	7	0
1985			1	9	9.0	9	0
Career			11	63	5.7	30t	1
Playoffs			1	2	2.0		0

Don Currivan

Year	Team		No	Yds	Avg	Lg	TD
1947	BOS	N	1	0	0.0	0	0
1949	LA	N	5	31	6.2	16	0
Career			6	31	5.2	16	0
Playoffs			2	0	0.0		0

Buddy Curry

Year	Team		No	Yds	Avg	Lg	TD
1980	ATL	N	3	13	4.3	9	0
1981			1	35	35.0	35t	1
1982			1	0	0.0	0	0
1985			1	0	0.0	0	0
1986			1	32	32.0	32	0
Career			7	80	11.4	35t	1

Craig Curry

Year	Team		No	Yds	Avg	Lg	TD
1986	TB	N	2	0	0.0	0	0
1987	IND	N	1	0	0.0	0	0
Career			3	0	0.0	0	0

Mike Curtis

Year	Team		No	Yds	Avg	Lg	TD
1967	BAL	N	1	6	6.0	6	0
1968			2	38	19.0	38t	1
1970			5	50	10.0	18	0
1971			3	44	14.7	31	0
1972			4	74	18.5	33	1
1973			2	9	4.5	7	0
1974			3	24	8.0	11	0
1975			1	3	3.0	3	0
1976	SEA	N	2	40	20.0	26	0
1977	WAS	N	1	1	1.0	1	0
1978			1	0	0.0	0	0
Career			25	289	11.6	38t	2
Playoffs			3	13	4.3		0

Tom Curtis

Year	Team		No	Yds	Avg	Lg	TD
1970	BAL	N	1	0	0.0	0	0

Travis Curtis

Year	Team		No	Yds	Avg	Lg	TD
1987	STL	N	5	65	13.0	31	0
1988	PHX	N	1	18	18.0	18	0
1990	NYJ	N	2	45	22.5	23	0
Career			8	128	16.0	31	0

Gary Cutsinger

Year	Team		No	Yds	Avg	Lg	TD
1962	HOU	A	1	3	3.0	3	0
1965			1	72	72.0	72	0
Career			2	75	37.5	72	0

Carlton Dabney

Year	Team		No	Yds	Avg	Lg	TD
1968	ATL	N	1	3	3.0	3	0

Bill Daddio

Year	Team		No	Yds	Avg	Lg	TD
1942	CHIC	N	1	4	4.0	4	0

Jeff Dale

Year	Team		No	Yds	Avg	Lg	TD
1985	SD	N	2	83	41.5	47t	1
1986			4	153	38.3	50	0
Career			6	236	39.3	50	1

Boley Dancewicz

Year	Team		No	Yds	Avg	Lg	TD
1946	BOS	N	1	4	4.0	4	0

Eugene Daniel

Year	Team		No	Yds	Avg	Lg	TD
1984	IND	N	6	25	4.2	18	0
1985			8	53	6.6	29	0
1986			3	11	3.7	5	0
1987			2	34	17.0	34	0
1988			2	44	22.0	41t	0
1989			1	34	34.0	34	0
1991			3	22	7.3	12	0
1992			1	0	0.0	0	0
1993			1	17	17.0	17	0
1994			2	6	3.0	6	0
1995			3	142	47.3	97t	1
1996			3	35	11.7	35t	1
Career			35	423	12.1	97t	3
Playoffs			2	72	36.0		1

Kenny Daniel

Year	Team		No	Yds	Avg	Lg	TD
1986	IND	N	1	0	0.0	0	0

Willie Daniel

Year	Team		No	Yds	Avg	Lg	TD
1961	PIT	N	3	76	25.3	41	0
1962			5	85	17.0	49t	1
1964			2	4	2.0	4	0
1965			1	9	9.0	9	0
1967	LA	N	2	45	22.5	35	0
1969			1	13	13.0	13	0
Career			14	232	16.6	49t	1

Calvin Daniels

Year	Team		No	Yds	Avg	Lg	TD
1984	KC	N	2	11	5.5	11	0
1986	WAS	N	1	4	4.0	4	0
Career			3	15	5.0	11	0

Clem Daniels

Year	Team		No	Yds	Avg	Lg	TD
1960	DAL	A	3	10	3.3		0

Dick Daniels

Year	Team		No	Yds	Avg	Lg	TD
1968	DAL	N	2	25	12.5	17	0
1969	CHI	N	3	37	12.3	32	0
1970			2	29	14.5	16	0
Career			7	91	13.0	32	0

Ed Danowski

Year	Team		No	Yds	Avg	Lg	TD
Playoffs			2	0	0.0		0

Matt Darby

Year	Team		No	Yds	Avg	Lg	TD
1993	BUF	N	2	32	16.0	32	0
1994			4	20	5.0	20	0
1995			2	37	18.5	37	0
Career			8	89	11.1	37	0
Playoffs			1	3	3.0		0

Thom Darden

Year	Team		No	Yds	Avg	Lg	TD
1972	CLE	N	3	64	21.3	20	0
1973			1	36	36.0	36	0
1974			8	105	13.1	31	0
1976			7	73	10.4	21	0
1977			6	107	17.8	49	1
1978			10	200	20.0	46	0
1979			5	125	25.0	39t	1
1980			2	42	21.0	23	0
1981			3	68	22.7	45	0
Career			45	820	18.2	49	2

Dick Daugherty

Year	Team		No	Yds	Avg	Lg	TD
1957	LA	N	1	32	32.0	32t	1
1958			1	12	12.0	12t	1
Career			2	44	22.0	32t	2

Lou Daukas

Year	Team		No	Yds	Avg	Lg	TD
1947	BKN	AA	1	1	1.0	1	0

Nick Daukas

Year	Team		No	Yds	Avg	Lg	TD
1946	BKN	AA	1	5	5.0	5	0

Red Daum

Year	Team		No	Yds	Avg	Lg	TD
1922	AKR	N					1

Jimmy David

Year	Team		No	Yds	Avg	Lg	TD
1952	DET	N	7	48	6.9	15	0
1953			4	50	12.5	21	0
1954			7	74	10.6	25	0
1955			3	44	14.7	28	0
1956			7	4	0.6	3	0
1957			3	20	6.7	17	0
1958			3	12	4.0	7	0
1959			2	7	3.5	7	0
Career			36	259	7.2	28	0
Playoffs			3	43	14.3		0

Bill Davidson

Year	Team		No	Yds	Avg	Lg	TD
1937	PIT	N					1

Kenny Davidson

Year	Team		No	Yds	Avg	Lg	TD
1993	PIT	N	1	6	6.0	6	0
1995	HOU	N	1	3	3.0	3	0
Career			2	9	4.5	6	0

Anthony Davis

Year	Team		No	Yds	Avg	Lg	TD
1995	KC	N	1	11	11.0	11	0
1996			2	37	18.5	30	0
Career			3	48	16.0	30	0

Ben Davis

Year	Team		No	Yds	Avg	Lg	TD
1967	CLE	N	1	9	9.0	9	0
1968			8	162	20.3	44	0
1970			1	0	0.0	0	0
1971			2	18	9.0	15	0
1972			3	10	3.3	10	0
1973			2	33	16.5	20	0
1974	DET	N	1	14	14.0	14	0
1975			1	67	67.0	67t	1
Career			19	313	16.5	67t	1
Playoffs			2	3	1.5		0

Bob Davis

Year	Team		No	Yds	Avg	Lg	TD
1942	PHI	N	2	35	17.5	35	0
1944	BOS	N	4	48	12.0	20	0
1945			6	28	4.7	10	0
1946			7	129	18.4	34	0
Career			19	240	12.6	35	0

Brian Davis

Year	Team		No	Yds	Avg	Lg	TD
1988	WAS	N	1	11	11.0	11	0
1989			4	40	10.0	15	0
1991	SEA	N	1	40	40.0	40t	1
1992			2	36	18.0	36	0
1993	SD	N	1	0	0.0	0	0
Career			9	127	14.1	40t	1
Playoffs			2	23	11.5		0

Butch Davis

Year	Team		No	Yds	Avg	Lg	TD
1970	CHI	N	1	0	0.0	0	0

Corby Davis

Year	Team		No	Yds	Avg	Lg	TD
1942	CLE	N	1	3	3.0	3	0

Dexter Davis

Year	Team		No	Yds	Avg	Lg	TD
1992	PHX	N	2	27	13.5	27	0

Eric Davis

Year	Team		No	Yds	Avg	Lg	TD
1990	SF	N	1	13	13.0	13	0
1992			3	52	17.3	37	0
1993			4	45	11.3	41t	1
1994			1	8	8.0	8	0
1995			3	84	28.0	86t	1
1996	CAR	N	5	57	11.4	36	0
Career			17	259	15.2	86t	2
Playoffs			6	50	8.3		1

Harper Davis

Year	Team		No	Yds	Avg	Lg	TD
1949	LA	AA	2	5	2.5		0
1950	CHIB	N	5	59	11.8	41	0

Year	Team		No	Yds	Avg	Lg	TD

Harper Davis *continued*

Year	Team		No	Yds	Avg	Lg	TD
1951	GB	N	4	37	9.3	25	0
Career			11	101	9.2	41	0

Henry Davis

1972	PIT	N	2	32	16.0	28	0
1973			2	23	11.5	15	0
Career			4	55	13.8	28	0

James Davis

1982	LARI	N	2	107	53.5	55	1
1983			1	10	10.0	10	0
1984			1	8	8.0	8	0
Career			4	125	31.3	55	1

Jeff Davis

1984	TB	N	1	0	0.0	0	0
1985			1	22	22.0	22	0
1986			1	0	0.0	0	0
Career			3	22	7.3	22	0

Jerry Davis

1948	CHIC	N	4	47	11.8	18	0
1949			6	63	10.5	27	0
1950			9	40	4.4	15	0
1951			2	36	18.0	36	0
1952	DAL	N	3	118	39.3	66t	1
Career			24	304	12.7	66t	1

Lamar Davis

1946	MIA	AA	4	40	10.0		
1947	BAL	AA	1	12	12.0	12	0
1948			5	110	22.0	54	0
1949			1	35	35.0	35	0
Career			11	197	17.9	54	0

Lee Davis

1987	IND	N	1	7	7.0	7	0

Mike Davis

1978	OAK	N	1	0	0.0	0	0
1979			2	22	11.0	11	0
1980			3	88	29.3	49	0
1981			1	0	0.0	0	0
1982	LARI	N	1	56	56.0	56t	1
1983			1	3	3.0	3	0
1984			2	11	5.5	11	0
Career			11	180	16.4	56t	1
Playoffs			3	2	0.7		0

Milt Davis

1957	BAL	N	10	219	21.9	75t	2
1958			4	40	10.0	28	0
1959			7	119	17.0	57t	1
1960			6	32	5.3	19	0
Career			27	410	15.2	75t	3

Oliver Davis

1977	CLE	N	3	71	23.7	32	0
1978			6	65	10.8	33	1
1979			1	33	33.0	33	0
1980			1	70	70.0	70	0
Career			11	239	21.7	70	1

Paul Davis

1948	PIT	N	1	7	7.0	7	0

Preston Davis

1984	IND	N	1	3	3.0	3	0
1985			2	14	7.0	14	0
Career			3	17	5.7	14	0

Reuben Davis

1989	TB	N	1	13	13.0	13t	1

Ricky Davis

1975	CIN	N	1	26	26.0	26	0

Ted Davis

1966	BAL	N	1	15	15.0	15	0
1970	MIA	N	1	15	15.0	15	0
Career			2	30	15.0	15	0

Travis Davis

1996	JAC	N	2	0	0.0	0	0

Van Davis

1948	NY	AA	1	5	5.0	5	0

Wayne Davis

1985	SD	N	2	29	14.5	28	0
1987	BUF	N	1	0	0.0	0	0
1988			1	3	3.0	3	0
1989	WAS	N	1	11	11.0	11	0
Career			5	43	8.6	28	0

Wendell Davis

1996	DAL	N	0	0		0L	0

Willie Davis

1965	GB	N	1	21	21.0	21	0
1969			1	0	0.0	0	0
Career			2	21	10.5	21	0

Brian Dawkins

1996	PHI	N	3	41	13.7	30	0

Mike Dawson

1982	STL	N	1	0	0.0	0	0

Tom Day

1965	BUF	A	1	0	0.0	0	0

Fred Dean

1977	SD	N	1	22	22.0	22t	1

Hal Dean

1948	LA	N	1	0	0.0	0	0

Vernon Dean

1982	WAS	N	3	62	20.7	26	0
1983			5	54	10.8	26	0
1984			7	114	16.3	36t	2
1985			5	8	1.6	8	0
1986			1	5	5.0	5	0
1988	SEA	N	1	31	31.0	31	0
Career			22	274	12.5	36t	2
Playoffs			2	21	10.5		0

Art DeCarlo

1953	PIT	N	5	83	16.6	27	0
1956	WAS	N	1	11	11.0	11	0
1957	BAL	N	1	14	14.0	14	0
Career			7	108	15.4	27	0

Bill deCorrevont

1947	CHIC	N	1	0	0.0	0	0
1948	CHIB	N	5	37	7.4	17	0
1949			4	53	13.3	40	0
Career			10	90	9.0	40	0

Bob Dee

1960	BOS	A	1	14	14.0	14	0
Playoffs			2	0	0.0		0

Bob DeFruiter

1947	DET	N	3	8	2.7	7	0

Dick Degen

1965	SD	A	2	6	3.0	6	0
1966			1	7	7.0	7	0
Career			3	13	4.3	7	0

Al Dekdebrun

1946	BUF	AA	3	19	6.3		0
1948	NY	AA	1	16	16.0	16	0
Career			4	35	8.8	16	0

Jeff Delaney

1980	LA	N	2	42	21.0	27	0
1983	BAL	N	2	16	8.0	11	0
Career			4	58	14.5	27	0

Spiro Dellerba

1948	BAL	AA	2	18	9.0		0

Keith DeLong

1989	SF	N	1	1	1.0	1	0
1992			1	2	2.0	2	0
Career			2	3	1.5	2	0

Steve DeLong

1970	SD	N	1	5	5.0	5	0

Jack Del Rio

1985	NO	N	2	13	6.5	11	0
1988	KC	N	1	0	0.0	0	0
1992	MIN	N	2	92	46.0	84t	1
1993			4	3	0.8	3	0
1994			3	5	1.7	5	0
1995			1	15	15.0	15	0
Career			13	128	9.8	84t	1

Al DeMao

1945	WAS	N	1	44	44.0	44	0
1946			2	28	14.0	11	0
1947			2	35	17.5	21	0
1948			1	22	22.0	22	0
1949			1	3	3.0	3	0
1951			1	0	0.0	0	0
Career			8	132	16.5	44	0

Frank Dempsey

1952	CHIB	N	1	13	13.0	13	0

Vern Den Herder

1972	MIA	N	1	24	24.0	24	0

Mike Dennis

1980	NYG	N	5	68	13.6	28	0
1983			1	0	0.0	0	0
Career			6	68	11.3	28	0

Rick Dennison

1986	DEN	N	1	5	5.0	5	0
1987			1	10	10.0	10	0
1988			1	29	29.0	29	0
1989			1	1	1.0	1	0
Career			4	45	11.3	29	0

Burnell Dent

1989	GB	N	1	53	53.0	53	0

Richard Dent

1985	CHI	N	2	10	5.0	9	1
1989			1	30	30.0	30	0
1990			3	21	7.0	15	0
1991			1	4	4.0	4	0
1993			1	24	24.0	24	0
Career			8	89	11.1	30	1

Steve DeOssie

1989	NYG	N	1	10	10.0	10	0

Dean Derby

1958	PIT	N	4	0	0.0	0	0
1959			7	127	18.1	24	0
1960			3	40	13.3	25	0
1961	MIN	N	3	73	24.3	30	0
1962			4	0	0.0	0	0
Career			21	240	11.4	30	0

Dan DeRose

1987	NYG	N	1	10	10.0	10	0

Dan DeSantis

1941	PHI	N	2	37	18.5	34	0

Chuck DeShane

1945	DET	N	3	75	25.0	46t	1
1946			1	3	3.0	3	0
1949			1	0	0.0	0	0
Career			5	78	15.6	46t	1

Chuck Detwiler

1973	STL	N	1	0	0.0	0	0

Chris Devlin

1976	CIN	N	1	2	2.0	2	0

Year	Team	No	Yds	Avg	Lg	TD

Jim Dewar
Year	Team		No	Yds	Avg	Lg	TD
1947	CLE	AA	1	50	50.0	50	0

Dorne Dibble
| 1951 | DET | N | 1 | 26 | 26.0 | 26 | 0 |

Dan Dickel
| 1974 | BAL | N | 1 | 5 | 5.0 | 5 | 0 |

Anthony Dickerson
1980	DAL	N	2	46	23.0	34	0
1982			1	4	4.0	4	0
1983			1	8	8.0	8	0
1984			1	0	0.0	0	0
Career			5	58	11.6	34	0
Playoffs			1	0	0.0		0

Wally Diehl
| 1928 | FRA | N | | | | | 1 |

Bobby Dillon
1952	GB	N	4	35	8.8	17	0
1953			9	112	12.4	49t	1
1954			7	111	15.9	50t	1
1955			9	153	17.0	61	0
1956			7	244	34.9	45	1
1957			9	180	20.0	55t	1
1958			6	134	22.3	46	1
1959			1	7	7.0	7	0
Career			52	976	18.8	61	5

Lavern Dilweg
1927	GB	N					1
1930							1
Career							2

Babe Dimancheff
1945	BOS	N	1	0	0.0	0	0
1946			1	7	7.0	7	0
Career			2	7	3.5	7	0

Charles Dimry
1989	ATL	N	2	72	36.0	40	0
1990			3	16	5.3	13	0
1991	DEN	N	3	35	11.7	26t	1
1992			1	2	2.0	2	0
1993			1	0	0.0	0	0
1994	TB	N	1	0	0.0	0	0
1995			1	0	0.0	0	0
1996			2	1	0.5	1	0
Career			14	126	9.0	40	1

Tom Dinkel
| 1978 | CIN | N | 1 | 1 | 1.0 | 1 | 0 |

Cris Dishman
1989	HOU	N	4	31	7.8	31	0
1990			4	50	12.5	42	0
1991			6	61	10.2	43	0
1992			3	34	11.3	17	0
1993			6	74	12.3	30	0
1994			4	74	18.5	36	1
1995			3	17	5.7	17	0
1996			1	7	7.0	7	0
Career			31	348	11.2	43	1

Ernest Dixon
| 1995 | NO | N | 2 | 17 | 8.5 | 11 | 0 |

Gerald Dixon
1995	CLE	N	2	48	24.0	30	1
1996	CIN	N	1	10	10.0	10	0
Career			3	58	19.3	30	1

Hanford Dixon
1982	CLE	N	4	22	5.5	22	0
1983			3	41	13.7	35	0
1984			5	31	6.2	18	0
1985			3	65	21.7	37	0
1986			5	35	7.0	19	0
1987			3	5	1.7	6	0
1988			2	24	12.0	24	0

Hanford Dixon *continued*
1989			1	2	2.0	2	0
Career			26	225	8.7	37	0
Playoffs			1	0	0.0		0

Randy Dixon
1988	CIN	N	1	13	13.0	13	0
1989			3	47	15.7	28	0
1991			2	62	31.0	47	0
Career			6	122	20.3	47	0

Glenn Dobbs
1946	BKN	AA	2	44	22.0		0
1947	LA	AA	5	44	8.8		0
1948			1	32	32.0	32	0
Career			8	120	15.0	32	0

Bob Dobelstein
| 1948 | NYG | N | 1 | 20 | 20.0 | 20t | 1 |

John Dockery
1969	NY	A	5	98	19.6	35	0
1971	NYJ	N	2	13	6.5	13	0
1973	PIT	N	1	0	0.0	0	0
Career			8	111	13.9	35	0

Dedrick Dodge
1992	SEA	N	1	13	13.0	13	0
1995	SF	N	1	13	13.0	13	0
1996			3	27	9.0	26	0
Career			5	53	10.6	26	0

Dale Dodrill
1953	PIT	N	1	3	3.0	3	0
1954			3	28	9.3	16	0
1955			2	25	12.5	25	0
1956			1	1	1.0	1	0
1957			2	50	25.0	44	0
1958			1	13	13.0	13	0
Career			10	120	12.0	44	0

Chris Doleman
1985	MIN	N	1	5	5.0	5	0
1986			1	59	59.0	59t	1
1990			1	30	30.0	30	0
1992			1	27	27.0	27t	1
1993			1	-3	-3.0	-3	0
1994	ATL	N	1	2	2.0	2	0
1996	SF	N	2	1	0.5	1	0
Career			8	121	15.1	59t	2

Don Doll
1949	DET	N	11	301	27.4	95t	1
1950			12	163	13.6	38	1
1951			1	0	0.0	0	0
1952			2	0	0.0	0	0
1953	WAS	N	10	102	10.2	28	0
1954	LA	N	5	51	10.2	26	0
Career			41	617	15.0	95t	2

Paul Dombroski
1980	KC	N	1	6	6.0	6	0
1984	NE	N	1	23	23.0	23	0
Career			2	29	14.5	23	0

Joe Domnanovich
1947	BOS	N	1	16	16.0	16	0
1948			1	6	6.0	6	0
1949	NYB	N	1	28	28.0	28	0
Career			3	50	16.7	28	0

Tom Domres
| 1970 | HOU | N | 0 | 13 | | 13L | 0 |

Jeff Donaldson
1986	HOU	N	1	0	0.0	0	0
1987			4	16	4.0	9	0
1988			4	29	7.3	23	0
1989			0	14		14	0
1990	KC	N	3	28	9.3	14	0
Career			12	87	7.3	23	0

John Donaldson
| 1949 | CHI | AA | 0 | 23 | | 23L | 0 |

Al Donelli
| 1941 | PIT | N | 1 | 18 | 18.0 | 18 | 0 |

Roger Donnahoo
| 1960 | NY | A | 5 | 89 | 17.8 | | 0 |

George Donnelly
| 1966 | SF | N | 2 | 16 | 8.0 | 16 | 0 |

Jim Dooley
| 1952 | CHIB | N | 5 | 30 | 6.0 | 12 | 0 |

Jim Doran
| 1951 | DET | N | 1 | 38 | 38.0 | 38 | 0 |

Torin Dorn
1992	LARI	N	1	7	7.0	7	0
1995	STL	N	1	24	24.0	24t	1
1996			1	40	40.0	40	0
Career			3	71	23.7	40	1
Playoffs			1	1	1.0		0

Noble Doss
| 1947 | PHI | N | 2 | 31 | 15.5 | 23 | 0 |

Bob Dougherty
1957	LA	N	1	6	6.0	6	0
1961	OAK	A	2	12	6.0	9	0
Career			3	18	6.0	9	0

Phil Dougherty
| 1938 | CHIC | N | | | | | 1 |

John Douglas
| 1967 | NO | N | 1 | 19 | 19.0 | 19 | 0 |

John Douglas
1972	NYG	N	1	0	0.0	0	0
1973			1	0	0.0	0	0
Career			2	0	0.0	0	0

Maurice Douglass
1987	CHI	N	2	0	0.0	0	0
1988			1	35	35.0	35	0
1989			1	0	0.0	0	0
1994			1	18	18.0	18	0
1996	NYG	N	1	32	32.0	32t	1
Career			6	85	14.2	35	1
Playoffs			1	47	47.0		0

Mike Douglass
1979	GB	N	3	73	24.3	46	0
1981			3	20	6.7	13	0
1982			2	55	27.5	30	0
1985			2	126	63.0	80t	1
Career			10	274	27.4	80t	1

Bob Dove
| 1950 | CHIC | N | 1 | 0 | 0.0 | 0 | 0 |

Eddie Dove
1959	SF	N	1	6	6.0	6	0
1960			3	29	9.7	29	0
1961			3	41	13.7	28	0
1962			1	0	0.0	0	0
1963	NYG	N	2	75	37.5	75	0
Career			10	151	15.1	75	0

Jerome Dove
1977	SD	N	1	32	32.0	32	0
1978			1	4	4.0	4	0
Career			2	36	18.0	32	0

Jerry Dowd
| 1939 | CLE | N | | | | | 1 |

Harry Dowda
1949	WAS	N	3	36	12.0	36	0
1950			4	28	7.0	28t	1
1952			2	34	17.0	29	0

Year	Team		No	Yds	Avg	Lg	TD

Harry Dowda *continued*

Year	Team		No	Yds	Avg	Lg	TD
1953			5	67	13.4	23t	1
1954	PHI	N	2	34	17.0	34	0
Career			16	199	12.4	36	2

Corey Dowden

Year	Team		No	Yds	Avg	Lg	TD
1996	GB	N	1	5	5.0	5	0

Mike Dowdle

Year	Team		No	Yds	Avg	Lg	TD
1961	DAL	N	1	14	14.0	14	0
1962			1	7	7.0	7	0
1963	SF	N	2	6	3.0	6	0
1964			1	14	14.0	14	0
1966			1	27	27.0	27t	1
Career			6	68	11.3	27t	1

Michael Downs

Year	Team		No	Yds	Avg	Lg	TD
1981	DAL	N	7	81	11.6	25	0
1982			1	22	22.0	22	0
1983			4	80	20.0	28	0
1984			7	126	18.0	27t	1
1985			3	11	3.7	11	0
1986			6	54	9.0	31	0
1987			4	56	14.0	27	0
1988			2	3	1.5	3	0
1989	PHX	N	1	37	37.0	37	0
Career			35	470	13.4	37	1
Playoffs			1	21	21.0		0

Dick Doyle

Year	Team		No	Yds	Avg	Lg	TD
1955	PIT	N	1	4	4.0	4	0
1960	DEN	A	1	24	24.0	24	0
Career			2	28	14.0	24	0

Ted Doyle

Year	Team		No	Yds	Avg	Lg	TD
1945	PIT	N	1	50	50.0	50t	1

Johnny Drake

Year	Team		No	Yds	Avg	Lg	TD
1941	CLE	N	2	66	33.0	54	0

Tyronne Drakeford

Year	Team		No	Yds	Avg	Lg	TD
1994	SF	N	1	6	6.0	6	0
1995			5	54	10.8	37	0
1996			1	11	11.0	11	0
Career			7	71	10.1	37	0

Dwight Drane

Year	Team		No	Yds	Avg	Lg	TD
1989	BUF	N	1	25	25.0	25	0

Chuck Drazenovich

Year	Team		No	Yds	Avg	Lg	TD
1950	WAS	N	2	43	21.5	35	0
1951			2	27	13.5	20	0
1952			3	58	19.3	38	0
1954			1	5	5.0	5	0
1955			2	10	5.0	6	0
1957			2	6	3.0	4	0
1958			2	16	8.0	12	0
1959			1	0	0.0	0	0
Career			15	165	11.0	38	0

Wally Dreyer

Year	Team		No	Yds	Avg	Lg	TD
1950	GB	N	5	62	12.4	34	1

Paddy Driscoll

Year	Team		No	Yds	Avg	Lg	TD
1925	CHIC	N					1

Shane Dronett

Year	Team		No	Yds	Avg	Lg	TD
1993	DEN	N	2	13	6.5	7	0

Chuck Drulis

Year	Team		No	Yds	Avg	Lg	TD
1942	CHIB	N	1	41	41.0	41	0
1946			1	8	8.0	8	0
1948			1	2	2.0	2	0
1949			1	0	0.0	0	0
Career			4	51	12.8	41	0

Fred Dryer

Year	Team		No	Yds	Avg	Lg	TD
1975	LA	N	1	20	20.0	20t	1

Walt Dubzinski

Year	Team		No	Yds	Avg	Lg	TD
1943	NYG	N	1	0	0.0	0	0

Bill Dudley

Year	Team		No	Yds	Avg	Lg	TD
1942	PIT	N	3	60	20.0	25	0
1945			2	47	23.5	26	0
1946			10	242	24.2	80t	1
1947	DET	N	5	104	20.8	41t	1
1948			1	3	3.0	3	0
1950	WAS	N	2	3	1.5	3	0
Career			23	459	20.0	80t	2

Dave Duerson

Year	Team		No	Yds	Avg	Lg	TD
1984	CHI	N	1	9	9.0	9	0
1985			5	53	10.6	20	0
1986			6	139	23.2	38	0
1987			3	0	0.0	0	0
1988			2	18	9.0	18	0
1989			1	2	2.0	2	0
1990	NYG	N	1	0	0.0	0	0
1991	PHX	N	1	5	5.0	5	0
Career			20	226	11.3	38	0

Don Dufek

Year	Team		No	Yds	Avg	Lg	TD
1977	SEA	N	2	26	13.0	27	0
1982			1	16	16.0	16	0
Career			3	42	14.0	27	0

Gil Duggan

Year	Team		No	Yds	Avg	Lg	TD
1942	CHIC	N	1	0		0	0

Jack Dugger

Year	Team		No	Yds	Avg	Lg	TD
1947	DET	N	1	6	6.0	6	0

Paul Duhart

Year	Team		No	Yds	Avg	Lg	TD
1944	GB	N	4	23	5.8	14	0
Playoffs			1	0	0.0		0

A.J. Duhe

Year	Team		No	Yds	Avg	Lg	TD
1981	MIA	N	1	11	11.0	11	0
1982			1	0	0.0	0	0
1984			1	7	7.0	7	0
Career			3	18	6.0	11	0
Playoffs			4	36	9.0		1

Mike Dukes

Year	Team		No	Yds	Avg	Lg	TD
1960	HOU	A	2	34	17.0	29	0
1961			2	10	5.0	5	0
1962			2	11	5.5	6	0
1963			1	4	4.0	4	0
1964	BOS	A	1	6	6.0	6	0
1965			1	10	10.0	10	0
Career			9	75	8.3	29	0
Playoffs			1	8	8.0		0

Mike Dumas

Year	Team		No	Yds	Avg	Lg	TD
1991	HOU	N	1	19	19.0	19	0
1992			1	0	0.0	0	0
1995	JAC	N	1	0	0.0	0	0
Career			3	19	6.3	19	0

Billy DuMoe

Year	Team		No	Yds	Avg	Lg	TD
1921	GB	A					1

Jim Dunaway

Year	Team		No	Yds	Avg	Lg	TD
1967	BUF	A	1	8	8.0	8	0

Frank Duncan

Year	Team		No	Yds	Avg	Lg	TD
1981	SD	N	1	0	0.0	0	0

Jim Duncan

Year	Team		No	Yds	Avg	Lg	TD
1951	NYG	N	2	19	9.5	13	0
1952			2	24	12.0	24	0
1953			3	39	13.0	31	0
Career			7	82	11.7	31	0

Jim Duncan

Year	Team		No	Yds	Avg	Lg	TD
1970	BAL	N	2	56	28.0	30	0

Speedy Duncan

Year	Team		No	Yds	Avg	Lg	TD
1964	SD	A	1	3	3.0	3	0
1965			4	30	7.5	26	0
1966			7	67	9.6	31	0
1967			2	100	50.0	100t	1
1968			1	4	4.0	4	0
1969			6	118	19.7	72t	1
1971	WAS	N	1	46	46.0	46t	1

Speedy Duncan *continued*

Year	Team		No	Yds	Avg	Lg	TD
1972			1	8	8.0	8	0
1973			1	6	6.0	6	0
Career			24	382	15.9	100t	3

Tony Dungy

Year	Team		No	Yds	Avg	Lg	TD
1977	PIT	N	3	37	12.3	29	0
1978			6	95	15.8	65	0
Career			9	132	14.7	65	0

Lenny Dunlap

Year	Team		No	Yds	Avg	Lg	TD
1972	SD	N	5	67	13.4	25	0

Gary Dunn

Year	Team		No	Yds	Avg	Lg	TD
Playoffs			1	5	5.0		0

Don Durdan

Year	Team		No	Yds	Avg	Lg	TD
1946	SF	AA	2	38	19.0		0

Clarence Duren

Year	Team		No	Yds	Avg	Lg	TD
1973	STL	N	2	13	6.5	13	0
1974			2	29	14.5	20	0
1975			1	23	23.0	23	0
1976			1	8	8.0	8	0
1977	SD	N	4	45	11.3	25	0
Career			10	118	11.8	25	0

Sandy Durko

Year	Team		No	Yds	Avg	Lg	TD
1971	CIN	N	4	46	11.5	25	0
1973	NE	N	3	26	8.7	16	0
Career			7	72	10.3	25	0

Jeff Durkota

Year	Team		No	Yds	Avg	Lg	TD
1948	LA	AA	1	18	18.0	18	0

Mark Dusbabek

Year	Team		No	Yds	Avg	Lg	TD
1989	MIN	N	1	2	2.0	2	0

Brad Dusek

Year	Team		No	Yds	Avg	Lg	TD
1976	WAS	N	1	0	0.0	0	0
1977			1	0	0.0	0	0
1978			1	11	11.0	11	0
1979			1	0	0.0	0	0
Career			4	11	2.8	11	0

John Dutton

Year	Team		No	Yds	Avg	Lg	TD
1980	DAL	N	1	38	38.0	38t	1

Dan Dworsky

Year	Team		No	Yds	Avg	Lg	TD
1949	LA	AA	1	3	3.0	3	0

Jack Dwyer

Year	Team		No	Yds	Avg	Lg	TD
1951	WAS	N	1	14	14.0	14	0
1952	LA	N	4	48	12.0	23	0
1953			2	31	15.5	31t	1
1954			4	90	22.5	76t	1
Career			11	183	16.6	76t	2

Ken Dyer

Year	Team		No	Yds	Avg	Lg	TD
1970	CIN	N	3	45	15.0	22	0

Donald Dykes

Year	Team		No	Yds	Avg	Lg	TD
1980	NYJ	N	5	1	0.2	1	0
Playoffs			1	22	22.0		0

Kay Eakin

Year	Team		No	Yds	Avg	Lg	TD
1941	NYG	N	2	33	16.5	33	0
1946	MIA	AA	2	31	15.5		0
Career			4	64	16.0	33	0

Kenny Easley

Year	Team		No	Yds	Avg	Lg	TD
1981	SEA	N	3	155	51.7	82t	1
1982			4	48	12.0	44	0
1983			7	106	15.1	48	0
1984			10	126	12.6	58t	2
1985			2	22	11.0	16	0
1986			2	34	17.0	24	0
1987			4	47	11.8	22	0
Career			32	538	16.8	82t	3
Playoffs			1	21	21.0		0

Ricky Easmon

Year	Team		No	Yds	Avg	Lg	TD
1986	TB	N	1	0	0.0	0	0

Bo Eason

Year	Team		No	Yds	Avg	Lg	TD
1984	HOU	N	1	20	20.0	20	0
1985			3	55	18.3	55	0
1986			2	16	8.0	11	0
Career			6	91	15.2	55	0

Ray Easterling

Year	Team		No	Yds	Avg	Lg	TD
1975	ATL	N	3	32	10.7	15	0
1976			3	33	11.0	19	0
1977			4	46	11.5	36	0
1978			1	1	1.0	1	0
1979			2	5	2.5	5	0
Career			13	117	9.0	36	0

Scott Eaton

Year	Team		No	Yds	Avg	Lg	TD
1967	NYG	N	2	7	3.5	7	0
1968			4	20	5.0	16	0
1969			2	23	11.5	23t	1
1970			2	8	4.0	8	0
1971			1	0	0.0	0	0
Career			11	58	5.3	23t	1

Tracey Eaton

Year	Team		No	Yds	Avg	Lg	TD
1989	HOU	N	3	33	11.0	20	0
1993	ATL	N	1	0	0.0	0	0
Career			4	33	8.3	20	0
Playoffs			1	0	0.0		0

John Ebersole

Year	Team		No	Yds	Avg	Lg	TD
1973	NYJ	N	1	0	0.0	0	0
1974			3	48	16.0	41	0
1975			2	21	10.5	18	0
1976			1	0	0.0	0	0
1977			1	0	0.0	0	0
Career			8	69	8.6	41	0

Ox Eckhardt

Year	Team		No	Yds	Avg	Lg	TD
1928	NYG	N					1

Booker Edgerson

Year	Team		No	Yds	Avg	Lg	TD
1962	BUF	A	6	111	18.5	40	0
1963			1	0	0.0	0	0
1964			4	130	32.5	91	0
1965			5	55	11.0	19	0
1967			2	25	12.5	25	0
1968			4	100	25.0	45t	2
1969			1	0	0.0	0	0
Career			23	421	18.3	91	2

Randy Edmunds

Year	Team		No	Yds	Avg	Lg	TD
1968	MIA	A	1	1	1.0	1	0

Brad Edwards

Year	Team		No	Yds	Avg	Lg	TD
1988	MIN	N	2	47	23.5	37t	1
1989			1	18	18.0	18	0
1990	WAS	N	2	33	16.5	33	0
1991			4	52	13.0	27	0
1992			6	157	26.2	53t	1
1993			1	17	17.0	17	0
1996	ATL	N	2	15	7.5	15	0
Career			18	339	18.8	53t	2
Playoffs			3	62	20.7		0

Dave Edwards

Year	Team		No	Yds	Avg	Lg	TD
1963	DAL	N	1	17	17.0	17	0
1964			1	1	1.0	1	0
1965			2	0	0.0	0	0
1966			1	12	12.0	12	0
1967			3	34	11.3	26t	1
1969			1	0	0.0	0	0
1970			2	2	1.0	2	0
1971			2	0	0.0	0	0
Career			13	66	5.1	26t	1
Playoffs			1	6	6.0		0

Dave Edwards

Year	Team		No	Yds	Avg	Lg	TD
1987	PIT	N	1	0	0.0	0	0

Dixon Edwards

Year	Team		No	Yds	Avg	Lg	TD
1991	DAL	N	1	36	36.0	36t	1
1996	MIN	N	1	18	18.0	18	0
Career			2	54	27.0	36t	1

Donnie Edwards

Year	Team		No	Yds	Avg	Lg	TD
1996	KC	N	1	22	22.0	22	0

Eddie Edwards

Year	Team		No	Yds	Avg	Lg	TD
1978	CIN	N	1	2	2.0	2	0

Glen Edwards

Year	Team		No	Yds	Avg	Lg	TD
1971	PIT	N	1	20	20.0	20	0
1972			1	14	14.0	14	0
1973			6	186	31.0	86t	1
1974			5	153	30.6	59	1
1975			3	68	22.7	47	0
1976			6	95	15.8	55	0
1977			3	116	38.7	51	0
1978	SD	N	3	43	14.3	24	0
1979			4	99	24.8	53	0
1980			5	122	24.4	68t	1
1981			2	45	22.5	39	0
Career			39	961	24.6	86t	3
Playoffs			6	151	25.2		0

Herman Edwards

Year	Team		No	Yds	Avg	Lg	TD
1977	PHI	N	6	9	1.5	6	0
1978			7	59	8.4	25	0
1979			3	6	2.0	6	0
1980			3	12	4.0	9	0
1981			3	1	0.3	1	0
1982			5	3	0.6	3	0
1983			1	0	0.0	0	0
1984			2	0	0.0	0	0
1985			3	8	2.7	3t	1
Career			33	98	3.0	25	1
Playoffs			5	40	8.0		0

Doug Eggers

Year	Team		No	Yds	Avg	Lg	TD
1954	BAL	N	3	18	6.0	10	0
1956			1	6	6.0	6	0
Career			4	24	6.0	10	0

Tom Ehlers

Year	Team		No	Yds	Avg	Lg	TD
1976	PHI	N	1	27	27.0	27	0

Clyde Ehrhardt

Year	Team		No	Yds	Avg	Lg	TD
1946	WAS	N	1	38	38.0	38	0
1948			2	29	14.5	15	0
Career			3	67	22.3	38	0

Joe Ehrmann

Year	Team		No	Yds	Avg	Lg	TD
1980	BAL	N	1	5	5.0	5	0

Larry Eisenhauer

Year	Team		No	Yds	Avg	Lg	TD
1963	BOS	A	1	0	0.0	0	0

Carl Ekern

Year	Team		No	Yds	Avg	Lg	TD
1982	LARM	N	1	9	9.0	9	0
1983			1	1	1.0	1	0
1985			2	55	27.5	33t	1
1987			1	7	7.0	7	0
Career			5	72	14.4	33t	1

Donnie Elder

Year	Team		No	Yds	Avg	Lg	TD
1988	TB	N	3	9	3.0	9	0
1989			1	0	0.0	0	0
1990	SD	N	1	0	0.0	0	0
1991			1	0	0.0	0	0
Career			6	9	1.5	9	0

Chief Elkins

Year	Team		No	Yds	Avg	Lg	TD
1928	FRA	N					1

Carl Eller

Year	Team		No	Yds	Avg	Lg	TD
1975	MIN	N	1	1	1.0	1	0

Don Ellersick

Year	Team		No	Yds	Avg	Lg	TD
1960	LA	N	2	12	6.0	12	0

Allan Ellis

Year	Team		No	Yds	Avg	Lg	TD
1973	CHI	N	1	12	12.0	12	0
1974			3	32	10.7	19	0
1975			2	4	2.0	4	0
1976			6	47	7.8	22t	1
1977			6	23	3.8	11	0
1979			3	67	22.3	24	0

Allan Ellis *continued*

Year	Team		No	Yds	Avg	Lg	TD
1980			1	0	0.0	0	0
Career			22	185	8.4	24	1
Playoffs			1	25	25.0		0

Clarence Ellis

Year	Team		No	Yds	Avg	Lg	TD
1972	ATL	N	3	13	4.3	13	0
1973			2	90	45.0	48	0
1974			3	11	3.7	6	0
Career			8	114	14.3	48	0

Ken Ellis

Year	Team		No	Yds	Avg	Lg	TD
1970	GB	N	3	69	23.0	60	0
1971			6	10	1.7	5	0
1972			4	106	26.5	40	1
1973			3	53	17.7	47t	1
1974			3	56	18.7	38t	1
1975			1	0	0.0	0	0
1976	MIA	N	2	40	20.0	40	0
Career			22	334	15.2	60	3

Ray Ellis

Year	Team		No	Yds	Avg	Lg	TD
1983	PHI	N	1	18	18.0	18	0
1984			7	119	17.0	31	0
1985			4	32	8.0	18	0
1986	CLE	N	2	12	6.0	7	0
Career			14	181	12.9	31	0

Roger Ellis

Year	Team		No	Yds	Avg	Lg	TD
1960	NY	A	1	0	0.0	0	0

Riki Ellison

Year	Team		No	Yds	Avg	Lg	TD
1990	LARI	N	1	7	7.0	7	0
Playoffs			3	20	6.7		0

Percy Ellsworth

Year	Team		No	Yds	Avg	Lg	TD
1996	NYG	N	3	62	20.7	33	0

Dave Elmendorf

Year	Team		No	Yds	Avg	Lg	TD
1971	LA	N	2	32	16.0	32	0
1972			3	29	9.7	15	0
1973			1	16	16.0	16	0
1974			7	186	26.6	57t	2
1975			4	48	12.0	26	0
1976			2	0	0.0	0	0
1977			2	51	25.5	27	0
1978			3	20	6.7	12	0
1979			3	39	13.0	32	0
Career			27	421	15.6	57t	2
Playoffs			3	15	5.0		0

Doug Elmore

Year	Team		No	Yds	Avg	Lg	TD
1962	WAS	N	2	28	14.0	24	0

Jimbo Elrod

Year	Team		No	Yds	Avg	Lg	TD
1976	KC	N	1	3	3.0	3	0

Earl Elsey

Year	Team		No	Yds	Avg	Lg	TD
1946	LA	AA	2	2	1.0		0

Art Elston

Year	Team		No	Yds	Avg	Lg	TD
1946	SF	AA	1	34	34.0	34	0
1947			2	13	6.5		0
1948			1	0	0.0	0	0
Career			4	47	11.8	34	0

Larry Ely

Year	Team		No	Yds	Avg	Lg	TD
1975	CHI	N	1	2	2.0	2	0

Frank Emanuel

Year	Team		No	Yds	Avg	Lg	TD
1966	MIA	A	1	14	14.0	14	0
1967			1	24	24.0	24	0
1968			2	8	4.0	6	0
Career			4	46	11.5	24	0

Steve Emtman

Year	Team		No	Yds	Avg	Lg	TD
1992	IND	N	1	90	90.0	90t	1

Tiny Engebretsen

Year	Team		No	Yds	Avg	Lg	TD
Playoffs			1	4	4.0		0

Wuert Engelmann

Year	Team		No	Yds	Avg	Lg	TD
1932	GB	N					1

Wuert Engelmann *continued*

Year	Team		No	Yds	Avg	Lg	TD
1933							1
Career							2

Dick Erdlitz

Year	Team		No	Yds	Avg	Lg	TD
1942	PHI	N	1	0	0.0	0	0
1945			1	3	3.0	3	0
1946	MIA	AA	1	12	12.0	12	0
Career			3	15	5.0	12	0

Bernie Erickson

Year	Team		No	Yds	Avg	Lg	TD
1967	SD	A	1	17	17.0	17	0

Hal Erickson

Year	Team		No	Yds	Avg	Lg	TD
1925	CHIC	N					1
1928							1
Career							2

Tom Erlandson

Year	Team		No	Yds	Avg	Lg	TD
1962	DEN	A	1	3	3.0	3	0
1965			1	3	3.0	3	0
1966	MIA	A	3	31	10.3	26	1
1967			1	37	37.0	37	0
1968	SD	A	2	22	11.0	16	0
Career			8	96	12.0	37	1

Len Eshmont

Year	Team		No	Yds	Avg	Lg	TD
1947	SF	AA	6	72	12.0		0
1948			1	0	0.0	0	0
1949			3	56	18.7		0
Career			10	128	12.8	0	0

Mike Esposito

Year	Team		No	Yds	Avg	Lg	TD
1977	ATL	N	1	55	55.0	55	0

Don Ettinger

Year	Team		No	Yds	Avg	Lg	TD
1948	NYG	N	2	14	7.0	12	0
1949			2	7	3.5	6	0
Career			4	21	5.3	12	0

Byron Evans

Year	Team		No	Yds	Avg	Lg	TD
1987	PHI	N	1	12	12.0	12	0
1989			3	23	7.7	15	0
1990			1	43	43.0	43t	1
1991			2	46	23.0	31	0
1992			4	76	19.0	43	0
1993			1	8	8.0	7	0
1994			1	6	6.0	6	0
Career			13	214	16.5	43t	1

Doug Evans

Year	Team		No	Yds	Avg	Lg	TD
1993	GB	N	1	0	0.0	0	0
1994			1	0	0.0	0	0
1995			2	24	12.0	24	0
1996			5	102	20.4	63	1
Career			9	126	14.0	63	1
Playoffs			2	0	0.0		0

Fred Evans

Year	Team		No	Yds	Avg	Lg	TD
1946	CLE	AA	1	21	21.0	21	0

Greg Evans

Year	Team		No	Yds	Avg	Lg	TD
1995	BUF	N	1	18	18.0	18	0
Playoffs			1	19	19.0		0

Larry Evans

Year	Team		No	Yds	Avg	Lg	TD
1977	DEN	N	1	0	0.0	0	0
1980			1	13	13.0	13	0
1981			1	1	1.0	1	0
Career			3	14	4.7	13	0

Eric Everett

Year	Team		No	Yds	Avg	Lg	TD
1988	PHI	N	1	0	0.0	0	0
1989			4	64	16.0	30t	1
1990	TB	N	3	28	9.3	23	0
Career			8	92	11.5	30t	1
Playoffs			2	38	19.0		0

Thomas Everett

Year	Team		No	Yds	Avg	Lg	TD
1987	PIT	N	3	22	7.3	21	0
1988			3	31	10.3	29	0
1989			3	68	22.7	32	0
1990			3	2	0.7	2	0
1991			4	53	13.3	27	0
1992	DAL	N	2	28	14.0	17	0
1993			2	25	12.5	17	0
1994	TB	N	1	26	26.0	26	0
Career			21	255	12.1	32	0
Playoffs			4	62	15.5		

Dick Evey

Year	Team		No	Yds	Avg	Lg	TD
1965	CHI	N	1	15	15.0	15	0
1968			1	6	6.0	6	0
Career			2	21	10.5	15	0

Jim Fahnhorst

Year	Team		No	Yds	Avg	Lg	TD
1984	SF	N	2	9	4.5	9	0
1986			4	52	13.0	46	0
1987			1	0	0.0	0	0
Career			7	61	8.7	46	0

Richard Fain

Year	Team		No	Yds	Avg	Lg	TD
1991	CIN	N	1	1	1.0	1	0

Art Faircloth

Year	Team		No	Yds	Avg	Lg	TD
1948	NYG	N	3	5	1.7	3	0

Earl Faison

Year	Team		No	Yds	Avg	Lg	TD
1961	SD	A	2	14	7.0	8	0
1962			1	30	30.0	30	0
1964			1	42	42.0	42t	1
1965			1	24	24.0	24t	1
1966	MIA	A	1	26	26.0	26	0
Career			6	136	22.7	42t	2

Nello Falaschi

Year	Team		No	Yds	Avg	Lg	TD
1941	NYG	N	1	10	10.0	10	0

Gary Famiglietti

Year	Team		No	Yds	Avg	Lg	TD
1940	CHIB	N	4	18	4.5		
1942			1	10	10.0	10	0
Career			5	28	5.6	10	0

Ken Fantetti

Year	Team		No	Yds	Avg	Lg	TD
1980	DET	N	1	10	10.0	10	0
1981			2	18	9.0	17	0
1983			2	0	0.0	0	0
1984			1	1	1.0	1	0
Career			6	29	4.8	17	0

Chris Farasopoulas

Year	Team		No	Yds	Avg	Lg	TD
1972	NYJ	N	2	48	24.0	25	0
1973			1	1	1.0	1	0
1974	NO	N	1	14	14.0	14	0
Career			4	63	15.8	25	0

Andy Farkas

Year	Team		No	Yds	Avg	Lg	TD
1941	WAS	N	4	27	6.8	26	0
1942			3	26	8.7	18	0
1944			3	31	10.3	21	0
Career			10	84	8.4	26	0

Dale Farley

Year	Team		No	Yds	Avg	Lg	TD
1972	BUF	N	1	42	42.0	42	0

Dick Farman

Year	Team		No	Yds	Avg	Lg	TD
1940	WAS	N	1	0	0.0	0	0

Lonnie Farmer

Year	Team		No	Yds	Avg	Lg	TD
1965	BOS	A	1	16	16.0	16	0

Ray Farmer

Year	Team		No	Yds	Avg	Lg	TD
1996	PHI	N	1	0	0.0	0	0

Tom Farmer

Year	Team		No	Yds	Avg	Lg	TD
1947	WAS	N	6	27	4.5	22	0

D'Marco Farr

Year	Team		No	Yds	Avg	Lg	TD
1995	STL	N	1	5	5.0	5	0
1996			1	5	5.0	5	0
Career			2	10	5.0	5	0

Miller Farr

Year	Team		No	Yds	Avg	Lg	TD
1965	DEN	A	2	22	11.0	17	0
1966	SD	A	3	68	22.7	35	0

Miller Farr *continued*

Year	Team		No	Yds	Avg	Lg	TD
1967	HOU	A	10	264	26.4	67	3
1968			3	104	34.7	52t	2
1969			6	48	8.0	35	0
1970	STL	N	5	38	7.6	19t	1
1971			2	13	6.5	13	0
1972			3	21	7.0	21	0
1973	DET	N	1	0	0.0	0	0
Career			35	578	16.5	67	6
Playoffs			1	0	0.0		0

Tom Farris

Year	Team		No	Yds	Avg	Lg	TD
1946	CHIB	N	4	43	10.8	16	0
1947			1	2	2.0	2	0
Career			5	45	9.0	16	0

Chuck Faucette

Year	Team		No	Yds	Avg	Lg	TD
1988	SD	N	1	2	2.0	2	0

Wilson Faumina

Year	Team		No	Yds	Avg	Lg	TD
1978	ATL	N	1	7	7.0	7	0

Calvin Favron

Year	Team		No	Yds	Avg	Lg	TD
1981	STL	N	1	42	42.0	42	0

Jake Fawcett

Year	Team		No	Yds	Avg	Lg	TD
1946	LA	N	1	5	5.0	5	0

Tom Fears

Year	Team		No	Yds	Avg	Lg	TD
1948	LA	N	2	37	18.5	35t	1

John Federovich

Year	Team		No	Yds	Avg	Lg	TD
1941	CHIB	N	1	8	8.0	8	0

Joe Federspiel

Year	Team		No	Yds	Avg	Lg	TD
1973	NO	N	1	1	1.0	1	0
1974			1	9	9.0	9	0
1978			2	12	6.0	12	0
1979			1	4	4.0	4	0
Career			5	26	5.2	12	0

Howard Feggins

Year	Team		No	Yds	Avg	Lg	TD
1989	NE	N	1	4	4.0	4	0

Bernie Feibish

Year	Team		No	Yds	Avg	Lg	TD
1941	PHI	N	1	9	9.0	9	0

Ron Fellows

Year	Team		No	Yds	Avg	Lg	TD
1983	DAL	N	5	139	27.8	58t	1
1984			3	3	1.0	3	0
1985			4	52	13.0	29	0
1986			5	46	9.2	34t	1
1988	LARI	N	2	14	7.0	14	0
Career			19	254	13.4	58t	2

Dick Felt

Year	Team		No	Yds	Avg	Lg	TD
1960	NY	A	2	7	3.5		0
1961			4	88	22.0	55	1
1962	BOS	A	5	73	14.6	22	0
1963			3	81	27.0	35	0
1964			2	10	5.0	8	0
1966			2	35	17.5	32	0
Career			18	294	16.3	55	1

Eric Felton

Year	Team		No	Yds	Avg	Lg	TD
1978	NO	N	1	0	0.0	0	0
1979			4	53	13.3	53	0
Career			5	53	10.6	53	0

Ralph Felton

Year	Team		No	Yds	Avg	Lg	TD
1954	WAS	N	2	7	3.5	7	0
1957			1	6	6.0	6	0
1959			2	6	3.0	6	0
1961	BUF	A	2	15	7.5	15	0
1962			0	1		1L	0
Career			7	35	5.0	15	0

Gary Fencik

Year	Team		No	Yds	Avg	Lg	TD
1977	CHI	N	4	33	8.3	23	0
1978			4	77	19.3	59	0
1979			6	31	5.2	17	0
1980			1	8	8.0	8	0
1981			6	121	20.2	69t	1

Year	Team		No	Yds	Avg	Lg	TD

Gary Fencik *continued*

Year	Team		No	Yds	Avg	Lg	TD
1982			2	2	1.0	2	0
1983			2	34	17.0	20	0
1984			5	102	20.4	61	0
1985			5	43	8.6	22	0
1986			3	37	12.3	24	0
Career			38	488	12.8	69t	1
Playoffs			2	5	2.5		0

Chuck Fenenbock

Year	Team		No	Yds	Avg	Lg	TD
1943	DET	N	1	28	28.0	28	0
1945			1	10	10.0	10	0
Career			2	38	19.0	28	0

Bob Fenimore

Year	Team		No	Yds	Avg	Lg	TD
1947	CHIB	N	2	83	41.5	71	0

Keith Ferguson

Year	Team		No	Yds	Avg	Lg	TD
1986	DET	N	1	7	7.0	7	0

Jack Ferrante

Year	Team		No	Yds	Avg	Lg	TD
1945	PHI	N	1	15	15.0	15	0

Neil Ferris

Year	Team		No	Yds	Avg	Lg	TD
1952	PHI	N	0	3		3L	0

Jim Fetherton

Year	Team		No	Yds	Avg	Lg	TD
1968	SD	A	1	0	0.0	0	0

Ross Fichtner

Year	Team		No	Yds	Avg	Lg	TD
1962	CLE	N	7	76	10.9	31	0
1963			2	75	37.5	39	1
1964			2	67	33.5	64	0
1965			4	98	24.5	48	1
1966			8	152	19.0	58	1
1967			4	113	28.3	88	0
Career			27	581	21.5	88	3

Floyd Fields

Year	Team		No	Yds	Avg	Lg	TD
1992	SD	N	1	0	0.0	0	0

George Fields

Year	Team		No	Yds	Avg	Lg	TD
1960	OAK	A	2	7	3.5		0

Cedric Figaro

Year	Team		No	Yds	Avg	Lg	TD
1989	SD	N	1	2	2.0	2	0
1991	CLE	N	1	9	9.0	9	0
Career			2	11	5.5	9	0

George Figner

Year	Team		No	Yds	Avg	Lg	TD
1953	CHIB	N	1	4	4.0	4	0

Deon Figures

Year	Team		No	Yds	Avg	Lg	TD
1993	PIT	N	1	78	78.0	78	0
1996			2	13	6.5	13	0
Career			3	91	30.3	78	0

Frank Filchock

Year	Team		No	Yds	Avg	Lg	TD
1940	WAS	N	4	1	0.3		0
1945			1	0	0.0	0	0
1946	NYG	N	1	19	19.0	19	0
Career			6	20	3.3	19	0

Jim Files

Year	Team		No	Yds	Avg	Lg	TD
1970	NYG	N	1	8	8.0	8	0
1971			1	29	29.0	29	0
1972			2	46	23.0	37t	1
1973			1	22	22.0	22	0
Career			5	105	21.0	37t	1

Steve Filipowicz

Year	Team		No	Yds	Avg	Lg	TD
1946	NYG	N	4	52	13.0	31t	1

Jim Finks

Year	Team		No	Yds	Avg	Lg	TD
1949	PIT	N	1	14	14.0	14	0
1950			3	24	8.0	24	0
1951			3	46	15.3	25t	1
Career			7	84	12.0	25t	1

Al Fiorentino

Year	Team		No	Yds	Avg	Lg	TD
1944	WAS	N	1	0	0.0	0	0

Bill Fischer

Year	Team		No	Yds	Avg	Lg	TD
1949	CHIC	N	1	3	3.0	3	0

Clete Fischer

Year	Team		No	Yds	Avg	Lg	TD
1949	NYG	N	2	10	5.0	7	0

Pat Fischer

Year	Team		No	Yds	Avg	Lg	TD
1962	STL	N	3	41	13.7	25	0
1963			8	169	21.1	55	0
1964			10	164	16.4	39t	2
1965			3	30	10.0	16	0
1966			1	40	40.0	40	0
1967			4	85	21.3	69t	1
1968	WAS	N	2	14	7.0	13	0
1969			2	28	14.0	27	0
1970			2	13	6.5	10	0
1971			3	103	34.3	53t	0
1972			4	61	15.3	35	0
1973			3	99	33.0	67	0
1974			3	52	17.3	30	0
1975			3	4	1.3	4	0
1976			5	38	7.6	32	0
Career			56	941	16.8	69t	4
Playoffs			1	17	17.0		0

Jeff Fisher

Year	Team		No	Yds	Avg	Lg	TD
1981	CHI	N	2	3	1.5	3	0
1982			3	19	6.3	19	0
Career			5	22	4.4	19	0

Jason Fisk

Year	Team		No	Yds	Avg	Lg	TD
1996	MIN	N	1	0	0.0	0	0

Galen Fiss

Year	Team		No	Yds	Avg	Lg	TD
1956	CLE	N	1	4	4.0	4	0
1957			1	15	15.0	15	0
1959			1	9	9.0	9	0
1960			1	19	19.0	10	0
1961			1	13	13.0	13	0
1962			4	81	20.3	40	0
1963			2	8	4.0	6	0
1964			1	24	24.0	24	0
1965			1	5	5.0	5	0
Career			13	178	13.7	40	0

Fitzgerald

Year	Team		No	Yds	Avg	Lg	TD
1920	DET	A					1

Mike Fitzgerald

Year	Team		No	Yds	Avg	Lg	TD
1966	MIN	N	1	18	18.0	18	0

Dick Flanagan

Year	Team		No	Yds	Avg	Lg	TD
1951	DET	N	2	0	0.0	0	0
1952			1	14	14.0	14	0
1953	PIT	N	2	23	11.5	23	0
1954			3	0	0.0	0	0
Career			8	37	4.6	23	0

Hoot Flanagan

Year	Team		No	Yds	Avg	Lg	TD
1925	POT	N					2

Jim Flanigan

Year	Team		No	Yds	Avg	Lg	TD
1971	NO	N	1	10	10.0	10	0

Don Fleming

Year	Team		No	Yds	Avg	Lg	TD
1960	CLE	N	5	85	17.0	30	0
1961			3	62	20.7	41	0
1962			2	13	6.5	13	0
Career			10	160	16.0	41	0

Chris Fletcher

Year	Team		No	Yds	Avg	Lg	TD
1971	SD	N	3	63	21.0	36t	1
1974			4	74	18.5	31	0
1975			6	100	16.7	45	0
Career			13	237	18.2	45	1

Simon Fletcher

Year	Team		No	Yds	Avg	Lg	TD
1988	DEN	N	1	4	4.0	4	0
1994			1	4	4.0	4	0
Career			2	8	4.0	4	0

Judson Flint

Year	Team		No	Yds	Avg	Lg	TD
1981	CLE	N	2	33	16.5	33	0

Judson Flint *continued*

Year	Team		No	Yds	Avg	Lg	TD
1982			1	0	0.0	0	0
Career			3	33	11.0	33	0

Bob Flowers

Year	Team		No	Yds	Avg	Lg	TD
1943	GB	N	1	0	0.0	0	0
1947			1	12	12.0	12	0
1948			4	21	5.3	19	0
Career			6	33	5.5	19	0

Keith Flowers

Year	Team		No	Yds	Avg	Lg	TD
1952	DAL	N	1	16	16.0	16	0

Larry Flowers

Year	Team		No	Yds	Avg	Lg	TD
1981	NYG	N	1	9	9.0	9	0
1983			1	19	19.0	19	0
Career			2	28	14.0	19	0

Richmond Flowers

Year	Team		No	Yds	Avg	Lg	TD
1971	NYG	N	1	0	0.0	0	0
1972			4	30	7.5	20	0
1973			1	0	0.0	0	0
Career			6	30	5.0	20	0

Don Floyd

Year	Team		No	Yds	Avg	Lg	TD
1962	HOU	A	4	50	12.5	28	1
1964			0	8		8L	0
Career			4	58	14.5	28	1

Don Flynn

Year	Team		No	Yds	Avg	Lg	TD
1960	DAL	A	3	65	21.7		1
1961			2	9	4.5	9	0
Career			5	74	14.8	9	1

Tom Flynn

Year	Team		No	Yds	Avg	Lg	TD
1984	GB	N	9	106	11.8	31	0
1985			1	7	7.0	7	0
1986			1	0	0.0	0	0
Career			11	113	10.3	31	0

Steve Foley

Year	Team		No	Yds	Avg	Lg	TD
1976	DEN	N	4	95	23.8	34	0
1977			3	22	7.3	22	0
1978			6	84	14.0	30	0
1979			6	14	2.3	7	0
1980			4	115	28.8	36	0
1981			5	81	16.2	24	0
1983			5	28	5.6	16	0
1984			6	97	16.2	40t	1
1985			3	47	15.7	29	0
1986			2	39	19.5	24	0
Career			44	622	14.1	40t	1

Tim Foley

Year	Team		No	Yds	Avg	Lg	TD
1971	MIA	N	4	14	3.5	18	0
1972			3	25	8.3	15	0
1973			2	22	11.0	15	0
1974			2	-2	-1.0	0	0
1977			3	17	5.7	17	0
1978			6	12	2.0	8	0
1979			2	8	4.0	8	0
Career			22	96	4.4	18	0

Wayne Fontes

Year	Team		No	Yds	Avg	Lg	TD
1962	NY	A	4	145	36.3	83	1

Adrian Ford

Year	Team		No	Yds	Avg	Lg	TD
1926	PHI	A					1

Charlie Ford

Year	Team		No	Yds	Avg	Lg	TD
1971	CHI	N	5	46	9.2	24	0
1972			7	104	14.9	43	0
1973			2	50	25.0	41	0
1975	BUF	N	1	19	19.0	19	0
Career			15	219	14.6	43	0

Henry Ford

Year	Team		No	Yds	Avg	Lg	TD
1956	PIT	N	1	17	17.0	17	0

Len Ford

Year	Team		No	Yds	Avg	Lg	TD
1948	LA	AA	1	0	0.0	0	0
1949			1	45	45.0	45	0

Year	Team		No	Yds	Avg	Lg	TD

Len Ford *continued*

Year	Team		No	Yds	Avg	Lg	TD
1953	CLE	N	1	0	0.0	0	0
Career			3	45	15.0	45	0
Playoffs			3	46	15.3		0

Bill Forester

1953	GB	N	1	0	0.0	0	0
1954			1	21	21.0	21	0
1955			4	32	8.0	17	0
1956			4	35	8.8	13	0
1957			4	79	19.8	37	0
1959			2	48	24.0	34	0
1960			2	18	9.0	15	0
1961			2	33	16.5	33	0
1963			1	13	13.0	13	0
Career			21	279	13.3	37	0

Fred Forsberg

1968	DEN	A	1	6	6.0	6	0
1971	DEN	N	3	75	25.0	40t	1
1973			1	7	7.0	7	0
Career			5	88	17.6	40t	1

Bob Forte

1946	GB	N	2	23	11.5	16	0
1947			9	140	15.6	68t	1
1948			5	56	11.2	40	0
1949			2	17	8.5	17	0
1950			1	5	5.0	5	0
1952			4	50	12.5	25	0
Career			23	291	12.7	68t	1

Danny Fortmann

1940	CHIB	N	1	7	7.0	7	0
1941			3	7	2.3	5	0
1942			4	40	10.0	20	0
Career			8	54	6.8	20	0
Playoffs			1	2	2.0		0

Joe Fortunato

1956	CHIB	N	2	30	15.0	27t	1
1958			1	5	5.0	5	0
1959			2	10	5.0	6	0
1961	CHI	N	3	34	11.3	16	0
1962			3	44	14.7	36	0
1963			2	30	15.0	19	0
1965			2	0	0.0	0	0
1966			1	3	3.0	3	0
Career			16	156	9.8	36	1

Elbert Foules

1983	PHI	N	1	0	0.0	0	0
1984			4	27	6.8	20	0
1986			1	14	14.0	14	0
1987			4	6	1.5	6	0
Career			10	47	4.7	20	0

Sid Fournet

| 1956 | LA | N | 1 | 29 | 29.0 | 29 | 0 |

Aubrey Fowler

| 1948 | BAL | AA | 3 | 0 | 0.0 | | 0 |

Tim Fox

1976	NE	N	3	67	22.3	29	0
1977			3	39	13.0	27	0
1978			2	10	5.0	10	0
1979			2	38	19.0	25	0
1980			4	41	10.3	23	0
1981			3	20	6.7	20	0
1982	SD	N	4	103	25.8	35	0
1983			2	14	7.0	14	0
1984			1	36	36.0	36	0
1985	LARM	N	2	8	4.0	8	0
Career			26	376	14.5	36	0
Playoffs			2	18	9.0		0

Gene Francis

| 1926 | CHIC | N | | | | | 1 |

James Francis

| 1990 | CIN | N | 1 | 17 | 17.0 | 17t | 1 |
| 1991 | | | 1 | 0 | 0.0 | 0 | 0 |

James Francis *continued*

Year	Team		No	Yds	Avg	Lg	TD
1992			3	108	36.0	66t	1
1993			2	12	6.0	12	0
1996			3	61	20.3	42t	1
Career			10	198	19.8	66t	3

Ron Francis

1987	DAL	N	2	18	9.0	18t	1
1988			1	29	29.0	29	0
1989			1	2	2.0	2	0
Career			4	49	12.3	29	1

Sam Francis

| 1937 | CHIB | N | | | | | 1 |

George Franck

1941	NYG	N	4	94	23.5	45	0
1947			1	0	0.0	0	0
Career			5	94	18.8	45	0

Tom Franckhauser

1959	LA	N	3	2	0.7	2	0
1960	DAL	N	3	11	3.7	9	0
1961			1	23	23.0	23	0
1962	MIN	N	4	27	6.8	24	0
1963			2	59	29.5	32	0
Career			13	122	9.4	32	0

Donald Frank

1990	SD	N	2	8	4.0	4	0
1991			1	71	71.0	71t	1
1992			4	37	9.3	33	0
1993			3	119	39.7	102t	1
1994	LARI	N	1	8	8.0	8	0
1995	MIN	N	3	72	24.0	42	0
Career			14	315	22.5	102t	2

Ike Frankian

| Playoffs | | | 1 | 0 | 0.0 | | 0 |

Bobby Franklin

1960	CLE	N	8	131	16.4	37t	2
1961			2	20	10.0	20	0
1962			1	10	10.0	10	0
1963			2	26	13.0	14	0
Career			13	187	14.4	37t	2

Jim Fraser

1962	DEN	A	1	2	2.0	2	0
1964			1	1	1.0	1	0
1966	BOS	A	1	3	3.0	3	0
Career			3	6	2.0	3	0

Derrick Frazier

| 1995 | PHI | N | 1 | 3 | 3.0 | 3 | 0 |

Guy Frazier

| 1985 | BUF | N | 1 | 8 | 8.0 | 8 | 0 |

Leslie Frazier

1982	CHI	N	2	0	0.0	0	0
1983			7	135	19.3	58	1
1984			5	89	17.8	33	0
1985			6	119	19.8	33	1
Career			20	343	17.1	58	2
Playoffs			1	-3	-3.0		0

Rob Frederickson

| 1995 | OAK | N | 1 | 14 | 14.0 | 14 | 0 |

Bobby Freeman

1957	CLE	N	3	46	15.3	25	0
1958			3	21	7.0	19	0
1959	GB	N	2	22	11.0	22	0
1960	PHI	N	4	67	16.8	48	0
1962	WAS	N	3	48	16.0	40	0
Career			15	204	13.6	48	0

Mike Freeman

| 1970 | ATL | N | 1 | 3 | 3.0 | 3 | 0 |

Steve Freeman

| 1975 | BUF | N | 2 | 44 | 22.0 | 30t | 1 |

Steve Freeman *continued*

Year	Team		No	Yds	Avg	Lg	TD
1977			1	4	4.0	4	0
1979			3	62	20.7	50t	1
1980			7	107	15.3	47t	1
1982			3	27	9.0	14	0
1983			3	40	13.3	29	0
1984			3	45	15.0	45	0
1986			1	0	0.0	0	0
Career			23	329	14.3	50t	3
Playoffs			1	30	30.0		0

Jess Freitas

1946	SF	AA	2	40	20.0		0
1947			1	11	11.0	11	0
Career			3	51	17.0	11	0

Bob Friedman

| 1944 | PHI | N | 1 | 2 | 2.0 | 2 | 0 |

Sherwood Fries

| 1943 | GB | N | 2 | 6 | 3.0 | 4 | 0 |

Ted Fritsch

1944	GB	N	6	115	19.2	50	1
1945			1	69	69.0	69t	1
1946			1	15	15.0	15	0
1947			1	12	12.0	12	0
1948			1	52	52.0	52	0
Career			10	263	26.3	69t	2

William Frizzell

1985	DET	N	1	3	3.0	3	0
1988	PHI	N	3	19	6.3	13	0
1989			4	58	14.5	27	0
1990			3	91	30.3	37	1
Career			11	171	15.5	37	1

Ken Frost

| 1961 | DAL | N | 1 | 0 | 0.0 | 0 | 0 |

Wes Fry

1926	NY	A					2
1927	NYY	N					1
Career							3

David Frye

| 1985 | ATL | N | 1 | 20 | 20.0 | 20 | 0 |

Bill Fulcher

| 1956 | WAS | N | 1 | 0 | 0.0 | 0 | 0 |

David Fulcher

1986	CIN	N	4	20	5.0	15	0
1987			3	30	10.0	28	0
1988			5	38	7.6	16t	1
1989			8	87	10.9	22	0
1990			4	20	5.0	18	0
1991			4	51	12.8	27t	1
1992			3	0	0.0	0	0
Career			31	246	7.9	28	2
Playoffs			3	54	18.0		0

Corey Fuller

1995	MIN	N	1	0	0.0	0	0
1996			3	3	1.0	2	0
Career			4	3	0.8	2	0

James Fuller

| 1996 | PHI | N | 1 | 4 | 4.0 | 4 | 0 |

Jeff Fuller

1984	SF	N	1	38	38.0	38	0
1985			1	4	4.0	4	0
1986			4	44	11.0	26	0
1988			4	18	4.5	10	0
Career			10	104	10.4	38	0
Playoffs			2	48	24.0		1

Joe Fuller

| 1990 | SD | N | 1 | 5 | 5.0 | 5 | 0 |

Johnny Fuller

| 1968 | SF | N | 2 | 3 | 1.5 | 3 | 0 |

Johnny Fuller *continued*

Year	Team		No	Yds	Avg	Lg	TD
1969			1	31	31.0	31	0
1970			1	20	20.0	20	0
1971			2	57	28.5	57	0
1972			1	0	0.0	0	0
1974	NO	N	1	16	16.0	16	0
Career			8	127	15.9	57	0

Mike Fuller

Year	Team		No	Yds	Avg	Lg	TD
1975	SD	N	1	1	1.0	1	0
1976			1	0	0.0	0	0
1977			5	61	12.2	37	0
1978			4	44	11.0	23	1
1979			4	39	9.8	23	0
1981	CIN	N	1	31	31.0	31	0
1982			1	0	0.0	0	0
Career			17	176	10.4	37	1
Playoffs			1	20	20.0		0

Randy Fuller

Year	Team		No	Yds	Avg	Lg	TD
1996	PIT	N	1	0	0.0	0	0

William Fuller

Year	Team		No	Yds	Avg	Lg	TD
1988	HOU	N	1	9	9.0	9	0

Darrell Fullington

Year	Team		No	Yds	Avg	Lg	TD
1988	MIN	N	3	57	19.0	40	0
1989			1	0	0.0	0	0
1990			1	10	10.0	10	0
1991	TB	N	2	13	6.5	10	0
1992			3	25	8.3	16	0
Career			10	105	10.5	40	0

Tony Furst

Year	Team		No	Yds	Avg	Lg	TD
1941	DET	N	1	0	0.0	0	0

Bobby Futrell

Year	Team		No	Yds	Avg	Lg	TD
1987	TB	N	2	46	23.0	23	0
1988			1	26	26.0	26	0
1989			1	1	1.0	1	0
Career			4	73	18.3	26	0

Mike Gaechter

Year	Team		No	Yds	Avg	Lg	TD
1962	DAL	N	5	136	27.2	100t	1
1963			3	140	46.7	86	0
1965			2	21	10.5	19	0
1966			3	28	9.3	23	0
1967			2	0	0.0	0	0
1968			3	23	7.7	17	0
1969			3	72	24.0	37	0
Career			21	420	20.0	100t	1

Monk Gafford

Year	Team		No	Yds	Avg	Lg	TD
1946	MIA-BKN	AA	4	88	22.0	51	0
1947	BKN	AA	3	16	5.3		0
Career			7	104	14.9	51	0

Bobby Gage

Year	Team		No	Yds	Avg	Lg	TD
1949	PIT	N	5	58	11.6	16	0
1950			4	64	16.0	23	0
Career			9	122	13.6	23	0

Steve Gage

Year	Team		No	Yds	Avg	Lg	TD
1987	WAS	N	1	7	7.0	7	0

Bob Gain

Year	Team		No	Yds	Avg	Lg	TD
1960	CLE	N	1	22	22.0	22t	1

Greg Gaines

Year	Team		No	Yds	Avg	Lg	TD
1984	SEA	N	1	18	18.0	18	0
1986			1	8	8.0	8	0
Career			2	26	13.0	18	0

Wentford Gaines

Year	Team		No	Yds	Avg	Lg	TD
1978	CHI	N	1	0	0.0	0	0
1979			1	38	38.0	38	0
Career			2	38	19.0	38	0

Blane Gaison

Year	Team		No	Yds	Avg	Lg	TD
1981	ATL	N	1	0	0.0	0	0
1982			1	0	0.0	0	0
Career			2	0	0.0	0	0

Dave Gallagher

Year	Team		No	Yds	Avg	Lg	TD
1976	NYG	N	1	7	7.0	7	0

Hugh Gallarneau

Year	Team		No	Yds	Avg	Lg	TD
1941	CHIB	N	1	46	46.0	46t	1
1945			2	6	3.0	5	0
1947			1	9	9.0	9	0
Career			4	61	15.3	46t	1

David Galloway

Year	Team		No	Yds	Avg	Lg	TD
1983	STL	N	1	17	17.0	17	0

Duane Galloway

Year	Team		No	Yds	Avg	Lg	TD
1986	DET	N	4	58	14.5	36	0
1987			3	46	15.3	30	0
Career			7	104	14.9	36	0

Kenny Gamble

Year	Team		No	Yds	Avg	Lg	TD
1988	KC	N	1	2	2.0	2	0

Sonny Gandee

Year	Team		No	Yds	Avg	Lg	TD
1953	DET	N	1	0	0.0	0	0
1954			3	29	9.7	17	0
Career			4	29	7.3	17	0

Mike Gann

Year	Team		No	Yds	Avg	Lg	TD
1991	ATL	N	1	0	0.0	0	0

Brian Gant

Year	Team		No	Yds	Avg	Lg	TD
1987	TB	N	1	5	5.0	5	0

Kenneth Gant

Year	Team		No	Yds	Avg	Lg	TD
1990	DAL	N	1	26	26.0	26	0
1991			1	0	0.0	0	0
1992			3	19	6.3	11	0
1993			1	0	0.0	0	0
1994			1	0	0.0	0	0
Career			7	45	6.4	26	0

Milt Gantenbein

Year	Team		No	Yds	Avg	Lg	TD
Playoffs			1	5	5.0		0

Don Garlin

Year	Team		No	Yds	Avg	Lg	TD
1949	SF	AA	1	0	0.0	0	0

John Garlington

Year	Team		No	Yds	Avg	Lg	TD
1968	CLE	N	1	0	0.0	0	0
1969			2	4	2.0	4	0
1970			1	6	6.0	6	0
1971			1	0	0.0	0	0
1972			1	10	10.0	10	0
1973			1	10	10.0	10	0
1974			2	33	16.5	28	0
Career			9	63	7.0	28	0

Bob Garner

Year	Team		No	Yds	Avg	Lg	TD
1960	LA	A	2	2	1.0		0
1961	OAK	A	2	14	7.0	11	0
1962			3	31	10.3	11	0
Career			7	47	6.7	11	0

Drake Garrett

Year	Team		No	Yds	Avg	Lg	TD
1968	DEN	A	2	6	3.0	6	0

Thurman Garrett

Year	Team		No	Yds	Avg	Lg	TD
1947	CHIB	N	1	2	2.0	2	0

Leon Garror

Year	Team		No	Yds	Avg	Lg	TD
1973	BUF	N	1	0	0.0	0	0

Russell Gary

Year	Team		No	Yds	Avg	Lg	TD
1981	NO	N	1	0	0.0	0	0
1982			2	25	12.5	19	0
1983			3	70	23.3	26	0
1986			1	14	14.0	14	0
Career			7	109	15.6	26	0

Thane Gash

Year	Team		No	Yds	Avg	Lg	TD
1989	CLE	N	3	65	21.7	36t	2
1990			1	16	16.0	16	0
Career			4	81	20.3	36t	2

Frank Gatski

Year	Team		No	Yds	Avg	Lg	TD
1946	CLE	AA	1	35	35.0	35t	1

Frank Gatski *continued*

Year	Team		No	Yds	Avg	Lg	TD
1947			2	0	0.0		0
Career			3	35	11.7	35t	1

Dennis Gaubatz

Year	Team		No	Yds	Avg	Lg	TD
1963	DET	N	1	55	55.0	55	0
1964			1	16	16.0	16	0
1965	BAL	N	1	5	5.0	5	0
1966			2	12	6.0	10	0
1967			2	10	5.0	5	0
1968			2	15	7.5	10	0
1969			1	11	11.0	11	0
Career			10	124	12.4	55	0

Charlie Gauer

Year	Team		No	Yds	Avg	Lg	TD
1943	P-P	N	1	0	0.0	0	0
1944	PHI	N	1	2	2.0	2	0
Career			2	2	1.0	2	0

Chuck Gavin

Year	Team		No	Yds	Avg	Lg	TD
1962	DEN	A	1	35	35.0	35	0

William Gay

Year	Team		No	Yds	Avg	Lg	TD
1982	DET	N	1	7	7.0	7	0
1985			1	7	7.0	7	0
Career			2	14	7.0	7	0

Shaun Gayle

Year	Team		No	Yds	Avg	Lg	TD
1984	CHI	N	1	-1	-1.0	-1	0
1986			1	13	13.0	13	0
1987			1	20	20.0	20t	1
1988			1	0	0.0	0	0
1989			3	39	13.0	20	0
1990			2	5	2.5	5	0
1991			1	11	11.0	11	0
1992			2	39	19.5	30	0
1994			2	33	16.5	33	0
1995	SD	N	2	99	49.5	99t	1
Career			16	258	16.1	99t	2
Playoffs			1	27	27.0		0

Bob Geddes

Year	Team		No	Yds	Avg	Lg	TD
1974	NE	N	2	32	16.0	29t	1

Ken Geddes

Year	Team		No	Yds	Avg	Lg	TD
1974	LA	N	2	15	7.5	15	0
1975			1	4	4.0	4	0
1977	SEA	N	3	9	3.0	6	0
Career			6	28	4.7	15	0

Fred Gehrke

Year	Team		No	Yds	Avg	Lg	TD
1945	CLE	N	4	16	4.0	14	0
1946	LA	N	3	63	21.0	41	0
1947			1	0	0.0	0	0
1948			2	29	14.5	21	0
1950	CHIC	N	3	23	7.7	23	0
Career			13	131	10.1	41	0

Chuck Gelatka

Year	Team		No	Yds	Avg	Lg	TD
1938	NYG	N					1

Curtis Gentry

Year	Team		No	Yds	Avg	Lg	TD
1966	CHI	N	1	0	0.0	0	0
1967			4	25	6.3	17	0
1968			1	7	7.0	7	0
Career			6	32	5.3	17	0

Lee Gentry

Year	Team		No	Yds	Avg	Lg	TD
1941	WAS	N	1	9	9.0	9	0

Bill George

Year	Team		No	Yds	Avg	Lg	TD
1954	CHIB	N	2	9	4.5	6	0
1955			2	13	6.5	13	0
1956			2	9	4.5	9	0
1958			1	5	5.0	5	0
1959			2	20	10.0	20	0
1960	CHI	N	1	12	12.0	12	0
1961			3	18	6.0	13	0
1962			2	26	13.0	15	0
1963			1	4	4.0	4	0
1964			2	28	14.0	20	0
Career			18	144	8.0	20	0

Year	Team		No	Yds	Avg	Lg	TD

Ed Gerber
Year	Team		No	Yds	Avg	Lg	TD
1942	PHI	N	1	0	0.0	0	0

Willie Germany
| 1975 | HOU | N | 2 | 15 | 7.5 | 15 | 0 |

Carl Gersbach
1973	SD	N	1	9	9.0	9	0
1974			1	0	0.0	0	0
1975	CHI	N	1	4	4.0	4	0
Career			3	13	4.3	9	0

Bill Geyer
| 1943 | CHIB | N | 2 | 0 | 0.0 | 0 | 0 |

Vern Ghersanich
| 1943 | CHIC | N | 1 | 19 | 19.0 | 19 | 0 |

Antonio Gibson
1986	NO	N	2	43	21.5	43	0
1987			1	17	17.0	17	0
Career			3	60	20.0	43	0

Claude Gibson
1961	SD	A	5	43	8.6	23	0
1962			8	85	10.6	37	1
1963	OAK	A	3	18	6.0	18	0
1964			2	74	37.0	39	0
1965			4	53	13.3	22	0
Career			22	273	12.4	39	1

Dennis Gibson
1987	DET	N	1	5	5.0	5	0
1989			1	10	10.0	10	0
1993			1	0	0.0	0	0
Career			3	15	5.0	10	0

Ernest Gibson
1984	NE	N	2	4	2.0	4	0
1987			2	17	8.5	17	0
Career			4	21	5.3	17	0

Joe Gibson
| 1947 | BKN | AA | 1 | 0 | 0.0 | 0 | 0 |

Paul Gibson
| 1949 | BUF | AA | 1 | 9 | 9.0 | 9 | 0 |

Frank Gifford
1952	NYG	N	1	46	46.0	46	0
1953			1	66	66.0	50	1
Career			2	112	56.0	50	1

Freddie Gilbert
| Playoffs | | | 1 | 0 | 0.0 | | 0 |

Wally Gilbert
| 1924 | DUL | N | | | | | 1 |

Sloko Gill
| 1942 | DET | N | 1 | 9 | 9.0 | 9 | 0 |

Jim Gillette
1944	CLE	N	3	29	9.7	15	0
1945			4	8	2.0	4	0
1946	BOS	N	1	5	5.0	5	0
1948	DET	N	6	17	2.8	10	0
Career			14	59	4.2	15	0

Horace Gillom
| 1947 | CLE | AA | 1 | 29 | 29.0 | 29 | 0 |

Harry Gilmer
| 1951 | WAS | N | 5 | 79 | 15.8 | 30 | 0 |

Earl Girard
1948	GB	N	1	34	34.0	34	0
1949			1	41	41.0	41	0
1950			1	6	6.0	6	0
1951			5	25	5.0	15	0
Career			8	106	13.3	41	0

Chet Gladchuk
| 1941 | NYG | N | 1 | 16 | 16.0 | 16 | 0 |

Nesby Glasgow
1979	BAL	N	1	-1	-1.0	-1	0
1980			4	65	16.3	29	0
1981			2	35	17.5	31	0
1983			3	35	11.7	18	0
1984	IND	N	1	8	8.0	8	0
1987			1	0	0.0	0	0
1988	SEA	N	2	19	9.5	19	0
1991			1	28	28.0	28	0
Career			15	189	12.6	31	0

Bill Glass
1965	CLE	N	1	0	0.0	0	0
1967			1	0	0.0	0	0
1968			2	21	10.5	17t	0
Career			4	21	5.3	17t	0

Glen Glass
1963	PIT	N	1	29	29.0	29	0
1964	PHI	N	1	18	18.0	18	0
Career			2	47	23.5	29	0

Charles Glaze
| 1987 | SEA | N | 2 | 53 | 26.5 | 53 | 0 |

Bob Glazebrook
1980	ATL	N	2	6	3.0	6	0
1981			2	21	10.5	18	0
1982			1	10	10.0	10	0
1983			3	30	10.0	25	0
Career			8	67	8.4	25	0
Playoffs			1	35	35.0		1

Aaron Glenn
1995	NYJ	N	1	17	17.0	17	0
1996			4	113	28.3	100t	2
Career			5	130	26.0	100t	2

Kerry Glenn
1985	NYJ	N	4	15	3.8	15t	1
1989			1	0	0.0	0	0
1990	MIA	N	2	31	15.5	31t	1
Career			7	46	6.6	31t	2

Vencie Glenn
1986	SD	N	2	31	15.5	31	0
1987			4	166	41.5	10t	1
1988			1	0	0.0	0	0
1989			4	52	13.0	31	0
1990			1	0	0.0	0	0
1991	NO	N	4	35	8.8	18	0
1992	MIN	N	5	65	13.0	39	0
1993			5	49	9.8	23	0
1994			4	55	13.8	32	0
1995	NYG	N	5	91	18.2	75t	1
Career			35	544	15.5	75t	2
Playoffs			1	0	0.0		0

Fred Glick
1961	HOU	A	4	28	7.0	11	0
1962			3	53	17.7	31	0
1963			12	180	15.0	45	1
1964			5	54	10.8	27	0
1965			2	18	9.0	18	0
1966			4	57	14.3	41	0
Career			30	390	13.0	45	1
Playoffs			1	0	0.0		0

Gary Glick
1957	PIT	N	2	0	0.0	0	0
1958			2	60	30.0	20	0
1959	WAS	N	2	35	17.5	35	0
1960			3	4	1.3	3	0
1961	BAL	N	4	18	4.5	10	0
1963	SD	A	1	13	13.0	13	0
Career			14	130	9.3	35	0

Larry Glueck
| 1963 | CHI | N | 1 | 14 | 14.0 | 14 | 0 |

Les Goble
| 1954 | CHIC | N | 1 | 3 | 3.0 | 3 | 0 |

Bill Godwin
| 1947 | BOS | N | 2 | 27 | 13.5 | 16 | 0 |

Keith Goganious
| 1995 | JAC | N | 2 | 11 | 5.5 | 6 | 0 |

Marshall Goldberg
1941	CHIC	N	7	54	7.7	16	0
1942			3	39	13.0	21	0
1943			1	0	0.0	0	0
1946			4	46	11.5	14	0
1948			2	9	4.5	5	0
Career			17	148	8.7	21	0

Buckets Goldenberg
1933	GB	N					1
1937							1
1941			1	0	0.0	0	0
1942			4	31	7.8	15	0
1943			2	37	18.5	30	0
Career			7	68	9.7	30	2

Joe Golding
1947	BOS	N	5	87	17.4	28	0
1948			4	205	51.3	89t	2
1949	NYB	N	1	65	65.0	65t	1
1950	NYY	N	7	145	20.7	46	1
1951			2	9	4.5	9	0
Career			19	511	26.9	89t	4

John Goldsberry
| 1949 | CHIC | N | 1 | 36 | 36.0 | 36 | 0 |

Bob Golic
| 1983 | CLE | N | 1 | 7 | 7.0 | 7t | 1 |

Mike Golic
1989	PHI	N	1	23	23.0	23	0
1990			1	12	12.0	12	0
1991			1	13	13.0	13	0
Career			3	48	16.0	23	0

Bill Gompers
| 1948 | BUF | AA | 2 | 74 | 37.0 | 58 | 0 |

George Gonda
| 1942 | PIT | N | 1 | 37 | 37.0 | 37 | 0 |

Goose Gonsoulin
1960	DEN	A	11	98	8.9		0
1961			6	76	12.7	38	0
1962			7	88	12.6	64	1
1963			6	64	10.7	42	1
1964			7	125	17.9	36	0
1965			6	91	15.2	32	0
1967	SF	N	3	9	3.0	5	0
Career			46	551	12.0	64	2

Chris Goode
1988	IND	N	2	53	26.5	35	0
1990			1	10	10.0	10	0
1991			2	27	13.5	27	0
1992			2	93	46.5	47	0
Career			7	183	26.1	47	0

Don Goode
1975	SD	N	1	37	37.0	37	0
1976			6	82	13.7	27	0
1978			1	0	0.0	0	0
1979			1	0	0.0	0	0
1981	CLE	N	1	1	1.0	1	0
Career			10	120	12.0	37	0

Rob Goode
1949	WAS	N	2	25	12.5	25	0
1950			2	29	14.5	20	0
Career			4	54	13.5	25	0

Owen Goodnight
| 1941 | CLE | N | 2 | 13 | 6.5 | 11 | 0 |

Alex Gordon
| 1989 | NYJ | N | 1 | 2 | 2.0 | 2 | 0 |

Bobby Gordon

Year	Team		No	Yds	Avg	Lg	TD
1958	CHIC	N	2	27	13.5	27	0
1960	HOU	A	3	45	15.0	27	0
Career			5	72	14.4	27	0
Playoffs			1	27	27.0		0

Cornell Gordon

Year	Team		No	Yds	Avg	Lg	TD
1965	NY	A	2	7	3.5	7	0
1967			1	14	14.0	14	0
1968			2	0	0.0	0	0
1969			4	23	5.8	20	0
1970	DEN	N	3	26	8.7	24	0
1971			2	21	10.5	21	0
Career			14	91	6.5	24	0

Darrien Gordon

Year	Team		No	Yds	Avg	Lg	TD
1993	SD	N	1	3	3.0	3	0
1994			4	32	8.0	23	0
1996			2	55	27.5	55	0
Career			7	90	12.9	55	0

Larry Gordon

Year	Team		No	Yds	Avg	Lg	TD
1977	MIA	N	1	27	27.0	27	0
1978			3	35	11.7	22	0
1979			2	33	16.5	33	0
1980			1	11	11.0	11	0
1982			1	15	15.0	15	0
Career			8	121	15.1	33	0

Tim Gordon

Year	Team		No	Yds	Avg	Lg	TD
1987	ATL	N	2	28	14.0	27	0
1988			2	10	5.0	7	0
1989			4	60	15.0	34	0
Career			8	98	12.3	34	0

Ken Gorgal

Year	Team		No	Yds	Avg	Lg	TD
1950	CLE	N	6	23	3.8	13	0
1953			4	25	6.3	19	0
1954			1	53	53.0	53t	1
1955	CHIB	N	6	107	17.8	34	0
1956	GB	N	2	2	1.0	2	0
Career			19	210	11.1	53t	1
Playoffs			3	40	13.3		0

Kurt Gouveia

Year	Team		No	Yds	Avg	Lg	TD
1989	WAS	N	1	1	1.0	1	0
1991			1	22	22.0	22	0
1992			3	43	14.3	28	0
1993			1	59	59.0	59t	1
1994			1	7	7.0	7	0
1995	PHI	N	1	20	20.0	20	0
1996	SD	N	3	41	13.7	21	0
Career			11	193	17.5	59t	1
Playoffs			4	70	17.5		0

Cornell Gowdy

Year	Team		No	Yds	Avg	Lg	TD
1987	PIT	N	2	50	25.0	45t	1
1988			1	24	24.0	24	0
Career			3	74	24.7	45t	1

Randy Gradishar

Year	Team		No	Yds	Avg	Lg	TD
1975	DEN	N	3	77	25.7	44t	1
1976			3	44	14.7	31t	1
1977			3	56	18.7	28	0
1978			4	19	4.8	8	0
1980			2	96	48.0	93t	1
1981			4	38	9.5	16	0
1983			1	5	5.0	5	0
Career			20	335	16.8	93t	3

Dave Graf

Year	Team		No	Yds	Avg	Lg	TD
1975	CLE	N	1	19	19.0	19	0

Rick Graf

Year	Team		No	Yds	Avg	Lg	TD
1988	MIA	N	1	14	14.0	14	0
1992	HOU	N	1	0	0.0	0	0
Career			2	14	7.0	14	0

Bill Graham

Year	Team		No	Yds	Avg	Lg	TD
1984	DET	N	3	22	7.3	15	0
1985			3	22	7.3	22	0
Career			6	44	7.3	22	0

Kenny Graham

Year	Team		No	Yds	Avg	Lg	TD
1964	SD	A	4	24	6.0	9	0
1965			5	108	21.6	51	1
1966			5	70	14.0	32	1
1967			2	76	38.0	68t	1
1968			5	87	17.4	42	0
1969			4	112	28.0	65t	2
1970	CIN	N	3	31	10.3	31	0
Career			28	508	18.1	68t	5

Lyle Graham

Year	Team		No	Yds	Avg	Lg	TD
1941	PHI	N	2	39	19.5	18	0

Mike Graham

Year	Team		No	Yds	Avg	Lg	TD
1948	LA	AA	1	20	20.0	20	0

Otto Graham

Year	Team		No	Yds	Avg	Lg	TD
1946	CLE	AA	5	102	20.4		1
1947			1	0	0.0	0	0
1948			1	0	0.0	0	0
Career			7	102	14.6		1
Playoffs			1	4	4.0		0

Tom Graham

Year	Team		No	Yds	Avg	Lg	TD
1972	DEN	N	2	10	5.0	7	0
1975	SD	N	2	5	2.5	4	0
1976			3	55	18.3	25	0
Career			7	70	10.0	25	0

Red Grange

Year	Team		No	Yds	Avg	Lg	TD
1925	CHIB	N					1
1926	NY	A					1
Career							2
Playoffs			1	11	11.0		0

Alan Grant

Year	Team		No	Yds	Avg	Lg	TD
1990	IND	N	1	25	25.0	25t	1
1993	CIN	N	1	17	17.0	17	0
1994	WAS	N	1	0	0.0	0	0
Career			3	42	14.0	25t	1

Bob Grant

Year	Team		No	Yds	Avg	Lg	TD
1969	BAL	N	3	0	0.0	0	0
1970			2	39	19.5	27t	1
Career			5	39	7.8	27t	1

Darryl Grant

Year	Team		No	Yds	Avg	Lg	TD
1989	WAS	N	2	0	0.0	0	0
Playoffs			1	10	10.0		1

David Grant

Year	Team		No	Yds	Avg	Lg	TD
1991	CIN	N	1	0	0.0	0	0

Steve Grant

Year	Team		No	Yds	Avg	Lg	TD
1995	IND	N	1	9	9.0	9	0
Playoffs			1	13	13.0		0

Larry Grantham

Year	Team		No	Yds	Avg	Lg	TD
1960	NY	A	5	13	2.6		0
1961			1	30	30.0	30	0
1962			2	2	1.0	2	0
1963			3	89	29.7	41	0
1964			2	32	16.0	22	0
1965			1	0			0
1966			1	14	14.0	14	0
1967			5	77	15.4	36	0
1970	NYJ	N	3	51	17.0	41t	1
1971			1	0	0.0	0	0
Career			24	308	12.8	41t	1

Ray Graves

Year	Team		No	Yds	Avg	Lg	TD
1942	PHI	N	1	0	0.0	0	0
1943	P-P	N	1	15	15.0	15	0
Career			2	15	7.5	15	0

White Graves

Year	Team		No	Yds	Avg	Lg	TD
1965	BOS	A	2	0	0.0	0	0
1966			1	0	0.0	0	0
Career			3	0	0.0	0	0

Carlton Gray

Year	Team		No	Yds	Avg	Lg	TD
1993	SEA	N	3	33	11.0	16	0
1994			2	0	0.0	0	0
1995			4	45	11.3	26	0

Carlton Gray *continued*

Year	Team		No	Yds	Avg	Lg	TD
1996			0	3		3L	0
Career			9	81	9.0	26	0

David Gray

Year	Team		No	Yds	Avg	Lg	TD
1979	NO	N	1	32	32.0	32	0

Derwin Gray

Year	Team		No	Yds	Avg	Lg	TD
1995	IND	N	1	10	10.0	10	0

Hector Gray

Year	Team		No	Yds	Avg	Lg	TD
1981	DET	N	1	0	0.0	0	0
1982			1	5	5.0	5	0
Career			2	5	2.5	5	0

Jerry Gray

Year	Team		No	Yds	Avg	Lg	TD
1986	LARM	N	8	101	12.6	28	0
1987			2	35	17.5	35	0
1988			3	83	27.7	47t	1
1989			6	48	8.0	27t	1
1991			3	83	27.7	59t	1
1992	HOU	N	6	24	4.0	22	0
Career			28	374	13.4	59t	3
Playoffs			1	10	10.0		0

Johnnie Gray

Year	Team		No	Yds	Avg	Lg	TD
1975	GB	N	1	7	7.0	7	0
1976			4	101	25.3	67	1
1977			1	12	12.0	12	0
1978			3	66	22.0	66	0
1979			5	66	13.2	35	0
1980			5	54	10.8	21	0
1982			1	21	21.0	21	0
1983			2	5	2.5	5	0
Career			22	332	15.1	67	1

Tim Gray

Year	Team		No	Yds	Avg	Lg	TD
1976	KC	N	4	19	4.8	11	0
1977			2	16	8.0	11	0
1978			6	118	19.7	61	0
1979	SF	N	1	20	20.0	20	0
Career			13	173	13.3	61	0

Dave Grayson

Year	Team		No	Yds	Avg	Lg	TD
1961	DAL	A	4	100	25.0	99	1
1962			4	6	1.5	6	0
1963	KC	A	5	17	3.4	11	0
1964			7	**187**	26.7	56	0
1965	OAK	A	3	145	48.3	79	2
1966			3	64	21.3	24	0
1967			4	63	15.8	23	0
1968			10	195	19.5	54	1
1969			8	132	16.5	76t	1
1970	OAK	N	1	25	25.0	25	0
Career			49	934	19.1	99	5
Playoffs			1	20	20.0		

David Grayson

Year	Team		No	Yds	Avg	Lg	TD
1989	CLE	N	2	25	12.5	14t	1
1990			1	3	3.0	3	0
Career			3	28	9.3	14t	1

Dick Grecni

Year	Team		No	Yds	Avg	Lg	TD
1961	MIN	N	1	16	16.0	16	0

Alex Green

Year	Team		No	Yds	Avg	Lg	TD
1987	DAL	N	1	0	0.0	0	0

Bubba Green

Year	Team		No	Yds	Avg	Lg	TD
1981	BAL	N	1	3	3.0	3	0

Chris Green

Year	Team		No	Yds	Avg	Lg	TD
1993	MIA	N	2	0	0.0	0	0

Cornell Green

Year	Team		No	Yds	Avg	Lg	TD
1963	DAL	N	7	211	30.1	55	0
1965			3	49	16.3	43	0
1966			4	88	22.0	41t	1
1967			7	52	7.4	28	0
1968			4	74	18.5	55t	1
1969			2	0	0.0	0	0
1970			1	59	59.0	59	0
1971			2	16	8.0	12	0

Year	Team		No	Yds	Avg	Lg	TD

Cornell Green *continued*

Year	Team		No	Yds	Avg	Lg	TD
1972			2	1	0.5	1	0
1974			2	2	1.0	2	0
Career			34	552	16.2	59	2
Playoffs			1	60	60.0		1

Darrell Green

Year	Team		No	Yds	Avg	Lg	TD
1983	WAS	N	2	7	3.5	7	0
1984			5	101	20.2	50	1
1985			2	0	0.0	0	0
1986			5	9	1.8	7	0
1987			3	65	21.7	56	0
1988			1	12	12.0	12	0
1989			2	0	0.0	0	0
1990			4	20	5.0	18t	1
1991			5	47	9.4	24	0
1992			1	15	15.0	15	0
1993			4	10	2.5	6	0
1994			3	32	10.7	27t	1
1995			3	42	14.0	22	1
1996			3	84	28.0	68t	1
Career			43	444	10.3	68t	5
Playoffs			5	121	24.2		2

Gary Green

Year	Team		No	Yds	Avg	Lg	TD
1977	KC	N	3	19	6.3	19	0
1978			1	0	0	0	0
1979			5	148	29.6	57	0
1980			2	25	12.5	25	0
1981			5	37	7.4	16	0
1982			2	42	21.0	42t	1
1983			6	59	9.8	25	0
1984	LARM	N	3	88	29.3	60	0
1985			6	84	14.0	41t	1
Career			33	502	15.2	60	2
Playoffs			1	1	1.0		0

Hugh Green

Year	Team		No	Yds	Avg	Lg	TD
1981	TB	N	2	56	28.0	50	0
1982			1	31	31.0	31	0
1983			2	54	27.0	33t	2
1985	MIA	N	1	28	28.0	28	0
Career			6	169	28.2	50	2

Jacob Green

Year	Team		No	Yds	Avg	Lg	TD
1983	SEA	N	1	73	73.0	73t	1
1985			1	19	19.0	19t	1
1991			1	-2	-2.0	-2	0
Career			3	90	30.0	73t	2

Mike Green

Year	Team		No	Yds	Avg	Lg	TD
1983	SD	N	1	3	3.0	3	0
1985			2	17	8.5	12	0
Career			3	20	6.7	12	0

Roy Green

Year	Team		No	Yds	Avg	Lg	TD
1980	STL	N	1	10	10.0	10	0
1981			3	44	14.7	29	0
Career			4	54	13.5	29	0

Sammy Green

Year	Team		No	Yds	Avg	Lg	TD
1977	SEA	N	1	9	9.0	9	0
1978			1	0	0.0	0	0
1979			1	91	91.0	91t	1
Career			3	100	33.3	91t	1

Van Green

Year	Team		No	Yds	Avg	Lg	TD
1974	CLE	N	2	56	28.0	36t	1
1975			1	0	0.0	0	0
Career			3	56	18.7	36t	1

Victor Green

Year	Team		No	Yds	Avg	Lg	TD
1995	NYJ	N	1	2	2.0	2	0
1996			2	27	13.5	18	0
Career			3	29	9.7	18	0

Doug Greene

Year	Team		No	Yds	Avg	Lg	TD
1979	BUF	N	1	21	21.0	21	0

Joe Greene

Year	Team		No	Yds	Avg	Lg	TD
1974	PIT	N	1	26	26.0	26	0
Playoffs			1	10	10.0		0

John Greene

Year	Team		No	Yds	Avg	Lg	TD
1944	DET	N	2	22	11.0	15	0
1945			3	65	21.7	37	0
Career			5	87	17.4	37	0

Ken Greene

Year	Team		No	Yds	Avg	Lg	TD
1979	STL	N	3	37	12.3	21	0
1980			4	41	10.3	26	0
1981			7	111	15.9	47	0
1982			1	2	2.0	2	0
Career			15	191	12.7	47	0

Kevin Greene

Year	Team		No	Yds	Avg	Lg	TD
1987	LARM	N	1	25	25.0	25t	1
1988			1	10	10.0	10	0
1995	PIT	N	1	0	0.0	0	0
Career			3	35	11.7	25t	1

Ted Greene

Year	Team		No	Yds	Avg	Lg	TD
1960	DAL	A	3	26	8.7		0
1961			1	30	30.0	30	0
Career			4	56	14.0	30	0

Tiger Greene

Year	Team		No	Yds	Avg	Lg	TD
1985	ATL	N	2	27	13.5	27	0
1986	GB	N	2	0	0.0	0	0
1987			1	11	11.0	11	0
1989			1	0	0.0	0	0
Career			6	38	6.3	27	0

Tony Greene

Year	Team		No	Yds	Avg	Lg	TD
1972	BUF	N	3	45	15.0	39t	1
1973			1	0	0.0	0	0
1974			9	157	17.4	38	0
1975			6	81	13.5	37	0
1976			5	135	27.0	101t	1
1977			9	144	16.0	47	0
1978			3	56	18.7	29	0
1979			1	10	10.0	10	0
Career			37	628	17.0	101t	2

David Greenwood

Year	Team		No	Yds	Avg	Lg	TD
1985	TB	N	5	15	3.0	7	0

Don Greenwood

Year	Team		No	Yds	Avg	Lg	TD
1946	CLE	AA	2	56	28.0		0
1947			4	19	4.8		0
Career			6	75	12.5		0

Charles Greer

Year	Team		No	Yds	Avg	Lg	TD
1968	DEN	A	4	18	4.5	14	0
1969			2	13	6.5	13	0
1970	DEN	N	4	20	5.0	15	0
1971			3	32	10.7	30	0
1972			2	18	9.0	17	0
1973			1	1	1.0	1	0
1974			1	23	23.0	23	0
Career			17	125	7.4	30	0

Bob Gregor

Year	Team		No	Yds	Avg	Lg	TD
1981	SD	N	2	11	5.5	11	0
1982			1	6	6.0	6	0
1984			1	12	12.0	12	0
Career			4	29	7.3	12	0

Bill Gregory

Year	Team		No	Yds	Avg	Lg	TD
1975	DAL	N	1	3	3.0	3	0
1978	SEA	N	1	3	3.0	3	0
Career			2	6	3.0	3	0

Glynn Gregory

Year	Team		No	Yds	Avg	Lg	TD
1961	DAL	N	1	21	21.0	21	0

Jack Gregory

Year	Team		No	Yds	Avg	Lg	TD
1969	CLE	N	1	12	12.0	12	0

Hank Gremminger

Year	Team		No	Yds	Avg	Lg	TD
1956	GB	N	2	36	18.0	21	0
1957			5	93	18.6	45	0
1958			3	15	5.0	14	0
1959			1	45	45.0	45	0
1960			3	52	17.3	21	0
1961			5	54	10.8	41	0
1962			5	88	17.6	35	0

Hank Gremminger *continued*

Year	Team		No	Yds	Avg	Lg	TD
1963			3	25	8.3	16	0
1964			1	13	13.0	13	0
1966	LA	N	1	0	0.0	0	0
Career			29	421	14.5	45	0
Playoffs			1	13	13.0		0

Visco Grgich

Year	Team		No	Yds	Avg	Lg	TD
1950	SF	N	1	37	37.0	37	0

Bob Griffin

Year	Team		No	Yds	Avg	Lg	TD
1955	LA	N	1	20	20.0	20	0

Bobby Griffin

Year	Team		No	Yds	Avg	Lg	TD
1951	NYY	N	4	27	6.8	13	0

Don Griffin

Year	Team		No	Yds	Avg	Lg	TD
1946	CHI	AA	1	19	19.0	19	0

Don Griffin

Year	Team		No	Yds	Avg	Lg	TD
1986	SF	N	3	0	0.0	0	0
1987			5	1	0.2	1	0
1989			2	6	3.0	3	0
1990			3	32	10.7	23	0
1991			1	0	0.0	0	0
1992			5	4	0.8	2	0
1993			3	6	2.0	3	0
1994	CLE	N	2	2	1.0	2	0
1995			1	0	0.0	0	0
Career			25	51	2.0	23	0
Playoffs			1	0	0.0		0

James Griffin

Year	Team		No	Yds	Avg	Lg	TD
1983	CIN	N	1	41	41.0	41t	1
1984			1	57	57.0	57t	1
1985			7	116	16.6	33	1
1986	DET	N	2	34	17.0	21	0
1987			6	130	21.7	29	0
1988			2	31	15.5	31	0
Career			19	409	21.5	57t	3

Jeff Griffin

Year	Team		No	Yds	Avg	Lg	TD
1981	STL	N	1	4	4.0	4	0
1982			1	8	8.0	8	0
1984			2	0	0.0	0	0
Career			4	12	3.0	8	0

John Griffin

Year	Team		No	Yds	Avg	Lg	TD
1965	DEN	A	4	109	27.3	44	1

Larry Griffin

Year	Team		No	Yds	Avg	Lg	TD
1987	PIT	N	2	2	1.0	2	0
1988			2	63	31.5	33	0
1989			1	15	15.0	15	0
1990			4	75	18.8	36	0
1991			1	22	22.0	22	0
1992			3	98	32.7	65t	1
Career			13	275	21.2	65t	1

Ray Griffin

Year	Team		No	Yds	Avg	Lg	TD
1979	CIN	N	4	167	41.8	97t	1
1980			2	80	40.0	52t	2
1982			1	21	21.0	21	0
1983			2	24	12.0	24	0
1984			2	13	6.5	13	0
Career			11	305	27.7	97t	3

Robert Griffith

Year	Team		No	Yds	Avg	Lg	TD
1996	MIN	N	4	67	16.8	41	0

Johnny Grigas

Year	Team		No	Yds	Avg	Lg	TD
1943	CHIC	N	5	42	8.4	27	0
1944	C-P	N	1	2	2.0	2	0
1945	BOS	N	1	3	3.0	3	0
1946			1	0	0.0	0	0
Career			8	47	5.9	27	0

Tex Grigg

Year	Team		No	Yds	Avg	Lg	TD
1921	CAN	A					1

Anthony Griggs

Year	Team		No	Yds	Avg	Lg	TD
1983	PHI	N	3	61	20.3	32	0

David Griggs

Year	Team		No	Yds	Avg	Lg	TD
1994	SD	N	1	11	11.0	11	0

Frank Grigonis

Year	Team		No	Yds	Avg	Lg	TD
1942	DET	N	1	26	26.0	26	0

George Grimes

Year	Team		No	Yds	Avg	Lg	TD
1948	DET	N	1	26	26.0	26	0

John Grimsley

Year	Team		No	Yds	Avg	Lg	TD
1988	HOU	N	1	9	9.0	9	0

Mel Groomes

Year	Team		No	Yds	Avg	Lg	TD
1949	DET	N	1	25	25.0	25	0

Elois Grooms

Year	Team		No	Yds	Avg	Lg	TD
1979	NO	N	1	-2	-2.0	-2	0
1980			1	37	37.0	37	0
1983	STL	N	1	10	10.0	10	0
Career			3	45	15.0	37	0

Al Gross

Year	Team		No	Yds	Avg	Lg	TD
1983	CLE	N	1	18	18.0	18	0
1984			5	103	20.6	47	0
1985			5	109	21.8	37t	1
Career			11	230	20.9	47	1

Rex Grossman

Year	Team		No	Yds	Avg	Lg	TD
1948	BAL	AA	2	13	6.5		0

Monty Grow

Year	Team		No	Yds	Avg	Lg	TD
1994	KC	N	1	21	21.0	21	0
1995	JAC	N	1	2	2.0	2	0
Career			2	23	11.5	21	0

Al Grygo

Year	Team		No	Yds	Avg	Lg	TD
1944	CHIB	N	4	79	19.8	29	0
1945			3	9	3.0	6	0
Career			7	88	12.6	29	0

Pete Gudauskas

Year	Team		No	Yds	Avg	Lg	TD
1944	CHIB	N	1	26	26.0	26	0
1945			1	0	0.0	0	0
Career			2	26	13.0	26	0

Scotty Gudmundson

Year	Team		No	Yds	Avg	Lg	TD
1945	BOS	N	2	23	11.5	17	0

Neal Guggemos

Year	Team		No	Yds	Avg	Lg	TD
1987	MIN	N	1	26	26.0	26	0

Paul Guidry

Year	Team		No	Yds	Avg	Lg	TD
1968	BUF	A	1	21	21.0	21	0
1969			2	39	19.5	39	0
1971	BUF	N	1	13	13.0	13	0
1972			1	0	0.0	0	0
Career			5	73	14.6	39	0

John Guillory

Year	Team		No	Yds	Avg	Lg	TD
1969	CIN	A	1	0	0.0	0	0

George Gulyanics

Year	Team		No	Yds	Avg	Lg	TD
1947	CHIB	N	2	36	18.0	22	0

Jimmy Gunn

Year	Team		No	Yds	Avg	Lg	TD
1971	CHI	N	1	5	5.0	5	0
1975			1	5	5.0	5	0
Career			2	10	5.0	5	0

Riley Gunnels

Year	Team		No	Yds	Avg	Lg	TD
1966	PIT	N	1	2	2.0	2	0

Harry Gunner

Year	Team		No	Yds	Avg	Lg	TD
1968	CIN	A	1	20	20.0	20	0
1969			1	70	70.0	70t	1
Career			2	90	45.0	70t	1

Joe Guyon

Year	Team		No	Yds	Avg	Lg	TD
1921	CLE	A					1
1922	OOR	N					1
1923							1
Career							3

Myron Guyton

Year	Team		No	Yds	Avg	Lg	TD
1989	NYG	N	2	27	13.5	14	0
1990			1	0	0.0	0	0
1993			2	34	17.0	19	0
1994	NE	N	2	18	9.0	15	0
1995			3	68	22.7	45	0
Career			10	147	14.7	45	0

Dale Hackbart

Year	Team		No	Yds	Avg	Lg	TD
1961	WAS	N	6	128	21.3	48t	2
1962			3	49	16.3	23	0
1963			1	7	7.0	7	0
1966	MIN	N	5	73	14.6	41t	1
1967			2	45	22.5	24	1
1971	STL	N	1	11	11.0	11	0
1972			1	22	22.0	22	0
Career			19	335	17.6	48t	4

Dino Hackett

Year	Team		No	Yds	Avg	Lg	TD
1986	KC	N	1	0	0.0	0	0

Elmer Hackney

Year	Team		No	Yds	Avg	Lg	TD
1943	DET	N	2	94	47.0	63	0
1944			3	41	13.7	20	0
Career			5	135	27.0	63	0

Wayne Haddix

Year	Team		No	Yds	Avg	Lg	TD
1990	TB	N	7	**231**	33.0	65t	3

Dave Hadley

Year	Team		No	Yds	Avg	Lg	TD
1971	KC	N	1	0	0.0	0	0

Rudy Hagberg

Year	Team		No	Yds	Avg	Lg	TD
1930	BKN	N					1

Britt Hager

Year	Team		No	Yds	Avg	Lg	TD
1993	PHI	N	1	19	19.0	19	0
1994			1	0	0.0	0	0
1995	DEN	N	1	19	19.0	19	0
Career			3	38	12.7	19	0

John Hagy

Year	Team		No	Yds	Avg	Lg	TD
1990	BUF	N	2	23	11.5	23	0

Carl Hairston

Year	Team		No	Yds	Avg	Lg	TD
1980	PHI	N	1	0	0.0	0	0
1987	CLE	N	0	40		40L	0
Career			1	40	40.0	40L	0

George Halas

Year	Team		No	Yds	Avg	Lg	TD
1927	CHIB	N					1

Chris Hale

Year	Team		No	Yds	Avg	Lg	TD
1991	BUF	N	1	0	0.0	0	0

Charles Haley

Year	Team		No	Yds	Avg	Lg	TD
1986	SF	N	1	8	8.0	8	0
1994	DAL	N	1	1	1.0	1	0
Career			2	9	4.5	8	0
Playoffs			1	0	0.0	0	

Dick Haley

Year	Team		No	Yds	Avg	Lg	TD
1959	WAS	N	1	15	15.0	15	0
1961	PIT	N	1	0	0.0	0	0
1962			4	26	6.5	18	0
1963			6	65	10.8	37	1
1964			2	11	5.5	8	0
Career			14	117	8.4	37	1

Al Hall

Year	Team		No	Yds	Avg	Lg	TD
1961	LA	N	0	10		10L	0
1962			1	0	0.0	0	0
Career			1	10	10.0	10L	0

Alvin Hall

Year	Team		No	Yds	Avg	Lg	TD
1981	DET	N	1	60	60.0	60t	1
1982			1	2	2.0	2	0
1983			2	18	9.0	18	0
1984			2	64	32.0	36	0
1987			1	0	0.0	0	0
Career			7	144	20.6	60t	1

Charlie Hall

Year	Team		No	Yds	Avg	Lg	TD
1972	CLE	N	1	12	12.0	12	0

Charlie Hall *continued*

Year	Team		No	Yds	Avg	Lg	TD
1974			3	54	18.0	29t	1
1975			2	28	14.0	19	0
1976			1	12	12.0	12	0
1977			1	2	2.0	2	0
1978			1	6	6.0	6	0
1979			2	14	7.0	11	0
1980			2	3	1.5	3	0
Career			13	131	10.1	29t	1

Charlie Hall

Year	Team		No	Yds	Avg	Lg	TD
1974	GB	N	2	22	11.0	19	0

Dana Hall

Year	Team		No	Yds	Avg	Lg	TD
1992	SF	N	2	34	17.0	34	0
1994			2	0	0.0	0	0
1995	CLE	N	2	41	20.5	36	0
1996	JAC	N	1	20	20.0	20	0
Career			7	95	13.6	36	0

Darryl Hall

Year	Team		No	Yds	Avg	Lg	TD
1993	DEN	N	1	0	0.0	0	0

Delton Hall

Year	Team		No	Yds	Avg	Lg	TD
1987	PIT	N	3	29	9.7	25t	1
1989			1	6	6.0	6	0
1990			1	0	0.0	0	0
Career			5	35	7.0	25t	1

Johnny Hall

Year	Team		No	Yds	Avg	Lg	TD
1940	CHIC	N					1
1942	DET	N	1	9	9.0	9	0
1943	CHIC	N	2	49	24.5	44	0
Career			3	58	19.3	44	1

Parker Hall

Year	Team		No	Yds	Avg	Lg	TD
1941	CLE	N	2	0	0.0	0	0
1942			3	60	20.0	25	0
Career			5	60	12.0	25	0

Rhett Hall

Year	Team		No	Yds	Avg	Lg	TD
1996	PHI	N	0	0		0L	0

Ronnie Hall

Year	Team		No	Yds	Avg	Lg	TD
1959	PIT	N	1	0	0.0	0	0
1961	BOS	A	2	12	6.0	12	0
1962			3	94	31.3	47	1
1963			3	24	8.0	14	0
1964			11	148	13.5	50	0
1965			3	35	11.7	29	0
1966			6	159	26.5	87	0
1967			1	4	4.0	4	0
Career			30	476	15.9	87	1

Tom Hall

Year	Team		No	Yds	Avg	Lg	TD
1963	DET	N	3	45	15.0	36	0

Willie Hall

Year	Team		No	Yds	Avg	Lg	TD
1976	OAK	N	2	17	8.5	12	0
1977			1	0	0.0	0	0
1978			2	18	9.0	15	0
Career			5	35	7.0	15	0
Playoffs			2	41	20.5		

Windlan Hall

Year	Team		No	Yds	Avg	Lg	TD
1972	SF	N	1	0	0.0	0	0
1973			1	0	0.0	0	0
Career			2	0	0.0	0	0

Dean Halverson

Year	Team		No	Yds	Avg	Lg	TD
1974	PHI	N	1	0	0.0	0	0

Jack Ham

Year	Team		No	Yds	Avg	Lg	TD
1971	PIT	N	2	4	2.0	4	0
1972			7	83	11.9	32t	1
1973			2	30	15.0	27	0
1974			5	13	2.6	10	0
1975			1	2	2.0	2	0
1976			2	13	6.5	13	0
1977			4	17	4.3	9	0
1978			3	7	2.3	7	0
1979			2	8	4.0	6	0
1980			2	16	8.0	15	0

Jack Ham *continued*

Year	Team		No	Yds	Avg	Lg	TD
1981			1	23	23.0	23	0
1982			1	2	2.0	2	0
Career			32	218	6.8	32t	1
Playoffs			5	25	5.0		0

Johnny Haman

Year	Team		No	Yds	Avg	Lg	TD
1940	CLE	N					1
1941			1	6	6.0	6	0
Career			1	6	6.0	6	1

Tex Hamer

Year	Team		No	Yds	Avg	Lg	TD
1925	FRA	N					1

Conrad Hamilton

Year	Team		No	Yds	Avg	Lg	TD
1996	NYG	N	1	29	29.0	29	0

Harry Hamilton

Year	Team		No	Yds	Avg	Lg	TD
1985	NYJ	N	2	14	7.0	14	0
1986			1	29	29.0	29	0
1987			3	25	8.3	25	0
1988	TB	N	6	123	20.5	58	0
1989			6	70	11.7	30	0
1990			5	39	7.8	27	0
Career			23	300	13.0	58	0

Alonzo Hampton

Year	Team		No	Yds	Avg	Lg	TD
1991	TB	N	1	12	12.0	12	0

Chris Hanburger

Year	Team		No	Yds	Avg	Lg	TD
1965	WAS	N	1	14	14.0	14	0
1966			1	1	1.0	1	0
1968			2	53	26.5	30t	1
1970			1	12	12.0	12	0
1971			1	17	17.0	17	0
1972			4	98	24.5	41t	1
1973			1	45	45.0	45	0
1974			4	6	1.5	5	0
1975			3	81	27.0	37	0
1976			1	20	20.0	20	0
Career			19	347	18.3	45	2
Playoffs			1	15	15.0		0

Jon Hand

Year	Team		No	Yds	Avg	Lg	TD
1986	IND	N	1	8	8.0	8	0

Larry Hand

Year	Team		No	Yds	Avg	Lg	TD
1967	DET	N	2	6	3.0	4t	2
1970			1	62	62.0	62t	1
1975			1	38	38.0	38	0
1976			1	4	4.0	4	0
Career			5	110	22.0	62t	3

Merton Hanks

Year	Team		No	Yds	Avg	Lg	TD
1992	SF	N	2	5	2.5	4	0
1993			3	104	34.7	67t	1
1994			7	93	13.3	38	0
1995			5	31	6.2	23	0
1996			4	7	1.8	8	0
Career			21	240	11.4	67t	1
Playoffs			1	31	31.0		0

Bob Hanlon

Year	Team		No	Yds	Avg	Lg	TD
1948	CHIC	N	1	25	25.0	25	0
1949	PIT	N	3	29	9.7	19	0
Career			4	54	13.5	25	0

Dave Hanner

Year	Team		No	Yds	Avg	Lg	TD
1953	GB	N	1	2	2.0	2	0
1961			1	1	1.0	1	0
1962			1	0	0.0	0	0
1963			1	0	0.0	0	0
Career			4	3	0.8	2	0

Tom Hannon

Year	Team		No	Yds	Avg	Lg	TD
1978	MIN	N	2	0	0.0	0	0
1979			4	85	21.3	52	0
1980			4	89	22.3	41t	1
1981			4	28	7.0	28	0
1984			1	0	0.0	0	0
Career			15	202	13.5	52	1
Playoffs			1	0	0.0		0

Frank Hanny

Year	Team		No	Yds	Avg	Lg	TD
1924	CHIB	N					1
1925							1
1928	PRO	N					1
Career							3

Don Hansen

Year	Team		No	Yds	Avg	Lg	TD
1969	ATL	N	2	51	25.5	40	0
1970			1	15	15.0	15	0
1971			3	56	18.7	40t	1
1972			1	0	0.0	0	0
1973			1	0	0.0	0	0
1974			1	0	0.0	0	0
1975			1	1	1.0	1	0
Career			10	123	12.3	40t	1

Phil Hansen

Year	Team		No	Yds	Avg	Lg	TD
Playoffs			1	0	0.0		0

Wayne Hansen

Year	Team		No	Yds	Avg	Lg	TD
1954	CHIB	N	1	57	57.0	57	0
1956			1	11	11.0	11	0
1957			1	34	34.0	34	0
1958			1	12	12.0	12	0
1960	DAL	N	2	14	7.0	14	0
Career			6	128	21.3	57	0

Merle Hapes

Year	Team		No	Yds	Avg	Lg	TD
1942	NYG	N	3	49	16.3	28	0

Billy Hardee

Year	Team		No	Yds	Avg	Lg	TD
1977	NYJ	N	1	0	0.0	0	0

Bobby Harden

Year	Team		No	Yds	Avg	Lg	TD
1991	MIA	N	2	39	19.5	22	0

Mike Harden

Year	Team		No	Yds	Avg	Lg	TD
1981	DEN	N	2	34	17.0	38	0
1982			2	3	1.5	3	0
1983			4	127	31.8	48	0
1984			6	79	13.2	45t	1
1985			5	100	20.0	42t	1
1986			6	179	29.8	52	2
1987			4	85	21.3	32	0
1988			4	36	9.0	34	0
1989	LARI	N	2	1	0.5	1	0
1990			3	19	6.3	15	0
Career			38	663	17.4	52	4

Roger Harding

Year	Team		No	Yds	Avg	Lg	TD
1945	CLE	N	1	16	16.0	16	0
1946	LA	N	1	14	14.0	14	0
1949	GB	N	1	5	5.0	5	0
Career			3	35	11.7	16	0

Jim Hardy

Year	Team		No	Yds	Avg	Lg	TD
1946	LA	N	1	8	8.0	8	0

Kevin Hardy

Year	Team		No	Yds	Avg	Lg	TD
1996	JAC	N	2	19	9.5	13	0

Cecil Hare

Year	Team		No	Yds	Avg	Lg	TD
1941	WAS	N	1	4	4.0	4	0

Ray Hare

Year	Team		No	Yds	Avg	Lg	TD
1942	WAS	N	1	0	0.0	0	0
1943			3	13	4.3	11	0
1944	BKN	N	1	12	12.0	12	0
Career			5	25	5.0	12	0
Playoffs			1	0	0.0		0

Jimmy Hargrove

Year	Team		No	Yds	Avg	Lg	TD
1967	MIN	N	1	3	3.0	3	0

Andy Harmon

Year	Team		No	Yds	Avg	Lg	TD
1994	PHI	N	1	0	0.0	0	0

Tommy Harmon

Year	Team		No	Yds	Avg	Lg	TD
1946	LA	N	3	97	32.3	85t	1
1947			8	136	17.0	36	1
Career			11	233	21.2	85t	2

Alvin Harper

Year	Team		No	Yds	Avg	Lg	TD
1992	DAL	N	1	1	1.0	1	0

Dwayne Harper

Year	Team		No	Yds	Avg	Lg	TD
1989	SEA	N	2	15	7.5	15	0
1990			3	69	23.0	47	0
1991			4	84	21.0	43	0
1992			3	74	24.7	41	0
1993			1	0	0.0	0	0
1994	SD	N	3	28	9.3	15	0
1995			4	12	3.0	15	0
1996			1	0	0.0	0	0
Career			21	282	13.4	47	0

Mark Harper

Year	Team		No	Yds	Avg	Lg	TD
1986	CLE	N	1	31	31.0	31	0
1987			2	16	8.0	16	0
1988			2	13	6.5	8	0
1989			3	8	2.7	8	0
Career			8	68	8.5	31	0
Playoffs			3	17	5.7		0

Maurice Harper

Year	Team		No	Yds	Avg	Lg	TD
1937	PHI	N					1

Roger Harper

Year	Team		No	Yds	Avg	Lg	TD
1994	ATL	N	1	22	22.0	22	0
1995			1	0	0.0	0	0
1996	DAL	N	2	30	15.0	15	0
Career			4	52	13.0	22	0

Willie Harper

Year	Team		No	Yds	Avg	Lg	TD
1977	SF	N	1	6	6.0	6	0
1982			1	0	0.0	0	0
1983			1	37	37.0	37	0
Career			3	43	14.3	37	0

James Harrell

Year	Team		No	Yds	Avg	Lg	TD
1985	DET	N	1	20	20.0	20	0

Al Harris

Year	Team		No	Yds	Avg	Lg	TD
1981	CHI	N	1	44	44.0	44t	1
1984			1	34	34.0	34	0
1989	PHI	N	2	18	9.0	11	0
Career			4	96	24.0	44t	1

Bo Harris

Year	Team		No	Yds	Avg	Lg	TD
1976	CIN	N	2	-3	-1.5	0	0
1977			2	17	8.5	10	0
1981			2	92	46.0	49	0
1982			1	62	62.0	62t	1
Career			7	168	24.0	62t	1
Playoffs			1	16	16.0		0

Bob Harris

Year	Team		No	Yds	Avg	Lg	TD
1983	STL	N	3	10	3.3	10	0

Cliff Harris

Year	Team		No	Yds	Avg	Lg	TD
1970	DAL	N	2	66	33.0	60	0
1971			2	0	0.0	0	0
1972			3	40	13.3	23	0
1973			2	9	4.5	5	0
1974			3	8	2.7	8	0
1975			3	58	19.3	27t	1
1976			3	32	10.7	29	0
1977			5	7	1.4	7	0
1978			4	26	6.5	23	0
1979			2	35	17.5	20	0
Career			29	281	9.7	60	1
Playoffs			6	103	17.2		0

Corey Harris

Year	Team		No	Yds	Avg	Lg	TD
1995	SEA	N	3	-5	-1.7	0	0
1996			1	25	25.0	25	0
Career			4	20	5.0	25	0

Dick Harris

Year	Team		No	Yds	Avg	Lg	TD
1960	LA	A	5	56	11.2	42t	1
1961	SD	A	7	140	20.0	36	3
1962			5	52	10.4	36	0
1963			8	83	10.4	22	1
1964			3	82	27.3	44	0
1965			1	0	0.0	0	0
Career			29	413	14.2	44	5

Eric Harris

Year	Team		No	Yds	Avg	Lg	TD
1980	KC	N	7	54	7.7	41	0

Eric Harris *continued*

Year	Team		No	Yds	Avg	Lg	TD
1981			7	109	15.6	43	0
1982			3	66	22.0	56t	1
1983	LARM	N	4	100	25.0	45	0
Career			21	329	15.7	56t	1

James Harris

Year	Team		No	Yds	Avg	Lg	TD
1994	MIN	N	1	21	21.0	21	0

Jimmy Harris

Year	Team		No	Yds	Avg	Lg	TD
1957	PHI	N	3	99	33.0	65t	1
1958	LA	N	4	51	12.8	14	0
1960	DAL	A	2	29	14.5		0
1961	DAL	N	2	13	6.5	12	0
Career			11	192	17.5	65t	1

Joe Harris

Year	Team		No	Yds	Avg	Lg	TD
1981	LA	N	1	7	7.0	7	0

John Harris

Year	Team		No	Yds	Avg	Lg	TD
1961	OAK	A	3	81	27.0	32	0

John Harris

Year	Team		No	Yds	Avg	Lg	TD
1978	SEA	N	4	65	16.3	28	0
1979			2	30	15.0	25	0
1980			6	28	4.7	15	0
1981			10	155	15.5	42t	2
1982			4	33	8.3	18	0
1983			2	15	7.5	10	0
1984			6	79	13.2	29	0
1985			7	20	2.9	17	0
1986	MIN	N	3	69	23.0	28	0
1987			3	20	6.7	14	0
1988			3	46	15.3	27	0
Career			50	560	11.2	42t	2
Playoffs			5	60	12.0		0

Odie Harris

Year	Team		No	Yds	Avg	Lg	TD
1988	TB	N	2	26	13.0	24	0
1989			1	19	19.0	19	0
1995	HOU	N	2	0	0.0	0	0
Career			5	45	9.0	24	0

Rickie Harris

Year	Team		No	Yds	Avg	Lg	TD
1965	WAS	N	1	34	34.0	34t	1
1966			1	0	0.0	0	0
1967			1	0	0.0	0	0
1968			2	3	1.5	3	0
1969			4	81	20.3	47	0
1970			3	67	22.3	25	0
1972	NE	N	3	45	15.0	32	0
Career			15	230	15.3	47	1

Walt Harris

Year	Team		No	Yds	Avg	Lg	TD
1996	CHI	N	2	0	0.0	0	0

Wendell Harris

Year	Team		No	Yds	Avg	Lg	TD
1962	BAL	N	2	52	26.0	38	0
1964			1	20	20.0	20	0
1965			3	77	25.7	36	0
1966	NYG	N	1	20	20.0	20	0
1967			1	0	0.0	0	0
Career			8	169	21.1	38	0

Anthony Harrison

Year	Team		No	Yds	Avg	Lg	TD
1987	GB	N	1	0	0.0	0	0

Bob Harrison

Year	Team		No	Yds	Avg	Lg	TD
1960	SF	N	1	6	6.0	6	0
1961			2	14	7.0	9	0
1962	PHI	N	2	14	7.0	12	0
Career			5	34	6.8	12	0

Bob Harrison

Year	Team		No	Yds	Avg	Lg	TD
1961	BAL	N	3	43	14.3	27	0

Dennis Harrison

Year	Team		No	Yds	Avg	Lg	TD
1978	PHI	N	1	12	12.0	12	0

Dwight Harrison

Year	Team		No	Yds	Avg	Lg	TD
1973	BUF	N	5	117	23.4	38	1
1974			1	24	24.0	24	0
1975			8	99	12.4	40	0

Dwight Harrison *continued*

Year	Team		No	Yds	Avg	Lg	TD
1976			1	18	18.0	18	0
1977			2	0	0.0	0	0
1979	BAL	N	2	6	3.0	6	0
Career			19	264	13.9	40	1

Martin Harrison

Year	Team		No	Yds	Avg	Lg	TD
1995	MIN	N	1	15	15.0	15	0

Rodney Harrison

Year	Team		No	Yds	Avg	Lg	TD
1995	SD	N	5	22	4.4	17	0
1996			5	56	11.2	29	0
Career			10	78	7.8	29	0

Ben Hart

Year	Team		No	Yds	Avg	Lg	TD
1967	NO	N	1	21	21.0	21	0

Douglas Hart

Year	Team		No	Yds	Avg	Lg	TD
1964	GB	N	1	0	0.0	0	0
1965			4	29	7.3	24	0
1966			1	40	40.0	40t	1
1968			1	24	24.0	24	0
1969			3	156	52.0	85t	1
1970			3	114	38.0	76t	1
1971			2	73	36.5	69	0
Career			15	436	29.1	85t	3

Leon Hart

Year	Team		No	Yds	Avg	Lg	TD
1951	DET	N	2	22	11.0	20	0

Tommy Hart

Year	Team		No	Yds	Avg	Lg	TD
1970	SF	N	1	0	0.0	0	0
1972			1	0	0.0	0	0
Career			2	0	0.0	0	0

Mike Hartenstine

Year	Team		No	Yds	Avg	Lg	TD
1976	CHI	N	0	12		12tL	1

Howard Hartley

Year	Team		No	Yds	Avg	Lg	TD
1948	WAS	N	3	76	25.3	53	0
1949	PIT	N	6	63	10.5	41	0
1950			5	84	16.8	38	0
1951			10	69	6.9	23	0
1952			4	51	12.8	24	0
Career			28	343	12.3	53	0

Fred Hartman

Year	Team		No	Yds	Avg	Lg	TD
1947	CHIB	N	1	16	16.0	16t	1

Carter Hartwig

Year	Team		No	Yds	Avg	Lg	TD
1979	HOU	N	2	24	12.0	24	0
1980			1	0	0.0	0	0
1981			3	78	26.0	38	0
1984			3	23	7.7	19	0
Career			9	125	13.9	38	0

Ken Harvey

Year	Team		No	Yds	Avg	Lg	TD
1996	WAS	N	1	2	2.0	2	0

Maurice Harvey

Year	Team		No	Yds	Avg	Lg	TD
1980	DEN	N	1	18	18.0	18	0
1981	GB	N	6	217	36.2	53	0
1982			2	32	16.0	17	0
Career			9	267	29.7	53	0

Jim Haslett

Year	Team		No	Yds	Avg	Lg	TD
1979	BUF	N	2	15	7.5	11	0
1980			2	30	15.0	17	0
1985			1	40	40.0	40	0
1987	NYJ	N	1	9	9.0	9	0
Career			6	94	15.7	40	0

James Hasty

Year	Team		No	Yds	Avg	Lg	TD
1988	NYJ	N	5	20	4.0	16	0
1989			5	62	12.4	34t	1
1990			2	0	0.0	0	0
1991			3	39	13.0	39	0
1992			2	18	9.0	18	0
1993			2	22	11.0	22	0
1994			5	90	18.0	40	0
1995	KC	N	3	89	29.7	64t	1
Career			27	340	12.6	64t	2

Derrick Hatchett

Year	Team		No	Yds	Avg	Lg	TD
1981	BAL	N	2	8	4.0	8	0
1982			1	0	0.0	0	0
1983			4	36	9.0	25	0
Career			7	44	6.3	25	0

Mike Hawkins

Year	Team		No	Yds	Avg	Lg	TD
1979	NE	N	2	35	17.5	35t	1
1980			2	5	2.5	5	0
1981			1	16	16.0	16	0
Career			5	56	11.2	35t	1

Rip Hawkins

Year	Team		No	Yds	Avg	Lg	TD
1961	MIN	N	5	70	14.0	34	0
1962			1	3	3.0	3	0
1963			1	6	6.0	6	0
1964			2	85	42.5	56t	2
1965			3	68	22.7	35t	1
Career			12	232	19.3	56t	3

Ken Hayden

Year	Team		No	Yds	Avg	Lg	TD
1942	PHI	N	1	5	5.0	5	0

Ed Hayes

Year	Team		No	Yds	Avg	Lg	TD
1970	PHI	N	1	2	2.0	2	0

Lester Hayes

Year	Team		No	Yds	Avg	Lg	TD
1977	OAK	N	1	27	27.0	27	0
1978			4	86	21.5	52	0
1979			7	100	14.3	52t	2
1980			**13**	**273**	21.0	62	1
1981			3	0	0.0	0	0
1982	LARI	N	2	0	0.0	0	0
1983			2	49	24.5	28	0
1984			1	3	3.0	3	0
1985			4	27	6.8	27t	1
1986			2	7	3.5	7	0
Career			39	572	14.7	62	4
Playoffs			8	107	13.4		2

Tom Hayes

Year	Team		No	Yds	Avg	Lg	TD
1971	ATL	N	3	27	9.0	27	0
1972			5	10	2.0	8	0
1973			4	142	35.5	65t	2
1974			1	2	2.0	2	0
1975			4	16	4.0	7	0
1976	SD	N	2	37	18.5	37t	1
Career			19	234	12.3	65t	3

Alvin Haymond

Year	Team		No	Yds	Avg	Lg	TD
1965	BAL	N	3	47	15.7	30t	1
1966			4	88	22.0	52t	1
1967			2	33	16.5	33	0
1968	PHI	N	1	10	10.0	10	0
Career			10	178	17.8	52t	2

Hall Haynes

Year	Team		No	Yds	Avg	Lg	TD
1950	WAS	N	4	77	19.3	40t	1
1954	LA	N	1	0	0.0	0	0
Career			5	77	15.4	40t	1

James Haynes

Year	Team		No	Yds	Avg	Lg	TD
1986	NO	N	1	17	17.0	17t	1

Mark Haynes

Year	Team		No	Yds	Avg	Lg	TD
1980	NYG	N	1	6	6.0	6	0
1981			1	9	9.0	9	0
1982			1	0	0.0	0	0
1983			3	18	6.0	23	0
1984			7	90	12.9	22	0
1987	DEN	N	3	39	13.0	25	0
1988			1	0	0.0	0	0
Career			17	162	9.5	25	1
Playoffs			1	57	57.0		0

Mike Haynes

Year	Team		No	Yds	Avg	Lg	TD
1976	NE	N	8	90	11.3	28	0
1977			5	54	10.8	22	0
1978			6	123	20.5	50	1
1979			3	66	22.0	33	0
1980			1	31	31.0	31	0
1981			1	3	3.0	3	0
1982			4	26	6.5	26	0
1983	LARI	N	1	0	0.0	0	0

Mike Haynes *continued*

Year	Team		No	Yds	Avg	Lg	TD
1984			6	**220**	36.7	97t	1
1985			4	8	2.0	8	0
1986			2	28	14.0	22	0
1987			2	9	4.5	7	0
1988			3	30	10.0	30	0
Career			46	688	15.0	97t	2
Playoffs			1	0	0.0		0

Tommy Haynes

Year	Team		No	Yds	Avg	Lg	TD
1987	DAL	N	3	7	2.3	7	0

George Hays

Year	Team		No	Yds	Avg	Lg	TD
1952	PIT	N	1	1	1.0	1t	1

Tracy Hayworth

Year	Team		No	Yds	Avg	Lg	TD
1991	DET	N	1	0	0.0	0	0

Matt Hazeltine

Year	Team		No	Yds	Avg	Lg	TD
1956	SF	N	1	7	7.0	7	0
1957			2	22	11.0	14	0
1958			3	30	10.0	17	1
1961			1	26	26.0	26	0
1962			2	24	12.0	17	0
1964			1	1	1.0	1	0
1965			1	6	6.0	6	0
1966			1	8	8.0	8	0
1970	NYG	N	1	6	6.0	6	0
Career			13	130	10.0	26	1

Andy Headen

Year	Team		No	Yds	Avg	Lg	TD
1984	NYG	N	1	4	4.0	4	0
1985			2	7	3.5	7	0
1986			1	1	1.0	1	0
1987			2	25	12.5	20	0
Career			6	37	6.2	20	0

Sherrill Headrick

Year	Team		No	Yds	Avg	Lg	TD
1960	DAL	A	2	9	4.5		0
1961			2	89	44.5	56	2
1962			3	30	10.0	11	0
1963	KC	A	2	49	24.5	38	1
1964			1	0	0.0		0
1965			1	1	1.0	1	0
1966			2	22	11.0	15	0
1967			1	7	7.0	7	0
1968	CIN	A	1	0	0.0	0	0
Career			15	207	13.8	56	3

Don Healy

Year	Team		No	Yds	Avg	Lg	TD
1961	DAL	N	1	11	11.0	11	0

Walt Heap

Year	Team		No	Yds	Avg	Lg	TD
1947	LA	AA	5	107	21.4	55t	1
1948			5	94	18.8	53	1
Career			10	201	20.1	55t	2

JoJo Heath

Year	Team		No	Yds	Avg	Lg	TD
1987	NYJ	N	1	35	35.0	35	0

Bud Hebert

Year	Team		No	Yds	Avg	Lg	TD
1980	NYG	N	1	0	0.0	0	0

Ralph Heck

Year	Team		No	Yds	Avg	Lg	TD
1968	ATL	N	1	9	9.0	9	0
1969	NYG	N	2	31	15.5	20	0
1970			1	3	3.0	3	0
1971			1	17	17.0	17	0
Career			5	60	12.0	20	0

Norb Hecker

Year	Team		No	Yds	Avg	Lg	TD
1951	LA	N	3	74	24.7	36	0
1952			1	50	50.0	50	0
1953			7	91	13.0	24	0
1955	WAS	N	6	52	8.7	26	0
1956			8	26	3.3	14	0
1957			3	39	13.0	22	0
Career			28	332	11.9	50	0
Playoffs			1	7	7.0		0

Pat Heenan

Year	Team		No	Yds	Avg	Lg	TD
1960	WAS	N	1	25	25.0	25	0

Victor Heflin

Year	Team		No	Yds	Avg	Lg	TD
1984	STL	N	1	19	19.0	19	0

Larry Hefner

Year	Team		No	Yds	Avg	Lg	TD
1973	GB	N	1	3	3.0	3	0

Mike Hegman

Year	Team		No	Yds	Avg	Lg	TD
1977	DAL	N	1	0	0.0	0	0
1980			2	2	1.0	2	0
1984			3	3	1.0	3	0
1985			1	7	7.0	7	0
Career			7	12	1.7	7	0

Jim Heidel

Year	Team		No	Yds	Avg	Lg	TD
1967	NO	N	1	2	2.0	2	0

Mel Hein

Year	Team		No	Yds	Avg	Lg	TD
1938	NYG	N					1
1941			1	9	9.0	9	0
1942			1	2	2.0	2	0
1943			1	31	31.0	31	0
1944			3	14	4.7	10	0
1945			2	7	3.5	7	0
Career			8	63	7.9	31	1
Playoffs			1	-3	-3.0		0

Ken Heineman

Year	Team		No	Yds	Avg	Lg	TD
1943	BKN	N	2	3	1.5	3	0

Jerry Helluin

Year	Team		No	Yds	Avg	Lg	TD
1957	GB	N	1	0	0.0	0	0

John Helwig

Year	Team		No	Yds	Avg	Lg	TD
1954	CHIB	N	3	22	7.3	12	0

Jerome Henderson

Year	Team		No	Yds	Avg	Lg	TD
1991	NE	N	2	2	1.0	2	0
1992			3	43	14.3	34	0
1996			2	7	3.5	7	0
Career			7	52	7.4	34	0

Reuben Henderson

Year	Team		No	Yds	Avg	Lg	TD
1981	CHI	N	4	84	21.0	39	0

Thomas Henderson

Year	Team		No	Yds	Avg	Lg	TD
1977	DAL	N	3	79	26.3	79t	1
1980	HOU	N	1	3	3.0	3	0
Career			4	82	20.5	79t	1
Playoffs			2	69	34.5		1

Wymon Henderson

Year	Team		No	Yds	Avg	Lg	TD
1987	MIN	N	4	33	8.3	17	0
1988			1	13	13.0	13	0
1989	DEN	N	3	58	19.3	25	0
1990			2	71	35.5	49t	1
1991			2	53	26.5	53	0
1992			4	79	19.8	46t	1
Career			16	307	19.2	53	2

Ted Hendricks

Year	Team		No	Yds	Avg	Lg	TD
1970	BAL	N	1	31	31.0	31	0
1971			5	70	14.0	40	0
1972			2	13	6.5	13	0
1973			3	33	11.0	24	0
1974	GB	N	5	74	14.8	44	0
1975	OAK	N	2	40	20.0	33	0
1976			1	9	9.0	9	0
1978			3	29	9.7	16	0
1979			1	23	23.0	23t	1
1980			3	10	3.3	5	0
Career			26	332	12.8	44	1

Steve Hendrickson

Year	Team		No	Yds	Avg	Lg	TD
1993	SD	N	1	16	16.0	16	0

Manny Hendrix

Year	Team		No	Yds	Avg	Lg	TD
1988	DAL	N	1	0	0.0	0	0
1990			1	0	0.0	0	0
Career			2	0	0.0		0

John Hendy

Year	Team		No	Yds	Avg	Lg	TD
1985	SD	N	4	139	34.8	75t	1

Darryl Henley

Year	Team		No	Yds	Avg	Lg	TD
1989	LARM	N	1	10	10.0	10	0
1990			1	0	0.0	0	0
1991			3	22	7.3	22	0
1992			4	41	10.3	25	0
1994			3	46	15.3	23	0
Career			12	119	9.9	25	0

Tom Hennessey

Year	Team		No	Yds	Avg	Lg	TD
1965	BOS	A	2	14	7.0	14	0
1966			6	99	16.5	33	0
Career			8	113	14.1	33	0

Mike Hennigan

Year	Team		No	Yds	Avg	Lg	TD
1978	NYJ	N	3	76	25.3	53	0

Kevin Henry

Year	Team		No	Yds	Avg	Lg	TD
1993	PIT	N	1	10	10.0	10	0

Mike Henry

Year	Team		No	Yds	Avg	Lg	TD
1959	PIT	N	2	42	21.0	33	0
1961			1	8	8.0	8	0
1962	LA	N	1	10	10.0	10	0
1963			5	43	8.6	28	0
Career			9	103	11.4	33	0

Pete Henry

Year	Team		No	Yds	Avg	Lg	TD
1920	CAN	A					1

Steve Henry

Year	Team		No	Yds	Avg	Lg	TD
1980	NYG	N	1	0	0.0	0	0

Lonnie Hepburn

Year	Team		No	Yds	Avg	Lg	TD
1972	BAL	N	1	14	14.0	14	0
1974	DEN	N	0	22		22L	0
Career			1	36	36.0	22L	0

Arnie Herber

Year	Team		No	Yds	Avg	Lg	TD
1932	GB	N					1

Bill Herchman

Year	Team		No	Yds	Avg	Lg	TD
1957	SF	N	1	54	54.0	54t	1

Joe Hergert

Year	Team		No	Yds	Avg	Lg	TD
1960	BUF	A	1	29	29.0	29t	1
1961			1	0	0.0	0	0
Career			2	29	14.5	29t	1

Hal Herring

Year	Team		No	Yds	Avg	Lg	TD
1949	BUF	AA	1	1	1.0	1	0
1950	CLE	N	2	12	6.0	9	0
1951			1	28	28.0	28	0
Career			4	41	10.3	28	0
Playoffs			1				0

Jeff Herrod

Year	Team		No	Yds	Avg	Lg	TD
1990	IND	N	1	12	12.0	12	0
1991			1	25	25.0	25	0
1992			1	4	4.0	4	0
1993			1	29	29.0	29	0
1996			1	68	68.0	68t	1
Career			5	138	27.6	68t	1
Playoffs			1	17	17.0		0

Bryan Hicks

Year	Team		No	Yds	Avg	Lg	TD
1980	CIN	N	1	8	8.0	8	0

Cliff Hicks

Year	Team		No	Yds	Avg	Lg	TD
1987	LARM	N	1	9	9.0	9	0
1989			2	27	13.5	27	0
1990	BUF	N	1	0	0.0	0	0
1991			1	0	0.0	0	0
Career			5	36	7.2	27	0
Playoffs			2	31	15.5		0

Dwight Hicks

Year	Team		No	Yds	Avg	Lg	TD
1979	SF	N	5	57	11.4	29	0
1980			4	73	18.3	44	0
1981			9	**239**	26.6	72	1
1982			3	5	1.7	3	0
1983			2	102	51.0	62t	2
1984			3	42	14.0	29	0
1985			4	68	17.0	25	0

Dwight Hicks *continued*

Year	Team		No	Yds	Avg	Lg	TD
1986	IND	N	2	16	8.0	16	0
Career			32	602	18.8	72	3
Playoffs			3	49	16.3		0

Tom Hicks

Year	Team		No	Yds	Avg	Lg	TD
1977	CHI	N	1	9	9.0	9	0
1979			3	85	28.3	66t	1
1980			1	8	8.0	8	0
Career			5	102	20.4	66t	1

W.K. Hicks

Year	Team		No	Yds	Avg	Lg	TD
1964	HOU	A	5	89	17.8	62	0
1965			**9**	156	17.3	31	0
1966			3	12	4.0	12	0
1967			3	122	40.7	62	0
1968			3	42	14.0	28	0
1969			4	36	9.0	20	0
1970	NYJ	N	8	99	12.4	35	0
1971			4	46	11.5	26	0
1972			1	43	43.0	43	0
Career			40	645	16.1	62	0

Ed Hiemstra

Year	Team		No	Yds	Avg	Lg	TD
1942	NYG	N	1	9	9.0	9	0

Ben Hightower

Year	Team		No	Yds	Avg	Lg	TD
1943	DET	N	1	9	9.0	9	0

Wally Hilgenberg

Year	Team		No	Yds	Avg	Lg	TD
1970	MIN	N	2	33	16.5	17	0
1971			2	6	3.0	6	0
1972			1	17	17.0	14t	1
1973			1	6	6.0	6	0
1974			1	0	0.0	0	0
1975			1	0	0.0	0	0
Career			8	62	7.8	17	1
Playoffs			2	11	5.5		0

Greg Hill

Year	Team		No	Yds	Avg	Lg	TD
1984	KC	N	2	-1	-0.5	0	0
1985			3	37	12.3	37	0
1986			3	64	21.3	26t	1
1988			1	24	24.0	24	0
Career			9	124	13.8	37	1

Harlon Hill

Year	Team		No	Yds	Avg	Lg	TD
1961	CHI	N	3	52	17.3	24	0

Jim Hill

Year	Team		No	Yds	Avg	Lg	TD
1969	SD	A	7	92	13.1	42	0
1971	SD	N	2	7	3.5	7	0
1972	GB	N	4	37	9.3	21	0
1973			3	53	17.7	20	0
1974			2	47	23.5	24	0
1975	CLE	N	1	56	56.0	56t	1
Career			19	292	15.4	56t	1

Jimmy Hill

Year	Team		No	Yds	Avg	Lg	TD
1952	DET	N	1	15	15.0	15	0
1955	PIT	N	1	9	9.0	9	0
Career			2	24	12.0	15	0

Jimmy Hill

Year	Team		No	Yds	Avg	Lg	TD
1955	CHIC	N	0	0		0L	0
1956			5	21	4.2	12	0
1957			3	53	17.7	31	0
1959			2	4	2.0	4	0
1961	STL	N	4	92	23.0	35t	1
1962			2	15	7.5	15	0
1963			3	126	42.0	58t	1
1965	DET	N	1	9	9.0	9	0
Career			20	320	16.0	58t	2

Kenny Hill

Year	Team		No	Yds	Avg	Lg	TD
1985	NYG	N	2	30	15.0	30	0
1986			3	25	8.3	23	0
1987			1	1	1.0	1	0
1989	KC	N	1	3	3.0	3	0
Career			7	59	8.4	30	0

Rod Hill

Year	Team		No	Yds	Avg	Lg	TD
1983	DAL	N	2	12	6.0	12	0

Rod Hill *continued*

Year	Team		No	Yds	Avg	Lg	TD
1985	BUF	N	2	17	8.5	17	0
Career			4	29	7.3	17	0

Sean Hill

Year	Team		No	Yds	Avg	Lg	TD
1996	MIA	N	1	0	0.0	0	0

Jerry Hillebrand

Year	Team		No	Yds	Avg	Lg	TD
1963	NYG	N	5	54	10.8	34	1
1964			1	9	9.0	9	0
1965			2	25	12.5	25t	1
1966			1	31	31.0	31t	1
1968	PIT	N	2	32	16.0	32	0
1969			1	14	14.0	14	0
1970			2	14	7.0	14	0
Career			14	179	12.8	34	3

Billy Hillenbrand

Year	Team		No	Yds	Avg	Lg	TD
1946	CHI	AA	3	37	12.3		0
1947	BAL	AA	1	48	48.0	48	0
Career			4	85	21.3	48	0

Randy Hilliard

Year	Team		No	Yds	Avg	Lg	TD
1991	CLE	N	1	19	19.0	19	0
1993			1	54	54.0	54	0
1994	DEN	N	2	8	4.0	8	0
1996			1	27	27.0	27	0
Career			5	108	21.6	54	0

Roy Hilton

Year	Team		No	Yds	Avg	Lg	TD
1968	BAL	N	1	13	13.0	13t	1

Stan Hindman

Year	Team		No	Yds	Avg	Lg	TD
1968	SF	N	1	25	25.0	25t	1

Bryan Hinkle

Year	Team		No	Yds	Avg	Lg	TD
1983	PIT	N	1	14	14.0	14t	1
1984			3	77	25.7	43	0
1986			3	7	2.3	6	0
1987			3	15	5.0	8	0
1988			1	1	1.0	1	0
1989			1	4	4.0	4	0
1990			1	19	19.0	19	0
1991			2	68	34.0	57t	1
Career			15	205	13.7	57t	2

Clarke Hinkle

Year	Team		No	Yds	Avg	Lg	TD
1941	GB	N	1	2	2.0	2	0

Jack Hinkle

Year	Team		No	Yds	Avg	Lg	TD
1943	P-P	N	4	98	24.5	91	0
1944	PHI	N	2	62	31.0	50t	1
1945			1	17	17.0	17	0
1946			2	37	18.5	34	0
Career			9	214	23.8	91	1

Chuck Hinton

Year	Team		No	Yds	Avg	Lg	TD
1964	PIT	N	1	8	8.0	8t	1
1969			1	7	7.0	7	0
Career			2	15	7.5	8t	1

Claude Hipps

Year	Team		No	Yds	Avg	Lg	TD
1952	PIT	N	3	48	16.0	17	0
1953			2	0	0.0	0	0
Career			5	48	9.6	17	0

Ed Hirsch

Year	Team		No	Yds	Avg	Lg	TD
1947	BUF	AA	3	73	24.3		1
Playoffs			1	20	20.0		1

Elroy Hirsch

Year	Team		No	Yds	Avg	Lg	TD
1946	CHI	AA	6	97	16.2		0
1948			2	59	29.5		0
1949	LA	N	2	55	27.5	32	0
1950			4	28	7.0	23	0
1954			1	12	12.0	12	0
Career			15	251	16.7	32	0
Playoffs			2	16	8.0		0

Jimmy Hitchcock

Year	Team		No	Yds	Avg	Lg	TD
1996	NE	N	2	14	7.0	14	0

Terry Hoage

Year	Team		No	Yds	Avg	Lg	TD
1985	NO	N	4	79	19.8	52t	1
1986	PHI	N	1	18	18.0	18	0
1987			2	3	1.5	3	0
1988			8	116	14.5	38	0
1990			1	0	0.0	0	0
1994	ARI	N	3	64	21.3	41	0
1995			2	0	0.0	0	0
Career			21	280	13.3	52t	1
Playoffs			2	12	6.0		0

Joe Hoague

Year	Team		No	Yds	Avg	Lg	TD
1942	PIT	N	1	15	15.0	15	0
1946	BOS	N	1	8	8.0	8	0
Career			2	23	11.5	15	0

Liffort Hobley

Year	Team		No	Yds	Avg	Lg	TD
1987	MIA	N	2	7	3.5	7	0
1989			1	22	22.0	22	0
1990			1	15	15.0	15	0
1993			1	17	17.0	17	0
Career			5	61	12.2	22	0

Herman Hodges

Year	Team		No	Yds	Avg	Lg	TD
1939	BKN	N					1

Dick Hoerner

Year	Team		No	Yds	Avg	Lg	TD
1948	LA	N	1	6	6.0	6	0

Bob Hoernschemeyer

Year	Team		No	Yds	Avg	Lg	TD
1946	CHI	AA	1	10	10.0	10	0
1947	BKN	AA	1	8	8.0	8	0
Career			2	18	9.0	10	0

George Hoey

Year	Team		No	Yds	Avg	Lg	TD
1972	NE	N	1	25	25.0	25	0
1974	SD	N	1	20	20.0	20	0
Career			2	45	22.5	25	0

Bob Hoffman

Year	Team		No	Yds	Avg	Lg	TD
1940	WAS	N	1	6	6.0	6	0
1947	LA	N	1	14	14.0	14	0
1949	LA	AA	1	7	7.0	7	0
Career			3	27	9.0	14	0

Jack Hoffman

Year	Team		No	Yds	Avg	Lg	TD
1952	CHIB	N	1	7	7.0	7	0
1958			1	4	4.0	4	0
Career			2	11	5.5	7	0

John Hoffman

Year	Team		No	Yds	Avg	Lg	TD
1950	CHIB	N	1	39	39.0	39t	1
1952			2	54	27.0	54	0
1953			1	27	27.0	27	0
Career			4	120	30.0	54	1

Darrell Hogan

Year	Team		No	Yds	Avg	Lg	TD
1949	PIT	N	1	5	5.0	5	0
1950			1	3	3.0	3	0
1951			1	3	3.0	3	0
1952			4	50	12.5	21	0
Career			7	61	8.7	21	0

Marc Hogan

Year	Team		No	Yds	Avg	Lg	TD
1987	NYJ	N	1	5	5.0	5	0

Bob Hohn

Year	Team		No	Yds	Avg	Lg	TD
1967	PIT	N	2	0	0.0	0	0
1969			5	64	12.8	24	0
Career			7	64	9.1	24	0

Jimmy Holifield

Year	Team		No	Yds	Avg	Lg	TD
1969	NYG	N	1	5	5.0	5	0

Bobby Holladay

Year	Team		No	Yds	Avg	Lg	TD
1956	SF	N	1	0	0.0	0	0

Johnny Holland

Year	Team		No	Yds	Avg	Lg	TD
1987	GB	N	2	4	2.0	4	0
1989			1	26	26.0	26	0
1990			1	32	32.0	32	0
1992			3	27	9.0	22	0

Year	Team		No	Yds	Avg	Lg	TD

Johnny Holland *continued*

Year	Team		No	Yds	Avg	Lg	TD
1993			2	41	20.5	30	0
Career			9	130	14.4	32	0

Hugo Hollas

1970	NO	N	5	79	15.8	29	0
1971			5	56	11.2	25	0
1972			1	14	14.0	14	0
Career			11	149	13.5	29	0

Ed Holler

| 1964 | PIT | N | 1 | 2 | 2.0 | 2 | 0 |

Dwight Hollier

1994	MIA	N	1	36	36.0	36	0
1996			1	11	11.0	11	0
Career			2	47	23.5	36	0

Lamont Hollinquest

1994	WAS	N	1	39	39.0	39	0
1996	GB	N	1	2	2.0	2	0
Career			2	41	20.5	39	0

David Hollis

| 1988 | SEA | N | 2 | 32 | 16.0 | 30 | 0 |

Gus Holloman

1968	DEN	A	1	16	16.0	16	0
1969			1	0	0.0	0	0
1970	NYJ	N	3	11	3.7	9	0
1971			2	2	1.0	2	0
1972			1	25	25.0	25	0
Career			8	54	6.8	25	0

Cornell Holloway

| 1991 | IND | N | 1 | 4 | 4.0 | 4 | 0 |

Johnny Holloway

| 1986 | DAL | N | 1 | 1 | 1.0 | 1 | 0 |

Randy Holloway

| 1982 | MIN | N | 1 | 6 | 6.0 | 6 | 0 |

Walt Holmer

| 1930 | CHIB | N | | | | | 1 |

Clayton Holmes

1994	DAL	N	0	3		3L	0
1995			1	0	0.0	0	0
Career			1	3	3.0	3L	0

Darryl Holmes

| 1987 | NE | N | 1 | 4 | 4.0 | 4 | 0 |

Jerry Holmes

1981	NYJ	N	1	0	0.0	0	0
1982			3	2	0.7	2	0
1983			3	107	35.7	43t	1
1986			6	29	4.8	28	0
1987			1	20	20.0	20	0
1988	DET	N	1	32	32.0	32	0
1989			6	77	12.8	36	1
1990	GB	N	3	39	13.0	24	0
1991			1	0	0.0	0	0
Career			25	306	12.2	43t	2
Playoffs			2	0	0.0		0

Mike Holmes

| 1974 | SF | N | 3 | 26 | 8.7 | 14 | 0 |

Pat Holmes

| 1973 | KC | N | 1 | 17 | 17.0 | 17 | 0 |

Tom Holmoe

1986	SF	N	3	149	49.7	78t	2
1987			1	0	0.0	0	0
1988			2	0	0.0	0	0
1989			1	23	23.0	23	0
Career			7	172	24.6	78t	2

Mike Holovak

| 1948 | CHIB | N | 1 | 18 | 18.0 | 18 | 0 |

Issiac Holt

1985	MIN	N	1	0	0.0	0	0
1986			8	54	6.8	27	0
1987			2	7	3.5	7	0
1988			2	15	7.5	15	0
1989			1	90	90.0	90t	1
1990	DAL	N	3	72	24.0	64t	0
1991			4	2	0.5	2	0
1992			2	11	5.5	8	0
Career			23	251	10.9	90t	2
Playoffs			1	0	0.0		0

John Holt

1981	TB	N	1	13	13.0	13	0
1983			3	43	14.3	25	0
1984			1	25	25.0	25	0
1985			1	3	3.0	3	0
1986	IND	N	1	80	80.0	80	0
Career			7	164	23.4	80	0
Playoffs			1	0	0.0		0

E.J. Holub

1961	DAL	A	1	0	0.0	0	0
1962			2	8	4.0	8	0
1963	KC	A	5	60	12.0	24	0
1965			1	8	8.0	8	0
Career			9	76	8.4	24	0
Playoffs			1	43	43.0		0

Gordy Holz

| 1963 | DEN | A | 1 | 0 | 0.0 | 0 | 0 |

Tom Homco

| 1993 | LARM | N | 1 | 6 | 6.0 | 6 | 0 |

Estus Hood

1978	GB	N	3	18	6.0	18	0
1979			2	8	4.0	6	0
1980			1	0	0.0	0	0
1981			3	59	19.7	41t	1
1982			1	0	0.0	0	0
1984			1	8	8.0	8	0
Career			11	93	8.5	41t	1
Playoffs			1	0	0.0		0

Trell Hooper

| 1987 | MIA | N | 2 | 11 | 5.5 | 11 | 0 |

Jerry Hopkins

1963	DEN	A	1	21	21.0	21	0
1964			2	11	5.5	9	0
1965			1	7	7.0	7	0
1966			2	9	4.5	9	0
Career			6	48	8.0	21	0
Playoffs			1	7	7.0		0

Wes Hopkins

1984	PHI	N	5	107	21.4	33	0
1985			6	36	6.0	24t	1
1988			5	21	4.2	11	0
1990			5	45	9.0	21	0
1991			5	26	5.2	14	0
1992			3	6	2.0	4	0
1993			1	0	0.0	0	0
Career			30	241	8.0	33	1

Harry Hopp

1941	DET	N	1	3	3.0	3	0
1942			1	0	0.0	0	0
1943			2	40	20.0	40t	1
1947	LA	AA	1	16	16.0	16	0
Career			5	59	11.8	40t	1

Alvin Horn

| 1987 | CLE | N | 1 | 28 | 28.0 | 28 | 0 |

Bob Horn

1976	SD	N	1	6	6.0	6	0
1977			1	12	12.0	12	0
1978			1	0	0.0	0	0
1979			2	44	22.0	30	0
1981			1	12	12.0	12	0
1982	SF	N	1	19	19.0	19	0
Career			7	93	13.3	30	0

Ronnie Hornsby

| 1974 | NYG | N | 1 | 2 | 2.0 | 2 | 0 |

Ray Horton

1983	CIN	N	5	121	24.2	55t	1
1984			3	48	16.0	48t	1
1985			2	3	1.5	3	0
1986			1	4	4.0	4	0
1988			3	13	4.3	11	0
1989	DAL	N	1	0	0.0	0	0
1990			1	0	0.0	0	0
1991			1	65	65.0	65t	1
1992			2	15	7.5	15t	1
Career			19	269	14.2	65t	4

Les Horvath

1948	LA	N	2	14	7.0	9	0
1949	CLE	AA	2	4	2.0		0
Career			4	18	4.5	9	0

Derrick Hoskins

1993	LARI	N	2	34	17.0	20	0
1995	OAK	N	1	26	26.0	26	0
Career			3	60	20.0	26	0

Bobby Houston

1992	NYJ	N	1	20	20.0	20t	1
1993			1	0	0.0	0	0
1996			2	3	1.5	3	0
Career			4	23	5.8	20t	1

Jim Houston

1963	CLE	N	1	0	0.0	0	0
1964			2	86	43.0	44	1
1965			2	32	16.0	28	0
1966			2	27	13.5	21	0
1967			3	97	32.3	79t	2
1968			3	11	3.7	7	0
1970			1	25	25.0	25	0
Career			14	278	19.9	79t	3
Playoffs			1	35	35.0		0

Ken Houston

1967	HOU	A	4	151	37.8	78	2
1968			5	160	32.0	66t	2
1969			4	87	21.8	51t	1
1970	HOU	N	3	32	10.7	9	0
1971			9	220	24.4	48t	4
1973	WAS	N	6	32	5.3	22	0
1974			2	40	20.0	37	0
1975			4	33	8.3	19	0
1976			4	25	6.3	12	0
1977			5	69	13.8	31	0
1978			2	29	14.5	29	0
1979			1	20	20.0	20	0
Career			49	898	18.3	78	9
Playoffs			1	8	8.0		0

Bobby Howard

1968	SD	A	1	0	0.0	0	0
1969			6	50	8.3	19	0
1970	SD	N	2	19	9.5	19	0
1971			4	47	11.8	29	0
1973			5	25	5.0	25	0
1974			3	52	17.3	23	0
1975	NE	N	3	52	17.3	44t	1
1976			3	28	9.3	15	0
1977			4	10	2.5	6	0
1978	PHI	N	3	15	5.0	15	0
1979			3	34	11.3	34	0
Career			37	332	9.0	44t	1
Playoffs			2	29	14.5		0

Carl Howard

1987	NYJ	N	3	29	9.7	29	0
1988			2	0	0.0	0	0
Career			5	29	5.8	29	0

David Howard

1987	MIN	N	1	1	1.0	1	0
1988			3	16	5.3	10	0
1992	NE	N	1	1	1.0	1	0
Career			5	18	3.6	10	0

Gene Howard

Year	Team		No	Yds	Avg	Lg	TD
1968	NO	N	3	51	17.0	35	0
1969			2	0	0.0	0	0
1971	LA	N	6	99	16.5	35	0
1972			3	26	8.7	24t	1
Career			14	176	12.6	35	1

Thomas Howard

Year	Team		No	Yds	Avg	Lg	TD
1977	KC	N	1	0	0.0	0	0
1978			1	0	0.0	0	0
1979			1	19	19.0	19	0
1982			2	10	5.0	5	0
1984	STL	N	2	-4	-2.0	1	0
Career			7	25	3.6	19	0

Sherman Howard

Year	Team		No	Yds	Avg	Lg	TD
1949	B-NY	AA	1	26	26.0	26	0
1953	CLE	N	1	3	3.0	3	0
Career			2	29	14.5	26	0

Clarence Howell

Year	Team		No	Yds	Avg	Lg	TD
1948	SF	AA	1	5	5.0	5	0

Delles Howell

Year	Team		No	Yds	Avg	Lg	TD
1970	NO	N	3	28	9.3	28	0
1971			5	120	24.0	60	0
1972			1	6	6.0	6	0
1973	NYJ	N	4	76	19.0	41	0
1974			2	23	11.5	16	0
1975			2	19	9.5	10	0
Career			17	272	16.0	60	0

Mike Howell

Year	Team		No	Yds	Avg	Lg	TD
1966	CLE	N	8	62	7.8	29	0
1967			3	20	6.7	20	0
1968			6	55	9.2	24	0
1969			6	21	3.5	11	0
1970			1	0	0.0	0	0
1971			2	93	46.5	68	0
1972			1	1	1.0	1	0
Career			27	252	9.3	68	0
Playoffs			1	20	20.0		

Chuck Howley

Year	Team		No	Yds	Avg	Lg	TD
1958	CHIB	N	1	4	4.0	4	0
1961	DAL	N	1	5	5.0	5	0
1962			2	33	16.5	21	0
1963			2	3	1.5	3	0
1964			2	27	13.5	21	0
1967			1	28	28.0	28t	1
1968			6	115	19.2	58	1
1969			2	37	18.5	28	0
1970			2	18	9.0	17	0
1971			5	122	24.4	53	0
1972			1	7	7.0	7	0
Career			25	399	16.0	58	2
Playoffs			4	89	22.3		

John Huard

Year	Team		No	Yds	Avg	Lg	TD
1967	DEN	A	2	12	6.0	9	0
1968			2	35	17.5	26	0
1969			2	18	9.0	18	0
Career			6	65	10.8	26	0

Cal Hubbard

Year	Team		No	Yds	Avg	Lg	TD
1935	GB	N					1

Frank Hubbell

Year	Team		No	Yds	Avg	Lg	TD
1949	LA	N	1	21	21.0	21t	1

Floyd Hudlow

Year	Team		No	Yds	Avg	Lg	TD
1967	ATL	N	2	25	12.5	21	0

Billy Hudson

Year	Team		No	Yds	Avg	Lg	TD
1961	SD	A	1	5	5.0	5t	1

Bob Hudson

Year	Team		No	Yds	Avg	Lg	TD
1953	PHI	N	3	74	24.7	42	0
1954			8	89	11.1	32	0
1955			3	48	16.0	25	0
1958			1	15	15.0	15	0
1960	DAL	A	1	0	0.0	0	0
1961	DEN	A	3	16	5.3	13	0
Career			19	242	12.7	42	0

Chris Hudson

Year	Team		No	Yds	Avg	Lg	TD
1996	JAC	N	2	25	12.5	21	0

Jim Hudson

Year	Team		No	Yds	Avg	Lg	TD
1966	NY	A	3	39	13.0	18	0
1967			4	38	9.5	18	0
1968			5	96	19.2	45	0
1969			2	22	11.0	22	0
Career			14	195	13.9	45	0
Playoffs			1	9	9.0		0

Charles Huff

Year	Team		No	Yds	Avg	Lg	TD
1987	ATL	N	2	14	7.0	14	0

Sam Huff

Year	Team		No	Yds	Avg	Lg	TD
1956	NYG	N	3	49	16.3	27	0
1957			1	6	6.0	6	0
1958			2	23	11.5	15	0
1959			1	21	21.0	21	0
1960			3	45	15.0	17	0
1961			3	13	4.3	13	0
1962			1	4	4.0	4	0
1963			4	47	11.8	36t	1
1964	WAS	N	4	34	8.5	14	0
1965			2	49	24.5	29	0
1966			1	17	17.0	17	0
1967			2	8	4.0	5	0
1969			3	65	21.7	32	0
Career			30	381	12.7	36t	2
Playoffs			1				

Dick Huffman

Year	Team		No	Yds	Avg	Lg	TD
1950	LA	N	0	6		6L	0

Vern Huffman

Year	Team		No	Yds	Avg	Lg	TD
1937	DET	N					1

Bill Hughes

Year	Team		No	Yds	Avg	Lg	TD
1941	CHIB	N	1	3	3.0	3	0

Ed Hughes

Year	Team		No	Yds	Avg	Lg	TD
1954	LA	N	2	24	12.0	24	0
1956	NYG	N	1	38	38.0	38	0
Career			3	62	20.7	38	0
Playoffs			1	0	0.0		0

Pat Hughes

Year	Team		No	Yds	Avg	Lg	TD
1972	NYG	N	2	4	2.0	3	0
1973			3	13	4.3	11	0
1974			2	4	2.0	4	0
1976			1	5	5.0	5	0
1977	NO	N	1	2	2.0	2	0
1978			2	11	5.5	7	0
1979			4	62	15.5	40	0
Career			15	101	6.7	40	0

Randy Hughes

Year	Team		No	Yds	Avg	Lg	TD
1975	DAL	N	2	33	16.5	33t	1
1976			1	0	0.0	0	0
1977			2	19	9.5	11	0
1978			2	80	40.0	56	0
1979			2	91	45.5	68	0
Career			9	223	24.8	68	1
Playoffs			3	1	0.3		0

Tyrone Hughes

Year	Team		No	Yds	Avg	Lg	TD
1994	NO	N	2	31	15.5	31	0
1995			2	19	9.5	19	0
Career			4	50	12.5	31	0

Bill Hull

Year	Team		No	Yds	Avg	Lg	TD
Playoffs			1	23	23.0		0

Don Hultz

Year	Team		No	Yds	Avg	Lg	TD
1963	MIN	N	1	35	35.0	35t	1
1965	PHI	N	1	6	6.0	6	0
1967			1	16	16.0	16t	1
1971			1	4	4.0	4	0
Career			4	61	15.3	35t	2

Dick Humbert

Year	Team		No	Yds	Avg	Lg	TD
1941	PHI	N	1	0	0.0	0	0
1947			2	12	6.0	12	0
1948			4	35	8.8	20	0

Dick Humbert *continued*

Year	Team		No	Yds	Avg	Lg	TD
1949			7	69	9.9	37	0
Career			14	116	8.3	37	0

Weldon Humble

Year	Team		No	Yds	Avg	Lg	TD
1947	CLE	AA	2	31	15.5		0
1948			1	11	11.0	11	0
1949			2	55	27.5		0
Career			5	97	19.4	11	0

Bobby Humphery

Year	Team		No	Yds	Avg	Lg	TD
1988	NYJ	N	1	0	0.0	0	0
1990	LARM	N	4	52	13.0	44t	1
Career			5	52	10.4	44t	1

Claude Humphrey

Year	Team		No	Yds	Avg	Lg	TD
1970	ATL	N	1	5	5.0	5	0
1973			1	6	6.0	6	0
Career			2	11	5.5	6	0

Leonard Humphries

Year	Team		No	Yds	Avg	Lg	TD
1994	IND	N	1	1	1.0	1	0

Ricky Hunley

Year	Team		No	Yds	Avg	Lg	TD
1986	DEN	N	1	22	22.0	22	0
1987			2	64	32.0	52t	1
Career			3	86	28.7	52t	1
Playoffs			1	14	14.0		0

Bobby Hunt

Year	Team		No	Yds	Avg	Lg	TD
1962	DAL	A	8	101	12.6	17	0
1963	KC	A	6	228	38.0	66	0
1964			7	133	19.0	59	1
1965			1	28	28.0	28	0
1966			10	113	11.3	33	0
1967			5	71	14.2	39	0
1968	CIN	A	1	15	15.0	15	0
1969			4	66	16.5	27	0
Career			42	755	18.0	66	1

Byron Hunt

Year	Team		No	Yds	Avg	Lg	TD
1981	NYG	N	1	7	7.0	7	0
1984			1	14	14.0	14	0
Career			2	21	10.5	14	0

Jim Hunt

Year	Team		No	Yds	Avg	Lg	TD
1963	BOS	A	1	78	78.0	78t	1

Mike Hunt

Year	Team		No	Yds	Avg	Lg	TD
1978	GB	N	1	10	10.0	10	0
1979			1	13	13.0	13	0
Career			2	23	11.5	13	0

Sam Hunt

Year	Team		No	Yds	Avg	Lg	TD
1974	NE	N	3	66	22.0	27	0
1976			2	106	53.0	68t	1
1977			2	17	8.5	10	0
Career			7	189	27.0	68t	1

Daniel Hunter

Year	Team		No	Yds	Avg	Lg	TD
1985	DEN	N	1	20	20.0	20	0

James Hunter

Year	Team		No	Yds	Avg	Lg	TD
1976	DET	N	7	120	17.1	39t	1
1977			6	104	17.3	26	0
1978			2	-4	-2.0	0	0
1979			3	6	2.0	6	0
1980			6	20	3.3	13	0
1981			1	-3	-3.0	-3	0
1982			2	36	18.0	36	0
Career			27	279	10.3	39t	1

Monty Hunter

Year	Team		No	Yds	Avg	Lg	TD
Playoffs			1	19	19.0		1

Patrick Hunter

Year	Team		No	Yds	Avg	Lg	TD
1987	SEA	N	1	3	3.0	3	0
1990			1	0	0.0	0	0
1991			1	32	32.0	32t	1
1992			2	0	0.0	0	0
1993			4	54	13.5	34	0
1994			3	85	28.3	51	0

Year	Team		No	Yds	Avg	Lg	TD

Patrick Hunter *continued*

Year	Team		No	Yds	Avg	Lg	TD
1995	ARI	N	2	21	10.5	21	0
Career			14	195	13.9	51	1

Tom Hupke
Year	Team		No	Yds	Avg	Lg	TD
1937	DET	N					1

Bill Hurley
Year	Team		No	Yds	Avg	Lg	TD
1982	NO	N	1	26	26.0	26	0

Maurice Hurst
Year	Team		No	Yds	Avg	Lg	TD
1989	NE	N	5	31	6.2	16t	1
1990			4	61	15.3	36	0
1991			3	21	7.0	21	0
1992			3	29	9.7	27	0
1993			4	53	13.3	24	0
1994			7	68	9.7	24	0
1995			1	0	0.0	0	0
Career			27	263	9.7	36	1

Don Hutson
Year	Team		No	Yds	Avg	Lg	TD
1940	GB	N	6	24	4.0		0
1941			1	32	32.0	32	0
1942			7	71	10.1	27	0
1943			8	197	24.6	84	1
1944			4	50	12.5	43	0
1945			4	15	3.8	15	0
Career			30	389	13.0	84	1

Paul Hynes
Year	Team		No	Yds	Avg	Lg	TD
1962	NY	A	2	2	1.0	2	0

Bob Ingalls
Year	Team		No	Yds	Avg	Lg	TD
1942	GB	N	1	23	23.0	23t	1

Tony Ippolito
Year	Team		No	Yds	Avg	Lg	TD
1943	CHIB	N	1	5	5.0	5	0

Gerald Irons
Year	Team		No	Yds	Avg	Lg	TD
1972	OAK	N	2	18	9.0	11	0
1973			2	19	9.5	10	0
1974			2	23	11.5	12	0
1975			1	9	9.0	9	0
1976	CLE	N	1	1	1.0	1	0
1977			3	99	33.0	53t	1
1978			2	9	4.5	9	0
Career			13	178	13.7	53t	1

Ken Irvin
Year	Team		No	Yds	Avg	Lg	TD
Playoffs			1	0	0.0		0

LeRoy Irvin
Year	Team		No	Yds	Avg	Lg	TD
1980	LA	N	2	80	40.0	80	0
1981			3	18	6.0	18	0
1983	LARM	N	4	42	10.5	22	0
1984			5	166	33.2	81t	2
1985			6	83	13.8	34t	1
1986			6	150	25.0	50t	1
1987			2	47	23.5	47t	1
1988			3	25	8.3	22	0
1989			3	43	14.3	18	0
1990	DET	N	1	22	22.0	22	0
Career			35	676	19.3	81t	5
Playoffs			4	149	37.3		

Cecil Isbell
Year	Team		No	Yds	Avg	Lg	TD
1941	GB	N	1	0	0.0	0	0
1942			6	47	7.8	19	0
Career			7	47	6.7	19	0

Ray Isom
Year	Team		No	Yds	Avg	Lg	TD
1987	TB	N	2	67	33.5	38	0

Steve Israel
Year	Team		No	Yds	Avg	Lg	TD
1996	SF	N	1	3	3.0	3	0

Jack Itzel
Year	Team		No	Yds	Avg	Lg	TD
1945	PIT	N	1	13	13.0	13	0

Duke Iverson
Year	Team		No	Yds	Avg	Lg	TD
1948	NY	AA	1	1	1.0	1	0
1949	B-NY	AA	1	8	8.0	8	0

Duke Iverson *continued*
Year	Team		No	Yds	Avg	Lg	TD
1950	NYY	N	3	26	8.7	10t	1
Career			5	35	7.0	10t	1

Pop Ivy
Year	Team		No	Yds	Avg	Lg	TD
1941	CHIC	N	1	20	20.0	20t	1
1945			1	0	0.0	0	0
1946			1	22	22.0	22	0
Career			3	42	14.0	22	1

Alfred Jackson
Year	Team		No	Yds	Avg	Lg	TD
1991	CLE	N	1	0	0.0	0	0
1995	MIN	N	2	46	23.0	37t	1
1996			2	4	2.0	4	0
Career			5	50	10.0	37t	1

Bernie Jackson
Year	Team		No	Yds	Avg	Lg	TD
1972	CIN	N	1	0	0.0	0	0
1973			1	0	0.0	0	0
1974			1	17	17.0	17	0
1975			5	97	19.4	34	0
1976			1	0	0.0	0	0
1977	DEN	N	1	13	13.0	13	0
1978			6	128	21.3	38	0
1979			0	13		13L	0
1980			1	11	11.0	11	0
Career			17	279	16.4	38	0
Playoffs			1	15	15.0		

Bobby Jackson
Year	Team		No	Yds	Avg	Lg	TD
1978	NYJ	N	5	26	5.2	13	0
1979			4	63	15.8	58t	1
1980			1	7	7.0	7	0
1982			5	84	16.8	77t	1
1983			2	8	4.0	8	0
1985			4	8	2.0	8	0
Career			21	196	9.3	77t	2
Playoffs			1	10	10.0		0

Calvin Jackson
Year	Team		No	Yds	Avg	Lg	TD
1995	MIA	N	1	23	23.0	23	0
1996			3	82	27.3	61t	1
Career			4	105	26.3	61t	1

Charles Jackson
Year	Team		No	Yds	Avg	Lg	TD
1984	KC	N	1	16	16.0	16	0

Charlie Jackson
Year	Team		No	Yds	Avg	Lg	TD
1958	CHIC	N	1	13	13.0	13	0

Ernie Jackson
Year	Team		No	Yds	Avg	Lg	TD
1972	NO	N	3	41	13.7	31	0
1973			3	40	13.3	23	0
1974			4	53	13.3	28	0
1975			2	48	24.0	46	0
1976			2	5	2.5	5	0
1977			1	0	0.0	0	0
Career			15	187	12.5	46	0

Gerald Jackson
Year	Team		No	Yds	Avg	Lg	TD
1979	KC	N	1	4	4.0	4	0

Greg Jackson
Year	Team		No	Yds	Avg	Lg	TD
1990	NYG	N	5	8	1.6	5	0
1991			1	3	3.0	3	0
1992			4	71	17.8	36	0
1993			4	32	8.0	29	0
1994	PHI	N	6	86	14.3	55t	1
1995			1	18	18.0	18	0
1996	NO	N	3	24	8.0	10	0
Career			24	242	10.1	55t	1
Playoffs			1	31	31.0		0

Honor Jackson
Year	Team		No	Yds	Avg	Lg	TD
1972	NE	N	4	133	33.3	55	0
1973			1	0	0.0	0	0
Career			5	133	26.6	55	0

Jeff Jackson
Year	Team		No	Yds	Avg	Lg	TD
1984	ATL	N	1	35	35.0	35t	1

Jim Jackson
Year	Team		No	Yds	Avg	Lg	TD
1967	SF	N	1	22	22.0	22	0

Johnnie Jackson
Year	Team		No	Yds	Avg	Lg	TD
1989	SF	N	2	35	17.5	19	0
1991			1	11	11.0	11	0
Career			3	46	15.3	19	0
Playoffs			1	0	0.0		

Kirby Jackson
Year	Team		No	Yds	Avg	Lg	TD
1987	LARM	N	1	36	36.0	36	0
1989	BUF	N	2	43	21.5	40t	1
1990			3	16	5.3	14	0
1991			4	31	7.8	15	0
Career			10	126	12.6	40t	1
Playoffs			3	10	3.3		0

Michael Jackson
Year	Team		No	Yds	Avg	Lg	TD
1980	SEA	N	2	9	4.5	5	0
1981			2	51	25.5	33	0
1982			2	29	14.5	28	0
Career			6	89	14.8	33	0

Monte Jackson
Year	Team		No	Yds	Avg	Lg	TD
1975	LA	N	2	13	6.5	10	0
1976			10	173	17.3	46t	3
1977			5	73	14.6	33	0
1978	OAK	N	2	25	12.5	25	0
1979			2	5	2.5	5	0
1980			1	0	0.0	0	0
1982	LARI	N	1	0	0.0	0	0
Career			23	289	12.6	46t	3
Playoffs			2	0	0.0		

Ray Jackson
Year	Team		No	Yds	Avg	Lg	TD
1996	BUF	N	1	0	0.0	0	0

Rickey Jackson
Year	Team		No	Yds	Avg	Lg	TD
1982	NO	N	1	32	32.0	32	0
1983			1	0	0.0	0	0
1984			1	14	14.0	14	0
1986			1	1	1.0	1	0
1987			2	4	2.0	4	0
1988			1	16	16.0	16	0
1995	SF	N	1	1	1.0	1	0
Career			8	68	8.5	32	0

Robert Jackson
Year	Team		No	Yds	Avg	Lg	TD
1980	CLE	N	2	15	7.5	9	0

Robert Jackson
Year	Team		No	Yds	Avg	Lg	TD
1983	CIN	N	2	21	10.5	15	0
1984			4	32	8.0	28t	1
1985			6	100	16.7	57t	1
1987			3	49	16.3	29	0
Career			15	202	13.5	57t	2

Roger Jackson
Year	Team		No	Yds	Avg	Lg	TD
1983	DEN	N	1	15	15.0	15	0
1984			1	23	23.0	23	0
Career			2	38	19.0	23	0

Stephen Jackson
Year	Team		No	Yds	Avg	Lg	TD
1966	WAS	N	1	0	0.0	0	0

Steve Jackson
Year	Team		No	Yds	Avg	Lg	TD
1977	OAK	N	1	33	33.0	33	0

Steve Jackson
Year	Team		No	Yds	Avg	Lg	TD
1992	HOU	N	3	18	6.0	18	0
1993			5	54	10.8	22t	1
1994			1	0	0.0	0	0
1995			2	0	0.0	0	0
Career			11	72	6.5	22t	1
Playoffs			1	14	14.0		

Terry Jackson
Year	Team		No	Yds	Avg	Lg	TD
1978	NYG	N	7	115	16.4	51	1
1979			3	10	3.3	10	0
1980			1	5	5.0	5	0
1981			3	57	19.0	32t	1
1982			4	75	18.8	37	0
1983			6	20	3.3	17	0
1984	SEA	N	4	78	19.5	62t	1
Career			28	360	12.9	62t	3

Year	Team		No	Yds	Avg	Lg	TD

Tom Jackson

Year	Team		No	Yds	Avg	Lg	TD
1974	DEN	N	1	39	39.0	39	0
1975			2	0	0.0	0	0
1976			7	136	19.4	46t	1
1977			4	95	23.8	73t	1
1978			3	28	9.3	28t	1
1979			1	34	34.0	34	0
1982			1	8	8.0	8	0
1983			1	0	0.0	0	0
Career			20	340	17.0	73t	3
Playoffs			2	49	24.5		0

Vestee Jackson

Year	Team		No	Yds	Avg	Lg	TD
1986	CHI	N	3	0	0.0	0	0
1987			1	0	0.0	0	0
1988			8	94	11.8	46	0
1989			2	16	8.0	16	0
1990			1	45	45.0	45t	1
1992	MIA	N	3	63	21.0	30t	1
Career			18	218	12.1	46	2
Playoffs			1	51	51.0		0

Harry Jacobs

Year	Team		No	Yds	Avg	Lg	TD
1960	BOS	A	4	26	6.5		0
1963	BUF	A	1	8	8.0	8	0
1964			2	13	6.5	13	0
1965			1	0	0.0	0	0
1966			2	15	7.5	15	0
1969			2	13	6.5	12	0
Career			12	75	6.3	15	0
Playoffs			1	12	12.0		0

Jack Jacobs

Year	Team		No	Yds	Avg	Lg	TD
1942	CLE	N	4	22	5.5	22	0
1946	WAS	N	2	56	28.0	42	0
1947	GB	N	4	64	16.0	29	0
1949			2	26	13.0	26	0
Career			12	168	14.0	42	0

Tim Jacobs

Year	Team		No	Yds	Avg	Lg	TD
1994	CLE	N	2	9	4.5	8	0

Harry Jacunski

Year	Team		No	Yds	Avg	Lg	TD
1943	GB	N	1	7	7.0	7	0

Harry Jagielski

Year	Team		No	Yds	Avg	Lg	TD
1961	OAK	A	1	7	7.0	7	0

Van Jakes

Year	Team		No	Yds	Avg	Lg	TD
1986	NO	N	2	6	3.0	4	0
1987			3	32	10.7	27	0
1988			3	61	20.3	39	0
1989	GB	N	1	0	0.0	0	0
Career			9	99	11.0	39	0

Dick James

Year	Team		No	Yds	Avg	Lg	TD
1957	WAS	N	2	3	1.5	3	0
1958			4	43	10.8	23	0
1959			3	47	15.7	25	0
1961			1	28	28.0	28	0
1963			2	21	10.5	21	0
Career			12	142	11.8	28	0

Robert James

Year	Team		No	Yds	Avg	Lg	TD
1971	BUF	N	4	25	6.3	25	0
1972			1	0	0.0	0	0
1973			1	0	0.0	0	0
1974			3	13	4.3	8	0
Career			9	38	4.2	25	0

Roland James

Year	Team		No	Yds	Avg	Lg	TD
1980	NE	N	4	32	8.0	19	0
1981			2	29	14.5	21	0
1982			3	12	4.0	12	0
1983			5	99	19.8	46	0
1984			2	14	7.0	14	0
1985			4	51	12.8	39	0
1986			2	39	19.5	21	0
1987			1	27	27.0	27	0
1988			4	30	7.5	22	0
1989			2	50	25.0	28	0
Career			29	383	13.2	46	0

Tommy James

Year	Team		No	Yds	Avg	Lg	TD
1948	CLE	AA	4	37	9.3		0
1949			4	64	16.0		1
1950	CLE	N	9	69	7.7	34	0
1951			2	1	0.5	1	0
1952			4	40	10.0	18	0
1953			5	21	4.2	11	0
1954			4	57	14.3	36	0
1955			2	20	10.0	16	0
Career			34	309	9.1	36	1
Playoffs			4	47	11.8		0

Tory James

Year	Team		No	Yds	Avg	Lg	TD
1996	DEN	N	2	15	7.5	15	0

George Jamison

Year	Team		No	Yds	Avg	Lg	TD
1988	DET	N	3	56	18.7	52t	1
1991			3	52	17.3	19	0
1993			2	48	24.0	35t	1
Career			8	156	19.5	52t	2

Bobby Jancik

Year	Team		No	Yds	Avg	Lg	TD
1962	HOU	A	2	33	16.5	24	0
1963			3	31	10.3	19	0
1964			3	16	5.3	16	0
1965			4	90	22.5	36	0
1966			2	36	18.0	35	0
1967			1	4	4.0	4	0
Career			15	210	14.0	36	0

Charlie Janerette

Year	Team		No	Yds	Avg	Lg	TD
1963	NY	A	1	6	6.0	6	0
1965	DEN	A	1	0	0.0	0	0
Career			2	6	3.0	6	0

Len Janiak

Year	Team		No	Yds	Avg	Lg	TD
1941	CLE	N	1	19	19.0	19	0

Tommy Janik

Year	Team		No	Yds	Avg	Lg	TD
1963	DEN	A	2	32	16.0	31	0
1964			1	22	22.0	22t	1
1966	BUF	A	8	136	17.0	37	2
1967			10	222	22.2	46	2
1968			3	137	45.7	100	1
1969	BOS	A	1	8	8.0	8	0
Career			25	557	22.3	100	6

Ed Jankowski

Year	Team		No	Yds	Avg	Lg	TD
1937	GB	N					1
1941			1	33	33.0	33	0
Career			1	33	33.0	33	1

Jon Jaqua

Year	Team		No	Yds	Avg	Lg	TD
1970	WAS	N	1	25	25.0	25	0

Pete Jaquess

Year	Team		No	Yds	Avg	Lg	TD
1964	HOU	A	8	141	17.6	98	1
1966	MIA	A	3	27	9.0	27	1
1968	DEN	A	5	64	12.8	28	0
Career			16	232	14.5	98	2

Mike Jarmoluk

Year	Team		No	Yds	Avg	Lg	TD
1948	BOS	N	2	13	6.5	10	0
1949	PHI	N	1	3	3.0	3	0
1951			1	9	9.0	9	0
1952			2	48	24.0	45t	1
1953			1	2	2.0	2	0
Career			7	75	10.7	45t	1

Toimi Jarvi

Year	Team		No	Yds	Avg	Lg	TD
1944	PHI	N	1	0	0.0	0	0

Dick Jauron

Year	Team		No	Yds	Avg	Lg	TD
1973	DET	N	4	208	52.0	95t	1
1974			1	26	26.0	26	0
1975			4	39	9.8	38	0
1976			2	0	0.0	0	0
1977			3	55	18.3	28	0
1978	CIN	N	4	52	13.0	24t	1
1979			6	41	6.8	12	0
1980			1	11	11.0	11	0
Career			25	432	17.3	95t	2

Garth Jax

Year	Team		No	Yds	Avg	Lg	TD
1990	PHX	N	2	5	2.5	4	0

Jim Jeffcoat

Year	Team		No	Yds	Avg	Lg	TD
1985	DAL	N	1	65	65.0	65t	1
1987			1	26	26.0	26t	1
Career			2	91	45.5	65t	2

Billy Jefferson

Year	Team		No	Yds	Avg	Lg	TD
1941	DET	N	1	12	12.0	12	0

James Jefferson

Year	Team		No	Yds	Avg	Lg	TD
1990	SEA	N	1	0	0.0	0	0
1993			1	12	12.0	12	0
Career			2	12	6.0	12	0

Greg Jeffries

Year	Team		No	Yds	Avg	Lg	TD
1996	DET	N	1	0	0.0	0	0

Jon Jelacic

Year	Team		No	Yds	Avg	Lg	TD
1962	OAK	A	1	0	0.0	0	0
1963			1	1	1.0	1t	1
Career			2	1	0.5	1t	1

Carlos Jenkins

Year	Team		No	Yds	Avg	Lg	TD
1992	MIN	N	1	19	19.0	19t	1
1993			2	7	3.5	4	0
1996	STL	N	1	-3	-3.0	-3	0
Career			4	23	5.8	19t	1

Izel Jenkins

Year	Team		No	Yds	Avg	Lg	TD
1989	PHI	N	4	58	14.5	22	0
Playoffs			1	33	33.0		0

Jack Jenkins

Year	Team		No	Yds	Avg	Lg	TD
1946	WAS	N	3	57	19.0	38	0
1947			1	7	7.0	7	0
Career			4	64	16.0	38	0

Melvin Jenkins

Year	Team		No	Yds	Avg	Lg	TD
1987	SEA	N	3	46	15.3	34	0
1988			3	41	13.7	21	0
1990			1	0	0.0	0	0
1992	DET	N	4	34	8.5	14	0
Career			11	121	11.0	34	0
Playoffs			3	84	28.0		2

Mark Jerue

Year	Team		No	Yds	Avg	Lg	TD
1986	LARM	N	2	23	11.5	22t	1
1988			1	0	0.0	0	0
Career			3	23	7.7	22t	1

Bob Jeter

Year	Team		No	Yds	Avg	Lg	TD
1965	GB	N	1	21	21.0	21	0
1966			5	142	28.4	75t	2
1967			8	78	9.8	25	0
1968			3	35	11.7	29	0
1969			3	30	10.0	30	0
1970			3	27	9.0	18	0
1971	CHI	N	1	0	0.0	0	0
1972			2	0	0.0	0	0
Career			26	333	12.8	75t	2

Dan Jilek

Year	Team		No	Yds	Avg	Lg	TD
1976	BUF	N	2	33	16.5	28	0

Bill Jobko

Year	Team		No	Yds	Avg	Lg	TD
1959	LA	N	1	0	0.0	0	0
1960			1	7	7.0	7	0
1961			1	16	16.0	16	0
1966	ATL	N	2	5	2.5	3	0
Career			5	28	5.6	16	0

A.J. Johnson

Year	Team		No	Yds	Avg	Lg	TD
1989	WAS	N	4	94	23.5	59t	1
1990			1	0	0.0	0	0
1992			3	38	12.7	29	0
1993			1	69	69.0	69t	1
Career			9	201	22.3	69t	2
Playoffs			1	0	0.0		0

Alonzo Johnson

Year	Team		No	Yds	Avg	Lg	TD
1986	PHI	N	3	6	2.0	9	0

Benny Johnson

Year	Team		No	Yds	Avg	Lg	TD
1972	HOU	N	1	34	34.0	34	0

Bert Johnson

Year	Team		No	Yds	Avg	Lg	TD
1941	CHIC	N	1	30	30.0	30	0

Bill Johnson

Year	Team		No	Yds	Avg	Lg	TD
1948	SF	AA	1	0	0.0	0	0
1949			1	16	16.0	16t	1
Career			2	16	8.0	16t	1

Billy Johnson

Year	Team		No	Yds	Avg	Lg	TD
1968	BOS	A	2	33	16.5	19	0

Bobby Johnson

Year	Team		No	Yds	Avg	Lg	TD
1983	NO	N	2	80	40.0	70t	1
1984			1	7	7.0	7	0
Career			3	87	29.0	70t	1

Cecil Johnson

Year	Team		No	Yds	Avg	Lg	TD
1943	BKN	N	1	14	14.0	14	0

Cecil Johnson

Year	Team		No	Yds	Avg	Lg	TD
1977	TB	N	1	0	0.0	0	0
1978			2	5	2.5	4	0
1981			5	84	16.8	36	0
1985			1	12	12.0	12	0
Career			9	101	11.2	36	0

Charles Johnson

Year	Team		No	Yds	Avg	Lg	TD
1980	SF	N	1	15	15.0	15	0
1981	STL	N	1	19	19.0	19	0
Career			2	34	17.0	19	0

Charles Johnson

Year	Team		No	Yds	Avg	Lg	TD
1979	GB	N	1	0	0.0	0	0

Charlie Johnson

Year	Team		No	Yds	Avg	Lg	TD
1980	PHI	N	3	9	3.0	9	0
1981			1	0	0.0	0	0
1983	MIN	N	1	2	2.0	2	0
Career			5	11	2.2	9	0

Curtis Johnson

Year	Team		No	Yds	Avg	Lg	TD
1970	MIA	N	3	29	9.7	21	0
1971			2	34	17.0	34	0
1972			3	20	6.7	13	0
1973			2	19	9.5	17	0
1975			4	41	10.3	17	0
1976			1	14	14.0	14	0
1977			4	35	8.8	19	0
1978			3	-2	-0.7	0	0
Career			22	190	8.6	34	0
Playoffs			3	43	14.3		

Daryl Johnson

Year	Team		No	Yds	Avg	Lg	TD
1968	BOS	A	1	11	11.0	11	0
1969			2	23	11.5	23	0
1970	BOS	N	2	51	25.5	42	0
Career			5	85	17.0	42	0

Demetrious Johnson

Year	Team		No	Yds	Avg	Lg	TD
1985	DET	N	3	39	13.0	19	0
1986			2	18	9.0	18	0
Career			5	57	11.4	19	0

Dennis Johnson

Year	Team		No	Yds	Avg	Lg	TD
1975	WAS	N	1	57	57.0	57	0
1976			1	2	2.0	2	0
Career			2	59	29.5	57	0

D.J. Johnson

Year	Team		No	Yds	Avg	Lg	TD
1989	PIT	N	1	0	0.0	0	0
1990			2	60	30.0	34	1
1991			1	0	0.0	0	0
1992			5	67	13.4	35	0
1993			3	51	17.0	26	0
1994	ATL	N	5	0	0.0	0	0
1995			2	4	2.0	2	0
Career			19	182	9.6	35	1

Eddie Johnson

Year	Team		No	Yds	Avg	Lg	TD
1984	CLE	N	2	3	1.5	3	0
1985			1	6	6.0	6	0

Eddie Johnson *continued*

Year	Team		No	Yds	Avg	Lg	TD
1987			1	11	11.0	11	0
1988			2	0	0.0	0	0
Career			6	20	3.3	11	0

Filmel Johnson

Year	Team		No	Yds	Avg	Lg	TD
Playoffs			1	2	2.0		0

Frank Johnson

Year	Team		No	Yds	Avg	Lg	TD
1920	AKR	A					1

Gary Johnson

Year	Team		No	Yds	Avg	Lg	TD
1978	SD	N	1	52	52.0	52t	1
1981			1	41	41.0	41	1
Career			2	93	46.5	52t	2

Gene Johnson

Year	Team		No	Yds	Avg	Lg	TD
1959	PHI	N	1	22	22.0	22	0
1960			3	34	11.3	33	0
Career			4	56	14.0	33	0

Greg Johnson

Year	Team		No	Yds	Avg	Lg	TD
1977	TB	N	1	0	0.0	0t	1

Greggory Johnson

Year	Team		No	Yds	Avg	Lg	TD
Playoffs			2	0	0.0		0

Harvey Johnson

Year	Team		No	Yds	Avg	Lg	TD
1949	B-NY	AA	1	1	1.0	1	0

Holbert Johnson

Year	Team		No	Yds	Avg	Lg	TD
1987	LARM	N	1	49	49.0	49	0

Howard Johnson

Year	Team		No	Yds	Avg	Lg	TD
1941	GB	N	1	10	10.0	10	0

Jack Johnson

Year	Team		No	Yds	Avg	Lg	TD
1957	CHIB	N	4	36	9.0	20	0
1958			1	5	5.0	5	0
1959			1	0	0.0	0	0
1960	BUF	A	2	1	0.5		0
Career			8	42	5.3	20	0

Jimmy Johnson

Year	Team		No	Yds	Avg	Lg	TD
1961	SF	N	5	116	23.2	63	0
1963			2	36	18.0	36	0
1964			3	65	21.7	43	0
1965			6	47	7.8	26	0
1966			4	57	14.3	35t	1
1967			2	68	34.0	38	0
1968			1	25	25.0	25	0
1969			5	18	3.6	18	0
1970			2	36	18.0	36t	1
1971			3	16	5.3	10	0
1972			4	18	4.5	15	0
1973			4	46	11.5	30	0
1974			3	50	16.7	37	0
1975			2	0	0.0	0	0
1976			1	17	17.0	17	0
Career			47	615	13.1	63	2

John Johnson

Year	Team		No	Yds	Avg	Lg	TD
1992	SF	N	1	56	56.0	56t	1
1993			1	0	0.0	0	0
Career			2	56	28.0	56t	1

John Henry Johnson

Year	Team		No	Yds	Avg	Lg	TD
1955	SF	N	1	29	29.0	29	0

Johnnie Johnson

Year	Team		No	Yds	Avg	Lg	TD
1980	LA	N	3	102	34.0	99t	1
1982	LARM	N	1	7	7.0	7	0
1983			4	115	28.8	60t	2
1984			2	21	10.5	21	0
1985			5	96	19.2	46	1
1986			1	13	13.0	13	0
1987			1	0	0.0	0	0
1988			4	18	4.5	11	0
1989	SEA	N	1	18	18.0	18	0
Career			22	390	17.7	99t	4

Kenny Johnson

Year	Team		No	Yds	Avg	Lg	TD
1987	GB	N	1	2	2.0	2	0

Kenny Johnson

Year	Team		No	Yds	Avg	Lg	TD
1980	ATL	N	4	49	12.3	33	0
1981			3	35	11.7	23	0
1982			2	30	15.0	30	0
1983			2	57	28.5	31t	2
1984			5	75	15.0	28	0
1988	HOU	N	1	51	51.0	51	0
Career			17	297	17.5	51	2

Keshon Johnson

Year	Team		No	Yds	Avg	Lg	TD
1994	GB	N	1	3	3.0	3	0

Lawrence Johnson

Year	Team		No	Yds	Avg	Lg	TD
1980	CLE	N	1	3	3.0	3	0
1982			4	17	4.3	17	0
1983			2	0	0.0	0	0
1984			1	0	0.0	0	0
1985	BUF	N	1	0	0.0	0	0
Career			9	20	2.2	17	0

Levi Johnson

Year	Team		No	Yds	Avg	Lg	TD
1973	DET	N	5	82	16.4	38	0
1974			5	139	27.8	55t	2
1975			3	71	23.7	45	0
1976			6	**206**	34.3	76	1
1977			2	51	25.5	32	0
Career			21	549	26.1	76	3

Marv Johnson

Year	Team		No	Yds	Avg	Lg	TD
1952	GB	N	2	22	11.0	22	0
1953			4	39	9.8	36	0
Career			6	61	10.2	36	0
Playoffs			1	35	35.0		0

Melvin Johnson

Year	Team		No	Yds	Avg	Lg	TD
1995	TB	N	1	0	0.0	0	0
1996			2	24	12.0	24	0
Career			3	24	8.0	24	0

Mike Johnson

Year	Team		No	Yds	Avg	Lg	TD
1967	DAL	N	5	88	17.6	49	0
1968			3	3	1.0	3	0
Career			8	91	11.4	49	0

Mike Johnson

Year	Team		No	Yds	Avg	Lg	TD
1987	CLE	N	1	3	3.0	3	0
1988			2	36	18.0	31	0
1989			3	43	14.3	23	0
1990			1	64	64.0	64t	1
1991			1	0	0.0	0	0
1992			1	0	0.0	0	0
1993			1	0	0.0	0	0
1994	DET	N	1	48	48.0	48t	1
1995			2	23	11.5	14	0
Career			13	217	16.7	64t	2

Monte Johnson

Year	Team		No	Yds	Avg	Lg	TD
1974	OAK	N	1	17	17.0	17	0
1975			1	57	57.0	57	0
1976			4	40	10.0	22	0
1977			2	15	7.5	15	0
1978			1	6	6.0	6	0
1979			1	0	0.0	0	0
Career			10	135	13.5	57	0
Playoffs			2	11	5.5		0

Pepper Johnson

Year	Team		No	Yds	Avg	Lg	TD
1986	NYG	N	1	13	13.0	13	0
1988			1	33	33.0	33t	1
1989			3	60	20.0	39t	1
1990			1	0	0.0	0	0
1991			2	5	2.5	5	0
1992			2	42	21.0	38	0
1995	CLE	N	2	22	11.0	22	0
Career			12	175	14.6	39t	2
Playoffs			2	30	15.0		0

Richard Johnson

Year	Team		No	Yds	Avg	Lg	TD
1986	HOU	N	2	6	3.0	6	0
1987			1	0	0.0	0	0
1988			3	0	0.0	0	0
1989			1	0	0.0	0	0
1990			8	100	12.5	35	1
Career			15	106	7.1	35	1
Playoffs			2	25	12.5		

Ron Johnson

Year	Team		No	Yds	Avg	Lg	TD
1978	PIT	N	4	24	6.0	21	0
1979			1	20	20.0	20	0
1980			1	19	19.0	19	0
1981			2	8	4.0	8	0
1982			2	5	2.5	5	0
1983			3	84	28.0	34t	1
Career			13	160	12.3	34t	1
Playoffs			1	34	34.0		0

Sidney Johnson

Year	Team		No	Yds	Avg	Lg	TD
1991	WAS	N	2	5	2.5	5	0
1992			1	12	12.0	12	0
Career			3	17	5.7	12	0

Ted Johnson

Year	Team		No	Yds	Avg	Lg	TD
1996	NE	N	1	0	0.0	0	0

Tim Johnson

Year	Team		No	Yds	Avg	Lg	TD
1991	WAS	N	1	14	14.0	14	0

Vaughan Johnson

Year	Team		No	Yds	Avg	Lg	TD
1986	NO	N	1	15	15.0	15	0
1987			1	0	0.0	0	0
1988			1	34	34.0	34	0
1991			1	19	19.0	19	0
Career			4	68	17.0	34	0

Walter Johnson

Year	Team		No	Yds	Avg	Lg	TD
1970	CLE	N	1	4	4.0	4	0
1972			1	1	1.0	1	0
Career			2	5	2.5	4	0

Luke Johnsos

Year	Team		No	Yds	Avg	Lg	TD
1932	CHIB	N					1

Jimmy Johnston

Year	Team		No	Yds	Avg	Lg	TD
1940	WAS	N	1	65	65.0	65t	1
1946	CHIC	N	1	20	20.0	20	0
Career			2	85	42.5	65t	1

Mark Johnston

Year	Team		No	Yds	Avg	Lg	TD
1960	HOU	A	4	42	10.5	33	0
1961			3	54	18.0	27	0
1962			4	31	7.8	27	0
1963			1	90	90.0	90t	1
1964	NY	A	1	3	3.0	3	0
Career			13	220	16.9	90t	1
Playoffs			1	0	0.0		0

Preston Johnston

Year	Team		No	Yds	Avg	Lg	TD
1946	BUF	AA	1	15	15.0	15	0

Mike Jolly

Year	Team		No	Yds	Avg	Lg	TD
1980	GB	N	2	2	1.0	2	0
1983			1	0	0.0	0	0
Career			3	2	0.7	2	0

Aaron Jones

Year	Team		No	Yds	Avg	Lg	TD
1990	PIT	N	1	3	3.0	3	0

Art Jones

Year	Team		No	Yds	Avg	Lg	TD
1941	PIT	N	7	35	5.0	12	0
1945			1	17	17.0	17	0
Career			8	52	6.5	17	0

Bruce Jones

Year	Team		No	Yds	Avg	Lg	TD
1928	GB	N					1

Bryant Jones

Year	Team		No	Yds	Avg	Lg	TD
1987	IND	N	2	26	13.0	23	0

Calvin Jones

Year	Team		No	Yds	Avg	Lg	TD
1973	DEN	N	4	69	17.3	31	0
1974			5	19	3.8	11	0
1975			1	0	0.0	0	0
1976			2	7	3.5	7	0
Career			12	95	7.9	31	0

Dante Jones

Year	Team		No	Yds	Avg	Lg	TD
1993	CHI	N	4	52	13.0	22	0

Deacon Jones

Year	Team		No	Yds	Avg	Lg	TD
1963	LA	N	1	0	0.0	0	0

Deacon Jones *continued*

Year	Team		No	Yds	Avg	Lg	TD
1966			1	50	50.0	50	0
Career			2	50	25.0	50	0

Doug Jones

Year	Team		No	Yds	Avg	Lg	TD
1974	KC	N	1	13	13.0	13	0
1976	BUF	N	3	5	1.7	5	0
1977			2	30	15.0	24t	1
Career			6	48	8.0	24t	1

Dub Jones

Year	Team		No	Yds	Avg	Lg	TD
1947	BKN	AA	2	35	17.5		0

Earl Jones

Year	Team		No	Yds	Avg	Lg	TD
1980	ATL	N	1	0	0.0	0	0
1981			2	42	21.0	39	0
1983			1	19	19.0	19	0
Career			4	61	15.3	39	0

Ed Jones

Year	Team		No	Yds	Avg	Lg	TD
1975	BUF	N	3	13	4.3	13	0

Ed Jones

Year	Team		No	Yds	Avg	Lg	TD
1975	DAL	N	1	2	2.0	2	0
1982			1	0	0.0	0	0
1983			1	12	12.0	12	0
Career			3	14	4.7	12	0
Playoffs			1	0	0.0		0

Edgar Jones

Year	Team		No	Yds	Avg	Lg	TD
1946	CLE	AA	2	16	8.0		

Elmer Jones

Year	Team		No	Yds	Avg	Lg	TD
1946	BUF	AA	2	7	3.5		

Ernie Jones

Year	Team		No	Yds	Avg	Lg	TD
1977	NYG	N	1	0	0.0	0	0
1978			3	100	33.3	52	0
1979			2	42	21.0	31t	1
Career			6	142	23.7	52	1

Gary Jones

Year	Team		No	Yds	Avg	Lg	TD
1991	PIT	N	1	0	0.0	0	0
1993			2	11	5.5	11	0
1994			1	0	0.0	0	0
1995	NYJ	N	2	51	25.5	49t	1
Career			6	62	10.3	49t	1

Harvey Jones

Year	Team		No	Yds	Avg	Lg	TD
1944	CLE	N	3	71	23.7	32	0
1945			2	73	36.5	53	0
Career			5	144	28.8	53	0

Henry Jones

Year	Team		No	Yds	Avg	Lg	TD
1992	BUF	N	8	263	32.9	82t	2
1993			2	92	46.0	85t	1
1994			2	45	22.5	45	0
1995			1	10	10.0	10	0
Career			13	410	31.5	85t	3
Playoffs			2	30	15.0		0

James Jones

Year	Team		No	Yds	Avg	Lg	TD
1991	CLE	N	1	20	20.0	20t	1

Jock Jones

Year	Team		No	Yds	Avg	Lg	TD
1992	PHX	N	1	27	27.0	27	0

Joe Jones

Year	Team		No	Yds	Avg	Lg	TD
1977	CLE	N	1	0	0.0	0	0

Leroy Jones

Year	Team		No	Yds	Avg	Lg	TD
1976	SD	N	1	11	11.0	11	0
1977			1	17	17.0	17t	1
1981			1	6	6.0	6	0
Career			3	34	11.3	17t	1

Lew Jones

Year	Team		No	Yds	Avg	Lg	TD
1943	BKN	N	1	4	4.0	4	0

Mike Jones

Year	Team		No	Yds	Avg	Lg	TD
1995	OAK	N	1	23	23.0	23	0

Ray Jones

Year	Team		No	Yds	Avg	Lg	TD
1970	PHI	N	2	17	8.5	17	0

Reggie Jones

Year	Team		No	Yds	Avg	Lg	TD
1991	NO	N	3	61	20.3	51	0
1992			2	71	35.5	71t	1
1993			1	12	12.0	12	0
Career			6	144	24.0	71t	1

Robert Jones

Year	Team		No	Yds	Avg	Lg	TD
1996	STL	N	1	0	0.0	0	0

Rod Jones

Year	Team		No	Yds	Avg	Lg	TD
1986	TB	N	1	0	0.0	0	0
1987			2	9	4.5	9	0
1988			1	0	0.0	0	0
1992	CIN	N	2	14	7.0	14	0
1993			1	0	0.0	0	0
1995			1	24	24.0	24	0
1996			2	2	1.0	2	0
Career			10	49	4.9	24	0

Roger Jones

Year	Team		No	Yds	Avg	Lg	TD
1995	CIN	N	1	17	17.0	17t	1
1996			1	30	30.0	30	0
Career			2	47	23.5	30	1

Rondell Jones

Year	Team		No	Yds	Avg	Lg	TD
1994	DEN	N	2	9	4.5	9	0

Sean Jones

Year	Team		No	Yds	Avg	Lg	TD
1992	HOU	N	1	0	0.0	0	0

Selwyn Jones

Year	Team		No	Yds	Avg	Lg	TD
1993	CLE	N	3	0	0.0	0	0
1995	SEA	N	1	0	0.0	0	0
Career			4	0	0.0	0	0

Victor Jones

Year	Team		No	Yds	Avg	Lg	TD
1990	DET	N	1	0	0.0	0	0

Brian Jordan

Year	Team		No	Yds	Avg	Lg	TD
1990	ATL	N	3	14	4.7	14	0
1991			2	3	1.5	3	0
Career			5	17	3.4	14	0
Playoffs			1	4	4.0		0

Curtis Jordan

Year	Team		No	Yds	Avg	Lg	TD
1976	TB	N	2	10	5.0	10	0
1977			1	0	0.0	0	0
1978			3	23	7.7	22	0
1983	WAS	N	1	20	20.0	20	0
1984			2	18	9.0	16	0
1985			5	88	17.6	36	0
1986			3	46	15.3	20	0
Career			17	205	12.1	36	0

Darin Jordan

Year	Team		No	Yds	Avg	Lg	TD
1988	PIT	N	1	28	28.0	28t	1

Henry Jordan

Year	Team		No	Yds	Avg	Lg	TD
1962	GB	N	1	0	0.0	0	0

Jeff Jordan

Year	Team		No	Yds	Avg	Lg	TD
1965	MIN	N	4	45	11.3	18	0

Lee Roy Jordan

Year	Team		No	Yds	Avg	Lg	TD
1963	DAL	N	3	41	13.7	23	0
1964			1	3	3.0	3	0
1966			1	49	49.0	49t	1
1967			3	85	28.3	40	1
1968			3	17	5.7	7	0
1969			2	38	19.0	38	0
1970			1	6	6.0	6	0
1971			2	34	17.0	23	0
1972			2	18	9.0	12	0
1973			6	78	13.0	31t	1
1974			2	23	11.5	13	0
1975			6	80	13.3	38	0
Career			32	472	14.8	49t	3
Playoffs			4	34	8.5		0

Tim Jordan

Year	Team		No	Yds	Avg	Lg	TD
1988	NE	N	1	31	31.0	31	0

Year	Team		No	Yds	Avg	Lg	TD

Dwayne Joseph
| 1995 | CHI | N | 2 | 31 | 15.5 | 31 | 0 |

Vance Joseph
| 1995 | NYJ | N | 2 | 39 | 19.5 | 39 | 0 |

Don Joyce
| 1957 | BAL | N | 1 | 0 | 0.0 | 0 | 0 |

Seth Joyner
1986	PHI	N	1	4	4.0	4	0
1987			2	42	21.0	29	0
1988			4	96	24.0	30	0
1989			1	0	0.0	0	0
1990			1	9	9.0	9	0
1991			3	41	13.7	41	0
1992			4	88	22.0	43t	2
1993			1	6	6.0	6	0
1994	ARI	N	3	2	0.7	2	0
1995			3	9	3.0	11	0
1996			1	10	10.0	10	0
Career			24	307	12.8	43t	2
Playoffs			3	23	7.7		0

William Judson
1983	MIA	N	6	60	10.0	29	0
1984			4	121	30.3	60t	1
1985			4	88	22.0	61t	1
1986			2	0	0.0	0	0
1987			2	11	5.5	10	0
1988			4	57	14.3	52	0
1989			2	31	15.5	28	0
Career			24	368	15.3	61t	2
Playoffs			1	34	34.0		0

Fred Julian
| 1960 | NY | A | 6 | 27 | 4.5 | | 0 |

Harold Jungmichel
| 1946 | MIA | AA | 1 | 21 | 21.0 | 21 | 0 |

E.J. Junior
1981	STL	N	1	5	5.0	5	0
1983			3	27	9.0	19	0
1984			1	18	18.0	18	0
1985			5	109	21.8	53	0
1987			1	25	25.0	25	0
1988	PHX	N	1	2	2.0	2	0
Career			12	186	15.5	53	0

Ed Justice
1940	WAS	N	1	14	14.0	14	0
1941			2	13	6.5	13	0
1942			1	2	2.0	2	0
Career			4	29	7.3	14	0

Kerry Justin
1979	SEA	N	1	0	0.0	0	0
1980			1	0	0.0	0	0
1983			1	2	2.0	2	0
1986			4	29	7.3	18	0
Career			7	31	4.4	18	0
Playoffs			2	45	22.5		0

Sid Justin
| 1979 | LA | N | 1 | 13 | 13.0 | 13 | 0 |

Steve Juzwik
| 1946 | BUF | AA | 5 | 108 | 21.6 | | 1 |

Mike Kabealo
| 1944 | CLE | N | 2 | 9 | 4.5 | 9 | 0 |

Mike Kaczmarek
| 1973 | BAL | N | 1 | 2 | 2.0 | 2 | 0 |

Mark Kafentzis
| 1984 | IND | N | 1 | 59 | 59.0 | 59t | 1 |

Carl Kammerer
1962	SF	N	1	13	13.0	13	0
1963	WAS	N	2	1	0.5	1	0
Career			3	14	4.7	13	0

Al Kaporch
1943	DET	N	1	0	0.0	0	0
1944			1	1	1.0	1	0
1945			1	14	14.0	14	0
Career			3	15	5.0	14	0

Emil Karas
1959	WAS	N	1	0	0.0	0	0
1961	SD	A	3	21	7.0	11	0
1962			2	8	4.0	8	0
1963			2	30	15.0	30	0
Career			8	59	7.4	30	0

Carl Karilivacz
1954	DET	N	2	66	33.0	30t	1
1955			2	33	16.5	23	0
1956			1	0	0.0	0	0
1957			5	54	10.8	30	0
1958	NYG	N	3	15	5.0	15	0
Career			13	168	12.9	30t	1
Playoffs			2	22	11.0		0

Abe Karnofsky
| 1945 | PHI | N | 1 | 27 | 27.0 | 27 | 0 |

Alex Karras
1962	DET	N	1	28	28.0	28	0
1964			2	7	3.5	5	0
1969			1	22	22.0	22	0
Career			4	57	14.3	28	0

Karl Kassulke
1964	MIN	N	3	4	1.3	4	0
1965			2	31	15.5	16	0
1966			2	30	15.0	30	0
1967			2	10	5.0	10	0
1968			1	0	0.0	0	0
1969			2	36	18.0	20	0
1970			3	22	7.3	11	0
1971			2	29	14.5	27	0
1972			2	25	12.5	22	0
Career			19	187	9.8	30	0

Jim Katcavage
| 1962 | NYG | N | 1 | 4 | 4.0 | 4 | 0 |

Mel Kaufman
1981	WAS	N	2	25	12.5	25	0
1983			2	93	46.5	70t	1
1985			3	10	3.3	10	0
Career			7	128	18.3	70t	1
Playoffs			2	12	6.0		0

Ken Kavanaugh
| 1941 | CHIB | N | 1 | 6 | 6.0 | 6 | 0 |

Eddie Kawal
| 1935 | CHIB | N | | | | | 1 |
| Playoffs | | | 2 | 19 | 9.5 | | 0 |

Bill Kay
1981	HOU	N	2	47	23.5	30	0
1983			2	31	15.5	27	0
Career			4	78	19.5	30	0

Rick Kay
| 1976 | LA | N | 1 | 0 | 0.0 | 0 | 0 |

Tom Keane
1950	LA	N	6	50	8.3	25t	1
1951			2	2	1.0	2	0
1952	DAL	N	10	93	9.3	39	0
1953	BAL	N	11	118	10.7	35	0
1954			5	22	4.4	9	0
1955	CHIC	N	6	64	10.7	32	0
Career			40	349	8.7	39	1
Playoffs			1	16	16.0		0

Jim Kearney
1968	KC	A	3	23	7.7	23	0
1969			5	143	28.6	60t	1
1970	KC	N	4	28	7.0	15	0
1971			3	46	15.3	29	0
1972			5	**192**	38.4	65t	4

Jim Kearney *continued*
1973			3	30	10.0	24	0
Career			23	462	20.1	65t	5
Playoffs			1	17	17.0		0

Tim Kearney
1976	STL	N	1	0	0.0	0	0
1978			1	8	8.0	8	0
1980			1	22	22.0	22	0
Career			3	30	10.0	22	0

Chris Keating
1982	BUF	N	1	14	14.0	14	0
1983			2	20	10.0	17	0
Career			3	34	11.3	17	0

Bob Keene
| 1944 | DET | N | 2 | 14 | 7.0 | 14 | 0 |

Louie Kelcher
1978	SD	N	1	0	0.0	0	0
1980			1	2	2.0	2	0
Career			2	2	1.0	2	0

Bill Kellagher
| 1947 | CHI | AA | 6 | 77 | 12.8 | | 0 |

Larry Keller
1976	NYJ	N	1	31	31.0	31	0
1977			1	36	36.0	36	0
1978			1	4	4.0	4	0
Career			3	71	23.7	36	0

Ernie Kellerman
1966	CLE	N	3	23	7.7	12	0
1967			1	9	9.0	9	0
1968			6	29	4.8	12	0
1969			3	40	13.3	40t	1
1970			1	18	18.0	18	0
1971			3	0	0.0	0	0
1973	BUF	N	2	23	11.5	19	0
Career			19	142	7.5	40t	1
Playoffs			1	0	0.0		0

Brian Kelley
1974	NYG	N	1	31	31.0	21	0
1975			3	30	10.0	23	0
1977			1	17	17.0	17	0
1978			1	20	20.0	20	0
1979			3	41	13.7	16	0
1981			2	43	21.5	27	0
1982			3	27	9.0	14	0
1983			1	17	17.0	17	0
Career			15	226	15.1	27	0

Gordon Kelley
1960	SF	N	2	10	5.0	10	0
1961			1	0	0.0	0	0
1962	WAS	N	2	11	5.5	11	0
Career			5	21	4.2	11	0

Ike Kelley
| 1967 | PHI | N | 1 | 18 | 18.0 | 18 | 0 |

Les Kelley
| 1968 | NO | N | 1 | 0 | 0.0 | 0 | 0 |

Marv Kellum
1974	PIT	N	1	0	0.0	0	0
1977	STL	N	1	14	14.0	14	0
Career			2	14	7.0	14	0

Bill Kelly
| 1928 | NYY | N | | | | | 1 |

Bob Kelly
1947	LA	AA	2	47	23.5		0
1948			3	14	4.7		0
1949	BAL	AA	3	24	8.0		0
Career			8	85	10.6		0

Joe Kelly
| 1986 | CIN | N | 1 | 6 | 6.0 | 6 | 0 |

Joe Kelly *continued*

Year	Team		No	Yds	Avg	Lg	TD
1989			1	25	25.0	25	0
1991	NYJ	N	2	6	3.0	6	0
1994	LARM	N	1	31	31.0	31	0
1995	GB	N	1	0	0.0	0	0
Career			6	68	11.3	31	0

Larry Kelm

Year	Team		No	Yds	Avg	Lg	TD
1988	LARM	N	2	15	7.5	9	0
1992			1	16	16.0	16	0
Career			3	31	10.3	16	0

Mark Kelso

Year	Team		No	Yds	Avg	Lg	TD
1987	BUF	N	6	25	4.2	12	0
1988			7	**180**	25.7	78t	1
1989			6	101	16.8	43	0
1990			2	0	0.0	0	0
1991			2	0	0.0	0	0
1992			7	21	3.0	13	0
Career			30	327	10.9	78t	1
Playoffs			4	53	13.3		0

Bobby Kemp

Year	Team		No	Yds	Avg	Lg	TD
1982	CIN	N	1	0	0.0	0	0
1983			3	26	8.7	26	0
1984			4	27	6.8	14	0
1985			1	0	0.0	0	0
1987	TB	N	1	11	11.0	11	0
Career			10	64	6.4	26	0
Playoffs			1	24	24.0		0

Chuck Kendall

Year	Team		No	Yds	Avg	Lg	TD
1960	HOU	A	2	10	5.0		0

Bob Kennedy

Year	Team		No	Yds	Avg	Lg	TD
1949	LA	AA	1	33	33.0	33	0

Bob Kennedy

Year	Team		No	Yds	Avg	Lg	TD
1946	NY	AA	3	35	11.7		0
1947			2	66	33.0		0
1948			4	49	12.3		0
1949	B-NY	AA	2	2	1.0		0
1950	NYY	N	1	11	11.0	11	0
Career			12	163	13.6	11	0

Mike Kennedy

Year	Team		No	Yds	Avg	Lg	TD
1983	BUF	N	1	22	22.0	22t	1

Ralph Kercheval

Year	Team		No	Yds	Avg	Lg	TD
1936	BKN	N					1

Rex Kern

Year	Team		No	Yds	Avg	Lg	TD
1973	BAL	N	2	22	11.0	22	0

Marlon Kerner

Year	Team		No	Yds	Avg	Lg	TD
1996	BUF	N	1	6	6.0	6	0

Bill Kerr

Year	Team		No	Yds	Avg	Lg	TD
1946	LA	AA	1	34	34.0	34	0

Jim Kerr

Year	Team		No	Yds	Avg	Lg	TD
1961	WAS	N	7	93	13.3	38	0
1962			1	12	12.0	12	0
Career			8	105	13.1	38	0

Ken Keuper

Year	Team		No	Yds	Avg	Lg	TD
1946	GB	N	3	22	7.3	15	0
1947			2	41	20.5	26	0
1948	NYG	N	1	30	30.0	30	0
Career			6	93	15.5	30	0

Leroy Keyes

Year	Team		No	Yds	Avg	Lg	TD
1971	PHI	N	6	31	5.2	17	0
1972			2	0	0.0	0	0
Career			8	31	3.9	17	0

Brady Keys

Year	Team		No	Yds	Avg	Lg	TD
1961	PIT	N	2	21	10.5	12	0
1962			3	16	5.3	13	0
1964			2	11	5.5	11	0
1965			1	20	20.0	20	0
1966			4	0	0.0	0	0

Brady Keys *continued*

Year	Team		No	Yds	Avg	Lg	TD
1967	PIT-MIN	N	3	38	12.7	30	0
1968	STL	N	1	8	8.0	8	0
Career			16	114	7.1	30	0

Eddie Khayat

Year	Team		No	Yds	Avg	Lg	TD
1959	PHI	N	1	0	0.0	0	0

Carl Kidd

Year	Team		No	Yds	Avg	Lg	TD
1996	OAK	N	1	1	1.0	1	0

Frank Kilroy

Year	Team		No	Yds	Avg	Lg	TD
1946	PHI	N	1	0	0.0	0	0
1954			4	29	7.3	19	0
Career			5	29	5.8	19	0

Elbert Kimbrough

Year	Team		No	Yds	Avg	Lg	TD
1963	SF	N	1	45	45.0	45	0
1964			2	3	1.5	3	0
1965			2	5	2.5	5	0
1966			3	60	20.0	44	0
1968	NO	N	1	15	15.0	15	0
Career			9	128	14.2	45	0

Billy Kinard

Year	Team		No	Yds	Avg	Lg	TD
1960	BUF	A	4	29	7.3		0

Frank Kinard

Year	Team		No	Yds	Avg	Lg	TD
1944	BKN	N	1	26	26.0	26	0

Terry Kinard

Year	Team		No	Yds	Avg	Lg	TD
1983	NYG	N	3	49	16.3	25	0
1984			2	29	14.5	29	0
1985			5	100	20.0	31	0
1986			4	52	13.0	25	0
1987			5	163	32.6	70t	1
1988			3	46	15.3	39	0
1989			5	135	27.0	58t	1
1990	HOU	N	4	75	18.8	47	0
Career			31	649	20.9	70t	2
Playoffs			1	15	15.0		0

Howard Kindig

Year	Team		No	Yds	Avg	Lg	TD
1966	SD	A	1	0	0.0	0	0

Don Kindt

Year	Team		No	Yds	Avg	Lg	TD
1947	CHIB	N	3	19	6.3	10	0
1948			1	21	21.0	21	0
1949			2	3	1.5	3	0
1951			4	56	14.0	39	0
1952			3	49	16.3	26	0
1953			6	172	28.7	67t	1
1954			2	28	14.0	25	0
Career			21	348	16.6	67t	1

George Kinek

Year	Team		No	Yds	Avg	Lg	TD
1954	CHIC	N	2	0	0.0	0	0

Steve Kiner

Year	Team		No	Yds	Avg	Lg	TD
1970	DAL	N	1	28	28.0	28	0
1971	NE	N	4	25	6.3	14	0
1974	HOU	N	1	34	34.0	34	0
1975			2	7	3.5	7	0
1977			1	17	17.0	17	0
1978			1	3	3.0	3	0
Career			10	114	11.4	34	0

Andy King

Year	Team		No	Yds	Avg	Lg	TD
1922	AKR	N					1

Charley King

Year	Team		No	Yds	Avg	Lg	TD
1966	BUF	A	1	0	0.0	0	0
1968	CIN	A	1	32	32.0	32t	1
Career			2	32	16.0	32t	1

Don King

Year	Team		No	Yds	Avg	Lg	TD
1960	DEN	A	2	18	9.0		0

Joe King

Year	Team		No	Yds	Avg	Lg	TD
1992	TB	N	2	24	12.0	24	0
1993			3	29	9.7	28	0
Career			5	53	10.6	28	0

Linden King

Year	Team		No	Yds	Avg	Lg	TD
1978	SD	N	1	3	3.0	3	0
1981			1	28	28.0	28	0
1983			1	19	19.0	19	0
1984			2	52	26.0	37	0
1985			2	8	4.0	5	0
1987	LARI	N	1	8	8.0	8	0
Career			8	118	14.8	37	0

Shawn King

Year	Team		No	Yds	Avg	Lg	TD
1996	CAR	N	1	1	1.0	1	0

Steve King

Year	Team		No	Yds	Avg	Lg	TD
1974	NE	N	1	9	9.0	9	0

Ellsworth Kingery

Year	Team		No	Yds	Avg	Lg	TD
1954	CHIC	N	1	19	19.0	19	0

Wayne Kingery

Year	Team		No	Yds	Avg	Lg	TD
1949	BAL	AA	1	0	0.0	0	0

Rick Kingrea

Year	Team		No	Yds	Avg	Lg	TD
1975	NO	N	1	14	14.0	14	0

Carl Kinscherf

Year	Team		No	Yds	Avg	Lg	TD
1944	NYG	N	1	3	3.0	3	0

Ernie Kirk

Year	Team		No	Yds	Avg	Lg	TD
1977	HOU	N	1	2	2.0	2	0

Levon Kirkland

Year	Team		No	Yds	Avg	Lg	TD
1994	PIT	N	2	0	0.0	0	0
1996			4	12	3.0	6	0
Career			6	12	2.0	6	0
Playoffs			2	4	2.0		0

Ben Kish

Year	Team		No	Yds	Avg	Lg	TD
1941	BKN	N	1	9	9.0	9	0
1943	P-P	N	5	114	22.8	86	1
1944	PHI	N	4	52	13.0	15	0
1945			1	0	0.0	0	0
1946			1	13	13.0	13	0
1947			1	37	37.0	37	0
1948			3	32	10.7	22	0
Career			16	257	16.1	86	1

Ed Kissell

Year	Team		No	Yds	Avg	Lg	TD
1952	PIT	N	5	71	14.2	37	0
1954			1	15	15.0	15	0
Career			6	86	14.3	37	0

Vito Kissell

Year	Team		No	Yds	Avg	Lg	TD
1949	BUF	AA	1	14	14.0	14	0
1950	BAL	N	2	7	3.5	5	0
Career			3	21	7.0	14	0

Paul Kittredge

Year	Team		No	Yds	Avg	Lg	TD
1929	BOS	N					1

Tony Klimek

Year	Team		No	Yds	Avg	Lg	TD
1951	CHIC	N	3	39	13.0	22	0
1952			2	5	2.5	5	0
Career			5	44	8.8	22	0

Leander Knight

Year	Team		No	Yds	Avg	Lg	TD
1990	HOU	N	1	0	0.0	0	0

Pat Knight

Year	Team		No	Yds	Avg	Lg	TD
1954	NYG	N	3	41	13.7	30	0
1955			2	29	14.5	18	0
Career			5	70	14.0	30	0

Kurt Knoff

Year	Team		No	Yds	Avg	Lg	TD
1978	HOU	N	1	6	6.0	6	0
1979	MIN	N	2	25	12.5	15	0
1980			3	87	29.0	67t	0
1981			3	24	8.0	20	0
1982			1	4	4.0	4	0
Career			10	146	14.6	67t	1

Johnny Knolla

Year	Team		No	Yds	Avg	Lg	TD
1942	CHIC	N	1	28	28.0	28	0

Oscar Knop

Year	Team		No	Yds	Avg	Lg	TD
1923	CHIB	N					1

Bill Knox

Year	Team		No	Yds	Avg	Lg	TD
1974	CHI	N	2	26	13.0	21	0

George Koch

Year	Team		No	Yds	Avg	Lg	TD
1947	BUF	AA	3	24	8.0		0

Joe Kodba

Year	Team		No	Yds	Avg	Lg	TD
1947	BAL	AA	1	2	2.0	2	0

Mike Kolen

Year	Team		No	Yds	Avg	Lg	TD
1972	MIA	N	1	14	14.0	14	0
1973			2	54	27.0	29	0
1974			1	3	3.0	3	0
1975			1	14	14.0	14	0
Career			5	85	17.0	29	0
Playoffs			2	16	8.0		0

Bill Koman

Year	Team		No	Yds	Avg	Lg	TD
1958	PHI	N	1	5	5.0	5	0
1960	STL	N	1	5	5.0	5	0
1961			1	8	8.0	8	0
1962			1	6	6.0	6	0
1964			2	1	0.5	1	0
1965			1	2	2.0	2	0
Career			7	27	3.9	8	0

Floyd Konetsky

Year	Team		No	Yds	Avg	Lg	TD
1947	BAL	AA	1	15	15.0	15	0

Kenny Konz

Year	Team		No	Yds	Avg	Lg	TD
1953	CLE	N	5	15	3.0	9	0
1954			7	133	19.0	54	2
1955			5	32	6.4	15t	1
1956			4	34	8.5	28	0
1957			4	20	5.0	16	0
1958			4	123	30.8	46t	1
1959			1	35	35.0	35	0
Career			30	392	13.1	54	4
Playoffs			4	40	10.0		0

George Koonce

Year	Team		No	Yds	Avg	Lg	TD
1995	GB	N	1	12	12.0	12	0
1996			3	84	28.0	75t	1
Career			4	96	24.0	75t	1

Ed Korisky

Year	Team		No	Yds	Avg	Lg	TD
1944	BOS	N	1	1	1.0	1	0

R.J. Kors

Year	Team		No	Yds	Avg	Lg	TD
1991	NYJ	N	1	0	0.0	0	0
1992			1	16	16.0	16	0
Career			2	16	8.0	16	0

Kelvin Korver

Year	Team		No	Yds	Avg	Lg	TD
1973	OAK	N	1	12	12.0	12	0

Eddie Kotal

Year	Team		No	Yds	Avg	Lg	TD
1925	GB	N					1

Marty Kottler

Year	Team		No	Yds	Avg	Lg	TD
1933	PIT	N					1

Ed Kovac

Year	Team		No	Yds	Avg	Lg	TD
1962	NY	A	1	21	21.0	21	0

Jim Kovach

Year	Team		No	Yds	Avg	Lg	TD
1980	NO	N	1	0	0.0	0	0
1981			1	13	13.0	13	0
1984			1	16	16.0	16	0
1985			1	53	53.0	53	0
Career			4	82	20.5	53	0

Walt Kowalczyk

Year	Team		No	Yds	Avg	Lg	TD
1958	PHI	N	1	2	2.0	2	0

Andy Kowalski

Year	Team		No	Yds	Avg	Lg	TD
1943	BKN	N	1	9	9.0	9	0

Mike Kozlowski

Year	Team		No	Yds	Avg	Lg	TD
1981	MIA	N	3	37	12.3	29	0
1982			1	36	36.0	36	0

Mike Kozlowski *continued*

Year	Team		No	Yds	Avg	Lg	TD
1983			2	73	36.5	38t	2
1984			1	26	26.0	26	0
1986			1	0	0.0	0	0
Career			8	172	21.5	38t	2

George Kracum

Year	Team		No	Yds	Avg	Lg	TD
1941	BKN	N	1	27	27.0	27	0

Greg Kragen

Year	Team		No	Yds	Avg	Lg	TD
1995	CAR	N	1	29	29.0	29	0
Playoffs			1	0	0.0		0

Merv Krakau

Year	Team		No	Yds	Avg	Lg	TD
1974	BUF	N	1	37	37.0	37	0
1975			1	2	2.0	2	0
1976			1	0	0.0	0	0
Career			3	39	13.0	37	0

Joe Krakoski

Year	Team		No	Yds	Avg	Lg	TD
1961	WAS	N	4	13	3.3	11	0
1963	OAK	A	4	39	9.8	30	0
Career			8	52	6.5	30	0

Kyle Kramer

Year	Team		No	Yds	Avg	Lg	TD
1989	CLE	N	1	12	12.0	12	0

Max Krause

Year	Team		No	Yds	Avg	Lg	TD
Playoffs			1	13	13.0		0

Paul Krause

Year	Team		No	Yds	Avg	Lg	TD
1964	WAS	N	12	140	11.7	35t	1
1965			6	118	19.7	43	0
1966			2	0	0.0	0	0
1967			8	75	9.4	32	0
1968	MIN	N	7	82	11.7	29	0
1969			5	82	16.4	77t	1
1970			6	90	15.0	40	0
1971			6	112	18.7	31	0
1972			6	109	18.2	35	1
1973			4	28	7.0	24	0
1974			2	53	26.5	45	0
1975			10	201	20.1	81	0
1976			2	21	10.5	19	0
1977			2	25	12.5	25	0
1979			3	49	16.3	18	0
Career			81	1185	14.6	81	3
Playoffs			3	14	4.7		0

Barry Krauss

Year	Team		No	Yds	Avg	Lg	TD
1981	BAL	N	1	10	10.0	10	0
1984	IND	N	3	20	6.7	18	0
1985			1	0	0.0	0	0
1988			1	3	3.0	3	0
Career			6	33	5.5	18	0

Rich Kraynak

Year	Team		No	Yds	Avg	Lg	TD
1985	PHI	N	1	26	26.0	26	0

Ken Kremer

Year	Team		No	Yds	Avg	Lg	TD
1984	KC	N	1	1	1.0	1	0

Al Krueger

Year	Team		No	Yds	Avg	Lg	TD
1941	WAS	N	1	12	12.0	12	0

Charlie Krueger

Year	Team		No	Yds	Avg	Lg	TD
1969	SF	N	1	0	0.0	0	0

Todd Krumm

Year	Team		No	Yds	Avg	Lg	TD
1988	CHI	N	2	14	7.0	14	0

Joe Kuharich

Year	Team		No	Yds	Avg	Lg	TD
1941	CHIC	N	1	20	20.0	20	0

Vic Kulbitski

Year	Team		No	Yds	Avg	Lg	TD
1946	BUF	AA	1	20	20.0	20	0
1947			1	14	14.0	14	0
Career			2	34	17.0	20	0

Mike Kullman

Year	Team		No	Yds	Avg	Lg	TD
1987	PHI	N	2	25	12.5	13	0

Eric Kumerow

Year	Team		No	Yds	Avg	Lg	TD
1990	MIA	N	1	5	5.0	5	0

Rod Kush

Year	Team		No	Yds	Avg	Lg	TD
1981	BUF	N	1	19	19.0	19	0
1984			1	15	15.0	15	0
1985	HOU	N	2	6	3.0	6	0
Career			4	40	10.0	19	0

Mal Kutner

Year	Team		No	Yds	Avg	Lg	TD
1946	CHIC	N	4	29	7.3	24	0
1947			3	56	18.7	56t	1
1948			2	35	17.5	31	0
1950			3	31	10.3	26	0
Career			12	151	12.6	56t	1

Fulton Kuykendall

Year	Team		No	Yds	Avg	Lg	TD
1981	ATL	N	1	20	20.0	20t	1
1982			2	22	11.0	22	0
Career			3	42	14.0	22	1

Aaron Kyle

Year	Team		No	Yds	Avg	Lg	TD
1977	DAL	N	1	9	9.0	9	0
1978			3	20	6.7	17	0
1979			2	0	0.0	0	0
1981	DEN	N	2	40	20.0	40	0
1982			3	26	8.7	14	0
Career			11	95	8.6	40	0
Playoffs			2	34	17.0		0

Steve Lach

Year	Team		No	Yds	Avg	Lg	TD
1942	CHIC	N	4	52	13.0	26	0
1946	PIT	N	1	10	10.0	10	0
Career			5	62	12.4	26	0

Ernie Ladd

Year	Team		No	Yds	Avg	Lg	TD
1968	KC	A	1	3	3.0	3	0

Jeff Lageman

Year	Team		No	Yds	Avg	Lg	TD
1993	NYJ	N	1	15	15.0	15	0

Thomas Lahey

Year	Team		No	Yds	Avg	Lg	TD
1946	CHI	AA	1	4	4.0	4	0

Warren Lahr

Year	Team		No	Yds	Avg	Lg	TD
1949	CLE	AA	4	32	8.0		0
1950	CLE	N	8	99	12.4	30t	2
1951			5	95	19.0	29	2
1952			5	51	10.2	14	0
1953			5	119	23.8	42	0
1954			5	44	8.8	27t	1
1955			5	52	10.4	24	0
1956			3	33	11.0	18	0
1957			2	12	6.0	10	0
1958			1	25	25.0	25	0
1959			1	0	0.0	0	0
Career			44	562	12.8	42	5
Playoffs			5				1

Bruce Laird

Year	Team		No	Yds	Avg	Lg	TD
1972	BAL	N	1	31	31.0	31	0
1974			1	15	15.0	15	0
1975			3	46	15.3	28	0
1977			3	56	18.7	22	0
1979			3	101	33.7	68	0
1980			5	71	14.2	18	0
1981			3	59	19.7	24	0
Career			19	379	19.9	68	0
Playoffs			3	96	32.0		1

Carnell Lake

Year	Team		No	Yds	Avg	Lg	TD
1989	PIT	N	1	0	0.0	0	0
1990			1	0	0.0	0	0
1993			4	31	7.8	26	0
1994			1	2	2.0	2	0
1995			1	32	32.0	32t	1
1996			1	47	47.0	47t	1
Career			9	112	12.4	47t	2
Playoffs			1	3	3.0		0

Peter Lamana

Year	Team		No	Yds	Avg	Lg	TD
1946	CHI	AA	1	16	16.0	16	0
1948			1	0	0.0	0	0
Career			2	16	8.0	16	0

Year	Team		No	Yds	Avg	Lg	TD

Mack Lamb

Year	Team		No	Yds	Avg	Lg	TD
1968	MIA	A	1	0	0.0	0	0

Dion Lambert

Year	Team		No	Yds	Avg	Lg	TD
1993	NE	N	1	0	0.0	0	0

Jack Lambert

Year	Team		No	Yds	Avg	Lg	TD
1974	PIT	N	2	19	9.5	13	0
1975			2	35	17.5	24	0
1976			2	32	16.0	22	0
1977			1	5	5.0	5	0
1978			4	41	10.3	24	0
1979			6	29	4.8	23	0
1980			2	1	0.5	1	0
1981			6	76	12.7	31	0
1982			1	6	6.0	6	0
1983			2	-1	-0.5	0	0
Career			28	243	8.7	31	0
Playoffs			1	16	16.0		0

Pat Lamberti

Year	Team		No	Yds	Avg	Lg	TD
1961	DEN	A	1	5	5.0	5	0

Chuck Lamson

Year	Team		No	Yds	Avg	Lg	TD
1962	MIN	N	1	0	0.0	0	0
1963			1	7	7.0	7	0
1965	LA	N	2	0	0.0	0	0
1966			5	59	11.8	44t	1
1967			2	18	9.0	10	0
Career			11	84	7.6	44t	1
Playoffs			1	24	24.0		0

Dan Land

Year	Team		No	Yds	Avg	Lg	TD
1992	LARI	N	1	0	0.0	0	0

Tom Landry

Year	Team		No	Yds	Avg	Lg	TD
1949	B-NY	AA	1	44	44.0	44	0
1950	NYG	N	2	0	0.0	0	0
1951			8	121	15.1	55t	2
1952			8	99	12.4	30t	1
1953			3	55	18.3	30	0
1954			8	71	8.9	27	0
1955			2	14	7.0	10	0
Career			32	404	12.6	55t	3

Mort Landsberg

Year	Team		No	Yds	Avg	Lg	TD
1941	PHI	N	2	45	22.5	37	0

Night Train Lane

Year	Team		No	Yds	Avg	Lg	TD
1952	LA	N	14	298	21.3	80t	2
1953			3	9	3.0	8	0
1954	CHIC	N	10	181	18.1	64	0
1955			6	69	11.5	26	0
1956			7	206	29.4	66t	1
1957			2	47	23.5	33	0
1958			2	0	0.0	0	0
1959			3	125	41.7	69	1
1960	DET	N	5	102	20.4	80t	1
1961			6	73	12.2	32	0
1962			4	16	4.0	13	0
1963			5	70	14.0	33	0
1964			1	11	11.0	11	0
Career			68	1207	17.8	80t	5

Le-Lo Lang

Year	Team		No	Yds	Avg	Lg	TD
1990	DEN	N	1	5	5.0	5	0
1991			1	30	30.0	30	0
1992			1	26	26.0	26	0
1993			2	4	2.0	4	0
Career			5	65	13.0	30	0

Jevon Langford

Year	Team		No	Yds	Avg	Lg	TD
1996	CIN	N	1	0	0.0	0	0

Antonio Langham

Year	Team		No	Yds	Avg	Lg	TD
1994	CLE	N	2	2	1.0	2	0
1995			2	29	14.5	29	0
1996	BAL	N	5	59	11.8	28	0
Career			9	90	10.0	29	0

Willie Lanier

Year	Team		No	Yds	Avg	Lg	TD
1968	KC	A	4	120	30.0	75t	1
1969			4	70	17.5	44	0
1970	KC	N	2	2	1.0	2	0

Willie Lanier *continued*

Year	Team		No	Yds	Avg	Lg	TD
1971			2	38	19.0	21	0
1972			2	2	1.0	2	0
1973			3	47	15.7	29	1
1974			2	28	14.0	14	0
1975			5	105	21.0	61	0
1976			3	28	9.3	14	0
Career			27	440	16.3	75t	2
Playoffs			2	26	13.0		0

Paul Lankford

Year	Team		No	Yds	Avg	Lg	TD
1983	MIA	N	1	10	10.0	10	0
1984			3	25	8.3	22	0
1985			4	10	2.5	6	0
1987			3	44	14.7	44	0
1988			1	0	0.0	0	0
1989			1	0	0.0	0	0
Career			13	89	6.8	44	0
Playoffs			1	2	2.0		0

Bob Laraba

Year	Team		No	Yds	Avg	Lg	TD
1960	LA	A	1	17	17.0	17	0
1961	SD	A	5	151	30.2	60	2
Career			6	168	28.0	60	2

Jack Laraway

Year	Team		No	Yds	Avg	Lg	TD
1961	HOU	A	1	30	30.0	30	0

Yale Lary

Year	Team		No	Yds	Avg	Lg	TD
1952	DET	N	4	61	15.3	53	0
1953			5	98	19.6	32	0
1956			8	182	22.8	73t	1
1957			2	64	32.0	63	0
1958			3	70	23.3	31	0
1959			3	0	0.0	0	0
1960			3	44	14.7	22	0
1961			6	95	15.8	42	0
1962			8	51	6.4	32	0
1963			2	21	10.5	21t	1
1964			6	101	16.8	30	0
Career			50	787	15.7	73t	2

Greg Lasker

Year	Team		No	Yds	Avg	Lg	TD
1986	NYG	N	1	0	0.0	0	0

Bill Laskey

Year	Team		No	Yds	Avg	Lg	TD
1969	OAK	A	3	66	22.0	32	0
1970	OAK	N	1	0	0.0	0	0
1973	DEN	N	2	3	1.5	3	0
1974			1	3	3.0	3	0
Career			7	72	10.3	32	0

Jim Laslavic

Year	Team		No	Yds	Avg	Lg	TD
1974	DET	N	1	14	14.0	14	0
1975			2	12	6.0	10	0
1976			2	13	6.5	13	0
1977			1	14	14.0	14	0
1980	SD	N	2	11	5.5	11	0
Career			8	64	8.0	14	0

Dick Lasse

Year	Team		No	Yds	Avg	Lg	TD
1960	WAS	N	3	17	5.7	17	0

Ike Lassiter

Year	Team		No	Yds	Avg	Lg	TD
1966	OAK	A	1	10	10.0	10	0

Kwamie Lassiter

Year	Team		No	Yds	Avg	Lg	TD
1996	ARI	N	1	20	20.0	20	0

Lamar Lathon

Year	Team		No	Yds	Avg	Lg	TD
1991	HOU	N	3	77	25.7	52t	1

Al Latimer

Year	Team		No	Yds	Avg	Lg	TD
1983	DET	N	1	0	0.0	0	0

Don Latimer

Year	Team		No	Yds	Avg	Lg	TD
1980	DEN	N	1	15	15.0	15t	1

Tony Latone

Year	Team		No	Yds	Avg	Lg	TD
1925	POT	N					1

Jim Laughlin

Year	Team		No	Yds	Avg	Lg	TD
1980	ATL	N	1	7	7.0	7	0

Jim Laughlin *continued*

Year	Team		No	Yds	Avg	Lg	TD
1983	GB	N	1	22	22.0	22	0
Career			2	29	14.5	22	0

Ted Laux

Year	Team		No	Yds	Avg	Lg	TD
1943	P-P	N	1	24	24.0	24	0

Al Lavan

Year	Team		No	Yds	Avg	Lg	TD
1969	ATL	N	2	0	0.0	0	0
1970			3	11	3.7	8	0
Career			5	11	2.2	8	0

Joe Lavender

Year	Team		No	Yds	Avg	Lg	TD
1974	PHI	N	1	37	37.0	37t	1
1975			3	59	19.7	36t	1
1976	WAS	N	8	77	9.6	28	0
1977			4	36	9.0	31	0
1978			1	0	0.0	0	0
1979			6	77	12.8	27	0
1980			6	96	16.0	51t	1
1981			4	52	13.0	30	0
Career			33	434	13.2	51t	3

Hubbard Law

Year	Team		No	Yds	Avg	Lg	TD
1942	PIT	N	1	13	13.0	13	0

Ty Law

Year	Team		No	Yds	Avg	Lg	TD
1995	NE	N	3	47	15.7	38	0
1996			3	45	15.0	38t	1
Career			6	92	15.3	38t	1

Jimmy Lawrence

Year	Team		No	Yds	Avg	Lg	TD
Playoffs			1	0	0.0		0

Rolland Lawrence

Year	Team		No	Yds	Avg	Lg	TD
1973	ATL	N	1	81	81.0	81	0
1974			1	0	0.0	0	0
1975			9	163	18.1	87t	1
1976			6	43	7.2	22	0
1977			7	138	19.7	36	0
1978			6	76	12.7	44	0
1979			6	120	20.0	38	0
1980			3	37	12.3	37	0
Career			39	658	16.9	87t	1
Playoffs			1	0	0.0		0

Joe Laws

Year	Team		No	Yds	Avg	Lg	TD
1938	GB	N					1
1941			2	36	18.0	36	0
1942			3	67	22.3	38	0
1943			7	67	9.6	17	0
1944			3	36	12.0	16	0
1945			3	60	20.0	35	0
Career			18	266	14.8	38	1
Playoffs			3	28	9.3		0

Pete Layden

Year	Team		No	Yds	Avg	Lg	TD
1948	NY	AA	3	63	21.0		0
1949	B-NY	AA	7	137	19.6		1
1950	NYY	N	3	40	13.3	19	0
Career			13	240	18.5	19	1

Milan Lazetich

Year	Team		No	Yds	Avg	Lg	TD
1949	LA	N	2	47	23.5	29	0

Scott Leach

Year	Team		No	Yds	Avg	Lg	TD
1987	NO	N	1	10	10.0	10	0

Les Lear

Year	Team		No	Yds	Avg	Lg	TD
1946	LA	N	1	0	0.0	0	0

Tom Leary

Year	Team		No	Yds	Avg	Lg	TD
1930	NEW	N					2

Dick LeBeau

Year	Team		No	Yds	Avg	Lg	TD
1960	DET	N	4	58	14.5	43	0
1961			3	45	15.0	33	0
1962			4	67	16.8	31t	1
1963			5	158	31.6	70t	1
1964			5	45	9.0	18	0
1965			7	84	12.0	30t	1
1966			4	66	16.5	37	0
1967			4	29	7.3	27	0

Year	Team		No	Yds	Avg	Lg	TD

Dick LeBeau *continued*

Year	Team		No	Yds	Avg	Lg	TD
1968			5	23	4.6	16	0
1969			6	15	2.5	8	0
1970			9	96	10.7	43	0
1971			6	76	12.7	40	0
Career			62	762	12.3	70t	3

Bob Leberman
| 1954 | BAL | N | 2 | 0 | 0.0 | 0 | 0 |

Bill Leckonby
| 1941 | BKN | N | 3 | 22 | 7.3 | 12 | 0 |

Jim LeClair
1975	CIN	N	3	25	8.3	21	0
1976			1	9	9.0	9	0
1977			2	8	4.0	8	0
1978			1	11	11.0	11	0
1979			1	0	0.0	0	0
1981			1	0	0.0	0	0
1982			1	11	11.0	11	0
Career			10	64	6.4	21	0

Roger LeClerc
| 1963 | CHI | N | 1 | 2 | 2.0 | 2 | 0 |

Bivian Lee
1972	NO	N	4	65	16.3	32	0
1973			3	23	7.7	12	0
1975			2	22	11.0	19	0
Career			9	110	12.2	32	0

Carl Lee
1983	MIN	N	1	31	31.0	31	0
1984			1	0	0.0	0	0
1985			3	68	22.7	35	0
1986			3	10	3.3	10	0
1987			3	53	17.7	36	0
1988			8	118	14.8	58t	2
1989			2	0	0.0	0	0
1990			2	29	14.5	25	0
1991			1	0	0.0	0	0
1992			2	20	10.0	20	0
1993			3	20	6.7	19	0
1994	NO	N	2	3	1.5	3	0
Career			31	352	11.4	58t	2
Playoffs			1	-5	-5.0		0

Gene Lee
| 1946 | BOS | N | 1 | 31 | 31.0 | 31 | 0 |

Keith Lee
| 1981 | NE | N | 1 | 0 | 0.0 | 0 | 0 |

Ken Lee
| 1972 | BUF | N | 6 | 155 | 25.8 | 61 | 1 |

Mark Lee
1981	GB	N	6	50	8.3	25	0
1982			1	40	40.0	40	0
1983			4	23	5.8	15	0
1984			3	33	11.0	14	0
1985			1	23	23.0	23	0
1986			9	33	3.7	11	0
1987			1	0	0.0	0	0
1988			3	37	12.3	27	0
1989			2	10	5.0	10	0
1990			1	0	0.0	0	0
1991	SF	N	1	5	5.0	5	0
Career			32	254	7.9	40	0
Playoffs			1	22	22.0		1

Monte Lee
| 1961 | STL | N | 1 | 7 | 7.0 | 7 | 0 |

Shawn Lee
1991	MIA	N	1	14	14.0	14	0
1996	SD	N	1	-1	-1.0	-1	0
Career			2	13	6.5	14	0

Zeph Lee
| 1988 | LARI | N | 1 | 20 | 20.0 | 20 | 0 |

Tuffy Leemans
| 1941 | NYG | N | 3 | 35 | 11.7 | 26 | 0 |

Clyde LeForce
1947	DET	N	3	13	4.3	10	0
1948			1	0	0.0	0	0
Career			4	13	3.3	10	0

Tyrone Legette
| 1995 | NO | N | 1 | 43 | 43.0 | 43 | 0 |

Earl Leggett
| 1960 | CHI | N | 1 | 11 | 11.0 | 11 | 0 |

Jake Leicht
| 1948 | BAL | AA | 5 | 91 | 18.2 | 59 | 0 |

Frank LeMaster
1975	PHI	N	4	133	33.3	89t	1
1978			3	22	7.3	9t	1
1980			1	7	7.0	7	0
1981			2	28	14.0	22	0
Career			10	190	19.0	89t	2
Playoffs			1	7	7.0		0

Jack Lentz
1967	DEN	A	4	72	18.0	47	0
1968			1	0	0.0	0	0
Career			5	72	14.4	47	0

Tony Leon
| 1944 | BKN | N | 1 | 14 | 14.0 | 14 | 0 |

Bill Leonard
| 1949 | BAL | AA | 1 | 7 | 7.0 | 7 | 0 |

Tony Leonard
1977	SF	N	1	0	0.0	0	0
1978			4	44	11.0	30t	1
Career			5	44	8.8	30t	1

Bobby Leopold
1980	SF	N	2	23	11.5	13	0
1983			2	13	6.5	9	0
1986	GB	N	1	21	21.0	21	0
Career			5	57	11.4	21	0
Playoffs			1	5	5.0		0

Leon Lett
| Playoffs | | | 1 | -1 | -1.0 | | 0 |

Verne Lewellen
| 1929 | GB | N | | | | | 1 |

Albert Lewis
1983	KC	N	4	42	10.5	34	0
1984			4	57	14.3	31	0
1985			8	59	7.4	16	0
1986			4	18	4.5	13	0
1987			1	0	0.0	0	0
1988			1	19	19.0	19	0
1989			4	37	9.3	22	0
1990			2	15	7.5	15	0
1991			3	21	7.0	21	0
1992			1	0	0.0	0	0
1993			6	61	10.2	24	0
1996	OAK	N	2	0	0.0	0	0
Career			40	329	8.2	34	0

Cliff Lewis
1946	CLE	AA	5	41	8.2		0
1947			4	19	4.8		0
1948			9	103	11.4		0
1949			6	53	8.8		0
1950	CLE	N	1	4	4.0	4	0
1951			5	46	9.2	20	0
Career			30	266	8.9	20	0

Darryll Lewis
1991	HOU	N	1	33	33.0	33t	1
1993			1	47	47.0	47t	1
1994			5	57	11.4	20	0
1995			6	145	24.2	98t	1

Darryll Lewis *continued*
| 1996 | | | 5 | 103 | 20.6 | 53 | 1 |
| Career | | | 18 | 385 | 21.4 | 98t | 4 |

Dave Lewis
1977	TB	N	2	55	27.5	42	0
1978			3	24	8.0	13	0
1979			2	19	9.5	11	0
1980			1	0	0.0	0	0
1981			2	12	6.0	10	0
Career			10	110	11.0	42	0

D.D. Lewis
1971	DAL	N	1	0	0.0	0	0
1972			1	15	15.0	15	0
1974			2	45	22.5	27	0
1977			1	29	29.0	29	0
1979			2	8	4.0	5	0
1981			1	0	0.0	0	0
Career			8	97	12.1	29	0
Playoffs			4	64	16.0		0

Eddie Lewis
| 1978 | SF | N | 3 | 17 | 5.7 | 11 | 0 |

Ernie Lewis
| 1946 | CHI | AA | 1 | 10 | 10.0 | 10 | 0 |

Garry Lewis
| 1992 | TB | N | 1 | 0 | 0.0 | 0 | 0 |
| Playoffs | | | 1 | 0 | 0.0 | | 0 |

Joe Lewis
| 1958 | PIT | N | 1 | 8 | 8.0 | 8 | 0 |

Kevin Lewis
1990	SF	N	1	28	28.0	28	0
1991			2	20	10.0	20	0
Career			3	48	16.0	28	0

Mike Lewis
| 1972 | ATL | N | 1 | 3 | 3.0 | 3 | 0 |

Mo Lewis
1992	NYJ	N	1	1	1.0	1	0
1993			2	4	2.0	3	0
1994			4	106	26.5	67t	2
1995			2	22	11.0	15t	1
Career			9	133	14.8	67t	3

Reggie Lewis
| 1983 | NO | N | 1 | 27 | 27.0 | 27t | 1 |

Rich Lewis
| 1974 | BUF | N | 1 | 33 | 33.0 | 33 | 0 |

Rod Lewis
| 1996 | BAL | N | 1 | 0 | 0.0 | 0 | 0 |

Rodney Lewis
| 1982 | NO | N | 1 | 12 | 12.0 | 12 | 0 |

Tim Lewis
1983	GB	N	5	111	22.2	46	0
1984			7	151	21.6	99t	1
1985			4	4	1.0	4	0
Career			16	266	16.6	99t	1

Woodley Lewis
1950	LA	N	12	**275**	22.9	36	0
1951			3	34	11.3	20	0
1952			1	20	20.0	20	0
1953			7	87	12.4	45t	1
1956	CHIC	N	1	0	0.0	0	0
1957			2	34	17.0	30	0
Career			26	450	17.3	45t	1
Playoffs			1	28	28.0		0

Frank Liebel
| 1944 | NYG | N | 1 | 8 | 8.0 | 8 | 0 |
| 1945 | | | 1 | 17 | 17.0 | 17 | 0 |

Year	Team		No	Yds	Avg	Lg	TD

Frank Liebel *continued*

Year	Team		No	Yds	Avg	Lg	TD
1946			5	117	23.4	44	0
Career			7	142	20.3	44	0

Elvin Liles

Year	Team		No	Yds	Avg	Lg	TD
1944	DET	N	1	14	14.0	14	0
1945	CLE	N	1	6	6.0	6	0
Career			2	20	10.0	14	0

Bob Lilly

Year	Team		No	Yds	Avg	Lg	TD
1965	DAL	N	1	17	17.0	17t	1

Tony Lilly

Year	Team		No	Yds	Avg	Lg	TD
1984	DEN	N	1	5	5.0	5	0
1985			2	4	2.0	4	0
1986			3	22	7.3	15	0
1987			3	29	9.7	24	0
Career			9	60	6.7	24	0

Verl Lillywhite

Year	Team		No	Yds	Avg	Lg	TD
1948	SF	AA	3	26	8.7		0
1949			1	9	9.0	9	0
1950	SF	N	1	11	11.0	11	0
1951			3	47	15.7	24	0
Career			8	93	11.6	24	0

Jeremy Lincoln

Year	Team		No	Yds	Avg	Lg	TD
1993	CHI	N	3	109	36.3	80t	1
1994			1	5	5.0	5	0
1995			1	32	32.0	32	0
1996	STL	N	1	3	3.0	3	0
Career			6	149	24.8	80t	1
Playoffs			1	12	12.0		0

Dale Lindsey

Year	Team		No	Yds	Avg	Lg	TD
1965	CLE	N	1	11	11.0	11	0
1967			1	5	5.0	5	0
1968			1	0	0.0	0	0
1969			1	3	3.0	3	0
1970			2	65	32.5	56t	1
1971			2	50	25.0	29	0
Career			8	134	16.8	56t	1
Playoffs			1	27	27.0		1

Vic Lindskog

Year	Team		No	Yds	Avg	Lg	TD
1944	PHI	N	1	65	65.0	65t	1
1945			1	22	22.0	22	0
1946			1	10	10.0	10	0
1947			1	15	15.0	15	0
Career			4	112	28.0	65t	1

Ray Lininger

Year	Team		No	Yds	Avg	Lg	TD
1950	DET	N	3	20	6.7	15	0

Augie Lio

Year	Team		No	Yds	Avg	Lg	TD
1941	DET	N	3	12	4.0	8	0
1942			1	9	9.0	9	0
1943			1	-2	-2.0	-2	0
1944	BOS	N	2	13	6.5	10	0
1945			3	42	14.0	29	0
Career			10	74	7.4	29	0

Ronnie Lippett

Year	Team		No	Yds	Avg	Lg	TD
1984	NE	N	3	23	7.7	13	0
1985			3	93	31.0	58	0
1986			8	76	9.5	43	0
1987			3	103	34.3	45t	2
1988			1	4	4.0	4	0
1990			4	94	23.5	73	0
1991			2	27	13.5	27	0
Career			24	420	17.5	73	2
Playoffs			2	1	0.5		0

Gene Lipscomb

Year	Team		No	Yds	Avg	Lg	TD
1959	BAL	N	1	49	49.0	49	0

Paul Lipscomb

Year	Team		No	Yds	Avg	Lg	TD
1951	WAS	N	1	0	0.0	0	0
1952			1	7	7.0	7	0
Career			2	7	3.5	7	0

David Little

Year	Team		No	Yds	Avg	Lg	TD
1985	PIT	N	2	0	0.0	3	0

David Little *continued*

Year	Team		No	Yds	Avg	Lg	TD
1988			1	0	0.0	0	0
1989			3	23	7.7	13	0
1990			1	35	35.0	35	0
1991			1	5	5.0	5	0
1992			2	6	3.0	6	0
Career			10	69	6.9	35	0

Virgil Livers

Year	Team		No	Yds	Avg	Lg	TD
1975	CHI	N	2	40	20.0	40t	1
1976			3	34	11.3	18	0
1977			2	29	14.5	29	0
1978			3	86	28.7	60t	1
1979			2	41	20.5	30	0
Career			12	230	19.2	60t	2
Playoffs			1	8	8.0		0

Cliff Livingston

Year	Team		No	Yds	Avg	Lg	TD
1959	NYG	N	2	25	12.5	16	0
1960			1	0	0.0	0	0
1961			3	0	0.0	0	0
1963	LA	N	1	13	13.0	13	0
1965			1	8	8.0	8	0
Career			8	46	5.8	16	0

Howie Livingston

Year	Team		No	Yds	Avg	Lg	TD
1944	NYG	N	9	172	19.1	40	1
1945			3	65	21.7	38	0
1946			4	69	17.3	33	0
1947			4	69	17.3	40	0
1949	WAS	N	4	53	13.3	21	0
1950	WAS-SF	N	5	126	25.2	35t	1
Career			29	554	19.1	40	3
Playoffs			3	10	3.3		0

Warren Livingston

Year	Team		No	Yds	Avg	Lg	TD
1961	DAL	N	1	3	3.0	3	0
1963			3	31	10.3	29	0
1964			1	27	27.0	27	0
1965			3	5	1.7	5	0
1966			2	13	6.5	13	0
Career			10	79	7.9	29	0

Bob Livingstone

Year	Team		No	Yds	Avg	Lg	TD
1949	BUF	AA	1	6	6.0	6	0
1950	BAL	N	3	61	20.3	56	0
Career			4	67	16.8	56	0
Playoffs			2	14	7.0		0

Dan Lloyd

Year	Team		No	Yds	Avg	Lg	TD
1979	NYG	N	2	10	5.0	7	0

Dave Lloyd

Year	Team		No	Yds	Avg	Lg	TD
1963	PHI	N	3	30	10.0	14	0
1964			3	68	22.7	27	0
1965			2	35	17.5	21	0
1966			3	46	15.3	24	0
1967			1	1	1.0	1	0
1969			2	22	11.0	14	0
Career			14	202	14.4	27	0

Greg Lloyd

Year	Team		No	Yds	Avg	Lg	TD
1989	PIT	N	3	49	16.3	31	0
1990			1	9	9.0	9	0
1991			1	0	0.0	0	0
1992			1	35	35.0	35	0
1994			1	8	8.0	8	0
1995			3	85	28.3	52	0
Career			10	186	18.6	52	0

Spider Lockhart

Year	Team		No	Yds	Avg	Lg	TD
1965	NYG	N	4	117	29.3	39	0
1966			6	20	3.3	14	0
1967			5	38	7.6	28	0
1968			8	130	16.3	72t	2
1969			2	0	0.0	0	0
1970			4	51	12.8	25	0
1971			3	60	20.0	31	0
1972			4	56	14.0	29t	1
1973			2	3	1.5	2	0
1974			2	0	0.0	0	0

Spider Lockhart *continued*

Year	Team		No	Yds	Avg	Lg	TD
1975			1	0	0.0	0	0
Career			41	475	11.6	72t	3

Eugene Lockhart

Year	Team		No	Yds	Avg	Lg	TD
1984	DAL	N	1	32	32.0	32	0
1985			1	19	19.0	19t	1
1986			1	5	5.0	5	0
1987			1	13	13.0	13	0
1989			2	14	7.0	12	0
Career			6	83	13.8	32	1

Steve Lofton

Year	Team		No	Yds	Avg	Lg	TD
1996	CAR	N	1	42	42.0	42	0

Dave Logan

Year	Team		No	Yds	Avg	Lg	TD
1981	CLE	N	1	0	0.0	0	0

Dave Logan

Year	Team		No	Yds	Avg	Lg	TD
1984	TB	N	1	27	27.0	27t	1

Jerry Logan

Year	Team		No	Yds	Avg	Lg	TD
1963	BAL	N	1	15	15.0	15	0
1964			6	91	15.2	30	1
1965			2	74	37.0	38t	2
1966			3	13	4.3	13	0
1967			4	22	5.5	11	0
1968			3	9	3.0	9	0
1969			1	6	6.0	6	0
1970			6	92	15.3	33t	2
1971			4	28	7.0	23	0
1972			4	47	11.8	20	0
Career			34	397	11.7	38t	5
Playoffs			5	66	13.2		0

Obert Logan

Year	Team		No	Yds	Avg	Lg	TD
1965	DAL	N	3	5	1.7	3	0
1966			2	44	22.0	22	0
1967	NO	N	3	21	7.0	18	0
Career			8	70	8.8	22	0

Randy Logan

Year	Team		No	Yds	Avg	Lg	TD
1973	PHI	N	5	38	7.6	30	0
1974			2	2	1.0	2	0
1975			1	4	4.0	4	0
1976			1	38	38.0	38	0
1977			5	124	24.8	45	0
1978			2	15	7.5	9	0
1979			3	57	19.0	35	0
1980			1	16	16.0	16	0
1981			2	-1	-0.5	0	0
1983			1	0	0.0	0	0
Career			23	293	12.7	45	0

Al Lolotai

Year	Team		No	Yds	Avg	Lg	TD
1945	WAS	N	1	0	0.0	0	0

Bob Long

Year	Team		No	Yds	Avg	Lg	TD
1956	DET	N	2	47	23.5	40	0
1957			1	3	3.0	3	0
1958			2	28	14.0	25	0
1960	LA	N	1	23	23.0	23	0
1961			1	10	10.0	10	0
Career			7	111	15.9	40	0
Playoffs			1	17	17.0		0

Cutter Long

Year	Team		No	Yds	Avg	Lg	TD
1953	NYG	N	3	59	19.7	26	0

Howie Long

Year	Team		No	Yds	Avg	Lg	TD
1988	LARI	N	1	73	73.0	73	0
1991			1	11	11.0	11	0
Career			2	84	42.0	73	0

Tom Longo

Year	Team		No	Yds	Avg	Lg	TD
1969	NYG	N	2	31	15.5	26	0
1970			2	33	16.5	33	0
Career			4	64	16.0	33	0

Ace Loomis

Year	Team		No	Yds	Avg	Lg	TD
1951	GB	N	4	103	25.8	66	0
1952			4	115	28.8	45t	1

Ace Loomis *continued*

Year	Team		No	Yds	Avg	Lg	TD
1953			4	39	9.8	27	0
Career			12	257	21.4	66	1

Don Looney

Year	Team		No	Yds	Avg	Lg	TD
1940	PHI	N					1

Karl Lorch

Year	Team		No	Yds	Avg	Lg	TD
1979	WAS	N	1	31	31.0	31t	1

Billy Lothridge

Year	Team		No	Yds	Avg	Lg	TD
1968	ATL	N	3	76	25.3	44	0

Ronnie Lott

Year	Team		No	Yds	Avg	Lg	TD
1981	SF	N	7	117	16.7	41t	3
1982			2	95	47.5	83t	1
1983			4	22	5.5	22	0
1984			4	26	6.5	15	0
1985			6	68	11.3	25	0
1986			**10**	134	13.4	57t	1
1987			5	62	12.4	34	0
1988			5	59	11.8	44	0
1989			5	34	6.8	28	0
1990			3	26	8.7	15	0
1991	LARI	N	**8**	52	6.5	27	0
1992			1	0	0.0	0	0
1993	NYJ	N	3	35	11.7	29	0
Career			63	730	11.6	83t	5
Playoffs			**9**	187	20.8		2

Fletcher Louallen

Year	Team		No	Yds	Avg	Lg	TD
1987	MIN	N	1	16	16.0	16	0

Rommie Loudd

Year	Team		No	Yds	Avg	Lg	TD
1960	LA	A	3	17	5.7		0
1961	BOS	A	1	12	12.0	12	0
Career			4	29	7.3	12	0

Tom Louderback

Year	Team		No	Yds	Avg	Lg	TD
1960	OAK	A	2	7	3.5		0
1961			1	46	46.0	46	1
Career			3	53	17.7	46	1

Gary Lowe

Year	Team		No	Yds	Avg	Lg	TD
1956	WAS	N	1	30	30.0	30	0
1957	DET	N	1	3	3.0	3	0
1958			2	25	12.5	25	0
1959			5	**130**	26.0	42	0
1960			2	49	24.5	22	0
1961			5	16	3.2	11	0
1962			2	20	10.0	20	0
1963			2	14	7.0	14	0
Career			20	287	14.4	42	0

Lloyd Lowe

Year	Team		No	Yds	Avg	Lg	TD
1953	CHIB	N	1	6	6.0	6	0

Woodrow Lowe

Year	Team		No	Yds	Avg	Lg	TD
1976	SD	N	1	8	8.0	8	0
1977			1	28	28.0	28	0
1978			1	16	16.0	16	0
1979			5	150	30.0	77t	2
1980			3	72	24.0	28	1
1981			3	0	0.0	0	0
1982			1	2	2.0	2	0
1984			3	61	20.3	32t	1
1985			3	6	2.0	4	0
Career			21	343	16.3	77t	4

Russ Lowther

Year	Team		No	Yds	Avg	Lg	TD
1944	DET	N	1	32	32.0	32	0

Richie Lucas

Year	Team		No	Yds	Avg	Lg	TD
1961	BUF	A	2	0	0.0	0	0

Tim Lucas

Year	Team		No	Yds	Avg	Lg	TD
1987	DEN	N	1	11	11.0	11	0

Mike Lucci

Year	Team		No	Yds	Avg	Lg	TD
1966	DET	N	5	118	23.6	63t	1
1967			2	47	23.5	31t	1
1968			1	1	1.0	1	0
1970			2	18	9.0	12	0

Mike Lucci *continued*

Year	Team		No	Yds	Avg	Lg	TD
1971			5	74	14.8	27t	2
1972			2	0	0.0	0	0
1973			4	50	12.5	21	0
Career			21	308	14.7	63t	4

Derrel Luce

Year	Team		No	Yds	Avg	Lg	TD
1976	BAL	N	2	7	3.5	7	0
1978			1	15	15.0	15	0
Career			3	22	7.3	15	0

Sid Luckman

Year	Team		No	Yds	Avg	Lg	TD
1939	CHIB	N					1
1940			3	17	5.7		0
1941			3	52	17.3	37	0
1942			4	96	24.0	54	1
1943			4	85	21.3	27	0
1944			2	36	18.0	35	0
1946			1	24	24.0	24	0
Career			17	310	18.2	54	2
Playoffs			3	42	14.0		0

Johnny Lujack

Year	Team		No	Yds	Avg	Lg	TD
1948	CHIB	N	8	131	16.4	43	0
1950			1	15	15.0	15	0
1951			3	44	14.7	31	0
Career			12	190	15.8	43	0

Steve Luke

Year	Team		No	Yds	Avg	Lg	TD
1976	GB	N	2	30	15.0	15	0
1977			4	9	2.3	7	0
1978			2	91	45.5	63t	1
1979			1	10	10.0	10	0
1980			1	9	9.0	9	0
Career			10	149	14.9	63t	1

Roy Lumpkin

Year	Team		No	Yds	Avg	Lg	TD
1934	DET	N					1

Sean Lumpkin

Year	Team		No	Yds	Avg	Lg	TD
1994	NO	N	1	1	1.0	1	0
1995			1	47	47.0	47t	1
Career			2	48	24.0	47t	1

Bobby Luna

Year	Team		No	Yds	Avg	Lg	TD
1955	SF	N	2	0	0.0	0	0
1959	PIT	N	3	53	17.7	32	0
Career			5	53	10.6	32	0

Bill Lund

Year	Team		No	Yds	Avg	Lg	TD
1946	CLE	AA	1	12	12.0	12	0
1947			2	36	18.0		1
Career			3	48	16.0	12	1

Ken Lunday

Year	Team		No	Yds	Avg	Lg	TD
1941	NYG	N	1	5	5.0	5	0

Lamar Lundy

Year	Team		No	Yds	Avg	Lg	TD
1960	LA	N	1	25	25.0	25t	1
1964			1	14	14.0	14t	1
1966			1	33	33.0	33t	1
Career			3	72	24.0	33t	3

Bob Lurtsema

Year	Team		No	Yds	Avg	Lg	TD
1968	NYG	N	1	39	39.0	39	0

Allen Lyday

Year	Team		No	Yds	Avg	Lg	TD
1984	HOU	N	1	12	12.0	12	0
1986			3	24	8.0	24	0
Career			4	36	9.0	24	0

Todd Lyght

Year	Team		No	Yds	Avg	Lg	TD
1991	LARM	N	1	0	0.0	0	0
1992			3	80	26.7	39	0
1993			2	0	0.0	0	0
1994			1	14	14.0	14	0
1995	STL	N	4	34	8.5	29t	1
1996			5	43	8.6	25t	1
Career			16	171	10.7	39	2

Garry Lyle

Year	Team		No	Yds	Avg	Lg	TD
1969	CHI	N	1	10	10.0	10	0

Garry Lyle *continued*

Year	Team		No	Yds	Avg	Lg	TD
1971			1	29	29.0	29	0
1972			2	52	26.0	35	0
1973			5	62	12.4	24	0
1974			3	57	19.0	36	0
Career			12	210	17.5	36	0

Keith Lyle

Year	Team		No	Yds	Avg	Lg	TD
1994	LARM	N	2	1	0.5	1	0
1995	STL	N	3	42	14.0	31	0
1996			**9**	152	16.9	68	0
Career			14	195	13.9	68	0

Lenny Lyles

Year	Team		No	Yds	Avg	Lg	TD
1963	BAL	N	2	36	18.0	36t	1
1964			2	40	20.0	23	0
1965			1	28	28.0	28	0
1966			1	6	6.0	6	0
1967			5	59	11.8	36t	1
1968			5	32	6.4	11	0
Career			16	201	12.6	36t	2

Lester Lyles

Year	Team		No	Yds	Avg	Lg	TD
1986	NYJ	N	5	36	7.2	22	0
1988	PHX	N	2	0	0.0	0	0
1989	SD	N	2	28	14.0	28	0
1990			1	19	19.0	19	0
Career			10	83	8.3	28	0

Robert Lyles

Year	Team		No	Yds	Avg	Lg	TD
1986	HOU	N	2	0	0.0	0	0
1987			2	42	21.0	27	0
1988			2	3	1.5	3	0
1989			4	66	16.5	48	0
Career			10	111	11.1	48	0

Dick Lynch

Year	Team		No	Yds	Avg	Lg	TD
1958	WAS	N	2	24	12.0	13	0
1959	NYG	N	1	0	0.0	0	0
1960			3	61	20.3	32	1
1961			**9**	60	6.7	36	0
1962			5	90	18.0	27	0
1963			**9**	**251**	27.9	82t	3
1964			4	68	17.0	37	0
1965			4	38	9.5	23	0
Career			37	592	16.0	82t	4

Jim Lynch

Year	Team		No	Yds	Avg	Lg	TD
1967	KC	A	1	26	26.0	26	0
1968			3	73	24.3	49	1
1969			3	18	6.0	14	0
1970	KC	N	3	40	13.3	27	0
1971			1	10	10.0	10	0
1973			1	9	9.0	9	0
1976			2	7	3.5	7	0
1977			3	8	2.7	6	0
Career			17	191	11.2	49	1
Playoffs			1	0	0.0		0

John Lynch

Year	Team		No	Yds	Avg	Lg	TD
1995	TB	N	3	3	1.0	3	0
1996			3	26	8.7	25	0
Career			6	29	4.8	25	0

Lorenzo Lynch

Year	Team		No	Yds	Avg	Lg	TD
1989	CHI	N	3	55	18.3	41	0
1991	PHX	N	3	59	19.7	35t	1
1993			3	13	4.3	13	0
1994	ARI	N	2	35	17.5	23	0
1995			1	72	72.0	72t	1
1996	OAK	N	3	75	25.0	35	0
Career			15	309	20.6	72t	2

Johnny Lynn

Year	Team		No	Yds	Avg	Lg	TD
1979	NYJ	N	2	46	23.0	32	0
1981			3	76	25.3	67	0
1982			1	3	3.0	3	0
1983			3	70	23.3	42t	1
1984			2	16	8.0	16	0
1985			1	24	24.0	24	0
1986			5	36	7.2	26	0
Career			17	271	15.9	67	1
Playoffs			2	40	20.0		0

Dicky Lyons

Year	Team		No	Yds	Avg	Lg	TD
1970	NO	N	1	12	12.0	12	0

Robert Lyons

Year	Team		No	Yds	Avg	Lg	TD
1989	CLE	N	1	0	0.0	0	0

Cedric Mack

Year	Team		No	Yds	Avg	Lg	TD
1983	STL	N	3	25	8.3	13	0
1985			2	10	5.0	10	0
1986			4	42	10.5	24	0
1987			2	0	0.0	0	0
1988	PHX	N	3	33	11.0	12	0
1989			4	15	3.8	9	0
1990			2	53	26.5	39	0
Career			20	178	8.9	39	0

Milton Mack

Year	Team		No	Yds	Avg	Lg	TD
1987	NO	N	4	32	8.0	26	0
1988			1	19	19.0	19	0
1989			2	0	0.0	0	0
1992	TB	N	3	0	0.0	0	0
1993			1	27	27.0	27t	1
1994	DET	N	1	0	0.0	0	0
Career			12	78	6.5	27t	1

Earsell Mackbee

Year	Team		No	Yds	Avg	Lg	TD
1966	MIN	N	2	27	13.5	17	0
1967			5	98	19.6	40	1
1968			2	55	27.5	36	0
1969			6	100	16.7	38	0
Career			15	280	18.7	40	1

Bob MacLeod

Year	Team		No	Yds	Avg	Lg	TD
1939	CHIB	N					1

Tom MacLeod

Year	Team		No	Yds	Avg	Lg	TD
1973	GB	N	2	8	4.0	8	0
1975	BAL	N	1	50	50.0	50	0
1977			2	37	18.5	33	0
Career			5	95	19.0	50	0

Eddie Macon

Year	Team		No	Yds	Avg	Lg	TD
1960	OAK	A	9	105	11.7	42	1

Elmer Madarik

Year	Team		No	Yds	Avg	Lg	TD
1945	DET	N	1	40	40.0	40	0
1946			3	75	25.0	31	0
Career			4	115	28.8	40	0

Mark Maddox

Year	Team		No	Yds	Avg	Lg	TD
1994	BUF	N	1	11	11.0	11	0

George Maderos

Year	Team		No	Yds	Avg	Lg	TD
1955	SF	N	2	23	11.5	19	0
1956			2	2	1.0	2	0
Career			4	25	6.3	19	0

Jim Magee

Year	Team		No	Yds	Avg	Lg	TD
1945	BOS	N	1	6	6.0	6	0

Archie Maggiolo

Year	Team		No	Yds	Avg	Lg	TD
1948	BUF	AA	1	7	7.0	7	0
1949	DET	N	3	46	15.3	23	0
1950	BAL	N	8	165	20.6	50	0
Career			12	218	18.2	50	0
Playoffs			1	2	2.0		0

Joe Magliolo

Year	Team		No	Yds	Avg	Lg	TD
1948	NY	AA	1	12	12.0	12	0

Dante Magnani

Year	Team		No	Yds	Avg	Lg	TD
1941	CLE	N	2	6	3.0	4	0
1943	CHIB	N	2	23	11.5	14	0
1946			1	35	35.0	35	0
Career			5	64	12.8	35	0
Playoffs			2	49	24.5		1

Paul Maguire

Year	Team		No	Yds	Avg	Lg	TD
1960	LA	A	3	37	12.3	15	0
1961	SD	A	1	2	2.0	2	0
1962			1	13	13.0	13	0
1963			4	47	11.8	38	0
Career			9	99	11.0	38	0
Playoffs			1	10	10.0		0

George Magulick

Year	Team		No	Yds	Avg	Lg	TD
1944	C-P	N	2	12	6.0	12	0

Drew Mahalic

Year	Team		No	Yds	Avg	Lg	TD
1975	SD	N	1	3	3.0	3	0
1978	PHI	N	1	5	5.0	5	0
Career			2	8	4.0	5	0

Bruce Maher

Year	Team		No	Yds	Avg	Lg	TD
1960	DET	N	1	19	19.0	19	0
1961			1	8	8.0	8	0
1963			1	0	0.0	0	0
1964			2	28	14.0	28	0
1965			4	76	19.0	35	0
1966			5	90	18.0	56	0
1967			2	14	7.0	14	0
1968	NYG	N	1	89	89.0	89	0
1969			5	112	22.4	48	0
Career			22	436	19.8	89	0

Gene Malinowski

Year	Team		No	Yds	Avg	Lg	TD
1948	BOS	N	1	9	9.0	9	0

John Mallory

Year	Team		No	Yds	Avg	Lg	TD
1969	ATL	N	1	22	22.0	22	0
1970			1	9	9.0	9	0
Career			2	31	15.5	22	0

Larry Mallory

Year	Team		No	Yds	Avg	Lg	TD
1976	NYG	N	1	0	0.0	0	0
1977			1	9	9.0	9	0
Career			2	9	4.5	9	0

Ray Mallouf

Year	Team		No	Yds	Avg	Lg	TD
1946	CHIC	N	1	15	15.0	15	0
1949	NYG	N	1	0	0.0	0	0
Career			2	15	7.5	15	0

Darrell Malone

Year	Team		No	Yds	Avg	Lg	TD
1994	MIA	N	1	0	0.0	0	0

Van Malone

Year	Team		No	Yds	Avg	Lg	TD
1995	DET	N	1	0	0.0	0	0
1996			1	5	5.0	5	0
Career			2	5	2.5	5	0

Jack Manders

Year	Team		No	Yds	Avg	Lg	TD
1934	CHIB	N					1
1937							1
1940			1	27	27.0	27	0
Career			1	27	27.0	27	2
Playoffs			1	27	27.0		0

Pug Manders

Year	Team		No	Yds	Avg	Lg	TD
1941	BKN	N	4	73	18.3	65	1
1942			2	23	11.5	17	0
1944			1	4	4.0	4	0
1945	BOS	N	3	5	1.7	5	0
Career			10	105	10.5	65	1

Dino Mangiero

Year	Team		No	Yds	Avg	Lg	TD
1980	KC	N	1	0	0.0	0	0

John Mangum

Year	Team		No	Yds	Avg	Lg	TD
1991	CHI	N	1	5	5.0	5	0
1993			1	0	0.0	0	0
1995			1	2	2.0	2	0
Career			3	7	2.3	5	0
Playoffs			1	9	9.0		0

Joe Maniaci

Year	Team		No	Yds	Avg	Lg	TD
1940	CHIB	N	2	38	19.0		1
Playoffs			2	26	13.0		0

Dexter Manley

Year	Team		No	Yds	Avg	Lg	TD
1982	WAS	N	1	-2	-2.0	-2	0
1983			1	1	1.0	1	0
Career			2	-1	-0.5	1	0

Brison Manor

Year	Team		No	Yds	Avg	Lg	TD
1981	DEN	N	1	16	16.0	16	0

Von Mansfield

Year	Team		No	Yds	Avg	Lg	TD
1987	GB	N	1	14	14.0	14	0

Ed Manske

Year	Team		No	Yds	Avg	Lg	TD
1937	CHIB	N					1

Frank Manumaleuga

Year	Team		No	Yds	Avg	Lg	TD
1979	KC	N	1	17	17.0	17	0
1980			3	44	14.7	22t	1
1981			2	17	8.5	12	0
Career			6	78	13.0	22t	1

Bap Manzini

Year	Team		No	Yds	Avg	Lg	TD
1944	PHI	N	1	16	16.0	16	0

Bobby Maples

Year	Team		No	Yds	Avg	Lg	TD
1965	HOU	A	1	0	0.0	0	0

Gino Marchetti

Year	Team		No	Yds	Avg	Lg	TD
1959	BAL	N	1	1	1.0	1	0

Andrew Marefos

Year	Team		No	Yds	Avg	Lg	TD
1941	NYG	N	2	48	24.0	40	0
1942			1	11	11.0	11	0
Career			3	59	19.7	40	0

Bob Margarita

Year	Team		No	Yds	Avg	Lg	TD
1944	CHIB	N	3	34	11.3	36	0
1945			6	79	13.2	26	0
Career			9	113	12.6	36	0

Brock Marion

Year	Team		No	Yds	Avg	Lg	TD
1993	DAL	N	1	2	2.0	2	0
1994			1	11	11.0	11	0
1995			6	40	6.7	32t	1
Career			8	53	6.6	32t	1
Playoffs			1	0	0.0		0

Frank Marion

Year	Team		No	Yds	Avg	Lg	TD
1980	NYG	N	1	7	7.0	7	0

Fred Marion

Year	Team		No	Yds	Avg	Lg	TD
1983	NE	N	2	4	2.0	4	0
1984			2	39	19.5	26	0
1985			7	**189**	27.0	83	0
1986			2	56	28.0	37t	0
1987			4	53	13.3	25	0
1988			4	47	11.8	22	0
1989			2	19	9.5	18	0
1990			4	17	4.3	16	0
1991			2	33	16.5	33	0
Career			29	457	15.8	83	1
Playoffs			3	71	23.7		0

Duke Maronic

Year	Team		No	Yds	Avg	Lg	TD
1944	PHI	N	1	32	32.0	32	0
1946			1	7	7.0	7	0
Career			2	39	19.5	32	0

Jim Marsalis

Year	Team		No	Yds	Avg	Lg	TD
1969	KC	A	2	33	16.5	28	0
1970	KC		4	26	6.5	26	0
1971			3	0	0.0	0	0
1972			2	20	10.0	19	0
1973			2	36	18.0	36	0
1975			1	1	1.0	1	0
1977	NO	N	1	0	0.0	0	0
Career			15	116	7.7	36	0
Playoffs			3	65	21.7		0

Anthony Marshall

Year	Team		No	Yds	Avg	Lg	TD
1995	CHI	N	1	0	0.0	0	0
1996			2	20	10.0	20	0
Career			3	20	6.7	20	0

James Marshall

Year	Team		No	Yds	Avg	Lg	TD
1980	NO	N	2	17	8.5	17	0

Jim Marshall

Year	Team		No	Yds	Avg	Lg	TD
1969	MIN	N	1	30	30.0	30	0

Leonard Marshall

Year	Team		No	Yds	Avg	Lg	TD
1985	NYG	N	1	3	3.0	3	0
1986			1	0	0.0	0	0
Career			2	3	1.5	3	0

Year	Team		No	Yds	Avg	Lg	TD

Wilber Marshall

Year	Team		No	Yds	Avg	Lg	TD
1985	CHI	N	4	23	5.8	14	0
1986			5	68	13.6	58t	1
1988	WAS	N	3	61	20.3	43	0
1989			1	18	18.0	18	0
1990			1	6	6.0	6	0
1991			5	75	15.0	54t	1
1992			2	20	10.0	20t	1
1994	ARI	N	0	13		13L	0
1995	NYJ	N	2	20	10.0	20	0
Career			23	304	13.2	58t	3

Paul Martha

Year	Team		No	Yds	Avg	Lg	TD
1966	PIT	N	3	44	14.7	35	0
1967			4	41	10.3	23	0
1968			3	43	14.3	23	0
1969			5	37	7.4	15	0
1970	DEN	N	6	99	16.5	50	0
Career			21	264	12.6	50	0

Aaron Martin

Year	Team		No	Yds	Avg	Lg	TD
1964	LA	N	2	107	53.5	71t	1
1965			2	60	30.0	37t	1
1966	PHI	N	1	47	47.0	47	0
1967			2	8	4.0	8	0
1968	WAS	N	4	23	5.8	18	0
Career			11	245	22.3	71t	2

Amos Martin

Year	Team		No	Yds	Avg	Lg	TD
1974	MIN	N	3	39	13.0	28	0

Bob Martin

Year	Team		No	Yds	Avg	Lg	TD
1976	NYJ	N	2	15	7.5	12	0
1977			1	0	0.0	0	0
1978			2	32	16.0	26	0
Career			5	47	9.4	26	0

Chris Martin

Year	Team		No	Yds	Avg	Lg	TD
1991	KC	N	1	0	0.0	0	0

D'Artagnan Martin

Year	Team		No	Yds	Avg	Lg	TD
1971	NO	N	3	51	17.0	26	0

Derrick Martin

Year	Team		No	Yds	Avg	Lg	TD
1987	SF	N	1	12	12.0	12	0

Doug Martin

Year	Team		No	Yds	Avg	Lg	TD
1982	MIN	N	1	0	0.0	0	0

Emanuel Martin

Year	Team		No	Yds	Avg	Lg	TD
1996	BUF	N	2	35	17.5	31	0

Frank Martin

Year	Team		No	Yds	Avg	Lg	TD
1943	BKN	N	2	22	11.0	14	0
1944			1	0	0.0	0	0
1945	NYG	N	1	0	0.0	0	0
Career			4	22	5.5	14	0

George Martin

Year	Team		No	Yds	Avg	Lg	TD
1977	NYG	N	1	30	30.0	30t	1
1985			1	56	56.0	56t	1
1986			1	78	78.0	78t	1
Career			3	164	54.7	78t	3

Harvey Martin

Year	Team		No	Yds	Avg	Lg	TD
1976	DAL	N	1	0	0.0	0	0
1978			1	7	7.0	7	0
Career			2	7	3.5	7	0

Jack Martin

Year	Team		No	Yds	Avg	Lg	TD
1947	LA	N	1	0	0.0	0	0

Jim Martin

Year	Team		No	Yds	Avg	Lg	TD
1950	CLE	N	2	15	7.5	14	0
1953	DET	N	1	0	0.0	0	0
1957			1	22	22.0	22	0
1959			2	33	16.5	19	0
Career			6	70	11.7	22	0

John Martin

Year	Team		No	Yds	Avg	Lg	TD
1941	CHIC	N	1	2	2.0	2	0
1942			6	45	7.5	25	0
1943			1	35	35.0	35	0
1944	BOS	N	3	46	15.3	26	0

John Martin *continued*

Year	Team		No	Yds	Avg	Lg	TD
1945			1	10	10.0	10	0
Career			12	138	11.5	35	0

Rod Martin

Year	Team		No	Yds	Avg	Lg	TD
1980	OAK	N	2	15	7.5	15	0
1981			1	7	7.0	7	0
1982	LARI	N	3	60	20.0	39t	1
1983			4	81	20.3	40t	2
1984			2	31	15.5	17	1
1985			1	16	16.0	16	0
1986			1	15	15.0	15	0
Career			14	225	16.1	40t	4
Playoffs			3	44	14.7		0

Saladin Martin

Year	Team		No	Yds	Avg	Lg	TD
1981	SF	N	1	0	0.0	0	0

Wayne Martin

Year	Team		No	Yds	Avg	Lg	TD
1995	NO	N	1	12	12.0	12	0

John Martinelli

Year	Team		No	Yds	Avg	Lg	TD
1946	BUF	AA	1	12	12.0	12	0

Lonnie Marts

Year	Team		No	Yds	Avg	Lg	TD
1992	KC	N	1	36	36.0	36t	1
1993			1	20	20.0	20	0
1995	TB	N	1	8	8.0	8	0
Career			3	64	21.3	36t	1
Playoffs			2	19	9.5		0

Eugene Marve

Year	Team		No	Yds	Avg	Lg	TD
1982	BUF	N	1	0	0.0	0	0
1988	TB	N	1	29	29.0	29	0
1991			1	1	1.0	1	0
Career			3	30	10.0	29	0

Len Masini

Year	Team		No	Yds	Avg	Lg	TD
1947	SF	AA	1	0	0.0	0	0

Carlton Massey

Year	Team		No	Yds	Avg	Lg	TD
1955	CLE	N	1	24	24.0	24	0

Robert Massey

Year	Team		No	Yds	Avg	Lg	TD
1989	NO	N	5	26	5.2	22	0
1992	PHX	N	5	147	29.4	46t	3
1994	DET	N	4	25	6.3	17	0
Career			14	198	14.1	46t	3

Bob Masterson

Year	Team		No	Yds	Avg	Lg	TD
1941	WAS	N	1	0	0.0	0	0
1946	NY	AA	1	0	0.0	0	0
Career			2	0	0.0	0	0

Ed Matesic

Year	Team		No	Yds	Avg	Lg	TD
1934	PHI						1

Bob Matheson

Year	Team		No	Yds	Avg	Lg	TD
1967	CLE	N	1	0	0.0	0	0
1968			2	44	22.0	30	0
1970			1	11	11.0	11	0
1974	MIA	N	1	10	10.0	10	0
1975			3	32	10.7	22	0
1976			2	34	17.0	34	0
1977			1	7	7.0	7	0
1979			1	28	28.0	28	0
Career			12	166	13.8	34	0
Playoffs			1	29	29.0		0

Jack Matheson

Year	Team		No	Yds	Avg	Lg	TD
1944	DET	N	1	21	21.0	21	0
1946			1	8	8.0	8	0
Career			2	29	14.5	21	0

Riley Matheson

Year	Team		No	Yds	Avg	Lg	TD
1941	CLE	N	1	1	1.0	1	0
1942			1	13	13.0	13	0
1944			3	12	4.0	6	0
1945			2	49	24.5	45	0
1946	LA	N	4	11	2.8	7	0
1947			1	5	5.0	5	0
1948	SF	AA	2	4	2.0		0
Career			14	95	6.8	45	0

Ned Mathews

Year	Team		No	Yds	Avg	Lg	TD
1941	DET	N	5	128	25.6	51	1
1943			4	44	11.0	22	0
1945	BOS	N	3	42	14.0	18	0
1946	CHI	AA	2	8	4.0		0
1947	SF	AA	4	149	37.3	52	1
Career			18	371	20.6	52	2

Ray Mathews

Year	Team		No	Yds	Avg	Lg	TD
1951	PIT	N	1	0	0.0	0	0
1953			1	17	17.0	17	0
Career			2	17	8.5	17	0

Mark Mathis

Year	Team		No	Yds	Avg	Lg	TD
1987	STL	N	1	4	4.0	4	0

Reggie Mathis

Year	Team		No	Yds	Avg	Lg	TD
1980	NO	N	1	15	15.0	15	0

John Matisi

Year	Team		No	Yds	Avg	Lg	TD
1943	BKN	N	1	13	13.0	13	0

Ollie Matson

Year	Team		No	Yds	Avg	Lg	TD
1952	CHIC	N	2	51	25.5	30	0
1954			1	0	0.0	0	0
Career			3	51	17.0	30	0

Archie Matsos

Year	Team		No	Yds	Avg	Lg	TD
1960	BUF	A	8	142	17.8	33	1
1961			2	12	6.0	12	0
1963	OAK	A	4	39	9.8	19	0
1964			2	50	25.0	27	0
1965			3	52	17.3	47	0
1966	DEN-SD	A	3	16	5.3	6	0
Career			22	311	14.1	47	1

Al Matthews

Year	Team		No	Yds	Avg	Lg	TD
1971	GB	N	1	20	20.0	20	0
1972			2	8	4.0	8	0
1973			2	58	29.0	58t	0
1974			3	41	13.7	32	0
1975			2	42	21.0	40	0
1976	SEA	N	3	60	20.0	40t	1
Career			13	229	17.6	58t	1

Bill Matthews

Year	Team		No	Yds	Avg	Lg	TD
1980	NE	N	1	5	5.0	5	0

Clay Matthews

Year	Team		No	Yds	Avg	Lg	TD
1955	SF	N	1	19	19.0	19	0

Clay Matthews

Year	Team		No	Yds	Avg	Lg	TD
1978	CLE	N	1	5	5.0	5	0
1979			1	30	30.0	30	0
1980			1	6	6.0	6	0
1981			2	14	7.0	8	0
1986			2	12	6.0	8	0
1987			3	62	20.7	36	1
1989			1	25	25.0	25	0
1991			1	35	35.0	35	0
1992			1	6	6.0	6	0
1993			1	10	10.0	10	0
1995	ATL	N	2	1	0.5	1	0
Career			16	206	12.9	36	1
Playoffs			1	0	0.0		0

Fran Mattingly

Year	Team		No	Yds	Avg	Lg	TD
1947	CHI	AA	1	1	1.0	1	0

Marv Matuszak

Year	Team		No	Yds	Avg	Lg	TD
1953	PIT	N	1	0	0.0	0	0
1955			1	7	7.0	7	0
1956			2	28	14.0	26	0
1958	SF	N	1	0	0.0	0	0
1959	BAL	N	1	23	23.0	23	0
1962	BUF	A	6	46	7.7	25	0
1964	DEN	A	2	16	8.0	8	0
Career			14	120	8.6	26	0

Al Matuza

Year	Team		No	Yds	Avg	Lg	TD
1941	CHIB	N	2	9	4.5	9	0
1942			2	8	4.0	4	0
Career			4	17	4.3	9	0

Year	Team		No	Yds	Avg	Lg	TD

Stan Mauldin
Year	Team		No	Yds	Avg	Lg	TD
1947	CHIC	N	1	11	11.0	11	0

Brett Maxie
Year	Team		No	Yds	Avg	Lg	TD
1986	NO	N	2	15	7.5	15	0
1987			3	17	5.7	10	0
1989			3	41	13.7	26t	1
1990			2	88	44.0	50t	1
1991			3	33	11.0	31t	1
1992			2	12	6.0	8	0
1995	CAR	N	6	59	9.8	49	0
1996			1	35	35.0	35	0
Career			22	300	13.6	50t	3

Tommy Maxwell
Year	Team		No	Yds	Avg	Lg	TD
1969	BAL	N	3	37	12.3	22	0
1970			0	9		9L	0
1974	HOU	N	2	30	15.0	15	0
Career			5	76	15.2	22	0

Vernon Maxwell
Year	Team		No	Yds	Avg	Lg	TD
1983	BAL	N	1	31	31.0	31	0

Ray May
Year	Team		No	Yds	Avg	Lg	TD
1968	PIT	N	3	31	10.3	25t	1
1969			2	4	2.0	4	0
1970	BAL	N	1	18	18.0	18	0
1971			1	46	46.0	46	0
1972			2	43	21.5	37	0
1973	DEN	N	1	1	1.0	1	0
1974			2	40	20.0	25	0
1975			1	0	0.0	0	0
Career			13	183	14.1	46	1
Playoffs			1	0	0.0		0

James Mayberry
Year	Team		No	Yds	Avg	Lg	TD
1979	ATL	N	1	6	6.0	6t	1

Mike Mayes
Year	Team		No	Yds	Avg	Lg	TD
1990	NYJ	N	1	0	0.0	0	0

Martin Mayhew
Year	Team		No	Yds	Avg	Lg	TD
1990	WAS	N	7	20	2.9	15	0
1991			3	31	10.3	31t	1
1992			3	58	19.3	33	0
1994	TB	N	2	4	2.0	4	0
1995			5	81	16.2	40	0
1996			1	5	5.0	5	0
Career			21	199	9.5	40	1
Playoffs			2	46	23.0		0

Alvoid Mays
Year	Team		No	Yds	Avg	Lg	TD
1991	WAS	N	1	0	0.0	0	0
1992			2	18	9.0	13	0
1995	PIT	N	2	35	17.5	32t	1
Career			5	53	10.6	32t	1

Jerry Mays
Year	Team		No	Yds	Avg	Lg	TD
1961	DAL	A	1	7	7.0	7	0

Frank Maznicki
Year	Team		No	Yds	Avg	Lg	TD
1942	CHIB	N	4	13	3.3	9	0
1946			2	17	8.5	9	0
1947	BOS	N	4	46	11.5	19	0
Career			10	76	7.6	19	0

Vince Mazza
Year	Team		No	Yds	Avg	Lg	TD
1947	BUF	AA	1	26	26.0	26	0
1948			0	5		5L	1
Career			1	31	31.0	26	1

Dean McAdams
Year	Team		No	Yds	Avg	Lg	TD
1941	BKN	N	1	0	0.0	0	0
1943			3	34	11.3	14	0
Career			4	34	8.5	14	0

George McAfee
Year	Team		No	Yds	Avg	Lg	TD
1940	CHIB	N	4	50	12.5		0
1941			6	78	13.0	56	1
1945			1	7	7.0	7	0
1946			3	18	6.0	18	0
1947			1	49	49.0	49	0
1948			2	35	17.5	25	0
1949			6	76	12.7	54t	1

George McAfee *continued*
Year	Team		No	Yds	Avg	Lg	TD
1950			2	31	15.5	19	0
Career			25	344	13.8	56	2
Playoffs			4	69	17.3		1

Ken McAlister
Year	Team		No	Yds	Avg	Lg	TD
1984	KC	N	2	33	16.5	22	0

Kevin McArthur
Year	Team		No	Yds	Avg	Lg	TD
1988	NYJ	N	1	3	3.0	3	0
Playoffs			1	21	21.0		1

Gerald McBurrows
Year	Team		No	Yds	Avg	Lg	TD
1996	STL	N	1	3	3.0	3	0

Richie McCabe
Year	Team		No	Yds	Avg	Lg	TD
1955	PIT	N	3	29	9.7	25	0
1959	WAS	N	1	8	8.0	8	0
1960	BUF	A	4	0	0.0		0
1961			1	17	17.0	17	0
Career			9	54	6.0	25	0

Keith McCants
Year	Team		No	Yds	Avg	Lg	TD
1994	ARI	N	1	46	46.0	46t	1

Jim McCarthy
Year	Team		No	Yds	Avg	Lg	TD
1946	BKN	AA	1	3	3.0	3	0

Thomas McCauley
Year	Team		No	Yds	Avg	Lg	TD
1970	ATL	N	1	32	32.0	32	0
1971			1	0	0.0	0	0
Career			2	32	16.0	32	0

Clint McClain
Year	Team		No	Yds	Avg	Lg	TD
1941	NYG	N	1	34	34.0	34	0

Dewey McClain
Year	Team		No	Yds	Avg	Lg	TD
1976	ATL	N	1	13	13.0	13	0

Randy McClanahan
Year	Team		No	Yds	Avg	Lg	TD
1980	OAK	N	1	7	7.0	7	0

Mike McClellan
Year	Team		No	Yds	Avg	Lg	TD
1962	PHI	N	3	2	0.7	2	0
1963			1	0	0.0	0	0
Career			4	2	0.5	2	0

J.J. Mc Cleskey
Year	Team		No	Yds	Avg	Lg	TD
1995	NO	N	1	0	0.0	0	0

Kent McCloughan
Year	Team		No	Yds	Avg	Lg	TD
1965	OAK	A	3	22	7.3	16	0
1966			4	62	15.5	58	0
1967			2	7	3.5	7	0
1968			1	0	0.0	0	0
1970	OAK	N	5	5	1.0	5	0
Career			15	96	6.4	58	0

Milt McColl
Year	Team		No	Yds	Avg	Lg	TD
1981	SF	N	1	22	22.0	22	0
1987			1	0	0.0	0	0
Career			2	22	11.0	22	0

Dewey McConnell
Year	Team		No	Yds	Avg	Lg	TD
1954	PIT	N	3	117	39.0	30	0

Darris McCord
Year	Team		No	Yds	Avg	Lg	TD
1961	DET	N	1	11	11.0	11	0
1963			1	5	5.0	5	0
1967			1	15	15.0	15	0
Career			3	31	10.3	15	0

Mike McCormack
Year	Team		No	Yds	Avg	Lg	TD
1954	CLE	N	1	14	14.0	14	0

Len McCormick
Year	Team		No	Yds	Avg	Lg	TD
1948	BAL	AA	1	5	5.0	5	0

Mike McCoy
Year	Team		No	Yds	Avg	Lg	TD
1974	GB	N	1	5	5.0	5	0

Mike McCoy
Year	Team		No	Yds	Avg	Lg	TD
1977	GB	N	4	2	0.5	2	0

Mike McCoy *continued*
Year	Team		No	Yds	Avg	Lg	TD
1978			3	34	11.3	23	0
1979			3	60	20.0	38	0
1980			1	0	0.0	0	0
1981			2	20	10.0	16	0
Career			13	116	8.9	38	0

Hurdis McCrary
Year	Team		No	Yds	Avg	Lg	TD
1929	GB	N					1

Bruce McCray
Year	Team		No	Yds	Avg	Lg	TD
1987	CHI	N	1	23	23.0	23t	1

Prentice McCray
Year	Team		No	Yds	Avg	Lg	TD
1974	NE	N	3	61	20.3	33	0
1976			5	182	36.4	63t	2
1977			4	61	15.3	48	0
1979			3	48	16.0	26	0
Career			15	352	23.5	63t	2

Ed McDaniel
Year	Team		No	Yds	Avg	Lg	TD
1962	DEN	A	4	37	9.3	18	0
1963			2	12	6.0	10	0
1964	NY	A	3	60	20.0	38	1
1965			1	7	7.0	7	0
1966	MIA	A	2	20	10.0	20	0
1967			1	15	15.0	15	0
Career			13	151	11.6	38	1

Ed McDaniel
Year	Team		No	Yds	Avg	Lg	TD
1994	MIN	N	1	0	0.0	0	0
1995			1	3	3.0	3	0
Career			2	3	1.5	3	0

LeCharls McDaniel
Year	Team		No	Yds	Avg	Lg	TD
1982	WAS	N	1	7	7.0	7	0

Terry McDaniel
Year	Team		No	Yds	Avg	Lg	TD
1989	LARI	N	3	21	7.0	20	0
1990			3	20	6.7	15	0
1992			4	180	45.0	67	0
1993			5	87	17.4	36t	1
1994			7	103	14.7	35	2
1995	OAK	N	6	46	7.7	42t	1
1996			5	150	30.0	56t	1
Career			33	607	18.4	67	5

Lloyd McDermott
Year	Team		No	Yds	Avg	Lg	TD
1951	CHIC	N	1	5	5.0	5	0

Ron McDole
Year	Team		No	Yds	Avg	Lg	TD
1964	BUF	A	1	0	0.0	0	0
1965			1	24	24.0	24	0
1966			1	4	4.0	4	0
1967			1	5	5.0	5	0
1968			2	47	23.5	42	0
1971	WAS	N	3	18	6.0	18t	1
1977			2	15	7.5	15	0
1978			1	2	2.0	2	0
Career			12	115	9.6	42	1

Don McDonald
Year	Team		No	Yds	Avg	Lg	TD
1944	PHI	N	1	14	14.0	14	0

Ricardo McDonald
Year	Team		No	Yds	Avg	Lg	TD
1992	CIN	N	1	0	0.0	0	0

Tim McDonald
Year	Team		No	Yds	Avg	Lg	TD
1988	PHX	N	2	11	5.5	11	0
1989			7	170	24.3	53t	1
1990			4	63	15.8	38	0
1991			5	36	7.2	13	0
1992			2	35	17.5	20	0
1993	SF	N	3	23	7.7	21	0
1994			2	79	39.5	73t	1
1995			4	135	33.8	52t	2
1996			2	14	7.0	14	0
Career			31	566	18.3	73t	4
Playoffs			2	4	2.0		0

Walt McDonald
Year	Team		No	Yds	Avg	Lg	TD
1946	BKN	AA	2	31	15.5		0

Walt McDonald *continued*

Year	Team	No	Yds	Avg	Lg	TD
1948		3	21	7.0		0
Career		5	52	10.4		0

Bubba McDowell

Year	Team	No	Yds	Avg	Lg	TD
1989	HOU N	4	65	16.3	21	0
1990		2	11	5.5	11	0
1991		4	31	7.8	23	0
1992		3	52	17.3	26t	1
1993		3	31	10.3	13	0
1995	CAR N	1	33	33.0	33	0
Career		17	223	13.1	33	1
Playoffs		2	59	29.5		1

Ray McElroy

Year	Team	No	Yds	Avg	Lg	TD
Playoffs		2	0	0.0		0

Vann McElroy

Year	Team	No	Yds	Avg	Lg	TD
1982	LARI N	1	0	0.0	0	0
1983		8	68	8.5	28	0
1984		4	42	10.5	31	0
1985		2	23	11.5	23	0
1986		7	105	15.0	28	0
1987		4	41	10.3	35t	1
1988		3	17	5.7	13	0
1989		2	0	0.0	0	0
Career		31	296	9.5	35t	1
Playoffs		1	-6	-6.0		0

Doug McEnulty

Year	Team	No	Yds	Avg	Lg	TD
1943	CHIB N	1	11	11.0	11	0
1944		1	34	34.0	34	0
Career		2	45	22.5	34	0

Bud McFadin

Year	Team	No	Yds	Avg	Lg	TD
1953	LA N	1	0	0.0	0	0

Ben McGee

Year	Team	No	Yds	Avg	Lg	TD
1967	PIT N	1	21	21.0	21t	1

Ed McGee

Year	Team	No	Yds	Avg	Lg	TD
1944	BOS N	1	15	15.0	15	0

John McGeever

Year	Team	No	Yds	Avg	Lg	TD
1962	DEN A	2	63	31.5	48	1
1963		0	18		18L	0
1964		6	60	10.0	19	0
1965		1	36	36.0	36	0
1966	MIA A	2	15	7.5	15	0
Career		11	192	17.5	48	1

Charlie McGibbony

Year	Team	No	Yds	Avg	Lg	TD
1944	BKN N	1	6	6.0	6	0

Lenny McGill

Year	Team	No	Yds	Avg	Lg	TD
1994	GB N	2	16	8.0	16	0

Mike McGill

Year	Team	No	Yds	Avg	Lg	TD
1971	STL N	1	19	19.0	19	0
1972		2	28	14.0	26	0
Career		3	47	15.7	26	0

Ralph McGill

Year	Team	No	Yds	Avg	Lg	TD
1974	SF N	5	71	14.2	45	0
1975		1	27	27.0	27	0
1977		1	30	30.0	30	0
1979	NO N	1	6	6.0	6	0
Career		8	134	16.8	45	0

Willie McGinest

Year	Team	No	Yds	Avg	Lg	TD
1996	NE N	1	46	46.0	46t	1

Chester McGlockton

Year	Team	No	Yds	Avg	Lg	TD
1993	LARI N	1	19	19.0	19	0

Thurman McGraw

Year	Team	No	Yds	Avg	Lg	TD
1950	DET N	1	4	4.0	4	0
1953		1	2	2.0	2	0
Career		2	6	3.0	4	0

Larry McGrew

Year	Team	No	Yds	Avg	Lg	TD
1983	NE N	1	3	3.0	3	0
1985		1	0	0.0	0	0
1986		2	44	22.0	27	0
1988		1	6	6.0	6	0
1989		1	-4	-4.0	-4	0
Career		6	49	8.2	27	0

Lamar McGriggs

Year	Team	No	Yds	Avg	Lg	TD
1993	MIN N	1	63	63.0	63t	1
1994		1	1	1.0	1	0
Career		2	64	32.0	63t	1

Mike McGruder

Year	Team	No	Yds	Avg	Lg	TD
1993	SF N	5	89	17.8	37	1
1994	TB N	1	0	0.0	0	0
Career		6	89	14.8	37	1

Pat McHugh

Year	Team	No	Yds	Avg	Lg	TD
1947	PHI N	3	52	17.3	48	0
1948		2	27	13.5	15	0
1949		6	89	14.8	36	1
1950		4	34	8.5	27	0
1951		1	19	19.0	19	0
Career		16	221	13.8	48	1

Dan McIlhany

Year	Team	No	Yds	Avg	Lg	TD
1965	LA N	2	7	3.5	7	0

Roy McKay

Year	Team	No	Yds	Avg	Lg	TD
1945	GB N	3	33	11.0	18	0
1946		1	20	20.0	20	0
Career		4	53	13.3	20	0

Marlin McKeever

Year	Team	No	Yds	Avg	Lg	TD
1962	LA N	2	1	0.5	1	0
1969	WAS N	1	3	3.0	3	0
1971	LA N	4	38	9.5	15	0
1972		2	8	4.0	8	0
Career		9	50	5.6	15	0

Vito McKeever

Year	Team	No	Yds	Avg	Lg	TD
1986	TB N	3	12	4.0	10	0

Reggie McKenzie

Year	Team	No	Yds	Avg	Lg	TD
1986	LARI N	1	9	9.0	9	0
1988		1	26	26.0	26	0
Career		2	35	17.5	26	0

Mike McKibben

Year	Team	No	Yds	Avg	Lg	TD
1979	NYJ N	1	5	5.0	5	0

Odis McKinney

Year	Team	No	Yds	Avg	Lg	TD
1978	NYG N	1	11	11.0	11	0
1979		1	25	25.0	25	0
1980	OAK N	3	22	7.3	22	0
1981		3	38	12.7	34	0
1983	LARI N	1	0	0.0	0	0
1984		1	0	0.0	0	0
1985		1	22	22.0	22	0
Career		11	118	10.7	34	0

Tim McKyer

Year	Team	No	Yds	Avg	Lg	TD
1986	SF N	6	33	5.5	21t	1
1987		2	0	0.0	0	0
1988		7	11	1.6	7	0
1989		1	18	18.0	18	0
1990	MIA N	4	40	10.0	21	0
1991	ATL N	6	24	4.0	24	0
1992		1	0	0.0	0	0
1993	DET N	2	10	5.0	10	0
1995	CAR N	3	99	33.0	96t	1
Career		32	235	7.3	96t	2
Playoffs		4	89	22.3		0

Ray McLean

Year	Team	No	Yds	Avg	Lg	TD
1940	CHIB N	1	5	5.0	5	0
1941		3	79	26.3	45	0
1942		3	74	24.7	30	0
1943		4	20	5.0	11	0
1944		3	42	14.0	36	0
1945		1	0	0.0	0	0
1946		2	26	13.0	20	0
1947		1	12	12.0	12	0
Career		18	258	14.3	45	0
Playoffs		2	22	11.0		0

Dana McLemore

Year	Team	No	Yds	Avg	Lg	TD
1984	SF N	2	54	27.0	54t	1
1985		1	0	0.0	0	0
1987		2	35	17.5	25	0
Career		5	89	17.8	54t	1

Mike McLeod

Year	Team	No	Yds	Avg	Lg	TD
1984	GB N	1	0	0.0	0	0

Harold McLinton

Year	Team	No	Yds	Avg	Lg	TD
1972	WAS N	2	22	11.0	19	0
1974		1	14	14.0	14t	1
1976		1	8	8.0	8	0
Career		4	44	11.0	19	1

Art McMahon

Year	Team	No	Yds	Avg	Lg	TD
1968	BOS A	2	27	13.5	27	0
1970	BOS N	1	72	72.0	72	0
Career		3	99	33.0	72	0

Steve McMichael

Year	Team	No	Yds	Avg	Lg	TD
1986	CHI N	1	5	5.0	5	0
1993		1	0	0.0	0	0
Career		2	5	2.5	5	0

Eddie McMillan

Year	Team	No	Yds	Avg	Lg	TD
1973	LA N	4	20	5.0	15	0
1975		3	64	21.3	31	0
1976	SEA N	1	0	0.0	0	0
1977		4	157	39.3	57	0
Career		12	241	20.1	57	0

Erik McMillan

Year	Team	No	Yds	Avg	Lg	TD
1988	NYJ N	8	168	21.0	55t	2
1989		6	180	30.0	92t	1
1990		5	92	18.4	25	0
1991		3	168	56.0	83t	2
Career		22	608	27.6	92t	5
Playoffs		1	0	0.0		0

Audrey McMillian

Year	Team	No	Yds	Avg	Lg	TD
1990	MIN N	3	20	6.7	20	0
1991		4	5	1.3	3	0
1992		8	157	19.6	51t	2
1993		4	45	11.3	22t	1
Career		19	227	11.9	51t	3

Mark McMillian

Year	Team	No	Yds	Avg	Lg	TD
1992	PHI N	1	0	0.0	0	0
1993		2	25	12.5	17	0
1994		2	2	1.0	5	0
1995		3	27	9.0	19	0
1996	NO N	2	4	2.0	4	0
Career		10	58	5.8	19	0
Playoffs		2	50	25.0		0

Jim McMillin

Year	Team	No	Yds	Avg	Lg	TD
1961	DEN A	5	56	11.2	26	0
1962		4	117	29.3	48	1
1963	OAK A	4	62	15.5	62	1
1964	DEN A	1	3	3.0	3	0
Career		14	238	17.0	62	2

Frank McNally

Year	Team	No	Yds	Avg	Lg	TD
1933	CHIC N					1

Bob McNamara

Year	Team	No	Yds	Avg	Lg	TD
1960	DEN A	4	63	15.8		0
1961		3	85	28.3	34	0
Career		7	148	21.1	34	0

Don McNeal

Year	Team	No	Yds	Avg	Lg	TD
1980	MIA N	5	17	3.4	15	0
1982		4	42	10.5	23	1
1984		3	41	13.7	30	0
1986		2	46	23.0	29	0
1988		1	23	23.0	23	0
1989		3	-6	-2.0	0	0
Career		18	163	9.1	30	2
Playoffs		2	36	18.0		0

Charlie McNeil

Year	Team	No	Yds	Avg	Lg	TD
1960	LA A	3	47	15.7		0
1961	SD A	9	349	38.8	76	2
1962		1	36	36.0	36	0

Charlie McNeil *continued*

Year	Team		No	Yds	Avg	Lg	TD
1963			4	40	10.0	21	0
1964			2	30	15.0	17	0
Career			19	502	26.4	76	2
Playoffs			2	15	7.5		0

Fred McNeil

Year	Team		No	Yds	Avg	Lg	TD
1975	MIN	N	1	0	0.0	0	0
1977			1	0	0.0	0	0
1978			2	1	0.5	1	0
1981			2	26	13.0	14	0
1984			1	0	0.0	0	0
Career			7	27	3.9	14	0

Ryan McNeil

Year	Team		No	Yds	Avg	Lg	TD
1993	DET	N	2	19	9.5	16	0
1994			1	14	14.0	14	0
1995			2	26	13.0	21	0
1996			5	14	2.8	15	0
Career			10	73	7.3	21	0

Bruce McNorton

Year	Team		No	Yds	Avg	Lg	TD
1983	DET	N	7	30	4.3	15	0
1984			2	0	0.0	0	0
1985			2	14	7.0	10	0
1986			4	10	2.5	10	0
1987			3	20	6.7	20	0
1988			1	4	4.0	4	0
1990			1	33	33.0	33	0
Career			20	111	5.5	33	0

Paul McNulty

Year	Team		No	Yds	Avg	Lg	TD
1925	CHIC	N					1

Hal McPhail

Year	Team		No	Yds	Avg	Lg	TD
1934	BOS	N					1

Miles McPherson

Year	Team		No	Yds	Avg	Lg	TD
1983	SD	N	1	0	0.0	0	0
1985			1	30	30.0	30	0
Career			2	30	15.0	30	0

Bennie McRae

Year	Team		No	Yds	Avg	Lg	TD
1962	CHI	N	1	47	47.0	47	0
1963			6	90	15.0	44	1
1964			2	44	22.0	26	0
1965			4	116	29.0	89t	1
1966			3	53	17.7	53	0
1967			5	94	18.8	34t	2
1968			4	41	10.3	22	0
1969			1	0	0.0	0	0
1970			1	0	0.0	0	0
Career			27	485	18.0	89t	4
Playoffs			1	0	0.0		0

Rod McSwain

Year	Team		No	Yds	Avg	Lg	TD
1985	NE	N	1	0	0.0	0	0
1986			1	3	3.0	3	0
1987			1	17	17.0	17	0
1988			2	51	25.5	42	0
1989			1	18	18.0	18	0
Career			6	89	14.8	42	0
Playoffs			1	2	2.0		0

Tom McWilliams

Year	Team		No	Yds	Avg	Lg	TD
1949	LA	AA	2	35	17.5		0
1950	PIT	N	2	31	15.5	27	0
Career			4	66	16.5	27	0

Jack Mead

Year	Team		No	Yds	Avg	Lg	TD
1946	NYG	N	1	33	33.0	33	0

Jim Meade

Year	Team		No	Yds	Avg	Lg	TD
1940	WAS	N	1	0	0.0	0	0

Eddie Meador

Year	Team		No	Yds	Avg	Lg	TD
1959	LA	N	3	3	1.0	3	0
1960			4	46	11.5	26t	1
1961			1	34	34.0	34	0
1962			1	0	0.0	0	0
1963			6	38	6.3	20	0
1964			3	50	16.7	29	0
1965			2	57	28.5	29	0
1966			5	60	12.0	31	0

Eddie Meador *continued*

Year	Team		No	Yds	Avg	Lg	TD
1967			8	103	12.9	30t	2
1968			6	37	6.2	20	0
1969			5	97	19.4	38t	2
1970			2	22	11.0	12	0
Career			46	547	11.9	38t	5
Playoffs			1	15	15.0		0

Johnny Meads

Year	Team		No	Yds	Avg	Lg	TD
1990	HOU	N	1	32	32.0	32	0

Karl Mecklenburg

Year	Team		No	Yds	Avg	Lg	TD
1984	DEN	N	2	105	52.5	63	0
1987			3	23	7.7	16	0
Career			5	128	25.6	63	0
Playoffs			1	18	18.0		0

Ron Medved

Year	Team		No	Yds	Avg	Lg	TD
1967	PHI	N	2	23	11.5	23	0
1968			1	0	0.0	0	0
Career			3	23	7.7	23	0

Lance Mehl

Year	Team		No	Yds	Avg	Lg	TD
1981	NYJ	N	3	17	5.7	10	0
1982			2	38	19.0	38	0
1983			7	57	8.1	34t	1
1985			3	33	11.0	18	0
Career			15	145	9.7	38	1
Playoffs			2	20	10.0		0

Dale Meinert

Year	Team		No	Yds	Avg	Lg	TD
1960	STL	N	3	17	5.7	17	0
1961			2	68	34.0	41	0
1962			1	12	12.0	12	0
1964			2	24	12.0	18t	1
1967			1	5	5.0	5	0
Career			9	126	14.0	41	1

Darrell Meisenheimer

Year	Team		No	Yds	Avg	Lg	TD
1951	NYY	N	3	26	8.7	26	0

Greg Meisner

Year	Team		No	Yds	Avg	Lg	TD
1988	LARM	N	1	20	20.0	20	0

Jim Melka

Year	Team		No	Yds	Avg	Lg	TD
1987	GB	N	1	0	0.0	0	0

Jim Mello

Year	Team		No	Yds	Avg	Lg	TD
1947	BOS	N	1	0	0.0	0	0
1949	DET	N	3	61	20.3	28	0
Career			4	61	15.3	28	0

Don Menasco

Year	Team		No	Yds	Avg	Lg	TD
1952	NYG	N	4	5	1.3	5	0
1953			1	5	5.0	5	0
Career			5	10	2.0	5	0

John Mendenhall

Year	Team		No	Yds	Avg	Lg	TD
1976	NYG	N	1	3	3.0	3	0

Dudley Meredith

Year	Team		No	Yds	Avg	Lg	TD
1967	BUF	A	1	8	8.0	8	0

Jim Merlo

Year	Team		No	Yds	Avg	Lg	TD
1973	NO	N	3	25	8.3	16	0
1976			4	142	35.5	83t	2
1977			1	57	57.0	57t	1
Career			8	224	28.0	83t	3

Mike Merriweather

Year	Team		No	Yds	Avg	Lg	TD
1983	PIT	N	3	55	18.3	31t	1
1984			2	9	4.5	8	0
1985			2	36	18.0	35t	1
1986			2	14	7.0	11	0
1987			2	26	13.0	15	0
1989	MIN	N	3	29	9.7	15t	1
1990			3	108	36.0	73	0
1991			1	22	22.0	22t	1
Career			18	299	16.6	73	4

Scott Mersereau

Year	Team		No	Yds	Avg	Lg	TD
1989	NYJ	N	1	4	4.0	4	0
1991			2	0	0.0	0	0
Career			3	4	1.3	4	0

Jerry Mertens

Year	Team		No	Yds	Avg	Lg	TD
1959	SF	N	2	56	28.0	30t	1
1960			2	0	0.0	0	0
1962			2	0	0.0	0	0
Career			6	56	9.3	30t	1

Bus Mertes

Year	Team		No	Yds	Avg	Lg	TD
1946	LA	AA	1	14	14.0	14	0
1958	SF	N	2	16	8.0	12	0
Career			3	30	10.0	14	0

Dale Messer

Year	Team		No	Yds	Avg	Lg	TD
1962	SF	N	1	35	35.0	35	0

Max Messner

Year	Team		No	Yds	Avg	Lg	TD
1960	DET	N	1	26	26.0	26	0
1965	PIT	N	1	14	14.0	14	0
Career			2	40	20.0	26	0

Russ Method

Year	Team		No	Yds	Avg	Lg	TD
1926	DUL	N					1

John Meyers

Year	Team		No	Yds	Avg	Lg	TD
1965	PHI	N	2	12	6.0	10	0

Rich Miano

Year	Team		No	Yds	Avg	Lg	TD
1985	NYJ	N	2	9	4.5	6	0
1987			3	24	8.0	21	0
1988			2	0	0.0	0	0
1991	PHI	N	3	30	10.0	18	0
1992			1	39	39.0	39	0
1993			4	26	6.5	16	0
Career			15	128	8.5	39	0

Lou Michaels

Year	Team		No	Yds	Avg	Lg	TD
1958	LA	N	2	6	3.0	6t	1
1961	PIT	N	1	30	30.0	30	0
1963			1	0	0.0	0	0
Career			4	36	9.0	30	1

Walt Michaels

Year	Team		No	Yds	Avg	Lg	TD
1952	CLE	N	4	26	6.5	18	0
1953			1	34	34.0	34t	1
1954			1	20	20.0	20	0
1955			1	25	25.0	25t	1
1957			1	10	10.0	10	0
1959			1	7	7.0	7	0
1961			2	17	8.5	15	0
Career			11	139	12.6	34t	2
Playoffs			2	22	11.0		0

Mike Michalske

Year	Team		No	Yds	Avg	Lg	TD
1931	GB	N					1

Mike Micka

Year	Team		No	Yds	Avg	Lg	TD
1944	WAS	N	1	5	5.0	5	0
1945	BOS	N	1	0	0.0	0	0
1946			2	40	20.0	40t	0
1947			2	46	23.0	46	0
1948			3	9	3.0	5	0
Career			9	100	11.1	46	1

Rick Middleton

Year	Team		No	Yds	Avg	Lg	TD
1975	NO	N	1	0	0.0	0	0
1978	SD	N	1	2	2.0	2	0
Career			2	2	1.0	2	0

Jack Mildren

Year	Team		No	Yds	Avg	Lg	TD
1974	NE	N	3	51	17.0	41	0

Jack Milks

Year	Team		No	Yds	Avg	Lg	TD
1966	SD	A	1	13	13.0	13	0

Keith Millard

Year	Team		No	Yds	Avg	Lg	TD
1986	MIN	N	1	17	17.0	17	0
1989			1	48	48.0	48	0
Career			2	65	32.5	48	0

Matt Millen

Year	Team		No	Yds	Avg	Lg	TD
1980	OAK	N	2	17	8.5	9	0
1982	LARI	N	3	77	25.7	60	0
1983			1	14	14.0	14	0
1987			1	6	6.0	6	0
1989	SF	N	1	10	10.0	10	0

Year	Team		No	Yds	Avg	Lg	TD

Matt Millen *continued*

Year	Team		No	Yds	Avg	Lg	TD
1990			1	8	8.0	8	0
Career			9	132	14.7	60	0
Playoffs			1	13	13.0		0

Bob Miller

Year	Team		No	Yds	Avg	Lg	TD
1953	DET	N	1	0	0.0	0	0

Clark Miller

1967	SF	N	1	3	3.0	3	0

Corey Miller

1992	NYG	N	2	10	5.0	10	0
1993			2	18	9.0	11	0
1994			2	6	3.0	6	0
Career			6	34	5.7	11	0

Darrin Miller

1988	SEA	N	1	7	7.0	7	0

Eddie Miller

Playoffs			1	27	27.0		0

Paul Miller

1954	LA	N	1	0	0.0	0	0

Shawn Miller

1989	LARM	N	1	3	3.0	3	0

Tom Miller

1943	P-P	N	1	0	0.0	0	0
1944	PHI	N	1	35	35.0	35t	1
Career			2	35	17.5	35t	1

Lawyer Milloy

1996	NE	N	2	14	7.0	14	0
Playoffs			1	0	0.0		

Sam Mills

1991	NO	N	2	13	6.5	8	0
1992			1	10	10.0	10	0
1994			1	10	10.0	10	0
1995	CAR	N	5	58	11.6	36t	1
1996			1	10	10.0	10	0
Career			10	101	10.1	36t	1
Playoffs			2	34	17.0		0

Stan Mills

1924	AKR	N					1

Charles Milner

1947	CHIB	N	1	7	7.0	7	0

Rich Milot

1980	WAS	N	4	-8	-2.0	2	0
1983			2	20	10.0	20	0
1984			3	42	14.0	27	0
1985			2	33	16.5	22	0
1986			2	33	16.5	31	0
Career			13	120	9.2	31	0

Charley Milstead

1961	HOU	A	2	25	12.5	22	0

Charles Mincy

1992	KC	N	4	128	32.0	39	2
1993			5	44	8.8	20	0
1994			3	49	16.3	31	0
1995	MIN	N	3	37	12.3	20	0
1996	TB	N	1	26	26.0	26	0
Career			16	284	17.8	39	2
Playoffs			1	12	12.0		0

Kevin Miniefield

1995	CHI	N	3	37	12.3	37	0

Frank Minini

1947	CHIB	N	1	3	3.0	3	0

Tony Minisi

1948	NYG	N	2	10	5.0	10	0

Frank Minnifield

Year	Team		No	Yds	Avg	Lg	TD
1984	CLE	N	1	26	26.0	26	0
1985			1	3	3.0	3	0
1986			3	20	6.7	20	0
1987			4	24	6.0	27	0
1988			4	16	4.0	13	0
1989			3	29	9.7	25	0
1990			2	0	0.0	0	0
1992			2	6	3.0	5	0
Career			20	124	6.2	27	0
Playoffs			1	48	48.0		1

Vic Minor

1980	SEA	N	1	0	0.0	0	0

Barry Minter

1995	CHI	N	1	2	2.0	2t	1
1996			1	5	5.0	5	0
Career			2	7	3.5	5	1
Playoffs			1	7	7.0		0

Ed Mioduszewski

1953	BAL	N	1	0	0.0	0	0

Aaron Mitchell

1979	DAL	N	1	36	36.0	36	0
1980			3	56	18.7	56	0
Career			4	92	23.0	56	0
Playoffs			2	12	6.0		0

Bob Mitchell

1946	LA	AA	1	32	32.0	32	0
1947			2	24	12.0		0
1948			3	1	0.3		0
Career			6	57	9.5	32	0

Brian Mitchell

1992	ATL	N	1	0	0.0	0	0

Charlie Mitchell

1946	GB	N	1	18	18.0	18	0

Charlie Mitchell

1963	DEN	A	1	0	0.0	0	0

Devon Mitchell

1986	DET	N	5	41	8.2	17	0
1988			3	107	35.7	90t	1
Career			8	148	18.5	90t	1

Fondren Mitchell

1946	MIA	AA	1	2	2.0	2	0

Jim Mitchell

1972	DET	N	1	0	0.0	0	0

Leroy Mitchell

1967	BOS	A	3	9	3.0	9	0
1968			7	41	5.9	20	0
1970	HOU	N	2	35	17.5	35	0
1971	DEN	N	2	0	0.0	0	0
1972			3	27	9.0	27	0
1973			2	43	21.5	40t	1
Career			19	155	8.2	40t	1

Mike Mitchell

1987	WAS	N	1	17	17.0	17	0

Roland Mitchell

1988	PHX	N	1	0	0.0	0	0
1990	ATL	N	2	16	8.0	16	0
1992	GB	N	2	40	20.0	35	0
1993			1	0	0.0	0	0
Career			6	56	9.3	35	0

Willie Mitchell

1964	KC	A	1	0	0.0	0	0
1965			2	44	22.0	37	1
1966			3	97	32.3	60	1
1967			4	88	22.0	55	0
1968			5	46	9.2	46	0
1969			1	27	27.0	27	0
Career			16	302	18.9	60	3
Playoffs			1	0			0

Bob Mitinger

Year	Team		No	Yds	Avg	Lg	TD
1963	SD	A	3	26	8.7	18	0
Playoffs			1	5	5.0		0

Alonzo Mitz

1991	CIN	N	1	8	8.0	8	0
1992			1	3	3.0	3	0
Career			2	11	5.5	8	0

Billy Mixon

1954	SF	N	2	6	3.0	3	0

John Mobley

1996	DEN	N	1	8	8.0	8	0

Rudy Mobley

1947	BAL	AA	2	8	4.0		0

Dicky Moegle

1955	SF		6	50	8.3	37	0
1956			6	75	12.5	31t	1
1957			8	107	13.4	40	0
1960	PIT	N	6	49	8.2	31	0
1961	DAL	N	2	31	15.5	25	0
Career			28	312	11.1	40	1
Playoffs			1	17	17.0		0

Alex Molden

1996	NO	N	2	2	1.0	2	0

Frank Molden

1965	LA	N	1	59	59.0	59	0

Bo Molenda

1935	NYG	N					1
Playoffs			1	10	10.0		0

Tommy Mont

1947	WAS	N	1	7	7.0	7	0
1948			2	21	10.5	19	0
Career			3	28	9.3	19	0

Alton Montgomery

1990	DEN	N	2	43	21.5	24	0
1995	ATL	N	1	71	71.0	71t	1
Career			3	114	38.0	71t	1

Randy Montgomery

1972	DEN	N	1	20	20.0	20	0
1974	CHI	N	2	56	28.0	33	0
Career			3	76	25.3	33	0

Sankar Montoute

1987	TB	N	1	0	0.0	0	0

Keith Moody

1976	BUF	N	3	63	21.0	44	0

Tipp Mooney

1944	CHIB	N	1	35	35.0	35	0

Derland Moore

1973	NO	N	1	0	0.0	0	0

Henry Moore

1957	BAL	N	1	0	0.0	0	0

Jerry Moore

1972	CHI	N	1	5	5.0	5	0
1974	NO	N	1	0	0.0	0	0
Career			2	5	2.5	5	0

Leroy Moore

1962	BUF	A	1	3	3.0	3t	0
1964	DEN	A	1	70	70.0	70	0
Career			2	73	36.5	70	1

McNeil Moore

1954	CHIB	N	3	76	25.3	50	0
1956			3	30	10.0	22	0
1957			2	28	14.0	20	0
Career			8	134	16.8	50	0

Robert Moore

Year	Team		No	Yds	Avg	Lg	TD
1986	ATL	N	1	0	0.0	0	0
1987			2	23	11.5	18	0
1988			5	56	11.2	47t	1
Career			8	79	9.9	47t	1

Stevon Moore

Year	Team		No	Yds	Avg	Lg	TD
1995	CLE	N	5	55	11.0	28	0
1996	BAL	N	1	10	10.0	10	0
Career			6	65	10.8	28	0

Wilbur Moore

Year	Team		No	Yds	Avg	Lg	TD
1940	WAS	N	1	0	0.0	0	0
1942			3	23	7.7	15	0
1943			2	46	23.0	44	0
1944			5	53	10.6	35	0
1946			2	45	22.5	42	0
Career			13	167	12.8	44	0
Playoffs			1	14	14.0		0

Zeke Moore

Year	Team		No	Yds	Avg	Lg	TD
1969	HOU	A	4	71	17.8	51t	1
1970	HOU	N	6	85	14.2	32	0
1971			3	29	9.7	26	0
1974			2	38	19.0	22t	1
1975			5	137	27.4	74	0
1976			1	28	28.0	28	0
1977			3	56	18.7	34	0
Career			24	444	18.5	74	2
Playoffs			1	0	0.0		0

Gonzalo Morales

Year	Team		No	Yds	Avg	Lg	TD
1947	PIT	N	1	5	5.0	5	0
1948			1	11	11.0	11	0
Career			2	16	8.0	11	0

John Morelli

Year	Team		No	Yds	Avg	Lg	TD
1945	BOS	N	1	10	10.0	10	0

Melvin Morgan

Year	Team		No	Yds	Avg	Lg	TD
1977	CIN	N	1	0	0.0	0	0
1978			1	64	64.0	64	0
1979	SF	N	1	0	0.0	0	0
Career			3	64	21.3	64	0

Mike Morgan

Year	Team		No	Yds	Avg	Lg	TD
1965	PHI	N	1	1	1.0	1	0
1966			1	5	5.0	5	0
1967			1	0	0.0	0	0
1968	WAS	N	2	23	11.5	14	0
1970	NO	N	1	7	7.0	7	0
Career			6	36	6.0	14	0

Bobby Morris

Year	Team		No	Yds	Avg	Lg	TD
1947	NYG	N	1	0	0.0	0	0

Dennit Morris

Year	Team		No	Yds	Avg	Lg	TD
1960	HOU	A	4	32	8.0	26	0
1961			1	31	31.0	31	0
Career			5	63	12.6	31	0

George Morris

Year	Team		No	Yds	Avg	Lg	TD
1942	CLE	N	2	7	3.5	4	0

Jack Morris

Year	Team		No	Yds	Avg	Lg	TD
1958	LA	N	6	152	25.3	44t	1
1961	MIN	N	2	90	45.0	65	0
Career			8	242	30.3	65	1

Jim Bob Morris

Year	Team		No	Yds	Avg	Lg	TD
1987	GB	N	3	135	45.0	73	0

Larry Morris

Year	Team		No	Yds	Avg	Lg	TD
1957	LA	N	1	0	0.0	0	0
1959	CHIB	N	1	14	14.0	14	0
1960	CHI	N	1	5	5.0	5	0
1961			1	25	25.0	25	0
1962			2	9	4.5	9	0
Career			6	53	8.8	25	0
Playoffs			2	83	41.5		0

Reilly Morris

Year	Team		No	Yds	Avg	Lg	TD
1961	OAK	A	3	79	26.3	35	1

Darryl Morrison

Year	Team		No	Yds	Avg	Lg	TD
1996	WAS	N	1	4	4.0	4	0

Joe Morrison

Year	Team		No	Yds	Avg	Lg	TD
1961	NYG	N	2	30	15.0	18	0

Steve Morrison

Year	Team		No	Yds	Avg	Lg	TD
1996	IND	N	1	20	20.0	20	0

Jim Morrissey

Year	Team		No	Yds	Avg	Lg	TD
1988	CHI	N	3	13	4.3	13	0
1989			2	0	0.0	0	0
1990			2	12	6.0	12	0
1991			1	5	5.0	5	0
1992			1	22	22.0	22	0
Career			9	52	5.8	22	0
Playoffs			1	47	47.0		

Bob Morrow

Year	Team		No	Yds	Avg	Lg	TD
1941	CHIC	N	1	0	0.0	0	0
1943			2	49	24.5	44	0
Career			3	49	16.3	44	0

Jim Morrow

Year	Team		No	Yds	Avg	Lg	TD
1921	CAN	A					1

Tommy Morrow

Year	Team		No	Yds	Avg	Lg	TD
1962	OAK	A	10	141	14.1	36	0
1963			9	104	11.6	35	0
1964			4	101	25.3	77	0
Career			23	346	15.0	77	0

Jack Morton

Year	Team		No	Yds	Avg	Lg	TD
1946	LA	AA	1	11	11.0	11	0

John Morton

Year	Team		No	Yds	Avg	Lg	TD
1953	SF	N	2	16	8.0	9	0

Mike Morton

Year	Team		No	Yds	Avg	Lg	TD
1996	OAK	N	2	13	6.5	13	0

Dom Moselle

Year	Team		No	Yds	Avg	Lg	TD
1951	GB	N	1	0	0.0	0	0
1952			3	2	0.7	2	0
Career			4	2	0.5	2	0

Russ Mosley

Year	Team		No	Yds	Avg	Lg	TD
1945	GB	N	1	20	20.0	20	0
1946			1	20	20.0	20	0
Career			2	40	20.0	20	0

Gary Moss

Year	Team		No	Yds	Avg	Lg	TD
1987	ATL	N	1	18	18.0	18	0

Winston Moss

Year	Team		No	Yds	Avg	Lg	TD
1990	TB	N	1	31	31.0	31	0
1995	SEA	N	1	0	0.0	0	0
1996			1	1	1.0	1	0
Career			3	32	10.7	31	0

Rich Mostardi

Year	Team		No	Yds	Avg	Lg	TD
1961	MIN	N	2	22	11.0	21	0

Kelley Mote

Year	Team		No	Yds	Avg	Lg	TD
1947	DET	N	1	0	0.0	0	0
1950	NYG	N	1	10	10.0	10	0
Career			2	10	5.0	10	0

Marion Motley

Year	Team		No	Yds	Avg	Lg	TD
1946	CLE	AA	1	0	0.0	0	0
1947			1	48	48.0	48t	1
Career			2	48	24.0	48t	1

Alex Moyer

Year	Team		No	Yds	Avg	Lg	TD
1985	MIA	N	1	4	4.0	4	0

Paul Moyer

Year	Team		No	Yds	Avg	Lg	TD
1983	SEA	N	1	19	19.0	19t	1
1986			3	38	12.7	20	0
1987			1	0	0.0	0	0
1988			6	79	13.2	34	0
Career			11	136	12.4	34	1

Jerry Muckensturm

Year	Team		No	Yds	Avg	Lg	TD
1979	CHI	N	1	5	5.0	5	0
1980			2	2	1.0	2	0
Career			3	7	2.3	5	0

Joe Muha

Year	Team		No	Yds	Avg	Lg	TD
1946	PHI	N	1	8	8.0	8	0
1949			2	31	15.5	28t	1
1950			2	40	20.0	21	1
Career			5	79	15.8	28t	2

Mark Mullaney

Year	Team		No	Yds	Avg	Lg	TD
1985	MIN	N	1	15	15.0	15	0

Davlin Mullen

Year	Team		No	Yds	Avg	Lg	TD
1984	NYJ	N	1	25	25.0	25	0
1985			3	14	4.7	14	0
Career			4	39	9.8	25	0

Noah Mullins

Year	Team		No	Yds	Avg	Lg	TD
1946	CHIB	N	3	96	32.0	64	0
1947			6	113	18.8	51	0
1948			7	99	14.1	33t	1
1949	NYG	N	3	26	8.7	19	0
Career			19	334	17.6	64	1

Nick Mumley

Year	Team		No	Yds	Avg	Lg	TD
1960	NY	A	1	26	26.0	26	0

Lloyd Mumphord

Year	Team		No	Yds	Avg	Lg	TD
1969	MIA	A	5	102	20.4	51	0
1970	MIA	N	5	35	7.0	32t	0
1972			4	50	12.5	28t	1
1975	BAL	N	4	58	14.5	28	0
1976			1	22	22.0	22	0
1978			2	20	10.0	19	0
Career			21	287	13.7	51	2
Playoffs			2	67	33.5		

Fred Mundee

Year	Team		No	Yds	Avg	Lg	TD
1943	CHIB	N	1	8	8.0	8	0
1944			1	0	0.0	0	0
Career			2	8	4.0	8	0

Marc Munford

Year	Team		No	Yds	Avg	Lg	TD
1989	DEN	N	2	16	8.0	10	0

Lyle Munn

Year	Team		No	Yds	Avg	Lg	TD
1926	KC	N					1

Nelson Munsey

Year	Team		No	Yds	Avg	Lg	TD
1975	BAL	N	3	36	12.0	30t	1
1976			1	10	10.0	10	0
1977			3	25	8.3	14	0
Career			7	71	10.1	30t	1

Kevin Murphy

Year	Team		No	Yds	Avg	Lg	TD
1988	TB	N	1	35	35.0	35t	1

Mark Murphy

Year	Team		No	Yds	Avg	Lg	TD
1979	WAS	N	3	29	9.7	16	0
1980			6	58	9.7	28	0
1981			7	68	9.7	29	0
1982			2	0	0.0	0	0
1983			9	127	14.1	48	0
Career			27	282	10.4	48	0
Playoffs			1	0	0.0		0

Mark Murphy

Year	Team		No	Yds	Avg	Lg	TD
1981	GB	N	3	57	19.0	50	0
1984			1	4	4.0	4	0
1985			2	50	25.0	50t	0
1988			5	19	3.8	9	0
1989			3	31	10.3	20	0
1990			3	6	2.0	4	0
1991			3	27	9.0	16	0
Career			20	194	9.7	50t	1
Playoffs			1	22	22.0		0

Neal Musser

Year	Team		No	Yds	Avg	Lg	TD
1981	ATL	N	1	0	0.0	0	0

Najee Mustafaa

Year	Team		No	Yds	Avg	Lg	TD
1988	MIN	N	3	63	21.0	36	0

Najee Mustafaa continued

Year	Team	No	Yds	Avg	Lg	TD
1989		2	7	3.5	7	0
1990		2	21	10.5	16	0
1991		3	104	34.7	97t	1
1993	CLE N	1	97	97.0	97t	1
Career		11	292	26.5	97t	2
Playoffs		2	45	22.5		1

Chet Mutryn

Year	Team	No	Yds	Avg	Lg	TD
1947	BUF AA	1	11	11.0	11	0

Greg Myers

Year	Team	No	Yds	Avg	Lg	TD
1996	CIN N	2	10	5.0	10	0

Jack Myers

Year	Team	No	Yds	Avg	Lg	TD
1948	PHI N	2	9	4.5	8	0

Tommy Myers

Year	Team	No	Yds	Avg	Lg	TD
1972	NO N	3	0	0.0	0	0
1973		3	33	11.0	20	0
1974		3	43	14.3	21	0
1975		5	83	16.6	29	0
1976		1	0	0.0	0	0
1977		1	2	2.0	2	0
1978		6	167	27.8	97t	1
1979		7	127	18.1	52t	1
1980		5	96	19.2	48	0
1981		2	70	35.0	54	0
Career		36	621	17.3	97t	2

Godfrey Myles

Year	Team	No	Yds	Avg	Lg	TD
1992	DAL N	1	13	13.0	13	0
1995		1	15	15.0	15	0
Career		2	28	14.0	15	0

Chip Myrtle

Year	Team	No	Yds	Avg	Lg	TD
1967	DEN A	1	1	1.0	1	0
1971	DEN N	3	64	21.3	30	0
Career		4	65	16.3	30	0

Roland Nabors

Year	Team	No	Yds	Avg	Lg	TD
1948	NY AA	1	10	10.0	10	0

Ross Nagel

Year	Team	No	Yds	Avg	Lg	TD
1951	NYY N	1	27	27.0	27	0

Rob Nairne

Year	Team	No	Yds	Avg	Lg	TD
1980	DEN N	1	2	2.0	2	0
1981	NO N	1	18	18.0	18	0
1982		1	1	1.0	1	0
Career		3	21	7.0	18	0

Joe Nash

Year	Team	No	Yds	Avg	Lg	TD
1993	SEA N	1	13	13.0	13t	1

Fred Naumetz

Year	Team	No	Yds	Avg	Lg	TD
1946	LA N	1	1	1.0	1	0
1947		1	9	9.0	9	0
1948		4	75	18.8	68	0
1950		1	13	13.0	13	0
Career		7	98	14.0	68	0
Playoffs		1	11	11.0		0

Paul Naumoff

Year	Team	No	Yds	Avg	Lg	TD
1968	DET N	1	3	3.0	3	0
1972		1	4	4.0	4	0
1974		1	8	8.0	8	0
1975		2	11	5.5	9	0
1978		1	12	12.0	12	0
Career		6	38	6.3	12	0

Bobby Neff

Year	Team	No	Yds	Avg	Lg	TD
1966	MIA A	1	22	22.0	22	0
1967		1	32	32.0	17	0
Career		2	54	27.0	22	0

Fred Negus

Year	Team	No	Yds	Avg	Lg	TD
1948	CHI AA	5	30	6.0		0
1949		2	28	14.0		0
Career		7	58	8.3		0

Steve Neils

Year	Team	No	Yds	Avg	Lg	TD
1978	STL N	1	18	18.0	18	0

Mike Nelms

Year	Team	No	Yds	Avg	Lg	TD
1981	WAS N	1	3	3.0	3	0

Al Nelson

Year	Team	No	Yds	Avg	Lg	TD
1965	PHI N	2	23	11.5	16	0
1966		1	0	0.0	0	0
1968		3	7	2.3	7	0
1969		3	10	3.3	10	0
1970		2	45	22.5	45	0
1971		2	63	31.5	44	1
Career		13	148	11.4	45	1

Andy Nelson

Year	Team	No	Yds	Avg	Lg	TD
1957	BAL N	5	29	5.8	13	0
1958		8	**199**	24.9	69	1
1959		6	33	5.5	33t	1
1960		6	47	7.8	22	0
1962		4	20	5.0	10	0
1963		3	37	12.3	26t	1
1964	NYG N	1	13	13.0	13	0
Career		33	378	11.5	69	3
Playoffs		1	17	17.0		0

Benny Nelson

Year	Team	No	Yds	Avg	Lg	TD
1964	HOU A	1	45	45.0	45t	1

Bob Nelson

Year	Team	No	Yds	Avg	Lg	TD
1941	DET N	1	41	41.0	41	0
1945		1	0	0.0	0	0
1946	LA AA	1	5	5.0	5	0
1947		2	52	26.0		1
1948		1	0	0.0	0	0
Career		6	98	16.3	41	1

Bob Nelson

Year	Team	No	Yds	Avg	Lg	TD
1980	OAK N	1	0	0.0	0	0

Frank Nelson

Year	Team	No	Yds	Avg	Lg	TD
1948	BOS N	1	28	28.0	28	0
1949	NYB N	1	10	10.0	10	0
Career		2	38	19.0	28	0

Jimmy Nelson

Year	Team	No	Yds	Avg	Lg	TD
1946	MIA AA	2	8	4.0		0

Lee Nelson

Year	Team	No	Yds	Avg	Lg	TD
1977	STL N	4	37	9.3	26	0
1978		1	-3	-3.0	-3	0
1982		1	7	7.0	7	0
1983		1	8	8.0	8	0
Career		7	49	7.0	26	0

Shane Nelson

Year	Team	No	Yds	Avg	Lg	TD
1978	BUF N	3	69	23.0	40	0
1979		1	13	13.0	13	0
1981		1	9	9.0	9	0
Career		5	91	18.2	40	0

Steve Nelson

Year	Team	No	Yds	Avg	Lg	TD
1975	NE N	2	8	4.0	4	0
1976		2	32	16.0	34	0
1978		5	104	20.8	37	0
1979		1	18	18.0	18	0
1980		3	37	12.3	33	0
1983		1	6	6.0	6	0
1984		1	0	0.0	0	0
1986		2	21	10.5	17	0
Career		17	226	13.3	37	0

Dick Nesbitt

Year	Team	No	Yds	Avg	Lg	TD
1931	CHIB N					1

Al Nesser

Year	Team	No	Yds	Avg	Lg	TD
1923	AKR N					1

Doug Nettles

Year	Team	No	Yds	Avg	Lg	TD
1974	BAL N	1	0	0.0	0	0
1977		1	30	30.0	30	0
1978		1	0	0.0	0	0
1979		2	30	15.0	30	0
Career		5	60	12.0	30	0

Jim Nettles

Year	Team	No	Yds	Avg	Lg	TD
1965	PHI N	3	84	28.0	56t	1

Jim Nettles continued

Year	Team	No	Yds	Avg	Lg	TD
1966		3	57	19.0	34t	1
1967		4	52	13.0	34	0
1969	LA N	2	37	18.5	25	0
1970		3	54	18.0	32	0
1971		5	97	19.4	44	1
1972		6	168	28.0	43	0
Career		26	549	21.1	56t	3

Elijah Nevett

Year	Team	No	Yds	Avg	Lg	TD
1969	NO N	3	20	6.7	20	0
1970		3	49	16.3	47	0
Career		6	69	11.5	47	0

Anthony Newman

Year	Team	No	Yds	Avg	Lg	TD
1988	LARM N	2	27	13.5	27	0
1990		2	0	0.0	0	0
1991		1	58	58.0	58	0
1992		4	33	8.3	17	0
1994		2	46	23.0	24	1
1996	NO N	3	40	13.3	21	0
Career		14	204	14.6	58	1

Tony Newsom

Year	Team	No	Yds	Avg	Lg	TD
1987	HOU N	1	-3	-3.0	-3	0

Billy Newsome

Year	Team	No	Yds	Avg	Lg	TD
1971	BAL N	2	19	9.5	19t	1
1973	NO N	1	1	1.0	1	0
Career		3	20	6.7	19t	1

Craig Newsome

Year	Team	No	Yds	Avg	Lg	TD
1995	GB N	1	3	3.0	3	0
1996		2	22	11.0	20	0
Career		3	25	8.3	20	0
Playoffs		4	40	10.0		0

Vince Newsome

Year	Team	No	Yds	Avg	Lg	TD
1984	LARM N	1	31	31.0	31	0
1985		3	20	6.7	20	0
1986		3	45	15.0	34	0
1988		0	3		3L	0
1989		1	81	81.0	81t	1
1990		4	47	11.8	22	0
1991	CLE N	1	31	31.0	31	0
1992		3	55	18.3	29	0
Career		16	313	19.6	81t	1

Tim Newton

Year	Team	No	Yds	Avg	Lg	TD
1985	MIN N	2	63	31.5	63	0

Ham Nichols

Year	Team	No	Yds	Avg	Lg	TD
1947	CHIC N	1	41	41.0	41	0

Mark Nichols

Year	Team	No	Yds	Avg	Lg	TD
1978	SF N	1	0	0.0	0	0

Hardy Nickerson

Year	Team	No	Yds	Avg	Lg	TD
1988	PIT N	1	0	0.0	0	0
1993	TB N	1	6	6.0	6	0
1994		2	9	4.5	10	0
1996		2	24	12.0	17	0
Career		6	39	6.5	17	0

George Nicksich

Year	Team	No	Yds	Avg	Lg	TD
1950	PIT N	3	31	10.3	18	0

Rob Niehoff

Year	Team	No	Yds	Avg	Lg	TD
1987	CIN N	1	19	19.0	19	0

Ray Nitschke

Year	Team	No	Yds	Avg	Lg	TD
1958	GB N	1	2	2.0	2	0
1960		3	90	30.0	43t	1
1961		2	41	20.5	14	0
1962		4	56	14.0	28	0
1963		2	8	4.0	5	0
1964		2	36	18.0	29	0
1965		1	21	21.0	21	0
1966		2	44	22.0	22	0
1967		3	35	11.7	20t	1
1968		2	20	10.0	11	0
1969		2	32	16.0	20	0

Ray Nitschke *continued*

Year	Team		No	Yds	Avg	Lg	TD
1971			1	0	0.0	0	0
Career			25	385	15.4	43t	2
Playoffs			1	9	9.0		0

Doyle Nix

Year	Team		No	Yds	Avg	Lg	TD
1955	GB	N	5	33	6.6	12	0
1958	WAS	N	3	5	1.7	5	0
1959			1	19	19.0	19	0
1960	LA	A	4	30	7.5		1
1961	DAL	A	3	58	19.3	25	0
Career			16	145	9.1	25	1

Emery Nix

Year	Team		No	Yds	Avg	Lg	TD
1943	NYG	N	2	13	6.5	13	0

Jeff Nixon

Year	Team		No	Yds	Avg	Lg	TD
1979	BUF	N	6	81	13.5	43	0
1980			5	81	16.2	50t	1
Career			11	162	14.7	50t	1

Tory Nixon

Year	Team		No	Yds	Avg	Lg	TD
1986	SF	N	2	106	53.0	88t	1
1987			1	5	5.0	5	0
Career			3	111	37.0	88t	1

Leo Nobile

Year	Team		No	Yds	Avg	Lg	TD
1949	PIT	N	1	7	7.0	7	0

Tommy Nobis

Year	Team		No	Yds	Avg	Lg	TD
1967	ATL	N	3	57	19.0	41t	1
1968			1	0	0.0	0	0
1969			1	0	0.0	0	0
1970			2	36	18.0	19	0
1972			3	74	24.7	37	1
1974			1	10	10.0	10	0
1976			1	5	5.0	5	0
Career			12	182	15.2	41t	2

Brian Noble

Year	Team		No	Yds	Avg	Lg	TD
1987	GB	N	1	10	10.0	10	0
1989			2	10	5.0	10	0
Career			3	20	6.7	10	0

John Nocera

Year	Team		No	Yds	Avg	Lg	TD
1961	PHI	N	0	3		3L	0
1962			1	0	0.0	0	0
Career			1	3	3.0	3L	0

Al Noga

Year	Team		No	Yds	Avg	Lg	TD
1990	MIN	N	1	26	26.0	26t	1

Niko Noga

Year	Team		No	Yds	Avg	Lg	TD
1989	DET	N	1	0	0.0	0	0

Pete Noga

Year	Team		No	Yds	Avg	Lg	TD
1987	STL	N	1	60	60.0	60t	1

Dick Nolan

Year	Team		No	Yds	Avg	Lg	TD
1954	NYG	N	6	48	8.0	17	0
1955			1	20	20.0	20	0
1956			2	17	8.5	17	0
1957			1	12	12.0	12	0
1958	CHIC	N	5	30	6.0	13	0
1959	NYG	N	5	57	11.4	34	0
1960			3	32	10.7	20	0
Career			23	216	9.4	34	0

Don Nolander

Year	Team		No	Yds	Avg	Lg	TD
1946	LA	AA	1	13	13.0	13	0

Chuck Noll

Year	Team		No	Yds	Avg	Lg	TD
1955	CLE	N	5	74	14.8	24	1
1956			1	13	13.0	13	0
1959			2	5	2.5	5	0
Career			8	92	11.5	24	1

Ray Nolting

Year	Team		No	Yds	Avg	Lg	TD
1939	CHIB	N					1
1940			3	18	6.0		0
1943			1	5	5.0	5	0
Career			4	23	5.8	5	1
Playoffs			2	10	5.0		0

Danny Noonan

Year	Team		No	Yds	Avg	Lg	TD
1988	DAL	N	1	17	17.0	17t	1

Hank Norberg

Year	Team		No	Yds	Avg	Lg	TD
1946	SF	AA	1	22	22.0	22	0

Keith Nord

Year	Team		No	Yds	Avg	Lg	TD
1983	MIN	N	1	0	0.0	0	0

Joe Norman

Year	Team		No	Yds	Avg	Lg	TD
1980	SEA	N	1	0	0.0	0	0

Jon Norris

Year	Team		No	Yds	Avg	Lg	TD
1987	CHI	N	1	6	6.0	6	0

John North

Year	Team		No	Yds	Avg	Lg	TD
1948	BAL	AA	1	25	25.0	25	0

Jerry Norton

Year	Team		No	Yds	Avg	Lg	TD
1954	PHI	N	5	110	22.0	69t	1
1955			1	0	0.0	0	0
1956			2	34	17.0	23	0
1957			4	155	38.8	99t	1
1958			1	0	0.0	0	0
1959	CHIC	N	3	35	11.7	30	0
1960	STL	N	**10**	96	9.6	26	0
1961			7	136	19.4	47t	2
1962	DAL	N	2	21	10.5	21	0
Career			35	587	16.8	99t	4

Jim Norton

Year	Team		No	Yds	Avg	Lg	TD
1960	HOU	A	1	0	0.0	0	0
1961			9	150	16.7	36	0
1962			8	75	9.4	36	0
1963			6	86	14.3	37	0
1964			2	31	15.5	31	0
1965			7	52	7.4	18	0
1966			4	125	31.3	56	0
1967			6	73	12.2	26	1
1968			2	0	0.0	0	0
Career			45	592	13.2	56	1

Jim Norton

Year	Team		No	Yds	Avg	Lg	TD
1967	ATL	N	1	0	0.0	0	0

Ken Norton

Year	Team		No	Yds	Avg	Lg	TD
1993	DAL	N	1	25	25.0	25	0
1994	SF	N	1	0	0.0	0	0
1995			3	102	34.0	46	2
Career			5	127	25.4	46	2
Playoffs			1	14	14.0		0

Marty Norton

Year	Team		No	Yds	Avg	Lg	TD
1925	GB	N					1

Bob Nowaskey

Year	Team		No	Yds	Avg	Lg	TD
1946	LA	AA	1	35	35.0	35t	1
1947			2	15	7.5		0
1949	BAL	AA	1	9	9.0	9	0
Career			4	59	14.8	35t	1

Tom Nowatzke

Year	Team		No	Yds	Avg	Lg	TD
1971	BAL	N	1	29	29.0	29	0

Phil Nugent

Year	Team		No	Yds	Avg	Lg	TD
1961	DEN	A	7	77	11.0	30	0

Frank Nunley

Year	Team		No	Yds	Avg	Lg	TD
1967	SF	N	1	7	7.0	7	0
1969			1	7	7.0	7	0
1970			3	42	14.0	24	0
1971			1	7	7.0	7	0
1972			1	12	12.0	12	0
1973			1	13	13.0	13	0
1974			4	30	7.5	20	0
1975			1	6	6.0	6	0
1976			1	12	12.0	12	0
Career			14	136	9.7	24	0

Bob Nussbaumer

Year	Team		No	Yds	Avg	Lg	TD
1946	GB	N	3	31	10.3	16	0
1947	WAS	N	1	0	0.0	0	0
1949	CHIC	N	**12**	157	13.1	68	0
Career			16	188	11.8	68	0

Jerry Nuzum

Year	Team		No	Yds	Avg	Lg	TD
1948	PIT	N	1	3	3.0	3	0

Bernie Nygren

Year	Team		No	Yds	Avg	Lg	TD
1946	LA	AA	2	30	15.0		0

Tom Oberg

Year	Team		No	Yds	Avg	Lg	TD
1968	DEN	A	3	17	5.7	16	0

Ed O'Bradovich

Year	Team		No	Yds	Avg	Lg	TD
Playoffs			1	10	10.0		0

Grattan O'Connell

Year	Team		No	Yds	Avg	Lg	TD
1926	HAR	N					1

Cliff Odom

Year	Team		No	Yds	Avg	Lg	TD
1991	MIA	N	1	0	0.0	0	0

Ricky Odom

Year	Team		No	Yds	Avg	Lg	TD
1978	SF	N	2	19	9.5	19	0

Sammy Odom

Year	Team		No	Yds	Avg	Lg	TD
1964	HOU	A	2	22	11.0	22	0

Nate Odomes

Year	Team		No	Yds	Avg	Lg	TD
1988	BUF	N	1	0	0.0	0	0
1989			5	20	4.0	13	0
1990			1	0	0.0	0	0
1991			5	120	24.0	48	1
1992			5	19	3.8	10	0
1993			**9**	65	7.2	25	0
Career			26	224	8.6	48	1
Playoffs			5	62	12.4		0

John Offerdahl

Year	Team		No	Yds	Avg	Lg	TD
1986	MIA	N	1	14	14.0	14	0
1988			2	2	1.0	2	0
1990			1	28	28.0	28	0
Career			4	44	11.0	28	0

Ross O'Hanley

Year	Team		No	Yds	Avg	Lg	TD
1960	BOS	A	3	1	0.3		0
1962			5	83	16.6	28	0
1963			3	79	26.3	61	0
1964			3	120	40.0	47	1
1965			1	5	5.0	5	0
Career			15	288	19.2	61	1
Playoffs			2	13	6.5		0

Doug Oldershaw

Year	Team		No	Yds	Avg	Lg	TD
1940	NYG	N	4	48	12.0		0
1941			1	26	26.0	26t	1
Career			5	74	14.8	26t	1

Chris Oldham

Year	Team		No	Yds	Avg	Lg	TD
1990	DET	N	1	28	28.0	28	0
1993	PHX	N	1	0	0.0	0	0
1995	PIT	N	1	12	12.0	12	0
Career			3	40	13.3	28	0

Ray Oldham

Year	Team		No	Yds	Avg	Lg	TD
1973	BAL	N	2	10	5.0	7	0
1974			1	3	3.0	3	0
1975			2	23	11.5	13	0
1976			2	40	20.0	33	0
1979	NYG	N	2	4	2.0	4	0
1980	DET	N	3	39	13.0	29t	1
1981			1	10	10.0	10	0
1982			1	35	35.0	35t	1
Career			14	164	11.7	35t	2

Chip Oliver

Year	Team		No	Yds	Avg	Lg	TD
1969	OAK	A	1	29	29.0	29t	1

Louis Oliver

Year	Team		No	Yds	Avg	Lg	TD
1989	MIA	N	4	32	8.0	23	0
1990			5	87	17.4	35	0
1991			5	80	16.0	37	0
1992			5	200	40.0	103t	1
1993			2	60	30.0	56t	1
1994	CIN	N	3	36	12.0	19	0
1996	MIA	N	3	110	36.7	60	0
Career			27	605	22.4	103t	2
Playoffs			2	21	10.5		0

Year	Team		No	Yds	Avg	Lg	TD

Muhammad Oliver
| 1994 | MIA | N | 1 | 0 | 0.0 | 0 | 0 |

Neal Olkewicz
1979	WAS	N	1	4	4.0	4	0
1981			2	22	11.0	12	1
1983			1	14	14.0	14	0
1985			1	21	21.0	21	0
1986			1	15	15.0	15	0
Career			6	76	12.7	21	1

Jerry Olsavsky
| 1996 | PIT | N | 1 | 5 | 5.0 | 5 | 0 |
| Playoffs | | | 1 | 5 | 5.0 | | 0 |

Merlin Olsen
| 1962 | LA | N | 1 | 20 | 20.0 | 20t | 1 |

Jim O'Malley
| 1975 | DEN | N | 1 | 38 | 38.0 | 38 | 0 |

Leslie O'Neal
| 1986 | SD | N | 2 | 22 | 11.0 | 17 | 1 |
| Playoffs | | | 1 | 3 | 3.0 | | 0 |

Ed O'Neil
1976	DET	N	1	16	16.0	16	0
1978			4	49	12.3	31	0
Career			5	65	13.0	31	0

Johnny O'Quinn
| 1950 | CHIB | N | 3 | 73 | 24.3 | 38 | 1 |

Bo Orlando
1991	HOU	N	4	18	4.5	18	0
1993			3	68	22.7	38t	1
1995	SD	N	0	37		37L	0
1996	CIN	N	2	0	0.0	0	0
Career			9	123	13.7	38t	1
Playoffs			2	31	15.5		0

Dan Orlich
| 1950 | GB | N | 1 | 0 | 0.0 | 0 | 0 |

Charlie O'Rourke
1942	CHIB	N	3	15	5.0	10	0
1946	LA	AA	0	7		7L	0
Career			3	22	7.3	10	0
Playoffs			1	0	0.0		0

Ralph Ortega
1977	ATL	N	4	15	3.8	6	0
1980	MIA	N	1	17	17.0	17	0
Career			5	32	6.4	17	0

Chuck Ortmann
| 1951 | PIT | N | 1 | 62 | 62.0 | 62 | 0 |

Clancy Osborne
1961	MIN	N	4	35	8.8	10	0
1963	OAK	A	2	64	32.0	48	0
1964			2	50	25.0	44	0
Career			8	149	18.6	48	0

Bill Osmanski
1941	CHIB	N	3	19	6.3	19	0
1946			1	13	13.0	13	0
Career			4	32	8.0	19	0
Playoffs			1	0	0.0		0

Dwayne O'Steen
1979	LA	N	4	42	10.5	36	0
1980	OAK	N	3	10	3.3	14	0
1981			1	2	2.0	2	0
Career			8	54	6.8	36	0

Chet Ostrowski
1954	WAS	N	1	5	5.0	5	0
1956			1	2	2.0	2	0
Career			2	7	3.5	5	0

Gus Otto
| 1965 | OAK | A | 3 | 131 | 43.7 | 68 | 2 |
| 1967 | | | 1 | 0 | 0.0 | 0 | 0 |

Gus Otto *continued*
| 1969 | | | 2 | 4 | 2.0 | 4 | 0 |
| Career | | | 6 | 135 | 22.5 | 68 | 2 |

John Outlaw
1971	NE	N	3	89	29.7	60t	1
1973	PHI	N	2	48	24.0	45t	1
1974			2	22	11.0	22	0
1975			5	23	4.6	23	0
1976			2	19	9.5	19	0
1977			2	41	20.5	38	0
Career			16	242	15.1	60t	2

Brig Owens
1966	WAS	N	7	165	23.6	60t	1
1967			1	68	68.0	68t	1
1968			8	109	13.6	38	0
1969			3	24	8.0	15	0
1970			4	86	21.5	32	0
1971			2	27	13.5	19	0
1972			1	0	0.0	0	0
1973			5	123	24.6	27	1
1974			4	59	14.8	24	0
1975			1	25	25.0	25	0
Career			36	686	19.1	68t	3
Playoffs			1	0	0.0		0

Burgess Owens
1973	NYJ	N	1	27	27.0	27	0
1974			3	68	22.7	39	1
1975			3	3	1.0	3	0
1977			3	18	6.0	12	0
1978			5	156	31.2	49	1
1979			6	41	6.8	15	0
1980	OAK	N	3	59	19.7	58t	1
1981			2	30	15.0	30t	1
1982	LARI	N	4	56	14.0	35	0
Career			30	458	15.3	58t	4
Playoffs			3	30	10.0		0

Dan Owens
| 1993 | DET | N | 1 | 1 | 1.0 | 1 | 0 |

Jim Owens
| 1950 | BAL | N | 1 | 25 | 25.0 | 25t | 0 |

Joe Owens
| 1973 | NO | N | 1 | 3 | 3.0 | 3 | 0 |

Mel Owens
1984	LARM	N	1	-4	-4.0	-4	0
1987			1	26	26.0	26	0
1988			1	11	11.0	11	0
1989			1	4	4.0	4	0
Career			4	37	9.3	26	0

Alan Page
1969	MIN	N	0	15		15Lt	1
1970			1	27	27.0	27	0
1980	CHI	N	1	0	0.0	0	0
Career			2	42	21.0	27	1
Playoffs			1	29	29.0		0

Shane Pahukoa
| 1995 | NO | N | 2 | 12 | 6.0 | 12 | 0 |

John Paluck
1961	WAS	N	1	0	0.0	0	0
1963			1	23	23.0	23	0
Career			2	23	11.5	23	0

Sam Palumbo
| 1957 | GB | N | 1 | 11 | 11.0 | 11 | 0 |
| Playoffs | | | 1 | 10 | 10.0 | | 0 |

Don Panciera
| 1950 | DET | N | 1 | 1 | 1.0 | 1 | 0 |

John Panelli
1949	DET	N	1	2	2.0	2	0
1952	CHIC	N	3	5	1.7	5	0
1953			1	22	22.0	22	0
Career			5	29	5.8	22	0

Ernie Pannell
| 1941 | GB | N | 1 | 0 | 0.0 | 0 | 0 |

Jack Pardee
1960	LA	N	1	10	10.0	10	0
1961			1	2	2.0	2	0
1963			2	5	2.5	5	0
1964			1	32	32.0	32	0
1966			2	0	0.0	0	0
1967			6	95	15.8	40t	2
1968			2	75	37.5	46t	2
1969			1	19	19.0	19	0
1970			1	9	9.0	9	0
1971	WAS	N	5	58	11.6	20t	1
Career			22	305	13.9	46t	5

Don Parish
| 1970 | STL | N | 1 | 41 | 41.0 | 41t | 0 |

Ace Parker
1938	BKN	N					1
1940			6	146	24.3		1
1941			1	5	5.0	5	0
Career			7	151	21.6	5	2

Anthony Parker
1992	MIN	N	3	23	7.7	23	0
1993			1	1	1.0	1	0
1994			4	99	24.8	44t	2
1995	STL	N	2	-5	-2.5	3	0
1996			4	128	32.0	92t	2
Career			14	246	17.6	92t	4
Playoffs			1	10	10.0		0

Artimus Parker
1975	PHI	N	4	15	3.8	11	0
1977	NYJ	N	1	45	45.0	45	0
Career			5	60	12.0	45	0

Buddy Parker
| 1941 | CHIC | N | 2 | 8 | 4.0 | 7 | 0 |
| Playoffs | | | 1 | 23 | 23.0 | | 0 |

Jim Parmer
1948	PHI	N	1	6	6.0	6	0
1949			2	12	6.0	12	0
Career			3	18	6.0	12	0

Bernie Parrish
1959	CLE	N	5	83	16.6	37t	1
1960			6	238	39.7	92t	1
1961			7	40	5.7	15	0
1962			2	37	18.5	37	0
1964			4	98	24.5	54t	1
1965			4	45	11.3	35	0
1966	CLE-HOU	N-A	3	16	5.3	16	0
Career			31	557	18.0	92t	3

Lemar Parrish
1970	CIN	N	5	28	5.6	19	0
1971			7	105	15.0	65t	1
1972			5	90	18.0	33t	2
1973			2	10	5.0	10	0
1975			1	26	26.0	26	0
1976			2	0	0.0	0	0
1977			3	95	31.7	47t	1
1978	WAS	N	4	21	5.3	23	0
1979			9	65	7.2	23	0
1980			7	13	1.9	9	0
1981			1	1	1.0	1	0
1982	BUF	N	1	8	8.0	8	0
Career			47	462	9.8	65t	4

Ara Parseghian
| 1948 | CLE | AA | 1 | 56 | 56.0 | 56 | 0 |

Lou Partlow
| 1924 | DAY | N | | | | | 1 |

George Paskvan
| 1941 | GB | N | 2 | 6 | 3.0 | 4 | 0 |

Jack Patera

Year	Team		No	Yds	Avg	Lg	TD
1955	BAL	N	1	8	8.0	8	0
1956			2	10	5.0	10	0
1957			1	16	16.0	16	0
1959	CHIC	N	1	21	21.0	21	0
1960	DAL	N	1	21	21.0	21	0
Career			6	76	12.7	21	0

John Patrick

Year	Team		No	Yds	Avg	Lg	TD
1941	PIT	N	1	25	25.0	25	0

Craig Patterson

Year	Team		No	Yds	Avg	Lg	TD
1991	PHX	N	1	0	0.0	0	0

Elvis Patterson

Year	Team		No	Yds	Avg	Lg	TD
1985	NYG	N	6	88	14.7	29t	1
1986			2	26	13.0	26	0
1987	SD	N	1	75	75.0	75t	1
1988			1	0	0.0	0	0
1989			2	44	22.0	34	0
Career			12	233	19.4	75t	2
Playoffs			1	9	9.0		

Paul Patterson

Year	Team		No	Yds	Avg	Lg	TD
1949	CHI	AA	3	104	34.7	55	0

Shawn Patterson

Year	Team		No	Yds	Avg	Lg	TD
1990	GB	N	1	9	9.0	9t	1

Cliff Patton

Year	Team		No	Yds	Avg	Lg	TD
1951	CHIC	N	3	31	10.3	19	0

Jerry Patton

Year	Team		No	Yds	Avg	Lg	TD
1974	PHI	N	1	4	4.0	4	0

Jimmy Patton

Year	Team		No	Yds	Avg	Lg	TD
1955	NYG	N	1	0	0.0	0	0
1956			1	2	2.0	2	0
1957			3	50	16.7	50t	1
1958			11	183	16.6	42	0
1959			5	13	2.6	12	0
1960			6	100	16.7	34	0
1961			8	163	20.4	51t	1
1962			7	125	17.9	45	0
1963			6	46	7.7	20	0
1964			2	0	0.0	0	0
1965			1	27	27.0	27	0
1966			1	3	3.0	3	0
Career			52	712	13.7	51t	2
Playoffs			1	28	28.0		

Marvcus Patton

Year	Team		No	Yds	Avg	Lg	TD
1993	BUF	N	2	0	0.0	0	0
1994			2	8	4.0	8	0
1995	WAS	N	2	7	3.5	6	0
1996			2	26	13.0	23	0
Career			8	41	5.1	23	0

Don Paul

Year	Team		No	Yds	Avg	Lg	TD
1949	LA	N	2	23	11.5	19	0
1950			3	44	14.7	32	0
1951			1	16	16.0	16	0
1952			2	40	20.0	30	0
1953			3	50	16.7	32	0
Career			11	173	15.7	32	0
Playoffs			2	30	15.0		

Don Paul

Year	Team		No	Yds	Avg	Lg	TD
1950	CHIC	N	4	90	22.5	41	0
1951			3	52	17.3	36	0
1953			5	62	12.4	38	0
1954	CLE	N	3	42	14.0	23	0
1955			4	49	12.3	19	0
1956			7	190	27.1	42	1
1957			4	28	7.0	12	0
1958			4	80	20.0	36	0
Career			34	593	17.4	42	1
Playoffs			2	96	48.0		

Markus Paul

Year	Team		No	Yds	Avg	Lg	TD
1989	CHI	N	1	20	20.0	20	0
1990			2	49	24.5	26	0
1991			3	21	7.0	10	0

Markus Paul *continued*

Year	Team		No	Yds	Avg	Lg	TD
1992			1	10	10.0	10	0
Career			7	100	14.3	26	0

Tito Paul

Year	Team		No	Yds	Avg	Lg	TD
1995	ARI	N	1	4	4.0	4	0

Whitney Paul

Year	Team		No	Yds	Avg	Lg	TD
1977	KC	N	1	6	6.0	6	0
1978			3	21	7.0	10	0
1979			1	28	28.0	28	0
1980			1	0	0.0	0	0
1981			2	30	15.0	25	0
1982	NO	N	1	14	14.0	14	0
1983			2	3	1.5	3	0
Career			11	102	9.3	28	0

Dainard Paulson

Year	Team		No	Yds	Avg	Lg	TD
1961	NY	A	1	0	0.0	0	0
1962			3	0	0.0	0	0
1963			6	114	19.0	47	0
1964			12	157	13.1	42	1
1965			7	72	10.3	22	0
Career			29	343	11.8	47	1

Bryce Paup

Year	Team		No	Yds	Avg	Lg	TD
1993	GB	N	1	8	8.0	8	0
1994			3	47	15.7	30	1
1995	BUF	N	2	0	0.0	0	0
Career			6	55	9.2	30	1
Playoffs			1	34	34.0		

Johnny Peacock

Year	Team		No	Yds	Avg	Lg	TD
1969	HOU	A	2	56	28.0	39	0
1970	HOU	N	3	24	8.0	12	0
Career			5	80	16.0	39	0
Playoffs			1	0	0.0		

J.C. Pearson

Year	Team		No	Yds	Avg	Lg	TD
1988	KC	N	2	8	4.0	7	0
1990			1	10	10.0	10	0
1991			3	43	14.3	43	0
1993	MIN	N	1	0	0.0	0	0
Career			7	61	8.7	43	0

Win Pedersen

Year	Team		No	Yds	Avg	Lg	TD
1941	NYG	N	1	3	3.0	3	0

Bob Pellegrini

Year	Team		No	Yds	Avg	Lg	TD
1958	PHI	N	4	90	22.5	40	0
1959			3	42	14.0	39	0
1962	WAS	N	4	43	10.8	16	0
1963			2	37	18.5	37	0
Career			13	212	16.3	40	0

Bill Pellington

Year	Team		No	Yds	Avg	Lg	TD
1953	BAL	N	2	22	11.0	22	0
1955			2	17	8.5	12	0
1956			1	4	4.0	4	0
1958			4	44	11.0	21	0
1959			4	99	24.8	30t	0
1960			1	4	4.0	4	0
1961			3	9	3.0	4	0
1962			2	29	14.5	21	0
1964			2	20	10.0	13	0
Career			21	248	11.8	30t	1

Jesse Penn

Year	Team		No	Yds	Avg	Lg	TD
1987	DAL	N	1	21	21.0	21	0

Robert Pennywell

Year	Team		No	Yds	Avg	Lg	TD
1977	ATL	N	2	30	15.0	20t	1
1979			1	39	39.0	39t	1
Career			3	69	23.0	39t	2

Leon Pense

Year	Team		No	Yds	Avg	Lg	TD
1945	PIT	N	3	39	13.0	30	0

Bob Perina

Year	Team		No	Yds	Avg	Lg	TD
1946	NY	AA	2	24	12.0		0
1947	BKN	AA	4	40	10.0		0
1948	CHI	AA	6	87	14.5		0

Bob Perina *continued*

Year	Team		No	Yds	Avg	Lg	TD
1949	CHIB	N	6	23	3.8	17	0
Career			18	174	9.7	17	0

Don Perkins

Year	Team		No	Yds	Avg	Lg	TD
1944	GB	N	2	123	61.5	83t	2

John Perko

Year	Team		No	Yds	Avg	Lg	TD
1944	C-P	N	1	10	10.0	10	0

Benny Perrin

Year	Team		No	Yds	Avg	Lg	TD
1982	STL	N	1	35	35.0	35	0
1983			4	50	12.5	30	0
1984			4	22	5.5	22	0
Career			9	107	11.9	35	0

Darren Perry

Year	Team		No	Yds	Avg	Lg	TD
1992	PIT	N	6	69	11.5	34	0
1993			4	61	15.3	30	0
1994			7	112	16.0	42	0
1995			4	71	17.8	26	0
1996			5	115	23.0	28	1
Career			26	428	16.5	42	1
Playoffs			1	0	0.0	0	0

Jerry Perry

Year	Team		No	Yds	Avg	Lg	TD
Playoffs			1	0	0.0		0

Joe Perry

Year	Team		No	Yds	Avg	Lg	TD
1948	SF	AA	1	24	24.0	24	0

Marlo Perry

Year	Team		No	Yds	Avg	Lg	TD
1996	BUF	N	1	6	6.0	6	0
Playoffs			1	3	3.0		0

Rod Perry

Year	Team		No	Yds	Avg	Lg	TD
1976	LA	N	8	79	9.9	43	0
1977			1	0	0.0	0	0
1978			8	117	14.6	44t	3
1980			5	115	23.0	83t	1
1981			3	18	6.0	10	0
1982	LARM	N	3	57	19.0	33	0
1983	CLE	N	1	21	21.0	21	0
1984			1	17	17.0	17	0
Career			30	424	14.1	83t	4
Playoffs			1	-1	-1.0		

Scott Perry

Year	Team		No	Yds	Avg	Lg	TD
1978	CIN	N	3	59	19.7	39t	2
1979			1	11	11.0	11	0
Career			4	70	17.5	39t	2

Vernon Perry

Year	Team		No	Yds	Avg	Lg	TD
1979	HOU	N	3	33	11.0	24	0
1980			5	85	17.0	42	0
1981			2	46	23.0	34	0
1982			1	8	8.0	8	0
Career			11	172	15.6	42	0
Playoffs			6	75	12.5		1

Jim Perryman

Year	Team		No	Yds	Avg	Lg	TD
1987	IND	N	1	0	0.0	0	0

Dick Pesonen

Year	Team		No	Yds	Avg	Lg	TD
1961	MIN	N	1	28	28.0	28	0
1962	NYG	N	2	24	12.0	17	0
1963			1	1	1.0	1	0
Career			4	53	13.3	28	0

John Petchel

Year	Team		No	Yds	Avg	Lg	TD
1944	CLE	N	1	25	25.0	25	0
1945	PIT	N	1	4	4.0	4	0
Career			2	29	14.5	25	0

Floyd Peters

Year	Team		No	Yds	Avg	Lg	TD
1962	CLE	N	1	9	9.0	9	0
1967	PHI	N	1	3	3.0	3	0
1968			1	0	0.0	0	0
Career			3	12	4.0	9	0

Forest Peters

Year	Team		No	Yds	Avg	Lg	TD
1930	PRO	N					1

Tony Peters

Year	Team		No	Yds	Avg	Lg	TD
1975	CLE	N	1	0	0.0	0	0
1977			2	29	14.5	25	0
1978			2	7	3.5	7	0
1979	WAS	N	1	-4	-4.0	-4	0
1980			4	59	14.8	37	0
1981			3	0	0.0	0	0
1982			1	14	14.0	14	0
1985			2	21	10.5	12	0
Career			16	126	7.9	37	0

Bill Peterson

Year	Team		No	Yds	Avg	Lg	TD
1969	CIN	A	4	23	5.8	17	0
1971	CIN	N	1	16	16.0	16	0
Career			5	39	7.8	17	0

Cal Peterson

Year	Team		No	Yds	Avg	Lg	TD
1975	DAL	N	1	19	19.0	19	0
1976	TB	N	1	15	15.0	15	0
Career			2	34	17.0	19	0

Joe Peterson

Year	Team		No	Yds	Avg	Lg	TD
1987	NE	N	1	0	0.0	0	0

Johnny Petitbon

Year	Team		No	Yds	Avg	Lg	TD
1952	DAL	N	5	42	8.4	24	0
1955	CLE	N	2	11	5.5	7	0
1957	GB	N	1	0	0.0	0	0
Career			8	53	6.6	24	0

Richie Petitbon

Year	Team		No	Yds	Avg	Lg	TD
1959	CHIB	N	3	52	17.3	33t	1
1960	CHI	N	2	0	0.0	0	0
1961			5	71	14.2	43	0
1962			6	212	35.3	101t	1
1963			8	161	20.1	66t	1
1965			2	22	11.0	18	0
1966			4	34	8.5	20	0
1967			5	73	14.6	35	0
1968			2	18	9.0	8	0
1969	LA	N	5	46	9.2	25	0
1970			1	10	10.0	10	0
1971	WAS	N	5	102	20.4	42	0
Career			48	801	16.7	101t	3
Playoffs			2	4	2.0		0

Bob Petrella

Year	Team		No	Yds	Avg	Lg	TD
1967	MIA	A	3	67	22.3	28	0
1968			1	4	4.0	4	0
1969			1	33	33.0	33	0
Career			5	104	20.8	33	0

John Petrella

Year	Team		No	Yds	Avg	Lg	TD
1945	PIT	N	1	8	8.0	8	0

Bob Petrich

Year	Team		No	Yds	Avg	Lg	TD
1964	SD	A	1	11	11.0	11	0

Bill Petrilas

Year	Team		No	Yds	Avg	Lg	TD
1944	NYG	N	5	144	28.8	67	2
1945			2	1	0.5	1	0
Career			7	145	20.7	67	2

Stan Petry

Year	Team		No	Yds	Avg	Lg	TD
1990	KC	N	3	33	11.0	33t	1
1991	NO	N	1	4	4.0	4	0
Career			4	37	9.3	33t	1

John Petty

Year	Team		No	Yds	Avg	Lg	TD
1942	CHIB	N	1	7	7.0	7	0

Don Phelps

Year	Team		No	Yds	Avg	Lg	TD
1950	CLE	N	1	9	9.0	9	0

Roman Phifer

Year	Team		No	Yds	Avg	Lg	TD
1992	LARM	N	1	3	3.0	3	0
1994			2	7	3.5	7	0
1995	STL	N	3	52	17.3	25	0
Career			6	62	10.3	25	0

Gerry Philbin

Year	Team		No	Yds	Avg	Lg	TD
1969	NY	A	1	18	18.0	18	0

Anthony Phillips

Year	Team		No	Yds	Avg	Lg	TD
1994	ATL	N	1	0	0.0	0	0
1995			1	43	43.0	43	0
Career			2	43	21.5	43	0

Charles Phillips

Year	Team		No	Yds	Avg	Lg	TD
1975	OAK	N	6	45	7.5	23	0
1976			1	11	11.0	11	0
1977			2	35	17.5	29	0
1978			6	121	20.2	42t	1
1979			4	92	23.0	30	0
Career			19	304	16.0	42t	1

Jess Phillips

Year	Team		No	Yds	Avg	Lg	TD
1968	CIN	A	3	26	8.7	23	0

Joe Phillips

Year	Team		No	Yds	Avg	Lg	TD
1995	KC	N	1	2	2.0	2	0

Loyd Phillips

Year	Team		No	Yds	Avg	Lg	TD
1968	CHI	N	2	23	11.5	17	0

Mel Phillips

Year	Team		No	Yds	Avg	Lg	TD
1967	SF	N	1	0	0.0	0	0
1970			3	49	16.3	35t	1
1972			1	0	0.0	0	0
1973			1	13	13.0	13	0
1974			1	27	27.0	27	0
1975			1	3	3.0	3	0
1976			2	14	7.0	14	0
1977			2	23	11.5	23	0
Career			12	129	10.8	35t	1

Ray Phillips

Year	Team		No	Yds	Avg	Lg	TD
1981	PHI	N	1	0	0.0	0	0

Reggie Phillips

Year	Team		No	Yds	Avg	Lg	TD
1986	CHI	N	1	6	6.0	6	0
1987			2	1	0.5	1	0
Career			3	7	2.3	6	0
Playoffs			1	28	28.0		1

Ed Philpott

Year	Team		No	Yds	Avg	Lg	TD
1968	BOS	A	4	31	7.8	17	0
1969			4	37	9.3	16	0
1970	BOS	N	1	23	23.0	23	0
Career			9	91	10.1	23	0

Alex Piasecky

Year	Team		No	Yds	Avg	Lg	TD
1943	WAS	N	1	0	0.0	0	0

Bill Piccolo

Year	Team		No	Yds	Avg	Lg	TD
1944	NYG	N	2	5	2.5	3	0

Bruce Pickens

Year	Team		No	Yds	Avg	Lg	TD
1992	ATL	N	2	16	8.0	16	0

Damon Pieri

Year	Team		No	Yds	Avg	Lg	TD
1996	CAR	N	1	0	0.0	0	0

Bob Pifferini

Year	Team		No	Yds	Avg	Lg	TD
1949	DET	N	3	3	1.0	3	0

Bert Piggott

Year	Team		No	Yds	Avg	Lg	TD
1947	LA	AA	1	9	9.0	9	0

Pete Pihos

Year	Team		No	Yds	Avg	Lg	TD
1951	PHI	N	2	30	15.0	30	0

Lawrence Pillers

Year	Team		No	Yds	Avg	Lg	TD
1983	SF	N	1	16	16.0	16	0

Erny Pinckert

Year	Team		No	Yds	Avg	Lg	TD
1933	BOS	N					1
1940	WAS	N	2	26	13.0		0
Career			2	26	13.0		1
Playoffs			1	17	17.0		0

Ed Pine

Year	Team		No	Yds	Avg	Lg	TD
1962	SF	N	2	16	8.0	13	0
1963			1	1	1.0	1	0
Career			3	17	5.7	13	0

Reggie Pinkney

Year	Team		No	Yds	Avg	Lg	TD
1977	DET	N	2	61	30.5	48t	1
1978			1	22	22.0	22	0
1981	BAL	N	1	0	0.0	0	0
Career			4	83	20.8	48t	1

Hank Piro

Year	Team		No	Yds	Avg	Lg	TD
1941	PHI	N	1	0	0.0	0	0

Rocco Pirro

Year	Team		No	Yds	Avg	Lg	TD
1941	PIT	N	1	2	2.0	2	0

Hugh Pitts

Year	Team		No	Yds	Avg	Lg	TD
1956	LA	N	3	22	7.3	16	0

John Pitts

Year	Team		No	Yds	Avg	Lg	TD
1968	BUF	A	2	21	10.5	17	0
1969			2	40	20.0	38	0
1970	BUF	N	1	11	11.0	11	0
1971			2	12	6.0	12	0
1972			1	10	10.0	10	0
1974	DEN	N	1	2	2.0	2	0
1975	CLE	N	1	0	0.0	0	0
Career			10	96	9.6	38	0

Mike Pitts

Year	Team		No	Yds	Avg	Lg	TD
1985	ATL	N	1	1	1.0	1	0

Ron Pitts

Year	Team		No	Yds	Avg	Lg	TD
1987	BUF	N	3	19	6.3	12	0
1988	GB	N	2	56	28.0	31	0
1989			1	37	37.0	37	0
1990			1	0	0.0	0	0
Career			7	112	16.0	37	0

Doug Plank

Year	Team		No	Yds	Avg	Lg	TD
1975	CHI	N	2	50	25.0	29	0
1976			4	31	7.8	15	0
1977			4	32	8.0	20	0
1978			1	0	0.0	0	0
1979			3	33	11.0	22	0
1980			1	20	20.0	20	0
Career			15	166	11.1	29	0

George Platukas

Year	Team		No	Yds	Avg	Lg	TD
1942	CLE	N	1	12	12.0	12	0

Bruce Plummer

Year	Team		No	Yds	Avg	Lg	TD
1989	IND	N	1	18	18.0	18	0
1990	DEN	N	1	16	16.0	16	0
Career			2	34	17.0	18	0

Gary Plummer

Year	Team		No	Yds	Avg	Lg	TD
1987	SD	N	1	2	2.0	2	0
1992			2	40	20.0	38	0
1993			2	7	3.5	6	0
1994	SF	N	1	1	1.0	1	0
Career			6	50	8.3	38	0

Tony Plummer

Year	Team		No	Yds	Avg	Lg	TD
1973	ATL	N	1	39	39.0	39	0

Bobby Ply

Year	Team		No	Yds	Avg	Lg	TD
1962	DAL	N	7	144	20.6	41	0
1964	KC	A	1	12	12.0	12	0
1966			1	0	0.0	0	0
Career			9	156	17.3	41	0

Johnnie Poe

Year	Team		No	Yds	Avg	Lg	TD
1981	NO	N	1	0	0.0	0	0
1983			7	146	20.9	31t	0
1984			1	16	16.0	16	0
1985			3	63	21.0	40t	1
1986			4	42	10.5	30	0
1987			1	0	0.0	0	0
Career			17	267	15.7	40t	2

Dick Poillon

Year	Team		No	Yds	Avg	Lg	TD
1947	WAS	N	2	28	14.0	16	0

John Polanski

Year	Team		No	Yds	Avg	Lg	TD
1942	DET	N	1	20	20.0	20	0
1946	LA	AA	1	50	50.0	50	0
Career			2	70	35.0	50	0

Year	Team		No	Yds	Avg	Lg	TD

Darryl Pollard
1989	SF	N	1	12	12.0	12	0
1990			1	0	0.0	0	0
1992	TB	N	2	99	49.5	75	0
Career			4	111	27.8	75	0
Playoffs			1	0	0.0		0

Randy Poltl
| 1976 | DEN | N | 1 | 0 | 0.0 | 0 | 0 |
| Playoffs | | | 1 | 16 | 16.0 | | 0 |

David Pool
1990	BUF	N	1	0	0.0	0	0
1992	NE	N	2	54	27.0	41t	1
Career			3	54	18.0	41t	1

Hamp Pool
| Playoffs | | | 1 | 15 | 15.0 | | 1 |

Barney Poole
| 1949 | B-NY | AA | 1 | 0 | 0.0 | 0 | 0 |

Jim Poole
1941	NYG	N	1	16	16.0	16	0
1945	CHIC	N	1	28	28.0	28	0
Career			2	44	22.0	28	0

Ray Poole
1947	NYG	N	1	0	0.0	0	0
1950			1	8	8.0	8	0
1952			1	6	6.0	6	0
Career			3	14	4.7	8	0

Tyrone Poole
1995	CAR	N	2	8	4.0	4	0
1996			1	35	35.0	35	0
Career			3	43	14.3	35	0

Marquez Pope
1993	SD	N	2	14	7.0	12	0
1994	LARM	N	3	66	22.0	51	0
1995	SF	N	1	-7	-7.0	-7	0
1996			6	98	16.3	55t	1
Career			12	171	14.3	55t	1
Playoffs			1	0	0.0		0

Milt Popovich
| 1942 | CHIC | N | 1 | 6 | 6.0 | 6 | 0 |

Kevin Porter
| 1990 | KC | N | 1 | 13 | 13.0 | 13 | 0 |

Ron Porter
1967	BAL	N	1	0	0.0	0	0
1972	PHI	N	2	10	5.0	7	0
Career			3	10	3.3	7	0

Rufus Porter
1991	SEA	N	1	0	0.0	0	0
1993			1	4	4.0	4	0
1994			1	33	33.0	33	0
Career			3	37	12.3	33	0

Steve Potter
| 1983 | KC | N | 1 | 0 | 0.0 | 0 | 0 |

Myron Pottios
1961	PIT	N	2	40	20.0	22	0
1963			4	78	19.5	38	0
1964			1	8	8.0	8	0
1967	LA	N	1	24	24.0	24	0
1969			1	16	16.0	16	0
1970			2	27	13.5	14	0
1971	WAS	N	1	31	31.0	31	0
Career			12	224	18.7	38	0

Darryl Pounds
1995	WAS	N	1	26	26.0	26	0
1996			2	11	5.5	11	0
Career			3	37	12.3	26	0

Art Powell
| 1959 | PHI | N | 3 | 17 | 5.7 | 17 | 0 |

Charley Powell
| 1955 | SF | N | 0 | 7 | | 7L | 0 |

Clyde Powers
1975	NYG	N	3	0	0.0	0	0
1976			1	11	11.0	11	0
1977			1	1	1.0	1	0
Career			5	12	2.4	11	0

Jim Powers
1950	SF	N	5	42	8.4	26	0
1951			4	73	18.3	28	0
1952			2	37	18.5	23	0
Career			11	152	13.8	28	0

Warren Powers
1964	OAK	A	5	65	13.0	33	0
1965			5	56	11.2	21	0
1966			5	88	17.6	35	0
1967			6	154	25.7	70	2
1968			1	3	3.0	3	0
Career			22	366	16.6	70	2

Steve Preece
1969	NO	N	1	6	6.0	6	0
1970	PHI	N	2	19	9.5	19	0
1972	DEN	N	1	30	30.0	30	0
1973	LA	N	2	25	12.5	25	0
1974			3	38	12.7	17	0
1976			1	6	6.0	6	0
1977	SEA	N	4	55	13.8	29	0
Career			14	179	12.8	30	0

Merv Pregulman
1947	DET	N	2	9	4.5	9	0
1948			1	6	6.0	6	0
Career			3	15	5.0	9	0

Hal Prescott
| 1947 | PHI | N | 3 | 5 | 1.7 | 5 | 0 |

Jim Prestel
| 1964 | MIN | N | 1 | 26 | 26.0 | 26t | 1 |

Ray Preston
1979	SD	N	5	121	24.2	35	0
1983			1	13	13.0	13	0
Career			6	134	22.3	35	0

Felton Prewitt
1946	BUF	AA	4	89	22.3		0
1947			2	20	10.0		0
Career			6	109	18.2		0

Charley Price
| 1945 | DET | N | 1 | 16 | 16.0 | 16 | 0 |

Dennis Price
1988	LARI	N	2	18	9.0	18	0
1992	NYJ	N	1	0	0.0	0	0
Career			3	18	6.0	18	0

Elex Price
| 1976 | NO | N | 1 | 23 | 23.0 | 23t | 1 |

Jim Price
| 1963 | NY | A | 1 | 15 | 15.0 | 15 | 0 |

Mitchell Price
1990	CIN	N	1	0	0.0	0	0
1991			1	0	0.0	0	0
Career			2	0	0.0	0	0

Danny Pride
| 1969 | CHI | N | 1 | 1 | 1.0 | 1 | 0 |

Tom Pridemore
1978	ATL	N	1	0	0.0	0	0
1979			2	20	10.0	20	0
1980			2	2	1.0	2	0
1981			7	221	31.6	101t	1
1982			1	28	28.0	28	0
1983			4	56	14.0	25	0
1984			2	0	0.0	0	0

Tom Pridemore *continued*
1985			2	45	22.5	36	0
Career			21	372	17.7	101t	1
Playoffs			1	22	22.0		0

Mike Prior
1987	IND	N	6	57	9.5	38	0
1988			3	46	15.3	23	0
1989			6	88	14.7	58t	1
1990			3	66	22.0	36	0
1991			3	50	16.7	37	0
1992			6	44	7.3	19	0
1993	GB	N	1	1	1.0	1	0
1995			1	9	9.0	9	0
1996			1	7	7.0	7	0
Career			30	368	12.3	58t	1
Playoffs			2	12	6.0		0

Bosh Pritchard
1942	PHI	N	3	23	7.7	10	0
1946			3	7	2.3	4	0
1947			1	12	12.0	12	0
Career			7	42	6.0	12	0

Ron Pritchard
1970	HOU	N	2	28	14.0	17	0
1976	CIN	N	1	0	0.0	0	0
Career			3	28	9.3	17	0

Steve Pritko
| 1944 | CLE | N | 1 | 3 | 3.0 | 3 | 0 |

Dewey Proctor
| 1947 | NY | AA | 1 | 32 | 32.0 | 32 | 0 |

Rex Proctor
| 1953 | CHIB | N | 1 | 4 | 4.0 | 4 | 0 |

Eddie Prokop
1946	NY	AA	1	14	14.0	14	0
1947			3	57	19.0		0
Career			4	71	17.8	14	0
Playoffs			1	16	16.0		0

Bob Prout
| 1975 | NYJ | N | 1 | 10 | 10.0 | 10 | 0 |

Mickey Pruitt
| Playoffs | | | 1 | 0 | 0.0 | | 0 |

Jim Psaltis
1953	CHIC	N	2	43	21.5	43	0
1955			4	42	10.5	21	1
Career			6	85	14.2	43	1

Jethro Pugh
| 1970 | DAL | N | 1 | 0 | 0.0 | 0 | 0 |

Craig Puki
| 1980 | SF | N | 1 | 0 | 0.0 | 0 | 0 |

Andy Puplis
| 1943 | CHIC | N | 1 | 19 | 19.0 | 19 | 0 |

Jim Purnell
1971	LA	N	2	32	16.0	17	0
1972			1	2	2.0	2	0
Career			3	34	11.3	17	0

Johnny Pyeatt
| 1960 | DEN | A | 4 | 60 | 15.0 | | 1 |

Frank Quillen
| 1946 | CHI | AA | 1 | 9 | 9.0 | 9 | 0 |

Bill Quinlan
1959	GB	N	1	5	5.0	5	0
1962			1	4	4.0	4	0
1964	DET	N	1	0	0.0	0	0
Career			3	9	3.0	5	0

Ed Quirk
| 1950 | WAS | N | 2 | 5 | 2.5 | 5 | 0 |

Year	Team		No	Yds	Avg	Lg	TD

Frank Racis
Year	Team		No	Yds	Avg	Lg	TD
1930	PRO	N					1

George Radachowsky
| 1987 | NYJ | N | 2 | 45 | 22.5 | 45 | 0 |

John Rade
1985	ATL	N	2	42	21.0	38t	1
1986			1	6	6.0	6	0
Career			3	48	16.0	38t	1

Scott Radecic
1984	KC	N	2	54	27.0	35	1
1985			1	21	21.0	21	0
1986			1	20	20.0	20	0
1987	BUF	N	2	4	2.0	4	0
1991	IND	N	1	26	26.0	26	0
1992			1	0	0.0	0	0
Career			8	125	15.6	35	1

Bill Rademacher
| 1964 | NY | A | 1 | 16 | 16.0 | 16 | 0 |

Phil Ragazzo
| 1945 | NYG | N | 1 | 7 | 7.0 | 7 | 0 |

Garrard Ramsey
1946	CHIC	N	1	6	6.0	6	0
1947			4	29	7.3	74	0
1948			1	13	13.0	13	0
1949			1	0	0.0	0	0
1950			1	0	0.0	0	0
Career			8	48	6.0	74	0
Playoffs			1	41	41.0		0

Nate Ramsey
1963	PHI	N	1	0	0.0	0	0
1964			5	31	6.2	17	0
1965			6	74	12.3	24	0
1966			1	0	0.0	0	0
1968			2	0	0.0	0	0
1969			2	26	13.0	26t	1
1970			1	0	0.0	0	0
1972			3	14	4.7	10	0
Career			21	145	6.9	26t	1

Ray Ramsey
1947	CHI	AA	5	66	13.2		0
1948	BKN	AA	7	124	17.7		0
1949	CHI	AA	2	79	39.5		0
1951	CHIC	N	5	90	18.0	39	0
1952			5	67	13.4	23	0
1953			10	237	23.7	46	1
Career			34	663	19.5	46	1

Ervin Randle
| 1985 | TB | N | 1 | 0 | 0.0 | 0 | 0 |

Tate Randle
1983	BAL	N	1	41	41.0	41	0
1984	IND	N	3	66	22.0	54	0
1985			1	0	0.0	0	0
1987	MIA	N	2	16	8.0	11	0
Career			7	123	17.6	54	0

Al Randolph
1966	SF	N	3	138	46.0	94t	1
1968			4	60	15.0	40	0
1969			2	10	5.0	5	0
1970			1	0	0.0	0	0
1971	GB	N	1	34	34.0	34	0
Career			11	242	22.0	94t	1

Thomas Randolph
1994	NYG	N	1	0	0.0	0	0
1995			2	15	7.5	15	0
Career			3	15	5.0	15	0

Walt Rankin
1943	CHIC	N	3	30	10.0	15	0
1944	C-P	N	2	9	4.5	7	0
1945	CHIC	N	1	0	0.0	0	0
1946			2	14	7.0		0
Career			8	53	6.6	15	0

Year	Team		No	Yds	Avg	Lg	TD

Wayne Rasmussen
1965	DET	N	5	122	24.4	50t	2
1966			3	14	4.7	8	0
1970			2	21	10.5	14	0
1971			4	31	7.8	19	0
1972			2	1	0.5	1	0
Career			16	189	11.8	50t	2

Nick Rassas
| 1968 | ATL | N | 1 | 18 | 18.0 | 18 | 0 |

John Rauch
| 1949 | NYB | N | 2 | 4 | 2.0 | 3 | 0 |

Bob Ravensburg
| 1948 | CHIC | N | 1 | 0 | 0.0 | 0 | 0 |

Baby Ray
| 1946 | GB | N | 1 | 2 | 2.0 | 2 | 0 |

Darrol Ray
1980	NYJ	N	6	132	22.0	71t	1
1981			7	227	32.4	94t	2
1982			3	91	30.3	44	0
1983			3	77	25.7	42	0
1984			2	54	27.0	28	0
Career			21	581	27.7	94t	3
Playoffs			1	98	98.0		1

Ricky Ray
| 1981 | NO | N | 1 | 33 | 33.0 | 33 | 0 |

Terry Ray
1993	NE	N	1	0	0.0	0	0
1994			1	2	2.0	2	0
1995			1	21	21.0	21	0
1996			1	43	43.0	43	0
Career			4	66	16.5	43	0

Corey Raymond
1993	NYG	N	2	11	5.5	11	0
1994			1	0	0.0	0	0
1995	DET	N	6	44	7.3	18	0
1996			1	24	24.0	24t	1
Career			10	79	7.9	24t	1

Rick Razzano
| 1981 | CIN | N | 1 | 11 | 11.0 | 11 | 0 |

Frank Reagan
1941	NYG	N	1	28	28.0	28	0
1947			10	203	20.3	71	0
1948			9	145	16.1	45	0
1949	PHI	N	7	146	20.9	52	0
1950			4	132	33.0	47	1
1951			4	60	15.0	44	0
Career			35	714	20.4	71	1
Playoffs			1	0	0.0		0

Kerry Reardon
1973	KC	N	2	17	8.5	17	0
1974			4	0	0.0		0
1975			3	40	13.3	28	0
1976			5	26	5.2	22	0
Career			14	83	5.9	28	0

Gary Reasons
1984	NYG	N	2	26	13.0	26	0
1985			1	10	10.0	10	0
1986			2	28	14.0	18	0
1988			1	20	20.0	20	0
1989			1	40	40.0	40	0
1990			3	13	4.3	10	0
Career			10	137	13.7	40	0
Playoffs			3	48	16.0		0

Ken Reaves
1966	ATL	N	1	16	16.0	16	0
1967			7	153	21.9	42	0
1968			1	90	90.0	90t	1
1969			3	14	4.7	14	0
1970			6	44	7.3	28	0
1971			6	43	7.2	31	0

Year	Team		No	Yds	Avg	Lg	TD

Ken Reaves continued
1972			3	59	19.7	28	0
1973			2	20	10.0	11	0
1974	STL	N	1	54	54.0	54	0
1975			3	7	2.3	9	0
1976			2	41	20.5	25	0
1977			2	17	8.5	10	0
Career			37	558	15.1	90t	1

Bert Rechichar
1952	CLE	N	6	79	13.2	25	0
1953	BAL	N	7	64	9.1	36t	0
1954			2	27	13.5	21	0
1955			6	109	18.2	40	0
1956			4	63	15.8	42	0
1957			5	33	6.6	21	0
1960	PIT	N	1	10	10.0	10	0
Career			31	385	12.4	42	1

Glen Redd
1981	NO	N	1	7	7.0	7	0
1985			1	25	25.0	25	0
Career			2	32	16.0	25	0

Rick Redman
1965	SD	A	1	11	11.0	11	0
1966			2	7	3.5	7	0
1967			2	26	13.0	23	0
1969			1	3	3.0	3	0
1971	SD	N	1	0	0.0	0	0
1972			1	14	14.0	14	0
1973			1	1	1.0	1	0
Career			9	62	6.9	23	0

Rudy Redmond
1969	ATL	N	5	50	10.0	32	0
1970			1	12	12.0	12	0
1972	DET	N	2	91	45.5	88t	1
Career			8	153	19.1	88t	1

Beasley Reece
1979	NYG	N	1	3	3.0	3	0
1980			3	24	8.0	10	0
1981			4	84	21.0	32	0
1982			1	0	0.0	0	0
1983	NYG-TB		8	103	12.9	29	0
1984	TB	N	1	12	12.0	12	0
Career			18	226	12.6	32	0

Danny Reece
| 1978 | TB | N | 1 | 13 | 13.0 | 13 | 0 |

Don Reece
| 1946 | MIA | AA | 1 | 17 | 17.0 | 17 | 0 |

Frank Reed
1976	ATL	N	3	48	16.0	42	0
1978			1	38	38.0	38	0
1979			2	0	0.0	0	0
Career			6	86	14.3	42	0

Henry Reed
1971	NYG	N	1	11	11.0	11	0
1973			1	36	36.0	36	0
Career			2	47	23.5	36	0

Booker Reese
| 1983 | TB | N | 2 | 11 | 5.5 | 11 | 0 |

John Reger
1955	PIT	N	2	11	5.5	9	0
1956			2	33	16.5	33	0
1958			1	3	3.0	3	0
1960			1	18	18.0	18	0
1961			1	17	17.0	17	0
1962			1	0	0.0	0	0
1963			1	16	16.0	16	0
1964	WAS	N	3	37	12.3	19	1
1966			3	27	9.0	13	0
Career			15	162	10.8	33	1

Steve Rehage
| 1987 | NYG | N | 1 | 14 | 14.0 | 14 | 0 |

Mike Reichenbach

Year	Team		No	Yds	Avg	Lg	TD
1985	PHI	N	1	10	10.0	10	0
1991	MIA	N	1	2	2.0	2	0
Career			2	12	6.0	10	0

Joe Reid

Year	Team		No	Yds	Avg	Lg	TD
1952	DAL	N	1	0	0.0	0	0

Kevin Reilly

Year	Team		No	Yds	Avg	Lg	TD
1975	NE	N	1	54	54.0	54	0

Mike Reinfeldt

Year	Team		No	Yds	Avg	Lg	TD
1976	HOU	N	1	19	19.0	19	0
1977			5	78	15.6	30	0
1978			1	0	0.0	0	0
1979			12	205	17.1	39	0
1980			4	36	9.0	23	0
1981			2	18	9.0	16	0
1983			1	19	19.0	19	0
Career			26	375	14.4	39	0
Playoffs			3	35	11.7		

Billy Reinhard

Year	Team		No	Yds	Avg	Lg	TD
1947	LA	AA	1	7	7.0	7	0
1948			4	52	13.0		1
Career			5	59	11.8	7	1

Bob Reinhard

Year	Team		No	Yds	Avg	Lg	TD
1947	LA	AA	1	0	0.0	0	0

Albie Reisz

Year	Team		No	Yds	Avg	Lg	TD
1944	CLE	N	3	72	24.0	25	0
1945			2	55	27.5	55	0
Career			5	127	25.4	55	0
Playoffs			1	16	16.0		0

Johnny Rembert

Year	Team		No	Yds	Avg	Lg	TD
1986	NE	N	1	37	37.0	37	0
1987			1	1	1.0	1	0
1988			2	10	5.0	6	0
1989			1	0	0.0	0	0
1990			2	22	11.0	11	0
Career			7	70	10.0	37	0
Playoffs			1	0	0.0		0

Mel Renfro

Year	Team		No	Yds	Avg	Lg	TD
1964	DAL	N	7	110	15.7	39t	1
1965			2	92	46.0	90t	1
1966			2	57	28.5	33	0
1967			7	38	5.4	30	0
1968			3	5	1.7	5	0
1969			10	118	11.8	41	0
1970			4	3	0.8	3	0
1971			4	11	2.8	7	0
1972			1	0	0.0	0	0
1973			2	65	32.5	35	1
1974			1	6	6.0	6	0
1975			4	70	17.5	22	0
1976			3	23	7.7	23	0
1977			2	28	14.0	25	0
Career			52	626	12.0	90t	3
Playoffs			4	32	8.0		0

Pug Rentner

Year	Team		No	Yds	Avg	Lg	TD
1936	BOS	N					1
Playoffs			1	5	5.0		0

Jack Reynolds

Year	Team		No	Yds	Avg	Lg	TD
1973	LA	N	2	52	26.0	49	0
1975			1	15	15.0	15	0
1980			1	20	20.0	20	0
1981	SF	N	1	0	0.0	0	0
1982			1	0	0.0	0	0
Career			6	87	14.5	49	0
Playoffs			2	16	8.0		0

Jim Reynolds

Year	Team		No	Yds	Avg	Lg	TD
1946	MIA	AA	2	33	16.5		0

Ricky Reynolds

Year	Team		No	Yds	Avg	Lg	TD
1988	TB	N	4	7	1.8	7	0
1989			5	87	17.4	68t	0
1990			3	70	23.3	46	0
1991			2	7	3.5	7	0

Ricky Reynolds *continued*

Year	Team		No	Yds	Avg	Lg	TD
1992			2	0	0.0	0	0
1993			1	3	3.0	3	0
1994	NE	N	1	11	11.0	11t	1
1995			3	6	2.0	4	0
1996			2	7	3.5	7	0
Career			23	198	8.6	68t	2

Floyd Rhea

Year	Team		No	Yds	Avg	Lg	TD
1944	BKN	N	1	0	0.0	0	0

Jay Rhodemyre

Year	Team		No	Yds	Avg	Lg	TD
1948	GB	N	1	24	24.0	24	0
1949			4	12	3.0	9	0
Career			5	36	7.2	24	0

Bruce Rhodes

Year	Team		No	Yds	Avg	Lg	TD
1976	SF	N	3	42	14.0	30	0
1978	DET	N	1	24	24.0	24	0
Career			4	66	16.5	30	0

Ray Rhodes

Year	Team		No	Yds	Avg	Lg	TD
1977	NYG	N	2	59	29.5	40	0
1978			3	74	24.7	41	0
1979			2	0	0.0	0	0
1980	SF	N	1	25	25.0	25	0
Career			8	158	19.8	41	0

Earnie Rhone

Year	Team		No	Yds	Avg	Lg	TD
1975	MIA	N	2	2	1.0	2	0
1978			2	4	2.0	4	0
1979			2	17	8.5	10	0
1980			3	33	11.0	12	0
1981			3	35	11.7	16	0
1982			1	4	4.0	4	0
1983			1	15	15.0	15	0
Career			14	110	7.9	16	0

Jim Ricca

Year	Team		No	Yds	Avg	Lg	TD
1955	DET	N	1	33	33.0	33	0

Floyd Rice

Year	Team		No	Yds	Avg	Lg	TD
1973	SD	N	1	8	8.0	8	0
1974			3	44	14.7	15	0
1975			1	0	0.0	0	0
1977	OAK	N	2	5	2.5	3	0
Career			7	57	8.1	15	0
Playoffs			1	11	11.0		0

Rodney Rice

Year	Team		No	Yds	Avg	Lg	TD
1990	TB	N	2	7	3.5	4	0

Herb Rich

Year	Team		No	Yds	Avg	Lg	TD
1950	BAL	N	3	45	15.0	45t	1
1951	LA	N	3	11	3.7	6	0
1952			8	201	25.1	97t	1
1953			3	95	31.7	53t	1
1954	NYG	N	5	56	11.2	19	0
1955			6	61	10.2	53	0
1956			1	0	0.0	0	0
Career			29	469	16.2	97t	3

Stanley Richard

Year	Team		No	Yds	Avg	Lg	TD
1991	SD	N	2	5	2.5	3	0
1992			3	26	8.7	20	0
1993			1	-2	-2.0	-2	0
1994			4	224	56.0	99t	2
1995	WAS	N	3	24	8.0	24	0
1996			3	47	15.7	42	0
Career			16	324	20.3	99t	2

Jim Richards

Year	Team		No	Yds	Avg	Lg	TD
1969	NY	A	3	48	16.0	37	0

Al Richardson

Year	Team		No	Yds	Avg	Lg	TD
1980	ATL	N	7	139	19.9	52	0
1981			1	9	9.0	9	0
1983			1	38	38.0	38	0
Career			9	186	20.7	52	0

Jerry Richardson

Year	Team		No	Yds	Avg	Lg	TD
1964	LA	N	5	146	29.2	41	0
1965			1	33	33.0	33	0

Jerry Richardson *continued*

Year	Team		No	Yds	Avg	Lg	TD
1966	ATL	N	5	68	13.6	20	0
Career			11	247	22.5	41	0

Jesse Richardson

Year	Team		No	Yds	Avg	Lg	TD
1954	PHI	N	1	10	10.0	10	0

Mike Richardson

Year	Team		No	Yds	Avg	Lg	TD
1983	CHI	N	5	9	1.8	6	0
1984			2	7	3.5	7	0
1985			4	174	43.5	90	1
1986			7	69	9.9	32	0
1988			2	15	7.5	15	0
Career			20	274	13.7	90	1
Playoffs			3	43	14.3		0

Pete Richardson

Year	Team		No	Yds	Avg	Lg	TD
1969	BUF	A	2	17	8.5	17	0
1970	BUF	N	5	46	9.2	22	0
1971			1	0	0.0	0	0
Career			8	63	7.9	22	0

Frank Richter

Year	Team		No	Yds	Avg	Lg	TD
1967	DEN	A	2	6	3.0	6	0

Les Richter

Year	Team		No	Yds	Avg	Lg	TD
1954	LA	N	1	24	24.0	24	0
1955			2	23	11.5	20	0
1957			4	60	15.0	25	0
1958			3	26	8.7	16	0
1960			2	29	14.5	20	0
1961			4	44	11.0	17	0
Career			16	206	12.9	25	0

Louis Riddick

Year	Team		No	Yds	Avg	Lg	TD
Playoffs			1	16	16.0		0

Jimmy Ridlon

Year	Team		No	Yds	Avg	Lg	TD
1958	SF	N	4	10	2.5	3	0
1962			1	8	8.0	8	0
1964	DAL	N	4	121	30.3	74t	1
Career			9	139	15.4	74t	1

Bill Rieth

Year	Team		No	Yds	Avg	Lg	TD
1944	CLE	N	1	12	12.0	12	0

Charley Rieves

Year	Team		No	Yds	Avg	Lg	TD
1964	HOU	A	1	3	3.0	3	0

Chuck Riffle

Year	Team		No	Yds	Avg	Lg	TD
1948	NY	AA	1	11	11.0	11	0

Dick Riffle

Year	Team		No	Yds	Avg	Lg	TD
1941	PIT	N	6	93	15.5	29	0
1942			4	59	14.8	51	0
Career			10	152	15.2	51	0

Bob Riggle

Year	Team		No	Yds	Avg	Lg	TD
1966	ATL	N	3	71	23.7	62t	1

Avon Riley

Year	Team		No	Yds	Avg	Lg	TD
1983	HOU	N	1	0	0.0	0	0
1985			1	14	14.0	14	0
1987	PIT	N	1	4	4.0	4	0
Career			3	18	6.0	14	0

Ken Riley

Year	Team		No	Yds	Avg	Lg	TD
1969	CIN	A	4	66	16.5	66	0
1970	CIN	N	4	17	4.3	14	0
1971			5	22	4.4	21	0
1972			3	0	0.0	0	0
1973			2	2	1.0	5	0
1974			5	33	6.6	19	0
1975			6	76	12.7	30t	1
1976			9	141	15.7	53t	1
1977			2	14	7.0	14	0
1978			3	33	11.0	17	0
1979			1	0	0.0	0	0
1980			3	9	3.0	9	0
1981			5	6	1.2	6	0
1982			5	88	17.6	56t	1
1983			8	89	11.1	42t	2
Career			65	596	9.2	66	5
Playoffs			3	34	11.3		0

Year	Team		No	Yds	Avg	Lg	TD

Lee Riley

Year	Team		No	Yds	Avg	Lg	TD
1955	DET	N	2	38	19.0	23	0
1956	PHI	N	3	57	19.0	31	0
1958			1	8	8.0	8	0
1959			1	0	0.0	0	0
1960	NYG	N	1	2	2.0	2	0
1961	NY	A	4	59	14.8	41	0
1962			11	122	11.1	30	0
Career			23	286	12.4	41	0

Del Ritchhart

Year	Team		No	Yds	Avg	Lg	TD
1936	DET	N					1

Ron Rivera

Year	Team		No	Yds	Avg	Lg	TD
1985	CHI	N	1	4	4.0	4	0
1987			2	19	9.5	15	0
1988			2	0	0.0	0	0
1989			2	1	0.5	1	0
1990			2	13	6.5	13	0
Career			9	37	4.1	15	0

Jamie Rivers

Year	Team		No	Yds	Avg	Lg	TD
1968	STL	N	2	22	11.0	14	0
1973			1	11	11.0	11	0
1974	NYJ	N	1	0	0.0	0	0
Career			4	33	8.3	14	0

Don Rives

Year	Team		No	Yds	Avg	Lg	TD
1978	CHI	N	2	8	4.0	8	0

Joe Rizzo

Year	Team		No	Yds	Avg	Lg	TD
1976	DEN	N	1	8	8.0	8	0
1977			3	49	16.3	38	0
1978			3	10	3.3	10	0
1979			2	25	12.5	25	0
Career			9	92	10.2	38	0

Joe Robb

Year	Team		No	Yds	Avg	Lg	TD
1961	STL	N	1	3	3.0	3	0

Randy Robbins

Year	Team		No	Yds	Avg	Lg	TD
1984	DEN	N	2	62	31.0	62t	1
1985			1	3	3.0	3	0
1987			3	9	3.0	9	0
1988			2	66	33.0	39	0
1989			2	18	9.0	18t	0
1991			1	35	35.0	35	0
1992	NE	N	2	27	13.5	20	0
Career			13	220	16.9	62t	2

Vern Roberson

Year	Team		No	Yds	Avg	Lg	TD
1977	MIA	N	1	0	0.0	0	0
1978	SF	N	1	31	31.0	31	0
Career			2	31	15.5	31	0

Guy Roberts

Year	Team		No	Yds	Avg	Lg	TD
1973	HOU	N	4	55	13.8	27	0
1976	ATL	N	1	7	7.0	7	0
Career			5	62	12.4	27	0

Larry Roberts

Year	Team		No	Yds	Avg	Lg	TD
1992	SF	N	1	19	19.0	19	0

Bobbie Robertson

Year	Team		No	Yds	Avg	Lg	TD
1942	BKN	N	2	30	15.0	30	0

Isiah Robertson

Year	Team		No	Yds	Avg	Lg	TD
1971	LA	N	4	32	8.0	20	0
1973			3	57	19.0	49t	1
1974			2	11	5.5	6	0
1975			4	118	29.5	76t	1
1976			4	28	7.0	14	0
1977			1	20	20.0	20	0
1979	BUF	N	2	29	14.5	23t	1
1980			2	39	19.5	39	0
1981			2	15	7.5	15	0
1982			1	0	0.0	0	0
Career			25	349	14.0	76t	3
Playoffs			2	74	37.0		1

Marcus Robertson

Year	Team		No	Yds	Avg	Lg	TD
1992	HOU	N	1	27	27.0	27	0
1993			7	137	19.6	69	0
1994			3	90	30.0	41	0

Marcus Robertson *continued*

Year	Team		No	Yds	Avg	Lg	TD
1996			4	44	11.0	27	0
Career			15	298	19.9	69	0

Tom Robertson

Year	Team		No	Yds	Avg	Lg	TD
1942	BKN	N	1	2	2.0	2	0

Dave Robinson

Year	Team		No	Yds	Avg	Lg	TD
1965	GB	N	3	141	47.0	87	0
1966			5	60	12.0	23	0
1967			4	16	4.0	12	0
1968			2	18	9.0	18	0
1970			2	33	16.5	20	0
1971			3	44	14.7	23	0
1972			2	10	5.0	7	0
1973	WAS	N	4	98	24.5	39	1
1974			2	29	14.5	29	0
Career			27	449	16.6	87	1

DeJuan Robinson

Year	Team		No	Yds	Avg	Lg	TD
1987	CLE	N	1	0	0.0	0	0

Eddie Robinson

Year	Team		No	Yds	Avg	Lg	TD
1995	HOU	N	1	49	49.0	49t	1
1996			1	2	2.0	2	0
Career			2	51	25.5	49t	1

Eugene Robinson

Year	Team		No	Yds	Avg	Lg	TD
1985	SEA	N	2	47	23.5	47	0
1986			3	39	13.0	25	0
1987			3	75	25.0	44	0
1988			1	0	0.0	0	0
1989			5	24	4.8	20	0
1990			5	89	29.7	39	0
1991			5	56	11.2	27	0
1992			7	126	18.0	49	0
1993			9	80	8.9	28	0
1994			3	18	6.0	18	0
1995			1	32	32.0	32	0
1996	GB	N	6	107	17.8	39	0
Career			48	693	14.4	49	0
Playoffs			2	0	0.0		0

Frank Robinson

Year	Team		No	Yds	Avg	Lg	TD
1993	DEN	N	1	13	13.0	13	0

Freddie Robinson

Year	Team		No	Yds	Avg	Lg	TD
1987	IND	N	2	86	43.0	68	0
Playoffs			1	0	0.0		0

Jerry Robinson

Year	Team		No	Yds	Avg	Lg	TD
1980	PHI	N	2	13	6.5	13	0
1981			1	3	3.0	3	0
1982			3	19	6.3	12	0
1986	LARI	N	4	42	10.5	32t	1
1989			1	25	25.0	25	0
1990			1	5	5.0	5t	1
Career			12	107	8.9	32t	2
Playoffs			1	37	37.0		0

Johnny Robinson

Year	Team		No	Yds	Avg	Lg	TD
1962	DAL	A	4	25	6.3	20	0
1963	KC	A	3	41	13.7	19	0
1964			2	17	8.5	17	0
1965			5	99	19.8	50	0
1966			10	136	13.6	29	1
1967			5	17	3.4	10	0
1968			6	40	6.7	16	0
1969			8	158	19.8	33	0
1970	KC	N	10	155	15.5	57	0
1971			4	53	13.3	29	0
Career			57	741	13.0	57	1
Playoffs			4	131	32.8		0

Larry Robinson

Year	Team		No	Yds	Avg	Lg	TD
1987	NYJ	N	1	38	38.0	38	0

Mark Robinson

Year	Team		No	Yds	Avg	Lg	TD
1985	KC	N	1	20	20.0	20	0
1987			2	42	21.0	25	0
1988	TB	N	2	28	14.0	28	0
1989			6	44	7.3	16	0

Mark Robinson *continued*

Year	Team		No	Yds	Avg	Lg	TD
1990			4	81	20.3	27	0
Career			15	215	14.3	28	0

Rafael Robinson

Year	Team		No	Yds	Avg	Lg	TD
1994	SEA	N	1	0	0.0	0	0

Shelton Robinson

Year	Team		No	Yds	Avg	Lg	TD
1983	SEA	N	1	18	18.0	18	0

Wayne Robinson

Year	Team		No	Yds	Avg	Lg	TD
1954	PHI	N	4	41	10.3	18	0
1955			1	20	20.0	20	0
Career			5	61	12.2	20	0

Marshall Robnett

Year	Team		No	Yds	Avg	Lg	TD
1944	C-P	N	1	48	48.0	48	0

Frank Robotti

Year	Team		No	Yds	Avg	Lg	TD
1961	BOS	A	2	18	9.0	11	0

Andy Robustelli

Year	Team		No	Yds	Avg	Lg	TD
1952	LA	N	1	14	14.0	14t	1
1955			1	10	10.0	10t	1
Career			2	24	12.0	14t	2

Chris Rockins

Year	Team		No	Yds	Avg	Lg	TD
1984	CLE	N	1	0	0.0	0	0
1985			1	8	8.0	8	0
1986			2	41	20.5	24	0
1987			2	25	12.5	15	0
Career			6	74	12.3	24	0

Hank Rockwell

Year	Team		No	Yds	Avg	Lg	TD
1941	CLE	N	1	9	9.0	9	0
1942			1	58	58.0	58	0
Career			2	67	33.5	58	0

Don Rogers

Year	Team		No	Yds	Avg	Lg	TD
1984	CLE	N	1	39	39.0	39	0
1985			1	3	3.0	3	0
Career			2	42	21.0	39	0
Playoffs			1	45	45.0		0

Mel Rogers

Year	Team		No	Yds	Avg	Lg	TD
1973	SD	N	1	3	3.0	3	0

Herm Rohrig

Year	Team		No	Yds	Avg	Lg	TD
1941	GB	N	1	17	17.0	17	0
1946			5	134	26.8	51	0
1947			5	80	16.0	28	0
Career			11	231	21.0	51	0

Henry Rolling

Year	Team		No	Yds	Avg	Lg	TD
1990	SD	N	1	67	67.0	67	0
1991			2	54	27.0	47	0
1993	LARM	N	2	21	10.5	12	0
Career			5	142	28.4	67	0

Nick Roman

Year	Team		No	Yds	Avg	Lg	TD
1972	CLE	N	1	36	36.0	36t	1

Bill Romanowski

Year	Team		No	Yds	Avg	Lg	TD
1989	SF	N	1	13	13.0	13	0
1991			1	7	7.0	7	0
1994	PHI	N	2	8	4.0	8	0
1995			2	5	2.5	7	0
1996	DEN	N	3	1	0.3	1	0
Career			9	34	3.8	13	0
Playoffs			1	0	0.0		0

Rudy Romboli

Year	Team		No	Yds	Avg	Lg	TD
1946	BOS	N	1	12	12.0	12	0
1947			1	14	14.0	14	0
Career			2	26	13.0	14	0

Charles Romes

Year	Team		No	Yds	Avg	Lg	TD
1978	BUF	N	2	95	47.5	85t	1
1979			1	0	0.0	0	0
1980			2	41	20.5	30	0
1981			4	113	28.3	35	0
1982			1	8	8.0	8	0
1983			2	27	13.5	27	0

Year	Team		No	Yds	Avg	Lg	TD

Charles Romes *continued*

Year	Team		No	Yds	Avg	Lg	TD
1984			5	130	26.0	55	0
1985			7	56	8.0	21	0
1986			4	23	5.8	23	0
Career			28	493	17.6	85t	1

Al Romine

1958	GB	N	1	0	0.0	0	0
1960	DEN	A	3	69	23.0		0
Career			4	69	17.3	0	0

Gene Ronzani

| 1944 | CHIB | N | 3 | 19 | 6.3 | 11 | 0 |
| Playoffs | | | 2 | 36 | 18.0 | | 0 |

Joe Rooney

| 1924 | DUL | N | | | | | 1 |

John Roper

| 1989 | CHI | N | 2 | 46 | 23.0 | 43 | 0 |

Durwood Roquemore

1982	KC	N	1	17	17.0	17	0
1983			4	117	29.3	42t	1
Career			5	134	26.8	42t	1

Donovan Rose

| 1986 | MIA | N | 2 | 63 | 31.5 | 36 | 0 |

George Rose

1964	MIN	N	6	48	8.0	32t	1
1965			1	6	6.0	6	0
1966			1	17	17.0	17	0
1967	NO	N	1	15	15.0	15	0
Career			9	86	9.6	32t	1

Ken Rose

| 1987 | NYJ | N | 1 | 1 | 1.0 | 1 | 0 |

Rocky Rosema

| 1969 | STL | N | 1 | 3 | 3.0 | 3 | 0 |

Ken Roskie

| 1948 | GB | N | 1 | 12 | 12.0 | 12 | 0 |

Kevin Ross

1984	KC	N	6	124	20.7	71t	1
1985			3	47	15.7	27	0
1986			4	66	16.5	35	0
1987			3	40	13.3	40	0
1988			1	0	0.0	0	0
1989			4	29	7.3	23	0
1990			5	97	19.4	40	0
1991			1	0	0.0	0	0
1992			1	99	99.0	99t	1
1993			2	49	24.5	48	0
1994	ATL	N	3	26	8.7	16	0
1995			3	70	23.3	33	0
1996	SD	N	2	7	3.5	7	0
Career			38	654	17.2	99t	2

George Rosso

| 1954 | WAS | N | 4 | 9 | 2.3 | 7 | 0 |

Tim Rossovich

1971	PHI	N	1	24	24.0	24	0
1972	SD	N	1	0	0.0	0	0
1973			1	9	9.0	9	0
Career			3	33	11.0	24	0

Tom Roussel

| 1972 | NO | N | 2 | 15 | 7.5 | 11 | 0 |

Bob Rowe

| 1969 | STL | N | 2 | 19 | 9.5 | 18t | 1 |

Harmon Rowe

1947	NY	AA	2	20	10.0		0
1949	B-NY	AA	3	53	17.7		0
1950	NYG	N	3	48	16.0	32	0
1951			2	19	9.5	19	0
1952			1	22	22.0	22	0
Career			11	162	14.7	32	0

Justin Rowland

| 1961 | MIN | N | 1 | 4 | 4.0 | 4 | 0 |

John Rowser

1970	PIT	N	3	27	9.0	12	0
1971			4	94	23.5	70t	1
1972			4	30	7.5	23	0
1973			6	131	21.8	71t	1
1974	DEN	N	4	56	14.0	33	0
1975			1	2	2.0	2	0
1976			4	104	26.0	41t	2
Career			26	444	17.1	71t	4

Aubrey Rozelle

| 1957 | PIT | N | 1 | 4 | 4.0 | 4 | 0 |

Dave Rozumek

| 1978 | KC | N | 2 | 5 | 2.5 | 3 | 0 |

Karl Rubke

1957	SF	N	1	16	16.0	16	0
1961	MIN	N	1	12	12.0	12	0
Career			2	28	14.0	16	0

Martin Ruby

| 1949 | B-NY | AA | 1 | 19 | 19.0 | 19t | 1 |

Eddie Rucinski

| 1944 | C-P | | 4 | 35 | 8.8 | 22 | 0 |

Council Rudolph

| 1975 | STL | N | 1 | 18 | 18.0 | 18 | 0 |

Jack Rudolph

1960	BOS	A	2	13	6.5		0
1966	MIA	A	1	3	3.0	3	0
Career			3	16	5.3	3	0

Paul Rudzinski

| 1980 | GB | N | 1 | 14 | 14.0 | 14 | 0 |

Howie Ruetz

| 1951 | GB | N | 1 | 11 | 11.0 | 11 | 0 |

Joe Ruetz

| 1946 | CHI | AA | 2 | 13 | 6.5 | | 0 |

Marion Rushing

1966	ATL	N	3	5	1.7	5	0
1967			1	2	2.0	2	0
Career			4	7	1.8	5	0

Roy Ruskusky

| 1947 | NY | AA | 1 | 8 | 8.0 | 8 | 0 |

Andy Russell

1963	PIT	N	3	20	6.7	10	0
1967			3	50	16.7	42	0
1968			2	2	1.0	1	0
1969			2	48	24.0	26	0
1970			3	64	21.3	37	0
1973			3	54	18.0	45t	1
1974			1	0	0.0	0	0
1976			1	0	0.0	0	0
Career			18	238	13.2	45t	1
Playoffs			1	0	0.0		0

Jack Russell

1947	NY	AA	1	33	33.0	33	0
1948			1	0	0.0	0	0
1949	B-NY	AA	1	5	5.0	5	0
Career			3	38	12.7	33	0

Ralph Ruthstrom

1945	CLE	N	1	46	46.0	46	0
1949	BAL	AA	1	15	15.0	15	0
Career			2	61	30.5	46	0

Dave Ryan

1945	DET	N	3	90	30.0	42	0
1946			4	105	26.3	44	0
Career			7	195	27.9	44	0

Jim Ryan

1980	DEN	N	1	21	21.0	21	0
1984			1	13	13.0	13	0
1987			3	7	2.3	5	0
Career			5	41	8.2	21	0
Playoffs			1	26	26.0		0

John Ryan

1956	PHI	N	1	17	17.0	17	0
1958			1	38	38.0	38	0
Career			2	55	27.5	38	0

Kent Ryan

| 1940 | DET | N | 6 | 65 | 10.8 | | 0 |

Julie Rykovich

1947	BUF	AA	2	61	30.5	56	0
1948	CHI	AA	3	65	21.7		0
Career			5	126	25.2	56	0

Lou Rymkus

| 1943 | WAS | N | 1 | 21 | 21.0 | 21t | 1 |

Lou Saban

1946	CLE	AA	4	32	8.0		0
1947			2	2	1.0		0
1948			5	41	8.2		0
1949			2	35	17.5		1
Career			13	110	8.5		1
Playoffs			2	75	37.5		1

Joe Sabasteanski

1947	BOS	N	1	0	0.0	0	0
1948			2	38	19.0	38	0
Career			3	38	12.7	38	0

Dwayne Sabb

1994	NE	N	2	6	3.0	5	0
1996			1	0	0.0	0	0
Career			3	6	2.0	5	0

Lenny Sachs

| 1921 | CHIC | A | | | | | 1 |

Frankie Sachse

| 1945 | BOS | N | 2 | 25 | 12.5 | 22 | 0 |

Nick Sacrinty

| 1947 | CHIB | N | 1 | 7 | 7.0 | 7 | 0 |

Rod Saddler

| 1987 | STL | N | 1 | 0 | 0.0 | 0 | 0 |

Eddie Saenz

1946	WAS	N	1	0	0.0	0	0
1950			1	0	0.0	0	0
Career			2	0	0.0	0	0

Floyd Sagely

| 1957 | CHIC | N | 1 | 7 | 7.0 | 7 | 0 |

George Saimes

1963	BUF	A	4	29	7.3	16	0
1964			6	56	9.3	32	0
1965			4	24	6.0	20	0
1966			1	32	32.0	32	0
1967			2	14	7.0	14	0
1968			2	36	18.0	19	0
1969			3	47	15.7	28	0
Career			22	238	10.8	32	0

Dan Saleaumua

1989	KC	N	1	21	21.0	21	0
1993			1	13	13.0	13	0
1995			1	0	0.0	0	0
Career			3	34	11.3	21	0

Eddie Salem

| 1951 | WAS | N | 5 | 26 | 5.2 | 21 | 0 |

Bryant Salter

1971	SD	N	6	48	8.0	44	0
1972			7	111	15.9	31	0
1973			1	20	20.0	20	0

Bryant Salter *continued*

Year	Team		No	Yds	Avg	Lg	TD
1974	WAS	N	1	0	0.0	0	0
1975			1	17	17.0	17	0
1976	MIA	N	1	0	0.0	0	0
Career			17	196	11.5	44	0

Johnny Sample

Year	Team		No	Yds	Avg	Lg	TD
1959	BAL	N	1	10	10.0	10	0
1960			4	27	6.8	18	0
1961	PIT	N	8	141	17.6	42	0
1962			0	21		21L	0
1963	WAS	N	1	0	0.0	0	0
1964			4	31	7.8	16	1
1965			6	57	9.5	28	0
1966	NY	A	6	32	5.3	21	0
1967			4	53	13.3	41t	1
1968			7	88	12.6	39	1
Career			41	460	11.2	42	4
Playoffs			3	76	25.3		1

Don Samuel

Year	Team		No	Yds	Avg	Lg	TD
1949	PIT	N	1	4	4.0	4	0

Carl Samuelson

Year	Team		No	Yds	Avg	Lg	TD
1948	PIT	N	1	33	33.0	33	0

Johnny Sanchez

Year	Team		No	Yds	Avg	Lg	TD
1947	WAS	N	1	0	0.0	0	0

Lupe Sanchez

Year	Team		No	Yds	Avg	Lg	TD
1986	PIT	N	3	71	23.7	67t	1
1988			1	0	0.0	0	0
Career			4	71	17.8	67t	1

Deion Sanders

Year	Team		No	Yds	Avg	Lg	TD
1989	ATL	N	5	52	10.4	22	0
1990			3	153	51.0	82t	2
1991			6	119	19.8	55t	1
1992			3	105	35.0	55	0
1993			7	91	13.0	41	0
1994	SF	N	6	**303**	50.5	93t	3
1995	DAL	N	2	34	17.0	34	0
1996			2	3	1.5	2	0
Career			34	860	25.3	93t	6
Playoffs			5	80	16.0		

Jack Sanders

Year	Team		No	Yds	Avg	Lg	TD
1942	PIT	N	1	8	8.0	8	0

John Sanders

Year	Team		No	Yds	Avg	Lg	TD
1974	NE	N	5	57	11.4	23t	1
1975			1	18	18.0	18	0
1977	PHI	N	6	122	20.3	45	0
1978			5	43	8.6	24	1
Career			17	240	14.1	45	2

Lonnie Sanders

Year	Team		No	Yds	Avg	Lg	TD
1963	WAS	N	3	46	15.3	38	0
1964			2	4	2.0	4	0
1965			4	121	30.3	42	0
1968	STL	N	3	6	2.0	6	0
Career			12	177	14.8	42	0

Spec Sanders

Year	Team		No	Yds	Avg	Lg	TD
1946	NY	AA	2	71	35.5	50t	0
1947			3	63	21.0		0
1948			1	24	24.0	24	0
1950	NYY	N	13	199	15.3	29	0
Career			19	357	18.8	50t	0

Dan Sandifer

Year	Team		No	Yds	Avg	Lg	TD
1948	WAS	N	13	**258**	19.8	5	2
1949			5	82	16.4	59	0
1950	DET	N	2	27	13.5	27	0
1951	PHI	N	1	28	28.0	28	0
1952	GB	N	2	25	12.5	17	0
Career			23	420	18.3	59	2

Curt Sandig

Year	Team		No	Yds	Avg	Lg	TD
1942	PIT	N	5	94	18.8	42	0

Leo Sanford

Year	Team		No	Yds	Avg	Lg	TD
1951	CHIC	N	1	20	20.0	20	

Leo Sanford *continued*

Year	Team		No	Yds	Avg	Lg	TD
1952			2	5	2.5	5	0
1953			2	56	28.0	48t	1
1954			2	2	1.0	2	0
1955			3	97	32.3	92t	1
1956			5	24	4.8	19	0
1957			1	2	2.0	2	0
1958	BAL	N	1	7	7.0	7	0
Career			17	213	12.5	92t	2

Lucius Sanford

Year	Team		No	Yds	Avg	Lg	TD
1978	BUF	N	1	41	41.0	41	0
1979			2	44	22.0	25	0
1983			2	39	19.5	20	0
Career			5	124	24.8	41	0

Rick Sanford

Year	Team		No	Yds	Avg	Lg	TD
1979	NE	N	1	39	39.0	39	0
1980			1	0	0.0	0	0
1981			3	28	9.3	21	0
1982			2	105	52.5	99t	1
1983			7	24	3.4	16	0
1984			2	2	1.0	2	0
Career			16	198	12.4	99t	1

Dom Sanzotta

Year	Team		No	Yds	Avg	Lg	TD
1942	DET	N	2	16	8.0	10	0

Warren Sapp

Year	Team		No	Yds	Avg	Lg	TD
1995	TB	N	1	5	5.0	5t	0

Doug Satcher

Year	Team		No	Yds	Avg	Lg	TD
1968	BOS	A	1	1	1.0	1	0

George Sauer

Year	Team		No	Yds	Avg	Lg	TD
1935	GB	N					1

Bill Saul

Year	Team		No	Yds	Avg	Lg	TD
1964	PIT	N	1	13	13.0	13	0
1966			2	21	10.5	13	0
1967			1	0	0.0	0	0
Career			4	34	8.5	13	0

Corey Sawyer

Year	Team		No	Yds	Avg	Lg	TD
1994	CIN	N	2	0	0.0	0	0
1995			2	61	30.5	61	0
1996			2	0	0.0	0	0
Career			6	61	10.2	61	0

Joe Scarpati

Year	Team		No	Yds	Avg	Lg	TD
1964	PHI	N	3	41	13.7	24t	1
1965			3	4	1.3	3	0
1966			8	**182**	22.8	32	0
1967			4	99	24.8	67t	1
1968			2	22	11.0	17	0
1969			4	54	13.5	34t	1
1970	NO	N	1	4	4.0	4	0
Career			25	406	16.2	67t	3

Mike Scarry

Year	Team		No	Yds	Avg	Lg	TD
1944	CLE	N	1	5	5.0	5	0
1945			4	32	8.0	18	0
1946	CLE	AA	2	0	0.0	0	0
Career			7	37	5.3	18	0

Pete Schabarum

Year	Team		No	Yds	Avg	Lg	TD
1954	SF	N	1	9	9.0	9	0

Joe Schaffer

Year	Team		No	Yds	Avg	Lg	TD
1960	BUF	A	1	19	19.0	19	0

Francis Schammel

Year	Team		No	Yds	Avg	Lg	TD
1937	GB	N					1

Scott Schankweiler

Year	Team		No	Yds	Avg	Lg	TD
1987	BUF	N	1	7	7.0	7	0

Bernie Scherer

Year	Team		No	Yds	Avg	Lg	TD
1936	GB	N					1

Johnny Schiechl

Year	Team		No	Yds	Avg	Lg	TD
1941	PIT	N	1	0	0.0	0	0
1946	CHIB	N	3	26	8.7	15	0

Johnny Schiechl *continued*

Year	Team		No	Yds	Avg	Lg	TD
1947	SF	AA	2	45	22.5		0
Career			6	71	11.8	15	0

Maury Schleicher

Year	Team		No	Yds	Avg	Lg	TD
1960	LA	A	1	5	5.0	5	0

Hank Schmidt

Year	Team		No	Yds	Avg	Lg	TD
1964	SD	A	1	58	58.0	58t	1

Joe Schmidt

Year	Team		No	Yds	Avg	Lg	TD
1953	DET	N	2	51	25.5	39	0
1954			2	13	6.5	13	0
1956			1	7	7.0	7	0
1957			1	8	8.0	8	0
1958			6	69	11.5	25	0
1959			1	17	17.0	17	0
1960			2	46	23.0	29	0
1961			4	38	9.5	26	1
1962			1	3	3.0	3	0
1965			4	42	10.5	14	0
Career			24	294	12.3	39	2
Playoffs			3	32	10.7		0

Terry Schmidt

Year	Team		No	Yds	Avg	Lg	TD
1974	NO	N	4	27	6.8	24t	0
1975			1	37	37.0	37	0
1978	CHI	N	2	23	11.5	23	0
1979			6	44	7.3	20t	1
1980			1	0	0.0	0	0
1981			2	4	2.0	4	0
1982			4	39	9.8	29	0
1983			5	31	6.2	32t	0
1984			1	0	0.0	0	0
Career			26	205	7.9	37	1

Bob Schmitz

Year	Team		No	Yds	Avg	Lg	TD
1962	PIT	N	3	65	21.7	24t	1

Otto Schnellbacher

Year	Team		No	Yds	Avg	Lg	TD
1948	NY	AA	11	239	21.7	51	1
1949	B-NY	AA	4	26	6.5		0
1950	NYG	N	8	99	12.4	37	0
1951			**11**	**194**	17.6	46t	2
Career			34	558	16.4	51	3

Bruce Scholtz

Year	Team		No	Yds	Avg	Lg	TD
1982	SEA	N	1	31	31.0	31t	0
1983			1	8	8.0	8	0
1984			1	15	15.0	15	0
1986			2	10	5.0	10	0
Career			5	64	12.8	31t	0
Playoffs			1	8	8.0		0

Marty Schottenheimer

Year	Team		No	Yds	Avg	Lg	TD
1966	BUF	A	1	20	20.0	20	0
1967			3	88	29.3	45t	1
1968			1	22	22.0	22	0
1969	BOS	A	1	3	3.0	3	0
Career			6	133	22.2	45t	1

Bill Schroeder

Year	Team		No	Yds	Avg	Lg	TD
1946	CHI	AA	1	4	4.0	4	0
1947			4	148	37.0	62	2
Career			5	152	30.4	62	2

Gene Schroeder

Year	Team		No	Yds	Avg	Lg	TD
1951	CHIB	N	5	62	12.4	22	0

Bill Schroll

Year	Team		No	Yds	Avg	Lg	TD
1949	BUF	AA	1	4	4.0	4	0
1950	DET	N	2	8	4.0	7	0
Career			3	12	4.0	7	0

Ken Schroy

Year	Team		No	Yds	Avg	Lg	TD
1979	NYJ	N	1	4	4.0	4	0
1980			8	91	11.4	82t	1
1981			2	58	29.0	39	0
1982			1	34	34.0	34	0
1983			2	6	3.0	4	0
1984			2	13	6.5	13	0
Career			16	206	12.9	82t	1
Playoffs			2	1	0.5		0

Charles Schuette

Year	Team		No	Yds	Avg	Lg	TD
1948	BUF	AA	4	97	24.3		1
1950	GB	N	1	0	0.0	0	0
Career			5	97	19.4	0	1

Jeff Schuh

Year	Team		No	Yds	Avg	Lg	TD
1984	CIN	N	1	0	0.0	0	0

Jody Schulz

Year	Team		No	Yds	Avg	Lg	TD
1986	PHI	N	1	11	11.0	11	0

Kurt Schulz

Year	Team		No	Yds	Avg	Lg	TD
1995	BUF	N	6	48	8.0	32t	1
1996			4	24	6.0	19	0
Career			10	72	7.2	32t	1

Don Schwartz

Year	Team		No	Yds	Avg	Lg	TD
1979	NO	N	2	31	15.5	22	0

Elmer Schwartz

Year	Team		No	Yds	Avg	Lg	TD
1931	POR	N					1

John Schweder

Year	Team		No	Yds	Avg	Lg	TD
1951	PIT	N	1	20	20.0	20	0

Dick Schweidler

Year	Team		No	Yds	Avg	Lg	TD
1946	CHIB	N	1	31	31.0	31	0

Wilson Schwenk

Year	Team		No	Yds	Avg	Lg	TD
1942	CHIC	N	1	21	21.0	21	0

John Sciarra

Year	Team		No	Yds	Avg	Lg	TD
1978	PHI	N	1	21	21.0	21	0
1979			2	47	23.5	34	0
1981			1	0	0.0	0	0
Career			4	68	17.0	34	0

Nick Scollard

Year	Team		No	Yds	Avg	Lg	TD
1949	NYB	N	1	5	5.0	5	0

Clarence Scott

Year	Team		No	Yds	Avg	Lg	TD
1970	BOS	N	1	18	18.0	18	0

Clarence Scott

Year	Team		No	Yds	Avg	Lg	TD
1971	CLE	N	4	47	11.8	21	0
1973			5	71	14.2	45t	1
1974			4	42	10.5	25	0
1975			2	4	2.0	4	0
1976			4	11	2.8	5	0
1977			3	72	24.0	49t	1
1978			3	15	5.0	7	0
1979			3	56	18.7	29	0
1980			2	14	7.0	9	0
1981			4	46	11.5	26	0
1982			3	29	9.7	24	0
1983			2	0	0.0	0	0
Career			39	407	10.4	49t	2
Playoffs			1	25	25.0		0

Clyde Scott

Year	Team		No	Yds	Avg	Lg	TD
1952	PHI	N	1	0	0.0	0	0

Jake Scott

Year	Team		No	Yds	Avg	Lg	TD
1970	MIA	N	5	112	22.4	47	0
1971			7	34	4.9	21	0
1972			5	73	14.6	31	0
1973			4	71	17.8	29	0
1974			8	75	9.4	30	0
1975			6	60	10.0	38	0
1976	WAS	N	4	12	3.0	6	0
1977			3	42	14.0	25	0
1978			7	72	10.3	39	0
Career			49	551	11.2	47	0
Playoffs			5	93	18.6		0

Joe Scott

Year	Team		No	Yds	Avg	Lg	TD
1948	NYG	N	5	10	2.0	10	0
1949			1	16	16.0	16	0
Career			6	26	4.3	16	0

Johnny Scott

Year	Team		No	Yds	Avg	Lg	TD
1921	BUF	A					1

Kevin Scott

Year	Team		No	Yds	Avg	Lg	TD
1992	DET	N	4	35	8.8	26	0

Prince Scott

Year	Team		No	Yds	Avg	Lg	TD
1946	MIA	AA	1	0	0.0	0	0

Randy Scott

Year	Team		No	Yds	Avg	Lg	TD
1983	GB	N	1	12	12.0	12	0
1985			2	50	25.0	30	0
Career			3	62	20.7	30	0

Todd Scott

Year	Team		No	Yds	Avg	Lg	TD
1992	MIN	N	5	79	15.8	35t	1
1993			2	26	13.0	26	0
Career			7	105	15.0	35t	1
Playoffs			1	21	21.0		0

Tom Scott

Year	Team		No	Yds	Avg	Lg	TD
1956	PHI	N	1	12	12.0	12	0
1958			2	15	7.5	10	0
1960	NYG	N	1	14	14.0	14t	1
1961			1	65	65.0	65t	1
1962			1	0	0.0	0	0
1964			2	31	15.5	31	0
Career			8	137	17.1	65t	2

Victor Scott

Year	Team		No	Yds	Avg	Lg	TD
1984	DAL	N	1	5	5.0	5	0
1985			2	26	13.0	26t	1
1986			1	31	31.0	31	0
1987			1	1	1.0	1	0
Career			5	63	12.6	31	1

Ben Scotti

Year	Team		No	Yds	Avg	Lg	TD
1960	WAS	N	4	76	19.0	30	0
1961			1	10	10.0	10	0
1962	PHI	N	4	72	18.0	39	0
1963			1	17	17.0	17	0
Career			10	175	17.5	39	0

Tracy Scroggins

Year	Team		No	Yds	Avg	Lg	TD
1993	DET	N	1	0	0.0	0	0

Joe Scudero

Year	Team		No	Yds	Avg	Lg	TD
1954	WAS	N	1	26	26.0	26	0
1955			5	60	12.0	39	0
1956			2	26	13.0	24	0
1958			2	25	12.5	14	0
Career			10	137	13.7	39	0

Mike Scurlock

Year	Team		No	Yds	Avg	Lg	TD
1995	STL	N	1	13	13.0	13	0

Stan Scuzerk

Year	Team		No	Yds	Avg	Lg	TD
1965	CLE	N	1	10	10.0	10	0

Charlie Seabright

Year	Team		No	Yds	Avg	Lg	TD
1946	PIT	N	1	3	3.0	3	0
1947			3	80	26.7	39t	1
1948			1	16	16.0	16	0
Career			5	99	19.8	39t	1

Eugene Seale

Year	Team		No	Yds	Avg	Lg	TD
1987	HOU	N	1	73	73.0	73t	1
1988			1	46	46.0	46	0
Career			2	119	59.5	73t	1

Sam Seale

Year	Team		No	Yds	Avg	Lg	TD
1985	LARI	N	1	38	38.0	38t	1
1986			4	2	0.5	2	0
1989	SD	N	4	47	11.8	25	0
1990			2	14	7.0	14	0
Career			11	101	9.2	38t	1

George Seals

Year	Team		No	Yds	Avg	Lg	TD
1970	CHI	N	1	0	0.0	0	0

Leon Seals

Year	Team		No	Yds	Avg	Lg	TD
1990	BUF	N	1	0	0.0	0	0

Ray Seals

Year	Team		No	Yds	Avg	Lg	TD
1993	TB	N	1	0	0.0	0t	1
1995	PIT	N	1	0	0.0	0	0
Career			2	0	0.0	0t	1

Jimmy Sears

Year	Team		No	Yds	Avg	Lg	TD
1960	LA	A	2	73	36.5		0

Vic Sears

Year	Team		No	Yds	Avg	Lg	TD
1952	PHI	N	1	9	9.0	9t	1

Junior Seau

Year	Team		No	Yds	Avg	Lg	TD
1992	SD	N	2	51	25.5	29	0
1993			2	58	29.0	42	0
1995			2	5	2.5	3	0
1996			2	18	9.0	10	0
Career			8	132	16.5	42	0
Playoffs			1	0	0.0		0

Len Sedbrook

Year	Team		No	Yds	Avg	Lg	TD
1928	DET	N					1
1930	NYG	N					1
Career							2

Jason Sehorn

Year	Team		No	Yds	Avg	Lg	TD
1996	NYG	N	5	61	12.2	24	1

Champ Seibold

Year	Team		No	Yds	Avg	Lg	TD
1942	CHIC	N	1	3	3.0	3t	1

Clarence Self

Year	Team		No	Yds	Avg	Lg	TD
1949	CHIC	N	1	0	0.0	0	0
1950	DET	N	3	84	28.0	50t	1
1952	GB	N	1	0	0.0	0	0
1954			2	23	11.5	23	0
Career			7	107	15.3	50t	1

Andy Selfridge

Year	Team		No	Yds	Avg	Lg	TD
1974	NYG	N	1	12	12.0	12	0

Goldie Sellers

Year	Team		No	Yds	Avg	Lg	TD
1966	DEN	A	3	24	8.0	24	0
1967			7	78	11.1	47	1
1968	KC	A	3	19	6.3	19	0
Career			13	121	9.3	47	1

Dewey Selmon

Year	Team		No	Yds	Avg	Lg	TD
1977	TB	N	2	29	14.5	20	0
1978			1	0	0.0	0	0
Career			3	29	9.7	20	0

Bernie Semes

Year	Team		No	Yds	Avg	Lg	TD
1944	C-P	N	1	0	0.0	0	0

Frank Seno

Year	Team		No	Yds	Avg	Lg	TD
1943	WAS	N	1	0	0.0	0	0
1944			2	27	13.5	15	0
1945	CHIC	N	1	0	0.0	0	0
1946			4	33	8.3	14	0
1947	BOS	N	10	100	10.0	38	0
1948			1	0	0.0	0	0
Career			19	160	8.4	38	0

Mike Sensibaugh

Year	Team		No	Yds	Avg	Lg	TD
1972	KC	N	8	65	8.1	35	0
1973			3	58	19.3	27	0
1974			4	85	21.3	33	0
1975			5	123	24.6	38	0
1976	STL	N	4	60	15.0	35t	1
1977			3	110	36.7	79t	1
Career			27	501	18.6	79t	2

Tom Sestak

Year	Team		No	Yds	Avg	Lg	TD
1962	BUF	A	1	6	6.0	6t	1
1964			1	15	15.0	15t	1
Career			2	21	10.5	15t	2

Joe Setcavage

Year	Team		No	Yds	Avg	Lg	TD
1943	BKN	N	1	10	10.0	10	0

Jeff Severson

Year	Team		No	Yds	Avg	Lg	TD
1973	HOU	N	4	24	6.0	19	0
1974			1	0	0.0	0	0
1977	STL	N	1	0	0.0	0	0
Career			6	24	4.0	19	0

Harley Sewell

Year	Team		No	Yds	Avg	Lg	TD
1953	DET	N	1	4	4.0	4	0

Lin Sexton

Year	Team		No	Yds	Avg	Lg	TD
1948	LA	AA	1	30	30.0	30	0

Bob Seymour

Year	Team		No	Yds	Avg	Lg	TD
1940	WAS	N	1	13	13.0	13	0
1941			2	36	18.0	20	0
1942			3	39	13.0	22	0
1943			2	5	2.5	5	0
1944			2	20	10.0	15	0
1945			4	28	7.0	8	0
1946	LA	AA	4	34	8.5		0
Career			18	175	9.7	22	0
Playoffs			1	18	18.0		

Leland Shaffer

Year	Team		No	Yds	Avg	Lg	TD
1940	NYG	N	4	14	3.5		0
1941			1	4	4.0	4	0
1943			1	18	18.0	18	0
Career			6	36	6.0	18	0

Bobby Shann

Year	Team		No	Yds	Avg	Lg	TD
1967	PHI	N	1	8	8.0	8	0

Carver Shannon

Year	Team		No	Yds	Avg	Lg	TD
1962	LA	N	4	33	8.3	20	0

Ed Sharkey

Year	Team		No	Yds	Avg	Lg	TD
1949	B-NY	AA	1	0	0.0	0	0
1950	NYY	N	1	7	7.0	7	0
1954	PHI	N	1	4	4.0	4	0
1956	SF	N	1	4	4.0	4	0
Career			4	15	3.8	7	0

Ed Sharockman

Year	Team		No	Yds	Avg	Lg	TD
1962	MIN	N	6	92	15.3	32	0
1963			5	93	18.6	47t	1
1964			1	22	22.0	22	0
1965			6	118	19.7	40t	1
1966			1	38	38.0	38	0
1967			3	94	31.3	37	0
1968			4	70	17.5	22	0
1969			1	36	36.0	36	0
1970			7	132	18.9	43	1
1971			6	109	18.2	33	0
Career			40	804	20.1	47t	3
Playoffs			1	21	21.0		

Pete Shaw

Year	Team		No	Yds	Avg	Lg	TD
1978	SD	N	2	0	0.0	0	0
1979			3	54	18.0	30	0
1980			4	50	12.5	25	0
1981			3	50	16.7	23	0
Career			12	154	12.8	30	0

Terrance Shaw

Year	Team		No	Yds	Avg	Lg	TD
1995	SD	N	1	31	31.0	31	0
1996			3	78	26.0	36	0
Career			4	109	27.3	36	0

Chris Sheffield

Year	Team		No	Yds	Avg	Lg	TD
1987	PIT	N	1	2	2.0	2	0

Ron Shegog

Year	Team		No	Yds	Avg	Lg	TD
1987	NE	N	1	7	7.0	7	0

Donnie Shell

Year	Team		No	Yds	Avg	Lg	TD
1974	PIT	N	1	0	0.0	0	0
1975			1	29	29.0	29	0
1976			1	4	4.0	4	0
1977			3	14	4.7	8	0
1978			3	21	7.0	20	0
1979			5	10	2.0	8	0
1980			7	135	19.3	67	0
1981			5	52	10.4	25	0
1982			5	27	5.4	18	0
1983			5	18	3.6	18	0
1984			7	61	8.7	52t	1
1985			4	40	10.0	26	0
1986			3	29	9.7	17	0
1987			1	50	50.0	50t	1
Career			51	490	9.6	67	2
Playoffs			2	23	11.5		

Todd Shell

Year	Team		No	Yds	Avg	Lg	TD
1984	SF	N	3	81	27.0	53t	1
1985			1	33	33.0	33	0
1987			1	1	1.0	1	0
Career			5	115	23.0	53t	1

Elbert Shelley

Year	Team		No	Yds	Avg	Lg	TD
1989	ATL	N	1	31	31.0	31	0

Anthony Shelton

Year	Team		No	Yds	Avg	Lg	TD
1991	SD	N	1	19	19.0	19	0

Richard Shelton

Year	Team		No	Yds	Avg	Lg	TD
1991	PIT	N	3	57	19.0	57t	1
1992			0	15		15L	0
Career			3	72	24.0	57t	1

Bill Shepherd

Year	Team		No	Yds	Avg	Lg	TD
1937	DET	N					1

Stan Sheriff

Year	Team		No	Yds	Avg	Lg	TD
1954	PIT	N	1	18	18.0	18	0

Jerry Sherk

Year	Team		No	Yds	Avg	Lg	TD
1971	CLE	N	2	3	1.5	3	0
1976			1	0	0.0	0	0
Career			3	3	1.0	3	0

Allie Sherman

Year	Team		No	Yds	Avg	Lg	TD
1944	PHI	N	2	34	17.0	29	0

Bob Sherman

Year	Team		No	Yds	Avg	Lg	TD
1965	PIT	N	1	35	35.0	35	0

Solly Sherman

Year	Team		No	Yds	Avg	Lg	TD
1939	CHIB	N					1
1940			2	0	0.0		
Career			2	0	0.0		1

Will Sherman

Year	Team		No	Yds	Avg	Lg	TD
1952	DAL	N	1	23	23.0	23	0
1954	LA	N	6	70	11.7	28	0
1955			11	101	9.2	36	0
1956			4	122	30.5	95t	1
1957			1	51	51.0	51	0
1958			5	171	34.2	70t	2
1960			1	0	0.0	0	0
Career			29	538	18.6	95t	3

Rhoten Shetley

Year	Team		No	Yds	Avg	Lg	TD
1941	BKN	N	1	22	22.0	22	0
1942			1	7	7.0	7	0
Career			2	29	14.5	22	0

Burrell Shields

Year	Team		No	Yds	Avg	Lg	TD
1954	PIT	N	1	8	8.0	8	0

Don Shinnick

Year	Team		No	Yds	Avg	Lg	TD
1957	BAL	N	2	31	15.5	22	0
1958			3	23	7.7	16	0
1959			7	70	10.0	23	0
1960			5	40	8.0	11	0
1961			2	15	7.5	15	0
1962			5	16	3.2	7	0
1963			2	20	10.0	18	0
1964			3	10	3.3	9	0
1965			1	4	4.0	4	0
1966			3	4	1.3	4	0
1967			3	20	6.7	17	0
1968			1	2	2.0	2	0
Career			37	255	6.9	23	0
Playoffs			1	14	14.0		

Jerry Shipkey

Year	Team		No	Yds	Avg	Lg	TD
1949	PIT	N	3	76	25.3	50	0
1950			2	34	17.0	30	0
1951			6	113	18.8	58	1
1952			2	15	7.5	9	0
Career			13	238	18.3	58	1

Jackie Shipp

Year	Team		No	Yds	Avg	Lg	TD
1985	MIA	N	1	7	7.0	7	0

Rex Shiver

Year	Team		No	Yds	Avg	Lg	TD
1956	LA	N	1	0	0.0	0	0

Sanders Shiver

Year	Team		No	Yds	Avg	Lg	TD
1979	BAL	N	4	85	21.3	52	0
1980			1	34	34.0	34t	1
Career			5	119	23.8	52	1

Rod Shoate

Year	Team		No	Yds	Avg	Lg	TD
1979	NE	N	1	0	0.0	0	0
1980			3	50	16.7	42t	1
1981			1	0	0.0	0	0
Career			5	50	10.0	42t	1

Hal Shoener

Year	Team		No	Yds	Avg	Lg	TD
1950	SF	N	1	14	14.0	14	0

Del Shofner

Year	Team		No	Yds	Avg	Lg	TD
1957	LA	N	2	27	13.5	15	0
1960			1	19	19.0	19	0
Career			3	46	15.3	19	0

Jim Shofner

Year	Team		No	Yds	Avg	Lg	TD
1958	CLE	N	1	0	0.0	0	0
1959			2	50	25.0	30	0
1960			8	75	9.4	23	0
1961			5	8	1.6	5	0
1962			4	86	21.5	35	0
Career			20	219	10.9	35	0

John Shonk

Year	Team		No	Yds	Avg	Lg	TD
1941	PHI	N	1	1	1.0	1	0

Chuck Shonta

Year	Team		No	Yds	Avg	Lg	TD
1960	BOS	A	2	101	50.5		
1961			1	12	12.0	12	0
1962			2	0	0.0	0	0
1963			3	15	5.0	12	0
1964			1	21	21.0	21	0
1965			2	46	23.0	27	0
1966			1	9	9.0	9	0
1967			3	57	19.0	28	0
Career			15	261	17.4	28	0

Jim Shorter

Year	Team		No	Yds	Avg	Lg	TD
1964	WAS	N	1	2	2.0	2	0
1965			2	20	10.0	20	0
1966			5	123	24.6	54	0
1967			4	32	8.0	21	0
1969	PIT	N	3	47	15.7	23	0
Career			15	224	14.9	54	0

Clyde Shugart

Year	Team		No	Yds	Avg	Lg	TD
1943	WAS	N	1	8	8.0	8	0

Don Shula

Year	Team		No	Yds	Avg	Lg	TD
1951	CLE	N	4	23	5.8	16	0
1953	BAL	N	3	46	15.3	35	0
1954			5	84	16.8	25	0
1955			5	64	12.8	31	0
1956			1	2	2.0	2	0
1957	WAS	N	3	48	16.0	30	0
Career			21	267	12.7	35	0

Ron Shumon

Year	Team		No	Yds	Avg	Lg	TD
1978	CIN	N	1	48	48.0	48	0

Johnny Siegal

Year	Team		No	Yds	Avg	Lg	TD
1940	CHIB	N	1	20	20.0	20	0

Herb Siegert

Year	Team		No	Yds	Avg	Lg	TD
1949	WAS	N	2	16	8.0	9	0

Jeff Siemon

Year	Team		No	Yds	Avg	Lg	TD
1972	MIN	N	2	23	11.5	23	0
1973			2	24	12.0	21	0
1974			2	24	12.0	22	0
1975			3	24	8.0	14	0
1976			1	9	9.0	9	0
1977			1	9	9.0	9	0
Career			11	104	9.5	23	0
Playoffs			1	0	0.0		

Tracy Simien

Year	Team		No	Yds	Avg	Lg	TD
1992	KC	N	3	18	6.0	10	0
1996			1	2	2.0	2	0
Career			4	20	5.0	10	0

Clyde Simmons

Year	Team		No	Yds	Avg	Lg	TD
1989	PHI	N	1	60	60.0	60t	1
1993			1	0	0.0	0	0
1995	ARI	N	1	25	25.0	25t	1
Career			3	85	28.3	60t	2
Playoffs			1	20	20.0		1

Dave Simmons

Year	Team		No	Yds	Avg	Lg	TD
1967	NO	N	1	12	12.0	12	0
1968	DAL	N	1	8	8.0	8	0
Career			2	20	10.0	12	0

John Simmons

Year	Team		No	Yds	Avg	Lg	TD
1984	CIN	N	2	43	21.5	43t	1

Wayne Simmons

Year	Team		No	Yds	Avg	Lg	TD
1993	GB	N	2	21	10.5	19	0
1996			1	0	0.0	0	0
Career			3	21	7.0	19	0

Len Simonetti

Year	Team		No	Yds	Avg	Lg	TD
1947	CLE	AA	1	22	22.0	22	0

Ed Simonini

Year	Team		No	Yds	Avg	Lg	TD
1977	BAL	N	1	0	0.0	0	0
1978			2	4	2.0	3	0
Career			3	4	1.3	3	0

Bill Simpson

Year	Team		No	Yds	Avg	Lg	TD
1974	LA	N	1	0	0.0	0	0
1975			6	90	15.0	29	0
1976			4	62	15.5	30	0
1977			6	157	26.2	42	0
1978			5	82	16.4	28	0
1980	BUF	N	4	36	9.0	14	0
1981			4	42	10.5	42	0
1982			4	45	11.3	24	0
Career			34	514	15.1	42	0
Playoffs			9	149	16.6		1

Jackie Simpson

Year	Team		No	Yds	Avg	Lg	TD
1961	PIT	N	2	46	23.0	27	0

Jackie Simpson

Year	Team		No	Yds	Avg	Lg	TD
1962	OAK	A	3	20	6.7	13	0
1963			2	19	9.5	12	0
Career			5	39	7.8	13	0

Keith Simpson

Year	Team		No	Yds	Avg	Lg	TD
1978	SEA	N	2	40	20.0	40t	1
1979			4	72	18.0	41	0
1980			3	15	5.0	10	0
1981			2	34	17.0	21	0
1983			4	39	9.8	14	0
1984			4	138	34.5	76t	2
Career			19	338	17.8	76t	3

Mike Simpson

Year	Team		No	Yds	Avg	Lg	TD
1971	SF	N	1	15	15.0	15	0
1972			2	32	16.0	32t	1
Career			3	47	15.7	32t	1

George Sims

Year	Team		No	Yds	Avg	Lg	TD
1949	LA	N	9	78	8.7	27	1
1950			1	5	5.0	5	0
Career			10	83	8.3	27	1

Mike Singletary

Year	Team		No	Yds	Avg	Lg	TD
1981	CHI	N	1	-3	-3.0	-3	0
1983			1	0	0.0	0	0
1984			1	4	4.0	4	0
1985			1	23	23.0	23	0
1986			1	3	3.0	3	0
1988			1	13	13.0	13	0
1992			1	4	4.0	4	0
Career			7	44	6.3	23	0

Chris Singleton

Year	Team		No	Yds	Avg	Lg	TD
1992	NE	N	1	82	82.0	82t	1

Chris Singleton *continued*

Year	Team		No	Yds	Avg	Lg	TD
1995	MIA	N	1	3	3.0	3	0
Career			2	85	42.5	82t	1

Frank Sinkovitz

Year	Team		No	Yds	Avg	Lg	TD
1947	PIT	N	3	57	19.0	47t	1
1948			1	65	65.0	65	0
1949			1	54	54.0	54	0
1950			2	24	12.0	17	0
1951			2	6	3.0	6	0
1952			1	5	5.0	5	0
Career			10	211	21.1	65	1

Frankie Sinkwich

Year	Team		No	Yds	Avg	Lg	TD
1943	DET	N	1	39	39.0	39t	1
1944			3	28	9.3	18	0
Career			4	67	16.8	39t	1

Otis Sistrunk

Year	Team		No	Yds	Avg	Lg	TD
1972	OAK	N	1	0	0.0	0	0
1974			1	2	2.0	2	0
1977			1	0	0.0	0	0
Career			3	2	0.7	2	0

John Skorupan

Year	Team		No	Yds	Avg	Lg	TD
1975	BUF	N	1	0	0.0	0	0
1976			1	13	13.0	13	0
Career			2	13	6.5	13	0

Lou Slaby

Year	Team		No	Yds	Avg	Lg	TD
1964	NYG	N	2	32	16.0	26	0

Chris Slade

Year	Team		No	Yds	Avg	Lg	TD
1996	NE	N	1	2	2.0	2	0

Duke Slater

Year	Team		No	Yds	Avg	Lg	TD
1929	CHIC	N					1

Howie Slater

Year	Team		No	Yds	Avg	Lg	TD
1926	MIL	N					1

Walt Slater

Year	Team		No	Yds	Avg	Lg	TD
1947	PIT	N	4	38	9.5	38	0

Steve Slivinski

Year	Team		No	Yds	Avg	Lg	TD
1941	WAS	N	1	20	20.0	20	0
1943			1	2	2.0	2	0
Career			2	22	11.0	20	0

Phil Slosburg

Year	Team		No	Yds	Avg	Lg	TD
1949	NYB	N	1	0	0.0	0	0

Donovan Small

Year	Team		No	Yds	Avg	Lg	TD
1987	HOU	N	1	3	3.0	3	0

Eldridge Small

Year	Team		No	Yds	Avg	Lg	TD
1974	NYG	N	1	0	0.0	0	0

Gerald Small

Year	Team		No	Yds	Avg	Lg	TD
1978	MIA	N	4	157	39.3	46t	1
1979			5	74	14.8	40	0
1980			7	46	6.6	22	0
1982			2	41	20.5	21	0
1983			5	60	12.0	28	0
1984	ATL	N	1	2	2.0	2	0
Career			24	380	15.8	46t	1
Playoffs			4	64	16.0		0

Joel Smeenge

Year	Team		No	Yds	Avg	Lg	TD
1995	JAC	N	1	12	12.0	12	0

Fred Smerlas

Year	Team		No	Yds	Avg	Lg	TD
1984	BUF	N	1	25	25.0	25	0
1986			1	3	3.0	3	0
Career			2	28	14.0	25	0

Al Smith

Year	Team		No	Yds	Avg	Lg	TD
1991	HOU	N	1	16	16.0	16	0
1992			1	26	26.0	26	0
Career			2	42	21.0	26	0

Ben Smith

Year	Team		No	Yds	Avg	Lg	TD
1990	PHI	N	3	1	0.3	1	0

Ben Smith *continued*

Year	Team		No	Yds	Avg	Lg	TD
1991			2	6	3.0	6	0
1994	DEN	N	1	0	0.0	0	0
Career			6	7	1.2	6	0

Billy Ray Smith

Year	Team		No	Yds	Avg	Lg	TD
1965	BAL	N	1	5	5.0	5	0

Billy Ray Smith

Year	Team		No	Yds	Avg	Lg	TD
1984	SD	N	3	41	13.7	21	0
1985			1	0	0.0	0	0
1987			5	28	5.6	12	0
1988			1	9	9.0	9	0
1989			1	9	9.0	9	0
1990			2	12	6.0	12	0
1991			2	0	0.0	0	0
Career			15	99	6.6	21	0

Bobby Smith

Year	Team		No	Yds	Avg	Lg	TD
1962	LA	N	1	47	47.0	47	0
1963			2	11	5.5	11	0
1964			2	97	48.5	97t	1
Career			5	155	31.0	97t	1

Bruce Smith

Year	Team		No	Yds	Avg	Lg	TD
1993	BUF	N	1	0	0.0	0	0
1994			1	0	0.0	0	0
Career			2	0	0.0	0	0

Charley Smith

Year	Team		No	Yds	Avg	Lg	TD
1956	SF	N	1	0	0.0	0	0

Charlie Smith

Year	Team		No	Yds	Avg	Lg	TD
1947	CHIC	N	1	5	5.0	5	0

Chuck Smith

Year	Team		No	Yds	Avg	Lg	TD
1994	ATL	N	1	36	36.0	36t	1
1996			1	21	21.0	21	0
Career			2	57	28.5	36t	1

Darrin Smith

Year	Team		No	Yds	Avg	Lg	TD
1994	DAL	N	2	13	6.5	13t	1

Daryl Smith

Year	Team		No	Yds	Avg	Lg	TD
1987	CIN	N	2	0	0.0	0	0

Dennis Smith

Year	Team		No	Yds	Avg	Lg	TD
1981	DEN	N	1	65	65.0	65	0
1982			1	29	29.0	29	0
1983			4	39	9.8	23	0
1984			3	13	4.3	10	0
1985			3	46	15.3	39	0
1986			1	0	0.0	0	0
1987			2	21	10.5	15	0
1989			2	78	39.0	50	0
1990			1	13	13.0	13	0
1991			5	60	12.0	39	0
1992			4	10	2.5	8	0
1993			3	57	19.0	36	0
Career			30	431	14.4	65	0
Playoffs			2	13	6.5		0

Dick Smith

Year	Team		No	Yds	Avg	Lg	TD
1967	WAS	N	3	0	0.0	0	0
1968			1	0	0.0	0	0
Career			4	0	0.0	0	0

Doug Smith

Year	Team		No	Yds	Avg	Lg	TD
1988	HOU	N	1	20	20.0	20	0

Ed Smith

Year	Team		No	Yds	Avg	Lg	TD
1949	NYB	N	2	21	10.5	18	0

Ed Smith

Year	Team		No	Yds	Avg	Lg	TD
1974	DEN	N	1	2	2.0	2	0

Ed Smith

Year	Team		No	Yds	Avg	Lg	TD
1981	BAL	N	2	11	5.5	8	0

Fletcher Smith

Year	Team		No	Yds	Avg	Lg	TD
1967	KC	A	6	150	25.0	57	0
1968	CIN	A	1	16	16.0	16	0
1969			4	67	16.8	29	0

Year	Team		No	Yds	Avg	Lg	TD

Fletcher Smith *continued*

Year	Team		No	Yds	Avg	Lg	TD
1970	CIN	N	3	17	5.7	17	0
1971			1	0	0	0	0
Career			15	250	16.7	57	0

Frankie Smith

			No	Yds	Avg	Lg	TD
Playoffs			1	14	14.0		0

Gaylon Smith

Year	Team		No	Yds	Avg	Lg	TD
1941	CLE	N	1	16	16.0	16	0
1942			4	20	5.0	12	0
1946	CLE	AA	1	0	0	0	0
Career			6	36	6.0	16	0

George Smith

Year	Team		No	Yds	Avg	Lg	TD
1943	WAS	N	2	40	20.0	34	0
1944	BKN	N	1	8	8.0	8	0
1945	BOS	N	2	23	11.5	13	0
1947	SF	AA	1	10	10.0	10	0
Career			6	81	13.5	34	0

J.D. Smith

Year	Team		No	Yds	Avg	Lg	TD
1957	SF	N	2	17	8.5	12	0

Jeff Smith

Year	Team		No	Yds	Avg	Lg	TD
1966	NYG	N	1	0	0.0	0	0

Jim Smith

Year	Team		No	Yds	Avg	Lg	TD
1948	BUF-BKN	AA	4	29	7.3		0
1949	DET	N	9	218	24.2	102t	1
1950			5	128	25.6	41	1
1951			3	70	23.3	42	0
1952			9	184	20.4	90	1
1953			3	119	39.7	73	0
Career			33	748	22.7	102t	3

Joe Smith

Year	Team		No	Yds	Avg	Lg	TD
1948	BAL	AA	1	0	0.0	0	0

Kevin Smith

Year	Team		No	Yds	Avg	Lg	TD
1992	DAL	N	2	10	5.0	7	0
1993			6	56	9.3	32t	1
1994			2	11	5.5	11	0
1996			5	45	9.0	24	0
Career			15	122	8.1	32t	1
Playoffs			1	2	2.0		0

Leonard Smith

Year	Team		No	Yds	Avg	Lg	TD
1984	STL	N	2	31	15.5	25t	1
1985			2	73	36.5	67	0
1986			1	13	13.0	13	0
1988	PHX-BUF	N	2	29	14.5	15	0
1989	BUF	N	2	46	23.0	24	0
1990			2	39	19.5	39t	1
1991			3	22	7.3	22	0
Career			14	253	18.1	67	2
Playoffs			2	24	12.0		0

Lucious Smith

Year	Team		No	Yds	Avg	Lg	TD
1983	KC	N	3	99	33.0	58t	1
1984	BUF	N	1	7	7.0	7	0
Career			4	106	26.5	58t	1
Playoffs			1	7	7.0		0

Neil Smith

Year	Team		No	Yds	Avg	Lg	TD
1992	KC	N	1	22	22.0	22t	1
1993			1	3	3.0	3	0
1994			1	41	41.0	41	0
Career			3	66	22.0	41	1

Otis Smith

Year	Team		No	Yds	Avg	Lg	TD
1991	PHI	N	2	74	37.0	74t	1
1992			1	0	0.0	0	0
1993			1	0	0.0	0	0
1995	NYJ	N	6	101	16.8	49t	1
1996	NE	N	2	20	10.0	11	0
Career			12	195	16.3	74t	2

Paul Smith

Year	Team		No	Yds	Avg	Lg	TD
1977	DEN	N	1	6	6.0	6	0
1980	WAS	N	1	8	8.0	8	0
Career			2	14	7.0	8	0

Perry Smith

Year	Team		No	Yds	Avg	Lg	TD
1975	GB	N	6	97	16.2	61	0
1976			1	0	0.0	0	0
1978	STL	N	3	6	2.0	6	0
1979			1	22	22.0	22	0
1980	DEN	N	2	3	1.5	3	0
Career			13	128	9.8	61	0

Ray Gene Smith

Year	Team		No	Yds	Avg	Lg	TD
1954	CHIB	N	2	0	0.0	0	0
1955			2	12	6.0	12	0
1956			4	90	22.5	41	0
1957			1	22	22.0	22	0
Career			9	124	13.8	41	0

Ricky Smith

Year	Team		No	Yds	Avg	Lg	TD
1984	WAS	N	1	37	37.0	37	0
1987	DET	N	1	34	34.0	34t	1
Career			2	71	35.5	37	1

Riley Smith

Year	Team		No	Yds	Avg	Lg	TD
1937	WAS	N					1
Playoffs			1	10	10.0		0

Rod Smith

Year	Team		No	Yds	Avg	Lg	TD
1992	NE	N	1	0	0.0	0	0
1994			2	10	5.0	10	0
Career			3	10	3.3	10	0

Ron Smith

Year	Team		No	Yds	Avg	Lg	TD
1966	ATL	N	2	6	3.0	6	0
1968	LA	N	3	28	9.3	19	0
1969			3	70	23.3	24t	1
1971	CHI		3	48	16.0	27	0
1972			1	2	2.0	2	0
1973	SD	N	1	4	4.0	4	0
Career			13	158	12.2	27	1

Thomas Smith

Year	Team		No	Yds	Avg	Lg	TD
1994	BUF	N	1	4	4.0	4	0
1995			2	23	11.5	13	0
1996			1	0	0.0	0	0
Career			4	27	6.8	13	0
Playoffs			1	0	0.0		0

Tody Smith

Year	Team		No	Yds	Avg	Lg	TD
1974	HOU	N	1	34	34.0	34	0

Wayne Smith

Year	Team		No	Yds	Avg	Lg	TD
1980	DET	N	1	23	23.0	23	0
1982			1	10	10.0	10	0
1983	STL	N	2	3	1.5	3	0
1984			4	35	8.8	23	0
1986			1	35	35.0	35	0
1987	MIN	N	1	24	24.0	24	0
Career			10	130	13.0	35	0

Bob Sneddon

Year	Team		No	Yds	Avg	Lg	TD
1944	WAS	N	1	20	20.0	20	0
1946	LA	AA	1	15	15.0	15	0
Career			2	35	17.5	20	0

Jim Sniadecki

Year	Team		No	Yds	Avg	Lg	TD
1973	SF	N	1	11	11.0	11	0
Playoffs			1	5	5.0		0

Ron Snidow

Year	Team		No	Yds	Avg	Lg	TD
1965	WAS	N	1	3	3.0	3	0
1971	CLE	N	0	3		3L	0
Career			1	6	6.0	3L	0
Playoffs			1	1	1.0		0

Angelo Snipes

Year	Team		No	Yds	Avg	Lg	TD
1989	KC	N	1	16	16.0	16	0

Percy Snow

Year	Team		No	Yds	Avg	Lg	TD
1990	KC	N	1	0	0.0	0	0

Bob Snyder

Year	Team		No	Yds	Avg	Lg	TD
1941	CHIB	N	1	24	24.0	24	0
1943			1	8	8.0	8	0
Career			2	32	16.0	24	0

Hank Soar

Year	Team		No	Yds	Avg	Lg	TD
1937	NYG	N					1
1939							1
1941			2	31	15.5	31	0
1942			3	30	10.0	22	0
1943			3	43	14.3	23	0
1944			1	18	18.0	18	0
1946			3	35	11.7	21	0
Career			12	157	13.1	31	2
Playoffs			1				

John Sodaski

Year	Team		No	Yds	Avg	Lg	TD
1973	PHI	N	1	0	0.0	0	0

Jesse Solomon

Year	Team		No	Yds	Avg	Lg	TD
1986	MIN	N	2	34	17.0	18	0
1987			1	30	30.0	30	0
1988			4	84	21.0	78t	1
1992	ATL	N	1	13	13.0	13	0
Career			8	161	20.1	78t	1

Bob Soltis

Year	Team		No	Yds	Avg	Lg	TD
1960	BOS	A	2	33	16.5		0

Robert Sowell

Year	Team		No	Yds	Avg	Lg	TD
1984	MIA	N	1	7	7.0	7	0
1987			1	29	29.0	29	0
Career			2	36	18.0	29	0

Rich Sowells

Year	Team		No	Yds	Avg	Lg	TD
1972	NYJ	N	2	14	7.0	14	0
1973			3	55	18.3	30t	0
1974			2	0	0.0	0	0
1975			1	0	0.0	0	0
1976			2	46	23.0	27	0
Career			10	115	11.5	30t	1

Vic Spadaccini

Year	Team		No	Yds	Avg	Lg	TD
1940	CLE	N					1

Gary Spani

Year	Team		No	Yds	Avg	Lg	TD
1980	KC	N	1	47	47.0	47t	1
1986			1	24	24.0	24	0
Career			2	71	35.5	47t	1

Frank Spaniel

Year	Team		No	Yds	Avg	Lg	TD
1950	BAL	N	1	29	29.0	9t	1

Phillippi Sparks

Year	Team		No	Yds	Avg	Lg	TD
1992	NYG	N	1	0	0.0	0	0
1994			3	4	1.3	4	0
1995			5	11	2.2	6	0
1996			3	23	7.7	19	0
Career			12	38	3.2	19	0

Jim Spavital

Year	Team		No	Yds	Avg	Lg	TD
1949	LA	AA	4	58	14.5		0

Cliff Speegle

Year	Team		No	Yds	Avg	Lg	TD
1945	CHIC	N	2	13	6.5	13	0

Del Speer

Year	Team		No	Yds	Avg	Lg	TD
1993	CLE	N	1	22	22.0	22	0

Alonzo Spellman

Year	Team		No	Yds	Avg	Lg	TD
1994	CHI	N	1	31	31.0	31	0

Julian Spence

Year	Team		No	Yds	Avg	Lg	TD
1956	CHIC	N	1	7	7.0	7	0
1960	HOU	A	4	5	1.3		0
1961			1	23	23.0	23	0
Career			6	35	5.8	23	0
Playoffs			1	0	0.0		0

Jimmy Spencer

Year	Team		No	Yds	Avg	Lg	TD
1994	NO	N	5	24	4.8	11	0
1995			4	11	2.8	9	0
1996	CIN	N	5	48	9.6	34	0
Career			14	83	5.9	34	0

Joe Spencer

Year	Team		No	Yds	Avg	Lg	TD
1950	GB	N	1	0	0.0	0	0

Year	Team		No	Yds	Avg	Lg	TD

Maurice Spencer

Year	Team		No	Yds	Avg	Lg	TD
1975	NO	N	0	11		11L	0
1976			1	0	0.0	0	0
1978			4	83	20.8	37	0
Career			5	94	18.8	37	0

Rob Spicer

| 1973 | NYJ | N | 1 | 12 | 12.0 | 12 | 0 |

Chris Spielman

1990	DET	N	1	12	12.0	12	0
1993			2	-2	-1.0	0	0
1995			1	4	4.0	4	0
1996	BUF	N	1	14	14.0	14	0
Career			5	28	5.6	14	0
Playoffs			1	0	0.0		0

Phil Spiller

| 1967 | STL | N | 2 | 13 | 6.5 | 13 | 0 |

Marc Spindler

| 1996 | NYJ | N | 1 | -1 | -1.0 | -1 | 0 |

Bobby Spitulski

| 1994 | SEA | N | 1 | 7 | 7.0 | 7 | 0 |

Mike Spivey

| 1981 | NO | N | 1 | 0 | 0.0 | 0 | 0 |

Kirk Springs

1981	NYJ	N	2	5	2.5	5	0
1982			1	0	0.0	0	0
1984			1	13	13.0	13	0
Career			4	18	4.5	13	0

Ed Sprinkle

1944	CHIB	N	1	15	15.0	15	0
1946			1	34	34.0	34	0
1951			1	0	0.0	0	0
1954			1	6	6.0	6	0
Career			4	55	13.8	34	0

Jack Squirek

| 1985 | LARI | N | 1 | 3 | 3.0 | 3 | 0 |
| Playoffs | | | 1 | 5 | 5.0 | | 1 |

Billy Stacy

1959	CHIC	N	5	114	22.8	36	0
1960	STL	N	4	42	10.5	25	0
1961			4	95	23.8	39t	2
1962			6	72	12.0	53	0
1963			1	0	0.0	0	0
Career			20	323	16.1	53	2

Jeff Staggs

1968	SD	A	2	2	1.0	2	0
1972	STL	N	1	7	7.0	7	0
Career			3	9	3.0	7	0

Jerry Stalcup

| 1960 | LA | N | 1 | 12 | 12.0 | 12 | 0 |

Larry Stallings

1964	STL	N	2	31	15.5	18	0
1966			1	0	0.0	0	0
1970			1	9	9.0	9	0
1971			1	26	26.0	26t	1
1973			1	0	0.0	0	0
1974			2	13	6.5	13	0
1975			1	-3	-3.0	-3	0
Career			9	76	8.4	26t	1

Frank Stams

1989	LARM	N	1	20	20.0	20	0
1994	CLE	N	1	7	7.0	7	0
Career			2	27	13.5	20	0

Norm Standlee

| 1941 | CHIB | N | 2 | 31 | 15.5 | 27 | 0 |
| Playoffs | | | 1 | 11 | 11.0 | | 0 |

Bill Stanfill

| 1969 | MIA | A | 2 | 32 | 16.0 | 17t | 2 |

Tony Stargell

1990	NYJ	N	2	-3	-1.5	0	0
1992	IND	N	2	26	13.0	15	0
1994	TB	N	1	0	0.0	0	0
1996	KC	N	1	9	9.0	9	0
Career			6	32	5.3	15	0

Marshall Starks

1963	NY	A	0	19		19L	0
1964			1	20	20.0	20	0
Career			1	39	39.0	20	0

Ben Starrett

1943	GB	N	1	4	4.0	4	0
1945			1	27	27.0	27	0
Career			2	31	15.5	27	0

Leo Stasica

1943	WAS	N	1	0	0.0	0	0
1944	BOS	N	1	15	15.0	15	0
Career			2	15	7.5	15	0

Ernie Stautner

1954	PIT	N	1	3	3.0	3	0
1962			1	2	2.0	2	0
Career			2	5	2.5	3	0

Ernie Steele

1942	PHI	N	2	49	24.5	29	0
1944			6	113	18.8	62	0
1945			1	15	15.0	15	0
1946			3	69	23.0	30	0
1947			6	103	17.2	42	0
1948			6	55	9.2	33	0
Career			24	404	16.8	62	0
Playoffs			1	0	0.0		0

Jim Steffen

1961	WAS	N	1	11	11.0	11	0
1962			4	37	9.3	36	0
1963			5	140	28.0	47t	1
1964			4	20	5.0	11	0
1965			3	56	18.7	25	0
Career			17	264	15.5	47t	1

Bob Stein

1971	KC	N	1	5	5.0	5	0
1973	LA	N	1	6	6.0	6	0
Career			2	11	5.5	6	0

Rebel Steiner

1950	GB	N	7	190	27.1	94t	1
1951			3	4	1.3	3	0
Career			10	194	19.4	94t	1

Gil Steinke

1946	PHI	N	6	72	12.0	52t	1
1947			1	17	17.0	17	0
Career			7	89	12.7	52t	1

Ken Steinmetz

| 1945 | BOS | N | 1 | 0 | 0.0 | 0 | 0 |

Greg Stemrick

1976	HOU	N	1	0	0.0	0	0
1977			1	18	18.0	18	0
1978			3	65	21.7	38	0
1979			2	50	25.0	50	0
1980			4	25	6.3	15	0
1981			3	94	31.3	38	0
1983	NO	N	1	26	26.0	26	0
Career			15	278	18.5	50	0
Playoffs			2	0	0.0		0

Brian Stenger

| 1969 | PIT | N | 3 | 36 | 12.0 | 19 | 0 |

Mike Stensrud

1985	HOU	N	1	0	0.0	0	0
1988	KC	N	1	5	5.0	5	0
Career			2	5	2.5	5	0

Scott Stephen

| 1989 | GB | N | 2 | 16 | 8.0 | 8 | 0 |

Scott Stephen continued

Year	Team		No	Yds	Avg	Lg	TD
1990			2	26	13.0	26	0
1991			1	23	23.0	23	0
Career			5	65	13.0	26	0

Larry Stephens

| 1960 | CLE | N | 1 | 34 | 34.0 | 34t | 1 |

Rod Stephens

| 1996 | WAS | N | 1 | 0 | 0.0 | 0 | 0 |

Tom Stephens

| 1963 | BOS | A | 1 | 22 | 22.0 | 22 | 0 |

Bob Steuber

| 1946 | CLE | AA | 1 | 52 | 52.0 | 52 | 0 |

Matt Stevens

| 1996 | BUF | N | 2 | 0 | 0.0 | 0 | 0 |

Michael Stewart

1988	LARM	N	2	61	30.5	43	0
1989			2	76	38.0	41t	1
1991			2	8	4.0	8	0
1993			1	30	30.0	30	0
1994	MIA	N	3	11	3.7	11	0
1995			1	0	0.0	0	0
Career			11	186	16.9	43	1
Playoffs			2	29	14.5		0

Ryan Stewart

| 1996 | DET | N | 1 | 14 | 14.0 | 14 | 0 |

Jim Stienke

1975	NYG	N	2	41	20.5	27	0
1976			2	0	0.0	0	0
Career			4	41	10.3	27	0

Art Still

| 1989 | BUF | N | 1 | 10 | 10.0 | 10 | 0 |

Jim Still

| 1948 | BUF | AA | 1 | 37 | 37.0 | 37 | 0 |

Ken Stills

1986	GB	N	1	58	58.0	58t	1
1988			3	29	9.7	17	0
1989			3	20	6.7	12	0
Career			7	107	15.3	58t	1

Tom Stincic

| 1970 | DAL | N | 1 | 11 | 11.0 | 11 | 0 |

Jim Stinnette

| 1961 | DEN | A | 1 | 40 | 40.0 | 40 | 0 |

Lemuel Stinson

1989	CHI	N	4	59	14.8	29t	1
1990			6	66	11.0	30	0
1991			4	69	17.3	34t	1
1992			2	46	23.0	46	0
Career			16	240	15.0	46	2

Bill Stits

1954	DET	N	6	73	12.2	23	0
1955			3	7	2.3	7t	1
1956			1	11	11.0	11	0
1957	SF	N	2	28	14.0	20	0
1958			3	3	1.0	2	0
Career			15	122	8.1	23	1

Hust Stockton

| 1928 | FRA | N | | | | | 1 |

Fred Stokes

| 1991 | WAS | N | 1 | 0 | 0.0 | 0 | 0 |

Tommy Stolhandske

| 1955 | SF | N | 1 | 6 | 6.0 | 6 | 0 |

Billy Stone

| 1950 | BAL | N | 6 | 56 | 9.3 | 20 | 0 |
| 1951 | CHIB | N | 4 | 20 | 5.0 | 9 | 0 |

Billy Stone *continued*

Year	Team		No	Yds	Avg	Lg	TD
1952			1	13	13.0	13	0
Career			11	89	8.1	20	0

Ken Stone

Year	Team		No	Yds	Avg	Lg	TD
1973	BUF	N	0	31		31L	0
1974	WAS	N	5	95	19.0	31	0
1976	TB	N	2	47	23.5	26	0
1978	STL	N	9	139	15.4	33	0
1979			6	70	11.7	30	0
1980			5	63	12.6	20	0
Career			27	445	16.5	33	0
Playoffs			1	7	7.0		0

Steve Stonebreaker

Year	Team		No	Yds	Avg	Lg	TD
1965	BAL	N	1	0	0.0	0	0
1966			1	8	8.0	8	0
Career			2	8	4.0	8	0

Pete Stout

Year	Team		No	Yds	Avg	Lg	TD
1949	WAS	N	1	8	8.0	8	0
1950			1	9	9.0	9	0
Career			2	17	8.5	9	0

Dick Stovall

Year	Team		No	Yds	Avg	Lg	TD
1947	DET	N	1	0			0

Jerry Stovall

Year	Team		No	Yds	Avg	Lg	TD
1963	STL	N	1	0	0.0	0	0
1964			3	71	23.7	40	1
1965			2	30	15.0	18	0
1966			3	43	14.3	22	1
1967			4	6	1.5	6	0
1969			1	28	28.0	28	0
1970			2	45	22.5	27	0
1971			2	20	10.0	20	0
Career			18	243	13.5	40	2

Stewart Stover

Year	Team		No	Yds	Avg	Lg	TD
1960	DAL	A	1	10	10.0	10	0
1961			2	44	22.0	36	0
1964	KC	A	2	11	5.5	7	0
1966			1	6	6.0	6	0
Career			6	71	11.8	36	0

Tyronne Stowe

Year	Team		No	Yds	Avg	Lg	TD
1994	WAS	N	1	2	2.0	2	0

Michael Strahan

Year	Team		No	Yds	Avg	Lg	TD
1995	NYG	N	2	56	28.0	56	0

Mike Stramiello

Year	Team		No	Yds	Avg	Lg	TD
1931	BKN	N					1

Mike Stratton

Year	Team		No	Yds	Avg	Lg	TD
1962	BUF	A	6	99	16.5	18	0
1963			3	31	10.3	26	1
1964			1	0	0.0	0	0
1965			2	19	9.5	19	0
1966			3	37	12.3	23	0
1967			1	3	3.0	3	0
1968			1	15	15.0	15	0
1972	BUF	N	1	0	0.0	0	0
1973	SD	N	3	46	15.3	23	0
Career			21	250	11.9	26	1
Playoffs			1	0	0.0		0

Tony Stricker

Year	Team		No	Yds	Avg	Lg	TD
1963	NY	A	1	6	6.0	6	0

Fred Strickland

Year	Team		No	Yds	Avg	Lg	TD
1989	LARM	N	2	56	28.0	29	0
1994	GB	N	1	7	7.0	7	0
1996	DAL	N	1	0	0.0	0	0
Career			4	63	15.8	29	0

Art Stringer

Year	Team		No	Yds	Avg	Lg	TD
1977	HOU	N	1	20	20.0	20	0
1978			1	20	20.0	20	0
1979			2	21	10.5	21	0
Career			4	61	15.3	21	0

Bob Stringer

Year	Team		No	Yds	Avg	Lg	TD
1952	PHI	N	1	9	9.0	9	0
1953			1	7	7.0	7	0
Career			2	16	8.0	9	0

Hal Stringert

Year	Team		No	Yds	Avg	Lg	TD
1976	SD	N	1	24	24.0	24	0
1977			4	64	16.0	29	0
1978			2	4	2.0	2	0
1980			1	0	0.0	0	0
Career			8	92	11.5	29	0

George Strohmeyer

Year	Team		No	Yds	Avg	Lg	TD
1948	BKN	AA	4	79	19.8	50	0
1949	CHI	AA	3	9	3.0		0
Career			7	88	12.6	50	0

Ken Strong

Year	Team		No	Yds	Avg	Lg	TD
1933	NYG	N					1

George Strugar

Year	Team		No	Yds	Avg	Lg	TD
1961	LA	N	1	4	4.0	4	0

Art Strutt

Year	Team		No	Yds	Avg	Lg	TD
1935	PIT	N					1

Johnny Strzykalski

Year	Team		No	Yds	Avg	Lg	TD
1946	SF	AA	3	55	18.3		0
1947			2	25	12.5		0
1948			3	21	7.0		0
Career			8	101	12.6		0

Roy Stuart

Year	Team		No	Yds	Avg	Lg	TD
1942	CLE	N	1	25	25.0	25	0

Dana Stubblefield

Year	Team		No	Yds	Avg	Lg	TD
1995	SF	N	1	12	12.0	12	0
1996			1	15	15.0	15	0
Career			2	27	13.5	15	0

Henry Stuckey

Year	Team		No	Yds	Avg	Lg	TD
1973	MIA	N	1	4	4.0	4	0
1974			1	21	21.0	21	0
Career			2	25	12.5	21	0

Scott Studwell

Year	Team		No	Yds	Avg	Lg	TD
1977	MIN	N	1	4	4.0	4	0
1979			1	18	18.0	18	0
1980			1	4	4.0	4	0
1982			1	3	3.0	3	0
1984			1	20	20.0	20	0
1985			2	20	10.0	13	0
1986			1	2	2.0	2	0
1987			2	26	13.0	14	0
1989			1	0	0.0	0	0
Career			11	97	8.8	20	0
Playoffs			1	0	0.0		0

Charlie Stukes

Year	Team		No	Yds	Avg	Lg	TD
1967	BAL	N	2	13	6.5	13	0
1968			1	60	60.0	60t	1
1969			1	6	6.0	6	0
1970			3	52	17.3	47	0
1971			8	95	11.9	40	0
1972			5	23	4.6	11	0
1973	LA	N	5	104	20.8	42	0
1974			7	90	12.9	41	0
Career			32	443	13.8	60t	1
Playoffs			2	23	11.5		0

Joe Stydahar

Year	Team		No	Yds	Avg	Lg	TD
1941	CHIB	N	1	55	55.0	55	0

Bob Suci

Year	Team		No	Yds	Avg	Lg	TD
1962	HOU	A	1	22	22.0	22	0
1963	BOS	A	8	294	36.8	98	2
Career			9	316	35.1	98	2

Leo Sugar

Year	Team		No	Yds	Avg	Lg	TD
1955	CHIC	N	1	29	29.0	29	0

Shafer Suggs

Year	Team		No	Yds	Avg	Lg	TD
1976	NYJ	N	1	12	12.0	12	0
1978			3	61	20.3	32	

Shafer Suggs *continued*

Year	Team		No	Yds	Avg	Lg	TD
1979			3	41	13.7	32t	1
Career			7	114	16.3	32t	1

Joe Sulatis

Year	Team		No	Yds	Avg	Lg	TD
1947	NYG	N	1	18	18.0	18	0
1953			1	6	6.0	6	0
Career			2	24	12.0	18	0

Bob Sullivan

Year	Team		No	Yds	Avg	Lg	TD
1948	SF	AA	1	6	6.0	6	0

Ivory Sully

Year	Team		No	Yds	Avg	Lg	TD
1985	TB	N	1	20	20.0	20	0

Pat Summerall

Year	Team		No	Yds	Avg	Lg	TD
1955	CHIC	N	1	26	26.0	26t	0

Bob Summerhays

Year	Team		No	Yds	Avg	Lg	TD
1950	GB	N	1	0	0.0	0	0
1951			2	112	56.0	88t	1
Career			3	112	37.3	88t	1

Charlie Sumner

Year	Team		No	Yds	Avg	Lg	TD
1955	CHIB	N	7	162	23.1	63	0
1958			6	67	11.2	17	0
1959			3	22	7.3	15	0
1961	MIN	N	2	6	3.0	6	0
1962			3	46	15.3	32	0
Career			21	303	14.4	63	0

Walt Sumner

Year	Team		No	Yds	Avg	Lg	TD
1969	CLE	N	4	82	20.5	40t	0
1970			4	85	21.3	34	0
1971			5	35	7.0	25	0
1973			2	4	2.0	4	0
Career			15	206	13.7	40t	1
Playoffs			1	88	88.0		1

Len Supulski

Year	Team		No	Yds	Avg	Lg	TD
1942	PHI	N	1	5	5.0	5	0

Don Sutherin

Year	Team		No	Yds	Avg	Lg	TD
1960	PIT	N	1	0	0.0	0	0

Ed Sutton

Year	Team		No	Yds	Avg	Lg	TD
1957	WAS	N	1	11	11.0	11	0

Joe Sutton

Year	Team		No	Yds	Avg	Lg	TD
1950	PHI	N	8	67	8.4	32	0
1951			2	8	4.0	8	0
1952			3	54	18.0	30	0
Career			13	129	9.9	32	0

Mickey Sutton

Year	Team		No	Yds	Avg	Lg	TD
1986	LARM	N	2	25	12.5	20	0
1987			1	4	4.0	4	0
1988			1	1	1.0	1	0
1989	BUF	N	1	3	3.0	3	0
Career			5	33	6.6	20	0

Reggie Sutton

Year	Team		No	Yds	Avg	Lg	TD
1987	NO	N	5	68	13.6	26	0
1988			3	32	10.7	34	0
Career			8	100	12.5	34	0

Harland Svare

Year	Team		No	Yds	Avg	Lg	TD
1953	LA	N	1	9	9.0	9	0
1955	NYG	N	2	19	9.5	19	0
1957			1	21	21.0	21	0
1958			1	25	25.0	25	0
1959			3	118	39.3	70t	1
1960			1	37	37.0	37	0
Career			9	229	25.4	70t	1

Earl Svendsen

Year	Team		No	Yds	Avg	Lg	TD
1941	BKN	N	1	1	1.0	1	0
1942			1	18	18.0	18	0
1943			1	20	20.0	20	0
Career			3	39	13.0	20	0
Playoffs			1	15	15.0		

Year	Team		No	Yds	Avg	Lg	TD

George Svendsen
1941	GB	N	1	42	42.0	42	0

Bill Svoboda
1952	CHIC	N	2	2	1.0	2	0
1953			1	0	0.0	0	0
1954	NYG	N	1	30	30.0	30	0
1955			1	24	24.0	24	0
1956			2	3	1.5	3	0
1957			2	43	21.5	43	0
Career			9	102	11.3	43	0
Playoffs			1	20	20.0		0

Bill Swain
1967	NYG	N	1	0	0.0	0	0
1968	DET	N	1	50	50.0	50t	1
Career			2	50	25.0	50t	1

John Swain
1981	MIN	N	2	18	9.0	18	0
1982			2	20	10.0	16	0
1983			6	12	2.0	11	0
1984			2	20	10.0	11	0
1985	PIT	N	2	4	2.0	4	0
1986			0	9		9L	0
Career			14	83	5.9	18	0
Playoffs			1	0	0.0		0

Eric Swann
| 1994 | ARI | N | 1 | 0 | 0.0 | 0 | 0 |

Bob Sweiger
1946	NY	AA	4	82	20.5		0
1947			2	51	25.5		1
1949	CHI	AA	1	21	21.0	21	0
Career			7	154	22.0	21	1

Bob Swenson
1975	DEN	N	1	4	4.0	4	0
1976			2	26	13.0	26	0
1977			1	0	0.0	0	0
1978			1	0	0.0	0	0
1979			3	0	0.0	0	0
1981			3	53	17.7	32	0
Career			11	83	7.5	32	0
Playoffs			3	18	6.0		0

Doug Swift
1971	MIA	N	1	12	12.0	12	0
1972			3	5	1.7	4	0
1973			1	0	0.0	0	0
Career			5	17	3.4	12	0
Playoffs			2	19	9.5		0

Pat Swilling
1987	NO	N	1	10	10.0	10	0
1989			1	14	14.0	14	0
1991			1	39	39.0	39t	1
1993	DET	N	3	16	5.3	14	0
Career			6	79	13.2	39t	1

Bob Swisher
1941	CHIB	N	1	60	60.0	60t	1
1945			1	0	0.0	0	0
Career			2	60	30.0	60t	1

Craig Swoope
| 1986 | TB | N | 1 | 23 | 23.0 | 23 | 0 |

Gene Sykes
1964	BUF	A	2	36	18.0	22	0
1967	DEN	A	2	29	14.5	29	0
Career			4	65	16.3	29	0

Johnny Sylvester
| 1948 | BAL | AA | 1 | 0 | 0.0 | 0 | 0 |

John Symank
1957	GB	N	9	198	22.0	36	0
1958			1	23	23.0	23	0
1959			2	46	23.0	25	0
1960			1	0	0.0	0	0
1961			5	99	19.8	41	0

John Symank *continued*
1963	STL	N	1	21	21.0	21t	1
Career			19	387	20.4	41	1
Playoffs			1	0	0.0		0

Dick Szymanski
1945	DET	N	1	11	11.0	11	0
1959	BAL	N	5	24	4.8	15t	1
1960			1	15	15.0	15	0
Career			7	50	7.1	15t	1

Doyle Tackett
1946	BKN	AA	1	16	16.0	16	0
1947			1	17	17.0	17	0
Career			2	33	16.5	17	0

George Taliaferro
| 1951 | NYY | N | 4 | 74 | 18.5 | 34 | 0 |

Darryl Talley
1984	BUF	N	1	0	0.0	0	0
1990			2	60	30.0	60t	1
1991			5	45	9.0	13	0
1993			3	74	24.7	61t	1
1996	MIN	N	1	10	10.0	10	0
Career			12	189	15.8	61t	2
Playoffs			2	48	24.0		1

Steve Tannen
1970	NYJ	N	2	16	8.0	16	0
1972			7	125	17.9	32	0
1973			1	30	30.0	30	0
1974			2	33	16.5	19	0
Career			12	204	17.0	32	0

Bob Tanner
| 1930 | FRA | N | | | | | 1 |

George Tarasovic
1956	PIT	N	3	60	20.0	31	0
1957			2	21	10.5	11	0
1960			1	8	8.0	8	0
1961			1	16	16.0	16	0
1962			4	55	13.8	37	0
1965	PHI	N	1	40	40.0	40t	1
Career			12	200	16.7	40t	1

Carl Taseff
1953	BAL	N	2	36	18.0	29	0
1954			2	15	7.5	15	0
1955			1	0	0.0	0	0
1956			2	13	6.5	8	0
1957			1	7	7.0	7	0
1958			7	52	7.4	17	0
1959			2	60	30.0	33	0
1961			1	15	15.0	15	0
1962	BUF	A	2	21	10.5	17	0
Career			20	219	10.9	33	0

Damon Tassos
1945	DET	N	3	49	16.3	22	0
1946			1	30	30.0	30	0
1949	GB	N	1	10	10.0	10	0
Career			5	89	17.8	30	0

David Tate
1988	CHI	N	4	35	8.8	17	0
1989			1	0	0.0	0	0
1991			2	35	17.5	28	0
1993	NYG	N	1	12	12.0	12	0
1994	IND	N	3	51	17.0	30	0
Career			11	133	12.1	30	0

Jack Tatum
1971	OAK	N	4	136	34.0	66	0
1972			4	91	22.8	56	0
1973			1	26	26.0	26	0
1974			4	84	21.0	40	0
1975			4	67	16.8	28	0
1976			2	0	0.0	0	0
1977			6	146	24.3	41	0
1978			3	60	20.0	27	0
1979			2	26	13.0	13	0

Jack Tatum *continued*
1980	HOU	N	7	100	14.3	35	0
Career			37	736	19.9	66	0
Playoffs			2	8	4.0		0

Terry Tautolo
| 1980 | SF | N | 1 | 0 | 0.0 | 0 | 0 |

Bobby Taylor
1995	PHI	N	2	52	26.0	35	0
1996			3	-1	-0.3	0	0
Career			5	51	10.2	35	0

Bruce Taylor
1970	SF	N	3	70	23.3	70	0
1971			3	68	22.7	49	0
1972			2	4	2.0	2	0
1973			6	30	5.0	22	0
1974			1	0	0.0	0	0
1975			3	29	9.7	15	0
Career			18	201	11.2	70	0
Playoffs			1	0	0.0		0

Corky Taylor
| 1955 | LA | N | 2 | 55 | 27.5 | 55t | 1 |

Ed Taylor
1976	NYJ	N	2	22	11.0	22	0
1977			1	0	0.0	0	0
1978			2	0	0.0	0	0
1980	MIA	N	3	55	18.3	44	0
Career			8	77	9.6	44	0

Jay Taylor
1990	PHX	N	3	50	16.7	34	0
1993	KC	N	1	0	0.0	0	0
1994			1	0	0.0	0	0
Career			5	50	10.0	34	0

Jim Taylor
| 1958 | CHIC | N | 1 | 5 | 5.0 | 5 | 0 |

Joe Taylor
1967	CHI	N	1	27	27.0	27	0
1968			1	0	0.0	0	0
1969			3	37	12.3	23	0
1970			2	18	9.0	18	0
1971			3	69	23.0	39	0
1972			4	0	0.0	0	0
1974			1	27	27.0	27	0
Career			15	178	11.9	39	0

Keith Taylor
1989	IND	N	7	225	32.1	80t	1
1990			2	51	25.5	40	0
1991			0	-2		-2L	0
1992	NO	N	2	20	10.0	20	0
1993			2	32	16.0	30	0
Career			13	326	25.1	80t	1

Kenny Taylor
1985	CHI	N	3	28	9.3	18	0
1986	SD	N	1	0	0.0	0	0
Career			4	28	7.0	18	0

Lawrence Taylor
1981	NYG	N	1	1	1.0	1	0
1982			1	97	97.0	97t	1
1983			2	10	5.0	10	0
1984			1	-1	-1.0	-1	0
1987			3	16	5.3	15	0
1990			1	11	11.0	11t	1
Career			9	134	14.9	97t	2
Playoffs			1	34	34.0		1

Mike Taylor
| 1972 | NYJ | N | 1 | 2 | 2.0 | 2 | 0 |

Rosey Taylor
1962	CHI	N	2	64	32.0	43t	1
1963			9	172	19.1	46	1
1964			2	45	22.5	26	0
1965			1	3	3.0	3	0

Year	Team		No	Yds	Avg	Lg	TD

Rosey Taylor *continued*

Year	Team		No	Yds	Avg	Lg	TD
1966			1	15	15.0	15	0
1967			5	19	3.8	10	0
1968			3	96	32.0	96t	1
1969	SF	N	2	15	7.5	15	0
1970			3	27	9.0	19	0
1971			3	13	4.3	13	0
1972	WAS	N	1	17	17.0	17	0
Career			32	486	15.2	96t	3
Playoffs			1	17	17.0		0

Terry Taylor

Year	Team		No	Yds	Avg	Lg	TD
1984	SEA	N	3	63	21.0	37	0
1985			4	75	18.8	75t	1
1986			2	0	0	0	0
1987			1	11	11.0	11	0
1988			5	53	10.6	27t	1
1989	DET	N	1	0	0.0	0	0
1991			4	26	6.5	23	0
1992	CLE	N	1	0	0.0	0	0
1994	SEA	N	1	0	0.0	0	0
1995	ATL	N	3	31	10.3	31	0
Career			25	259	10.4	75t	2

George Teague

Year	Team		No	Yds	Avg	Lg	TD
1993	GB	N	1	22	22.0	22	0
1994			3	33	11.0	16	0
1995			2	100	50.0	74	0
1996	DAL	N	4	47	11.8	22	0
Career			10	202	20.2	74	0
Playoffs			3	160	53.3		2

Willie Teal

Year	Team		No	Yds	Avg	Lg	TD
1981	MIN	N	4	23	5.8	15	0
1982			4	15	3.8	13	0
1983			3	26	8.7	12	0
1984			1	53	53.0	53t	1
1985			3	6	2.0	6	0
Career			15	123	8.2	53t	1

Jim Temp

Year	Team		No	Yds	Avg	Lg	TD
1959	GB	N	1	13	13.0	13	0

Lou Tepe

Year	Team		No	Yds	Avg	Lg	TD
1954	PIT	N	3	67	22.3	29	0

Joe Tereshinski

Year	Team		No	Yds	Avg	Lg	TD
1952	WAS	N	1	31	31.0	31	0

George Terlep

Year	Team		No	Yds	Avg	Lg	TD
1947	BUF	AA	1	0	0.0	0	0

Pat Terrell

Year	Team		No	Yds	Avg	Lg	TD
1990	LARM	N	1	6	6.0	6	0
1991			1	4	4.0	4	0
1993			2	1	0.5	1	0
1995	CAR	N	3	33	11.0	21	0
1996			3	6	2.0	6	0
Career			10	50	5.0	21	0
Playoffs			1	49	49.0		0

Ray Terrell

Year	Team		No	Yds	Avg	Lg	TD
1946	CLE	AA	3	101	33.7	76t	1
1947	BAL	AA	1	12	12.0	12	0
Career			4	113	28.3	76t	1

Doug Terry

Year	Team		No	Yds	Avg	Lg	TD
1992	KC	N	1	9	9.0	9	0
1993			1	21	21.0	21	0
Career			2	30	15.0	21	0

Deral Teteak

Year	Team		No	Yds	Avg	Lg	TD
1952	GB	N	1	0	0.0	0	0
1954			1	23	23.0	23	0
1955			2	41	20.5	32	0
1956			2	20	10.0	18	0
Career			6	84	14.0	32	0

Lee Tevis

Year	Team		No	Yds	Avg	Lg	TD
1947	BKN	AA	2	9	4.5		0

Tom Tharp

Year	Team		No	Yds	Avg	Lg	TD
1960	NY	A	2	19	9.5		0

James Thaxton

Year	Team		No	Yds	Avg	Lg	TD
1974	CLE	N	1	0	0.0	0	0

Broderick Thomas

Year	Team		No	Yds	Avg	Lg	TD
1992	TB	N	2	81	40.5	56t	1

Carl Thomas

Year	Team		No	Yds	Avg	Lg	TD
1922	BUF						1

Clendon Thomas

Year	Team		No	Yds	Avg	Lg	TD
1960	LA	N	1	0	0.0	0	0
1961			3	11	3.7	7	0
1962	PIT	N	7	48	6.9	15	0
1963			8	122	15.3	32	0
1964			1	0	0.0	0	0
1966			2	24	12.0	24	0
1967			2	39	19.5	33	0
1968			3	0	0.0	0	0
Career			27	244	9.0	33	0

Dave Thomas

Year	Team		No	Yds	Avg	Lg	TD
1996	JAC	N	2	7	3.5	8	0

Earlie Thomas

Year	Team		No	Yds	Avg	Lg	TD
1970	NYJ	N	2	46	23.0	36t	1
1972			1	14	14.0	14	0
1973			2	25	12.5	25	0
1975	DEN	N	2	66	33.0	36	0
Career			7	151	21.6	36t	1

Emmitt Thomas

Year	Team		No	Yds	Avg	Lg	TD
1967	KC	A	4	60	15.0	57t	1
1968			4	25	6.3	14	0
1969			9	146	16.2	45t	1
1970	KC	N	5	87	17.4	39	0
1971			8	145	18.1	36	1
1972			2	46	23.0	26	0
1973			3	65	21.7	33	0
1974			12	214	17.8	73t	2
1975			6	119	19.8	36	0
1976			2	30	15.0	29	0
1977			1	0	0.0	0	0
1978			2	0	0.0	0	0
Career			58	937	16.2	73t	5
Playoffs			5	101	20.2		0

Eric Thomas

Year	Team		No	Yds	Avg	Lg	TD
1987	CIN	N	1	3	3.0	3	0
1988			7	61	8.7	37	0
1989			4	18	4.5	18t	1
1991			3	0	0.0	0	0
1993	NYJ	N	2	20	10.0	20	0
Career			17	102	6.0	37	1
Playoffs			2	26	13.0		0

Henry Thomas

Year	Team		No	Yds	Avg	Lg	TD
1987	MIN	N	1	0	0.0	0	0
1988			1	7	7.0	7	0
Career			2	7	3.5	7	0

Ike Thomas

Year	Team		No	Yds	Avg	Lg	TD
1975	BUF	N	2	74	37.0	58	0

Jesse Thomas

Year	Team		No	Yds	Avg	Lg	TD
1955	BAL	N	1	23	23.0	23	0
1956			2	36	18.0	23	0
1957			1	0	0.0	0	0
Career			4	59	14.8	23	0

J.T. Thomas

Year	Team		No	Yds	Avg	Lg	TD
1973	PIT	N	1	10	10.0	10	0
1974			5	22	4.4	14	0
1975			3	44	14.7	33	0
1976			2	43	21.5	38	0
1977			2	10	5.0	12	0
1980			2	0	0.0	0	0
1981			4	18	4.5	16	0
1982	DEN	N	1	0	0.0	0	0
Career			20	147	7.3	38	0
Playoffs			2	72	36.0		0

Norris Thomas

Year	Team		No	Yds	Avg	Lg	TD
1977	MIA	N	3	23	7.7	23	0
1978			2	63	31.5	53t	1

Norris Thomas *continued*

Year	Team		No	Yds	Avg	Lg	TD
1979			2	29	14.5	24	0
1980	TB	N	1	0	0.0	0	0
1982			1	0	0.0	0	0
Career			9	115	12.8	53t	1

Orlanda Thomas

Year	Team		No	Yds	Avg	Lg	TD
1995	MIN	N	9	108	12.0	45t	1
1996			5	57	11.4	34	0
Career			14	165	11.8	45t	1
Playoffs			1	4	4.0		0

Pat Thomas

Year	Team		No	Yds	Avg	Lg	TD
1977	LA	N	5	97	19.4	30	0
1978			8	96	12.0	33t	1
1979			3	5	1.7	5	0
1980			3	14	4.7	14	0
1981			4	80	20.0	64	0
1982	LARM	N	3	0	0.0	0	0
Career			26	292	11.2	64	1
Playoffs			1	6	6.0		0

Rodney Thomas

Year	Team		No	Yds	Avg	Lg	TD
1988	MIA	N	1	48	48.0	48	0
1989			2	4	2.0	4	0
Career			3	52	17.3	48	0

Russ Thomas

Year	Team		No	Yds	Avg	Lg	TD
1946	DET	N	1	1	1.0	1	0

Skip Thomas

Year	Team		No	Yds	Avg	Lg	TD
1973	OAK	N	2	24	12.0	12	0
1974			6	70	11.7	34	1
1975			6	86	14.3	48	0
1976			2	26	13.0	14	0
1977			1	16	16.0	16	0
Career			17	222	13.1	48	1
Playoffs			1	18	18.0		0

William Thomas

Year	Team		No	Yds	Avg	Lg	TD
1992	PHI	N	2	4	2.0	4	0
1993			2	39	19.5	21	0
1994			1	7	7.0	7	0
1995			7	104	14.9	37t	1
1996			3	47	15.7	37	0
Career			15	201	13.4	37t	1
Playoffs			1	30	30.0		0

Zach Thomas

Year	Team		No	Yds	Avg	Lg	TD
1996	MIA	N	3	64	21.3	27	1

Bennie Thompson

Year	Team		No	Yds	Avg	Lg	TD
1990	NO	N	2	0	0.0	0	0
1991			1	14	14.0	14	0
1992	KC	N	4	26	6.5	25	0
Career			7	40	5.7	25	0

Billy Thompson

Year	Team		No	Yds	Avg	Lg	TD
1969	DEN	A	3	92	30.7	57t	1
1970	DEN	N	2	65	32.5	33	0
1971			5	83	16.6	42	0
1972			1	4	4.0	4	0
1973			3	96	32.0	59t	1
1974			5	105	21.0	38t	1
1975			2	97	48.5	49	0
1977			5	122	24.4	38	0
1978			4	0	0.0	0	0
1979			4	57	14.3	36	0
1980			2	49	24.5	36	0
1981			4	14	3.5	14	0
Career			40	784	19.6	59t	3
Playoffs			1	18	18.0		0

Bobby Lee Thompson

Year	Team		No	Yds	Avg	Lg	TD
1964	DET	N	3	45	15.0	24	0
1965			2	3	1.5	2	0
1966			4	52	13.0	26	0
1969	NO	N	1	2	2.0	2	0
Career			10	102	10.2	26	0

Don Thompson

Year	Team		No	Yds	Avg	Lg	TD
1926	LA	N					2

Norm Thompson

Year	Team		No	Yds	Avg	Lg	TD
1971	STL	N	4	45	11.3	25	0
1972			1	5	5.0	5	0
1974			6	190	31.7	56t	1
1975			7	141	20.1	61t	1
1976			4	83	20.8	38	0
1977	BAL	N	3	39	13.0	20	0
1978			6	52	8.7	31	0
1979			2	38	19.0	26	0
Career			33	593	18.0	61t	2

Reyna Thompson

Year	Team		No	Yds	Avg	Lg	TD
1992	NYG	N	2	69	34.5	69t	1
1993	NE	N	1	4	4.0	4	0
Career			3	73	24.3	69t	1

Ted Thompson

Year	Team		No	Yds	Avg	Lg	TD
1984	HOU	N	0	5		5L	0

Tommy Thompson

Year	Team		No	Yds	Avg	Lg	TD
1941	PHI	N	3	24	8.0	14	0
1942			4	28	7.0	22	0
1945			2	33	16.5	25	0
Career			9	85	9.4	25	0

Tommy Thompson

Year	Team		No	Yds	Avg	Lg	TD
1949	CLE	AA	1	9	9.0	9	0
1951	CLE	N	2	23	11.5	17	0
1952			1	21	21.0	21	0
1953			2	13	6.5	8	0
Career			6	66	11.0	21	0
Playoffs			1	0	0.0		0

Art Thoms

Year	Team		No	Yds	Avg	Lg	TD
1972	OAK	N	1	0	0.0	0	0
1975			1	0	0.0	0	0
Career			2	0	0.0	0	0

Bruce Thornton

Year	Team		No	Yds	Avg	Lg	TD
1979	DAL	N	1	3	3.0	3	0

Wilfred Thorpe

Year	Team		No	Yds	Avg	Lg	TD
1941	CLE	N	1	5	5.0	5	0
1942			1	5	5.0	5	0
Career			2	10	5.0	5	0

Cliff Thrift

Year	Team		No	Yds	Avg	Lg	TD
1980	SD	N	1	0	0.0	0	0
1982			2	16	8.0	9	0
Career			3	16	5.3	9	0

Bob Thurbon

Year	Team		No	Yds	Avg	Lg	TD
1943	P-P	N	1	3	3.0	3	0
1944	C-P	N	2	14	7.0	8	0
Career			3	17	5.7	8	0

Dennis Thurman

Year	Team		No	Yds	Avg	Lg	TD
1978	DAL	N	2	35	17.5	23	0
1979			1	0	0.0	0	0
1980			5	114	22.8	78t	1
1981			9	187	20.8	96	0
1982			3	75	25.0	60t	1
1983			6	49	8.2	34	0
1984			5	81	16.2	43	1
1985			5	21	4.2	21t	1
Career			36	562	15.6	96	4
Playoffs			7	126	18.0		1

Glenn Tidd

Year	Team		No	Yds	Avg	Lg	TD
1924	DAY						1

Pete Tinsley

Year	Team		No	Yds	Avg	Lg	TD
1941	GB	N	1	24	24.0	24	0
1942			1	3	3.0	3	0
1943			1	8	8.0	8	0
1945			1	6	6.0	6	0
Career			4	41	10.3	24	0

Sid Tinsley

Year	Team		No	Yds	Avg	Lg	TD
1945	PIT	N	1	-2	-2.0	-2	0

Andre Tippett

Year	Team		No	Yds	Avg	Lg	TD
1986	NE	N	0	32		32L	0

Andre Tippett *continued*

Year	Team		No	Yds	Avg	Lg	TD
1991			1	10	10.0	10	0
Career			1	42	42.0	32L	0

Kenny Tippins

Year	Team		No	Yds	Avg	Lg	TD
1991	ATL	N	1	35	35.0	35	0
1995			1	0	0.0	0	0
Career			2	35	17.5	35	0

Bob Titchenal

Year	Team		No	Yds	Avg	Lg	TD
1941	WAS	N	2	3	1.5	3	0
1942			1	19	19.0	19	0
Career			3	22	7.3	19	0

Si Titus

Year	Team		No	Yds	Avg	Lg	TD
1941	BKN	N	2	5	2.5	2	0

Dick Todd

Year	Team		No	Yds	Avg	Lg	TD
1940	WAS	N	2	3	1.5		0
1942			2	39	19.5	36	0
1945			4	35	8.8	22	0
1946			4	26	6.5	0	0
1947			4	59	14.8	50	0
Career			16	162	10.1	50	0

Loren Toews

Year	Team		No	Yds	Avg	Lg	TD
1973	PIT	N	2	13	6.5	8	0
1978			1	12	12.0	12	0
1982			1	20	20.0	20	0
Career			4	45	11.3	20	0
Playoffs			1	35	35.0		0

Jim Tolbert

Year	Team		No	Yds	Avg	Lg	TD
1966	SD	A	1	0	0.0	0	0
1967			1	9	9.0	9	0
1968			2	42	21.0	22	0
1970	SD	N	2	19	9.5	19	0
1973	STL	N	2	34	17.0	26	0
1974			2	22	11.0	22	0
Career			10	126	12.6	26	0

Tony Tolbert

Year	Team		No	Yds	Avg	Lg	TD
1994	DAL	N	1	54	54.0	54t	1

Lou Tomasetti

Year	Team		No	Yds	Avg	Lg	TD
1941	DET	N	1	13	13.0	13	0
1942	PHI	N	1	23	23.0	23	0
1946	BUF	AA	1	0	0.0	0	0
1947			1	44	44.0	44t	1
Career			4	80	20.0	44t	1

Andy Tomasic

Year	Team		No	Yds	Avg	Lg	TD
1942	PIT	N	2	75	37.5	41	0

Bob Toneff

Year	Team		No	Yds	Avg	Lg	TD
1954	SF	N	1	15	15.0	15	0
1958			1	5	5.0	5	0
Career			2	20	10.0	15	0

Tom Toner

Year	Team		No	Yds	Avg	Lg	TD
1973	GB	N	1	1	1.0	1	0
1975			1	0	0.0	0	0
1976			1	28	28.0	28	0
1977			1	10	10.0	10	0
Career			4	39	9.8	28	0

Clayton Tonnemaker

Year	Team		No	Yds	Avg	Lg	TD
1950	GB	N	1	1	1.0	1	0
1954			1	1	1.0	1	0
Career			2	2	1.0	1	0

Charley Toogood

Year	Team		No	Yds	Avg	Lg	TD
1951	LA	N	1	0	0.0	0	0
1953			1	0	0.0	0	0
1954			1	3	3.0	3	0
Career			3	3	1.0	3	0

Pat Toomay

Year	Team		No	Yds	Avg	Lg	TD
1973	DAL	N	1	35	35.0	35	0
1975	BUF	N	1	44	44.0	44t	1
Career			2	79	39.5	44t	1

Stacey Toran

Year	Team		No	Yds	Avg	Lg	TD
1985	LARI	N	1	76	76.0	76t	1
1986			2	28	14.0	19	0
1987			3	48	16.0	48t	1
Career			6	152	25.3	76t	2

LaVerne Torczon

Year	Team		No	Yds	Avg	Lg	TD
1963	NY	A	1	2	2.0	2	0
1964			1	40	40.0	40t	1
Career			2	42	21.0	40t	1

LaVern Torgeson

Year	Team		No	Yds	Avg	Lg	TD
1951	DET	N	1	0	0.0	0	0
1952			5	100	20.0	34	1
1953			5	27	5.4	10	0
1954			2	33	16.5	33	0
1955	WAS	N	3	45	15.0	20	0
1956			1	0	0.0	0	0
1957			1	6	6.0	6	0
Career			18	211	11.7	34	1
Playoffs			1	0	0.0		0

Steve Tovar

Year	Team		No	Yds	Avg	Lg	TD
1993	CIN	N	1	0	0.0	0	0
1994			1	14	14.0	14	0
1995			1	13	13.0	13	0
1996			4	42	10.5	24	0
Career			7	69	9.9	24	0

Steve Towle

Year	Team		No	Yds	Avg	Lg	TD
1975	MIA	N	1	16	16.0	16	0
1978			1	14	14.0	14	0
1979			1	0	0.0	0	0
Career			3	30	10.0	16	0

Greg Townsend

Year	Team		No	Yds	Avg	Lg	TD
1988	LARI	N	1	86	86.0	86t	1
1990			1	0	0.0	0	0
1991			1	31	31.0	31	0
Career			3	117	39.0	86t	1

John Tracey

Year	Team		No	Yds	Avg	Lg	TD
1960	STL	N	1	14	14.0	14	0
1963	BUF	A	5	22	4.4	15	0
1964			3	12	4.0	6	0
1965			1	8	8.0	8	0
1966			1	0	0.0	0	0
1967			1	3	3.0	3	0
Career			12	59	4.9	15	0

James Trapp

Year	Team		No	Yds	Avg	Lg	TD
1993	LARI	N	1	7	7.0	7	0
1996	OAK	N	1	23	23.0	23	0
Career			2	30	15.0	23	0

Orville Trask

Year	Team		No	Yds	Avg	Lg	TD
1961	HOU	A	1	17	17.0	17	0

Ivan Trebotich

Year	Team		No	Yds	Avg	Lg	TD
1945	DET	N	3	46	15.3	28	0

Bill Triplett

Year	Team		No	Yds	Avg	Lg	TD
1962	STL	N	1	24	24.0	24	0

Paul Tripoli

Year	Team		No	Yds	Avg	Lg	TD
1987	TB	N	3	17	5.7	15t	1

Charley Trippi

Year	Team		No	Yds	Avg	Lg	TD
1947	CHIC	N	1	59	59.0	59t	1
1954			3	34	11.3	23	0
Career			4	93	23.3	59t	1

Eddie Tryon

Year	Team		No	Yds	Avg	Lg	TD
1926	NY	A					1
1927	NYY	N					2
Career							3

Esera Tuaolo

Year	Team		No	Yds	Avg	Lg	TD
1991	GB	N	1	23	23.0	23	0

Natu Tuatagaloa

Year	Team		No	Yds	Avg	Lg	TD
1992	SEA	N	1	0	0.0	0	0

Jerry Tubbs

Year	Team		No	Yds	Avg	Lg	TD
1959	SF	N	2	32	16.0	21	0
1960	DAL	N	1	5	5.0	5	0
1961			3	33	11.0	33	0
1962			4	35	8.8	21	0
1963			2	61	30.5	44	0
1964			2	27	13.5	26	0
1965			2	9	4.5	8	0
1966			1	6	6.0	6	0
Career			17	208	12.2	44	0

Winfred Tubbs

Year	Team		No	Yds	Avg	Lg	TD
1994	NO	N	1	0	0.0	0	0
1995			1	6	6.0	6	0
1996			1	11	11.0	11	0
Career			3	17	5.7	11	0

Jessie Tuggle

Year	Team		No	Yds	Avg	Lg	TD
1991	ATL	N	1	21	21.0	21	0
1992			1	1	1.0	1	0
1994			1	0	0.0	0	0
1995			3	84	28.0	49	1
Career			6	106	17.7	49	1

Manu Tuiasosopo

Year	Team		No	Yds	Avg	Lg	TD
1986	SF	N	1	22	22.0	22	0

Willie Tullis

Year	Team		No	Yds	Avg	Lg	TD
1983	HOU	N	5	65	13.0	44	0
1984			4	48	12.0	22	0
1985	NO	N	2	22	11.0	22	0
1987	IND	N	3	0	0.0	0	0
1988			4	36	9.0	20	0
Career			18	171	9.5	44	0

Emlen Tunnell

Year	Team		No	Yds	Avg	Lg	TD
1948	NYG	N	7	116	16.6	43t	1
1949			10	251	25.1	55t	2
1950			7	167	23.9	35	0
1951			9	74	8.2	30	0
1952			7	149	21.3	40	0
1953			6	117	19.5	44	0
1954			8	108	13.5	43	0
1955			7	76	10.9	26	0
1956			6	87	14.5	23	0
1957			6	87	14.5	52t	1
1958			1	8	8.0	8	0
1959	GB	N	2	20	10.0	18	0
1960			3	22	7.3	22	0
Career			79	1282	16.2	55t	4

Godwin Turk

Year	Team		No	Yds	Avg	Lg	TD
1975	NYJ	N	2	20	10.0	12	0
1978	DEN	N	2	36	18.0	22	0
Career			4	56	14.0	22	0

Renaldo Turnbull

Year	Team		No	Yds	Avg	Lg	TD
1993	NO	N	1	2	2.0	2	0

Bulldog Turner

Year	Team		No	Yds	Avg	Lg	TD
1940	CHIB	N	1	9	9.0	9	0
1941			1	12	12.0	12	0
1942			8	96	12.0	42	1
1944			2	44	22.0	38	0
1946			1	15	15.0	15	0
1947			2	103	51.5	96t	1
1948			2	19	9.5	14	0
Career			17	298	17.5	96t	2
Playoffs			4	51	12.8		1

Eric Turner

Year	Team		No	Yds	Avg	Lg	TD
1991	CLE	N	2	42	21.0	42t	1
1992			1	6	6.0	6	0
1993			5	25	5.0	19	0
1994			9	199	22.1	93t	1
1996	BAL	N	5	1	0.2	1	0
Career			22	273	12.4	93t	2
Playoffs			1	28	28.0		0

Jimmy Turner

Year	Team		No	Yds	Avg	Lg	TD
1984	CIN	N	1	4	4.0	4	0
1985			1	40	40.0	40	0
Career			2	44	22.0	40	0

John Turner

Year	Team		No	Yds	Avg	Lg	TD
1978	MIN	N	1	15	15.0	15	0
1979			2	48	24.0	36	0
1980			6	22	3.7	13	0
1982			2	43	21.5	33t	1
1983			6	37	6.2	14	0
1984	SD	N	2	43	21.5	43	0
1985	MIN	N	5	62	12.4	25	0
Career			24	270	11.3	43	1
Playoffs			3	25	8.3		0

Keena Turner

Year	Team		No	Yds	Avg	Lg	TD
1980	SF	N	2	15	7.5	11	0
1981			1	0	0.0	0	0
1984			4	51	12.8	21	0
1986			1	9	9.0	9	0
1987			1	15	15.0	15	0
1988			1	2	2.0	2	0
1989			1	42	42.0	42	0
Career			11	134	12.2	42	0
Playoffs			2	26	13.0		0

Marcus Turner

Year	Team		No	Yds	Avg	Lg	TD
1990	PHX	N	1	70	70.0	70	2
1992	NYJ	N	2	15	7.5	14	0
1994			5	155	31.0	90t	1
Career			8	240	30.0	90t	3

Scott Turner

Year	Team		No	Yds	Avg	Lg	TD
1995	WAS	N	1	0	0.0	0	0
1996			2	16	8.0	12	0
Career			3	16	5.3	12	0

Vince Turner

Year	Team		No	Yds	Avg	Lg	TD
1964	NY	A	1	0	0.0	0	0

Wylie Turner

Year	Team		No	Yds	Avg	Lg	TD
1980	GB	N	2	13	6.5	13	0

Maurice Tyler

Year	Team		No	Yds	Avg	Lg	TD
1972	BUF	N	4	61	15.3	27	0
1974	DEN	N	1	0	0.0	0	0
Career			5	61	12.2	27	0

Olen Underwood

Year	Team		No	Yds	Avg	Lg	TD
1965	NYG	N	1	20	20.0	20	0
1967	HOU	A	1	8	8.0	8	0
1968			1	0	0.0	0	0
1969			1	2	2.0	2	0
1971	DEN	N	1	5	5.0	5	0
Career			5	35	7.0	20	0

Marv Upshaw

Year	Team		No	Yds	Avg	Lg	TD
1969	CLE	N	1	0	0.0	0	0
1974	KC	N	1	52	52.0	2	1
Career			2	52	26.0	2	1

Andy Uram

Year	Team		No	Yds	Avg	Lg	TD
1941	GB	N	2	37	18.5	28	0
1942			2	18	9.0	18	0
1943			2	40	20.0	22	0
Career			6	95	15.8	28	0
Playoffs			1	10	10.0		0

Gasper Urban

Year	Team		No	Yds	Avg	Lg	TD
1948	CHI	AA	1	5	5.0	5	0

Luke Urban

Year	Team		No	Yds	Avg	Lg	TD
1923	BUF	N					1

Emil Uremovich

Year	Team		No	Yds	Avg	Lg	TD
1948	CHI	AA	1	1	1.0	1	0

Ted Vactor

Year	Team		No	Yds	Avg	Lg	TD
1972	WAS	N	1	28	28.0	28	0
1973			1	34	34.0	34t	1
Career			2	62	31.0	34t	1

Vern Valdez

Year	Team		No	Yds	Avg	Lg	TD
1960	LA	N	1	0	0.0	0	0
1961	BUF	A	2	54	27.0	50	0
1962	OAK	A	4	47	11.8	36	0
Career			7	101	14.4	50	0

Ebert Van Buren

Year	Team		No	Yds	Avg	Lg	TD
1951	PHI	N	1	23	23.0	23	0
1953			1	13	13.0	13	0
Career			2	36	18.0	23	0

Steve Van Buren

Year	Team		No	Yds	Avg	Lg	TD
1944	PHI	N	5	47	9.4	13	0
1945			1	2	2.0	2	0
1947			1	0	0.0	0	0
1948			2	32	16.0	20	0
Career			9	81	9.0	20	0

Skip Vanderbundt

Year	Team		No	Yds	Avg	Lg	TD
1970	SF	N	3	18	6.0	18	0
1971			1	10	10.0	10	0
1972			2	58	29.0	37t	2
1973			1	7	7.0	7	0
1974			2	22	11.0	18	0
1975			2	36	18.0	21	0
1976			2	8	4.0	8	0
1977			1	6	6.0	6	0
Career			14	165	11.8	37t	2
Playoffs			2	4	2.0		0

Hal Van Every

Year	Team		No	Yds	Avg	Lg	TD
1941	GB	N	3	104	34.7	91	1

Sean Vanhorse

Year	Team		No	Yds	Avg	Lg	TD
1992	SD	N	1	11	11.0	11	0
1993			2	0	0.0	0	0
1994			2	56	28.0	50t	1
1995	DET	N	1	0	0.0	0	0
Career			6	67	11.2	50t	1

Brad Van Pelt

Year	Team		No	Yds	Avg	Lg	TD
1974	NYG	N	2	22	11.0	13	0
1975			3	8	2.7	5	0
1976			2	13	6.5	7	0
1977			2	9	4.5	9	0
1978			3	32	10.7	20	0
1980			3	3	1.0	3	0
1981			1	10	10.0	10	0
1983			2	7	3.5	6	0
1984	LARI	N	1	9	9.0	9	0
1985			1	22	22.0	22	0
Career			20	135	6.8	22	0

Art Van Tone

Year	Team		No	Yds	Avg	Lg	TD
1943	DET	N	2	29	14.5	24	0
1944			4	16	4.0	11	0
1946	BKN	AA	1	5	5.0	5	0
Career			7	50	7.1	24	0

Johnny Vardian

Year	Team		No	Yds	Avg	Lg	TD
1947	BAL	AA	3	48	16.0		0

Larry Vargo

Year	Team		No	Yds	Avg	Lg	TD
1963	DET	N	1	42	42.0	42t	1
1964	MIN	N	1	0	0.0	0	0
1965			3	18	6.0	18	0
1966	NYG	N	1	1	1.0	1	0
Career			6	61	10.2	42t	1

Vic Vasicek

Year	Team		No	Yds	Avg	Lg	TD
1950	LA	N	1	52	52.0	52	0

Tommy Vaughn

Year	Team		No	Yds	Avg	Lg	TD
1966	DET	N	1	16	16.0	16	0
1967			1	0	0.0	0	0
1968			3	33	11.0	24	0
1969			2	0	0.0	0	0
1970			1	0	0.0	0	0
1971			1	8	8.0	8	0
Career			9	57	6.3	24	0

Craig Veasey

Year	Team		No	Yds	Avg	Lg	TD
1994	MIA	N	1	7	7.0	7	0

Garin Veris

Year	Team		No	Yds	Avg	Lg	TD
Playoffs			1	18	18.0		0

Joe Vetrano

Year	Team		No	Yds	Avg	Lg	TD
1946	SF	AA	3	32	10.7		0

Year	Team		No	Yds	Avg	Lg	TD

Phil Villapiano

Year	Team		No	Yds	Avg	Lg	TD
1971	OAK	N	2	25	12.5	14	0
1972			3	97	32.3	82t	1
1973			1	6	6.0	6	0
1975			2	32	16.0	19	0
1976			1	0	0.0	0	0
1978			2	0	0.0	0	0
Career			11	160	14.5	82t	1
Playoffs			3	23	7.7		0

Shawn Vincent

Year	Team		No	Yds	Avg	Lg	TD
1991	PIT	N	2	52	26.0	27	0

Troy Vincent

Year	Team		No	Yds	Avg	Lg	TD
1992	MIA	N	2	47	23.5	32	0
1993			2	29	14.5	23	0
1994			5	113	22.6	58t	1
1995			5	95	19.0	69t	1
1996	PHI	N	3	144	48.0	90t	1
Career			17	428	25.2	90t	3
Playoffs			3	2	0.7		0

Paul Vinnola

Year	Team		No	Yds	Avg	Lg	TD
1946	LA	AA	1	4	4.0	4	0

Larry Visnic

Year	Team		No	Yds	Avg	Lg	TD
1944	NYG	N	2	56	28.0	41	0
1945			1	3	3.0	3	0
Career			3	59	19.7	41	0

Rick Volk

Year	Team		No	Yds	Avg	Lg	TD
1967	BAL	N	6	145	24.2	94t	1
1968			6	154	25.7	90	0
1969			4	36	9.0	23	0
1970			4	61	15.3	31	0
1971			4	36	9.0	21	0
1972			4	86	21.5	23	0
1973			1	0	0.0	0	0
1974			2	0	0.0	0	0
1976	NYG	N	2	14	7.0	11	0
1977	MIA	N	1	0	0.0	0	0
1978			4	42	10.5	24	0
Career			38	574	15.1	94t	1
Playoffs			5	112	22.4		0

Lloyd Voss

Year	Team		No	Yds	Avg	Lg	TD
1967	PIT	N	1	4	4.0	4	0

Ray Waddy

Year	Team		No	Yds	Avg	Lg	TD
1979	WAS	N	1	6	6.0	6	0

Bob Wade

Year	Team		No	Yds	Avg	Lg	TD
1969	WAS	N	0	14		14L	0
1970	DEN	N	1	10	10.0	10	0
Career			1	24	24.0	14L	0

Jim Wade

Year	Team		No	Yds	Avg	Lg	TD
1949	NYB	N	1	12	12.0	12	0

Lowell Wagner

Year	Team		No	Yds	Avg	Lg	TD
1948	NY	AA	1	31	31.0	31	0
1949	SF	AA	6	121	20.2	66t	1
1950	SF	N	4	12	3.0	8	0
1951			9	115	12.8	40	0
1952			6	69	11.5	30	0
1953			6	135	22.5	32	0
Career			32	483	15.1	66t	1

Mike Wagner

Year	Team		No	Yds	Avg	Lg	TD
1971	PIT	N	2	53	26.5	27	0
1972			6	77	12.8	35	0
1973			8	134	16.8	38	0
1974			2	13	6.5	9	0
1975			4	122	30.5	65	0
1976			2	0	0.0	0	0
1978			2	34	17.0	20	0
1979			4	31	7.8	19	0
1980			6	27	4.5	17	0
Career			36	491	13.6	65	0
Playoffs			5	91	18.2		0

Jim Wagstaff

Year	Team		No	Yds	Avg	Lg	TD
1960	BUF	A	6	93	15.5		1

Jim Wagstaff *continued*

Year	Team		No	Yds	Avg	Lg	TD
1961			3	25	8.3	19	0
Career			9	118	13.1	19	1

Jim Wahler

Year	Team		No	Yds	Avg	Lg	TD
1989	PHX	N	1	5	5.0	5	0

Van Waiters

Year	Team		No	Yds	Avg	Lg	TD
1990	CLE	N	1	15	15.0	15	0

Bracey Walker

Year	Team		No	Yds	Avg	Lg	TD
1995	CIN	N	4	56	14.0	23	0
1996			2	35	17.5	35	0
Career			6	91	15.2	35	0

Chuck Walker

Year	Team		No	Yds	Avg	Lg	TD
1973	ATL	N	1	0	0.0	0	0

Darnell Walker

Year	Team		No	Yds	Avg	Lg	TD
1993	ATL	N	3	7	2.3	7	0
1994			3	105	35.0	44t	1
1996			1	0	0.0	0	0
Career			7	112	16.0	44t	1

Doak Walker

Year	Team		No	Yds	Avg	Lg	TD
1950	DET	N	1	40	40.0	40	0
1955			1	20	20.0	20	0
Career			2	60	30.0	40	0

Donnie Walker

Year	Team		No	Yds	Avg	Lg	TD
1973	BUF	N	1	22	22.0	22	0

Fulton Walker

Year	Team		No	Yds	Avg	Lg	TD
1981	MIA	N	1	0	0.0	0	0
1982			3	54	18.0	30	0
1983			1	7	7.0	7	0
Career			5	61	12.2	30	0
Playoffs			0	9			0

Kevin Walker

Year	Team		No	Yds	Avg	Lg	TD
1987	TB	N	2	30	15.0	30t	1

Marquis Walker

Year	Team		No	Yds	Avg	Lg	TD
1996	STL	N	1	0	0.0	0	0

Paul Walker

Year	Team		No	Yds	Avg	Lg	TD
1948	NYG	N	1	5	5.0	5	0

Val Joe Walker

Year	Team		No	Yds	Avg	Lg	TD
1953	GB	N	4	74	18.5	54t	1
1954			4	83	20.8	44	0
1955			6	77	12.8	36	0
1956			1	0	0.0	0	0
1957	SF	N	2	20	10.0	12	0
Career			17	254	14.9	54t	1

Wayne Walker

Year	Team		No	Yds	Avg	Lg	TD
1958	DET	N	1	33	33.0	33t	1
1960			1	21	21.0	21	0
1961			2	16	8.0	12	0
1962			1	47	47.0	47	0
1963			1	17	17.0	17	0
1964			1	14	14.0	14	0
1965			2	0	0.0	0	0
1966			1	3	3.0	3	0
1968			1	0	0.0	0	0
1969			1	0	0.0	0	0
1971			2	12	6.0	8	0
Career			14	163	11.6	47	1

Jackie Wallace

Year	Team		No	Yds	Avg	Lg	TD
1974	MIN	N	1	3	3.0	3	0
1975	BAL	N	4	126	31.5	42t	2
1976			5	105	21.0	41	0
1977	LA	N	1	23	23.0	23	0
Career			11	257	23.4	42t	2

Stan Wallace

Year	Team		No	Yds	Avg	Lg	TD
1954	CHIB	N	4	63	15.8	51	0
1956			1	7	7.0	7	0
1957			2	23	11.5	21	0

Stan Wallace *continued*

Year	Team		No	Yds	Avg	Lg	TD
1958			3	16	5.3	9	0
Career			10	109	10.9	51	0

Fred Wallner

Year	Team		No	Yds	Avg	Lg	TD
1951	CHIC	N	1	10	10.0	10	0
1955			2	4	2.0	4	0
Career			3	14	4.7	10	0

Everson Walls

Year	Team		No	Yds	Avg	Lg	TD
1981	DAL	N	11	133	12.1	33	0
1982			7	61	8.7	37	0
1983			4	70	17.5	37	0
1984			3	12	4.0	12	0
1985			9	31	3.4	19	0
1986			3	46	15.3	24	0
1987			5	38	7.6	30	0
1988			2	0	0.0	0	0
1990	NYG	N	6	80	13.3	40	1
1991			4	7	1.8	5	0
1992	NYG-CLE	N	3	26	8.7	24	0
Career			57	504	8.8	40	1
Playoffs			4	57	14.3		0

Mike Walter

Year	Team		No	Yds	Avg	Lg	TD
1985	SF	N	1	0	0.0	0	0
1987			1	16	16.0	16	0
Career			2	16	8.0	16	0
Playoffs			1	4	4.0		0

Danny Walters

Year	Team		No	Yds	Avg	Lg	TD
1983	SD	N	7	55	7.9	33	0
1985			5	71	14.2	30	0
Career			12	126	10.5	33	0

Les Walters

Year	Team		No	Yds	Avg	Lg	TD
1958	WAS	N	1	19	19.0	19	0

Tommy Walters

Year	Team		No	Yds	Avg	Lg	TD
1964	WAS	N	2	36	18.0	29	0
1965			1	63	63.0	63t	1
Career			3	99	33.0	63t	1

Len Walterscheid

Year	Team		No	Yds	Avg	Lg	TD
1978	CHI	N	1	0	0.0	0	0
1979			1	15	15.0	15	0
1980			4	84	21.0	36t	1
1981			1	0	0.0	0	0
Career			7	99	14.1	36t	1

Alvin Walton

Year	Team		No	Yds	Avg	Lg	TD
1987	WAS	N	3	28	9.3	24	0
1988			3	54	18.0	29	0
1989			4	58	14.5	29t	1
1990			2	118	59.0	61	1
Career			12	258	21.5	61	2
Playoffs			1	16	16.0		0

Joe Walton

Year	Team		No	Yds	Avg	Lg	TD
1957	WAS	N	1	55	55.0	55	0

Carl Ward

Year	Team		No	Yds	Avg	Lg	TD
1967	CLE	N	1	0	0.0	0	0

Charley Warner

Year	Team		No	Yds	Avg	Lg	TD
1963	KC	A	1	12	12.0	12	0
1964	BUF	A	1	30	30.0	30	0
1965			5	84	16.8	23	1
Career			7	126	18.0	30	1
Playoffs			1	8	8.0		0

Buist Warren

Year	Team		No	Yds	Avg	Lg	TD
1945	PIT	N	1	19	19.0	19	0

Frank Warren

Year	Team		No	Yds	Avg	Lg	TD
1983	NO	N	1	6	6.0	6	0

Jimmy Warren

Year	Team		No	Yds	Avg	Lg	TD
1964	SD	A	2	28	14.0	28	0
1965			5	43	8.6	26	0
1966	MIA	A	5	198	39.6	70	1
1967			4	22	5.5	17	0

Jimmy Warren *continued*

Year	Team		No	Yds	Avg	Lg	TD
1968			2	27	13.5	18	0
1970	OAK	N	2	26	13.0	26	0
1971			2	114	57.0	59t	2
1973			1	0	0.0	0	0
1974			2	58	29.0	34	0
Career			25	516	20.6	70	3
Playoffs			1	0	0.0		0

Lonnie Warwick

Year	Team		No	Yds	Avg	Lg	TD
1966	MIN	N	2	27	13.5	23	0
1967			2	36	18.0	19	0
1969			4	46	11.5	19	0
1970			3	30	10.0	23	0
1972			1	6	6.0	6	0
Career			12	145	12.1	23	0

Anthony Washington

Year	Team		No	Yds	Avg	Lg	TD
1981	PIT	N	3	46	15.3	35	0
1983	WAS	N	4	12	3.0	8	0
1984			1	25	25.0	25	0
Career			8	83	10.4	35	0
Playoffs			1	0	0.0		0

Brian Washington

Year	Team		No	Yds	Avg	Lg	TD
1988	CLE	N	3	104	34.7	75t	1
1990	NYJ	N	3	22	7.3	13	0
1991			1	0	0.0	0	0
1992			6	59	9.8	23t	1
1993			6	128	21.3	62t	1
1994			2	-3	-1.5	0	0
1995	KC	N	3	100	33.3	74t	1
1996			3	39	13.0	34	0
Career			27	449	16.6	75t	4

Charles Washington

Year	Team		No	Yds	Avg	Lg	TD
1991	KC	N	1	34	34.0	34	0

Chris Washington

Year	Team		No	Yds	Avg	Lg	TD
1986	TB	N	1	12	12.0	12	0

Clyde Washington

Year	Team		No	Yds	Avg	Lg	TD
1960	BOS	A	3	13	4.3		0
1961			4	45	11.3	33	0
1963	NY	A	2	2	1.0	1	0
Career			9	60	6.7	33	0

Dave Washington

Year	Team		No	Yds	Avg	Lg	TD
1971	DEN	N	1	8	8.0	8	0
1972	BUF	N	1	4	4.0	4	0
1974			2	72	36.0	72t	1
1977	SF	N	2	68	34.0	50	0
Career			6	152	25.3	72t	1

Dewayne Washington

Year	Team		No	Yds	Avg	Lg	TD
1994	MIN	N	3	135	45.0	81t	2
1995			1	25	25.0	25	0
1996			2	27	13.5	27t	1
Career			6	187	31.2	81t	3

James Washington

Year	Team		No	Yds	Avg	Lg	TD
1988	LARM	N	1	7	7.0	7	0
1990	DAL	N	3	24	8.0	13	0
1991			2	9	4.5	9	0
1992			3	31	10.3	16	0
1993			1	38	38.0	38	0
1994			5	43	8.6	25	0
1995	WAS	N	2	35	17.5	21	0
Career			17	187	11.0	38	0
Playoffs			3	46	15.3		0

Kenny Washington

Year	Team		No	Yds	Avg	Lg	TD
1948	LA	N	2	45	22.5	40	0

Lionel Washington

Year	Team		No	Yds	Avg	Lg	TD
1983	STL	N	8	92	11.5	26	0
1984			5	42	8.4	18	0
1985			1	48	48.0	48t	1
1986			2	19	9.5	19	0
1988	LARI	N	1	0	0.0	0	0
1989			3	46	15.3	32t	1
1990			1	2	2.0	2	0
1991			5	22	4.4	16	0

Lionel Washington *continued*

Year	Team		No	Yds	Avg	Lg	TD
1992			2	21	10.5	18	0
1993			2	0	0.0	0	0
1994			3	65	21.7	31t	1
1996	DEN	N	2	17	8.5	23	0
Career			35	374	10.7	48t	3

Mark Washington

Year	Team		No	Yds	Avg	Lg	TD
1970	DAL	N	1	0	0.0	0	0
1973			1	0	0.0	0	0
1974			1	0	0.0	0	0
1975			4	26	6.5	23	0
1976			4	49	12.3	22	0
1977			2	32	16.0	21	0
Career			13	107	8.2	23	0
Playoffs			1	27	27.0		0

Marvin Washington

Year	Team		No	Yds	Avg	Lg	TD
1994	NYJ	N	1	7	7.0	7	0

Mickey Washington

Year	Team		No	Yds	Avg	Lg	TD
1991	NE	N	2	0	0.0	0	0
1993	BUF	N	1	27	27.0	27t	1
1994			3	63	21.0	36	0
1995	JAC	N	1	48	48.0	48t	1
1996			1	1	1.0	1	0
Career			8	139	17.4	48t	2

Mike Washington

Year	Team		No	Yds	Avg	Lg	TD
1977	TB	N	5	71	14.2	45t	1
1978			5	43	8.6	24	0
1979			3	64	21.3	49t	1
1980			4	30	7.5	16	0
1981			6	156	26.0	34	1
1982			3	13	4.3	13	0
1983			2	41	20.5	25	0
Career			28	418	14.9	49t	3

Sam Washington

Year	Team		No	Yds	Avg	Lg	TD
1983	PIT	N	1	25	25.0	25	0
1984			6	138	23.0	69t	2
Career			7	163	23.3	69t	2

Ted Washington

Year	Team		No	Yds	Avg	Lg	TD
1975	HOU	N	3	30	10.0	23	0
1977			3	26	8.7	19	0
1981			1	19	19.0	19	0
Career			7	75	10.7	23	0

Ted Washington

Year	Team		No	Yds	Avg	Lg	TD
1994	DEN	N	1	5	5.0	5	0

Lloyd Wasserbach

Year	Team		No	Yds	Avg	Lg	TD
1946	CHI	AA	1	0	0.0	0	0

Bob Waterfield

Year	Team		No	Yds	Avg	Lg	TD
1945	CLE	N	6	92	15.3	29	0
1946	LA	N	5	72	14.4	28	0
1947			5	56	11.2	35	0
1948			4	8	2.0	5	0
Career			20	228	11.4	35	0

Andre Waters

Year	Team		No	Yds	Avg	Lg	TD
1986	PHI	N	6	39	6.5	21	0
1987			3	63	21.0	63	0
1988			3	19	6.3	14	0
1989			1	20	20.0	20	0
1991			1	0	0.0	0	0
1992			1	23	23.0	23	0
Career			15	164	10.9	63	0

Charlie Waters

Year	Team		No	Yds	Avg	Lg	TD
1970	DAL	N	5	45	9.0	20	0
1971			2	37	18.5	30	0
1972			6	132	22.0	56	1
1973			5	112	22.4	44	0
1974			2	26	13.0	24	0
1975			3	55	18.3	35	1
1976			3	6	2.0	5	0
1977			3	11	3.7	6	0
1978			4	61	15.3	22	0
1980			5	78	15.6	29	0

Charlie Waters *continued*

Year	Team		No	Yds	Avg	Lg	TD
1981			3	21	7.0	21	0
Career			41	584	14.2	56	2
Playoffs			9	124	13.8		0

Bobby Watkins

Year	Team		No	Yds	Avg	Lg	TD
1982	DET	N	5	22	4.4	20	0
1983			4	48	12.0	31	0
1984			6	0	0.0	0	0
1985			5	15	3.0	8	0
Career			20	85	4.3	31	0
Playoffs			1	24	24.0		0

Joe Watson

Year	Team		No	Yds	Avg	Lg	TD
1950	DET	N	1	5	5.0	5	0

Joe Watt

Year	Team		No	Yds	Avg	Lg	TD
1947	DET	N	2	32	16.0	25	0
1948			4	39	9.8	22	0
1949	NYB	N	1	5	5.0	5	0
Career			7	76	10.9	25	0

Frank Wattelet

Year	Team		No	Yds	Avg	Lg	TD
1981	NO	N	3	16	5.3	16	0
1983			2	33	16.5	24	0
1984			2	52	26.0	35t	1
1985			2	0	0.0	0	0
1986			3	34	11.3	22	0
Career			12	135	11.3	35t	1

Orlando Watters

Year	Team		No	Yds	Avg	Lg	TD
1994	SEA	N	3	39	13.0	35t	1

Damon Watts

Year	Team		No	Yds	Avg	Lg	TD
1994	IND	N	1	0	0.0	0	0
1995			1	9	9.0	9	0
1996			1	21	21.0	21	0
Career			3	30	10.0	21	0

Elbert Watts

Year	Team		No	Yds	Avg	Lg	TD
1986	GB	N	1	6	6.0	6	0

Ted Watts

Year	Team		No	Yds	Avg	Lg	TD
1981	OAK	N	1	12	12.0	12	0
1982	LARI	N	1	0	0.0	0	0
1983			1	13	13.0	13	0
1984			1	0	0.0	0	0
1985	NYG	N	1	0	0.0	0	0
Career			5	25	5.0	13	0

Dave Waymer

Year	Team		No	Yds	Avg	Lg	TD
1981	NO	N	4	54	13.5	31	0
1984			4	9	2.3	9	0
1985			6	49	8.2	28	0
1986			9	48	5.3	17	0
1987			5	78	15.6	35	0
1988			3	91	30.3	44	0
1989			6	66	11.0	42	0
1990	SF	N	7	64	9.1	24	0
1991			4	77	19.3	42	0
Career			48	536	11.2	44	0

Jim Weatherford

Year	Team		No	Yds	Avg	Lg	TD
1969	ATL	N	1	18	18.0	18	0

Gerry Weatherly

Year	Team		No	Yds	Avg	Lg	TD
1950	CHIB	N	2	58	29.0	35t	2
1952			3	13	4.3	12	0
1953			1	13	13.0	13	0
1954			2	56	28.0	40	0
Career			8	140	17.5	40	2

Curtis Weathers

Year	Team		No	Yds	Avg	Lg	TD
1985	CLE	N	1	9	9.0	9	0

Charlie Weaver

Year	Team		No	Yds	Avg	Lg	TD
1972	DET	N	1	0	0.0	0	0
1973			2	32	16.0	27	0
1974			3	4	1.3	3	0
1975			1	31	31.0	31	0
1976			2	24	12.0	19	0
1977			1	0	0.0	0	0
1978			3	32	10.7	22	0

Charlie Weaver *continued*

Year	Team		No	Yds	Avg	Lg	TD
1979			1	17	17.0	17	0
1980			1	-3	-3.0	-3	0
Career			15	137	9.1	31	0

Allan Webb

Year	Team		No	Yds	Avg	Lg	TD
1962	NYG	N	3	24	8.0	21	0
1963			3	34	11.3	21	0
1964			1	0	0.0	0	0
Career			7	58	8.3	21	0

Don Webb

Year	Team		No	Yds	Avg	Lg	TD
1961	BOS	A	5	153	30.6	59	2
1964			6	43	7.2	25	0
1965			2	45	22.5	45	0
1966			1	0	0.0	0	0
1967			4	91	22.8	41	0
1969			2	32	16.0	32	0
1970	BOS	N	1	2	2.0	2	0
Career			21	366	17.4	59	2

Chuck Weber

Year	Team		No	Yds	Avg	Lg	TD
1956	CHIC	N	1	19	19.0	19	0
1959	PHI	N	2	8	4.0	8	0
1960			6	48	8.0	13	0
1961			1	15	15.0	15	0
Career			10	90	9.0	19	0

Cornell Webster

Year	Team		No	Yds	Avg	Lg	TD
1977	SEA	N	1	-4	-4.0	-4	0
1978			5	9	1.8	14	0
1979			1	0	0.0	0	0
1980			1	0	0.0	0	0
Career			8	5	0.6	14	0

Dave Webster

Year	Team		No	Yds	Avg	Lg	TD
1960	DAL	A	6	156	26.0	80t	2
1961			5	50	10.0	15	0
Career			11	206	18.7	80t	2

George Webster

Year	Team		No	Yds	Avg	Lg	TD
1967	HOU	A	1	23	23.0	23	0
1968			1	9	9.0	9	0
1969			2	35	17.5	26	0
1975	NE	N	1	0	0.0	0	0
Career			5	67	13.4	26	0

Mike Weger

Year	Team		No	Yds	Avg	Lg	TD
1968	DET	N	5	50	10.0	18	0
1969			3	44	14.7	25	0
1970			5	52	10.4	29t	0
1971			1	16	16.0	16	0
1973			2	20	10.0	12	0
1975			1	23	23.0	23	0
Career			17	205	12.1	29t	1
Playoffs			1	31	31.0		0

Ray Wehba

Year	Team		No	Yds	Avg	Lg	TD
1944	GB	N	1	7	7.0	7	0

Roger Wehrli

Year	Team		No	Yds	Avg	Lg	TD
1969	STL	N	3	44	14.7	44	0
1970			6	50	8.3	41	0
1971			2	11	5.5	6	0
1973			1	0	0.0	0	0
1974			2	54	27.0	53t	1
1975			6	31	5.2	31	0
1976			4	31	7.8	26	0
1977			5	44	8.8	41	0
1978			4	3	0.8	3	0
1979			2	8	4.0	9t	1
1980			1	25	25.0	25	0
1981			4	8	2.0	6	0
Career			40	309	7.7	53t	2
Playoffs			1	10	10.0		0

Ed Weisacosky

Year	Team		No	Yds	Avg	Lg	TD
1969	MIA	A	3	10	3.3	7	0

Clayton Weishuhn

Year	Team		No	Yds	Avg	Lg	TD
1983	NE	N	0	27		27tL	1

Gibby Welch

Year	Team		No	Yds	Avg	Lg	TD
1928	NYY	N					1

Herb Welch

Year	Team		No	Yds	Avg	Lg	TD
1985	NYG	N	2	8	4.0	8	0
1986			2	22	11.0	16	0
1987			2	7	3.5	7	0
1990	DET	N	1	16	16.0	16	0
Career			7	53	7.6	16	0
Playoffs			1	0	0.0		0

Jim Welch

Year	Team		No	Yds	Avg	Lg	TD
1962	BAL	N	1	30	30.0	30	0
1963			4	49	12.3	15	0
Career			5	79	15.8	30	0

Bub Weller

Year	Team		No	Yds	Avg	Lg	TD
1927	CHIC	N					1

Harold Wells

Year	Team		No	Yds	Avg	Lg	TD
1966	PHI	N	1	8	8.0	8	0
1967			1	17	17.0	17	0
1968			2	0	0.0	0	0
Career			4	25	6.3	17	0

Clyde Werner

Year	Team		No	Yds	Avg	Lg	TD
1972	KC	N	1	11	11.0	11	0
1974			1	7	7.0	7	0
Career			2	18	9.0	11	0

Charlie West

Year	Team		No	Yds	Avg	Lg	TD
1970	MIN	N	1	0	0.0	0	0
1971			7	236	33.7	89	0
1972			3	7	2.3	8	0
1974	DET	N	1	0	0.0	0	0
1976			1	0	0.0	0	0
1977			1	7	7.0	7	0
1979	DEN	N	1	26	26.0	26	0
Career			15	276	18.4	89	0

Pat West

Year	Team		No	Yds	Avg	Lg	TD
1947	LA	N	1	24	24.0	24	0
Playoffs			1	19	19.0		0

Stan West

Year	Team		No	Yds	Avg	Lg	TD
1953	LA	N	1	10	10.0	10	0
1954			1	0	0.0	0	0
Career			2	10	5.0	10	0
Playoffs			1	15	15.0		0

Troy West

Year	Team		No	Yds	Avg	Lg	TD
1987	PHI	N	1	0	0.0	0	0

Walt West

Year	Team		No	Yds	Avg	Lg	TD
1944	CLE	N	2	5	2.5	3	0

Willie West

Year	Team		No	Yds	Avg	Lg	TD
1961	STL	N	1	14	14.0	14	0
1962	BUF	A	3	24	8.0	24	0
1963			5	57	11.4	23	0
1964	DEN-NY	A	2	0	0.0	0	0
1965	NY	A	6	57	9.5	28	0
1966	MIA	A	8	62	7.8	31	0
1967			1	16	16.0	16	0
1968			4	102	25.5	32	0
Career			30	332	11.1	32	0

Greg Westbrooks

Year	Team		No	Yds	Avg	Lg	TD
1975	NO	N	1	21	21.0	21	0

Bob Westfall

Year	Team		No	Yds	Avg	Lg	TD
1944	DET	N	1	30	30.0	30	0

Dick Westmoreland

Year	Team		No	Yds	Avg	Lg	TD
1964	SD	A	6	51	8.5	38	0
1965			1	28	28.0	28	0
1966	MIA	A	4	104	26.0	42	1
1967			10	127	12.7	29	1
1968			1	0	0.0	0	0
Career			22	310	14.1	42	2

Chet Wetterlund

Year	Team		No	Yds	Avg	Lg	TD
1942	DET	N	1	0	0.0	0	0

Tom Wham

Year	Team		No	Yds	Avg	Lg	TD
1949	CHIC	N	1	46	46.0	46t	1

Leonard Wheeler

Year	Team		No	Yds	Avg	Lg	TD
1992	CIN	N	1	12	12.0	12	0
1993			0	24		24L	0
Career			1	36	36.0	24L	0

Larry Whigham

Year	Team		No	Yds	Avg	Lg	TD
1994	NE	N	1	21	21.0	21	0

Adrian White

Year	Team		No	Yds	Avg	Lg	TD
1988	NYG	N	1	29	29.0	29	0
1989			2	8	4.0	9	0
1991			1	30	30.0	30	0
Career			4	67	16.8	30	0

Bob White

Year	Team		No	Yds	Avg	Lg	TD
1951	SF	N	1	11	11.0	11	0

David White

Year	Team		No	Yds	Avg	Lg	TD
1995	BUF	N	1	9	9.0	9	0

Dwight White

Year	Team		No	Yds	Avg	Lg	TD
1973	PIT	N	2	10	5.0	8	0
1977			2	27	13.5	19	0
Career			4	37	9.3	19	0

Freeman White

Year	Team		No	Yds	Avg	Lg	TD
1967	NYG	N	2	53	26.5	45	0

Gene White

Year	Team		No	Yds	Avg	Lg	TD
1954	GB	N	1	20	20.0	20	0

James White

Year	Team		No	Yds	Avg	Lg	TD
1983	MIN	N	1	22	22.0	22	0

Jeris White

Year	Team		No	Yds	Avg	Lg	TD
1976	MIA	N	2	4	2.0	4	0
1977	TB	N	4	61	15.3	32	0
1978			5	56	11.2	31	0
1979			3	39	13.0	39	0
1980	WAS	N	2	1	0.5	1	0
1982			3	4	1.3	4	0
Career			19	165	8.7	39	0
Playoffs			2	77	38.5		1

Jim White

Year	Team		No	Yds	Avg	Lg	TD
1947	NYG	N	1	16	16.0	16	0

Leon White

Year	Team		No	Yds	Avg	Lg	TD
1989	CIN	N	1	22	22.0	22	0
1990			1	21	21.0	21	0
1992	LARM	N	2	49	24.5	40	0
Career			4	92	23.0	40	0

Paul White

Year	Team		No	Yds	Avg	Lg	TD
1947	PIT	N	2	22	11.0	15	0

Phil White

Year	Team		No	Yds	Avg	Lg	TD
1925	KC	N					1

Randy White

Year	Team		No	Yds	Avg	Lg	TD
1987	DAL	N	1	0	0.0	0	0
Playoffs			1	0	0.0		0

Ray White

Year	Team		No	Yds	Avg	Lg	TD
1976	STL	N	2	20	10.0	16	0

Reggie White

Year	Team		No	Yds	Avg	Lg	TD
1990	PHI	N	1	33	33.0	33	0
1991			1	0	0.0	0	0
1996	GB	N	1	46	46.0	46	0
Career			3	79	26.3	46	0

Sheldon White

Year	Team		No	Yds	Avg	Lg	TD
1988	NYG	N	4	70	17.5	39	0
1989			2	18	9.0	18	0
1991	DET	N	1	18	18.0	18t	1
1992			2	26	13.0	20	0
1993	CIN	N	2	19	9.5	14	0
Career			11	151	13.7	39	1

Year	Team		No	Yds	Avg	Lg	TD

Sherman White
1976	BUF	N	1	5	5.0	5	0
1980			1	0	0.0	0	0
Career			2	5	2.5	5	0

Stan White
1973	BAL	N	4	40	10.0	19t	1
1974			1	40	40.0	40	0
1975			8	135	16.9	32	1
1976			3	26	8.7	15	0
1977			7	84	12.0	19	0
1978			1	12	12.0	12	0
1979			1	11	11.0	11	0
1980	DET	N	2	22	11.0	15	0
1981			4	37	9.3	16	0
1982			3	21	7.0	18	0
Career			34	428	12.6	40	2

Whizzer White
| 1941 | DET | N | 1 | 82 | 82.0 | 82t | 1 |

William White
1989	DET	N	1	0	0.0	0	0
1990			5	120	24.0	48	1
1991			2	35	17.5	28	0
1992			4	54	13.5	28	0
1993			1	5	5.0	5	0
1994	KC	N	2	0	0.0	0	0
1995			2	48	24.0	30	0
Career			17	262	15.4	48	1

Marv Whited
| 1945 | WAS | N | 1 | 12 | 12.0 | 12 | 0 |

Bud Whitehead
1961	SD	A	1	0	0.0	0	0
1962			1	18	18.0	18	0
1963			1	0	0.0	0	0
1964			3	43	14.3	33	0
1965			7	127	18.1	35	1
1966			2	89	44.5	61	0
Career			15	277	18.5	61	1
Playoffs			2	45	22.5		0

Wilson Whitley
| 1979 | CIN | N | 1 | 2 | 2.0 | 2 | 0 |

Ken Whitlow
| 1946 | MIA | AA | 2 | 20 | 10.0 | | 0 |

S.J. Whitman
1951	CHIC	N	7	102	14.6	31	0
1952			3	27	9.0	18	0
1953	CHIC-CHIB	N	3	39	13.0	30	0
1954	CHIB	N	5	117	23.4	38	1
Career			18	285	15.8	38	1

David Whitmore
1991	SF	N	1	5	5.0	5	0
1992			1	0	0.0	0	0
Career			2	5	2.5	5	0
Playoffs			1	2	2.0		0

Nat Whitmyer
| 1963 | LA | N | 1 | 27 | 27.0 | 27 | 0 |

Dave Whitsell
1958	DET	N	1	29	29.0	29	0
1961	CHI	N	6	123	20.5	52	0
1962			5	45	9.0	26	0
1963			6	61	10.2	39t	1
1964			2	57	28.5	41	0
1965			4	67	16.8	32	1
1966			3	44	14.7	21	0
1967	NO	N	10	178	17.8	41t	2
1968			6	50	8.3	32	0
1969			3	14	4.7	11	0
Career			46	668	14.5	52	4
Playoffs			1	0	0.0		0

Jesse Whittenton
1956	LA	N	3	83	27.7	32	1
1957			1	31	31.0	31	0
1958	GB	N	1	0	0.0	0	0

Year	Team		No	Yds	Avg	Lg	TD

Jesse Whittenton *continued*
1960			6	101	16.8	34	0
1961			5	98	19.6	41t	1
1962			3	40	13.3	36	0
1963			4	90	22.5	33	0
1964			1	0	0.0	0	0
Career			24	443	18.5	41t	2
Playoffs			1	0			0

Fred Whittingham
1966	PHI	N	1	0	0.0	0	0
1967	NO	N	1	8	8.0	8	0
1968			1	16	16.0	16	0
Career			3	24	8.0	16	0

C.L. Whittington
1975	HOU	N	1	5	5.0	5	0
1976			5	103	20.6	50	0
1978			1	6	6.0	6	0
Career			7	114	16.3	50	0

Mike Whitwell
| 1983 | CLE | N | 3 | 67 | 22.3 | 28 | 0 |

Ossie Wiberg
| 1927 | CLE | N | | | | | 1 |

Corey Widmer
| 1996 | NYG | N | 2 | 8 | 4.0 | 4 | 0 |

Bob Wiese
| 1947 | DET | N | 5 | 54 | 10.8 | 19 | 0 |

Ray Wietecha
| 1953 | NYG | N | 1 | 0 | 0.0 | 0 | 0 |

John Wiethe
| 1941 | DET | N | 2 | 8 | 4.0 | 8 | 0 |

Paul Wiggin
1960	CLE	N	1	20	20.0	20t	1
1963			1	2	2.0	2	0
1966			1	0	0.0	0	0
Career			3	22	7.3	20t	1

Bill Wightkin
| 1952 | CHIB | N | 0 | 9 | | 9L | 0 |

Barry Wilburn
1985	WAS	N	1	10	10.0	10	0
1986			2	14	7.0	14	0
1987			9	135	15.0	100t	1
1988			4	24	6.0	14	0
1989			3	13	4.3	13	0
1995	PHI	N	1	0	0.0	0	0
Career			20	196	9.8	100t	1
Playoffs			5	37	7.4		0

Mike Wilcher
1985	LARM	N	1	0	0.0	0	0
1986			1	0	0.0	0	0
1987			1	11	11.0	11	0
1989			1	4	4.0	4	0
Career			4	15	3.8	11	0

Solomon Wilcots
1987	CIN	N	1	37	37.0	37	0
1988			1	6	6.0	6	0
Career			2	43	21.5	37	0
Playoffs			1	0	0.0		0

Dave Wilcox
1964	SF	N	1	6	6.0	6	0
1965			1	16	16.0	16	0
1967			2	17	8.5	17	0
1969			2	17	8.5	17	0
1970			2	46	23.0	35	0
1972			3	12	4.0	9	0
1973			2	14	7.0	10	0
1974			1	21	21.0	21t	1
Career			14	149	10.6	35	1

Year	Team		No	Yds	Avg	Lg	TD

Ned Wilcox
| 1926 | FRA | N | | | | | 1 |

Reggie Wilkes
1979	PHI	N	2	0	0.0	0	0
1980			1	0	0.0	0	0
1981			2	18	9.0	11	0
1984			1	6	6.0	6	0
1986	ATL	N	2	11	5.5	10	0
Career			8	35	4.4	11	0

Willie Wilkin
| 1946 | CHI | AA | 0 | 18 | | 18L | 0 |

Bob Wilkinson
| 1951 | NYG | N | 1 | 12 | 12.0 | 12 | 0 |

Dan Wilkinson
| 1996 | CIN | N | 1 | 7 | 7.0 | 7 | 0 |

Norm Willey
1950	PHI	N	1	41	41.0	41t	1
1952			1	0	0.0	0	0
Career			2	41	20.5	41t	1

Aeneas Williams
1991	PHX	N	6	60	10.0	32	0
1992			3	25	8.3	23	0
1993			2	87	43.5	46t	1
1994	ARI	N	9	89	9.9	43	0
1995			6	86	14.3	48t	1
1996			6	89	14.8	65t	1
Career			32	436	13.6	65t	4

Ben Williams
1981	BUF	N	1	0	0.0	0	0
1982			1	20	20.0	20	0
Career			2	20	10.0	20	0

Bobby Ray Williams
1967	STL	N	2	21	10.5	19	0
1970	DET	N	1	0	0.0	0	0
Career			3	21	7.0	19	0

Brian Williams
| Playoffs | | | 1 | 16 | 16.0 | | 0 |

Chris Williams
| 1983 | BUF | N | 3 | 6 | 2.0 | 4 | 0 |

Clancy Williams
1966	LA	N	8	97	12.1	32t	1
1967			4	75	18.8	29	0
1968			7	51	7.3	36	0
1969			4	97	24.3	40	1
1970			5	108	21.6	65t	0
Career			28	428	15.3	65t	2

Clarence Williams
| 1974 | GB | N | 1 | 23 | 23.0 | 23 | 0 |

Dan Williams
| 1994 | DEN | N | 1 | -3 | -3.0 | -3 | 0 |

Darryl Williams
1992	CIN	N	4	65	16.3	30	0
1993			2	126	63.0	97t	1
1994			2	45	22.5	33	0
1995			1	1	1.0	1	0
1996	SEA	N	5	148	29.6	79t	1
Career			14	385	27.5	97t	2

Ed Williams
| 1987 | NE | N | 1 | 51 | 51.0 | 51 | 0 |

Eric Williams
1978	STL	N	1	24	24.0	24	0
1979			1	25	25.0	25	0
1980			2	31	15.5	20	0
1981			1	17	17.0	17	0
Career			5	97	19.4	25	0

Eric Williams
| 1984 | PIT | N | 3 | 49 | 16.3 | 44 | 0 |

Eric Williams *continued*

Year	Team		No	Yds	Avg	Lg	TD
1985			4	47	11.8	29	0
1986			3	44	14.7	25	0
Career			10	140	14.0	44	0
Playoffs			1	29	29.0		

Eric Williams

Year	Team		No	Yds	Avg	Lg	TD
1986	DET	N	1	2	2.0	2	0

Eugene Williams

Year	Team		No	Yds	Avg	Lg	TD
1983	SEA	N	1	0	0.0	0	0

Fred Williams

Year	Team		No	Yds	Avg	Lg	TD
1952	CHIB	N	1	54	54.0	54	0
1956			1	11	11.0	11	0
Career			2	65	32.5	54	0

Gerard Williams

Year	Team		No	Yds	Avg	Lg	TD
1977	WAS	N	4	25	6.3	25	0
1978			4	51	12.8	20	0
1979	SF	N	4	38	9.5	22	0
1980			1	28	28.0	28	0
Career			13	142	10.9	28	0

Greg Williams

Year	Team		No	Yds	Avg	Lg	TD
1983	WAS	N	2	25	12.5	25	0

Henry Williams

Year	Team		No	Yds	Avg	Lg	TD
1979	OAK	N	3	37	12.3	33	0

Howie Williams

Year	Team		No	Yds	Avg	Lg	TD
1964	OAK	A	1	0	0.0	0	0
1965			2	23	11.5	21	0
1966			3	51	17.0	36	0
1967			4	96	24.0	37	0
1968			2	66	33.0	41	0
1969			2	4	2.0	2	0
Career			14	240	17.1	41	0

Jack Williams

Year	Team		No	Yds	Avg	Lg	TD
1946	MIA	AA	1	3	3.0	3	0

James Williams

Year	Team		No	Yds	Avg	Lg	TD
1990	BUF	N	2	0	0.0	0	0
1991			1	0	0.0	0	0
1992			2	15	7.5	15	0
1993			2	11	5.5	6	0
1994	ARI	N	4	48	12.0	29	0
Career			11	74	6.7	29	0
Playoffs			2	0	0.0		

James Williams

Year	Team		No	Yds	Avg	Lg	TD
1994	NO	N	2	42	21.0	33t	1
1995	JAC	N	2	19	9.5	16	0
Career			4	61	15.3	33t	1

Jarvis Williams

Year	Team		No	Yds	Avg	Lg	TD
1988	MIA	N	4	62	15.5	23	0
1989			2	43	21.5	24	0
1990			5	82	16.4	42t	1
1991			1	0	0.0	0	0
1992			2	29	14.5	25	0
1994	NYG	N	2	10	5.0	10	0
Career			16	226	14.1	42t	1
Playoffs			2	0	0.0		

Jerrol Williams

Year	Team		No	Yds	Avg	Lg	TD
1992	PIT	N	1	4	4.0	4	0

Jerry Williams

Year	Team		No	Yds	Avg	Lg	TD
1949	LA	N	5	42	8.4	25t	1
1950			3	39	13.0	23	0
1951			3	53	17.7	21	1
1952			4	41	10.3	22	0
Career			15	175	11.7	25t	2
Playoffs			1	15	15.0		

Jimmy Williams

Year	Team		No	Yds	Avg	Lg	TD
1982	DET	N	1	4	4.0	4	0
1986			2	12	6.0	11	0
1987			2	51	25.5	48	0
1988			1	5	5.0	5	0
1989			5	15	3.0	9	0

Jimmy Williams *continued*

Year	Team		No	Yds	Avg	Lg	TD
1992	TB	N	2	4	2.0	3	0
Career			13	91	7.0	48	0

Joel Williams

Year	Team		No	Yds	Avg	Lg	TD
1980	ATL	N	2	55	27.5	32	0
1981			1	25	25.0	25	0
1986			2	18	9.0	14t	1
Career			5	98	19.6	32	1

Johnny Williams

Year	Team		No	Yds	Avg	Lg	TD
1952	WAS	N	5	97	19.4	38t	1
1953			6	26	4.3	7	0
1954	SF	N	3	28	9.3	15	0
Career			14	151	10.8	38t	1

Kendall Williams

Year	Team		No	Yds	Avg	Lg	TD
1983	BAL	N	1	32	32.0	32	0

Lee Williams

Year	Team		No	Yds	Avg	Lg	TD
1984	SD	N	1	66	66.0	66t	1
1985			1	17	17.0	17	0
Career			2	83	41.5	66t	1

Mike Williams

Year	Team		No	Yds	Avg	Lg	TD
1975	SD	N	4	67	16.8	40	0
1976			4	76	19.0	35	0
1977			3	36	12.0	36	0
1978			3	23	7.7	23	0
1979			4	55	13.8	50	0
1980			1	0	0.0	0	0
1981			3	0	0.0	0	0
1982			2	12	6.0	6	0
Career			24	269	11.2	50	0
Playoffs			1	0	0.0		0

Perry Williams

Year	Team		No	Yds	Avg	Lg	TD
1984	NYG	N	3	7	2.3	7	0
1985			2	28	14.0	28	0
1986			4	31	7.8	15	0
1987			1	-5	-5.0	-5	0
1988			1	0	0.0	0	0
1989			3	14	4.7	14	0
1990			3	4	1.3	4	0
1992			1	0	0.0	0	0
Career			18	79	4.4	28	0

Perry Williams

Year	Team		No	Yds	Avg	Lg	TD
1987	NE	N	1	0	0.0	0	0

Ray Williams

Year	Team		No	Yds	Avg	Lg	TD
1987	PIT	N	1	0	0.0	0	0

Reggie Williams

Year	Team		No	Yds	Avg	Lg	TD
1976	CIN	N	1	17	17.0	17	0
1977			3	67	22.3	54t	1
1978			1	11	11.0	11	0
1979			2	5	2.5	3	0
1980			2	8	4.0	8	0
1981			4	33	8.3	14	0
1982			1	20	20.0	20	0
1984			2	33	16.5	33	0
Career			16	194	12.1	54t	1

Robert Williams

Year	Team		No	Yds	Avg	Lg	TD
1988	DAL	N	2	18	9.0	12	0
1990			1	0	0.0	0	0
1991			1	24	24.0	24	0
Career			4	42	10.5	24	0

Sam Williams

Year	Team		No	Yds	Avg	Lg	TD
1962	DET	N	1	22	22.0	22t	1

Sam Williams

Year	Team		No	Yds	Avg	Lg	TD
1974	SD	N	1	25	25.0	25	0
1975			1	0	0.0	0	0
Career			2	25	12.5	25	0

Sid Williams

Year	Team		No	Yds	Avg	Lg	TD
1965	CLE	N	1	0	0.0	0	0

Stan Williams

Year	Team		No	Yds	Avg	Lg	TD
1952	DAL	N	5	84	16.8	62	0

Ted Williams

Year	Team		No	Yds	Avg	Lg	TD
1944	BOS	N	1	54	54.0	54	0

Tyrone Williams

Year	Team		No	Yds	Avg	Lg	TD
Playoffs			1	0	0.0		0

Walt Williams

Year	Team		No	Yds	Avg	Lg	TD
1946	CHI	AA	2	148	74.0	97t	1

Walt Williams

Year	Team		No	Yds	Avg	Lg	TD
1978	DET	N	1	2	2.0	2	0
1979			2	39	19.5	36t	1
1980			1	19	19.0	19	0
Career			4	60	15.0	36t	1

Willie Williams

Year	Team		No	Yds	Avg	Lg	TD
1965	NYG	N	1	0	0.0	0	0
1967			1	44	44.0	44	0
1968			10	103	10.3	24	0
1969			4	19	4.8	19	0
1970			6	114	19.0	52	0
1971			5	58	11.6	24	0
1972			4	42	10.5	18	0
1973			4	82	20.5	35	0
Career			35	462	13.2	52	0

Willie Williams

Year	Team		No	Yds	Avg	Lg	TD
1995	PIT	N	7	122	17.4	63t	1
1996			1	1	1.0	1	0
Career			8	123	15.4	63t	1
Playoffs			1	0	0.0		0

Carlton Williamson

Year	Team		No	Yds	Avg	Lg	TD
1981	SF	N	4	44	11.0	28	0
1983			4	51	12.8	26	0
1984			2	42	21.0	26	0
1985			3	137	45.7	82	1
1986			3	3	1.0	2	0
1987			1	17	17.0	17	0
Career			17	294	17.3	82	1
Playoffs			2	2	1.0		0

Fred Williamson

Year	Team		No	Yds	Avg	Lg	TD
1961	OAK	A	4	32	8.0	12	0
1962			8	151	18.9	91	1
1963			6	43	7.2	17	0
1964			6	40	6.7	28	0
1965	KC	A	6	89	14.8	51	0
1966			4	20	5.0	19	0
1967			1	77	77.0	77t	1
Career			35	452	12.9	91	2

Greg Williamson

Year	Team		No	Yds	Avg	Lg	TD
1987	LARM	N	1	28	28.0	28	0

John Williamson

Year	Team		No	Yds	Avg	Lg	TD
1967	OAK	A	2	9	4.5	6	0
1970	BOS	N	1	2	2.0	2	0
Career			3	11	3.7	6	0

Bill Willis

Year	Team		No	Yds	Avg	Lg	TD
1949	CLE	AA	1	6	6.0	6	0

James Willis

Year	Team		No	Yds	Avg	Lg	TD
1994	GB	N	2	20	10.0	17	0
1996	PHI	N	1	14	14.0	14	0
Career			3	34	11.3	17	0

Keith Willis

Year	Team		No	Yds	Avg	Lg	TD
1990	PIT	N	1	5	5.0	5	0

Bernard Wilson

Year	Team		No	Yds	Avg	Lg	TD
1979	PHI	N	4	70	17.5	50	0
1980			6	79	13.2	41	0
1981			5	73	14.6	26	0
1982			1	0	0.0	0	0
1984			1	28	28.0	28	0
Career			17	250	14.7	50	0

Don Wilson

Year	Team		No	Yds	Avg	Lg	TD
1985	BUF	N	2	23	11.5	23	0

Gene Wilson

Year	Team		No	Yds	Avg	Lg	TD
1948	GB	N	2	13	6.5	13	0

George Wilson

Year	Team		No	Yds	Avg	Lg	TD
1942	CHIB	N	1	2	2.0	2t	1
1943			2	15	7.5	13	0
Career			3	17	5.7	13	1
Playoffs			3	9	3.0		0

Jack Wilson

Year	Team		No	Yds	Avg	Lg	TD
1946	LA	N	1	32	32.0	32	0

J.C. Wilson

Year	Team		No	Yds	Avg	Lg	TD
1978	HOU	N	2	10	5.0	10	0
1979			6	135	22.5	66	1
1980			2	26	13.0	26	0
1981			1	1	1.0	1	0
Career			11	172	15.6	66	1
Playoffs			1	3	3.0		0

Larry Wilson

Year	Team		No	Yds	Avg	Lg	TD
1960	STL	N	2	4	2.0	4	0
1961			3	36	12.0	25	0
1962			2	59	29.5	57t	1
1963			4	67	16.8	36	0
1964			3	44	14.7	42t	1
1965			6	153	25.5	96t	1
1966			10	180	18.0	91t	2
1967			4	75	18.8	44	0
1968			4	14	3.5	8	0
1969			2	15	7.5	15	0
1970			5	72	14.4	22	0
1971			4	46	11.5	23	0
1972			3	35	11.7	24	0
Career			52	800	15.4	96t	5

Mule Wilson

Year	Team		No	Yds	Avg	Lg	TD
1927	NYG	N					1

Nemiah Wilson

Year	Team		No	Yds	Avg	Lg	TD
1965	DEN	A	3	118	39.3	65	1
1966			1	2	2.0	2	0
1967			4	153	38.3	70t	2
1969	OAK	A	2	25	12.5	22	0
1970	OAK	N	2	7	3.5	7	0
1971			5	70	14.0	22	0
1972			4	48	12.0	32	0
1973			3	28	9.3	20	0
1974			3	35	11.7	34	0
Career			27	486	18.0	70t	3
Playoffs			4	58	14.5		0

Otis Wilson

Year	Team		No	Yds	Avg	Lg	TD
1980	CHI	N	2	4	2.0	4	0
1982			2	39	19.5	39t	1
1983			1	6	6.0	6	0
1985			3	35	11.7	23t	1
1986			2	31	15.5	21	0
Career			10	115	11.5	39t	2

Steve Wilson

Year	Team		No	Yds	Avg	Lg	TD
1980	DAL	N	4	82	20.5	35	0
1981			2	0	0.0	0	0
1982	DEN	N	2	22	11.0	16	0
1983			5	91	18.2	36	0
1984			4	59	14.8	22	0
1985			3	8	2.7	8	0
1986			1	-5	-5.0	-5	0
1988			1	7	7.0	7	0
Career			22	264	12.0	36	0
Playoffs			2	8	4.0		0

Troy Wilson

Year	Team		No	Yds	Avg	Lg	TD
1987	CLE	N	1	0	0.0	0	0

Ab Wimberly

Year	Team		No	Yds	Avg	Lg	TD
1949	LA	AA	1	16	16.0	16t	1
1950	GB	N	1	0	0.0	0	0
1952			1	5	5.0	5	0
Career			3	21	7.0	16t	1

Rich Wingo

Year	Team		No	Yds	Avg	Lg	TD
1979	GB	N	2	13	6.5	13	0
1981			1	38	38.0	38	0
1982			1	0	0.0		0
Career			4	51	12.8	38	0

Ben Winkleman

Year	Team		No	Yds	Avg	Lg	TD
1923	MIL	N					1

Joe Winkler

Year	Team		No	Yds	Avg	Lg	TD
1945	CLE	N	1	5	5.0	5	0

Dennis Winston

Year	Team		No	Yds	Avg	Lg	TD
1977	PIT	N	2	7	3.5	7	0
1979			3	48	16.0	41t	1
1981			1	1	1.0	1	0
1982	NO	N	2	-2	-1.0	0	0
1983			3	21	7.0	15	0
1984			2	90	45.0	47t	2
1985			0	8		8L	0
Career			13	173	13.3	47t	3
Playoffs			1	3	3.0		0

Roy Winston

Year	Team		No	Yds	Avg	Lg	TD
1963	MIN	N	1	0	0.0	0	0
1964			3	24	8.0	15	0
1969			3	17	5.7	17	0
1970			1	13	13.0	13	0
1971			1	29	29.0	29t	1
1972			3	55	18.3	23	0
Career			12	138	11.5	29t	1

Bill Winter

Year	Team		No	Yds	Avg	Lg	TD
1963	NYG	N	1	38	38.0	38	0

Denny Wirgowski

Year	Team		No	Yds	Avg	Lg	TD
1973	PHI	N	1	0	0.0	0	0

Phil Wise

Year	Team		No	Yds	Avg	Lg	TD
1971	NYJ	N	1	33	33.0	33	0
1975			2	17	8.5	14	0
1977	MIN	N	1	4	4.0	4	0
1978			2	21	10.5	14	0
Career			6	75	12.5	33	0

Pete Wismann

Year	Team		No	Yds	Avg	Lg	TD
1949	SF	AA	1	12	12.0	12	0
1950	SF	N	1	5	5.0	5	0
1951			2	12	6.0	10	0
Career			4	29	7.3	12	0

Al Wistert

Year	Team		No	Yds	Avg	Lg	TD
1946	PHI	N	1	27	27.0	27	0

Al Witcher

Year	Team		No	Yds	Avg	Lg	TD
1960	HOU	A	1	0	0.0	0	0

Mel Witt

Year	Team		No	Yds	Avg	Lg	TD
1968	BOS	A	1	4	4.0	4t	1

Alex Wizbicki

Year	Team		No	Yds	Avg	Lg	TD
1948	BUF	AA	3	49	16.3		0
1949			1	1	1.0	1	0
1950	GB	N	2	38	19.0	34	0
Career			6	88	14.7	34	0

Johnny Woitt

Year	Team		No	Yds	Avg	Lg	TD
1969	SF	N	1	57	57.0	57t	1

Alex Wojciechowicz

Year	Team		No	Yds	Avg	Lg	TD
1940	DET	N					1
1942			2	5	2.5	4	0
1943			2	14	7.0	14	0
1944			7	88	12.6	50	0
1947	PHI	N	1	3	3.0	3	0
1948			1	2	2.0	2	0
1949			2	26	13.0	16	0
1950			1	4	4.0	4	0
Career			16	142	8.9	50	1

Duane Wood

Year	Team		No	Yds	Avg	Lg	TD
1960	DAL	A	4	85	21.3		1
1961			4	31	7.8	31	0
1962			4	81	20.3	33	0
1963	KC	A	3	23	7.7	23	0
1964			5	27	5.4	12	0
Career			20	247	12.4	33	1

Richard Wood

Year	Team		No	Yds	Avg	Lg	TD
1977	TB	N	4	86	21.5	30t	1

Richard Wood *continued*

Year	Team		No	Yds	Avg	Lg	TD
1979			2	37	18.5	24	0
1980			3	76	25.3	55t	1
Career			9	199	22.1	55t	2

Willie Wood

Year	Team		No	Yds	Avg	Lg	TD
1961	GB	N	5	52	10.4	21	0
1962			9	132	14.7	37	0
1963			5	67	13.4	22	0
1964			3	73	24.3	42t	1
1965			6	65	10.8	28	0
1966			3	38	12.7	20	1
1967			4	60	15.0	25	0
1968			2	54	27.0	35	0
1969			3	40	13.3	21	0
1970			7	110	15.7	24	0
1971			1	8	8.0	8	0
Career			48	699	14.6	42t	2
Playoffs			2	65	32.5		0

Lee Woodall

Year	Team		No	Yds	Avg	Lg	TD
1995	SF	N	2	0	0.0	0	0

Ken Woodard

Year	Team		No	Yds	Avg	Lg	TD
1984	DEN	N	1	27	27.0	27t	1
1985			1	18	18.0	18	0
Career			2	45	22.5	27t	1

Dennis Woodberry

Year	Team		No	Yds	Avg	Lg	TD
1986	ATL	N	2	14	7.0	9	0
Playoffs			1	0	0.0		0

Shawn Wooden

Year	Team		No	Yds	Avg	Lg	TD
1996	MIA	N	2	15	7.5	15	0

Terry Wooden

Year	Team		No	Yds	Avg	Lg	TD
1992	SEA	N	1	3	3.0	3	0
1994			3	78	26.0	69t	1
1995			1	9	9.0	9	0
1996			1	13	13.0	13	0
Career			6	103	17.2	69t	2

Howie Woodin

Year	Team		No	Yds	Avg	Lg	TD
1931	GB	N					1

Doug Woodlief

Year	Team		No	Yds	Avg	Lg	TD
1967	LA	N	2	24	12.0	15	0
1969			4	29	7.3	10	0
Career			6	53	8.8	15	0

Dwayne Woodruff

Year	Team		No	Yds	Avg	Lg	TD
1979	PIT	N	1	31	31.0	31	0
1980			1	0	0.0	0	0
1981			1	17	17.0	17	0
1982			5	53	10.6	30	0
1983			3	85	28.3	47	0
1984			5	56	11.2	42t	1
1985			5	80	16.0	33	0
1987			5	91	18.2	33t	1
1988			4	109	27.3	78t	1
1989			4	57	14.3	35	0
1990			3	110	36.7	59	0
Career			37	689	18.6	78t	3
Playoffs			2	0	0.0		0

Lee Woodruff

Year	Team		No	Yds	Avg	Lg	TD
1933	PHI	N					1

Mike Woods

Year	Team		No	Yds	Avg	Lg	TD
1980	BAL	N	1	13	13.0	13	0

Rick Woods

Year	Team		No	Yds	Avg	Lg	TD
1982	PIT	N	1	12	12.0	12	0
1983			5	53	10.6	31	0
1984			2	0	0.0	0	0
1986			3	26	8.7	23	0
1987	TB	N	2	63	31.5	42	0
Career			13	154	11.8	42	0

Abe Woodson

Year	Team		No	Yds	Avg	Lg	TD
1958	SF	N	1	44	44.0	44	0
1959			4	20	5.0	14	0
1960			2	0	0.0	0	0

Year	Team		No	Yds	Avg	Lg	TD

Abe Woodson *continued*

Year	Team		No	Yds	Avg	Lg	TD
1961			1	2	2.0	2	0
1962			2	31	15.5	31	0
1963			3	61	20.3	61	0
1964			2	1	0.5	1	0
1966	STL	N	4	47	11.8	26	0
Career			19	206	10.8	61	0

Darren Woodson

Year	Team		No	Yds	Avg	Lg	TD
1994	DAL	N	5	140	28.0	94t	1
1995			2	46	23.0	37t	1
1996			5	43	8.6	21	0
Career			12	229	19.1	94t	2
Playoffs			2	5	2.5		0

Marv Woodson

Year	Team		No	Yds	Avg	Lg	TD
1965	PIT	N	3	87	29.0	61t	1
1966			4	91	22.8	56t	1
1967			7	49	7.0	24	0
1968			3	23	7.7	12	0
1969			1	0	0.0	0	0
Career			18	250	13.9	61t	2

Rod Woodson

Year	Team		No	Yds	Avg	Lg	TD
1987	PIT	N	1	45	45.0	45t	1
1988			4	98	24.5	29	0
1989			3	39	13.0	39	0
1990			5	67	13.4	34	0
1991			3	72	24.0	41	0
1992			4	90	22.5	57	0
1993			8	138	17.3	63t	1
1994			4	109	27.3	37t	2
1996			6	121	20.2	43t	1
Career			38	779	20.5	63t	5
Playoffs			1	6	6.0		0

Dick Woodward

Year	Team		No	Yds	Avg	Lg	TD
1949	LA	AA	2	39	19.5		1
1950	NYG	N	1	11	11.0	11	0
1951			2	13	6.5	7	0
1953			1	10	10.0	10	0
Career			6	73	12.2	11	1

Donnell Woolford

Year	Team		No	Yds	Avg	Lg	TD
1989	CHI	N	3	0	0.0	0	0
1990			3	18	6.0	9	0
1991			2	21	10.5	16	0
1992			7	67	9.6	32	0
1993			2	18	9.0	18	0
1994			5	30	6.0	25	0
1995			4	21	5.3	16	0
1996			6	37	6.2	28t	1
Career			32	212	6.6	32	1

Gary Woolford

Year	Team		No	Yds	Avg	Lg	TD
1980	NYG	N	2	0	0.0	0	0

Rolly Woolsey

Year	Team		No	Yds	Avg	Lg	TD
1976	SEA	N	4	19	4.8	13	0
1977	CLE	N	1	0	0.0	0	0
Career			5	19	3.8	13	0

Tito Wooten

Year	Team		No	Yds	Avg	Lg	TD
1995	NYG	N	1	38	38.0	38	0
1996			1	35	35.0	35	0
Career			2	73	36.5	38	0

Roscoe Word

Year	Team		No	Yds	Avg	Lg	TD
1974	NYJ	N	2	19	9.5	19	0
1975			1	0	0.0	0	0
Career			3	19	6.3	19	0

John Wozniak

Year	Team		No	Yds	Avg	Lg	TD
1948	BKN	AA	1	7	7.0	7	0

Darryl Wren

Year	Team		No	Yds	Avg	Lg	TD
1993	NE	N	3	-7	-2.3	2	0

Junior Wren

Year	Team		No	Yds	Avg	Lg	TD
1956	CLE	N	1	0	0.0	0	0
1957			2	73	36.5	43	0
1958			3	36	12.0	29	0
1959			5	39	7.8	22	0

Junior Wren *continued*

Year	Team		No	Yds	Avg	Lg	TD
1960	PIT	N	2	0	0.0	0	0
1961	NY	A	1	2	2.0	2	0
Career			14	150	10.7	43	0
Playoffs			1	14	14.0		0

Eric Wright

Year	Team		No	Yds	Avg	Lg	TD
1981	SF	N	3	26	8.7	26	0
1982			1	31	31.0	31	0
1983			7	164	23.4	60t	2
1984			2	0	0.0	0	0
1985			1	0	0.0	0	0
1988			2	-2	-1.0	0	0
1989			2	37	18.5	23	0
Career			18	256	14.2	60t	2
Playoffs			3	25	8.3		0

Felix Wright

Year	Team		No	Yds	Avg	Lg	TD
1985	CLE	N	2	11	5.5	10	0
1986			3	33	11.0	33	0
1987			4	152	38.0	68	1
1988			5	126	25.2	53	0
1989			9	91	10.1	27t	1
1990			3	56	18.7	36	0
1991	MIN	N	2	3	1.5	3	0
1992			1	20	20.0	20	0
Career			29	492	17.0	68	2
Playoffs			3	45	15.0		0

James Wright

Year	Team		No	Yds	Avg	Lg	TD
1964	DEN	A	1	11	11.0	11	0

Jeff Wright

Year	Team		No	Yds	Avg	Lg	TD
1972	MIN	N	3	31	10.3	31	0
1973			3	31	10.3	25	0
1974			4	60	15.0	27	0
1976			1	5	5.0	5	0
1977			1	5	5.0	5	0
Career			12	132	11.0	31	0
Playoffs			3	34	11.3		0

Jeff Wright

Year	Team		No	Yds	Avg	Lg	TD
1989	BUF	N	1	0	0.0	0	0

John Wright

Year	Team		No	Yds	Avg	Lg	TD
1947	BAL	AA	1	5	5.0	5	0

Lonnie Wright

Year	Team		No	Yds	Avg	Lg	TD
1966	DEN	A	1	15	15.0	15	0
1967			4	22	5.5	8	0
Career			5	37	7.4	15	0

Louis Wright

Year	Team		No	Yds	Avg	Lg	TD
1975	DEN	N	2	9	4.5	9	0
1976			0	32		32L	0
1977			3	128	42.7	59	1
1978			2	2	1.0	2	0
1979			2	20	10.0	15	0
1982			2	18	9.0	18	0
1983			6	50	8.3	34	0
1984			1	1	1.0	1	0
1985			5	44	8.8	24	0
1986			3	56	18.7	56	0
Career			26	360	13.8	59	1

Nate Wright

Year	Team		No	Yds	Avg	Lg	TD
1969	STL	N	2	41	20.5	21	0
1970			1	0	0.0	0	0
1972	MIN	N	1	10	10.0	10	0
1973			3	6	2.0	6	0
1974			6	91	15.2	44	0
1976			7	47	6.7	21	0
1977			3	0	0.0	0	0
1978			5	58	11.6	30	0
1979			4	44	11.0	32	0
1980			2	16	8.0	10	0
Career			34	313	9.2	44	0
Playoffs			3	26	8.7		0

Toby Wright

Year	Team		No	Yds	Avg	Lg	TD
1995	STL	N	6	79	13.2	27	0
1996			1	19	19.0	19t	1
Career			7	98	14.0	27	1

Al Wukits

Year	Team		No	Yds	Avg	Lg	TD
1943	P-P	N	1	7	7.0	7	0
1946	MIA	AA	2	26	13.0		0
Career			3	33	11.0	7	0

Jim Wulff

Year	Team		No	Yds	Avg	Lg	TD
1961	WAS	N	3	11	3.7	7	0

Alvin Wyatt

Year	Team		No	Yds	Avg	Lg	TD
1971	BUF	N	1	30	30.0	30	0
1972			4	52	13.0	49t	1
Career			5	82	16.4	49t	1

Doug Wyatt

Year	Team		No	Yds	Avg	Lg	TD
1970	NO	N	4	45	11.3	25	0
1971			4	84	21.0	55t	1
Career			8	129	16.1	55t	1

Doug Wycoff

Year	Team		No	Yds	Avg	Lg	TD
1927	NYG	N					1
1931							1
Career							2

Frank Wydo

Year	Team		No	Yds	Avg	Lg	TD
1957	PHI	N	1	25	25.0	25	0

Dave Wyman

Year	Team		No	Yds	Avg	Lg	TD
1990	SEA	N	2	24	12.0	22	0
1993	DEN	N	1	9	9.0	9	0
Career			3	33	11.0	22	0

Pete Wysocki

Year	Team		No	Yds	Avg	Lg	TD
1979	WAS	N	1	9	9.0	9	0

Jeff Yeates

Year	Team		No	Yds	Avg	Lg	TD
1980	ATL	N	1	5	5.0	5	0

Billy Yelverton

Year	Team		No	Yds	Avg	Lg	TD
1960	DEN	A	1	20	20.0	20t	1

Mack Yoho

Year	Team		No	Yds	Avg	Lg	TD
1960	BUF	A	1	15	15.0	15t	1
1961			1	0	0.0	0	0
Career			2	15	7.5	15t	1

John Yonakor

Year	Team		No	Yds	Avg	Lg	TD
1948	CLE	AA	1	1	1.0	1	0
1950	NYY	N	1	10	10.0	10	0
Career			2	11	5.5	10	0

Wally Yonamine

Year	Team		No	Yds	Avg	Lg	TD
1947	SF	AA	1	20	20.0	20	0

Jim Youel

Year	Team		No	Yds	Avg	Lg	TD
1946	WAS	N	2	0	0.0	0	0

Len Younce

Year	Team		No	Yds	Avg	Lg	TD
1941	NYG	N	2	25	12.5	18	0
1943			1	30	30.0	30t	1
1944			3	16	5.3	10	0
1946			1	0	0.0	0	0
1947			3	44	14.7	24	0
Career			10	115	11.5	30t	1
Playoffs			1	5	5.0		0

Adrian Young

Year	Team		No	Yds	Avg	Lg	TD
1969	PHI	N	1	0	0.0	0	0
1970			2	19	9.5	13	0
Career			3	19	6.3	13	0

Andre Young

Year	Team		No	Yds	Avg	Lg	TD
1982	SD	N	2	9	4.5	9	0
1983			2	49	24.5	40t	1
1984			2	31	15.5	31	0
Career			6	89	14.8	40t	1

Anthony Young

Year	Team		No	Yds	Avg	Lg	TD
1985	IND	N	1	0	0.0	0	0

Fredd Young

Year	Team		No	Yds	Avg	Lg	TD
1987	SEA	N	1	50	50.0	50t	1
1989	IND	N	2	2	1.0	6	0
Career			3	52	17.3	50t	1

Year	Team		No	Yds	Avg	Lg	TD

Glen Young
| 1996 | SD | N | 1 | -1 | -1.0 | -1 | 0 |

Lonnie Young
1985	STL	N	3	0	0.0	0	0
1987			1	0	0.0	0	0
1988	PHX	N	1	2	2.0	2	0
1989			1	32	32.0	32	0
1990			2	8	4.0	5	0
1991	NYJ	N	1	15	15.0	15	0
1993			1	6	6.0	6	0
1996			1	0	0.0	0	0
Career			11	63	5.7	32	0

Roynell Young
1980	PHI	N	4	27	6.8	26	0
1981			4	35	8.8	33	0
1982			4	0	0.0	0	0
1983			1	0	0.0	0	0
1985			1	0	0.0	0	0
1986			6	9	1.5	9	0
1987			1	30	30.0	30	0
1988			2	5	2.5	5	0
Career			23	106	4.6	33	0
Playoffs			3	5	1.7		0

Wilbur Young
1971	KC	N	1	3	3.0	3	0
1974			1	52	52.0	52t	1
Career			2	55	27.5	52t	1

George Youngblood
| 1969 | CHI | N | 3 | 22 | 7.3 | 22t | 1 |

Jack Youngblood
| Playoffs | | | 1 | 47 | 47.0 | | 1 |

Jim Youngblood
1973	LA	N	1	15	15.0	15	0
1976			2	28	14.0	26	0
1977			2	27	13.5	25t	1
1978			2	50	25.0	36	0
1979			5	89	17.8	34t	2
1980			1	33	33.0	33t	1
1981			1	20	20.0	20	0
Career			14	262	18.7	36	4
Playoffs			1	10	10.0		0

Tank Younger
| 1951 | LA | N | 1 | 0 | 0.0 | 0 | 0 |

Tank Younger *continued*
| 1952 | | | 2 | 0 | 0.0 | 0 | 0 |
| Career | | | 3 | 0 | 0.0 | 0 | 0 |

Swede Youngstrom
| 1926 | FRA | N | | | | | 1 |

Steve Zabel
1971	PHI	N	1	4	4.0	4	0
1973			2	13	6.5	7	0
1974			2	12	6.0	7	0
1978	NE	N	1	0	0.0	0	0
Career			6	29	4.8	7	0

Tony Zackery
| 1989 | ATL | N | 1 | 3 | 3.0 | 3 | 0 |

Bert Zagers
1957	WAS	N	2	29	14.5	22	0
1958			2	59	29.5	34	0
Career			4	88	22.0	34	0

Ernie Zalejski
| 1950 | BAL | N | 2 | 81 | 40.5 | 81t | 1 |

John Zamberlin
| 1981 | NE | N | 1 | 11 | 11.0 | 11 | 0 |

Carl Zander
1986	CIN	N	1	18	18.0	18	0
1988			1	3	3.0	3	0
1990			1	12	12.0	12	0
Career			3	33	11.0	18	0

Roger Zatkoff
1954	GB	N	1	0	0.0	0	0
1955			3	25	8.3	15	0
Career			4	25	6.3	15	0
Playoffs			1	0	0.0		0

Joe Zeller
| 1938 | CHIB | N | | | | | 1 |

Bob Zeman
1960	LA	A	2	25	12.5		0
1961	SD	A	8	89	11.1	21	0
1962	DEN	A	6	133	22.2	55	1

Bob Zeman *continued*
1963			1	23	23.0	23	0
Career			17	270	15.9	55	1
Playoffs			2	0	0.0		0

Joe Zeno
| 1946 | BOS | N | 1 | 0 | 0.0 | 0 | 0 |

Frank Ziegler
| 1949 | PHI | N | 1 | 16 | 16.0 | 16 | 0 |

Roy Zimmerman
1943	P-P	N	5	19	3.8	10	0
1944	PHI	N	4	36	9.0	14	0
1945			7	90	12.9	23	0
1946			3	58	19.3	37	0
Career			19	203	10.7	37	0

Lou Zontini
1944	CLE	N	2	14	7.0	10	0
1946	BUF	AA	1	2	2.0	2	0
Career			3	16	5.3	10	0

John Zook
1969	ATL	N	2	22	11.0	15	0
1970			1	24	24.0	24	0
1974			1	14	14.0	14	0
Career			4	60	15.0	24	0

Mike Zordich
1988	NYJ	N	1	35	35.0	35t	1
1989	PHX	N	1	16	16.0	16t	1
1990			1	25	25.0	25	0
1991			1	27	27.0	27	0
1992			3	37	12.3	23	0
1993			1	0	0.0	0	0
1994	PHI	N	4	39	9.8	18t	1
1995			1	10	10.0	10	0
1996			4	54	13.5	28	0
Career			17	243	14.3	35t	3
Playoffs			1	15	15.0		0

George Zorich
| 1944 | CHIB | N | 1 | 4 | 4.0 | 4 | 0 |

Vic Zucco
1957	CHIB	N	3	20	6.7	14	0
1958			3	13	4.3	13	0
1960	CHI	N	2	52	26.0	44	0
Career			8	85	10.6	44	0

PUNTING REGISTER

Year	Team		No	Bl	Yds	Avg	Lg	NetAvg
Rohn Stark								
1982	BAL	N	46	0	2044	44.4	60	34.3
1983			91	0	**4124**	**45.3**	68	36.3
1984	IND	N	**98**	0	4383	44.7	72	37.2
1985			78	2	3584	**45.9**	68	34.2
1986			76	0	3432	**45.2**	63	37.2
1987			61	2	2440	40.0	63	30.9
1988			64	0	2784	43.5	65	34.5
1989			79	1	3392	42.9	64	32.9
1990			71	1	3084	43.4	61	37.4
1991			82	0	3492	42.6	65	34.8
1992			83	0	3716	44.8	64	39.3
1993			83	0	3595	43.3	65	35.9
1994			73	1	3092	42.4	60	34.1
1995	PIT	N	59	0	2368	40.1	64	33.3
1996	CAR	N	77	0	3128	40.6	60	36.0
Career			1121	7	48658	43.4	72	
Playoffs			22	0	851	38.7		

Key

Team	The team (and league) the player played for.
No	Number of punts
Bl	Punts Blocked
Yds	Yards
Avg	Average length of punt
Lg	Longest punt of the season
NetAvg	Average length of punt with punt return factored in

In addition, boldface numbers indicate that the player led the league in that category that season. For example, Stark's 98 punts in 1984 are boldfaced, meaning that he led the league in punting that year.

John Adams

Year	Team		No	Bl	Yds	Avg	Lg	NetAvg
1961	CHI	N	2	0	56	28.0	43	
1963	LA	N	4	0	121	30.3	42	
Career			6	0	177	29.5	43	

Louie Aguiar

Year	Team		No	Bl	Yds	Avg	Lg	NetAvg
1991	NYJ	N	64	0	2521	39.4	61	34.6
1992			73	0	2993	41.0	65	37.6
1993			73	0	2806	38.4	71	34.4
1994	KC	N	85	0	3582	42.1	61	34.5
1995			91	0	3990	43.8	65	36.5
1996			88	0	3667	41.7	68	33.8
Career			474	0	19559	41.3	71	
Playoffs			8	0	299	37.4		

Joe Aguirre

Year	Team		No	Bl	Yds	Avg	Lg	NetAvg
1944	WAS	N	2	0	87	43.5	44	
1946	LA	AA	2	0	91	45.5		
Career			4	0	178	44.5	44	

Frank Akins

Year	Team		No	Bl	Yds	Avg	Lg	NetAvg
1943	WAS	N	2	1	54	27.0	33	
1944			1	0	39	39.0	39	
Career			3	1	93	31.0	39	

Frankie Albert

Year	Team		No	Bl	Yds	Avg	Lg	NetAvg
1946	SF	AA	54	0	2214	41.0	73	
1947			39	1	1759	45.1	69	
1948			35	0	1568	44.8	82	
1949			31	0	1495	**48.2**	72	
1950	SF	N	36	1	1423	39.5	64	
1951			34	0	1506	44.3	66	
1952			68	0	2899	42.6	70	
Career			297	2	12864	43.3	82	
Playoffs			15	0	683	45.5		

Harold Alexander

Year	Team		No	Bl	Yds	Avg	Lg	NetAvg
1993	ATL	N	72	0	3114	43.3	75	37.6
1994			71	0	2836	39.9	61	34.8
Career			143	0	5950	41.6	75	

Eddie Allen

Year	Team		No	Bl	Yds	Avg	Lg	NetAvg
1947	CHIB	N	8	0	299	37.4	46	

Ermal Allen

Year	Team		No	Bl	Yds	Avg	Lg	NetAvg
1947	CLE	AA	4	0	135	33.8		

Jim Allison

Year	Team		No	Bl	Yds	Avg	Lg	NetAvg
1965	SD	A	2	0	72	36.0	39	
Playoffs			2	0	28	14.0		

Bill Anderson

Year	Team		No	Bl	Yds	Avg	Lg	NetAvg
1962	WAS	N	7	0	235	33.6	46	

Billy Anderson

Year	Team		No	Bl	Yds	Avg	Lg	NetAvg
1953	CHIB	N	1	0	46	46.0	46	

Dick Anderson

Year	Team		No	Bl	Yds	Avg	Lg	NetAvg
1969	MIA	A	5	0	188	37.6	49	
1972	MIA	N	4	0	147	36.8	45	
Career			9	0	335	37.2	49	

Donny Anderson

Year	Team		No	Bl	Yds	Avg	Lg	NetAvg
1966	GB	N	2	0	89	44.5	49	
1967			64	1	2378	37.2	63	
1968			59	0	2359	40.0	65	
1969			58	0	2329	40.2	58	
1970			81	0	3302	40.8	62	
1971			50	0	2022	40.4	58	
1972	STL	N	72	0	2847	39.5	61	
Career			386	1	15326	39.7	65	
Playoffs			20	0	670	33.5		

Zenon Andrusyshyn

Year	Team		No	Bl	Yds	Avg	Lg	NetAvg
1978	KC	N	79	1	3247	41.1	61	32.1

Leo Araguz

Year	Team		No	Bl	Yds	Avg	Lg	NetAvg
1996	OAK	N	13	0	534	41.1	52	34.5

Evan Arapostathis

Year	Team		No	Bl	Yds	Avg	Lg	NetAvg
1986	STL	N	30	0	1140	38.0	50	32.5

Charlie Armstrong

Year	Team		No	Bl	Yds	Avg	Lg	NetAvg
1946	BKN	AA	6	0	231	38.5		

Jay Arnold

Year	Team		No	Bl	Yds	Avg	Lg	NetAvg
1939	PHI	N	1		42	42.0	42	

Jim Arnold

Year	Team		No	Bl	Yds	Avg	Lg	NetAvg
1983	KC	N	93	0	3710	39.9	64	32.6
1984			**98**	0	**4397**	**44.9**	63	37.5
1985			93	2	3827	41.2	62	32.4
1986	DET	N	36	1	1533	42.6	60	32.1
1987			46	0	2007	43.6	60	**39.6**
1988			97	0	**4110**	42.4	69	35.9
1989			82	1	3538	43.1	64	36.0
1990			63	0	2560	40.6	59	35.3
1991			75	0	3092	41.2	63	35.4
1992			65	1	2846	43.8	71	34.7
1993			72	0	3207	44.5	68	36.8
1994	MIA	N	46	0	1810	39.3	53	33.5
Career			866	5	36637	42.3	71	
Playoffs			11	0	517	47.0		

Jim Asmus

Year	Team		No	Bl	Yds	Avg	Lg	NetAvg
1987	SF	N	12	0	384	32.0	51	28.0

Billy Atkins

Year	Team		No	Bl	Yds	Avg	Lg	NetAvg
1958	SF	N	25	0	983	39.3	51	
1960	BUF	A	**89**	0	**3468**	39.0	58	
1961			**84**		**3783**	**45.0**	70	
1962	NY	A	21		969	46.1	63	
Career			219	0	9203	42.0	70	

Clarence Avinger

Year	Team		No	Bl	Yds	Avg	Lg	NetAvg
1953	NYG	N	41	1	1600	39.0	69	

Chris Bahr

Year	Team		No	Bl	Yds	Avg	Lg	NetAvg
1977	CIN	N	2	0	88	44.0	45	47.5
1978			4	0	108	27.0	41	20.5
1981	OAK	N	2	0	43	21.5	32	11.5
Career			8	0	239	29.9	45	

Matt Bahr

Year	Team		No	Bl	Yds	Avg	Lg	NetAvg
1995	NE	N	1	0	29	29.0	29	9.0

Dave Baker

Year	Team		No	Bl	Yds	Avg	Lg	NetAvg
1960	SF	N	3	0	143	47.7	55	

Sam Baker

Year	Team		No	Bl	Yds	Avg	Lg	NetAvg
1953	WAS	N	17	0	614	36.1	51	
1956			59	0	2510	42.5	56	
1957			50	0	2139	42.8	63	
1958			48	0	2181	**45.4**	64	
1959			49	0	2229	45.5	66	
1960	CLE	N	55	0	2309	42.0	64	
1961			53	0	2296	43.3	62	
1962	DAL	N	57	0	2589	45.4	72	
1963			71	0	3138	44.2	64	
1964	PHI	N	48	1	2073	43.2	61	
1965			37	0	1551	41.9	60	
1966			42	0	1762	41.1	63	
1967			60	1	2335	38.9	53	
1968			55	0	2248	40.9	57	
Career			701	2	29974	42.8	72	

Jim Bakken

Year	Team		No	Bl	Yds	Avg	Lg	NetAvg
1965	STL	N	26	0	1098	42.2	56	
1966			29	0	960	33.1	49	
1971			5	0	207	41.4	44	
1972			1	0	26	26.0	26	
1978			4	0	147	36.8	42	31.3
Career			65	0	2438	37.5	56	

Frank Balazs

Year	Team		No	Bl	Yds	Avg	Lg	NetAvg
1939	GB	N	1	0	35	35.0	35	
1941	CHIC	N	7	0	259	37.0	55	
Career			8	0	294	36.8	55	

Lou Baldacci

Year	Team		No	Bl	Yds	Avg	Lg	NetAvg
1956	PIT	N	26	0	1010	38.8	64	

Emil Banjavic

Year	Team		No	Bl	Yds	Avg	Lg	NetAvg
1942	DET	N	5	0	235	47.0	58	

Jack Banta

Year	Team		No	Bl	Yds	Avg	Lg	NetAvg
1941	PHI	N	9	0	410	45.6	67	
1944			9	0	398	44.2	56	
1946	LA	N	1	0	44	44.0	44	

Jack Banta *continued*

Year	Team		No	Bl	Yds	Avg	Lg	NetAvg
1947			3	0	125	41.7	45	
1948			17	0	639	37.6	55	
Career			39	0	1616	41.4	67	

Bryan Barker

Year	Team		No	Bl	Yds	Avg	Lg	NetAvg
1990	KC	N	64	0	2479	38.7	56	33.4
1991			57	0	2303	40.4	57	35.0
1992			75	1	3245	43.3	65	35.3
1993			76	1	3240	42.6	59	35.4
1994	PHI	N	66	0	2696	40.8	67	36.3
1995	JAC	N	82	0	3591	43.8	63	**38.6**
1996			69	0	3016	43.7	62	35.6
Career			489	2	20570	42.1	67	
Playoffs			51	0	2167	42.5		

Bruce Barnes

Year	Team		No	Bl	Yds	Avg	Lg	NetAvg
1973	NE	N	55	0	2134	38.8	53	
1974			45	0	1604	35.6	50	
Career			100	0	3738	37.4	53	

Joe Barnes

Year	Team		No	Bl	Yds	Avg	Lg	NetAvg
1974	CHI	N	1	0	27	27.0	27	

Larry Barnes

Year	Team		No	Bl	Yds	Avg	Lg	NetAvg
1957	SF	N	19	0	894	47.1	88	

Lem Barney

Year	Team		No	Bl	Yds	Avg	Lg	NetAvg
1967	DET	N	47	0	1757	37.4	55	
1969			65	1	2249	34.6	53	
Career			112	1	4006	35.8	55	

Tommy Barnhardt

Year	Team		No	Bl	Yds	Avg	Lg	NetAvg
1987	NO-CHI	N	17	0	719	42.3	52	35.2
1988	WAS	N	15	0	628	41.9	55	34.3
1989	NO	N	55	0	2179	39.6	56	35.0
1990			70	1	2990	42.7	65	36.2
1991			86	1	**3743**	43.5	61	35.3
1992			67	0	2947	44.0	62	37.7
1993			77	0	3356	43.6	58	37.5
1994			67	0	2920	43.6	57	33.5
1995	CAR	N	95	0	3906	41.1	54	35.2
1996	TB	N	70	1	3015	43.1	62	37.8
Career			619	3	26403	42.7	65	
Playoffs			13	0	533	41.0		

Len Barnum

Year	Team		No	Bl	Yds	Avg	Lg	NetAvg
1939	NYG	N	29		1189	41.0	60	
1940			39		1560	40.0	64	
1941	PHI	N	41	0	1788	43.6	68	
1942			50	0	1905	38.1	65	
Career			159	0	6442	40.5	68	
Playoffs			3	0	105	35.0		

Mike Basca

Year	Team		No	Bl	Yds	Avg	Lg	NetAvg
1941	PHI	N	10	0	348	34.8	45	

Marv Bateman

Year	Team		No	Bl	Yds	Avg	Lg	NetAvg
1972	DAL	N	51	0	1949	38.2	61	
1973			53	2	2290	43.2	62	
1974	DAL-BUF	N	67	0	2712	40.5	66	
1975	BUF	N	59	2	2536	43.0	74	
1976			86	1	3678	**42.8**	78	29.0
1977			81	2	3229	39.9	75	29.2
Career			397	7	16394	41.3	78	
Playoffs			29	0	1235	42.6		

Cliff Battles

Year	Team		No	Bl	Yds	Avg	Lg	NetAvg
Playoffs			1	0	12	12.0	12	

Sammy Baugh

Year	Team		No	Bl	Yds	Avg	Lg	NetAvg
1939	WAS	N	25	1	998	39.9	69	
1940			35	0	1799	**52.9**	85	
1941			30	0	1462	**48.7**	75	
1942			37	0	1725	**46.6**	74	
1943			47	3	2295	**48.8**	81	
1944			43	1	1780	41.4	76	
1945			33	0	1429	**43.3**	57	
1946			32	1	1488	46.5	60	
1947			33	2	1530	**46.4**	67	
1949			1	0	53	53.0	53	
1950			8	1	352	44.0	58	
1951			4	0	221	55.3	58	

Sammy Baugh continued

Year	Team		No	Bl	Yds	Avg		Lg	NetAvg
1952			1	0	48	48.0		48	
Career			329	9	15180	46.1		85	
Playoffs			13	1	539	41.5			

Chuck Bednarik

Year	Team		No	Bl	Yds	Avg		Lg	NetAvg
1953	PHI	N	12	0	484	40.3		54	

Keith Beebe

1944	NYG	N	7	0	210	30.0		45	

Bill Bell

1971	ATL	N	16	0	577	36.1		48	

Darren Bennett

1995	SD	N	72	0	3221	44.7		66	36.6
1996			87	0	3967	45.6		66	37.2
Career			159	0	7188	45.2		66	
Playoffs			2	0	109	54.5			

Mitch Berger

1994	PHI	N	25	0	951	38.0		57	31.3
1996	MIN	N	88	2	3616	41.1		63	32.4
Career			113	2	4567	40.4		63	
Playoffs			2	0	79	39.5			

Louis Berry

1987	ATL	N	7	0	258	36.9		51	31.9

Rex Berry

1954	SF	N	0	1	0			0	

Angelo Bertelli

1946	LA	AA	2	0	96	48.0			

David Beverly

1974	HOU	N	79	0	3100	39.2		69	
1975	HOU-GB	N	78	0	2941	37.7		55	
1976	GB	N	83	1	3074	37.0		60	32.2
1977			85	1	3391	39.9		59	33.7
1978			106	0	3759	35.5		57	31.1
1979			69	0	2785	40.4		65	34.8
1980			86	0	3294	38.3		55	32.9
Career			586	2	22344	38.1		69	

Carl Birdsong

1981	STL	N	69	0	2883	41.8		75	35.5
1982			54	0	2365	43.8		65	36.2
1983			85	0	3529	41.5		59	36.3
1984			67	1	2594	38.7		59	32.3
1985			85	2	3545	41.7		67	33.7
Career			360	3	14916	41.4		75	

Mike Black

1983	DET	N	71	1	2911	41.0		60	33.7
1984			76	0	3164	41.6		63	32.7
1985			73	0	3054	41.8		60	34.7
1986			46	1	1819	39.5		57	31.3
1987			6	0	233	38.8		47	36.8
Career			272	2	11181	41.1		63	
Playoffs			2	0	73	36.5			

Hal Blackwell

1945	CHIC	N	17	0	661	38.9		52	

Bill Blackburn

1946	CHIC	N	35	0	1467	41.9		60	
1947			1	0	19	19.0		19	
Career			36	0	1486	41.3		60	

Tom Blanchard

1971	NYG	N	66	0	2681	40.6		57	
1972			46	1	2006	43.6		58	
1973			55	1	2347	42.7		62	
1974	NO	N	88	0	3704	42.1		71	
1975			89	3	3776	42.4		61	
1976			101	0	3974	39.3		63	31.0
1977			82	2	3474	42.4		66	31.5
1978			84	2	3532	42.0		61	32.5
1979	TB	N	93	2	3679	39.6		58	30.6
1980			88	1	3722	42.3		62	33.2
1981			22	0	899	40.9		58	27.3
Career			814	12	33794	41.5		71	
Playoffs			13	0	510	39.2			

George Blanda

Year	Team		No	Bl	Yds	Avg		Lg	NetAvg
1949	CHIB	N	19	0	747	39.3		57	
1950			1	1	30	30.0		30	
1956			1	0	33	33.0		33	
Career			21	1	810	38.6		57	

Scott Blanton

1996	WAS	N	2	0	84	42.0		45	26.5

Chris Boniol

1995	DAL	N	2	0	77	38.5		56	38.5

Dick Booth

1941	DET	N	1	0	25	25.0		25	

Lew Bostick

1939	CLE	N	1	0	55	55.0		55	

Barry Bowman

1987	SEA	N	3	0	104	34.7		36	30.7

Mike Boyda

1949	NYB	N	56	0	2475	44.2		61	

Don Bracken

1985	GB	N	26	0	1052	40.5		54	33.3
1986			55	2	2203	40.1		63	32.8
1987			72	1	2947	40.9		65	34.2
1988			85	1	3287	38.7		62	31.8
1989			66	0	2682	40.6		63	31.0
1990			64	1	2431	38.0		59	32.7
1992	LARM	N	76	0	3122	41.1		59	33.2
1993			17	0	651	38.3		51	33.2
Career			461	5	18375	39.9		65	

Bill Bradley

1969	PHI	N	74	0	2942	39.8		60	
1970			61	0	2246	36.8		56	
1971			2	0	76	38.0		45	
1972			56	0	2250	40.2		60	
1973			18	0	735	40.8		61	
1974			2	0	67	33.5		35	
Career			213	0	8316	39.0		61	

Jim Bradshaw

1963	PIT	N	2	0	70	35.0		38	

Terry Bradshaw

1970	PIT	N	2	1	52	26.0		39	
1980			5	0	173	34.6		44	34.6
Career			7	1	225	32.1		44	

Pat Brady

1952	PIT	N	77	0	3328	43.2		69	
1953			80	0	3752	46.9		64	
1954			66	0	2852	43.2		72	
Career			223	0	9932	44.5		72	

Mike Bragg

1968	WAS	N	74	2	3288	44.4		64	
1969			68	2	2957	43.5		63	
1970			60	1	2493	41.5		66	
1971			57	1	2348	41.2		59	
1972			59	0	2273	38.5		62	
1973			64	0	2581	40.3		61	
1974			73	1	2823	38.7		57	
1975			72	0	2924	40.6		63	
1976			90	0	3503	38.9		56	32.9
1977			91	0	3502	38.5		58	35.1
1978			103	1	4056	39.4		56	33.9
1979			78	0	2998	38.4		74	34.1
1980	BAL	N	82	2	3203	39.1		59	32.5
Career			971	10	38949	40.1		74	
Playoffs			35	0	1382	39.5			

Zeke Bratkowski

1954	CHIB	N	39	0	1599	41.0		70	
1957			16	0	618	38.6		52	
1958			14	0	554	39.6		52	
1960	CHI	N	7	0	252	36.0		47	
1961	LA	N	12	0	458	38.2		51	
Career			88	0	3481	39.6		70	

Jim Breech

Year	Team		No	Bl	Yds	Avg		Lg	NetAvg
1980	CIN	N	2	0	67	33.5		37	22.5
1985			5	0	153	30.6		43	26.8
1988			3	0	64	21.3		30	14.7
1989			2	0	58	29.0		32	19.0
1990			1	0	34	34.0		34	14.0
1991			1	0	33	33.0		33	13.0
Career			14	0	409	29.2		43	

Monte Brethauer

1955	BAL	N	55	0	2161	39.3		50	

Lou Brock

1940	GB	N	3		126	42.0		52	
1941			3	0	128	42.7		48	
1942			32	0	1219	38.1		52	
1943			31	1	1165	37.6		72	
1944			14	0	490	35.0		50	
Career			83	1	3128	37.7		72	
Playoffs			6	0	231	38.5			

Steve Broussard

1975	GB	N	26	3	922	35.5		51	

Dave Brown

1994	NYG	N	2	0	57	28.5		33	18.5
1995			1	0	15	15.0		15	15.0
Career			3	0	72	24.0		33	

Ed Brown

1954	CHIB	N	18	0	684	38.0		60	
1955			43	1	1764	41.0		59	
1956			41	1	1644	40.1		53	
1957			33	1	1363	41.3		62	
1958			27	0	1139	42.2		57	
1959			64	0	2634	41.2		66	
1960	CHI	N	54	2	2231	41.3		65	
1961			58	0	2448	42.2		69	
1962	PIT	N	60	0	2400	40.0		78	
1963			57	0	2256	39.6		57	
1964			31	0	1346	43.4		54	
1965	BAL	N	2	0	80	40.0		49	
Career			488	5	19994	41.0		78	
Playoffs			7	1	272	38.9			

Hardy Brown

1949	CHI	AA	10	0	397	39.7			
1954	SF	N	10	0	384	38.4		58	
Career			20	0	781	39.0		58	

Kevin Brown

1987	CHI	N	18	1	742	41.2		58	29.2

Pete Brown

1954	SF	N	49	0	1837	37.5		51	

Ray Brown

1958	BAL	N	41	0	1635	39.3		60	
1959			2	0	89	44.5		55	
1960			52	0	2001	38.5		55	
Career			95	0	3735	39.2		60	
Playoffs			4	0	191	47.8			

Boyd Brumbaugh

1939	BKN-PIT	N	1		34	34.0		34	
1940	PIT	N	6		192	32.0		44	
Career			7		226	32.3		44	

Dave Bruno

1987	MIN	N	13	0	464	35.7		53	32.5

John Bruno

1987	PIT	N	16	1	619	38.7		56	30.4

Maury Buford

1982	SD	N	21	2	868	41.3		71	31.4
1983			63	0	2763	43.9		60	36.6
1984			66	0	2773	42.0		60	35.1
1985	CHI	N	68	1	2870	42.2		69	34.6
1986			69	1	2663	38.6		59	36.9
1988	NYG	N	73	0	3012	41.3		66	33.5
1989	CHI	N	72	0	2844	39.5		60	33.4
1990			76	2	3073	40.4		59	33.5

Maury Buford *continued*

Year	Team		No	Bl	Yds	Avg	Lg	NetAvg
1991			69	1	2814	40.8	64	35.0
Career			577	9	23867	41.4	71	
Playoffs			34	1	1315	38.7		

Joe Bukant

Year	Team		No	Bl	Yds	Avg	Lg	NetAvg
1939	**PHI**	**N**	1		54	54.0	54	
1940			15		570	38.0	52	
1943	**CHIC**	**N**	5	0	181	36.2	46	
Career			21	0	805	38.3	54	

Jerry Burch

Year	Team		No	Bl	Yds	Avg	Lg	NetAvg
1961	**OAK**	**A**	11		315	28.6	41	

Adrian Burk

Year	Team		No	Bl	Yds	Avg	Lg	NetAvg
1950	**BAL**	**N**	80	1	3243	40.5	68	
1951	**PHI**	**N**	67	0	2646	39.5	60	
1952			81	2	3335	41.2	68	
1953			41	0	1763	43.0	66	
1954			**73**	0	2918	40.0	58	
1955			61	0	2615	42.9	75	
1956			67	1	2843	42.4	62	
Career			470	4	19363	41.2	75	

Mike Burke

Year	Team		No	Bl	Yds	Avg	Lg	NetAvg
1974	**LA**	**N**	46	0	1701	37.0	51	
Playoffs			10	0	434	43.4		

Jeff Burkett

Year	Team		No	Bl	Yds	Avg	Lg	NetAvg
1947	**CHIC**	**N**	11	0	521	47.4	53	

Ode Burrell

Year	Team		No	Bl	Yds	Avg	Lg	NetAvg
1969	**HOU**	**A**	29	0	1066	36.8	56	
Playoffs			11	0	455	41.4		

Young Bussey

Year	Team		No	Bl	Yds	Avg	Lg	NetAvg
1941	**CHIB**	**N**	2	0	74	37.0	41	

Johnny Butler

Year	Team		No	Bl	Yds	Avg	Lg	NetAvg
1943	**P-P**	**N**	11	0	407	37.0	45	
1944	**BKN-BOS**	**N**	12	1	485	37.3	56	
Career			23	1	892	37.2	56	

Skip Butler

Year	Team		No	Bl	Yds	Avg	Lg	NetAvg
1972	**HOU**	**N**	3	0	105	35.0	47	
1973			36	0	1344	37.3	55	
1976			11	1	370	33.6	39	25.6
Career			50	1	1819	36.4	55	

George Cafego

Year	Team		No	Bl	Yds	Avg	Lg	NetAvg
1940	**BKN**	**N**	1		18	18.0	18	
1943	**BKN-WAS**	**N**	20	1	720	36.0	68	
1944	**BOS**	**N**	16	0	582	36.4	57	
1945			6	0	213	35.5	39	
Career			43	1	1533	35.7	68	
Playoffs			3	0	125	41.7		

Ronnie Cahill

Year	Team		No	Bl	Yds	Avg	Lg	NetAvg
1943	**CHIC**	**N**	3	0	88	29.3	36	

Jim Callahan

Year	Team		No	Bl	Yds	Avg	Lg	NetAvg
1946	**DET**	**N**	4	0	182	45.5	63	

Bill Callihan

Year	Team		No	Bl	Yds	Avg	Lg	NetAvg
1942	**DET**	**N**	1	0	44	44.0	44	

Rich Camarillo

Year	Team		No	Bl	Yds	Avg	Lg	NetAvg
1981	**NE**	**N**	47	0	1959	41.7	75	33.4
1982			49	0	2140	43.7	76	37.7
1983			81	0	3615	44.6	70	**37.1**
1984			48	0	2020	42.1	61	34.7
1985			92	0	**3953**	43.0	75	33.6
1986			89	3	3746	42.1	64	33.1
1987			62	1	2489	40.1	73	31.7
1988	**LARM**	**N**	40	0	1579	39.5	57	34.8
1989	**PHX**	**N**	76	0	3298	**43.4**	58	37.5
1990			67	0	2865	42.8	63	37.4
1991			76	1	3445	45.3	60	**38.9**
1992			54	0	2317	42.9	73	**39.6**
1993			73	0	3189	43.7	61	37.8
1994	**HOU**	**N**	96	0	**4115**	42.9	58	36.4
1995			77	1	3165	41.1	60	34.8
Career			1027	6	43895	42.7	76	
Playoffs			35	1	1559	44.5		

Tony Canadeo

Year	Team		No	Bl	Yds	Avg	Lg	NetAvg
1941	**GB**	**N**	10	0	405	40.5	62	
1942			18	0	644	35.8	47	
1943			3	0	102	34.0	39	
1944			13	0	478	36.8	46	
1948			1	0	38	38.0	38	
Career			45	0	1667	37.0	62	

Leo Cantor

Year	Team		No	Bl	Yds	Avg	Lg	NetAvg
1942	**NYG**	**N**	19	1	762	40.1	63	
1945	**CHIC**	**N**	5	0	166	33.2	38	
Career			24	1	928	38.7	63	

John Carney

Year	Team		No	Bl	Yds	Avg	Lg	NetAvg
1993	**SD**	**N**	4	0	155	38.8	46	34.8

Reg Carolan

Year	Team		No	Bl	Yds	Avg	Lg	NetAvg
1967	**KC**	**A**	1	0	42	42.0	42	
1968			2	0	101	50.5	52	
Career			3	0	143	47.7	52	

Duane Carrell

Year	Team		No	Bl	Yds	Avg	Lg	NetAvg
1974	**DAL**	**N**	40	0	1591	39.8	59	
1975	**LA**	**N**	73	0	2874	39.4	57	
1976	**NYJ**	**N**	81	0	3218	39.7	72	32.6
1977	**NYJ-STL**	**N**	63	0	2314	36.7	56	30.9
Career			257	0	9997	38.9	72	
Playoffs			12	0	406	33.8		

Joe Carter

Year	Team		No	Bl	Yds	Avg	Lg	NetAvg
1944	**BKN**	**N**	9	0	325	36.1	45	

Rick Casares

Year	Team		No	Bl	Yds	Avg	Lg	NetAvg
1956	**CHIB**	**N**	1	0	51	51.0	51	
1957			2	0	67	33.5	41	
1959			3	0	139	46.3	71	
1960	**CHI**	**N**	1	0	60	60.0	60	
Career			7	0	317	45.3	71	

Ernie Case

Year	Team		No	Bl	Yds	Avg	Lg	NetAvg
1947	**BAL**	**AA**	4	1	152	38.0		

Tom Casey

Year	Team		No	Bl	Yds	Avg	Lg	NetAvg
1948	**NY**	**AA**	6	0	242	40.3		

Greg Cater

Year	Team		No	Bl	Yds	Avg	Lg	NetAvg
1980	**BUF**	**N**	73	1	2828	38.7	61	31.1
1981			80	0	3175	39.7	71	33.9
1982			35	0	1328	37.9	61	36.5
1983			89	0	3533	39.7	60	33.6
1986	**STL**	**N**	61	1	2271	37.2	52	33.2
1987			39	1	1470	37.7	68	30.7
Career			377	3	14605	38.7	71	
Playoffs			13	0	568	43.7		

Bob Celeri

Year	Team		No	Bl	Yds	Avg	Lg	NetAvg
1951	**NYY**	**N**	5	0	224	44.8	54	
1952	**DAL**	**N**	21	0	876	41.7	57	
Career			26	0	1100	42.3	57	

Don Chandler

Year	Team		No	Bl	Yds	Avg	Lg	NetAvg
1956	**NYG**	**N**	59	0	2473	41.9	63	
1957			60	0	2673	**44.5**	61	
1958			**65**	0	2859	44.0	67	
1959			55	0	2565	46.6	62	
1960			31	0	1257	40.5	58	
1961			66	2	2984	45.2	66	
1962			53	2	2233	42.1	65	
1963			59	0	2648	44.9	64	
1964			73	0	3328	45.6	74	
1965	**GB**	**N**	74	0	3176	42.9	90	
1966			60	0	2452	40.9	58	
1967			1	0	31	31.0	31	
Career			656	4	28679	43.7	90	
Playoffs			50	0	2168	43.4		

Wes Chandler

Year	Team		No	Bl	Yds	Avg	Lg	NetAvg
1979	**NO**	**N**	8	0	248	31.0	40	26.4
1986	**SD**	**N**	5	0	167	33.4	38	33.0
Career			13	0	415	31.9	40	

Dave Chapple

Year	Team		No	Bl	Yds	Avg	Lg	NetAvg
1971	**BUF**	**N**	3	0	101	33.7	47	
1972	**LA**	**N**	53	0	2344	44.2	70	

Dave Chapple *continued*

Year	Team		No	Bl	Yds	Avg	Lg	NetAvg
1973			50	1	2079	41.6	65	
1974	**LA-NE**	**N**	55	1	1995	36.3	57	
Career			161	2	6519	40.5	70	
Playoffs			5	0	218	43.6		

George Chesser

Year	Team		No	Bl	Yds	Avg	Lg	NetAvg
1966	**MIA**	**A**	7	0	233	33.3	39	

John Chickerneo

Year	Team		No	Bl	Yds	Avg	Lg	NetAvg
1942	**NYG**	**N**	8	0		37.7	45	

Bob Cifers

Year	Team		No	Bl	Yds	Avg	Lg	NetAvg
1946	**DET**	**N**	30	0	1368	**45.6**	73	
1947	**PIT**	**N**	66	2	2796	42.4	74	
1948			62	0	2454	39.6	66	
1949	**GB**	**N**	1	0	49	49.0	49	
Career			159	2	6667	41.9	74	
Playoffs			8	1	360	45.0		

Neil Clabo

Year	Team		No	Bl	Yds	Avg	Lg	NetAvg
1975	**MIN**	**N**	71	2	2997	42.2	62	
1976			69	0	2678	38.8	55	30.9
1977			83	0	3302	39.8	69	31.3
Career			223	2	8977	40.3	69	
Playoffs			44	0	1703	38.7		

Beryl Clark

Year	Team		No	Bl	Yds	Avg	Lg	NetAvg
1940	**CHIC**	**N**	28		924	33.0	44	

Harry Clark

Year	Team		No	Bl	Yds	Avg	Lg	NetAvg
1940	**CHIB**	**N**	1	0	30	30.0	30	

Ken Clark

Year	Team		No	Bl	Yds	Avg	Lg	NetAvg
1979	**LA**	**N**	93	2	3731	40.1	60	33.5
Playoffs			15	0	613	40.9		

Leroy Clark

Year	Team		No	Bl	Yds	Avg	Lg	NetAvg
1976	**HOU**	**N**	10	0	335	33.5	47	27.3

Walt Clay

Year	Team		No	Bl	Yds	Avg	Lg	NetAvg
1946	**CHI**	**AA**	1	0	45	45.0	45	

Johnny Clement

Year	Team		No	Bl	Yds	Avg	Lg	NetAvg
1941	**CHIC**	**N**	4	0	125	31.3	38	
1946	**PIT**	**N**	9	0	315	35.0	52	
Career			13	0	440	33.8	52	

Ray Clemons

Year	Team		No	Bl	Yds	Avg	Lg	NetAvg
1939	**DET**	**N**	15		645	43.0	57	

Red Cochran

Year	Team		No	Bl	Yds	Avg	Lg	NetAvg
1947	**CHIC**	**N**	1	0	25	25.0	25	
1948			6	0	229	38.2	56	
1949			52	0	2186	42.0	66	
Career			59	0	2440	41.4	66	

Don Cockroft

Year	Team		No	Bl	Yds	Avg	Lg	NetAvg
1968	**CLE**	**N**	61	0	2397	39.3	59	
1969			56	1	2138	38.2	55	
1970			70	1	3023	43.2	71	
1971			60	2	2508	41.8	59	
1972			81	0	**3498**	43.2	65	
1973			81	1	3321	41.0	71	
1974			90	0	3643	40.5	64	
1975			81	1	3317	41.0	67	
1976			64	3	2487	38.9	51	28.4
1977			1	0	30	30.0	30	10.0
Career			645	9	26362	40.9	71	
Playoffs			26	1	965	37.1		

Lewis Colbert

Year	Team		No	Bl	Yds	Avg	Lg	NetAvg
1986	**KC**	**N**	99	0	4033	40.7	56	33.7
1987			10	0	377	37.7	47	31.8
1989	**SD**	**N**	8	0	266	33.3	46	27.9
Career			117	0	4676	40.0	56	
Playoffs			3	0	124	41.3		

John Cole

Year	Team		No	Bl	Yds	Avg	Lg	NetAvg
1940	**PHI**	**N**	10		340	34.0	66	

Tom Colella

Year	Team		No	Bl	Yds	Avg	Lg	NetAvg
1942	**DET**	**N**	16	0	610	38.1	63	
1943			6	0	280	46.7	55	

Tom Colella *continued*

Year	Team	No	Bl	Yds	Avg	Lg	NetAvg
1944	CLE N	33	0	1247	37.8	63	
1946	CLE AA	47	0	1895	40.3		
1947		1	0	16	16.0	16	
1948		49	0	1716	35.0		
1949	BUF AA	43	1	1554	36.1		
Career		195	1	7318	37.5	63	
Playoffs		4	0	139	34.8		

Greg Coleman

Year	Team	No	Bl	Yds	Avg	Lg	NetAvg
1977	CLE N	61	0	2389	39.2	58	29.4
1978	MIN N	51	1	1991	39.0	61	30.6
1979		90	1	3551	39.5	70	33.2
1980		81	0	3139	38.8	65	33.6
1981		88	0	3646	41.4	73	34.4
1982		**58**	0	2384	41.1	67	36.0
1983		91	0	3780	41.5	65	36.5
1984		82	0	3473	42.4	62	38.6
1985		67	0	2867	42.8	62	36.7
1986		67	0	2774	41.4	69	34.9
1987		45	1	1786	39.7	54	30.5
1988	WAS N	39	0	1505	38.6	53	29.2
Career		820	3	33285	40.6	73	
Playoffs		19	1	765	40.3		

Gary Collins

Year	Team	No	Bl	Yds	Avg	Lg	NetAvg
1962	CLE N	45	0	1926	42.8	64	
1963		54	0	2160	40.0	73	
1964		48	0	2016	42.0	58	
1965		65	0	3035	**46.7**	71	
1966		57	0	2223	39.0	60	
1967		55	2	2078	37.8	52	
1968		2	0	52	26.0	28	
1969		3	0	112	37.3	59	
1971		5	0	162	32.4	42	
Career		334	2	13764	41.2	73	
Playoffs		14	0	595	42.5		

Rip Collins

Year	Team	No	Bl	Yds	Avg	Lg	NetAvg
1949	CHI AA	41	0	1725	42.1		
1950	BAL N	2	0	91	45.5	46	
1951	GB N	2	0	81	40.5	49	
Career		45	0	1897	42.2	49	

Mickey Colmer

Year	Team	No	Bl	Yds	Avg	Lg	NetAvg
1947	BKN AA	56	0	2504	44.7	69	
1948		54	2	2382	44.1	72	
1949	B-NY AA	5	0	232	46.4		
Career		115	2	5118	44.5	72	

Craig Colquitt

Year	Team	No	Bl	Yds	Avg	Lg	NetAvg
1978	PIT N	66	0	2642	40.0	58	**35.2**
1979		68	0	2733	40.2	61	33.8
1980		61	0	2483	40.7	54	35.5
1981		84	0	3641	43.3	74	35.3
1983		80	0	3352	41.9	58	34.9
1984		70	0	2883	41.2	62	34.7
1987	IND N	2	1	61	30.5	33	18.0
Career		431	1	17795	41.3	74	
Playoffs		26	1	1094	42.1		

Jimmy Colquitt

Year	Team	No	Bl	Yds	Avg	Lg	NetAvg
1985	SEA N	12	0	481	40.1	55	34.3

Irv Comp

Year	Team	No	Bl	Yds	Avg	Lg	NetAvg
1943	GB N	12	0	454	37.8	46	

Dick Compton

Year	Team	No	Bl	Yds	Avg	Lg	NetAvg
1963	DET N	2	0	85	42.5	44	

Merl Condit

Year	Team	No	Bl	Yds	Avg	Lg	NetAvg
1940	PIT N	12		456	38.0	59	
1941	BKN N	1	0	38	38.0	38	
1942		7	0	315	45.0	55	
1943		19	0	724	38.1	58	
Career		39	0	1533	39.3	59	

Fred Cone

Year	Team	No	Bl	Yds	Avg	Lg	NetAvg
1951	GB N	1	0	47	47.0	47	

Charlie Conerly

Year	Team	No	Bl	Yds	Avg	Lg	NetAvg
1948	NYG N	17	0	678	39.9	53	
1949		2	0	70	35.0	36	
1950		20	0	760	38.0	54	

Charlie Conerly *continued*

Year	Team	No	Bl	Yds	Avg	Lg	NetAvg
1951		72	0	2858	39.7	55	
1956		1	0	33	33.0	33	
1960		18	0	634	35.2	59	
Career		130	0	5033	38.7	59	
Playoffs						72	

Mike Connell

Year	Team	No	Bl	Yds	Avg	Lg	NetAvg
1978	SF N	96	1	3583	37.3	59	31.6
1980	WAS N	85	0	3331	39.2	57	33.4
1981		73	0	2923	40.0	57	33.4
Career		254	1	9837	38.7	59	

Ollie Cordill

Year	Team	No	Bl	Yds	Avg	Lg	NetAvg
1967	SD A	3	0	145	48.3	52	
1969	NO N	41	1	1719	41.9	58	
Career		44	1	1864	42.4	58	

Ollie Cordill

Year	Team	No	Bl	Yds	Avg	Lg	NetAvg
1940	CLE N	5		225	45.0	47	

Fred Cox

Year	Team	No	Bl	Yds	Avg	Lg	NetAvg
1963	MIN N	70	0	2707	38.7	57	

Frank Corral

Year	Team	No	Bl	Yds	Avg	Lg	NetAvg
1980	LA N	76	1	3002	39.5	65	33.1
1981		89	0	3735	42.0	67	35.9
Career		165	1	6537	40.8	67	
Playoffs		6	0	236	39.3		

Billy Cox

Year	Team	No	Bl	Yds	Avg	Lg	NetAvg
1951	WAS N	28	0	1120	40.0	61	
1952		5	0	177	35.4	51	
Career		33	0	1297	39.3	61	

Steve Cox

Year	Team	No	Bl	Yds	Avg	Lg	NetAvg
1981	CLE N	68	2	2884	42.4	66	34.2
1982		48	1	1877	39.1	52	31.4
1984		74	2	3213	43.4	69	33.7
1985	WAS N	52	0	2175	41.8	57	32.4
1986		75	0	3271	43.6	58	36.4
1987		63	1	2571	40.8	77	35.0
1988		6	1	221	36.8	55	22.4
Career		386	7	16212	42.0	77	
Playoffs		43	0	1729	40.2		

Milt Crain

Year	Team	No	Bl	Yds	Avg	Lg	NetAvg
1944	BOS N	1	0	40	40.0	40	

Ray Criswell

Year	Team	No	Bl	Yds	Avg	Lg	NetAvg
1987	TB N	26	0	1046	40.2	61	33.8
1988		68	0	2477	36.4	62	32.4
Career		94	0	3523	37.5	62	

Steve Crosby

Year	Team	No	Bl	Yds	Avg	Lg	NetAvg
1974	NYG N	1	0	60	60.0	60	
1975		1	0	28	28.0	28	
Career		2	0	88	44.0	60	

Wayne Crow

Year	Team	No	Bl	Yds	Avg	Lg	NetAvg
1960	OAK A	76	0	2958	38.9		
1961		61		2613	42.8	77	
1962	BUF A	75		2929	39.1	59	
1963		10	0	424	42.4	57	
Career		222	0	8924	40.2	77	

Jim Cunningham

Year	Team	No	Bl	Yds	Avg	Lg	NetAvg
1961	WAS N	1	0	46	46.0	46	

Randall Cunningham

Year	Team	No	Bl	Yds	Avg	Lg	NetAvg
1986	PHI N	2	0	54	27.0	39	25.5
1988		3	0	167	55.7	58	49.7
1989		6	0	319	53.2	91	51.7
1994		1	0	80	80.0	80	80.0
Career		12	0	620	51.7	91	
Playoffs		1	0	20	20.0	20	

Bill Daley

Year	Team	No	Bl	Yds	Avg	Lg	NetAvg
1948	NY AA	1	0	41	41.0	41	

Brad Daluiso

Year	Team	No	Bl	Yds	Avg	Lg	NetAvg
1992	DEN N	10	0	467	46.7	67	40.7

Boley Dancewicz

Year	Team	No	Bl	Yds	Avg	Lg	NetAvg
1947	BOS N	1	0	40	40.0	40	

Ed Danowski

Year	Team	No	Bl	Yds	Avg	Lg	NetAvg
1939	NYG N	29		1102	38.0	56	
1941		2	0	73	36.5	40	
Career		31	0	1125	37.9	56	
Playoffs		10	1	407	40.7		

Cotton Davidson

Year	Team	No	Bl	Yds	Avg	Lg	NetAvg
1954	BAL N	71	1	2680	37.7	55	
1957		47	0	1664	35.4	56	
1960	DAL A	58	0	2287	39.4	66	
1961		61	1	2479	40.6	62	
1962	OAK A	40	1	1569	39.2	64	
Career		277	3	10679	38.6	66	

Bob Davis

Year	Team	No	Bl	Yds	Avg	Lg	NetAvg
1944	BOS N	3	0	60	20.0	26	
1945		3	0	123	41.0	56	
Career		6	0	183	30.5	56	

Corby Davis

Year	Team	No	Bl	Yds	Avg	Lg	NetAvg
1939	CLE N	10		390	39.0	58	
1941		2	0	75	37.5	38	
1942		7	0	275	39.3	49	
Career		19	0	740	38.9	58	

Greg Davis

Year	Team	No	Bl	Yds	Avg	Lg	NetAvg
1987	ATL N	6	0	191	31.8	55	27.5
1992	PHX N	4	0	167	41.8	52	36.8
Career		10	0	358	35.8	55	

Tommy Davis

Year	Team	No	Bl	Yds	Avg	Lg	NetAvg
1959	SF N	59	0	2694	45.7	71	
1960		62	0	2737	44.1	74	
1961		50	0	2269	45.4	67	
1962		48	0	2188	45.6	82	
1963		71	2	3311	46.6	64	
1964		79	0	3599	45.6	68	
1965		54	0	2471	45.8	65	
1966		63	0	2609	41.4	60	
1969		23	0	955	41.5	55	
Career		509	2	22833	44.9	82	

Eagle Day

Year	Team	No	Bl	Yds	Avg	Lg	NetAvg
1960	WAS N	59	0	2476	42.0	56	

Case deBruijn

Year	Team	No	Bl	Yds	Avg	Lg	NetAvg
1982	KC N	5	0	174	34.8	56	16.6

Bill deCorrevont

Year	Team	No	Bl	Yds	Avg	Lg	NetAvg
1946	DET N	5	0	293	58.6	81	

Al Del Greco

Year	Team	No	Bl	Yds	Avg	Lg	NetAvg
1995	HOU N	1	0	15	15.0	15	15.0

Jerry DePoyster

Year	Team	No	Bl	Yds	Avg	Lg	NetAvg
1968	DET N	71	0	2868	40.4	60	
1971	OAK N	51	0	2013	39.5	56	
1972		52	3	2031	39.1	57	
Career		174	3	6912	39.7	60	
Playoffs		7	0	316	45.1		

Dan DeSantis

Year	Team	No	Bl	Yds	Avg	Lg	NetAvg
1941	PHI N	7	0	206	29.4	45	

Dick Deschaine

Year	Team	No	Bl	Yds	Avg	Lg	NetAvg
1955	GB N	56	0	2420	43.2	73	
1956		62	0	2649	42.7	57	
1957		61	2	2645	43.4	71	
1958	CLE N	50	0	2063	41.3	63	
Career		229	2	9777	42.7	73	
Playoffs		8	0	304	38.0		

Bucky Dilts

Year	Team	No	Bl	Yds	Avg	Lg	NetAvg
1977	DEN N	90	0	3525	39.2	63	33.6
1978		96	0	3494	36.4	73	32.8
1979	BAL N	99	2	3657	36.9	53	32.3
Career		285	2	10676	37.5	73	
Playoffs		19	0	708	37.3		

Joe DiVito

Year	Team	No	Bl	Yds	Avg	Lg	NetAvg
1968	DEN A	7	1	242	34.6	47	

Glenn Dobbs

Year	Team		No	Bl	Yds	Avg	Lg	NetAvg
1946	BKN	AA	78	2	3824	**49.0**	78	
1947	BKN-LA	AA	42	2	1909	45.5		
1948	LA	AA	65	3	**3336**	**51.3**	80	
1949			39	0	1650	42.3		
Career			224	7	10719	47.9	80	

Les Dodson

Year	Team		No	Bl	Yds	Avg	Lg	NetAvg
1941	PIT	N	1	0	34	34.0	34	

Al Donelli

Year	Team		No	Bl	Yds	Avg	Lg	NetAvg
1941	PIT	N	1	0	41	41.0	41	

Rick Donnelly

Year	Team		No	Bl	Yds	Avg	Lg	NetAvg
1985	ATL	N	59	0	2574	43.6	68	37.5
1986			78	1	3421	43.9	71	35.0
1987			61	2	2686	**44.0**	62	32.1
1988			**98**	0	3920	40.0	61	35.7
1990	SEA	N	67	0	2722	40.6	54	34.4
1991			13	0	505	38.8	57	33.8
Career			376	3	15828	42.1	71	

Dan Doornink

Year	Team		No	Bl	Yds	Avg	Lg	NetAvg
1982	SEA	N	1	0	54	54.0	54	54.0

Al Dorow

Year	Team		No	Bl	Yds	Avg	Lg	NetAvg
1960	NY	A	6		264	44.0		

Boyd Dowler

Year	Team		No	Bl	Yds	Avg	Lg	NetAvg
1960	GB	N	16	2	690	43.1	61	
1961			38	0	1676	44.1	75	
1962			36	0	1550	43.1	75	
1969			1	0	34	34.0	34	
Career			91	2	3950	43.4	75	
Playoffs			5	0	208	41.6		

Doug Dressler

Year	Team		No	Bl	Yds	Avg	Lg	NetAvg
1971	CIN	N	1	0	34	34.0	34	
1975	KC	N	4	0	100	25.0	30	
Career			5	0	134	26.8	34	

Bill Dudley

Year	Team		No	Bl	Yds	Avg	Lg	NetAvg
1942	PIT	N	17	1	576	33.9	52	
1945			2	1	36	18.0	36	
1946			59	1	2408	40.8	69	
1947	DET	N	15	0	657	43.8	62	
1948			23	0	826	35.9	68	
1949			31	1	1277	41.2	55	
1950	WAS	N	14	0	585	41.8	60	
1951			27	0	942	34.9	46	
Career			188	4	7307	38.9	69	

Dave Dunaway

Year	Team		No	Bl	Yds	Avg	Lg	NetAvg
1969	NYG	N	13	0	497	38.2	52	

Ken Duncan

Year	Team		No	Bl	Yds	Avg	Lg	NetAvg
1971	GB	N	6	0	216	36.0	47	

Rick Duncan

Year	Team		No	Bl	Yds	Avg	Lg	NetAvg
1968	PHI	N	5	0	228	45.6	55	
1969	DET	N	3	0	77	25.7	29	
Career			8	0	305	38.1	55	

L.G. Dupre

Year	Team		No	Bl	Yds	Avg	Lg	NetAvg
1956	BAL	N	25	0	952	38.1	54	
1957			3	0	75	25.0	38	
1958			1	0	0	0.0	0	
Career			29	0	1027	35.4	54	

Don Durdan

Year	Team		No	Bl	Yds	Avg	Lg	NetAvg
1946	SF	AA	6	0	239	39.8	66	

Kay Eakin

Year	Team		No	Bl	Yds	Avg	Lg	NetAvg
1940	NYG	N	11		451	41.0	68	
1941			20	0	948	47.4	71	
1946	MIA	AA	36	1	1532	42.6	67	
Career			67	1	2931	43.7	71	

Vic Eaton

Year	Team		No	Bl	Yds	Avg	Lg	NetAvg
1955	PIT	N	66	0	2522	38.2	57	

Shayne Edge

Year	Team		No	Bl	Yds	Avg	Lg	NetAvg
1996	PIT	N	17	0	675	39.7	48	34.1

Charley Eikenberg

Year	Team		No	Bl	Yds	Avg	Lg	NetAvg
1948	CHIC	N	2	0	72	36.0	38	

Mike Eischeid

Year	Team		No	Bl	Yds	Avg	Lg	NetAvg
1966	OAK	A	64	1	2703	42.2	56	
1967			75	1	3364	44.9	62	
1968			64	0	2788	43.6	72	
1969			69	0	2944	42.7	58	
1970	OAK	N	78	1	3121	40.0	57	
1971			11	0	461	41.9	57	
1972	MIN	N	61	1	2651	43.5	61	
1973			66	0	2628	39.8	57	
1974			72	1	2636	36.6	50	
Career			560	5	23296	41.6	72	
Playoffs			72	1	2978	41.4		

Jason Elam

Year	Team		No	Bl	Yds	Avg	Lg	NetAvg
1995	DEN	N	1	0	17	17.0	17	17.0

Jim Elliott

Year	Team		No	Bl	Yds	Avg	Lg	NetAvg
1967	PIT	N	70	2	2744	39.2	55	

Doug Elmore

Year	Team		No	Bl	Yds	Avg	Lg	NetAvg
1962	WAS	N	54	0	1860	34.4	52	

John Elway

Year	Team		No	Bl	Yds	Avg	Lg	NetAvg
1987	DEN	N	1	0	31	31.0	31	31.0
1988			3	0	117	39.0	40	39.0
1989			1	0	34	34.0	34	14.0
1990			1	0	37	37.0	37	17.0
1991			1	0	34	34.0	34	14.0
Career			7	0	253	36.1	40	
Playoffs			4	0	85	21.3		

Rick Engels

Year	Team		No	Bl	Yds	Avg	Lg	NetAvg
1976	SEA	N	80	2	3067	38.3	55	29.9
1977	SEA-PIT	N	9	1	306	34.0	48	25.3
1978	PHI	N	33	1	1307	39.6	53	30.6
Career			122	4	4680	38.4	55	
Playoffs			5	1	204	40.8		

Keith English

Year	Team		No	Bl	Yds	Avg	Lg	NetAvg
1990	LARM	N	68	1	2663	39.2	56	31.9

Russell Erxleben

Year	Team		No	Bl	Yds	Avg	Lg	NetAvg
1979	NO	N	4	0	148	37.0	40	31.5
1980			89	0	3499	39.3	57	33.1
1981			66	0	2672	40.5	60	34.4
1982			46	0	1976	43.0	60	35.2
1983			74	0	3034	41.0	60	30.9
1987	DET	N	1	0	52	52.0	52	52.0
Career			280	0	11381	40.6	60	

Len Eshmont

Year	Team		No	Bl	Yds	Avg	Lg	NetAvg
1941	NYG	N	11	0	340	30.9	66	

Boomer Esiason

Year	Team		No	Bl	Yds	Avg	Lg	NetAvg
1986	CIN	N	1	0	31	31.0	31	31.0
1987			2	0	68	34.0	41	28.0
1988			1	0	21	21.0	21	21.0
Career			4	0	120	30.0	41	

Sam Etcheverry

Year	Team		No	Bl	Yds	Avg	Lg	NetAvg
1962	STL	N	58	1	2259	38.9	61	

Fred Evans

Year	Team		No	Bl	Yds	Avg	Lg	NetAvg
1946	CLE	AA	8	0	296	37.0		
1947	CHI	AA	2	0	73	36.5		
Career			10	0	369	36.9		

Johnny Evans

Year	Team		No	Bl	Yds	Avg	Lg	NetAvg
1978	CLE	N	79	0	3089	39.1	65	32.4
1979			69	2	2844	41.2	59	32.2
1980			66	0	2530	38.3	56	32.5
Career			214	2	8463	39.5	65	
Playoffs			6	0	237	39.5		

Ray Evans

Year	Team		No	Bl	Yds	Avg	Lg	NetAvg
1948	PIT	N	0	1	0		0	

Julian Fagan

Year	Team		No	Bl	Yds	Avg	Lg	NetAvg
1970	NO	N	75	2	3269	43.6	64	
1971			77	0	3188	41.4	64	
1972			70	1	2899	41.4	71	

Julian Fagan *continued*

Year	Team		No	Bl	Yds	Avg	Lg	NetAvg
1973	NYJ	N	72	2	2744	38.1	58	
Career			294	5	12100	41.2	71	

Art Faircloth

Year	Team		No	Bl	Yds	Avg	Lg	NetAvg
1947	NYG	N	4	0	159	39.8	45	

George Faust

Year	Team		No	Bl	Yds	Avg	Lg	NetAvg
1939	CHIC	N	25		1100	**44.0**	63	

Jeff Feagles

Year	Team		No	Bl	Yds	Avg	Lg	NetAvg
1988	NE	N	91	0	3482	38.3	74	34.1
1989			63	1	2392	38.0	64	31.3
1990	PHI	N	72	2	3026	42.0	60	35.5
1991			**87**	1	3640	41.8	77	34.0
1992			82	0	3459	42.2	68	36.9
1993			83	0	3323	40.0	60	35.3
1994	ARI	N	**98**	0	3997	40.8	54	36.0
1995			72	0	3150	43.8	60	38.2
1996			76	1	3328	43.8	68	36.4
Career			724	5	29797	41.2	77	
Playoffs			19	0	816	42.9		

Beattie Feathers

Year	Team		No	Bl	Yds	Avg	Lg	NetAvg
Playoffs			1	0	56	56.0	56	

Chuck Fenenbock

Year	Team		No	Bl	Yds	Avg	Lg	NetAvg
1943	DET	N	4	0	184	46.0	56	
1945			29	0	1079	37.2	57	
Career			33	0	1263	38.3	57	

Frank Filchock

Year	Team		No	Bl	Yds	Avg	Lg	NetAvg
1941	WAS	N	1	0	35	35.0	35	

Jim Finks

Year	Team		No	Bl	Yds	Avg	Lg	NetAvg
1952	PIT	N	4	0	156	39.0	50	

Dave Finzer

Year	Team		No	Bl	Yds	Avg	Lg	NetAvg
1984	CHI	N	83	2	3328	40.1	87	35.3
1985	SEA	N	68	0	2766	40.7	61	34.6
Career			151	2	6094	40.4	87	
Playoffs			12	0	499	41.6		

Lee Folkins

Year	Team		No	Bl	Yds	Avg	Lg	NetAvg
1964	DAL	N	15	0	497	33.1	48	

Bob Forte

Year	Team		No	Bl	Yds	Avg	Lg	NetAvg
1950	GB	N	3	0	107	35.7	39	

Terry Fox

Year	Team		No	Bl	Yds	Avg	Lg	NetAvg
1946	MIA	AA	2	0	88	44.0		

Sam Francis

Year	Team		No	Bl	Yds	Avg	Lg	NetAvg
1939	PIT-BKN	N	13		494	38.0	52	
1940	BKN	N	16		720	45.0	69	
Career			29		1214	41.9	69	
Playoffs			1	0	63	63.0	63	

George Franck

Year	Team		No	Bl	Yds	Avg	Lg	NetAvg
1941	NYG	N	18	0	716	39.8	70	
1945			22	0	832	37.8	57	
1946			16	0	624	39.0	53	
1947			7	0	297	42.4	54	
Career			63	0	2467	39.2	70	

Bobby Franklin

Year	Team		No	Bl	Yds	Avg	Lg	NetAvg
1964	CLE	N	1	0	36	36.0	36	
1965			4	0	118	29.5	31	
Career			5	0	154	30.8	36	

Tony Franklin

Year	Team		No	Bl	Yds	Avg	Lg	NetAvg
1979	PHI	N	1	0	32	32.0	32	32.0
1981			1	0	13	13.0	13	13.0
Career			2	0	45	22.5	32	

Jim Fraser

Year	Team		No	Bl	Yds	Avg	Lg	NetAvg
1962	DEN	A	54	1	2400	**44.4**	75	
1963			**78**	3	**3595**	**46.1**	66	
1964			72	1	3225	**44.8**	67	
1965	KC	A	3	0	81	27.0	37	
1966	BOS	A	53		2044	38.6	68	
1968	NO	N	11	0	391	35.5	56	
Career			271	5	11736	43.3	75	

Jess Freitas

Year	Team	No	Bl	Yds	Avg	Lg	NetAvg
1947	SF AA	8	0	336	42.0		

Ted Fritsch

Year	Team	No	Bl	Yds	Avg	Lg	NetAvg
1942	GB N	3	0	122	40.7	54	
1943		5	0	151	30.2	47	
1944		10	0	408	40.8	54	
1946		1	0	52	52.0	52	
Career		19	0	733	38.6	54	
Playoffs		4	0	164	41.0		

Kenny Fryer

Year	Team	No	Bl	Yds	Avg	Lg	NetAvg
1944	BKN N	7	0	273	39.0	66	

Dom Fucci

Year	Team	No	Bl	Yds	Avg	Lg	NetAvg
1955	DET N	2	0	72	36.0	55	

Scott Fulhage

Year	Team	No	Bl	Yds	Avg	Lg	NetAvg
1987	CIN N	52	0	2168	41.7	58	35.6
1988		44	2	1672	38.0	53	29.4
1989	ATL N	84	1	3472	41.3	65	33.3
1990		70	0	2913	41.6	59	36.0
1991		81	0	3470	42.8	60	36.6
1992		68	1	2818	41.4	56	33.0
Career		399	4	16513	41.4	65	
Playoffs		5	0	211	42.2		

Monk Gafford

Year	Team	No	Bl	Yds	Avg	Lg	NetAvg
1946	MIA-BKN AA	13	0	524	40.3		

Bobby Gage

Year	Team	No	Bl	Yds	Avg	Lg	NetAvg
1949	PIT N	3	1	163	54.3	63	
1950		3	0	146	48.7	74	
Career		6	1	309	51.5	74	

Hugh Gallarneau

Year	Team	No	Bl	Yds	Avg	Lg	NetAvg
1941	CHIB N	0	1	0		0	

John Galvin

Year	Team	No	Bl	Yds	Avg	Lg	NetAvg
1947	BAL AA	64	2	2377	37.1		

Vince Gamache

Year	Team	No	Bl	Yds	Avg	Lg	NetAvg
1986	SEA N	79	0	3048	38.6	55	33.0
1987	LARI N	13	1	519	39.9	53	33.6
Career		92	1	3567	38.8	55	

Greg Gantt

Year	Team	No	Bl	Yds	Avg	Lg	NetAvg
1974	NYJ N	75	0	2689	35.9	59	
1975		56	3	2156	38.5	71	
Career		131	3	4845	37.0	71	

Frank Garcia

Year	Team	No	Bl	Yds	Avg	Lg	NetAvg
1981	SEA N	2	0	74	37.0	41	37.0
1983	TB N	95	1	4008	42.2	64	33.0
1984		68	0	2849	41.9	60	34.7
1985		77	2	3233	42.0	61	32.8
1986		77	0	3089	40.1	60	32.7
1987		62	0	2409	38.9	58	28.3
Career		381	3	15662	41.1	64	

Chris Gardocki

Year	Team	No	Bl	Yds	Avg	Lg	NetAvg
1992	CHI N	79	0	3393	42.9	61	36.2
1993		80	0	3080	38.5	58	36.6
1994		76	0	2871	37.8	57	32.4
1995	IND N	63	0	2681	42.6	69	33.4
1996		68	0	3105	45.7	61	39.0
Career		366	0	15130	41.3	69	
Playoffs		30	0	1208	40.3		

Mike Garrett

Year	Team	No	Bl	Yds	Avg	Lg	NetAvg
1981	BAL N	78	0	3071	39.4	57	33.7

Roy Gerela

Year	Team	No	Bl	Yds	Avg	Lg	NetAvg
1969	HOU A	41	0	1656	40.4	70	
1972	PIT N	1	0	29	29.0	29	
Career		42	0	1685	40.1	70	

Joe Geri

Year	Team	No	Bl	Yds	Avg	Lg	NetAvg
1949	PIT N	43	0	1856	43.2	82	
1950		55	0	2237	40.7	60	
1951		73	0	2787	38.2	72	
1952	CHIC N	29	0	1093	37.7	47	
Career		200	0	7973	39.9	82	

Ralph Giacomarro

Year	Team	No	Bl	Yds	Avg	Lg	NetAvg
1983	ATL N	70	1	2823	40.3	57	35.0
1984		68	2	2855	42.0	58	32.6
1985		29	0	1157	39.9	52	33.1
1987	DEN N	18	0	757	42.1	50	27.7
Career		185	3	7592	41.0	58	

Donnie Gibbs

Year	Team	No	Bl	Yds	Avg	Lg	NetAvg
1974	NO N	3	0	99	33.0	35	

Tom Gilburg

Year	Team	No	Bl	Yds	Avg	Lg	NetAvg
1961	BAL N	42	0	1804	43.0	61	
1962		57	0	2384	41.8	62	
1963		52	0	2173	41.8	64	
1964		27	0	1106	41.0	58	
1965		54	0	2139	39.6	66	
Career		232	0	9606	41.4	66	
Playoffs		12	0	465	38.8		

Johnny Gildea

Year	Team	No	Bl	Yds	Avg	Lg	NetAvg
Playoffs		1	0	55	55.0		

Horace Gillom

Year	Team	No	Bl	Yds	Avg	Lg	NetAvg
1947	CLE AA	47	0	2096	44.6	74	
1948		6	0	227	37.8		
1949		53	1	2011	37.9		
1950	CLE N	65	1	2849	43.8	75	
1951		73	0	3321	45.5	66	
1952		60	1	2787	46.5	73	
1953		63	0	2760	43.8	67	
1954		52	0	2230	42.9	80	
1955		55	3	2389	43.4	56	
1956		12	0	537	44.8	53	
Career		486	6	21207	43.6	80	
Playoffs		43	0	1780	41.4		

Earl Girard

Year	Team	No	Bl	Yds	Avg	Lg	NetAvg
1948	GB N	8	0	320	40.0	49	
1949		66	3	2691	40.8	72	
1950		69	2	2715	39.3	63	
1951		52	0	2101	40.4	66	
1954	DET N	63	0	2585	41.0	65	
1955		56	0	2310	41.3	65	
1956		10	0	448	44.8	54	
1957	PIT N	68	0	2754	40.5	56	
Career		392	5	15924	40.6	72	

Fred Glatz

Year	Team	No	Bl	Yds	Avg	Lg	NetAvg
1956	PIT N	25	0	984	39.4	60	

Pete Gogolak

Year	Team	No	Bl	Yds	Avg	Lg	NetAvg
1969	NYG N	12	0	491	40.9	61	

Marshall Goldberg

Year	Team	No	Bl	Yds	Avg	Lg	NetAvg
1940	CHIC N	1	0	47	47.0	47	

Kelly Goodburn

Year	Team	No	Bl	Yds	Avg	Lg	NetAvg
1987	KC N	59	0	2412	40.9	55	32.4
1988		76	0	3059	40.3	59	31.9
1989		67	0	2688	40.1	54	33.8
1990	KC-WAS N	28	0	1030	36.8	58	30.7
1991	WAS N	52	3	2070	39.8	61	33.1
1992		64	1	2555	39.9	56	32.7
1993		5	0	197	39.4	49	39.4
Career		351	4	14011	39.9	61	
Playoffs		29	0	1069	36.9		

Owen Goodnight

Year	Team	No	Bl	Yds	Avg	Lg	NetAvg
1941	CLE N	16	0	637	39.8	74	

John Goodson

Year	Team	No	Bl	Yds	Avg	Lg	NetAvg
1982	PIT N	49	0	1981	40.4	66	35.1
Playoffs		2	0	65	32.5		

Bobby Gordon

Year	Team	No	Bl	Yds	Avg	Lg	NetAvg
1958	CHIC N	55	0	2089	38.0	66	

Stacy Gore

Year	Team	No	Bl	Yds	Avg	Lg	NetAvg
1987	MIA N	14	0	502	35.9	60	34.4

Bruce Gossett

Year	Team	No	Bl	Yds	Avg	Lg	NetAvg
1974	SF N	2	0	56	28.0	31	

Jeff Gossett

Year	Team	No	Bl	Yds	Avg	Lg	NetAvg
1981	KC N	29	0	1141	39.3	55	32.9
1982		33	0	1366	41.4	56	30.9
1983	CLE N	70	0	2854	40.8	60	34.1
1985		81	0	3261	40.3	64	34.5
1986		83	0	3423	41.2	61	35.6
1987	CLE-HOU N	44	1	1777	40.4	55	31.6
1988	LARI N	91	0	3804	41.8	58	35.7
1989		67	0	2711	40.5	60	33.9
1990		60	2	2315	38.6	57	33.6
1991		67	0	2961	44.2	61	38.5
1992		77	0	3255	42.3	56	36.5
1993		71	0	2971	41.8	61	35.1
1994		77	0	3377	43.9	65	35.2
1995	OAK N	75	1	3089	41.2	60	34.7
1996		57	0	2264	39.7	64	34.6
Career		982	4	40569	41.3	65	
Playoffs		42	0	1643	39.1		

Paul Governali

Year	Team	No	Bl	Yds	Avg	Lg	NetAvg
1946	BOS N	11	0	481	43.7	65	
1947	NYG N	4	0	142	35.5	42	
Career		15	0	623	41.5	65	

Allen Green

Year	Team	No	Bl	Yds	Avg	Lg	NetAvg
1961	DAL N	60	1	2236	37.3	53	

Bobby Joe Green

Year	Team	No	Bl	Yds	Avg	Lg	NetAvg
1960	PIT N	63	1	2829	44.9	75	
1961		73	0	3431	47.0	71	
1962	CHI N	69	0	3018	43.7	72	
1963		64	0	2974	46.5	66	
1964		71	0	3161	44.5	62	
1965		58	0	2479	42.7	66	
1966		80	0	3358	42.0	69	
1967		79	0	3392	42.9	68	
1968		26	1	1142	43.9	58	
1969		75	1	2964	39.5	59	
1970		83	0	3395	40.9	56	
1971		77	0	3095	40.2	60	
1972		67	0	2758	41.2	58	
1973		82	0	3321	40.5	62	
Career		967	3	41317	42.7	75	
Playoffs		7	0	293	41.9		

Dave Green

Year	Team	No	Bl	Yds	Avg	Lg	NetAvg
1973	HOU N	22	0	868	39.5	61	
1974	CIN N	66	0	2701	40.9	53	
1975		67	1	2655	39.3	57	
1976	TB N	92	0	3619	39.3	56	30.5
1977		98	1	3948	40.3	70	33.9
1978		100	2	4092	40.9	61	33.0
Career		445	4	17883	40.2	70	
Playoffs		6	0	215	35.8		

Johnny Green

Year	Team	No	Bl	Yds	Avg	Lg	NetAvg
1962	NY A	3		121	40.3	55	

Tom Greene

Year	Team	No	Bl	Yds	Avg	Lg	NetAvg
1960	BOS A	59		2235	37.9		

Russell Griffith

Year	Team	No	Bl	Yds	Avg	Lg	NetAvg
1987	SEA N	11	0	386	35.1	51	29.9

Johnny Grigas

Year	Team	No	Bl	Yds	Avg	Lg	NetAvg
1944	C-P N	12	0	421	35.1	64	
1946	BOS N	1	0	45	45.0	45	
Career		13	0	466	35.8	64	

George Grimes

Year	Team	No	Bl	Yds	Avg	Lg	NetAvg
1948	DET N	27	1	969	35.9	56	

Rex Grossman

Year	Team	No	Bl	Yds	Avg	Lg	NetAvg
1949	BAL AA	28	0	1087	38.8	68	

Bob Grupp

Year	Team	No	Bl	Yds	Avg	Lg	NetAvg
1979	KC N	89	1	3883	43.6	74	37.2
1980		84	1	3317	39.5	57	33.7
1981		41	0	1556	38.0	57	33.4
Career		214	2	8756	40.9	74	

Al Grygo

Year	Team	No	Bl	Yds	Avg	Lg	NetAvg
1944	CHIB N	4	0	123	30.8	39	

Al Grygo *continued*

Year	Team		No	Bl	Yds	Avg	Lg	NetAvg
1945			2	0	86	43.0	46	
Career			6	0	209	34.8	46	

Scotty Gudmundson

Year	Team		No	Bl	Yds	Avg	Lg	NetAvg
1944	**BOS**	**N**	11	1	402	36.5	55	
1945			17	0	612	36.0	52	
Career			28	1	1014	36.2	55	

George Gulyanics

Year	Team		No	Bl	Yds	Avg	Lg	NetAvg
1947	**CHIB**	**N**	23	0	1031	44.8	56	
1948			55	0	2242	40.8	70	
1949			29	0	1369	**47.2**	69	
1950			5	1	201	40.2	51	
Career			112	1	4843	43.2	70	

Ray Guy

Year	Team		No	Bl	Yds	Avg	Lg	NetAvg
1973	**OAK**	**N**	69	0	3127	45.3	72	
1974			74	0	3124	42.2	66	
1975			68	0	2979	43.8	64	
1976			67	0	2785	41.6	66	33.1
1977			59	0	2552	**43.3**	74	34.8
1978			81	2	3462	42.7	69	34.6
1979			69	1	2939	42.6	71	33.8
1980			71	0	3099	43.6	66	35.9
1981			96	0	4195	43.7	69	35.2
1982	**LARI**	**N**	47	0	1839	39.1	57	36.3
1983			78	0	3336	42.8	67	35.9
1984			91	0	3809	41.9	63	35.4
1985			89	0	3627	40.8	68	36.3
1986			90	0	3620	40.2	64	33.8
Career			1049	3	44493	42.4	74	
Playoffs			**111**	1	**4705**	**42.4**		

Dale Hackbart

Year	Team		No	Bl	Yds	Avg	Lg	NetAvg
1962	**WAS**	**N**	2	0	78	39.0	42	

John Hadl

Year	Team		No	Bl	Yds	Avg	Lg	NetAvg
1963	**SD**	**A**	2	0	75	37.5	38	
1964			62	0	2447	39.5	71	
1965			38	0	1544	40.6	65	
1967			2	0	70	35.0	46	
1970	**SD**	**N**	1	0	30	30.0	30	
Career			105	0	4166	39.7	71	
Playoffs			10	0	439	43.9		

Ali Haji-Sheikh

Year	Team		No	Bl	Yds	Avg	Lg	NetAvg
1984	**NYG**	**N**	0	1	0		0	

Irv Hall

Year	Team		No	Bl	Yds	Avg	Lg	NetAvg
1942	**PHI**	**N**	1	0	36	36.0	36	

Ken Hall

Year	Team		No	Bl	Yds	Avg	Lg	NetAvg
1960	**HOU**	**A**	6	0	210	35.0		
1961			8	0	238	29.8	50	
Career			14	0	448	32.0	50	

Parker Hall

Year	Team		No	Bl	Yds	Avg	Lg	NetAvg
1939	**CLE**	**N**	**58**		2366	40.8	80	
1940			**57**		2297	43.0	75	
1941			**49**	0	1965	40.1	67	
1942			36	0	1397	38.8	67	
Career			200	0	8025	40.1	80	

Chuck Hanneman

Year	Team		No	Bl	Yds	Avg	Lg	NetAvg
1939	**DET**	**N**	1	0	31	31.0	31	

Brian Hansen

Year	Team		No	Bl	Yds	Avg	Lg	NetAvg
1984	**NO**	**N**	69	1	3020	43.8	66	33.3
1985			89	0	3763	42.3	58	36.5
1986			81	1	3456	42.7	66	36.6
1987			52	0	2104	40.5	60	35.6
1988			72	1	2913	40.5	64	34.3
1990	**NE**	**N**	**90**	2	**3752**	41.7	69	33.6
1991	**CLE**	**N**	80	0	3397	42.5	65	36.1
1992			74	1	3083	41.7	73	36.1
1993			82	2	3632	44.3	72	35.6
1994	**NYJ**	**N**	84	0	3534	42.1	64	36.1
1995			**99**	1	**4090**	41.3	67	31.9
1996			74	0	3311	44.7	69	36.8
Career			946	9	40055	42.3	73	
Playoffs			6	0	265	44.2		

Jason Hanson

Year	Team		No	Bl	Yds	Avg	Lg	NetAvg
1995	**DET**	**N**	1	0	34	34.0	34	14.0
1996			1	0	24	24.0	24	24.0
Career			2	0	58	29.0	34	

Merle Hapes

Year	Team		No	Bl	Yds	Avg	Lg	NetAvg
1942	**NYG**	**N**	15	0	557	37.1	52	
1946			11	1	479	43.5	60	
Career			26	1	1036	39.8	60	

Jim Hardy

Year	Team		No	Bl	Yds	Avg	Lg	NetAvg
1946	**LA**	**N**	5	0	209	41.8	47	
1947			10	0	263	26.3	45	
1948			3	0	151	50.3	77	
1949	**CHIC**	**N**	5	0	180	36.0	51	
1950			55	1	2206	40.1	76	
Career			78	1	3009	38.1	77	

Eddie Hare

Year	Team		No	Bl	Yds	Avg	Lg	NetAvg
1979	**NE**	**N**	83	1	3038	36.6	58	29.8

Ken Hartley

Year	Team		No	Bl	Yds	Avg	Lg	NetAvg
1981	**NE**	**N**	9	0	266	29.6	41	25.0

Dale Hatcher

Year	Team		No	Bl	Yds	Avg	Lg	NetAvg
1985	**LARM**	**N**	87	1	3761	43.2	67	**38.0**
1986			97	1	3740	38.6	57	32.9
1987			76	1	**3140**	41.3	62	35.6
1988			36	0	1424	39.6	54	33.4
1989			73	1	2834	38.8	54	32.1
1991			63	0	2403	38.1	52	32.9
1993	**MIA**	**N**	58	0	2304	39.7	56	32.2
Career			490	4	19606	40.0	67	
Playoffs			44	0	1672	38.0		

Jeff Hayes

Year	Team		No	Bl	Yds	Avg	Lg	NetAvg
1982	**WAS**	**N**	51	1	1937	38.0	58	33.3
1983			72	0	2796	38.8	56	32.6
1984			72	1	2834	39.4	59	34.9
1985			16	0	685	42.8	55	36.1
1986	**CIN**	**N**	56	2	1965	35.1	52	29.7
1987	**MIA**	**N**	7	1	274	39.1	51	30.1
Career			274	5	10491	38.3	59	
Playoffs			35	1	1282	36.6		

Hall Haynes

Year	Team		No	Bl	Yds	Avg	Lg	NetAvg
1950	**WAS**	**N**	19	0	756	39.8	52	

Bob Hazelhurst

Year	Team		No	Bl	Yds	Avg	Lg	NetAvg
1948	**BOS**	**N**	2	0	101	50.5	68	

Ken Heineman

Year	Team		No	Bl	Yds	Avg	Lg	NetAvg
1940	**CLE**	**N**	2		64	32.0	34	
1943	**BKN**	**N**	14	0	484	34.6	54	
Career			16	0	548	34.3	54	

Barry Helton

Year	Team		No	Bl	Yds	Avg	Lg	NetAvg
1988	**SF**	**N**	78	1	3069	39.3	53	32.2
1989			55	1	2226	40.5	56	31.2
1990			69	1	2537	36.8	56	30.9
1991	**LARM**	**N**	11	1	453	41.2	46	29.3
Career			213	4	8285	38.9	56	
Playoffs			35	0	1288	36.8		

Craig Hentrich

Year	Team		No	Bl	Yds	Avg	Lg	NetAvg
1994	**GB**	**N**	81	0	3351	41.4	70	35.5
1995			65	2	2740	42.2	61	34.6
1996			68	0	2886	42.4	65	36.3
Career			214	2	8977	41.9	70	
Playoffs			36	0	1511	42.0		

Arnie Herber

Year	Team		No	Bl	Yds	Avg	Lg	NetAvg
1939	**GB**	**N**	24		960	40.0	74	
1940			13		507	39.0	55	
1944	**NYG**	**N**	1	0	39	39.0	39	
1945			1	0	51	51.0	51	
Career			39	0	1557	39.9	74	
Playoffs			6	0	231	38.5		

Alan Herline

Year	Team		No	Bl	Yds	Avg	Lg	NetAvg
1987	**NE**	**N**	25	1	861	34.4	50	27.6

Efren Herrera

Year	Team		No	Bl	Yds	Avg	Lg	NetAvg
1976	**DAL**	**N**	2	0	49	24.5	27	24.5
1977			2	0	44	22.0	28	22.0
1978	**SEA**	**N**	3	0	73	24.3	30	24.3
1979			1	0	36	36.0	36	16.0
1980			1	0	29	29.0	29	29.0
Career			9	0	231	25.7	36	

George Herring

Year	Team		No	Bl	Yds	Avg	Lg	NetAvg
1960	**DEN**	**A**	70		2610	37.3		
1961			80	0	3149	39.4	63	
Career			150	0	5759	38.4	63	

Ralph Heywood

Year	Team		No	Bl	Yds	Avg	Lg	NetAvg
1946	**CHI**	**AA**	2	0	57	28.5		
1948	**DET-BO**	**N**	46	0	1766	38.4	53	
1949	**NYB**	**N**	20	0	698	34.9	53	
Career			68	0	2521	37.1	53	

King Hill

Year	Team		No	Bl	Yds	Avg	Lg	NetAvg
1959	**CHIC**	**N**	3	0	118	39.3	47	
1960	**STL**	**N**	5	0	198	39.6	50	
1961	**PHI**	**N**	55	0	2403	43.7	64	
1962			64	0	2747	42.9	80	
1963			69	0	2972	43.1	62	
1964			24	0	968	40.3	56	
1965			19	0	813	42.8	55	
1966			23	0	862	37.5	51	
1968	**MIN**	**N**	33	0	1354	41.0	53	
1969	**STL**	**N**	72	1	2746	38.1	57	
Career			367	1	15181	37.1	80	
Playoffs			6	0	238	39.7		

Clarke Hinkle

Year	Team		No	Bl	Yds	Avg	Lg	NetAvg
1939	**GB**	**N**	43	0	1750	40.7	65	
1940			22	0	818	37.2	59	
1941			22	0	979	44.5	63	
Career			87	0	3597	40.8	65	
Playoffs			11	3	397	36.1		

Jack Hinkle

Year	Team		No	Bl	Yds	Avg	Lg	NetAvg
1943	**P-P**	**N**	2	2	78	39.0	45	

Joe Hoague

Year	Team		No	Bl	Yds	Avg	Lg	NetAvg
1941	**PIT**	**N**	17	0	631	37.1	55	
1942			2	0	88	44.0	45	
Career			19	0	719	37.8	55	

Billy Joe Hobert

Year	Team		No	Bl	Yds	Avg	Lg	NetAvg
1996	**OAK**	**N**	9	0	371	41.2	53	35.1

Dick Hoerner

Year	Team		No	Bl	Yds	Avg	Lg	NetAvg
1949	**LA**	**N**	1	0	43	43.0	43	

Bob Hoernschemeyer

Year	Team		No	Bl	Yds	Avg	Lg	NetAvg
1946	**CHI**	**AA**	11	0	484	44.0	72	
1947	**BKN**	**AA**	1	1	56	56.0		
1948			1	0	40	40.0	40	
1949	**CHI**	**AA**	4	0	195	48.8		
1950	**DET**	**N**	4	0	147	36.8	42	
Career			21	1	922	43.9	72	

Ed Holler

Year	Team		No	Bl	Yds	Avg	Lg	NetAvg
1964	**PIT**	**N**	31	0	1334	43.0	64	

Gus Holloman

Year	Team		No	Bl	Yds	Avg	Lg	NetAvg
1969	**DEN**	**A**	46	1	1868	40.6	57	

Mitch Hoopes

Year	Team		No	Bl	Yds	Avg	Lg	NetAvg
1975	**DAL**	**N**	67	1	2676	39.9	55	
1976	**SD-HOU**	**N**	49	2	1849	37.7	57	25.6
1977	**DET**	**N**	6	1	235	39.2	48	19.6
Career			122	4	4760	39.0	57	
Playoffs			16	1	615	38.4		

Harry Hopp

Year	Team		No	Bl	Yds	Avg	Lg	NetAvg
1941	**DET**	**N**	2	0	84	42.0	50	
1942			27	0	1099	40.7	52	
1943			42	0	1643	39.1	60	
1946	**BUF**	**AA**	13	2	461	35.5		
Career			84	2	3287	39.1	60	

Mike Horan

Year	Team		No	Bl	Yds	Avg	Lg	NetAvg
1984	PHI	N	92	0	3880	42.2	69	35.6
1985			91	0	3777	41.5	75	34.2
1986	DEN	N	21	0	864	41.1	50	34.5
1987			44	2	1807	41.1	61	33.1
1988			65	0	2861	44.0	70	**37.8**
1989			77	0	3111	40.4	63	34.3
1990			58	1	2575	**44.4**	67	**38.9**
1991			72	1	3012	41.8	71	36.7
1992			37	1	1681	45.4	62	40.2
1993	NYG	N	44	0	1882	42.8	60	**39.9**
1994			85	2	3521	41.4	63	35.3
1995			72	0	3063	42.5	60	36.2
1996			**102**	0	**4289**	42.0	63	35.9
Career			860	7	36323	42.2	75	
Playoffs			58	0	2361	40.7		

Dick Horn

Year	Team		No	Bl	Yds	Avg	Lg	NetAvg
1958	BAL	N	19	0	613	32.3	48	

Greg Horne

Year	Team		No	Bl	Yds	Avg	Lg	NetAvg
1987	CIN-STL	N	43	0	1730	40.2	57	31.5
1988	PHX	N	79	1	3228	40.9	66	32.9
Career			122	1	4958	40.6	66	

Sam Horner

Year	Team		No	Bl	Yds	Avg	Lg	NetAvg
1960	WAS	N	1	0	48	48.0	48	
1961			63	0	2409	38.2	62	
Career			64	0	2457	38.4	62	

Chuck Howley

Year	Team		No	Bl	Yds	Avg	Lg	NetAvg
1964	DAL	N	1	0	37	37.0	37	

Mike Hubach

Year	Team		No	Bl	Yds	Avg	Lg	NetAvg
1980	NE	N	63	0	2392	38.0	69	33.6
1981			19	0	726	38.2	56	31.1
Career			82	0	3118	38.0	69	

George Hunt

Year	Team		No	Bl	Yds	Avg	Lg	NetAvg
1975	NYG	N	9	0	218	24.2	35	

Jackie Hunt

Year	Team		No	Bl	Yds	Avg	Lg	NetAvg
1945	CHIB	N	2	0	54	27.0	34	

Michael Husted

Year	Team		No	Bl	Yds	Avg	Lg	NetAvg
1994	TB	N	2	0	53	26.5	32	22.0

Bill Hutchinson

Year	Team		No	Bl	Yds	Avg	Lg	NetAvg
1942	NYG	N	2	0	65	32.5	39	

Tom Hutton

Year	Team		No	Bl	Yds	Avg	Lg	NetAvg
1995	PHI	N	85	1	3682	43.3	63	33.7
1996			73	1	3107	42.6	60	35.1
Career			158	2	6789	43.0	63	
Playoffs			17	0	681	40.1		

Hank Ilesic

Year	Team		No	Bl	Yds	Avg	Lg	NetAvg
1989	SD	N	76	0	3049	40.1	64	32.9

Cecil Isbell

Year	Team		No	Bl	Yds	Avg	Lg	NetAvg
1939	GB	N	4		124	31.0	39	
1940			2		64	32.0	37	
1942			4	0	141	35.3	46	
Career			10	0	329	32.9	46	
Playoffs			0	1	0			

Rusty Jackson

Year	Team		No	Bl	Yds	Avg	Lg	NetAvg
1976	LA	N	77	2	3006	39.0	61	33.0
1978	BUF	N	87	2	3373	38.8	70	30.9
1979			96	0	3671	38.2	60	30.2
Career			260	4	10050	38.7	70	
Playoffs			13	3	459	35.3		

Dave Jacobs

Year	Team		No	Bl	Yds	Avg	Lg	NetAvg
1987	PHI	N	10	1	369	36.9	44	30.5

Jack Jacobs

Year	Team		No	Bl	Yds	Avg	Lg	NetAvg
1942	CLE	N	33	0	1066	42.3	66	
1945			1	0	43	43.0	43	
1946	WAS	N	10	0	428	42.8	61	
1947	GB	N	56	1	2480	44.3	74	
1948			68	1	2782	40.9	78	
1949			17	0	757	44.5	58	
Career			185	2	7556	40.8	78	

Dick James

Year	Team		No	Bl	Yds	Avg	Lg	NetAvg
1961	WAS	N	6	0	210	35.0	51	
1964	NYG	N	1	0	35	35.0	35	
Career			7	0	245	35.0	51	

John James

Year	Team		No	Bl	Yds	Avg	Lg	NetAvg
1972	ATL	N	61	0	2609	42.8	59	
1973			63	0	2682	42.6	72	
1974			95	1	**3891**	41.0	61	
1975			88	1	3696	42.0	75	
1976			**101**	0	**4253**	42.1	67	**36.2**
1977			**105**	0	**4349**	41.4	61	34.0
1978			**109**	1	**4227**	38.8	57	34.0
1979			83	1	3296	39.7	62	35.2
1980			79	0	3087	39.1	59	34.3
1981			87	1	3543	40.7	62	32.6
1982	DET-HOU	N	43	0	1741	40.5	56	34.1
1983	HOU	N	79	1	3136	39.7	53	32.8
1984			88	0	3482	39.6	55	31.4
Career			1081	6	43992	40.7	75	
Playoffs			17	0	601	35.4		

Len Janiak

Year	Team		No	Bl	Yds	Avg	Lg	NetAvg
1940	CLE	N	1	0	30	30.0	30	

Tommy Janik

Year	Team		No	Bl	Yds	Avg	Lg	NetAvg
1964	DEN	A	10		374	37.4	49	
1969	BOS	A	70	0	2903	41.5	56	
1970	BOS	N	85	1	3364	39.6	57	
1971	NE	N	87	0	3249	37.3	58	
Career			252	1	9890	39.2	58	

Vic Janowicz

Year	Team		No	Bl	Yds	Avg	Lg	NetAvg
1954	WAS	N	1	0	32	32.0	32	

Toimi Jarvi

Year	Team		No	Bl	Yds	Avg	Lg	NetAvg
1945	PIT	N	2	0	69	34.5	38	

Billy Jefferson

Year	Team		No	Bl	Yds	Avg	Lg	NetAvg
1941	DET	N	20	0	750	37.5	72	
1942	BKN-DET	N	2	0	99	49.5	50	
Career			22	0	849	38.6	72	

Dave Jennings

Year	Team		No	Bl	Yds	Avg	Lg	NetAvg
1974	NYG	N	66	2	2709	41.0	64	
1975			76	0	3107	40.9	64	
1976			74	3	3054	41.3	61	30.6
1977			100	0	3993	39.9	58	32.3
1978			95	0	3995	42.1	68	33.2
1979			**104**	0	**4445**	42.7	72	36.7
1980			94	0	**4211**	**44.8**	63	**36.6**
1981			97	0	4198	43.3	62	35.0
1982			49	0	2096	42.8	73	37.3
1983			84	1	3386	40.3	68	35.3
1984			90	3	3598	40.0	54	31.4
1985	NYJ	N	74	0	2978	40.2	68	33.8
1986			85	0	3353	39.4	55	36.1
1987			64	0	2444	38.2	58	34.8
Career			1152	9	47567	41.3	73	
Playoffs			40	1	1574	39.4		

Billy Jessup

Year	Team		No	Bl	Yds	Avg	Lg	NetAvg
1956	SF	N	14	0	563	40.2	63	
1957			38	0	1656	43.6	62	
1958			23	0	856	37.2	59	
Career			75	0	3075	41.0	63	
Playoffs			3	0	103	34.3		

John Jett

Year	Team		No	Bl	Yds	Avg	Lg	NetAvg
1993	DAL	N	56	0	2342	41.8	59	37.7
1994			70	0	2935	41.9	58	35.4
1995			53	0	2166	40.9	58	34.5
1996			74	0	3150	42.6	60	36.8
Career			253	0	10593	41.9	60	
Playoffs			33	1	1415	42.9		

Al Johnson

Year	Team		No	Bl	Yds	Avg	Lg	NetAvg
1948	PHI	N	1	0	5	5.0	5	

Bert Johnson

Year	Team		No	Bl	Yds	Avg	Lg	NetAvg
1939	CHIB-CHIC	N	14		518	37.0	63	
1940	CHIC	N	1	0	19	19.0	19	
Career			15	0	537	35.8	63	

Bill Johnson

Year	Team		No	Bl	Yds	Avg	Lg	NetAvg
1970	NYG	N	42	1	1700	40.5	68	

Cecil Johnson

Year	Team		No	Bl	Yds	Avg	Lg	NetAvg
1943	BKN	N	10	0	349	34.9	46	
1944			23	0	980	**42.6**	76	
Career			33	0	1329	40.3	76	

Curley Johnson

Year	Team		No	Bl	Yds	Avg	Lg	NetAvg
1960	DAL	A	3	0	110	36.7	58	
1961	NY	A	65	0	2821	43.4	70	
1962			50	0	1998	40.0	63	
1963			71	1	3033	42.7	64	
1964			77	2	3261	42.4	61	
1965			72	0	3260	45.3	73	
1966			62	0	2633	42.5	63	
1967			65	0	2734	42.1	60	
1968			67	1	2977	44.4	65	
1969	NYG	N	20	2	823	41.1	66	
Career			552	6	23650	42.8	73	
Playoffs			14	0	570	40.7		

Jack Johnson

Year	Team		No	Bl	Yds	Avg	Lg	NetAvg
1957	CHIB	N	11	0	398	36.2	50	
1958			17	1	626	36.8	47	
1959			1	0	32	32.0	32	
Career			29	1	1056	36.4	50	

Lee Johnson

Year	Team		No	Bl	Yds	Avg	Lg	NetAvg
1985	HOU	N	83	0	3464	41.7	65	35.7
1986			88	0	3623	41.2	66	35.7
1987	HOU-CLE	N	50	0	1969	39.4	66	32.8
1988	CLE-CIN	N	31	0	1237	39.9	61	33.4
1989	CIN	N	61	2	2446	40.1	62	30.2
1990			64	0	2705	42.3	70	34.3
1991			64	0	2795	43.7	62	34.7
1992			76	0	3196	42.1	64	35.9
1993			90	0	3954	43.9	60	36.6
1994			79	1	3461	43.8	64	35.3
1995			68	0	2861	42.1	61	38.6
1996			80	1	3630	45.4	67	34.4
Career			834	4	35341	42.4	70	
Playoffs			28	0	1244	44.4		

Norm Johnson

Year	Team		No	Bl	Yds	Avg	Lg	NetAvg
1991	ATL	N	1	0	21	21.0	21	21.0
1992			1	0	37	37.0	37	37.0
Career			2	0	58	29.0	37	

Chet Johnston

Year	Team		No	Bl	Yds	Avg	Lg	NetAvg
1939	PIT	N	10		470	47.0	52	
1940			8		320	40.0	50	
Career			18		790	43.9	52	

Jimmy Johnston

Year	Team		No	Bl	Yds	Avg	Lg	NetAvg
1939	WAS	N	8		312	39.0	46	
1940			3		120	40.0	55	
Career			11		432	39.3	55	

Preston Johnston

Year	Team		No	Bl	Yds	Avg	Lg	NetAvg
1946	MIA-BUF	AA	27	1	1112	41.2		

Art Jones

Year	Team		No	Bl	Yds	Avg	Lg	NetAvg
1941	PIT	N	47	0	1772	37.7	51	

Jim Jones

Year	Team		No	Bl	Yds	Avg	Lg	NetAvg
1946	DET	N	1	0	-9	-9.0	-9	

Spike Jones

Year	Team		No	Bl	Yds	Avg	Lg	NetAvg
1970	HOU	N	83	1	3559	42.9	73	
1971	BUF	N	72	1	2966	41.2	62	
1972			79	1	3104	39.3	67	
1973			66	0	2660	40.3	62	
1974			35	0	1305	37.3	56	
1975	PHI	N	68	0	2742	40.3	64	
1976			94	3	3445	36.6	57	29.9
1977			93	2	3463	37.2	58	32.8
Career			590	8	23244	39.4	73	

Terry Joyce

Year	Team		No	Bl	Yds	Avg	Lg	NetAvg
1976	STL	N	64	2	2331	36.4	54	27.1
1977			22	1	851	38.7	58	33.8
Career			86	3	3182	37.0	58	

Charlie Justice

Year	Team	No	Bl	Yds	Avg	Lg	NetAvg
1950	WAS N	22	0	909	41.3	57	
1952		11	0	431	39.2	68	
1954		61	0	2461	40.3	63	
Career		94	0	3801	40.4	68	

Jim Karcher

Year	Team	No	Bl	Yds	Avg	Lg	NetAvg
1939	WAS N	8		312	39.0	52	

John Kasay

Year	Team	No	Bl	Yds	Avg	Lg	NetAvg
1995	CAR N	1	0	32	32.0	32	32.0
1996		1	0	30	30.0	30	10.0
Career		2	0	62	31.0	32	

Jim Keane

Year	Team	No	Bl	Yds	Avg	Lg	NetAvg
1946	CHIB N	2	0	79	39.5	47	

Tom Keane

Year	Team	No	Bl	Yds	Avg	Lg	NetAvg
1953	BAL N	18	0	753	41.8	56	

Rex Keeling

Year	Team	No	Bl	Yds	Avg	Lg	NetAvg
1968	CIN A	6	0	170	28.3	35	

Bob Keene

Year	Team	No	Bl	Yds	Avg	Lg	NetAvg
1944	DET N	1	0	30	30.0	30	

Gary Keithley

Year	Team	No	Bl	Yds	Avg	Lg	NetAvg
1973	STL N	65	1	2478	38.1	55	

Bill Kellagher

Year	Team	No	Bl	Yds	Avg	Lg	NetAvg
1946	CHI AA	1	0	56	56.0	56	

Bobby Kellogg

Year	Team	No	Bl	Yds	Avg	Lg	NetAvg
1940	CHIC N	2		54	27.0	33	

Leroy Kelly

Year	Team	No	Bl	Yds	Avg	Lg	NetAvg
1967	CLE N	10	0	407	40.7	51	

Jack Kemp

Year	Team	No	Bl	Yds	Avg	Lg	NetAvg
1957	PIT N	2	0	55	27.5	33	

Bob Kennedy

Year	Team	No	Bl	Yds	Avg	Lg	NetAvg
1946	NY AA	6	1	259	43.2		
1947		2	3	126	63.0		
1948		7	3	237	33.9		
Career		15	4	622	41.5		
Playoffs		6	0	216	36.0		

Ralph Kercheval

Year	Team	No	Bl	Yds	Avg	Lg	NetAvg
1939	BKN N	28		1092	39.0	60	
1940		8		368	46.0	66	
Career		36		1460	40.6	66	

Merritt Kersey

Year	Team	No	Bl	Yds	Avg	Lg	NetAvg
1974	PHI N	80	2	2959	37.0	59	
1975		15	0	489	32.6	50	
Career		95	2	3448	36.3	59	

Ken Keuper

Year	Team	No	Bl	Yds	Avg	Lg	NetAvg
1945	GB N	1	0	12	12.0	12	

John Kidd

Year	Team	No	Bl	Yds	Avg	Lg	NetAvg
1984	BUF N	88	2	3696	42.0	63	32.7
1985		92	0	3818	41.5	67	35.9
1986		75	0	3031	40.4	57	34.5
1987		64	0	2495	39.0	67	34.5
1988		62	0	2451	39.5	60	35.3
1989		65	2	2564	39.4	60	32.2
1990	SD N	61	1	2442	40.0	59	36.6
1991		76	1	3064	40.3	60	34.8
1992		68	0	2899	42.6	65	36.4
1993		57	0	2431	42.6	67	35.9
1994	SD-MIA N	21	0	848	40.4	58	30.1
1995	MIA N	57	0	2433	42.7	56	36.3
1996		78	0	3611	46.3	63	38.8
Career		864	6	35783	41.4	67	
Playoffs		37	0	1612	43.6		

Blair Kiel

Year	Team	No	Bl	Yds	Avg	Lg	NetAvg
1986	IND N	5	0	190	38.0	43	31.8
1987		12	0	440	36.7	50	33.7
Career		17	0	630	37.1	50	

Jon Kilgore

Year	Team	No	Bl	Yds	Avg	Lg	NetAvg
1965	LA N	24	0	999	41.6	56	
1966		71	0	3037	42.8	58	
1967		66	2	2872	43.5	68	
1968	CHI N	33	2	1231	37.3	50	
1969	SF N	36	0	1451	40.3	72	
Career		230	4	9590	41.7	72	
Playoffs		6	0	236	39.3		

Billy Kilmer

Year	Team	No	Bl	Yds	Avg	Lg	NetAvg
1961	SF N	9	0	814	90.4	64	
1966		7	0	234	33.4	45	
Career		16	0	1048	65.5	64	

Wayne Kingery

Year	Team	No	Bl	Yds	Avg	Lg	NetAvg
1949	BAL AA	3	0	109	36.3		

Carl Kinscherf

Year	Team	No	Bl	Yds	Avg	Lg	NetAvg
1943	NYG N	32	0	1299	40.6	72	

Matt Kinzer

Year	Team	No	Bl	Yds	Avg	Lg	NetAvg
1987	DET N	7	0	238	34.0	42	29.0

Ben Kish

Year	Team	No	Bl	Yds	Avg	Lg	NetAvg
1940	BKN N	3		132	44.0	50	
1941		1	0	35	35.0	35	
1943	P-P N	1	0	42	42.0	42	
1944	PHI N	4	0	182	45.5	65	
1946		4	0	163	40.8	50	
1947		8	0	301	37.6	47	
Career		21	0	855	40.7	65	

Mike Klotovich

Year	Team	No	Bl	Yds	Avg	Lg	NetAvg
1945	NYG N	11	0	422	38.4	54	

Johnny Knolla

Year	Team	No	Bl	Yds	Avg	Lg	NetAvg
1945	CHIC N	2	0	66	33.0	34	

Elmer Kolberg

Year	Team	No	Bl	Yds	Avg	Lg	NetAvg
1940	PHI N	10		400	40.0	50	

Kenny Konz

Year	Team	No	Bl	Yds	Avg	Lg	NetAvg
1957	CLE N	60	1	2396	39.9	63	
Playoffs		4	0	142	35.5		

Ernie Koy

Year	Team	No	Bl	Yds	Avg	Lg	NetAvg
1965	NYG N	55	0	2268	41.2	67	
1966		49	0	1932	39.4	55	
1967		40	0	1509	37.7	54	
1968		44	0	1649	37.5	65	
1969		26	0	933	35.9	54	
1970		11	0	369	33.5	44	
Career		225	0	8660	38.5	67	

Joe Krol

Year	Team	No	Bl	Yds	Avg	Lg	NetAvg
1945	DET N	2	0	74	37.0	44	

Gary Kubiak

Year	Team	No	Bl	Yds	Avg	Lg	NetAvg
1989	DEN N	2	0	43	21.5	29	21.5

Joe Kuharich

Year	Team	No	Bl	Yds	Avg	Lg	NetAvg
1941	CHIC N	1	0	45	45.0	45	

Steve Lach

Year	Team	No	Bl	Yds	Avg	Lg	NetAvg
1942	CHIC N	31	0	1243	40.1	59	

Warren Lahr

Year	Team	No	Bl	Yds	Avg	Lg	NetAvg
1949	CLE AA	3	1	125	41.7		

Ron Lamb

Year	Team	No	Bl	Yds	Avg	Lg	NetAvg
1969	CIN A	1	0	29	29.0	29	

Frank Lambert

Year	Team	No	Bl	Yds	Avg	Lg	NetAvg
1965	PIT N	77	1	3518	45.7	69	
1966		78	0	3284	42.1	63	
Career		155	1	6802	43.9	69	

Daryle Lamonica

Year	Team	No	Bl	Yds	Avg	Lg	NetAvg
1963	BUF A	51	1	2071	40.6	57	
Playoffs		8	0	281	35.1		

Sean Landeta

Year	Team	No	Bl	Yds	Avg	Lg	NetAvg
1985	NYG N	81	0	3472	42.9	68	36.4
1986		79	0	3539	44.8	61	37.1

Sean Landeta *continued*

Year	Team	No	Bl	Yds	Avg	Lg	NetAvg
1987		65	1	2773	42.7	64	31.0
1988		6	0	222	37.0	53	35.8
1989		70	0	3019	43.1	71	37.8
1990		75	0	3306	44.1	67	35.3
1991		64	0	2768	43.3	61	35.3
1992		53	2	2317	43.7	71	31.5
1993	NYG-LARMN	75	1	3215	42.9	66	33.8
1994	LARM N	78	0	3494	44.8	62	34.3
1995	STL N	83	0	3679	44.3	63	36.7
1996		78	0	3491	44.8	70	36.1
Career		807	4	35295	43.7	71	
Playoffs		45	0	1832	40.7		

Tom Landry

Year	Team	No	Bl	Yds	Avg	Lg	NetAvg
1949	B-NY AA	49	2	2249	45.9		
1950	NYG N	57	1	2136	37.5	61	
1951		15	0	637	42.5	59	
1952		81	1	3363	41.5	61	
1953		44	0	1771	40.3	60	
1954		64	0	2720	42.5	61	
1955		74	1	3022	40.8	69	
Career		384	5	15898	41.4	69	
Playoffs		10	0	550	55.0		

Bob Laraba

Year	Team	No	Bl	Yds	Avg	Lg	NetAvg
1960	LA A	15	0	558	37.2	55	
Playoffs		4	0	164	41.0		

Yale Lary

Year	Team	No	Bl	Yds	Avg	Lg	NetAvg
1952	DET N	5	0	181	36.2	43	
1953		28	0	1064	39.7	61	
1956		42	0	1698	40.4	61	
1957		54	0	2156	39.9	66	
1958		58	1	2524	43.5	62	
1959		45	0	2121	47.1	67	
1960		62	2	2802	45.2	63	
1961		52	0	2519	48.4	71	
1962		51	1	2402	47.1	68	
1963		35	0	1713	48.9	73	
1964		67	0	3099	46.3	74	
Career		499	4	22279	42.5	74	
Playoffs		12	0	515	42.9	72	

Chuck Latourette

Year	Team	No	Bl	Yds	Avg	Lg	NetAvg
1967	STL N	62	0	2532	40.8	67	
1968		65	0	2701	41.6	55	
1970		65	0	2659	40.9	59	
1971		55	1	2157	39.2	55	
Career		247	1	10049	40.7	67	

Hank Lauricella

Year	Team	No	Bl	Yds	Avg	Lg	NetAvg
1952	DAL N	57	1	2036	35.7	60	

Ted Laux

Year	Team	No	Bl	Yds	Avg	Lg	NetAvg
1944	PHI N	1	0	18	18.0	18	

Jimmy Lawrence

Year	Team	No	Bl	Yds	Avg	Lg	NetAvg
1939	CHIC-GB N	3		114	38.0	55	

Pete Layden

Year	Team	No	Bl	Yds	Avg	Lg	NetAvg
1948	NY AA	21	0	884	42.1		
1949	B-NY AA	15	0	626	41.7		
Career		36	0	1510	41.9		

Bobby Layne

Year	Team	No	Bl	Yds	Avg	Lg	NetAvg
1948	CHIB N	1	0	24	24.0	24	

Pat Leahy

Year	Team	No	Bl	Yds	Avg	Lg	NetAvg
1990	NYJ N	1	0	12	12.0	12	12.0

Eddie Le Baron

Year	Team	No	Bl	Yds	Avg	Lg	NetAvg
1952	WAS N	51	0	2152	42.2	63	
1953		50	1	2004	40.1	60	
1955		62	0	2581	41.6	57	
1956		4	0	161	40.3	47	
1960	DAL N	3	0	99	33.0	34	
Career		170	1	5997	41.2	63	

Bill Leckonby

Year	Team	No	Bl	Yds	Avg	Lg	NetAvg
1940	BKN N	2		54	27.0	34	
1941		15	0	588	39.2	48	
Career		17	0	642	37.8	48	

Bob Lee

Year	Team	Lg	No	Bl	Yds	Avg	Lg	NetAvg
1969	MIN	N	67	0	2680	40.0	58	
1971			**89**	0	**3515**	39.5	58	
Career			156	0	6195	39.7	58	
Playoffs			13	0	526	40.5		

David Lee

Year	Team	Lg	No	Bl	Yds	Avg	Lg	NetAvg
1966	BAL	N	49	0	2233	**45.6**	64	
1967			49	0	2075	42.3	68	
1968			47	1	1935	41.2	50	
1969			57	0	2580	**45.3**	66	
1970			62	1	2819	45.5	62	
1971			62	0	2542	41.0	76	
1972			56	1	2400	42.9	60	
1973			60	2	2402	40.0	60	
1974			70	1	2634	37.6	58	
1975			85	1	3402	40.0	62	
1976			59	0	2342	39.7	56	34.8
1977			82	2	3142	38.3	59	29.5
1978			92	2	3513	38.2	67	30.6
Career			830	11	34019	41.0	76	
Playoffs			60	1	2397	40.0		

Jack Lee

Year	Team	Lg	No	Bl	Yds	Avg	Lg	NetAvg
1939	PIT	N	1	0	44	44.0	44	

Cliff Lewis

Year	Team	Lg	No	Bl	Yds	Avg	Lg	NetAvg
1948	CLE	AA	1	0	18	18.0	18	

Dave Lewis

Year	Team	Lg	No	Bl	Yds	Avg	Lg	NetAvg
1970	CIN	N	79	0	3651	**46.2**	63	
1971			72	0	3229	44.8	56	
1972			66	0	2777	42.1	60	
1973			68	0	2790	41.0	60	
Career			285	0	12447	43.7	63	
Playoffs			15	0	567	37.8		

Ernie Lewis

Year	Team	Lg	No	Bl	Yds	Avg	Lg	NetAvg
1946	CHI	AA	49	1	2085	42.6	76	
1947			61	4	**2549**	41.8		
1948			60	0	2680	44.7		
1949			15	1	680	45.3	73	
Career			185	6	7994	43.2	76	

Verl Lillywhite

Year	Team	Lg	No	Bl	Yds	Avg	Lg	NetAvg
1948	SF	AA	3	0	76	25.3		
1949			4	0	202	50.5	68	
1950	SF	N	26	0	1017	39.1	57	
1951			20	0	848	42.4	75	
Career			53	0	2143	40.4	75	

Augie Lio

Year	Team	Lg	No	Bl	Yds	Avg	Lg	NetAvg
1941	DET	N	1	0	28	28.0	28	

Steve Little

Year	Team	Lg	No	Bl	Yds	Avg	Lg	NetAvg
1978	STL	N	46	1	1749	38.0	54	28.0
1979			79	2	3060	38.7	63	31.6
Career			125	3	4809	38.5	63	

Dale Livingston

Year	Team	Lg	No	Bl	Yds	Avg	Lg	NetAvg
1968	CIN	A	70	0	3036	43.4	66	
1969			69	1	2769	40.1	55	
1970	GB	N	6	0	199	33.2	52	
Career			145	1	6004	41.4	66	

Howie Livingston

Year	Team	Lg	No	Bl	Yds	Avg	Lg	NetAvg
1944	NYG	N	2	0	79	39.5	47	
1945			13	0	481	37.0	62	
Career			15	0	560	37.3	62	

Spider Lockhart

Year	Team	Lg	No	Bl	Yds	Avg	Lg	NetAvg
1965	NYG	N	6	0	267	44.5	53	
1966	NY	N	4	0	131	32.8	42	
1968	NYG	N	3	0	110	36.7	49	
Career			13	0	508	39.1	53	

Jerry Logan

Year	Team	Lg	No	Bl	Yds	Avg	Lg	NetAvg
1963	BAL	N	4	0	121	30.3	55	

Chip Lohmiller

Year	Team	Lg	No	Bl	Yds	Avg	Lg	NetAvg
1988	WAS	N	6	0	208	34.7	42	30.5

Bill Long

Year	Team	Lg	No	Bl	Yds	Avg	Lg	NetAvg
1949	PIT	N	30	0	1127	37.6	52	

Johnny Long

Year	Team	Lg	No	Bl	Yds	Avg	Lg	NetAvg
1944	CHIB	N	7	0	249	35.6	52	
1945			1	0	42	42.0	42	
Career			8	0	291	36.4	52	

Joe Don Looney

Year	Team	Lg	No	Bl	Yds	Avg	Lg	NetAvg
1964	BAL	N	32	0	1358	42.4	64	

Tony Lorick

Year	Team	Lg	No	Bl	Yds	Avg	Lg	NetAvg
1968	NO	N	1	0	36	36.0	36	

Billy Lothridge

Year	Team	Lg	No	Bl	Yds	Avg	Lg	NetAvg
1964	DAL	N	62	0	2501	40.3	75	
1965	LA	N	41	1	1619	39.5	55	
1966	ATL	N	73	0	2968	40.7	60	
1967			**87**	0	**3801**	**43.7**	62	
1968			75	0	**3324**	44.3	70	
1969			69	0	2846	41.2	57	
1970			76	0	2944	38.7	59	
1971			43	1	1639	38.1	58	
1972	MIA	N	4	0	150	37.5	42	
Career			530	2	21792	41.1	75	

Nick Lowery

Year	Team	Lg	No	Bl	Yds	Avg	Lg	NetAvg
1992	KC	N	4	0	141	35.3	39	32.8

Russ Lowther

Year	Team	Lg	No	Bl	Yds	Avg	Lg	NetAvg
1944	DET	N	5	0	205	41.0	58	
1945	PIT	N	1	0	35	35.0	35	
Career			6	0	240	40.0	58	

Mick Luckhurst

Year	Team	Lg	No	Bl	Yds	Avg	Lg	NetAvg
1985	ATL	N	1	0	26	26.0	26	26.0
1987			1	0	37	37.0	37	17.0
Career			2	0	63	31.5	37	

Sid Luckman

Year	Team	Lg	No	Bl	Yds	Avg	Lg	NetAvg
1939	CHIB	N	27		1170	43.3	67	
1940			27		1148	42.5	70	
1941			13	0	534	41.1	52	
1942			24	0	976	40.7	60	
1943			33	1	1220	37.0	78	
1944			20	0	685	34.3	63	
1945			36	0	1297	36.0	61	
1946			33	0	1235	37.4	69	
1947			5	0	177	35.4	42	
1948			10	0	384	38.4	49	
1949			1	0	16	16.0	16	
Career			229	1	8842	38.6	78	
Playoffs			14	0	593	42.4		

Johnny Lujack

Year	Team	Lg	No	Bl	Yds	Avg	Lg	NetAvg
1949	CHIB	N	3	0	123	41.0	48	

Bobby Luna

Year	Team	Lg	No	Bl	Yds	Avg	Lg	NetAvg
1955	SF	N	60	3	2558	42.6	63	
1959	PIT	N	63	0	2528	40.1	61	
Career			123	3	5086	41.3	63	

Garry Lyle

Year	Team	Lg	No	Bl	Yds	Avg	Lg	NetAvg
1968	CHI	N	5	0	134	26.8	39	
1970			1	0	29	29.0	29	
Career			6	0	163	27.2	39	

Archie Maggiolo

Year	Team	Lg	No	Bl	Yds	Avg	Lg	NetAvg
1948	BUF	AA	2	0	95	47.5		

Dante Magnani

Year	Team	Lg	No	Bl	Yds	Avg	Lg	NetAvg
1940	CLE	N	1	0	33	33.0	33	

Paul Maguire

Year	Team	Lg	No	Bl	Yds	Avg	Lg	NetAvg
1960	LA	A	43	0	1743	**40.5**	61	
1961	SD	A	62	1	2615	42.2	82	
1962			**79**	0	**3289**	41.6	66	
1963			58	0	2242	38.7	60	
1964	BUF	A	65	0	2777	42.7	64	
1965			80	0	3437	43.0	68	
1966			69	0	2841	41.2	61	
1967			77	0	3320	43.1	64	
1968			99	1	**4175**	42.2	61	
1969			77	1	**3471**	**45.1**	78	
1970	BUF	N	82	1	3228	39.4	58	
Career			791	4	30438	38.5	82	
Playoffs			25	0	1020	40.8	64	

Howie Maley

Year	Team	Lg	No	Bl	Yds	Avg	Lg	NetAvg
1946	BOS	N	59	1	2363	40.1	61	
1947			89	3	3731	41.9	66	
Career			148	4	6094	41.2	66	

Bill Malinchak

Year	Team	Lg	No	Bl	Yds	Avg	Lg	NetAvg
1969	DET	N	5	0	184	36.8	47	

Ray Mallouf

Year	Team	Lg	No	Bl	Yds	Avg	Lg	NetAvg
1941	CHIC	N	28	0	1148	41.0	57	
1946			15	0	518	34.5	47	
1947			43	0	1716	39.9	62	
1948			45	0	1755	39.0	61	
1949	NYG	N	56	1	2129	38.0	50	
Career			187	1	7266	38.9	62	
Playoffs			16	0	555	34.7		

Dave Mann

Year	Team	Lg	No	Bl	Yds	Avg	Lg	NetAvg
1955	CHIC	N	42	1	1723	41.0	60	
1956			35	1	1346	38.5	53	
1957			59	0	2509	42.5	67	
Career			136	2	5578	41.0	67	

Errol Mann

Year	Team	Lg	No	Bl	Yds	Avg	Lg	NetAvg
1974	DET	N	1	0	18	18.0	18	
1975			1	0	34	34.0	34	
Career			2	0	52	26.0	34	

Chester Marcol

Year	Team	Lg	No	Bl	Yds	Avg	Lg	NetAvg
1980	GB	N	1	0	33	33.0	33	13.0

Joe Marconi

Year	Team	Lg	No	Bl	Yds	Avg	Lg	NetAvg
1959	LA	N	2	0	81	40.5	44	
1960			9	1	408	45.3	62	
1961			6	0	265	44.2	50	
Career			17	1	754	44.4	62	

Bob Margarita

Year	Team	Lg	No	Bl	Yds	Avg	Lg	NetAvg
1944	CHIB	N	1	0	34	34.0	34	
1945			1	0	29	29.0	29	
Career			2	0	63	31.5	34	

Billy Martin

Year	Team	Lg	No	Bl	Yds	Avg	Lg	NetAvg
1968	MIN	N	28	0	1046	37.4	49	

Frank Martin

Year	Team	Lg	No	Bl	Yds	Avg	Lg	NetAvg
1944	BKN	N	1	0	2	2.0	2	

John Martin

Year	Team	Lg	No	Bl	Yds	Avg	Lg	NetAvg
1941	CHIC	N	24	0	958	39.9	60	
1942			36	0	1415	39.3	64	
1943			30	0	1187	39.6	59	
1944	C-P-BOS	N	41	0	1492	36.4	47	
1945	BOS	N	14	0	575	41.1	58	
Career			145	0	5627	38.8	64	

Walt Masters

Year	Team	Lg	No	Bl	Yds	Avg	Lg	NetAvg
1943	CHIC	N	10	0	368	36.8	49	
1944	C-P	N	2	0	91	45.5	52	
Career			12	0	459	38.3	52	

Bob Masterson

Year	Team	Lg	No	Bl	Yds	Avg	Lg	NetAvg
1944	BKN	N	4	0	136	34.0	46	

Ned Mathews

Year	Team	Lg	No	Bl	Yds	Avg	Lg	NetAvg
1941	DET	N	1	0	26	26.0	26	
1943			1	0	35	35.0	35	
Career			2	0	61	30.5	35	

Lew Mayne

Year	Team	Lg	No	Bl	Yds	Avg	Lg	NetAvg
1946	BKN	AA	3	0	109	36.3		

Dave Mays

Year	Team	Lg	No	Bl	Yds	Avg	Lg	NetAvg
1976	CLE	N	2	0	91	45.5	54	38.5

Dean McAdams

Year	Team	Lg	No	Bl	Yds	Avg	Lg	NetAvg
1941	BKN	N	16	0	782	47.6	70	
1942			51	1	2148	42.1	74	
1943			35	1	1354	38.7	60	
Career			102	2	4264	41.8	74	

George McAfee

Year	Team	Lg	No	Bl	Yds	Avg	Lg	NetAvg
1940	CHIB	N	22		858	39.0	79	
1941			11	1	430	39.1	55	

Year	Team		No	Bl	Yds	Avg	Lg	NetAvg

George McAfee *continued*

Year	Team		No	Bl	Yds	Avg	Lg	NetAvg
1945			2	0	62	31.0	33	
1947			2	0	71	35.5	40	
1948			1	0	18	18.0	18	
Career			38	1	1439	37.9	79	
Playoffs			1	0	38	38.0	38	

Wes McAfee

| 1941 | PHI | N | 1 | 0 | 32 | 32.0 | 32 | |

Jim McCann

1971	SF	N	48	1	1897	39.5	54	
1972			63	1	2542	40.3	63	
1973	NYG	N	9	3	294	32.7	50	
1975	KC	N	13	1	493	37.9	52	
Career			133	6	5226	39.3	63	
Playoffs			6	0	224	37.3		

John McCarthy

| 1944 | C-P | N | 23 | 1 | 802 | 34.9 | 52 | |

Shawn McCarthy

1991	NE	N	66	2	2650	40.2	93	35.7
1992			103	0	4227	41.0	61	35.4
Career			169	2	6877	40.7	93	

John McCormick

1962	MIN	N	46	0	1795	39.0	53	
1965	DEN	A	1	0	45	45.0	45	
Career			47	0	1840	39.1	53	

Hal McCullough

| 1942 | BKN | N | 12 | 0 | 422 | 35.2 | 71 | |

Hugh McCullough

1939	PIT	N	31		1023	33.0	52	
1940	CHIC	N	30		1200	40.0	68	
1941			3	0	122	40.7	43	
1945	BOS	N	2	0	64	32.0	37	
Career			66	0	2409	36.5	68	

Ed McDaniel

1962	DEN	A	5	0	173	34.6	39	
1966	MIA	A	32	1	1222	38.2	54	
Career			37	1	1395	37.7	54	

Coley McDonough

1939	CHIC-PIT	N	10		370	37.0	49	
1940	PIT	N	4		160	40.0	47	
1941			7	0	260	37.1	65	
Career			21	0	790	37.6	65	

Doug McEnulty

1943	CHIB	N	4	0	187	46.8	59	
1944			25	0	995	39.8	60	
Career			29	0	1182	40.8	60	

Max McGee

1954	GB	N	72	0	2999	41.7	63	
1958			62	0	2625	42.3	61	
1959			63	1	2716	43.1	61	
1960			30	1	1291	43.0	58	
1961			13	0	521	40.1	51	
1962			14	0	496	35.4	56	
Career			254	2	10648	41.9	63	
Playoffs			10	1	386	38.6		

Charlie McGibbony

| 1944 | BKN | N | 8 | 0 | 294 | 36.8 | 55 | |

Lamar McHan

1954	CHIC	N	4	0	159	39.8	49	
1956			8	0	285	35.6	42	
1958			2	0	65	32.5	54	
1962	BAL	N	1	0	22	22.0	22	
Career			15	0	531	35.4	54	

Pat McInally

1976	CIN	N	76	0	2999	39.5	61	33.6
1977			67	1	2802	41.8	67	**36.4**
1978			91	0	3919	**43.1**	65	34.7
1979			89	2	3678	41.3	61	34.2
1980			83	2	3390	40.8	61	31.5

Pat McInally *continued*

Year	Team		No	Bl	Yds	Avg	Lg	NetAvg
1981			72	1	3272	**45.4**	62	36.1
1982			31	0	1201	38.7	53	34.0
1983			67	2	2804	41.9	60	33.5
1984			67	0	2832	42.3	61	35.3
1985			57	1	2410	42.3	64	29.9
Career			700	9	29307	41.9	67	
Playoffs			12	0	487	40.6		

Paul McJulien

1991	GB	N	86	0	3473	40.4	62	34.4
1992			36	2	1386	38.5	67	30.2
1993	LARM	N	21	0	795	37.9	56	28.2
Career			143	2	5654	39.5	67	

Roy McKay

1944	GB	N	8	0	297	37.1	55	
1945			44	0	1813	41.2	73	
1946			63	1	2735	43.4	64	
1947			8	0	350	43.8	54	
Career			123	1	5195	47.2	73	

Jim McMahon

1982	CHI	N	1	0	59	59.0	59	59.0
1983			1	0	36	36.0	36	36.0
Career			2	0	95	47.5	59	

John McMichael

| 1944 | BKN | N | 2 | 0 | 85 | 42.5 | 51 | |

Tom McNeill

1967	NO	N	74	0	3174	42.9	66	
1968			48	1	2009	41.9	58	
1969			7	0	312	44.6	81	
1970	MIN	N	61	0	2309	37.9	64	
1971	PHI	N	72	1	3063	42.5	64	
1972			7	0	290	41.4	51	
1973			46	0	1881	40.9	66	
Career			315	2	13038	41.4	81	
Playoffs			7	0	276	39.4		

Tom McWilliams

| 1950 | PIT | N | 3 | 0 | 135 | 45.0 | 67 | |

Jim Meade

1939	WAS	N	8		296	37.0	50	
1940			9		360	40.0	55	
Career			17		656	38.6	55	

Dan Melville

| 1979 | SF | N | 71 | 1 | 2626 | 37.0 | 53 | 30.1 |

Mike Mercer

1961	MIN	N	61	2	2458	40.3	59	
1962			19	0	827	43.5	77	
1963	OAK	A	75	0	3007	40.1	53	
1964			58	1	2446	42.2	67	
1965			75	0	3079	41.1	70	
1966			9	0	373	41.4	59	
1970	SD	N	8	0	283	35.4	42	
Career			305	3	12473	40.9	77	

Guido Merkens

1983	NO	N	4	0	144	36.0	45	30.5
1987	PHI	N	2	1	61	30.5	38	20.3
Career			6	1	205	34.2	45	

Mike Michel

1977	MIA	N	35	0	1338	38.2	61	32.5
1978	PHI	N	58	0	2078	35.8	52	30.9
Career			93	0	3416	36.7	61	
Playoffs			9	0	303	33.7		

Mike Micka

| 1944 | WAS | N | 2 | 0 | 42 | 21.0 | 25 | |

Nick Mike-Mayer

| 1977 | ATL | N | 1 | 0 | 23 | 23.0 | 23 | 23.0 |

Eddie Miller

1939	NYG	N	5		185	37.0	47	
1940			19		741	39.0	52	
Career			24		926	38.6	52	

Jim Miller

1980	SF	N	77	0	3152	40.9	65	32.8
1981			93	0	3858	41.5	65	31.1
1982			44	1	1676	38.1	80	30.9
1983	DAL	N	5	0	178	35.6	43	21.2
1984			5	0	173	34.6	41	29.2
1987	NYG	N	10	0	345	34.5	53	27.4
Career			234	1	9382	40.1	80	
Playoffs			12	0	498	41.5		

Josh Miller

| 1996 | PIT | N | 55 | 0 | 2256 | 41.0 | 61 | 33.6 |
| Playoffs | | | 11 | 0 | 461 | 41.9 | | |

Charley Milstead

| 1960 | HOU | A | 66 | 0 | 2365 | 35.8 | 59 | |
| Playoffs | | | 5 | 0 | 170 | 34.0 | | |

John Misko

1982	LARM	N	45	1	1961	43.6	59	33.0
1983			82	1	3301	40.3	67	33.9
1984			74	0	2866	38.7	58	33.6
1987	DET	N	6	0	242	40.3	51	36.5
Career			207	2	8370	40.4	67	
Playoffs			17	0	612	36.0		

Bob Mitchell

| 1946 | LA | AA | 1 | 0 | 44 | 44.0 | 44 | |

Kelly Moan

| 1939 | CLE | N | 1 | 0 | 30 | 30.0 | 30 | |

Chris Mohr

1989	TB	N	84	2	3311	39.4	58	32.1
1991	BUF	N	54	0	2085	38.6	58	36.1
1992			60	0	2531	42.2	61	36.8
1993			74	0	2991	40.4	58	36.0
1994			67	0	2799	41.8	71	36.0
1995			86	0	3473	40.4	60	36.2
1996			101	0	4194	41.5	80	36.5
Career			526	2	21384	40.7	80	
Playoffs			54	0	2041	37.8		

Ralf Mojsiejenko

1985	SD	N	68	0	2881	42.4	67	35.7
1986			72	2	3026	42.0	62	32.9
1987			67	0	2875	42.9	57	33.5
1988			85	1	3745	44.1	62	34.5
1989	WAS	N	62	1	2663	43.0	74	33.3
1990			43	1	1687	39.2	53	34.2
1991	SF	N	16	0	656	41.0	55	29.7
Career			413	5	17533	42.5	74	

Greg Montgomery

1988	HOU	N	65	0	2523	38.8	61	34.1
1989			56	2	2422	43.3	63	36.1
1990			34	0	1530	45.0	60	36.6
1991			48	2	2105	43.9	60	36.8
1992			53	2	2487	**46.9**	66	37.3
1993			54	0	2462	**45.6**	77	39.1
1994	DET	N	63	1	2782	44.2	64	34.2
1996	BAL	N	68	1	2980	43.8	67	37.8
Career			441	8	19291	43.7	77	
Playoffs			35	2	1441	41.2		

Mike Montgomery

| 1973 | DAL | N | 4 | 0 | 158 | 39.5 | 48 | |

Dana Moore

| 1987 | NYG | N | 14 | 1 | 486 | 34.7 | 46 | 22.1 |

Earl Morrall

1956	SF	N	45	0	1705	37.9	57	
1958	DET	N	1	0	25	25.0	25	
1959			11	0	481	43.7	66	
1961			3	0	113	37.7	43	
1962			1	0	48	48.0	48	
1963			29	0	1143	39.4	55	
1964			1	0	8	8.0	8	
1967	NYG	N	14	1	472	33.7	43	
Career			105	1	3995	38.0	66	

Fred Morrison

| 1950 | CHIB | N | 57 | 0 | 2470 | 43.3 | 65 | |

Fred Morrison *continued*

Year	Team		No	Bl	Yds	Avg	Lg	NetAvg
1951			56	1	2227	39.8	67	
1952			63	1	2707	43.0	65	
1953			63	2	2766	43.9	65	
1956	CLE	N	38	0	1560	41.1	70	
Career			277	4	11730	42.3	70	
Playoffs			7	0	308	44.0		

Tommy Morrow

Year	Team		No	Bl	Yds	Avg	Lg	NetAvg
1962	OAK	A	45		1654	36.8	59	

Emmett Mortell

Year	Team		No	Bl	Yds	Avg	Lg	NetAvg
1939	PHI	N	23		989	43.0	62	

Mark Moseley

Year	Team		No	Bl	Yds	Avg	Lg	NetAvg
1970	PHI	N	10	0	350	35.0	56	

Rudy Mucha

Year	Team		No	Bl	Yds	Avg	Lg	NetAvg
1941	CLE	N	11	0	488	44.4	52	
1946	CHIB	N	22	1	897	40.8	53	
Career			33	1	1385	40.8	53	

Frank Muehlheuser

Year	Team		No	Bl	Yds	Avg	Lg	NetAvg
1948	BOS	N	1	0	46	46.0	46	
1949	NYB	N	0	1	0		0	
Career			1	1	46	46.0	46	

Joe Muha

Year	Team		No	Bl	Yds	Avg	Lg	NetAvg
1946	PHI	N	22	0	843	38.3	64	
1947			53	0	2303	43.5	75	
1948			57	0	2692	**47.2**	82	
1949			44	1	1802	41.0	59	
1950			1	1	48	48.0	48	
Career			177	2	7688	43.4	82	
Playoffs			25	0	895	35.8	69	

Horst Muhlmann

Year	Team		No	Bl	Yds	Avg	Lg	NetAvg
1969	CIN	A	1	1	38	38.0	38	

Noah Mullins

Year	Team		No	Bl	Yds	Avg	Lg	NetAvg
1948	CHIB	N	2	0	88	44.0	45	

Eddie Murray

Year	Team		No	Bl	Yds	Avg	Lg	NetAvg
1986	DET	N	1	0	37	37.0	37	17.0
1987			4	0	155	38.8	46	28.0
Career			5	0	192	38.4	46	

Franny Murray

Year	Team		No	Bl	Yds	Avg	Lg	NetAvg
1939	PHI	N	33		1221	37.0	54	
1940			30		1110	37.0	50	
Career			63		2331	37.0	54	

Dick Nardi

Year	Team		No	Bl	Yds	Avg	Lg	NetAvg
1939	PIT	N	1	0	19	19.0	19	

Johnny Naumu

Year	Team		No	Bl	Yds	Avg	Lg	NetAvg
1948	LA	AA	1	0	34	34.0	34	

Chuck Nelson

Year	Team		No	Bl	Yds	Avg	Lg	NetAvg
1986	MIN	N	3	0	72	24.0	31	24.0

Jimmy Nelson

Year	Team		No	Bl	Yds	Avg	Lg	NetAvg
1946	MIA	AA	16	0	635	39.7		

Steve Nemeth

Year	Team		No	Bl	Yds	Avg	Lg	NetAvg
1946	CHI	AA	2	0	92	46.0		
1947	BAL	AA	3	0	126	42.0		
Career			5	0	218	43.6		

Harry Newsome

Year	Team		No	Bl	Yds	Avg	Lg	NetAvg
1985	PIT	N	78	1	3088	39.6	59	32.5
1986			86	3	3447	40.1	64	32.2
1987			64	1	2678	41.8	57	31.5
1988			65	6	2950	**45.4**	62	32.8
1989			82	1	3368	41.1	57	34.1
1990	MIN	N	78	1	3299	42.3	61	33.2
1991			68	0	3095	45.5	65	36.3
1992			72	1	3243	45.0	64	35.7
1993			90	0	3862	42.9	64	35.4
Career			683	14	29030	42.5	65	
Playoffs			22	1	842	38.3		

Walt Nielson

Year	Team		No	Bl	Yds	Avg	Lg	NetAvg
1940	NYG	N	1	0	42	42.0	42	

John Nies

Year	Team		No	Bl	Yds	Avg	Lg	NetAvg
1990	BUF	N	5	0	174	34.8	39	27.4

Ray Nolting

Year	Team		No	Bl	Yds	Avg	Lg	NetAvg
1939	CHIB	N	12		468	39.0	47	
1940			2	0	68	34.0	38	
Career			14	0	536	38.3	47	
Playoffs			4	0	180	45.0		

John Noppenberg

Year	Team		No	Bl	Yds	Avg	Lg	NetAvg
1940	PIT	N	4		136	34.0	50	
1941	DET	N	7	0	270	38.6	44	
Career			11	0	406	36.9	50	

Chris Norman

Year	Team		No	Bl	Yds	Avg	Lg	NetAvg
1984	DEN	N	96	0	3850	40.1	83	35.4
1985			92	2	3764	40.9	61	34.0
1986			30	1	1168	38.9	57	32.1
Career			218	3	8782	40.3	83	
Playoffs			4	0	169	42.3		

Jerry Norton

Year	Team		No	Bl	Yds	Avg	Lg	NetAvg
1957	PHI	N	67	1	2798	41.8	63	
1959	CHIC	N	59	0	2650	44.9	60	
1960	STL	N	39	0	1777	**45.6**	62	
1961			84	1	3802	45.3	78	
1963	GB	N	51	0	2279	44.7	61	
1964			56	0	2365	42.2	61	
Career			356	2	15671	44.0	78	

Jim Norton

Year	Team		No	Bl	Yds	Avg	Lg	NetAvg
1961	HOU	A	48	0	1952	40.7	63	
1962			55	1	2298	41.8	64	
1963			65	0	2792	43.0	68	
1964			53	2	2267	42.8	79	
1965			**84**	1	**3711**	44.2	65	
1966			69	0	2908	42.1	65	
1967			70	1	3025	43.2	68	
1968			71	2	3008	42.4	64	
Career			515	7	21961	42.6	79	
Playoffs			18	0	707	39.3		

Mike Nott

Year	Team		No	Bl	Yds	Avg	Lg	NetAvg
1976	KC	N	1	0	35	35.0	35	24.0

Davey O'Brien

Year	Team		No	Bl	Yds	Avg	Lg	NetAvg
1939	PHI	N	3		120	40.0	64	
1940			6		246	41.0	56	
Career			9		366	40.7	64	

Ken O'Brien

Year	Team		No	Bl	Yds	Avg	Lg	NetAvg
1990	NYJ	N	1	0	23	23.0	23	11.0

Tom O'Connor

Year	Team		No	Bl	Yds	Avg	Lg	NetAvg
1987	NYJ	N	18	0	602	33.4	47	28.9

Steve O'Neal

Year	Team		No	Bl	Yds	Avg	Lg	NetAvg
1969	NY	A	54	0	2393	44.3	98	
1970	NYJ	N	72	1	2925	40.6	64	
1971			78	0	3026	38.8	58	
1972			50	1	2006	40.1	57	
1973	NO	N	81	0	3375	41.7	71	
Career			335	2	13725	41.0	98	
Playoffs			5	0	186	37.2		

Pat O'Neill

Year	Team		No	Bl	Yds	Avg	Lg	NetAvg
1994	NE	N	69	0	2841	41.2	67	35.7
1995	NE-CHI	N	44	0	1603	36.4	57	30.9
Career			113	0	4444	39.3	67	
Playoffs			4	0	169	42.3		

Tom Orosz

Year	Team		No	Bl	Yds	Avg	Lg	NetAvg
1981	MIA	N	83	0	3386	40.8	61	34.7
1982			35	0	1353	38.7	61	34.2
1983	SF	N	65	1	2552	39.3	61	32.6
1984			5	0	195	39.0	55	36.2
Career			188	1	7486	39.8	61	
Playoffs			37	0	1351	36.5		

Charlie O'Rourke

Year	Team		No	Bl	Yds	Avg	Lg	NetAvg
1942	CHIB	N	23	0	817	35.5	57	
1946	LA	AA	8	0	312	39.0		
1948	BAL	AA	65	1	2546	39.2	76	

Charlie O'Rourke *continued*

Year	Team		No	Bl	Yds	Avg	Lg	NetAvg
1949			28	0	1098	39.2		
Career			124	1	4773	38.5	76	
Playoffs			5	0	212	42.4		

Jimmy Orr

Year	Team		No	Bl	Yds	Avg	Lg	NetAvg
1958	PIT	N	51	0	2023	39.7	62	
1959			8	0	302	37.8	46	
Career			59	0	2325	39.4	62	

Chuck Ortmann

Year	Team		No	Bl	Yds	Avg	Lg	NetAvg
1951	PIT	N	6	1	302	50.3	72	

Bob Paffrath

Year	Team		No	Bl	Yds	Avg	Lg	NetAvg
1946	MIA	AA	1	0	50	50.0	50	

Joe Pagliei

Year	Team		No	Bl	Yds	Avg	Lg	NetAvg
1959	PHI	N	1	0	45	45.0	45	
1960	NY	A	48		1779	37.1		
Career			49	0	1824	37.2	45	

Les Palmer

Year	Team		No	Bl	Yds	Avg	Lg	NetAvg
1948	PHI	N	4	0	148	37.0	47	

Babe Parilli

Year	Team		No	Bl	Yds	Avg	Lg	NetAvg
1952	GB	N	65	0	2645	40.7	63	
1953			19	0	685	36.1	58	
1964	BOS	A	5	0	180	36.0	45	
Career			89	0	3510	39.4	63	

Ace Parker

Year	Team		No	Bl	Yds	Avg	Lg	NetAvg
1939	BKN	N	40		1680	42.0	65	
1940			49		1862	38.0	59	
1941			27	0	1067	39.5	49	
1945	BOS	N	7	0	224	32.0	51	
1946	NY	AA	25	2	910	36.4		
Career			148	2	5743	38.8	65	
Playoffs			4	0	116	29.0		

Daren Parker

Year	Team		No	Bl	Yds	Avg	Lg	NetAvg
1992	DEN	N	12	0	491	40.9	61	31.9

Cliff Parsley

Year	Team		No	Bl	Yds	Avg	Lg	NetAvg
1977	HOU	N	77	2	3030	39.4	55	31.8
1978			91	1	3539	38.9	59	31.5
1979			93	0	3777	40.6	59	31.7
1980			67	0	2727	40.7	57	32.4
1981			79	0	3137	39.7	62	34.4
1982			24	0	926	38.6	51	31.3
Career			431	3	17136	39.8	62	
Playoffs			40	0	1607	40.2		

Bob Parsons

Year	Team		No	Bl	Yds	Avg	Lg	NetAvg
1973	CHI	N	4	0	106	26.5	33	
1974			89	1	3408	38.3	59	
1975			**93**	0	3625	39.0	60	
1976			99	1	3726	37.6	62	32.2
1977			80	2	3232	40.4	58	35.1
1978			96	0	3549	37.0	54	32.2
1979			92	1	3486	37.9	54	31.8
1980			79	0	3207	40.6	61	32.8
1981			**114**	0	**4531**	39.7	55	33.3
1982			**58**	0	**2394**	41.3	81	34.8
1983			79	0	2916	36.9	54	32.3
Career			883	5	34180	38.7	81	
Playoffs			12	0	489	40.8		

Dennis Partee

Year	Team		No	Bl	Yds	Avg	Lg	NetAvg
1968	SD	A	56	0	2281	40.7	60	
1969			71	0	3169	44.6	62	
1970	SD	N	64	1	2852	44.6	62	
1971			55	0	2392	43.5	73	
1972			45	0	1813	40.3	65	
1973			69	3	2958	42.9	62	
1974			76	0	3042	40.0	65	
1975			78	1	2910	37.3	56	
Career			514	5	21417	41.7	73	

Rick Partridge

Year	Team		No	Bl	Yds	Avg	Lg	NetAvg
1979	NO	N	57	0	2330	40.9	61	35.5
1980	SD	N	60	1	2347	39.1	55	31.6
1987	BUF	N	18	1	678	37.7	52	31.9
Career			135	2	5355	39.7	61	
Playoffs			5	1	192	38.4		

Bill Paschal

Year	Team		No	Bl	Yds	Avg	Lg	NetAvg
1943	NYG	N	12	0	420	35.0	59	
1944			1	0	6	6.0	6	
1946			1	0	47	47.0	47	
1948	BOS	N	2	0	80	40.0	40	
Career			16	0	553	34.6	59	

Dan Pastorini

Year	Team		No	Bl	Yds	Avg	Lg	NetAvg
1971	HOU	N	75	0	3044	40.6	62	
1972			81	1	3381	41.7	63	
1973			27	0	1087	40.3	59	
1975			62	0	2447	39.5	68	
1976			70	0	2571	36.7	74	28.3
Career			315	1	12530	39.8	74	

Frank Patrick

Year	Team		No	Bl	Yds	Avg	Lg	NetAvg
1939	CHIC	N	16		640	40.0	70	

Mike Patrick

Year	Team		No	Bl	Yds	Avg	Lg	NetAvg
1975	NE	N	83	0	3223	38.8	62	
1976			67	0	2688	40.1	52	32.2
1977			65	3	2354	36.2	64	28.9
1978			7	0	216	30.9	47	27.9
Career			222	3	8481	38.2	64	
Playoffs			3	0	132	44.0		

Billy Patterson

Year	Team		No	Bl	Yds	Avg	Lg	NetAvg
1939	CHIB	N	8		304	38.0	53	
1940	PIT	N	43		1677	39.0	68	
Career			51		1981	38.8	68	

Dainard Paulson

Year	Team		No	Bl	Yds	Avg	Lg	NetAvg
1962	NY	A	3	0	113	37.7	48	

Walter Payton

Year	Team		No	Bl	Yds	Avg	Lg	NetAvg
1975	CHI	N	1	0	39	39.0	39	

Doug Pelfrey

Year	Team		No	Bl	Yds	Avg	Lg	NetAvg
1995	CIN	N	2	0	52	26.0	27	26.0
1996			1	0	4	4.0	4	
Career			3	0	56	18.7	27	

Ray Pelfrey

Year	Team		No	Bl	Yds	Avg	Lg	NetAvg
1951	GB	N	5	0	220	44.0	46	

Bob Perina

Year	Team		No	Bl	Yds	Avg	Lg	NetAvg
1946	NY	AA	11	0	413	37.5		
1947	BKN	AA	5	2	209	41.8		
Career			16	2	622	38.9		

Don Perkins

Year	Team		No	Bl	Yds	Avg	Lg	NetAvg
1944	GB	N	1	0	34	34.0	34	
1945			1	0	13	13.0	13	
Career			2	0	47	23.5	34	

John Petty

Year	Team		No	Bl	Yds	Avg	Lg	NetAvg
1942	CHIB	N	2	0	114	57.0	53	

Milt Piepul

Year	Team		No	Bl	Yds	Avg	Lg	NetAvg
1941	DET	N	1	0	35	35.0	35	

Johnny Pingel

Year	Team		No	Bl	Yds	Avg	Lg	NetAvg
1939	DET	N	32		1376	43.0	65	

Dick Poillon

Year	Team		No	Bl	Yds	Avg	Lg	NetAvg
1942	WAS	N	11	0	424	38.5	55	
1947			15	0	533	35.5	49	
1948			50	1	2150	43.0	76	
1949			65	1	2699	40.9	59	
Career			141	2	5806	41.2	76	

Fran Polsfoot

Year	Team		No	Bl	Yds	Avg	Lg	NetAvg
1951	CHIC	N	47	0	1913	40.7	56	

Milt Popovich

Year	Team		No	Bl	Yds	Avg	Lg	NetAvg
1939	CHIC	N	27		891	33.0	48	
1940			5		210	42.0	48	
1942			3		109	36.3	40	
Career			35		1210	34.6	48	

Jim Powers

Year	Team		No	Bl	Yds	Avg	Lg	NetAvg
1953	SF	N	41	1	1706	41.6	55	

Luke Prestridge

Year	Team		No	Bl	Yds	Avg	Lg	NetAvg
1979	DEN	N	89	0	3555	39.9	63	33.0
1980			70	0	3075	43.9	57	35.9
1981			86	0	3478	40.4	67	34.8
1982			45	0	2026	45.0	65	37.8
1983			87	0	3620	41.6	60	34.0
1984	NE	N	44	0	1884	42.8	89	35.4
Career			421	0	17638	41.9	89	
Playoffs			10	0	467	46.7		

Charley Price

Year	Team		No	Bl	Yds	Avg	Lg	NetAvg
1940	DET	N	9		369	41.0	55	
1941			5	0	191	38.2	60	
1945			4	0	148	37.0	46	
1946	MIA	AA	3	1	105	35.0		
Career			21	1	813	38.7	60	

Dom Principe

Year	Team		No	Bl	Yds	Avg	Lg	NetAvg
1942	NYG	N	1	0	32	32.0	32	

Bosh Pritchard

Year	Team		No	Bl	Yds	Avg	Lg	NetAvg
1942	CLE-PHI	N	19	0	659	34.7	45	
1946	PHI	N	7	0	242	34.6	64	
1947			2	0	64	32.0	36	
Career			28	0	965	34.5	64	

Joe Prokop

Year	Team		No	Bl	Yds	Avg	Lg	NetAvg
1985	GB	N	56	0	2210	39.5	66	32.6
1987	SD	N	17	0	654	38.5	50	35.1
1988	NYJ	N	85	0	3310	38.9	64	34.2
1989			87	0	3426	39.4	76	35.5
1990			59	0	2363	40.1	58	34.7
1991	SF	N	40	0	1541	38.5	58	34.6
1992	MIA-NYG	N	32	0	1164	36.4	56	28.9
Career			376	0	14668	39.0	76	

Cal Purdin

Year	Team		No	Bl	Yds	Avg	Lg	NetAvg
1943	CHIC	N	7	1	341	48.7	72	

Chuck Ramsey

Year	Team		No	Bl	Yds	Avg	Lg	NetAvg
1977	NYJ	N	62	0	2298	37.1	61	29.6
1978			74	0	2964	40.1	79	29.9
1979			73	0	2979	40.8	64	34.5
1980			73	1	3096	42.4	59	34.1
1981			81	0	3290	40.6	65	35.6
1982			35	1	1348	38.5	54	32.1
1983			81	1	3218	39.7	56	33.5
1984			74	1	2935	39.7	64	33.8
Career			553	4	22128	40.0	79	
Playoffs			15	1	552	36.8		

Frank Reagan

Year	Team		No	Bl	Yds	Avg	Lg	NetAvg
1941	NYG	N	12	1	488	40.7	54	
1946			20	0	856	42.8	58	
1947			60	1	2613	43.5	67	
1948			60	1	2330	38.8	64	
1949	PHI	N	8	0	362	45.3	63	
1950			54	0	2770	51.3	68	
1951			10	0	367	36.7	48	
Career			224	3	9786	43.7	68	

Bert Rechichar

Year	Team		No	Bl	Yds	Avg	Lg	NetAvg
1956	BAL	N	33	0	1277	38.7	56	
1957			5	0	157	31.4	51	
Career			38	0	1434	37.7	56	

Rick Redman

Year	Team		No	Bl	Yds	Avg	Lg	NetAvg
1965	SD	A	29	0	1145	39.5	59	
1966			66	0	2442	37.0	54	
1967			58	0	2147	37.0	56	
Career			153	0	5734	37.5	59	

Bob Reinhard

Year	Team		No	Bl	Yds	Avg	Lg	NetAvg
1946	LA	AA	43	1	1996	46.4	67	
1947			27	1	1279	47.4	81	
1948			6	0	204	34.0		
Career			76	2	3479	45.8	81	

Albie Reisz

Year	Team		No	Bl	Yds	Avg	Lg	NetAvg
1944	CLE	N	24	0	960	40.0	66	
1945			7	0	241	34.4	51	
1947	BUF	AA	57	0	2107	37.0		
Career			88	0	3308	37.6	66	

Bill Renner

Year	Team		No	Bl	Yds	Avg	Lg	NetAvg
1986	GB	N	15	3	622	41.5	50	30.6
1987			20	0	712	35.6	49	31.2
Career			35	3	1334	38.1	50	

Bill Reynolds

Year	Team		No	Bl	Yds	Avg	Lg	NetAvg
1945	CHIC	N	38	0	1383	36.4	48	

Jim Reynolds

Year	Team		No	Bl	Yds	Avg	Lg	NetAvg
1946	MIA	AA	1	0	39	39.0	39	

Benny Ricardo

Year	Team		No	Bl	Yds	Avg	Lg	NetAvg
1976	DET	N	1	0	16	16.0	16	16.0

Kink Richards

Year	Team		No	Bl	Yds	Avg	Lg	NetAvg
1939	NYG	N	1		39	39.0	39	

Pat Richter

Year	Team		No	Bl	Yds	Avg	Lg	NetAvg
1963	WAS	N	53	0	2210	41.7	61	
1964			91	0	3749	41.2	63	
1965			54	0	2364	43.8	72	
1966			68	0	2884	42.4	60	
1967			72	0	2976	41.3	58	
Career			338	0	14183	42.0	72	

Colin Ridgway

Year	Team		No	Bl	Yds	Avg	Lg	NetAvg
1965	DAL	N	13	0	510	39.2	44	

Dick Riffle

Year	Team		No	Bl	Yds	Avg	Lg	NetAvg
1939	PHI	N	17		680	40.0	51	
1940			14		476	34.0	48	
1941	PIT	N	6	1	246	35.2	51	
1942			1	0	40	40.0	40	
Career			38	1	1446	37.9	51	

John Roach

Year	Team		No	Bl	Yds	Avg	Lg	NetAvg
1956	CHIC	N	11	0	449	40.8	54	

Jack Robbins

Year	Team		No	Bl	Yds	Avg	Lg	NetAvg
1939	CHIC	N	2			41.0	53	

George Roberts

Year	Team		No	Bl	Yds	Avg	Lg	NetAvg
1978	MIA	N	81	0	3263	40.3	59	34.3
1979			69	1	2772	40.2	68	34.6
1980			77	2	3279	42.6	71	35.2
1981	SD	N	62	1	2540	41.0	61	35.4
1982	ATL	N	17	0	690	40.6	54	30.1
Career			306	4	12544	41.0	71	
Playoffs			20	0	821	41.0		

Hal Roberts

Year	Team		No	Bl	Yds	Avg	Lg	NetAvg
1974	STL	N	81	0	3131	38.7	57	
Playoffs			7	0	255	36.4		

Bobbie Robertson

Year	Team		No	Bl	Yds	Avg	Lg	NetAvg
1942	BKN	N	1	0	32	32.0	32	

Marshall Robnett

Year	Team		No	Bl	Yds	Avg	Lg	NetAvg
1944	C-P	N	1	0	14	14.0	14	

Reggie Roby

Year	Team		No	Bl	Yds	Avg	Lg	NetAvg
1983	MIA	N	74	1	3189	43.1	64	36.5
1984			51	0	2281	44.7	69	38.1
1985			59	0	2576	43.7	63	34.7
1986			56	0	2476	44.2	73	37.4
1987			32	0	1371	42.8	77	38.3
1988			64	0	2754	43.0	64	35.3
1989			58	1	2458	42.4	58	35.3
1990			72	0	3022	42.0	62	35.6
1991			54	1	2466	45.7	64	36.4
1992			35	0	1443	41.2	60	34.3
1993	WAS	N	78	0	3447	44.2	60	37.2
1994			82	0	3639	44.4	65	36.1
1995	TB	N	77	1	3296	42.8	61	36.2
1996	HOU	N	67	1	2973	44.4	68	38.0
Career			859	5	37391	43.5	77	
Playoffs			40	0	1622	40.5		

Ruben Rodriguez

Year	Team		No	Bl	Yds	Avg	Lg	NetAvg
1987	SEA	N	47	0	1880	40.0	63	34.0
1988			70	0	2858	40.8	68	36.8
1989			75	1	2995	39.9	59	32.9

Ruben Rodriguez *continued*

Year	Team		No	Bl	Yds	Avg	Lg	NetAvg
1992	DEN-NYG	N	46	1	1907	41.5	55	34.5
Career			238	2	9640	40.5	68	
Playoffs			13	0	575	44.2		

Herm Rohrig

Year	Team		No	Bl	Yds	Avg	Lg	NetAvg
1941	GB	N	5	0	214	42.8	52	

Tobin Rote

Year	Team		No	Bl	Yds	Avg	Lg	NetAvg
1951	GB	N	1	0	55	55.0	55	
1953			1	0	57	57.0	57	
Career			2	0	112	56.0	57	

Tom Rouen

Year	Team		No	Bl	Yds	Avg	Lg	NetAvg
1993	DEN	N	67	1	3017	45.0	62	37.1
1994			76	0	3258	42.9	59	37.1
1995			52	1	2192	42.2	61	37.6
1996			65	0	2714	41.8	57	36.2
Career			260	2	11181	43.0	62	
Playoffs			9	0	348	38.7		

Brad Rowland

Year	Team		No	Bl	Yds	Avg	Lg	NetAvg
1951	CHIB	N	1	0	18	18.0	18	

Mark Royals

Year	Team		No	Bl	Yds	Avg	Lg	NetAvg
1987	STL-PHI	N	11	0	431	39.2	48	23.3
1990	TB	N	72	0	2902	40.3	62	34.0
1991			84	0	3389	40.3	56	32.3
1992	PIT	N	73	1	3119	42.7	58	35.6
1993			89	0	3781	42.5	61	34.2
1994			97	0	3849	39.7	64	35.7
1995	DET	N	57	2	2393	42.0	69	31.0
1996			69	1	3020	43.8	60	33.4
Career			552	4	22884	41.5	69	
Playoffs			24	1	980	40.8		

Max Runager

Year	Team		No	Bl	Yds	Avg	Lg	NetAvg
1979	PHI	N	74	1	2927	39.6	57	34.8
1980			75	1	2947	39.3	58	33.7
1981			63	0	2567	40.7	64	34.9
1982			44	0	1784	40.5	53	32.9
1983			59	0	2459	41.7	55	34.2
1984	SF	N	56	1	2341	41.8	59	33.8
1985			86	1	3422	39.8	57	33.9
1986			83	2	3450	41.6	62	34.3
1987			55	1	2157	39.2	56	33.0
1988	SF-CLE	N	49	2	1959	40.0	52	33.7
1989	PHI	N	17	0	568	33.4	52	30.5
Career			661	9	26581	40.2	64	
Playoffs			63	0	2466	39.1		

Clive Rush

Year	Team		No	Bl	Yds	Avg	Lg	NetAvg
1953	GB	N	60	0	2265	37.8	60	

Doug Russell

Year	Team		No	Bl	Yds	Avg	Lg	NetAvg
1939	CHIC-CLE	N	8		328	41.0	56	

Roger Ruzek

Year	Team		No	Bl	Yds	Avg	Lg	NetAvg
1989	DAL	N	1	0	28	28.0	28	28.0

Dave Ryan

Year	Team		No	Bl	Yds	Avg	Lg	NetAvg
1945	DET	N	17	0	668	39.3	50	

Kent Ryan

Year	Team		No	Bl	Yds	Avg	Lg	NetAvg
1939	DET	N	3		111	37.0	40	
1940			9		351	39.0	53	
Career			12		462	38.5	53	

Julie Rykovich

Year	Team		No	Bl	Yds	Avg	Lg	NetAvg
1950	CHIB	N	1	0	48	48.0	48	

Jack Salschneider

Year	Team		No	Bl	Yds	Avg	Lg	NetAvg
1949	NYG	N	14	0	495	35.4	46	

Spec Sanders

Year	Team		No	Bl	Yds	Avg	Lg	NetAvg
1946	NY	AA	31	2	1208	39.0	63	
1947			44	2	1938	44.0	84	
1948			42	0	1707	40.6		
1950	NYY	N	69	2	3001	43.5	63	
Career			186	6	7854	42.2	84	
Playoffs			1	0	45	45.0	45	

Curt Sandig

Year	Team		No	Bl	Yds	Avg	Lg	NetAvg
1942	PIT	N	37	0	1436	38.8	63	

Curt Sandig *continued*

Year	Team		No	Bl	Yds	Avg	Lg	NetAvg
1946	BUF	AA	4	0	155	38.8		
Career			41	0	1591	38.8	63	

Dom Sanzotta

Year	Team		No	Bl	Yds	Avg	Lg	NetAvg
1942	DET	N	1	0	42	42.0	42	

Rick Sapienza

Year	Team		No	Bl	Yds	Avg	Lg	NetAvg
1960	NY	A	8		259	32.4		

Charley Sarratt

Year	Team		No	Bl	Yds	Avg	Lg	NetAvg
1948	DET	N	5	0	166	33.2	43	

Larry Sartori

Year	Team		No	Bl	Yds	Avg	Lg	NetAvg
1942	DET	N	1	0	42	42.0	42	

Todd Sauerbrun

Year	Team		No	Bl	Yds	Avg	Lg	NetAvg
1995	CHI	N	55	0	2080	37.8	61	31.1
1996			78	0	3491	44.8	72	34.9
Career			133	0	5571	41.9	72	

Buzzy Sawyer

Year	Team		No	Bl	Yds	Avg	Lg	NetAvg
1987	DAL	N	16	0	639	39.9	54	31.4

John Sawyer

Year	Team		No	Bl	Yds	Avg	Lg	NetAvg
1976	HOU	N	1	0	32	32.0	32	35.0

Mike Saxon

Year	Team		No	Bl	Yds	Avg	Lg	NetAvg
1985	DAL	N	81	1	3396	41.9	57	35.5
1986			86	1	3498	40.7	58	34.4
1987			68	0	2685	39.5	63	34.2
1988			80	0	3271	40.9	55	34.2
1989			79	2	3233	40.9	56	34.3
1990			79	0	3413	43.2	62	35.6
1991			57	0	2426	42.6	64	36.8
1992			61	0	2620	43.0	58	33.5
1993	NE	N	73	3	3096	42.4	59	34.8
1994	MIN	N	77	0	3301	42.9	67	36.2
1995			72	0	2948	40.9	60	33.1
Career			813	7	33887	41.7	67	
Playoffs			30	1	1262	42.1		

Jimmy Saxton

Year	Team		No	Bl	Yds	Avg	Lg	NetAvg
1962	DAL	A	3	0	139	46.3	51	
Playoffs			2	0	58	29.0		

Bob Scarpitto

Year	Team		No	Bl	Yds	Avg	Lg	NetAvg
1965	DEN	A	67	0	2833	42.3	74	
1966			**76**	1	**3480**	**45.8**	70	
1967			104	1	**4713**	**45.3**	73	
1968	BOS	A	32	2	1382	43.2	87	
Career			279	4	12408	44.5	87	

Ivan Schottel

Year	Team		No	Bl	Yds	Avg	Lg	NetAvg
1946	DET	N	5	0	208	41.6	60	

Jay Schroeder

Year	Team		No	Bl	Yds	Avg	Lg	NetAvg
1985	WAS	N	4	0	132	33.0	44	25.5

Wilson Schwenk

Year	Team		No	Bl	Yds	Avg	Lg	NetAvg
1942	CHIC	N	3	0	114	38.0	41	

Bobby Scott

Year	Team		No	Bl	Yds	Avg	Lg	NetAvg
1977	NO	N	3	0	95	31.7	34	31.7

Bucky Scribner

Year	Team		No	Bl	Yds	Avg	Lg	NetAvg
1983	GB	N	69	1	2869	41.6	70	33.5
1984			85	0	3596	42.3	61	35.2
1987	MIN	N	20	0	827	41.4	54	36.4
1988			84	2	3387	40.3	55	32.6
1989			72	0	2864	39.8	55	33.4
Career			330	3	13543	41.0	70	
Playoffs			36	1	1304	36.2		

John Seedborg

Year	Team		No	Bl	Yds	Avg	Lg	NetAvg
1965	WAS	N	6	1	247	41.2	49	

Larry Seiple

Year	Team		No	Bl	Yds	Avg	Lg	NetAvg
1967	MIA	A	69	1	2909	42.2	70	
1968			75	0	3044	40.6	60	
1969			78	2	3263	41.8	66	
1970	MIA	N	58	0	2392	41.2	67	
1971			51	1	2087	40.9	73	
1972			36	0	1437	39.9	54	

Larry Seiple *continued*

Year	Team		No	Bl	Yds	Avg	Lg	NetAvg
1973			48	0	2031	42.3	57	
1974			65	0	2511	38.6	60	
1975			65	0	2506	38.6	61	
1976			62	0	2366	38.2	56	32.2
1977			22	1	801	36.4	54	31.1
Career			629	5	25347	40.3	73	
Playoffs			50	0	2000	40.0		

Rafael Septien

Year	Team		No	Bl	Yds	Avg	Lg	NetAvg
1981	DAL	N	2	0	62	31.0	33	31.0

Bob Seymour

Year	Team		No	Bl	Yds	Avg	Lg	NetAvg
1944	WAS	N	10	0	355	35.5	51	

Charley Shepard

Year	Team		No	Bl	Yds	Avg	Lg	NetAvg
1956	PIT	N	26	0	931	35.8	49	

Bill Shepherd

Year	Team		No	Bl	Yds	Avg	Lg	NetAvg
1939	DET	N	23		851	37.0	54	
1940			1		40	40.0	40	
Career			24		891	37.1	54	

Dave Sherer

Year	Team		No	Bl	Yds	Avg	Lg	NetAvg
1959	BAL	N	51	0	2140	42.0	60	
1960	DAL	N	56	1	2420	43.2	67	
Career			107	1	4560	42.6	67	
Playoffs			6	0	218	36.3		

Allie Sherman

Year	Team		No	Bl	Yds	Avg	Lg	NetAvg
1944	PHI	N	1	0	27	27.0	27	

Del Shofner

Year	Team		No	Bl	Yds	Avg	Lg	NetAvg
1957	LA	N	2	0	97	48.5	52	
1958			49	0	2018	41.2	62	
1959			47	1	2004	42.6	66	
1960			53	1	2301	43.4	63	
Career			151	2	6420	42.5	66	

Jim Shofner

Year	Team		No	Bl	Yds	Avg	Lg	NetAvg
1959	CLE	N	23	0	860	37.4	48	

Don Silvestri

Year	Team		No	Bl	Yds	Avg	Lg	NetAvg
1995	NYJ	N	5	0	238	47.6	61	33.6

Jack Simmons

Year	Team		No	Bl	Yds	Avg	Lg	NetAvg
1953	CHIC	N	22	0	843	38.3	61	

Frankie Sinkwich

Year	Team		No	Bl	Yds	Avg	Lg	NetAvg
1943	DET	N	12	0	551	45.9	64	
1944			45	0	1845	41.0	73	
1947	NY-BAL	AA	6	1	260	43.3		
Career			63	1	2656	42.2	73	

Tom Skladany

Year	Team		No	Bl	Yds	Avg	Lg	NetAvg
1978	DET	N	86	1	3654	42.5	63	35.0
1979			10	0	406	40.6	52	40.1
1980			72	1	3036	42.2	67	35.3
1981			64	0	2784	43.5	74	**37.3**
1982			36	0	1483	41.2	59	34.0
1983	PHI	N	27	0	1062	39.3	51	31.5
Career			295	2	12425	42.1	74	
Playoffs			3	0	115	38.3		

Dwight Sloan

Year	Team		No	Bl	Yds	Avg	Lg	NetAvg
1939	DET	N	1		43	43.0	43	
1940			2		54	27.0	32	
Career			3		97	32.3	43	

Marty Slovak

Year	Team		No	Bl	Yds	Avg	Lg	NetAvg
1939	CLE	N	1	0	15	15.0	15	

Dave Smigelsky

Year	Team		No	Bl	Yds	Avg	Lg	NetAvg
1982	ATL	N	26	0	1000	38.5	54	33.9

Bill Smith

Year	Team		No	Bl	Yds	Avg	Lg	NetAvg
1939	CHIC	N	1	0	36	36.0	36	

Fletcher Smith

Year	Team		No	Bl	Yds	Avg	Lg	NetAvg
1968	CIN	A	8	0	230	28.8	45	

Gaylon Smith

Year	Team		No	Bl	Yds	Avg	Lg	NetAvg
1940	CLE	N	11		396	36.0	62	

Gaylon Smith *continued*

Year	Team		No	Bl	Yds	Avg	Lg	NetAvg
1941			1	0	23	23.0	23	
Career			12	0	419	34.9	62	

George Smith

Year	Team		No	Bl	Yds	Avg	Lg	NetAvg
1944	BKN	N	6	0	223	37.2	52	
1945	BOS	N	9	0	355	39.4	47	
Career			15	0	578	38.5	52	

Jackie Smith

Year	Team		No	Bl	Yds	Avg	Lg	NetAvg
1964	STL	N	41	0	1658	40.4	64	
1965			38	1	1532	40.3	62	
1966			46	1	1781	37.9	56	
Career			125	2	4971	39.8	64	

Jim Smith

Year	Team		No	Bl	Yds	Avg	Lg	NetAvg
1948	BUF-BKN	AA	13	1	538	41.4		
1950	DET	N	32	0	1280	40.0	60	
1951			48	1	2082	43.4	73	
1952			61	0	2729	44.7	66	
1953			40	0	1648	41.2	57	
Career			194	2	8277	42.7	73	
Playoffs			11	0	464	42.2		

Riley Smith

Year	Team		No	Bl	Yds	Avg	Lg	NetAvg
Playoffs			10	2	356	35.6		

Tim Smith

Year	Team		No	Bl	Yds	Avg	Lg	NetAvg
1985	HOU	N	1	0	26	26.0	26	26.0

Dave Smukler

Year	Team		No	Bl	Yds	Avg	Lg	NetAvg
1939	PHI	N	10		480	48.0	62	
1944	BOS	N	2	0	49	24.5	33	
Career			12	0	529	44.0	62	

Ron Snidow

Year	Team		No	Bl	Yds	Avg	Lg	NetAvg
1965	WAS	N	9	0	336	37.3	53	

Bob Snyder

Year	Team		No	Bl	Yds	Avg	Lg	NetAvg
1939	CHIB	N	7		294	42.0	46	
1940			5		175	35.0	48	
1941			2	0	76	38.0	38	
1943			10	0	378	37.8	48	
Career			24	0	923	38.5	48	

Hank Soar

Year	Team		No	Bl	Yds	Avg	Lg	NetAvg
1942	NYG	N	3	0	126	42.0	46	

Ronnie South

Year	Team		No	Bl	Yds	Avg	Lg	NetAvg
1968	NO	N	14	0	387	27.6	44	

Mac Speedie

Year	Team		No	Bl	Yds	Avg	Lg	NetAvg
1946	CLE	AA	3	0	84	28.0		

Johnny Spirida

Year	Team		No	Bl	Yds	Avg	Lg	NetAvg
1939	WAS	N	10		390	39.0	54	

Ron Springs

Year	Team		No	Bl	Yds	Avg	Lg	NetAvg
1986	TB	N	1	0	43	43.0	43	39.0

Steve Spurrier

Year	Team		No	Bl	Yds	Avg	Lg	NetAvg
1967	SF	N	72	1	2745	38.1	61	
1968			68	0	2651	39.0	54	
1969			12	0	468	39.0	57	
1970			75	0	2877	38.4	58	
1971			2	0	77	38.5	40	
Career			229	1	8818	38.5	61	
Playoffs			28	1	1041	37.2		

Ray Stachowicz

Year	Team		No	Bl	Yds	Avg	Lg	NetAvg
1981	GB	N	82	2	3330	40.6	72	31.4
1982			42	0	1687	40.2	53	32.4
1983	CHI	N	12	2	447	37.3	48	27.6
Career			136	4	5464	40.2	72	
Playoffs			5	0	196	39.2		

Norm Standlee

Year	Team		No	Bl	Yds	Avg	Lg	NetAvg
1941	CHIB	N	2	0	126	63.0	70	
1946	SF	AA	1	0	34	34.0	34	
1949			7	1	276	39.4		
Career			10	1	436	43.6	70	

Rohn Stark

Year	Team		No	Bl	Yds	Avg	Lg	NetAvg
1982	BAL	N	46	0	2044	44.4	60	34.3

Rohn Stark *continued*

Year	Team		No	Bl	Yds	Avg	Lg	NetAvg
1983			91	0	**4124**	**45.3**	68	36.3
1984	IND	N	**98**	0	4383	44.7	72	37.2
1985			78	2	3584	**45.9**	68	34.2
1986			76	0	3432	**45.2**	63	37.2
1987			61	2	2440	40.0	63	30.9
1988			64	0	2784	43.5	65	34.5
1989			79	1	3392	42.9	64	32.9
1990			71	1	3084	43.4	61	37.4
1991			82	0	3492	42.6	65	34.8
1992			83	0	3716	44.8	64	39.3
1993			83	0	3595	43.3	65	35.9
1994			73	1	3092	42.4	60	34.1
1995	PIT	N	59	0	2368	40.1	64	33.3
1996	CAR	N	77	0	3128	40.6	60	36.0
Career			1121	7	48658	43.4	72	
Playoffs			22	0	851	38.7		

John Starnes

Year	Team		No	Bl	Yds	Avg	Lg	NetAvg
1987	ATL	N	6	0	203	33.8	49	30.7

Paul Staroba

Year	Team		No	Bl	Yds	Avg	Lg	NetAvg
1973	GB	N	12	0	373	31.1	49	

Ben Starrett

Year	Team		No	Bl	Yds	Avg	Lg	NetAvg
1942	GB	N	1	0	43	43.0	43	
1944			2	0	66	33.0	43	
Career			3	0	109	36.3	43	

Leo Stasica

Year	Team		No	Bl	Yds	Avg	Lg	NetAvg
1943	WAS	N	1	0	38	38.0	38	
1944	BOS	N	1	0	38	38.0	38	
Career			2	0	76	38.0	38	

Ernie Steele

Year	Team		No	Bl	Yds	Avg	Lg	NetAvg
1942	PHI	N	2	0	61	30.5	51	

Ken Steinmetz

Year	Team		No	Bl	Yds	Avg	Lg	NetAvg
1944	BOS	N	1	0	17	17.0	17	
1945			8	1	240	30.0	46	
Career			9	1	257	28.6	46	

Jan Stenerud

Year	Team		No	Bl	Yds	Avg	Lg	NetAvg
1976	KC	N	1	0	28	28.0	28	28.0

Bob Steuber

Year	Team		No	Bl	Yds	Avg	Lg	NetAvg
1948	BUF	AA	1	0	40	40.0	40	

Dean Steward

Year	Team		No	Bl	Yds	Avg	Lg	NetAvg
1943	P-P	N	2	0	84	42.0	47	

Kordell Stewart

Year	Team		No	Bl	Yds	Avg	Lg	NetAvg
Playoffs			1	0	41	41.0	41	

Vaughn Stewart

Year	Team		No	Bl	Yds	Avg	Lg	NetAvg
1944	BKN	N	1	0	58	58.0	58	

Jim Still

Year	Team		No	Bl	Yds	Avg	Lg	NetAvg
1948	BUF	AA	47	0	1825	38.8		
1949			16	0	614	38.4		
Career			63	0	2439	38.7		
Playoffs			6	0	255	42.5		

Ken Stofer

Year	Team		No	Bl	Yds	Avg	Lg	NetAvg
1946	BUF	AA	3	0	108	36.0		

Eddie Stofko

Year	Team		No	Bl	Yds	Avg	Lg	NetAvg
1945	PIT	N	3	0	109	36.3	46	

Avatus Stone

Year	Team		No	Bl	Yds	Avg	Lg	NetAvg
1958	BAL	N	1	0	28	28.0	28	

Jerry Stovall

Year	Team		No	Bl	Yds	Avg	Lg	NetAvg
1963	STL	N	65	0	2647	40.7	69	
1964			15	0	632	42.1	60	
1965			2	0	80	40.0	43	
1966			5	0	139	27.8	35	
Career			87	0	3498	40.2	69	

Pete Stoyanovich

Year	Team		No	Bl	Yds	Avg	Lg	NetAvg
1991	MIA	N	2	0	85	42.5	49	38.5
1992			2	0	90	45.0	48	45.0
Career			4	0	175	43.8	49	

Joe Stringfellow

Year	Team		No	Bl	Yds	Avg	Lg	NetAvg
1942	DET	N	9	0	363	40.3	49	

Don Strock

Year	Team		No	Bl	Yds	Avg	Lg	NetAvg
1987	MIA	N	9	0	277	30.8	44	30.8

Ken Strong

Year	Team		No	Bl	Yds	Avg	Lg	NetAvg
1939	NYG	N	5		275	55.0	69	
1944			1	0	44	44.0	44	
1945			3	0	134	44.7	51	
Career			9	0	453	50.3	69	

Dan Stryzinski

Year	Team		No	Bl	Yds	Avg	Lg	NetAvg
1990	PIT	N	65	1	2454	37.8	51	34.1
1991			74	1	2996	40.5	63	36.3
1992	TB	N	74	0	3015	40.7	57	36.2
1993			**93**	1	3772	40.6	57	35.3
1994			72	0	2800	38.9	53	35.9
1995	ATL	N	67	0	2759	41.2	64	36.2
1996			75	0	3152	42.0	58	35.5
Career			520	3	20948	40.3	64	
Playoffs			5	0	183	36.6		

Pat Studstill

Year	Team		No	Bl	Yds	Avg	Lg	NetAvg
1961	DET	N	1	0	32	32.0	32	
1965			**78**	0	3335	42.8	69	
1966			72	0	2956	41.1	66	
1967			36	0	1602	44.5	78	
1968	LA	N	**81**	0	3207	39.6	58	
1969			**80**	0	**3259**	40.7	60	
1970			67	0	2618	39.1	53	
1971			70	0	2896	41.4	60	
1972	NE	N	74	1	2859	38.6	57	
Career			559	1	22764	40.7	78	
Playoffs			3	0	110	36.7		

Kent Sullivan

Year	Team		No	Bl	Yds	Avg	Lg	NetAvg
1991	HOU	N	3	0	106	35.3	37	32.3
1992	KC	N	6	0	247	41.2	59	38.2
1993	HOU-SD	N	15	0	614	40.9	50	37.4
Career			24	0	967	40.3	59	

Wilbur Summers

Year	Team		No	Bl	Yds	Avg	Lg	NetAvg
1977	DET	N	93	1	3420	36.8	51	30.5

Steve Superick

Year	Team		No	Bl	Yds	Avg	Lg	NetAvg
1987	HOU	N	8	0	269	33.6	45	28.0

Terry Swanson

Year	Team		No	Bl	Yds	Avg	Lg	NetAvg
1967	BOS	A	65	0	2632	40.5	62	
1968			60	2	2449	40.8	57	
1969	CIN	A	12	0	459	38.3	55	
Career			137	2	5540	40.4	62	

Bob Sweiger

Year	Team		No	Bl	Yds	Avg	Lg	NetAvg
1946	NY	AA	1	0	52	52.0	52	

Larry Swider

Year	Team		No	Bl	Yds	Avg	Lg	NetAvg
1979	DET	N	88	0	3523	40.0	72	33.5
1980	STL	N	**99**	1	4111	41.5	66	31.7
1981	TB	N	58	2	2476	42.7	62	33.1
1982			39	1	1620	41.5	59	32.7
Career			284	4	11730	41.3	72	
Playoffs			11	0	453	41.2		

Bob Swisher

Year	Team		No	Bl	Yds	Avg	Lg	NetAvg
1939	CHIB	N	3		93	31.0	36	

Johnny Sylvester

Year	Team		No	Bl	Yds	Avg	Lg	NetAvg
1947	NY	AA	1	0	42	42.0	42	

George Taliaferro

Year	Team		No	Bl	Yds	Avg	Lg	NetAvg
1949	LA	AA	25	2	982	39.3		
1950	NYY	N	1	0	39	39.0	39	
1951			75	1	2881	38.4	72	
1953	BAL	N	65	0	2437	37.5	61	
Career			166	3	6339	38.2	72	

Stan Talley

Year	Team		No	Bl	Yds	Avg	Lg	NetAvg
1987	LARI	N	56	1	2277	40.7	63	34.6

John Teltschik

Year	Team		No	Bl	Yds	Avg	Lg	NetAvg
1986	PHI	N	**108**	1	**4493**	41.6	62	33.6
1987			**82**	1	3131	38.2	60	32.0

John Teltschik continued

Year	Team	No	Bl	Yds	Avg	Lg	NetAvg
1988		**98**	3	3958	40.4	70	33.9
1989		57	0	2246	39.4	58	35.3
Career		345	5	13828	40.1	70	
Playoffs		4	0	130	32.5		

George Terlep

Year	Team	No	Bl	Yds	Avg	Lg	NetAvg
1946	BUF AA	1	0	31	31.0	31	

Lee Tevis

Year	Team	No	Bl	Yds	Avg	Lg	NetAvg
1947	BKN AA	5	0	246	49.2		
1948		5	0	214	42.8		
Career		10	0	460	46.0		

Joe Theismann

Year	Team	No	Bl	Yds	Avg	Lg	NetAvg
1985	WAS N	1	0	1	1.0	1	1.0

Clendon Thomas

Year	Team	No	Bl	Yds	Avg	Lg	NetAvg
1958	LA N	2	0	66	33.0	34	

Tommy Thompson

Year	Team	No	Bl	Yds	Avg	Lg	NetAvg
1941	PHI N	1	0	43	43.0	43	

Tommy Thompson

Year	Team	No	Bl	Yds	Avg	Lg	NetAvg
1995	SF N	57	0	2312	40.6	65	33.7
1996		73	2	3217	44.1	65	38.2
Career		130	2	5529	42.5	65	
Playoffs		17	0	658	38.7		

Bob Thurbon

Year	Team	No	Bl	Yds	Avg	Lg	NetAvg
1944	C-P N	15	1	450	30.0	43	

Sid Tinsley

Year	Team	No	Bl	Yds	Avg	Lg	NetAvg
1945	PIT N	56	1	2262	40.4	58	

Dick Todd

Year	Team	No	Bl	Yds	Avg	Lg	NetAvg
1939	WAS N	5		160	32.0	41	
1940		12		432	36.0	53	
1941		10	0	435	43.5	61	
1942		11	0	442	40.2	69	
Career		38	0	1469	38.7	69	
Playoffs		1	0	35	35.0	35	

Lou Tomasetti

Year	Team	No	Bl	Yds	Avg	Lg	NetAvg
1939	PIT N	3		111	37.0	46	

Andy Tomasic

Year	Team	No	Bl	Yds	Avg	Lg	NetAvg
1942	PIT N	16	1	604	35.5	58	
1946		1	0	56	56.0	56	
Career		17	1	660	38.8	58	

Mario Tonelli

Year	Team	No	Bl	Yds	Avg	Lg	NetAvg
1940	CHIC N	1	0	15	15.0	15	

Charley Trippi

Year	Team	No	Bl	Yds	Avg	Lg	NetAvg
1948	CHIC N	13	0	564	43.4	56	
1949		8	0	292	36.5	46	
1950		2	0	94	47.0	56	
1951		12	0	446	37.2	48	
1952		16	0	589	36.8	47	
1953		54	0	2316	42.9	63	
1954		59	0	2308	39.1	62	
1955		32	0	1301	40.7	53	
Career		196	0	7910	40.4	63	

Frank Tripucka

Year	Team	No	Bl	Yds	Avg	Lg	NetAvg
1949	DET N	27	1	1075	39.8	50	
1950	CHIC N	18	0	790	43.9	63	
1951		10	1	319	29.0	56	
1952	CHIC-DAL N	34	2	1321	38.8	65	
Career		89	4	3505	39.4	65	

Bob Trocolor

Year	Team	No	Bl	Yds	Avg	Lg	NetAvg
1942	NYG N	16	0	661	41.3	61	
1943		5	0	155	31.0	41	
1944	BKN N	1	0	10	10.0	10	
Career		22	0	826	37.5	61	

Tom Tupa

Year	Team	No	Bl	Yds	Avg	Lg	NetAvg
1989	PHX N	6	0	280	46.7	51	39.8
1994	CLE N	80	0	3211	40.1	65	35.4
1995		65	0	2831	43.6	64	36.2

Tom Tupa continued

Year	Team	No	Bl	Yds	Avg	Lg	NetAvg
1996	NE N	63	0	2739	43.5	62	36.0
Career		214	0	9061	42.3	65	
Playoffs		29	0	1207	41.6		

Matt Turk

Year	Team	No	Bl	Yds	Avg	Lg	NetAvg
1995	WAS N	74	0	3140	42.4	60	37.7
1996		75	0	3386	45.1	63	**39.2**
Career		149	0	6526	43.8	63	

Bake Turner

Year	Team	No	Bl	Yds	Avg	Lg	NetAvg
1969	NY A	2	0	89	44.5	46	

Jay Turner

Year	Team	No	Bl	Yds	Avg	Lg	NetAvg
1939	WAS N	1		33	33.0	33	

Rick Tuten

Year	Team	No	Bl	Yds	Avg	Lg	NetAvg
1989	PHI N	7	0	256	36.6	45	33.6
1990	BUF N	53	0	2107	39.8	55	34.2
1991	SEA N	49	0	2106	43.0	60	36.9
1992		**108**	0	**4760**	44.1	65	38.7
1993		90	1	**4007**	44.5	64	37.3
1994		91	0	3905	42.9	64	36.7
1995		83	0	3735	**45.0**	73	36.5
1996		85	1	3746	44.1	66	34.5
Career		566	2	24622	43.5	73	
Playoffs		17	0	662	38.9		

Scott Tyner

Year	Team	No	Bl	Yds	Avg	Lg	NetAvg
1994	ATL N	8	0	285	35.6	46	31.8

Norm Van Brocklin

Year	Team	No	Bl	Yds	Avg	Lg	NetAvg
1949	LA N	2	0	91	45.5	46	
1950		11	0	466	42.4	51	
1951		47	1	1992	42.4	62	
1952		29	0	1270	43.8	66	
1953		60	0	2529	42.1	57	
1954		44	0	1874	42.6	61	
1955		60	0	2676	**44.6**	61	
1956		48	0	2070	**43.1**	72	
1957		54	0	2392	44.3	71	
1958	PHI N	53	1	2225	42.0	58	
1959		52	1	2263	43.5	59	
1960		60	0	2585	43.1	70	
Career		520	3	22433	43.1	72	
Playoffs		16	0	601	37.6		

Steve Van Buren

Year	Team	No	Bl	Yds	Avg	Lg	NetAvg
1944	PHI N	1	0	35	35.0	35	
1946		1	0	41	41.0	41	
Career		2	0	76	38.0	41	

Hal Van Every

Year	Team	No	Bl	Yds	Avg	Lg	NetAvg
1940	GB N	17		612	36.0	50	
1941		13	0	506	38.9	65	
Career		30	0	1118	37.3	65	

Billy Van Heusen

Year	Team	No	Bl	Yds	Avg	Lg	NetAvg
1968	DEN A	88	0	3853	43.8	68	
1969		25	0	1021	40.8	61	
1970	DEN N	87	0	3732	42.9	64	
1971		75	0	3176	42.3	62	
1972		59	1	2408	40.8	60	
1973		69	0	3114	45.1	78	
1974		74	1	3024	40.9	61	
1975		63	0	2515	39.9	64	
1976		31	0	1093	35.3	52	28.3
Career		571	4	23936	41.9	78	

Art Van Tone

Year	Team	No	Bl	Yds	Avg	Lg	NetAvg
1944	DET N	2	0	94	47.0	50	

Joe Vetrano

Year	Team	No	Bl	Yds	Avg	Lg	NetAvg
1946	SF AA	6	0	236	39.3		
1948		1	0	38	38.0	38	
Career		7	0	274	39.1	38	

Danny Villanueva

Year	Team	No	Bl	Yds	Avg	Lg	NetAvg
1961	LA N	46	0	1845	40.1	53	
1962		86	1	3960	46.0	65	
1963		81	0	3678	45.4	68	
1964		82	0	3616	44.1	58	
1965	DAL	60	0	2505	41.8	58	
1966		64	1	2551	39.9	58	

Danny Villanueva continued

Year	Team	No	Bl	Yds	Avg	Lg	NetAvg
1967		67	0	2707	40.4	57	
Career		486	2	20862	42.9	68	
Playoffs		14	0	531	37.9		

Adam Vinatieri

Year	Team	No	Bl	Yds	Avg	Lg	NetAvg
1996	NE N	1	0	27	27.0	27	27.0

Uwe von Schamann

Year	Team	No	Bl	Yds	Avg	Lg	NetAvg
1979	MIA N	1	0	31	31.0	31	11.0

Bryan Wagner

Year	Team	No	Bl	Yds	Avg	Lg	NetAvg
1987	CHI N	36	1	1461	40.6	71	32.1
1988		79	0	3282	41.5	70	33.4
1989	CLE N	**97**	0	**3817**	39.4	60	33.8
1990		74	4	2879	38.9	65	30.9
1991	NE N	14	0	548	39.1	54	29.1
1992	GB N	30	0	1222	40.7	52	35.0
1993		74	0	3174	42.9	60	36.3
1994	SD N	65	0	2705	41.6	59	35.3
1995	NE N	37	0	1557	42.1	57	35.4
Career		506	5	20645	40.8	71	
Playoffs		38	0	1509	39.7		

Alex Waits

Year	Team	No	Bl	Yds	Avg	Lg	NetAvg
1991	SEA N	14	0	474	33.9	50	33.6

Bobby Walden

Year	Team	No	Bl	Yds	Avg	Lg	NetAvg
1964	MIN N	72	0	3341	**46.4**	73	
1965		51	0	2146	42.1	61	
1966		60	0	2463	41.0	70	
1967		75	0	3117	41.6	76	
1968	PIT N	68	0	2745	40.4	57	
1969		77	0	3254	42.3	61	
1970		75	0	3393	45.2	66	
1971		79	0	3455	43.7	57	
1972		63	2	2846	45.2	72	
1973		61	1	2548	41.8	57	
1974		78	0	3040	39.0	65	
1975		68	1	2717	40.0	67	
1976		76	0	2982	39.2	58	33.1
1977		67	1	2482	37.0	65	29.4
Career		970	5	40529	41.8	76	
Playoffs		48	1	1991	41.5		

Doak Walker

Year	Team	No	Bl	Yds	Avg	Lg	NetAvg
1950	DET N	31	1	1277	41.2	61	
1951		9	0	316	35.1	50	
1955		9	0	362	40.2	49	
Career		49	1			61	

Glen Walker

Year	Team	No	Bl	Yds	Avg	Lg	NetAvg
1977	LA N	73	0	2568	35.2	56	31.4
1978		83	2	3069	37.0	61	32.3
Career		156	2	5637	36.1	61	
Playoffs		13	1	507	39.0		

Randy Walker

Year	Team	No	Bl	Yds	Avg	Lg	NetAvg
1974	GB N	69	0	2648	38.4	58	

Wayne Walker

Year	Team	No	Bl	Yds	Avg	Lg	NetAvg
1967	KC A	19	0	736	38.7	56	

Beverly Wallace

Year	Team	No	Bl	Yds	Avg	Lg	NetAvg
1947	SF AA	2	0	78	39.0		
1948		5	0	192	38.4		
1949		1	0	30	30.0	30	
Career		8	0	300	37.5	30	

Dale Walters

Year	Team	No	Bl	Yds	Avg	Lg	NetAvg
1987	CLE N	11	0	400	36.4	56	32.0

John Warren

Year	Team	No	Bl	Yds	Avg	Lg	NetAvg
1983	DAL N	39	0	1551	39.8	54	32.0
1984		21	0	799	38.0	48	33.0
Career		60	0	2350	39.2	54	

Clyde Washington

Year	Team	No	Bl	Yds	Avg	Lg	NetAvg
1960	BOS A	17		539	31.7		

Bob Waterfield

Year	Team	No	Bl	Yds	Avg	Lg	NetAvg
1945	CLE N	38	1	1588	41.8	68	
1946	LA N	39	1	1743	44.7	65	
1947		58	1	2500	43.1	86	

Bob Waterfield *continued*

Year	Team		No	Bl	Yds	Avg	Lg	NetAvg
1948			43	0	1843	42.9	88	
1949			48	1	2177	45.4	61	
1950			50	2	2087	41.7	61	
1951			4	0	166	41.5	52	
1952			30	0	1276	42.5	59	
Career			310	5	13380	43.2	88	
Playoffs			35	1	1490	42.6		

Foster Watkins

Year	Team		No	Bl	Yds	Avg	Lg	NetAvg
1940	**PHI**	**N**	2			23.0	35	

Herman Weaver

Year	Team		No	Bl	Yds	Avg	Lg	NetAvg
1970	**DET**	**N**	61	1	2483	40.7	65	
1971			40	2	1752	43.8	63	
1972			43	0	1734	40.3	55	
1973			53	1	2333	44.0	66	
1974			70	2	2772	39.6	61	
1975			79	1	3361	42.5	61	
1976			83	1	3280	39.5	69	34.3
1977	**SEA**	**N**	58	1	2293	39.5	59	31.8
1978			66	0	2440	37.0	59	29.5
1979			66	3	2651	40.2	60	33.4
1980			67	2	2798	41.8	62	31.6
Career			686	14	27897	40.7	69	
Playoffs			8	0	391	48.9		

Dick Weber

Year	Team		No	Bl	Yds	Avg	Lg	NetAvg
1945	**DET**	**N**	1	0	42	42.0	42	

Herman Wedemeyer

Year	Team		No	Bl	Yds	Avg	Lg	NetAvg
1948	**LA**	**AA**	1	0	10	10.0	10	
1949	**BAL**	**AA**	3	0	54	18.0		
Career			4	0	64	16.0	10	

Norris Weese

Year	Team		No	Bl	Yds	Avg	Lg	NetAvg
1976	**DEN**	**N**	52	0	1852	35.6	55	30.9
1977			1	0	38	38.0	38	38.0
Career			53	0	1890	35.7	55	

Jack Weil

Year	Team		No	Bl	Yds	Avg	Lg	NetAvg
1986	**DEN**	**N**	34	0	1344	39.5	55	32.8
1987	**WAS**	**N**	14	0	482	34.4	51	30.3
Career			48	0	1826	38.0	55	

Jeff West

Year	Team		No	Bl	Yds	Avg	Lg	NetAvg
1975	**STL**	**N**	63	1	2412	38.3	58	
1976	**SD**	**N**	38	0	1548	40.7	57	32.2
1977			72	1	2707	37.6	59	31.1
1978			73	2	2720	37.3	59	29.4
1979			75	0	2736	36.5	62	31.4
1981	**SEA**	**N**	66	0	2578	39.1	68	36.1
1982			48	0	1835	38.2	52	35.5
1983			79	0	3118	39.5	56	34.6
1984			95	0	3567	37.5	60	33.3
1985			11	0	420	38.2	52	28.3
Career			620	4	23641	38.1	68	
Playoffs			35	0	1318	37.7		

Bob Westfall

Year	Team		No	Bl	Yds	Avg	Lg	NetAvg
1944	**DET**	**N**	1	0	11	11.0	11	

Chet Wetterlund

Year	Team		No	Bl	Yds	Avg	Lg	NetAvg
1942	**CHIC-DET**	**N**	11	0	449	40.8	56	

Ernie Wheeler

Year	Team		No	Bl	Yds	Avg	Lg	NetAvg
1939	**PIT-CHIC**	**N**	10		460	46.0	75	
1942	**CHIC**	**N**	1	0	40	40.0	40	
Career			11	0	500	45.5	75	

Danny White

Year	Team		No	Bl	Yds	Avg	Lg	NetAvg
1976	**DAL**	**N**	70	2	2690	38.4	54	30.5
1977			80	1	3171	39.6	57	33.2
1978			76	1	3076	40.5	56	33.1
1979			76	0	3168	41.7	73	36.0
1980			71	0	2903	40.9	58	34.8
1981			79	0	3222	40.8	60	36.1
1982			37	0	1542	41.7	56	37.4
1983			38	1	1643	43.2	50	32.1
1984			82	0	3151	38.4	54	34.6

Danny White *continued*

Year	Team		No	Bl	Yds	Avg	Lg	NetAvg
1985			1	0	43	43.0	43	23.0
Career			610	5	24609	40.3	73	
Playoffs			84	0	3061	36.4		

Jeff White

Year	Team		No	Bl	Yds	Avg	Lg	NetAvg
1973	**NE**	**N**	6	0	163	27.2	51	

Whizzer White

Year	Team		No	Bl	Yds	Avg	Lg	NetAvg
1940	**DET**	**N**	52		2132	41.0	61	
1941			48	0	1997	41.6	63	
Career			100	0	4129	41.3	63	

Bud Whitehead

Year	Team		No	Bl	Yds	Avg	Lg	NetAvg
1964	**SD**	**A**	1	0	30	30.0	30	
1965			1	0	40	40.0	40	
Career			2	0	70	35.0	40	

Ron Widby

Year	Team		No	Bl	Yds	Avg	Lg	NetAvg
1968	**DAL**	**N**	59	0	2415	40.9	84	
1969			63	0	2729	43.3	62	
1970			68	1	2847	41.9	59	
1971			55	1	2329	42.3	59	
1972	**GB**	**N**	63	2	2714	43.1	64	
1973			56	0	2414	43.1	60	
Career			364	4	15448	42.4	84	
Playoffs			59	0	2370	40.2		

Bob Wiese

Year	Team		No	Bl	Yds	Avg	Lg	NetAvg
1947	**DET**	**N**	1	0	61	61.0	61	

Bobby Williams

Year	Team		No	Bl	Yds	Avg	Lg	NetAvg
1951	**CHIB**	**N**	4	0	145	36.3	50	
1952			2	0	90	45.0	48	
1955			13	0	508	39.1	59	
Career			19	0	743	39.1	59	

Walt Williams

Year	Team		No	Bl	Yds	Avg	Lg	NetAvg
1946	**CHI**	**AA**	23	1	998	43.4		

Willie Williams

Year	Team		No	Bl	Yds	Avg	Lg	NetAvg
1968	**NYG**	**N**	9	1	291	32.3	43	

Klaus Wilmsmeyer

Year	Team		No	Bl	Yds	Avg	Lg	NetAvg
1992	**SF**	**N**	49	0	1918	39.1	58	34.7
1993			42	0	1718	40.9	61	34.5
1994			54	0	2235	41.4	60	35.8
1995	**NO**	**N**	73	1	2965	40.6	53	35.6
1996			87	0	3551	40.8	63	32.5
Career			305	1	12387	40.6	63	
Playoffs			22	0	917	41.7		

Camp Wilson

Year	Team		No	Bl	Yds	Avg	Lg	NetAvg
1946	**DET**	**N**	21	1	768	36.6	69	

Eddie Wilson

Year	Team		No	Bl	Yds	Avg	Lg	NetAvg
1962	**DAL**	**A**	47	1	1681	35.8	51	
1963	**KC**	**A**	1	0	43	43.0	43	
1964			1	0	32	32.0	32	
1965	**BOS**	**A**	5	1	194	38.8	49	
Career			54	2	1950	36.1	51	
Playoffs			6	0	192	32.0		

George Wilson

Year	Team		No	Bl	Yds	Avg	Lg	NetAvg
1966	**MIA**	**A**	42		1772	42.2	63	

Jerrel Wilson

Year	Team		No	Bl	Yds	Avg	Lg	NetAvg
1963	**KC**	**A**	60	1	2628	43.8	72	
1964			**78**	0	**3326**	42.6	70	
1965			68	1	3132	**46.1**	64	
1966			61	1	2715	44.5	69	
1967			40	1	1739	43.5	59	
1968			63	0	2841	**45.1**	70	
1969			68	0	3022	44.4	62	
1970	**KC**	**N**	76	0	3415	44.9	68	
1971			63	1	2864	**45.5**	68	
1972			65	1	2960	**45.5**	69	
1973			79	1	**3642**	**46.1**	68	
1974			81	2	3462	**42.7**	64	
1975			53	1	2233	42.1	64	
1976			65	1	2729	42.0	62	33.4
1977			88	1	3510	39.9	59	30.4

Jerrel Wilson *continued*

Year	Team		No	Bl	Yds	Avg	Lg	NetAvg
1978	**NE**	**N**	54	0	1921	35.6	57	29.4
Career			1062	12	46139	43.4	72	
Playoffs			43	0	1786	41.5		

Wade Wilson

Year	Team		No	Bl	Yds	Avg	Lg	NetAvg
1986	**MIN**	**N**	2	1	76	38.0	46	24.3

George Winslow

Year	Team		No	Bl	Yds	Avg	Lg	NetAvg
1987	**CLE**	**N**	18	0	616	34.2	45	31.4
1989	**NO**	**N**	16	0	595	37.2	50	31.6
Career			34	0	1211	35.6	50	

Tom Wittum

Year	Team		No	Bl	Yds	Avg	Lg	NetAvg
1973	**SF**	**N**	79	0	3455	43.7	62	
1974			67	1	2800	41.8	67	
1975			64	3	2804	**43.8**	64	
1976			89	2	3634	40.8	68	33.9
1977			77	3	2801	36.4	54	28.5
Career			376	9	15494	41.2	68	

Mike Wood

Year	Team		No	Bl	Yds	Avg	Lg	NetAvg
1978	**MIN-STL**	**N**	82	2	3019	36.8	81	29.0

Junior Wren

Year	Team		No	Bl	Yds	Avg	Lg	NetAvg
1958	**CLE**	**N**	1	0	38	38.0	38	
1959			27	0	996	38.9	55	
1961	**NY**	**A**	8	0	271	33.9	53	
Career			36	0	1305	36.3	55	

Tom Yewcic

Year	Team		No	Bl	Yds	Avg	Lg	NetAvg
1961	**BOS**	**A**	62	0	2406	38.8	64	
1962			68	1	2634	38.7	56	
1963			73	2	2880	39.5	65	
1964			72	1	2787	38.7	63	
1965			74	2	3094	41.8	70	
1966			20	1	732	36.6	49	
Career			369	7	14533	39.4	70	
Playoffs			14	0	554	39.6	68	

Jim Youel

Year	Team		No	Bl	Yds	Avg	Lg	NetAvg
1946	**WAS**	**N**	2	0	68	34.0	36	
1947			1	1	35	35.0	35	
1948	**BOS**	**N**	2	0	65	32.5	40	
Career			5	1	168	33.6	40	

Len Younce

Year	Team		No	Bl	Yds	Avg	Lg	NetAvg
1943	**NYG**	**N**	20	0	850	42.5	74	
1944			48	0	1937	40.4	72	
1946			1	0	10	10.0	10	
1947			1	0	43	43.0	43	
Career			70	0	2840	40.6	74	
Playoffs			10	0	397	39.7		

John Yurchey

Year	Team		No	Bl	Yds	Avg	Lg	NetAvg
1940	**PIT**	**N**	3		120	40.0	41	

Tony Zendejas

Year	Team		No	Bl	Yds	Avg	Lg	NetAvg
1986	**HOU**	**N**	1	0	36	36.0	36	36.0

Roy Zimmerman

Year	Team		No	Bl	Yds	Avg	Lg	NetAvg
1940	**WAS**	**N**	7		259	37.0	47	
1941			13	1	594	45.7	65	
1942			4	0	202	50.5	52	
1943	**P-P**	**N**	42	2	1522	36.2	53	
1944	**PHI**	**N**	39	0	1531	39.3	61	
1945			46	1	1777	38.6	64	
1946			23	0	890	38.7	52	
1947	**DET**	**N**	47	2	2078	44.2	62	
1948	**BOS**	**N**	51	0	2215	43.4	67	
Career			272	6	11068	40.7	67	
Playoffs			1	0	61	61.0	61	

Joe Zombek

Year	Team		No	Bl	Yds	Avg	Lg	NetAvg
1955	**PIT**	**N**	5	0	201	40.2	45	

Lou Zontini

Year	Team		No	Bl	Yds	Avg	Lg	NetAvg
1940	**CHIC**	**N**	2		92	46.0	60	
1941			12	0	445	37.1	55	
1946	**BUF**	**AA**	44	0	1597	36.3		
Career			58	0	2134	36.8	60	

PART NINE

Head Coaches Register

Key

Don Coryell
Coryell, Donald David
  B. Oct. 17, 1924, Seattle, WA
  Washington

Year	Team	Lg	C	D	Games	W	L	T	Pct	APct	Fin	Seq	Pos
1973	STL	N	N	E	14	4	9	1	.321	.321	4		HC
1974					14	10	4	0	.714	.714	1		HC
1975					14	11	3	0	.786	.786	1		HC
1976					14	10	4	0	.714	.714	2		HC
1977	ST	N	N	E	14	7	7	0	.500	.500	3		HC
1978	SD	N	A	W	12	8	4	0	.667	.667	4/2	2/2	HC
1979					16	12	4	0	.750	.750	1		HC
1980					16	11	5	0	.688	.688	1		HC
1981					16	10	6	0	.625	.625	1		HC
1982				—	9	6	3	0	.667	.667	5		HC
1983				W	16	6	10	0	.375	.375	4		HC
1984					16	7	9	0	.438	.438	5		HC
1985					16	8	8	0	.500	.500	3		HC
1986					8	1	7	0	.125	.125	5/5	1/2	HC
14 yrs.					195	111	83	1		.572			
Playoffs													
1974					1	0	1						HC
1975					1	0	1						HC
1979					1	0	1						HC
1980					2	1	1						HC
1981					2	1	1						HC
1982					2	1	1						HC
6 yrs.					9	3	6			.333			

The Coaches register is an alphabetical listing of every man who has managed a professional football team. Included are facts about the managers and their year-by-year managerial records and lifetime totals for the regular season and playoffs.

Team Lg C D	The team, league, conference, and division for which each individual coached. For example, in 1978 Don Coryell coached the San Diego Chargers (SD) of the NFL (N) in the Western division (W) of the American Football Conference (A).
Games	Games coached
W	Games won
L	Games lost
T	Games tied
Pct	Winning percentage
APct	Actual winning percentage (does not factor in ties)
Fin	Place the team finished in that year. If there are two numbers separated by a slash, as in 1978, the first number signifies the place the team occupied when the coach took over the team, and the second number signifies the place the team occupied when the season was over or when the coach left. For example, in 1978 the Chargers were in fourth place (4) when Coryell took over the team and finished in second place (2) under him.
Seq	Signifies when more than one coach has directed a team in the same season. The first number shows what order coaches took over a team. The second number is the total number of coaches the team had that year. For example, in 1978 Coryell was the second head coach of the Chargers (2) that year. The second 2 signifies that only 2 men were head coaches that year.
Pos	HC—Head coach. CHC—Co-head coach.

Year	Team	Lg	C	D	Games	W	L	T	Pct	APct	Fin	Seq	Pos

Fay Abbott
Abbott, Lafayette (Hack)
B. Aug. 16, 1895
D. Jan., 1965, Dayton, OH
Syracuse

Year	Team	Lg	C	D	Games	W	L	T	Pct	APct	Fin	Seq	Pos
1928	DAY	N			7	0	7	0	.000	.000	10		HC
1929					6	0	6	0	.000	.000	12		HC
2 yrs.					13	0	13	0		.000			

Frankie Albert
Albert, Frank Cullen
B. Jan. 27, 1920, Chicago, IL
Stanford

Year	Team	Lg	C	D	Games	W	L	T	Pct	APct	Fin	Seq	Pos
1956	SF	N	W		12	5	6	1	.455	.458	3		HC
1957					12	8	4	0	.667	.667	1		HC
1958					12	6	6	0	.500	.500	4		HC
3 yrs.					36	19	16	1		.542			
Playoffs													
1957					1	0	1			.000			HC

George Allen
Allen, George Herbert
B. Apr. 29, 1922, Detroit, MI
D. Dec. 31, 1990, Palos Verdes, CA
Marquette/Alma/Michigan

Year	Team	Lg	C	D	Games	W	L	T	Pct	APct	Fin	Seq	Pos
1966	LA	N	W		14	8	6	0	.571	.571	3		HC
1967				CO	14	11	1	2	.917	.857	1		HC
1968					14	10	3	1	.769	.750	2		HC
1969					14	11	3	0	.786	.786	1		HC
1970		N	W		14	9	4	1	.692	.679	2		HC
1971	WAS	N	N	E	14	9	4	1	.692	.679	2		HC
1972					14	11	3	0	.786	.786	1		HC
1973					14	10	4	0	.714	.714	2		HC
1974					14	10	4	0	.714	.714	2		HC
1975					14	8	6	0	.571	.571	3		HC
1976					14	10	4	0	.714	.714	2		HC
1977					14	9	5	0	.643	.643	2		HC
12 yrs.					168	116	47	5		.705			
Playoffs													
1967					1	0	1						HC
1969					1	0	1						HC
1971					1	0	1						HC
1972					3	2	1						HC
1973					1	0	1						HC
1974					1	0	1						HC
1976					1	0	1						HC
7 yrs.					9	2	7			.222			

Hunk Anderson
Anderson, Heartley William
B. Sep. 22, 1898, Calumet, MI
D. Apr. 24, 1978, West Palm Beach, FL
Notre Dame

Year	Team	Lg	C	D	Games	W	L	T	Pct	APct	Fin	Seq	Pos
1942	CHIB	N		W	6	6	0	0	1.000	1.000	1/1	2/2	CHC
1943					10	8	1	1	.889	.850	1		CHC
1944					10	6	3	1	.667	.650	2		CHC
1945					10	3	7	0	.300	.300	4		CHC
4 yrs.					36	23	11	2		.667			
Playoffs													
1942					1	0	1						CHC
1943					1	1	0						CHC
2 yrs.					2	1	1			.500			

Roy Andrews
Andrews, LeRoy (Bull)
B. Jun., 1896, Osage Township, KS
Pittsburg State

Year	Team	Lg	C	D	Games	W	L	T	Pct	APct	Fin	Seq	Pos
1924	KC	N			9	2	7	0	.222	.222	15		HC
1925					8	2	5	1	.286	.313	13		HC
1926					11	8	3	0	.727	.727	4		HC
1927	CLE	N			13	8	4	1	.667	.654	4		HC
1928	DET	N			10	7	2	1	.778	.750	3		HC
1929	NY	N			15	13	1	1	.929	.900	2		HC
1930					15	11	4	0	.733	.733	2/2	1/2	HC
1931	CHIC	N			1	0	1	0	.000	.000	7/4	1/2	HC
8 yrs.					82	51	27	4		.646			

Dunc Annan
Annan, Duncan Colin
B. Aug. 10, 1895
D. Jun., 1981, Fort Pierce, FL
Brown/Chicago

Year	Team	Lg	C	D	Games	W	L	T	Pct	APct	Fin	Seq	Pos
1926	HAM	N			4	0	4	0	.000	.000	21		HC

Johnny Armstrong
Armstrong, John A.
B. 1894
Deceased
Dubuque

Year	Team	Lg	C	D	Games	W	L	T	Pct	APct	Fin	Seq	Pos
1926	RI	A			8	1	6	1	.143	.188	1/7	2/2	HC

Neill Armstrong
Armstrong, Neill Ford (Bird)
B. Mar. 9, 1926, Tishomingo, OK
Oklahoma State

Year	Team	Lg	C	D	Games	W	L	T	Pct	APct	Fin	Seq	Pos
1978	CHI	N	N	C	16	7	9	0	.438	.438	3		HC
1979					16	10	6	0	.625	.625	2		HC
1980					16	7	9	0	.438	.438	3		HC
1981					16	6	10	0	.375	.375	5		HC
4 yrs.					64	30	34	0		.469			
Playoffs													
1979					1	0	1			.000			HC

Bill Arnsparger
Arnsparger, William Stephen
B. Dec. 16, 1926, Paris, KY
Miami (Ohio)

Year	Team	Lg	C	D	Games	W	L	T	Pct	APct	Fin	Seq	Pos
1974	NYG	N	N	E	14	2	12	0	.143	.143	5		HC
1975					14	5	9	0	.357	.357	4		HC
1976					7	0	7	0	.000	.000	5/5	1/2	HC
3 yrs.					35	7	28	0		.200			

Bill Austin
Austin, William Lee
B. Oct. 28, 1928, San Pedro, CA
Oregon State

Year	Team	Lg	C	D	Games	W	L	T	Pct	APct	Fin	Seq	Pos
1966	PIT	N		E	14	5	8	1	.385	.393	6		HC
1967				CE	14	4	9	1	.308	.321	4		HC
1968					14	2	11	1	.154	.179	4		HC
1970	WAS	N	N	E	14	6	8	0	.429	.429	4		HC
4 yrs.					56	17	36	3		.330			

Joe Bach
Bach, Joseph Anthony
B. Jan. 7, 1901, Tower, MN
D. Oct. 24, 1966, Pittsburgh, PA
Carleton/Minnesota/Notre Dame

Year	Team	Lg	C	D	Games	W	L	T	Pct	APct	Fin	Seq	Pos
1935	PIT	N		E	12	4	8	0	.333	.333	3		HC
1936					12	6	6	0	.500	.500	2		HC
1952					12	5	7	0	.417	.417	4		HC
1953					12	6	6	0	.500	.500	4		HC
4 yrs.					48	21	27	0		.438			

Herman Ball
Ball, Herman
B. May 9, 1910, Kingsville, WV
Davis & Elkins

Year	Team	Lg	C	D	Games	W	L	T	Pct	APct	Fin	Seq	Pos
1949	WAS	N		E	5	1	4	0	.200	.200	3/4	2/2	HC
1950					12	3	9	0	.250	.250	6		HC
1951					3	0	3	0	.000	.000	5/3	1/2	HC
3 yrs.					20	4	16	0		.200			

Shorty Barr
Barr, Wallace C.
B. May 28, 1896
D. Mar., 1980, Chenequa, WI
Wisconsin

Year	Team	Lg	C	D	Games	W	L	T	Pct	APct	Fin	Seq	Pos
1926	RAC	N			3	1	2	0	.333	.333	15/16	1/2	HC

Norm Barry

Barry, Norman Christopher
B. Dec. 25, 1897, Chicago, IL
D. Oct. 12, 1988, Chicago, IL
Notre Dame

Year	Team	Lg	C	D	Games	W	L	T	Pct	APct	Fin	Seq	Pos
1925	CHIC	N			14	11	2	1	.846	.821	1		HC
1926					12	5	6	1	.455	.458	10		HC
2 yrs.					26	16	8	2	.654				

Dim Batterson

Batterson, George W.
B. Oct., 1882, NY
None

Year	Team	Lg	C	D	Games	W	L	T	Pct	APct	Fin	Seq	Pos
1927	BUF	N			5	0	5	0	.000	.000	12		HC

Cliff Battles

Battles, Clifford Franklyn (Gyp)
B. May 1, 1910, Akron, OH
D. Apr. 28, 1981, Clearwater, FL
West Virginia Wesleyan

Year	Team	Lg	C	D	Games	W	L	T	Pct	APct	Fin	Seq	Pos
1946	BKN	AA	E		7	1	6	0	.143	.143	2/2	2/2	HC
1947					14	3	10	1	.231	.250	3		HC
2 yrs.					21	4	16	1	.214				

Sammy Baugh

Baugh, Samuel Adrian (Slingin' Sam)
B. Mar. 17, 1914, Temple, TX
Texas Christian

Year	Team	Lg	C	D	Games	W	L	T	Pct	APct	Fin	Seq	Pos
1960	NY	A		E	14	7	7	0	.500	.500	2		HC
1961					14	7	7	0	.500	.500	3		HC
1964	HOU	A		E	14	4	10	0	.296	.296	4		HC
3 yrs.					42	18	24	0	.429				

Bull Behman

Behman, Russell J.
B. Jan. 15, 1900, Steelton, PA
D. Mar. 24, 1950, Harrisburg, PA
Lebanon Valley/Dickinson

Year	Team	Lg	C	D	Games	W	L	T	Pct	APct	Fin	Seq	Pos
1929	FRA	N			19	10	4	5	.714	.658	3		HC
1930					18	4	13	1	.235	.250	9		HC
1931					8	1	6	1	.143	.188	10		HC
3 yrs.					45	15	23	7	.411				

Bill Belichick

Belichick, William
B. Apr. 16, 1952, Nashville, TN
Wesleyan

Year	Team	Lg	C	D	Games	W	L	T	Pct	APct	Fin	Seq	Pos
1991	CLE	N	A	C	16	6	10	0	.375	.375	3		HC
1992					16	7	9	0	.438	.438	3		HC
1993					16	7	9	0	.438	.438	3		HC
1994					16	11	5	0	.688	.688	2		HC
1995					16	5	11	0	.313	.313	4		HC
5 yrs.					80	36	44	0	.450				
Playoffs													
1994					2	1	1			.500			HC

Bert Bell

Bell, DeBenneville
B. Feb. 25, 1895, Philadelphia, PA
D. Oct. 11, 1959, Philadelphia, PA
Pennsylvania

Year	Team	Lg	C	D	Games	W	L	T	Pct	APct	Fin	Seq	Pos
1936	PHI	N		E	12	1	11	0	.083	.083	5		HC
1937					11	2	8	1	.200	.227	5		HC
1938					11	5	6	0	.455	.455	4		HC
1939					11	1	9	1	.100	.136	4		HC
1940					11	1	10	0	.091	.091	5		HC
1941	PIT	N		E	2	0	2	0	.100	.136	5/5	1/3	HC
6 yrs.					58	10	46	2	.190				

Phil Bengtston

Bengtston, John Phillip
B. Jul.17, 1913, Rosseau, MN
D. Dec. 18, 1994, San Diego, CA
Minnesota

Year	Team	Lg	C	D	Games	W	L	T	Pct	APct	Fin	Seq	Pos
1968	GB	N	W	C	14	6	7	1	.462	.464	3		HC

Phil Bengtston *continued*

Year	Team	Lg	C	D	Games	W	L	T	Pct	APct	Fin	Seq	Pos
1969					14	8	6	0	.571	.571	3		HC
1970		N		C	14	6	8	0	.429	.429	3		HC
1972	NE	N	A	E	5	1	4	0	.200	.200	3/5	2/2	HC
4 yrs.					47	21	25	1	.457				

Leeman Bennett

Bennett, Leeman
B. Jun. 20, 1938, Paducah, KY
Kentucky

Year	Team	Lg	C	D	Games	W	L	T	Pct	APct	Fin	Seq	Pos
1977	ATL	N	N	W	14	7	7	0	.500	.500	2		HC
1978					16	9	7	0	.563	.563	2		HC
1979					16	6	10	0	.375	.375	3		HC
1980					16	12	4	0	.750	.750	1		HC
1981					16	7	9	0	.438	.438	2		HC
1982		—			9	5	4	0	.556	.556	5		HC
1985	TB	N	N	C	16	2	14	0	.125	.125	5		HC
1986					16	2	14	0	.125	.125	5		HC
8 yrs.					119	50	69	0	.420				
Playoffs													
1978					2	1	1						HC
1980					1	0	1						HC
1982					1	0	1						HC
3 yrs.					4	1	3			.250			

Arthur Bergman

Bergman, Arthur H. (Dutch)
B. Feb. 23, 1895, Peru, IN
D. Aug. 18, 1972, Washington, DC
Notre Dame

Year	Team	Lg	C	D	Games	W	L	T	Pct	APct	Fin	Seq	Pos
1943	WAS	N		E	10	6	3	1	.667	.650	1		HC
Playoffs													
1943					2	1	1			.500			HC

Raymond Berry

Berry, Raymond Emmett
B. Feb. 27, 1933, Corpus Christi, TX
Southern Methodist

Year	Team	Lg	C	D	Games	W	L	T	Pct	APct	Fin	Seq	Pos
1984	NE	N	A	E	8	4	4	0	.500	.500	3/2	2/2	HC
1985					16	11	5	0	.688	.688	2		HC
1986					16	11	5	0	.688	.688	1		HC
1987					15	8	7	0	.533	.533	2		HC
1988					16	9	7	0	.563	.563	2		HC
1989					16	5	11	0	.313	.313	4		HC
6 yrs.					87	48	39	0	.552				
Playoffs													
1985					4	3	1						HC
1986					1	0	1						HC
2 yrs.					5	3	2			.600			

Bob Berryman

Berryman, Robert L. (Punk)
B. Dec. 13, 1893
D. May 20, 1988, Philadelphia, PA
Penn State

Year	Team	Lg	C	D	Games	W	L	T	Pct	APct	Fin	Seq	Pos
1924	FRA	N			14	11	2	1	.846	.821	3		HC
1926	BKN	N			11	3	8	0	.273	.273	14		HC
2 yrs.					25	14	10	1	.580				

Tom Bettis

Bettis, Thomas W.
B. Mar. 17, 1933, Chicago, IL
Purdue

Year	Team	Lg	C	D	Games	W	L	T	Pct	APct	Fin	Seq	Pos
1977	KC	N	A	W	7	1	6	0	.143	.143	5/5	2/2	HC

Hugo Bezdek

Bezdek, Hugo Francis
B. Apr. 1, 1883, Prague, Austria-Hungary
D. Sep. 19, 1952, Atlantic City, NJ
Chicago

Year	Team	Lg	C	D	Games	W	L	T	Pct	APct	Fin	Seq	Pos
1937	CLE	N		W	11	1	10	0	.091	.091	5		HC

Scotty Bierce
Bierce, Bruce W.
B. Sep. 3, 1896, Kearney, NE
D. Apr. 26, 1982, Medina, OH
Akron

Year	Team	Lg	C	D	Games	W	L	T	Pct	APct	Fin	Seq	Pos
1925	AKR	N			8	4	2	2	.667	.625	4		HC

Ed Biles
Biles, Edward G.
B. Oct. 18, 1931, Reading, OH
Miami (Ohio)

Year	Team	Lg	C	D	Games	W	L	T	Pct	APct	Fin	Seq	Pos
1981	HOU	N	A	C	16	7	9	0	.438	.438	3		HC
1982	—				9	1	8	0	.111	.111	13		HC
1983				C	6	0	6	0	.000	.000	4/4	1/2	HC
3 yrs.					31	8	23	0	.258				

Lisle Blackbourn
Blackbourn, Lisle William
B. Jun. 3, 1899, Beetown, WI
D. Jun. 14, 1963, Lancaster, WI
Lawrence

Year	Team	Lg	C	D	Games	W	L	T	Pct	APct	Fin	Seq	Pos
1954	GB	N	W		12	4	8	0	.333	.333	5		HC
1955					12	6	6	0	.500	.500	3		HC
1956					12	4	8	0	.333	.333	5		HC
1957					12	3	9	0	.250	.250	6		HC
4 yrs.					48	17	31	0	.354				

Johnny Blood
McNally, John Victor
B. Nov. 27, 1903, New Richmond, WI
D. Nov. 28, 1985, Palm Springs, CA
Wisc.-River Falls/St. John's (Minnesota)

Year	Team	Lg	C	D	Games	W	L	T	Pct	APct	Fin	Seq	Pos
1937	PIT	N		E	11	4	7	0	.364	.364	3		HC
1938					11	2	9	0	.182	.182	5		HC
1939					3	0	3	0	.000	.000	4/4	1/2	HC
3 yrs.					25	6	19	0	.240				

Pat Boland
Boland, Patrick H.
B. Sep. 25, 1910
D. Aug., 1976, Bronx, NY
Minnesota

Year	Team	Lg	C	D	Games	W	L	T	Pct	APct	Fin	Seq	Pos
1946	CHI	AA		W	6	2	3	1	.400	.417	3/4	3/3	HC

Wes Bradshaw
Bradshaw, Wesley W.
B. Nov. 26, 1898
Deceased
Trinity (Texas)/Baylor

Year	Team	Lg	C	D	Games	W	L	T	Pct	APct	Fin	Seq	Pos
1926	RI	A			1	1	0	0	1.000	1.000	1/7	1/2	HC

Joe Brandy
Brandy, Joseph H., Jr.
B. Nov. 6, 1897, Ogdensburg, NY
D. Jul., 1971, Ogdensburg, NY
Notre Dame

Year	Team	Lg	C	D	Games	W	L	T	Pct	APct	Fin	Seq	Pos
1924	MIN	N			6	0	6	0	.000	.000	16		HC

Wayne Brenkert
Brenkert, Wayne D.
B. Mar. 5, 1898
D. Aug. 1, 1979, Altamonte Springs, FL
Washington & Jefferson

Year	Team	Lg	C	D	Games	W	L	T	Pct	APct	Fin	Seq	Pos
1924	AKR	N			8	2	6	0	.250	.250	13		HC

Brooke Brewer
Brewer, Edward Brooke (Untz)
B. Nov. 21, 1894, Washington, DC
D. Feb., 1970, Rockville, MD
Maryland

Year	Team	Lg	C	D	Games	W	L	T	Pct	APct	Fin	Seq	Pos
1922	AKR	N			6	3	2	1	.600	.583	6/	1/2	HC

Charlie Brickley
Brickley, Charles Edward
B. Nov. 24, 1891, Boston, MA
D. Dec. 28, 1949, New York, NY
Harvard

Year	Team	Lg	C	D	Games	W	L	T	Pct	APct	Fin	Seq	Pos
1921	NY	A			2	0	2	0	.000	.000	18		HC

Frank Bridges
Bridges, Frank D.
B. Jul. 4, 1890
D. Jun. 10, 1970, San Antonio, TX
Baylor

Year	Team	Lg	C	D	Games	W	L	T	Pct	APct	Fin	Seq	Pos
1944	BKN	N		E	5	0	5	0	.000	.000	5/5	2/2	CHC

Marty Brill
Brill, Martin
B. Mar. 13, 1906
D. Apr. 30, 1973, Whittier, CA
Notre Dame

Year	Team	Lg	C	D	Games	W	L	T	Pct	APct	Fin	Seq	Pos
1931	SI	N			2	2	0	0	1.000	1.000	8/7	2/2	HC

Rich Brooks
Brooks, Richard L.
B. Aug. 20, 1941, Forest, CA
Oregon State

Year	Team	Lg	C	D	Games	W	L	T	Pct	APct	Fin	Seq	Pos
1995	STL	N	N	W	16	7	9	0	.438	.438	3		HC
1996					16	6	10	0	.375	.375	3		HC
2 yrs.					32	13	19	0	.406				

Paul Brown
Brown, Paul Eugene
B. Sep. 7, 1908, Norwalk, OH
D. Sep. 7, 1991, Cincinnati, OH
Miami (Ohio)/Ohio State

Year	Team	Lg	C	D	Games	W	L	T	Pct	APct	Fin	Seq	Pos
1946	CLE	AA		W	14	12	2	0	.857	.857	1		HC
1947					14	12	1	1	.923	.893	1		HC
1948					14	14	0	0	1.000	1.000	1		HC
1949					12	9	1	2	.900	.833	1		HC
1950	CLE	N	A		12	10	2	0	.833	.833	1		HC
1951					12	11	1	0	.917	.917	1		HC
1952					12	8	4	0	.667	.667	1		HC
1953					12	11	1	0	.917	.917	1		HC
1954					12	9	3	0	.750	.750	1		HC
1955					12	9	2	1	.818	.792	1		HC
1956					12	5	7	0	.417	.417	4		HC
1957					12	9	2	1	.818	.792	1		HC
1958					12	9	3	0	.750	.750	1		HC
1959					12	7	5	0	.583	.583	2		HC
1960					12	8	3	1	.727	.708	2		HC
1961					14	8	5	1	.615	.607	3		HC
1962					14	7	6	1	.538	.536	3		HC
1968	CIN	A		W	14	3	11	0	.214	.214	4		HC
1969					14	4	9	1	.308	.321	5		HC
1970	CIN	N	A	C	14	8	6	0	.571	.571	1		HC
1971					14	4	10	0	.286	.286	4		HC
1972					14	8	6	0	.571	.571	3		HC
1973					14	10	4	0	.714	.714	1		HC
1974					14	7	7	0	.500	.500	2		HC
1975					14	11	3	0	.786	.786	2		HC
25 yrs.					326	213	104	9	.667				
Playoffs													
1946					1	1	0						HC
1947					1	1	0						HC
1948					1	1	0						HC
1949					2	2	0						HC
1950					2	2	0						HC
1951					1	0	1						HC
1952					1	0	1						HC
1953					1	0	1						HC
1954					1	1	0						HC
1955					1	0	1						HC
1957					1	0	1						HC
1958					1	0	1						HC
1970					1	0	1						HC
1973					1	0	1						HC
1975					1	0	1						HC
15 yrs.					17	9	8		.529				

Year	Team	Lg	C	D	Games	W	L	T	Pct	APct	Fin	Seq	Pos

Fred Bruney
Bruney, Frederick K.
B. Dec. 30, 1931, Martins Ferry, OH
Ohio State

Year	Team	Lg	C	D	Games	W	L	T	Pct	APct	Fin	Seq	Pos
1985	PHI	N	N	E	1	1	0	0	1.000	1.000	4/4	2/2	HC

Johnny Bryan
Bryan, John Frederick (Red)
B. Feb. 28, 1897, Chicago, IL
D. Jul. 1, 1966, Fort Collins, CO
Dartmouth/Chicago

Year	Team	Lg	C	D	Games	W	L	T	Pct	APct	Fin	Seq	Pos
1925	MIL	N			6	0	6	0	.000	.000	16		HC
1926					9	2	7	0	.222	.222	15		HC
2 yrs.					15	2	13	0		.133			

Joe Bugel
Bugel, Joseph John
B. Mar. 10, 1940, Pittsburgh, PA
Western Kentucky

Year	Team	Lg	C	D	Games	W	L	T	Pct	APct	Fin	Seq	Pos
1990	PHX	N	N	E	16	5	11	0	.313	.313	5		HC
1991					16	4	12	0	.250	.250	5		HC
1992					16	4	12	0	.250	.250	5		HC
1993					16	7	9	0	.438	.438	4		HC
4 yrs.					64	20	44	0		.313			

Hank Bullough
Bullough, Henry Charles
B. Jan. 24, 1934, Scranton, PA
Michigan State

Year	Team	Lg	C	D	Games	W	L	T	Pct	APct	Fin	Seq	Pos
1978	NE	N	A	E	1	0	0	0	.000	.000	1/1	2/2	CHC
1985	BUF	N	A	E	12	2	10	0	.167	.167	5/5	2/2	HC
1986					9	2	7	0	.222	.222	4/4	1/2	HC
3 yrs.					22	4	18	0		.182			
Playoffs													
1978					1	0	1			.000			CHC

Jerry Burns
Burns, Jerome Monahan
B. Jan. 24, 1927, Detroit, MI
Michigan

Year	Team	Lg	C	D	Games	W	L	T	Pct	APct	Fin	Seq	Pos
1986	MIN	N	N	C	16	9	7	0	.563	.563	2		HC
1987					15	8	7	0	.533	.533	2		HC
1988					16	11	5	0	.688	.688	2		HC
1989					16	10	6	0	.625	.625	1		HC
1990					16	6	10	0	.375	.375	5		HC
1991					16	8	8	0	.500	.500	3		HC
6 yrs.					95	52	43	0		.547			
Playoffs													
1987					3	2	1						HC
1988					2	1	1						HC
1989					1	0	1						HC
3 yrs.					6	3	3			.500			

Hugh Campbell
Campbell, Hugh Thomas
B. May 21, 1941, San Jose, CA
Washington State

Year	Team	Lg	C	D	Games	W	L	T	Pct	APct	Fin	Seq	Pos
1984	HOU	N	A	C	16	3	13	0	.188	.188	4		HC
1985					14	5	9	0	.313	.313	4/4	1/2	HC
2 yrs.					30	8	22	0		.267			

Marion Campbell
Campbell, Francis Marion
B. May 25, 1929, Chester, SC
Georgia

Year	Team	Lg	C	D	Games	W	L	T	Pct	APct	Fin	Seq	Pos
1974	ATL	N	N	W	6	1	5	0	.167	.167	4/4	2/2	HC
1975					14	4	10	0	.286	.286	3		HC
1976					5	1	4	0	.250	.250	4/3	1/2	HC
1983	PHI	N	N	E	16	5	11	0	.313	.313	4		HC
1984					16	6	9	1	.406	.406	3		HC
1985					15	6	9	0	.438	.438	4/4	1/2	HC
1987	ATL	N	N	W	15	3	12	0	.200	.200	4		HC
1988					16	5	11	0	.313	.313	4		HC
1989					12	3	9	0	.250	.250	4/4	1/2	HC
9 yrs.					115	34	80	1		.300			

Dom Capers
Capers, Dominic
B. Aug. 7, 1950, Cambridge, OH
Mount Union

Year	Team	Lg	C	D	Games	W	L	T	Pct	APct	Fin	Seq	Pos
1995	CAR	N	N	W	16	7	9	0	.438	.438	3		HC
1996					16	12	4	0	.750	.750	1		HC
2 yrs.					32	19	13	0		.594			
Playoffs													
1996					2	1	1			.500			HC

Pete Carroll
Carroll, Pete
B. Sep. 15, 1951, San Francisco, CA
Pacific

Year	Team	Lg	C	D	Games	W	L	T	Pct	APct	Fin	Seq	Pos
1994	NYJ	N	A	E	16	6	10	0	.375	.375	5		HC

Bud Carson
Carson, Leon H.
B. Apr. 28, 1931, Freeport, PA
North Carolina

Year	Team	Lg	C	D	Games	W	L	T	Pct	APct	Fin	Seq	Pos
1989	CLE	N	A	C	16	9	6	1	.594	.594	1		HC
1990					9	2	7	0	.222	.222	4/4	1/2	HC
2 yrs.					25	11	13	1		.460			
Playoffs													
1989					2	1	1						HC

Eddie Casey
Casey, Edward Lawrence
B. May 16, 1894, Natick, MA
D. July 26, 1966, Boston, MA
Harvard

Year	Team	Lg	C	D	Games	W	L	T	Pct	APct	Fin	Seq	Pos
1935	BOS	N		E	11	2	8	1	.200	.227	4		HC

Pete Cawthon
Cawthon, Peter Willis
B. Mar. 24, 1898, Houston, TX
D. Dec. 31, 1962, Houston, TX
Southwestern (Texas)

Year	Team	Lg	C	D	Games	W	L	T	Pct	APct	Fin	Seq	Pos
1943	BKN	N		E	10	2	8	0	.200	.200	4		HC
1944					5	0	5	0	.000	.000	5/	1/2	HC
2 yrs.					15	2	13	0		.133			

Guy Chamberlin
Chamberlin, Berlin Guy (Champ)
B. Jan. 16, 1894, Blue Springs, NE
D. Apr. 4, 1967, Lincoln, NE
Nebraska Wesleyan/Nebraska

Year	Team	Lg	C	D	Games	W	L	T	Pct	APct	Fin	Seq	Pos
1922	CAN	N			12	10	0	2	1.000	.917	1		HC
1923					12	11	0	1	1.000	.958	1		HC
1924	CLE	N			9	7	1	1	.875	.833	1		HC
1925	FRA	N			20	13	7	0	.650	.650	6		HC
1926					17	14	1	2	.933	.882	1		HC
1927	CHIC	N			11	3	7	1	.300	.318	9		HC
6 yrs.					81	58	16	7		.759			

Coonie Checkaye
Checkaye, Severin J.
B. Jan. 6, 1893, Muncie, IN
D. Nov. 18, 1970, Muncie, IN

Year	Team	Lg	C	D	Games	W	L	T	Pct	APct	Fin	Seq	Pos
1921	MUN	A			2	0	2	0	.000	.000	18		HC

Jack Chevigny
Chevigny, Jack
B. Aug. 14, 1906
D. Feb. 19, 1945, Iwo Jima
Notre Dame

Year	Team	Lg	C	D	Games	W	L	T	Pct	APct	Fin	Seq	Pos
1932	CHIC	N			10	2	6	2	.250	.300	7		HC

Jack Christiansen
Christiansen, John Leroy
B. Dec. 20, 1928, Sublette, KS
D. Jun. 29, 1986, Stanford, CA
Colorado State

Year	Team	Lg	C	D	Games	W	L	T	Pct	APct	Fin	Seq	Pos
1963	SF	N		W	11	2	9	0	.182	.182	6/7	2/2	HC

Year	Team	Lg	C	D	Games	W	L	T	Pct	APct	Fin	Seq	Pos

Jack Christiansen *continued*

Year	Team	Lg	C	D	Games	W	L	T	Pct	APct	Fin	Seq	Pos
1964					14	4	10	0	.286	.286	7		HC
1965					14	7	6	1	.538	.536	4		HC
1966					14	6	6	2	.500	.500	4		HC
1967			CO		14	7	7	0	.500	.500	3		HC
5 yrs.					67	26	38	3		.410			

Algy Clark
Clark, Myers Algernon
B. 1904
Ohio State

Year	Team	Lg	C	D	Games	W	L	T	Pct	APct	Fin	Seq	Pos
1934	C-S	N		W	8	0	8	0	.000	.000	5/5	1/2	HC

Dutch Clark
Clark, Earl Harry
B. Oct. 11, 1906, Fowler, CO
D. Aug. 5, 1978, Canon City, CO
Colorado College

Year	Team	Lg	C	D	Games	W	L	T	Pct	APct	Fin	Seq	Pos
1937	DET	N		W	11	7	4	0	.636	.636	3		HC
1938					11	7	4	0	.636	.636	2		HC
1939	CLE	N		W	11	5	5	1	.500	.500	4		HC
1940					11	4	6	1	.400	.409	4		HC
1941					11	2	9	0	.182	.182	5		HC
1942					11	5	6	0	.455	.455	3		HC
6 yrs.					66	30	34	2		.470			

Jim Clark
Clark, Jim
Montana

Year	Team	Lg	C	D	Games	W	L	T	Pct	APct	Fin	Seq	Pos
1926	LA	A			14	6	6	2	.500	.500	4		HC

Monte Clark
Clark, Monte Dale
B. Jan. 24, 1937, Fillmore, CA
Southern California

Year	Team	Lg	C	D	Games	W	L	T	Pct	APct	Fin	Seq	Pos
1976	SF	N	N	W	14	8	6	0	.571	.571	2		HC
1978	DET	N	N	C	16	7	9	0	.438	.438	3		HC
1979					16	2	14	0	.125	.125	5		HC
1980					16	9	7	0	.563	.563	2		HC
1981					16	8	8	0	.500	.500	2		HC
1982		—			9	4	5	0	.444	.444	8		HC
1983			C		16	9	7	0	.553	.563	1		HC
1984					16	4	11	1	.281	.281	4		HC
8 yrs.					119	51	67	1		.433			
Playoffs													
1982					1	0	1						HC
1983					1	0	1						HC
2 yrs.					2	0	2			.000			

Potsy Clark
Clark, George M.
B. 1893
D. Nov. 8, 1972, La Jolla, CA
Illinois

Year	Team	Lg	C	D	Games	W	L	T	Pct	APct	Fin	Seq	Pos
1931	POR	N			14	11	3	0	.796	.796	2		HC
1932					12	6	2	4	.750	.667	3		HC
1933				W	11	6	5	0	.545	.545	2		HC
1934	DET	N		W	13	10	3	0	.769	.769	2		HC
1935					12	7	3	2	.700	.667	1		HC
1936					12	8	4	0	.667	.667	3		HC
1937	BKN	N		E	11	3	7	1	.300	.318	4		HC
1938					11	4	4	3	.500	.500	3		HC
1939					11	4	6	1	.400	.409	3		HC
1940	DET	N		W	11	5	5	1	.500	.500	3		HC
10 yrs.					118	64	42	12		.593			
Playoffs													
1935					1	1	0			1.000			HC

Stan Cofall
Cofall, Stanley Bingham
B. May 5, 1894, Cleveland, OH
D. Sep. 21, 1961, Cleveland, OH
Notre Dame

Year	Team	Lg	C	D	Games	W	L	T	Pct	APct	Fin	Seq	Pos
1920	CLE	A			3	0	2	1	.200	.286	10/9	1/2	HC

Blanton Collier
Collier, Blanton L.
B. Jul. 2, 1906, Millersburg, KY
Georgetown (Kentucky)

Year	Team	Lg	C	D	Games	W	L	T	Pct	APct	Fin	Seq	Pos
1963	CLE	N	N	E	14	10	4	0	.714	.714	2		HC
1964					14	10	3	1	.769	.750	1		HC
1965					14	11	3	0	.786	.786	1		HC
1966					14	9	5	0	.643	.643	2		HC
1967			CE		14	9	5	0	.643	.643	1		HC
1968					14	10	4	0	.714	.714	1		HC
1969					14	10	3	1	.769	.750	1		HC
1970		A		C	14	7	7	0	.500	.500	2		HC
8 yrs.					112	76	34	2		.688			
Playoffs													
1965					1	0	1						HC
1967					1	0	1						HC
1968					2	1	1						HC
1969					2	1	1						HC
4 yrs.					6	2	4			.333			

Joe Collier
Collier, Joel D.
B. June 7, 1932, Rock Island, IL
Northwestern

Year	Team	Lg	C	D	Games	W	L	T	Pct	APct	Fin	Seq	Pos
1966	BUF	A		E	14	9	4	1	.692	.679	1		HC
1967					14	4	10	0	.286	.286	3		HC
1968					2	0	2	0	.000	.000	4/5	1/2	HC
3 yrs.					30	13	16	1		.450			
Playoffs													
1966					1	0	1			.000			HC

Bill Conkright
Conkright, William F. (Red)
B. Apr. 17, 1914, Beggs, OK
D. Oct. 27, 1980, Houston, TX
Oklahoma

Year	Team	Lg	C	D	Games	W	L	T	Pct	APct	Fin	Seq	Pos
1962	OAK	A		W	9	1	8	0	.111	.111	4/4	2/2	HC

Jimmy Conzelman
Conzelman, James Gleason
B. Mar. 6, 1898, St. Louis, MO
D. July 31, 1970, St. Louis, MO
Washington (Missouri)

Year	Team	Lg	C	D	Games	W	L	T	Pct	APct	Fin	Seq	Pos
1921	RI	A			5	4	1	0	.800	.800	16/5	2/2	HC
1922	RI	N			7	4	2	1	.667	.643	5		HC
1923	MIL	N			13	7	2	4	.778	.692	3		HC
1925	DET	N			12	8	2	2	.800	.750	3		HC
1926					12	4	6	2	.400	.416	12		HC
1927	PRO	N			14	8	5	1	.615	.607	5		HC
1928					11	8	1	2	.889	.818	1		HC
1929					12	4	6	2	.400	.417	7		HC
1930					11	6	4	1	.600	.591	5		HC
1940	CHIC	N		W	11	2	7	2	.222	.273	5		HC
1941					11	3	7	1	.300	.227	4		HC
1942					11	3	8	0	.273	.273	4		HC
1946					11	6	5	0	.545	.545	3		HC
1947					12	9	3	0	.750	.750	1		HC
1948					12	11	1	0	.917	.917	1		HC
15 yrs.					165	87	60	18		.582			
Playoffs													
1947					1	1	0						HC
1948					1	0	1						HC
2 yrs.					2	1	1			.500			

Al Cornsweet
Cornsweet, Albert Charles
B. Jul. 16, 1906
D. Oct. 16, 1991, Arlington, VA
Brown

Year	Team	Lg	C	D	Games	W	L	T	Pct	APct	Fin	Seq	Pos
1931	CLE	N			10	2	8	0	.200	.200	8		CHC

Don Coryell
Coryell, Donald David
B. Oct. 17, 1924, Seattle, WA
Washington

Year	Team	Lg	C	D	Games	W	L	T	Pct	APct	Fin	Seq	Pos
1973	STL	N	N	E	14	4	9	1	.321	.321	4		HC
1974					14	10	4	0	.714	.714	1		HC

Year Team Lg C D	Games	W	L	T	Pct	APct	Fin	Seq	Pos
Don Coryell *continued*									
1975	14	11	3	0	.786	.786	1		HC
1976	14	10	4	0	.714	.714	2		HC
1977 ST N N E	14	7	7	0	.500	.500	3		HC
1978 SD N A W	12	8	4	0	.667	.667	4/2	2/2	HC
1979	16	12	4	0	.750	.750	1		HC
1980	16	11	5	0	.688	.688	1		HC
1981	16	10	6	0	.625	.625	1		HC
1982 —	9	6	3	0	.667	.667	5		HC
1983 W	16	6	10	0	.375	.375	4		HC
1984	16	7	9	0	.438	.438	5		HC
1985	16	8	8	0	.500	.500	3		HC
1986	8	1	7	0	.125	.125	5/5	1/2	HC
14 yrs.	195	111	83	1		.572			
Playoffs									
1974	1	0	1						HC
1975	1	0	1						HC
1979	1	0	1						HC
1980	2	1	1						HC
1981	2	1	1						HC
1982	2	1	1						HC
6 yrs.	9	3	6			.333			

Bruce Coslet

Coslet, Bruce Noel
B. Aug. 5, 1946, Oakdale, CA
Pacific

Year Team Lg C D	Games	W	L	T	Pct	APct	Fin	Seq	Pos
1990 NYJ N A E	16	6	10	0	.375	.375	4		HC
1991	16	8	8	0	.500	.500	2		HC
1992	16	4	12	0	.250	.250	4		HC
1993	16	8	8	0	.500	.500	3		HC
1996 CIN N A C	9	7	2	0	.778	.778	5/3	2/2	HC
5 yrs.	73	33	40	0		.452			
Playoffs									
1991 NYJ N	1	0	1			.000			HC

Frank Coughlin

Coughlin, Frank E.
B. Mar., 1896
Deceased
Notre Dame

Year Team Lg C D	Games	W	L	T	Pct	APct	Fin	Seq	Pos
1921 RI A	2	0	1	1	.000	.250	16/5	1/2	HC

Tom Coughlin

Coughlin, Tom
B. Aug. 31, 1946, Waterloo, NY
Syracuse

Year Team Lg C D	Games	W	L	T	Pct	APct	Fin	Seq	Pos
1995 JAC N A C	16	4	12	0	.250	.250	5		HC
1996	16	9	7	0	.563	.563	2		HC
2 yrs.	32	13	19	0		.406			
Playoffs									
1996	3	2	1			.667			HC

Bill Cowher

Cowher, William Laird
B. May 8, 1957, Pittsburgh, PA
North Carolina State

Year Team Lg C D	Games	W	L	T	Pct	APct	Fin	Seq	Pos
1992 PIT N A C	16	11	5	0	.688	.688	1		HC
1993	16	9	7	0	.563	.563	2		HC
1994	16	12	4	0	.750	.750	1		HC
1995	16	11	5	0	.688	.688	1		HC
1996	16	10	6	0	.625	.625	1		HC
5 yrs.	80	53	27	0		.662			
Playoffs									
1992	1	0	1						HC
1993	1	0	1						HC
1994	2	1	1						HC
1995	3	2	1						HC
1996	2	1	1						HC
5 yrs.	9	4	5			.444			

Carl Cramer

Cramer, Carl (Curley)
B. Dec. 20, 1897
D. Feb., 1978, Canal Fulton, OH
Hamline

Year Team Lg C D	Games	W	L	T	Pct	APct	Fin	Seq	Pos
1923 AKR N	2	1	1	0	.500	.500	16/16	2/2	HC

Milan Creighton

Creighton, Milan S.
B. Jan. 21, 1908, Gothenburg, NE
Arkansas

Year Team Lg C D	Games	W	L	T	Pct	APct	Fin	Seq	Pos
1935 CHIC N W	12	6	4	2	.600	.583	3		HC
1936	12	3	8	1	.273	.292	4		HC
1937	11	5	5	1	.500	.500	4		HC
1938	11	2	9	0	.182	.182	5		HC
4 yrs.	46	16	26	4		.391			

Clem Crowe

Crowe, Clem F.
B. Oct. 18, 1903, Lafayette, IN
D. Apr. 13, 1983, Rochester, NY
Notre Dame

Year Team Lg C D	Games	W	L	T	Pct	APct	Fin	Seq	Pos
1949 BUF AA	7	4	2	1	.667	.643	6/4	2/2	HC
1950 BAL N N	12	1	11	0	.083	.083	7		HC
2 yrs.	19	5	13	1		.289			

Jim Crowley

Crowley, James Harold (Sleepy Jim)
B. Sep. 10, 1902, Chicago, IL
D. Jan. 15, 1986, Scranton, PA
Notre Dame

Year Team Lg C D	Games	W	L	T	Pct	APct	Fin	Seq	Pos
1947 CHI AA W	13	1	12	0	.077	.077	4/4	1/2	HC

Russ Daugherty

Daugherty, Russell S. (Pug)
B. Jan. 31, 1902
Deceased
Illinois

Year Team Lg C D	Games	W	L	T	Pct	APct	Fin	Seq	Pos
1927 FRA N	1	0	0	1	.000	.500	8/5	4/4	CHC

Al Davis

Davis, Allen R.
B. Jul. 4, 1929, Brockton, MA
Wittenberg/Syracuse

Year Team Lg C D	Games	W	L	T	Pct	APct	Fin	Seq	Pos
1963 OAK A W	14	10	4	0	.714	.714	2		HC
1964	14	5	7	2	.417	.429	3		HC
1965	14	8	5	1	.615	.607	2		HC
3 yrs.	42	23	16	3		.583			

Lowell Dawson

Dawson, Lowell P. (Red)
B. Dec. 20, 1906, River Falls, WI
D. Jun. 10, 1983
Tulane

Year Team Lg C D	Games	W	L	T	Pct	APct	Fin	Seq	Pos
1946 BUF AA E	14	3	10	1	.231	.250	3		HC
1947	14	8	4	2	.667	.643	2		HC
1948	14	7	7	0	.500	.500	1		HC
1949	5	1	3	1	.250	.300	6/4	1/2	HC
4 yrs.	47	19	24	4		.447			
Playoffs									
1948	2	1	1						HC
1949	1	0	1						HC
2 yrs.	3	1	2			.333			

Dudley De Groot

DeGroot, Dudley S.
B. Nov. 20, 1899, Chicago, IL
Deceased
Stanford

Year Team Lg C D	Games	W	L	T	Pct	APct	Fin	Seq	Pos
1944 WAS N E	10	6	3	1	.667	.650	3		HC
1945	10	8	2	0	1.000	1.000	1		HC
1946 LA AA W	14	7	5	2	.583	.571	3		HC
1947	10	5	5	0	.500	.500	3/3	1/2	HC
4 yrs.	44	26	15	3		.625			
Playoffs									
1945	1	0	1			.000			HC

Herb Dell

Dell, Herbert
B. Jan., 1889, OH
Deceased
None

Year Team Lg C D	Games	W	L	T	Pct	APct	Fin	Seq	Pos
1922 COL N	7	0	7	0	.000	.000	15		HC

Year	Team	Lg	C	D		Games	W	L	T	Pct	APct		Fin	Seq		Pos

Jack Depler
Depler, John C. (Fat)
B. Jan. 6, 1899
D. Dec., 1970, Lewiston, ID
Illinois

Year	Team	Lg	C	D	Games	W	L	T	Pct	APct	Fin	Seq	Pos
1929	ORA	N			12	3	5	4	.375	.417	8		HC
1931	BKN	N			14	2	12	0	.143	.143	9		HC
2 yrs.					26	5	17	4		.269			

Dan Devine
Devine, Daniel John
B. Dec. 23, 1924, Augusta, WI
Minnesota-Duluth

Year	Team	Lg	C	D	Games	W	L	T	Pct	APct	Fin	Seq	Pos
1971	GB	N	N C		14	4	8	2	.333	.357	4		HC
1972					14	10	4	0	.714	.714	1		HC
1973					14	5	7	2	.429	.429	3		HC
1974					14	6	8	0	.429	.429	3		HC
4 yrs.					56	25	27	4		.482			
Playoffs													
1972					1	0	1						HC

Hugh Devore
Devore, Hugh John
B. Nov. 25, 1910, Newark, NJ
D. Dec. 8, 1992
Notre Dame

Year	Team	Lg	C	D	Games	W	L	T	Pct	APct	Fin	Seq	Pos
1953	GB	N	W		2	0	2	0	.000	.000	6/6	2/2	CHC
1956	PHI	N	E		12	3	8	1	.273	.292	6		HC
1957					12	4	8	0	.333	.333	5		HC
3 yrs.					26	7	18	1		.288			

William Dietz
Dietz, William (Lone Star)
B. Aug. 17, 1884
D. Jul. 20, 1964
Carlisle Indian

Year	Team	Lg	C	D	Games	W	L	T	Pct	APct	Fin	Seq	Pos
1933	BOS	N	E		12	5	5	2	.500	.500	3		HC
1934					12	6	6	0	.500	.500	2		HC
2 yrs.					24	11	11	2		.500			

Luby Di Meolo
DiMeolo, Albert
B. Oct. 27, 1903
D. Jun., 1966
Pittsburgh

Year	Team	Lg	C	D	Games	W	L	T	Pct	APct	Fin	Seq	Pos
1934	PIT	N	E	12	2	10	0	.167	.167	5		HC

Mike Ditka
Ditka, Michael Keller
B. Oct. 18, 1939, Carnegie, PA
Pittsburgh

Year	Team	Lg	C	D	Games	W	L	T	Pct	APct	Fin	Seq	Pos
1982	CHI	N	N	—	9	3	6	0	.333	.333	12		HC
1983				C	16	8	8	0	.500	.500	2		HC
1984					16	10	6	0	.625	.625	1		HC
1985					16	15	1	0	.938	.938	1		HC
1986					16	14	2	0	.875	.875	1		HC
1987					15	11	4	0	.733	.733	1		HC
1988					9	7	2	0	.778	.778	1/1	1/3	HC
1988					5	3	2	0	.600	.600	1/1	3/3	HC
1989					16	6	10	0	.375	.375	4		HC
1990					16	11	5	0	.688	.688	1		HC
1991					16	11	5	0	.688	.688	2		HC
1992					16	5	11	0	.313	.313	4		HC
11 yrs.					166	104	62	0		.627			
Playoffs													
1984					2	1	1						HC
1985					3	3	0						HC
1986					1	0	1						HC
1987					1	0	1						HC
1988					2	1	1						HC
1990					2	1	1						HC
1991					1	0	1						HC
7 yrs.					12	6	6			.500			

Bill Doherty
Doherty, William
B. 1883
Deceased
None

Year	Team	Lg	C	D	Games	W	L	T	Pct	APct	Fin	Seq	Pos
1921	CIN	A			4	1	3	0	.250	.250	13		HC

Aldo Donelli
Donelli, Aldo T. (Buff)
B. Jun. 22, 1907, Morgan, PA
D. Aug. 9, 1994, Fort Lauderdale, FL
Duquesne

Year	Team	Lg	C	D	Games	W	L	T	Pct	APct	Fin	Seq	Pos
1941	PIT	N	E		5	0	5	0	.000	.000	5/5	2/3	HC
1944	CLE	N	W		10	4	6	0	.400	.400	4		HC
2 yrs.					15	4	11	0		.267			

Jim Dooley
Dooley, James William
B. Feb. 8, 1930, Stoutsville, MO
Miami (Florida)

Year	Team	Lg	C	D	Games	W	L	T	Pct	APct	Fin	Seq	Pos
1968	CHI	N	W C		14	7	7	0	.500	.500	2		HC
1969					14	1	13	0	.071	.071	4		HC
1970			N C		14	6	8	0	.429	.429	3		HC
1971					14	6	8	0	.429	.429	3		HC
4 yrs.					56	20	36	0		.357			

Gus Dorais
Dorais, Charles Emile
B. Jul. 2, 1891, Chippewa Falls, WI
D. Jan. 3, 1954, Birmingham, AL
Notre Dame

Year	Team	Lg	C	D	Games	W	L	T	Pct	APct	Fin	Seq	Pos
1943	DET	N	W		10	3	6	1	.333	.350	3		HC
1944					10	6	3	1	.667	.650	2		HC
1945					10	7	3	0	.700	.700	2		HC
1946					11	1	10	0	.091	.091	5		HC
1947					12	3	9	0	.250	.250	5		HC
5 yrs.					53	20	31	2		.396			

Forrest Douds
Douds, Forrest M. (Jap)
B. Apr. 21, 1905
D. Aug. 16, 1979, Sewickley, PA
Washington & Jefferson

Year	Team	Lg	C	D	Games	W	L	T	Pct	APct	Fin	Seq	Pos
1933	PIT	N	E		11	3	6	2	.333	.364	5		HC

Bob Dove
Dove, Robert Leo Patrick
B. Feb. 21, 1921, Youngstown, OH
Notre Dame

Year	Team	Lg	C	D	Games	W	L	T	Pct	APct	Fin	Seq	Pos
1946	CHI	AA	W		5	2	2	1	.500	.500	3/3	2/3	CHC

Rod Dowhower
Dowhower, Rodney Douglas
B. Apr. 15, 1943, Ord, NE
San Diego State

Year	Team	Lg	C	D	Games	W	L	T	Pct	APct	Fin	Seq	Pos
1985	IND	N	A E		16	5	11	0	.313	.313	4		HC
1986					13	0	13	0	.000	.000	5/5	1/2	HC
2 yrs.					29	5	24	0		.172			

Paddy Driscoll
Driscoll, John Leo
B. Jan. 11, 1895, Evanston, IL
D. Jun. 29, 1968, Chicago, IL
Northwestern

Year	Team	Lg	C	D	Games	W	L	T	Pct	APct	Fin	Seq	Pos
1920	CHIC	A			6	3	2	1	.600	.583	6		HC
1922	CHIC	N			11	8	3	0	.727	.727	3		HC
1956	CHIB	N	W		12	9	2	1	.818	.792	1		HC
1957					12	5	7	0	.417	.417	5		HC
4 yrs.					41	25	14	2		.634			
Playoffs													
1956					1	0	1			.000			HC

Year	Team	Lg	C	D	Games	W	L	T	Pct	APct	Fin	Seq	Pos

Walt Driskill

Driskill, Walter

Maryland

Year	Team	Lg	C	D	Games	W	L	T	Pct	APct	Fin	Seq	Pos
1949	BAL	AA			8	1	7	0	.125	.125	6/7	2/2	HC

Chuck Drulis

Drulis, Charles John

B. Mar. 18, 1918, Girardville, PA

D. Aug. 23, 1972

Temple

Year	Team	Lg	C	D	Games	W	L	T	Pct	APct	Fin	Seq	Pos
1961	STL	N	E		2	2	0	0	1.000	1.000	4/4	2/2	CHC

Bill Edwards

Edwards, William M.

B. Jun. 21, 1905, Massillon, OH

D. Sep. 12, 1987, Springfield, OH

Ohio State/Wittenberg

Year	Team	Lg	C	D	Games	W	L	T	Pct	APct	Fin	Seq	Pos
1941	DET	N		W	11	4	6	1	.400	.409	3		HC
1942					3	0	3	0	.000	.000	5/5	1/2	HC
2 yrs.					14	4	9	1	.321				

Howard Edwards

Edwards, Howard (Cap, Horse)

B. May, 1888, South Bend, IN

D. 1944

Notre Dame

Year	Team	Lg	C	D	Games	W	L	T	Pct	APct	Fin	Seq	Pos
1921	CAN	A			10	5	2	3	.714	.650	4		HC
1923	CLE	N			7	3	1	3	.750	.643	5		HC
1925					14	5	8	1	.385	.393	12		HC
3 yrs.					31	13	11	7	.532				

Turk Edwards

Edwards, Albert Glen

B. Sep. 28, 1907, Clarkston, WA

D. Jan. 10, 1973, Seattle, WA

Washington State

Year	Team	Lg	C	D	Games	W	L	T	Pct	APct	Fin	Seq	Pos
1946	WAS	N		E	11	5	5	1	.500	.500	3		HC
1947					12	4	8	0	.333	.333	4		HC
1948					12	7	5	0	.583	.583	2		HC
3 yrs.					35	16	18	1	.471				

Eddie Erdelatz

Erdelatz, Edward J.

B. San Francisco, CA

St. Mary's (California)

Year	Team	Lg	C	D	Games	W	L	T	Pct	APct	Fin	Seq	Pos
1960	OAK	A		W	14	6	8	0	.429	.429	3		HC
1961					2	0	2	0	.000	.000	3/4	1/2	HC
2 yrs.					16	6	10	0	.375				

Ron Erhardt

Erhardt, Ronald Peter

B. Feb. 27, 1931, Mandan, ND

Jamestown (North Dakota)

Year	Team	Lg	C	D	Games	W	L	T	Pct	APct	Fin	Seq	Pos
1978	NE	N	A	E	1	0	1	0	.000	.000	1/1	2/2	CHC
1979					16	9	7	0	.563	.563	2		HC
1980					16	10	6	0	.625	.625	2		HC
1981					16	2	14	0	.125	.125	4		HC
4 yrs.					49	21	28	0	.429				
Playoffs													
1978					1	0	1		.000				CHC

Dennis Erickson

Erickson, Dennis

B. Mar. 24, 1947, Everett, WA

Montana State

Year	Team	Lg	C	D	Games	W	L	T	Pct	APct	Fin	Seq	Pos
1995	SEA	N	A	W	16	8	8	0	.500	.500	3		HC
1996					16	7	9	0	.438	.438	5		HC
2 yrs.					32	15	17	0	.469				

Hal Erickson

Erickson, Harold (Swede)

B. Mar. 10, 1899, Maynard, MN

D. Jan. 28, 1962

St. Olaf/Washington & Jefferson

Year	Team	Lg	C	D	Games	W	L	T	Pct	APct	Fin	Seq	Pos
1924	MIL	N			13	5	8	0	.385	.385	12		HC

Charley Ewart

Ewart, Charles Diven

B. Oct. 16, 1915

D. Apr. 30, 1990

Yale

Year	Team	Lg	C	D	Games	W	L	T	Pct	APct	Fin	Seq	Pos
1949	NYB	N		E	12	1	10	1	.091	.125	5		HC

Weeb Ewbank

Ewbank, Wilbur Charles

B. May 6, 1907, Richmond, IN

Miami (Ohio)

Year	Team	Lg	C	D	Games	W	L	T	Pct	APct	Fin	Seq	Pos
1954	BAL	N		W	12	3	9	0	.250	.250	6		HC
1955					12	5	6	1	.455	.458	4		HC
1956					12	5	7	0	.417	.417	4		HC
1957					12	7	5	0	.583	.583	3		HC
1958					12	9	3	0	.750	.750	1		HC
1959					12	9	3	0	.750	.750	1		HC
1960					12	6	6	0	.500	.500	4		HC
1961					14	8	6	0	.571	.571	3		HC
1962					14	7	7	0	.500	.500	4		HC
1963	NY	A		E	14	5	8	1	.385	.393	4		HC
1964					14	5	8	1	.385	.393	3		HC
1965					14	5	8	1	.385	.393	2		HC
1966					14	6	6	2	.500	.500	3		HC
1967					14	8	5	1	.615	.607	2		HC
1968					14	11	3	0	.786	.786	1		HC
1969					14	10	4	0	.714	.714	1		HC
1970	NYJ	N	A	E	14	4	10	0	.286	.286	3		HC
1971					14	6	8	0	.429	.429	3		HC
1972					14	7	7	0	.500	.500	2		HC
1973					14	4	10	0	.286	.286	4		HC
20 yrs.					266	130	129	7	.502				
Playoffs													
1958					1	1	0						HC
1959					1	1	0						HC
1968					2	2	0						HC
1969					1	0	1						HC
4 yrs.					5	4	1		.800				

Chuck Fairbanks

Fairbanks, Charles Leo

B. Jun. 10, 1933, Detroit, MI

Michigan State

Year	Team	Lg	C	D	Games	W	L	T	Pct	APct	Fin	Seq	Pos
1973	NE	N	A	E	14	5	9	0	.357	.357	3		HC
1974					14	7	7	0	.500	.500	3		HC
1975					14	3	11	0	.214	.214	4		HC
1976					14	11	3	0	.786	.786	2		HC
1977					14	9	5	0	.643	.643	3		HC
1978					15	11	4	0	.733	.733	1/1	1/2	HC
6 yrs.					85	46	39	0	.541				
Playoffs													
1976					1	0	1		.000				HC

Guil Falcon

Falcon, Guilford W. (Hawk)

B. Dec. 16, 1892, Evanston, IN

D. Jul., 1982, Hallandale, FL

Year	Team	Lg	C	D	Games	W	L	T	Pct	APct	Fin	Seq	Pos
1920	CHIT	A			7	1	5	1	.167	.214	10		HC
1922	TOL	N			9	5	2	2	.714	.667	4		HC
1923					8	3	3	2	.500	.500	10		HC
3 yrs.					24	9	10	5	.479				

Jack Faulkner

Faulkner, Jack T.

B. Apr. 4, 1926, Youngstown, OH

Miami (Ohio)

Year	Team	Lg	C	D	Games	W	L	T	Pct	APct	Fin	Seq	Pos
1962	DEN	A		W	14	7	7	0	.500	.500	2		HC
1963					14	2	11	1	.154	.179	4		HC
1964					4	0	4	0	.000	.000	3/4	1/2	HC
3 yrs.					32	9	22	1	.297				

Frank Fausch

Fausch, Franklin L. (Whitey, Fox)

B. Jun. 13, 1895

Deceased

Kalamazoo

Year	Team	Lg	C	D	Games	W	L	T	Pct	APct	Fin	Seq	Pos
1921	EVA	A			5	3	2	0	.600	.600	6		HC

Frank Fausch continued

Year	Team	Lg	C	D	Games	W	L	T	Pct	APct	Fin	Seq	Pos
1922	EVA	N			3	0	3	0	.000	.000	15		HC
2 yrs.					8	3	5	0		.375			

Tom Fears
Fears, Thomas Jesse
B. Dec. 3, 1923, Los Angeles, CA
Santa Clara/UCLA

Year	Team	Lg	C	D	Games	W	L	T	Pct	APct	Fin	Seq	Pos
1967	NO	N	E	CA	14	3	11	0	.214	.214	4		HC
1968			CE		14	4	9	1	.308	.321	3		HC
1969			CA		14	5	9	0	.357	.357	3		HC
1970		N	W		7	1	5	1	.167	.214	4/4	1/2	HC
4 yrs.					49	13	34	2		.286			

Marty Feldman
Feldman, Marty
B. Sep. 12, 1922, Los Angeles, CA
Oregon/Stanford

Year	Team	Lg	C	D	Games	W	L	T	Pct	APct	Fin	Seq	Pos
1961	OAK	A		W	12	2	10	0	.167	.167	3/4	2/2	HC
1962					5	0	5	0	.000	.000	4/4	1/2	HC
2 yrs.					17	2	15	0		.118			

Frank Filchock
Filchock, Frank Joseph (Frankie)
B. Oct. 18, 1916, Crucible, PA
Indiana

Year	Team	Lg	C	D	Games	W	L	T	Pct	APct	Fin	Seq	Pos
1960	DEN	A		W	14	4	9	1	.308	.321	4		HC
1961					14	3	11	0	.214	.214	3		HC
2 yrs.					28	7	20	1		.268			

Jack Fish
Fish, Jack
None

Year	Team	Lg	C	D	Games	W	L	T	Pct	APct	Fin	Seq	Pos
1930	NEW	N			12	1	10	1	.091	.125	11		CHC

Jeff Fisher
Fisher, Jeffrey Michael
B. Feb. 25, 1958, Culver City, CA
Southern California

Year	Team	Lg	C	D	Games	W	L	T	Pct	APct	Fin	Seq	Pos
1994	HOU	N	A	C	6	1	5	0	.167	.167	4/4	2/2	HC
1995					16	7	9	0	.438	.438	2		HC
1996					16	8	8	0	.500	.500	4		HC
3 yrs.					38	16	22	0		.421			

Ray Flaherty
Flaherty, Raymond Paul
B. Sep. 1, 1904, Spokane, WA
D. Jul. 19, 1994, Coeur d'Alene, ID
Gonzaga

Year	Team	Lg	C	D	Games	W	L	T	Pct	APct	Fin	Seq	Pos
1936	BOS	N	E		12	7	5	0	.583	.583	1		HC
1937	WAS	N	E		11	8	3	0	.727	.727	1		HC
1938					11	6	3	2	.667	.636	2		HC
1939					11	8	2	1	.800	.773	2		HC
1940					11	9	2	0	.818	.818	1		HC
1941					11	6	5	0	.545	.545	3		HC
1942					11	10	1	0	.909	.909	1		HC
1946	NY	AA	E		14	10	3	1	.769	.750	1		HC
1947					14	11	2	1	.846	.821	1		HC
1948					8	2	6	0	.250	.250	3/3	1/2	HC
1949	CHI	AA			12	4	8	0	.333	.333	5		HC
11 yrs.					126	81	40	5		.663			
Playoffs													
1936					1	0	1						HC
1937					1	1	0						HC
1940					1	0	1						HC
1942					1	1	0						HC
1946					1	0	1						HC
1947					1	0	1						HC
6 yrs.					6	2	4			.333			

Tom Flores
Flores, Thomas Raymond
B. Mar. 21, 1937, Fresno, CA
Pacific

Year	Team	Lg	C	D	Games	W	L	T	Pct	APct	Fin	Seq	Pos
1979	OAK	N	A	W	16	9	7	0	.563	.563	3		HC
1980					16	11	5	0	.688	.688	2		HC

Tom Flores continued

Year	Team	Lg	C	D	Games	W	L	T	Pct	APct	Fin	Seq	Pos
1981					16	7	9	0	.438	.438	4		HC
1982	LARI	N	A	—	9	8	1	0	.889	.889	1		HC
1983				W	16	12	4	0	.750	.750	1		HC
1984					16	11	5	0	.688	.688	3		HC
1985					16	12	4	0	.750	.750	1		HC
1986					16	8	8	0	.500	.500	4		HC
1987					15	5	10	0	.333	.333	4		HC
1992	SEA	N	A	W	16	2	14	0	.125	.125	5		HC
1993					16	6	10	0	.375	.375	5		HC
1994					16	6	10	0	.375	.375	5		HC
12 yrs.					184	97	87	0		.527			
Playoffs													
1980					4	4	0						HC
1982					2	1	1						HC
1983					3	3	0						HC
1984					1	0	1						HC
1985					1	0	1						HC
5 yrs.					11	8	3			.727			

Bob Folwell
Folwell, Bob
Deceased
Pennsylvania

Year	Team	Lg	C	D	Games	W	L	T	Pct	APct	Fin	Seq	Pos
1925	NY	N			12	8	4	0	.667	.667	4		HC
1926	PHI	A			10	8	2	0	.800	.800	1		HC
2 yrs.					22	16	6	0		.727			

Wayne Fontes
Fontes, Wayne Howard Joseph
B. Feb. 2, 1940, New Bedford, MA
Michigan State

Year	Team	Lg	C	D	Games	W	L	T	Pct	APct	Fin	Seq	Pos
1988	DET	N	N	C	5	2	3	0	.400	.400	4/4	2/2	HC
1989					16	7	9	0	.438	.438	3		HC
1990					16	6	10	0	.375	.375	3		HC
1991					16	12	4	0	.750	.750	1		HC
1992					16	5	11	0	.313	.313	5		HC
1993					16	10	6	0	.625	.625	1		HC
1994					16	9	7	0	.563	.563	3		HC
1995					16	10	6	0	.625	.625	2		HC
1996					16	5	11	0	.313	.313	5		HC
9 yrs.					133	66	67	0		.496			
Playoffs													
1991					2	1	1						HC
1993					1	0	1						HC
1994					1	0	1						HC
1995					1	0	1						HC
4 yrs.					5	1	4			.200			

Jack Forsyth
Forsyth, Jack
B. May 10, 1898
D. Jul., 1978, Alden, NY
Rochester

Year	Team	Lg	C	D	Games	W	L	T	Pct	APct	Fin	Seq	Pos
1920	ROC	A			1	0	1	0	.000	.000	11		HC
1921					6	3	3	0	.500	.500	8		HC
2 yrs.					7	3	4	0		.429			

Rick Forzano
Forzano, Rick
B. Nov. 20, 1928, Akron, OH
*Kent State**

Year	Team	Lg	C	D	Games	W	L	T	Pct	APct	Fin	Seq	Pos
1974	DET	N	N	C	14	7	7	0	.500	.500	2		HC
1975					14	7	7	0	.500	.500	2		HC
1976					4	1	3	0	.250	.250	3/3	1/2	HC
3 yrs.					32	15	17	0		.469			

Benny Friedman
Friedman, Benjamin
B. Mar. 18, 1905, Cleveland, OH
D. Nov. 23, 1982, New York, NY
Michigan

Year	Team	Lg	C	D	Games	W	L	T	Pct	APct	Fin	Seq	Pos
1930	NY	N			2	2	0	0	1.000	1.000	2/2	2/2	HC
1932	BKN	N			12	3	9	0	.250	.250	6		HC
2 yrs.					14	5	9	0		.357			

Year	Team	Lg	C	D	Games	W	L	T	Pct	APct	Fin	Seq	Pos

Frank Gansz
Gansz, Francis von Rensselaer
B. Nov. 22, 1938, Altoona, PA
Navy

Year	Team	Lg	C	D	Games	W	L	T	Pct	APct	Fin	Seq	Pos
1987	KC	N	A	W	15	4	11	0	.267	.267	5		HC
1988					16	4	11	1	.281	.281	5		HC
2 yrs.					31	8	22	1		.274			

Al Garrett
Garrett, Alfred T. (Budge)
B. 1893
D. Jun. 7, 1950
Rutgers

Year	Team	Lg	C	D	Games	W	L	T	Pct	APct	Fin	Seq	Pos
1922	MIL	N			9	2	4	3	.333	.389	11		HC

Mike Getto
Getto, Michael
B. Sep. 18, 1905, Jeannette, PA
D. Aug., 1960
Pittsburgh

Year	Team	Lg	C	D	Games	W	L	T	Pct	APct	Fin	Seq	Pos
1942	BKN	N		E	11	3	8	0	.273	.273	4		HC

Joe Gibbs
Gibbs, Joe Jackson
B. Nov. 25, 1940, Mocksville, NC
San Diego State

Year	Team	Lg	C	D	Games	W	L	T	Pct	APct	Fin	Seq	Pos
1981	WAS	N	N	E	16	8	8	0	.500	.500	4		HC
1982		—			9	8	1	0	.889	.889	1		HC
1983				E	16	14	2	0	.875	.875	1		HC
1984					16	11	5	0	.688	.688	1		HC
1985					16	10	6	0	.625	.625	3		HC
1986					16	12	4	0	.750	.750	2		HC
1987					15	11	4	0	.733	.733	1		HC
1988					16	7	9	0	.438	.438	3		HC
1989					16	10	6	0	.625	.625	3		HC
1990					16	10	6	0	.625	.625	3		HC
1991					16	14	2	0	.875	.875	1		HC
1992					16	9	7	0	.563	.563	3		HC
12 yrs.					184	124	60	0		.674			
Playoffs													
1982					4	4	0						HC
1983					3	2	1						HC
1984					1	0	1						HC
1986					3	2	1						HC
1987					3	3	0						HC
1990					2	1	1						HC
1991					3	3	0						HC
1992					2	1	1						HC
8 yrs.					21	16	5			.762			

Abe Gibron
Gibron, Abe
B. Sep. 22, 1925, Michigan City, IN
Valparaiso/Purdue

Year	Team	Lg	C	D	Games	W	L	T	Pct	APct	Fin	Seq	Pos
1972	CHI	N	N	C	14	4	9	1	.321	.321	4		HC
1973					14	3	11	0	.214	.214	4		HC
1974					14	4	10	0	.286	.286	4		HC
3 yrs.					42	11	30	1		.274			

George Gibson
Gibson, George F.
B. Oct. 2, 1905, Kendaia, NY
Minnesota

Year	Team	Lg	C	D	Games	W	L	T	Pct	APct	Fin	Seq	Pos
1930	MIN	N			9	1	7	1	.125	.167	10		HC

Fred Gillies
Gillies, Frederick M. (Boo)
B. Dec. 9, 1895
D. May 8, 1974, Flossmoor, IL
Cornell

Year	Team	Lg	C	D	Games	W	L	T	Pct	APct	Fin	Seq	Pos
1928	CHIC	N			6	1	5	0	.167	.167	9		HC

Sid Gillman
Gillman, Sidney
B. Oct. 26, 1911, Minneapolis, MN
Ohio State

Year	Team	Lg	C	D	Games	W	L	T	Pct	APct	Fin	Seq	Pos
1955	LA	N		W	12	8	3	1	.727	.708	1		HC
1956					12	4	8	0	.333	.333	5		HC
1957					12	6	6	0	.500	.500	4		HC
1958					12	8	4	0	.667	.667	2		HC
1959					12	2	10	0	.167	.167	6		HC
1960	LA	A		W	14	10	4	0	.714	.714	1		HC
1961	SD	A		W	14	12	2	0	.857	.857	1		HC
1962					14	4	10	0	.286	.286	3		HC
1963					14	11	3	0	.786	.786	1		HC
1964					14	8	5	1	.615	.607	1		HC
1965					14	9	2	3	.818	.750	1		HC
1966					14	7	6	1	.538	.536	3		HC
1967					14	8	5	1	.615	.607	3		HC
1968					14	9	5	0	.643	.643	3		HC
1969					9	4	5	0	.444	.444	4	1/2	HC
1971	SD	N	A	W	10	4	6	0	.400	.400	3/3	1/2	HC
1973	HOU	N	A	C	9	1	8	0	.111	.111	4/4	2/2	HC
1974					14	7	7	0	.500	.500	3		HC
18 yrs.					228	122	99	7		.550			
Playoffs													
1955					1	0	1						HC
1960					1	0	1						HC
1961					1	0	1						HC
1963					1	1	0						HC
1964					1	0	1						HC
1965					1	0	1						HC
6 yrs.					6	1	5			.167			

Hank Gillo
Gillo, Henry Charles
B. Oct. 5, 1894, Milwaukee, WI
D. Sep. 6, 1948
Colgate

Year	Team	Lg	C	D	Games	W	L	T	Pct	APct	Fin	Seq	Pos
1923	RAC	N			10	4	4	2	.500	.500	10		HC

Harry Gilmer
Gilmer, Harry V., Jr.
B. Apr. 14, 1926, Birmingham, AL
Alabama

Year	Team	Lg	C	D	Games	W	L	T	Pct	APct	Fin	Seq	Pos
1965	DET	N		W	14	6	7	1	.462	.464	6		HC
1966					14	4	9	1	.308	.321	6		HC
2 yrs.					28	10	16	2		.393			

Jerry Glanville
Glanville, Jerry Michael
B. Oct. 14, 1941, Detroit, MI
Northern Michigan

Year	Team	Lg	C	D	Games	W	L	T	Pct	APct	Fin	Seq	Pos
1985	HOU	N	A	C	2	0	2	0	.000	.000	4/4	2/2	HC
1986					16	5	11	0	.313	.313	4		HC
1987					15	9	6	0	.600	.600	2		HC
1988					16	10	6	0	.625	.625	2		HC
1989					16	9	7	0	.563	.563	2		HC
1990	ATL	N	N	W	16	5	11	0	.313	.313	4		HC
1991					16	10	6	0	.625	.625	2		HC
1992					16	6	10	0	.375	.375	3		HC
1993					16	6	10	0	.375	.375	3		HC
9 yrs.					129	60	69	0		.465			
Playoffs													
1987					2	1	1						HC
1988					2	1	1						HC
1989					1	0	1						HC
1991					2	1	1						HC
4 yrs.					7	3	4			.429			

Archie Golembeski
Golembeski, Anthony
B. May 25, 1900
D. Mar. 9, 1976, Worcester, MA
Holy Cross

Year	Team	Lg	C	D	Games	W	L	T	Pct	APct	Fin	Seq	Pos
1925	PRO	N			12	6	5	1	.545	.542	10		HC

Otto Graham
Graham, Otto Everett, Jr. (Automatic Otto)
B. Dec. 6, 1921, Waukegan, IL
Northwestern

Year	Team	Lg	C	D	Games	W	L	T	Pct	APct	Fin	Seq	Pos
1966	WAS	N	E		14	7	7	0	.500	.500	5		HC
1967			CA		14	5	6	3	.455	.464	3		HC
1968					14	5	9	0	.357	.357	3		HC
3 yrs.					42	17	22	3		.440			

Bud Grant
Grant, Harold Peter
B. May 20, 1927, Superior, WI
Minnesota

Year	Team	Lg	C	D	Games	W	L	T	Pct	APct	Fin	Seq	Pos
1967	MIN	N	W	C	14	3	8	3	.273	.321	4		HC
1968					14	8	6	0	.571	.571	1		HC
1969					14	12	2	0	.857	.857	1		HC
1970			N	C	14	12	2	0	.857	.857	1		HC
1971					14	11	3	0	.786	.786	1		HC
1972					14	7	7	0	.500	.500	3		HC
1973					14	12	2	0	.857	.857	1		HC
1974					14	10	4	0	.714	.714	1		HC
1975					14	12	2	0	.857	.857	1		HC
1976					14	11	2	1	.821	.821	1		HC
1977					14	9	5	0	.643	.643	1		HC
1978					16	8	7	1	.531	.531	1		HC
1979					16	7	9	0	.438	.438	3		HC
1980					16	9	7	0	.563	.563	1		HC
1981					16	7	9	0	.438	.438	4		HC
1982			—		9	5	4	0	.556	.556	4		HC
1983			C		16	8	8	0	.500	.500	2		HC
1985					16	7	9	0	.438	.438	3		HC
18 yrs.					259	158	96	5		.620			
Playoffs													
1968					1	0	1						HC
1969					3	2	1						HC
1970					1	0	1						HC
1971					1	0	1						HC
1973					3	2	1						HC
1974					3	2	1						HC
1975					1	0	1						HC
1976					3	2	1						HC
1977					2	1	1						HC
1978					1	0	1						HC
1980					1	0	1						HC
1982					2	1	1						HC
12 yrs.					22	10	12			.455			

Dennis Green
Green, Dennis
B. Feb. 17, 1949, Harrisburg, PA
Iowa

Year	Team	Lg	C	D	Games	W	L	T	Pct	APct	Fin	Seq	Pos
1992	MIN	N	N	C	16	11	5	0	.688	.688	1		HC
1993					16	9	7	0	.563	.563	2		HC
1994					16	10	6	0	.625	.625	1		HC
1995					16	8	8	0	.500	.500	4		HC
1996					16	9	7	0	.563	.563	2		HC
5 yrs.					80	47	33	0		.588			
Playoffs													
1992					1	0	1						HC
1993					1	0	1						HC
1994					1	0	1						HC
1996					1	0	1						HC
4 yrs.					4	0	4			.000			

Forrest Gregg
Gregg, Alvis Forrest
B. Oct. 18, 1933, Birthright, TX
Southern Methodist

Year	Team	Lg	C	D	Games	W	L	T	Pct	APct	Fin	Seq	Pos
1975	CLE	N	A	C	14	3	11	0	.214	.214	4		HC
1976					14	9	5	0	.643	.643	3		HC
1977					13	6	7	0	.429	.429	4/4	1/2	HC
1980	CIN	N	A	C	16	6	10	0	.375	.375	4		HC
1981					16	12	4	0	.750	.750	1		HC
1982			—		9	7	2	0	.778	.778	3		HC
1983			C		16	7	9	0	.438	.438	3		HC
1984	GB	N	N	C	16	8	8	0	.500	.500	2		HC
1985					16	8	8	0	.500	.500	2		HC
1986					16	4	12	0	.250	.250	4		HC

Forrest Gregg *continued*

Year	Team	Lg	C	D	Games	W	L	T	Pct	APct	Fin	Seq	Pos
1987					15	5	9	1	.367	.367	3		HC
11 yrs.					161	75	85	1		.469			
Playoffs													
1981	CIN	N			3	2	1						HC
1982					1	0	1						HC
2 yrs.					4	2	2			.500			

Hal Griffen
Griffen, Harold W. (Tubby)
B. Mar., 1902
Deceased
Iowa

Year	Team	Lg	C	D	Games	W	L	T	Pct	APct	Fin	Seq	Pos
1930	POR	N			14	5	6	3	.455	.464	7		HC

Tex Grigg
Grigg, Cecil
B. Feb. 15, 1891, Nashville, TN
D. Sep. 5, 1968, Houston, TX
Austin

Year	Team	Lg	C	D	Games	W	L	T	Pct	APct	Fin	Seq	Pos
1925	ROC	N			7	0	6	1	.000	.071	16		HC

Hinkey Haines
Haines, Henry Luther
B. Dec. 23, 1898, Red Lion, PA
D. Jan. 9, 1979, Sharon Hills, PA
Lebanon Valley/Penn State

Year	Team	Lg	C	D	Games	W	L	T	Pct	APct	Fin	Seq	Pos
1931	SI	N			9	2	6	1	.250	.278	8/7	1/2	HC

George Halas
Halas, George Stanley (Papa Bear)
B. Feb. 2, 1895, Chicago, IL
D. Oct. 31, 1983, Chicago, IL
Illinois

Year	Team	Lg	C	D	Games	W	L	T	Pct	APct	Fin	Seq	Pos
1920	DEC	A			8	5	1	2	.833	.750	2		HC
1921					11	9	1	1	.900	.864	1		HC
1922	CHIB	N			12	9	3	0	.750	.750	2		CHC
1923					13	9	2	2	.818	.769	2		HC
1924					11	6	1	4	.857	.727	2		CHC
1925					17	9	5	3	.643	.617	7		HC
1926					16	12	1	3	.923	.844	2		HC
1927					14	9	3	2	.750	.714	3		HC
1928					13	7	5	1	.583	.577	5		HC
1929					15	4	9	2	.308	.333	9		HC
1933					13	10	2	1	.833	.808	1		HC
1934					13	13	0	0	1.000	1.000	1		HC
1935					12	6	4	2	.600	.583	4		HC
1936					12	9	3	0	.750	.750	2		HC
1937					11	9	1	1	.900	.864	1		HC
1938					11	6	5	0	.545	.545	3		HC
1939					11	8	3	0	.727	.727	2		HC
1940					11	8	3	0	.727	.727	1		HC
1941					11	10	1	0	.909	.909	1		HC
1942					5	5	0	0	1.000	1.000	1/1	1/2	HC
1946					11	8	2	1	.800	.773	1		HC
1947					12	8	4	0	.667	.667	2		HC
1948					12	10	2	0	.833	.833	2		HC
1949					12	9	3	0	.750	.750	2		HC
1950					12	9	3	0	.750	.750	1		HC
1951					12	7	5	0	.583	.583	4		HC
1952					12	5	7	0	.417	.417	5		HC
1953					12	3	8	1	.273	.292	4		HC
1954					12	8	4	0	.667	.667	2		HC
1955					12	8	4	0	.667	.667	2		HC
1958					12	8	4	0	.667	.667	2		HC
1959					12	8	4	0	.667	.667	2		HC
1960	CHI	N	W		12	5	6	1	.455	.458	5		HC
1961					14	8	6	0	.571	.571	3		HC
1962					14	9	5	0	.643	.643	3		HC
1963					14	11	1	2	.917	.857	1		HC
1964					14	5	9	0	.357	.357	6		HC
1965					14	9	5	0	.643	.643	3		HC
1966					14	5	7	2	.417	.429	5		HC
1967			C		14	7	6	1	.538	.536	2		HC
40 yrs.					493	313	148	32		.667			

Year	Team	Lg	C	D	Games	W	L	T	Pct	APct	Fin	Seq	Pos

George Halas continued

Playoffs

Year	Team	Lg	C	D	Games	W	L	T	Pct	APct	Fin	Seq	Pos
1933					1	1	0						HC
1934					1	0	1						HC
1937					1	0	1						HC
1940					1	1	0						HC
1941					2	2	0						HC
1946					1	1	0						HC
1950					1	0	1						HC
1963					1	1	0						HC
8 yrs.					9	6	3		.667				

Phil Handler

Handler, Philip Jacob (Motsy)
B. Jul. 21, 1908, Fort Worth, TX
D. Dec. 8, 1968, Skokie, IL
Texas Christian

Year	Team	Lg	C	D	Games	W	L	T	Pct	APct	Fin	Seq	Pos
1943	CHIC	N		W	10	0	10	0	.000	.000	4		HC
1944	C-P	N		W	10	0	10	0	.000	.000	5		CHC
1945	CHIC	N		W	10	1	9	0	.100	.100	5		CHC
1949					6	2	4	0	.333	.333	3/	1/2	CHC
1951					2	1	1	0	.500	.500	6/6	2/2	CHC
5 yrs.					38	4	34	0	.105				

Ray Handley

Handley, Robert Ray
B. Oct. 8, 1944, Artesia, NM
Stanford

Year	Team	Lg	C	D	Games	W	L	T	Pct	APct	Fin	Seq	Pos
1991	NYG	N	N	E	16	8	8	0	.500	.500	4		HC
1992					16	6	10	0	.375	.375	4		HC
2 yrs.					32	14	18	0	.438				

Jim Hanifan

Hanifan, James Martin Michael
B. Sep. 21, 1933, Compton, CA
California

Year	Team	Lg	C	D	Games	W	L	T	Pct	APct	Fin	Seq	Pos
1980	STL	N	N	E	16	5	11	0	.313	.313	4		HC
1981					16	7	9	0	.438	.438	5		HC
1982				—	9	5	4	0	.556	.556	6		HC
1983				E	16	8	7	1	.531	.531	3		HC
1984					16	9	7	0	.563	.563	2		HC
1985					16	5	11	0	.313	.313	5		HC
1989	ATL	N	N	W	4	0	4	0	.000	.000	4/4	2/2	HC
7 yrs.					93	39	53	1	.425				

Playoffs

Year	Team	Lg	C	D	Games	W	L	T	Pct	APct	Fin	Seq	Pos
1982					1	0	1						HC

Bo Hanley

Hanley, G.
B. Dec. 14, 1887
D. Sep., 1980, Milwaukee, WI
Marquette

Year	Team	Lg	C	D	Games	W	L	T	Pct	APct	Fin	Seq	Pos
1924	KEN	N			5	0	4	1	.000	.100	16		HC

Dick Hanley

Hanley, Richard E.
B. Nov. 19, 1894, Cloquet, MN
D. Dec. 16, 1970, Palo Alto, CA
Washington State

Year	Team	Lg	C	D	Games	W	L	T	Pct	APct	Fin	Seq	Pos
1946	CHI	AA		W	3	1	1	1	.500	.500	3/4	1/3	HC

Hal Hansen

Hansen, Harlan C. (King Hal)
B. Sep. 3, 1892
D. Sep., 1977, Des Moines, IA
Minnesota

Year	Team	Lg	C	D	Games	W	L	T	Pct	APct	Fin	Seq	Pos
1926	NEW	A			5	0	3	2	.000	.200	9		HC
1932	SI	N			12	2	7	3	.222	.292	8		HC
2 yrs.					17	2	10	5	.265				

Norb Hecker

Hecker, Norbert Earl
B. May 26, 1927, Berea, OH
Baldwin-Wallace

Year	Team	Lg	C	D	Games	W	L	T	Pct	APct	Fin	Seq	Pos
1966	ATL	N	E		14	3	11	0	.214	.214	7		HC
1967			W	CO	14	1	12	1	.077	.107	4		HC

Norb Hecker continued

Year	Team	Lg	C	D	Games	W	L	T	Pct	APct	Fin	Seq	Pos
1968					3	0	3	0	.000	.000	4/4	1/2	HC
3 yrs.					31	4	26	1	.145				

Ernie Hefferle

Hefferle, Ernie
B. Jan. 12, 1915, Herminie, PA
Duquesne

Year	Team	Lg	C	D	Games	W	L	T	Pct	APct	Fin	Seq	Pos
1975	NO	N	N	W	8	1	7	0	.125	.125	4/4	2/2	HC

Jack Hegarty

Hegarty, John Edward
B. Jun. 9, 1888, Newburyport, MA
Deceased
Holy Cross/Georgetown

Year	Team	Lg	C	D	Games	W	L	T	Pct	APct	Fin	Seq	Pos
1921	WAS	A			4	2	2	0	.500	.500	8		HC

Mel Hein

Hein, Melvin John
B. Aug. 22, 1909, Redding, CA
D. Feb. 1, 1992, San Clemente, CA
Washington State

Year	Team	Lg	C	D	Games	W	L	T	Pct	APct	Fin	Seq	Pos
1947	LA	AA		W	4	2	2	0	.500	.500	3/3	2/2	CHC

John Heldt

Heldt, John
B. Dec. 2, 1899
D. Oct., 1975, Mallard, IA
Iowa

Year	Team	Lg	C	D	Games	W	L	T	Pct	APct	Fin	Seq	Pos
1926	COL	N			7	1	6	0	.143	.143	19		HC

Gus Henderson

Henderson, Elmer C.
B. Mar. 10, 1889, Oberlin, OH
D. Dec. 16, 1965
Oberlin

Year	Team	Lg	C	D	Games	W	L	T	Pct	APct	Fin	Seq	Pos
1939	DET	N		W	11	6	5	0	.545	.545	3		HC

Dutch Hendrian

Hendrian, Oscar G.
B. 1897
Deceased
DePauw/Detroit/Pittsburgh*/Princeton*

Year	Team	Lg	C	D	Games	W	L	T	Pct	APct	Fin	Seq	Pos
1923	AKR	N			5	0	5	0	.000	.000	16/16	1/2	HC

Dan Henning

Henning, Daniel Ernest
B. Jun. 21, 1942, Bronx, NY
William & Mary

Year	Team	Lg	C	D	Games	W	L	T	Pct	APct	Fin	Seq	Pos
1983	ATL	N	N	W	16	7	9	0	.438	.438	4		HC
1984					16	4	12	0	.250	.250	4		HC
1985					16	4	12	0	.250	.250	4		HC
1986					16	7	8	1	.469	.469	3		HC
1989	SD	N	A	W	16	6	10	0	.375	.375	5		HC
1990					16	6	10	0	.375	.375	4		HC
1991					16	4	12	0	.250	.250	5		HC
7 yrs.					112	38	73	1	.344				

Pete Henry

Henry, Wilbur Francis (Fats)
B. Oct. 31, 1897, Mansfield, OH
D. Feb. 7, 1952, Washington, PA
Washington & Jefferson

Year	Team	Lg	C	D	Games	W	L	T	Pct	APct	Fin	Seq	Pos
1926	CAN	N			13	1	9	3	.100	.192	20		HC
1928	POT	N			10	2	8	0	.200	.200	8		HC
2 yrs.					23	3	17	3	.196				

Wally Hess

Hess, Walter
B. Oct. 28, 1894
D. Aug., 1963
Indiana

Year	Team	Lg	C	D	Games	W	L	T	Pct	APct	Fin	Seq	Pos
1922	HAM	N			6	0	5	1	.000	.083	15		HC

Wally Hess *continued*

Year	Team	Lg	C	D	Games	W	L	T	Pct	APct	Fin	Seq	Pos
1923					7	1	5	1	.167	.214	15		HC
1924					5	2	2	1	.500	.500	10		HC
3 yrs.					18	3	12	3		.250			

Red Hickey
Hickey, Howard W.
B. Feb. 14, 1917, Clarksville, AR
Arkansas

Year	Team	Lg	C	D	Games	W	L	T	Pct	APct	Fin	Seq	Pos
1959	SF	N	W		12	7	5	0	.583	.583	3		HC
1960					12	7	5	0	.583	.583	2		HC
1961					14	7	6	1	.538	.536	5		HC
1962					14	6	8	0	.429	.429	5		HC
1963					3	0	3	0	.000	.000	6/7	1/2	HC
5 yrs.					55	27	27	1		.500			

Eddie Hicks
Hicks, Eddie
None

Year	Team	Lg	C	D	Games	W	L	T	Pct	APct	Fin	Seq	Pos
1920	HAM	A			3	0	3	0	.000	.000	11		HC

Max Hicks
Hicks, Max
B. 1894
Deceased
Geneva

Year	Team	Lg	C	D	Games	W	L	T	Pct	APct	Fin	Seq	Pos
1921	HAM	A			5	1	3	1	.250	.300	13		HC

Austin Higgins
Higgins, Austin
B. Nov. 29, 1897
D. Mar., 1976, Kingsley, KY

Year	Team	Lg	C	D	Games	W	L	T	Pct	APct	Fin	Seq	Pos
1921	LOU	A			2	0	2	0	.000	.000	18		HC

Joe Hoeffel
Hoeffel, J. Merrill
Wisconsin

Year	Team	Lg	C	D	Games	W	L	T	Pct	APct	Fin	Seq	Pos
1921	GB	A			6	3	2	1	.600	.583	6		HC

Bill Hollenback
Hollenback, William
Pennsylvania

Year	Team	Lg	C	D	Games	W	L	T	Pct	APct	Fin	Seq	Pos
1922	RAC	N			11	6	4	1	.600	.591	6		HC

Bob Hollway
Hollway, Robert
B. Jan. 29, 1926, Ann Arbor, MI
Michigan

Year	Team	Lg	C	D	Games	W	L	T	Pct	APct	Fin	Seq	Pos
1971	STL	N	N	E	14	4	9	1	.308	.321	4		HC
1972					14	4	9	1	.321	.321	4		HC
2 yrs.					28	8	18	2		.321			

Mike Holmgren
Holmgren, Michael George
B. Jun. 15, 1948, San Francisco, CA
Southern California

Year	Team	Lg	C	D	Games	W	L	T	Pct	APct	Fin	Seq	Pos
1992	GB	N	N	C	16	9	7	0	.563	.563	2		HC
1993					16	9	7	0	.563	.563	3		HC
1994					16	9	7	0	.563	.563	2		HC
1995					16	11	5	0	.688	.688	1		HC
1996					16	13	3	0	.813	.813	1		HC
5 yrs.					80	51	29	0		.637			
Playoffs													
1993					2	1	1						HC
1994					2	1	1						HC
1995					3	2	1						HC
1996					3	3	0						HC
4 yrs.					10	7	3			.700			

Mike Holovak
Holovak, Michael Joseph
B. Sep. 19, 1919, Lansford, PA
Boston College

Year	Team	Lg	C	D	Games	W	L	T	Pct	APct	Fin	Seq	Pos
1961	BOS	A		E	9	7	1	1	.875	.833	2/2	2/2	HC

Mike Holovak *continued*

Year	Team	Lg	C	D	Games	W	L	T	Pct	APct	Fin	Seq	Pos
1962					14	9	4	1	.692	.679	2		HC
1963					14	7	6	1	.538	.536	1		HC
1964					14	10	3	1	.769	.750	2		HC
1965					14	4	8	2	.333	.357	3		HC
1966					14	8	4	2	.667	.643	2		HC
1967					14	3	10	1	.231	.250	5		HC
1968					14	4	10	0	.286	.286	4		HC
1976	NYJ	N	A	E	1	0	1	0	.000	.000	4/4	2/2	HC
9 yrs.					108	52	47	9		.523			
Playoffs													
1963					2	1	1						HC

Lou Holtz
Holtz, Lou
B. Jan. 6, 1937, Follansbee, WV
Kent State

Year	Team	Lg	C	D	Games	W	L	T	Pct	APct	Fin	Seq	Pos
1976	NYJ	N	A	E	13	3	10	0	.231	.231	4/4	1/2	HC

Arnie Horween
Horowitz, Arnold (played as McMahon)
B. Jul. 7, 1898, Chicago, IL
D. Aug. 5, 1985, Chicago, IL
Harvard

Year	Team	Lg	C	D	Games	W	L	T	Pct	APct	Fin	Seq	Pos
1923	CHIC	N			12	8	4	0	.667	.667	6		HC
1924					10	5	4	1	.556	.550	8		HC
2 yrs.					22	13	8	1		.614			

Jim Lee Howell
Howell, James Lee
B. Sep. 27, 1914, Lonoke, AR
D. Jan. 4, 1995, Lonoke, AR
Arkansas

Year	Team	Lg	C	D	Games	W	L	T	Pct	APct	Fin	Seq	Pos
1954	NY	N		E	12	7	5	0	.583	.583	3		HC
1955					12	6	5	1	.545	.542	3		HC
1956					12	8	3	1	.727	.708	1		HC
1957					12	7	5	0	.583	.583	2		HC
1958					12	9	3	0	.750	.750	1		HC
1959					12	10	2	0	.833	.833	1		HC
1960					12	6	4	0	.600	.583	3		HC
7 yrs.					84	53	27	4		.655			
Playoffs													
1956					1	1	0						HC
1958					2	1	1						HC
1959					1	0	1						HC
3 yrs.					4	2	2			.500			

Tommy Hudspeth
Hudspeth, Tommy
B. Sep. 14, 1931, Cherryvale, KS
Tulsa

Year	Team	Lg	C	D	Games	W	L	T	Pct	APct	Fin	Seq	Pos
1976	DET	N	N	C	10	5	5	0	.500	.500	3/3	2/2	HC
1977					14	6	8	0	.429	.429	3		HC
2 yrs.					24	11	13	0		.458			

Ken Huffine
Huffine, Kenneth W.
B. Dec. 22, 1897
D. Sep. 26, 1977, Bradenton, FL
Purdue

Year	Team	Lg	C	D	Games	W	L	T	Pct	APct	Fin	Seq	Pos
1920	MUN	A			1	0	1	0	.000	.000	11		HC

Ed Hughes
Hughes, Edward D.
B. Oct. 23, 1927, Buffalo, NY
North Carolina State/Tulsa

Year	Team	Lg	C	D	Games	W	L	T	Pct	APct	Fin	Seq	Pos
1971	HOU	N	A	C	14	4	9	1	.308	.321	3		HC

Tommy Hughitt
Hughitt, Ernest Thomas (Tiny)
B. Dec. 27, 1892, Genoa, B.C.
Deceased
Michigan

Year	Team	Lg	C	D	Games	W	L	T	Pct	APct	Fin	Seq	Pos
1920	BUF	A			6	4	1	1	.800	.750	3		HC
1921					12	9	1	2	.900	.833	2		HC

Year	Team	Lg	C	D	Games	W	L	T	Pct	APct	Fin	Seq	Pos

Tommy Hughitt *continued*

Year	Team	Lg	C	D	Games	W	L	T	Pct	APct	Fin	Seq	Pos
1922	BUF	N			10	5	4	1	.556	.550	9		HC
1923					12	5	4	3	.556	.542	8		HC
1924					11	6	5	0	.545	.545	9		HC
5 yrs.					51	29	15	7		.637			

Hal Hunter

Hunter, Hal
B. Jun. 3, 1934, Canonsburg, PA
Pittsburgh

Year	Team	Lg	C	D	Games	W	L	T	Pct	APct	Fin	Seq	Pos
1984	IND	N	A	E	1	0	1	0	.000	.000	4/4	2/2	HC

Tut Imlay

Imlay, Talma W.
B. Mar. 20, 1902
D. Mar. 20, 1976, Del Monte Forest, CA
California

Year	Team	Lg	C	D	Games	W	L	T	Pct	APct	Fin	Seq	Pos
1926	LA	N			10	6	3	1	.667	.650	6		CHC

Lindy Infante

Infante, Gelindo
B. May 27, 1940, Miami, FL
Florida

Year	Team	Lg	C	D	Games	W	L	T	Pct	APct	Fin	Seq	Pos
1988	GB	N	N	C	16	4	12	0	.250	.250	4		HC
1989					16	10	6	0	.625	.625	2		HC
1990					16	6	10	0	.375	.375	4		HC
1991					16	4	12	0	.250	.250	4		HC
1996	IND	N	A	E	16	9	7	0	.563	.563	3		HC
5 yrs.					80	33	47	0		.412			
Playoffs													
1996					1	0	1			.000			HC

Cecil Isbell

Isbell, Cecil F.
B. Jul. 11, 1915, Iola, TX
D. Jun. 23, 1985, Hammond, IN
Purdue

Year	Team	Lg	C	D	Games	W	L	T	Pct	APct	Fin	Seq	Pos
1947	BAL	AA		E	14	2	11	1	.154	.179	4		HC
1948					14	7	7	0	.500	.500	1		HC
1949					4	0	4	0	.000	.000	6/7	1/2	HC
1951	CHIC	N	A		2	1	1	0	.500	.500	6/6	2/2	CHC
4 yrs.					34	10	23	1		.309			
Playoffs													
1948					1	0	1			.000			HC

Pop Ivy

Ivy, Lee Frank
B. Jan. 25, 1916, Skiatook, OK
Oklahoma

Year	Team	Lg	C	D	Games	W	L	T	Pct	APct	Fin	Seq	Pos
1958	CHIC	N	E		12	2	9	1	.182	.208	5		HC
1959					12	2	10	0	.167	.167	6		HC
1960	STL	N	E		12	6	5	1	.545	.542	4		HC
1961					12	5	7	0	.417	.417	4/4	1/2	HC
1962	HOU	A		E	14	11	3	0	.786	.786	1		HC
1963					14	6	8	0	.429	.429	3		HC
6 yrs.					76	32	42	2		.434			
Playoffs													
1962					1	0	1			.000			HC

Herb Joesting

Joesting, Herbert W. (The Owatonna Thunderbolt)
B. Apr. 17, 1905, Little Falls, MN
D. Oct. 2, 1963, Shoreview, MN
Minnesota

Year	Team	Lg	C	D	Games	W	L	T	Pct	APct	Fin	Seq	Pos
1929	MIN	N			10	1	9	0	.100	.100	11		HC

Bill Johnson

Johnson, William Levi, Sr. (Tiger)
B. Jul. 14, 1926, Tyler, TX
Texas A&M/Tyler JC

Year	Team	Lg	C	D	Games	W	L	T	Pct	APct	Fin	Seq	Pos
1976	CIN	N	A	C	14	10	4	0	.714	.714	2		HC
1977					14	8	6	0	.571	.571	2		HC
1978					5	0	5	0	.000	.000	4/4	1/2	HC
3 yrs.					33	18	15	0		.545			

Harvey Johnson

Johnson, Harvey P. (Stud)
B. Jun. 22, 1919, Bridgeton, NJ
D. Aug. 8, 1983, Orchard Park, NY
William & Mary

Year	Team	Lg	C	D	Games	W	L	T	Pct	APct	Fin	Seq	Pos
1968	BUF	A		E	12	1	10	1	.091	.125	4/5	2/2	HC
1971	BUF	N	A	E	14	1	13	0	.071	.071	5		HC
2 yrs.					26	2	23	1		.096			

Jimmy Johnson

Johnson, James William
B. Jul. 16, 1943, Port Arthur, TX
Arkansas

Year	Team	Lg	C	D	Games	W	L	T	Pct	APct	Fin	Seq	Pos
1989	DAL	N	N	E	16	1	15	0	.063	.063	5		HC
1990					16	7	9	0	.438	.438	4		HC
1991					16	11	5	0	.688	.688	2		HC
1992					16	13	3	0	.813	.813	1		HC
1993					16	12	4	0	.750	.750	1		HC
1996	MIA	N	A	E	16	8	8	0	.500	.500	4		HC
6 yrs.					96	52	44	0		.542			
Playoffs													
1991					2	1	1						HC
1992					3	3	0						HC
1993					3	3	0						HC
3 yrs.					8	7	1			.875			

Luke Johnsos

Johnsos, Luke A.
B. Dec. 6, 1905, Chicago, IL
D. Dec. 10, 1984, Evanston, IL
Northwestern

Year	Team	Lg	C	D	Games	W	L	T	Pct	APct	Fin	Seq	Pos
1942	CHIB	N		W	6	6	0	0	1.000	1.000	1/1	2/2	CHC
1943					10	8	1	1	.889	.850	1		CHC
1944					10	6	3	1	.667	.650	2		CHC
1945					10	3	7	0	.300	.300	4		CHC
4 yrs.					36	23	11	2		.667			
Playoffs													
1942					1	0	1						CHC
1943					1	1	0						CHC
2 yrs.					2	1	1			.500			

Al Jolley

Jolley, Alvin Jay (Rocky)
B. Sep. 29, 1899, Onaga, KS
D. Aug. 26, 1948, Marietta, OH
Marietta/Tulsa/Kansas State

Year	Team	Lg	C	D	Games	W	L	T	Pct	APct	Fin	Seq	Pos
1929	BUF	N			9	1	7	1	.125	.167	10		HC
1930	BKN	N			12	7	4	1	.636	.625	4		HC
1933	CIN	N		W	3	0	3	0	.000	.000	5/4	1/2	HC
3 yrs.					24	8	14	2		.375			

June Jones

Jones, June Sheldon, III
B. Feb. 19, 1953, Portland, OR
Oregon/Hawaii/Portland State

Year	Team	Lg	C	D	Games	W	L	T	Pct	APct	Fin	Seq	Pos
1994	ATL	N	N	W	16	7	9	0	.438	.438	3		HC
1995					16	9	7	0	.563	.563	2		HC
1996					16	3	13	0	.188	.188	4		HC
3 yrs.					48	19	29	0		.396			
Playoffs													
1995					1	0	1			.000			HC

Ralph Jones

Jones, Ralph
Wabash

Year	Team	Lg	C	D	Games	W	L	T	Pct	APct	Fin	Seq	Pos
1930	CHIB	N			14	9	4	1	.692	.679	3		HC
1931					13	8	5	0	.615	.615	3		HC
1932					14	7	1	6	.875	.714	1		HC
3 yrs.					41	24	10	7		.671			

Bull Karcis

Karcis, John
B. Dec. 3, 1908, Monaca, PA
D. Sep. 4, 1973, Pittsburgh, PA
Carnegie-Mellon

Year	Team	Lg	C	D	Games	W	L	T	Pct	APct	Fin	Seq	Pos
1942	DET	N		W	8	0	8	0	.000	.000	5/5	2/2	HC

Jim Kendrick

Kendrick, James M.
B. Aug. 22, 1893
Texas A&M

Year	Team	Lg	C	D	Games	W	L	T	Pct	APct	Fin	Seq	Pos
1923	LOU	N			3	0	3	0	.000	.000	19		HC
1926	BUF	N			10	4	4	2	.500	.500	9		HC
2 yrs.					13	4	7	2	.385				

Jack Keough

Keough, John Joseph
B. Jun. 17, 1886, South Hadley Falls, PA
Pennsylvania

Year	Team	Lg	C	D	Games	W	L	T	Pct	APct	Fin	Seq	Pos
1926	HAR	N			9	3	6	0	.333	.333	15/13	2/2	HC

Eddie Khayat

Khayat, Edward Michael
B. Sep. 14, 1935, Moss Point, MS
Millsaps/Tulane

Year	Team	Lg	C	D	Games	W	L	T	Pct	APct	Fin	Seq	Pos
1971	PHI	N	N	E	11	6	4	1	.600	.591	5/3	2/2	HC
1972					14	2	11	1	.179	.179	5		HC
2 yrs.					25	8	15	2	.360				

Walt Kiesling

Kiesling, Walter Andrew
B. Mar. 27, 1903, St. Paul, MN
D. Mar. 2, 1962, Pittsburgh, PA
St. Thomas (Minnesota)

Year	Team	Lg	C	D	Games	W	L	T	Pct	APct	Fin	Seq	Pos
1939	PIT	N		E	8	1	6	1	.143	.188	4/4	2/2	HC
1940					11	2	7	2	.222	.273	4		HC
1941					4	1	2	1	.333	.375	5/5	3/3	HC
1942					11	7	4	0	.636	.636	2		HC
1943	P-P	N		E	10	5	4	1	.556	.550	3		CHC
1944	C-P	N		W	10	0	10	0	.000	.000	5		CHC
1954	PIT	N	E		12	5	7	0	.417	.417	4		HC
1955					12	4	8	0	.333	.333	6		HC
1956					12	5	7	0	.417	.417	4		HC
9 yrs.					90	30	55	5	.361				

Chuck Knox

Knox, Charles Robert, Sr.
B. Apr. 27, 1932, Sewickley, PA
Juniata

Year	Team	Lg	C	D	Games	W	L	T	Pct	APct	Fin	Seq	Pos
1973	LA	N	N	W	14	12	2	0	.857	.857	1		HC
1974					14	10	4	0	.714	.714	1		HC
1975					14	12	2	0	.857	.857	1		HC
1976					14	10	3	1	.750	.750	1		HC
1977					14	10	4	0	.714	.714	1		HC
1978	BUF	N	A	E	16	5	11	0	.313	.313	4		HC
1979					16	7	9	0	.438	.438	4		HC
1980					16	11	5	0	.688	.688	1		HC
1981					16	10	6	0	.625	.625	3		HC
1982				—	9	4	5	0	.444	.444	9		HC
1983	SEA	N	A	W	16	9	7	0	.563	.563	2		HC
1984					16	12	4	0	.750	.750	2		HC
1985					16	8	8	0	.500	.500	3		HC
1986					16	10	6	0	.625	.625	3		HC
1987					15	9	6	0	.600	.600	2		HC
1988					16	9	7	0	.563	.563	1		HC
1989					16	7	9	0	.438	.438	4		HC
1990					16	9	7	0	.563	.563	3		HC
1991					16	7	9	0	.438	.438	4		HC
1992	LARM	N	N	W	16	6	10	0	.375	.375	4		HC
1993					16	5	11	0	.313	.313	4		HC
1994					16	4	12	0	.250	.250	4		HC
22 yrs.					334	186	147	1	.558				

Playoffs

Year	Team	Lg	C	D	Games	W	L	T	Pct	APct	Fin	Seq	Pos
1973					1	0	1						HC
1974					2	1	1						HC
1975					2	1	1						HC
1976					2	1	1						HC
1977					1	0	1						HC
1980					1	0	1						HC
1981					2	1	1						HC
1983					3	2	1						HC
1984					2	1	1						HC
1987					1	0	1						HC
1988					1	0	1						HC
11 yrs.					18	7	11		.389				

Herb Kopf

Kopf, Herbert M.
B. Feb. 3, 1895, Winsted, CT
D. Jan., 1967, Caldwell, NJ
Washington & Jefferson

Year	Team	Lg	C	D	Games	W	L	T	Pct	APct	Fin	Seq	Pos
1944	BOS	N		E	10	2	8	0	.200	.200	4		HC
1945					10	3	6	1	.333	.350	4		HC
1946					11	2	8	1	.200	.227	5		HC
3 yrs.					31	7	22	2	.258				

Walt Koppisch

Koppisch, Walter Frederic
B. 1902
D. Nov. 5, 1953
Columbia

Year	Team	Lg	C	D	Games	W	L	T	Pct	APct	Fin	Seq	Pos
1925	BUF	N			9	1	6	2	.143	.222	15		HC

Rich Kotite

Kotite, Richard Edward
B. Oct. 13, 1942, Brooklyn, NY
Wagner

Year	Team	Lg	C	D	Games	W	L	T	Pct	APct	Fin	Seq	Pos
1991	PHI	N	N	E	16	10	6	0	.625	.625	3		HC
1992					16	11	5	0	.688	.688	2		HC
1993					16	8	8	0	.500	.500	3		HC
1994					16	7	9	0	.438	.438	4		HC
1995	NYJ	N	A	E	16	3	13	0	.188	.188	5		HC
1996					16	1	15	0	.063	.063	5		HC
6 yrs.					96	40	56	0	.417				

Playoffs

Year	Team	Lg	C	D	Games	W	L	T	Pct	APct	Fin	Seq	Pos
1992					2	1	1			.500			HC

Ollie Kraehe

Kraehe, Oliver R.
B. Aug. 22, 1898, St. Louis, MO
D. Nov. 2, 1969, St. Louis, MO
Washington (Missouri)

Year	Team	Lg	C	D	Games	W	L	T	Pct	APct	Fin	Seq	Pos
1923	STL	N			7	1	4	2	.200	.286	14		HC

Ed Kubale

Kubale, Edwin
B. Nov. 12, 1899
D. Feb., 1971, Danville, KY
Centre

Year	Team	Lg	C	D	Games	W	L	T	Pct	APct	Fin	Seq	Pos
1944	BKN	N		E	5	0	5	0	.000	.000	5/5	2/2	CHC

Joe Kuharich

Kuharich, Joseph Lawrence
B. Apr. 14, 1917, South Bend, IN
D. Jan. 25, 1981, Philadelphia, PA
Notre Dame

Year	Team	Lg	C	D	Games	W	L	T	Pct	APct	Fin	Seq	Pos
1952	CHIC	N	A		12	4	8	0	.333	.333	5		HC
1954	WAS	N		E	12	3	9	0	.250	.250	5		HC
1955					12	8	4	0	.667	.667	2		HC
1956					12	6	6	0	.500	.500	3		HC
1957					12	5	6	1	.455	.458	4		HC
1958					12	4	7	1	.364	.375	4		HC
1964	PHI	N		E	14	6	8	0	.429	.429	3		HC
1965					14	5	9	0	.357	.357	5		HC
1966					14	9	5	0	.643	.643	2		HC
1967				CA	14	6	7	1	.462	.464	2		HC
1968					14	2	12	0	.143	.143	4		HC
11 yrs.					142	58	81	3	.419				

Hank Kuhlmann

Kuhlmann, Henry Norman
B. Oct. 6, 1937, Webster Groves, MO
Missouri

Year	Team	Lg	C	D	Games	W	L	T	Pct	APct	Fin	Seq	Pos
1989	PHX	N	N	E	5	0	5	0	.000	.000	3/4	2/2	HC

Frank Kush

Kush, Frank Joseph
B. Jan. 20, 1929, Windber, PA
Michigan State

Year	Team	Lg	C	D	Games	W	L	T	Pct	APct	Fin	Seq	Pos
1982	BAL	N	A	—	9	0	8	1	.056	.056	14		HC
1983				E	16	7	9	0	.438	.438	4		HC

Year	Team	Lg	C	D	Games	W	L	T	Pct	APct	Fin	Seq	Pos

Frank Kush *continued*

Year	Team	Lg	C	D	Games	W	L	T	Pct	APct	Fin	Seq	Pos
1984	IND	N	A	E	15	4	11	0	.267	.267	4/4	1/2	HC
3 yrs.					40	11	28	1		.287			

Jim Laird

Laird, James T.
B. Sep. 10, 1897
D. Aug. 16, 1970, Lebanon, CT
Colgate

Year	Team	Lg	C	D	Games	W	L	T	Pct	APct	Fin	Seq	Pos
1926	PRO	N			13	5	7	1	.417	.423	11		HC

Curly Lambeau

Lambeau, Earl Louis
B. Apr. 9, 1898, Green Bay, WI
D. Jun. 1, 1965, Sturgeon Bay, WI
Wisconsin/Notre Dame

Year	Team	Lg	C	D	Games	W	L	T	Pct	APct	Fin	Seq	Pos
1922	GB	N			10	4	3	3	.571	.550	7		HC
1923					10	7	2	1	.778	.750	3		HC
1924					11	7	4	0	.636	.636	6		HC
1925					13	8	5	0	.615	.615	9		HC
1926					13	7	3	3	.700	.654	5		HC
1927					10	7	2	1	.778	.750	2		HC
1928					13	6	4	3	.600	.577	4		HC
1929					13	12	0	1	1.000	.962	1		HC
1930					14	10	3	1	.769	.750	1		HC
1931					14	12	2	0	.857	.857	1		HC
1932					14	10	3	1	.769	.750	2		HC
1933			W		13	5	7	1	.417	.423	3		HC
1934					13	7	6	0	.538	.538	3		HC
1935					12	8	4	0	.667	.667	2		HC
1936					12	10	1	1	.909	.875	1		HC
1937					11	7	4	0	.636	.636	2		HC
1938					11	8	3	0	.727	.727	1		HC
1939					11	9	2	0	.818	.818	1		HC
1940					11	6	4	0	.600	.591	2		HC
1941					11	10	1	0	.909	.909	1		HC
1942					11	8	2	1	.800	.773	2		HC
1943					10	7	2	1	.778	.750	2		HC
1944					10	8	2	0	.800	.800	1		HC
1945					10	6	4	0	.600	.600	3		HC
1946					11	6	5	0	.545	.545	3		HC
1947					12	6	5	1	.545	.542	3		HC
1948					12	3	9	0	.250	.250	4		HC
1949					12	2	10	0	.167	.167	5		HC
1950	CHIC	N	A		12	5	7	0	.417	.417	5		HC
1951					10	2	8	0	.200	.200	6/6	1/2	HC
1952	WAS	N	A		12	4	8	0	.333	.333	5		HC
1953					12	6	5	1	.545	.542	3		HC
32 yrs.					374	223	130	21		.624			
Playoffs													
1936					1	1	0						HC
1938					1	0	1						HC
1939					1	1	0						HC
1941					1	0	1						HC
1944					1	1	0						HC
5 yrs.					5	3	2			.600			

Tom Landry

Landry, Thomas Wade
B. Sep. 11, 1924, Mission, TX
Texas

Year	Team	Lg	C	D	Games	W	L	T	Pct	APct	Fin	Seq	Pos
1960	DAL	N	W		12	0	11	1	.000	.042	7		HC
1961			E		14	4	9	1	.308	.321	6		HC
1962					14	5	8	1	.385	.393	5		HC
1963					14	4	10	0	.286	.286	5		HC
1964					14	5	8	1	.385	.393	5		HC
1965					14	7	7	0	.500	.500	2		HC
1966					14	10	3	1	.769	.750	1		HC
1967			CA		14	9	5	0	.643	.643	1		HC
1968					14	12	2	0	.857	.857	1		HC
1969					14	11	2	1	.846	.821	1		HC
1970			N	E	14	10	4	0	.714	.714	1		HC
1971					14	11	3	0	.786	.786	1		HC
1972					14	10	4	0	.714	.714	2		HC
1973					14	10	4	0	.714	.714	1		HC
1974					14	8	6	0	.571	.571	3		HC
1975					14	10	4	0	.714	.714	2		HC
1976					14	11	3	0	.786	.786	1		HC
1977					14	12	2	0	.857	.857	1		HC

Tom Landry *continued*

Year	Team	Lg	C	D	Games	W	L	T	Pct	APct	Fin	Seq	Pos
1978					16	12	4	0	.750	.750	1		HC
1979					16	11	5	0	.688	.688	1		HC
1980					16	12	4	0	.750	.750	2		HC
1981					16	12	4	0	.750	.750	1		HC
1982			—		9	6	3	0	.667	.667	2		HC
1983			E		16	12	4	0	.750	.750	2		HC
1984					16	9	7	0	.563	.563	2		HC
1985					16	10	6	0	.625	.625	1		HC
1986					16	7	9	0	.438	.438	3		HC
1987					15	7	8	0	.467	.467	2		HC
1988					16	3	13	0	.188	.188	5		HC
29 yrs.					418	250	162	6		.605			
Playoffs													
1966					1	0	1						HC
1967					2	1	1						HC
1968					1	0	1						HC
1969					1	0	1						HC
1970					3	2	1						HC
1971					3	3	0						HC
1972					2	1	1						HC
1973					2	1	1						HC
1975					3	2	1						HC
1976					1	0	1						HC
1977					3	3	0						HC
1978					3	2	1						HC
1979					1	0	1						HC
1980					3	2	1						HC
1981					2	1	1						HC
1982					3	2	1						HC
1983					1	0	1						HC
1985					1	0	1						HC
18 yrs.					36	20	16			.556			

Wally Lemm

Lemm, Walter H.
B. Oct. 23, 1919, Chicago, IL
Carroll (Wisconsin)

Year	Team	Lg	C	D	Games	W	L	T	Pct	APct	Fin	Seq	Pos
1961	HOU	A		E	9	9	0	0	1.000	1.000	4/1	2/2	HC
1962	STL	N	E		14	4	9	1	.308	.321	6		HC
1963					14	9	5	0	.643	.643	3		HC
1964					14	9	3	2	.750	.714	2		HC
1965					14	5	9	0	.357	.357	5		HC
1966	HOU	A		E	14	3	11	0	.214	.214	4		HC
1967					14	9	4	1	.692	.679	1		HC
1968					14	7	7	0	.500	.500	2		HC
1969					14	6	6	2	.500	.500	2		HC
1970	HOU	N	A	C	14	3	10	1	.231	.250	4		HC
10 yrs.					135	64	64	7		.500			
Playoffs													
1961					1	1	0						HC
1967					1	0	1						HC
1969					1	0	1						HC
3 yrs.					3	1	2			.333			

Jim Leonard

Leonard, James R., Sr. (Big Jim)
B. Feb. 14, 1910, Philadelphia, PA
D. Nov. 28, 1993, Woodbury, NJ
Notre Dame

Year	Team	Lg	C	D	Games	W	L	T	Pct	APct	Fin	Seq	Pos
1945	PIT	N		E	10	2	8	0	.200	.200	5		HC

Marv Levy

Levy, Marvin Daniel
B. Aug. 3, 1928, Chicago, IL
Coe

Year	Team	Lg	C	D	Games	W	L	T	Pct	APct	Fin	Seq	Pos
1978	KC	N	A	W	16	4	12	0	.250	.250	5		HC
1979					16	7	9	0	.438	.438	5		HC
1980					16	8	8	0	.500	.500	3		HC
1981					16	9	7	0	.563	.563	3		HC
1982			—		9	3	6	0	.333	.333	11		HC
1986	BUF	N	A	E	7	2	5	0	.286	.286	4/4	2/2	HC
1987					15	7	8	0	.467	.467	4		HC
1988					16	12	4	0	.750	.750	1		HC
1989					16	9	7	0	.563	.563	2		HC
1990					16	13	3	0	.813	.813	1		HC
1991					16	13	3	0	.813	.813	1		HC
1992					16	11	5	0	.688	.688	2		HC
1993					16	12	4	0	.750	.750	1		HC

Marv Levy *continued*

Year	Team	Lg	C	D	Games	W	L	T	Pct	APct	Fin	Seq	Pos
1994					16	7	9	0	.438	.438	4		HC
1995					6	5	1	0	.833	.833	1/1	1/3	HC
1995					7	4	3	0	.571	.571	1/1	3/3	HC
1996					16	10	6	0	.625	.625	2		HC
16 yrs.					236	136	100	0		.576			
Playoffs													
1988					2	1	1						HC
1989					1	0	1						HC
1990					3	2	1						HC
1991					3	2	1						HC
1992					4	3	1						HC
1993					3	2	1						HC
1995					2	1	1						HC
1996					1	0	1						HC
8 yrs.					19	11	8			.579			

Art Lewis

Lewis, Arthur E. (Pappy)
B. Feb. 8, 1911, Middleport, OH
D. Jun. 13, 1962
Ohio University

Year	Team	Lg	C	D	Games	W	L	T	Pct	APct	Fin	Seq	Pos
1938	CLE	N		W	8	4	4	0	.500	.500	5/4	2/2	HC

Vince Lombardi

Lombardi, Vincent Thomas
B. Jun. 11, 1913, Brooklyn, NY
D. Sep. 3, 1970, Washington, DC
Fordham

Year	Team	Lg	C	D	Games	W	L	T	Pct	APct	Fin	Seq	Pos
1959	GB	N		W	12	7	5	0	.583	.583	3		HC
1960					12	8	4	0	.667	.667	1		HC
1961					14	11	3	0	.786	.786	1		HC
1962					14	13	1	0	.929	.929	1		HC
1963					14	11	2	1	.846	.821	2		HC
1964					14	8	5	1	.615	.607	2		HC
1965					14	10	3	1	.769	.750	1		HC
1966					14	12	2	0	.857	.857	1		HC
1967			C		14	9	4	1	.692	.679	1		HC
1969	WAS	N	E	CA	14	7	5	2	.583	.571	2		HC
10 yrs.					136	96	34	6		.728			
Playoffs													
1960					1	0	1						HC
1961					1	1	0						HC
1962					1	1	0						HC
1965					2	2	0						HC
1966					2	2	0						HC
1967					3	3	0						HC
6 yrs.					10	9	1			.900			

Leo Lyons

Lyons, Leo V.
B. 1893
Deceased
None

Year	Team	Lg	C	D	Games	W	L	T	Pct	APct	Fin	Seq	Pos
1923	ROC	N			4	0	4	0	.000	.000	19		HC

John Mackovic

Mackovic, John
B. Oct. 1, 1943, Barberton, OH
Wake Forest

Year	Team	Lg	C	D	Games	W	L	T	Pct	APct	Fin	Seq	Pos
1983	KC	N	A	W	16	6	10	0	.375	.375	4		HC
1984					16	8	8	0	.500	.500	4		HC
1985					16	6	10	0	.375	.375	5		HC
1986					16	10	6	0	.625	.625	2		HC
4 yrs.					64	30	34	0		.469			
Playoffs													
1986					1	0	1						HC

Dick MacPherson

MacPherson, Richard F.
B. Nov. 4, 1930
Springfield

Year	Team	Lg	C	D	Games	W	L	T	Pct	APct	Fin	Seq	Pos
1991	NE	N	A	E	16	6	10	0	.375	.375	4		HC
1992					8	0	8	0	.000	.000	5/5	1/3	HC
1992					1	0	1	0	.000	.000	5/5	3/3	HC
2 yrs.					25	6	19	0		.240			

John Madden

Madden, John Earl
B. Apr. 10, 1936, Austin, MN
California Poly (San Luis Obispo)

Year	Team	Lg	C	D	Games	W	L	T	Pct	APct	Fin	Seq	Pos
1969	OAK	A		W	14	12	1	1	.923	.893	1		HC
1970	OAK	N	A	W	14	8	4	2	.667	.643	1		HC
1971					14	8	4	2	.667	.643	2		HC
1972					14	10	3	1	.750	.750	1		HC
1973					14	9	4	1	.679	.679	1		HC
1974					14	12	2	0	.857	.857	1		HC
1975					14	11	3	0	.786	.786	1		HC
1976					14	13	1	0	.929	.929	1		HC
1977					14	11	3	0	.786	.786	2		HC
1978					16	9	7	0	.563	.563	2		HC
10 yrs.					142	103	32	7		.750			
Playoffs													
1969					2	1	1						HC
1970					2	1	1						HC
1972					1	0	1						HC
1973					2	1	1						HC
1974					2	1	1						HC
1975					2	1	1						HC
1976					3	3	0						HC
1977					2	1	1						HC
8 yrs.					16	9	7			.563			

Lou Mahrt

Mahrt, Louis R.
B. Jul. 30, 1904
D. Aug., 1962, Dayton, OH
Dayton

Year	Team	Lg	C	D	Games	W	L	T	Pct	APct	Fin	Seq	Pos
1927	DAY	N			8	1	6	1	.143	.188	10		HC

Ray Malavasi

Malavasi, Raymondo Giuseppi Giovanni Baptiste
B. Nov. 8, 1930, Passaic, NJ
Army/Mississippi State

Year	Team	Lg	C	D	Games	W	L	T	Pct	APct	Fin	Seq	Pos
1966	DEN	A		W	12	4	8	0	.333	.333	4/4	2/2	HC
1978	LA	N	N	W	16	12	4	0	.750	.750	1		HC
1979					16	9	7	0	.563	.563	1		HC
1980					16	11	5	0	.688	.688	2		HC
1981					16	6	10	0	.375	.375	3		HC
1982	LARM	N	N	—	9	2	7	0	.222	.222	14		HC
6 yrs.					85	44	41	0		.518			
Playoffs													
1978	LA	N			2	1	1						HC
1979					3	2	1						HC
1980					1	0	1						HC
3 yrs.					6	3	3			.500			

Ted Marchibroda

Marchibroda, Theodore Joseph
B. Mar. 15, 1931, Franklin, PA
Detroit/St. Bonaventure

Year	Team	Lg	C	D	Games	W	L	T	Pct	APct	Fin	Seq	Pos
1975	BAL	N	A	E	14	10	4	0	.714	.714	1		HC
1976					14	11	3	0	.786	.786	1		HC
1977					14	10	4	0	.714	.714	1		HC
1978					16	5	11	0	.313	.313	4		HC
1979					16	5	11	0	.313	.313	5		HC
1992	IND	N	A	E	16	9	7	0	.563	.563	3		HC
1993					16	4	12	0	.250	.250	5		HC
1994					16	8	8	0	.500	.500	3		HC
1995					16	9	7	0	.563	.563	2		HC
1996	BAL	N	A	C	16	4	12	0	.250	.250	5		HC
10 yrs.					154	75	79	0		.487			
Playoffs													
1975					1	0	1						HC
1976					1	0	1						HC
1977					1	0	1						HC
1995					3	2	1						HC
4 yrs.					6	2	4			.333			

Billy Marshall

Marshall, William H.

Year	Team	Lg	C	D	Games	W	L	T	Pct	APct	Fin	Seq	Pos
1920	DET	A			4	1	3	0	.250	.250	8		HC
1921					7	1	5	1	.167	.214	16		HC
2 yrs.					11	2	8	1		.227			

Year	Team	Lg	C	D	Games	W	L	T	Pct	APct	Fin	Seq	Pos

Ned Mathews

Mathews, Ned A.
B. Aug. 11, 1918, Provo, UT
UCLA

Year	Team	Lg	C	D	Games	W	L	T	Pct	APct	Fin	Seq	Pos
1946	CHI	AA		W	5	2	2	1	.500	.500	3/3	2/3	CHC

John Mazur

Mazur, John
B. Jun. 17, 1930, Plymouth, PA
Notre Dame

Year	Team	Lg	C	D	Games	W	L	T	Pct	APct	Fin	Seq	Pos
1970	BOS	N	A	E	7	1	6	0	.143	.143	4/5	2/2	HC
1971	NE	N	A	E	14	6	8	0	.429	.429	3		HC
1972					9	2	7	0	.222	.222	3/5	1/2	HC
3 yrs.					30	9	21	0		.300			

Don McCafferty

McCafferty, Donald William
B. Mar. 12, 1921, Cleveland, OH
D. Jul. 28, 1974
Ohio State

Year	Team	Lg	C	D	Games	W	L	T	Pct	APct	Fin	Seq	Pos
1970	BAL	N	A	E	14	11	2	1	.846	.821	1		HC
1971					14	10	4	0	.714	.714	2		HC
1972					5	1	4	0	.200	.200	5/3	1/2	HC
1973	DET	N	N	C	14	6	7	1	.464	.464	2		HC
4 yrs.					47	28	17	2		.617			
Playoffs													
1970					3	3	0						HC
1971					2	1	1						HC
2 yrs.					5	4	1			.800			

Ernie McCann

McCann, Ernest H.
B. Aug. 5, 1902
D. Nov. 25, 1971, Acton, CA
Penn State

Year	Team	Lg	C	D	Games	W	L	T	Pct	APct	Fin	Seq	Pos
1926	HAR	N			1	0	1	0	.000	.000	15/13	1/2	HC

Mike McCormack

McCormack, Michael Joseph, Jr.
B. Jun. 21, 1930, Chicago, IL
Kansas

Year	Team	Lg	C	D	Games	W	L	T	Pct	APct	Fin	Seq	Pos
1973	PHI	N	N	E	14	5	8	1	.393	.393	3		HC
1974					14	7	7	0	.500	.500	4		HC
1975					14	4	10	0	.286	.286	5		HC
1980	BAL	N	A	E	16	7	9	0	.438	.438	4		HC
1981					16	2	14	0	.125	.125	4		HC
1982	SEA	N	A	—	7	4	3	0	.571	.571	13/10	2/2	HC
6 yrs.					81	29	51	1		.364			

Pete McCulley

McCulley, Peter
B. Nov. 29, 1931, Franklin County, MS
Louisiana Tech

Year	Team	Lg	C	D	Games	W	L	T	Pct	APct	Fin	Seq	Pos
1978	SF	N	N	W	9	1	8	0	.111	.111	4/4	1/2	HC

Cap McEwan

McEwan, John James
B. Feb. 18, 1893, Alexandria, MN
D. Aug. 9, 1970, New York, NY
Minnesota/Army

Year	Team	Lg	C	D	Games	W	L	T	Pct	APct	Fin	Seq	Pos
1933	BKN	N		E	10	5	4	1	.556	.550	2		HC
1934					11	4	7	0	.364	.364	3		HC
2 yrs.					21	9	11	1		.452			

Wally McIllwain

McIllwain, Wallace W.
B. Jan. 20, 1903
D. Jun., 1963
Illinois

Year	Team	Lg	C	D	Games	W	L	T	Pct	APct	Fin	Seq	Pos
1926	RAC	N			2	0	2	0	.000	.000	15/16	2/2	HC

John McKay

McKay, John Harvey
B. Jul. 5, 1923, Everettsville, WV
Purdue/Oregon

Year	Team	Lg	C	D	Games	W	L	T	Pct	APct	Fin	Seq	Pos
1976	TB	N	A	W	14	0	14	0	.000	.000	5		HC
1977			N	C	14	2	12	0	.143	.143	5		HC
1978					16	5	11	0	.313	.313	5		HC
1979					16	10	6	0	.625	.625	1		HC
1980					16	5	10	1	.344	.344	4		HC
1981					16	9	7	0	.563	.563	1		HC
1982					9	5	4	0	.556	.556	7		HC
1983					16	2	14	0	.125	.125	5		HC
1984					16	6	10	0	.375	.375	3		HC
9 yrs.					133	44	88	1		.335			
Playoffs													
1979					2	1	1						HC
1981					1	0	1						HC
1982					1	0	1						HC
3 yrs.					4	1	3			.250			

Ed McKeever

McKeever, Edward C.
B. Aug. 25, 1910, San Antonio, TX
D. Sep. 12, 1974, Baton Rouge, LA
Notre Dame/Texas Tech

Year	Team	Lg	C	D	Games	W	L	T	Pct	APct	Fin	Seq	Pos
1948	CHI	AA		W	14	1	13	0	.071	.071	4		HC

Ray McLean

McLean, Raymond (Scooter)
B. Dec. 6, 1915, Lowell, MA
D. Mar. 4, 1964, Ann Arbor, MI
St. Anselm's

Year	Team	Lg	C	D	Games	W	L	T	Pct	APct	Fin	Seq	Pos
1953	GB	N		W	2	0	2	0	.000	.000	6/6	2/2	CHC
1958					12	1	10	1	.091	.125	6		HC
2 yrs.					14	1	12	1		.107			

Bo McMillin

McMillin, Alvin Nugent
B. Jan. 12, 1895, Prairie Hill, TX
D. Mar. 31, 1952, Bloomington, IN
Centre

Year	Team	Lg	C	D	Games	W	L	T	Pct	APct	Fin	Seq	Pos
1948	DET	N		W	12	2	10	0	.167	.167	5		HC
1949					12	4	8	0	.333	.333	4		HC
1950					12	6	6	0	.500	.500	4		HC
1951	PHI	N	A		2	2	0	0	1.000	1.000	1/5	1/2	HC
4 yrs.					38	14	24	0		.368			

Eddie McNeely

McNeely, Eddie
None

Year	Team	Lg	C	D	Games	W	L	T	Pct	APct	Fin	Seq	Pos
1926	BKN	A			4	1	3	0	.250	.250	7		HC

Bill McPeak

McPeak, William Patrick
B. Jul. 24, 1926, New Castle, PA
D. May 7, 1991, Foxboro, MA
Pittsburgh

Year	Team	Lg	C	D	Games	W	L	T	Pct	APct	Fin	Seq	Pos
1961	WAS	N		E	14	1	12	1	.077	.107	7		HC
1962					14	5	7	2	.417	.428	4		HC
1963					14	3	11	0	.214	.214	6		HC
1964					14	6	8	0	.429	.429	3		HC
1965					14	6	8	0	.429	.429	4		HC
5 yrs.					70	21	46	3		.321			

John McVay

McVay, John E.
B. Jan. 5, 1931, Bellaire, OH
Miami (Ohio)

Year	Team	Lg	C	D	Games	W	L	T	Pct	APct	Fin	Seq	Pos
1976	NYG	N	N	E	7	3	4	0	.429	.429	5/5	2/2	HC
1977					14	5	9	0	.357	.357	4		HC
1978					16	6	10	0	.375	.375	4		HC
3 yrs.					37	14	23	0		.378			

Year	Team	Lg	C	D	Games	W	L	T	Pct	APct	Fin	Seq	Pos

Jack Meagher
Meagher, John J.
B. Oct. 1, 1896, Chicago, IL
D. Nov. 7, 1968, San Francisco, CA
Notre Dame

Year	Team	Lg	C	D	Games	W	L	T	Pct	APct	Fin	Seq	Pos
1946	MIA	AA		E	6	1	5	0	.167	.167	3/4	1/2	HC

Harry Mehre
Mehre, Harry James (Red)
B. Sep. 18, 1901, Lincoln, IN
D. Sep. 26, 1978, Atlanta, GA
Notre Dame

Year	Team	Lg	C	D	Games	W	L	T	Pct	APct	Fin	Seq	Pos
1923	MIN	N			9	2	5	2	.296	.333	13		HC

Ken Meyer
Meyer, Ken
B. Jul. 14, 1926, Erie, PA
Denison

Year	Team	Lg	C	D	Games	W	L	T	Pct	APct	Fin	Seq	Pos
1977	SF	N	N	W	14	5	9	0	.357	.357	3		HC

Ron Meyer
Meyer, Ronald Shaw
B. Feb. 17, 1941, Columbus, OH
Purdue

Year	Team	Lg	C	D	Games	W	L	T	Pct	APct	Fin	Seq	Pos
1982	NE	N	A	—	9	5	4	0	.556	.556	7		HC
1983				E	16	8	8	0	.500	.500	2		HC
1984					8	5	3	0	.625	.625	3/2	1/2	HC
1986	IND	N	A	E	3	3	0	0	1.000	1.000	5/5	2/2	HC
1987					15	9	6	0	.600	.600	1		HC
1988					16	9	7	0	.563	.563	2		HC
1989					16	8	8	0	.500	.500	2		HC
1990					16	7	9	0	.438	.438	3		HC
1991					5	0	5	0	.000	.000	5/5	1/2	HC
9 yrs.					104	54	50	0		.519			
Playoffs													
1982					1	0	1						HC
1987					1	0	1						HC
2 yrs.					2	0	2			.000			

Walt Michaels
Michaels, Walter
B. Oct. 16, 1929, Swoyersville, PA
Washington & Lee

Year	Team	Lg	C	D	Games	W	L	T	Pct	APct	Fin	Seq	Pos
1977	NYJ	N	A	E	14	3	11	0	.214	.214	4		HC
1978					16	8	8	0	.500	.500	3		HC
1979					16	8	8	0	.500	.500	3		HC
1980					16	4	12	0	.250	.250	5		HC
1981					16	10	5	1	.656	.656	2		HC
1982				—	9	6	3	0	.667	.667	6		HC
6 yrs.					87	39	47	1		.454			
Playoffs													
1981					1	0	1						HC
1982					3	2	1						HC
2 yrs.					4	2	2			.500			

Johnny Michelosen
Michelosen, John P.
B. Feb. 21, 1916, Ambridge, PA
D. Oct. 17, 1982, San Diego, CA
Pittsburgh

Year	Team	Lg	C	D	Games	W	L	T	Pct	APct	Fin	Seq	Pos
1948	PIT	N		E	12	4	8	0	.333	.333	3		HC
1949					12	6	5	1	.545	.542	2		HC
1950					12	6	6	0	.500	.500	3		HC
1951					12	4	7	1	.364	.375	4		HC
4 yrs.					48	20	26	2		.438			

Red Miller
Miller, Robert N.
B. Oct. 31, 1927, Macomb, IL
Western Illinois

Year	Team	Lg	C	D	Games	W	L	T	Pct	APct	Fin	Seq	Pos
1977	DEN	N	A	W	14	12	2	0	.857	.857	1		HC
1978					16	10	6	0	.625	.625	1		HC
1979					16	10	6	0	.625	.625	2		HC
1980					16	8	8	0	.500	.500	3		HC
4 yrs.					62	40	22	0		.645			

Red Miller *continued*

Year	Team	Lg	C	D	Games	W	L	T	Pct	APct	Fin	Seq	Pos
Playoffs													
1977					3	2	1						HC
1978					1	0	1						HC
1979					1	0	1						HC
3 yrs.					5	2	3			.400			

Wayne Millner
Millner, Wayne Vernal
B. Jan. 31, 1913, Roxbury, MA
D. Nov. 19, 1976, Falls Church, VA
Notre Dame

Year	Team	Lg	C	D	Games	W	L	T	Pct	APct	Fin	Seq	Pos
1951	PHI	N	A		10	2	8	0	.200	.200	1/5	2/2	HC

Dick Modzelewski
Modzelewski, Richard Blair (Little Mo)
B. Jan. 16, 1931, West Natrona, PA
Maryland

Year	Team	Lg	C	D	Games	W	L	T	Pct	APct	Fin	Seq	Pos
1977	CLE	N	A	C	1	0	1	0	.000	.000	4/4	2/2	HC

Bo Molenda
Molenda, John J.
B. Feb. 20, 1905, Oglesby, IL
D. Jul. 20, 1986, Banning, CA
Michigan

Year	Team	Lg	C	D	Games	W	L	T	Pct	APct	Fin	Seq	Pos
Playoffs													
1939	NY	N		E	1	0	1			.000			HC

Keith Molesworth
Molesworth, Keith Frank
B. Oct. 20, 1905, Washington, IA
D. Mar. 12, 1966
Monmouth (Illinois)

Year	Team	Lg	C	D	Games	W	L	T	Pct	APct	Fin	Seq	Pos
1953	BAL	N		W	12	3	9	0	.250	.250	5		HC

Jim Mora
Mora, James Ernest
B. May 24, 1935, Glendale, CA
Occidental

Year	Team	Lg	C	D	Games	W	L	T	Pct	APct	Fin	Seq	Pos
1986	NO	N	N	W	16	7	9	0	.438	.438	4		HC
1987					15	12	3	0	.800	.800	2		HC
1988					16	10	6	0	.625	.625	3		HC
1989					16	9	7	0	.563	.563	3		HC
1990					16	8	8	0	.500	.500	2		HC
1991					16	11	5	0	.688	.688	1		HC
1992					16	12	4	0	.750	.750	2		HC
1993					16	8	8	0	.500	.500	2		HC
1994					16	7	9	0	.438	.438	2		HC
1995					16	7	9	0	.438	.438	3		HC
1996					8	2	6	0	.250	.250	4/	1/2	HC
11 yrs.					167	93	74	0		.557			
Playoffs													
1987					1	0	1						HC
1990					1	0	1						HC
1991					1	0	1						HC
1992					1	0	1						HC
4 yrs.					4	0	4			.000			

Charley Moran
Moran, Charles Berthell (Uncle Charley)
B. Feb. 22, 1878, Nashville, TN
D. Jun. 14, 1949, Horse Cave, KY
Tennessee

Year	Team	Lg	C	D	Games	W	L	T	Pct	APct	Fin	Seq	Pos
1927	FRA	N			6	2	4	0	.333	.333	9/10	2/4	HC

Tom Moran
Moran, Thomas
B. 1898
Deceased
Centre

Year	Team	Lg	C	D	Games	W	L	T	Pct	APct	Fin	Seq	Pos
1927	FRA	N			2	0	1	1	.000	.250	9/10	1/4	HC

Year	Team	Lg	C	D	Games	W	L	T	Pct	APct	Fin	Seq	Pos

Brick Muller
Muller, Harold Powers
B. Jun. 12, 1901, Dunsmuir, CA
D. May 17, 1962, Berkeley, CA
California

Year	Team	Lg	C	D	Games	W	L	T	Pct	APct	Fin	Seq	Pos
1926	LA	N			10	6	3	1	.667	.650	6		CHC

Greasy Neale
Neale, Alfred Earle
B. Nov. 5, 1891, Parkersburg, WV
D. Nov. 2, 1973, Lake Worth, FL
West Virginia Wesleyan

Year	Team	Lg	C	D	Games	W	L	T	Pct	APct	Fin	Seq	Pos
1941	PHI	N	E		11	2	8	1	.200	.227	4		HC
1942					11	2	9	0	.182	.182	5		HC
1943	P-P	N	E		10	5	4	1	.556	.550	3		CHC
1944	PHI	N	E		10	7	1	2	.875	.800	2		HC
1945					10	7	3	0	.700	.700	2		HC
1946					11	6	5	0	.545	.545	2		HC
1947					12	8	4	0	.667	.667	1		HC
1948					12	9	2	1	.818	.792	1		HC
1949					12	11	1	0	.917	.917	1		HC
1950					12	6	6	0	.500	.500	3		HC
10 yrs.					111	63	43	5	.590				
Playoffs													
1947					2	1	1						HC
1948					1	1	0						HC
1949					1	1	0						HC
3 yrs.					4	3	1		.750				

Andy Nemecek
Nemecek, Andrew J.
B. May 6, 1896
D. May, 1984, Cleveland, OH
Ohio State

Year	Team	Lg	C	D	Games	W	L	T	Pct	APct	Fin	Seq	Pos
1924	COL	N			8	4	4	0	.500	.500	10		HC

Al Nesser
Nesser, Alfred (Nappy, Whitey)
B. Jun. 6, 1893, Columbus, OH
D. Mar. 11, 1967, Akron, OH
none

Year	Team	Lg	C	D	Games	W	L	T	Pct	APct	Fin	Seq	Pos
1926	AKR	N			2	0	1	1	.000	.250	15/16	1/2	HC

Ted Nesser
Nesser, Theodore, Jr.
B. Apr. 5, 1883
Deceased
none

Year	Team	Lg	C	D	Games	W	L	T	Pct	APct	Fin	Seq	Pos
1920	COL	A			5	0	5	0	.000	.000	11		HC
1921					9	1	8	0	.111	.111	17		HC
2 yrs.					14	1	13	0	.071				

Ernie Nevers
Nevers, Ernest Alonzo
B. Jun. 11, 1903, Willow River, MN
D. May 3, 1976, San Rafael, CA
Stanford

Year	Team	Lg	C	D	Games	W	L	T	Pct	APct	Fin	Seq	Pos
1926	DUL	N			14	6	5	3	.545	.536	8		HC
1927					9	1	8	0	.111	.111	11		HC
1930	CHIC	N			13	5	6	2	.455	.462	7		HC
1931					8	5	3	0	.625	.625	7/4	2/2	HC
1939			W		11	1	10	0	.091	.136	5		HC
5 yrs.					55	18	32	5	.373				

Frank Nied
Nied, Francis Theodore
B. Aug. 14, 1894, Akron, OH
none

Year	Team	Lg	C	D	Games	W	L	T	Pct	APct	Fin	Seq	Pos
1926	AKR	N			6	1	3	2	.250	.333	15/16	2/2	HC

Mike Nixon
Nicksick, Michael Regis
B. Nov. 12, 1911, Masontown, PA
Pittsburgh

Year	Team	Lg	C	D	Games	W	L	T	Pct	APct	Fin	Seq	Pos
1959	WAS	N	E		12	3	9	0	.250	.250	5		HC

Mike Nixon *continued*

Year	Team	Lg	C	D	Games	W	L	T	Pct	APct	Fin	Seq	Pos
1960					12	1	9	2	.100	.167	6		HC
1965	PIT	N	E		14	2	12	0	.143	.143	7		HC
3 yrs.					38	6	30	2	.184				

Dick Nolan
Nolan, Richard Charles
B. Mar. 26, 1932, Pittsburgh, PA
Maryland

Year	Team	Lg	C	D	Games	W	L	T	Pct	APct	Fin	Seq	Pos
1968	SF	N	W	CO	14	7	6	1	.538	.536	3		HC
1969					14	4	8	2	.333	.357	4		HC
1970		N	W		14	10	3	1	.789	.750	1		HC
1971					14	9	5	0	.643	.643	1		HC
1972					14	8	5	1	.607	.607	1		HC
1973					14	5	9	0	.357	.357	3		HC
1974					14	6	8	0	.429	.429	2		HC
1975					14	5	9	0	.357	.357	2		HC
1978	NO	N	N	W	16	7	9	0	.438	.438	3		HC
1979					16	8	8	0	.500	.500	2		HC
1980					12	0	12	0	.000	.000	4/4	1/2	HC
11 yrs.					156	69	82	5	.458				
Playoffs													
1970					2	1	1						HC
1971					2	1	1						HC
1972					1	0	1						HC
3 yrs.					5	2	3		.400				

Chuck Noll
Noll, Charles Henry
B. Jan. 5, 1932, Cleveland, OH
Dayton

Year	Team	Lg	C	D	Games	W	L	T	Pct	APct	Fin	Seq	Pos
1969	PIT	N	E	CE	14	1	13	0	.071	.071	4		HC
1970		A	C		14	5	9	0	.357	.357	3		HC
1971					14	6	8	0	.429	.429	2		HC
1972					14	11	3	0	.786	.786	1		HC
1973					14	10	4	0	.714	.714	2		HC
1974					14	10	3	1	.750	.750	1		HC
1975					14	12	2	0	.857	.857	1		HC
1976					14	10	4	0	.714	.714	1		HC
1977					14	9	5	0	.643	.643	1		HC
1978					16	14	2	0	.875	.875	1		HC
1979					16	12	4	0	.750	.750	1		HC
1980					16	9	7	0	.563	.563	3		HC
1981					16	8	8	0	.500	.500	2		HC
1982		—			9	6	3	0	.667	.667	4		HC
1983			C		16	10	6	0	.625	.625	1		HC
1984					16	9	7	0	.563	.563	1		HC
1985					16	7	9	0	.438	.438	2		HC
1986					16	6	10	0	.375	.375	3		HC
1987					15	8	7	0	.533	.533	3		HC
1988					16	5	11	0	.313	.313	4		HC
1989					16	9	7	0	.563	.563	2		HC
1990					16	9	7	0	.563	.563	3		HC
1991					16	7	9	0	.438	.438	2		HC
23 yrs.					342	193	148	1	.566				
Playoffs													
1972					2	1	1						HC
1973					1	0	1						HC
1974					3	3	0						HC
1975					3	3	0						HC
1976					2	1	1						HC
1977					1	0	1						HC
1978					3	3	0						HC
1979					3	3	0						HC
1982					1	0	1						HC
1983					1	0	1						HC
1984					2	1	1						HC
1989					2	1	1						HC
12 yrs.					24	16	8		.667				

Jerry Noonan
Noonan, Gerald
B. Oct. 13, 1898
D. Nov., 1967, San Francisco, CA
Fordham

Year	Team	Lg	C	D	Games	W	L	T	Pct	APct	Fin	Seq	Pos
1924	ROC	N			7	0	7	0	.000	.000	16		HC

John North

North, John Puckett
B. Jun. 17, 1921, Old Hickory, TN
Vanderbilt

Year	Team	Lg	C	D	Games	W	L	T	Pct	APct	Fin	Seq	Pos
1973	NO	N	N	W	14	5	9	0	.357	.357	3		HC
1974					14	5	9	0	.357	.357	3		HC
1975					6	1	5	0	.167	.167	4/4	1/2	HC
3 yrs.					34	11	23	0		.324			

Fred O'Connor

O'Connor, Fred
B. Sep. 1, 1939, Brooklyn, NY
East Stroudsburg State

Year	Team	Lg	C	D	Games	W	L	T	Pct	APct	Fin	Seq	Pos
1978	SF	N	N	W	7	1	6	0	.143	.143	4/4	2/2	HC

Steve Owen

Owen, Stephen Joseph
B. Apr. 21, 1898, Cleo Springs, OK
D. May 17, 1964, New York, NY
Phillips

Year	Team	Lg	C	D	Games	W	L	T	Pct	APct	Fin	Seq	Pos
1931	NYG	N			14	7	6	1	.538	.536	5		HC
1932					12	4	6	2	.400	.417	5		HC
1933				E	14	11	3	0	.786	.786	1		HC
1934					13	8	5	0	.615	.615	1		HC
1935					12	9	3	0	.750	.750	1		HC
1936					12	5	6	1	.455	.458	3		HC
1937					11	6	3	2	.667	.636	2		HC
1938					11	8	2	1	.800	.773	1		HC
1939					11	9	1	1	.900	.864	1	1/2	HC
1940					11	6	4	1	.600	.591	3		HC
1941					11	8	3	0	.727	.727	1		HC
1942					11	5	5	1	.500	.500	3		HC
1943					10	6	3	1	.667	.650	1		HC
1944					10	8	1	1	.889	.850	1		HC
1945					10	3	6	1	.333	.350	3		HC
1946					11	7	3	1	.700	.682	1		HC
1947					12	2	8	2	.200	.250	5		HC
1948					12	4	8	0	.333	.333	3		HC
1949					12	6	6	0	.500	.500	3		HC
1950					12	10	2	0	.833	.833	1		HC
1951					12	9	2	1	.818	.792	2		HC
1952		A			12	7	5	0	.583	.583	2		HC
1953					12	3	9	0	.250	.250	5		HC
23 yrs.					268	151	100	17		.595			
Playoffs													
1933					1	0	1						HC
1934					1	1	0						HC
1935					1	0	1						HC
1938					1	1	0						HC
1941					1	0	1						HC
1943					1	0	1						HC
1944					1	0	1						HC
1946					1	0	1						HC
1950					1	0	1						HC
9 yrs.					9	2	7			.222			

Mike Palm

Palm, Myron
B. Nov. 24, 1899
D. Apr. 8, 1974, Washington, DC
Penn State

Year	Team	Lg	C	D	Games	W	L	T	Pct	APct	Fin	Seq	Pos
1933	CIN	N		W	7	3	3	1	.500	.500	5/4	2/2	HC

Bill Parcells

Parcells, Duane Charles (Tuna)
B. Aug. 22, 1941, Engelwood, NJ
Wichita State

Year	Team	Lg	C	D	Games	W	L	T	Pct	APct	Fin	Seq	Pos
1983	NYG	N	N	E	16	3	12	1	.219	.219	5		HC
1984					16	9	7	0	.563	.563	2		HC
1985					16	10	6	0	.625	.625	2		HC
1986					16	14	2	0	.875	.875	1		HC
1987					15	6	9	0	.400	.400	5		HC
1988					16	10	6	0	.625	.625	2		HC
1989					16	12	4	0	.750	.750	1		HC
1990					16	13	3	0	.813	.813	1		HC
1993	NE	N	N	A	E	16	5	11	0	.313	.313	4		HC
1994					16	10	6	0	.625	.625	2		HC

Bill Parcells continued

Year	Team	Lg	C	D	Games	W	L	T	Pct	APct	Fin	Seq	Pos
1995					16	6	10	0	.375	.375	4		HC
1996					16	11	5	0	.688	.688	1		HC
12 yrs.					191	109	81	1		.573			
Playoffs													
1984					2	1	1						HC
1985					2	1	1						HC
1986					3	3	0						HC
1989					1	0	1						HC
1990					3	3	0						HC
1994					1	0	1						HC
1996					3	2	1						HC
7 yrs.					15	10	5			.667			

Jack Pardee

Pardee, John Perry
B. Apr. 19, 1936, Exira, IA
Texas A&M

Year	Team	Lg	C	D	Games	W	L	T	Pct	APct	Fin	Seq	Pos
1975	CHI	N	N	C	14	4	10	0	.286	.286	3		HC
1976					14	7	7	0	.500	.500	2		HC
1977					14	9	5	0	.643	.643	2		HC
1978	WAS	N	N	E	16	8	8	0	.500	.500	3		HC
1979					16	10	6	0	.625	.625	3		HC
1980					16	6	10	0	.375	.375	3		HC
1990	HOU	N	A	C	16	9	7	0	.563	.563	2		HC
1991					16	11	5	0	.688	.688	1		HC
1992					16	10	6	0	.625	.625	2		HC
1993					16	12	4	0	.750	.750	1		HC
1994					10	1	9	0	.125	.125	4/4	1/2	HC
11 yrs.					164	87	77	0		.530			
Playoffs													
1977					1	0	1						HC
1990					1	0	1						HC
1991					2	1	1						HC
1992					1	0	1						HC
1993					1	0	1						HC
5 yrs.					6	1	5			.167			

Buddy Parker

Parker, Raymond Klein
B. Dec. 16, 1913, Slaton, TX
D. Mar. 22, 1982, Kaufman, TX
North Texas/Centenary

Year	Team	Lg	C	D	Games	W	L	T	Pct	APct	Fin	Seq	Pos
1949	CHIC	N		W	6	2	4	0	.333	.333	3/3	1/2	CHC
1949					6	4	1	1	.800	.750	3/3	2/2	HC
1951	DET	N	N		12	7	4	1	.636	.625	2		HC
1952					12	9	3	0	.750	.750	1		HC
1953					12	10	2	0	.833	.833	1		HC
1954					12	9	2	1	.818	.792	1		HC
1955					12	3	9	0	.250	.250	6		HC
1956					12	9	3	0	.750	.750	2		HC
1957	PIT	N	E		12	6	6	0	.500	.500	3		HC
1958					12	7	4	1	.636	.625	3		HC
1959					12	6	5	1	.545	.542	4		HC
1960					12	5	6	1	.455	.458	5		HC
1961					14	6	8	0	.429	.429	5		HC
1962					14	9	5	0	.643	.643	2		HC
1963					14	7	4	3	.636	.607	4		HC
1964					14	5	9	0	.357	.357	6		HC
15 yrs.					188	104	75	9		.577			
Playoffs													
1952					2	2	0						HC
1953					1	1	0						HC
1954					1	0	1						HC
3 yrs.					4	3	1			.750			

Jack Patera

Patera, John Arlen
B. Aug. 1, 1933, Bismarck, ND
Oregon

Year	Team	Lg	C	D	Games	W	L	T	Pct	APct	Fin	Seq	Pos
1976	SEA	N	N	W	14	2	12	0	.143	.143	5		HC
1977			A	W	14	5	9	0	.357	.357	4		HC
1978					16	9	7	0	.563	.563	2		HC
1979					16	9	7	0	.563	.563	3		HC
1980					16	4	12	0	.250	.250	5		HC
1981					16	6	10	0	.375	.375	5		HC
1982			—		2	0	2	0	.000	.000	13/10	1/2	HC
7 yrs.					94	35	59	0		.372			

Pat Peppler
Peppler, Albert
Michigan State

Year	Team	Lg	C	D	Games	W	L	T	Pct	APct	Fin	Seq	Pos
1976	ATL	N	N	W	9	3	6	0	.333	.333	4/3	2/2	HC

Ray Perkins
Perkins, Walter Ray
B. Dec. 6, 1941, Mount Olive, MS
Alabama

Year	Team	Lg	C	D	Games	W	L	T	Pct	APct	Fin	Seq	Pos
1979	NYG	N	N	E	16	6	10	0	.375	.375	4		HC
1980					16	4	12	0	.250	.250	5		HC
1981					16	9	7	0	.563	.563	3		HC
1982					9	4	5	0	.444	.444	10		HC
1987	TB	N	N	C	15	4	11	0	.267	.267	4		HC
1988					16	5	11	0	.313	.313	3		HC
1989					16	5	11	0	.313	.313	5		HC
1990					13	5	8	0	.385	.385	4/2	1/2	HC
8 yrs.					117	42	75	0		.359			
Playoffs													
1981					2	1	1						HC

Bill Peterson
Peterson, William E.
B. May 14, 1923, Toronto, OH
Ohio Northern

Year	Team	Lg	C	D	Games	W	L	T	Pct	APct	Fin	Seq	Pos
1972	HOU	N	A	C	14	1	13	0	.071	.071	4		HC
1973					5	0	5	0	.000	.000	4/4	1/2	HC
2 yrs.					19	1	18	0		.053			

Richie Petitbon
Petitbon, Richard Alvin
B. Apr. 18, 1938, New Orleans, LA
Tulane

Year	Team	Lg	C	D	Games	W	L	T	Pct	APct	Fin	Seq	Pos
1993	WAS	N	N	E	16	4	12	0	.250	.250	5		HC

Jimmy Phelan
Phelan, James Michael
B. Dec. 5, 1893
D. Nov. 14, 1974, Honolulu, HI
Notre Dame

Year	Team	Lg	C	D	Games	W	L	T	Pct	APct	Fin	Seq	Pos
1948	LA	AA		W	14	7	7	0	.500	.500	3		HC
1949					12	4	8	0	.333	.333	5		HC
1951	NYY	N	N		12	1	9	2	.100	.167	6		HC
1952	DAL	N	N		12	1	11	0	.083	.083	6		HC
4 yrs.					50	13	35	2		.280			

Bum Phillips
Phillips, Oail Andrews
B. Sep. 29, 1923, Orange, TX
Stephen F. Austin

Year	Team	Lg	C	D	Games	W	L	T	Pct	APct	Fin	Seq	Pos
1975	HOU	N	A	C	14	10	4	0	.714	.714	3		HC
1976					14	5	9	0	.357	.357	4		HC
1977					14	8	6	0	.571	.571	2		HC
1978					16	10	6	0	.625	.625	2		HC
1979					16	11	5	0	.688	.688	2		HC
1980					16	11	5	0	.688	.688	2		HC
1981	NO	N	N	W	16	4	12	0	.250	.250	4		HC
1982				—	9	4	5	0	.444	.444	9		HC
1983				W	16	8	8	0	.500	.500	3		HC
1984					16	7	9	0	.438	.438	3		HC
1985					12	4	8	0	.333	.333	3/3	1/2	HC
11 yrs.					159	82	77	0		.516			
Playoffs													
1978					3	2	1						HC
1979					3	2	1						HC
1980					1	0	1						HC
3 yrs.					7	4	3			.571			

Wade Phillips
Phillips, Wade
B. Jun. 21, 1947, Orange, TX
Houston

Year	Team	Lg	C	D	Games	W	L	T	Pct	APct	Fin	Seq	Pos
1985	NO	N	N	W	4	1	3	0	.250	.250	3/3	2/2	HC
1993	DEN	N	A	W	16	9	7	0	.563	.563	3		HC
1994					16	7	9	0	.438	.438	4		HC
3 yrs.					36	17	19	0		.472			

Wade Phillips *continued*
Playoffs

Year	Team	Lg	C	D	Games	W	L	T	Pct	APct	Fin	Seq	Pos
1993					1	0	1		.000				HC

Al Pierotti
Pierotti, Albert Felix
B. Oct. 24, 1895, Boston, MA
D. Feb. 12, 1964, Everett, MA
Washington & Lee

Year	Team	Lg	C	D	Games	W	L	T	Pct	APct	Fin	Seq	Pos
1920	CLE	A			4	1	2	1	.333	.375	10/9	2/2	HC

Elijah Pitts
Pitts, Elijah Eugene
B. Feb. 3, 1938, Mayflower, AR
Philander Smith

Year	Team	Lg	C	D	Games	W	L	T	Pct	APct	Fin	Seq	Pos
1995	BUF	N	A	E	3	1	2	0	.333	.333	1/1	2/3	HC

Fritz Pollard
Pollard, Frederick Douglass
B. Jan. 27, 1894, Chicago, IL
D. May 11, 1986, Silver Spring, MD
Bates/Brown

Year	Team	Lg	C	D	Games	W	L	T	Pct	APct	Fin	Seq	Pos
1925	HAM	N			4	1	3	0	.250	.250	12/14	1/2	HC

Hamp Pool
Pool, J. Hampton
B. Mar. 11, 1915, San Miguel, CA
California/Stanford

Year	Team	Lg	C	D	Games	W	L	T	Pct	APct	Fin	Seq	Pos
1946	MIA	AA		E	8	2	6	0	.250	.250	3/4	2/2	HC
1947	CHI	AA		W	1	0	1	0	.000	.000	4/4	2/2	HC
1952	LA	N	N		11	9	2	0	.818	.818	3/1	2/2	HC
1953					12	8	3	1	.727	.708	3		HC
1954					12	6	5	1	.545	.542	4		HC
5 yrs.					44	25	17	2		.591			
Playoffs													
1952					1	0	1		.000				HC

Earl Potteiger
Potteiger, William Earl
B. Jan. 11, 1891
D. Aug., 1962
Ursinus

Year	Team	Lg	C	D	Games	W	L	T	Pct	APct	Fin	Seq	Pos
1927	NYG	N			13	11	1	1	.917	.885	1		HC
1928	HC	6			13	4	7	2	.364	.385	6		HC
2 yrs.					26	15	8	3		.635			

Ray Prochaska
Prochaska, Raymond
B. Aug. 9, 1919, Ulysses, NE
Nebraska

Year	Team	Lg	C	D	Games	W	L	T	Pct	APct	Fin	Seq	Pos
1961	STL	N		E	2	2	0	0	1.000	1.000	4/4	2/2	CHC

Tommy Prothro
Prothro, James Thompson
B. Jul. 20, 1920, Memphis, TN
D. May 14, 1995, Memphis, TN
Duke

Year	Team	Lg	C	D	Games	W	L	T	Pct	APct	Fin	Seq	Pos
1971	LA	N	N	W	14	8	5	1	.615	.607	2		HC
1972					14	6	7	1	.464	.464	3		HC
1974	SD	N	A	W	14	5	9	0	.357	.357	4		HC
1975					14	2	12	0	.143	.143	4		HC
1976					14	6	8	0	.429	.429	3		HC
1977					14	7	7	0	.500	.500	3		HC
1978					4	1	3	0	.250	.250	4/2	1/2	HC
7 yrs.					88	35	51	2		.409			

Mike Purdy
Purdy, Clair J., Jr.
B. 1895, Auburn, NY
D. Jan. 10, 1950, Auburn, NY
Brown

Year	Team	Lg	C	D	Games	W	L	T	Pct	APct	Fin	Seq	Pos
1921	SYR	A			3	0	2	1	.000	.167	18		HC

Year	Team	Lg	C	D	Games	W	L	T	Pct	APct	Fin	Seq	Pos

John Ralston
Ralston, John R.
B. Apr. 26, 1927, Oakland, CA
California

Year	Team	Lg	C	D	Games	W	L	T	Pct	APct	Fin	Seq	Pos
1972	DEN	N	A	W	14	5	9	0	.357	.357	3		HC
1973					14	7	5	2	.571	.571	2		HC
1974					14	7	6	1	.536	.536	2		HC
1975					14	6	8	0	.429	.429	2		HC
1976					14	9	5	0	.643	.643	2		HC
5 yrs.					70	34	33	3		.507			

Garrard Ramsey
Ramsey, Garrard S. (Buster)
B. Mar. 16, 1920, Townsend, TN
William & Mary

Year	Team	Lg	C	D	Games	W	L	T	Pct	APct	Fin	Seq	Pos
1960	BUF	A		E	14	5	8	1	.385	.393	3		HC
1961					14	6	8	0	.429	.429	4		HC
2 yrs.					28	11	16	1		.411			

Art Ranney
Ranney, Arthur
B. 1889
Deceased
Akron

Year	Team	Lg	C	D	Games	W	L	T	Pct	APct	Fin	Seq	Pos
1922	AKR	N			4	0	3	1	.000	.125	6/10	2/2	HC

Dick Rauch
Rauch, Richard
B. Jul. 15, 1893
D. Oct., 1970, Harrisburg, PA
Penn State

Year	Team	Lg	C	D	Games	W	L	T	Pct	APct	Fin	Seq	Pos
1925	POT	N			12	10	2	0	.833	.833	2		HC
1926					14	10	2	2	.833	.786	3		HC
1927					13	5	8	0	.385	.385	8		HC
1928	NYY	N			13	4	8	1	.333	.346	7		HC
1929	BOS	N			8	4	4	0	.500	.500	5		HC
5 yrs.					60	33	24	3		.575			

John Rauch
Rauch, John
B. Aug. 20, 1927, Philadelphia, PA
Georgia

Year	Team	Lg	C	D	Games	W	L	T	Pct	APct	Fin	Seq	Pos
1966	OAK	A		W	14	8	5	1	.615	.607	2		HC
1967					14	13	1	0	.929	.929	1		HC
1968					14	12	2	0	.857	.857	1		HC
1969	BUF	A		E	14	4	10	0	.286	.286	3		HC
1970	BUF	N	A	E	14	3	10	1	.231	.250	4		HC
5 yrs.					70	40	28	2		.586			
Playoffs													
1967					2	1	1			.500			HC
1968					2	1	1			.500			HC
2 yrs.					4	2	2			.500			

Dan Reeves
Reeves, Daniel Edward
B. Jan. 19, 1944, Rome, GA
South Carolina

Year	Team	Lg	C	D	Games	W	L	T	Pct	APct	Fin	Seq	Pos
1981	DEN	N	A	W	16	10	6	0	.625	.625	2		HC
1982		—			9	2	7	0	.222	.222	12		HC
1983				W	16	9	7	0	.563	.563	2		HC
1984					16	13	3	0	.813	.813	1		HC
1985					16	11	5	0	.688	.688	2		HC
1986					16	11	5	0	.688	.688	1		HC
1987					15	10	4	1	.700	.700	1		HC
1988					16	8	8	0	.500	.500	2		HC
1989					16	11	5	0	.688	.688	1		HC
1990					16	5	11	0	.313	.313	5		HC
1991					16	12	4	0	.750	.750	1		HC
1992					16	8	8	0	.500	.500	3		HC
1993	NYG	N	N	E	16	11	5	0	.688	.688	2		HC
1994					16	9	7	0	.563	.563	2		HC
1995					16	5	11	0	.313	.313	4		HC
1996					16	6	10	0	.375	.375	5		HC
16 yrs.					248	141	106	1		.571			

Dan Reeves *continued*

Year	Team	Lg	C	D	Games	W	L	T	Pct	APct	Fin	Seq	Pos
Playoffs													
1983					1	0	1						HC
1984					1	0	1						HC
1986					3	2	1						HC
1987					3	2	1						HC
1989					3	2	1						HC
1991					2	1	1						HC
1993					2	1	1						HC
7 yrs.					15	8	7			.533			

Ray Rhodes
Rhodes, Raymond Earl
B. Oct. 20, 1950, Mexia, TX
Texas Christian/Tulsa

Year	Team	Lg	C	D	Games	W	L	T	Pct	APct	Fin	Seq	Pos
1995	PHI	N	N	E	16	10	6	0	.625	.625	2		HC
1996					16	10	6	0	.625	.625	2		HC
2 yrs.					32	20	12	0		.625			
Playoffs													
1995					2	1	1						HC
1996					1	0	1						HC
2 yrs.					3	1	2			.333			

Homer Rice
Rice, Homer C.
B. Feb. 20, 1927, Bellevue, KY
Centre

Year	Team	Lg	C	D	Games	W	L	T	Pct	APct	Fin	Seq	Pos
1978	CIN	N	A	C	11	4	7	0	.364	.364	4/4	2/2	HC
1979					16	4	12	0	.250	.250	4		HC
2 yrs.					27	8	19	0		.296			

Ray Richards
Richards, Raymond W.
B. Jul. 16, 1906, Liberty, NE
D. Sep. 18, 1974, La Habra, CA
Nebraska

Year	Team	Lg	C	D	Games	W	L	T	Pct	APct	Fin	Seq	Pos
1955	CHIC	N		E	12	4	7	1	.364	.375	4		HC
1956					12	7	5	0	.583	.583	2		HC
1957					12	3	9	0	.250	.250	6		HC
3 yrs.					36	14	21	1		.403			

Jim Ringo
Ringo, James Stephen
B. Nov. 21, 1932, Orange, NJ
Syracuse

Year	Team	Lg	C	D	Games	W	L	T	Pct	APct	Fin	Seq	Pos
1976	BUF	N	A	E	9	0	9	0	.000	.000	3/5	2/2	HC
1977					14	3	11	0	.214	.214	5		HC
2 yrs.					23	3	20	0		.130			

Harry Robb
Robb, Harry D.
B. May 11, 1897
D. Dec., 1971, Greenville, PA
Penn State/Columbia

Year	Team	Lg	C	D	Games	W	L	T	Pct	APct	Fin	Seq	Pos
1925	CAN	N			8	4	4	0	.500	.500	11		HC

J.D. Roberts
Roberts, John David
B. Oct. 24, 1932, Oklahoma City, OK
Oklahoma

Year	Team	Lg	C	D	Games	W	L	T	Pct	APct	Fin	Seq	Pos
1970	NO	N	N	W	7	1	6	0	.143	.143	4/4	2/2	HC
1971					14	4	8	2	.333	.357	4		HC
1972					14	2	11	1	.179	.179	4		HC
3 yrs.					35	7	25	3		.243			

Ed Robinson
Robinson, Edward N.
B. Oct. 15, 1903, Lynn, MA
D. Mar. 10, 1945
Brown

Year	Team	Lg	C	D	Games	W	L	T	Pct	APct	Fin	Seq	Pos
1931	PRO	N			11	4	4	3	.500	.500	6		HC

John Robinson

Robinson, John Alexander
B. Jul. 25, 1935, Chicago, IL
Oregon

Year	Team	Lg	C	D	Games	W	L	T	Pct	APct	Fin	Seq	Pos
1983	LARM	N	N	W	16	9	7	0	.563	.563	2		HC
1984					16	10	6	0	.625	.625	2		HC
1985					16	11	5	0	.688	.688	1		HC
1986					16	10	6	0	.625	.625	2		HC
1987					15	6	9	0	.400	.400	3		HC
1988					16	10	6	0	.625	.625	2		HC
1989					16	11	5	0	.688	.688	2		HC
1990					16	5	11	0	.313	.313	3		HC
1991					16	3	13	0	.188	.188	4		HC
9 yrs.					143	75	68	0		.524			
Playoffs													
1983					2	1	1						HC
1984					1	0	1						HC
1985					2	1	1						HC
1986					1	0	1						HC
1988					1	0	1						HC
1989					3	2	1						HC
6 yrs.					10	4	6			.400			

Charley Rogers

Rogers, Charles S.
B. 1904
D. Jun. 26, 1986
Pennsylvania

Year	Team	Lg	C	D	Games	W	L	T	Pct	APct	Fin	Seq	Pos
1927	FRA	N			1	0	0	1	.000	.500	8/5	4/4	CHC

Darryl Rogers

Rogers, Darryl D.
B. May 28, 1935, Los Angeles, CA
Fresno State

Year	Team	Lg	C	D	Games	W	L	T	Pct	APct	Fin	Seq	Pos
1985	DET	N	N	C	16	7	9	0	.438	.438	3		HC
1986					16	5	11	0	.313	.313	3		HC
1987					15	4	11	0	.267	.267	4		HC
1988					11	2	9	0	.250	.250	4/4	1/2	HC
4 yrs.					58	18	40	0		.310			

Milt Romney

Romney, Milton Addas
B. Jun. 20, 1899, Salt Lake City, UT
D. Nov. 10, 1975, North Little Rock, AR
Utah/Chicago

Year	Team	Lg	C	D	Games	W	L	T	Pct	APct	Fin	Seq	Pos
1924	RAC	N			10	4	3	3	.571	.550	7		HC

Gene Ronzani

Ronzani, Eugene
B. Mar. 28, 1909, Iron Mountain, MI
D. Sep. 12, 1975, Lac du Flambeau, WI
Marquette

Year	Team	Lg	C	D	Games	W	L	T	Pct	APct	Fin	Seq	Pos
1950	GB	N	N		12	3	9	0	.250	.250	5		HC
1951					12	3	9	0	.250	.250	5		HC
1952					12	6	6	0	.500	.500	4		HC
1953					10	2	7	1	.222	.250	6/6	1/2	HC
4 yrs.					46	14	31	1		.315			

Tam Rose

Rose, Walter S.
B. Jun. 20, 1889
D. Dec., 1965
Syracuse

Year	Team	Lg	C	D	Games	W	L	T	Pct	APct	Fin	Seq	Pos
1921	TON	A			2	0	1	1	.000	.250	18		HC

Bobby Ross

Ross, Robert Joseph
B. Dec. 23, 1936, Richmond, VA
Virginia Military Institute

Year	Team	Lg	C	D	Games	W	L	T	Pct	APct	Fin	Seq	Pos
1992	SD	N	A	W	16	11	5	0	.688	.688	1		HC
1993					16	8	8	0	.500	.500	4		HC
1994					16	11	5	0	.688	.688	1		HC
1995					16	9	7	0	.563	.563	2		HC
1996					16	8	8	0	.500	.500	3		HC
5 yrs.					80	47	33	0		.588			

Bobby Ross *continued*

Year	Team	Lg	C	D	Games	W	L	T	Pct	APct	Fin	Seq	Pos
Playoffs													
1992					2	1	1						HC
1994					3	2	1						HC
1995					1	0	1						HC
3 yrs.					6	3	3			.500			

Clive Rush

Rush, Clive H.
B. Feb. 14, 1931, De Graff, OH
D. Aug. 22, 1980, London, OH
Miami (Ohio)

Year	Team	Lg	C	D	Games	W	L	T	Pct	APct	Fin	Seq	Pos
1969	BOS	A		E	14	4	10	0	.286	.286	3		HC
1970	BOS	N	A	E	7	1	6	0	.143	.143	4/5	1/2	HC
2 yrs.					21	5	16	0		.238			

Rod Rust

Rust, Rodney A.
B. Aug. 2, 1928, Webster City, IA
Iowa State

Year	Team	Lg	C	D	Games	W	L	T	Pct	APct	Fin	Seq	Pos
1990	NE	N	A	E	16	1	15	0	.063	.063	5		HC

Sam Rutigliano

Rutigliano, Sam
B. Jul. 1, 1932, Brooklyn, NY
Tulsa

Year	Team	Lg	C	D	Games	W	L	T	Pct	APct	Fin	Seq	Pos
1978	CLE	N	A	C	16	8	8	0	.500	.500	3		HC
1979					16	9	7	0	.563	.563	3		HC
1980					16	11	5	0	.688	.688	1		HC
1981					16	5	11	0	.313	.313	4		HC
1982			—		9	4	5	0	.444	.444	8		HC
1983			C		16	9	7	0	.563	.563	2		HC
1984					8	1	7	0	.125	.125	3/3	1/2	HC
7 yrs.					97	47	50	0		.485			
Playoffs													
1980					1	0	1						HC
1982					1	0	1						HC
2 yrs.					2	0	2			.000			

Buddy Ryan

Ryan, James David
B. Feb. 17, 1934, Frederick, OK
Oklahoma State

Year	Team	Lg	C	D	Games	W	L	T	Pct	APct	Fin	Seq	Pos
1986	PHI	N	N	E	16	5	10	1	.344	.344	4		HC
1987					15	7	8	0	.467	.467	2		HC
1988					16	10	6	0	.625	.625	1		HC
1989					16	11	5	0	.688	.688	2		HC
1990					16	10	6	0	.625	.625	2		HC
1994	ARI	N	N	E	16	8	8	0	.500	.500	3		HC
1995					16	4	12	0	.250	.250	5		HC
7 yrs.					111	55	55	1		.500			
Playoffs													
1988					1	0	1						HC
1989					1	0	1						HC
1990					1	0	1						HC
3 yrs.					3	0	3			.000			

Lou Rymkus

Rymkus, Louis J.
B. Nov. 6, 1919, Royalton, IL
Notre Dame

Year	Team	Lg	C	D	Games	W	L	T	Pct	APct	Fin	Seq	Pos
1960	HOU	A		E	14	10	4	0	.714	.714	1		HC
1961					5	1	3	1	.250	.300	4/1	1/2	HC
2 yrs.					19	11	7	1		.605			
Playoffs													
1960					1	1	0			1.000			HC

Lou Saban

Saban, Louis H.
B. Oct. 13, 1921, Brookfield, IL
Indiana

Year	Team	Lg	C	D	Games	W	L	T	Pct	APct	Fin	Seq	Pos
1960	BOS	A		E	14	5	9	0	.357	.357	4		HC
1961					5	2	3	0	.400	.400	2/2	1/2	HC
1962	BUF	A		E	14	7	6	1	.538	.536	3		HC
1963					14	7	6	1	.538	.536	1		HC
1964					14	12	2	0	.857	.857	1		HC

Year Team	Lg	C	D	Games	W	L	T	Pct	APct	Fin	Seq	Pos

Lou Saban *continued*

Year Team	Lg	C	D	Games	W	L	T	Pct	APct	Fin	Seq	Pos
1965				14	10	3	1	.769	.750	1		HC
1967 DEN	A		W	14	3	11	0	.214	.214	4		HC
1968				14	5	9	0	.357	.357	4		HC
1969				14	5	8	1	.385	.393	4		HC
1970 DEN	N	A	W	14	5	8	1	.385	.393	4		HC
1971				9	2	6	1	.250	.250	4/4	1/2	HC
1972 BUF	N	A	E	14	4	9	1	.321	.321	4		HC
1973				14	9	5	0	.643	.643	2		HC
1974				14	9	5	0	.643	.643	2		HC
1975				14	8	6	0	.571	.571	3		HC
1976				5	2	3	0	.400	.400	3/5	1/2	HC
16 yrs.				201	95	99	7		.490			
Playoffs												
1963				1	0	1						HC
1964				1	1	0						HC
1965				1	1	0						HC
1974				1	0	1						HC
4 yrs.				4	2	2			.500			

Lenny Sachs
Sachs, Leonard David
B. Aug. 7, 1897, Chicago, IL
D. Oct. 27, 1942, Chicago, IL
Loyola (Illinois)/DePaul

Year Team	Lg	C	D	Games	W	L	T	Pct	APct	Fin	Seq	Pos
1926 LOU	N			4	0	4	0	.000	.000	21		HC

Andy Salata
Salata, Andrew J.
B. 1904
Deceased
Pittsburgh

Year Team	Lg	C	D	Games	W	L	T	Pct	APct	Fin	Seq	Pos
1930 NEW	N			12	1	10	1	.091	.125	11		CHC

John Sandusky
Sandusky, John T.
B. Dec. 28, 1925, Philadelphia, PA
Villanova

Year Team	Lg	C	D	Games	W	L	T	Pct	APct	Fin	Seq	Pos
1972 BAL	N	A	E	9	4	5	0	.444	.444	5/3	2/2	HC

Al Saunders
Saunders, Alan Keith
B. Feb. 1, 1947, London, England
San Jose State

Year Team	Lg	C	D	Games	W	L	T	Pct	APct	Fin	Seq	Pos
1986 SD	N	A	W	8	3	5	0	.375	.375	5/5	2/2	HC
1987				15	8	7	0	.533	.533	3		HC
1988				16	6	10	0	.375	.375	4		HC
3 yrs.				39	17	22	0		.436			

Dewey Scanlon
Scanlon, Dewey D.
B. Aug. 16, 1899
Deceased
Valparaiso

Year Team	Lg	C	D	Games	W	L	T	Pct	APct	Fin	Seq	Pos
1924 DUL	N			6	5	1	0	.833	.833	4		HC
1925				3	0	3	0	.000	.000	16		HC
1929 CHIC	N			13	6	6	1	.500	.500	4		HC
3 yrs.				22	11	10	1		.523			

Dante Scarnecchia
Scarnecchia, Dante
B. Feb. 15, 1948, Los Angeles, CA
U.S. International

Year Team	Lg	C	D	Games	W	L	T	Pct	APct	Fin	Seq	Pos
1992 NE	N	A	E	7	2	5	0	.286	.286	5/5	2/3	HC

Paul Schissler
Schissler, Paul J., Jr.
B. Nov. 11, 1893, Hastings, NE
D. Apr. 17, 1968, Hastings, NE
Doane/Hastings/St. Viator

Year Team	Lg	C	D	Games	W	L	T	Pct	APct	Fin	Seq	Pos
1933 CHIC	N		W	11	1	9	1	.100	.136	5		HC
1934				11	5	6	0	.455	.455	4		HC
1935 BKN	N		E	12	5	6	1	.455	.458	2		HC

Paul Schissler *continued*

Year Team	Lg	C	D	Games	W	L	T	Pct	APct	Fin	Seq	Pos
1936				12	3	8	1	.273	.292	4		HC
4 yrs.				46	14	29	3		.337			

Joe Schmidt
Schmidt, Joseph Paul
B. Jan. 18, 1932, Pittsburgh, PA
Pittsburgh

Year Team	Lg	C	D	Games	W	L	T	Pct	APct	Fin	Seq	Pos
1967 DET	N	W	C	14	5	7	2	.417	.429	3		HC
1968				14	4	8	2	.333	.357	4		HC
1969				14	9	4	1	.692	.679	2		HC
1970		N	C	14	10	4	0	.714	.714	2		HC
1971				14	7	6	1	.538	.536	2		HC
1972				14	8	5	1	.607	.607	2		HC
6 yrs.				84	43	34	7		.554			
Playoffs												
1970				1	0	1						HC

Howard Schnellenberger
Schnellenberger, Howard
B. Mar. 16, 1934, Louisville, KY
Kentucky

Year Team	Lg	C	D	Games	W	L	T	Pct	APct	Fin	Seq	Pos
1973 BAL	N	A	E	14	4	10	0	.286	.286	4		HC
1974				3	0	3	0	.000	.000	5/5	1/2	HC
2 yrs.				17	4	13	0		.235			

Marty Schottenheimer
Schottenheimer, Martin Edward
B. Sep. 23, 1943, Canonsburg, PA
Pittsburgh

Year Team	Lg	C	D	Games	W	L	T	Pct	APct	Fin	Seq	Pos
1984 CLE	N	A	C	8	4	4	0	.500	.500	3/3	2/2	HC
1985				16	8	8	0	.500	.500	1		HC
1986				16	12	4	0	.750	.750	1		HC
1987				15	10	5	0	.667	.667	1		HC
1988				16	10	6	0	.625	.625	2		HC
1989 KC	N	A	W	16	8	7	1	.531	.531	2		HC
1990				16	11	5	0	.688	.688	2		HC
1991				16	10	6	0	.625	.625	2		HC
1992				16	10	6	0	.625	.625	2		HC
1993				16	11	5	0	.688	.688	1		HC
1994				16	9	7	0	.563	.563	2		HC
1995				16	13	3	0	.813	.813	1		HC
1996				16	9	7	0	.563	.563	2		HC
13 yrs.				199	125	73	1		.631			
Playoffs												
1980				1	0	1						HC
1985				1	0	1						HC
1986				2	1	1						HC
1987				2	1	1						HC
1988				1	0	1						HC
1991				2	1	1						HC
1992				1	0	1						HC
1993				3	2	1						HC
1994				1	0	1						HC
1995				1	0	1						HC
10 yrs.				15	5	10			.333			

Ralph Scott
Scott, Ralph V.
B. Sep., 1897, Dewey Township, WI
D. Aug. 16, 1936, Hardin, MT
Wisconsin

Year Team	Lg	C	D	Games	W	L	T	Pct	APct	Fin	Seq	Pos
1926 NY	A			15	10	5	0	.667	.667	2		HC
1927 NYY	N			16	7	8	1	.467	.469	6		HC
2 yrs.				31	17	13	1		.565			

George Seifert
Seifert, George Gerald
B. Jan. 22, 1940, San Francisco, CA
Utah

Year Team	Lg	C	D	Games	W	L	T	Pct	APct	Fin	Seq	Pos
1989 SF	N	N	W	16	14	2	0	.875	.875	1		HC
1990				16	14	2	0	.875	.875	1		HC
1991				16	10	6	0	.625	.625	3		HC
1992				16	14	2	0	.875	.875	1		HC
1993				16	10	6	0	.625	.625	1		HC
1994				16	13	3	0	.813	.813	1		HC
1995				16	11	5	0	.688	.688	1		HC

Year	Team	Lg	C	D	Games	W	L	T	Pct	APct	Fin	Seq	Pos

George Seifert continued

Year	Team	Lg	C	D	Games	W	L	T	Pct	APct	Fin	Seq	Pos
1996					16	12	4	0	.750	.750	2		HC
8 yrs.					128	98	30	0		.766			
Playoffs													
1990					2	1	1						HC
1992					2	1	1						HC
1993					2	1	1						HC
1994					3	3	0						HC
1995					1	0	1						HC
1996					2	1	1						HC
6 yrs.					12	7	5			.583			

Mike Shanahan

Shanahan, Michael Edward
B. Aug. 24, 1952, Oak Park, IL
Eastern Illinois

Year	Team	Lg	C	D	Games	W	L	T	Pct	APct	Fin	Seq	Pos
1988	LARI	N	A	W	16	7	9	0	.438	.438	3		HC
1989					4	1	3	0	.250	.250	4/3	1/2	HC
1995	DEN	N	A	W	16	8	8	0	.500	.500	3		HC
1996					16	13	3	0	.813	.813	1		HC
4 yrs.					52	29	23	0		.558			
Playoffs													
1996					1	0	1						HC

Clark Shaughnessy

Shaughnessy, Clark David
B. Mar. 6, 1892, St. Cloud, MN
D. May 15, 1970, Santa Monica, CA
Minnesota

Year	Team	Lg	C	D	Games	W	L	T	Pct	APct	Fin	Seq	Pos
1948	LA	N		W	12	6	5	1	.545	.542	3		HC
1949					12	8	2	2	.800	.750	1		HC
2 yrs.					24	14	7	3		.646			
Playoffs													
1949					1	0	1						HC

Buck Shaw

Shaw, Lawrence Timothy
B. Mar. 28, 1899, Mitchellville, IA
D. Mar. 19, 1977, Menlo Park, CA
Notre Dame

Year	Team	Lg	C	D	Games	W	L	T	Pct	APct	Fin	Seq	Pos
1946	SF	AA		W	14	9	5	0	.643	.643	2		HC
1947					14	8	4	2	.667	.643	2		HC
1948					14	12	2	0	.857	.857	2		HC
1949					12	9	3	0	.750	.750	2		HC
1950	SF	N		N	12	3	9	0	.250	.250	5		HC
1951					12	7	4	1	.636	.625	2		HC
1952					12	7	5	0	.583	.583	3		HC
1953					12	9	3	0	.750	.750	2		HC
1954					12	7	4	1	.636	.625	3		HC
1958	PHI	N		E	12	2	9	1	.182	.208	5		HC
1959					12	7	5	0	.583	.583	2		HC
1960					12	10	2	0	.833	.833	1		HC
12 yrs.					150	90	55	5		.617			
Playoffs													
1949					2	1	1						HC
1960					1	1	0						HC
2 yrs.					3	2	1			.667			

Art Shell

Shell, Arthur
B. Nov. 26, 1946, Charleston, SC
Maryland-Eastern Shore

Year	Team	Lg	C	D	Games	W	L	T	Pct	APct	Fin	Seq	Pos
1989	LARI	N	A	W	12	7	5	0	.583	.583	4/3	2/2	HC
1990					16	12	4	0	.750	.750	1		HC
1991					16	9	7	0	.563	.563	3		HC
1992					16	7	9	0	.438	.438	4		HC
1993					16	10	6	0	.625	.625	2		HC
1994					16	9	7	0	.563	.563	3		HC
6 yrs.					92	54	38	0		.587			
Playoffs													
1990					2	1	1						HC
1991					1	0	1						HC
1993					2	1	1						HC
3 yrs.					5	2	3			.400			

Allie Sherman

Sherman, Alexander
B. Feb. 10, 1923, Brooklyn, NY
Brooklyn College

Year	Team	Lg	C	D	Games	W	L	T	Pct	APct	Fin	Seq	Pos
1961	NY	N		E	14	10	3	1	.769	.750	1		HC
1962					14	12	2	0	.857	.857	1		HC
1963					14	11	3	0	.786	.786	1		HC
1964					14	2	10	2	.167	.214	7		HC
1965					14	7	7	0	.500	.500	2		HC
1966					14	1	12	1	.077	.107	8		HC
1967			CE		14	7	7	0	.500	.500	2		HC
1968			CA		14	7	7	0	.500	.500	2		HC
8 yrs.					112	57	51	4		.527			
Playoffs													
1962					1	0	1						HC
1963					1	0	1						HC
2 yrs.					2	0	2			.000			

Ted Shipkey

Shipkey, Theodore E.
B. Sep. 28, 1904, Great Falls, MT
D. Jul. 18, 1978, Placentia, CA
Stanford

Year	Team	Lg	C	D	Games	W	L	T	Pct	APct	Fin	Seq	Pos
1947	LA	AA		W	4	2	2	0	.500	.500	3/3	2/2	CHC

Ken Shipp

Shipp, Ken
B. Feb. 3, 1929, Old Hickory, TN
Middle Tennessee State

Year	Team	Lg	C	D	Games	W	L	T	Pct	APct	Fin	Seq	Pos
1975	NYJ	N	A	E	5	1	4	0	.250	.250	5/4	2/2	HC

Jim Shofner

Shofner, James
B. Dec. 18, 1935, Grapevine, TX
Texas Christian

Year	Team	Lg	C	D	Games	W	L	T	Pct	APct	Fin	Seq	Pos
1990	CLE	N	A	C	7	1	6	0	.143	.143	4/4	2/2	HC

Dave Shula

Shula, David Donald
B. May 28, 1959, Lexington, KY
Dartmouth

Year	Team	Lg	C	D	Games	W	L	T	Pct	APct	Fin	Seq	Pos
1992	CIN	N	A	C	16	5	11	0	.313	.313	4		HC
1993					16	3	13	0	.188	.188	4		HC
1994					16	3	13	0	.188	.188	3		HC
1995					16	7	9	0	.438	.438	2		HC
1996					7	1	6	0	.143	.143	5/3	1/2	HC
5 yrs.					71	19	52	0		.268			

Don Shula

Shula, Donald Francis
B. Jan. 4, 1930, Painesville, OH
John Carroll

Year	Team	Lg	C	D	Games	W	L	T	Pct	APct	Fin	Seq	Pos
1963	BAL	N		W	14	8	6	0	.571	.571	3		HC
1964					14	12	2	0	.857	.857	1		HC
1965					14	10	3	1	.769	.750	1		HC
1966					14	9	5	0	.643	.643	2		HC
1967			CO		14	11	1	2	.917	.857	1		HC
1968					14	13	1	0	.929	.929	1		HC
1969					14	8	5	1	.615	.607	2		HC
1970	MIA	N	A	E	14	10	4	0	.714	.714	2		HC
1971					14	10	3	1	.769	.750	1		HC
1972					14	14	0	0	1.000	1.000	1		HC
1973					14	12	2	0	.857	.857	1		HC
1974					14	11	3	0	.786	.786	1		HC
1975					14	10	4	0	.714	.714	2		HC
1976					14	6	8	0	.429	.429	3		HC
1977					14	10	4	0	.714	.714	2		HC
1978					16	11	5	0	.688	.688	2		HC
1979					16	10	6	0	.625	.625	1		HC
1980					16	8	8	0	.500	.500	3		HC
1981					16	11	4	1	.719	.719	1		HC
1982			—		9	7	2	0	.778	.778	2		HC
1983				E	16	12	4	0	.750	.750	1		HC
1984					16	14	2	0	.875	.875	1		HC
1985					16	12	4	0	.750	.750	1		HC
1986					16	8	8	0	.500	.500	3		HC

Year Team	Lg	C	D	Games	W	L	T	Pct	APct	Fin	Seq	Pos

Don Shula *continued*

Year	Team	Lg	C	D	Games	W	L	T	Pct	APct	Fin	Seq	Pos
1987					15	8	7	0	.533	.533	2		HC
1988					16	6	10	0	.375	.375	5		HC
1989					16	8	8	0	.500	.500	2		HC
1990					16	12	4	0	.750	.750	2		HC
1991					16	8	8	0	.500	.500	3		HC
1992					16	11	5	0	.688	.688	1		HC
1993					16	9	7	0	.563	.563	2		HC
1994					16	10	6	0	.625	.625	1		HC
1995					16	9	7	0	.563	.563	2		HC
33 yrs.					490	328	156	6		.676			

Playoffs

Year	Games	W	L	T	Pct	APct	Fin	Seq	Pos
1964	1	0	1						HC
1965	1	0	1						HC
1968	3	2	1						HC
1970	1	0	1						HC
1971	3	2	1						HC
1972	3	3	0						HC
1973	3	3	0						HC
1974	1	0	1						HC
1978	1	0	1						HC
1979	1	0	1						HC
1981	1	0	1						HC
1982	4	3	1						HC
1983	1	0	1						HC
1984	3	2	1						HC
1985	2	1	1						HC
1990	2	1	1						HC
1992	2	1	1						HC
1994	2	1	1						HC
1995	1	0	1						HC
19 yrs.	36	19	17			.528			

Herb Sies
Sies, Dale Herbert
B. 1893
Deceased
Pittsburgh

Year	Team	Lg	Games	W	L	T	Pct	APct	Fin	Pos
1923	RI	N	8	2	3	3	.400	.438	12	HC

Nick Skorich
Skorich, Nicholas L.
B. Jun. 26, 1921, Bellaire, OH
Cincinnati

Year	Team	Lg	C	D	Games	W	L	T	Pct	APct	Fin	Pos
1961	PHI	N	E		14	10	4	0	.714	.714	2	HC
1962					14	3	10	1	.231	.250	7	HC
1963					14	2	10	2	.167	.214	7	HC
1971	CLE	N	A	C	14	9	5	0	.643	.643	1	HC
1972					14	10	4	0	.714	.714	2	HC
1973					14	7	5	2	.571	.571	3	HC
1974					14	4	10	0	.286	.286	4	HC
7 yrs.					98	45	48	5		.485		

Playoffs

Year	Games	W	L	Pct	Pos
1971	1	0	1		HC
1972	1	0	1		HC
2 yrs.	2	0	2	.000	

Clipper Smith
Smith, Maurice J.
B. Oct. 15, 1898, Manteno, IL
D. Mar. 18, 1984, Laguna Beach, CA
Notre Dame

Year	Team	Lg		Games	W	L	T	Pct	APct	Fin	Pos
1947	BOS	N	E	12	4	7	1	.364	.375	3	HC
1948				12	3	9	0	.250	.250	4	HC
2 yrs.				24	7	16	1		.313		

Jerry Smith
Smith, Jerome A.
B. Sep. 9, 1930, Dayton, OH
Wisconsin

Year	Team	Lg	C	D	Games	W	L	T	Pct	APct	Fin	Seq	Pos
1971	DEN	N	A	W	5	2	3	0	.400	.400	4/4	2/2	HC

Martin Smith
Smith, Martin
None

Year	Team	Lg	Games	W	L	T	Pct	APct	Fin	Seq	Pos
1921	CHI	A	5	2	1	2	.667	.600	16/8	2/2	HC

Bob Snyder
Snyder, Robert A.
B. Feb. 6, 1913, Fremont, OH
D. Nov. 13, 1990
Ohio University

Year	Team	Lg			Games	W	L	T	Pct	APct	Fin	Pos
1947	LA	N		W	12	6	6	0	.500	.500	4	HC

Mac Speedie
Speedie, Mac Curtis
B. Jan. 12, 1920, Odell, IL
D. Mar. 12, 1993, Laguna Hills, CA
Utah

Year	Team	Lg			Games	W	L	T	Pct	APct	Fin	Seq	Pos
1964	DEN	A		W	10	2	7	1	.222	.250	3/4	2/2	HC
1965					14	4	10	0	.286	.286	4		HC
1966					2	0	2	0	.000	.000	4/4	1/2	HC
3 yrs.					26	6	19	1		.250			

Gene Stallings
Stallings, Eugene Clifton
B. Mar. 2, 1935, Paris, TX
Texas A&M

Year	Team	Lg	C	D	Games	W	L	T	Pct	APct	Fin	Pos
1986	STL	N	N	E	16	4	11	1	.281	.281	5	HC
1987					15	7	8	0	.467	.467	2	HC
1988	PHX	N	N	E	16	7	9	0	.438	.438	3	HC
1989					11	5	6	0	.455	.455	3/4	1/2	HC
4 yrs.					58	23	34	1		.405		

Dick Stanfel
Stanfel, Richard Anthony
B. Jul. 20, 1927, San Francisco, CA
San Francisco

Year	Team	Lg	C	D	Games	W	L	T	Pct	APct	Fin	Seq	Pos
1980	NO	N	N	W	4	1	3	0	.250	.250	4/4	2/2	HC

Bart Starr
Starr, Bryan Bartlett
B. Jan. 9, 1934, Montgomery, AL
Alabama

Year	Team	Lg	C	D	Games	W	L	T	Pct	APct	Fin	Pos
1975	GB	N	N	C	14	4	10	0	.286	.286	3	HC
1976					14	5	9	0	.357	.357	4	HC
1977					14	4	10	0	.286	.286	4	HC
1978					16	8	7	1	.531	.531	2	HC
1979					16	5	11	0	.313	.313	4	HC
1980					16	5	10	1	.344	.344	4	HC
1981					16	8	8	0	.500	.500	2	HC
1982	—				9	5	3	1	.611	.611	3	HC
1983			C		16	8	8	0	.500	.500	2	HC
9 yrs.					131	52	76	3		.408		

Playoffs

Year	Games	W	L	T	Pct	Pos
1982	2	1	1		.500	HC

Les Steckel
Steckel, Leslie Todd
B. Jul. 1, 1946, North Hampton, PA
Kansas

Year	Team	Lg	C	D	Games	W	L	T	Pct	APct	Fin	Pos
1984	MIN	N	N	C	16	3	13	0	.188	.188	5	HC

Kay Stephenson
Stephenson, George Kay
B. Dec. 17, 1944, De Funiak Springs, FL
Florida

Year	Team	Lg	C	D	Games	W	L	T	Pct	APct	Fin	Seq	Pos
1983	BUF	N	A	E	16	8	8	0	.500	.500	2		HC
1984					16	2	14	0	.125	.125	5		HC
1985					4	0	4	0	.000	.000	5/5	1/2	HC
3 yrs.					36	10	26	0		.278			

Ed Sternaman
Sternaman, Edward Carl (Dutch)
B. Feb. 9, 1895, Chicago, IL
D. Feb. 1, 1973, Chicago, IL
Illinois

Year	Team	Lg	Games	W	L	T	Pct	APct	Fin	Pos
1922	CHIB	N	12	9	3	0	.750	.750	2	CHC
1924			11	6	1	4	.857	.727	2	CHC
2 yrs.			23	15	4	4		.739		

Year	Team	Lg	C	D	Games	W	L	T	Pct	APct	Fin	Seq	Pos

Joey Sternaman

Sternaman, Joseph Theodore
B. Feb. 1, 1900, Springfield, IL
D. Mar. 10, 1988, Oak Park, IL
Illinois

Year	Team	Lg	C	D	Games	W	L	T	Pct	APct	Fin	Seq	Pos
1923	DUL	N			7	4	3	0	.571	.571	7		HC
1926	CHI	A			14	5	6	3	.455	.464	5		HC
2 yrs.					21	9	9	3		.500			

Mal Stevens

Stevens, Marvin Allen
B. Apr. 14, 1900, Stockton, KS
D. Dec. 6, 1979, New York, NY
Washburn/Yale

Year	Team	Lg	C	D	Games	W	L	T	Pct	APct	Fin	Seq	Pos
1946	BKN	AA	E		7	2	4	1	.333	.357	2/2	1/2	HC

Pete Stinchcomb

Stinchcomb, Gaylord R.
B. Jun. 24, 1895, Fostoria, OH
D. Aug. 24, 1973, Findlay, OH
Ohio State

Year	Team	Lg	C	D	Games	W	L	T	Pct	APct	Fin	Seq	Pos
1923	COL	N			4	1	2	1	.333	.375	12/8	1/2	HC

Carl Storck

Storck, Carl L.
B. Nov. 14, 1892, Dayton, OH
D. Mar. 13, 1950, Dayton, OH
None

Year	Team	Lg	C	D	Games	W	L	T	Pct	APct	Fin	Seq	Pos
1922	DAY	N			8	4	3	1	.571	.563	7		HC
1923					7	0	6	1	.000	.071	1/16	2/2	HC
1924					8	2	6	0	.250	.250	13		HC
1925					8	0	7	1	.000	.063	16		HC
1926					6	1	4	1	.200	.250	16		HC
5 yrs.					37	7	26	4		.243			

Red Strader

Strader, Norman Parker
B. Dec. 21, 1904, Newton, NJ
D. May 26, 1956
St. Mary's (California)

Year	Team	Lg	C	D	Games	W	L	T	Pct	APct	Fin	Seq	Pos
1948	NY	AA	E		6	4	2	0	.667	.667	3/3	2/2	HC
1949	B-NY	AA			12	8	4	0	.667	.667	3		HC
1950	NYY	N	N		12	7	5	0	.583	.583	3		HC
1955	SF	N	W		12	4	8	0	.333	.333	5		HC
4 yrs.					42	23	19	0		.548			
Playoffs													
1949	B, NY	AA			1	0	1			.000			HC

Hank Stram

Stram, Henry Louis
B. Jan. 3, 1924, Chicago, IL
Purdue

Year	Team	Lg	C	D	Games	W	L	T	Pct	APct	Fin	Seq	Pos
1960	DAL	A		W	14	8	6	0	.571	.571	2		HC
1961					14	6	8	0	.429	.429	2		HC
1962					14	11	3	0	.786	.786	1		HC
1963	KC	A		W	14	5	7	2	.417	.429	3		HC
1964					14	7	7	0	.500	.500	2		HC
1965					14	7	5	2	.583	.571	3		HC
1966					14	11	2	1	.846	.821	1		HC
1967					14	9	5	0	.643	.643	2		HC
1968					14	12	2	0	.857	.857	1		HC
1969					14	11	3	0	.786	.786	2		HC
1970	KC	N	A	W	14	7	5	2	.583	.571	2		HC
1971					14	10	3	1	.769	.750	1		HC
1972					14	8	6	0	.571	.571	2		HC
1973					14	7	5	2	.571	.571	3		HC
1974					14	5	9	0	.357	.357	3		HC
1976	NO	N	N	W	14	4	10	0	.286	.286	3		HC
1977					14	3	11	0	.214	.214	4		HC
17 yrs.					238	131	97	10		.571			
Playoffs													
1962					1	1	0						HC
1966					2	1	1						HC
1968					1	0	1						HC
1969					3	3	0						HC

Hank Stram *continued*

Year	Team	Lg	C	D	Games	W	L	T	Pct	APct	Fin	Seq	Pos
1971					1	0	1						HC
5 yrs.					8	5	3			.625			

Chuck Studley

Studley, Chuck
B. Jan. 17, 1929, Maywood, IL
Illinois

Year	Team	Lg	C	D	Games	W	L	T	Pct	APct	Fin	Seq	Pos
1983	HOU	N	A	C	10	2	8	0	.200	.200	4/4	2/2	HC

Joe Stydahar

Stydahar, Joseph Lee
B. Mar. 16, 1912, Kaylor, PA
D. Mar. 23, 1977, Beckley, WV
Pittsburgh/West Virginia

Year	Team	Lg	C	D	Games	W	L	T	Pct	APct	Fin	Seq	Pos
1950	LA	N	N		12	9	3	0	.750	.750	1		HC
1951					12	8	4	0	.667	.667	1		HC
1952					1	0	1	0	.000	.000	3/1	1/2	HC
1953	CHIC	N	E		12	1	10	1	.091	.125	6		HC
1954					12	2	10	0	.167	.167	6		HC
5 yrs.					49	20	28	1		.418			
Playoffs													
1950					2	1	1						HC
1951					1	1	0						HC
2 yrs.					3	2	1			.667			

Jock Sutherland

Sutherland, John Bain
B. Mar. 21, 1889, Coupar, Angus, Scotland
D. Apr. 11, 1948, Pittsburgh, PA
Pittsburgh

Year	Team	Lg	C	D	Games	W	L	T	Pct	APct	Fin	Seq	Pos
1940	BKN	N		E	11	8	3	0	.727	.727	2		HC
1941					11	7	4	0	.636	.636	2		HC
1946	PIT	N		E	11	5	5	1	.500	.500	4		HC
1947					12	8	4	0	.667	.667	1		HC
4 yrs.					45	28	16	1		.633			
Playoffs													
1947					1	0	1						HC

Harland Svare

Svare, Harland James (Swede)
B. Nov. 15, 1930, Clarksville, MN
Washington State

Year	Team	Lg	C	D	Games	W	L	T	Pct	APct	Fin	Seq	Pos
1962	LA	N		W	6	0	5	1	.000	.083	7/7	2/2	HC
1963					14	5	9	0	.357	.357	6		HC
1964					14	5	7	2	.417	.429	5		HC
1965					14	4	10	0	.286	.286	7		HC
1971	SD	N	A	W	4	2	2	0	.500	.500	3/3	2/2	HC
1972					14	4	9	1	.321	.321	4		HC
1973					8	1	6	1	.188	.188	4/4	1/2	HC
7 yrs.					74	21	48	5		.318			

Barry Switzer

Switzer, Barry
B. Oct. 5, 1937, Crossett, AR
Arkansas

Year	Team	Lg	C	D	Games	W	L	T	Pct	APct	Fin	Seq	Pos
1994	DAL	N	N	E	16	12	4	0	.750	.750	1		HC
1995					16	12	4	0	.750	.750	1		HC
1996					16	10	6	0	.625	.625	1		HC
3 yrs.					48	34	14	0		.708			
Playoffs													
1994					2	1	1						HC
1995					3	3	0						HC
1996					2	1	1						HC
3 yrs.					7	5	2			.714			

Nelson Talbott

Talbott, Nelson S. (Bud)
B. Jun., 1892, OH
Deceased
Yale

Year	Team	Lg	C	D	Games	W	L	T	Pct	APct	Fin	Seq	Pos
1920	DAY	A			8	4	2	2	.667	.625	4		HC
1921	HC	8			9	4	4	1	.500	.500	8		HC
1923	DAY	N			1	1	0	0	1.000	1.000	1/16	1/2	HC
3 yrs.					18	9	6	3		.583			

Year	Team	Lg	C	D	Games	W	L	T	Pct	APct	Fin	Seq	Pos

Hugh Taylor

Taylor, Hugh Wilson (Bones)
B. Jul. 6, 1923, Wynne, AR
D. Oct. 31, 1992, Wynne, AR
Tulane/Oklahoma City

Year	Team	Lg	C	D	Games	W	L	T	Pct	APct	Fin	Seq	Pos
1965	HOU	A		E	14	4	10	0	.286	.286	4		HC

Gus Tebell

Tebell, Gustave Kenneth
B. Sep. 6, 1897, St. Charles, IL
D. May 28, 1969
Wisconsin

Year	Team	Lg	C	D	Games	W	L	T	Pct	APct	Fin	Seq	Pos
1923	COL	N			6	4	2	0	.667	.667	12/8	2/2	HC

Joe Thomas

Thomas, Joe
B. Mar. 18, 1921, Warren, OH
Ohio Northern

Year	Team	Lg	C	D	Games	W	L	T	Pct	APct	Fin	Seq	Pos
1974	BAL	N	A	E	11	2	9	0	.182	.182	5/5	2/2	HC

Jim Thorpe

Thorpe, James Francis (Bright Path)
B. May 28, 1887, Prague, OK
D. Mar. 28, 1953, Long Beach, CA
Carlisle

Year	Team	Lg	C	D	Games	W	L	T	Pct	APct	Fin	Seq	Pos
1920	CAN	A			8	4	3	1	.571	.563	7		HC
1921	CLE	A			8	3	5	0	.375	.375	12		HC
1922	OOR	N			9	3	6	0	.333	.333	12		HC
1923					11	1	10	0	.091	.091	18		HC
4 yrs.					36	11	24	1		.319			

Elgie Tobin

Tobin, Elgin W. (Yegg)
B. May, 1885
Deceased
Penn State

Year	Team	Lg	C	D	Games	W	L	T	Pct	APct	Fin	Seq	Pos
1920	AKR	A			9	6	0	3	1.000	.833	1		HC
1921					12	8	3	1	.727	.708	3		HC
2 yrs.					21	14	3	4		.762			

Vince Tobin

Tobin, Vincent Michael
B. Sep. 29, 1943, Burlington Junction, MO
Missouri

Year	Team	Lg	C	D	Games	W	L	T	Pct	APct	Fin	Seq	Pos
1988	CHI	N	N	C	2	2	0	0	1.000	1.000	1/1	2/3	HC
1996	ARI	N	N	E	16	7	9	0	.438	.438	4		HC
2 yrs.					18	9	9	0		.500			

Dick Todd

Todd, Richard S.
B. Oct. 2, 1914, Thrall, TX
Texas A&M

Year	Team	Lg	C	D	Games	W	L	T	Pct	APct	Fin	Seq	Pos
1951	WAS	N	A		9	5	4	0	.556	.556	5/3	2/2	HC

Russell Tollefson

Tollefson, Russell I.
B. 1892
Deceased
Minnesota

Year	Team	Lg	C	D	Games	W	L	T	Pct	APct	Fin	Seq	Pos
1922	MIN	N			4	1	3	0	.250	.250	13		HC

Herb Treat

Treat, C. Herbert
B. Dec. 16, 1900, Cambridge, MA
Boston College/Princeton

Year	Team	Lg	C	D	Games	W	L	T	Pct	APct	Fin	Seq	Pos
1926	BOS	A			6	2	4	0	.333	.333	6		HC

Jim Trimble

Trimble, James William (Big Jim)
B. May 29, 1918, McKeesport, PA
Indiana

Year	Team	Lg	C	D	Games	W	L	T	Pct	APct	Fin	Seq	Pos
1952	PHI	N	A		12	7	5	0	.583	.583	2		HC
1953					12	7	4	1	.636	.625	2		HC
1954					12	7	4	1	.636	.625	2		HC

Jim Trimble *continued*

Year	Team	Lg	C	D	Games	W	L	T	Pct	APct	Fin	Seq	Pos
1955					12	4	7	1	.364	.375	4		HC
4 yrs.					48	25	20	3		.552			

Norv Turner

Turner, Norval Eugene
B. May 17, 1952, Lejeune, CA
Oregon

Year	Team	Lg	C	D	Games	W	L	T	Pct	APct	Fin	Seq	Pos
1994	WAS	N	N	E	16	3	13	0	.188	.188	5		HC
1995					16	6	10	0	.375	.375	3		HC
1996					16	9	7	0	.563	.563	3		HC
3 yrs.					48	18	30	0		.375			

Rube Ursella

Ursella, Reuben
B. Jan. 11, 1890
D. Feb., 1980, Minneapolis, MN

Year	Team	Lg	C	D	Games	W	L	T	Pct	APct	Fin	Seq	Pos
1920	RI	A			7	4	2	1	.667	.643	4		HC
1921	MIN	A			5	1	3	1	.250	.300	13		HC
1924	RI	N			9	5	2	2	.714	.667	5		HC
1925					11	5	3	3	.625	.591	8		HC
4 yrs.					32	15	10	7		.578			

Norm Van Brocklin

Van Brocklin, Norman (The Dutchman)
B. Mar. 15, 1926, Eagle Butte, SD
D. May 2, 1983, Social Circle, GA
Oregon

Year	Team	Lg	C	D	Games	W	L	T	Pct	APct	Fin	Seq	Pos
1961	MIN	N	W		14	3	11	0	.214	.214	7		HC
1962					14	2	11	1	.154	.179	6		HC
1963					14	5	8	1	.385	.393	4		HC
1964					14	8	5	1	.615	.607	2		HC
1965					14	7	7	0	.500	.500	5		HC
1966					14	4	9	1	.308	.321	6		HC
1968	ATL	N	W	CO	11	2	9	0	.182	.182	4/4	2/2	HC
1969					14	6	8	0	.429	.429	3		HC
1970		N	W		14	4	8	2	.333	.357	3		HC
1971					14	7	6	1	.538	.536	3		HC
1972					14	7	7	0	.500	.500	2		HC
1973					14	9	5	0	.643	.643	2		HC
1974					8	2	6	0	.250	.250	4/4	1/2	HC
13 yrs.					173	66	100	7		.402			

Rick Venturi

Venturi, Rick
B. Feb. 23, 1946, Taylorville, IL
Northwestern

Year	Team	Lg	C	D	Games	W	L	T	Pct	APct	Fin	Seq	Pos
1991	IND	N	A	E	11	1	10	0	.091	.091	5/5	2/2	HC
1996	NO	N	N	W	8	1	7	0	.125	.125	4/5	2/2	HC
2 yrs.					19	2	17	0		.105			

Dick Vermeil

Vermeil, Richard Albert
B. Oct. 30, 1936, Calistoga, CA
San Jose State

Year	Team	Lg	C	D	Games	W	L	T	Pct	APct	Fin	Seq	Pos
1976	PHI	N	N	E	14	4	10	0	.286	.286	4		HC
1977					14	5	9	0	.357	.357	4		HC
1978					16	9	7	0	.563	.563	2		HC
1979					16	11	5	0	.688	.688	2		HC
1980					16	12	4	0	.750	.750	1		HC
1981					16	10	6	0	.625	.625	2		HC
1982		—			9	3	6	0	.333	.333	13		HC
7 yrs.					101	54	47	0		.535			
Playoffs													
1978					1	0	1						HC
1979					2	1	1						HC
1980					3	2	1						HC
1981					1	0	1						HC
4 yrs.					7	3	4			.429			

Carl Voyles

Voyles, Carl M. (Dutch)
B. Aug. 11, 1902, McLoud, OK
Oklahoma State

Year	Team	Lg	C	D	Games	W	L	T	Pct	APct	Fin	Seq	Pos
1948	BKN	AA		E	14	2	12	0	.143	.143	4		HC

Year	Team	Lg	C	D	Games	W	L	T	Pct	APct	Fin	Seq	Pos

Charlie Waller

Waller, Charlie
B. Dec. 26, 1921, Griffin, GA
Oglethorpe

Year	Team	Lg	C	D	Games	W	L	T	Pct	APct	Fin	Seq	Pos
1969	SD	A		W	5	4	1	0	.800	.800	4/3	2/2	HC
1970	SD	N	A	W	14	5	6	3	.455	.464	3		HC
2 yrs.					19	9	7	3		.553			

Ron Waller

Waller, Ronald
B. Feb. 14, 1933, Hastings, FL
Maryland

Year	Team	Lg	C	D	Games	W	L	T	Pct	APct	Fin	Seq	Pos
1973	SD	N	A	W	6	1	5	0	.167	.167	4/4	2/2	HC

Adam Walsh

Walsh, Adam J.
B. Dec. 4, 1901, Churchville, IA
D. Jan. 13, 1985, Los Angeles, CA
Notre Dame

Year	Team	Lg	C	D	Games	W	L	T	Pct	APct	Fin	Seq	Pos
1945	CLE	N		W	10	9	1	0	.900	.900	1		HC
1946	LA	N		W	11	6	4	1	.600	.591	2		HC
2 yrs.					21	15	5	1		.738			
Playoffs													
1945					1	1	0						HC

Bill Walsh

Walsh, William Ernest
B. Nov. 30, 1931, Los Angeles, CA
San Jose State

Year	Team	Lg	C	D	Games	W	L	T	Pct	APct	Fin	Seq	Pos
1979	SF	N	N	W	16	2	14	0	.125	.125	4		HC
1980					16	6	10	0	.375	.375	3		HC
1981					16	13	3	0	.813	.813	1		HC
1982			—		9	3	6	0	.333	.333	11		HC
1983				W	16	10	6	0	.625	.625	1		HC
1984					16	15	1	0	.938	.938	1		HC
1985					16	10	6	0	.625	.625	2		HC
1986					16	10	5	1	.656	.656	1		HC
1987					15	13	2	0	.867	.867	1		HC
1988					16	10	6	0	.625	.625	1		HC
10 yrs.					152	92	59	1		.609			
Playoffs													
1981					3	3	0						HC
1983					2	1	1						HC
1984					3	3	0						HC
1985					1	0	1						HC
1986					1	0	1						HC
1987					1	0	1						HC
1988					3	3	0						HC
7 yrs.					14	10	4			.714			

Chile Walsh

Walsh, Charles Francis
B. Feb. 4, 1903, Des Moines, IA
D. Sep. 4, 1971, Hollywood, CA
Notre Dame

Year	Team	Lg	C	D	Games	W	L	T	Pct	APct	Fin	Seq	Pos
1934	C-S	N		W	3	1	2	0	.333	.333	5/5	2/2	HC

Joe Walton

Walton, Joseph Frank
B. Dec. 15, 1935, Beaver Falls, PA
Pittsburgh

Year	Team	Lg	C	D	Games	W	L	T	Pct	APct	Fin	Seq	Pos
1983	NYJ	N	A	E	16	7	9	0	.438	.438	4		HC
1984					16	7	9	0	.438	.438	3		HC
1985					16	11	5	0	.688	.688	2		HC
1986					16	10	6	0	.625	.625	2		HC
1987					15	6	9	0	.400	.400	5		HC
1988					16	8	7	1	.531	.531	4		HC
1989					16	4	12	0	.250	.250	5		HC
7 yrs.					111	53	57	1		.482			
Playoffs													
1985					1	0	1						HC
1986					2	1	1						HC
2 yrs.					3	1	2			.333			

Dave Wannstedt

Wannstedt, David Raymond
B. May 21, 1952, Pittsburgh, PA
Pittsburgh

Year	Team	Lg	C	D	Games	W	L	T	Pct	APct	Fin	Seq	Pos
1993	CHI	N	N	C	16	7	9	0	.438	.438	4		HC
1994					16	9	7	0	.563	.563	4		HC
1995					16	9	7	0	.563	.563	3		HC
1996					16	7	9	0	.438	.438	3		HC
4 yrs.					64	32	32	0		.500			
Playoffs													
1994					2	1	1						HC

Bob Waterfield

Waterfield, Robert Stanton (Rifle)
B. Jul. 26, 1920, Elmira, NY
D. Mar. 25, 1983, Burbank, CA
UCLA

Year	Team	Lg	C	D	Games	W	L	T	Pct	APct	Fin	Seq	Pos
1960	LA	N		W	12	4	7	1	.364	.375	6		HC
1961					14	4	10	0	.286	.286	6		HC
1962					8	1	7	0	.125	.125	7/7	1/2	HC
3 yrs.					34	9	24	1		.279			

Ray Watts

Watts, Raymond E.
Otterbein

Year	Team	Lg	C	D	Games	W	L	T	Pct	APct	Fin	Seq	Pos
1926	CLE	A			5	3	2	0	.600	.600	3		HC

Jim Weaver

Weaver, James Redwick (Red)
B. Jul. 19, 1897
D. Nov. 23, 1968, Mayfield, KY
Centre

Year	Team	Lg	C	D	Games	W	L	T	Pct	APct	Fin	Seq	Pos
1925	COL	N			9	0	9	0	.000	.000	16		HC

Alex Webster

Webster, Alexander (Big Red)
B. Apr. 19, 1931, Kearny, NJ
North Carolina State

Year	Team	Lg	C	D	Games	W	L	T	Pct	APct	Fin	Seq	Pos
1969	NY	N	E	CE	14	6	8	0	.429	.429	2		HC
1970	NYG	N	N	E	14	9	5	0	.643	.643	2		HC
1971					14	4	10	0	.286	.286	5		HC
1972					14	8	6	0	.571	.571	3		HC
1973					14	2	11	1	.179	.179	5		HC
5 yrs.					70	29	40	1		.421			

Ed Weir

Weir, Edward S.
B. Mar. 14, 1903, Superior, WI
D. May 15, 1991, Lincoln, NE
Nebraska

Year	Team	Lg	C	D	Games	W	L	T	Pct	APct	Fin	Seq	Pos
1927	FRA	N			1	0	0	1	.000	.500	8/5	4/4	CHC
1928					16	11	3	2	.786	.750	2		HC
2 yrs.					17	11	3	3		.735			

John Whelchel

Whelchel, John E.
B. Apr. 1, 1898, Hogansville, GA
Deceased
Navy

Year	Team	Lg	C	D	Games	W	L	T	Pct	APct	Fin	Seq	Pos
1949	WAS	N		E	7	3	3	1	.500	.500	3/4	1/2	HC

Mike White

White, Mike
B. Jan. 4, 1936, Berkeley, CA
California

Year	Team	Lg	C	D	Games	W	L	T	Pct	APct	Fin	Seq	Pos
1995	OAK	N	A	W	16	8	8	0	.500	.500	3		HC
1996					16	7	9	0	.438	.438	4		HC
2 yrs.					32	15	17	0		.469			

Paul Wiggin

Wiggin, Paul David
B. Nov. 18, 1934, Modesto, CA
Stanford

Year	Team	Lg	C	D	Games	W	L	T	Pct	APct	Fin	Seq	Pos
1975	KC	N	A	W	14	5	9	0	.357	.357	3		HC

Year	Team	Lg	C	D	Games	W	L	T	Pct	APct	Fin	Seq	Pos

Paul Wiggin *continued*

Year	Team	Lg	C	D	Games	W	L	T	Pct	APct	Fin	Seq	Pos
1976					14	5	9	0	.357	.357	4		HC
1977					7	1	6	0	.143	.143	5/5	1/2	HC
3 yrs.					35	11	24	0		.314			

Hubert Wiggs
Wiggs, Hubert
B. 1896
Deceased
Vanderbilt

Year	Team	Lg	C	D	Games	W	L	T	Pct	APct	Fin	Seq	Pos
1922	LOU	N			4	1	3	0	.250	.250	13		HC

Willie Wilkin
Wilkin, Wilbur B. (Wee Willie)
B. Apr. 21, 1916, Bingham, UT
D. May 16, 1973, Palo Alto, CA
St. Mary's (California)

Year	Team	Lg	C	D	Games	W	L	T	Pct	APct	Fin	Seq	Pos
1946	CHI	AA	W		5	2	2	1	.500	.500	3/3	2/3	CHC

Bud Wilkinson
Wilkinson, Charles Burnham
B. Apr. 23, 1916, Minneapolis, MN
D. Feb. 9, 1994, St. Louis, MO
Minnesota

Year	Team	Lg	C	D	Games	W	L	T	Pct	APct	Fin	Seq	Pos
1978	STL	N	N	E	16	6	10	0	.375	.375	4		HC
1979					13	3	10	0	.231	.231	5/5	1/2	HC
2 yrs.					29	9	20	0		.310			

Jerry Williams
Williams, Jerome Ralph
B. Nov. 1, 1923, Spokane, WA
Washington State

Year	Team	Lg	C	D	Games	W	L	T	Pct	APct	Fin	Seq	Pos
1969	PHI	N	E	CA	14	4	9	1	.308	.321	4		HC
1970			N	E	14	3	10	1	.231	.250	5		HC
1971					3	0	3	0	.000	.000	5/3	1/2	HC
3 yrs.					31	7	22	2		.258			

Richard Williamson
Williamson, Richard
B. Apr. 13, 1941, Fort Deposit, AL
Alabama

Year	Team	Lg	C	D	Games	W	L	T	Pct	APct	Fin	Seq	Pos
1990	TB	N	N	C	3	1	2	0	.333	.333	4/2	2/2	HC
1991					16	3	13	0	.188	.188	5		HC
2 yrs.					19	4	15	0		.211			

Ray Willsey
Willsey, Ray
B. Sep. 30, 1929, Regina, Sask.
California

Year	Team	Lg	C	D	Games	W	L	T	Pct	APct	Fin	Seq	Pos
1961	STL	N	E		2	2	0	0	1.000	1.000	4/4	2/2	CHC

George Wilson
Wilson, George William
B. Feb. 3, 1914, Chicago, IL
D. Nov. 23, 1978, Detroit, MI
Northwestern

Year	Team	Lg	C	D	Games	W	L	T	Pct	APct	Fin	Seq	Pos
1957	DET	N	W		12	8	4	0	.667	.667	1		HC
1958					12	4	7	1	.364	.375	5		HC
1959					12	3	8	1	.273	.292	5		HC
1960					12	7	5	0	.583	.583	2		HC
1961					14	8	5	1	.615	.607	2		HC
1962					14	11	3	0	.786	.786	2		HC
1963					14	5	8	1	.385	.393	4		HC
1964					14	7	5	2	.583	.571	4		HC
1966	MIA	A		E	14	3	11	0	.214	.214	4		HC
1967					14	4	10	0	.286	.286	4		HC
1968					14	5	8	1	.385	.393	3		HC
1969					14	3	10	1	.231	.250	5		HC
12 yrs.					160	68	84	8		.450			
Playoffs													
1957					2	2	0			1.000			HC

Larry Wilson
Wilson, Lawrence Frank
B. Mar. 24, 1938, Rigby, ID
Utah

Year	Team	Lg	C	D	Games	W	L	T	Pct	APct	Fin	Seq	Pos
1979	STL	N	N	E	3	2	1	0	.667	.667	5/5	2/2	HC

Charley Winner
Winner, Charles H.
B. Jul. 2, 1924, Somerville, NJ
Southeast Missouri State/Washington (Missouri)

Year	Team	Lg	C	D	Games	W	L	T	Pct	APct	Fin	Seq	Pos
1966	STL	N		E	14	8	5	1	.615	.607	4		HC
1967				CE	14	6	7	1	.462	.464	3		HC
1968					14	9	4	1	.692	.679	2		HC
1969					14	4	9	1	.308	.321	3		HC
1970			N	E	14	8	5	1	.615	.607	3		HC
1974	NYJ	N	A	E	14	7	7	0	.500	.500	3		HC
1975					9	2	7	0	.222	.222	5/4	1/2	HC
7 yrs.					93	44	44	5		.500			

Harry Workman
Workman, Harry Hall (Hoge)
B. Sep. 25, 1899, Huntington, WV
D. May 20, 1972, Fort Myers, FL
Ohio State

Year	Team	Lg	C	D	Games	W	L	T	Pct	APct	Fin	Seq	Pos
1931	CLE	N			10	2	8	0	.200	.200	8		CHC

Lud Wray
Wray, James R. Ludlow
B. Feb. 7, 1894, Philadelphia, PA
D. Jul. 24, 1967, Philadelphia, PA
Pennsylvania

Year	Team	Lg	C	D	Games	W	L	T	Pct	APct	Fin	Seq	Pos
1932	BOS	N			10	4	4	2	.500	.500	4		HC
1933	PHI	N		E	9	3	5	1	.375	.389	4		HC
1934					11	4	7	0	.364	.364	4		HC
1935					11	2	9	0	.182	.182	5		HC
4 yrs.					41	13	25	3		.354			

Sam Wyche
Wyche, Samuel David
B. Jan. 5, 1945, Atlanta, GA
Furman

Year	Team	Lg	C	D	Games	W	L	T	Pct	APct	Fin	Seq	Pos
1984	CIN	N	A	C	16	8	8	0	.500	.500	2		HC
1985					16	7	9	0	.438	.438	2		HC
1986					16	10	6	0	.625	.625	2		HC
1987					15	4	11	0	.267	.267	4		HC
1988					16	12	4	0	.750	.750	1		HC
1989					16	8	8	0	.500	.500	4		HC
1990					16	9	7	0	.563	.563	1		HC
1991					16	3	13	0	.188	.188	4		HC
1992	TB	N	N	C	16	5	11	0	.313	.313	3		HC
1993					16	5	11	0	.313	.313	5		HC
1994					16	6	10	0	.375	.375	5		HC
1995					16	7	9	0	.438	.438	5		HC
12 yrs.					191	84	107	0		.440			
Playoffs													
1988					3	2	1						HC
1990					2	1	1						HC
2 yrs.					5	3	2			.600			

Doug Wycoff
Wycoff, Stephen Douglas
B. Sep. 6, 1903, St. Louis, MO
D. Oct., 1981, Atlanta, GA
Georgia Tech

Year	Team	Lg	C	D	Games	W	L	T	Pct	APct	Fin	Seq	Pos
1929	SI	N			10	3	4	3	.429	.450	6		HC
1930					12	5	5	2	.500	.500	6		HC
2 yrs.					22	8	9	5		.477			

Doc Young
Young, Alva Andrew
B. Dec. 18, 1891, Hamilton City, IN
D. Aug. 9, 1942, Chicago, IL
Indiana University Medical College

Year	Team	Lg	C	D	Games	W	L	T	Pct	APct	Fin	Seq	Pos
1925	HAM	N			1	0	1	0	.000	.000	12/14	2/2	HC

Year	Team	Lg	C	D		Games	W	L	T	Pct	APct		Fin	Seq		Pos

Year	Team	Lg	C	D		Games	W	L	T	Pct	APct		Fin	Seq		Pos

Swede Youngstrom
Youngstrom, Adolph F.
B. May 24, 1897, Waltham, MA
D. Aug. 5, 1968, Lexington, MA
Dartmouth

Year	Team	Lg	C	D		Games	W	L	T	Pct	APct		Fin	Seq		Pos
1927	**FRA**	N				9	4	4	1	.500	.500		10/8	3/4		**HC**

PART TEN

Other Leagues

1936 AFL

	W	L	T	PCT	PTS	OPP	COACH
Boston Shamrocks	8	3	0	.727	133	97	George Kenneally
Cleveland Rams	5	2	2	.714	123	77	Buzz Wetzel
New York Yankees	5	3	2	.625	75	74	Jack McBride
Pittsburgh Americans	3	2	1	.600	78	65	Rudy Comstock
Syracuse/Rochester Braves	1	6	0	.143	41	113	Red Badgro/Don Irwin
Brooklyn/Rochester Tigers	0	6	1	.000	58	82	Mike Palm

1937 AFL

	W	L	T	PCT	PTS	OPP	COACH
Los Angeles Bulldogs	9	0	0	1.000	233	72	Gus Henderson
Rochester Tigers	3	3	1	.500	94	115	Mike Palm
New York Yankees	2	3	1	.400	57	115	Jack McBride/ Jim Mooney
Cincinnati Bengals	2	4	2	.333	105	103	Hal Pennington
Boston Shamrocks	2	5	0	.286	76	98	George Kenneally
Pittsburgh Americans	0	3	0	.000	7	69	Jess Quatse

ALL-AFL TEAM

E	*Bill Moore, Los Angeles*
T	*Bill Steinkemper, Cincinnati*
G	*Pete Mehringer, Los Angeles*
C	*Lee Mulleneaux, Cincinnati*
G	*Alex Drobnitch, New York*
T	*Harry Fields, Los Angeles*
E	*Red Fleming, Boston*
QB	*Harry Newman, Rochester*
HB	*Don Geyer, Cincinnati*
HB	*Al Nichelini, Los Angeles*
FB	*Gordon Gore, Los Angeles*

1940 AFL

	W	L	T	PCT	PTS	OPP	COACH
Columbus Bullies	8	1	1	.889	134	69	Phil Bucklew
Milwaukee Chiefs	7	2	0	.778	180	59	Ivan (Tiny) Cahoon
Boston Bears	5	4	1	.556	120	79	Eddie Casey
New York Yankees	4	5	0	.444	137	138	Jack McBride
Buffalo Indians	2	8	0	.200	44	137	Red Seick/Ole Nesmith
Cincinnati Bengals	1	7	0	.125	53	186	Dana King

ALL-AFL TEAM

E	*Sherman Barnes, Milwaukee*
T	*Ed Karp, Buffalo*
G	*Jim Karcher, Columbus*
C	*Joe Aleskus, Columbus*
G	*Alex Drobnitch, Buffalo*
T	*Bob Eckl, Milwaukee*
E	*Harlan Gustafson, New York*
QB	*Andy Karpus, Boston*
HB	*Bill Hutchinson, New York*
HB	*Nelson Peterson, Columbus*
FB	*Al Novakofski, Milwaukee*

1941 AFL

	W	L	T	PCT	PTS	OPP	COACH
Columbus Bullies	5	1	2	.833	142	55	Phil Bucklew
New York Americans	5	2	1	.714	116	73	Jack McBride
Milwaukee Chiefs	4	3	1	.571	115	84	Ivan (Tiny) Cahoon
Buffalo Tigers	2	6	0	.333	72	172	Tiny Engebretsen
Cincinnati Bengals	1	5	2	.167	69	120	Dana King

ALL-AFL TEAM

E	*Earl Ohlgren, Milwaukee*
T	*Alec Shellogg, Buffalo*
G	*Ted Livingston, Columbus*
C	*Paul Humphrey, Milwaukee*
G	*Tex Akin, Milwaukee*
T	*Bob Eckl, Milwaukee*
E	*Joe Kruse, Cincinnati*
QB	*Bob Davis, Columbus*
HB	*Charley Armstrong, New York*
HB	*Bill McGannon, Cincinnati*
FB	*John Kimbrough, New York*

1974 WORLD FOOTBALL LEAGUE

EASTERN DIVISION	W	L	T	PCT	PTS	OPP	COACH
Florida Blazers	14	6	0	.700	419	280	Jack Pardee
N.Y. Stars/ Charlotte Hornets	10	10	0	.500	467	350	Babe Parilli
Philadelphia Bell	9	11	0	.450	493	413	Ron Waller
Jacksonville Sharks	4	10	0	.286	258	358	Bud Asher/Charlie Tate

CENTRAL DIVISION	W	L	T	PCT	PTS	OPP	COACH
Memphis Southmen	17	3	0	.850	629	365	John McVay
Birmingham Americans	15	5	0	.750	503	394	Jack Gotta
Chicago Fire	7	13	0	.350	446	622	Jim Spavital
Detroit Wheels	1	13	0	.071	209	358	Dan Boisture

WESTERN DIVISION	W	L	T	PCT	PTS	OPP	COACH
Southern California Sun	13	7	0	.650	486	441	Tom Fears
The Hawaiians	9	11	0	.450	413	425	Mike Giddings
Portland Storm	7	12	1	.375	264	426	Dick Coury
Houston Texans/ Shreveport Steamers	7	12	1	.375	240	415	Jim Garrett/ Henry Lee Walker/ Marshall Taylor

FIRST-ROUND PLAYOFFS

Hawaii 32, Southern California 14

Florida 18, Philadelphia 3

SECOND-ROUND PLAYOFFS

Birmingham 22, Hawaii 19

Florida 18, Memphis 15

WORLD BOWL

Birmingham 22, Florida 21

ALL-WFL TEAM

Offense		**Defense**	
WR	*Tim Delaney, Hawaii*	DE	*Gerry Philbin, N.Y./Charlotte*
WR	*Alfred Jenkins, Birmingham*	DE	*Larry Ross, Florida*
TE	*Ed Marshall, Memphis*	DT	*Mike McBath, Florida*
T	*Dave Roller, So. California*	DT	*John Elliott, N.Y./Charlotte*
T	*Bob Wolfe, Birmingham*	LB	*Ross Brupbacher, Birmingham*
G	*Dave Bradley, Chicago*	LB	*Rudy Kuechenberg, Chicago*
G	*Buddy Brown, Birmingham*	LB	*John Villapiano, Hou./Shreve.*
C	*Bob Kuziel, N.Y./Charlotte*	CB	*Ron Mabra, Philadelphia*
QB	*Tony Adams, So. California*	CB	*Miller Farr, Florida*
RB	*Tommy Reamon, Florida*	S	*Dave Thomas, Memphis*
RB	*J.J. Jennings, Memphis*	S	*Jeff Woodcock, N.Y./Charlotte*
K	*Grant Guthrie, Jacks.-Birm.*	P	*Ken Clark, Portland*

1975 WORLD FOOTBALL LEAGUE

EASTERN DIVISION	W	L	T	PCT	PTS	OPP	COACH
Birmingham Vulcans	9	3	0	.750	257	186	Marvin Bass
Memphis Southmen	7	4	0	.636	254	206	John McVay

	W	L	T	PCT	PTS	OPP	COACH
Charlotte Hornets	6	5	0	.545	225	199	Bob Gibson
Jacksonville Express	6	5	0	.545	227	247	Charlie Tate
Philadelphia Bell	4	7	0	.364	195	237	Willie Wood

WESTERN DIVISION	W	L	T	PCT	PTS	OPP	COACH
Southern California Sun	7	5	0	.583	354	341	Tom Fears
San Antonio Wings	7	6	0	.538	364	268	Perry Moss
Shreveport Steamer	5	7	0	.417	276	313	Marshall Taylor
The Hawaiians	4	7	0	.364	210	281	Mike Giddings
Portland Thunder	4	7	0	.364	213	239	Greg Barton
Chicago Winds	1	4	0	.200	67	124	Abe Gibron

1983 UNITED STATES FOOTBALL LEAGUE

ATLANTIC DIVISION	W	L	T	PCT	PTS	OPP	COACH
Philadelphia Stars	15	3	0	.833	379	204	Jim Mora
Boston Breakers	11	7	0	.611	399	334	Dick Coury
New Jersey Generals	6	12	0	.333	314	443	Chuck Fairbanks
Washington Federals	4	14	0	.222	297	442	Ray Jauch

CENTRAL DIVISION	W	L	T	PCT	PTS	OPP	COACH
Michigan Panthers	12	6	0	.667	451	337	Jim Stanley
Chicago Blitz	12	6	0	.667	456	271	George Allen
Tampa Bay Bandits	11	7	0	.611	363	378	Steve Spurrier
Birmingham Stallions	9	9	0	.500	343	326	Rollie Dotsch

PACIFIC DIVISION	W	L	T	PCT	PTS	OPP	COACH
Oakland Invaders	9	9	0	.500	319	317	John Ralston
Los Angeles Express	8	10	0	.444	296	370	Hugh Campbell
Denver Gold	7	11	0	.389	284	304	Red Miller/ Charlie Armey/ Craig Morton
Arizona Wranglers	4	14	0	.222	261	442	Doug Shively

DIVISIONAL PLAYOFFS
Philadelphia 44, Chicago 38 (OT)
Michigan 37, Oakland 21

CHAMPIONSHIP
Michigan 24, Philadelphia 22

ALL-USFL TEAM
Offense

WR	Trumaine Johnson, Chicago
WR	Eric Truvillion, Tampa Bay
TE	Raymond Chester, Oakland
T	Irv Eatman, Philadelphia
T	Ray Pinney, Michigan
G	Buddy Aydelette, Birmingham
G	Thom Dornbrook, Michigan
C	Bob Van Duyne, Tampa Bay
QB	Bobby Hebert, Michigan
RB	Herschel Walker, New Jersey
RB	Kelvin Bryant, Philadelphia
K	Tim Mazzetti, Boston
KR	Eric Robinson, Washington

Defense

DE	Mike Raines, Birmingham
DE	Kit Lathrop, Chicago
NT	Fred Nordgren, Tampa Bay
LB	John Corker, Michigan
LB	Stan White, Chicago
LB	Sam Mills, Philadelphia
LB	Marcus Marek, Boston
CB	Jeff George, Tampa Bay
CB	David Martin, Denver
S	Luther Bradley, Chicago
S	Scott Woerner, Philadelphia
P	Stan Talley, Oakland
PR	David Martin, Denver

1984 UNITED STATES FOOTBALL LEAGUE
EASTERN CONFERENCE

ATLANTIC DIVISION	W	L	T	PCT	PTS	OPP	COACH
Philadelphia Stars	16	2	0	.889	479	225	Jim Mora
New Jersey Generals	14	4	0	.778	430	312	Walt Michaels
Pittsburgh Maulers	3	15	0	.167	259	379	Joe Pendry
Washington Federals	3	15	0	.167	270	492	Ray Jauch

SOUTHERN DIVISION	W	L	T	PCT	PTS	OPP	COACH
Birmingham Stallions	14	4	0	.778	557	316	Rollie Dotsch
Tampa Bay Bandits	14	4	0	.778	498	337	Steve Spurrier
New Orleans Breakers	8	10	0	.444	348	395	Dick Coury
Memphis Showboats	7	11	0	.389	320	455	Pepper Rodgers
Jacksonville Bulls	6	12	0	.333	327	455	Lindy Infante

WESTERN CONFERENCE

WESTERN DIVISION	W	L	T	PCT	PTS	OPP	COACH
Houston Gamblers	13	5	0	.722	618	400	Jack Pardee
Michigan Panthers	10	8	0	.556	400	382	Jim Stanley
San Antonio Gunslingers	7	11	0	.389	309	325	Gil Steinke
Oklahoma Outlaws	6	12	0	.333	251	459	Woody Widenhofer
Chicago Blitz	5	13	0	.278	340	466	Marv Levy

PACIFIC DIVISION	W	L	T	PCT	PTS	OPP	COACH
Los Angeles Express	10	8	0	.556	338	373	John Hadl
Arizona Wranglers	10	8	0	.556	502	284	George Allen
Denver Gold	9	9	0	.500	356	413	Craig Morton
Oakland Invaders	7	11	0	.389	242	348	John Ralston

QUARTERFINALS
Philadelphia 28, New Jersey 7
Los Angeles 27, Michigan 21 (OT)
Birmingham 36, Tampa Bay 17
Arizona 17, Houston 16

SEMIFINALS
Arizona 35, Los Angeles 23
Philadelphia 20, Birmingham 10

CHAMPIONSHIP
Philadelphia 23, Arizona 3

ALL-USFL TEAM
Offense

WR	Richard Johnson, Houston
WR	Trumaine Johnson, Arizona
TE	Dan Ross, New Orleans
T	Irv Eatman, Philadelphia
T	Pat Phenix, Birmingham
G	Chuck Commiskey, Philadelphia
G	Buddy Aydelette, Birmingham
C	Bart Oates, Philadelphia
QB	Jim Kelly, Houston
RB	Joe Cribbs, Birmingham
RB	Kelvin Bryant, Philadelphia
K	Toni Fritsch, Houston
KR	Derrick Crawford, Memphis
PR	David Martin, Denver

Defense

DE	John Lee, Arizona
DE	Pete Catan, Houston
DT	Kit Lathrop, Arizona
DT	Pete Kugler, Philadelphia
LB	Kiki DeAyala, Houston
LB	Sam Mills, Philadelphia
LB	Jim LeClair, New Jersey
LB	Ed Smith, Arizona
CB	Peter Raeford, San Antonio
CB	Garcia Lane, Philadelphia
S	Marcus Quinn, Oakland
S	Mike Lush, Philadelphia
P	Stan Talley, Oakland

1985 UNITED STATES FOOTBALL LEAGUE

EASTERN CONFERENCE	W	L	T	PCT	PTS	OPP	COACH
Birmingham Stallions	13	5	0	.722	436	299	Rollie Dotsch
New Jersey Generals	11	7	0	.611	418	377	Walt Michaels
Memphis Showboats	11	7	0	.611	428	337	Pepper Rodgers
Baltimore Stars	10	7	1	.583	368	260	Jim Mora
Tampa Bay Bandits	10	8	0	.556	405	422	Steve Spurrier
Jacksonville Bulls	9	9	0	.500	407	402	Lindy Infante
Orlando Renegades	5	13	0	.278	308	481	Lee Corso

WESTERN CONFERENCE	W	L	T	PCT	PTS	OPP	COACH
Oakland Invaders	13	4	1	.750	473	359	Charlie Sumner
Denver Gold	11	7	0	.611	433	389	Mouse Davis

Houston Gamblers	10	8	0	.556	544	388	Jack Pardee
Arizona Wranglers	8	10	0	.444	376	405	Frank Kush
Portland Breakers	6	12	0	.333	275	422	Dick Coury
San Antonio Gunslingers	5	13	0	.278	296	436	Jim Bates
Los Angeles Express	3	15	0	.167	266	456	John Hadl

QUARTERFINALS

Birmingham 22, Houston 20
Memphis 48, Denver 7
Oakland 48, Tampa Bay 27
Baltimore 20, New Jersey 17

SEMIFINALS

Baltimore 28, Birmingham 14
Oakland 28, Memphis 19

CHAMPIONSHIP

Baltimore 28, Oakland 24

ALL-USFL TEAM

Offense		**Defense**	
WR	Jim Smith, Birmingham	DE	James Lockette, New Jersey
WR	Richard Johnson, Houston	DE	Bruce Thornton, Denver
TE	Marvin Harvey, Tampa Bay	DT	Reggie White, Memphis
T	Irv Eatman, Philadelphia	LB	Dave Tipton, Arizona
T	Ray Pinney, Oakland	LB	Sam Mills, Baltimore
G	Buddy Aydelette, Birmingham	LB	Kiki DeAyala, Houston
G	Pat Saindon, Birmingham	LB	Angelo Snipes, Oakland
C	Kent Hull, New Jersey	CB	Kerry Justin, New Jersey
QB	Jim Kelly, Houston	CB	David Martin, Arizona
RB	Herschel Walker, New Jersey	S	Chuck Clanton, Birmingham
RB	Gary Anderson, Tampa Bay	S	Mike Lush, Baltimore
K	Brian Franco, Jacksonville	P	Stan Talley, Oakland
KR	Clarence Verdin, Houston	PR	Gerald McNeil, Houston